# British Companies Legislation 2000

CCH NEW LAW

## Disclaimer

This publication is intended to provide accurate information in regard to the subject matter covered. Readers entering into transactions on the basis of such information should seek the services of a competent professional adviser as this publication is sold on the understanding that the publisher is not engaged in rendering legal or accounting advice or other professional services. The publisher, its editors and any authors, consultants or general editors expressly disclaim all and any liability and responsibility to any person, whether a purchaser or reader of this publication or not, in respect of anything and of the consequences of anything done or omitted to be done by any such person in reliance, whether wholly or partially, upon the whole or any part of the contents of this publication.

## Legislative and other material

While copyright in all statutory and other materials resides in the Crown or other relevant body, copyright in the remaining material in this publication is vested in the publisher. In particular, copyright in any indexes, annotations and in the table of destinations relating to the 1985 companies legislation, in the tables to the Companies Act 1989, in the table relating to EC directive implementation and in the four lists to statutory instruments is vested in the publisher.

The publisher advises that any statutory or other materials issued by the Crown or other relevant bodies and reproduced in this publication are not the authorised official versions of those statutory or other materials. In their preparation, however, the greatest care has been taken to ensure exact conformity with the law as enacted or other materials as issued.

Crown copyright material is reproduced with the permission of the Controller of HMSO.

## Ownership of Trade Mark

The trade mark **CCH © NEW LAW** is the property of

Croner.CCH Group Ltd

ISBN 0 86325 553 1
ISSN 0268-9588

CCH.New Law (a division of Croner.CCH Group Ltd, 145 London Road, Kingston upon Thames, Surrey KT2 6SR, part of the Wolters Kluwer Group) Telford Road, Bicester, Oxfordshire OX26 4LB Telephone (01869) 253300, Facsimile (01869) 874700.

First Edition, July 1985
Revised impression, August 1985
Second Edition, June 1986
Third Edition, April 1987
Fourth Edition, August 1988
Fifth Edition, September 1990
Sixth Edition, September 1991
Seventh Edition, September 1992
Eighth Edition, September 1993
Ninth Edition, September 1994
Tenth Edition, August 1995
Eleventh Edition, August 1996
Twelfth Edition, August 1997
Thirteenth Edition, September 1998
Fourteenth Edition, September 1999
Fifteenth Edition, September 2000



Typeset in the UK by Croner.CCH Group Ltd.
Printed and bound in the UK by Clays Ltd, St. Ives plc.

# Introduction

The fifteenth edition of *British Companies Legislation* comprises one volume containing the texts of the following eight main statutes:

the *Companies Act* 1985;

the *Business Names Act* 1985;

the *Companies Consolidation (Consequential Provisions) Act* 1985;

the *Insolvency Act* 1986;

the *Company Directors Disqualification Act* 1986;

the *Financial Services Act* 1986;

the *Companies Act* 1989; and

the *Financial Services and Markets Act* 2000.

In addition, certain ancillary legislation (including the insider dealing provisions in the *Criminal Justice Act* 1993), the *Insolvency Rules* 1986 (as amended) and other subordinate legislation relating to company law are reproduced.

**1985 companies consolidation**

The first three of the above statutes (together with the now repealed *Company Securities (Insider Dealing) Act* 1985 – see 'Insider dealing' below) represent the consolidation of the Companies Acts 1948 to 1983, operative from 1 July 1985. The *Companies Act* 1985 has been significantly amended by the *Companies Act* 1989 (see below) and other legislation.

**Insolvency and director disqualification**

The *Insolvency Act* 1986 and the *Company Directors Disqualification Act* 1986 (in force from 29 December 1986) are the consolidation of the *Insolvency Act* 1985 with over 200 sections of the *Companies Act* 1985 relating to receivership and companies winding up. The *Insolvency Act* 1985 represented the most comprehensive revision of corporate and individual insolvency law in more than a century. Provisions relating to disqualification and personal liability of directors and others were the only substantive provisions of the 1985 Act ever to come into force (28 April 1986).

However, although the *Insolvency Act* 1985 was superseded by the 1986 statutes, it made many amendments to other legislation – as did the *Insolvency Act* 1986. These are covered throughout the publication as relevant. It is to be noted that the commencement date of the two 1986 Acts was tied to the last commencement date for the *Insolvency Act* 1985 (see IA 1986, s. 443, CDDA 1986, s. 25 and SI 1986/1924 (C 71)).

*Insolvency Bill*

An Insolvency Bill was introduced into the House of Lords on 3 February 2000. When enacted and in force it will effect amendments to the *Insolvency Act* 1986, primarily by amending Pt. I of the Act to allow a moratorium at the outset for company voluntary arrangements (a recommendation suggested by the Cork Report, *Report of the Review Committee on Insolvency Law and Practice* (Cmnd 8558, 1982) and resurrected in several consultation exercises throughout the 1990s), amend the *Company Directors Disqualification Act* 1986 to introduce formal undertakings not to act as a director in lieu of a disqualification order and allow the Secretary of State for Trade and Industry to make regulations for the purpose of giving effect to the model law on cross-border insolvency contained in Annex 1 of the report of the 30th session of the United Nations Commission on International Trade Law (UNCITRAL).

*Insolvency proceedings regulation*

The EU Council of Ministers on 29 May 2000 adopted a regulation on insolvency proceedings (1346/2000, OJ 2000 L160/1) under art. 61(c) of the EC Treaty. The objective of the regulation is to define common rules on cross-border insolvency proceedings – an area not covered by the 1968 Brussels Convention on Jurisdiction and Enforcement of Judgments in Civil and Commercial Matters – so that these proceedings can operate more efficiently. The application of the regulation will also reduce transfers of assets or of judicial proceedings from one member state to another. The regulation has direct applicability, i.e. does not have to be implemented by domestic legislation, and comes into force on 31 May 2002.

**Financial services**

The *Financial Services Act* 1986 received Royal Assent on 7 November 1986 and set up a new system of self-regulation intended to give greater protection to both private and professional investors. The Act's key provision is s. 3 which came into force on 29 April 1988 making it an offence to carry on investment business without authorisation or exemption. The Financial Services Act made a large number of amendments to companies legislation. Because of the close relationship with much of the legislation in this book that statute has been included in full text in a separate division. Operative amendments from the Act are included throughout the publication. There are also many amendments to the Act by the *Companies Act* 1989 (see below) and other legislation.

As at the time of writing there have been 14 commencement orders to the Financial Services Act. The last two of these have been reproduced immediately after the Act in the same division. The penultimate (i.e. thirteenth) order includes a note with details of previous commencements.

Part V of the Financial Services Act, which was to regulate offers of unlisted securities replacing Pt. III of and Sch. 3 to the *Companies Act* 1985 relating to prospectuses, was never brought into force. The *Public Offers of Securities Regulations* 1995 from 19 June 1995 repealed Pt. V and replaced Pt. III of the Companies Act which is largely repealed from the same date as a result of the thirteenth commencement order mentioned above. It is the above regulations, made under the *European Communities Act* 1972, which now provide for the preparation and publication of prospectuses when transferable securities are offered to the public, and for the mutual recognition of prospectuses and listing particulars (implementing Directives 89/298 and 80/390, as amended). The regulations made many amendments to Pt. IV of the Financial Services Act relating to prospectuses and listing particulars. These and other amendments are covered to the extent that they are relevant to this publication. Of significant interest is the new Sch. 11A inserted into the Financial

Services Act defining what is an offer to the public for the purposes of Pt. IV. The *Public Offers of Securities Regulations* 1995 were intended amongst other things to increase cross-border offers of securities, but the first years of their operation witnessed little of this activity and so the regulations were amended in May 1999 to promote mutual recognition of prospectuses throughout the EU.

On the subject of investor protection, the *Investment Services Regulations* 1995 are included in 'Rules and Regulations' (see below). These implement two EU directives, the investment services directive and the capital adequacy directive, which permit firms to conduct investment business throughout the EEA on the basis of their home-state authorisation.

*Reform of financial services regulation*

The system of regulation under the *Financial Services Act* 1986 was criticised from its inception. Attempts at simplifying the system were made without great success, and in May 1997 it was announced that the system was to be fundamentally reformed. This will involve a move away from self-regulation in favour of the centralisation of regulatory power within a single body, the Financial Services Authority ('FSA') (previously the Securities and Investments Board ('SIB')). The other regulators under the SIB will be closed down. The FSA was launched by renaming the SIB in October 1997, but it will have far wider power than the the SIB. In addition to regulating financial services as understood under the 1986 Act, the FSA will also regulate insurance companies, building societies, friendly societies, credit unions and other bodies. A major step in the reforming process occurred on 1 June 1998 when the FSA took over supervision of banks from the Bank of England under the *Bank of England Act* 1998. From that date the latter Act effected many amendments to companies and related legislation. A draft Financial Services and Markets Bill was published on 30 July 1998 and immediately was subjected to a barrage of criticism, especially in relation to the FSA's proposed disciplinary and enforcement powers, where the perception was that the FSA was potentially being made regulator, prosecutor, judge, jury, appeal body and gaoler! Members of the legal community threatened that the legislation could be in breach of the *Human Rights Act* 1998 (s. 19 of which requires a minister introducing a bill into Parliament to state whether it is compatible with the Act) and the government in late 1998 agreed to appoint a joint committee of both Houses of Parliament to scrutinise the draft legislation. The committee reported in May 1999 and, amongst other things, recommended that marketing and provision of advice on mortgage services should be brought within the FSA's regulatory responsibilities.

The Financial Services and Markets Bill was introduced into Parliament on 17 June 1999. It did not include mortgages within the scope of FSA regulation but aspects of mortgage provision were added to the Bill during its passage through Parliament. The Bill had a tortuous passage through Parliament which took almost a year. It apparently was subjected to the second highest number of amendments of any Bill. During the debates in the House of Lords, Lord Saatchi memorably stated that sight of the Bill had been known to make grown men weep. The Bill eventually received the Royal Assent on 14 June 2000. The *Financial Services and Markets Act* 2000 contains 433 sections, 22 schedules and the HMSO print version is 301 pages in length. The Treasury announced on 18 July 2000 that it had set a target of 'about a year's time' for the arrangements to be ready for the Act to come fully into force, and so mid-July 2001 is the target date.

The Act provides the framework within which the FSA as single regulator for the financial services industry will operate. It also creates the Financial Services and Markets Tribunal and establishes the framework for single ombudsman and compensation schemes to provide further protection for consumers. The framework of the Act provides, amongst other things, for the constitution and accountability of the FSA, the definition of the scope of regulated activities, the control of financial promotion, powers of the FSA to authorise, regulate, investigate and discipline authorised persons, the recognition of investment exchanges and clearing houses, arrangements for the approval of controllers and the performance of regulated activities, the oversight of financial services provided by members of the professions, regulation and marketing of collective investment schemes, certain criminal offences, powers to impose penalties for market abuse, and the transfer to the FSA of registration functions in respect of building societies, friendly societies, industrial and provident societies and certain other mutual societies.

The regulatory scope of the *Financial Services and Markets Act* 2000 when fully in force is far wider than that under the *Financial Services Act* 1986. Businesses to be authorised and regulated under the 2000 Act include banks, building societies, insurance companies, friendly societies, credit unions, Lloyd's, investment and pensions advisers, stockbrokers, professional firms offering certain types of investment services, fund managers, derivatives traders and mortgage lenders. All these are to be regulated by the FSA, which from 1 May 2000 is also the competent authority for Official Listing of securities.

Quite remarkably, the Financial Services and Markets Act contains only a few amendments and repeals, and these are largely consequential. It does not contain amendments and repeals in particular to the *Companies Act* 1985, the *Companies Act* 1989 and the *Financial Services Act* 1986. It is difficult to predict whether the 1986 Act will be repealed in its entirety (subject to transitional provisions), or whether some of its provisions will continue. Presumably the amendments and repeals will have to be effected by delegated legislation. Over 90 statutory instruments are expected to be made under the 2000 Act. The FSA's Handbook of principles, codes, rules and guidance will be vast.

## Companies Act 1989

The *Companies Act* 1989 could be described as the most reforming Companies Act for over 40 years. The 1989 Act received Royal Assent on 16 November 1989 after a protracted passage through Parliament and comprised 216 sections and 24 Schedules. It contains provisions altering the law in regard to company accounts, regulation of auditors, investigations and powers to obtain information, registration of company charges, mergers, financial markets and insolvency and the transfer of securities. There are also many provisions which effect miscellaneous amendments to company law, including the reform of the ultra vires rule, and numerous amendments to the *Financial Services Act* 1986.

Only a small number of provisions of the 1989 Act came into force on Royal Assent (see s. 215 for details). Since then there have been 17 commencement orders. All relevant operative amendments to other legislation in *British Companies Legislation* have been covered. The fifteenth of these commencement orders (SI 1995/1352 (C 27)) is included in 'Rules and Regulations' with a note providing details of all previous commencements.

The main area of the 1989 Act still not in force is Pt. IV (registration of company charges). The Department of Trade and Industry (DTI) has advised that it is likely that this will never be brought into force in its current form – a working party was set up and a further consultation document was published in November 1994. The DTI confirmed in 1996 that s. 133 (the issue of redeemable shares) is unlikely to be brought into force.

Statutory instruments supporting provisions introduced by the 1989 Act are included in the 'Rules and Regulations' division (see below).

The 1989 Act has its own division. It should be noted that provisions which are in force and have amended other legislative provisions elsewhere in the publication are not reproduced. Included with the 1989 Act are two CCH tables – one indicates the main effect of each 1989 Act provision and the other lists the legislative provisions in this edition affected by the 1989 Act.

**Ancillary legislation**

The 'Ancillary Acts' division (see p. 2,901ff.) includes provisions of the following statutes: the *Partnership Act* 1890, the *Limited Partnerships Act* 1907, the *Stock Transfer Act* 1963, the *Theft Act* 1968, the *Fair Trading Act* 1973, the *Criminal Justice Act* 1987 (relating to the Serious Fraud Office), the *Charities Act* 1993, the *Insolvency Act* 1994 and the *Insolvency (No. 2) Act* 1994 (the last two amending the *Insolvency Act* 1986) and the insider dealing provisions from the *Criminal Justice Act* 1993 (see 'Insider dealing' below). Also included are provisions contained in the *Pension Schemes Act* 1993 and in the *Employment Rights Act* 1996 concerning certain rights of employees of insolvent employer companies. Major extracts from the *Bank of England Act* 1998 are reproduced and amendments effected by the Act to companies and financial services legislation (including statutory instruments) are covered. The *Companies and Business Names (Chamber of Commerce, etc.) Act* 1999 is also reproduced, although at the time of writing it has still not been brought into force.

Relevant provisions of the *Competition Act* 1998 have been included in this edition. These exempt company mergers and concentrations from the effects of the new competition regime in force from 1 March 2000. In particular transactions within the scope of the EC merger regulation are specifically excluded.

The most recent substantive statute to be inserted into 'Ancillary Acts' is the *Limited Liability Partnerships Act* 2000, enacted on 20 July 2000 and which, when in force, will allow the establishment of a new type of enterprise which is basically a hybrid between a partnership and a company. The Act will be brought into force by statutory instrument. The concept of limited liability partnership ('LLP') is already popular in the US with law and accounting firms. Under the 2000 Act an LLP will be a body corporate incorporated by registration with the registrar of companies (in England and Wales or in Scotland) under the Act, have unlimited capacity and have limited liability for its members (the Act does not refer to them as 'partners'). Members are constituted agents for the company but under the Act will only bind the company if authorised to do so in dealing with another person. Changes in membership will require notice to the registrar. A schedule to the Act contains provisions for names and registered offices of LLPs.

The Act contains regulation-making powers for provision, with modifications, for parts of the *Companies Act* 1985 and the *Insolvency Act* 1986 to apply to LLPs. The draft versions of the regulations issued in a consultation exercise indicate that the amount of legislation involved will be formidable and, not being free-standing, it is in less than user-friendly appearance. The regulations are expected to be made in October 2000 and the first LLPs to be in operation early in 2001.

**Stamp duty**

The various Finance Act provisions relating to stamp duty and stamp duty reserve tax that have appeared in previous editions of this book are this year available only on the CD-ROM version of the product which accompanies *British Companies Legislation 2000*.

**Insider dealing**

The *Criminal Justice Act* 1993 contains, amongst other things, in Pt. V, provisions on insider dealing, changing the scope of the previous legislation in a number of ways. There are a number of amendments to other legislation and the *Company Securities (Insider Dealing) Act* 1985 is repealed. Part V came into force on 1 March 1994 (as a result of the fifth commencement order to the Criminal Justice Act) together with two ancillary statutory instruments (both reproduced in 'Rules and Regulations'): the *Insider Dealing (Securities and Regulated Markets) Order* 1994 (as most recently amended) and the *Traded Securities (Disclosure) Regulations* 1994. The relevant provisions (as already noted) are in 'Ancillary Acts' and the repealed 1985 Insider Dealing Act is reproduced in a note immediately afterwards. Appropriate amendments from the Criminal Justice Act have been made throughout the publication.

**Subordinate legislation**

The fifteenth edition also contains the *Insolvency Rules* 1986 and much other subordinate legislation.

The *Insolvency Rules* 1986 are reproduced in full text at p. 2,801ff. They provide the procedural gloss to the framework of the *Insolvency Act* 1986. Like the Act, they operate from 29 December 1986. There have been seven sets of amendments to the 1986 rules (the most recent operative from March 1999) and these amendments have been included at appropriate places.

The 'Rules and Regulations' division contains subordinate legislation remade in light of the 1985 companies legislation and operative from 1 July 1985, such as the *Companies (Tables A to F) Regulations* 1985 which include the revised form of Table A articles of association. The former Table A (as contained in the First Schedule to the repealed *Companies Act* 1948) is reproduced after the 1985 Regulations as it is still relevant for many companies incorporated before 1 July 1985.

In addition to the Insolvency Rules, the 'Rules and Regulations' division contains other subordinate legislation relevant for the *Insolvency Act* 1986 and the *Company Directors Disqualification Act* 1986, including that relating specifically to Scotland. The division contains the *Companies (Fees) Regulations* 1991 (as amended, most recently in March 1999) and the *Insolvency Fees Order* 1986 (as amended). As already noted, the fifteenth commencement order to the *Companies Act* 1989 is reproduced in the division (including a note about previous commencements – the two subsequent commencement orders do not contain such a note), as are two insider dealing statutory instruments which came into force at the same time as Pt. V of the *Criminal Justice Act* 1993.

Also in the division are the *Insolvent Partnerships Order* 1994 (as amended), the *Insolvency Regulations* 1994, the *Public Offers of Securities Regulations* 1995, the *Companies (Summary Financial Statement) Regulations* 1995, the *Uncertificated Securities Regulations* 1995, the *Open-Ended Investment Companies (Investment Companies with Variable Capital) Regulations* 1996, which from 6 January 1997 introduced open-ended investment companies as a new form of investment vehicle in the UK, and the *Companies Act 1985 (Accounts of Small and Medium-Sized Companies and Minor Accounting Amendments) Regulations* 1997.

Of considerable importance to litigators was the implementation on 26 April 1999 of the *Civil Procedure Rules* 1998 ('the CPR'). These replace the Rules of the Supreme Court and the County Court Rules as part of the reform of civil litigation based on recommendations of the final *Access to Justice* report by Lord Woolf MR. The CPR have revolutionised litigation in the civil courts. Amongst other things the terminology has been made more user-friendly (e.g. 'plaintiff' has become 'claimant' and 'writ' has become a 'claim form': logically now one has a claim by a claimant using a claim form). The CPR are expressed not to apply to insolvency proceedings (since the procedure for these is governed by the *Insolvency Rules* 1986 which are amended by the CPR) but they do apply to proceedings under the Companies Acts of 1985 and 1989. Extracts from the CPR in relation to companies are reproduced in this edition and a number of consequential amendments to other legislation covered. Extracts from new fees orders in relation to companies for the county courts and the Supreme Court consequent on the CPR are also reproduced.

Audit exemption was introduced by regulations amending the *Companies Act* 1985 in 1994. The turnover threshold was increased in 1997 (and a system of partial exemption subject to an accountant's report was scrapped for all but qualifying charitable companies) and this was increased again by the *Companies Act 1985 (Audit Exemption) Regulations* 2000 to £1m for financial periods ending on or after 26 July 2000. The Department of Trade and Industry has indicated that it will increase the figure to the maximum permitted under EU law of £4.2m if the consultation under the Company Law Review (see below) comments favourably on this.

In this fifteenth edition several statutory instruments have been inserted or their effects covered. These include the *Financial Markets and Insolvency (Settlement Finality) Regulations* 1999 which from 11 December 1999 implement the EC settlement finality directive to reduce the risk in payment and securities settlement systems on the insolvency of a participant in such a system, and the *Official Listing of Securities (Change of Competent Authority) Regulations* 2000 which from 1 May 2000 transferred Listing Authority status for the UK to the Financial Services Authority. Amending delegated legislation covered relates to audit exemption (see above), the Crest paperless trading system, contents of company annual returns, distribution of profits by investment companies, stamp duty and stamp duty reserve tax in relation to open-ended investment companies and payments by liquidators into the Insolvency Services Account.

**Company law reform**

The Department of Trade and Industry (DTI) has carried out several consultation exercises in recent years and has stated that it intends to introduce legislation in a number of areas, but other legislative priorities have meant no primary legislation on company law in the first three years of the Labour government formed after the General Election of May 1997. In the longer term, the DTI is carrying out a review of the whole of 'core' company law (i.e. excluding insolvency and financial services) (see 'Company Law Review' below). It now appears in light of developments in the Company Law Review in 1999/2000 that many of the proposals mentioned below are being subsumed within the review and so legislation effecting them will not appear for a few more years.

Recent consultation exercises for which legislation is ultimately hoped for include: shareholders' rights to table amendments at an annual general meeting at the company's expense; implementation of the revised thirteenth company law directive on takeover bids; and reform of financial assistance for acquisition by a company of its shares (the DTI has stated that separate regimes will have to apply for public and private companies, as its objective to produce an overall scheme was producing even more complex and obscure draft legislation than under the existing system).

The Law Commission in 1996–97 held a detailed consultation exercise on reforming shareholders' remedies (with particular reference to derivative actions and the remedy against unfairly prejudicial conduct in s. 459–461 of the *Companies Act* 1985). The DTI commenced a short consultation of some specific aspects of remedies in December 1998.

Simplification of Pt. VI of the *Companies Act* 1985 on the disclosure of interests in the shares of public companies is also a proposed subject for reform.

Other consultation exercises likely to result in legislation include redenomination of share capital in light of the single European currency (the euro), giving companies a substantive right to purchase and resell their own shares (without having to cancel the shares as is currently required, so that the shares cannot be resold) and regulation of political donations by companies so that directors will need advance authorisation to make donations (this latter is contained in a Political Parties, Elections and Referendums Bill introduced into the House of Commons on 10 January 2000).

**Company Law Review**

On 4 March 1998 the DTI published a consultative document entitled *Modern Company Law for a Competitive Economy*. This heralds a fundamental review of company law, to be the first overview of the whole of 'core' company law (i.e. without financial services and insolvency) since the 'modern' system of companies legislation was introduced in the mid-nineteenth century. The terms of reference for the review, which is to be carried out by working groups overseen by a steering group, are to make recommendations having:

(1) considered how core company law can be modernised in order to provide a simple, efficient and cost-effective framework for carrying out business activity which provides the maximum freedom and flexibility while protecting those involved in the enterprise and is drafted in clear, concise and unambiguous language that can be readily understood by those involved in business;
(2) considered whether company law, partnership law and other legislation together provide an adequate choice of legal vehicle for business at all levels;
(3) considered the proper relationship between company law and non-statutory standards of corporate behaviour; and
(4) reviewed the extent to which foreign companies operating in Great Britain should be regulated under British company law.

The review is clearly ambitious and wide-ranging. The timetable for the review is lengthy. The steering group was launched in June 1998 and in February 1999 published for consultation a strategic framework for the review. A major element in the review is consideration of separate provisions for economically small and closely held companies, in order to reduce the regulatory burdens on these companies which represent a large proportion of the total number of companies and have a significant impact on enterprise and job creation. It is unlikely that there would be separate, free-standing legislation for these small companies as the steering group favours an integrated approach.

The steering group published three consultation documents simultaneously in October 1999 and a further document, *Developing the Framework*, in March 2000, following up the earlier strategic framework document. A shorter document was issued in June 2000, specifically seeking technical comments on the subject of maintenance of capital in light of responses to one of the October 1999 consultation documents.

The steering group expects to publish one more consultative document late in 2000 prior to its final report to government in spring 2001. This will be followed by a government White Paper in 2001. Reforming legislation, in the form of a new Companies Act (or Acts), is not anticipated before 2003.

**Miscellaneous**

Throughout the statutes and the various rules and regulations, repealed or revoked provisions and some amending provisions have been omitted. In the case of certain more recent repeals and amendments history notes have been inserted to indicate the previous wording. Additional notes have also been included referring to other relevant provisions, and to incidental matters.

The publisher advises that the legislation in this fifteenth edition is not the authorised version. In its preparation, however, the greatest care has been taken to ensure exact conformity with the law as enacted. Some changes in printing style have been adopted for convenience and to improve readability. For example, marginal notes appearing in the official statutes have been reproduced in bold type above the section to which they relate. CCH.New Law has also added its own subsection notes in square brackets, thus [ ].

As with the fourteenth edition, several useful lists of statutory instruments are included. The first is an alphabetical list of statutory instruments covered in the publication (see p. 4,903). There are also lists of statutory instruments relevant to forms and fees (see p. 4,917 and p. 4,927 respectively). There are three more useful lists. The first (see p. 4,929) relates to the numbered EU company law directives and notes of the relevant implementing legislation are included. The second (see p. 4,931) covers other relevant EU measures and directives. Finally, at p. 4,933 the accounting standards and guidance list itemises the financial reporting standards, statements of recommended practice and urgent issues task force abstracts issued by the relevant accounting bodies.

A comprehensive Index to all the legislation in the main body of the publication is at the back of the volume commencing on p. 5,005. The index references are to provisions of the *Companies Act* 1985 except where they show prefix letters as explained on p. 5,003.

CCH.New Law
August 2000

# About the Publisher

CCH.New Law is a division of Croner.CCH Group Ltd, part of the Wolters Kluwer Group. Wolters Kluwer is the leading international professional publisher specialising in tax, business and law publishing throughout Europe, the US and the Asia Pacific region. The group produces a wide range of information services in different media for the accounting and legal professions and for businesses.

All CCH.New Law publications are designed to provide practical, authoritative reference works and useful guides, and are written by our highly qualified and experienced editorial team and specialist outside authors.

CCH.New Law publishes information packages including electronic products, loose-leaf reporting services, newsletters and books on UK and European legal topics for distribution world-wide. The UK operation also acts as distributor of the publications of the overseas affiliates.

CCH.New Law
Telford Road
Bicester
Oxfordshire
OX26 4LB
Telephone : (01869) 253300

A division of Croner.CCH Group Ltd,
Croner House, London Road, Kingston upon Thames,
Surrey, KT2 6SR, 020 8547 3333
Part of the Wolters Kluwer Group

# Table of Contents

## Table of Contents

## Table of Contents

# COMPANIES ACT 1985

## Table of Contents

# COMPANIES ACT 1985

(1985 Chapter 6)

# ARRANGEMENT OF SECTIONS

## PART I – FORMATION AND REGISTRATION OF COMPANIES; JURIDICAL STATUS AND MEMBERSHIP

### CHAPTER I – COMPANY FORMATION



### CHAPTER II – COMPANY NAMES

SECTION

*Dormant companies*

250. Resolution not to appoint auditors

*Listed public companies*

251. Provision of summary financial statement to shareholders

*Private companies*

252. Election to dispense with laying of accounts and reports before general meeting
253. Right of shareholder to require laying of accounts

*Unlimited companies*

254. Exemption from requirement to deliver accounts and reports

*Banking and insurance companies and groups*

255. Special provisions for banking and insurance companies
255A. Special provisions for banking and insurance groups
255B. Modification of disclosure requirements in relation to banking company or group
255C. (Omitted by the Companies Act 1985 (Insurance Companies Accounts) Regulations 1993 (SI 1993/3246), reg. 1, 5, Sch. 2, para. 3)
255D. Power to apply provisions to banking partnerships

*Welsh private companies*

255E. (Ceased to have effect and repealed by Welsh Language Act 1993, s. 30(1), (5), 35(1) and Sch. 2)

## CHAPTER III – SUPPLEMENTARY PROVISIONS

*Accounting standards*

256. Accounting standards

*Power to alter accounting requirements*

257. Power of Secretary of State to alter accounting requirements

*Parent and subsidiary undertakings*

258. Parent and subsidiary undertakings

*Other interpretation provisions*

259. Meaning of "undertaking" and related expressions
260. Participating interests
261. Notes to the accounts
262. Minor definitions
262A. Index of defined expressions

# PART VIII – DISTRIBUTION OF PROFITS AND ASSETS

*Limits of company's power of distribution*

263. Certain distributions prohibited
264. Restriction on distribution of assets
265. Other distributions by investment companies
266. Meaning of "investment company"
267. Extension of s. 265, 266 to other companies
268. Realised profits of insurance company with long term business
269. Treatment of development costs

*Relevant accounts*

270. Distribution to be justified by reference to company's accounts

SECTION

## PART XXVI – INTERPRETATION



## PART XXVII – FINAL PROVISIONS



## SCHEDULES

8. Form and content of accounts prepared by small companies
8A. Form and content of abbreviated accounts of small companies delivered to registrar
9. Special provisions for banking companies and groups
9A. Form and content of accounts of insurance companies and groups
10. (Omitted by the Companies Act 1985 (Insurance Companies Accounts) Regulations 1993 (SI 1993/3246), reg. 1, 5 and Sch. 2, para. 7)
10A. Parent and subsidiary undertakings: supplementary provisions
11. Modifications of Part VIII where company's accounts prepared in accordance with special provisions for banking or insurance companies
12. (Repealed by Company Directors Disqualification Act 1986, s. 23(2) and Sch. 4)
13. Provisions supplementing and interpreting s. 324 to 328
14. Overseas branch registers
15. (Repealed by Companies Act 1989, s. 212 and Sch. 24)
15A. Written resolutions of private companies
15B. Provisions subject to which s. 425–427 have effect in their application to mergers and divisions of public companies
16. (Repealed by Insolvency Act 1986, s. 438 and Sch. 12)
17–19. (Repealed by Insolvency Act 1985, s. 235 and Sch. 10, Pt. II)
20. Vesting of disclaimed property; protection of third parties
21. Effect of registration under s. 680
21A. Branch registration under the Eleventh Company Law Directive (89/666/EEC)
21B. Change in registration regime: transitional provisions
21C. Delivery of reports and accounts: credit and financial institutions to which the Bank Branches Directive (89/117/EEC) applies
21D. Delivery of reports and accounts: companies to which the Eleventh Company Law Directive applies
22. Provisions of this Act applying to unregistered companies
23. Form of statement to be published by certain companies under s. 720
24. Punishment of offences under this Act
25. Companies Act 1981, s. 38, as originally enacted

# COMPANIES ACT 1985

(1985 Chapter 6)

An Act to consolidate the greater part of the Companies Acts.

[*11th March 1985*]

# PART I – FORMATION AND REGISTRATION OF COMPANIES; JURIDICAL STATUS AND MEMBERSHIP

## Chapter I – Company Formation

MEMORANDUM OF ASSOCIATION

### 1 Mode of forming incorporated company

**1(1) [Formation]** Any two or more persons associated for a lawful purpose may, by subscribing their names to a memorandum of association and otherwise complying with the requirements of this Act in respect of registration, form an incorporated company, with or without limited liability.

**1(2) [Types of company]** A company so formed may be either–

(a) a company having the liability of its members limited by the memorandum to the amount, if any, unpaid on the shares respectively held by them (**"a company limited by shares"**);

(b) a company having the liability of its members limited by the memorandum to such amount as the members may respectively thereby undertake to contribute to the assets of the company in the event of its being wound up (**"a company limited by guarantee"**); or

(c) a company not having any limit on the liability of its members (**"an unlimited company"**).

**1(3) [Classification as public or private]** A **"public company"** is a company limited by shares or limited by guarantee and having a share capital, being a company–

(a) the memorandum of which states that it is to be a public company, and

(b) in relation to which the provisions of this Act or the former Companies Acts as to the registration or re-registration of a company as a public company have been complied with on or after 22nd December 1980;

and a **"private company"** is a company that is not a public company.

**1(3A) [Formation by one person]** Notwithstanding subsection (1), one person may, for a lawful purpose, by subscribing his name to a memorandum of association and otherwise complying with the requirements of this Act in respect of registration, form an incorporated company being a private company limited by shares or by guarantee.

**History**
S. 1(3A) inserted by the Companies (Single Member Private Limited Companies) Regulations 1992 (SI 1992/1699), reg. 2 and Sch. para. 1 as from 15 July 1992.

**Note**
The Companies (Single Member Private Limited Companies) Regulations 1992 (SI 1992/1699) implemented the Twelfth EC Company Law Directive (89/667).

**1(4) [Restriction on types]** With effect from 22nd December 1980, a company cannot be formed as, or become, a company limited by guarantee with a share capital.

### 2 Requirements with respect to memorandum

**2(1) [Contents of memorandum]** The memorandum of every company must state–

(a) the name of the company;

(b) whether the registered office of the company is to be situated in England and Wales, or in Scotland;

(c) the objects of the company.

**Note**

S. 2(1)(a): see s. 25ff. re company names.

**2(2) [Registered office in Wales]** Alternatively to subsection (1)(b), the memorandum may contain a statement that the company's registered office is to be situated in Wales; and a company whose registered office is situated in Wales may by special resolution alter its memorandum so as to provide that its registered office is to be so situated.

**2(3) [Limited liability]** The memorandum of a company limited by shares or by guarantee must also state that the liability of its members is limited.

**2(4) [Limited by guarantee]** The memorandum of a company limited by guarantee must also state that each member undertakes to contribute to the assets of the company if it should be wound up while he is a member, or within one year after he ceases to be a member, for payment of the debts and liabilities of the company contracted before he ceases to be a member, and of the costs, charges and expenses of winding up, and for adjustment of the rights of the contributories among themselves, such amount as may be required, not exceeding a specified amount.

**2(5) [Company having a share capital]** In the case of a company having a share capital–

(a) the memorandum must also (unless it is an unlimited company) state the amount of the share capital with which the company proposes to be registered and the division of the share capital into shares of a fixed amount;

(b) no subscriber of the memorandum may take less than one share; and

(c) there must be shown in the memorandum against the name of each subscriber the number of shares he takes.

**2(6) [Signing and attestation]** The memorandum must be signed by each subscriber in the presence of at least one witness, who must attest the signature.

**History**

In s. 2(6) the words "; and that attestation is sufficient in Scotland as well as in England and Wales" repealed by Requirements of Writing (Scotland) Act 1995, s. 14(2), 15 and Sch. 5 as from 1 August 1995.

**2(7) [Restriction on alteration]** A company may not alter the conditions contained in its memorandum except in the cases, in the mode and to the extent, for which express provision is made by this Act.

## 3 Forms of memorandum

**3(1) [Form]** Subject to the provisions of sections 1 and 2, the form of the memorandum of association of–

(a) a public company, being a company limited by shares,

(b) a public company, being a company limited by guarantee and having a share capital,

(c) a private company limited by shares,

(d) a private company limited by guarantee and not having a share capital,

(e) a private company limited by guarantee and having a share capital, and

(f) an unlimited company having a share capital,

shall be as specified respectively for such companies by regulations made by the Secretary of State, or as near to that form as circumstances admit.

**3(2) [Regulations]** Regulations under this section shall be made by statutory instrument subject to annulment in pursuance of a resolution of either House of Parliament.

## 3A Statement of company's objects: general commercial company

**3A** Where the company's memorandum states that the object of the company is to carry on business as a general commercial company–

(a) the object of the company is to carry on any trade or business whatsoever, and

(b) the company has power to do all such things as are incidental or conducive to the carrying on of any trade or business by it.

**History**
S. 3A inserted by CA 1989, s. 110(1) as from 4 February 1991 (see SI 1990/2569 (C 68), art. 4(a)).

# 4 Resolution to alter objects

**4(1) [Power to alter memorandum]** A company may by special resolution alter its memorandum with respect to the statement of the company's objects.

**4(2) [Application under s. 5]** If an application is made under the following section, an alteration does not have effect except in so far as it is confirmed by the court.

**History**
S. 4 substituted by CA 1989, s. 110(2) as from 4 February 1991 (see SI 1990/2569 (C 68), art. 4(a)); s. 4 formerly read as follows:

"A company may by special resolution alter its memorandum with respect to the objects of the company, so far as may be required to enable it–

(a) to carry on its business more economically or more efficiently; or
(b) to attain its main purpose by new or improved means; or
(c) to enlarge or change the local area of its operations; or
(d) to carry on some business which under existing circumstances may conveniently or advantageously be combined with the business of the company; or
(e) to restrict or abandon any of the objects specified in the memorandum; or
(f) to sell or dispose of the whole or any part of the undertaking of the company; or
(g) to amalgamate with any other company or body of persons;

but if an application is made under the following section, the alteration does not have effect except in so far as it is confirmed by the court."

# 5 Procedure for objecting to alteration

**5(1) [Application to court]** Where a company's memorandum has been altered by special resolution under section 4, application may be made to the court for the alteration to be cancelled.

**5(2) [Applicants]** Such an application may be made–

(a) by the holders of not less in the aggregate than 15 per cent in nominal value of the company's issued share capital or any class of it or, if the company is not limited by shares, not less than 15 per cent of the company's members; or

(b) by the holders of not less than 15 per cent of the company's debentures entitling the holders to object to an alteration of its objects;

but an application shall not be made by any person who has consented to or voted in favour of the alteration.

**5(3) [Time for application]** The application must be made within 21 days after the date on which the resolution altering the company's objects was passed, and may be made on behalf of the persons entitled to make the application by such one or more of their number as they may appoint in writing for the purpose.

**5(4) [Orders by court]** The court may on such an application make an order confirming the alteration either wholly or in part and on such terms and conditions as it thinks fit, and may–

(a) if it thinks fit, adjourn the proceedings in order that an arrangement may be made to its satisfaction for the purchase of the interests of dissentient members, and

(b) give such directions and make such orders as it thinks expedient for facilitating or carrying into effect any such arrangement.

**5(5) [Order for purchase of shares]** The court's order may (if the court thinks fit) provide for the purchase by the company of the shares of any members of the company, and for the reduction accordingly of its capital, and may make such alterations in the company's memorandum and articles as may be required in consequence of that provision.

**5(6) [Order for no alteration]** If the court's order requires the company not to make any, or any specified, alteration in its memorandum or articles, the company does not then have power without the leave of the court to make any such alteration in breach of that requirement.

**5(7) [Effect of alteration by order]** An alteration in the memorandum or articles of a company made by virtue of an order under this section, other than one made by resolution of the

Company, is of the same effect as if duly made by resolution; and this Act applies accordingly to the memorandum or articles as so altered.

**5(8) [Debentures entitling holders to object]** The debentures entitling the holders to object to an alteration of a company's objects are any debentures secured by a floating charge which were issued or first issued before 1st December 1947 or form part of the same series as any debentures so issued; and a special resolution altering a company's objects requires the same notice to the holders of any such debentures as to members of the company.

In the absence of provisions regulating the giving of notice to any such debenture holders, the provisions of the company's articles regulating the giving of notice to members apply.

## 6 Provisions supplementing s. 4, 5

**6(1) [Requirements made where resolution altering objects]** Where a company passes a resolution altering its objects, then–

(a) if with respect to the resolution no application is made under section 5, the company shall within 15 days from the end of the period for making such an application deliver to the registrar of companies a printed copy of its memorandum as altered; and

(b) if such an application is made, the company shall–

(i) forthwith give notice (in the prescribed form) of that fact to the registrar, and

(ii) within 15 days from the date of any order cancelling or confirming the alteration, deliver to the registrar an office copy of the order and, in the case of an order confirming the alteration, a printed copy of the memorandum as altered.

**Note**

Re s. 6(1)(b)(i) see the Companies (Forms) (Amendment) Regulations 1995 (SI 1995/736).

**6(2) [Extension of time for delivery of documents]** The court may by order at any time extend the time for the delivery of documents to the registrar under subsection (1)(b) for such period as the court may think proper.

**6(3) [Penalty in default]** If a company makes default in giving notice or delivering any document to the registrar of companies as required by subsection (1), the company and every officer of it who is in default is liable to a fine and, for continued contravention, to a daily default fine.

**6(4) [Validity of alteration of objects]** The validity of an alteration of a company's memorandum with respect to the objects of the company shall not be questioned on the ground that it was not authorised by section 4, except in proceedings taken for the purpose (whether under section 5 or otherwise) before the expiration of 21 days after the date of the resolution in that behalf.

**6(5) [Where proceedings otherwise than under s. 5]** Where such proceedings are taken otherwise than under section 5, subsections (1) to (3) above apply in relation to the proceedings as if they had been taken under that section, and as if an order declaring the alteration invalid were an order cancelling it, and as if an order dismissing the proceedings were an order confirming the alteration.

ARTICLES OF ASSOCIATION

## 7 Articles prescribing regulations for companies

**7(1) [Articles signed by subscribers]** There may in the case of a company limited by shares, and there shall in the case of a company limited by guarantee or unlimited, be registered with the memorandum articles of association signed by the subscribers to the memorandum and prescribing regulations for the company.

**7(2) [Articles of unlimited company]** In the case of an unlimited company having a share capital, the articles must state the amount of share capital with which the company proposes to be registered.

**7(3) [Printing, numbering and signing]** Articles must–

(a) be printed,

(b) be divided into paragraphs numbered consecutively, and
(c) be signed by each subscriber to the memorandum in the presence of at least one witness who must attest the signature.

**History**
In s. 7(3)(c) the words "(which attestation is sufficient in Scotland as well as in England and Wales)" repealed by Requirements of Writing (Scotland) Act 1995, s. 14(2), 15 and Sch. 5 as from 1 August 1995.

## 8 Tables A, C, D and E

**8(1) [Table A]** Table A is as prescribed by regulations made by the Secretary of State; and a company may for its articles adopt the whole or any part of that Table.

**8(2) [Articles not registered]** In the case of a company limited by shares, if articles are not registered or, if articles are registered, in so far as they do not exclude or modify Table A, that Table (so far as applicable, and as in force at the date of the company's registration) constitutes the company's articles, in the same manner and to the same extent as if articles in the form of that Table had been duly registered.

**8(3) [If Table A altered]** If in consequence of regulations under this section Table A is altered, the alteration does not affect a company registered before the alteration takes effect, or repeal as respects that company any portion of the Table.

**8(4) [Tables C, D and E]** The form of the articles of association of–
(a) a company limited by guarantee and not having a share capital,
(b) a company limited by guarantee and having a share capital, and
(c) an unlimited company having a share capital,

shall be respectively in accordance with Table C, D or E prescribed by regulations made by the Secretary of State, or as near to that form as circumstances admit.

**8(5) [Regulations]** Regulations under this section shall be made by statutory instrument subject to annulment in pursuance of a resolution of either House of Parliament.

**Note**
See the Companies (Tables A to F) Regulations 1985 (SI 1985/805).

## 9 Alteration of articles by special resolution

**9(1) [Special resolution]** Subject to the provisions of this Act and to the conditions contained in its memorandum, a company may by special resolution alter its articles.

**9(2) [Effect of alteration]** Alterations so made in the articles are (subject to this Act) as valid as if originally contained in them, and are subject in like manner to alteration by special resolution.

REGISTRATION AND ITS CONSEQUENCES

## 10 Documents to be sent to registrar

**10(1) [Memorandum and articles]** The company's memorandum and articles (if any) shall be delivered–
(a) to the registrar of companies for England and Wales, if the memorandum states that the registered office of the company is to be situated in England and Wales, or that it is to be situated in Wales; and
(b) to the registrar of companies for Scotland, if the memorandum states that the registered office of the company is to be situated in Scotland.

**10(2) [Statement of directors and secretary]** With the memorandum there shall be delivered a statement in the prescribed form containing the names and requisite particulars of–
(a) the person who is, or the persons who are, to be the first director or directors of the company; and
(b) the person who is, or the persons who are, to be the first secretary or joint secretaries of the company;

and the requisite particulars in each case are those set out in Schedule 1.

**Note**
See the Companies (Forms) Regulations 1985 (SI 1985/854), the Companies (Forms Amendment No. 2 and Company's Type and Principal Business Activities) Regulations 1990 (SI 1990/1766), the Companies (Welsh Language Forms and Documents) (Amendment) Regulations 1995 (SI 1995/734) and the Companies (Forms) (Amendment) Regulations 1995 (SI 1995/736).

**10(3) [Signing of s. 10(2) statement]** The statement shall be signed by or on behalf of the subscribers of the memorandum and shall contain a consent signed by each of the persons named in it as a director, as secretary or as one of joint secretaries, to act in the relevant capacity.

**10(4) [Where statement delivered by agent]** Where a memorandum is delivered by a person as agent for the subscribers, the statement shall specify that fact and the person's name and address.

**10(5) [Appointment by articles also to be in statement]** An appointment by any articles delivered with the memorandum of a person as director or secretary of the company is void unless he is named as a director or secretary in the statement.

**10(6) [Registered office]** There shall in the statement be specified the intended situation of the company's registered office on incorporation.

# 11 Minimum authorised capital (public companies)

**11** When a memorandum delivered to the registrar of companies under section 10 states that the association to be registered is to be a public company, the amount of the share capital stated in the memorandum to be that with which the company proposes to be registered must not be less than the authorised minimum (defined in section 118).

# 12 Duty of registrar

**12(1) [Registrar to be satisfied re requirements]** The registrar of companies shall not register a company's memorandum delivered under section 10 unless he is satisfied that all the requirements of this Act in respect of registration and of matters precedent and incidental to it have been complied with.

**12(2) [Registration]** Subject to this, the registrar shall retain and register the memorandum and articles (if any) delivered to him under that section.

**12(3) [Statutory declaration of compliance]** A statutory declaration in the prescribed form by–

(a) a solicitor engaged in the formation of a company, or

(b) a person named as a director or secretary of the company in the statement delivered under section 10(2),

that those requirements have been complied with shall be delivered to the registrar of companies, and the registrar may accept such a declaration as sufficient evidence of compliance.

**Note**
See the Companies (Welsh Language Forms and Documents) (Amendment) Regulations 1995 (SI 1995/734), the Companies (Forms) (Amendment) Regulations 1995 (SI 1995/736) and the Companies (Welsh Language Forms and Documents) (No. 2) Regulations 1995 (SI 1995/1480).

# 13 Effect of registration

**13(1) [Certification registration]** On the registration of a company's memorandum, the registrar of companies shall give a certificate that the company is incorporated and, in the case of a limited company, that it is limited.

**13(2) [Certificate to be signed or sealed]** The certificate may be signed by the registrar, or authenticated by his official seal.

**13(3) [Effect]** From the date of incorporation mentioned in the certificate, the subscribers of the memorandum, together with such other persons as may from time to time become members of the company, shall be a body corporate by the name contained in the memorandum.

**13(4) [Capability of body corporate]** That body corporate is then capable forthwith of exercising all the functions of an incorporated company, but with such liability on the part of its members to contribute to its assets in the event of its being wound up as is provided by this Act and the Insolvency Act.



CCH.New Law
bbcl ca 1985a Mp 126—bcl98 2b

This is subject, in the case of a public company, to section 117 (additional certificate as to amount of allotted share capital).

**History**
In s. 13(4) the words "and the Insolvency Act" added by Insolvency Act 1986, s. 439(1) and Sch. 13 as from 29 December 1986 (see IA 1986 s. 443 and SI 1986/1924 (C 71)).

**13(5) [First directors and secretary]** The persons named in the statement under section 10 as directors, secretary or joint secretaries are, on the company's incorporation, deemed to have been respectively appointed as its first directors, secretary or joint secretaries.

**13(6) [Statement in certificate re public company]** Where the registrar registers an association's memorandum which states that the association is to be a public company, the certificate of incorporation shall contain a statement that the company is a public company.

**13(7) [Effect of certificate of incorporation]** A certificate of incorporation given in respect of an association is conclusive evidence–

(a) that the requirements of this Act in respect of registration and of matters precedent and incidental to it have been complied with, and that the association is a company authorised to be registered, and is duly registered, under this Act, and

(b) if the certificate contains a statement that the company is a public company, that the company is such a company.

## 14 Effect of memorandum and articles

**14(1) [Company and members bound]** Subject to the provisions of this Act, the memorandum and articles, when registered, bind the company and its members to the same extent as if they respectively had been signed and sealed by each member, and contained covenants on the part of each member to observe all the provisions of the memorandum and of the articles.

**14(2) [Debt by member]** Money payable by a member to the company under the memorandum or articles is a debt due from him to the company, and in England and Wales is of the nature of a specialty debt.

## 15 Memorandum and articles of company limited by guarantee

**15(1) [Provision re right to profits void]** In the case of a company limited by guarantee and not having a share capital, every provision in the memorandum or articles, or in any resolution of the company purporting to give any person a right to participate in the divisible profits of the company otherwise than as a member, is void.

**15(2) [Provisions dividing into shares]** For purposes of provisions of this Act relating to the memorandum of a company limited by guarantee, and for those of section 1(4) and this section, every provision in the memorandum or articles, or in any resolution, of a company so limited purporting to divide the company's undertaking into shares or interests is to be treated as a provision for a share capital, notwithstanding that the nominal amount or number of the shares or interests is not specified by the provision.

## 16 Effect of alteration on company's members

**16(1) [Alterations not binding on members]** A member of a company is not bound by an alteration made in the memorandum or articles after the date on which he became a member, if and so far as the alteration–

(a) requires him to take or subscribe for more shares than the number held by him at the date on which the alteration is made; or

(b) in any way increases his liability as at that date to contribute to the company's share capital or otherwise to pay money to the company.

**16(2) [Exception]** Subsection (1) operates notwithstanding anything in the memorandum or articles; but it does not apply in a case where the member agrees in writing, either before or after the alteration is made, to be bound by the alteration.

## 17 Conditions in memorandum which could have been in articles

**17(1) [Alteration by special resolution]** A condition contained in a company's memorandum which could lawfully have been contained in articles of association instead of in the memorandum may be altered by the company by special resolution; but if an application is made to the court for the alteration to be cancelled, the alteration does not have effect except in so far as it is confirmed by the court.

**17(2) [Application of section]** This section–

(a) is subject to section 16, and also to Part XVII (court order protecting minority), and

(b) does not apply where the memorandum itself provides for or prohibits the alteration of all or any of the conditions above referred to, and does not authorise any variation or abrogation of the special rights of any class of members.

**17(3) [Application of parts of s. 5, 6]** Section 5 (except subsections (2)(b) and (8)) and section 6(1) to (3) apply in relation to any alteration and to any application made under this section as they apply in relation to alterations and applications under sections 4 to 6.

## 18 Amendments of memorandum or articles to be registered

**18(1) [Printed copy to registrar]** Where an alteration is made in a company's memorandum or articles by any statutory provision, whether contained in an Act of Parliament or in an instrument made under an Act, a printed copy of the Act or instrument shall, not later than 15 days after that provision comes into force, be forwarded to the registrar of companies and recorded by him.

**18(2) [Also printed copy of memorandum or articles as altered]** Where a company is required (by this section or otherwise) to send to the registrar any document making or evidencing an alteration in the company's memorandum or articles (other than a special resolution under section 4), the company shall send with it a printed copy of the memorandum or articles as altered.

**18(3) [Penalty on default]** If a company fails to comply with this section, the company and any officer of it who is in default is liable to a fine and, for continued contravention, to a daily default fine.

**Note**

S. 18 was previously European Communities Act 1972, s. 9(5) which in part implemented the First EC Company Law Directive (68/151).

## 19 Copies of memorandum and articles to be given to members

**19(1) [Copies to member on request]** A company shall, on being so required by any member, send to him a copy of the memorandum and of the articles (if any), and a copy of any Act of Parliament which alters the memorandum, subject to payment–

(a) in the case of a copy of the memorandum and of the articles, of 5 pence or such less sum as the company may prescribe, and

(b) in the case of a copy of an Act, of such sum not exceeding its published price as the company may require.

**19(2) [Penalty on default]** If a company makes default in complying with this section, the company and every officer of it who is in default is liable for each offence to a fine.

## 20 Issued copy of memorandum to embody alterations

**20(1) [Copies in accordance with alteration]** Where an alteration is made in a company's memorandum, every copy of the memorandum issued after the date of the alteration shall be in accordance with the alteration.

**20(2) [Penalty on default]** If, where any such alteration has been made, the company at any time after the date of the alteration issues any copies of the memorandum which are not in

(a) in the opinion of the Secretary of State would be likely to give the impression that the company is connected in any way with Her Majesty's Government or with any local authority; or

(b) includes any word or expression for the time being specified in regulations under section 29.

**"Local authority"** means any local authority within the meaning of the Local Government Act 1972 or the Local Government (Scotland) Act 1973, the Common Council of the City of London or the Council of the Isles of Scilly.

**26(3) [Determination of same name]** In determining for purposes of subsection (1)(c) whether one name is the same as another, there are to be disregarded–

(a) the definite article, where it is the first word of the name;

(b) the following words and expressions where they appear at the end of the name, that is to say–
"company" or its Welsh equivalent ("cwmni"),
"and company" or its Welsh equivalent ("a'r cwmni"),
"company limited" or its Welsh equivalent ("cwmni cyfyngedig"),
"and company limited" or its Welsh equivalent ("a'r cwmni cyfyngedig"),
"limited" or its Welsh equivalent ("cyfyngedig"),
"unlimited" or its Welsh equivalent ("anghyfyngedig"),
"public limited company" or its Welsh equivalent ("cwmni cyfyngedig cyhoeddus"), and
"investment company with variable capital" or its Welsh equivalent ("cwmni buddsoddi â chyfalaf newidiol");

(c) abbreviations of any of those words or expressions where they appear at the end of the name; and

(d) type and case of letters, accents, spaces between letters and punctuation marks;

and "and" and "&" are to be taken as the same.

**History**
In s. 26(3)(b) the words from "and "investment company"" to the end inserted and the former word "and" appearing after the word "anghyfyngedig" omitted by the Open-Ended Investment Companies (Investment Companies with Variable Capital) Regulations 1996 (SI 1996/2827), reg. 1, 75 and Sch. 8, para. 4 as from 6 January 1997.

## 27 Alternatives of statutory designations

**27(1) [Specified alternative abbreviations]** A company which by any provision of this Act is either required or entitled to include in its name, as its last part, any of the words specified in subsection (4) below may, instead of those words, include as the last part of the name the abbreviations there specified as alternatives in relation to those words.

**27(2) [Reference to name of company]** A reference in this Act to the name of a company or to the inclusion of any of those words in a company's name includes a reference to the name including (in place of any of the words so specified) the appropriate alternative, or to the inclusion of the appropriate alternative, as the case may be.

**27(3) [Reference to company not including words in name]** A provision of this Act requiring a company not to include any of those words in its name also requires it not to include the abbreviated alternative specified in subsection (4).

**27(4) [Abbreviations]** For the purposes of this section–

(a) the alternative of "limited" is "ltd.";

(b) the alternative of "public limited company" is "p.l.c.";

(c) the alternative of "cyfyngedig" is "cyf."; and

(d) the alternative of "cwmni cyfyngedig cyhoeddus" is "c.c.c.".

## 28 Change of name

**28(1) [Change by special resolution]** A company may by special resolution change its name (but subject to section 31 in the case of a company which has received a direction under subsection (2) of that section from the Secretary of State).

**28(2) [Direction to change same or similar name]** Where a company has been registered by a name which–

(a) is the same as or, in the opinion of the Secretary of State, too like a name appearing at the time of the registration in the registrar's index of company names, or

(b) is the same as or, in the opinion of the secretary of State, too like a name which should have appeared in that index at that time,

the Secretary of State may within 12 months of that time, in writing, direct the company to change its name within such period as he may specify.

Section 26(3) applies in determining under this subsection whether a name is the same as or too like another.

**28(3) [Direction where misleading information given]** If it appears to the Secretary of State that misleading information has been given for the purpose of a company's registration with a particular name, or that undertakings or assurances have been given for that purpose and have not been fulfilled, he may within 5 years of the date of its registration with that name in writing direct the company to change its name within such period as he may specify.

**28(4) [Extension of time for direction under s. 28(2), (3)]** Where a direction has been given under subsection (2) or (3), the Secretary of State may by a further direction in writing extend the period within which the company is to change its name, at any time before the end of that period.

**28(5) [Daily default]** A company which fails to comply with a direction under this section, and any officer of it who is in default, is liable to a fine and, for continued contravention, to a daily default fine.

**28(6) [New company name]** Where a company changes its name under this section, the registrar of companies shall (subject to section 26) enter the new name on the register in place of the former name, and shall issue a certificate of incorporation altered to meet the circumstances of the case; and the change of name has effect from the date on which the altered certificate is issued.

**28(7) [Effect of change of name]** A change of name by a company under this section does not affect any rights or obligations of the company or render defective any legal proceedings by or against it; and any legal proceedings that might have been continued or commenced against it by its former name may be continued or commenced against it by its new name.

# 29 Regulations about names

**29(1) [Regulations by Secretary of State]** The Secretary of State may by regulations–

(a) specify words or expressions for the registration of which as or as part of a company's corporate name his approval is required under section 26(2)(b), and

(b) in relation to any such word or expression, specify a Government department or other body as the relevant body for purposes of the following subsection.

**29(2) [Request to relevant body under s. 29(1)(b)]** Where a company proposes to have as, or as part of, its corporate name any such word or expression and a Government department or other body is specified under subsection (1)(b) in relation to that word or expression, a request shall be made (in writing) to the relevant body to indicate whether (and if so why) it has any objections to the proposal; and the person to make the request is–

(a) in the case of a company seeking to be registered under this Part, the person making the statutory declaration required by section 12(3),

(b) in the case of a company seeking to be registered under section 680, the persons making the statutory declaration required by section 686(2), and

(c) in any other case, a director or secretary of the company concerned.

**29(3) [Statement re request in s. 29(2) to registrar]** The person who has made that request to the relevant body shall submit to the registrar of companies a statement that it has been made and a copy of any response received from that body, together with–

(a) the requisite statutory declaration, or

(b) a copy of the special resolution changing the company's name,

according as the case is one or other of those mentioned in subsection (2).

**29(4) [Non-application of s. 709, 710]** Sections 709 and 710 (public rights of inspection of documents kept by registrar of companies) do not apply to documents sent under subsection (3) of this section.

**29(5) [Transitional provisions etc.]** Regulations under this section may contain such transitional provisions and savings as the Secretary of State thinks appropriate and may make different provision for different cases or classes of case.

**29(6) [Approval of regulations etc.]** The regulations shall be made by statutory instrument, to be laid before Parliament after it is made; and the regulations shall cease to have effect at the end of 28 days beginning with the day on which the regulations were made (but without prejudice to anything previously done by virtue of them or to the making of new regulations), unless during that period they are approved by resolution of each House. In reckoning that period, no account is to be taken of any time during which Parliament is dissolved or prorogued or during which both Houses are adjourned for more than 4 days.

**Note**
See the Company and Business Names Regulations 1981 (SI 1981/1685), as amended.

## 30 Exemption from requirement of "limited" as part of the name

**30(1) [Certain companies exempt]** Certain companies are exempt from requirements of this Act relating to the use of "limited" as part of the company name.

**30(2) [Exempt companies]** A private company limited by guarantee is exempt from those requirements, and so too is a company which on 25th February 1982 was a private company limited by shares with a name which, by virtue of a licence under section 19 of the Companies Act 1948, did not include "limited"; but in either case the company must, to have the exemption, comply with the requirements of the following subsection.

**30(3) [Requirements for exemption]** Those requirements are that–

(a) the objects of the company are (or, in the case of a company about to be registered, are to be) the promotion of commerce, art, science, education, religion, charity or any profession, and anything incidental or conducive to any of those objects; and

(b) the company's memorandum or articles–
   (i) require its profits (if any) or other income to be applied in promoting its objects,
   (ii) prohibit the payment of dividends to its members, and
   (iii) require all the assets which would otherwise be available to its members generally to be transferred on its winding up either to another body with objects similar to its own or to another body the objects of which are the promotion of charity and anything incidental or conducive thereto (whether or not the body is a member of the company).

**30(4) [Statutory declaration to registrar]** A statutory declaration that a company complies with the requirements of subsection (3), may be delivered to the registrar of companies, who may accept the declaration as sufficient evidence of the matters stated in it; and the registrar may refuse to register a company by a name which does not include the word "limited" unless such a declaration has been delivered to him.

**30(5) [Requirements for statutory declaration in s. 30(4)]** The statutory declaration must be in the prescribed form and be made–

(a) in the case of a company to be formed, by a solicitor engaged in its formation or by a person named as director or secretary in the statement delivered under section 10(2);

(b) in the case of a company to be registered in pursuance of section 680, by two or more directors or other principal officers of the company; and

(c) in the case of a company proposing to change its name so that it ceases to have the word "limited" as part of its name, by a director or secretary of the company.

**Note**
See the Companies (Forms) (Amendment) Regulations 1995 (SI 1995/736).

**30(6) [References to "limited"]** References in this section to the word "limited" include (in an appropriate case) its Welsh equivalent ("cyfyngedig"), and the appropriate alternative ("ltd." or "cyf.", as the case may be).

**30(7) [Additional exemption]** A company which is exempt from requirements relating to the use of "limited" and does not include that word as part of its name, is also exempt from the requirements of this Act relating to the publication of its name and the sending of lists of members to the registrar of companies.

**Note**
See the Companies (Welsh Language Forms and Documents) (No. 2) Regulations 1995 (SI 1995/1480).

## 31 Provisions applying to company exempt under s. 30

**31(1) [Memorandum and articles of exempt company not to be altered]** A company which is exempt under section 30 and whose name does not include "limited" shall not alter its memorandum or articles of association so that it ceases to comply with the requirements of subsection (3) of that section.

**31(2) [Exempt company contravening requirements]** If it appears to the Secretary of State that such a company–

(a) has carried on any business other than the promotion of any of the objects mentioned in that subsection, or

(b) has applied any of its profits or other income otherwise than in promoting such objects, or

(c) has paid a dividend to any of its members,

he may, in writing, direct the company to change its name by resolution of the directors within such period as may be specified in the direction, so that its name ends with "limited".

A resolution passed by the directors in compliance with a direction under this subsection is subject to section 380 of this Act (copy to be forwarded to the registrar of companies within 15 days).

**31(3) [Company directed under s. 31(2)]** A company which has received a direction under subsection (2) shall not thereafter be registered by a name which does not include "limited", without the approval of the Secretary of State.

**31(4) [References to "limited"]** References in this section to the word "limited" include (in an appropriate case) its Welsh equivalent ("cyfyngedig"), and the appropriate alternative ("ltd." or "cyf.", as the case may be).

**31(5) [Penalty for contravention of s. 31(1)]** A company which contravenes subsection (1), and any officer of it who is in default, is liable to a fine and, for continued contravention, to a daily default fine.

**31(6) [Failure to comply with s. 31(2) direction]** A company which fails to comply with a direction by the Secretary of State under subsection (2), and any officer of the company who is in default, is liable to a fine and, for continued contravention, to a daily default fine.

## 32 Power to require company to abandon misleading name

**32(1) [Direction to change name]** If in the Secretary of State's opinion the name by which a company is registered gives so misleading an indication of the nature of its activities as to be likely to cause harm to the public, he may direct it to change its name.

**32(2) [Time for compliance with direction]** The direction must, if not duly made the subject of an application to the court under the following subsection, be complied with within a period of 6 weeks from the date of the direction or such longer period as the Secretary of State may think fit to allow.

**32(3) [Application to court to set aside direction]** The company may, within a period of 3 weeks from the date of the direction, apply to the court to set it aside; and the court may set the direction aside or confirm it and, if it confirms the direction, shall specify a period within which it must be complied with.

**32(4) [Penalty for non-compliance with direction]** If a company makes default in complying with a direction under this section, it is liable to a fine and, for continued contravention, to a daily default fine.

**32(5) [New certificate of incorporation on change of name]** Where a company changes its name under this section, the registrar shall (subject to section 26) enter the new name on the register in place of the former name, and shall issue a certificate of incorporation altered to meet the circumstances of the case; and the change of name has effect from the date on which the altered certificate is issued.

**32(6) [Effect of change of name]** A change of name by a company under this section does not affect any of the rights or obligations of the company, or render defective any legal proceedings by or against it; and any legal proceedings that might have been continued or commended against it by its former name may be continued or commenced against it by its new name.

## 33 Prohibition on trading under misleading name

**33(1) [Non-public company using misleading title]** A person who is not a public company is guilty of an offence if he carries on any trade, profession or business under a name which includes, as its last part, the words "public limited company" or their equivalent in Welsh ("cwmni cyfyngedig cyhoeddus").

**33(2) [Public company giving false impression]** A public company is guilty of an offence if, in circumstances in which the fact that it is a public company is likely to be material to any person, it uses a name which may reasonably be expected to give the impression that it is a private company.

**33(3) [Penalty]** A person guilty of an offence under subsection (1) or (2) and, if that person is a company, any officer of the company who is in default, is liable to a fine and, for continued contravention, to a daily default fine.

## 34 Penalty for improper use of "limited" or "cyfyngedig"

**34** If any person trades or carries on business under a name or title of which "limited" or "cyfyngedig", or any contraction or imitation of either of those words, is the last word, that person, unless duly incorporated with limited liability, is liable to a fine and, for continued contravention, to a daily default fine.

# Chapter III – A Company's Capacity; Formalities of Carrying on Business

## 35 A company's capacity not limited by its memorandum

**35(1) [Validity of company's acts]** The validity of an act done by a company shall not be called into question on the ground of lack of capacity by reason of anything in the company's memorandum.

**35(2) [Proceedings by member]** A member of a company may bring proceedings to restrain the doing of an act which but for subsection (1) would be beyond the company's capacity; but no such proceedings shall lie in respect of an act to be done in fulfilment of a legal obligation arising from a previous act of the company.

**35(3) [Directors' duty]** It remains the duty of the directors to observe any limitations on their powers flowing from the company's memorandum; and action by the directors which but for subsection (1) would be beyond the company's capacity may only be ratified by the company by special resolution.

A resolution ratifying such action shall not affect any liability incurred by the directors or any other person; relief from any such liability must be agreed to separately by special resolution.

**35(4) [Restriction]** The operation of this section is restricted by section 65(1) of the Charities Act 1993 and section 112(3) of the Companies Act 1989 in relation to companies which are charities; and section 322A below (invalidity of certain transactions to which directors or their associates are parties) has effect notwithstanding this section.

**History**

In s. 35(4) the words "section 65(1) of the Charities Act 1993" substituted for the former words "section 30B(1) of the Charities Act 1960" by Charities Act 1993, s. 98(1), 99(1) and Sch. 6, para. 20(1), (2) as from 1 August 1993.
See also history note after s. 35B.

**Note**

S. 35 in its original form (see history note after s. 35B) was previously European Communities Act 1972, s. 9(1) which in part implemented the First EC Company Law Directive (68/151).

## 35A Power of directors to bind the company

**35A(1) [Power free of limitation under constitution]** In favour of a person dealing with a company in good faith, the power of the board of directors to bind the company, or authorise others to do so, shall be deemed to be free of any limitation under the company's constitution.

**35A(2) [Interpretation]** For this purpose–

(a) a person "deals with" a company if he is a party to any transaction or other act to which the company is a party;

(b) a person shall not be regarded as acting in bad faith by reason only of his knowing that an act is beyond the powers of the directors under the company's constitution; and

(c) a person shall be presumed to have acted in good faith unless the contrary is proved.

**35A(3) [Limitations on directors' powers]** The references above to limitations on the directors' powers under the company's constitution include limitations deriving–

(a) from a resolution of the company in general meeting or a meeting of any class of shareholders, or

(b) from any agreement between the members of the company or of any class of shareholders.

**35A(4) [Right of member to bring proceedings]** Subsection (1) does not affect any right of a member of the company to bring proceedings to restrain the doing of an act which is beyond the powers of the directors; but no such proceedings shall lie in respect of an act to be done in fulfilment of a legal obligation arising from a previous act of the company.

**35A(5) [Liability of directors]** Nor does that subsection affect any liability incurred by the directors, or any other person, by reason of the directors' exceeding their powers.

**35A(6) [Restriction]** The operation of this section is restricted by section 65(1) of the Charities Act 1993 and section 112(3) of the Companies Act 1989 in relation to companies which are charities; and section 322A below (invalidity of certain transactions to which directors or their associates are parties) has effect notwithstanding this section.

**History**

In s. 35A(6) the words "section 65(1) of the Charities Act 1993" substituted for the former words "section 30B(1) of the Charities Act 1960" by Charities Act 1993, s. 98(1), 99(1) and Sch. 6, para. 20(1), (2) as from 1 August 1993.
See also history note after s. 35B.

## 35B No duty to enquire as to capacity of company or authority of directors

**35B** A party to a transaction with a company is not bound to enquire as to whether it is permitted by the company's memorandum or as to any limitation on the powers of the board of directors to bind the company or authorise others to do so.

**History**

S. 35–35B substituted for the former s. 35 by CA 1989, s. 108 as from 4 February 1991 subject to transitional and saving provisions (see SI 1990/2569 (C 68), art. 4(a), 7); the former s. 35 read as follows:

"**35 Company's capacity: power of directors to bind it**

**35(1)** In favour of a person dealing with a company in good faith, any transaction decided on by the directors is deemed to be one which it is within the capacity of the company to enter into, and the power of the directors to bind the company is deemed to be free of any limitation under the memorandum or articles.

**(2)** A party to a transaction so decided on is not bound to enquire as to the capacity of the company to enter into it or as to any such limitation on the powers of the directors, and is presumed to have acted in good faith unless the contrary is proved."

**Note**
See note to s. 35 above.

## 36 Company contracts: England and Wales

**36** Under the law of England and Wales a contract may be made–

(a) by a company, by writing under its common seal, or

(b) on behalf of a company, by any person acting under its authority, express or implied;

and any formalities required by law in the case of a contract made by an individual also apply, unless a contrary intention appears, to a contract made by or on behalf of a company.

**History**
S. 36 substituted by CA 1989, s. 130(1) as from 31 July 1990 (see SI 1990/1392 (C 41), art. 2(b)); s. 36 formerly read as follows:

**"36 Form of company contracts**

**36(1)** Contracts on behalf of a company may be made as follows–

(a) a contract which if made between private persons would be by law required to be in writing, and if made according to the law of England and Wales to be under seal, may be made on behalf of the company in writing under the company's common seal;

(b) a contract which if made between private persons would be by law required to be in writing, signed by the parties to be charged therewith, may be made on behalf of the company in writing signed by any person acting under its authority, express or implied;

(c) a contract which if made between private persons would by law be valid although made by parol only, and not reduced into writing, may be made by parol on behalf of the company by any person acting under its authority, express or implied.

**(2)** A contract made according to this section–

(a) is effectual in law, and binds the company and its successors and all other parties to it;

(b) may be varied or discharged in the same manner in which it is authorised by this section to be made.

**(3)** A deed to which a company is a party is held to be validly executed according to the law of Scotland on behalf of the company if it is executed in accordance with this Act or is sealed with the company's common seal and subscribed on behalf of the company by two of the directors, or by a director and the secretary; and such subscription on behalf of the company is binding whether attested by witnesses or not.

**(4)** Where a contract purports to be made by a company, or by a person as agent for a company, at a time when the company has not been formed, then subject to any agreement to the contrary the contract has effect as one entered into by the person purporting to act for the company or as agent for it, and he is personally liable on the contract accordingly."

**Note**
S. 36(4) in the original section (see above) was previously European Communities Act 1972, s. 9(2) which in part implemented the First EC Company Law Directive (68/151).
See note after s. 36C re application to companies incorporated outside Great Britain.

## 36A Execution of documents: England and Wales

**36A(1) [Application]** Under the law of England and Wales the following provisions have effect with respect to the execution of documents by a company.

**36A(2) [Execution by common seal]** A document is executed by a company by the affixing of its common seal.

**36A(3) [Common seal not necessary]** A company need not have a common seal, however, and the following subsections apply whether it does or not.

**36A(4) [Execution by director(s), secretary]** A document signed by a director and the secretary of a company, or by two directors of a company, and expressed (in whatever form of words) to be executed by the company has the same effect as if executed under the common seal of the company.

**36A(5) [Execution as deed]** A document executed by a company which makes it clear on its face that it is intended by the person or persons making it to be a deed has effect, upon delivery, as a deed; and it shall be presumed, unless a contrary intention is proved, to be delivered upon its being so executed.

**36A(6) [Deemed execution in favour of purchaser]** In favour of a purchaser a document shall be deemed to have been duly executed by a company if it purports to be signed by a director and the secretary of the company, or by two directors of the company, and, where it makes it clear on its face that it is intended by the person or persons making it to be a deed, to have been delivered upon its being executed.

A **"purchaser"** means a purchaser in good faith for valuable consideration and includes a lessee, mortgagee or other person who for valuable consideration acquires an interest in property.

**History**
S. 36A inserted by CA 1989, s. 130(2) as from 31 July 1990 (see SI 1990/1392 (C 41), art. 2(b)).
**Note**
See note after s. 36C re application to companies incorporated outside Great Britain.

## 36B Execution of documents by companies

**36B(1) [Company seal not necessary]** Notwithstanding the provisions of any enactment, a company need not have a company seal.

**36B(2) [Reference to execution by common seal]** For the purposes of any enactment–

(a) providing for a document to be executed by a company by affixing its common seal; or

(b) referring (in whatever terms) to a document so executed,

a document signed or subscribed by or on behalf of the company in accordance with the provisions of the Requirements of Writing (Scotland) Act 1995 shall have effect as if so executed.

**36B(3) ["Enactment"]** In this section **"enactment"** includes an enactment contained in a statutory instrument.

**History**
S. 36B substituted by Requirements of Writing (Scotland) Act 1995, s. 14(1), 15 and Sch. 4, para. 51 as from 1 August 1995; s. 36B formerly read as follows:

**"36B Execution of documents: Scotland**

**36B(1)** This section has effect in relation to the execution of any document by a company under the law of Scotland on or after 31 July 1990.

**(2)** For any purpose other than those mentioned in subsection (3) below, a document is validly executed by a company if it is signed on behalf of the company by a director or the secretary of the company or by a person authorised to sign the document on its behalf.

**(3)** For the purposes of any enactment or rule of law relating to the authentication of documents under the law of Scotland, a document is validly executed by a company if it is subscribed on behalf of the company by–
(a) two of the directors of the company;
(b) a director and the secretary of the company; or
(c) two persons authorised to subscribe the document on behalf of the company,
notwithstanding that such subscription is not attested by witnesses and the document is not sealed with the company's common seal.

**(4)** A document which bears to be executed by a company in accordance with subsection (3) above is, in relation to such execution, a probative document.

**(5)** Notwithstanding the provisions of any enactment (including an enactment contained in this section) a company need not have a common seal.

**(6)** For the purposes of any enactment providing for a document to be executed by a company by affixing its common seal or referring (in whatever terms) to a document so executed, a document signed or subscribed on behalf of the company by–
(a) two directors of the company;
(b) a director and the secretary of the company; or
(c) two persons authorised to sign or subscribe the document on behalf of the company,
shall have effect as if executed under the common seal of the company.

**(7)** In this section **"enactment"** includes an enactment contained in a statutory instrument.

**(8)** Subsections (2) and (3) above are–
(a) without prejudice to any other method of execution of documents by companies permitted by any enactment or rule of law; and
(b) subject to any other enactment making express provision, in relation to companies, as to the execution of a particular type of document."

(Previously s. 36B substituted by Law Reform (Miscellaneous Provisions) (Scotland) Act 1990, s. 72(1) as from 1 December 1990 (see SI 1990/2328 (C 60) (S 197), art. 3, Sch.); originally s. 36B – inserted by CA 1989, s. 130(2) as from 31 July 1990 (see SI 1990/1392 (C 41), art. 2(b)) – read as follows:

**"36B(1)** Under the law of Scotland the following provisions have effect with respect to the execution of documents by a company.

**(2)** A document–
(a) is signed by a company if it is signed on its behalf by a director, or by the secretary, of the company or by a person authorised to sign the document on its behalf, and
(b) is subscribed by a company if it is subscribed on its behalf by being signed in accordance with the provisions of paragraph (a) at the end of the last page.

**(3)** A document shall be presumed, unless the contrary is shown, to have been subscribed by a company in accordance with subsection (2) if–
(a) it bears to have been subscribed on behalf of the company by a director, or by the secretary, of the company or by a person bearing to have been authorised to subscribe the document on its behalf; and
(b) it bears–
(i) to have been signed by a person as a witness of the subscription of the director, secretary or other person subscribing on behalf of the company; or

(ii) (if the subscription is not so witnessed) to have been sealed with the common seal of the company.

**(4)** A presumption under subsection (3) as to subscription of a document does not include a presumption–

(a) that a person bearing to subscribe the document as a director or the secretary of the company was such director or secretary; or

(b) that a person subscribing the document on behalf of the company bearing to have been authorised to do so was authorised to do so.

**(5)** Notwithstanding subsection (3)(b)(ii), a company need not have a common seal.

**(6)** Any reference in any enactment (including an enactment contained in a subordinate instrument) to a probative document shall, in relation to a document executed by a company after the commencement of section 130 of the Companies Act 1989, be construed as a reference to a document which is presumed under subsection (3) above to be subscribed by the company.

**(7)** Subsections (1) to (4) above do not apply where an enactment (including an enactment contained in a subordinate instrument) provides otherwise.")

**Note**

See note after s. 36C re application to companies incorporated outside Great Britain.

# 36C Pre-incorporation contracts, deeds and obligations

**36C(1) [Contract by company not formed]** A contract which purports to be made by or on behalf of a company at a time when the company has not been formed has effect, subject to any agreement to the contrary, as one made with the person purporting to act for the company or as agent for it, and he is personally liable on the contract accordingly.

**36C(2) [Application of s. 36C(1)]** Subsection (1) applies–

(a) to the making of a deed under the law of England and Wales, and

(b) to the undertaking of an obligation under the law of Scotland,

as it applies to the making of a contract.

**History**

S. 36C inserted by CA 1989, s. 130(4) as from 31 July 1990 (see SI 1990/1392 (C 41), art. 2(b)).

**Note**

For application of s. 36–36C to companies incorporated outside Great Britain, see the Foreign Companies (Execution of Documents) Regulations 1994 (SI 1994/950).

# 37 Bills of exchange and promissory notes

**37** A bill of exchange or promissory note is deemed to have been made, accepted or endorsed on behalf of a company if made, accepted or endorsed in the name of, or by or on behalf or on account of, the company by a person acting under its authority.

# 38 Execution of deeds abroad

**38(1) [Execution by attorney]** A company may, by writing under its common seal, empower any person, either generally or in respect of any specified matters, as its attorney, to execute deeds on its behalf in any place elsewhere than in the United Kingdom.

**History**

In s. 38(1) the words "under the law of England and Wales" formerly appearing after the words "a company may" ceased to have effect and repealed by Law Reform (Miscellaneous Provisions) (Scotland) Act 1990, s. 74, Sch. 8, para. 33 (1), (2) and Sch. 9 as from 1 December 1990 (see SI 1990/2328 (C 60) (S 197), art. 3, Sch.); those words previously inserted by CA 1989, s. 130(7) and Sch. 17, para. 1(1), (2) as from 31 July 1990 (see SI 1990/1392 (C 41), art. 2(b)).

**38(2) [Effect]** A deed executed by such an attorney on behalf of the company has the same effect as if it were executed under the company's common seal.

**History**

S. 38(2) substituted by CA 1989, s. 130(7) and Sch. 17, para. 1(1), (3) as from 31 July 1990 (see SI 1990/1392 (C 41), art. 2(b)); s. 38(2) formerly read as follows:

"A deed signed by such an attorney on behalf of the company and under his seal binds the company and has the same effect as if it were under the company's common seal."

**38(3) [Extent]** This section does not extend to Scotland.

**History**

S. 38(3) inserted by Requirements of Writing (Scotland) Act 1995, s. 14(1), 15 and sch. 4, para. 52 as from 1 August 1995.

# 39 Power of company to have official seal for use abroad

**39(1) [Official seal]** A company which has a common seal whose objects require or comprise the transaction of business in foreign countries may, if authorised by its articles, have for use in any territory, district, or place elsewhere than in the United Kingdom, an official seal, which shall be a facsimile of its common seal, with the addition on its face of the name of every territory, district or place where it is to be used.

**History**
In s. 39(1) the words "which has a common seal" inserted and the words "its common seal" substituted for the former words "the common seal of the company" by CA 1989, s. 130(7) and Sch. 17, para. 2(1), (2) as from 31 July 1990 (see SI 1990/1392 (C 41), art. 2(b)).

**39(2) [Effect]** The official seal when duly affixed to a document has the same effect as the company's common seal.

**History**
S. 39(1) substituted by CA 1989, s. 130(7) and Sch. 17, para. 2(1), (3) as from 31 July 1990 (see SI 1990/1392 (C 41), art. 2(b)); s. 39(2) formerly read as follows:
"A deed or other document to which the official seal is duly affixed binds the company as if it had been sealed with the company's common seal."

**39(2A) [Extent]** Subsection (2) does not extend to Scotland.

**History**
S. 39(2A) inserted by Requirements of Writing (Scotland) Act 1995, s. 14(1), 15 and Sch. 4, para. 53(a) as from 1 August 1995.

**39(3) [Authority to agent to affix official seal]** A company having an official seal for use in any such territory, district or place may, by writing under its common seal or as respects Scotland by writing subscribed in accordance with the Requirements of Writing (Scotland) Act 1995 authorise any person appointed for the purpose in that territory, district or place to affix the official seal to any deed or other document to which the company is party in that territory, district or place.

**History**
In s. 39(3) the words "or as respects Scotland by writing subscribed in accordance with the Requirements of Writing (Scotland) Act 1995" inserted by Requirements of Writing (Scotland) Act 1995, s. 14(1), 15 and Sch. 4, para. 53(b) as from 1 August 1995. Previously in s. 39(3) the words "or, in the case of a company registered in Scotland, subscribed in accordance with section 36B," formerly appearing after the words "by writing under its common seal" ceased to have effect and repealed by Law Reform (Miscellaneous Provisions) (Scotland) Act 1990, s. 74, Sch. 8, para. 33 (1), (3) and Sch. 9 as from 1 December 1990 (see SI 1990/2328 (C 60) (S 197), art. 3, Sch.); those words originally inserted by CA 1989, s. 130(7) and Sch. 17, para. 2(1), (4) as from 31 July 1990 (see SI 1990/1392 (C 41), art. 2(b)).

**39(4) [Duration of agent's authority]** As between the company and a person dealing with such an agent, the agent's authority continues during the period (if any) mentioned in the instrument conferring the authority, or if no period is there mentioned, then until notice of the revocation or determination of the agent's authority has been given to the person dealing with him.

**39(5) [Certificate or deed etc.]** The person affixing the official seal shall certify in writing on the deed or other instrument to which the seal is affixed the date on which and the place at which it is affixed.

## 40 Official seal for share certificates, etc.

**40(1) [Facsimile of common seal]** A company which has a common seal may have, for use for sealing securities issued by the company and for sealing documents creating or evidencing securities so issued, an official seal which is a facsimile of its common seal with the addition on its face of the word "Securities".

The official seal when duly affixed to a document has the same effect as the company's common seal.

**History**
In s. 40(1) the words "which has a common seal" inserted, the words "its common seal" substituted for the former words "the company's common seal" and the words "The official" to the end added by CA 1989, s. 130(7) and Sch. 17, para. 3 as from 31 July 1990 (see SI 1990/1392 (C 41), art. 2(b)).

**40(2) [Scotland]** Nothing in this section shall affect the right of a company registered in Scotland to subscribe such securities and documents in accordance with the Requirements of Writing (Scotland) Act 1995.

**History**
S. 40(2) inserted by Requirements of Writing (Scotland) Act 1995, s. 14(1), 15 and Sch. para. 54 as from 1 August 1995.

## 41 Authentication of documents

**41** A document or proceeding requiring authentication by a company is sufficiently authenticated for the purposes of the law of England and Wales by the signature of a director, secretary or other authorised officer of the company.

**History**
In s. 41 the words "is sufficiently authenticated" to the end substituted by CA 1989, s. 130(7) and Sch. 17, para. 4 as from 31 July 1990 (see SI 1990/1392 (C 41), art. 2(b)); the former words read as follows: "may be signed by a director, secretary or other authorised officer of the company, and need not be under the company's common seal."

## 42 Events affecting a company's status

**42(1) [Official notification etc.]** A company is not entitled to rely against other persons on the happening of any of the following events–

(a) the making of a winding-up order in respect of the company, or the appointment of a liquidator in a voluntary winding up of the company, or

(b) any alteration of the company's memorandum or articles, or

(c) any change among the company's directors, or

(d) (as regards service of any document on the company) any change in the situation of the company's registered office,

if the event had not been officially notified at the material time and is not shown by the company to have been known at that time to the person concerned, or if the material time fell on or before the 15th day after the date of official notification (or, where the 15th day was a non-business day, on or before the next day that was not) and it is shown that the person concerned was unavoidably prevented from knowing of the event at that time.

**42(2) [Definitions]** In subsection (1)–

(a) **"official notification"** and **"officially notified"** have the meanings given by section 711(2) (registrar of companies to give public notice of the issue or receipt by him of certain documents), and

(b) **"non-business day"** means a Saturday or Sunday, Christmas Day, Good Friday and any other day which is a bank holiday in the part of Great Britain where the company is registered.

**Note**
S. 42 was previously European Communities Act 1972, s. 9 (3), (4) which in part implemented the First EC Company Law Directive (68/151).

# PART II – RE-REGISTRATION AS A MEANS OF ALTERING A COMPANY'S STATUS

### PRIVATE COMPANY BECOMING PUBLIC

## 43 Re-registration of private company as public

**43(1) [Requirements for re-registration]** Subject to this and the following five sections, a private company (other than a company not having a share capital) may be re-registered as a public company if–

(a) a special resolution that it should be so re-registered is passed; and

(b) an application for re-registration is delivered to the registrar of companies, together with the necessary documents.

A company cannot be re-registered under this section if it has previously been re-registered as unlimited.

**43(2) [Special resolution]** The special resolution must–

(a) alter the company's memorandum so that it states that the company is to be a public company; and

(b) make such other alterations in the memorandum as are necessary to bring it (in substance and in form) into conformity with the requirements of this Act with respect to the memorandum of a public company (the alterations to include compliance with section 25(1) as regards the company's name); and

(c) make such alterations in the company's articles as are requisite in the circumstances.

**43(3) [Requirements for application under s. 43(1)(b)]** The application must be in the prescribed form and be signed by a director or secretary of the company; and the documents to be delivered with it are the following–

(a) a printed copy of the memorandum and articles as altered in pursuance of the resolution;

(b) a copy of a written statement by the company's auditors that in their opinion the relevant balance sheet shows that at the balance sheet date the amount of the company's net assets (within the meaning given to that expression by section 264(2)) was not less than the aggregate of its called-up share capital and undistributable reserves;

(c) a copy of the relevant balance sheet, together with a copy of an unqualified report (defined in section 46) by the company's auditors in relation to that balance sheet;

(d) if section 44 applies, a copy of the valuation report under subsection (2)(b) of that section; and

(e) a statutory declaration in the prescribed form by a director or secretary of the company–
   (i) that the special resolution required by this section has been passed and that the conditions of the following two sections (so far as applicable have been satisfied, and
   (ii) that, between the balance sheet date and the application for re-registration, there has been no change in the company's financial position that has resulted in the amount of its net assets becoming less than the aggregate of its called-up share capital and undistributable reserves.

**Note**
See the Companies (Forms) (Amendment) Regulations 1995 (SI 1995/736).

**43(4) ["Relevant balance sheet"] "Relevant balance sheet"** means a balance sheet prepared as at a date not more than 7 months before the company's application under this section.

**43(5) [Change of company name]** A resolution that a company be re-registered as a public company may change the company name by deleting the word "company" or the words "and company", or its or their equivalent in Welsh ("cwmni", "a'r cwmni"), including any abbreviation of them.

# 44 Consideration for shares recently allotted to be valued

**44(1) [Application of section]** The following applies if shares have been allotted by the company between the date as at which the relevant balance sheet was prepared and the passing of the special resolution under section 43, and those shares were allotted as fully or partly paid up as to their nominal value or any premium on them otherwise than in cash.

**44(2) [Conditions for s. 43 application]** Subject to the following provisions, the registrar of companies shall not entertain an application by the company under section 43 unless beforehand–

(a) the consideration for the allotment has been valued in accordance with section 108, and

(b) a report with respect to the value of the consideration has been made to the company (in accordance with that section) during the 6 months immediately preceding the allotment of the shares.

**44(3) [Consideration for the allotment]** Where an amount standing to the credit of any of the company's reserve accounts, or of its profit and loss account, has been applied in paying up (to any extent) any of the shares allotted or any premium on those shares, the amount applied does not count as consideration for the allotment, and accordingly subsection (2) does not apply to it.

**44(4) [Non-application of s. 44(2)]** Subsection (2) does not apply if the allotment is in connection with an arrangement providing for it to be on terms that the whole or part of the consideration for the shares allotted is to be provided by the transfer to the company or the cancellation of all or some of the shares, or of all or some of the shares of a particular class, in another company (with or without the issue to the company applying under section 43 of shares, or of shares of any particular class, in that other company).

**44(5) [Qualification to s. 44(4)]** But subsection (4) does not exclude the application of subsection (2), unless under the arrangement it is open to all the holders of the shares of the other

(c) the provisions of this Act apply accordingly to the memorandum and articles as altered.

**50(3) [Certificate conclusive evidence]** The certificate is conclusive evidence that the requirements of section 49 in respect of re-registration and of matters precedent and incidental to it have been complied with, and that the company was authorised to be re-registered under this Act in pursuance of that section and was duly so re-registered.

UNLIMITED COMPANY BECOMING LIMITED

# 51 Re-registration of unlimited company as limited

**51(1) [Re-registration – special resolution etc.]** Subject as follows, a company which is registered as unlimited may be re-registered as limited if a special resolution that it should be so re-registered is passed, and the requirements of this section are complied with in respect of the resolution and otherwise.

**51(2) [Limitations]** A company cannot under this section be re-registered as a public company; and a company is excluded from registering under it if it is unlimited by virtue of re-registration under section 43 of the Companies Act 1967 or section 49 of this Act.

**51(3) [Requirements for special resolution]** The special resolution must state whether the company is to be limited by shares or by guarantee and–

(a) if it is to be limited by shares, must state what the share capital is to be and provide for the making of such alterations in the memorandum as are necessary to bring it (in substance and in form) into conformity with the requirements of this Act with respect to the memorandum of a company so limited, and such alterations in the articles as are requisite in the circumstances;

(b) if it is to be limited by guarantee, must provide for the making of such alterations in its memorandum and articles as are necessary to bring them (in substance and in form) into conformity with the requirements of this Act with respect to the memorandum and articles of a company so limited.

**51(4) [Time limit for documents to registrar]** The special resolution is subject to section 380 of this Act (copy to be forwarded to registrar within 15 days); and an application for the company to be re-registered as limited, framed in the prescribed form and signed by a director or by the secretary of the company, must be lodged with the registrar of companies, together with the necessary documents, not earlier than the day on which the copy of the resolution forwarded under section 380 is received by him.

**Note**
See the Companies (Forms) (Amendment) Regulations 1995 (SI 1995/736).

**51(5) [Documents to be lodged with registrar]** The documents to be lodged with the registrar are–

(a) a printed copy of the memorandum as altered in pursuance of the resolution; and

(b) a printed copy of the articles as so altered.

**51(6) [Non-application of section]** This section does not apply in relation to the re-registration of an unlimited company as a public company under section 43.

# 52 Certification of re-registration under s. 51

**52(1) [Certificate from registrar]** The registrar shall retain the application and other documents lodged with him under section 51, and shall issue to the company a certificate of incorporation appropriate to the status to be assumed by the company by virtue of that section.

**52(2) [Effect of issue of certificate]** On the issue of the certificate–

(a) the status of the company is, by virtue of the issue, changed from unlimited to limited; and

(b) the alterations in the memorandum specified in the resolution and the alterations in, and additions to, the articles so specified take effect.

**52(3) [Certificate conclusive evidence]** The certificate is conclusive evidence that the requirements of section 51 in respect of re-registration and of matters precedent and incidental to it have been complied with, and that the company was authorised to be re-registered in pursuance of that section and was duly so re-registered.

PUBLIC COMPANY BECOMING PRIVATE

## 53 Re-registration of public company as private

**53(1) [Requirements for re-registration]** A public company may be re-registered as a private company if–

(a) a special resolution complying with subsection (2) below that it should be so re-registered is passed and has not been cancelled by the court under the following section;

(b) an application for the purpose in the prescribed form and signed by a director or the secretary of the company is delivered to the registrar of companies, together with a printed copy of the memorandum and articles of the company as altered by the resolution; and

(c) the period during which an application for the cancellation of the resolution under the following section may be made has expired without any such application having been made; or

(d) where such an application has been made, the application has been withdrawn or an order has been made under section 54(5) confirming the resolution and a copy of that order has been delivered to the registrar.

**Note**
See the Companies (Forms) (Amendment) Regulations 1995 (SI 1995/736).

**53(2) [Alteration to memorandum etc.]** The special resolution must alter the company's memorandum so that it no longer states that the company is to be a public company and must make such other alterations in the company's memorandum and articles as are requisite in the circumstances.

**53(3) [Extent of section]** A company cannot under this section be re-registered otherwise than as a company limited by shares or by guarantee.

## 54 Litigated objection to resolution under s. 53

**54(1) [Application for cancellation of resolution]** Where a special resolution by a public company to be re-registered under section 53 as a private company has been passed, an application may be made to the court for the cancellation of that resolution.

**54(2) [Applicants]** The application may be made–

(a) by the holders of not less in the aggregate than 5 per cent in nominal value of the company's issued share capital or any class thereof;

(b) if the company is not limited by shares, by not less than 5 per cent of its members; or

(c) by not less than 50 of the company's members;

but not by a person who has consented to or voted in favour of the resolution.

**54(3) [Time limit etc. for application]** The application must be made within 28 days after the passing of the resolution and may be made on behalf of the persons entitled to make the application by such one or more of their number as they may appoint in writing for the purpose.

**54(4) [Notice to registrar]** If such an application is made, the company shall forthwith give notice in the prescribed form of that fact to the registrar of companies.

**Note**
See the Companies (Forms) (Amendment) Regulations 1995 (SI 1995/736).

**54(5) [Court order]** On the hearing of the application, the court shall make an order either cancelling or confirming the resolution and–

(a) may make that order on such terms and conditions as it thinks fit, and may (if it thinks fit) adjourn the proceedings in order that an arrangement may be made to the satisfaction of the court for the purchase of the interests of dissentient members; and

(b) may give such directions and make such orders as it thinks expedient for facilitating or carrying into effect any such arrangement.

**54(6) [Extent of court order]** The court's order may, if the court thinks fit, provide for the purchase by the company of the shares of any of its members and for the reduction accordingly of the company's capital, and may make such alterations in the company's memorandum and articles as may be required in consequence of that provision.

**54(7) [Office copy of order to registrar]** The company shall, within 15 days from the making of the court's order, or within such longer period as the court may at any time by order direct, deliver to the registrar of companies an office copy of the order.

**54(8) [If order requires no alteration to memorandum or articles]** If the court's order requires the company not to make any, or any specified, alteration in its memorandum or articles, the company has not then power without the leave of the court to make any such alteration in breach of the requirement.

**54(9) [Alteration by virtue of order]** An alteration in the memorandum or articles made by virtue of an order under this section, if not made by resolution of the company, is of the same effect as if duly made by resolution; and this Act applies accordingly to the memorandum or articles as so altered.

**54(10) [Penalty on default]** A company which fails to comply with subsection (4) or subsection (7), and any officer of it who is in default, is liable to a fine and, for continued contravention, to a daily default fine.

## 55 Certificate of re-registration under s. 53

**55(1) [Obligations of registrar]** If the registrar of companies is satisfied that a company may be re-registered under section 53, he shall–

(a) retain the application and other documents delivered to him under that section; and

(b) issue the company with a certificate of incorporation appropriate to a private company.

**55(2) [Effect of issue of certificate]** On the issue of the certificate–

(a) the company by virtue of the issue becomes a private company; and

(b) the alterations in the memorandum and articles set out in the resolution under section 53 take effect accordingly.

**55(3) [Certificate conclusive evidence]** The certificate is conclusive evidence–

(a) that the requirements of section 53 in respect of re-registration and of matters precedent and incidental to it have been complied with; and

(b) that the company is a private company.

# PART III – CAPITAL ISSUES

(Repealed by Financial Services Act 1986, s. 212(3) and Sch. 17, Pt. I as from 12 January 1987, 16 February 1987, 29 April 1988, 1 July 1988 and 19 June 1995 subject to exceptions in relation to s. 58–60 and s. 62.)

**History**

The repeal of Pt. III has effect as follows:

- as from 12 January 1987 re any investment listed or the subject of a listing application under Financial Services Act 1986, Pt. IV for all purposes relating to the admission of securities offered by or on behalf of a Minister of the Crown or a body corporate controlled by a Minister of the Crown or a subsidiary of such a body corporate to the Official List in respect of which an application is made after that date (see SI 1986/2246 (C 88));
- as from 16 February 1987 re any investment listed or the subject of a listing application under Financial Services Act 1986, Pt. IV for purposes relating to the admission of securities in respect of which an application is made after that date other than those referred to in the preceding paragraph and otherwise for all purposes (see SI 1986/2246 (C 88));
- as from 29 April 1988 as far as Pt. III would apply to a prospectus offering for subscription, or to any form of application for units in a body corporate which is a recognised scheme (see SI 1988/740 (C 22));
- as from 1 July 1988 as far as Pt. III would apply to a prospectus offering for subscription, or to any application form for, units in a body corporate which is an open-ended investment company (see SI 1988/740 (C 22));
- as from 19 June 1995 for all remaining purposes except CA 1985, s. 58, 59, 60, in so far as is necessary for the purposes of CA 1985, s. 81, 83, 246, 248, 744; and CA 1985, Sch. 3, para. 2, in so far as it is necessary for the purposes of CA 1985, s. 83(1)(a); and CA 1985, s. 62, in so far as is necessary for the purposes of CA 1985, s. 744 (see SI 1995/1538 (C 33)).

S. 56 and 57 formerly read as follows:

"Chapter I – Issues by Companies Registered, or to be Registered, in Great Britain

THE PROSPECTUS

**56 Matters to be stated, and reports to be set out, in prospectus**

**56(1)** Every prospectus issued by or on behalf of a company, or by or on behalf of any person who is or has been engaged or interested in the formation of the company, must comply–

(a) with Part I of Schedule 3 to this Act, as respects the matters to be stated in the prospectus, and

(b) with Part II of that Schedule, as respects the reports to be set out.

**(2)** It is unlawful to issue any form of application for shares in or debentures of a company unless the form is issued with a prospectus which complies with the requirements of this section.

**(3)** Subsection (2) does not apply if it is shown that the form of application was issued either–

(a) in connection with a bona fide invitation to a person to enter into an underwriting agreement with respect to the shares or debentures, or

(b) in relation to shares or debentures which were not offered to the public.

**(4)** If a person acts in contravention of subsection (2), he is liable to a fine.

**(5)** This section does not apply–

(a) to the issue to existing members or debenture holders of a company of a prospectus or form of application relating to shares in or debentures of the company, whether an applicant for shares or debentures will or will not have the right to renounce in favour of other persons, or

(b) to the issue of a prospectus or form of application relating to shares or debentures which are or are to be in all respects uniform with shares or debentures previously issued and for the time being listed on a prescribed stock exchange;

but subject to this, it applies to a prospectus or a form of application whether issued on or with reference to the formation of a company or subsequently.

**57 Attempted evasion of s. 56 to be void**

57 A condition requiring or binding an applicant for shares in or debentures of a company to waive compliance with any requirement of section 56, or purporting to affect him with notice of any contract, document or matter not specifically referred to in the prospectus, is void."

## 58 Document offering shares etc. for sale deemed a prospectus

**58(1) [Deemed prospectus]** If a company allots or agrees to allot its shares or debentures with a view to all or any of them being offered for sale to the public, any document by which the offer for sale to the public is made is deemed for all purposes a prospectus issued by the company.

**58(2) [Application of prospectus rules]** All enactments and rules of law as to the contents of prospectuses, and to liability in respect of statements in and omissions from prospectuses, or otherwise relating to prospectuses, apply and have effect accordingly, as if the shares or debentures had been offered to the public for subscription and as if persons accepting the offer in respect of any shares or debentures were subscribers for those shares or debentures.

This is without prejudice to the liability (if any) of the persons by whom the offer is made, in respect of mis-statements in the document or otherwise in respect of it.

**58(3) [Allotment with view to offer to public]** For purposes of this Act it is evidence (unless the contrary is proved) that an allotment of, or an agreement to allot, shares or debentures was made with a view to their being offered for sale to the public if it is shown–

(a) than an offer of the shares or debentures (or of any of them) for sale to the public was made within 6 months after the allotment or agreement to allot, or

(b) that at the date when the offer was made the whole consideration to be received by the company in respect of the shares or debentures had not been so received.

**58(4) [Effect of s. 56]** Section 56 as applied by this section has effect as if it required a prospectus to state, in addition to the matters required by that section–

(a) the net amount of the consideration received or to be received by the company in respect of the shares or debentures to which the offer relates, and

(b) the place and time at which the contract under which those shares or debentures have been or are to be allotted may be inspected.

**History**

See history note after s. 60.

## 59 Rule governing what is an "offer to the public"

**59(1) [Offering shares or deentures to public]** Subject to the next section, any reference in this Act to offering shares or debentures to the public is to be read (subject to any provision to the contrary) as including a reference to offering them to any section of the public, whether selected as members or debenture holders of the company concerned, or as clients of the person issuing the prospectus, or in any other manner.

**59(2) [Invitation to public to subscribe]** The same applies to any reference in this Act, or in a company's articles, to an invitation to the public to subscribe for shares or debentures.

**History**
See history note after s. 60.

## 60 Exceptions from rule in s. 59

**60(1) [Offers not treated as made to public]** Section 59 does not require an offer or invitation to be treated as made to the public if it can properly be regarded, in all the circumstances, as not being calculated to result, directly or indirectly, in the shares or debentures becoming available for subscription or purchase by persons other than those receiving the offer or invitation, or otherwise as being a domestic concern of the persons receiving and making it.

**60(2) [Provision in articles]** In particular, a provision in a company's articles prohibiting invitations to the public to subscribe for shares or debentures is not to be taken as prohibiting the making to members or debenture holders of an invitation which can properly be regarded as falling within the preceding subsection.

**60(3) [Where offer a domestic concern]** For purposes of that subsection, an offer of shares in or debentures of a private company, or an invitation to subscribe for such shares or debentures, is to be regarded (unless the contrary is proved) as being a domestic concern of the persons making and receiving the offer or invitation if it falls within any of the following descriptions.

**60(4) [Where offer is domestic concern]** It is to be so regarded if it is made to–

(a) an existing member of the company making the offer or invitation,

(b) an existing employee of that company,

(c) a member of the family of such a member or employee, or

(d) an existing debenture holder.

**60(5) [Members of family under s. 60(4)(c)]** For purposes of subsection (4)(c) , the members of a person's family are–

(a) the person's husband or wife, widow or widower and children (including stepchildren) and their descendants, and

(b) any trustee (acting in his capacity as such) of a trust the principal beneficiary of which is the person him or herself, or any of those relatives.

**60(6) [Employees' share scheme]** The offer or invitation is also to be so regarded if it is to subscribe for shares or debentures to be held under an employees' share scheme.

**60(7) [Renounceable rights]** The offer or invitation is also to be so regarded if it falls within subsection (4) or (6) and it is made on terms which permit the person to whom it is made to renounce his right to the allotment of shares or issue of debentures, but only in favour–

(a) of such a person as is mentioned in any of the paragraphs of subsection (4), or

(b) where there is an employees' share scheme, of a person entitled to hold shares or debentures under the scheme.

**60(8) [Where application to Stock Exchange Official List]** Where application has been made to the competent authority for the purposes of Part IV of the Financial Services Act 1986 for admission of any securities to the Official List of the Stock Exchange, then an offer of those securities for subscription or sale to a person whose ordinary business it is to buy or sell shares or debentures (whether as principal or agent) is not deemed an offer to the public for purposes of this Part.

**History**
S. 58–60 repealed together with the rest of Pt. III (see history note at beginning of Pt. III) except in so far as is necessary for the purposes of CA 1985, s. 81, 83, 246, 248, 744 (see SI 1995/1538 (C 33)).
In s. 60(8) the words "the competent authority for the purposes of Part IV of the Financial Services Act 1986" substituted for the former words "the Council of The Stock Exchange" by the Official Listing of Security (Change of Competent Authority) Regulations 1991 (SI 1991/2000), reg. 5(1) as from 2 October 1991.

**"61 Prospectus containing statement by expert**

**61(1)** A prospectus inviting persons to subscribe for a company's shares or debentures and including a statement purporting to be made by an expert shall not be issued unless–

.(a) he (the expert) has given and has not, before delivery of a copy of the prospectus for registration, withdrawn his written consent to its issue with the statement included in the form and context in which it is in fact included; and

(b) a statement that he has given and not withdrawn that consent appears in the prospectus.

**(2)** If a prospectus is issued in contravention of this section, the company and every person who is knowingly a party to the issue of the prospectus is liable to a fine."

# 62 Meaning of "expert"

62 The expression **"expert"**, in both Chapters of this Part, includes engineer, valuer, accountant and any other person whose profession gives authority to a statement made by him.

**History**

S. 62 repealed together with the rest of Pt. III (see history note at beginning of Pt. III) except in so far as is necessary for the purposes of s. 744 (see SI 1995/1538 (C 33)).

**63 Prospectus to be dated**

63 A prospectus issued by or on behalf of a company, or in relation to an intended company, shall be dated; and that date shall, unless the contrary is proved, be taken as its date of publication.

REGISTRATION OF PROSPECTUS

**64 Registration requirement applicable in all cases**

**64(1)** No prospectus shall be issued by or on behalf of a company, or in relation to an intended company, unless on or before the date of its publication there has been delivered to the registrar of companies for registration a copy of the prospectus–

(a) signed by every person who is named in it as a director or proposed director of the company, or by his agent authorised in writing, and

(b) having endorsed on or attached to it any consent to its issue required by section 61 from any person as an expert.

**(2)** Where the prospectus is such a document as is referred to in section 58, the signatures required by subsection (1) above include those of every person making the offer, or his agent authorised in writing.

Where the offer is made by a company or a firm, it is sufficient for the purposes of this subsection if the document is signed on its behalf by two directors or (as the case may be) not less than half of the partners; and a director or partner may sign by his agent authorised in writing.

**(3)** Every prospectus shall on its face–

(a) state that a copy has been delivered for registration as required by this section, and

(b) specify, or refer to statements in the prospectus specifying, any documents required by this or the following section to be endorsed on or attached to the copy delivered.

**(4)** The registrar shall not register a prospectus unless it is dated and the copy of it signed as required by this section and unless it has endorsed on or attached to it the documents (if any) specified in subsection (3)(b).

**(5)** If a prospectus is issued without a copy of it being delivered to the registrar as required by this section, or without the copy so delivered having the required documents endorsed on or attached to it, the company and every person who is knowingly a party to the issue of the prospectus is liable to a fine and, for continued contravention, to a daily default fine.

**65 Additional requirements in case of prospectus issued generally**

**65(1)** In the case of a prospectus issued generally (that is, to persons who are not existing members or debenture holders of the company), the following provisions apply in addition to those of section 64.

**(2)** The copy of the prospectus delivered to the registrar of companies must also have endorsed on or attached to it a copy of any contract required by paragraph 11 of Schedule 3 to be stated in the prospectus or, in the case of a contract not reduced into writing, a memorandum giving full particulars of it.

**(3)** In the case of a contract wholly or partly in a foreign language–

(a) the copy required by subsection (2) to be endorsed on or attached to the prospectus must be a copy of a translation of the contract into English or (as the case may be) a copy embodying a translation into English of the parts in a foreign language, and

(b) the translation must be certified in the prescribed manner to be a correct translation.

**(4)** If the persons making any report required by Part II of Schedule 3 have made in the report, or have (without giving reasons) indicated in it, any such adjustments as are mentioned in paragraph 21 of the Schedule (profits, losses, assets, liabilities), the copy of the prospectus delivered to the registrar must have endorsed on or attached to it a written statement signed by those persons setting out the adjustments and giving the reasons for them.

LIABILITIES AND OFFENCES IN CONNECTION WITH PROSPECTUS

**66 Directors, etc. exempt from liability in certain cases**

**66(1)** In the event of non-compliance with or contravention of section 56, a director or other person responsible for the prospectus does not incur any liability by reason of that non-compliance or contravention if–

(a) as regards any matter not disclosed, he proves that he was not cognisant of it, or

(b) he proves that the non-compliance or contravention arose from an honest mistake of fact on his part, or

(c) the non-compliance or contravention was in respect of matters which, in the opinion of the court dealing with the case, were immaterial or was otherwise such as ought (in the court's opinion, having regard to all the circumstances of the case) reasonably to be excused.

**(2)** In the event of failure to include in a prospectus a statement with respect to the matters specified in paragraph 13 of Schedule 3 (disclosure of directors' interests), no director or other person incurs any liability in respect of the failure unless it is proved that he had knowledge of the matters not disclosed.

**(3)** Nothing in section 56 or 57 or this section limits or diminishes any liability which a person may incur under the general law or this Act apart from those provisions.

ordinary resolution; but it is in any case subject to section 380 of this Act (copy to be forwarded to registrar within 15 days).

**80(9) [Penalty]** A director who knowingly and wilfully contravenes, or permits or authorises a contravention of, this section is liable to a fine.

**80(10) [Validity of allotment]** Nothing in this section affects the validity of any allotment.

**80(11) [Non-application of section]** This section does not apply to any allotment of relevant securities by a company, other than a public company registered as such on its original incorporation, if it is made in pursuance of an offer or agreement made before the earlier of the following two dates–

(a) the date of the holding of the first general meeting of the company after its registration or re-registration as a public company, and

(b) 22nd June 1982;

but any resolution to give, vary or revoke an authority for the purposes of section 14 of the Companies Act 1980 or this section has effect for those purposes if passed at any time after the end of April 1980.

## 80A Election by private company as to duration of authority

**80A(1) [Power of private company re authority]** A private company may elect (by elective resolution in accordance with section 379A) that the provisions of this section shall apply, instead of the provisions of section 80(4) and (5), in relation to the giving or renewal, after the election, of an authority under that section.

**80A(2) [Authority]** The authority must state the maximum amount of relevant securities that may be allotted under it and may be given–

(a) for an indefinite period, or

(b) for a fixed period, in which case it must state the date on which it will expire.

**80A(3) [Revocation or variation of authority]** In either case an authority (including an authority contained in the articles) may be revoked or varied by the company in general meeting.

**80A(4) [Renewal of authority]** An authority given for a fixed period may be renewed or further renewed by the company in general meeting.

**80A(5) [Resolution renewing authority]** A resolution renewing an authority–

(a) must state, or re-state, the amount of relevant securities which may be allotted under the authority or, as the case may be, the amount remaining to be allotted under it, and

(b) must state whether the authority is renewed for an indefinite period or for a fixed period, in which case it must state the date on which the renewed authority will expire.

**80A(6) [Maximum amount of relevant securities allotted]** The references in this section to the maximum amount of relevant securities that may be allotted shall be construed in accordance with section 80(6).

**80A(7) [If election ceases to have effect]** If an election under this section ceases to have effect, an authority then in force which was given for an indefinite period or for a fixed period of more than five years–

(a) if given five years or more before the election ceases to have effect, shall expire forthwith, and

(b) otherwise, shall have effect as if it had been given for a fixed period of five years.

**History**

S. 80A inserted by CA 1989, s. 115(1) as from 1 April 1990 subject to transitional and saving provisions (see SI 1990/355 (C 13), art. 4(a) and also art. 10).

## 81 Restriction on public offers by private company

**81(1) [Offence by private company]** A private limited company (other than a company limited by guarantee and not having a share capital) commits an offence if it–

(a) offers to the public (whether for cash or otherwise) any shares in or debentures of the company; or

(b) allots or agrees to allot (whether for cash or otherwise) any shares in or debentures of the company with a view to all or any of those shares or debentures being offered for sale to the public (within the meaning given to that expression by sections 58 to 60).

**81(2) [Penalty]** A company guilty of an offence under this section, and any officer of it who is in default, is liable to a fine.

**81(3) [Validity of allotment]** Nothing in this section affects the validity of any allotment or sale of shares or debentures, or of any agreement to allot or sell shares or debentures.

**Note**

S. 81 repealed by Financial Services Act 1986, s. 212(3) and Sch. 17, Pt. I to the extent to which it would apply re any investment listed or the subject of a listing application under Financial Services Act 1986, Pt. IV and commencing:

- on 12 January 1987 for all purposes relating to the admission of securities offered by or on behalf of a Minister of the Crown or a body corporate controlled by a Minister of the Crown or a subsidiary of such a body corporate to the Official List in respect of which an application is made after that date;
- on 16 February 1987 for purposes relating to the admission of securities in respect of which an application is made after that date other than those referred to in the preceding paragraph and otherwise for all purposes.

(See SI 1986/2246 (C 88).)

The section also repealed by Financial Services Act 1986, s. 212(3) and Sch. 17, Pt. I as from 29 April 1988 as far as it would apply to a prospectus offering for subscription, or to any form of application for units in a body corporate which is a recognised scheme (see SI 1988/740 (C 22)).

## 82 Application for, and allotment of, shares and debentures

**82(1) [Allotment re prospectus issued generally]** No allotment shall be made of a company's shares or debentures in pursuance of a prospectus issued generally, and no proceedings shall be taken on applications made in pursuance of a prospectus so issued, until the beginning of the third day after than on which the prospectus is first so issued or such later time (if any) as may be specified in the prospectus.

**82(2) [Definition]** The beginning of that third day, or that later time, is "the time of the opening of the subscription lists".

**82(3) [First issue of prospectus in s. 82(1)]** In subsection (1), the reference to the day on which the prospectus is first issued generally is to the day when it is first so issued as a newspaper advertisement; and if it is not so issued as a newspaper advertisement before the third day after that on which it is first so issued in any other manner, the reference is to the day on which it is first so issued in any manner.

**82(4) [Interpretation]** In reckoning for this purpose the third day after another day–

(a) any intervening day which is a Saturday or Sunday, or is a bank holiday in any part of Great Britain, is to be disregarded; and

(b) if the third day (as so reckoned) is itself a Saturday or Sunday, or a bank holiday, there is to be substituted the first day after that which is none of them.

**82(5) [Validity of allotment, penalty]** The validity of an allotment is not affected by any contravention of subsections (1) to (4); but in the event of contravention, the company and every officer of it who is in default is liable to a fine.

**82(6) [Prospectus offering shares, etc. for sale]** As applying to a prospectus offering shares or debentures for sale, the above provisions are modified as follows–

(a) for references to allotment, substitute references to sale; and

(b) for the reference to the company and every officer of it who is in default, substitute a reference to any person by or through whom the offer is made and who knowingly and wilfully authorises or permits the contravention.

**82(7) [Revocation of application re prospectus issued generally]** An application for shares in or debentures of a company which is made in pursuance of a prospectus issued generally is not revocable until after the expiration of the third day after the time of the opening of the subcription lists, or the giving before the expiration of that day of the appropriate public notice; and that notice is one given by some person responsible under sections 67 to 69 for the prospectus and having the effect under those sections of excluding or limiting the responsibility of the giver.

(c) contain or be accompanied by a note as to the matters mentioned in section 108(6)(a) to (c); and
(d) contain or be accompanied by a note that on the basis of the valuation the value of the consideration to be received by the company is not less than the value of the consideration to be given by it.

**109(3) [Reference to consideration]** A reference in section 104 or this section to consideration given for the transfer of an asset includes consideration given partly for its transfer; but–
(a) the value of any consideration partly so given is to be taken as the proportion of the consideration properly attributable to its transfer;
(b) the valuer shall carry out or arrange for such valuations of anything else as will enable him to determine that proportion; and
(c) his report for purposes of section 104 shall state what valuation has been made under this subsection and also the reason for and method and date of any such valuation and any other matters which may be relevant to that determination.

## 110 Entitlement of valuer to full disclosure

**110(1) [Information from company officers]** A person carrying out a valuation or making a report under section 103 or 104, with respect to any consideration proposed to be accepted or given by a company, is entitled to require from the officers of the company such information and explanation as he thinks necessary to enable him to carry out the valuation or make the report and provide a note under section 108(6) or (as the case may be) section 109(2)(c).

**110(2) [Penalty for misleading statement etc.]** A person who knowingly or recklessly makes a statement which–
(a) is misleading, false or deceptive in a material particular, and
(b) is a statement to which this subsection applies,
is guilty of an offence and liable to imprisonment or a fine, or both.

**110(3) [Application of s. 110(2)]** Subsection (2) applies to any statement made (whether orally or in writing) to a person carrying out a valuation or making a report under section 108 or 109, being a statement which conveys or purports to convey any information or explanation which that person requires, or is entitled to require, under subsection (1) of this section.

## 111 Matters to be communicated to registrar

**111(1) [Report under s. 108 to registrar]** A company to which a report is made under section 108 as to the value of any consideration for which, or partly for which, it proposes to allot shares shall deliver a copy of the report to the registrar of companies for registration at the same time that it files the return of the allotments of those shares under section 88.

**111(2) [Resolution under s. 104 to registrar]** A company which has passed a resolution under section 104 with respect to the transfer of an asset shall, within 15 days of so doing, deliver to the registrar of companies a copy of the resolution together with the valuer's report required by that section.

**111(3) [Penalty for contravening s. 111(1)]** If default is made in complying with subsection (1), every officer of the company who is in default is liable to a fine and, for continued contravention, to a daily default fine; but this is subject to the same exception as is made by section 88(6) (relief on application to the court) in the case of default in complying with that section.

**111(4) [Penalty for contravening s. 111(2)]** If a company fails to comply with subsection (2), it and every officer of it who is in default is liable to a fine and, for continued contravention, to a daily default fine.

### OTHER MATTERS ARISING OUT OF ALLOTMENT ETC.

## 111A Right to damages, etc. not affected

**111A** A person is not debarred from obtaining damages or other compensation from a company by reason only of his holding or having held shares in the company or any right to apply or subscribe for shares or to be included in the company's register in respect of shares.

**History**
S. 111A inserted by CA 1989, s. 131(1) as from 1 April 1990 subject to a saving provision (see SI 1990/355 (C 13), art. 4(b) and also art. 11).

## 112 Liability of subsequent holders of shares allotted

**112(1) [Subsequent holder of shares liable]** If a person becomes a holder of shares in respect of which–

(a) there has been a contravention of section 99, 100, 101 or 103; and
(b) by virtue of that contravention, another is liable to pay any amount under the section contravened,

that person is also liable to pay that amount (jointly and severally with any other person so liable), unless he is exempted from liability by subsection (3) below.

**112(2) [Where agreement in contravention of s. 104]** If a company enters into an agreement in contravention of section 104 and–

(a) the agreement is or includes an agreement for the allotment of shares in the company; and
(b) a person becomes a holder of shares allotted under the agreement; and
(c) by virtue of the agreement and allotment under it, another person is liable to pay any amount under section 105,

the person who becomes the holder of the shares is also liable to pay that amount (jointly and severally with any other person so liable), unless he is exempted from liability by the following subsection; and this applies whether or not the agreement also contravenes section 103.

**112(3) [Exemption from liability under s. 112(1), (2)]** A person otherwise liable under subsection (1) or (2) is exempted from that liability if either–

(a) he is a purchaser for value and, at the time of the purchase, he did not have actual notice of the contravention concerned; or
(b) he derived title to the shares (directly or indirectly) from a person who became a holder of them after the contravention and was not liable under subsection (1) or (as the case may be) subsection (2).

**112(4) [References to holder]** References in this section to a holder, in relation to shares in a company, include any person who has an unconditional right to be included in the company's register of members in respect of those shares or to have an instrument of transfer of the shares executed in his favour.

**112(5) [Further application of s. 112(1), (3)]** As subsections (1) and (3) apply in relation to the contraventions there mentioned, they also apply–

(a) to a contravention of section 102; and
(b) to a failure to carry out a term of a contract as mentioned in subsections (5) and (6) of that section.

## 113 Relief in respect of certain liabilities under s. 99ff.

**113(1) [Application for exemption from liability]** Where a person is liable to a company under–

(a) section 99, 102, 103 or 105;
(b) section 112(1) by reference to a contravention of section 99 or 103; or
(c) section 112(2) or (5),

in relation to payment in respect of any shares in the company, or is liable by virtue of an undertaking given to it in, or in connection with, payment for any such shares, the person so liable may make an application to the court to be exempted in whole or in part from the liability.

**113(2) [Limitation on court's power to exempt]** If the liability mentioned in subsection (1) arises in relation to payment in respect of any shares, the court may, on an application under that subsection, exempt the applicant from the liability only–

**144(2) [Failure by nominee to pay up]** Subject to that section, if a person is called on to pay any amount for the purpose of paying up, or paying any premium on, any shares in such a company which were issued to him, or which he otherwise acquired, as the company's nominee and he fails to pay that amount within 21 days from being called on to do so, then–

(a) if the shares were issued to him as subscriber to the memorandum by virtue of an undertaking of his in the memorandum, the other subscribers to the memorandum, or

(b) if the shares were otherwise issued to or acquired by him, the directors of the company at the time of the issue or acquisition,

are jointly and severally liable with him to pay that amount.

**144(3) [Relief of nominee from liability]** If in proceedings for the recovery of any such amount from any such subscriber or director under this section it appears to the court–

(a) that he is or may be liable to pay that amount, but

(b) that he has acted honestly and reasonably and, having regard to all the circumstances of the case, he ought fairly to be excused from liability,

the court may relieve him, either wholly or partly, from his liability on such terms as the court thinks fit.

**144(4) [Relief for subscriber or director]** Where any such subscriber or director has reason to apprehend that a claim will or might be made for the recovery of any such amount from him, he may apply to the court for relief; and the court has the same power to relieve him as it would have had in proceedings for the recovery of that amount.

## 145 Exceptions from s. 144

**145(1) [Non-application of s. 144(1)]** Section 144(1) does not apply to shares acquired otherwise than by subscription by a nominee of a public company, where a person acquires shares in the company with financial assistance given to him directly or indirectly by the company for the purpose of or in connection with the acquisition, and the company has a beneficial interest in the shares.

**145(2) [Non-application of s. 144(1), (2)]** Section 144(1) and (2) do not apply–

(a) to shares acquired by a nominee of a company when the company has no beneficial interest in those shares, or

(b) to shares issued in consequence of an application made before 22nd December 1980, or transferred in pursuance of an agreement to acquire them made before that date.

**145(3) [Effect of Sch. 2]** Schedule 2 to this Act has effect for the interpretation of references in this section to a company having, or not having, a beneficial interest in shares.

## 146 Treatment of shares held by or for public company

**146(1) [Application]** Except as provided by section 148, the following applies to a public company–

(a) where shares in the company are forfeited, or surrendered to the company in lieu, in pursuance of the articles, for failure to pay any sum payable in respect of the shares;

(b) where shares in the company are acquired by it (otherwise than by any of the methods mentioned in section 143(3)(a) to (d)) and the company has a beneficial interest in the shares;

(c) where the nominee of the company acquires shares in the company from a third person without financial assistance being given directly or indirectly by the company and the company has a beneficial interest in the shares; or

(d) where a person acquires shares in the company with financial assistance given to him directly or indirectly by the company for the purpose of or in connection with the acquisition, and the company has a beneficial interest in the shares.

Schedule 2 to this Act has effect for the interpretation of references in this subsection to the company having a beneficial interest in shares.

**146(2) [Shares or any interest in company not previously disposed of]** Unless the shares or any interest of the company in them are previously disposed of, the company must not later than the end of the relevant period from their forfeiture or surrender or, in a case within subsection (1)(b), (c) or (d), their acquisition–

(a) cancel them and diminish the amount of the share capital by the nominal value of the shares cancelled, and

(b) where the effect of cancelling the shares will be that the nominal value of the company's allotted share capital is brought below the authorised minimum, apply for re-registration as a private company, stating the effect of the cancellation.

**146(3) ["The relevant period"]** For this purpose "the relevant period" is–

(a) 3 years in the case of shares forfeited or surrendered to the company in lieu of forfeiture, or acquired as mentioned in subsection (1)(b) or (c);

(b) one year in the case of shares acquired as mentioned in subsection (1)(d).

**146(4) [Prohibition on voting rights]** The company and, in a case within subsection (1)(c) or (d), the company's nominee or (as the case may be) the other shareholder must not exercise any voting rights in respect of the shares; and any purported exercise of those rights is void.

## 147 Matters arising out of compliance with s. 146(2)

**147(1) [Not necessary to comply with s. 135, 136]** The directors may take such steps as are requisite to enable the company to carry out its obligations under section 146(2) without complying with sections 135 and 136 (resolution to reduce share capital; application to court for approval).

**147(2) [Alterations in resolution]** The steps taken may include the passing of a resolution to alter the company's memorandum so that it no longer states that the company is to be a public company; and the resolution may make such other alterations in the memorandum as are requisite in the circumstances.

Such a resolution is subject to section 380 (copy to be forwarded to registrar within 15 days).

**147(3) [S. 146(2)(b) application for re-registration]** The application for re-registration required by section 146(2)(b) must be in the prescribed form and be signed by a director or secretary of the company, and must be delivered to the registrar of companies together with a printed copy of the memorandum and articles of the company as altered by the resolution.

**147(4) [Issue of appropriate certificate of incorporation]** If the registrar is satisfied that the company may be re-registered under section 146, he shall retain the application and other documents delivered with it and issue the company with a certificate of incorporation appropriate to a company that is not a public company; and–

(a) the company by virtue of the issue of the certificate becomes a private company, and the alterations in the memorandum and articles set out in the resolution take effect accordingly, and

(b) the certificate is conclusive evidence that the requirements of sections 146 to 148 in respect of re-registration and of matters precedent and incidental to it have been complied with, and that the company is a private company.

## 148 Further provisions supplementing s. 146, 147

**148(1) [Private company re-registering as public company]** Where, after shares in a private company–

(a) are forfeited in pursuance of the company's articles or are surrendered to the company in lieu of forfeiture, or

(b) are acquired by the company (otherwise than by such surrender or forfeiture, and otherwise than by any of the methods mentioned in section 143(3)), the company having a beneficial interest in the shares, or

# Chapter VII – Redeemable Shares; Purchase by a Company of its Own Shares

## REDEMPTION AND PURCHASE GENERALLY

### 159 Power to issue redeemable shares

**159(1) [Power]** Subject to the provisions of this Chapter, a company limited by shares or limited by guarantee and having a share capital may, if authorised to do so by its articles, issue shares which are to be redeemed or are liable to be redeemed at the option of the company or the shareholder.

**159(2) [Must be non-redeemable shares in issue]** No redeemable shares may be issued at a time when there are no issued shares of the company which are not redeemable.

**159(3) [Shares must be fully paid; payment on redemption]** Redeemable shares may not be redeemed unless they are fully paid; and the terms of redemption must provide for payment on redemption.

### 160 Financing, etc. of redemption

**160(1) [From distributable profits of company]** Subject to the next subsection and to sections 171 (private companies redeeming or purchasing own shares out of capital) and 178(4) (terms of redemption or purchase enforceable in a winding up)–

(a) redeemable shares may only be redeemed out of distributable profits of the company or out of the proceeds of a fresh issue of shares made for the purposes of the redemption; and

(b) any premium payable on redemption must be paid out of distributable profits of the company.

**160(2) [Premiums payable on redemption]** If the redeemable shares were issued at a premium, any premium payable on their redemption may be paid out of the proceeds of a fresh issue of shares made for the purposes of the redemption, up to an amount equal to–

(a) the aggregate of the premiums received by the company on the issue of the shares redeemed, or

(b) the current amount of the company's share premium account (including any sum transferred to that account in respect of premiums on the new shares),

whichever is the less; and in that case the amount of the company's share premium account shall be reduced by a sum corresponding (or by sums in the aggregate corresponding) to the amount of any payment made by virtue of this subsection out of the proceeds of the issue of the new shares.

**160(3) [Redemption in accordance with articles]** Subject to the following provisions of this Chapter, redemption of shares may be effected on such terms and in such manner as may be provided by the company's articles.

**160(4) [Shares redeemed treated as cancelled]** Shares redeemed under this section shall be treated as cancelled on redemption, and the amount of the company's issued share capital shall be diminished by the nominal value of those shares accordingly; but the redemption of shares by a company is not to be taken as reducing the amount of the company's authorised share capital.

**160(5) [Extent of power to issue shares]** Without prejudice to subsection (4), where a company is about to redeem shares, it has power to issue shares up to the nominal value of the shares to be redeemed as if those shares had never been issued.

### 161 Stamp duty on redemption of shares

**161** (Repealed by Finance Act 1988, s. 148 and Sch. 14, Pt. XI as from 22 March 1988.)

**History**
S. 161 formerly read as follows:
"**161(1)** For the purposes of section 47 of the Finance Act 1973, the issue of shares by a company in place of shares redeemed under section 160 constitutes a chargeable transaction if, and only if, the actual value of the shares so issued exceeds the value of the shares redeemed at the date of their redemption.

**(2)** Where the issue of the shares does constitute a chargeable transaction for those purposes, the amount on which stamp duty on the relevant document relating to that transaction is chargeable under section 47(5) of the Finance Act 1973 is the difference between–

(a) the amount on which that duty would be so chargeable if the shares had not been issued in place of shares redeemed under section 160; and
(b) the value of the shares redeemed at the date of their redemption.

**(3)** Subject to the following subsection, for the purposes of subsections (1) and (2) shares issued by a company–

(a) up to the nominal amount of any shares which the company has redeemed under section 160; or
(b) in pursuance of section 160(5) before the redemption of shares which the company is about to redeem under that section,

are to be regarded as issued in place of the shares redeemed or (as the case may be) about to be redeemed.

**(4)** Shares issued in pursuance of section 160(5) are not to be regarded for purposes of subsections (1) and (2) of this section as issued in place of the shares about to be redeemed, unless those shares are redeemed within one month after the issue of the new shares."

## 162 Power of company to purchase own shares

**162(1) [Power]** Subject to the following provisions of this Chapter, a company limited by shares or limited by guarantee and having a share capital may, if authorised to do so by its articles, purchase its own shares (including any redeemable shares).

**162(2) [Application of s. 159–161]** Sections 159 to 161 apply to the purchase by a company under this section of its own shares as they apply to the redemption of redeemable shares, save that the terms and manner of purchase need not be determined by the articles as required by section 160(3).

**162(3) [Limitation on purchase]** A company may not under this section purchase its shares if as a result of the purchase there would no longer be any member of the company holding shares other than redeemable shares.

## 163 Definitions of "off-market" and "market" purchase

**163(1) ["Off-market" purchase]** A purchase by a company of its own shares is **"off-market"** if the shares either–

(a) are purchased otherwise than on a recognised investment exchange, or
(b) are purchased on a recognised investment exchange but are not subject to a marketing arrangement on that investment exchange.

**History**
In s. 163(1) the words "a recognised investment exchange" substituted for the former words "a recognised stock exchange" in both places where they appear and the words "that investment exchange" substituted for the former words "that stock exchange" by Financial Services Act 1986, s. 212(2) and Sch. 16, para. 17(a), (b) as from 29 April 1988 (see SI 1988/740 (C 22)).

**163(2) [Interpretation of s. 163(1)]** For this purpose, a company's shares are subject to a marketing arrangement on a recognised investment exchange if either–

(a) they are listed under Part IV of the Financial Services Act 1986; or
(b) the company has been afforded facilities for dealings in those shares to take place on that investment exchange without prior permission for individual transactions from the authority governing that investment exchange and without limit as to the time during which those facilities are to be available.

**History**
In s. 163(2) the words "a recognised investment exchange" substituted for the former words "a recognised stock exchange" by Financial Services Act 1986, s. 212(2) and Sch. 16, para. 17(a) as from 29 April 1988 (see SI 1988/740 (C 22)), in para. (a) the words "under Part IV of the Financial Services Act 1986" substituted for the former words "on that stock exchange" by Financial Services Act 1986, s. 212(2) and Sch. 16, para. 17(c) as from 12 January 1987 (see SI 1986/2246 (C 88)), and in para. (b) the words "that investment exchange" substituted for the former words "that stock exchange" in both places where they occur by Financial Services Act 1986, s. 212(2) and Sch. 16, para. 17(a), (c) as from 29 April 1988 (see SI 1988/740 (C 22)).

**163(3) ["Market" purchase]** A purchase by a company of its own shares is a **"market purchase"** if it is a purchase made on a recognised investment exchange, other than a purchase which is an off-market purchase by virtue of subsection (1)(b).

is equal to the price of redemption or purchase; and the payment permissible under this subsection is referred to below in this Chapter as the permissible capital payment for the shares.

**171(4) [Transfer to capital redemption reserve]** Subject to subsection (6), if the permissible capital payment for shares redeemed or purchased is less than their nominal amount, the amount of the difference shall be transferred to the company's capital redemption reserve.

**171(5) [Permissible capital payment exceeding nominal amount of shares]** Subject to subsection (6), if the permissible capital payment is greater than the nominal amount of the shares redeemed or purchased–

(a) the amount of any capital redemption reserve, share premium account or fully paid share capital of the company, and

(b) any amount representing unrealised profits of the company for the time being standing to the credit of any reserve maintained by the company in accordance with paragraph 34 of Schedule 4 or paragraph 34 of Schedule 8 (revaluation reserve),

may be reduced by a sum not exceeding (or by sums not in the aggregate exceeding) the amount by which the permissible capital payment exceeds the nominal amount of the shares.

**History**

In s. 171(5) the words "or paragraph 34 of Schedule 8" appearing after the words "paragraph 34 of Schedule 4" inserted by the Companies Act 1985 (Accounts of Small and Medium-sized Companies and Minor Accounting Amendments) Regulations 1997 (SI 1997/220), reg . 1, 7(1) as from 1 March 1997.

**171(6) [Proceeds of fresh issue]** Where the proceeds of a fresh issue are applied by a company in making any redemption or purchase of its own shares in addition to a payment out of capital under this section, the references in subsections (4) and (5) to the permissible capital payment are to be read as referring to the aggregate of that payment and those proceeds.

## 172 Availability of profits for purposes of s. 171

**172(1) [Reference to available profits of the company]** The reference in section 171(3)(a) to available profits of the company is to the company's profits which are available for distribution (within the meaning of Part VIII); but the question whether a company has any profits so available and the amount of any such profits are to be determined for purposes of that section in accordance with the following subsections, instead of sections 270 to 275 in that Part.

**172(2) [Determination of amount of profits]** Subject to the next subsection, that question is to be determined by reference to–

(a) profits, losses, assets and liabilities,

(b) provisions of any of the kinds mentioned in paragraphs 88 and 89 of Schedule 4 (depreciation, diminution in value of assets, retentions to meet liabilities, etc.), and

(c) share capital and reserves (including undistributable reserves),

as stated in the relevant accounts for determining the permissible capital payment for shares.

**172(3) [The relevant accounts in s. 172(2)]** The relevant accounts for this purpose are such accounts, prepared as at any date within the period for determining the amount of the permissible capital payment, as are necessary to enable a reasonable judgment to be made as to the amounts of any of the items mentioned in subsection (2)(a) to (c) above.

**172(4) [Determination of amount of permissible capital payment]** For purposes of determining the amount of the permissible capital payment for shares, the amount of the company's available profits (if any) determined in accordance with subsections (2) and (3) is treated as reduced by the amount of any distributions lawfully made by the company after the date of the relevant accounts and before the end of the period for determining the amount of that payment.

**172(5) [Lawful distributions in s. 172(4)]** The reference in subsection (4) to distributions lawfully made by the company includes–

(a) financial assistance lawfully given out of distributable profits in a case falling within section 154 or 155,

(b) any payment lawfully made by the company in respect of the purchase by it of any shares in the company (except a payment lawfully made otherwise than out of distributable profits), and

(c) a payment of any description specified in section 168(1) lawfully made by the company.

**172(6) [Period for determining the amount of permissible capital payment]** References in this section to the period for determining the amount of the permissible capital payment for shares are to the period of 3 months ending with the date on which the statutory declaration of the directors purporting to specify the amount of that payment is made in accordance with subsection (3) of the section next following.

## 173 Conditions for payment out of capital

**173(1) [Requirements for payment by private company]** Subject to any order of the court under section 177, a payment out of capital by a private company for the redemption or purchase of its own shares is not lawful unless the requirements of this and the next two sections are satisfied.

**173(2) [Approval by special resolution]** The payment out of capital must be approved by a special resolution of the company.

**173(3) [Statutory declaration by directors]** The company's directors must make a statutory declaration specifying the amount of the permissible capital payment for the shares in question and stating that, having made full inquiry into the affairs and prospects of the company, they have formed the opinion–

(a) as regards its initial situation immediately following the date on which the payment out of capital is proposed to be made, that there will be no grounds on which the company could then be found unable to pay its debts, and

(b) as regards its prospects for the year immediately following that date, that, having regard to their intentions with respect to the management of the company's business during that year and to the amount and character of the financial resources which will in their view be available to the company during that year, the company will be able to continue to carry on business as a going concern (and will accordingly be able to pay its debts as they fall due) throughout that year.

**173(4) [Directors' opinion in s. 173(3)(a)]** In forming their opinion for purposes of subsection (3)(a), the directors shall take into account the same liabilities (including prospective and contingent liabilities) as would be relevant under section 122 of the Insolvency Act (winding up by the court) to the question whether a company is unable to pay its debts.

**History**

In s. 173(4) the words "section 122 of the Insolvency Act" substituted for the former words "section 517" by Insolvency Act 1986, s. 439(1) and Sch. 13 as from 29 December 1986 (see IA 1986, s. 443 and SI 1986/1924 (C 71)).

**173(5) [Form and content of statutory declaration, auditors' report]** The directors' statutory declaration must be in the prescribed form and contain such information with respect to the nature of the company's business as may be prescribed, and must in addition have annexed to it a report addressed to the directors by the company's auditors stating that–

(a) they have inquired into the company's state of affairs; and

(b) the amount specified in the declaration as the permissible capital payment for the shares in question is in their view properly determined in accordance with sections 171 and 172; and

(c) they are not aware of anything to indicate that the opinion expressed by the directors in the declaration as to any of the matters mentioned in subsection (3) is unreasonable in all the circumstances.

**173(6) [Penalty for unreasonable declaration]** A director who makes a declaration under this section without having reasonable grounds for the opinion expressed in the declaration is liable to imprisonment or a fine, or both.

## 174 Procedure for special resolution under s. 173

**174(1) [Dates for special resolution and payment out of capital]** The resolution required by section 173 must be passed on, or within the week immediately following, the date on which the directors make the statutory declaration required by that section; and the payment out of capital must be made no earlier than 5 nor more than 7 weeks after the date of the resolution.

SUPPLEMENTARY

## 178 Effect of company's failure to redeem or purchase

**178(1) [Effect]** This section has effect where a company has, on or after 15th June 1982,–

(a) issued shares on terms that they are or are liable to be redeemed, or

(b) agreed to purchase any of its own shares.

**178(2) [Company not liable in damages]** The company is not liable in damages in respect of any failure on its part to redeem or purchase any of the shares.

**178(3) [Qualification to s. 178(2)]** Subsection (2) is without prejudice to any right of the holder of the shares other than his right to sue the company for damages in respect of its failure; but the court shall not grant an order for specific performance of the terms of redemption or purchase if the company shows that it is unable to meet the costs of redeeming or purchasing the shares in question out of distributable profits.

**178(4) [Enforcement of terms of redemption or purchase]** If the company is wound up and at the commencement of the winding up any of the shares have not been redeemed or purchased, the terms of redemption or purchase may be enforced against the company; and when shares are redeemed or purchased under this subsection, they are treated as cancelled.

**178(5) [Non-application of s. 178(4)]** However, subsection (4) does not apply if–

(a) the terms provided for the redemption or purchase to take place at a date later than that of the commencement of the winding up, or

(b) during the period beginning with the date on which the redemption or purchase was to have taken place and ending with the commencement of the winding up the company could not at any time have lawfully made a distribution equal in value to the price at which the shares were to have been redeemed or purchased.

**178(6) [Priority payments]** There shall be paid in priority to any amount which the company is liable under subsection (4) to pay in respect of any shares–

(a) all other debts and liabilities of the company (other than any due to members in their character as such),

(b) if other shares carry rights (whether as to capital or as to income) which are preferred to the rights as to capital attaching to the first-mentioned shares, any amount due in satisfaction of those preferred rights;

but, subject to that, any such amount shall be paid in priority to any amounts due to members in satisfaction of their rights (whether as to capital or income) as members.

**178(7)** (Repealed by Insolvency Act 1985, s. 235 and Sch. 10, Pt. II as from 29 December 1986.)

**History**

In regard to the date of the above repeal, see SI 1986/1924 (C 71); s. 178(7) formerly read as follows:

"Where by virtue of section 66 of the Bankruptcy Act 1914 (payment of interest on debts) as applied by section 612 (application of bankruptcy rules to insolvent companies in England and Wales) a creditor of a company is entitled to payment of any interest only after payment of all other debts of the company, the company's debts and liabilities for purposes of subsection (6) of this section include the liability to pay that interest."

## 179 Power for Secretary of State to modify this Chapter

**179(1) [Regulations modifying provisions of Ch. VII]** The Secretary of State may by regulations made by statutory instrument modify the provisions of this Chapter with respect to any of the following matters–

(a) the authority required for a purchase by a company of its own shares,

(b) the authority required for the release by a company or its rights under a contract for the purchase of its own shares or a contract under which the company may (subject to any conditions) become entitled or obliged to purchase its own shares,

(c) the information to be included in a return delivered by a company to the registrar of companies in accordance with section 169(1),

(d) the matters to be dealt with in the statutory declaration of the directors under section 173 with a view to indicating their opinion of their company's ability to make a proposed payment out of capital with due regard to its financial situation and prospects, and

(e) the contents of the auditors' report required by that section to be annexed to that declaration.

**179(2) [Further regulations]** The Secretary of State may also by regulations so made make such provision (including modification of the provisions of this Chapter) as appears to him to be appropriate–

(a) for wholly or partly relieving companies from the requirement of section 171(3)(a) that any available profits must be taken into account in determining the amount of the permissible capital payment for shares under that section, or

(b) for permitting a company's share premium account to be applied, to any extent appearing to the Secretary of State to be appropriate, in providing for the premiums payable on the redemption or purchase by the company of any of its own shares.

**179(3) [Content of regulations]** Regulations under this section–

(a) may make such further modification of any provisions of this Chapter as appears to the Secretary of State to be reasonably necessary in consequence of any provision made under such regulations by virtue of subsection (1) or (2),

(b) may make different provision for different cases or classes of case, and

(c) may contain such further consequential provisions, and such incidental and supplementary provisions, as the Secretary of State thinks fit.

**179(4) [Approval of regulations]** No regulations shall be made under this section unless a draft of the instrument containing them has been laid before Parliament and approved by resolution of each House.

## 180 Transitional cases arising under this Chapter; and savings

**180(1) [Certain preference shares issued before 15 June 1982]** Any preference shares issued by a company before 15th June 1982 which could but for the repeal by the Companies Act 1981 of section 58 of the Companies Act 1948 (power to issue redeemable preference shares) have been redeemed under that section are subject to redemption in accordance with the provisions of this Chapter.

**180(2) [Where s. 159, 160 apply]** In a case to which sections 159 and 160 apply by virtue of this section, any premium payable on redemption may, notwithstanding the repeal by the 1981 Act of any provision of the 1948 Act, be paid out of the share premium account instead of out of profits, or partly out of that account and partly out of profits (but subject to the provisions of this Chapter so far as payment is out of profits).

**180(3) [Capital redemption reserve fund before 15 June 1982]** Any capital redemption reserve fund established before 15th June 1982 by a company for the purposes of section 58 of the Act of 1948 is to be known as the company's capital redemption reserve and be treated as if it had been established for the purposes of section 170 of this Act; and accordingly, a reference in any enactment or in the articles of any company, or in any other instrument, to a company's capital redemption reserve fund is to be construed as a reference to the company's capital redemption reserve.

## 181 Definitions for Chapter VII

**181** In this Chapter–

(a) **"distributable profits"**, in relation to the making of any payment by a company, means those profits out of which it could lawfully make a distribution (within the meaning given by section 263(2)) equal in value to the payment, and

(b) **"permissible capital payment"** means the payment permitted by section 171;

and references to payment out of capital are to be construed in accordance with section 171.

# Chapter VIII – Miscellaneous Provisions about Shares and Debentures

## SHARE AND DEBENTURE CERTIFICATES, TRANSFERS AND WARRANTS

## 182 Nature, transfer and numbering of shares

**182(1) [Nature, transfer]** The shares or other interest of any member in a company–

(a) are personal estate or, in Scotland, moveable property and are not in the nature of real estate or heritage,

(b) are transferable in manner provided by the company's articles, but subject to the Stock Transfer Act 1963 (which enables securities of certain descriptions to be transferred by a simplified process) and to regulations made under section 207 of the Companies Act 1989 (which enable title to securities to be evidenced and transferred without a written instrument).

**History**
In s. 182(1)(b) the words "and to regulations" to the end inserted by the Uncertificated Securities Regulations 1995 (SI 1995/3272), reg. 1, 40(1) as from 19 December 1995.

**182(2) [Numbering]** Each share in a company having a share capital shall be distinguished by its appropriate number; except that, if at any time all the issued shares in a company, or all the issued shares in it of a particular class, are fully paid up and rank pari passu for all purposes, none of those shares need thereafter have a distinguishing number so long as it remains fully paid up and ranks pari passu for all purposes with all shares of the same class for the time being issued and fully paid up.

## 183 Transfer and registration

**183(1) [Conditions for registration of transfer]** It is not lawful for a company to register a transfer of shares in or debentures of the company unless a proper instrument of transfer has been delivered to it, or the transfer is an exempt transfer within the Stock Transfer Act 1982 or is in accordance with regulations made under section 207 of the Companies Act 1989.

This applies notwithstanding anything in the company's articles.

**History**
In s. 183(1) the words "or is in accordance with regulations made under section 207 of the Companies Act 1989" inserted by the Uncertificated Securities Regulations 1995 (SI 1995/3272), reg. 1, 40(2)(a) as from 19 December 1995.

**183(2) [Where shares transmitted by operation of law]** Subsection (1) does not prejudice any power of the company to register as shareholder or debenture holder a person to whom the right to any shares in or debentures of the company has been transmitted by operation of law.

**183(3) [Transfer by personal representative]** A transfer of the share or other interest of a deceased member of a company made by his personal representative, although the personal representative is not himself a member of the company, is as valid as if he had been such a member at the time of the execution of the instrument of transfer.

**183(4) [Registration of transfer at request of transferor]** On the application of the transferor of any share or interest in a company, the company shall enter in its register of members the name of the transferee in the same manner and subject to the same conditions as if the application for the entry were made by the transferee.

**Note**
In accordance with the Uncertificated Securities Regulations 1995 (SI 1995/3272), reg. 1, 40(2)(b), s. 183(4) shall not apply.

**183(5) [Notice of refusal to register transfer]** If a company refuses to register a transfer of shares or debentures, the company shall, within 2 months after the date on which the transfer was lodged with it, send to the transferee notice of the refusal.

**183(6) [Penalty re s. 183(5)]** If default is made in complying with subsection (5), the company and every officer of it who is in default is liable to a fine and, for continued contravention, to a daily default fine.

## 184 Certification of transfers

**184(1) [Effect of certification by company]** The certification by a company of any instrument of transfer of any shares in, or debentures of, the company is to be taken as a representation by the company to any person acting on the faith of the certification that there have been produced to the company such documents as on their face show a prima facie title to the shares or debentures in the transferor named in the instrument.

However, the certification is not to be taken as a representation that the transferor has any title to the shares or debentures.

**184(2) [Liability of company for negligently made false certification]** Where a person acts on the faith of a false certification by a company made negligently, the company is under the same liability to him as if the certification had been made fraudulently.

**184(3) [Interpretation]** For purposes of this section–

(a) an instrument of transfer is deemed certificated if it bears the words "certificate lodged" (or words to the like effect);

(b) the certification of an instrument of transfer is deemed made by a company if–
  (i) the person issuing the instrument is a person authorised to issue certificated instruments of transfer on the company's behalf, and
  (ii) the certification is signed by a person authorised to certificate transfers on the company's behalf or by an officer or servant either of the company or of a body corporate so authorised;

(c) a certification is deemed signed by a person if–
  (i) it purports to be authenticated by his signature or initials (whether handwritten or not), and
  (ii) it is not shown that the signature or initials was or were placed there neither by himself nor by a person authorised to use the signature or initials for the purpose of certificating transfers on the company's behalf.

## 185 Duty of company as to issue of certificates

**185(1) [General obligations of company]** Subject to the following provisions, every company shall–

(a) within 2 months after the allotment of any of its shares, debentures or debenture stock, and

(b) within 2 months after the date on which a transfer of any such shares, debentures or debenture stock is lodged with the company,

complete and have ready for delivery the certificates of all shares, the debentures and the certificates of all debenture stock allotted or transferred (unless the conditions of issue of the shares, debentures or debenture stock otherwise provide).

**185(2) ["Transfer"]** For this purpose, **"transfer"** means a transfer duly stamped and otherwise valid, or an exempt transfer within the Stock Transfer Act 1982, and does not include such a transfer as the company is for any reason entitled to refuse to register and does not register.

**185(3) [Non-application of s. 185(1)]** Subsection (1) does not apply in the case of a transfer to any person where, by virtue of regulations under section 3 of the Stock Transfer Act 1982, he is not entitled to a certificate or other document of or evidencing title in respect of the securities transferred; but if in such a case the transferee–

(a) subsequently becomes entitled to such a certificate or other document by virtue of any provision of those regulations, and

(b) gives notice in writing of that fact to the company,

this section has effect as if the reference in subsection (1)(b) to the date of the lodging of the transfer were a reference to the date of the notice.

**185(4) [Exception to s. 185(1) for clearing house or nominee]** A company of which shares or debentures are allotted or debenture stock is allotted to a recognised clearing house or a nominee of a recognised clearing house or of a recognised investment exchange, or with which a transfer is lodged for transferring any shares, debentures or debenture stock of the company to such a clearing house or nominee, is not required, in consequence of the allotment or the lodging of the transfer, to comply with subsection (1); but no person shall be a nominee for the purposes of this section unless he is a person designated for the purposes of this section in the rules of the recognised investment exchange in question.

**"Recognised clearing house"** means a recognised clearing house within the meaning of the Financial Services Act 1986 acting in relation to a recognised investment exchange and **"recognised investment exchange"** has the same meaning as in that Act.

**History**
In s. 185(4):
- the words "a recognised clearing house or a nominee of a recognised clearing house or of a recognised investment exchange" substituted for the former words "a stock exchange nominee";
- the words "such a clearing house or nominee" substituted for the former words "a stock exchange nominee";
- the words from "; but no person shall be a nominee" to the end of the paragraph inserted; and
- the second paragraph substituted for the former words "**"stock exchange nominee"** means any person whom the Secretary of State designates, by order in a statutory instrument, as a nominee of The Stock Exchange for the purposes of this section"

by Financial Services Act 1986, s. 195(5) as from 29 April 1988 (see SI 1988/740 (C 22)).

**Note**
See also the Stock Exchange (Designation of Nominees) Order 1985 (SI 1985/806).

**185(5) [Penalty re s. 185(1)]** If default is made in complying with subsection (1), the company and every officer of it who is in default is liable to a fine and, for continued contravention, to a daily default fine.

**185(6) [Application to court on continuing default]** If a company on which a notice has been served requiring it to make good any default in complying with subsection (1) fails to make good the default within 10 days after service of the notice, the court may, on the application of the person entitled to have the certificates or the debentures delivered to him, exercise the power of the following subsection.

**185(7) [Court order re default]** The court may make an order directing the company and any officer of it to make good the default within such time as may be specified in the order; and the order may provide that all costs of and incidental to the application shall be borne by the company or by an officer of it responsible for the default.

## 186 Certificate to be evidence of title

**186(1) [Certificate as evidence]** A certificate, under the common seal of the company specifying any shares held by a member is –

(a) in England and Wales, prima facie evidence, and

(b) in Scotland, sufficient evidence unless the contrary is shown,

of his title to the shares.

**History**
S. 186(1) renumbered as sub by Requirements of Writing (Scotland) Act 1995, s. 14(1), 15 and Sch. 4, para. 55 as from 1 August 1995. Previously in what was then s. 186 the words "(or, in the case of a company registered in Scotland, subscribed in accordance with section 36B)" formerly appearing after the words "common seal of the company" ceased to have effect and repealed by Law Reform (Miscellaneous Provisions) (Scotland) Act 1990, s. 74, Sch. 8, para. 33 (1), (4) and Sch. 9 as from 1 December 1990 (see SI 1990/2328 (C 60) (S 197), art. 3, Sch.); previously to that s. 186 substituted by CA 1989, s. 130(7) and Sch. 17, para. 5 as from 31 July 1990 (see SI 1990/1392 (C 41), art. 2(b)); s. 186 originally read as follows:

"A certificate under the common seal of the company or the seal kept by the company by virtue of section 40, specifying any shares held by a member, is prima facie evidence of his title to the shares."

**186(2) [Scotland]** Without prejudice to subsection (1), as respects Scotland a certificate specifying any shares held by a member and subscribed by the company in accordance with the Requirements of Writing (Scotland) Act 1995 is, unless the contrary is shown, sufficient evidence of his title to the shares.

**History**
S. 186(2) inserted by Requirements of Writing (Scotland) Act 1995, s. 14(1), 15 and Sch. 4, para. 55 as from 1 August 1995.

## 187 Evidence of grant of probate or confirmation as executor

**187** The production to a company of any document which is by law sufficient evidence of probate of the will, or letters of administration of the estate, or confirmation as executor, of a deceased person having been granted to some person shall be accepted by the company as sufficient evidence of the grant.

This has effect notwithstanding anything in the company's articles.

## 188 Issue and effect of share warrant to bearer

**188(1) [Issue of warrant]** A company limited by shares may, if so authorised by its articles, issue with respect to any fully paid shares a warrant (a "share warrant") stating that the bearer of the warrant is entitled to the shares specified in it.

**188(2) [Effect]** A share warrant issued under the company's common seal (or, in the case of a company registered in Scotland, subscribed in accordance with the Requirements of Writing (Scotland) Act 1995) entitles the bearer to the shares specified in it: and the shares may be transferred by delivery of the warrant.

**History**

In s. 188(2) the words "(or, in the case of a company registered in Scotland, subscribed in accordance with the Requirements of Writing (Scotland) Act 1995)" inserted by Requirements of Writing (Scotland) Act 1995, s. 14(1), 15 and Sch. 4, para. 56 as from 1 August 1995. Previously in s. 188(2) the words "(or, in the case of a company registered in Scotland, subscribed in accordance with section 36B)" originally appearing after the words "company's common seal" ceased to have effect and repealed by Law Reform (Miscellaneous Provisions) (Scotland) Act 1990, s. 74, Sch. 8, para. 33(1), (5) and Sch. 9 as from 1 December 1990 (see SI 1990/2328 (C 60) (S 197), art. 3, Sch.)

**188(3) [Provision for payment of future dividends]** A company which issues a share warrant may, if so authorised by its articles, provide (by coupons or otherwise) for the payment of the future dividends on the shares included in the warrant.

**History**

S. 188 substituted by CA 1989, s. 130(7) and Sch. 17, para. 6 as from 31 July 1990 (see SI 1990/1392 (C 41), art. 2(b)); s. 188 formerly read as follows:

"**188(1)** A company limited by shares, if so authorised by its articles, may, with respect to any fully paid-up shares, issue under its common seal a warrant stating that the bearer of the warrant is entitled to the shares specified in it, and may provide (by coupons or otherwise) for the payment of the future dividends on the shares included in the warrant.

**(2)** Such a warrant is termed a "share warrant" and entitles the bearer to the shares specified in it: and the shares may be transferred by delivery of the warrant."

## 189 Offences in connection with share warrants (Scotland)

**189(1) [Offence re defrauding warrant etc., penalty]** If in Scotland a person–

(a) with intent to defraud, forges or alters, or offers, utters, disposes of, or puts off, knowing the same to be forged or altered, any share warrant or coupon, or any document purporting to be a share warrant or coupon, issued in pursuance of this Act; or

(b) by means of any such forged or altered share warrant, coupon, or document, purporting as aforesaid, demands or endeavours to obtain or receive any share or interest in any company under this Act, or to receive any dividend or money payable in respect thereof, knowing the warrant, coupon, or document to be forged or altered;

he is on conviction thereof liable to imprisonment or a fine, or both.

**189(2) [Offence re making warrants, penalty]** If in Scotland a person without lawful authority or excuse (proof whereof lies on him)–

(a) engraves or makes on any plate, wood, stone, or other material, any share warrant or coupon purporting to be–
   (i) a share warrant or coupon issued or made by any particular company in pursuance of this Act; or
   (ii) a blank share warrant or coupon so issued or made; or
   (iii) a part of such a share warrant or coupon; or

(b) uses any such plate, wood, stone, or other material, for the making or printing of any such share warrant or coupon, or of any such blank share warrant or coupon, or any part thereof respectively; or

(c) knowingly has in his custody or possession any such plate, wood, stone, or other material;

he is on conviction thereof liable to imprisonment or a fine, or both.

DEBENTURES

## 190 Register of debenture holders

**190(1) [Scottish register not needed for English or Welsh companies]** A company registered in England and Wales shall not keep in Scotland any register of holders of debentures of the company or any duplicate of any such register or part of any such register which is kept outside Great Britain.

**190(2) [English or Welsh register not needed for Scottish companies]** A company registered in Scotland shall not keep in England and Wales any such register as above-mentioned.

**190(3) [Location of register]** Neither a register of holders of debentures of a company nor a duplicate of any such register or part of any such register which is kept outside Great Britain shall be kept in England and Wales (in the case of a company registered in England and Wales) or in Scotland (in the case of a company registered in Scotland) elsewhere than–

(a) at the company's registered office; or

(b) at any office of the company at which the work of making it up is done; or

(c) if the company arranges with some other person for the making up of the register or duplicate to be undertaken on its behalf by that other person, at the office of that other person at which the work is done.

**190(4) [Register and duplicate to be at same place]** Where a company keeps (in England and Wales or in Scotland, as the case may be) both such a register and such a duplicate, it shall keep them at the same place.

**190(5) [Notice to registrar]** Every company which keeps any such register or duplicate in England and Wales or Scotland shall send to the registrar of companies notice (in the prescribed form) of the place where the register or duplicate is kept and of any change in that place.

**Note**

See the Companies (Forms) Regulations 1991 (SI 1991/879), the Companies (Forms) (No. 2) Regulations 1991 (SI 1991/1259) and the Companies (Forms) (Amendment) Regulations 1995 (SI 1995/736).

**190(6) [No s. 190(5) notice if always at registered office]** But a company is not bound to send notice under sub-section (5) where the register or duplicate has, at all times since it came into existence, been kept at the company's registered office.

## 191 Right to inspect register

**191(1) [Inspection of register]** Every register of holders of debentures of a company shall, except when duly closed, be open to the inspection–

(a) of the registered holder of any such debentures or any holder of shares in the company without fee; and

(b) of any other person on payment of such fee as may be prescribed.

**History**

In s. 191(1) the words "(but subject to such reasonable restrictions as the company may impose in general meeting, so that not less than 2 hours in each day shall be allowed for inspection)" formerly appearing after the words "except when duly closed" omitted and repealed and the words "such fee as may be prescribed" substituted for the former words "a fee of 5 pence or such less sum as may be prescribed by the company" by CA 1989, s. 143(4)(a), 212 and Sch. 24 as from 1 November 1991 (see SI 1991/1996 (C 57), art. 2(2)(b), (c)).

**Note**

See note after s. 191(3).

**191(2) [Copy of register]** Any such registered holder of debentures or holder of shares, or any other person, may require a copy of the register of the holders of debentures of the company or any part of it, on payment of such fee as may be prescribed.

**History**

In s. 191(2) the words "such fee as may be prescribed" substituted for the former words "10 pence (or such less sum as may be prescribed by the company) for every 100 words, or fractional part of 100 words, required to be copied" by CA 1989 s. 143(4)(b) as from 1 November 1991 (see SI 1991/1996 (C 57), art. 2(2)(b)).

**Note**

See note after s. 191(3).

**191(3) [Copy on request of trust deed securing issue of debentures]** A copy of any trust deed for securing an issue of debentures shall be forwarded to every holder of any such debentures at his request on payment of such fee as may be prescribed.

**History**
In s. 191(3) the words "of such fee as may be prescribed" inserted and para. (a) and (b) formerly appearing after the words "on payment" omitted and repealed by CA 1989, s. 143(4)(c), 212 and Sch. 24 as from 1 November 1991 (see SI 1991/1996 (C 57), art. 2(2)(b), (c)); former para. (a) and (b) read as follows:

"(a) in the case of a printed trust deed, of 20 pence (or such less sum as may be prescribed by the company), or
(b) where the trust deed has not been printed, of 10 pence (or such less sum as may be so prescribed), for every 100 words, or fractional part of 100 words, required to be copied."

**Note**
Re s. 191(1)–(3) see the Companies (Inspection and Copying of Registers, Indices and Documents) Regulations 199 (SI 1991/1998).

**191(4) [Penalty re refusal of inspection]** If inspection is refused, or a copy is refused or not forwarded, the company and every officer of it who is in default is liable to a fine and, for continued contravention, to a daily default fine.

**191(5) [Court may compel inspection]** Where a company is in default as above-mentioned, the court may by order compel an immediate inspection of the register or direct that the copies required be sent to the person requiring them.

**191(6) [Closure of register]** For purposes of this section, a register is deemed to be duly closed if closed in accordance with provisions contained in the articles or in the debentures or, in the case of debenture stock, in the stock certificates, or in the trust deed or other document securing the debentures or debenture stock, during such period or periods, not exceeding in the whole 30 days in any year, as may be therein specified.

**191(7) [Time limit re liability for deletion etc.]** Liability incurred by a company from the making or deletion of an entry in its register of debenture holders, or from a failure to make or delete any such entry, is not enforceable more than 20 years after the date on which the entry was made or deleted or, in the case of any such failure, the failure first occurred.

This is without prejudice to any lesser period of limitation.

**Note**
Re application of s. 191 in regard to uncertificated debentures see the Uncertificated Securities Regulations 1992 (SI 1992/225), Sch. 2, para. 1.

## 192 Liability of trustees of debentures

**192(1) [Certain provisions in trust deed exempting trustees void]** Subject to this section, any provision contained–

(a) in a trust deed for securing an issue of debentures, or
(b) in any contract with the holders of debentures secured by a trust deed,

is void in so far as it would have the effect of exempting a trustee of the deed from, or indemnifying him against, liability for breach of trust where he fails to show the degree of care and diligence required of him as trustee, having regard to the provisions of the trust deed conferring on him any powers, authorities or discretions.

**192(2) [Releases etc.]** Subsection (1) does not invalidate–

(a) a release otherwise validly given in respect of anything done or omitted to be done by a trustee before the giving of the release; or
(b) any provision enabling such a release to be given–
   (i) on the agreement thereto of a majority of not less than three-fourths in value of the debenture holders present and voting in person or, where proxies are permitted, by proxy at a meeting summoned for the purpose, and
   (ii) either with respect to specific acts or omissions or on the trustee dying or ceasing to act.

**192(3) [Exceptions to s. 192(1)]** Subsection (1) does not operate–

(a) to invalidate any provision in force on 1st July 1948 so long as any person then entitled to the benefit of that provision or afterwards given the benefit of that provision under the following subsection remains a trustee of the deed in question; or
(b) to deprive any person of any exemption or right to be indemnified in respect of anything done or omitted to be done by him while any such provision was in force.

**192(4) [Benefits of s. 192(3)]** While any trustee of a trust deed remains entitled to the benefit of a provision save by subsection (3), the benefit of that provision may be given either–

See also history note after s. 209(13).

**209(11) [Conditions in s. 209(10)(c)]** The conditions referred to in subsection (10)(c) are, in relation to a settlement–

(a) that it is irrevocable, and

(b) that the settlor (within the meaning of section 670 of the Income and Corporation Taxes Act 1988) has no interest in any income arising under, or property comprised in, the settlement.

**History**

See history note after s. 209(13).

**209(12) [Extent of s. 208(4)(b)]** A person is not by virtue of section 208(4)(b) taken to be interested in shares by reason only that he has been appointed a proxy to vote at a specified meeting of a company or of any class of its members and at any adjournment of that meeting, or has been appointed by a corporation to act as its representative at any meeting of a company or of any class of its members.

**History**

See history note after s. 209(13).

**209(13) [Application of s. 209(1)(a) to Scottish trust property]** In the application of subsection (1)(a) to property held on trust according to the law of Scotland, for the words "or remainder or an interest of a bare trustee" there shall be substituted "or in fee or an interest of a simple trustee".

**History**

S. 209 substituted by the Disclosure of Interests in Shares (Amendment) Regulations 1993 (SI 1993/1819), reg. 1, 2, 8 as from 18 September 1993 (see transitional provisions in reg. 11); s. 209 formerly read as follows:

"**209(1)** The following interests in shares are disregarded for purposes of sections 198 to 202–

(a) where property is held on trust according to the law of England and Wales and an interest in shares is comprised in that property, an interest in reversion or remainder or of a bare trustee or a custodian trustee, and any discretionary interest;

(b) where property is held on trust according to the law of Scotland and an interest in shares is comprised in that property, an interest in fee or of a simple trustee and any discretionary interest;

(c) an interest which subsists by virtue of an authorised unit trust scheme within the meaning of the Financial Services Act 1986, a scheme made under section 22 or 22A of the Charities Act 1960 or section 24 or 25 of the Charities Act 1993, section 11 of the Trustee Investments Act 1961 or section 1 of the Administration of Justice Act 1965 or the scheme set out in the Schedule to the Church Funds Investment Measure 1958;

(d) an interest of the Church of Scotland General Trustees or of the Church of Scotland Trust in shares held by them or of any other person in shares held by those Trustees or that Trust otherwise than as simple trustees;

(e) an interest for the life of himself or another of a person under a settlement in the case of which the property comprised in the settlement consists of or includes shares, and the conditions mentioned in subsection (3) below are satisfied;

(f) an exempt interest held by a recognised jobber or market maker;

(g) an exempt security interest;

(h) an interest of the President of the Family Division of the High Court subsisting by virtue of section 9 of the Administration of Estates Act 1925;

(i) an interest of the Accountant General of the Supreme Court in shares held by him.

**(2)** A person is not by virtue of section 208(4)(b) taken to be interested in shares by reason only that he has been appointed a proxy to vote at a specified meeting of a company or of any class of its members and at any adjournment of that meeting, or has been appointed by a corporation to act as its representative at any meeting of a company or of any class of its members.

**(3)** The conditions referred to in subsection (1)(e) are, in relation to a settlement–

(a) that it is irrevocable, and

(b) that the settlor (within the meaning of section 670 of the Income and Corporation Taxes Act 1988) has no interest in any income arising under, or property comprised in, the settlement.

**(4)** A person is a recognised jobber for purposes of subsection (1)(f) if he is a member of The Stock Exchange recognised by the Council of The Stock Exchange as carrying on the business of a jobber; and an interest of such a person in shares is an exempt interest for those purposes if–

(a) he carries on that business in the United Kingdom, and

(b) he holds the interest for the purposes of that business.

**(4A)** A person is a market maker for the purposes of subsection (1)(f) if–

(a) he holds himself out at all normal times in compliance with the rules of a recognised investment exchange other than an overseas investment exchange (within the meaning of the Financial Services Act 1986) as willing to buy and sell securities at prices specified by him; and

(b) is recognised as doing so by that investment exchange;

and an interest of such a person in shares is an exempt interest if he carries on business as a market maker in the United Kingdom, is subject to such rules in the carrying on of that business and holds the interest for the purposes of that business.

**(5)** An interest in shares is an exempt security interest for purposes of subsection (1)(g) if–

(a) it is held by a person who is–

(i) a banking company or an insurance company to which Part II of the Insurance Companies Act 1982 applies, or

(ii) a trustee savings bank (within the Trustee Savings Banks Act 1981), or
(iii) a member of The Stock Exchange carrying on business in the United Kingdom as a stock broker, and
(b) it is held by way of security only for the purposes of a transaction entered into in the ordinary course of his business as such a person,

or if it is held by way of security only either by the Bank of England or by the Post Office for the purposes of a transaction entered into in the ordinary course of that part of the business of the Post Office which consists of the provision of banking services."

Previously (former) s. 209 amended as follows:

- in s. 209(1)(c) the words "the Financial Services Act 1986" substituted for the original words "the Prevention of Fraud (Investments) Act 1958" by Financial Services Act 1986, s. 212(2) and Sch. 16, para. 18, the words "or 22A" inserted by Charities Act 1992, s. 78(1) and Sch. 6, para. 11 as from 1 September 1992 (see SI 1992/1900 (C 64), art. 2 and Sch. 1), the words "or section 24 or 25 of the Charities Act 1993" inserted by Charities Act 1993, s. 98(1), 99(1) and Sch. 6, para. 20 (1), (3) as from 1 August 1993; in s. 209(1)(f) the words "or market maker" inserted by Financial Services Act 1986, s. 197(1)(a) as from 29 April 1988 (see SI 1988/740 (C 22)); and s. 209(1)(j) originally appearing at the end repealed by CA 1989, s. 212 and Sch. 24 as from 31 May 1990 (see SI 1990/713 (C 22), art. 3(ii)); s. 209(1)(j) originally read as follows:

"(j) such interests, or interests of such a class, as may be prescribed for purposes of this paragraph by regulations made by the Secretary of State by statutory instrument."

(in regard to any regulations under original s. 209(1)(j), see CA 1985, s. 210A(1) below and CA 1989, s. 134(6));

- in s. 209(3)(b) the words "670 of the Income and Corporation Taxes Act" substituted for the original words "444 of the Income and Corporation Taxes Act 1970" by Income and Corporation Taxes Act 1988, s. 844 and Sch. 29, para. 32 for companies' accounting periods ending after 5 April 1988 (see s. 843(1));
- s. 209(4A) inserted by Financial Services Act 1986, s. 197(1)(b) as from 29 April 1988 (see SI 1988/740 (C 22)); and
- in s. 209(5)(a) the words "a banking company" substituted for the previous words "an authorised institution" by CA 1989, s. 23and Sch. 10, para. 2 as from 1 April 1990 subject to transitional and saving provisions (see SI 1990/355 (C 13), art. 3, Sch. 1 and also see art. 6–9); previously the words "an authorised institution" substituted for the original words "a recognised bank or licensed institution within the meaning of the Banking Act 1979" by Banking Act 1987, s. 108(1) and Sch. 6, para. 18(1) as from 1 October 1987 (see SI 1987/1664 (C 50)).

# 210 Other provisions about notification under this Part

**210(1) [Notification by agent of shares acquired or disposed of]** Where a person authorises another ("the agent") to acquire or dispose of, on his behalf, interests in shares comprised in relevant share capital of a public company, he shall secure that the agent notifies him immediately of acquisitions or disposals effected by the agent which will or may give rise to any obligation of disclosure imposed on him by this Part with respect to his interest in that share capital.

**210(2) [Particulars of person making notification]** An obligation of disclosure imposed on a person by any provision of sections 198 to 202 is treated as not being fulfilled unless the notice by means of which it purports to be fulfilled identifies him and gives his address and, in a case where he is a director of the company, is expressed to be given in fulfilment of that obligation.

**210(3) [Offences]** A person who–

(a) fails to fulfil, within the proper period, an obligation of disclosure imposed on him by this Part, or
(b) in purported fulfilment of any such obligation makes to a company a statement which he knows to be false, or recklessly makes to a company a statement which is false, or
(c) fails to fulfil, within the proper period, an obligation to give another person a notice required by section 206, or
(d) fails without reasonable excuse to comply with subsection (1) of this section,

is guilty of an offence and liable to imprisonment or a fine, or both.

**210(4) [Defence to s. 210(3) offences]** It is a defence for a person charged with an offence under subsection (3)(c) to prove that it was not possible for him to give the notice to the other person required by section 206 within the proper period, and either–

(a) that it has not since become possible for him to give the notice so required, or
(b) that he gave the notice as soon after the end of that period as it became possible for him to do so.

**210(5) [Directions by Secretary of State where person convicted of offence]** Where a person is convicted of an offence under this section (other than an offence relating to his ceasing to be interested in a company's shares), the Secretary of State may by order direct that the shares in relation to which the offence was committed shall, until further order, be subject to the

**218(3) [Penalty]** If default is made in complying with subsection (1) or (2), the company and every officer of it who is in default is liable to a fine and, for continued contravention of subsection (2), to a daily default fine.

# 219 Inspection of register and reports

**219(1) [Inspection]** Any register of interests in shares and any report which is required by section 215(7) to be available for inspection in accordance with this section shall be open to the inspection of any member of the company or of any other person without charge.

**History**
In s. 219(1) the words "during business hours (subject to such reasonable restrictions as the company may in general meeting impose, but so that not less than 2 hours in each day are allowed for inspection)" formerly appearing after the words "this section shall" omitted and repealed by CA 1989, s. 143(5)(a), 212 and Sch. 24 as from 1 November 1991 (see SI 1991/1996 (C 57), art. 2(2)(b), (c)).

**Note**
See the Companies (Inspection and Copying of Registers, Indices and Documents) Regulations 1991 (SI 1991/1998).

**219(2) [Copy of register or report]** Any such member or other person may require a copy of any such register or report, or any part of it, on payment of such fee as may be prescribed; and the company shall cause any copy so required by a person to be sent to him before the expiration of the period of 10 days beginning with the day next following that on which the requirement is received by the company.

**History**
In s. 219(2) the words "such fee as may be prescribed" substituted for the former words "10 pence or such less sum as the company may prescribe, for every 100 words or fractional part of 100 words required to be copied" by CA 1989, s. 143(5)(b) as from 1 November 1991 (see SI 1991/1996(C 57), art. 2(2)(b)).

**Note**
See the Companies (Inspection and Copying of Registers, Indices and Documents) Regulations 1991 (SI 1991/1998).

**219(3) [Penalty]** If an inspection required under this section is refused or a copy so required is not sent within the proper period, the company and every officer of it who is in default is liable to a fine and, for continued contravention, to a daily default fine.

**219(4) [Power of court to compel inspection or copy]** In the case of a refusal of an inspection required under this section of any register or report, the court may by order compel an immediate inspection of it; and in the case of failure to send a copy required under this section, the court may by order direct that the copy required shall be sent to the person requiring it.

**219(5) [Regulations]** The Secretary of State may by regulations made by statutory instrument substitute a sum specified in the regulations for the sum for the time being mentioned in subsection (2).

SUPPLEMENTARY

# 220 Definitions for Part VI

**220(1) [Definitions]** In this Part of this Act–

**"associated index"**, in relation to a register, means the index kept in relation to that register in pursuance of section 211(6);

**"authorised credit institution"** means a credit institution as defined in Article 1 of Council Directive 77/780/EEC which is authorised to carry on the business of a credit institution by a competent authority of a member State other than the United Kingdom;

**"authorised insurance undertaking"** means an insurance undertaking which has been authorised in accordance with Article 6 or 23 of Council Directive 73/239/EEC or Article 6 or 27 of Council Directive 79/267/EEC, or is authorised under the law of a member State to carry on insurance business restricted to re-insurance;

**"authorised unit trust scheme"** has the same meaning as in Chapter VIII of Part I of the Financial Services Act 1986;

**"depositary receipt"** means a certificate or other record (whether or not in the form of a document)–

(a) which is issued by or on behalf of a person who holds shares or who holds evidence of the right to receive shares, or has an interest in shares, in a particular company; and

(b) which evidences or acknowledges that another person is entitled to rights in relation to those shares or shares of the same kind, which shall include the right to receive such shares (or evidence of the right to receive such shares) from the person mentioned in paragraph (a);

**"derivatives"** means–

(a) options to acquire or dispose of shares; and

(b) rights under a contract falling within paragraph 8 of Schedule 1 to the Financial Services Act 1986 (futures), where the property in question is shares;

**"designated agency"** has the same meaning as in the Financial Services Act 1986;

**"investment company with variable capital"** has the same meaning as in the Open-Ended Investment Companies (Investment Companies with Variable Capital) Regulations 1996;

**"listed company"** means a company any of the shares in which are officially listed on a relevant stock exchange and "listed" shall be construed accordingly;

**"material interest"** shall be construed in accordance with section 199(2A);

**"operator"**, in relation to a collective investment scheme, shall be construed in accordance with section 75(8) of the Financial Services Act 1986;

**"recognised clearing house"**, **"recognised professional body"**, **"recognised scheme"**, and **"recognised self-regulating organisation"** have the same meaning as in the Financial Services Act 1986;

**"register of interests in shares"** means the register kept in pursuance of section 211 including, except where the context otherwise requires, that part of the register kept in pursuance of section 213;

**"relevant investment exchange"** means an exchange situated or operating in a member State on which derivatives are traded;

**"relevant share capital"** has the meaning given by section 198(2);

**"relevant stock exchange"** means a stock exchange situated or operating in a member State;

**"UCITS"** has the meaning given by section 199(8);

**"units"** has the same meaning as in section 75 of the Financial Services Act 1986.

**History**

S. 220(1) substituted by the Disclosure of Interests in Shares (Amendment) Regulations 1993 (SI 1993/1819), reg. 1, 2, 9 as from 18 September 1993 (see transitional provisions in reg. 11); s. 220(1) formerly read as follows:

"In this Part of this Act–

**'associated index'**, in relation to a register, means the index kept in relation to that register in pursuance of section 211(6),

**'register of interests in shares'** means the register kept in pursuance of section 211 including, except where the context otherwise requires, that part of the register kept in pursuance of section 213, and

**'relevant share capital'** has the meaning given by section 198(2)."

Definition of **"investment company with variable capital"** inserted by the Open-Ended Investment Companies (Investment Companies with Variable Capital) Regulations 1996 (SI 1996/2827), reg. 1, 75, and Sch. 8, para. 7 as from 6 January 1997.

**220(2) [Calculation of time]** Where the period allowed by any provision of this Part for fulfilling an obligation is expressed as a number of days, any day that is a Saturday or Sunday or a bank holiday in any part of Great Britain is to be disregarded in reckoning that period.

# PART VII – ACCOUNTS AND AUDIT

**Note**

Pt. VII (in its original form) was previously CA 1980, Pt. I which implemented the Fourth EC Company Law Directive (78/660).

## Chapter I – Provisions Applying to Companies Generally

### ACCOUNTING RECORDS

### 221 Duty to keep accounting records

**221(1) [Duty of company]** Every company shall keep accounting records which are sufficient to show and explain the company's transactions and are such as to–

(a) disclose with reasonable accuracy, at any time, the financial position of the company at that time, and

(b) enable the directors to ensure that any balance sheet and profit and loss account prepared under this Part complies with the requirements of this Act.

**221(2) [Contents]** The accounting records shall in particular contain–

(a) entries from day to day of all sums of money received and expended by the company, and the matters in respect of which the receipt and expenditure takes place, and

(b) a record of the assets and liabilities of the company.

**221(3) [Where business re goods]** If the company's business involves dealing in goods, the accounting records shall contain–

(a) statements of stock held by the company at the end of each financial year of the company,

(b) all statements of stocktakings from which any such statement of stock as is mentioned in paragraph (a) has been or is to be prepared, and

(c) except in the case of goods sold by way of ordinary retail trade, statements of all goods sold and purchased, showing the goods and the buyers and sellers in sufficient detail to enable all these to be identified.

**221(4) [Duty of parent company]** A parent company which has a subsidiary undertaking in relation to which the above requirements do not apply shall take reasonable steps to secure that the undertaking keeps such accounting records as to enable the directors of the parent company to ensure that any balance sheet and profit and loss account prepared under this Part complies with the requirements of this Act.

**221(5) [Offence]** If a company fails to comply with any provision of this section, every officer of the company who is in default is guilty of an offence unless he shows that he acted honestly and that in the circumstances in which the company's business was carried on the default was excusable.

**221(6) [Penalty]** A person guilty of an offence under this section is liable to imprisonment or a fine, or both.

**History**
See history note after s. 262A.

# 222 Where and for how long records to be kept

**222(1) [Location, inspection]** A company's accounting records shall be kept at its registered office or such other place as the directors think fit, and shall at all times be open to inspection by the company's officers.

**222(2) [If records outside Great Britain]** If accounting records are kept at a place outside Great Britain, accounts and returns with respect to the business dealt with in the accounting records so kept shall be sent to, and kept at, a place in Great Britain, and shall at all times be open to such inspection.

**222(3) [Accounts and records sent to Great Britain]** The accounts and returns to be sent to Great Britain shall be such as to–

(a) disclose with reasonable accuracy the financial position of the business in question at intervals of not more than six months, and

(b) enable the directors to ensure that the company's balance sheet and profit and loss account comply with the requirements of this Act.

**222(4) [Offence]** If a company fails to comply with any provision of subsections (1) to (3), every officer of the company who is in default is guilty of an offence, and liable to imprisonment or a fine or both, unless he shows that he acted honestly and that in the circumstances in which the company's business was carried on the default was excusable.

**222(5) [Preservation of records]** Accounting records which a company is required by section 221 to keep shall be preserved by it–

(a) in the case of a private company, for three years from the date on which they are made, and

(b) in the case of a public company, for six years from the date on which they are made.

This is subject to any provision contained in rules made under section 411 of the Insolvency Act 1986 (company insolvency rules).

**222(6) [Offence, penalty re s. 222(5)]** An officer of a company is guilty of an offence, and liable to imprisonment or a fine or both, if he fails to take all reasonable steps for securing compliance by the company with subsection (5) or intentionally causes any default by the company under that subsection.

**History**

See history note after s. 262A.

## A COMPANY'S FINANCIAL YEAR AND ACCOUNTING REFERENCE PERIODS

## 223 A company's financial year

**223(1) ["Financial year"]** A company's "financial year" is determined as follows.

**223(2) [First financial year]** Its first financial year begins with the first day of its first accounting reference period and ends with the last day of that period or such other date, not more than seven days before or after the end of that period, as the directors may determine.

**223(3) [Subsequent financial years]** Subsequent financial years begin with the day immediately following the end of the company's previous financial year and end with the last day of its next accounting reference period or such other date, not more than seven days before or after the end of that period, as the directors may determine.

**223(4) [Undertaking not a company]** In relation to an undertaking which is not a company, references in this Act to its financial year are to any period in respect of which a profit and loss account of the undertaking is required to be made up (by its constitution or by the law under which it is established), whether that period is a year or not.

**223(5) [Subsidiary undertakings]** The directors of a parent company shall secure that, except where in their opinion there are good reasons against it, the financial year of each of its subsidiary undertakings coincides with the company's own financial year.

**History**

See history note after s. 262A.

## 224 Accounting reference periods and accounting reference date

**224(1) [Determination of periods]** A company's accounting reference periods are determined according to its accounting reference date.

**224(2) [Notice by company]** A company incorporated before 1st April 1996 may, at any time before the end of the period of nine months beginning with the date of its incorporation, by notice in the prescribed form given to the registrar specify its accounting reference date, that is, the date on which its accounting reference period ends in each calendar year.

**History**

In s. 224(2) the words "incorporated before 1st April 1996" inserted by the Companies Act 1985 (Miscellaneous Accounting Amendments) Regulations 1996 (SI 1996/189), reg. 1(2), 2(1), (2) as from 1 April 1996, subject to reg. 16(1)–(3).

**Note**

See note after s. 225(1).

**224(3) [Where no s. 224(2) notice]** Failing such notice, the accounting reference date of such a company is–

(a) in the case of a company incorporated before 1st April 1990, 31st March;

(b) in the case of a company incorporated after 1st April 1990, the last day of the month in which the anniversary of its incorporation falls.

**History**

In s. 224(3) the words "the accounting reference date of such a company" substituted for the former words "a company's accounting reference date" by the Companies Act 1985 (Miscellaneous Accounting Amendments) Regulations 1996 (SI 1996/189), reg. 1(2), 2(1), (3) as from 1 April 1996, subject to reg. 16(1)–(3); and the words "1st April 1990" (appearing twice) substituted for the former words "the commencement of section 3 of the Companies Act 1989" and "the commencement of that section" respectively by SI 1990/355 (C 13), art. 15 as from 1 April 1990.

**224(3A) [Accounting reference date]** The accounting reference date of a company incorporated on or after 1st April 1996 is the last day of the month in which the anniversary of its incorporation falls.

**History**
S. 224(3A) inserted by the Companies Act 1985 (Miscellaneous Accounting Amendments) Regulations 1996 (SI 1996/189), reg. 1(2), 2(1), (4) as from 1 April 1996, subject to reg. 16(1)–(3).

**224(4) [First accounting reference period]** A company's first accounting reference period is the period of more than six months, but not more than 18 months, beginning with the date of its incorporation and ending with its accounting reference date.

**224(5) [Subsequent periods]** Its subsequent accounting reference periods are successive periods of twelve months beginning immediately after the end of the previous accounting reference period and ending with its accounting reference date.

**224(6) [Effect of s. 225]** This section has effect subject to the provisions of section 225 relating to the alteration of accounting reference dates and the consequences of such alteration.

**History**
See history note after s. 262A.

# 225 Alteration of accounting reference date

**225(1) [Notice by company re current and subsequent periods]** A company may by notice in the prescribed form given to the registrar specify a new accounting reference date having effect in relation to–

(a) the company's current accounting reference period and subsequent periods; or

(b) the company's previous accounting reference period and subsequent periods.

A company's **"previous accounting reference period"** means that immediately preceding its current accounting reference period.

**History**
In s. 225(1) the words "having effect in relation to–" to the end substituted for the former words "having effect in relation to the company's current accounting reference period and subsequent periods." by the Companies Act 1985 (Miscellaneous Accounting Amendments) Regulations 1996 (SI 1996/189), reg. 1(2), 3(1), (2) as from 1 April 1996, subject to reg. 16(1)–(3).

**Note**
Re s. 224(2), 225(1), (2) see the Companies (Forms) (Amendment) Regulations 1996 (SI 1996/594).

**225(2)** (Repealed by the Companies Act 1985 (Miscellaneous Accounting Amendments) Regulations 1996 (SI 1996/189), reg. 1(2), 3(1), (3) as from 1 April 1996, subject to reg. 16(1)–(3).)

**History**
S. 225(2) formerly read as follows:

"A company may by notice in the prescribed form given to the registrar specify a new accounting reference date having effect in relation to the company's previous accounting reference period and subsequent periods if–

(a) the company is a subsidiary undertaking or parent undertaking of another company and the new accounting reference date coincides with the accounting reference date of that other company, or

(b) an administration order under Part II of the Insolvency Act 1986 is in force.

A company's **"previous accounting reference period"** means that immediately preceding its current accounting reference period."

**Note**
See note after s. 225(1).

**225(3) [Contents of s. 225(1) notice]** The notice shall state whether the current or previous accounting reference period–

(a) is to be shortened, so as to come to an end on the first occasion on which the new accounting reference date falls or fell after the beginning of the period, or

(b) is to be extended, so as to come to an end on the second occasion on which that date falls or fell after the beginning of the period.

**225(4) [Time for s. 225(1) notice]** A notice under subsection (1) stating that the current or previous accounting reference period is to be extended is ineffective, except as mentioned below, if given less than five years after the end of an earlier accounting reference period of the company which was extended by virtue of this section.

This subsection does not apply–

(a) to a notice given by a company which is a subsidiary undertaking or parent undertaking of another EEA undertaking if the new accounting reference date coincides with that of the other EEA undertaking or, where that undertaking is not a company, with the last day of its financial year, or

(b) where an administration order is in force under Part II of the Insolvency Act 1986, or where the Secretary of State directs that it should not apply, which he may do with respect to a notice which has been given or which may be given.

**History**

In s. 225(4) the words "or previous" inserted after the word "current" and para. (a) substituted by the Companies Act 1985 (Miscellaneous Accounting Amendments) Regulations 1996 (SI 1996/189), reg. 1(2), 3(1), (4) as from 1 April 1996, subject to reg. 16(1)–(3); para. (a) formerly read as follows:

"(a) to a notice given by a company which is a subsidiary undertaking or parent undertaking of another company and the new accounting reference date coincides with that of the other company, or".

**225(5) [Where no s. 225(1) notice]** A notice under subsection (1) may not be given in respect of a previous accounting reference period if the period allowed for laying and delivering accounts and reports in relation to that period has already expired.

**History**

In s. 225(5) the words "subsection (1)" substituted for the former words "subsection (2)(a)", the words "in respect of a previous accounting reference period" inserted after the word "given", and the words "that period" substituted for the former words "the previous accounting reference period" by the Companies Act 1985 (Miscellaneous Accounting Amendments) Regulations 1996 (SI 1996/189), reg. 1(2), 3(1), (5) as from 1 April 1996, subject to reg. 16(1)–(3).

**225(6) [Limit on extension of accounting reference period]** An accounting reference period may not in any case, unless an administration order is in force under Part II of the Insolvency Act 1986, be extended so as to exceed 18 months and a notice under this section is ineffective if the current or previous accounting reference period as extended in accordance with the notice would exceed that limit.

**225(7) ["EEA undertaking"]** In this section **"EEA undertaking"**means an undertaking established under the law of any part of the United Kingdom or the law of any other EEA State.

**History**

S. 225(7) inserted by the Companies Act 1985 (Miscellaneous Accounting Amendments) Regulations 1996 (SI 1996/189), reg. 1(2), 3(1), (6) as from 1 April 1996, subject to reg. 16(1)–(3).
See history note after s. 262A.

### ANNUAL ACCOUNTS

## 226 Duty to prepare individual company accounts

**226(1) [Duty of directors]** The directors of every company shall prepare for each financial year of the company–

(a) a balance sheet as at the last day of the year, and

(b) a profit and loss account.

Those accounts are referred to in this Part as the company's "individual accounts".

**226(2) [Requirements for true and fair view]** The balance sheet shall give a true and fair view of the state of affairs of the company as at the end of the financial year; and the profit and loss account shall give a true and fair view of the profit or loss of the company for the financial year.

**226(3) [Compliance with Sch. 4]** A company's individual accounts shall comply with the provisions of Schedule 4 as to the form and content of the balance sheet and profit and loss account and additional information to be provided by way of notes to the accounts.

**226(4) [Additional information]** Where compliance with the provisions of that Schedule, and the other provisions of this Act as to the matters to be included in a company's individual accounts or in notes to those accounts, would not be sufficient to give a true and fair view, the necessary additional information shall be given in the accounts or in a note to them.

**226(5) [Special circumstances]** If in special circumstances compliance with any of those provisions is inconsistent with the requirement to give a true and fair view, the directors shall depart from that provision to the extent necessary to give a true and fair view.

Particulars of any such departure, the reasons for it and its effect shall be given in a note to the accounts.

**History**

See history note after s. 262A.

## 227 Duty to prepare group accounts

**227(1) [Directors' duty]** If at the end of a financial year a company is a parent company the directors shall, as well as preparing individual accounts for the year, prepare group accounts.

**227(2) [Contents of group accounts]** Group accounts shall be consolidated accounts comprising–

(a) a consolidated balance sheet dealing with the state of affairs of the parent company and its subsidiary undertakings, and

(b) a consolidated profit and loss account dealing with the profit or loss of the parent company and its subsidiary undertakings.

**227(3) [Requirements for true and fair view]** The accounts shall give a true and fair view of the state of affairs as at the end of the financial year, and the profit or loss for the financial year, of the undertakings included in the consolidation as a whole, so far as concerns members of the company.

**227(4) [Compliance with Sch. 4A]** A company's group accounts shall comply with the provisions of Schedule 4A as to the form and content of the consolidated balance sheet and consolidated profit and loss account and additional information to be provided by way of notes to the accounts.

**227(5) [Additional information]** Where compliance with the provisions of that Schedule, and the other provisions of this Act, as to the matters to be included in a company's group accounts or in notes to those accounts, would not be sufficient to give a true and fair view, the necessary additional information shall be given in the accounts or in a note to them.

**227(6) [Special circumstances]** If in special circumstances compliance with any of those provisions is inconsistent with the requirement to give a true and fair view, the directors shall depart from that provision to the extent necessary to give a true and fair view.

Particulars of any such departure, the reasons for it and its effect shall be given in a note to the accounts.

**History**
See history note after s. 262A.

# 228 Exemption for parent companies included in accounts of larger group

**228(1) [Exemption from requirement to prepare group accounts]** A company is exempt from the requirement to prepare group accounts if it is itself a subsidiary undertaking and its immediate parent undertaking is established under the law of a member State of the European Economic Community, in the following cases–

(a) where the company is a wholly-owned subsidiary of that parent undertaking;

(b) where that parent undertaking holds more than 50 per cent of the shares in the company and notice requesting the preparation of group accounts has not been served on the company by shareholders holding in aggregate–
  (i) more than half of the remaining shares in the company, or
  (ii) 5 per cent of the total shares in the company.

Such notice must be served not later than six months after the end of the financial year before that to which it relates.

**228(2) [Conditions for exemption]** Exemption is conditional upon compliance with all of the following conditions–

(a) that the company is included in consolidated accounts for a larger group drawn up to the same date, or to an earlier date in the same financial year, by a parent undertaking established under the law of a member State of the European Economic Community;

(b) that those accounts are drawn up and audited, and that parent undertaking's annual report is drawn up, according to that law, in accordance with the provisions of the Seventh Directive (83/349/EEC) (where applicable as modified by the provisions of the Bank Accounts Directive (86/635/EEC) or the Insurance Accounts Directive (91/674/EEC));

(c) that the company discloses in its individual accounts that it is exempt from the obligation to prepare and deliver group accounts;

(d) that the company states in its individual accounts the name of the parent undertaking which draws up the group accounts referred to above and–
(i) if it is incorporated outside Great Britain, the country in which it is incorporated,
(iii) if it is unincorporated, the address of its principal place of business;
(e) that the company delivers to the registrar, within the period allowed for delivering its individual accounts, copies of those group accounts and of the parent undertaking's annual report, together with the auditors' report on them; and
(f) (subject to section 710B(6) (delivery of certain Welsh documents without a translation)) that if any document comprised in accounts and reports delivered in accordance with paragraph (e) is in a language other than English, there is annexed to the copy of that document delivered a translation of it into English, certified in the prescribed manner to be a correct translation.

**History**
In s. 228(2)(b) the words in parentheses "where applicable" to "Bank Accounts Directive (86/635/EEC)" inserted by the Companies Act 1985 (Disclosure of Branches and Bank Accounts) Regulations 1992 (SI 1992/3178), reg. 1, 4 as from 1 January 1993 and the words "or the Insurance Accounts Directive (91/674/EEC)" inserted by the Companies Act 1985 (Insurance Companies Accounts) Regulations 1993 (SI 1993/3246), reg. 1, 5, Sch. 2, para. 1 as from 19 December 1993 subject to exemption in reg. 6 and transitional provisions in reg. 7.
S. 228(2)(d)(ii) repealed by the Companies Act 1985 (Miscellaneous Accounting Amendments) Regulations 1996 (SI 1996/189), reg. 1(1), 4 as from 2 February 1996, subject to reg. 16(1), (2); s. 228(2)(d)(ii) formerly read as follows:
"(ii) if it is incorporated in Great Britain, whether it is registered in England and Wales or in Scotland, and"
In s. 228(2)(f) the words in parentheses "(subject to" to "without a translation))" inserted by Welsh Language Act 1993, s. 30 (1), (3) as from 1 February 1994 (see SI 1994/115 (C 5), art. 2(2)).

**228(3) [No exemption for certain listed companies]** The exemption does not apply to a company any of whose securities are listed on a stock exchange in any member State of the European Economic Community.

**228(4) [Interpretation re s. 228(1)(a)]** Shares held by directors of a company for the purpose of complying with any share qualification requirement shall be disregarded in determining for the purposes of subsection (1)(a) whether the company is a wholly-owned subsidiary.

**228(5) [Interpretation re s. 228(1)(b)]** For the purposes of subsection (1)(b) shares held by a wholly-owned subsidiary of the parent undertaking, or held on behalf of the parent undertaking or a wholly-owned subsidiary, shall be attributed to the parent undertaking.

**228(6) ["Securities" in s. 228(3)]** In subsection (3) **"securities"** includes–
(a) shares and stock,
(b) debentures, including debenture stock, loan stock, bonds, certificates of deposit and other instruments creating or acknowledging indebtedness,
(c) warrants or other instruments entitling the holder to subscribe for securities falling within paragraph (a) or (b), and
(d) certificates or other instruments which confer–
(i) property rights in respect of a security falling within paragraph (a), (b) or (c),
(ii) any right to acquire, dispose of, underwrite or convert a security, being a right to which the holder would be entitled if he held any such security to which the certificate or other instrument relates, or
(iii) a contractual right (other than an option) to acquire any such security otherwise than by subscription.

**History**
See history note after s. 262A.

# 229 Subsidiary undertakings included in the consolidation

**229(1) [All subsidiaries to be in consolidation]** Subject to the exceptions authorised or required by this section, all the subsidiary undertakings of the parent company shall be included in the consolidation.

**229(2) [Exclusion if not material]** A subsidiary undertaking may be excluded from consolidation if its inclusion is not material for the purpose of giving a true and fair view; but two or more undertakings may be excluded only if they are not material taken together.

**229(3) [Further grounds for exclusion]** In addition, a subsidiary undertaking may be excluded from consolidation where–

(a) severe long-term restrictions substantially hinder the exercise of the rights of the parent company over the assets or management of that undertaking, or

(b) the information necessary for the preparation of group accounts cannot be obtained without disproportionate expense or undue delay, or

(c) the interest of the parent company is held exclusively with a view to subsequent resale and the undertaking has not previously been included in consolidated group accounts prepared by the parent company.

The reference in paragraph (a) to the rights of the parent company and the reference in paragraph (c) to the interest of the parent company are, respectively, to rights and interests held by or attributed to the company for the purposes of section 258 (definition of "parent undertaking") in the absence of which it would not be the parent company.

**229(4) [Where subsidiaries' activities so different]** Where the activities of one or more subsidiary undertakings are so different from those of other undertakings to be included in the consolidation that their inclusion would be incompatible with the obligation to give a true and fair view, those undertakings shall be excluded from consolidation.

This subsection does not apply merely because some of the undertakings are industrial, some commercial and some provide services, or because they carry on industrial or commercial activities involving different products or provide different services.

**229(5) [Where all subsidiaries within exclusions]** Where all the subsidiary undertakings of a parent company fall within the above exclusions, no group accounts are required.

**History**
See history note after s. 262A.

## 230 Treatment of individual profit and loss account where group accounts prepared

**230(1) [Application]** The following provisions apply with respect to the individual profit and loss account of a parent company where–

(a) the company is required to prepare and does prepare group accounts in accordance with this Act, and

(b) the notes to the company's individual balance sheet show the company's profit or loss for the financial year determined in accordance with this Act.

**230(2) [Profit and loss account need not have certain information]** The profit and loss account need not contain the information specified in paragraphs 52 to 57 of Schedule 4 (information supplementing the profit and loss account).

**230(3) [Approval, omission]** The profit and loss account must be approved in accordance with section 233(1) (approval by board of directors) but may be omitted from the company's annual accounts for the purposes of the other provisions below in this Chapter.

**230(4) [Disclosure re exemption]** The exemption conferred by this section is conditional upon its being disclosed in the company's annual accounts that the exemption applies.

**History**
See history note after s. 262A.

## 231 Disclosure required in notes to accounts: related undertakings

**231(1) [Information in Sch. 5]** The information specified in Schedule 5 shall be given in notes to a company's annual accounts.

**231(2) [Sch. 5, Pt. I, II]** Where the company is not required to prepare group accounts, the information specified in Part I of that Schedule shall be given; and where the company is required to prepare group accounts, the information specified in Part II of that Schedule shall be given.

**231(3) [Information need not be disclosed re certain foreign undertakings]** The information required by Schedule 5 need not be disclosed with respect to an undertaking which–

(a) is established under the law of a country outside the United Kingdom, or

(b) carries on business outside the United Kingdom,

if in the opinion of the directors of the company the disclosure would be seriously prejudicial to the business of that undertaking, or to the business of the company or any of its subsidiary undertakings, and the Secretary of State agrees that the information need not be disclosed.

This subsection does not apply in relation to the information required under paragraph 6, 9A, 20 or 28A of that Schedule.

**History**

In s. 231(3) the words "5(2)" formerly appearing before the words "6, 9A, 20" repealed by the Companies Act 1985 (Miscellaneous Accounting Amendments) Regulations 1996 (SI 1996/189), reg. 1(1), 15(1) as from 2 February 1996, subject to reg. 16(1), (2). Previously the words "paragraph 5(2), 6, 9A, 20 or 28A" substituted for the former words "paragraph 5(2), 6 or 20" by the Partnerships and Unlimited Companies (Accounts) Regulations 1993 (SI 1993/1820), reg. 1(2), 11(1) as from 21 July 1993.

**231(4) [Where advantage taken of s. 231(3)]** Where advantage is taken of subsection (3), that fact shall be stated in a note to the company's annual accounts.

**231(5) [Where information of excessive length]** If the directors of the company are of the opinion that the number of undertakings in respect of which the company is required to disclose information under any provision of Schedule 5 to this Act is such that compliance with that provision would result in information of excessive length being given, the information need only be given in respect of–

(a) the undertakings whose results or financial position, in the opinion of the directors, principally affected the figures shown in the company's annual accounts, and

(b) undertakings excluded from consolidation under section 229(3) or (4).

**History**

In s. 231(5) the words "This subsection does not apply in relation to the information required under paragraph 10 or 29 of that Schedule", formerly appearing at the end, repealed by the Companies Act 1985 (Miscellaneous Accounting Amendments) Regulations 1996 (SI 1996/189), reg. 1(2), 15(1) as from 2 February 1996, subject to reg. 16(1), (2).

**231(6) [Where advantage taken of s. 231(5)]** If advantage is taken of subsection (5)–

(a) there shall be included in the notes to the company's annual accounts a statement that the information is given only with respect to such undertakings as are mentioned in that subsection, and

(b) the full information (both that which is disclosed in the notes to the accounts and that which is not) shall be annexed to the company's next annual return.

For this purpose the **"next annual return"** means that next delivered to the registrar after the accounts in question have been approved under section 233.

**231(7) [Penalty re non-compliance with s. 231(6)(b)]** If a company fails to comply with subsection (6)(b), the company and every officer of it who is in default is liable to a fine and, for continued contravention, to a daily default fine.

**History**

See history note after s. 262A.

## 232 Disclosure required in notes to accounts: emoluments and other benefits of directors and others

**232(1) [Information in Sch. 6]** The information specified in Schedule 6 shall be given in notes to a company's annual accounts.

**232(2) [Sch. 6, Pt. I–III]** In that Schedule–

Part I relates to the emoluments of directors (including emoluments waived), pensions of directors and past directors, compensation for loss of office to directors and past directors and sums paid to third parties in respect of directors' services,

Part II relates to loans, quasi-loans and other dealings in favour of directors and connected persons, and

Part III relates to transactions, arrangements and agreements made by the company or a subsidiary undertaking for officers of the company other than directors.

**232(3) [Notice by directors and others]** It is the duty of any director of a company, and any person who is or has at any time in the preceding five years been an officer of the company, to give notice to the company of such matters relating to himself as may be necessary for the purposes of Part I of Schedule 6.

**232(4) [Offence re s. 232(3)]** A person who makes default in complying with subsection (3) commits an offence and is liable to a fine.

**History**
See history note after s. 262A.

## APPROVAL AND SIGNING OF ACCOUNTS

# 233 Approval and signing of accounts

**233(1) [Approval, signing]** A company's annual accounts shall be approved by the board of directors and signed on behalf of the board by a director of the company.

**233(2) [Signature on balance sheet]** The signature shall be on the company's balance sheet.

**233(3) [Every balance sheet to state name of signatory]** Every copy of the balance sheet which is laid before the company in general meeting, or which is otherwise circulated, published or issued, shall state the name of the person who signed the balance sheet on behalf of the board.

**233(4) [Signatory of balance sheet delivered to registrar]** The copy of the company's balance sheet which is delivered to the registrar shall be signed on behalf of the board by a director of the company.

**233(5) [Offence, penalty re non-compliance]** If annual accounts are approved which do not comply with the requirements of this Act, every director of the company who is party to their approval and who knows that they do not comply or is reckless as to whether they comply is guilty of an offence and liable to a fine.

For this purpose every director of the company at the time the accounts are approved shall be taken to be a party to their approval unless he shows that he took all reasonable steps to prevent their being approved.

**Note**
S. 233(5) in force from 7 January 1991 subject to transitional and saving provisions (see SI 1990/2569 (C 68), art. 3, 6).

**233(6) [Further offence, penalty]** If a copy of the balance sheet–

(a) is laid before the company, or otherwise circulated, published or issued, without the balance sheet having been signed as required by this section or without the required statement of the signatory's name being included, or

(b) is delivered to the registrar without being signed as required by this section,

the company and every officer of it who is in default is guilty of an offence and liable to a fine.

**History**
See history note after s. 262A but note that s. 233(5) not in force at same time as rest of section.

## DIRECTORS' REPORT

# 234 Duty to prepare directors' report

**234(1) [Duty of directors]** The directors of a company shall for each financial year prepare a report–

(a) containing a fair review of the development of the business of the company and its subsidiary undertakings during the financial year and of their position at the end of it, and

(b) stating the amount (if any) which they recommend should be paid as dividend.

**History**
In s. 234(1)(b) the words "and the amount (if any) which they propose to carry to reserves" formerly appearing after the word "dividend" repealed by the Companies Act 1985 (Miscellaneous Accounting Amendments) Regulations 1996 (SI 1996/189), reg. 1(1), 5(1), (2) as from 2 February 1996, subject to reg. 16(1), (2).

**234(2) [Contents of report]** The report shall state the names of the persons who, at any time during the financial year, were directors of the company, and the principal activities of the company and its subsidiary undertakings in the course of the year and any significant change in those activities in the year.

**234(3) [Compliance with Sch. 7]** The report shall also comply with Schedule 7 as regards the disclosure of the matters mentioned there.

**234(4) [Sch. 7, Pt. I–V]** In Schedule 7–

Part I relates to matters of a general nature, including changes in asset values, directors' shareholdings and other interests and contributions for political and charitable purposes,
Part II relates to the acquisition by a company of its own shares or a charge on them,
Part III relates to the employment, training and advancement of disabled persons,
Part V relates to the involvement of employees in the affairs, policy and performance of the company,
Part VI relates to the company's policy and practice on the payment of creditors.

**History**
In s. 234(4) the words "and practice" appearing before the words "on the payment of creditors." inserted by the Companies Act 1985 (Directors' Report) (Statement of Payment Practice) Regulations 1997 (SI 1997/571), reg. 1, 2(1) as from 4 March 1997. Previously in s. 234(4) the words "Part IV relates to the health, safety and welfare at work of the company's employees, and" formerly appearing before "Part V"omitted, and the words "Part VI" to the end inserted by the Companies Act 1985 (Miscellaneous Accounting Amendments) Regulations 1995 (SI 1996/189), reg. 1(1), 5(1), (3) as from 2 February 1996, subject to reg. 16(1), (2).

**234(5) [Offence, penalty]** In the case of any failure to comply with the provisions of this Part as to the preparation of a directors' report and the contents of the report, every person who was a director of the company immediately before the end of the period for laying and delivering accounts and reports for the financial year in question is guilty of an offence and liable to a fine.

**234(6) [Defence]** In proceedings against a person for an offence under this section it is a defence for him to prove that he took all reasonable steps for securing compliance with the requirements in question.

**History**
See history note after s. 262A.

## 234A Approval and signing of directors' report

**234A(1) [Approval, signing]** The directors' report shall be approved by the board of directors and signed on behalf of the board by a director or the secretary of the company.

**234A(2) [Every report to state name of signatory]** Every copy of the directors' report which is laid before the company in general meeting, or which is otherwise circulated, published or issued, shall state the name of the person who signed it on behalf of the board.

**234A(3) [Signatory of report sent to registrar]** The copy of the directors' report which is delivered to the registrar shall be signed on behalf of the board by a director or the secretary of the company.

**234A(4) [Offence, penalty]** If a copy of the directors' report–

(a) is laid before the company, or otherwise circulated, published or issued, without the report having been signed as required by this section or without the required statement of the signatory's name being included, or

(b) is delivered to the registrar without being signed as required by this section,

the company and every officer of it who is in default is guilty of an offence and liable to a fine.

**History**
See history note after s. 262A.

### AUDITORS' REPORT

## 235 Auditors' report

**235(1) [Duty of auditors]** A company's auditors shall make a report to the company's members on all annual accounts of the company of which copies are to be laid before the company in general meeting during their tenure of office.

**235(2) [Contents of report]** The auditors' report shall state whether in the auditors' opinion the annual accounts have been properly prepared in accordance with this Act, and in particular whether a true and fair view is given–

(a) in the case of an individual balance sheet, of the state of affairs of the company as at the end of the financial year,

(b) in the case of an individual profit and loss account, of the profit or loss of the company for the financial year,

| *Length of period* | *Public company* | *Private company* |
|---|---|---|
| Not more than 3 months. | £500 | £100 |
| More than 3 months but not more than 6 months. | £1,000 | £250 |
| More than 6 months but not more than 12 months. | £2,000 | £500 |
| More than 12 months. | £5,000 | £1,000 |

**242A(3) [Recovery and payment of penalty]** The penalty may be recovered by the registrar and shall be paid by him into the Consolidated Fund.

**242A(4) [Not a defence]** It is not a defence in proceedings under this section to prove that the documents in question were not in fact prepared as required by this Part.

**History**
S. 242A inserted by CA 1989, s. 1 and 11 as from 1 July 1992 subject to a transitional provision (see SI 1991/2945 (C 92)).

## 242B Delivery and publication of accounts in ECUs

**242B(1) [Amounts translated into ECUs]** The amounts set out in the annual accounts of a company may also be shown in the same accounts translated into ECUs.

**242B(2) [Delivery of copy to registrar]** When complying with section 242, the directors of a company may deliver to the registrar an additional copy of the company's annual accounts in which the amounts have been translated into ECUs.

**242B(3) [Exchange rate]** In both cases–

(a) the amounts must have been translated at the relevant exchange rate prevailing on the balance sheet date, and

(b) that rate must be disclosed in the notes to the accounts.

**242B(4) [Copy treated as statutory accounts]** For the purposes of section 240 any additional copy of the company's annual accounts delivered to the registrar under subsection (2) shall be treated as statutory accounts of the company and, in the case of such a copy, references in section 240 to the auditors' report under section 235 shall be read as references to the auditors' report on the annual accounts of which it is a copy.

**242B(5) [Definitions]** In this section–

**"ECU"** means a unit with a value equal to the value of the unit of account known as the ecu used in the European Monetary System, and

**"relevant exchange rate"** means the rate of exchange used for translating the value of the ecu for the purposes of that System.

**History**
S. 242B inserted by the Companies Act 1985 (Accounts of Small and Medium-Sized Enterprises and Publication of Accounts in ECUs) Regulations 1992 (SI 1992/2452), reg. 1, 3 as from 16 November 1992.

## 243 Accounts of subsidiary undertakings to be appended in certain cases

**243(1) [Application]** The following provisions apply where at the end of the financial year a parent company has as a subsidiary undertaking–

(a) a body corporate incorporated outside Great Britain which does not have an established place of business in Great Britain, or

(b) an unincorporated undertaking,

which is excluded from consolidation in accordance with section 229(4) (undertaking with activities different from the undertakings included in the consolidation).

**243(2) [Documents to be appended]** There shall be appended to the copy of the company's annual accounts delivered to the registrar in accordance with section 242 a copy of the undertaking's latest individual accounts and, if it is a parent undertaking, its latest group accounts.

If the accounts appended are required by law to be audited, a copy of the auditors' report shall also be appended.

**243(3) [Period for accounts]** The accounts must be for a period ending not more than twelve months before the end of the financial year for which the parent company's accounts are made up.

**243(4) [Documents not in English]** If any document required to be appended is in a language other than English, then, subject to section 710B(6) (delivery of certain Welsh documents without a translation), the directors shall annex to the copy of that document delivered a translation of it into English, certified in the prescribed manner to be a correct translation.

**History**

In s. 243(4) the words "Subject to section 255E (delivery of accounting documents in Welsh only)," formerly appearing at the beginning repealed by Welsh Language Act 1993, s. 35(1) and Sch. 2 as from 1 February 1994 (see SI 1994/115 (C 5), art. 2(2)); these words were previously inserted by the Companies Act 1985 (Welsh Language Accounts) Regulations 1992 (SI 1992/1083), reg. 1(1), 2(1), (3) as from 1 June 1992.

Also in s. 243(4) the words "then, subject to section 710B(6) (delivery of certain Welsh documents without a translation)," inserted by Welsh Language Act 1993, s. 30 (1), (4)(a) as from 1 February 1994 (see SI 1994/115 (C 5), art. 2(2)).

**243(5) [Qualifications]** The above requirements are subject to the following qualifications–

(a) an undertaking is not required to prepare for the purposes of this section accounts which would not otherwise be prepared, and if no accounts satisfying the above requirements are prepared none need be appended;

(b) a document need not be appended if it would not otherwise be required to be published, or made available for public inspection, anywhere in the world, but in that case the reason for not appending it shall be stated in a note to the company's accounts;

(c) where an undertaking and all its subsidiary undertakings are excluded from consolidation in accordance with section 229(4), the accounts of such of the subsidiary undertakings of that undertaking as are included in its consolidated group accounts need not be appended.

**243(6) [Application of s. 242(2)–(4)]** Subsections (2) to (4) of section 242 (penalties, etc. in case of default) apply in relation to the requirements of this section as they apply in relation to the requirements of subsection (1) of that section.

**History**

See history note after s. 262A.

## 244 Period allowed for laying and delivering accounts and reports

**244(1) [Usual relevant period]** The period allowed for laying and delivering accounts and reports is–

(a) for a private company, 10 months after the end of the relevant accounting reference period, and

(b) for a public company, 7 months after the end of that period.

This is subject to the following provisions of this section.

**244(2) [If first accounting reference period is more than 12 months]** If the relevant accounting reference period is the company's first and is a period of more than 12 months, the period allowed is–

(a) 10 months or 7 months, as the case may be, from the first anniversary of the incorporation of the company, or

(b) 3 months from the end of the accounting reference period,

whichever last expires.

**244(3) [Notice where foreign business]** Where a company carries on business, or has interests, outside the United Kingdom, the Channel Islands and the Isle of Man, the directors may, in respect of any financial year, give to the registrar before the end of the period allowed by subsection (1) or (2) a notice in the prescribed form–

(a) stating that the company so carries on business or has such interests, and

(b) claiming a 3 month extension of the period allowed for laying and delivering accounts and reports;

**245B(5) [Matters to be considered for order]** Where the court makes an order under subsection (4) it shall have regard to whether the directors party to the approval of the defective accounts knew or ought to have known that the accounts did not comply with the requirements of this Act, and it may exclude one or more directors from the order or order the payment of different amounts by different directors.

**245B(6) [Order or notice to registrar]** On the conclusion of proceedings on an application under this section, the applicant shall give to the registrar for registration an office copy of the court order or, as the case may be, notice that the application has failed or been withdrawn.

**245B(7) [Revised accounts]** The provisions of this section apply equally to revised annual accounts, in which case the references to revised accounts shall be read as references to further revised accounts.

**History**

See history note after s. 262A.

## 245C Other persons authorised to apply to court

**245C(1) [Power of Secretary of State]** The Secretary of State may authorise for the purposes of section 245B any person appearing to him–

(a) to have an interest in, and to have satisfactory procedures directed to securing, compliance by companies with the accounting requirements of this Act,

(b) to have satisfactory procedures for receiving and investigating complaints about the annual accounts of companies, and

(c) otherwise to be a fit and proper person to be authorised.

**245C(2) [Scope of authorisation]** A person may be authorised generally or in respect of particular classes of case, and different persons may be authorised in respect of different classes of case.

**245C(3) [Refusal to authorise]** The Secretary of State may refuse to authorise a person if he considers that his authorisation is unnecessary having regard to the fact that there are one or more other persons who have been or are likely to be authorised.

**245C(4) [Authorisation by statutory instrument]** Authorisation shall be by order made by statutory instrument which shall be subject to annulment in pursuance of a resolution of either House of Parliament.

**245C(5) [Revocation of authorisation]** Where authorisation is revoked, the revoking order may make such provision as the Secretary of State thinks fit with respect to pending proceedings.

**245C(6) [Limit on liability for damages]** Neither a person authorised under this section, nor any officer, servant or member of the governing body of such a person, shall be liable in damages for anything done or purporting to be done for the purposes of or in connection with–

(a) the taking of steps to discover whether there are grounds for an application to the court,

(b) the determination whether or not to make such an application, or

(c) the publication of its reasons for any such decision,

unless the act or omission is shown to have been in bad faith.

**History**

See history note after s. 262A.

**Note**

See the Companies (Defective Accounts) (Authorised Person) Order 1991 (SI 1991/13).

# Chapter II – Exemptions, Exceptions and Special Provisions

SMALL AND MEDIUM-SIZED COMPANIES AND GROUPS

## 246 Special provisions for small companies

**246(1) [Application of s. 246]** Subject to section 247A, this section applies where a company qualifies as a small company in relation to a financial year.

**246(2) [Compliance with Sch. 8]** If the company's individual accounts for the year–

(a) comply with the provisions of Schedule 8, or

(b) fail to comply with those provisions only in so far as they comply instead with one or more corresponding provisions of Schedule 4,

they need not comply with the provisions or, as the case may be, the remaining provisions of Schedule 4; and where advantage is taken of this subsection, references in section 226 to compliance with the provisions of Schedule 4 shall be construed accordingly.

**246(3) [Information needed in company's accounts]** The company's individual accounts for the year–

(a) may give the total of the aggregates required by paragraphs (a), (c) and (d) of paragraph 1(1) of Schedule 6 (emoluments and other benefits etc. of directors) instead of giving those aggregates individually; and

(b) need not give the information required by–
  (i) paragraph 4 of Schedule 5 (financial years of subsidiary undertakings);
  (ii) paragraph 1(2)(b) of Schedule 6 (numbers of directors exercising share options and receiving shares under long term incentive schemes);
  (iii) paragraph 2 of Schedule 6 (details of highest paid director's emoluments etc.); or
  (iv) paragraph 7 of Schedule 6 (excess retirement benefits of directors and past directors).

**History**

S. 246(3) substituted by the Company Accounts (Disclosure of Directors' Emoluments) Regulations 1997 (SI 1997/570), reg. 1, 6(1) as from 31 March 1997 and effective as respects companies' financial years ending on or after that date. The former s. 246(3) read as follows:

"The company's individual accounts for the year need not give the information required by–
(a) paragraph 4 of Schedule 5 (financial years of subsidiary undertakings);
(b) paragraph 1(3) of Schedule 6 (breakdown of aggregate amount of directors' emoluments);
(c) paragraphs 2 to 5 of Schedule 6 (details of chairman's and directors' emoluments); or
(d) paragraph 7 of Schedule 6 (pensions of directors and past directors)."

**246(4) [Information not needed in directors' report]** The directors' report for the year need not give the information required by–

(a) section 234(1)(a) and (b) (fair review of business and amount to be paid as dividend);

(b) paragraph 1(2) of Schedule 7 (statement of market value of fixed assets where substantially different from balance sheet amount);

(c) paragraph 6 of Schedule 7 (miscellaneous disclosures); or

(d) paragraph 11 of Schedule 7 (employee involvement).

**246(5) [Delivery to registrar not needed]** Notwithstanding anything in section 242(1), the directors of the company need not deliver to the registrar any of the following, namely–

(a) a copy of the company's profit and loss account for the year;

(b) a copy of the directors' report for the year; and

(c) if they deliver a copy of a balance sheet drawn up as at the last day of the year which complies with the requirements of Schedule 8A, a copy of the company's balance sheet drawn up as at that day.

**246(6) [Information not needed in accounts or balance sheet]** Neither a copy of the company's accounts for the year delivered to the registrar under section 242(1), nor a copy of a balance sheet delivered to the registrar under subsection (5)(c), need give the information required by–

(a) paragraph 4 of Schedule 5 (financial years of subsidiary undertakings);

(b) paragraph 6 of Schedule 5 (shares of company held by subsidiary undertakings);

(c) Part I of Schedule 6 (directors' and chairman's emoluments, pensions and compensation for loss of office); or

(d) section 390A(3) (amount of auditors' remuneration).

**246(7) [Application of s. 233]** The provisions of section 233 as to the signing of the copy of the balance sheet delivered to the registrar apply to a copy of a balance sheet delivered under subsection (5)(c).

**246(8) [Statement of preparation in accordance with s. 246]** Subject to subsection (9), each of the following, namely–

(a) accounts prepared in accordance with subsection (2) or (3),

(b) a report prepared in accordance with subsection (4), and

(c) a copy of accounts delivered to the registrar in accordance with subsection (5) or (6),

shall contain a statement in a prominent position on the balance sheet, in the report or, as the case may be, on the copy of the balance sheet, above the signature required by subsection 233, 234A or subsection (7), that they are prepared in accordance with the special provisions of this Part relating to small companies.

**246(9) [Non-application of s. 246(8)]** Subsection (8) does not apply where the directors of the company have taken advantage of the exemption from audit conferred by section 249AA (dormant companies).

**History**

In s. 246(9) the words "the directors of the company" to the end substituted for the former words "the company is exempt by virtue of section 250 (dormant companies) from the obligation to appoint auditors" by the Companies Act 1985 (Audit Exemption) (Amendment) Regulations 2000 (SI 2000/1430), reg. 1, 8(1) as from 26 May 2000 in relation to annual accounts and reports in respect of financial years ending on or after 26 July 2000.

S. 246 substituted by the Companies Act 1985 (Accounts of Small and Medium-sized Companies and Minor Accounting Amendments) Regulations 1997 (SI 1997/220), reg. 1, 2(1), as from 1 March 1997. Previous to that, s. 246 substituted by the Companies Act 1989, s. 13(1).

Previous s. 246 read as follows:

"**246 Exemptions for small and medium-sized companies**

**246(1)** A company which qualifies as a small or medium-sized company in relation to a financial year–

(a) is exempt from the requirements of paragraph 36A of Schedule 4 (disclosure with respect to compliance with accounting standards), and

(b) is entitled to the exemptions provided by Part III of Schedule 8 with respect to the delivery to the registrar under section 242 of individual accounts and other documents for that financial year.

**(1A)** A company which qualifies as a small company in relation to a financial year is entitled to the exemptions provided by Part I of Schedule 8 with respect to the preparation of annual accounts for that year if its balance sheet contains, above the signature required by section 233–

(a) a statement to the effect that advantage has been taken, in the preparation of the accounts, of special exemptions applicable to small companies, and

(b) a statement of the grounds on which, in the directors' opinion, the company is entitled to those exemptions.

**(1B)** A company which qualifies as a small company in relation to a financial year is entitled to the exemptions provided by Part II of Schedule 8 with respect to the preparation of a directors' report for that year if the report contains, above the signature required by section 234A–

(a) a statement to the effect that advantage has been taken, in the preparation of the report, of special exemptions applicable to small companies, and

(b) where the company's balance sheet for that year does not contain a statement under subsection (1A)(b), a statement of the grounds on which, in the directors' opinion, the company is entitled to those exemptions.

**(2)** (Repealed by the Companies Act 1985 (Accounts of Small and Medium-Sized Enterprises and Publication of Accounts in ECUs) Regulations 1992 (SI 1992/2452), reg. 1, 4(2)(b) as from 16 November 1992.)"

S. 246(2) formerly read as follows:

"In that Schedule–

Part I relates to small companies,
Part II relates to medium-sized companies, and
Part III contains supplementary provisions."

"**(3)** A company is not entitled to the exemptions mentioned in subsections (1), (1A) and (1B) if it is, or was at any time within the financial year to which the accounts relate–

(a) a public company,

(b) a banking or insurance company, or

(c) an authorised person under the Financial Services Act 1986,

or if it is or was at any time during that year a member of an ineligible group.

**(4)** A group is ineligible if any of its members is–

(a) a public company or a body corporate which (not being a company) has power under its constitution to offer its shares or debentures to the public and may lawfully exercise that power,

(b) an authorised institution under the Banking Act 1987,

(c) an insurance company to which Part II of the Insurance Companies Act 1982 applies, or

(d) an authorised person under the Financial Services Act 1986.

**(5)** A parent company shall not be treated as qualifying as a small company in relation to a financial year unless the group headed by it qualifies as a small group, and shall not be treated as qualifying as a medium-sized company in relation to a financial year unless that group qualifies as a medium-sized group (see section 249)."

See also history note after s. 262A.

## 246A Special provisions for medium-sized companies

**246A(1) [Application]** Subject to section 247A, this section applies where a company qualifies as a medium-sized company in relation to a financial year.

**246A(2) [Non-compliance with Sch. 4, para. 36A]** The company's individual accounts for the year need not comply with the requirements of paragraph 36A of Schedule 4 (disclosure with respect to compliance with accounting standards).

**246A(3) [Delivery of accounts]** The company may deliver to the registrar a copy of the company's accounts for the year–

(a) which includes a profit and loss account in which the following items listed in the profit and loss account formats set out in Part I of Schedule 4 are combined as one item under the heading "gross profit or loss"–
Items 1, 2, 3 and 6 in Format 1;
Items 1 to 5 in Format 2;
Items A.1, B.1 and B.2 in Format 3;
Items A.1, A.2 and B.1 to B.4 in Format 4;

(b) which does not contain the information required by paragraph 55 of Schedule 4 (particulars of turnover).

**246A(4) [Statement of preparation in accordance with s. 246A]** A copy of accounts delivered to the registrar in accordance with subsection (3) shall contain a statement in a prominent position on the copy of the balance sheet, above the signature required by section 233, that the accounts are prepared in accordance with the special provisions of this Part relating to medium-sized companies.

**History**

S. 246A inserted by the Companies Act 1985 (Accounts of Small and Medium-sized Companies and Minor Accounting Amendments) Regulations 1997 (SI 1997/220), reg. 1, 3 as from 1 March 1997.

## 247 Qualification of company as small or medium-sized

**247(1) [Time for meeting qualifying conditions]** A company qualifies as small or medium-sized in relation to a financial year if the qualifying conditions are met–

(a) in the case of the company's first financial year, in that year, and

(b) in the case of any subsequent financial year, in that year and the preceding year.

**247(2) [Relevant financial year for qualification]** A company shall be treated as qualifying as small or medium-sized in relation to a financial year–

(a) if it so qualified in relation to the previous financial year under subsection (1) above or was treated as so qualifying under paragraph (b) below; or

(b) if it was treated as so qualifying in relation to the previous year by virtue of paragraph (a) and the qualifying conditions are met in the year in question.

**History**

In s. 247(2)(a) the words "subsection (1) above or was treated as so qualifying under paragraph (b) below" substituted for the former words "subsection (1)" by the Companies Act 1985 (Accounts of Small and Medium- Sized Enterprises and Publication of Accounts in ECUs) Regulations 1992 (SI 1992/2452), reg. 1, 5(1), (2) as from 16 November 1992.

**247(3) [Qualification requirements]** The qualifying conditions are met by a company in a year in which it satisfies two or more of the following requirements–

| *Small company* | |
|---|---|
| 1. Turnover | Not more than £2.8 million |
| 2. Balance sheet total | Not more than £1.4 million |
| 3. Number of employees | Not more than 50 |
| *Medium-sized company* | |
| 1. Turnover | Not more than £11.2 million |
| 2. Balance sheet total | Not more than £5.6 million |
| 3. Number of employees | Not more than 250. |

**History**

In s. 247(3) under the heading "Small company" the words "Not more than £2.8 million" substituted for the former words "Not more than £2 million" and the words "Not more than £1.4 million" substituted for the former words "Not more than £975,000"; and under the heading "Medium-sized company" the words "Not more than £11.2 million" substituted for the former words "Not more than £8 million" and the words "Not more from £5.6 million" substituted for the former words "Not more than £3.9 million" by the Companies Act 1985 (Accounts of Small and Medium-Sized Enterprises and Publication of Accounts in ECUs) Regulations 1992 (SI 1992/2452), reg. 1, 5(1), (3), (4) as from 16 November 1992.

**247(4) [Where financial year not a year]** For a period which is a company's financial year but not in fact a year the maximum figures for turnover shall be proportionately adjusted.

(b) is preparing group accounts in respect of the same year.

**248A(2) [Compliance of group accounts]** If the group accounts–

(a) comply with the provisions of Schedule 8, or

(b) fail to comply with those provisions only in so far as they comply instead with one or more corresponding provisions of Schedule 4,

they need not comply with the provisions or, as the case may be, the remaining provisions of Schedule 4; and where advantage is taken of this subsection, references in Schedule 4A to compliance with the provisions of Schedule 4 shall be construed accordingly.

**248A(3) [Effect of s. 248A on Sch. 8]** For the purposes of this section, Schedule 8 shall have effect as if, in each balance sheet format set out in that Schedule, for item B.III there were substituted the following item–

"B.III Investments

(1) Shares in group undertakings
(2) Interests in associated undertakings
(3) Other participating interests
(4) Loans to group undertakings and undertakings in which a participating interest is held
(5) Other investments other than loans
(6) Others."

**248A(4) [Information not needed in group accounts]** The group accounts need not give the information required by the provisions specified in section 246(3).

**248A(5) [Statement of preparation in accordance with s. 248A]** Group accounts prepared in accordance with this section shall contain a statement in a prominent position on the balance sheet, above the signature required by section 233, that they are prepared in accordance with the special provisions of this Part relating to small companies.

**History**
S. 248A inserted by the Companies Act 1985 (Accounts of Small and Medium-sized Companies and Minor Accounting Amendments) Regulations 1997 (SI 1997/220), reg. 1, 6 as from 1 March 1997.

# 249 Qualification of group as small or medium-sized

**249(1) [Time for meeting qualifying conditions]** A group qualifies as small or medium-sized in relation to a financial year if the qualifying conditions are met–

(a) in the case of the parent company's first financial year, in that year, and

(b) in the case of any subsequent financial year, in that year and the preceding year.

**249(2) [Relevant financial year for qualification]** A group shall be treated as qualifying as small or medium-sized in relation to a financial year–

(a) if it so qualified in relation to the previous financial year under subsection (1) above or was treated as so qualifying under paragraph (b) below; or

(b) if it was treated as so qualifying in relation to the previous year by virtue of paragraph (a) and the qualifying conditions are met in the year in question.

**History**
In s. 249(2)(a) the words "subsection (1) above or was treated as so qualifying under paragraph (b) below" substituted for the former words "subsection 1" by the Companies Act 1985 (Accounts of Small and Medium-Sized Enterprises and Publication of Accounts in ECUs) Regulations 1992 (SI 1992/2452), reg. 1, 6(1), (2) as from 16 November 1992.

**249(3) [Qualification requirements]** The qualifying conditions are met by a group in a year in which it satisfies two or more of the following requirements–

| | *Small group* |
|---|---|
| 1. Aggregate turnover | Not more than £2.8 million net (or £3.36 million gross) |
| 2. Aggregate balance sheet total | Not more than £1.4 million net (or £1.68 million gross) |
| 3. Aggregate number of employees | Not more than 50 |

*Medium-sized group*

| | |
|---|---|
| 1. Aggregate turnover | Not more than £11.2 million net (or £13.44 million gross) |
| 2. Aggregate balance sheet total | Not more than £5.6 million net (or £6.72 million gross) |
| 3. Aggregate number of employees | Not more than 250. |

**History**

In s. 249(3) under the heading "Small group" the words "Not more than £2.8 million net (or £3.36 million gross)" substituted for the former words "Not more than £2 million net (or £2.4 million gross)"; the words "Not more than £1.4 million net (or £1.68 million gross)" substituted for the former words "Not more than £1 million net (or £1.2 million gross)"; and under the heading "Medium-sized group" the words "Not more than £11.2 million net (or £13.44 million gross)" substituted for the former words "Not more than £8 million net (or £9.6 million gross)"; and the words "Not more than £5.6 million net (or £6.72 million gross)" substituted for the former words "Not more than £3.9 million net (or £4.7 million gross)" by the Companies Act 1985 (Accounts of Small and Medium-Sized Enterprises and Publication of Accounts in ECUs) Regulations 1992 (SI 1992/2452), reg. 1, 6(1), (3), (4) as from 16 November 1992.

**249(4) [Aggregate figures]** The aggregate figures shall be ascertained by aggregating the relevant figures determined in accordance with section 247 for each member of the group.

In relation to the aggregate figures for turnover and balance sheet total, **"net"** means with the set-offs and other adjustments required by Schedule 4A in the case of group accounts and **"gross"** means without those set-offs and other adjustments; and a company may satisfy the relevant requirement on the basis of either the net or the gross figure.

**249(5) [Figures for each subsidiary]** The figures for each subsidiary undertaking shall be those included in its accounts for the relevant financial year, that is–

(a) if its financial year ends with that of the parent company, that financial year, and

(b) if not, its financial year ending last before the end of the financial year of the parent company.

**249(6) [Expense, delay re figures]** If those figures cannot be obtained without disproportionate expense or undue delay, the latest available figures shall be taken.

**History**

See history note after s. 262A.

## EXEMPTIONS FROM AUDIT FOR CERTAIN CATEGORIES OF SMALL COMPANY

# 249A Exemptions from audit

**249A(1) [Total exemption]** Subject to section 249B, a company which meets the total exemption conditions set out below in respect of a financial year is exempt from the provisions of this Part relating to the audit of accounts in respect of that year.

**249A(2) [Exemption where report by reporting accountant]** Subject to section 249B, a company which is a charity and which meets the report conditions set out below in respect of a financial year is exempt from the provisions of this Part relating to the audit of accounts in respect of that year if the directors cause a report in respect of the company's individual accounts for that year to be prepared in accordance with section 249C and made to the company's members.

**History**

In s. 249A(2) the words "a company which is a charity and" substituted for the former words "a company" by the Companies Act 1985 (Audit Exemption) (Amendment) Regulations 1997 (SI 1997/936), reg. 1, 2(1), 2(2) as from 15 April 1997 and apply to the annual accounts of any company for any financial year ending on or after 15 June 1997.

**Note**

See the Companies Act 1985 (Audit Exemption) (Amendment) Regulations 1995 (SI 1995/589), in particular reg. 3(1).

**249A(3) [Total exemption conditions]** The total exemption conditions are met by a company in respect of a financial year if–

(a) it qualifies as a small company in relation to that year for the purposes of section 246,

(b) its turnover in that year is not more than £1 million, and

(c) its balance sheet total for that year is not more than £1.4 million.

**History**

In s. 249A(3)(b) the words "£1 million" substituted for the former words "£350,000" by the Companies Act 1985 (Audit Exemption) (Amendment) Regulations 2000 (SI 2000/1430), reg. 1, 2(1), (2) as from 26 May 2000 in relation to annual accounts and reports in respect of financial years ending on or after 26 July 2000.

Previously, "£350,000" substituted for former words "£90,000" by the Companies Act 1985 (Audit Exemption) (Amendment) Regulations 1997 (SI 1997/936), reg. 1, 2(1), 2(3) as from 15 April 1997 and applied to the annual accounts of any company for any financial year ending on or after 15 June 1997.

**249A(3A) [Company which is a charity]** In relation to any company which is a charity, subsection (3)(b) shall have effect with the substitution–

(a) for the reference to turnover of a reference to gross income, and

(b) for the reference to £1 million of a reference to £90,000.

**History**
In s. 249A(3A)(b) the words "£1 million" substituted for the former words "£350,000" by the Companies Act 1985 (Audit Exemption) (Amendment) Regulations 2000 (SI 2000/1430), reg. 1, 2(1), (2) as from 26 May 2000 in relation to annual accounts and reports in respect of financial years ending on or after 26 July 2000.
S. 249A(3A) inserted by the Companies Act 1985 (Audit Exemption) (Amendment) Regulations 1997 (SI 1997/936), reg. 1, 2(1), 2(4) as from 15 April 1997, and applies to the annual accounts of any company for any financial year ending on or after 15 June 1997.

**249A(4) [Report conditions]** The report conditions are met by a company which is a charity in respect of a financial year if–

(a) it qualifies as a small company in relation to that year for the purposes of section 246,

(b) its gross income in that year is more than £90,000 but not more than £250,000, and

(c) its balance sheet total for that year is not more than £1.4 million.

**History**
In s. 249A(4) the words "a company which is a charity" substituted for the former words "a company" by the Companies Act 1985 (Audit Exemption) (Amendment) Regulations 1997 (SI 1997/936), reg. 1, 2(1), 2(5)(a) as from 15 April 1997; in s. 249A(4)(b) the words "gross income" substituted for the former word "turnover" and the words "£250,000" substituted for the former words "£350,000" by the Companies Act 1985 (Audit Exemption ) (Amendment) Regulations 1997 (SI 1997/936), reg. 1, 2(1), 2(5)(b)(i) and (ii) respectively as from 15 April 1997 and apply to the annual accounts of any company for any financial year ending on or after 15 June 1997.

**249A(5)** (Repealed by the Companies Act 1985 (Audit Exemption) (Amendment) Regulations 1997 (SI 1997/936), reg. 1, 2(1), 2(6) as from 15 April 1997, subject to reg. 1(2).)

**History**
The above repeal applies to the annual accounts of any companyfor any financial year ending on or after 15 June 1997.
S. 249A(5) formerly read as follows:

"In relation to any company which is a charity–

(a) subsection (3)(b) shall have effect with the substitution for the reference to turnover of a reference to gross income, and

(b) subsection (4)(b) shall have effect with the substitution–

(i) for the reference to turnover of a reference to a gross income, and

(ii) for the reference to £350,000 of a reference to £250,000."

**249A(6) [Where financial year not a year]** For a period which is a company's financial year but not in fact a year the maximum figures for turnover or gross income shall be proportionately adjusted.

**249A(6A) [Entitlement to exemption]** A company is entitled to the exemption conferred by subsection (1) or (2) notwithstanding that it falls within paragraph (a) or (b) of section 249AA(1).

**History**
In s. 249A(6A) the words "section 249AA(1)" substituted for the former words "250(1)" by the Companies Act 1985 (Audit Exemption) (Amendment) Regulations 2000 (SI 2000/1430), reg. 1, 2(1), (3) as from 26 May 2000 in relation to annual accounts and reports in respect of financial years ending on or after 26 July 2000.
S. 249A(6A) inserted by the Companies Act 1985 (Audit Exemption) (Amendment) Regulations 1997 (SI 1997/936), reg. 1, 2(1), 2(7) as from 15 April 1997 and applies to the annual accounts of any company for any financial year ending on or after 15 June 1997.

**249A(7) ["Balance sheet total", "gross income"]** In this section–

**"balance sheet total"** has the meaning given by section 247(5), and

**"gross income"** means the company's income from all sources, as shown in the company's income and expenditure account.

**History**
See history note after s. 249E.

# 249AA Dormant companies

**249AA(1) [Exemption from audit]** Subject to section 249B(2) to (5), a company is exempt from the provisions of this Part relating to the audit of accounts in respect of a financial year if–

(a) it has been dormant since its formation, or

(b) it has been dormant since the end of the previous financial year and subsection (2) applies.

**249AA(2) [Requirements for exemption]** This subsection applies if the company–

(a) is entitled in respect of its individual accounts for the financial year in question to prepare accounts in accordance with section 246, or would be so entitled but for the application of section 247A(1)(a)(i) or (b), and

(b) is not required to prepare group accounts for that year.

**249AA(3) [Cases where exemption not applicable]** Subsection (1) does not apply if at any time in the financial year in question the company was–

(a) a banking or insurance company, or

(b) an authorised person for the purposes of the Financial Services Act 1986.

**249AA(4) ["Dormant"]** A company is **"dormant"** during any period in which it has no significant accounting transaction.

**249AA(5) ["Significant accounting transaction"] "Significant accounting transaction"** means a transaction which–

(a) is required by section 221 to be entered in the company's accounting records; but

(b) is not a transaction to which subsection (6) or (7) applies.

**249AA(6) [Transaction not a significant accounting transaction]** This subsection applies to a transaction arising from the taking of shares in the company by a subscriber to the memorandum as a result of an undertaking of his in the memorandum.

**249AA(7) [Certain payments not a significant accounting transaction]** This subsection applies to a transaction consisting of the payment of–

(a) a fee to the registrar on a change of name under section 28 (change of name),

(b) a fee to the registrar on the re-registration of a company under Part II (re-registration as a means of altering a company's status),

(c) a penalty under section 242A (penalty for failure to deliver accounts), or

(d) a fee to the registrar for the registration of an annual return under Chapter III of Part XI.

**History**

S. 249AA inserted by the Companies Act 1985 (Audit Exemption) (Amendment) Regulations 2000 (SI 2000/1430), reg. 1, 3 as from 26 May 2000 in relation to annual accounts and reports in respect of financial years ending on or after 26 July 2000.

## 249B Cases where exemptions not available

**249B(1) [Cases where not available]** Subject to subsections (1A) to (1C), a company is not entitled to the exemption conferred by subsection (1) or (2) of section 249A in respect of a financial year if at any time within that year–

(a) it was a public company,

(b) it was a banking or insurance company,

(c) it was enrolled in the list maintained by the Insurance Brokers Registration Council under section 4 of the Insurance Brokers (Registration) Act 1977,

(d) it was an authorised person or an appointed representative under the Financial Services Act 1986,

(e) it was a special register body as defined in section 117(1) of the Trade Union and Labour Relations (Consolidation) Act 1992 or an employers' association as defined in section 122 of that Act, or

(f) it was a parent company or a subsidiary undertaking.

**History**

In s. 249B(1) the words "subsections (1A) to (1C)" substituted for the former words "subsection (1A)" by the Companies Act 1985 (Audit Exemption) (Amendment) Regulations 1997 (SI 1997/936), reg. 1, 3(1), 3(2) as from 15 April 1997 and apply to the annual accounts of any company for any financial year ending on or after 15 June 1997.

Previously in s. 249B(1) the words "Subject to subsection (1A)" inserted by the Companies Act 1985 (Miscellaneous Accounting Amendments) Regulations 1996 (SI 1996/189), reg. 1(1), 10(1), (2) as from 2 February 1996, subject to reg. 16(1), (2), (5).

**249B(1A) [Parent or subsidiary dormant]** A company which, apart from this subsection, would fall within subsection (1)(f) by virtue of its being a subsidiary undertaking for any period within a financial year shall not be treated as so falling if it is dormant (within the meaning of section 249AA) throughout that period.

**History**

In s. 249B(1A) the words "section 249AA" substituted for the former words "section 250" by the Companies Act 1985 (Audit Exemption) (Amendment) Regulations 2000 (SI 2000/1430), reg. 1, 4(1), (2) as from 26 May 2000 in relation to annual accounts and reports in respect of financial years ending on or after 26 July 2000.

S. 249B(1A) inserted by the Companies Act 1985 (Miscellaneous Accounting Amendments) Regulations 1996 (SI 1996/189), reg. 1(1), 10(1), (3) as from 2 February 1996, subject to reg. 16(1), (2), (5).

**249B(1B) [Parent or subsidiary not falling under s. 249B(1)(f)]** A company which, apart from this subsection, would fall within subsection (1)(f) by virtue of its being a parent company or a subsidiary undertaking for any period within a financial year, shall not be treated as so falling if throughout that period it was a member of a group meeting the conditions set out in subsection (1C).

**249B(1C) [Conditions referred to in s. 249B(1B)]** The conditions referred to in subsection (1B) are–

(a) that the group qualifies as a small group, in relation to the financial year within which the period falls, for the purposes of section 249 (or if all bodies corporate in such group were companies, would so qualify) and is not, and was not at any time within that year, an ineligible group within the meaning of section 248(2),

(b) that the group's aggregate turnover in that year (calculated in accordance with section 249), where the company referred to in subsection (1B) is a charity, is not more than £350,00 net (or £420,000 gross) or, where the company so referred to is not a charity, not more than £1 million net (or £1.2 million gross), and

(c) that the group's aggregate balance sheet total for that year (calculated in accordance with section 249) is not more than £1.4 million net (or £1.68 million gross).

**History**

In s. 249B(1C)(a) the words "(or if all bodies corporate in such group were companies, would so qualify)", and in s. 249B(1C)(b) the words ", where the company referred to in subsection (1B) is a charity," and "or, where the company so referred to is not a charity, not more than £1 million net (or £1.2 million gross)", inserted by the Companies Act 1985 (Audit Exemption) (Amendment) Regulations 2000 (SI 2000/1430), reg. 1, 4(1), (3) as from 26 May 2000 in relation to annual accounts and reports in respect of financial years ending on or after 26 July 2000.

S. 249B(1B), (1C) inserted by the Companies Act 1985 (Audit Exemption) (Amendment) Regulations 1997 (SI 1997/936), reg. 1, 3(1), 3(3) as from 15 April 1997 and apply to the annual accounts of any company for any financial year ending on or after 15 June 1997.

**249B(2) [Members' right to require audit]** Any member or members holding not less in the aggregate than 10 per cent in nominal value of the company's issued share capital or any class of it or, if the company does not have a share capital, not less than 10 per cent in number of the members of the company, may, by notice in writing deposited at the registered office of the company during a financial year but not later than one month before then end of that year, require the company to obtain an audit of its accounts for that year.

**249B(3) [Exemption not available where members require audit]** Where a notice has been deposited under subsection (2), the company is not entitled to the exemption conferred by subsection (1) or (2) of section 249A or by subsection (1) of section 249AA in respect of the financial year to which the notice relates.

**History**

In s. 249B(3) the words "or by subsection (1) of section 249AA" inserted by the Companies Act 1985 (Audit Exemption) (Amendment) Regulations 2000 (SI 2000/1430), reg. 1, 4(1), (4) as from 26 May 2000 in relation to annual accounts and reports in respect of financial years ending on or after 26 July 2000.

**249B(4) [Balance sheet statement]** A company is not entitled to the exemption conferred by subsection (1) or (2) of section 249A or by subsection (1) of section 249AA unless its balance sheet contains a statement by the directors–

(a) to the effect that for the year in question the company was entitled to exemption under subsection (1) or (2) of section 249A or subsection (1) of section 249AA,

(b) to the effect that members have not required the company to obtain an audit of its accounts for the year in question in accordance with subsection (2) of this section, and

(c) to the effect that the directors acknowledge their responsibilities for–

(i) ensuring that the company keeps accounting records which comply with section 221, and

(ii) preparing accounts which give a true and fair view of the state of affairs of the company as at the end of the financial year and of its profit or loss for the financial year in accordance with the requirements of section 226, and which otherwise comply with the requirements of this Act relating to accounts, so far as applicable to the company.

**History**

In s. 249B(4)the words "or by subsection (1) of section 249AA" inserted, in s. 249B(4)(a) the words "(as the case may be)" formerly appearing after the words "under subsection (1) or (2)" omitted and the words "or subsection (1) of section 249AA" inserted, and s. 249B(4)(b) substituted, by the Companies Act 1985 (Audit Exemption) (Amendment) Regulations 2000 (SI 2000/1430), reg. 1, 4(1), (5) as from 26 May 2000 in relation to annual accounts and reports in respect of financial years ending on or after 26 July 2000. S. 249B(4)(b) formerly read as follows:

"(b) to the effect that no notice has been deposited under subsection (2) of this section in relation to its accounts for the financial year, and".

Previously in s. 249B(4)(a)–(c) the words "to the effect" inserted at the beginning of each para. by the Companies Act 1985 (Miscellaneous Accounting Amendments) Regulations 1996 (SI 1996/189), reg. 1(1), 10(1), (4) as from 2 February 1996, subject to reg. 16(1), (2).

**249B(5) [Position of balance sheet statement]** The statement required by subsection (4) shall appear in the balance sheet above the signature required by section 233.

**History**

In s. 249B(5) the words "above the signature required by section 233" substituted for the former words "immediately above the signature required by section 246(1A) or by paragraph 23 of Schedule 8" by the Companies Act 1985 (Miscellaneous Accounting Amendments) Regulations 1996 (SI 1996/189), reg. 1(1), 10(1), (5) as from 2 February 1996, subject to reg. 16(1), (2).

See history note after s. 249E.

# 249C The report required for the purposes of section 249A(2)

**249C(1) [Report to be prepared by reporting accountant]** The report required for the purposes of section 249A(2) shall be prepared by a person (referred to in this Part as "the reporting accountant") who is eligible under section 249D.

**249C(2) [Opinion of reporting accountant]** The report shall state whether in the opinion of the reporting accountant making it–

(a) the accounts of the company for the financial year in question are in agreement with the accounting records kept by the company under section 221, and

(b) having regard only to, and on the basis of, the information contained in those accounting records, those accounts have been drawn up in a manner consistent with the provisions of this Act specified in subsection (6), so far as applicable to the company.

**249C(3) [Report also to state]** The report shall also state that in the opinion of the reporting accountant, having regard only to, and on the basis of, the information contained in the accounting records kept by the company under section 221, the company satisfied the requirements of subsection (4) of section 249A for the financial year in question, and did not fall within section 249B(1)(a) to (f) at any time within that financial year.

**History**

In s. 249C(3) the words "(or, where the company is a charity, of that subsection as modified by subsection (5) of that section)" formerly appearing after the words "of subsection (4) of section 249A" omitted by the Companies Act 1985 (Audit Exemption) (Amendment) Regulations 2000 (SI 2000/1430), reg. 1, 8(3) as from 26 May 2000 in relation to annual accounts and reports in respect of financial years ending on or after 26 July 2000.

**249C(4) [Name and signature of reporting accountant]** The report shall state the name of the reporting accountant and be signed by him.

**249C(5) [Where reporting accountant a company or partnership]** Where the reporting accountant is a body corporate or partnership, any reference to signature of the report, or any copy of the report, by the reporting accountant is a reference to signature in the name of the body corporate or partnership by a person authorised to sign on its behalf.

**249C(6) [Accounts consistent with provisions]** The provisions referred to in subsection (2)(b) are–

(a) section 226(3) and Schedule 4,

(b) section 231 and paragraphs 7 to 9A and 13(1), (3) and (4) of Schedule 5, and

(c) section 232 and Schedule 6,

where appropriate as modified by section 246(2) and (3).

**History**
In s. 249C(6) the words "section 246(2) and (3)" appearing after the words "where appropriate as modified by" substituted for former words "section 246(1)(a) and (1A) and Section A of Part I of Schedule 8" by the Companies Act 1985 (Accounts of Small and Medium-sized Companies and Minor Accounting Amendments) Regulations 1997 (SI 1997/220), reg. 1, 7(3) as from 1 March 1997.

# 249D The reporting accountant

**249D(1) [Qualification]** The reporting acountant shall be either–

(a) any member of a body listed in subsection (3) who, under the rules of the body–
  (i) is entitled to engage in public practice, and
  (ii) is not ineligible for appointment as a reporting accountant, or

(b) any person (whether or not a member of any such body) who–
  (i) is subject to the rules of any such body in seeking appointment or acting as auditor under Chapter V of Part XI, and
  (ii) under those rules, is eligible for appointment as auditor under that Chapter.

**History**
See history note after s. 249D(1A).

**249D(1A) [Interpretation of s. 249D(1)]** In subsection (1), references to the rules of a body listed in subsection (3) are to the rules (whether or not laid down by the body itself) which the body has power to enforce and which are relevant for the purposes of Part II of the Companies Act 1989 or this section.

This includes rules relating to the admission and expulsion of members of the body, so far as relevant for the purposes of that Part or this section.

**History**
S. 249D(1), (1A) substituted for the former s. 240D(1) by the Companies Act 1985 (Audit Exemption) (Amendment) Regulations 1995 (SI 1995/589), reg. 1, 2(1), (2) as from 30 March 1995 (see also reg. 3); former s. 249D(1) read as follows:
"The reporting accountant shall be a person who is a member of a body listed in subsection (3) and who, under the rules of the body, is either–
(a) entitled to engage in public practice and not ineligible for appointment as a reporting accountant, or
(b) eligible for appointment as a company auditor."

**249D(2) [Individual, company or partnership]** An individual, a body corporate or a partnership may be appointed as a reporting accountant, and section 26 of the Companies Act 1989 (effect of appointment of partnership) shall apply to the appointment as reporting accountant of a partnership constituted under the law of England and Wales or Northern Ireland, or under the law of any other country or territory in which a partnership is not a legal person.

**249D(3) [Professional bodies]** The bodies referred to in subsections (1) and (1A) are–

(a) the Institute of Chartered Accountants in England and Wales,
(b) the Institute of Chartered Accountants of Scotland,
(c) the Institute of Chartered Accountants in Ireland,
(d) the Association of Chartered Certified Accountants,
(e) the Association of Authorised Public Accountants,
(f) the Association of Accounting Technicians,
(g) the Association of International Accountants, and
(h) the Chartered Institute of Management Accountants.

**History**
In s. 249D(3) the words "the Association of Chartered Certified Accountants" substituted for the former words "the Chartered Association of Certified Accountants" by the Companies Act 1985 (Audit Exemption) (Amendment) Regulations 1997 (SI 1997/936), reg. 1, 4(1), 4(2) as from 15 April 1997, subject to reg. 1(2). Previously in s. 249D(3) the word "and" appearing at the end of para. (d) omitted and para. (f), (g) and (h) inserted by the Companies Act 1985 (Audit Exemption) (Amendment) Regulations 1996 (SI 1996/3080) as from 1 January 1997. Previously to that in s. 249D(3) the words "subsections (1) and (1A)" substituted for the former words "subsection (1)" by the Companies Act 1985 (Audit Exemption) (Amendment) Regulations 1995 (SI 1995/589), reg. 1, 2(1), (3) as from 30 March 1995 (see also reg. 3).

**249D(4) [Person ineligible]** A person is ineligible for appointment by a company as reporting accountant if he would be ineligible for appointment as an auditor of that company under section 27 of the Companies Act 1989 (ineligibility on ground of lack of independence).

**History**
See history note after s. 249E.

## 249E Effect of exemptions

**249E(1) [Effect where total exemption]** Where the directors of a company have taken advantage of the exemption conferred by section 249A(1) or section 249AA(1)–

(a) sections 238 and 239 (right to receive or demand copies of accounts and reports) shall have effect with the omission of references to the auditors' report;

(b) no copy of an auditors' report need be delivered to the registrar or laid before the company in general meeting;

(c) subsections (3) to (5) of section 271 (accounts by reference to which distribution to be justified) shall not apply.

**History**
In s. 249E(1) the words "or section 249AA()1)" inserted by the Companies Act 1985 (Audit Exemption) (Amendment) Regulations 2000 (SI 2000/1430), reg. 1, 8(4) as from 26 May 2000 in relation to annual accounts and reports in respect of financial years ending on or after 26 July 2000.

**249E(1A) [Effect for dormant company in ineligible group]** Where the directors of a company have taken advantage of the exemption conferred by section 249AA, then for the purposes of that section the company shall be treated as a company entitled to prepare accounts in accordance with section 246 even though it is a member of an ineligible group.

**History**
S. 249E(1A) inserted by the Companies Act 1985 (Audit Exemption) (Amendment) Regulations 2000 (SI 2000/1430), reg. 1, 8(5) as from 26 May 2000 and applies to annual accounts and reports in respect of financial years ending on or after 26 July 2000.

**249E(2) [Effect where report]** Where the directors of a company have taken advantage of the exemption conferred by section 249A(2)—

(a) subsections (2) to (4) of section 236 (which require copies of the auditors' report to state the names of the auditors) shall have effect with the substitution for references to the auditors and the auditors' report of references to the reporting accountant and the report made for the purposes of section 249A(2) respectively;

(b) sections 238 and 239 (right to receive or demand copies of accounts and reports), section 241 (accounts and reports to be laid before company in general meeting) and section 242 (accounts and reports to be delivered to the registrar) shall have effect with the substitution for references to the auditors' report of references to the report made for the purposes of section 249A(2);

(c) subsections (3) to (5) of section 271 (accounts by reference to which distribution to be justified) shall not apply;

(d) section 389A(1) and (2) (rights to information) shall have effect with the substitution for references to the auditors of references to the reporting accountant.

**History**
S. 249A–E inserted by the Companies Act 1985 (Audit Exemption) Regulations 1994 (SI 1994/1935), reg. 2 as from 11 August 1994 subject to transitional provisions in reg. 6.

DORMANT COMPANIES

## 250 Resolution not to appoint auditors

**250** (Repealed by the Companies Act 1985 (Audit Exemption) (Amendment) Regulations 2000 (SI 2000/1430), reg. 1, 8(6) as from 26 May 2000 in relation to annual accounts and reports in respect of financial years ending on or after 26 July 2000.)

**History**
S. 250 formerly read as follows:

"**250(1)** A company may by special resolution make itself exempt from the provisions of this Part relating to the audit of accounts in the following cases–

(a) if the company has been dormant from the time of its formation,
(b) if the company has been dormant since the end of the previous financial year and–
  (i) is entitled in respect of its individual accounts for that year to prepare accounts in accordance with section 246(2), or would be so entitled but for the application of subsection (1)(a)(i) or (b) of section 247A, and
  (ii) is not required to prepare group accounts for that year,

by a special resolution passed at a general meeting of the company at any time after copies of the annual accounts and reports for that year have been sent out in accordance with section 238(1)."

(relationship between specific requirements and duty to give true and fair view) shall be read as references to the provisions of Part I of Schedule 9, in the case of the accounts of banking companies, or to the provisions of Part I of Schedule 9A, in the case of the accounts of insurance companies.

**255(5)** (Omitted by the Companies Act 1985 (Insurance Companies Accounts) Regulations 1993 (SI 1993/3246), reg. 1, 2(2) as from 19 December 1993 subject to exemption in reg. 6 and transitional provisions in reg. 7.)

**History**
S. 255(5) formerly read as follows:

"The Secretary of State may, on the application or with the consent of the directors of an insurance company which prepares individual accounts in accordance with the special provisions of this Part relating to insurance companies, modify in relation to the company any of the requirements of this Part, other than the duty to give a true and fair view, for the purpose of adapting them to the circumstances of the company."

**History to s. 255**
See note after s. 255B.

# 255A Special provisions for banking and insurance groups

**255A(1) [Banking groups]** The parent company of a banking group shall prepare group accounts in accordance with the provisions of this Part as modified by Part II of Schedule 9.

**255A(2) [Insurance groups]** The parent company of an insurance group shall prepare group accounts in accordance with the provisions of this Part as modified by Part II of Schedule 9A.

**History**
In s. 255A(2) the word "shall" substituted for the former word "may" by the Companies Act 1985 (Insurance Companies Accounts) Regulations 1993 (SI 1993/3246), reg. 1, 3(1) as from 19 December 1993 subject to exemption in reg. 6 and transitional provisions in reg. 7.

**255A(3) [Statement in accounts]** Accounts so prepared shall contain a statement that they are prepared in accordance with the special provisions of this Part relating to banking groups or to insurance groups, as the case may be.

**255A(4) [References to banking group]** References in this Part to a banking group are to a group where the parent company is a banking company or where–

(a) the parent company's principal subsidiary undertakings are wholly or mainly credit institutions, and

(b) the parent company does not itself carry on any material business apart from the acquisition, management and disposal of interests in subsidiary undertakings.

**History**
See history note after s. 255A(5A).

**255A(5) [References to insurance group]** References in this Part to an insurance group are to a group where the parent company is an insurance company or where–

(a) the parent company's principal subsidiary undertakings are wholly or mainly insurance companies, and

(b) the parent company does not itself carry on any material business apart from the acquisition, management and disposal of interests in subsidiary undertakings.

**History**
See history note after s. 255A(5A).

**255A(5A) [Interpretation of s. 255A(4), (5)]** For the purposes of subsections (4) and (5) above–

(a) a parent company's principal subsidiary undertakings are the subsidiary undertakings of the company whose results or financial position would principally afect the figures shown in the group accounts, and

(b) the management of interests in subsidiary undertakings includes the provision of services to such undertakings.

**History**
S. 255A(4)–(5A) substituted for the former s. 255A(4), (5) by the Companies Act 1985 (Insurance Companies Accounts) Regulations 1993 (SI 1993/3246), reg. 1, 3(2) as from 19 December 1993 subject to exemption in reg. 6 and transitional provisions in reg. 7; former s. 255A(4), (5) read as follows:

"**255A(4)** References in this Part to a banking group are to a group where–
(a) the parent company is a banking company, or
(b) the parent company:

(i) does not itself carry on any material business apart from the acquisition, management and disposal of interests in subsidiary undertakings; and
(ii) its principal subsidiary undertakings are wholly or mainly credit institutions.
For the purposes of (b) the management of interests in subsidiary undertakings includes the provision of services to such undertakings, and a parent company's principal subsidiary undertakings are those subsidiary undertakings of the company whose results or financial position would principally affect the figures shown in the group accounts."

(In s. 255A(4)(b)(ii) the words "credit institutions" substituted for the former words "banking companies" by the Companies Act 1985 (Disclosure of Branches and Bank Accounts) Regulations 1992 (SI 1992/3178), reg. 5 as from 1 January 1993 (subject to transitional provisions in reg. 8).)

"**(5)** References in this Part to an insurance group are to a group where–
(a) the parent company is an insurance company, or
(b) the predominant activity of the group is insurance business and activities which are a direct extension of or ancillary to insurance business."

**255A(6) [References to group accounts]** In relation to the preparation of group accounts in accordance with the special provisions of this Part:

(a) the references to the provisions of Schedule 4A in section 227(5) and (6) (relationship between specific requirements and duty to give true and fair view) shall be read as references to those provisions as modified by Part II of Schedule 9, in the case of the group accounts of a banking group, or Part II of Schedule 9A, in the case of the group accounts of an insurance group; and

(b) the reference to paragraphs 52 to 57 of Schedule 4 in section 230(2) (relief from obligation to comply with those paragraphs where group accounts prepared) shall be read as a reference to paragraphs 75 to 77, 80 and 81 of Part I of Schedule 9, in the case of the group accounts of a banking group, and as a reference to paragraphs 73, 74, 79 and 80 of Part I of Schedule 9A, in the case of the group accounts of an insurance group.

**History**
In s. 255A(6)(b) the words "75 to 77" substituted for the former words "74 to 77" by the Companies Act 1985 (Miscellaneous Accounting Amendments) Regulations 1996 (SI 1996/189), reg. 1(1), 15(2) as from 2 February 1996, subject to reg. 16(1), (2); and at the end the words ", and as a reference to paragraphs 73," to the end inserted by the Companies Act 1985 (Insurance Companies Accounts) Regulations 1993 (SI 1993/3246), reg. 1, 3(3) as from 19 December 1993 subject to exemption in reg. 6 and transitional provisions in reg. 7.

**255A(7)** (Omitted by the Companies Act 1985 (Insurance Companies Accounts) Regulations 1993 (SI 1993/3246), reg. 1, 3(4) as from 19 December 1993 subject to exemption in reg. 6 and transitional provisions in reg. 7.)

**History**
S. 255A(7) formerly read as follows:
"The Secretary of State may, on the application or with the consent of the directors of a company which prepares group accounts in accordance with the special provisions of this Part relating to insurance groups, modify in relation to the company any of the requirements of this Part for the purpose of adapting them to the circumstances of the company."

**History to s. 255A**
See note after s. 255B.

# 255B Modification of disclosure requirements in relation to banking company or group

**255B(1) [Sch. 5]** In relation to a banking company, or the parent company of a banking group, the provisions of Schedule 5 (Disclosure of information: related undertakings) have effect subject to Part III of Schedule 9.

**History**
In s. 255B(1) the words "parent company of a banking group" substituted for the former words "parent company of a banking company" by the Companies Act 1985 (Disclosure of Branches and Bank Accounts) Regulations 1992 (SI 1992/3178), reg. 6 as from 1 January 1993 (subject to transitional provisions in reg. 8).

**255B(2) [Sch. 6]** In relation to a banking company, or the holding company of a credit institution, the provisions of Schedule 6 (Disclosure of information: emoluments and other benefits of directors and others) have effect subject to Part IV of Schedule 9.

**History**
In s. 255B the words "holding company of a credit institution" substituted for the former words "parent company of a banking company" by the Companies Act 1985 (Bank Accounts) Regulations 1994 (SI 1994/233), reg. 1, 3 as from 28 February 1994 subject to any transitional provisions in reg. 7, 8.
Previously s. 255–255B inserted by the Companies Act 1985 (Bank Accounts) Regulations 1991 (SI 1991/2705), reg. 3 as from 2 December 1991 (subject to transitional provisions in reg. 9); the former s. 255–255B (but for original provisions see history note after s. 262A) read as follows:

"**255 Special provisions for banking and insurance companies**

**255(1)** A banking or insurance company may prepare its individual accounts in accordance with Part I of Schedule 9 rather than Schedule 4.

**(2)** Accounts so prepared shall contain a statement that they are prepared in accordance with the special provisions of this Part relating to banking companies or insurance companies, as the case may be.

**(3)** In relation to the preparation of individual accounts in accordance with the special provisions of this Part relating to banking or insurance companies, the references to the provisions of Schedule 4 in section 226(4) and (5) (relationship between specific requirements and duty to give true and fair view) shall be read as references to the provisions of Part I of Schedule 9.

**(4)** The Secretary of State may, on the application or with the consent of the directors of a company which prepares individual accounts in accordance with the special provisions of this Part relating to banking or insurance companies, modify in relation to the company any of the requirements of this Part for the purpose of adapting them to the circumstances of the company.

This does not affect the duty to give a true and fair view.

**255A Special provisions for banking and insurance groups**

**255A(1)** The parent company of a banking or insurance group may prepare group accounts in accordance with the provisions of this Part as modified by Part II of Schedule 9.

**(2)** Accounts so prepared shall contain a statement that they are prepared in accordance with the special provisions of this Part relating to banking groups or insurance groups, as the case may be.

**(3)** References in this Part to a banking group are to a group where–

(a) the parent company is a banking company, or

(b) at least one of the undertakings in the group is an authorised institution under the Banking Act 1987 and the predominant activities of the group are such as to make it inappropriate to prepare group accounts in accordance with the formats in Part I of Schedule 4.

**(4)** References in this Part to an insurance group are to a group where–

(a) the parent company is an insurance company, or

(b) the predominant activity of the group is insurance business and activities which are a direct extension of or ancillary to insurance business.

**(5)** In relation to the preparation of group accounts in accordance with the special provisions of this Part relating to banking or insurance groups, the references to the provisions of Schedule 4A in section 227(5) and (6) (relationship between specific requirements and duty to give true and fair view) shall be read as references to those provisions as modified by Part II of Schedule 9.

**(6)** The Secretary of State may, on the application or with the consent of the directors of a company which prepares group accounts in accordance with the special provisions of this Part relating to banking or insurance groups, modify in relation to the company any of the requirements of this Part for the purpose of adapting them to the circumstances of the company.

**255B Modification of disclosure requirements in relation to banking company or group**

**255B(1)** In relation to a company which prepares accounts in accordance with the special provisions of this Part relating to banking companies or groups, the provisions of Schedule 5 (additional disclosure: related undertakings) have effect subject to Part III of Schedule 9.

**(2)** In relation to a banking company, or the parent company of a banking company, the provisions of Schedule 6 (disclosure: emoluments and other benefits of directors and others) have effect subject to Part IV of Schedule 9."

## 255C Directors' report where accounts prepared in accordance with special provisions relating to insurance companies or groups

**255C** (Omitted by the Companies Act 1985 (Insurance Companies Accounts) Regulations 1993 (SI 1993/3246). reg. 1, 5, Sch. 2, para. 3 as from 19 December 1993 subject to exemption in reg. 6 and transitional provisions in reg. 7.)

**History**

S. 255C formerly read as follows:

"**255C(1)** The following provisions apply in relation to the directors' report of a company for a financial year in respect of which it prepares accounts in accordance with the special provisions of this Part relating to insurance companies or groups."

(In s. 255C(1) the words "banking or" formerly appearing before the words "insurance companies as groups" deleted by the Companies Act 1985 (Bank Accounts) Regulations 1991 (SI 1991/2705), reg. 4(b) as from 2 December 1991 (subject to transitional provisions in reg. 9).)

"**(2)** The information required to be given by paragraph 6, 8 or 13 of Part I of Schedule 9A (which is allowed to be given in a statement or report annexed to the accounts), may be given in the directors' report instead.

Information so given shall be treated for the purposes of audit as forming part of the accounts."

(In s. 255C(2) the words "Schedule 9A" substituted for the former words "Schedule 9" by the Companies Act 1985 (Bank Accounts) Regulations 1991 (SI 1991/2705), reg. 4(c) as from 2 December 1991 (subject to transitional provisions in reg. 9).)

"**(3)** The reference in section 234(1)(b) to the amount proposed to be carried to reserves shall be construed as a reference to the amount proposed to be carried to reserves within the meaning of Part I of Schedule 9A."

(In s. 255C(3) the words "Schedule 9A" substituted for the former words "Schedule 9" by the Companies Act 1985 (Bank Accounts) Regulations 1991 (SI 1991/2705), reg. 4(c) as from 2 December 1991 (subject to transitional provisions in reg. 9).)

"**(4)** If the company takes advantage, in relation to its individual or group accounts, of the exemptions conferred by paragraph 28 of Part I of Schedule 9A, paragraph 1 of Schedule 7 (disclosure of asset values) does not apply."

(In s. 255C(4) the words "27 or" formerly appearing after the words "conferred by paragraph" deleted and the words "Schedule 9A" substituted for the former words "Schedule 9" by the Companies Act 1985 (Bank Accounts) Regulations 1991 (SI 1991/2705), reg. 4(c), (d) as from 2 December 1991 (subject to transitional provisions in reg. 9).)

"**(5)** The directors' report shall, in addition to complying with Schedule 7, also comply with Schedule 10 (which specifies additional matters to be disclosed)."

See also history note after s. 262A.

## 255D Power to apply provisions to banking partnerships

**255D(1) [Power to make regulations]** The Secretary of State may by regulations apply to banking partnerships, subject to such exceptions, adaptations and modifications as he considers appropriate, the provisions of this Part applying to banking companies.

**255D(2) ["Banking partnership"]** A **"banking partnership"** means a partnership which is an authorised institution under the Banking Act 1987.

**255D(3) [Regulations by statutory instrument]** Regulations under this section shall be made by statutory instrument.

**255D(4) [Approval by Parliament]** No regulations under this section shall be made unless a draft of the instrument containing the regulations has been laid before Parliament and approved by a resolution of each House.

**History**

See history note after s. 262A.

### WELSH PRIVATE COMPANIES

## 255E Delivery of accounting documents in Welsh only

255E (Ceased to have effect and repealed by Welsh Language Act 1993, s. 30(1), (5), 35(1) and Sch. 2 as from 1 February 1994.)

**History**

In regard to the date of the above cessation of effect and repeal, see SI 1994/115 (C 5), art. 2(2); s. 255E formerly read as follows:

**"255E(1)** The directors of a private company whose memorandum states that its registered office is to be situated in Wales may deliver to the registrar a copy of any document to which this section applies in Welsh without annexing to the copy a translation of the document into English.

**(2)** This section applies to any document required to be delivered to the registrar by the following provision of this Part–

(a) section 242(1) (accounts and reports to be delivered to the registrar);
(b) section 243 (accounts of subsidiary undertakings to be appended in certain cases); and
(c) paragraph 7 of Part II of Schedule 9 (banking groups: information as to undertaking in which shares held as a result of financial assistance operation).

**(3)** The registrar shall, having received any document in Welsh under this section, obtain a translation of it into English; and the translation shall be regarded as a document delivered to the registrar for the purposes of sections 707A and 709 and shall be registered by him accordingly."

(Previously s. 255E inserted by the Companies Act 1985 (Welsh Language Accounts) Regulations 1992 (SI 1992/1083), reg. 1(1), 2(1), (4) as from 1 June 1992.)

# Chapter III – Supplementary Provisions

### ACCOUNTING STANDARDS

## 256 Accounting standards

**256(1) ["Accounting standards"]** In this Part **"accounting standards"** means statements of standard accounting practice issued by such body or bodies as may be prescribed by regulations.

**Note**

The Accounting Standards Board Limited is prescribed for the purposes of s. 256(1) – see the Accounting Standards (Prescribed Body) Regulations 1990 (SI 1990/1667).

**256(2) [Interpretation]** References in this Part to accounting standards applicable to a company's annual accounts are to such standards as are, in accordance with their terms, relevant to the company's circumstances and to the accounts.

**256(3) [Power of Secretary of State to make grants]** The Secretary of State may make grants to or for the purposes of bodies concerned with–

(a) issuing accounting standards,
(b) overseeing and directing the issuing of such standards, or
(c) investigating departures from such standards or from the accounting requirements of this Act and taking steps to secure compliance with them.

**256(4) [Content of regulations]** Regulations under this section may contain such transitional and other supplementary and incidental provisions as appear to the Secretary of State to be appropriate.

**History**

See history note after s. 262A.

POWER TO ALTER ACCOUNTING REQUIREMENTS

## 257 Power of Secretary of State to alter accounting requirements

**257(1) [Power to make regulations]** The Secretary of State may by regulations made by statutory instrument modify the provisions of this Part.

**257(2) [Certain regulations require approval by Parliament]** Regulations which–

(a) add to the classes of documents required to be prepared, laid before the company in general meeting or delivered to the registrar,

(b) restrict the classes of company which have the benefit of any exemption, exception or special provision,

(c) require additional matter to be included in a document of any class, or

(d) otherwise render the requirements of this Part more onerous,

shall not be made unless a draft of the instrument containing the regulations has been laid before Parliament and approved by a resolution of each House.

**257(3) [Other regulations subject to annulment]** Otherwise, a statutory instrument containing regulations under this section shall be subject to annulment in pursuance of a resolution of either House of Parliament.

**257(4) [Scope of regulations]** Regulations under this section may–

(a) make different provision for different cases or classes of case,

(b) repeal and re-enact provisions with modifications of form or arrangement, whether or not they are modified in substance,

(c) make consequential amendments or repeals in other provisions of this Act, or in other enactments, and

(d) contain such transitional and other incidental and supplementary provisions as the Secretary of State thinks fit.

**257(5) [Enactments outside the Companies Acts]** Any modification by regulations under this section of section 258 or Schedule 10A (parent and subsidiary undertakings) does not apply for the purposes of enactments outside the Companies Acts unless the regulations so provide.

**History**
See history note after s. 262A.

**Note**
See the Companies Act 1985 (Bank Accounts) Regulations 1991 (SI 1991/2705) (see also the Bank Accounts Directive (Miscellaneous Banks) Regulations 1991 (SI 1991/2704)); the Companies Act 1985 (Welsh Language Accounts) Regulations 1992 (SI 1992/1083); the Companies Act 1985 (Accounts of Small and Medium-Sized Enterprises and Publication of Accounts in ECUs) Regulations 1992 (SI 1992/2452); the Companies Act 1985 (Amendment of Section 250 and 251) Regulations 1992 (SI 1992/3003); the Companies Act 1985 (Disclosure of Branches and Bank Accounts) Regulations 1992 (SI 1992/3178); the Partnerships and Unlimited Companies (Accounts) Regulations 1993 (SI 1993/1820); the Companies Act 1985 (Insurance Companies Accounts) Regulations 1993 (SI 1993/3246); the Companies Act 1985 (Bank Accounts) Regulations 1994 (SI 1994/233); the Companies Act 1985 (Audit Exemption) Regulations 1994 (SI 1994/1935), as amended; the Companies Act 1985 (Audit Exemption) (Amendment) Regulations 1995 (SI 1995/589); the Companies Act 1985 (Miscellaneous Accounting Amendments) Regulations 1996 (SI 1996/189), the Companies Act 1985 (Accounts of Small and Medium-sized Companies and Minor Accounting Amendments) Regulations 1997 (SI 1997/220), the Companies Act 1985 (Audit Exemption) (Amendment) Regulations 1996 (SI 1996/3080), the Company Accounts (Disclosure of Directors' Emoluments) Regulations 1997 (SI 1997/570), the Companies Act 1985 (Directors' Report) (Statement of Payment Practice) Regulations 1997 (SI 1997/571) and the Companies Act 1985 (Audit Exemption) (Amendment) Regulations 1997 (SI 1997/936).

PARENT AND SUBSIDIARY UNDERTAKINGS

## 258 Parent and subsidiary undertakings

**258(1) [Construction]** The expressions **"parent undertaking"** and **"subsidiary undertaking"** in this Part shall be construed as follows; and a **"parent company"** means a parent undertaking which is a company.

**258(2) [Parent undertaking]** An undertaking is a parent undertaking in relation to another undertaking, a subsidiary undertaking, if–

(a) it holds a majority of the voting rights in the undertaking, or

(b) it is a member of the undertaking and has the right to appoint or remove a majority of its board of directors, or

(c) it has the right to exercise a dominant influence over the undertaking–

(i) by virtue of provisions contained in the undertaking's memorandum or articles, or

(ii) by virtue of a control contract, or

(d) it is a member of the undertaking and controls alone, pursuant to an agreement with other shareholders or members, a majority of the voting rights in the undertaking.

**Note**

See the Financial Institutions (Prudential Supervision) Regulations 1996 (SI 1996/1669), reg. 2(3), Sch. 1, para. 1, 2(1) for the insertion of s. 258(2A) for the purpose of determining any question arising under reg. 2(2) of those Regulations as from 18 July 1996.

**258(3) [Member of another undertaking]** For the purposes of subsection (2) an undertaking shall be treated as a member of another undertaking–

(a) if any of its subsidiary undertakings is a member of that undertaking, or

(b) if any shares in that other undertaking are held by a person acting on behalf of the undertaking or any of its subsidiary undertakings.

**Note**

See the Financial Institutions (Prudential Supervision) Regulations 1996 (SI 1996/1669), reg. 2(3), Sch. 1, para. 1, 2(2), 3(1) and for modification to s. 258(3) and the insertion of s. 258(3A) and s. 258(3B) for the purposes of determining any question arising under reg. 2(2) of those Regulations as from 18 July 1996.

**258(4) [Another parent undertaking]** An undertaking is also a parent undertaking in relation to another undertaking, a subsidiary undertaking, if it has a participating interest in the undertaking and–

(a) it actually exercises a dominant influence over it, or

(b) it and the subsidiary undertaking are managed on a unified basis.

**258(5) [Treatment as parent undertaking]** A parent undertaking shall be treated as the parent undertaking of undertakings in relation to which any of its subsidiary undertakings are, or are to be treated as, parent undertakings; and references to its subsidiary undertakings shall be construed accordingly.

**Note**

See the Financial Institutions (Prudential Supervision) Regulations 1996 (SI 1996/1669), reg. 2(3), Sch. 1, para. 1, 3(2) for the insertion of s. 258(5A) for the purposes of determining any question arising under reg. 2(2) of those Regulations as from 18 July 1996.

**258(6) [Sch. 10A]** Schedule 10A contains provisions explaining expressions used in this section and otherwise supplementing this section.

**History**

See history note after s. 262A.

## OTHER INTERPRETATION PROVISIONS

# 259 Meaning of "undertaking" and related expressions

**259(1) ["Undertaking"]** In this Part **"undertaking"** means–

(a) a body corporate or partnership, or

(b) an unincorporated association carrying on a trade or business, with or without a view to profit.

**259(2) [References to shares]** In this Part references to shares–

(a) in relation to an undertaking with a share capital, are to allotted shares;

(b) in relation to an undertaking with capital but no share capital, are to rights to share in the capital of the undertaking; and

(c) in relation to an undertaking without capital, are to interests–

(i) conferring any right to share in the profits or liability to contribute to the losses of the undertaking, or

(ii) giving rise to an obligation to contribute to the debts or expenses of the undertaking in the event of a winding up.

**259(3) [Other expressions appropriate to companies]** Other expressions appropriate to companies shall be construed, in relation to an undertaking which is not a company, as

| | |
|---|---|
| long term fund (in Schedule 9A) | paragraph 81 of Part I of that Schedule |
| notes to the accounts | section 261(1) |
| parent undertaking (and parent company) | section 258 and Schedule 10A |
| participating interest | section 260 |
| pension costs | |
| — in Schedule 4 | paragraph 94(2) of that Schedule |
| — in Schedule 8 | paragraph 59(2) of that Schedule |
| — in Schedule 9 | paragraph 87(b) of Part I of that Schedule |
| — in Schedule 9A | paragraph 86(b) of Part I of that Schedule |
| period allowed for laying and delivering accounts and reports | section 244 |
| policy holder (in Schedule 9A) | paragraph 81 of Part I of that Schedule |
| profit and loss account | |
| (includes notes) | section 261(2) |
| (in relation to a company not trading for profit) | section 262(2) |
| provision for unexpired risks (in Schedule 9A) | paragraph 81 of Part I of that Schedule |
| provision | |
| — in Schedule 4 | paragraphs 88 and 89 of that Schedule |
| — in Schedule 8 | paragraphs 57 and 58 of that Schedule |
| — in Schedule 9 | paragraph 85 of Part I of that Schedule |
| — in Schedule 9A | paragraph 84 of Part I of that Schedule |
| purchase price | section 262(1) |
| qualified | section 262(1) |
| realised losses and realised profits | section 262(3) |
| repayable on demand (in Schedule 9) | paragraph 82 of Part I of that Schedule |
| reporting accountant | section 249C(1) |
| reserve (in Schedule 9A) | paragraph 32 of that Schedule |
| sale and repurchase transaction (in Schedule 9) | paragraph 82 of Part I of that Schedule |
| sale and option to resell transaction (in Schedule 9) | paragraph 82 of Part I of that Schedule |
| shares | section 259(2) |
| social security costs | |
| — in Schedule 4 | paragraph 94(1) and (3) of that Schedule |
| — in Schedule 8 | paragraph 59(1) and (3) of that Schedule |
| — in Schedule 9 | paragraph 87(a) and (c) of Part I of that Schedule |

| | |
|---|---|
| — in Schedule 9A | paragraph 86(a) and (c) of Part I of that Schedule |
| special provisions for banking and insurance companies and groups | sections 255 and 255A |
| subsidiary undertaking | section 258 and Schedule 10A |
| the 1982 Act (in Schedule 9A) | paragraph 81 of Part I of that Schedule |
| true and fair view | section 262(1) |
| turnover | section 262(1) |
| undertaking and related expressions | section 259(1) to (3) |

**History to s. 262A**

In s. 262A the entry relating to "EEA State" omitted by the Companies (Membership of Holding Company) (Dealers in Securities) Regulations 1997 (SI 1997/2306), reg. 1, 4(4) as from 20 October 1997. The former entry read as follows:

"EEA State section 262(1)"

Previously to that s. 262A amended by the Companies Act 1985 (Accounts of Small and Medium-sized Companies and Minor Accounting Amendments) Regulations 1997 (SI 1997/220), reg . 1, 7(6) as from 1 March 1997 as follows:

- in entry relating to "historical cost accounting rules" words relating to Sch. 8 inserted;
- in entry r elating to "listed investment" words relating to Sch. 8 inserted;
- entry relating to "pension costs" substituted– the former entry read as follows:
  "pension costs
  - — in Schedule 4 paragraph 94(2) and (3) of that Schedule
  - — in Schedule 9 paragraph 87(b) and (c) of Part I of that Schedule
  - — in Schedule 9A paragraph 86(b) and (c) of Part I of that Schedule"
- in entry relating to "provision" words relating to Sch. 8 inserted;
- in entry relating to "social security costs" words relating to Sch. 8 inserted.

Previously to that in s. 262A the entry relating to "EEA State" inserted by the Companies Act 1985 (Miscellaneous Accounting Amendments) Regulations 1996 (SI 1996/189), reg. 1(1), 12(2) as from 2 February 1996, subject to reg. 16(1), (2). Previously in s. 262A the entry relating to "reporting accountant" inserted by the Companies Act 1985 (Audit Exemption) Regulations 1994 (SI 1994/1935), reg. 4 and Sch. 1, para. 3 as from 11 August 1994.

Previously to that in s. 262A the entries relating to the expressions "banking activities" and "banking transactions", formerly appearing after "balance sheet date" and "banking group" respectively, repealed by the Companies Act 1985 (Bank Accounts) Regulations 1994 (SI 1994/233), reg. 1, 4(2) as from 11 February 1994 subject to transitional provisions in reg. 7, 8; the entries formerly read as follows:

"banking activities (in Schedule 9) paragraph 82 of Part I of that Schedule"
"banking transactions (in Schedule 9) paragraph 82 of Part I of that Schedule"

Previously to that s. 262A amended by the Companies Act 1985 (Insurance Companies Accounts) Regulations 1993 (SI 1993/3246), reg. 1, 5, Sch. 2, para. 5 as from 19 December 1993 (subject to exemption in reg. 6 and transitional provisions in reg. 7) as follows:

- entry relating to "general business" inserted;
- in entry relating to "historical cost accounting rules" words relating to Sch. 9A inserted;
- in entry relating to "land of freehold tenure and land of leasehold tenure" words relating to Sch. 9A substituted; the former words read as follows:
  "— in Schedule 9A paragraph 36 of that Schedule"
- in entry relating to "lease, long lease and short lease" words relating to Sch. 9A substituted; the former words read as follows:
  "— in Schedule 9A paragraph 34 of that Schedule"
- in entry relating to "listed investment" words relating to Sch. 9A substituted; the former words read as follows:
  "— in Schedule 9A paragraph 33 of that Schedule"
- entries relating to "long term business" and "long term fund" inserted;
- in entry relating to "pension costs" words relating to Sch. 9A inserted;
- entry relating to "policy holder" inserted;
- entry relating to "provision for unexpired risks" inserted;
- in entry relating to "provision" words relating to Sch. 9A substituted; the former words read as follows:
  "— in Schedule 9A paragraph 32 of that Schedule"
- in entry relating to "social security costs" words relating to Sch. 9A inserted;
- entry relating to "the 1982 Act" inserted.

Previously to that s. 262A amended by the Companies Act 1985 (Bank Accounts) Regulations 1991 (SI 1991/2705), reg. 6 and Sch. 2, para. 3 as from 2 December 1991 (subject to transitional provisions in reg. 9) as follows:

- entry relating to "banking activities" inserted;
- in entry relating to "banking group" the words "section 255A(4)" substituted for the former words "section 255A(3)";
- entries relating to "banking transactions" and "financial fixed assets" inserted;
- entry relating to "historical cost accounting rules" substituted – the former entry read as follows:

"historical cost accounting rules (in Schedule 4) paragraph 29 of that Schedule"

- in entry relating to "insurance group" the words "section 255A(5)" substituted for the former words "section 255A(4)";
- in entry relating to "land of freehold tenure and land of leasehold tenure (in relation to Scotland)" reference to Sch. 9 inserted and the words "Schedule 9A" substituted for the former words "Schedule 9";
- in entry relating to "lease, long lease and short lease" reference to Sch. 9 inserted and the words "Schedule 9A" substituted for the former words "Schedule 9";
- in entry relating to "listed investment" the words "Schedule 9A" substituted for the former words "Schedule 9";
- entry relating to "listed security" inserted;
- entry relating to "pension costs" substituted – the former entry read as follows:
  "pension costs (in Schedule 4) paragraph 94(2) and (3) of that Schedule"
- in entry relating to "provision" reference to Sch. 9 inserted and the words "Schedule 9A" substituted for the former words "Schedule 9";
- entry relating to "repayable on demand" inserted;
- in entry relating to "reserve" the words "Schedule 9A" substituted for the former words "Schedule 9";
- entries relating to "sale and repurchase transaction" and "sale and option to resell transaction" inserted; and
- entry relating to "social security costs" substituted – the former entry read as follows:
  "social security costs (in Schedule 4) paragraph 94(1) and (3) of that Schedule".

**Note to s. 221–262A**
CA 1989, Pt. I (i.e. s. 1–23) which inserts the above provisions implements the Eighth EC Company Law Directive (84/253).

**History to s. 221–262A**
S. 221–244, 246–262A inserted by CA 1989, s. 1–11, 13–22 as from 1 April 1990 (with the exception of s. 233(5), 242A, 249A–E, 251, 255–255B – see history notes after s. 233(5), 242, 249E, 251 and 255B) subject to transitional and saving provisions (see SI 1990/355 (C 13), art. 3, Sch. 1 and also art. 6–9).
S. 245–245C inserted by CA 1989, s. 12 as from 7 January 1991 subject to transitional and saving provisions (see SI 1990/2569 (C 68), art. 3, 6).
S. 249A–E inserted by the Companies Act 1985 (Audit Exemption) Regulations 1994 (SI 1994/1935), reg. 2 as from 11 August 1994 subject to transitional provisions in reg. 6.
Original s. 221–262 read as follows:

"ACCOUNTING RECORDS

**221 Companies to keep accounting records**

**221(1)** Every company shall cause accounting records to be kept in accordance with this section.

**(2)** The accounting records shall be sufficient to show and explain the company's transactions, and shall be such as to–
(a) disclose with reasonable accuracy, at any time, the financial position of the company at that time, and
(b) enable the directors to ensure that any balance sheet and profit and loss account prepared under this Part comply with the requirements of this Act as to the form and content of company accounts and otherwise.

**(3)** The accounting records shall in particular contain–
(a) entries from day to day of all sums of money received and expended by the company, and the matters in respect of which the receipt and expenditure takes place, and
(b) a record of the assets and liabilities of the company.

**(4)** If the company's business involves dealing in goods, the accounting records shall contain–
(a) statements of stock held by the company at the end of each financial year of the company,
(b) all statements of stocktakings from which any such statement of stock as is mentioned in paragraph (a) has been or is to be prepared, and
(c) except in the case of goods sold by way of ordinary retail trade, statements of all goods sold and purchased, showing the goods and the buyers and sellers in sufficient detail to enable all these to be identified.

**222 Where and for how long records to be kept**

**222(1)** Subject as follows, a company's accounting records shall be kept at its registered office or such other place as the directors think fit, and shall at all times be open to inspection by the company's officers.

**(2)** If accounting records are kept at a place outside Great Britain, accounts and returns with respect to the business dealt with in the accounting records so kept shall be sent to, and kept at, a place in Great Britain, and shall at all times be open to such inspection.

**(3)** The accounts and returns to be sent to Great Britain in accordance with subsection (2) shall be such as to–
(a) disclose with reasonable accuracy the financial position of the business in question at intervals of not more than 6 months, and
(b) enable the directors to ensure that the company's balance sheet and profit and loss account comply with the requirements of this Act as to the form and content of company accounts and otherwise.

**(4)** Accounting records which a company is required by section 221 to keep shall be preserved by it–
(a) in the case of a private company, for 3 years from the date on which they are made, and
(b) in the case of a public company, for 6 years from that date.
This is subject to any provision contained in rules made under section 411 of the Insolvency Act."

(In s. 222(4) previously the words "section 411 of the Insolvency Act" substituted for the former words "section 106 of the Insolvency Act 1985" by Insolvency Act 1986, s. 439(1) and Sch. 13 as from 29 December 1986 (see IA 1986, s. 443 and SI 1986/1924 (C 71)) – that substitution repealed by CA 1989, s. 212 and Sch. 24 as from 1 April 1990 (see SI 1990/355 (C 13), art. 5(1)(d)). Immediately before this the words "provision contained in rules made under section 106 of the Insolvency Act 1985" substituted for the original words "direction with respect to the disposal of records given under winding-up rules under section 663": see SI 1986/1924 (C 71) – that substitution by the Insolvency Act 1985 was repealed by CA 1989, s. 212 and Sch. 24 as from 1 April 1990 (see SI 1990/355 (C 13), art. 5(1)(c)).)

**"223 Penalties for non-compliance with s. 221, 222**

**223(1)** If a company fails to comply with any provision of section 221 or 222(1) or (2), every officer of the company who is in default is guilty of an offence unless he shows that he acted honestly and that in the circumstances in which the company's business was carried on the default was excusable.

**(2)** An officer of a company is guilty of an offence if he fails to take all reasonable steps for securing compliance by the company with section 222(4), or has intentionally caused any default by the company under it.

**(3)** A person guilty of an offence under this section is liable to imprisonment or a fine, or both.

A COMPANY'S ACCOUNTING REFERENCE PERIODS AND FINANCIAL YEAR

**224 Accounting reference period and date**

**224(1)** A company's accounting reference periods are determined according to its accounting reference date.

**(2)** A company may give notice in the prescribed form to the registrar of companies specifying a date in the calendar year as being the date on which in each successive calendar year an accounting reference period of the company is to be treated as coming to an end; and the date specified in the notice is then the company's accounting reference date.

**(3)** However, no such notice has effect unless it is given before the end of 6 months beginning with the date of the company's incorporation; and, failing such notice, the company's accounting reference date is 31st March.

**(4)** A company's first accounting reference period is such period ending with its accounting reference date as begins on the date of its incorporation and is a period of more than 6 months and not more than 18 months; and each successive period of 12 months beginning after the end of the first accounting reference period and ending with the accounting reference date is also an accounting reference period of the company.

**(5)** This section is subject to section 225, under which in certain circumstances a company may alter its accounting reference date and accounting reference periods.

**225 Alteration of accounting reference period**

**225(1)** At any time during a period which is an accounting reference period of a company by virtue of section 224 or 226 the company may give notice in the prescribed form to the registrar of companies specifying a date in the calendar year ("the new accounting reference date") on which that accounting reference period ("the current accounting reference period") and each subsequent accounting reference period of the company is to be treated as coming to an end or (as the case may require) as having come to an end.

**(2)** At any time after the end of a period which was an accounting reference period of a company by virtue of section 224 or 226 the company may give notice in the prescribed form to the registrar of companies specifying a date in the calendar year ("the new accounting reference date") on which that accounting reference period ("the previous accounting reference period") and each subsequent accounting reference period of the company is to be treated as coming or (as the case may require) as having come to an end.

**(3)** But a notice under subsection (2)–

(a) has no effect unless the company is a subsidiary or holding company of another company and the new accounting reference date coincides with the accounting reference date of that other company, and

(b) has no effect if the period allowed (under section 242) for laying and delivering accounts in relation to the previous accounting reference period has already expired at the time when the notice is given.

**(4)** A notice under this section shall state whether the current or previous accounting reference period of the company–

(a) is to be treated as shortened, so as to come to an end or (as the case may require) be treated as having come to an end on the new accounting reference date on the first occasion on which that date falls or fell after the beginning of that accounting reference period, or

(b) is to be treated as extended, so as to come to an end or (as the case may require) be treated as having come to an end on the new accounting reference date on the second occasion on which that date falls or fell after the beginning of that accounting reference period.

**(5)** A notice which states that the current or previous accounting reference period is to be extended has no effect if the current or previous accounting reference period, as extended in accordance with the notice, would exceed 18 months.

**(6)** Subject to any direction given by the Secretary of State under the next subsection, a notice which states that the current or previous accounting reference period is to be extended has no effect unless–

(a) no earlier accounting reference period of the company has been extended by virtue of a previous notice given by the company under this section, or

(b) the notice is given not less than 5 years after the date on which any earlier accounting reference period of the company which was so extended came to an end, or

(c) the company is a subsidiary or holding company of another company and the new accounting reference date coincides with the accounting reference date of that other company.

**(7)** The Secretary of State may, if he thinks fit, direct that subsection (6) shall not apply to a notice already given by a company under this section or (as the case may be) in relation to a notice which may be so given.

**(8)** At any time when an administration order under Part II of the Insolvency Act is in force, this section has effect as if subsections (3) and (5) to (7) were omitted."

(S. 225(8) previously added by Insolvency Act 1986, s. 439(1) and Sch. 13 as from 29 December 1986 (see IA 1986, s. 443 and SI 1986/1924 (C 71)) – that addition repealed by CA 1989, s. 212 and Sch. 24 as from 1 April 1990 (see SI 1990/355 (C 13), art. 5(d)).)

**"226 Consequence of giving notice under s. 225**

**226(1)** Where a company has given notice with effect in accordance with section 225, and that notice has not been superseded by a subsequent notice by the company which has such effect, the new date specified in the notice is the company's accounting reference date, in substitution for that which, by virtue of section 224 or this section, was its accounting reference date at the time when the notice was given.

**(2)** Where by virtue of such a notice one date is substituted for another as the accounting reference date of a company–

(a) the current or previous accounting reference period, shortened or extended (as the case may be) in accordance with the notice, and

(b) each successive period of 12 months beginning after the end of that accounting reference period (as so shortened or extended) and ending with the new accounting reference date,

is or (as the case may require) is to be treated as having been an accounting reference period of the company, instead of any period which would be an accounting reference period of the company if the notice had not been given.

**(3)** Section 225 and this section do not affect any accounting reference period of the company which–
- (a) in the case of a notice under section 225(1), is earlier than the current accounting reference period, or
- (b) in the case of a notice under section 225(2), is earlier than the previous accounting reference period.

### 227 Directors' duty to prepare annual accounts

**227(1)** In the case of every company, the directors shall in respect of each accounting reference period of the company prepare a profit and loss account for the financial year or, if it is a company not trading for profit, an income and expenditure account.

**(2)** Where it is the company's first accounting reference period, the financial year begins with the first day of that period and ends with–
- (a) the date on which the accounting reference period ends, or
- (b) such other date, not more than 7 days before or more than 7 days after the end of that period, as the directors may determine;

and after that the financial year begins with the day after the date to which the last preceding profit and loss account was made up and ends as mentioned in paragraphs (a) and (b) above.

**(3)** The directors shall prepare a balance sheet as at the last day of the financial year.

**(4)** In the case of a holding company, the directors shall secure that, except where in their opinion there are good reasons against it, the financial year of each of its subsidiaries coincides with the company's own financial year.

## FORM AND CONTENT OF COMPANY INDIVIDUAL AND GROUP ACCOUNTS

### 228 Form and content of individual accounts

**228(1)** A company's accounts prepared under section 227 shall comply with the requirements of Schedule 4 (so far as applicable) with respect to the form and content of the balance sheet and profit and loss account and any additional information to be provided by way of notes to the accounts.

**(2)** The balance sheet shall give a true and fair view of the state of affairs of the company as at the end of the financial year; and the profit and loss account shall give a true and fair view of the profit or loss of the company for the financial year.

**(3)** Subsection (2) overrides–
- (a) the requirements of Schedule 4, and
- (b) all other requirements of this Act as to the matters to be included in a company's accounts or in notes to those accounts;

and accordingly the following two subsections have effect.

**(4)** If the balance sheet or profit and loss account drawn up in accordance with those requirements would not provide sufficient information to comply with subsection (2), any necessary additional information must be provided in that balance sheet or profit and loss account, or in a note to the accounts.

**(5)** If, owing to special circumstances in the case of any company, compliance with any such requirement in relation to the balance sheet or profit and loss account would prevent compliance with subsection (2) (even if additional information were provided in accordance with subsection (4)), the directors shall depart from that requirement in preparing the balance sheet or profit and loss amount (so far as necessary in order to comply with subsection (2)).

**(6)** If the directors depart from any such requirement, particulars of the departure, the reasons for it and its effect shall be given in a note to the accounts.

**(7)** Subsections (1) to (6) do not apply to group accounts prepared under the next section; and subsections (1) and (2) do not apply to a company's profit and loss account (or require the notes otherwise required in relation to that account) if–
- (a) the company has subsidiaries, and
- (b) the profit and loss account is framed as a consolidated account dealing with all or any of the company's subsidiaries as well as the company, and–
  - (i) complies with the requirements of this Act relating to consolidated profit and loss accounts, and
  - (ii) shows how much of the consolidated profit or loss for the financial year is dealt with in the company's individual accounts.

If group accounts are prepared, and advantage is taken of this subsection, that fact shall be disclosed in a note to the group accounts.

### 229 Group accounts of holding company

**229(1)** If at the end of its financial year a company has subsidiaries, the directors shall, as well as preparing individual accounts for that year, also prepare group accounts, being accounts or statements which deal with the state of affairs and profit or loss of the company and the subsidiaries.

**(2)** This does not apply if the company is at the end of the financial year the wholly-owned subsidiary of another body corporate incorporated in Great Britain.

**(3)** Group accounts need not deal with a subsidiary if the company's directors are of opinion that–
- (a) it is impracticable, or would be of no real value to the company's members, in view of the insignificant amounts involved, or
- (b) it would involve expense or delay out of proportion to the value to members, or
- (c) the result would be misleading, or harmful to the business of the company or any of its subsidiaries, or
- (d) the business of the holding company and that of the subsidiary are so different that they cannot reasonably be treated as a single undertaking;

and, if the directors are of that opinion about each of the company's subsidiaries, group accounts are not required.

**(4)** However, the approval of the Secretary of State is required for not dealing in group accounts with a subsidiary on the ground that the result would be harmful or on the ground of difference between the business of the holding company and that of the subsidiary.

**(5)** A holding company's group accounts shall be consolidated accounts comprising–
- (a) a consolidated balance sheet dealing with the state of affairs of the company and all the subsidiaries to be dealt with in group accounts, and
- (b) a consolidated profit and loss account dealing with the profit or loss of the company and those subsidiaries.

**(6)** However, if the directors are of opinion that it is better for the purpose of presenting the same or equivalent information about the state of affairs and profit or loss of the company and those subsidiaries, and of so presenting it that it may be readily appreciated by the company's members, the group accounts may be prepared in other than consolidated form, and in particular may consist–

(a) of more than one set of consolidated accounts dealing respectively with the company and one group of subsidiaries and with other groups of subsidiaries, or
(b) of separate accounts dealing with each of the subsidiaries, or
(c) of statements expanding the information about the subsidiaries in the company's individual accounts,

or of any combination of those forms.

**(7)** The group accounts may be wholly or partly incorporated in the holding company's individual balance sheet and profit and loss account.

**230 Form and content of group accounts**

**230(1)** A holding company's group accounts shall comply with the requirements of Schedule 4 (so far as applicable to group accounts in the form in which those accounts are prepared) with respect to the form and content of those accounts and any additional information to be provided by way of notes to those accounts.

**(2)** Group accounts (together with any notes to them) shall give a true and fair view of the state of affairs and profit or loss of the company and the subsidiaries dealt with by those accounts as a whole, so far as concerns members of the company.

**(3)** Subsection (2) overrides–

(a) the requirements of Schedule 4, and
(b) all other requirements of this Act as to the matters to be included in group accounts or in notes to those accounts,

and accordingly the following two subsections have effect.

**(4)** If group accounts drawn up in accordance with those requirements would not provide sufficient information to comply with subsection (2), any necessary additional information must be provided in, or in a note to, the group accounts.

**(5)** If, owing to special circumstances in the case of any company, compliance with any such requirement in relation to its group accounts would prevent those accounts from complying with subsection (2) (even if additional information were provided in accordance with subsection (4)), the directors shall depart from that requirement in preparing the group accounts (so far as necessary to comply with subsection (2)).

**(6)** If the directors depart from any such requirement, particulars of that departure, the reason for it and its effect shall be given in a note to the group accounts.

**(7)** If the financial year of a subsidiary does not coincide with that of the holding company, the group accounts shall (unless the Secretary of State, on the application or with the consent of the holding company's directors, otherwise directs) deal with the subsidiary's state of affairs as at the end of its relevant financial year, that is–

(a) if its financial year ends with that of the holding company, that financial year, and
(b) if not, the subsidiary's financial year ending last before the end of the financial year of the holding company dealt with in the group accounts,

and with the subsidiary's profit or loss for its relevant financial year.

**(8)** The Secretary of State may, on the application or with the consent of a company's directors, modify the requirements of Schedule 4 as they have effect in relation to that company by virtue of subsection (1), for the purpose of adapting them to the company's circumstances; and references above in this section to the requirements of Schedule 4 are then to be read in relation to that company as references to those requirements as modified.

**231 Additional disclosure required in notes to accounts**

**231(1)** Schedule 5 has effect with respect to additional matters which must be disclosed in company accounts for a financial year; and in that Schedule, where a thing is required to be stated or shown, or information is required to be given, it means that the thing is to be stated or shown, or the information is to be given, in a note to those accounts.

**(2)** In Schedule 5–

(a) Parts I and II are concerned, respectively, with the disclosure of particulars of the company's subsidiaries and of its other shareholdings,
(b) Part III is concerned with the disclosure of financial information relating to subsidiaries,
(c) Part IV requires a company which is itself a subsidiary to disclose its ultimate holding company,
(d) Part V is concerned with the emoluments of directors (including emoluments waived), pensions of directors and past directors and compensation for loss of office to directors and past directors, and
(e) Part VI is concerned with disclosure of the number of the company's employees who are remunerated at higher rates.

**(3)** Whenever it is stated in Schedule 5 that this subsection applies to certain particulars or information, it means that the particulars or information shall be annexed to the annual return first made by the company after copies of its accounts have been laid before it in general meeting; and if a company fails to satisfy an obligation thus imposed, the company and every officer of it who is in default is liable to a fine and, for continued contravention, to a daily default fine.

**(4)** It is the duty of any director of a company to give notice to the company of such matters relating to himself as may be necessary for purposes of Part V of Schedule 5; and this applies to persons who are or have at any time in the preceding 5 years been officers, as it applies to directors.

A person who makes default in complying with this subsection is liable to a fine.

**232 Loans in favour of directors and connected persons**

**232(1)** A holding company's group accounts for a financial year shall comply with Part I of Schedule 6 (so far as applicable) as regards the disclosure of transactions, arrangements and agreements there mentioned (loans, quasi-loans and other dealings in favour of directors).

**(2)** In the case of a company other than a holding company, its individual accounts shall comply with Part I of Schedule 6 (so far as applicable) as regards disclosure of those matters.

**(3)** Particulars which are required by Part I of Schedule 6 to be contained in any accounts shall be given by way of notes to the accounts, and are required in respect of shadow directors as well as directors.

**(4)** Where by virtue of section 229(2) or (3) a company does not prepare group accounts for a financial year, subsection (1) of this section requires disclosure of such matters in its individual accounts as would have been disclosed in group accounts.

**(5)** The requirements of this section apply with such exceptions as are mentioned in Part I of Schedule 6 (including in particular exceptions for and in respect of authorised institutions)."

(In s. 232(5) previously the words "authorised institutions" substituted for the former words "recognised banks" by Banking Act 1987, s. 108(1) and Sch. 6, para. 18(2) as from 1 October 1987 (see SI 1987/1664 (C 50)).)

**"233 Loans etc. to company's officers; statement of amounts outstanding**

**233(1)** A holding company's group accounts for a financial year shall comply with Part II of Schedule 6 (so far as applicable) as regards transactions, arrangements and agreements made by the company or a subsidiary of it for persons who at any time during that financial year were officers of the company (but not directors).

**(2)** In the case of a company other than a holding company, its individual accounts shall comply with Part II of Schedule 6 (so far as applicable) as regards those matters.

**(3)** Subsections (1) and (2) do not apply in relation to any transaction, arrangement or agreement made by an authorised institution for any officer of the institution or for any officer of its holding company unless the officer is a chief executive or manager within the meaning of the Banking Act 1987; and references to officers in Part II of Schedule 6 shall be construed accordingly."

(S. 233(3) previously substituted by Banking Act 1987, s. 90(1) as from 1 October 1987 (see SI 1987/1664 (C 50)); s. 233(3) formerly read as follows:

"Subsections (1) and (2) do not apply in relation to any transaction, arrangement or agreement made by a recognised bank for any of its officers or for any of the officers of its holding company.)"

**"(4)** Particulars required by Part II of Schedule 6 to be contained in any accounts shall be given by way of notes to the accounts.

**(5)** Where by virtue of section 229(2) or (3) a company does not prepare group accounts for a financial year, subsection (1) of this section requires such matters to be stated in its individual accounts as would have been stated in group accounts.

**234 Authorised institutions: disclosure of dealings with and for directors**

**234(1)** The group accounts of a company which is, or is the holding company of, an authorised institution, and the individual accounts of any other company which is an authorised institution, shall comply with Part III of Schedule 6 (so far as applicable) as regards transactions, arrangements and agreements made by the company preparing the accounts (if it is an authorised institution) and, in the case of a holding company, by any of its subsidiaries which is an authorised institution, for persons who at any time during the financial year were directors of the company or connected with a director of it."

(In s. 234(1) previously the words "an authorised institution", wherever they occurred, substituted for the former words "a recognised bank" by Banking Act 1987, s. 108(1) and Sch. 6, para. 18(3) as from 1 October 1987 (see SI 1981/1664 (C 50). Also in heading to s. 234 the words "authorised institutions" substituted for the words "Recognised banks" by CCH to reflect the amendment by the Banking Act 1987 noted above.)

**"(2)** Particulars required by Part III of Schedule 6 to be contained in any accounts shall be given by way of notes to those accounts, and are required in respect of shadow directors as well as directors.

**(3)** Where by virtue of section 229(2) or (3) a company does not prepare group accounts for a financial year, subsection (1) of this section requires such matters to be stated in its individual accounts as would have been stated in group accounts.

## DIRECTORS' AND AUDITORS' REPORTS

**235 Directors' report**

**235(1)** In the case of every company there shall for each financial year be prepared a report by the directors–

(a) containing a fair review of the development of the business of the company and its subsidiaries during the financial year and of their position at the end of it, and

(b) stating the amount (if any) which they recommend should be paid as dividend and the amount (if any) which they propose to carry to reserves.

**(2)** The directors' report shall state the names of the persons who, at any time during the financial year, were directors of the company, and the principal activities of the company and its subsidiaries in the course of the year and any significant change in those activities in the year.

**(3)** The report shall also state the matters, and give the particulars, required by Part I of Schedule 7 (changes in asset values, directors' shareholdings and other interests, contributions for political and charitable purposes, etc.).

**(4)** Part II of Schedule 7 applies as regards the matters to be stated in the directors' report in the circumstances there specified (company acquiring its own shares or a permitted charge on them).

**(5)** Parts III, IV and V of Schedule 7 apply respectively as regards the matters to be stated in the directors' report relative to the employment, training and advancement of disabled persons; the health, safety and welfare at work of the company's employees; and the involvement of employees in the affairs, policy and performance of the company.

**(6)** If the company's individual accounts are accompanied by group accounts which are special category, the directors' report shall, in addition to complying with Schedule 7, also comply with paragraphs 2 to 6 of Schedule 10 (turnover and profitability; size of labour force and wages paid).

**(7)** In respect of any failure to comply with the requirements of this Act as to the matters to be stated, and the particulars to be given, in the directors' report, every person who was a director of the company immediately before the end of the relevant period (meaning whatever is under section 242 the period for laying and delivering accounts) is guilty of an offence and liable to a fine.

In proceedings for an offence under this subsection, it is a defence for the person to prove that he took all reasonable steps for securing compliance with the requirements in question.

**236 Auditors' report**

**236(1)** A company's auditors shall make a report to its members on the accounts examined by them, and on every balance sheet and profit and loss account, and on all group accounts, copies of which are to be laid before the company in general meeting during the auditors' tenure of office.

**(2)** The auditors' report shall state–

(a) whether in the auditors' opinion the balance sheet and profit and loss account and (if it is a holding company submitting group accounts) the group accounts have been properly prepared in accordance with this Act; and

(b) without prejudice to the foregoing, whether in their opinion a true and fair view is given–

(i) in the balance sheet, of the state of the company's affairs at the end of the financial year,

(ii) in the profit and loss account (if not framed as a consolidated account), of the company's profit or loss for the financial year, and

(iii) in the case of group accounts, of the state of affairs and profit or loss of the company and its subsidiaries dealt with by those accounts, so far as concerns members of the company.

**237 Auditors' duties and powers**

**237(1)** It is the duty of the company's auditors, in preparing their report, to carry out such investigations as will enable them to form an opinion as to the following matters–

(a) whether proper accounting records have been kept by the company and proper returns adequate for their audit have been received from branches not visited by them,

(b) whether the company's balance sheet and (if not consolidated) its profit and loss account are in agreement with the accounting records and returns.

**(2)** If the auditors are of opinion that proper accounting records have not been kept, or that proper returns adequate for their audit have not been received from branches not visited by them, or if the balance sheet and (if not consolidated) the profit and loss account are not in agreement with the accounting records and returns, the auditors shall state that fact in their report.

**(3)** Every auditor of a company has a right of access at all times to the company's books, accounts and vouchers, and is entitled to require from the company's officers such information and explanations as he thinks necessary for the performance of the auditor's duties.

**(4)** If the auditors fail to obtain all the information and explanations which, to the best of their knowledge and belief, are necessary for the purposes of their audit, they shall state that fact in their report.

**(5)** If the requirements of Parts V and VI of Schedule 5 and Parts I to III of Schedule 6 are not complied with in the accounts, it is the auditors' duty to include in their report, so far as they are reasonably able to do so, a statement giving the required particulars.

**(6)** It is the auditors' duty to consider whether the information given in the directors' report for the financial year for which the accounts are prepared is consistent with those accounts; and if they are of opinion that it is not, they shall state that fact in their report.

PROCEDURE ON COMPLETION OF ACCOUNTS

**238 Signing of balance sheet; documents to be annexed**

**238(1)** A company's balance sheet, and every copy of it which is laid before the company in general meeting or delivered to the registrar of companies, shall be signed on behalf of the board by two of the directors of the company or, if there is only one director, by that one.

**(2)** If a copy of the balance sheet–

(a) is laid before the company or delivered to the registrar without being signed as required by this section, or

(b) not being a copy so laid or delivered, is issued, circulated or published in a case where the balance sheet has not been signed as so required or where (the balance sheet having been so signed) the copy does not include a copy of the signatures or signature, as the case may be,

the company and every officer of it who is in default is liable to a fine.

**(3)** A company's profit and loss account and, so far as not incorporated in its individual balance sheet or profit and loss account, any group accounts of a holding company shall be annexed to the balance sheet, and the auditors' report shall be attached to it.

**(4)** Any accounts so annexed shall be approved by the board of directors before the balance sheet is signed on their behalf.

**239 Documents to be included in company's accounts**

**239** For the purposes of this Part, a company's accounts for a financial year are to be taken as comprising the following documents–

(a) the company's profit and loss account and balance sheet,

(b) the directors' report,

(c) the auditors' report, and

(d) where the company has subsidiaries and section 229 applies, the company's group accounts.

**240 Persons entitled to receive accounts as of right**

**240(1)** In the case of every company, a copy of the company's accounts for the financial year shall, not less than 21 days before the date of the meeting at which they are to be laid in accordance with the next section, be sent to each of the following persons–

(a) every member of the company (whether or not entitled to receive notice of general meetings),

(b) every holder of the company's debentures (whether or not so entitled), and

(c) all persons other than members and debenture holders, being persons so entitled.

**(2)** In the case of a company not having a share capital, subsection (1) does not require a copy of the accounts to be sent to a member of the company who is not entitled to receive notices of general meetings of the company, or to a holder of the company's debentures who is not so entitled.

**(3)** Subsection (1) does not require copies of the accounts to be sent–

(a) to a member of the company or a debenture holder, being in either case a person who is not entitled to receive notices of general meetings, and of whose address the company is unaware, or

(b) to more than one of the joint holders of any shares or debentures none of whom are entitled to receive such notices, or

(c) in the case of joint holders of shares or debentures some of whom are, and some not, entitled to receive such notices, to those who are not so entitled.

**(4)** If copies of the accounts are sent less than 21 days before the date of the meeting, they are, notwithstanding that fact, deemed to have been duly sent if it is so agreed by all the members entitled to attend and vote at the meeting.

**(5)** If default is made in complying with subsection (1), the company and every officer of it who is in default is liable to a fine.

**241 Directors' duty to lay and deliver accounts**

**241(1)** In respect of each financial year of a company the directors shall lay before the company in general meeting copies of the accounts of the company for that year.

**(2)** The auditors' report shall be read before the company in general meeting, and be open to the inspection of any member of the company.

**(3)** In respect of each financial year the directors–
(a) shall deliver to the registrar of companies a copy of the accounts for the year, and
(b) if any document comprised in the accounts is in a language other than English, shall annex to the copy of that document delivered a translation of it into English, certified in the prescribed manner to be a correct translation.

**(4)** In the case of an unlimited company, the directors are not required by subsection (3) to deliver a copy of the accounts if–
(a) at no time during the accounting reference period has the company been, to its knowledge, the subsidiary of a company that was then limited and at no such time, to its knowledge, have there been held or been exercisable, by or on behalf of two or more companies that were then limited, shares or powers which, if they had been held or been exercisable by one of them, would have made the company its subsidiary, and
(b) at no such time has the company been the holding company of a company which was then limited, and
(c) at no such time has the company been carrying on business as the promoter of a trading stamp scheme within the Trading Stamps Act 1964.

References here to a company that was limited at a particular time are to a body corporate (under whatever law incorporated) the liability of whose members was at that time limited.

**242 Period allowed for laying and delivery**

**242(1)** The period allowed for laying and delivering a company's accounts for a financial year is as follows in this section, being determined by reference to the end of the relevant accounting reference period (that is, the accounting reference period in respect of which the financial year of the company is ascertained).

**(2)** Subject to the following subsections, the period allowed is–
(a) for a private company, 10 months after the end of the relevant accounting reference period, and
(b) for a public company, 7 months after the end of that period.

**(3)** If a company carries on business, or has interests, outside the United Kingdom, the Channel Islands and the Isle of Man and in respect of a financial year the directors (before the end of the period allowed by subsection (2)) give to the registrar of companies notice in the prescribed form–
(a) stating that the company so carries on business or has such interests, and
(b) claiming an extension of the period so allowed by a further 3 months,
the period allowed in relation to that financial year is then so extended.

**(4)** Where a company's first accounting reference period–
(a) begins on the date of its incorporation, and
(b) is a period of more than 12 months,
the period otherwise allowed for laying and delivering accounts is reduced by the number of days by which the relevant accounting reference period is longer than 12 months.

However, the period allowed is not by this provision reduced to less than 3 months after the end of that accounting reference period.

**(5)** Where a company's relevant accounting reference period has been shortened under section 226 (in consequence of notice by the company under section 225), the period allowed for laying and delivering accounts is–
(a) the period allowed in accordance with subsections (2) to (4) above, or
(b) the period of 3 months beginning with the date of the notice under section 225,
whichever of those periods last expires.

**(6)** If for any special reason the Secretary of State thinks fit to do so, he may by notice in writing to a company extend, by such further period as may be specified in the notice, the period otherwise allowed for laying and delivering accounts for any financial year of the company.

**243 Penalty for non-compliance with s. 241**

**243(1)** If for a financial year of a company any of the requirements of section 241(1) or (3) is not complied with before the end of the period allowed for laying and delivering accounts, every person who immediately before the end of that period was a director of the company is, in respect of each of those subsections which is not so complied with, guilty of an offence and liable to a fine and, for continued contravention, to a daily default fine.

**(2)** If a person is charged with that offence in respect of any of the requirements of section 241(1) or (3), it is a defence for him to prove that he took all reasonable steps for securing that those requirements would be complied with before the end of the period allowed for laying and delivering accounts.

**(3)** If in respect of the company's financial year any of the requirements of section 241(3) is not complied with before the end of the period allowed for laying and delivering accounts, the company is liable to a penalty, recoverable in civil proceedings by the Secretary of State.

**(4)** The amount of the penalty is determined by reference to the length of the period between the end of the accounting reference period and the earliest day by which all those requirements have been complied with, and is–
(a) £20 where the period is not more than one month,
(b) £50 where the period is more than 1 month but not more than 3 months,
(c) £100 where the period is more than 3 months but not more than 6 months,
(d) £200 where the period is more than 6 months but not more than 12 months, and
(e) £450 where the period is more than 12 months.

**(5)** In proceedings under this section with respect to a requirement to lay a copy of a document before a company in general meeting, or to deliver a copy of a document to the registrar of companies, it is not a defence to prove that the document in question was not in fact prepared as required by this Part.

**(6)** Subsections (3) and (4) of this section do not come into force unless and until made to do so by an order of the Secretary of State in a statutory instrument."
(There appear to have been no statutory instruments under s. 243(6).)

**"244 Default order in case of non-compliance**

**244(1)** If–

(a) in respect of a company's financial year any of the requirements of section 241(3) has not been complied with before the end of the period allowed for laying and delivering accounts, and

(b) the directors of the company fail to make good the default within 14 days after the service of a notice on them requiring compliance,

the court may, on application by any member or creditor of the company, or by the registrar of companies, make an order directing the directors (or any of them) to make good the default within such time as may be specified in the order.

**(2)** The court's order may provide that all costs of and incidental to the application shall be borne by the directors.

**(3)** Nothing in this section prejudices section 243.

**245 Penalty for laying or delivering defective accounts**

**245(1)** If any accounts of a company of which a copy is laid before the company in general meeting or delivered to the registrar of companies do not comply with the requirements of this Act as to the matters to be included in, or in a note to, those accounts, every person who at the time when the copy is so laid or delivered is a director of the company is guilty of an offence and, in respect of each offence, liable to a fine.

This subsection does not apply to a company's group accounts.

**(2)** If any group accounts of which a copy is laid before a company in general meeting or delivered to the registrar of companies do not comply with section 229(5) to (7) or section 230, and with the other requirements of this Act as to the matters to be included in or in a note to those accounts, every person who at the time when the copy was so laid or delivered was a director of the company is guilty of an offence and liable to a fine.

**(3)** In proceedings against a person for an offence under this section, it is a defence for him to prove that he took all reasonable steps for securing compliance with the requirements in question.

**246 Shareholders' right to obtain copies of accounts**

**246(1)** Any member of a company, whether or not he is entitled to have sent to him copies of the company's accounts, and any holder of the company's debentures (whether or not so entitled) is entitled to be furnished (on demand and without charge) with a copy of its last accounts.

**(2)** If, when a person makes a demand for a document with which he is entitled by this section to be furnished, default is made in complying with the demand within 7 days after its making, the company and every officer of it who is in default is liable to a fine and, for continued contravention, to a daily default fine (unless it is proved that the person has already made a demand for, and been furnished with, a copy of the document).

MODIFIED ACCOUNTS

**247 Entitlement to deliver accounts in modified form**

**247(1)** In certain cases a company's directors may, in accordance with Part I of Schedule 8, deliver modified accounts in respect of a financial year; and whether they may do so depends on the company qualifying, in particular financial years, as small or medium-sized.

**(2)** Modified accounts for a financial year may not be delivered in the case of a company which is, or was at any time in that year–

(a) a public company,

(b) a special category company (Chapter II of this Part), or

(c) subject to the next-but-one subsection, a member of a group which is ineligible for this purpose.

**(3) "Group"** here means a holding company and its subsidiaries together; and a group is ineligible if any of its members is–

(a) a public company or a special category company, or

(b) a body corporate (other than a company) which has power under its constitution to offer its shares or debentures to the public and may lawfully exercise that power, or

(c) a body corporate (other than a company) which is either an authorised institution or an insurance company to which Part II of the Insurance Companies Act 1982 applies."

(In s. 247(3)(c) previously the words "an authorised institution" substituted for the former words "a recognised bank or licensed institution within the Banking Act 1979" by Banking Act 1987, s. 108(2) and Sch. 6, para. 18(4) as from 1 October 1987 (see SI 1987/1664 (C 50)).)

"**(4)** Notwithstanding subsection (2)(c), modified accounts for a financial year may be delivered if the company is exempt under section 252 (dormant companies) from the obligation to appoint auditors and either–

(a) was so exempt throughout that year, or

(b) became so exempt by virtue of a special resolution under that section passed during that year.

**(5)** For purposes of sections 247 to 250 and Schedule 8, **"deliver"** means deliver to the registrar of companies under this Chapter; and for purposes of subsection (3)(b), **"shares"** and **"debentures"** have the same meaning as when used in relation to a company.

**248 Qualification of company as small or medium-sized**

**248(1)** A company qualifies as small in a financial year if for that year two or more of the following conditions are satisfied–

(a) the amount of its turnover for the year is not more than £2 million;

(b) its balance sheet total is not more than £975,000;

(c) the average number of persons employed by the company in the year (determined on a weekly basis) does not exceed 50."

(In s. 248(1) previously the figure "£2 million" substituted for the former figure "£1.4 million", and the figure "£975,000" substituted for the former figure "£700,000" by the Companies (Modified Accounts) Amendment Regulations 1986 (SI 1986/1865), reg. 2 as from 30 November 1986.)

"**(2)** A company qualifies as medium-sized in a financial year if for that year two or more of the following conditions are satisfied–

(a) the amount of its turnover for the year is not more than £8 million;

(b) its balance sheet total is not more than £3.9 million;

(c) the average number of persons employed by the company in the year (determined on a weekly basis) does not exceed 250."

(In s. 248(2) previously the figure "£8 million" substituted for the former figure "£5.75 million", and the figure "£3.9 million" substituted for the former figure "£2.8 million" by the Companies (Modified Accounts) Amendment Regulations 1986 (SI 1986/1865), reg. 3 as from 30 November 1986.)

"**(3)** In subsections (1) and (2), **"balance sheet total"** means, in relation to a company's financial year–

(a) where in the company's accounts Format 1 of the balance sheet formats set out in Part I of Schedule 4 is adopted, the aggregate of the amounts shown in the balance sheet under the headings corresponding to items A to D in that Format, and

(b) where Format 2 is adopted, the aggregate of the amounts shown under the general heading "Assets".

**(4)** The average number of persons employed as mentioned in subsections (1)(c) and (2)(c) is determined by applying the method of calculation prescribed by paragraph 56(2) and (3) of Schedule 4 for determining the number required by sub-paragraph (1)(a) of that paragraph to be stated in a note to the company's accounts.

**(5)** In applying subsections (1) and (2) to a period which is a company's financial year but not in fact a year, the maximum figures for turnover in paragraph (a) of each subsection are to be proportionately adjusted.

**249 Modified individual accounts**

**249(1)** This section specifies the cases in which a company's directors may (subject to section 250, where the company has subsidiaries) deliver individual accounts modified as for a small or a medium-sized company; and Part I of Schedule 8 applies with respect to the delivery of accounts so modified.

**(2)** In respect of the company's first financial year the directors may–

(a) deliver accounts modified as for a small company, if in that year it qualifies as small,

(b) deliver accounts modified as for a medium-sized company, if in that year it qualifies as medium-sized.

**(3)** The next three subsections are concerned only with a company's financial year subsequent to the first.

**(4)** The directors may in respect of a financial year–

(a) deliver accounts modified as for a small company if in that year the company qualifies as small and it also so qualified in the preceding year,

(b) deliver accounts modified as for a medium-sized company if in that year the company qualifies as medium-sized and it also so qualified in the preceding year.

**(5)** The directors may in respect of a financial year–

(a) deliver accounts modified as for a small company (although not qualifying in that year as small), if in the preceding year it so qualified and the directors were entitled to deliver accounts so modified in respect of that year, and

(b) deliver accounts modified as for a medium-sized company (although not qualifying in that year as medium-sized), if in the preceding year it so qualified and the directors were entitled to deliver accounts so modified in respect of that year.

**(6)** The directors may in respect of a financial year–

(a) deliver accounts modified as for a small company, if in that year the company qualifies as small and the directors were entitled under subsection (5)(a) to deliver accounts so modified for the preceding year (although the company did not in that year qualify as small), and

(b) deliver accounts modified as for a medium-sized company if in that year the company qualifies as medium-sized and the directors were entitled under subsection (5)(b) to deliver accounts so modified for the preceding year (although the company did not in that year qualify as medium-sized).

**250 Modified accounts of holding company**

**250(1)** This section applies to a company ("the holding company") where in respect of a financial year section 229 requires the preparation of group accounts for the company and its subsidiaries.

**(2)** The directors of the holding company may not under section 249–

(a) deliver accounts modified as for a small company, unless the group (meaning the holding company and its subsidiaries together) is in that year a small group,

(b) deliver accounts modified as for a medium-sized company, unless in that year the group is medium-sized;

and the group is small or medium-sized if it would so qualify under section 248 (applying that section as directed by subsections (3) and (4) below), if it were all one company.

**(3)** The figures to be taken into account in determining whether the group is small or medium-sized (or neither) are the group account figures, that is–

(a) where the group accounts are prepared as consolidated accounts, the figures for turnover, balance sheet total and numbers employed which are shown in those accounts, and

(b) where not, the corresponding figures given in the group accounts, with such adjustment as would have been made if the accounts had been prepared in consolidated form,

aggregated in either case with the relevant figures for the subsidiaries (if any) omitted from the group accounts (excepting those for any subsidiary omitted under section 229(3)(a) on the ground of impracticability).

**(4)** In the case of each subsidiary omitted from the group accounts, the figures relevant as regards turnover, balance sheet total and numbers employed are those which are included in the accounts of that subsidiary prepared in respect of its relevant financial year (with such adjustment as would have been made if those figures had been included in group accounts prepared in consolidated form).

**(5)** For the purposes of subsection (4), the relevant financial year of the subsidiary is–

(a) if its financial year ends with that of the holding company to which the group accounts relate, that financial year, and

(b) if not, the subsidiary's financial year ending last before the end of the financial year of the holding company.

**(6)** If the directors are entitled to deliver modified accounts (whether as for a small or a medium-sized company), they may also deliver modified group accounts; and this means that the group accounts–

(a) if consolidated, may be in accordance with Part II of Schedule 8 (while otherwise comprising or corresponding with group accounts prepared under section 229), and

(b) if not consolidated, may be such as (together with any notes) give the same or equivalent information as required by paragraph (a) above;

and Part III of the Schedule applies to modified group accounts, whether consolidated or not.

**251 Power of Secretary of State to modify s. 247–250 and Sch. 8**

**251(1)** The Secretary of State may by regulations in a statutory instrument modify the provisions of section 247(1) to (3), 248 to 250 and Schedule 8; and those provisions then apply as modified by regulations for the time being in force.

**(2)** Regulations under this section reducing the classes of companies which have the benefit of those provisions, or rendering the requirements of those provisions more onerous, shall not be made unless a draft of the instrument containing the regulations has been laid before Parliament and approved by a resolution of each House.

**(3)** Otherwise, a statutory instrument containing such regulations is subject to annulment in pursuance of a resolution of either House.

DORMANT COMPANIES

**252 Company resolution not to appoint auditors**

**252(1)** In certain circumstances a company may, with a view to the subsequent laying and delivery of unaudited accounts, pass a special resolution making itself exempt from the obligation to appoint auditors as otherwise required by section 384.

**(2)** Such a resolution may be passed at a general meeting of the company at which its accounts for a financial year are laid as required by section 241 (if it is not a year for which the directors are required to lay group accounts); but the following conditions must be satisfied–

(a) the directors must be entitled under section 249 to deliver, in respect of that financial year, accounts modified as for a small company (or would be so entitled but for the company being, or having at any time in the financial year been, a member of an ineligible group within section 247(3)), and

(b) the company must have been dormant since the end of the financial year.

**(3)** A company may by such a resolution make itself exempt from the obligation to appoint auditors if the resolution is passed at some time before the first general meeting of the company at which accounts are laid as required by section 241, provided that the company has been dormant from the time of its formation until the resolution is passed.

**(4)** A company may not under subsection (3) pass such a resolution if it is a public company or a special category company.

**(5)** For purposes of this and the next section, a company is **"dormant"** during any period in which no transaction occurs which is for the company a significant accounting transaction; and–

(a) this means a transaction which is required by section 221 to be entered in the company's accounting records (disregarding any which arises from the taking of shares in the company by a subscriber to the memorandum in pursuance of an undertaking of his in the memorandum), and

(b) a company which has been dormant for any period ceases to be so on the occurrence of any such transaction.

**(6)** A company which has under this section made itself exempt from the obligation to appoint auditors loses that exemption if–

(a) it ceases to be dormant, or

(b) it would no longer qualify (for any other reason) to exclude that obligation by passing a resolution under this section.

**(7)** Where the exemption is lost, the directors may, at any time before the next meeting of the company at which accounts are to be laid, appoint an auditor or auditors, to hold office until the conclusion of that meeting; and if they fail to exercise that power, the company in general meeting may exercise it.

**253 Laying and delivery of unaudited accounts**

**253(1)** The following applies in respect of a company's accounts for a financial year if the company is exempt under section 252 from the obligation to appoint auditors and either–

(a) was so exempt throughout that year, or

(b) became so exempt by virtue of a special resolution passed during that year, and retained the exemption until the end of that year.

**(2)** A report by the company's auditors need not be included (as otherwise required by preceding provisions of this Chapter) with the accounts laid before the company in general meeting and delivered to the registrar of companies.

**(3)** If the auditors' report is omitted from the accounts so delivered, then–

(a) the balance sheet shall contain a statement by the directors (in a position immediately above their signatures to the balance sheet) that the company was dormant throughout the financial year, and

(b) if the accounts delivered to the registrar are modified as permitted by sections 247 to 249–

(i) the modified balance sheet need not contain the statement otherwise required by paragraph 9 of Schedule 8, and

(ii) the modified accounts need not include the special report of the auditors otherwise required by paragraph 10 of that Schedule.

PUBLICATION OF ACCOUNTS

**254 Publication of full company accounts**

**254(1)** This section applies to the publication by a company of full individual or group accounts, that is to say the accounts required by section 241 to be laid before the company in general meeting and delivered to the registrar of companies (including the directors' report, unless dispensed with under paragraph 3 of Schedule 8).

**(2)** If a company publishes individual accounts (modified or other) for a financial year, it shall publish with them the relevant auditors' report.

**(3)** If a company required by section 229 to prepare group accounts for a financial year publishes individual accounts for that year, it shall also publish with them its group accounts (modified or other).

**(4)** If a company publishes group accounts (modified or other), otherwise than together with its individual accounts, it shall publish with them the relevant auditors' report.

**(5)** References above to the relevant auditors' report are to the auditors' report under section 236 or, in the case of modified accounts (individual or group), the auditors' special report under paragraph 10 of Schedule 8.

**(6)** A company which contravenes any provision of this section, and any officer of it who is in default, is liable to a fine.

**255 Publication of abridged accounts**

**255(1)** This section applies to the publication by a company of abridged accounts, that is to say any balance sheet or profit and loss account relating to a financial year of the company or purporting to deal with any such financial year, otherwise than as part of full accounts (individual or group) to which section 254 applies.

**(2)** The reference above to a balance sheet or profit and loss account, in relation to accounts published by a holding company, includes an account in any form purporting to be a balance sheet or profit and loss account for the group consisting of the holding company and its subsidiaries.

**(3)** If the company publishes abridged accounts, it shall publish with those accounts a statement indicating–
(a) that the accounts are not full accounts,
(b) whether full individual or full group accounts (according as the abridged accounts deal solely with the company's own affairs or with the affairs of the company and any subsidiaries) have been delivered to the registrar of companies or, in the case of an unlimited company exempt under section 241(4) from the requirement to deliver accounts, that the company is so exempt,
(c) whether the company's auditors have made a report under section 236 on the company's accounts for any financial year with which the abridged accounts purport to deal, and
(d) whether any report so made was unqualified (meaning that it was a report, without qualification, to the effect that in the opinion of the person making it the company's accounts had been properly prepared).

**(4)** Where a company publishes abridged accounts, it shall not publish with those accounts any such report of the auditors as is mentioned in subsection (3)(c).

**(5)** A company which contravenes any provision of this section, and any officer of it who is in default, is liable to a fine.

SUPPLEMENTARY

**256 Power of Secretary of State to alter accounting requirements**

**256(1)** The Secretary of State may by regulations in a statutory instrument–
(a) add to the classes of documents–
(i) to be comprised in a company's accounts for a financial year to be laid before the company in general meeting as required by section 241, or
(ii) to be delivered to the registrar of companies under that section,
and make provision as to the matters to be included in any document to be added to either class;
(b) modify the requirements of this Act as to the matters to be stated in a document of any such class;
(c) reduce the classes of documents to be delivered to the registrar of companies under section 241.

**(2)** In particular, the Secretary of State may by such regulations alter or add to the requirements of Schedule 4 and Schedule 9 (special category companies); and any reference in this Act to a provision of it then refers to that provision as it has effect subject to regulations in force under this section.

**(3)** Where regulations made under subsection (1)(a) add to either class of documents there mentioned documents dealing with the state of affairs and profit or loss of a company and other bodies, the regulations may also–
(a) extend the provisions of this Act relating to group accounts (or such of those provisions as may be specified) to such documents,
(b) exempt that company from the requirement to prepare group accounts in respect of any period for which it has prepared such a document.

**(4)** Regulations under this section may make different provision for different cases or classes of case, and may contain such incidental and supplementary provisions as the Secretary of State thinks fit.

**(5)** Regulations under subsection (1)(a), or extending the classes of company to which any requirement mentioned in subsection (1)(b) applies or rendering those requirements more onerous, shall not be made unless a draft of the instrument containing them has been laid before Parliament and approved by a resolution of each House.

**(6)** Otherwise, a statutory instrument containing such regulations is subject to annulment in pursuance of a resolution of either House.

**Chapter II – Accounts of Banking, Shipping and Insurance Companies**

**257 Special category companies and their accounts**

**257(1)** For purposes of this Act, **"special category companies"** are banking companies, shipping companies and insurance companies; and–
(a) **"banking company"** means a company which is an authorised insitution;
(b) **"insurance company"** means an insurance company to which Part II of the Insurance Companies Act 1982 applies; and
(c) **"shipping company"** means a company which, or a subsidiary of which, owns ships or includes among its activities the management or operation of ships and which satisfies the Secretary of State that it ought in the national interest to be treated under this Part of this Act as a shipping company."

(In s. 257(1) previously para. (a) substituted by Banking Act 1987, s. 108(1) and Sch. 6, para. 18(5) as from 1 October 1987 (see SI 1987/1664 (C 50)); the former para. (a) read as follows:

"(a) **"banking company"** means a company which is a recognised bank for the purposes of the Banking Act 1979 or is a licensed institution within that Act;".)

"**(2)** Except as otherwise provided below, Chapter I of this Part applies to a special category company and its accounts as it applies to, and to the accounts of, any other company.

**(3)** The individual accounts of a special category company, and the group accounts of a holding company which is, or has as its subsidiary, a special category company, may be prepared under this Chapter and not under Chapter I, and contain a statement that they are so prepared; and a reference in this Act to a company's accounts (individual or group) being "special category" is to their being so prepared and containing that statement.

**(4)** Subject as follows, a reference in any enactment or other document to section 228 or 230 of this Act or to Schedule 4 is, in relation to special category accounts, to be read as a reference to section 258 or 259 or Schedule 9 (as the case may require); but this is subject to any contrary context.

**258 Special category individual accounts**

**258(1)** Where a company's individual accounts are special category, section 228 and Schedule 4 do not apply, but–
(a) the balance sheet shall give a true and fair view of the state of affairs of the company as at the end of the financial year, and
(b) the profit and loss account shall give a true and fair view of the company's profit or loss for the financial year.

**(2)** The balance sheet and profit and loss account shall comply with the requirements of Schedule 9, so far as applicable.

**(3)** Except as expressly provided by this section or Part III of Schedule 9, the requirements of subsection (2) and that Schedule are without prejudice to the general requirements of sub-section (1) or to any other requirements of this Act.

**(4)** The Secretary of State may, on the application or with the consent of the company's directors, modify in relation to that company any of the requirements of this Chapter as to the matters to be stated in a company's balance sheet or profit and loss account (except the requirements of subsection (1) above), for the purpose of adapting them to the circumstances of the company.

**(5)** So much of subsections (1) and (2) as relates to the profit and loss account does not apply if–

(a) the company has subsidiaries, and

(b) the profit and loss account is framed as a consolidated account dealing with all or any of the company's subsidiaries as well as the company and–

(i) complies with the requirements of this Act relating to consolidated profit and loss accounts (as those requirements apply in the case of special category companies), and

(ii) shows how much of the consolidated profit or loss for the financial year is dealt with in the company's accounts.

**259 Special category group accounts**

**259(1)** Where a holding company's group accounts are special category, those accounts shall give a true and fair view of the state of affairs and profit or loss of the company and the subsidiaries dealt with by those accounts as a whole, so far as concerns members of the company.

**(2)** Where the financial year of a subsidiary does not coincide with that of the holding company, the group accounts shall (unless the Secretary of State on the application or with the consent of the holding company's directors otherwise directs) deal with the subsidiary's state of affairs as at the end of its relevant financial year, that is–

(a) if its financial year ends with that of the holding company, that financial year, and

(b) if not, the subsidiary's financial year ending last before the end of the financial year of the holding company dealt with in the group accounts,

and with the subsidiary's profit or loss for its relevant financial year

**(3)** Without prejudice to subsection (1), the group accounts, if prepared as consolidated accounts, shall comply with the requirements of Schedule 9 (so far as applicable), and if not so prepared shall give the same or equivalent information.

**(4)** However, the Secretary of State may, on the application or with the consent of the holding company's directors, modify the requirements of Schedule 9 in relation to that company for the purpose of adapting them to the company's circumstances.

**260 Notes to special category accounts**

**260(1)** In Schedule 5 (matters to be dealt with in notes to accounts–

(a) paragraph 8 in Part II (disclosure of shareholdings in other bodies corporate, not being subsidiaries), and

(b) Part III (financial information about subsidiaries),

do not apply in the case of special category accounts.

**(2)** Where an item is given in a note to special category accounts, to comply with Part V or VI of Schedule 5 (directors' emoluments, pensions etc.; emoluments of higher-paid employees), the corresponding amount for the immediately preceding financial year shall be included in the note.

**(3)** If a person, being a director of a company preparing special category accounts, fails to take all reasonable steps to secure compliance with subsection (2), he is in respect of each offence liable to a fine; but in proceedings against a person for that offence it is a defence to prove that he had reasonable ground to believe, and did believe, that a competent and reliable person was charged with the duty of seeing that subsection (2) was complied with and was in a position to discharge that duty.

**261 Directors' report**

**261(1)** Where a company's individual accounts are special category, the following applies with respect to the directors' report accompanying the accounts.

**(2)** Paragraphs (a) and (b) of section 235(1) do not apply as regards the contents of the report; but the report shall deal with the company's state of affairs, the amount (if any) which the directors recommend should be paid as dividend, and the amount (if any) which they propose to carry to reserves (within the meaning of Schedule 9).

**(3)** Information which is otherwise required to be given in the accounts, and allowed to be given in a statement annexed, may be given in the directors' report instead of in the accounts.

If any information is so given, the report is treated as forming part of the accounts for the purposes of audit, except that the auditors shall report on it only so far as it gives that information.

**(4)** Where advantage is taken of subsection (3) to show an item in the directors' report instead of in the accounts, the report shall also show the corresponding amount for (or, as the case may require, as at the end of) the immediately preceding financial year of that item, except where the amount would not have had to be shown had the item been shown in the accounts.

**(5)** Schedule 7 applies to the directors' report only in respect of the matters to be stated, and the information to be given, under paragraphs 1 to 5 (but excluding paragraph 2(3)) and 9, 10 and 11; and paragraph 1 of the Schedule does not apply if the company has the benefit of any provision of Part III of Schedule 9.

**(6)** The report shall, in addition to complying with those paragraphs of Schedule 7, also comply with Schedule 10, where and so far as applicable (disclosure of recent share and debenture issues; turnover and profitability; size of labour force and wages paid; and other general matters); but in that Schedule paragraphs 2 to 4 and 6 do not apply to a directors' report attached to any accounts unless the documents required to be comprised in those accounts include group accounts which are special category.

**(7)** Section 237(6) does not apply.

**262 Auditors' report**

**262(1)** The following applies where a company is entitled to avail itself, and has availed itself, of the benefit of any of the provisions of Part III of Schedule 9.

**(2)** In that case section 236(2) does not apply; and the auditors' report shall state whether in their opinion the company's balance sheet and profit and loss account and (if it is a holding company submitting group accounts) the group accounts have been properly prepared in accordance with this Act."

# PART VIII – DISTRIBUTION OF PROFITS AND ASSETS

**Note**

Pt. IV, V (excluding Ch. VIII) and VIII (in their original forms) were previously CA 1980, Pt. I, II and III and CA 1981, Pt. III which implemented the Second EC Company Law Directive (77/91).

## LIMITS OF COMPANY'S POWER OF DISTRIBUTION

## 263 Certain distributions prohibited

**263(1) [Distribution only out of profits]** A company shall not make a distribution except out of profits available for the purpose.

**263(2) ["Distribution"]** In this Part, **"distribution"** means every description of distribution of a company's assets to its members, whether in cash or otherwise, except distribution by way of–

(a) an issue of shares as fully or partly paid bonus shares,

(b) the redemption or purchase of any of the company's own shares out of capital (including the proceeds of any fresh issue of shares) or out of unrealised profits in accordance with Chapter VII of Part V,

(c) the reduction of share capital by extinguishing or reducing the liability of any of the members on any of the company's shares in respect of share capital not paid up, or by paying off paid up share capital, and

(d) a distribution of assets to members of the company on its winding-up.

**263(3) [Profits available for distribution]** For purposes of this Part, a company's profits available for distribution are its accumulated, realised profits, so far as not previously utilised by distribution or capitalisation, less its accumulated, realised losses, so far as not previously written off in a reduction or reorganisation of capital duly made.

This is subject to the provision made by sections 265 and 266 for investment and other companies.

**263(4) [Unrealised profits not to be applied etc.]** A company shall not apply an unrealised profit in paying up debentures, or any amounts unpaid on its issued shares.

**263(5) [Some profits treated as realised]** Where the directors of a company are, after making all reasonable enquiries, unable to determine whether a particular profit made before 22nd December 1980 is realised or unrealised, they may treat the profit as realised; and where after making such enquiries they are unable to determine whether a particular loss so made is realised or unrealised, they may treat the loss as unrealised.

## 264 Restriction on distribution of assets

**264(1) [Distribution by public company]** A public company may only make a distribution at any time–

(a) if at that time the amount of its net assets is not less than the aggregate of its called-up share capital and undistributable reserves, and

(b) if, and to the extent that, the distribution does not reduce the amount of those assets to less than that aggregate.

This is subject to the provision made by sections 265 and 266 for investment and other companies.

**264(2) ["Net assets" in s. 264(1)]** In subsection (1), **"net assets"** means the aggregate of the company's assets less the aggregate of its liabilities ("liabilities" to include any provision for liabilities or charges within paragraph 89 of Schedule 4).

**264(3) [Company's undistributable reserves]** A company's undistributable reserves are–

(a) the share premium account,

(b) the capital redemption reserve,

(c) the amount by which the company's accumulated, unrealised profits, so far as not previously utilised by capitalisation of a description to which this paragraph applies, exceed its accumulated, unrealised losses (so far as not previously written off in a reduction or reorganisation of capital duly made), and

(d) any other reserve which the company is prohibited from distributing by any enactment (other than one contained in this Part) or by its memorandum or articles;

and paragraph (c) applies to every description of capitalisation except a transfer of profits of the company to its capital redemption reserve on or after 22nd December 1980.

**264(4) [Uncalled share capital not to be asset]** A public company shall not include any uncalled share capital as an asset in any accounts relevant for purposes of this section.

# 265 Other distributions by investment companies

**265(1) [Distribution out of profits]** Subject to the following provisions of this section, an investment company (defined in section 266) may also make a distribution at any time out of its accumulated, realised revenue profits, so far as not previously utilised by distribution or capitalisation, less its accumulated revenue losses (whether realised or unrealised), so far as not previously written off in a reduction or reorganisation of capital duly made–

(a) if at that time the amount of its assets is at least equal to one and a half times the aggregate of its liabilities, and

(b) if, and to the extent that, the distribution does not reduce that amount to less than one and a half times that aggregate.

**265(2) ["Liabilities" in s. 265(1)(a)]** In subsection (1)(a), **"liabilities"** includes any provision for liabilities or charges (within the meaning of paragraph 89 of Schedule 4).

**265(3) [Uncalled share capital not to be asset]** The company shall not include any uncalled share capital as an asset in any accounts relevant for purposes of this section.

**265(4) [Conditions for s. 265(1) distribution]** An investment company may not make a distribution by virtue of subsection (1) unless–

(a) its shares are listed on a recognised investment exchange other than an overseas investment exchange within the meaning of the Financial Services Act 1986, and

(b) during the relevant period it has not–

(i) distributed any of its capital profits otherwise than by way of the redemption or purchase of any of the ompany's own shares in accordance with section 160 or 162 in Chapter VII of Part V, or

(ii) applied any unrealised profits or any capital profits (realised or unrealised) in paying up debentures or amounts unpaid on its issued shares.

**History**

In s. 265(4)(a) the words "recognised investment exchange other than an overseas investment exchange within the meaning of the Financial Services Act 1986" substituted for the former words "recognised stock exchange" by Financial Services Act 1986, s. 212(2) and Sch. 16, para. 19 as from 29 April 1988 (see SI 1988/740 (C 22)).

In s. 265(4)(b)(i) the words after "capital profits" added by the Companies (Investment Companies) (Distribution of Profits) Regulations 1999 (SI 1999/2770), reg. 1, 2 as from 8 November 1999, subject to transitional provision in reg. 4.

**265(5) ["Relevant period" under s. 265(4)]** The "relevant period" under subsection (4) is the period beginning with–

(a) the first day of the accounting reference period immediately preceding that in which the proposed distribution is to be made, or

(b) where the distribution is to be made in the company's first accounting reference period, the first day of that period,

and ending with the date of the distribution.

**265(6) [Requisite notice to registrar before s. 265(1) distribution]** An investment company may not make a distribution by virtue of subsection (1) unless the company gave to the registrar of companies the requisite notice (that is, notice under section 266(1)) of the company's intention to carry on business as an investment company–

(a) before the beginning of the relevant period under subsection (4), or

(b) in the case of a company incorporated on or after 22nd December 1980, as soon as may have been reasonably practicable after the date of its incorporation.

## 266 Meaning of "investment company"

**266(1) ["Investment company" in s. 265]** In section 265 **"investment company"** means a public company which has given notice in the prescribed form (which has not been revoked) to the registrar of companies of its intention to carry on business as an investment company, and has since the date of that notice complied with the requirements specified below.

**Note**
See note to s. 266(3).

**266(2) [Requirements in s. 266(1)]** Those requirements are–

(a) that the business of the company consists of investing its funds mainly in securities, with the aim of spreading investment risk and giving members of the company the benefit of the results of the management of its funds,

(b) that none of the company's holdings in companies (other than those which are for the time being investment companies) represents more than 15 per cent by value of the investing company's investments,

(c) that subject to subsection (2A) distribution of the company's capital profits is prohibited by its memorandum or articles of association,

(d) that the company has not retained, otherwise than in compliance with this Part, in respect of any accounting reference period more than 15 per cent of the income it derives from securities.

**History**
See history note after s. 266(2A).

**266(2A) [Investment companies – redemption or purchase of shares]** An investment company need not be prohibited by its memorandum or articles from redeeming or purchasing its own shares in accordance with section 160 or 162 in Chapter VII of Part V out of its capital profits.

**History**
In s. 266(2)(c) the words "subject to subsection (2A)" and s. 266(2A) inserted by Companies (Investment Companies) (Distribution of Profits) Regulations 1999 (SI 1999/2770), reg. 1, 2 as from 8 November 1999.

**266(3) [Revocation of s. 266(1) notice]** Notice to the registrar of companies under subsection (1) may be revoked at any time by the company on giving notice in the prescribed form to the registrar that is no longer wishes to be an investment company within the meaning of this section; and, on giving such notice, the company ceases to be such a company.

**Note**
See the Companies (Forms) (Amendment) Regulations 1995 (SI 1995/736).

**266(4) [Application of tax legislation]** Subsections (1A) to (3) of section 842 of the Income and Corporation Taxes Act 1988 apply for the purposes of subsection (2)(b) above as for those of subsection (1)(b) of that section.

**History**
S. 266(4) substituted by Finance Act 1988, s. 117(3), (4) for companies' accounting periods ending after 5 April 1988; s. 266(4) formerly read as follows:

"Section 359(2) and (3) of the Income and Corporation Taxes Act 1970 and section 93(6)(b) of the Finance Act 1972 apply for purposes of subsection (2)(b) as for those of section 359(1)(b) of the Act first mentioned."

There were also some amendments by Income and Corporation Taxes Act 1988, s. 844 and Sch. 29, para. 32 which did not take effect.

## 267 Extension of s. 265, 266 to other companies

**267(1) [Regulations]** The Secretary of State may by regulations in a statutory instrument extend the provisions of sections 265 and 266 (with or without modifications) to companies whose principal business consists of investing their funds in securities, land or other assets with the aim of spreading investment risk and giving their members the benefit of the results of the management of the assets.

**267(2) [Scope and approval of regulations]** Regulations under this section–

(a) may make different provision for different classes of companies and may contain such transitional and supplemental provisions as the Secretary of State considers necessary, and

(b) shall not be made unless a draft of the statutory instrument containing them has been laid before Parliament and approved by a resolution of each House.

## 268 Realised profits of insurance company with long term business

**268(1) [Realised profits and losses]** Where an insurance company to which Part II of the Insurance Companies Act 1982 applies carries on long term business–

(a) any amount included in the relevant part of the balance sheet of the company which represents a surplus in the fund or funds maintained by it in respect of that business and which has not been allocated to policy holders in accordance with section 30(1) of that Act or carried forward unappropriated as mentioned in section 30(7) of that Act, and

(b) any deficit in that fund or those funds,

are to be (respectively) treated, for purposes of this Part, as a realised profit and a realised loss; and, subject to this, any profit or loss arising in that business is to be left out of account for those purposes.

**History**

S. 268(1)(a) substituted by the Companies Act 1985 (Miscellaneous Accounting Amendments) Regulations 1996 (SI 1996/189), reg. 1(1), 13(1), (2) as from 2 February 1996, subject to reg. 16(1), (2), (6); s. 268(1)(a) formerly read as follows:

"(a) any amount included in the profit and loss account of the company which represents a surplus in the fund or funds maintained by it in respect of that business and which has not been allocated to policy holders under section 30 of that Act, and".

Previously s. 268(1)(a) substituted by the Companies Act 1985 (Insurance Companies Accounts) Regulations 1993 (SI 1993/3246), reg. 1, 5, Sch. 2, para. 6 as from 19 December 1993 subject to exemption in reg. 6 and transitional provisions in reg. 7; s. 268(1)(a) originally read as follows:

"(a) any amount properly transferred to the profit and loss account of the company from a surplus in the fund or funds maintained by it in respect of that business, and".

**268(2) [Surplus and deficit in s. 268(1)]** In subsection (1)–

(aa) the reference to the relevant part of the balance sheet is to that part of the balance sheet which represents Liabilities item A.V (profit and loss account) in the balance sheet format set out in section B of Chapter I of Part I of Schedule 9A,

(a) the reference to a surplus in any fund or funds of an insurance company is to an excess of the assets representing that fund or those funds over the liabilities of the company attributable to its long term business, as shown by an actuarial investigation, and

(b) the reference to a deficit in any such fund or funds is to the excess of those liabilities over those assets, as so shown.

**History**

S. 268(2)(aa) inserted by the Companies Act 1985 (Miscellaneous Accounting Amendments) Regulations 11996 (SI 1996/189), reg. 1(1), 13(1), (3) as from 2 February 1996, subject to reg. 16(1), (2), (6).

**268(3) [Definitions]** In this section–

(a) **"actuarial investigation"**means an investigation to which section 18 of the Insurance Companies Act 1982 (periodic actuarial investigation of company with long term business) applies or which is made in pursuance of a requirement imposed by section 42 of that Act (actuarial investigation required by Secretary of State); and

(b) **"long term business"** has the same meaning as in that Act.

## 269 Treatment of development costs

**269(1) [Realised loss, realised revenue loss]** Subject as follows, where development costs are shown as an asset in a company's accounts, any amount shown in respect of those costs is to be treated–

(a) under section 263, as a realised loss, and

(b) under section 265, as a realised revenue loss.

**269(2) [Non-application]** This does not apply to any part of that amount representing an unrealised profit made on revaluation of those costs; nor does it apply if–

(a) there are special circumstances in the company's case justifying the directors in deciding that the amount there mentioned is not to be treated as required by subsection (1), and

(b) the note to the accounts required by paragraph 20 of Schedule 4, paragraph 20 of Schedule 8 (reasons for showing development costs as an asset) states that the amount is not to be so treated and explains the circumstances relied upon to justify the decision of the directors to that effect.

**History**
In s. 269(2)(b) the words "paragraph 20 of Schedule 8" appearing after the words "paragraph 20 of Schedule 4" inserted by the Companies Act 1985 (Accounts of Small and Medium-sized Companies and Minor Accounting Amendments) Regulations 1997 (SI 1997/220), reg . 1, 7(7) as from 1 March 1997.

## RELEVANT ACCOUNTS

## 270 Distribution to be justified by reference to company's accounts

**270(1) [Distribution without contravening s. 263–265]** This section and sections 271 to 276 below are for determining the question whether a distribution may be made by a company without contravening section 263, 264 or 265.

**270(2) [Determination of amount of distribution]** The amount of a distribution which may be made is determined by reference to the following items as stated in the company's accounts–

(a) profits, losses, assets and liabilities,

(b) provisions of any of the kinds mentioned in paragraphs 88 and 89 of Schedule 4 (depreciation, diminution in value of assets, retentions to meet liabilities, etc.), and

(c) share capital and reserves (including undistributable reserves).

**270(3) [Relevant accounts]** Except in a case falling within the next subsection, the company's accounts which are relevant for this purpose are its last annual accounts, that is to say those prepared under Part VII which were laid in respect of the last preceding accounting reference period in respect of which accounts so prepared were laid; and for this purpose accounts are laid if section 241(1) has been complied with in relation to them.

**270(4) [Exception – interim and initial accounts]** In the following two cases–

(a) where the distribution would be found to contravene the relevant section if reference were made only to the company's last annual accounts, or

(b) where the distribution is proposed to be declared during the company's first accounting reference period, or before any accounts are laid in respect of that period,

the accounts relevant under this section (called "interim accounts" in the first case, and "initial accounts" in the second) are those necessary to enable a reasonable judgment to be made as to the amounts of the items mentioned in subsection (2) above.

**270(5) [Contravention]** The relevant section is treated as contravened in the case of a distribution unless the statutory requirements about the relevant accounts (that is, the requirements of this and the following three sections, as and where applicable) are complied with in relation to that distribution.

## 271 Requirements for last annual accounts

**271(1) [If last annual accounts only relevant accounts]** If the company's last annual accounts constitute the only accounts relevant under section 270, the statutory requirements in respect of them are as follows.

**271(2) [Requirements for last annual accounts]** The accounts must have been properly prepared in accordance with this Act, or have been so prepared subject only to matters which are not material for determining, by reference to items mentioned in section 270(2), whether the distribution would contravene the relevant section; and, without prejudice to the foregoing–

(a) so much of the accounts as consists of a balance sheet must give a true and fair view of the state of the company's affairs as at the balance sheet date, and

(b) so much of the accounts as consists of a profit and loss account must give a true and fair view of the company's profit or loss for the period in respect of which the accounts were prepared.

**271(3) [Auditors must have made report]** The auditors must have made their report on the accounts under section 235; and the following subsection applies if the report is a qualified report, that is to say, it is not a report without qualification to the effect that in the auditors' opinion the accounts have been properly prepared in accordance with this Act.

**History**
In s. 271(3) the words "section 235" substituted for the former words "section 236" by CA 1989, s. 23 and Sch. 10, para. 4 as from 1 April 1990 subject to transitional and saving provisions (see SI 1990/355 (C 13), art. 3, Sch. 1 and also art. 6–9).

**271(4) [Statement if qualified auditors' report]** The auditors must in that case also have stated in writing (either at the time of their report or subsequently) whether, in their opinion, the matter in respect of which their report is qualified is material for determining, by reference to items mentioned in section 270(2), whether the distribution would contravene the relevant section; and a copy of the statement must have been laid before the company in general meeting.

**271(5) [S. 271(4) statement]** A statement under subsection (4) suffices for purposes of a particular distribution not only if it relates to a distribution which has been proposed but also if it relates to distributions of any description which includes that particular distribution, notwithstanding that at the time of the statement it has not been proposed.

# 272 Requirements for interim accounts

**272(1) [Statutory requirements]** The following are the statutory requirements in respect of interim accounts prepared for a proposed distribution by a public company.

**272(2) [Accounts to have been properly prepared]** The accounts must have been properly prepared, or have been so prepared subject only to matters which are not material for determining, by reference to items mentioned in section 270(2), whether the proposed distribution would contravene the relevant section.

**272(3) ["Properly prepared"] "Properly prepared"** means that the accounts must comply with section 226 (applying that section and Schedule 4 with such modifications as are necessary because the accounts are prepared otherwise than in respect of an accounting reference period) and any balance sheet comprised in the accounts must have been signed in accordance with section 233; and, without prejudice to the foregoing–

(a) so much of the accounts as consists of a balance sheet must give a true and fair view of the state of the company's affairs as at the balance sheet date, and

(b) so much of the accounts as consists of a profit and loss account must give a true and fair view of the company's profit or loss for the period in respect of which the accounts were prepared.

**History**

In s. 272(3) the words "section 226" and "section 233" substituted for the former words "section 228" and "section 238" respectively by CA 1989, s. 23 and Sch. 10, para. 5 as from 1 April 1990 subject to transitional and saving provisions (see SI 1990/355 (C 13), art. 3, Sch. 1 and also art. 6–9).

**272(4) [Copy of accounts to registrar]** A copy of the accounts must have been delivered to the registrar of companies.

**272(5) [Certified translation of accounts etc.]** If the accounts are in a language other than English and the second sentence of section 242(1) (translation) does not apply, then, subject to section 710B(6) (delivery of certain Welsh documents without a translation), a translation into English of the accounts, certified in the prescribed manner to be a correct translation, must also have been delivered to the registrar.

**History**

In s. 272(5) the words "the second sentence of section 242(1)" substituted for the former words "section 241(3)(b)" by CA 1989, s. 23 and Sch. 10, para. 6 as from 1 April 1990 subject to transitional and saving provisions (see SI 1990/355 (C 13), art. 3, Sch. 1 and also art. 6–9); and the words "then, subject to section 710B(6) (delivery of certain Welsh documents without a translation)," inserted by Welsh Language Act 1993, s. 30(1), (4)(b) as from 1 February 1994 (see SI 1994/115 (C 5) art. 2(2)).

# 273 Requirements for initial accounts

**273(1) [Statutory requirements]** The following are the statutory requirements in respect of initial accounts prepared for a proposed distribution by a public company.

**273(2) [Accounts to have been properly prepared]** The accounts must have been properly prepared, or they must have been so prepared subject only to matters which are not material for determining, by reference to items mentioned in section 270(2), whether the proposed distribution would contravene the relevant section.

**273(3) ["Properly prepared"]** Section 272(3) applies as respects the meaning of **"properly prepared"**.

**273(4) [Auditors must have made report]** The company's auditors must have made a report stating whether in their opinion the accounts have been properly prepared; and the following subsection applies if their report is a qualified report, that is to say it is not a report without qualification to the effect that in the auditors' opinion the accounts have been so prepared.

**273(5) [Statement if qualified report]** The auditors must in that case also have stated in writing whether, in their opinion, the matter in respect of which their report is qualified is material for determining, by reference to items mentioned in section 270(2), whether the distribution would contravene the relevant section.

**273(6) [Copies of accounts, auditors report, statement to registrar]** A copy of the accounts, of the auditors' report under subsection (4) and of the auditors' statement (if any) under subsection (5) must have been delivered to the registrar of companies.

**273(7) [Certified translation of accounts etc.]** If the accounts are, or the auditors' report under subsection (4) or their statement (if any) under subsection (5) is, in a language other than English and the second sentence of section 242(1) (translation) does not apply, then, subject to section 710B(6) (delivery of certain Welsh documents without a translation), a translation into English of the accounts, the report or the statement (as the case may be), certified in the prescribed manner to be a correct translation, must also have been delivered to the registrar.

**History**

In s. 273(7) the words "the second sentence of section 242(1)" substituted for the former words "section 241(3)(b)" by CA 1989, s. 23 and Sch. 10, para. 6 as from 1 April 1990 subject to transitional and saving provisions (see SI 1990/355 (C 13), art. 3, Sch. 1 and also art. 6–9); and the words "then, subject to section 710B(6) (delivery of certain Welsh documents without a translation)," inserted by Welsh Language Act 1993, s. 30(1), (4)(b) as from 1 February 1994 (see SI 1994/115 (C 5) art. 2(2)).

## 274 Method of applying s. 270 to successive distributions

**274(1) [Effect of s. 270]** For the purpose of determining by reference to particular accounts whether a proposed distribution may be made by a company, section 270 has effect, in a case where one or more distributions have already been made in pursuance of determinations made by reference to those same accounts, as if the amount of the proposed distribution was increased by the amount of the distributions so made.

**274(2) [Application of s. 274(1)]** Subsection (1) of this section applies (if it would not otherwise do so) to–

(a) financial assistance lawfully given by a public company out of its distributable profits in a case where the assistance is required to be so given by section 154,

(b) financial assistance lawfully given by a private company out of its distributable profits in a case where the assistance is required to be so given by section 155(2),

(c) financial assistance given by a company in contravention of section 151, in a case where the giving of that assistance reduces the company's net assets or increases its net liabilities,

(d) a payment made by a company in respect of the purchase by it of shares in the company (except a payment lawfully made otherwise than out of distributable profits), and

(e) a payment of any description specified in section 168 (company's purchase of right to acquire its own shares, etc.),

being financial assistance given or payment made since the relevant accounts were prepared, as if any such financial assistance or payment were a distribution already made in pursuance of a determination made by reference to those accounts.

**274(3) [Definitions]** In this section the following definitions apply–

**"financial assistance"** means the same as in Chapter VI of Part V;

**"net assets"** has the meaning given by section 154(2)(a); and

**"net liabilities"**, in relation to the giving of financial assistance by a company, means the amount by which the aggregate amount of the company's liabilities (within the meaning of section 154(2)(b)) exceeds the aggregate amount of its assets, taking the amount of the assets and liabilities to be as stated in the company's accounting records immediately before the financial assistance is given.

**274(4) [Regulations]** Subsections (2) and (3) of this section are deemed to be included in Chapter VII of Part V for purposes of the Secretary of State's power to make regulations under section 179.

## 275 Treatment of assets in the relevant accounts

**275(1) [Certain provisions treated as realised loss]** For purposes of sections 263 and 264, a provision of any kind mentioned in paragraphs 88 and 89 of Schedule 4, other than one in respect of a diminution in value of a fixed asset appearing on a revaluation of all the fixed assets of the company, or of all of its fixed assets other than goodwill, is treated as a realised loss.

**275(2) [Realised profit on revaluation]** If, on the revaluation of a fixed asset, an unrealised profit is shown to have been made and, on or after the revaluation, a sum is written off or retained for depreciation of that asset over a period, then an amount equal to the amount by which that sum exceeds the sum which would have been so written off or retained for the depreciation of that asset over that period, if that profit had not been made, is treated for purposes of sections 263 and 264 as a realised profit made over that period.

**275(3) [Where no record of original cost of asset]** Where there is no record of the original cost of an asset, or a record cannot be obtained without unreasonable expense or delay, then for the purpose of determining whether the company has made a profit or loss in respect of that asset, its cost is taken to the value ascribed to it in the earliest available record of its value made on or after its acquisition by the company.

**275(4) [Consideration by directors of value of fixed asset]** Subject to subsection (6), any consideration by the directors of the value at a particular time of a fixed asset is treated as a revaluation of the asset for the purposes of determining whether any such revaluation of the company's fixed assets as is required for purposes of the exception from subsection (1) has taken place at that time.

**275(5) [Application of s. 275(4) exception]** But where any such assets which have not actually been revalued are treated as revalued for those purposes under subsection (4), that exception applies only if the directors are satisfied that their aggregate value at that time in question is not less than the aggregate amount at which they are for the time being stated in the company's accounts.

**275(6) [Non-application of s. 275(4), (5)]** Where section 271(2), 272(2) or 273(2) applies to the relevant accounts, subsections (4) and (5) above do not apply for the purpose of determining whether a revaluation of the company's fixed assets affecting the amount of the relevant items (that is, the items mentioned in section 270(2)) as stated in those accounts has taken place, unless it is stated in a note to the accounts–

(a) that the directors have considered the value at any time of any fixed assets of the company, without actually revaluing those assets,

(b) that they are satisfied that the aggregate value of those assets at the time in question is or was not less than the aggregate amount at which they are or were for the time being stated in the company's accounts, and

(c) that the relevant items in question are accordingly stated in the relevant accounts on the basis that a revaluation of the company's fixed assets which by virtue of subsections (4) and (5) included the assets in question took place at that time.

## 276 Distributions in kind

**276** Where a company makes a distribution of or including a non-cash asset, and any part of the amount at which that asset is stated in the accounts relevant for the purposes of the distribution in accordance with sections 270 to 275 represents an unrealised profit, that profit is to be treated as a realised profit–

(a) for the purpose of determining the lawfulness of the distribution in accordance with this Part (whether before or after the distribution takes place), and

(b) for the purpose of the application of paragraphs 12(a) and 34(3)(a) of Schedule 4 or paragraphs 12(a) and 34(3)(a) of Schedule 8 (only realised profits to be included in or transferred to the profit and loss account) in relation to anything done with a view to or in connection with the making of that distribution.

**History**
In s. 276(b) the words " or paragraphs 12(a) and 34(3)(a) of Schedule 8" appearing after the words "of Schedule 4" inserted by the Companies Act 1985 (Accounts of Small and Medium-sized Companies and Minor Accounting Amendments) Regulations 1997 (SI 1997/220), reg . 1, 7(8) as from 1 March 1997.

Previously in s. 276(b) "34(3)(a)" substituted for the former "34(4)(b)" by CA 1989, s. 23 and Sch. 10, para. 7 as from 1 April 1990 subject to transitional and saving provisions (see SI 1990/355 (C 13), art. 3, Sch. 1 and also art. 6–9).

## SUPPLEMENTARY

## 277 Consequences of unlawful distribution

**277(1) [Penalty etc.]** Where a distribution, or part of one, made by a company to one of its members is made in contravention of this Part and, at the time of the distribution, he knows or has reasonable grounds for believing that it is so made, he is liable to repay it (or that part of it, as the case may be) to the company or (in the case of a distribution made otherwise than in cash) to pay the company a sum equal to the value of the distribution (or part) at that time.

**277(2) [Without prejudice to general repayment obligation]** The above is without prejudice to any obligation imposed apart from this section on a member of a company to repay a distribution unlawfully made to him; but this section does not apply in relation to–

(a) financial assistance given by a company in contravention of section 151, or

(b) any payment made by a company in respect of the redemption or purchase by the company of shares in itself.

**277(3)** Subsection (2) of this section is deemed included in Chapter VII of Part V for purposes of the Secretary of State's power to make regulations under section 179.

## 278 Saving for provision in articles operative before Act of 1980

**278** Where immediately before 22nd December 1980 a company was authorised by a provision of its articles to apply its unrealised profits in paying up in full or in part unissued shares to be allotted to members of the company as fully or partly paid bonus shares, that provision continues (subject to any alteration of the articles) as authority for those profits to be so applied after that date.

## 279 Distributions by banking or insurance companies

**279** Where a company's accounts relevant for the purposes of this Part are prepared in accordance with the special provisions of Part VII relating to banking or insurance companies, sections 264 to 275 apply with the modifications shown in Schedule 11.

**History**
S. 279 substituted by CA 1989, s. 23 and Sch. 10, para. 8 as from 1 April 1990 subject to transitional and saving provisions (see SI 1990/355 (C 13), art. 3, Sch. 1 and also art. 6–9); s. 279 formerly read as follows:

"**279 Distributions by special category companies**
Where a company's accounts relevant for the purposes of this Part are special category, sections 265 to 275 apply with the modifications shown in Schedule 11."

## 280 Definitions for Part VIII

**280(1) [Interpretation]** The following has effect for the interpretation of this Part.

**280(2) ["Capitalisation"] "Capitalisation"**, in relation to a company's profits, means any of the following operations (whenever carried out)–

(a) applying the profits in wholly or partly paying up unissued shares in the company to be allotted to members of the company as fully or partly paid bonus shares, or

(b) transferring the profits to capital redemption reserve.

**280(3) [References to profits and losses etc.]** References to profits and losses of any description are (respectively) to profits and losses of that description made at any time and, except where the context otherwise requires, are (respectively) to revenue and capital profits and revenue and capital losses.

## 281 Saving for other restraints on distribution

**281** The provisions of this Part are without prejudice to any enactment or rule of law, or any provision of a company's memorandum or articles, restricting the sums out of which, or the cases in which, a distribution may be made.

# PART IX – A COMPANY'S MANAGEMENT; DIRECTORS AND SECRETARIES; THEIR QUALIFICATIONS, DUTIES AND RESPONSIBILITIES

## OFFICERS AND REGISTERED OFFICE

## 282 Directors

**282(1) [Public company on or after 1 November 1929]** Every company registered on or after 1st November 1929 (other than a private company) shall have at least two directors.

**282(2) [Public company before 1 November 1929]** Every company registered before that date (other than a private company) shall have at least one director.

**282(3) [Private company]** Every private company shall have at least one director.

## 283 Secretary

**283(1) [Obligation]** Every company shall have a secretary.

**283(2) [Not sole director]** A sole director shall not also be secretary.

**283(3) [If office vacant]** Anything required or authorised to be done by or to the secretary may, if the office is vacant or there is for any other reason no secretary capable of acting, be done by or to any assistant or deputy secretary or, if there is no assistant or deputy secretary capable of acting, by or to any officer of the company authorised generally or specially in that behalf by the directors.

**283(4) [Certain persons not to be sole director or secretary]** No company shall–

(a) have as secretary to the company a corporation the sole director of which is a sole director of the company;

(b) have as sole director of the company a corporation the sole director of which is secretary to the company.

## 284 Acts done by person in dual capacity

**284** A provision requiring or authorising a thing to be done by or to a director and the secretary is not satisfied by its being done by or to the same person acting both as director and as, or in place of, the secretary.

## 285 Validity of acts of directors

**285** The acts of a director or manager are valid notwithstanding any defect that may afterwards be discovered in his appointment or qualification; and this provision is not excluded by section 292(2) (void resolution to appoint).

## 286 Qualifications of company secretaries

**286(1) [Duty of directors to secure appropriate secretary]** It is the duty of the directors of a public company to take all reasonable steps to secure that the secretary (or each joint secretary) of the company is a person who appears to them to have the requisite knowledge and experience to discharge the functions of secretary of the company and who–

(a) on 22nd December 1980 held the office of secretary or assistant or deputy secretary of the company; or

(b) for at least 3 of the 5 years immediately preceding his appointment as secretary held the office of secretary of a company other than a private company; or

(c) is a member of any of the bodies specified in the following subsection; or

(d) is a barrister, advocate or solicitor called or admitted in any part of the United Kingdom; or

(e) is a person who, by virtue of his holding or having held any other position or his being a member of any other body, appears to the directors to be capable of discharging those functions.

**286(2) [Bodies specified in s. 286(1)(c)]** The bodies referred to in subsection (1)(c) are–

(a) the Institute of Chartered Accountants in England and Wales;
(b) the Institute of Chartered Accountants of Scotland;
(c) the Chartered Association of Certified Accountants;
(d) the Institute of Chartered Accountants in Ireland;
(e) the Institute of Chartered Secretaries and Administrators;
(f) the Institute of Cost and Management Accountants;
(g) the Chartered Institute of Public Finance and Accountancy.

# 287 Registered office

**287(1) [Duty to have registered office]** A company shall at all times have a registered office to which all communications and notices may be addressed.

**287(2) [Situation on incorporation]** On incorporation the situation of the company's registered office is that specified in the statement sent to the registrar under section 10.

**287(3) [Change of registered office]** The company may change the situation of its registered office from time to time by giving notice in the prescribed form to the registrar.

**Note**

See the Companies (Forms Amendment No. 2 and Company's Type and Principal Business Activities) Regulations 1990 (SI 1990/1766); the Companies (Forms) (No. 2) Regulations 1991 (SI 1991/1259); the Companies (Welsh Language Forms and Documents) Regulations 1994 (SI 1994/117); the Companies (Welsh Language Forms and Documents) (Amendment) Regulations 1995 (SI 1995/734); the Companies (Forms) (Amendment) Regulations 1995 (SI 1995/736); and the Companies (Forms) (Amendment) Regulations 1998 (SI 1998/1702).

**287(4) [Effective date of change]** The change takes effect upon the notice being registered by the registrar, but until the end of the period of 14 days beginning with the date on which it is registered a person may validly serve any document on the company at its previous registered office.

**287(5) [Date of change re company's duties]** For the purposes of any duty of a company–

(a) to keep at its registered office, or make available for public inspection there, any register, index or other document, or

(b) to mention the address of its registered office in any document,

a company which has given notice to the registrar of a change in the situation of its registered office may act on the change as from such date, not more than 14 days after the notice is given, as it may determine.

**287(6) [Where no failure to comply with s. 287(5) duty]** Where a company unavoidably ceases to perform at its registered office any such duty as is mentioned in subsection (5)(a) in circumstances in which it was not practicable to give prior notice to the registrar of a change in the situation of its registered office, but–

(a) resumes performance of that duty at other premises as soon as practicable, and

(b) gives notice accordingly to the registrar of a change in the situation of its registered office within 14 days of doing so,

it shall not be treated as having failed to comply with that duty.

**287(7) [Onus in proceedings for failure to comply]** In proceedings for an offence of failing to comply with any such duty as is mentioned in subsection (5), it is for the person charged to show that by reason of the matters referred to in that subsection or subsection (6) no offence was committed.

**History**

S. 287 substituted by CA 1989, s. 136 as from 1 April 1990 subject to a transitional and saving provision (see SI 1990/355 (C 13), art. 4(d) and also art. 12); s. 287 formerly read as follows:

**"287 Registered office**

**287(1)** A company shall at all times have a registered office to which all communications and notices may be addressed.

(2) Notice (in the prescribed form) of any change in the situation of a company's registered office shall be given within 14 days of the change to the registrar of companies, who shall record the new situation.

(3) If default is made in complying with subsection (1) or (2), the company and every officer of it who is in default is liable to a fine and, for continued contravention, to a daily default fine."

## 288 Register of directors and secretaries

**288(1) [Obligation to keep register]** Every company shall keep at its registered office a register of its directors and secretaries; and the register shall, with respect to the particulars to be contained in it of those persons, comply with sections 289 and 290 below.

**288(2) [Notification of change etc. to registrar]** The company shall, within the period of 14 days from the occurrence of–

(a) any change among its directors or in its secretary, or

(b) any change in the particulars contained in the register,

send to the registrar of companies a notification in the prescribed form of the change and of the date on which it occurred; and a notification of a person having become a director or secretary, or one of joint secretaries, of the company shall contain a consent, signed by that person, to act in the relevant capacity.

**Note**

See the Companies (Forms Amendment No. 2 and Company's Type and Principal Business Activities) Regulations 1990 (SI 1990/1766); the Companies (Forms) (No. 2) Regulations 1991 (SI 1991/1259); the Companies (Welsh Language Forms and Documents) Regulations 1994 (SI 1994/117); the Companies (Welsh Language Forms and Documents) (Amendment) Regulations 1995 (SI 1995/734); the Companies (Forms) (Amendment) Regulations 1995 (SI 1995/736); and the Companies (Forms) (Amendment) Regulations 1998 (SI 1998/1702).

**288(3) [Inspection of register]** The register shall be open to the inspection of any member of the company without charge and of any other person on payment of such fee as may be prescribed.

**History**

In s. 288(3) the words "during business hours (subject to such reasonable restrictions as the company may by its articles or in general meeting impose, so that not less than 2 hours in each day be allowed for inspection)" formerly appearing after the word "shall" omitted and repealed and the words "such fee as may be prescribed" substituted for the former words "5 pence or such less sum as the company may prescribe, for each inspection" by CA 1989, s. 143(6), 212 and Sch. 24 as from 1 November 1991 (see SI 1991/1996 (C 57), art. 2(2)(b), (c)).

**Note**

See the Companies (Inspection and Copying of Registers, Indices and Documents) Regulations 1991 (SI 1991/1998).

**288(4) [Penalty for refusal of inspection]** If an inspection required under this section is refused, or if default is made in complying with subsection (1) or (2), the company and every officer of it who is in default is liable to a fine and, for continued contravention, to a daily default fine.

**288(5) [Compelling inspection]** In the case of a refusal of inspection of the register, the court may by order compel an immediate inspection of it.

**288(6) [Shadow director]** For purposes of this and the next section, a shadow director of a company is deemed a director and officer of it.

## 289 Particulars of directors to be registered under s. 288

**289(1) [Particulars]** Subject to the provisions of this section, the register kept by a company under section 288 shall contain the following particulars with respect to each director–

(a) in the case of an individual–

(i) his present name,

(ii) any former name,

(iii) his usual residential address,

(iv) his nationality,

(v) his business occupation (if any),

(vi) particulars of any other directorships held by him or which have been held by him, and

(vii) the date of his birth;

(b) in the case of a corporation or Scottish firm, its corporate or firm name and registered or principal office.

**History**
In s. 289(1)(a)(i) the word "name" substituted for the former words "Christian name and surname," in s. 289(1)(a)(ii) the word "name" substituted for the former words "Christian name or surname," s. 289(1)(a)(vii) substituted and in s. 289(1)(b) the words "or Scottish firm" and "or firm" inserted by CA 1989, s. 145 and Sch. 19, para. 2(1)–(3) as from 1 October 1990 subject to transitional and saving provisions (see SI 1990/1707 (C 46), art. 2(b) and also art. 6); s. 289(1)(a)(vii) formerly read as follows:
"in the case of a company subject to section 293 (age-limit), the date of his birth;".

**289(2) [Interpretation of s. 289(1)(a)]** In subsection (1)(a)–

(a) **"name"** means a person's Christian name (or other forename) and surname, except that in the case of a peer, or an individual usually known by a title, the title may be stated instead of his Christian name (or other forename) and surname, or in addition to either or both of them; and

(b) the reference to a former name does not include–
  (i) in the case of a peer, or an individual normally known by a British title, the name by which he was known previous to the adoption of or succession to the title, or
  (ii) in the case of any person, a former name which was changed or disused before he attained the age of 18 years or which has been changed or disused for 20 years or more, or
  (iii) in the case of a married woman, the name by which she was known previous to the marriage.

**History**
S. 289(2) substituted by CA 1989, s. 145 and Sch. 19, para. 2(1), (4) as from 1 October 1990 subject to transitional and saving provisions (see SI 1990/1707 (C 46), art. 2(b) and also art. 6); s. 289(2) formerly read as follows:
"In subsection (1)–
(a) **"Christian name"** includes a forename,
(b) **"surname"**, in the case of a peer or a person usually known by a title different from his surname, means that title, and
(c) the reference to a former Christian name or surname does not include–
  (i) in the case of a peer or a person usually known by a British title different from his surname, the name by which he was known previous to the adoption of or succession to the title, or
  (ii) in the case of any person, a former Christian name or surname where that name or surname was changed or disused before the person bearing the name attained the age of 18, or has been changed or disused for a period of not less than 20 years, or
  (iii) in the case of a married woman, the name or surname by which she was known previous to the marriage."

**289(3) [Particulars not required to be registered]** It is not necessary for the register to contain on any day particulars of a directorship–

(a) which has not been held by a director at any time during the 5 years preceding that day,

(b) which is held by a director in a company which–
  (i) is dormant or grouped with the company keeping the register, and
  (ii) if he also held that directorship for any period during those 5 years, was for the whole of that period either dormant or so grouped,

(c) which was held by a director for any period during those 5 years in a company which for the whole of that period was either dormant or grouped with the company keeping the register.

**289(4) ["Company" in s. 289(3)]** For purposes of subsection (3), **"company"** includes any body corporate incorporated in Great Britain; and–

(a) section 249AA(3) applies as regards whether and when a company is or has been dormant, and

(b) a company is to be regarded as being, or having been, grouped with another at any time if at that time it is or was a company of which the other is or was a wholly-owned subsidiary, or if it is or was a wholly-owned subsidiary of the other or of another company of which that other is or was a wholly-owned subsidiary.

**History**
In s. 289(4)(a) the words "section 249AA(3)" substituted for the former words "section 250(3)" by the Companies Act 1985 (Audit Exemption) (Amendment) Regulations 2000 (SI 2000/1430), reg. 1, 8(7) as from 26 May 2000 in relation to annual accounts and reports in respect of financial years ending on or after 26 July 2000.
Previously in s. 289(4) the words "section 250(3)" substituted for the former words "section 252(5)" by CA 1989, s. 23 and Sch. 10, para. 9 as from 1 April 1990 subject to transitional and saving provisions (see SI 1990/355 (C 13), art. 3, Sch. 1 and also art. 6–9).

## 290 Particulars of secretaries to be registered under s. 288

**290(1) [Particulars]** The register to be kept by a company under section 288 shall contain the following particulars with respect to the secretary or, where there are joint secretaries, with respect to each of them–

(a) in the case of an individual, his present name, any former name and his usual residential address, and

(b) in the case of a corporation or a Scottish firm, its corporate or firm name and registered or principal office.

**History**

In s. 290(1)(a) the word "name" (occurring twice) substituted for the words "Christian name and surname" and "Christian name or surname" respectively by CA 1989, s. 145 and Sch. 19, para. 3(1), (2) as from 1 October 1990 (see SI 1990/1707 (C 46), art. 2(b)).

**290(2) [Partners joint secretaries]** Where all the partners in a firm are joint secretaries, the name and principal office of the firm may be stated instead of the particulars specified above.

**290(3) [Application of s. 289(2)(a), (b)]** Section 289(2)(a) and (b) apply for the purposes of the obligation under subsection (1)(a) of this section to state the name or former name of an individual.

**History**

S. 290(3) substituted by CA 1989, s. 145 and Sch. 19, para. 3(1), (3) as from 1 October 1990 (see SI 1990/1707 (C 46), art. 2(b)); s. 290(3) formerly read as follows:

"Section 289(2) applies as regards the meaning of **"Christian name"**, **"surname"** and **"former Christian name or surname"**."

PROVISIONS GOVERNING APPOINTMENT OF DIRECTORS

## 291 Share qualification of directors

**291(1) [Director to obtain required share qualification]** It is the duty of every director who is by the company's articles required to hold a specified share qualification, and who is not already qualified, to obtain his qualification within 2 months after his appointment, or such shorter time as may be fixed by the articles.

**291(2) [Bearer of share warrant not holder of shares]** For the purpose of any provision of the articles requiring a director or manager to hold any specified share qualification, the bearer of a share warrant is not deemed the holder of the shares specified in the warrant.

**291(3) [Vacation of office of director]** The office of director of a company is vacated if the director does not within 2 months from the date of his appointment (or within such shorter time as may be fixed by the articles) obtain his qualification, or if after the expiration of that period or shorter time he ceases at any time to hold his qualification.

**291(4) [No re-appointment unless has share qualification]** A person vacating office under this section is incapable of being reappointed to be a director of the company until he has obtained his qualification.

**291(5) [Penalty]** If after the expiration of that period or shorter time any unqualified person acts as a director of the company, he is liable to a fine and, for continued contravention, to a daily default fine.

## 292 Appointment of directors to be voted on individually

**292(1) [Directors appointed by single resolution]** At a general meeting of a public company, a motion for the appointment of two or more persons as directors of the company by a single resolution shall not be made, unless a resolution that it shall be so made has first been agreed to by the meeting without any vote being given against it.

**292(2) [Resolution in contravention of s. 292]** A resolution moved in contravention of this section is void, whether or not its being so moved was objected to at the time; but where a resolution so moved is passed, no provision for the auto- matic reappointment of retiring directors in default of another appointment applies.

**292(3) [Interpretation]** For purposes of this section, a motion for approving a person's appointment, or for nominating a person for appointment, is to be treated as a motion for his appointment.

**292(4) [Non-application of section]** Nothing in this section applies to a resolution altering the company's articles.

## 293 Age limit for directors

**293(1) [Application]** A company is subject to this section if–

(a) it is a public company, or

(b) being a private company, it is a subsidiary of a public company or of a body corporate registered under the law relating to companies for the time being in force in Northern Ireland as a public company.

**293(2) [Age limit of 70]** No person is capable of being appointed a director of a company which is subject to this section if at the time of his appointment he has attained the age of 70.

**293(3) [Vacation of office at next annual general meeting after turning 70]** A director of such a company shall vacate his office at the conclusion of the annual general meeting commencing next after he attains the age of 70; but acts done by a person as director are valid notwithstanding that it is afterwards discovered that his appointment had terminated under this subsection.

**293(4) [Vacancy of retiring director under s. 293(3) may be filled casually]** Where a person retires under subsection (3), no provision for the automatic reappointment of retiring directors in default of another appointment applies; and if at the meeting at which he retires the vacancy is not filled, it may be filled as a casual vacancy.

**293(5) [No age limit if approval by general meeting etc.]** Nothing in subsections (2) to (4) prevents the appointment of a director at any age, or requires a director to retire at any time, if his appointment is or was made or approved by the company in general meeting; but special notice is required of a resolution appointing or approving the appointment of a director for it to have effect under this subsection, and the notice of the resolution given to the company, and by the company to its members, must state, or have stated, the age of the person to whom it relates.

**293(6) [Commencement of re-appointed director]** A person reappointed director on retiring under subsection (3), or appointed in place of a director so retiring, is to be treated, for the purpose of determining the time at which he or any other director is to retire, as if he had become director on the day on which the retiring director was last appointed before his retirement.

Subject to this, the retirement of a director out of turn under subsection (3) is to be disregarded in determining when any other directors are to retire.

**293(7) [Extent of effect of section]** In the case of a company first registered after the beginning of 1947, this section has effect subject to the provisions of the company's articles; and in the case of a company first registered before the beginning of that year–

(a) this section has effect subject to any alterations of the company's articles made after the beginning of that year; and

(b) if at the beginning of that year the company's articles contained provision for retirement of directors under an age limit, or for preventing or restricting appointments of directors over a given age, this section does not apply to directors to whom that provision applies.

**Note**

S. 293 does not apply in relation to a director of a company if he had attained the age of 70 before the commencement of CA 1989, s. 144(1) (1 November 1990), and the company became a subsidiary of a public company by reason only of the commencement of that section (CA 1989, Sch. 18, para. 34).

## 294 Duty of director to disclose his age

**294(1) [Notice of age]** A person who is appointed or to his knowledge proposed to be appointed director of a company subject to section 293 at a time when he has attained any retiring age applicable to him under that section or under the company's articles shall give notice of his age to the company.

**294(2) [Companies deemed subject to s. 293]** For purposes of this section, a company is deemed subject to section 293 notwithstanding that all or any of the section's provisions are excluded or modified by the company's articles.

**294(3) [Non-application of s. 294(1)]** Subsection (1) does not apply in relation to a person's reappointment on the termination of a previous appointment as director of the company.

**294(4) [Penalty]** A person who–

(a) fails to give notice of his age as required by this section; or

(b) acts as director under any appointment which is invalid or has terminated by reason of his age,

is liable to a fine and, for continued contravention, to a daily default fine.

**294(5) [Interpretation of s. 294(4)]** For purposes of subsection (4), a person who has acted as director under an appointment which is invalid or has terminated is deemed to have continued so to act throughout the period from the invalid appointment or the date on which the appointment terminated (as the case may be), until the last day on which he is shown to have acted thereunder.

## DISQUALIFICATION

**295-299** (Repealed by Company Directors Disqualification Act 1986, s. 23(2) and Sch. 4 as from 29 December 1986.)

**History**

In regard to the date of the above repeal, see Company Directors Disqualification Act 1986, s. 25, Insolvency Act 1986, s. 443 and SI 1986/1924 (C 71). S. 295 had previously been amended by Insolvency Act 1985, s. 109 and Sch. 6, para. 1 as from 28 April 1986: see SI 1986/463 (C 14); s. 295–299 (including these Insolvency Act 1985 amendments) formerly read as follows:

**"295 Disqualification orders: introductory**

**295(1)** In the circumstances specified in sections 296 to 299, a court may make against a person a disqualification order, that is to say an order that he shall not, without leave of the court–

(a) be a director of a company, or

(b) be a liquidator or administrator of a company, or

(c) be a receiver or manager of a company's property, or

(d) in any way, whether directly or indirectly, be concerned or take part in the promotion, formation or management of a company,

for a specified period beginning with the date of the order.

**(2)** The maximum period to be so specified is–

(a) in the case of an order made under section 297 or made by a court of summary jurisdiction, 5 years, and

(b) in any other case, 15 years; and where a disqualification order is made against a person who is already subject to such an order the periods specified in those orders shall run concurrently.

**(3)** In this section and sections 296 to 299, **"company"** includes any company which may be wound up under Part XXI.

**(4)** A disqualification order may be made on grounds which are or include matters other than criminal convictions, notwithstanding that the person in respect of whom it is to be made may be criminally liable in respect of those matters.

**(5)** In sections 296 to 299, any reference to provisions, or to a particular provision, of this Act or the Consequential Provisions Act includes the corresponding provision or provisions of the former Companies Acts.

**(6)** Part I of Schedule 12 has effect with regard to the procedure for obtaining a disqualification order, and to applications for leave under such an order; and Part III of that Schedule has effect–

(a) in connection with certain transitional cases arising under sections 93 and 94 of the Companies Act 1981, so as to limit the power to make a disqualification order, or to restrict the duration of an order, by reference to events occurring or things done before those sections came into force, and

(b) to preserve orders made under section 28 of the Companies Act 1976 (repealed by the Act of 1981).

**(7)** If a person acts in contravention of a disqualification order, he is in respect of each offence liable to imprisonment or a fine, or both.

**296 Disqualification on conviction of indictable offence**

**296(1)** The court may make a disqualification order against a person where he is convicted of an indictable offence (whether on indictment or summarily) in connection with the promotion, formation, management or liquidation of a company, or with the receivership or management of a company's property.

**(2) "The court"** for this purpose means–

(a) any court having jurisdiction to wind up the company in relation to which the offence was committed, or

(b) the court by or before which the person is convicted of the offence, or

(c) in the case of a summary conviction in England and Wales, any other magistrates' court acting for the same petty sessions area;

and for purposes of this section the definition of **"indictable offence"** in Schedule 1 to the Interpretation Act 1978 applies in relation to Scotland as it does in relation to England and Wales.

**297 Disqualification for persistent default under Companies Acts**

**297(1)** The court may make a disqualification order against a person where it appears to it that he has been persistently in default in relation to provisions of this Act or the Consequential Provisions Act requiring any return, account or other document to be filed with, delivered or sent, or notice of any matter to be given, to the registrar of companies.

**(2)** On an application to the court for an order to be made under this section, the fact that a person has been persistently in default in relation to such provisions as are mentioned above may (without prejudice to its proof in any other manner) be conclusively proved by showing that in the 5 years ending with the date of the application he has been adjudged guilty (whether or not on the same occasion) of three or more defaults in relation to those provisions.

**(3)** A person is treated under subsection (2) as being adjudged guilty of a default in relation to any such provision if–
- (a) he is convicted (whether on indictment or summarily) of an offence consisting in a contravention of or failure to comply with that provision (whether on his own part or on the part of any company), or
- (b) a default order is made against him, that is to say an order under–
  - (i) section 244 (order requiring delivery of company accounts), or
  - (ii) section 499 (enforcement of receiver's or manager's duty to make returns), or
  - (iii) section 636 (corresponding provision for liquidator in winding-up), or
  - (iv) section 713 (enforcement of company's duty to make returns),

in respect of any such contravention of or failure to comply with that provision (whether on his own part or on the part of any company).

**(4)** In this section **"the court"** means any court having jurisdiction to wind up any of the companies in relation to which the offence or other default has been or is alleged to have been committed.

**298** Disqualification for fraud, etc. in winding-up

**298(1)** The court may make a disqualification order against a person if, in the course of the winding-up of a company, it appears that he–
- (a) has been guilty of an offence for which he is liable (whether he has been convicted or not) under section 458 (fraudulent trading), or
- (b) has otherwise been guilty, while an officer or liquidator of the company or receiver or manager of its property, of any fraud in relation to the company or of any breach of his duty as such officer, liquidator, receiver or manager.

**(2)** In this section **"the court"** means the same as in section 297; and **"officer"** includes a shadow director.

**299 Disqualification on summary conviction**

**299(1)** An offence counting for the purposes of this section is one of which a person is convicted (either on indictment or summarily) in consequence of a contravention of, or failure to comply with, any provision of this Act or the Consequential Provisions Act requiring a return, account or other document to be filed with, delivered or sent, or notice of any matter to be given, to the registrar of companies (whether the contravention or failure is on the person's own part or on the part of any company).

**(2)** Where a person is convicted of a summary offence counting for those purposes, the court by which he is convicted (or, in England and Wales, any other magistrates' court acting for the same petty sessions area) may make a disqualification order against him if the circumstances specified in the next subsection are present.

**(3)** Those circumstances are that, during the 5 years ending with the date of the conviction, the person has had made against him, or has been convicted of, in total not less than 3 default orders and offences counting for the purposes of this section; and those offences may include that of which he is convicted as mentioned in subsection (2) and any other offence of which he is convicted on the same occasion.

**(4)** For the purposes of this section–
- (a) the definition of **"summary offence"** in Schedule 1 to the Interpretation Act 1978 applies for Scotland as for England and Wales, and
- (b) **"default order"** means the same as in section 297(3)(b)."

# 300 Disqualification by reference to association with insolvent companies

**300** (Repealed by Insolvency Act 1985, s. 235 and Sch. 10, Pt. II as from 28 April 1986.)

**History**

In regard to the date of the above repeal see SI 1986/463 (C 14); s. 300 formerly read as follows:

"**300(1)** The court may make a disqualification order against a person where, on an application under this section, it appears to it that he–
- (a) is or has been a director of a company which has at any time gone into liquidation (whether while he was a director or subsequently) and was insolvent at that time, and
- (b) is or has been a director of another such company which has gone into liquidation within 5 years of the date on which the first-mentioned company went into liquidation,

and that his conduct as director of any of those companies makes him unfit to be concerned in the management of a company.

**(2)** In the case of a person who is or has been a director of a company which has gone into liquidation as above-mentioned and is being wound up by the court, **"the court"** in subsection (1) means the court by which the company is being wound up; and in any other case it means the High Court or, in Scotland, the Court of Session.

**(3)** The Secretary of State may require the liquidator or former liquidator of a company–
- (a) to furnish him with such information with respect to the company's affairs, and
- (b) to produce and permit inspection of such books or documents of or relevant to the company,

as the Secretary of State may reasonably require for the purpose of determining whether to make an application under this section in respect of a person who is or has been a director of that company; and if a person makes default in complying with such a requirement, the court may, on the Secretary of State's application, make an order requiring that person to make good the default within such time as may be specified.

**(4)** For purposes of this section, a shadow director of a company is deemed a director of it; and a company goes into liquidation–
- (a) if it is wound up by the court, on the date of the winding-up order, and
- (b) in any other case, on the date of the passing of the resolution for voluntary winding-up."

**Note**

For current provisions see Company Directors Disqualification Act 1986, s. 6–8 and Insolvency Act 1986, s. 214, 215. See also SI 1986/463 (C 14).

## 301 Register of disqualification orders

**301** (Repealed by Company Directors Disqualification Act 1986, s. 23(2) and Sch. 4 as from 29 December 1986.)

**History**

In regard to the date of the above repeal see Company Directors Disqualification Act 1986, s. 25, Insolvency Act 1986, s. 443 and SI 1986/1924 (C 71).

S. 301 (as previously amended by Insolvency Act 1985, s. 109 and Sch. 6, para. 2 as from 28 April 1986: see SI 1986/463 (C 14)) formerly read as follows:

"**301(1)** The Secretary of State may make regulations requiring officers of courts to furnish him with such particulars as the regulations may specify of cases in which–

(a) a disqualification order is made under any of sections 296 to 299, or

(b) any action is taken by a court in consequence of which such an order is varied or ceases to be in force, or

(c) leave is granted by a court for a person subject to such an order to do any thing which otherwise the order prohibits him from doing;

and the regulations may specify the time within which, and the form and manner in which, such particulars are to be furnished.

**(2)** The Secretary of State shall, from the particulars so furnished, continue to maintain the register of orders, and of cases in which leave has been granted as mentioned in subsection (1)(c), which was set up by him under section 29 of the Companies Act 1976.

**(3)** When an order of which entry is made in the register ceases to be in force, the Secretary of State shall delete the entry from the register and all particulars relating to it which have been furnished to him under this section.

**(4)** The register shall be open to inspection on payment of such fee as may be specified by the Secretary of State in regulations.

**(5)** Regulations under this section shall be made by statutory instrument subject to annulment in pursuance of a resolution of either House of Parliament."

**Note**

For current provision, see Company Directors Disqualification Act 1986, s. 18.
See also the Companies (Disqualification Orders) Regulations 1986 (SI 1986/2067).

## 302 Provision against undischarged bankrupt acting as director etc.

**302** (Repealed by Company Directors Disqualification Act 1986, s. 23(2) and Sch. 4 as from 29 December 1986.)

**History**

In regard to the date of the above repeal see Company Directors Disqualification Act 1986, s. 25, Insolvency Act 1986, s. 443 and SI 1986/1924 (C 71). Immediately prior to the repeal there was an amendment by Insolvency Act 1985, s. 235 and Sch. 10. S. 302 originally read as follows:

"**302(1)** If any person being an undischarged bankrupt acts as director or liquidator of, or directly or indirectly takes part in or is concerned in the promotion, formation or management of, a company except with the leave of the court, he is liable to imprisonment or a fine, or both.

**(2) "the court"** for this purpose is the court by which the person was adjudged bankrupt or, in Scotland, sequestration of his estates was awarded.

**(3)** In England and Wales, the leave of the court shall not be given unless notice of intention to apply for it has been served on the official receiver in bankruptcy; and it is the latter's duty, if he is of opinion that it is contrary to the public interest that the application should be granted, to attend on the hearing of the application and oppose it.

**(4)** In this section **"company"** includes an unregistered company and a company incorporated outside Great Britain which has an established place of business in Great Britain."

**Note**

For current provisions, see Company Directors Disqualification Act 1986, s. 11, 13, 22(2)(a).

### REMOVAL OF DIRECTORS

## 303 Resolution to remove director

**303(1) [Removal by ordinary resolution]** A company may by ordinary resolution remove a director before the expiration of his period of office, notwithstanding anything in its articles or in any agreement between it and him.

**303(2) [Special notice]** Special notice is required of a resolution to remove a director under this section or to appoint somebody instead of a director so removed at the meeting at which he is removed.

**303(3) [Filling of vacancy]** A vacancy created by the removal of a director under this section, if not filled at the meeting at which he is removed, may be filled as a casual vacancy.

**303(4) [Person appointed director in place of removed director]** A person appointed director in place of a person removed under this section is treated, for the purpose of determining the time at which he or any other director is to retire, as if he had become director on the day on which the person in whose place he is appointed was last appointed a director.

**303(5) [Compensation, damages for termination etc.]** This section is not to be taken as depriving a person removed under it of compensation or damages payable to him in respect of the termination of his appointment as director or of any appointment terminating with that as director, or as derogating from any power to remove a director which may exist apart from this section.

## 304 Director's right to protest removal

**304(1) [Copy of removal notice under s. 303 to director]** On receipt of notice of an intended resolution to remove a director under section 303, the company shall forthwith send a copy of the notice to the director concerned; and he (whether or not a member of the company) is entitled to be heard on the resolution at the meeting.

**304(2) [Company to circulate director's representations]** Where notice is given of an intended resolution to remove a director under that section, and the director concerned makes with respect to it representations in writing to the company (not exceeding a reasonable length) and requests their notification to members of the company, the company shall, unless the representations are received by it too late for it to do so–

(a) in any notice of the resolution given to members of the company state the fact of the representations having been made; and

(b) send a copy of the representations to every member of the company to whom notice of the meeting is sent (whether before or after receipt of the representations by the company).

**304(3) [If representations not sent as in s. 304(2)]** If a copy of the representations is not sent as required by subsection (2) because received too late or because of the company's default, the director may (without prejudice to his right to be heard orally) require that the representations shall be read out at the meeting.

**304(4) [Exception where court satisfied there is abuse of rights]** But copies of the representations need not be sent out and the representations need not be read out at the meeting if, on the application either of the company or of any other person who claims to be aggrieved, the court is satisfied that the rights conferred by this section are being abused to secure needless publicity for defamatory matter.

**304(5) [Company's costs]** The court may order the company's costs on an application under this section to be paid in whole or in part by the director, notwithstanding that he is not a party to the application.

### OTHER PROVISIONS ABOUT DIRECTORS AND OFFICERS

## 305 Directors' names on company correspondence, etc.

**305(1) [Reference to directors]** A company to which this section applies shall not state, in any form, the name of any of its directors (otherwise than in the text or as a signatory) on any business letter on which the company's name appears unless it states on the letter in legible characters the name of every director of the company.

**History**
In s. 305(1) the words "the name of every director of the company" substituted for the former words "the Christian name (or its initials) and surname of every director of the company who is an individual and the corporate name of every corporate director" by CA 1989, s. 145 and Sch. 19, para. 3(1), (2) as from 1 October 1990 (see SI 1990/1707 (C 46), art. 2(b)).

**305(2) [Application]** This section applies to–

(a) every company registered under this Act or under the former Companies Acts (except a company registered before 23rd November 1916); and

(b) every company incorporated outside Great Britain which has an established place of business within Great Britain, unless it had established such a place of business before that date.

**305(3) [Penalty on default]** If a company makes default in complying with this section, every officer of the company who is in default is liable for each offence to a fine; and for this purpose, where a corporation is an officer of the company, any officer of the corporation is deemed an officer of the company.

**305(4) ["Name" in s. 305(1)]** For the purposes of the obligation under subsection (1) to state the name of every director of the company, a person's **"name"** means–

(a) in the case of an individual, his Christian name (or other forename) and surname; and

(b) in the case of a corporation or Scottish firm, its corporate or firm name.

**History**
See history note after s. 305(7).

**305(5) [Initial or abbreviation]** The initial or a recognised abbreviation of a person's Christian name or other forename may be stated instead of the full Christian name or other forename.

**History**
See history note after s. 305(7).

**305(6) [Peer or individual known by title]** In the case of a peer, or an individual usually known by a title, the title may be stated instead of his Christian name (or other forename) and surname or in addition to either or both of them.

**History**
See history note after s. 305(7).

**305(7) ["Director", "officer"]** In this section **"director"** includes a shadow director and the reference in subsection (3) to an **"officer"** shall be construed accordingly.

**History**
S. 305(4)–(7) substituted for the former s. 305(4) by CA 1989, s. 45 and Sch. 19, para. 4(1), (3) as from 1 October 1990 (see SI 1990/1707 (C 46), art. 2(b)); former s. 305(4) read as follows:

"For purposes of this section–

(a) **"director"** includes shadow director, and **"officer"** is to be construed accordingly;
(b) **"Christian name"** includes a forename;
(c) **"initials"** includes a recognised abbreviation of a Christian name; and
(d) in the case of a peer or a person usually known by a title different from his surname, **"surname"** means that title."

## 306 Limited company may have directors with unlimited liability

**306(1) [Liability of directors etc. may be limited]** In the case of a limited company the liability of the directors or managers, or of the managing director, may, if so provided by the memorandum, be unlimited.

**306(2) [Statement re liability for proposed director etc.]** In the case of a limited company in which the liability of a director or manager is unlimited, the directors and any managers of the company and the member who proposes any person for election or appointment to the office of director or manager, shall add to that proposal a statement that the liability of the person holding that office will be unlimited.

**306(3) [Notice re liability to proposed director]** Before the person accepts the office or acts in it, notice in writing that his liability will be unlimited shall be given to him by the following or one of the following persons, namely–

(a) the promoters of the company,

(b) the directors of the company,

(c) any managers of the company,

(d) the company secretary.

**306(4) [Penalty on default]** If a director, manager or proposer makes default in adding such a statement, or if a promoter, director, manager or secretary makes default in giving the notice required by subsection (3), then–

(a) he is liable to a fine, and

(b) he is also liable for any damage which the person so elected or appointed may sustain from the default;

but the liability of the person elected or appointed is not affected by the default.

## 307 Special resolution making liability of directors unlimited

**307(1) [Special resolution]** A limited company, if so authorised by its articles, may by special resolution alter its memorandum so as to render unlimited the liability of its directors or managers, or of any managing director.

**307(2) [Effect of special resolution]** When such a special resolution is passed, its provisions are as valid as if they had been originally contained in the memorandum.

## 308 Assignment of office by directors

**308** If provision is made by a company's articles, or by any agreement entered into between any person and the company, for empowering a director or manager of the company to assign his office as such to another person, any assignment of office made in pursuance of that provision is (notwithstanding anything to the contrary contained in the provision) of no effect unless and until it is approved by a special resolution of the company.

## 309 Directors to have regard to interests of employees

**309(1) [Interests of company's employees in general]** The matters to which the directors of a company are to have regard in the performance of their functions include the interests of the company's employees in general, as well as the interests of its members.

**309(2) [Duty owed to company]** Accordingly, the duty imposed by this section on the directors is owed by them to the company (and the company alone) and is enforceable in the same way as any other fiduciary duty owed to a company by its directors.

**309(3) [Shadow directors]** This section applies to shadow directors as it does to directors.

## 310 Provisions exempting officers and auditors from liability

**310(1) [Application]** This section applies to any provision, whether contained in a company's articles or in any contract with the company or otherwise, for exempting any officer of the company or any person (whether an officer or not) employed by the company as auditor from, or indemnifying him against, any liability which by virtue of any rule of law would otherwise attach to him in respect of any negligence, default, breach of duty or breach of trust of which he may be guilty in relation to the company.

**310(2) [Provisions as in s. 310(1) void]** Except as provided by the following subsection, any such provision is void.

**310(3) [Insurance, indemnity by company]** This section does not prevent a company–

(a) from purchasing and maintaining for any such officer or auditor insurance against any such liability, or

(b) from indemnifying any such officer or auditor against any liability incurred by him–
  (i) in defending any proceedings (whether civil or criminal) in which judgment is given in his favour or he is acquitted, or
  (ii) in connection with any application under section 144(3) or (4) (acquisition of shares by innocent nominee) or section 727 (general power to grant relief in case of honest and reasonable conduct) in which relief is granted to him by the court.

**History**
S. 310(3) substituted by CA 1989, s. 137(1) as from 1 April 1990 (see SI 1990/355 (C 13), art. 4(e)(i)); s. 310(3) formerly read as follows:

"A company may, in pursuance of such a provision, indemnify any such officer or auditor against any liability incurred by him in defending any proceedings (whether civil or criminal) in which judgment is given in his favour or he is acquitted, or in connection with any application under section 144(3) or (4) (acquisition of shares by innocent nominee) or section 727 (director in default, but not dishonest or unreasonable), in which relief is granted to him by the court."

# PART X – ENFORCEMENT OF FAIR DEALING BY DIRECTORS

## RESTRICTIONS ON DIRECTORS TAKING FINANCIAL ADVANTAGE

### 311 Prohibition on tax-free payments to directors

**311(1) [No tax-free remuneration]** It is not lawful for a company to pay a director remuneration (whether as director or otherwise) free of income tax, or otherwise calculated by reference to or varying with the amount of his income tax, or to or with any rate of income tax.

**311(2) [Effect of certain provisions in articles and contracts]** Any provision contained in a company's articles, or in any contract, or in any resolution of a company or a company's directors, for payment to a director of remuneration as above mentioned has effect as if it provided for payment, as a gross sum subject to income tax, of the net sum for which it actually provides.

### 312 Payment to director for loss of office, etc.

**312** It is not lawful for a company to make to a director of the company any payment by way of compensation for loss of office, or as consideration for or in connection with his retirement from office, without particulars of the proposed payment (including its amount) being disclosed to members of the company and the proposal being approved by the company.

### 313 Company approval for property transfer

**313(1) [Disclosure and approval]** It is not lawful, in connection with the transfer of the whole or any part of the undertaking or property of a company, for any payment to be made to a director of the company by way of compensation for loss of office, or as consideration for or in connection with his retirement from office, unless particulars of the proposed payment (including its amount) have been disclosed to members of the company and the proposal approved by the company.

**313(2) [Unlawful payment deemed on trust for company]** Where a payment unlawful under this section is made to a director, the amount received is deemed to be received by him in trust for the company.

### 314 Director's duty of disclosure on takeover, etc.

**314(1) [Application]** This section applies where, in connection with the transfer to any persons of all or any of the shares in a company, being a transfer resulting from–

(a) an offer made to the general body of shareholders; or

(b) an offer made by or on behalf of some other body corporate with a view to the company becoming its subsidiary or a subsidiary of its holding company; or

(c) an offer made by or on behalf of an individual with a view to his obtaining the right to exercise or control the exercise of not less than one-third of the voting power at any general meeting of the company; or

(d) any other offer which is conditional on acceptance to a given extent,

a payment is to be made to a director of the company by way of compensation for loss of office, or as consideration for or in connection with his retirement from office.

**314(2) [Director to give full particulars re s. 314(1) payment in notice of offer]** It is in those circumstances the director's duty to take all reasonable steps to secure that particulars of the proposed payment (including its amount) are included in or sent with any notice of the offer made for their shares which is given to any shareholders.

**314(3) [Penalty on default]** If–

(a) the director fails to take those steps, or

(b) any person who has been properly required by the director to include those particulars in or send them with the notice required by subsection (2) fails to do so, he is liable to a fine.

## 315 Consequences of non-compliance with s. 314

**315(1) [Deemed trust for shareholders]** If in the case of any such payment to a director as is mentioned in section 314(1)–

(a) his duty under that section is not complied with, or

(b) the making of the proposed payment is not, before the transfer of any shares in pursuance of the offer, approved by a meeting (summoned for the purpose) of the holders of the shares to which the offer relates and of other holders of shares of the same class as any of those shares,

any sum received by the director on account of the payment is deemed to have been received by him in trust for persons who have sold their shares as a result of the offer made; and the expenses incurred by him in distributing that sum amongst those persons shall be borne by him and not retained out of that sum.

**315(2) [Where shareholders in s. 315(1)(b) not all members]** Where–

(a) the shareholders referred to in subsection (1)(b) are not all the members of the company, and

(b) no provision is made by the articles for summoning or regulating the meeting referred to in that paragraph,

the provisions of this Act and of the company's articles relating to general meetings of the company apply (for that purpose) to the meeting either without modification or with such modifications as the Secretary of State on the application of any person concerned may direct for the purpose of adapting them to the circumstances of the meeting.

**315(3) [Where no quorum at meeting]** If at a meeting summoned for the purpose of approving any payment as required by subsection (1)(b) a quorum is not present and, after the meeting has been adjourned to a later date, a quorum is again not present, the payment is deemed for the purposes of that subsection to have been approved.

## 316 Provisions supplementing s. 312 to 315

**316(1) [Payments deemed in trust]** Where in proceedings for the recovery of any payment as having, by virtue of section 313(2) or 315(1) been received by any person in trust, it is shown that–

(a) the payment was made in pursuance of any arrangement entered into as part of the agreement for the transfer in question, or within one year before or two years after that agreement or the offer leading to it; and

(b) the company or any person to whom the transfer was made was privy to that arrangement,

the payment is deemed, except in so far as the contrary is shown, to be one to which the provisions mentioned above in this subsection apply.

**316(2) [Excess consideration]** If in connection with any such transfer as is mentioned in any of sections 313 to 315–

(a) the price to be paid to a director of the company whose office is to be abolished or who is to retire from office for any shares in the company held by him is in excess of the price which could at the time have been obtained by other holders of the like shares; or

(b) any valuable consideration is given to any such director,

the excess or the money value of the consideration (as the case may be) is deemed for the purposes of that section to have been a payment made to him by way of compensation for loss of office or as consideration for or in connection with his retirement from office.

**316(3) [Interpretation]** References in sections 312 to 315 to payments made to a director by way of compensation for loss of office or as consideration for or in connection with his retirement from office, do not include any bona fide payment by way of damages for breach of contract or by way of pension in respect of past services.

**"Pension"** here includes any superannuation allowance, superannuation gratuity or similar payment.

**316(4) [Rules of law re disclosure etc.]** Nothing in sections 313 to 315 prejudices the operation of any rule of law requiring disclosure to be made with respect to such payments as are there mentioned, or with respect to any other like payments made or to be made to a company's directors.

## 317 Directors to disclose interest in contracts

**317(1) [Duty to declare interest at directors' meeting]** It is the duty of a director of a company who is in any way, whether directly or indirectly, interested in a contract or proposed contract with the company to declare the nature of his interest at a meeting of the directors of the company.

**317(2) [Declaration of interest re proposed contract]** In the case of a proposed contract, the declaration shall be made–

(a) at the meeting of the directors at which the question of entering into the contract is first taken into consideration; or

(b) if the director was not at the date of that meeting interested in the proposed contract, at the next meeting of the directors held after he became so interested;

and, in a case where the director becomes interested in a contract after it is made, the declaration shall be made at the first meeting of the directors held after he becomes so interested.

**317(3) [General notice deemed sufficient declaration of interest re contracts]** For purposes of this section, a general notice given to the directors of a company by a director to the effect that–

(a) he is a member of a specified company or firm and is to be regarded as interested in any contract which may, after the date of the notice, be made with that company or firm; or

(b) he is to be regarded as interested in any contract which may after the date of the notice be made with a specified person who is connected with him (within the meaning of section 346 below),

is deemed a sufficient declaration of interest in relation to any such contract.

**317(4) [Requirements for s. 317(3) notice to be of effect]** However, no such notice is of effect unless either it is given at a meeting of the directors or the director takes reasonable steps to secure that it is brought up and read at the next meeting of the directors after it is given.

**317(5) [Interpretation]** A reference in this section to a contract includes any transaction or arrangement (whether or not constituting a contract) made or entered into on or after 22nd December 1980.

**317(6) [Further interpretation]** For purposes of this section, a transaction or arrangement of a kind described in section 330 (prohibition of loans, quasi-loans etc. to directors) made by a company for a director of the company or a person connected with such a director is treated (if it would not otherwise be so treated, and whether or not it is prohibited by that section) as a transaction or arrangment in which that director is interested.

**317(7) [Penalty on default]** A director who fails to comply with this section is liable to a fine.

**317(8) [Application to shadow director]** This section applies to a shadow director as it applies to a director, except that a shadow director shall declare his interest, not at a meeting of the directors, but by a notice in writing to the directors which is either–

(a) a specific notice given before the date of the meeting at which, if he had been a director, the declaration would be required by subsection (2) to be made; or

(b) a notice which under subsection (3) falls to be treated as a sufficient declaration of that interest (or would fall to be so treated apart from subsection (4)).

**317(9) [Rules of law etc.]** Nothing in this section prejudices the operation of any rule of law restricting directors of a company from having an interest in contracts with the company.

## 318 Directors' service contracts to be open to inspection

**318(1) [Particulars of contracts etc. to be kept at appropriate place]** Subject to the following provisions, every company shall keep at an appropriate place–

(a) in the case of each director whose contract of service with the company is in writing, a copy of that contract;
(b) in the case of each director whose contract of service with the company is not in writing, a written memorandum setting out its terms; and
(c) in the case of each director who is employed under a contract of service with a subsidiary of the company, a copy of that contract or, if it is not in writing, a written memorandum setting out its terms.

**318(2) [Copies etc. at same place]** All copies and memoranda kept by a company in pursuance of subsection (1) shall be kept at the same place.

**318(3) [Appropriate places for s. 318(1)]** The following are appropriate places for the purposes of subsection (1)–
(a) the company's registered office;
(b) the place where its register of members is kept (if other than its registered office);
(c) its principal place of business, provided that is situated in that part of Great Britain in which the company is registered.

**318(4) [Notice to registrar re place under s. 318(1), changes etc.]** Every company shall send notice in the prescribed form to the registrar of companies of the place where copies and memoranda are kept in compliance with subsection (1), and of any change in that place, save in a case in which they have at all times been kept at the company's registered office.

**Note**
See the Companies (Forms) (Amendment) Regulations 1995 (SI 1995/736).

**318(5) [Where director working outside UK]** Subsection (1) does not apply to a director's contract of service with the company or with a subsidiary of it if that contract required him to work wholly or mainly outside the United Kingdom; but the company shall keep a memorandum–
(a) in the case of a contract of service with the company, giving the director's name and setting out the provisions of the contract relating to its duration;
(b) in the case of a contract of service with a subsidiary, giving the director's name and the name and place of incorporation of the subsidiary, and setting out the provisions of the contract relating to its duration,

at the same place as copies and memoranda are kept by the company in pursuance of subsection (1).

**318(6) [Shadow director]** A shadow director is treated for purposes of this section as a director.

**318(7) [Inspection]** Every copy and memorandum required by subsection (1) or (5) to be kept shall be open to inspection of any member of the company without charge.

**History**
In s. 318(7) the words ", during business hours (subject to such reasonable restrictions as the company may in general meeting impose, so that not less than 2 hours in each day be allowed for inspection)" formerly appearing after the word "shall" omitted and repealed by CA 1989, s. 143(7), 212 and Sch. 24 as from 1 November 1991 (see SI 1991/1996 (C 57), art. 2(2)(b), (c)).

**Note**
See the Companies (Inspection and Copying of Registers, Indices and Documents) Regulations 1991 (SI 1991/1998).

**318(8) [Offence, penalty]** If–
(a) default is made in complying with subsection (1) or (5), or
(b) an inspection required under subsection (7) is refused, or
(c) default is made for 14 days in complying with subsection (4),

the company and every officer of it who is in default is liable to a fine and, for continued contravention, to a daily default fine.

**318(9) [Compelling inspection]** In the case of a refusal of an inspection required under subsection (7) of a copy or memorandum, the court may by order compel an immediate inspection of it.

**318(10) [Variation of director's contract]** Subsections (1) and (5) apply to a variation of a director's contract of service as they apply to the contract.

**318(11) [Exception]** This section does not require that there be kept a copy of, or memorandum setting out the terms of, a contract (or its variation) at a time when the unexpired portion of the term for which the contract is to be in force is less than 12 months, or at a time at which the contract can, within the next ensuing 12 months, be terminated by the company without payment of compensation.

## 319 Director's contract of employment for more than 5 years

**319(1) [Application]** This section applies in respect of any term of an agreement whereby a director's employment with the company of which he is a director or, where he is the director of a holding company, his employment within the group is to continue, or may be continued, otherwise than at the instance of the company (whether under the original agreement or under a new agreement entered into in pursuance of it), for a period of more than 5 years during which the employment–

(a) cannot be terminated by the company by notice; or

(b) can be so terminated only in specified circumstances.

**319(2) [Further application]** In any case where–

(a) a person is or is to be employed with a company under an agreement which cannot be terminated by the company by notice or can be so terminated only in specified circumstances; and

(b) more than 6 months before the expiration of the period for which he is or is to be so employed, the company enters into a further agreement (otherwise than in pursuance of a right conferred by or under the original agreement on the other party to it) under which he is to be employed with the company or, where he is a director of a holding company, within the group,

this section applies as if to the period for which he is to be employed under that further agreement there were added a further period equal to the unexpired period of the original agreement.

**319(3) [Approval by general meeting]** A company shall not incorporate in an agreement such a term as is mentioned in subsection (1), unless the term is first approved by a resolution of the company in general meeting and, in the case of a director of a holding company, by a resolution of that company in general meeting.

**319(4) [Bodies corporate covered by section]** No approval is required to be given under this section by any body corporate unless it is a company within the meaning of this Act, or is registered under section 680, or if it is a wholly-owned subsidiary of any body corporate, wherever incorporated.

**319(5) [Memorandum re agreement to be available at meeting]** A resolution of a company approving such a term as is mentioned in subsection (1) shall not be passed at a general meeting of the company unless a written memorandum setting out the proposed agreement incorporating the term is available for inspection by members of the company both–

(a) at the company's registered office for not less than 15 days ending with the date of the meeting; and

(b) at the meeting itself.

**319(6) [Contravening term in agreement void]** A term incorporated in an agreement in contravention of this section is, to the extent that it contravenes the section, void; and that agreement and, in a case where subsection (2) applies, the original agreement are deemed to contain a term entitling the company to terminate it at any time by the giving of reasonable notice.

**319(7) [Interpretation]** In this section–

(a) **"employment"** includes employment under a contract for services; and

(b) **"group"**, in relation to a director of a holding company, means the group which consists of that company and its subsidiaries;

and for purposes of this section a shadow director is treated as a director.

## 320 Substantial property transactions involving directors, etc.

**320(1) [Prohibition unless approved by general meeting]** With the exceptions provided by the section next following, a company shall not enter into an arrangement–

(a) whereby a director of the company or its holding company, or a person connected with such a director, acquires or is to acquire one or more non-cash assets of the requisite value from the company; or

(b) whereby the company acquires or is to acquire one or more non-cash assets of the requisite value from such a director or a person so connected,

unless the arrangement is first approved by a resolution of the company in general meeting and, if the director or connected person is a director of its holding company or a person connected with such a director, by a resolution in general meeting of the holding company.

**320(2) [Non-cash asset of requisite value in s. 320(1)]** For this purpose a non-cash asset is of the requisite value if at the time the arrangement in question is entered into its value is not less than £2,000 but (subject to that) exceeds £100,000 or 10 per cent of the company's asset value, that is–

(a) except in a case falling within paragraph (b) below, the value of the company's net assets determined by reference to the accounts prepared and laid under Part VII in respect of the last preceding financial year in respect of which such accounts were so laid; and

(b) where no accounts have been so prepared and laid before that time, the amount of the company's called-up share capital.

**History**

In s. 320(2) "£2,000" and "£100,000" substituted for the former "£1,000" and "£50,000" respectively by the Companies (Fair Dealing by Directors) (Increase in Financial Limits) Order 1990 (SI 1990/1393), art. 2(a) as from 31 July 1990.

**320(3) [Shadow director]** For purposes of this section and sections 321 and 322, a shadow director is treated as a director.

## 321 Exceptions from s. 320

**321(1) [Bodies corporate covered by s. 320]** No approval is required to be given under section 320 by any body corporate unless it is a company within the meaning of this Act or registered under section 680 or, if it is a wholly-owned subsidiary of any body corporate, wherever incorporated.

**321(2) [Exception to s. 320(1)]** Section 320(1) does not apply to an arrangement for the acquisition of a non-cash asset–

(a) if the asset is to be acquired by a holding company from any of its wholly-owned subsidiaries or from a holding company by any of its wholly-owned subsidiaries, or by one wholly-owned subsidiary of a holding company from another wholly-owned subsidiary of that same holding company, or

(b) if the arrangement is entered into by a company which is being wound up, unless the winding-up is a members' voluntary winding-up.

**321(3) [Exception to s. 320(1)(a)]** Section 320(1)(a) does not apply to an arrangement whereby a person is to acquire an asset from a company of which he is a member, if the arrangement is made with that person in his character as a member.

**321(4) [Exception to s. 320(1) re independent brokers]** Section 320(1) does not apply to a transaction on a recognised investment exchange which is effected by a director, or a person connected with him, through the agency of a person who in relation to the transaction acts as an independent broker.

For this purpose an **"independent broker"** means–

(a) in relation to a transaction on behalf of a director, a person who independently of the director selects the person with whom the transaction is to be effected, and

(b) in relation to a transaction on behalf of a person connected with a director, a person who independently of that person or the director selects the person with whom the transaction is to be effected;

and **"recognised"**, in relation to an investment exchange, means recognised under the Financial Services Act 1986.

**History**
S. 321(4) inserted by CA 1989, s. 145 and Sch. 19, para. 8 as from 1 March 1990 (see SI 1990/142 (C 5), art. 5).

## 322 Liabilities arising from contravention of s. 320

**322(1) [Arrangement in contravention of s. 320 voidable]** An arrangement entered into by a company in contravention of section 320, and any transaction entered into in pursuance of the arrangement (whether by the company or any other person) is voidable at the instance of the company unless one or more of the conditions specified in the next subsection is satisfied.

**322(2) [Conditions for exemption to s. 322(1)]** Those conditions are that–

(a) restitution of any money or other asset which is the subject-matter of the arrangement or transaction is no longer possible or the company has been indemnified in pursuance of this section by any other person for the loss or damage suffered by it; or

(b) any rights acquired bona fide for value and without actual notice of the contravention by any person who is not a party to the arrangement or transaction would be afffected by its avoidance; or

(c) the arrangement is, within a reasonable period, affirmed by the company in general meeting and, if it is an arrangement for the transfer of an asset to or by a director of its holding company or a person who is connected with such a director, is so affirmed with the approval of the holding company given by a resolution in general meeting.

**322(3) [Directors liable to account to or indemnify company]** If an arrangement is entered into with a company by a director of the company or its holding company or a person connected with him in contravention of section 320, that director and the person so connected, and any other director of the company who authorised the arrangement or any transaction entered into in pursuance of such an arrangement, is liable–

(a) to account to the company for any gain which he has made directly or indirectly by the arrangement or transaction, and

(b) (jointly and severally with any other person liable under this subsection) to indemnify the company for any loss or damage resulting from the arrangement or transaction.

**322(4) [Extent of s. 322(3)]** Subsection (3) is without prejudice to any liability imposed otherwise than by that subsection, and is subject to the following two subsections; and the liability under subsection (3) arises whether or not the arrangement or transaction entered into has been avoided in pursuance of subsection (1).

**322(5) [Exception to s. 322(3) – all reasonable steps taken etc.]** If an arrangement is entered into by a company and a person connected with a director of the company or its holding company in contravention of section 320, that director is not liable under subsection (3) if he shows that he took all reasonable steps to secure the company's compliance with that section.

**322(6) [Exception to s. 322(3) – no knowledge]** In any case, a person so connected and any such other director as is mentioned in subsection (3) is not so liable if he shows that, at the time the arrangement was entered into, he did not know the relevant circumstances constituting the contravention.

## 322A Invalidity of certain transactions involving directors, etc.

**322A(1) [Application]** This section applies where a company enters into a transaction to which the parties include–

(a) a director of the company or of its holding company, or

(b) a person connected with such a director or a company with whom such a director is associated,

and the board of directors, in connection with the transaction, exceed any limitation on their powers under the company's constitution.

**322A(2) [Transaction voidable]** The transaction is voidable at the instance of the company.

**322A(3) [Liability of directors and associates]** Whether or not it is avoided, any such party to the transaction as is mentioned in subsection (1)(a) or (b), and any director of the company who authorised the transaction, is liable–

(a) to account to the company for any gain which he has made directly or indirectly by the transaction, and

(b) to indemnify the company for any loss or damage resulting from the transaction.

**322A(4) [Construction of above provisions]** Nothing in the above provisions shall be construed as excluding the operation of any other enactment or rule of law by virtue of which the transaction may be called in question or any liability to the company may arise.

**322A(5) [Cessation of voidability]** The transaction ceases to be voidable if–

(a) restitution of any money or other asset which was the subject-matter of the transaction is no longer possible, or

(b) the company is indemnified for any loss or damage resulting from the transaction, or

(c) rights acquired bona fide for value and without actual notice of the directors' exceeding their powers by a person who is not party to the transaction would be affected by the avoidance, or

(d) the transaction is ratified by the company in general meeting, by ordinary or special resolution or otherwise as the case may require.

**322A(6) [Defence to s. 322A(3) liability]** A person other than a director of the company is not liable under subsection (3) if he shows that at the time the transaction was entered into he did not know that the directors were exceeding their powers.

**322A(7) [Effect on s. 35A]** This section does not affect the operation of section 35A in relation to any party to the transaction not within subsection (1)(a) or (b).

But where a transaction is voidable by virtue of this section and valid by virtue of that section in favour of such a person, the court may, on the application of that person or of the company, make such order affirming, severing or setting aside the transaction, on such terms, as appear to the court to be just.

**322A(8) [Interpretation]** In this section **"transaction"** includes any act; and the reference in subsection (1) to limitations under the company's constitution includes limitations deriving–

(a) from a resolution of the company in general meeting or a meeting of any class of shareholders, or

(b) from any agreement between the members of the company or of any class of shareholders.

**History**

S. 322A inserted by CA 1989, s. 109(1) as from 4 February 1991 subject to transitional and saving provisions (see SI 1991/2569 (C 68), art. 4(a), 7).

## 322B Contracts with sole members who are directors

**322B(1) [Duty of company]** Subject to subsection (2), where a private company limited by shares or by guarantee having only one member enters into a contract with the sole member of the company and the sole member is also a director of the company, the company shall, unless the contract is in writing, ensure that the terms of the contract are either set out in a written memorandum or are recorded in the minutes of the first meeting of the directors of the company following the making of the contract.

**322B(2) [Non-application of s. 322B(1)]** Subsection (1) shall not apply to contracts entered into in the ordinary course of the company's business.

**322B(3) [Shadow director]** For the purposes of this section a sole member who is a shadow director is treated as a director.

**322B(4) [Offence, penalty]** If a company fails to comply with subsection (1), the company and every officer of it who is in default is liable to a fine.

**322B(5) [Effect]** Subject to subsection (6), nothing in this section shall be construed as excluding the operation of any other enactment or rule of law applying to contracts between a company and a director of that company.

**322B(6) [Validity of contracts]** Failure to comply with subsection (1) with respect to a contract shall not affect the validity of that contract.

**History**

S. 322B inserted by the Companies (Single Member Private Limited Companies) Regulations 1992 (SI 1992/1699), reg. 2, Sch., para. 3(1) as from 15 July 1992.

**Note**

The Companies (Single Member Private Limited Companies) Regulations 1992 (SI 1992/1699) implement the Twelfth EC Company Law Directive (89/667).

## SHARE DEALINGS BY DIRECTORS AND THEIR FAMILIES

## 323 Prohibition on directors dealing in share options

**323(1) [Offence]** It is an offence for a director of a company to buy–

(a) a right to call for delivery at a specified price and within a specified time of a specified number of relevant shares or a specified amount of relevant debentures; or

(b) a right to make delivery at a specified price and within a specified time of a specified number of relevant shares or a specified amount of relevant debentures; or

(c) a right (as he may elect) to call for delivery at a specified price and within a specified time or to make delivery at a specified price and within a specified time of a specified number of relevant shares or a specified amount of relevant debentures.

**323(2) [Penalty]** A person guilty of an offence under subsection (1) is liable to imprisonment or a fine, or both.

**323(3) [Definitions]** In subsection (1)–

(a) **"relevant shares"**, in relation to a director of a company, means shares in the company or in any other body corporate, being the company's subsidiary or holding company, or a subsidiary of the company's holding company, being shares as respects which there has been granted a listing on a stock exchange (whether in Great Britain or elsewhere);

(b) **"relevant debentures"**, in relation to a director of a company, means debentures of the company or of any other body corporate, being the company's subsidiary or holding company or a subsidiary of the company's holding company, being debentures as respects which there has been granted such a listing; and

(c) **"price"** includes any consideration other than money.

**323(4) [Shadow director]** This section applies to a shadow director as to a director.

**323(5) [Extent of section]** This section is not to be taken as penalising a person who buys a right to subscribe for shares in, or debentures of, a body corporate or buys debentures of a body corporate that confer upon the holder of them a right to subscribe for, or to convert the debentures (in whole or in part) into, shares of that body.

## 324 Duty of director to disclose shareholdings in own company

**324(1) [Duty to notify re certain interests etc.]** A person who becomes a director of a company and at the time when he does so is interested in shares in, or debentures of, the company or any other body corporate, being the company's subsidiary or holding company or a subsidiary of the company's holding company, is under obligation to notify the company in writing–

(a) of the subsistence of his interests at that time; and

(b) of the number of shares of each class in, and the amount of debentures of each class of, the company or other such body corporate in which each interest of his subsists at that time.

**324(2) [Duty to notify re certain events]** A director of a company is under obligation to notify the company in writing of the occurrence, while he is a director, of any of the following events–

(a) any event in consequence of whose occurrence he becomes, or ceases to be, interested in shares in, or debentures of, the company or any other body corporate, being the company's subsidiary or holding company or a subsidiary of the company's holding company;

(b) the entering into by him of a contract to sell any such shares or debentures;

(c) the assignment by him of a right granted to him by the company to subscribe for shares in, or debentures of, the company; and

(d) the grant to him by another body corporate, being the company's subsidiary or holding company or a subsidiary of the company's holding company, of a right to subscribe for shares in, or debentures of, that other body corporate, the exercise of such a right granted to him and the assignment by him of such a right so granted;

and notification to the company must state the number or amount, and class, of shares or debentures involved.

**324(3) [Effect of Sch. 13, Pt. I, II, III; exceptions to s. 324(1), (2)]** Schedule 13 has effect in connection with subsections (1) and (2) above; and of that Schedule–

(a) Part I contains rules for the interpretation of, and otherwise in relation to, those subsections and applies in determining, for purposes of those subsections, whether a person has an interest in shares or debentures;

(b) Part II applies with respect to the periods within which obligations imposed by the subsections must be fulfilled; and

(c) Part III specifies certain circumstances in which obligations arising from subsection (2) are to be treated as not discharged;

and subsections (1) and (2) are subject to any exceptions for which provision may be made by regulations made by the Secretary of State by statutory instrument.

**Note**
See the Companies (Disclosure of Directors' Interests) (Exceptions) Regulations 1985 (SI 1985/802).

**324(4) [Qualification to s. 324(2)]** Subsection (2) does not require the notification by a person of the occurrence of an event whose occurrence comes to his knowledge after he has ceased to be a director.

**324(5) [Notice must refer to obligation]** An obligation imposed by this section is treated as not discharged unless the notice by means of which it purports to be discharged is expressed to be given in fulfilment of that obligation.

**324(6) [Shadow directors, wholly-owned subsidiary]** This section applies to shadow directors as to directors; but nothing in it operates so as to impose an obligation with respect to shares in a body corporate which is the wholly-owned subsidiary of another body corporate.

**324(7) [Offence, penalty]** A person who–

(a) fails to discharge, within the proper period, an obligation to which he is subject under subsection (1) or (2), or

(b) in purported discharge of an obligation to which he is so subject, makes to the company a statement which he knows to be false, or recklessly makes to it a statement which is false,

is guilty of an offence and liable to imprisonment or a fine, or both.

**324(8) [Application of s. 732]** Section 732 (restriction on prosecutions) applies to an offence under this section.

## 325 Register of directors' interests notified under s. 324

**325(1) [Register for s. 324 purposes]** Every company shall keep a register for the purposes of section 324.

**325(2) [Particulars to be entered in register]** Whenever a company receives information from a director given in fulfilment of an obligation imposed on him by that section, it is under obligation to enter in the register, against the director's name, the information received and the date of the entry.

**325(3) [Rights of directors to be entered]** The company is also under obligation, whenever it grants to a director a right to subscribe for shares in, or debentures of, the company to enter in the register against his name–

(a) the date on which the right is granted,

(b) the period during which, or time at which, it is exercisable,

(c) the consideration for the grant (or, if there is no consideration, that fact), and

(d) the description of shares or debentures involved and the number or amount of them, and the price to be paid for them (or the consideration, if otherwise than in money).

**325(4) [Further details re s. 325(3)]** Whenever such a right as is mentioned above is exercised by a director, the company is under obligation to enter in the register against his name that fact (identifying the right), the number or amount of shares or debentures in respect of which it is exercised and, if they were registered in his name, that fact and, if not, the name or names of the person or persons in whose name or names they were registered, together (if they were registered in the names of two persons or more) with the number or amount of the shares or debentures registered in the name of each of them.

**325(5) [Effect of Sch. 13, Pt. IV, inspection etc.]** Part IV of Schedule 13 has effect with respect to the register to be kept under this section, to the way in which entries in it are to be made, to the right of inspection, and generally.

**325(6) [Shadow director]** For purposes of this section, a shadow director is deemed a director.

**Note**

See the Companies (Forms) (Amendment) Regulations 1995 (SI 1995/736).

# 326 Sanctions for non-compliance

**326(1) [Application]** The following applies with respect to defaults in complying with, and to contraventions of, section 325 and Part IV of Schedule 13.

**326(2) [Default re s. 325(1), (2), (3), (4); Sch. 13, para. 21, 22, 28]** If default is made in complying with any of the following provisions–

(a) section 325(1), (2), (3) or (4), or

(b) Schedule 13, paragraph 21, 22 or 28,

the company and every officer of it who is in default is liable to a fine and, for continued contravention, to a daily default fine.

**326(3) [Refusal of inspection of register etc.]** If an inspection of the register required under paragraph 25 of the Schedule is refused, or a copy required under paragraph 26 is not sent within the proper period, the company and every officer of it who is in default is liable to a fine and, for contined contravention, to a daily default fine.

**326(4) [Default re notice of where register kept]** If default is made for 14 days in complying with paragraph 27 of the Schedule (notice to registrar of where register is kept), the company and every officer of it who is in default is liable to a fine and, for continued contravention, to a daily default fine.

**326(5) [Default re producing register]** If default is made in complying with paragraph 29 of the Schedule (register to be produced at annual general meeting), the company and every officer of it who is in default is liable to a fine.

**326(6) [Compelling inspection of register etc.]** In the case of a refusal of an inspection of the register required under paragraph 25 of the Schedule, the court may by order compel an immediate inspection of it; and in the case of failure to send within the proper period a copy required under paragraph 26, the court may by order direct that the copy be sent to the person requiring it.

# 327 Extension of s. 323 to spouses and children

**327(1) [Application to spouse etc; defence]** Section 323 applies to–

(a) the wife or husband of a director of a company (not being herself or himself a director of it), and

(b) an infant son or infant daughter of a director (not being himself or herself a director of the company),

as it applies to the director; but it is a defence for a person charged by virtue of this section with an offence under section 323 to prove that he (she) had no reason to believe that his (her) spouse or, as the case may be, parent was a director of the company in question.

**327(2) [Interpretation]** For purposes of this section–

(a) **"son"** includes step-son, and **"daughter"** includes step-daughter ("parent" being construed accordingly),

(b) **"infant"** means, in relation to Scotland, person under the age of 18 years, and

(c) a shadow director of a company is deemed a director of it.

**History**
In s. 327(2)(b) the words "person under the age of 18 years" substituted for the former words "pupil or minor" by the Age of Legal Capacity (Scotland) Act 1991, s. 10(1), 11(2), Sch. 1, para. 39 as from 25 September 1991.

## 328 Extension of s. 324 to spouses and children

**328(1) [Interest of spouse, children treated as director's interest]** For the purposes of section 324–

(a) an interest of the wife or husband of a director of a company (not being herself or himself a director of it) in shares or debentures is to be treated as the director's interest; and

(b) the same applies to an interest of an infant son or infant daughter of a director of a company (not being himself or herself a director of it) in shares or debentures.

**328(2) [Contract etc. of spouse, children treated as that of director]** For those purposes–

(a) a contract, assignment or right of subscription entered into, exercised or made by, or a grant made to, the wife or husband of a director of a company (not being herself or himself a director of it) is to be treated as having been entered into, exercised or made by, or (as the case may be) as having been made to, the director; and

(b) the same applies to a contract, assignment or right of subscription entered into, exercised or made by, or grant made to, an infant son or infant daughter of a director of a company (not being himself or herself a director of it).

**328(3) [Directors to notify company re certain events]** A director of a company is under obligation to notify the company in writing of the occurrence while he or she is a director, of either of the following events, namely–

(a) the grant by the company to his (her) spouse, or to his or her infant son or infant daughter, of a right to subscribe for shares in, or debentures of, the company; and

(b) the exercise by his (her) spouse or by his or her infant son or infant daughter of such a right granted by the company to the wife, husband, son or daughter.

**328(4) [Contents of s. 328(3) notice]** In a notice given to the company under subsection (3) there shall be stated–

(a) in the case of the grant of a right, the like information as is required by section 324 to be stated by the director on the grant to him by another body corporate of a right to subscribe for shares in, or debentures of, that other body corporate; and

(b) in the case of the exercise of a right, the like information as is required by that section to be stated by the director on the exercise of a right granted to him by another body corporate to subscribe for shares in, or debentures of, that other body corporate.

**328(5) [Time for fulfilment of s. 328(3) obligation]** An obligation imposed by subsection (3) on a director must be fulfilled by him before the end of 5 days beginning with the day following that on which the occurrence of the event giving rise to it comes to his knowledge; but in reckoning that period of days there is disregarded any Saturday or Sunday, and any day which is a bank holiday in any part of Great Britain.

**328(6) [Offence, penalty]** A person who–

(a) fails to fulfil, within the proper period, an obligation to which he is subject under subsection (3), or

(b) in purported fulfilment of such an obligation, makes to a company a statement which he knows to be false, or recklessly makes to a company a statement which is false,

is guilty of an offence and liable to imprisonment or a fine, or both.

**328(7) [Interpretation]** The rules set out in Part I of Schedule 13 have effect for the interpretation of, and otherwise in relation to, subsections (1) and (2); and subsections (5), (6) and (8) of section 324 apply with any requisite modification.

**328(8) [Definitions]** In this section, **"son"** includes step-son, **"daughter"** includes step-daughter, and **"infant"** means, in relation to Scotland, person under the age of 18 years.

**History**

In s. 328(8) the words "person under the age of 18 years" substituted for the former words "pupil or minor" by the Age of Legal Capacity (Scotland) Act 1991, s. 10(1), 11(2), Sch. 1, para. 39 as from 25 September 1991.

# 329 Duty to notify stock exchange of matters notified under preceding sections

**329(1) [Obligation for company to notify]** Whenever a company whose shares or debentures are listed on a recognised investment exchange other than an overseas investment exchange within the meaning of the Financial Services Act 1986 is notified of any matter by a director in consequence of the fulfilment of an obligation imposed by section 324 or 328, and that matter relates to shares or debentures so listed, the company is under obligation to notify that investment exchange of that matter; and the investment exchange may publish, in such manner as it may determine, any information received by it under this subsection.

**History**

In s. 329(1) the words "recognised investment exchange other than an overseas investment exchange within the meaning of the Financial Services Act 1986", "that investment exchange" and "the investment exchange" substituted respectively for the former words "recognised stock exchange", "that stock exchange" and "the stock exchange" by Financial Services Act 1986, s. 212 and Sch. 16, para. 20 as from 29 April 1988 (see SI 1988/740 (C 22)).

**329(2) [Time for fulfilling s. 329(1) obligation]** An obligation imposed by subsection (1) must be fulfilled before the end of the day next following that on which it arises; but there is disregarded for this purpose a day which is a Saturday or a Sunday or a bank holiday in any part of Great Britain.

**329(3) [Penalty on default]** If default is made in complying with this section, the company and every officer of it who is in default is guilty of an offence and liable to a fine and, for continued contravention, to a daily default fine.

Section 732 (restriction on prosecutions) applies to an offence under this section.

## RESTRICTIONS ON A COMPANY'S POWER TO MAKE LOANS ETC. TO DIRECTORS AND PERSONS CONNECTED WITH THEM

# 330 General restrictions on loans etc. to directors and persons connected with them

**330(1) [Prohibitions, exceptions]** The prohibitions listed below in this section are subject to the exceptions in sections 332 to 338.

**330(2) [Loans etc.]** A company shall not–

(a) make a loan to a director of the company or of its holding company;

(b) enter into any guarantee or provide any security in connection with a loan made by any person to such a director.

**330(3) [Quasi-loans etc.]** A relevant company shall not–

(a) make a quasi-loan to a director of the company or of its holding company;

(b) make a loan or a quasi-loan to a person connected with such a director;

(c) enter into a guarantee or provide any security in connection with a loan or quasi-loan made by any other person for such a director or a person so connected.

**330(4) [Credit transactions etc.]** A relevant company shall not–

(a) enter into a credit transaction as creditor for such a director or a person so connected;

(b) enter into any guarantee or provide any security in connection with a credit transaction made by any other person for such a director or a person so connected.

**330(5) [Shadow director]** For purposes of sections 330 to 346, a shadow director is treated as a director.

**330(6) [Prohibition of certain assignments]** A company shall not arrange for the assignment to it, or the assumption by it, of any rights, obligations or liabilities under a transaction which, if it had been entered into by the company, would have contravened subsection (2), (3) or (4); but for the purposes of sections 330 to 347 the transaction is to be treated as having been entered into on the date of the arrangement.

**330(7) [Prohibition of further arrangements]** A company shall not take part in any arrangement whereby–

(a) another person enters into a transaction which, if it had been entered into by the company, would have contravened any of subsections (2), (3), (4) or (6); and

(b) that other person, in pursuance of the arrangement, has obtained or is to obtain any benefit from the company or its holding company or a subsidiary of the company or its holding company.

# 331 Definitions for s. 330ff.

**331(1) [Interpretation of s. 330–346]** The following subsections apply for the interpretation of sections 330 to 346.

**331(2) ["Guarantee"] "Guarantee"** includes indemnity, and cognate expressions are to be construed accordingly.

**331(3) [Quasi-loans]** A quasi-loan is a transaction under which one party ("the creditor") agrees to pay, or pays otherwise than in pursuance of an agreement, a sum for another ("the borrower") or agrees to reimburse, or reimburses otherwise than in pursuance of an agreement, expenditure incurred by another party for another ("the borrower")–

(a) on terms that the borrower (or a person on his behalf) will reimburse the creditor; or

(b) in circumstances giving rise to a liability on the borrower to reimburse the creditor.

**331(4) [Borrower under quasi-loan]** Any reference to the person to whom a quasi-loan is made is a reference to the borrower; and the liabilities of a borrower under a quasi-loan include the liabilities of any person who has agreed to reimburse the creditor on behalf of the borrower.

**331(5)** (Repealed by Banking Act 1987, s. 108(2) and Sch. 7, Pt. I as from 1 October 1987)

**History**

In regard to the date of the above repeal, see SI 1987/1664 (C 50): s. 331(5) formerly read as follows:

""**Recognised bank**" means a company which is recognised as a bank for the purposes of the Banking Act 1979."

**331(6) ["Relevant company"] "Relevant company"** means a company which–

(a) is a public company, or

(b) is a subsidiary of a public company, or

(c) is a subsidiary of a company which has as another subsidiary a public company, or

(d) has a subsidiary which is a public company.

**331(7) [Credit transactions]** A credit transaction is a transaction under which one party ("the creditor")–

(a) supplies any goods or sells any land under a hire-purchase agreement or a conditional sale agreement;

(b) leases or hires any land or goods in return for periodical payments;

(c) otherwise disposes of land or supplies goods or services on the understanding that payment (whether in a lump sum or instalments or by way of periodical payments or otherwise) is to be deferred.

**331(8) ["Services"] "Services"** means anything other than goods or land.

**331(9) [Transactions etc. for a person]** A transaction or arrangement is made "for" a person if–

(a) in the case of a loan or quasi-loan, it is made to him;

(b) in the case of a credit transaction, he is the person to whom goods or services are supplied, or land is sold or otherwise disposed of, under the transaction;

(c) in the case of a guarantee or security, it is entered into or provided in connection with a loan or quasi-loan made to him or a credit transaction made for him;

(d) in the case of an arrangement within subsection (6) or (7) of section 330, the transaction to which the arrangement relates was made for him; and

(e) in the case of any other transaction or arrangement for the supply or transfer of, or of any interest in, goods, land or services, he is the person to whom the goods, land or services (or the interest) are supplied or transferred.

**331(10) ["Conditional sale agreement"] "Conditional sale agreement"** means the same as in the Consumer Credit Act 1974.

# 332 Short-term quasi-loans

**332(1) [Certain quasi-loans possible to directors]** Subsection (3) of section 330 does not prohibit a company ("the creditor") from making a quasi-loan to one of its directors or to a director of its holding company if–

(a) the quasi-loan contains a term requiring the director or a person on his behalf to reimburse the creditor his expenditure within 2 months of its being incurred; and

(b) the aggregate of the amount of that quasi-loan and of the amount outstanding under each relevant quasi-loan does not exceed £5,000.

**History**
In s. 332(1)(b) "£5,000" substituted for the former "£1,000" by CA 1989, s. 138(a) as from 31 July 1990 subject to a saving provision (see SI 1990/1392 (C 41), art. 2(c) and also art. 5).

**332(2) [Quasi-loan relevant for s. 332(1)]** A quasi-loan is relevant for this purpose if it was made to the director by virtue of this section by the creditor or its subsidiary or, where the director is a director of the creditor's holding company, any other subsidiary of that company; and **"the amount outstanding"** is the amount of the outstanding liabilities of the person to whom the quasi-loan was made.

# 333 Inter-company loans in same group

**333** In the case of a relevant company which is a member of a group of companies (meaning a holding company and its subsidiaries), paragraphs (b) and (c) of section 330(3) do not prohibit the company from–

(a) making a loan or quasi-loan to another member of that group; or

(b) entering into a guarantee or providing any security in connection with a loan or quasi-loan made by any person to another member of the group,

by reason only that a director of one member of the group is associated with another.

# 334 Loans of small amounts

**334** Without prejudice to any other provision of sections 332 to 338, paragraph (a) of section 330(2) does not prohibit a company from making a loan to a director of the company or of its holding company if the aggregate of the relevant amounts does not exceed £5,000.

**History**
In s. 334 "£5,000" substituted for the former "£2,500" by CA 1989, s. 138(b) as from 31 July 1990 subject to a saving provision (see SI 1990/1392 (C 41), art. 2(c) and also art. 5).

# 335 Minor and business transactions

**335(1) [Exception to s. 330(4)]** Section 330(4) does not prohibit a company from entering into a transaction for a person if the aggregate of the relevant amounts does not exceed £10,000.

**History**
In s. 335(1) "£10,000" substituted for the former "£5,000" by the Companies (Fair Dealing by Directors) (Increase in Financial Limits) Order 1990 (SI 1990/1393), art. 2(b) as from 31 July 1990.

**335(2) [Conditions for exception]** Section 330(4) does not prohibit a company from entering into a transaction for a person if–

(a) the transaction is entered into by the company in the ordinary course of its business; and

(b) the value of the transaction is not greater, and the terms on which it is entered into are no more favourable, in respect of the person for whom the transaction is made, than that or those which it is reasonable to expect the company to have offered to or in respect of a person of the same financial standing but unconnected with the company.

## 336 Transactions at behest of holding company

**336** The following transactions are excepted from the prohibitions of section 330–

(a) a loan or quasi-loan by a company to its holding company, or a company entering into a guarantee or providing any security in connection with a loan or quasi-loan made by any person to its holding company;

(b) a company entering into a credit transaction as creditor for its holding company, or entering into a guarantee or providing any security in connection with a credit transaction made by any other person for its holding company.

## 337 Funding of director's expenditure on duty to company

**337(1) [Exception to s. 330]** A company is not prohibited by section 330 from doing anything to provide a director with funds to meet expenditure incurred or to be incurred by him for the purposes of the company or for the purpose of enabling him properly to perform his duties as an officer of the company.

**337(2) [Extension of s. 337(1)]** Nor does the section prohibit a company from doing anything to enable a director to avoid incurring such expenditure.

**337(3) [Conditions for s. 337(1), (2)]** Subsections (1) and (2) apply only if one of the following conditions is satisfied–

(a) the thing in question is done with prior approval of the company given at a general meeting at which there are disclosed all the matters mentioned in the next subsection;

(b) that thing is done on condition that, if the approval of the company is not so given at or before the next annual general meeting, the loan is to be repaid, or any other liability arising under any such transaction discharged, within 6 months from the conclusion of that meeting;

but those subsections do not authorise a relevant company to enter into any transaction if the aggregate of the relevant amounts exceeds £20,000.

**History**

In s. 337(3) "£20,000" substituted for the former "£10,000" by the Companies (Fair Dealing by Directors) (Increase in Financial Limits) Order 1990 (SI 1990/1393), art. 8(c) as from 31 July 1990.

**337(4) [Matters to be disclosed under s. 337(3)(a)]** The matters to be disclosed under subsection (3)(a) are–

(a) the purpose of the expenditure incurred or to be incurred, or which would otherwise be incurred, by the director,

(b) the amount of the funds to be provided by the company, and

(c) the extent of the company's liability under any transaction which is or is connected with the thing in question.

## 338 Loan or quasi-loan by money-lending company

**338(1) [Exception to s. 330]** There is excepted from the prohibitions in section 330–

(a) a loan or quasi-loan made by a money-lending company to any person; or

(b) a money-lending company entering into a guarantee in connection with any other loan or quasi-loan.

**338(2) ["Money-lending company"] "Money-lending company"** means a company whose ordinary business includes the making of loans or quasi-loans, or the giving of guarantees in connection with loans or quasi-loans.

**338(3) [Conditions for s. 338(1)]** Subsection (1) applies only if both the following conditions are satisfied–

(a) the loan or quasi-loan in question is made by the company, or it enters into the guarantee, in the ordinary course of the company's business; and

(b) the amount of the loan or quasi-loan, or the amount guaranteed, is not greater, and the terms of the loan, quasi-loan or guarantee are not more favourable, in the case of the person to whom the loan or quasi-loan is made or in respect of whom the guarantee is entered into, than that or those which it is reasonable to expect that company to have offered to or in respect of a person of the same financial standing but unconnected with the company.

**338(4) [No authorisation in s. 338(1) if amounts over £100,000]** But subsection (1) does not authorise a relevant company (unless it is a banking company) to enter into any transaction if the aggregate of the relevant amounts exceeds £100,000.

**History**

In s. 338(4) the words "a banking company" substituted for the former words "an authorised institution" by CA 1989, s. 23 and Sch. 10, para. 10 as from 1 April 1990 subject to transitional and saving provisions (see SI 1990/355 (C 13), art. 3, Sch. 1 and also art. 6–9); previously the words "an authorised institution" substituted for the original words "a recognised bank" by Banking Act 1987, s. 108(2) and Sch. 6, para. 18(6) as from 1 October 1987 (see SI 1987/1664 (C 50). Also in s. 338(4) "£100,000" substituted for the former "£50,000" by CA 1989, s. 138(c) as from 31 July 1990 subject to a saving provision (see SI 1990/1392 (C 41), art. 2(c) and also art. 5).

**338(5) [Determination of s. 338(4) aggregate]** In determining that aggregate, a company which a director does not control is deemed not to be connected with him.

**338(6) [Extent of condition in s. 338(3)(b)]** The condition specified in subsection (3)(b) does not of itself prevent a company from making a loan to one of its directors or a director of its holding company–

(a) for the purpose of facilitating the purchase, for use as that director's only or main residence, of the whole or part of any dwelling-house together with any land to be occupied and enjoyed with it;

(b) for the purpose of improving a dwelling-house or part of a dwelling-house so used or any land occupied and enjoyed with it;

(c) in substitution for any loan made by any person and falling within paragraph (a) or (b) of this subsection,

if loans of that description are ordinarily made by the company to its employees and on terms no less favourable than those on which the transaction in question is made, and the aggregate of the relevant amounts does not exceed £100,000.

**History**

In s. 338(6) "£100,000" substituted for the former figure "£50,000" by CA 1989, s. 138(c) as from 31 July 1990 subject to saving provision (see SI 1990/1392 (C 41), art. 2(c), 5).

## 339 "Relevant amounts" for purposes of s. 334ff.

**339(1) [Defining relevant amount for exceptions]** This section has effect for defining the "relevant amounts" to be aggregated under sections 334, 335(1), 337(3) and 338(4); and in relation to any proposed transaction or arrangement and the question whether it falls within one or other of the exceptions provided by those sections, **"the relevant exception"** is that exception; but where the relevant exception is the one provided by section 334 (loan of small amount), references in this section to a person connected with a director are to be disregarded.

**339(2) [Relevant amounts for proposed transaction or arrangement]** Subject as follows, the relevant amounts in relation to a proposed transaction or arrangement are–

(a) the value of the proposed transaction or arrangement,

(b) the value of any existing arrangement which–

 (i) falls within subsection (6) or (7) of section 330, and

 (ii) also falls within subsection (3) of this section, and

 (iii) was entered into by virtue of the relevant exception by the company or by a subsidiary of the company or, where the proposed transaction or arrangement is to be made for a director of its holding company or a person connected with such a director, by that holding company or any of its subsidiaries;

(c) the amount outstanding under any other transaction–

 (i) falling within subsection (3) below, and

 (ii) made by virtue of the relevant exception, and

(iii) made by the company or by a subsidiary of the company or, where the proposed transaction or arrangement is to be made for a director of its holding company or a person connected with such a director by that holding company or any of its subsidiaries.

**339(3) [Transactions under s. 339(2)]** A transaction falls within this subsection if it was made–

(a) for the director for whom the proposed transaction or arrangement is to be made, or for any person connected with that director; or

(b) where the proposed transaction or arrangement is to be made for a person connected with a director of a company, for that director or any person connected with him;

and an arrangement also falls within this subsection if it relates to a transaction which does so.

**339(4) [S. 338 transaction – banking company]** But where the proposed transaction falls within section 338 and is one which a banking company proposes to enter into under subsection (6) of that section (housing loans, etc.), any other transaction or arrangement which apart from this subsection would fall within subsection (3) of this section does not do so unless it was entered into in pursuance of section 338(6).

**History**

In s. 339(4) the words "a banking company" substituted for the former words "an authorised institution" by CA 1989, s. 23 and Sch. 10, para. 10 as from 1 April 1990 subject to transitional and saving provisions (see SI 1990/355 (C 13), art. 3, Sch. 1, and also art. 6–9); previously the words "an authorised institution" substituted for the original words "a recognised bank" by Banking Act 1987, s. 108(1) and Sch. 6, para. 18(6) as from 1 October 1987 (see SI 1987/1664 (C 50)).

**339(5) [Exception to s. 339(3) re certain subsidiaries etc.]** A transaction entered into by a company which is (at the time of that transaction being entered into) a subsidiary of the company which is to make the proposed transaction, or is a subsidiary of that company's holding company, does not fall within subsection (3) if at the time when the question arises (that is to say, the question whether the proposed transaction or arrangement falls within any relevant exception), it no longer is such a subsidiary.

**339(6) [Values under s. 339(2)]** Values for purposes of subsection (2) of this section are to be determined in accordance with the section next following; and **"the amount outstanding"** for purposes of subsection (2)(c) above is the value of the transaction less any amount by which that value has been reduced.

## 340 "Value" of transactions and arrangements

**340(1) [Application]** This section has effect for determining the value of a transaction or arrangement for purposes of sections 330 to 339.

**340(2) [Loan]** The value of a loan is the amount of its principal.

**340(3) [Quasi-loan]** The value of a quasi-loan is the amount, or maximum amount, which the person to whom the quasi-loan is made is liable to reimburse the creditor.

**340(4) [Guarantee or security]** The value of a guarantee or security is the amount guaranteed or secured.

**340(5) [S. 330(6) or (7) arrangement]** The value of an arrangement to which section 330(6) or (7) applies is the value of the transaction to which the arrangement relates less any amount by which the liabilities under the arrangement or transaction of the person for whom the transaction was made have been reduced.

**340(6) [Arrangement not under s. 340(2)–(5)]** The value of a transaction or arrangement not falling within subsections (2) to (5) above is the price which it is reasonable to expect could be obtained for the goods, land or services to which the transaction or arrangement relates if they had been supplied (at the time the transaction or arrangement is entered into) in the ordinary course of business and on the same terms (apart from price) as they have been supplied, or are to be supplied, under the transaction or arrangement in question.

**340(7) [Where value not able to be expressed as specific sum]** For purposes of this section, the value of a transaction or arrangement which is not capable of being expressed as a specific sum of money (because the amount of any liability arising under the transaction or arrangement is unascertainable, or for any other reason), whether or not any liability under the transaction or arrangement has been reduced, is deemed to exceed £100,000.

**History**
In s. 340(7) "£100,000" substituted for the former "£50,000" by the Companies (Fair Dealing by Directors) (Increase in Financial Limits) Order 1990 (SI 1990/1393), art. 2(d) as from 31 July 1990.

## 341 Civil remedies for breach of s. 330

**341(1) [Contravening provision voidable]** If a company enters into a transaction or arrangement in contravention of section 330, the transaction or arrangement is voidable at the instance of the company unless–

(a) restitution of any money or any other asset which is the subject matter of the arrangement or transaction is no longer possible, or the company has been indemnified in pursuance of subsection (2)(b) below for the loss or damage suffered by it, or

(b) any rights acquired bona fide for value and without actual notice of the contravention by a person other than the person for whom the transaction or arrangement was made would be affected by its avoidance.

**341(2) [Liability of director and connected person to account or indemnify]** Where an arrangement or transaction is made by a company for a director of the company or its holding company or a person connected with such a director in contravention of section 330, that director and the person so connected and any other director of the company who authorised the transaction or arrangement (whether or not it has been avoided in pursuance of subsection (1)) is liable–

(a) to account to the company for any gain which he has made directly or indirectly by the arrangement or transaction; and

(b) (jointly and severally with any other person liable under this subsection) to indemnify the company for any loss or damage resulting from the arrangement or transaction.

**341(3) [Extent of s. 341(2)]** Subsection (2) is without prejudice to any liability imposed otherwise than by that subsection, but is subject to the next two subsections.

**341(4) [Exception to s. 341(2) – all reasonable steps taken etc.]** Where an arrangement or transaction is entered into by a company and a person connected with a director of the company or its holding company in contravention of section 330, that director is not liable under subsection (2) of this section if he shows that he took all reasonable steps to secure the company's compliance with that section.

**341(5) [Exception to s. 341(2) – no knowledge]** In any case, a person so connected and any such other director as is mentioned in subsection (2) is not so liable if he shows that, at the time the arrangement or transaction was entered into, he did not know the relevant circumstances constituting the contravention.

## 342 Criminal penalties for breach of s. 330

**342(1) [Offence by director]** A director of a relevant company who authorises or permits the company to enter into a transaction or arrangement knowing or having reasonable cause to believe that the company was thereby contravening section 330 is guilty of an offence.

**342(2) [Offence by relevant company]** A relevant company which enters into a transaction or arrangement for one of its directors or for a director of its holding company in contravention of section 330 is guilty of an offence.

**342(3) [Offence of procuring contravention by relevant company]** A person who procures a relevant company to enter into a transaction or arrangement knowing or having reasonable cause to believe that the company was thereby contravening section 330 is guilty of an offence.

**342(4) [Penalty]** A person guilty of an offence under this section is liable to imprisonment or a fine, or both.

**342(5) [Exception for relevant company]** A relevant company is not guilty of an offence under subsection (2) if it shows that, at the time the transaction or arrangement was entered into, it did not know the relevant circumstances.

# 343 Record of transactions not disclosed in company accounts

**343(1) [Application re banking companies and s. 344 exceptions]** The following provisions of this section–

(a) apply in the case of a company which is a banking company, or is the holding company of a credit institution, and

(b) are subject to the exceptions provided by section 344.

**History**

In s. 343(1)(a) the words "a banking company, or is the holding company of a credit institution," substituted for the former words ", or is the holding company of, a banking company," by the Companies Act 1985 (Bank Accounts) Regulations 1994 (SI 1994/233), reg. 1, 6(1), (2) as from 28 February 1994 subject to transitional provisions in reg. 7, 8; previously the words "a banking company" substituted for the former words "an authorised institution" by CA 1989, s. 23 and Sch. 10, para. 10 as from 1 April 1990 subject to transitional and saving provisions (see SI 1990/355 (C 13), art. 3, Sch. 1 and also art. 6–9); originally the words "an authorised institution" substituted for the words "a recognised bank" by Banking Act 1987, s. 108(1) and Sch. 6, para. 18(6) as from 1 October 1987 (see SI 1987/1664 (C 50)).

**343(2) [Register of transactions etc. to be kept]** Where such a company takes advantage of the provisions of paragraph 2 of Part IV of Schedule 9 in relation to a financial year, that company shall keep a register containing a copy of every transaction, arrangement or agreement of which particulars would, but for that paragraph, be required to be disclosed in the company's accounts or group accounts for that financial year and for each financial year in the preceding 10 in relation to which the company has taken advantage of the provisions of that paragraph.

**History**

S. 343(2) substituted by the Companies Act 1985 (Bank Accounts) Regulations 1994 (SI 1994/233), reg. 1, 6(1), (3) as from 28 February 1994 subject to transitional provisions in reg. 7, 8; s. 343(2) formerly read as follows:

"Such a company shall maintain a register containing a copy of every transaction, arrangement or agreement of which particulars would, but for paragraph 2 of Part IV of Schedule 9, be required to be disclosed in the company's accounts or group accounts for the current financial year and for each of the preceding 10 financial years."

In that former s. 343(2) the words "paragraph 2 of Part IV of Schedule 9, be required" substituted for the original words "paragraph 4 of Schedule 6, be required by section 232" by CA 1989, s. 23 and Sch. 10, para. 11 as from 1 April 1990 subject to transitional and saving provisions (see SI 1990/355 (C 13), art. 3, Sch. 1 and also art. 6–9).

**343(3) [Transactions etc. not in writing]** In the case of a transaction, arrangement or agreement which is not in writing, there shall be contained in the register a written memorandum setting out its terms.

**343(4) [Statement re transactions etc. at registered office]** Where such a company takes advantage of the provisions of paragraph 2 of Part IV of Schedule 9 in relation to the last complete financial year preceding its annual general meeting, that company shall before that meeting make available at its registered office for not less than 15 days ending with the date of the meeting a statement containing the particulars of transactions, arrangements and agreements which the company would, but for that paragraph, be required to disclose in its accounts or group accounts for that financial year.

**History**

S. 343(4) substituted by the Companies Act 1985 (Bank Accounts) Regulations 1994 (SI 1994/233), reg. 1, 6(1), (4) as from 28 February 1994 subject to transitional provisions in reg. 7, 8; s. 343(4) formerly read as follows:

"Such a company shall before its annual general meeting make available at its registered office for not less than 15 days ending with the date of the meeting a statement containing the particulars of transactions, arrangements and agreements which the company would, but for paragraph 2 of Part IV of Schedule 9, be required to disclose in its accounts or group accounts for the last complete financial year preceding that meeting."

In that former s. 343(4) the words "paragraph 2 of Part IV of Schedule 9, be required" substituted for the original words "paragraph 4 of Schedule 6, be required by section 232" by CA 1989, s. 23 and Sch. 10, para. 11 as from 1 April 1990 subject to transitional and saving provisions (see SI 1990/355 (C 13), art. 3, Sch. 1 and also art. 6–9).

**343(5) [Inspection by members]** The statement shall be so made available for inspection by members of the company; and such a statement shall also be made available for their inspection at the annual general meeting.

**343(6) [Auditors' report on statement]** It is the duty of the company's auditors to examine the statement before it is made available to members of the company and to make a report to the members on it; and the report shall be annexed to the statement before it is made so available.

**343(7) [Statement in auditors' report etc.]** The auditors' report shall state whether in their opinion the statement contains the particulars required by subsection (4); and, where their opinion is that it does not, they shall include in the report, so far as they are reasonably able to do so, a statement giving the required particulars.

**343(8) [Offence, penalty, defence: shadow director]** If a company fails to comply with any provision of subsections (2) to (5), every person who at the time of the failure is a director of it is guilty of an offence and liable to a fine; but–

(a) it is a defence in proceedings against a person for this offence to prove that he took all reasonable steps for securing compliance with the subsection concerned, and

(b) a person is not guilty of the offence by virtue only of being a shadow director of the company.

**343(9) [Application to certain loans and quasi-loans]** For purposes of the application of this section to loans and quasi-loans made by a company to persons connected with a person who at any time is a director of the company or of its holding company, a company which a person does not control is not connected with him.

## 344 Exceptions from s. 343

**344(1) [Certain transactions etc. less than £2,000]** Section 343 does not apply in relation to–

(a) transactions or arrangements made or subsisting during a financial year by a company or by a subsidiary of a company for a person who was at any time during that year a director of the company or of its holding company or was connected with such a director, or

(b) an agreement made or subsisting during that year to enter into such a transaction or arrangement,

if the aggregate of the values of each transaction or arrangement made for that person, and of each agreement for such a transaction or arrangement, less the amount (if any) by which the value of those transactions, arrangements and agreements has been reduced, did not exceed £2,000 at any time during the financial year.

For purposes of this subsection, values are to be determined as under section 340.

**History**

In s. 344(1) "£2,000" substituted for the former "£1,000" by the Companies (Fair Dealing by Directors) (Increase in Financial Limits) Order 1990 (SI 1990/1393), art. 2(e) as from 31 July 1990.

**344(2) [Certain UK subsidiary banking companies]** Section 343(4) and (5) do not apply to a banking company which is the wholly-owned subsidiary of a company incorporated in the United Kingdom.

**History**

In s. 344(2) the words "a banking company" substituted for the former words "an authorised institution" by CA 1989, s. 23 and Sch. 10, para. 10 as from 1 April 1990 subject to transitional and saving provisions (see SI 1990/355 (C 13), art. 3, Sch. 1 and also art. 6–9); previously the words "an authorised institution" substituted for the original words "a recognised bank" by Banking Act 1987, s. 108(1) and Sch. 6, para. 18(6) as from 1 October 1987 (see SI 1987/1664 (C 50)).

### SUPPLEMENTARY

## 345 Power to increase financial limits

**345(1) [Larger sum]** The Secretary of State may by order in a statutory instrument substitute for any sum of money specified in this Part a larger sum specified in the order.

**Note**

See the Companies (Fair Dealing by Directors) (Increase in Financial Limits) Order 1990 (SI 1990/1393).

**345(2) [Annulment of order]** An order under this section is subject to annulment in pursuance of a resolution of either House of Parliament.

**345(3) [No effect on things done before]** Such an order does not have effect in relation to anything done or not done before its coming into force; and accordingly, proceedings in respect of any liability (whether civil or criminal) incurred before that time may be continued or instituted as if the order had not been made.

## 346 "Connected persons", etc.

**346(1) [Application]** This section has effect with respect to references in this Part to a person being "connected" with a director of a company, and to a director being "associated with" or "controlling" a body corporate.

"Every company shall have its name engraved in legible characters on its seal; and if a company fails to comply with this subsection, it is liable to a fine."

**350(2) [Officer using seal without name]** If an officer of a company or a person on its behalf uses or authorises the use of any seal purporting to be a seal of the company on which its name is not engraved as required by subsection (1), he is liable to a fine.

## 351 Particulars in correspondence, etc.

**351(1) [Particulars in business letters and order forms]** Every company shall have the following particulars mentioned in legible characters in all business letters and order forms of the company, that is to say–

(a) the company's place of registration and the number with which it is registered,

(b) the address of its registered office,

(c) in the case of an investment company (as defined in section 266), the fact that it is such a company, and

(d) in the case of a limited company exempt from the obligation to use the word "limited" as part of its name, the fact that it is a limited company.

**Note**
See note after s. 351(5).

**351(2) [Reference to share capital]** If in the case of a company having a share capital there is on the stationery used for any such letters, or on the company's order forms, a reference to the amount of share capital, the reference must be to paid-up share capital.

**Note**
See note after s. 351(5).

**351(3), (4)** (Ceased to have effect and repealed by Welsh Language Act 1993, s. 31, 35(1) and Sch. 2 as from 1 February 1994.)

**History**
In regard to the date of the above cessation of effect and repeal, see SI 1994/115 (C 5), art. 2(2); s. 351(3), (4) formerly read as follows:

"**351(3)** Where the name of a public company includes, as its last part, the equivalent in Welsh of the words "public limited company" ("cwmni cyfyngedig cyhoeddus"), the fact that the company is a public limited company shall be stated in English and in legible characters–

(a) in all prospectuses, bill-heads, letter paper, notices and other official publications of the company, and
(b) in a notice conspicuously displayed in every place in which the company's business is carried on.

**(4)** Where the name of a limited company has "cyfyngedig" as the last word, the fact that the company is a limited company shall be stated in English and in legible characters–

(a) in all prospectuses, bill-heads, letter paper, notices and other official publications of the company, and
(b) in a notice conspicuously displayed in every place in which the company's business is carried on."

**351(5) [Contraventions]** As to contraventions of this section, the following applies–

(a) if a company fails to comply with subsection (1) or (2), it is liable to a fine,

(b) if an officer of a company or a person on its behalf issues or authorises the issue of any business letter or order form not complying with those subsections, he is liable to a fine.

**History**
S. 351(5)(c) and the word "and" immediately preceding it, repealed by Welsh Language Act 1993, s. 35(1) and Sch. 2 as from 1 February 1994 (see SI 1994/115 (C 5) art. 2(2)); s. 351(5)(c) formerly read as follows:

"(c) if subsection (3) or (4) is contravened, the company and every officer of it who is in default is liable to a fine and, in the case of subsection (3), to a daily default fine for continued contravention."

**Note**
S. 351(1), (2), (5)(a), (b) were previously European Communities Act 1972, s. 9(7) which in part implemented the First EC Company Law Directive (68/151).

# Chapter II – Register of Members

## 352 Obligation to keep and enter up register

**352(1) [Obligation on every company]** Every company shall keep a register of its members and enter in it the particulars required by this section.

**352(2) [Matters to be entered]** There shall be entered in the register–

(a) the names and addresses of the members;

(b) the date on which each person was registered as a member; and

(c) the date at which any person ceased to be a member.

**352(3) [Company with share capital]** The following applies in the case of a company having a share capital–

(a) with the names and addresses of the members there shall be entered a statement–
  (i) of the shares held by each member, distinguishing each share by its number (so long as the share has a number) and, where the company has more than one class of issued shares, by its class, and
  (ii) of the amount paid or agreed to be considered as paid on the shares of each member;

(b) where the company has converted any of its shares into stock and given notice of the conversion to the registrar of companies, the register shall show the amount and class of stock held by each member, instead of the amount of shares and the particulars relating to shares specified in paragraph (a).

**352(4) [Company not having share capital]** In the case of a company which does not have a share capital but has more than one class of members, there shall be entered in the register, with the names and addresses of the members, the class to which each member belongs.

**352(5) [Penalty on default]** If a company makes default in complying with this section, the company and every officer of it who is in default is liable to a fine and, for continued contravention, to a daily default fine.

**Note**

Re application of s. 352(5) to default under the Uncertificated Securities Regulations 1995 (SI 1995/3272) see reg. 19(4) of those Regulations.

**352(6) [Removal of entries re former member]** An entry relating to a former member of the company may be removed from the register after the expiration of 20 years from the date on which he ceased to be a member.

**352(7) [Liability of company re deletions]** Liability incurred by a company from the making or deletion of an entry in its register of members, or from a failure to make or delete any such entry, is not enforceable more than 20 years after the date on which the entry was made or deleted or, in the case of any such failure, the failure first occurred.

This is without prejudice to any lesser period of limitation.

**Note**

See the Companies (Inspection and Copying of Registers, Indices and Documents) Regulations 1991 (SI 1991/1998).

## 352A Statement that company has only one member

**352A(1) [Fall in number of members to one]** If the number of members of a private company limited by shares or by guarantee falls to one there shall upon the occurrence of that event be entered in the company's register of members with the name and address of the sole member–

(i) a statement that the company has only one member, and

(ii) the date on which the company became a company having only one member.

**352A(2) [Increase in number of members to two or more]** If the membership of a private company limited by shares or by guarantee increases from one to two or more members there shall upon the occurrence of that event be entered in the company's register of members, with the name and address of the person who was formerly the sole member, a statement that the company has ceased to have only one member together with the date on which that event occurred.

**352A(3) [Offence, penalty]** If a company makes default in complying with this section, the company and every officer of it who is in default is liable to a fine and, for continued contravention, to a daily default fine.

**History**

S. 352A inserted by the Companies (Single Member Private Limited Companies) Regulations 1992 (SI 1992/1699), reg. 2 and Sch., para. 4(1) as from 15 July 1992.

**Note**

The Companies (Single Member Private Limited Companies) Regulations 1992 (SI 1992/1699) implement the Twelfth EC Company Law Directive (89/667).

## 353 Location of register

**353(1) [Usually at registered office]** A company's register of members shall be kept at its registered office, except that–

(a) if the work of making it up is done at another office of the company, it may be kept there; and

(b) if the company arranges with some other person for the making up of the register to be undertaken on its behalf by that other, it may be kept at the office of the other at which the work is done;

but it must not be kept, in the case of a company registered in England and Wales, at any place elsewhere than in England and Wales or, in the case of a company registered in Scotland, at any place elsewhere than in Scotland.

**353(2) [Notice to registrar re location and change]** Subject as follows, every company shall send notice in the prescribed form to the registrar of companies of the place where its register of members is kept, and of any change in that place.

**Note**

See the Companies (Forms) Regulations 1991 (SI 1991/879); the Companies (Forms) (No. 2) Regulations 1991 (SI 1991/1259); and the Companies (Forms) (Amendment) Regulations 1995 (SI 1995/736).

**353(3) [Notice not necessary if always at registered office]** The notice need not be sent if the register has, at all times since it came into existence (or, in the case of a register in existence on 1st July 1948, at all times since then) been kept at the company's registered office.

**353(4) [Penalty on default]** If a company makes default for 14 days in complying with subsection (2), the company and every officer of it who is in default is liable to a fine and, for continued contravention, to a daily default fine.

## 354 Index of members

**354(1) [Index if more than 50 members]** Every company having more than 50 members shall, unless the register of members is in such a form as to constitute in itself an index, keep an index of the names of the members of the company and shall, within 14 days after the date on which any alteration is made in the register of members, make any necessary alteration in the index.

**354(2) [Requirement for entry]** The index shall in respect of each member contain a sufficient indication to enable the account of that member in the register to be readily found.

**354(3) [Location of index]** The index shall be at all times kept at the same place as the register of members.

**354(4) [Penalty on default]** If default is made in complying with this section, the company and every officer of it who is in default is liable to a fine and, for continued contravention, to a daily default fine.

**Note**

See the Companies (Inspection and Copying of Registers, Indices and Documents) Regulations 1991 (SI 1991/1998).

## 355 Entries in register in relation to share warrants

**355(1) [Amendment of register on issue of share warrant]** On the issue of a share warrant the company shall strike out of its register of members the name of the member then entered in it as holding the shares specified in the warrant as if he had ceased to be a member, and shall enter in the register the following particulars, namely–

(a) the fact of the issue of the warrant;

(b) a statement of the shares included in the warrant, distinguishing each share by its number so long as the share has a number; and

(c) the date of the issue of the warrant.

**355(2) [Entitlement to re-entry on cancellation of share warrant]** Subject to the company's articles, the bearer of a share warrant is entitled, on surrendering it for cancellation, to have his name entered as a member in the register of members.

**355(3) [Company responsible for loss]** The company is responsible for any loss incurred by any person by reason of the company entering in the register the name of a bearer of a share warrant in respect of the shares specified in it without the warrant being surrendered and cancelled.

**355(4) [S. 355(1) particulars sufficient until surrender]** Until the warrant is surrendered, the particulars specified in subsection (1) are deemed to be those required by this Act to be entered in the register of members; and, on the surrender, the date of the surrender must be entered.

**355(5) [Status of bearer of share warrant]** Except as provided by section 291(2) (director's share qualification), the bearer of a share warrant may, if the articles of the company so provide, be deemed a member of the company within the meaning of this Act, either to the full extent or for any purposes defined in the articles.

## 356 Inspection of register and index

**356(1) [Open for inspection]** Except when the register of members is closed under the provisions of this Act, the register and the index of members' names shall be open to the inspection of any member of the company without charge, and of any other person on payment of such fee as may be prescribed.

**History**

In s. 356(1) the words "during business hours" formerly appearing after the words "index of members' names shall" omitted and repealed and the words "such fee as may be prescribed" substituted for the former words "the appropriate charge" by CA 1989, s. 143(8)(a), 212 and Sch. 24 as from 1 November 1991 (see SI 1991/1996 (C 57), art. 2(2)(b), (c)).

**Note**

See the Companies (Inspection and Copying of Registers, Indices and Documents) Regulations 1991 (SI 1991/1998).

**356(2)** (Omitted and repealed by Companies Act 1989, s. 143(8)(b), 212 and Sch. 24 as from 1 November 1991.)

**History**

In regard to the date of the above omission and repeal see SI 1991/1996 (C 57), art. 2(2)(b), (c); s. 356(2) formerly read as follows:

"The reference to business hours is subject to such reasonable restrictions as the company in general meeting may im'pose, but so that not less than 2 hours in each day is to be allowed for inspection."

**356(3) [Copies of register for charge etc.]** Any member of the company or other person may require a copy of the register, or of any part of it, on payment of such fee as may be prescribed; and the company shall cause any copy so required by a person to be sent to him within 10 days beginning with the day next following that on which the requirement is received by the company.

**History**

In s. 356(3) the words "such fee as may be prescribed" substituted for the former words "the appropriate charge" by CA 1989, s. 143(8)(c) as from 1 November 1991 (see SI 1991/1996 (C 57), art. 2(2)(b)).

**Note**

See the Companies (Inspection and Copying of Registers, Indices and Documents) Regulations 1991 (SI 1991/1998).

**356(4)** (Omitted and repealed by Companies Act 1989, s. 143(8)(d), 212 and Sch. 24 as from 1 November 1991.)

**History**

In regard to the date of the above omission and repeal see SI 1991/1996 (C 57), art. 2(2)(b), (c); s. 356(4) formerly read as follows:

"The appropriate charge is–

(a) under subsection (1), 5 pence or such less sum as the company may prescribe, for each inspection; and

(b) under subsection (3), 10 pence or such less sum as the company may prescribe, for every 100 words (or fraction of 100 words) required to be copied."

**356(5) [Penalty for refusal of inspection etc.]** If an inspection required under this section is refused, or if a copy so required is not sent within the proper period, the company and every officer of it who is in default is liable in respect of each offence to a fine.

**356(6) [Compelling of inspection etc.]** In the case of such refusal or default, the court may by order compel an immediate inspection of the register and index, or direct that the copies required be sent to the persons requiring them.

## 357 Non-compliance with s. 353, 354, 356; agent's default

**357** Where under section 353(1)(b), the register of members is kept at the office of some person other than the company, and by reason of any default of his the company fails to comply with–

section 353(2) (notice to registrar),
section 354(3) (index to be kept with register), or
section 356 (inspection),

or with any requirement of this Act as to the production of the register, that other person is liable to the same penalties as if he were an officer of the company who was in default, and the power of the court under section 356(6) extends to the making of orders against that other and his officers and servants.

## 358 Power to close register

**358** A company may, on giving notice by advertisement in a newspaper circulating in the district in which the company's registered office is situated, close the register of members for any time or times not exceeding in the whole 30 days in each year.

## 359 Power of court to rectify register

**359(1) [Application for rectification]** If–

(a) the name of any person is, without sufficient cause, entered in or omitted from a company's register of members, or

(b) default is made or unnecessary delay takes place in entering on the register the fact of any person having ceased to be a member,

the person aggrieved, or any member of the company, or the company, may apply to the court for rectification of the register.

**359(2) [Court may refuse application or grant rectification]** The court may either refuse the application or may order rectification of the register and payment by the company of any damages sustained by any party aggrieved.

**359(3) [Court may decide on other matters]** On such an application the court may decide any question relating to the title of a person who is a party to the application to have his name entered in or omitted from the register, whether the question arises between members or alleged members, or between members or alleged members on the one hand and the company on the other hand, and generally may decide any question necessary or expedient to be decided for rectification of the register.

**359(4) [Notice to be given of rectification to registrar]** In the case of a company required by this Act to send a list of its members to the registrar of companies, the court, when making an order for rectification of the register, shall by its order direct notice of the rectification to be given to the registrar.

## 360 Trusts not to be entered on register in England and Wales

**360** No notice of any trust, expressed, implied or constructive, shall be entered on the register, or be receivable by the registrar, in the case of companies registered in England and Wales.

## 361 Register to be evidence

**361** The register of members is prima facie evidence of any matters which are by this Act directed or authorised to be inserted in it.

## 362 Overseas branch registers

**362(1) [Branch register]** A company having a share capital whose objects comprise the transaction of business in any of the countries or territories specified in Part I of Schedule 14 to this Act may cause to be kept in any such country or territory in which it transacts business a branch register of members resident in that country or territory.

**362(2) ["Overseas branch register", references to dominion register etc.]** Such a branch register is to be known as an **"overseas branch register"**; and–

(a) any dominion register kept by a company under section 119 of the Companies Act 1948 is to become known as an overseas branch register of the company;

(b) where any Act or instrument (including in particular a company's articles) refers to a company's dominion register, that reference is to be read (unless the context otherwise requires) as being to an overseas branch register kept under this section; and

(c) references to a colonial register occurring in articles registered before 1st November 1929 are to be read as referring to an overseas branch register.

**362(3) [Sch. 14, Pt. II, III]** Part II of Schedule 14 has effect with respect to overseas branch registers kept under this section; and Part III of the Schedule enables corresponding facilities in Great Britain to be accorded to companies incorporated in other parts of the world.

**362(4) [Foreign Jurisdiction Act]** The Foreign Jurisdiction Act 1890 has effect as if subsection (1) of this section, and Part II of Schedule 14, were included among the enactments which by virtue of section 5 of that Act may be applied by Order in Council to foreign countries in which for the time being Her Majesty has jurisdiction.

**362(5) [Possible extension]** Her Majesty may by Order in Council direct that subsection (1) above and Part II of Schedule 14 shall extend, with such exceptions, modifications or adaptations (if any) as may be specified in the Order, to any territories under Her Majesty's protection to which those provisions cannot be extended under the Foreign Jurisdiction Act 1890.

# Chapter III – Annual Return

## 363 Duty to deliver annual returns

**363(1) [Returns up to "return date"]** Every company shall deliver to the registrar successive annual returns each of which is made up to a date not later than the date which is from time to time the company's "return date", that is–

(a) the anniversary of the company's incorporation, or

(b) if the company's last return delivered in accordance with this Chapter was made up to a different date, the anniversary of that date.

**363(2) [Requirements for return]** Each return shall–

(a) be in the prescribed form,

(b) contain the information required by or under the following provisions of this Chapter, and

(c) be signed by a director or the secretary of the company;

and it shall be delivered to the registrar within 28 days after the date to which it is made up.

**Note**

See the Companies (Forms Amendment No. 2 and Company's Type and Principal Business Activities) Regulations 1990 (SI 1990/1766) (for Form 363a until 1 April 1996), the Companies (Forms) (No. 2) Regulations 1991 (SI 1991/1259), the Companies (Welsh Language Forms and Documents) Regulations 1994 (SI 1994/117), the Companies (Welsh Language Forms and Documents) (Amendment) Regulations 1995 (SI 1995/734), the Companies (Forms) (Amendment) Regulations 1995 (SI 1995/736), the Companies (Forms) (Amendment) Regulations 1999 (SI 1999/2356) subject to transitional provision in reg. 3(2) and the Companies (Welsh Language Forms) (Amendment) Regulations 1999 (SI 1999/2357) subject to transitional provision in reg. 3(2).

**363(3) [Offence by company, penalty]** If a company fails to deliver an annual return in accordance with this Chapter before the end of the period of 28 days after a return date, the company is guilty of an offence and liable to a fine and, in the case of continued contravention, to a daily default fine.

The contravention continues until such time as an annual return made up to that return date and complying with the requirements of subsection (2) (except as to date of delivery) is delivered by the company to the registrar.

**363(4) [Offence by director or secretary]** Where a company is guilty of an offence under subsection (3), every director or secretary of the company is similarly liable unless he shows that he took all reasonable steps to avoid the commission or continuation of the offence.

**363(5) [Delivered "in accordance with this Chapter"]** The references in this section to a return being delivered "in accordance with this Chapter" are–

(a) in relation to a return made on or after 1st October 1990, to a return with respect to which all the requirements of subsection (2) are complied with;

(b) in relation to a return made before 1st October 1990, to a return with respect to which the formal and substantive requirements of this Chapter as it then had effect were complied with, whether or not the return was delivered in time.

**History**

In s. 363(5)(a), (b) the words "on or after 1st October 1990" and "1st October 1990" substituted for the former words "after the commencement of section 139 of the Companies Act 1989" and "that commencement" respectively by SI 1990/1707 (C 46), art. 7 as from 1 October 1990.

See also history note after s. 365.

## 364 Contents of annual return: general

**364(1) [Information in return]** Every annual return shall state the date to which it is made up and shall contain the following information–

(a) the address of the company's registered office;

(b) the type of company it is and its principal business activities;

(c) the name and address of the company secretary;

(d) the name and address of every director of the company;

(e) in the case of each individual director–

 (i) his nationality, date of birth and business occupation,

(g) if the register of members is not kept at the company's registered office, the address of the place where it is kept;

(h) if any register of debenture holders (or a duplicate of any such register or a part of it) is not kept at the company's registered office, the address of the place where it is kept.

**History**

In s. 364(1) para. (e)(ii), (f) and (i), and the word "and" immediately preceding former s. 364(1)(e)(ii), repealed by the Companies (Contents of Annual Return) Regulations 1999 (SI 1999/2322), reg. 1 and 2 as from 13 September 1999; para. (e)(ii), (f) and (i) formerly read as follows:

"(e)(ii) such particulars of other directorships and former names as are required to be contained in the company's register of directors;

(f) in the case of any corporate director, such particulars of other directorships as would be required to be contained in that register in the case of an individual;

(i) if the company has elected–

 (i) to dispense under section 252 with the laying of accounts and reports before the company in general meeting, or

 (ii) to dispense under section 366A with the holding of annual general meetings,

a statement to that effect."

**364(2) [Information as to company's type]** The information as to the company's type shall be given by reference to the classification scheme prescribed for the purposes of this section.

**Note**

See note after s. 364(3).

**364(3) [Information as to company's principal business activities]** The information as to the company's principal business activities may be given by reference to one or more categories of any prescribed system of classifying business activities.

**Note**

Re s. 364(2), (3) see the Companies (Forms Amendment No. 2 and Company's Type and Principal Business Activities) Regulations 1990 (SI 1990/1766) and the Companies (Forms) (No. 2) Regulations 1991 (SI 1991/1259). Re s. 364(3) see the Companies (Principal Business Activities) (Amendment) Regulations 1996 (SI 1996/1105).

**364(4) ["Name", "address"]** A person's **"name"** and **"address"** mean, respectively–

(a) in the case of an individual, his Christian name (or other forename) and surname and his usual residential address:

(b) in the case of a corporation or Scottish firm, its corporate or firm name and its registered or principal office.

**364(5) [Name of peer et al.]** In the case of a peer, or an individual usually known by a title, the title may be stated instead of his Christian name (or other forename) and surname or in addition to either or both of them.

**364(6) [Where all partners joint secretaries]** Where all the partners in a firm are joint secretaries, the name and principal office of the firm may be stated instead of the names and addresses of the partners.

**History**

See history note after s. 365.

## 364A Contents of annual return: particulars of share capital and shareholders

**364A(1) [Information in return]** The annual return of a company having a share capital shall contain the following information with respect to its share capital and members.

**364A(2) [Total number and value of issued shares]** The return shall state the total number of issued shares of the company at the date to which the return is made up and the aggregate nominal value of those shares.

**364A(3) [Information re classes of shares]** The return shall state with respect to each class of shares in the company–

(a) the nature of the class, and

(b) the total number and aggregate nominal value of issued shares of that class at the date to which the return is made up.

**364A(4) [List re members et al., index]** The return shall contain a list of the names and addresses of every person who

(a) is a member of the company on the date to which the return is made up, or

(b) has ceased to be a member of the company since the date to which the last return was made up (or, in the case of the first return, since the incorporation of the company);

and if the names are not arranged in alphabetical order the return shall have annexed to it an index sufficient to enable the name of any person in the list to be easily found.

**364A(5) [Shares held by each member et al.]** The return shall also state–

(a) the number of shares of each class held by each member of the company at the date to which the return is made up, and

(b) the number of shares of each class transferred since the date to which the last return was made up (or, in the case of the first return, since the incorporation of the company) by each member or person who has ceased to be a member, and the dates of registration of the transfers.

**364A(6) [Only particulars that have changed since last return]** The return may, if either of the two immediately preceding returns has given the full particulars required by subsections (4) and (5), give only such particulars as relate to persons ceasing to be or becoming members since the date of the last return and to shares transferred since that date.

**364A(7) [Particulars in overseas branch register]** Subsections (4) and (5) do not require the inclusion of particulars entered in an overseas branch register if copies of those entries have not been recieved at the company's registered office by the date to which the return is made up.

Those particulars shall be included in the company's next annual return after they are received.

**364A(8) [Where shares converted into stock]** Where the company has converted any of its shares into stock, the return shall give the corresponding information in relation to that stock, stating the amount of stock instead of the number or nominal value of shares.

**History**
See history note after s. 365.

## 365 Supplementary provisions: regulations and interpretation

**365(1) [Power of Secretary of State]** The Secretary of State may be regulations make further provision as to the information to be given in a company's annual return, which may amend or repeal the provisions of sections 364 and 364A.

**365(2) [Form of regulations]** Regulations under this section shall be made by statutory instrument which shall be subject to annulment in pursuance of a resolution of either House of Parliament.

**365(3) [Shadow director]** For the purposes of this Chapter, except section 363(2)(c) (signature of annual return), a shadow director shall be deemed to be a director.

**History**
S. 363–365 substituted by CA 1989, s. 139(1) as from 1 October 1990 subject to transitional and saving provisions (see SI 1990/1707 (C 46), art. 2(a) and also art. 4 and 5; the former s. 363–365 read as follows:

**"363 Annual return (company having a share capital)**

**363(1)** Subject to the provisions of this section, every company having a share capital shall, at least once in every year, make a return containing with respect to the company's registered office, registers of members and debenture holders, shares and debentures, indebtedness, past and present members and directors and secretary, the matters specified in Schedule 15.

**(2)** The annual return shall be in the prescribed form.

**(3)** A company need not make a return under subsection (1) either in the year of its incorporation or, if it is not required by this Act to hold an annual general meeting during the following year, in that year.

**(4)** Where the company has converted any of its shares into stock and given notice of the conversion to the registrar of companies, the list referred to in paragraph 5 of Schedule 15 must state the amount of stock held by each of the existing members instead of the amount of shares and the particulars relating to shares required by that paragraph.

**(5)** The return may, in any year, if the return for either of the two immediately preceding years has given (as at the date of that return) the full particulars required by that paragraph of the Schedule, give only such of those particulars as relate to persons ceasing to be or becoming members since the date of the last return and to shares transferred since that date or to changes as compared with that date in the amount of stock held by a member.

**(6)** The following applies to a company keeping an overseas branch register–
- (a) references in subsection (5) to the particulars required by paragraph 5 are to be taken as not including any such particulars contained in the overseas branch register, in so far as copies of the entries containing those particulars are not received at the company's registered office before the date when the return in question is made;
- (b) if an annual return is made between the date when entries are made in the overseas branch register and the date when copies of those entries are received at the company's registered office, the particulars contained in those entries (so far as relevant to an annual return) shall be included in the next or a subsequent annual return, as may be appropriate having regard to the particulars included in that return with respect to the company's register of members.

**(7)** If a company fails to comply with this section, the company and every officer of it who is in default is liable to a fine and, for continued contravention, to a daily default fine.

**(8)** For purposes of this section and Schedule 15, a shadow director is deemed a director and officer.

**364 Annual return (company not having a share capital)**

**364(1)** Every company not having a share capital shall once at least in every calendar year make a return in the prescribed form stating–
- (a) the address of the company's registered office;
- (b) if the register of members is under provisions of this Act kept elsewhere than at that office, the address of the place where it is kept;
- (c) if any register of holders of debentures of the company or any duplicate of any such register or part of it is under provisions of this Act kept elsewhere than at the company's registered office, the address of the place where it is kept;
- (d) all such particulars with respect to the persons who at the date of the return are the directors of the company, and any person who at that date is its secretary, as are by this Act required to be contained (with respect to directors and the secretary respectively) in the company's register of directors and secretaries.

**(2)** A company need not make a return under subsection (1) either in the year of its incorporation or, if it is not required by this Act to hold an annual general meeting during the following year, in that year.

**(3)** There shall be included in the return a statement containing particulars of the total amount of the company's indebtedness in respect of all mortgages and charges (whenever created) of any description specified in section 396(1) or, in the case of a company registered in Scotland, section 410(4).

**(4)** If a company fails to comply with this section, the company and every officer of it who is in default is liable to a fine and, for continued contravention, to a daily default fine.

**(5)** For purposes of this section, a shadow director is deemed a director and officer.

**365 Time for completion of annual return**

**365(1)** A company's annual return must be completed within 42 days after the annual general meeting for the year, whether or not that meeting is the first or only ordinary general meeting, or the first or only general meeting of the company in that year.

**(2)** The company must forthwith forward to the registrar of companies a copy of the return signed both by a director and by the secretary of the company.

**(3)** If a company fails to comply with this section, the company and every officer of it who is in default is liable to a fine and, for continued contravention, to a daily default fine; and for this purpose a shadow director is deemed an officer."

# Chapter IV – Meetings and Resolutions

## MEETINGS

## 366 Annual general meeting

**366(1) [Annual general meeting each year]** Every company shall in each year hold a general meeting as its annual general meeting in addition to any other meetings in that year, and shall specify the meeting as such in the notices calling it.

**366(2) [Qualification to s. 366(1)]** However, so long as a company holds its first annual general meeting within 18 months of its incorporation, it need not hold it in the year of its incorporation or in the following year.

**366(3) [Time between annual general meetings]** Not more than 15 months shall elapse between the date of one annual general meeting of a company and that of the next.

**366(4) [Penalty on default]** If default is made in holding a meeting in accordance with this section, the company and every officer of it who is in default is liable to a fine.

# 366A Election by private company to dispense with annual general meetings

**366A(1) [Power of private company]** A private company may elect (by elective resolution in accordance with section 379A) to dispense with the holding of annual general meetings.

**366A(2) [Effect of election]** An election has effect for the year in which it is made and subsequent years, but does not affect any liability already incurred by reason of default in holding an annual general meeting.

**366A(3) [Power of member to require meeting]** In any year in which an annual general meeting would be required to be held but for the election, and in which no such meeting has been held, any member of the company may, by notice to the company not later than three months before the end of the year, require the holding of an annual general meeting in that year.

**366A(4) [If s. 366A(3) notice given]** If such a notice is given, the provisions of section 366(1) and (4) apply with respect to the calling of the meeting and the consequences of default.

**366A(5) [If election ceases to have effect]** If the election ceases to have effect, the company is not obliged under section 366 to hold an annual general meeting in that year if, when the election ceases to have effect, less than three months of the year remains.

This does not affect any obligation of the company to hold an annual general meeting in that year in pursuance of a notice given under subsection (3).

**History**

S. 366A inserted by CA 1989, s. 115(2) as from 1 April 1990 subject to transitional and saving provisions (see SI 1990/355 (C 13), art. 4(a) and also art. 10).

# 367 Secretary of State's power to call meeting in default

**367(1) [Power of Secretary of State on application by member]** If default is made in holding a meeting in accordance with section 366, the Secretary of State may, on the application of any member of the company, call, or direct the calling of, a general meeting of the company and give such ancillary or consequential directions as he thinks expedient, including directions modifying or supplementing, in relation to the calling, holding and conduct of the meeting, the operation of the company's articles.

**367(2) [S. 367(1) directions]** The directions that may be given under subsection (1) include a direction that one member of the company present in person or by proxy shall be deemed to constitute a meeting.

**367(3) [Penalty for not complying with directions]** If default is made in complying with directions of the Secretary of State under subsection (1), the company and every officer of it who is in default is liable to a fine.

**367(4) [Status of general meeting under section]** A general meeting held under this section shall, subject to any directions of the Secretary of State, be deemed to be an annual general meeting of the company; but, where a meeting so held is not held in the year in which the default in holding the company's annual general meeting occurred, the meeting so held shall not be treated as the annual general meeting for the year in which it is held unless at that meeting the company resolves that it be so treated.

**367(5) [Copy of resolution to registrar]** Where a company so resolves, a copy of the resolution shall, within 15 days after its passing, be forwarded to the registrar of companies and recorded by him; and if default is made in complying with this subsection, the company and every officer of it who is in default is liable to a fine and, for continued contravention, to a daily default fine.

## 368 Extraordinary general meeting on members' requisition

**368(1) [Directors to convene meeting]** The directors of a company shall, on a members' requisition, forthwith proceed duly to convene an extraordinary general meeting of the company.

This applies notwithstanding anything in the company's articles.

**368(2) [Members' requisition]** A members' requisition is a requisition of–

(a) members of the company holding at the date of the deposit of the requisition not less than one-tenth of such of the paid-up capital of the company as at that date carries the right of voting at general meetings of the company; or

(b) in the case of a company not having a share capital, members of it representing not less than one-tenth of the total voting rights of all the members having at the date of deposit of the requisition a right to vote at general meetings.

**368(3) [Requirements of requisition]** The requisition must state the objects of the meeting, and must be signed by the requisitionists and deposited at the registered office of the company, and may consist of several documents in like form each signed by one or more requisitionists.

**368(4) [Where directors fail to convene meeting within 21 days]** If the directors do not within 21 days from the date of the deposit of the requisition proceed duly to convene a meeting, the requisitionists, or any of them representing more than one half of the total voting rights of all of them, may themselves convene a meeting, but any meeting so convened shall not be held after the expiration of 3 months from that date.

**368(5) [Convening of meeting]** A meeting convened under this section by requisitionists shall be convened in the same manner, as nearly as possible, as that in which meetings are to be convened by directors.

**368(6) [Reasonable expenses to be repaid by company]** Any reasonable expenses incurred by the requisitionists by reason of the failure of the directors duly to convene a meeting shall be repaid to the requisitionists by the company, and any sum so repaid shall be retained by the company out of any sums due or to become due from the company by way of fees or other remuneration in respect of their services to such of the directors as were in default.

**368(7) [Where s. 378(2) notice not given]** In the case of a meeting at which a resolution is to be proposed as a special resolution, the directors are deemed not to have duly convened the meeting if they do not give the notice required for special resolutions by section 378(2).

**368(8) [Where meeting not duly convened]** The directors are deemed not to have duly convened a meeting if they convene a meeting for a date more than 28 days after the date of the notice convening the meeting.

**History**
S. 368(8) added by CA 1989, s. 145 and Sch. 19, para. 9 as from 1 March 1990 (see SI 1990/142 (C 5), art. 5).

## 369 Length of notice for calling meetings

**369(1) [Minimum notice for meetings]** A provision of a company's articles is void in so far as it provides for the calling of a meeting of the company (other than an adjourned meeting) by a shorter notice than–

(a) in the case of the annual general meeting, 21 days' notice in writing; and

(b) in the case of a meeting other than an annual general meeting or a meeting for the passing of a special resolution–
   (i) 7 days' notice in writing in the case of an unlimited company, and
   (ii) otherwise, 14 days' notice in writing.

**369(2) [Usual notice]** Save in so far as the articles of a company make other provision in that behalf (not being a provision avoided by subsection (1)), a meeting of the company (other than an adjourned meeting) may be called–

(a) in the case of the annual general meeting, by 21 days' notice in writing; and

(b) in the case of a meeting other than an annual general meeting or a meeting for the passing of a special resolution–

(i) by 7 days' notice in writing in the case of an unlimited company, and
(ii) otherwise, 14 days' notice in writing.

**369(3) [Agreement to short notice]** Notwithstanding that a meeting is called by shorter notice than that specified in subsection (2) or in the company's articles (as the case may be), it is deemed to have been duly called if it is so agreed–

(a) in the case of a meeting called as the annual general meeting, by all the members entitled to attend and vote at it; and

(b) otherwise, by the requisite majority.

**369(4) [Requisite majority in s. 369(3)(b)]** The requisite majority for this purpose is a majority in number of the members having a right to attend and vote at the meeting, being a majority–

(a) together holding not less than 95 per cent in nominal value of the shares giving a right to attend and vote at the meeting; or

(b) in the case of a company not having a share capital, together representing not less than 95 per cent of the total voting rights at that meeting of all the members.

A private company may elect (by elective resolution in accordance with section 379A) that the above provisions shall have effect in relation to the company as if for the references to 95 per cent there were substituted references to such lesser percentage, but not less than 90 per cent, as may be specified in the resolution or subsequently determined by the company in general meeting.

**History**

In s. 369(4) the words from "A private company may elect" to the end inserted by CA 1989, s. 115(3) as from 1 April 1990 subject to transitional and saving provisions (see SI 1990/355 (C 13), art. 4(a) and also art. 10).

## 370 General provisions as to meetings and votes

**370(1) [If articles do not provide otherwise]** The following provisions have effect in so far as the articles of the company do not make other provision in that behalf.

**370(2) [Service of notice of meeting]** Notice of the meeting of a company shall be served on every member of it in the manner in which notices are required to be served by Table A (as for the time being in force).

**370(3) [Members calling meeting]** Two or more members holding not less than one-tenth of the issued share capital or, if the company does not have a share capital, not less than 5 per cent in number of the members of the company may call a meeting.

**370(4) [Quorum]** Two members personally present are a quorum.

**370(5) [Chairman]** Any member elected by the members present at a meeting may be chairman of it.

**370(6) [Votes]** In the case of a company originally having a share capital, every member has one vote in respect of each share or each £10 of stock held by him; and in any other case every member has one vote.

## 370A Quorum at meetings of the sole member

**370A** Notwithstanding any provisions to the contrary in the articles of a private company limited by shares or by guarantee having only one member, one member present in person or by proxy shall be a quorum.

**History**

S. 370A inserted by the Companies (Single Member Private Limited Companies) Regulations 1992 (SI 1992/1699), reg. 2, Sch., para. 5 as from 15 July 1992.

**Note**

The Companies (Single Member Private Limited Companies) Regulations 1992 (SI 1992/1699) implement the Twelfth EC Company Law Directive (89/667).

## 371 Power of court to order meeting

**371(1) [Impracticable to call meeting in accordance with Act]** If for any reason it is impracticable to call a meeting of a company in any manner in which meetings of that company may be called, or to conduct the meeting in manner prescribed by the articles or this Act, the court may, either of its own motion or on the application–

(a) of any director of the company, or

(b) of any member of the company who would be entitled to vote at the meeting,

order a meeting to be called, held and conducted in any manner the court thinks fit.

**371(2) [Ancillary directions]** Where such an order is made, the court may give such ancillary or consequential directions as it thinks expedient; and these may include a direction that one member of the company present in person or by proxy be deemed to constitute a meeting.

**371(3) [Status of meeting]** A meeting called, held and conducted in accordance with an order under subsection (1) is deemed for all purposes a meeting of the company duly called, held and conducted.

## 372 Proxies

**372(1) [Entitlement to appoint proxy]** Any member of a company entitled to attend and vote at a meeting of it is entitled to appoint another person (whether a member or not) as his proxy to attend and vote instead of him; and in the case of a private company a proxy appointed to attend and vote instead of a member has also the same right as the member to speak at the meeting.

**372(2) [Limitations re proxy]** But, unless the articles otherwise provide–

(a) subsection (1) does not apply in the case of a company not having a share capital; and

(b) a member of a private company is not entitled to appoint more than one proxy to attend on the same occasion; and

(c) a proxy is not entitled to vote except on a poll.

**372(3) [Statement re proxy in notice re meeting]** In the case of a company having a share capital, in every notice calling a meeting of the company there shall appear with reasonable prominence a statement that a member entitled to attend and vote is entitled to appoint a proxy or, where that is allowed, one or more proxies to attend and vote instead of him, and that a proxy need not also be a member.

**372(4) [Penalty on default re s. 372(3)]** If default is made in complying with subsection (3) as respects any meeting, every officer of the company who is in default is liable to a fine.

**372(5) [Certain provisions in articles void]** A provision contained in a company's articles is void in so far as it would have the effect of requiring the instrument appointing a proxy, or any other document necessary to show the validity of, or otherwise relating to, the appointment of a proxy, to be received by the company or any other person more than 48 hours before a meeting or adjourned meeting in order that the appointment may be effective.

**372(6) [Issue of invitations to appoint proxy to some members only]** If for the purpose of any meeting of a company invitations to appoint as proxy a person or one of a number of persons specified in the invitations are issued at the company's expense to some only of the members entitled to be sent a notice of the meeting and to vote at it by proxy, then every officer of the company who knowingly and wilfully authorises or permits their issue in that manner is liable to a fine.

However, an officer is not so liable by reason only of the issue to a member at his request in writing of a form of appointment naming the proxy, or of a list of persons willing to act as proxy, if the form or list is available on request in writing to every member entitled to vote at the meeting by proxy.

**372(7) [Application]** This section applies to meetings of any class of members of a company as it applies to general meetings of the company.

## 373 Right to demand a poll

**373(1) [Certain provisions in articles re excluding poll etc. void]** A provision contained in a company's articles is void in so far as it would have the effect either–

(a) of excluding the right to demand a poll at a general meeting on any question other than the election of the chairman of the meeting or the adjournment of the meeting; or

(b) of making ineffective a demand for a poll on any such question which is made either–
  (i) by not less than 5 members having the right to vote at the meeting; or
  (ii) by a member or members representing not less than one-tenth of the total voting rights of all the members having the right to vote at the meeting; or
  (iii) by a member or members holding shares in the company conferring a right to vote at the meeting, being shares on which an aggregate sum has been paid up equal to not less than one-tenth of the total sum paid up on all the shares conferring that right.

**373(2) [Proxy may demand poll]** The instrument appointing a proxy to vote at a meeting of a company is deemed also to confer authority to demand or join in demanding a poll; and for the purposes of subsection (1) a demand by a person as proxy for a member is the same as a demand by the member.

# 374 Voting on a poll

**374** On a poll taken at a meeting of a company or a meeting of any class of members of a company, a member entitled to more than one vote need not, if he votes, use all his votes or cast all the votes he uses in the same way.

# 375 Representation of corporations at meetings

**375(1) [Corporation as member or creditor]** A corporation, whether or not a company within the meaning of this Act, may–

(a) if it is a member of another corporation, being such a company, by resolution of its directors or other governing body authorise such person as it thinks fit to act as its representative at any meeting of the company or at any meeting of any class of members of the company;

(b) if it is a creditor (including a holder of debentures) of another corporation, being such a company, by resolution of its directors or other governing body authorise such person as it thinks fit to act as its representative at any meeting of creditors of the company held in pursuance of this Act or of rules made under it, or in pursuance of the provisions contained in any debenture or trust deed, as the case may be.

**375(2) [Person authorised under s. 375(1)]** A person so authorised is entitled to exercise the same powers on behalf of the corporation which he represents as that corporation could exercise if it were an individual shareholder, creditor or debenture-holder of the other company.

RESOLUTIONS

# 376 Circulation of members' resolutions

**376(1) [Company to supply details of proposed resolutions etc.]** Subject to the section next following, it is the duty of a company, on the requisition in writing of such number of members as is specified below and (unless the company otherwise resolves) at the expense of the requisitionists–

(a) to give to members of the company entitled to receive notice of the next annual general meeting notice of any resolution which may properly be moved and is intended to be moved at that meeting;

(b) to circulate to members entitled to have notice of any general meeting sent to them any statement of not more than 1,000 words with respect to the matter referred to in any proposed resolution or the business to be dealt with at that meeting.

**376(2) [Number of members for s. 376(1) requisition]** The number of members necessary for a requisition under subsection (1) is–

(a) any number representing not less than one-twentieth of the total voting rights of all the members having at the date of the requisition a right to vote at the meeting to which the requisition relates; or

(b) not less than 100 members holding shares in the company on which there has been paid up an average sum, per member, of not less than £100.

**376(3) [Service of notice re resolution to members entitled to notice]** Notice of any such resolution shall be given, and any such statement shall be circulated, to members of the company entitled to have notice of the meeting sent to them, by serving a copy of the resolution or statement on each such member in any manner permitted for service of notice of the meeting.

**376(4) [Notice to other members]** Notice of any such resolution shall be given to any other member of the company by giving notice of the general effect of the resolution in any manner permitted for giving him notice of meetings of the company.

**376(5) [Compliance with s. 376(3), (4)]** For compliance with subsections (3) and (4), the copy must be served, or notice of the effect of the resolution be given (as the case may be), in the same manner and (so far as practicable) at the same time as notice of the meeting; and, where it is not practicable for it to be served or given at the same time, it must be served or given as soon as practicable thereafter.

**376(6) [Business at annual general meeting]** The business which may be dealt with at an annual general meeting includes any resolution of which notice is given in accordance with this section; and for purposes of this subsection notice is deemed to have been so given notwithstanding the accidental omission, in giving it, of one or more members. This has effect notwithstanding anything in the company's articles.

**376(7) [Penalty on default]** In the event of default in complying with this section, every officer of the company who is in default is liable to a fine.

## 377 In certain cases, compliance with s. 376 not required

**377(1) [Situations where company bound under s. 376]** A company is not bound under section 376 to give notice of a resolution or to circulate a statement unless–

(a) a copy of the requisition signed by the requisitionists (or two or more copies which between them contain the signatures of all the requisitionists) is deposited at the registered office of the company–
  (i) in the case of a requisition requiring notice of a resolution, not less than 6 weeks before the meeting, and
  (ii) otherwise, not less than one week before the meeting; and

(b) there is deposited or tendered with the requisition a sum reasonably sufficient to meet the company's expenses in giving effect to it.

**377(2) [Extension of s. 377(1)]** But if, after a copy of a requisition requiring notice of a resolution has been deposited at the company's registered office, an annual general meeting is called for a date 6 weeks or less after the copy has been deposited, the copy (though not deposited within the time required by subsection (1)) is deemed properly deposited for the purposes of that subsection.

**377(3) [Exception to s. 376 where rights abused to secure publicity etc.]** The company is also not bound under section 376 to circulate a statement if, on the application either of the company or of any other person who claims to be aggrieved, the court is satisfied that the rights conferred by that section are being abused to secure needless publicity for defamatory matter; and the court may order the company's costs on such an application to be paid in whole or in part by the requisitionists, notwithstanding that they are not parties to the application.

## 378 Extraordinary and special resolutions

**378(1) [Extraordinary resolution]** A resolution is an extraordinary resolution when it has been passed by a majority of not less than three-fourths of such members as (being entitled to do so) vote in person or, where proxies are allowed, by proxy, at a general meeting of which notice specifying the intention to propose the resolution as an extraordinary resolution has been duly given.

**378(2) [Special resolution]** A resolution is a special resolution when it has been passed by such a majority as is required for the passing of an extraordinary resolution and at a general meeting of which not less than 21 days' notice, specifying the intention to propose the resolution as a special resolution, has been duly given.

**378(3) [Agreement to short notice re special resolution]** If it is so agreed by a majority in number of the members having the right to attend and vote at such a meeting, being a majority–

(a) together holding not less than 95 per cent in nominal value of the shares giving that right; or

(b) in the case of a company not having a share capital, together representing not less than 95 per cent of the total voting rights at that meeting of all the members,

a resolution may be proposed and passed as a special resolution at a meeting of which less than 21 days' notice has been given.

A private company may elect (by elective resolution in accordance with section 379A) that the above provisions shall have effect in relation to the company as if for the references to 95 per cent there were substituted references to such lesser percentage, but not less than 90 per cent, as may be specified in the resolution or subsequently determined by the company in general meeting.

**History**

In s. 378(3) the words from "A private company may elect" to the end inserted by CA 1989, s. 115(3) as from 1 April 1990 subject to transitional and saving provisions (see SI 1990/355 (C 13), art. 4(a) and also art. 10).

**378(4) [Declaration of chairman conclusive evidence]** At any meeting at which an extraordinary resolution or a special resolution is submitted to be passed, a declaration by the chairman that the resolution is carried is, unless a poll is demanded, conclusive evidence of the fact without proof of the number or proportion of the votes recorded in favour of or against the resolution.

**378(5) [Majority on poll]** In computing the majority on a poll demanded on the question that an extraordinary resolution or a special resolution be passed, reference is to be had to the number of votes cast for and against the resolution.

**378(6) [Notice of meeting]** For purposes of this section, notice of a meeting is deemed duly given, and the meeting duly held, when the notice is given and the meeting held in the manner provided by this Act or the company's articles.

## 379 Resolution requiring special notice

**379(1) [28 days' notice of intention to move]** Where by any provision of this Act special notice is required of a resolution, the resolution is not effective unless notice of the intention to move it has been given to the company at least 28 days before the meeting at which it is moved.

**379(2) [Notice to members of resolution]** The company shall give its members notice of any such resolution at the same time and in the same manner as it gives notice of the meeting or, if that is not practicable, shall give them notice either by advertisement in a newspaper having an appropriate circulation or in any other mode allowed by the company's articles, at least 21 days before the meeting.

**379(3) [Where notice deemed properly given]** If, after notice of the intention to move such a resolution has been given to the company, a meeting is called for a date 28 days or less after the notice has been given, the notice is deemed properly given, though not given within the time required.

## 379A Elective resolution of private company

**379A(1) ["Elective resolution"]** An election by a private company for the purposes of–

(a) section 80A (election as to duration of authority to allot shares),

(b) section 252 (election to dispense with laying of accounts and reports before general meeting),

(c) section 366A (election to dispense with holding of annual general meeting),

(d) section 369(4) or 378(3) (election as to majority required to authorise short notice of meeting), or

(e) section 386 (election to dispense with appointment of auditors annually),

shall be made by resolution of the company in general meeting in accordance with this section.

Such a resolution is referred to in this Act as an "elective resolution".

**379A(2) [Conditions for resolution to be effective]** An elective resolution is not effective unless–

(a) at least 21 days' notice in writing is given of the meeting, stating that an elective resolution is to be proposed and stating the terms of the resolution, and

(b) the resolution is agreed to at the meeting, in person or by proxy, by all the members entitled to attend and vote at the meeting.

**379A(2A) [Agreement of members]** An elective resolution is effective notwithstanding the fact that less than 21 days' notice in writing of the meeting is given if all the members entitled to attend and vote at the meeting so agree.

**History**
S. 379A(2A) inserted by the Deregulation (Resolutions of Private Companies) Order 1996 (SI 1996/1471), art. 1, 2 as from 19 June 1996.

**379A(3) [Revocation of resolution]** The company may revoke an elective resolution by passing an ordinary resolution to that effect.

**379A(4) [Effect of re-registration as public company]** An elective resolution shall cease to have effect if the company is re-registered as a public company.

**379A(5) [Contrary provision in memorandum or articles]** An elective resolution may be passed or revoked in accordance with this section, and the provisions referred to in subsection (1) have effect, notwithstanding any contrary provision in the company's articles of association.

**History**
S. 379A inserted by CA 1989, s. 116(1), (2) as from 1 April 1990 (see SI 1990/355 (C 13), art. 4(a)).

**Note**
See CA 1989, s. 117 for Secretary of State's power to make further provision by regulations.

# 380 Registration, etc. of resolutions and agreements

**380(1) [Copies of resolutions etc. to registrar within 15 days]** A copy of every resolution or agreement to which this section applies shall, within 15 days after it is passed or made, be forwarded to the registrar of companies and recorded by him; and it must be either a printed copy or else a copy in some other form approved by the registrar.

**380(2) [Copies of resolution etc. to be attached to articles]** Where articles have been registered, a copy of every such resolution or agreement for the time being in force shall be embodied in or annexed to every copy of the articles issued after the passing of the resolution or the making of the agreement.

**380(3) [Where articles in s. 380(2) not registered]** Where articles have not been registered, a printed copy of every such resolution or agreement shall be forwarded to any member at his request on payment of 5 pence or such less sum as the company may direct.

**380(4) [Application]** This section applies to–

(a) special resolutions;

(b) extraordinary resolutions;

(bb) an elective resolution or a resolution revoking such a resolution;

(c) resolutions or agreements which have been agreed to by all the members of a company but which, if not so agreed to, would not have been effective for their purpose unless (as the case may be) they had been passed as special resolutions or as extraordinary resolutions;

(d) resolutions or agreements which have been agreed to by all the members of some class of shareholders but which, if not so agreed to, would not have been effective for their purpose unless they had been passed by some particular majority or otherwise in some particular manner, and all resolutions or agreements which effectively bind all the members of any class of shareholders though not agreed to by all those members;

(e) a resolution passed by the directors of a company in compliance with a direction under section 31(2) (change of name on Secretary of State's direction);

(f) a resolution of a company to give, vary, revoke or renew an authority to the directors for the purposes of section 80 (allotment of relevant securities);

(g) a resolution of the directors passed under section 147(2) (alteration of memorandum on company ceasing to be a public company, following acquisition of its own shares);

(h) a resolution conferring, varying, revoking or renewing authority under section 166 (market purchase of company's own shares);

(j) a resolution for voluntary winding up, passed under section 84(1)(a) of the Insolvency Act;

(k) a resolution passed by the directors of an old public company, under section 2(1) of the Consequential Provisions Act, that the company should be re-registered as a public company;

(l) a resolution of the directors passed by virtue of regulation 16(2) of the Uncertificated Securities Regulations 1995 (which allow title to a company's shares to be evidenced and transferred without written instrument); and

(m) a resolution of a company passed by virtue of regulation 16(6) of the Uncertificated Securities Regulations 1995 (which prevents or reverses a resolution of the directors under regulation 16(2) of those Regulations).

**History**

S. 380(4)(bb) inserted by CA 1989, s. 116(1), (3) as from 1 April 1990 (see SI 1990/355 (C 13), art. 4(a)); in s. 380(4)(j) the words "section 84(1)(a) of the Insolvency Act" substituted for the former words "section 572(1)(a)" by Insolvency Act 1986, s. 439(1) and Sch. 13 as from 29 December 1986 (see IA 1986, s. 443 and SI 1986/1924 (C 71)); and s. 380(4)(l), (m) added by the Uncertificated Securities Regulations 1995 (SI 1995/3272), reg. 1, 40(3) as from 19 December 1995.

**380(5) [Penalty on default re s. 380(1)]** If a company fails to comply with subsection (1), the company and every officer of it who is in default is liable to a fine and, for continued contravention, to a daily default fine.

**380(6) [Penalty on default re s. 380(2), (3)]** If a company fails to comply with subsection (2) or (3), the company and every officer of it who is in default is liable to a fine.

**380(7) [Liquidator officer]** For purposes of subsections (5) and (6), a liquidator of a company is deemed an officer of it.

# 381 Resolution passed at adjourned meeting

**381** Where a resolution is passed at an adjourned meeting of–

(a) a company;

(b) the holders of any class of shares in a company;

(c) the directors of a company;

the resolution is for all purposes to be treated as having been passed on the date on which it was in fact passed, and is not to be deemed passed on any earlier date.

WRITTEN RESOLUTIONS OF PRIVATE COMPANIES

# 381A Written resolutions of private companies

**381A(1) [Matters may be done by written resolution]** Anything which in the case of a private company may be done–

(a) by resolution of the company in general meeting, or

(b) by resolution of a meeting of any class of members of the company,

may be done, without a meeting and without any previous notice being required, by resolution in writing signed by or on behalf of all the members of the company who at the date of the resolution would be entitled to attend and vote at such meeting.

**381A(2) [Signatures]** The signatures need not be on a single document provided each is on a document which accurately states the terms of the resolution.

**381A(3) [Date of resolution]** The date of the resolution means when the resolution is signed by or on behalf of the last member to sign.

**381A(4) [Effect of resolution]** A resolution agreed to in accordance with this section has effect as if passed–

(a) by the company in general meeting, or

(b) by a meeting of the relevant class of members of the company,

as the case may be; and any reference in any enactment to a meeting at which a resolution is passed or to members voting in favour of a resolution shall be construed accordingly.

**381A(5) [Reference to date of passing of resolution]** Any reference in any enactment to the date of passing of a resolution is, in relation to a resolution agreed to in accordance with this section, a reference to the date of the resolution.

**History**

In s. 381A(5) words formerly appearing after "reference to the date of the resolution" omitted and repealed by the Deregulation (Resolutions of Private Companies) Order 1996 (SI 1996/1471), art. 1, 3(2)(a) as from 19 June 1996; the former words read as follows:

"unless section 381B(4) applies in which case it shall be construed as a reference to the date from which the resolution has effect."

**381A(6) [Types of resolutions otherwise required]** A resolution may be agreed to in accordance with this section which would otherwise be required to be passed as a special, extraordinary or elective resolution; and any reference in any enactment to a special, extraordinary or elective resolution includes such a resolution.

**381A(7) [Sch. 15A: exceptions, procedure]** This section has effect subject to the exceptions specified in Part I of Schedule 15A; and in relation to certain descriptions of resolution under this section the procedural requirements of this Act have effect with the adaptations specified in Part II of that Schedule.

**History**

See history note after s. 381C.

## 381B Duty to notify auditors of proposed written resolution

**381B(1) [Copy of proposed resolution to auditors]** If a director or secretary of a company–

(a) knows that it is proposed to seek agreement to a resolution in accordance with section 381A, and

(b) knows the terms of the resolution,

he shall, if the company has auditors, secure that a copy of the resolution is sent to them, or that they are otherwise notified of its contents, at or before the time the resolution is supplied to a member for signature.

**381B(2) [Penalty on default]** A person who fails to comply with subsection (1) is liable to a fine.

**381B(3) [Defence]** In any proceedings for an offence under this section it is a defence for the accused to prove–

(a) that the circumstances were such that it was not practicable for him to comply with subsection (1), or

(b) that he believed on reasonable grounds that a copy of the resolution had been sent to the company's auditors or that they had otherwise been informed of its contents.

**381B(4) [Effect on resolutions]** Nothing in this section affects the validity of any resolution.

**History**

S. 381B substituted by the Deregulation (Resolutions of Private Companies) Order 1996 (SI 1996/1471), art. 1, 3 as from 19 June 1996; s. 381B formerly read as follows:

"**381B Right of auditors in relation to written resolution**

**381B(1)** A copy of any written resolution proposed to be agreed to in accordance with section 381A shall be sent to the company's auditors.

**(2)** If the resolution concerns the auditors as auditors, they may within seven days from the day on which they receive the copy give notice to the company stating their opinion that the resolution should be considered by the company in general meeting or, as the case may be, by a meeting of the relevant class of members of the company.

**(3)** A written resolution shall not have effect unless–

(a) the auditors notify the company that in their opinion the resolution–

(i) does not concern them as auditors, or

(ii) does so concern them but need not be considered by the company in general meeting or, as the case may be, by a meeting of the relevant class of members of the company, or

(b) the period for giving a notice under subsection (2) expires without any notice having been given in accordance with that subsection.

**(4)** A written resolution previously agreed to in accordance with section 381A shall not have effect until that notification is given or, as the case may be, that period expires."

For original provisions, see history note after s. 381C.

## 381C Written resolutions: supplementary provisions

**381C(1) [Provision in memorandum or articles]** Sections 381A and 381B have effect notwithstanding any provision of the company's memorandum or articles, but do not prejudice any power conferred by any such provision.

**History**
In s. 381C the words from ", but do not prejudice" to the end inserted by the Deregulation (Resolutions of Private Companies) Order 1996 (SI 1996/1471), art. 1, 4 as from 19 June 1996.

**381C(2) [Things not affected by s. 381A, 381B]** Nothing in those sections affects any enactment of rule of law–

(a) things done otherwise than by passing a resolution, or

(b) cases in which a resolution is treated as having been passed, or a person is precluded from alleging that a resolution has not been duly passed.

**History**
S. 381A–381C inserted by CA 1989, s. 113(1), (2) as from 1 April 1990 (see SI 1990/355 (C 13), art. 4(a)).

RECORDS OF PROCEEDINGS

# 382 Minutes of meetings

**382(1) [Minutes to be entered in books]** Every company shall cause minutes of all proceedings of general meetings, all proceedings at meetings of its directors and, where there are managers, all proceedings at meetings of its managers to be entered in books kept for that purpose.

**382(2) [Minutes signed by chairman evidence]** Any such minute, if purporting to be signed by the chairman of the meeting at which the proceedings were had, or by the chairman of the next succeeding meeting, is evidence of the proceedings.

**382(3) [Where shadow director declaring interest by s. 317(8)]** Where a shadow director by means of a notice required by section 317(8) declares an interest in a contract or proposed contract, this section applies–

(a) if it is a specific notice under paragraph (a) of that subsection, as if the declaration had been made at the meeting there referred to, and

(b) otherwise, as if it had been made at the meeting of the directors next following the giving of the notice;

and the making of the declaration is in either case deemed to form part of the proceedings at the meeting.

**382(4) [Where minutes kept meeting deemed held, etc.]** Where minutes have been made in accordance with this section of the proceedings at any general meeting of the company or meeting of directors or managers, then, until the contrary is proved, the meeting is deemed duly held and convened, and all proceedings had at the meeting to have been duly had; and all appointments of directors, managers or liquidators are deemed valid.

**382(5) [Penalty on default re s. 382(1)]** If a company fails to comply with subsection (1), the company and every officer of it who is in default is liable to a fine and, for continued contravention, to a daily default fine.

# 382A Recording of written resolutions

**382A(1) [Duty of company to make record]** Where a written resolution is agreed to in accordance with section 381A which has effect as if agreed by the company in general meeting, the company shall cause a record of the resolution (and of the signatures) to be entered in a book in the same way as minutes of proceedings of a general meeting of the company.

**382A(2) [Record evidence, deemed compliance]** Any such record, if purporting to be signed by a director of the company or by the company secretary, is evidence of the proceedings in agreeing to the resolution; and where a record is made in accordance with this section, then, until the contrary is proved, the requirements of this Act with respect to those proceedings shall be deemed to be complied with.

**382A(3) [Penalty, inspection]** Section 382(5) (penalties) applies in relation to a failure to comply with subsection (1) above as it applies in relation to a failure to comply with subsection (1) of that section; and section 383 (inspection of minute books) applies in relation to a record made in accordance with this section as it applies in relation to the minutes of a general meeting.

**History**
S. 382A inserted by CA 1989, s. 113(1), (3) as from 1 April 1990 (see SI 1990/355 (C 13), art. 4(a)).

## 382B Recording of decisions by the sole member

**382B(1) [Duty to provide written record]** Where a private company limited by shares or by guarantee has only one member and he takes any decision which may be taken by the company in general meeting and which has effect as if agreed by the company in general meeting, he shall (unless that decision is taken by way of a written resolution) provide the company with a written record of that decision.

**382B(2) [Offence, penalty]** If the sole member fails to comply with subsection (1) he shall be liable to a fine.

**382B(3) [Effect of non-compliance within s. 382B(1)]** Failure by the sole member to comply with subsection (1) shall not affect the validity of any decision referred to in that subsection.

**History**
S. 382B inserted by the Companies (Single Member Private Limited Companies) Regulations 1992 (SI 1992/1699), reg. 2, Sch., para. 6(1) as from 15 July 1992.

**Note**
The Companies (Single Member Private Limited Companies) Regulations 1992 (SI 1992/1699) implement the Twelfth EC Company Law Directive (89/667).

## 383 Inspection of minute books

**383(1) [Books at registered office and open to inspection]** The books containing the minutes of proceedings of any general meeting of a company held on or after 1st November 1929 shall be kept at the company's registered office, and shall be open to the inspection of any member without charge.

**History**
In s. 383(1) the words "during business hours" formerly appearing after the words "and shall" omitted and repealed by CA 1989, s. 143(9)(a), 212 and Sch. 24 as from 1 November 1991 (see SI 1991/1996 (C 57), art. 2(2)(b), (c)).

**383(2)** (Omitted and repealed by Companies Act 1989, s. 143(9)(b), 212 and Sch. 24 as from 1 November 1991.)

**History**
In regard to the date of the above omission and repeal see SI 1991/1996 (C 57), art. 2(2)(c); s. 383(2) formerly read as follows:

"The reference to business hours is subject to such reasonable restrictions as the company may by its articles or in general meeting impose, but so that not less than 2 hours in each day be allowed for inspection."

**383(3) [Copy of minutes]** Any member shall be entitled on payment of such fee as may be prescribed to be furnished, within 7 days after he has made a request in that behalf to the company, with a copy of any such minutes as are referred to above.

**History**
In s. 383(3) the words "on payment of such fee as may be prescribed" inserted and the words "at a charge of not more than $2^1/_2$ pence for every 100 words" formerly appearing at the end omitted and repealed by CA 1989, s. 143(9)(c), 212 and Sch. 24 as from 1 November 1991 (see SI 1991/1996 (C 57), art. 2(2)(b), (c)).

**Note**
See the Companies (Inspection and Copying of Registers, Indices and Documents) Regulations 1991 (SI 1991/1998).

**383(4) [Penalty re refusal of inspection etc.]** If an inspection required under this section is refused or if a copy required under this section is not sent within the proper time, the company and every officer of it who is in default is liable in respect of each offence to a fine.

**383(5) [Court may compel inspection etc.]** In the case of any such refusal or default, the court may by order compel an immediate inspection of the books in respect of all proceedings of general meetings, or direct that the copies required be sent to the persons requiring them.

# Chapter V – Auditors

### APPOINTMENT OF AUDITORS

## 384 Duty to appoint auditors

**384(1) [Every company to have auditor(s)]** Every company shall appoint an auditor or auditors in accordance with this Chapter.

This is subject to section 388A (certain companies exempt from obligation to appoint auditors).

**History**
In s. 384(1) the words "certain companies" substituted for the former words "dormant company" by the Companies Act 1985 (Audit Exemption) Regulations 1994 (SI 1994/1935), reg. 4 and Sch. 1, para. 4 as from 11 August 1994.

**384(2) [Appointment]** Auditors shall be appointed in accordance with section 385 (appointment at general meeting at which accounts are laid), except in the case of a private company which has elected to dispense with the laying of accounts in which case the appointment shall be made in accordance with section 385A.

**384(3) [End of time for appointing auditors]** References in this Chapter to the end of the time for appointing auditors are to the end of the time within which an appointment must be made under section 385(2) or 385A(2), according to whichever of those sections applies.

**384(4) [Private companies may dispense with auditors]** Sections 385 and 385A have effect subject to section 386 under which a private company may elect to dispense with the obligation to appoint auditors annually.

**History**
See history note after s. 394A.

## 385 Appointment at general meeting at which accounts laid

**385(1) [Application]** This section applies to every public company and to a private company which has not elected to dispense with the laying of accounts.

**385(2) [Duty of company]** The company shall, at each general meeting at which accounts are laid, appoint an auditor or auditors to hold office from the conclusion of that meeting until the conclusion of the next general meeting at which accounts are laid.

**385(3) [First auditors]** The first auditors of the company may be appointed by the directors at any time before the first general meeting of the company at which accounts are laid; and auditors so appointed shall hold office until the conclusion of that meeting.

**385(4) [If directors fail to exercise powers]** If the directors fail to exercise their powers under subsection (3), the powers may be exercised by the company in general meeting.

**History**
See history note after s. 394A.

## 385A Appointment by private company which is not obliged to lay accounts

**385A(1) [Application]** This section applies to a private company which has elected in accordance with section 252 to dispense with the laying of accounts before the company in general meeting.

**385A(2) [Appointment]** Auditors shall be appointed by the company in general meeting before the end of the period of 28 days beginning with the day on which copies of the company's annual accounts for the previous financial year are sent to members under section 238 or, if notice is given under section 253(2) requiring the laying of the accounts before the company in general meeting, the conclusion of that meeting.

Auditors so appointed shall hold office from the end of that period or, as the case may be, the conclusion of that meeting until the end of the time for appointing auditors for the next financial year.

**385A(3) [First auditors]** The first auditors of the company may be appointed by the directors at any time before–

(a) the end of the period of 28 days beginning with the day on which copies of the company's first annual accounts are sent to members under section 238, or

(b) if notice is given under section 253(2) requiring the laying of the accounts before the company in general meeting, the beginning of that meeting;

and auditors so appointed shall hold office until the end of that period or, as the case may be, the conclusion of that meeting.

**385A(4) [If directors fail to exercise powers]** If the directors fail to exercise their powers under subsection (3), the powers may be exercised by the company in general meeting.

**385A(5) [Continuation of office]** Auditors holding office when the election is made shall, unless the company in general meeting determines otherwise, continue to hold office until the end of the time for appointing auditors for the next financial year; and auditors holding office when an election ceases to have effect shall continue to hold office until the conclusion of the next general meeting of the company at which accounts are laid.

**History**
See history note after s. 394A.

## 386 Election by private company to dispense with annual appointment

**386(1) [Power of private company]** A private company may elect (by elective resolution in accordance with section 379A) to dispense with the obligation to appoint auditors annually.

**386(2) [Deemed re-appointment]** When such an election is in force the company's auditors shall be deemed to be re-appointed for each succeeding financial year on the expiry of the time for appointing auditors for that year, unless–

(a) the directors of the company have taken advantage of the exemption conferred by section 249A or 249AA, or

(b) a resolution has been passed under section 393 to the effect that their appointment should be brought to an end.

**History**
S. 386(2)(a) substituted by the Companies Act 1985 (Audit Exemption) (Amendment) Regulations 2000 (SI 2000/1430), reg. 1, 8(8) as from 26 May 2000 in relation to annual accounts and reports in respect of financial years ending on or after 26 July 2000; s. 386(2)(a) formerly read as follows:

"(a) a resolution has been passed under section 250 by virtue of which the company is exempt from the obligation to appoint auditors, or".

**386(3) [If election ceases]** If the election ceases to be in force, the auditors then holding office shall continue to hold office–

(a) where section 385 then applies, until the conclusion of the next general meeting of the company at which accounts are laid;

(b) where section 385A then applies, until the end of the time for appointing auditors for the next financial year under that section.

**386(4) [Compensation or damages for loss of office]** No account shall be taken of any loss of the opportunity of further deemed re-appointment under this section in ascertaining the amount of any compensation or damages payable to an auditor on his ceasing to hold office for any reason.

**History**
See history note after s. 394A.

## 387 Appointment by Secretary of State in default of appointment by company

**387(1) [Power of Secretary of State]** If in any case no auditors are appointed, re-appointed or deemed to be re-appointed before the end of the time for appointing auditors, the Secretary of State may appoint a person to fill the vacancy.

**387(2) [Notice by company – offence, penalty]** In such a case the company shall within one week of the end of the time for appointing auditors give notice to the Secretary of State of his power having become exercisable.

If a company fails to give the notice required by this subsection, the company and every officer of it who is in default is guilty of an offence and liable to a fine and, for continued contravention, to a daily default fine.

**History**
See history note after s. 394A.

## 388 Filling of casual vacancies

**388(1) [Power of directors, general meeting]** The directors, or the company in general meeting, may fill a casual vacancy in the office of auditor.

**388(2) [Continuation to act in vacancy]** While such a vacancy continues, any surviving or continuing auditor or auditors may continue to act.

**388(3) [Special notice for certain resolutions]** Special notice is required for a resolution at a general meeting of a company–

(a) filling a casual vacancy in the office of auditor, or

(b) re-appointing as auditor a retiring auditor who was appointed by the directors to fill a casual vacancy.

**388(4) [Duty of company on receipt of notice]** On receipt of notice of such an intended resolution the company shall forthwith send a copy of it–

(a) to the person proposed to be appointed, and

(b) if the casual vacancy was caused by the resignation of an auditor, to the auditor who resigned.

**History**

See history note after s. 394A.

## 388A Certain companies exempt from obligation to appoint auditors

**388A(1) [Extended exemption]** A company which by virtue of section 249A (certain categories of small company) or section 249AA (dormant companies) is exempt from the provisions of Part VII relating to the audit of accounts is also exempt from the obligation to appoint auditors.

**History**

In s. 388A(1) the words "section 249AA" substituted for the former words "section 250" by the Companies Act 1985 (Audit Exemption) (Amendment) Regulations 2000 (SI 2000/1430), reg. 1, 8(9) as from 26 May 2000 in relation to annual accounts and reports in respect of financial years ending on or after 26 July 2000.

**388A(2) [Cessation of exemption]** The following provisions apply if a company which has been exempt from those provisions ceases to be so exempt.

**388A(3) [Appointment where accounts being laid]** Where section 385 applies (appointment at general meeting at which accounts are laid), the directors may appoint auditors at any time before the next meeting of the company at which accounts are to be laid; and auditors so appointed shall hold office until the conclusion of that meeting.

**388A(4) [Appointment where accounts not being laid]** Where section 385A applies (appointment by private company not obliged to lay accounts), the directors may appoint auditors at any time before–

(a) the end of the period of 28 days beginning with the day on which copies of the company's annual accounts are next sent to members under section 238, or

(b) if notice is given under section 253(2) requiring the laying of the accounts before the company in general meeting, the beginning of that meeting;

and auditors so appointed shall hold office until the end of that period or, as the case may be, the conclusion of that meeting.

**388A(5) [Directors' failure to appoint]** If the directors fail to exercise their powers under subsection (3) or (4), the powers may be exercised by the company in general meeting.

**History**

S. 388A substituted by the Companies Act 1989 (Audit Exemption) Regulations 1994 (SI 1994/1935), reg. 3 as from 11 August 1994; former s. 388A, inserted by CA 1989, s. 119 as from 1 April 1990 subject to transitional and saving provisions (see SI 1990/355 (C 13), art. 4(a), 10 and Sch. 4), read as follows:

"**388A** Dormant company exempt from obligation to appoint auditors

**388A(1)** A company which by virtue of section 250 (dormant companies: exemption from provisions as to audit of accounts) is exempt from the provisions of Part VII relating to the audit of accounts is also exempt from the obligation to appoint auditors.

**(2)** The following provisions apply if the exemption ceases.

**(3)** Where section 385 applies (appointment at general meeting at which accounts are laid), the directors may appoint auditors at any time before the next meeting of the company at which accounts are to be laid; and auditors so appointed shall hold office until the conclusion of that meeting.

**(4)** Where section 385A applies (appointment by private company not obliged to lay accounts), the directors may appoint auditors at any time before–

(a) the end of the period of 28 days beginning with the day on which copies of the company's annual accounts are next sent to members under section 238, or

(b) if notice is given under section 253(2) requiring the laying of the accounts before the company in general meeting, the beginning of that meeting;

and auditors so appointed shall hold office until the end of that period or, as the case may be, the conclusion of that meeting.

**(5)** If the directors fail to exercise their powers under subsection (3) or (4), the powers may be exercised by the company in general meeting."

See also history note after s. 394A.

# 389 Qualification for appointment as auditor

**389** (Repealed by Companies Act 1989, s. 212 and Sch. 24 as from 1 October 1991.)

**History**

In regard to the date of the above repeal see SI 1991/1996 (C 57), art. 2(1)(c)(i); s. 389 formerly read as follows:

"**389(1)** Subject to the next subsection, a person is not qualified for appointment as auditor of a company unless either–

(a) he is a member of a body of accountants established in the United Kingdom and for the time being recognised for the purposes of this provision by the Secretary of State; or

(b) he is for the time being authorised by the Secretary of State to be so appointed, as having similar qualifications obtained outside the United Kingdom or else he retains an authorisation formerly granted by the Board of Trade or the Secretary of State under section 161(1)(b) of the Companies Act 1948 (adequate knowledge and experience, or pre-1947 practice).

**(2)** Subject to subsections (6) to (8) below, a person is qualified for appointment as auditor of an unquoted company if he retains an authorisation granted by the Board of Trade or the Secretary of State under section 13(1) of the Companies Act 1967.

In this subsection–

(a) **"unquoted company"** means a company in the case of which, at the time of the person's appointment, the following condition is satisfied, namely, that no shares or debentures of the company, or of a body corporate of which it is the subsidiary, have been quoted on a stock exchange (whether in Great Britain or elsewhere) to the public for subscription or purchase, and

(b) **"company"** does not include a company that carries on business as the promoter of a trading stamp scheme within the meaning of the Trading Stamps Act 1964.

**(3)** Subject to the next subsection, the bodies of accountants recognised for the purposes of subsection (1)(a) are–

(a) the Institute of Chartered Accountants in England and Wales,

(b) the Institute of Chartered Accountants of Scotland,

(c) the Chartered Association of Certified Accountants, and

(d) the Institute of Chartered Accountants in Ireland.

**(4)** The Secretary of State may by regulations in a statutory instrument amend subsection (3) by adding or deleting any body, but shall not make regulations–

(a) adding any body, or

(b) deleting any body which has not consented in writing to its deletion,

unless he has published notice of his intention to do so in the London and Edinburgh Gazettes at least 4 months before making the regulations.

**(5)** The Secretary of State may refuse an authorisation under subsection (1)(b) to a person as having qualifications obtained outside the United Kingdom if it appears to him that the country in which the qualifications were obtained does not confer on persons qualified in the United Kingdom privileges corresponding to those conferred by that subsection.

**(6)** None of the following persons is qualified for appointment as auditor of a company–

(a) an officer or servant of the company;

(b) a person who is a partner of or in the employment of an officer or servant of the company;

(c) a body corporate;

and for this purpose an auditor of a company is not to be regarded as either officer or servant of it.

**(7)** A person is also not qualified for appointment as auditor of a company if he is, under subsection (6), disqualified for appointment as auditor of any other body corporate which is that company's subsidiary or holding company or a subsidiary of that company's holding company, or would be so disqualified if the body corporate were a company.

**(8)** Notwithstanding subsections (1), (6) and (7), a Scottish firm is qualified for appointment as auditor of a company if, but only if, all the partners are qualified for appointment as auditor of it.

**(9)** No person shall act as auditor of a company at a time when he knows that he is disqualified for appointment to that office; and if an auditor of a company to his knowledge becomes so disqualified during his term of office he shall thereupon vacate his office and give notice in writing to the company that he has vacated it by reason of that disqualification.

**(10)** A person who acts as auditor in contravention of subsection (9), or fails without reasonable excuse to give notice of vacating his office as required by that subsection, is guilty of an offence and liable to a fine and, for continued contravention, to a daily default fine."

**Note**

See now CA 1989, Pt. II.

## RIGHTS OF AUDITORS

# 389A Rights to information

**389A(1) [Auditors' right of access]** The auditors of a company have a right of access at all times to the company's books, accounts and vouchers, and are entitled to require from the company's officers such information and explanations as they think necessary for the performance of their duties as auditors.

**389A(2) [Offence, penalty]** An officer of a company commits an offence if he knowingly or recklessly makes to the company's auditors a statement (whether written or oral) which–

(a) conveys or purports to convey any information or explanations which the auditors require, or are entitled to require, as auditors of the company, and
(b) is misleading, false or deceptive in a material particular.

A person guilty of an offence under this subsection is liable to imprisonment or a fine, or both.

**389A(3) [Duty of subsidiary undertaking, offence and penalty]** A subsidiary undertaking which is a body corporate incorporated in Great Britain, and the auditors of such an undertaking, shall give to the auditors of any parent company of the undertaking such information and explanations as they may reasonably require for the purposes of their duties as auditors of that company.

If a subsidiary undertaking fails to comply with this subsection, the undertaking and every officer of it who is in default is guilty of an offence and liable to a fine; and if an auditor fails without reasonable excuse to comply with this subsection he is guilty of an offence and liable to a fine.

**389A(4) [Duty of parent where subsidiary not GB body corporate, offence and penalty]** A parent company having a subsidiary undertaking which is not a body corporate incorporated in Great Britain shall, if required by its auditors to do so, take all such steps as are reasonably open to it to obtain from the subsidiary undertaking such information and explanations as they may reasonably require for the purposes of their duties as auditors of that company.

If a parent company fails to comply with this subsection, the company and every officer of it who is in default is guilty of an offence and liable to a fine.

**389A(5) [Application of s. 734]** Section 734 (criminal proceedings against unincorporated bodies) applies to an offence under subsection (3).

**History**
See history note after s. 394A.

# 390 Right to attend company meetings, etc.

**390(1) [Auditors' rights of attendance, etc.]** A company's auditors are entitled–

(a) to receive all notices of, and other communications relating to, any general meeting which a member of the company is entitled to receive;
(b) to attend any general meeting of the company; and
(c) to be heard at any general meeting which they attend on any part of the business of the meeting which concerns them as auditors.

**390(2) [Rights re s. 381A written resolution]** In relation to a written resolution proposed to be agreed to by a private company in accordance with section 381A, the company's auditors are entitled–

(a) to receive all such communications relating to the resolution as, by virtue of any provision of Schedule 15A, are required to be supplied to a member of the company.

**History**
In s. 390(2) para. (b)–(d) repealed by the Deregulation (Resolutions of Private Companies) Order 1996 (SI 1996/1471), art. 1, 3(2)(b) as from 19 June 1996; para. (b)–(d) formerly read as follows:

"(b) to give notice in accordance with section 381B of their opinion that the resolution concerns them as auditors and should be considered by the company in general meeting or, as the case may be, by a meeting of the relevant class of members of the company,
(c) to attend any such meeting, and
(d) to be heard at any such meeting which they attend on any part of the business of the meeting which concerns them as auditors."

For original provisions, see history note after s. 394A.

**390(3) [Exercise of rights by corporate or partnership auditors]** The right to attend or be heard at a meeting is exercisable in the case of a body corporate or partnership by an individual authorised by it in writing to act as its representative at the meeting.

**History**
See history note after s. 394A.

REMUNERATION OF AUDITORS

## 390A Remuneration of auditors

**390A(1) [Auditors appointed by general meeting]** The remuneration of auditors appointed by the company in general meeting shall be fixed by the company in general meeting or in such manner as the company in general meeting may determine.

**390A(2) [Auditors appointed by directors, Secretary of State]** The remuneration of auditors appointed by the directors or the Secretary of State shall be fixed by the directors or the Secretary of State, as the case may be.

**390A(3) [Note to accounts re remuneration]** There shall be stated in a note to the company's annual accounts the amount of the remuneration of the company's auditors in their capacity as such.

**390A(4) ["Remuneration"]** For the purposes of this section "remuneration" includes sums paid in respect of expenses.

**390A(5) [Application]** This section applies in relation to benefits in kind as to payments in cash, and in relation to any such benefit references to its amount are to its estimated money value.

The nature of any such benefit shall also be disclosed.

**History**
See history note after s. 394A.

## 390B Remuneration of auditors or their associates for non-audit work

**390B(1) [Power of Secretary of State to make regulations]** The Secretary of State may make provision by regulations for securing the disclosure of the amount of any remuneration received or receivable by a company's auditors or their associates in respect of services other than those of auditors in their capacity as such.

**390B(2) [Scope of regulations]** The regulations may–

(a) provide that "remuneration" includes sums paid in respect of expenses,

(b) apply in relation to benefits in kind as to payments in cash, and in relation to any such benefit require disclosure of its nature and its estimated money value,

(c) define "associate" in relation to an auditor,

(d) require the disclosure of remuneration in respect of services rendered to associated undertakings of the company, and

(e) define "associated undertaking" for that purpose.

**390B(3) [Regulations may require disclosure of certain information]** The regulations may require the auditors to disclose the relevant information in their report or require the relevant information to be disclosed in a note to the company's accounts and require the auditors to supply the directors of the company with such information as is necessary to enable that disclosure to be made.

**390B(4) [Different provision for different cases]** The regulations may make different provision for different cases.

**390B(5) [Annulment by Parliament]** Regulations under this section shall be made by statutory instrument which shall be subject to annulment in pursuance of a resolution of either House of Parliament.

**History**
See history note after s. 394A.

**Note**
See the Companies Act 1985 (Disclosure of Remuneration for Non-Audit Work) Regulations 1991 (SI 1991/2128), as amended.

REMOVAL, RESIGNATION, ETC. OF AUDITORS

## 391 Removal of auditors

**391(1) [Power of company]** A company may by ordinary resolution at any time remove an auditor from office, notwithstanding anything in any agreement between it and him.

**391(2) [Notice of resolution removing auditors, offence and penalty]** Where a resolution removing an auditor is passed at a general meeting of a company, the company shall within 14 days give notice of that fact in the prescribed form to the registrar.

If a company fails to give the notice required by this subsection, the company and every officer of it who is in default is guilty of an offence and liable to a fine and, for continued contravention, to a daily default fine.

**Note**
See the Companies (Forms) (Amendment) Regulations 1995 (SI 1995/736).

**391(3) [Compensation or damages]** Nothing in this section shall be taken as depriving a person removed under it of compensation or damages payable to him in respect of the termination of his appointment as auditor or of any appointment terminating with that as auditor.

**391(4) [Removed auditor still has s. 390 rights]** An auditor of a company who has been removed has, notwithstanding his removal, the rights conferred by section 390 in relation to any general meeting of the company–

(a) at which his term of office would otherwise have expired, or

(b) at which it is proposed to fill the vacancy caused by his removal.

In such a case the references in that section to matters concerning the auditors as auditors shall be construed as references to matters concerning him as a former auditor.

**History**
See history note after s. 394A.

## 391A Rights of auditors who are removed or not re-appointed

**391A(1) [Special notice]** Special notice is required for a resolution at a general meeting of a company–

(a) removing an auditor before the expiration of his term of office, or

(b) appointing as auditor a person other than a retiring auditor.

**391A(2) [Copy of notice to relevant persons]** On receipt of notice of such an intended resolution the company shall forthwith send a copy of it to the person proposed to be removed or, as the case may be, to the person proposed to be appointed and to the retiring auditor.

**391A(3) [Representations by relevant persons]** The auditor proposed to be removed or (as the case may be) the retiring auditor may make with respect to the intended resolution representations in writing to the company (not exceeding a reasonable length) and request their notification to members of the company.

**391A(4) [Duty of company]** The company shall (unless the representations are received by it too late for it to do so)–

(a) in any notice of the resolution given to members of the company, state the fact of the representations having been made, and

(b) send a copy of the representations to every member of the company to whom notice of the meeting is or has been sent.

**391A(5) [Where copies of representations not sent or sent too late]** If a copy of any such representations is not sent out as required because received too late or because of the company's default, the auditor may (without prejudice to his right to be heard orally) require that the representations be read out at the meeting.

**391A(6) [Power of court on application]** Copies of the representations need not be sent out and the representations need not be read at the meeting if, on the application either of the company or of any other person claiming to be aggrieved, the court is satisfied that the rights conferred by this section are being abused to secure needless publicity for defamatory matter; and the court may order the company's costs on the application to be paid in whole or in part by the auditor, notwithstanding that he is not a party to the application.

**History**
See history note after s. 394A.

## 392 Resignation of auditors

**392(1) [Resignation by notice]** An auditor of a company may resign his office by depositing a notice in writing to that effect at the company's registered office.

The notice is not effective unless it is accompanied by the statement required by section 394.

**392(2) [Effect of notice]** An effective notice of resignation operates to bring the auditor's term of office to an end as of the date on which the notice is deposited or on such later date as may be specified in it.

**392(3) [Copy of notice to registrar, offence and penalty]** The company shall within 14 days of the deposit of a notice of resignation send a copy of the notice to the registrar of companies.

If default is made in complying with this subsection, the company and every officer of it who is in default is guilty of an offence and liable to a fine and, for continued contravention, a daily default fine.

**History**
See history note after s. 394A.

## 392A Rights of resigning auditors

**392A(1) [Application]** This section applies where an auditor's notice of resignation is accompanied by a statement of circumstances which he considers should be brought to the attention of members or creditors of the company.

**392A(2) [Signed requisition may accompany notice]** He may deposit with the notice a signed requisition calling on the directors of the company forthwith duly to convene an extraordinary general meeting of the company for the purpose of receiving and considering such explanation of the circumstances connected with his resignation as he may wish to place before the meeting.

**392A(3) [Right of auditor to request circulation of statement]** He may request the company to circulate to its members–

(a) before the meeting convened on his requisition, or

(b) before any general meeting at which his term of office would otherwise have expired or at which it is proposed to fill the vacancy caused by his resignation,

a statement in writing (not exceeding a reasonable length) of the circumstances connected with his resignation.

**392A(4) [Duty of company re statement]** The company shall (unless the statement is received too late for it to comply)–

(a) in any notice of the meeting given to members of the company, state the fact of the statement having been made, and

(b) send a copy of the statement to every member of the company to whom notice of the meeting is or has been sent.

**392A(5) [Offence, penalty]** If the directors do not within 21 days from the date of the deposit of a requisition under this section proceed duly to convene a meeting for a day not more than 28 days after the date on which the notice convening the meeting is given, every director who failed to take all reasonable steps to secure that a meeting was convened as mentioned above is guilty of an offence and liable to a fine.

**392A(6) [Right of auditor where statement not sent]** If a copy of the statement mentioned above is not sent out as required because received too late or because of the company's default, the auditor may (without prejudice to his right to be heard orally) require that the statement be read out at the meeting.

**392A(7) [Power of court on application]** Copies of a statement need not be sent out and the statement need not be read out at the meeting if, on the application either of the company or of any other person who claims to be aggrieved, the court is satisfied that the rights conferred by this section are being abused to secure needless publicity for defamatory matter; and the court may order the company's costs on such an application to be paid in whole or in part by the auditor, notwithstanding that he is not a party to the application.

**392A(8) [Resigning auditor still has s. 390 rights]** An auditor who has resigned has, notwithstanding his resignation, the rights conferred by section 390 in relation to any such general meeting of the company as is mentioned in subsection (3)(a) or (b).

In such a case the references in that section to matters concerning the auditors as auditors shall be construed as references to matters concerning him as a former auditor.

**History**
See history note after s. 394A.

# 393 Termination of appointment of auditors not appointed annually

**393(1) [Notice by member]** When an election is in force under section 386 (election by private company to dispense with annual appointment), any member of the company may deposit notice in writing at the company's registered office proposing that the appointment of the company's auditors be brought to an end.

No member may deposit more than one such notice in any financial year of the company.

**393(2) [Duty of directors]** If such a notice is deposited it is the duty of the directors–

(a) to convene a general meeting of the company for a date not more than 28 days after the date on which the notice was given, and

(b) to propose at the meeting a resolution in a form enabling the company to decide whether the appointment of the company's auditors should be brought to an end.

**393(3) [If general meeting decided auditors' appointment ended]** If the decision of the company at the meeting is that the appointment of the auditors should be brought to an end, the auditors shall not be deemed to be re-appointed when next they would be and, if the notice was deposited within the period immediately following the distribution of accounts, any deemed re-appointment for the financial year following that to which those accounts relate which has already occurred shall cease to have effect.

The period immediately following the distribution of accounts means the period beginning with the day on which copies of the company's annual accounts are sent to members of the company under section 238 and ending 14 days after that day.

**393(4) [Where directors do not call meeting]** If the directors do not within 14 days from the date of the deposit of the notice proceed duly to convene a meeting, the member who deposited the notice (or, if there was more than one, any of them) may himself convene the meeting; but any meeting so convened shall not be held after the expiration of three months from that date.

**393(5) [Meeting called by member]** A meeting convened under this section by a member shall be convened in the same manner, as nearly as possible, as that in which meetings are to be convened by directors.

**393(6) [Reasonable expenses re member calling meeting]** Any reasonable expenses incurred by a member by reason of the failure of the directors duly to convene a meeting shall be made good to him by the company; and any such sums shall be recouped by the company from such of the directors as were in default out of any sums payable, or to become payable, by the company by way of fees or other remuneration in respect of their services.

**393(7) [Provision in agreement, compensation or damages]** This section has effect notwithstanding anything in any agreement between the company and its auditors; and no compensation or damages shall be payable by reason of the auditors' appointment being terminated under this section.

**History**
See history note after s. 394A.

# 394 Statement by person ceasing to hold office as auditor

**394(1) [Duty of auditor to deposit statement]** Where an auditor ceases for any reason to hold office, he shall deposit at the company's registered office a statement of any circumstances connected with his ceasing to hold office which he considers should be brought to the attention of the members or creditors of the company or, if he considers that there are no such circumstances, a statement that there are none.

**394(2) [Time for depositing statement]** In the case of resignation, the statement shall be deposited along with the notice of resignation; in the case of failure to seek re-appointment, the statement shall be deposited not less than 14 days before the end of the time allowed for next appointing auditors; in any other case, the statement shall be deposited not later than the end of the period of 14 days beginning with the date on which he ceases to hold office.

**394(3) [Duty of company if there are certain circumstances]** If the statement is of circumstances which the auditor considers should be brought to the attention of the members or creditors of the company, the company shall within 14 days of the deposit of the statement either–

(a) send a copy of it to every person who under section 238 is entitled to be sent copies of the accounts, or

(b) apply to the court.

**394(4) [Notice to auditor re application to court]** The company shall if it applies to the court notify the auditor of the application.

**394(5) [If no notice of application auditors must send copy of statement to registrar]** Unless the auditor receives notice of such an application before the end of the period of 21 days beginning with the day on which he deposited the statement, he shall within a further seven days send a copy of the statement to the registrar.

**394(6) [Power of court where statement used for publicity]** If the court is satisfied that the auditor is using the statement to secure needless publicity for defamatory matter–

(a) it shall direct that copies of the statement need not be sent out, and

(b) it may further order the company's costs on the application to be paid in whole or in part by the auditor, notwithstanding that he is not a party to the application;

and the company shall within 14 days of the court's decision send to the persons mentioned in subsection (3)(a) a statement setting out the effect of the order.

**394(7) [Power of court where statement not so used]** If the court is not so satisfied, the company shall within 14 days of the court's decision–

(a) send copies of the statement to the persons mentioned in subsection (3)(a), and

(b) notify the auditor of the court's decision;

and the auditor shall within seven days of receiving such notice send a copy of the statement to the registrar.

**History**

See history note after s. 394A.

## 394A Offences of failing to comply with s. 394

**394A(1) [Offence, penalty]** If a person ceasing to hold office as auditor fails to comply with section 394 he is guilty of an offence and liable to a fine.

**394A(2) [Defence]** In proceedings for an offence under subsection (1) it is a defence for the person charged to show that he took all reasonable steps and exercised all due diligence to avoid the commission of the offence.

**394A(3) [Application of s. 733, 734];** Sections 733 (liability of individuals for corporate default) and 734 (criminal proceedings against unincorporated bodies) apply to an offence under subsection (1).

**394A(4) [Offence re company, penalty]** If a company makes default in complying with section 394, the company and every officer of it who is in default is guilty of an offence and liable to a fine and, for continued contravention, to a daily default fine.

**History**

S. 384–388A, 389A–394A inserted by CA 1989, s. 118, 119–124 as from 1 April 1990 subject to transitional and saving provisions (see SI 1990/355 (C 13), art. 4(a) and also art. 10) – see also notes to s. 388A, 389; the former s. 384–388, 390–394 read as follows:

"**384 Annual appointment of auditors**

**384(1)** Every company shall, at each general meeting of the company at which accounts are laid in accordance with section 241, appoint an auditor or auditors to hold office from the conclusion of that meeting until the conclusion of the next general meeting at which the requirements of section 241 are complied with.

This is subject to section 252 (exemption for dormant companies).

**(2)** The first auditors of a company may be appointed wby the directors at any time before the first general meeting of the company at which accounts are laid; and auditors so appointed shall hold office until the conclusion of that meeting.

**(3)** If the directors fail to exercise their powers under subsection (2), those powers may be exercised by the company in general meeting.

**(4)** The directors, or the company in general meeting, may fill any casual vacancy in the office of auditor; but while any such vacancy continues, the surviving or continuing auditor or auditors (if any) may act.

**(5)** If at any general meeting of a company at which accounts are laid as required by section 241 no auditors are appointed or reappointed, the Secretary of State may appoint a person to fill the vacancy; and the company shall, within one week of that power of the Secretary of State becoming exercisable, give to him notice of that fact.

If a company fails to give the notice required by this subsection, the company and every officer of it who is in default is guilty of an offence and liable to a fine and, for continued contravention, to a daily default fine.

**385 Remuneration of auditors**

**385(1)** The remuneration of a company's auditors shall be fixed by the company in general meeting, or in such manner as the company in general meeting may determine.

**(2)** This does not apply in the case of auditors appointed by the directors or by the Secretary of State; and in that case their remuneration may be fixed by the directors or by the Secretary of State (as the case may be).

**(3)** For the purpose of this section, **"remuneration"** includes any sums paid by the company in respect of the auditor's expenses.

**386 Removal of auditors**

**386(1)** A company may by ordinary resolution remove an auditor before the expiration of his term of office, notwithstanding anything in any agreement between it and him.

**(2)** Where a resolution removing an auditor is passed at a general meeting of a company, the company shall within 14 days give notice of that fact in the prescribed form to the registrar of companies
If a company fails to give the notice required by this subsection, the company and every officer of it who is in default is guilty of an offence and liable to a fine and, for continued contravention, to a daily default fine.

**(3)** Nothing in this section is to be taken as depriving a person removed under it of compensation or damages payable to him in respect of the termination of his appointment as auditor or of any appointment terminating with that as auditor.

**387 Auditors' right to attend company meetings**

**387(1)** A company's auditors are entitled to attend any general meeting of the company and to receive all notices of, and other communications relating to, any general meeting which a member of the company is entitled to receive, and to be heard at any general meeting which they attend on any part of the business of the meeting which concerns them as auditors.

**(2)** An auditor of a company who has been removed is entitled to attend–

(a) the general meeting at which his term of office would otherwise have expired, and
(b) any general meeting at which it is proposed to fill the vacancy caused by his removal,

and to receive all notices of, and other communications relating to, any such meeting which any member of the company is entitled to receive, and to be heard at any such meeting which he attends on any part of the business of the meeting which concerns him as former auditor of the company.

**388 Supplementary provisions as to auditors**

**388(1)** Special notice is required for a resolution at a general meeting of a company–

(a) appointing as auditor a person other than a retiring auditor; or
(b) filling a casual vacancy in the office of auditor; or
(c) reappointing as auditor a retiring auditor who was appointed by the directors to fill a casual vacancy; or
(d) removing an auditor before the expiration of his term of office.

**(2)** On receipt of notice of such an intended resolution as is mentioned above the company shall forthwith send a copy of it–

(a) to the person proposed to be appointed or removed, as the case may be;
(b) in a case within subsection (1)(a), to the retiring auditor; and
(c) where, in a case within subsection (1) (b) or (c), the casual vacancy was caused by the resignation of an auditor, to the auditor who resigned.

**(3)** Where notice is given of such a resolution as is mentioned in subsection (1)(a) or (d), and the retiring auditor or (as the case may be) the auditor proposed to be removed makes with respect to the intended resolution representations in writing to the company (not exceeding a reasonable length) and requests their notification to members of the company, the company shall (unless the representations are received by it too late for it to do so)–

(a) in any notice of the resolution given to members of the company state the fact of the representations having been made, and
(b) send a copy of the representations to every member of the company to whom notice of the meeting is or has been sent.

**(4)** If a copy of any such representations is not sent out as required by subsection (3) because received too late or because of the company's default, the auditor may (without prejudice to his right to be heard orally) require that the representations shall be read out at the meeting.

**(5)** Copies of the representations need not be sent out and the representations need not be read out at the meeting if, on the application either of the company or of any other person claiming to be aggrieved, the court is satisfied that the rights conferred by this section are being abused to secure needless publicity for defamatory matter; and the court may order the company's costs on the application to be paid in whole or in part by the auditor, notwithstanding that he is not a party to the application.

**390 Resignation of auditors**

**390(1)** An auditor of a company may resign his office by depositing a notice in writing to that effect at the company's registered office; and any such notice operates to bring his term of office to an end on the date on which the notice is deposited, or on such later date as may be specified in it.

**(2)** An auditor's notice of resignation is not effective unless it contains either–

(a) a statement to the effect that there are no circumstances connected with his resignation which he considers should be brought to the notice of the members or creditors of the company; or
(b) a statement of any such circumstances as are mentioned above.

**(3)** Where a notice under this section is deposited at a company's registered office, the company shall within 14 days send a copy of the notice–
(a) to the registrar of companies; and
(b) if the notice contained a statement under subsection (2)(b), to every person who under section 240 is entitled to be sent copies of the accounts.

**(4)** The company or any person claiming to be aggrieved may, within 14 days of the receipt by the company of a notice containing a statement under subsection (2)(b), apply to the court for an order under the next subsection.

**(5)** If on such an application the court is satisfied that the auditor is using the notice to secure needless publicity for defamatory matter, it may by order direct that copies of the notice need not be sent out; and the court may further order the company's costs on the application to be paid in whole or in part by the auditor, notwithstanding that he is not a party to the application.

**(6)** The company shall, within 14 days of the court's decision, send to the persons mentioned in subsection (3)–
(a) if the court makes an order under subsection (5), a statement setting out the effect of the order;
(b) if not, a copy of the notice containing the statement under subsection (2)(b).

**(7)** If default is made in complying with subsection (3) or (6), the company and every officer of it who is in default is liable to a fine and, for continued contravention, to a daily default fine.

**391 Right of resigning auditor to requisition company meeting**

**391(1)** Where an auditor's notice of resignation contains a statement under section 390(2)(b) there may be deposited with the notice a requisition signed by the auditor calling on the directors of the company forthwith duly to convene an extraordinary general meeting of the company for the purpose of receiving and considering such explanation of the circumstances connected with his resignation as he may wish to place before the meeting.

**(2)** Where an auditor's notice of resignation contains such a statement, the auditor may request the company to circulate to its members–
(a) before the general meeting at which his term of office would otherwise have expired; or
(b) before any general meeting at which it is proposed to fill the vacancy caused by his resignation or convened on his requisition,

a statement in writing (not exceeding a reasonable length) of the circumstances connected with his resignation.

**(3)** The company shall in that case (unless the statement is received by it too late for it to comply)–
(a) in any notice of the meeting given to members of the company state the fact of the statement having been made, and
(b) send a copy of the statement to every member of the company to whom notice of the meeting is or has been sent.

**(4)** If the directors do not within 21 days from the date of the deposit of a requisition under this section proceed duly to convene a meeting for a day not more than 28 days after the date on which the notice convening the meeting is given, every director who failed to take all reasonable steps to secure that a meeting was convened as mentioned above is guilty of an offence and liable to a fine.

**(5)** If a copy of the statement mentioned in subsection (2) is not sent out as required by subsection (3) because received too late or because of the company's default, the auditor may (without prejudice to his right to be heard orally) require that the statement shall be read out at the meeting.

**(6)** Copies of a statement need not be sent out and the statement need not be read out at the meeting if, on the application either of the company or of any other person who claims to be aggrieved, the court is satisfied that the rights conferred by this section are being abused to secure needless publicity for defamatory matter; and the court may order the company's costs on such an application to be paid in whole or in part by the auditor, notwithstanding that he is not a party to the application.

**(7)** An auditor who has resigned his office is entitled to attend any such meeting as is mentioned in subsection (2)(a) or (b) and to receive all notices of, and other communications relating to, any such meeting which any member of the company is entitled to receive, and to be heard at any such meeting which he attends on any part of the business of the meeting which concerns him as former auditor of the company.

**392 Powers of auditors in relation to subsidiaries**

**392(1)** Where a company ("the holding company") has a subsidiary, then–
(a) if the subsidiary is a body corporate incorporated in Great Britain, it is the duty of the subsidiary and its auditors to give to the auditors of the holding company such information and explanation as those auditors may reasonably require for the purposes of their duties as auditors of the holding company;
(b) in any other case, it is the duty of the holding company, if required by its auditors to do so, to take all such steps as are reasonably open to it to obtain from the subsidiary such information and explanation as are mentioned above.

**(2)** If a subsidiary or holding company fails to comply with subsection (1), the subsidiary or holding company and every officer of it who is in default is guilty of an offence and liable to a fine; and if an auditor fails without reasonable excuse to comply with paragraph (a) of the subsection, he is guilty of an offence and so liable.

**393 False statements to auditors**

**393** An officer of a company commits an offence if he knowingly or recklessly makes to a company's auditors a statement (whether written or oral) which–
(a) conveys or purports to convey any information or explanation which the auditors require, or are entitled to require, as auditors of the company, and
(b) is misleading, false or deceptive in a material particular.

A person guilty of an offence under this section is liable to imprisonment or a fine, or both.

**394 Auditors of trade unions**

**394(1)** Subject as follows, this section applies to every body which is both a company and a trade union or an employers' association to which section 11 of the Trade Union and Labour Relations Act 1974 applies.

**(2)** Section 11(3) of the Act of 1974 and paragraphs 6 to 15 of Schedule 2 to that Act (qualifications, appointment and removal of auditors) do not have effect in relation to bodies to which this section applies.

(3) The rights and powers conferred, and the duties imposed, by paragraphs 16 to 21 of that Schedule on the auditors of a body to which this section applies belong to the auditors from time to time appointed by or on behalf of that body under section 384 of this Act."

# PART XII – REGISTRATION OF CHARGES

## Chapter I – Registration of Charges (England and Wales)

### 395 Certain charges void if not registered

**395(1) [Void against liquidator or administrator and creditors]** Subject to the provisions of this Chapter, a charge created by a company registered in England and Wales and being a charge to which this section applies is, so far as any security on the company's property or undertaking is conferred by the charge, void against the liquidator or administrator and any creditor of the company, unless the prescribed particulars of the charge together with the instrument (if any) by which the charge is created or evidenced, are delivered to or received by the registrar of companies for registration in the manner required by this Chapter within 21 days after the date of the charge's creation.

**History**
In s. 395(1) the words "or administrator" appearing after the word "liquidator" inserted by Insolvency Act 1985, s. 109 and Sch. 6, para. 10 as from 29 December 1986 (see SI 1986/1924 (C 71)).

**395(2) [Contracts for repayment etc.]** Subsection (1) is without prejudice to any contract or obligation for repayment of the money secured by the charge; and when a charge becomes void under this section, the money secured by it immediately becomes payable.

### 396 Charges which have to be registered

**396(1) [Application of s. 395]** Section 395 applies to the following charges–

(a) a charge for the purpose of securing any issue of debentures,
(b) a charge on uncalled share capital of the company,
(c) a charge created or evidenced by an instrument which, if executed by an individual, would require registration as a bill of sale,
(d) a charge on land (wherever situated) or any interest in it, but not including a charge for any rent or other periodical sum issuing out of the land,
(e) a charge on book debts of the company,
(f) a floating charge on the company's undertaking or property,
(g) a charge on calls made but not paid,
(h) a charge on a ship or aircraft, or any share in a ship,
(j) a charge on goodwill, or on any intellectual property.

**History**
In s. 396(1)(j) the words "or an any intellectual property" substituted for the former words "on a patent or a licence under a patent, on a trademark or on a copyright or a licence under a copyright" by the Copyright, Designs and Patents Act 1988, s. 303(1), Sch. 7, para. 31(1),(2) as from 1 August 1989 (see SI 1989/816).

**396(2) [Negotiable instrument securing payment of book debts]** Where a negotiable instrument has been given to secure the payment of any book debts of a company, the deposit of the instrument for the purpose of securing an advance to the company is not, for purposes of section 395, to be treated as a charge on those book debts.

**396(3) [Holding of debentures entitling holder to charge on land]** The holding of debentures entitling the holder to a charge on land is not for purposes of this section deemed to be an interest in land.

**396(3A) [Intellectual property]** The following are "intellectual property" for the purposes of this section–

(a) any patent, trade mark, registered design, copyright or design right;
(b) any licence under or in respect of any such right.

**History**
S. 396(3A) inserted by the Copyright, Designs and Patents Act 1988, s. 303(1), Sch. 7, para. 31(1), (2) as from 1 August 1989 (see SI 1989/816). In s. 396(3A)(a) the words "service mark," formerly appearing before the words "registered design," repealed by Trade Marks Act 1994, s. 106(2), Sch. 5 as from 31 October 1994 (see Trade Marks Act 1994 (Commencement) Order 1994 (SI 1994/2550)).

**Note**
The reference to a trade mark in s. 396(3A) is construed a as reference to a trade mark within the meaning of the Trade Marks Act 1994 by virtue of s. 106(1), Sch. 4, para. 1 of that Act as from 31 October 1994 (SI 1994/2550).

**396(4) ["Charge"]** In this Chapter, **"charge"** includes mortgage.

# 397 Formalities of registration (debentures)

**397(1) [Required particulars re series of debentures]** Where a series of debentures containing, or giving by reference to another instrument, any charge to the benefit of which the debenture holders of that series are entitled pari passu is created by a company, it is for purposes of section 395 sufficient if there are delivered to or received by the registrar, within 21 days after the execution of the deed containing the charge (or, if there is no such deed, after the execution of any debentures of the series), the following particulars in the prescribed form–

(a) the total amount secured by the whole series, and

(b) the dates of the resolutions authorising the issue of the series and the date of the covering deed (if any) by which the security is created or defined, and

(c) a general description of the property charged, and

(d) the names of the trustees (if any) for the debenture holders,

together with the deed containing the charge or, if there is no such deed, one of the debentures of the series:

Provided that there shall be sent to the registrar of companies, for entry in the register, particulars in the prescribed form of the date and amount of each issue of debentures of the series, but any omission to do this does not affect the validity of any of those debentures.

**397(2) [Required particulars where commission etc. paid]** Where any commission, allowance or discount has been paid or made either directly or indirectly by a company to a person in consideration of his–

(a) subscribing or agreeing to subscribe, whether absolutely or conditionally, for debentures of the company, or

(b) procuring or agreeing to procure subscriptions, whether absolute or conditional, for such debentures,

the particulars required to be sent for registration under section 395 shall include particulars as to the amount or rate per cent of the commission, discount or allowance so paid or made, but omission to do this does not affect the validity of the debentures issued.

**397(3) [Interpretation in s. 397(2)]** The deposit of debentures as security for a debt of the company is not, for the purposes of subsection (2), treated as the issue of the debentures at a discount.

# 398 Verification of charge on property outside United Kingdom

**398(1) [Charge created outside UK re property within UK]** In the case of a charge created out of the United Kingdom comprising property situated outside the United Kingdom, the delivery to and the receipt by the registrar of companies of a copy (verified in the prescribed manner) of the instrument by which the charge is created or evidenced has the same effect for purposes of sections 395 to 398 as the delivery and receipt of the instrument itself.

**398(2) [Timing]** In that case, 21 days after the date on which the instrument or copy could, in due course of post (and if despatched with due diligence), have been received in the United Kingdom are substituted for the 21 days mentioned in section 395(1) (or as the case may be, section 397(1)) as the time within which the particulars and instrument or copy are to be delivered to the registrar.

**398(3) [Charge created in UK re property outside UK]** Where a charge is created in the United Kingdom but comprises property outside the United Kingdom, the instrument creating or purporting to create the charge may be sent for registration under section 395 notwithstanding that further proceedings may be necessary to make the charge valid or effectual according to the law of the country in which the property is situated.

**398(4) [Charge re property in Scotland or Northern Ireland]** Where a charge comprises property situated in Scotland or Northern Ireland and registration in the country where the property is situated is necessary to make the charge valid or effectual according to the law of that country, the delivery to and the receipt by the registrar of a copy (verified in the prescribed manner) of the instrument by which the charge is created or evidenced, together with a certificate in the prescribed form stating that the charge was presented for registration in Scotland or Northern Ireland (as the case may be) on the date on which it was so presented has, for purposes of sections 395 to 398, the same effect as the delivery and receipt of the instrument itself.

## 399 Company's duty to register charges it creates

**399(1) [Company's obligation]** It is a company's duty to send to the registrar of companies for registration the particulars of every charge created by the company and of the issues of debentures of a series requiring registration under sections 395 to 398; but registration of any such charge may be effected on the application of any person interested in it.

**399(2) [Where registration by person other than company]** Where registration is effected on the application of some person other than the company, that person is entitled to recover from the company the amount of any fees properly paid by him to the registrar on the registration.

**399(3) [Penalty on default re s. 399(1)]** If a company fails to comply with subsection (1), then, unless the registration has been effected on the application of some other person, the company and every officer of it who is in default is liable to a fine and, for continued contravention, to a daily default fine.

## 400 Charges existing on property acquired

**400(1) [Application]** This section applies where a company registered in England and Wales acquires property which is subject to a charge of any such kind as would, if it had been created by the company after the acquisition of the property, have been required to be registered under this Chapter.

**400(2) [Particulars and copy of instrument to registrar within 21 days]** The company shall cause the prescribed particulars of the charge, together with a copy (certified in the prescribed manner to be a correct copy) of the instrument (if any) by which the charge was created or is evidenced, to be delivered to the registrar of companies for registration in manner required by this Chapter within 21 days after the date on which the acquisition is completed.

**400(3) [If property and charge outside Great Britain]** However, if the property is situated and the charge was created outside Great Britain, 21 days after the date on which the copy of the instrument could in due course of post, and if despatched with due diligence, have been received in the United Kingdom is substituted for the 21 days above-mentioned as the time within which the particulars and copy of the instrument are to be delivered to the registrar.

**400(4) [Penalty on default]** If default is made in complying with this section, the company and every officer of it who is in default is liable to a fine and, for continued contravention, to a daily default fine.

## 401 Register of charges to be kept by registrar of companies

**401(1) [Matters to be entered in register]** The registrar of companies shall keep, with respect to each company, a register in the prescribed form of all the charges requiring registration under this Chapter; and he shall enter in the register with respect to such charges the following particulars–

(a) in the case of a charge to the benefit of which the holders of a series of debentures are entitled, the particulars specified in section 397(1),

(b) in the case of any other charge–

(i) if it is a charge created by the company, the date of its creation, and if it is a charge which was existing on property acquired by the company, the date of the acquisition of the property, and
(ii) the amount secured by the charge, and
(iii) short particulars of the property charged, and
(iv) the persons entitled to the charge.

**401(2) [Issue of certificate by registrar]** The registrar shall give a certificate of the registration of any charge registered in pursuance of this Chapter, stating the amount secured by the charge.

The certificate–

(a) shall be either signed by the registrar, or authenticated by his official seal, and
(b) is conclusive evidence that the requirements of this Chapter as to registration have been satisfied.

**401(3) [Inspection of register]** The register kept in pursuance of this section shall be open to inspection by any person.

## 402 Endorsement of certificate on debentures

**402(1) [Company to endorse debenture etc.]** The company shall cause a copy of every certificate of registration given under section 401 to be endorsed on every debenture or certificate of debenture stock which is issued by the company and the payment of which is secured by the charge so registered.

**402(2) [No endorsement before charge created]** But this does not require a company to cause a certificate or registration of any charge so given to be endorsed on any debenture or certificate of debenture stock issued by the company before the charge was created.

**402(3) [Offence, penalty]** If a person knowingly and wilfully authorises or permits the delivery of a debenture or certificate of debenture stock which under this section is required to have endorsed on it a copy of a certificate of registration without the copy being so endorsed upon it, he is liable (without prejudice to any other liability) to a fine.

## 403 Entries of satisfaction and release

**403(1) [Entry by registrar]** The registrar of companies, on receipt of a statutory declaration in the prescribed form verifying, with respect to a registered charge,–

(a) that the debt for which the charge was given has been paid or satisfied in whole or in part, or
(b) that part of the property or undertaking charged has been released from the charge or has ceased to form part of the company's property or undertaking,

may enter on the register a memorandum of satisfaction in whole or in part, or of the fact that part of the property or undertaking has been released from the charge or has ceased to form part of the company's property or undertaking (as the case may be).

**403(2) [Copy of memorandum of satisfaction in whole]** Where the registrar enters a memorandum of satisfaction in whole, he shall if required furnish the company with a copy of it.

## 404 Rectification of register of charges

**404(1) [Application]** The following applies if the court is satisfied that the omission to register a charge within the time required by this Chapter or that the omission or mis-statement of any particular with respect to any such charge or in a memorandum of satisfaction was accidental, or due to inadvertence or to some other sufficient cause, or is not of a nature to prejudice the position of creditors or shareholders of the company, or that on other grounds it is just and equitable to grant relief.

**404(2) [Order by court]** The court may, on the application of the company or a person interested, and on such terms and conditions as seem to the court just and expedient, order that the time for registration shall be extended or, as the case may be, that the omission or mis-statement shall be rectified.

## 405 Registration of enforcement of security

**405(1) [Notice to registrar re appointment of receiver etc.]** If a person obtains an order for the appointment of a receiver or manager of a company's property, or appoints such a receiver or manager under powers contained in an instrument, he shall within 7 days of the order or of the appointment under those powers, give notice of the fact to the registrar of companies; and the registrar shall enter the fact in the register of charges.

**405(2) [Receiver to notify registrar of ceasing to act]** Where a person appointed receiver or manager of a company's property under powers contained in an instrument ceases to act as such receiver or manager, he shall, on so ceasing, give the registrar notice to that effect, and the registrar shall enter the fact in the register of charges.

**405(3) [Form of notice]** A notice under this section shall be in the prescribed form.

**405(4) [Penalty on default]** If a person makes default in complying with the requirements of this section, he is liable to a fine and, for continued contravention, to a daily default fine.

## 406 Companies to keep copies of instruments creating charges

**406(1) [Copies to be kept at registered office]** Every company shall cause a copy of every instrument creating a charge requiring registration under this Chapter to be kept at its registered office.

**406(2) [Series of uniform debentures]** In the case of a series of uniform debentures, a copy of one debenture of the series is sufficient.

## 407 Company's register of charges

**407(1) [Register at registered office]** Every limited company shall keep at its registered office a register of charges and enter in it all charges specificially affecting property of the company and all floating charges on the company's undertaking or any of its property.

**407(2) [Details of entries]** The entry shall in each case give a short description of the property charged, the amount of the charge and, except in the case of securities to bearer, the names of the persons entitled to it.

**407(3) [Offence, penalty]** If an officer of the company knowingly and wilfully authorises or permits the omission of an entry required to be made in pursuance of this section, he is liable to a fine.

## 408 Right to inspect instruments which create charges, etc.

**408(1) [Open to inspection free to creditor or member]** The copies of instruments creating any charge requiring registration under this Chapter with the registrar of companies, and the register of charges kept in pursuance of section 407, shall be open during business hours (but subject to such reasonable restrictions as the company in general meeting may impose, so that not less than 2 hours in each day be allowed for inspection) to the inspection of any creditor or member of the company without fee.

**408(2) [Open to inspection to others for fee]** The register of charges shall also be open to the inspection of any other person on payment of such fee, not exceeding 5 pence, for each inspection, as the company may prescribe.

**408(3) [Penalty re refusal of inspection]** If inspection of the copies referred to, or of the register, is refused, every officer of the company who is in default is liable to a fine and, for continued contravention, to a daily default fine.

**408(4) [Court may compel inspection]** If such a refusal occurs in relation to a company registered in England and Wales, the court may by order compel an immediate inspection of the copies or register.

## 409 Charges on property in England and Wales created elsewhere

**409(1) [Extent of Chapter I]** This Chapter extends to charges on property in England and Wales which are created, and to charges on property in England and Wales which is acquired, by a company (whether a company within the meaning of this Act or not) incorporated outside Great Britain which has an established place of business in England and Wales.

**409(2) [Application of s. 406, 407]** In relation to such a company, sections 406 and 407 apply with the substitution, for the reference to the company's registered office, of a reference to its principal place of business in England and Wales.

# Chapter II – Registration of Charges (Scotland)

## 410 Charges void unless registered

**410(1) [Application]** The following provisions of this Chapter have effect for the purpose of securing the registration in Scotland of charges created by companies.

**410(2) [Particulars etc. to registrar within 21 days]** Every charge created by a company, being a charge to which this section applies, is, so far as any security on the company's property or any part of it is conferred by the charge, void against the liquidator or administrator and any creditor of the company unless the prescribed particulars of the charge, together with a copy (certified in the prescribed manner to be a correct copy) of the instrument (if any) by which the charge is created or evidenced, are delivered to or received by the registrar of companies for registration in the manner required by this Chapter within 21 days after the date of the creation of the charge.

**History**

In s. 410(2) the words "or administrator" appearing after the word "liquidator" inserted by Insolvency Act 1985, s. 109 and Sch. 6, para. 10 as from 29 December 1986 (see SI 1986/1924 (C 71)).

**410(3) [Extent of s. 410(2)]** Subsection (2) is without prejudice to any contract or obligation for repayment of the money secured by the charge; and when a charge becomes void under this section the money secured by it immediately becomes payable.

**410(4) [Charges covered]** This section applies to the following charges–

(a) a charge on land wherever situated, or any interest in such land (not including a charge for any rent, ground annual or other periodical sum payable in respect of the land, but including a charge created by a heritable security within the meaning of section 9(8) of the Conveyancing and Feudal Reform (Scotland) Act 1970),

(b) a security over the uncalled share capital of the company,

(c) a security over incorporeal moveable property of any of the following categories–
   (i) the book debts of the company,
   (ii) calls made but not paid,
   (iii) goodwill,
   (iv) a patent or a licence under a patent,
   (v) a trademark,
   (vi) a copyright or a licence under a copyright,
   (vii) a registered design or a licence in respect of such a design,
   (viii) a design or a licence under a design right,

(d) a security over a ship or aircraft or any share in a ship, and

(e) a floating charge.

**History**

S. 410(4)(c)(vii), (viii) inserted by the Copyright, Designs and Patents Act 1988, s. 303(1), Sch. 7, para. 31(3) as from 1 August 1989 (see SI 1989/816); the amendment purports to be made to s. 410(3)(c).

**Note**

The reference to a trade mark in s. 410(4)(c)(v) is construed as a reference to a trade mark within the meaning of the Trade Marks Act 1994 by virtue of s. 106(1), Sch. 4, para. 1 of that Act as from 31 October 1994 (SI 1994/2550).

**410(5) ["Company"]** In this Chapter **"company"** (except in section 424) means an incorporated company registered in Scotland; "registrar of companies" means the registrar or other officer performing under this Act the duty of registration of companies in Scotland; and references to the date of creation of a charge are–

(a) in the case of a floating charge, the date on which the instrument creating the floating charge was executed by the company creating the charge, and

(b) in any other case, the date on which the right of the person entitled to the benefit of the charge was constituted as a real right.

## 411 Charges on property outside United Kingdom

**411(1) [Charge created outside United Kingdom]** In the case of a charge created out of the United Kingdom comprising property situated outside the United Kingdom, the period of 21 days after the date on which the copy of the instrument creating it could (in due course of post, and if despatched with due diligence) have been received in the United Kingdom is substituted for the period of 21 days after the date of the creation of the charge as the time within which, under section 410(2), the particulars and copy are to be delivered to the registrar.

**411(2) [Charge created in United Kingdom]** Where a charge is created in the United Kingdom but comprises property outside the United Kingdom, the copy of the instrument creating or purporting to create the charge may be sent for registration under section 410 notwithstanding that further proceedings may be necessary to make the charge valid or effectual according to the law of the country in which the property is situated.

## 412 Negotiable instrument to secure book debts

**412** Where a negotiable instrument has been given to secure the payment of any book debts of a company, the deposit of the instrument for the purpose of securing an advance to the company is not, for purposes of section 410, to be treated as a charge on those book debts.

## 413 Charges associated with debentures

**413(1) [Holding of debentures entitling holder to charge on land]** The holding of debentures entitling the holder to a charge on land is not, for the purposes of section 410, deemed to be an interest in land.

**413(2) [Required particulars re series of debentures]** Where a series of debentures containing, or giving by reference to any other instrument, any charge to the benefit of which the debenture-holders of that series are entitled pari passu, is created by a company, it is sufficient for purposes of section 410 if there are delivered to or received by the registrar of companies within 21 days after the execution of the deed containing the charge or, if there is no such deed, after the execution of any debentures of the series, the following particulars in the prescribed form–

(a) the total amount secured by the whole series,

(b) the date of the resolutions authorising the issue of the series and the date of the covering deed (if any) by which the security is created or defined,

(c) a general description of the property charged,

(d) the names of the trustees (if any) for the debenture holders, and

(e) in the case of a floating charge, a statement of any provisions of the charge and of any instrument relating to it which prohibit or restrict or regulate the power of the company to grant further securities ranking in priority to, or pari passu with, the floating charge, or which vary or otherwise regulate the order of ranking of the floating charge in relation to subsisting securities,

together with a copy of the deed containing the charge or, if there is no such deed, of one of the debentures of the series:

Provided that, where more than one issue is made of debentures in the series, there shall be sent to the registrar of companies for entry in the register particulars (in the prescribed form) of the date and amount of each issue of debentures of the series, but any omission to do this does not affect the validity of any of those debentures.

**413(3) [Required particulars where commission paid for subscription]** Where any commission, allowance or discount has been paid or made, either directly or indirectly, by a company to any person in consideration of his subscribing or agreeing to subscribe, whether absolutely or conditionally, for any debentures of the company, or procuring or agreeing to procure subscriptions (whether absolute or conditional) for any such debentures, the particulars required to be sent for registration under section 410 include particulars as to the amount or rate per cent of the commission, discount or allowance so paid or made; but any omission to do this does not affect the validity of the debentures issued.

The deposit of any debentures as security for any debt of the company is not, for purposes of this subsection, treated as the issue of the debentures at a discount.

## 414 Charge by way of ex facie absolute disposition, etc.

**414(1) [Effect of compliance with s. 410(2)]** For the avoidance of doubt, it is hereby declared that, in the case of a charge created by way of an ex facie absolute disposition or assignation qualified by a back letter or other agreement, or by a standard security qualified by an agreement, compliance with section 410(2) does not of itself render the charge unavailable as security for indebtedness incurred after the date of compliance.

**414(2) [Increase of charge]** Where the amount secured by a charge so created is purported to be increased by a further back letter or agreement, a further charge is held to have been created by the ex facie absolute disposition or assignation or (as the case may be) by the standard security, as qualified by the further back letter or agreement; and the provisions of this Chapter apply to the further charge as if–

(a) references in this Chapter (other than in this section) to the charge were references to the further charge, and

(b) references to the date of the creation of the charge were references to the date on which the further back letter or agreement was executed.

## 415 Company's duty to register charges created by it

**415(1) [Company to send details of charge]** It is a company's duty to send to the registrar of companies for registration the particulars of every charge created by the company and of the issues of debentures of a series requiring registration under sections 410 to 414; but registration of any such charge may be effected on the application of any person interested in it.

**415(2) [Fees recoverable by other persons effecting registration]** Where registration is effected on the application of some person other than the company, that person is entitled to recover from the company the amount of any fees properly paid by him to the registrar on the registration.

**415(3) [Penalty on default]** If a company makes default in sending to the registrar for registration the particulars of any charge created by the company or of the issues of debentures of a series requiring registration as above mentioned, then, unless the registration has been effected on the application of some other person, the company and every officer of it who is in default is liable to a fine and, for continued contravention, to a daily default fine.

## 416 Duty to register charges existing on property acquired

**416(1) [Particulars etc. to registrar within 21 days]** Where a company acquires any property which is subject to a charge of any kind as would, if it had been created by the company after the acquisition of the property, have been required to be registered under this Chapter, the company shall cause the prescribed particulars of the charge, together with a copy (certified in the prescribed manner to be a correct copy) of the instrument (if any) by which the charge was created or is evidenced, to be delivered to the registrar of companies for registration in the manner required by this Chapter within 21 days after the date on which the transaction was settled.

**416(2) [If property and charge outside Great Britain]** If, however, the property is situated and the charge was created outside Great Britain, 21 days after the date on which the copy of the instrument could (in due course of post, and if despatched with due diligence) have been received in the United Kingdom are substituted for 21 days after the settlement of the transaction as the time within which the particulars and the copy of the instrument are to be delivered to the registrar.

**416(3) [Penalty on default]** If default is made in complying with this section, the company and every officer of it who is in default is liable to a fine and, for continued contravention, to a daily default fine.

## 417 Register of charges to be kept by registrar of companies

**417(1) [Register to be kept]** The registrar of companies shall keep, with respect to each company, a register in the prescribed form of all the charges requiring registration under this Chapter, and shall enter in the register with respect to such charges the particulars specified below.

**417(2) [Charge re holders of series of debentures]** In the case of a charge to the benefit of which the holders of a series of debentures are entitled, there shall be entered in the register the particulars specified in section 413(2).

**417(3) [Details of entries]** In the case of any other charge, there shall be entered–

(a) if it is a charge created by the company, the date of its creation, and if it was a charge existing on property acquired by the company, the date of the acquisition of the property,

(b) the amount secured by the charge,

(c) short particulars of the property charged,

(d) the persons entitled to the charge, and

(e) in the case of a floating charge, a statement of any of the provisions of the charge and of any instrument relating to it which prohibit or restrict or regulate the company's power to grant further securities ranking in priority to, or pari passu with, the floating charge, or which vary or otherwise regulate the order of ranking of the floating charge in relation to subsisting securities.

**417(4) [Inspection of register]** The register kept in pursuance of this section shall be open to inspection by any person.

## 418 Certificate of registration to be issued

**418(1) [Registrar to give certificate]** The registrar of companies shall give a certificate of the registration of any charge registered in pursuance of this Chapter.

**418(2) [Details re certificate; conclusive evidence]** The certificate–

(a) shall be either signed by the registrar, or authenticated by his official seal,

(b) shall state the name of the company and the person first-named in the charge among those entitled to the benefit of the charge (or, in the case of a series of debentures, the name of the holder of the first such debenture to be issued) and the amount secured by the charge, and

(c) is conclusive evidence that the requirements of this Chapter as to registration have been complied with.

## 419 Entries of satisfaction and relief

**419(1) [Memorandum of satisfaction may be entered on register]** The registrar of companies, on application being made to him in the prescribed form, and on receipt of a statutory declaration in the prescribed form verifying, with respect to any registered charge–

(a) that the debt for which the charge was given has been paid or satisfied in whole or in part, or

(b) that part of the property charged has been released from the charge or has ceased to form part of the company's property,

may enter on the register a memorandum of satisfaction (in whole or in part) regarding that fact.

**419(2) [Copy to registrar]** Where the registrar enters a memorandum of satisfaction in whole, he shall, if required, furnish the company with a copy of the memorandum.

by members of the transferor company or transferor companies, with or without any cash payment to members,

sections 425 to 427 shall, as regards that compromise or arrangement, have effect subject to the provisions of this section and Schedule 15B.

**History**

In s. 427A(1) "15B" substituted for the former "15A" by CA 1989, s. 114(2) as from 1 April 1990 (see SI 1990/355 (C 13), art. 4(a)).

**427A(2) [Cases referred to in s. 427A(1)]** The Cases referred to in subsection (1) are as follows–

*Case 1*

Where under the scheme the undertaking, property and liabilities of the company in respect of which the compromise or arrangement in question is proposed are to be transferred to another public company, other than one formed for the purpose of, or in connection with, the scheme.

*Case 2*

Where under the scheme the undertaking, property and liabilities of each of two or more public companies concerned in the scheme, including the company in respect of which the compromise or arrangement in question is proposed, are to be transferred to a company (whether or not a public company) formed for the purpose of, or in connection with, the scheme.

*Case 3*

Where under the scheme the undertaking, property and liabilities of the company in respect of which the compromise or arrangement in question is proposed are to be divided among and transferred to two or more companies each of which is either–

(a) a public company, or

(b) a company (whether or not a public company) formed for the purposes of, or in connection with, the scheme.

**427A(3) [Application to court for meeting]** Before sanctioning any compromise or arrangement under section 425(2) the court may, on the application of any pre-existing transferee company or any member or creditor of it or, an administration order being in force in relation to the company, the administrator, order a meeting of the members of the company or any class of them or of the creditors of the company or any class of them to be summoned in such manner as the court directs.

**427A(4) [Exception if company is winding up]** This section does not apply where the company in respect of which the compromise or arrangement is proposed is being wound up.

**427A(5) [Exception if application under s. 425(1)]** This section does not apply to compromises or arrangements in respect of which an application has been made to the court for an order under section 425(1) before 1 January 1988.

**427A(6) [Application if transferee is Northern Ireland company]** Where section 427 would apply in the case of a scheme but for the fact that the transferee company or any of the transferee companies is a company within the meaning of Article 3 of the Companies (Northern Ireland) Order 1986 (and thus not within the definition of "company" in subsection (6) of section 427), section 427 shall apply notwithstanding that fact.

**427A(7) [Registrar of Companies, Northern Ireland]** In the case of a scheme mentioned in subsection (1), for a company within the meaning of Article 3 of the Companies (Northern Ireland) Order 1986, the reference in section 427(5) to the registrar of companies shall have effect as a reference to the registrar as defined in Article 2 of that Order.

**427A(8) [Definitions]** In this section and Schedule 15B–

**"transferor company"** means a company whose undertaking, property and liabilities are to be transferred by means of a transfer envisaged in any of the Cases specified in subsection (2);

**"transferee company"** means a company to which a transfer envisaged in any of those Cases is to be made;

**"pre-existing transferee company"** means a transferee company other than one formed for the purpose of, or in connection with, the scheme;

**"compromise or arrangement"** means a compromise or arrangement to which subsection (1) applies;

**"the scheme"** means the scheme mentioned in subsection (1)(a);

**"company"** includes only a company as defined in section 735(1) except that, in the case of a transferee company, it also includes a company as defined in Article 3 of the Companies (Northern Ireland) Order 1986 (referred to in these definitions as a **"Northern Ireland company"**);

**"public company"** means, in relation to a transferee company which is a Northern Ireland company, a public company within the meaning of Article 12 of the Companies (Northern Ireland) Order 1986;

**"the registrar of companies"** means, in relation to a transferee company which is a Northern Ireland company, the registrar as defined in Article 2 of the Companies (Northern Ireland) Order 1986;

**"the Gazette"** means, in relation to a transferee company which is a Northern Ireland company, the Belfast Gazette;

**"Case 1 Scheme"**, **"Case 2 Scheme"** and **"Case 3 Scheme"** mean a scheme of a kind described in Cases 1, 2 and 3 of subsection (2) respectively;

**"property"** and **"liabilities"** have the same meaning as in section 427.

**History**

In s. 427A(8) "15B" substituted for the former "15A" by CA 1989, s. 114(2) as from 1 April 1990 (see SI 1990/355 (C 13), art. 4(a)).

S. 427A inserted by the Companies (Mergers and Divisions) Regulations 1987 (SI 1987/1991), reg. 2(a) and Sch., Pt. I, as from 1 January 1988.

**Note**

The Companies (Mergers and Divisions) Regulations 1987 (SI 1987/1991) (referred to above) implemented the Third and Sixth EC Company Law Directives (78/855, 82/891).

# PART XIIIA – TAKEOVER OFFERS

**Note**

Nothing in CA 1989, s. 144(1) (inserting new s. 736, 736A in CA 1985) affects the operation of Pt. XIIIA in relation to a take-over offer made before the commencement of that provision – 1 November 1990 (CA 1989, Sch. 18, para. 35).

## 428 "Takeover offers"

**428(1) ["A takeover offer"]** In this Part of this Act **"a takeover offer"** means an offer to acquire all the shares, or all the shares of any class or classes, in a company (other than shares which at the date of the offer are already held by the offeror), being an offer on terms which are the same in relation to all the shares to which the offer relates or, where those shares include shares of different classes, in relation to all the shares of each class.

**428(2) ["Shares" in s. 428(1)]** In subsection (1) **"shares"** means shares which have been allotted on the date of the offer but a takeover offer may include among the shares to which it relates all or any shares that are subsequently allotted before a date specified in or determined in accordance with the terms of the offer.

**428(3) [Terms re shares]** The terms offered in relation to any shares shall for the purposes of this section be treated as being the same in relation to all the shares or, as the case may be, all the shares of a class to which the offer relates notwithstanding any variation permitted by subsection (4).

**428(4) [Where variation permitted]** A variation is permitted by this subsection where–

(a) the law of a country or territory outside the United Kingdom precludes an offer of consideration in the form or any of the forms specified in the terms in question or precludes it except after compliance by the offeror with conditions with which he is unable to comply or which he regards as unduly onerous; and

(b) the variation is such that the persons to whom an offer of consideration in that form is precluded are able to receive consideration otherwise than in that form but of substantially equivalent value.

**428(5) [Shares already held by offeror in s. 428(1)]** The reference in subsection (1) to shares already held by the offeror includes a reference to shares which he has contracted to acquire but that shall not be construed as including shares which are the subject of a contract binding the holder to accept the offer when it is made, being a contract entered into by the holder either for no consideration and under seal or for no consideration other than a promise by the offeror to make the offer.

**428(6) [Application of s. 428(5) to Scotland]** In the application of subsection (5) to Scotland, the words "and under seal" shall be omitted.

**428(7) [Revision of terms of offer]** Where the terms of an offer make provision for their revision and for acceptances on the previous terms to be treated as acceptances on the revised terms, the revision shall not be regarded for the purposes of this Part of this Act as the making of a fresh offer and references in this Part of this Act to the date of the offer shall accordingly be construed as references to the date on which the original offer was made.

**428(8) ["The offeror", "the company"]** In this Part of this Act **"the offeror"** means, subject to section 430D, the person making a takeover offer and **"the company"** means the company whose shares are the subject of the offer.

**History**
See history note after s. 430F.

# 429 Right of offeror to buy out minority shareholders

**429(1) [Notice to shareholders]** If, in a case in which a takeover offer does not relate to shares of different classes, the offeror has by virtue of acceptances of the offer acquired or contracted to acquire not less than nine-tenths in value of the shares to which the offer relates he may give notice to the holder of any shares to which the offer relates which the offeror has not acquired or contracted to acquire that he desires to acquire those shares.

**429(2) [Notice where shares of different classes]** If, in a case in which a takeover offer relates to shares of different classes, the offeror has by virtue of acceptances of the offer acquired or contracted to acquire not less than nine-tenths in value of the shares of any class to which the offer relates, he may give notice to the holder of any shares of that class which the offeror has not acquired or contracted to acquire that he desires to acquire those shares.

**429(3) [Condition for s. 429(1), (2) notice]** No notice shall be given under subsection (1) or (2) unless the offeror has acquired or contracted to acquire the shares necessary to satisfy the minimum specified in that subsection before the end of the period of four months beginning with the date of the offer; and no such notice shall be given after the end of the period of two months beginning with the date on which he has acquired or contracted to acquire shares which satisfy that minimum.

**429(4) [Form of notice]** Any notice under this section shall be given in the prescribed manner; and when the offeror gives the first notice in relation to an offer he shall send a copy of it to the company together with a statutory declaration by him in the prescribed form stating that the conditions for the giving of the notice are satisfied.

**Note**
See also reg. 4 of the Companies (Forms) (Amendment) Regulations 1987 (SI 1987/752).

**429(5) [Statutory declaration where offeror company]** Where the offeror is a company (whether or not a company within the meaning of this Act) the statutory declaration shall be signed by a director.

**429(6) [Penalty for non-compliance]** Any person who fails to send a copy of a notice or a statutory declaration as required by subsection (4) or makes such a declaration for the purposes of that subsection knowing it to be false or without having reasonable grounds for believing it to be true shall be liable to imprisonment or a fine, or both, and for continued failure to send the copy or declaration, to a daily default fine.

**429(7) [Defence re s. 429(4) offence]** If any person is charged with an offence for failing to send a copy of a notice as required by subsection (4) it is a defence for him to prove that he took reasonable steps for securing compliance with that subsection.

**429(8) [Acquisition other than by acceptances of offer]** Where during the period within which a takeover offer can be accepted the offeror acquires or contracts to acquire any of the shares to which the offer relates but otherwise than by virtue of acceptances of the offer, then, if–

(a) the value of the consideration for which they are acquired or contracted to be acquired ("the acquisition consideration") does not at that time exceed the value of the consideration specified in the terms of the offer; or

(b) those terms are subsequently revised so that when the revision is announced the value of the acquisition consideration, at the time mentioned in paragraph (a) above, no longer exceeds the value of the consideration specified in those terms,

the offeror shall be treated for the purposes of this section as having acquired or contracted to acquire those shares by virtue of acceptances of the offer; but in any other case those shares shall be treated as excluded from those to which the offer relates.

**History**
See history note after s. 430F.

## 430 Effect of notice under s. 429

**430(1) [Application]** The following provisions shall, subject to section 430C, have effect where a notice is given in respect of any shares under section 429.

**430(2) [Right and duty of offeror]** The offeror shall be entitled and bound to acquire those shares on the terms of the offer.

**430(3) [Notice to include details re choice of consideration]** Where the terms of an offer are such as to give the holder of any shares a choice of consideration the notice shall give particulars of the choice and state–

(a) that the holder of the shares may within six weeks from the date of the notice indicate his choice by a written communication sent to the offeror at an address specified in the notice; and

(b) which consideration specified in the offer is to be taken as applying in default of his indicating a choice as aforesaid;

and the terms of the offer mentioned in subsection (2) shall be determined accordingly.

**430(4) [Application of s. 430(3)]** Subsection (3) applies whether or not any time-limit or other conditions applicable to the choice under the terms of the offer can still be complied with; and if the consideration chosen by the holder of the shares–

(a) is not cash and the offeror is no longer able to provide it; or

(b) was to have been provided by a third party who is no longer bound or able to provide it,

the consideration shall be taken to consist of an amount of cash payable by the offeror which at the date of the notice is equivalent to the chosen consideration.

**430(5) [Copy of notice to company etc.]** At the end of six weeks from the date of the notice the offeror shall forthwith–

(a) send a copy of the notice to the company; and

(b) pay or transfer to the company the consideration for the shares to which the notice relates.

**430(6) [If shares registered]** If the shares to which the notice relates are registered the copy of the notice sent to the company under subsection (5)(a) shall be accompanied by an instrument of transfer executed on behalf of the shareholder by a person appointed by the offeror; and on receipt of that instrument the company shall register the offeror as the holder of those shares.

**430(7) [If shares transferable by delivery of warrants]** If the shares to which the notice relates are transferable by the delivery of warrants or other instruments the copy of the notice sent to the company under subsection (5)(a) shall be accompanied by a statement to that effect; and the company shall on receipt of the statement issue the offeror with warrants or other instruments in respect of the shares and those already in issue in respect of the shares shall become void.

**430(8) [S. 430(5) consideration]** Where the consideration referred to in paragraph (b) of subsection (5) consists of shares or securities to be allotted by the offeror the reference in that paragraph to the transfer of the consideration shall be construed as a reference to the allotment of the shares or securities to the company.

**430(9) [Sums under s. 430(5) to be held on trust]** Any sum received by a company under paragraph (b) of subsection (5) and any other consideration received under that paragraph shall be held by the company on trust for the person entitled to the shares in respect of which the sum or other consideration was received.

**430(10) [S. 430(5) sums to be paid into separate bank account]** Any sum received by a company under paragraph (b) of subsection (5), and any dividend or other sum accruing from any other consideration received by a company under that paragraph, shall be paid into a separate bank account, being an account the balance on which bears interest at an appropriate rate and can be withdrawn by such notice (if any) as is appropriate.

**430(11) [Where person entitled to consideration unable to be found]** Where after reasonable enquiry made at such intervals as are reasonable the person entitled to any consideration held on trust by virtue of subsection (9) cannot be found and twelve years have elapsed since the consideration was received or the company is wound up the consideration (together with any interest, dividend or other benefit that has accrued from it) shall be paid into court.

**430(12) [Company registered in Scotland]** In relation to a company registered in Scotland, subsections (13) and (14) shall apply in place of subsection (11).

**430(13) [Termination of trust etc. re s. 430(11)]** Where after reasonable enquiry made at such intervals as are reasonable the person entitled to any consideration held on trust by virtue of subsection (9) cannot be found and twelve years have elapsed since the consideration was received or the company is wound up–

(a) the trust shall terminate;

(b) the company or, as the case may be, the liquidator shall sell any consideration other than cash and any benefit other than cash that has accrued from the consideration; and

(c) a sum representing–
   (i) the consideration so far as it is cash;
   (ii) the proceeds of any sale under paragraph (b) above; and
   (iii) any interest, dividend or other benefit that has accrued from the consideration,

shall be deposited in the name of the Accountant of Court in a bank account such as is referred to in subsection (10) and the receipt for the deposit shall be transmitted to the Accountant of Court.

**430(14) [Application of Bankruptcy (Scotland) Act 1985]** Section 58 of the Bankruptcy (Scotland) Act 1985 (so far as consistent with this Act) shall apply with any necessary modifications to sums deposited under subsection (13) as that section applies to sums deposited under section 57(1)(a) of that Act.

**430(15) [Expenses of s. 430(11), (13) enquiry]** The expenses of any such enquiry as is mentioned in subsection (11) or (13) may be defrayed out of the money or other property held on trust for the person or persons to whom the enquiry relates.

**History**
See history note after s. 430F.

## 430A Right of minority shareholder to be bought out by offeror

**430A(1) [Shareholder may require acquisition]** If a takeover offer relates to all the shares in a company and at any time before the end of the period within which the offer can be accepted–

(a) the offeror has by virtue of acceptances of the offer acquired or contracted to acquire some (but not all) of the shares to which the offer relates; and

(b) those shares, with or without any other shares in the company which he has acquired or contracted to acquire, amount to not less than nine-tenths in value of all the shares in the company, the holder of any shares to which the offer relates who has not accepted the offer may by a written communication addressed to the offeror require him to acquire those shares.

**430A(2) [Right re classes of shares]** If a takeover offer relates to shares of any class or classes and at any time before the end of the period within which the offer can be accepted–

(a) the offeror has by virtue of acceptances of the offer acquired or contracted to acquire some (but not all) of the shares of any class to which the offer relates; and

(b) those shares, with or without any other shares of that class which he has acquired or contracted to acquire, amount to not less than nine-tenths in value of all the shares of that class,

the holder of any shares of that class who has not accepted the offer may by a written communication addressed to the offeror require him to acquire those shares.

**430A(3) [Notice within one month of s. 430A(1), (2) time]** Within one month of the time specified in subsection (1) or, as the case may be, subsection (2) the offeror shall give any shareholder who has not accepted the offer notice in the prescribed manner of the rights that are exercisable by him under that subsection; and if the notice is given before the end of the period mentioned in that subsection it shall state that the offer is still open for acceptance.

**Note**

See also reg. 4 of the Companies (Forms) (Amendment) Regulations 1987 (SI 1987/752).

**430A(4) [S. 430A(3) may specify period]** A notice under subsection (3) may specify a period for the exercise of the rights conferred by this section and in that event the rights shall not be exercisable after the end of that period; but no such period shall end less than three months after the end of the period within which the offer can be accepted.

**430A(5) [Non-application of s. 430A(3)]** Subsection (3) does not apply if the offeror has given the shareholder a notice in respect of the shares in question under section 429.

**430A(6) [Penalty on default]** If the offeror fails to comply with subsection (3) he and, if the offeror is a company, every officer of the company who is in default or to whose neglect the failure is attributable, shall be liable to a fine and, for continued contravention, to a daily default fine.

**430A(7) [Defence]** If an offeror other than a company is charged with an offence for failing to comply with subsection (3) it is a defence for him to prove that he took all reasonable steps for securing compliance with that subsection.

**History**

See history note after s. 430F.

# 430B Effect of requirement under s. 430A

**430B(1) [Application]** The following provisions shall, subject to section 430C, have effect where a shareholder exercises his rights in respect of any shares under section 430A.

**430B(2) [Right and duty re aquisition of shares]** The offeror shall be entitled and bound to acquire those shares on the terms of the offer or on such other terms as may be agreed.

**430B(3) [Indication of choice re consideration]** Where the terms of an offer are such as to give the holder of shares a choice of consideration the holder of the shares may indicate his choice when requiring the offeror to acquire them and the notice given to the holder under section 430A(3)–

(a) shall give particulars of the choice and of the rights conferred by this subsection; and

(b) may state which consideration specified in the offer is to be taken as applying in default of his indicating a choice;

and the terms of the offer mentioned in subsection (2) shall be determined accordingly.

**430B(4) [Application of s. 430B(3)]** Subsection (3) applies whether or not any time-limit or other conditions applicable to the choice under the terms of the offer can still be complied with; and if the consideration chosen by the holder of the shares–

(a) is not cash and the offeror is no longer able to provide it; or

(b) was to have been provided by a third party who is no longer bound or able to provide it, the consideration shall be taken to consist of an amount of cash payable by the offeror which at the date when the holder of the shares requires the offeror to acquire them is equivalent to the chosen consideration.

**History**
See history note after s. 430F.

## 430C Applications to the court

**430C(1) [Order by court]** Where a notice is given under section 429 to the holder of any shares the court may, on an application made by him within six weeks from the date on which the notice was given–

(a) order that the offeror shall not be entitled and bound to acquire the shares; or

(b) specify terms of acquisition different from those of the offer.

**430C(2) [Where s. 430C application pending]** If an application to the court under subsection (1) is pending at the end of the period mentioned in subsection (5) of section 430 that subsection shall not have effect until the application has been disposed of.

**430C(3) [Where s. 430A rights exercised]** Where the holder of any shares exercises his rights under section 430A the court may, on an application made by him or the offeror, order that the terms on which the offeror is entitled and bound to acquire the shares shall be such as the court thinks fit.

**430C(4) [Order for costs, expenses]** No order for costs or expenses shall be made against a shareholder making an application under subsection (1) or (3) unless the court considers–

(a) that the application was unnecessary, improper or vexatious; or

(b) that there has been unreasonable delay in making the application or unreasonable conduct on his part in conducting the proceedings on the application.

**430C(5) [Where not sufficient acceptance for s. 429 notices]** Where a takeover offer has not been accepted to the extent necessary for entitling the offeror to give notices under subsection (1) or (2) of section 429 the court may, on the application of the offeror, make an order authorising him to give notices under that subsection if satisfied–

(a) that the offeror has after reasonable enquiry been unable to trace one or more of the persons holding shares to which the offer relates;

(b) that the shares which the offeror has acquired or contracted to acquire by virtue of acceptances of the offer, together with the shares held by the person or persons mentioned in paragraph (a), amount to not less than the minimum specified in that subsection; and

(c) that the consideration offered is fair and reasonable;

but the court shall not make an order under this subsection unless it considers that it is just and equitable to do so having regard, in particular, to the number of shareholders who have been traced but who have not accepted the offer.

**History**
See history note after s. 430F.

## 430D Joint offers

**430D(1) [Making of joint offers]** A takeover offer may be made by two or more persons jointly and in that event this Part of this Act has effect with the following modifications.

**430D(2) [Satisfaction of s. 429, 430A conditions]** The conditions for the exercise of the rights conferred by sections 429 and 430A shall be satisfied by the joint offerors acquiring or contracting to acquire the necessary shares jointly (as respects acquisitions by virtue of acceptances of the offer) and either jointly or separately (in other cases); and, subject to the following provisions, the rights and obligations of the offeror under those sections and sections 430 and 430B shall be respectively joint rights and joint and several obligations of the joint offerors.

**430D(3) [Sufficient compliance with s. 429, 430A]** It shall be a sufficient compliance with any provision of those sections requiring or authorising a notice or other document to be given or sent by or to the joint offerors that it is given or sent by or to any of them; but the statutory declaration required by section 429(4) shall be made by all of them and, in the case of a joint offeror being a company, signed by a director of that company.

**430D(4) [References to offeror in s. 428, 430(8), 430E]** In sections 428, 430(8) and 430E references to the offeror shall be construed as references to the joint offerors or any of them.

**430D(5) [References to offeror in s. 430(6), (7)]** In section 430(6) and (7) references to the offeror shall be construed as references to the joint offerors or such of them as they may determine.

**430D(6) [References in s. 430(4)(a), 430B(4)(a)]** In sections 430(4)(a) and 430B(4)(a) references to the offeror being no longer able to provide the relevant consideration shall be construed as references to none of the joint offerors being able to do so.

**430D(7) [References to offeror in s. 430C]** In section 430C references to the offeror shall be construed as references to the joint offerors except that any application under subsection (3) or (5) may be made by any of them and the reference in subsection (5)(a) to the offeror having been unable to trace one or more of the persons holding shares shall be construed as a reference to none of the offerors having been able to do so.

**History**
See history note after s. 430F.

## 430E Associates

**430E(1) [Satisfaction re s. 428(1) requirement]** The requirement in section 428(1) that a takeover offer must extend to all the shares, or all the shares of any class or classes, in a company shall be regarded as satisfied notwithstanding that the offer does not extend to shares which associates of the offeror hold or have contracted to acquire; but, subject to subsection (2), shares which any such associate holds or has contracted to acquire, whether at the time when the offer is made or subsequently, shall be disregarded for the purposes of any reference in this Part of this Act to the shares to which a takeover offer relates.

**430E(2) [Acquisition by associate of offeror]** Where during the period within which a takeover offer can be accepted any associate of the offeror acquires or contracts to acquire any of the shares to which the offer relates, then, if the condition specified in subsection (8)(a) or (b) of section 429 is satisfied as respects those shares they shall be treated for the purposes of that section as shares to which the offer relates.

**430E(3) [Interpretation re s. 430A(1)(b), (2)(b)]** In section 430A(1)(b) and (2)(b) the reference to shares which the offeror has acquired or contracted to acquire shall include a reference to shares which any associate of his has acquired or contracted to acquire.

**430E(4) ["Associate"]** In this section "**associate**", in relation to an offeror means–

(a) a nominee of the offeror;

(b) a holding company, subsidiary or fellow subsidiary of the offeror or a nominee of such a holding company, subsidiary or fellow subsidiary;

(c) a body corporate in which the offeror is substantially interested; or

(d) any person who is, or is a nominee of, a party to an agreement with the offeror for the acquisition of, or of an interest in, the shares which are the subject of the takeover offer, being an agreement which includes provisions imposing obligations or restrictions such as are mentioned in section 204(2)(a).

**430E(5) [Interpretation re s. 430E(4)(b)]** For the purposes of subsection (4)(b) a company is a fellow subsidiary of another body corporate if both are subsidiaries of the same body corporate but neither is a subsidiary of the other.

**430E(6) [Interpretation re s. 430E(4)(c)]** For the purposes of subsection (4)(c) an offeror has a substantial interest in a body corporate if–

(a) that body or its directors are accustomed to act in accordance with his directions or instructions; or

(b) he is entitled to exercise or control the exercise of one-third or more of the voting power at general meetings of that body.

**430E(7) [Application of other sections to s. 430E(4)(d), (6)]** Subsections (5) and (6) of section 204 shall apply to subsection (4)(d) above as they apply to that section and subsections (3) and (4) of section 203 shall apply for the purposes of subsection (6) above as they apply for the purposes of subsection (2)(b) of that section.

**430E(8) [Spouse et al. of offeror]** Where the offeror is an individual his associates shall also include his spouse and any minor child or step-child of his.

# 430F Convertible securities

**430F(1) [Securities to be treated as shares]** For the purposes of this Part of this Act securities of a company shall be treated as shares in the company if they are convertible into or entitle the holder to subscribe for such shares; and references to the holder of shares or a shareholder shall be construed accordingly.

**430F(2) [Qualification to s. 430F(1)]** Subsection (1) shall not be construed as requiring any securities to be treated–

(a) as shares of the same class as those into which they are convertible or for which the holder is entitled to subscribe; or

(b) as shares of the same class as other securities by reason only that the shares into which they are convertible or for which the holder is entitled to subscribe are of the same class.

**History**

S. 428–430F (Pt. XIIIA) substituted by Financial Services Act 1986, s. 172 and Sch. 12 as from 30 April 1987 (see SI 1986/2246 (C 88)); but note the exception in s. 172(2) for offers made before that date. The former s. 428–430 read as follows:

**"428 Power to acquire shares of dissenting minority**

**428(1)** This section applies where a scheme or contract involving the transfer of shares or any class of shares in a company ("the transferor company") to another company, whether or not a company as defined in section 735(1) ("the transferee company") has, within 4 months after the making of the offer in that behalf by the transferee company, been approved by the holders of not less than nine-tenths in value of the shares whose transfer is involved (other than shares already held at the date of the offer by, or by a nominee for, the transferee company or its subsidiary).

**(2)** In those circumstances, the transferee company may, at any time within 2 months after the expiration of the 4 months mentioned above, give notice in the prescribed manner to any dissenting shareholder that it desires to acquire his shares.

**(3)** The expression **"dissenting shareholder"** includes a shareholder who has not assented to the scheme or contract, and any shareholder who has failed or refused to transfer his shares to the transferee company in accordance with the scheme or contract.

**(4)** If such a notice is given, the transferee company is then (unless on an application made by the dissenting shareholder within one month from the date on which the notice was given, the court thinks fit to order otherwise) entitled and bound to acquire those shares on the terms on which, under the scheme or contract, the shares of the approving shareholders are to be transferred to the transferee company.

**(5)** But where shares in the transferor company of the same class or classes as the shares whose transfer is involved are already held (at the date of the offer) by, or by a nominee for, the transferee company or its subsidiary to a value greater than one-tenth of the aggregate of their value and that of the shares (other than those already so held) whose transfer is involved, subsections (2) and (4) do not apply unless–

(a) the transferee company offers the same terms to all holders of the shares (other than those already so held) whose transfer is involved or, where those shares include shares of different classes, of each class of them, and

(b) the holders who approve the scheme or contract, besides holding not less than nine-tenths in value of the shares (other than those so held) whose transfer is involved, are not less than three-fourths in number of the holders of those shares.

**429 Dissentient's right to compel acquisition of his shares**

**429(1)** This section applies where, in pursuance of such a scheme or contract as is mentioned in section 428(1), shares in a company are transferred to another company or its nominee, and those shares (together with any other shares in the first-mentioned company held by, or by a nominee for, the transferee company or its subsidiary at the date of the transfer) comprise or include nine-tenths in value of the shares in the first-mentioned company or of any class of those shares.

**(2)** The transferee company shall within one month from the date of the transfer (unless on a previous transfer in pursuance of the scheme or contract it has already complied with this requirement) give notice of that fact in the prescribed manner to the holders of the remaining shares or of the remaining shares of that class (as the case may be) who have not assented to the scheme or contract.

**(3)** Any such holder may, within 3 months from the giving of that notice to him, himself give notice (in the prescribed form) requiring the transferee company to acquire the shares in question.

**(4)** If a shareholder gives notice under subsection (3) with respect to any shares, the transferee company is then entitled and bound to acquire those shares on the terms on which under the scheme or contract the shares of the approving shareholders were transferred to it, or on such other terms as may be agreed or as the court on the application of either the transferee company or the shareholder thinks fit to order.

**430 Provisions supplementing s. 428, 429**

**430(1)** Where notice has been given by the transferee company under section 428(2) and the court has not, on an application made by the dissenting shareholder, ordered to the contrary, the two following subsections apply.

**(2)** The transferee company shall, on expiration of one month from the date on which the notice has been given (or, if an application to the court by the dissenting shareholder is then pending, after that application has been disposed of) transmit a copy of the notice to the transferor company together with an instrument of transfer executed on behalf of the shareholder by any person appointed by the transferee company and on its own behalf by the transferee company.

An instrument of transfer is not required for any share for which a share warrant is for the time being outstanding.

**(3)** The transferee company shall also pay or transfer to the transferor company the amount or other consideration representing the price payable by the transferee company for the shares which by virtue of section 428(4) that company is entitled to acquire; and the transferor company shall thereupon register the transferee company as the holder of those shares.

**(4)** Any sums received by the transferor company under this section shall be paid into a separate bank account, and any such sums and any other consideration so received shall be held by that company on trust for the several persons entitled to the shares in respect of which those sums, or that other consideration, were respectively received."

# PART XIV – INVESTIGATION OF COMPANIES AND THEIR AFFAIRS; REQUISITION OF DOCUMENTS

## APPOINTMENT AND FUNCTIONS OF INSPECTORS

## 431 Investigation of a company on its own application or that of its members

**431(1) [Appointment of inspectors]** The Secretary of State may appoint one or more competent inspectors to investigate the affairs of a company and to report on them in such manner as he may direct.

**431(2) [Appointment made on application]** The appointment may be made–

(a) in the case of a company having a share capital, on the application either of not less than 200 members or of members holding not less than one-tenth of the shares issued,

(b) in the case of a company not having a share capital, on the application of not less than one-fifth in number of the persons on the company's register of members, and

(c) in any case, on application of the company.

**431(3) [Supporting evidence to application]** The application shall be supported by such evidence as the Secretary of State may require for the purpose of showing that the applicant or applicants have good reason for requiring the investigation.

**431(4) [Applicants may be required to give security etc.]** The Secretary of State may, before appointing inspectors, require the applicant or applicants to give security, to an amount not exceeding £5,000, or such other sum as he may by order specify, for payment of the costs of the investigation.

An order under this subsection shall be made by statutory instrument subject to annulment in pursuance of a resolution of either House of Parliament.

## 432 Other company investigations

**432(1) [Appointment of inspectors]** The Secretary of State shall appoint one or more competent inspectors to investigate the affairs of a company and report on them in such manner as he directs, if the court by order declares that its affairs ought to be so investigated.

**432(2) [Circumstances when appointment may be made]** The Secretary of State may make such an appointment if it appears to him that there are circumstances suggesting–

(a) that the company's affairs are being or have been conducted with intent to defraud its creditors or the creditors of any other person, or otherwise for a fraudulent or unlawful purpose, or in a manner which is unfairly prejudicial to some part of its members, or

(b) that any actual or proposed act or omission of the company (including an act or omission on its behalf) is or would be so prejudicial, or that the company was formed for any fraudulent or unlawful purpose, or

(c) that persons concerned with the company's formation or the management of its affairs have in connection therewith been guilty of fraud, misfeasance or other misconduct towards it or towards its members, or

(d) that the company's members have not been given all the information with respect to its affairs which they might reasonably expect.

**432(2A) [Terms of appointment]** Inspectors may be appointed under subsection (2) on terms that any report they may make is not for publication; and in such a case, the provisions of section 437(3)(availability and publication of inspectors' reports) do not apply.

**History**

S. 432(2A) inserted by CA 1989, s. 55 as from 21 February 1990 (see SI 1990/142 (C 5), art. 4).

**432(3) [Extent of powers under s. 432(1), (2)]** Subsections (1) and (2) are without prejudice to the powers of the Secretary of State under section 431; and the power conferred by subsection (2) is exercisable with respect to a body corporate notwithstanding that it is in course of being voluntarily wound up.

**432(4) [Interpretation of s. 432(2)(a)]** The reference in subsection (2)(a) to a company's members includes any person who is not a member but to whom shares in the company have been transferred or transmitted by operation of law.

## 433 Inspectors' powers during investigation

**433(1) [Investigation of connected body corporate]** If inspectors appointed under section 431 or 432 to investigate the affairs of a company think it necessary for the purposes of their investigation to investigate also the affairs of another body corporate which is or at any relevant time has been the company's subsidiary or holding company, or a subsidiary of its holding company or a holding company of its subsidiary, they have power to do so; and they shall report on the affairs of the other body corporate so far as they think that the results of their investigation of its affairs are relevant to the investigation of the affairs of the company first mentioned above.

**433(2)** (Omitted by Financial Services Act 1986, s. 182 and Sch. 13, para. 7 as from 15, 27 November 1986 and repealed by s. 212(3) and Sch. 17 as from 27 November 1986.)

**History**

In regard to the dates of the above omission and repeal see SI 1986/1940 (C 69) and SI 1986/2031 (C 76); s. 433(2) formerly read as follows:

"Inspectors appointed under either section may at any time in the course of their investigation, without the necessity of making an interim report, inform the Secretary of State of matters coming to their knowledge as a result of the investigation tending to show that an offence has been committed."

## 434 Production of documents and evidence to inspectors

**434(1) [Duty of company officers et al.]** When inspectors are appointed under section 431 or 432, it is the duty of all officers and agents of the company, and of all officers and agents of any other body corporate whose affairs are investigated under section 433(1)–

(a) to produce to the inspectors all documents of or relating to the company or, as the case may be, the other body corporate which are in their custody or power,

(b) to attend before the inspectors when required to do so, and

(c) otherwise to give the inspectors all assistance in connection with the investigation which they are reasonably able to give.

**History**

In s. 434(1) the word "documents" substituted for the former words "books and documents" by CA 1989, s. 56(1), (2) as from 21 February 1990 (see SI 1990/142 (C 5), art. 4).

**434(2) [Power of inspectors re production etc.]** If the inspectors consider that an officer or agent of the company or other body corporate, or any other person, is or may be in possession of information relating to a matter which they believe to be relevant to the investigation, they may require him–

(a) to produce to them any documents in his custody or power relating to that matter,

(b) to attend before them, and

(c) otherwise to give them all assistance in connection with the investigation which he is reasonably able to give;

and it is that person's duty to comply with the requirement.

**History**
S. 434(2) substituted by CA 1989, s. 56(1), (3) as from 21 February 1990 (see SI 1990/142(C 5), art. 4); s. 434(2) formerly read as follows:

"If the inspectors consider that a person other than an officer or agent of the company or other body corporate is or may be in possession of information concerning its affairs, they may require that person to produce to them any books or documents in his custody or power relating to the company or other body corporate, to attend before them and otherwise to give them all assistance in connection with the investigation which he is reasonably able to give; and it is that person's duty to comply with the requirement."

**434(3) [Examination on oath]** An inspector may for the purposes of the investigation examine any person on oath, and may administer an oath accordingly.

**History**
S. 434(3) substituted by CA 1989, s. 56(1), (4) as from 21 February 1990 (see SI 1990/142 (C 5), art. 4); s. 434(3) formerly read as follows:

"An inspector may examine on oath the officers and agents of the company or other body corporate, and any such person as is mentioned in subsection (2), in relation to the affairs of the company or other body, and may administer an oath accordingly."

**434(4) [Interpretation]** In this section a reference to officers or to agents includes past, as well as present, officers or agents (as the case may be); and **"agents"**, in relation to a company or other body corporate, includes its bankers and solicitors and persons employed by it as auditors, whether these persons are or are not officers of the company or other body corporate.

**Note**
In regard to the interpretation of the reference to "solicitors" in s. 434(4) see the Solicitors' Incorporated Practices Order 1991 (SI 1991/2684).

**434(5) [Answer can be used in evidence]** An answer given by a person to a question put to him in exercise of powers conferred by this section (whether as it has effect in relation to an investigation under any of sections 431 to 433, or as applied by any other section in this Part) may be used in evidence against him.

**434(5A) [Limits on use of answer in criminal proceedings]** However, in criminal proceedings in which that person is charged with an offence to which this subsection applies–

(a) no evidence relating to the answer may be adduced, and

(b) no question relating to it may be asked,

by or on behalf of the prosecution, unless evidence relating to it is adduced, or a question relating to it is asked, in the proceedings by or on behalf of that person.

**History**
S. 434(5A) inserted by Youth Justice and Criminal Evidence Act 1999, s. 59, 68(3) and Sch. 3, para. 5, with effect from 14 April 2000 (see Youth Justice and Criminal Evidence Act 1999 (Commencement No. 2) Order 2000 (SI 2000/1034 (C. 27)), art. 2(a)).

**434(5B) [Offences to which s. 434(5A) applies]** Subsection (5A) applies to any offence other than–

(a) an offence under section 2 or 5 of the Perjury Act 1911 (false statements made on oath otherwise than in judicial proceedings or made otherwise than on oath); or

(b) an offence under section 44(1) or (2) of the Criminal Law (Consolidation) (Scotland) Act 1995 (false statements made on oath or otherwise than on oath).

**History**
S. 434(5B) inserted by Youth Justice and Criminal Evidence Act 1999, s. 59, 68(3) and Sch. 3, para. 5, with effect from 14 April 2000 (see Youth Justice and Criminal Evidence Act 1999 (Commencement No. 2) Order 2000 (SI 2000/1034 (C. 27)), art. 2(a)).

**434(6) ["Documents"]** In this section **"documents"** includes information recorded in any form; and, in relation to information recorded otherwise than in legible form, the power to require its production includes power to require the production of a copy of the information in legible form.

**History**
S. 434(6) inserted by CA 1989, s. 56(1), (5) as from 21 February 1990 (see SI 1990/142 (C 5), art. 4).

**Note**
See the the Open-Ended Investment Companies (Investment Companies with Variable Capital) Regulations 1996 (SI 1996/2827), reg. 22(3), (4) for modifications to s. 434 for the purpose of those Regulations.

## 435 Power of inspector to call for directors' bank accounts

435 (Repealed by Companies Act 1989, s. 212 and Sch. 24 as from 21 February 1990.)

**History**
In regard to the date of the above repeal see SI 1990/142 (C 5), art. 7(d); s. 435 formerly read as follows:

**442(3C) [Alternative investigation under s. 444]** If on an application under subsection (3) it appears to the Secretary of State that the powers conferred by section 444 are sufficient for the purposes of investigating the matters which inspectors would be appointed to investigate, he may instead conduct the investigation under that section.

**History**
S. 442(3)–(3C) substituted for the former s. 442(3) by CA 1989, s. 62 as from 21 February 1990 (see SI 1990/142 (C 5), art. 4); the former s. 442(3) read as follows:

"If application for an investigation under this section with respect to particular shares or debentures of a company is made to the Secretary of State by members of the company, and the number of applicants or the amount of the shares held by them is not less than that required for an application for the appointment of inspectors under section 431(2)(a) and (b)–

(a) the Secretary of State shall appoint inspectors to conduct the investigation (unless he is satisfied that the application is vexatious), and

(b) the inspectors' appointment shall not exclude from the scope of their investigation any matter which the application seeks to have included, except in so far as the Secretary of State is satisfied that it is unreasonable for that matter to be investigated."

**442(4) [Powers of inspectors]** Subject to the terms of their appointment, the inspectors' powers extend to the investigation of any circumstances suggesting the existence of an arrangement or understanding which, though not legally binding, is or was observed or likely to be observed in practice and which is relevant to the purposes of the investigation.

## 443 Provisions applicable on investigation under s. 442

**443(1) [Application of s. 433(1), 434, 436, 437]** For purposes of an investigation under section 442, sections 433(1), 434, 436 and 437 apply with the necessary modifications of references to the affairs of the company or to those of any other body corporate, subject however to the following subsections.

**443(2) [How those sections apply]** Those sections apply to–

(a) all persons who are or have been, or whom the inspector has reasonable cause to believe to be or have been, financially interested in the success or failure or the apparent success or failure of the company or any other body corporate whose membership is investigated with that of the company, or able to control or materially influence its policy (including persons concerned only on behalf of others), and

(b) any other person whom the inspector has reasonable cause to believe possesses information relevant to the investigation,

as they apply in relation to officers and agents of the company or the other body corporate (as the case may be).

**443(3) [Parts of report need not be disclosed]** If the Secretary of State is of opinion that there is good reason for not divulging any part of a report made by virtue of section 442 and this section, he may under section 437 disclose the report with the omission of that part; and he may cause to be kept by the registrar of companies a copy of the report with that part omitted or, in the case of any other such report, a copy of the whole report.

**443(4)** (Repealed by Companies Act 1989, s. 212 and Sch. 24 as from 21 February 1990.)

**History**
In regard to the date of the above repeal see SI 1990/142 (C 5), art. 7(d); s. 443(4) formerly read as follows:

"The expenses of an investigation under section 442 shall be defrayed by the Secretary of State out of money provided by Parliament."

**Note**
See the Companies (Inspectors' Reports) (Fees) Regulations 1981 (SI 1981/1686).

## 444 Power to obtain information as to those interested in shares, etc.

**444(1) [Secretary of State may require persons to produce information]** If it appears to the Secretary of State that there is good reason to investigate the ownership of any shares in or debentures of a company and that it is unnecessary to appoint inspectors for the purpose, he may require any person whom he has reasonable cause to believe to have or to be able to obtain any information as to the present and past interests in those shares or debentures and the names and addresses of the persons interested and of any persons who act or have acted on their behalf in relation to the shares or debentures to give any such information to the Secretary of State.

**444(2) [Interpretation]** For this purpose a person is deemed to have an interest in shares or debentures if he has any right to acquire or dispose of them or of any interest in them, or to vote in respect of them, or if his consent is necessary for the exercise of any of the rights of other persons interested in them, or if other persons interested in them can be required, or are accustomed, to exercise their rights in accordance with his instructions.

**444(3) [Failure to give information etc.]** A person who fails to give information required of him under this section, or who in giving such information makes any statement which he knows to be false in a material particular, or recklessly makes any statement which is false in a material particular, is liable to imprisonment or a fine, or both.

# 445 Power to impose restrictions on shares and debentures

**445(1) [Secretary may impose restrictions]** If in connection with an investigation under either section 442 or 444 it appears to the Secretary of State that there is difficulty in finding out the relevant facts about any shares (whether issued or to be issued), he may by order direct that the shares shall until further order be subject to the restrictions of Part XV of this Act.

**445(1A) [Directions by Secretary of State to protect third parties' rights]** If the Secretary of State is satisfied that an order under subsection (1) may unfairly affect the rights of third parties in respect of shares then the Secretary of State, for the purpose of protecting such rights and subject to such terms as he thinks fit, may direct that such acts by such persons or descriptions of persons and for such purposes as may be set out in the order, shall not constitute a breach of the restrictions of Part XV of this Act.

**History**

S. 445(1A) inserted by the Companies (Disclosure of Interests in Shares) (Orders imposing restrictions on shares) Regulations 1991 (SI 1991/1646), reg. 5(a) as from 18 July 1991.

**445(2) [Application of s. 445 and Pt. XV re debentures]** This section, and Part XV in its application to orders under it, apply in relation to debentures as in relation to shares save that subsection (1A) shall not so apply.

**History**

In s. 445(2) the words "save that subsection (1A) shall not so apply" at the end inserted by the Companies (Disclosure of Interests in Shares) (Orders imposing restrictions on shares) Regulations 1991 (SI 1991/1646), reg. 5(b) as from 18 July 1991.

# 446 Investigation of share dealings

**446(1) [Inspectors may be appointed by Secretary of State]** If it appears to the Secretary of State that there are circumstances suggesting that contraventions may have occurred, in relation to a company's shares or debentures, of section 323 or 324 (taken with Schedule 13), or of subsections (3) to (5) of section 328 (restrictions on share dealings by directors and their families; obligation of director to disclose shareholding in his own company), he may appoint one or more competent inspectors to carry out such investigations as are requisite to establish whether or not such contraventions have occurred and to report the result of their investigations to him.

**446(2) [Limits of investigation]** The appointment of inspectors under this section may limit the period to which their investigation is to extend or confine it to shares or debentures of a particular class, or both.

**446(3) [Application of s. 434–437]** For purposes of an investigation under this section, sections 434 to 437 apply–

(a) with the substitution, for references to any other body corporate whose affairs are investigated under section 433(1), of a reference to any other body corporate which is, or has at any relevant time been, the company's subsidiary or holding company, or a subsidiary of its holding company.

**History**

In s. 446(3) the words "to 437" substituted for the former words "to 436" by Financial Services Act 1986, s. 182 and Sch. 7, para. 8 as from 27 November 1986 – see SI 1986/2031 (C 76). Also para. (b) and the word "and" preceding it repealed by CA 1989, s. 212 and Sch. 24 as from 21 February 1990 (see SI 1990/142 (C 5), art. 7(d)); the former para. (b) read as follows:

"(b) with the necessary modification of references in section 436 to the affairs of the company or other body corporate."

**446(4) [How s. 434–436 apply]** Sections 434 to 436 apply under the preceding subsection–

(a) to any individual who is an authorised person within the meaning of the Financial Services Act 1986;

(b) to any individual who holds a permission granted under paragraph 23 of Schedule 1 to that Act;

(c) to any officer (whether past or present) of a body corporate which is such an authorised person or holds such a permission;

(d) to any partner (whether past or present) in a partnership which is such an authorised person or holds such a permission;

(e) to any member of the governing body or officer (in either case whether past or present) of an unincorporated association which is such an authorised person or holds such a permission

as they apply to officers of the company or of the other body corporate.

**History**

In s. 446(4), para. (a) to (e) substituted for former para. (a) to (c) by Financial Services Act 1986, s. 212(2) and Sch. 16, para. 21 as from 29 April 1988 (see SI 1988/740 (C 22)); the former para. (a) to (c) read as follows:

"(a) to members of a recognised stock exchange or of a recognised association of dealers in securities who are individuals and to officers (past as well as present) of members of such an exchange or association being bodies corporate,

(b) to holders of licences granted under section 3 of the Prevention of Fraud (Investments) Act 1958 who are individuals and to officers (past as well as present) of holders of licences so granted being bodies corporate, and

(c) to any individual declared by an order of the Secretary of State for the time being in force to be an exempted dealer for purposes of that Act and to officers (past as well as present) of any body corporate declared by an order of the Secretary of State for the time being in force to be such a dealer,".

**Note**

Concerning references in s. 446(4)(c)–(e) to an authorised person within the meaning of the Financial Services Act 1986, these have effect as from 1 January 1993 as if they included a reference to a European institution carrying on home-regulated investment business in the UK: see the Banking Coordination (Second Council Directive) Regulations 1992 (SI 1992/3218), reg. 1(2), reg. 82 and Sch. 10, para. 16. The references also have effect as from 1 January 1996 as if they included a reference to a European investment firm carrying on home-regulated investment business in the UK: see the Investment Services Regulations 1995 (SI 1995/3275), reg. 1(2), 57(1) and Sch. 10, para. 4.

**446(5)** (Omitted and repealed by Financial Services Act 1986, s. 182, 212(3), Sch. 13, para. 8 and Sch. 17, Pt. I as from 27 November 1986.)

**History**

In regard to the date of the above repeal see SI 1986/2031 (C 76). The subsection formerly read as follows:

"The inspectors may, and if so directed by the Secretary of State shall, make interim reports to him; and, on conclusion of the investigation, they shall make to him a final report.

Any such report shall be written or printed, as the Secretary of State may direct; and he may cause it to be published."

**446(6)** (Repealed by Financial Services Act 1986, s. 212(3) and Sch. 17, Pt. I as from 29 April 1988.)

**History**

In regard to the date of the above repeal see SI 1988/740 (C 22); s. 446(6) read as follows:

""**Recognised association of dealers in securities**" means any body of persons which is for the time being such an association for purposes of the Prevention of Fraud (Investments) Act 1958."

**446(7)** (Repealed by Companies Act 1989, s. 212 and Sch. 24 as from 21 February 1990.)

**History**

In regard to the date of the above repeal, see SI 1990/142 (C 5), art. 7(d); s. 446(7) formerly read as follows:

"The expenses of an investigation under this section shall be defrayed by the Secretary of State out of money provided by Parliament."

## REQUISITION AND SEIZURE OF BOOKS AND PAPERS

# 447 Secretary of State's power to require production of documents

**447(1)** (Omitted and repealed by Companies Act 1989, s. 63(1), (2), 212 and Sch. 24 as from 21 February 1990.)

**History**

In regard to the date of the above repeal, see SI 1990/142 (C 5), art. 4, 7(d); s. 447(1) formerly read as follows:

"The powers of this section are exercisable in relation to the following bodies–

(a) a company, as defined by section 735(1);

(b) a company to which this Act applies by virtue of section 676 or which is registered under section 680;

(c) a body corporate incorporated in, and having a principal place of business in, Great Britain, being a body to which any of the provisions of this Act with respect to prospectuses and allotments apply by virtue of section 718 (unregistered companies); and

(d) a body corporate incorporated outside Great Britain which is carrying on business in Great Britain or has at any time carried on business there."

**447(2)** **[Directions to produce]** The Secretary of State may at any time, if he thinks there is good reason to do so, give directions to a company requiring it, at such time and place as may be specified in the directions, to produce such documents as may be so specified.

**History**
In s. 447(2) the words "a company" substituted for the former words "any such body" and the word "documents" substituted for the former words "books or papers" by CA 1989, s. 63(1), (2)(a), (3) as from 21 February 1990 (see SI 1990/142 (C 5), art. 4).

**447(3) [Secretary of State may authorise officer to produce etc.]** The Secretary of State may at any time, if he thinks there is good reason to do so, authorise an officer of his or any other competent person, on producing (if so required) evidence of his authority, to require a company to produce to him (the officer or other person) forthwith any documents which he (the officer or other person) may specify.

**History**
In s. 447(3) the words "a company" substituted for the former words "any such body" and the word "documents" substituted for the former words "books or papers" by CA 1989, s. 63(1), (2)(a), (3) and the words "or any other competent person" and "or other person" inserted and the words "he (the officer or other person)" substituted for the former words "the officer" by CA 1989, s. 63(1), (4) as from 21 February 1990 (see SI 1990/142(C 5), art. 4).

**447(4) [Production from other persons]** Where by virtue of subsection (2) or (3) the Secretary of State or an officer of his or other person has power to require the production of documents from a company, he or the officer or other person has the like power to require production of those documents from any person who appears to him or the officer or other person to be in possession of them; but where any such person claims a lien on documents produced by him, the production is without prejudice to the lien.

**History**
In s. 447(4) the words "a company" substituted for the former words "any body", the words "or other person" (appearing three times) inserted and the word "documents" (appearing three times) substituted for the former words "books or papers" by CA 1989, s. 63(1), (2)(b), (3), (5) as from 21 February 1990 (see SI 1990/142 (C 5), art. 4).

**447(5) [Powers included]** The power under this section to require a company or other person to produce documents includes power–

(a) if the documents are produced–
  (i) to take copies of them or extracts from them, and
  (ii) to require that person, or any other person who is a present or past officer of, or is or was at any time employed by, the company in question, to provide an explanation of any of them;

(b) if the documents are not produced, to require the person who was required to produce them to state, to the best of his knowledge and belief, where they are.

**History**
In s. 447(5) the words "a company" substituted for the former words "a body", the words "the company" substituted for the former words "the body" and the word "documents" (appearing three times) substituted for the former words "books and papers" by CA 1989, s. 63(1), 2(b), (c), (3) as from 21 February 1990 (see SI 1990/142 (C 5), art. 4).

**447(6) [Offence re non-production, penalty]** If the requirement to produce documents or provide an explanation or make a statement is not complied with, the company or other person on whom the requirement was so imposed is guilty of an offence and liable to a fine.

Sections 732 (restriction on prosecutions), 733 (liability of individuals for corporate default) and 734 (criminal proceedings against unincorporated bodies) apply to this offence.

**History**
In s. 447(6) the words "the company" substituted for the former words "the body", the word "documents" substituted for the former words "books and papers" and the second sentence substituted by CA 1989, s. 63(1), (2)(c), (3), (6) as from 21 February 1990 (see SI 1990/142 (C 5), art. 4); the second sentence formerly read as follows:

"Sections 732 (restriction on prosecutions) and 733(2) and (4) (liability of individuals for corporate default) apply to this offence."

**447(7) [Defence]** However, where a person is charged with an offence under subsection (6) in respect of a requirement to produce any documents, it is a defence to prove that they were not in his possession or under his control and that it was not reasonably practicable for him to comply with the requirement.

**History**
In s. 447(7) the word "documents" substituted for the former words "books or papers" by CA 1989, s. 63(3) as from 21 February 1990 (see SI 1990/142 (C 5), art. 4).

**447(8) [Evidence]** A statement made by a person in compliance with such a requirement may be used in evidence against him.

**447(8A) [Limits on use of statement in criminal proceedings]** However, in criminal proceedings in which that person is charged with an offence to which this subsection applies–

(a) no evidence relating to the statement may be adduced, and

(b) no question relating to it may be asked,

by or on behalf of the prosecution, unless evidence relating to it is adduced, or a question relating to it is asked, in the proceedings by or on behalf of that person.

**History**
S. 447(8A) inserted by Youth Justice and Criminal Evidence Act 1999, s. 59, 68(3) and Sch. 3, para. 6, with effect from 14 April 2000 (see Youth Justice and Criminal Evidence Act 1999 (Commencement No. 2) Order 2000 (SI 2000/1034 (C. 27)), art. 2(a)).

**447(8B) [Offences to which s. 447(8A) applies]** Subsection (8A) applies to any offence other than–

(a) an offence under subsection (6) or section 451;

(b) an offence under section 5 of the Perjury Act 1911 (false statements made otherwise than on oath); or

(c) an offence under section 44(2) of the Criminal Law (Consolidation) (Scotland) Act 1995 (false statements made otherwise than on oath).

**History**
S. 447(8B) inserted by Youth Justice and Criminal Evidence Act 1999, s. 59, 68(3) and Sch. 3, para. 6, with effect from 14 April 2000 (see Youth Justice and Criminal Evidence Act 1999 (Commencement No. 2) Order 2000 (SI 2000/1034 (C. 27)), art. 2(a)).

**447(9) ["Documents"]** In this section **"documents"** includes information recorded in any form; and, in relation to information recorded otherwise than in legible form, the power to require its production includes power to require the production of a copy of it in legible form.

**History**
S. 447(9) inserted by CA 1989, s. 63(1), (7) as from 21 February 1990 (see SI 1990/142 (C 5), art. 4).

**Note**
For provision re disqualification of directors see Company Directors Disqualification Act 1986, s. 8.

# 448 Entry and search of premises

**448(1) [Power of JP to issue warrant]** A justice of the peace may issue a warrant under this section if satisfied on information on oath given by or on behalf of the Secretary of State, or by a person appointed or authorised to exercise powers under this Part, that there are reasonable grounds for believing that there are on any premises documents whose production has been required under this Part and which have not been produced in compliance with the requirement.

**448(2) [Further warrant power]** A justice of the peace may also issue a warrant under this section if satisfied on information on oath given by or on behalf of the Secretary of State, or by a person appointed or authorised to exercise powers under this Part–

(a) that there are reasonable grounds for believing that an offence has been committed for which the penalty on conviction on indictment is imprisonment for a term of not less than two years and that there are on any premises documents relating to whether the offence has been committed,

(b) that the Secretary of State, or the person so appointed or authorised, has power to require the production of the documents under this Part, and

(c) that there are reasonable grounds for believing that if production was so required the documents would not be produced but would be removed from the premises, hidden, tampered with or destroyed.

**448(3) [Extent of warrant]** A warrant under this section shall authorise a constable, together with any other person named in it and any other constables–

(a) to enter the premises specified in the information, using such force as is reasonably necessary for the purpose;

(b) to search the premises and take possession of any documents appearing to be such documents as are mentioned in subsection (1) or (2), as the case may be, or to take, in relation to any such documents, any other steps which may appear to be necessary for preserving them or preventing interference with them;

(c) to take copies of any such documents; and

(d) to require any person named in the warrant to provide an explanation of them or to state where they may be found.

**448(4) [Where re s. 448(2) warrant – other documents]** If in the case of a warrant under subsection (2) the justice of the peace is satisfied on information on oath that there are reasonable grounds for believing that there are also on the premises other documents relevant to the investigation, the warrant shall also authorise the actions mentioned in subsection (3) to be taken in relation to such documents.

**448(5) [Duration of warrant]** A warrant under this section shall continue in force until the end of the period of one month beginning with the day on which it is issued.

**448(6) [Retention of documents]** Any documents of which possession is taken under this section may be retained–

(a) for a period of three months; or

(b) if within that period proceedings to which the documents are relevant are commenced against any person for any criminal offence, until the conclusion of those proceedings.

**448(7) [Offence]** Any person who intentionally obstructs the exercise of any rights conferred by a warrant issued under this section or fails without reasonable excuse to comply with any requirement imposed in accordance with subsection (3)(d) is guilty of an offence and liable to a fine.

Sections 732 (restriction on prosecutions), 733 (liability of individuals for corporate default) and 734 (criminal proceedings against unincorporated bodies) apply to this offence.

**448(8) [Interpretation re s. 449, 451A]** For the purposes of sections 449 and 451A (provision for security of information) documents obtained under this section shall be treated as if they had been obtained under the provision of this Part under which their production was or, as the case may be, could have been required.

**448(9) [Application to Scotland]** In the application of this section to Scotland for the references to a justice of the peace substitute references to a justice of the peace or a sheriff, and for the references to information on oath substitute references to evidence on oath.

**448(10) ["Document"]** In this section **"document"** includes information recorded in any form.

**History**

S. 448 substituted by CA 1989, s. 64(1) as from 21 February 1990 (see SI 1990/142 (C 5), art. 4); s.448 formerly read as follows:

**"448 Entry and search of premises**

**448(1)** The following applies if a justice of the peace is satisfied on information on oath laid by an officer of the Secretary of State, or laid under the Secretary of State's authority, that there are reasonable grounds for suspecting that there are on any premises any books or papers of which production has been required under section 447 and which have not been produced in compliance with that requirement.

**(2)** The justice may issue a warrant authorising any constable, together with any other persons named in the warrant and any other constables, to enter the premises specified in the information (using such force as is reasonably necessary for the purpose) and to search the premises and take possession of any books or papers appearing to be such books or papers as are mentioned above, or to take, in relation to any books or papers so appearing, any other steps which may appear to be necessary for preserving them and preventing interference with them.

**(3)** A warrant so issued continues in force until the end of one month after the date on which it is issued.

**(4)** Any books or papers of which possession is taken under this section may be retained–

(a) for a period of 3 months, or

(b) if within that period there are commenced any such criminal proceedings as are mentioned in subsection (1)(a) or (b) of the next following section (being proceedings to which the books or papers are relevant), until the conclusion of those proceedings.

**(5)** A person who obstructs the exercise of a right of entry or search conferred by a warrant issued under this section, or who obstructs the exercise of a right so conferred to take possession of any books or papers, is guilty of an offence and liable to a fine.

Sections 732 (restriction on prosecutions) and 733(2) and (4) (liability of individuals for corporate default) apply to this offence.

**(6)** In the application of this section to Scotland, the reference to a justice of the peace includes the sheriff and a magistrate."

**Note**

For provision re disqualification of directors see Company Directors Disqualification Act 1986, s. 8.

## 449 Provision for security of information obtained

**449(1) [Limitation on publication or disclosure of information]** No information or document relating to a company which has been obtained under section 447 shall, without the previous consent in writing of that company, be published or disclosed, except to a competent authority, unless the publication or disclosure is required–

(a) with a view to the institution of or otherwise for the purposes of criminal proceedings,

(ba) with a view to the institution of, or otherwise for the purposes of any proceedings on an application under section 6, 7 or 8 of the Company Directors Disqualification Act 1986,

(c) for the purposes of enabling or assisting any inspector appointed under this Part, or under section 94 or 177 of the Financial Services Act 1986, to discharge his functions,

(cc) for the purpose of enabling or assisting any person authorised to exercise powers or appointed under section 43A or 44 of the Insurance Companies Act 1982, section 447 of this Act, section 106 of the Financial Services Act 1986 or section 84 of the Companies Act 1989 to discharge his functions,

(d) for the purpose of enabling or assisting the Secretary of State or the Treasury to exercise any of their functions under this Act, the insider dealing legislation, the Prevention of Fraud (Investments) Act 1958, the Insurance Companies Act 1982, the Insolvency Act 1986, the Company Directors Disqualification Act 1986, the Financial Services Act 1986 or Part II, III or VII of the Companies Act 1989,

(dd) for the purpose of enabling or assisting the Department of Economic Development for Northern Ireland to exercise any powers conferred on it by the enactments relating to companies or insolvency or for the purpose of enabling or assisting any inspector appointed by it under the enactments relating to companies to discharge his functions,

(de) for the purpose of enabling or assisting the Chief Registrar of friendly societies or the Assistant Registrar of friendly societies for Scotland to discharge his functions under the enactments relating to friendly societies,

(df) for the purpose of enabling or assisting the Friendly Societies Commission to discharge its functions under the Financial Services Act 1986,

(dg) for the purpose of enabling or assisting the Occupational Pensions Regulatory Authority to discharge their functions under the Pension Schemes Act 1993 or the Pensions Act 1995 or any enactment in force in Northern Ireland corresponding to either of them,

(e) (Omitted and repealed by Companies Act 1989, s. 65(1), (2)(e), 212 and Sch. 24 as from 21 February 1990),

(f) for the purpose of enabling or assisting the Bank of England to discharge its functions,

(fa) for the purpose of enabling or assisting the Financial Services Authority to discharge–
- (i) any functions under the Financial Services Act 1986, other than as a designated agency within the meaning of that Act,
- (ii) its functions under the Banking Act 1987, or
- (iii) its functions under section 171 of the Companies Act 1989.

(g) for the purpose of enabling or assisting the Deposit Protection Board to discharge its functions under that Act,

(h) for any purpose mentioned in section 180(1)(b), (e), (h) or (n) of the Financial Services Act 1986,

(hh) for the purpose of enabling or assisting a body established by order under section 46 of the Companies Act 1989 to discharge its functions under Part II of that Act, or of enabling or assisting a recognised supervisory or qualifying body within the meaning of that Part to discharge its functions as such,

(i) for the purpose of enabling or assisting the Industrial Assurance Commissioner or the Industrial Assurance Commissioner for Northern Ireland to discharge his functions under the enactments relating to industrial assurance,

(j) for the purpose of enabling or assisting the Insurance Brokers Registration Council to discharge its functions under the Insurance Brokers (Registration) Act 1977,

(k) for the purpose of enabling or assisting an official receiver to discharge his functions under the enactments relating to insolvency or for the purpose of enabling or assisting a body which is for the time being a recognised professional body for the purposes of section 391 of the Insolvency Act 1986 to discharge its functions as such,

(l) with a view to the institution of, or otherwise for the purposes of, any disciplinary proceedings relating to the exercise by a solicitor, auditor, accountant, valuer or actuary of his professional duties,

(ll) with a view to the institution of, or otherwise for the purposes of, any disciplinary proceedings relating to the discharge by a public servant of his duties,

(m) for the purpose of enabling or assisting an overseas regulatory authority to exercise its regulatory functions.

**History**

In s. 449(1):

- in the opening words "company" (appearing twice) substituted for the former word "body" and the words "or 448" repealed by CA 1989, s. 65(1), (2), 212 and Sch. 24 as from 21 February 1990 (see SI 1990/142 (C 5), art. 4);
- para. (a) substituted for the former para. (a) and (b) by Financial Services Act 1986, s. 182 and Sch. 13, para. 9(1)(a) as from 15 November 1986 for certain purposes (see SI 1986/1940 (C 69)) and as from 27 November 1986 for remaining purposes (see SI 1986/2031 (C 76)); the former para. (a) and (b) read as follows:

"(a) with a view to the institution of, or otherwise for the purposes of, any criminal proceedings pursuant to, or arising out of, this Act, the Insider Dealing Act or the Insurance Companies Act 1982, or any criminal proceedings for an offence entailing misconduct in connection with the management of the body's affairs or misapplication or wrongful retainer of its property;

(b) with a view to the institution of, or otherwise for the purposes of, any criminal proceedings pursuant to, or arising out of, the Exchange Control Act 1947,";

- para. (ba) inserted by Insolvency Act 1985, s. 109 and Sch. 6, para. 4 as from 28 April 1986 (see SI 1986/463 (C 14)). In that paragraph the words "section 6, 7 or 8 of the Company Directors Disqualification Act 1986" substituted for the former words "section 12 or 13 of the Insolvency Act 1985" by Insolvency Act 1986, s. 439(1) and Sch. 13 as from 29 December 1986 (see IA 1986, s. 443 and SI 1986/1924 (C 71));
- para. (c) substituted (see immediately below in regard to para. (cc);
- in para. (cc) the words "or appointed under section 43A or 44" substituted for the former words "under section 44" by the Insurance Companies (Third Insurance Directives) Regulations 1994 (SI 1994/1696), reg. 1, 68, Sch. 8, para. 9(2) as from 1 July 1994; previously para. (c) substituted and para. (cc) inserted by CA 1989, s. 65(1), (2)(b), (c) as from 21 February 1990 (see SI 1990/142 (C 5), art. 4); para. (c) formerly read as follows:

"(c) for the purposes of the examination of any person by inspectors appointed under section 431, 432, 442 or 446 in the course of their investigation,";

- in para. (d) the words "Secretary of State or the Treasury to exercise any of their functions" substituted for the former words "Secretary of State to exercise any of his functions" by the Transfer of Functions (Financial Services) Order 1992 (SI 1992/1315), art. 10(1) and Sch. 4, para. 1, as from 7 June 1992; the words "the insider dealing legislation" substituted for the former words "the Insider Dealing Act" by Criminal Justice Act 1993, s. 79(13) and Sch. 5, para. 4(2) as from 1 March (see SI 1994/242 (C 7), art. 2, Sch.); the words ", the Financial Services Act 1986 or Part II, III or VII of the Companies Act 1989," substituted for the former words "or the Financial Services Act 1986" by CA 1989, s. 65(1), (2)(d) as from 21 February 1990 except in regard to the reference to CA 1989, Pt. VII (see SI 1990/142 (C 5), art. 4(b)) and in regard to the reference to CA 1989, Pt. VII as from 25 April 1991 (see SI 1991/878 (C 21), art. 2, Sch.); para. (d) and (dd) previously substituted for the original para. (d) by Financial Services Act 1986, s. 182 and Sch. 13, para. 9(1)(b) as from 15 November 1986 for certain purposes (see SI 1986/1940 (C 69)) and as from 27 November 1986 for remaining purposes (see SI 1986/2031 (C 76)); the original para. (d) read as follows:

"(d) for the purpose of enabling the Secretary of State to exercise, in relation to that or any other body, any of his functions under this Act, the Insider Dealing Act, the Prevention of Fraud (Investments) Act 1958 and the Insurance Companies Act 1982,";

- para. (de), (df) inserted by Friendly Societies Act 1992, s. 120(1) and Sch. 21, para. 7(1) as from 1 February 1993 (see SI 1993/16 (C 1), art. 2 and Sch. 3);
- para. (dg) inserted by the Pensions Act 1995, s. 122 and Sch. 3, para. 12 as from 6 April 1997 (see SI 1997/664 (C 23), art. 2(3), Sch., Pt. II);
- in regard to the date of the omission and repeal of para. (e) see SI 1990/142 (C 5), art. 4; para. (e) formerly read as follows:

"for the purposes of proceedings under section 448,";

- para. (f), (fa) substituted for the former para. (f) by the Bank of England Act 1998, s. 23(1), 45 and Sch. 5, para. 62(1), (2) as from 1 June 1998 (see SI 1998/1120 (C 25), art. 2). The former para. (f) read as follows:

"for the purpose of enabling or assisting the Bank of England to discharge its functions under the Banking Act 1987 or any other functions,"

- para. (f)–(m) (not including (hh) and (ll) originally inserted by Financial Services Act 1986, s. 182 and Sch. 13, para. 9(1)(c) as from 15 November 1986 for certain purposes (see SI 1986/1940 (C 69)) and as from 27 November 1986 for remaining purposes (see SI 1986/2031 (C 76));
- previously in para. (f) the words "the Banking Act 1987" substituted for the former words "the Banking Act 1979" by Banking Act 1987, s. 108(1) and Sch. 6, para. 18(7) as from 1 October 1987 (see SI 1987/1664 (C 50));
- in para. (h) the words "or (n)" substituted for the former words "(n) or (p)" by CA 1989, s. 63(1), (2)(f) as from 21 February 1990 (see SI 1990/142 (C 5), art. 4);
- para. (hh) inserted by CA 1989, s. 65(1), (2)(g) as from 21 February 1990 except in regard to the reference to a body established by order under CA 1989, s. 46 (see SI 1990/142 (C 5), art. 4(a));
- para. (ll) inserted by CA 1989, s. 65(1), (2)(b) as from 21 February 1990 (see SI 1990/142 (C 5), art. 4);
- para. (m) substituted by CA 1989, s. 65(1), (2)(i) as from 21 February 1990 (see SI 1990/142 (C 5), art. 4); para (m) formerly read as follows:

"(m) for the purpose of enabling or assisting an authority in a country or territory outside the United Kingdom to exercise corresponding supervisory functions.".

**Note**

In s. 449(1)(d) the words "the Prevention of Fraud (Investments) Act 1958" repealed by Financial Services Act 1986, s. 212(3) and Sch. 17, Pt. I as from 29 April 1988 as far as they would apply to a prospectus offering for subscription, or to any form of application for units in a body corporate which is a recognised scheme (see SI 1988/740 (C 22)).

**449(1A) [Definitions]** In subsection (1)–

(a) in paragraph (ll) **"public servant"** means an officer or servant of the Crown or of any public or other authority for the time being designated for the purposes of that paragraph by the Secretary of State by order made by statutory instrument; and

(b) in paragraph (m) **"overseas regulatory authority"** and **"regulatory functions"** have the same meaning as in section 82 of the Companies Act 1989.

**History**

S. 449(1A) substituted by CA 1989, s. 65(1), (3) as from 21 February 1990 (see SI 1990/142 (C 5), art. 4); s. 449(1A) formerly read as follows:

"In subsection (1) above "**corresponding supervisory functions**" means functions corresponding to those of the Secretary of State or the competent authority under the Financial Services Act 1986 or to those of the Secretary of State under the Insurance Companies Act 1982 or to those of the Bank of England under the Banking Act 1987 or any other functions in connection with rules of law corresponding to the provisions of the Insider Dealing Act or Part VII of the Financial Services Act 1986."

In that former s. 449(1A) the words "the Banking Act 1987" substituted for the original words "the Banking Act 1979" by Banking Act 1987, s. 108(1) and Sch. 6, para. 18(7) as from 1 October 1987 (see SI 1987/1664 (C 50)).

**449(1B) [Exception to s. 449(1) limitation]** Subject to subsection (1C), subsection (1) shall not preclude publication or disclosure for the purpose of enabling or assisting any public or other authority for the time being designated for the purposes of this subsection by the Secretary of State by an order in a statutory instrument to discharge any functions which are specified in the order.

**History**

In s. 449(1B) the words "designated for the purposes of this subsection" substituted for the former words "designated for the purposes of this section" by CA 1989, s. 65(1), (4) as from 21 February 1990 (see SI 1990/142 (C 5), art. 4).

**Note**

See note after s. 449(1C).

**449(1C) [Qualification to s. 449(1B)]** An order under subsection (1B) designating an authority for the purpose of that subsection may–

(a) impose conditions subject to which the publication or disclosure of any information or document is permitted by that subsection; and

(b) otherwise restrict the circumstances in which that subsection permits publication or disclosure.

**Note**

The following orders have been made under s. 449(1B), (1C): the Financial Services (Disclosure of Information) (Designated Authorities) Order 1986 (SI 1986/2046) in operation from 28 November 1986; the Financial Services (Disclosure of Information) (Designated Authorities No. 2) Order 1987 (SI 1987/859) in operation from 13 May 1987; the Financial Services (Disclosure of Information) (Designated Authorities) (No. 3) Order 1987 (SI 1987/1141) in operation from 4 July 1987; the Financial Services (Disclosure of Information) (Designated Authorities) (No. 4) Order 1988 (SI 1988/1058) in operation from 17 June 1988, the Companies (Disclosure of Information) (Designated Authorities) Order 1988 (SI 1988/1334) in operation from 19 August 1988, the Financial Services (Disclosure of Information) (Designated Authorities) (No. 5) Order 1989 (SI 1989/940) in operation from 7 June 1989, the Financial Services (Disclosure of Information) (Designated Authorities) (No. 6) Order 1989 (SI 1989/2009) in operation from 28 November 1989, the Financial Services (Disclosure of Information) (Designated Authorities) (No. 7) Order 1993 (SI 1993/1826) in operation from 16 August 1993 and the Financial Services (Disclosure of Information) (Designated Authorities) (No. 8) Order 1994 (SI 1994/340) in operation from 10 March 1994.

**449(1D) [Further exception to s. 449(1) limitation]** Subsection (1) shall not preclude the publication or disclosure of any such information as is mentioned in section 180(5) of the Financial Services Act 1986 by any person who by virtue of that section is not precluded by section 179 of that Act from disclosing it.

**History**

S. 449(1A)–(1D) inserted by Financial Services Act 1986, s. 182 and Sch. 13, para. 9(2) as from 15 November 1986 for certain purposes (see SI 1986/1940 (C 69)) and as from 27 November 1986 for remaining purposes (see SI 1986/2031 (C 76)).

**449(2) [Offence, penalty]** A person who publishes or discloses any information or document in contravention of this section is guilty of an offence and liable to imprisonment or a fine, or both.

Sections 732 (restrictions on prosecutions), 733 (liability of individuals for corporate default) and 734 (criminal proceedings against unincorporated bodies) apply to this offence.

**History**
In s. 449(2) second sentence substituted by CA 1989, s. 65(1), (5) as from 21 February 1990 (see SI 1990/142 (C 5), art. 4); the second sentence formerly read as follows:
"Sections 732 (restriction on prosecutions) and 733(2) and (4) (liability of individuals for corporate default) apply to this offence."

**449(3) [Competent authorities]** For the purposes of this section each of the following is a competent authority–

(a) the Secretary of State,
(b) an inspector appointed under this Part or under section 94 or 177 of the Financial Services Act 1986,
(c) any person authorised to exercise powers under section 44 of the Insurance Companies Act 1982, section 447 of this Act, section 106 of the Financial Services Act 1986 or section 84 of the Companies Act 1989,
(d) the Department of Economic Development in Northern Ireland,
(e) the Treasury,
(f) the Bank of England,
(g) the Lord Advocate,
(h) the Director of Public Prosecutions, and the Director of Public Prosecutions for Northern Ireland,
(ha) the Financial Services Authority, other than its capacity as a designated agency within the meaning of the Financial Services Act 1986.
(i) any designated agency or transferee body within the meaning of the Financial Services Act 1986, and any body administering a scheme under section 54 of or paragraph 18 of Schedule 11 to that Act (schemes for compensation of investors),
(j) the Chief Registrar of friendly societies,
(jj) the Friendly Societies Commission,
(k) the Industrial Assurance Commissioner,
(l) any constable,
(m) any procurator fiscal,
(n) the Scottish Ministers.

**History**
S. 449(3)(ha) inserted by the Bank of England Act 1998, s. 23(1), 45 and Sch. 5, para. 62(1), (2) as from 1 June 1998 (see SI 1998/1120 (C 25), art. 2).
In s. 449(3)(j) the words "and the Registrar of Friendly Societies for Northern Ireland" formerly appearing at the end, and in para. (k) the words "and the Industrial Assurance Commission for Northern Ireland" formerly appearing at the end repealed by Friendly Societies Act 1992, s. 120 and Sch. 22, Pt. I as from 1 January 1994 (see SI 1993/3226 (C 65), art. 2, Sch. 2, subject to any transitional and saving provisions in art. 3–9).
S. 449(3)(jj) inserted by Friendly Societies Act 1992, s. 120(1) and Sch. 21, para. 7(2) as from 1 February 1993 (see SI 1993/16 (C 1), art. 2 and Sch. 3).
S. 449(3)(n) inserted by the Scotland Act 1998 (Consequential Modifications) (No. 2) Order 1999 (SI 1999/1820), art. 1(2), 4, Sch. 2, Pt. I, para. 78 as from 1 July 1999.
See also history note after s. 449(3A).

**449(3A) [Disclosure to officers or servants]** Any information which may by virtue of this section be disclosed to a competent authority may be disclosed to any officer or servant of the authority.

**History**
S. 449(3), (3A) substituted for the former s. 449(3) by CA 1989, s. 65(1), (6) as from 21 February 1990 (see SI 1990/142 (C 5), art. 4); the former s. 449(3) read as follows:
"For the purposes of this section each of the following is a competent authority–
(a) the Secretary of State,
(b) the Department of Economic Development for Northern Ireland and any officer of that Department,
(c) an inspector appointed under this Part by the Secretary of State,
(d) the Treasury and any officer of the Treasury,
(e) the Bank of England and any officer or servant of the Bank,
(f) the Lord Advocate,
(g) the Director of Public Prosecutions, and the Director of Public Prosecutions for Northern Ireland,
(h) any designated agency or transferee body within the meaning of the Financial Services Act 1986 and any officer or servant of such an agency or body,
(i) any person appointed or authorised to exercise any powers under section 94, 106 or 177 of the Financial Services Act 1986 and any officer or servant of such a person,
(j) the body administering a scheme under section 54 of or paragraph 18 of Schedule 11 to that Act and any officer or servant of such a body,

(k) the Chief Registrar of friendly societies and the Registrar of Friendly Societies for Northern Ireland and any officer or servant of either of them,
(l) the Industrial Assurance Commissioner and the Industrial Assurance Commissioner for Northern Ireland and any officer of either of them,
(m) any constable,
(n) any procurator fiscal."

Previously s. 449(3), (4) substituted for the original s. 449(3) by Financial Services Act 1986, s. 182 and Sch. 13, para. 9(3) as from 15 November 1986 for certain purposes (see SI 1986/1940 (C 69)) and as from 27 November 1986 for remaining purposes (see SI 1986/2031 (C 76)); the original s. 449(3) read as follows:

"For purposes of this section–
(a) in relation to information or a document relating to a body other than one carrying on industrial assurance business (as defined by section 1(2) of the Industrial Assurance Act 1923), each of the following is a competent authority–
(i) the Secretary of State for Trade and Industry, and any officer of his,
(ii) an inspector appointed under this Part by the Secretary of State,
(iii) the Treasury, and any officer of the Treasury,
(iv) the Lord Advocate,
(v) the Director of Public Prosecutions,
(vi) any constable, and
(vii) any procurator fiscal;
(b) in relation to information or a document relating to a body carrying on industrial assurance business (as so defined), all the same persons as above specified are competent authorities, and also the Industrial Assurance Commissioner and any officer of his."

**449(4) [Order under s. 449(1B)]** A statutory instrument containing an order under subsection (1A)(a) or (1B) is subject to annulment in pursuance of a resolution of either House of Parliament.

**History**
In s. 449(4) the words "subsection (1A)(a) or (1B)" substituted for the former words "subsection (1B)" by CA 1989 s. 65(1), (7) as from 21 February 1990 (see SI 1990/142 (C 5), art. 4); originally s. 449(4) was substituted, with s. 449(3), for the original s. 449(3) – see history note to s. 449(3) above.

**Note**
Re s. 449(4) see Financial Services (Disclosure of Information) (Designated Authorities) Order 1986 (SI 1986/2046) in operation from 28 November 1986.

# 450 Punishment for destroying, mutilating etc. company documents

**450(1) [Offence of destruction etc.]** An officer of the company, or an insurance company to which Part II of the Insurance Companies Act 1982 applies, who–
(a) destroys, mutilates or falsifies, or is privy to the destruction, mutilation or falsification of a document affecting or relating to the company's property or affairs, or
(b) makes, or is privy to the making of, a false entry in such a document,

is guilty of an offence, unless he proves that he had no intention to conceal the state of affairs of the company or to defeat the law.

**History**
In s. 450(1) the words "An officer of the company, or an insurance company" substituted for the former words "A person, being an officer of any such body as is mentioned in paragraphs (a) to (d) of section 447(1) or a body other than as there mentioned, being an insurance company", the word "company's" substituted for the former word "body's" and the word "the company" substituted for the former word "the body" by CA 1989, s. 66(1), (2) as from 21 February 1990 (see SI 1990/142 (C 5), art. 4).

**Note**
The reference to the insurance company in s. 450(1) includes a reference to an EC company lawfully carrying on insurance business in the UK: the Insurance Companies (Third Insurance Directives) Regulations 1994 (SI 1994/1696), reg. 68, Sch. 8, para. 9(1).

**450(2) [Offence re fraudulent omissions etc.]** Such a person as above mentioned who fraudulently either parts with, alters or makes an omission in any such document or is privy to fraudulent parting with, fraudulent altering or fraudulent making of an omission in, any such document, is guilty of an offence.

**450(3) [Penalty]** A person guilty of an offence under this section is liable to imprisonment or a fine, or both.

**450(4) [Application of s. 732–734]** Sections 732 (restriction on prosecutions), 733 (liability of individuals for corporate default) and 734 (criminal proceedings against unincorporated bodies) apply to an offence under this section.

**History**
S. 450(4) substituted by CA 1989, s. 66(1), (3) as from 21 February 1990 (see SI 1990/142 (C 5), art. 4); s. 450(4) formerly read as follows:

"Sections 732 (restriction on prosecutions) and 733(2) and (4) (liability of individuals for corporate default) apply to an offence under this section."

**450(5) ["Document"]** In this section **"document"** includes information recorded in any form.

**History**

S. 450(5) inserted by CA 1989, s. 66(1), (4) as from 21 February 1990 (see SI 1990/142 (C 5), art. 4).

# 451 Punishment for furnishing false information

**451** A person who, in purported compliance with a requirement imposed under section 447 to provide an explanation or make a statement, provides or makes an explanation or statement which he knows to be false in a material particular or recklessly provides or makes an explanation or statement which is so false, is guilty of an offence and liable to imprisonment or a fine, or both.

Sections 732 (restriction on prosecutions) and 733 (liability of individuals for corporate default) and 734 (criminal proceedings against unincorporated bodies) apply to this offence.

**History**

In s. 451 second sentence substituted by CA 1989, s. 67 as from 21 February 1990 (see SI 1990/142 (C 5), art. 4); the second sentence formerly read as follows:

"Sections 732 (restriction on prosecutions) and 733(2) and (4) (liability of individuals for corporate default) apply to this offence."

# 451A Disclosure of information by Secretary of State or inspector

**451A(1) [Application]** This section applies to information obtained under sections 434 to 446.

**451A(2) [Power of Secretary of State]** The Secretary of State may, if he thinks fit–

(a) disclose any information to which this section applies to any person to whom, or for any purpose for which, disclosure is permitted under section 449, or

(b) authorise or require an inspector appointed under this Part to disclose such information to any such person or for any such purpose.

**451A(3) [Limit on disclosure]** Information to which this section applies may also be disclosed by an inspector appointed under this Part to–

(a) another inspector appointed under this Part or an inspector appointed under section 94 or 177 of the Financial Services Act 1986, or

(b) a person authorised to exercise powers or appointed under section 43A or 44 of the Insurance Companies Act 1982, section 447 of this Act, section 106 of the Financial Services Act 1986 or section 84 of the Companies Act 1989.

**History**

In s. 451A(3) the words "or appointed under section 43A or 44" substituted for the former words "under section 44" by the Insurance Companies (Third Insurance Directives) Regulations 1994 (SI 1994/1696), reg. 1, 68, Sch. 8, para. 9(3) as from 1 July 1994.

**451A(4) [Disclosure to officer or servant]** Any information which may by virtue of subsection (3) be disclosed to any person may be disclosed to any officer or servant of that person.

**451A(5) [Further power of Secretary of State]** The Secretary of State may, if he thinks fit, disclose any information obtained under section 444 to–

(a) the company whose ownership was the subject of the investigation,

(b) any member of the company,

(c) any person whose conduct was investigated in the course of the investigation,

(d) the auditors of the company, or

(e) any person whose financial interests appear to the Secretary of State to be affected by matters covered by the investigation.

**History**

S. 451A substituted by CA 1989, s. 68 as from 21 February 1990 (see SI 1990/142 (C 5), art. 4); s. 451A formerly read as follows:

"**451A Disclosure of information by Secretary of State**

**451A** The Secretary of State may, if he thinks fit, disclose any information obtained under this Part of this Act–

(a) to any person who is a competent authority for the purposes of section 449, or

(b) in any circumstances in which or for any purpose for which that section does not preclude the disclosure of the information to which it applies."

S. 451A originally inserted by Financial Services Act 1986, s. 182 and Sch. 13, para. 10 as from 15 November 1986 for certain purposes (see SI 1986/1940 (C 69)) and as from 27 November 1986 for remaining purposes (see SI 1986/2031 (C 76)).

## SUPPLEMENTARY

# 452 Privileged information

**452(1) [Privilege re legal proceedings – s. 431–446]** Nothing in sections 431 to 446 requires the disclosure to the Secretary of State or to an inspector appointed by him–

(a) by any person of information which he would in an action in the High Court or the Court of Session be entitled to refuse to disclose on grounds of legal professional privilege except, if he is a lawyer, the name and address of his client,

(b) (omitted and repealed by Companies Act 1989, s. 69(1), (2), 212 and Sch. 24 as from 21 February 1990).

**History**
In regard to the date of the above omission and repeal see SI 1990/142 (C 5); para. (b) formerly read as follows:
"(b) by a company's bankers (as such) of information as to the affairs of any of their customers other than the company."

**452(1A) [Qualification re privilege]** Nothing in section 434, 443 or 446 requires a person (except as mentioned in subsection (1B) below) to disclose information or produce documents in respect of which he owes an obligation of confidence by virtue of carrying on the business of banking unless–

(a) the person to whom the obligation of confidence is owed is the company or other body corporate under investigation,

(b) the person to whom the obligation of confidence is owed consents to the disclosure or production, or

(c) the making of the requirement is authorised by the Secretary of State.

**History**
See history note after s. 452(1B).

**452(1B) [Non-application of s. 452(1A)]** Subsection (1A) does not apply where the person owing the obligation of confidence is the company or other body corporate under investigation under section 431, 432 or 433.

**History**
S. 452(1A), (1B) inserted by CA 1989, s. 69(1), (3) as from 21 February 1990 (see SI 1990/142 (C 5), art. 4).

**452(2) [Legal proceedings – s. 447–451]** Nothing in sections 447 to 451 compels the production by any person of a document which he would in an action in the High Court or the Court of Session be entitled to refuse to produce on grounds of legal professional privilege, or authorises the taking of possession of any such document which is in the person's possession.

**452(3) [Bankers – s. 447]** The Secretary of State shall not under section 447 require, or authorise an officer of his or other person to require, the production by a person carrying on the business of banking of a document relating to the affairs of a customer of his unless either it appears to the Secretary of State that it is necessary to do so for the purpose of investigating the affairs of the first-mentioned person or the customer is a person on whom a requirement has been imposed under that section, or under section 43A or 44(2) to (4) of the Insurance Companies Act 1982 (provision corresponding to section 447).

**History**
In s. 452(3) the words "or other person" inserted by CA 1989, s. 69(1), (4) as from 21 February 1990 (see SI 1990/142 (C 5), art. 4); and the words "section 43A or 44(2) to (4)" substituted for the former words "section 44(2) to (4)" by the Insurance Companies (Third Insurance Directives) Regulations 1994 (SI 1994/1696) reg. 1, 68, Sch. 8, para. 9(3) as from 1 July 1994.

# 453 Investigation of oversea companies

**453(1) [Companies covered by Pt. XIV]** The provisions of this Part apply to bodies corporate incorporated outside Great Britain which are carrying on business in Great Britain, or have at any time carried on business there, as they apply to companies under this Act; but subject to the following exceptions, adaptations and modifications.

**453(1A) [Provisions not applying to s. 453(1A) bodies]** The following provisions do not apply to such bodies–

(a) section 431 (investigation on application of company or its members),
(b) section 438 (power to bring civil proceedings on the company's behalf),
(c) sections 442 to 445 (investigation of company ownership and power to obtain information as to those interested in shares, etc.), and
(d) section 446 (investigation of share dealings).

**453(1B) [Other provisions of Pt. XIV]** The other provisions of this Part apply to such bodies subject to such adaptations and modifications as may be specified by regulations made by the Secretary of State.

**History**
S. 453(1)–(1B) substituted for the former s. 453(1) by CA 1989, s. 70 as from 21 February 1990; the former s. 453(1) read as follows:
"Sections 432 to 437, 439, 441 and 452(1) apply to all bodies corporate incorporated outside Great Britain which are carrying on business in Great Britain or have at any time carried on business there as if they were companies under this Act, but subject to such (if any) adaptations and modifications as may be specified by regulations made by the Secretary of State."

**453(2) [Regulations]** Regulations under this section shall be made by statutory instrument subject to annulment in pursuance of a resolution of either House of Parliament.

# PART XV – ORDERS IMPOSING RESTRICTIONS ON SHARES (SECTIONS 210, 216, 445)

## 454 Consequence of order imposing restrictions

**454(1) [Effect of restrictions]** So long as any shares are directed to be subject to the restrictions of this Part then, subject to any directions made in relation to an order pursuant to sections 210(5A), 216(1B), 445(1A) or 456(1A) or subject in the case of an interim order pursuant to section 216(1A) to the terms of that order–
(a) any transfer of those shares or, in the case of unissued shares, any transfer of the right to be issued with them, and any issue of them, is void;
(b) no voting rights are exercisable in respect of the shares;
(c) no further shares shall be issued in right of them or in pursuance of any offer made to their holder; and
(d) except in a liquidation, no payment shall be made of any sums due from the company on the shares, whether in respect of capital or otherwise.

**History**
In s. 454(1) the words from "then, subject to any directions" to "the terms of that order" inserted by the Companies (Disclosure of Interests in Shares) (Orders imposing restrictions on shares) Regulations 1991 (SI 1991/1646), reg. 6(a) as from 18 July 1991.

**454(2) [Effect of s. 454(1)(a) restriction]** Where shares are subject to the restrictions of subsection (1)(a), any agreement to transfer the shares or, in the case of unissued shares, the right to be issued with them is void (except such agreement or right as may be made or exercised under the terms of directions made by the Secretary of State or the court under sections 210(5A), 216(1B), 445(1A), 456(1A) or of an interim order made under section 216(1A) or an agreement to transfer the shares on the making of an order under section 456(3)(b) below).

**History**
In s. 454(2) the word "transfer" substituted for the former word "sell" by CA 1989, s. 145 and Sch. 19, para. 10(2) as from 7 January 1991 (see SI 1990/2569 (C 68), art. 4(d)) and the words from "such agreement or right as may be made" to "interim order made under section 216(1A) or" inserted by the Companies (Disclosure of Interests in Shares) (Orders imposing restrictions on shares) Regulations 1991 (SI 1991/1646), reg. 6(b) as from 18 July 1991.

**454(3) [Effect of s. 454(1)(c), (d)]** Where shares are subject to the restrictions of subsection (1)(c) or (d), an agreement to transfer any right to be issued with other shares in right of those shares, or to receive any payment on them (otherwise than in a liquidation) is void (except such agreement or right as may be made or exercised under the terms of directions made by the Secretary of State or the court under sections 210(5A), 216(1B), 445(1A), 456(1A) or of an interim order made under section 216(1A) or an agreement to transfer any such right on the transfer of the shares on the making of an order under section 456(3)(b) below).

**History**
In s. 454(3) the word "transfer" substituted for the former word "sale" by CA 1989, s. 145 and Sch. 19, para. 10(2) as from 7 January 1991 (see SI 1990/2569 (C 68), art. 4(d)) and the words from "such agreement or right as may be made" to "interim order made under section 216(1A) or" inserted by the Companies (Disclosure of Interests in Shares) (Orders imposing restrictions on shares) Regulations 1991 (SI 1991/1646), reg. 16(c) as from 18 July 1991.

# 455 Punishment for attempted evasion of restrictions

**455(1) [Offence by person]** Subject to the terms of any directions made under sections 210(5A), 216(1B) or 445 (1A) or 456 or of an interim order made under section 216(1A) a person is liable to a fine if he–

(a) exercises or purports to exercise any right to dispose of any shares which, to his knowledge, are for the time being subject to the restrictions of this Part or of any right to be issued with any such shares, or

(b) votes in respect of any such shares (whether as holder or proxy), or appoints a proxy to vote in respect of them, or

(c) being the holder of any such shares, fails to notify of their being subject to those restrictions any person whom he does not know to be aware of that fact but does know to be entitled (apart from the restrictions) to vote in respect of those shares whether as holder or as proxy, or

(d) being the holder of any such shares, or being entitled to any right to be issued with other shares in right of them, or to receive any payment on them (otherwise than in a liquidation), enters into any agreement which is void under section 454(2) or (3).

**History**
In s. 455(1) the words at the beginning from "Subject to the terms of any directions" to "interim order made under section 216(1A)" inserted by the Companies (Disclosure of Interests in Shares) (Orders imposing restrictions on shares) Regulations 1991 (SI 1991/1646), reg. 7(a) as from 18 July 1991.

**455(2) [Offence by company]** Subject to the terms of any directions made under sections 210(5A), 216(1B), 445(1A) or 456 or of an interim order made under section 216(1A) if shares in a company are issued in contravention of the restrictions, the company and every officer of it who is in default is liable to a fine.

**History**
In s. 455(2) the words at the beginning from "Subject to the terms of any directions" to "interim order made under section 216(1A)" inserted by the Companies (Disclosure of Interests in Shares) (Orders imposing restrictions on shares) Regulations 1991 (SI 1991/1646), reg. 7(b) as from 18 July 1991.

**455(3) [Application of s. 732]** Section 732 (restriction on prosecutions) applies to an offence under this section.

# 456 Relaxation and removal of restrictions

**456(1) [Application to court]** Where shares in a company are by order made subject to the restrictions of this Part, application may be made to the court for an order directing that the shares be no longer so subject.

**456(1A) [Court order to protect third parties' rights]** Where the court is satisfied that an order subjecting the shares to the restrictions of this Part unfairly affects the rights of third parties in respect of shares then the court, for the purpose of protecting such rights and subject to such terms as it thinks fit and in addition to any order it may make under subsection (1), may direct on an application made under that subsection that such acts by such persons or descriptions of persons and for such purposes, as may be set out in the order, shall not constitute a breach of the restrictions of Part XV of this Act.

Subsection (3) does not apply to an order made under this subsection.

**History**
S. 456(1A) inserted by the Companies (Disclosure of Interests in Shares) (Orders imposing restrictions on shares) Regulations 1991 (SI 1991/1646), reg. 8(a) as from 18 July 1991.

**456(2) [Persons entitled to make application]** If the order applying the restrictions was made by the Secretary of State, or he has refused to make an order disapplying them, the application may be made by any person aggrieved; and if the order was made by the court under section 216 (non-disclosure of share holding), it may be made by any such person or by the company.

**456(3) [Conditions for order by court or Secretary of State]** Subject as follows, an order of the court or the Secretary of State directing that shares shall cease to be subject to the restrictions may be made only if–

(a) the court or (as the case may be) the Secretary of State is satisfied that the relevant facts about the shares have been disclosed to the company and no unfair advantage has accrued to any person as a result of the earlier failure to make that disclosure, or

(b) the shares are to be transferred for valuable consideration and the court (in any case) or the Secretary of State (if the order was made under section 210 or 445) approves the transfer.

**History**

In s. 456(3)(b) the words "transferred for valuable consideration" and "transfer" substituted for the former words "sold" and "sale" respectively by CA 1989, s. 145 and Sch. 10, para. 10(1) as from 7 January 1991 (see SI 1990/2569 (C 68), art. 4(e)).

**456(4) [Order re sale of shares etc.]** Without prejudice to the power of the court to give directions under subsection (1A), where shares in a company are subject to the restrictions, the court may on application order the shares to be sold, subject to the court's approval as to the sale, and may also direct that the shares shall cease to be subject to the restrictions.

An application to the court under this subsection may be made by the Secretary of State (unless the restrictions were imposed by court order under section 216), or by the company.

**History**

In s. 456(4) the words at the beginning from "Without prejudice" to "under subsection (1A)," inserted by the Companies (Disclosure of Interests in Shares) (Orders imposing restrictions on shares) Regulations 1991 (SI 1991/1646), reg. 8(b) as from 18 July 1991.

**456(5) [Further order when order made under s. 456(4)]** Where an order has been made under subsection (4), the court may on application make such further order relating to the sale or transfer of the shares as it thinks fit.

An application to the court under this subsection may be made–

(a) by the Secretary of State (unless the restrictions on the shares were imposed by court order under section 216), or

(b) by the company, or

(c) by the person appointed by or in pursuance of the order to effect the sale, or

(d) by any person interested in the shares.

**456(6) [Continuation of certain restrictions]** An order (whether of the Secretary of State or the court) directing that shares shall cease to be subject to the restrictions of this Part, if it is–

(a) expressed to be made with a view to permitting a transfer of the shares, or

(b) made under subsection (4) of this section,

may continue the restrictions mentioned in paragraphs (c) and (d) of section 454(1), either in whole or in part, so far as they relate to any right acquired or offer made before the transfer.

**456(7) [Non-application of s. 456(3)]** Subsection (3) does not apply to an order directing that shares shall cease to be subject to any restrictions which have been continued in force in relation to those shares under subsection (6).

## 457 Further provisions on sale by court order of restricted shares

**457(1) [Proceeds of sale of shares under s. 456(4)]** Where shares are sold in pursuance of an order of the court under section 456(4) the proceeds of sale, less the costs of the sale, shall be paid into court for the benefit of the persons who are beneficially interested in the shares; and any such person may apply to the court for the whole or part of those proceeds to be paid to him.

**457(2) [Application under s. 457(1) for payment of proceeds etc.]** On application under subsection (1) the court shall (subject as provided below) order the payment to the applicant of the whole of the proceeds of sale together with any interest thereon or, if any other person had a beneficial interest in the shares at the time of their sale, such proportion of those proceeds and interest as is equal to the proportion which the value of the applicant's interest in the shares bears to the total value of the shares.

**457(3) [Order re applicant's costs]** On granting an application for an order under section 456(4) or (5) the court may order that the applicant's costs be paid out of the proceeds of sale; and if that order is made, the applicant is entitled to payment of his costs out of those proceeds before any person interested in the shares in question receives any part of those proceeds.

# PART XVI – FRAUDULENT TRADING BY A COMPANY

## 458 Punishment for fraudulent trading

**458** If any business of a company is carried on with intent to defraud creditors of the company or creditors of any other person, or for any fraudulent purpose, every person who was knowingly a party to the carrying on of the business in that manner is liable to imprisonment or a fine, or both.

This applies whether or not the company has been, or is in the course of being, wound up.

# PART XVII – PROTECTION OF COMPANY'S MEMBERS AGAINST UNFAIR PREJUDICE

## 459 Order on application of company member

**459(1) [Application for order that affairs conducted in unfairly prejudicial way]** A member of a company may apply to the court by petition for an order under this Part on the ground that the company's affairs are being or have been conducted in a manner which is unfairly prejudicial to the interests of its members generally or of some part of its members (including at least himself) or that any actual or proposed act or omission of the company (including an act or omission on its behalf) is or would be so prejudicial.

**History**

In s. 459(1) the words "unfairly prejudicial to the interests of its members generally or of some part of its members" substituted for the former words "unfairly prejudicial to the interests of some part of the members" by CA 1989, s. 145 and Sch. 19, para. 11 as from 4 February 1991 (see SI 1990/2569 (C 68), art. 4(e)).

**459(2) [Application to certain non-members]** The provisions of this Part apply to a person who is not a member of a company but to whom shares in the company have been transferred or transmitted by operation of law, as those provisions apply to a member of the company; and references to a member or members are to be construed accordingly.

**459(3) ["Company" to include statutory water company]** In this section (and so far as applicable for the purposes of this section, in section 461(2)) **"company"** means any company within the meaning of this Act or any company which is not such a company but is a statutory water company within the meaning of the Statutory Water Companies Act 1991.

**History**

In s. 459(3) the words "the Statutory Water Companies Act 1991" substituted for the former words "the Water Act 1989" by the Water Consolidation (Consequential Provisions) Act 1991, s. 2, 4(2) and Sch. 1, para. 40(2) as from 1 December 1991.

S. 459(3) previously inserted by Water Act 1989, s. 190(1) and Sch. 25, para. 71(3) as from 1 September 1989 (see Water Act 1989, s. 4, 194(4) and SI 1989/1146 (C 37) – see also SI 1989/1530 (C 51)).

## 460 Order on application of Secretary of State

**460(1) [Secretary of State may apply for order]** If in the case of any company–

(a) the Secretary of State has received a report under section 437, or exercised his powers under section 447 or 448 of this Act or section 43A or 44(2) to (6) of the Insurance Companies Act 1982, and

(b) it appears to him that the company's affairs are being or have been conducted in a manner which is unfairly prejudicial to the interests of its members generally or of some part of its members, or that any actual or proposed act or omission of the company (including an act or omission on its behalf) is or would be so prejudicial, he may himself (in addition to or instead of presenting a petition for the winding up of the company) apply to the court by petition for an order under this Part.

**History**

In s. 460(1) the words "section 43A or 44(2) to (6)" in para. (a) substituted for the former words "section 44(2) to (6)" by the Insurance Companies (Third Insurance Directives) Regulations 1994 (SI 1994/1696), reg. 1, 68, Sch. 8, para. 9(5) as from 1 July 1994; the words "(inspection of company's books and papers)" formerly appearing in para. (a) after the words "Insurance Companies Act 1982" and the words "under section 440" formerly appearing after the words "presenting a petition" repealed by CA 1989, s. 212 and Sch. 24 as from 1 October 1991 (see SI 1991/1996 (C 57), art. 2(1)(c)(ii)).

Previously in s. 460(1) the words "unfairly prejudicial to the interests of its members generally or of some part of its members" substituted for the former words "unfairly prejudicial to the interests of some part of the members" by CA 1989, s. 145 and Sch. 19, para. 11 as from 4 February 1991 (see SI 1990/2569 (C 68), art. 4(e)).

**460(2) ["Company"]** In this section (and, so far as applicable for its purposes, in the section next following) **"company"** means any body corporate which is liable to be wound up under this Act.

## 461 Provisions as to petitions and orders under this Part

**461(1) [Order by court]** If the court is satisfied that a petition under this Part is well founded, it may make such order as it thinks fit for giving relief in respect of the matters complained of.

**461(2) [Scope of order]** Without prejudice to the generality of subsection (1), the court's order may–

(a) regulate the conduct of the company's affairs in the future,

(b) require the company to refrain from doing or continuing an act complained of by the petitioner or to do an act which the petitioner has complained it has omitted to do,

(c) authorise civil proceedings to be brought in the name and on behalf of the company by such person or persons and on such terms as the court may direct,

(d) provide for the purchase of the shares of any members of the company by other members or by the company itself and, in the case of a purchase by the company itself, the reduction of the company's capital accordingly.

**461(3) [Order forbidding alteration of memorandum or articles]** If an order under this Part requires the company not to make any, or any specified, alteration in the memorandum or articles, the company does not then have power without leave of the court to make any such alteration in breach of that requirement.

**461(4) [Effect of alteration by court order]** Any alteration in the company's memorandum or articles made by virtue of an order under this Part is of the same effect as if duly made by resolution of the company, and the provisions of this Act apply to the memorandum or articles as so altered accordingly.

**461(5) [Copy of order re alteration etc. to registrar, penalty on default]** An office copy of an order under this Part altering, or giving leave to alter, a company's memorandum or articles shall, within 14 days from the making of the order or such longer period as the court may allow, be delivered by the company to the registrar of companies for registration; and if a company makes default in complying with this subsection, the company and every officer of it who is in default is liable to a fine and, for continued contravention, to a daily default fine.

**461(6) [Power under Insolvency Act, s. 411]** The power under section 411 of the Insolvency Act to make rules shall, so far as it relates to a winding-up petition, apply for the purposes of a petition under this Part.

**History**

In s. 461(6) the words "section 411 of the Insolvency Act" substituted for the former words "section 106 of the Insolvency Act 1985" by Insolvency Act 1986, s. 439(1) and Sch. 13 as from 29 December 1986 (see IA 1986, s. 443 and SI 1986/1924 (C 71)), in addition s. 461(6) was previously substituted by Insolvency Act 1985, s. 109 and Sch. 6, para. 24 – it originally read as follows:

"Section 663 (winding-up rules) applies in relation to a petition under this Part as in relation to a winding-up petition."

It should be noted that the amendment by the Insolvency Act 1985 was in force as from 1 March 1986 in regard to the making of rules under s. 106 of Insolvency Act 1985 – see SI 1986/185 (C 7).

# PART XVIII – FLOATING CHARGES AND RECEIVERS (SCOTLAND)

## Chapter I – Floating Charges

### 462 Power of incorporated company to create floating charge

**462(1) [Securing of debt by floating charge]** It is competent under the law of Scotland for an incorporated company (whether a company within the meaning of this Act or not), for the purpose of securing any debt or other obligation (including a cautionary obligation) incurred or to be incurred by, or binding upon, the company or any other person, to create in favour of the creditor in the debt or obligation a charge, in this Part referred to as a floating charge, over all or any part of the property (including uncalled capital) which may from time to time be comprised in its property and undertaking.

**462(2)** (Ceased to have effect and repealed by Law Reform (Miscellaneous Provisions) (Scotland) Act 1990, s. 74, Sch. 8, para. 33(1), (6) and Sch. 9 as from 1 December 1990).

**History**

In regard to the date of the above cesser and repeal see SI 1990/2328 (C 60) (S 197), art. 3, Sch.; s. 462(2) formerly read as follows:

"In the case of a company which the Court of Session has jurisdiction to wind up, a floating charge may be created only by a written instrument which is presumed under section 36B to be subscribed by the company."

Previously s. 462(2) substituted for the original s. 462(2), (3) by CA 1989, s. 130(7) and Sch. 17, para. 8 as from 31 July 1990 (see SI 1990/1392 (C 41), art. 2(b)); the original s. 462(2), (3) read as follows:

"**462(2)** A floating charge may be created, in the case of a company which the Court of Session has jurisdiction to wind up, only by the execution, under the seal of the company, of an instrument or bond or other written acknowledgment of debt or obligation which purports to create such a charge.

**(3)** Execution in accordance with this section includes execution by an attorney authorised for such purpose by the company by writing under its common seal; and any such execution on behalf of the company binds the company."

**462(4) [Interpretation]** References in this Part to the instrument by which a floating charge was created are, in the case of a floating charge created by words in a bond or other written acknowledgment, references to the bond or, as the case may be, the other written acknowledgment.

**462(5) [Effect re heritable property in Scotland]** Subject to this Act, a floating charge has effect in accordance with this Part and Part III of the Insolvency Act 1986 in relation to any heritable property in Scotland to which it relates, notwithstanding that the instrument creating it is not recorded in the Register of Sasines or, as appropriate, registered in accordance with the Land Registration (Scotland) Act 1979.

**History**

In s. 462(5) the words "and Part III of the Insolvency Act 1986" inserted by Insolvency Act 1986, s. 439(1) and Sch. 13 as from 29 December 1986 (see IA 1986, s. 443 and SI 1986/1924 (C 71)).

### 463 Effect of floating charge on winding up

**463(1) [Attachment on liquidation]** Where a company goes into liquidation within the meaning of section 247(2) of the Insolvency Act 1986, a floating charge created by the company attaches to the property then comprised in the company's property and undertaking or, as the case may be, in part of that property and undertaking, but does so subject to the rights of any person who–

(a) has effectually executed diligence on the property or any part of it; or

(b) holds a fixed security over the property or any part of it ranking in priority to the floating charge; or

(c) holds over the property or any part of it another floating charge so ranking.

**History**

In s. 463(1) the words "Where a company goes into liquidation" to "the Insolvency Act 1986," substituted for the former words "On the commencement of the winding up of a company," by CA 1989, s. 140(1) as from 3 July 1995 subject to transitional provision (see SI 1995/1352 (C 27), art. 3(a), 4).

**463(2) [Application of Pt. XX to floating charge]** The provisions of Part IV of the Insolvency Act (except section 185) have effect in relation to a floating charge, subject to subsection (1), as if the charge were a fixed security over the property to which it has attached in respect of the principal of the debt or obligation to which it relates and any interest due or to become due thereon.

**History**

In s. 463(2) the words "Part IV of the Insolvency Act (except section 185)" substituted for the former words "Part XX (except section 623(4))" by Insolvency Act 1986, s. 439(1) and Sch. 13 as from 29 December 1986 (see IA 1986, s. 443 and SI 1986/1924 (C 71)).

**463(3) [Operation of Insolvency Act]** Nothing in this section derogates from the provisions of sections 53(7) and 54(6) of the Insolvency Act (attachment of floating charge on appointment of receiver), or prejudices the operation of sections 175 and 176 of that Act (payment of preferential debts in winding up).

**History**

S. 463(3) substituted by Insolvency Act 1986, s. 439(1) and Sch. 13 as from 29 December 1986 (see IA 1986, s. 443 and SI 1986/1924 (C 71)); s. 463(3) (as previously amended by Insolvency Act 1985, s. 109 and Sch. 6, para. 18) read as follows:

"Nothing in this section–

(a) prejudices the operation of section 89 of the Insolvency Act 1985;
(b) derogates from the provisions of sections 469(7) and 470(6) in this Part."

The original wording of s. 463(3)(a) was: "prejudices the operation of section 614(2)".

**463(4) [Accrual of interest]** Interest accrues, in respect of a floating charge which after 16th November 1972 attaches to the property of the company, until payment of the sum due under the charge is made.

**History**

In s. 463(4) the words "Subject to section 617", formerly appearing at the beginning repealed by Insolvency Act 1986, s. 438 and Sch. 12 as from 29 December 1986 (see IA 1986, s. 443 and SI 1986/1924 (C 71)).

## 464 Ranking of floating charges

**464(1) [Contents of instrument creating floating charge]** Subject to subsection (2), the instrument creating a floating charge over all or any part of the company's property under section 462 may contain–

(a) provisions prohibiting or restricting the creation of any fixed security or any other floating charge having priority over, or ranking pari passu with, the floating charge; or
(b) with the consent of the holder of any subsisting floating charge or fixed security which would be adversely affected, provisions regulating the order in which the floating charge shall rank with any other subsisting or future floating charges or fixed securities over that property or any part of it.

**History**

In s. 464(1)(b) the words "with the consent of" to "adversely affected," inserted by CA 1989, s. 140(2), (3) as from 3 July 1995 subject to transitional provision (see SI 1995/1352 (C 27), art. 3(a), 5).

**464(1A) [Priority of floating charge under s. 464(1)(a)]** Where an instrument creating a floating charge contains any such provision as is mentioned in subsection (1)(a), that provision shall be effective to confer priority on the floating charge over any fixed security or floating charge created after the date of the instrument.

**History**

S, 464(1A) inserted by CA 1989, s. 140(2), (4) as from 3 July 1995 subject to transitional provision (see SI 1995/1352 (C 27), art. 3(a), 6).

**464(2) [Priority of fixed security by operation of law]** Where all or any part of the property of a company is subject both to a floating charge and to a fixed security arising by operation of law, the fixed security has priority over the floating charge.

**464(3) [Priority with other floating charges and fixed securities]** The order of ranking of the floating charge with any other subsisting or future floating charges or fixed securities over all or any part of the company's property is determined in accordance with the provisions of subsections (4) and (5) except where it is determined in accordance with any provision such as is mentioned in paragraph (a) or (b) of subsection (1).

**History**

S. 464(3) substituted by CA 1989, s. 140(2), (5) as from 3 July 1995 subject to transitional provision (see SI 1995/1352 (C 27), art. 3(a), 7); s. 464(3) formerly read as follows:

"Where the order of ranking of the floating charge with any other subsisting or future floating charges or fixed securities over all or any part of the company's property is not regulated by provisions contained in the instrument creating the floating charge, the order of ranking is determined in accordance with the following provisions of this section."

**464(4) [Rules of priority]** Subject to the provisions of this section–

(a) a fixed security, the right to which has been constituted as a real right before a floating charge has attached to all or any part of the property of the company, has priority of ranking over the floating charge;

(b) floating charges rank with one another according to the time of registration in accordance with Chapter II of Part XII;

(c) floating charges which have been received by the registrar for registration by the same postal delivery rank with one another equally.

**464(5) [Restriction of priority of one floating charge over another]** Where the holder of a floating charge over all or any part of the company's property which has been registered in accordance with Chapter II of Part XII has received intimation in writing of the subsequent registration in accordance with that Chapter of another floating charge over the same property or any part thereof, the preference in ranking of the first-mentioned floating charge is restricted to security for–

(a) the holder's present advances;

(b) future advances which he may be required to make under the instrument creating the floating charge or under any ancillary document;

(c) interest due or to become due on all such advances;

(d) any expenses or outlays which may reasonably be incurred by the holder; and

(e) (in the case of a floating charge to secure a contingent liability other than a liability arising under any further advances made from time to time) the maximum sum to which that contingent liability is capable of amounting whether or not it is contractually limited.

**History**
The word "and" at the end of s. 464(5)(c) repealed and s. 464(5)(e) inserted together with the preceding "; and" by CA 1989, s. 140(2), (6), 212 and Sch. 24 as from 3 July 1995 subject to transitional provision (see SI 1995/1352 (C 27), art. 3(a), (c)(i), 8).

**464(6) [S. 175, 176 of Insolvency Act]** This section is subject to sections 175 and 176 of the Insolvency Act.

**History**
In s. 464(6) the words "sections 175 and 176 of the Insolvency Act" substituted by Insolvency Act 1986, s. 439(1) and Sch. 13 as from 29 December 1986 (see IA 1986, s. 443 and SI 1986/1924 (C 71)). The former words were "section 89 of the Insolvency Act 1985", themselves substituted briefly by Insolvency Act 1985, s. 109 and Sch. 6, para. 19 for the original words "section 614(2) (preferential debts in winding up)" (see SI 1986/1924 (C 71)).

# 465 Continued effect of certain charges validated by Act of 1972

**465(1) [Subsisting floating charges]** Any floating charge which–

(a) purported to subsist as a floating charge on 17th November 1972, and

(b) if it had been created on or after that date, would have been validly created by virtue of the Companies (Floating Charges and Receivers) (Scotland) Act 1972,

is deemed to have subsisted as a valid floating charge as from the date of its creation.

**465(2) [Subsisting provisions]** Any provision which–

(a) is contained in an instrument creating a floating charge or in any ancillary document executed prior to, and still subsisting at, the commencement of that Act,

(b) relates to the ranking of charges, and

(c) if it had been made after the commencement of that Act, would have been a valid provision,

is deemed to have been a valid provision as from the date of its making.

# 466 Alteration of floating charges

**466(1) [Alteration by execution of instrument of alteration by company et al.]** The instrument creating a floating charge under section 462 or any ancillary document may be altered by the execution of an instrument of alteration by the company, the holder of the charge and the holder of any other charge (including a fixed security) which would be adversely affected by the alteration.

**466(2) [Valid execution of instrument of alteration]** Without prejudice to any enactment or rule of law regarding the execution of documents, such an instrument of alteration is validly executed if it is executed–

(b) where trustees for debenture-holders are acting under and in accordance with a trust deed, by those trustees; or

(c) where, in the case of a series of secured debentures, no such trustees are acting, by or on behalf of–

(i) a majority in nominal value of those present or represented by proxy and voting at a meeting of debenture-holders at which the holders of at least one-third in nominal value of the outstanding debentures of the series are present or so represented; or

(ii) where no such meeting is held, the holders of at least one-half in nominal value of the outstanding debentures of the series.

**History**

In s. 466(2) the words at the beginning "Without prejudice to any enactment or rule of law regarding the execution of documents," inserted, former para. (a) omitted, the word "or" at the end of para. (b) inserted and former para. (d) and the former word "or" preceding it omitted by CA 1989, s. 130(7) and Sch. 17, para. 9 as from 31 July 1990 (see SI 1990/1392 (C 41), art. 2(b)) – former para. (a) and (d) and the word "or" preceding the latter also repealed by CA 1989, s. 212 and Sch. 24 as from 1 October 1990 (see SI 1990/1707 (C 46), art. 3(a)), former para. (a) and (d) read as follows:

"(a) in the case of a company, under its common seal or by an attorney authorised for such purpose by the company by a writing under its common seal;

(d) in such manner as may be provided for in the instrument creating the floating charge or any ancillary document."

**466(3) [Application of s. 464]** Section 464 applies to an instrument of alteration under this section as it applies to an instrument creating a floating charge.

**466(4) [Application of s. 410(2), (3), 420]** Subject to the next subsection, section 410(2) and (3) and section 420 apply to an instrument of alteration under this section which–

(a) prohibits or restricts the creation of any fixed security or any other floating charge having priority over, or ranking pari passu with, the floating charge; or

(b) varies, or otherwise regulates the order of, the ranking of the floating charge in relation to fixed securities or to other floating charges; or

(c) releases property from the floating charge; or

(d) increases the amount secured by the floating charge.

**466(5) [Interpretation re s. 466(4)]** Section 410(2) and (3) and section 420 apply to an instrument of alteration falling under subsection (4) of this section as if references in the said sections to a charge were references to an alteration to a floating charge, and as if in section 410(2) and (3)–

(a) references to the creation of a charge were references to the execution of such alteration; and

(b) for the words from the beginning of subsection (2) to the word "applies" there were substituted the words "Every alteration to a floating charge created by a company".

**466(6) [Reference to floating charge includes reference to floating charge as altered]** Any reference (however expressed) in any enactment, including this Act, to a floating charge is, for the purposes of this section and unless the context otherwise requires, to be construed as including a reference to the floating charge as altered by an instrument of alteration falling under subsection (4) of this section.

# Chapter II – Receivers

**467-485** (Repealed by Insolvency Act 1986, s. 438 and Sch. 12 as from 29 December 1986.)

**History**

In regard to the date of the above repeal, see IA 1986, s. 443 and SI 1986/1924 (C 71). These were some previous amendments and repeals by Insolvency Act 1985 which only came into force briefly – see IA 1985, Sch. 6, 10 and the above SI (note in particular art. 4(b)). S. 467–485 originally read as follows:

"**467 Power to appoint receiver**

**467(1)** It is competent under the law of Scotland for the holder of a floating charge over all or any part of the property (including uncalled capital), which may from time to time be comprised in the property and undertaking of an incorporated company (whether a company within the meaning of this Act or not) which the Court of Session has jurisdiction to wind up, to appoint a receiver of such part of the property of the company as is subject to the charge.

**(2)** It is competent under the law of Scotland for the court, on the application of the holder of such a floating charge, to appoint a receiver of such part of the property of the company as is subject to the charge.

**(3)** The following are disqualified from being appointed as receiver–
(a) a body corporate;
(b) an undischarged bankrupt; and
(c) a firm according to the law of Scotland.

**(4)** A body corporate or a firm according to the law of Scotland which acts as a receiver is liable to a fine.

**(5)** An undischarged bankrupt who so acts is liable to imprisonment or a fine, or both.

**(6)** In this section, **"receiver"** includes joint receivers.

**468 Circumstances justifying appointment**

**468(1)** A receiver may be appointed under section 467(1) by the holder of the floating charge on the occurrence of any event which, by the provisions of the instrument creating the charge, entitles the holder of the charge to make that appointment and, in so far as not otherwise provided for by the instrument, on the occurrence of any of the following events, namely–
(a) the expiry of a period of 21 days after the making of a demand for payment of the whole or any part of the principal sum secured by the charge, without payment having been made;
(b) the expiry of a period of two months during the whole of which interest due and payable under the charge has been in arrears;
(c) the making of an order or the passing of a resolution to wind up the company;
(d) the appointment of a receiver by virtue of any other floating charge created by the company.

**(2)** A receiver may be appointed by the court under section 467(2) on the occurrence of any event which, by the provisions of the instrument creating the floating charge, entitles the holder of the charge to make that appointment and, in so far as not otherwise provided for by the instrument, on the occurrence of any of the following events, namely–
(a) where the court, on the application of the holder of the charge, pronounces itself satisfied that the position of the holder of the charge is likely to be prejudiced if no such appointment is made;
(b) any of the events referred to in paragraphs (a) to (c) of subsection (1) above.

**469 Mode of appointment by holder of charge**

**469(1)** The appointment of a receiver by the holder of the floating charge under section 467(1) shall be by means of a validly executed instrument in writing (referred to as the "instrument of appointment"), a copy (certified in the prescribed manner to be a correct copy) whereof shall be delivered by or on behalf of the person making the appointment to the registrar of companies for registration within 7 days of its execution and shall be accompanied by a notice in the prescribed form.

**(2)** If any person without reasonable excuse makes default in complying with the requirements of subsection (1), he is liable to a fine and, for continued contravention, to a daily default fine.

**(3)** The instrument of appointment is validly executed–
(a) by a company, if it is executed in accordance with the provisions of section 36 of this Act as if it were a contract; and
(b) by any other person, if it is executed in the manner required or permitted by the law of Scotland in the case of an attested deed.

**(4)** The instrument may be executed on behalf of the holder of the floating charge by virtue of which the receiver is to be appointed–
(a) by any person duly authorised in writing by the holder to execute the instrument; and
(b) in the case of an appointment of a receiver by the holders of a series of secured debentures, by any person authorised by resolution of the debenture-holders to execute the instrument.

**(5)** On receipt of the certified copy of the instrument of appointment in accordance with subsection (1) of this section, the registrar shall, on payment of the prescribed fee, enter the particulars of the appointment in the register of charges.

**(6)** The receiver is to be regarded as having been appointed on the date of the execution of the instrument of his appointment.

**(7)** On the appointment of a receiver under this section, the floating charge by virtue of which he was appointed attaches to the property then subject to the charge; and such attachment has effect as if the charge was a fixed security over the property to which it has attached.

**470 Appointment by court**

**470(1)** Application for the appointment of a receiver by the court under section 467(2) shall be by petition to the court, which shall be served on the company.

**(2)** On such application, the court shall, if it thinks fit, issue an interlocutor making the appointment of the receiver on such terms as to caution as it may think fit.

**(3)** A copy (certified by the clerk of the court to be a correct copy) of the court's interlocutor making the appointment shall be delivered by or on behalf of the petitioner to the registrar of companies for registration, accompanied by a notice in the prescribed form, within 7 days of the date of the interlocutor or such longer period as the court may allow.
If any person without reasonable excuse makes default in complying with the requirements of this subsection he is liable to a fine and, for continued contravention, to a daily default fine.

**(4)** On receipt of the certified copy interlocutor in accordance with subsection (3), and on receipt of a certificate by the appropriate officer of the court that caution as ordered by the court has been found, the registrar shall, on payment of the prescribed fee, enter the particulars of the appointment in the register of charges.

**(5)** The receiver is to be regarded as having been appointed on the date of his being appointed by the court.

**(6)** On the appointment of a receiver under this section, the floating charge by virtue of which he was appointed attaches to the property then subject to the charge; and such attachment has effect as if the charge were a fixed security over the property to which it has attached.

**(7)** In making rules of court for the purposes of this section, the Court of Session shall have regard to the need for special provision for cases which appear to the court to require to be dealt with as a matter of urgency.

**471 Powers of receiver**

**471(1)** Subject to subsection (2) below, a receiver has in relation to such part of the property of the company as is attached by the floating charge by virtue of which he was appointed, the powers, if any, given to him by the instrument creating that charge and, in addition, he has under this Part the following powers as respects that property, in so far as these are not inconsistent with any provision contained in that instrument, namely–

(a) power to take possession of, collect and get in the property from the company or a liquidator thereof or any other person, and for that purpose, to take such proceedings as may seem to him expedient;
(b) power to sell, feu, hire out or otherwise dispose of the property by public roup or private bargain and with or without advertisement;
(c) power to borrow money and grant security therefor over the property;
(d) power to appoint a solicitor or accountant or other professionally qualified person to assist him in the performance of his functions;
(e) power to apply to the court for directions in connection with the performance of his functions;
(f) power to bring or defend any action or other legal proceedings in the name and on behalf of the company;
(g) power to refer to arbitration all questions affecting the company;
(h) power to effect and maintain insurances in respect of the business and property of the company;
(i) power to use the company's seal;
(j) power to do all acts and to execute in the name and on behalf of the company any deed, receipt or other document;
(k) power to draw, accept, make and endorse any bill of exchange or promissory note in the name and on behalf of the company;
(l) power to appoint any agent to do any business which he is unable to do himself or which can more conveniently be done by an agent and power to employ and discharge servants;
(m) power to have carried out to the best advantage any work on the property of the company and in general to do all such other things as may be necessary for the realisation of the property;
(n) power to make any payment which is necessary or incidental to the performance of his functions;
(o) power to carry on the business of the company so far as he thinks it desirable to do so;
(p) power to grant any lease of the property, and to input and output tenants, and to take on lease any property required or convenient for the business of the company;
(q) power to rank and claim in the bankruptcy, insolvency, sequestration or liquidation of any person or company indebted to the company and to receive dividends, and to accede to trust deeds for creditors of any such person;
(r) power to present or defend a petition for the winding up of the company; and
(s) power to do all other things incidental to the exercise of the powers mentioned in this subsection.

**(2)** Subsection (1) applies–

(a) subject to the rights of any person who has effectually executed diligence on all or any part of the property of the company prior to the appointment of the receiver; and
(b) subject to the rights of any person who holds over all or any part of the property of the company a fixed security or floating charge having priority over, or ranking pari passu with, the floating charge by virtue of which the receiver was appointed.

**(3)** A person transacting with a receiver shall not be concerned to inquire whether any event has happened to authorise the receiver to act.

**472 Precedence among receivers**

**472(1)** Where there are two or more floating charges subsisting over all or any part of the property of the company, a receiver may be appointed under this Chapter by virtue of each such charge, but a receiver appointed by, or on the application of, the holder of a floating charge having priority of ranking over any other floating charge by virtue of which a receiver has been appointed has the powers given to a receiver by section 471 to the exclusion of any other receiver.

**(2)** Where two or more floating charges rank with one another equally, and two or more receivers have been appointed by virtue of such charges, the receivers so appointed are deemed to have been appointed as joint receivers.

**(3)** Receivers appointed, or deemed to have been appointed, as joint receivers shall act jointly unless the instrument of appointment or respective instruments of appointment otherwise provide.

**(4)** Subject to subsection (5) below, the powers of a receiver appointed by, or on the application of, the holder of a floating charge are suspended by, and as from the date of, the appointment of a receiver by, or on the application of, the holder of a floating charge having priority of ranking over that charge to such extent as may be necessary to enable the receiver second mentioned to exercise his powers under section 471; and any powers so suspended take effect again when the floating charge having priority of ranking ceases to attach to the property then subject to the charge, whether such cessation is by virtue of section 478(6) or otherwise.

**(5)** The suspension of the powers of a receiver under subsection (4) does not have the effect of requiring him to release any part of the property (including any letters or documents) of the company from his control until he receives from the receiver superseding him a valid indemnity (subject to the limit of the value of such part of the property of the company as is subject to the charge by virtue of which he was appointed) in respect of any expenses, charges and liabilities he may have incurred in the performance of his functions as receiver.

**(6)** The suspension of the powers of a receiver under subsection (4) does not cause the floating charge by virtue of which he was appointed to cease to attach to the property to which it attached by virtue of section 469(7) or 470(6).

**(7)** Nothing in this section prevents the same receiver being appointed by virtue of two or more floating charges.

**473 Agency and liability of receiver for contracts**

**473(1)** A receiver is deemed to be the agent of the company in relation to such property of the company as is attached by the floating charge by virtue of which he was appointed.

**(2)** Subject to subsection (1), a receiver (including a receiver whose powers are subsequently suspended under section 472) is personally liable on any contract entered into by him in the performance of his functions, except in so far as the contract otherwise provides.

**(3)** A receiver who is personally liable by virtue of subsection (2) is entitled to be indemnified out of the property in respect of which he was appointed.

**(4)** Any contract entered into by or on behalf of the company prior to the appointment of a receiver continues in force (subject to its terms) notwithstanding that appointment, but the receiver does not by virtue only of his appointment incur any personal liability on any such contract.

**(5)** Any contract entered into by a receiver in the performance of his functions continues in force (subject to its terms) although the powers of the receiver are subsequently suspended under section 472.

**474 Remuneration of receiver**

**474(1)** The remuneration to be paid to a receiver is to be determined by agreement between the receiver and the holder of the floating charge by virtue of which he was appointed.

**(2)** Where the remuneration to be paid to the receiver has not been determined under subsection (1) or where it has been so determined but is disputed by any of the persons mentioned in paragraphs (a) to (d), it may be fixed instead by the Auditor of the Court of Session on application made to him by–

(a) the receiver;
(b) the holder of any floating charge or fixed security over all or any part of the property of the company;
(c) the company; or
(d) the liquidator of the company.

**(3)** Application to the Auditor of the Court of Session under subsection (2) shall be made in writing not later than one month after the sending of the abstract of receipts and payments of the receiver mentioned below in this Chapter which discloses the remuneration, if any, payable to the receiver.

**(4)** Where the receiver has been paid or has retained for his remuneration for any period before the remuneration has been fixed by the Auditor of the Court of Session under subsection (2) any amount in excess of the remuneration so fixed for that period, the receiver or his personal representatives shall account for the excess.

**475 Priority of debts**

**475(1)** Where a receiver is appointed and the company is not at the time of the appointment in course of being wound up, the debts which fall under subsection (2) of this section shall be paid out of any assets coming to the hands of the receiver in priority to any claim for principal or interest by the holder of the floating charge by virtue of which the receiver was appointed.

**(2)** Debts falling under this subsection are debts which satisfy the conditions of this subsection, that is to say, they are debts–

(a) which in every winding up are, under the provisions of Part XX relating to preferential payments, to be paid in priority to all other debts; and
(b) which, by the end of a period of six months after advertisement by the receiver for claims in the Edinburgh Gazette and in a newspaper circulating in the district where the company carries on business, either–
  (i) have been intimated to him; or
  (ii) have become known to him.

**(3)** In the application of Part XX, section 614 and Schedule 19 are to be read as if the provision for payment of accrued holiday remuneration becoming payable on the termination of employment before or by the effect of the winding-up order or resolution were a provision for payment of such remuneration becoming payable on the termination of employment before or by the effect of the appointment of the receiver.

**(4)** The periods of time mentioned in Schedule 19 are to be reckoned from the date of the appointment of the receiver under section 469(6) or 470(5).

**(5)** Any payments made under this section shall be recouped as far as may be out of the assets of the company available for payment of ordinary creditors.

**476 Distribution of monies**

**476(1)** Subject to section 477, and to the rights of any of the following categories of persons, namely–

(a) the holder of any fixed security which is over property subject to the floating charge and which ranks prior to, or pari passu with, the floating charge;
(b) all persons who have effectually executed diligence on any part of the property of the company which is subject to the charge by virtue of which the receiver was appointed;
(c) creditors in respect of all liabilities, charges and expenses incurred by or on behalf of the receiver;
(d) the receiver in respect of his liabilities, expenses and remuneration; and
(e) the preferential creditors entitled to payment under section 475,

the receiver shall pay monies received by him to the holder of the floating charge by virtue of which the receiver was appointed in or towards satisfaction of the debt secured by the floating charge.

**(2)** Any balance of monies remaining after the provisions of subsection (1) of this section and section 477 have been satisfied shall be paid in accordance with their respective rights and interests to the following persons, as the case may require, namely–

(a) any other receiver;
(b) the holder of a fixed security which is over property subject to the floating charge;
(c) the company or its liquidator, as the case may be.

**(3)** Where any question arises as to the person entitled to a payment under this section, or where a receipt or a discharge of a security cannot be obtained in respect of any such payment, the receiver shall consign the amount of such payment in any joint stock bank of issue in Scotland in name of the Accountant of Court for behoof of the person or persons entitled thereto.

**477 Disposal of interest in property**

**477(1)** Where the receiver sells or disposes, or is desirous of selling or disposing, of any property or interest in property of the company which is subject to the floating charge by virtue of which the receiver was appointed and which is–

(a) subject to any security or interest of, or burden or encumbrance in favour of, a creditor the ranking of which is prior to, pari passu with, or postponed to the floating charge; or
(b) property or an interest in property affected or attached by effectual diligence executed by any person;

and the receiver is unable to obtain the consent of such creditor or, as the case may be, such person to such a sale or disposal, the receiver may apply to the court for authority to sell or dispose of the property or interest in property free of such security, interest, burden, encumbrance or diligence.

**(2)** On such an application, the court may, if it thinks fit, authorise the sale or disposal of the property or interest in question free of such security, interest, burden, encumbrance or diligence, and such authorisation may be on such terms or conditions as the court thinks fit:

But that authorisation shall not be given where a fixed security over the property or interest in question which ranks prior to the floating charge has not been met or provided for in full.

**(3)** Where any sale or disposal is effected in accordance with the authorisation of the court under subsection (2) of this section, the receiver shall grant to the purchaser or disponee an appropriate document of transfer or conveyance of the property or interest in question, and that document has the effect, or, where recording, intimation or registration of that document is a legal requirement for completion of title to the property or interest, then that recording, intimation or registration, as the case may be, has the effect, of–

(a) disencumbering the property or interest of the security, interest, burden or encumbrance affecting it; and
(b) freeing the property or interest from the diligence executed upon it.

**(4)** Nothing in this section prejudices the right of any creditor of the company to rank for his debt in the winding up of the company.

**478 Cessation of appointment of receiver**

**478(1)** A receiver appointed by the holder of a floating charge under section 467(1) may resign on giving one month's notice thereof to–

(a) the holders of floating charges over all or any part of the property of the company;
(b) the company or its liquidator; and
(c) the holders of any fixed security over property of the company which is subject to the floating charge by virtue of which the receiver was appointed.

**(2)** A receiver appointed by the court under section 467(2) may resign only with the authority of the court and on such terms and conditions, if any, as may be laid down by the court.

**(3)** Subject to subsection (4) below, a receiver may, on application to the court by the holder of the floating charge by virtue of which he was appointed, be removed by the court on cause shown.

**(4)** Where a receiver ceases to act as such, then, in respect of any expenses, charges or other liabilities he may have incurred in the performance of his functions as receiver, he is entitled to be indemnified out of the property which is subject to the floating charge by virtue of which he was appointed.

**(5)** When a receiver ceases to act as such otherwise than by death he shall, and, when a receiver is removed by the court, the holder of the floating charge by virtue of which he was appointed shall, within 7 days of the cessation or removal, as the case may be, give the registrar of companies notice to that effect, and the registrar shall enter the notice in the register of charges.

If the receiver or the holder of the floating charge, as the case may require, makes default in complying with the requirements of this subsection, he is liable to a fine and, for continued contravention, to a daily default fine.

**(6)** If by the expiry of a period of one month following upon the removal of the receiver or his ceasing to act as such no other receiver has been appointed, the floating charge by virtue of which the receiver was appointed–

(a) thereupon ceases to attach to the property then subject to the charge; and
(b) again subsists as a floating charge.

**479 Powers of court**

**479(1)** A holder of a floating charge by virtue of which a receiver was appointed may apply to the court for directions in any matter arising in connection with the performance by the receiver of his functions.

**(2)** Where a floating charge by virtue of which a person is purported to have been appointed receiver is discovered to be invalid, the court may, if it thinks fit, in whole or in part relieve that person from personal liability in respect of anything done or omitted to be done which, had he been validly appointed, would have been properly done or omitted.

**(3)** The court may, if it thinks fit, make the person by whom the invalid appointment was made personally liable in respect of anything done or omitted to be done to the extent to which the person purported to have been appointed receiver has been relieved of personal liability.

**480 Notification that receiver appointed**

**480(1)** Where a receiver has been appointed, every invoice, order for goods or business letter issued by or on behalf of the company or the receiver or the liquidator of the company, being a document on or in which the name of the company appears, shall contain a statement that a receiver has been appointed.

**(2)** If default is made in complying with the requirements of this section, the company and any of the following persons who knowingly and wilfully authorises or permits the default, namely, any officer of the company, any liquidator of the company and any receiver, is liable to a fine.

**481 Provisions as to information where receiver appointed**

**481(1)** Where a receiver is appointed then, subject to the provisions of this section and the section next following–

(a) he shall forthwith send notice to the company of his appointment; and
(b) there shall, within 14 days after receipt of the notice, or such longer period as may be allowed by the court or in writing by the receiver, be made out and submitted to the receiver in accordance with section 482 a statement in the prescribed form as to the affairs of the company; and
(c) the receiver shall, within 2 months after receipt of the statement, send–
  (i) to the registrar of companies and to the court, a copy of the statement and of any comments he sees fit to make thereon and, in the case of the registrar of companies, also a summary of the statement and of his comments (if any) thereon; and
  (ii) to the company, a copy of any such comments or, if he does not see fit to make any comment, a notice to that effect; and
  (iii) to the holder of the floating charge by virtue of which he was appointed, to any trustees for the debenture-holders on whose behalf he was appointed and, so far as he is aware of their addresses, to all such debenture-holders, a copy of the said summary.

**(2)** The receiver shall, within two months, or such longer period as the court may allow, after the expiration of the period of 12 months from the date of his appointment and of every subsequent period of twelve months, and within two months, or such longer period as the court may allow, after he ceases to act as receiver, send to–

(a) the registrar of companies;
(b) the company;
(c) the holder of the floating charge by virtue of which he was appointed;

(d) any trustees for the debenture-holders of the company on whose behalf he was appointed;
(e) all such debenture-holders (so far as he is aware of their addresses); and
(f) the holders of all other floating charges or fixed securities over property of the company,

an abstract in the prescribed form showing his receipts and payments during that period of twelve months, or, where he ceases to act as receiver, during the period from the end of the period to which the last preceding abstract related (or, if no preceding abstract has been sent under this section, from the date of his appointment) up to the date of his so ceasing, and the aggregate amounts of his receipts and of his payments during all preceding periods since his appointment.

**(3)** Where the receiver is appointed by the holder of the floating charge under section 467, this section has effect–
(a) with the omission of the references to the court in subsection (1); and
(b) with the substitution for the references to the court in subsection (2) of references to the Secretary of State;

and, in any other case, references to the court shall be taken as referring to the court by which the receiver was appointed.

**(4)** Subsection (1) does not apply in relation to the appointment of a receiver to act with an existing receiver or in place of a receiver dying or ceasing to act, except that, where that subsection applies to a receiver who dies or ceases to act before it has been fully complied with, the references in paragraphs (b) and (c) of the subsection include (subject to subsection (5)) reference to his successor and to any continuing receiver.

Nothing in this subsection shall be taken as limiting the meaning of the expression "the receiver" where used in, or in relation to, subsection (2).

**(5)** Where the company is being wound up, this section and section 482 shall apply notwithstanding that the receiver and the liquidator are the same person, but with any necessary modifications arising from that fact.

**(6)** Nothing in subsection (2) above prejudices the duty of the receiver to render proper accounts of his receipts and payments to the persons to whom, and at the times at which, he may be required to do so apart from that subsection.

**(7)** If the receiver makes default in complying with the requirements of this section, he is liable to a fine and, for continued contravention, to a daily default fine.

**482 Special provisions as to statement submitted to receiver**

**482(1)** The statement as to the affairs of a company required by section 481 to be submitted to the receiver (or his successor) shall show as at the date of the receiver's appointment the particulars of the company's assets, debts and liabilities, the names, residences and occupations of its creditors, the securities held by them respectively, the dates when the securities were respectively given and such further or other information as may be prescribed.

**(2)** The statement shall be submitted by, and be verified by the statutory declaration of, one or more of the persons who are at the date of the receiver's appointment the directors, and by the person who is at that date the secretary, of the company, or by such of the persons mentioned below in this subsection as the receiver (or his successor), subject to the direction of the court, may require to submit and verify the statement, that is to say, persons–
(a) who are or have been officers of the company;
(b) who have taken part in the formation of the company at any time within one year before the date of the receiver's appointment;
(c) who are in the employment of the company, or have been in its employment within that year, and are, in the opinion of the receiver, capable of giving the information required;
(d) who are, or have been within that year, officers of, or in the employment of, a company which is, or within that year was, an officer of the company to which the statement relates.

**(3)** Any person making the statement and statutory declaration shall be allowed, and shall be paid by the receiver (or his successor) out of his receipts, such costs and expenses incurred in the preparation and making of the statement and statutory declaration as the receiver (or his successor) may consider reasonable, subject to an appeal to the court.

**(4)** Where the receiver is appointed by the holder of the floating charge under section 467(1), this section has effect with the substitution for the references to the court in subsections (2) and (3) of references to the Secretary of State; and in any other case references to the court are to be taken as referring to the court by which the receiver was appointed.

**(5)** If any person without reasonable excuse makes default in complying with the requirements of this section, he is liable to a fine and, for continued contravention, to a daily default fine.

**(6)** References in this section to the receiver's successor include a continuing receiver.

**483 Enforcement of receiver's duty to make returns, etc.**

**483(1)** If any receiver–
(a) having made default in filing, delivering or making any return, account or other document, or in giving any notice, which a receiver is by law required to file, deliver, make or give, fails to make good the default within 14 days after the service on him of a notice requiring him to do so; or
(b) has, after being required at any time by the liquidator of the company so to do, failed to render proper accounts of his receipts and payments and to vouch the same and to pay over to the liquidator the amount properly payable to him,

the court may, on an application made for the purpose, make an order directing the receiver to make good the default within such time as may be specified in the order.

**(2)** In the case of any such default as is mentioned in subsection (1)(a), an application for the purposes of this section may be made by any member or creditor of the company or by the registrar of companies, and, in the case of any such default as is mentioned in subsection (1)(b) the application shall be made by the liquidator, and, in either case, the order may provide that all expenses of and incidental to the application shall be borne by the receiver.

**(3)** Nothing in this section prejudices the operation of any enactments imposing penalties on receivers in respect of any such default as is mentioned in subsection (1).

**484 Interpretation for Chapter II**

**484(1)** In this Chapter, unless the contrary intention appears, the following expressions have the following meanings respectively assigned to them, that is to say–

**"company"** means an incorporated company (whether a company within the meaning of this Act or not) which the Court of Session has jurisdiction to wind up;

**"secured debenture"** means a bond, debenture, debenture stock or other security which, either itself or by reference to any other instrument, creates a floating charge over all or any part of the property of the company, but does not include a security which creates no charge other than a fixed security;

**"series of secured debentures"** means two or more secured debentures created as a series by the company in such a manner that the holders thereof are entitled pari passu to the benefit of the floating charge.

**(2)** Where a floating charge, secured debenture or series of secured debentures has been created by the company, then, except where the context otherwise requires, any reference in this Chapter to the holder of the floating charge shall–

(a) where the floating charge, secured debenture or series of secured debentures provides for a receiver to be appointed by any person or body, be construed as a reference to that person or body;

(b) where, in the case of a series of secured debentures, no such provision has been made therein but–

(i) there are trustees acting for the debenture-holders under and in accordance with a trust deed, be construed as a reference to those trustees; and

(ii) where no such trustees are acting, be construed as a reference to–

(aa) a majority in nominal value of those present or represented by proxy and voting at a meeting of debenture-holders at which the holders of at least one-third in nominal value of the outstanding debentures of the series are present or so represented; or

(bb) where no such meeting is held, the holders of at least one-half in nominal value of the outstanding debentures of the series.

**(3)** Any reference in this Chapter to a floating charge, secured debenture, series of secured debentures or instrument creating a charge includes, except where the context otherwise requires, a reference to that floating charge, debenture, series of debentures or instrument as varied by any instrument.

**485 Prescription of forms etc., and regulations**

**485(1)** The notice referred to in section 478(5) and the notice referred to in section 481(1)(a) and the statutory declaration referred to in section 482(2) shall be in such form as may be prescribed.

**(2)** Any power conferred by this Part on the Secretary of State to make regulations is exercisable by statutory instrument; and a statutory instrument made in the exercise of any power so conferred to prescribe a fee is subject to annulment in pursuance of a resolution of either House of Parliament."

# Chapter III – General

## 486 Interpretation for Part XVIII generally

**486(1) [Definitions]** In this Part, unless the context otherwise requires, the following expressions have the following meanings respectively assigned to them, that is to say–

**"ancillary document"** means–

(a) a document which relates to the floating charge and which was executed by the debtor or creditor in the charge before the registration of the charge in accordance with Chapter II of Part XII; or

(b) an instrument of alteration such as is mentioned in section 466 in this Part;

**"company"** means an incorporated company (whether a company within the meaning of this Act or not);

**"fixed security"** in relation to any property of a company, means any security, other than a floating charge or a charge having the nature of a floating charge, which on the winding up of the company in Scotland would be treated as an effective security over that property, and (without prejudice to that generality) includes a security over that property, being a heritable security within the meaning of section 9(8) of the Conveyancing and Feudal Reform (Scotland) Act 1970;

**"Register of Sasines"** means the appropriate division of the General Register of Sasines.

**History**

In s. 486(1):

- in the definition of "company" the words "other than in Chapter II of this part" formerly appearing before the word "means" repealed by Insolvency Act 1986, s. 438 and Sch. 12 as from 29 December 1986;
- the definitions of "instrument of appointment", "prescribed", "receiver"; and "register of changes" formerly appearing after the definition of "fixed security" repealed by Insolvency Act 1986, s. 438 and Sch. 12 as from 29 December 1986; these definitions formerly read as follows:

  "**"instrument of appointment"** has the meaning given by section 469(1);

  **"prescribed"** means prescribed by regulations made under this Part by the Secretary of State;

  **"receiver"** means a receiver of such part of the property of the company as is subject to the floating charge by virtue of which he has been appointed under section 467;

  **"register of charges"** means the register kept by the registrar of companies for the purposes of Chapter II of Part XII;".

In regard to the date of the above repeals, see IA 1986, s. 443 and SI 1986/1924 (C 71).

## 487 Extent of Part XVIII

**487** This Part extends to Scotland only.

# PART XIX – RECEIVERS AND MANAGERS (ENGLAND AND WALES)

**488-500** (Repealed by Insolvency Act 1986, s. 438 and Sch. 12 as from 29 December 1986.)

**History**

In regard to the date of the above repeal, see Insolvency Act 1986, s. 443 and SI 1986/1924 (C 71). There were some amendments and repeals by Insolvency Act 1985 which very briefly came into force – see Insolvency Act 1985, Sch. 6,10 and SI 1986/1924 (C 71). S. 488–500 originally read as follows:

**"488 Extent of this Part**

**488** This Part does not apply to receivers under Part XVIII.

**489 Disqualification of body corporate from acting as receiver**

**489** A body corporate is not qualified for appointment as receiver of the property of a company, and any body corporate which acts as such a receiver is liable to a fine.

**490 Disqualification of undischarged bankrupt**

**490** If a person being an undischarged bankrupt acts as receiver or manager of the property of a company on behalf of debenture holders, he is liable to imprisonment or a fine, or both.
This does not apply to a receiver or manager acting under an appointment made by the court.

**491 Power for court to appoint official receiver**

**491** Where application is made to the court to appoint a receiver on behalf of the debenture holders or other creditors of a company which is being wound up by the court, the official receiver may be appointed.

**492 Receivers and managers appointed out of court**

**492(1)** A receiver or manager of the property of a company appointed under powers contained in an instrument may apply to the court for directions in relation to any particular matter arising in connection with the performance of his functions.

**(2)** On such an application, the court may give such directions, or may make such order declaring the rights of persons before the court or otherwise, as it thinks just.

**(3)** A receiver or manager so appointed is, to the same extent as if he had been appointed by order of a court–

(a) personally liable on any contract entered into by him in the performance of his functions (except in so far as the contract otherwise provides), and

(b) entitled in respect of that liability to indemnity out of the assets;

but this subsection does not limit any right to indemnity which the receiver or manager would have apart from it, nor limit his liability on contracts entered into without authority, nor confer any right to indemnity in respect of that liability.

**493 Notification that receiver or manager appointed**

**493(1)** When a receiver or manager of the property of a company has been appointed, every invoice, order for goods or business letter issued by or on behalf of the company or the receiver or manager or the liquidator of the company, being a document on or in which the company's name appears, shall contain a statement that a receiver or manager has been appointed.

**(2)** If default is made in complying with this section, the company and any of the following persons, who knowingly and wilfully authorises or permits the default, namely, any officer of the company, any liquidator of the company and any receiver or manager, is liable to a fine.

**494 Court's power to fix remuneration of receiver or manager**

**494(1)** The court may, on an application made by the liquidator of a company, by order fix the amount to be paid by way of remuneration to a person who, under powers contained in an instrument, has been appointed receiver or manager of the company's property.

**(2)** The court's power under subsection (1), where no previous order has been made with respect thereto under the subsection–

(a) extends to fixing the remuneration for any period before the making of the order or the application for it, and

(b) is exercisable notwithstanding that the receiver or manager has died or ceased to act before the making of the order or the application, and

(c) where the receiver or manager has been paid or has retained for his remuneration for any period before the making of the order any amount in excess of that so fixed for that period, extends to requiring him or his personal representative to account for the excess or such part of it as may be specified in the order.

But the power conferred by paragraph (c) shall not be exercised as respects any period before the making of the application for the order under this section, unless in the court's opinion there are special circumstances making it proper for the power to be exercised.

**(3)** The court may from time to time on an application made either by the liquidator or by the receiver or manager, vary or amend an order made under subsection (1).

**495 Information to be given by and to receiver on appointment**

**495(1)** The following applies where, in the case of a company registered in England and Wales, a receiver or manager of the whole (or substantially the whole) of the company's property is appointed on behalf of the holders of any debentures of the company secured by a floating charge.

In this and the following two sections, he is referred to as "the receiver".

**(2)** Subject to the following provisions of this section, and to sections 496 and 497–

(a) the receiver shall forthwith send to the company notice of his appointment in the prescribed form, and

(b) there shall within 14 days after receipt of the notice (or such longer period as may be allowed by the court or by the receiver) be made out and submitted to the receiver in accordance with section 496 a statement in the prescribed form as to the affairs of the company.

**(3)** The receiver shall, within 2 months after receipt of the statement, send–

(a) to the registrar of companies and to the court, a copy of the statement and of any comments he sees fit to make on it and, in the case of the registrar of companies, also a summary of the statement and of his comments (if any) on it; and

(b) to the company, a copy of any such comments as above-mentioned or, if he does not see fit to make any comments, a notice to that effect; and

(c) to any trustees for the debenture holders on whose behalf he was appointed and, so far as he is aware of their addresses, to all such debenture holders a copy of the summary.

**(4)** If the receiver is appointed under powers contained in an instrument, subsections (2) and (3) have effect with the omission of references to the court; and in any other case references to the court are to the court by which the receiver was appointed.

**(5)** This section does not apply in relation to the appointment of a receiver or manager to act–

(a) with an existing receiver or manager, or
(b) in place of a receiver or manager dying or ceasing to act,

except that, where it applies to a receiver or manager who dies or ceases to act before it has been fully complied with, the references in subsection (2)(b) and (3) to the receiver include (subject to the next subsection) his successor and any continuing receiver or manager.

**(6)** If the company is being wound up, this section and section 496 apply notwithstanding that the receiver or manager and the liquidator are the same person, but with any necessary modifications arising from that fact.

**(7)** If the receiver makes default in complying with this section, he is liable to a fine and, for continued contravention, to a daily default fine.

**496 Company's statement of affairs**

**496(1)** The company's statement of affairs required by section 495 to be submitted to the receiver (or his successor) shall show as at the date of the receiver's appointment–

(a) the particulars of the company's assets, debts and liabilities,
(b) the names, residences and occupations of its creditors,
(c) the securities held by them respectively,
(d) the dates when the securities were respectively given, and
(e) such further or other information as may be prescribed.

**(2)** The statement shall be submitted by, and be verified by affidavit of, one or more of the persons who are at the date of the receiver's appointment the directors and by the person who is at that date the secretary of the company, or by such of the persons mentioned in the next subsection as the receiver (or his successor), subject to the direction of the court, may require to submit and verify the statement.

**(3)** The persons referred to above are those–

(a) who are or have been officers of the company,
(b) who have taken part in the company's formation at any time within one year before the date of the receiver's appointment,
(c) who are in the company's employment, or have been in its employment during that year and are in the receiver's opinion capable of giving the information required,
(d) who are or have been during that year officers of or in the employment of a company which is, or within that year was, an officer of the company to which the statement relates.

**(4)** A person making the statement and affidavit shall be allowed, and shall be paid by the receiver (or his successor) out of his receipts, such costs and expenses incurred in and about the preparation and making of the statement and affidavit as the receiver (or his successor) may consider reasonable, subject to an appeal to the court.

**(5)** Where the receiver is appointed under powers contained in an instrument, this section applies with the substitution for references to the court of references to the Secretary of State, and for references to an affidavit of references to a statutory declaration; and in any other case references to the court are to the court by which the receiver was appointed.

**(6)** If a person without reasonable excuse makes default in complying with the requirements of this section, he is liable to a fine and, for continued contravention, to a daily default fine.

**(7)** References in this section to the receiver's successor include a continuing receiver or manager.

**497 Subsequent returns by receiver**

**497(1)** In the case mentioned in section 495(1), the receiver shall–

(a) within 2 months (or such longer period as the court may allow) after the expiration of 12 months from the date of his appointment and of every subsequent period of 12 months, and
(b) within 2 months (or such longer period as the court may allow) after he ceases to act as receiver or manager of the company's property,

send the requisite accounts of his receipts and payments to the registrar of companies, to any trustees for the debenture holders on whose behalf he was appointed, to the company and (so far as he is aware of their addresses) to all such debenture holders.

**(2)** The requisite accounts shall be an abstract in the prescribed form showing–

(a) receipts and payments during the relevant period of 12 months, or
(b) where the receiver ceases to act, receipts and payments during the period from the end of the period of 12 months to which the last preceding abstract related (or, if no preceding abstract has been sent under this section, from the date of his appointment) up to the date of his so ceasing, and the aggregate amount of receipts and payments during all preceding periods since his appointment.

**(3)** Nothing in section 495(5) is to be taken as limiting the meaning of the expression "the receiver" where used in, or in relation to, subsection (1) or (2) above.

**(4)** Where the receiver is appointed under powers contained in an instrument, this section has effect with the substitution of the Secretary of State for the court; and in any other case references to the court are to the court by which the receiver was appointed.

**(5)** This section applies, where the company is being wound up, notwithstanding that the receiver or manager and the liquidator are the same person, but with any necessary modifications arising from that fact.

**(6)** This section does not prejudice the receiver's duty to render proper accounts of his receipts and payments to the persons to whom, and at the times at which, he may be required to do so apart from this section.

**(7)** If the receiver makes default in complying with the requirements of this section, he is liable to a fine and, for continued contravention, to a daily default fine.

**498 Receivership accounts to be delivered to registrar**

**498(1)** Except where section 497 applies, every receiver or manager of a company's property who has been appointed under powers contained in an instrument shall deliver to the registrar of companies for registration the requisite accounts of his receipts and payments.

**(2)** The accounts shall be delivered within one month (or such longer period as the registrar may allow) after the expiration of 6 months from the date of his appointment and of every subsequent period of 6 months, and also within one month after he ceases to act as receiver or manager.

**(3)** The requisite accounts shall be an abstract in the prescribed form showing–

(a) receipts and payments during the relevant period of 6 months, or

(b) where the receiver or manager ceases to act, receipts and payments during the period from the end of the period of 6 months to which the last preceding abstract related (or, if no preceding abstract has been delivered under this section, from the date of his appointment) up to the date of his so ceasing, and the aggregate amount of receipts and payments during all preceding periods since his appointment.

**(4)** A receiver or manager who makes default in complying with this section is liable to a fine and, for continued contravention, to a daily default fine.

**499 Enforcement of duty of receivers to make returns**

**499(1)** If a receiver or manager of a company's property–

(a) having made default in filing, delivering or making any return, account or other document, or in giving any notice, which a receiver or manager is by law required to file, deliver, make or give, fails to make good the default within 14 days after the service on him of a notice requiring him to do so, or

(b) having been appointed under powers contained in an instrument, has, after being required at any time by the liquidator of the company to do so, failed to render proper accounts of his receipts and payments and to vouch them and pay over to the liquidator the amount properly payable to him,

the court may, on an application made for the purpose, make an order directing the receiver or manager (as the case may be) to make good the default within such time as may be specified in the order.

**(2)** In the case of the default mentioned in subsection (1)(a), application to the court may be made by any member or creditor of the company or by the registrar of companies; and in the case of the default mentioned in subsection (1)(b), the application shall be made by the liquidator.

In either case the court's order may provide that all costs of and incidental to the application shall be borne by the receiver or manager, as the case may be.

**(3)** Nothing in this section prejudices the operation of any enactment imposing penalties on receivers in respect of any such default as is mentioned in subsection (1).

**500 Construction of references to receivers and managers**

**500** It is hereby declared that, except where the context otherwise requires–

(a) any reference in this Act to a receiver or manager of the property of a company, or to a receiver of it, includes a reference to a receiver or manager, or (as the case may be) to a receiver of part only of that property and to a receiver only of the income arising from the property or from part of it, and

(b) any reference in this Act to the appointment of a receiver or manager under powers contained in an instrument includes a reference to an appointment made under powers which, by virtue of any enactment, are implied in and have effect as if contained in an instrument."

# PART XX – WINDING UP OF COMPANIES REGISTERED UNDER THIS ACT OR THE FORMER COMPANIES ACTS

**501-650** (Repealed by Insolvency Act 1986, s. 438 and Sch. 12 as from 29 December 1986.)

**History**

In regard to the date of the above repeal, see Insolvency Act 1986, s. 443 and SI 1986/1924 (C 71). There were some amendments and repeals by Insolvency Act 1985 – some of which came into force (see SI 1986/185 (C 7), SI 1986/463 (C 14)) and some of which came into force only briefly – for complete details see Insolvency Act 1985, Sch. 6, 10 and SI 1986/1924 (C 71). Similarly s. 613, 615A, 615B, 623, 643 had been effected by Bankruptcy (Scotland) Act 1985 (see also SI 1985/1924) and s. 638 by Finance Act 1985. Immediately before the Insolvency Act 1986 repeals s. 501–650 read as follows:

"**Chapter I – Preliminary**

MODES OF WINDING UP

**501 The three modes in which a company may be wound up**

**501(1)** The winding up of a company may be either–

(a) by the court, or

(b) voluntary, or

(c) subject to the supervision of the court.

**(2)** This Part applies, unless the contrary appears, to the winding up of a company in any of those modes.

CONTRIBUTORIES

**502 Liability as contributories of present and past members**

**502(1)** When a company is wound up, every present and past member is liable to contribute to its assets to any amount sufficient for payment of its debts and liabilities, and the costs, charges and expenses of the winding up, and for the adjustment of the rights of the contributories among themselves.

**(2)** This is subject as follows–

(a) a past member is not liable to contribute if he has ceased to be a member for one year or more before the commencement of the winding up;

(b) a past member is not liable to contribute in respect of any debt or liability of the company contracted after he ceased to be a member;

(c) a past member is not liable to contribute unless it appears to the court that the existing members are unable to satisfy the contributions required to be made by them in pursuance of this Act;

(d) in the case of a company limited by shares, no contribution is required from any member exceeding the amount (if any) unpaid on the shares in respect of which he is liable as a present or past member;

(e) nothing in this Act invalidates any provision contained in a policy of insurance or other contract whereby the liability of individual members on the policy or contract is restricted, or whereby the funds of the company are alone made liable in respect of the policy or contract;

(f) a sum due to any member of the company (in his character of a member) by way of dividends, profits or otherwise is not deemed to be a debt of the company, payable to that member in a case of competition between himself and any other creditor not a member of the company, but any such sum may be taken into account for the purpose of the final adjustment of the rights of the contributories among themselves.

**(3)** In the case of a company limited by guarantee, no contribution is required from any member exceeding the amount undertaken to be contributed by him to the company's assets in the event of its being wound up; but if it is a company with a share capital, every member of it is liable (in addition to the amount so undertaken to be contributed to the assets), to contribute to the extent of any sums unpaid on shares held by him.

**503 Directors, etc., with unlimited liability**

**503(1)** In the winding up of a limited company, any director or manager (whether past or present) whose liability is under this Act unlimited, is liable, in addition to his liability (if any) to contribute as an ordinary member, to make a further contribution as if he were at the commencement of the winding up a member of an unlimited company.

**(2)** However–

(a) a past director or manager is not liable to make such further contribution if he has ceased to hold office for a year or more before the commencement of the winding up;

(b) a past director or manager is not liable to make such further contribution in respect of any debt or liability of the company contracted after he ceased to hold office;

(c) subject to the company's articles, a director or manager is not liable to make such further contribution unless the court deems it necessary to require that contribution in order to satisfy the company's debts and liabilities and the costs, charges and expenses of the winding up.

**504 Liability of past directors and shareholders**

**504(1)** This section applies where a company is being wound up and–

(a) it has under Chapter VII of Part V made a payment out of capital in respect of the redemption or purchase of any of its own shares (the payment being referred to below as "the relevant payment"), and

(b) the aggregate amount of the company's assets and the amounts paid by way of contribution to its assets (apart from this section) is not sufficient for payment of its debts and liabilities and the costs, charges and expenses of the winding up.

**(2)** If the winding up commenced within one year of the date on which the relevant payment was made, then–

(a) the person from whom the shares were redeemed or purchased, and

(b) the directors who signed the statutory declaration made in accordance with section 173(3) for purposes of the redemption or purchase (except a director who shows that he had reasonable grounds for forming the opinion set out in the declaration),

are, so as to enable that insufficiency to be met, liable to contribute to the following extent to the company's assets.

**(3)** A person from whom any of the shares were redeemed or purchased is liable to contribute an amount not exceeding so much of the relevant payment as was made by the company in respect of his shares; and the directors are jointly and severally liable with that person to contribute that amount.

**(4)** A person who has contributed any amount to the assets in pursuance of this section may apply to the court for an order directing any other person jointly and severally liable in respect of that amount to pay him such amount as the court thinks just and equitable.

**(5)** Sections 502 and 503 above do not apply in relation to liability accruing by virtue of this section.

**(6)** This section is deemed included in Chapter VII of Part V for the purposes of the Secretary of State's power to make regulations under section 179.

**505 Limited company formerly unlimited**

**505(1)** This section applies in the case of a company being wound up which was at some former time registered as unlimited but has re-registered–

(a) as a public company under section 43 of this Act (or the former corresponding provision, section 5 of the Companies Act 1980), or

(b) as a limited company under section 51 of this Act (or the former corresponding provision, section 44 of the Companies Act 1967).

**(2)** Notwithstanding section 502(2)(a) above, a past member of the company who was a member of it at the time of re-registration, if the winding up commences within the period of 3 years beginning with the day on which the company was re-registered, is liable to contribute to the assets of the company in respect of debts and liabilities contracted before that time.

**(3)** If no persons who were members of the company at that time are existing members of it, a person who at that time was a present or past member is liable to contribute as above notwithstanding that the existing members have satisfied the contributions required to be made by them under this Act.

This applies subject to section 502(2)(a) above and to subsection (2) of this section, but notwithstanding section 502(2)(c).

**(4)** Notwithstanding section 502(2)(d) and (3), there is no limit on the amount which a person who, at that time, was a past or present member of the company is liable to contribute as above.

**506 Unlimited company formerly limited**

**506(1)** This section applies in the case of a company being wound up which was at some former time registered as limited but has been re-registered as unlimited under section 49 (or the former corresponding provision, section 43 of the Companies Act 1967).

**(2)** A person who, at the time when the application for the company to be re-registered was lodged, was a past member of the company and did not after that again become a member of it is not liable to contribute to the assets of the company more than he would have been liable to contribute had the company not been re-registered.

**507 Meaning of "contributory"**

**507(1)** In this Act, the expression **"contributory"** means every person liable to contribute to the assets of a company in the event of its being wound up (other than a person so liable by virtue of a declaration under section 630 below or section 15 of the Insolvency Act 1985), and for the purposes of all proceedings for determining, and all proceedings prior to the final determination of, the persons who are to be deemed contributories, includes any person alleged to be a contributory.

**(2)** A reference in a company's articles to a contributory does not (unless the context requires) include a person who is a contributory only by virtue of section 504.
This subsection is deemed included in Chapter VII of Part V for the purposes of the Secretary of State's power to make regulations under section 179.

**508 Nature of contributory's liability**

**508** The liability of a contributory creates a debt (in England and Wales in the nature of a specialty) accruing due from him at the time when his liability commenced, but payable at the times when calls are made for enforcing the liability.

**509 Contributories in case of death of a member**

**509(1)** If a contributory dies either before or after he has been placed on the list of contributories, his personal representatives, and the heirs and legatees of heritage of his heritable estate in Scotland, are liable in a due course of administration to contribute to the assets of the company in discharge of his liability and are contributories accordingly.

**(2)** Where the personal representatives are placed on the list of contributories, the heirs or legatees of heritage need not be added, but they may be added as and when the court thinks fit.

**(3)** If in England and Wales the personal representatives make default in paying any money ordered to be paid by them, proceedings may be taken for administering the estate of the deceased contributory and for compelling payment out of it of the money due.

**510 Effect of contributory's bankruptcy**

**510(1)** The following applies if a contributory becomes bankrupt, either before or after he has been placed on the list of contributories.

**(2)** His trustee in bankruptcy represents him for all purposes of the winding up, and is a contributory accordingly.

**(3)** The trustee may be called on to admit to proof against the bankrupt's estate, or otherwise allow to be paid out of the bankrupt's assets in due course of law, any money due from the bankrupt in respect of his liability to contribute to the company's assets.

**(4)** There may be proved against the bankrupt's estate the estimated value of his liability to future calls as well as calls already made.

**511 Companies registered under Part XXII, Chapter II**

**511(1)** The following applies in the event of a company being wound up which has been registered under section 680 (or the previous corresponding provision).

**(2)** Every person is a contributory, in respect of the company's debts and liabilities contracted before registration, who is liable–

(a) to pay or contribute to the payment of any debt or liability so contracted, or
(b) to pay or contribute to the payment of any sum for the adjustment of the rights of the members among themselves in respect of any such debt or liability, or
(c) to pay or contribute to the payment of the costs and expenses of winding up the company, so far as relates to the debts or liabilities above-mentioned.

**(3)** Every contributory is liable to contribute to the assets of the company, in the course of the winding up, all sums due from him in respect of any such liability.

**(4)** In the event of the death, bankruptcy or insolvency of any contributory, provisions of this Act with respect to the personal representatives, to the heirs and legatees of heritage of the heritable estate in Scotland of deceased contributories and to the trustees of bankrupt or insolvent contributories respectively, apply.

## Chapter II – Winding up by the Court

### JURISDICTION (ENGLAND AND WALES)

**512 High Court and county court jurisdiction**

**512(1)** The High Court has jurisdiction to wind up any company registered in England and Wales.

**(2)** Where the amount of a company's share capital paid up or credited as paid up does not exceed £120,000, then (subject to the provisions of this section) the county court of the district in which the company's registered office is situated has concurrent jurisdiction with the High Court to wind up the company.

**(3)** The money sum for the time being specified in subsection (2) is subject to increase or reduction by regulations under section 664; but no reduction of it affects any case in which proceedings were begun before the coming into force of the reduction.

**(4)** The Lord Chancellor may by order in a statutory instrument exclude a county court from having winding-up jurisdiction, and for the purposes of that jurisdiction may attach its district, or any part thereof, to any other county court, and may by statutory instrument revoke or vary any such order.
In exercising the powers of this section, the Lord Chancellor shall provide that a county court is not to have winding-up jurisdiction unless it has for the time being jurisdiction in bankruptcy.

**(5)** Every court in England and Wales having winding-up jurisdiction has for the purposes of that jurisdiction all the powers of the High Court; and every prescribed officer of the court shall perform any duties which an officer of the High Court may discharge by order of a judge of that court or otherwise in relation to winding-up.

**(6)** For purposes of this section, a company's **"registered office"** is the place which has longest been its registered office during the 6 months immediately preceding the presentation of the petition for winding up.

**513 Proceedings taken in wrong court**

**513(1)** Nothing in section 512 invalidates a proceeding by reason of its being taken in the wrong court.

**(2)** The winding up of a company by the court in England and Wales, or any proceedings in the winding up, may be retained in the court in which the proceedings were commenced, although it may not be the court in which they ought to have been commenced.

**514 Proceedings in county court: case stated for High Court**

**514** If any question arises in any winding up proceedings in a county court which all the parties to the proceeding, or which one of them and the judge of the court, desire to have determined in the first instance in the High Court, the judge shall state the facts in the form of a special case for the opinion of the High Court; and thereupon the special case and the proceedings (or such of them as may be required) shall be transmitted to the High Court for the purposes of the determination.

JURISDICTION (SCOTLAND)

**515 Court of Session and sheriff's court jurisdiction**

**515(1)** The Court of Session has jurisdiction to wind up any company registered in Scotland.

**(2)** When the Court of Session is in vacation, the jurisdiction conferred on that court by this section may (subject to the provisions of this Part) be exercised by the judge acting as vacation judge in pursuance of section 4 of the Administration of Justice (Scotland) Act 1933.

**(3)** Where the amount of a company's share capital paid up or credited as paid up does not exceed £120,000, the sheriff court of the sheriffdom in which the company's registered office is situated has concurrent jurisdiction with the Court of Session to wind up the company; but–

(a) the Court of Session may, if it thinks expedient having regard to the amount of the company's assets to do so–
  (i) remit to a sheriff court any petition presented to the Court of Session for winding up such a company, or
  (ii) require such a petition presented to a sheriff court to be remitted to the Court of Session; and

(b) the Court of Session may require any such petition as above-mentioned presented to one sheriff court to be remitted to another sheriff court; and

(c) in a winding up in the sheriff court it is lawful for the sheriff to submit a stated case for the opinion of the Court of Session on any question of law arising in that winding up.

**(4)** For the purposes of this section, the expression **"registered office"** means the place which has longest been the company's registered office during the 6 months immediately preceding the presentation of the petition for winding up.

**(5)** The money sum for the time being specified in subsection (3) is subject to increase or reduction by regulations under section 664; but no reduction of it affects any case in which proceedings were begun before the coming into force of the reduction.

**516 Power to remit winding up to Lord Ordinary**

**516(1)** The Court of Session may, by Act of Sederunt, make provision for the taking of proceedings in a winding up before one of the Lords Ordinary; and, where provision is so made, the Lord Ordinary has, for the purposes of the winding up, all the powers and jurisdiction of the court.

**(2)** However, the Lord Ordinary may report to the Inner House any matter which may arise in the course of a winding up.

GROUNDS AND EFFECT OF WINDING-UP PETITION

**517 Circumstances in which company may be wound up by the court**

**517(1)** A company may be wound up by the court if–

(a) the company has by special resolution resolved that the company be wound up by the court,

(b) being a public company which was registered as such on its original incorporation, the company has not been issued with a certificate under section 117 (public company share capital requirements) and more than a year has expired since it was so registered,

(c) it is an old public company, within the meaning of section 1 of the Consequential Provisions Act,

(d) the company does not commence its business within a year from its incorporation or suspends its business for a whole year,

(e) the number of members is reduced below 2,

(f) the company is unable to pay its debts,

(g) the court is of the opinion that it is just and equitable that the company should be wound up.

**(2)** In Scotland, a company which the Court of Session has jurisdiction to wind up may be wound up by the Court if there is subsisting a floating charge over property comprised in the company's property and undertaking, and the court is satisfied that the security of the creditor entitled to the benefit of the floating charge is in jeopardy.

For this purpose a creditor's security is deemed to be in jeopardy if the Court is satisfied that events have occurred or are about to occur which render it unreasonable in the creditor's interests that the company should retain power to dispose of the property which is subject to the floating charge.

**518 Definition of inability to pay debts**

**518(1)** A company is deemed unable to pay its debts–

(a) if a creditor (by assignment or otherwise) to whom the company is indebted in a sum exceeding £750 then due has served on the company, by leaving it at the company's registered office, a written demand requiring the company to pay the sum so due and the company has for 3 weeks thereafter neglected to pay the sum or to secure or compound for it to the reasonable satisfaction of the creditor, or

(b) if, in England and Wales, execution or other process issued on a judgment, decree or order of any court in favour of a creditor of the company is returned unsatisfied in whole or in part, or

(c) if, in Scotland, the induciae of a charge for payment on an extract decree, or an extract registered bond, or an extract registered protest, have expired without payment being made, or

(d) if, in Northern Ireland, a certificate of unenforceability has been granted in respect of a judgment against the company, or

(e) if it is proved to the satisfaction of the court that the company is unable to pay its debts (and, in determining that question, the court shall take into account the company's contingent and prospective liabilities).

**(2)** The money sum for the time being specified in subsection (1)(a) is subject to increase or reduction by regulations under section 664; but no increase of it affects any case in which the winding-up petition was presented before the coming into force of the increase.

**519 Application for winding up**

**519(1)** Subject to the provisions of this section, an application to the court for the winding up of a company shall be by petition presented either by the company or by any creditor or creditors (including any contingent or prospective creditor or creditors), contributory or contributories, or by all or any of those parties, together or separately.

**(2)** Except as mentioned below, a contributory is not entitled to present a winding-up petition unless either–

(a) the number of members is reduced below 2, or

(b) the shares in respect of which he is a contributory, or some of them, either were originally allotted to him, or have been held by him, and registered in his name, for at least 6 months during the 18 months before the commencement of the winding up, or have devolved on him through the death of a former holder.

**(3)** A person who is liable under section 504 to contribute to a company's assets in the event of its being wound up may petition on either of the grounds set out in section 517(1)(f) and (g), and subsection (2) above does not then apply; but unless the person is a contributory otherwise than under section 504 he may not in his character as contributory petition on any other ground.

This subsection is deemed included in Chapter VII of Part V for the purposes of the Secretary of State's power to make regulations under section 179.

**(4)** If the ground of the petition is that in section 517(1)(b) or (c), a winding-up petition may be presented by the Secretary of State.

**(5)** The court shall not hear a petition presented by a contingent or prospective creditor until such security for costs has been given as the court thinks reasonable (or until caution is found, if so ordered by a Scottish court) and until a prima facie case for winding up has been established to the satisfaction of the court.

**(6)** In a case falling within section 440 (expedient in the public interest, following report of inspectors, etc.) a winding-up petition may be presented by the Secretary of State.

**(7)** Where a company is being wound up voluntarily or subject to supervision in England and Wales, a winding-up petition may be presented by the official receiver attached to the court as well as by any other person authorised in that behalf under the other provisions of this section; but the court shall not make a winding-up order on the petition unless it is satisfied that the voluntary winding up or winding up subject to supervision cannot be continued with due regard to the interests of the creditors or contributories.

**520 Powers of court on hearing of petition**

**520(1)** On hearing a winding-up petition the court may dismiss it, or adjourn the hearing conditionally or unconditionally, or make an interim order, or any other order that it thinks fit; but the court shall not refuse to make a winding-up order on the ground only that the company's assets have been mortgaged to an amount equal to or in excess of those assets or that the company has no assets.

**(2)** If the petition is presented by members of the company as contributories on the ground that it is just and equitable that the company should be wound up, the court, if it is of opinion–

(a) that the petitioners are entitled to relief either by winding up the company or by some other means, and

(b) that in the absence of any other remedy it would be just and equitable that the company should be wound up,

shall make a winding-up order; but this does not apply if the court is also of the opinion both that some other remedy is available to the petitioners and that they are acting unreasonably in seeking to have the company wound up instead of pursuing that other remedy.

**521 Power to stay or restrain proceedings against company**

**521(1)** At any time after the presentation of a winding-up petition and before a winding-up order has been made, the company, or any creditor or contributory, may–

(a) where any action or proceeding against the company is pending in the High Court or Court of Appeal in England and Wales or Northern Ireland, apply to the court in which the action or proceeding is pending for a stay of proceedings therein, and

(b) where any other action or proceeding is pending against the company, apply to the court having jurisdiction to wind up the company to restrain further proceedings in the action or proceeding,

and the court to which application is so made may (as the case may be) stay, sist or restrain the proceedings accordingly on such terms as it thinks fit.

**(2)** In the case of a company registered under section 680, where the application to stay, sist or restrain is by a creditor, this section extends to actions and proceedings against any contributory of the company.

**522 Avoidance of property dispositions, etc.**

**522** In a winding up by the court, any disposition of the company's property, and any transfer of shares, or alteration in the status of the company's members, made after the commencement of the winding up is, unless the court otherwise orders, void.

**523 Avoidance of attachments, etc.**

**523(1)** Where a company registered in England and Wales is being wound up by the court, any attachment, sequestration, distress or execution put in force against the estate or effects of the company after the commencement of the winding up is void.

**(2)** This section, so far as relates to any estate or effects of the company situated in England and Wales, applies in the case of a company registered in Scotland as it applies in the case of a company registered in England and Wales.

COMMENCEMENT OF WINDING UP

**524 Commencement of winding up**

**524(1)** If, before the presentation of a petition for the winding up of a company by the court, a resolution has been passed by the company for voluntary winding up, the winding up of the company is deemed to have commenced at the time of the passing of the resolution; and unless the court, on proof of fraud or mistake, directs otherwise, all proceedings taken in the voluntary winding up are deemed to have been validly taken.

**(2)** In any other case, the winding up of a company by the court is deemed to commence at the time of the presentation of the petition for winding up.

**525 Consequences of winding-up order**

**525(1)** On the making of a winding-up order, a copy of the order must forthwith be forwarded by the company (or otherwise as may be prescribed) to the registrar of companies, who shall enter it in his records relating to the company.

**(2)** When a winding-up order has been made or a provisional liquidator has been appointed, no action or proceeding shall be proceeded with or commenced against the company except by leave of the court and subject to such terms as the court may impose.

**(3)** When an order has been made for winding up a company registered under section 680, no action or proceeding shall be commenced or proceeded with against the company or any contributory of the company, in respect of any debt of the company, except by leave of the court, and subject to such terms as the court may impose.

**(4)** An order for winding up a company operates in favour of all the creditors and of all contributories of the company as if made on the joint petition of a creditor and of a contributory.

THE OFFICIAL RECEIVER (ENGLAND AND WALES ONLY)

**526 The official receiver**

**526(1)** For the purposes of this Act as it relates to the winding up of companies by the court in England and Wales, the term **"official receiver"** means the official receiver (if any) attached to the court for bankruptcy purposes or, if there is more than one such official receiver, then such one of them as the Secretary of State may appoint or, if there is no such official receiver, then an officer appointed for the purpose by the Secretary of State.

**(2)** Any such officer shall, for the purpose of his duties under this Act, be styled "the official receiver".

**527 Appointment of official receiver by court in certain cases**

**527(1)** If in the case of the winding up of a company by the court in England and Wales it appears to the court desirable, with a view to securing the more convenient and economical conduct of the winding up, that some officer other than the person who would under section 526 be the official receiver should be the official receiver for the purposes of that winding up, the court may appoint that other officer to act.

**(2)** The officer so appointed is then deemed, for all purposes of this Act, to be the official receiver in that winding up.

**528 Statement of company's affairs**

**528(1)** Where the court in England and Wales has made a winding-up order or appointed a provisional liquidator, there shall (unless the court otherwise orders) be made out and submitted to the official receiver a statement as to the affairs of the company in the prescribed form.

**(2)** The statement shall be verified by affidavit and show particulars of the company's assets, its debts and liabilities, the names, residences and occupations of its creditors, the securities held by them respectively, the dates when the securities were respectively given, and such further or other information as may be prescribed or as the official receiver may require.

**(3)** The statement shall be submitted and verified by one or more of the persons who are at the relevant date the directors and by the person who at that date is the secretary of the company, or by such of the persons mentioned in the following subsection as the official receiver (subject to the direction of the court) may require to submit and verify the statement.

**(4)** The persons referred to above are–

(a) those who are or have been officers of the company,

(b) those who have taken part in the formation of the company at any time within one year before the relevant date,

(c) those who are in the employment of the company, or have been in its employment within the year just mentioned, and are in the opinion of the official receiver capable of giving the information required, and

(d) those who are or have been within that year officers of or in the employment of a company which is, or within that year was, an officer of the company to which the statement relates.

**(5)** For purposes of this section, **"the relevant date"** is–

(a) in a case where a provisional liquidator is appointed, the date of his appointment, and

(b) in a case where no such appointment is made, the date of the winding-up order.

**(6)** The statement of affairs required by this section shall be submitted within 14 days from the relevant date, or within such extended time as the official receiver or the court may for special reasons appoint.

**(7)** If a person, without reasonable excuse, makes default in complying with the requirements of this section, he is liable to a fine and, for continued contravention, to a daily default fine.

**529 Further provisions as to statement etc. under s. 528**

**529(1)** A person making or concurring in the making of the statement and affidavit required by section 528 shall be allowed, and shall be paid by the official receiver or provisional liquidator (as the case may be) out of the company's assets such costs and expenses incurred in and about the preparation and making of the statement and affidavit as the official receiver may consider reasonable, subject to an appeal to the court.

**(2)** A person stating himself in writing to be a creditor or contributory of the company is entitled by himself or by his agent at all reasonable times, on payment of the prescribed fee, to inspect the statement submitted under section 528, and to a copy of or extract from it.

**(3)** A person untruthfully so stating himself to be a creditor or contributory is guilty of a contempt of court and, on the application of the official receiver or the liquidator, punishable accordingly.

**(4)** The statement required by section 528 may be used in evidence against any person making or concurring in making it.

**530 Report by official receiver**

**530(1)** When a winding-up order is made, the official receiver shall, as soon as practicable after the receipt of the statement to be submitted under section 528 (or, in a case where the court orders that no statement shall be submitted, as soon as practicable after the date of the order) submit a preliminary report to the court–

(a) as to the amount of capital issued, subscribed and paid up, and the estimated amount of assets and liabilities, and

(b) if the company has failed, as to the causes of the failure, and

(c) whether in his opinion further enquiry is desirable as to any matter relating to the promotion, formation or failure of the company or the conduct of its business.

**(2)** The official receiver may also, if he thinks fit, make further reports (one or more) stating the manner in which the company was formed and whether in his opinion any fraud has been committed by any person in its promotion or formation, or by any officer of the company in relation to it since its formation, and any other matter which in his opinion it is desirable to bring to the notice of the court.

**(3)** If the official receiver states in any such further report that in his opinion a fraud has been committed as above-mentioned, the court has the further powers provided in sections 563 and 564 (public examination of promoters and officers).

LIQUIDATORS

**531 Power of court to appoint liquidators**

**531** For the purpose of conducting the proceedings in winding up a company and performing such duties in reference thereto as the court may impose, the court may appoint a liquidator or liquidators.

**532 Appointment and powers of provisional liquidator**

**532(1)** Subject to the provisions of this section, the court may, at any time after the presentation of a winding-up petition, appoint a liquidator provisionally.

**(2)** In England and Wales, the appointment of a provisional liquidator may be made at any time before the making of a winding-up order, and either the official receiver or any other fit person may be appointed.

**(3)** In Scotland, such an appointment may be made at any time before the first appointment of liquidators.

**(4)** When a liquidator is provisionally appointed by the court, his powers may be limited by the order appointing him.

**533 Appointment, style, etc., of liquidators in England and Wales**

**533(1)** The following provisions with respect to liquidators have effect on a winding-up order being made in England and Wales.

**(2)** The official receiver by virtue of his office becomes the provisional liquidator and shall continue to act as such until he or another person becomes liquidator and is capable of acting as such.

**(3)** The official receiver shall summon separate meetings of the company's creditors and contributories for the purpose of determining whether or not an application is to be made to the court for appointing a liquidator in the place of the official receiver.

**(4)** The court may make any appointment and order required to give effect to that determination; and, if there is a difference between the determinations of the meetings of the creditors and contributories in respect of the matter in question, the court shall decide the difference and make such order thereon as it may think fit.

**(5)** If a liquidator is not appointed by the court, the official receiver shall be the liquidator of the company.

**(6)** The official receiver is, ex officio, the liquidator during any vacancy.

**(7)** A liquidator shall be described, where a person other than the official receiver is liquidator, by the style of "the liquidator" and, where the official receiver is liquidator, by the style of "the official receiver and liquidator", of the particular company in respect of which he is appointed (and not by his individual name).

**534 Liquidator other than official receiver**

**534** If in the winding up of a company by the court in England and Wales a person other than the official receiver is appointed liquidator, that person–

(a) cannot act as liquidator until he has notified his appointment to the registrar of companies and given security in the prescribed manner to the satisfaction of the Secretary of State,

(b) shall give the official receiver such information, and such access to and facilities for inspecting the company's books and documents, and generally such aid as may be requisite for enabling that officer to perform his duties under this Act.

**535 Liquidators in Scotland**

**535(1)** The following provisions with respect to liquidators have effect in a winding up by the court in Scotland.

**(2)** The court may determine whether any and what caution is to be found by a liquidator on his appointment.

**(3)** A liquidator shall be described by the style of "the official liquidator" of the particular company in respect of which he is appointed (and not by his individual name).

**(4)** Where an order has been made for winding up a company subject to supervision and an order is afterwards made for winding up by the court, the court may by the last-mentioned or by a subsequent order appoint any person who is then liquidator, either provisionally or permanently, and either with or without any other person, to be liquidator in the winding up by the court.

**536 General provisions as to liquidators**

**536(1)** A liquidator appointed by the court may resign or, on cause shown, be removed by the court.

**(2)** Where a person other than the official receiver is appointed liquidator, he shall receive such salary or remuneration by way of percentage or otherwise as the court may direct; and, if more such persons than one are appointed liquidators, their remuneration shall be distributed among them in such proportions as the court directs.

**(3)** A vacancy in the office of a liquidator appointed by the court shall be filled by the court.

**(4)** If more than one liquidator is appointed by the court, the court shall declare whether any act required or authorised by this Act to be done by the liquidator is to be done by all or any one or more of the persons appointed.

**(5)** Subject to section 634 (disqualification of bodies corporate for appointment as liquidator), the acts of a liquidator are valid notwithstanding any defects that may afterwards be discovered in his appointment or qualification.

**537 Custody of company's property**

**537(1)** When a winding-up order has been made, or where a provisional liquidator has been appointed, the liquidator or the provisional liquidator (as the case may be) shall take into his custody or under his control all the property and things in action to which the company is or appears to be entitled.

**(2)** In a winding up by the court in Scotland, if and so long as there is no liquidator, all the property of the company is deemed to be in the custody of the court.

**538 Vesting of company property in liquidator**

**538(1)** When a company is being wound up by the court, the court may on the application of the liquidator by order direct that all or any part of the property of whatsoever description belonging to the company or held by trustees on its behalf shall vest in the liquidator by his official name; and thereupon the property to which the order relates vests accordingly.

**(2)** The liquidator may, after giving such indemnity (if any) as the court may direct, bring or defend in his official name any action or other legal proceeding which relates to that property or which it is necessary to bring or defend for the purpose of effectually winding up the company and recovering its property.

**539 Powers of liquidator**

**539(1)** The liquidator in a winding up by the court has power, with the sanction either of the court or of the committee of inspection–

(a) to bring or defend any action or other legal proceeding in the name and on behalf of the company,

(b) to carry on the business of the company so far as may be necessary for its beneficial winding up,

(c) to appoint a solicitor to assist him in the performance of his duties,

(d) to pay any class of creditors in full,

(e) to make any compromise or arrangement with creditors or persons claiming to be creditors, or having or alleging themselves to have any claim (present or future, certain or contingent, ascertained or sounding only in damages) against the company, or whereby the company may be rendered liable,

(f) to compromise all calls and liabilities to calls, debts and liabilities capable of resulting in debts, and all claims (present or future, certain or contingent, ascertained or sounding only in damages) subsisting or supposed to subsist between the company and a contributory or alleged contributory or other debtor or person apprehending liability to the company, and all questions in any way relating to or affecting the assets or the winding up of the company, on such terms as may be agreed, and take any security for the discharge of any such call, debt, liability or claim and give a complete discharge in respect of it.

**(2)** The liquidator in a winding up by the court has the power–

(a) to sell any of the company's property by public auction or private contract, with power to transfer the whole thereof to any person or to sell the same in parcels,

(b) to do all acts and to execute, in the name and on behalf of the company, all deeds, receipts and other documents and for that purpose to use, when necessary, the company's seal,

(c) to prove, rank and claim in the bankruptcy, insolvency or sequestration of any contributory for any balance against his estate, and to receive dividends in the bankruptcy, insolvency or sequestration in respect of that balance, as a separate debt due from the bankrupt or insolvent, and rateably with the other separate creditors,

(d) to draw, accept, make and indorse any bill of exchange or promissory note in the name and on behalf of the company, with the same effect with respect to the company's liability as if the bill or note had been drawn, accepted, made or indorsed by or on behalf of the company in the course of its business,

(e) to raise on the security of the assets of the company any money requisite,

(f) to take out in his official name letters of administration to any deceased contributory, and to do in his official name any other act necessary for obtaining payment of any money due from a contributory or his estate which cannot conveniently be done in the name of the company (and in all such cases the money due is deemed, for the purpose of enabling the liquidator to take out the letters of administration or recover the money, to be due to the liquidator himself),

(g) to appoint an agent to do any business which the liquidator is unable to do himself,

(h) to do all such other things as may be necessary for winding up the company's affairs and distributing its assets.

**(3)** The exercise by the liquidator in a winding up by the court of the powers conferred by this section is subject to the control of the court, and any creditor or contributory may apply to the court with respect to any exercise or proposed exercise of any of those powers.

**(4)** In the case of a winding up in Scotland, the court may provide by order that the liquidator may, where there is no committee of inspection, exercise any of the powers mentioned in subsection (1)(a) or (b) without the sanction or intervention of the court.

**(5)** In a winding up by the court in Scotland, the liquidator has (subject to general rules), the same powers as a trustee on a bankrupt estate.

## PROVISIONS ABOUT LIQUIDATORS APPLYING IN ENGLAND AND WALES ONLY

### 540 Exercise and control of liquidator's powers

**540(1)** Subject to the provisions of this Act, the liquidator of a company which is being wound up by the court in England and Wales shall, in the administration of the company's assets and their distribution among its creditors, have regard to any directions that may be given by resolution of the creditors or contributories at any general meeting or by the committee of inspection.

**(2)** Directions given by the creditors or contributories at any general meeting are, in case of conflict, deemed to override any directions given by the committee of inspection.

**(3)** The liquidator may summon general meetings of the creditors or contributories for the purpose of ascertaining their wishes; and it is his duty to summon meetings at such times as the creditors or contributories by resolution (either at the meeting appointing the liquidator or otherwise) may direct, or whenever requested in writing to do so by one tenth in value of the creditors or contributories (as the case may be).

**(4)** The liquidator may apply to the court (in the prescribed manner) for directions in relation to any particular matter arising in the winding up.

**(5)** Subject to the provisions of this Act, the liquidator shall use his own discretion in the management of the estate and its distribution among the creditors.

**(6)** If any person is aggrieved by any act or decision of the liquidator, that person may apply to the court; and the court may confirm, reverse or modify the act or decision complained of, and make such order in the case as it thinks just.

### 541 Books to be kept by liquidator

**541(1)** Every liquidator of a company which is being wound up by the court in England and Wales shall keep, in the prescribed manner, proper books in which he shall cause to be made entries or minutes of proceedings at meetings, and of such other matters as may be prescribed.

**(2)** Any creditor or contributory may, subject to the control of the court, personally or by his agent inspect any such books.

### 542 Payments by liquidator into bank

**542(1)** The following applies to a liquidator of a company which is being wound up by the court in England and Wales.

**(2)** Subject to the next subsection, the liquidator shall, in such manner and at such times as the Secretary of State (with the concurrence of the Treasury) directs, pay the money received by him to the Insolvency Services Account at the Bank of England; and the Secretary of State shall furnish him with a certificate of receipt of the money so paid.

**(3)** However, if the committee of inspection satisfies the Secretary of State that for the purpose of carrying on the company's business or of obtaining advances, or for any other reason, it is for the advantage of the creditors or contributories that the liquidator should have an account at any other bank, the Secretary of State shall, on the application of the committee of inspection, authorise the liquidator to make his payments into and out of such other bank as the committee may select, and thereupon those payments shall be made in the prescribed manner.

**(4)** If the liquidator at any time retains for more than 10 days a sum exceeding £100 or such other amount as the Secretary of State in any particular case authorises him to retain, then unless he explains the retention to the Secretary of State's satisfaction, he shall pay interest on the amount so retained in excess at the rate of 20 per cent per annum, and is liable to disallowance of all or such part of his remuneration as the Secretary of State thinks just, and to be removed from his office by the Secretary of State, and is liable to pay any expenses occasioned by reason of his default.

**(5)** The liquidator shall not pay any sums received by him as liquidator into his private banking account.

**(6)** The money sum for the time being specified in subsection (4) is subject to increase or reduction by regulations under section 664.

**543 Submission of liquidator's accounts for audit**

**543(1)** The following applies in the case of a company which is being wound up by the court in England and Wales.

**(2)** The liquidator shall, at such times as may be prescribed but not less than twice in each year during his tenure of office, send to the Secretary of State (or as he directs) an account of his receipts and payments as liquidator.

**(3)** The account shall be in the prescribed form, shall be made in duplicate, and shall be verified by a statutory declaration in the prescribed form; and the Secretary of State may cause the account to be audited.

**(4)** The liquidator shall furnish the Secretary of State with such vouchers and information as he requires, and the Secretary of State may at any time require the production of, and inspect, any books or accounts kept by the liquidator.
This applies whether or not the Secretary of State decides to cause the account to be audited, and extends to production and inspection at the liquidator's premises.

**(5)** After the account has been audited (or, as the case may be, forthwith if the Secretary of State decides not to have an audit) one copy of the account shall be filed by the Secretary of State, to be retained by him, and the other copy shall be delivered to the court for filing, each copy when filed to be open to inspection by any person on payment of the prescribed fee.

**(6)** The liquidator shall, when the account has been audited (alternatively, when he has been notified of the Secretary of State's decision not to have an audit), cause the account, or a summary of it, to be printed, and shall send a printed copy by post to every creditor or contributory.
The Secretary of State may in any case dispense with compliance with this subsection.

**544 Control of liquidators by Secretary of State**

**544(1)** The Secretary of State shall take cognizance of the conduct of liquidators of companies which are being wound up by the court in England and Wales; and–

(a) if a liquidator does not faithfully perform his duties and duly observe all the requirements imposed on him by statute, rules or otherwise with respect to the performance of his duties, or

(b) if any complaint is made to the Secretary of State by any creditor or contributory in regard thereto,

the Secretary of State shall inquire into the matter, and take such action on it as he thinks expedient.

**(2)** The Secretary of State may at any time require the liquidator to answer any inquiry in relation to a winding up in which he is engaged and may, if the Secretary of State thinks fit, apply to the court to examine him or any other person on oath concerning the winding up.

**(3)** The Secretary of State may also direct a local investigation to be made of the liquidator's books and vouchers.

**545 Release of liquidators**

**545(1)** The following applies to the liquidator of a company which is being wound up by the court in England and Wales.

**(2)** When the liquidator has realised all the company's property, or so much of it as can (in his opinion) be realised without needlessly protracting the liquidation, and has distributed a final dividend (if any) to the creditors, and adjusted the rights of the contributories among themselves, and made a final return (if any) to the contributories, or has resigned, or has been removed from his office, the following subsection has effect.

**(3)** The Secretary of State shall, on the liquidator's application, cause a report on the latter's accounts to be prepared and, on his complying with all the Secretary of State's requirements, shall take into consideration the report and any objection which may be urged by any creditor or contributory or person interested against the release of the liquidator, and shall either grant or withhold the release accordingly, subject nevertheless to an appeal to the High Court.

**(4)** If the release of the liquidator is withheld, the court may, on the application of any creditor or contributory or person interested, make such order as it thinks just, charging the liquidator with the consequences of any act or default which he may have done or made contrary to his duty.

**(5)** An order of the Secretary of State releasing the liquidator discharges him from all liability in respect of any act done or default made by him in the administration of the company's affairs or otherwise in relation to his conduct as liquidator; but any such order may be revoked on proof that it was obtained by fraud or by suppression or concealment of any material fact.

**(6)** If the liquidator has not previously resigned or been removed, his release operates as removal of him from his office.

## COMMITTEES OF INSPECTION

**546 Decision whether committee of inspection to be appointed**

**546(1)** When a winding-up order has been made by the court in England and Wales, and separate meetings of creditors and contributories have been summoned for the purpose of determining whether an application should be made to the court for the appointment of a liquidator in place of the official receiver, it is the business of those meetings to determine further whether or not an application is to be made to the court for the appointment of a committee of inspection to act with the liquidator, and who are to be members of the committee if appointed.

**(2)** In Scotland, when a winding-up order has been made by the court, the liquidator shall summon separate meetings of the company's creditors and contributories for the purpose of determining whether or not an application is to be made to the court for the appointment of a committee of inspection and who are to be the members of the committee if appointed. However, if the winding-up order has been made on the ground that the company is unable to pay its debts, it is not necessary for the liquidator to summon a meeting of the contributories.

**(3)** The court may make the appointment and order required to give effect to such determination; and if there is a difference between the determinations of the meetings of the creditors and contributories in respect of the matters referred to above, the court shall decide the difference and make such order on those matters as the court may think fit.

**547 Constitution and proceedings of committee of inspection**

**547(1)** Subject as follows, the committee of inspection (if appointed) shall consist of creditors and contributories of the company or persons holding general powers of attorney from creditors and contributories in such proportions as may be agreed on by the meetings of creditors and contributories or as, in case of difference, may be determined by the court.

(2) In Scotland–

(a) if a winding-up order has been made on the ground that the company is unable to pay its debts, the committee shall consist of creditors or persons holding general powers of attorney from creditors, and

(b) the committee has, in addition to the powers and duties conferred and imposed on it by this Act, such of the powers and duties of commissioners on a bankrupt estate as may be conferred and imposed on committees of inspection by general rules.

(3) Schedule 17 has effect with respect to the committee of inspection and its proceedings.

**548 Power of Secretary of State to in place of committee**

**548** If in the case of a winding up in England and Wales there is no committee of inspection, the Secretary of State may, on the application of the liquidator, do any act or thing or give any direction or permission which is by this Act authorised or required to be done or given by the committee.

GENERAL POWERS OF COURT IN CASE OF WINDING UP BY THE COURT

**549 Power to stay or sist winding up**

**549(1)** The court may at any time after an order for winding up, on the application either of the liquidator or the official receiver or any creditor or contributory, and on proof to the satisfaction of the court that all proceedings in the winding up ought to be stayed or sisted, make an order staying or sisting the proceedings, either altogether or for a limited time, on such terms and conditions as the court thinks fit.

**(2)** The court may, before making an order, require the official receiver to furnish to the court a report with respect to any facts or matters which are in his opinion relevant to the application.

**(3)** A copy of every order made under this section shall forthwith be forwarded by the company, or otherwise as may be prescribed, to the registrar of companies, who shall enter it in his records relating to the company.

**550 Settlement of list of contributories and application of assets**

**550(1)** As soon as may be after making a winding-up order, the court shall settle a list of contributories, with power to rectify the register of members in all cases where rectification is required in pursuance of this Act, and shall cause the company's assets to be collected, and applied in discharge of its liabilities.

**(2)** If it appears to the court that it will not be necessary to make calls on or adjust the rights of contributories, the court may dispense with the settlement of a list of contributories.

**(3)** In settling the list, the court shall distinguish between persons who are contributories in their own right and persons who are contributories as being representatives of or liable for the debts of others.

**551 Delivery of property to liquidator**

**551** The court may, at any time after making a winding-up order, require any contributory for the time being on the list of contributories and any trustee, receiver, banker, agent or officer of the company to pay, deliver, convey, surrender or transfer forthwith (or within such time as the court directs) to the liquidator any money, property or books and papers in his hands to which the company is prima facie entitled.

**552 Debts due from contributory to company**

**552(1)** The court may, at any time after making a winding-up order, make an order on any contributory for the time being on the list of contributories to pay, in manner directed by the order, any money due from him (or from the estate of the person whom he represents) to the company, exclusive of any money payable by him or the estate by virtue of any call in pursuance of this Act.

**(2)** The court in making such an order may–

(a) in the case of an unlimited company, allow to the contributory by way of set-off any money due to him or the estate which he represents from the company on any independent dealing or contract with the company, but not any money due to him as a member of the company in respect of any dividend or profit, and

(b) in the case of a limited company, make to any director or manager whose liability is unlimited or to his estate the like allowance.

**(3)** In the case of any company, whether limited or unlimited, when all the creditors are paid in full, any money due on any account whatever to a contributory from the company may be allowed to him by way of set-off against any subsequent call.

**553 Power to make calls**

**553(1)** The court may, at any time after making a winding-up order, and either before or after it has ascertained the sufficiency of the company's assets, make calls on all or any of the contributories for the time being settled on the list of the contributories to the extent of their liability, for payment of any money which the court considers necessary to satisfy the company's debts and liabilities, and the costs, charges and expenses of winding up, and for the adjustment of the rights of the contributories among themselves, and make an order for payment of any calls so made.

**(2)** In making a call the court may take into consideration the probability that some of the contributories may partly or wholly fail to pay it.

**554 Payment into bank of money due to company**

**554(1)** The court may order any contributory, purchaser or other person from whom money is due to the company to pay the amount due into the Bank of England (or any branch of it) to the account of the liquidator instead of to the liquidator, and any such order may be enforced in the same manner as if it had directed payment to the liquidator.

**(2)** All money and securities paid or delivered into the Bank of England (or branch) in the event of a winding up by the court are subject in all respects to the orders of the court.

**555 Order on contributory to be conclusive evidence**

**555(1)** An order made by the court on a contributory is conclusive evidence that the money (if any) thereby appearing to be due or ordered to be paid is due, but subject to any right of appeal.

**(2)** All other pertinent matters stated in the order are to be taken as truly stated as against all persons and in all proceedings, except proceedings in Scotland against the heritable estate of a deceased contributory; and in that case the order is only prima facie evidence for the purpose of charging his heritable estate, unless his heirs or legatees of heritage were on the list of contributories at the time of the order being made.

**556 Appointment of special manager (England and Wales)**

**556(1)** Where in proceedings in England and Wales the official receiver becomes the liquidator of a company, whether provisionally or otherwise, he may, if satisfied that the nature of the company's estate or business, or the interests of the creditors of contributories generally, require the appointment of a special manager of the estate or business other than himself, apply to the court.

**(2)** The court may on the application appoint a special manager of the company's estate or business to act during such time as the court may direct, with such powers (including any of the powers of a receiver or manager) as may be entrusted to him by the court.

**(3)** The special manager shall give such security and account in such manner as the Secretary of State directs, and shall receive such remuneration as may be fixed by the court.

**557 Power to exclude creditors not proving in time**

**557** The court may fix a time or times within which creditors are to prove their debts or claims or to be excluded from the benefit of any distribution made before those debts are proved.

**558 Adjustment of rights of contributories**

**558** The court shall adjust the rights of the contributories among themselves and distribute any surplus among the persons entitled to it.

**559 Inspection of books by creditors and contributories**

**559(1)** The court may, at any time after making a winding-up order, make such order for inspection of the company's books and papers by creditors and contributories as the court thinks just; and any books and papers in the company's possession may be inspected by creditors and contributories accordingly, but not further or otherwise.

**(2)** Nothing in this section excludes or restricts any statutory rights of a government department or person acting under the authority of a government department.

**560 Costs of winding up may be made payable out of assets**

**560** The court may, in the event of the assets being insufficient to satisfy the liabilities, make an order as to the payment out of the assets of the costs, charges and expenses incurred in the winding up in such order of priority as the court thinks just.

**561 Summoning of persons suspected of having company property, etc.**

**561(1)** The court may, at any time after the appointment of a provisional liquidator or the making of a winding-up order, summon before it any officer of the company or any person known or suspected to have in his possession any property of the company or supposed to be indebted to the company, or any person whom the court deems capable of giving information concerning the promotion, formation, trade, dealings, affairs or property of the company.

**(2)** The court may examine the officer or other person summoned on oath concerning those matters either by word of mouth or on written interrogatories, and may reduce his answers to writing and require him to sign them.

**(3)** The court may require him to produce any books and papers in his custody or power relating to the company; but if he claims any lien on books or papers produced by him, the production is without prejudice to that lien, and the court has jurisdiction in the winding up to determine all questions relating to that lien.

**(4)** If a person so summoned, after being tendered a reasonable sum for his expenses, refuses to come before the court at the time appointed, not having a lawful impediment (made known to the court at the time of its sitting and allowed by it), the court may cause him to be apprehended and brought before the court for examination.

**562 Attendance at company meetings (Scotland)**

**562** In the winding up by the court of a company registered in Scotland, the court has power to require the attendance of any officer of the company at any meeting of creditors or of contributories, or of a committee of inspection, for the purpose of giving information as to the trade, dealings, affairs or property of the company.

**563 Public examination of promoters and officers (England and Wales)**

**563(1)** Where an order has been made in England and Wales for winding up a company by the court, and the official receiver has made a further report under this Act stating that in his opinion a fraud has been committed by any person in the promotion or formation of the company, or by any officer of the company in relation to it since its formation, the following applies.

**(2)** The court may, after consideration of the report, direct that that person or officer shall attend before the court on a day appointed by the court for that purpose and be publicly examined as to the promotion or formation of the company, or the conduct of its business, or as to the conduct or dealings of that person as an officer of it.

**(3)** The official receiver shall take part in the examination and for that purpose may, if specially authorised by the Secretary of State in that behalf, employ a solicitor with or without counsel.

**(4)** The liquidator (where the official receiver is not the liquidator) and any creditor or contributory may also take part in the examination either personally or by solicitor or counsel.

**564 Procedure under s. 563**

**564(1)** On a public examination ordered by the court under section 563, the court may put such questions to the person examined as it thinks fit.

**(2)** The person examined shall be examined on oath and shall answer all such questions as the court may put or allow to be put to him.

**(3)** The person shall at his own cost, before his examination, be furnished with a copy of the official receiver's report, and may at his own cost employ a solicitor with or without counsel, who is at liberty to put to him such questions as the court may deem just for the purpose of enabling him to explain or qualify any answers given by him.

**(4)** If the person applies to the court to be exculpated from any charges made or suggested against him, it is the duty of the official receiver to appear on the hearing of the application and call the court's attention to any matters which appear to him to be relevant; and if the court, after hearing evidence given or witnesses called by the official receiver, grants the application, the court may allow the applicant such costs as in its discretion it thinks fit.

**(5)** Notes of a person's public examination shall be taken down in writing, and shall be read over to or by, and signed by, him and may thereafter be used in evidence against him, and shall be open to the inspection of any creditor or contributory at all reasonable times.

**(6)** The court may, if it thinks fit, adjourn the examination from time to time.

**(7)** The examination may, if the court so directs (and subject to general rules) be held before any Circuit judge, or before any officer of the Supreme Court being an official referee, master or registrar in bankruptcy, or before a district registrar of the High Court named for the purpose by the Lord Chancellor; and the powers of the court under this section may be exercised by the person before whom the examination is held.

**565 Power to arrest absconding contributory**

**565** The court, at any time either before or after making a winding-up order, on proof of probable cause for believing that a contributory is about to quit the United Kingdom or otherwise to abscond or to remove or conceal any of his property for the purpose of evading payment of calls or of avoiding examination respecting the company's affairs, may cause the contributory to be arrested and his books and papers and movable personal property to be seized and him and them to be kept safely until such time as the court may order.

**566 Powers of court to be cumulative**

**566** Powers conferred by this Act on the court are in addition to and not in restriction of any existing powers of instituting proceedings against a contributory or debtor of the company, or the estate of any contributory or debtor, for the recovery of any call or other sums.

**567 Delegation of powers to liquidator (England and Wales)**

**567(1)** Provision may be made by general rules for enabling or requiring all or any of the powers and duties conferred and imposed on the court in England and Wales by this Act in respect of the following matters–

- (a) the holding and conducting of meetings to ascertain the wishes of creditors and contributories,
- (b) the settling of lists of contributories and the rectifying of the register of members where required, and the collection and application of the assets,
- (c) the payment, delivery, conveyance, surrender or transfer of money, property, books or papers to the liquidator,
- (d) the making of calls,
- (e) the fixing of a time within which debts and claims must be proved,

to be exercised or performed by the liquidator as an officer of the court, and subject to the court's control.

**(2)** But the liquidator shall not, without the special leave of the court, rectify the register of members, and shall not make any call without either that special leave or the sanction of the committee of inspection.

**568 Dissolution of company**

**568(1)** When the company's affairs have been completely wound up, the court (if the liquidator makes an application in that behalf) shall make an order that the company be dissolved from the date of the order, and the company is then dissolved accordingly.

**(2)** A copy of the order shall within 14 days from its date be forwarded by the liquidator to the registrar of companies who shall record the company's dissolution.

**(3)** If the liquidator makes default in complying with the requirements of subsection (2), he is liable to a fine and, for continued contravention, to a daily default fine.

ENFORCEMENT OF, AND APPEAL FROM, ORDERS

**569 Orders for calls on contributories (Scotland)**

**569(1)** In Scotland, where an order, interlocutor or decree has been made for winding up a company by the court, it is competent to the court, on production by the liquidators of a list certified by them of the names of the contributories liable in payment of any calls, and of the amount due by each contributory, and of the date when that amount became due, to pronounce forthwith a decree against those contributories for payment of the sums so certified to be due, with interest from that date until payment (at 5 per cent per annum) in the same way and to the same effect as if they had severally consented to registration for execution, on a charge of 6 days, of a legal obligation to pay those calls and interest.

**(2)** The decree may be extracted immediately, and no suspension of it is competent, except on caution or consignation, unless with special leave of the court.

**570 Enforcement throughout United Kingdom of orders made in winding up**

**570** (Repealed by Insolvency Act 1985, s. 235 and Sch. 10, Pt. IV as from 1 April 1986.)

**571 Appeals from orders in Scotland**

**571(1)** Subject to the provisions of this section and to rules of court, an appeal from any order or decision made or given in the winding up of a company by the court in Scotland under this Act lies in the same manner and subject to the same conditions as an appeal from an order or decision of the court in cases within its ordinary jurisdiction.

**(2)** In regard to orders or judgments pronounced by the judge acting as vacation judge in pursuance of section 4 of the Administration of Justice (Scotland) Act 1933–

- (a) none of the orders specified in Part I of Schedule 16 to this Act are subject to review, reduction, suspension or stay of execution, and
- (b) every other order or judgment (except as mentioned below) may be submitted to review by the Inner House by reclaiming motion enrolled within 14 days from the date of the order or judgment.

**(3)** However, an order being one of those specified in Part II of the Schedule shall, from the date of the order and notwithstanding that it has been submitted to review as above, be carried out and receive effect until the Inner House have disposed of the matter.

**(4)** In regard to orders or judgments pronounced in Scotland by a Lord Ordinary before whom proceedings in a winding up are being taken, any such order or judgment may be submitted to review by the Inner House by reclaiming motion enrolled within 14 days from its date; but should it not be so submitted to review during session, the provisions of this section in regard to orders or judgments pronounced by the judge acting as vacation judge apply.

**(5)** Nothing in this section affects provisions of this Act in reference to decrees in Scotland for payment of calls in the winding up of companies, whether voluntary or by, or subject to the supervision of, the court.

**Chapter III – Voluntary Winding Up**

RESOLUTIONS FOR, AND COMMENCEMENT OF, VOLUNTARY WINDING UP

**572 Circumstances in which company may be wound up voluntarily**

**572(1)** A company may be wound up voluntarily–

(a) when the period (if any) fixed for the duration of the company by the articles expires, or the event (if any) occurs, on the occurrence of which the articles provide that the company is to be dissolved, and the company in general meeting has passed a resolution requiring it to be wound up voluntarily;
(b) if the company resolves by special resolution that it be wound up voluntarily;
(c) if the company resolves by extraordinary resolution to the effect that it cannot by reason of its liabilities continue its business, and that it is advisable to wind up.

**(2)** In this Act the expression **"a resolution for voluntary winding up"** means a resolution passed under any of the paragraphs of subsection (1).

**(3)** A resolution passed under paragraph (a) of subsection (1), as well as a special resolution under paragraph (b) and an extraordinary resolution under paragraph (c), is subject to section 380 (copy of resolution to be forwarded to registrar of companies within 15 days).

**573 Notice of resolution to wind up voluntarily**

**573(1)** When a company has passed a resolution for voluntary winding up, it shall, within 14 days after the passing of the resolution, give notice of the resolution by advertisement in the Gazette.

**(2)** If default is made in complying with this section, the company and every officer of it who is in default is liable to a fine and, for continued contravention, to a daily default fine.

For purposes of this subsection the liquidator is deemed an officer of the company.

**574 Commencement of voluntary winding up**

**574** A voluntary wnding up is deemed to commence at the time of the passing of the resolution for voluntary winding up.

CONSEQUENCES OF VOLUNTARY WINDING UP

**575 Effect on business and status of company**

**575(1)** In case of a voluntary winding up, the company shall from the commencement of the winding up cease to carry on its business, except so far as may be required for its beneficial winding up.

**(2)** However, the corporate state and corporate powers of the company, notwithstanding anything to the contrary in its articles, continue until the company is dissolved.

**576 Avoidance of share transfers etc., other winding up resolution**

**576** Any transfer of shares, not being a transfer made to or with the sanction of the liquidator, and any alteration in the status of the company's members, made after the commencement of a voluntary winding up is void.

DECLARATION OF SOLVENCY

**577 Statutory declaration of solvency**

**577(1)** Where it is proposed to wind up a company voluntarily, the directors (or, in the case of a company having more than two directors, the majority of them) may at a directors' meeting make a statutory declaration to the effect that they have made a full inquiry into the company's affairs and that, having done so, they have formed the opinion that the company will be able to pay its debts in full within such period, not exceeding 12 months from the commencement of the winding up, as may be specified in the declaration.

**(2)** Such a declaration by the directors has no effect for purposes of this Act unless–
(a) it is made within the 5 weeks immediately preceding the date of the passing of the resolution for winding up, or on that date but before the passing of the resolution, and
(b) it embodies a statement of the company's assets and liabilities as at the latest practicable date before the making of the declaration.

**(3)** The declaration shall be delivered to the registrar of companies before the expiration of 15 days immediately following the date on which the resolution for winding up is passed.

**(4)** A director making a declaration under this section without having reasonable grounds for the opinion that the company will be able to pay its debts in full within the period specified is liable to imprisonment or a fine, or both.

**(5)** If the company is wound up in pursuance of a resolution passed within 5 weeks after the making of the declaration, and its debts are not paid or provided for in full within the period specified, it is to be presumed (unless the contrary is shown) that the director did not have reasonable grounds for his opinion.

**(6)** If a declaration required by subsection (3) to be delivered to the registrar is not so delivered within the time prescribed by that subsection, the company and every officer in default is liable to a fine and, for continued contravention, to a daily default fine.

**578 Distinction between "members" and "creditors" voluntary winding up**

**578** A winding up in the case of which a directors' statutory declaration under section 577 has been made is a "members" voluntary winding up'; and a winding up in the case of which such a declaration has not been made is a "creditors" voluntary winding up'.

PROVISIONS APPLICABLE TO A MEMBERS' VOLUNTARY WINDING UP

**579 Introduction to next 7 sections**

**579** The provisions contained in sections 580 to 586 apply in relation to a members' voluntary winding up.

**580 Company's power to appoint and fix remuneration of liquidator**

**580(1)** The company in general meeting shall appoint one or more liquidators for the purpose of winding up the company's affairs and distributing its assets, and may fix the remuneration to be paid to him or them.

**(2)** On the appointment of a liquidator all the powers of the directors cease, except so far as the company in general meeting or the liquidator sanctions their continuance.

**581 Power to fill vacancy in office of liquidator**

**581(1)** If a vacancy occurs by death, resignation or otherwise in the office of liquidator appointed by the company, the company in general meeting may, subject to any arrangement with its creditors, full the vacancy.

**(2)** For that purpose a general meeting may be convened by any contributory or, if there were more liquidators than one, by the continuing liquidators.

**(3)** The meeting shall be held in manner provided by this Act or by the articles, or in such manner as may, on application by any contributory or by the continuing liquidators, be determined by the court.

**582 Liquidator accepting shares as consideration for sale of company property**

**582(1)** The following applies where a company is proposed to be, or is being, wound up altogether voluntarily, and the whole or part of its business or property is proposed to be transferred or sold to another company ("the transferee company"), whether or not this latter is a company within the meaning of this Act.

**(2)** The liquidator of the company to be, or being, wound up ("the transferor company") may, with the sanction of a special resolution of that company, conferring either a general authority on himself or an authority in respect of any particular arrangement, receive, in compensation or part compensation for the transfer or sale, shares, policies or other like interests in the transferee company for distribution among the members of the transferor company.

**(3)** Alternatively, the liquidator may (with that sanction) enter into any other arrangement whereby the members of the transferor company may, in lieu of receiving cash, shares, policies or other like interests (or in addition thereto) participate in the profits of, or receive any other benefit from, the transferee company.

**(4)** A sale or arrangement in pursuance of this section is binding on members of the transferor company.

**(5)** If a member of the transferor company who did not vote in favour of the special resolution expresses his dissent from it in writing addressed to the liquidator, and left at the company's registered office within 7 days after the passing of the resolution, he may require the liquidator either to abstain from carrying the resolution into effect or to purchase his interest at a price to be determined by agreement or by arbitration in manner provided by this section.

**(6)** If the liquidator elects to purchase the member's interest, the purchase money must be paid before the company is dissolved and be raised by the liquidator in such manner as may be determined by special resolution.

**(7)** A special resolution is not invalid for purposes of this section by reason that it is passed before or concurrently with a resolution for voluntary winding up or for appointing liquidators; but, if an order is made within a year for winding up the company by or subject to the supervision of the court, the special resolution is not valid unless sanctioned by the court.

**(8)** For purposes of an arbitration under this section, the provisions of the Companies Clauses Consolidation Act 1845 or, in the case of a winding up in Scotland, the Companies Clauses Consolidation (Scotland) Act 1845 with respect to the settlement of disputes by arbitration are incorporated with this Act, and–

(a) in the construction of those provisions this Act is deemed the special Act and **"the company"** means the transferor company, and

(b) any appointment by the incorporated provisions directed to be made under the hand of the secretary or any two of the directors may be made in writing by the liquidator (or, if there is more than one liquidator, then any two or more of them).

**583 Creditors' meeting in case of insolvency**

**583(1)** If the liquidator is at any time of opinion that the company will not be able to pay its debts in full within the period stated in the directors' declaration under section 577, he shall forthwith summon a meeting of the creditors, and shall lay before the meeting a statement of the company's assets and liabilities.

**(2)** If the liquidator fails to comply with this section, he is liable to a fine.

**584 General company meeting at each year's end**

**584(1)** Subject to section 586, in the event of the winding up continuing for more than one year, the liquidator shall summon a general meeting of the company at the end of the first year from the commencement of the winding up, and of each succeeding year, or at the first convenient date within 3 months from the end of the year or such longer period as the Secretary of State may allow, and shall lay before the meeting an account of his acts and dealings and of the conduct of the winding up during the preceding year.

**(2)** If the liquidator fails to comply with this section, he is liable to a fine.

**585 Final meeting and dissolution**

**585(1)** As soon as the company's affairs are fully wound up, the liquidator shall make up an account of the winding up, showing how it has been conducted and the company's property has been disposed of, and thereupon shall call a general meeting of the company for the purpose of laying before it the account, and giving an explanation of it.

**(2)** The meeting shall be called by advertisement in the Gazette, specifying its time, place and object and published at least one month before the meeting.

**(3)** Within one week after the meeting, the liquidator shall send to the registrar of companies a copy of the account, and shall make a return to him of the holding of the meeting and of its date; and if the copy is not sent or the return is not made in accordance with this subsection the liquidator is liable to a fine and, for continued contravention, to a daily default fine.

**(4)** If a quorum is not present at the meeting, the liquidator shall, in lieu of the return mentioned above, make a return that the meeting was duly summoned and that no quorum was present; and upon such a return being made, the provisions of subsection (3) as to the making of the return and deemed complied with.

**(5)** The registrar on receiving the account and either of these returns shall forthwith register them, and on the expiration of 3 months from the registration of the return the company is deemed to be dissolved; but the court may, on the application of the liquidator or of any other person who appears to the court to be interested, make an order deferring the date at which the dissolution of the company is to take effect for such time as the court thinks fit.

**(6)** It is the duty of the person on whose application an order of the court under this section is made within 7 days after the making of the order to deliver to the registrar an office copy of the order for registration; and if that person fails to do so he is liable to a fine and, for continued contravention, to a daily default fine.

**(7)** If the liquidator fails to call a general meeting of the company as required by subsection (1), he is liable to a fine.

**586 Alternative provision as to company meetings in case of insolvency**

**586(1)** Where section 583 has effect, sections 594 and 595 apply to the winding up to the exclusion of sections 584 and 585, as if the winding up were a creditors' voluntary winding up and not a members' voluntary winding up.

**(2)** However, the liquidator is not required to summon a meeting of creditors under seciton 594 at the end of the first year from the commencement of the winding up, unless the meeting held under section 583 is held more than 3 months before the end of that year.

## PROVISIONS APPLICABLE TO A CREDITORS' VOLUNTARY WINDING UP

**587 Introduction to next 8 sections**

**587** The provisions contained in sections 588 to 595 apply in relation to a creditors' voluntary winding up.

**588 Meeting of creditors**

**588(1)** The company shall give at least 7 days' notice of the company meeting at which the resolution for voluntary winding up is to be proposed.

This applies notwithstanding any power of the members, or of any particular majority of the members, to exclude or waive any other requirement of this Act or the company's articles with respect to the period of notice to be given of any company meeting.

**(2)** The company shall in addition–

(a) cause a meeting of its creditors to be summoned for the day, or the day next following the day, on which the company meeting is to be held,

(b) cause the notices of the creditors' meeting to be sent by post to the creditors simultaneously with the sending of the notices of the company meeting, and

(c) cause notice of the creditors' meeting to be advertised once in the Gazette and once at least in two local newspapers circulating in the district in which the company's registered office or its principal place of business is situated.

**(3)** The directors of the company shall–

(a) cause a full statement of the position of the company's affairs, together with a list of its creditors and the estimated amount of their claims, to be laid before the creditors' meeting, and

(b) appoint one of their number to preside at the meeting;

and it is the duty of the director so appointed to attend the meeting and preside at it.

**(4)** If the company meeting at which the resolution for voluntary winding up is to be proposed is adjourned and the resolution is passed at an adjourned meeting, any resolution passed at the creditors' meeting held under subsection (2) has effect as if it had been passed immediately after the passing of the resolution for voluntary winding up.

**(5)** If default is made–

(a) by the company in complying with subsections (1) and (2),

(b) by the directors in complying with subsection (3),

(c) by any director in complying with that subsection, so far as requiring him to attend and preside at the creditors' meeting,

the company, the directors or the director (as the case may be) is or are liable to a fine; and, in the case of default by the company, every officer of the company who is in default is also so liable.

**(6)** Failure to give notice of the company meeting as required by subsection (1) does not affect the validity of any resolution passed or other thing done at that meeting which would be valid apart from that subsection.

**589 Appointment of liquidator**

**589(1)** The creditors and the company at their respective meetings mentioned in section 588 may nominate a person to be liquidator for the purpose of winding up the company's affairs and distributing its assets.

**(2)** If the creditors and the company nominate different persons, the person nominated by the creditors shall be liquidator; and if no person is nominated by the creditors the person (if any) nominated by the company shall be liquidator.

**(3)** In the case of different persons being nominated, any director, member or creditor of the company may, within 7 days after the date on which the nomination was made by the creditors, apply to the court for an order either–

(a) directing that the person nominated as liquidator by the company shall be liquidator instead of or jointly with the person nominated by the creditors, or

(b) appointing some other person to be liquidator instead of the person nominated by the creditors.

**590 Appointment of committee of inspection**

**590(1)** The creditors at the meeting to be held under section 588 or at any subsequent meeting may, if they think fit, appoint a committee of inspection consisting of not more than 5 persons.

**(2)** If such a committee is appointed, the company may, either at the meeting at which the resolution for voluntary winding up is passed or at any time subsequently in general meeting, appoint such number of persons as they think fit to act as members of the committee, not exceeding 5.

**(3)** However, the creditors may, if they think fit, resolve that all or any of the persons so appointed by the company ought not to be members of the committee of inspection; and if the creditors so resolve–

(a) the persons mentioned in the resolution are not then, unless the court otherwise directs, qualified to act as members of the committee, and

(b) on any application to the court under this provision the court may, if it thinks fit, appoint other persons to act as such members in place of the persons mentioned in the resolution.

**(4)** Schedule 17 has effect with respect to a committee of inspection appointed under this section and its proceedings.

**(5)** In Scotland, such a committee has, in addition to the powers and duties conferred and imposed on it by this Act, such of the powers and duties of commissioners on a bankrupt estate as may be conferred and imposed on committees of inspection by general rules.

**591 Remuneration of liquidator; cesser of directors' powers**

**591(1)** The committee of inspection or, if there is no such committee, the creditors may fix the remuneration to be paid to the liquidator or liquidators.

**(2)** On the appointment of a liquidator, all the powers of the directors cease, except so far as the committee of inspection (or, if there is no such committee, the creditors) sanction their continuance.

**592 Vacancy in office of liquidator**

**592** If a vacancy occurs, by death, resignation or otherwise, in the office of a liquidator (other than a liquidator appointed by, or by the direction of, the court), the creditors may fill the vacancy.

**593 Application of s. 582 to creditors' voluntary winding up**

**593** Section 582 applies in the case of a creditors' voluntary winding up as in the case of a members' voluntary winding up, with the modification that the liquidator's powers under that section are not to be exercised except with the sanction either of the court or of the committee of inspection.

**594 Meetings of company and creditors at end of each year**

**594(1)** If the winding up continues for more than one year, the liquidator shall summon a general meeting of the company and a meeting of the creditors at the end of the first year from the commencement of the winding up, and of each succeeding year, or at the first convenient date within 3 months from the end of the year or such longer period as the Secretary of State may allow, and shall lay before the meetings an account of his acts and dealings and of the conduct of the winding up during the preceding year.

**(2)** If the liquidator fails to comply with this section, he is liable to a fine.

**595 Final meeting and dissolution**

**595(1)** As soon as the company's affairs are fully wound up, the liquidator shall make up an account of the winding up, showing how it has been conducted and the company's property has been disposed of, and thereupon shall call a general meeting of the company and a meeting of the creditors for the purpose of laying the account before the meetings and giving an explanation of it.

**(2)** Each such meeting shall be called by advertisement in the Gazette specifying the time, place and object of the meeting, and published at least one month before it.

**(3)** Within one week after the date of the meetings (or, if they are not held on the same date, after the date of the later one) the liquidator shall send to the registrar of companies a copy of the account, and shall make a return to him of the holding of the meetings and of their dates.

**(4)** If the copy is not sent or the return is not made in accordance with subsection (3), the liquidator is liable to a fine and, for continued contravention, to a daily default fine.

**(5)** However, if a quorum is not present at either such meeting, the liquidator shall, in lieu of the return required by subsection (3), make a return that the meeting was duly summoned and that no quorum was present; and upon such return being made the provisions of that subsection as to the making of the return are, in respect of that meeting, deemed complied with.

**(6)** The registrar on receiving the account and, in respect of each such meeting, either of the returns mentioned above, shall forthwith register them, and on the expiration of 3 months from their registration the company is deemed to be dissolved; but the court may, on the application of the liquidator or of any other person who appears to the court to be interested, make an order deferring the date at which the dissolution of the company is to take effect for such time as the court thinks fit.

**(7)** It is the duty of the person on whose application an order of the court under this section is made, within 7 days after the making of the order, to deliver to the registrar an office copy of the order for registration; and if that person fails to do so he is liable to a fine and, for continued contravention, to a daily default fine.

**(8)** If the liquidator fails to call a general meeting of the company or a meeting of the creditors as required by this section, he is liable to a fine.

## PROVISIONS APPLICABLE TO EVERY VOLUNTARY WINDING UP

**596 Introduction to next 9 sections**

**596** The provisions of sections 597 to 605 apply to every voluntary winding up, whether a members' or a creditors' winding up.

**597 Distribution of company's property**

**597** Subject to the provisions of this Act as to preferential payments, the company's property shall on the winding up be applied in satisfaction of the company's liabilities pari passu and, subject to that application, shall (unless the articles otherwise provide) be distributed among the members according to their rights and interests in the company.

**598 Powers and duties of liquidator in voluntary winding up**

**598(1)** The liquidator may –

(a) in the case of a members' voluntary winding up, with the sanction of an extraordinary resolution of the company, and

(b) in the case of a creditors' voluntary winding up, with the sanction of the court or the committee of inspection (or, if there is no such committee, a meeting of the creditors),

exercise any of the powers given by paragraphs (d), (e) and (f) of section 539(1) to a liquidator in a winding up by the court.

**(2)** The liquidator may, without sanction, exercise any of the other powers given by this Act to the liquidator in a winding up by the court.

**(3)** The liquidator may –

(a) exercise the court's power of settling a list of contributories (and the list of contributories is prima facie evidence of the liability of the persons named in it to be contributories),

(b) exercise the court's power of making calls,

(c) summon general meetings of the company for the purpose of obtaining its sanction by special or extraordinary resolution or for any other purpose he may think fit.

**(4)** The liquidator shall pay the company's debts and adjust the rights of the contributories among themselves.

**(5)** When several liquidators are appointed, any power given by this Act may be exercised by such one or more of them as may be determined at the time of their appointment or, in default of such determination, by any number not less than two.

**599 Appointment or removal of liquidator by the court**

**599(1)** If from any cause whatever there is no liquidator acting, the court may appoint a liquidator.

**(2)** The court may, on cause shown, remove a liquidator and appoint another.

**600 Notice by liquidator of his appointment**

**600(1)** The liquidator shall, within 14 days after his appointment, publish in the Gazette and deliver to the registrar of companies for registration a notice of his appointment in the prescribed form.

**(2)** If the liquidator fails to comply with this section he is liable to a fine and, for continued contravention, to a daily default fine.

**601 Arrangement when binding on creditors**

**601(1)** Any arrangement entered into between a company about to be, or in the course of being, wound up and its creditors is (subject to the right of appeal under this section) binding –

(a) on the company, if sanctioned by an extraordinary resolution, and
(b) on the creditors, if acceded to by three-fourths in number and value of them.

**(2)** Any creditor or contributory may, within 3 weeks from the completion of the arrangement, appeal to the court against it; and the court may thereupon, as it thinks just, amend, vary or confirm the arrangement.

**602 Reference of questions and powers to court**

**602(1)** The liquidator or any contributory or creditor may apply to the court to determine any question arising in the winding up of a company, or to exercise, as respects the enforcing of calls or any other matter, all or any of the powers which the court might exercise if the company were being wound up by the court.

**(2)** The court, if satisfied that the determination of the question or the required exercise of power will be just and beneficial, may accede wholly or partially to the application on such terms and conditions as it thinks fit or may make such other order on the application as it thinks just.

**(3)** A copy of an order made by virtue of this section staying the proceedings in the winding up shall forthwith be forwarded by the company, or otherwise as may be prescribed, to the registrar of companies, who shall enter it in his records relating to the company.

**603 Court's power to control proceedings (Scotland)**

**603** If the court, on the application of the liquidator in the winding up of a company registered in Scotland, so directs, no action or proceeding shall be proceeded with or commenced against the company except by leave of the court and subject to such terms as the court may impose.

**604 Costs of voluntary winding up**

**604** All costs, charges and expenses properly incurred in the winding up, including the remuneration of the liquidator, are payable out of the company's assets in priority to all other claims.

**605 Saving for rights of creditors and contributories**

**605** The winding up of a company under this Chapter does not bar the right of any creditor or contributory to have it wound up by the court; but in the case of an application by a contributory the court must be satisfied that the rights of the contributories will be prejudiced by a voluntary winding up.

## Chapter IV – Winding Up Subject to Supervision of Court

**606 Power to order winding up under supervision**

**606** When a company has passed a resolution for voluntary winding up, the court may make an order that the voluntary winding up shall continue but subject to such supervision of the court, and with such liberty for creditors, contributories or others to apply to the court, and generally on such terms and conditions, as the court thinks just.

**607 Effect of petition for court supervision**

**607** A petition for the continuance of a voluntary winding up subject to the supervision of the court is deemed, for the purpose of giving jurisdiction to the court over actions, to be a petition for winding up by the court.

**608 Application of s. 522, 523**

**608** A winding up subject to the supervision of the court is deemed for the purposes of sections 522 and 523 (avoidance of dispositions of property, etc.) to be a winding up by the court.

**609 Appointment and removal of liquidators**

**609(1)** Where an order is made for a winding up subject to supervision, the court may by that or any subsequent order appoint an additional liquidator.

**(2)** A liquidator so appointed has the same powers, is subject to the same obligations, and in all respects stands in the same position, as if he had been duly appointed in accordance with provisions of this Act with respect to the appointment of liquidators in a voluntary winding up.

**(3)** The court may remove a liquidator so appointed by the court, or any liquidator continued under the supervision order, and fill any vacancy occasioned by the removal, or by death or resignation.

**610 Effect of supervision order**

**610(1)** Where an order is made for a winding up subject to supervision, the liquidator may (subject to any restrictions imposed by the court) exercise all his powers, without the court's sanction or intervention, in the same manner as if the company were being wound up altogether voluntarily.

**(2)** However, the powers specified in paragraphs (d), (e) and (f) of section 539(1) shall not be exercised by the liquidator except with the sanction of the court or, in a case where before the order the winding up was a creditors' voluntary winding up, with the sanction of the court or the committee of inspection or (if there is no such committee) a meeting of the creditors.

**(3)** A winding up subject to the supervision of the court is not a winding up by the court for the purposes of the provisions of this Act specified in Schedule 18, nor for those of section 491 (power in England and Wales to appoint official receiver as receiver for debenture holders or creditors); but, subject to this, an order for a winding up subject to supervision is deemed to be for all purposes an order for winding up by the court.

**(4)** But where the order for winding up subject to supervision was made in relation to a creditors' voluntary winding up in which a committee of inspection had been appointed, the order is deemed an order for winding up by the court for the purposes of section 547(2)(b) and Schedule 17, except in so far as the operation of those provisions is excluded in a voluntary winding up by general rules.

## Chapter V – Provisions Applicable to Every Mode of Winding Up

### PROOF AND RANKING OF CLAIMS

**611 Debts of all descriptions may be proved**

**611(1)** In every winding up (subject, in the case of insolvent companies, to the application in accordance with this Act of the law of bankruptcy) all debts payable on a contingency, and all claims against the company, present or future, certain or contingent, ascertained or sounding only in damages, are admissible to proof against the company.

**(2)** A just estimate is to be made (so far as possible) of the value of such debts or claims as may be subject to any contingency or sound only in damages, or for some other reason do not bear a certain value.

**612 Application of bankruptcy rules (England and Wales)**

**612(1)** In the winding up of an insolvent company registered in England and Wales the same rules prevail and are to be observed with regard to the respective rights of secured and unsecured creditors, and to debts provable and to the valuation of annuities and future and contingent liabilities, as are in force for the time being under the law of bankruptcy in England and Wales with respect to the estates of persons adjudged bankrupt.

**(2)** All those who in any such case would be entitled to prove for and receive dividends out of the company's assets may come in under the winding up and make such claims against the company as they respectively are entitled to by virtue of this section.

**613 Ranking of claims (Scotland)**

**613(1)** In the winding up of a company registered in Scotland, the following enactments–

(a) sections 22 (except subsection (8)), 23(1) and (2), 48 (except in so far as it relates to the application of section 22(8)), 49 and 50 of, and Schedule 1 to, the Bankruptcy (Scotland) Act 1985 (claims by creditors for voting and payment of dividends);

(b) paragraphs 11 and 13 of Schedule 6 to that Act (voting at meetings);

(c) section 60 of that Act (liabilities and rights of co-obligants); and

(d) sections 8(5) and 22(8) of that Act (including section 22(8) as applied by section 48(7) of that Act);

apply, so far as is consistent with this Act, in like manner as they apply in the sequestration of a bankrupt's estate, with the substitutions specified below, and with any other necessary modifications.

**(2)** The substitutions to be made in those sections of the Act of 1985 are as follows–

(a) for references to sequestration, substitute references to winding up,

(b) for references to the sheriff, substitute references to the court,

(c) for references to the interim or permanent trustee, substitute references to the liquidator, and

(d) for references to the debtor, substitute references to the company.

**614 Preferential payments**

**614(1)** In a winding up the preferential debts listed in Schedule 19 shall be paid in priority to all other debts, but with the exceptions and reservations specified in that Schedule.

**(2)** The preferential debts shall–

(a) rank equally among themselves and be paid in full, unless the assets are insufficient to meet them, in which case they shall abate in equal proportions, and

(b) so far as the assets of the company available for payment of general creditors are insufficient to meet them, have priority over the claims of holders of debentures under any floating charge created by the company, and be paid accordingly out of any property comprised in or subject to that charge.

**(3)** Subject to the retention of such sums as may be necessary for the costs and expenses of the winding up, the preferential debts shall be discharged forthwith so far as the assets are sufficient to meet them; and in the case of the debts to which priority is given by paragraph 8 of Schedule 19 (social security payments), formal proof of them is not required except in so far as is otherwise provided by general rules.

**(4)** In the event of a landlord or other person distraining or having distrained on any goods or effects of the company within 3 months next before the date of a winding-up order, the preferential debts are a first charge on the goods or effects so distrained on, or the proceeds of their sale; but in respect of any money paid under such a charge, the landlord or other person has the same rights of priority as the person to whom the payment is made.

## EFFECT OF WINDING UP ON ANTECEDENT AND OTHER TRANSACTIONS

**615 Fraudulent preference**

**615(1)** Any conveyance, mortgage, delivery of goods, payment, execution or other act relating to property made or done by or against a company within 6 months before the commencement of its winding up which, had it been made or done by or against an individual within 6 months before the presentation of a bankruptcy petition on which he is adjudged bankrupt, would be deemed in his bankruptcy a fraudulent preference, is in the event of the company being wound up deemed a fraudulent preference of its creditors and invalid accordingly.

**(2)** Any conveyance or assignment by a company of all its property to trustees for the benefit of all its creditors is void to all intents.

**(3)** In the application of this section to Scotland, **"bankruptcy petition"** means petition for sequestration.

**615A Gratuitous alienations**

**615A(1)** Where this subsection applies and–

(a) the winding up of a company has commenced, an alienation by the company is challengeable by–

(i) any creditor who is a creditor by virtue of a debt incurred on or before the date of such commencement; or

(ii) the liquidator;

(iii) an administration order is in force in relation to a company, an alienation by the company is challengeable by the administrator.

**(2)** Subsection (1) applies where–

(a) by the alienation, whether before or after the coming into force of section 75 of the Bankruptcy (Scotland) Act 1985, any part of the company's property is transferred or any claim or right of the company is discharged or renounced; and

(b) the alienation takes place on a relevant day.

**(3)** For the purposes of subsection (2)(b), the day on which an alienation takes place is the day on which it becomes completely effectual; and in that subsection **"relevant day"** means, if the alienation has the effect of favouring–

(a) a person who is an associate (within the meaning of the Bankruptcy (Scotland) Act 1985) of the company, a day not earlier than 5 years before the date on which–

(b) the winding up of the company commences; or

(c) as the case may be, the administration order is made; or

(d) any other person, a day not earlier than 2 years before such date.

**(4)** Subsections (4) to (6) and (8) of section 34 of the Bankruptcy (Scotland) Act 1985 (challenge of gratuitous alienation) apply for the purposes of this section as they apply for the purposes of that section but as if–

(a) for any reference to the debtor there is substituted a reference to the company; and

(b) in subsection (8) for the words from the beginning to "1889" there are substituted the words

"A liquidator and, after the coming into force of Chapter III of Part II of the Insolvency Act 1985, an administrator appointed thereunder."

**(5)** In subsections (1) to (3) above, any reference to an administrator or to an administration order–
(a) shall be construed in accordance with Chapter III of Part II of the Insolvency Act 1985; and
(b) shall be of no effect until the coming into force of that Chapter.

**(6)** This section extends to Scotland only.

**615B Unfair preferences**

**615B(1)** Section 36 of the Bankruptcy (Scotland) Act 1985 (unfair preferences) applies for the purposes of this Act as it applies for the purposes of that Act but as if–
(a) for any reference to a debtor there is substituted a reference to a company;
(b) in subsection (1), for paragraphs (a) to (c) there are substituted the words "the commencement of the winding up of the company or the making of an administration order in relation to the company.";
(c) in subsection (4) for paragraphs (a) and (b) there are substituted the following paragraphs–
"(a) in the case of a winding up–
(i) any creditor who is a creditor by virtue of a debt incurred on or before the date of commencement of the winding up; or
(ii) the liquidator; and
(b) in the case of an administration order, the administrator.";
(d) in subsection (6), for the words from the beginning to "1889" there are substituted the words "A liquidator and an administrator"; and
(e) for subsection (7) there is substituted the following subsection–
"(7) This section shall be construed as one with Part XX of the Companies Act 1985; and subsection (5) of section 615A of that Act shall apply in relation to the foregoing provisions of this section as it applies in relation to subsections (1) to (3) of that section.".

**(2)** This section applies to Scotland only.

**616 Liabilities and rights of those fraudulently preferred (England and Wales)**

**616(1)** Where in the case of a company wound up in England and Wales anything made or done is void under section 615 as a fraudulent preference of a person interested in property mortgaged or charged to secure the company's debt, then (without prejudice to any rights or liabilities arising apart from this provision) the person preferred is subject to the same liabilities, and has the same rights, as if he had undertaken to be personally liable as surety for the debt to the extent of the charge on the property or the value of his interest, whichever is the less.

**(2)** The value of the person's interest is determined as at the date of the transaction constituting the fraudulent preference, and as if the interest were free of all incumbrances other than those to which the charge for the company's debt was then subject.

**(3)** On an application made to the court with respect to any payment on the ground that the payment was a fraudulent preference of a surety or guarantor, the court has jurisdiction to determine any question with respect to the payment arising between the person to whom the payment was made and the surety or guarantor, and to grant relief in respect of it.

**(4)** The court's jurisdiction under subsection (3) is exercisable notwithstanding that the determination of the question is not necessary for the purposes of the winding up; and the court may for the purposes of that subsection give leave to bring in the surety or guarantor as a third party as in the case of an action for the recovery of the sum paid.

**(5)** Subsections (3) and (4) apply, with the necessary modifications, in relation to transactions other than the payment of money as they apply in relation to payments.

**617 Effect of floating charge**

**617(1)** Where a company is being wound up, a floating charge on its undertaking or property created within 12 months of the commencement of the winding up is invalid (unless it is proved that the company immediately after the creation of the charge was solvent), except to the amount of any cash paid to the company at the time of or subsequently to the creation of, and in consideration for, the charge, together with interest on that amount.

**(2)** Interest under this section is at the rate of 5 per cent per annum or such other rate as may for the time being be prescribed by order of the Treasury in a statutory instrument subject to annulment in pursuance of a resolution of either House of Parliament.

**(3)** Where a company is being wound up in Scotland, a floating charge over all or any part of its property is not to be held an alienation or preference voidable by statute (other than by the provisions of this section) or at common law on the ground of insolvency or notour bankruptcy.

**618 Disclaimer of onerous property (England and Wales)**

**618(1)** Where any part of the property of a company which is being wound up consists of land (of any tenure) burdened with onerous covenants, of shares or stock in companies, of unprofitable contracts, or of any other property that is unsaleable, or not readily saleable, by reason of its binding its possessor to the performance of any onerous act or to the payment of any sum of money, the liquidator may, with the leave of the court and subject to the provisions of this section and the next, disclaim the property.

**(2)** The power to disclaim is exercisable notwithstanding that the liquidator has endeavoured to sell or has taken possession of the property or exercised any act of ownership in relation to it; and the disclaimer must be in writing signed by him.

**(3)** The power is exercisable at any time within 12 months after the commencement of the winding up or such extended period as may be allowed by the court; but where any such property has not come to the liquidator's knowledge within one month after the commencement of the winding up, he may disclaim at any time within 12 months after he has become aware of it or such extended period as may be so allowed.

**(4)** The disclaimer operates to determine, as from the date of disclaimer, the rights, interests and liabilities of the company, and the company's property, in or in respect of the property disclaimed; but it does not (except so far as is necessary for the purpose of releasing the company and its property from liability) affect the rights or liabilities of any other person.

**(5)** This section does not apply in the case of a winding up in Scotland.

**619 Further provisions about disclaimer under s. 618**

**619(1)** The court, before or on granting leave to disclaim under section 618, may require such notices to be given to persons interested, and impose such terms as a condition of granting leave, and make such other order in the matter, as the court thinks just.

(2) The liquidator is not entitled to disclaim property under section 618 in a case where application in writing has been made to him by persons interested in the property requiring him to decide whether he will or will not disclaim and he has not within 28 days after the receipt of the application (or such further period as may be allowed by the court) given notice to the applicant that he intends to apply to the court for leave to disclaim.

(3) In the case of a contract, if the liquidator after such an application does not within that period or further period disclaim the contract, the company is deemed to have adopted it.

(4) The court may, on the application of a person who is, as against the liquidator, entitled to the benefit or subject to the burden of a contract made with the company, make an order rescinding the contract on such terms as to payment by or to either party of damages for the non-performance of the contract, or otherwise as the court thinks just; and any damages payable under the order to such a person may be proved by him as a debt in the winding up.

(5) The court may, on an application by a person who either claims an interest in disclaimed property or is under a liability not discharged by this Act in respect of disclaimed property, and on hearing any such persons as it thinks fit, make an order for the vesting of the property in or its delivery to any persons entitled to it, or to whom it may seem just that the property should be delivered by way of compensation for such liability, or a trustee for him, and on such terms as the court thinks just.

(6) On such a vesting order being made, the property comprised in it vests accordingly in the person named in that behalf in the order, without conveyance or assignment for that purpose.

(7) Part I of Schedule 20 has effect for the protection of third parties where the property disclaimed is of a leasehold nature.

(8) A person injured by the operation of a disclaimer under section 618 and this section is deemed a creditor of the company to the amount of the injury, and may accordingly prove the debt in the winding up.

**620 Liability for rentchange on company's land after disclaimer**

**620(1)** Where on a disclaimer under section 618 land in England and Wales vests subject to a rentcharge in the Crown or any other person, that does not impose on the Crown or that other person, or on its or his successors in title, any personal liability in respect of the rentcharge.

(2) But this section does not affect any liability in respect of sums accruing due after the Crown or other person, or some person claiming through or under it or him, has taken possession or control of the land or has entered into occupation of it.

(3) This section applies to land whenever vesting, and to sums whenever accrued.

**621 Effect of execution or attachment (England and Wales)**

**621(1)** Where a creditor has issued execution against the goods or land of a company or has attached any debt due to it, and the company is subsequently wound up, he is not entitled to retain the benefit of the execution or attachment against the liquidator in the winding up unless he has completed the execution or attachment before the commencement of the winding up.

(2) However –

(a) if a creditor has had notice of a meeting having been called at which a resolution for voluntary winding up is to be proposed, the date on which he had notice is substituted, for the purpose of subsection (1), for the date of commencement of the winding up,

(b) a person who purchases in good faith under a sale by the sheriff any goods of a company on which execution has been levied in all cases acquires a good title to them against the liquidator, and

(c) the rights conferred by subsection (1) on the liquidator may be set aside by the court in favour of the creditor to such extent and subject to such terms as the court thinks fit.

(3) For purposes of this Act –

(a) an execution against goods is completed by seizure and sale, or by the making of a charging order under section 1 of the Charging Orders Act 1979,

(b) an attachment of a debt is completed by receipt of the debt; and

(c) an execution against land is completed by seizure, by the appointment of a receiver, or by the making of a charging order under section 1 of the Act above-mentioned.

(4) In this section, **"goods"** includes all chattels personal; and **"the sheriff"** includes any officer charged with the execution of a writ or other process.

(5) This section does not apply in the case of a winding up in Scotland.

**622 Duties of sheriff where goods seized in execution (England and Wales)**

**622(1)** The following applies where a company's goods are taken in execution and, before their sale or the completion of the execution (by the receipt or recovery of the full amount of the levy), notice is served on the sheriff that a provisional liquidator has been appointed or that a winding-up order has been made, or that a resolution for voluntary winding up has been passed.

(2) The sheriff shall, on being so required, deliver the goods and any money seized or received in part satisfaction of the execution to the liquidator; but the costs of execution are a first charge on the goods or money so delivered, and the liquidator may sell the goods, or a sufficient part of them, for the purpose of satisfying the charge.

(3) If under an execution in respect of a judgment for a sum exceeding £250 a company's goods are sold or money is paid in order to avoid sale, the sheriff shall deduct the costs of the execution from the proceeds of sale or the money paid and retain the balance for 14 days.

(4) If within that time notice is served on the sheriff of a petition for the winding up of the company having been presented, or of a meeting having been called at which there is to be proposed a resolution for voluntary winding up, and an order is made or a resolution passed (as the case may be), the sheriff shall pay the balance to the liquidator, who is entitled to retain it as against the execution creditor.

(5) The rights conferred by this section on the liquidator may be set aside by the court in favour of the creditor to such extent and subject to such terms as the court thinks fit.

(6) In this section, **"goods"** includes all chattels personal; and **"the sheriff"** includes any officer charged with the execution of a writ or other process.

(7) The money sum for the time being specified in subsection (3) is subject to increase or reduction by regulations under section 664; but no increase or reduction of its affects any case where the goods are sold, or the payment to avoid sale is made, before the coming into force of the increase or reduction.

**(8)** This section does not apply in the case of a winding up in Scotland.

**623 Effect of diligence within 60 days of winding up**

**623(1)** In the winding up of a company registered in Scotland, the following provisions of the Bankruptcy (Scotland) Act 1985–
- (a) subsections (1) to (6) of section 37 (effect of sequestration on diligence); and
- (b) subsections (3), (4), (7) and (8) of section 39 (realisation of estate),

apply, so far as is consistent with this Act, in like manner as they apply in the sequestration of a debtor's estate, with the substitutions specified below and with any other necessary modifications.

**(2)** The substitutions to be made in those sections of the Act of 1985 are as follows–
- (a) for references to the debtor, substitute references to the company,
- (b) for references to the sequestration, substitute references to the winding up,
- (c) for references to the date of sequestration, substitute references to the commencement of the winding up of the company, and
- (d) for references to the permanent trustee, substitute references to the liquidator.

**(3)** In this section, **"the commencement of the winding up of the company"** means, where it is being wound up by the court, the day on which the winding up order is made.

**(4), (5)** (S. 623(1)–(3) substituted for former 623(1)–(5) by Bankruptcy (Scotland) Act 1985, s. 75(1) and Sch. 7 as from 1 April 1986 (see SI 1985/1924).

**(6)** This section, so far as relating to any estate or effects of the company situated in Scotland, applies in the case of a company registered in England as in the case of one registered in Scotland.

OFFENCES OF FRAUD, DECEPTION, ETC. BEFORE AND IN COURSE OF WINDING UP; FRAUDULENT TRADING AND ITS CONSEQUENCES

**624 Fraud, etc. in anticipation of winding up**

**624(1)** When a company is ordered to be wound up by the court, or passes a resolution for voluntary winding up, any person, being a past or present officer of the company, is deemed to have committed an offence if, within the 12 months immediately preceding the commencement of the winding up, he has–
- (a) concealed any part of the company's property to the value of £120 or more, or concealed any debt due to or from the company,
- (b) fraudulently removed any part of the company's property to the value of £120 or more, or
- (c) concealed, destroyed, mutilated or falsified any book or paper affecting or relating to the company's property or affairs, or
- (d) made any false entry in any book or paper affecting or relating to the company's property or affairs, or
- (e) fraudulently parted with, altered or made any omission in any document affecting or relating to the company's property or affairs, or
- (f) pawned, pledged or disposed of any property of the company which has been obtained on credit and has not been paid for (unless the pawning, pledging or disposal was in the ordinary way of the company's business).

**(2)** Such a person is deemed to have committed an offence if within the period above mentioned he has been privy to the doing by others of any of the things mentioned in paragraphs (c), (d) and (e) of subsection (1); and he commits an offence if, at any time after the commencement of the winding up, he does any of the things mentioned in paragraphs (a) to (f) of that subsection, or is privy to the doing by others of any of the things mentioned in paragraphs (c) to (e) of it.

**(3)** For purposes of this section, **"officer"** includes a shadow director.

**(4)** It is a defence –
- (a) for a person charged under paragraph (a) or (f) of subsection (1) (or under subsection (2) in respect of the things mentioned in either of those paragraphs) to prove that he had no intent to defraud, and
- (b) for a person charged under paragraph (c) or (d) of subsection (1) (or under subsection (2) in respect of the things mentioned in either of those two paragraphs) to prove that he had no intent to conceal the state of affairs of the company or to defeat the law.

**(5)** Where a person pawns, pledges or disposes of any property in circumstances which amount to an offence under subsection (1)(f), every person who takes in pawn or pledge, or otherwise receives the property knowing it to be pawned, pledged or disposed of in such circumstances, is guilty of an offence.

**(6)** A person guilty of an offence under this section is liable to imprisonment or a fine, or both.

**(7)** The money sums specified in paragraphs (a) and (b) of subsection (1) are subject to increase or reduction by regulations under section 664.

**625 Transactions in fraud of creditors**

**625(1)** When a company is ordered to be wound up by the court or passes a resolution for voluntary winding up, a person is deemed to have committed an offence if he, being at the time an officer of the company –
- (a) with intent to defraud creditors of the company, has made or caused to be made any gift or transfer of, or charge on, or has caused or connived at the levying of any execution against, the company's property, or
- (b) with that intent, has concealed or removed any part of the company's property since, or within 2 months before, the date of any unsatisfied judgment or order for the payment of money obtained against the company.

**(2)** A person guilty of an offence under this section is liable to imprisonment or a fine, or both.

**626 Misconduct in course of winding up**

**626(1)** When a company is being wound up, whether by or under the supervision of the court or voluntarily, any person, being a past or present officer of the company, commits an offence if he –
- (a) does not to the best of his knowledge and belief fully and truly discover to the liquidator all the company's property, and how and to whom and for what consideration and when the company disposed of any part of that property (except such part as has been disposed of in the ordinary way of the company's business), or
- (b) does not deliver up to the liquidator (or as he directs) all such part of the company's property as is in his custody or under his control, and which he is required by law to deliver up, or
- (c) does not deliver up to the liquidator (or as he directs) all books and papers in his custody or under his control belonging to the company and which he is required by law to deliver up, or
- (d) knowing or believing that a false debt has been proved by any person in the winding up, fails for the period of a month to inform the liquidator of it, or

(e) after the commencement of the winding up, prevents the production of any book or paper affecting or relating to the company's property or affairs.

**(2)** Such a person commits an offence if after the commencement of the winding up he attempts to account for any part of the company's property by fictitious losses or expenses; and he is deemed to have committed that offence if he has so attempted at any meeting of the company's creditors within the 12 months immediately preceding the commencement of the winding up.

**(3)** For purposes of this section, **"officer"** includes a shadow director.

**(4)** It is a defence –

(a) for a person charged under paragraph (a), (b) or (c) of subsection (1) to prove that he had no intent to defraud, and

(b) for a person charged under paragraph (e) of that subsection to prove that he had no intent to conceal the state of affairs of the company or to defeat the law.

**(5)** A person guilty of an offence under this section is liable to imprisonment or a fine, or both.

**627 Falsification of company's books**

**627(1)** When a company is being wound up, an officer or contributory of the company commits an offence if he destroys, mutilates, alters or falsifies any books, papers or securities, or makes or is privy to the making of any false or fraudulent entry in any register, book or account or document belonging to the company with intent to defraud or deceive any person.

**(2)** A person guilty of an offence under this section is liable to imprisonment or a fine, or both.

**628 Material omissions from statements relating to company affairs**

**628(1)** When a company is being wound up, whether by or under the supervision of the court or voluntarily, any person, being a past or present officer of the company, commits an offence if he makes any material omission in any statement relating to the company's affairs.

**(2)** When a company has been ordered to be wound up by the court, or has passed a resolution for voluntary winding up, any such person is deemed to have committed that offence if, prior to the winding up, he has made any material omission in any such statement.

**(3)** For purposes of this section, **"officer"** includes a shadow director.

**(4)** It is a defence for a person charged under this section to prove that he had no intent to defraud.

**(5)** A person guilty of an offence under this section is liable to imprisonment or a fine, or both.

**629 False representations to creditors**

**629(1)** When a company is being wound up, whether by or under the supervision of the court or voluntarily, any person, being a past or present officer of the company –

(a) commits an offence if he makes any false representation or commits any other fraud for the purpose of obtaining the consent of the company's creditors or any of them to an agreement with reference to the company's affairs or to the winding up, and

(b) is deemed to have committed that offence if, prior to the winding up, he has made any false representation, or committed any other fraud, for that purpose.

**(2)** For purposes of this section, **"officer"** includes a shadow director.

**(3)** A person guilty of an offence under this section is liable to imprisonment or a fine, or both.

**630 Responsibility of individuals for company's fraudulent trading**

**630(1)** If in the course of the winding up of a company it appears that any business of the company has been carried on with intent to defraud creditors of the company or creditors of any other person, or for any fraudulent purpose, the following has effect.

**(2)** The court, on the application of the liquidator, may declare that any persons who were knowingly parties to the carrying on of the business in the manner above mentioned are to be liable to make such contributions (if any) to the company's assets as the court thinks proper.

**(3)** On the hearing of the application, the liquidator may himself give evidence or call witnesses.

**(4)** Where the court makes such a declaration, it may give such further directions as it thinks proper for giving effect to the declaration; and in particular, the court may –

(a) provide for the liability of any person under the declaration to be a charge on any debt or obligation due from the company to him, or on any mortgage or charge or any interest in a mortgage or charge on assets of the company held by or vested in him, or any person on his behalf, or any person claiming as assignee from or through the person liable or any person acting on his behalf, and

(b) from time to time make such further order as may be necessary for enforcing any charge imposed under this subsection.

**(5)** For purposes of subsection (4), **"assignee"** –

(a) includes a person to whom or in whose favour, by the directions of the person made liable, the debt, obligation, mortgage or charge was created, issued or transferred or the interest created, but

(b) does not include an assignee for valuable consideration (not including consideration by way of marriage) given in good faith and without notice of any of the matters on the ground of which the declaration is made.

**(5A)** Where the court makes a declaration under subsection (2) above in relation to a person who is a creditor of the company, it may direct that the whole or any part of any debt owed by the company to that person and any interest thereon shall rank in priority after all other debts owed by the company and after any interest on those debts.

**(6)** This section has effect notwithstanding that the person concerned may be criminally liable in respect of matters on the ground of which the declaration under subsection (2) is to be made: and where the declaration is made in the case of a winding up in England and Wales, it is deemed a final judgment within section 1(1)(g) of the Bankruptcy Act 1914.

**631 Assessment of damages against delinquent directors, etc.**

**631(1)** The following applies if in the course of winding up a company it appears that a person who has taken part in its formation or promotion, or any past or present director, manager or liquidator, or an officer of the company, has misapplied or retained or become liable or accountable for any money or property of the company, or been guilty of any misfeasance or breach of trust in relation to the company.

**(2)** The court may, on the application of the official receiver or the liquidator, or of any creditor or contributory, examine into the conduct of the promoter, director, manager, liquidator or officer and compel him—

(a) to repay or restore the money or property, or any part of it, respectively with interest at such rate as the court thinks just, or

(b) to contribute such sum to the company's assets by way of compensation in respect of the misapplication, retainer, misfeasance or breach of trust as the court thinks just.

**(3)** This section has effect notwithstanding that the offence is one for which the offencer may be criminally liable.

**(4)** If in the case of a winding up in England and Wales an order for payment of money is made under this section, the order is deemed a final judgment within section 1(1)(g) of the Bankruptcy Act 1914.

**632 Prosecution of delinquent officers and members of company**

**632(1)** If it appears to the court in the course of a winding up by, or subject to the supervision of, the court that any past or present officer, or any member, of the company has been guilty of any offence in relation to the company for which he is criminally liable, the court may (either on the application of a person interested in the winding up or of its own motion) direct the liquidator to refer the matter to the prosecuting authority.

**(2)** **"The prosecuting authority"** means –

(a) in the case of a winding up in England and Wales, the Director of Public Prosecutions, and

(b) in the case of a winding up in Scotland, the Lord Advocate.

**(3)** If it appears to the liquidator in the course of a voluntary winding up that any past or present officer of the company, or any member of it, has been guilty of any offence in relation to the company for which he is criminally liable, he shall –

(a) forthwith report the matter to the prosecuting authority, and

(b) furnish to that authority such information and give to him such access to and facilities for inspecting and taking copies of documents (being information or documents in the possession or under the control of the liquidator and relating to the matter in question) as the authority requires.

**(4)** Where a report is made to him under subsection (3), the prosecuting authority may, if he thinks fit, refer the matter to the Secretary of State for further enquiry; and the Secretary of State –

(a) shall thereupon investigate the matter, and

(b) for the purpose of his investigation may exercise any of the powers which are exercisable by inspectors appointed under section 431 or 432 to investigate a company's affairs.

**(5)** If it appears to the court in the course of a voluntary winding up that any past or present officer of the company, or any member of it, has been guilty as above-mentioned, and that no report with respect to the matter has been made by the liquidator to the prosecuting authority under subsection (3), the court may (on the application of any person interested in the winding up or of its own motion) direct the liquidator to make such a report; and on a report being made accordingly this section has effect as though the report had been made in pursuance of subsection (3).

**633 Obligations arising under s. 632**

**633(1)** For the purpose of an investigation by the Secretary of State under section 632(4), any obligation imposed on a person by any provision of this Act to produce documents or give information to, or otherwise to assist, inspectors appointed as mentioned in that subsection is to be regarded as an obligation similarly to assist the Secretary of State in his investigation.

**(2)** An answer given by a person to a question put to him in exercise of the powers conferred by section 632(4) may be used in evidence against him.

**(3)** Where criminal proceedings are instituted by the prosecuting authority or the Secretary of State following any report or reference under section 632, it is the duty of the liquidator and every officer and agent of the company past and present (other than the defendant or defender) to give to that authority or the Secretary of State (as the case may be) all assistance in connection with the prosecution which he is reasonably able to give.
For this purpose **"agent"** includes any banker or solicitor of the company and any person employed by the company as auditor, whether that person is or is not an officer of the company.

**(4)** If a person fails or neglects to give assistance in the manner required by subsection (3), the court may, on the application of the prosecuting authority or the Secretary of State (as the case may be) direct the person to comply with that subsection; and if the application is made with respect to a liquidator, the court may (unless it appears that the failure or neglect to comply was due to the liquidator not having in his hands sufficient assets of the company to enable him to do so) direct that the costs shall be borne by the liquidator personally.

SUPPLEMENTARY PROVISIONS AS TO WINDING UP

**634 Disqualification for appointment as liquidator**

**634(1)** A body corporate is not qualified for appointment as liquidator of a company, whether in a winding up by or under the supervision of the court or in a voluntary winding up.

**(2)** Any appointment made in contravention of this section is void; and a body corporate which acts as liquidator of a company is liable to a fine.

**635 Corrupt inducement affecting appointment as liquidator**

**635** A person who gives or agrees or offers to give to any member or creditor of a company any valuable consideration with a view to securing his own appointment or nomination, or to securing or preventing the appointment or nomination of some person other than himself, as the company's liquidator is liable to a fine.

**636 Enforcement of liquidator's duty to make returns, etc.**

**636(1)** If a liquidator who has made any default –

(a) in filing, delivering or making any return, account or other document, or

(b) in giving any notice which he is by law required to file, deliver, make or give,

fails to make good the default within 14 days after the service on him of a notice requiring him to do so, the court has the following powers.

**(2)** On an application made by any creditor or contributory of the company, or by the registrar of companies, the court may make an order directing the liquidator to make good the default within such time as may be specified in the order.

**(3)** The court's order may provide that all costs of and incidental to the application shall be borne by the liquidator.

**(4)** Nothing in this section prejudices the operation of any enactment imposing penalties on a liquidator in respect of any such default as is mentioned above.

**637 Notification that company is in liquidation**

**637(1)** When a company is being wound up, whether by or under supervision of the court or voluntarily, every invoice, order for goods or business letter issued by or on behalf of the company, or a liquidator of the company, or a receiver or manager of the company's property, being a document on or in which the name of the company appears, shall contain a statement that the company is being wound up.

**(2)** If default is made in complying with this section, the company and any of the following persons who knowingly and wilfully authorises or permits the default, namely, any officer of the company, any liquidator of the company and any receiver or manager, is liable to a fine.

**638 In a winding up, certain documents exempt from stamp duty**

**638(1)** In the case of a winding up by the court, or of a creditors' voluntary winding up, the following has effect as regards exemption from duties chargeable under the enactments relating to stamp duties.

**(2)** If the company is registered in England and Wales, the following documents are exempt from stamp duty –

(a) every assurance relating solely to freehold or leasehold property, or to any estate, right or interest in, any real or personal property, which forms part of the company's assets and which, after the execution of the assurance, either at law or in equity, is or remains part of those assets, and

(b) every writ, order, certificate, or other instrument or writing relating solely to the property of any company which is being wound up as mentioned in subsection (1), or to any proceeding under such a winding up.

"**Assurance**" here includes deed, conveyance, assignment and surrender.

**(3)** If the company is registered in Scotland, the following documents are exempt from stamp duty –

(a) every conveyance relating solely to property which forms part of the company's assets and which, after the execution of the conveyance, is or remains the company's property for the benefit of its creditors,

(b) every articles of roup or sale, submission and every other instrument and writing whatsoever relating solely to the company's property, and

(c) every deed or writing forming part of the proceedings in the winding up.

"**Conveyance**" here includes assignation, instrument, discharge, writing and deed.

**639 Company's books to be evidence**

**639** Where a company is being wound up, all books and papers of the company and of the liquidators are, as between the contributories of the company, prima facie evidence of the truth of all matters purporting to be recorded in them.

**640 Disposal of books and papers**

**640(1)** When a company has been wound up and is about to be dissolved, its books and papers and those of the liquidators may be disposed of as follows –

(a) in the case of a winding up by or subject to the supervision of the court, in such way as the court directs;

(b) in the case of a members' voluntary winding up, in such way as the company by extraordinary resolution directs, and

(c) in the case of a creditors' voluntary winding up, in such way as the committee of inspection or, if there is no such committee, the company's creditors may direct.

**(2)** After 5 years from the company's dissolution no responsibility rests on the company, the liquidators, or any person to whom the custody of the books and papers has been committed, by reason of any book or paper not being forthcoming to a person claiming to be interested in it.

**(3)** Provision may be made by general rules –

(a) for enabling the Secretary of State to prevent, for such period as he thinks proper (but not exceeding 5 years from the company's dissolution), the destruction of the books and papers of a company which has been wound up, and

(b) for enabling any creditor or contributory of the company to make representations to the Secretary of State and to appeal to the court from any direction which may be given by the Secretary of State in the matter.

**(4)** If a person acts in contravention of general rules made for the purposes of this section, or of any direction of the Secretary of State under them, he is liable to a fine.

**641 Information as to pending liquidations**

**641(1)** If the winding up of a company is not concluded within one year after its commencement, the liquidator shall, at such intervals as may be prescribed, until the winding up is concluded, send to the registrar of companies a statement in the prescribed form and containing the prescribed particulars with respect to the proceedings in, and position of, the liquidation.

**(2)** If a liquidator fails to comply with this section, he is liable to a fine and, for continued contravention, to a daily default fine.

**642 Unclaimed assets (England and Wales)**

**642(1)** This section applies if, where a company is being wound up in England and Wales, it appears (either from any statement sent to the registrar under section 641 or otherwise) that a liquidator has in his hands or under his control any money –

(a) representing unclaimed or undistributed assets of the company which have remained unclaimed or undistributed for 6 months after the date of their receipt, or

(b) held by the company in trust in respect of dividends or other sums due to any person as a member of the company.

**(2)** The liquidator shall forthwith pay the money in question to the Insolvency Services Account at the Bank of England, and is entitled to the prescribed certificate of receipt for the money so paid, and that certificate is an effectual discharge to him in respect of it.

**(3)** For the purpose of ascertaining and getting in any money payable into the Bank of England in pursuance of this section, the like powers may be exercised, and by the like authority, as are exercisable under section 153 of the Bankruptcy Act 1914 for the purpose of ascertaining and getting in the sums, funds and dividends referred to in that section.

**(4)** Any person claiming to be entitled to money paid into the Bank of England under this section may apply to the Secretary of State for payment; and the Secretary of State may, on a certificate by the liquidator that the person claiming is entitled, make an order for payment to that person of the sum due.

**(5)** Any person dissatisfied with a decision of the Secretary of State in respect of a claim made under this section may appeal to the High Court.

**643 Unclaimed dividends, etc. (Scotland)**

**643(1)** The following applies where a company registered in Scotland has been wound up, and is about to be dissolved.

**(2)** The liquidator shall lodge in an appropriate bank or institution as defined in section 73(1) (interpretation) of the Bankruptcy (Scotland) Act 1985 (not being a bank or institution in or of which the liquidator is acting partner, manager, agent or cashier) in the name of the Accountant of Court the whole unclaimed dividends and unapplied or undistributable balances, and the deposit receipts shall be transmitted to the Accountant of Court.

**(3)** The provisions of section 58 of the Bankruptcy (Scotland) Act 1985 (so far as consistent with this Act) apply with any necessary modifications to sums lodged in a bank or institution under this section as they apply to sums deposited under that section.

**644 Resolutions passed at adjourned meetings**

**644** Where a resolution is passed at an adjourned meeting of a company's creditors or contributories, the resolution is treated for all purposes as having been passed on the date on which it was in fact passed, and not as having been passed on any earlier date.

SUPPLEMENTARY POWERS OF COURT

**645 Meetings to ascertain wishes of creditors or contributories**

**645(1)** The court may –

(a) as to all matters relating to the winding up of a company, have regard to the wishes of the creditors or contributories (as proved to it by any sufficient evidence), and

(b) if it thinks fit, for the purpose of ascertaining those wishes, direct meetings of the creditors or contributories to be called, held and conducted in such manner as the court directs, and appoint a person to act as chairman of any such meeting and report the result of it to the court.

**(2)** In the case of creditors, regard shall be had to the value of each creditor's debt.

**(3)** In the case of contributories, regard shall be had to the number of votes conferred on each contributory by this Act or the articles.

**646 Judicial notice of signature of court officers**

**646** In all proceedings under this Part, all courts, judges and persons judicially acting, and all officers, judicial or ministerial, of any court, or employed in enforcing the process of any court shall take judicial notice –

(a) of the signature of any officer of the High Court or of a county court in England and Wales, or of the Court of Session or a sheriff court in Scotland, or of the High Court in Northern Ireland, and also

(b) of the official seal or stamp of the several offices of the High Court in England and Wales or Northern Ireland, or of the Court of Session, appended to or impressed on any document made, issued or signed under the provisions of this Act, or any official copy of such a document.

**647 Commission for receiving evidence**

**647(1)** When a company is wound up in England and Wales or in Scotland, the court may refer the whole or any part of the examination of witnesses –

(a) to a specified county court in England and Wales, or

(b) to the sheriff principal for a specified sheriffdom in Scotland, or

(c) to the High Court in Northern Ireland or a specified Northern Ireland County Court,

(**"specified"** meaning specified in the order of the winding-up court).

**(2)** Any person exercising jurisdiction as a judge of the court to which the reference is made (or, in Scotland, the sheriff principal to whom it is made) shall then, by virtue of this section, be a commissioner for the purpose of taking the evidence of those witnesses.

**(3)** The judge or sheriff principal has in the matter referred the same power of summoning and examining witnesses, of requiring the production and delivery of documents, of punishing defaults by witnesses, and of allowing costs and expenses to witnesses, as the court which made the winding-up order.

These powers are in addition to any which the judge or sheriff principal might lawfully exercise apart from this section.

**(4)** The examination so taken shall be returned or reported to the court which made the order in such manner as that court requests.

**(5)** This section extends to Northern Ireland.

**648 Court order for examination of persons in Scotland**

**648(1)** The court may direct the examination in Scotland of any person for the time being in Scotland (whether a contributory of the company or not), in regard to the trade, dealings, affairs or property of any company in course of being wound up, or of any person being a contributory of the company, so far as the company may be interested by reason of his being a contributory.

**(2)** The order or commission to take the examination shall be directed to the sheriff principal of the sheriffdom in which the person to be examined is residing or happens to be for the time; and the sheriff principal shall summon the person to appear before him at a time and place to be specified in the summons for examination on oath as a witness or as a haver, and to produce any books or papers called for which are in his possession or power.

**(3)** The sheriff principal may take the examination either orally or on written interrogatories, and shall report the same in writing in the usual form to the court, and shall transmit with the report the books and papers produced, if the originals are required and specified by the order or commission, or otherwise copies or extracts authenticated by the sheriff.

**(4)** If a person so summoned fails to appear at the time and place specified, or refuses to be examined or to make the production required, the sheriff principal shall proceed against him as a witness or haver duly cited; and failing to appear or refusing to give evidence or make production may be proceeded against by the law of Scotland.

**(5)** The sheriff principal is entitled to such fees, and the witness is entitled to such allowances, as sheriffs principal when acting as commissioners under appointment from the Court of Session and as witnesses and havers are entitled to in the like cases according to the law and practice of Scotland.

**(6)** If any objection is stated to the sheriff principal by the witness, either on the ground of his incompetency as a witness, or as to the production required, or on any other ground, the sheriff principal may, if he thinks fit, report the objection to the court, and suspend the examination of the witness until it has been disposed of by the court.

**649 Costs of application for leave to proceed (Scottish companies)**

**649** Where a petition or application for leave to proceed with an action or proceeding against a company which is being wound up in Scotland is unopposed and is granted by the court, the costs of the petition or application shall, unless the court otherwise directs, be added to the amount of the petitioner's or applicant's claim against the company.

**650 Affidavits, etc., in United Kingdom and overseas**

**650(1)** An affidavit required to be sworn under or for the purposes of this Part may be sworn in the United Kingdom or elsewhere in Her Majesty's dominions, before any court, judge or person lawfully authorised to take and receive affidavits, or before any of Her Majesty's consuls or vice-consuls in any place outside Her dominions.

**(2)** All courts, judges, justices, commissioners and persons acting judicially shall take judicial notice of the seal or stamp or signature (as the case may be) of any such court, judge, person, consul or vice-consul attached, appended or subscribed to any such affidavit, or to any other document to be used for the purposes of this Part."

# Chapter VI – Matters Arising Subsequent to Winding Up

## 651 Power of court to declare dissolution of company void

**651(1) [Declaration by court, on application]** Where a company has been dissolved, the court may, on an application made for the purpose by the liquidator of the company or by any other person appearing to the court to be interested, make an order, on such terms as the court thinks fit, declaring the dissolution to have been void.

**History**

In s. 651(1) the words "at any time within 2 years of the date of the dissolution" formerly appearing after the words "the court may" omitted by CA 1989, s. 141(2) as from 16 November 1989 (see CA 1989, s. 215(1)(a)) and repealed by CA 1989, s. 212 and Sch. 24 as from 31 July 1990 (see SI 1990/1392 (C 41), art. 4(b)(i)). Previously the words "12 years" were to have been substituted for the words "2 years" by Insolvency Act 1985, s. 109 and Sch. 6, para. 45 from a day to be appointed (see SI 1986/1924 (C 71), art. 4(a)) but such day was never appointed and from 1 April 1990 Insolvency Act 1986, Sch. 6, para. 45 repealed by CA 1989, s. 212 and Sch. 24 (see SI 1990/355 (C 13), art. 5(1)(c)).

**651(2) [Proceedings]** Thereupon such proceedings may be taken as might have been taken if the company had not been dissolved.

**651(3) [Copy of order to registrar, penalty on default]** It is the duty of the person on whose application the order was made, within 7 days after its making (or such further time as the court may allow), to deliver to the registrar of companies for registration an office copy of the order.

If the person fails to do so, he is liable to a fine and, for continued contravention, to a daily default fine.

**651(4) [Timing of application]** Subject to the following provisions, an application under this section may not be made after the end of the period of two years from the date of the dissolution of the company.

**651(5) [Applications for damages]** An application for the purpose of bringing proceedings against the company–

(a) for damages in respect of personal injuries (including any sum claimed by virtue of section 1(2)(c) of the Law Reform (Miscellaneous Provisions) Act 1934 (funeral expenses)), or

(b) for damages under the Fatal Accidents Act 1976 or the Damages (Scotland) Act 1976,

may be made at any time; but no order shall be made on such an application if it appears to the court that the proceedings would fail by virtue of any enactment as to the time within which proceedings must be brought.

**651(6) [Qualification to s. 651(5)]** Nothing in subsection (5) affects the power of the court on making an order under this section to direct that the period between the dissolution of the company and the making of the order shall not count for the purposes of any such enactment.

**651(7) ["Personal injuries" in s. 651(5)(a)]** In subsection (5)(a) **"personal injuries"** includes any disease and any impairment of a person's physical or mental condition.

**History**

S. 651(4)–(7) added by CA 1989, s. 141(3) as from 16 November 1989 (see CA 1989, s. 215(1)(a)).

## 652 Registrar may strike defunct company off register

**652(1) [Registrar's letter]** If the registrar of companies has reasonable cause to believe that a company is not carrying on business or in operation, he may send to the company by post a letter inquiring whether the company is carrying on business or in operation.

**652(2) [Where no answer to registrar's letter]** If the registrar does not within one month of sending the letter receive any answer to it, he shall within 14 days after the expiration of that month send to the company by post a registered letter referring to the first letter, and stating that no answer to it has been received, and that if an answer is not received to the second letter within one month from its date, a notice will be published in the Gazette with a view to striking the company's name off the register.

**652(3) [Notice of proposed dissolution]** If the registrar either receives an answer to the effect that the company is not carrying on business or in operation, or does not within one month after sending the second letter receive any answer, he may publish in the Gazette, and send to the company by post, a notice that at the expiration of 3 months from the date of that notice the name of the company mentioned in it will, unless cause is shown to the contrary, be struck off the register and the company will be dissolved.

**652(4) [Notice if no liquidator etc.]** If, in a case where a company is being wound up, the registrar has reasonable cause to believe either that no liquidator is acting, or that the affairs of the company are fully wound up, and the returns required to be made by the liquidator have not been made for a period of 6 consecutive months, the registrar shall publish in the Gazette and send to the company or the liquidator (if any) a like notice as is provided in subsection (3).

**652(5) [Striking name off register, notice in Gazette]** At the expiration of the time mentioned in the notice the registrar may, unless cause to the contrary is previously shown by the company, strike its name off the register, and shall publish notice of this in the Gazette; and on the publication of that notice in the Gazette the company is dissolved.

**652(6) [Qualification to s. 652(5)]** However –

(a) the liability (if any) of every director, managing officer and member of the company continues and may be enforced as if the company had not been dissolved, and

(b) nothing in subsection (5) affects the power of the court to wind up a company the name of which has been struck off the register.

**652(7) [Addresses for notices]** A notice to be sent to a liquidator under this section may be addressed to him at his last known place of business; and a letter or notice to be sent under this section to a company may be addressed to the company at its registered office or, if no office has been registered, to the care of some officer of the company.

If there is no officer of the company whose name and address are known to the registrar of companies, the letter or notice may be sent to each of the persons who subscribed the memorandum, addressed to him at the address mentioned in the memorandum.

# 652A Registrar may strike private company off register on application

**652A(1) [Application by private company]** On application by a private company, the registrar of companies may strike the company's name off the register.

**652A(2) [Requirements for application]** An application by a company under this section shall–

(a) be made on its behalf by its directors or by a majority of them,

(b) be in the prescribed form, and

(c) contain the prescribed information.

**History**

See the Companies (Forms) (No. 2) Regulations 1995 (SI 1995/1479) and the Companies (Welsh Language Forms and Documents) (No. 2) Regulations 1995 (SI 1995/1480).

**652A(3) [Striking name off register 3 months after notice in Gazette]** The registrar shall not strike a company off under this section until after the expiration of 3 months from the publication by him in the Gazette of a notice–

(a) stating that he may exercise his power under this section in relation to the company, and

(b) inviting any person to show cause why he should not do so.

**652A(4) [Notice in Gazette]** Where the registrar strikes a company off under this section, he shall publish notice of that fact in the Gazette.

**652A(5) [Effect of notice]** On the publication in the Gazette of a notice under subsection (4), the company to which the notice relates is dissolved.

**652A(6) [Continuing liability of company personnel]** However, the liability (if any) of every director, managing officer and member of the company continues and may be enforced as if the company had not been dissolved.

**652A(7) [Court's power to wind up company]** Nothing in this section affects the power of the court to wind up a company the name of which has been struck off the register.

**History**
See history note after s. 652F.

# 652B Duties in connection with making application under s. 652A

**652B(1) [Where application not to be made under s. 652A]** A person shall not make an application under section 652A on behalf of a company if, at any time in the previous 3 months, the company has–

(a) changed its name,

(b) traded or otherwise carried on business,

(c) made a disposal for value of property or rights which, immediately before ceasing to trade or otherwise carry on business, it held for the purpose of disposal for gain in the normal course of trading or otherwise carrying on business, or

(d) engaged in any other activity, except one which is–

 (i) necessary or expedient for the purpose of making an application under section 652A, or deciding whether to do so,

 (ii) necessary or expedient for the purpose of concluding the affairs of the company,

 (iii) necessary or expedient for the purpose of complying with any statutory requirement, or

 (iv) specified by the Secretary of State by order for the purposes of this sub-paragraph.

**652B(2) [Trading under s. 652B(1)]** For the purposes of subsection (1), a company shall not be treated as trading or otherwise carrying on business by virtue only of the fact that it makes a payment in respect of a liability incurred in the course of trading or otherwise carrying on business.

**652B(3) [Further situations where application not to be made under s. 652A]** A person shall not make an application under section 652A on behalf of a company at a time when any of the following is the case–

(a) an application has been made to the court under section 425 on behalf of the company for the sanctioning of a compromise or arrangement and the matter has not been finally concluded;

(b) a voluntary arrangement in relation to the company has been proposed under Part I of the Insolvency Act 1986 and the matter has not been finally concluded;

(c) an administration order in relation to the company is in force under Part II of that Act or a petition for such an order has been presented and not finally dealt with or withdrawn;

(d) the company is being wound up under Part IV of that Act, whether voluntarily or by the court, or a petition under that Part for the winding up of the company by the court has been presented and not finally dealt with or withdrawn;

(e) there is a receiver or manager of the company's property;

(f) the company's estate is being administered by a judicial factor.

**652B(4) [Final conclusion of matter under s. 652B(3)(a)]** For the purposes of subsection (3)(a), the matter is finally concluded if–

(a) the application has been withdrawn,

(b) the application has been finally dealt with without a compromise or arrangement being sanctioned by the court, or

(c) a compromise or arrangement has been sanctioned by the court and has, together with anything required to be done under any provision made in relation to the matter by order of the court, been fully carried out.

**652B(5) [Final conclusion of matter under s. 652B(3)(b)]** For the purposes of subsection (3)(b), the matter is finally concluded if–

(a) no meetings are to be summoned under section 3 of the Insolvency Act 1986,

(b) meetings summoned under that section fail to approve the arrangement with no, or the same, modifications,

(c) an arrangement approved by meetings summoned under that section, or in consequence of a direction under section 6(4)(b) of that Act, has been fully implemented, or

(d) the court makes an order under subsection (5) of section 6 of that Act revoking approval given at previous meetings and, if the court gives any directions under subsection (6) of that section, the company has done whatever it is required to do under those directions.

**652B(6) [Persons to receive copy of s. 652A application]** A person who makes an application under section 652A on behalf of a company shall secure that a copy of the application is given, within 7 days from the day on which the application is made, to every person who, at any time on that day, is–

(a) a member of the company,

(b) an employee of the company,

(c) a creditor of the company,

(d) a director of the company,

(e) a manager or trustee of any pension fund established for the benefit of employees of the company, or

(f) a person of a description specified for the purposes of this paragraph by regulations made by the Secretary of State.

**652B(7) [Extent of s. 652B(6)]** Subsection (6) shall not require a copy of the application to be given to a director who is a party to the application.

**652B(8) [When s. 652B(6) duty ceases]** The duty imposed by subsection (6) shall cease to apply if the application is withdrawn before the end of the period for giving the copy application.

**652B(9) [Amendment of s. 652B(1)]** The Secretary of State may by order amend subsection (1) for the purpose of altering the period in relation to which the doing of the things mentioned in paragraphs (a) to (d) of that subsection is relevant.

**History**
See history note after s. 652F.

## 652C Directors' duties following application under s. 652A

**652C(1) [Application of s. 652C(2)]** Subsection (2) applies in relation to any time after the day on which a company makes an application under section 652A and before the day on which the application is finally dealt with or withdrawn.

**652C(2) [Persons to receive copy of s. 652A application]** A person who is a director of the company at the end of a day on which a person other than himself becomes–

(a) a member of the company,

(b) an employee of the company,

(c) a creditor of the company,

(d) a director of the company,

(e) a manager or trustee of any pension fund established for the benefit of employees of the company, or

(f) a person of a description specified for the purposes of this paragraph by regulations made by the Secretary of State,

shall secure that a copy of the application is given to that person within 7 days from that day.

**652C(3) [When s. 652C(2) duty ceases]** The duty imposed by subsection (2) shall cease to apply if the application is finally dealt with or withdrawn before the end of the period for giving the copy application.

**652C(4) [Application of s. 652C(5)]** Subsection (5) applies where, at any time on or after the day on which a company makes an application under section 652A and before the day on which the application is finally dealt with or withdrawn–

(a) the company–
  (i) changes its name,
  (ii) trades or otherwise carries on business,
  (iii) makes a disposal for value of any property or rights other than those which it was necessary or expedient for it to hold for the purpose of making, or proceeding with, an application under section 652A, or
  (iv) engages in any other activity, except one to which subsection (6) applies;

(b) an application is made to the court under section 425 on behalf of the company for the sanctioning of a compromise or arrangement;

(c) a voluntary arrangement in relation to the company is proposed under Part I of the Insolvency Act 1986;

(d) a petition is presented for the making of an administration order under Part II of that Act in relation to the company;

(e) there arise any of the circumstances in which, under section 84(1) of that Act, the company may be voluntarily wound up;

(f) a petition is presented for the winding up of the company by the court under Part IV of that Act;

(g) a receiver or manager of the company's property is appointed; or

(h) a judicial factor is appointed to administer the company's estate.

**652C(5) [Withdrawal by s. 652C(4)(a)–(b) persons]** A person who, at the end of a day on which an event mentioned in any of paragraphs (a) to (h) of subsection (4) occurs, is a director of the company shall secure that the company's application is withdrawn forthwith.

**652C(6) [Activities for s. 652C(4)(a)(iv)]** This subsection applies to any activity which is–

(a) necessary or expedient for the purpose of making, or proceeding with, an application under section 652A,

(b) necessary or expedient for the purpose of concluding affairs of the company which are outstanding because of what has been necessary or expedient for the purpose of making, or proceeding with, such an application,

(c) necessary or expedient for the purpose of complying with any statutory requirement, or

(d) specified by the Secretary of State by order for the purposes of this subsection.

**652C(7) [Trading under s. 652C(4)(a)]** For the purposes of subsection (4)(a), a company shall not be treated as trading or otherwise carrying on business by virtue only of the fact that it makes a payment in respect of a liability incurred in the course of trading or otherwise carrying on business.

**History**
See history note after s. 652F.

## 652D Sections 652B and 652C: supplementary provisions

**652D(1) [Giving of document under s. 652B(6), 652C(2)]** For the purposes of sections 652B(6) and 652C(2), a document shall be treated as given to a person if it is delivered to him or left at his proper address or sent by post to him at that address.

**652D(2) [Proper address for s. 652D(1)]** For the purposes of subsection (1) and section 7 of the Interpretation Act 1978 (which relates to the service of documents by post) in its application to that subsection, the proper address of any person shall be his last known address, except that–

(a) in the case of a body corporate, other than one to which subsection (3) applies, it shall be the address of its registered or principal office,

(b) in the case of a partnership, other than one to which subsection (3) applies, it shall be the address of its principal office, and

(c) in the case of a body corporate or partnership to which subsection (3) applies, it shall be the address of its principal office in the United Kingdom.

**652D(3) [Exceptions under s. 652D(2)]** This subsection applies to a body corporate or partnership which–

(a) is incorporated or formed under the law of a country or territory outside the United Kingdom, and

(b) has a place of business in the United Kingdom.

**652D(4) [Where creditor of company has more than one place of business]** Where a creditor of the company has more than one place of business, subsection (l) shall have effect, so far as concerns the giving of a document to him, as if for the words from "delivered" to the end there were substituted "left, or sent by post to him, at each place of business of his with which the company has had dealings in relation to a matter by virtue of which he is a creditor of the company."

**652D(5) [Extent of regulations under s. 652B or 652C]** Any power to make an order or regulations under section 652B or 652C shall–

(a) include power to make different provision for different cases or classes of case,

(b) include power to make such transitional provisions as the Secretary of State considers appropriate, and

(c) be exercisable by statutory instrument subject to annulment in pursuance of a resolution of either House of Parliament.

**652D(6) [Withdrawal of notice under s. 652B and 652C]** For the purposes of sections 652B and 652C, an application under section 652A is withdrawn if notice of withdrawal in the prescribed form is given to the registrar of companies.

**Note**

See the Companies (Forms) (No. 2) Regulations 1995 (SI 1995/1479) and the Companies (Welsh Language Forms and Documents) (No. 2) Regulations 1995 (SI 1995/1480).

**652D(7) ["Disposal"]** In sections 652B and 652C, **"disposal"** includes part disposal.

**652D(8) ["Creditor"]** In sections 652B and 652C and this section, **"creditor"** includes a contingent or prospective creditor.

**History**

See history note after s. 652F.

## 652E Sections 652B and 652C: enforcement

**652E(1) [Offence, penalty under s. 652B or 652C]** A person who breaches or fails to perform a duty imposed on him by section 652B or 652C is guilty of an offence and liable to a fine.

**652E(2) [Further offence, penalty under s. 652B(6) or 652C(2)]** A person who fails to perform a duty imposed on him by section 652B(6) or 652C(2) with the intention of concealing the making of the application in question from the person concerned is guilty of an offence and liable to imprisonment or a fine, or both.

**652E(3) [Defence under s. 652B(1) or (3)]** In any proceedings for an offence under subsection (1) consisting of breach of a duty imposed by section 652B(l) or (3), it shall be a defence for the accused to prove that he did not know, and could not reasonably have known, of the existence of the facts which led to the breach.

**652E(4) [Defence under s. 652B(6)]** In any proceedings for an offence under subsection (l) consisting of failure to perform the duty imposed by section 652B(6), it shall be a defence for the accused to prove that he took all reasonable steps to perform the duty.

**652E(5) [Defence for failure under s. 652C(2) or (5)]** In any proceedings for an offence under subsection (1) consisting of failure to perform a duty imposed by section 652C(2) or (5), it shall be a defence for the accused to prove–

(a) that at the time of the failure he was not aware of the fact that the company had made an application under section 652A, or

(b) that he took all reasonable steps to perform the duty.

**History**
See history note after s. 652F.

## 652F Other offences connected with s. 652A

**652F(1) [Offence, penalty re false information re s. 652A application]** Where a company makes an application under section 652A, any person who, in connection with the application, knowingly or recklessly furnishes any information to the registrar of companies which is false or misleading in a material particular is guilty of an offence and liable to a fine.

**652F(2) [Offence, penalty re false s. 652A application]** Any person who knowingly or recklessly makes an application to the registrar of companies which purports to be an application under section 652A, but which is not, is guilty of an offence and liable to a fine.

**History**
S. 652A–F inserted by Deregulation and Contracting Out Act 1994, s. 13(1) and Sch. 5, para. 1, 2 as from 1 July 1995 (see SI 1995/1433 (C 31), art. 2, 3(a)).

## 653 Objection to striking off by person aggrieved

**653(1) [Application]** Subsection (2) applies if a company or any member or creditor of it feels aggrieved by the company having been struck off the register under section 652.

**History**
In s. 653(1) the words "Subsection 2" substituted for the former words "The following" and the words "under section 652" inserted by Deregulation and Contracting Out Act 1994, s. 13(1) and Sch. 5, para. 1, 3(1), (2)(a)(b) as from 1 July 1995 (see SI 1995/1433 (C 31), art. 2, 3(a)).

**653(2) [On application court may order restoration of name to register]** The court, on an application by the company or the member or creditor made before the expiration of 20 years from publication in the Gazette of notice under section 652, may, if satisfied that the company was at the time of the striking off carrying on business or in operation, or otherwise that it is just that the company be restored to the register, order the company's name to be restored.

**653(2A) [Application of s. 653(2B), (2D)]** Subsections (2B) and (2D) apply if a company has been struck off the register under section 652A.

**History**
See history note after s. 653(2D).

**653(2B) [Power of court]** The court, on an application by a notifiable person made before the expiration of 20 years from publication in the Gazette of notice under section 652A(4), may, if satisfied–

(a) that any duty under section 652B or 652C with respect to the giving to that person of a copy of the company's application under section 652A was not performed,

(b) that the making of the company's application under section 652A involved a breach of duty under section 652B(1) or (3), or

(c) that it is for some other reason just to do so,

order the company's name to be restored to the register.

**History**
See history note after s. 653(2D).

**653(2C) ["Notifiable person"]** In subsection (2B), **"notifiable person"** means a person to whom a copy of the company's application under section 652A was required to be given under section 652B or 652C.

**History**
See history note after s. 653(2D).

**653(2D) [Further power of court]** The court, on an application by the Secretary of State made before the expiration of 20 years from publication in the Gazette of notice under section 652A(4), may, if satisfied that it is in the public interest to do so, order the company's name to be restored.

**History**
S. 653(2A)–653(2D) inserted by Deregulation and Contracting Out Act 1994, s. 13(1) and Sch. 5, para. 1 and 3(1), (3) as from 1 July (see SI 1995/1433 (C 31), art. 2, 3(a).

**653(3) [Effect of order etc.]** On an office copy of an order under subsection (2), (2B) or (2D) being delivered to the registrar of companies for registration the company to which the order relates is deemed to have continued in existence as if its name had not been struck off; and the court may by the order give such directions and make such provisions as seem just for placing the company and all other persons in the same position (as nearly as may be) as if the company's name had not been struck off.

**History**

In s. 653(3) the words "an order under subsection (2), (2B) or (2D)" substituted for the former words "the order" and the words "to which the order relates" inserted by Deregulation and Contracting Out Act 1994, s. 13(1) and Sch. 5, para. 1, 3(4)(a)(b) as from 1 July 1995 (see SI 1995/1433 (C 31), art. 2, 3(a)).

# 654 Property of dissolved company to be bona vacantia

**654(1) [All property and rights vested in Crown etc.]** When a company is dissolved, all property and rights whatsoever vested in or held on trust for the company immediately before its dissolution (including leasehold property, but not including property held by the company on trust for any other person) are deemed to be bona vacantia and –

(a) accordingly belong to the Crown, or to the Duchy of Lancaster or to the Duke of Cornwall for the time being (as the case may be), and

(b) vest and may be dealt with in the same manner as other bona vacantia accruing to the Crown, to the Duchy of Lancaster or to the Duke of Cornwall.

**654(2) [Orders under s. 651, 653]** Except as provided by the section next following, the above has effect subject and without prejudice to any order made by the court under section 651 or 653.

# 655 Effect on s. 654 of company's revival after dissolution

**655(1) [Disposition of interest once s. 654 order made]** The person in whom any property or right is vested by section 654 may dispose of, or of an interest in, that property or right notwithstanding that an order may be made under section 651 or 653.

**655(2) [Effect of s. 654 order]** Where such an order is made –

(a) it does not affect the disposition (but without prejudice to the order so far as it relates to any other property or right previously vested in or held on trust for the company) and

(b) the Crown or, as the case may be, the Duke of Cornwall shall pay to the company an amount equal to –

(i) the amount of any consideration received for the property or right, or interest therein, or

(ii) the value of any such consideration at the time of the disposition,

or, if no consideration was received, an amount equal to the value of the property, right or interest disposed of, as at the date of the disposition.

**655(3) [Where liability accrued to Duchy of Lancaster before order under s. 651, 653]** Where a liability accrues under subsection (2) in respect of any property or right which, before the order under section 651 or 653 was made, had accrued as bona vacantia to the Duchy of Lancaster, the Attorney General of the Duchy shall represent Her Majesty in any proceedings arising in connection with that liability.

**655(4) [Where liability accrued to Duchy of Cornwall before order under s. 651, 653]** Where a liability accrues under subsection (2) in respect of any property or right which, before the order under section 651 or 653 was made, had accrued as bona vacantia to the Duchy of Cornwall, such persons as the Duke of Cornwall (or other possessor for the time being of the Duchy) may appoint shall represent the Duke (or other possessor) in any proceedings arising out of that liability.

**655(5) [Application]** This section applies in relation to the disposition of any property, right or interest on or after 22nd December 1981, whether the company concerned was dissolved before, on or after that day.

# 656 Crown disclaimer of property vesting as bona vacantia

**656(1) [Disclaimer by notice]** Where property vests in the Crown under section 654, the Crown's title to it under that section may be disclaimed by a notice signed by the Crown representative, that is to say the Treasury Solicitor, or, in relation to property in Scotland, the Queen's and Lord Treasurer's Remembrancer.

**656(2) [Waiver of right to execute notice]** The right to execute a notice of disclaimer under this section may be waived by or on behalf of the Crown either expressly or by taking possession or other act envincing that intention.

**656(3) [Requirements for notice of disclaimer to be of effect]** A notice of disclaimer under this section is of no effect unless it is executed –

(a) within 12 months of the date on which the vesting of the property under section 654 came to the notice of the Crown representative, or

(b) if an application in writing is made to the Crown representative by any person interested in the property requiring him to decide whether he will or will not disclaim, within a period of 3 months after the receipt of the application or such further period as may be allowed by the court which would have had jurisdiction to wind up the company if it had not been dissolved.

**656(4) [Statements in notice sufficient evidence]** A statement in a notice of disclaimer of any property under this section that the vesting of it came to the notice of the Crown representative on a specified date, or that no such application as above mentioned was received by him with respect to the property before a specified date, is sufficient evidence of the fact stated, until the contrary is proved.

**656(5) [Notice to registrar, publication in Gazette, distribution]** A notice of disclaimer under this section shall be delivered to the registrar of companies and retained and registered by him; and copies of it shall be published in the Gazette and sent to any persons who have given the Crown representative notice that they claim to be interested in the property.

**656(6) [Application]** This section applies to property vested in the Duchy of Lancaster or the Duke of Cornwall under section 654 as if for references to the Crown and the Crown representative there were respectively substituted references to the Duchy of Lancaster and to the Solicitor to that Duchy, or to the Duke of Cornwall and to the Solicitor to the Duchy of Cornwall, as the case may be.

## 657 Effect of Crown disclaimer under s. 656

**657(1) [Effect of disclaimer]** Where notice of disclaimer is executed under section 656 as respects any property, that property is deemed not to have vested in the Crown under section 654.

**657(2) [Property in England and Wales]** As regards property in England and Wales, section 178(4) and sections 179 to 182 of the Insolvency Act shall apply as if the property had been disclaimed by the liquidator under the said section 91 immediately before the dissolution of the company.

**History**
S. 657(2) substituted by Insolvency Act 1985, s. 109(1) and Sch. 6, para. 46 and further amended by Insolvency Act 1986, s. 439(1) and Sch. 13, Pt. I as from 29 December 1986 (see SI 1986/1924 (C 71)).

**Note**
The reference to s. 91 should be to s. 178 to 180.

**657(3) [Re property in Scotland]** As regards property in Scotland, the following 4 subsections apply.

**657(4) [Operation in Scotland]** The Crown's disclaimer operates to determine, as from the date of the disclaimer, the rights, interests and liabilities of the company, and the property of the company, in or in respect of the property disclaimed; but it does not (except so far as is necessary for the purpose of releasing the company and its property from liability) affect the rights or liabilities of any other person.

**657(5) [Scotland – court order on application]** The court may, on application by a person who either claims an interest in disclaimed property or is under a liability not discharged by this Act in respect of disclaimed property, and on hearing such persons as it thinks fit, make an order for the vesting of the property in or its delivery to any persons entitled to it, or to whom it may seem just that the property should be delivered by way of compensation for such liability, or a trustee for him, and on such terms as the court thinks just.

**657(6) [Effect of s. 657(5) order]** On such a vesting order being made, the property comprised in it vests accordingly in the person named in that behalf in the order, without conveyance or assignation for that purpose.

**657(7) [Protection of third parties re lease in Scotland]** Part II of Schedule 20 has effect for the protection of third parties where the property disclaimed is held under a lease.

## 658 Liability for rentcharge on company's land after dissolution

**658(1) [Application of Insolvency Act, s. 180]** Section 180 of the Insolvency Act shall apply to land in England and Wales which by operation of law vests subject to a rentcharge in the crown or any other person on the dissolution of a company as it applies to land so vesting on a disclaimer under that section.

**History**
S. 658(1) substituted by Insolvency 1985, s. 109(1) and Sch. 6, para. 47 and further amended by Insolvency Act 1986, s. 439(1) and Sch. 13, Pt. I as from 29 December 1986 (see SI 1986/1924 (C 71)).

**658(2) ["Company"]** In this section **"company"** includes any body corporate.

# Chapter VII – Miscellaneous Provisions About Winding Up

**659-664** (Repealed by Insolvency Act 1986, s. 438 and Sch. 12 as from 29 December 1986.

**History**
In regard to the date of the above repeal, see Insolvency Act 1986, s. 443 and SI 1986/1924 (C 71). There were some amendments and repeals by Insolvency Act 1985 which very briefly came into force (see SI 1986/1924 (C 71)) – except the repeal of s. 663 for England and Wales from 1 March 1986 (see SI 1986/185 (C 7)). See Insolvency Act 1985, Sch. 6, 10 for details. S. 659–664 originally read as follows:

**"659 Power to make over assets to employees**

**659(1)** On the winding up of a company (whether by the court or voluntarily), the liquidator may, subject to the following provisions of this section, make any payment which the company has, before the commencement of the winding up, decided to make under section 719 (power to provide for employees or former employees on cessation or transfer of business).

**(2)** The power which a company may exercise by virtue only of that section may be exercised by the liquidator after the winding up has commenced if, after the company's liabilities have been fully satisfied and provision has been made for the costs of the winding up, the exercise of that power has been sanctioned by such a resolution of the company as would be required of the company itself by section 719(3) before that commencement, if paragraph (b) of that subsection were omitted and any other requirement applicable to its exercise by the company had been met.

**(3)** Any payment which may be made by a company under this section (that is, a payment after the commencement of its winding up) may be made out of the company's assets which are available to the members on the winding up.

**(4)** On a winding up by the court, the exercise by the liquidator of his powers under this section is subject to the court's control, and any creditor or contributory may apply to the court with respect to any exercise or proposed exercise of the power.

**(5)** Subsections (1) and (2) above have effect notwithstanding anything in any rule of law or in section 597 of this Act (property of company after satisfaction of liabilities to be distributed among members).

**660 Separate accounts of particular estates (England and Wales)**

**660(1)** An account shall be kept by the Secretary of State of the receipts and payments in the winding up of each company in England and Wales.

**(2)** When the cash balance standing to the credit of the account of any company is in excess of the amount which, in the opinion of the committee of inspection, is required for the time being to answer demands in respect of the company's estate, the Secretary of State shall on the request of the committee invest the amount not so required in Government securities, to be placed to the credit of that account for the company's benefit.

**(3)** When any part of the money so invested is, in the opinion of the committee of inspection, required to answer any demands in respect of the company's estate, the Secretary of State shall, on the committee's request, raise such sum as may be required by the sale of such part of those securities as may be necessary.

**(4)** The dividends on investments under this section shall be paid to the credit of the company.

**(5)** When the balance at the credit of a company's account in the hands of the Secretary of State exceeds £2,000, and the liquidator gives notice to him that the excess is not required for the purposes of the liquidation, the company is entitled to interest on the excess at such rate as may for the time being be prescribed by order of the Treasury.

**(6)** The Treasury's power to make orders under this section is exercisable by statutory instrument subject to annulment in pursuance of a resolution of either House of Parliament.

**661 Officers and remuneration (England and Wales)**

**661(1)** The Secretary of State may, with the approval of the Treasury, appoint such additional officers as may be required by him for the execution of this Part as respects England and Wales, and may remove any person so appointed.

**(2)** The Secretary of State, with the concurrence of the Treasury, shall direct whether any and what remuneration is to be allowed to any officer of, or person attached to, his department performing any duties under this Part in relation to the winding up of companies in England and Wales, and may vary, increase or diminish that remuneration as he (the Secretary of State) thinks fit.

**662 Returns by officers in winding up (England and Wales)**

**662** The officers of the courts acting in the winding up of companies in England and Wales shall make to the Secretary of State such returns of the business of their respective courts and offices at such times, and in such manner and form, as may be prescribed; and from these returns the Secretary of State shall cause books to be prepared which shall (under regulations made by him) be open for public information and searches.

**663 Rules and fees**

**663(1)** The Lord Chancellor may, with the concurrence of the Secretary of State, make general rules for carrying into effect the objects of this Act so far as relates to the winding up of companies in England and Wales.

**(2)** The Court of Session may by Act of Sederunt make general rules for carrying into effect the objects of this Act so far as relates to the winding up of companies in Scotland.

**(3)** An answer given by a person to a question put to him in exercise of powers conferred by general rules may be used in evidence against him.

**(4)** There shall be paid in respect of proceedings under this Act in relation to the winding up of companies in England and Wales such fees as the Lord Chancellor may, with the sanction of the Treasury, direct; and the Treasury may direct by whom and in what manner the fees are to be collected and accounted for.

**(5)** The powers conferred by this section on the Lord Chancellor, the Court of Session and the Treasury are exercisable by statutory instrument; and a statutory instrument containing general rules shall be laid before Parliament after being made.

**(6)** Fees in respect of proceedings under this Act in relation to the winding up of companies shall be paid into the Consolidated Fund.

**664 Power to increase monetary limits**

**664(1)** The Secretary of State may by regulations in a statutory instrument increase or reduce any of the money sums for the time being specified in the following provisions of this Part –

section 512(2),
section 515(3),
section 518(1)(a),
section 542(4),
section 622(3),
section 624(1)(a) and (b), and paragraph 12 of Schedule 19.

**(2)** Regulations shall not be made under this section unless a draft of the statutory instrument containing them has been approved by resolution of each House of Parliament."

# PART XXI – WINDING UP OF UNREGISTERED COMPANIES

## 665-674 (Repealed by Insolvency Act 1986, s. 438 and Sch. 12 as from 29 December 1986.)

**History**

In regard to the date of the above repeal, see Insolvency Act 1986, s. 443 and SI 1986/1924 (C 71).

There were some previous repeals to s. 665 by Bankruptcy (Scotland) Act 1985, s. 75(2) and Sch. 8 as from 1 April 1986 (see SI 1985/1924 (C 71)) and to s. 665 and 666(6) by Trustee Savings Bank Act 1985, s. 4(3), 7(3) and Sch. 4 as from 21 July 1986 (see SI 1986/1223 (C 36)). There were other amendments and repeals by Insolvency Act 1985 which were very briefly in force – see Insolvency Act 1985, Sch. 6, 10 and SI 1986/1924 (C 71) for details. Prior to the Insolvency Act 1986 repeals the s. 665–674 read as follows:

**"665 Meaning of "unregistered company"**

**665** For the purposes of this Part, the expression **"unregistered company"** includes any partnership, any association and any company, with the following exceptions –

(a) a railway company incorporated by Act of Parliament,
(b) a company registered in any part of the United Kingdom under the Joint Stock Companies Acts or under the legislation (past or present) relating to companies in Great Britain,
(c) a partnership, association or company which consists of less than 8 members and is not a foreign partnership, association or company,
(d) limited partnership.

**666 Winding up of unregistered companies**

**666(1)** Subject to the provisions of this Part, any unregistered company may be wound up under this Act; and all the provisions of this Act about winding up apply to an unregistered company, with the exceptions and additions mentioned in the following subsections.

**(2)** If an unregistered company has a principal place of business situated in Northern Ireland, it shall not be wound up under this Part unless it has a principal place of business situated in England and Wales or Scotland, or in both England and Wales and Scotland.

**(3)** For the purpose of determining a court's winding-up jurisdiction, an unregistered company is deemed –

(a) to be registered in England and Wales or Scotland, according as its principal place of business is situated in England and Wales or Scotland, or
(b) if it has a principal place of business situated in both countries, to be registered in both countries;

and the principal place of business situated in that part of Great Britain in which proceedings are being instituted is, for all purposes of the winding up, deemed to be the registered office of the company.

**(4)** No unregistered company shall be wound up under this Act voluntarily or subject to supervision.

**(5)** The circumstances in which an unregistered company may be wound up are as follows –

(a) if the company is dissolved, or has ceased to carry on business, or is carrying on business only for the purpose of winding up its affairs;
(b) if the company is unable to pay its debts;
(c) if the court is of opinion that it is just and equitable that the company should be wound up.

**(6)** (Repealed by Trustee Savings Bank Act 1985, s. 4(3), 7(3) and Sch. 4 from 21 July 1986 (see SI 1986/1223 (C 36)).

**(7)** In the case of a limited partnership, the provisions of this Act about winding up apply with such modifications (if any) as may be provided by rules made by statutory instrument by the Lord Chancellor with the concurrence of the Secretary of State, and with the substitution of general partners for directors.

**(8)** In Scotland, an unregistered company which the Court of Session has jurisdiction to wind up may be wound up by the court if there is subsisting a floating charge over property comprised in the company's property and undertaking, and the court is satisfied that the security of the creditor entitled to the benefit of the floating charge is in jeopardy.

For this purpose a creditor's security is deemed to be in jeopardy if the court is satisfied that events have occurred or are about to occur which render it unreasonable in the creditor's interests that the company should retain power to dispose of the property which is subject to the floating charge.

**667 Inability to pay debts: unpaid creditor for £750 or more**

**667(1)** An unregistered company is deemed (for purposes of section 666) unable to pay its debts if there is a creditor, by assignment or otherwise, to whom the company is indebted in a sum exceeding £750 then due and –
(a) the creditor has served on the company, by leaving at its principal place of business, or by delivering to the secretary or some director, manager or principal officer of the company, or by otherwise serving in such manner as the court may approve or direct, a written demand requiring the company to pay the sum due, and
(b) the company has for 3 weeks after the service of the demand neglected to pay the sum or to secure or compound for it to the creditor's satisfaction.

**(2)** The Secretary of State may by regulations in a statutory instrument increase or reduce the money sum for the time being specified in subsection (1); but –
(a) such regulations shall not be made unless a draft of the statutory instrument containing them has been approved by resolution of each House of Parliament, and
(b) no increase in the sum so specified affects any case in which the winding-up petition was presented before the coming into force of the increase.

**668 Inability to pay debts: debt remaining unsatisfied after action brought**

**668** An unregistered company is deemed (for purposes of section 666) unable to pay its debts if an action or other proceeding has been instituted against any member for any debt or demand due, or claimed to be due, from the company, or from him in his character of member, and –
(a) notice in writing of the institution of the action or proceeding has been served on the company by leaving it at the company's principal place of business (or by delivering it to the secretary, or some director, manager or principal officer of the company, or by otherwise serving it in such manner as the court may approve or direct), and
(b) the company has not within 10 days after service of the notice paid, secured or compounded for the debt or demand, or procured the action or proceeding to be stayed or sisted, or indemnified the defendant or defender to his reasonable satisfaction against the action or proceeding, and against all costs, damages and expenses to be incurred by him because of it.

**669 Inability to pay debts: other cases**

**669** An unregistered company is deemed (for purposes of section 666) unable to pay its debts –
(a) if in England and Wales execution or other process issued on a judgment, decree or order obtained in any court in favour of a creditor against the company, or any member of it as such, or any person authorised to be sued as nominal defendant on behalf of the company, is returned unsatisfied;
(b) if in Scotland the inducia of a charge for payment on an extract decree,or an extract registered bond, or an extract registered protest, have expired without payment being made;
(c) if in Northern Ireland a certificate of unenforceability has been granted in respect of any judgment, decree or order obtained as mentioned in paragraph (a);
(d) if it is otherwise proved to the satisfaction of the court that the company is unable to pay its debts.

**670 Oversea company may be wound up, though dissolved**

**670** Where a company incorporated outside Great Britain which has been carrying on business in Great Britain ceases to carry on business in Great Britain, it may be wound up as an unregistered company under this Act, notwithstanding that it has been dissolved or otherwise ceased to exist as a company under or by virtue of the laws of the country under which it was incorporated.

**671 Contributories in winding up of unregistered company**

**671(1)** In the event of an unregistered company being wound up, every person is deemed a contributory who is liable to pay or contribute to the payment of any debt or liability of the company, or to pay or contribute to the payment of any sum for the adjustment of the rights of members among themselves, or to pay or contribute to the payment of the costs and expenses of winding up the company.

**(2)** Every contributory is liable to contribute to the company's assets all sums due from him in respect of any such liability as is mentioned above.

**(3)** In the case of an unregistered company engaged in or formed for working mines within the stannaries, a past member is not liable to contribute to the assets if he has ceased to be a member for 2 years or more either before the mine ceased to be worked or before the date of the winding up order.

**(4)** In the event of the death, bankruptcy or insolvency of any contributory, the provisions of this Act with respect to the personal representatives, to the heirs and legatees of heritage of the heritable estate in Scotland of deceased contributories, and to the trustees of bankrupt or insolvent contributories, respectively apply.

**672 Power of court to stay, sist or restrain proceedings**

**672** The provisions of this Part with respect to staying, sisting or restraining actions and proceedings against a company at any time after the presentation of a petition for winding up and before the making of a winding up order extend, in the case of an unregistered company, where the application to stay, sist or restrain is presented by a creditor, to actions and proceedings against any contributory of the company.

**673 Actions stayed on winding up order**

**673** Where an order has been made for winding up an unregistered company, no action or proceeding shall be proceeded with or commenced against any contributory of the company in respect of any debt of the company, except by leave of the court, and subject to such terms as the court may impose.

**674 Provisions of this Part to be cumulative**

**674(1)** The provisions of this Part with respect to unregistered companies are in addition to and not in restriction of any provisions in Part XX with respect to winding up companies by the court; and the court or liquidator may exercise any powers or do any act in the case of unregistered companies which might be exercised or done by it or him in winding up companies formed and registered under this Act.

**(2)** However, an unregistered company is not, except in the event of its being wound up, deemed to be a company under this Act, and then only to the extent provided by this Part."

# PART XXII – BODIES CORPORATE SUBJECT, OR BECOMING SUBJECT, TO THIS ACT (OTHERWISE THAN BY ORIGINAL FORMATION UNDER PART I)

## Chapter I – Companies Formed or Registered under Former Companies Acts

### 675 Companies formed and registered under former Companies Acts

**675(1) [Application to existing companies]** In its application to existing companies, this Act applies in the same manner –

(a) in the case of a limited company (other than a company limited by guarantee) as if the company had been formed and registered under Part I of this Act as a company limited by shares,

(b) in the case of a company limited by guarantee, as if the company had been formed and registered under that Part as a company limited by guarantee, and

(c) in the case of a company other than a limited company, as if the company had been formed and registered under that Part as an unlimited company.

**675(2) [Reference to date of registration]** But reference, express or implied, to the date of registration is to be read as the date at which the company was registered under the Joint Stock Companies Acts, the Companies Act 1862, the Companies (Consolidation) Act 1908, the Companies Act 1929, or the Companies Act 1948.

### 676 Companies registered but not formed under former Companies Acts

**676(1) [Application of this Act]** This Act applies to every company registered but not formed under the Joint Stock Companies Acts, the Companies Act 1862, the Companies (Consolidation) Act 1908, the Companies Act 1929, or the Companies Act 1948, in the same manner as it is in Chapter II of this Part declared to apply to companies registered but not formed under this Act.

**676(2) [Reference to date of registration]** But reference, express or implied, to the date of registration is to be read as referring to the date at which the company was registered under the Joint Stock Companies Acts, the Companies Act 1862, the Companies (Consolidation) Act 1908, the Companies Act 1929, or the Companies Act 1948.

### 677 Companies re-registered with altered status under former Companies Acts

**677(1) [Application of this Act]** This Act applies to every unlimited company registered or re-registered as limited in pursuance of the Companies Act 1879, section 57 of the Companies (Consolidation) Act 1908, section 16 of the Companies Act 1929, section 16 of the Companies

Act 1948 or section 44 of the Companies Act 1967 as it (this Act) applies to an unlimited company re-registered as limited in pursuance of Part II of this Act.

**677(2) [Reference to date of registration]** But reference, express or implied, to the date of registration or re-registration is to be read as referring to the date at which the company was registered or re-registered as a limited company under the relevant enactment.

## 678 Companies registered under Joint Stock Companies Acts

**678(1) [Transfer of shares]** A company registered under the Joint Stock Companies Acts may cause its shares to be transferred in manner hitherto in use, or in such other manner as the company may direct.

**678(2) [Power of altering articles under s. 9]** The power of altering articles under section 9 of this Act extends, in the case of an unlimited company formed and registered under the Joint Stock Companies Acts, to altering any regulations relating to the amount of capital or to its distribution into shares, notwithstanding that those regulations are contained in the memorandum.

## 679 Northern Ireland and Irish companies

**679** Nothing in sections 675 to 678 applies to companies registered in Northern Ireland or the Republic of Ireland.

# Chapter II – Companies not Formed under Companies Legislation, but Authorised to Register

## 680 Companies capable of being registered under this Chapter

**680(1) [Application in prescribed form]** With the exceptions and subject to the provisions contained in this section and the next –

(a) any company consisting of two or more members, which was in existence on 2nd November 1862, including any company registered under the Joint Stock Companies Acts, and

(b) any company formed after that date (whether before or after the commencement of this Act), in pursuance of any Act of Parliament (other than this Act), or of letters patent, or being otherwise duly constituted according to law, and consisting of two or more members,

may at any time, on making application in the prescribed form, register under this Act as an unlimited company, or as a company limited by shares, or as a company limited by guarantee; and the registration is not invalid by reason that it has taken place with a view to the company's being wound up.

**680(1A) [One member companies]** A company shall not be prevented from registering under this Act as a private company limited by shares or by guarantee solely because it has only one member.

**History**

S. 680(1A) inserted by the Companies (Single Member Private Limited Companies) Regulations 1992 (SI 1992/1699), reg. 2, Sch., para. 7 as from 15 July 1992.

**Note**

The Companies (Single Member Private Limited Companies) Regulations 1992 (SI 1992/1699) implement the Twelfth EC Company Law Directive (89/667).

**680(2) [Companies registered in UK]** A company registered in any part of the United Kingdom under the Companies Act 1862, the Companies (Consolidation) Act 1908, the Companies Act 1929 or the Companies Act 1948 shall not register under this section.

**680(3) [Limited companies]** A company having the liability of its members limited by Act of Parliament or letters patent, and not being a joint stock company, shall not register under this section.

**680(4) [Limited companies becoming unlimited or limited by guarantee]** A company having the liability of its members limited by Act of Parliament or letters patent shall not register in pursuance of this section as an unlimited company or as a company limited by guarantee.

**680(5) [Joint stock companies]** A company that is not a joint stock company shall not register under this section as a company limited by shares.

## 681 Procedural requirements for registration

**681(1) [Assent of general meeting]** A company shall not register under section 680 without the assent of a majority of such of its members as are present in person or by proxy (in cases where proxies are allowed) at a general meeting summoned for the purpose.

**681(2) [Company reregistering as limited]** Where a company not having the liability of its members limited by Act of Parliament or letters patent is about to register as a limited company, the majority required to assent as required by subsection (1) shall consist of not less than three-fourths of the members present in person or by proxy at the meeting.

**681(3) [Computation of majority]** In computing any majority under this section when a poll is demanded, regard is to be had to the number of votes to which each member is entitled according to the company's regulations.

**681(4) [Resolution to accompany assent]** Where a company is about to register (under section 680) as a company limited by guarantee, the assent to its being so registered shall be accompanied by a resolution declaring that each member undertakes to contribute to the company's assets, in the event of its being wound up while he is a member, or within one year after he ceases to be a member, for payment of the company's debts and liabilities contracted before he ceased to be a member, and of the costs and expenses of winding up and for the adjustment of the rights of the contributories among themselves, such amount as may be required, not exceeding a specified amount.

**681(5) [Documents to registrar]** Before a company is registered under section 680, it shall deliver to the registrar of companies –

(a) a statement that the registered office of the company is to be situated in England, or in Wales, or in Scotland (as the case may be),

(b) a statement specifying the intended situation of the company's registered office after registration, and

(c) in an appropriate case, if the company wishes to be registered with the Welsh equivalent of "public limited company" or, as the case may be, "limited" as the last words or word of its name, a statement to that effect.

**681(6) [S. 681(5) statements]** Any statement delivered to the registrar under subsection (5) shall be made in the prescribed form.

## 682 Change of name on registration

**682(1) [If existing name precluded etc.]** Where the name of a company seeking registration under section 680 is a name by which it is precluded from registration by section 26 of this Act, either because it falls within subsection (1) of that section or, if it falls within subsection (2), because the Secretary of State would not approve the company's being registered with that name, the company may change its name with effect from the date on which it is registered under this Chapter.

**682(2) [Assent as in s. 681]** A change of name under this section requires the like assent of the company's members as is required by section 681 for registration.

## 683 Definition of "joint stock company"

**683(1) ["Joint stock company"]** For purposes of this Chapter, as far as relates to registration of companies as companies limited by shares, **"joint stock company"** means a company –

(a) having a permanent paid-up or nominal share capital of fixed amount divided into shares, also of fixed amount, or held and transferable as stock, or divided and held partly in one way and partly in the other, and

(b) formed on the principle of having for its members the holders of those shares or that stock, and no other persons.

**683(2) [Deemed company limited by shares]** Such a company when registered with limited liability under this Act is deemed a company limited by shares.

## 684 Requirements for registration by joint stock companies

**684(1) [Documents to registrar]** Before the registration under section 680 of a joint stock company, there shall be delivered to the registrar of companies the following documents –

(a) a statement in the prescribed form specifying the name with which the company is proposed to be registered,

(b) a list in the prescribed form showing the names and addresses of all persons who on a day named in the list (not more than 28 clear days before the day of registration) were members of the company, with the addition of the shares or stock held by them respectively (distinguishing, in cases where the shares are numbered, each share by its number), and

(c) a copy of any Act of Parliament, royal charter, letters patent, deed of settlement, contract of copartnery or other instrument constituting or regulating the company.

**History**

In s. 684(1)(b) the words "(not more than 28 clear days before the day of registration)" substituted for the former words "(not more than 6 clear days before the day of registration)" by CA 1989, s. 145 and Sch. 19, para. 12 as from 1 March 1990 (see SI 1990/142 (C 5), art. 5).

**684(2) [Statements to be registered as limited]** If the company is intended to be registered as a limited company, there shall also be delivered to the registrar of companies a statement in the prescribed form specifying the following particulars –

(a) the nominal share capital of the company and the number of shares into which it is divided, or the amount of stock of which it consists, and

(b) the number of shares taken and the amount paid on each share.

## 685 Registration of joint stock company as public company

**685(1) [Application for registration]** A joint stock company applying to be registered under section 680 as a company limited by shares may, subject to –

(a) satisfying the conditions set out in section 44(2)(a) and (b) (where applicable) and section 45(2) to (4) as applied by this section, and

(b) complying with subsection (4) below,

apply to be so registered as a public company.

**685(2) [Application of s. 44, 45]** Sections 44 and 45 apply for this purpose as in the case of a private company applying to be re-registered under section 43, but as if a reference to the special resolution required by section 43 were to the joint stock company's resolution that it be a public company.

**685(3) [Change of name]** The resolution may change the company's name by deleting the word "company" or the words "and company", or its or their equivalent in Welsh ("cwmni", "a'r cwmni"), including any abbreviation of them.

**685(4) [Documents to registrar]** The joint stock company's application shall be made in the form prescribed for the purpose, and shall be delivered to the registrar of companies together with the following documents (as well as those required by section 684), namely –

(a) a copy of the resolution that the company be a public company,

(b) a copy of a written statement by an accountant with the appropriate qualifications that in his opinion a relevant balance sheet shows that at the balance sheet date the amount of the company's net assets was not less than the aggregate of its called up share capital and undistributable reserves,

(c) a copy of the relevant balance sheet, together with a copy of an unqualified report (by an accountant with such qualifications) in relation to that balance sheet,

(d) a copy of any valuation report prepared under section 44(2)(b) as applied by this section, and

(e) a statutory declaration in the prescribed form by a director or secretary of the company–
   (i) that the conditions set out in section 44(2)(a) and (b) (where applicable) and section 45(2) to (4) have been satisfied, and
   (ii) that, between the balance sheet date referred to in paragraph (b) of this subsection and the joint stock company's application, there has been no change in the company's financial position that has resulted in the amount of its net assets becoming less than the aggregate of its called up share capital and undistributable reserves.

**685(5)** **[Section 685(4)(e) declaration sufficient evidence]** The registrar may accept a declaration under subsection (4)(e) as sufficient evidence that the conditions referred to in that paragraph have been satisfied.

**685(6)** **[Definitions]** In this section –

**"accountant with the appropriate qualifications"** means a person who would be eligible for appointment as the company's auditor, if it were a company registered under this Act,

**"relevant balance sheet"** means a balance sheet prepared as at a date not more than 7 months before the joint stock company's application to be registered as a public company limited by shares, and

**"undistributable reserves"** has the meaning given by section 264(3);

and section 46 applies (with necessary modifications) for the interpretation of the reference in subsection (4)(c) above to an unqualified report by the accountant.

**History**
In s. 685(6), in the definition of "accountant with appropriate qualifications" the words "a person who would be eligible" substituted for the former words "a person who would be qualified under section 389(1)" by the Companies Act 1989 (Eligibility for Appointment as Company Auditor) (Consequential Amendments) Regulations 1991 (SI 1991/1997), reg. 2 and Sch., para. 53(1), (2) as from 1 October 1991.

## 686 Other requirements for registration

**686(1)** **[Documents to registrar]** Before the registration in pursuance of this Chapter of any company (not being a joint stock company), there shall be delivered to the registrar of companies –

(a) a statement in the prescribed form specifying the name with which the company is proposed to be registered,

(b) a list showing with respect to each director or manager of the company–
   (i) in the case of an individual, his name, address, occupation and date of birth,
   (ii) in the case of a corporation or Scottish firm, its corporate or firm name and registered or principal office,

(c) a copy of any Act of Parliament, letters patent, deed of settlement, contract of copartnery or other instrument constituting or regulating the company, and

(d) in the case of a company intended to be registered as a company limited by guarantee, a copy of the resolution declaring the amount of the guarantee.

**History**
S. 686(1)(b) substituted by CA 1989, s. 145 and Sch. 19, para. 5(1), (2) as from 1 October 1990 (see SI 1990/1707 (C 46), art. 2(b)); s. 686(1)(b) formerly read as follows:

"(b) a list showing the names, addresses and occupations of the directors or other managers (if any) of the company,"

**686(1A)** **["Name" in s. 686(1)(b)]** For the purposes of subsection (1)(b)(i) a person's **"name"** means his Christian name (or other forename) and surname, except that in the case of a peer, or an individual usually known by a title, the title may be stated instead of his Christian name (or other forename) and surname or in addition to either or both of them.

**History**
S. 686(1A) inserted by CA 1989, s. 145 and Sch. 19, para. 5(1), (3) as from 1 October 1990 (see SI 1990/1707 (C 46), art. 2(b)).

**686(2)** **[Verification by statutory declaration]** The lists of members and directors and any other particulars relating to the company which are required by this Chapter to be delivered to the registrar shall be verified by a statutory declaration in the prescribed form made by any two or more directors or other principal officers of the company.

**686(3) [Evidence re whether joint stock company]** The registrar may require such evidence as he thinks necessary for the purpose of satisfying himself whether a company proposing to be registered is or is not a joint stock company as defined by section 683).

# 687 Name of company registering

**687(1) [Applications]** The following applies with respect to the name of a company registering under this Chapter (whether a joint stock company or not).

**687(2) [Public company]** If the company is to be registered as a public company, its name must end with the words "public limited company" or, if it is stated that the company's registered office is to be situated in Wales, with those words or their equivalent in Welsh ("cwmni cyfyngedig cyhoeddus"); and those words or that equivalent may not be preceded by the word "limited" or its equivalent in Welsh ("cyfyngedig").

**687(3) [Company limited by shares or guarantee]** In the case of a company limited by shares or by guarantee (not being a public company), the name must have "limited" as its last word (or, if the company's registered office is to be situated in Wales, "cyfyngedig"); but this is subject to section 30 (exempting a company, in certain circumstances, from having "limited" as part of the name).

**687(4) [Addition to name of company with limited liability]** If the company is registered with limited liability, then any additions to the company's name set out in the statements delivered under section 684(1)(a) or 686(1)(a) shall form and be registered as the last part of the company's name.

# 688 Certificate of registration under this Chapter

**688(1) [Issue of certificate]** On compliance with the requirements of this Chapter with respect to registration, the registrar of companies shall give a certificate (which may be signed by him, or authenticated by his official seal) that the company applying for registration is incorporated as a company under this Act and, in the case of a limited company, that it is limited.

**688(2) [Effect of issue]** On the issue of the certificate, the company shall be so incorporated; and a banking company in Scotland so incorporated is deemed a bank incorporated, constituted or established by or under Act of Parliament.

**688(3) [Certificate conclusive evidence]** The certificate is conclusive evidence that the requirements of this Chapter in respect of registration, and of matters precedent and incidental to it, have been complied with.

**688(4) [Joint stock company registered as public limited company]** Where on an application by a joint stock company to register as a public company limited by shares the registrar of companies is satisfied that the company may be registered as a public company so limited, the certificate of incorporation given under this section shall state that the company is a public company; and that statement is conclusive evidence that the requirement of section 685 have been complied with and that the company is a public company so limited.

# 689 Effect of registration

**689** Schedule 21 to this Act has effect with respect to the consequences of registration under this Chapter, the vesting of property, savings for existing liabilities, continuation of existing actions, status of the company following registration, and other connected matters.

# 690 Power to substitute memorandum and articles for deed of settlement

**690(1) [Alteration of constitution by special resolution]** Subject as follows, a company registered in pursuance of this Chapter may by special resolution alter the form of its constitution by substituting a memorandum and articles for a deed of settlement.

**690(2) [Application of s. 4–6]** The provisions of sections 4 to 6 of this Act with respect to applications to the court for cancellation of alterations of the objects of a company and matters consequential on the passing of resolutions for such alterations (so far as applicable) apply, but with the following modifications–

(a) there is substituted for the printed copy of the altered memorandum required to be delivered to the registrar of companies a printed copy of the substituted memorandum and articles, and

(b) on the delivery to the registrar of the substituted memorandum and articles or the date when the alteration is no longer liable to be cancelled by order of the court (whichever is the later) –
  (i) the substituted memorandum and articles apply to the company in the same manner as if it were a company registered under Part I with that memorandum and those articles, and
  (ii) the company's deed of settlement ceases to apply to the company.

**690(3) [Alteration of objects]** An alteration under this section may be made either with or without alteration of the company's objects.

**690(4) ["Deed of settlement"]** In this section **"deed of settlement"** includes any contract of copartnery or other instrument constituting or regulating the company, not being an Act of Parliament, a royal charter or letters patent.

# PART XXIII – OVERSEA COMPANIES

**Note**

Pt. XXIII has been amended by the Oversea Companies and Credit and Financial Institutions (Branch Disclosure) Regulations 1992 (SI 1992/3179) – which implement the Eleventh EC Company Law Directive (89/666) and the Bank Branches Directive (89/117). See also s. 262 and Sch. 7.

## Chapter I – Registration, etc.

### 690A Branch registration under the Eleventh Company Law Directive (89/666/EEC)

**690A(1) [Application]** This section applies to any limited company which–

(a) is incorporated outside the United Kingdom and Gibraltar, and

(b) has a branch in Great Britain.

**690A(2) [Schedule 21A]** Schedule 21A to this Act (Branch registration under the Eleventh Company Law Directive (89/666/EEC)) shall have effect in relation to any company to which this section applies.

**History**

See history note after s. 690B.

### 690B Scope of sections 691 and 692

**690B** Sections 691 and 692 shall not apply to any limited company which–

(a) is incorporated outside the United Kingdom and Gibraltar, and

(b) has a branch in the United Kingdom.

**History**

S. 690A, 690B inserted by the Oversea Companies and Credit and Financial Institutions (Branch Disclosure) Regulations 1992 (SI 1992/3179) reg. 1(3), 3(1) and Sch. 2, para. 2 as from 1 January 1993.

**Note**

See also note after s. 692.

### 691 Documents to be delivered to registrar

**691(1) [Documents to registrar]** When a company incorporated outside Great Britain establishes a place of business in Great Britain, it shall within one month of doing so deliver to the registrar of companies for registration –

(a) a certified copy of the charter, statutes or memorandum and articles of the company or other instrument constituting or defining the company's constitution, and, if the instrument is not written in the English language, a certified translation of it; and

(b) a return in the prescribed form containing –

(i) a list of the company's directors and secretary, containing the particulars specified in the next subsection,

(ii) a list of the names and addresses of some one or more persons resident in Great Britain authorised to accept on the company's behalf service of process and any notices required to be served on it,

(iii) a list of the documents delivered in compliance with paragraph (a) of this subsection, and

(iv) a statutory declaration (made by a director or secretary of the company or by any person whose name and address are given in the list required by sub-paragraph (ii)), stating the date on which the company's place of business in Great Britain was established.

**Note**
Re s. 691(1)(b) see the Companies (Forms Amendment No. 2 and Company's Type and Principal Business Activities) Regulations 1990 (SI 1990/1766) and the Companies (Forms) (Amendment) Regulations 1992 (SI 1992/3006).

**691(2) [Particulars re directors in list in s. 691(1)(b)(i)]** The list referred to in subsection (1)(b)(i) shall contain the following particulars with respect to each director–

(a) in the case of an individual–

(i) his name,

(ii) any former name,

(iii) his usual residential address,

(iv) his nationality,

(v) his business occupation (if any),

(vi) if he has no business occupation but holds other directorships, particulars of them, and

(vii) his date of birth;

(b) in the case of a corporation or Scottish firm, its corporate or firm name and registered or principal office.

**History**
See history note after s. 691(4).

**691(3) [Particulars re secretary in list]** The list referred to in subsection (1)(b)(i) shall contain the following particulars with respect to the secretary (or, where there are joint secretaries, with respect to each of them)–

(a) in the case of an individual, his name, any former name and his usual residential address;

(b) in the case of a corporation or Scottish firm, its corporate or firm name and registered or principal office.

Where all the partners in a firm are joint secretaries of the company, the name and principal office of the firm may be stated instead of the particulars required by paragraph (a).

**History**
See history note after s. 691(4).

**691(4) ["Name", former name in s. 691(2)(a), (3)(a)]** In subsections (2)(a) and (3)(a) above–

(a) **"name"** means a person's Christian name (or other forename) and surname, except that in the case of a peer, or an individual usually known by a title, the title may be stated instead of his Christian name (or other forename) and surname, or in addition to either or both of them; and

(b) the reference to a former name does not include–

(i) in the case of a peer, or an individual normally known by a British title, the name by which he was known previous to the adoption of or succession to the title, or

(ii) in the case of any person, a former name which was changed or disused before he attained the age of 18 years or which has been changed or disused for 20 years or more, or

(iii) in the case of a married woman, the name by which she was known previous to the marriage.

**History**

S. 691(2)–(4) substituted for the former s. 691(2) by CA 1989, s. 145 and Sch. 19, para. 6 as from 1 October 1990 subject to transitional and saving provisions (see SI 1990/1707 (C 46), art. 2(b) and also art. 6); former s. 691(2) read as follows:

"The list referred to in subsection (1)(b)(i) shall contain the following particulars –

(a) with respect to each director–

(i) in the case of an individual, his present Christian name and surname and any former Christian name or surname, his usual residential address, his nationality and his business occupation (if any), or, if he has no business occupation but holds other directorships, particulars of any of them,

(ii) in the case of a corporation, its corporate name and registered or principal office;

(b) with respect to the secretary (or, where there are joint secretaries, with respect to each of them)–

(i) in the case of an individual, his present Christian name and surname, any former Christian name and surname and his usual residential address,

(ii) in the case of a corporation or a Scottish firm, its corporate or firm name and registered or principal office.

Where all the partners in a firm are joint secretaries of the company, the name and principal office of the firm may be stated instead of the particulars mentioned in paragraph (b).

Section 289(2) applies for the purposes of the construction of references above to present and former Christian names and surnames."

**Note**

See note after s. 692.

# 692 Registration of altered particulars

**692(1) [Return re alterations]** If any alteration is made in –

(a) the charter, statutes, or memorandum and articles of an oversea company or any such instrument as is mentioned above, or

(b) the directors or secretary of an oversea company or the particulars contained in the list of the directors and secretary, or

(c) the names or addresses of the persons authorised to accept service on behalf of an oversea company,

the company shall, within the time specified below, deliver to the registrar of companies for registration a return containing the prescribed particulars of the alteration.

**Note**

Re s. 692(1)(b) see the Companies (Forms Amendment No. 2 and Company's Type and Principal Business Activities) Regulations 1990 (SI 1990/1766).

**692(2) [Return re change of name]** If any change is made in the corporate name of an oversea company, the company shall, within the time specified below, deliver to the registrar of companies for registration a return containing the prescribed particulars of the change.

**692(3) [Time for delivery of returns]** The time for delivery of the returns required by subsections (1) and (2) is –

(a) in the case of an alteration to which subsection (1)(c) applies, 21 days after the making of the alteration, and

(b) otherwise, 21 days after the date on which notice of the alteration or change in question could have been received in Great Britain in due course of post (if despatched with due diligence).

**Note**

Re s. 691, 692 see the Oversea Companies and Credit and Financial Institutions (Branch Disclosure) Regulations 1992 (SI 1992/3179), reg. 1(3), 5 and Sch. 4 for transitional provisions re continued operation until s. 690B relevant.

# 692A Change in registration regime

**692A(1) [Where s. 690A ceases to apply]** Where a company ceases to be a company to which section 690A applies and, immediately after ceasing to be such a company–

(a) continues to have in Great Britain a place of business which it had immediately before ceasing to be such a company, and

(b) does not have a branch in Northern Ireland,

it shall be treated for the purposes of section 691 as having established the place of business on the date when it ceased to be a company to which section 690A applies.

**692A(2) [Where company ceases to have NI branch]** Where a limited company incorporated outside the United Kingdom and Gibraltar–

(a) ceases to have a branch in Northern Ireland, and

(b) both immediately before and immediately after ceasing to do so, has a place of business, but not a branch, in Great Britain,

it shall be treated for the purposes of section 691 as having established the place of business on the date when it ceased to have a branch in Northern Ireland.

**692A(3) [Where s. 690A applies]** Where a company–

(a) becomes a company to which section 690A applies,

(b) immediately after becoming such a company, has in a part of Great Britain an established place of business but no branch, and

(c) immediately before becoming such a company, had an established place of business in that part,

sections 691 and 692 shall, in relation to that part, continue to apply to the company (notwithstanding section 690B) until such time as it gives notice to the registrar for that part that it is a company to which that section applies.

**692A(4) [Sch. 21B]** Schedule 21B to this Act (transitional provisions in relation to change in registration regime) shall have effect.

**History**

S. 692A inserted by the Oversea Companies and Credit and Financial Institutions (Branch Disclosure) Regulations 1992 (SI 1992/3179), reg. 1(3), 3(1) and Sch. 2, para. 4 as from 1 January 1993.

## 693 Obligation to state name and other particulars

**693(1) [Disclosure by oversea company]** Every oversea company shall –

(a) in every prospectus inviting subscriptions for its shares or debentures in Great Britain, state the country in which the company is incorporated,

(b) conspicuously exhibit on every place where it carries on business in Great Britain the company's name and the country in which it is incorporated,

(c) cause the company's name and the country in which it is incorporated to be stated in legible characters in all bill-heads and letter paper, and in all notices and other official publications of the company, and

(d) if the liability of the members of the company is limited, cause notice of that fact to be stated in legible characters in every such prospectus as above mentioned and in all bill-heads, letter paper, notices and other official publications of the company in Great Britain, and to be affixed on every place where it carries on its business.

**History**

S. 693 renumbered s. 693(1) and s. 693(2)–(4) inserted by the Oversea Companies and Credit and Financial Institutions (Branch Disclosure) Regulations 1992 (SI 1992/3179), reg. 1(3), 3(1) and Sch. 2, para. 6 as from 1 January 1993.

In s. 693(1), formerly s. 693, para. (a) and in para. (d) the words "in every such prospectus as above mentioned" repealed by Financial Services Act 1986, s. 212(3) and Sch. 17, Pt. I to the extent to which they would apply re any investment listed as the subject of a listing application under Financial Services Act 1986, Pt. IV and commencing:

- on 12 January 1987 for all purposes relating to the admission of securities offered by or on behalf of a Minister of the Crown or a body corporate controlled by a Minister of the Crown or a subsidiary of such a body corporate to the Official List in respect of which an application is made after that date;
- on 16 February 1987 for the purposes relating to the admission of securities in respect of which an application is made after that date other than those referred to in the preceding paragraph and otherwise for all purposes.

(See SI 1986/2246 (C 88).)

Para. (a) and the above words in para. (d) also repealed by Financial Services Act 1986, s. 212(3) and Sch. 17, Pt. I as from 29 April 1988 as far as they would apply to a prospectus offering for subscription, or to any form of application for units in a body corporate which is a recognised scheme; and as from 1 July 1988 as far as they would apply to a prospectus offering for subscription, or to any application form for, units in a body corporate which is an open-ended investment company (see SI 1988/740 (C 22)).

**693(2) [General obligation re s. 690A company]** Every company to which section 690A applies shall, in the case of each branch of the company registered under paragraph 1 of Schedule 21A, cause the following particulars to be stated in legible characters in all letter paper and order forms used in carrying on the business of the branch–

(a) the place of registration of the branch, and

(b) the registered number of the branch.

**History**
S. 693 renumbered s. 693(1) and s. 693(2)–(4) inserted by the Oversea Companies and Credit and Financial Institutions (Branch Disclosure) Regulations 1992 (SI 1992/3179), reg. 1(3), 3(1) and Sch. 2, para. 6 as from 1 January 1993.

**693(3) [Non-member state company with home registration]** Every company to which section 690A applies, which is not incorporated in a Member State and which is required by the law of the country in which it is incorporated to be registered shall, in the case of each branch of the company registered under paragraph 1 of Schedule 21A, cause the following particulars to be stated in legible characters in all letter paper and order forms used in carrying on the business of the branch–

(a) the identity of the registry in which the company is registered in its country of incorporation, and
(b) the number with which it is registered.

**History**
S. 693 renumbered s. 693(1) and s. 693(2)–(4) inserted by the Oversea Companies and Credit and Financial Institutions (Branch Disclosure) Regulations 1992 (SI 1992/3179), reg. 1(3), 3(1) and Sch. 2, para. 6 as from 1 January 1993.

**693(4) [Non-member state company]** Every company to which section 690A applies and which is not incorporated in a Member State shall, in the case of each branch of the company registered under paragraph 1 of Schedule 21A, cause the following particulars to be stated in legible characters in all letter paper and order forms used in carrying on the business of the branch–

(a) the legal form of the company,
(b) the location of its head office, and
(c) if applicable, the fact that it is being wound up.

**History**
S. 693 renumbered s. 693(1) and s. 693(2)–(4) inserted by the Oversea Companies and Credit and Financial Institutions (Branch Disclosure) Regulations 1992 (SI 1992/3179), reg. 1(3), 3(1) and Sch. 2, para. 6 as from 1 January 1993.

## 694 Regulation of oversea companies in respect of their names

**694(1) [Notice re non-registration of name]** If it appears to the Secretary of State that the corporate name of an oversea company is a name by which the company, had it been formed under this Act, would on the relevant date (determined in accordance with subsections (3A) and (3B)) have been precluded from being registered by section 26 either–

(a) because it falls within subsection (1) of that section, or
(b) if it falls within subsection (2) of that section, because the Secretary of State would not approve the company's being registered with that name,

the Secretary of State may serve a notice on the company, stating why the name would not have been registered.

**History**
In s. 694(1) the words "(determined in accordance with subsections (3A) and (3B))" substituted for the former words "(defined below in subsection (3))" by the Oversea Companies and Credit and Financial Institutions (Branch Disclosure) Regulations 1992 (SI 1992/3179), reg. 3(1) and Sch. 2, para. 7(1), (2) as from 1 January 1993.

**694(2) [Name too similar]** If the corporate name of an oversea company is in the Secretary of State's opinion too like a name appearing on the relevant date in the index of names kept by the registrar of companies under section 714 or which should have appeared in that index on that date, or is the same as a name which should have so appeared, the Secretary of State may serve a notice on the company specifying the name in the index which the company's name is too like or which is the same as the company's name.

**694(3) [Time for notice under s. 694(1), (2)]** No notice shall be served on a company under subsection (1) or (2) later than 12 months after the relevant date.

**History**
In s. 694(3) the following words formerly appearing at the end repealed by the Oversea Companies and Credit and Financial Institutions (Branch Disclosure) Regulations 1992 (SI 1992/3179), reg. 3(1) and Sch. 2, para. 7(1), (3) as from 1 January 1993:

"being the date on which the company has complied with –
(a) section 691 in this Part, or
(b) if there has been a change in the company's corporate name, section 692(2)."

**694(3A) [Relevant date]** For the purposes of subsections (1) to (3), the relevant date, in relation to a company, is the date on which it has complied with paragraph 1 of Schedule 21A or section

691(1) or, if there is more than one date, the first date on which it has complied with that paragraph or that subsection since becoming an oversea company.

**History**

See history note after s. 694(3B).

**694(3B) [Relevant date following change of name]** But where the company's corporate name has changed since the date ascertained in accordance with subsection (3A), the relevant date is the date on which the company has, in respect of the change or, if more than one, the latest change, complied with paragraph 7(1) of Schedule 21A or section 692(2), as the case may be.

**History**

S. 694(3A), (3B) inserted by the Oversea Companies and Credit and Financial Institutions (Branch Disclosure) Regulations 1992 (SI 1992/3179), reg. 1(3), 3(1) and Sch. 2, para. 7(1), (4) as from 1 January 1993.

**694(4) [Statement by oversea company re alternative name]** An oversea company on which a notice is served under subsection (1) or (2) –

(a) may deliver to the registrar of companies for registration a statement in the prescribed form specifying a name approved by the Secretary of State other than its corporate name under which it proposes to carry on business in Great Britain, and

(b) may, after that name has been registered, at any time deliver to the registrar for registration a statement in the prescribed form specifying a name approved by the Secretary of State (other than its corporate name) in substitution for the name previously registered.

**Note**

See the Companies (Forms) (Amendment) Regulations 1992 (SI 1992/3006).

**694(5) [Name under s. 694(4)]** The name by which an oversea company is for the time being registered under subsection (4) is, for all purposes of the law applying in Great Britain (including this Act and the Business Names Act 1985), deemed to be the company's corporate name; but–

(a) this does not affect references to the corporate name in this section, or any rights or obligations of the company, or render defective any legal proceedings by or against the company, and

(b) any legal proceedings that might have been continued or commenced against the company by its corporate name or its name previously registered under this section may be continued or commenced against it by its name for the time being so registered.

**694(6) [Prohibition of carrying on business]** An oversea company on which a notice is served under subsection (1) or (2) shall not at any time after the expiration of 2 months from the service of that notice (or such longer period as may be specified in that notice) carry on business in Great Britain under its corporate name.

Nothing in this subsection, or in section 697(2) (which imposes penalties for its contravention) invalidates any transaction entered into by the company.

**694(7) [Withdrawal of s. 694(1), (2) notice]** The Secretary of State may withdraw a notice served under subsection (1) or (2) at any time before the end of the period mentioned in subsection (6); and that subsection does not apply to a company served with a notice which has been withdrawn.

## 694A Service of documents: companies to which section 690A applies

**694A(1) [Application]** This section applies to any company to which section 690A applies.

**694A(2) [Sufficient service]** Any process or notice required to be served on a company to which this section applies in respect of the carrying on of the business of a branch registered by it under paragraph 1 of Schedule 21A is sufficiently served if–

(a) addressed to any person whose name has, in respect of the branch, been delivered to the registrar as a person falling within paragraph 3(e) of that Schedule, and

(b) left at or sent by post to the address for that person which has been so delivered.

**694A(3) [Service on place of business]** Where–

(a) a company to which this section applies makes default, in respect of a branch, in delivering to the registrar the particulars mentioned in paragraph 3(e) of Schedule 21A, or

(b) all the persons whose names have, in respect of a branch, been delivered to the registrar as persons falling within paragraph 3(e) of that Schedule are dead or have ceased to reside in Great Britain, or refuse to accept service on the company's behalf or for any reason cannot be served,

a document may be served on the company in respect of the carrying on of the business of the branch by leaving it at, or sending it by post to, any place of business established by the company in Great Britain.

**694A(4) [Where more than one branch]** Where a company to which this section applies has more than one branch in Great Britain, any notice or process required to be served on the company which is not required to be served in respect of the carrying on of the business of one branch rather than another shall be treated for the purposes of this section as required to be served in respect of carrying on the business of each of its branches.

**History**

S. 694A inserted by the Oversea Companies and Credit and Financial Institutions (Branch Disclosure) Regulations 1992 (SI 1992/3179), reg. 1(3), 3(1) and Sch. 2, para. 8 as from 1 January 1993.

## 695 Service of documents on oversea company

**695(1) [Usual service]** Any process or notice required to be served on an oversea company to which section 691 applies is sufficiently served if addressed to any person whose name has been delivered to the registrar under preceding sections in this Part and left at or sent by post to the address which has been so delivered.

**History**

In s. 695(1) the words "to which section 691 applies" inserted by the Oversea Companies and Credit and Financial Institutions (Branch Disclosure) Regulations 1992 (SI 1992/3179), reg. 1(3), 3(1) and Sch. 2, para. 9 as from 1 January 1993.

**695(2) [Other service]** However –

(a) where such a company makes default in delivering to the registrar the name and address of a person resident in Great Britain who is authorised to accept on behalf of the company service of process or notices, or

(b) if at any time all the persons whose names and addresses have been so delivered are dead or have ceased so to reside, or refuse to accept service on the company's behalf, or for any reason cannot be served,

a document may be served on the company by leaving it at, or sending it by post to, any place of business established by the company in Great Britain.

## 695A Registrar to whom documents to be delivered: companies to which section 690A applies

**695A(1) [Interpretation]** References to the registrar, in relation to a company to which section 690A applies, (except references in Schedule 21C) shall be construed in accordance with the following provisions.

**695A(2) [Delivery of documents to registrar]** The documents which a company is required to deliver to the registrar shall be delivered–

(a) to the registrar for England and Wales, if required to be delivered in respect of a branch in England and Wales, and

(b) to the registrar for Scotland, if required to be delivered in respect of a branch in Scotland.

**695A(3) [Notice of closure of branch]** If a company closes a branch in a part of Great Britain, it shall forthwith give notice of that fact to the registrar for that part; and from the date on which notice is so given it is no longer obliged to deliver documents to that registrar in respect of that branch.

**695A(4) [Transfer of branch]** In subsection (3) above, the reference to closing a branch in either part of Great Britain includes a reference to a branch ceasing to be situated in that part on becoming situated elsewhere.

**History**

S. 695A inserted by the Oversea Companies and Credit and Financial Institutions (Branch Disclosure) Regulations 1992 (SI 1992/3179), reg. 3(1) and Sch. 2, para. 10 as from 1 January 1993.

## 696 Office where documents to be filed

**696(1) [Delivery to registrar]** Any document which an oversea company to which section 691 applies is required to deliver to the registrar of companies shall be delivered to the registrar at the registration office in England and Wales or Scotland, according to where the company has established a place of business.

**History**

In s. 696(1) the words "to which section 691 applies" inserted by the Oversea Companies and Credit and Financial Institutions (Branch Disclosure) Regulations 1992 (SI 1992/3179), reg. 3(1) and Sch. 2 para. 11(a) as from 1 January 1993.

**696(2) [If places of business in England and Wales and in Scotland]** If the company has established a place of business both in England and Wales and in Scotland, the document shall be delivered at the registration office both in England and Wales and in Scotland.

**696(3) [Interpretation]** References in this Part (except references in Schedule 21C) to the registrar of companies, in relation to a company to which section 691 applies, are to be construed in accordance with the above subsections.

**History**

In s. 696(3) the words ", in relation to a company to which section 691 applies," and the words "(except references in Schedule 21C)" inserted by the Oversea Companies and Credit and Financial Institutions (Branch Disclosure) Regulations 1992 (SI 1992/3179), reg. 3(1) and Sch. 2, para. 11(b) and reg. 1(3), 4 and Sch. 3, para. 4 respectively as from 1 January 1993.

**696(4) [Notice re cessation of place of business in Great Britain]** If an oversea company to which section 691 applies ceases to have a place of business in either part of Great Britain, it shall forthwith give notice of that fact to the registrar of companies for that part; and as from the date on which notice is so given the obligation of the company to deliver any document to the registrar ceases.

**History**

In s. 696(4) the words "to which section 691 applies" inserted by the Oversea Companies and Credit and Financial Institutions (Branch Disclosure) Regulations 1992 (SI 1992/3179), reg. 3(1) and Sch. 2, para. 11(c) as from 1 January 1993.

## 697 Penalties for non-compliance

**697(1) [Non-compliance with s. 691–693, 696]** If an oversea company fails to comply with any of sections 691 to 693 and 696, the company, and every officer or agent of the company who knowingly and wilfully authorises or permits the default, is liable to a fine and, in the case of a continuing offence, to a daily default fine for continued contravention.

**697(2) [Contravention of s. 694(6)]** If an oversea company contravenes section 694(6), the company and every officer or agent of it who knowingly and wilfully authorises or permits the contravention is guilty of an offence and liable to a fine and, for continued contravention, to a daily default fine.

**697(3) [Non-compliance with s. 695A or Sch. 21A]** If an oversea company fails to comply with section 695A or Schedule 21A, the company, and every officer or agent of the company who knowingly and wilfully authorises or permits the default, is liable to a fine and, in the case of a continuing offence, to a daily default fine for continued contravention.

**History**

S. 697(3) inserted by the Oversea Companies and Credit and Financial Institutions (Branch Disclosure) Regulations1992 (SI 1992/3179), reg. 1(3), 3(1) and Sch. 2, para. 12 as from 1 January 1993.

## 698 Definitions for this Chapter

**698(1) [Definitions]** For purposes of this Chapter –

**"certified"** means certified in the prescribed manner to be a true copy or a correct translation;

**"director"**, in relation to an oversea company, includes shadow director; and

**"secretary"** includes any person occupying the position of secretary by whatever name called.

**History**

See history note after s. 698(2).

**698(2) [Interpretation]** For the purposes of this Part (except section 699A and Schedule 21C):

(a) where a branch comprises places of business in more than one part of the United Kingdom, the branch shall be treated as being situated in that part of the United Kingdom where its principal place of business is situated; and

(b) **"branch"** means a branch within the meaning of the Council Directive concerning disclosure requirements in respect of branches opened in a Member State by certain types of company governed by the law of another State (the Eleventh Company Law Directive, 89/666/EEC).

**History**
S. 698 renumbered s. 698(1) and s. 698(2) inserted by the Oversea Companies and Credit and Financial Institutions (Branch Disclosure) Regulations 1992 (SI 1992/3179), reg. 1(3), 3(1) and Sch. 2, para. 13 as from 1 January 1993.

## 699 Channel Islands and Isle of Man companies

**699(1) [Application of other provisions]** With the exceptions specified in subsection (3) below, the provisions of this Act requiring documents to be forwarded or delivered to or filed with the registrar of companies and applying to companies formed and registered under Part I apply also (if they would not otherwise) to an oversea company to which section 691 applies incorporated in the Channel Islands or the Isle of Man.

**History**
In s. 699(1) the words "to which section 691 applies" inserted by the Oversea Companies and Credit and Financial Institutions (Branch Disclosure) Regulations 1992 (SI 1992/3179), reg. 1(3), 3(1) and Sch. 2, para. 14 as from 1 January 1993.

**699(2) [Where such provisions apply]** Those provisions apply to such a company –

(a) if it has established a place of business in England and Wales, as if it were registered in England and Wales,

(b) if it has established a place of business in Scotland, as if it were registered in Scotland, and

(c) if it has established a place of business both in England and Wales and in Scotland, as if it were registered in both England and Wales and Scotland,

with such modifications as may be necessary and, in particular, apply in a similar way to documents relating to things done outside Great Britain as if they had been done in Great Britain.

**699(3) [Exceptions]** The exceptions are –

section 6(1) (resolution altering company's objects),
section 18 (alteration of memorandum or articles by statute or statutory instrument),
section 242(1) (directors' duty to file accounts),
section 288(2) (notice to registrar of change of directors or secretary), and
section 380 (copies of certain resolutions and agreements to be sent to registrar within 15 days), so far as applicable to a resolution altering a company's memorandum or articles.

**History**
In s. 699(3) the words "section 242(1)" substituted for the former words "section 241(3)" by CA 1989, s. 213 and Sch. 10, para. 12 as from 1 April 1990 subject to transitional and saving provisions (see SI 1990/355 (C 13), art. 3, Sch. 1 and also art. 6–9.)

# Chapter II – Delivery of Accounts and Reports

## 699A Credit and financial institutions to which the Bank Branches Directive (89/117/EEC) applies

**699A(1) [Application]** This section applies to any credit or financial institution–

(a) which is incorporated or otherwise formed outside the UK and Gibraltar,

(b) whose head office is outside the UK and Gibraltar, and

(c) which has a branch in Great Britain.

**699A(2) [Sch. 21C]** Schedule 21C (delivery of accounts and reports) shall have effect in relation to any institution to which this section applies.

**699A(3) [Interpretation]** In this section–

**"branch"**, in relation to a credit or financial institution, means a place of business which forms a legally dependent part of the institution and which conducts directly all or some of the operations inherent in its business;

**"credit institution"** means a credit institution as defined in article 1 of the First Council Directive on the co-ordination of laws, regulations and administrative provisions relating to the taking up and pursuit of the business of credit institutions (77/780/EEC), that is to say an undertaking whose business is to receive deposits or other repayable funds from the public and to grant credits for its own account;

**"financial institution"** means a financial institution within the meaning of Article 1 of the Council Directive on the obligations of branches established in a Member State of credit and financial institutions having their head offices outside that Member State regarding the publication of annual accounting documents (the Bank Branches Directive, 89/117/EEC); and

**"undertaking"** has the same meaning as in Part VII.

**History**
S. 699A inserted by the Oversea Companies and Credit and Financial Institutions (Branch Disclosure) Regulations 1992 (SI 1992/3179), reg. 1(3), 2 as from 1 January 1993.

## 699AA Companies to which the Eleventh Company Law Directive applies

**699AA(1) [Application]** This section applies to any limited company which–

(a) is incorporated outside the United Kingdom and Gibraltar,

(b) has a branch in Great Britain, and

(c) is not an institution to which section 699A applies.

**699AA(2) [Sch. 21D]** Schedule 21D to this Act (delivery of accounts and reports) shall have effect in relation to any company to which this section applies.

**History**
S. 699AA inserted by the Oversea Companies and Credit and Financial Institutions (Branch Disclosure) Regulations 1992 (SI 1992/3179), reg. 1(3), 3(1) and Sch. 2, para. 16 as from 1 January 1993.

## 699B Scope of sections 700 to 703

**699B** Sections 700 to 703 shall not apply to any institution to which section 699A applies or to any limited company which is incorporated outside the United Kingdom and Gibraltar and has a branch in the United Kingdom.

**History**
S. 699B inserted by the Oversea Companies and Credit and Financial Institutions (Branch Disclosure) Regulations 1992 (SI 1992/3179), reg. 1(3), 2 as from 1 January 1993; and in s. 699B the words "or to any limited company" to the end inserted by reg. 3(1) and Sch. 2, para. 17 from the same date.

**Note**
See note after s. 703.

## 700 Preparation of accounts and reports by oversea companies

**700(1) [Same duties as other companies]** Every oversea company shall in respect of each financial year of the company prepare the like accounts and directors' report, and cause to be prepared such an auditors' report, as would be required if the company were formed and registered under this Act.

**700(2) [Order by Secretary of State]** The Secretary of State may by order–

(a) modify the requirements referred to in subsection (1) for the purpose of their application to oversea companies;

(b) exempt an oversea company from those requirements or from such of them as may be specified in the order.

**700(3) [Scope of order]** An order may make different provision for different cases or classes of case and may contain such incidental and supplementary provisions as the Secretary of State thinks fit.

**Note**
Re s. 700(2), (3) see the Oversea Companies (Accounts) (Modifications and Exemptions) Order 1990 (SI 1990/440).

**700(4) [Annulment of order]** An order under this section shall be made by statutory instrument which shall be subject to annulment in pursuance of a resolution of either House of Parliament.

**History**
See history note after s. 703.

# 701 Oversea company's financial year and accounting reference periods

**701(1) [Application of s. 223–225]** Sections 223 to 225 (financial year and accounting reference periods) apply to an oversea company, subject to the following modifications.

**701(2) [Interpretation]** For the references to the incorporation of the company substitute references to the company establishing a place of business in Great Britain.

**701(3) [Omission of s. 225(4)]** Omit section 225(4) (restriction on frequency with which current accounting reference period may be extended).

**History**
See history note after s. 703.

**Note**
Re s. 701(3) see note after s. 703. Re s. 701 see the Companies (Forms) (Amendment) Regulations 1996 (SI 1996/594).

# 702 Delivery to registrar of accounts and reports of oversea company

**702(1) [Duty of oversea company]** An oversea company shall in respect of each financial year of the company deliver to the registrar copies of the accounts and reports prepared in accordance with section 700.

If any document comprised in those accounts or reports is in a language other than English, the directors shall annex to the copy delivered a translation of it into English, certified in the prescribed manner to be a correct translation.

**702(2) [Period for delivering accounts and reports]** In relation to an oversea company the period allowed for delivering accounts and reports is 13 months after the end of the relevant accounting reference period.

This is subject to the following provisions of this section.

**702(3) [If accounting reference period first]** If the relevant accounting reference period is the company's first and is a period of more than 12 months, the period allowed is 13 months from the first anniversary of the company's establishing a place of business in Great Britain.

**702(4) [If accounting reference period shortened]** If the relevant accounting period is treated as shortened by virtue of a notice given by the company under section 225 (alteration of accounting reference date), the period allowed is that applicable in accordance with the above provisions or three months from the date of the notice under that section, whichever last expires.

**702(5) [Power of Secretary of State to extend period]** If for any special reason the Secretary of State thinks fit he may, on an application made before the expiry of the period otherwise allowed, by notice in writing to an oversea company extend that period by such further period as may be specified in the notice.

**702(6) ["The relevant accounting reference period"]** In this section **"the relevant accounting reference period"** means the accounting reference period by reference to which the financial year for the accounts in question was determined.

**History**
See history note after s. 703.

**Note**
See note after s. 703.

# 703 Penalty for non-compliance

**703(1) [Offence, penalty]** If the requirements of section 702(1) are not complied with before the end of the period allowed for delivering accounts and reports, or if the accounts and reports delivered do not comply with the requirements of this Act, the company and every person who immediately before the end of that period was a director of the company is guilty of an offence and liable to a fine and, for continued contravention, to a daily default fine.

**703(2) [Defence]** It is a defence for a person charged with such an offence to prove that he took all reasonable steps for securing that the requirements in question would be complied with.

**703(3) [Not a defence]** It is not a defence in relation to a failure to deliver copies to the registrar to prove that the documents in question were not in fact prepared as required by this Act.

**Note**

Re s. 700–703 see the Oversea Companies and Credit and Financial Institutions (Branch Disclosure) Regulations 1992 (SI 1992/3179), reg. 1(3), 5 and Sch. 4 for transitional provisions re continued operation until s. 699B relevant.

**History**

Ch. II (s. 700–703) substituted by CA 1989, s. 23 and Sch. 10, para. 13 as from 1 April 1990 subject to transitional and saving provisions (see SI 1990/355 (C 13), art. 3, Sch. 1 and also art. 6–9); Ch. II formerly read as follows:

**"Chapter II – Delivery of Accounts**

**700 Preparation and delivery of accounts by oversea companies**

**700(1)** Every oversea company shall in respect of each accounting reference period of the company prepare such accounts, made up by reference to such date or dates, and in such form, containing such particulars and having annexed to them such documents, as would have been required if it were a company formed and registered under this Act.

**(2)** An oversea company shall, in respect of each accounting reference period of the company, deliver to the registrar of companies copies of the accounts and other documents required by subsection (1); and, if such an account or other document is in a language other than English, there shall be annexed to the copy so delivered a translation of it into English certified in the prescribed manner to be a correct translation.

**(3)** If in relation to an accounting reference period the company's directors would be exempt under section 241(4) from compliance with subsection (3) of that section (independent company with unlimited liability), if the company were otherwise subject to that section, compliance with this section is not required in respect of that accounting reference period.

**(4)** The Secretary of State may by order in a statutory instrument–

(a) modify the requirements referred to in subsection (1) for the purpose of their application to oversea companies,

(b) exempt an oversea company from those requirements or from such of them as may be specified in the order.

**(5)** An order under subsection (4) may make different provision in relation to different cases or classes of case and may contain such incidental and supplementary provisions as the Secretary of State thinks fit; and a statutory instrument containing an order so made is subject to annulment in pursuance of a resolution of either House of Parliament.

**701 Oversea company's accounting reference period and date**

**701(1)** An oversea company's accounting reference periods are determined according to its accounting reference date.

**(2)** The company may give notice in the prescribed form to the registrar of companies specifying a date in the calendar year as being the date on which in each successive calendar year an accounting reference period of the company is to be treated as coming to an end; and the date specified in the notice is then the company's accounting reference date.

**(3)** No such notice has effect unless it is given before the end of 6 months beginning with the date on which a place of business in Great Britain is or was established by the company; and, failing such a notice, the company's accounting reference date is 31st March.

**(4)** The company's first accounting reference period is such period ending with its accounting reference date as–

(a) begins or began on a date determined by the company, but not later than that on which a place of business is or was established in Great Britain, and

(b) is a period exceeding 6 months and not exceeding 18 months.

**(5)** Each successive period of 12 months beginning after the end of the first accounting reference period and ending with the company's accounting reference date is also an accounting reference period of the company.

**(6)** Subsections (2) to (5) are subject to section 225 of this Act, under which in certain circumstances a company's accounting reference period may be altered, and which applies to oversea companies as well as to companies subject to Part VII, but omitting subsections (6) and (7).

**702 Period allowed for delivering accounts**

**702(1)** In the case of an oversea company, the period allowed for delivering accounts in relation to an accounting reference period is 13 months after the end of the period.

**(2)** Where the company's first accounting reference period–

(a) begins or began on the date determined by the company for the purposes of section 701(4)(a) and

(b) is or was a period of more than 12 months,

the period which would otherwise be allowed for delivering accounts in relation to that accounting reference period is treated as reduced by the number of days by which the accounting reference period is or was longer than 12 months.

**(3)** But the period allowed in relation to a company's first accounting reference period is not by subsection (2) reduced to less than 3 months after the end of that accounting reference period.

**(4)** In relation to an accounting reference period of an oversea company as respects which notice is given by the company under section 225 (as applied) and which by virtue of that section is treated as shortened in accordance with the notice, the period allowed for delivering accounts is–

(a) the period allowed in relation to that accounting reference period in accordance with the preceding subsections, or

(b) the period of 3 months beginning with the date of the notice,

whichever of those periods last expires.

**(5)** If for any special reason the Secretary of State thinks fit to do so, he may by notice in writing to an oversea company extend, by such further period as may be specified in the notice, the period which in accordance with the preceding subsections is the period allowed for delivering accounts in relation to any accounting reference period of the company.

**703 Penalty for non-compliance**

**703(1)** If in respect of an accounting reference period of an oversea company any of the requirements of section 700(2) is not complied with before the end of the period allowed for delivering accounts, the company and every officer or agent of it who knowingly and wilfully authorises or permits the default is, in respect of the company's failure to comply with the requirements in question, guilty of an offence and liable to a fine and, for continued contravention, to a daily default fine.

**(2)** For purposes of any proceedings under this section with respect to a requirement to deliver a copy of a document to the registrar of companies, it is not a defence to prove that the document in question was not in fact prepared as required by section 700."

# Chapter III – Registration of Charges

**Note**

Prospective insertion of s. 703(A)–(N) by CA 1989, s. 105 and Sch. 15.

# Chapter IV – Winding up etc.

## 703O Scope of Chapter

**703O** This Chapter applies to any company to which section 690A applies.

**History**

See history note after s. 703R.

## 703P Particulars to be delivered to the registrar: winding up

**703P(1) [Delivery of return]** Subject to subsection (8), where a company to which this Chapter applies is being wound up, it shall deliver to the registrar for registration a return in the prescribed form containing the following particulars–

(a) the name of the company;

(b) whether the company is being wound up by an order of a court and, if so, the name and address of the court and the date of the order;

(c) if the company is not being so wound up, as a result of what action the winding up has commenced;

(d) whether the winding up has been instigated by:
  (i) the company's members;
  (ii) the company's creditors; or
  (iii) some other person or persons,

and, in the case of (iii) the identity of that person or those persons shall be given; and

(e) the date on which the winding up became or will become effective.

**Note**

See note after s. 703P(5).

**703P(2) [Period allowed re s. 703P(1)]** The period allowed for delivery of a return under subsection (1) above is 14 days from the date on which the winding up begins.

**703P(3) [Liquidator's return on appointment]** Subject to subsection (8), a person appointed to be the liquidator of a company to which this Chapter applies shall deliver to the registrar for registration a return in the prescribed form containing the following particulars–

(a) his name and address,

(b) the date of his appointment, and

(c) a description of such of his powers, if any, as are derived otherwise than from the general law or the company's constitution.

**Note**

See note after s. 703P(5).

**703P(4) [Period allowed re s. 703P(3)]** The period allowed for delivery of a return under subsection (3) above is 14 days from the date of the liquidator's appointment.

**703P(5) [Liquidator's return on termination of winding up and company ceasing to be registered]** Subject to subsection (8), the liquidator of a company to which this Chapter applies shall deliver to the registrar for registration a return in the prescribed form upon the occurrence of the following events–

(a) the termination of the winding up of the company, and

(b) the company ceasing to be registered, in circumstances where ceasing to be registered is an event of legal significance.

The following particulars shall be given:

(i) in the case of (a), the name of the company and the date on which the winding up terminated; and

(ii) in the case of (b), the name of the company and the date on which the company ceased to be registered.

**Note**
See the Companies (Forms) (Amendment) Regulations 1992 (SI 1992/3006).

**703P(6) [Period allowed re s. 703P(5)]** The period allowed for delivery of a return under subsection (5) is 14 days from the date of the event concerned.

**703P(7) [Return of each branch]** The obligation to deliver a return under subsection (1), (3) or (5) above shall apply in respect of each branch which the company has in Great Britain (though where the company has more than one branch in a part of Great Britain a return which gives the branch numbers of two or more such branches is to be regarded as a return in respect of each branch whose number is given).

**703P(8) [Unregistered companies]** No return is required under subsection (1), (3), or (5) above in respect of a winding up under Part V of the Insolvency Act 1986.

**History**
See history note after s. 703R.

## 703Q Particulars to be delivered to the registrar: insolvency proceedings etc.

**703Q(1) [Return where company becomes subject to proceedings]** Where a company to which this Chapter applies becomes subject to any of the following proceedings (other than proceedings for the winding up of the company), that is to say, insolvency proceedings or an arrangement or composition or any analogous proceedings, it shall deliver to the registrar for registration a return in the prescribed form containing the following particulars–

(a) the name of the company;

(b) whether the proceedings are by order of a court and, if so, the name and address of the court and the date of the order;

(c) if the proceedings are not by order of a court, as a result of what action the proceedings have been commenced;

(d) whether the proceedings have been instigated by:
  (i) the company's members;
  (ii) the company's creditors; or
  (iii) some other person or persons,
  and, in the case of (iii) the identity of that person or those persons shall be given; and

(e) the date on which the proceedings became or will become effective.

**Note**
See note after s. 703Q(2).

**703Q(2) [Return where company no longer subject to proceedings]** Where a company to which this Chapter applies ceases to be subject to any of the proceedings mentioned in subsection (1) it shall deliver to the registrar for registration a return in the prescribed form containing the following particulars:

(a) the name of the company; and

(b) the date on which it ceased to be subject to the proceedings.

**Note**
See the Companies (Forms) (Amendment) Regulations 1992 (SI 1992/3006).

**703Q(3) [Period allowed re s. 703Q(1), (2)]** The period allowed for delivery of a return under subsection (1) or (2) is 14 days from the date on which the company becomes subject, or (as the case may be) ceases to be subject to the proceedings concerned.

**703Q(4) [Return for each branch]** The obligation to deliver a return under subsection (1) or (2) shall apply in respect of each branch which the company has in Great Britain (though where the company has more than one branch in a part of Great Britain a return which gives the branch numbers of two or more such branches is to be regarded as a return in respect of each branch whose number is given).

**History**

See history note after s. 703R.

## 703R Penalty for non-compliance

**703R(1) [Offence, penalty for default of company]** If a company fails to comply with section 703P(1) or 703Q(1) or (2) within the period allowed for compliance, it, and every person who immediately before the end of that period was a director of it, is guilty of an offence and liable to a fine and, for continued contravention, to a daily default fine.

**703R(2) [Offence, penalty where liquidator defaults]** If a liquidator fails to comply with section 703P(3) or (5) within the period allowed for compliance, he is guilty of an offence and liable to a fine and, for continued contravention, to a daily default fine.

**703R(3) [Defence]** It is a defence for a person charged with an offence under this section to prove that he took all reasonable steps for securing compliance with the requirements concerned.

**History**

Ch. IV (s. 703O–703R) inserted by the Oversea Companies and Credit and Financial Institutions (Branch Disclosure) Regulations 1992 (SI 1992/3179), reg. 1(3), 3(1), Sch. 2, para. 19 as from 1 January 1993.

# PART XXIV – THE REGISTRAR OF COMPANIES, HIS FUNCTIONS AND OFFICES

## 704 Registration offices

**704(1) [Offices in England, Wales and Scotland]** For the purposes of the registration of companies under the Companies Acts, there shall continue to be offices in England and Wales and in Scotland, at such places as the Secretary of State thinks fit.

**704(2) [Officers appointed]** The Secretary of State may appoint such registrars, assistant registrars, clerks and servants as he thinks necessary for that purpose, and may make regulations with respect to their duties, and may remove any persons so appointed.

**Note**

S. 704(2) has effect as if the purpose referred to included the purpose of carrying out functions under the Registration of Political Parties Act 1998. A register of political parties is to be maintained by the registrar or other officer who performs the duty of registration of companies in England and Wales under the Companies Act 1985 (see the Registration of Political Parties Act 1998, s. 1(2) and Sch. 3, para. 2).

**704(3) [Salaries of officers]** The salaries of the persons so appointed continue to be fixed by the Secretary of State, with the concurrence of the Treasury, and shall be paid out of money provided by Parliament.

**704(4) [Seal for authentication of documents]** The Secretary of State may direct a seal or seals to be prepared for the authentication of documents required for or in connection with the registration of companies; and any seal so prepared is referred to in this Act as the registrar's official seal.

**704(5) [Things to be done by registrar]** Wherever any act is by the Companies Acts directed to be done to or by the registrar of companies, it shall (until the Secretary of State otherwise directs) be done to or by the existing registrar of companies in England and Wales or in Scotland (as the case may be), or to or by such person as the Secretary of State may for the time being authorise.

**704(6) [Alteration of constitution of offices]** In the event of the Secretary of State altering the constitution of the existing registration offices or any of them, any such act shall be done to or by such officer and at such place with reference to the local situation of the registered offices of the companies to be registered as the Secretary of State may appoint.

**704(7) [Application of s. 704(8)]** Subsection (8) below applies where by virtue of an order made under section 69 of the Deregulation and Contracting Out Act 1994 a person is authorised by the registrar of companies to accept delivery of any class of documents which are under any provision of the Companies Acts to be delivered to the registrar.

**History**
See history note after s. 704(8).

**704(8) [Delivery of documents]** If–

(a) the registrar directs that documents of that class shall be delivered to a specified address of the authorised person; and

(b) the direction is printed and made available to the public (with or without payment),

any document of that class which is delivered to an address other than the specified address shall be treated for the purposes of those Acts as not having been delivered.

**History**
S. 704(7), (8) inserted by the Deregulation and Contracting Out Act 1994, s. 76, 82(2)(f) and Sch. 16 , para. 8 as from 3 January 1995.

# 705 Companies' registered numbers

**705(1) [Allocation of numbers]** The registrar shall allocate to every company a number, which shall be known as the company's registered number.

**705(2) [Form of numbers]** Companies' registered numbers shall be in such form, consisting of one or more sequences of figures or letters, as the registrar may from time to time determine.

**705(3) [Changes of existing numbers]** The registrar may upon adopting a new form of registered number make such changes of existing registered numbers as appear to him necessary.

**705(4) [Date of change]** A change of a company's registered number has effect from the date on which the company is notified by the registrar of the change; but for a period of three years beginning with the date on which that notification is sent by the registrar the requirement of section 351(1)(a) as to the use of the company's registered number on business letters and order forms is satisfied by the use of either the old number or the new.

**705(5) ["Company"]** In this section **"company"** includes–

(za) any oversea company which has complied with paragraph 1 of Schedule 21A other than a company which appears to the registrar not to have a branch in Great Britain;

(a) any oversea company which has complied with section 691 (delivery of statutes to registrar, etc.), other than a company which appears to the registrar not to have a place of business in Great Britain; and

(b) any body to which any provision of this Act applies by virtue of section 718 (unregistered companies).

**History**
S. 705(5)(za) inserted by the Oversea Companies and Credit and Financial Institutions (Branch Disclosure) Regulations 1992 (SI 1992/3179), reg. 1(3), 4 and Sch. 3, para. 5 as from 1 January 1993.
Previously s. 705 substituted by CA 1989, s. 145 and Sch. 19, para. 14 as from 1 October 1990 (see SI 1990/1707 (C 46), art. 2(b)); s. 705 originally read as follows:

"**705(1)** The registrar of companies shall allocate to every company a number, which shall be known as the company's registered number; and he may in addition allocate to any such company a letter, which is then deemed for all purposes to be part of the registered number.

**(2) "Company"** here includes –

(a) an oversea company which has complied with section 691 (delivery of statutes to registrar of companies, etc.) and which does not appear to the registrar not to have a place of business in Great Britain, and

(b) any incorporated or unincorporated body to which any provision of this Act applies by virtue of section 718 (unregistered companies)."

# 705A Registration of branches of oversea companies

**705A(1) [Register]** For each company to which section 690A applies the registrar, shall keep, in such form as he thinks fit, a register of the branches registered by the company under paragraph 1 of Schedule 21A.

**705A(2) [Registered number]** The registrar shall allocate to every branch registered by him under this section a number, which shall be known as the branch's registered number.

**705A(3) [Form]** Branches' registered numbers shall be in such form, consisting of one or more sequences of figures or letters, as the registrar may from time to time determine.

**705A(4) [Change of number]** The registrar may upon adopting a new form of registered number make such changes of existing registered numbers as appear to him necessary.

**705A(5) [Transitional provision]** A change of a branch's registered number has effect from the date on which the company is notified by the registrar of the change; but for a period of three years beginning with the date on which that notification is sent by the registrar the requirement of section 693(2) as to the use of the branch's registered number on business letters and order forms is satisfied by the use of either the old number or the new.

**705A(6) [Register for each branch]** Where an oversea company to which section 690A applies files particulars, in any circumstances permitted by this Act, by:

(i) adopting particulars already filed in respect of another branch; or

(ii) including in one document particulars which are to relate to two or more branches,

the registrar shall ensure that the particulars concerned become part of the registered particulars of each branch concerned.

**History**
S. 705A inserted by the Oversea Companies and Credit and Financial Institutions (Branch Disclosure) Regulations 1992 (SI 1992/3179), reg. 1(3), 3(2) as from 1 January 1993.

# 706 Delivery to the registrar of documents in legible form

**706(1) [Application]** This section applies to the delivery to the registrar under any provision of the Companies Acts of documents in legible form.

**706(2) [Requirements for document]** The document must–

(a) state in a prominent position the registered number of the company to which it relates and, if the document is delivered under sections 695A(3), 703P or 703Q or Schedules 21A or 21D the registered number of the branch to which it relates,

(b) satisfy any requirements prescribed by regulations for the purposes of this section, and

(c) conform to such requirements as the registrar may specify for the purpose of enabling him to copy the document.

**History**
In s. 706(2)(a) the words "and, if the document" to the end inserted by the Oversea Companies and Credit and Financial Institutions (Branch Disclosure) Regulations 1992 (SI 1992/3179), reg. 1(3), 4 and Sch. 3, para. 6 as from 1 January 1993.

**706(3) [Notice re non-compliance]** If a document is delivered to the registrar which does not comply with the requirements of this section, he may serve on the person by whom the document was delivered (or, if there are two or more such persons, on any of them) a notice indicating the respect in which the document does not comply.

**706(4) [Effect of s. 706(3) notice]** Where the registrar serves such a notice, then, unless a replacement document–

(a) is delivered to him within 14 days after the service of the notice, and

(b) complies with the requirements of this section (or section 707) or is not rejected by him for failure to comply with those requirements,

the original document shall be deemed not to have been delivered to him.

But for the purposes of any enactment imposing a penalty for failure to deliver, so far as it imposes a penalty for continued contravention, no account shall be taken of the period between the delivery of the original document and the end of the period of 14 days after service of the registrar's notice.

**706(5) [Regulations]** Regulations made for the purposes of this section may make different provision with respect to different descriptions of document.

**History**
See history note after s. 707.

# 707 Delivery to the registrar of documents otherwise than in legible form

**707(1) [Application]** This section applies to the delivery to the registrar under any provision of the Companies Acts of documents otherwise than in legible form.

**707(2) [Satisfaction of relevant requirement]** Any requirement to deliver a document to the registrar, or to deliver a document in the prescribed form, is satisfied by the communication to the registrar of the requisite information in any non-legible form prescribed for the purposes of this section by regulations or approved by the registrar.

**707(3) [Where document to be signed or sealed]** Where the document is required to be signed or sealed, it shall instead be authenticated in such manner as may be prescribed by regulations or approved by the registrar.

**707(4) [Requirements for document]** The document must–

(a) contain in a prominent position the registered number of the company to which it relates and, if the document is delivered under sections 695A(3), 703P or 703Q or Schedules 21A or 21D the registered number of the branch to which it relates,

(b) satisfy any requirements prescribed by regulations for the purposes of this section, and

(c) be furnished in such manner, and conform to such requirements, as the registrar may specify for the purpose of enabling him to read and copy the document.

**History**

In s. 707(4)(a) the words "and, if the document" to the end inserted by the Oversea Companies and Credit and Financial Institutions (Branch Disclosure) Regulations 1992 (SI 1992/3179), reg. 1(3), 4 and Sch. 3, para. 6 as from 1 January 1993.

**707(5) [Notice re non-compliance]** If a document is delivered to the registrar which does not comply with the requirements of this section, he may serve on the person by whom the document was delivered (or, if there are two or more such persons, on any of them) a notice indicating the respect in which the document does not comply.

**707(6) [Effect of s. 707(5) notice]** Where the registrar serves such a notice, then, unless a replacement document–

(a) is delivered to him within 14 days after the service of the notice, and

(b) complies with the requirements of this section (or section 706) or is not rejected by him for failure to comply with those requirements,

the original document shall be deemed not to have been delivered to him.

But for the purposes of any enactment imposing a penalty for failure to deliver, so far as it imposes a penalty for continued contravention, no account shall be taken of the period between the delivery of the original document and the end of the period of 14 days after service of the registrar's notice.

**707(7) [Regulations re instantaneous forms of communication]** The Secretary of State may by regulations make further provision with respect to the application of this section in relation to instantaneous forms of communication.

**707(8) [Scope of Regulations]** Regulations made for the purposes of this section may make different provision with respect to different descriptions of document and different forms of communication, and as respects delivery to the registrar for England and Wales and delivery to the registrar for Scotland.

**History**

S. 706, 707 substituted by CA 1989, s. 125(1), (2) as from 7 January 1991 (see SI 1990/2569 (C 68), art. 4(b)); s. 706, 707 formerly read as follows:

**"706 Size, durability, etc. of documents delivered to registrar**

**706(1)** For the purpose of securing that documents delivered to the registrar of companies under the Companies Acts are of standard size, durable and easily legible, regulations made by the Secretary of State by statutory instrument may prescribe such requirements (whether as to size, weight, quality or colour of paper, size, type or colouring of lettering, or otherwise) as he may consider appropriate; and different requirements may be so prescribed for different documents or classes of documents.

**(2)** If under any such provision there is delivered to the registrar a document (whether an original document or a copy) which in the registrar's opinion does not comply with such requirements prescribed under this section as are applicable to it, the registrar may serve on any person by whom under that provision the document was required to be delivered (or, if there are two or more such persons, may serve on any of them) a notice stating his opinion to that effect and indicating the requirements so prescribed with which in his opinion the document does not comply.

**(3)** Where the registrar serves such a notice with respect to a document delivered under any such provision, then, for the purposes of any enactment which enables a penalty to be imposed in respect of any omission to deliver to the registrar of companies a document required to be delivered under that provision (and, in particular, for the purposes of any such enactment whereby such a penalty may be imposed by reference to each day during which the omission continues) –

(a) any duty imposed by that provision to deliver such a document to the registrar is to be treated as not having been discharged by the delivery of that document, but

(b) no account is to be taken of any days falling within the period mentioned in the following subsection.

**(4)** That period begins with the day on which the document was delivered to the registrar as mentioned in subsection (2) and ends with the 14th day after the date of service of the notice under subsection (2) by virtue of which subsection (3) applies.

**(5)** In this section any reference to delivering a document includes sending, forwarding, producing or (in the case of a notice) giving it.

**707 Power of registrar to accept information on microfilm, etc.**

**707(1)** The registrar of companies may, if he thinks fit, accept under any provision of the Companies Acts requiring a document to be delivered to him any material other than a document which contains the information in question and is of a kind approved by him.

**(2)** The delivery to the registrar of material so accepted is sufficient compliance with the provision in question.

**(3)** In this section any reference to delivering a document includes sending, forwarding, producing or (in the case of a notice) giving it."

# 707A The keeping of company records by the registrar

**707A(1) [Form in which information kept]** The information contained in a document delivered to the registrar under the Companies Acts may be recorded and kept by him in any form he thinks fit, provided it is possible to inspect the information and to produce a copy of it in legible form.

This is sufficient compliance with any duty of his to keep, file or register the document.

**707A(2) [Keeping of originals]** The originals of documents delivered to the registrar in legible form shall be kept by him for ten years, after which they may be destroyed.

**707A(3) [Where company dissolved]** Where a company has been dissolved, the registrar may, at any time after the expiration of two years from the date of the dissolution, direct that any records in his custody relating to the company may be removed to the Public Record Office; and records in respect of which such a direction is given shall be disposed of in accordance with the enactments relating to that Office and the rules made under them.

This subsection does not extend to Scotland.

**707A(4) ["Company"]** In subsection (3) **"company"** includes a company provisionally or completely registered under the Joint Stock Companies Act 1844.

**History**

S. 707A inserted by CA 1989, s. 126(1) as from 1 July 1991 (see SI 1991/488 (C 11), art. 2(1)).

# 708 Fees payable to registrar

**708(1) [Regulations re fees]** The Secretary of State may by regulations made by statutory instrument require the payment to the registrar of companies of such fees as may be specified in the regulations in respect of –

(a) the performance by the registrar of such functions under the Companies Acts as may be so specified, including the receipt by him of any document which under those Acts is required to be delivered to him.

(b) the inspection of documents kept by him under those Acts.

**History**

In s. 708(1), in para. (a) the words "any document which under those Acts is required to be delivered to him" substituted for the former words "any notice or other document which under those Acts is required to be given, delivered, sent or forwarded to him" and in para (b) the words "or other material" omitted and repealed by CA 1989, s. 127(2), 212 and Sch. 24 as from 7 January 1991 (see SI 1990/2569 (C 68), art. 4(b), 5(a)).

**Note**

See the Companies (Fees) Regulations 1991 (SI 1991/1206); the Companies (Fees) (Amendment) Regulations 1992 (SI 1992/2876); the Companies Fees (Amendment) Regulations 1994 (SI 1994/2217); the Companies (Fees) (Amendment) Regulations 1995 (SI 1995/1423); and the Companies (Fees) (Amendment) Regulations 1996 (SI 1996/1444).

**708(2) [Approval of certain regulations]** A statutory instrument containing regulations under this section requiring the payment of a fee in respect of a matter for which no fee was previously payable, or increasing a fee, shall be laid before Parliament after being made and shall cease to have effect at the end of the period of 28 days beginning with the day on which the regulations were made (but without prejudice to anything previously done under the regulations or to the making of further regulations) unless in that period the regulations are approved by resolution of each House of Parliament.

In reckoning that period of 28 days no account is to be taken of any time during which Parliament is dissolved or prorogued or during which both Houses are adjourned for more than 4 days.

**Note**
See the Companies (Fees) Regulations 1991 (SI 1991/1206); the Companies (Fees) (Amendment) Regulations 1992 (SI 1992/2876); the Companies Fees (Amendment) Regulations 1994 (SI 1994/2217); the Companies (Fees) (Amendment) Regulations 1995 (SI 1995/1423); and the Companies (Fees) (Amendment) Regulations 1996 (SI 1996/1444).

**708(3) [Annulment]** A statutory instrument containing regulations under this section, where subsection (2) does not apply, is subject to annulment in pursuance of a resolution of either House of Parliament.

**708(4) [Fees into Consolidated Fund]** Fees paid to the registrar under the Companies Acts shall be paid into the Consolidated Fund.

**708(5) [Fees for other services]** It is hereby declared that the registrar may charge a fee for any services provided by him otherwise than in pursuance of an obligation imposed on him by law.

# 709 Inspection etc. of records kept by the registrar

**709(1) [Inspection, copies]** Any person may inspect any records kept by the registrar for the purposes of the Companies Acts and may require–

(a) a copy, in such form as the registrar considers appropriate, of any information contained in those records, or

(b) a certified copy of, or extract from, any such record.

**Note**
See note after s. 709(3).

**709(2) [Extent of right of inspection]** The right of inspection extends to the originals of documents delivered to the registrar in legible form only where the record kept by the registrar of the contents of the document is illegible or unavailable.

**Note**
See note after s. 709(3).

**709(3) [Status of certified copy]** A copy of or extract from a record kept at any of the offices for the registration of companies in England and Wales or Scotland, certified in writing by the registrar (whose official position it is unnecessary to prove) to be an accurate record of the contents of any document delivered to him under the Companies Acts, is in all legal proceedings admissible in evidence as of equal validity with the original document and as evidence of any fact stated therein of which direct oral evidence would be admissible.

**History**
In s. 709(3), final paragraph repealed by the Youth Justice and Criminal Evidence Act 1999, s. 67(3), 68(3) and Sch. 6 with effect from 14 April 2000 (see Youth Justice and Criminal Evidence Act 1999 (Commencement No. 2) Order 2000 (SI 2000/1034 (C. 27)), art. 2(c)). The paragraph formerly read as follows:

"In England and Wales this is subject to compliance with any applicable rules of court under section 5 of the Civil Evidence Act 1968 or section 69(2) of the Police and Criminal Evidence Act 1984 (which relate to evidence from computer records)."

As a result of a transitional provision in SI 1991/488 (C 11), art. 3, s. 709(2), (3) as originally enacted (and reproduced below) shall continue in effect to the extent that the repeal of s. 709(2), (3) by the Financial Services Act 1986 had not been brought into force, with the modification that the original s. 709(2) shall be read as if the reference to the "rights conferred by subsection (1) of this section" was a reference to the rights conferred by the (new) s. 709(1) as inserted by CA 1989 and the reference to those rights in s. 709(3), as originally enacted, shall be construed accordingly. S. 709(2), (3) as originally enacted, are:

"**709(2)** In relation to documents delivered to the registrar with a prospectus in pursuance of section 65(2), the rights conferred by subsection (1) of this section are exercisable only during the 14 days beginning with the date of publication of the prospectus, or with the permission of the Secretary of State.

**(3)** In relation to documents so delivered in pursuance of section 77(3)(b) and (4) (prospectus of oversea company), those rights are exercisable only during the 14 days beginning with the date of the prospectus, or with that permission."

S. 709(2), (3) repealed by Financial Services Act 1986, s. 212(3) and Sch. 17, Pt. I to the extent to which they would apply re any investment listed or the subject of a listing application under Financial Services Act 1986, Pt. IV commencing:

- on 12 January 1987 for all purposes relating to the admission of securities offered by or on behalf of a Minister of the Crown or a body corporate controlled by a Minister of the Crown or a subsidiary of such a body corporate to the Official List in respect of which an application is made after that date;
- on 16 February 1987 for purposes relating to the admission of securities in respect of which an application is made after that date other than those referred to in the preceding paragraph and otherwise for all purposes. (See SI 1986/2246 (C 88).)

S. 709(2), (3) also repealed by Financial Services Act 1986, s. 212(3) and Sch. 17, Pt. I as from 29 April 1988 as far as they would apply to a prospectus offering for subscription, or to any form of application for units in a body corporate which is a recognised scheme (see SI 1988/740 (C 22)).)

**709(4) [Sealed copies]** Copies of or extracts from records furnished by the registrar may, instead of being certified by him in writing to be an accurate record, be sealed with his official seal.

**709(5) [Process of court compelling production]** No process for compelling the production of a record kept by the registrar shall issue from any court except with the leave of the court; and any such process shall bear on it a statement that it is issued with the leave of the court.

**History**

See history note after s. 710A.

# 710 Certificate of incorporation

**710** Any person may require a certificate of the incorporation of a company, signed by the registrar or authenticated by his official seal.

**History**

See history note after s. 710A.

# 710A Provision and authentication by registrar of documents in non-legible form

**710A(1) [Communication by registrar]** Any requirement of the Companies Acts as to the supply by the registrar of a document may, if the registrar thinks fit, be satisfied by the communication by the registrar of the requisite information in any non-legible form prescribed for the purposes of this section by regulations or approved by him.

**710A(2) [Authentication]** Where the document is required to be signed by him or sealed with his official seal, it shall instead be authenticated in such manner as may be prescribed by regulations or approved by the registrar.

**History**

S. 709–710A substituted for the former s. 709 (but see note after new s. 709(3) above) and 710 by CA 1989, s. 126(2) as from 1 July 1991 subject to a transitional provision (see SI 1991/488 (C 11), art. 2(1), 3); the former s. 709 and 710 read as follows:

"**709 Inspection of documents kept by registrar**

**709(1)** Subject to the provisions of this section, any person may –

(a) inspect a copy of any document kept by the registrar of companies or, if the copy is illegible or unavailable, the document itself,

(b) require a certificate of the incorporation of any company, or a certified copy or extract of any other document or any part of any other document.

A certificate given under paragraph (b) may be signed by the registrar, or authenticated by his official seal."

**(2), (3)** (See note after new s. 709(3) above.)

**(4)** (Repealed by Insolvency Act 1986, s. 438 and Sch. 12 as from 29 December 1986.)

In regard to the date of the above repeal, see Insolvency Act 1986, s. 443 and SI 1986/1924 (C 71); s. 709(4) formerly read as follows:

"The right conferred by subsection (1)(a) of this section does not extend to any copy sent to the registrar under section 495 (information to be given by receiver or manager following his appointment) of a statement as to the affairs of a company, or of any comments of the receiver or his successor, or a continuing receiver or manager, on the statement, but only to the summary of it, except where the person claiming the right either is or is the agent of a person stating himself in writing to be a member or creditor of the company to which the statement relates.

The rights conferred by subsection (1)(b) are similarly limited.")

"**710 Additional provisions about inspection**

**710(1)** No process for compelling the production of any document kept by the registrar shall issue from any court except with the leave of that court; and any such process if issued shall bear on it a statement that it is issued with leave of the court.

**(2)** A copy of, or extract from, any document kept and registered at any of the offices for the registration of companies in England and Wales or Scotland, certified in writing by the registrar (whose official position it is unnecessary to prove) to be a true copy, is in all legal proceedings admissible in evidence as of equal validity with the original document.

**(3)** Copies or extracts of documents or parts of documents furnished by the registrar under section 709 may, instead of being certified by him in writing to be true copies, be sealed with his official seal."

"**(4)** (Repealed by Insolvency Act 1986, s. 438 and Sch. 12 as from 29 December 1986.)"

(In regard to the date of the above repeal, see Insolvency Act 1986, s. 443 and SI 1986/1924 (C 71); s. 710(4) formerly read as follows:

"Any person untruthfully stating himself in writing for the purposes of section 709(4) to be a member or creditor of a company is liable to a fine.")

"**(5)** For purposes of section 709 and this section, a copy is to be taken to be the copy of a document notwithstanding that it is taken from a copy or other reproduction of the original; and in both sections **"document"** includes any material which contains information kept by the registrar of companies for purposes of the Companies Acts."

# 710B Documents relating to Welsh companies

**710B(1) [Application]** This section applies to any document which –

(a) is delivered to the registrar under this Act or the Insolvency Act 1986, and

(b) relates to a company (whether already registered or to be registered) whose memorandum states that its registered office is to be situated in Wales.

**710B(2) [In Welsh but with English translation]** A document to which this section applies may be in Welsh but, subject to subsection (3), shall on delivery to the registrar be accompanied by a certified translation into English.

**710B(3) [Non-application of s. 710B(2)]** The requirement for a translation imposed by subsection (2) shall not apply –

(a) to documents of such descriptions as may be prescribed for the purposes of this paragraph, or

(b) to documents in a form prescribed in Welsh (or partly in Welsh and partly in English) by virtue of section 26 of the Welsh Language Act 1993.

**Note**

See the Companies (Welsh Language Forms and Documents) Regulations 1994 (SI 1994/117) as amended by SI 1994/727 and SI 1995/734.

**710B(4) [Where registrar has no certified translation]** Where by virtue of subsection (3) the registrar receives a document in Welsh without a certified translation into English, he shall, if that document is to be available for inspection, himself obtain such a translation; and that translation shall be treated as delivered to him in accordance with the same provision as the original.

**710B(5) [Company whose memorandum refers to registered office in Wales]** A company whose memorandum states that its registered office is to be situated in Wales may deliver to the registrar a certified translation into Welsh of any document in English which relates to the company and which is or has been delivered to the registrar.

**710B(6) [Non-application of provisions in s. 710B(7)]** The provisions within subsection (7) (which require certified translations into English of certain documents delivered to the registrar) shall not apply where a translation is required by subsection (2) or would be required but for subsection (3).

**710B(7) [Provisions referred to in s. 710B(6)]** The provisions within this subsection are section 228(2)(f), the second sentence of section 242(1), sections 243(4), 272(5) and 273(7) and paragraph 7(3) of Part II of Schedule 9.

**710B(8) ["Certified translation"]** In this section **"certified translation"** means a translation certified in the prescribed manner to be a correct translation.

**History**

S. 710B inserted by Welsh Language Act, s. 30(6) as from 25 January 1994 for certain purposes and as from 1 February 1994 for all remaining purposes (see SI 1994/115 (C 5), art. 2).

# 711 Public notice by registrar of receipt and issue of certain documents

**711(1) [Relevant documents]** The registrar of companies shall cause to be published in the Gazette notice of the issue or receipt by him of documents of any of the following descriptions (stating in the notice the name of the company, the description of document and the date of issue or receipt) –

(a) any certificate of incorporation of a company,

(b) any document making or evidencing an alteration in a company's memorandum or articles,

(c) any notification of a change among the directors of a company,

(d) any copy of a resolution of a public company which gives, varies, revokes or renews an authority for the purposes of section 80 (allotment of relevant securities),

(e) any copy of a special resolution of a public company passed under section 95(1), (2) or (3) (disapplication of pre-emption rights),

(f) any report under section 103 or 104 as to the value of a non-cash asset,
(g) any statutory declaration delivered under section 117 (public company share capital requirements),
(h) any notification (given under section 122) of the redemption of shares,
(j) any statement or notice delivered by a public company under section 128 (registration of particulars of special rights),
(k) any documents delivered by a company under section 242(1) (accounts and reports),
(l) a copy of any resolution or agreement to which section 380 applies and which –
(i) states the rights attached to any shares in a public company, other than shares which are in all respects uniform (for purposes of section 128) with shares previously allotted, or
(ii) varies rights attached to any shares in a public company, or
(iii) assigns a name or other designation, or a new name or designation, to any class of shares in a public company,
(m) any return of allotments of a public company,
(n) any notice of a change in the situation of a company's registered office,
(p) any copy of a winding-up order in respect of a company,
(q) any order for the dissolution of a company on a winding up,
(r) any return by a liquidator of the final meeting of a company on a winding up,
(s) any copy of a draft of the terms of a scheme delivered to the registrar of companies under paragraph 2(1) of Schedule 15B,
(t) any copy of an order under section 425(2) or section 427 in respect of a compromise or arrangement to which section 427A(1) applies,
(u) any return delivered under paragraph 1, 7 or 8 of Schedule 21A (branch registration),
(v) any document delivered under paragraph 1 or 8 of that Schedule,
(w) any notice under section 695A(3) of the closure of a branch,
(x) any document delivered under Schedule 21C (accounts and reports of foreign credit and financial institutions),
(y) any document delivered under Schedule 21D (accounts and reports of oversea companies subject to branch registration, other than credit and financial institutions),
(z) any return delivered under section 703P (particulars of winding up of oversea companies subject to branch registration).

**History**

In s. 711(1)(k) the words "section 242(1) (accounts and reports)" substituted for the former words "section 241 (annual accounts)" by CA 1989, s. 23 and Sch. 10, para. 14 as from 1 April 1990 subject to transitional and saving provisions (see SI 1990/355 (C 13), art. 3, Sch. 1 and also art. 6–9). S. 711(1)(s), (t) added by the Companies Mergers and Divisions) Regulations 1987 (SI 1987/1991), reg. 2(b) as from 1 January 1988.

S. 711(u)–(z) inserted by the Oversea Companies and Credit and Financial Institutions (Branch Disclosure) Regulations 1992 (SI 1992/3179), reg. 1(3), 4 and Sch. 3, para. 7 as from 1 January 1993.

**Note**

The Companies (Mergers and Divisions) Regulations 1987 (SI 1987/1991) (referred to above) implement the Third and Sixth EC Company Law Directives (78/855, 82/891).

**CCH Note**

In s. 711(1)(s) the previous reference altered from "Schedule 15A" to "Schedule 15B" because of the amendment made by CA 1989, s. 114(2).

**711(2) ["Official notification"]** In section 42 **"official notification"** means–
(a) in relation to anything stated in a document of any of the above descriptions, the notification of that document in the Gazette under this section, and
(b) in relation to the appointment of a liquidator in a voluntary winding up, the notification of it in the Gazette under section 109 of the Insolvency Act;

and **"officially notified"** is to be construed accordingly.

**History**

In s. 711(2)(b) the words "section 109 of the Insolvency Act" substituted for the words "section 600" by Insolvency Act 1986, s. 439(1) and Sch. 13 as from 29 December 1986 (see SI 1986/1924 (C 71)).

**Note**

S. 711 (in its original form) was previously part of European Communities Act 1972, s. 9(3) which in part implemented the First EC Company Law Directive (68/151).

See the the Open-Ended Investment Companies (Investment Companies with Variable Capital) Regulations 1996 (SI 1996/2827) Sch. 1, para. 6 for modifications to s. 711 for the purpose of those Regulations.

## 712 Removal of documents to Public Record Office

**712** (Omitted and repealed by Companies Act 1989, s. 127(3), 212 and Sch. 24 as from 1 July 1991.)

**History**

In regard to the above date see SI 1991/488 (C 11), art. 2(1); s. 712 formerly read as follows:

"**712(1)** Where a company has been dissolved, whether under this Act or otherwise, the registrar may, at any time after the expiration of 2 years from the date of the dissolution, direct that any documents in his custody relating to that company may be removed to the Public Record Office; and documents in respect of which such a direction is given shall be disposed of in accordance with the enactments relating to that Office and the rules made under them.

**(2)** In this section **"company"** includes a company provisionally or completely registered under the Joint Stock Companies Act 1844.

**(3)** This section does not extend to Scotland."

## 713 Enforcement of company's duty to make returns

**713(1) [Order by court on application]** If a company, having made default in complying with any provision of the Companies Acts which requires it to deliver a document to the registrar of companies, or to give notice to him of any matter, fails to make good the default within 14 days after the service of a notice on the company requiring it to do so, the court may, on an application made to it by any member or creditor of the company or by the registrar of companies, make an order directing the company and any officer of it to make good the default within such time as may be specified in the order.

**History**

In s. 713(1) the words "deliver a document to the registrar of companies" substituted for the former words "file with, deliver or send to the registrar of companies any return, account or other document" by CA 1989, s. 127(4) as from 7 January 1991 (see SI 1990/2569 (C 68)).

**713(2) [Costs]** The court's order may provide that all costs of and incidental to the application shall be borne by the company or by any officers of it responsible for the default.

**713(3) [Other enactments imposing penalties]** Nothing in this section prejudices the operation of any enactment imposing penalties on a company or its officers in respect of any such default as is mentioned above.

## 714 Registrar's index of company and corporate names

**714(1) [Index to be kept re certain bodies]** The registrar of companies shall keep an index of the names of the following bodies –

(a) companies as defined by this Act,

(aa) companies incorporated outside the United Kingdom and Gibraltar which have complied with paragraph 1 of Schedule 21A and which do not appear to the registrar of companies not to have a branch in Great Britain,

(b) companies incorporated outside Great Britain which have complied with section 691 and which do not appear to the registrar of companies not to have a place of business in Great Britain,

(c) incorporated and unincorporated bodies to which any provision of this Act applies by virtue of section 718 (unregistered companies),

(d) limited partnerships registered under the Limited Partnerships Act 1907,

(e) companies within the meaning of the Companies Act (Northern Ireland) 1960,

(f) companies incorporated outside Northern Ireland which have complied with section 356 of that Act (which corresponds with section 691 of this Act), and which do not appear to the registrar not to have a place of business in Northern Ireland, and

(g) societies registered under the Industrial and Provident Societies Act 1965 or the Industrial and Provident Societies Act (Northern Ireland) 1969.

**History**
S. 714(1)(aa) inserted by the Oversea Companies and Credit and Financial Institutions (Branch Disclosure) Regulations 1992 (SI 1992/3179), reg. 1(3), 4 and Sch. 3, para. 8 as from 1 January 1993.

**Note**
See the Open-Ended Investment Companies (Investment Companies with Variable Capital) Regulations 1996 (SI 1996/2827) Sch. 1, para. 7 for modifications to s. 714(1) for the purpose of those Regulations.

**714(2) [Variation or deletion re s. 714(1)]** The Secretary of State may by order in a statutory instrument vary subsection (1) by the addition or deletion of any class of body, except any within paragraph (a) or (b) of the subsection, whether incorporated or unincorporated; and any such statutory instrument is subject to annulment in pursuance of a resolution of either House of Parliament.

## 715 Destruction of old records

**715** (Omitted and repealed by Companies Act 1989, s. 127(3), 212 and Sch. 24 as from 1 July 1991.)

**History**
In regard to the above date see SI 1991/488 (C 11), art. 2(1); s. 715 formerly read as follows:

"**715(1)** The registrar of companies may destroy any documents or other material which he has kept for over 10 years and which were, or were comprised in or annexed or attached to, the accounts or annual returns of any company.

**(2)** The registrar shall retain a copy of any document or other material destroyed in pursuance of subsection (1); and sections 709 and 710 apply in relation to any such copy as if it were the original."

## 715A Interpretation

**715A(1) ["Document", "legible"]** In this Part–

**"document"** includes information recorded in any form; and

**"legible"**, in the context of documents in legible or non-legible form, means capable of being read with the naked eye.

**715A(2) [References to delivering document]** References in this Part to delivering a document include sending, forwarding, producing or (in the case of a notice) giving it.

**History**
S. 715A inserted by CA 1989, s. 127(1) as from 7 January 1991 (see SI 1990/2569 (C 68), art. 4(b)).

# PART XXV – MISCELLANEOUS AND SUPPLEMENTARY PROVISIONS

## 716 Prohibition of partnerships with more than 20 members

**716(1) [Requirement of registration]** No company, association or partnership consisting of more than 20 persons shall be formed for the purpose of carrying on any business that has for its object the acquisition of gain by the company, association or partnership, or by its individual members, unless it is registered as a company under this Act, or is formed in pursuance of some other Act of Parliament, or of letters patent.

**Note**
See list of regulations in note to s. 716(2).

**716(2) [Qualification to s. 716(1)]** However, this does not prohibit the formation–

(a) for the purpose of carrying on practice as solicitors, of a partnership consisting of persons each of whom is a solicitor;

(b) for the purpose of carrying on practice as accountants, of a partnership which is eligible for appointment as a company auditor under section 25 of the Companies Act 1989;

(c) for the purpose of carrying on business as members of a recognised stock exchange, of a partnership consisting of persons each of whom is a member of that stock exchange;

(d) for any purpose prescribed by regulations (which may include a purpose mentioned above), of a partnership of a description so prescribed;

(e) of an investment company with variable capital within the meaning of the Open-Ended Investment Companies (Investment Companies with Variable Capital) Regulations 1996.

**History**
In s. 716(2)(b) the words "a partnership which is eligible for appointment as a company auditor under section 25 of the Companies Act 1989" substituted for the former words "a partnership consisting of persons each of whom falls within either paragraph (a) or (b) of section 389(1) (qualifications of company auditors)" by the Companies Act 1989 (Eligibility for Appointment as Company Auditor) (Consequential Amendments) Regulations 1991 (SI 1991/1997), reg. 2 and Sch., para. 53(1), (3) as from 1 October 1991.

S. 716(2)(d) inserted and words formerly appearing at the end omitted and repealed by CA 1989, s. 145, 212, Sch. 19, para. 15(1), (2) and Sch. 24 as from 1 April 1990 (see SI 1990/355 (C 13), art. 4(f), 5(1)(b), (2) and also relevant transitional or saving provisions in that S.I.); the former words were originally inserted by Financial Services Act 1986, s. 212(2) and Sch. 16, para. 22 as from 29 April 1988 (see SI 1988/740 (C 22)) (but now repealed by CA 1989, s. 212 and Sch. 24 – see SI 1990/355 (C 13), art. 5(1)(e)) and read as follows:

"and in this subsection **"recognised stock exchange"** means The Stock Exchange and any other stock exchange which is declared to be a recognised stock exchange for the purposes of this section by an order in a statutory instrument made by the Secretary of State which is for the time being in force."

S. 716(2)(e) inserted by the Open-Ended Investment Companies (Investment Companies with Variable Capital) Regulations 1996 (SI 1996/2827), reg. 1, 75, and Sch. 8, para. 8 as from 6 January 1997.

**Note**
In regard to s. 716(2)(d) see the Partnerships (Unrestricted Size) No. 6 Regulations 1990 (SI 1990/1581) and the Partnership (Unrestricted Size) No. 7 Regulations 1990 (SI 1990/1969) (both previous regulations made under former s. 716(3)), the Partnerships (Unrestricted Size) No. 8 Regulations 1991 (SI 1991/2729) and the Partnerships (Unrestricted Size) No. 9 Regulations 1992 (SI 1992/1028); the Partnerships (Unrestricted Size) No. 10 Regulations 1991 (SI 1992/1439); the Partnerships (Unrestricted Size) No. 11 Regulations 1994 (SI 1994/644); the Partnerships (Unrestricted Size) No. 11 Regulations 1996 (SI 1996/262); the Partnerships (Unrestricted Size) No. 12 Regulations 1997 (SI 1997/1937); the Partnerships (Unrestricted Size) No. 13 Regulations 1999 (SI 1999/2464); and the Partnership (Unrestricted Size) No. 14 Regulations 2000 (SI 2000/486).

**716(3) ["Solicitor"]** In subsection (2)(a) **"solicitor"**–

(a) in relation to England and Wales, means solicitor of the Supreme Court, and

(b) in relation to Scotland, means a person enrolled or deemed enrolled as a solicitor in pursuance of the Solicitors (Scotland) Act 1980.

**History**
See history note after s. 716(4).

**716(4) ["Recognised stock exchange"]** In subsection (2)(c) **"recognised stock exchange"** means–

(a) The International Stock Exchange of the United Kingdom and the Republic of Ireland Limited, and

(b) any other stock exchange for the time being recognised for the purposes of this section by the Secretary of State by order made by statutory instrument.

**History**
S. 716(3), (4) substituted by CA 1989, s. 145 and Sch. 19, para. 15(1), (3) as from 1 April 1990 (see SI 1990/355 (C 13), art. 4(f)); s. 716(3), (4) formerly read as follows:

"**716(3)** The Secretary of State may by regulations in a statutory instrument provide that subsection (1) shall not apply to the formation (otherwise than as permitted by subsection (2)), for a purpose specified in the regulations, of a partnership of a description so specified.

**(4)** In this section **"solicitor"**–
(a) in relation to England and Wales, means solicitor of the Supreme Court, and
(b) in relation to Scotland, means a person enrolled or deemed enrolled as a solicitor in pursuance of the Solicitors (Scotland) Act 1980."

**716(5) [Non-application of s. 716(1)]** Subsection (1) does not apply in relation to any body of persons for the time being approved for the purposes of the Marine and Aviation Insurance (War Risks) Act 1952 by the Secretary of State, being a body the objects of which are or include the carrying on of business by way of the re-insurance of risks which may be re-insured under any agreement for the purpose mentioned in section 1(1)(b) of that Act.

# 717 Limited partnerships: limit on number of members

**717(1) [Exceptions to Limited Partnerships Act 1907]** So much of the Limited Partnerships Act 1907 as provides that a limited partnership shall not consist of more than 20 persons does not apply–

(a) to a partnership carrying on practice as solicitors and consisting of persons each of whom is a solicitor,

(b) to a partnership carrying on practice as accountants which is eligible for appointment as a company auditor under section 25 of the Companies Act 1989,

(c) to a partnership carrying on business as members of a recognised stock exchange and consisting of persons each of whom is a member of that exchange;

(d) to a partnership carrying on business of any description prescribed by regulations (which may include a business of any description mentioned above), of a partnership of a description so prescribed.

**History**

In s. 717(1)(b) the words "which is eligible for appointment as a company auditor under section 25 of the Companies Act 1989" substituted for the former words "and consisting of persons each of whom falls within either paragraph (a) or (b) of section 389(1) of this Act (qualification of company auditors)" by the Companies Act 1989 (Eligibility for Appointment as Company Auditor) (Consequential Amendments) Regulations 1991 (SI 1991/1997), reg. 2 and Sch., para. 53(1), (4) as from 1 October 1991 (an error in para. 53 was corrected by the Companies Act 1989 Part II (Consequential Amendments) Regulations 1995 (SI 1995/1163), reg. 1, 2).

S. 717(1)(d) inserted and words formerly appearing at the end of s. 717(1) omitted and repealed as from 1 April 1990 by CA 1989, s. 145, 212, Sch. 19, para. 16(1), (2) and Sch. 24 as from 1 April 1990 (see SI 1990/355 (C 13), art. 4(f), 5(1)(b), (2) and also relevant transitional or saving provisions in that S.I.); the former words were originally inserted by Financial Services Act 1986, s. 212(2) and Sch. 16, para. 22 as from 29 April 1988 (see SI 1988/740 (C 22)) (but now repealed by CA 1989, s. 212 and Sch. 24 – see SI 1990/355 (C 13), art. 5(1)(e) and read as follows:

"and in this subsection **"recognised stock exchange"** means The Stock Exchange and any other stock exchange which is declared to be a recognised stock exchange for the purposes of this section by an order in a statutory instrument made by the Secretary of State which is for the time being in force."

**Note**

In regard to s. 717(1)(d) see the Limited Partnerships (Unrestricted Size) No. 2 Regulations 1990 (SI 1990/1580) – previous regulations made under former s. 717(2) – and also the Limited Partnerships (Unrestricted Size) No. 3 Regulations 1992 (SI 1992/1027).

**717(2) ["Solicitor"]** In subsection (1)(a) **"solicitor"**–

(a) in relation to England and Wales, means solicitor of the Supreme Court, and

(b) in relation to Scotland, means a person enrolled or deemed enrolled as a solicitor in pursuance of the Solicitors (Scotland) Act 1980.

**History**

See history note after s. 717(3).

**717(3) ["Recognised stock exchange"]** In subsection (1)(c) **"recognised stock exchange"** means–

(a) The International Stock Exchange of the United Kingdom and the Republic of Ireland Limited, and

(b) any other stock exchange for the time being recognised for the purposes of this section by the Secretary of State by order made by statutory instrument.

**History**

S. 717(2), (3) substituted by CA 1989, s. 145 and Sch. 19, para. 16(1), (3) as from 1 April 1990 (see SI 1990/355 (C 13), art. 4(f)); s. 717(2), (3) formerly read as follows:

"**717(2)** The Secretary of State may by regulations in a statutory instrument provide that so much of section 4(2) of the Act of 1907 as provides that a limited partnership shall not consist of more than 20 persons shall not apply to a partnership (other than one permitted by subsection (1) of this section) carrying on business of a description specified in the regulations, being a partnership of a description so specified.

**(3)** In this section **"solicitor"** means the same as in section 716."

# 718 Unregistered companies

**718(1) [Application of provisions to certain unregistered companies]** The provisions of this Act specified in the first column of Schedule 22 (relating respectively to the matters specified in the second column of the Schedule) apply to all bodies corporate incorporated in and having a principal place of business in Great Britain, other than those mentioned in subsection (2) below, as if they were companies registered under this Act, but subject to any limitations mentioned in relation to those provisions respectively in the third column and to such adaptations and modifications (if any) as may be specified by regulations made by the Secretary of State.

**718(2) [Exception to application of s. 718(1)]** Those provisions of this Act do not apply by virtue of this section to any of the following–

(a) any body incorporated by or registered under any public general Act of Parliament,

(b) any body not formed for the purpose of carrying on a business which has for its object the acquisition of gain by the body or its individual members,

(c) any body for the time being exempted by direction of the Secretary of State (or before him by the Board of Trade),

(d) any investment company with variable capital within the meaning of the Open-Ended Investment Companies (Investment Companies with Variable Capital) Regulations 1996.

**History**
S. 718(2)(d) inserted by the Open-Ended Investment Companies (Investment Companies with Variable Capital) Regulations 1996 (SI 1996/2827), reg. 1, 75, and Sch. 8, para. 9 as from 6 January 1997.

**718(3) [Application by regulations]** Where against any provision of this Act specified in the first column of Schedule 22 there appears in the third column the entry **"Subject to section 718(3)"**, it means that the provision is to apply by virtue of this section so far only as may be specified by regulations made by the Secretary of State and to such bodies corporate as may be so specified.

**718(4) [Certain unincorporated bodies, etc.]** The provisions specified in the first column of the Schedule also apply in like manner in relation to any unincorporated body of persons entitled by virtue of letters patent to any of the privileges conferred by the Chartered Companies Act 1837 and not registered under any other public general Act of Parliament, but subject to the like exceptions as are provided for in the case of bodies corporate by paragraphs (b) and (c) of subsection (2).

**718(5) [Operation of section]** This section does not repeal or revoke in whole or in part any enactment, royal charter or other instrument constituting or regulating any body in relation to which those provisions are applied by virtue of this section, or restrict the power of Her Majesty to grant a charter in lieu of or supplementary to any such charter as above mentioned; but, in relation to any such body, the operation of any such enactment, charter or instrument is suspended in so far as it is inconsistent with any of those provisions as they apply for the time being to that body.

**718(6) [Regulations]** The power to make regulations conferred by this section (whether regulations under subsection (1) or subsection (3)) is exercisable by statutory instrument subject to annulment in pursuance of a resolution of either House of Parliament.

**Note**
Re s. 718 see the Companies (Unregistered Companies) Regulations 1985 (SI 1985/680), as amended.

# 719 Power of company to provide for employees on cessation or transfer of business

**719(1) [For benefit of employees]** The powers of a company include (if they would not otherwise do so apart from this section) power to make the following provision for the benefit of persons employed or formerly employed by the company or any of its subsidiaries, that is to say, provision in connection with the cessation or the transfer to any person of the whole or part of the undertaking of the company or that subsidiary.

**719(2) [Exercise of s. 719(1) power]** The power conferred by subsection (1) is exercisable notwithstanding that its exercise is not in the best interests of the company.

**719(3) [Sanctions for exercise of power]** The power which a company may exercise by virtue only of subsection (1) shall only be exercised by the company if sanctioned –

(a) in a case not falling within paragraph (b) or (c) below, by an ordinary resolution of the company, or

(b) if so authorised by the memorandum or articles, a resolution of the directors, or

(c) if the memorandum or articles require the exercise of the power to be sanctioned by a resolution of the company of some other description for which more than a simple majority of the members voting is necessary, with the sanction of a resolution of that description;

and in any case after compliance with any other requirements of the memorandum or articles applicable to its exercise.

**719(4) [Source of payment]** Any payment which may be made by a company under this section may, if made before the commencement of any winding up of the company, be made out of profits of the company which are available for dividend.

**Note**
For the purposes of s. 719 a company which immediately before the commencement of CA 1989, s. 144(1) (inserting new s. 736, 736A) (1 November 1990) was a subsidiary of another company shall not be treated as ceasing to be such a subsidiary by reason of that provision coming into force (CA 1989, Sch. 18, para. 36).

## 720 Certain companies to publish periodical statement

**720(1) [Statement in form of Sch. 23]** Every company, being an insurance company or a deposit, provident or benefit society, shall before it commences business, and also on the first Monday in February and the first Tuesday in August in every year during which it carries on business, make a statement in the form set out in Schedule 23, or as near to it as circumstances admit.

**720(2) [Copy of statement in registered office, etc.]** A copy of the statement shall be put up in a conspicuous place in the company's registered office, and in every branch office or place where the business of the company is carried on.

**720(3) [Entitlement to copy]** Every member and every creditor of the company is entitled to a copy of the statement, on payment of a sum not exceeding $2^1/_2$ pence.

**720(4) [Penalty on default]** If default is made in complying with this section, the company and every officer of it who is in default is liable to a fine and, for continued contravention, to a daily default fine.

**720(5) [Deemed insurance company]** For purposes of this Act, a company which carries on the business of insurance in common with any other business or businesses is deemed an insurance company.

**720(6) [Exception re certain insurance companies]** In the case of an insurance company to which Part II of the Insurance Companies Act 1982 applies, this section does not apply if the company complies with provisions of that Act as to the accounts and balance sheet to be prepared annually and deposited by such a company.

**720(7) [Regulations]** The Secretary of State may, by regulations in a statutory instrument (subject to annulment in pursuance of a resolution of either House of Parliament), alter the form in Schedule 23.

**Note**

S. 720 does not apply to an EC company if it complies relevant law of the home state re preparation and of annual accounts and balance sheet: see the Insurance Companies (Third Insurance Directives) Regulations 1994 (SI 1994/1696), reg. 9(6).

## 721 Production and inspection of books where offence suspected

**721(1) [Application re possible offence in company management, etc.]** The following applies if on an application made–

(a) in England and Wales, to a judge of the High Court by the Director of Public Prosecutions, the Secretary of State or a chief officer of police, or

(b) in Scotland, to one of the Lords Commissioners of Justiciary by the Lord Advocate,

there is shown to be reasonable cause to believe that any person has, while an officer of a company, committed an offence in connection with the management of the company's affairs and that evidence of the commission of the offence is to be found in any books or papers of or under the control of the company.

**721(2) [Court order for inspection or production]** An order may be made–

(a) authorising any person named in it to inspect the books or papers in question, or any of them, for the purpose of investigating and obtaining evidence of the offence, or

(b) requiring the secretary of the company or such other officer of it as may be named in the order to produce the books or papers (or any of them) to a person named in the order at a place so named.

**721(3) [Application of s. 721(1), (2) to bankers]** The above applies also in relation to any books or papers of a person carrying on the business of banking so far as they relate to the company's affairs, as it applies to any books or papers of or under the control of the company, except that no such order as is referred to in subsection (2)(b) shall be made by virtue of this subsection.

**721(4) [No appeal from court decision]** The decision of a judge of the High Court or of any of the Lords Commissioners of Justiciary on an application under this section is not appealable.

## 722 Form of company registers, etc.

**722(1) [Form]** Any register, index, minute book or accounting records required by the Companies Acts to be kept by a company may be kept either by making entries in bound books or by recording the matters in question in any other manner.

**722(2) [Precautions against falsification, etc.]** Where any such register, index, minute book or accounting record is not kept by making entries in a bound book, but by some other means, adequate precautions shall be taken for guarding against falsification and facilitating its discovery.

**722(3) [Penalty on default re s. 722(2)]** If default is made in complying with subsection (2), the company and every officer of it who is in default is liable to a fine and, for continued contravention, to a daily default fine.

## 723 Use of computers for company records

**723(1) [Records otherwise than in legible form]** The power conferred on a company by section 722(1) to keep a register or other record by recording the matters in question otherwise than by making entries in bound books includes power to keep the register or other record by recording those matters otherwise than in a legible form, so long as the recording is capable of being reproduced in a legible form.

**723(2) [Certain provisions in instrument before 12 February 1979]** Any provision of an instrument made by a company before 12th February 1979 which requires a register of holders of the company's debentures to be kept in a legible form is to be read as requiring the register to be kept in a legible or non-legible form.

**723(3) [Extension of duty re inspection, etc.]** If any such register or other record of a company as is mentioned in section 722(1), or a register of holders of a company's debentures, is kept by the company by recording the matters in question otherwise than in a legible form, any duty imposed on the company by this Act to allow inspection of, or to furnish a copy of, the register or other record or any part of it is to be treated as a duty to allow inspection of, or to furnish, a reproduction of the recording or of the relevant part of it in a legible form.

**723(4) [Additional provisions in regulations]** The Secretary of State may by regulations in a statutory instrument make such provision in addition to subsection (3) as he considers appropriate in connection with such registers or other records as are mentioned in that subsection, and are kept as so mentioned; and the regulations may make modifications of provisions of this Act relating to such registers or other records.

**Note**
See the Companies (Registers and other Records) Regulations 1985 (SI 1985/724).

**723(5) [Annulment of s. 723(4) statutory instrument]** A statutory instrument under subsection (4) is subject to annulment in pursuance of a resolution of either House of Parliament.

## 723A Obligations of company as to inspection of registers, etc.

**723A(1) [Power of Secretary of State to make regulations]** The Secretary of State may make provision by regulations as to the obligations of a company which is required by any provision of this Act–

(a) to make available for inspection any register, index or document, or

(b) to provide copies of any such register, index or document, or part of it;

and a company which fails to comply with the regulations shall be deemed to have refused inspection or, as the case may be, to have failed to provide a copy.

**723A(2) [Time, duration and manner]** The regulations may make provision as to the time, duration and manner of inspection, including the circumstances in which and extent to which the copying of information is permitted in the course of inspection.

**723A(3) [Extracting or presenting information]** The regulations may define what may be required of the company as regards the nature, extent and manner of extracting or presenting any information for the purposes of inspection or the provision of copies.

**723A(4)** **[Fees]** Where there is power to charge a fee, the regulations may make provision as to the amount of the fee and the basis of its calculation.

**723A(5)** **[Different provisions for different cases]** Regulations under this section may make different provision for different classes of case.

**723A(6)** **[More extensive facilities]** Nothing in any provision of this Act or in the regulations shall be construed as preventing a company from affording more extensive facilities than are required by the regulations or, where a fee may be charged, from charging a lesser fee than that prescribed or no fee at all.

**723A(7)** **[Regulations by statutory instrument]** Regulations under this section shall be made by statutory instrument which shall be subject to annulment in pursuance of a resolution of either House of Parliament.

**History**

S. 723A inserted by CA 1989, s. 143(1) as from 1 November 1991 (see SI 1991/1996 (C 57), art. 2(2)(b)).

**Note**

See the Companies (Inspection and Copying of Registers, Indices and Documents) Regulations 1991 (SI 1991/1998).

## 724 Cross-border operation of receivership provisions

**724** (Repealed by Insolvency Act 1986, s. 438 and Sch. 12 as from 29 December 1986.)

**History**

In regard to the date of the above repeal see Insolvency Act 1986, s. 443 and SI 1986/1924 (C 71); s. 724 formerly read as follows:

"**724(1)** A receiver appointed under the law of either part of Great Britain in respect of the whole or any part of any property or undertaking of a company and in consequence of the company having created a charge which, as created, was a floating charge may exercise his powers in the other part of Great Britain so far as their exercise is not inconsistent with the law applicable there.

**(2)** In subsection (1) **"receiver"** includes a manager and a person who is appointed both receiver and manager."

## 725 Service of documents

**725(1)** **[Usual service]** A document may be served on a company by leaving it at, or sending it by post to, the company's registered office.

**725(2)** **[Scottish registered company carrying on business in England, Wales]** Where a company registered in Scotland carries on business in England and Wales, the process of any court in England and Wales may be served on the company by leaving it at, or sending it by post to, the company's principal place of business in England and Wales, addressed to the manager or other head officer in England and Wales of the company.

**725(3)** **[Copy to registered office if s. 725(2) service]** Where process is served on a company under subsection (2), the person issuing out the process shall send a copy of it by post to the company's registered office.

## 726 Costs and expenses in actions by certain limited companies

**726(1)** **[Security for costs – England and Wales]** Where in England and Wales a limited company is plaintiff in an action or other legal proceeding, the court having jurisdiction in the matter may, if it appears by credible testimony that there is reason to believe that the company will be unable to pay the defendant's costs if successful in his defence, require sufficient security to be given for those costs, and may stay all proceedings until the security is given.

**726(2)** **[Caution for costs – Scotland]** Where in Scotland a limited company is pursuer in an action or other legal proceeding, the court having jurisdiction in the matter may, if it appears by credible testimony that there is reason to believe that the company will be unable to pay the defender's expenses if successful in his defence, order the company to find caution and sist the proceedings until caution is found.

## 727 Power of court to grant relief in certain cases

**727(1)** **[Relief of officers from liability]** If in any proceedings for negligence, default, breach of duty or breach of trust against an officer of a company or a person employed by a company as auditor (whether he is or is not an officer of the company) it appears to the court hearing the case that that officer or person is or may be liable in respect of the negligence, default, breach of duty or breach of trust, but that he has acted honestly and reasonably, and that having regard to all the circumstances of the case (including those connected with his appointment) he ought fairly to be excused for the negligence, default, breach of duty or breach of trust, that court may relieve him, either wholly or partly, from his liability on such terms as it thinks fit.

**727(2) [Application by officer for relief]** If any such officer or person as above-mentioned has reason to apprehend that any claim will or might be made against him in respect of any negligence, default, breach of duty or breach of trust, he may apply to the court for relief; and the court on the application has the same power to relieve him as under this section it would have had if it had been a court before which proceedings against that person for negligence, default, breach of duty or breach of trust had been brought.

**727(3) [Withdrawal of case from jury]** Where a case to which subsection (1) applies is being tried by a judge with a jury, the judge, after hearing the evidence, may, if he is satisfied that the defendant or defender ought in pursuance of that subsection to be relieved either in whole or in part from the liability sought to be enforced against him, withdraw the case in whole or in part from the jury and forthwith direct judgment to be entered for the defendant or defender on such terms as to costs or otherwise as the judge may think proper.

## 728 Enforcement of High Court orders

**728** Orders made by the High Court under this Act may be enforced in the same manner as orders made in an action pending in that court.

## 729 Annual report by Secretary of State

**729** The Secretary of State shall cause a general annual report of matters within the Companies Acts to be prepared and laid before both Houses of Parliament.

## 730 Punishment of offences

**730(1) [Sch. 24]** Schedule 24 to this Act has effect with respect to the way in which offences under this Act are punishable on conviction.

**730(2) [First, second and third columns of Schedule]** In relation to an offence under a provision of this Act specified in the first column of the Schedule (the general nature of the offence being described in the second column), the third column shows whether the offence is punishable on conviction on indictment, or on summary conviction, or either in the one way or the other.

**730(3) [Fourth column]** The fourth column of the Schedule shows, in relation to an offence, the maximum punishment by way of fine or imprisonment under this Act which may be imposed on a person convicted of the offence in the way specified in relation to it in the third column (that is to say, on indictment or summarily), a reference to a period of years or months being to a term of imprisonment of that duration.

**730(4) [Fifth column]** The fifth column shows (in relation to an offence for which there is an entry in that column) that a person convicted of the offence after continued contravention is liable to a daily default fine; that is to say, he is liable on a second or subsequent summary conviction of the offence to the fine specified in that column for each day on which the contravention is continued (instead of the penalty specified for the offence in the fourth column of the Schedule).

**730(5) ["Officer who is in default"]** For the purpose of any enactment in the Companies Acts which provides that an officer of a company or other body who is in default is liable to a fine or penalty, the expression **"officer who is in default"** means any officer of the company or other body who knowingly and wilfully authorises or permits the default, refusal or contravention mentioned in the enactment.

**History**

In s. 730(5) the words "or other body" (appearing twice) inserted by CA 1989, s. 145 and Sch. 19, para. 17 as from 1 April 1990 (see SI 1990/355 (C 13), art. 4(f)).

## 731 Summary proceedings

**731(1) [Taking of summary proceedings]** Summary proceedings for any offence under the Companies Acts may (without prejudice to any jurisdiction exercisable apart from this subsection) be taken against a body corporate at any place at which the body has a place of business, and against any other person at any place at which he is for the time being.

**731(2) [Time for laying information]** Notwithstanding anything in section 127(1) of the Magistrates' Courts Act 1980, an information relating to an offence under the Companies Acts which is triable by a magistrates' court in England and Wales may be so tried if it is laid at any time within 3 years after the commission of the offence and within 12 months after the date on which evidence sufficient in the opinion of the Director of Public Prosecutions or the Secretary of State (as the case may be) to justify the proceedings comes to his knowledge.

**731(3) [Time for commencement of summary proceedings in Scotland]** Summary proceedings in Scotland for an offence under the Companies Acts shall not be commenced after the expiration of 3 years from the commission of the offence.

Subject to this (and notwithstanding anything in section 331 of the Criminal Procedure (Scotland) Act 1975), such proceedings may (in Scotland) be commenced at any time within 12 months after the date on which evidence sufficient in the Lord Advocate's opinion to justify the proceedings came to his knowledge or, where such evidence was reported to him by the Secretary of State, within 12 months after the date on which it came to the knowledge of the latter; and subsection (3) of that section applies for the purpose of this subsection as it applies for the purpose of that section.

**731(4) [Certificate by DPP et al. conclusive evidence]** For purposes of this section, a certificate of the Director of Public Prosecutions, the Lord Advocate or the Secretary of State (as the case may be) as to the date on which such evidence as is referred to above came to his knowledge is conclusive evidence.

## 732 Prosecution by public authorities

**732(1) [Institution of proceedings only with consent]** In respect of an offence under any of sections 210, 324, 329, 447 to 451 and 455, proceedings shall not, in England and Wales, be instituted except by or with the consent of the appropriate authority.

**732(2) [Authority under s. 732(1)]** That authority is–

(a) for an offence under any of sections 210, 324 and 329, the Secretary of State or the Director of Public Prosecutions,

(b) for an offence under any of sections 447 to 451, either one of those two persons or the Industrial Assurance Commissioner, and

(c) for an offence under section 455, the Secretary of State.

**732(3) [Legal professional privilege]** Where proceedings are instituted under the Companies Acts against any person by the Director of Public Prosecutions or by or on behalf of the Secretary of State or the Lord Advocate, nothing in those Acts is to be taken to require any person to disclose any information which he is entitled to refuse to disclose on grounds of legal professional privilege.

## 733 Offences by bodies corporate

**733(1) [Application]** The following applies to offences under any of sections 210, 216(3), 394A(1) and 447 to 451.

**History**

In s. 733(1) "295(7)" inserted by Insolvency Act 1985, s. 109 and Sch. 6, para. 7(2) as from 28 April 1986; and omitted by Insolvency Act 1986, s. 439(1) and Sch. 13 as from 29 December 1986 (see IA 1986, s. 443 and SI 1986/1924 (C 71)). Also in s. 733(1) ", 394A(1)" inserted by CA 1989, s. 123(3) as from 1 April 1990 subject to transitional and saving provisions (see SI 1990/355 (C 13), art. 4(a) and also art. 10).

**733(2) [Offence re officer]** Where a body corporate is guilty of such an offence and it is proved that the offence occurred with the consent or connivance of, or was attributable to any neglect on the part of any director, manager, secretary or other similar officer of the body, or any person who was purporting to act in any such capacity, he as well as the body corporate is guilty of that offence and is liable to be proceeded against and punished accordingly.

**733(3) [Where managers are members]** Where the affairs of a body corporate are managed by its members, subsection (2) above applies in relation to the acts and defaults of a member in connection with his functions of management as if he were a director of the body corporate.

**History**

In s. 733(3) the words "210, 216(3) or 295(7)" substituted for the former words "210 or 216(3)" by Insolvency Act 1985, s. 109 and Sch. 6, para. 7(3) as from 28 April 1986. In addition the words "or 216(3)" substituted for the former words "216(3) or 295(7)" by Insolvency Act 1986, s. 439(1) and Sch. 13 as from 29 December 1986 (see IA 1986, s. 443 and SI 1986/1924 (C 71)).

Also in s. 733(3) the words "then in the case of an offence under section 210, or 216(3)" formerly appearing after the words "by its members," repealed by CA 1989, s. 212 and Sch. 24 as from 1 October 1990 (see SI 1990/1707 (C 46), art. 3(a)) and the former substitution by Insolvency Act 1986, s. 439(1) and Sch. 13 (referred to above) repealed by CA 1989, s. 212 and Sch. 24 from the same date (see SI 1990/1707 (C 46), art. 3(b)).

**733(4) ["Director"]** In this section **"director"**, in relation to an offence under any of sections 447 to 451, includes a shadow director.

## 734 Criminal proceedings against unincorporated bodies

**734(1) [Offences by unincorporated body]** Proceedings for an offence alleged to have been committed under section 389A(3) or section 394A(1) or any of sections 447 to 451 by an unincorporated body shall be brought in the name of that body (and not in that of any of its members), and for the purposes of any such proceedings, any rules of court relating to the service of documents apply as if that body were a corporation.

**History**

In s. 734(1) the words "section 389A(3) or" and "section 394A(1) or" inserted by CA 1989, s. 120(2), 123(4) as from 1 April 1990 subject to transitional and saving provisions (see SI 1990/355 (C 13), art. 4(a) and also art. 10).

**734(2) [Payment of fine]** A fine imposed on an unincorporated body on its conviction of such an offence shall be paid out of the funds of that body.

**734(3) [Application of Criminal Justice Act, etc.]** In a case in which an unincorporated body is charged in England and Wales with such an offence, section 33 of the Criminal Justice Act 1925 and Schedule 3 to the Magistrates' Courts Act 1980 (procedure on charge of an offence against a corporation) have effect in like manner as in the case of a corporation so charged.

**734(4) [Scotland: application of Criminal Procedure (Scotland) Act]** In relation to proceedings on indictment in Scotland for such an offence alleged to have been committed by an unincorporated body, section 74 of the Criminal Procedure (Scotland) Act 1975 (proceedings on indictment against bodies corporate) has effect as if that body were a body corporate.

**734(5) [Offence by partner]** Where such an offence committed by a partnership is proved to have been committed with the consent or connivance of, or to be attributable to any neglect on the part of, a partner, he as well as the partnership is guilty of the offence and liable to be proceeded against and punished accordingly.

**734(6) [Offence by member of unincorporated body]** Where such an offence committed by an unincorporated body (other than a partnership) is proved to have been committed with the consent or connivance of, or to be attributable to any neglect on the part of, any officer of the body or any member of its governing body, he as well as the body is guilty of the offence and liable to be proceeded against and punished accordingly.

**History**

S. 734(5), (6) added by CA 1989, s. 145 and Sch. 19, para. 18 as from 1 April 1990 (see SI 1990/355 (C 13), art. 4(f)).

# PART XXVI – INTERPRETATION

## 735 "Company", etc.

**735(1) ["Company", "existing company", etc.]** In this Act –

(a) **"company"** means a company formed and registered under this Act, or an existing company;

(b) **"existing company"** means a company formed and registered under the former

Companies Acts, but does not include a company registered under the Joint Stock Companies Acts, the Companies Act 1862 or the Companies (Consolidation) Act 1908 in what was then Ireland;

(c) **"the former Companies Acts"** means the Joint Stock Companies Acts, the Companies Act 1862, the Companies (Consolidation) Act 1908, the Companies Act 1929 and the Companies Acts 1948 to 1983.

**735(2) ["Public company", "private company"] "Public company"** and **"private company"** have the meanings given by section 1(3).

**735(3) ["The Joint Stock Companies Acts"] "The Joint Stock Companies Acts"** means the Joint Stock Companies Act 1856, the Joint Stock Companies Acts 1856, 1857, the Joint Stock Banking Companies Act 1857 and the Act to enable Joint Stock Banking Companies to be formed on the principle of limited liability, or any one or more of those Acts (as the case may require), but does not include the Joint Stock Companies Act 1844.

**735(4) [Application of definitions]** The definitions in this section apply unless the contrary intention appears.

## 735A Relationship of this Act to Insolvency Act

**735A(1) ["The Insolvency Act"]** In this Act **"the Insolvency Act"** means the Insolvency Act 1986; and in the following provisions of this Act, namely, sections 375(1)(b), 425(6)(a), 460(2), 675, 676, 677, 699(1), 728 and Schedule 21, paragraph 6(1), the words "this Act" are to be read as including Parts I to VII of that Act, sections 411, 413, 414, 416 and 417 in Part XV of that Act, and also the Company Directors Disqualification Act 1986.

**History**
In s. 735A(1) the words "440, 449(1)(a) and (d)" formerly appearing after "425(6)(a)", repealed by CA 1989, s. 212 and Sch. 24 as from 21 February 1990 (see SI 1990/142 (C 5), art. 7(d)).

**735A(2) [Interpretation]** In sections 704(5), (7) and (8), 706(1), 707(1), 707A(1), 708(1)(a) and (4), 709(1) and (3), 710A, 713(1), 729 and 732(3) references to the Companies Acts include Parts I to VII of the Insolvency Act, sections 411, 413, 414, 416 and 417 in Part XV of that Act, and also the Company Directors Disqualification Act 1986.

**History**
In s. 735A(2) the words "sections 704(5), (7) and (8)" substituted for the former words "sections 704(5)" by the Deregulation and Contracting Out Act 1994, s. 76, 82(2)(f) and Sch. 16, para. 9 as from 3 January 1995.
Previously in s. 735A(2) "707A(1)," and "709(1) and (3)," inserted and "710A" substituted for the former "710(5)" by CA 1989, s. 127(5) or from 1 July 1991 (see SI 1991/488 (C 11), art. 2(1)).

**735A(3) [Application of s. 735A(1), (2)]** Subsections (1) and (2) apply unless the contrary intention appears.

**History**
S. 735A inserted by Insolvency Act 1986, s. 439(1) and Sch. 13, Pt. II as from 29 December 1986 (see IA 1986, s. 443 and SI 1986/1924 (C 71)).

## 735B Relationship of this Act to Parts IV and V of the Financial Services Act 1986

**735B** In sections 704(5), (7) and (8), 706(1), 707(1), 707A(1), 708(1)(a) and (4), 709(1) and (3), 710A and 713(1) references to the Companies Acts include Parts IV and V of the Financial Services Act 1986.

**History**
In s. 735B the words "sections 704(5), (7) and (8)" substituted for the former words "sections 704(5)" by the Deregulation and Contracting Out Act 1994, s. 76, 82(2)(f) and Sch. 16, para. 10 as from 3 January 1995.
S. 735B inserted by CA 1989, s. 127(6) as from 1 July 1991 (see SI 1991/488 (C 11)).

## 736 "Subsidiary", "holding company" and "wholly-owned subsidiary"

**736(1) ["Subsidiary", "holding company"]** A company is a **"subsidiary"** of another company, its **"holding company"**, if that other company–

(a) holds a majority of the voting rights in it, or

(b) is a member of it and has the right to appoint or remove a majority of its board of directors, or

(c) is a member of it and controls alone, pursuant to an agreement with other shareholders or members, a majority of the voting rights in it,

or if it is a subsidiary of a company which is itself a subsidiary of that other company.

**736(2) ["Wholly-owned subsidiary"]** A company is a **"wholly-owned subsidiary"** of another company if it has no members except that other and that other's wholly-owned subsidiaries or persons acting on behalf of that other or its wholly-owned subsidiaries.

**736(3) ["Company"]** In this section **"company"** includes any body corporate.

**History**

See history note after s. 736A.

## 736A Provisions supplementing s. 736

**736A(1) [Extent]** The provisions of this section explain expressions used in section 736 and otherwise supplement that section.

**736A(2) [Reference to voting rights in s. 736(1)(a), (c)]** In section 736(1)(a) and (c) the references to the voting rights in a company are to the rights conferred on shareholders in respect of their shares or, in the case of a company not having a share capital, on members, to vote at general meetings of the company on all, or substantially all, matters.

**736A(3) [Reference to right to appoint/remove majority of board in s. 736(1)(b)]** In section 736(1)(b) the reference to the right to appoint or remove a majority of the board of directors is to the right to appoint or remove directors holding a majority of the voting rights at meetings of the board on all, or substantially all, matters; and for the purposes of that provision–

(a) a company shall be treated as having the right to appoint to a directorship if–

 (i) a person's appointment to it follows necessarily from his appointment as director of the company, or

 (ii) the directorship is held by the company itself; and

(b) a right to appoint or remove which is exercisable only with the consent or concurrence of another person shall be left out of account unless no other person has a right to appoint or, as the case may be, remove in relation to that directorship.

**736A(4) [Other rights to be taken into account]** Rights which are exercisable only in certain circumstances shall be taken into account only–

(a) when the circumstances have arisen, and for so long as they continue to obtain, or

(b) when the circumstances are within the control of the person having the rights;

and rights which are normally exercisable but are temporarily incapable of exercise shall continue to be taken into account.

**736A(5) [Rights held in fiduciary capacity]** Rights held by a person in a fiduciary capacity shall be treated as not held by him.

**736A(6) [Rights held as nominee]** Rights held by a person as nominee for another shall be treated as held by the other; and rights shall be regarded as held as nominee for another if they are exercisable only on his instructions or with his consent or concurrence.

**736A(7) [Rights held by way of security]** Rights attached to shares held by way of security shall be treated as held by the person providing the security–

(a) where apart from the right to exercise them for the purpose of preserving the value of the security, or of realising it, the rights are exercisable only in accordance with his instructions;

(b) where the shares are held in connection with the granting of loans as part of normal business activities and apart from the right to exercise them for the purpose of preserving the value of the security, or of realising it, the rights are exercisable only in his interests.

**736A(8) [Rights held by subsidiaries]** Rights shall be treated as held by a company if they are held by any of its subsidiaries; and nothing in subsection (6) or (7) shall be construed as requiring rights held by a company to be treated as held by any of its subsidiaries.

**736A(9) [Interpretation re s. 736A(7)]** For the purposes of subsection (7) rights shall be treated as being exercisable in accordance with the instructions or in the interests of a company if they are exercisable in accordance with the instructions of or, as the case may be, in the interests of–

(a) any subsidiary or holding company of that company, or
(b) any subsidiary of a holding company of that company.

**736A(10) [Reduction of voting rights]** The voting rights in a company shall be reduced by any rights held by the company itself.

**736A(11) [Reference in s. 736A(5)–(10) to rights held by a person]** References in any provision of subsections (5) to (10) to rights held by a person include rights falling to be treated as held by him by virtue of any other provision of those subsections but not rights which by virtue of any such provision are to be treated as not held by him.

**736A(12) ["Company"]** In this section **"company"** includes any body corporate.

**History**

S. 736, 736A substituted for the former s. 736 by CA 1989, s. 144(1) as from 1 November 1990 subject to transitional provisions (see SI 1990/1392 (C 41), art. 2(d) and also art. 6); the former s. 736 read as follows:

**"736 "Holding company", "subsidiary" and "wholly-owned subsidiary"**

**736(1)** For the purposes of this Act, a company is deemed to be a subsidiary of another if (but only if) –
(a) that other either –
(i) is a member of it and controls the composition of its board of directors, or
(ii) holds more than half in nominal value of its equity share capital, or
(b) the first-mentioned company is a subsidiary of any company which is that other's subsidiary.
The above is subject to subsection (4) below in this section.

**(2)** For purposes of subsection (1), the composition of a company's board of directors is deemed to be controlled by another company if (but only if) that other company by the exercise of some power exercisable by it without the consent or concurrence of any other person can appoint or remove the holders of all or a majority of the directorships.

**(3)** For purposes of this last provision, the other company is deemed to have power to appoint to a directorship with respect to which any of the following conditions is satisfied –
(a) that a person cannot be appointed to it without the exercise in his favour by the other company of such a power as is mentioned above, or
(b) that a person's appointment to the directorship follows necessarily from his appointment as director of the other company, or
(c) that the directorship is held by the other company itself or by a subsidiary of it.

**(4)** In determining whether one company is a subsidiary of another –
(a) any shares held or power exercisable by the other in a fiduciary capacity are to be treated as not held or exercisable by it,
(b) subject to the two following paragraphs, any shares held or power exercisable–
(i) by any person as nominee for the other (except where the other is concerned only in a fiduciary capacity), or
(ii) by, or by a nominee for, a subsidiary of the other (not being a subsidiary which is concerned only in a fiduciary capacity),
are to be treated as held or exercisable by the other,
(c) any shares held or power exercisable by any person by virtue of the provisions of any debentures of the first-mentioned company or of a trust deed for securing any issue of such debentures are to be disregarded,
(d) any shares held or power exercisable by, or by a nominee for, the other or its subsidiary (not being held or exercisable as mentioned in paragraph (c)) are to be treated as not held or exercisable by the other if the ordinary business of the other or its subsidiary (as the case may be) includes the lending of money and the shares are held or the power is exercisable as above mentioned by way of security only for the purposes of a transaction entered into in the ordinary course of that business.

**(5)** For purposes of this Act–
(a) a company is deemed to be another's holding company if (but only if) the other is its subsidiary, and
(b) a body corporate is deemed the wholly-owned subsidiary of another if it has no members except that other and that other's wholly-owned subsidiaries and its or their nominees.

**(6)** In this section **"company"** includes any body corporate."

## 736B Power to amend s. 736 and 736A

**736B(1) [Amendment by regulations]** The Secretary of State may by regulations amend sections 736 and 736A so as to alter the meaning of the expressions "holding company", "subsidiary" or "wholly-owned subsidiary".

**736B(2) [Different provisions for different cases etc.]** The regulations may make different provision for different cases or classes of case and may contain such incidental and supplementary provisions as the Secretary of State thinks fit.

**736B(3) [Annulment by Parliament]** Regulations under this section shall be made by statutory instrument which shall be subject to annulment in pursuance of a resolution of either House of Parliament.

**736B(4) [Application of amendments]** Any amendment made by regulations under this section does not apply for the purposes of enactments outside the Companies Acts unless the regulations so provide.

**736B(5) [Interpretation Act, s. 23(3)]** So much of section 23(3) of the Interpretation Act 1978 as applies section 17(2)(a) of that Act (effect of repeal and re-enactment) to deeds, instruments and documents other than enactments shall not apply in relation to any repeal and re-enactment effected by regulations made under this section.

**History**

S. 736B inserted by CA 1989, s. 144(3) as from 1 November 1990 subject to transitional provisions (see SI 1990/1392 (C 41), art. 2(d) and also art. 6).

# 737 "Called-up share capital"

**737(1) ["Called-up share capital"]** In this Act, **"called-up share capital"** in relation to a company, means so much of its share capital as equals the aggregate amount of the calls made on its shares (whether or not those calls have been paid), together with any share capital paid up without being called and any share capital to be paid on a specified future date under the articles, the terms of allotment of the relevant shares or any other arrangements for payment of those shares.

**737(2) ["Uncalled share capital"] "Uncalled share capital"** is to be construed accordingly.

**737(3) [Application of definitions]** The definitions in this section apply unless the contrary intention appears.

# 738 "Allotment" and "paid up"

**738(1) [Where share allotted]** In relation to an allotment of shares in a company, the shares are to be taken for the purposes of this Act to be allotted when a person acquires the unconditional right to be included in the company's register of members in respect of those shares.

**738(2) [Where share paid up in cash, or allotted in cash]** For purposes of this Act, a share in a company is deemed paid up (as to its nominal value or any premium on it) in cash, or allotted for cash, if the consideration for the allotment or payment up is cash received by the company, or is a cheque received by it in good faith which the directors have no reason for suspecting will not be paid, or is a release of a liability of the company for a liquidated sum, or is an undertaking to pay cash to the company at a future date.

**738(3) [References to consideration other than cash, etc.]** In relation to the allotment or payment up of any shares in a company, references in this Act (except sections 89 to 94) to consideration other than cash and to the payment up of shares and premiums on shares otherwise than in cash include the payment of, or any undertaking to pay, cash to any person other than the company.

**738(4) ["Cash"]** For the purpose of determining whether a share is or is to be allotted for cash, or paid up in cash, **"cash"** includes foreign currency.

# 739 "Non-cash asset"

**739(1) ["Non-cash asset"]** In this Act **"non-cash asset"** means any property or interest in property other than cash; and for this purpose **"cash"** includes foreign currency.

**739(2) [Reference to transfer of non-cash asset, etc.]** A reference to the transfer or acquisition of a non-cash asset includes the creation or extinction of an estate or interest in, or a right over, any property and also the discharge of any person's liability, other than a liability for a liquidated sum.

# 740 "Body corporate" and "corporation"

**740** References in this Act to a body corporate or to a corporation do not include a corporation sole, but include a company incorporated elsewhere than in Great Britain.

Such references to a body corporate do not include a Scottish firm.

# 741 "Director" and "shadow director"

**741(1) ["Director"]** In this Act, **"director"** includes any person occupying the position of director, by whatever name called.

**741(2) ["Shadow director"]** In relation to a company, **"shadow director"** means a person in accordance with whose directions or instructions the directors of the company are accustomed to act.

However, a person is not deemed a shadow director by reason only that the directors act on advice given by him in a professional capacity.

**741(3) [Where body corporate not shadow director of subsidiary]** For the purposes of the following provisions of this Act, namely –

section 309 (directors' duty to have regard to interests of employees),
section 319 (directors' long-term contracts of employment),
sections 320 to 322 (substantial property transactions involving directors),
section 322B (contracts with sole members who are directors), and
sections 330 to 346 (general restrictions on power of companies to make loans, etc., to directors and others connected with them),

(being provisions under which shadow directors are treated as directors), a body corporate is not to be treated as a shadow director of any of its subsidiary companies by reason only that the directors of the subsidiary are accustomed to act in accordance with its directions or instructions.

**History**
In s. 741(3) the word "and" formerly appearing after the words "involving directors)," deleted and the words "section 322B (contracts with sole members who are directors), and" inserted by the Companies (Single Member Private Limited Companies) Regulations 1992 (SI 1992/1699), reg. 2 and Sch., para. 3(2) as from 15 July 1992.

**Note**
The Companies (Single Member Private Limited Companies) Regulations 1992 (SI 1992/1699) implement the Twelfth EC Company Law Directive (89/667).

## 742 Expressions used in connection with accounts

**742(1) [Definitions]** In this Act, unless a contrary intention appears, the following expressions have the same meaning as in Part VII (accounts)–

**"annual accounts"**,
**"accounting reference date"** and **"accounting reference period"**,
**"balance sheet"** and **"balance sheet date"**,
**"current assets"**,
**"financial year"**, in relation to a company,
**"fixed assets"**,
**"parent company"** and **"parent undertaking"**,
**"profit and loss account"**, and
**"subsidiary undertaking"**.

**742(2) [References to "realised profits", "realised losses"]** References in this Act to "realised profits" and "realised losses", in relation to a company's accounts, shall be construed in accordance with section 262(3).

**History**
S. 742 substituted by CA 1989, s. 23 and Sch. 10, para. 15 as from 1 April 1990 subject to transitional and saving provisions (see SI 1990/355 (C 13), art. 3, Sch. 1 and also art. 6–9); s. 742 formerly read as follows:

**"742 Expressions used in connection with accounts**

**742(1)** In this Act, unless the contrary intention appears–
(a) **"accounting reference period"** has the meaning given by sections 224 to 226;
(b) **"accounts"** includes a company's group accounts (within the meaning of section 229), whether prepared in the form of accounts or not;
(c) **"balance sheet date"**, in relation to a balance sheet, means the date as at which the balance sheet was prepared;
(d) **"financial year"** –
(i) in relation to a body corporate to which Part VII applies, means a period in respect of which a profit and loss account under section 227 in that Part is made up, and
(ii) in relation to any other body corporate, means a period in respect of which a profit and loss account of the body laid before it in general meeting is made up,
(whether, in either case, that period is a year or not);
(e) any reference to a profit and loss account, in the case of a company not trading for profit, is to its income and expenditure account, and references to profit or loss and, if the company has subsidiaries, references to a consolidated profit and loss account are to be construed accordingly.

**(2)** Except in relation to special category accounts, any reference to a balance sheet or profit and loss account includes any notes to the account in question giving information which is required by any provision of this Act, and required or allowed by any such provision to be given in a note to company accounts.

(3) In relation to special category accounts, any reference to a balance sheet or profit and loss account includes any notes thereon or document annexed thereto giving information which is required by this Act and is thereby allowed to be so given.

(4) References to special category companies and special category accounts are to be construed in accordance with Chapter II of Part VII.

(5) For the purposes of Part VII, a body corporate is to be regarded as publishing any balance sheet or other account if it publishes, issues or circulates it or otherwise makes it available for public inspection in a manner calculated to invite members of the public generally, or any class of members of the public, to read it.

(6) Expressions which, when used in Schedule 4, fall to be construed in accordance with any provision of Part VII of that Schedule have the same meaning (unless the contrary intention appears) 802when used in any provision of this Act."

# 743 "Employees' share scheme"

**743** For purposes of this Act, an employees' share scheme is a scheme for encouraging or facilitating the holding of shares or debentures in a company by or for the benefit of–

(a) the bona fide employees or former employees of the company, the company's subsidiary or holding company or a subsidiary of the company's holding company, or

(b) the wives, husbands, widows, widowers or children or step-children under the age of 18 of such employees or former employees.

**Note**

For the purposes of s. 743 a company which immediately before the commencement of CA 1989, s. 144(1) (inserting new s. 736, 736A) (1 November 1990) was a subsidiary of another company shall not be treated as ceasing to be such a subsidiary by reason of that provision coming into force.

# 743A Meaning of "office copy" in Scotland

**743A** References in this Act to an office copy of a court order shall be construed, as respects Scotland, as references to a certified copy interlocutor.

**History**

S. 743A inserted by CA 1989, s. 145 and Sch. 19, para. 19 as from 1 March 1990 (see SI 1990/142 (C 5), art. 5).

# 744 Expressions used generally in this Act

**744** In this Act, unless the contrary intention appears, the following definitions apply –

**"agent"** does not include a person's counsel acting as such;

**"articles"** means, in relation to a company, its articles of association, as originally framed or as altered by resolution, including (so far as applicable to the company) regulations contained in or annexed to any enactment relating to companies passed before this Act, as altered by or under any such enactment;

**"authorised minimum"** has the meaning given by section 118;

**"bank holiday"** means a holiday under the Banking and Financial Dealings Act 1971;

**"banking company"** means a company which is authorised under the Banking Act 1987;

**"books and papers"** and **"books or papers"** include accounts, deeds, writings and documents;

**"the Companies Acts"** means this Act, the insider dealing legislation and the Consequential Provisions Act;

**"the Consequential Provisions Act"** means the Companies Consolidation (Consequential Provisions) Act 1985;

**"the court"**, in relation to a company, means the court having jurisdiction to wind up the company;

**"debenture"** includes debenture stock, bonds and any other securities of a company, whether constituting a charge on the assets of the company or not;

**"document"** includes summons, notice, order, and other legal process, and registers;

**"EEA State"** means a State which is a Contracting Party to the Agreement on the European Economic Area signed at Oporto on 2nd May 1992 as adjusted by the Protocol signed at Brussels on 17th March 1993;

**"equity share capital"** means, in relation to a company, its issued share capital excluding any part of that capital which, neither as respects dividends nor as respects capital, carries any right to participate beyond a specified amount in a distribution;

**"expert"** has the meaning given by section 62;

**"floating charge"** includes a floating charge within the meaning given by section 462;
**"the Gazette"** means, as respects companies registered in England and Wales, the London Gazette and, as respects companies registered in Scotland, the Edinburgh Gazette;
**"hire-purchase agreement"** has the same meaning as in the Consumer Credit Act 1974;
**"the insider dealing legislation"** means Part V of the Criminal Justice Act 1993 (insider dealing);
**"insurance company"** means the same as in the Insurance Companies Act 1982;
**"joint stock company"** has the meaning given by section 683;
**"memorandum"**, in relation to a company, means its memorandum of association, as originally framed or as altered in pursuance of any enactment;
**"number"**, in relation to shares, includes amount, where the context admits of the reference to shares being construed to include stock;
**"officer"**, in relation to a body corporate, includes a director, manager or secretary;
**"official seal"**, in relation to the registrar of companies, means a seal prepared under section 704(4) for the authentication of documents required for or in connection with the registration of companies;
**"oversea company"** means –

(a) a company incorporated elsewhere than in Great Britain which, after the commencement of this Act, establishes a place of business in Great Britain, and
(b) a company so incorporated which has, before that commencement, established a place of business and continues to have an established place of business in Great Britain at that commencement;

**"place of business"** includes a share transfer or share registration office;
**"prescribed"** means –

(a) as respects provisions of this Act relating to winding up, prescribed by general rules, and
(b) otherwise, prescribed by statutory instrument made by the Secretary of State;

**"prospectus"** means any prospectus, notice, circular, advertisement, or other invitation, offering to the public for subscription or purchase any shares in or debentures of a company;
**"prospectus issued generally"** means a prospectus issued to persons who are not existing members of the company or holders of its debentures;
**"the registrar of companies"** and **"the registrar"** mean the registrar or other officer performing under this Act the duty of registration of companies in England and Wales or in Scotland, as the case may require;
**"share"** means share in the share capital of a company, and includes stock (except where a distinction between shares and stock is express or implied); and
**"undistributable reserves"** has the meaning given by section 264(3).

**History**
In s. 744:

- the definition of "EEA State" inserted by the Companies (Membership of Holding Company) (Dealers in Securities) Regulations 1997 (SI 1997/2306), reg. 1, 4(1) as from 20 October 1997.
- the definition of "annual return" formerly appearing repealed by CA 1989, s. 212 and Sch. 24 as from 3 July 1995 (see SI 1995/1352 (C 27), art. 3(c)); the former definition read as follows:
  "**"annual return"** means the return to be made by a company under section 363 or 364 (as the case may be);"
- the definition of "banking company" inserted and the definition of "authorised institution" formerly appearing omitted by CA 1989, s. 23, 212, Sch. 10, para. 16 and Sch. 24 as from 1 April 1990 subject to transitional and saving provisions (see SI 1990/355 (C 13), art 3, 5(1)(b), (2), Sch. 1 and also art. 6–9); the former definition of "authorised institution" read as follows:
  "**"authorised institution"** means a company which is an institution authorised under the Banking Act 1987;".
  Previously the definition of "authorised institution" inserted and the definition of "recognised bank" formerly appearing omitted by Banking Act 1987, s. 108(1) and Sch. 6, para. 18(8) as from 1 October 1987 (the latter definition also repealed by s. 108(2) and Sch. 7, Pt. I of that Act from the same date) (see SI 1987/1664 (C 50)); the former definition of "recognised bank" read as follows:
  "**"recognised bank"** means a company which is recognised as a bank for the purposes of the Banking Act 1979;".
- the definition "**"general rules"** means general rules made under section 663, and includes forms;", and in the definition "prescribed" the words "under section 663" formerly appearing after the words "general rules" repealed by Insolvency Act 1985, s. 235 and Sch. 10, Pt. II as from 1 March 1986 as far as they relate to the meaning of general rules in relation to England and Wales (see SI 1986/185 (C 7)), and otherwise from 29 December 1986 (see IA 1986, s. 443 and SI 1986/1924 (C 71)).

- the definition of "the insider dealing legislation" substituted by Criminal Justice Act 1993, s. 79(13) and Sch. 5, para. 4 as from 1 March 1994 (see SI 1994/242 (C 7), art. 2, Sch.); the former definition read as follows:
  "**"the Insider Dealing Act"** means the Company Securities (Insider Dealing) Act 1985;"
- the definition of "recognised stock exchange" formerly appearing repealed by Financial Services Act 1986, s. 212(3) and Sch. 17, Pt. I as from 29 April 1986 (see SI 1988/740 (C 22)); the former definition read as follows:
  "**"recognised stock exchange"** means any body of persons which is for the time being a recognised stock exchange for the purposes of the Prevention of Fraud (Investments) Act 1958;".
- the definition of "prospectus issued generally" repealed by Financial Services Act 1986, s. 212(3) and Sch. 17, Pt. I as from 29 April 1988 as far as they would apply to a prospectus offering for subscription, or to any form of application for units in a body corporate which is a recognised scheme (see SI 1988/740 (C 22)).

**Note**

See the Companies (Welsh Language Forms and Documents) Regulations 1994 (SI 1994/117) and the Companies (Forms) (Amendment) Regulations 1998 (SI 1998/1702).

Under the Transfer of Functions (Financial Services) Order 1992 (SI 1992/1315), art. 10(1) and Sch. 4, para. 2 as from 7 June 1992: s. 744 shall have effect in relation to any provision of the Companies Act 1985 conferring a function transferred to the Treasury by the above order as if "prescribed" in s. 744 meant prescribed by statutory instrument made by the Treasury.

# 744A Index of defined expressions

**744A** The following Table shows provisions defining or otherwise explaining expressions for the purposes of this Act generally–

| | |
|---|---|
| accounting reference date, accounting reference period | sections 224 and 742(1) |
| acquisition (in relation to a non-cash asset) | section 739(2) |
| agent | section 744 |
| allotment (and related expressions) | section 738 |
| annual accounts | sections 261(2), 262(1) and 742(1) |
| annual general meeting | section 366 |
| annual return | section 363 |
| articles | section 744 |
| authorised minimum | section 118 |
| balance sheet and balance sheet date | sections 261(2), 262(1) and 742(1) |
| bank holiday | section 744 |
| banking company | section 744 |
| body corporate | section 740 |
| books and papers, books or papers | section 744 |
| called-up share capital | section 737(1) |
| capital redemption reserve | section 170(1) |
| the Companies Acts | section 744 |
| companies charges register | section 397 |
| company | section 735(1) |
| the Consequential Provisions Act | section 744 |
| corporation | section 740 |
| the court (in relation to a company) | section 744 |
| current assets | sections 262(1) and 742(1) |
| debenture | section 744 |
| director | section 741(1) |
| document | section 744 |
| EEA State | section 744 |
| elective resolution | section 379A |
| employees' share scheme | section 743 |
| equity share capital | section 744 |
| existing company | section 735(1) |
| extraordinary general meeting | section 368 |
| extraordinary resolution | section 378(1) |
| financial year (of a company) | sections 223 and 742(1) |
| fixed assets | sections 262(1) and 742(1) |
| floating charge (in Scotland) | section 462 |
| the former Companies Acts | section 735(1) |

| | |
|---|---|
| the Gazette | section 744 |
| hire-purchase agreement | section 744 |
| holding company | section 736 |
| the insider dealing legislation | section 744 |
| the Insolvency Act | section 735A(1) |
| insurance company | section 744 |
| the Joint Stock Companies Acts | section 735(3) |
| limited company | section 1(2) |
| member (of a company) | section 22 |
| memorandum (in relation to a company) | section 744 |
| non-cash asset | section 739(1) |
| number (in relation to shares) | section 744 |
| office copy (in relation to a court order in Scotland) | section 743A |
| officer (in relation to a body corporate) | section 744 |
| official seal (in relation to the registrar of companies) | section 744 |
| oversea company | section 744 |
| overseas branch register | section 362 |
| paid up (and related expressions) | section 738 |
| parent company and parent undertaking | sections 258 and 742(1) |
| place of business | section 744 |
| prescribed | section 744 |
| private company | section 1(3) |
| profit and loss account | sections 261(2), 262(1) and 742(1) |
| prospectus | section 744 |
| public company | section 1(3) |
| realised profits or losses | sections 262(3) and 742(2) |
| registered number (of a company) | section 705(1) |
| registered office (of a company) | section 287 |
| registrar and registrar of companies | section 744 |
| resolution for reducing share capital | section 135(3) |
| shadow director | section 741(2) and (3) |
| share | section 744 |
| share premium account | section 130(1) |
| share warrant | section 188 |
| special notice (in relation to a resolution) | section 379 |
| special resolution | section 378(2) |
| subsidiary | section 736 |
| subsidiary undertaking | sections 258 and 742(1) |
| transfer (in relation to a non-cash asset) | section 739(2) |
| uncalled share capital | section 737(2) |
| undistributable reserves | section 264(3) |
| unlimited company | section 1(2) |
| unregistered company | section 718 |
| wholly-owned subsidiary | section 736(2) |

**History**
In s. 744A the entry relating to "EEA State" inserted by the Companies (Membership of Holding Company) (Dealers in Securities) Regulations 1997 (SI 1997/2306), reg. 1, 4(3) as from 20 October 1997. Originally, s. 744A inserted by CA 1989, s. 145 and Sch. 19, para. 20 as from 3 July 1995 (see SI 1995/1352 (C 27), art. 3(b)).

# PART XXVII – FINAL PROVISIONS

## 745 Northern Ireland

**745(1) [Application only when expressly provided]** Except where otherwise expressly provided, nothing in this Act (except provisions relating expressly to companies registered or incorporated in Northern Ireland or outside Great Britain) applies to or in relation to companies so registered or incorporated.

**745(2)** **[Not usually applicable]** Subject to any such provision, and to any express provision as to extent, this Act does not extend to Northern Ireland.

## 746 Commencement

**746** This Act comes into force on 1st July 1985.

**History**
In s. 746 the words "Except as provided by section 243(6)," formerly appearing at the beginning repealed by CA 1989, s. 212 and Sch. 24 as from 1 April 1990 subject to any relevant transitional or saving provisions (see SI 1990/355 (C 13), art. 5(1)(b), (2)).

## 747 Citation

**747** This Act may be cited as the Companies Act 1985.

# SCHEDULES

# Schedule 1 – Particulars of Directors etc. to be Contained in Statement Under Section 10

Section 10

DIRECTORS

**1** Subject as provided below, the statement under section 10(2) shall contain the following particulars with respect to each person named as director –

(a) in the case of an individual, his present name, any former name, his usual residential address, his nationality, his business occupation (if any), particulars of any other directorships held by him, or which have been held by him and his date of birth;

(b) in the case of a corporation or Scottish firm, its corporate or firm name and registered or principal office.

**History**
In para. 1(a) the word "name" (appearing twice) substituted for the former words "Christian name and surname" and "Christian name or surname" respectively and the words "and his date of birth" substituted for the former words "and, in the case of a company subject to section 293, the date of his birth" and in para. 1(b) the words "or Scottish firm" and "or firm" inserted by CA 1989, s. 145 and Sch. 19, para. 7(1)–(3) as from 1 October 1990 (see SI 1990/1707 (C 46), art. 2(b)).

**2(1)** It is not necessary for the statement to contain particulars of a directorship –

(a) which has not been held by a director at any time during the 5 years preceding the date on which the statement is delivered to the registrar,

(b) which is held by a director in a company which –

(i) is dormant or grouped with the company delivering the statement, and

(ii) if he also held that directorship for any period during those 5 years, was for the whole of that period either dormant or so grouped,

(c) which was held by a director for any period during those 5 years in a company which for the whole of that period was either dormant or grouped with the company delivering the statement.

**2(2)** For these purposes, **"company"** includes any body corporate incorporated in Great Britain; and –

(a) section 249AA(3) applies as regards whether and when a company is or has been "dormant", and

(b) a company is treated as being or having been at any time grouped with another company if at that time it is or was a company of which that other is or was a wholly-owned subsidiary, or if it is or was a wholly-owned subsidiary of the other or of another company of which that other is or was a wholly-owned subsidiary.

**History**

In para. 2(2)(a) the words "section 249AA(3)" substituted for the former words "section 250(3)" by the Companies Act 1985 (Audit Exemption) (Amendment) Regulations 2000 (SI 2000/1430), reg. 1, 8(10) as from 26 May 2000 in relation to annual accounts and reports in respect of financial years ending on or after 26 July 2000.

Previously in para. 2(2)(a) the words "section 250(3)" substituted for the former words "section 252(5)" by CA 1989, s. 23 and Sch. 10, para. 17 as from 1 April 1990 subject to transitional and saving provisions (see SI 1990/355 (C 13), art. 3, Sch. 1 and also art. 6–9).

### SECRETARIES

**3(1)** The statement shall contain the following particulars with respect to the person named as secretary or, where there are to be joint secretaries, with respect to each person named as one of them –

(a) in the case of an individual, his present name, any former name and his usual residential address,

(b) in the case of a corporation or a Scottish firm, its corporate or firm name and registered or principal office.

**History**

In para. 3(1)(a) the word "name" (appearing twice) substituted for the former words "Christian name and surname" and "Christian name or surname" respectively by CA 1989, s. 145 and Sch. 19, para. 7(1), (4) as from 1 October 1990 (see SI 1990/1707 (C 46), art. 2(b)).

**3(2)** However, if all the partners in a firm are joint secretaries, the name and principal office of the firm may be stated instead of the particulars otherwise required by this paragraph.

### INTERPRETATION

**4** In paragraphs 1(a) and 3(1)(a) above–

(a) **"name"** means a person's Christian name (or other forename) and surname, except that in the case of a peer, or an individual usually known by a title, the title may be stated instead of his Christian name (or other forename) and surname or in addition to either or both of them; and

(b) the reference to a former name does not include–

(i) in the case of a peer, or a person usually known by a British title, the name by which he was known previous to the adoption of or succession to the title, or

(ii) in the case of any person, a former name which was changed or disused before he attained the age of 18 or which has been changed or disused for 20 years or more, or

(iii) in the case of a married woman, the name by which she was known previous to the marriage.

**History**

Para. 4 substituted by CA 1989, s. 145 and Sch. 19, para. 7(1), (5) as from 1 October 1990 (see SI 1990/1707 (C 46), art. 2(b)); para. 4 formerly read as follows:

"In paragraphs 1 and 3 above –

(a) **"Christian name"** includes a forename,

(b) **"surname"**, in the case of a peer or a person usually known by a title different from his surname, means that title,

(c) the reference to a former Christian name or surname does not include –

(i) in the case of a peer or a person usually known by a British title different from his surname, the name by which he was known previous to the adoption of or succession to the title, or

(ii) in the case of any person, a former Christian name or surname where that name or surname was changed or disused before the person bearing the name attained the age of 18 or has been changed or disused for a period of not less than 20 years, or

(iii) in the case of a married woman, the name or surname by which she was known previous to the marriage."

# Schedule 2 – Interpretation of References to "Beneficial Interest"

Sections 23, 145, 146, 148

## Part I – References in Sections 23, 145, 146 and 148

**History**

The heading "Part I – References in Sections 23, 145, 146 and 148" inserted by CA 1989, s. 23 and Sch. 10, para. 18(1), (2), as from 1 April 1990 subject to transitional and saving provisions (see SI 1990/355 (C 13), art. 3, Sch. 1 and also art. 6–9).

## RESIDUAL INTERESTS UNDER PENSION AND EMPLOYEES' SHARE SCHEMES

**1(1)** Where shares in a company are held on trust for the purposes of a pension scheme or an employees' share scheme, there is to be disregarded any residual interest which has not vested in possession, being an interest of the company or, as this paragraph applies for the purposes of section 23(2), of any subsidiary of the company.

**History**

In para. 1(1) the words "paragraph 60(2) of Schedule 4, or paragraph 19(3) of Schedule 9," formerly appearing after the words "section 23(4)," omitted and repealed by CA 1989, s. 23, 212, Sch. 10, para. 18(1), (3)(a) and Sch. 24 as from 1 April 1990 subject to transitional and saving provisions (see SI 1990/355 (C 13), art. 3, 5(1)(a), (2), Sch. 1 and also art. 6–9).
Also in para. 1(1) the words "as this paragraph applies for the purposes of section 23(2)" substituted for the former words "as respects section 23(4)" by CA 1989, s. 129(2) as from 1 November 1990 (see SI 1990/1392 (C 41), art. 2(a)).

**1(2)** In this paragraph, **"a residual interest"** means a right of the company or subsidiary in question ("the residual beneficiary") to receive any of the trust property in the event of –

(a) all the liabilities arising under the scheme having been satisfied or provided for, or

(b) the residual beneficiary ceasing to participate in the scheme, or

(c) the trust property at any time exceeding what is necessary for satisfying the liabilities arising or expected to arise under the scheme.

**1(3)** In sub-paragraph (2), references to a right include a right dependent on the exercise of a discretion vested by the scheme in the trustee or any other person; and references to liabilities arising under a scheme include liabilities that have resulted or may result from the exercise of any such discretion.

**1(4)** For purposes of this paragraph, a residual interest vests in possession –

(a) in a case within (a) of sub-paragraph (2), on the occurrence of the event there mentioned, whether or not the amount of the property receivable pursuant to the right mentioned in that sub-paragraph is then ascertained, and

(b) in a case within (b) or (c) of that sub-paragraph, when the residual beneficiary becomes entitled to require the trustee to transfer to that beneficiary any of the property receivable pursuant to that right.

**1(5)** (Omitted and repealed by Companies Act 1989, s. 23, 212, Sch. 10, para. 18(1), (3)(b) and Sch. 24 as from 1 April 1990.)

**History**

In regard to the date of the above omission and repeal see SI 1990/355 (C 13), art. 3, 5(1)(b), (2), Sch. 1 and also note transitional and saving provisions in art. 6–9; para. 1(5) formerly read as follows:

"As respects paragraph 60(2) of Schedule 4 and paragraph 19(3) of Schedule 9, sub-paragraph (1) has effect as if references to shares included debentures."

**2(1)** The following has effect as regards the operation of sections 144, 145 and 146 to 149 in cases where a residual interest vests in possession.

**History**

In para. 2(1) "23," formerly appearing before "144, 145" repealed by CA 1989, s. 212 and Sch. 24 as from 1 April 1990 subject to transitional and saving provisions (see SI 1990/355 (C 13), art. 4, 5(1)(b), (2) and also art. 6–9).

**2(2)** (Repealed by Companies Act 1989, s. 212 and Sch. 24 as from 1 April 1990.)

**History**

In regard to the date of the above repeal see SI 1990/355 (C 13), art. 5(1)(b), (2) and also note transitional and saving provisions in art. 6–9; para. 2(2) formerly read as follows:

"Where by virtue of the vesting in possession of a residual interest a subsidiary ceases to be exempt from section 23, that section does not prevent the subsidiary from continuing to be a member of its holding company; but subject to subsection (4) of that section, the subsidiary has no right from the date of vesting to vote at meetings of the holding company or any class of its members."

**2(3)** Where by virtue of paragraph 1 of this Schedule any shares are exempt from section 144 or 145 at the time when they are issued or acquired but the residual interest in question vests in possession before they are disposed of or fully paid up, those sections apply to the shares as if they had been issued or acquired on the date on which that interest vests in possession.

**2(4)** Where by virtue of paragraph 1 any shares are exempt from sections 146 to 149 at the time when they are acquired but the residual interest in question vests in possession before they are disposed of, those sections apply to the shares as if they had been acquired on the date on which that interest vests in possession.

**2(5)** The above sub-paragraphs apply irrespective of the date on which the residual interest vests or vested in possession; but where the date on which it vested was before 26th July 1983 (the passing of the Companies (Beneficial Interests) Act 1983), they have effect as if the vesting had occurred on that date.

## EMPLOYER'S CHARGES AND OTHER RIGHTS OF RECOVERY

**3(1)** Where shares in a company are held on trust, there are to be disregarded –

(a) if the trust is for the purposes of a pension scheme, any such rights as are mentioned in the following sub-paragraph, and

(b) if the trust is for the purposes of an employees' share scheme, any such rights as are mentioned in (a) of the sub-paragraph,

being rights of the company or, as this paragraph applies for the purposes of section 23(2) of any subsidiary of the company.

**History**

In para. 3(1) the words ", paragraph 60(2) of Schedule 4 or paragraph 19(3) of Schedule 9" formerly appearing after the words "section 23(4)," omitted and repealed by CA 1989, s. 23, 212, Sch. 10, para. 18(1), (4)(a) and Sch. 24 as from 1 April 1990 subject to transitional and saving provisions (see SI 1990/355 (C 13), art. 3, 5(1)(a), (2), Sch. 1 and also art. 6–9).
Also in para. 3(1) the words "as this paragraph applies for the purposes of section 23(2)" substitued for the former words "as respects section 23(4)" by CA 1989, s. 129(2) as from 1 November 1990 (see SI 1990/1392 (C 41), art. 2(a)).

**3(2)** The rights referred to are –

(a) any charge or lien on, or set-off against, any benefit or other right or interest under the scheme for the purpose of enabling the employer or former employer of a member of the scheme to obtain the discharge of a monetary obligation due to him from the member, and

(b) any right to receive from the trustee of the scheme, or as trustee of the scheme to retain, an amount that can be recovered or retained under section 61 of the Pension Schemes Act 1993 (deduction of contributions equivalent premium from refund of scheme contributions) or otherwise as reimbursement or partial reimbursement for any contributions equivalent premium paid in connection with the scheme under Part III of that Act.

**History**

In para. 3(2)(b) the words "contributions equivalent premium" substituted for the former words "state scheme premiums" by the Pensions Act 1995, s. 151 and Sch. 5, para. 11 as from 6 April 1997 (see SI 1997/644 (C 23), art. 2(3), Sch., Pt. II).
Previously in para. 3(2)(b) the words "section 61 of the Pension Schemes Act 1993 (deduction of contributions equivalent premium from refund of scheme contributions)" substituted for the former words "section 47 of the Social Security Pensions Act 1975 (deduction of premium from refund of contributions)" by Pension Schemes Act 1993, s. 190 and Sch. 8, para. 16(b) as from 7 February 1994 (see SI 1994/86 (C 3), art. 2).

**3(3)** (Omitted and repealed by Companies Act 1989, s. 23, 212, Sch. 10, para. 18(1), (4)(b) and Sch. 24 as from 1 April 1990.)

**History**

In regard to the date of the above omission and repeal see SI 1990/355 (C 13), art. 3, 5(1)(b), (2), Sch. 1 and also note transitional and saving provisions in art. 6–9; para. 3(3) formerly read as follows:

"As respects paragraph 60(2) of Schedule 4 and paragraph 19(3) of Schedule 9, sub-paragraph (1) has effect as if references to shares included debentures."

## TRUSTEE'S RIGHT TO EXPENSES, REMUNERATION, INDEMNITY, ETC.

**4(1)** Where a company is a trustee, there are to be disregarded any rights which the company has in its capacity as trustee including, in particular, any right to recover its expenses or be remunerated out of the trust property and any right to be indemnified out of that property for any liability incurred by reason of any act or omission of the company in the performance of its duties as trustee.

**History**

In para. 4(1) the words "(whether as personal representative or otherwise)" formerly appearing after the words "is a trustee" omitted and repealed by CA 1989, s. 23, 212, Sch. 10, para. 18(1), (5)(a) and Sch. 24 as from 1 April 1990 subject to transitional and saving provisions (see SI 1990/355 (C 13), art. 3, 5(1)(b), (2), Sch. 1 and also art. 6–9).

**4(2)** As this paragraph applies for the purposes of section 23(2), sub-paragraph (1) has effect as if references to a company included any body corporate which is a subsidiary of a company.

**History**

In para. 4(2) the words ", paragraph 60(2) of Schedule 4 and paragraph 19(3) of Schedule 9" formerly appearing after the words "section 23(4)" omitted and repealed by CA 1989, s. 23, 212, Sch. 10, para. 18(1), (5)(b) and Sch. 24 as from 1 April 1990 subject to transitional and saving provisions (see SI 1990/355 (C 13), art. 3, 5(1)(a), (2), Sch. 1 and also art. 6–9). Also in para. 4(2) the words "As this paragraph applies for the purposes of section 23(2)" substituted for the former words "As respects section 23(4)" by CA 1989, s. 129(2) as from 1 November 1990 (see SI 1990/1392 (C 41), art. 2(a)).

**4(3)** As respects sections 145, 146 and 148, sub-paragraph (1) above applies where a company is a personal representative as it applies where a company is a trustee.

**History**

Para. 4(3) added by CA 1989, s. 23 and Sch. 10, para. 18(1), (5) as from 1 April 1990 subject to transitional and saving provisions (see SI 1990/355 (C 13), art. 3, Sch. 1 and also art. 6–9).

## SUPPLEMENTARY

**5(1)** The following applies for the interpretation of this Part of this Schedule.

**History**

In para. 5(1) the words "this Part of this Schedule" substituted for the former words "this Schedule" by CA 1989, s. 23 and Sch. 10, para. 18(1), (6) as from 1 April 1990 subject to transitional and saving provisions (see SI 1990/355 (C 13), art. 3, Sch. 1 and also art. 6–9).

**5(2)** **"Pension scheme"** means any scheme for the provision of benefits consisting of or including relevant benefits for or in respect of employees or former employees; and **"relevant benefits"** means any pension, lump sum, gratuity or other like benefit given or to be given on retirement or on death or in anticipation of retirement or, in connection with past service, after retirement or death.

**5(3)** In sub-paragraph (2) of this paragraph, and in paragraph 3(2)(a), **"employer"** and **"employee"** are to be read as if a director of a company were employed by it.

# Part II – References in Schedule 5

## RESIDUAL INTERESTS UNDER PENSION AND EMPLOYEES' SHARE SCHEMES

**6(1)** Where shares in an undertaking are held on trust for the purposes of a pension scheme or an employees' share scheme, there shall be disregarded any residual interest which has not vested in possession, being an interest of the undertaking or any of its subsidiary undertakings.

**6(2)** In this paragraph a **"residual interest"** means a right of the undertaking in question (the "residual beneficiary") to receive any of the trust property in the event of –

(a) all the liabilities arising under the scheme having been satisfied or provided for, or

(b) the residual beneficiary ceasing to participate in the scheme, or

(c) the trust property at any time exceeding what is necessary for satisfying the liabilities arising or expected to arise under the scheme.

**6(3)** In sub-paragraph (2) references to a right include a right dependent on the exercise of a discretion vested by the scheme in the trustee or any other person; and references to liabilities arising under a scheme include liabilities that have resulted or may result from the exercise of any such discretion.

**6(4)** For the purposes of this paragraph a residual interest vests in possession –

(a) in a case within sub-paragraph (2)(a), on the occurrence of the event there mentioned, whether or not the amount of the property receivable pursuant to the right mentioned in that sub-paragraph is then ascertained;

(b) in a case within sub-paragraph (2)(b) or (c), when the residual beneficiary becomes entitled to require the trustee to transfer to that beneficiary any of the property receivable pursuant to that right.

## EMPLOYER'S CHARGES AND OTHER RIGHTS OF RECOVERY

**7(1)** Where shares in an undertaking are held on trust, there shall be disregarded –

(a) if the trust is for the purposes of a pension scheme, any such rights as are mentioned in sub-paragraph (2) below;

(b) if the trust is for the purposes of an employees' share scheme, any such rights as are mentioned in paragraph (a) of that sub-paragraph,

being rights of the undertaking or any of its subsidiary undertakings.

**7(2)** The rights referred to are–

(a) any charge or lien on, or set-off against, any benefit or other right or interest under the scheme for the purpose of enabling the employer or former employer of a member of the scheme to obtain the discharge of a monetary obligation due to him from the member, and

(b) any right to receive from the trustee of the scheme, or as trustee of the scheme to retain, an amount that can be recovered or retained under section 61 of the Pension Schemes Act 1993 (deduction of contributions equivalent premium from refund of scheme contributions) or otherwise as reimbursement or partial reimbursement for any state scheme premium paid in connection with the scheme under Chapter III of Part III of that Act.

**History**

In para. 7(2)(b) the words "section 61 of the Pension Schemes Act 1993 (deduction of contributions equivalent premium from refund of scheme contributions)" substituted for the former words "section 47 of the Social Security Pensions Act 1975 (deduction of premium from refund of pension contributions)" and the words "Chapter III of Part III" substituted for the former words "Part III" by Pension Schemes Act 1993, s. 190 and Sch. 8, para. 16(b) as from 7 February 1994 (see SI 1994/86 (C 3), art. 2).

## TRUSTEE'S RIGHT TO EXPENSES, REMUNERATION, INDEMNITY, ETC.

**8** Where an undertaking is a trustee, there shall be disregarded any rights which the undertaking has in its capacity as trustee including, in particular, any right to recover its expenses or be remunerated out of the trust property and any right to be indemnified out of that property for any liability incurred by reason of any act or omission of the undertaking in the performance of its duties as trustee.

## SUPPLEMENTARY

**9(1)** The following applies for the interpretation of this Part of this Schedule.

**9(2)** "Undertaking", and "shares" in relation to an undertaking, have the same meaning as in Part VII.

**9(3)** This Part of this Schedule applies in relation to debentures as it applies in relation to shares.

**9(4)** **"Pension scheme"** means any scheme for the provision of benefits consisting of or including relevant benefits for or in respect of employees or former employees; and **"relevant benefits"** means any pension, lump sum, gratuity or other like benefit given or to be given on retirement or on death or in anticipation of retirement or, in connection with past service, after retirement or death.

**9(5)** In sub-paragraph (4) of this paragraph and in paragraph 7(2) "employee" and "employer" shall be read as if a director of an undertaking were employed by it.

**History**

Pt. II (para. 6–9) inserted by CA 1989, s. 23 and Sch. 10, para. 18(1), (7) as from 1 April 1990 subject to transitional and saving provisions (see SI 1990/355 (C 13), art. 3, Sch. 1 and also art. 6–9).

# Schedule 3 – Mandatory Contents of Prospectus

(Repealed by Financial Services Act 1986, s. 212(3) and Sch. 17, Pt. I as from 12 January 1987, 16 February 1987, 29 April 1988, 1 July 1988 and 19 June 1995.)

**History**

This repeal has effect as follows:

- as from 12 January 1987 re any investment listed or the subject of a listing application under Financial Services Act 1986, Pt. IV for all purposes relating to the admission of securities offered by or on behalf of a Minister of the Crown or a body corporate controlled by a Minister of the Crown or a subsidiary of such a body corporate to the Official List in respect of which an application is made after that date (see SI 1986/2246 (C 88));
- as from 16 February 1987 re any investment listed or the subject of a listing application under Financial Services

Act 1986, Pt. IV for purposes relating to the admission of securities in respect of which an application is made after that date other than those referred to in the preceding paragraph and otherwise for all purposes (see SI 1986/2246 (C 88));

- as from 29 April 1988 as far as Sch. 3 would apply to a prospectus offering for subscription, or to any form of application for units in a body corporate which is a recognised scheme (see SI 1988/740 (C 22));
- as from 1 July 1988 as far as Sch. 3 would apply to a prospectus offering for subscription, or to any application form for , units in a body corporate which is an open-ended investment company (see SI 1988/740 (C 22));
- as from 19 June 1995 for all remaining purposes except CA 1985, s. 58, 59, 60, in so far as Sch. 3 is necessary for the purposes of CA 1985, s. 81, 83, 246, 248, 744; and CA 1985, Sch. 3, para. 2, in so far as it is necessary for the purposes of CA 1985, s. 83(1)(a); and CA 1985, s. 62, in so far as it is necessary for the purposes of CA 1985, s. 744 (see SI 1995/1538 (C 33)).

Sch. 3 formerly read as follows:

Section 57, et passim in Part III

"**Part I – Matters to be Stated**

THE COMPANY'S PROPRIETORSHIP, MANAGEMENT AND ITS CAPITAL REQUIREMENT

**1(1)** The prospectus must state –

(a) the number of founders or management or deferred shares (if any) and the nature and extent of the interest of the holders in the property and profits of the company;

(b) the number of shares (if any) fixed by the company's articles as the qualification of a director, and any provision in the articles as to the remuneration of directors; and

(c) the names, descriptions and addresses of the directors or proposed directors.

**(2)** As this paragraph applies for the purposes of section 72(3), sub-paragraph (1)(b) is to be read with the substitution for the reference to the company's articles of a reference to its constitution.

**(3)** Sub-paragraphs (1)(b) and (1)(c) do not apply in the case of a prospectus issued more than 2 years after the date at which the company is entitled to commence business.

**2** Where shares are offered to the public for subscription, the prospectus must give particulars as to –

(a) the minimum amount which, in the opinion of the directors, must be raised by the issue of those shares in order to provide the sums (or, if any part of them is to be defrayed in any other manner, the balance of the sums) required to be provided in respect of each of the following –

(i) the purchase price of any property purchased or to be purchased which is to be defrayed in whole or in part out of the proceeds of the issue,

(ii) any preliminary expenses payable by the company, and any commission so payable to any person in consideration of his agreeing to subscribe for, or of his procuring or agreeing to procure subscriptions for, any shares in the company,

(iii) the repayment of any money borrowed by the company in respect of any of the foregoing matters,

(iv) working capital, and

(b) the amounts to be provided in respect of the matters above mentioned otherwise than out of the proceeds of the issue and the sources out of which those amounts are to be provided.

DETAILS RELATING TO THE OFFER

**3(1)** The prospectus must state –

(a) the time of the opening of the subscription lists, and

(b) the amount payable on application and allotment on each share (including the amount, if any, payable by way of premium).

**(2)** In the case of a second or subsequent offer of shares, there must also be stated the amount offered for subscription on each previous allotment made within the 2 preceding years, the amount actually allotted and the amount (if any) paid on the shares so allotted, including the amount (if any) paid by way of premium.

**4(1)** There must be stated the number, description and amount of any shares in or debentures of the company which any person has, or is entitled to be given, an option to subscribe for.

**(2)** The following particulars of the option must be given –

(a) the period during which it is exercisable,

(b) the price to be paid for shares or debentures subscribed for under it,

(c) the consideration (if any) given or to be given for it or the right to it,

(d) the names and addresses of the persons to whom it or the right to it was given or, if given to existing shareholders or debenture holders as such, the relevant shares or debentures.

**(3)** References in this paragraph to subscribing for shares or debentures include acquiring them from a person to whom they have been allotted or agreed to be allotted with a view to his offering them for sale.

**5** The prospectus must state the number and amount of shares and debentures which within the 2 preceding years have been issued, or agreed to be issued, as fully or partly paid up otherwise than in cash; and –

(a) in the latter case the extent to which they are so paid up, and

(b) in either case the consideration for which those shares or debentures have been issued or are proposed or intended to be issued.

PROPERTY ACQUIRED OR TO BE ACQUIRED BY THE COMPANY

**6(1)** For purposes of the following two paragraphs, **"relevant property"** is property purchased or acquired by the company, or proposed so to be purchased or acquired,

(a) which is to be paid for wholly or partly out of the proceeds of the issue offered for subscription by the prospectus, or

(b) the purchase or acquisition of which has not been completed at the date of the issue of the prospectus.

**(2)** But those two paragraphs do not apply to property –

(a) the contract for whose purchase or acquisition was entered into in the ordinary course of the company's business, the contract not being made in contemplation of the issue nor the issue in consequence of the contract, or

(b) as respects which the amount of the purchase money is not material.

**7** As respects any relevant property, the prospectus must state –

(a) the names and addresses of the vendors,
(b) the amount payable in cash, shares or debentures to the vendor and, where there is more than one separate vendor, or the company is a sub-purchaser, the amount so payable to each vendor,
(c) short particulars of any transaction relating to the property completed within the 2 preceding years in which any vendor of the property to the company or any person who is, or was at the time of the transaction, a promoter or a director or proposed director of the company had any interest direct or indirect.

**8** There must be stated the amount (if any) paid or payable as purchase money in cash, shares or debentures for any relevant property, specifying the amount (if any) payable for goodwill.

**9(1)** The following applies for the interpretation of paragraphs 6, 7 and 8.

**(2)** Every person is deemed a vendor who has entered into any contract (absolute or conditional) for the sale or purchase, or for any option of purchase, of any property to be acquired by the company, in any case where –
(a) the purchase money is not fully paid at the date of the issue of the prospectus,
(b) the purchase money is to be paid or satisfied wholly or in part out of the proceeds of the issue offered for subscription by the prospectus,
(c) the contract depends for its validity or fulfilment on the result of that issue.

**(3)** Where any property to be acquired by the company is to be taken on lease, paragraphs 6, 7 and 8 apply as if "vendor" included the lessor, "purchase money" included the consideration for the lease, and "sub-purchaser" included a sub-lessee.

**(4)** For purposes of paragraph 7, where the vendors or any of them are a firm, the members of the firm are not to be treated as separate vendors.

COMMISSIONS, PRELIMINARY EXPENSES, ETC.

**10(1)** The prospectus must state –
(a) the amount (if any) paid within the 2 preceding years, or payable, as commission (but not including commission to sub-underwriters) for subscribing or agreeing to subscribe, or procuring or agreeing to procure subscriptions, for any shares in or debentures of the company, or the rate of any such commission,
(b) the amount or estimated amount of any preliminary expenses and the persons by whom any of those expenses have been paid or are payable, and the amount or estimated amount of the expenses of the issue and the persons by whom any of those expenses have been paid or are payable,
(c) any amount or benefit paid or given within the 2 preceding years or intended to be paid or given to any promoter, and the consideration for the payment or the giving of the benefit.

**(2)** Sub-paragraph (1)(b) above, so far as it relates to preliminary expenses, does not apply in the case of a prospectus issued more than 2 years after the date at which the company is entitled to commence business.

CONTRACTS

**11(1)** The prospectus must give the dates of, parties to and general nature of every material contract.

**(2)** This does not apply to a contract entered into in the ordinary course of the business carried on or intended to be carried on by the company, or a contract entered into more than 2 years before the date of issue of the prospectus.

AUDITORS

**12** The prospectus must state the names and addresses of the company's auditors (if any).

INTERESTS OF DIRECTORS

**13(1)** The prospectus must give full particulars of –
(a) the nature and extent of the interest (if any) of every director in the promotion of, or in the property proposed to be acquired by, the company, or
(b) where the interest of such a director consists in being a partner in a firm, the nature and extent of the interest of the firm.

**(2)** With the particulars under sub-paragraph (1)(b) must be provided a statement of all sums paid or agreed to be paid to the director or the firm in cash or shares or otherwise by any person either to induce him to become, or to qualify him as, a director, or otherwise for services rendered by him or the firm in connection with the promotion or formation of the company.

**(3)** This paragraph does not apply in the case of a prospectus issued more than 2 years after the date at which the company is entitled to commence business.

OTHER MATTERS

**14** If the prospectus invites the public to subscribe for shares in the company and the company's share capital is divided into different classes of shares, the prospectus must state the right of voting at meetings of the company conferred by, and the rights in respect of capital and dividends attached to, the several classes of shares respectively.

**15** In the case of a company which has been carrying on business, or of a business which has been carried on for less than 3 years, the prospectus must state the length of time during which the business of the company (or the business to be acquired, as the case may be) has been carried on.

**Part II – Auditors' and Accountants' Reports to be Set Out in Prospectus**

AUDITORS' REPORT

**16(1)** The prospectus shall set out a report by the company's auditors with respect to –
(a) profits and losses and assets and liabilities, in accordance with sub-paragraphs (2) and (3) below, as the case requires, and
(b) the rates of the dividends (if any) paid by the company in respect of each class of shares in respect of each of the 5 financial years immediately preceding the issue of the prospectus, giving particulars of each such class of shares on which such dividends have been paid and particulars of the cases in which no dividends have been paid in respect of any class of shares in respect of any of those years.

If no accounts have been made up in respect of any part of the 5 years ending on a date 3 months before the issue of the prospectus, the report shall contain a statement of that fact.

**(2)** If the company has no subsidiary undertakings, the report shall–
(a) deal with profits and losses of the company in respect of each of the 5 financial years immediately preceding the issue of the prospectus, and
(b) deal with the assets and liabilities of the company at the last date to which the company's accounts were made up."

(In para. 16(2) the words "subsidiary undertakings" substituted for the former words "subsidiaries" by CA 1989, s. 23 and Sch. 10, para. 19(1), (2) as from 1 August 1990 subject to transitional and saving provisions (see SI 1990/355 (C 13), art. 3, Sch. 1 and also art. 6–9).)

"**(3)** If the company has subsidiary undertakings, the report shall –

(a) deal separately with the company's profits or losses as provided by sub-paragraph (2), and in addition deal either –

(i) as a whole with the combined profits or losses of its subsidiary undertakings, so far as they concern members of the company, or

(ii) individually with the profits or losses of each of its subsidiary undertakings, so far as they concern members of the company,

or, instead of dealing separately with the company's profits or losses, deal as a whole with the profits or losses of the company and (so far as they concern members of the company) with the combined profits and losses of its subsidiary undertakings; and

(b) deal separately with the company's assets and liabilities as provided by sub-paragraph (2), and in addition deal either –

(i) as a whole with the combined assets and liabilities of its subsidiary undertakings, with or without the company's assets and liabilities, or

(ii) individually with the assets and liabilities of each of its subsidiary undertakings,

indicating, as respects the assets and liabilities of its subsidiary undertakings, the allowance to be made for persons other than members of the company."

(Para. 16(3) substituted by CA 1989, s. 23 and Sch. 10, para. 19(1), (2) as from 1 August 1990 subject to transitional and saving provisions (see SI 1990/355 (C 13), art. 3, Sch. 1 and also art. 6–9); para. 16(3) formerly read as follows:

"If the company has subsidiaries, the report shall –

(a) deal separately with the company's profits or losses as provided by sub-paragraph (2), and in addition deal either –

(i) as a whole with the combined profits or losses of its subsidiaries, so far as they concern members of the company, or

(ii) individually with the profits or losses of each subsidiary, so far as they concern members of the company,

or, instead of dealing separately with the company's profits or losses, deal as a whole with the profits or losses of the company and (so far as they concern members of the company) with the combined profits and losses of its subsidiaries; and

(b) deal separately with the company's assets and liabilities as provided by sub-paragraph (2), and in addition deal either–

(i) as a whole with the combined assets and liabilities of its subsidiaries, with or without the company's assets and liabilities, or

(ii) individually with the assets and liabilities of each subsidiary,

indicating, as respects the assets and liabilities of the subsidiaries, the allowance to be made for persons other than members of the company.")

"ACCOUNTANTS' REPORTS

**17** If the proceeds of the issue of the shares or debentures are to be applied directly or indirectly in the purchase of any business, or any part of the proceeds of the issue is to be so applied, there shall be set out in the prospectus a report made by accountants upon–

(a) the profits or losses of the business in respect of each of the 5 financial years immediately preceding the issue of the prospectus, and

(b) the assets and liabilities of the business at the last date to which the accounts of the business were made up.

**18(1)** The following provisions apply if–

(a) the proceeds of the issue are to be applied directly or indirectly in any manner resulting in the acquisition by the company of shares in any other undertaking, or any part of the proceeds is to be so applied, and

(b) by reason of that acquisition or anything to be done in consequence of or in connection with it, that undertaking will become a subsidiary undertaking of the company.

**(2)** There shall be set out in the prospectus a report made by accountants upon–

(a) the profits or losses of the other undertaking in respect of each of the five financial years immediately preceding the issue of the prospectus, and

(b) the assets and liabilities of the other undertaking at the last date to which its accounts were made up.

**(3)** The report shall–

(a) indicate how the profits or losses of the other undertaking would in respect of the shares to be acquired have concerned members of the company and what allowance would have fallen to be made, in relation to assets and liabilities so dealt with, for holders of other shares, if the company had at all material times held the shares to be acquired, and

(b) where the other undertaking is a parent undertaking, deal with the profits or losses and the assets and liabilities of the undertaking and its subsidiary undertakings, in the manner provided by paragraph 16(3) above in relation to the company and its subsidiary undertakings.

**(4)** In this paragraph **"undertaking"** and **"shares"**, in relation to an undertaking, have the same meaning as in Part VII."

(Para. 18 substituted by CA 1989, s. 23 and Sch. 10, para. 19(1), (3) as from 1 August 1990 subject to transitional and saving provisions (see SI 1990/355 (C 13), art. 3, Sch. 1 and also art. 6–9); para. 18 formerly read as follows:

"**18(1)** The following applies if–

(a) the proceeds of the issue are to be applied directly or indirectly in any manner resulting in the acquisition by the company of shares in any other body corporate, or any part of the proceeds is to be so applied, and

(b) by reason of that acquisition or anything to be done in consequence of or in connection with it, that body corporate will become a subsidiary of the company.

**(2)** There shall be set out in the prospectus a report made by accountants upon–

(a) the profits or losses of the other body corporate in respect of each of the 5 financial years immediately preceding the issue of the prospectus, and

(b) the assets and liabilities of the other body corporate at the last date to which its accounts were made up.

**(3)** The accountants' report required by this paragraph shall–

(a) indicate how the profits of losses of the other body corporate dealt with by the report would, in respect of the shares to be acquired, have concerned members of the company and what allowance would have fallen to be made, in relation to assets and liabilities so dealt with, for holders of other shares, if the company had at all material times held the shares to be acquired, and

(b) where the other body corporate has subsidiaries, deal with the profits or losses and the assets and liabilities of the body corporate and its subsidiaries in the manner provided by paragraph 16(3) above in relation to the company and its subsidiaries.")

"PROVISIONS INTERPRETING PRECEDING PARAGRAPHS, AND MODIFYING THEM IN CERTAIN CASES

**19** If in the case of a company which has been carrying on business, or of a business which has been carried on for less than 5 years, the accounts of the company or business have only been made up in respect of 4 years, 3 years, 2 years or one year, the preceding paragraphs of this Part have effect as if references to 4 years, 3 years, 2 years or one year (as the case may be) were substituted for references to 5 years.

**20** The expression **"financial year"** in this Part means the year in respect of which the accounts of the company or of the business (as the case may be) are made up; and where by reason of any alteration of the date on which the financial year of the company or business terminates the accounts have been made up for a period greater or less than one year, that greater or less period is for purposes of this Part deemed to be a financial year.

**21** Any report required by this Part shall either indicate by way of note any adjustments as respects the figures of any profits or losses or assets and liabilities dealt with by the report which appear to the persons making the report necessary, or shall make those adjustments and indicate that adjustments have been made.

**22(1)** A report required by paragraph 17 or 18 shall be made by accountants qualified under this Act for appointment as auditors of a company.

**(2)** Such a report shall not be made by an accountant who is an officer or servant, or a partner of or in the employment of an officer or servant, of–

(a) the company or any of its subsidiary undertakings,

(b) a parent undertaking of the company or any subsidiary undertaking of such an undertaking."

(Para. 22(2) substituted by CA 1989, s. 23 and Sch. 10, para. 19(1), (4) as from 1 August 1990 subject to transitional and saving provisions (see SI 1990/355 (C 13), art. 3, Sch. 1 and also art. 6–9); para. 22(2) formerly read as follows:

"Such a report shall not be made by any accountant who is an officer or servant, or a partner of or in the employment of an officer or servant, of the company or the company's subsidiary or holding company or of a subsidiary of the company's holding company.

In this paragraph, **"officer"** includes a proposed director, but not an auditor.")

"**(3)** The accountants making any report required for purposes of paragraph 17 or 18 shall be named in the prospectus."

# Schedule 4 – Form and Content of Company Accounts

[Companies Act 1985, s. 226;
Companies Act 1989, s. 1, 4(2), Sch. 1]

## Part I – General Rules and Formats

### SECTION A – GENERAL RULES

**1(1)** Subject to the following provisions of this Schedule–

(a) every balance sheet of a company shall show the items listed in either of the balance sheet formats set out below in section B of this Part; and

(b) every profit and loss account of a company shall show the items listed in any one of the profit and loss account formats so set out;

in either case in the order and under the headings and sub-headings given in the format adopted.

**1(2)** Sub-paragraph (1) above is not to be read as requiring the heading or sub-heading for any item to be distinguished by any letter or number assigned to that item in the format adopted.

**2(1)** Where in accordance with paragraph 1 a company's balance sheet or profit and loss account for any financial year has been prepared by reference to one of the formats set out in section B below, the directors of the company shall adopt the same format in preparing the accounts for subsequent financial years of the company unless in their opinion there are special reasons for a change.

**2(2)** Particulars of any change in the format adopted in preparing a company's balance sheet or profit and loss account in accordance with paragraph 1 shall be disclosed, and the reasons for the change shall be explained, in a note to the accounts in which the new format is first adopted.

**3(1)** Any item required in accordance with paragraph 1 to be shown in a company's balance sheet or profit and loss account may be shown in greater detail than required by the format adopted.

**3(2)** A company's balance sheet or profit and loss account may include an item representing or covering the amount of any asset or liability, income or expenditure not otherwise covered by any of the items listed in the format adopted, but the following shall not be treated as assets in any company's balance sheet–

(a) preliminary expenses;

(b) expenses of and commission on any issue of shares or debentures; and

(c) costs of research.

**3(3)** In preparing a company's balance sheet or profit and loss account the directors of the company shall adapt the arrangement and headings and sub-headings otherwise required by paragraph 1 in respect of items to which an Arabic number is assigned in the format adopted, in any case where the special nature of the company's business requires such adaptation.

**3(4)** Items to which Arabic numbers are assigned in any of the formats set out in section B below may be combined in a company's accounts for any financial year if either–

(a) their individual amounts are not material to assessing the state of affairs or profit or loss of the company for that year; or

(b) the combination facilitates that assessment;

but in a case within paragraph (b) the individual amounts of any items so combined shall be disclosed in a note to the accounts.

**3(5)** Subject to paragraph 4(3) below, a heading or sub-heading corresponding to an item listed in the format adopted in preparing a company's balance sheet or profit and loss account shall not be included if there is no amount to be shown for that item in respect of the financial year to which the balance sheet or profit and loss account relates.

**3(6)** Every profit and loss account of a company shall show the amount of the company's profit or loss on ordinary activities before taxation.

**3(7)** Every profit and loss account of a company shall show separately as additional items–

(a) any amount set aside or proposed to be set aside to, or withdrawn or proposed to be withdrawn from, reserves;

(b) the aggregate amount of any dividends paid and proposed;

(c) if it is not shown in the notes to the accounts, the aggregate amount of any dividends proposed.

**History**

In para. 3(7), the word "and" formerly appearing at the end of para. (a) omitted, and para. (c) inserted by the Companies Act 1985 (Miscellaneous Accounting Amendments) Regulations 1996 (SI 1996/189, reg. 1(1), 14(1) and Sch. 1, para. 1, 2 as from 2 February 1996, subject to reg. 16(1), (2).

**4(1)** In respect of every item shown in a company's balance sheet or profit and loss account the corresponding amount for the financial year immediately preceding that to which the balance sheet or profit and loss account relates shall also be shown.

**4(2)** Where that corresponding amount is not comparable with the amount to be shown for the item in question in respect of the financial year to which the balance sheet or profit and loss account relates, the former amount shall be adjusted and particulars of the adjustment and the reasons for it shall be disclosed in a note to the accounts.

**4(3)** Paragraph 3(5) does not apply in any case where an amount can be shown for the item in question in respect of the financial year immediately preceding that to which the balance sheet or profit and loss account relates, and that amount shall be shown under the heading or sub-heading required by paragraph 1 for that item.

**5** Amounts in respect of items representing assets or income may not be set off against amounts in respect of items representing liabilities or expenditure (as the case may be), or vice versa.

## SECTION B – THE REQUIRED FORMATS FOR ACCOUNTS

### Preliminary

**6** References in this Part of this Schedule to the items listed in any of the formats set out below are to those items read together with any of the notes following the formats which apply to any of those items, and the requirement imposed by paragraph 1 to show the items listed in any such format in the order adopted in the format is subject to any provision in those notes for alternative positions for any particular items.

**7** A number in brackets following any item in any of the formats set out below is a reference to the note of that number in the notes following the formats.

**8** In the notes following the formats–

(a) the heading of each note gives the required heading or sub-heading for the item to which it applies and a reference to any letters and numbers assigned to that item in the formats set out below (taking a reference in the case of Format 2 of the balance sheet formats to the item listed under "Assets" or under "Liabilities" as the case may require); and

(b) references to a numbered format are to the balance sheet format or (as the case may require) to the profit and loss account format of that number set out below.

### Balance Sheet Formats

#### *Format 1*

A. Called up share capital not paid *(1)*

B. Fixed assets

I Intangible assets

1. Development costs
2. Concessions, patents, licences, trade marks and similar rights and assets *(2)*
3. Goodwill *(3)*
4. Payments on account

II Tangible assets

1. Land and buildings
2. Plant and machinery
3. Fixtures, fittings, tools and equipment
4. Payments on account and assets in course of construction

III Investments

1. Shares in group undertakings
2. Loans to group undertakings
3. Participating interests
4. Loans to undertakings in which the company has a participating interest
5. Other investments other than loans
6. Other loans
7. Own shares *(4)*

C. Current assets

I Stocks

1. Raw materials and consumables
2. Work in progress
3. Finished goods and goods for resale
4. Payments on account

II Debtors *(5)*

1. Trade debtors
2. Amounts owed by group undertakings
3. Amounts owed by undertakings in which the company has a participating interest
4. Other debtors

5. Called up share capital not paid *(1)*
6. Prepayments and accrued income *(6)*

III Investments

1. Shares in group undertakings
2. Own shares *(4)*
3. Other investments

IV Cash at bank and in hand

D. Prepayments and accrued income *(6)*

E. Creditors: amounts falling due within one year

1. Debenture loans *(7)*
2. Bank loans and overdrafts
3. Payments received on account *(8)*
4. Trade creditors
5. Bills of exchange payable
6. Amounts owed to group undertakings
7. Amounts owed to undertakings in which the company has a participating interest
8. Other creditors including taxation and social security *(9)*
9. Accruals and deferred income *(10)*

F. Net current assets (liabilities) *(11)*

G. Total assets less current liabilities

H. Creditors: amounts falling due after more than one year

1. Debenture loans *(7)*
2. Bank loans and overdrafts
3. Payments received on account *(8)*
4. Trade creditors
5. Bills of exchange payable
6. Amounts owed to group undertakings
7. Amounts owed to undertakings in which the company has a participating interest
8. Other creditors including taxation and social security *(9)*
9. Accruals and deferred income *(10)*

I. Provisions for liabilities and charges

1. Pensions and similar obligations
2. Taxation, including deferred taxation
3. Other provisions

J. Accruals and deferred income *(10)*

K. Capital and reserves

I Called up share capital *(12)*

II Share premium account

III Revaluation reserve

IV Other reserves

1. Capital redemption reserve
2. Reserve for own shares
3. Reserves provided for by the articles of association
4. Other reserves

V Profit and loss account

**Note**

See history note at end of Pt. I.

## Balance Sheet Formats

*Format 2*

ASSETS

A. Called up share capital not paid *(1)*

B. Fixed assets

I Intangible assets

1. Development costs
2. Concessions, patents, licences, trade marks and similar rights and assets *(2)*
3. Goodwill *(3)*
4. Payments on account

II Tangible assets

1. Land and buildings
2. Plant and machinery
3. Fixtures, fittings, tools and equipment
4. Payments on account and assets in course of construction

III Investments

1. Shares in group undertakings
2. Loans to group undertakings
3. Participating interests
4. Loans to undertakings in which the company has a participating interest
5. Other investments other than loans
6. Other loans
7. Own shares *(4)*

C. Current assets

I Stocks

1. Raw materials and consumables
2. Work in progress
3. Finished goods and goods for resale
4. Payments on account

II Debtors *(5)*

1. Trade debtors
2. Amounts owed by group undertakings
3. Amounts owed by undertakings in which the company has a participating interest
4. Other debtors
5. Called up share capital not paid *(1)*
6. Prepayments and accrued income *(6)*

III Investments

1. Shares in group undertakings
2. Own shares *(4)*
3. Other investments

IV Cash at bank and in hand

D. Prepayments and accrued income *(6)*

LIABILITIES

A. Capital and reserves

I Called up share capital *(12)*

II Share premium account

III Revaluation reserve

IV Other reserves

1. Capital redemption reserve
2. Reserve for own shares
3. Reserves provided for by the articles of association
4. Other reserves

V Profit and loss account

B. Provisions for liabilities and charges

1. Pensions and similar obligations
2. Taxation including deferred taxation
3. Other provisions

C. Creditors *(13)*

1. Debenture loans *(7)*
2. Bank loans and overdrafts
3. Payments received on account *(8)*
4. Trade creditors
5. Bills of exchange payable
6. Amounts owed to group undertakings
7. Amounts owed to undertakings in which the company has a participating interest
8. Other creditors including taxation and social security *(9)*
9. Accruals and deferred income *(10)*

D. Accruals and deferred income *(10)*

**History**
See history note at end of Pt. I.

## Notes on the balance sheet formats

*(1) Called up share capital not paid* – (Formats 1 and 2, items A and C.II.5.)

This item may be shown in either of the two positions given in Formats 1 and 2.

*(2) Concessions, patents, licences, trade marks and similar rights and assets* – (Formats 1 and 2, item B.I.2.)

Amounts in respect of assets shall only be included in a company's balance sheet under this item if either–

(a) the assets were acquired for valuable consideration and are not required to be shown under goodwill; or

(b) the assets in question were created by the company itself.

*(3) Goodwill* – (Formats 1 and 2, item B.I.3.)

Amounts representing goodwill shall only be included to the extent that the goodwill was acquired for valuable consideration.

*(4) Own shares* – (Formats 1 and 2, items B.III.7 and C.III.2.)

The nominal value of the shares held shall be shown separately.

*(5) Debtors* – (Formats 1 and 2, items C.II.1 to 6.)

The amount falling due after more than one year shall be shown separately for each item included under debtors.

*(6) Prepayments and accrued income* – (Formats 1 and 2, items C.II.6 and D.)

This item may be shown in either of the two positions given in Formats 1 and 2.

*(7) Debenture loans* – (Format 1, items E.1 and H.1 and Format 2, item C.1.)

The amount of any convertible loans shall be shown separately.

*(8) Payments received on account* – (Format 1, items E.3 and H.3 and Format 2, item C.3.)

Payments received on account of orders shall be shown for each of these items in so far as they are not shown as deductions from stocks.

*(9) Other creditors including taxation and social security* – (Format 1, items E.8 and H.8 and Format 2, item C.8.)

The amount for creditors in respect of taxation and social security shall be shown separately from the amount for other creditors.

*(10) Accruals and deferred income* – (Format 1, items E.9, H.9 and J and Format 2, items C.9 and D.)

The two positions given for this item in Format 1 at E.9 and H.9 are an alternative to the position at J, but if the item is not shown in a position corresponding to that at J it may be shown in either or both of the other two positions (as the case may require).

The two positions given for this item in Format 2 are alternatives.

*(11) Net current assets (liabilities)* – (Format 1, item F.)

In determining the amount to be shown for this item any amounts shown under "prepayments and accrued income" shall be taken into account wherever shown.

*(12) Called up share capital* – (Format 1, item K.I and Format 2, item A.I.)

The amount of allotted share capital and the amount of called up share capital which has been paid up shall be shown separately.

*(13) Creditors* – (Format 2, items C.1 to 9.)

Amounts falling due within one year and after one year shall be shown separately for each of these items and for the aggregate of all of these items.

**History**

See history note at end of Pt. I.

## Profit and loss account formats

### *Format 1*

(see note *(17)* below)

1. Turnover
2. Cost of sales *(14)*
3. Gross profit or loss
4. Distribution costs *(14)*
5. Administrative expenses *(14)*
6. Other operating income
7. Income from shares in group undertakings
8. Income from participating interests
9. Income from other fixed asset investments *(15)*
10. Other interest receivable and similar income *(15)*
11. Amounts written off investments
12. Interest payable and similar charges *(16)*
13. Tax on profit or loss on ordinary activities
14. Profit or loss on ordinary activities after taxation
15. Extraordinary income
16. Extraordinary charges
17. Extraordinary profit or loss
18. Tax on extraordinary profit or loss
19. Other taxes not shown under the above items
20. Profit or loss for the financial year

**History**

See history note at end of Pt. I.

## Profit and loss account formats

### *Format 2*

1. Turnover
2. Change in stocks of finished goods and in work in progress
3. Own work capitalised
4. Other operating income
5. (a) Raw materials and consumables
   (b) Other external charges
6. Staff costs:

(a) wages and salaries
(b) social security costs
(c) other pension costs

7. (a) Depreciation and other amounts written off tangible and intangible fixed assets
   (b) Exceptional amounts written off current assets
8. Other operating charges
9. Income from shares in group undertakings
10. Income from participating interests
11. Income from other fixed asset investments *(15)*
12. Other interest receivable and similar income *(15)*
13. Amounts written off investments
14. Interest payable and similar charges *(16)*
15. Tax on profit or loss on ordinary activities
16. Profit or loss on ordinary activities after taxation
17. Extraordinary income
18. Extraordinary charges
19. Extraordinary profit or loss
20. Tax on extraordinary profit or loss
21. Other taxes not shown under the above items
22. Profit or loss for the financial year

**History**
See history note at end of Pt. I.

## Profit and loss account formats

*Format 3*

(see note *(17)* below)

A. Charges

1. Cost of sales *(14)*
2. Distribution costs *(14)*
3. Administrative expenses *(14)*
4. Amounts written off investments
5. Interest payable and similar charges *(16)*
6. Tax on profit or loss on ordinary activities
7. Profit or loss on ordinary activities after taxation
8. Extraordinary charges
9. Tax on extraordinary profit or loss
10. Other taxes not shown under the above items
11. Profit or loss for the financial year

B. Income

1. Turnover
2. Other operating income
3. Income from shares in group undertakings
4. Income from participating interests
5. Income from other fixed asset investments *(15)*
6. Other interest receivable and similar income *(15)*
7. Profit or loss on ordinary activities after taxation
8. Extraordinary income
9. Profit or loss for the financial year

**History**
See history note at end of Pt. I.

## Profit and loss account formats

*Format 4*

A. Charges

1. Reduction in stocks of finished goods and in work in progress
2. (a) Raw materials and consumables
   (b) Other external charges
3. Staff costs:
   (a) wages and salaries
   (b) social security costs
   (c) other pension costs
4. (a) Depreciation and other amounts written off tangible and intangible fixed assets
   (b) Exceptional amounts written off current assets
5. Other operating charges
6. Amounts written off investments
7. Interest payable and similar charges *(16)*
8. Tax on profit or loss on ordinary activities
9. Profit or loss on ordinary activities after taxation
10. Extraordinary charges
11. Tax on extraordinary profit or loss
12. Other taxes not shown under the above items
13. Profit or loss for the financial year

B. Income

1. Turnover
2. Increase in stocks of finished goods and in work in progress
3. Own work capitalised
4. Other operating income
5. Income from shares in group undertakings
6. Income from participating interests
7. Income from other fixed asset investments *(15)*
8. Other interest receivable and similar income *(15)*
9. Profit or loss on ordinary activities after taxation
10. Extraordinary income
11. Profit or loss for the financial year

**History**
See history note at end of Pt. I.

## Notes on the profit and loss account formats

*(14) Cost of sales: distribution costs: administrative expenses* – (Format 1, items 2, 4 and 5 and Format 3, items A.1, 2 and 3.)

These items shall be stated after taking into account any necessary provisions for depreciation or diminution in value of assets.

*(15) Income from other fixed asset investments: other interest receivable and similar income* – (Format 1, items 9 and 10: Format 2, items 11 and 12: Format 3, items B.5 and 6: Format 4, items B.7 and 8.)

Income and interest derived from group undertakings shall be shown separately from income and interest derived from other sources.

*(16) Interest payable and similar charges* – (Format 1, item 12: Format 2, item 14: Format 3, item A.5: Format 4, item A.7.)

The amount payable to group undertakings shall be shown separately.

*(17) Formats 1 and 3*

The amount of any provisions for depreciation and diminution in value of tangible and intangible fixed assets falling to be shown under items 7(a) and A.4(a) respectively in Formats

2 and 4 shall be disclosed in a note to the accounts in any case where the profit and loss account is prepared by reference to Format 1 or Format 3.

**History**

In note (13) to the balance sheet formats the words "and for the aggregate of all of these items" substituted for the former words "and their aggregate shall be shown separately for all of these items" by the Companies Act 1985 (Miscellaneous Accounting Amendments) Regulations 1996 (SI 1996/189), reg. 1(1), 14(1) and Sch. 1, para. 1, 3 as from 2 February 1996, subject to reg. 16(1), (2). Previously in the balance sheet formats, profit and loss account formats and notes (15) and (16) to the latter, the words "group undertakings", "participating interests" and "undertakings in which the company has a participating interest" wherever they occur, substituted for the former words "group companies", "shares in related companies" and "related companies" respectively by CA 1989, s. 1, 4(2) and Sch. 1, para. 1–4 as from 1 April 1990 subject to transitional and saving provisions (see SI 1990/355 (C 13), art. 3, Sch. 1 and also art. 6–9).

# Part II – Accounting Principles and Rules

## SECTION A – ACCOUNTING PRINCIPLES

### Preliminary

**9** Subject to paragraph 15 below, the amounts to be included in respect of all items shown in a company's accounts shall be determined in accordance with the principles set out in paragraphs 10 to 14.

### Accounting principles

**10** The company shall be presumed to be carrying on business as a going concern.

**11** Accounting policies shall be applied consistently within the same accounts and from one financial year to the next.

**History**

Para. 11 substituted by CA 1989, s. 1, 4(2) and Sch. 1, para. 1, 5 as from 1 April 1990 subject to transitional and saving provisions (see SI 1990/355 (C 13), art. 3, Sch. 1 and also art. 6–9); para. 11 formerly read as follows:

"Accounting policies shall be applied consistently from one financial year to the next."

**12** The amount of any item shall be determined on a prudent basis, and in particular–

(a) only profits realised at the balance sheet date shall be included in the profit and loss account; and

(b) all liabilities and losses which have arisen or are likely to arise in respect of the financial year to which the accounts relate or a previous financial year shall be taken into account, including those which only become apparent between the balance sheet date and the date on which it is signed on behalf of the board of directors in pursuance of section 233 of this Act.

**History**

In para. 12(b) the words "section 233" substituted for the former words "section 238" by CA 1989, s. 23 and Sch. 10, para. 20 as from 1 April 1990 subject to transitional and saving provisions (see SI 1990/355 (C 13), art. 3, Sch. 1 and also art. 6–9).

**13** All income and charges relating to the financial year to which the accounts relate shall be taken into account, without regard to the date of receipt or payment.

**14** In determining the aggregate amount of any item the amount of each individual asset or liability that falls to be taken into account shall be determined separately.

### Departure from the accounting principles

**15** If it appears to the directors of a company that there are special reasons for departing from any of the principles stated above in preparing the company's accounts in respect of any financial year they may do so, but particulars of the departure, the reasons for it and its effect shall be given in a note to the accounts.

## SECTION B – HISTORICAL COST ACCOUNTING RULES

### Preliminary

**16** Subject to section C of this Part of this Schedule, the amounts to be included in respect of all items shown in a company's accounts shall be determined in accordance with the rules set out in paragraphs 17 to 28.

## Fixed assets

*General rules*

**17** Subject to any provision for depreciation or diminution in value made in accordance with paragraph 18 or 19 the amount to be included in respect of any fixed asset shall be its purchase price or production cost.

**18** In the case of any fixed asset which has a limited useful economic life, the amount of–

(a) its purchase price or production cost; or

(b) where it is estimated that any such asset will have a residual value at the end of the period of its useful economic life, its purchase price or production cost less that estimated residual value;

shall be reduced by provisions for depreciation calculated to write off that amount systematically over the period of the asset's useful economic life.

**19(1)** Where a fixed asset investment of a description falling to be included under item B.III of either of the balance sheet formats set out in Part I of this Schedule has diminished in value provisions for diminution in value may be made in respect of it and the amount to be included in respect of it may be reduced accordingly; and any such provisions which are not shown in the profit and loss account shall be disclosed (either separately or in aggregate) in a note to the accounts.

**19(2)** Provisions for diminution in value shall be made in respect of any fixed asset which has diminished in value if the reduction in its value is expected to be permanent (whether its useful economic life is limited or not), and the amount to be included in respect of it shall be reduced accordingly; and any such provisions which are not shown in the profit and loss account shall be disclosed (either separately or in aggregate) in a note to the accounts.

**19(3)** Where the reasons for which any provision was made in accordance with sub-paragraph (1) or (2) have ceased to apply to any extent, that provision shall be written back to the extent that it is no longer necessary; and any amounts written back in accordance with this sub-paragraph which are not shown in the profit and loss account shall be disclosed (either separately or in aggregate) in a note to the accounts.

*Rules for determining particular fixed asset items*

**20(1)** Notwithstanding that an item in respect of "development costs" is included under "fixed assets" in the balance sheet formats set out in Part I of this Schedule, an amount may only be included in a company's balance sheet in respect of development costs in special circumstances.

**20(2)** If any amount is included in a company's balance sheet in respect of development costs the following information shall be given in a note to the accounts–

(a) the period over which the amount of those costs originally capitalised is being or is to be written off; and

(b) the reasons for capitalising the development costs in question.

**21(1)** The application of paragraphs 17 to 19 in relation to goodwill (in any case where goodwill is treated as an asset) is subject to the following provisions of this paragraph.

**21(2)** Subject to sub-paragraph (3) below, the amount of the consideration for any goodwill acquired by a company shall be reduced by provisions for depreciation calculated to write off that amount systematically over a period chosen by the directors of the company.

**21(3)** The period chosen shall not exceed the useful economic life of the goodwill in question.

**21(4)** In any case where any goodwill acquired by a company is shown or included as an asset in the company's balance sheet the period chosen for writing off the consideration for that goodwill and the reasons for choosing that period shall be disclosed in a note to the accounts.

## Current assets

**22** Subject to paragraph 23, the amount to be included in respect of any current asset shall be its purchase price or production cost.

**23(1)** If the net realisable value of any current asset is lower than its purchase price or production cost the amount to be included in respect of that asset shall be the net realisable value.

**23(2)** Where the reasons for which any provision for diminution in value was made in accordance with sub-paragraph (1) have ceased to apply to any extent, that provision shall be written back to the extent that it is no longer necessary.

## Miscellaneous and supplementary provisions

*Excess of money owed over value received as an asset item*

**24(1)** Where the amount repayable on any debt owed by a company is greater than the value of the consideration received in the transaction giving rise to the debt, the amount of the difference may be treated as an asset.

**24(2)** Where any such amount is so treated–

(a) it shall be written off by reasonable amounts each year and must be completely written off before repayment of the debt; and

(b) if the current amount is not shown as a separate item in the company's balance sheet it must be disclosed in a note to the accounts.

*Assets included at a fixed amount*

**25(1)** Subject to the following sub-paragraph, assets which fall to be included–

(a) amongst the fixed assets of a company under the item "tangible assets"; or

(b) amongst the current assets of a company under the item "raw materials and consumables";

may be included at a fixed quantity and value.

**25(2)** Sub-paragraph (1) applies to assets of a kind which are constantly being replaced, where–

(a) their overall value is not material to assessing the company's state of affairs; and

(b) their quantity, value and composition are not subject to material variation.

*Determination of purchase price or production cost*

**26(1)** The purchase price of an asset shall be determined by adding to the actual price paid any expenses incidental to its acquisition.

**26(2)** The production cost of an asset shall be determined by adding to the purchase price of the raw materials and consumables used the amount of the costs incurred by the company which are directly attributable to the production of that asset.

**26(3)** In addition, there may be included in the production cost of an asset–

(a) a reasonable proportion of the costs incurred by the company which are only indirectly attributable to the production of that asset, but only to the extent that they relate to the period of production; and

(b) interest on capital borrowed to finance the production of that asset, to the extent that it accrues in respect of the period of production;

provided, however, in a case within paragraph (b) above, that the inclusion of the interest in determining the cost of that asset and the amount of the interest so included is disclosed in a note to the accounts.

**26(4)** In the case of current assets distribution costs may not be included in production costs.

**27(1)** Subject to the qualification mentioned below, the purchase price or production cost of–

(a) any assets which fall to be included under any item shown in a company's balance sheet under the general item "stocks"; and

(b) any assets which are fungible assets (including investments);

may be determined by the application of any of the methods mentioned in sub-paragraph (2) below in relation to any such assets of the same class.

The method chosen must be one which appears to the directors to be appropriate in the circumstances of the company.

**27(2)** Those methods are–

(a) the method known as "first in, first out" (FIFO);

(b) the method known as "last in, first out" (LIFO);

(c) a weighted average price; and

(d) any other method similar to any of the methods mentioned above.

**27(3)** Where in the case of any company–

(a) the purchase price or production cost of assets falling to be included under any item shown in the company's balance sheet has been determined by the application of any method permitted by this paragraph; and

(b) the amount shown in respect of that item differs materially from the relevant alternative amount given below in this paragraph;

the amount of that difference shall be disclosed in a note to the accounts.

**27(4)** Subject to sub-paragraph (5) below, for the purposes of sub-paragraph (3)(b) above, the relevant alternative amount, in relation to any item shown in a company's balance sheet, is the amount which would have been shown in respect of that item if assets of any class included under that item at an amount determined by any method permitted by this paragraph had instead been included at their replacement cost as at the balance sheet date.

**27(5)** The relevant alternative amount may be determined by reference to the most recent actual purchase price or production cost before the balance sheet date of assets of any class included under the item in question instead of by reference to their replacement cost as at that date, but only if the former appears to the directors of the company to constitute the more appropriate standard of comparison in the case of assets of that class.

**27(6)** For the purposes of this paragraph, assets of any description shall be regarded as fungible if assets of that description are substantially indistinguishable one from another.

*Substitution of original stated amount where price or cost unknown*

**28** Where there is no record of the purchase price or production cost of any asset of a company or of any price, expenses or costs relevant for determining its purchase price or production cost in accordance with paragraph 26, or any such record cannot be obtained without unreasonable expense or delay, its purchase price or production cost shall be taken for the purposes of paragraphs 17 to 23 to be the value ascribed to it in the earliest available record of its value made on or after its acquisition or production by the company.

## SECTION C – ALTERNATIVE ACCOUNTING RULES

### Preliminary

**29(1)** The rules set out in section B are referred to below in this Schedule as the historical cost accounting rules.

**29(2)** Those rules, with the omission of paragraphs 16, 21 and 25 to 28, are referred to below in this Part of this Schedule as the depreciation rules; and references below in this Schedule to the historical cost accounting rules do not include the depreciation rules as they apply by virtue of paragraph 32.

**30** Subject to paragraphs 32 to 34, the amounts to be included in respect of assets of any description mentioned in paragraph 31 may be determined on any basis so mentioned.

### Alternative accounting rules

**31(1)** Intangible fixed assets, other than goodwill, may be included at their current cost.

**31(2)** Tangible fixed assets may be included at a market value determined as at the date of their last valuation or at their current cost.

**31(3)** Investments of any description falling to be included under item B.III of either of the balance sheet formats set out in Part I of this Schedule may be included either–

(a) at a market value determined as at the date of their last valuation; or

(b) at a value determined on any basis which appears to the directors to be appropriate in the circumstances of the company;

but in the latter case particulars of the method of valuation adopted and of the reasons for adopting it shall be disclosed in a note to the accounts.

**31(4)** Investments of any description falling to be included under item C.III of either of the balance sheet formats set out in Part I of this Schedule may be included at their current cost.

**31(5)** Stocks may be included at their current cost.

## Application of the depreciation rules

**32(1)** Where the value of any asset of a company is determined on any basis mentioned in paragraph 31, that value shall be, or (as the case may require) be the starting point for determining, the amount to be included in respect of that asset in the company's accounts, instead of its purchase price or production cost or any value previously so determined for that asset; and the depreciation rules shall apply accordingly in relation to any such asset with the substitution for any reference to its purchase price or production cost of a reference to the value most recently determined for that asset on any basis mentioned in paragraph 31.

**32(2)** The amount of any provision for depreciation required in the case of any fixed asset by paragraph 18 or 19 as it applies by virtue of sub-paragraph (1) is referred to below in this paragraph as the adjusted amount, and the amount of any provision which would be required by that paragraph in the case of that asset according to the historical cost accounting rules is referred to as the historical cost amount.

**32(3)** Where sub-paragraph (1) applies in the case of any fixed asset the amount of any provision for depreciation in respect of that asset–

(a) included in any item shown in the profit and loss account in respect of amounts written off assets of the description in question; or

(b) taken into account in stating any item so shown which is required by note (14) of the notes on the profit and loss account formats set out in Part I of this Schedule to be stated after taking into account any necessary provisions for depreciation or diminution in value of assets included under it;

may be the historical cost amount instead of the adjusted amount, provided that the amount of any difference between the two is shown separately in the profit and loss account or in a note to the accounts.

## Additional information to be provided in case of departure from historical cost accounting rules

**33(1)** This paragraph applies where the amounts to be included in respect of assets covered by any items shown in a company's accounts have been determined on any basis mentioned in paragraph 31.

**33(2)** The items affected and the basis of valuation adopted in determining the amounts of the assets in question in the case of each such item shall be disclosed in a note to the accounts.

**33(3)** In the case of each balance sheet item affected (except stocks) either–

(a) the comparable amounts determined according to the historical cost accounting rules; or

(b) the differences between those amounts and the corresponding amounts actually shown in the balance sheet in respect of that item;

shall be shown separately in the balance sheet or in a note to the accounts.

**33(4)** In sub-paragraph (3) above, references in relation to any item to the comparable amounts determined as there mentioned are references to–

(a) the aggregate amount which would be required to be shown in respect of that item if the amounts to be included in respect of all the assets covered by that item were determined according to the historical cost accounting rules; and

(b) the aggregate amount of the cumulative provisions for depreciation or diminution in value which would be permitted or required in determining those amounts according to those rules.

### Revaluation reserve

**34(1)** With respect to any determination of the value of an asset of a company on any basis mentioned in paragraph 31, the amount of any profit or loss arising from that determination (after allowing, where appropriate, for any provisions for depreciation or diminution in value made otherwise than by reference to the value so determined and any adjustments of any such provisions made in the light of that determination) shall be credited or (as the case may be) debited to a separate reserve ("the revaluation reserve").

**34(2)** The amount of the revaluation reserve shall be shown in the company's balance sheet under a separate sub-heading in the position given for the item "revaluation reserve" in Format 1 or 2 of the balance sheet formats set out in Part I of this Schedule, but need not be shown under that name.

**34(3)** An amount may be transferred

(a) from the revaluation reserve–
  (i) to the profit and loss account, if the amount was previously charged to that account or represents realised profit, or
  (ii) on capitalisation,

(b) to or from the revaluation reserve in respect of the taxation relating to any profit or loss credited or debited to the reserve;

and the revaluation reserve shall be reduced to the extent that the amounts transferred to it are no longer necessary for the purposes of the valuation method used.

**History**
In para. 34(3) subpara. (a) and (b) substituted by the Companies Act 1985 (Miscellaneous Accounting Amendments) Regulations 1996 (SI 1996/189), reg. 1(1), 14(1) and Sch. 1, para. 1, 4(1), (2) as from 2 February 1996, subject to reg. 16(1), (2); the former words read as follows:

"from the revaluation reserve–
(a) to the profit and loss account, if the amount was previously charged to that account or represents realised profit, or
(b) on capitalisation;".

See also history note after para. 34(3B).

**34(3A)** In sub-paragraph (3)(a)(ii) **"capitalisation"**, in relation to an amount standing to the credit of the revaluation reserve, means applying it in wholly or partly paying up unissued shares in the company to be allotted to members of the company as fully or partly paid shares.

**History**
In para. 34(3A) the words "sub-paragraph (3)(a)(ii)" substituted for the former words "sub-paragraph (3)(b)" by the Companies Act (Miscellaneous Accounting Amendments) Regulations 1996 (SI 1996/189), reg. 1(1), 14(1) and Sch. 1, para. 1, 4(1), (3) as from 2 February 1996, subject to reg. 16(1), (2).
See also history note after para. 34(3B).

**34(3B)** The revaluation reserve shall not be reduced except as mentioned in this paragraph.

**History**
Para. 34(3), (3A) and (3B) substituted for the former para. 34(3) by CA 1989, s. 1, 4(2) and Sch. 1, para. 6 as from 1 April 1990 subject to transitional and saving provisions (see SI 1990/355 (C 13), art. 3, Sch. 1 and also art. 6–9); former para. 34(3) read as follows:

"The revaluation reserve shall be reduced to the extent that the amounts standing to the credit of the reserve are in the opinion of the directors of the company no longer necessary for the purpose of the accounting policies adopted by the company; but an amount may only be transferred from the reserve to the profit and loss account if either–
(a) the amount in question was previously charged to that account; or
(b) it represents realised profit."

**34(4)** The treatment for taxation purposes of amounts credited or debited to the revaluation reserve shall be disclosed in a note to the accounts.

# Part III – Notes to the Accounts

### Preliminary

**35** Any information required in the case of any company by the following provisions of this Part of this Schedule shall (if not given in the company's accounts) be given by way of a note to those accounts.

## Disclosure of accounting policies

**36** The accounting policies adopted by the company in determining the amounts to be included in respect of items shown in the balance sheet and in determining the profit or loss of the company shall be stated (including such policies with respect to the depreciation and diminution in value of assets).

**36A** It shall be stated whether the accounts have been prepared in accordance with applicable accounting standards and particulars of any material departure from those standards and the reasons for it shall be given.

**History**
Para. 36A inserted by CA 1989, s. 1, 4(2) and Sch. 1, para. 1, 7 as from 1 April 1990 subject to transitional and saving provisons (see SI 1990/355 (C 13), art. 3, Sch. 1 and also art. 6–9).

## Information supplementing the balance sheet

**37** Paragraphs 38 to 51 require information which either supplements the information given with respect to any particular items shown in the balance sheet or is otherwise relevant to assessing the company's state of affairs in the light of the information so given.

*Share capital and debentures*

**38(1)** The following information shall be given with respect to the company's share capital–

(a) the authorised share capital; and

(b) where shares of more than one class have been allotted, the number and aggregate nominal value of shares of each class allotted.

**38(2)** In the case of any part of the allotted share capital that consists of redeemable shares, the following information shall be given–

(a) the earliest and latest dates on which the company has power to redeem those shares;

(b) whether those shares must be redeemed in any event or are liable to be redeemed at the option of the company or of the shareholder; and

(c) whether any (and, if so, what) premium is payable on redemption.

**39** If the company has allotted any shares during the financial year, the following information shall be given–

(b) the classes of shares allotted; and

(c) as respects each class of shares, the number allotted, their aggregate nominal value, and the consideration received by the company for the allotment.

**History**
Para. 39(a) repealed by the Companies Act 1985 (Miscellaneous Accounting Amendments) Regulations 1996 (SI 1996/189), reg. 1(1), 14(1) and Sch. 1, para. 1, 5 as from 2 February 1996, subject to reg. 16(1), (2); para. 39(a) formerly read as follows:
"(a) the reason for making the allotment;".

**40(1)** With respect to any contingent right to the allotment of shares in the company the following particulars shall be given–

(a) the number, description and amount of the shares in relation to which the right is exercisable;

(b) the period during which it is exercisable; and

(c) the price to be paid for the shares allotted.

**40(2)** In sub-paragraph (1) above **"contingent right to the allotment of shares"** means any option to subscribe for shares and any other right to require the allotment of shares to any person whether arising on the conversion into shares of securities of any other description or otherwise.

**41(1)** If the company has issued any debentures during the financial year to which the accounts relate, the following information shall be given–

(b) the classes of debentures issued; and

(c) as respects each class of debentures, the amount issued and the consideration received by the company for the issue.

**History**
Para. 41(1)(a) repealed by the Companies Act 1985 (Miscellaneous Accounting Amendments) Regulations 1996 (SI 1996/189), reg. 1(1), 14(1) and Sch. 1, para. 1, 6 as from 2 February 1996, subject to reg. 16(1), (2); para. 41(1)(a) formerly read as follows:
"(a) the reason for making the issue;".

**41(2)** (Repealed by the Companies Act 1985 (Miscellaneous Accounting Amendments) Regulations 1996 (SI 1996/189), reg. 1(1), 14(1) and Sch. 1, para. 1, 6 as from 2 February 1996, subject to reg. 16(1), (2).)

**History**
Para. 41(2) formerly read as follows:
"Particulars of any redeemed debentures which the company has power to reissue shall also be given."

**41(3)** Where any of the company's debentures are held by a nominee of or trustee for the company, the nominal amount of the debentures and the amount at which they are stated in the accounting records kept by the company in accordance with section 221 of this Act shall be stated.

*Fixed assets*

**42(1)** In respect of each item which is or would but for paragraph 3(4)(b) be shown under the general item "fixed assets" in the company's balance sheet the following information shall be given–

(a) the appropriate amounts in repect of that item as at the date of the beginning of the financial year and as at the balance sheet date respectively;
(b) the effect on any amount shown in the balance sheet in respect of that item of–
   (i) any revision of the amount in respect of any assets included under that item made during that year on any basis mentioned in paragraph 31;
   (ii) acquisitions during that year of any assets;
   (iii) disposals during that year of any assets; and
   (iv) any transfers of assets of the company to and from that item during that year.

**42(2)** The reference in sub-paragraph (1)(a) to the appropriate amounts in respect of any item as at any date there mentioned is a reference to amounts representing the aggregate amounts determined, as at that date, in respect of assets falling to be included under that item on either of the following bases, that is to say–

(a) on the basis of purchase price or production cost (determined in accordance with paragraphs 26 and 27); or
(b) on any basis mentioned in paragraph 31,

(leaving out of account in either case any provisions for depreciation or diminution in value).

**42(3)** In respect of each item within sub-paragraph (1)–

(a) the cumulative amount of provisions for depreciation or diminution in value of assets included under that item as at each date mentioned in sub-paragraph (1)(a);
(b) the amount of any such provisions made in respect of the financial year;
(c) the amount of any adjustments made in respect of any such provisions during that year in consequence of the disposal of any assets; and
(d) the amount of any other adjustments made in respect of any such provisions during that year;

shall also be stated.

**43** Where any fixed assets of the company (other than listed investments) are included under any item shown in the company's balance sheet at an amount determined on any basis mentioned in paragraph 31, the following information shall be given–

(a) the years (so far as they are known to the directors) in which the assets were severally valued and the several values; and
(b) in the case of assets that have been valued during the financial year, the names of the persons who valued them or particulars of their qualifications for doing so and (whichever is stated) the bases of valuation used by them.

**44** In relation to any amount which is or would but for paragraph 3(4)(b) be shown in respect of the item "land and buildings" in the company's balance sheet there shall be stated–

(a) how much of that amount is ascribable to land of freehold tenure and how much to land of leasehold tenure; and

(b) how much of the amount ascribable to land of leasehold tenure is ascribable to land held on long lease and how much to land held on short lease.

*Investments*

**45(1)** In respect of the amount of each item which is or would but for paragraph 3(4)(b) be shown in the company's balance sheet under the general item "investments" (whether as fixed assets or as current assets) there shall be stated–

(a) how much of that amount is ascribable to listed investments.

**History**

Para. 45(1)(b) and the word "and" immediately preceding it repealed by the Companies Act 1985 (Miscellaneous Accounting Amendments) Regulations 1996 (SI 1996/189), reg. 1(1), 14(1) and Sch. 1, para. 1, 7 as from 2 February 1996, subject to reg. 16(1), (2); para 45(1)(b) formerly read as follows:

"(b) how much of any amount so ascribable is ascribable to investments as respects which there has been granted a listing on a recognised investment exchange other than an overseas investment exchange within the meaning of the Financial Services Act 1986 and how much to other listed investments."

Previously in para. 45(1)(b) the words "recognised investment exchange other than an overseas investment exchange within the meaning of the Financial Services Act 1986" substituted for the former words "recognised stock exchange" by Financial Services Act 1986, s. 212(2) and Sch. 16, para. 23(a) as from 29 April 1988 (see SI 1988/740 (C 22)).

**45(2)** Where the amount of any listed investments is stated for any item in accordance with sub-paragraph (1)(a), the following amounts shall also be stated–

(a) the aggregate market value of those investments where it differs from the amount so stated; and

(b) both the market value and the stock exchange value of any investments of which the former value is, for the purposes of the accounts, taken as being higher than the latter.

*Reserves and provisions*

**46(1)** Where any amount is transferred–

(a) to or from any reserves; or

(b) to any provisions for liabilities and charges; or

(c) from any provision for liabilities and charges otherwise than for the purpose for which the provision was established;

and the reserves or provisions are or would but for paragraph 3(4)(b) be shown as separate items in the company's balance sheet, the information mentioned in the following sub-paragraph shall be given in respect of the aggregate of reserves or provisions included in the same item.

**46(2)** That information is–

(a) the amount of the reserves or provisions as at the date of the beginning of the financial year and as at the balance sheet date respectively;

(b) any amounts transferred to or from the reserves or provisions during that year; and

(c) the source and application respectively of any amounts so transferred.

**46(3)** Particulars shall be given of each provision included in the item "other provisions" in the company's balance sheet in any case where the amount of that provision is material.

*Provision for taxation*

**47** The amount of any provision for deferred taxation shall be stated separately from the amount of any provision for other taxation.

**History**

Para. 47 substituted by CA 1989, s. 1, 4(2) and Sch. 1, para. 1, 8 as from 1 April 1990 subject to transitional and saving provisions (see SI 1990/355 (C 13), art. 3, Sch. 1 and also art. 6–9); para. 47 formerly read as follows:

"The amount of any provisions for taxation other than deferred taxation shall be stated."

*Details of indebtedness*

**48(1)** In respect of each item shown under "creditors" in the company's balance sheet there shall be stated the aggregate of the following amounts, that is to say–

(a) the amount of any debts included under that item which are payable or repayable otherwise than by instalments and fall due for payment or repayment after the end of the period of five years beginning with the day next following the end of the financial year; and

(b) in the case of any debts so included which are payable or repayable by instalments, the amount of any instalments which fall due for payment after the end of that period.

**History**

Para. 48(1)(b) substituted by the Companies Act 1985 (Accounts of Small and Medium-sized Companies and Minor Accounting Amendments) Regulations 1997 (SI 1997/220), reg . 1, 7(9) as from 1 March 1997. The former para. 48(1)(b) read as follows:

" the amount of any debts so included which are payable or repayable by instalments any of which fall due for payment after the end of that period."

Para. 48(1) substituted by the Companies Act 1985 (Miscellaneous Accounting Amendments) Regulations 1996 (SI 1996/189), reg. 1(1), 14(1) and Sch. 1, para. 1, 8 as from 2 February 1996, subject to reg. 16(1), (2); para. 48(1) formerly read as follows:

"In respect of each item shown under "creditors" in the company's balance sheet there shall be stated–

(a) the aggregate amount of any debts included under that item which are payable or repayable otherwise than by instalments and fall due for payment or repayment after the end of the period of five years beginning with the day next following the end of the financial year; and

(b) the aggregate amount of any debts so included which are payable or repayable by instalments any of which fall due for payment after the end of that period;

and in the case of debts within paragraph (b) above the aggregate amount of instalments falling due after the end of that period shall also be disclosed for each such item."

**48(2)** Subject to sub-paragraph (3), in relation to each debt falling to be taken into account under sub-paragraph (1), the terms of payment or repayment and the rate of any interest payable on the debt shall be stated.

**48(3)** If the number of debts is such that, in the opinion of the directors, compliance with sub-paragraph (2) would result in a statement of excessive length, it shall be sufficient to give a general indication of the terms of payment or repayment and the rates of any interest payable on the debts.

**48(4)** In respect of each item shown under "creditors" in the company's balance sheet there shall be stated–

(a) the aggregate amount of any debts included under that item in respect of which any security has been given by the company; and

(b) an indication of the nature of the securities so given.

**48(5)** References above in this paragraph to an item shown under "creditors" in the company's balance sheet include references, where amounts falling due to creditors within one year and after more than one year are distinguished in the balance sheet–

(a) in a case within sub-paragraph (1), to an item shown under the latter of those categories; and

(b) in a case within sub-paragraph (4), to an item shown under either of those categories;

and references to items shown under "creditors" include references to items which would but for paragraph 3(4)(b) be shown under that heading.

**49** If any fixed cumulative dividends on the company's shares are in arrear, there shall be stated–

(a) the amount of the arrears; and

(b) the period for which the dividends or, if there is more than one class, each class of them are in arrear.

*Guarantees and other financial commitments*

**50(1)** Particulars shall be given of any charge on the assets of the company to secure the liabilities of any other person, including, where practicable, the amount secured.

**50(2)** The following information shall be given with respect to any other contingent liability not provided for–

(a) the amount or estimated amount of that liability;

(b) its legal nature; and

(c) whether any valuable security has been provided by the company in connection with that liability and if so, what.

**50(3)** There shall be stated, where practicable–

(a) the aggregate amount or estimated amount of contracts for capital expenditure, so far as not provided for.

**History**

Para. 50(3)(b) and the word "and" immediately preceding it repealed by the Companies Act 1985 (Miscellaneous Accounting Amendments) Regulations 1996 (SI 1996/189), reg. 1(1), 14(1) and Sch. 1, para. 1, 9 as from 2 February 1996, subject to reg. 16(1), (2); para. 50(3)(b) formerly read as follows:

"(b) the aggregate amount or estimated amount of capital expenditure authorised by the directors which has not been contracted for."

**50(4)** Particulars shall be given of–

(a) any pension commitments included under any provision shown in the company's balance sheet; and

(b) any such commitments for which no provision has been made;

and where any such commitment relates wholly or partly to pensions payable to past directors of the company separate particulars shall be given of that commitment so far as it relates to such pensions.

**50(5)** Particulars shall also be given of any other financial commitments which–

(a) have not been provided for; and

(b) are relevant to assessing the company's state of affairs.

**50(6)** (Repealed by Companies Act 1989, s. 221 and Sch. 24 as from 1 April 1990.)

**History**

In regard to the date of the above repeal see SI 1990/355 (C 13), art. 5(1)(b), (2) and art. 6–9 for transitional and saving provisions; para. 50(6) formerly read as follows:

"Commitments within any of the preceding sub-paragraphs undertaken on behalf of or for the benefit of–

(a) any holding company or fellow subsidiary of the company; or

(b) any subsidiary of the company;

shall be stated separately from the other commitments within that sub-paragraph (and commitments within paragraph (a) shall also be stated separately from those within paragraph (b)."

*Miscellaneous matters*

**51(1)** Particulars shall be given of any case where the purchase price or production cost of any asset is for the first time determined under paragraph 28.

**51(2)** Where any outstanding loans made under the authority of section 153(4)(b), (bb) or (c) or section 155 of this Act (various cases of financial assistance by a company for purchase of its own shares) are included under any item shown in the company's balance sheet, the aggregate amount of those loans shall be disclosed for each item in question.

**History**

In para. 51(2) ", (bb)" inserted after "153(4)(b)" by CA 1989, s. 1, 4(2) and Sch. 1, para. 1, 9 as from 1 April 1990 subject to transitional and saving provisions (see SI 1990/355 (C 13), art. 3, Sch. 1 and also art. 6–9).

**51(3)** (Repealed by the Companies Act 1985 (Miscellaneous Accounting Amendments) Regulations 1996 (SI 1996/189), reg. 1(1), 14(1) and Sch. 1, para. 1, 10 as from 2 February 1996, subject to reg. 16(1), (2).)

**History**

Para. 51(3) formerly read as follows:

"The aggregate amount which is recommended for distribution by way of dividend shall be stated."

## Information supplementing the profit and loss account

**52** Paragraphs 53 to 57 require information which either supplements the information given with respect to any particular items shown in the profit and loss account or otherwise provides particulars of income or expenditure of the company or of circumstances affecting the items shown in the profit and loss account.

*Separate statement of certain items of income and expenditure*

**53(1)** Subject to the following provisions of this paragraph, each of the amounts mentioned below shall be stated.

**53(2)** The amount of the interest on or any similar charges in respect of–

(a) bank loans and overdrafts; and

(b) loans of any other kind made to the company.

This sub-paragraph does not apply to interest or charges on loans to the company from group undertakings, but, with that exception, it applies to interest or charges on all loans, whether made on the security of debentures or not.

**History**

In para. 53(2)(a) the former words repealed by the Companies Act 1985 (Miscellaneous Accounting Amendments) Regulations 1996 (SI 1996/189), reg. 1(1), 14(1) and Sch. 1, para. 1, 11(1), (2) as from 2 February 1996, subject to reg. 16(1), (2); the former words read as follows:

"and loans made to the company (other than bank loans and overdrafts) which–

(i) are repayable otherwise than by instalments and fall due for repayment before the end of the period of five years beginning with the day next following the end of the financial year; or

(ii) are repayable by instalments the last of which falls due for payment before the end of that period".

Previously in para. 53(2) the words "group undertakings" substituted for the former words "group companies" by CA 1989, s. 1, 4(2) and Sch. 1, para. 1, 2(1)(e) as from 1 April 1990 subject to transitional and saving provisions (see SI 1990/355 (C 13), art. 3, Sch. 1 and also art. 6–9).

**53(3)–(6)** (Repealed by the Companies Act 1985 (Miscellaneous Accounting Amendments) Regulations 1996 (SI 1996/189), reg. 1(1), 14(1) and Sch. 1, para. 1, 11(3) as from 2 February 1996, subject to reg. 16(1), (2).)

**History**

Para. 53(3)–(6) formerly read as follows:

"**53(3)** The amounts respectively set aside for redemption of share capital and for redemption of loans.

**(4)** The amount of income from listed investments.

**(5)** The amount of rents from land (after deduction of ground rents, rates and other outgoings).
This amount need only be stated if a substantial part of the company's revenue for the financial year consists of rents from land.

**(6)** The amount charged to revenue in respect of sums payable in respect of the hire of plant and machinery."

**53(7)** (Repealed by Companies Act 1989, s. 212 and Sch. 24 as from 1 April 1990.)

**History**

In regard to the date of the above repeal see the Companies Act 1989 (Commencement No. 4 and Transitional and Saving Provisions) Order 1990 (SI 1990/355) (C 13), art. 5(1)(b), (2) and art. 6–9 for transitional and saving provisions; para. 53(7) formerly read as follows:

"The amount of the remuneration of the auditors (taking **"remuneration"**, for the purposes of this sub-paragraph, as including any sums paid by the company in respect of the auditors' expenses)."

*Particulars of tax*

**54(1)** (Repealed by the Companies Act 1985 (Miscellaneous Accounting Amendments) Regulations 1996 (SI 1996/189), reg. 1(1), 14(1) and Sch. 1, para. 1, 12 as from 2 February 1996, subject to reg. 16(1), (2).)

**History**

Para. 54(1) formerly read as follows:

"The basis on which the charge for United Kingdom corporation tax and United Kingdom income tax is computed shall be stated."

**54(2)** Particulars shall be given of any special circumstances which affect liability in respect of taxation of profits, income or capital gains for the financial year or liability in respect of taxation of profits, income or capital gains for succeeding financial years.

**54(3)** The following amounts shall be stated–

(a) the amount of the charge for United Kingdom corporation tax;

(b) if that amount would have been greater but for relief from double taxation, the amount which it would have been but for such relief;

(c) the amount of the charge for United Kingdom income tax; and

(d) the amount of the charge for taxation imposed outside the United Kingdom of profits, income and (so far as charged to revenue) capital gains.

These amounts shall be stated separately in respect of each of the amounts which is or would but for paragraph 3(4)(b) be shown under the following items in the profit and loss account, that is to say "tax on profit or loss on ordinary activities" and "tax on extraordinary profit or loss".

*Particulars of turnover*

**55(1)** If in the course of the financial year the company has carried on business of two or more classes that, in the opinion of the directors, differ substantially from each other, there shall be stated in respect of each class (describing it)–

(a) the amount of the turnover attributable to that class.

**History**
Para. 55(1)(b) and the word "and" immediately preceding it, repealed by the Companies Act 1985 (Miscellaneous Accounting Amendments) Regulations 1996 (SI 1996/189), reg. 1(1), 14(1) and Sch. 1, para. 1, 13(1), (2) as from 2 February 1996, subject to reg. 16(1), (2); para. 55(1)(b) formerly read as follows:
"(b) the amount of the profit or loss of the company before taxation which is in the opinion of the directors attributable to that class."

**55(2)** If in the course of the financial year the company has supplied markets that, in the opinion of the directors, differ substantially from each other, the amount of the turnover attributable to each such market shall also be stated.

In this paragraph **"market"** means a market delimited by geographical bounds.

**55(3)** In analysing for the purposes of this paragraph the source (in terms of business or in terms of market) of turnover, the directors of the company shall have regard to the manner in which the company's activities are organised.

**History**
In para. 55(3) the words "or (as the case may be) of profit and loss" formerly appearing after the word "turnover" omitted by the Companies Act 1985 (Miscellaneous Accounting Amendments) Regulations 1996 (SI 1996/189), reg. 1(1), 14(1) and Sch. 1, para. 1, 13(1), (3) as from 2 February 1996, subject to reg. 16(1), (2).

**55(4)** For the purposes of this paragraph–

(a) classes of business which, in the opinion of the directors, do not differ substantially from each other shall be treated as one class; and

(b) markets which, in the opinion of the directors, do not differ substantially from each other shall be treated as one market;

and any amounts properly attributable to one class of business or (as the case may be) to one market which are not material may be included in the amount stated in respect of another.

**55(5)** Where in the opinion of the directors the disclosure of any information required by this paragraph would be seriously prejudicial to the interests of the company, that information need not be disclosed, but the fact that any such information has not been disclosed must be stated.

*Particulars of staff*

**56(1)** The following information shall be given with respect to the employees of the company–

(a) the average number of persons employed by the company in the financial year; and

(b) the average number of persons so employed within each category of persons employed by the company.

**56(2)** The average number required by sub-paragraph (1)(a) or (b) shall be determined by dividing the relevant annual number by the number of months in the financial year.

**History**
See history note after para. 56(3).

**56(3)** The relevant annual number shall be determined by ascertaining for each month in the financial year–

(a) for the purposes of sub-paragraph (1)(a), the number of persons employed under contracts of service by the company in that month (whether throughout the month or not);

(b) for the purposes of sub-paragraph (1)(b), the number of persons in the category in question of persons so employed;

and, in either case, adding together all the monthly numbers.

**History**
In para. 56(2) the word "months" substituted for the former word "weeks", and in para. 56(3) the word "month" substituted for the former word "week" in three places where the word occurred and the word "monthly" substituted for the former word "weekly" by the Companies Act 1985 (Miscellaneous Accounting Amendments) Regulations 1996 (SI 1996/189), reg. 1(1), 14(1) and Sch. 1, para. 1, 14 as from 2 February 1996, subject to reg. 16(1), (2).

**56(4)** In respect of all persons employed by the company during the financial year who are taken into account in determining the relevant annual number for the purposes of sub-paragraph (1)(a) there shall also be stated the aggregate amounts respectively of–

(a) wages and salaries paid or payable in respect of that year to those persons;

(b) social security costs incurred by the company on their behalf; and

(c) other pension costs so incurred;

save in so far as those amounts or any of them are stated in the profit and loss account.

**56(5)** The categories of persons employed by the company by reference to which the number required to be disclosed of sub-paragraph (1)(b) is to be determined shall be such as the directors may select, having regard to the manner in which the company's activities are organised.

*Miscellaneous matters*

**57(1)** Where any amount relating to any preceding financial year is included in any item in the profit and loss account, the effect shall be stated.

**57(2)** Particulars shall be given of any extraordinary income or charges arising in the financial year.

**57(3)** The effect shall be stated of any transactions that are exceptional by virtue of size or incidence though they fall within the ordinary activities of the company.

## General

**58(1)** Where sums originally denominated in foreign currencies have been brought into account under any items shown in the balance sheet or profit and loss account, the basis on which those sums have been translated into sterling shall be stated.

**58(2)** Subject to the following sub-paragraph, in respect of every item stated in a note to the accounts the corresponding amount for the financial year immediately preceding that to which the accounts relate shall also be stated and where the corresponding amount is not comparable, it shall be adjusted and particulars of the adjustment and the reasons for it shall be given.

**58(3)** Sub-paragraph (2) does not apply in relation to any amounts stated by virtue of any of the following provisions of this Act–

(a) paragraph 13 of Schedule 4A (details of accounting treatment of acquisitions),

(b) paragraphs 2, 8(3), 16, 21(1)(d), 22(4) and (5), 24(3) and (4) and 27(3) and (4) of Schedule 5 (shareholdings in other undertakings),

(c) Parts II and III of Schedule 6 (loans and other dealings in favour of directors and others), and

(d) paragraphs 42 and 46 above (fixed assets and reserves and provisions).

**History**

Para. 58(3)(a)–(d) substituted for former para. 58(3)(a)–(c) by CA 1989, s. 1, 4(2) and Sch. 1, para. 1, 10 as from 1 April 1990 subject to transitional and saving provisions (see SI 1990/355 (C 13), art. 3, Sch. 1 and also art. 6–9); the former para. 58(3)(a)–(c) read as follows:

"(a) section 231 as applying Parts I and II of Schedule 5 (proportion of share capital of subsidiaries and other bodies corporate held by the company, etc.),

(b) sections 232 to 234 and Schedule 6 (particulars of loans to directors, etc.), and

(c) paragraphs 42 and 46 above."

## Dormant companies acting as agents

**58A** Where the directors of a company take advantage of the exemption conferred by section 249AA, and the company has during the financial year in question acted as an agent for any person, the fact that it has so acted must be stated.

**History**

Para. 58A inserted by the Companies Act 1985 (Audit Exemption) (Amendment) Regulations 2000 (SI 2000/1430), reg. 1, 5 as from 26 May 2000 in relation to annual accounts and reports in respect of financial years ending on or after 26 July 2000.

# Part IV – Special Provisions Where Company is a Parent or Subsidiary Undertaking

**History**

The heading to Pt. IV substituted by CA 1989, s. 1, 4(2) and Sch. 1, para. 1, 11(1) as from 1 April 1990 subject to transitional and saving provisions (see SI 1990/355 (C 13), art. 3, Sch. 1 and also art. 6–9); heading formerly read as follows:

"Part IV – Special Provisions Where the Company is a Holding or Subsidiary Company"

## Company's own accounts

*Dealings with or interests in group undertakings*

**59** (Repealed by the Companies Act 1985 (Miscellaneous Accounting Amendments) Regulations 1996 (SI 1996/189), reg. 1(1), 14(1) and Sch. 1, para. 1, 15 as from 2 February 1996, subject to reg. 16(1), (2).)

**History**

Para. 59 formerly read as follows:

"Where a company is a parent company or a subsidiary undertaking and any item required by Part I of this Schedule to be shown in the company's balance sheet in relation to group undertakings includes–

(a) amounts attributable to dealings with or interests in any parent undertaking or fellow subsidiary undertaking, or
(b) amounts attributable to dealings with or interests in any subsidiary undertaking of the company,

the aggregate amounts within paragraphs (a) and (b) respectively shall be shown as separate items, either by way of subdivision of the relevant item in the balance sheet or in a note to the company's accounts."

Previously para. 59 substituted by CA 1989, s. 1, 4(2) and Sch. 1, para. 1, 11(2) as from 1 April 1990 subject to transitional and saving provisions (see SI 1990/355 (C 13), art. 3, Sch. 1 and also art. 6–9); para. 59 originally read as follows:

"Where a company is a holding company or a subsidiary of another body corporate and any item required by Part I of this Schedule to be shown in the company's balance sheet in relation to group companies includes–

(a) amounts attributable to dealings with or interests in any holding company or fellow subsidiary of the company; or
(b) amounts attributable to dealings with or interests in any subsidiary of the company;

the aggregate amounts within paragraphs (a) and (b) respectively shall be shown as separate items, either by way of subdivision of the relevant item in the balance sheet or in a note to the company's accounts."

*Guarantees and other financial commitments in favour of group undertakings*

**59A** Commitments within any of sub-paragraphs (1) to (5) of paragraph 50 (guarantees and other financial commitments) which are undertaken on behalf of or for the benefit of–

(a) any parent undertaking or fellow subsidiary undertaking, or

(b) any subsidiary undertaking of the company,

shall be stated separately from the other commitments within that sub-paragraph, and commitments within paragraph (a) shall also be stated separately from those within paragraph (b).

**History**

Para. 59A inserted by CA 1989, s. 1, 4(2) and Sch. 1, para. 1, 11(3) as from 1 April 1990 subject to transitional and saving provisions (see SI 1990/355 (C 13), art. 3, Sch. 1 and also art. 6–9).

**60–70** (Repealed by Companies Act 1989, s. 212 and Sch. 24 as from 1 April 1990.)

**History**

In regard to the date of the above repeal see SI 1990/355 (C 13), art. 5(1)(b), (2) and art. 6–9 for transitional and saving provisions; para. 60–70 formerly read as follows:

"**60(1)** Subject to the following sub-paragraph, where the company is a holding company, the number, description and amount of the shares in and debentures of the company held by its subsidiaries or their nominees shall be disclosed in a note to the company's accounts.

**(2)** Sub-paragraph (1) does not apply in relation to any shares or debentures–

(a) in the case of which the subsidiary is concerned as personal representative; or
(b) in the case of which it is concerned as trustee;

provided that in the latter case neither the company nor any subsidiary of the company is beneficially interested under the trust, otherwise than by way of security only for the purposes of a transaction entered into by it in the ordinary course of a business which includes the lending of money.

Schedule 2 to this Act has effect for the interpretation of the reference in this sub-paragraph to a beneficial interest under a trust.

**Consolidated accounts of holding company and subsidiaries**

**61** Subject to paragraphs 63 and 66, the consolidated balance sheet and profit and loss account shall combine the information contained in the separate balance sheets and profit and loss accounts of the holding company and of the subsidiaries dealt with by the consolidated accounts, but with such adjustments (if any) as the directors of the holding company think necessary.

**62** Subject to paragraphs 63 to 66, and to Part V of this Schedule, the consolidated accounts shall, in giving the information required by paragraph 61, comply so far as practicable with the requirements of this Schedule and with the other requirements of this Act as if they were the accounts of an actual company.

63 The following provisions of this Act, namely–
(a) section 231 as applying Schedule 5, but only Parts II, III, V and VI of that Schedule, and
(b) sections 232 to 234 and Schedule 6, so far as relating to accounts other than group accounts,
do not, by virtue of paragraphs 61 and 62, apply for the purposes of the consolidated accounts.

64 Paragraph 62 is without prejudice to any requirement of this Act which applies (otherwise than by virtue of paragraph 61 or 62) to group accounts.

65(1) Notwithstanding paragraph 62, the consolidated accounts prepared by a holding company may deal with an investment of any member of the group in the shares of any other body corporate by way of the equity method of accounting in any case where it appears to the directors of the holding company that that body corporate is so closely associated with any member of the group as to justify the use of that method in dealing with investments by that or any other member of the group in the shares of that body corporate.

(2) In this paragraph, references to the group, in relation to consolidated accounts prepared by a holding company, are references to the holding company and the subsidiaries dealt with by the accounts.

66 Notwithstanding paragraphs 61 and 62, paragraphs 17 to 19 and 21 do not apply to any amount shown in the consolidated balance sheet in respect of goodwill arising on consolidation.

67 In relation to any subsidiaries of the holding company not dealt with by the consolidated accounts paragraphs 59 and 60 apply for the purpose of those accounts as if those accounts were the accounts of an actual company of which they were subsidiaries.

**Group accounts not prepared as consolidated accounts**

68 Group accounts which are not prepared as consolidated accounts, together with any notes to those accounts, shall give the same or equivalent information as that required to be given by consolidated accounts by virtue of paragraphs 61 to 67.

**Provisions of general application**

69(1) This paragraph applies where the company is a holding company and either–
(a) does not prepare group accounts; or
(b) prepares group accounts which do not deal with one or more of its subsidiaries;
and references below in this paragraph to the company's subsidiaries shall be read in a case within paragraph (b) as references to such of the company's subsidiaries as are excluded from the group accounts.

(2) Subject to the following provisions of this paragraph–
(a) the reasons why the subsidiaries are not dealt with in group accounts; and
(b) a statement showing any qualifications contained in the reports of the auditors of the subsidiaries on their accounts for their respective financial years ending with or during the financial year of the company, and any note or saving contained in those accounts to call attention to a matter which, apart from the note or saving, would properly have been referred to in such a qualification, in so far as the matter which is the subject of the qualification or note is not covered by the company's own accounts and is material from the point of view of its members,
shall be given in a note to the company's accounts.

(3) Subject to the following provisions of this paragraph, the aggregate amount of the total investment of the holding company in the shares of the subsidiaries shall be stated in a note to the company's accounts by way of the equity method of valuation.

(4) Sub-paragraph (3) does not apply where the company is a wholly owned subsidiary of another body corporate incorporated in Great Britain if there is included in a note to the company's accounts a statement that in the opinion of the directors of the company the aggregate value of the assets of the company consisting of shares in, or amounts owing (whether on account of a loan or otherwise) from, the company's subsidiaries is not less than the aggregate of the amounts at which those assets are stated or included in the company's balance sheet.

(5) In so far as information required by any of the preceding provisions of this paragraph to be stated in a note to the company's accounts is not obtainable, a statement to that effect shall be given instead in a note to those accounts.

(6) The Secretary of State may, on the application or with the consent of the company's directors, direct that in relation to any subsidiary sub-paragraphs (2) and (3) shall not apply, or shall apply only to such extent as may be provided by the direction.

(7) Where in any case within sub-paragraph (1)(b) the group accounts are consolidated accounts, references above in this paragraph to the company's accounts and the company's balance sheet respectively shall be read as references to the consolidated accounts and the consolidated balance sheet.

70 Where a company has subsidiaries whose financial years did not end with that of the company, the following information shall be given in relation to each such subsidiary (whether or not dealt with in any group accounts prepared by the company) by way of a note to the company's accounts or (where group accounts are prepared) to the group accounts, that is to say–
(a) the reasons why the company's directors consider that the subsidiaries' financial years should not end with that of the company; and
(b) the dates on which the subsidiaries' financial years ending last before that of the company respectively ended or the earliest and latest of those dates."

# Part V – Special Provisions where the Company is an Investment Company

71(1) Paragraph 34 does not apply to the amount of any profit or loss arising from a determination of the value of any investments of an investment company on any basis mentioned in paragraph 31(3).

71(2) Any provisions made by virtue of paragraph 19(1) or (2) in the case of an investment company in respect of any fixed asset investments need not be charged to the company's profit and loss account provided they are either–

(a) charged against any reserve account to which any amount excluded by sub-paragraph (1) from the requirements of paragraph 34 has been credited; or

(b) shown as a separate item in the company's balance sheet under the sub-heading "other reserves".

**71(3)** For the purposes of this paragraph, as it applies in relation to any company, **"fixed asset investment"** means any asset falling to be included under any item shown in the company's balance sheet under the subdivision "investments" under the general item "fixed assets".

**72(1)** Any distribution made by an investment company which reduces the amount of its net assets to less than the aggregate of its called-up share capital and undistributable reserves shall be disclosed in a note to the company's accounts.

**72(2)** For purposes of this paragraph, a company's net assets are the aggregate of its assets less the aggregate of its liabilities (including any provision for liabilities or charges within paragraph 89); and **"undistributable reserves"** has the meaning given by section 264(3) of this Act.

**73** A company shall be treated as an investment company for the purposes of this Part of this Schedule in relation to any financial year of the company if–

(a) during the whole of that year it was an investment company as defined by section 266 of this Act, and

(b) it was not at any time during that year prohibited under section 265(4) of this Act (no distribution where capital profits have been distributed, etc.) from making a distribution by virtue of that section.

**74** (Repealed by Companies Act 1989, s. 212 and Sch. 24 as from 1 April 1990.)

**History**

In regard to the date of the above repeal see SI 1990/355 (C 13), art. 5(1)(b), (2) and art. 6–9 for transitional and saving provisions; para. 74 formerly read as follows:

"Where a company entitled to the benefit of any provision contained in this Part of this Schedule is a holding company, the reference in paragraph 62 to consolidated accounts complying with the requirements of this Act shall, in relation to consolidated accounts of that company, be construed as referring to those requirements in so far only–

(a) as they apply to the individual accounts of that company; and

(b) as they apply otherwise than by virtue of paragraphs 61 and 62 to any group accounts prepared by that company."

# Part VI – Special Provisions Where the Company has Entered into Arrangements Subject to Merger Relief

**75** (Repealed by Companies Act 1989, s. 212 and Sch. 24 as from 1 April 1990.)

**History**

In regard to the date of the above repeal see SI 1990/355 (C 13), art. 5(1)(b), (2) and art. 6–9 for transitional and saving provisons; para. 75 formerly read as follows:

"**75(1)** Where during the financial year the company has allotted shares in consideration for the issue, transfer or cancellation of shares in another body corporate ("the other company") in circumstances where by virtue of section 131(2) of this Act (merger relief) section 130 did not apply to the premiums on those shares, the following information shall be given by way of a note to the company's accounts–

(a) the name of the other company;

(b) the number, nominal value and class of shares so allotted;

(c) the number, nominal value and class of shares in the other company so issued, transferred or cancelled;

(d) particulars of the accounting treatment adopted in the company's accounts (including any group accounts) in respect of such issue, transfer or cancellation; and

(e) where the company prepares group accounts, particulars of the extent to which and manner in which the profit or loss for the year of the group which appears in those accounts is affected by any profit or loss of the other company or any of its subsidiaries which arose at any time before the allotment.

**(2)** Where the company has during the financial year or during either of the two financial years immediately preceding it made such an allotment of shares as is mentioned in sub-paragraph (1) above and there is included in the company's consolidated profit and loss account or, if it has no such account, in its individual profit and loss account, any profit or loss (or part thereof) to which this sub-paragraph applies then the net amount of any such profit or loss (or part thereof) shall be shown in a note to the accounts together with an explanation of the transactions to which that information relates.

**(3)** Sub-paragraph (2) applies–

(a) to any profit or loss realised during the financial year by the company, or any of its subsidiaries, on the disposal of any shares in the other company or of any assets which were fixed assets of the other company, or of any of its subsidiaries, at the time of the allotment; and

(b) to any part of any profit or loss realised during the financial year by the company, or any of its subsidiaries, on the disposal of any shares (not being shares in the other company), which was attributable to the fact that at the time of the disposal there were amongst the assets of the company which issued those shares, or any of its subsidiaries, such shares or assets as are described in sub-paragraph (a) above.

(4) Where in pursuance of the arrangement in question shares are allotted on different dates, the time of allotment for the purposes of sub-paragraphs (1)(e) and (3)(a) above is taken to be–

(a) if the other company becomes a subsidiary of the company as a result of the arrangement–
  (i) if the arrangement becomes binding only upon the fulfilment of a condition, the date on which that condition is fulfilled, and
  (ii) in any other case, the date on which the other company becomes a subsidiary of the company;

(b) if the other company is a subsidiary of the company when the arrangement is proposed, the date of the first allotment pursuant to that arrangement."

# Part VII – Interpretation of Schedule

**76** The following paragraphs apply for the purposes of this Schedule and its interpretation.

**77–81** (Repealed by Companies Act 1989, s. 212 and Sch. 24 as from 1 April 1990.)

**History**

In regard to the date of the above repeal see SI 1990/355 (C 13), art. 5(1)(b), (2) and art. 6–9 for transitional and saving provisions; para. 77–81 formerly read as follows:

"*Assets: fixed or current*

**77** Assets of a company are taken to be fixed assets if they are intended for use on a continuing basis in the company's activities, and any assets not intended for such use shall be taken to be current assets.

*Balance sheet date*

**78 "Balance sheet date"**, in relation to a balance sheet, means the date as at which the balance sheet was prepared.

*Capitalisation*

**79** References to capitalising any work or costs are to treating that work or those costs as a fixed asset.

*Fellow subsidiary*

**80** A body corporate is treated as a fellow subsidiary of another body corporate if both are subsidiaries of the same body corporate but neither is the other's.

*Group companies*

**81 "Group company"**, in relation to any company, means any body corporate which is that company's subsidiary or holding company, or a subsidiary of that company's holding company."

*Historical cost accounting rules*

**82** References to the historical cost accounting rules shall be read in accordance with paragraph 29.

*Leases*

**83(1)** **"Long lease"** means a lease in the case of which the portion of the term for which it was granted remaining unexpired at the end of the financial year is not less than 50 years.

**83(2)** **"Short lease"** means a lease which is not a long lease.

**83(3)** **"Lease"** includes an agreement for a lease.

*Listed investments*

**84** **"Listed investment"** means an investment as respects which there has been granted a listing on a recognised investment exchange other than an overseas investment exchange within the meaning of the Financial Services Act 1986 or on any stock exchange of repute outside Great Britain.

**History**

In para. 84 the words from "on a recognised investment exchange" to the end substituted for the former words "on a recognised stock exchange, or on any stock exchange of repute (other than a recognised stock exchange) outside Great Britain" by Financial Services Act 1986, s. 212(2) and Sch. 16, para. 23(b) as from 29 April 1988 (see SI 1988/740 (C 22)).

*Loans*

**85** A loan is treated as falling due for repayment, and an instalment of a loan is treated as falling due for payment, on the earliest date on which the lender could require repayment or (as the case may be) payment, if he exercised all options and rights available to him.

*Materiality*

**86** Amounts which in the particular context of any provision of this Schedule are not material may be disregarded for the purposes of that provision.

**87** (Repealed by Companies Act 1989, s. 212 and Sch. 24 as from 1 April 1990.)

**History**
In regard to the date of the above repeal see SI 1990/355 (C 13), art. 5(1)(b), (2) and art. 6–9 for transitional and saving provisions; para. 87 formerly read as follows:

"*Notes to the accounts*

**87** Notes to a company's accounts may be contained in the accounts or in a separate document annexed to the accounts."

*Provisions*

**88(1)** References to provisions for depreciation or diminution in value of assets are to any amount written off by way of providing for depreciation or diminution in value of assets.

**88(2)** Any reference in the profit and loss account formats set out in Part I of this Schedule to the depreciation of, or amounts written off, assets of any description is to any provision for depreciation or diminution in value of assets of that description.

**89** References to provisions for liabilities or charges are to any amount retained as reasonably necessary for the purpose of providing for any liability or loss which is either likely to be incurred, or certain to be incurred but uncertain as to amount or as to the date on which it will arise.

**90–92** (Repealed by Companies Act 1989, s. 212 and Sch. 24 as from 1 April 1990.)

**History**
In regard to the date of the above repeal see SI 1990/355 (C 13), art. 5(1)(b), (2) and art. 6–9 for transitional and saving provisions; para. 90–92 formerly read as follows:

"*Purchase price*

**90** References (however expressed) to the purchase price of any asset of a company or of any raw materials or consumables used in the production of any such asset include any consideration (whether in cash or otherwise) given by the company in respect of that asset or in respect of those materials or consumables (as the case may require).

*Realised profits*

**91** Without prejudice to–
- (a) the construction of any other expression (where appropriate) by reference to accepted accounting principles or practice, or
- (b) any specific provision for the treatment of profits of any description as realised,

it is hereby declared for the avoidance of doubt that references in this Schedule to realised profits, in relation to a company's accounts, are to such profits of the company as fall to be treated as realised profits for the purposes of those accounts in accordance with principles generally accepted with respect to the determination for accounting purposes of realised profits at the time when those accounts are prepared.

*Related companies*

**92(1) "Related company"**, in relation to any company, means any body corporate (other than one which is a group company in relation to that company) in which that company holds on a long-term basis a qualifying capital interest for the purpose of securing a contribution to that company's own activities by the exercise of any control or influence arising from that interest.

(2) In this paragraph **"qualifying capital interest"** means, in relation to any body corporate, an interest in shares comprised in the equity share capital of that body corporate of a class carrying rights to vote in all circumstances at general meetings of that body corporate.

(3) Where–
- (a) a company holds a qualifying capital interest in a body corporate; and
- (b) the nominal value of any relevant shares in that body corporate held by that company is equal to twenty per cent. or more of the nominal value of all relevant shares in that body corporate;

it shall be presumed to hold that interest on the basis and for the purpose mentioned in sub-paragraph (1), unless the contrary is shown.

In this sub-paragraph **"relevant shares"** means, in relation to any body corporate, any such shares in that body corporate as are mentioned in sub-paragraph (2)."

*Scots land tenure*

**93** In the application of this Schedule to Scotland, **"land of freehold tenure"** means land in respect of which the company is the proprietor of the *dominium utile* or, in the case of land not held on feudal tenure, is the owner; **"land of leasehold tenure"** means land of which the company is the tenant under a lease; and the reference to ground-rents, rates and other outgoings includes feu-duty and ground annual.

*Staff costs*

**94(1) "Social security costs"** means any contributions by the company to any state social security or pension scheme, fund or arrangement.

**94(2) "Pension costs"** includes any costs incurred by the company in respect of any pension scheme established for the purpose of providing pensions for persons currently or formerly employed by the company, any sums set aside for the future payment of pensions directly by the company to current or former employees and any pensions paid directly to such persons without having first been set aside.

**History**

Para. 94(2) substituted by the Companies Act 1985 (Miscellaneous Accounting Amendments) Regulations 1996 (SI 1996/189), reg. 1(1), 14(1) and Sch. 1, para. 1, 16(1), (2) as from 2 February 1996 subject to reg. 16(1), (2); para. 94(2) formerly read as follows:

"**"Pension costs"** includes any other contributions by the company for the purposes of any pension scheme established for the purpose of providing pensions for persons employed by the company, any sums set aside for that purpose and any amounts paid by the company in respect of pensions without first being so set aside."

**94(3)** Any amount stated in respect of the item "social security costs" or in respect of the item "wages and salaries" in the company's profit and loss account shall be determined by reference to payments made or costs incurred in respect of all persons employed by the company during the financial year who are taken into account in determining the relevant annual number for the purposes of paragraph 56(1)(a).

**History**

In para. 94(3) the words "the item "social security costs"" substituted for the former words "either of the above items" by the Companies Act 1985 (Miscellaneous Accounting Amendments) Regulations 1996 (SI 1996/189), reg. 1(1), 14(1) and Sch. 1, para. 1, 16(1), (3) as from 2 February 1996, subject to reg. 16(1), (2).

**95** (Repealed by Companies Act 1989, s. 212 and Sch. 24 as from 1 April 1990.)

**History**

In regard to the date of the above repeal see SI 1990/355 (C 13), art. 5(1)(b), (2) and art. 6–9 for transitional and saving provisions; para. 95 formerly read as follows:

"*Turnover*

**95 "Turnover"**, in relation to a company, means the amounts derived from the provision of goods and services falling within the company's ordinary activities, after deduction of–

(a) trade discounts,
(b) value added tax, and
(c) any other taxes based on the amounts so derived."

# Schedule 4A – Form and Content of Group Accounts

[Companies Act 1985, s. 227;
Companies Act 1989, s. 1, 5(2)]

## GENERAL RULES

**1(1)** Group accounts shall comply so far as practicable with the provisions of section 390A(3) (amount of auditors' remuneration) and Schedule 4 (form and content of company accounts) as if the undertakings included in the consolidation ("the group") were a single company.

**History**

In para. 1(1) the words "provisions of section 390A(3) (amount of auditors' remuneration) and Schedule 4 (form and content of company accounts)" substituted for the former words "provisions of Schedule 4" by the Companies Act 1985 (Miscellaneous Accounting Amendments) Regulations 1996 (SI 1996/189), reg. 1(1), 14(2) and Sch. 2, para. 1, 2 as from 2 February 1996, subject to reg. 16(1), (2).

**1(2)** (Repealed by the Companies Act 1985 (Accounts of Small and Medium-sized Companies and Minor Accounting Amendments) Regulations 1997 (SI 1997/220), reg . 1, 7(10)(a) as from 1 March 1997.)

**History**

Para. 1(2) formerly read as follows:

" In particular, for the purposes of paragraph 59 of that Schedule (dealings with or interests in group undertakings) as it applies to group accounts–

(a) any subsidiary undertakings of the parent company not included in the consolidation shall be treated as subsidiary undertakings of the group, and
(b) if the parent company is itself a subsidiary undertaking, the group shall be treated as a subsidiary undertaking of any parent undertaking of that company, and the reference to fellow-subsidiary undertakings shall be construed accordingly."

**1(3)** Where the parent company is treated as an investment company for the purposes of Part V of that Schedule (special provisions for investment companies) the group shall be similarly treated.

**2(1)** The consolidated balance sheet and profit and loss account shall incorporate in full the information contained in the individual accounts of the undertakings included in the consolidation, subject to the adjustments authorised or required by the following provisions of this Schedule and to such other adjustments (if any) as may be appropriate in accordance with generally accepted accounting principles or practice.

**2(2)** If the financial year of a subsidiary undertaking included in the consolidation does not end with that of the parent company, the group accounts shall be made up–

(a) from the accounts of the subsidiary undertaking for its financial year last ending before the end of the parent company's financial year, provided that year ended no more than three months before that of the parent company, or

(b) from interim accounts prepared by the subsidiary undertaking as at the end of the parent company's financial year.

**History**

In para. 2(2) the words "does not end with that of the parent company" substituted for the former words "differs from that of the parent company" by the Companies Act 1985 (Miscellaneous Accounting Amendments) Regulations 1996 (SI 1996/189), reg. 1(1), 14(2) and Sch. 2, para. 1, 3 as from 2 February 1996, subject to reg. 16(1), (2).

**3(1)** Where assets and liabilities to be included in the group accounts have been valued or otherwise determined by undertakings according to accounting rules differing from those used for the group accounts, the values or amounts shall be adjusted so as to accord with the rules used for the group accounts.

**3(2)** If it appears to the directors of the parent company that there are special reasons for departing from sub-paragraph (1) they may do so, but particulars of any such departure, the reasons for it and its effect shall be given in a note to the accounts.

**3(3)** The adjustments referred to in this paragraph need not be made if they are not material for the purpose of giving a true and fair view.

**4** Any differences of accounting rules as between a parent company's individual accounts for a financial year and its group accounts shall be disclosed in a note to the latter accounts and the reasons for the difference given.

**5** Amounts which in the particular context of any provision of this Schedule are not material may be disregarded for the purposes of that provision.

## ELIMINATION OF GROUP TRANSACTIONS

**6(1)** Debts and claims between undertakings included in the consolidation, and income and expenditure relating to transactions between such undertakings, shall be eliminated in preparing the group accounts.

**6(2)** Where profits and losses resulting from transactions between undertakings included in the consolidation are included in the book value of assets, they shall be eliminated in preparing the group accounts.

**6(3)** The elimination required by sub-paragraph (2) may be effected in proportion to the group's interest in the shares of the undertakings.

**6(4)** Sub-paragraphs (1) and (2) need not be complied with if the amounts concerned are not material for the purpose of giving a true and fair view.

## ACQUISITION AND MERGER ACCOUNTING

**7(1)** The following provisions apply where an undertaking becomes a subsidiary undertaking of the parent company.

**7(2)** That event is referred to in those provisions as an "acquisition", and references to the "undertaking acquired" shall be construed accordingly.

**8** An acquisition shall be accounted for by the acquisition method of accounting unless the conditions for accounting for it as a merger are met and the merger method of accounting is adopted.

**9(1)** The acquisition method of accounting is as follows.

**9(2)** The identifiable assets and liabilities of the undertaking acquired shall be included in the consolidated balance sheet at their fair values as at the date of acquisition.

In this paragraph the **"identifiable"** assets or liabilities of the undertaking acquired means the assets or liabilities which are capable of being disposed of or discharged separately, without disposing of a business of the undertaking.

**9(3)** The income and expenditure of the undertaking acquired shall be brought into the group accounts only as from the date of the acquisition.

**9(4)** There shall be set off against the acquisition cost of the interest in the shares of the undertaking held by the parent company and its subsidiary undertakings the interest of the parent company and its subsidiary undertakings in the adjusted capital and reserves of the undertaking acquired.

For this purpose–

**"the acquisition cost"** means the amount of any cash consideration and the fair value of any other consideration, together with such amount (if any) in respect of fees and other expenses of the acquisition as the company may determine, and

**"the adjusted capital and reserves"** of the undertaking acquired means its capital and reserves at the date of the acquisition after adjusting the identifiable assets and liabilities of the undertaking to fair values as at that date.

**9(5)** The resulting amount if positive shall be treated as goodwill, and if negative as a negative consolidation difference.

**10(1)** The conditions for accounting for an acquisition as a merger are–

(a) that at least 90 per cent of the nominal value of the relevant shares in the undertaking acquired is held by or on behalf of the parent company and its subsidiary undertakings,

(b) that the proportion referred to in paragraph (a) was attained pursuant to an arrangement providing for the issue of equity shares by the parent company or one or more of its subsidiary undertakings,

(c) that the fair value of any consideration other than the issue of equity shares given pursuant to the arrangement by the parent company and its subsidiary undertakings did not exceed 10 per cent of the nominal value of the equity shares issued, and

(d) that adoption of the merger method of accounting accords with generally accepted accounting principles or practice.

**10(2)** The reference in sub-paragraph (1)(a) to the "relevant shares" in an undertaking acquired is to those carrying unrestricted rights to participate both in distributions and in the assets of the undertaking upon liquidation.

**11(1)** The merger method of accounting is as follows.

**11(2)** The assets and liabilities of the undertaking acquired shall be brought into the group accounts at the figures at which they stand in the undertaking's accounts, subject to any adjustment authorised or required by this Schedule.

**11(3)** The income and expenditure of the undertaking acquired shall be included in the group accounts for the entire financial year, including the period before the acquisition.

**11(4)** The group accounts shall show corresponding amounts relating to the previous financial year as if the undertaking acquired had been included in the consolidation throughout that year.

**11(5)** There shall be set off against the aggregate of–

(a) the appropriate amount in respect of qualifying shares issued by the parent company or its subsidiary undertakings in consideration for the acquisition of shares in the undertaking acquired, and

(b) the fair value of any other consideration for the acquisition of shares in the undertaking acquired, determined as at the date when those shares were acquired,

the nominal value of the issued share capital of the undertaking acquired held by the parent company and its subsidiary undertakings.

**11(6)** The resulting amount shall be shown as an adjustment to the consolidated reserves.

**11(7)** In sub-paragraph (5)(a) **"qualifying shares"** means–

(a) shares in relation to which section 131 (merger relief) applies, in respect of which the appropriate amount is the nominal value; or

(b) shares in relation to which section 132 (relief in respect of group reconstructions) applies, in respect of which the appropriate amount is the nominal value together with any minimum premium value within the meaning of that section.

**12(1)** Where a group is acquired, paragraphs 9 to 11 apply with the following adaptations.

**12(2)** References to shares of the undertaking acquired shall be construed as references to shares of the parent undertaking of the group.

**12(3)** Other references to the undertaking acquired shall be construed as references to the group; and references to the assets and liabilities, income and expenditure and capital and reserves of the undertaking acquired shall be construed as references to the assets and liabilities, income and expenditure and capital and reserves of the group after making the set-offs and other adjustments required by this Schedule in the case of group accounts.

**13(1)** The following information with respect to acquisitions taking place in the financial year shall be given in a note to the accounts.

**13(2)** There shall be stated–

(a) the name of the undertaking acquired or, where a group was acquired, the name of the parent undertaking of that group, and

(b) whether the acquisition has been accounted for by the acquisition or the merger method of accounting;

and in relation to an acquisition which significantly affects the figures shown in the group accounts, the following further information shall be given.

**13(3)** The composition and fair value of the consideration for the acquisition given by the parent company and its subsidiary undertakings shall be stated.

**13(4)** (Repealed by the Companies Act 1985 (Miscellaneous Accounting Amendments) Regulations 1996 (SI 1996/189), reg. 1(1), 14(2) and Sch. 2, para. 1, 4(1), (2) as from 2 February 1996, subject to reg. 16(1), (2).)

**History**
Para. 13(4) formerly read as follows:

"The profit or loss of the undertaking or group acquired shall be stated–

(a) for the period from the beginning of the financial year of the undertaking or, as the case may be, of the parent undertaking of the group, up to the date of the acquisition, and

(b) for the previous financial year of that undertaking or parent undertaking;

and there shall also be stated the date on which the financial year referred to in paragraph (a) began."

**13(5)** Where the acquisition method of accounting has been adopted, the book values immediately prior to the acquisition, and the fair values at the date of acquisition, of each class of assets and liabilities of the undertaking or group acquired shall be stated in tabular form, including a statement of the amount of any goodwill or negative consolidation difference arising on the acquisition, together with an explanation of any significant adjustments made.

**13(6)** Where the merger method of accounting has been adopted, an explanation shall be given of any significant adjustments made in relation to the amounts of the assets and liabilities of the undertaking or group acquired, together with a statement of any resulting adjustment to the consolidated reserves (including the re-statement of opening consolidated reserves).

**13(7)** In ascertaining for the purposes of sub-paragraph (5) or (6) the profit or loss of a group, the book values and fair values of assets and liabilities of a group or the amount of the assets and liabilities of a group, the set-offs and other adjustments required by this Schedule in the case of group accounts shall be made.

**History**
In para. 13(7) the word "(4)" formerly appearing before "(5) or (6)" omitted by the Companies Act 1985 (Miscellaneous Accounting Amendments) Regulations 1996 (SI 1996/189), reg. 1(1), 14(2) and Sch. 2, para. 1, 4(1), (3) as from 2 February 1996, subject to reg. 16(1), (2).

**14(1)** There shall also be stated in a note to the accounts the cumulative amount of goodwill resulting from acquisitions in that and earlier financial years which has been written off otherwise than in the consolidated profit and loss account for that or any earlier financial year.

**History**
In para. 14(1) the words "otherwise than in the consolidated profit and loss account for that or any earlier financial year" inserted by the Companies Act 1985 (Miscellaneous Accounting Amendments) Regulations 1996 (SI 1996/189), reg. 1(1), 14(2) and Sch. 2, para. 1, 5 as from 2 February 1996, subject to reg. 16(1), (2).

**14(2)** That figure shall be shown net of any goodwill attributable to subsidiary undertakings or businesses disposed of prior to the balance sheet date.

**15** Where during the financial year there has been a disposal of an undertaking or group which significantly affects the figures shown in the group accounts, there shall be stated in a note to the accounts–

(a) the name of that undertaking or, as the case may be, of the parent undertaking of that group, and

(b) the extent to which the profit or loss shown in the group accounts is attributable to profit or loss of that undertaking or group.

**16** The information required by paragraph 13, 14 or 15 above need not be disclosed with respect to an undertaking which–

(a) is established under the law of a country outside the United Kingdom, or

(b) carries on business outside the United Kingdom,

if in the opinion of the directors of the parent company the disclosure would be seriously prejudicial to the business of that undertaking or to the business of the parent company or any of its subsidiary undertakings and the Secretary of State agrees that the information should not be disclosed.

## MINORITY INTERESTS

**17(1)** The formats set out in Schedule 4 have effect in relation to group accounts with the following additions.

**17(2)** In the Balance Sheet Formats a further item headed "Minority interests" shall be added–

(a) in Format 1, either after item J or at the end (after item K), and

(b) in Format 2, under the general heading "LIABILITIES", between items A and B;

and under that item shall be shown the amount of capital and reserves attributable to shares in subsidiary undertakings included in the consolidation held by or on behalf of persons other than the parent company and its subsidiary undertakings.

**17(3)** In the Profit and Loss Account Formats a further item headed "Minority interests" shall be added–

(a) in Format 1, between items 14 and 15,

(b) in Format 2, between items 16 and 17,

(c) in Format 3, between items 7 and 8 in both sections A and B, and

(d) in Format 4, between items 9 and 10 in both sections A and B;

and under that item shall be shown the amount of any profit or loss on ordinary activities attributable to shares in subsidiary undertakings included in the consolidation held by or on behalf of persons other than the parent company and its subsidiary undertakings.

**17(4)** In the Profit and Loss Account Formats a further item headed "Minority interests" shall be added–

(a) in Format 1, between items 18 and 19,

(b) in Format 2, between items 20 and 21,

(c) in Format 3, between items 9 and 10 in section A and between items 8 and 9 in section B, and

(d) in Format 4, between items 11 and 12 in section A and between items 10 and 11 in section B;

and under that item shall be shown the amount of any profit or loss on extraordinary activities attributable to shares in subsidiary undertakings included in the consolidation held by or on behalf of persons other than the parent company and its subsidiary undertakings.

**17(5)** For the purposes of paragraph 3(3) and (4) of Schedule 4 (power to adapt or combine items)–

(a) the additional item required by sub-paragraph (2) above shall be treated as one to which a letter is assigned, and

(b) the additional items required by sub-paragraphs (3) and (4) above shall be treated as ones to which an Arabic number is assigned.

## INTERESTS IN SUBSIDIARY UNDERTAKINGS EXCLUDED FROM CONSOLIDATION

**18** The interest of the group in subsidiary undertakings excluded from consolidation under section 229(4) (undertakings with activities different from those of undertakings included in the consolidation), and the amount of profit or loss attributable to such an interest, shall be shown in the consolidated balance sheet or, as the case may be, in the consolidated profit and loss account by the equity method of accounting (including dealing with any goodwill arising in accordance with paragraphs 17 to 19 and 21 of Schedule 4).

## JOINT VENTURES

**19(1)** Where an undertaking included in the consolidation manages another undertaking jointly with one or more undertakings not included in the consolidation, that other undertaking ("the joint venture") may, if it is not–

(a) a body corporate, or

(b) a subsidiary undertaking of the parent company,

be dealt with in the group accounts by the method of proportional consolidation.

**19(2)** The provisions of this Schedule relating to the preparation of consolidated accounts apply, with any necessary modifications, to proportional consolidation under this paragraph.

**History**

In para. 19(2) the words "this Schedule" appearing after the words "The provisions of" substituted for the the former words "this Part" by the Companies Act 1985 (Accounts of Small and Medium-sized Companies and Minor Accounting Amendments) Regulations 1997 (SI 1997/220), reg . 1, 7(10)(b) as from 1 March 1997.

## ASSOCIATED UNDERTAKINGS

**20(1)** An **"associated undertaking"** means an undertaking in which an undertaking included in the consolidation has a participating interest and over whose operating and financial policy it exercises a significant influence, and which is not–

(a) a subsidiary undertaking of the parent company, or

(b) a joint venture dealt with in accordance with paragraph 19.

**20(2)** Where an undertaking holds 20 per cent or more of the voting rights in another undertaking, it shall be presumed to exercise such an influence over it unless the contrary is shown.

**20(3)** The voting rights in an undertaking means the rights conferred on shareholders in respect of their shares or, in the case of an undertaking not having a share capital, on members, to vote at general meetings of the undertaking on all, or substantially all, matters.

**20(4)** The provisions of paragraphs 5 to 11 of Schedule 10A (rights to be taken into account and attribution of rights) apply in determining for the purposes of this paragraph whether an undertaking holds 20 per cent or more of the voting rights in another undertaking.

**21(1)** The formats set out in Schedule 4 have effect in relation to group accounts with the following modifications.

**21(2)** In the Balance Sheet Formats the items headed "Participating interests", that is–

(a) in Format 1, item B.III.3, and

(b) In Format 2, item B.III.3 under the heading "ASSETS",

shall be replaced by two items, "Interests in associated undertakings" and "Other participating interests".

**21(3)** In the Profit and Loss Account Formats, the items headed "Income from participating interests", that is–

(a) in Format 1, item 8,

(b) in Format 2, item 10,

(c) in Format 3, item B.4, and

(d) in Format 4, item B.6,

shall be replaced by two items, "Income from interests in associated undertakings" and "Income from other participating interests".

**22(1)** The interest of an undertaking in an associated undertaking, and the amount of profit or loss attributable to such an interest, shall be shown by the equity method of accounting (including dealing with any goodwill arising in accordance with paragraphs 17 to 19 and 21 of Schedule 4).

**22(2)** Where the associated undertaking is itself a parent undertaking, the net assets and profits or losses to be taken into account are those of the parent and its subsidiary undertakings (after making any consolidation adjustments).

**22(3)** The equity method of accounting need not be applied if the amounts in question are not material for the purpose of giving a true and fair view.

**History**
Sch. 4A inserted by CA 1989, s. 1, 5(2) and Sch. 2 as from 1 April 1990 subject to transitional and saving provisions (see SI 1990/355 (C 13), art. 3, Sch. 1 and also art. 6–9).

# Schedule 5 – Disclosure of Information: Related Undertakings

[Companies Act 1985, s. 231;
Companies Act 1989, s. 1, 6(2), Sch. 3]

# Part I – Companies not Required to Prepare Group Accounts

## SUBSIDIARY UNDERTAKINGS

**1(1)** The following information shall be given where at the end of the financial year the company has subsidiary undertakings.

**1(2)** The name of each subsidiary undertaking shall be stated.

**1(3)** There shall be stated with respect to each subsidiary undertaking–

(a) if it is incorporated outside Great Britain, the country in which it is incorporated;

(c) if it is unincorporated, the address of its principal place of business.

**History**
Para. 1(3)(b) repealed by the Companies Act 1985 (Miscellaneous Accounting Amendments) Regulations 1996 (SI 1996/189), reg. 1(1), 14(3) and Sch. 3, para. 1, 2 as from 2 February 1996, subject to reg. 16(1), (2); para. 1(3)(b) formerly read as follows:
"(b) if it is incorporated in Great Britain, whether it is registered in England and Wales or in Scotland;"

**1(4)** The reason why the company is not required to prepare group accounts shall be stated.

**1(5)** If the reason is that all the subsidiary undertakings of the company fall within the exclusions provided for in section 229, it shall be stated with respect to each subsidiary undertaking which of those exclusions applies.

## HOLDINGS IN SUBSIDIARY UNDERTAKINGS

**2(1)** There shall be stated in relation to shares of each class held by the company in a subsidiary undertaking–

(a) the identity of the class, and

(b) the proportion of the nominal value of the shares of that class represented by those shares.

**2(2)** The shares held by or on behalf of the company itself shall be distinguished from those attributed to the company which are held by or on behalf of a subsidiary undertaking.

## FINANCIAL INFORMATION ABOUT SUBSIDIARY UNDERTAKINGS

**3(1)** There shall be disclosed with respect to each subsidiary undertaking–

(a) the aggregate amount of its capital and reserves as at the end of its relevant financial year, and

(b) its profit or loss for that year.

**3(2)** That information need not be given if the company is exempt by virtue of section 228 from the requirement to prepare group accounts (parent company included in accounts of larger group).

**3(2A)** That information need not be given if the company's investment in the subsidiary undertaking is included in the company's accounts by way of the equity method of valuation.

**History**
Para. 3(2A) inserted by the Companies Act 1985 (Miscellaneous Accounting Amendments) Regulations 1996 (SI 1996/189), reg. 1(1), 14(3) and Sch. 3, para. 1, 3 as from 2 February 1996, subject to reg. 16(1), (2).

**3(3)** That information need not be given if–

(a) the subsidiary undertaking is not required by any provision of this Act to deliver a copy of its balance sheet for its relevant financial year and does not otherwise publish that balance sheet in Great Britain or elsewhere, and

(b) the company's holding is less than 50 per cent of the nominal value of the shares in the undertaking.

**3(4)** Information otherwise required by this paragraph need not be given if it is not material.

**3(5)** For the purposes of this paragraph the "relevant financial year" of a subsidiary undertaking is–

(a) if its financial year ends with that of the company, that year, and

(b) if not, its financial year ending last before the end of the company's financial year.

## FINANCIAL YEARS OF SUBSIDIARY UNDERTAKINGS

**4** Where–

(a) disclosure is made under paragraph 3(1) with respect to a subsidiary undertaking, and

(b) that undertaking's financial year does not end with that of the company,

there shall be stated in relation to that undertaking the date on which its last financial year ended (last before the end of the company's financial year).

**History**
Para. 4 substituted by the Companies Act 1985 (Miscellaneous Accounting Amendments) Regulations 1996 (SI 1996/189), reg. 1(1), 14(3) and Sch. 3, para. 1, 4 as from 2 February 1996, subject to reg. 16(1), (2); para. 4 formerly read as follows:

"Where the financial year of one or more subsidiary undertakings did not end with that of the company, there shall be stated in relation to each such undertaking–

(a) the reasons why the company's directors consider that its financial year should not end with that of the company, and

(b) the date on which its last financial year ended (last before the end of the company's financial year).

Instead of the dates required by paragraph (b) being given for each subsidiary undertaking the earliest and latest of those dates may be given."

## FURTHER INFORMATION ABOUT SUBSIDIARY UNDERTAKINGS

**5** (Repealed by the Companies Act 1985 (Miscellaneous Accounting Amendments) Regulations 1996 (SI 1996/189), reg. 1(1), 14(3) and Sch. 3, para. 1, 5 as from 2 February 1996, subject to reg. 16(1), (2).)

**History**
Para. 5 formerly read as follows:

"**5(1)** There shall be disclosed–

(a) any qualifications contained in the auditors' reports on the accounts of subsidiary undertakings for financial years ending with or during the financial year of the company, and

(b) any note or saving contained in such accounts to call attention to a matter which, apart from the note or saving, would properly have been referred to in such a qualification,

in so far as the matter which is the subject of the qualification or note is not covered by the company's own accounts and is material from the point of view of its members.

**(2)** The aggregate amount of the total investment of the company in the shares of subsidiary undertakings shall be stated by way of the equity method of valuation, unless–

(a) the company is exempt from the requirement to prepare group accounts by virtue of section 228 (parent company included in accounts of larger group), and

(b) the directors state their opinion that the aggregate value of the assets of the company consisting of shares in, or amounts owing (whether on account of a loan or otherwise) from, the company's subsidiary undertakings is not less than the aggregate of the amounts at which those assets are stated or included in the company's balance sheet.

**(3)** In so far as information required by this paragraph is not obtainable, a statement to that effect shall be given instead."

## SHARES AND DEBENTURES OF COMPANY HELD BY SUBSIDIARY UNDERTAKINGS

**6(1)** The number, description and amount of the shares in the company held by or on behalf of its subsidiary undertakings shall be disclosed.

**6(2)** Sub-paragraph (1) does not apply in relation to shares in the case of which the subsidiary undertaking is concerned as personal representative or, subject as follows, as trustee.

**6(3)** The exception for shares in relation to which the subsidiary undertaking is concerned as trustee does not apply if the company, or any subsidiary undertaking of the company, is beneficially interested under the trust, otherwise than by way of security only for the purposes of a transaction entered into by it in the ordinary course of a business which includes the lending of money.

**History**

In para. 6(1) the words "and debentures of" formerly appearing after the words "shares in" omitted, and in para. 6(2), (3) the words "or debentures" formerly appearing after the word "shares" omitted by the Companies Act 1985 (Miscellaneous Accounting Amendments) Regulations 1996 (SI 1996/189), reg. 1(1), 14(3) and Sch. 3, para. 1, 6 as from 2 February 1996, subject to reg. 16(1), (2).

**6(4)** Schedule 2 to this Act has effect for the interpretation of the reference in sub-paragraph (3) to a beneficial interest under a trust.

## SIGNIFICANT HOLDINGS IN UNDERTAKINGS OTHER THAN SUBSIDIARY UNDERTAKINGS

**7(1)** The information required by paragraphs 8 and 9 shall be given where at the end of the financial year the company has a significant holding in an undertaking which is not a subsidiary undertaking of the company.

**7(2)** A holding is significant for this purpose if–

(a) it amounts to 20 per cent or more of the nominal value of any class of shares in the undertaking, or

(b) the amount of the holding (as stated or included in the company's accounts) exceeds one-fifth of the amount (as so stated) of the company's assets.

**History**

In para. 7(2) the words "20 per cent" and "one-fifth" substituted for the former words "10 per cent" and "one-tenth" respectively by the Companies Act 1985 (Miscellaneous Accounting Amendments) Regulations 1996 (SI 1996/189), reg. 1(1), 14(3) and Sch. 3, para. 1, 7 as from 2 February 1996, subject to reg. 16(1), (2).

**8(1)** The name of the undertaking shall be stated.

**8(2)** There shall be stated–

(a) if the undertaking is incorporated outside Great Britain, the country in which it is incorporated;

(c) if it is unincorporated, the address of its principal place of business.

**History**

Para. 8(2)(b) repealed by the Companies Act 1985 (Miscellaneous Accounting Amendments) Regulations 1996 (SI 1996/189), reg. 1(1), 14(3) and Sch. 3, para. 1, 8 as from 2 February 1996, subject to reg. 16(1), (2); para. 8(2)(b) formerly read as follows:

"(b) if it is incorporated in Great Britain, whether it is registered in England and Wales or in Scotland;"

**8(3)** There shall also be stated–

(a) the identity of each class of shares in the undertaking held by the company, and

(b) the proportion of the nominal value of the shares of that class represented by those shares.

**9(1)** There shall also be stated–

(a) the aggregate amount of the capital and reserves of the undertaking as at the end of its relevant financial year, and

(b) its profit or loss for that year.

**History**

In para. 9(1) the words "Where the company has a significant holding in an undertaking amounting to 20 per cent or more of the nominal value of the shares in the undertaking," formerly appearing before the words "there shall also be stated–" omitted by the Companies Act 1985 (Miscellaneous Accounting Amendments) Regulations 1996 (SI 1996/189), reg. 1(1), 14(3) and Sch. 3, para. 1, 9 as from 2 February 1996, subject to reg. 16(1), (2).

**9(2)** That information need not be given if–

(a) the company is exempt by virtue of section 228 from the requirement to prepare group accounts (parent company included in accounts of larger group), and

(b) the investment of the company in all undertakings in which it has such a holding as is mentioned in sub-paragraph (1) is shown, in aggregate, in the notes to the accounts by way of the equity method of valuation.

**9(3)** That information need not be given in respect of an undertaking if–

(a) the undertaking is not required by any provision of this Act to deliver a copy of its balance sheet for its relevant financial year and does not otherwise publish that balance sheet in Great Britain or elsewhere, and

(b) the company's holding is less than 50 per cent of the nominal value of the shares in the undertaking.

**9(4)** Information otherwise required by this paragraph need not be given if it is not material.

**9(5)** For the purposes of this paragraph the "relevant financial year" of an undertaking is–

(a) if its financial year ends with that of the company, that year, and

(b) if not, its financial year ending last before the end of the company's financial year.

## MEMBERSHIP OF CERTAIN UNDERTAKINGS

**9A(1)** The information required by this paragraph shall be given where at the end of the financial year the company is a member of a qualifying undertaking.

**9A(2)** There shall be stated–

(a) the name and legal form of the undertaking, and

(b) the address of the undertaking's registered office (whether in or outside Great Britain) or, if it does not have such an office, its head office (whether in or outside Great Britain).

**9A(3)** Where the undertaking is a qualifying partnership there shall also be stated either–

(a) that a copy of the latest accounts of the undertaking has been or is to be appended to the copy of the company's accounts sent to the registrar under section 242 of this Act, or

(b) the name of at least one body corporate (which may be the company) in whose group accounts the undertaking has been or is to be dealt with on a consolidated basis.

**9A(4)** Information otherwise required by sub-paragraph (2) above need not be given if it is not material.

**9A(5)** Information otherwise required by sub-paragraph (3)(b) above need not be given if the notes to the company's accounts disclose that advantage has been taken of the exemption conferred by regulation 7 of the Partnerships and Unlimited Companies (Accounts) Regulations 1993.

**9A(6)** In this paragraph–

**"dealt with on a consolidated basis"**, **"member"**, **"qualifying company"** and **"qualifying partnership"** have the same meanings as in the Partnerships and Unlimited Companies (Accounts) Regulations 1993;

**"qualifying undertaking"** means a qualifying partnership or a qualifying company.

**History**
Para. 9A inserted by the Partnerships and Unlimited Companies (Accounts) Regulations 1993 (SI 1993/1820), reg. 1(2), 11(2) as from 21 July 1993.

## ARRANGEMENTS ATTRACTING MERGER RELIEF

**10** (Repealed by the Companies Act 1985 (Miscellaneous Accounting Amendments) Regulations 1996 (SI 1996/189), reg. 1(1), 14(3) and Sch. 3, para. 1, 10 as from 2 February 1996, subject to reg. 16(1), (2).)

**History**
Para. 10 formerly read as follows:

"**10(1)** This paragraph applies to arrangements attracting merger relief, that is, where a company allots shares in consideration for the issue, transfer or cancellation of shares in another body corporate ("the other company") in circumstances such that section 130 of this Act (share premium account) does not, by virtue of section 131(2) (merger relief), apply to the premiums on the shares.

**(2)** If the company makes such an arrangement during the financial year, the following information shall be given–
(a) the name of the other company,
(b) the number, nominal value and class of shares allotted,
(c) the number, nominal value and class of shares in the other company issued, transferred or cancelled, and
(d) particulars of the accounting treatment adopted in the company's accounts in respect of the issue, transfer or cancellation.

**(3)** Where the company made such an arrangement during the financial year, or during either of the two preceding financial years, and there is included in the company's profit and loss account–
(a) any profit or loss realised during the financial year by the company on the disposal of–
(i) any shares in the other company, or
(ii) any assets which were fixed assets of the other company or any of its subsidiary undertakings at the time of the arrangement, or
(b) any part of any profit or loss realised during the financial year by the company on the disposal of any shares (other than shares in the other company) which was attributable to the fact that there were at the time of the disposal amongst the assets of the company which issued the shares, or any of its subsidiary undertakings, such shares or assets as are described in paragraph (a) above,
then, the net amount of that profit or loss or, as the case may be, the part so attributable shall be shown, together with an explanation of the transactions to which the information relates.

**(4)** For the purposes of this paragraph the time of the arrangement shall be taken to be–
(a) where as a result of the arrangement the other company becomes a subsidiary undertaking of the company, the date on which it does so or, if the arrangement in question becomes binding only on the fulfilment of a condition, the date on which that condition is fulfilled;
(b) if the other company is already a subsidiary undertaking of the company, the date on which the shares are allotted or, if they are allotted on different days, the first day."

## PARENT UNDERTAKING DRAWING UP ACCOUNTS FOR LARGER GROUP

**11(1)** Where the company is a subsidiary undertaking, the following information shall be given with respect to the parent undertaking of–
(a) the largest group of undertakings for which group accounts are drawn up and of which the company is a member, and
(b) the smallest such group of undertakings.

**11(2)** The name of the parent undertaking shall be stated.

**11(3)** There shall be stated–
(a) if the undertaking is incorporated outside Great Britain, the country in which it is incorporated;
(c) if it is unincorporated, the address of its principal place of business.

**History**
Para. 11(3)(b) repealed by the Companies Act 1985 (Miscellaneous Accounting Amendments) Regulations 1996 (SI 1996/189), reg. 1(1), 14(3) and Sch. 3, para. 1, 11 as from 2 February 1996, subject to reg. 16(1), (2); para. 11(3)(b) formerly read as follows:
"(b) if it is incorporated in Great Britain, whether it is registered in England and Wales or in Scotland;"

**11(4)** If copies of the group accounts referred to in sub-paragraph (1) are available to the public, there shall also be stated the addresses from which copies of the accounts can be obtained.

## IDENTIFICATION OF ULTIMATE PARENT COMPANY

**12(1)** Where the company is a subsidiary undertaking, the following information shall be given with respect to the company (if any) regarded by the directors as being the company's ultimate parent company.

**12(2)** The name of that company shall be stated.

**12(3)** If known to the directors, there shall be stated–
(a) if that company is incorporated outside Great Britain, the country in which it is incorporated.

**History**
Para. 12(3)(b) repealed by the Companies Act 1985 (Miscellaneous Accounting Amendments) Regulations 1996 (SI 1996/189), reg. 1(1), 14(3) and Sch. 3, para. 1, 12 as from 2 February 1996, subject to reg. 16(1), (2); para. 12(3)(b) formerly read as follows:
"(b) if it is incorporated in Great Britain, whether it is registered in England and Wales or in Scotland."

**12(4)** In this paragraph **"company"** includes any body corporate.

## CONSTRUCTIONS OF REFERENCES TO SHARES HELD BY COMPANY

**13(1)** References in this Part of this Schedule to shares held by a company shall be construed as follows.

**13(2)** For the purposes of paragraphs 2 to 4 (information about subsidiary undertakings)–

(a) there shall be attributed to the company any shares held by a subsidiary undertaking, or by a person acting on behalf of the company or a subsidiary undertaking; but

(b) there shall be treated as not held by the company any shares held on behalf of a person other than the company or a subsidiary undertaking.

**History**
In para. 13(2) the words "paragraphs 2 to 4" substituted for the former words "paragraphs 2 to 5" by the Companies Act 1985 (Miscellaneous Accounting Amendments) Regulations 1996 (SI 1996/189), reg. 1(1), 14(3) and Sch. 3, para. 1, 13 as from 2 February 1996, subject to reg. 16(1), (2).

**13(3)** For the purposes of paragraphs 7 to 9 (information about undertakings other than subsidiary undertakings)–

(a) there shall be attributed to the company shares held on its behalf by any person; but

(b) there shall be treated as not held by a company shares held on behalf of a person other than the company.

**13(4)** For the purposes of any of those provisions, shares held by way of security shall be treated as held by the person providing the security–

(a) where apart from the right to exercise them for the purpose of preserving the value of the security, or of realising it, the rights attached to the shares are exercisable only in accordance with his instructions, and

(b) where the shares are held in connection with the granting of loans as part of normal business activities and apart from the right to exercise them for the purpose of preserving the value of the security, or of realising it, the rights attached to the shares are exercisable only in his interests.

# Part II – Companies Required to Prepare Group Accounts

## INTRODUCTORY

**14** In this Part of this Schedule **"the group"** means the group consisting of the parent company and its subsidiary undertakings.

## SUBSIDIARY UNDERTAKINGS

**15(1)** The following information shall be given with respect to the undertakings which are subsidiary undertakings of the parent company at the end of the financial year.

**15(2)** The name of each undertaking shall be stated.

**15(3)** There shall be stated–

(a) if the undertaking is incorporated outside Great Britain, the country in which it is incorporated;

(c) if it is unincorporated, the address of its principal place of business.

**History**
Para. 15(3)(b) repealed by the Companies Act 1985 (Miscellaneous Accounting Amendments) Regulations 1996 (SI 1996/189), reg. 1(1), 14(3) and Sch. 3, para. 1, 14 as from 2 February 1996, subject to reg. 16(1), (2); para. 15(3)(b) formerly read as follows:
"(b) if it is incorporated in Great Britain, whether it is registered in England and Wales or in Scotland;"

**15(4)** It shall also be stated whether the subsidiary undertaking is included in the consolidation and, if it is not, the reasons for excluding it from consolidation shall be given.

**15(5)** It shall be stated with respect to each subsidiary undertaking by virtue of which of the conditions specified in section 258(2) or (4) it is a subsidiary undertaking of its immediate parent undertaking.

That information need not be given if the relevant condition is that specified in subsection (2)(a) of that section (holding of a majority of the voting rights) and the immediate parent undertaking holds the same proportion of the shares in the undertaking as it holds voting rights.

## HOLDINGS IN SUBSIDIARY UNDERTAKINGS

**16(1)** The following information shall be given with respect to the shares of a subsidiary undertaking held–

(a) by the parent company, and
(b) by the group;

and the information under paragraphs (a) and (b) shall (if different) be shown separately.

**16(2)** There shall be stated–
(a) the identity of each class of shares held, and
(b) the proportion of the nominal value of the shares of that class represented by those shares.

## FINANCIAL INFORMATION ABOUT SUBSIDIARY UNDERTAKINGS NOT INCLUDED IN THE CONSOLIDATION

**17(1)** There shall be shown with respect to each subsidiary undertaking not included in the consolidation–
(a) the aggregate amount of its capital and reserves as at the end of its relevant financial year, and
(b) its profit or loss for that year.

**17(2)** That information need not be given if the group's investment in the undertaking is included in the accounts by way of the equity method of valuation or if–
(a) the undertaking is not required by any provision of this Act to deliver a copy of its balance sheet for its relevant financial year and does not otherwise publish that balance sheet in Great Britain or elsewhere, and
(b) the holding of the group is less than 50 per cent of the nominal value of the shares in the undertaking.

**17(3)** Information otherwise required by this paragraph need not be given if it is not material.

**17(4)** For the purposes of this paragraph the "relevant financial year" of a subsidiary undertaking is–
(a) if its financial year ends with that of the company, that year, and
(b) if not, its financial year ending last before the end of the company's financial year.

## FURTHER INFORMATION ABOUT SUBSIDIARY UNDERTAKINGS EXCLUDED FROM CONSOLIDATION

**18(1)** The following information shall be given with respect to subsidiary undertakings excluded from consolidation.

**18(2)** There shall be disclosed–
(a) any qualifications contained in the auditors' reports on the accounts of the undertaking for financial years ending with or during the financial year of the company, and
(b) any note or saving contained in such accounts to call attention to a matter which, apart from the note or saving, would properly have been referred to in such a qualification,

in so far as the matter which is the subject of the qualification or note is not covered by the consolidated accounts and is material from the point of view of the members of the parent company.

**18(3)** In so far as information required by this paragraph is not obtainable, a statement to that effect shall be given instead.

## FINANCIAL YEARS OF SUBSIDIARY UNDERTAKINGS

**19** (Repealed by the Companies Act 1985 (Miscellaneous Accounting Amendments) Regulations 1996 (SI 1996/189), reg. 1(1), 14(3) and Sch. 3, para. 1, 15 as from 2 February 1996, subject to reg. 16(1), (2).)

**History**

Para. 19 formerly read as follows:

"Where the financial year of one or more subsidiary undertakings did not end with that of the company, there shall be stated in relation to each such undertaking–
(a) the reasons why the company's directors consider that its financial year should not end with that of the company, and
(b) the date on which its last financial year ended (last before the end of the company's financial year).

Instead of the dates required by paragraph (b) being given for each subsidiary undertaking the earliest and latest of those dates may be given."

## SHARES AND DEBENTURES OF COMPANY HELD BY SUBSIDIARY UNDERTAKINGS

**20(1)** The number, description and amount of the shares in the company held by or on behalf of its subsidiary undertakings shall be disclosed.

**History**
In para. 20(1) the words "and debentures of", formerly appearing after the words "shares in", omitted by the Companies Act 1985 (Miscellaneous Accounting Amendments) Regulations 1996 (SI 1996/189), reg. 1(1), 14(3) and Sch. 3, para. 1, 17(1), (2) as from 2 February 1996, subject to reg. 16(1), (2).

**20(2)** Sub-paragraph (1) does not apply in relation to shares in the case of which the subsidiary undertaking is concerned as personal representative or, subject as follows, as trustee.

**History**
See history note after para. 20(3).

**20(3)** The exception for shares in relation to which the subsidiary undertaking is concerned as trustee does not apply if the company or any of its subsidiary undertakings is beneficially interested under the trust, otherwise than by way of security only for the purposes of a transaction entered into by it in the ordinary course of a business which includes the lending of money.

**History**
In para. 20(2), (3) the words "or debentures", formerly appearing after the word "shares", omitted by the Companies Act 1985 (Miscellaneous Accounting Amendments) Regulations 1996 (SI 1996/189), reg. 1(1), 14(3) and Sch. 3, para. 1, 17(1), (3) as from 2 February 1996, subject to reg. 16(1), (2).

**20(4)** Schedule 2 to this Act has effect for the interpretation of the reference in sub-paragraph (3) to a beneficial interest under a trust.

## JOINT VENTURES

**21(1)** The following information shall be given where an undertaking is dealt with in the consolidated accounts by the method of proportional consolidation in accordance with paragraph 19 of Schedule 4A (joint ventures)–

(a) the name of the undertaking;
(b) the address of the principal place of business of the undertaking;
(c) the factors on which joint management of the undertaking is based; and
(d) the proportion of the capital of the undertaking held by undertakings included in the consolidation.

**21(2)** Where the financial year of the undertaking did not end with that of the company, there shall be stated the date on which a financial year of the undertaking last ended before that date.

## ASSOCIATED UNDERTAKINGS

**22(1)** The following information shall be given where an undertaking included in the consolidation has an interest in an associated undertaking.

**22(2)** The name of the associated undertaking shall be stated.

**22(3)** There shall be stated–

(a) if the undertaking is incorporated outside Great Britain, the country in which it is incorporated;
(c) if it is unincorporated, the address of its principal place of business.

**History**
Para. 22(3)(b) repealed by the Companies Act 1985 (Miscellaneous Accounting Amendments) Regulations 1996 (SI 1996/189), reg. 1(1), 14(3) and Sch. 3, para. 1, 18 as from 2 February 1996, subject to reg. 16(1), (2); para. 22(3)(b) formerly read as follows:

"(b) if it is incorporated in Great Britain, whether it is registered in England and Wales or in Scotland;"

**22(4)** The following information shall be given with respect to the shares of the undertaking held–

(a) by the parent company, and
(b) by the group;

and the information under paragraphs (a) and (b) shall be shown separately.

**22(5)** There shall be stated–

(a) the identity of each class of shares held, and

(b) the proportion of the nominal value of the shares of that class represented by those shares.

**22(6)** In this paragraph **"associated undertaking"** has the meaning given by paragraph 20 of Schedule 4A; and the information required by this paragraph shall be given notwithstanding that paragraph 22(3) of that Schedule (materiality) applies in relation to the accounts themselves.

## OTHER SIGNIFICANT HOLDINGS OF PARENT COMPANY OR GROUP

**23(1)** The information required by paragraphs 24 and 25 shall be given where at the end of the financial year the parent company has a significant holding in an undertaking which is not one of its subsidiary undertakings and does not fall within paragraph 21 (joint ventures) or paragraph 22 (associated undertakings).

**23(2)** A holding is significant for this purpose if–

(a) it amounts to 20 per cent or more of the nominal value of any class of shares in the undertaking, or

(b) the amount of the holding (as stated or included in the company's individual accounts) exceeds one-fifth of the amount of its assets (as so stated).

**History**

See history note after para. 26(2).

**24(1)** The name of the undertaking shall be stated.

**24(2)** There shall be stated–

(a) if the undertaking is incorporated outside Great Britain, the country in which it is incorporated;

(c) if it is unincorporated, the address of its principal place of business.

**History**

Para. 24(2)(b) repealed by the Companies Act 1985 (Miscellaneous Accounting Amendments) Regulations 1996 (SI 1996/189), reg. 1(1), 14(3) and Sch. 3, para. 1, 20 as from 2 February 1996, subject to reg. 16(1), (2); para. 24(2)(b) formerly read as follows:

"(b) if it is incorporated in Great Britain, whether it is registered in England and Wales or in Scotland;"

**24(3)** The following information shall be given with respect to the shares of the undertaking held by the parent company.

**24(4)** There shall be stated–

(a) the identity of each class of shares held, and

(b) the proportion of the nominal value of the shares of that class represented by those shares.

**25(1)** There shall also be stated–

(a) the aggregate amount of the capital and reserves of the undertaking as at the end of its relevant financial year, and

(b) its profit or loss for that year.

**History**

See history note after para. 28(1).

**25(2)** That information need not be given in respect of an undertaking if–

(a) the undertaking is not required by any provision of this Act to deliver a copy of its balance sheet for its relevant financial year and does not otherwise publish that balance sheet in Great Britain or elsewhere, and

(b) the company's holding is less than 50 per cent of the nominal value of the shares in the undertaking.

**25(3)** Information otherwise required by this paragraph need not be given if it is not material.

**25(4)** For the purposes of this paragraph the "relevant financial year" of an undertaking is–

(a) if its financial year ends with that of the company, that year, and

(b) if not, its financial year ending last before the end of the company's financial year.

**26(1)** The information required by paragraphs 27 and 28 shall be given where at the end of the financial year the group has a significant holding in an undertaking which is not a subsidiary undertaking of the parent company and does not fall within paragraph 21 (joint ventures) or paragraph 22 (associated undertakings).

**26(2)** A holding is significant for this purpose if–

(a) it amounts to 20 per cent or more of the nominal value of any class of shares in the undertaking, or

(b) the amount of the holding (as stated or included in the group accounts) exceeds one-fifth of the amount of the group's assets (as so stated).

**History**
In para. 23(2) and 26(2) the words "20 per cent" and "one-fifth" substituted for the former words "10 per cent" and "one-tenth" respectively by the Companies Act 1985 (Miscellaneous Accounting Amendments) Regulations 1996 (SI 1996/189), reg. 1(1), 14(3) and Sch. 3, para. 1, 19 as from 2 February 1996, subject to reg. 16(1), (2).

**27(1)** The name of the undertaking shall be stated.

**27(2)** There shall be stated–

(a) if the undertaking is incorporated outside Great Britain, the country in which it is incorporated;

(c) if it is unincorporated, the address of its principal place of business.

**History**
Para. 27(2)(b) repealed by the Companies Act 1985 (Miscellaneous Accounting Amendments) Regulations 1996 (SI 1996/189), reg. 1(1), 14(3) and Sch. 3, para. 1, 22 as from 2 February 1996, subject to reg. 16(1), (2); para. 27(2)(b) formerly read as follows:

"(b) if it is incorporated in Great Britain, whether it is registered in England and Wales or in Scotland;"

**27(3)** The following information shall be given with respect to the shares of the undertaking held by the group.

**27(4)** There shall be stated–

(a) the identity of each class of shares held, and

(b) the proportion of the nominal value of the shares of that class represented by those shares.

**28(1)** There shall also be stated–

(a) the aggregate amount of the capital and reserves of the undertaking as at the end of its relevant financial year, and

(b) its profit or loss for that year.

**History**
In para. 25(1) and 28(1) the words "Where the holding of the group amounts to 20 per cent or more of the nominal value of the shares in the undertaking," formerly appearing before the words "there shall also be stated–" omitted by the Companies Act 1985 (Miscellaneous Accounting Amendments) Regulations 1996 (SI 1996/189), reg. 1(1), 14(3) and Sch. 3, para. 1, 21 as from 2 February 1996, subject to reg. 16(1), (2).

**28(2)** That information need not be given if–

(a) the undertaking is not required by any provision of this Act to deliver a copy of its balance sheet for its relevant financial year and does not otherwise publish that balance sheet in Great Britain or elsewhere, and

(b) the holding of the group is less than 50 per cent of the nominal value of the shares in the undertaking.

**28(3)** Information otherwise required by this paragraph need not be given if it is not material.

**28(4)** For the purposes of this paragraph the "relevant financial year" of an outside undertaking is–

(a) if its financial year ends with that of the parent company, that year, and

(b) if not, its financial year ending last before the end of the parent company's financial year.

## PARENT COMPANY'S OR GROUP'S MEMBERSHIP OF CERTAIN UNDERTAKINGS

**28A(1)** The information required by this paragraph shall be given where at the end of the financial year the parent company or group is a member of a qualifying undertaking.

**28A(2)** There shall be stated–

(a) the name and legal form of the undertaking, and

(b) the address of the undertaking's registered office (whether in or outside Great Britain) or, if it does not have such an office, its head office (whether in or outside Great Britain).

**28A(3)** Where the undertaking is a qualifying partnership there shall also be stated either–

(a) that a copy of the latest accounts of the undertaking has been or is to be appended to the copy of the company's accounts sent to the registrar under section 242 of this Act, or

(b) the name of at least one body corporate (which may be the company) in whose group accounts the undertaking has been or is to be dealt with on a consolidated basis.

**28A(4)** Information otherwise required by sub-paragraph (2) above need not be given if it is not material.

**28A(5)** Information otherwise required by sub-paragraph (3)(b) above need not be given if the notes to the company's accounts disclose that advantage has been taken of the exemption conferred by regulation 7 of the Partnerships and Unlimited Companies (Accounts) Regulations 1993.

**28A(6)** In this paragraph–

**"dealt with on a consolidated basis"**, **"member"**, **"qualifying company"** and **"qualifying partnership"** have the same meanings as in the Partnerships and Unlimited Companies (Accounts) Regulations 1993;

**"qualifying undertaking"** means a qualifying partnership or a qualifying company.

**History**

Para. 28A inserted by the Partnerships and Unlimited Companies (Accounts) Regulations 1993 (SI 1993/1820), reg. 1(2), 11(3) as from 21 July 1993.

## ARRANGEMENTS ATTRACTING MERGER RELIEF

**29** (Repealed by the Companies Act 1985 (Miscellaneous Accounting Amendments) Regulations 1996 (SI 1996/189), reg. 1(1), 14(3) and Sch. 3, para. 1, 23 as from 2 February 1996, subject to reg. 16(1), (2).)

**History**

Para. 29 formerly read as follows:

"**29(1)** This paragraph applies to arrangements attracting merger relief, that is, where a company allots shares in consideration for the issue, transfer or cancellation of shares in another body corporate ("the other company") in circumstances such that section 130 of this Act (share premium account) does not, by virtue of section 131(2) (merger relief), apply to the premiums on the shares.

**(2)** If the parent company made such an arrangement during the financial year, the following information shall be given–

(a) the name of the other company,

(b) the number, nominal value and class of shares allotted,

(c) the number, nominal value and class of shares in the other company issued, transferred or cancelled, and

(d) particulars of the accounting treatment adopted in the parent company's individual and group accounts in respect of the issue, transfer or cancellation, and

(e) particulars of the extent to which and manner in which the profit or loss for the financial year shown in the group accounts is affected by any profit or loss of the other company, or any of its subsidiary undertakings, which arose before the time of the arrangement.

**(3)** Where the parent company made such an arrangement during the financial year, or during either of the two preceding financial years, and there is included in the consolidated profit and loss account–

(a) any profit or loss realised during the financial year on the disposal of–

(i) any shares in the other company, or

(ii) any assets which were fixed assets of the other company or any of its subsidiary undertakings at the time of the arrangement, or

(b) any part of any profit or loss realised during the financial year on the disposal of any shares (other than shares in the other company) which was attributable to the fact that there were at the time of the disposal amongst the assets of the company which issued the shares, or any of its subsidiary undertakings, such shares or assets as are described in paragraph (a) above,

then, the net amount of that profit or loss or, as the case may be, the part so attributable shall be shown, together with an explanation of the transactions to which the information relates.

**(4)** For the purposes of this paragraph the time of the arrangement shall be taken to be–

(a) where as a result of the arrangement the other company becomes a subsidiary undertaking of the company in question, the date on which it does so or, if the arrangement in question becomes binding only on the fulfilment of a condition, the date on which that condition is fulfilled;

(b) if the other company is already a subsidiary undertaking of that company, the date on which the shares are allotted or, if they are allotted on different days, the first day."

## PARENT UNDERTAKING DRAWING UP ACCOUNTS FOR LARGER GROUP

**30(1)** Where the parent company is itself a subsidiary undertaking, the following information shall be given with respect to that parent undertaking of the company which heads–

(a) the largest group of undertakings for which group accounts are drawn up and of which that company is a member, and

(b) the smallest such group of undertakings.

**30(2)** The name of the parent undertaking shall be stated.

**30(3)** There shall be stated–

(a) if the undertaking is incorporated outside Great Britain, the country in which it is incorporated;

(c) if it is unincorporated, the address of its principal place of business.

**History**

Para. 30(3)(b) repealed by the Companies Act 1985 (Miscellaneous Accounting Amendments) Regulations 1996 (SI 1996/189), reg. 1(1), 14(3) and Sch. 3, para. 1, 24 as from 2 February 1996, subject to reg. 16(1), (2); para. 30(3)(b) formerly read as follows:

"(b) if it is incorporated in Great Britain, whether it is registered in England and Wales or in Scotland;"

**30(4)** If copies of the group accounts referred to in sub-paragraph (1) are available to the public, there shall also be stated the addresses from which copies of the accounts can be obtained.

## IDENTIFICATION OF ULTIMATE PARENT COMPANY

**31(1)** Where the parent company is itself a subsidiary undertaking, the following information shall be given with respect to the company (if any) regarded by the directors as being that company's ultimate parent company.

**31(2)** The name of that company shall be stated.

**31(3)** If known to the directors, there shall be stated–

(a) if that company is incorporated outside Great Britain, the country in which it is incorporated.

**History**

Para. 31(3)(b) repealed by the Companies Act 1985 (Miscellaneous Accounting Amendments) Regulations 1996 (SI 1996/189), reg. 1(1), 14(3) and Sch. 3, para. 1, 25 as from 2 February 1996, subject to reg. 16(1), (2); para. 31(3)(b) formerly read as follows:

"(b) if it is incorporated in Great Britain, whether it is registered in England and Wales or in Scotland."

**31(4)** In this paragraph "company" includes any body corporate.

## CONSTRUCTION OF REFERENCES TO SHARES HELD BY PARENT COMPANY OR GROUP

**32(1)** References in this Part of this Schedule to shares held by the parent company or the group shall be construed as follows.

**32(2)** For the purposes of paragraphs 16, 22(4) and (5) and 23 to 25 (information about holdings in subsidiary and other undertakings)–

(a) there shall be attributed to the parent company shares held on its behalf by any person; but

(b) there shall be treated as not held by the parent company shares held on behalf of a person other than the company.

**32(3)** References to shares held by the group are to any shares held by or on behalf of the parent company or any of its subsidiary undertakings; but there shall be treated as not held by the group any shares held on behalf of a person other than the parent company or any of its subsidiary undertakings.

**32(4)** Shares held by way of security shall be treated as held by the person providing the security–

(a) where apart from the right to exercise them for the purpose of preserving the value of the security, or of realising it, the rights attached to the shares are exercisable only in accordance with his instructions, and

(b) where the shares are held in connection with the granting of loans as part of normal business activities and apart from the right to exercise them for the purpose of preserving the value of the security, or of realising it, the rights attached to the shares are exercisable only in his interests.

**History**

Sch. 5 substituted by CA 1989, s. 6(2) and Sch. 3 as from 1 April 1990 subject to transitional and saving provisions (see SI 1990/355 (C 13), art. 3, Sch. 1 and also art. 6–9); Sch. 5 formerly read as follows:

**"Schedule 5 – Miscellaneous Matters to be Disclosed in Notes to Company Accounts**

Section 231

Part I – Particulars of Subsidiaries

**1** If at the end of the financial year the company has subsidiaries, there shall in the case of each subsidiary be stated–

(a) the name of the subsidiary and–

(i) if it is incorporated in Great Britain and if it is registered in England and Wales and the company is registered in Scotland (or vice versa), the part of Great Britain in which it is registered, and

(ii) if it is incorporated outside Great Britain, the country in which it is incorporated; and

(b) in relation to shares of each class of the subsidiary held by the company, the identity of the class and the proportion of the nominal value of the allotted shares of that class represented by the shares held.

**2** The particulars required by paragraph 1 include, with reference to the proportion of the nominal value of the allotted shares of a class represented by shares held by the company, a statement of the extent (if any) to which it consists in shares held by, or by a nominee for, a subsidiary of the company and the extent (if any) to which it consists in shares held by, or by a nominee for, the company itself.

**3** Paragraph 1 does not require the disclosure of information with respect to a body corporate which is the subsidiary of another and is incorporated outside the United Kingdom or, being incorporated in the United Kingdom, carries on business outside it if the disclosure would, in the opinion of the directors of that other, be harmful to the business of that other or of any of its subsidiaries and the Secretary of State agrees that the information need not be disclosed.

**4** If at the end of its financial year the company has subsidiaries and the directors are of the opinion that the number of them is such that compliance with paragraph 1 would result in particulars of excessive length being given, compliance with that paragraph is required only in the case of the subsidiaries carrying on the businesses the results of the carrying on of which (in the opinion of the directors) principally affected the amount of the profit or loss of the company and its subsidiaries or the amount of the assets of the company and its subsidiaries.

**5** If advantage is taken of paragraph 4, there must be included in the statement required by this Part the information that it deals only with the subsidiaries carrying on such businesses as are referred to in that paragraph; and in that case section 231(3) (subsequent disclosure with annual return) applies to the particulars given in compliance with paragraph 1, together with those which (but for the fact that advantage is so taken) would have to be so given.

**6** For purposes of this Part, shares of a body corporate are treated as held, or not held, by another such body if they would, by virtue of section 736(4) of this Act, be treated as being held or (as the case may be) not held by that other body for the purpose of determining whether the first-mentioned body is its subsidiary.

Part II – Shareholdings in Companies etc. Other than Subsidiaries

**7** If at the end of its financial year the company holds shares of any class comprised in the equity share capital of another body corporate (not being its subsidiary) exceeding in nominal value one-tenth of the nominal value of the allotted shares of that class, there shall be stated–

(a) the name of that other body corporate and–

(i) if it is incorporated in Great Britain and if it is registered in England and Wales and the company is registered in Scotland (or vice versa), the part of Great Britain in which it is registered, and

(ii) if it is incorporated outside Great Britain, the country in which it is incorporated;

(b) the identity of the class and the proportion of the nominal value of the allotted shares of that class represented by the shares held; and

(c) if the company also holds shares in that other body corporate of another class (whether or not comprised in its equity share capital), or of other classes (whether or not so comprised), the like particulars as respects that other class or (as the case may be) those other classes.

**8** If at the end of its financial year the company holds shares comprised in the share capital of another body corporate (not being its subsidiary) exceeding in nominal value one-tenth of the allotted share capital of that other body, there shall be stated–

(a) with respect to that other body corporate, the same information as is required by paragraph 7(a), and

(b) the identity of each class of such shares held and the proportion of the nominal value of the allotted shares of that class represented by the shares of that class held by the company.

**9** If at the end of its financial year the company holds shares in another body corporate (not being its subsidiary) and the amount of all the shares in it which the company holds (as stated or included in the company's accounts) exceeds one-tenth of the amount of the company's assets (as so stated), there shall be stated–

(a) with respect to the other body corporate, the same information as is required by paragraph 7(a), and

(b) in relation to shares in that other body corporate of each class held, the identity of the class and the proportion of the nominal value of the allotted shares of that class represented by the shares held.

**10** None of the foregoing provisions of this Part requires the disclosure by a company of information with respect to another body corporate if that other is incorporated outside the United Kingdom or, being incorporated in the United Kingdom, carries on business outside it if the disclosure would, in the opinion of the company's directors, be harmful to the business of the company or of that other body and the Secretary of State agrees that the information need not be disclosed.

**11** If at the end of its financial year the company falls within paragraph 7 or 8 in relation to more bodies corporate than one, and the number of them is such that, in the directors' opinion, compliance with either or both of those paragraphs would result in particulars of excessive length being given, compliance with paragraph 7 or (as the case may be) paragraph 8 is not required except in the case of the bodies carrying on the businesses the results of the carrying on of which (in the directors' opinion) principally affected the amount of the profit or loss of the company or the amount of its assets.

**12** If advantage is taken of paragraph 11, there must be included in the statement dealing with the bodies last mentioned in that paragraph the information that it deals only with them; and section 231(3) of this Act (subsequent disclosure in annual return) applies to the particulars given in compliance with paragraph 7 or 8 (as the case may be), together with those which, but for the fact that advantage is so taken, would have to be so given.

**13** For purposes of this Part, shares of a body corporate are treated as held, or not held, by another such body if they would, by virtue of section 736(4) of this Act (but on the assumption that paragraph (b)(ii) were omitted from that subsection) be treated as being held or (as the case may be), not held by that other body for the purpose of determining whether the first-mentioned body is its subsidiary.

Part III – Financial Information About Subsidiaries

**14** If–

(a) at the end of its financial year the company has subsidiaries, and

(b) it is required by paragraph 1 in Part I above to disclose particulars with respect to any of those subsidiaries,

the additional information specified below shall be given with respect to each subsidiary to which the requirement under paragraph 1 applies.

**15** If–

(a) at the end of the financial year the company holds shares in another body corporate, and

(b) it is required by paragraph 8 in Part II above to disclose particulars with respect to that body corporate, and

(c) the shares held by the company in that body corporate exceed in nominal value one-fifth of the allotted share capital of that body,

the additional information specified below shall be given with respect to that body corporate.

**16** The information required by paragraphs 14 and 15 is, in relation to any body corporate (whether a subsidiary of the company or not) the aggregate amount of the capital and reserves of that body corporate as at the end of its relevant financial year, and its profit or loss for that year; and for this purpose the relevant financial year is–

(a) if the financial year of the body corporate ends with that of the company giving the information in a note to its accounts, that financial year, and

(b) if not, the body corporate's financial year ending last before the end of the financial year of the company giving that information.

This is subject to the exceptions and other provisions in the next paragraph.

**17(1)** The information otherwise required by paragraph 16 need not be given in respect of a subsidiary of a company if either–

(a) the company is exempt under this Act from the requirement to prepare group accounts, as being at the end of its financial year the wholly-owned subsidiary of another body corporate incorporated in Great Britain, or

(b) the company prepares group accounts and–

(i) the accounts of the subsidiary are included in the group accounts, or

(ii) the investment of the company in the shares of the subsidiary is included in, or in a note to, the company's accounts by way of the equity method of valuation.

**(2)** That information need not be given in respect of another body corporate in which the company holds shares if the company's investment in those shares is included in or in a note to the accounts by way of the equity method of valuation.

**(3)** That information need not be given in respect of any body corporate if–

(a) that body is not required by any provision of this Act to deliver a copy of its balance sheet for its relevant financial year mentioned in paragraph 16, and does not otherwise publish that balance sheet in Great Britain or elsewhere, and

(b) the shares held by the company in that body do not amount to at least one half in nominal value of the body's allotted share capital.

**(4)** Information otherwise required by paragraph 16 need not be given if it is not material.

**18** Where with respect to any subsidiary of the company or any other body corporate particulars which would otherwise be required by paragraph 1 in Part I or paragraph 8 in Part II of this Schedule to be stated in a note to the company's accounts are omitted by virtue of paragraph 4 or (as the case may be) paragraph 11, section 231(3) of this Act (subsequent disclosure in next annual return) applies–

(a) to any information with respect to any other subsidiary or body corporate which is given in or in a note to the company's accounts in accordance with this Part, and

(b) to any information which would have been required by this Part to be given in relation to a subsidiary or other body corporate but for the exemption under paragraph 4 or 11.

**19** For purposes of this Part, shares of a body corporate are treated as held, or not held, by the company if they would, by virtue of section 736(4) of this Act (but on the assumption that paragraph (b)(ii) were omitted from that subsection), be treated as being held or (as the case may be) not held by the company for the purpose of determining whether that body corporate is the company's subsidiary.

Part IV – Identification of Ultimate Holding Company

**20** If at the end of its financial year the company is the subsidiary of another body corporate, there shall be stated the name of the body corporate regarded by the directors as being the company's ultimate holding company and, if known to them, the country in which it is incorporated.

**21** Paragraph 20 does not require the disclosure by a company which carries on business outside the United Kingdom of information with respect to the body corporate regarded by the directors as being its ultimate holding company if the disclosure would, in their opinion, be harmful to the business of that holding company or of the first-mentioned company, or any other of that holding company's subsidiaries, and the Secretary of State agrees that the information need not be disclosed.

Part V – Chairman's and Directors' Emoluments, Pensions and Compensation for Loss of Office

EMOLUMENTS

**22(1)** There shall be shown the aggregate amount of the directors' emoluments.

**(2)** This amount–

(a) includes any emoluments paid to or receivable by a person in respect of his services as director of the company or in respect of his services, while director of the company, as director of any subsidiary of it or otherwise in connection with the management of the affairs of the company or any subsidiary of it; and

(b) shall distinguish between emoluments in respect of services as director, whether of the company or its subsidiary, and other emoluments.

**(3)** For purposes of this paragraph **"emoluments"**, in relation to a director, includes fees and percentages, any sums paid by way of expenses allowance (in so far as those sums are charged to United Kingdom income tax), any contributions paid in respect of him under any pension scheme and the estimated money value of any other benefits received by him otherwise than in cash.

**23** A company which is neither a holding company nor a subsidiary of another body corporate need not comply with paragraphs 24 to 27 below as respects a financial year in the case of which the amount shown in compliance with paragraph 22 above does not exceed £60,000.

**24(1)** The following applies as respects the emoluments of the company's chairman; and for this purpose **"chairman"** means the person elected by the directors to be chairman of their meetings and includes a person who, though not so elected, holds any office (however designated) which in accordance with the company's constitution carries with it functions substantially similar to those discharged by a person so elected.

**(2)** If one person has been chairman throughout the financial year, there shall be shown his emoluments, unless his duties as chairman were wholly or mainly discharged outside the United Kingdom.

**(3)** Otherwise, there shall be shown with respect to each person who has been chairman during the year his emoluments so far as attributable to the period during which he was chairman, unless his duties as chairman were wholly or mainly discharged outside the United Kingdom.

**25(1)** The following applies as respects the emoluments of directors.

**(2)** With respect to all the directors (other than any who discharged their duties as such wholly or mainly outside the United Kingdom), there shall be shown–

(a) the number (if any) who had no emoluments or whose several emoluments amounted to not more than £5,000; and

(b) by reference to each pair of adjacent points on a scale whereon the lowest point is £5,000 and the succeeding ones are successive integral multiples of £5,000, the number (if any) whose several emoluments exceeded the lower point but did not exceed the higher.

**(3)** If, of the directors (other than any who discharged their duties as such wholly or mainly outside the United Kingdom), the emoluments of one only exceed the relevant amount, his emoluments (so far as so ascertainable) shall also be shown.

**(4)** If, of the directors (other than any who discharged their duties as such wholly or mainly outside the United Kingdom), the emoluments of each of two or more exceed the relevant amount, the emoluments of him (or them, in the case of equality) who had the greater or, as the case may be, the greatest shall also be shown.

**(5) "The relevant amount"**–

(a) if one person has been chairman throughout the year, means the amount of his emoluments; and

(b) otherwise, means an amount equal to the aggregate of the emoluments, so far as attributable to the period during which he was chairman, of each person who has been chairman during the year.

**26** There shall under paragraphs 24 and 25 be brought into account as emoluments of a person all such amounts (other than contributions paid in respect of him under a pension scheme) as in his case are to be included in the amount shown under paragraph 22.

EMOLUMENTS WAIVED

**27(1)** There shall be shown–

(a) the number of directors who have waived rights to receive emoluments which, but for the waiver, would have fallen to be included in the amount shown under paragraph 22, and

(b) the aggregate amount of those emoluments.

**(2)** For these purposes–

(a) it is assumed that a sum not receivable in respect of a period would have been paid at the time at which it was due to be paid,

(b) a sum not so receivable that was payable only on demand, being a sum the right to receive which has been waived, is deemed to have been due to be paid at the time of the waiver.

PENSIONS OF DIRECTORS AND PAST DIRECTORS

**28(1)** There shall be shown the aggregate amount of directors' or past directors' pensions.

**(2)** This amount does not include any pension paid or receivable under a pension scheme if the scheme is such that the contributions under it are substantially adequate for the maintenance of the scheme; but, subject to this, it includes any pension paid or receivable in respect of any such services of a director or past director as are mentioned in paragraph 22(2), whether to or by him or, on his nomination or by virtue of dependence on or other connection with him, to or by any other person.

**(3)** The amount shown shall distinguish between pensions in respect of services as director, whether of the company or its subsidiary, and other pensions.

COMPENSATION TO DIRECTORS FOR LOSS OF OFFICE

**29(1)** There shall be shown the aggregate amount of any compensation to directors or past directors in respect of loss of office.

**(2)** This amount–

(a) includes any sums paid to or receivable by a director or past director by way of compensation for the loss of office as director of the company or for the loss, while director of the company or on or in connection with his ceasing to be a director of it, of any other office in connection with the management of the company's affairs or of any office as director or otherwise in connection with the management of the affairs of any subsidiary of the company; and

(b) lishall distinguish between compensation in respect of the office of director, whether of the company or its subsidiary, and compensation in respect of other offices.

**(3)** References to compensation for loss of office include sums paid as consideration for or in connection with a person's retirement from office.

SUPPLEMENTARY

**30(1)** The following applies with respect to the amounts to be shown under paragraphs 22, 28 and 29.

**(2)** The amount in each case includes all relevant sums paid by or receivable from–

(a) the company; and
(b) the company's subsidiaries; and
(c) any other person,

except sums to be accounted for to the company or any of its subsidiaries or, by virtue of sections 314 and 315 of this Act (duty of directors to make disclosure on company takeover; consequence of non-compliance), to past or present members of the company or any of its subsidiaries or any class of those members.

**(3)** The amount to be shown under paragraph 29 shall distinguish between the sums respectively paid by or receivable from the company, the company's subsidiaries and persons other than the company and its subsidiaries.

**31(1)** The amounts to be shown for any financial year under paragraphs 22, 28 and 29 are the sums receivable in respect of that year (whenever paid) or, in the case of sums not receivable in respect of a period, the sums paid during that year.

**(2)** But where–
(a) any sums are not shown in a note to the accounts for the relevant financial year on the ground that the person receiving them is liable to account for them as mentioned in paragraph 30(2), but the liability is thereafter wholly or partly released or is not enforced within a period of 2 years; or
(b) any sums paid by way of express allowances are charged to United Kingdom income tax after the end of the relevant financial year,

those sums shall, to the extent to which the liability is released or not enforced or they are charged as mentioned above (as the case may be), be shown in a note to the first accounts in which it is practicable to show them and shall be distinguished from the amounts to be shown apart from this provision.

**32** Where it is necessary to do so for the purpose of making any distinction required by the preceding paragraphs in an amount to be shown in compliance with this Part, the directors may apportion any payments between the matters in respect of which these have been paid or are receivable in such manner as they think appropriate.

INTERPRETATION

**33(1)** The following applies for the interpretation of paragraphs 22 to 32.

**(2)** A reference to the company's subsidiary–
(a) in relation to a person who is or was, while a director of the company, a director also, by virtue of the company's nomination (direct or indirect) of any other body corporate, includes (subject to the following sub-paragraph) that body corporate, whether or not it is or was in fact the company's subsidiary, and
(b) for purposes of paragraphs 22 to 28 (including any provision of this Part referring to paragraph 22) is to a subsidiary at the time the services were rendered, and for purposes of paragraph 29 to a subsidiary immediately before the loss of office as director.

**(3)** The following definitions apply–
(a) **"pension"** includes any superannuation allowance, superannuation gratuity or similar payment,
(b) **"pension scheme"** means a scheme for the provision of pensions in respect of services as director or otherwise which is maintained in whole or in part by means of contributions, and
(c) **"contribution"**, in relation to a pension scheme, means any payment (including an insurance premium) paid for the purposes of the scheme by or in respect of persons rendering services in respect of which pensions will or may become payable under the scheme, except that it does not include any payment in respect of two or more persons if the amount paid in respect of each of them is not ascertainable.

SUPPLEMENTARY

**34** This Part of this Schedule requires information to be given only so far as it is contained in the company's books and papers or the company has the right to obtain it from the persons concerned.

Part VI – Particulars Relating to Number of Employees Remunerated at Higher Rates

**35(1)** There shall be shown by reference to each pair of adjacent points on a scale where the lowest point is £30,000 and the succeeding ones are successive integral multiples of £5,000 beginning with that in the case of which the multiplier is 7, the number (if any) of persons in the company's employment whose several emoluments exceeded the lower point but did not exceed the higher.

**(2)** The persons whose emoluments are to be taken into account for this purpose do not include–
(a) directors of the company; or
(b) persons (other than directors of the company) who–
(i) if employed by the company throughout the financial year, worked wholly or mainly during that year outside the United Kingdom, or
(ii) if employed by the company for part only of that year, worked wholly or mainly during that part outside the United Kingdom.

**36(1)** For these purposes, a person's emoluments include any paid to or receivable by him from the company, the company's subsidiaries and any other person in respect of his services as a person in the employment of the company or a subsidiary of it or as a director of a subsidiary of the company (except sums to be accounted for to the company or any of its subsidiaries).

**(2)** **"Emoluments"** here includes fees and percentages, any sums paid by way of expenses allowance in so far as those sums are charged to United Kingdom income tax, and the estimated money value of any other benefits received by a person otherwise than in cash.

**(3)** The amounts to be brought into account for the purpose of complying with paragraph 35 are the sums receivable in respect of the financial year (whenever paid) or, in the case of sums not receivable in respect of a period, the sums paid during that year.

**(4)** But where–
(a) any sums are not brought into account for the financial year on the ground that the person receiving them is liable to account for them as mentioned in sub-paragraph (1), but the liability is wholly or partly released or is not enforced within a period of 2 years; or
(b) any sums paid to a person by way of expenses allowance are charged to United Kingdom income tax after the end of the financial year,

those sums shall, to the extent to which the liability is released or not enforced or they are charged as above mentioned (as the case may be), be brought into account for the purpose of complying with paragraph 35 on the first occasion on which it is practicable to do so.

**37** References in paragraph 36 to a company's subsidiary–

(a) in relation to a person who is or was, while employed by the company a director, by virtue of the company's nomination (direct or indirect), of any other body corporate, include that body corporate (but subject to the following sub-paragraph), whether or not it is or was in fact the company's subsidiary; and

(b) are to be taken as referring to a subsidiary at the time the services are rendered."

# Schedule 6 – Disclosure of Information: Emoluments and Other Benefits of Directors and Others

[Companies Act 1985, s. 232; Companies Act 1989, s. 1, 6, Sch. 4]

**History**
Heading substituted by CA 1989, s. 1, 6(4) and Sch. 4, para. 1, 2 as from 1 April 1990 subject to transitional and saving provisions (see SI 1990/355 (C 13), art. 3 and also art. 6–9); former heading read as follows:
"Particulars in Company Accounts of Loan and Other Transactions Favouring Directors and Officers".

## Part I – Chairman's and Directors' Emoluments, Pensions and Compensation for Loss of Office

### AGGREGATE AMOUNT OF DIRECTORS' EMOLUMENTS ETC.

**1(1)** Subject to sub-paragraph (2), the following shall be shown, namely–

(a) the aggregate amount of emoluments paid to or receivable by directors in respect of qualifying services;

(b) the aggregate of the amount of gains made by directors on the exercise of share options;

(c) the aggregate of the following, namely–

(i) the amount of money paid to or receivable by directors under long term incentive schemes in respect of qualifying services; and

(ii) the net value of assets (other than money and share options) received or receivable by directors under such schemes in respect of such services;

(d) the aggregate value of any company contributions paid, or treated as paid, to a pension scheme in respect of directors' qualifying services, being contributions by reference to which the rate or amount of any money purchase benefits that may become payable will be calculated; and

(e) in the case of each of the following, namely–

(i) money purchase schemes; and

(ii) defined benefit schemes,

the number of directors (if any) to whom retirement benefits are accruing under such schemes in respect of qualifying services.

**1(2)** In the case of a company which is not a listed company–

(a) sub-paragraph (1) shall have effect as if paragraph (b) were omitted and, in paragraph (c)(ii), "assets" did not include shares; and

(b) the number of each of the following (if any) shall be shown, namely–

(i) the directors who exercised share options; and

(ii) the directors in respect of whose qualifying services shares were received or receivable under long term incentive schemes.

**1(3)** In this paragraph **"emoluments"** of a director–

(a) includes salary, fees and bonuses, sums paid by way of expenses allowance (so far as they are chargeable to United Kingdom income tax) and, subject to paragraph (b), the estimated money value of any other benefits received by him otherwise than in cash; but

(b) does not include any of the following, namely–

(i) the value of any share options granted to him or the amount of any gains made on the exercise of any such options;

(ii) any company contributions paid, or treated as paid, in respect of him under any pension scheme or any benefits to which he is entitled under any such scheme; or

(iii) any money or other assets paid to or received or receivable by him under any long term incentive scheme.

**1(4)** In this paragraph "long term incentive scheme" means any agreement or arrangement under which money or other assets may become receivable by a director and which includes one or more qualifying conditions with respect to service or performance which cannot be fulfilled within a single financial year; and for this purpose the following shall be disregarded, namely–

(a) bonuses the amount of which falls to be determined by reference to service or performance within a single financial year;

(b) compensation for loss of office, payments for breach of contract and other termination payments; and

(c) retirement benefits.

**1(5)** In this paragraph–

**"amount"**, in relation to a gain made on the exercise of a share option, means the difference between–

(a) the market price of the shares on the day on which the option was exercised; and

(b) the price actually paid for the shares;

**"company contributions"**, in relation to a pension scheme and a director, means any payments (including insurance premiums) made, or treated as made, to the scheme in respect of the director by a person other than the director;

**"defined benefits"**means retirement benefits payable under a pension scheme which are not money purchase benefits;

**"defined benefit scheme"**, in relation to a director, means a pension scheme which is not a money purchase scheme;

**"listed company"**means a company–

(a) whose securities have been admitted to the Official List of the Stock Exchange in accordance with the provisions of Part IV of the Financial Services Act 1986; or

(b) dealings in whose securities are permitted on any exchange which is an approved exchange for the purposes of that Part;

**"money purchase benefits"**, in relation to a director, means retirement benefits payable under a pension scheme the rate or amount of which is calculated by reference to payments made, or treated as made, by the director or by any other person in respect of the director and which are not average salary benefits;

**"money purchase scheme"**, in relation to a director, means a pension scheme under which all of the benefits that may become payable to or in respect of the director are money purchase benefits;

**"net value"**, in relation to any assets received or receivable by a director, means value after deducting any money paid or other value given by the director in respect of those assets;

**"qualifying services"**, in relation to any person, means his services as a director of the company, and his services while director of the company–

(a) as director of any of its subsidiary undertakings; or

(b) otherwise in connection with the management of the affairs of the company or any of its subsidiary undertakings;

**"shares"**means shares (whether allotted or not) in the company, or any undertaking which is a group undertaking in relation to the company, and includes a share warrant as defined by section 188(1);

**"share option"**means a right to acquire shares;

**"value"**, in relation to shares received or receivable by a director on any day, means the market price of the shares on that day.

**1(6)** For the purposes of this paragraph–

(a) any information, other than the aggregate amount of gains made by directors on the exercise of share options, shall be treated as shown if it is capable of being readily ascertained from other information which is shown; and

(b) emoluments paid or receivable or share options granted in respect of a person's accepting office as a director shall be treated as emoluments paid or receivable or share options granted in respect of his services as a director.

**1(7)** Where a pension scheme provides for any benefits that may become payable to or in respect of any director to be whichever are the greater of–

(a) money purchase benefits as determined by or under the scheme; and

(b) defined benefits as so determined,

the company may assume for the purposes of this paragraph that those benefits will be money purchase benefits, or defined benefits, according to whichever appears more likely at the end of the financial year.

**1(8)** For the purpose of determining whether a pension scheme is a money purchase or defined benefit scheme, any death in service benefits provided for by the scheme shall be disregarded.

**History**

Para. 1 substituted by the Company Accounts (Disclosure of Directors' Emoluments) Regulations 1997 (SI 1997/570), reg. 1, 2 as from 31 March 1997 and effective as respects companies' financial years ending on or after that date. The former para. 1 read as follows:

"**1(1)** The aggregate amount of directors' emoluments shall be shown.

**(2)** This means the emoluments paid to or receivable by any person in respect of–

(a) his services as a director of the company, or

(b) services while director of the company–

(i) as director of any of its subsidiary undertakings, or

(ii) otherwise in connection with the management of the affairs of the company or any of its subsidiary undertakings.

**(3)** There shall also be shown, separately, the aggregate amount within sub-paragraph (2)(a) and (b)(i) and the aggregate amount within sub-paragraph (2)(b)(ii).

**(4)** For the purposes of this paragraph the "emoluments" of a person include–

(a) fees and percentages,

(b) sums paid by way of expenses allowance (so far as those sums are chargeable to United Kingdom income tax),

(c) contributions paid in respect of him under any pension scheme, and

(d) the estimated money value of any other benefits received by him otherwise than in cash,

and emoluments in respect of a person's accepting office as director shall be treated as emoluments in respect of his services as director."

## DETAILS OF HIGHEST PAID DIRECTOR'S EMOLUMENTS ETC.

**2(1)** Where the aggregates shown under paragraph 1(1)(a), (b) and (c) total £200,000 or more, the following shall be shown, namely–

(a) so much of the total of those aggregates as is attributable to the highest paid director; and

(b) so much of the aggregate mentioned in paragraph 1(1)(d) as is so attributable.

**2(2)** Where sub-paragraph (1) applies and the highest paid director has performed qualifying services during the financial year by reference to which the rate or amount of any defined benefits that may become payable will be calculated, there shall also be shown–

(a) the amount at the end of the year of his accrued pension; and

(b) where applicable, the amount at the end of the year of his accrued lump sum.

**2(3)** Subject to sub-paragraph (4), where sub-paragraph (1) applies in the case of a company which is not a listed company, there shall also be shown–

(a) whether the highest paid director exercised any share options; and

(b) whether any shares were received or receivable by that director in respect of qualifying services under a long term incentive scheme.

**2(4)** Where the highest paid director has not been involved in any of the transactions specified in sub-paragraph (3), that fact need not be stated.

**2(5)** In this paragraph–

**"accrued pension"** and **"accrued lump sum"**, in relation to any pension scheme and any director, mean respectively the amount of the annual pension, and the amount of the lump sum, which would be payable under the scheme on his attaining normal pension age if–

(a) he had left the company's service at the end of the financial year;

(b) there were no increase in the general level of prices in Great Britain during the period beginning with the end of that year and ending with his attaining that age;

(c) no question arose of any commutation of the pension or inverse commutation of the lump sum; and

(d) any amounts attributable to voluntary contributions paid by the director to the scheme, and any money purchase benefits which would be payable under the scheme, were disregarded;

**"the highest paid director"** means the director to whom is attributable the greatest part of the total of the aggregates shown under paragraph 1(1)(a), (b) and (c);

**"normal pension age"**, in relation to any pension scheme and any director, means the age at which the director will first become entitled to receive a full pension on retirement of an amount determined without reduction to take account of its payment before a later age (but disregarding any entitlement to pension upon retirement in the event of illness, incapacity or redundancy).

**2(6)** Sub-paragraphs (4) to (8) of paragraph 1 apply for the purposes of this paragraph as they apply for the purposes of that paragraph.

**History**

Para. 2 substituted for the former para. 2 to 6 by the Company Accounts (Disclosure of Directors' Emoluments) Regulations 1997 (SI 1997/570), reg. 1, 3(1) as from 31 March 1997 and effective as respects companies' financial years ending on or after that date. Former para. 2 to 6 read as follows:

"DETAILS OF CHAIRMAN'S AND DIRECTORS' EMOLUMENTS ETC

**2** Where the company is a parent company or a subsidiary undertaking, or where the amount shown in compliance with paragraph 1(1) is £60,000 or more, the information required by paragraphs 3 to 6 shall be given with respect to the emoluments of the chairman and directors, and emoluments waived.

**3(1)** The emoluments of the chairman shall be shown.

**(2)** The **"chairman"** means the person elected by the directors to be chairman of their meetings, and includes a person who, though not so elected, holds an office (however designated) which in accordance with the company's constitution carries with it functions substantially similar to those discharged by a person so elected.

**(3)** Where there has been more than one chairman during the year, the emoluments of each shall be stated so far as attributable to the period during which he was chairman.

**(4)** The emoluments of a person need not be shown if his duties as chairman were wholly or mainly discharged outside the United Kingdom.

**4(1)** The following information shall be given with respect to the emoluments of directors.

**(2)** There shall be shown the number of directors whose emoluments fell within each of the following bands–
not more than £5,000,
more than £5,000 but not more than £10,000,
more than £10,000 but not more than £15,000,
and so on.

**(3)** If the emoluments of any of the directors exceeded that of the chairman, there shall be shown the greatest amount of emoluments of any director.

**(4)** Where more than one person has been chairman during the year, the reference in sub-paragraph (3) to the emoluments of the chairman is to the aggregate of the emoluments of each person who has been chairman, so far as attributable to the period during which he was chairman.

**(5)** The information required by sub-paragraph (2) need not be given in respect of a director who discharged his duties as such wholly or mainly outside the United Kingdom; and any such director shall be left out of account for the purposes of sub-paragraph (3).

**5** In paragraphs 3 and 4 "emoluments" has the same meaning as in paragraph 1, except that it does not include contributions paid in respect of a person under a pension scheme.

EMOLUMENTS WAIVED

**6(1)** There shall be shown–

(a) the number of directors who have waived rights to receive emoluments which, but for the waiver, would have fallen to be included in the amount shown under paragraph 1(1), and

(b) the aggregate amount of those emoluments.

**(2)** For the purposes of this paragraph it shall be assumed that a sum not receivable in respect of a period would have been paid at the time at which it was due, and if such a sum was payable only on demand, it shall be deemed to have been due at the time of the waiver."

## EXCESS RETIREMENT BENEFITS OF DIRECTORS AND PAST DIRECTORS

**7(1)** Subject to sub-paragraph (2), there shall be shown the aggregate amount of–

(a) so much of retirement benefits paid to or receivable by directors under pension schemes; and

(b) so much of retirement benefits paid to or receivable by past directors under such schemes,

as (in each case) is in excess of the retirement benefits to which they were respectively entitled on the date on which the benefits first became payable or 31st March 1997, whichever is the later.

7(2) Amounts paid or receivable under a pension scheme need not be included in the aggregate amount if–

(a) the funding of the scheme was such that the amounts were or, as the case may be, could have been paid without recourse to additional contributions; and

(b) amounts were paid to or receivable by all pensioner members of the scheme on the same basis;

and in this sub-paragraph **"pensioner member"**, in relation to a pension scheme, means any person who is entitled to the present payment of retirement benefits under the scheme.

7(3) In this paragraph–

(a) references to retirement benefits include benefits otherwise than in cash; and

(b) in relation to so much of retirement benefits as consists of a benefit otherwise than in cash, references to their amount are to the estimated money value of the benefit;

and the nature of any such benefit shall also be disclosed.

**History**

Para. 7 substituted by the Company Accounts (Disclosure of Directors' Emoluments) Regulations 1997 (SI 1997/570), reg. 1, 4 as from 31 March 1997 and effective as respects companies' financial years ending on or after that date. Former para. 7 read as follows:

"PENSIONS OF DIRECTORS AND PAST DIRECTORS

**7(1)** There shall be shown the aggregate amount of directors' or past directors' pensions.

**(2)** This amount does not include any pension paid or receivable under a pension scheme if the scheme is such that the contributions under it are substantially adequate for the maintenance of the scheme; but, subject to this, it includes any pension paid or receivable in respect of any such services of a director or past director as are mentioned in paragraph 1(2), whether to or by him or, on his nomination or by virtue of dependence on or other connection with him, to or by any other person.

**(3)** The amount shown shall distinguish between pensions in respect of services as director, whether of the company or any of its subsidiary undertakings, and other pensions.

**(4)** References to pensions include benefits otherwise than in cash and in relation to so much of a pension as consists of such a benefit references to its amount are to the estimated money value of the benefit. The nature of any such benefit shall also be disclosed."

## COMPENSATION TO DIRECTORS FOR LOSS OF OFFICE

8(1) There shall be shown the aggregate amount of any compensation to directors or past directors in respect of loss of office.

8(2) This amount includes compensation received or receivable by a director or past director for–

(a) loss of office as director of the company, or

(b) loss, while director of the company or on or in connection with his ceasing to be a director of it, of–

(i) any other office in connection with the management of the company's affairs, or

(ii) any office as director or otherwise in connection with the management of the affairs of any subsidiary undertaking of the company;

**History**

In para. 8(2) the former words appearing at the end omitted by the Company Accounts (Disclosure of Directors' Emoluments) Regulations 1997 (SI 1997/570), reg. 1, 5(1) as from 31 March 1997 and effective as respects companies' financial years ending on or after that date. The former words read as follows:

"and shall distinguish between compensation in respect of the office of director, whether of the company or any of its subsidiary undertakings, and compensation in respect of other offices."

8(3) References to compensation include benefits otherwise than in cash; and in relation to such compensation references to its amount are to the estimated money value of the benefit.

The nature of any such compensation shall be disclosed.

8(4) In this paragraph, references to compensation for loss of office include the following, namely–

(a) compensation in consideration for, or in connection with, a person's retirement from office; and

(b) where such a retirement is occasioned by a breach of the person's contract with the company or with a subsidiary undertaking of the company–
  (i) payments made by way of damages for the breach; or
  (ii) payments made by way of settlement or compromise of any claim in respect of the breach.

**History**
Para. 8(4) substituted by the Company Accounts (Disclosure of Directors' Emoluments) Regulations 1997 (SI 1997/570), reg. 1, 5(2) as from 31 March 1997 and effective as respects companies' financial years ending on or after that date. Former para. 4 read as follows:
"**(4)** References to compensation for loss of office include compensation in consideration for, or in connection with, a person's retirement from office."

**8(5)** Sub-paragraph (6)(a) of paragraph 1 applies for the purposes of this paragraph as it applies for the purposes of that paragraph.

## SUMS PAID TO THIRD PARTIES IN RESPECT OF DIRECTORS' SERVICES

**9(1)** There shall be shown the aggregate amount of any consideration paid to or receivable by third parties for making available the services of any person–
(a) as a director of the company, or
(b) while director of the company–
  (i) as director of any of its subsidiary undertakings, or
  (ii) otherwise in connection with the management of the affairs of the company or any of its subsidiary undertakings.

**9(2)** The reference to consideration includes benefits otherwise than in cash; and in relation to such consideration the reference to its amount is to the estimated money value of the benefit.

The nature of any such consideration shall be disclosed.

**9(3)** The reference to third parties is to persons other than–
(a) the director himself or a person connected with him or body corporate controlled by him, and
(b) the company or any of its subsidiary undertakings.

## SUPPLEMENTARY

**10(1)** The following applies with respect to the amounts to be shown under this Part of this Schedule.

**History**
In para. 10(1) the words "this Part of this Schedule" appearing after the words "shown under" substituted for the former words "paragraphs 1, 7, 8 and 9" by the Company Accounts (Disclosure of Directors' Emoluments) Regulations 1997 (SI 1997/570), reg. 1, 6(2)(a) as from 31 March 1997.

**10(2)** The amount in each case includes all relevant sums paid by or receivable from–
(a) the company; and
(b) the company's subsidiary undertakings; and
(c) any other person,
except sums to be accounted for to the company or any of its subsidiary undertakings or, by virtue of sections 314 and 315 of this Act (duty of directors to make disclosure on company takeover; consequence of non-compliance), to past or present members of the company or any of its subsidiaries or any class of those members.

**10(3)** (Omitted by the Company Accounts (Disclosure of Directors' Emoluments) Regulations 1997 (SI 1997/570), reg. 1, 6(2)(b) as from 31 March 1997.)

**History**
Above omission effective as respects companies' financial years ending on or after 31 March 1997. Para. 10(3) formerly read as follows:
"The amount to be shown under paragraph 8 shall distinguish between the sums respectively paid by or receivable from the company, the company's subsidiary undertakings and persons other than the company and its subsidiary undertakings."

**10(4)** References to amounts paid to or receivable by a person include amounts paid to or receivable by a person connected with him or a body corporate controlled by him (but not so as to require an amount to be counted twice).

**11(1)** The amounts to be shown for any financial year under this Part of this Schedule are the sums receivable in respect of that year (whenever paid) or, in the case of sums not receivable in respect of a period, the sums paid during that year.

**History**
In para. 11(1) the words "this Part of this Schedule" appearing after the words "financial year under" substituted for the former words "paragraphs 1, 7, 8 and 9" by the Company Accounts (Disclosure of Directors' Emoluments) Regulations 1997 (SI 1997/570), reg. 1, 6(3) as from 31 March 1997.

**11(2)** But where–

(a) any sums are not shown in a note to the accounts for the relevant financial year on the ground that the person receiving them is liable to account for them as mentioned in paragraph 10(2), but the liability is thereafter wholly or partly released or is not enforced within a period of 2 years; or

(b) any sums paid by way of expenses allowance are charged to United Kingdom income tax after the end of the relevant financial year,

those sums shall, to the extent to which the liability is released or not enforced or they are charged as mentioned above (as the case may be), be shown in a note to the first accounts in which it is practicable to show them and shall be distinguished from the amounts to be shown apart from this provision.

**12** Where it is necessary to do so for the purpose of making any distinction required by the preceding paragraphs in an amount to be shown in compliance with this Part of this Schedule, the directors may apportion any payments between the matters in respect of which these have been paid or are receivable in such manner as they think appropriate.

## INTERPRETATION

**13(1)** The following applies for the interpretation of this Part of this Schedule.

**13(2)** A reference to a subsidiary undertaking of the company–

(a) in relation to a person who is or was, while a director of the company, a director also, by virtue of the company's nomination (direct or indirect) of any other undertaking, includes (subject to the following sub-paragraph) that undertaking, whether or not it is or was in fact a subsidiary undertaking of the company, and

(b) for the purposes of paragraphs 1 to 7 is to an undertaking which is a subsidiary undertaking at the time the services were rendered, and for the purposes of paragraph 8 to a subsidiary undertaking immediately before the loss of office as director.

**History**
In para. 13(2)(b) the former words "(including any provision of this Part of this Schedule referring to paragraph 1)" appearing after the words "paragraphs 1 to 7" omitted by the Company Accounts (Disclosure of Directors' Emoluments) Regulations 1997 (SI 1997/570), reg. 1, 6(4) as from 31 March 1997.

**13(3)** The following definitions apply–

(a) **"pension scheme"** has the meaning assigned to **"retirement benefits scheme"** by section 611 of the Income and Corporation Taxes Act 1988;

(b) **"retirement benefits"** has the meaning assigned to relevant benefits by section 612(1) of that Act.

**History**
Para. 13(3) substituted by the Company Accounts (Disclosure od Directors' Emoluments) Regulations 1997 (SI 1997/570), reg. 1, 6(5) as from 31 March 1997 and effective as respects companies' financial years ending on or after that date. The former para. 13(3) read as follows:

"The following definitions apply–

(a) **"pension"** includes any superannuation allowance, superannuation gratuity or similar payment,

(b) **"pension scheme"** means a scheme for the provision of pensions in respect of services as director or otherwise which is maintained in whole or in part by means of contributions, and

(c) **"contribution"**, in relation to a pension scheme, means any payment (including an insurance premium) paid for the purposes of the scheme by or in respect of persons rendering services in respect of which pensions will or may become payable under the scheme except that it does not include any payment in respect of two or more persons if the amount paid in respect of each of them is not ascertainable."

**13(4)** References in this Part of this Schedule to a person being "connected" with a director, and to a director "controlling" a body corporate, shall be construed in accordance with section 346.

SUPPLEMENTARY

**14** This Part of this Schedule requires information to be given only so far as it is contained in the company's books and papers or the company has the right to obtain it from the persons concerned.

**History**
Pt. I inserted by CA 1989, s. 6(4) and Sch. 4, para. 1, 3 as from 1 April 1990 subject to transitional and saving provisions (see SI 1990/355 (C 13), art. 3, Sch. 1 and also art. 6–9).

# Part II – Loans, Quasi-Loans and Other Dealings in Favour of Directors

**History**
Heading substituted for former heading of Pt. I by CA 1989, s. 1, 6(4) and Sch. 4, para. 1, 4(1) as from 1 April 1990 subject to transitional and saving provisions (see SI 1990/355 (C 13), art. 3, Sch. 1 and also art. 6–9); former Pt. I heading read as follows:
"Part I – Matters to be Disclosed Under Section 232."

**15** The group accounts of a holding company, or if it is not required to prepare group accounts its individual accounts, shall contain the particulars required by this Schedule of–

(a) any transaction or arrangement of a kind described in section 330 entered into by the company or by a subsidiary of the company for a person who at any time during the financial year was a director of the company or its holding company, or was connected with such a director;

(b) an agreement by the company or by a subsidiary of the company to enter into any such transaction or arrangement for a person who was at any time during the financial year a director of the company or its holding company, or was connected with such a director; and

(c) any other transaction or arrangement with the company or a subsidiary of it in which a person who at any time during the financial year was a director of the company or its holding company had, directly or indirectly, a material interest.

**History**
In para. 15 (formerly numbered 1 – in regard to renumbering of paragraphs in this Part see history note after para. 27) the words "The group accounts of" to "its individual accounts" substituted for the former words "Group accounts" by CA 1989, s. 1, 6(4) and Sch. 4, para. 1, 4(4) as from 1 April 1990 subject to transitional and saving provisions (see SI 1990/355 (C 13), art. 3, Sch. 1 and also art. 6–9).

**16** The accounts prepared by a company other than a holding company shall contain the particulars required by this Schedule of–

(a) any transaction or arrangement of a kind described in section 330 entered into by the company for a person who at any time during the financial year was a director of it or of its holding company or was connected with such a director;

(b) an agreement by the company to enter into any such transaction or arrangement for a person who at any time during the financial year was a director of the company or its holding company or was connected with such a director; and

(c) any other transaction or arrangement with the company in which a person who at any time during the financial year was a director of the company or of its holding company had, directly or indirectly, a material interest.

**17(1)** For purposes of paragraphs 15(c) and 16(c), a transaction or arrangement between a company and a director of it or of its holding company, or a person connected with such a director, is to be treated (if it would not otherwise be so) as a transaction, arrangement or agreement in which that director is interested.

**17(2)** An interest in such a transaction or arrangement is not **"material"** for purposes of those sub-paragraphs if in the board's opinion it is not so; but this is without prejudice to the question whether or not such an interest is material in a case where the board have not considered the matter.

**"The board"** here means the directors of the company preparing the accounts, or a majority of those directors, but excluding in either case the director whose interest it is.

**History**
Formerly appearing here was a paragraph (numbered 4 – in regard to renumbering of paragraphs in this Part see history note after para. 27) omitted by CA 1989, s. 1, 6(4) and Sch. 4, para. 1, 4(3) as from 1 April 1990 subject to transitional and saving provisions (see SI 1990/355 (C 13), art. 3, Sch. 1 and also art. 6–9); former para. 4 read as follows:
"Paragraphs 1 and 2 do not apply, for the purposes of accounts prepared by a company which is, or is the holding company of, an authorised institution, in relation to a transaction or arrangement of a kind described in section 330 or an agreement to enter into such a transaction or arrangement, to which that authorised institution is a party."
In former para. 4 the words "an authorised institution" and "that authorised institution" substituted respectively for the original words "a recognised bank" and "that recognised bank" by Banking Act 1987, s. 108(1) and Sch. 6, para. 18(9) as from 1 October 1987 (see SI 1987/1664 (C 50)).

**18** Paragraphs 15 and 16 do not apply in relation to the following transactions, arrangements and agreements–

(a) a transaction, arrangement or agreement between one company and another in which a director of the former or of its subsidiary or holding company is interested only by virtue of his being a director of the latter;

(b) a contract of service between a company and one of its directors or a director of its holding company, or between a director of a company and any of that company's subsidiaries:

(c) a transaction, arrangement or agreement which was not entered into during the financial year and which did not subsist at any time during that year.

**19** Paragraphs 15 and 16 apply whether or not–

(a) the transaction or arrangement was prohibited by section 330;

(b) the person for whom it was made was a director of the company or was connected with a director of it at the time it was made;

(c) in the case of a transaction or arrangement made by a company which at any time during a financial year is a subsidiary of another company, it was a subsidiary of that other company at the time the transaction or arrangement was made.

**20** Neither paragraph 15(c) nor paragraph 16(c) applies in relation to any transaction or arrangement if–

(a) each party to the transaction or arrangement which is a member of the same group of companies (meaning a holding company and its subsidiaries) as the company entered into the transaction or arrangment in the ordinary course of business, and

(b) the terms of the transaction or arrangement are not less favourable to any such party than it would be reasonable to expect if the interest mentioned in that sub-paragraph had not been an interest of a person who was a director of the company or of its holding company.

**21** Neither paragraph 15(c) nor paragraph 16(c) applies in relation to any transaction or arrangement if–

(a) the company is a member of a group of companies (meaning a holding company and its subsidiaries), and

(b) either the company is a wholly-owned subsidiary or no body corporate (other than the company or a subsidiary of the company) which is a member of the group of companies which includes the company's ultimate holding company was a party to the transaction or arrangement, and

(c) the director in question was at some time during the relevant period associated with the company, and

(d) the material interest of the director in question in the transaction or arrangement would not have arisen if he had not been associated with the company at any time during the relevant period.

## THE PARTICULARS REQUIRED BY THIS PART

**22(1)** Subject to the next paragraph, the particulars required by this Part are those of the principal terms of the transaction, arrangement or agreement.

**22(2)** Without prejudice to the generality of sub-paragraph (1), the following particulars are required–

(a) a statement of the fact either that the transaction, arrangement or agreement was made or subsisted (as the case may be) during the financial year;

(b) the name of the person for whom it was made and, where that person is or was connected with a director of the company or of its holding company, the name of that director;

(c) in a case where paragraph 15(c) or 16(c) applies, the name of the director with the material interest and the nature of that interest;

(d) in the case of a loan or an agreement for a loan or an arrangement within section 330(6) or (7) of this Act relating to a loan–
   (i) the amount of the liability of the person to whom the loan was or was agreed to be made, in respect of principal and interest, at the beginning and at the end of the financial year;
   (ii) the maximum amount of that liability during that year;
   (iii) the amount of any interest which, having fallen due, has not been paid; and
   (iv) the amount of any provision (within the meaning of Schedule 4 to this Act) made in respect of any failure or anticipated failure by the borrower to repay the whole or part of the loan or to pay the whole or part of any interest on it;

(e) in the case of a guarantee or security or an arrangement within section 330(6) relating to a guarantee or security–
   (i) the amount for which the company (or its subsidiary) was liable under the guarantee or in respect of the security both at the beginning and at the end of the financial year;
   (ii) the maximum amount for which the company (or its subsidiary) may become so liable; and
   (iii) any amount paid and any liability incurred by the company (or its subsidiary) for the purpose of fulfilling the guarantee or discharging the security (including any loss incurred by reason of the enforcement of the guarantee or security); and

(f) in the case of any transaction, arrangement or agreement other than those mentioned in sub-paragraphs (d) and (e), the value of the transaction or arrangement or (as the case may be) the value of the transaction or arrangement to which the agreement relates.

**23** In paragraph 22(2) above, sub-paragraphs (c) to (f) do not apply in the case of a loan or quasi-loan made or agreed to be made by a company to or for a body corporate which is either–

(a) a body corporate of which that company is a wholly-owned subsidiary, or

(b) a wholly-owned subsidiary of a body corporate of which that company is a wholly-owned subsidiary, or

(c) a wholly-owned subsidiary of that company,

if particulars of that loan, quasi-loan or agreement for it would not have been required to be included in that company's annual accounts if the first-mentioned body corporate had not been associated with a director of that company at any time during the relevant period.

## EXCLUDED TRANSACTIONS

**History**
Heading before para. 24 (formerly numbered 11 – in regard to renumbering of paragraphs in this Part see history note to Pt. II, after para. 27) substituted by CA 1989, s. 16(4) and Sch. 4, para. 1, 4(5) as from 1 April 1990 subject to transitional and saving provisons (see SI 1990/355(C 13), art. 3, Sch. 1 and also art. 6–9); former heading read as follows:

**24(1)** In relation to a company's accounts for a financial year, compliance with this Part is not required in the case of transactions of a kind mentioned in the following sub-paragraph which are made by the company or a subsidiary of it for a person who at any time during that financial year was a director of the company or of its holding company, or was connected with such a director, if the aggregate of the values of each transaction, arrangement or agreement so made for that director or any person connected with him, less the amount (if any) by which the liabilities of the person for whom the transaction or arrangement was made has been reduced, did not at any time during the financial year exceed £5,000.

**24(2)** The transactions in question are–

(a) credit transactions,

(b) guarantees provided or securities entered into in connection with credit transactions,
(c) arrangements within subsection (6) or (7) of section 330 relating to credit transactions,
(d) agreements to enter into credit transactions.

**25** In relation to a company's accounts for a financial year, compliance with this Part is not required by virtue of paragraph 15(c) or 16(c) in the case of any transaction or arrangement with a company or any of its subsidiaries in which a director of the company or its holding company had, directly or indirectly, a material interest if–

(a) the value of each transaction or arrangement within paragraph 15(c) or 16(c) (as the case may be) in which that director had (directly or indirectly) a material interest and which was made after the commencement of the financial year with the company or any of its subsidiaries, and

(b) the value of each such transaction or arrangement which was made before the commencement of the financial year less the amount (if any) by which the liabilities of the person for whom the transaction or arrangement was made have been reduced,

did not at any time during the financial year exceed in the aggregate £1,000 or, if more, did not exceed £5,000 or 1 per cent of the value of the net assets of the company preparing the accounts in question as at the end of the financial year, whichever is the less.

For this purpose a company's net assets are the aggregate of its assets, less the aggregate of its liabilities (**"liabilities"** to include any provision for liabilities or charges within paragraph 89 of Schedule 4).

**26** Section 345 of this Act (power of Secretary of State to alter sums by statutory instrument subject to negative resolution in Parliament) applies as if the money sums specified in paragraph 21 or 22 above were specified in Part X.

## INTERPRETATION

**27(1)** The following provisions of this Act apply for purposes of this Part of this Schedule–

(a) section 331(2), and (7), as regards the meaning of **"guarantee"**, and **"credit transaction"**;
(b) section 331(9), as to the interpretation of references to a transaction or arrangement being made **"for"** a person;
(c) section 340, in assigning values to transactions and arrangements, and
(d) section 346, as to the interpretation of references to a person being **"connected with"** a director of a company.

**27(2)** In this Part of this Schedule **"director"** includes a shadow director.

**History**

Para. 27(2) inserted and existing provision (para. 14, renumbered 27 – in regard to renumbering of paragraphs in Pt. II see history note below) made sub-paragraph (1) by CA 1989, s. 6(4) and Sch. 4, para. 1, 5 as from 1 April 1990 subject to transitional and saving provisions (see SI 1990/355 (C 13), art. 3, Sch. 1 and also art. 6–9).
In para. 14(a), renumbered 27(1)(a), the figure "(5)" formerly appearing after the figure "331(2)" and the words "**"recognised bank"**" formerly appearing after the word
"**"guarantee,"**" repealed by Banking Act 1987, s. 108(2) and Sch. 7, Pt. I as from 1 October 1987 (see SI 1987/1664 (C 50)).

**History note to Pt. II**

In Pt. II (in regard to its renumbering as Pt. II see history note above para. 15), para. 15–27 renumbered as such and internal cross-references renumbered accordingly by CA 1989, s. 1, 6(4) and Sch. 4, para. 1, 4(2) as from 1 April 1990 subject to transitional and saving provisions (see SI 1990/355 (C 13), art. 3, Sch. 1 and also art. 6–9); formerly the paragraphs were numbered 1–3 and 5–14 (in regard to omission of former para. 4 see history note above para. 18).

# Part III – Other Transactions, Arrangements and Agreements

**History**

Heading substituted for former heading of Pt. II by CA 1989, s. 1, 6(4) and Sch. 4, para. 1, 6(1) as from 1 April 1990 subject to transitional and saving provisons (see SI 1990/355 (C 13), art. 3, Sch. 1 and also art. 6–9); former Pt. II heading read as follows:

"Part II – Matters to be Disclosed under Section 233".

**28** This Part of this Schedule applies in relation to the following classes of transactions, arrangements and agreements–

(a) loans, guarantees and securities relating to loans, arrangements of a kind described in subsection (6) or (7) of section 330 of this Act relating to loans and agreements to enter into any of the foregoing transactions and arrangements;

(b) quasi-loans, guarantees and securities relating to quasi-loans arrangements of a kind described in either of those subsections relating to quasi-loans and agreements to enter into any of the foregoing transactions and arrangements;

(c) credit transactions, guarantees and securities relating to credit transactions, arrangements of a kind described in either of those subsections relating to credit transactions and agreements to enter into any of the foregoing transactions and arrangements.

**29(1)** To comply with this Part of this Schedule, the accounts must contain a statement, in relation to transactions, arrangements and agreements made by the company or a subsidiary of it for persons who at any time during the financial year were officers of the company (but not directors or shadow directors), of–

(a) the aggregate amounts outstanding at the end of the financial year under transactions, arrangements and agreements within sub-paragraphs (a), (b) and (c) respectively of paragraph 25 above, and

(b) the numbers of officers for whom the transactions, arrangements and agreements falling within each of those sub-paragraphs were made.

**History**

In para. 29(1) (formerly numbered 16(1) – in regard to renumbering of paragraphs in this Part see history note after para. 30) the words "made by the company or a subsidiary of it for persons who at any time during the financial year were officers of the company (but not directors or shadow directors)" substituted for the former words "made as mentioned in section 233(1)" by CA 1989, s. 6(4) and Sch. 4, para. 1, 6(3) as from 1 April 1990 subject to transactions and saving provisions (see SI 1990/355 (C 13), art. 3, Sch. 1 and also art. 6–9).

**29(2)** This paragraph does not apply to transactions, arrangements and agreements made by the company or any of its subsidiaries for an officer of the company if the aggregate amount outstanding at the end of the financial year under the transactions, arrangements and agreements so made for that officer does not exceed £2,500.

**29(3)** Section 345 of this Act (power of Secretary of State to alter money sums by statutory instrument subject to negative resolution in Parliament) applies as if the money sum specified above in this paragraph were specified in Part X.

**30** The following provisions of this Act apply for purposes of this Part–

(a) section 331(2), (3), and (7), as regards the meaning of **"guarantee"**, **"quasi-loan"**, and **"credit transaction"**, and

(b) section 331(9), as to the interpretation of references to a transaction or arrangement being made **"for"** a person;

and **"amount outstanding"** means the amount of the outstanding liabilities of the person for whom the transaction, arrangement or agreement was made or, in the case of a guarantee or security, the amount guaranteed or secured.

**History**

In para. 30(a) (previously numbered 17(a)), the figure "(5)" formerly appearing after the figure "(3)" and the words "recognised bank" formerly appearing after the word "quasi-loan," repealed by Banking Act 1987, s. 108(2) and Sch. 7, Pt. I as from 1 October 1987 (see SI 1987/1664 (C 50)).

**History note to Pt. III**

In Pt. III (in regard to its renumbering as Pt. III see history note above para. 28), para. 28–30 renumbered as such and internal cross-references renumbered accordingly by CA 1989, s. 6(4) and Sch. 4, para. 1, 6(2) as from 1 April 1990 subject to transitional and saving provisions (see SI 1990/355 (C 13), art. 3, Sch. 1 and also art. 6–9); formerly the paragraphs were numbered 15–17.

**History note to former Pt. III**

Former Pt. III ("Part III – Matters to be Disclosed under Section 234 (Authorised Institutions)") omitted by CA 1989, s. 1, 6(4) and Sch. 4, para. 1, 7 as from 1 April 1990 subject to transitional and saving provisions (see SI 1990/355 (C 13), art. 3, Sch. 1 and also art. 6–9). In the heading to former Pt. III the words "Authorised Institutions" substituted for the previous words "Recognised Banks" by Banking Act 1987, s. 108(1) and Sch. 6, para. 18(9) as from 1 October 1987 (see SI 1987/1664 (C 50)); former Pt. III read as follows:

"**18** This Part of this Schedule applies in relation to the same classes of transactions, arrangements and agreements as does Part II.

**19** To comply with this Part, the accounts must contain a statement, in relation to such transactions, arrangements and agreements made as mentioned in section 234(1), of–

(a) the aggregate amounts outstanding at the end of the financial year under transactions, arrangements and agreements within sub-paragraphs (a), (b) and (c) respectively of paragraph 15 of this Schedule, and

(b) the numbers of persons for whom the transactions, arrangements and agreements falling within each of those sub-paragraphs were made.

**20** For the purposes of the application of paragraph 16 in relation to loans and quasi-loans made by a company to persons connected with a person who at any time is a director of the company or of its holding company, a company which a person does not control is not connected with him.

**21** The following provisions of this Act apply for purposes of this Part–

(a) section 331(3), as regards the meaning of **"quasi-loan"**;

(b) section 331(9), as to the interpretation of references to a transaction or arrrangement being made **"for"** a person; and

(c) section 346, as to the interpretation of references to a person being connected with a director, or to a director controlling a company;

and **"amount outstanding"** means the amount of the outstanding liabilities of the person for whom the transaction, arrangement or agreement was made or, in the case of a guarantee or security, the amount guaranteed or secured."

# Schedule 7 – Matters to be Dealt With in Directors' Report

[Section 234(3), (4)]

## Part I – Matters of a General Nature

### ASSET VALUES

**1(1)** (Repealed by the Companies Act 1985 (Miscellaneous Accounting Amendments) Regulations 1996 (SI 1996/189), reg. 1(1), 14(4)(a) as from 2 February 1996, subject to reg. 16(1), (2).)

**History**

Para. 1(1) formerly read as follows:

"If significant changes in the fixed assets of the company or of any of its subsidiary undertakings have occurred in the financial year, the report shall contain particulars of the changes."

Previously in para. 1(1) the words "subsidiary undertakings" substituted for the former words "subsidiaries" by CA 1989, s. 1, 8(2) and Sch. 7, para. 1, (2)(1) as from 1 April 1990 subject to transitional and saving provisions (see SI 1990/355 (C 13), art. 3, Sch. 1 and also art. 6–9).

**1(2)** If, in the case of such of the fixed assets of the company or of any of its subsidiary undertakings as consist in interests in land, their market value (as at the end of the financial year) differs substantially from the amount at which they are included in the balance sheet, and the difference is, in the directors' opinion, of such significance as to require that the attention of members of the company or of holders of its debentures should be drawn to it, the report shall indicate the difference with such degree of precision as is practicable.

**History**

In para. 1(2) the words "such of the fixed assets of the company or of any of its subsidiary undertakings" substituted for the former words "such of those assets" by the Companies Act 1985 (Miscellaneous Accounting Amendments) Regulations 1996 (SI 1996/189), reg. 1(1), 15(3) as from 2 February 1996, subject to reg. 16(1), (2).

### DIRECTORS' INTERESTS

**2(1)** The information required by paragraphs 2A and 2B shall be given in the directors' report, or by way of notes to the company's annual accounts, with respect to each person who at the end of the financial year was a director of the company.

**2(2)** In those paragraphs–

(a) **"the register"** means the register of directors' interests kept by the company under section 325; and

(b) references to a body corporate being in the same group as the company are to its being a subsidiary or holding company, or another subsidiary of a holding company, of the company.

**History**

See history note after para. 2B.

**2A(1)** It shall be stated with respect to each director whether, according to the register, he was at the end of the financial year interested in shares in or debentures of the company or any other body corporate in the same group.

**2A(2)** If he was so interested, there shall be stated the number of shares in and amount of debentures of each body (specifying it) in which, according to the register, he was then interested.

**2A(3)** If a director was interested at the end of the financial year in shares in or debentures of the company or any other body corporate in the same group–

(a) it shall also be stated whether, according to the register, he was at the beginning of the financial year (or, if he was not then a director, when he became one) interested in shares in or debentures of the company or any other body corporate in the same group, and

(b) if he was so interested, there shall be stated the number of shares in and amount of debentures of each body (specifying it) in which, according to the register, he was then interested.

**2A(4)** In this paragraph references to an interest in shares or debentures have the same meaning as in section 324; and references to the interest of a director include any interest falling to be treated as his for the purposes of that section.

**2A(5)** The reference above to the time when a person became a director is, in the case of a person who became a director on more than one occasion, to the time when he first became a director.

**History**
See history note after para. 2B.

**2B(1)** It shall be stated with respect to each director whether, according to the register, any right to subscribe for shares in or debentures of the company or another body corporate in the same group was during the financial year granted to, or exercised by, the director or a member of his immediate family.

**2B(2)** If any such right was granted to, or exercised by, any such person during the financial year, there shall be stated the number of shares in and amount of debentures of each body (specifying it) in respect of which, according to the register, the right was granted or exercised.

**2B(3)** A director's **"immediate family"** means his or her spouse and infant children; and for this purpose "children" includes step-children, and **"infant"**, in relation to Scotland, means pupil or minor.

**Note**
In para. 2B(3) the words "pupil or minor" have not been substituted by the words "person under the age of 18 years" by the Age of Legal Capacity (Scotland) Act 1991, s. 10(1), 11(2) and Sch. 1, para. 39, although that amendment was effected where the words otherwise appeared in the Act, see s. 203(1), 327(2)(b) and 328(8), as from 25 September 1991. This was probably a drafting oversight and the words should be interpreted accordingly.

**2B(4)** The reference above to a member of the director's immediate family does not include a person who is himself or herself a director of the company.

**History**
Para. 2, 2A and 2B substituted for former para. 2 by CA 1989, s. 8(2) and Sch. 5, para. 1, 3 as from 1 April 1990 subject to transitional and saving provisions (see SI 1990/355 (C 13), art. 3, Sch. 1 and also art. 6–9); former para. 2 read as follows:

"**2(1)** The report shall state the following, with respect to each person who, at the end of the financial year, was a director of the company–

(a) whether or not, according to the register kept by the company for the purposes of sections 324 to 328 of this Act (director's obligation to notify his interests in the company and companies in the same group), he was at the end of that year interested in shares in, or debentures of, the company or any other body corporate, being the company's subsidiary or holding company or a subsidiary of the company's holding company;

(b) if he was so interested–

(i) the number and amount of shares in, and debentures of each body (specifying it) in which, according to that register, he was then interested,

(ii) whether or not (according to that register) he was, at the beginning of that year (or, if he was not then a director, when he became one), interested in shares in, or debentures of, the company or any other such body corporate, and

(iii) if he was, the number and amount of shares in, and debentures of, each body (specifying it) in which, according to that register, he was interested at the beginning of the financial year or (as the case may be) when he became a director.

**(2)** An interest in shares or debentures which, under sections 324 to 328, falls to be treated as being the interest of a director is so treated for the purposes of this paragraph; and the references above to the time when a person became a director, in the case of a person who became a director on more than one occasion, is to the time when he first became a director.

**(3)** The particulars required by this paragraph may be given by way of notes to the company's accounts in respect of the financial year, instead of being stated in the directors' report."

## POLITICAL AND CHARITABLE GIFTS

**3(1)** The following applies if the company (not being the wholly-owned subsidiary of a company incorporated in Great Britain) has in the financial year given money for political purposes or charitable purposes or both.

**3(2)** If the money given exceeded £200 in amount, there shall be contained in the directors' report for the year–

(a) in the case of each of the purposes for which money has been given, a statement of the amount of money given for that purpose, and

(b) in the case of political purposes for which money has been given, the following particulars (so far as applicable)–

(i) the name of each person to whom money has been given for those purposes exceeding £200 in amount and the amount of money given.

(ii) if money exceeding £200 in amount has been given by way of donation or subscription to a political party, the identity of the party and the amount of money given.

**4(1)** Paragraph 3 does not apply to a company which, at the end of the financial year, has subsidiaries which have, in that year, given money as mentioned above, but is not itself the wholly-owned subsidiary of a company incorporated in Great Britain.

**4(2)** But in such a case there shall (if the amount of money so given in that year by the company and the subsidiaries between them exceeds £200) be contained in the directors' report for the year–

(a) in the case of each of the purposes for which money has been given by the company and the subsidiaries between them, a statement of the amount of money given for that purpose, and

(b) in the case of political purposes for which money has been given, the like particulars (so far as applicable) as are required by paragraph 3.

**5(1)** The following applies for the interpretation of paragraphs 3 and 4.

**5(2)** A company is to be treated as giving money for political purposes if, directly or indirectly–

(a) it gives a donation or subscription to a political party of the United Kingdom or any part of it; or

(b) it gives a donation or subscription to a person who, to the company's knowledge, is carrying on, or proposing to carry on, any activities which can, at the time at which the donation or subscription was given, reasonably be regarded as likely to affect public support for such a political party as is mentioned above.

**5(3)** Money given for charitable purposes to a person who, when it was given, was ordinarily resident outside the United Kingdom is to be left out of account.

**5(4)** **"Charitable purposes"** means purposes which are exclusively charitable; and, as respects Scotland, **"charitable"** is to be construed as if it were contained in the Income Tax Acts.

## INSURANCE EFFECTED FOR OFFICERS OR AUDITORS

**5A** (Repealed by the Companies Act 1985 (Miscellaneous Accounting Amendments) Regulations 1996 (SI 1996/189), reg. 1(1), 14(4)(b) as from 2 February 1996, subject to reg. 16(1), (2).)

**History**

Para. 5A formerly read as follows:

"Where in the financial year the company has purchased or maintained any such insurance as is mentioned in section 310(3)(a) (insurance of officers or auditors against liabilities in relation to the company), that fact shall be stated in the report."

Previously para. 5A inserted by CA 1989, s. 137(2) as from 1 April 1990 for the purposes of a directors' report of a company (within the meaning of CA 1985, s. 735) but subject to a transitional provision (see SI 1990/355 (C 13), art. 4(e)(ii) and also art. 13).

## MISCELLANEOUS

**6** The directors' report shall contain–

(a) particulars of any important events affecting the company or any of its subsidiary undertakings which have occurred since the end of the financial year,

(b) an indication of likely future developments in the business of the company and of its subsidiary undertakings,

(c) an indication of the activities (if any) of the company and its subsidiary undertakings in the field of research and development, and

(d) (unless the company is an unlimited company) an indication of the existence of branches (as defined in section 698(2)) of the company outside the United Kingdom.

**History**

Para. 6(d) inserted by the Companies Act 1985 (Disclosure of Branches and Bank Accounts) Regulations 1992 (SI 1992/3178), reg. 1, 3 as from 1 January 1993.

In para. 6 the words "subsidiary undertakings" (occurring three times) substituted for the former word "subsidiary" by CA 1989, s. 1, 8(2) and Sch. 5, para. 1, 2(2) as from 1 April 1990 subject to transitional and saving provisions (see SI 1990/355 (C 13), art. 3, Sch. 1 and also art. 6–9).

# Part II – Disclosure Required by Company Acquiring its Own Shares, etc.

**7** This Part of this Schedule applies where shares in a company–

(a) are purchased by the company or are acquired by it by forfeiture or surrender in lieu of forfeiture, or in pursuance of section 143(3) of this Act (acquisition of own shares by company limited by shares), or

(b) are acquired by another person in circumstances where paragraph (c) or (d) of section 146(1) applies (acquisition by company's nominee, or by another with company financial assistance, the company having a beneficial interest), or

(c) are made subject to a lien or other charge taken (whether expressly or otherwise) by the company and permitted by section 150(2) or (4), or section 6(3) of the Consequential Provisions Act (exceptions from general rule against a company having a lien or charge on its own shares).

**8** The directors' report with respect to a financial year shall state–

(a) the number and nominal value of the shares so purchased, the aggregate amount of the consideration paid by the company for such shares and the reasons for their purchase;

(b) the number and nominal value of the shares so acquired by the company, acquired by another person in such circumstances and so charged respectively during the financial year;

(c) the maximum number and nominal value of shares which, having been so acquired by the company, acquired by another person in such circumstances or so charged (whether or not during that year) are held at any time by the company or that other person during that year;

(d) the number and nominal value of the shares so acquired by the company, acquired by another person in such circumstances or so charged (whether or not during that year) which are disposed of by the company or that other person or cancelled by the company during that year;

(e) where the number and nominal value of the shares of any particular description are stated in pursuance of any of the preceding sub-paragraphs, the percentage of the called-up share capital which shares of that description represent;

(f) where any of the shares have been so charged the amount of the charge in each case; and

(g) where any of the shares have been disposed of by the company or the person who acquired them in such circumstances for money or money's worth the amount or value of the consideration in each case.

# Part III – Disclosure Concerning Employment, etc., of Disabled Persons

**9(1)** This Part of this Schedule applies to the directors' report where the average number of persons employed by the company in each week during the financial year exceeded 250.

**9(2)** That average number is the quotient derived by dividing, by the number of weeks in the financial year, the number derived by ascertaining, in relation to each of those weeks, the number of persons who, under contracts of service, were employed in the week (whether throughout it or not) by the company, and adding up the numbers ascertained.

**9(3)** The directors' report shall in that case contain a statement describing such policy as the company has applied during the financial year–

(a) for giving full and fair consideration to applications for employment by the company made by disabled persons, having regard to their particular aptitude and abilities,

(b) for continuing the employment of, and for arranging appropriate training for, employees of the company who have become disabled persons during the period when they were employed by the company, and

(c) otherwise for the training, career development and promotion of disabled persons employed by the company.

**9(4)** In this Part–

(a) **"employment"** means employment other than employment to work wholly or mainly outside the United Kingdom, and **"employed"** and **"employee"** shall be construed accordingly; and

(b) **"disabled person"** means the same as in the Disability Discrimination Act 1995.

**History**

In para. 9(4)(b) the words "Disability Discrimination Act 1995" substituted for the former words "Disabled Persons (Employment) Act 1944" by the Disability Discrimination Act 1995, s. 70(4) and Sch. 6, para. 4 as from 2 December 1996.

# Part IV – Health, Safety and Welfare at Work of Company's Employees

**10** (Repealed by the Companies Act 1985 (Miscellaneous Accounting Amendments) Regulations 1996 (SI 1996/189), reg. 1(1), 14(4)(c) as from 2 February 1996, subject to reg. 16(1), (2).)

**History**

Part IV formerly read as follows:

"**10(1)** In the case of companies of such classes as may be prescribed by regulations made by the Secretary of State, the directors' report shall contain such information as may be so prescribed about the arrangements in force in the financial year for securing the health, safety and welfare at work of employees of the company and its subsidiaries, and for protecting other persons against risks to health or safety arising out of or in connection with the activities at work of those employees.

**(2)** Regulations under this Part may–

(a) make different provision in relation to companies of different classes,

(b) enable any requirements of the regulations to be dispensed with or modified in particular cases by any specified person or by any person authorised in that behalf by a specified authority,

(c) contain such transitional provisions as the Secretary of State thinks necessary or expedient in connection with any provision made by the regulations.

**(3)** The power to make regulations under this paragraph is exercisable by statutory instrument subject to annulment in pursuance of a resolution of either House of Parliament.

**(4)** Any expression used in sub-paragraph (1) above and in Part I of the Health and Safety at Work etc. Act 1974 has the same meaning here as it has in that Part of that Act; section 1(3) of that Act applies for interpreting that sub-paragraph; and in sub-paragraph (2) **"specified"** means specified in regulations made under that sub-paragraph."

# Part V – Employee Involvement

**11(1)** This Part of this Schedule applies to the directors' report where the average number of persons employed by the company in each week during the financial year exceeded 250.

**11(2)** That average number is the quotient derived by dividing by the number of weeks in the financial year the number derived by ascertaining, in relation to each of those weeks, the number of persons who, under contracts of service, were employed in the week (whether throughout it or not) by the company, and adding up the numbers ascertained.

**11(3)** The directors' report shall in that case contain a statement describing the action that has been taken during the financial year to introduce, maintain or develop arrangements aimed at–

(a) providing employees systematically with information on matters of concern to them as employees,

(b) consulting employees or their representatives on a regular basis so that the views of employees can be taken into account in making decisions which are likely to affect their interests,

(c) encouraging the involvement of employees in the company's performance through an employee's share scheme or by some other means,

(d) achieving a common awareness on the part of all employees of the financial and economic factors affecting the performance of the company.

**11(4)** In sub-paragraph (3) **"employee"** does not include a person employed to work wholly or mainly outside the United Kingdom; and for the purposes of sub-paragraph (2) no regard is to be had to such a person.

# Part VI – Policy and Practice on Payment of Creditors

**12(1)** This Part of this Schedule applies to the directors' report for a financial year if–

(a) the company was at any time within the year a public company, or

(b) the company did not qualify as small or medium-sized in relation to the year by virtue of section 247 and was at any time within the year a member of a group of which the parent company was a public company.

**12(2)** The report shall state, with respect to the next following financial year–

(a) whether in respect of some or all of its suppliers it is the company's policy to follow any code or standard on payment practice and, if so, the name of the code or standard and the place where information about, and copies of, the code or standard can be obtained,

(b) whether in respect of some or all of its suppliers it is the company's policy–

(i) to settle the terms of payment with those suppliers when agreeing the terms of each transaction,

(ii) to ensure that those suppliers are made aware of the terms of payment, and

(iii) to abide by the terms of payment,

(c) where the company's policy is not as mentioned in paragraph (a) or (b) in respect of some or all of its suppliers, what its policy is with respect to the payment of those suppliers;

and if the company's policy is different for different suppliers or classes of suppliers, the report shall identify the suppliers to which the different policies apply.

In this sub-paragraph references to the company's suppliers are references to persons who are or may become its suppliers.

**12(3)** The report shall also state the number of days which bears to the number of days in the financial year the same proportion as X bears to Y where–

X = the aggregate of the amounts which were owed to trade creditors at the end of the year; and

Y = the aggregate of the amounts in which the company was invoiced by suppliers during the year.

**12(4)** For the purposes of sub-paragraphs (2) and (3) a person is a supplier of the company at any time if–

(a) at that time, he is owed an amount in respect of goods or services supplied, and

(b) that amount would be included under the heading corresponding to item E.4 (trade creditors) in Format 1 if–

(i) the company's accounts fell to be prepared as at that time,

(ii) those accounts were prepared in accordance with Schedule 4, and

(iii) that Format were adopted.

**12(5)** For the purpose of sub-paragraph (3), the aggregate of the amounts which at the end of the financial year were owed to trade creditors shall be taken to be–

(a) where in the company's accounts Format 1 of the balance sheet formats set out in Part I of Schedule 4 is adopted, the amount shown under the heading corresponding to item E.4 (trade creditors) in that Format,

(b) where Format 2 is adopted, the amount which, under the heading corresponding to item C.4 (trade creditors) in that Format, is shown as falling due within one year, and

(c) where the company's accounts are prepared in accordance with Schedule 9 or 9A, the amount which would be shown under the heading corresponding to item E.4 (trade creditors) in Format 1 if the company's accounts were prepared in accordance with Schedule 4 and that Format were adopted.

**History**

Sch. 7 Pt. VI substituted by the Companies Act 1985 (Directors' Report) (Statement of Payment Practice) Regulations 1997 (SI 1997/571), reg. 1, 2(2) as from 4 March 1997. The former Pt. VI read as follows:

"Policy on the Payment of Creditors

**12(1)** This Part of this Schedule applies to a report by the directors of a company for a financial year if–

(a) the company was at any time within the financial year a public company, or

(b) the company did not qualify as small or medium-sized in relation to the financial year by virtue of section 247 and was at any time within the year a member of a group of which the parent company was a public company.

**(2)** The report shall, with respect to the financial year immediately following that covered by the report, state–

(a) whether in respect of some or all of its suppliers it is the company's policy to follow any code or standard on payment practice and, if so, the name of the code or standard and the place where information about, and copies of, the code or standard can be obtained,

(b) whether in respect of some or all of its suppliers it is the company's policy–

(i) to settle the terms of payment with those suppliers when agreeing the terms of each transaction,

(ii) to ensure that those suppliers are made aware of the terms of payment, and

(iii) to abide by the terms of payment,

(c) where the company's policy is not as mentioned in paragraph (a) or (b) in respect of some or all of its suppliers, what its policy is with respect to the payment of those suppliers.

**(3)** If the company's policy is different for different suppliers or classes of suppliers, the report shall identify the suppliers or classes of suppliers to which the different policies apply.

**(4)** For the purposes of this Part of this Schedule a supplier is any person whose claim on the reporting company in respect of goods or services supplied would be included under "trade creditors" within "Creditors; amounts falling due within one year" in a balance sheet drawn up in accordance with balance sheet format 1 in Schedule 4."

Pt. VI originally inserted by the Companies Act 1985 (Miscellaneous Accounting Amendments) Regulations 1996 (SI 1996/189), reg. 1(1), 14(5) as from 2 February 1996, subject to reg. 16(1), (2).

# Schedule 8 – Form and Content of Accounts Prepared by Small Companies

[Companies Act 1985, s. 246]

## Part I – General Rules and Formats

### SECTION A – GENERAL RULES

**1(1)** Subject to the following provisions of this Schedule–

(a) every balance sheet of a small company shall show the items listed in either of the balance sheet formats set out below in section B of this Part; and

(b) every profit and loss account of a small company shall show the items listed in any one of the profit and loss account formats so set out;

in either case in the order and under the headings and sub-headings given in the format adopted.

**1(2)** Sub-paragraph (1) above is not to be read as requiring the heading or sub-heading for any item to be distinguished by any letter or number assigned to that item in the format adopted.

**2(1)** Where in accordance with paragraph 1 a small company's balance sheet or profit and loss account for any financial year has been prepared by reference to one of the formats set out in section B below, the directors of the company shall adopt the same format in preparing the accounts for subsequent financial years of the company unless in their opinion there are special reasons for a change.

**2(2)** Particulars of any change in the format adopted in preparing a small company's balance sheet or profit and loss account in accordance with paragraph 1 shall be disclosed, and the reasons for the change shall be explained, in a note to the accounts in which the new format is first adopted.

**3(1)** Any item required in accordance with paragraph 1 to be shown in a small company's balance sheet or profit and loss account may be shown in greater detail than required by the format adopted.

**3(2)** A small company's balance sheet or profit and loss account may include an item representing or covering the amount of any asset or liability, income or expenditure not otherwise covered by any of the items listed in the format adopted, but the following shall not be treated as assets in any small company's balance sheet–

(a) preliminary expenses;

(b) expenses of and commission on any issue of shares or debentures; and

(c) costs of research.

**3(3)** In preparing a small company's balance sheet or profit and loss account the directors of the company shall adapt the arrangement and headings and sub-headings otherwise required by paragraph 1 in respect of items to which an Arabic number is assigned in the format adopted, in any case where the special nature of the company's business requires such adaptation.

**3(4)** Items to which Arabic numbers are assigned in any of the formats set out in section B below may be combined in a small company's accounts for any financial year if either–

(a) their individual amounts are not material to assessing the state of affairs or profit or loss of the company for that year; or

(b) the combination facilitates that assessment;

but in a case within paragraph (b) the individual amounts of any items so combined shall be disclosed in a note to the accounts.

**3(5)** Subject to paragraph 4(3) below, a heading or sub-heading corresponding to an item listed in the format adopted in preparing a small company's balance sheet or profit and loss account shall not be included if there is no amount to be shown for that item in respect of the financial year to which the balance sheet or profit and loss account relates.

**3(6)** Every profit and loss account of a small company shall show the amount of the company's profit or loss on ordinary activities before taxation.

**3(7)** Every profit and loss account of a small company shall show separately as additional items–

(a) any amount set aside or proposed to be set aside to, or withdrawn or proposed to be withdrawn from, reserves;

(b) the aggregate amount of any dividends paid and proposed.

**4(1)** In respect of every item shown in a small company's balance sheet or profit and loss account the corresponding amount for the financial year immediately preceding that to which the balance sheet or profit and loss account relates shall also be shown.

**4(2)** Where that corresponding amount is not comparable with the amount to be shown for the item in question in respect of the financial year to which the balance sheet or profit and loss account relates, the former amount shall be adjusted and particulars of the adjustment and the reasons for it shall be disclosed in a note to the accounts.

**4(3)** Paragraph 3(5) does not apply in any case where an amount can be shown for the item in question in respect of the financial year immediately preceding that to which the balance sheet or profit and loss account relates, and that amount shall be shown under the heading or sub-heading required by paragraph 1 for that item.

**5** Amounts in respect of items representing assets or income may not be set off against amounts in respect of items representing liabilities or expenditure (as the case may be), or vice versa.

## SECTION B – THE REQUIRED FORMATS FOR ACCOUNTS

### Preliminary

**6** References in this Part of this Schedule to the items listed in any of the formats set out below are to those items read together with any of the notes following the formats which apply to any of those items, and the requirement imposed by paragraph 1 to show the items listed in any such format in the order adopted in the format is subject to any provision in those notes for alternative positions for any particular items.

**7** A number in brackets following any item in any of the formats set out below is a reference to the note of that number in the notes following the formats.

**8** In the notes following the formats–

(a) the heading of each note gives the required heading or sub-heading for the item to which it applies and a reference to any letters and numbers assigned to that item in the formats set out below (taking a reference in the case of Format 2 of the balance sheet formats to the item listed under "Assets" or under "Liabilities" as the case may require); and

(b) references to a numbered format are to the balance sheet format or (as the case may require) to the profit and loss account format of that number set out below.

## Balance Sheet Formats

*Format 1*

A. Called up share capital not paid *(1)*

B. Fixed assets

I Intangible assets

1. Goodwill *(2)*
2. Other intangible assets *(3)*

II Tangible assets

1. Land and buildings
2. Plant and machinery etc.

III Investments

1. Shares in group undertakings and participating interests
2. Loans to group undertakings and undertakings in which the company has a participating interest
3. Other investments other than loans
4. Other investments *(4)*

C. Current assets

I Stocks

1. Stocks
2. Payments on account

II Debtors *(5)*

1. Trade debtors
2. Amounts owed by group undertakings and undertakings in which the company has a participating interest
3. Other debtors

III Investments

1. Shares in group undertakings
2. Other investments

IV Cash at bank and in hand

D. Prepayments and accrued income *(6)*

E. Creditors: amounts falling due within one year

1. Bank loans and overdrafts
2. Trade creditors
3. Amounts owed to group undertakings and undertakings in which the company has a participating interest
4. Other creditors *(7)*

F. Net current assets (liabilities) *(8)*

G. Total assets less current liabilities

H. Creditors: amounts falling due after more than one year

1. Bank loans and overdrafts
2. Trade creditors
3. Amounts owed to group undertakings and undertakings in which the company has a participating interest
4. Other creditors *(7)*

I. Provisions for liabilities and charges
J. Accruals and deferred income *(7)*
K. Capital and reserves
  I Called up share capital *(9)*
  II Share premium account
  III Revaluation reserve
  IV Other reserves
  V Profit and loss account

## Balance Sheet Formats

*Format 2*

ASSETS

A. Called up share capital not paid *(1)*

B. Fixed assets

  I Intangible assets
    1. Goodwill *(2)*
    2. Other intangible assets *(3)*
  II Tangible assets
    1. Land and buildings
    2. Plant and machinery etc.
  III Investments
    1. Shares in group undertakings and participating interests
    2. Loans to group undertakings and undertakings in which the company has a participating interest
    3. Other investments other than loans
    4. Other investments *(4)*

C. Current assets

  I Stocks
    1. Stocks
    2. Payments on account
  II Debtors *(5)*
    1. Trade debtors
    2. Amounts owed by group undertakings and undertakings in which the company has a participating interest
    3. Other debtors
  III Investments
    1. Shares in group undertakings
    2. Other investments
  IV Cash at bank and in hand

D. Prepayments and accrued income *(6)*

LIABILITIES

A. Capital and reserves

  I Called up share capital *(9)*
  II Share premium account
  III Revaluation reserve
  IV Other reserves

V Profit and loss account

B. Provisions for liabilities and charges

C. Creditors *(10)*

1. Bank loans and overdrafts
2. Trade creditors
3. Amounts owed to group undertakings and undertakings in which the company has a participating interest
4. Other creditors *(7)*

D. Accruals and deferred income *(7)*

## Notes on the balance sheet formats

*(1) Called up share capital not paid*

(Formats 1 and 2, items A and C.II.3.)

This item may either be shown at item A or included under item C.II.3 in Format 1 or 2.

*(2) Goodwill*

(Formats 1 and 2, item B.I.1.)

Amounts representing goodwill shall only be included to the extent that the goodwill was acquired for valuable consideration.

*(3) Other intangible assets*

(Formats 1 and 2, item B.I.2.)

Amounts in respect of concessions, patents, licences, trade marks and similar rights and assets shall only be included in a company's balance sheet under this item if either–

(a) the assets were acquired for valuable consideration and are not required to be shown under goodwill; or

(b) the assets in question were created by the company itself.

*(4) Others: Other investments*

(Formats 1 and 2, items B.III.4 and C.III.2.)

Where amounts in respect of own shares held are included under either of these items, the nominal value of such shares shall be shown separately.

*(5) Debtors*

(Formats 1 and 2, items C.II.1 to 3.)

The amount falling due after more than one year shall be shown separately for each item included under debtors unless the aggregate amount of debtors falling due after more than one year is disclosed in the notes to the accounts.

*(6) Prepayments and accrued income*

(Formats 1 and 2, item D.)

This item may alternatively be included under item C.II.3 in Format 1 or 2.

*(7) Other creditors*

(Format 1, items E.4, H.4 and J and Format 2, items C.4 and D.)

There shall be shown separately–

(a) the amount of any convertible loans, and

(b) the amount for creditors in respect of taxation and social security.

Payments received on account of orders shall be included in so far as they are not shown as deductions from stocks.

In Format 1, accruals and deferred income may be shown under item J or included under item E.4 or H.4, or both (as the case may require). In Format 2, accruals and deferred income may be shown under item D or within item C.4 under Liabilities.

*(8) Net current assets (liabilities)*

(Format 1, item F.)

In determining the amount to be shown under this item any prepayments and accrued income shall be taken into account wherever shown.

*(9) Called up share capital*

(Format 1, item K.I and Format 2, item A.I.)

The amount of allotted share capital and the amount of called up share capital which has been paid up shall be shown separately.

*(10) Creditors*

(Format 2, items C.1 to 4.)

Amounts falling due within one year and after one year shall be shown separately for each of these items and for the aggregate of all of these items unless the aggregate amount of creditors falling due within one year and the aggregate amount of creditors falling due after more than one year is disclosed in the notes to the accounts.

## Profit and loss account formats

*Format 1*

*(see note (14) below)*

1. Turnover
2. Cost of sales *(11)*
3. Gross profit or loss
4. Distribution costs *(11)*
5. Administrative expenses *(11)*
6. Other operating income
7. Income from shares in group undertakings
8. Income from participating interests
9. Income from other fixed asset investments *(12)*
10. Other interest receivable and similar income *(12)*
11. Amounts written off investments
12. Interest payable and similar charges *(13)*
13. Tax on profit or loss on ordinary activities
14. Profit or loss on ordinary activities after taxation
15. Extraordinary income
16. Extraordinary charges
17. Extraordinary profit or loss
18. Tax on extraordinary profit or loss
19. Other taxes not shown under the above items
20. Profit or loss for the financial year

## Profit and loss account formats

*Format 2*

1. Turnover
2. Change in stocks of finished goods and in work in progress
3. Own work capitalised
4. Other operating income
5. (a) Raw materials and consumables
   (b) Other external charges
6. Staff costs:
   (a) wages and salaries
   (b) social security costs
   (c) other pension costs
7. (a) Depreciation and other amounts written off tangible and intangible fixed assets
   (b) Exceptional amounts written off current assets
8. Other operating charges

9. Income from shares in group undertakings
10. Income from participating interests
11. Income from other fixed asset investments *(12)*
12. Other interest receivable and similar income *(12)*
13. Amounts written off investments
14. Interest payable and similar charges *(13)*
15. Tax on profit or loss on ordinary activities
16. Profit or loss on ordinary activities after taxation
17. Extraordinary income
18. Extraordinary charges
19. Extraordinary profit or loss
20. Tax on extraordinary profit or loss
21. Other taxes not shown under the above items
22. Profit or loss for the financial year

## Profit and loss account formats

*Format 3*

*(see note (14) below)*

A. Charges

1. Cost of sales *(11)*
2. Distribution costs *(11)*
3. Administrative expenses *(11)*
4. Amounts written off investments
5. Interest payable and similar charges *(13)*
6. Tax on profit or loss on ordinary activities
7. Profit or loss on ordinary activities after taxation
8. Extraordinary charges
9. Tax on extraordinary profit or loss
10. Other taxes not shown under the above items
11. Profit or loss for the financial year

B. Income

1. Turnover
2. Other operating income
3. Income from shares in group undertakings
4. Income from participating interests
5. Income from other fixed asset investments *(12)*
6. Other interest receivable and similar income *(12)*
7. Profit or loss on ordinary activities after taxation
8. Extraordinary income
9. Profit or loss for the financial year

## Profit and loss account formats

*Format 4*

A. Charges

1. Reduction in stocks of finished goods and in work in progress
2. (a) Raw materials and consumables
   (b) Other external charges
3. Staff costs:
   (a) wages and salaries
   (b) social security costs
   (c) other pension costs
4. (a) Depreciation and other amounts written off tangible and intangible fixed assets

(b) Exceptional amounts written off current assets
5. Other operating charges
6. Amounts written off investments
7. Interest payable and similar charges *(13)*
8. Tax on profit or loss on ordinary activities
9. Profit or loss on ordinary activities after taxation
10. Extraordinary charges
11. Tax on extraordinary profit or loss
12. Other taxes not shown under the above items
13. Profit or loss for the financial year

B. Income
1. Turnover
2. Increase in stocks of finished goods and in work in progress
3. Own work capitalised
4. Other operating income
5. Income from shares in group undertakings
6. Income from participating interests
7. Income from other fixed asset investments (12)
8. Other interest receivable and similar income (12)
9. Profit or loss on ordinary activities after taxation
10. Extraordinary income
11. Profit or loss for the financial year

## Notes on the profit and loss account formats

*(11) Cost of sales: distribution costs: administrative expenses*

(Format 1, items 2, 4 and 5 and Format 3, items A.1, 2 and 3.)

These items shall be stated after taking into account any necessary provisions for depreciation or diminution in value of assets.

*(12) Income from other fixed asset investments: other interest receivable and similar income*

(Format 1, items 9 and 10: Format 2, items 11 and 12: Format 3, items B.5 and 6: Format 4, items B.7 and 8.)

Income and interest derived from group undertakings shall be shown separately from income and interest derived from other sources.

*(13) Interest payable and similar charges*

(Format 1, item 12: Format 2, item 14: Format 3, item A.5: Format 4, item A.7.)

The amount payable to group undertakings shall be shown separately.

*(14) Formats 1 and 3*

The amount of any provisions for depreciation and diminution in value of tangible and intangible fixed assets falling to be shown under items 7(a) and A.4(a) respectively in Formats 2 and 4 shall be disclosed in a note to the accounts in any case where the profit and loss account is prepared by reference to Format 1 or Format 3.

# Part II – Accounting Principles and Rules

## SECTION A – ACCOUNTING PRINCIPLES

### Preliminary

**9** Subject to paragraph 15 below, the amounts to be included in respect of all items shown in a small company's accounts shall be determined in accordance with the principles set out in paragraphs 10 to 14.

## Accounting principles

**10** The company shall be presumed to be carrying on business as a going concern.

**11** Accounting policies shall be applied consistently within the same accounts and from one financial year to the next.

**12** The amount of any item shall be determined on a prudent basis, and in particular–

(a) only profits realised at the balance sheet date shall be included in the profit and loss account; and

(b) all liabilities and losses which have arisen or are likely to arise in respect of the financial year to which the accounts relate or a previous financial year shall be taken into account, including those which only become apparent between the balance sheet date and the date on which it is signed on behalf of the board of directors in pursuance of section 233 of this Act.

**13** All income and charges relating to the financial year to which the accounts relate shall be taken into account, without regard to the date of receipt or payment.

**14** In determining the aggregate amount of any item the amount of each individual asset or liability that falls to be taken into account shall be determined separately.

## Departure from the accounting principles

**15** If it appears to the directors of a small company that there are special reasons for departing from any of the principles stated above in preparing the company's accounts in respect of any financial year they may do so, but particulars of the departure, the reasons for it and its effect shall be given in a note to the accounts.

## SECTION B – HISTORICAL COST ACCOUNTING RULES

### Preliminary

**16** Subject to section C of this Part of this Schedule, the amounts to be included in respect of all items shown in a small company's accounts shall be determined in accordance with the rules set out in paragraphs 17 to 28.

### Fixed assets

*General rules*

**17** Subject to any provision for depreciation or diminution in value made in accordance with paragraph 18 or 19 the amount to be included in respect of any fixed asset shall be its purchase price or production cost.

**18** In the case of any fixed asset which has a limited useful economic life, the amount of–

(a) its purchase price or production cost; or

(b) where it is estimated that any such asset will have a residual value at the end of the period of its useful economic life, its purchase price or production cost less that estimated residual value;

shall be reduced by provisions for depreciation calculated to write off that amount systematically over the period of the asset's useful economic life.

**19(1)** Where a fixed asset investment of a description falling to be included under item B.III of either of the balance sheet formats set out in Part I of this Schedule has diminished in value provisions for diminution in value may be made in respect of it and the amount to be included in respect of it may be reduced accordingly; and any such provisions which are not shown in the profit and loss account shall be disclosed (either separately or in aggregate) in a note to the accounts.

**19(2)** Provisions for diminution in value shall be made in respect of any fixed asset which has diminished in value if the reduction in its value is expected to be permanent (whether its useful economic life is limited or not), and the amount to be included in respect of it shall be reduced accordingly; and any such provisions which are not shown in the profit and loss account shall be disclosed (either separately or in aggregate) in a note to the accounts.

**19(3)** Where the reasons for which any provision was made in accordance with sub-paragraph (1) or (2) have ceased to apply to any extent, that provision shall be written back to the extent that it is no longer necessary; and any amounts written back in accordance with this sub-paragraph which are not shown in the profit and loss account shall be disclosed (either separately or in aggregate) in a note to the accounts.

*Rules for determining particular fixed asset items*

**20(1)** Notwithstanding that an item in respect of "development costs" is included under "fixed assets" in the balance sheet formats set out in Part I of this Schedule, an amount may only be included in a small company's balance sheet in respect of development costs in special circumstances.

**20(2)** If any amount is included in a small company's balance sheet in respect of development costs the following information shall be given in a note to the accounts–

(a) the period over which the amount of those costs originally capitalised is being or is to be written off; and

(b) the reasons for capitalising the development costs in question.

**21(1)** The application of paragraphs 17 to 19 in relation to goodwill (in any case where goodwill is treated as an asset) is subject to the following provisions of this paragraph.

**21(2)** Subject to sub-paragraph (3) below, the amount of the consideration for any goodwill acquired by a small company shall be reduced by provisions for depreciation calculated to write off that amount systematically over a period chosen by the directors of the company.

**21(3)** The period chosen shall not exceed the useful economic life of the goodwill in question.

**21(4)** In any case where any goodwill acquired by a small company is shown or included as an asset in the company's balance sheet the period chosen for writing off the consideration for that goodwill and the reasons for choosing that period shall be disclosed in a note to the accounts.

## Current assets

**22** Subject to paragraph 23, the amount to be included in respect of any current asset shall be its purchase price or production cost.

**23(1)** If the net realisable value of any current asset is lower than its purchase price or production cost the amount to be included in respect of that asset shall be the net realisable value.

**23(2)** Where the reasons for which any provision for diminution in value was made in accordance with sub-paragraph (1) have ceased to apply to any extent, that provision shall be written back to the extent that it is no longer necessary.

## Miscellaneous and supplementary provisions

*Excess of money owed over value received as an asset item*

**24(1)** Where the amount repayable on any debt owed by a small company is greater than the value of the consideration received in the transaction giving rise to the debt, the amount of the difference may be treated as an asset.

**24(2)** Where any such amount is so treated–

(a) it shall be written off by reasonable amounts each year and must be completely written off before repayment of the debt; and

(b) if the current amount is not shown as a separate item in the company's balance sheet it must be disclosed in a note to the accounts.

*Assets included at a fixed amount*

**25(1)** Subject to the following sub-paragraph, assets which fall to be included–

(a) amongst the fixed assets of a small company under the item "tangible assets"; or

(b) amongst the current assets of a small company under the item "raw materials and consumables";

may be included at a fixed quantity and value.

**25(2)** Sub-paragraph (1) applies to assets of a kind which are constantly being replaced, where–

(a) their overall value is not material to assessing the company's state of affairs; and

(b) their quantity, value and composition are not subject to material variation.

*Determination of purchase price or production cost*

**26(1)** The purchase price of an asset shall be determined by adding to the actual price paid any expenses incidental to its acquisition.

**26(2)** The production cost of an asset shall be determined by adding to the purchase price of the raw materials and consumables used the amount of the costs incurred by the company which are directly attributable to the production of that asset.

**26(3)** In addition, there may be included in the production cost of an asset–

(a) a reasonable proportion of the costs incurred by the company which are only indirectly attributable to the production of that asset, but only to the extent that they relate to the period of production; and

(b) interest on capital borrowed to finance the production of that asset, to the extent that it accrues in respect of the period of production;

provided, however, in a case within paragraph (b) above, that the inclusion of the interest in determining the cost of that asset and the amount of the interest so included is disclosed in a note to the accounts.

**26(4)** In the case of current assets distribution costs may not be included in production costs.

**27(1)** Subject to the qualification mentioned below, the purchase price or production cost of–

(a) any assets which fall to be included under any item shown in a small company's balance sheet under the general item "stocks"; and

(b) any assets which are fungible assets (including investments);

may be determined by the application of any of the methods mentioned in sub-paragraph (2) below in relation to any such assets of the same class.

The method chosen must be one which appears to the directors to be appropriate in the circumstances of the company.

**27(2)** Those methods are–

(a) the method known as "first in, first out" (FIFO);

(b) the method known as "last in, first out" (LIFO);

(c) a weighted average price; and

(d) any other method similar to any of the methods mentioned above.

**27(3)** For the purposes of this paragraph, assets of any description shall be regarded as fungible if assets of that description are substantially indistinguishable one from another.

*Substitution of original stated amount where price or cost unknown*

**28** Where there is no record of the purchase price or production cost of any asset of a small company or of any price, expenses or costs relevant for determining its purchase price or production cost in accordance with paragraph 26, or any such record cannot be obtained without unreasonable expense or delay, its purchase price or production cost shall be taken for the purposes of paragraphs 17 to 23 to be the value ascribed to it in the earliest available record of its value made on or after its acquisition or production by the company.

## SECTION C – ALTERNATIVE ACCOUNTING RULES

### Preliminary

**29(1)** The rules set out in section B are referred to below in this Schedule as the historical cost accounting rules.

**29(2)** Those rules, with the omission of paragraphs 16, 21 and 25 to 28, are referred to below in this Part of this Schedule as the depreciation rules; and references below in this Schedule to the historical cost accounting rules do not include the depreciation rules as they apply by virtue of paragraph 32.

**30** Subject to paragraphs 32 to 34, the amounts to be included in respect of assets of any description mentioned in paragraph 31 may be determined on any basis so mentioned.

## Alternative accounting rules

**31(1)** Intangible fixed assets, other than goodwill, may be included at their current cost.

**31(2)** Tangible fixed assets may be included at a market value determined as at the date of their last valuation or at their current cost.

**31(3)** Investments of any description falling to be included under item B.III of either of the balance sheet formats set out in Part I of this Schedule may be included either–

(a) at a market value determined as at the date of their last valuation; or

(b) at a value determined on any basis which appears to the directors to be appropriate in the circumstances of the company;

but in the latter case particulars of the method of valuation adopted and of the reasons for adopting it shall be disclosed in a note to the accounts.

**31(4)** Investments of any description falling to be included under item C.III of either of the balance sheet formats set out in Part I of this Schedule may be included at their current cost.

**31(5)** Stocks may be included at their current cost.

## Application of the depreciation rules

**32(1)** Where the value of any asset of a small company is determined on any basis mentioned in paragraph 31, that value shall be, or (as the case may require) be the starting point for determining, the amount to be included in respect of that asset in the company's accounts, instead of its purchase price or production cost or any value previously so determined for that asset; and the depreciation rules shall apply accordingly in relation to any such asset with the substitution for any reference to its purchase price or production cost of a reference to the value most recently determined for that asset on any basis mentioned in paragraph 31.

**32(2)** The amount of any provision for depreciation required in the case of any fixed asset by paragraph 18 or 19 as it applies by virtue of sub-paragraph (1) is referred to below in this paragraph as the adjusted amount, and the amount of any provision which would be required by that paragraph in the case of that asset according to the historical cost accounting rules is referred to as the historical cost amount.

**32(3)** Where sub-paragraph (1) applies in the case of any fixed asset the amount of any provision for depreciation in respect of that asset–

(a) included in any item shown in the profit and loss account in respect of amounts written off assets of the description in question; or

(b) taken into account in stating any item so shown which is required by note *(11)* of the notes on the profit and loss account formats set out in Part I of this Schedule to be stated after taking into account any necessary provision for depreciation or diminution in value of assets included under it;

may be the historical cost amount instead of the adjusted amount, provided that the amount of any difference between the two is shown separately in the profit and loss account or in a note to the accounts.

## Additional information to be provided in case of departure from historical cost accounting rules

**33(1)** This paragraph applies where the amounts to be included in respect of assets covered by any items shown in a small company's accounts have been determined on any basis mentioned in paragraph 31.

**33(2)** The items affected and the basis of valuation adopted in determining the amounts of the assets in question in the case of each such item shall be disclosed in a note to the accounts.

**33(3)** In the case of each balance sheet item affected (except stocks) either–

(a) the comparable amounts determined according to the historical cost accounting rules; or

(b) the differences between those amounts and the corresponding amounts actually shown in the balance sheet in respect of that item;

shall be shown separately in the balance sheet or in a note to the accounts.

**33(4)** In sub-paragraph (3) above, references in relation to any item to the comparable amounts determined as there mentioned are references to–

(a) the aggregate amount which would be required to be shown in respect of that item if the amounts to be included in respect of all the assets covered by that item were determined according to the historical cost accounting rules; and

(b) the aggregate amount of the cumulative provisions for depreciation or diminution in value which would be permitted or required in determining those amounts according to those rules.

### Revaluation reserve

**34(1)** With respect to any determination of the value of an asset of a small company on any basis mentioned in paragraph 31, the amount of any profit or loss arising from that determination (after allowing, where appropriate, for any provisions for depreciation or diminution in value made otherwise than by reference to the value so determined and any adjustments of any such provisions made in the light of that determination) shall be credited or (as the case may be) debited to a separate reserve ("the revaluation reserve").

**34(2)** The amount of the revaluation reserve shall be shown in the company's balance sheet under a separate sub-heading in the position given for the item "revaluation reserve" in Format 1 or 2 of the balance sheet formats set out in Part I of this Schedule, but need not be shown under that name.

**34(3)** An amount may be transferred–

(a) from the revaluation reserve–

 (i) to the profit and loss account, if the amount was previously charged to that account or represents realised profit, or

 (ii) on capitalisation,

(b) to or from the revaluation reserve in respect of the taxation relating to any profit or loss credited or debited to the reserve;

and the revaluation reserve shall be reduced to the extent that the amounts transferred to it are no longer necessary for the purposes of the valuation method used.

**34(4)** In sub-paragraph (3)(a)(ii) "capitalisation", in relation to an amount standing to the credit of the revaluation reserve, means applying it in wholly or partly paying up unissued shares in the company to be allotted to members of the company as fully or partly paid shares.

**34(5)** The revaluation reserve shall not be reduced except as mentioned in this paragraph.

**34(6)** The treatment for taxation purposes of amounts credited or debited to the revaluation reserve shall be disclosed in a note to the accounts.

# Part III – Notes to the Accounts

### Preliminary

**35** Any information required in the case of any small company by the following provisions of this Part of this Schedule shall (if not given in the company's accounts) be given by way of a note to those accounts.

### Disclosure of accounting policies

**36** The accounting policies adopted by the company in determining the amounts to be included in respect of items shown in the balance sheet and in determining the profit or loss of the company shall be stated (including such policies with respect to the depreciation and diminution in value of assets).

## Information supplementing the balance sheet

**37** Paragraphs 38 to 47 require information which either supplements the information given with respect to any particular items shown in the balance sheet or is otherwise relevant to assessing the company's state of affairs in the light of the information so given.

*Share capital and debentures*

**38(1)** The following information shall be given with respect to the company's share capital–

(a) the authorised share capital; and

(b) where shares of more than one class have been allotted, the number and aggregate nominal value of shares of each class allotted.

**38(2)** In the case of any part of the allotted share capital that consists of redeemable shares, the following information shall be given–

(a) the earliest and latest dates on which the company has power to redeem those shares;

(b) whether those shares must be redeemed in any event or are liable to be redeemed at the option of the company or of the shareholder; and

(c) whether any (and, if so, what) premium is payable on redemption.

**39** If the company has allotted any shares during the financial year, the following information shall be given–

(a) the classes of shares allotted; and

(b) as respects each class of shares, the number allotted, their aggregate nominal value, and the consideration received by the company for the allotment.

*Fixed assets*

**40(1)** In respect of each item which is or would but for paragraph 3(4)(b) be shown under the general item "fixed assets" in the company's balance sheet the following information shall be given–

(a) the appropriate amounts in respect of that item as at the date of the beginning of the financial year and as at the balance sheet date respectively;

(b) the effect on any amount shown in the balance sheet in respect of that item of–

(i) any revision of the amount in respect of any assets included under that item made during that year on any basis mentioned in paragraph 31;

(ii) acquisitions during that year of any assets;

(iii) disposals during that year of any assets; and

(iv) any transfers of assets of the company to and from that item during that year.

**40(2)** The reference in sub-paragraph (1)(a) to the appropriate amounts in respect of any item as at any date there mentioned is a reference to amounts representing the aggregate amounts determined, as at that date, in respect of assets falling to be included under that item on either of the following bases, that is to say–

(a) on the basis of purchase price or production cost (determined in accordance with paragraphs 26 and 27); or

(b) on any basis mentioned in paragraph 31,

(leaving out of account in either case any provisions for depreciation or diminution in value).

**40(3)** In respect of each item within sub-paragraph–

(a) the cumulative amount of provisions for depreciation or diminution in value of assets included under that item as at each date mentioned in sub-paragraph (1)(a);

(b) the amount of any such provisions made in respect of the financial year;

(c) the amount of any adjustments made in respect of any such provisions during that year in consequence of the disposal of any assets; and

(d) the amount of any other adjustments made in respect of any such provisions during that year;

shall also be stated.

**41** Where any fixed assets of the company (other than listed investments) are included under any item shown in the company's balance sheet at an amount determined on any basis mentioned in paragraph 31, the following information shall be given–

(a) the years (so far as they are known to the directors) in which the assets were severally valued and the several values; and

(b) in the case of assets that have been valued during the financial year, the names of the persons who valued them or particulars of their qualifications for doing so and (whichever is stated) the bases of valuation used by them.

*Investments*

**42(1)** In respect of the amount of each item which is or would but for paragraph 3(4)(b) be shown in the company's balance sheet under the general item "investments" (whether as fixed assets or as current assets) there shall be stated how much of that amount is ascribable to listed investments.

**42(2)** Where the amount of any listed investments is stated for any item in accordance with sub-paragraph (1), the following amounts shall also be stated–

(a) the aggregate market value of those investments where it differs from the amount so stated; and

(b) both the market value and the stock exchange value of any investments of which the former value is, for the purposes of the accounts, taken as being higher than the latter.

*Reserves and provisions*

**43(1)** Where any amount is transferred–

(a) to or from any reserves; or

(b) to any provisions for liabilities and charges; or

(c) from any provision for liabilities and charges otherwise than for the purpose for which the provision was established;

and the reserves or provisions are or would but for paragraph 3(4)(b) be shown as separate items in the company's balance sheet, the information mentioned in the following sub-paragraph shall be given in respect of the aggregate of reserves or provisions included in the same item.

**43(2)** That information is–

(a) the amount of the reserves or provisions as at the date of the beginning of the financial year and as at the balance sheet date respectively;

(b) any amounts transferred to or from the reserves or provisions during that year; and

(c) the source and application respectively of any amounts so transferred.

**43(3)** Particulars shall be given of each provision included in the item "other provisions" in the company's balance sheet in any case where the amount of that provision is material.

*Details of indebtedness*

**44(1)** For the aggregate of all items shown under "creditors" in the company's balance sheet there shall be stated the aggregate of the following amounts, that is to say–

(a) the amount of any debts included under "creditors" which are payable or repayable otherwise than by instalments and fall due for payment or repayment after the end of the period of five years beginning with the day next following the end of the financial year; and

(b) in the case of any debts so included which are payable or repayable by instalments, the amount of any instalments which fall due for payment after the end of that period.

**44(2)** In respect of each item shown under "creditors" in the company's balance sheet there shall be stated the aggregate amount of any debts included under that item in respect of which any security has been given by the company.

**44(3)** References above in this paragraph to an item shown under "creditors" in the company's balance sheet include references, where amounts falling due to creditors within one year and after more than one year are distinguished in the balance sheet–

(a) in a case within sub-paragraph (1), to an item shown under the latter of those categories; and

(b) in a case within sub-paragraph (2), to an item shown under either of those categories;

and references to items shown under "creditors" include references to items which would but for paragraph 3(4)(b) be shown under that heading.

**45** If any fixed cumulative dividends on the company's shares are in arrear, there shall be stated–

(a) the amount of the arrears; and

(b) the period for which the dividends or, if there is more than one class, each class of them are in arrear.

*Guarantees and other financial commitments*

**46(1)** Particulars shall be given of any charge on the assets of the company to secure the liabilities of any other person, including, where practicable, the amount secured.

**46(2)** The following information shall be given with respect to any other contingent liability not provided for–

(a) the amount or estimated amount of that liability;

(b) its legal nature; and

(c) whether any valuable security has been provided by the company in connection with that liability and if so, what.

**46(3)** There shall be stated, where practicable, the aggregate amount or estimated amount of contracts for capital expenditure, so far as not provided for.

**46(4)** Particulars shall be given of–

(a) any pension commitments included under any provision shown in the company's balance sheet; and

(b) any such commitments for which no provision has been made;

and where any such commitment relates wholly or partly to pensions payable to past directors of the company separate particulars shall be given of that commitment so far as it relates to such pensions.

**46(5)** Particulars shall also be given of any other financial commitments which–

(a) have not been provided for; and

(b) are relevant to assessing the company's state of affairs.

**46(6)** Commitments within any of sub-paragraphs (1) to (5) which are undertaken on behalf of or for the benefit of–

(a) any parent undertaking or fellow subsidiary undertaking, or

(b) any subsidiary undertaking of the company,

shall be stated separately from the other commitments within that sub-paragraph, and commitments within paragraph (a) shall also be stated separately from those within paragraph (b).

*Miscellaneous matters*

**47** Particulars shall be given of any case where the purchase price or production cost of any asset is for the first time determined under paragraph 28.

## Information supplementing the profit and loss account

**48** Paragraphs 49 and 50 require information which either supplements the information given with respect to any particular items shown in the profit and loss account or otherwise provides particulars of income or expenditure of the company or of circumstances affecting the items shown in the profit and loss account.

*Particulars of turnover*

**49(1)** If the company has supplied geographical markets outside the United Kingdom during the financial year in question, there shall be stated the percentage of its turnover that, in the opinion of the directors, is attributable to those markets.

**49(2)** In analysing for the purposes of this paragraph the source of turnover, the directors of the company shall have regard to the manner in which the company's activities are organised.

*Miscellaneous matters*

**50(1)** Where any amount relating to any preceding financial year is included in any item in the profit and loss account, the effect shall be stated.

**50(2)** Particulars shall be given of any extraordinary income or charges arising in the financial year.

**50(3)** The effect shall be stated of any transactions that are exceptional by virtue of size or incidence though they fall within the ordinary activities of the company.

### General

**51(1)** Where sums originally denominated in foreign currencies have been brought into account under any items shown in the balance sheet or profit and loss account, the basis on which those sums have been translated into sterling shall be stated.

**51(2)** Subject to the following sub-paragraph, in respect of every item stated in a note to the accounts the corresponding amount for the financial year immediately preceding that to which the accounts relate shall also be stated and where the corresponding amount is not comparable, it shall be adjusted and particulars of the adjustment and the reasons for it shall be given.

**51(3)** Sub-paragraph (2) does not apply in relation to any amounts stated by virtue of any of the following provisions of this Act–

(a) paragraph 13 of Schedule 4A (details of accounting treatment of acquisitions),

(b) paragraphs 2, 8(3), 16, 21(1)(d), 22(4) and (5), 24(3) and (4) and 27(3) and (4) of Schedule 5 (shareholdings in other undertakings),

(c) Parts II and III of Schedule 6 (loans and other dealings in favour of directors and others), and

(d) paragraphs 40 and 43 above (fixed assets and reserves and provisions).

### Dormant companies acting as agents

**51A** Where the directors of a company take advantage of the exemption conferred by section 249AA, and the company has during the financial year in question acted as an agent for any person, the fact that it has so acted must be stated.

**History**

Para. 51A inserted by the Companies Act 1985 (Audit Exemption) (Amendment) Regulations 2000 (SI 2000/1430), reg. 1, 6 as from 26 May 2000 in relation to annual accounts and reports in respect of financial years ending on or after 26 July 2000.

## Part IV – Interpretation of Schedule

**52** The following paragraphs apply for the purposes of this Schedule and its interpretation.

*Historial cost accounting rules*

**53** References to the historical cost accounting rules shall be read in accordance with paragraph 29.

*Listed investments*

**54** "Listed investment" means an investment as respects which there has been granted a listing on a recognised investment exchange other than an overseas investment exchange within the meaning of the Financial Services Act 1986 or on any stock exchange of repute outside Great Britain.

*Loans*

**55** A loan is treated as falling due for repayment, and an instalment of a loan is treated as falling due for payment, on the earliest date on which the lender could require repayment or (as the case may be) payment, if he exercised all options and rights available to him.

*Materiality*

**56** Amounts which in the particular context of any provision of this Schedule are not material may be disregarded for the purposes of that provision.

*Provisions*

**57(1)** References to provisions for depreciation or diminution in value of assets are to any amount written off by way of providing for depreciation or diminution in value of assets.

**57(2)** Any reference in the profit and loss account formats set out in Part I of this Schedule to the depreciation of, or amounts written off, assets of any description is to any provision for depreciation or diminution in value of assets of that description.

**58** References to provisions for liabilities or charges are to any amount retained as reasonably necessary for the purpose of providing for any liability or loss which is either likely to be incurred, or certain to be incurred but uncertain as to amount or as to the date on which it will arise.

*Staff costs*

**59(1)** "Social security costs" means any contributions by the company to any state social security or pension scheme, fund or arrangement.

**59(2)** "Pension costs" includes any costs incurred by the company in respect of any pension scheme established for the purpose of providing pensions for persons currently or formerly employed by the company, any sums set aside for the future payment of pensions directly by the company to current or former employees and any pensions paid directly to such persons without having first been set aside.

**59(3)** Any amount stated in respect of the item "social security costs" or in respect of the item "wages and salaries" in the company's profit and loss account shall be determined by reference to payments made or costs incurred in respect of all persons employed by the company during the financial year under contracts of service.

**History**

Sch. 8 substituted for former Sch. 8 by the Companies Act 1985 (Accounts of Small and Medium-sized Companies and Minor Accounting Amendments) Regulations 1997 (SI 1997/220), reg. 1, 2(2) and Sch. 1 as from 1 March 1997.

Former Sch. 8 read as follows:

**"Schedule 8 – Exemptions for Small and Medium-sized Companies**

[CA 1985, s. 246; CA 1989, s. 1, 13(2), Sch. 6]

Part I – Exemptions with Respect to Preparation of Annual Accounts of Small Companies

Section A – Individual Accounts

**1** The following provisions of this Section of this Part of this Schedule apply to the individual accounts of a small company.

BALANCE SHEET

**2(1)** In preparing its balance sheet according to the balance sheet formats set out in Section B of Part I of Schedule 4, a small company may apply all or any of the modifications permitted by paragraphs 3 and 4 below.

**(2)** Where any such modifications are applied by a small company, Schedule 4 shall be read as if the balance sheet formats were the formats as modified and references to the formats and the items in them shall be construed accordingly.

**(3)** Subject to paragraph 5 below, the notes on the balance sheet formats shall continue to apply to items which have been renumbered or combined into other items by the modifications under paragraphs 3 or 4 below.

**(4)** For the purposes of paragraph 3(3) and (4) of Schedule 4 (power to adapt or combine items), any new item which may be included in a balance sheet by virtue of paragraphs 3 or 4 below shall be treated as one to which an Arabic number is assigned.

FORMAT 1

**3(1)** Format 1 may be modified as follows.

**(2)** Of the items (development costs etc.) required to be shown as sub-items of item B.I (intangible assets) there need only be shown the item "goodwill" and the other items may be combined in a new item "other intangible assets", to be shown after "goodwill".

**(3)** Of the items (land and buildings etc.) required to be shown as sub-items of item B.II (tangible assets) there need only be shown the item "land and buildings" and the other items may be combined in a new item "plant and machinery etc.", to be shown after "land and buildings".

**(4)** The following items (required to be shown as sub-items of item B.III (investments)) may be combined as follows–

(a) item B.III.1 (shares in group undertakings) may be combined with item B.III.3 (participating interests) in a new item under the heading "shares in group undertakings and participating interests", to be shown as the first item under the heading "investments",

(b) item B.III.2 (loans to group undertakings) may be combined with item B.III.4 (loans to undertakings in which the company has a participating interest) in a new item under the heading "loans to group undertakings and undertakings in which the company has a participating interest", to be shown after the new item mentioned in paragraph (a), and

(c) item B.III.6 (other loans) may be combined with item B.III.7 (own shares) in a new item under the heading "others", to be shown after item B.III.5 (other investments other than loans).

**(5)** Of the items (raw materials and consumables etc.) required to be shown as sub-items of item C.I (stocks) there need only be shown the item "payments on account" and the other items may be combined in a new item "stocks", to be shown before "payments on account".

**(6)** The following items (required to be shown as sub-items of item C.II (debtors)) may be combined as follows–

(a) item C.II.2 (amounts owed by group undertakings) may be combined with item C.II.3 (amounts owed by undertakings in which the company has a participating interest) in a new item under the heading "amounts owed by group undertakings and undertakings in which the company has a participating interest", to be shown after item C.II.1 (trade debtors),

(b) item C.II.4 (other debtors) may be combined together with item C.II.5 (called up share capital not paid) and item C.II.6 (prepayments and accrued income) in a new item under the heading "others", to be shown after the new item mentioned in paragraph (a).

**(7)** Of the items (shares in group undertakings etc.) required to be shown as sub-items of item C.III (investments) there need only be shown the item "shares in group undertakings and the other items may be combined in a new item other investments", to be shown after "shares in group undertakings".

**(8)** The following items (required to be shown as sub-items of item E (creditors: amounts falling due within one year)) may be combined as follows–

(a) item E.6 (amounts owed to group undertakings) may be combined with item E.7 (amounts owed to undertakings in which the company has a participating interest) in a new item under the heading "amounts owed to group undertakings and undertakings in which the company has a participating interest", to be shown after item E.2 (bank loans and overdrafts) and item E.4 (trade creditors), and

(b) item E.1 (debenture loans), item E.3 (payments received on account), item E.5 (bills of exchange payable), item E.8 (other creditors including taxation and social security) and item E.9 (accruals and deferred income) may be combined in a new item under the heading "other creditors", to be shown after the new item mentioned in paragraph (a).

**(9)** The following items (required to be shown as sub-items of item H (creditors: amounts falling due after more than one year)) may be combined as follows–

(a) item H.6 (amounts owed to group undertakings) may be combined with item H.7 (amounts owed to undertakings in which the company has a participating interest) in a new item under the heading "amounts owed to group undertakings and undertakings in which the company has a participating interest", to be shown after item H.2 (bank loans and overdrafts) and item H.4 (trade creditors), and

(b) item H.1 (debenture loans), item H.3 (payments received on account), item H.5 (bills of exchange payable), item H.8 (other creditors including taxation and social security) and item H.9 (accruals and deferred income) may be combined in a new item under the heading "other creditors", to be shown after the new item mentioned in paragraph (a).

**(10)** The items (pensions and similar obligations etc.) required to be shown as sub-items of item I (provisions for liabilities and charges) and the items (capital redemption reserve etc.) required to be shown as sub-items of item K.IV (other reserves) need not be shown.

FORMAT 2

**4(1)** Format 2 may be modified as follows.

**(2)** Of the items (development costs etc.) required to be shown as sub-items of item B.I (intangible assets) under the general heading "ASSETS" there need only be shown the item "goodwill" and the other items may be combined in a new item "other intangible assets", to be shown after "goodwill".

**(3)** Of the items (land and buildings etc.) required to be shown as sub-items of item B.II (tangible assets) under the general heading "ASSETS" there need only be shown the item "land and buildings" and the other items may be combined in a new item "plant and machinery etc.", to be shown after "land and buildings".

**(4)** The following items (required to be shown as sub-items of item B.III (investments) under the general heading "ASSETS") may be combined as follows–

(a) item B.III.1 (shares in group undertakings) may be combined with item B.III.3 (participating interests) in a new item under the heading "shares in group undertakings and participating interests", to be shown as the first item under the heading "investments",

(b) item B.III.2 (loans to group undertakings) may be combined with item B.III.4 (loans to undertakings in which the company has a participating interest) in a new item under the heading "loans to group undertakings and undertakings in which the company has a participating interest", to be shown after the new item mentioned in paragraph (a), and

(c) item B.III.6 (other loans) may be combined with item B.III.7 (own shares) in a new item under the heading "others", to be shown after item B.III.5 (other investments other than loans).

**(5)** Of the items (raw materials and consumables etc.) required to be shown as sub-items of item C.I (stocks) under the general heading "ASSETS" there need only be shown the item "payments on account" and the other items may be combined in a new item "stocks", to be shown before "payments on account".

**(6)** The following items (required to be shown as sub-items of item C.II (debtors) under the general heading "ASSETS") may be combined as follows–

(a) item C.II.2 (amounts owed by group undertakings) may be combined with item C.II.3 (amounts owed by undertakings in which the company has a participating interest) in a new item under the heading "amounts owed by group undertakings and undertakings in which the company has a participating interest", to be shown after item C.II.1 (trade debtors),

(b) item C.II.4 (other debtors) may be combined together with item C.II.5 (called up share capital not paid) and item C.II.6 (prepayments and accrued income) in a new item under the heading "others", to be shown after the new item mentioned in paragraph (a).

**(7)** Of the items (shares in group undertakings etc.) required to be shown as sub-items of item C.III (investments) under the general heading "ASSETS" there need only be shown the item "shares in group undertakings" and the other items may be combined in a new item "other investments", to be shown after "shares in group undertakings".

**(8)** The following items (required to be shown as sub-items of item C (creditors) under the general heading "LIABILITIES") may be combined as follows–

(a) item C.6 (amounts owed to group undertakings) may be combined with item C.7 (amounts owed to undertakings in which the company has a participating interest) in a new item under the heading "amounts owed to group undertakings and undertakings in which the company has a participating interest", to be shown after the items for "bank loans and overdrafts" and "trade creditors", and

(b) item C.1 (debenture loans), item C.3 (payments received on account), item C.5 (bills of exchange payable), item C.8 (other creditors including taxation and social security) and item C.9 (accruals and deferred income) may be combined in a new item under the heading "other creditors", to be shown after the new item mentioned in paragraph (a).

**(9)** The items (pensions and similar obligations etc.) required to be shown as sub-items of item B (provisions for liabilities and charges) under the general heading "LIABILITIES" and the items (capital redemption reserve etc.) required to be shown as sub-items of item A.IV (other reserves) under the general heading "LIABILITIES" need not be shown.

THE NOTES ON THE BALANCE SHEET FORMATS

**5** With regard to the notes on the balance sheet formats set out in Section B of Part I to Schedule 4, a small company–

(a) in the case both of Format 1 and of Format 2, need not comply with the requirements of note (5) if it discloses in the notes to its accounts the aggregate amount included under "debtors" (item C.II in Format 1 and item C.II under the general heading "ASSETS" in Format 2) falling due after more than one year, and

(b) in the case of Format 2, need not comply with the requirements of note (13) if it discloses in the notes to its accounts the aggregate amount included under "creditors" (item C under the general heading "LIABILITIES") falling due within one year and the aggregate amount falling due after one year.

THE NOTES TO THE ACCOUNTS

**6** A small company need not set out in the notes to its accounts any information required by the following paragraphs of Schedule 4–

40 contingent right to allotment of shares),
41 (debentures),
44 (land and buildings),
47 (provision for taxation),
48(2) (particulars of debts),
48(4)(b) (nature of security given for debts),
51(2) (loans provided by way of financial assistance for purchase of own shares),
51(3) (dividend),
53 (separate statement of certain items of income and expenditure),
54 (particulars of tax),
56 (particulars of staff).

**7** Where any assets are included in the accounts of a small company at a value determined by the application of a method permitted by paragraph 27 of Schedule 4, the notes to the accounts need not disclose any information required by paragraph 27(3).

**8** A small company may comply with paragraph 48(1) of Schedule 4 (disclosure of debts repayable in more than 5 years) as if that paragraph stated that the information required by it was to be given in aggregate for all items shown under "creditors" in the company's balance sheet rather than in respect of each such item.

**9(1)** Subject to sub-paragraph (2) below, a small company need not give the information required by paragraph 55 of Schedule 4 (particulars of turnover).

**(2)** If the company has supplied geographical markets outside the United Kingdom during the financial year in question, the notes to the accounts shall state the percentage of its turnover that, in the opinion of the company's directors, is attributable to those markets.

**(4)** Paragraph 55(3) of Schedule 4 shall apply for the purposes of sub-paragraph (2) above.

**10** A small company need not comply with paragraph 59 of Schedule 4 (dealings with or interests in group undertakings).

**11** A small company need not give the information required by paragraph 4 (financial years of subsidiary undertakings) or paragraph 5(2) (valuation of investment in subsidiary undertakings by equity method) of Schedule 5.

**12** A small company need not give the information required by paragraph 1(3) (breakdown of aggregate amount of directors' emoluments), paragraphs 2 to 5 (details of chairman's and directors' emoluments) or paragraph 7 (pensions of directors and past directors) of Schedule 6.

Section B – Group Accounts

**13(1)** Subject to sub-paragraph (2), where a small company–

(a) has prepared individual accounts for a financial year in accordance with any exemptions set out in Section A of this Part of this Schedule, and

(b) is preparing group accounts in respect of the same year,

it may prepare those group accounts in accordance with the exemptions set out in Section A of this Part of this Schedule.

**(2)** In preparing the consolidated balance sheet the company–

(a) when using either balance sheet format set out in Section B of Part I of Schedule 4, shall not combine item B.III.1 (shares in group undertakings) with item B.III.3 (participating interests), and

(b) when applying the exemptions set out in paragraphs 3(4)(b) and 4(4)(b) of Section A of this Part of this Schedule, shall read the reference in each paragraph to the new item mentioned in paragraph (a) as a reference to the two items which will in each case replace item B.III.3 by virtue of paragraph 21 of Schedule 4A.

**(3)** Paragraph 1(1) of Schedule 4A shall have effect subject to the exemptions in question.

Section C – Supplementary Provisions

**14(1)** This paragraph applies where a small company has prepared annual accounts in accordance with any exemptions set out in this Part of this Schedule.

**(2)** The annual accounts of the company shall not be deemed, by reason only of the fact that advantage has been taken of any exemptions set out in this Part of this Schedule, not to give a true and fair view as required by this Act.

**(3)** Where a company is entitled to, and has taken advantage of, any exemptions set out in this Part of this Schedule, section 235(2) only requires the auditors to state whether in their opinion the annual accounts have been properly prepared in accordance with the provisions of this Act applicable to small companies.

Part II – Exemptions with Respect to Directors' Report

**15** The directors' report of a small company need not give any of the information required by or under the following provisions–

(a) section 234(1)(a) and (b) (fair review of business, amount to be paid as dividend and amount to be carried to reserves),

(b) paragraph 1(2) of Schedule 7 (statement of market value of fixed assets where substantially different from balance sheet amount),

(f) paragraph 11 of Schedule 7 (employee involvement).

Part III – Exemptions with Respect to Delivery of Accounts

**16** In this Part of this Schedule–

Section A relates to small companies,
Section B relates to medium-sized companies, and
Section C contains supplementary provisions.

Section A – Small Companies

BALANCE SHEET

**17(1)** The company may deliver a copy of an abbreviated version of the full balance sheet, showing only those items to which a letter or Roman number is assigned in the balance sheet format adopted under Part I of Schedule 4, but in other respects corresponding to the full balance sheet.

**(2)** If a copy of an abbreviated balance sheet is delivered, there shall be disclosed in it or in a note to the company's accounts delivered–

(a) the aggregate of the amounts required by note (5) of the notes on the balance sheet formats set out in Part I of Schedule 4 to be shown separately for each item included under debtors (amounts falling due after one year), and

(b) the aggregate of the amounts required by note (13) of those notes to be shown separately for each item included under creditors in Format 2 (amounts falling due within one year or after more than one year).

**(3)** The provisions of section 233 as to the signing of the copy of the balance sheet delivered to the registrar apply to a copy of an abbreviated balance sheet delivered in accordance with this paragraph.

PROFIT AND LOSS ACCOUNT

**18** A copy of the company's profit and loss account need not be delivered.

DISCLOSURE OF INFORMATION IN NOTES TO ACCOUNTS

**19(1)** Of the information required by Part III of Schedule 4 (information to be given in notes to accounts if not given in the accounts themselves) only the information required by the following provisions need be given–

paragraph 36 (accounting policies),
paragraph 38 (share capital),
paragraph 39 (particulars of allotments),
paragraph 42 (fixed assets), so far as it relates to those items to which a letter or Roman number is assigned in the balance sheet format adopted,
paragraph 48(1) and (4)(a) (particulars of debts),
paragraph 58(1) (basis of conversion of foreign currency amounts into sterling),
paragraph 58(2) (corresponding amounts for previous financial year), so far as it relates to amounts stated in a note to the company's accounts by virtue of a requirement of Schedule 4 or under any other provision of this Act.

**(2)** Of the information required by Schedule 5 to be given in notes to the accounts, the information required by the following provisions need not be given–

paragraph 4 (financial years of subsidiary undertakings),
paragraph 5 (additional information about subsidiary undertakings),
paragraph 6 (shares and debentures of company held by subsidiary undertakings),
paragraph 10 (arrangements attracting merger relief).

**(3)** Of the information required by Schedule 6 to be given in notes to the accounts, the information required by Part I (directors' and chairman's emoluments, pensions and compensation for loss of office) need not be given.

**(4)** The information required by section 390A(3) (amount of auditors' remuneration) need not be given.

DIRECTORS' REPORT

**20** A copy of the directors' report need not be delivered.

Section B – Medium-sized Companies

PROFIT AND LOSS ACCOUNT

**21** The company may deliver a profit and loss account in which the following items listed in the profit and loss account formats set out in Part I of Schedule 4 are combined as one item under the heading "gross profit or loss"–

Items 1, 2, 3 and 6 in Format 1;
Items 1 to 5 in Format 2;
Items A.1, B.1 and B.2 in Format 3;
Items A.1, A.2 and B.1 to B.4 in Format 4.

DISCLOSURE OF INFORMATION IN NOTES TO ACCOUNTS

**22** The information required by paragraph 55 of Schedule 4 (particulars of turnover) need not be given.

Section C – Supplementary Provisions

STATEMENT THAT ADVANTAGE TAKEN OF EXEMPTIONS

**23(1)** Where the directors of a company take advantage of the exemptions conferred by Section A or Section B of this Part of this Schedule, the company's balance sheet shall contain–

(a) a statement that advantage is taken of the exemptions conferred by Section A or, as the case may be, Section B Part of this Schedule, and

(b) a statement of the grounds on which, in the directors' opinion, the company is entitled to those exemptions.

**(2)** The statements shall appear in the balance sheet above the signature required by section 233.

SPECIAL AUDITORS' REPORT

**24(1)** If the directors of a company propose to take advantage of the exemptions conferred by Section A or Section B of this Part of this Schedule, it is the auditors' duty to provide them with a report stating whether in their opinion the company is entitled to those exemptions and whether the documents to be proposed to be delivered in accordance with this Schedule are properly prepared.

**(2)** The accounts delivered shall be accompanied by a special report of the auditors stating that in their opinion–
- (a) the company is entitled to the exemptions claimed in the directors' statement, and
- (b) the accounts to be delivered are properly prepared in accordance with this Schedule.

**(3)** In such a case a copy of the auditors' report under section 235 need not be delivered separately, but the full text of it shall be reproduced in the special report; and if the report under section 235 is qualified there shall be included in the special report any further material necessary to understand the qualification.

**(4)** Section 236 (signature of auditors' report) applies to a special report under this paragraph as it applies to a report under section 235.

DORMANT COMPANIES

**25** Paragraphs 23 and 24 above do not apply where the company is exempt by virtue of section 250 (dormant companies) from the obligation to appoint auditors.

OTHER COMPANIES EXEMPT FROM AUDIT

**25A** Paragraph 24 above does not apply where the company is exempt by virtue of section 249A (certain categories of small companies) from the obligation to appoint auditors.

REQUIREMENTS IN CONNECTION WITH PUBLICATION OF ACCOUNTS

**26(1)** Where advantage is taken of the exemptions conferred by Section A or Section B or this Part of this Schedule, section 240 (requirements in connection with publication of accounts) has effect with the following adaptations.

**(2)** Accounts delivered in accordance with this Part of this Schedule and accounts in the form in which they would be required to be delivered apart from this Part of this Schedule are both "statutory accounts" for the purposes of that section.

**(3)** References in that section to the auditors' report under section 235 shall be read, in relation to accounts delivered in accordance with this Part of this Schedule, as references to the special report under paragraph 24 above."

Previously to that, Sch. 8 substituted by CA 1989, s. 1, 13(2) and Sch. 6 as from 1 April 1990 subject to transitional and saving provisions (see SI 1990/355 (C 13), art. 3, Sch. 1 and also art. 6–9); Sch. 8 originally read as follows:

**"Schedule 8 – Modified Accounts of Companies Qualifying as Small or Medium Sized**

[Companies Act 1985, s. 247, 249,250, 253, 254]

Part I – Modified Individual Accounts

INTRODUCTORY

**1** In this Part of this Schedule–
- (a) paragraphs 2 to 6 relate to a company's individual accounts modified as for a small company,
- (b) paragraphs 7 and 8 relate to a company's individual accounts modified as for a medium-sized company, and
- (c) paragraphs 9 to 11 relate to both cases.

ACCOUNTS MODIFIED AS FOR A SMALL COMPANY

**2(1)** In respect of the relevant financial year, there may be delivered a copy of a modified balance sheet, instead of the full balance sheet.

**(2)** The modified balance sheet shall be an abbreviated version of the full balance sheet, showing only those items to which a letter or Roman number is assigned in the balance sheet format adopted under Schedule 4, Part I, but in other respects corresponding to the full balance sheet.

**(3)** The copy of the modified balance sheet shall be signed as required by section 238.

**3** A copy of the company's profit and loss account need not be delivered, nor a copy of the directors' report otherwise required by section 241.

**4** The information required by Parts V and VI of Schedule 5 need not be given.

**5** The information required by Schedule 4 to be given in notes to the accounts need not be given, with the exception of any information required by the following provisions of that Schedule–

paragraph 36 (accounting policies),
paragraph 38 (share capital),
paragraph 39 (particulars of allotments),
paragraph 48(1) and (4) (particulars of debts),
paragraph 58(1) (basis of translation of foreign currency amounts into sterling), and
paragraph 58(2) (corresponding amounts for preceding financial year);

and the reference here to paragraph 58(2) includes that sub-paragraph as applied to any item stated in a note to the company's accounts, whether by virtue of a requirement of Schedule 4 or under any other provision of this Act.

**6** If a modified balance sheet is delivered, there shall be disclosed in it (or in a note to the company's accounts delivered)–
- (a) the aggregate of the amounts required by note (5) of the notes on the balance sheet formats set out in Schedule 4 Part I to be shown separately for each item included under debtors (amounts falling due after one year), and
- (b) the aggregate of the amounts required by note (13) of those notes to be shown separately for each item included under creditors in Format 2 (amounts falling due within one year or after more than one year).

ACCOUNTS MODIFIED AS FOR A MEDIUM-SIZED COMPANY

**7(1)** There may be delivered a copy of a modified profit and loss account, instead of the company's full profit and loss account (that is, the profit and loss account prepared as under section 227).

**(2)** The modified profit and loss account shall, save for one exception, correspond to the full profit and loss account; and that exception is the combination as one item, under the heading "gross profit or loss", of the following items listed in the profit and loss account formats set out in Schedule 4 Part I–

Items 1, 2, 3 and 6 in Format 1;
Items 1 to 5 in Format 2;

Items A.1, B.1 and B.2 in Format 3; and
Items A.1, A.2 and B.1 to B.4 in Format 4.

8 The information required by paragraph 55 of Schedule 4 (particulars of turnover) need not be given.

BOTH CASES

9 The company's balance sheet shall contain a statement by the directors that–

(a) they rely on sections 247 to 249 of this Act as entitling them to deliver modified accounts, and

(b) they do so on the ground that the company is entitled to the benefit of those sections as a small or (as the case may be) a medium-sized company;

and the statement shall appear in the balance sheet immediately above the signatures of the directors.

10(1) The accounts delivered shall be accompanied by a special report of the auditors stating that in their opinion–

(a) the directors are entitled to deliver modified accounts in respect of the financial year, as claimed in the directors' statement, and

(b) any accounts comprised in the documents delivered as modified accounts are properly prepared as such in accordance with this Schedule.

(2) A copy of the auditors' report under section 236 need not be delivered; but the full text of it shall be reproduced in the special report under this paragraph.

(3) If the directors propose to rely on sections 247 to 249 as entitling them to deliver modified accounts, it is the auditors' duty to provide them with a report stating whether in their opinion the directors are so entitled, and whether the documents to be delivered as modified accounts are properly prepared in accordance with this Act.

11 Subject as above, where the directors rely on sections 247 to 249 in delivering any documents, and–

(a) the company is entitled to the benefit of those sections on the ground claimed by the directors in their statement under paragraph 9, and

(b) the accounts comprised in the documents delivered as modified accounts are properly prepared in accordance with this Schedule,

then section 241(3) has effect as if any document which by virtue of this Part of this Schedule is included in or omitted from the document delivered as modified accounts were (or, as the case may be, were not) required by this Act to be comprised in the company's accounts in respect of the financial year.

Part II – Modified Group Accounts (in Consolidated Form)

INTRODUCTORY

12 In this Part of this Schedule–

(a) paragraphs 13 to 17 relate to modified accounts for a small group, and

(b) paragraphs 18 and 19 relate to modified accounts for a medium-sized group.

SMALL GROUPS

13(1) In respect of the relevant financial year, there may be delivered a copy of a modified balance sheet, instead of the full consolidated balance sheet.

(2) The modified balance sheet shall be an abbreviated version of the full consolidated balance sheet, showing only those items to which a letter or Roman numeral is assigned in the balance sheet format adopted under Schedule 4 Part I, but in other respects corresponding to the full consolidated balance sheet.

14 A copy of the profit and loss account need not be delivered, nor a copy of the directors' report otherwise required by section 241.

15 The information required by Schedule 4 to be given in notes to group accounts need not be given, with the exception of any information required by provisions of that Schedule listed in paragraph 5 above.

16 There shall be disclosed in the modified balance sheet, or in a note to the group accounts delivered, aggregate amounts corresponding to those specified in paragraph 6 above.

17 The information required by Parts V and VI of Schedule 5 need not be given.

MEDIUM-SIZED GROUPS

18(1) There may be delivered a copy of a modified profit and loss account, instead of a full consolidated profit and loss account prepared as under section 229.

(2) The modified profit and loss account shall, save for one exception, correspond to the full consolidated profit and loss account; and that exception is the combination as one item, under the heading "gross profit or loss", of the items listed in the profit and loss account formats set out in Schedule 4 Part I which are specified in paragraph 7(2) above.

19 The information required by paragraph 55 of Schedule 4 (particulars of turnover) need not be given.

Part III – Modified Group Accounts (Consolidated or Other)

20 If modified group accounts are delivered, the following paragraphs apply.

21 The directors' statement required by paragraph 9 to be contained in the balance sheet shall include a statement that the documents delivered include modified group accounts, in reliance on section 250.

22(1) The auditors' special report under paragraph 10 shall include a statement that in their opinion–

(a) the directors are entitled to deliver modified group accounts, as claimed in their statement in the balance sheet, and

(b) any accounts comprised in the documents delivered as modified group accounts are properly prepared as such in accordance with this Schedule.

(2) A copy of the auditors' report under section 236 need not be delivered; but the full text of it shall be reproduced in the special report under paragraph 10.

(3) If the directors propose to rely on section 250 as entitling them to deliver modified group accounts, it is the auditors' duty to provide them with a report stating whether in their opinion the directors are so entitled, and whether the documents to be delivered as modified group accounts are properly prepared in accordance with this Schedule.

23 Subject as above, where the directors rely on section 250 in delivering any documents, and

(a) the company is entitled to the benefit of that section on the ground claimed by the directors in their statement in the balance sheet, and

(b) the accounts comprised in the documents delivered as modified accounts are properly prepared in accordance with this Schedule,

then section 241(3) has effect as if any document which by virtue of this Schedule is included in or omitted from the documents delivered as modified group accounts were (or, as the case may be, were not) required by this Act to be comprised in the company's accounts in respect of the financial year."

# Schedule 8A – Form and Content of Abbreviated Accounts of Small Companies Delivered to Registrar

[Companies Act 1985, s. 246]

## Part I – Balance Sheet Formats

**1** A small company may deliver to the registrar a copy of the balance sheet showing the items listed in either of the balance sheet formats set out in paragraph 2 below in the order and under the headings and sub-headings given in the format adopted, but in other respects corresponding to the full balance sheet.

**2** The formats referred to in paragraph 1 are as follows–

**Balance Sheet Formats**

*Format 1*

A. Called up share capital not paid
B. Fixed assets
  I Intangible assets
  II Tangible assets
  III Investments
C. Current assets
  I Stocks
  II Debtors *(1)*
  III Investments
  IV Cash at bank and in hand
D. Prepayments and accrued income
E. Creditors: amounts falling due within one year
F. Net current assets (liabilities)
G. Total assets less current liabilities
H. Creditors: amounts falling due after more than one year
I. Provisions for liabilities and charges
J. Accruals and deferred income
K. Capital and reserves
I Called up share capital
II Share premium account
III Revaluation reserve
IV Other reserves
V Profit and loss account

**Balance Sheet Formats**

*Format 2*

ASSETS
A. Called up share capital not paid
B. Fixed assets
  I Intangible assets
  II Tangible assets
  III Investments
C. Current assets
  I Stocks
  II Debtors *(1)*
  III Investments
  IV Cash at bank and in hand
D. Prepayments and accrued income

LIABILITIES

A. Capital and reserves

I Called up share capital

II Share premium account

III Revaluation reserve

IV Other reserves

V Profit and loss account

B. Provisions for liabilities and charges

C. Creditors *(2)*

D. Accruals and deferred income

### Notes on the balance sheet formats

*(1) Debtors*

(Formats 1 and 2, item C.II.)

The aggregate amount of debtors falling due after more than one year shall be shown separately, unless it is disclosed in the notes to the accounts.

*(2) Creditors*

(Format 2, Liabilities item C.)

The aggregate amount of creditors falling due within one year and of creditors falling due after more than one year shall be shown separately, unless it is disclosed in the notes to the accounts.

## Part II – Notes to the Accounts

### Preliminary

**3** Any information required in the case of any small company by the following provisions of this Part of this Schedule shall (if not given in the company's accounts) be given by way of a note to those accounts.

### Disclosure of accounting policies

**4** The accounting policies adopted by the company in determining the amounts to be included in respect of items shown in the balance sheet and in determining the profit or loss of the company shall be stated (including such policies with respect to the depreciation and diminution in value of assets).

### Information supplementing the balance sheet

*Share capital and debentures*

**5(1)** The following information shall be given with respect to the company's share capital–

(a) the authorised share capital; and

(b) where shares of more than one class have been allotted, the number and aggregate nominal value of shares of each class allotted.

**5(2)** In the case of any part of the allotted share capital that consists of redeemable shares, the following information shall be given–

(a) the earliest and latest dates on which the company has power to redeem those shares;

(b) whether those shares must be redeemed in any event or are liable to be redeemed at the option of the company or of the shareholder; and

(c) whether any (and, if so, what) premium is payable on redemption.

**6** If the company has allotted any shares during the financial year, the following information shall be given–

(a) the classes of shares allotted; and

(b) as respects each class of shares, the number allotted, their aggregate nominal value, and the consideration received by the company for the allotment.

*Fixed assets*

**7(1)** In respect of each item to which a letter or Roman number is assigned under the general item "fixed assets" in the company's balance sheet the following information shall be given–

(a) the appropriate amounts in respect of that item as at the date of the beginning of the financial year and as at the balance sheet date respectively;

(b) the effect on any amount shown in the balance sheet in respect of that item of–

(i) any revision of the amount in respect of any assets included under that item made during that year on any basis mentioned in paragraph 31 of Schedule 8;

(ii) acquisitions during that year of any assets;

(iii) disposals during that year of any assets; and

(iv) any transfers of assets of the company to and from that item during that year.

**7(2)** The reference in sub-paragraph (1)(a) to the appropriate amounts in respect of any item as at any date there mentioned is a reference to amounts representing the aggregate amounts determined, as at that date, in respect of assets falling to be included under that item on either of the following bases, that is to say–

(a) on the basis of purchase price or production cost (determined in accordance with paragraphs 26 and 27 of Schedule 8); or

(b) on any basis mentioned in paragraph 31 of that Schedule,

(leaving out of account in either case any provisions for depreciation or diminution in value).

**7(3)** In respect of each item within sub-paragraph–

(a) the cumulative amount of provisions for depreciation or diminution in value of assets included under that item as at each date mentioned in sub-paragraph (1)(a);

(b) the amount of any such provisions made in respect of the financial year;

(c) the amount of any adjustments made in respect of any such provisions during that year in consequence of the disposal of any assets; and

(d) the amount of any other adjustments made in respect of any such provisions during that year;

shall also be stated.

*Details of indebtedness*

**8(1)** For the aggregate of all items shown under "creditors" in the company's balance sheet there shall be stated the aggregate of the following amounts, that is to say–

(a) the amount of any debts included under "creditors" which are payable or repayable otherwise than by instalments and fall due for payment or repayment after the end of the period of five years beginning with the day next following the end of the financial year; and

(b) in the case of any debts so included which are payable or repayable by instalments, the amount of any instalments which fall due for payment after the end of that period.

**8(2)** In respect of each item shown under "creditors" in the company's balance sheet there shall be stated the aggregate amount of any debts included under that item, in respect of which any security has been given by the company.

## General

**9(1)** Where sums originally denominated in foreign currencies have been brought into account under any items shown in the balance sheet or profit and loss account, the basis on which those sums have been translated into sterling shall be stated.

**9(2)** Subject to the following sub-paragraph, in respect of every item required to be stated in a note to the accounts by or under any provision of this Act, the corresponding amount for the financial year immediately preceding that to which the accounts relate shall also be stated and where the corresponding amount is not comparable, it shall be adjusted and particulars of the adjustment and the reasons for it shall be given.

**9(3)** Sub-paragraph (2) does not apply in relation to any amounts stated by virtue of any of the following provisions of this Act–

(a) paragraph 13 of Schedule 4A (details of accounting treatment of acquisitions),
(b) paragraphs 2, 8(3), 16, 21(1)(d), 22(4) and (5), 24(3) and (4) and 27(3) and (4) of Schedule 5 (shareholdings in other undertakings),
(c) Parts II and III of Schedule 6 (loans and other dealings in favour of directors and others), and
(d) paragraph 7 above (fixed assets).

**Dormant companies acting as agents**

**9A** Where the directors of a company take advantage of the exemption conferred by section 249AA, and the company has during the financial year in question acted as an agent for any person, the fact that it has so acted must be stated.

**History**
Para. 9A inserted by the Companies Act 1985 (Audit Exemption) (Amendment) Regulations 2000 (SI 2000/1430), reg. 1, 7 as from 26 May 2000 in relation to annual accounts and reports in respect of financial years ending on or after 26 July 2000.

**History**
Sch. 8A inserted by the Companies Act 1985 (Accounts of Small and Medium-sized Companies and Minor Accounting Amendments) Regulations 1997 (SI 1997/220), reg . 1, 2(3) and Sch. 2 as from 1 March 1997.

# Schedule 9 – Special Provisions for Banking Companies and Groups

[Sections 255, 255A]

**History**
Pt. I–III of Sch. 9 inserted (with the above title to Sch. 9) by the Companies Act 1985 (Bank Accounts) Regulations 1991 (SI 1991/2705), reg. 5(3), (4) and Sch. 1 as from 2 December 1991 (subject to transitional provisions in reg. 9); the former Pt. I and II are now in Sch. 9A and the former Pt. III is repealed.

## Part I – Individual Accounts

### Chapter I – General Rules and Formats

#### SECTION A – GENERAL RULES

**1(1)** Subject to the following provisions of this Part of this Schedule:
(a) every balance sheet of a company shall show the items listed in the balance sheet format set out below in section B of this Chapter of this Schedule; and
(b) every profit and loss account of a company shall show the items listed in either of the profit and loss account formats so set out;

in either case in the order and under the headings and sub-headings given in the format adopted.

**1(2)** Sub-paragraph (1) above is not to be read as requiring the heading or sub-heading for any item to be distinguished by any number or letter assigned to that item in the format adopted.

**1(3)** Where the heading of an item in the format adopted contains any wording in square brackets, that wording may be omitted if not applicable to the company.

**2(1)** Where in accordance with paragraph 1 a company's profit and loss account for any financial year has been prepared by reference to one of the formats set out in section B below, the directors of the company shall adopt the same format in preparing the profit and loss account for subsequent financial years of the company unless in their opinion there are special reasons for a change.

**2(2)** Particulars of any change in the format adopted in preparing a company's profit and loss account in accordance with paragraph 1 shall be disclosed, and the reasons for the change shall be explained, in a note to the accounts in which the new format is first adopted.

**3(1)** Any item required in accordance with paragraph 1 to be shown in a company's balance sheet or profit and loss account may be shown in greater detail than so required.

**3(2)** A company's balance sheet or profit and loss account may include an item representing or covering the amount of any asset or liability, income or expenditure not specifically covered by any of the items listed in the balance sheet format provided or the profit and loss account format adopted, but the following shall not be treated as assets in any company's balance sheet:

(i) preliminary expenses;

(ii) expenses of and commission on any issue of shares or debentures; and

(iii) costs of research.

**3(3)** Items to which lower case letters are assigned in any of the formats set out in section B below may be combined in a company's accounts for any financial year if either:

(a) their individual amounts are not material for the purpose of giving a true and fair view; or

(b) the combination facilitates the assessment of the state of affairs or profit or loss of the company for that year;

but in a case within paragraph (b) the individual amounts of any items so combined shall be disclosed in a note to the accounts and any notes required by this Schedule to the items so combined shall, notwithstanding the combination, be given.

**3(4)** Subject to paragraph 4(3) below, a heading or sub-heading corresponding to an item listed in the balance sheet format or the profit and loss account format adopted in preparing a company's balance sheet or profit and loss account shall not be included if there is no amount to be shown for that item in respect of the financial year to which the balance sheet or profit and loss account relates.

**4(1)** In respect of every item shown in the balance sheet or profit and loss account, there shall be shown or stated the corresponding amount for the financial year immediately preceding that to which the accounts relate.

**4(2)** Where the corresponding amount is not comparable with the amount to be shown for the item in question in respect of the financial year to which the balance sheet or profit and loss account relates, the former amount shall be adjusted and particulars of the adjustment and the reasons for it shall be given in a note to the accounts.

**4(3)** Paragraph 3(4) does not apply in any case where an amount can be shown for the item in question in respect of the financial year immediately preceding that to which the balance sheet or profit and loss account relates, and that amount shall be shown under the heading or sub-heading required by paragraph 1 for that item.

**5(1)** Subject to the following provisions of this paragraph and without prejudice to note (6) to the balance sheet format, amounts in respect of items representing assets or income may not be set off against amounts in respect of items representing liabilities or expenditure (as the case may be), or vice versa.

**5(2)** Charges required to be included in profit and loss account format 1, items 11(a) and 11(b) or format 2, items A7(a) and A7(b) may however be set off against income required to be included in format 1, items 12(a) and 12(b) or format 2, items B5(a) and B5(b) and the resulting figure shown as a single item (in format 2 at position A7 if negative and at position B5 if positive).

**5(3)** Charges required to be included in profit and loss account format 1, item 13 or format 2 item A8 may also be set off against income required to be included in format 1, item 14 or format 2, item B6 and the resulting figure shown as a single item (in format 2 at position A8 if negative and at position B6 if positive).

**6(1)** Assets shall be shown under the relevant balance sheet headings even where the company has pledged them as security for its own liabilities or for those of third parties or has otherwise assigned them as security to third parties.

**6(2)** A company shall not include in its balance sheet assets pledged or otherwise assigned to it as security unless such assets are in the form of cash in the hands of the company.

**7** Assets acquired in the name of and on behalf of third parties shall not be shown in the balance sheet.

**8** Every profit and loss account of a company shall show separately as additional items:

(a) any amount set aside or proposed to be set aside to, or withdrawn or proposed to be withdrawn from, reserves;

(b) the aggregate amount of any dividends paid and proposed;

(c) if it is not shown in the notes to the accounts, the aggregate amount of any dividends proposed.

**History**

In Pt. I, para. 8(a) the word "and" formerly appearing after the word "reserves" omitted and para. 8(c) inserted by the Companies Act 1985 (Miscellaneous Accounting Amendments) Regulations 1996 (SI 1996/189), reg. 1(1), 14(6) and Sch. 4, para. 1, 2 as from 2 February 1996, subject to reg. 16(1), (2).

## SECTION B – THE REQUIRED FORMATS FOR ACCOUNTS

### Preliminary

**9(1)** References in this Part of this Schedule to the balance sheet format or to profit and loss account formats are to the balance sheet format or profit and loss account formats set out below and references to the items listed in any of the formats are to those items read together with any of the notes following the formats which apply to any of those items.

**9(2)** The requirement imposed by paragraph 1 of this Part of this Schedule to show the items listed in any such format in the order adopted in the format is subject to any provision in the notes following the formats for alternative positions for any particular items.

**10** A number in brackets following any item in any of the formats set out below is a reference to the note of that number in the notes following the formats.

### Balance Sheet Format

ASSETS

1. Cash and balances at central [or post office] banks *(1)*
2. Treasury bills and other eligible bills *(20)*
   (a) Treasury bills and similar securities *(2)*
   (b) Other eligible bills *(3)*
3. Loans and advances to banks *(4), (20)*
   (a) Repayable on demand
   (b) Other loans and advances
4. Loans and advances to customers *(5),(20)*
5. Debt securities [and other fixed income securities] *(6), (20)*
   (a) Issued by public bodies
   (b) Issued by other issuers
6. Equity shares [and other variable-yield securities]
7. Participating interests
8. Shares in group undertakings
9. Intangible fixed assets *(7)*
10. Tangible fixed assets*(8)*
11. Called up capital not paid*(9)*
12. Own shares *(10)*
13. Other assets
14. Called up capital not paid *(9)*
15. Prepayments and accrued income

Total assets

LIABILITIES

1. Deposits by banks *(11), (20)*
   (a) Repayable on demand
   (b) With agreed maturity dates or periods of notice
2. Customer accounts *(12), (20)*
   (a) Repayable on demand

(b) With agreed maturity dates or periods of notice

3. Debt securities in issue *(13), (20)*
   (a) Bonds and medium term notes
   (b) Others
4. Other liabilities
5. Accruals and deferred income
6. Provisions for liabilities and charges
   (a) Provisions for pensions and similar obligations
   (b) Provisions for tax
   (c) Other provisions
7. Subordinated liabilities *(14), (20)*
8. Called up share capital *(15)*
9. Share premium account
10. Reserves
    (a) Capital redemption reserve
    (b) Reserve for own shares
    (c) Reserves provided for by the articles of association
    (d) Other reserves
11. Revaluation reserve
12. Profit and loss account

Total liabilities

MEMORANDUM ITEMS

1. Contingent liabilities *(16)*
   (1) Acceptances and endorsements
   (2) Guarantees and assets pledged as collateral security *(17)*
   (3) Other contingent liabilities
2. Commitments *(18)*
   (1) Commitments arising out of sale and option to resell transactions *(19)*
   (2) Other commitments

## Notes on the balance sheet format and memorandum items

*(1) Cash and balances at central [or post office] banks*

(Assets item 1)

Cash shall comprise all currency including foreign notes and coins.

Only those balances which may be withdrawn without notice and which are deposited with central or post office banks of the country or countries in which the company is established shall be included in this item. All other claims on central or post office banks must be shown under Assets items 3 or 4.

*(2) Treasury bills and other eligible bills: Treasury bills and similar securities*

(Assets item 2(a))

Treasury bills and similar securities shall comprise treasury bills and similar debt instruments issued by public bodies which are eligible for refinancing with central banks of the country or countries in which the company is established. Any treasury bills or similar debt instruments not so eligible shall be included under Assets item 5, sub-item (a).

*(3) Treasury bills and other eligible bills: Other eligible bills*

(Assets item 2(b))

Other eligible bills shall comprise all bills purchased to the extent that they are eligible, under national law, for refinancing with the central banks of the country or countries in which the company is established.

*(4) Loans and advances to banks*

(Assets item 3)

Loans and advances to banks shall comprise all loans and advances to domestic or foreign credit institutions made by the company arising out of banking transactions. However loans and advances to credit institutions represented by debt securities or other fixed income securities shall be included under Assets item 5 and not this item.

(5) *Loans and advances to customers*

(Assets item 4)

Loans and advances to customers shall comprise all types of assets in the form of claims on domestic and foreign customers other than credit institutions. However loans and advances represented by debt securities or other fixed income securities shall be included under Assets item 5 and not this item.

*(6) Debt securities [and other fixed income securities]*

(Assets item 5)

This item shall comprise transferable debt securities and any other transferable fixed income securities issued by credit institutions, other undertakings or public bodies. Debt securities and other fixed income securities issued by public bodies shall however only be included in this item if they may not be shown under Assets item 2.

Where a company holds its own debt securities these shall not be included under this item but shall be deducted from Liabilities item 3(a) or (b), as appropriate.

Securities bearing interest rates that vary in accordance with specific factors, for example the interest rate on the inter-bank market or on the Euromarket, shall also be regarded as fixed income securities to be included under this item.

*(7) Intangible fixed assets*

(Assets item 9)

This item shall comprise:

(a) development costs;
(b) concessions, patents, licences, trade marks and similar rights and assets;
(c) goodwill; and
(d) payments on account.

Amounts shall, however, be included in respect of (b) only if the assets were acquired for valuable consideration or the assets in question were created by the company itself.

Amounts representing goodwill shall only be included to the extent that the goodwill was acquired for valuable consideration.

There shall be disclosed, in a note to the accounts, the amount of any goodwill included in this item.

*(8) Tangible fixed assets*

(Assets item 10)

This item shall comprise:

– land and buildings;
– plant and machinery;
– fixtures and fittings, tools and equipment; and
– payments on account and assets in the course of construction.

There shall be disclosed in a note to the accounts the amount included in this item with respect to land and buildings occupied by the company for its own activities.

*(9) Called up capital not paid*

(Assets items 11 and 14)

The two positions shown for this item are alternatives.

*(10) Own shares*

(Assets item 12)

The nominal value of the shares held shall be shown separately under this item.

*(11) Deposits by banks*

(Liabilities item 1)

Deposits by banks shall comprise all amounts arising out of banking transactions owed to other domestic or foreign credit institutions by the company. However liabilities in the form of debt securities and any liabilities for which transferable certificates have been issued shall be included under Liabilities item 3 and not this item.

*(12) Customer accounts*

(Liabilities item 2)

This item shall comprise all amounts owed to creditors that are not credit institutions. However liabilities in the form of debt securities and any liabilities for which transferable certificates have been issued shall be shown under Liabilities item 3 and not this item.

*(13) Debt securities in issue*

(Liabilities item 3)

This item shall include both debt securities and debts for which transferable certificates have been issued, including liabilities arising out of own acceptances and promissory notes. (Only acceptances which a company has issued for its own refinancing and in respect of which it is the first party liable shall be treated as own acceptances.)

*(14) Subordinated liabilities*

(Liabilities item 7)

This item shall comprise all liabilities in respect of which there is a contractual obligation that, in the event of winding up or bankruptcy, they are to be repaid only after the claims of other creditors have been met.

This item shall include all subordinated liabilities, whether or not a ranking has been agreed between the subordinated creditors concerned.

*(15) Called up share capital*

(Liabilities item 8)

The amount of allotted share capital and the amount of called up share capital which has been paid up shall be shown separately.

*(16) Contingent liabilities*

(Memorandum item 1)

This item shall include all transactions whereby the company has underwritten the obligations of a third party.

Liabilities arising out of the endorsement of rediscounted bills shall be included in this item. Acceptances other than own acceptances shall also be included.

*(17) Contingent liabilities: Guarantees and assets pledged as collateral security*

(Memorandum item 1(2))

This item shall include all guarantee obligations incurred and assets pledged as collateral security on behalf of third parties, particularly in respect of sureties and irrevocable letters of credit.

*(18) Commitments*

(Memorandum item 2)

This item shall include every irrevocable commitment which could give rise to a credit risk.

*(19) Commitments: Commitments arising out of sale and option to resell transactions*

(Memorandum item 2(1))

This sub-item shall comprise commitments entered into by the company in the context of sale and option to resell transactions.

*(20) Claims on, and liabilities to, undertakings in which a participating interest is held or group undertakings*

(Assets items 2 to 5, Liabilities items 1 to 3 and 7)

The following information must be given either by way of subdivision of the relevant items or by way of notes to the accounts.

The amount of the following must be shown for each of Assets items 2 to 5:

(a) claims on group undertakings included therein; and

(b) claims on undertakings in which the company has a participating interest included therein.

The amount of the following must be shown for each of Liabilities items 1, 2, 3 and 7:

(i) liabilities to group undertakings included therein; and

(ii) liabilities to undertakings in which the company has a participating interest included therein.

## Special rules

*Subordinated assets*

**11(1)** The amount of any assets that are subordinated must be shown either as a subdivision of any relevant asset item or in the notes to the accounts; in the latter case disclosure shall be by reference to the relevant asset item or items in which the assets are included.

**11(2)** In the case of Assets items 2 to 5 in the balance sheet format, the amounts required to be shown by note (20) to the format as sub-items of those items shall be further subdivided so as to show the amount of any claims included therein that are subordinated.

**11(3)** For this purpose, assets are subordinated if there is a contractual obligation to the effect that, in the event of winding up or bankruptcy, they are to be repaid only after the claims of other creditors have been met, whether or not a ranking has been agreed between the subordinated creditors concerned.

*Syndicated loans*

**12(1)** Where a company is a party to a syndicated loan transaction the company shall include only that part of the total loan which it itself has funded.

**12(2)** Where a company is a party to a syndicated loan transaction and has agreed to reimburse (in whole or in part) any other party to the syndicate any funds advanced by that party or any interest thereon upon the occurrence of any event, including the default of the borrower, any additional liability by reason of such a guarantee shall be included as a contingent liability in Memorandum item 1, sub-item (2).

*Sale and repurchase transactions*

**13(1)** The following rules apply where a company is a party to a sale and repurchase transaction.

**13(2)** Where the company is the transferor of the assets under the transaction:

(a) the assets transferred shall, notwithstanding the transfer, be included in its balance sheet;

(b) the purchase price received by it shall be included in its balance sheet as an amount owed to the transferee; and

(c) the value of the assets transferred shall be disclosed in a note to its accounts.

**13(3)** Where the company is the transferee of the assets under the transaction it shall not include the assets transferred in its balance sheet but the purchase price paid by it to the transferor shall be so included as an amount owed by the transferor.

*Sale and option to resell transactions*

**14(1)** The following rules apply where a company is a party to a sale and option to resell transaction.

**14(2)** Where the company is the transferor of the assets under the transaction it shall not include in its balance sheet the assets transferred but it shall enter under Memorandum item 2 an amount equal to the price agreed in the event of repurchase.

**14(3)** Where the company is the transferee of the assets under the transaction it shall include those assets in its balance sheet.

*Managed funds*

**15(1)** For the purposes of this paragraph **"managed funds"** are funds which the company administers in its own name but on behalf of others and to which it has legal title.

**15(2)** The company shall, in any case where claims and obligations arising in respect of managed funds fall to be treated as claims and obligations of the company, adopt the following accounting treatment: claims and obligations representing managed funds are to be included in the company's balance sheet, with the notes to the accounts disclosing the total amount included with respect to such assets and liabilities in the balance sheet and showing the amount included under each relevant balance sheet item in respect of such assets or (as the case may be) liabilities.

## Profit and Loss Account Formats

### FORMAT 1

Vertical layout

1. Interest receivable *(1)*
   (1) Interest receivable and similar income arising from debt securities [and other fixed income securities]
   (2) Other interest receivable and similar income
2. Interest payable *(2)*
3. Dividend income
   (a) Income from equity shares [and other variable-yield securities]
   (b) Income from participating interests
   (c) Income from shares in group undertakings
4. Fees and commissions receivable *(3)*
5. Fees and commissions payable *(4)*
6. Dealing [profits] [losses] *(5)*
7. Other operating income
8. Administrative expenses
   (a) Staff costs
      (i) Wages and salaries
      (ii) Social security costs
      (iii) Other pension costs
   (b) Other administrative expenses
9. Depreciation and amortisation *(6)*
10. Other operating charges
11. Provisions
    (a) Provisions for bad and doubtful debts *(7)*
    (b) Provisions for contingent liabilities and commitments *(8)*
12. Adjustments to provisions
    (a) Adjustments to provisions for bad and doubtful debts*(9)*
    (b) Adjustments to provisions for contingent liabilities and commitments *(10)*
13. Amounts written off fixed asset investments *(11)*
14. Adjustments to amounts written off fixed asset investments *(12)*
15. [Profit] [loss] on ordinary activities before tax
16. Tax on [profit] [loss] on ordinary activities
17. [Profit] [loss] on ordinary activities after tax
18. Extraordinary income
19. Extraordinary charges
20. Extraordinary [profit] [loss]
21. Tax on extraordinary [profit] [loss]
22. Extraordinary [profit] [loss] after tax
23. Other taxes not shown under the preceding items
24. [Profit] [loss] for the financial year

### FORMAT 2

Horizontal layout

A. Charges

1. Interest payable *(2)*
2. Fees and commissions payable *(4)*
3. Dealing losses *(5)*
4. Administrative expenses
   (a) Staff costs
      (i) Wages and salaries
      (ii) Social security costs
      (iii) Other pension costs
   (b) Other administrative expenses
5. Depreciation and amortisation *(6)*
6. Other operating charges
7. Provisions
   (a) Provisions for bad and doubtful debts *(7)*
   (b) Provisions for contingent liabilities and commitments *(8)*
8. Amounts written off fixed asset investments *(11)*
9. Profit on ordinary activities before tax
10. Tax on [profit] [loss] on ordinary activities
11. Profit on ordinary activities after tax
12. Extraordinary charges
13. Tax on extraordinary [profit] [loss]
14. Extraordinary loss after tax
15. Other taxes not shown under the preceding items
16. Profit for the financial year

B. Income

1. Interest receivable *(1)*
   (1) Interest receivable and similar income arising from debt securities [and other fixed income securities]
   (2) Other interest receivable and similar income
2. Dividend income
   (a) Income from equity shares [and other variable-yield securities]
   (b) Income from participating interests
   (c) Income from shares in group undertakings
3. Fees and commissions receivable *(3)*
4. Dealing profits *(5)*
5. Adjustments to provisions
   (a) Adjustments to provisions for bad and doubtful debts *(9)*
   (b) Adjustments to provisions for contingent liabilities and commitments *(10)*
6. Adjustments to amounts written off fixed asset investments *(12)*
7. Other operating income
8. Loss on ordinary activities before tax
9. Loss on ordinary activities after tax
10. Extraordinary income
11. Extraordinary profit after tax
12. Loss for the financial year

## Notes on the profit and loss account formats

*(1) Interest receivable*

(Format 1, item 1; Format 2, item B1)

This item shall include all income arising out of banking activities, including:

(a) income from assets included in Assets items 1 to 5 in the balance sheet format, however calculated;

(b) income resulting from covered forward contracts spread over the actual duration of the contract and similar in nature to interest; and

(c) fees and commissions receivable similar in nature to interest and calculated on a time basis or by reference to the amount of the claim (but not other fees and commissions receivable).

*(2) Interest payable*

(Format 1, item 2; Format 2, item A1)

This item shall include all expenditure arising out of banking activities, including:

(a) charges arising out of liabilities included in Liabilities items 1, 2, 3 and 7 in the balance sheet format, however calculated;
(b) charges resulting from covered forward contracts, spread over the actual duration of the contract and similar in nature to interest; and
(c) fees and commissions payable similar in nature to interest and calculated on a time basis or by reference to the amount of the liability (but not other fees and commissions payable).

*(3) Fees and commissions receivable*

(Format 1, item 4; Format 2, item B3)

Fees and commissions receivable shall comprise income in respect of all services supplied by the company to third parties, but not fees or commissions required to be included under interest receivable (Format 1, item 1; Format 2, item B1).

In particular the following fees and commissions receivable must be included (unless required to be included under interest receivable):

– fees and commissions for guarantees, loan administration on behalf of other lenders and securities transactions;
– fees, commissions and other income in respect of payment transactions, account administration charges and commissions for the safe custody and administration of securities;
– fees and commissions for foreign currency transactions and for the sale and purchase of coin and precious metals; and
– fees and commissions charged for brokerage services in connection with savings and insurance contracts and loans.

*(4) Fees and commissions payable*

(Format 1, item 5; Format 2, item A2)

Fees and commissions payable shall comprise charges for all services rendered to the company by third parties but not fees or commissions required to be included under interest payable (Format 1, item 2; Format 2, item A1).

In particular the following fees and commissions payable must be included (unless required to be included under interest payable):

– fees and commissions for guarantees, loan administration and securities transactions;
– fees, commissions and other charges in respect of payment transactions, account administration charges and commissions for the safe custody and administration of securities;
– fees and commissions for foreign currency transactions and for the sale and purchase of coin and precious metals; and
– fees and commissions for brokerage services in connection with savings and insurance contracts and loans.

*(5) Dealing [profits] [losses]*

(Format 1, item 6; Format 2, items B4 and A3)

This item shall comprise:

(a) the net profit or net loss on transactions in securities which are not held as financial fixed assets together with amounts written off or written back with respect to such securities, including amounts written off or written back as a result of the application of paragraph 34(1) below;

(b) the net profit or loss on exchange activities, save in so far as the profit or loss is included in interest receivable or interest payable (Format 1, items 1 or 2; Format 2, items B1 or A1); and

(c) the net profits and losses on other dealing operations involving financial instruments, including precious metals.

*(6) Depreciation and amortisation*

(Format 1, item 9; Format 2, item A5)

This item shall comprise depreciation and other amounts written off in respect of balance sheet Assets items 9 and 10.

*(7) Provisions: Provisions for bad and doubtful debts*

(Format 1, item 11(a); Format 2, item A7(a))

Provisions for bad and doubtful debts shall comprise charges for amounts written off and for provisions made in respect of loans and advances shown under balance sheet Assets items 3 and 4.

*(8) Provisions: Provisions for contingent liabilities and commitments*

(Format 1, item 11(b); Format 2, item A7(b))

This item shall comprise charges for provisions for contingent liabilities and commitments of a type which would, if not provided for, be shown under Memorandum items 1 and 2.

*(9) Adjustments to provisions: Adjustments to provisions for bad and doubtful debts*

(Format 1, item 12(a); Format 2, item B5(a))

This item shall include credits from the recovery of loans that have been written off, from other advances written back following earlier write offs and from the reduction of provisions previously made with respect to loans and advances.

*(10) Adjustments to provisions: Adjustments to provisions for contingent liabilities and commitments*

(Format 1, item 12(b); Format 2, item B5(b))

This item comprises credits from the reduction of provisions previously made with respect to contingent liabilities and commitments.

*(11) Amounts written off fixed asset investments*

(Format 1, item 13; Format 2, item A8)

Amounts written off fixed asset investments shall comprise amounts written off in respect of assets which are transferable securities held as financial fixed assets, participating interests and shares in group undertakings and which are included in Assets items 5 to 8 in the balance sheet format.

*(12) Adjustments to amounts written off fixed asset investments*

(Format 1, item 14; Format 2, item B6)

Adjustments to amounts written off fixed asset investments shall include amounts written back following earlier write offs and provisions in respect of assets which are transferable securities held as financial fixed assets, participating interests and group undertakings and which are included in Assets items 5 to 8 in the balance sheet format.

## Chapter II – Accounting Principles and Rules

### SECTION A – ACCOUNTING PRINCIPLES

**16** Subject to paragraph 22 below, the amounts to be included in respect of all items shown in a company's accounts shall be determined in accordance with the principles set out in paragraphs 17 to 21.

## Accounting principles

**17** The company shall be presumed to be carrying on business as a going concern.

**18** Accounting policies shall be applied consistently within the same accounts and from one financial year to the next.

**19** The amount of any item shall be determined on a prudent basis, and in particular:

(a) only profits realised at the balance sheet date shall be included in the profit and loss account; and

(b) all liabilities and losses which have arisen or are likely to arise in respect of the financial year to which the accounts relate or a previous financial year shall be taken into account, including those which only become apparent between the balance sheet date and the date on which it is signed on behalf of the board of directors in pursuance of section 233 of this Act.

**20** All income and charges relating to the financial year to which the accounts relate shall be taken into account, without regard to the date of receipt or payment.

**21** In determining the aggregate amount of any item the amount of each individual asset or liability that falls to be taken into account shall be determined separately.

## Departure from the accounting principles

**22** If it appears to the directors of a company that there are special reasons for departing from any of the principles stated above in preparing the company's accounts in respect of any financial year they may do so, but particulars of the departure, the reasons for it and its effect shall be given in a note to the accounts.

# SECTION B – VALUATION RULES HISTORICAL COST ACCOUNTING RULES

## Preliminary

**23** Subject to paragraphs 39 to 44 of this Part of this Schedule, the amounts to be included in respect of all items shown in a company's accounts shall be determined in accordance with the rules set out in paragraphs 24 to 38 of this Part of this Schedule.

## Fixed assets

*General rules*

**24** Subject to any provision for depreciation or diminution in value made in accordance with paragraph 25 or 26 the amount to be included in respect of any fixed asset shall be its cost.

**25** In the case of any fixed asset which has a limited useful economic life, the amount of:

(a) its cost; or

(b) where it is estimated that any such asset will have a residual value at the end of the period of its useful economic life, its cost less that estimated residual value;

shall be reduced by provisions for depreciation calculated to write off that amount systematically over the period of the asset's useful economic life.

**26(1)** Where a fixed asset investment of a description falling to be included under Assets items 7 (Participating interests) or 8 (Shares in group undertakings) in the balance sheet format, or any other holding of securities held as a financial fixed asset, has diminished in value, provisions for diminution in value may be made in respect of it and the amount to be included in respect of it may be reduced accordingly; and any such provisions which are not shown in the profit and loss account shall be disclosed (either separately or in aggregate) in a note to the accounts.

**26(2)** Provisions for diminution in value shall be made in respect of any fixed asset which has diminished in value if the reduction in its value is expected to be permanent (whether its useful economic life is limited or not), and the amount to be included in respect of it shall be reduced accordingly; and any such provisions which are not shown in the profit and loss account shall be disclosed (either separately or in aggregate) in a note to the accounts.

**26(3)** Where the reasons for which any provision was made in accordance with sub-paragraph (1) or (2) have ceased to apply to any extent, that provision shall be written back to the extent that it is no longer necessary; and any amounts written back in accordance with this sub-paragraph which are not shown in the profit and loss account shall be disclosed (either separately or in aggregate) in a note to the accounts.

*Development costs*

**27(1)** Notwithstanding that amounts representing "development costs" may be included under Assets item 9 in the balance sheet format, an amount may only be included in a company's balance sheet in respect of development costs in special circumstances.

**27(2)** If any amount is included in a company's balance sheet in respect of development costs the following information shall be given in a note to the accounts:

(a) the period over which the amount of those costs originally capitalised is being or is to be written off; and

(b) the reasons for capitalising the development costs in question.

*Goodwill*

**28(1)** The application of paragraphs 24 to 26 in relation to goodwill (in any case where goodwill is treated as an asset) is subject to the following provisions of this paragraph.

**28(2)** Subject to sub-paragraph (3) below the amount of the consideration for any goodwill acquired by a company shall be reduced by provisions for depreciation calculated to write off that amount systematically over a period chosen by the directors of the company.

**28(3)** The period chosen shall not exceed the useful economic life of the goodwill in question.

**28(4)** In any case where any goodwill acquired by a company is included as an asset in the company's balance sheet the period chosen for writing off the consideration for that goodwill and the reasons for choosing that period shall be disclosed in a note to the accounts.

*Intangible and tangible fixed assets*

**29** Assets included in Assets items 9 (Intangible fixed assets) and 10 (Tangible fixed assets) in the balance sheet format shall be valued as fixed assets.

*Other fixed assets*

**30** Other assets falling to be included in the balance sheet shall be valued as fixed assets where they are intended for use on a continuing basis in the company's activities.

*Financial fixed assets*

**31(1)** Debt securities, including fixed income securities, held as financial fixed assets shall be included in the balance sheet at an amount equal to their maturity value plus any premium, or less any discount, on their purchase, subject to the following provisions of this paragraph.

**31(2)** The amount included in the balance sheet with respect to such securities purchased at a premium shall be reduced each financial year on a systematic basis so as to write the premium off over the period to the maturity date of the security and the amounts so written off shall be charged to the profit and loss account for the relevant financial years.

**31(3)** The amount included in the balance sheet with respect to such securities purchased at a discount shall be increased each financial year on a systematic basis so as to extinguish the discount over the period to the maturity date of the security and the amounts by which the amount is increased shall be credited to the profit and loss account for the relevant years.

**31(4)** The notes to the accounts shall disclose the amount of any unamortised premium or discount not extinguished which is included in the balance sheet by virtue of sub-paragraph (1).

**31(5)** For the purposes of this paragraph **"premium"** means any excess of the amount paid for a security over its maturity value and **"discount"** means any deficit of the amount paid for a security over its maturity value.

## Current assets

**32** The amount to be included in respect of loans and advances, debt or other fixed income securities and equity shares or other variable yield securities not held as financial fixed assets shall be their cost, subject to paragraphs 33 and 34 below.

**33(1)** If the net realisable value of any asset referred to in paragraph 32 is lower than its cost the amount to be included in respect of that asset shall be the net realisable value.

**33(2)** Where the reasons for which any provision for diminution in value was made in accordance with sub-paragraph (1) have ceased to apply to any extent, that provision shall be written back to the extent that it is no longer necessary.

**34(1)** Subject to paragraph 33 above, the amount to be included in the balance sheet in respect of transferable securities not held as financial fixed assets may be the higher of their cost or their market value at the balance sheet date.

**34(2)** The difference between the cost of any securities included in the balance sheet at a valuation under sub-paragraph (1) and their market value shall be shown (in aggregate) in the notes to the accounts.

## Miscellaneous and supplementary provisions

*Excess of money owed over value received as an asset item*

**35(1)** Where the amount repayable on any debt owed by a company is greater than the value of the consideration received in the transaction giving rise to the debt, the amount of the difference may be treated as an asset.

**35(2)** Where any such amount is so treated:

(a) it shall be written off by reasonable amounts each year and must be completely written off before repayment of the debt; and

(b) if the current amount is not shown as a separate item in the company's balance sheet it must be disclosed in a note to the accounts.

*Determination of cost*

**36(1)** The cost of an asset that has been acquired by the company shall be determined by adding to the actual price paid any expenses incidental to its acquisition.

**36(2)** The cost of an asset constructed by the company shall be determined by adding to the purchase price of the raw materials and consumables used the amount of the costs incurred by the company which are directly attributable to the construction of that asset.

**36(3)** In addition, there may be included in the cost of an asset constructed by the company:

(a) a reasonable proportion of the costs incurred by the company which are only indirectly attributable to the construction of that asset, but only to the extent that they relate to the period of construction; and

(b) interest on capital borrowed to finance the construction of that asset, to the extent that it accrues in respect of the period of construction;

provided, however, in a case within sub-paragraph (b) above, that the inclusion of the interest in determining the cost of that asset and the amount of the interest so included is disclosed in a note to the accounts.

**37(1)** Subject to the qualification mentioned below, the cost of any assets which are fungible assets (including investments) may be determined by the application of any of the methods mentioned in sub-paragraph (2) below in relation to any such assets of the same class.

The method chosen must be one which appears to the directors to be appropriate in the circumstances of the company.

**37(2)** Those methods are:

(a) the method known as "first in, first out" (FIFO);

(b) the method known as "last in, first out" (LIFO);

(c) a weighted average price; and

(d) any other method similar to any of the methods mentioned above.

**37(3)** Where in the case of any company:

(a) the cost of assets falling to be included under any item shown in the company's balance sheet has been determined by the application of any method permitted by this paragraph; and

(b) the amount shown in respect of that item differs materially from the relevant alternative amount given below in this paragraph;

the amount of that difference shall be disclosed in a note to the accounts.

**37(4)** Subject to sub-paragraph (5) below, for the purposes of sub-paragraph (3)(b) above, the relevant alternative amount, in relation to any item shown in a company's balance sheet, is the amount which would have been shown in respect of that item if assets of any class included under that item at an amount determined by any method permitted by this paragraph had instead been included at their replacement cost as at the balance sheet date.

**37(5)** The relevant alternative amount may be determined by reference to the most recent actual purchase price before the balance sheet date of assets of any class included under the item in question instead of by reference to their replacement cost as at that date, but only if the former appears to the directors of the company to constitute the more appropriate standard of comparison in the case of assets of that class.

*Substitution of original amount where price or cost unknown*

**38** Where there is no record of the purchase price of any asset acquired by a company or of any price, expenses or costs relevant for determining its cost in accordance with paragraph 36, or any such record cannot be obtained without unreasonable expense or delay, its cost shall be taken for the purposes of paragraphs 24 to 34 to be the value ascribed to it in the earliest available record of its value made on or after its acquisition by the company.

## ALTERNATIVE ACCOUNTING RULES

### Preliminary

**39(1)** The rules set out in paragraphs 24 to 38 are referred to below in this Schedule as the historical cost accounting rules.

**39(2)** Paragraphs 24 to 27 and 31 to 35 are referred to below in this section of this Part of this Schedule as the depreciation rules; and references below in this Schedule to the historical cost accounting rules do not include the depreciation rules as they apply by virtue of paragraph 42.

**40** Subject to paragraphs 42 to 44, the amounts to be included in respect of assets of any description mentioned in paragraph 41 may be determined on any basis so mentioned.

### Alternative accounting rules

**41(1)** Intangible fixed assets, other than goodwill, may be included at their current cost.

**41(2)** Tangible fixed assets may be included at a market value determined as at the date of their last valuation or at their current cost.

**41(3)** Investments of any description falling to be included under Assets items 7 (Participating interests) or 8 (Shares in group undertakings) of the balance sheet format and any other securities held as financial fixed assets may be included either:

(a) at a market value determined as at the date of their last valuation; or

(b) at a value determined on any basis which appears to the directors to be appropriate in the circumstances of the company;

but in the latter case particulars of the method of valuation adopted and of the reasons for adopting it shall be disclosed in a note to the accounts.

**41(4)** Securities of any description not held as financial fixed assets (if not valued in accordance with paragraph 34 above) may be included at their current cost.

## Application of the depreciation rules

**42(1)** Where the value of any asset ofa company is determined in accordance with paragraph 41, that value shall be, or (as the case may require) be the starting point for determining, the amount to be included in respect of that asset in the company's accounts, instead of its cost or any value previously so determined for that asset: and the depreciation rules shall apply accordingly in relation to any such asset with the substitution for any reference to its cost of a reference to the value most recently determined for that asset in accordance with paragraph 41.

**42(2)** The amount of any provision for depreciation required in the case of any fixed asset by paragraph 25 or 26 as it applies by virtue of sub-paragraph (1) is referred to below in this paragraph as the "adjusted amount", and the amount of any provision which would be required by that paragraph in the case of that asset according to the historical cost accounting rules is referred to as the "historical cost amount".

**42(3)** Where sub-paragraph (1) applies in the case of any fixed asset the amount of any provision for depreciation in respect of that asset included in any item shown in the profit and loss account in respect of amounts written off assets of the description in question may be the historical cost amount instead of the adjusted amount, provided that the amount of any difference between the two is shown separately in the profit and loss account or in a note to the accounts.

## Additional information to be provided in case of departure from historical cost accounting rules

**43(1)** This paragraph applies where the amounts to be included in respect of assets covered by any items shown in a company's accounts have been determined in accordance with paragraph 41.

**43(2)** The items affected and the basis of valuation adopted in determining the amounts of the assets in question in the case of each such item shall be disclosed in a note to the accounts.

**43(3)** In the case of each balance sheet item affected either:

(a) the comparable amounts determined according to the historical cost accounting rules; or

(b) the differences between those amounts and the corresponding amounts actually shown in the balance sheet in respect of that item;

shall be shown separately in the balance sheet or in a note to the accounts.

**43(4)** In sub-paragraph (3) above, references in relation to any item to the comparable amounts determined as there mentioned are references to:

(a) the aggregate amount which would be required to be shown in respect of that item if the amounts to be included in respect of all the assets covered by that item were determined according to the historical cost accounting rules; and

(b) the aggregate amount of the cumulative provisions for depreciation or diminution in value which would be permitted or required in determining those amounts according to those rules.

## Revaluation reserve

**44(1)** With respect to any determination of the value of an asset of a company in accordance with paragraph 41, the amount of any profit or loss arising from that determination (after allowing, where appropriate, for any provisions for depreciation or diminution in value made otherwise than by reference to the value so determined and any adjustments of any such provisions made in the light of that determination) shall be credited or (as the case may be) debited to a separate reserve ("the revaluation reserve").

**44(2)** The amount of the revaluation reserve shall be shown in the company's balance sheet under Liabilities item 11 in the balance sheet format, but need not be shown under that name.

**44(3)** An amount may be transferred

(a) from the revaluation reserve–

(i) to the profit and loss account, if the amount was previously charged to that account or represents realised profit, or

(ii) on capialisation,

(b) to or from the revaluation reserve in respect of the taxation relating to any profit or loss credited or debited to the reserve;

and the revaluation reserve shall be reduced to the extent that the amounts transferred to it are no longer necessary for the purposes of the valuation method used.

**History**

In Pt. I, para. 44(3) the words "(a) from the revaluation reserve–" to "debited to the reserve;" substituted by the Companies Act 1985 (Miscellaneous Accounting Amendments) Regulations 1996 (SI 1996/189), reg. 1(1), 14(6) and Sch. 4, para. 1, 3(1), (2) as from 2 February 1996, subject to reg. 16(1), (2); the former words read as follows:

"from the revaluation reserve:

(a) to the profit and loss account, if the amount was previously charged to that account or represents realised profit, or

(b) on capitalisation;".

**44(4)** In sub-paragraph (3)(a)(ii) **"capitalisation"**, in relation to an amount standing to the credit of the revaluation reserve, means applying it in wholly or partly paying up unissued shares in the company to be allotted to members of the company as fully or partly paid shares.

**History**

In Pt. I, para. 44(4) the words "sub-paragraph (3)(a)(ii)" substituted for the former words "sub-paragaph (3)(b)" by the Companies Act 1985 (Miscellaneous Accounting Amendments) Regulations 1996 (SI 1996/189), reg. 1(1), 14(6) and Sch. 4, para. 1, 3(1), (3) as from 2 February 1996, subject to reg. 16(1), (2).

**44(5)** The revaluation reserve shall not be reduced except as mentioned in this paragraph.

**44(6)** The treatment for taxation purposes of amounts credited or debited to the revaluation reserve shall be disclosed in a note to the accounts.

## ASSETS AND LIABILITIES DENOMINATED IN FOREIGN CURRENCIES

**45(1)** Subject to the following sub-paragraphs, amounts to be included in respect of assets and liabilities denominated in foreign currencies shall be in sterling (or the currency in which the accounts are drawn up) after translation at an appropriate spot rate of exchange prevailing at the balance sheet date.

**45(2)** An appropriate rate of exchange prevailing on the date of purchase may however be used for assets held as financial fixed assets and assets to be included under Assets items 9 (Intangible fixed assets) and 10 (Tangible fixed assets) in the balance sheet format, if they are not covered or not specifically covered in either the spot or forward currency markets.

**45(3)** An appropriate spot rate of exchange prevailing at the balance sheet date shall be used for translating uncompleted spot exchange transactions.

**45(4)** An appropriate forward rate of exchange prevailing at the balance sheet date shall be used for translating uncompleted forward exchange transactions.

**45(5)** This paragraph does not apply to any assets or liabilities held, or any transactions entered into, for hedging purposes or to any assets or liabilities which are themselves hedged.

**46(1)** Subject to sub-paragraph (2), any difference between the amount to be included in respect of an asset or liability under paragraph 45 and the book value, after translation into sterling (or the currency in which the accounts are drawn up) at an appropriate rate, of that asset or liability shall be credited or, as the case may be, debited to the profit and loss account.

**46(2)** In the case, however, of assets held as financial fixed assets, of assets to be included under Assets items 9 (Intangible fixed assets) and 10 (Tangible fixed assets) in the balance sheet format and of transactions undertaken to cover such assets, any such difference may be deducted from or credited to any non-distributable reserve available for the purpose.

# Chapter III – Notes to the Accounts

### Preliminary

**47(1)** Any information required in the case of a company by the following provisions of this Part of this Schedule shall (if not given in the company's accounts) be given by way of a note to the accounts.

**History**
In Pt. I, para. 47(1), the words "(if not given in the company's accounts)" inserted and the words ", unless otherwise provided" formerly appearing after the words "note to the accounts" omitted by the Companies Act 1985 (Miscellaneous Accounting Amendments) Regulations 1996 (SI 1996/189), reg. 1(1), 14(6) and Sch. 4, para. 1, 4 as from 2 February 1996, subject to reg. 16(1), (2).

**47(2)** Subject to the next sub-paragraph, in respect of every item stated in a note to the accounts the corresponding amount for the financial year immediately preceding that to which the accounts relate shall also be stated and where the corresponding amount is not comparable, it shall be adjusted and particulars of the adjustment and the reasons for it shall be given.

**47(3)** The last sub-paragraph does not apply to:
(a) paragraphs 55 and 59 of this Part of this Schedule;
(b) paragraph 13 of Schedule 4A;
(c) paragraphs 2, 8(3), 16, 21(1)(d), 22(4) and (5), 24(3) and (4) and 27(3) and (4) of Schedule 5; and
(d) Parts II and III of Schedule 6 as modified by Part IV of this Schedule (loans and other dealings in favour of directors).

## General

*Disclosure of accounting policies*

**48** The accounting policies adopted by the company in determining the amounts to be included in respect of items shown in the balance sheet and in determining the profit or loss of the company shall be stated (including such policies with respect to the depreciation and diminution in value of assets).

**49** It shall be stated whether the accounts have been prepared in accordance with applicable accounting standards and particulars of any material departure from those standards and the reasons for it shall be given.

*Sums denominated in foreign currencies*

**50** Where any sums originally denominated in foreign currencies have been brought into account under any items shown in the balance sheet format or the profit and loss account formats the basis on which those sums have been translated into sterling (or the currency in which the accounts are drawn up) shall be stated.

## Information supplementing the balance sheet

*Share capital and debentures*

**51(1)** The following information shall be given with respect to the company's share capital:
(a) the authorised share capital; and
(b) where shares of more than one class have been allotted, the number and aggregate nominal value of shares of each class allotted.

**51(2)** In the case of any part of the allotted share capital that consists of redeemable shares, the following information shall be given:
(a) the earliest and latest dates on which the company has power to redeem those shares;
(b) whether those shares must be redeemed in any event or are liable to be redeemed at the option of the company or of the shareholder; and
(c) whether any (and, if so, what) premium is payable on redemption.

**52** If the company has allotted any shares during the financial year, the following information shall be given:
(b) the classes of shares allotted; and
(c) as respects each class of shares, the number allotted, their aggregate nominal value and the consideration received by the company for the allotment.

**History**
Pt. I, para. 52(a) repealed by the Companies Act 1985 (Miscellaneous Accounting Amendments) Regulations 1996 (SI 1996/189), reg. 1(1), 14(6) and Sch. 4, para. 1, 5 as from 2 February 1996, subject to reg. 16(1), (2); para. 52(a) formerly read as follows:
"(a) the reason for making the allotment;"

**53(1)** With respect to any contingent right to the allotment of shares in the company the following particulars shall be given:

(a) the number, description and amount of the shares in relation to which the right is exercisable;

(b) the period during which it is exercisable; and

(c) the price to be paid for the shares allotted.

**53(2)** In sub-paragraph (1) above **"contingent right to the allotment of shares"** means any option to subscribe for shares and any other right to require the allotment of shares to any person whether arising on the conversion into shares of securities of any other description or otherwise.

**54(1)** If the company has issued any debentures during the financial year to which the accounts relate, the following nformation shall be given:

(b) the classes of debentures issued; and

(c) as respects each class of debentures, the amount issued and the consideration received by the company for the issue.

**History**

Pt. I, para. 54(1)(a) repealed by the Companies Act 1985 (Miscellaneous Accounting Amendments) Regulations 1996 (SI 1996/189), reg. 1(1), 14(6) and Sch. 4, para. 1, 6 as from 2 February 1996, subject to reg. 16(1), (2); para. 54(1)(a) formerly read as follows:

"(a) the reason for making the issue;"

**54(2)** (Repealed by the Companies Act 1985 (Miscellaneous Accounting Amendments) Regulations 1996 (SI 1996/189), reg. 1(1), 14(6) and Sch. 4, para. 1, 6 as from 2 February 1996, subject to reg. 16(1), (2).)

**History**

Pt. I, para. 54(2) formerly read as follows:

"Particulars of any redeemed debentures which the company has power to reissue shall also be given."

**54(3)** Where any of the company's debentures are held by a nominee of or trustee for the company, the nominal amount of the debentures and the amount at which they are stated in the accounting records kept by the company in accordance with section 221 of this Act shall be stated.

*Fixed assets*

**55(1)** In respect of any fixed assets of the company included in any assets item in the company's balance sheet the following information shall be given by reference to each such item:

(a) the appropriate amounts in respect of those assets included in the item as at the date of the beginning of the financial year and as at the balance sheet date respectively;

(b) the effect on any amount included in the item in respect of those assets of:

(i) any determination during that year of the value to be ascribed to any of those assets in accordance with paragraph 41 above;

(ii) acquisitions during that year of any fixed assets;

(iii) disposals during that year of any fixed assets; and

(iv) any transfers of fixed assets of the company to and from the item during that year.

**55(2)** The reference in sub-paragraph (1)(a) to the appropriate amounts in respect of any fixed assets (included in an assets item) as at any date there mentioned is a reference to amounts representing the aggregate amounts determined, as at that date, in respect of fixed assets falling to be included under the item on either of the following bases, that is to say:

(a) on the basis of cost (determined in accordance with paragraphs 36 and 37); or

(b) on any basis permitted by paragraph 41;

(leaving out of account in either case any provisions for depreciation or diminution in value).

**55(3)** In addition, in respect of any fixed assets of the company included in any assets item in the company's balance sheet, there shall be stated (by reference to each such item):

(a) the cumulative amount of provisions for depreciation or diminution in value of those assets included under the item as at each date mentioned in sub-paragraph (1)(a);

(b) the amount of any such provisions made in respect of the financial year;

(c) the amount of any adjustments made in respect of any such provisions during that year in consequence of the disposal of any of those assets; and

(d) the amount of any other adjustments made in respect of any such provisions during that year.

**55(4)** The requirements of this paragraph need not be complied with to the extent that a company takes advantage of the option of setting off charges and income afforded by paragraph 5(3) of this Part of this Schedule.

**56** Where any fixed assets of the company (other than listed investments) are included under any item shown in the company's balance sheet at an amount determined in accordance with paragraph 41, the following information shall be given:

(a) the years (so far as they are known to the directors) in which the assets were severally valued and the several values; and

(b) in the case of assets that have been valued during the financial year, the names of the persons who valued them or particulars of their qualifications for doing so and (whichever is stated) the bases of valuation used by them.

**57** In relation to any amount which is included under Assets item 10 in the balance sheet format (Tangible fixed assets) with respect to land and buildings there shall be stated:

(a) how much of that amount is ascribable to land of freehold tenure and how much to land of leasehold tenure; and

(b) how much of the amount ascribable to land of leasehold tenure is ascribable to land held on long lease and how much to land held on short lease.

**58** There shall be disclosed separately the amount of:

(a) any participating interests; and

(b) any shares in group undertakings that are held in credit institutions.

*Reserves and provisions*

**59(1)** Where any amount is transferred:

(a) to or from any reserves;

(b) to any provisions for liabilities and charges; or

(c) from any provision for liabilities and charges otherwise than for the purpose for which the provision was established;

and the reserves or provisions are or would but for paragraph 3(3) of this Part of this Schedule be shown as separate items in the company's balance sheet, the information mentioned in the following sub-paragraph shall be given in respect of the aggregate of reserves or provisions included in the same item.

**59(2)** That information is:

(a) the amount of the reserves or provisions as at the date of the beginning of the financial year and as at the balance sheet date respectively;

(b) any amounts transferred to or from the reserve or provisions during that year; and

(c) the source and application respectively of any amounts so transferred.

**59(3)** Particulars shall be given of each provision included in Liabilities item 6(c) (Other provisions) in the company's balance sheet in any case where the amount of that provision is material.

*Provision for taxation*

**60** The amount of any provision for deferred taxation shall be stated separately from the amount of any provision for other taxation.

*Maturity analysis*

**61(1)** A company shall disclose separately for each of Assets items 3(b) and 4 and Liabilities items 1(b), 2(b) and 3(b) the aggregate amount of the loans and advances and liabilities included in those items broken down into the following categories:

(a) those repayable in not more than three months
(b) those repayable in more than three months but not more than one year
(c) those repayable in more than one year but not more than five years
(d) those repayable in more than five years

from the balance sheet date.

**61(2)** A company shall also disclose the aggregate amounts of all loans and advances falling within Assets item 4 (Loans and advances to customers) which are:

(a) repayable on demand; or
(b) are for an indeterminate period, being repayable upon short notice.

**61(3)** For the purposes of sub-paragraph (1), where a loan or advance or liability is repayable by instalments, each such instalment is to be treated as a separate loan or advance or liability.

*Debt and other fixed income securities*

**62** A company shall disclose the amount of debt and fixed income securities included in Assets item 5 (Debt securities [and other fixed income securities]) and the amount of such securities included in Liabilities item 3(a) (Bonds and medium term notes) that (in each case) will become due within one year of the balance sheet date.

*Subordinated liabilities*

**63(1)** The following information must be disclosed in relation to any borrowing included in Liabilities item 7 (Subordinated liabilities) that exceeds 10 per cent of the total for that item:

(a) its amount;
(b) the currency in which it is denominated;
(c) the rate of interest and the maturity date (or the fact that it is perpetual);
(d) the circumstances in which early repayment may be demanded;
(e) the terms of the subordination; and
(f) the existence of any provisions whereby it may be converted into capital or some other form of liability and the terms of any such provisions.

**63(2)** The general terms of any other borrowings included in Liabilities item 7 shall also be stated.

*Fixed cumulative dividends*

**64** If any fixed cumulative dividends on the company's shares are in arrear, there shall be stated:

(a) the amount of the arrears; and
(b) the period for which the dividends or, if there is more than one class, each class of them are in arrear.

*Details of assets charged*

**65(1)** There shall be disclosed, in relation to each liabilities and memorandum item of the balance sheet format, the aggregate amount of any assets of the company which have been charged to secure any liability or potential liability included thereunder, the aggregate amount of the liabilities or potential liabilities so secured and an indication of the nature of the security given.

**65(2)** Particulars shall also be given of any other charge on the assets of the company to secure the liabilities of any other person, including, where practicable, the amount secured.

*Guarantees and other financial commitments*

**66(1)** There shall be stated, where practicable:

(a) the aggregate amount or estimated amount of contracts for capital expenditure, so far as not provided for.

**History**
Pt. I, para. 66(1)(b) and the word "and" immediately preceding it, repealed by the Companies Act 1985 (Miscellaneous Accounting Amendments) Regulations 1996 (SI 1996/189), reg. 1(1), 14(6) and Sch. 4, para. 1, 7 as from 2 February 1996, subject to reg. 16(1), (2); para. 66(1)(b) formerly read as follows:

"(b) the aggregate amount or estimated amount of capital expenditure authorised by the directors which has not been contracted for."

**66(2)** Particulars shall be given of:

(a) any pension commitments included under any provision shown in the company's balance sheet; and

(b) any such commitments for which no provision has been made;

and where any such commitment relates wholly or partly to pensions payable to past directors of the company separate particulars shall be given of that commitment so far as it relates to such pensions.

**66(3)** Particulars shall also be given of any other financial commitments, including any contingent liabilities, which:

(a) have not been provided for;

(b) have not been included in the memorandum items in the balance sheet format; and

(c) are relevant to assessing the company's state of affairs.

**66(4)** Commitments within any of the preceding sub-paragraphs undertaken on behalf of or for the benefit of:

(a) any parent company or fellow subsidiary undertaking of the company; or

(b) any subsidiary undertaking of the company;

shall be stated separately from the other commitments within that sub-paragraph (and commitments within paragraph (a) shall be stated separately from those within paragraph (b)).

**66(5)** There shall be disclosed the nature and amount of any contingent liabilities and commitments included in Memorandum items 1 and 2 which are material in relation to the company's activities.

*Memorandum items: Group undertakings*

**67(1)** With respect to contingent liabilities required to be included under Memorandum item 1 in the balance sheet format, there shall be stated in a note to the accounts the amount of such contingent liabilities incurred on behalf of or for the benefit of:

(a) any parent undertaking or fellow subsidiary undertaking; or

(b) any subsidiary undertaking

of the company; in addition the amount incurred in respect of the undertakings referred to in paragraph (a) shall be stated separately from the amount incurred in respect of the undertakings referred to in paragraph (b).

**67(2)** With respect to commitments required to be included under Memorandum item 2 in the balance sheet format, there shall be stated in a note to the accounts the amount of such commitments undertaken on behalf of or for the benefit of:

(a) any parent undertaking or fellow subsidiary undertaking; or

(b) any subsidiary undertaking

of the company; in addition the amount incurred in respect of the undertakings referred to in paragraph (a) shall be stated separately from the amount incurred in respect of the undertakings referred to in paragraph (b).

*Transferable securities*

**68(1)** There shall be disclosed for each of Assets items 5 to 8 in the balance sheet format the amount of transferable securities included under those items:

(a) that are listed and the amount of those that are unlisted.

**History**
Pt. I, para. 68(1)(b) and the word "and" immediately preceding it, repealed by the Companies Act 1985 (Miscellaneous Accounting Amendments) Regulations 1996 (SI 1996/189), reg. 1(1), 14(6) and Sch. 4, para. 1, 8 as from 2 February 1996, subject to reg. 16(1), (2); para. 68(1)(b) formerly read as follows:

"(b) that are listed on a recognised investment exchange other than an overseas investment exchange within the meaning of the Financial Services Act 1986 and the amount of those listed on other exchanges."

**68(2)** In the case of each amount shown in respect of listed securities under sub-paragraph (1)(a) above, there shall also be disclosed the aggregate market value of those securities, if different from the amount shown.

**68(3)** There shall also be disclosed for each of Assets items 5 and 6 the amount of transferable securities included under those items that are held as financial fixed assets and the amount of those that are not so held, together with the criterion used by the directors to distinguish those held as financial fixed assets.

*Leasing transactions*

**69** The aggregate amount of all property (other than land) leased by the company to other persons shall be disclosed, broken down so as to show the aggregate amount included in each relevant balance sheet item.

*Assets and liabilities denominated in a currency other than sterling (or the currency in which the accounts are drawn up)*

**70(1)** The aggregate amount, in sterling (or the currency in which the accounts are drawn up), of all assets denominated in a currency other than sterling (or the currency used), together with the aggregate amount, in sterling (or the currency used), of all liabilities so denominated, is to be disclosed.

**70(2)** For the purposes of this paragraph an appropriate rate of exchange prevailing at the balance sheet date shall be used to determine the amounts concerned.

*Sundry assets and liabilities*

**71** Where any amount shown under either of the following items is material, particulars shall be given of each type of asset or liability included therein, including an explanation of the nature of the asset or liability and the amount included with respect to assets or liabilities of that type:

(a) Assets item 13 (Other assets)

(b) Liabilities item 4 (Other liabilities).

*Unmatured forward transactions*

**72(1)** The following shall be disclosed with respect to unmatured forward transactions outstanding at the balance sheet date:

(a) the categories of such transactions, by reference to an appropriate system of classification;

(b) whether, in the case of each such category, they have been made, to any material extent, for the purpose of hedging the effects of fluctuations in interest rates, exchange rates and market prices or whether they have been made, to any material extent, for dealing purposes.

**72(2)** Transactions falling within sub-paragraph (1) shall include all those in relation to which income or expenditure is to be included in:

(a) format 1, item 6 or format 2, items B4 or A3 (Dealing [profits] [losses]),

(b) format 1, items 1 or 2, or format 2, items B1 or A1, by virtue of notes(1)(b) and (2)(b) to the profit and loss account formats (forward contracts, spread over the actual duration of the contract and similar in nature to interest).

*Miscellaneous matters*

**73(1)** Particulars shall be given of any case where the cost of any asset is for the first time determined under paragraph 38 of this Part of this Schedule.

**73(2)** Where any outstanding loans made under the authority of section 153(4)(b), (bb) or (c) or section 155 of this Act (various cases of financial assistance by a company for purchase of its own shares) are included under any item shown in the company's balance sheet, the aggregate amount of those loans shall be disclosed for each item in question.

**73(3)** (Repealed by the Companies Act 1985 (Miscellaneous Accounting Amendments) Regulations 1996 (SI 1996/189), reg. 1(1), 14(6) and Sch. 4, para. 1, 9 as from 2 February 1996, subject to reg. 16(1), (2).)

**History**
Pt. I, para. 73(3) formerly read as follows:
"The aggregate amount which is recommended for distribution by way of dividend shall be stated."

## Information supplementing the profit and loss account

*Separate statement of certain items of income and expenditure*

**74** (Repealed by the Companies Act 1985 (Miscellaneous Accounting Amendments) Regulations 1996 (SI 1996/189), reg. 1(1), 14(6) and Sch. 4, para. 1, 10 as from 2 February 1996, subject to reg. 16(1), (2).)

**History**
Pt. I, para. 74 formerly read as follows:
"**74(1)** The amount respectively set aside for redemption of share capital and for redemption of loans shall be stated.
**(2)** The amount of income from listed investments shall be stated.
**(3)** The amount charged to revenue in respect of sums payable in respect of the hire of plant and machinery shall be stated."

*Particulars of tax*

**75(1)** (Repealed by the Companies Act 1985 (Miscellaneous Accounting Amendments) Regulations 1996 (SI 1996/189), reg. 1(1), 14(6) and Sch. 4, para. 1, 11 as from 2 February 1996, subject to reg. 16(1), (2).)

**History**
Pt. I, para. 75(1) formerly read as follows:
"The basis on which the charge for United Kingdom corporation tax and United Kingdom income tax is computed shall be stated."

**75(2)** Particulars shall be given of any special circumstances which affect liability in respect of taxation of profits, income or capital gains for the financial year or liability in respect of taxation of profits, income or capital gains for succeeding financial years.

**75(3)** The following amounts shall be stated:

(a) the amount of the charge for United Kingdom corporation tax;

(b) if that amount would have been greater but for relief from double taxation, the amount which it would have been but for such relief;

(c) the amount of the charge for United Kingdom income tax; and

(d) the amount of the charge for taxation imposed outside the United Kingdom of profits, income and (so far as charged to revenue) capital gains.

These amounts shall be stated separately in respect of each of the amounts which is shown under the following items in the profit and loss account, that is to say format 1 item 16, format 2 item A10 (Tax on [profit] [loss] on ordinary activities) and format 1 item 21, format 2 item A13 (Tax on extraordinary [profit] [loss]).

*Particulars of income*

**76(1)** A company shall disclose, with respect to income included in the following items in the profit and loss account formats the amount of that income attributable to each of the geographical markets in which the company has operated during the financial year:

(a) format 1 item 1, format 2 item B1 (Interest receivable);

(b) format 1 item 3, format 2 item B2 (Dividend income);

(c) format 1 item 4, format 2 item B3 (Fees and commissions receivable);

(d) format 1 item 6, format 2 item B4 (Dealing profits); and

(e) format 1 item 7, format 2 item B7 (Other operating income).

**76(2)** In analysing for the purposes of this paragraph the source of any income, the directors shall have regard to the manner in which the company's activities are organised.

**76(3)** For the purposes of this paragraph, markets which do not differ substantially from each other shall be treated as one market.

**76(4)** Where in the opinion of the directors the disclosure of any information required by this paragraph would be seriously prejudicial to the interests of the company, that information need not be disclosed, but the fact that any such information has not been disclosed must be stated.

*Particulars of staff*

**77(1)** The following information shall be given with respect to the employees of the company:

(a) the average number of persons employed by the company in the financial year; and

(b) the average number of persons so employed within each category of persons employed by the company.

**77(2)** The average number required by sub-paragraph (1)(a) or (b) shall be determined by dividing the relevant annual number by the number of months in the financial year.

**History**

In Pt. I, para. 77(2) the word "months" substituted for the former word "weeks" by the Companies Act 1985 (Miscellaneous Accounting Amendments) Regulations 1996 (SI 1996/189), reg. 1(1), 14(6) and Sch. 4, para. 1, 12(1), (2) as from 2 February 1996, subject to reg. 16(1), (2).

**77(3)** The relevant annual number shall be determined by ascertaining for each month in the financial year:

(a) for the purposes of sub-paragraph (1)(a), the number of persons employed under contracts of service by the company in that month (whether throughout the month or not); and

(b) for the purposes of sub-paragraph (1)(b), the number of persons in the category in question of persons so employed;

and, in either case, adding together all the monthly numbers.

**History**

In Pt. I, para. 77(3) the words "month" and "monthly" substituted for the former words "week" and "weekly" respectively wherever those words occur by the Companies Act 1985 (Miscellaneous Accounting Amendments) Regulations 1996 (SI 1996/189), reg. 1(1), 14(6) and Sch. 4, para. 1, 12(1), (3) as from 2 February 1996, subject to reg. 16(1), (2).

**77(4)** In respect of all persons employed by the company during the financial year who are taken into account in determining the relevant annual number for the purposes of sub-paragraph (1)(a) there shall also be stated the aggregate amounts respectively of:

(a) wages and salaries paid or payable in respect of that year to those persons;

(b) social security costs incurred by the company on their behalf; and

(c) other pension costs so incurred,

save in so far as those amounts or any of them are stated in the profit and loss account.

**77(5)** The categories of persons employed by the company by reference to which the number required to be disclosed by sub-paragraph (1)(b) is to be determined shall be such as the directors may select, having regard to the manner in which the company's activities are organised.

*Management and agency services*

**78** A company providing any management and agency services to customers shall disclose that fact, if the scale of such services provided is material in the context of its business as a whole.

*Subordinated liabilities*

**79** Any amounts charged to the profit and loss account representing charges incurred during the year with respect to subordinated liabilities shall be disclosed.

*Sundry income and charges*

**80** Where any amount to be included in any of the following items is material, particulars shall be given of each individual component of the figure, including an explanation of their nature and amount:

(a) In format 1:

(i) Items 7 and 10 (Other operating income and charges)

(ii) Items 18 and 19 (Extraordinary income and charges);

(b) In format 2:
(i) Items A6 and B7 (Other operating charges and income)
(ii) Items A12 and B10 (Extraordinary charges and income).

*Miscellaneous matters*

**81(1)** Where any amount relating to any preceding financial year is included in any item in the profit and loss account, the effect shall be stated.

**81(2)** The effect shall be stated of any transactions that are exceptional by virtue of size or incidence though they fall within the ordinary activities of the company.

## Chapter IV – Interpretation of Part I

*General*

**82** The following definitions apply for the purposes of this Part of this Schedule and its interpretation:

**"Financial fixed assets"** means loans and advances and securities held as fixed assets; participating interests and shareholdings in group undertakings shall be regarded as financial fixed assets;

**"Fungible assets"** means assets of any description which are substantially indistinguishable one from another;

**"Lease"** includes an agreement for a lease;

**"Listed security"** means a security listed on a recognised stock exchange, or on any stock exchange of repute outside Great Britain and the expression **"unlisted security"** shall be construed accordingly;

**"Long lease"** means a lease in the case of which the portion of the term for which it was granted remaining unexpired at the end of the financial year is not less than 50 years;

**"Repayable on demand"**, in connection with deposits, loans or advances, means those amounts which can at any time be withdrawn or demanded without notice or for which a maturity or period of notice of not more than 24 hours or one working day has been agreed;

**"Sale and repurchase transaction"** means a transaction which involves the transfer by a credit institution or customer (**"the transferor"**) to another credit institution or customer (**"the transferee"**) of assets subject to an agreement that the same assets, or (in the case of fungible assets) equivalent assets, will subsequently be transferred back to the transferor at a specified price on a date specified or to be specified by the transferor; but the following shall not be regarded as sale and repurchase transactions: forward exchange transactions, options, transactions involving the issue of debt securities with a commitment to repurchase all or part of the issue before maturity or any similar transactions;

**"Sale and option to resell transaction"** means a transaction which involves the transfer by a credit institution or customer (**"the transferor"**) to another credit institution or customer (**"the transferee"**) of assets subject to an agreement that the transferee is entitled to require the subsequent transfer of the same assets, or (in the case of fungible assets) equivalent assets, back to the transferor at the purchase price or another price agreed in advance on a date specified or to be specified; and

**"Short lease"** means a lease which is not a long lease.

**History**

In para. 82 the definitions of "Banking activities" and "Banking transactions" formerly appearing at the beginning repealed by the Companies Act 1985 (Bank Accounts) Regulations 1994 (SI 1994/233), reg. 1, 4(1) as from 11 February 1994 subject to transitional provisions in reg. 7, 8; the definitions formerly read as follows:

""**Banking activities**" means activities forming part of a deposit-taking business within the meaning of the Banking Act 1987;

"**Banking transactions**" means transactions entered into in the normal course of a deposit-taking business within the meaning of the Banking Act 1987;".

*Loans*

**83** For the purposes of this Part of this Schedule a loan or advance (including a liability comprising a loan or advance) is treated as falling due for repayment, and an instalment of a loan or advance is treated as falling due for payment, on the earliest date on which the lender could require repayment or (as the case may be) payment, if he exercised all options and rights available to him.

*Materiality*

**84** For the purposes of this Part of this Schedule amounts which in the particular context of any provision of this Part are not material may be disregarded for the purposes of that provision.

*Provisions*

**85** For the purposes of this Part of this Schedule and its interpretation:

(a) references in this Part to provisions for depreciation or diminution in value of assets are to any amount written off by way of providing for depreciation or diminution in value of assets;

(b) any reference in the profit and loss account formats or the notes thereto set out in Section B of this Part to the depreciation of, or amounts written off, assets of any description is to any provision for depreciation or diminution in value of assets of that description; and

(c) references in this Part to provisions for liabilities or charges are to any amount retained as reasonably necessary for the purpose of providing for any liability or loss which is either likely to be incurred, or certain to be incurred but uncertain as to amount or as to the date on which it will arise.

*Scots land tenure*

**86** In the application of this Part of this Schedule to Scotland, **"land of freehold tenure"** means land in respect of which the company is the proprietor of the *dominium utile* or in the case of land not held on feudal tenure, is the owner; **"land of leasehold tenure"** means land of which the company is the tenant under a lease; and the reference to ground-rents, rates and other outgoings includes feu-duty and ground annual.

*Staff costs*

**87** For the purposes of this Part of this Schedule and its interpretation:

(a) **"Social security costs"** means any contributions by the company to any state social security or pension scheme, fund or arrangement;

(b) **"Pension costs"** includes any costs incurred by the company in respect of any pension scheme established for the purpose of providing pensions for persons currently or formerly employed by the company, any sums set aside for the future payment of pensions directly by the company to current or former employees and any pensions paid directly to such persons without having first been set aside; and

(c) any amount stated in respect of the item **"social security costs"** or in respect of the item **"wages and salaries"** in the company's profit and loss account shall be determined by reference to payments made or costs incurred in respect of all persons employed by the company during the financial year who are taken into account in determining the relevant annual number for the purposes of paragraph 77(1)(a).

**History**

Pt. I, para. 87(b) substituted by the Companies Act 1985 (Miscellaneous Accounting Amendments) Regulations 1996 (SI 1996/189), reg. 1(1), 14(6) and Sch. 4, para. 1, 13(1), (2) as from 2 February 1996, subject to reg. 16(1), (2); para. 87(b) formerly read as follows:

"(b) **"Pension costs"** includes any other contributions by the company for the purposes of any pension scheme established for the purpose of providing pensions for persons employed by the company, any sums set aside for that purpose and any amounts paid by the company in respect of pensions without first being so set aside; and".

**History to Pt. I**

In Pt. I, para. 87(c) the words "the item "social security costs"" substituted for the former words "either of the above items" by the Companies Act 1985 (Miscellaneous Accounting Amendments) Regulations 1996 (SI 1996/189), reg. 1(1), 14(6) and Sch. 4, para. 1, 13(1), (3) as from 2 February 1996, subject to reg. 16(1), (2).
See also history note after Pt. III.

# Part II – Consolidated Accounts

*Undertakings to be included in consolidation*

**1(1)** An undertaking (other than a credit institution) whose activities are a direct extension of or ancillary to banking business shall not be excluded from consolidation under section 229(4) (exclusion of undertakings whose activities are different from those of the undertakings consolidated).

**1(2)** For the purposes of this paragraph **"banking"** means the carrying on of a deposit taking business within the meaning of the Banking Act 1987.

*General application of provisions applicable to individual accounts*

**2(1)** In paragraph 1 of Schedule 4A (application to group accounts of provisions applicable to individual accounts), the reference in sub-paragraph (1) to the provisions of Schedule 4 shall be construed as a reference to the provisions of Part I of this Schedule; and accordingly:

(a) (Repealed by the Companies Act 1985 (Accounts of Small and Medium-sized Companies and Minor Accounting Amendments) Regulations 1997 (SI 1997/220), reg . 1, 7(11) as from 1 March 1997.)

(b) sub-paragraph (3) shall be omitted.

**History**
Para. 2(1)(a) formerly read as follows:
"the reference in sub-paragraph (2) to paragraph 59 of Schedule 4 shall be construed as a reference to note (20) on the balance sheet format set out in Section B of Chapter 1 of Part I of this Schedule and paragraphs 66(4) and 67 of Part I of this Schedule; and"

**2(2)** The general application of the provisions of Part I of this Schedule in place of those of Schedule 4 is subject to the following provisions.

*Minority interests and associated undertakings*

**3(1)** The provisions of this paragraph shall have effect so as to adapt paragraphs 17 and 21 of Schedule 4A (which require items in respect of "Minority interests" and associated undertakings to be added to the formats set out in Schedule 4) to the formats prescribed by Part I of this Schedule.

**3(2)** The item required to be added to the balance sheet format by paragraph 17(2) shall be added either between Liabilities items 7 and 8 or after Liabilities item 12.

**3(3)** The item required to be added to the profit and loss account format by paragraph 17(3) shall be added:

(a) in the case of format 1, between items 17 and 18; or

(b) in the case of format 2, between items A11 and A12 or between items B9 and B10.

**3(4)** The item required to be added to the profit and loss account format by paragraph 17(4) shall be added:

(a) in the case of format 1, between items 22 and 23; or

(b) in the case of format 2, between items A14 and A15 or between items B11 and B12.

**3(5)** Paragraph 17(5) shall not apply but for the purposes of paragraph 3(3) of Part I of this Schedule (power to combine items) the additional items required by the foregoing provisions of this paragraph shall be treated as items to which a letter is assigned.

**3(6)** Paragraph 21(2) shall apply with respect to a balance sheet prepared under this Schedule as if it required Assets item 7 (Participating interests) in the balance sheet format to be replaced by the two replacement items referred to in that paragraph.

**3(7)** Paragraph 21(3) shall not apply, but the following items in the profit and loss account formats, namely:

(a) format 1 item 3(b) (Income from participating interests)

(b) format 2 item B2(b) (Income from participating interests),

shall be replaced by the following two replacement items:

(i) "Income from participating interests other than associated undertakings", which shall be shown at position 3(b) in format 1 and position B2(b) in format 2; and

(ii) "Income from associated undertakings", which shall be shown at an appropriate position.

**4** Paragraphs 18 and 22(1) of Schedule 4A shall apply as if, in substitution for the references therein to paragraphs 17 to 19 and 21 of Schedule 4, they referred to paragraphs 24 to 26 and 28 of Part I of this Schedule.

*Foreign currency translation*

**5** Any difference between:

(a) the amount included in the consolidated accounts for the previous financial year with respect to any undertaking included in the consolidation or the group's interest in any associated undertaking, together with the amount of any transactions undertaken to cover any such interest; and

(b) the opening amount for the financial year in respect of those undertakings and in respect of any such transactions

arising as a result of the application of paragraph 45 of Part I of this Schedule may be credited to (where (a) is less than (b)), or deducted from (where (a) is greater than (b)), (as the case may be) consolidated reserves.

**6** Any income and expenditure of undertakings included in the consolidation and associated undertakings in a foreign currency may be translated for the purposes of the consolidated accounts at the average rates of exchange prevailing during the financial year.

*Information as to undertaking in which shares held as a result of financial assistance operation*

**7(1)** The following provisions apply where the parent company of a banking group has a subsidiary undertaking which:

(a) is a credit institution of which shares are held as a result of a financial assistance operation with a view to its reorganisation or rescue; and

(b) is excluded from consolidation under section 229(3)(c) (interest held with a view to resale).

**7(2)** Information as to the nature and terms of the operations shall be given in a note to the group accounts and there shall be appended to the copy of the group accounts delivered to the registrar in accordance with section 242 a copy of the undertaking's latest individual accounts and, if it is a parent undertaking, its latest group accounts.

If the accounts appended are required by law to be audited, a copy of the auditors' report shall also be appended.

**7(3)** If any document required to be appended is in a language other than English, then, subject to section 710B(6) (delivery of certain Welsh documents without a translation), the directors shall annex a translation of it into English, certified in the prescribed manner to be a correct translation.

**History**

In para. 7(3) the words "Subject to section 255E (delivery of accounting documents in Welsh only)," formerly appearing at the beginning repealed by Welsh Language Act 1993, s. 35(1) and Sch. 2 as from 1 February 1994 (see SI 1994/115/193 (C 5) art. 2(2)); these words were previously inserted by the Companies Act 1985 (Welsh Language Accounts) Regulations 1992 (SI 1992/1083), reg. 1(1), 2(1), (5) as from 1 June 1992.

Also in para. 7(3) the words "then, subject to section 710B(6) (delivery of certain Welsh documents without a translation)," inserted by Welsh Language Act 1993, s. 30(1)(4)(a) as from 1 February 1994 (see SI 1994/115 (C 5), art. 2(2)).

**7(4)** The above requirements are subject to the following qualifications:

(a) an undertaking is not required to prepare for the purposes of this paragraph accounts which would not otherwise be prepared, and if no accounts satisfying the above requirements are prepared none need be appended;

(b) the accounts of an undertaking need not be appended if they would not otherwise be required to be published, or made available for public inspection, anywhere in the world, but in that case the reason for not appending the accounts shall be stated in a note to the consolidated accounts.

**7(5)** Where a copy of an undertaking's accounts is required to be appended to the copy of the group accounts delivered to the registrar, that fact shall be stated in a note to the group accounts.

**7(6)** Sub-sections (2) to (4) of section 242 (penalties, etc. in case of default) apply in relation to the requirements of this paragraph as regards the delivery of documents to the registrar as they apply in relation to the requirements of sub-section (1) of that section.

**History**
See history note after Pt. III.

# Part III – Additional Disclosure: Related Undertakings

**1(1)** Where accounts are prepared in accordance with the special provisions of this Schedule relating to banking companies or groups:

(a) the information required by paragraphs 8 and 24 of Schedule 5 (information about significant holdings of the company in undertakings other than subsidiary undertakings) need only be given in respect of undertakings (otherwise falling within the class of undertakings in respect of which disclosure is required) in which the company has a significant holding amounting to 20 per cent or more of the nominal value of the shares in the undertaking; and

(b) the information required by paragraph 27 of Schedule 5 (information about significant holdings of the group in undertakings other than subsidiary undertakings) need only be given in respect of undertakings (otherwise falling within the class of undertakings in respect of which disclosure is required) in which the group has a significant holding amounting to 20 per cent or more of the nominal value of the shares in the undertaking.

In addition any information required by those paragraphs may be omitted if it is not material.

**1(2)** Paragraph 13(3) and (4) of Schedule 5 shall apply *mutatis mutandis* for the purposes of sub-paragraph (1)(a) above and paragraph 32(3) and (4) of that Schedule shall apply *mutatis mutandis* for the purposes of sub-paragraph (1)(b) above.

**History**
Pt. I–III inserted by the Companies Act 1985 (Bank Accounts) Regulations 1991 (SI 1991/2705), reg. 5(4) and Sch. 1 as from 2 December 1991 (subject to transitional provisions in reg. 9); for the former Pt. I–III see now Sch. 9A.

# Part IV – Additional Disclosure: Emoluments and Other Benefits of Directors and Others

**1** The provisions of this Part of this Schedule have effect with respect to the application of Schedule 6 (additional disclosure: emoluments and other benefits of directors and others) to a banking company or the holding company of a credit institution.

**History**
In para. 1 the words "the holding company of a credit institution" substituted for the former words "the holding company of such a company" by the Companies Act 1985 (Bank Accounts) Regulations 1994 (SI 1994/233), reg. 1, 5(1), (2) as from 28 February 1994 subject to transitional provisions in reg. 7, 8.
See also history note after para. 3.

## LOANS, QUASI-LOANS AND OTHER DEALINGS

**2** Where a banking company, or a company which is the holding company of a credit institution, prepares annual accounts for a financial year, it need not comply with the provisions of Part II of Schedule 6 (loans, quasi-loans and other dealings) in relation to a transaction or arrangement of a kind mentioned in section 330, or an agreement to enter into such a transaction or arrangement, to which that banking company or (as the case may be) credit institution is a party.

**History**
Para. 2 substituted by the Companies Act 1985 (Bank Accounts) Regulations 1994 (SI 1994/233), reg. 1, 5(1), (3) as from 28 February 1994 subject to transitional provisions in reg. 7, 8; para. 2 formerly read as follows:

"Part II of Schedule 6 (loans, quasi-loans and other dealings) does not apply for the purposes of accounts prepared by a banking company, or a company which is the holding company of a banking company, in relation to a transaction or arrangement of a kind mentioned in section 330, or an agreement to enter into such a transaction or arrangement, to which that banking company is a party."

See also history note after para. 3.

### OTHER TRANSACTIONS, ARRANGEMENTS AND AGREEMENTS

**3(1)** Where a banking company, or a company which is the holding company of a credit institution, takes advantage of the provisions of paragraph 2 of this Part of this Schedule for the purposes of its annual accounts for a financial year, then, in preparing those accounts, it shall comply with the provisions of Part III of Schedule 6 (other transactions, arrangements and agreements) only in relation to a transaction, arrangement or agreement made by that banking company or (as the case may be) credit institution for –

(a) a person who was a director of the company preparing the accounts, or who was connected with such a director, or

(b) a person who was a chief executive or manager (within the meaning of the Banking Act 1987) of that company or its holding company.

**History**
In para. 3(1) the words from the beginning to "as the case may be) credit institution for –" substituted by the Companies Act 1985 (Bank Accounts) Regulations 1994 (SI 1994/233), reg. 1, 5(1), (4) as from 28 February 1994 subject to transitional provisions in reg. 7, 8; the former words read as follows:

"Part III of Schedule 6 (other transactions, arrangements and agreements) applies for the purposes of accounts prepared by a banking company, or a company which is the holding company of a banking company, only in relation to a transaction, arrangement or agreement made by that banking company for –"

See also history note after para. 3(5).

**3(2)** References in that Part to officers of the company shall be construed accordingly as including references to such persons.

**3(3)** In this paragraph **"director"** includes a shadow director.

**3(4)** For the purposes of that Part as it applies by virtue of this paragraph, a body corporate which a person does not control shall not be treated as connected with him.

**History**
See history note after para. 3(5).

**3(5)** Section 346 of this Act applies for the purposes of this paragraph as regards the interpretation of references to a person being connected with a director or controlling a body corporate.

**History**
In para. 3(4), (5) the words "body corporate" substituted for the former word "company" by the Companies Act 1985 (Bank Accounts) Regulations 1994 (SI 1994/233), reg. 1, 5(1), (5) as from 28 February 1994 subject to transitional provisions in reg. 7, 8.

**History to Pt. IV**
Pt. IV originally inserted – see CA 1989, s. 18(3), (4), Sch. 7, preliminary para. (d) and Pt. II–IV – as from 1 April 1990 subject to transitional and saving provisions (see SI 1990/355 (C 13), art. 3, Sch. 1 and also art. 6–9).

# Schedule 9A – Form and Content of Accounts of Insurance Companies and Groups

## Part I – Individual Accounts

### Chapter I – General Rules and Formats

#### SECTION A – GENERAL RULES

**1(1)** Subject to the following provisions of this Part of this Schedule–

(a) every balance sheet of a company shall show the items listed in the balance sheet format set out below in section B of this Chapter; and

(b) every profit and loss account of a company shall show the items listed in the profit and loss account format so set out,

in either case in the order and under the headings and sub-headings given in the format.

**1(2)** Sub-paragraph (1) above is not to be read as requiring the heading or sub-heading for any item to be distinguished by any letter or number assigned to that item in the format.

**2(1)** Any item required in accordance with paragraph 1 above to be shown in a company's balance sheet or profit and loss account may be shown in greater detail than so required.

**2(2)** A company's balance sheet or profit and loss account may include an item representing or covering the amount of any asset or liability, income or expenditure not specifically covered by any of the items listed in the balance sheet or profit and loss account format set out in section B below, but the following shall not be treated as assets in any company's balance sheet–

(a) preliminary expenses;

(b) expenses of and commission on any issue of shares or debentures; and

(c) costs of research.

**2(3)** Items to which Arabic numbers are assigned in the balance sheet format set out in section B below (except for items concerning technical provisions and the reinsurers' share of technical provisions), and items to which lower case letters in parentheses are assigned in the profit and loss account format so set out (except for items within items I.1 and 4 and II.1, 5 and 6) may be combined in a company's accounts for any financial year if either–

(a) their individual amounts are not material for the purpose of giving a true and fair view; or

(b) the combination facilitates the assessment of the state of affairs or profit or loss of the company for that year;

but in a case within paragraph (b) above the individual amounts of any items so combined shall be disclosed in a note to the accounts and any notes required by this Schedule to the items so combined under that paragraph shall, notwithstanding the combination, be given.

**2(4)** Subject to paragraph 3(3) below, a heading or sub-heading corresponding to an item listed in the format adopted in preparing a company's balance sheet or profit and loss account shall not be included if there is no amount to be shown for that item in respect of the financial year to which the balance sheet or profit and loss account relates.

**3(1)** In respect of every item shown in the balance sheet or profit and loss account, there shall be shown or stated the corresponding amount for the financial year immediately preceding that to which the accounts relate.

**3(2)** Where the corresponding amount is not comparable with the amount to be shown for the item in question in respect of the financial year to which the balance sheet or profit and loss account relates, the former amount shall be adjusted and particulars of the adjustment and the reasons for it shall be given in a note to the accounts.

**3(3)** Paragraph 2(4) above does not apply in any case where an amount can be shown for the item in question in respect of the financial year immediately preceding that to which the balance sheet or profit and loss account relates, and that amount shall be shown under the heading or sub-heading required by paragraph 1 above for that item.

**4** Subject to the provisions of this Schedule, amounts in respect of items representing assets or income may not be set off against amounts in respect of items representing liabilities or expenditure (as the case may be), or vice versa.

**5** Every profit and loss account of a company shall show separately as additional items–

(a) any amount set aside or proposed to be set aside to, or withdrawn or proposed to be withdrawn from, reserves;

(b) the aggregate amount of any dividends paid and proposed;

(c) if it is not shown in the notes to the accounts, the aggregate amount of any dividends proposed.

**History**
In Pt. I, para. 5(a) the word "and" formerly appearing at the end of the paragraph omitted, and para. 5(c) inserted by the Companies Act 1985 (Miscellaneous Accounting Amendments) Regulations 1996 (SI 1996/189), reg. 1(1), 14(7) and Sch. 5, para. 1, 2 as from 2 February 1996, subject to reg. 16(1), (2).

**6** The provisions of this Schedule which relate to long term business shall apply, with necessary modifications, to business within Classes 1 and 2 of Schedule 2 to the 1982 Act which–

(a) is transacted exclusively or principally according to the technical principles of long term business, and

(b) is a significant amount of the business of the company.

## SECTION B – THE REQUIRED FORMATS FOR ACCOUNTS

### Preliminary

**7(1)** References in this Part of this Schedule to the balance sheet format or profit and loss account format are to the balance sheet format or profit and loss account format set out below, and references to the items listed in either of the formats are to those items read together with any of the notes following the formats which apply to any of those items.

**7(2)** The requirement imposed by paragraph 1 to show the items listed in either format in the order adopted in the format is subject to any provision in the notes following the format for alternative positions for any particular items.

**7(3)** Where in respect of any item to which an Arabic number is assigned in either format, the gross amount and reinsurance amount or reinsurers' share are required to be shown, a sub-total of those amounts shall also be given.

**7(4)** Where in respect of any item to which an Arabic number is assigned in the profit and loss account format, separate items are required to be shown, then a separate sub-total of those items shall also be given in addition to any sub-total required by sub-paragraph (3) above.

**8** A number in brackets following any item in either of the formats set out below is a reference to the note of that number in the notes following the format.

**9** In the profit and loss account format set out below–

(a) the heading "Technical account – General business" is for business within the classes of insurance specified in Schedule 2 to the 1982 Act; and

(b) the heading "Technical account – Long term business" is for business within the classes of insurance specified in Schedule 1 to that Act.

### Balance Sheet Format

ASSETS

A. *Called up share capital not paid (1)*

B. *Intangible assets*
  1. Development costs
  2. Concessions, patents, licences, trade marks and similar rights and assets *(2)*
  3. Goodwill *(3)*
  4. Payments on account

C. *Investments*
  I. Land and buildings *(4)*
  II. Investments in group undertakings and participating interests
    1. Shares in group undertakings
    2. Debt securities issued by, and loans to, group undertakings
    3. Participating interests
    4. Debt securities issued by, and loans to, undertakings in which the company has a participating interest
  III. Other financial investments
    1. Shares and other variable-yield securities and units in unit trusts
    2. Debt securities and other fixed income securities
    3. Participation in investment pools
    4. Loans secured by mortgages *(7)*

5. Other loans *(7)*
6. Deposits with credit institutions *(8)*
7. Other *(9)*

IV. Deposits with ceding undertakings *(10)*

D. *Assets held to cover linked liabilities (11)*

Da. *Reinsurers' share of technical provisions (12)*

1. Provision for unearned premiums
2. Long term business provision
3. Claims outstanding
4. Provisions for bonuses and rebates
5. Other technical provisions
6. Technical provisions for unit-linked liabilities

E. *Debtors (13)*

I. Debtors arising out of direct insurance operations

1. Policy holders
2. Intermediaries

II. Debtors arising out of reinsurance operations

III. Other debtors

IV. Called up share capital not paid *(1)*

F. *Other assets*

I. Tangible assets

1. Plant and machinery
2. Fixtures, fittings, tools and equipment
3. Payments on account (other than deposits paid on land and buildings) and assets (other than buildings) in course of construction

II. Stocks

1. Raw materials and consumables
2. Work in progress
3. Finished goods and goods for resale
4. Payments on account

III. Cash at bank and in hand

IV. Own shares *(14)*

V. Other *(15)*

G. *Prepayments and accrued income*

I. Accrued interest and rent *(16)*

II. Deferred acquisition costs *(17)*

III. Other prepayments and accrued income

LIABILITIES

A. *Capital and reserves*

I. Called up share capital or equivalent funds

II. Share premium account

III. Revaluation reserve

IV. Reserves

1. Capital redemption reserve
2. Reserve for own shares
3. Reserves provided for by the articles of association
4. Other reserves

V. Profit and loss account

B. *Subordinated liabilities (18)*

Ba. *Fund for future appropriations (19)*

C. *Technical provisions*

1. Provision for unearned premiums *(20)*

(a) gross amount
(b) reinsurance amount *(12)*

2. Long term business provision *(20) (21) (26)*
   (a) gross amount
   (b) reinsurance amount *(12)*
3. Claims outstanding *(22)*
   (a) gross amount
   (b) reinsurance amount *(12)*
4. Provision for bonuses and rebates *(23)*
   (a) gross amount
   (b) reinsurance amount *(12)*
5. Equalisation provision *(24)*
6. Other technical provisions *(25)*
   (a) gross amount
   (b) reinsurance amount *(12)*

D. *Technical provisions for linked liabilities (26)*

(a) gross amount
(b) reinsurance amount *(12)*

E. *Provisions for other risks and charges*

1. Provisions for pensions and similar obligations
2. Provisions for taxation
3. Other provisions

F. *Deposits received from reinsurers (27)*

G. *Creditors (28)*

I. Creditors arising out of direct insurance operations
II. Creditors arising out of reinsurance operations
III. Debenture loans *(29)*
IV. Amounts owed to credit institutions
V. Other creditors including taxation and social security

H. *Accruals and deferred income*

## Notes on the balance sheet format

*(1) Called up share capital not paid*

(Assets items A and E.IV)

This item may be shown in either of the positions given in the format.

*(2) Concessions, patents, licences, trade marks and similar rights and assets*

(Assets item B.2)

Amounts in respect of assets shall only be included in a company's balance sheet under this item if either–

(a) the assets were acquired for valuable consideration and are not required to be shown under goodwill; or

(b) the assets in question were created by the company itself.

*(3) Goodwill*

(Assets item B.3)

Amounts representing goodwill shall only be included to the extent that the goodwill was acquired for valuable consideration.

*(4) Land and buildings*

(Assets item C.I.)

The amount of any land and buildings occupied by the company for its own activities shall be shown separately in the notes to the accounts.

*(5) Debt securities and other fixed income securities*

(Assets item C.III.2)

This item shall comprise transferable debt securities and any other transferable fixed income securities issued by credit institutions, other undertakings or public bodies, in so far as they are not covered by Assets item C.II.2 or C.II.4.

Securities bearing interest rates that vary in accordance with specific factors, for example the interest rate on the inter-bank market or on the Euromarket, shall also be regarded as debt securities and other fixed income securities and so be included under this item.

*(6) Participation in investment pools*

(Assets item C.III.3)

This item shall comprise shares held by the company in joint investments constituted by several undertakings or pension funds, the management of which has been entrusted to one of those undertakings or to one of those pension funds.

*(7) Loans secured by mortgages and other loans*

(Assets items C.III.4 and C.III.5)

Loans to policy holders for which the policy is the main security shall be included under "Other loans" and their amount shall be disclosed in the notes to the accounts. Loans secured by mortgage shall be shown as such even where they are also secured by insurance policies. Where the amount of "Other loans" not secured by policies is material, an appropriate breakdown shall be given in the notes to the accounts.

*(8) Deposits with credit institutions*

(Assets item C.III.6)

This item shall comprise sums the withdrawal of which is subject to a time restriction. Sums deposited with no such restriction shall be shown under Assets item F.III even if they bear interest.

*(9) Other*

(Assets item C.III.7)

This item shall comprise those investments which are not covered by Assets items C.III. 1 to 6. Where the amount of such investments is significant, they must be disclosed in the notes to the accounts.

*(10) Deposits with ceding undertakings*

(Assets item C.IV)

Where the company accepts reinsurance this item shall comprise amounts, owed by the ceding undertakings and corresponding to guarantees, which are deposited with those ceding undertakings or with third parties or which are retained by those undertakings.

These amounts may not be combined with other amounts owed by the ceding insurer to the reinsurer or set off against amounts owed by the reinsurer to the ceding insurer.

Securities deposited with ceding undertakings or third parties which remain the property of the company shall be entered in the company's accounts as an investment, under the appropriate item.

*(11) Assets held to cover linked liabilities*

(Assets item D)

In respect of long term business, this item shall comprise investments made pursuant to long term policies under which the benefits payable to the policy holder are wholly or partly to be determined by reference to the value of, or the income from, property of any description (whether or not specified in the contract) or by reference to fluctuations in, or in an index of, the value of property of any description (whether or not so specified).

This item shall also comprise investments which are held on behalf of the members of a tontine and are intended for distribution among them.

*(12) Reinsurance amounts*

(Assets item Da: Liabilities items C.1(b), 2(b), 3(b), 4(b) and 6(b) and D(b))

The reinsurance amounts may be shown either under Assets item Da or under Liabilities items C.1(b), 2(b), 3(b), 4(b) and 6(b) and D(b).

The reinsurance amounts shall comprise the actual or estimated amounts which, under contractual reinsurance arrangements, are deducted from the gross amounts of technical provisions.

As regards the provision for unearned premiums, the reinsurance amounts shall be calculated according to the methods referred to in paragraph 44 above or in accordance with the terms of the reinsurance policy.

*(13) Debtors*

(Assets item E)

Amounts owed by group undertakings and undertakings in which the company has a participating interest shall be shown separately as sub-items of Assets items E.I, II and III.

*(14) Own shares*

(Assets item F.IV)

The nominal value of the shares shall be shown separately under this item.

*(15) Other*

(Assets item F.V)

This item shall comprise those assets which are not covered by Assets items F.I to IV. Where such assets are material they must be disclosed in the notes to the accounts.

*(16) Accrued interest and rent*

(Assets item G.I)

This item shall comprise those items that represent interest and rent that have been earned up to the balance-sheet date but have not yet become receivable.

*(17) Deferred acquisition costs*

(Assets item G.II)

This item shall comprise the costs of acquiring insurance policies which are incurred during a financial year but relate to a subsequent financial year ("deferred acquisition costs"), except in so far as–

(a) allowance has been made in the computation of the long term business provision made under paragraph 46 below and shown under Liabilities item C2 or D in the balance sheet, for–
   (i) the explicit recognition of such costs, or
   (ii) the implicit recognition of such costs by virtue of the anticipation of future income from which such costs may prudently be expected to be recovered, or

(b) allowance has been made for such costs in respect of general business policies by a deduction from the provision for unearned premiums made under paragraph 44 below and shown under Liabilities item C.I in the balance sheet.

Deferred acquisition costs arising in general business shall be distinguished from those arising in long term business.

In the case of general business, the amount of any deferred acquisition costs shall be established on a basis compatible with that used for unearned premiums.

There shall be disclosed in the notes to the accounts–

(a) how the deferral of acquisition costs has been treated (unless otherwise expressly stated in the accounts), and

(b) where such costs are included as a deduction from the provisions at Liabilities item C.I, the amount of such deduction, or

(c) where the actuarial method used in the calculation of the provisions at Liabilities item C.2 or D has made allowance for the explicit recognition of such costs, the amount of the costs so recognised.

*(18) Subordinated liabilities*

(Liabilities item B)

This item shall comprise all liabilities in respect of which there is a contractual obligation that, in the event of winding up or of bankruptcy, they are to be repaid only after the claims of all other creditors have been met (whether or not they are represented by certificates).

*(19) Fund for future appropriations*

(Liabilities item Ba)

This item shall comprise all funds the allocation of which either to policy holders or to shareholders has not been determined by the end of the financial year.

Transfers to and from this item shall be shown in item II.12a in the profit and loss account.

*(20) Provision for unearned premiums*

(Liabilities item C.1)

In the case of long term business the provision for unearned premiums may be included in Liabilities item C.2 rather than in this item.

The provision for unearned premiums shall comprise the amount representing that part of gross premiums written which is estimated to be earned in the following financial year or to subsequent financial years.

*(21) Long term business provision*

(Liabilities item C.2)

This item shall comprise the actuarially estimated value of the company's liabilities (excluding technical provisions included in Liabilities item D), including bonuses already declared and after deducting the actuarial value of future premiums.

This item shall also comprise claims incurred but not reported, plus the estimated costs of settling such claims.

*(22) Claims outstanding*

(Liabilities item C.3)

This item shall comprise the total estimated ultimate cost to the company of settling all claims arising from events which have occurred up to the end of the financial year (including, in the case of general business, claims incurred but not reported) less amounts already paid in respect of such claims.

*(23) Provision for bonuses and rebates*

(Liabilities item C.4)

This item shall comprise amounts intended for policy holders or contract beneficiaries by way of bonuses and rebates as defined in Note (5) on the profit and loss account format to the extent that such amounts have not been credited to policy holders or contract beneficiaries or included in Liabilities item Ba or in Liabilities item C.2.

*(24) Equalisation provision*

(Liabilities item C.5)

This item shall comprise the amount of any reserve maintained by the company under section 34A of the Insurance Companies Act 1982.

This item shall also comprise any amounts which, in accordance with Council Directive 87/343/EEC, are required to be set aside by a company to equalise fluctuations in loss ratios in future years or to provide for special risks.

A company which otherwise constitutes reserves to equalise fluctuations in loss ratios in future years or to provide for special risks shall disclose that fact in the notes to the accounts.

**History**

In Note (24) the words "This item shall comprise the amount of any reserve maintained by the company under section 34A of the Insurance Companies Act 1982." appearing at the start and the word "also" appearing after the words "This item shall" in the second paragraph inserted by the Insurance Companies (Reserves) Act 1995, s. 3(1), (2) as from 30 April 1996.

*(25) Other technical provisions*

(Liabilities item C.6)

This item shall comprise, inter alia, the provision for unexpired risks as defined in paragraph 81 below. Where the amount of the provision for unexpired risks is significant, it shall be disclosed separately either in the balance sheet or in the notes to the accounts.

*(26) Technical provisions for linked liabilities*

(Liabilities item D)

This item shall comprise technical provisions constituted to cover liabilities relating to investment in the context of long term policies under which the benefits payable to policy holders are wholly or partly to be determined by reference to the value of, or the income from, property of any description (whether or not specified in the contract) or by reference to fluctuations in, or in an index of, the value of property of any description (whether or not so specified).

Any additional technical provisions constituted to cover death risks, operating expenses or other risks (such as benefits payable at the maturity date or guaranteed surrender values) shall be included under Liabilities item C.2.

This item shall also comprise technical provisions representing the obligations of a tontine's organiser in relation to its members.

*(27) Deposits received from reinsurers*

(Liabilities item F)

Where the company cedes reinsurance, this item shall comprise amounts deposited by or withheld from other insurance undertakings under reinsurance contracts. These amounts may not be merged with other amounts owed to or by those other undertakings.

Where the company cedes reinsurance and has received as a deposit securities which have been transferred to its ownership, this item shall comprise the amount owed by the company by virtue of the deposit.

*(28) Creditors*

(Liabilities item G)

Amounts owed to group undertakings and undertakings in which the company has a participating interest shall be shown separately as sub-items.

*(29) Debenture loans*

(Liabilities item G.III)

The amount of any convertible loans shall be shown separately.

**Special rules for balance sheet format**

*Additional items*

**10(1)** Every balance sheet of a company which carries on long term business shall show separately as an additional item the aggregate of any amounts included in Liabilities item A (capital and reserves) which are required not to be treated as realised profits under section 268 of this Act.

**10(2)** A company which carries on long term business shall show separately, in the balance sheet or in the notes to the accounts, the total amount of assets representing the long term fund valued in accordance with the provisions of this Schedule.

*Managed funds*

**11(1)** For the purposes of this paragraph **"managed funds"** are funds of a group pension fund–

(a) which fall within Class VII of Schedule 1 to the 1982 Act, and

(b) which the company administers in its own name but on behalf of others, and

(c) to which it has legal title.

**11(2)** The company shall, in any case where assets and liabilities arising in respect of managed funds fall to be treated as assets and liabilities of the company, adopt the following accounting treatment: assets and liabilities representing managed funds are to be included in the company's balance sheet, with the notes to the accounts disclosing the total amount included with respect to such assets and liabilities in the balance sheet and showing the amount included under each relevant balance sheet item in respect of such assets or (as the case may be) liabilities.

*Deferred acquisition costs*

**12** The costs of acquiring insurance policies which are incurred during a financial year but which relate to a subsequent financial year shall be deferred in a manner specified in Note *(17)* on the balance sheet format.

## Profit and loss account format

I. *Technical account – General business*

1. Earned premiums, net of reinsurance
   - (a) gross premiums written *(1)*
   - (b) outward reinsurance premiums *(2)*
   - (c) change in the gross provision for unearned premiums
   - (d) change in the provision for unearned premiums, reinsurers' share

2. Allocated investment return transferred from the non-technical account (item III.6) *(10)*

2a. Investment income *(8) (10)*
   - (a) income from participating interests, with a separate indication of that derived from group undertakings
   - (b) income from other investments, with a separate indication of that derived from group undertakings
     - (aa) income from land and buildings
     - (bb) income from other investments
   - (c) value re-adjustments on investments
   - (d) gains on the realisation of investments

3. Other technical income, net of reinsurance

4. Claims incurred, net of reinsurance *(4)*
   - (a) claims paid
     - (aa) gross amount
     - (bb) reinsurers' share
   - (b) change in the provision for claims
     - (aa) gross amount
     - (bb) reinsurers' share

5. Changes in other technical provisions, net of reinsurance, not shown under other headings

6. Bonuses and rebates, net of reinsurance *(5)*

7. Net operating expenses
   - (a) acquisition costs *(6)*
   - (b) change in deferred acquisition costs
   - (c) administrative expenses *(7)*
   - (d) reinsurance commissions and profit participation

8. Other technical charges, net of reinsurance

8a. Investment expenses and charges *(8)*
   - (a) investment management expenses, including interest
   - (b) value adjustments on investments
   - (c) losses on the realisation of investments

9. Change in the equalisation provision

10. Sub-total (balance on the technical account for general business) (item III.1)

II *Technical account – Long term business*

1. Earned premiums, net of reinsurance
   - (a) gross premiums written *(1)*
   - (b) outward reinsurance premiums *(2)*
   - (c) change in the provision for unearned premiums, net of reinsurance *(3)*

2. Investment income *(8) (10)*
   - (a) income from participating interests, with a separate indication of that derived from group undertakings

(b) income from other investments, with a separate indication of that derived from group undertakings
   (aa) income from land and buildings
   (bb) income from other investments
(c) value re-adjustments on investments
(d) gains on the realisation of investments

3. Unrealised gains on investments *(9)*
4. Other technical income, net of reinsurance
5. Claims incurred, net of reinsurance *(4)*
   (a) claims paid
      (aa) gross amount
      (bb) reinsurers' share
   (b) change in the provision for claims
      (aa) gross amount
      (bb) reinsurers' share
6. Change in other technical provisions, net of reinsurance, not shown under other headings
   (a) long term business provision, net of reinsurance *(3)*
      (aa) gross amount
      (bb) reinsurers' share
   (b) other technical provisions, net of reinsurance
7. Bonuses and rebates, net of reinsurance *(5)*
8. Net operating expenses
   (a) acquisition costs *(6)*
   (b) change in deferred acquisition costs
   (c) administrative expenses *(7)*
   (d) reinsurance commissions and profit participation
9. Investment expenses and charges *(8)*
   (a) investment management expenses, including interest
   (b) value adjustments on investments
   (c) losses on the realisation of investments
10. Unrealised losses on investments *(9)*
11. Other technical charges, net of reinsurance
11a. Tax attributable to the long term business
12. Allocated investment return transferred to the non-technical account (item III.4)
12a. Transfers to or from the fund for future appropriations
13. Sub-total (balance on the technical account – long term business) (item III.2)

III. *Non-technical account*

1. Balance on the general business technical account – (item I.10)
2. Balance on the long term business technical account – (item II.13)
2a. Tax credit attributable to balance on the long term business technical account

**History**
Item 2a inserted by the Companies Act 1985 (Miscellaneous Accounting Amendments) Regulations 1996 (SI 1996/189), reg. 1(1), 14(7) and Sch. 5, para. 1, 3 as from 2 February 1996, subject to reg. 16(1), (2), (5).

3. Investment income *(8)*
   (a) income from participating interests, with a separate indication of that derived from group undertakings
   (b) income from other investments, with a separate indication of that derived from group undertakings
      (aa) income from land and buildings
      (bb) income from other investments
   (c) value re-adjustments on investments
   (d) gains on the realisation of investments

3a. Unrealised gains on investments *(9)*
4. Allocated investment return transferred from the long term business technical account (item II.12) *(10)*
5. Investment expenses and charges *(8)*
   (a) investment management expenses, including interest
   (b) value adjustments on investments
   (c) losses on the realisation of investments
5a. Unrealised losses on investments *(9)*
6. Allocated investment return transferred to the general business technical account (item 1.2) *(10)*
7. Other income
8. Other charges, including value adjustments
8a. Profit or loss on ordinary activities before tax
9. Tax on profit or loss on ordinary activities
10. Profit or loss on ordinary activities after tax
11. Extraordinary income
12. Extraordinary charges
13. Extraordinary profit or loss
14. Tax on extraordinary profit or loss
15. Other taxes not shown under the preceding items
16. Profit or loss for the financial year

## Notes on the profit and loss account format

*(1) Gross premiums written*

General business technical account: item I.1.(a)

Long term business technical account: item II.1.(a))

This item shall comprise all amounts due during the financial year in respect of insurance contracts entered into regardless of the fact that such amounts may relate in whole or in part to a later financial year, and shall include inter alia–

(i) premiums yet to be determined, where the premium calculation can be done only at the end of the year;
(ii) single premiums, including annuity premiums, and, in long term business, single premiums resulting from bonus and rebate provisions in so far as they must be considered as premiums under the terms of the contract;
(iii) additional premiums in the case of half-yearly, quarterly or monthly payments and additional payments from policy holders for expenses borne by the company;
(iv) in the case of co-insurance, the company's portion of total premiums;
(v) reinsurance premiums due from ceding and retroceding insurance undertakings, including portfolio entries,

after deduction of cancellations and portfolio withdrawals credited to ceding and retroceding insurance undertakings.

The above amounts shall not include the amounts of taxes or duties levied with premiums.

*(2) Outward reinsurance premiums*

(General business technical account: item I.1.(b)

Long term business technical account: item II.1.(b))

This item shall comprise all premiums paid or payable in respect of outward reinsurance contracts entered into by the company. Portfolio entries payable on the conclusion or amendment of outward reinsurance contracts shall be added; portfolio withdrawals receivable must be deducted.

*(3) Change in the provision for unearned premiums, net of reinsurance*

(Long term business technical account: items II.1.(c) and II.6.(a))

In the case of long term business, the change in unearned premiums may be included either in item II.1.(c) or in item II.6.(a) of the long term business technical account.

*(4) Claims incurred, net of reinsurance*

(General business technical account: item I.4
Long term business technical account: item II.5)

This item shall comprise all payments made in respect of the financial year with the addition of the provision for claims (but after deducting the provision for claims for the preceding financial year).

These amounts shall include annuities, surrenders, entries and withdrawals of loss provisions to and from ceding insurance undertakings and reinsurers and external and internal claims management costs and charges for claims incurred but not reported such as are referred to in paragraphs 47(2) and 49 below.

Sums recoverable on the basis of subrogation and salvage (within the meaning of paragraph 47 below) shall be deducted.

Where the difference between–

(a) the loss provision made at the beginning of the year for outstanding claims incurred in previous years, and

(b) the payments made during the year on account of claims incurred in previous years and the loss provision shown at the end of the year for such outstanding claims,

is material, it shall be shown in the notes to the accounts, broken down by category and amount.

*(5) Bonuses and rebates, net of reinsurance*

(General business technical account: item I.6

Long term business technical account: item II.7)

Bonuses shall comprise all amounts chargeable for the financial year which are paid or payable to policy holders and other insured parties or provided for their benefit, including amounts used to increase technical provisions or applied to the reduction of future premiums, to the extent that such amounts represent an allocation of surplus or profit arising on business as a whole or a section of business, after deduction of amounts provided in previous years which are no longer required.

Rebates shall comprise such amounts to the extent that they represent a partial refund of premiums resulting from the experience of individual contracts.

Where material, the amount charged for bonuses and that charged for rebates shall be disclosed separately in the notes to the accounts.

*(6) Acquisition costs*

(General business technical account: item I.7.(a)
Long term business technical account: item II.8.(a))

This item shall comprise the costs arising from the conclusion of insurance contracts. They shall cover both direct costs, such as acquisition commissions or the cost of drawing up the insurance document or including the insurance contract in the portfolio, and indirect costs, such as advertising costs or the administrative expenses connected with the processing of proposals and the issuing of policies.

In the case of long term business, policy renewal commissions shall be included under item II.8.(c) in the long term business technical account.

*(7) Administrative expenses*

(General business technical account: item I.7.(c)

Long term business technical account: item II.8.(c))

This item shall include the costs arising from premium collection, portfolio administration, handling of bonuses and rebates, and inward and outward reinsurance. They shall in particular include staff costs and depreciation provisions in respect of office furniture and equipment in so far as these need not be shown under acquisition costs, claims incurred or investment charges.

Item II.8.(c) shall also include policy renewal commissions.

*(8) Investment income, expenses and charges*

(General business technical account: items I.2a and 8a

Long term business technical account: items II.2 and 9

Non-technical account: items III.3 and 5)

Investment income, expenses and charges shall, to the extent that they arise in the long term fund, be disclosed in the long term business technical account. Other investment income, expenses and charges shall either be disclosed in the non-technical account or attributed between the appropriate technical and non-technical accounts. Where the company makes such an attribution it shall disclose the basis for it in the notes to the accounts.

*(9) Unrealised gains and losses on investments*

(Long term business technical account: items II.3 and 10

Non-technical account: items III.3a and 5a)

In the case of investments attributed to the long term fund, the difference between the valuation of the investments and their purchase price or, if they have previously been valued, their valuation as at the last balance sheet date, may be disclosed (in whole or in part) in item II.3 or II.10 (as the case may be) of the long term business technical account, and in the case of investments shown as assets under Assets item D (assets held to cover linked liabilities) shall be so disclosed.

In the case of other investments, the difference between the valuation of the investments and their purchase price or, if they have previously been valued, their valuation as at the last balance sheet date, may be disclosed (in whole or in part) in item III.3a or III.5a (as the case may require) of the non-technical account.

*(10) Allocated investment return*

(General business technical account: item I.2

Long term business technical account: item II.12

Non-technical account: items III.4 and 6)

The allocated return may be transferred from one part of the profit and loss account to another. Where part of the investment return is transferred to the general business technical account, the transfer from the non-technical account shall be deducted from item III.6 and added to item I.2.

Where part of the investment return disclosed in the long term business technical account is transferred to the non-technical account, the transfer to the non-technical account shall be deducted from item II.12 and added to item III.4.

The reasons for such transfers (which may consist of a reference to any relevant statutory requirement) and the bases on which they are made shall be disclosed in the notes to the accounts.

**History**

In the heading to note (10) the words "item I.2" substituted for the former words "items I.2 and 2a" by the Companies Act 1985 (Insurance Companies Accounts) (Minor Amendments) Regulations 1997 (SI 1997/2704), reg. 1, 2(1), (2)(i) as from 31 December 1997 and the words "item II.12" substituted for the former words "item II.2" by the Companies Act 1985 (Insurance Companies Accounts) (Minor Amendments) Regulations 1997 (SI 1997/2704), reg. 1, 2(1), (2)(i) and (ii) respectively as from 31 December 1997.

## Chapter II – Accounting Principles and Rules

### SECTION A – ACCOUNTING PRINCIPLES

#### Preliminary

**13** Subject to paragraph 19 below, the amounts to be included in respect of all items shown in a company's accounts shall be determined in accordance with the principles set out in paragraphs 14 to 18 below.

## Accounting principles

**14** The company shall be presumed to be carrying on business as a going concern.

**15** Accounting policies shall be applied consistently within the same accounts and from one financial year to the next.

**16** The amount of any item shall be determined on a prudent basis, and in particular–

(a) subject to note *(9)* on the profit and loss account format, only profits realised at the balance sheet date shall be included in the profit and loss account; and

(b) all liabilities and losses which have arisen or are likely to arise in respect of the financial year to which the accounts relate or a previous financial year shall be taken into account, including those which only become apparent between the balance sheet date and the date on which it is signed on behalf of the board of directors in pursuance of section 233 of this Act.

**17** All income and charges relating to the financial year to which the accounts relate shall be taken into account, without regard to the date of receipt or payment.

**18** In determining the aggregate amount of any item the amount of each individual asset or liability that falls to be taken into account shall be determined separately.

## Departure from accounting principles

**19** If it appears to the directors of a company that there are special reasons for departing from any of the principles stated above in preparing the company's accounts in respect of any financial year they may do so, but particulars of the departure, the reasons for it and its effect shall be given in a note to the accounts.

## SECTION B – CURRENT VALUE ACCOUNTING RULES

## Preliminary

**20** Subject to paragraphs 27 to 29 below–

(a) the amounts to be included in respect of assets of any description mentioned in paragraph 22 below shall be determined in accordance with that paragraph; and

(b) subject to paragraph 21 below, the amounts to be included in respect of assets of any description mentioned in paragraph 23 below may be determined in accordance with that paragraph or the rules set out in paragraphs 30 to 41 below ("the historical cost accounting rules").

**21** (Repealed by the Companies Act 1985 (Miscellaneous Accounting Amendments) Regulations 1996 (SI 1996/189), reg. 1(1), 14(7) and Sch. 5, para. 1, 4 as from 2 February 1996, subject to reg. 16(1), (2), (5).)

**History**
Pt. I, para. 21 formerly read as follows:
"The same valuation method shall be applied to all investments included in any item in the balance sheet format which is denoted by an arabic number."

## Valuation of assets: general

**22(1)** Subject to paragraph 24 below, investments falling to be included under Assets item C (investments) shall be included at their current value calculated in accordance with paragraphs 25 and 26 below.

**22(2)** Investments falling to be included under Assets item D (assets held to cover linked liabilities) shall be shown at their current value calculated in accordance with paragraphs 25 and 26 below.

**23(1)** Intangible assets other than goodwill may be shown at their current cost.

**23(2)** Assets falling to be included under Assets items F.I (tangible assets) and F.IV (own shares) in the balance sheet format may be shown at their current value calculated in accordance with paragraphs 25 and 26 below or at their current cost.

**23(3)** Assets falling to be included under Assets item F.II (stocks) may be shown at current cost.

### Alternative valuation of fixed-income securities

**24(1)** This paragraph applies to debt securities and other fixed-income securities shown as assets under Assets items C.II (investments in group undertakings and participating interests) and C.III (other financial investments).

**24(2)** Securities to which this paragraph applies may either be valued in accordance with paragraph 22 above or their amortised value may be shown in the balance sheet, in which case the provisions of this paragraph apply.

**24(3)** Subject to sub-paragraph (4) below, where the purchase price of securities to which this paragraph applies exceeds the amount repayable at maturity, the amount of the difference –

(a) shall be charged to the profit and loss account, and

(b) shall be shown separately in the balance sheet or in the notes to the accounts.

**24(4)** The amount of the difference referred to in sub-paragraph (3) above may be written off in instalments so that it is completely written off when the securities are repaid, in which case there shall be shown separately in the balance sheet or in the notes to the accounts the difference between the purchase price (less the aggregate amount written off) and the amount repayable at maturity.

**24(5)** Where the purchase price of securities to which this paragraph applies is less than the amount repayable at maturity, the amount of the difference shall be released to income in instalments over the period remaining until repayment, in which case there shall be shown separately in the balance sheet or in the notes to the accounts the difference between the purchase price (plus the aggregate amount released to income) and the amount repayable at maturity.

**24(6)** Both the purchase price and the current value of securities valued in accordance with this paragraph shall be disclosed in the notes to the accounts.

**24(7)** Where securities to which this paragraph applies which are not valued in accordance with paragraph 22 above are sold before maturity, and the proceeds are used to purchase other securities to which this paragraph applies, the difference between the proceeds of sale and their book value may be spread uniformly over the period remaining until the maturity of the original investment.

### Meaning of "current value"

**25(1)** Subject to sub-paragraph (5) below, in the case of investments other than land and buildings, current value shall mean market value determined in accordance with this paragraph.

**25(2)** In the case of listed investments, market value shall mean the value on the balance sheet date or, when the balance sheet date is not a stock exchange trading day, on the last stock exchange trading day before that date.

**25(3)** Where a market exists for unlisted investments, market value shall mean the average price at which such investments were traded on the balance sheet date or, when the balance sheet date is not a trading day, on the last trading day before that date.

**25(4)** Where, on the date on which the accounts are drawn up, listed or unlisted investments have been sold or are to be sold within the short term, the market value shall be reduced by the actual or estimated realisation costs.

**25(5)** Except where the equity method of accounting is applied, all investments other than those referred to in sub-paragraphs (2) and (3) above shall be valued on a basis which has prudent regard to the likely realisable value.

**26(1)** In the case of land and buildings, current value shall mean the market value on the date of valuation, where relevant reduced as provided in sub-paragraphs (4) and (5) below.

**26(2)** Market value shall mean the price at which land and buildings could be sold under private contract between a willing seller and an arm's length buyer on the date of valuation, it being assumed that the property is publicly exposed to the market, that market conditions permit orderly disposal and that a normal period, having regard to the nature of the property, is available for the negotiation of the sale.

**26(3)** The market value shall be determined through the separate valuation of each land and buildings item, carried out at least every five years in accordance with generally recognised methods of valuation.

**26(4)** Where the value of any land and buildings item has diminished since the preceding valuation under sub-paragraph (3), an appropriate value adjustment shall be made.

**26(5)** The lower value arrived at under sub-paragraph (4) shall not be increased in subsequent balance sheets unless such increase results from a new determination of market value arrived at in accordance with sub-paragraphs (2) and (3).

**26(6)** Where, on the date on which the accounts are drawn up, land and buildings have been sold or are to be sold within the short term, the value arrived at in accordance with sub-paragraphs (2) and (4) shall be reduced by the actual or estimated realisation costs.

**26(7)** Where it is impossible to determine the market value of a land and buildings item, the value arrived at on the basis of the principle of purchase price or production cost shall be deemed to be its current value.

## Application of the depreciation rules

**27(1)** Where–

(a) the value of any asset of a company is determined in accordance with paragraph 22 or 23 above, and

(b) in the case of a determination under paragraph 22 above, the asset falls to be included under Assets item C.I,

that value shall be, or (as the case may require) be the starting point for determining, the amount to be included in respect of that asset in the company's accounts, instead of its cost or any value previously so determined for that asset; and paragraphs 31 to 35 and 37 below shall apply accordingly in relation to any such asset with the substitution for any reference to its cost of a reference to the value most recently determined for that asset in accordance with paragraph 22 or 23 above (as the case may be).

**27(2)** The amount of any provision for depreciation required in the case of any asset by paragraph 32 or 33 below as it applies by virtue of sub-paragraph (1) is referred to below in this paragraph as the "adjusted amount", and the amount of any provision which would be required by that paragraph in the case of that asset according to the historical cost accounting rules is referred to as the "historical cost amount".

**27(3)** Where sub-paragraph (1) applies in the case of any asset the amount of any provision for depreciation in respect of that asset included in any item shown in the profit and loss account in respect of amounts written off assets of the description in question may be the historical cost amount instead of the adjusted amount, provided that the amount of any difference between the two is shown separately in the profit and loss account or in a note to the accounts.

## Additional information to be provided

**28(1)** This paragraph applies where the amounts to be included in respect of assets covered by any items shown in a company's accounts have been determined in accordance with paragraph 22 or 23 above.

**28(2)** The items affected and the basis of valuation adopted in determining the amounts of the assets in question in the case of each such item shall be disclosed in a note to the accounts.

**28(3)** The purchase price of investments valued in accordance with paragraph 22 above shall be disclosed in the notes to the accounts.

**28(4)** In the case of each balance sheet item valued in accordance with paragraph 23 above either–

(a) the comparable amounts determined according to the historical cost accounting rules (without any provision for depreciation or diminution in value); or

(b) the differences between those amounts and the corresponding amounts actually shown in the balance sheet in respect of that item, shall be shown separately in the balance sheet or in a note to the accounts.

**28(5)** In sub-paragraph (4) above, references in relation to any item to the comparable amounts determined as there mentioned are references to–

(a) the aggregate amount which would be required to be shown in respect of that item if the amounts to be included in respect of all the assets covered by that item were determined according to the historical cost accounting rules; and

(b) the aggregate amount of the cumulative provisions for depreciation or diminution in value which would be permitted or required in determining those amounts according to those rules.

### Revaluation reserve

**29(1)** Subject to sub-paragraph (7) below, with respect to any determination of the value of an asset of a company in accordance with paragraph 22 or 23 above, the amount of any profit or loss arising from that determination (after allowing, where appropriate, for any provisions for depreciation or diminution in value made otherwise than by reference to the value so determined and any adjustments of any such provisions made in the light of that determination) shall be credited or (as the case may be) debited to a separate reserve ("the revaluation reserve").

**29(2)** The amount of the revaluation reserve shall be shown in the company's balance sheet under Liabilities item A.III, but need not be shown under the name "revaluation reserve".

**29(3)** An amount may be transferred

(a) from the revaluation reserve–
  (i) to the profit and loss account, if the amount was previously charged to that account or represents realised profit, or
  (ii) on capitalisation,

(b) to or from the revaluation reserve in respect of the taxation relating to any profit or loss credited or debited to the reserve;

and the revaluation reserve shall be reduced to the extent that the amounts transferred to it are no longer necessary for the purposes of the valuation method used.

**History**
In Pt. I, para. 29(3) the words "(a) from the revaluation reserve–" to "debited to the reserve" substituted for the former words by the Companies Act 1985 (Miscellaneous Accounting Amendments) Regulations 1996 (SI 1996/189), reg. 1(1), 14(7) and Sch. 5, para. 1, 5(1), (2) as from 2 February 1996, subject to reg. 16(1), (2); the former words read as follows:

"from the revaluation reserve–
(a) to the profit and loss account, if the amount was previously charged to that account or represents realised profit, or
(b) on capitalisation;"

**29(4)** In sub-paragraph (3)(a)(ii) "capitalisation", in relation to an amount standing to the credit of the revaluation reserve, means applying it in wholly or partly paying up unissued shares in the company to be allotted to members of the company as fully or partly paid shares.

**History**
In Pt. I, para. 29(4) the words "sub-paragraph (3)(a)(ii)" substituted for the former words "sub-paragraph (3)(b)" by the Companies Act 1985 (Miscellaneous Accounting Amendments) Regulations 1996 (SI 1996/189), reg. 1(1), 14(7) and Sch. 5, para. 1, 5(1), (3) as from 2 February 1996, subject to reg. 16(1), (2).

**29(5)** The revaluation reserve shall not be reduced except as mentioned in this paragraph.

**29(6)** The treatment for taxation purposes of amounts credited or debited to the revaluation reserve shall be disclosed in a note to the accounts.

**29(7)** This paragraph does not apply to the difference between the valuation of investments and their purchase price or previous valuation shown in the long term business technical account or the non-technical account in accordance with note *(9)* on the profit and loss account format.

## SECTION C – HISTORICAL COST ACCOUNTING RULES

### Preliminary

**30** Subject to paragraphs 20 to 29 above, the amounts to be included in respect of all items shown in a company's accounts shall be determined in accordance with the rules set out in paragraphs 31 to 41 below.

## Valuation of assets

*General rules*

**31** Subject to any provision for depreciation or diminution in value made in accordance with paragraph 32 or 33 below, the amount to be included in respect of any asset in the balance sheet format shall be its cost.

**32** In the case of any asset included under Assets item B (intangible assets), C.I (land and buildings), F.I (tangible assets) or F.II (stocks) which has a limited useful economic life, the amount of–

(a) its cost; or

(b) where it is estimated that any such asset will have a residual value at the end of the period of its useful economic life, its cost less that estimated residual value,

shall be reduced by provisions for depreciation calculated to write off that amount systematically over the period of the asset's useful economic life.

**33(1)** This paragraph applies to any asset included under Assets item B (tangible assets), C (investments), F.I (tangible assets) or F.IV (own shares).

**33(2)** Where an asset to which this paragraph applies has diminished in value, provisions for diminution in value may be made in respect of it and the amount to be included in respect of it may be reduced accordingly; and any such provisions which are not shown in the profit and loss account shall be disclosed (either separately or in aggregate) in a note to the accounts.

**33(3)** Provisions for diminution in value shall be made in respect of any asset to which this paragraph applies if the reduction in its value is expected to be permanent (whether its useful economic life is limited or not), and the amount to be included in respect of it shall be reduced accordingly; and any such provisions which are not shown in the profit and loss account shall be disclosed (either separately or in aggregate) in a note to the accounts.

**33(4)** Where the reasons for which any provision was made in accordance with sub-paragraph (1) or (2) have ceased to apply to any extent, that provision shall be written back to the extent that it is no longer necessary; and any amounts written back in accordance with this sub-paragraph which are not shown in the profit and loss account shall be disclosed (either separately or in aggregate) in a note to the accounts.

**34(1)** This paragraph applies to assets included under Assets items E.I., II. and III. (debtors) and F.III (cash at bank and in hand) in the balance sheet.

**34(2)** If the net realisable value of an asset to which this paragraph applies is lower than its cost the amount to be included in respect of that asset shall be the net realisable value.

**34(3)** Where the reasons for which any provision for diminution in value was made in accordance with sub-paragraph (2) have ceased to apply to any extent, that provision shall be written back to the extent that it is no longer necessary.

*Development costs*

**35(1)** Notwithstanding that amounts representing "development costs" may be included under Assets item B (intangible assets) in the balance sheet format, an amount may only be included in a company's balance sheet in respect of development costs in special circumstances.

**35(2)** If any amount is included in a company's balance sheet in respect of development costs the following information shall be given in a note to the accounts–

(a) the period over which the amount of those costs originally capitalised is being or is to be written off; and

(b) the reasons for capitalising the development costs in question.

*Goodwill*

**36(1)** The application of paragraphs 31 to 33 above in relation to goodwill (in any case where goodwill is treated as an asset) is subject to the following provisions of this paragraph.

**36(2)** Subject to sub-paragraph (3) below, the amount of the consideration for any goodwill acquired by a company shall be reduced by provisions for depreciation calculated to write off that amount systematically over a period chosen by the directors of the company.

**36(3)** The period chosen shall not exceed the useful economic life of the goodwill in question.

**36(4)** In any case where any goodwill acquired by a company is included as an asset in the company's balance sheet the period chosen for writing off the consideration for that goodwill and the reasons for choosing that period shall be disclosed in a note to the accounts.

## Miscellaneous and supplemental

*Excess of money owed over value received as an asset item*

**37(1)** Where the amount repayable on any debt owed by a company is greater than the value of the consideration received in the transaction giving rise to the debt, the amount of the difference may be treated as an asset.

**37(2)** Where any such amount is so treated–

(a) it shall be written off by reasonable amounts each year and must be completely written off before repayment of the debt; and

(b) if the current amount is not shown as a separate item in the company's balance sheet it must be disclosed in a note to the accounts.

*Assets included at a fixed amount*

**38(1)** Subject to the following sub-paragraph, assets which fall to be included under Assets item F.I. (tangible assets) in the balance sheet format may be included at a fixed quantity and value.

**38(2)** Sub-paragraph (1) applies to assets of a kind which are constantly being replaced, where–

(a) their overall value is not material to assessing the company's state of affairs; and

(b) their quantity, value and composition are not subject to material variation.

*Determination of cost*

**39(1)** The cost of an asset that has been acquired by the company shall be determined by adding to the actual price paid any expenses incidental to its acquisition.

**39(2)** The cost of an asset constructed by the company shall be determined by adding to the purchase price of the raw materials and consumables used the amount of the costs incurred by the company which are directly attributable to the construction of that asset.

**39(3)** In addition, there may be included in the cost of an asset constructed by the company–

(a) a reasonable proportion of the costs incurred by the company which are only indirectly attributable to the construction of that asset, but only to the extent that they relate to the period of construction; and

(b) interest on capital borrowed to finance the construction of that asset, to the extent that it accrues in respect of the period of construction;

provided, however, in a case within sub-paragraph (b) above, that the inclusion of the interest in determining the cost of that asset and the amount of the interest so included is disclosed in a note to the accounts.

**40(1)** Subject to the qualification mentioned below, the cost of any assets which are fungible assets may be determined by the application of any of the methods mentioned in sub-paragraph (2) below in relation to any such assets of the same class.

The method chosen must be one which appears to the directors to be appropriate in the circumstances of the company.

**40(2)** Those methods are–

(a) the method known as "first in, first out" (FIFO);

(b) the method known as "last in, first out" (LIFO);

(c) a weighted average price; and

(d) any other method similar to any of the methods mentioned above.

**40(3)** Where in the case of any company–

(a) the cost of assets falling to be included under any item shown in the company's balance sheet has been determined by the application of any method permitted by this paragraph; and

(b) the amount shown in respect of that item differs materially from the relevant alternative amount given below in this paragraph;

the amount of that difference shall be disclosed in a note to the accounts.

**40(4)** Subject to sub-paragraph (5) below, for the purposes of sub-paragraph (3)(b) above, the relevant alternative amount, in relation to any item shown in a company's balance sheet, is the amount which would have been shown in respect of that item if assets of any class included under that item at an amount determined by any method permitted by this paragraph had instead been included at their replacement cost as at the balance sheet date.

**40(5)** The relevant alternative amount may be determined by reference to the most recent actual purchase price before the balance sheet date of assets of any class included under the item in question instead of by reference to their replacement cost as at that date, but only if the former appears to the directors of the company to constitute the more appropriate standard of comparison in the case of assets of that class.

*Substitution of original amount where price or cost unknown*

**41** Where there is no record of the purchase price of any asset acquired by a company or of any price, expenses or costs relevant for determining its cost in accordance with paragraph 39 above, or any such record cannot be obtained without unreasonable expense or delay, its cost shall be taken for the purposes of paragraphs 31 to 36 above to be the value ascribed to it in the earliest available record of its value made on or after its acquisition by the company.

## SECTION D – RULES FOR DETERMINING PROVISIONS

*Preliminary*

**42** Provisions which are to be shown in a company's accounts shall be determined in accordance with paragraphs 43 to 53 below.

*Technical provisions*

**43** The amount of technical provisions must at all times be sufficient to cover any liabilities arising out of insurance contracts as far as can reasonably be foreseen.

*Provision for unearned premiums*

**44(1)** The provision for unearned premiums shall in principle be computed separately for each insurance contract, save that statistical methods (and in particular proportional and flat rate methods) may be used where they may be expected to give approximately the same results as individual calculations.

**44(2)** Where the pattern of risk varies over the life of a contract, this shall be taken into account in the calculation methods.

*Provision for unexpired risks*

**45** The provision for unexpired risks (as defined in paragraph 81 below) shall be computed on the basis of claims and administrative expenses likely to arise after the end of the financial year from contracts concluded before that date, in so far as their estimated value exceeds the provision for unearned premiums and any premiums receivable under those contracts.

*Long term business provision*

**46(1)** The long term business provision shall in principle be computed separately for each long term contract, save that statistical or mathematical methods may be used where they may be expected to give approximately the same results as individual calculations.

**46(2)** A summary of the principal assumptions in making the provision under sub-paragraph (1) shall be given in the notes to the accounts.

**46(3)** The computation shall be made annually by a Fellow of the Institute or Faculty of Actuaries on the basis of recognised actuarial methods, with due regard to the actuarial principles laid down in Council Directive 92/96/EEC.

## Provisions for claims outstanding

*General business*

**47(1)** A provision shall in principle be computed separately for each claim on the basis of the costs still expected to arise, save that statistical methods may be used if they result in an adequate provision having regard to the nature of the risks.

**47(2)** This provision shall also allow for claims incurred but not reported by the balance sheet date, the amount of the allowance being determined having regard to past experience as to the number and magnitude of claims reported after previous balance sheet dates.

**47(3)** All claims settlement costs (whether direct or indirect) shall be included in the calculation of the provision.

**47(4)** Recoverable amounts arising out of subrogation or salvage shall be estimated on a prudent basis and either deducted from the provision for claims outstanding (in which case if the amounts are material they shall be shown in the notes to the accounts) or shown as assets.

**47(5)** In sub-paragraph (4) above, **"subrogation"** means the acquisition of the rights of policy holders with respect to third parties, and **"salvage"** means the acquisition of the legal ownership of insured property.

**47(6)** Where benefits resulting from a claim must be paid in the form of annuity, the amounts to be set aside for that purpose shall be calculated by recognised actuarial methods, and paragraph 48 below shall not apply to such calculations.

**47(7)** Implicit discounting or deductions, whether resulting from the placing of a current value on a provision for an outstanding claim which is expected to be settled later at a higher figure or otherwise effected, is prohibited.

**48(1)** Explicit discounting or deductions to take account of investment income is permitted, subject to the following conditions:

(a) the expected average interval between the date for the settlement of claims being discounted and the accounting date shall be at least four years;

(b) the discounting or deductions shall be effected on a recognised prudential basis;

(c) when calculating the total cost of settling claims, the company shall take account of all factors that could cause increases in that cost;

(d) the company shall have adequate data at its disposal to construct a reliable model of the rate of claims settlements;

(e) the rate of interest used for the calculation of present values shall not exceed a rate prudently estimated to be earned by assets of the company which are appropriate in magnitude and nature to cover the provisions for claims being discounted during the period necessary for the payment of such claims, and shall not exceed either–

  (i) a rate justified by the performance of such assets over the preceding five years, or

  (ii) a rate justified by the performance of such assets during the year preceding the balance sheet date.

**48(2)** When discounting or effecting deductions, the company shall, in the notes to the accounts, disclose–

(a) the total amount of provisions before discounting or deductions,

(b) the categories of claims which are discounted or from which deductions have been made,

(c) for each category of claims, the methods used, in particular the rates used for the estimates referred to in sub-paragraph (1)(d) and (e), and the criteria adopted for estimating the period that will elapse before the claims are settled.

*Long term business*

**49** The amount of the provision for claims shall be equal to the sums due to beneficiaries, plus the costs of settling claims.

*Equalisation provision*

**50** Any equalisation provision established under Part X of the Insurance Companies Regulations 1994 shall be valued in accordance with the provisions of those Regulations.

**History**

In para. 50 the words "Part X of the Insurance Companies Regulations 1994" substituted for the former words "the Insurance Companies (Credit Insurance) Regulations 1990" by the Insurance Companies Regulations 1994 (SI 1994/1516), reg. 1, 85 as from 1 July 1994.

*Accounting on a non-annual basis*

**51(1)** Either of the methods described in paragraph 52 and 53 below may be applied where, because of the nature of the class or type of insurance in question, information about premiums receivable or claims payable (or both) for the underwriting years is insufficient when the accounts are drawn up for reliable estimates to be made.

**51(2)** The use of either of the methods referred to in sub-paragraph (1) shall be disclosed in the notes to the accounts together with the reasons for adopting it.

**51(3)** Where one of the methods referred to in sub-paragraph (1) above is adopted, it shall be applied systematically in successive years unless circumstances justify a change.

**51(4)** In the event of a change in the method applied, the effect on the assets, liabilities, financial position and profit or loss shall be stated in the notes to the accounts.

**51(5)** For the purposes of this paragraph and paragraph 52 below, **"underwriting year"** means the financial year in which the insurance contracts in the class or type of insurance in question commenced.

**52(1)** The excess of the premiums written over the claims and expenses paid in respect of contracts commencing in the underwriting year shall form a technical provision included in the technical provision for claims outstanding shown in the balance sheet under Liabilities item C.3.

**52(2)** The provision may also be computed on the basis of a given percentage of the premiums written where such a method is appropriate for the type of risk insured.

**52(3)** If necessary, the amount of this technical provision shall be increased to make it sufficient to meet present and future obligations.

**52(4)** The technical provision constituted under this paragraph shall be replaced by a provision for claims outstanding estimated in accordance with paragraph 47 above as soon as sufficient information has been gathered and not later than the end of the third year following the underwriting year.

**52(5)** The length of time that elapses before a provision for claims outstanding is constituted in accordance with sub-paragraph (4) above shall be disclosed in the notes to the accounts.

**53(1)** The figures shown in the technical account or in certain items within it shall relate to a year which wholly or partly precedes the financial year (but by no more than 12 months).

**53(2)** The amounts of the technical provisions shown in the accounts shall if necessary be increased to make them sufficient to meet present and future obligations.

**53(3)** The length of time by which the earlier year to which the figures relate precedes the financial year and the magnitude of the transactions concerned shall be disclosed in the notes to the accounts.

## Chapter III – Notes to the Accounts

### Preliminary

**54(1)** Any information required in the case of any company by the following provisions of this Part of this Schedule shall (if not given in the company's accounts) be given by way of a note to those accounts.

**54(2)** Subject to sub-paragraph (3) below, in respect of every item stated in a note to the accounts–

(a) the corresponding amount for the financial year immediately preceding that to which the accounts relate shall also be stated, and

(b) where the corresponding amount is not comparable, that amount shall be adjusted and particulars of the adjustment and the reasons for it shall be given.

**54(3)** Sub-paragraph (2) above does not apply to–

(a) paragraphs 62 and 66 of this Part of this Schedule (assets and reserves and provisions),

(b) paragraph 13 of Schedule 4A (details of accounting treatment of acquisitions),

(c) paragraphs 2, 8(3), 16, 21(1)(d), 22(4) and (5), 24(3) and (4) and 27(3) and (4) of Schedule 5 (shareholdings in other undertakings), and

(d) Parts II and III of Schedule 6 (loans and other dealings in favour of directors and others).

**History**

Pt. I, para. 54 substituted by the Companies Act 1985 (Miscellaneous Accounting Amendments) Regulations 1996 (SI 1996/189), reg. 1(1), 14(7) and Sch. 5, para. 1, 6 as from 2 February 1996, subject to reg. 16(1), (2), (5); para. 54 formerly read as follows:

"Any information required in the case of any company by the following provisions of this Part of this Schedule shall be given by way of a note to those accounts, unless otherwise provided."

## General

*Disclosure of accounting policies*

**55** The accounting policies adopted by the company in determining the amounts to be included in respect of items shown in the balance sheet and in determining the profit or loss of the company shall be stated (including such accounting policies with respect to the depreciation and diminution in value of assets).

**56** It shall be stated whether the accounts have been prepared in accordance with applicable accounting standards and particulars of any material departure from those standards and the reasons for it shall be given.

*Sums denominated in foreign currencies*

**57** Where any sums originally denominated in foreign currencies have been brought into account under any items shown in the balance sheet or profit and loss account format, the basis on which those sums have been translated into sterling (or the currency in which the accounts are drawn up) shall be stated.

## Information supplementing the balance sheet

*Share capital and debentures*

**58(1)** The following information shall be given with respect to the company's share capital–

(a) the authorised share capital; and

(b) where shares of more than one class have been allotted, the number and aggregate nominal value of shares of each class allotted.

**58(2)** In the case of any part of the allotted share capital that consists of redeemable shares, the following information shall be given–

(a) the earliest and latest dates on which the company has power to redeem those shares;

(b) whether those shares must be redeemed in any event or are liable to be redeemed at the option of the company or of the shareholder; and

(c) whether any (and, if so, what) premium is payable on redemption.

**59** If the company has allotted any shares during the financial year, the following information shall be given–

(b) the classes of shares allotted; and

(c) as respects each class of shares, the number allotted, their aggregate nominal value and the consideration received by the company for the allotment.

**History**
Pt. I, para. 59(a) repealed by the Companies Act 1985 (Miscellaneous Accounting Amendments) Regulations 1996 (SI 1996/189), reg. 1(1), 14(7) and Sch. 5, para. 1, 7 as from 2 February 1996, subject to reg. 16(1), (2); para. 59(a) formerly read as follows:
"(a) the reason for making the allotment;".

**60(1)** With respect to any contingent right to the allotment of shares in the company the following particulars shall be given–

(a) the number, description and amount of the shares in relation to which the right is exercisable;

(b) the period during which it is exercisable; and

(c) the price to be paid for the shares allotted.

**60(2)** In sub-paragraph (1) above **"contingent right to the allotment of shares"** means any option to subscribe for shares and any other right to require the allotment of shares to any person whether arising on the conversion into shares of securities of any other description or otherwise.

**61(1)** If the company has issued any debentures during the financial year to which the accounts relate, the following information shall be given–

(b) the classes of debentures issued; and

(c) as respects each class of debentures, the amount issued and the consideration received by the company for the issue.

**History**
Pt. I, para. 61(1)(a) repealed by the Companies Act 1985 (Miscellaneous Accounting Amendments) Regulations 1996 (SI 1996/189), reg. 1(1), 14(7) and Sch. 5, para. 1, 8 as from 2 February 1996, subject to reg. 16(1), (2); para. 61(1)(a) formerly read as follows:
"(a) the reason for making the issue;"

**61(2)** (Repealed by the Companies Act 1985 (Miscellaneous Accounting Amendments) Regulations 1996 (SI 1996/189), reg. 1(1), 14(7) and Sch. 5, para. 1, 8 as from 2 February 1996, subject to reg. 16(1), (2).)

**History**
Pt. I, para. 61(2) formerly read as follows:
"Particulars of any redeemed debentures which the company has power to reissue shall also be given."

**61(3)** Where any of the company's debentures are held by a nominee of or trustee for the company, the nominal amount of the debentures and the amount at which they are stated in the accounting records kept by the company in accordance with section 221 of this Act shall be stated.

*Assets*

**62(1)** In respect of any assets of the company included in Assets items B (intangible assets), C.I (land and buildings) and C.II (investments in group undertakings and participating interests) in the company's balance sheet the following information shall be given by reference to each such item–

(a) the appropriate amounts in respect of those assets included in the item as at the date of the beginning of the financial year and as at the balance sheet date respectively;

(b) the effect on any amount included in Assets item B in respect of those assets of–

(i) any determination during that year of the value to be ascribed to any of those assets in accordance with paragraph 23 above;

(ii) acquisitions during that year of any assets;

(iii) disposals during that year of any assets; and

(iv) any transfers of assets of the company to and from the item during that year.

**62(2)** The reference in sub-paragraph (1)(a) to the appropriate amounts in respect of any assets (included in an assets item) as at any date there mentioned is a reference to amounts representing the aggregate amounts determined, as at that date, in respect of assets falling to be included under the item on either of the following bases, that is to say–

(a) on the basis of cost (determined in accordance with paragraphs 39 and 40 above); or

(b) on any basis permitted by paragraph 22 or 23 above,

(leaving out of account in either case any provisions for depreciation or diminution in value).

**62(3)** In addition, in respect of any assets of the company included in any assets item in the company's balance sheet, there shall be stated (by reference to each such item)–

(a) the cumulative amount of provisions for depreciation or diminution in value of those assets included under the item as at each date mentioned in sub-paragraph (1)(a);

(b) the amount of any such provisions made in respect of the financial year;

(c) the amount of any adjustments made in respect of any such provisions during that year in consequence of the disposal of any of those assets; and

(d) the amount of any other adjustments made in respect of any such provisions during that year.

**63** Where any assets of the company (other than listed investments) are included under any item shown in the company's balance sheet at an amount determined on any basis mentioned in paragraph 22 or 23 above, the following information shall be given–

(a) the years (so far as they are known to the directors) in which the assets were severally valued and the several values; and

(b) in the case of assets that have been valued during the financial year, the names of the persons who valued them or particulars of their qualifications for doing so and (whichever is stated) the bases of valuation used by them.

**64** In relation to any amount which is included under Assets item C.I. (land and buildings) there shall be stated–

(a) how much of that amount is ascribable to land of freehold tenure and how much to land of leasehold tenure; and

(b) how much of the amount ascribable to land of leasehold tenure is ascribable to land held on long lease and how much to land held on short lease.

*Investments*

**65** In respect of the amount of each item which is shown in the company's balance sheet under Assets item C (investments) there shall be stated–

(a) how much of that amount is ascribable to listed investments.

**History**

Pt. I, para. 65(b) and the word "and" immediately preceding it repealed by the Companies Act 1985 (Miscellaneous Accounting Amendments) Regulations 1996 (SI 1996/189), reg. 1(1), 14(7) and Sch. 5, para. 1, 9 as from 2 February 1996, subject to reg. 16(1), (2); para. 65(b) formerly read as follows:

"(b) how much of any amount so ascribable is ascribable to investments as respects which there has been granted a listing on a recognised investment exchange other than an overseas investment exchange within the meaning of the Financial Services Act 1986 and how much to other listed investments."

*Reserves and provisions*

**66(1)** Where any amount is transferred–

(a) to or from any reserves;

(b) to any provisions for other risks and charges; or

(c) from any provision for other risks and charges otherwise than for the purpose for which the provision was established;

and the reserves or provisions are or would but for paragraph 2(3) above be shown as separate items in the company's balance sheet, the information mentioned in the following sub-paragraph shall be given in respect of the aggregate of reserves or provisions included in the same item.

**History**

In Pt. I, para. 66(1) the words "provisions for other risks and charges" substituted for the former words "provisions for liabilities and charges" in both places where they occur by the Companies Act 1985 (Miscellaneous Accounting Amendments) Regulations 1996 (SI 1996/189), reg. 1(1), 14(7) and Sch. 5, para. 1, 10 as from 2 February 1996, subject to reg. 16(1), (2), (5).

**66(2)** That information is–

(a) the amount of the reserves or provisions as at the date of the beginning of the financial year and as at the balance sheet date respectively;

(b) any amounts transferred to or from the reserves or provisions during that year; and

(c) the source and application respectively of any amounts so transferred.

**66(3)** Particulars shall be given of each provision included in Liabilities item E.3 (other provisions) in the company's balance sheet in any case where the amount of that provision is material.

*Provision for taxation*

**67** The amount of any provision for deferred taxation shall be stated separately from the amount of any provision for other taxation.

*Details of indebtedness*

**68(1)** In respect of each item shown under "creditors" in the company's balance sheet there shall be stated the aggregate of the following amounts, that is to say–

(a) the amount of any debts included under that item which are payable or repayable otherwise than by instalments and fall due for payment or repayment after the end of the period of five years beginning with the day next following the end of the financial year; and

(b) in the case of any debts so included which are payable or repayable by instalments which fall due for payment after the end of that period.

**History**

Pt. I, para. 68(1) substituted by the Companies Act 1985 (Miscellaneous Accounting Amendments) Regulations 1996 (SI 1996/189), reg. 1(1), 14(7) and Sch. 5, para. 1, 11 as from 2 February 1996, subject to reg. 16(1), (2); para. 68(1) formerly read as follows:

"In respect of each item shown under "creditors" in the company's balance sheet there shall be stated–

(a) the aggregate amount of any debts included under that item which are payable or repayable otherwise than by instalments and fall due for payment or repayment after the end of the period of five years beginning with the day next following the end of the financial year; and

(b) the aggregate amount of any debts so included which are payable or repayable by instalments any of which fall due for payment after the end of that period;

and in the case of debts within sub-paragraph (b) above the aggregate amount of instalments falling due after the end of that period shall also be disclosed for each such item."

Para. 68(1)(b) substituted by the Companies Act 1985 (Accounts of Small and Medium-sized Companies and Minor Accounting Amendments) Regulations 1997 (SI 1997/220), reg . 1, 7(9) as from 1 March 1997. Para. 68 (1)(b) previously read as follows:

"the aggregate amount of any debts so included which are payable or repayable by instalments any of which fall due for payment after the end of that period."

**68(2)** Subject to sub-paragraph (3), in relation to each debt falling to be taken into account under sub-paragraph (1), the terms of payment or repayment and the rate of any interest payable on the debt shall be stated.

**68(3)** If the number of debts is such that, in the opinion of the directors, compliance with sub-paragraph (2) would result in a statement of excessive length, it shall be sufficient to give a general indication of the terms of payment or repayment and the rates of any interest payable on the debts.

**68(4)** In respect of each item shown under "creditors" in the company's balance sheet there shall be stated–

(a) the aggregate amount of any debts included under that item in respect of which any security has been given by the company; and

(b) an indication of the nature of the securities so given.

**68(5)** References above in this paragraph to an item shown under "creditors" in the company's balance sheet include references, where amounts falling due to creditors within one year and after more than one year are distinguished in the balance sheet–

(a) in a case within sub-paragraph (1), to an item shown under the latter of those categories; and

(b) in a case within sub-paragraph (4), to an item shown under either of those categories;

and references to items shown under "creditors" include references to items which would but for paragraph 2(3)(b) above be shown under that heading.

**69** If any fixed cumulative dividends on the company's shares are in arrear, there shall be stated–

(a) the amount of the arrears; and

(b) the period for which the dividends or, if there is more than one class, each class of them are in arrear.

*Guarantees and other financial commitments*

**70(1)** Particulars shall be given of any charge on the assets of the company to secure the liabilities of any other person, including, where practicable, the amount secured.

**70(2)** The following information shall be given with respect to any other contingent liability not provided for (other than a contingent liability arising out of an insurance contract)–

(a) the amount or estimated amount of that liability;

(b) its legal nature;

(c) whether any valuable security has been provided by the company in connection with that liability and if so, what.

**70(3)** There shall be stated, where practicable–

(a) the aggregate amount or estimated amount of contracts for capital expenditure, so far as not provided for.

**History**

Pt. I, para. 70(3)(b) and the word "and" immediately preceding it repealed by the Companies Act 1985 (Miscellaneous Accounting Amendments) Regulations 1996 (SI 1996/189), reg. 1(1), 14(7) and Sch. 5, para. 1, 12 as from 2 February 1996, subject to reg. 16(1), (2); para. 70(3)(b) formerly read as follows:

"(b) the aggregate amount or estimated amount of capital expenditure authorised by the directors which has not been contracted for."

**70(4)** Particulars shall be given of–

(a) any pension commitments included under any provision shown in the company's balance sheet; and

(b) any such commitments for which no provision has been made;

and where any such commitment relates wholly or partly to pensions payable to past directors of the company separate particulars shall be given of that commitment so far as it relates to such pensions.

**70(5)** Particulars shall also be given of any other financial commitments, other than commitments arising out of insurance contracts, which–

(a) have not been provided for; and

(b) are relevant to assessing the company's state of affairs.

**70(6)** Commitments within any of the preceding sub-paragraphs undertaken on behalf of or for the benefit of–

(a) any parent undertaking or fellow subsidiary undertaking, or

(b) any subsidiary undertaking of the company,

shall be stated separately from the other commitments within that sub-paragraph, and commitments within paragraph (a) shall also be stated separately from those within paragraph (b).

*Dealings with or interests in group undertakings*

**71** (Repealed by the Companies Act 1985 (Miscellaneous Accounting Amendments) Regulations 1996 (SI 1996/189), reg. 1(1), 14(7) and Sch. 5, para. 1, 13 as from 2 February 1996, subject to reg. 16(1), (2).)

**History**

Pt. I, para. 71 formerly read as follows:

"Where a company is a parent company or a subsidiary undertaking and any item required by Part I of this Schedule to be shown in the company's balance sheet in relation to group undertakings includes–

(a) amounts attributable to dealings with or interests in any parent undertaking or fellow subsidiary undertaking, or

(b) amounts attributable to dealings with or interests in any subsidiary undertaking of the company,

the aggregate amounts within paragraphs (a) and (b) respectively shall be shown as separate items, either by way of subdivision of the relevant item in the balance sheet or in a note to the company's accounts."

*Miscellaneous matters*

**72(1)** Particulars shall be given of any case where the cost of any asset is for the first time determined under paragraph 41 above.

**72(2)** Where any outstanding loans made under the authority of section 153(4)(b), (bb) or (c) or section 155 of this Act (various cases of financial assistance by a company for purchase of its own shares) are included under any item shown in the company's balance sheet, the aggregate amount of those loans shall be disclosed for each item in question.

**72(3)** (Repealed by the Companies Act 1985 (Miscellaneous Accounting Amendments) Regulations 1996 (SI 1996/189), reg. 1(1), 14(7) and Sch. 5, para. 1, 14 as from 2 February 1996, subject to reg. 16(1), (2).)

**History**
Pt. I, para. 72(3) formerly read as follows:
"The aggregate amount which is recommended for distribution by way of dividend shall be stated."

## Information supplementing the profit and loss account

*Separate statement of certain items of income and expenditure*

**73(1)** Subject to the following provisions of this paragraph, each of the amounts mentioned below shall be stated.

**73(2)** The amount of the interest on or any similar charges in respect of–

(a) bank loans and overdrafts, and

(b) loans of any other kind made to the company.

This sub-paragraph does not apply to interest or charges on loans to the company from group undertakings, but, with that exception, it applies to interest or charges on all loans, whether made on the security of debentures or not.

**History**
In Pt. I, para. 73(2)(a) the words formerly appearing after the word "overdrafts," repealed by the Companies Act 1985 (Miscellaneous Accounting Amendments) Regulations 1996 (SI 1996/189), reg. 1(1), 14(7) and Sch. 5, para. 1, 15(1), (2) as from 2 February 1996, subject to reg. 16(1), (2); the former words read as follows:

"and loans made to the company (other than bank loans and overdrafts) which–

(i) are repayable otherwise than by instalments and fall due for repayment before the end of the period of five years beginning with the day next following the end of the financial year; or

(ii) are repayable by instalments the last of which falls due for payment before the end of that period;".

**73(3)–(5)** (Repealed by the Companies Act 1985 (Miscellaneous Accounting Amendments) Regulations 1996 (SI 1996/189), reg. 1(1), 14(7) and Sch. 5, para. 1, 15(1), (3) as from 2 February 1996, subject to reg. 16(1), (2).)

**History**
Pt. I, para. 73(3)–(5) formerly read as follows:

"**73(3)** The amount respectively set aside for redemption of share capital and for redemption of loans.

**(4)** The amount of income from listed investments.

**(5)** The amount charged to revenue in respect of sums payable in respect of the hire of plant and machinery."

*Particulars of tax*

**74(1)** (Repealed by the Companies Act 1985 (Miscellaneous Accounting Amendments) Regulations 1996 (SI 1996/189), reg. 1(1), 14(7) and Sch. 5, para. 1, 16 as from 2 February 1996, subject to reg. 16(1), (2).)

**History**
Pt. I, para. 74(1) formerly read as follows:
"The basis on which the charge for United Kingdom corporation tax and United Kingdom income tax is computed shall be stated."

**74(2)** Particulars shall be given of any special circumstances which affect liability in respect of taxation of profits, income or capital gains for the financial year or liability in respect of taxation of profits, income or capital gains for succeeding financial years.

**74(3)** The following amounts shall be stated–

(a) the amount of the charge for United Kingdom corporation tax;

(b) if that amount would have been greater but for relief from double taxation, the amount which it would have been but for such relief;

(c) the amount of the charge for United Kingdom income tax; and
(d) the amount of the charge for taxation imposed outside the United Kingdom of profits, income and (so far as charged to revenue) capital gains.

Those amounts shall be stated separately in respect of each of the amounts which is shown under the following items in the profit and loss account, that is to say item III.9 (tax on profit or loss on ordinary activities) and item III.14 (tax on extraordinary profit or loss).

*Particulars of business*

**75(1)** As regards general business a company shall disclose–

(a) gross premiums written,
(b) gross premiums earned,
(c) gross claims incurred,
(d) gross operating expenses, and
(e) the reinsurance balance.

**75(2)** The amounts required to be disclosed by sub-paragraph (1) shall be broken down between direct insurance and reinsurance acceptances, if reinsurance acceptances amount to 10 per cent or more of gross premiums written.

**75(3)** Subject to sub-paragraph (4) below, the amounts required to be disclosed by sub-paragraphs (1) and (2) above with respect to direct insurance shall be further broken down into the following groups of classes–

(a) accident and health,
(b) motor (third party liability),
(c) motor (other classes),
(d) marine, aviation and transport,
(e) fire and other damage to property,
(f) third-party liability,
(g) credit and suretyship,
(h) legal expenses,
(i) assistance, and
(j) miscellaneous,

where the amount of the gross premiums written in direct insurance for each such group exceeds 10 million ECUs.

**75(4)** The company shall in any event disclose the amounts relating to the three largest groups of classes in its business.

**76(1)** As regards long term business, the company shall disclose–

(a) gross premiums written, and
(b) the reinsurance balance.

**76(2)** Subject to sub-paragraph (3) below–

(a) gross premiums written shall be broken down between those written by way of direct insurance and those written by way of reinsurance; and
(b) gross premiums written by way of direct insurance shall be broken down–
  (i) between individual premiums and premiums under group contracts;
  (ii) between periodic premiums and single premiums; and
  (iii) between premiums from non-participating contracts, premiums from participating contracts and premiums from contracts where the investment risk is borne by policy holders.

**76(3)** Disclosure of any amount referred to in sub-paragraph (2)(a) or (2)(b)(i), (ii) or (iii) above shall not be required if it does not exceed 10 per cent of the gross premiums written or (as the case may be) of the gross premiums written by way of direct insurance.

**77(1)** Subject to sub-paragraph (2) below, there shall be disclosed as regards both general and long term business the total gross direct insurance premiums resulting from contracts concluded by the company–

(a) in the member State of its head office,

(b) in the other member States, and

(c) in other countries.

**77(2)** Disclosure of any amount referred to in sub-paragraph (1) above shall not be required if it does not exceed 5 per cent of total gross premiums.

*Commissions*

**78** There shall be disclosed the total amount of commissions for direct insurance business accounted for in the financial year, including acquisition, renewal, collection and portfolio management commissions.

*Particulars of staff*

**79(1)** The following information shall be given with respect to the employees of the company–

(a) the average number of persons employed by the company in the financial year; and

(b) the average number of persons so employed within each category of persons employed by the company.

**79(2)** The average number required by sub-paragraph (1)(a) or (b) shall be determined by dividing the relevant annual number by the number of months in the financial year.

**History**

In Pt. I, para. 79(2), the word "months" substituted for the former word "weeks" by the Companies Act 1985 (Miscellaneous Accounting Amendments) Regulations 1996 (SI 1996/189), reg. 1(1), 14(7) and Sch. 5, para. 1, 17(1), (2) as from 2 February 1996, subject to reg. 16(1), (2).

**79(3)** The relevant annual number shall be determined by ascertaining for each month in the financial year–

(a) for the purposes of sub-paragraph (1)(a), the number of persons employed under contracts of service by the company in that month (whether throughout the month or not); and

(b) for the purposes of sub-paragraph (1)(b), the number of persons in the category in question of persons so employed;

and, in either case, adding together all the monthly numbers.

**History**

In Pt. I, para. 79(3) the word "month" substituted for the former word "week" wherever it occurs and the word "monthly" substituted for the former word "weekly"by the Companies Act 1985 (Miscellaneous Accounting Amendments) Regulations 1996 (SI 1996/189), reg. 1(1), 14(7) and Sch. 5, para. 1, 17(1), (3) as from 2 February 1996, subject to reg. 16(1), (2).

**79(4)** In respect of all persons employed by the company during the financial year who are taken into account in determining the relevant annual number for the purposes of sub-paragraph (1)(a) there shall also be stated the aggregate amounts respectively of–

(a) wages and salaries paid or payable in respect of that year to those persons;

(b) social security costs incurred by the company on their behalf; and

(c) other pension costs so incurred,

save in so far as those amounts or any of them are stated in the profit and loss account.

**79(5)** The categories of person employed by the company by reference to which the number required to be disclosed by sub-paragraph (1)(b) is to be determined shall be such as the directors may select, having regard to the manner in which the company's activities are organised.

*Miscellaneous matters*

**80(1)** Where any amount relating to any preceding financial year is included in any item in the profit and loss account, the effect shall be stated.

**80(2)** Particulars shall be given of any extraordinary income or charges arising in the financial year.

**80(3)** The effect shall be stated of any transactions that are exceptional by virtue of size or incidence though they fall within the ordinary activities of the company.

# Chapter IV – Interpretation of Part I

*General*

**81(1)** The following definitions apply for the purposes of this Part of this Schedule and its interpretation–

**"the 1982 Act"** means the Insurance Companies Act 1982;

**"fungible assets"** means assets of any description which are substantially indistinguishable one from another;

**"general business"** has the same meaning as in the 1982 Act;

**"lease"** includes an agreement for a lease;

**"listed investment"** means an investment listed on a recognised stock exchange, or on any stock exchange of repute outside Great Britain and the expression **"unlisted investment"** shall be construed accordingly;

**"long lease"** means a lease in the case of which the portion of the term for which it was granted remaining unexpired at the end of the financial year is not less than 50 years;

**"long term business"** has the same meaning as in the 1982 Act;

**"long term fund"** means the fund or funds maintained by a company in respect of its long term business in accordance with the provisions of the 1982 Act;

**"policy holder"** has the same meaning as in the 1982 Act;

**"provision for unexpired risks"** means the amount set aside in addition to unearned premiums in respect of risks to be borne by the company after the end of the financial year, in order to provide for all claims and expenses in connection with insurance contracts in force in excess of the related unearned premiums and any premiums receivable on those contracts;

**"short lease"** means a lease which is not a long lease.

**81(2)** In this Part of this Schedule the **"ECU"** means the unit of account of that name defined in Council Regulation (EEC) No. 3180/78 as amended.

The exchange rates as between the ECU and the currencies of the member states to be applied for each financial year shall be the rates applicable on the last day of the preceding October for which rates for the currencies of all the member States were published in the Official Journal of the Communities.

*Loans*

**82** For the purposes of this Part of this Schedule a loan or advance (including a liability comprising a loan or advance) is treated as falling due for repayment, and an instalment of a loan or advance is treated as falling due for payment, on the earliest date on which the lender could require repayment or (as the case may be) payment, if he exercised all options and rights available to him.

*Materiality*

**83** For the purposes of this Part of this Schedule amounts which in the particular context of any provision of this Part are not material may be disregarded for the purposes of that provision.

*Provisions*

**84** For the purposes of this Part of this Schedule and its interpretation–

(a) references in this Part to provisions for depreciation or diminution in value of assets are to any amount written off by way of providing for depreciation or diminution in value of assets;

(b) any reference in the profit and loss account format or the notes thereto set out in Section

B of this Part to the depreciation of, or amounts written off, assets of any description is to any provision for depreciation or diminution in value of assets of that description; and

(c) references in this Part to provisions for other risks or charges are to any amount retained as reasonably necessary for the purpose of providing for any liability or loss which is either likely to be incurred, or certain to be incurred but uncertain as to amount or as to the date on which it will arise.

**History**

In Pt. I, para. 84(c), the words "provisions for other risks and charges" substituted for the former words "provisions for liabilities and charges" and the words "(other than provisions referred to in paragraphs 43 to 53 above)" formerly appearing immediately after them omitted by the Companies Act 1985 (Miscellaneous Accounting Amendments) Regulations 1996 (SI 1996/189), reg. 1(1), 14(7) and Sch. 5, para. 1, 18 as from 2 February 1996, subject to reg. 16(1), (2).

*Scots land tenure*

**85** In the application of this Part of this Schedule to Scotland–

**"land of freehold tenure"** means land in respect of which the company is the proprietor of the *dominium utile* or, in the case of land not held on feudal tenure, is the owner;

**"land of leasehold tenure"** means land of which the company is the tenant under a lease;

and the reference to ground-rents, rates and other outgoings includes feu-duty and ground annual.

*Staff costs*

**86** For the purposes of this Part of this Schedule and its interpretation–

(a) **"Social security costs"** means any contributions by the company to any state social security or pension scheme, fund or arrangement;

(b) **"Pension costs"** includes any costs incurred by the company in respect of any pension scheme established for the purpose of providing pensions for persons currently or formerly employed by the company, any sums set aside for the future payment of pensions directly by the company to current or former employees and any pensions paid directly to such persons without having first been set aside; and

(c) any amount stated in respect of the item "social security costs" or in respect of the item "wages and salaries" in the company's profit and loss account shall be determined by reference to payments made or costs incurred in respect of all persons employed by the company during the financial year who are taken into account in determining the relevant annual number for the purposes of paragraph 79(1)(a) above.

**History**

Pt. I, para. 86(b) substituted by the Companies Act 1985 (Miscellaneous Accounting Amendments) Regulations 1996 (SI 1996/189), reg. 1(1), 16(7) and Sch. 5, para. 1, 19(1), (2) as from 2 February 1996, subject to reg. 16(1), (2); para. 86(b) formerly read as follows:

""**Pension costs**" includes any other contributions by the company for the purposes of any pension scheme established for the purpose of providing pensions for persons employed by the company, any sums set aside for that purpose and any amounts paid by the company in respect of pensions without first being so set aside; and".

In Pt. I, para. 86(c) the words "the item "social security costs"" substituted for the former words "either of the above items" by the Companies Act 1985 (Miscellaneous Accounting Amendments) Regulations 1996 (SI 1996/189), reg. 1(1), 14(7) and Sch. 5, para. 1, 19(1), (3) as from 2 February 1996, subject to reg. 16(1), (2).

# Part II – Consolidated Accounts

*Schedule 4A to apply Part I of this Schedule with modifications*

**1(1)** In its application to insurance groups, Schedule 4A shall have effect with the following modifications.

**1(2)** In paragraph 1–

(a) for the reference in sub-paragraph (1) to the provisions of Schedule 4 there shall be substituted a reference to the provisions of Part I of this Schedule modified as mentioned in paragraph 2 below;

(b) (Repealed by the Companies Act 1985 (Accounts of Small and Medium-sized Companies and Minor Accounting Amendments) Regulations 1997 (SI 1997/220), reg. 1, 7(12) as from 1 March 1997.)

(c) sub-paragraph (3) shall be omitted.

**History**
Para. 1(2)(b) formerly read as follows:
"for the reference in sub-paragraph (2) to paragraph 59 of Schedule 4 there shall be substituted a reference to paragraphs 70(6) and 71 of Part I of this Schedule; and"

**1(3)** In paragraph 2(2)(a), for the words "three months" there shall be substituted the words "six months".

**1(4)** In paragraph 3, after sub-paragraph (1) there shall be inserted the following sub-paragraphs–

"(1A) Sub-paragraph (1) shall not apply to those liabilities items the valuation of which by the undertakings included in a consolidation is based on the application of provisions applying only to insurance undertakings, nor to those assets items changes in the values of which also affect or establish policy holders' rights.

(1B) Where sub-paragraph (1A) applies, that fact shall be disclosed in the notes on the consolidated accounts."

**1(5)** For sub-paragraph (4) of paragraph 6 there shall be substituted the following sub-paragraph–

"(4) Sub-paragraphs (1) and (2) need not be complied with–

(a) where a transaction has been concluded according to normal market conditions and a policy holder has rights in respect of that transaction, or

(b) if the amounts concerned are not material for the purpose of giving a true and fair view.

(5) Where advantage is taken of sub-paragraph (4)(a) above that fact shall be disclosed in the notes to the accounts, and where the transaction in question has a material effect on the assets, liabilities, financial position and profit or loss of all the undertakings included in the consolidation that fact shall also be so disclosed."

**1(6)** In paragraph 17–

(a) in sub-paragraph (1), for the reference to Schedule 4 there shall be substituted a reference to Part I of this Schedule;

(b) in sub-paragraph (2), paragraph (a) and, in paragraph (b), the words "in Format 2" shall be omitted;

(c) in sub-paragraph (3), for paragraph (a) to (d) there shall be substituted the words "between items 10 and 11 in section III";

(d) in sub-paragraph (4), for paragraphs (a) to (d) there shall be substituted the words "between items 14 and 15 in section III"; and

(e) for sub-paragraph (5) there shall be substituted the following sub-paragraph–

"(5) Paragraph 2(3) of Part I of Schedule 9A (power to combine items) shall not apply in relation to the additional items required by the foregoing provisions of this paragraph."

**1(7)** In paragraph 18, for the reference to paragraphs 17 to 19 and 21 of Schedule 4 there shall be substituted a reference to paragraphs 31 to 33 and 36 of Part I of this Schedule.

**1(8)** In paragraph 21–

(a) in sub-paragraph (1), for the reference to Schedule 4 there shall be substituted a reference to Part I of this Schedule; and

(b) for sub-paragraphs (2) and (3) there shall be substituted the following sub-paragraphs–

"(2) In the Balance Sheet Format, Asset item C.II.3 (participating interests) shall be replaced by two items, "Interests in associated undertakings" and "Other participating interests".

(3) In the Profit and Loss Account Format, items II.2(a) and III.3(a) (income from

participating interests, with a separate indication of that derived from group undertakings) shall each be replaced by the following items–

(a) "Income from participating interests other than associated undertakings, with a separate indication of that derived from group undertakings", which shall be shown as items II.2(a) and III.3(a), and

(b) "Income from associated undertakings", which shall be shown as items II.2(aa) and III.3(aa)."

**1(9)** In paragraph 22(l), for the reference to paragraphs 17 to 19 and 21 of Schedule 4 there shall be substituted a reference to paragraphs 31 to 33 and 36 of Part I of this Schedule.

*Modifications of Part I of this Schedule for purposes of paragraph 1*

**2(1)** For the purposes of paragraph 1 above, Part I of this Schedule shall be modified as follows.

**2(2)** The information required by paragraph 10 need not be given.

**2(3)** In the case of general business, investment income, expenses and charges may be disclosed in the non-technical account rather than in the technical account.

**2(4)** In the case of subsidiary undertakings which are not authorised to carry on long term business in Great Britain, notes *(8)* and *(9)* to the profit and loss account format shall have effect as if references to investment income, expenses and charges arising in the long term fund or to investments attributed to the long term fund were references to investment income, expenses and charges or (as the case may be) investments relating to long term business.

**2(5)** In the case of subsidiary undertakings which do not have a head office in Great Britain, the computation required by paragraph 46 shall be made annually by an actuary or other specialist in the field on the basis of recognised actuarial methods.

**2(6)** The information required by paragraphs 75 to 78 need not be shown.

**History**

Sch. 9A substituted by the Companies Act 1985 (Insurance Companies Accounts) Regulations 1993 (SI 1993/3246), reg. 1, 4 as from 19 December 1993 subject to exemption in reg. 6 and transitional provisions in reg. 7; Sch. 9A formerly read as follows:

**""Schedule 9A – Special Provisions for Insurance Companies and Groups"**

[Sections 255, 255A]

(Pt. I and II were formerly Pt. I and II of Sch. 9 – they were formed into a new schedule (Sch. 9A) and renamed by the Companies Act 1985 (Bank Accounts) Regulations 1991 (SI 1991/2705), reg. 5(1) as from 2 December 1991 (subject to transitional provisions in reg. 9); the former heading (to Sch. 9) was "Special Provisions for Banking and Insurance Companies and Groups".

Previously heading to what was Sch. 9 substituted by CA 1989, s. 18(3) and Sch. 7, preliminary para. (a) as from 1 April 1990 subject to transitional and saving provisions (see SI 1990/355 (C 13), art. 3, Sch. 1 and also art. 6–9); original heading read "Form and Content of Special Category Accounts".

Also introductory paragraph and its heading formerly following the heading omitted and repealed by CA 1989, s. 18(3), 212, Sch. 7, preliminary para. (b) and Sch. 24 as from 1 April 1990 subject to transitional and saving provisions (see SI 1990/355 (C 13), art. 3, 5(1)(b), (2), Sch. 1 and also art. 6–9); the original paragraph and heading read as follows:

"PRELIMINARY

**1** Paragraphs 2 to 13 of this Schedule apply to the balance sheet and 14 to 18 to the profit and loss account, and are subject to the exceptions and modifications provided for by Part II of this Schedule in the case of a holding or subsidiary company and by Part III thereof in the case of companies of the classes there mentioned.")

"Part I – Form and Content of Accounts"

(Heading for Pt. I (of what was Sch. 9) substituted by CA 1989, s. 18(3) and Sch. 7, preliminary para. (c)(i) as from 1 April 1990 subject to transitional and saving provisions (see SI 1990/355 (C 13), art. 3, Sch. 1 and also art. 6–9); former heading read "General Provisions as to Balance Sheet and Profit and Loss Account". Note that former Part headings before para. 19, 27, 31 and 32 also omitted.)

"BALANCE SHEET

**2** The authorised share capital, issued share capital, liabilities and assets shall be summarised, with such particulars as are necessary to disclose the general nature of the assets and liabilities, and there shall be specified–

(a) any part of the issued capital that consists of redeemable shares, the earliest and latest dates on which the company has power to redeem those shares, whether those shares must be redeemed in any event or are liable to be redeemed at the option of the company or of the shareholder and whether any (and, if so, what) premium is payable on redemption;

(b) so far as the information is not given in the profit and loss account, any share capital on which interest has been paid out of capital during the financial year, and the rate at which interest has been so paid;

(c) the amount of the share premium account;

(d) particulars of any redeemed debentures which the company has power to re-issue.

**3** There shall be stated under separate headings, so far as they are not written off,–

(a) the preliminary expenses;

(b) any expenses incurred in connection with any issue of share capital or debentures;
(c) any sums paid by way of commission in respect of any shares or debentures;
(d) any sums allowed by way of discount in respect of any debentures; and
(e) the amount of the discount allowed on any issue of shares at a discount.

**4(1)** The reserves, provisions, liabilities and assets shall be classified under headings appropriate to the company's business: Provided that–
(a) where the amount of any class is not material, it may be included under the same heading as some other class; and
(b) where any assets of one class are not separable from assets of another class, those assets may be included under the same heading.

**(2)** Fixed assets, current assets and assets that are neither fixed nor current shall be separately identified.

**(3)** The method or methods used to arrive at the amount of the fixed assets under each heading shall be stated.

**5(1)** The method of arriving at the amount of any fixed asset shall, subject to the next following sub-paragraph, be to take the difference between–
(a) its cost or, if it stands in the company's books at a valuation, the amount of the valuation; and
(b) the aggregate amount provided or written off since the date of acquisition or valuation, as the case may be, for depreciation or diminution in value;

and for the purposes of this paragraph the net amount at which any assets stood in the company's books on 1st July 1948 (after deduction of the amounts previously provided or written off for depreciation or diminution in value) shall, if the figures relating to the period before that date cannot be obtained without unreasonable expense or delay, be treated as if it were the amount of a valuation of those assets made at that date and, where any of those assets are sold, the said net amount less the amount of the sales shall be treated as if it were the amount of a valuation so made of the remaining assets.

**(2)** The foregoing sub-paragraph shall not apply–
(a) to assets for which the figures relating to the period beginning with 1st July 1948 cannot be obtained without unreasonable expense or delay; or
(b) to assets the replacement of which is provided for wholly or partly–
(i) by making provision for renewals and charging the cost of replacement against the provision so made; or
(ii) by charging the cost of replacement direct to revenue; or
(c) to any listed investments or to any unlisted investments of which the value as estimated by the directors is shown either as the amount of the investments or by way of note; or
(d) to goodwill, patents or trade marks.

**(3)** For the assets under each heading whose amount is arrived at in accordance with sub-paragraph (1) of this paragraph, there shall be shown–
(a) the aggregate of the amounts referred to in paragraph (a) of that sub-paragraph; and
(b) the aggregate of the amounts referred to in paragraph (b) thereof.

**(4)** As respects the assets under each heading whose amount is not arrived at in accordance with the said sub-paragraph (1) because their replacement is provided for as mentioned in sub-paragraph (2)(b) of this paragraph, there shall be stated–
(a) the means by which their replacement is provided for; and
(b) the aggregate amount of the provision (if any) made for renewals and not used.

**6** In the case of unlisted investments consisting in equity share capital of other bodies corporate (other than any whose values as estimated by the directors are separately shown, either individually or collectively or as to some individually and as to the rest collectively, and are so shown either as the amount thereof, or by way of note), the matters referred to in the following heads shall, if not otherwise shown, be stated by way of note or in a statement or report annexed:–
(a) the aggregate amount of the company's income for the financial year that is ascribable to the investments;
(b) the amount of the company's share before taxation, and the amount of that share after taxation, of the net aggregate amount of the profits of the bodies in which the investments are held, being profits for the several periods to which accounts sent by them during the financial year to the company related, after deducting those bodies' losses for those periods (or vice versa);
(c) the amount of the company's share of the net aggregate amount of the undistributed profits accumulated by the bodies in which the investments are held since the time when the investments were acquired after deducting the losses accumulated by them since that time (or vice versa);
(d) the manner in which any losses incurred by the said bodies have been dealt with in the company's accounts.

**7** The aggregate amounts respectively of reserves and provisions (other than provisions for depreciation, renewals or diminution in value of assets) shall be stated under separate headings;
Provided that–
(a) this paragraph shall not require a separate statement of either of the said amounts which is not material; and
(b) the Secretary of State may direct that a separate statement shall not be required of the amount of provisions where he is satisfied that that is not required in the public interest and would prejudice the company, but subject to the condition that any heading stating an amount arrived at after taking into account a provision (other than as aforesaid) shall be so framed or marked as to indicate that fact.

**8(1)** There shall also be shown (unless it is shown in the profit and loss account or a statement or report annexed thereto, or the amount involved is not material)–
(a) where the amount of the reserves or of the provisions (other than provisions for depreciation, renewals or diminution in value of assets) shows an increase as compared with the amount at the end of the immediately preceding financial year, the source from which the amount of the increase has been derived; and
(b) where–
(i) the amount of the reserves shows a decrease as compared with the amount at the end of the immediately preceding financial year; or
(ii) the amount at the end of the immediately preceding financial year of the provisions (other than provisions for depreciation, renewals or diminution in value of assets) exceeded the aggregate of the sums since applied and amounts still retained for the purposes thereof;

the application of the amounts derived from the difference.

**(2)** Where the heading showing the reserves or any of the provisions aforesaid is divided into sub-headings, this paragraph shall apply to each of the separate amounts shown in the sub-headings instead of applying to the aggregate amount thereof.

**9** If an amount is set aside for the purpose of its being used to prevent undue fluctuations in charges for taxation, it shall be stated.

**10(1)** There shall be shown under separate headings–

(a) the aggregate amounts respectively of the company's listed investments and unlisted investments;

(b) if the amount of the goodwill and of any patents and trade marks or part of that amount is shown as a separate item in or is otherwise ascertainable from the books of the company, or from any contract for the sale or purchase of any property to be acquired by the company, or from any documents in the possession of the company relating to the stamp duty payable in respect of any such contract or the conveyance of any such property, the said amount so shown or ascertained as far as not written off or, as the case may be, the said amount so far as it is so shown or ascertainable and as so shown or ascertained, as the case may be;

(c) the aggregate amount of any outstanding loans made under the authority of section 153(4)(b), (bb) or (c) or 155 of this Act;

(d) the aggregate amount of bank loans and overdrafts and the aggregate amount of loans made to the company which–

(i) are repayable otherwise than by instalments and fall due for repayment after the expiration of the period of five years beginning with the day next following the expiration of the financial year; or

(ii) are repayable by instalments any of which fall due for payment after the expiration of that period;

not being, in either case, bank loans or overdrafts;

(e) the aggregate amount which is recommended for distribution by way of dividend."

(In para. 10(1)(c) ", (bb)" inserted by CA 1989, s. 18(3) and Sch. 7, Pt. I, para. 1 as from 1 April 1990 subject to transitional and saving provisions (see SI 1990/355 (C 13), art. 3, Sch. 1 and also art. 6–9).)

"**(2)** Nothing in head (b) of the foregoing sub-paragraph shall be taken as requiring the amount of the goodwill, patents and trade marks to be stated otherwise than as a single item.

**(3)** The heading showing the amount of the listed investments shall be subdivided, where necessary, to distinguish the investments as respects which there has, and those as respects which there has not, been granted a listing on a recognised investment exchange other than an overseas investment exchange within the meaning of the Financial Services Act 1986."

(In para. 10(3) the words from "recognised investment exchange" to the end substituted for the former words "recognised stock exchange" by Financial Services Act 1986, s. 212(2) and Sch. 16, para. 24 as from 29 April 1988 (see SI 1988/740 (C 22)).)

"**(4)** In relation to each loan falling within head (d) of sub-paragraph (1) of this paragraph (other than a bank loan or overdraft), there shall be stated by way of note (if not otherwise stated) the terms on which it is repayable and the rate at which interest is payable thereon:

Provided that if the number of loans is such that, in the opinion of the directors, compliance with the foregoing requirement would result in a statement of excessive length, it shall be sufficient to give a general indication of the terms on which the loans are repayable and the rates at which interest is payable thereon.

**11** Where any liability of the company is secured otherwise than by operation of law on any assets of the company, the fact that that liability is so secured shall be stated, but it shall not be necessary to specify the assets on which the liability is secured.

**12** Where any of the company's debentures are held by a nominee of or trustee for the company, the nominal amount of the debentures and the amount at which they are stated in the books of the company shall be stated.

**13(1)** The matters referred to in the following sub-paragraphs shall be stated by way of note, or in a statement or report annexed, if not otherwise shown.

**(2)** The number, description and amount of any shares in the company which any person has an option to subscribe for, together with the following particulars of the option, that is to say–

(a) the period during which it is exercisable;

(b) the price to be paid for shares subscribed for under it."

**(3)** (Omitted and repealed by Companies Act 1989, s. 18(3), 212 and Sch. 7, Pt. I, para. 2 and Sch. 24 as from 1 April 1990.)

(In regard to the date of the above omission and repeal see SI 1990/355 (C 13), art. 3, 5(1)(b), (2), Sch. 1 and art. 6–9) for transitional and saving provisions; para. 13(3) formerly read as follows:

"Where shares in a public company (other than an old public company within the meaning of section 1 of the Consequential Provisions Act) are purchased or are acquired by the company by forfeiture or surrender in lieu of forfeiture, or as expressly permitted by section 143(3) of this Act, or are acquired by another person in circumstances where paragraph (c) or (d) of section 146(1) applies or are made subject to a lien or charge taken (whether expressly or otherwise) by the company and permitted by section 150(2) or (4), or section 6(3) of the Consequential Provisions Act–

(a) the number and nominal value of the shares so purchased, the aggregate amount of the consideration paid by the company for such shares and the reasons for their purchase;

(b) the number and nominal value of the shares so acquired by the company, acquired by another person in such circumstances and so charged respectively during the financial year;

(c) the maximum number and nominal value of shares which, having been so acquired by the company, acquired by another person in such circumstances or so charged (whether or not during the financial year) are held at any time by the company or that other person during that year;

(d) the number and nominal value of shares so acquired by the company, acquired by another person in such circumstances or so charged (whether or not during that year) which are disposed of by the company or that other person or cancelled by the company during that year;

(e) where the number and nominal value of the shares of any particular description are stated in pursuance of any of the preceding paragraphs, the percentage of the called-up share capital which shares of that description represent;

(f) where any of the shares have been so charged, the amount of the charge in each case;

(g) where any of the shares have been disposed of by the company or the person who acquired them in such circumstances for money or money's worth, the amount or value of the consideration in each case."

"**(4)** Any distribution made by an investment company within the meaning of Part VIII of this Act which reduces the amount of its net assets to less than the aggregate of its called-up share capital and undistributable reserves.

For purposes of this sub-paragraph, a company's net assets are the aggregate of its assets less the aggregate of its liabilities; and **"undistributable reserves"** has the meaning given by section 264(3).

**(5)** The amount of any arrears of fixed cumulative dividends on the company's shares and the period for which the dividends or, if there is more than one class, each class of them are in arrear.

**(6)** Particulars of any charge on the assets of the company to secure the liabilities of any other person, including, where practicable, the amount secured.

**(7)** The general nature of any other contingent liabilities not provided for and, where practicable, the aggregate amount or estimated amount of those liabilities, if it is material.

**(8)** Where practicable the aggregate amount or estimated amount, if it is material, of contracts for capital expenditure, so far as not provided for and, where practicable, the aggregate amount or estimated amount, if it is material, of capital expenditure authorised by the directors which has not been contracted for.

**(9)** In the case of fixed assets under any heading whose amount is required to be arrived at in accordance with paragraph 5(1) of this Schedule (other than unlisted investments) and is so arrived at by reference to a valuation, the years (so far as they are known to the directors) in which the assets were severally valued and the several values, and, in the case of assets that have been valued during the financial year, the names of the persons who valued them or particulars of their qualifications for doing so and (whichever is stated) the bases of valuation used by them.

**(10)** If there are included amongst fixed assets under any heading (other than investments) assets that have been acquired during the financial year, the aggregate amount of the assets acquired as determined for the purpose of making up the balance sheet, and if during that year any fixed assets included under a heading in the balance sheet made up with respect to the immediately preceding financial year (other than investments) have been disposed of or destroyed, the aggregate amount thereof as determined for the purpose of making up that balance sheet.

**(11)** Of the amount of fixed assets consisting of land, how much is ascribable to land of freehold tenure and how much to land of leasehold tenure, and, of the latter, how much is ascribable to land held on long lease and how much to land held on short lease.

**(12)** If in the opinion of the directors any of the current assets have not a value, on realisation in the ordinary course of the company's business, at least equal to the amount at which they are stated, the fact that the directors are of that opinion.

**(13)** The aggregate market value of the company's listed investments where it differs from the amount of the investments as stated and the stock exchange value of any investments of which the market value is shown (whether separately or not) and is taken as being higher than their stock exchange value.

**(14)** If a sum set aside for the purpose of its being used to prevent undue fluctuations in charges for taxation has been used during the financial year for another purpose, the amount thereof and the fact that it has been so used.

**(15)** If the amount carried forward for stock in trade or work in progress is material for the appreciation by its members of the company's state of affairs or of its profit or loss for the financial year, the manner in which that amount has been computed.

**(16)** The basis on which foreign currencies have been converted into sterling, where the amount of the assets or liabilities affected is material.

**(17)** The basis on which the amount, if any, set aside for United Kingdom corporation tax is computed."

**(18)** (Repealed by Companies Act 1989, s. 212 and Sch. 24 as from 1 April 1990.)

(In regard to the date of the above repeal see SI 1990/355 (C 13), art. 5(1)(b), (2) and art. 6–9 for transitional and saving provisions; para. 13(18) formerly read as follows:

"The corresponding amounts at the end of the immediately preceding financial year for all items shown in the balance sheet other than any item the amount for which is shown–

(a) in pursuance of sub-paragraph (10) of this paragraph, or

(b) as an amount the source or application of which is required by paragraph 8 to be shown."

"PROFIT AND LOSS ACCOUNT

**14(1)** There shall be shown–

(a) the amount charged to revenue by way of provision for depreciation, renewals or diminution in value of fixed assets;

(b) the amount of the interest on loans of the following kinds made to the company (whether on the security of debentures or not), namely, bank loans, overdrafts and loans which, not being bank loans or overdrafts,–

(i) are repayable otherwise than by instalments and fall due for repayment before the expiration of the period of five years beginning with the day next following the expiration of the financial year; or

(ii) are repayable by instalments the last of which falls due for payment before the expiration of that period;

and the amount of the interest on loans of other kinds so made (whether on the security of debentures or not);

(c) the amount of the charge to revenue for United Kingdom corporation tax and, if that amount would have been greater but for relief from double taxation, the amount which it would have been but for such relief, the amount of the charge for United Kingdom income tax, and the amount of the charge for taxation imposed outside the United Kingdom of profits, income and (so far as charged to revenue) capital gains;

(d) the amounts respectively set aside for redemption of share capital and for redemption of loans;

(e) the amount, if material, set aside or proposed to be set aside to, or withdrawn from, reserves;

(f) subject to sub-paragraph (2) of this paragraph, the amount, if material, set aside to provisions other than provisions for depreciation, renewals, or diminution in value of assets or, as the case may be, the amount, if material, withdrawn from such provisions and not applied for the purposes thereof;

(g) the amounts respectively of income from listed investments and income from unlisted investments;

(h) if a substantial part of the company's revenue for the financial year consists in rents from land, the amount thereof (after deduction of ground-rents, rates and other outgoings);

(j) the amount, if material, charged to revenue in respect of sums payable in respect of the hire of plant and machinery;

(k) the aggregate amount of the dividends paid and proposed.

**(2)** The Secretary of State may direct that a company shall not be obliged to show an amount set aside to provisions in accordance with sub-paragraph (1)(f) of this paragraph, if he is satisfied that that is not required in the public interest and would prejudice the company, but subject to the condition that any heading stating an amount arrived at after taking into account the amount set aside as aforesaid shall be so framed or marked as to indicate that fact.

**(3)** If, in the case of any assets in whose case an amount is charged to revenue by way of provision for depreciation or diminution in value, an amount is also so charged by way of provision for renewal thereof, the last-mentioned amount shall be shown separately.

**(4)** If the amount charged to revenue by way of provision for depreciation or diminution in value of any fixed assets (other than investments) has been determined otherwise than by reference to the amount of those assets as determined for the purpose of making up the balance sheet, that fact shall be stated.

**15** The amount of any charge arising in consequence of the occurrence of an event in a preceding financial year and of any credit so arising shall, if not included in a heading relating to other matters, be stated under a separate heading."

**16** (Repealed by Companies Act 1989. s. 212 and Sch. 24 as from 1 April 1990.)

(In regard to the date of the above repeal see SI 1990/355 (C 13), art. 5(1)(b), (2) and art. 6–9 for transitional and saving provisions; para. 16 formerly read as follows:

"The amount of the remuneration of the auditors shall be shown under a separate heading, and for the purposes of this paragraph, any sums paid by the company in respect of the auditors' expenses shall be deemed to be included in the expression "remuneration"."

"**17(1)** The following matters shall be stated by way of note, if not otherwise shown.

**(2)** The turnover for the financial year."

(In para. 17(1) the words "except in so far as it is attributable to the business of banking or discounting or to business of such other class as may be prescribed for the purposes of this sub-paragraph" formerly appearing at the end of the paragraph omitted by the Companies Act 1985 (Bank Accounts) Regulations 1991 (SI 1991/2705), reg. 6 and Sch. 2, para. 4(a) as from 2 December 1991 (subject to the transitional provisions in reg. 9).)

"**(3)** If some or all of the turnover is omitted by reason of its being attributable as aforesaid, the fact that it is so omitted.

**(4)** The method by which turnover stated is arrived at.

**(5)** A company shall not be subject to the requirements of this paragraph if it is neither a parent company nor a subsidiary undertaking and the turnover which, apart from this sub-paragraph, would be required to be stated does not exceed £1 million."

(In para. 17(5) the words "neither a parent company nor a subsidiary undertaking" substituted for the former words "neither a holding company nor a subsidiary of another body corporate" by CA 1989, s. 18(3) and Sch. 7, Pt. I, para. 3 as from 1 April 1990 (see SI 1990/355 (C 13), art. 3, Sch. 1 and also art. 6–9).)

"**18(1)** The following matters shall be stated by way of note, if not otherwise shown.

**(2)** If depreciation or replacement of fixed assets is provided for by some method other than a depreciation charge or provision for renewals, or is not provided for, the method by which it is provided for or the fact that it is not provided for, as the case may be.

**(3)** The basis on which the charge for United Kingdom corporation tax and United Kingdom income tax is computed.

**(4)** Any special circumstances which affect liability in respect of taxation of profits, income or capital gains for the financial year or liability in respect of taxation of profits, income or capital gains for succeeding financial years."

**(5)** (Repealed by Companies Act 1989, s. 212 and Sch. 24 as from 1 April 1990.)

(In regard to the date of the above repeal see SI 1990/355 (C 13), art. 5(1)(b), (2) and art. 6–9 for transitional and saving provisions; para. 18(5) formerly read as follows:

"The corresponding amounts for the immediately preceding financial year for all items shown in the profit and loss account."

"**(6)** Any material respects in which items shown in the profit and loss account are affected–

(a) by transactions of a sort not usually undertaken by the company or otherwise by circumstances of an exceptional or non-recurrent nature; or
(b) by any change in the basis of accounting.

SUPPLEMENTARY PROVISIONS

**18A(1)** Accounting policies shall be applied consistently within the same accounts and from one financial year to the next.

**(2)** If it appears to the directors of a company that there are special reasons for departing from the principle stated in sub-paragraph (1) in preparing the company'saccounts in respect of any financial year, they may do so; but particulars of the departure, the reasons for it and its effect shall be given in a note to the accounts."

(See history note after para. 18C.)

"**18B** It shall be stated whether the accounts have been prepared in accordance with applicable accounting standards, and particulars of any material departure from those standards and the reasons for it shall be given."

(See history note after para. 18C.)

"**18C(1)** In respect of every item shown in the balance sheet or profit and loss account, or stated in a note to the accounts, there shall be shown or stated the corresponding amount for the financial year immediately preceding that to which the accounts relate, subject to sub-paragraph (3).

**(2)** Where the corresponding amount is not comparable, it shall be adjusted and particulars of the adjustment and the reasons for it shall be given in a note to the accounts.

**(3)** Sub-paragraph (1) does not apply in relation to an amount shown–

(a) as an amount the source or application of which is required by paragraph 8 above (reserves and provisions),
(b) in pursuance of paragraph 13(10) above (acquisitions and disposals of fixed assets),
(c) by virtue of paragraph 13 of Schedule 4A (details of accounting treatment of acquisitions),
(d) by virtue of paragraph 2, 8(3), 16, 21(1)(d), 22(4) or (5), 24(3) or (4) or 27(3) or (4) of Schedule 5 (shareholdings in other undertakings), or
(e) by virtue of Part II or III of Schedule 6 (loans and other dealings in favour of directors and others)."

(Para. 18A–18C inserted by CA 1989, s. 18(3) and Sch. 7, Pt. I, para. 4 as from 1 April 1990 subject to transitional and saving provisions (see SI 1990/355 (C 13), art. 3, Sch. 1 and also art. 6–9).)

"PROVISIONS WHERE COMPANY IS PARENT COMPANY OR SUBSIDIARY UNDERTAKING"

(Former Part heading before para. 19 omitted by CA 1989, s. 18(3) and Sch. 7, preliminary para. c(ii) and new heading inserted by CA 1989, s. 18(3) and Sch. 7, Pt. I, para. 5(1) as from 1 April 1990 subject to transitional and saving provisions (see SI 1990/355 (C 13), art. 3, Sch. 1 and also art. 6–9); former heading read "Part II – Special Provisions where the Company is a Holding or Subsidiary Company". It seems that the heading (appearing below in square brackets) was never actually omitted.)

[MODIFICATIONS OF AND ADDITIONS TO REQUIREMENTS AS TO COMPANY'S OWN ACCOUNTS]

"**19(1)** This paragraph applies where the company is a parent company."

(In para. 19(1) the words "is a parent company" substituted for the former words "is a holding company, whether or not it is itself a subsidiary of another body corporate" by CA 1989, s. 18(3) and Sch. 7, Pt. I, para. 5(1), (2) as from 1 April 1990 subject to transitional and saving provisions (see SI 1990/355 (C 13), art. 3, Sch. 1 and also art. 6–9).)

"**(2)** The aggregate amount of assets consisting of shares in, or amounts owing (whether on account of a loan or otherwise) from, the company's subsidiary undertakings, distinguishing shares from indebtedness, shall be set out in the balance sheet separately from all the other assets of the company, and the aggregate amount of indebtedness (whether on account of a loan or otherwise) to the company's subsidiary undertakings shall be so set out separately from all its other liabilities and–

(a) the references in paragraphs 5, 6, 10, 13 and 14 of this Schedule to the company's investments (except those in paragraphs 13(10) and 14(4)) shall not include investments in its subsidiary undertakings required by this paragraph to be separately set out; and

(b) paragraph 5, sub-paragraph (1)(a) of paragraph 14, and sub-paragraph (2) of paragraph 18 of this Schedule shall not apply in relation to fixed assets consisting of interests in the company's subsidiary undertakings."

(In para. 19(2) the words "subsidiary undertakings" (appearing four times) substituted for the former words "subsidiaries" and (in para. 19(2)(a)) the words "paragraphs 5, 6, 10, 13 and 14" substituted for the former words "Part I" by CA 1989, s. 18(3) and Sch. 7, Pt. I, para. 5(1), (3) as from 1 April 1990 subject to transitional and saving provisions (see SI 1990/355 (C 13), art. 3, Sch. 1 and also art. 6–9).)

**(3)–(7)** (Omitted and repealed by Companies Act 1989, s. 18(3), 212, Sch. 7, Pt. I, para. 5(1), (4) and Sch. 24 as from 1 April 1990.)

(In regard to the date of the above omission and repeal see SI 1990/355 (C 13), art. 3, 5(1)(b), (2), Sch. 1. See art. 6–9 for transitional and saving provisions; para. 19(3)–(7) formerly read as follows:

"**19(3)** There shall be shown by way of note on the balance sheet or in a statement or report annexed thereto the number, description and amount of the shares in and debentures of the company held by its subsidiaries or their nominees, but excluding any of those shares or debentures in the case of which the subsidiary is concerned as personal representative or in the case of which it is concerned as trustee and neither the company nor any subsidiary thereof is beneficially interested under the trust, otherwise than by way of security only for the purposes of a transaction entered into by it in the ordinary course of a business which includes the lending of money.

Schedule 2 has effect for the interpretation of the reference in this sub-paragraph to a beneficial interest under a trust.

**(4)** Where group accounts are not submitted, there shall be annexed to the balance sheet a statement showing–

(a) the reasons why subsidiaries are not dealt with in group accounts;

(b) the net aggregate amount, so far as it concerns members of the holding company and is not dealt with in the company's accounts, of the subsidiaries' profits after deducting the subsidiaries' losses (or vice versa)–

(i) for the respective financial years of the subsidiaries ending with or during the financial year of the company; and

(ii) for their previous financial years since they respectively became the holding company's subsidiary;

(c) the net aggregate amount of the subsidiaries' profits after deducting the subsidiaries' losses (or vice versa)–

(i) for the respective financial years of the subsidiaries ending with or during the financial year of the company; and

(ii) for their other financial years since they respectively became the holding company's subsidiary;

so far as those profits are dealt with, or provision is made for those losses, in the company's accounts;

(d) any qualifications contained in the report of the auditors of the subsidiaries on their accounts for their respective financial years ending as aforesaid, and any note or saving contained in those accounts to call attention to a matter which, apart from the note or saving, would properly have been referred to in such a qualification, in so far as the matter which is the subject of the qualification or note is not covered by the company's own accounts and is material from the point of view of its members;

or, in so far as the information required by this sub-paragraph is not obtainable, a statement that it is not obtainable:

Provided that the Secretary of State may, on the application or with the consent of the company's directors, direct that in relation to any subsidiary this sub-paragraph shall not apply or shall apply only to such extent as may be provided by the direction.

**(5)** Paragraphs (b) and (c) of the last foregoing sub-paragraph shall apply only to profits and losses of a subsidiary which may properly be treated in the holding company's accounts as revenue profits or losses, and the profits or losses attributable to any shares in a subsidiary for the time being held by the holding company or any other of its subsidiaries shall not (for the purposes of those paragraphs) be treated as aforesaid so far as they are profits or losses for the period before the date on or as from which the shares were acquired by the company or any of its subsidiaries, except that they may in a proper case be so treated where–

(a) the company is itself the subsidiary of another body corporate; and

(b) the shares were acquired from that body corporate or a subsidiary of it;

and for the purpose of determining whether any profits or losses are to be treated as profits or losses for the said period the profit or loss for any financial year of the subsidiary may, if it is not practicable to apportion it with reasonable accuracy by reference to the facts, be treated as accruing from day to day during that year and be apportioned accordingly.

The amendment of the previous corresponding provision by section 40(3) of the Companies Act 1981 (substituting "(for the purposes of those paragraphs)" for "(for that or any other purpose)") is without prejudice to any other restriction with respect to the manner in which a holding company may treat pre-acquisition profits or losses of a subsidiary in its accounts.

**(6)** Paragraphs (b) and (c) of sub-paragraph (4) above shall not apply where the company is a wholly-owned subsidiary of another body corporate incorporated in Great Britain if there is annexed to the balance sheet a statement that in the opinion of the directors of the company the aggregate value of the assets of the company consisting of shares in, or amounts owing (whether on account of a loan or otherwise) from, the company's subsidiaries is not less than the aggregate of the amounts at which those assets are stated or included in the balance sheet.

**(7)** Where group accounts are not submitted, there shall be annexed to the balance sheet a statement showing, in relation to the subsidiaries (if any) whose financial years did not end with that of the company–

(a) the reasons why the company's directors consider that the subsidiaries' financial years should not end with that of the company; and

(b) the dates on which the subsidiaries' financial years ending last before that of the company respectively ended or the earliest and latest of those dates.")

"**20(1)** This paragraph applies where the company is a subsidiary undertaking.

**(2)** The balance sheet of the company shall show –

(a) the aggregate amount of its indebtedness to undertakings of which it is a subsidiary undertaking or which are fellow subsidiary undertakings, and

(b) the aggregate amount of the indebtedness of all such undertakings, to it,

distinguishing in each case between indebtedness in respect of debentures and otherwise.

**(3)** The balance sheet shall also show the aggregate amount of assets consisting of shares in fellow subsidiary undertakings."

(Para. 20 substituted by CA 1989, s. 18(3) and Sch. 7, Pt. I, para. 6 as from 1 April 1990 subject to transitional and saving provisions (see SI 1990/355 (C 13), art. 3, Sch. 1 and also art. 6–9); para. 20 formerly read as follows:

"**20(1)** The balance sheet of a company which is a subsidiary of another body corporate, whether or not it is itself a holding company, shall show the aggregate amount of its indebtedness to all bodies corporate of which it is a subsidiary or a fellow subsidiary and the aggregate amount of indebtedness of all such bodies corporate to it, distinguishing in each case between indebtedness in respect of debentures and otherwise, and the aggregate amount of assets consisting of shares in fellow subsidiaries.

**(2)** For the purposes of this paragraph a company shall be deemed to be a fellow subsidiary of another body corporate if both are subsidiaries of the same body corporate but neither is the other's.")

"CONSOLIDATED ACCOUNTS OF HOLDING COMPANY AND SUBSIDIARIES"

**21–26** (Omitted and repealed by Companies Act 1989, s. 18(3), 212, Sch. 7, Pt. I, para. 7 and Sch. 24 as from 1 April 1990.) (In regard to the date of the above repeal see SI 1990/355 (C 13), art. 3, 5(1)(b), (2), Sch. 1 and art. 6–9 for transitional and saving provisions; para. 21–26 formerly read as follows:

"**21** Subject to the following paragraphs of this Part of this Schedule the consolidated balance sheet and profit and loss account shall combine the information contained in the separate balance sheets and profit and loss accounts of the holding company and of the subsidiaries dealt with by the consolidated accounts, but with such adjustments (if any) as the directors of the holding company think necessary.

**22** Subject as aforesaid and to Part III of this Schedule, the consolidated accounts shall, in giving the said information, comply so far as practicable, with the requirements of this Act as if they were the accounts of an actual company.

**23** The following provisions of this Act, namely–

(a) section 231 as applying Schedule 5, but only Parts II, V and VI of that Schedule, and

(b) sections 232 to 234 and Schedule 6, so far as relating to accounts other than group accounts,

do not by virtue of the two last foregoing paragraphs apply for the purpose of the consolidated accounts.

**24** Paragraph 22 above is without prejudice to any requirement of this Act which applies (otherwise than by virtue of paragraph 21 or 22) to group accounts.

**25** In relation to any subsidiaries of the holding company not dealt with by the consolidated accounts–

(a) sub-paragraphs (2) and (3) of paragraph 19 of this Schedule shall apply for the purpose of those accounts as if those accounts were the accounts of an actual company of which they were subsidiaries; and

(b) there shall be annexed the like statement as is required by sub-paragraph (4) of that paragraph where there are no group accounts, but as if references therein to the holding company's accounts were references to the consolidated accounts.

**26** In relation to any subsidiary (whether or not dealt with by the consolidated accounts), whose financial year did not end with that of the company, there shall be annexed the like statement as is required by sub-paragraph (7) of paragraph 19 of this Schedule where there are no group accounts.")

"EXCEPTIONS FOR CERTAIN COMPANIES"

(Former Part heading before para. 27 omitted by CA 1989, s. 18(3) and Sch. 7, preliminary para. c(ii) and new heading inserted by CA 1989, s. 18(3) and Sch. 7, Pt. I, para. 8(1) as from 1 April 1990 subject to transitional and saving provisions (see SI 1990/355 (C 13), art. 3, Sch. 1 and also art. 6–9); former heading read "Part III – Exceptions for Certain Special Category Companies".)

**27** (Repealed by the Companies Act 1985 (Bank Accounts) Regulations 1991 (SI 1991/2705), reg. 6 and Sch. 2, para. 4(b) as from 2 December 1991 (subject to the transitional provisions in reg. 9).)

(Para. 27 formerly read as follows:

"**27(1)** The following applies to a banking company (if not subject to the Banking Companies (Accounts) Regulations 1970) which satisfies the Secretary of State that it ought to have the benefit of this paragraph."

(The Banking Companies (Accounts) Regulations 1970 (SI 1970/327) were made under former CA 1948, s. 454(1) and former CA 1967, s. 12 – under those Regulations former CA 1948, Sch. 8A, para. 23 (exemption for banking and discount companies from certain accounting provisions) does not apply to the London Clearing Banks or to banks represented on the Committee of Scottish Bank General Managers.)

"**(2)** The company shall not be subject to the requirements of paragraphs 2 to 18 of this Schedule other than–

(a) as respects its balance sheet, those of paragraphs 2 and 3, paragraph 4 (so far as it relates to assets), paragraph 10 (except sub-paragraphs (1)(d) and (4)), paragraphs 11 and 12 and paragraph 13 (except sub-paragraphs (9), (10), (11), (13) and (14)); and

(b) as respects its profit and loss account, those of sub-paragraph (1)(h) and (k) of paragraph 14, and paragraph 15."

(In para. 27(2) previously the words "paragraphs 2 to 18 of this Schedule" substituted for the former words "Part I of this Schedule" and in para. 27(2)(b) the words "and paragraph 15" substituted for the former words "paragraphs 15 and 16 and sub-paragraphs (1) and (15) of paragraph 18" by CA 1989, s. 18(3) and Sch. 7, Pt. I, para. 8(1), (2) as from 1 April 1990 subject to transitional and saving provisions (see SI 1990/355 (C 13), art. 3, Sch. 1 and also art. 6–9.))

"**(3)** But, where in the company's balance sheet reserves or provisions (other than provisions for depreciation, renewals or diminution in value of assets) are not stated separately, any heading stating an amount arrived at after taking into account a reserve or such a provision shall be so framed or marked as to indicate that fact, and its profit and loss account shall indicate by appropriate words the manner in which the amount stated for the company's profit or loss has been arrived at.

**(4)** The company's accounts shall not be deemed, by reason only of the fact that they do not comply with any requirements from which the company is exempt by virtue of this paragraph, not to give the true and fair view required by this Act."

(In para. 27(4) previously the words "of the said Part I" formerly appearing after the words "any requirements" omitted and repealed by CA 1989, s. 18(3), 212 and Sch. 7, Pt. I, para. 8(1), (3) and Sch. 24 as from 1 April 1990 subject to transitional and saving provisions (see SI 1990/355 (C 13), art. 3, 5(1)(b), (2), Sch. 1 and also art. 6–9).))

"**28(1)** An insurance company to which Part II of the Insurance Companies Act 1982 applies shall not be subject to the following requirements of paragraphs 2 to 18 of this Schedule, that is to say–

(a) as respects its balance sheet, those of paragraphs 4 to 8 (both inclusive), sub-paragraphs (1)(a) and (3) of paragraph 10 and sub-paragraphs (6), (7) and (9) to (13) (both inclusive) of paragraph 13;

(b) as respects its profit and loss account, those of paragraph 14 (except sub-paragraph (1)(b), (c), (d) and (k)) and paragraph 18(2);

but, where in its balance sheet reserves or provisions (other than provisions for depreciation, renewals or diminution in value of assets) are not stated separately, any heading stating an amount arrived at after taking into account a reserve or such a provision shall be so framed or marked as to indicate that fact, and its profit and loss account shall indicate by appropriate words the manner in which the amount stated for the company's profit or loss has been arrived at:

Provided that the Secretary of State may direct that any such insurance company whose business includes to a substantial extent business other than insurance business shall comply with all the requirements of the said paragraphs 2 to 18 or such of them as may be specified in the direction and shall comply therewith as respects either the whole of its business or such part thereof as may be so specified."

(In para. 28(1) the words "paragraphs 2 to 18" (appearing twice) substituted for the former words "Part I" by CA 1989, s. 18(3) and Sch. 7, Pt. I, para. 9 as from 1 April 1990 subject to transitional and saving provisions (see SI 1990/355 (C 13), art. 3, Sch. 1 and also art. 6–9).)

"**(2)** The accounts of a company shall not be deemed, by reason only of the fact that they do not comply with any requirement of paragraphs 2 to 18 of this Schedule from which the company is exempt by virtue of this paragraph, not to give the true and fair view required by this Act."

(In para. 28(2) the words "paragraphs 2 to 18" substituted for the former words "Part I" by CA 1989, s. 18(3) and Sch. 7, Pt. I, para. 9 as from 1 April 1990 subject to transitional and saving provisions (see SI 1990/355 (C 13), art. 3, Sch. 1 and also art. 6–9) – the new reference must be to para. 2–18 of Part I. There appears to be a contradictory repeal from the same date by CA 1989, s. 212 and Sch. 24 of the words "of Part I of this Schedule" (see SI 1990/355 (C 13), art. 5(1)(b), (2)).)

"**28A** Where a company is entitled to, and has availed itself of, any of the provisons of paragraph 28 of this Schedule, section 235(2) only requires the auditors to state whether in their opinion the accounts have been properly prepared in accordance with this Act."

(In para. 28A the words "27 or" formerly appearing before "28" omitted by the Companies Act 1985 (Bank Accounts) Regulations 1991 (SI 1991/2705), reg. 6 and Sch. 2, para. 4(c) as from 2 December 1991 (subject to the transitional provisions in reg. 9).

Previously para. 28A inserted by CA 1989, s. 18(3) and Sch. 7, Pt. I, para. 10 as from 1 April 1990 subject to transitional and saving provisions (see SI 1990/355 (C 13), art. 3, Sch. 1 and also art. 6–9).)

**29–31** (Omitted and repealed by Companies Act 1989, s. 18(3), 212, Sch. 7, Pt. I, para. 11 and Sch. 24 as from 1 April 1990.)

(In regard to the date of the above omission and repeal see SI 1990/355 (C 13), art. 3, 5, Sch. 1 and art. 6–9 for transitional and saving provisions; also the Part heading before para. 31 omitted by CA 1989, s. 18(3) and Sch. 7, preliminary para. (c)(ii) as from the same date and subject to the same provisions; para. 29–31 (including the Part heading) formerly read as follows:

"**29(1)** A shipping company shall not be subject to the following requirements of Part I of this Schedule, that is to say–

(a) as respects its balance sheet, those of paragraph 4 (except so far as it relates to assets), paragraphs 5, 7 and 8 and sub-paragraphs (9) and (10) of paragraph 13;

(b) as respects its profit and loss account, those of sub-paragraph (1)(a), (e) and (f) and sub-paragraphs (3) and (4) of paragraph 14 and paragraph 17.

**(2)** The accounts of a company shall not be deemed, by reason only of the fact that they do not comply with any requirements of Part I of this Schedule from which the company is exempt by virtue of this paragraph, not to give the true and fair view required by this Act.

**30** Where a company entitled to the benefit of any provision contained in this Part of this Schedule is a holding company, the reference in Part II of this Schedule to consolidated accounts complying with the requirements of this Act shall, in relation to consolidated accounts of that company, be construed as referring to those requirements in so far only–

(a) as they apply to the individual accounts of that company, and

(b) as they apply (otherwise than by virtue of paragraphs 21 and 22) to the group accounts prepared by that company.

Part IV – Special Provisions Where the Company Has Entered into Arrangements Subject to Merger Relief

**31(1)** Where during the financial year the company has allotted shares in consideration for the issue, transfer or cancellation of shares in another body corporate ("the other company") in circumstances where by virtue of section 131(2) (merger relief) section 130 did not apply to the premiums on those shares, the following information shall be given by way of a note to the company's accounts–

(a) the name of the other company;

(b) the number, nominal value and class of shares so allotted;

(c) the number, nominal value and class of shares in the other company so issued, transferred or cancelled;

(d) particulars of the accounting treatment adopted in the company's accounts (including any group accounts) in respect of such issue, transfer or cancellation; and

(e) where the company prepares group accounts, particulars of the extent to which and manner in which the profit or loss for the year of the group which appears in those accounts is affected by any profit or loss of the other company or any of its subsidiaries which arose at any time before the allotment.

**(2)** Where the company has during the financial year or during either of the two financial years immediately preceding it made such an allotment of shares as is mentioned in sub-paragraph (1) above and there is included in the company's consolidated profit and loss account, or if it has no such account, in its individual profit and loss account, any profit or loss (or part thereof) to which this sub-paragraph applies then the net amount of any such profit or loss (or part thereof) shall be shown in a note to the accounts together with an explanation of the transactions to which that information relates.

**(3)** Sub-paragraph (2) applies–

(a) to any profit or loss realised during the financial year by the company, or any of its subsidiaries, on the disposal of any shares in the other company or of any assets which were fixed assets of the other company, or of any of its subsidiaries, at the time of the allotment; and

(b) to any part of any profit or loss realised during the financial year by the company, or any of its subsidiaries, on the disposal of any shares (not being shares in the other company), which was attributable to the fact that at the time of the disposal there were amongst the assets of the company which issued those shares, or any of its subsidiaries, such shares or assets as are described in paragraph (a) above.

**(4)** Where in pursuance of the arrangement in question shares are allotted on different dates, the time of allotment for the purposes of sub-paragraphs (1)(e) and (3)(a) above is taken to be–

(a) if the other company becomes a subsidiary of the company as a result of the arrangement–

(i) if the arrangement becomes binding only upon the fulfilment of a condition, the date on which that condition is fulfilled, and

(ii) in any other case, the date on which the other company becomes a subsidiary of the company;

(b) if the other company is a subsidiary of the company when the arrangement is proposed, the date of the first allotment pursuant to that arrangement.")

"INTERPRETATION"

(Former Part heading before para. 32 omitted by CA 1989, s. 18(3) and Sch. 7, preliminary para. (c)(ii) and new heading inserted by CA 1989, s. 18(3) and Sch. 7, Pt. I, para. 12 as from 1 April 1990 subject to transitional and saving provisions (see SI 1990/355 (C 13), art. 3, Sch. 1 and also art. 6–9); former heading read "Part V – Interpretation of Schedule".)

"**32(1)** For the purposes of this Part of this Schedule, unless the context otherwise requires,–

(a) the expression **"provision"** shall, subject to sub-paragraph (2) of this paragraph, mean any amount written off or retained by way of providing for depreciation, renewals or diminution in value of assets or retained by way of providing for any known liability of which the amount cannot be determined with substantial accuracy;

(b) the expression **"reserve"** shall not, subject as aforesaid, include any amount written off or retained by way of providing for depreciation, renewals or diminution in value of assets or retained by way of providing for any known liability or any sum set aside for the purpose of its being used to prevent undue fluctuations in charges for taxation;

and in this paragraph the expression **"liability"** shall include all liabilities in respect of expenditure contracted for and all disputed or contingent liabilities."

(In para. 32(1) the words "this Part of this Schedule" substituted for the former words "this Schedule" by CA 1989, s. 18(3) and Sch. 7, Pt. I, para. 12 as from 1 April 1990 (see SI 1990/355 (C 13), art. 3, Sch. 1 and also art. 6–9).)

"**(2)** Where–

(a) any amount written off or retained by way of providing for depreciation, renewals or diminution in value of assets; or

(b) any amount retained by way of providing for any known liability;

is in excess of that which in the opinion of the directors is reasonably necessary for the purpose, the excess shall be treated for the purposes of this Part of this Schedule as a reserve and not as a provision."

(In para. 32(2) the words "this Part of this Schedule" substituted for the former words "this Schedule" by CA 1989, s. 18(3) and Sch. 7, Pt. I, para. 12 as from 1 April 1990 (see SI 1990/355 (C 13), art. 3, Sch. 1 and also art. 6–9).)

"**33** For the purposes aforesaid, the expression **"listed investment"** means an investment as respects which there has been granted a listing on a recognised investment exchange other than an overseas investment exchange within the meaning of the Financial Services Act 1986, or on any stock exchange of repute outside Great Britain and the expression **"unlisted investment"** shall be construed accordingly."

(In para. 33 the words from "recognised investment exchange" to "Financial Services Act 1986" substituted for the former words "recognised stock exchange" by Financial Services Act 1986, s. 212(2) and Sch. 16, para. 24 as from 29 April 1988 (see SI 1988/740 (C 22)).)

"**34** For the purposes aforesaid, the expression **"long lease"** means a lease in the case of which the portion of the term for which it was granted remaining unexpired at the end of the financial year is not less than fifty years, the expression **"short lease"** means a lease which is not a long lease and the expression **"lease"** includes an agreement for a lease.

**35** For the purposes aforesaid, a loan shall be deemed to fall due for repayment, and an instalment of a loan shall be deemed to fall due for payment, on the earliest date on which the lender could require repayment or, as the case may be, payment if he exercised all options and rights available to him.

**36** In the application of this Part of this Schedule to Scotland, **"land of freehold tenure"** means land in respect of which the company is the proprietor of the *dominium utile* or, in the case of land not held on feudal tenure, is the owner; **"land of leasehold tenure"** means land of which the company is the tenant under a lease; and the reference to ground-rents, rates and other outgoings includes a reference to feu-duty and ground annual."

(In para. 36 the words "this Part of this Schedule" substituted for the former words "this Schedule" by CA 1989, s. 18(3) and Sch. 7, Pt. I, para. 12 as from 1 April 1990 (see SI 1990/355 (C 13), art. 3, Sch. 1 and also art. 6–9).)

"Part II – Accounts of Insurance Group"

(In heading to Pt. II the words "Banking or" omitted by the Companies Act 1985 (Bank Accounts) Regulations 1991 (SI 1991/2705), reg. 6 and Sch. 3, para. 4(d) as from 2 December 1991 (subject to the transitional provisions in reg. 9).)

"UNDERTAKINGS TO BE INCLUDED IN CONSOLIDATION

**1** An undertaking (other than one carrying on insurance business) whose activities are a direct extension of or ancillary to insurance business shall not be excluded from consolidation under section 229(4) (exclusion of undertakings whose activities are different from those of the undertakings consolidated)."

(Para. 1 substituted by the Companies Act 1985 (Bank Accounts) Regulations 1991 (SI 1991/2705), reg. 6 and Sch. 3, para. 4(e) as from 2 December 1991 (subject to the transitional provisions in reg. 9); para. 1 formerly read as follows:

"**1** The following descriptions of undertaking shall not be excluded from consolidation under section 229(4) (exclusion of undertakings whose activities are different from those of the undertakings consolidated)–

(a) in the case of a banking group, an undertaking (other than a credit institution) whose activities are a direct extension of or ancillary to banking business;

(b) in the case of an insurance group, an undertaking (other than one carrying on insurance business) whose activities are a direct extension of or ancillary to insurance business.

For the purposes of paragraph (a) **"banking"** means the carrying on of a deposit-taking business within the meaning of the Banking Act 1987."

See also history note after (former) Pt. III.))

"GENERAL APPLICATION OF PROVISIONS APPLICABLE TO INDIVIDUAL ACCOUNTS

**2(1)** In paragraph 1 of Schedule 4A (application to group accounts of provisions applicable to individual accounts), the reference in sub-paragraph (1) to the provisions of Schedule 4 shall be construed as a reference to the provisions of Part I of this Schedule; and accordingly –

(a) the reference in sub-paragraph (2) to paragraph 59 of Schedule 4 shall be construed as a reference to paragraphs 19(2) and 20 of Part I of this Schedule; and

(b) sub-paragraph (3) shall be omitted.

**(2)** The general application of the provisions of Part I of this Schedule in place of those of Schedule 4 is subject to the following provisions."

(See history note after (former) Pt. III.)

"TREATMENT OF GOODWILL

**3(1)** The rules in paragraph 21 of Schedule 4 relating to the treatment of goodwill, and the rules in paragraphs 17 to 19 of that Schedule (valuation of fixed assets) so far as they relate to goodwill, apply for the purpose of dealing with any goodwill arising on consolidation.

**(2)** Goodwill shall be shown as a separate item in the balance sheet under an appropriate heading; and this applies notwithstanding anything in paragraph 10(1)(b) or (2) of Part I of this Schedule (under which goodwill, patents and trade marks may be stated in the company's individual accounts as a single item)."

(See history note after (former) Pt. III.)

"MINORITY INTERESTS AND ASSOCIATED UNDERTAKINGS

**4** The information required by paragraphs 17 and 20 to 22 of Schedule 4A (minority interests and associated undertakings) to be shown under separate items in the formats set out in Part I of Schedule 4 shall be shown separately in the balance sheet and profit and loss account under appropriate headings."

(See history note after (former) Pt. III.)

"COMPANIES ENTITLED TO BENEFIT OF EXEMPTIONS

**5(1)** Where an insurance company is entitled to the exemptions conferred by paragraph 28 of Part I of this Schedule, a group headed by that company is similarly entitled."

(In para. 5(1) the word "an" substituted for the former words "a banking or" and the words "27 or" formerly appearing before "28" omitted by the Companies Act 1985 (Bank Accounts) Regulations 1991 (SI 1991/2705), reg. 6 and Sch. 3, para. 4(f) as from 2 December 1991 (subject to the transitional provisions in reg. 9).

"**(2)** Paragraphs 28(2) and 28A (accounts not to be taken to be other than true and fair; duty of auditors) apply accordingly where advantage is taken of those exemptions in relation to group accounts."

(In para. 5(2) "27(4)" formerly appearing after the word "Paragraphs" omitted by the Companies Act 1985 (Bank Accounts) Regulations 1991 (SI 1991/2705), reg. 6 and Sch. 3, para. 4(f) as from 2 December 1991 (subject to the transitional provisions in reg. 9).

See also history note after (former) Pt. III.)

"INFORMATION AS TO UNDERTAKING IN WHICH SHARES HELD AS RESULT OF FINANCIAL ASSISTANCE OPERATION"

**6** (Repealed by the Companies Act 1985 (Bank Accounts) Regulations 1991 (SI 1991/2705), reg. 6 and Sch. 2, para. 4(g) as from 2 December 1991 (subject to the transitional provisions in reg. 9).)

(Para. 6 formerly read as follows:

"**6(1)** The following provisions apply where the parent company of a banking group has a subsidiary undertaking which–

(a) is a credit institution of which shares are held as a result of a financial assistance operation with a view to its reorganisation or rescue, and

(b) is excluded from consolidation under section 229(3)(c) (interest held with a view to resale).

**(2)** Information as to the nature and terms of the operation shall be given in a note to the group accounts and there shall be appended to the copy of the group accounts delivered to the registrar in accordance with section 242 a copy of the undertaking's latest individual accounts and, if it is a parent undertaking, its latest group accounts.
If the accounts appended are required by law to be audited, a copy of the auditors' report shall also be appended.

**(3)** If any document required to be appended is in a language other than English, the directors shall annex to the copy of that document delivered a translation of it into English, certified in the prescribed manner to be a correct translation.

**(4)** The above requirements are subject to the following qualifications –

(a) an undertaking is not required to prepare for the purposes of this paragraph accounts which would not otherwise be prepared, and if no accounts satisfying the above requirements are prepared none need be appended;

(b) the accounts of an undertaking need not be appended if they would not otherwise be required to be published, or made available for public inspection, anywhere in the world, but in that case the reason for not appending the accounts shall be stated in a note to the consolidated accounts.

**(5)** Where a copy of an undertaking's accounts is required to be appended to the copy of the group accounts delivered to the registrar, that fact shall be stated in a note to the group accounts.

**(6)** Subsections (2) to (4) of section 242 (penalties, etc. in case of default) apply in relation to the requirements of this paragraph as regards the delivery of documents to the registrar as they apply in relation to the requirements of subsection (1) of that section."

See also history note after (former) Pt. III.)

"Part III – Additional Disclosure: Related Undertakings"

**1** (Repealed by the Companies Act 1985 (Bank Accounts) Regulations 1991 (SI 1991/2705), reg. 5(2) as from 2 December 1991 (subject to the transitional provisions in reg. 9).)

(Pt. III (of what was then Sch. 9) formerly read as follows:

"**1** Where accounts are prepared in accordance with the special provisions of this Part relating to banking companies or groups, there shall be disregarded for the purposes of –

(a) paragraphs 7(2)(a), 23(2)(a) and 26(2)(a) of Schedule 5 (information about significant holdings in undertakings other than subsidiary undertakings: definition of 10 per cent holding), and

(b) paragraphs 9(1), 25(1) and 28(1) of that Schedule (additional information in case of 20 per cent holding),

any holding of shares not comprised in the equity share capital of the undertaking in question."
Also note that Pt. II and III inserted (as part of Sch. 9 – see note at beginning of Sch. 9A) – see CA 1989, s. 18(3), (4), Sch. 7, preliminary para. (d) and Pt. II–IV – as from 1 April 1990 subject to transitional and saving provisions (see SI 1990/355 (C 13), art. 3, Sch. 1 and also art. 6–9).)"

# Schedule 10 – Directors' Report where Accounts Prepared in Accordance with Special Provisions for Insurance Companies or Groups

[Companies Act 1985, s. 255-255C;
Companies Act 1989, s. 1, 18(5), Sch. 8]

(Omitted by the Companies Act 1985 (Insurance Companies Accounts) Regulations 1993 (SI 1993/3246), reg. 1, 5 and Sch. 2, para. 7 as from 19 December 1993 subject to exemption in reg. 6 and transitional regulations in reg. 7.)

**History**

Sch. 10 formerly read as follows:

(In heading to Sch. 10 the words "Banking or" formerly appearing before the words "Insurance Companies" omitted by the Companies Act 1985 (Bank Accounts) Regulations 1991 (SI 1991/2705), reg. 6 and Sch. 2, para. 5(a) as from 2 December 1991 (subject to the transitional provisions in reg. 9).)

"RECENT ISSUES

**1(1)** This paragraph applies where a company prepares individual accounts in accordance with the special provisions of this Part relating to insurance companies."

(In para. 1(1) the words "banking or" formerly appearing before the words "insurance companies" omitted by the Companies Act 1985 (Bank Accounts) Regulations 1991 (SI 1991/2705), reg. 6 and Sch. 2, para. 5(a) as from 2 December 1991 (subject to the transitional provisions in reg. 9).)

"**(2)** If in the financial year to which the accounts relate the company has issued any shares or debentures, the directors' report shall state the reason for making the issue, the classes of shares or debentures issued and, as respects each class, the number of shares or amount of debentures issued and the consideration received by the company for the issue.

TURNOVER AND PROFITABILITY

**2(1)** This paragraph applies where a company prepares group accounts in accordance with the special provisions of this Part relating to insurance groups."

(In para. 2(1) the words "banking or" formerly appearing before the words "insurance groups" omitted by the Companies Act 1985 (Bank Accounts) Regulations 1991 (SI 1991/2705), reg. 6 and Sch. 2, para. 5(a) as from 2 December 1991 (subject to the transitional provisions in reg. 9).)

"**(2)** If in the course of the financial year to which the accounts relate the group carried on business of two or more classes that in the opinion of the directors differ substantially from each other, there shall be contained in the directors' report a statement of –

(a) the proportions in which the turnover for the financial year (so far as stated in the consolidated accounts) is divided amongst those classes (describing them), and

(b) as regards business of each class, the extent or approximate extent (expressed in money terms) to which, in the opinion of the directors, the carrying on of business of that class contributed to or restricted the profit or loss of the group for that year (before taxation)."

(In para. 2(2) the words "(other than banking or discounting or a class prescribed for the purposes of paragraph 17(2) of Part I of Schedule 9)" formerly appearing after the words "two or more classes" omitted by the Companies Act 1985 (Bank Accounts) Regulations 1991 (SI 1991/2705), reg. 6 and Sch. 2, para. 5(c) as from 2 December 1991 (subject to the transitional provisions in reg. 9).)

"**(3)** In sub-paragraph (2) "**the group**" means the undertakings included in the consolidation.

**(4)** For the purposes of this paragraph classes of business which in the opinion of the directors do not differ substantially from each other shall be treated as one class.

LABOUR FORCE AND WAGES PAID

**3(1)** This paragraph applies where a company prepares individual or group accounts in accordance with the special provisions of this Part relating to insurance companies or groups."

(In para. 3(1) the words "banking or" omitted by the Companies Act 1985 (Bank Accounts) Regulations 1991 (SI 1991/2705), reg. 6 and Sch. 2, para. 5(a) from 2 December 1991 (subject to the transitional provisions in reg. 9).)

"**3(2)** There shall be stated in the directors' report –

(a) the average number of persons employed by the company or, if the company prepares group accounts, by the company and its subsidiary undertakings, and

(b) the aggregate amount of the remuneration paid or payable to persons so employed.

**(3)** The average number of persons employed shall be determined by adding together the number of persons employed (whether throughout the week or not) in each week of the financial year and dividing that total by the number of weeks in the financial year.

**(4)** The aggregate amount of the remuneration paid or payable means the total amount of remuneration paid or payable in respect of the financial year; and for this purpose remuneration means gross remuneration and includes bonuses, whether payable under contract or not.

**(5)** The information required by this paragraph need not be given if the average number of persons employed is less than 100.

**(6)** No account shall be taken for the purposes of this paragraph of persons who worked wholly or mainly outside the United Kingdom.

**(7)** This paragraph does not apply to a company which is a wholly-owned subsidiary of a company incorporated in Great Britain."

(Previously Sch. 10 substituted by CA 1989, s. 1, 18(5) and Sch. 8 as from 1 April 1990 subject to transitional and saving provisions (see SI 1990/355 (C 13), art. 3, Sch. 1 and also art. 6–9); Sch. 10 originally read as follows:

**"Schedule 10 – Additional Matters to be Dealt with in Directors' Report Attached to Special Category Accounts**

RECENT ISSUES

**1(1)** If in the financial year to which the accounts relate the company has issued any shares, the directors' report shall state the reason for making the issue, the classes of shares issued and, as respects each class of shares, the number issued and the consideration received by the company for the issue.

**(2)** If in that year the company has issued any debentures, the report shall state the reason for making the issue, the classes of debentures issued, and, as respects each class of debentures, the amount issued and the consideration received by the company for the issue.

TURNOVER AND PROFITABILITY

**2** If in the course of the financial year the company (being one subject to the requirements of paragraph 17 of Schedule 9, but not one that has subsidiaries at the end of the year and submits in respect of that year group accounts prepared as consolidated accounts) has carried on business of two or more classes (other than banking or discounting or a class prescribed for the purpose of paragraph 17(2) of that Schedule) that, in the opinion of the directors, differ substantially from each other, there shall be contained in the directors' report a statement of–

(a) the proportions in which the turnover for the year (so far as stated in the accounts in respect of the year in pursuance of that Schedule) is divided amongst those classes (describing them), and

(b) as regards business of each class, the extent or approximate extent (expressed, in either case, in monetary terms) to which, in the opinion of the directors, the carrying on of business of that class contributed to, or restricted, the profit or loss of the company for that year before taxation.

**3(1)** This paragraph applies if–

(a) the company has subsidiaries at the end of the financial year and submits in respect of that year group accounts prepared as consolidated accounts, and

(b) the company and the subsidiaries dealt with by the accounts carried on between them in the course of the year business of two or more classes (other than banking or discounting or a class prescribed for the purposes of paragraph 17(2) of Schedule 9) that, in the opinion of the directors, differ substantially from each other.

**(2)** There shall be contained in the directors' report a statement of–

(a) the proportions in which the turnover for the financial year (so far as stated in the accounts for that year in pursuance of Schedule 9) is divided amongst those classes (describing them), and

(b) as regards business of each class, the extent or approximate extent (expressed, in either case, in monetary terms) to which, in the opinion of the directors of the company, the carrying on of business of that class contributed to, or restricted, the profit or loss for that year (before taxation) of the company and the subsidiaries dealt with by the accounts.

**4** For the purposes of the preceding two paragraphs, classes of business which, in the opinion of the directors, do not differ substantially from each other, are to be treated as one class.

LABOUR FORCE AND WAGES PAID

**5(1)** If at the end of the financial year the company does not have subsidiaries, there shall be contained in the directors' report a statement of–

(a) the average number of persons employed by the company in each week in the year, and

(b) the aggregate remuneration paid or payable in respect of the year to the persons by reference to whom the number stated under sub-paragraph (a) is ascertained.

**(2)** The number to be stated under that sub-paragraph is the quotient derived by dividing, by the number of weeks in the financial year, the number derived by ascertaining, in relation to each of those weeks, the number of persons who, under contracts of service, were employed in the week (whether throughout it or not) by the company and adding up the numbers ascertained.

**6(1)** If at the end of the financial year the company has subsidiaries, there shall be contained in the directors' report a statement of–

(a) the average number of persons employed between them in each week in that year by the company and the subsidiaries, and

(b) the aggregate remuneration paid or payable in respect of that year to the persons by reference to whom the number stated under sub-paragraph (a) is ascertained.

**(2)** The number to be stated under that sub-paragraph is the quotient derived by dividing, by the number of weeks in the financial year, the number derived by ascertaining, in relation to each of those weeks, the number of persons who, under contracts of service, were employed between them in the week (whether throughout it or not) by the company and its subsidiaries and adding up the numbers ascertained.

**7** The remuneration to be taken into account under sub-paragraphs 5(1)(b) and 6(1)(b) is the gross remuneration paid or payable in respect of the financial year; and for this purpose **"remuneration"** includes bonuses (whether payable under contract or not).

**8(1)** Paragraphs 5 and 6 are qualified as follows.

**(2)** Neither paragraph applies if the number that, apart from this sub-paragraph, would fall to be stated under paragraph 5(1)(a) or 6(1)(a) is less than 100.

**(3)** Neither paragraph applies to a company which is a wholly-owned subsidiary of a company incorporated in Great Britain.

**(4)** For purposes of both paragraphs, no regard is to be had to any person who worked wholly or mainly outside the United Kingdom.

GENERAL MATTERS

**9** The directors' report shall contain particulars of any matters (other than those required to be dealt with in it by section

261(5) and the preceding provisions of this Schedule) so far as they are material for the appreciation of the state of the company's affairs by its members, being matters the disclosure of which will not, in the opinion of the directors, be harmful to the business of the company or of any of its subsidiaries.").

# Schedule 10A – Parent and Subsidiary Undertakings: Supplementary Provisions

[Companies Act 1985, s. 258;
Companies Act 1989, s. 1, 21(2), Sch. 9]

## INTRODUCTION

**1** The provisions of this Schedule explain expressions used in section 258 (parent and subsidiary undertakings) and otherwise supplement that section.

## VOTING RIGHTS IN AN UNDERTAKING

**2(1)** In section 258(2)(a) and (d) the references to the voting rights in an undertaking are to the rights conferred on shareholders in respect of their shares or, in the case of an undertaking not having a share capital, on members, to vote at general meetings of the undertaking on all, or substantially all, matters.

**Note**

See the Financial Institutions (Prudential Supervision) Regulations 1996 (SI 1996/1669), reg. 2(3), Sch. 1, para. 1, 3(5) for an amendment to para. 2(1) for the purpose of determining any question arising under reg. 2(2) of those Regulations as from 18 July 1996.

**2(2)** In relation to an undertaking which does not have general meetings at which matters are decided by the exercise of voting rights, the references to holding a majority of the voting rights in the undertaking shall be construed as references to having the right under the constitution of the undertaking to direct the overall policy of the undertaking or to alter the terms of its constitution.

## RIGHT TO APPOINT OR REMOVE A MAJORITY OF THE DIRECTORS

**3(1)** In section 258(2)(b) the reference to the right to appoint or remove a majority of the board of directors is to the right to appoint or remove directors holding a majority of the voting rights at meetings of the board on all, or substantially all, matters.

**3(2)** An undertaking shall be treated as having the right to appoint to a directorship if –

(a) a person's appointment to it follows necessarily from his appointment as director of the undertaking, or

(b) the directorship is held by the undertaking itself.

**3(3)** A right to appoint or remove which is exercisable only with the consent or concurrence of another person shall be left out of account unless no other person has a right to appoint or, as the case may be, remove in relation to that directorship.

## RIGHT TO EXERCISE DOMINANT INFLUENCE

**4(1)** For the purposes of section 258(2)(c) an undertaking shall not be regarded as having the right to exercise a dominant influence over another undertaking unless it has a right to give directions with respect to the operating and financial policies of that other undertaking which its directors are obliged to comply with whether or not they are for the benefit of that other undertaking.

**4(2)** A **"control contract"** means a contract in writing conferring such a right which –

(a) is of a kind authorised by the memorandum or articles of the undertaking in relation to which the right is exercisable, and

(b) is permitted by the law under which that undertaking is established.

**4(3)** This paragraph shall not be read as affecting the construction of the expression "actually exercises a dominant influence" in section 258(4)(a).

## RIGHTS EXERCISABLE ONLY IN CERTAIN CIRCUMSTANCES OR TEMPORARILY INCAPABLE OF EXERCISE

**5(1)** Rights which are exercisable only in certain circumstances shall be taken into account only –

(a) when the circumstances have arisen, and for so long as they continue to obtain, or

(b) when the circumstances are within the control of the person having the rights.

**5(2)** Rights which are normally exercisable but are temporarily incapable of exercise shall continue to be taken into account.

## RIGHTS HELD BY ONE PERSON ON BEHALF OF ANOTHER

**6** Rights held by a person in a fiduciary capacity shall be treated as not held by him.

**7(1)** Rights held by a person as nominee for another shall be treated as held by the other.

**7(2)** Rights shall be regarded as held as nominee for another if they are exercisable only on his instructions or with his consent or concurrence.

## RIGHTS ATTACHED TO SHARES HELD BY WAY OF SECURITY

**8** Rights attached to shares held by way of security shall be treated as held by the person providing the security –

(a) where apart from the right to exercise them for the purpose of preserving the value of the security, or of realising it, the rights are exercisable only in accordance with his instructions, and

(b) where the shares are held in connection with the granting of loans as part of normal business activities and apart from the right to exercise them for the purpose of preserving the value of the security, or of realising it, the rights are exercisable only in his interests.

## RIGHTS ATTRIBUTED TO PARENT UNDERTAKING

**9(1)** Rights shall be treated as held by a parent undertaking if they are held by any of its subsidiary undertakings.

**9(2)** Nothing in paragraph 7 or 8 shall be construed as requiring rights held by a parent undertaking to be treated as held by any of its subsidiary undertakings.

**9(3)** For the purposes of paragraph 8 rights shall be treated as being exercisable in accordance with the instructions or in the interests of an undertaking if they are exercisable in accordance with the instructions of or, as the case may be, in the interests of any group undertaking.

## DISREGARD FOR CERTAIN RIGHTS

**10** The voting rights in an undertaking shall be reduced by any rights held by the undertaking itself.

## SUPPLEMENTARY

**11** References in any provision of paragraphs 6 to 10 to rights held by a person include rights falling to be treated as held by him by virtue of any other provision of those paragraphs but not rights which by virtue of any such provision are to be treated as not held by him.

**History**
Sch. 10A inserted by CA 1989, s. 1, 21(2) and Sch. 9 as from 1 April 1990 subject to transitional and saving provisions (see SI 1990/355 (C 13), art. 3, Sch. 1 and also art. 6–9).

# Schedule 11 – Modifications of Part VIII where Company's Accounts Prepared in Accordance with Special Provisions for Banking or Insurance Companies

Section 279

**History**
Heading substituted for former heading "Modifications of Part VIII where Company's Relevant Accounts are Special Category" by CA 1989, s. 23 and Sch. 10, para. 21(1), (2) as from 1 April 1990 subject to transitional and saving provisions (see SI 1990/355 (C 13), art. 3, Sch. 1 and also art. 6–9).

**1** Paragraphs 2 to 6 below apply where a company has prepared accounts in accordance with the special provisions of Part VII relating to banking companies and paragraphs 7 to 13 below apply where a company has prepared accounts in accordance with the special provisions of Part VII relating to insurance companies.

**History**
See history note after para. 6.

## MODIFICATIONS WHERE ACCOUNTS PREPARED IN ACCORDANCE WITH SPECIAL PROVISIONS FOR BANKING COMPANIES

**2** Section 264(2) shall apply as if the reference to paragraph 89 of Schedule 4 therein was a reference to paragraph 85(c) of Part I of Schedule 9.

**History**
See history note after para. 6.

**3** Section 269 shall apply as if:

(a) there were substituted for the words "are shown as an asset" in sub-section (1) the words "are included as an asset"; and

(b) the reference to paragraph 20 of Schedule 4 in sub-section (2)(b) was to paragraph 27 of Part I of Schedule 9.

**History**
See history note after para. 6.

**4** Sections 270(2) and 275 shall apply as if the references therein to paragraphs 88 and 89 of Schedule 4 were to paragraph 85 of Part I of Schedule 9.

**History**
See history note after para. 6.

**5** Sections 272 and 273 shall apply as if in section 272(3) there were substituted, for the references to section 226 and Schedule 4, references to section 255 and Part I of Schedule 9.

**History**
See history note after para. 6.

**6** Section 276 shall apply as if the references to paragraphs 12(a) and 34(3)(a) of Schedule 4 were to paragraphs 19(a) and 44(3)(a) of Schedule 9.

**History**
Para. 1–6 inserted by the Companies Act 1985 (Bank Accounts) Regulations 1991 (SI 1991/2705), reg. 7 and Sch. 3, para. 1 as from 2 December 1991 (subject to transitional provisions in reg. 9).

## MODIFICATIONS WHERE ACCOUNTS PREPARED IN ACCORDANCE WITH SPECIAL PROVISIONS FOR INSURANCE COMPANIES

**History**
Heading above para. 7 inserted by the Companies Act 1985 (Bank Accounts) Regulations 1991 (SI 1991/2705), reg. 7 and Sch. 3, para. 1(3) as from 2 December 1991 (subject to the transitional provisions in reg. 9).

**7** Section 264(2) shall apply as if for the words in parentheses there were substituted "("liabiities" to include any provision for other risks and charges within paragraph 84(c) of Part I of Schedule 9A and any amount included under Liabilities items Ba (fund for future appropriations), C (technical provisions) and D (technical provisions for linked liabilities) in a balance sheet drawn up in accordance with the balance sheet format set out in section B of Part I of Schedule 9A)."

**History**
Para. 7 substituted by the Companies Act 1985 (Miscellaneous Accounting Amendments) Regulations 1996 (SI 1996/189), reg. 1(1), 14(8) and Sch. 6, para. 1, 2 as from 2 February 1996, subject to reg. 16(1), (2), (6); para. 7 formerly read as follows:

"Section 264(2) shall apply as if the reference to paragraph 89 of Schedule 4 were a reference to paragraph 84(c) of Part I of Schedule 9A."

**8** Section 269 shall apply as if the reference to paragraph 20 of Schedule 4 in subsection (2)(b) were a reference to paragraph 35 of Part I of Schedule 9A.

**9** Sections 270(2) and 275 shall apply as if the reference to provisions of any of the kinds mentioned in paragraphs 88 and 89 of Schedule 4 were a reference to provisions of any of the kinds mentioned in paragraph 84 of Part I of Schedule 9A and to any amount included under Liabilities items Ba (fund for future appropriations), C (technical provisions) and D (technical provisions for linked liabilities) in a balance sheet drawn up in accordance with the balance sheet format set out in section B of Part I of Schedule 9A.

**History**
Para. 9 substituted by the Companies Act 1985 (Miscellaneous Accounting Amendments) Regulations 1996 (SI 1996/189), reg. 1(1), 14(8) and Sch. 6, para. 1, 3 as from 2 February 1996, subject to reg. 16(1), (2), (6); para. 9 formerly read as follows:
"Sections 270(2) and 275 shall apply as if the references to paragraphs 88 and 89 of Schedule 4 were references to paragraph 84 of Part I of Schedule 9A."

**10** Sections 272 and 273 shall apply as if the references in section 272(3) to section 226 and Schedule 4 were references to section 255 and Part I of Schedule 9A.

**11** Section 276 shall apply as if the references to paragraphs 12(a) and 34(3)(a) of Schedule 4(d) were references to paragraphs 16(a) and 29(3)(a) of Part I of Schedule 9A.

**History**
Para. 7–11 substituted for the former para. 7–13 by the Companies Act 1985 (Insurance Companies Accounts) Regulations 1993 (SI 1993/3246), reg. 1, 5 and Sch. 2, para. 8 as from 19 December 1993 subject to exemption in reg. 6 and transitional provisions in reg. 7; former para. 7–13 read as follows:

"**7** Section 264 applies as if in subsection (2) for the words following "the aggregate of its liabilities" there were substituted "("liabilities" to include any provision within the meaning of Part I of Schedule 9A, except to the extent that that provision is taken into account in calculating the value of any asset of the company)"."

(Former para. 7 renumbered as such (formerly it was 1) and the words "Schedule 9A" substituted for the former words "Schedule 9" by the Companies Act 1985 (Bank Accounts) Regulations 1991 (SI 1991/2705), reg. 7 and Sch. 3, para. 1(3) as from 2 December 1991 (subject to the transitional provisions in reg. 9).

Previously to that the words "Part I of Schedule 9" substituted for the original words "Schedule 9" by CA 1989, s. 23 and Sch. 10, para. 21(1), (3) as from 1 April 1990 subject to transitional and saving provisions (see SI 1990/355 (C 13), art. 3, Sch. 1 and also art. 6–9).)

"**8** Section 265 applies as if–

(a) for subsection (2) there were substituted–

"(2) In subsection (1)(a), "liabilities" includes any provision (within the meaning of Part I of Schedule 9A) except to the extent that that provision is taken into account for the purposes of that subsection in calculating the value of any asset of the company", and

(b) there were added at the end of the section–

"(7) In determining capital and revenue profits and losses, an asset which is not a fixed asset or a current asset is treated as a fixed asset"."

(Former para. 8 renumbered as such (formerly it was 2) and the words "Schedule 9A" substituted for the former words "Schedule 9" by the Companies Act 1985 (Bank Accounts) Regulations 1991 (SI 1991/2705), reg. 7 and Sch. 3, para. 1(3) as from 2 December 1991 (subject to the transitional provisions in reg. 9).

Previously to that the words "Part I of Schedule 9" substituted for the original words "Schedule 9" by CA 1989, s. 23 and Sch. 10, para. 21(1), (3) as from 1 April 1990 subject to transitional and saving provisions (see SI 1990/355 (C 13), art. 3, Sch. 1 and also art. 6–9).)

"**9** Section 269 does not apply."
(Former para. 9 renumbered as such (formerly it was 3) by the Companies Act 1985 (Bank Accounts) Regulations 1991 (SI 1991/2705), reg. 7 and Sch. 3, para. 1(3) as from 2 December 1991 (subject to the transitional provisions in reg. 9).)

"**10** Section 270 applies as if–

(a) in subsection (2) the following were substituted for paragraph (b)–

"(b) provisions (within the meaning of Part I of Schedule 9A)"."

(Former para. 10 renumbered as such (formerly it was 4) and the words "Schedule 9A" substituted for the former words "Schedule 9" by the Companies Act 1985 (Bank Accounts) Regulations 1991 (SI 1991/2705), reg. 7 and Sch. 3, para. 1(3) as from 2 December 1991 (subject to the transitional provisions in reg. 9).

Previously the words "Part I of Schedule 9" substituted for the original words "Schedule 9" and para. 4(b), (c) omitted and repealed by CA 1989, s. 23, 212, Sch. 10, para. 21(1), (4) and Sch. 24 as from 1 April 1990 subject to transitional and saving provisions (see SI 1990/355 (C 13), art. 3, 5(1)(b), (2), Sch. 1 and also art. 6–9); para. 4(b), (c) originally read as follows:

"(b) in subsection (3), for the words from "which were laid" onwards there were substituted–

"which were laid or filed in respect of the last preceding accounting reference period in respect of which accounts so prepared were laid or filed; and for this purpose accounts are laid or filed if section 241(1) or (as the case may be) (3) has been complied with in relation to them"; and

(c) in subsection (4)(b) the words "or filed" were inserted after "laid".")

"**11** Section 271 applies as if–

(a) in subsection (2), immediately before paragraph (a) there were inserted "except where the company is entitled to avail itself, and has availed itself, of any of the provisions of paragraph 28 of Schedule 9A"."

(Former para. 11 renumbered as such (formerly it was 5) and the words "27 or" formerly appearing before "28" omitted and the words "Schedule 9A" substituted for the former words "Schedule 9" by the Companies Act 1985 (Bank Accounts) Regulations 1991 (SI 1991/2705), reg. 7 and Sch. 3, para. 1(3) as from 2 December 1991 (subject to the transitional provisions in reg. 9).

Previously the words "paragraph 27 or 28 of Schedule 9" substituted for the original words "Part III of Schedule 9" and para. 5(b) omitted and repealed by CA 1989, s. 23, 212, Sch. 10, para. 21(1), (5) and Sch. 24 as from 1 April 1990 subject to transitional and saving provisions (see SI 1990/355 (C 13), art. 3, 5(1)(b), (2), Sch. 1 and also art. 6–9); para. 5(b) originally read as follows:

"(b) at the end of subsection (4) there were added the words "or delivered to the registrar of companies according as those accounts have been laid or filed".")

"**12** Sections 272 and 273 apply as if in section 272(3)–

(a) for the references to section 226 and Schedule 4 there were substituted references to section 255 and Part I of Schedule 9A, and

(b) immediately before paragraph (a) there were inserted "except where the company is entitled to avail itself, and has availed itself, of any of the provisions of paragraph 28 of Schedule 9A"."

(Former para. 12 renumbered as such (formerly it was 6) and the words "27 or" formerly appearing before "28" omitted and the words "Schedule 9A" (in both places where they appear) substituted for the former words "Schedule 9" by the Companies Act 1985 (Bank Accounts) Regulations 1991 (SI 1991/2705), reg. 7 and Sch. 3, para. 1(3) as from 2 December 1991 (subject to the transitional provisions in reg. 9).

Previously the words "section 226" and "section 255 and Part I of Schedule 9" substituted for the original words "section 228" and "section 258 and Schedule 9" respectively and in para. 6(b) the words "paragraph 27 or 28 of Schedule 9" substituted for the original words "Part III of Schedule 9" by CA 1989, s. 23 and Sch. 10, para. 21(1), (6) as from 1 April 1990 subject to transitional and saving provisions (see SI 1990/355 (C 13), art. 3, Sch. 1 and also art. 6–9).)

"**13** Section 275 applies as if–

(a) for subsection (1) there were substituted–

"(1) For purposes of section 263, any provision (within the meaning of Part I of Schedule 9A), other than one in respect of any diminution of value of a fixed asset appearing on a revaluation of all the fixed assets of the company, or of all its fixed assets other than goodwill, is to be treated as a realised loss"; and

(b) **"fixed assets"** were defined to include any other asset which is not a current asset."

(Former para. 13 renumbered as such (formerly it was 7) and the words "Schedule 9A" substituted for the former words "Schedule 9" by the Companies Act 1985 (Bank Accounts) Regulations 1991 (SI 1991/2705), reg. 7 and Sch. 3, para. 1(3) as from 2 December 1991 (subject to the transitional provisions in reg. 9).

Previously the words "Part I of Schedule 9" substituted for the original words "Schedule 9" by CA 1989, s. 23 and Sch. 10, para. 21(1), (7) as from 1 April 1990 subject to transitional and saving provisions (see SI 1990/355 (C 13), art. 3, Sch. 1 and also art. 6–9).)

# Schedule 12 – Supplementary Provisions in Connection with Disqualification Orders

Section 295

(Repealed by Company Directors Disqualification Act 1986, s. 23(2) and Sch. 4 as from 29 December 1986.)

**History**

In regard to the date of the above repeal, see Company Directors Disqualification Act 1986, s. 25, Insolvency Act 1986, s. 443 and SI 1986/1924 (C 71). The previous form of the schedule appears below (see IA 1985, Sch. 6, para. 14 for a small amendment to para. 4(3)):

**"Part I – Orders under Sections 296 to 299**

APPLICATION FOR ORDER

**1** A person intending to apply for the making of an order under any of sections 296 to 299 by the court having jurisdiction to wind up a company shall give not less than 10 days' notice of his intention to the person against whom the order is sought; and on the hearing of the application the last-mentioned person may appear and himself give evidence or call witnesses.

**2** An application to a court with jurisdiction to wind up companies for the making of such an order against any person may be made by the Secretary of State or the official receiver, or by the liquidator or any past or present member or creditor of any company in relation to which that person has committed or is alleged to have committed an offence or other default.

HEARING OF APPLICATION

**3** On the hearing of an application made by the Secretary of State or the official receiver or the liquidator the applicant shall appear and call the attention of the court to any matters which seem to him to be relevant, and may himself give evidence or call witnesses.

APPLICATION FOR LEAVE UNDER AN ORDER

**4(1)** As regards the court to which application must be made for leave under a disqualification order made under any of sections 296 to 299, the following applies.

**(2)** Where the application is for leave to promote or form a company, it is any court with jurisdiction to wind up companies.

**(3)** Where the application is for leave to be a liquidator or director of, or otherwise to take part in the management of a company, or to be a receiver or manager of a company's property, it is any court having jurisdiction to wind up that company.

**5** On the hearing of an application for leave made by a person against whom a disqualification order has been made on the application of the Secretary of State, the official receiver or the liquidator, the Secretary of State, official receiver or liquidator shall appear and call the attention of the court to any matters which seem to him to be relevant, and may himself give evidence or call witnesses.

**Part II – Orders under Section 300**

**6–8** (Repealed by Insolvency Act 1985, s. 235 and Sch. 10, Pt. II as from 28 April 1986.)"

(Para. 6–8 originally read as follows:

"APPLICATION FOR ORDER

**6(1)** In the case of a person who is or has been a director of a company which has gone into liquidation as mentioned in section 300(1) and is being wound up by the court, any application under that section shall be made by the official receiver or, in Scotland, the Secretary of State.

**(2)** In any other case an application shall be made by the Secretary of State.

**7** Where the official receiver or the Secretary of State intends to make an application under the section in respect of any person, he shall not give less than 10 days' notice of his intention to that person.

HEARING OF APPLICATION

**8** On the hearing of an application under section 300 by the official receiver or the Secretary of State, or of an application for leave by a person against whom an order has been made on the application of the official reciever or Secretary of State–

(a) the official receiver or Secretary of State shall appear and call the attention of the court to any matters which seem to him to be relevant, and may himself give evidence or call witnesses, and

(b) the person against whom the order is sought may appear and himself give evidence or call witnesses.")

**"Part III – Transitional Provisions and Savings from Companies Act 1981, s. 93, 94**

**9** Sections 296 and 298(1)(b) do not apply in relation to anything done before 15th June 1982 by a person in his capacity as liquidator of a company or as receiver or manager of a company's property.

**10** Subject to paragraph 9–

(a) section 296 applies in a case where a person is convicted on indictment of an offence which he committed (and, in the case of a continuing offence, has ceased to commit) before 15th June 1982; but in such a case a disqualification order under that section shall not be made for a period in excess of 5 years;

(b) that section does not apply in a case where a person is convicted summarily–

(i) in England and Wales, if he had consented so to be tried before that date, or

(ii) in Scotland, if the summary proceedings commenced before that date.

**11** Subject to paragraph 9, section 298 applies in relation to an offence committed or other thing done before 15th June 1982; but a disqualification order made on the grounds of such an offence or other thing done shall not be made for a period in excess of 5 years.

**12** The powers of a court under section 299 are not exercisable in a case where a person is convicted of an offence which he committed (and, in the case of a continuing offence, had ceased to commit) before 15th June 1982.

**13** For purposes of section 297(1) and section 299, no account is to be taken of any offence which was committed, or any default order which was made, before 1st June 1977.

**14** An order made under section 28 of the Companies Act 1976 has effect as if made under section 297 of this Act; and an application made before 15th June 1982 for such an order is to be treated as an application for an order under the section last mentioned.

**15, 16** (Repealed by Insolvency Act 1985, s. 235 and Sch. 10, Pt. II as from 28 April 1986.)"

**Note**

For current provisions, see Company Directors Disqualification Act 1986, s. 16, 17 and Sch. 2.

# Schedule 13 – Provisions Supplementing and Interpreting Sections 324 to 328

Sections 324, 325, 326, 328 and 346

## Part I – Rules for Interpretation of the Sections and also Section 346(4) and (5)

**1(1)** A reference to an interest in shares or debentures is to be read as including any interest of any kind whatsoever in shares or debentures.

**1(2)** Accordingly, there are to be disregarded any restraints or restrictions to which the exercise of any right attached to the interest is or may be subject.

**2** Where property is held on trust and any interest in shares or debentures is comprised in the property, any beneficiary of the trust who (apart from this paragraph) does not have an interest in the shares or debentures is to be taken as having such an interest; but this paragraph is without prejudice to the following provisions of this Part of this Schedule.

**3(1)** A person is taken to have an interest in shares or debentures if–

(a) he enters into a contract for their purchase by him (whether for cash or other consideration), or

(b) not being the registered holder, he is entitled to exercise any right conferred by the holding of the shares or debentures, or is entitled to control the exercise of any such right.

**3(2)** For purposes of sub-paragraph (1)(b), a person is taken to be entitled to exercise or control the exercise of a right conferred by the holding of shares or debentures if he–

(a) has a right (whether subject to conditions or not) the exercise of which would make him so entitled, or

(b) is under an obligation (whether or not so subject) the fulfilment of which would make him so entitled.

**3(3)** A person is not by virtue of sub-paragraph (1)(b) taken to be interested in shares or debentures by reason only that he–

(a) has been appointed a proxy to vote at a specified meeting of a company or of any class of its members and at any adjournment of that meeting, or

(b) has been appointed by a corporation to act as its representative at any meeting of a company or of any class of its members.

**4** A person is taken to be interested in shares or debentures if a body corporate is interested in them and–

(a) that body corporate or its directors are accustomed to act in accordance with his directions or instructions, or

(b) he is entitled to exercise or control the exercise of one-third or more of the voting power at general meetings of that body corporate.

As this paragraph applies for the purposes of section 346(4) and (5), "more than one-half" is substituted for "one-third or more".

**5** Where a person is entitled to exercise or control the exercise of one-third or more of the voting power at general meetings of a body corporate, and that body corporate is entitled to exercise or control the exercise of any of the voting power at general meetings of another body corporate ("the effective voting power"), then, for purposes of paragraph 4(b), the effective voting power is taken to be exercisable by that person.

As this paragraph applies for the purposes of section 346(4) and (5), "more than one-half" is substituted for "one-third or more".

**6(1)** A person is taken to have an interest in shares or debentures if, otherwise than by virtue of having an interest under a trust–

(a) he has a right to call for delivery of the shares or debentures to himself or to his order, or

(b) he has a right to acquire an interest in shares or debentures or is under an obligation to take an interest in shares or debentures;

whether in any case the right or obligation is conditional or absolute.

**6(2)** Rights or obligations to subscribe for shares or debentures are not to be taken, for purposes of sub-paragraph (1), to be rights to acquire, or obligations to take, an interest in shares or debentures.

This is without prejudice to paragraph 1.

**7** Persons having a joint interest are deemed each of them to have that interest.

**8** It is immaterial that shares or debentures in which a person has an interest are unidentifiable.

**9** So long as a person is entitled to receive, during the lifetime of himself or another, income from trust property comprising shares or debentures, an interest in the shares or debentures in reversion or remainder or (as regards Scotland) in fee, are to be disregarded.

**10** A person is to be treated as uninterested in shares or debentures if, and so long as, he holds them under the law in force in England and Wales as a bare trustee or as a custodian trustee, or under the law in force in Scotland, as a simple trustee.

**11** There is to be disregarded an interest of a person subsisting by virtue of–

(a) any unit trust scheme which is an authorised unit trust scheme within the meaning of the Financial Services Act 1986;

(b) a scheme made under section 22 or 22A of the Charities Act 1960 or section 24 or 25 of the Charities Act 1993, section 11 of the Trustee Investments Act 1961 or section 1 of the Administration of Justice Act 1965; or

(c) the scheme set out in the Schedule to the Church Funds Investment Measure 1958.

**History**

Para. 11(a) substituted by Financial Services Act 1986, s. 212(2) and Sch. 16, para. 25 as from 29 April 1988 (see SI 1988/740 (C 22)); para. 11(a) formerly read as follows:

"(a) any unit trust scheme declared by an order of the Secretary of State (or any predecessor of his) for the time being in force under the Prevention of Fraud (Investments) Act 1958 to be an authorised unit trust scheme for the purposes of that Act".

In para. 11(b) the words "or 22A" inserted by Charities Act 1992, s. 78(1) and Sch. 6, para. 11 as from 1 September 1992 (see SI 1992/1900 (C 64), art. 2 and Sch. 1) and the words "or section 24 or 25 of the Charities Act 1993" inserted by Charities Act 1993, s. 98(1), 99(1) and Sch. 6, para. 20(1), (3) as from 1 August 1993.

**12** There is to be disregarded any interest–

(a) of the Church of Scotland General Trustees or of the Church of Scotland Trust in shares or debentures held by them;

(b) of any other person in shares or debentures held by those Trustees or that Trust otherwise than as simple trustees.

**"The Church of Scotland General Trustees"** are the body incorporated by the order confirmed by the Church of Scotland (General Trustees) Order Confirmation Act 1921; and **"the Church of Scotland Trust"** is the body incorporated by the order confirmed by the Church of Scotland Trust Order Confirmation Act 1932.

**13** Delivery to a person's order of shares or debentures in fulfilment of a contract for the purchase of them by him or in satisfaction of a right of his to call for their delivery, or failure to deliver shares or debentures in accordance with the terms of such a contract or on which such a right falls to be satisfied, is deemed to constitute an event in consequence of the occurrence of which he ceases to be interested in them, and so is the lapse of a person's right to call for delivery of shares or debentures.

# Part II – Periods Within Which Obligations Imposed By Section 324 Must Be Fulfilled

**14(1)** An obligation imposed on a person by section 324(1) to notify an interest must, if he knows of the existence of the interest on the day on which he becomes a director, be fulfilled before the expiration of the period of 5 days beginning with the day following that day.

**14(2)** Otherwise, the obligation must be fulfilled before the expiration of the period of 5 days beginning with the day following that on which the existence of the interest comes to his knowledge.

**15(1)** An obligation imposed on a person by section 324(2) to notify the occurrence of an event must, if at the time at which the event occurs he knows of its occurrence and of the fact that its occurrence gives rise to the obligation, be fulfilled before the expiration of the period of 5 days beginning with the day following that on which the event occurs.

**15(2)** Otherwise, the obligation must be fufilled before the expiration of a period of 5 days beginning with the day following that on which the fact that the occurrence of the event gives rise to the obligation comes to his knowledge.

**16** In reckoning, for purposes of paragraphs 14 and 15, any period of days, a day that is a Saturday or Sunday, or a bank holiday in any part of Great Britain, is to be disregarded.

# Part III – Circumstances in Which Obligation Imposed by Section 324 is not Discharged

**17(1)** Where an event of whose occurrence a director is, by virtue of section 324(2)(a), under obligation to notify a company consists of his entering into a contract for the purchase by him of shares or debentures, the obligation is not discharged in the absence of inclusion in the notice of a statement of the price to be paid by him under the contract.

**17(2)** An obligation imposed on a director by section 324(2)(b) is not discharged in the absence of inclusion in the notice of the price to be received by him under the contract.

**18(1)** An obligation imposed on a director by virtue of section 324(2)(c) to notify a company is not discharged in the absence of inclusion in the notice of a statement of the consideration for the assignment (or, if it be the case that there is no consideration, that fact).

**18(2)** Where an event of whose occurrence a director is, by virtue of section 324(2)(d), under obligation to notify a company consists in his assigning a right, the obligation is not discharged in the absence of inclusion in the notice of a similar statement.

**19(1)** Where an event of whose occurrence a director is, by virtue of section 324(2)(d), under obligation to notify a company consists in the grant to him of a right to subscribe for shares or debentures, the obligation is not discharged in the absence of inclusion in the notice of a statement of–

(a) the date on which the right was granted,

(b) the period during which or the time at which the right is exercisable,

(c) the consideration for the grant (or, if it be the case that there is no consideration, that fact), and

(d) the price to be paid for the shares or debentures.

**19(2)** Where an event of whose occurrence a director is, by section 324(2)(d), under obligation to notify a company consists in the exercise of a right granted to him to subscribe for shares or debentures, the obligation is not discharged in the absence of inclusion in the notice of a statement of–

(a) the number of shares or amount of debentures in respect of which the right was exercised, and

(b) if it be the case that they were registered in his name, that fact, and, if not, the name or names of the person or persons in whose name or names they were registered, together (if they were registered in the names of 2 persons or more) with the number or amount registered in the name of each of them.

**20** In this Part, a reference to price paid or received includes any consideration other than money.

# Part IV – Provisions with Respect to Register of Directors' Interests to be Kept Under Section 325

**21** The register must be so made up that the entries in it against the several names appear in chronological order.

**22** An obligation imposed by section 325(2) to (4) must be fulfilled before the expiration of the period of 3 days beginning with the day after that on which the obligation arises; but in reckoning that period, a day which is a Saturday or Sunday or a bank holiday in any part of Great Britain is to be disregarded.

**23** The nature and extent of an interest recorded in the register of a director in any shares or debentures shall, if he so requires, be recorded in the register.

**24** The company is not, by virtue of anything done for the purposes of section 325 or this Part of this Schedule, affected with notice of, or put upon enquiry as to, the rights of any person in relation to any shares or debentures.

**25** The register shall–

(a) if the company's register of members is kept at its registered office, be kept there;

(b) if the company's register of members is not so kept, be kept at the company's registered office or at the place where its register of members is kept;

and shall be open to the inspection of any member of the company without charge and of any other person on payment of such fee as may be prescribed.

**History**

In para. 25 the words "during business hours (subject to such reasonable restrictions as the company in general meeting may impose, so that not less than 2 hours in each day be allowed for inspection)" formerly appearing after the words "and shall" omitted and repealed and the words "such fee as may be prescribed" substituted for the former words "5 pence, or such less sum as the company may prescribe, for each inspection" by CA 1989, s. 143(10)(a), 212 and Sch. 24 as from 1 November 1991 (see SI 1991/1996 (C 57), art. 2(2)(b), (c)).

**Note**

See the Companies (Inspection and Copying of Registers, Indices and Documents) Regulations 1991 (SI 1991/1998).

**26(1)** Any member of the company or other person may require a copy of the register, or of any part of it, on payment of such fee as may be prescribed.

**History**

In para. 26(1) the words "such fee as may be prescribed" substituted for the former words "10 pence, or such less sum as the company may prescribe, for every 100 words or fractional part of 100 words required to be copied" by CA 1989, s. 143(10)(b) as from 1 November 1991 (see SI 1991/1996 (C 57), art. 2(2)(b)).

**Note**
See the Companies (Inspection and Copying of Registers, Indices and Documents) Regulations 1991 (SI 1991/1998).

**26(2)** The company shall cause any copy so required by a person to be sent to him within the period of 10 days beginning with the day after that on which the requirement is received by the company.

**27** The company shall send notice in the prescribed form to the registrar of companies of the place where the register is kept and of any change in that place, save in a case in which it has at all times been kept at its registered office.

**Note**
See the Companies (Forms) (Amendment) Regulations 1995 (SI 1995/736).

**28** Unless the register is in such a form as to constitute in itself an index, the company shall keep an index of the names inscribed in it, which shall–

(a) in respect of each name, contain a sufficient indication to enable the information entered against it to be readily found; and

(b) be kept at the same place as the register;

and the company shall, within 14 days after the date on which a name is entered in the register, make any necessary alteration in the index.

**29** The register shall be produced at the commencement of the company's annual general meeting and remain open and accessible during the continuance of the meeting to any person attending the meeting.

# Schedule 14 – Overseas Branch Registers

Section 362

## Part I – Countries and Territories in Which Overseas Branch Register May be Kept

### NORTHERN IRELAND

Any part of Her Majesty's dominions outside the United Kingdom, the Channel Islands or the Isle of Man

Bangladesh
Cyprus
Dominica
The Gambia
Ghana
Guyana
The Hong Kong Special Administrative Region of the People's Republic of China
India
Kenya
Kiribati
Lesotho
Malawi
Malaysia
Malta
Nigeria
Pakistan
Republic of Ireland
Seychelles
Sierra Leone
Singapore
South Africa

Sri Lanka
Swaziland
Trinidad and Tobago
Uganda
Zimbabwe

**History**
In Pt. I the entry relating to Hong Kong inserted by the Companies Overseas Branch Registers (Hong Kong) Order 1997 (SI 1997/1313), art. 1, 2 as from 1 July 1997.

# Part II – General Provisions With Respect to Overseas Branch Registers

**1(1)** A company keeping an overseas branch register shall give to the registrar of companies notice in the prescribed form of the situation of the office where any overseas branch register is kept and of any change in its situation, and, if it is discontinued, of its discontinuance.

**1(2)** Any such notice shall be given within 14 days of the opening of the office or of the change or discontinuance, as the case may be.

**1(3)** If default is made in complying with this paragraph, the company and every officer of it who is in default is liable to a fine and, for continued contravention, to a daily default fine.

**2(1)** An overseas branch register is deemed to be part of the company's register of members ("the principal register").

**2(2)** It shall be kept in the same manner in which the principal register is by this Act required to be kept, except that the advertisement before closing the register shall be inserted in a newspaper circulating in the district where the overseas branch register is kept.

**3(1)** A competent court in a country or territory where an overseas branch register is kept may exercise the same jurisdiction of rectifying the register as is under this Act exercisable by the court in Great Britain; and the offences of refusing inspection or copies of the register, and of authorising or permitting the refusal, may be prosecuted summarily before any tribunal having summary criminal jurisdiction.

**3(2)** This paragraph extends only to those countries and territories where, immediately before the coming into force of this Act, provision to the same effect made by section 120(2) of the Companies Act 1948 had effect as part of the local law.

**4(1)** The company shall–

(a) transmit to its registered office a copy of every entry in its overseas branch register as soon as may be after the entry is made, and

(b) cause to be kept at the place where the company's principal register is kept a duplicate of its overseas branch register duly entered up from time to time.

Every such duplicate is deemed for all purposes of this Act to be part of the principal register.

**4(2)** If default is made in complying with sub-paragraph (1), the company and every officer of it who is in default is liable to a fine and, for continued contravention, to a daily default fine.

**4(3)** Where, by virtue of section 353(1)(b), the principal register is kept at the office of some person other than the company, and by reason of any default of his the company fails to comply with sub-paragraph (1)(b) above he is liable to the same penalty as if he were an officer of the company who was in default.

**5** Subject to the above provisions with respect to the duplicate register, the shares registered in an overseas branch register shall be distinguished from those registered in the principal register; and no transaction with respect to any shares registered in an overseas branch register shall, during the continuance of that registration, be registered in any other register.

**6** A company may discontinue to keep an overseas branch register, and thereupon all entries in that register shall be transferred to some other overseas branch register kept by the company in the same country or territory, or to the principal register.

7 Subject to the provisions of this Act, any company may, by its articles, make such provisions as it thinks fit respecting the keeping of overseas branch registers.

8 An instrument of transfer of a share registered in an overseas branch register (other than such a register kept in Northern Ireland) is deemed a transfer of property situated outside the United Kingdom and, unless executed in a part of the United Kingdom, is exempt from stamp duty chargeable in Great Britain.

**Note**
In para. 8 prospective repeal of the words "and, unless executed in a part of the United Kingdom, is exempt from stamp duty chargeable in Great Britain" by Finance Act 1990, s. 132 and Sch. 19, Pt. VI in accordance with s. 107, 108 of that Act and from a day to be appointed under s. 111(1).

## Part III – Provisions for Branch Registers of Oversea Companies to be Kept in Great Britain

**9(1)** If by virtue of the law in force in any country or territory to which this paragraph applies companies incorporated under that law have power to keep in Great Britain branch registers of their members resident in Great Britain, Her Majesty may by Order in Council direct that–

(a) so much of section 353 as requires a company's register of members to be kept at its registered office,

(b) section 356 (register to be open to inspection by members), and

(c) section 359 (power of court to rectify),

shall, subject to any modifications and adaptations specified in the Order, apply to and in relation to any such branch registers kept in Great Britain as they apply to and in relation to the registers of companies subject to those sections.

**9(2)** The countries and territories to which this paragraph applies are–

(a) all those specified in Part I of this Schedule, plus the Channel Islands and the Isle of Man,

(b) Botswana, Zambia and Tonga, and

(c) any territory for the time being under Her Majesty's protection or administered by the Government of the United Kingdom under the Trusteeship System of the United Nations.

# Schedule 15 – Contents of Annual Return of a Company having a Share Capital

Section 363

[Repealed by Companies Act 1989, s. 212 and Sch. 24 as from 7 January 1991.]

**History**
In regard to the date of the above repeal see SI 1990/2569 (C 68), art. 5(b): for relevant transitional and saving provisions, see SI 1990/1707 (C 46), art. 4, 5; Sch. 15 formerly read as follows:

"**1** The address of the registered office of the company.

**2(1)** If the register of members is, under the provisions of this Act, kept elsewhere than at the registered office of the company, the address of the place where it is kept.

**(2)** If any register of holders of debentures of the company or any duplicate of any such register or part of any such register is, under the provisions of this Act, kept, in England and Wales in the case of a company registered in England and Wales or in Scotland in the case of a company registered in Scotland, elsewhere than at the registered office of the company, the address of the place where it is kept.

**3** A summary, distinguishing between shares issued for cash and shares issued as fully or partly paid up otherwise than in cash, specifying the following particulars–

(a) the amount of the share capital of the company and the number of shares into which it is divided;
(b) the number of shares taken from the commencement of the company up to the date of the return;
(c) the amount called up on each share;
(d) the total amount of calls received;
(e) the total amount of calls unpaid;
(f) the total amount of the sums (if any) paid by way of commission in respect of any shares or debentures;
(g) the discount allowed on the issue of any shares issued at a discount or so much of that discount as has not been written off at the date on which the return is made;

(h) the total amount of the sums (if any) allowed by way of discount in respect of any debentures since the date of the last return;
(i) the total number of shares forfeited;
(j) the total number of shares for which share warrants are outstanding at the date of the return and of share warrants issued and surrendered respectively since the date of the last return, and the number of shares comprised in each warrant.

**4** Particulars of the total amount of the company's indebtedness in respect of all mortgages and charges (whenever created) of any description specified in section 396(1) or, in the case of a company registered in Scotland, section 410(4).

**5** A list–
(a) containing the names and addresses of all persons who, on the fourteenth day after the company's annual general meeting for the year, are members of the company, and of persons who have ceased to be members since the date of the last return or, in the case of the first return, since the incorporation of the company;
(b) stating the number of shares held by each of the existing members at the date of the return, specifying shares transferred since the date of the last return (or, in the case of the first return, since the incorporation of the company) by persons who are still members and have ceased to be members respectively and the dates of registration of the transfers;
(c) if the names are not arranged in alphabetical order, having annexed to it an index sufficient to enable the name of any person in the list to be easily found.

**6** All such particulars with respect to the persons who at the date of the return are the directors of the company and any person who at that date is the secretary of the company as are by this Act required to be contained with respect to directors and the secretary respectively in the register of the directors and secretaries of a company."

# Schedule 15A – Written Resolutions of Private Companies

## Part I – Exceptions

**1** Section 381A does not apply to–
(a) a resolution under section 303 removing a director before the expiration of his period of office, or
(b) a resolution under section 391 removing an auditor before the expiration of his term of office.

## Part II – Adaptation of Procedural Requirements

### INTRODUCTORY

**2(1)** In this Part of this Schedule (which adapts certain requirements of this Act in relation to proceedings under section 381A)–
(a) a **"written resolution"** means a resolution agreed to, or proposed to be agreed to, in accordance with that section, and
(b) a **"relevant member"** means a member by whom, or on whose behalf, the resolution is required to be signed in accordance with that section.

**2(2)** A written resolution is not effective if any of the requirements of this Part of this Schedule is not complied with.

### SECTION 95 (DISAPPLICATION OF PRE-EMPTION RIGHTS)

**3(1)** The following adaptations have effect in relation to a written resolution under section 95(2) (disapplication of pre-emption rights), or renewing a resolution under that provision.

**3(2)** So much of section 95(5) as requires the circulation of a written statement by the directors with a notice of meeting does not apply, but such a statement must be supplied to each relevant member at or before the time at which the resolution is supplied to him for signature.

**3(3)** Section 95(6) (offences) applies in relation to the inclusion in any such statement of matter which is misleading, false or deceptive in a material particular.

### SECTION 155 (FINANCIAL ASSISTANCE FOR PURCHASE OF COMPANY'S OWN SHARES OR THOSE OF HOLDING COMPANY)

**4** In relation to a written resolution giving approval under section 155(4) or (5) (financial assistance for purchase of company's own shares or those of holding company), section

157(4)(a) (documents to be available at meeting) does not apply, but the documents referred to in that provision must be supplied to each relevant member at or before the time at which the resolution is supplied to him for signature.

## SECTIONS 164, 165 AND 167 (AUTHORITY FOR OFF-MARKET PURCHASE OR CONTINGENT PURCHASE CONTRACT OF COMPANY'S OWN SHARES)

**5(1)** The following adaptations have effect in relation to a written resolution–

(a) conferring authority to make an off-market purchase of the company's own shares under section 164(2),

(b) conferring authority to vary a contract for an off-market purchase of the company's own shares under section 164(7), or

(c) varying, revoking or renewing any such authority under section 164(3).

**5(2)** Section 164(5) (resolution ineffective if passed by exercise of voting rights by member holding shares to which the resolution relates) does not apply; but for the purposes of section 381A(1) a member holding shares to which the resolution relates shall not be regarded as a member who would be entitled to attend and vote.

**5(3)** Section 164(6) (documents to be available at company's registered office and at meeting) does not apply, but the documents referred to in that provision and, where that provision applies by virtue of section 164(7), the further documents referred to in that provision must be supplied to each relevant member at or before the time at which the resolution is supplied to him for signature.

**5(4)** The above adaptations also have effect in relation to a written resolution in relation to which the provisions of section 164(3) to (7) apply by virtue of–

(a) section 165(2) (authority for contingent purchase contract), or

(b) section 167(2) (approval of release of rights under contract approved under section 164 or 165).

## SECTION 173 (APPROVAL FOR PAYMENT OUT OF CAPITAL)

**6(1)** The following adaptations have effect in relation to a written resolution giving approval under section 173(2) (redemption or purchase of company's own shares out of capital).

**6(2)** Section 174(2) (resolution ineffective if passed by exercise of voting rights by member holding shares to which the resolution relates) does not apply; but for the purposes of section 381A(1) a member holding shares to which the resolution relates shall not be regarded as a member who would be entitled to attend and vote.

**6(3)** Section 174(4) (documents to be available at meeting) does not apply, but the documents referred to in that provision must be supplied to each relevant member at or before the time at which the resolution is supplied to him for signature.

## SECTION 319 (APPROVAL OF DIRECTOR'S SERVICE CONTRACT)

**7** In relation to a written resolution approving any such term as is mentioned in section 319(1) (director's contract of employment for more than five years), section 319(5) (documents to be available at company's registered office and at meeting) does not apply, but the documents referred to in that provision must be supplied to each relevant member at or before the time at which the resolution is supplied to him for signature.

## SECTION 337 (FUNDING OF DIRECTOR'S EXPENDITURE IN PERFORMING HIS DUTIES)

**8** In relation to a written resolution giving approval under section 337(3)(a) (funding a director's expenditure in performing his duties), the requirement of that provision that certain matters be disclosed at the meeting at which the resolution is passed does not apply, but those matters must be disclosed to each relevant member at or before the time at which the resolution is supplied to him for signature.

**History**
Sch. 15A inserted by CA 1989, s. 114(1) as from 1 April 1990 (see SI 1990/355 (C 13), art. 4(a)).

# Schedule 15B – Provisions Subject to which Sections 425–427 have effect in their Application to Mergers and Divisions of Public Companies

Section 427A

## MEETING OF TRANSFEREE COMPANY

**1** Subject to paragraphs 10(1), 12(4) and 14(2), the court shall not sanction a compromise or arrangement under section 425(2) unless a majority in number representing three-fourths in value of each class of members of every pre-existing transferee company concerned in the scheme, present and voting either in person or by proxy at a meeting, agree to the scheme.

## DRAFT TERMS OF MERGER

**2(1)** The court shall not sanction the compromise or arrangement under section 425(2) unless–

(a) a draft of the proposed terms of the scheme (from here on referred to as the "draft terms") has been drawn up and adopted by the directors of all the transferor and pre-existing transferee companies concerned in the scheme,

(b) subject to paragraph 11(3), in the case of each of those companies the directors have delivered a copy of the draft terms to the registrar of companies and the registrar has published in the Gazette notice of receipt by him of a copy of the draft terms from that company, and

(c) subject to paragraphs 10 to 14, that notice was so published at least one month before the date of any meeting of that company summoned under section 425(1) or for the purposes of paragraph 1.

**2(2)** Subject to paragraph 12(2), the draft terms shall give particulars of at least the following matters–

(a) in respect of each transferor company and transferee company concerned in the scheme, its name, the address of its registered office and whether it is a company limited by shares or a company limited by guarantee and having a share capital;

(b) the number of shares in any transferee company to be allotted to members of any transferor company for a given number of their shares (from here on referred to as the "share exchange ratio") and the amount of any cash payment;

(c) the terms relating to the allotment of shares in any transferee company;

(d) the date from which the holding of shares in a transferee company will entitle the holders to participate in profits, and any special conditions affecting that entitlement;

(e) the date from which the transactions of any transferor company are to be treated for accounting purposes as being those of any transferee company;

(f) any rights or restrictions attaching to shares or other securities in any transferee company to be allotted under the scheme to the holders of shares to which any special rights or restrictions attach, or of other securities, in any transferor company, or the measures proposed concerning them;

(g) any amount or benefit paid or given or intended to be paid or given to any of the experts referred to in paragraph 5 or to any director of a transferor company or pre-existing transferee company, and the consideration for the payment of benefit.

**2(3)** Where the scheme is a Case 3 Scheme the draft terms shall also–

(a) give particulars of the property and liabilities to be transferred (to the extent these are known to the transferor company) and their allocation among the transferee companies;

(b) make provision for the allocation among and transfer to the transferee companies of any other property and liabilities which the transferor company has or may subsequently acquire; and

(c) specify the allocation to members of the transferor company of shares in the transferee companies and the criteria upon which that allocation is based.

## DOCUMENTS AND INFORMATION TO BE MADE AVAILABLE

**3** Subject to paragraphs 10 to 14, the court shall not sanction the compromise or arrangement under section 425(2) unless–

(a) in the case of each transferor company and each pre-existing transferee company the directors have drawn up and adopted a report complying with paragraph 4 (from here on referred to as a "directors' report");

(b) where the scheme is a Case 3 Scheme, the directors of the transferor company have reported to every meeting of the members or any class of members of that company summoned under section 425(1), and to the directors of each transferee company, any material changes in the property and liabilities of the transferor company between the date when the draft terms were adopted and the date of the meeting in question;

(c) where the directors of a transferor company have reported to the directors of a transferee company such a change as is mentioned in sub-paragraph (b) above, the latter have reported that change to every meeting of the members or any class of members of that transferee company summoned for the purposes of paragraph 1, or have sent a report of that change to every member who would have been entitled to receive a notice of such a meeting;

(d) a report complying with paragraph 5 has been drawn up on behalf of each transferor company and pre-existing transferee company (from here on referred to as an "expert's report");

(e) the members of any transferor company or transferee company were able to inspect at the registered office of that company copies of the documents listed in paragraph 6(1) in relation to every transferor company and pre-existing transferee company concerned in the scheme during a period beginning one month before, and ending on, the date of the first meeting of the members or any class of members of the first-mentioned transferor or transferee company summoned either under section 425(1) or for the purposes of paragraph 1 and those members were able to obtain copies of those documents or any part of them on request during that period free of charge; and

(f) the memorandum and articles of association of any transferee company which is not a pre-existing transferee company, or a draft thereof, has been approved by ordinary resolution of every transferor company concerned in the scheme.

## DIRECTORS' REPORT

**4(1)** The directors' report shall consist of–

(a) the statement required by section 426, and

(b) insofar as that statement does not contain the following matters, a further statement–

(i) setting out the legal and economic grounds for the draft terms, and in particular for the share exchange ratio, and, where the scheme is a Case 3 Scheme, for the criteria upon which the allocation to the members of the transferor company of shares in the transferee companies was based, and

(ii) specifying any special valuation difficulties.

**4(2)** Where the scheme is a Case 3 Scheme the directors' report shall also state whether a report has been made to the transferee company under section 103 (non-cash consideration to be valued before allotment) and, if so, whether that report has been delivered to the registrar of companies.

## EXPERT'S REPORT

**5(1)** Except where a joint expert is appointed under sub-paragraph (2) below, an expert's report shall consist of a separate written report on the draft terms to the members of one transferor company or pre-existing transferee company concerned in the scheme drawn up by a separate expert appointed on behalf of that company.

**5(2)** The court may, on the joint application of all the transferor companies and pre-existing transferee companies concerned in the scheme, approve the appointment of a joint expert to draw up a single report on behalf of all those companies.

**5(3)** An expert shall be independent of any of the companies concerned in the scheme, that is to say a person qualified at the time of the report to be appointed, or to continue to be, an auditor of those companies.

**5(4)** However, where it appears to an expert that a valuation is reasonably necessary to enable him to draw up the report, and it appears to him to be reasonable for that valuation, or part of it, to be made (or for him to accept such a valuation) by another person who–

(a) appears to him to have the requisite knowledge and experience to make the valuation or that part of it; and

(b) is not an officer or servant of any of the companies concerned in the scheme or any other body corporate which is one of those companies' subsidiary or holding company or a subsidiary of one of those companies' holding company or a partner or employee of such an officer or servant,

he may arrange for or accept such a valuation, together with a report which will enable him to make his own report under this paragraph.

**5(5)** The reference in sub-paragraph (4) above to an officer or servant does not include an auditor.

**5(6)** Where any valuation is made by a person other than the expert himself, the latter's report shall state that fact and shall also–

(a) state the former's name and what knowledge and experience he has to carry out the valuation, and

(b) describe so much of the undertaking, property and liabilities as were valued by the other person, and the method used to value them, and specify the date of the valuation.

**5(7)** An expert's report shall–

(a) indicate the method or methods used to arrive at the share exchange ratio proposed;

(b) give an opinion as to whether the method or methods used are reasonable in all the circumstances of the case, indicate the values arrived at using each such method and (if there is more than one method) give an opinion on the relative importance attributed to such methods in arriving at the value decided on;

(c) describe any special valuation difficulties which have arisen;

(d) state whether in the expert's opinion the share exchange ratio is reasonable; and

(e) in the case of a valuation made by a person other than himself, state that it appeared to himself reasonable to arrange for it to be so made or to accept a valuation so made.

**5(8)** Each expert has the right of access to all such documents of all the transferor companies and pre-existing transferee companies concerned in the scheme, and the right to require from the companies' officers all such information, as he thinks necessary for the purpose of making his report.

## INSPECTION OF DOCUMENTS

**6(1)** The documents referred to in paragraph 3(e) are, in relation to any company–

(a) the draft terms;

(b) the directors' report referred to in paragraph 4 above;

(c) the expert's report;

(d) the company's annual accounts, together with the relevant directors' report and auditors' report, for the last three financial years ending on or before the relevant date; and

(e) if the last of those financial years ended more than six months before the relevant date, an accounting statement in the form described in the following provisions.

In paragraphs (d) and (e) **"the relevant date"** means one month before the first meeting of the company summoned under section 425(1) or for the purposes of paragraph 1.

**History**
In para. 6(1)(b) the words "referred to in paragraph 4 above" inserted, para. 6(1)(d), (e) substituted and the words after para. 6(1)(e) added by CA 1989, s. 23 and Sch. 10, para. 22(1)–(4) as from 1 April 1990 subject to transitional and saving provisions (see SI 1990/355 (C 13), art. 3, Sch. 1 and also art. 6–9); para. 6(1)(d), (e) formerly read as follows:

"(d) the company's accounts within the meaning of section 239 for the last three complete financial years ending on or before a date one month earlier than the first meeting of the company summoned either under section 425(1) or for the purposes of paragraph 1 (in this paragraph referred to as the "relevant date");

(e) if the last complete financial year in respect of which accounts were prepared for the company ended more than 6 months before the relevant date, an accounting statement in the form described in the following sub-paragraph."

**6(2)** The accounting statement shall consist of–

(a) a balance sheet dealing with the state of the affairs of the company as at a date not more than three months before the draft terms were adopted by the directors, and

(b) where the company would be required to prepare group accounts if that date were the last day of a financial year, a consolidated balance sheet dealing with the state of affairs of the company and its subsidiary undertakings as at that date.

**History**
See history note after para. 6(5).

**6(3)** The requirements of this Act as to balance sheets forming part of a company's annual accounts, and the matters to be included in notes thereto, apply to any balance sheet required for the accounting statement, with such modifications as are necessary by reason of its being prepared otherwise than as at the last day of a financial year.

**History**
See history note after para. 6(5).

**6(4)** Any balance sheet required for the accounting statement shall be approved by the board of directors and signed on behalf of the board by a director of the company.

**History**
See history note after para. 6(5).

**6(5)** In relation to a company within the meaning of Article 3 of the Companies (Northern Ireland) Order 1986, the references in this paragraph to the requirements of this Act shall be construed as reference to the corresponding requirements of that Order.

**History**
Para. 6(2)–(5) substituted by CA 1989, s. 23 and Sch. 10, para. 22(1), (5) as from 1 April 1990 subject to transitional and saving provisions (see SI 1990/355 (C 13), art. 3, Sch. 1 and also art. 6–9); para. 6(2)–(5) formerly read as follows:

"**6(2)** The accounting statement shall consist of–

(a) a balance sheet dealing with the state of affairs of the company, and;

(b) where the company has subsidiaries and section 229 would apply if the relevant date were the end of the company's financial year, a further balance sheet or balance sheets dealing with the state of affairs of the company and the subsidiaries.

**(3)** Subject to sub-paragraph (4) below, any balance sheet required by sub-paragraph (2)(a) or (b) above shall comply with section 228 or section 230 (as appropriate) and with all other requirements of this Act as to the matters to be included in a company's balance sheet or in notes thereto (applying those sections and Schedule 4 and those other requirements with such modifications as are necessary because the balance sheet is prepared otherwise than as at the last day of the financial year) and must be signed in accordance with section 238.

**(4)** Notwithstanding sub-paragraph (3) above, any balance sheet required by sub-paragraph (2)(a) or (b) above shall deal with the state of affairs of the company or subsidiaries as at a date not earlier than the first day of the third month preceding the date when the draft terms were adopted by the directors, and the requirement in section 228 to give a true and fair view shall for the purposes of this paragraph have effect as a requirement to give a true and fair view of the state of affairs of the company as at the first-mentioned date.

**(5)** In sub-paragraphs (1) to (4) above, references to section 228, 229, 230, 238 and 239 and Schedule 4 shall, in the case of a company within the meaning of Article 3 of the Companies (Northern Ireland) Order 1986, have effect as references to Articles 236, 237, 238, 246 and 247 and Schedule 4 of that Order respectively, and references to the requirements of this Act shall have effect as references to the requirements of that Order."

## TRANSFEROR COMPANY HOLDING ITS OWN SHARES

**7** The court shall not sanction under section 425(2) a compromise or arrangement under which any shares in a transferee company are to be allotted to a transferor company or its nominee in respect of shares in that transferor company held by it or its nominee.

## SECURITIES OTHER THAN SHARES TO WHICH SPECIAL RIGHTS ARE ATTACHED

**8(1)** Where any security of a transferor company to which special rights are attached is held by a person other than as a member or creditor of the company, the court shall not sanction a compromise or arrangement under section 425(2) unless under the scheme that person is to receive rights in a transferee company of equivalent value.

**8(2)** Sub-paragraph (1) above shall not apply in the case of any such security where–

(a) the holder has agreed otherwise; or

(b) the holder is, or under the scheme is to be, entitled to have the security purchased by a transferee company involved in the scheme on terms which the court considers reasonable.

## DATE AND CONSEQUENCES OF THE COMPROMISE OR ARRANGEMENT

**9(1)** The following provisions of this paragraph shall apply where the court sanctions a compromise or arrangement.

**9(2)** The court shall in the order sanctioning the compromise or arrangement or in a subsequent order under section 427 fix a date on which the transfer or transfers to the transferee company or transferee companies of the undertaking, property and liabilities of the transferor company shall take place; and any such order which provide for the dissolution of the transferor company shall fix the same date for the dissolution.

**9(3)** If it is necessary for the transferor company to take any steps to ensure that the undertaking, property and liabilities are fully transferred, the court shall fix a date, not later than six months after the date fixed under sub-paragraph (2) above, by which such steps must be taken and for that purpose may postpone the dissolution of the transferor company until that date.

**9(4)** The court may postpone or further postpone the date fixed under sub-paragraph (3) above if it is satisfied that the steps there mentioned cannot be completed by the date (or latest date) fixed under that sub-paragraph.

## EXCEPTIONS

**10(1)** The court may sanction a compromise or arrangement under section 425(2) notwithstanding that–

(a) any meeting otherwise required by paragraph 1 has not been summoned by a pre-existing transferee company ("the relevant company"), and

(b) paragraphs 2(1)(c) and 3(e) have not been complied with in respect of that company,

if the court is satisfied that the conditions specified in sub-paragraph (2) below have been complied with.

**10(2)** Subject to paragraphs 11(3) and 12(3), the conditions mentioned in sub-paragraph (1) above are–

(a) that the publication of notice of receipt of the draft terms by the registrar of companies referred to in paragraph 2(1)(b) took place in respect of the relevant company at least one month before the date of any meeting of members of any transferor company concerned in the scheme summoned under section 425(1);

(b) that the members of the relevant company were able to inspect at the registered office of that company the documents listed in paragraph 6(1) in relation to every transferor company and transferee company concerned in the scheme during a period ("the relevant period") beginning one month before, and ending on, the date of any such meeting, and that they were able to obtain copies of those documents or any part of them on request during that period free of charge; and

(c) that one or more members of the relevant company, who together held not less than five per cent of the paid-up capital of that company which carried the right to vote at general meetings of the company, would have been able during the relevant period to require that a meeting of each class of members be called for the purpose of deciding whether or not to agree to the scheme but that no such requisition had been made.

**11(1)** The following sub-paragraphs apply where the scheme is a Case 3 Scheme.

**11(2)** Sub-paragraphs (a) to (d) of paragraph 3 shall not apply and sub-paragraph (e) of that paragraph shall not apply as regards the documents listed in paragraph 6(1)(b), (c) and (e), if all members holding shares in, and all persons holding other securities of, any of the transferor companies and pre-existing transferee companies concerned in the scheme on the date of the application to the court under section 425(1), being shares or securities which as at that date carry the right to vote in general meetings of the company, so agree.

**11(3)** The court may by order direct in respect of any transferor company or pre-existing transferee company that the requirements relating to–

(a) delivering copies of the draft terms and publication of notice of receipt of the draft terms under paragraph 2(1)(b) and (c), or

(b) inspection under paragraph 3(e),

shall not apply, and may by order direct that paragraph 10 shall apply to any pre-existing transferee company with the omission of sub-paragraph (2)(a) and (b) of that paragraph.

**11(4)** The court shall not make any order under sub-paragraph (3) above unless it is satisfied that the following conditions will be fulfilled–

(a) that the members of the company will have received or will have been able to obtain free of charge copies of the documents listed in paragraph 6(1) in time to examine them before the date of the first meeting of the members or any class of members of the company summoned under section 425(1) or for the purposes of paragraph 1;

(b) in the case of a pre-existing transferee company, where in the circumstances described in paragraph 10 no meeting is held, that the members of that company will have received or will have been able to obtain free of charge copies of those documents in time to require a meeting under paragraph 10(2)(c);

(c) that the creditors of the company will have received or will have been able to obtain free of charge copies of the draft terms in time to examine them before the date of the meeting of the members or any class of members of the company, or, in the circumstances referred to in paragraph (b) above, at the same time as the members of the company; and

(d) that no prejudice would be caused to the members or creditors of any transferor company or transferee company concerned in the scheme by making the order in question.

## TRANSFEREE COMPANY OR COMPANIES HOLDING SHARES IN THE TRANSFEROR COMPANY

**12(1)** Where the scheme is a Case 1 Scheme and in the case of every transferor company concerned–

(a) the shares in that company, and

(b) such securities of that company (other than shares) as carry the right to vote at general meetings of that company,

are all held by or on behalf of the transferee company, section 427A and this Schedule shall apply subject to the following sub-paragraphs.

**12(2)** The draft terms need not give particulars of the matters mentioned in paragraph 2(2)(b), (c) or (d).

**12(3)** Section 426 and sub-paragraphs (a) and (d) of paragraph 3 shall not apply, and sub-paragraph (e) of that paragraph shall not apply as regards the documents listed in paragraph 6(1)(b) and (c).

**12(4)** The court may sanction the compromise or arrangement under section 425(2) notwithstanding that–

(a) any meeting otherwise required by section 425 or paragraph 1 has not been summoned by any company concerned in the scheme, and

(b) paragraphs 2(1)(c) and 3(e) have not been complied with in respect of that company,

if it is satisfied that the conditions specified in the following sub-paragraphs have been complied with.

**12(5)** The conditions mentioned in the previous sub-paragraph are–

(a) that the publication of notice of receipt of the draft terms by the registrar of companies referred to in paragraph 2(1)(b) took place in respect of every transferor company and transferee company concerned in the scheme at least one month before the date of the order under section 425(2) ("the relevant date");

(b) that the members of the transferee company were able to inspect at the registered office of that company copies of the documents listed in paragraphs 6(1)(a), (d) and (e) in relation to every transferor company or transferee company concerned in the scheme during a period ("the relevant period") beginning one month before, and ending on, the relevant date and that they were able to obtain copies of those documents or any part of them on request during that period free of charge; and

(c) that one or more members of the transferee company who together held not less than five per cent of the paid-up capital of the company which carried the right to vote at general meetings of the company would have been able during the relevant period to require that a meeting of each class of members be called for the purpose of deciding whether or not to agree to the scheme but that no such requisition has been made.

**13(1)** Where the scheme is a Case 3 Scheme and–

(a) the shares in the transferor company, and

(b) such securities of that company (other than shares) as carry the right to vote at general meetings of that company,

are all held by or on behalf of one or more transferee companies, section 427A and this Schedule shall apply subject to the following sub-paragraphs.

**13(2)** The court may sanction a compromise or arrangement under section 425(2) notwithstanding that–

(a) any meeting otherwise required by section 425 has not been summoned by the transferor company, and

(b) paragraphs 2(1)(c) and 3(b) and (e) have not been complied with in respect of that company,

if it is satisfied that the conditions specified in the following sub-paragraph have been complied with.

**13(3)** The conditions referred to in the previous sub-paragraph are–

(a) the conditions set out in paragraph 12(5)(a) and (c);

(b) that the members of the transferor company and every transferee company concerned in the scheme were able to inspect at the registered office of the company of which they were members copies of the documents listed in paragraph 6(1) in relation to every such company during a period beginning one month before, and ending on, the date of the order under section 425(2) ("the relevant date"), and that they were able to obtain copies of those documents or any part of them on request during that period free of charge; and

(c) that the directors of the transferor company have sent to every member who would have been entitled to receive a notice of the meeting (had it been called), and to the directors of each transferee company, a report of any material changes in the property and liabilities of the transferor company between the date when the draft terms were adopted and a date one month before the relevant date.

**14(1)** Where the scheme is a Case 1 Scheme and in the case of every transferor company concerned ninety per cent or more (but not all) of–

(a) the shares in that company, and

(b) such securities of that company (other than shares) as carry the right to vote at general meetings of that company,

are held by or on behalf of the transferee company, section 427A and this Schedule shall apply subject to the following sub-paragraphs.

**14(2)** The court may sanction a compromise or arrangement under section 425(2) notwithstanding that–

(a) any meeting otherwise required by paragraph 1 has not been summoned by the transferee company, and

(b) paragraphs 2(1)(c) and 3(e) have not been complied with in respect of that company,

if the court is satisfied that the conditions specified in the following sub-paragraph have been complied with.

**14(3)** The conditions referred to in the previous sub-paragraph are the same conditions as those specified in paragraph 10(2), save that for this purpose the condition contained in paragraph 10(2)(b) shall be treated as referring only to the documents listed in paragraph 6(1)(a), (d) and (e).

### LIABILITY OF TRANSFEREE COMPANIES FOR THE DEFAULT OF ANOTHER

**15(1)** Where the scheme is a Case 3 Scheme, each transferee company shall be jointly and severally liable, subject to sub-paragraph (2) below, for any liability transferred to any other transferee company under the scheme to the extent that that other company has made default in satisfying that liability, but so that no transferee company shall be so liable for an amount greater than the amount arrived at by calculating the value at the time of the transfer of the property transferred to it under the scheme less the amount at that date of the liabilities so transferred.

**15(2)** If a majority in number representing three-fourths in value of the creditors or any class of creditors of the transferor company present and voting either in person or by proxy at a meeting summoned under section 425(1) so agree, sub-paragraph (1) above shall not apply in respect of the liabilities of the creditors or that class of creditors.

**History**
Sch. 15B renumbered as such by CA 1989, s. 114(2) as from 1 April 1990 (see SI 1990/355 (C 13), art. 4(a)) – the schedule was previously Sch. 15A and was inserted by the Companies (Mergers and Divisions) Regulations 1987 (SI 1987/1991), reg. 2(c) and Sch., Pt. II as from 1 January 1988.

**Note**
The Companies (Merger and Divisions) Regulations 1987 (SI 1987/1991) implement the Third and Sixth EC Company Law Directives (78/855, 82/891).

# Schedule 16 – Orders in Course of Winding Up Pronounced in Vacation (Scotland)

— Section 571

[Repealed by Insolvency Act 1986, s. 438 and Sch. 12 as from 29 December 1986.]

**History**
In regard to the date of the above repeal, see Insolvency Act 1986, s. 443 and SI 1986/1924 (C 71); Sch. 16 formerly read as follows:

**"Part I – Orders Which are to be Final**

Order under section 557, as to the time for proving debts and claims.

Orders under section 561, as to the attendance of, and production of documents by, persons indebted to, or having property of, or information as to the affairs or property of, a company.

Orders under section 645 as to meetings for ascertaining wishes of creditors or contributories.

Orders under section 648, as to the examination of witnesses in regard to the property or affairs of a company.

**Orders Which are to take Effect Until Matter Disposed of by Inner House**

Orders under section 521(1), 525(2) or (3), 549, 672 or 673, restraining or permitting the commencement or the continuance of legal proceedings.

Orders under section 532(4), limiting the powers of provisional liquidators.

Orders under section 536, 599 or 609, appointing a liquidator to fill a vacancy, or appointing (except to fill a vacancy caused by the removal of a liquidator by the court) a liquidator for a winding up voluntarily or subject to supervision.

Orders under section 539, sanctioning the exercise of any power by a liquidator, other than the powers specified in paragraphs (c), (d), (e) and (f) of subsection (1).

Orders under section 551, requiring the delivery of property or documents to the liquidator.

Orders under section 565, as to the arrest and detention of an absconding contributory and his property.

Orders under section 606, for continuance of winding up subject to supervision."

# Schedule 17 – Proceedings of Committee of Inspection

Section 547, 590

[Repealed by Insolvency Act 1985, s. 235 and Sch. 10, Pt. II as from 29 December 1986.]

**History**

In regard to the date of the above repeal, see SI 1986/1924 (C 71); Sch. 17 formerly read as follows:

"**1** The committee shall meet at such times as it may from time to time appoint and, failing such appointment, at least once a month; and the liquidator or any member of the committee may also call a meeting of the committee as and when he thinks necessary.

**2** The committee may act by a majority of its members present at a meeting, but shall not act unless a majority of the committee are present.

**3** A member of the committee may resign by notice in writing signed by him and delivered to the liquidator.

**4** If a member of the committee becomes bankrupt or compounds or arranges with his creditors or is absent from five consecutive meetings of the committee without leave of those members who together with himself represent the creditors or contributories (as the case may be), his office thereupon becomes vacant.

**5** A member of the committee may be removed by an ordinary resolution at a meeting of creditors (if he represents creditors) or of contributories (if he represents contributories) of which 7 days' notice has been given, stating the object of the meeting.

**6(1)** On a vacancy occurring in the committee the liquidator shall forthwith summon a meeting of creditors or of contributories (as the case may require) to fill the vacancy; and the meeting may, by resolution, reappoint the same or appoint another creditor or contributory to fill the vacancy.

**(2)** However, if the liquidator, having regard to the position in the winding up, is of the opinion that it is unnecessary for the vacancy to be filled, he may apply to the court; and the court may make an order that the vacancy be not filled, or be not filled except in circumstances specified by the order.

**(3)** The continuing members of the committee, if not less than two, may act notwithstanding any vacancy in the committee."

# Schedule 18 – Provisions of Part XX Not Applicable in Winding Up Subject to Supervision of the Court

Section 610

[Repealed by Insolvency Act 1985, s. 235 and Sch. 10, Pt. II as from 29 December 1986.]

**History**

In regard to the date of the above repeal, see SI 1986/1924 (C 71); Sch. 18 formerly read as follows:

| "*Section* | *Subject matter* |
|---|---|
| 528, 529 | Statement of company's affairs to be submitted to official receiver. |
| 530 | Report by official receiver. |
| 531 | Power of court to appoint liquidators. |
| 532 | Appointment and powers of provisional liquidator. |
| 533 | Appointment, style, etc. of liquidators in England and Wales. |
| 534 | Provisions where person other than official receiver is appointed liquidator. |
| 535 | Provision as to liquidators in Scotland. |
| 536 (except subs. (5)). | General provisions as to liquidators. |
| 540 | Exercise and control of liquidator's powers in England and Wales. |
| 541 | Books to be kept by liquidator (England and Wales). |
| 542 | Payments of liquidator into bank (England and Wales). |
| 543 | Audit of liquidator's accounts (England and Wales). |
| 544 | Control of Secretary of State over liquidators in England and Wales. |
| 545 | Release of liquidators (England and Wales). |
| 546 | Meetings of creditors and contributories to determine whether committee of inspection shall be appointed. |
| 547, 548 (with Sch. 17) | Constitution, proceedings, etc. of committee of inspection; powers of Secretary of State where no committee. |
| 556 | Appointment of special manager (England and Wales). |
| 563, 564 | Power to order public examination of promoters and officers (England and Wales). |
| 567 | Delegation to liquidator of certain powers of the court (England and Wales)." |

# Schedule 19 – Preference Among Creditors in Company Winding Up

Section 614

[Repealed by Insolvency Act 1985, s. 235 and Sch. 10, Pt. II as from 29 December 1986.]

**History**

In regard to the date of the above repeal, see SI 1986/1924 (C 71); Sch. 19 formerly read as follows:

""THE RELEVANT DATE"

1 For the purposes of this Schedule, **"the relevant date"** is–

(a) in the case of a company ordered to be wound up compulsorily, the date of the appointment (or first appointment) of a provisional liquidator or, if no such appointment has been made, the date of the winding-up order, unless in either case the company had commenced to be wound up voluntarily before that date, and

(b) otherwise, the date of the passing of the resolution for winding up the company.

DEBTS TO INLAND REVENUE

2 All income tax, corporation tax, capital gains tax and other assessed taxes, assessed on the company up to 5th April next before the relevant date, and not exceeding in the whole one year's assessment.

3 Any sums due at the relevant date from the company on account of tax deductions for the 12 months next before that date.

The sums here referred to–

(a) are those due by way of deduction of income tax from emoluments during the relevant period, which the company was liable to make under section 204 of the Income and Corporation Taxes Act 1970, less the amount of the repayments of income tax which the company was liable to make during the same period, and

(b) include amounts due from the company in respect of deductions required to be made by it under section 69 of the Finance (No. 2) Act 1975 (construction industry contract workers).

DEBTS DUE TO CUSTOMS & EXCISE

4 Any value added tax due at the relevant date from the company and having become due within the 12 months next before that date.

For purposes of this paragraph, the tax having become due within those 12 months in respect of any prescribed accounting period falling partly within and partly outside those 12 months is taken to be such part of the tax due for the whole of that accounting reference period as is proportionate to the part of the period falling within the 12 months.

5 The amount of any car tax due at the relevant date from the company and having become due within the 12 months next before that date.

6 Any amount due–

(a) by way of general betting duty or bingo duty, or

(b) under section 12(1) of the Betting and Gaming Duties Act 1981 (general betting duty and pool betting duty recoverable from agent collecting stakes), or

(c) under section 14 of, or Schedule 2 to, that Act (gaming licence duty),

from the company at the relevant date and which became due within the 12 months next before that date.

LOCAL RATES

7 All local rates due from the company at the relevant date and having become due and payable within 12 months next before that date.

SOCIAL SECURITY DEBTS

8 All the debts specified in section 153(2) of the Social Security Act 1975, Schedule 3 to the Social Security Pensions Act 1975, and any corresponding provisions in force in Northern Ireland.

(This does not apply if the company is being wound up voluntarily merely for the purposes of reconstruction or amalgamation with another company.)

DEBTS TO AND IN RESPECT OF COMPANY'S EMPLOYEES

9 All wages or salary (whether or not earned wholly or in part by way of commission) of any clerk or servant in respect of services rendered to the company during 4 months next before the relevant date, and all wages (whether payable for time or for piece work) of any workman or labourer in respect of services so rendered.

10 All accrued holiday remuneration becoming payable to any clerk, servant, workman or labourer (or in the case of his death to any other person in his right) on the termination of his employment before or by the effect of the winding-up order or resolution.

This includes, in relation to any person, all sums which, by virtue either of his contract of employment or of any enactment (including any order made or direction given under an Act), are payable on account of the remuneration which would, in the ordinary course, have become payable to him in respect of a period of holiday had his employment with the company continued until he became entitled to be allowed the holiday.

11 The following amounts owed by the company to an employee are treated as wages payable by it to him in respect of the period for which they are payable–

(a) a guarantee payment under section 12(1) of the Employment Protection (Consolidation) Act 1978 (employee without work to do for a day or part of a day),

(b) remuneration on suspension on medical grounds under section 19 of that Act,

(c) any payment for time off under section 27(3) (trade union duties), 31(3) (looking for work, etc.) or 31A(4) (ante-natal care) of that Act,

(d) statutory sick pay under Part I of the Social Security and Housing Benefits Act 1982, and

(e) remuneration under a protective award made by an industrial tribunal under section 101 of the Employment Protection Act 1975 (redundancy dismissal with compensation).

**12(1)** The remuneration to which priority is to be given under paragraph 9 shall not, in the case of any claimant, exceed £800:

Provided that where a claimant under paragraph 9 is a labourer in husbandry who has entered into a contract for the payment of a portion of his wages in a lump sum at the end of the year of hiring, he had priority in respect of the whole of that sum, or a part of it, as the court may decide to be due under the contract, proportionate to the time of service up to the relevant date.

**(2)** No increase or reduction of the money sum specified above in this paragraph affects any case where the relevant date (or, where provisions of this Schedule apply by virtue of section 196, the date referred to in subsection (4) of that section) occurred before the coming into force of the increase or reduction.

PRIORITY FOR THIRD PARTY ADVANCING FUNDS FOR WAGE-PAYMENTS, ETC.

13 Where any payment has been made–

(a) to any clerk, servant, workman or labourer in the employment of the company on account of wages or salary, or

(b) to any such clerk, servant, workman or labourer or, in case of his death, to any other person in his right, on account of accrued holiday remuneration,

out of money advanced by some person for that purpose, the person by whom the money was advanced has in the winding-up a right of priority in respect of the money so advanced and paid up to the amount by which the sum in respect of which the clerk, servant, workman or labourer, or other person in his right, would have been entitled to priority in the winding-up has been diminished by reason of the payment having been made.

INTERPRETATION FOR THE ABOVE PARAGRAPHS

14 For purposes of this Schedule–

(a) any remuneration in respect of a period of holiday or of absence from work through sickness or other good cause is deemed to be wages in respect of services rendered to the company in that period; and

(b) references to remuneration in respect of a period of holiday include any sums which, if they had been paid, would have been treated for purposes of the enactments relating to social security as earnings in respect of that period."

# Schedule 20 – Vesting of Disclaimed Property; Protection of Third Parties

Section 619

## Part I – Disclaimer by Liquidator under sections 618, 619; Crown Disclaimer under section 656 (England and Wales Only)

[Repealed by Insolvency Act 1985, s. 235 and Sch. 10, Pt. II as from 29 December 1986.]

**History**

In regard to the date of the above repeal see SI 1986/1924 (C 71); Sch. 20, Pt. I formerly read as follows:

"1 The court shall not under section 619 (including that section as applied by section 657(2)) make a vesting order, where the property disclaimed is of a leasehold nature, in favour of a person claiming under the company, except on the following terms.

2 The person must by the order be made subject–

(a) to the same liabilities and obligations as those to which the company was subject under the lease in respect of the property at the commencement of the winding up, or

(b) (if the court thinks fit) only to the same liabilities and obligations as if the lease had been assigned to him at that date;

and in either event (if the case so requires) the liabilities and obligations must be as if the lease had comprised only the property comprised in the vesting order.

3 A mortgagee or under-lessee declining to accept a vesting order on such terms is excluded from all interest in and security on the property.

4 If there is no person claiming under the company who is willing to accept an order on such terms, the court has power to vest the company's estate and interest in the property in any person liable (either personally or in a representative character, and either alone or jointly with the company) to perform the lessee's covenants in the lease, freed and discharged from all estates, incumbrances and interests created therein by the company."

## Part II – Crown Disclaimer under section 656 (Scotland Only)

5 The court shall not under section 657 make a vesting order, where the property disclaimed is held under a lease, in favour of a person claiming under the company (whether as sub-lessee or as creditor in a duly registered or, as appropriate, recorded heritable security over a lease), except on the following terms.

6 The person must by the order be made subject–

(a) to the same liabilities and obligations as those to which the company was subject under the lease in respect of the property at the commencement of the winding up, or

(b) (if the court thinks fit) only to the same liabilities and obligations as if the lease had been assigned to him at that date;

and in either event (if the case so requires) the liabilities and obligations must be as if the lease had comprised only the property comprised in the vesting order.

**7** A creditor or sub-lessee declining to accept a vesting order on such terms is excluded from all interest in and security over the property.

**8** If there is no person claiming under the company who is willing to accept an order on such terms, the court has power to vest the company's estate and interest in the property in any person liable (either personally or in a representative character, and either alone or jointly with the company) to perform the lessee's obligations under the lease, freed and discharged from all interests, rights and obligations created by the company in the lease or in relation to the lease.

**9** For the purposes of paragraph 5 above, a heritable security is duly recorded if it is recorded in the Register of Sasines and is duly registered if registered in accordance with the Land Registration (Scotland) Act 1979.

# Schedule 21 – Effect of Registration under section 680

Section 689

## INTERPRETATION

**1** In this Schedule–

**"registration"** means registration in pursuance of section 680 in Chapter II of Part XXII of this Act, and

**" registered"** has the corresponding meaning, and

**"instrument"** includes deed of settlement, contract of copartnery and letters patent.

## VESTING OF PROPERTY

**2** All property belonging to or vested in the company at the date of its registration passes to and vests in the company on registration for all the estate and interest of the company in the property.

## EXISTING LIABILITIES

**3** Registration does not affect the company's rights or liabilities in respect of any debt or obligation incurred, or contract entered into, by, to, with or on behalf of the company before registration.

## PENDING ACTIONS AT LAW

**4(1)** All actions and other legal proceedings which at the time of the company's registration are pending by or against the company, or the public officer or any member of it, may be continued in the same manner as if the registration had not taken place.

**4(2)** However, execution shall not issue against the effects of any individual member of the company on any judgment, decree or order obtained in such an action or proceeding; but in the event of the company's property and effects being insufficient to satisfy the judgment, decree or order, an order may be obtained for winding up the company.

## THE COMPANY'S CONSTITUTION

**5(1)** All provisions contained in any Act of Parliament or other instrument constituting or regulating the company are deemed to be conditions and regulations of the company, in the same manner and with the same incidents as if so much of them as would, if the company had been formed under this Act, have been required to be inserted in the memorandum, were contained in a registered memorandum, and the residue were contained in registered articles.

**5(2)** The provisions brought in under this paragraph include, in the case of a company registered as a company limited by guarantee, those of the resolution declaring the amount of the guarantee; and they include also the statement under section 681(5)(a), and any statement under section 684(2).

**6(1)** All the provisions of this Act apply to the company, and to its members, contributories and creditors, in the same manner in all respects as if it had been formed under this Act, subject as follows.

**6(2)** Table A does not apply unless adopted by special resolution.

**6(3)** Provisions relating to the numbering of shares do not apply to any joint stock company whose shares are not numbered.

**6(4)** Subject to the provisions of this Schedule, the company does not have power–

(a) to alter any provision contained in an Act of Parliament relating to the company,

(b) without the sanction of the Secretary of State, to alter any provision contained in letters patent relating to the company.

**6(5)** The company does not have power to alter any provision contained in a royal charter or letters patent with respect to the company's objects.

### CAPITAL STRUCTURE

**7** Provisions of this Act with respect to–

(a) the registration of an unlimited company as limited,

(b) the powers of an unlimited company on registration as a limited company to increase the nominal amount of its share capital and to provide that a portion of its share capital shall not be capable of being called up except in the event of winding up, and

(c) the power of a limited company to determine that a portion of its share capital shall not be capable of being called up except in that event, apply, notwithstanding any provisions contained in an Act of Parliament, royal charter or other instrument constituting or regulating the company.

### SUPPLEMENTARY

**8** Nothing in paragraphs 5 to 7 authorises a company to alter any such provisions contained in an instrument constituting or regulating the company as would, if the company had originally been formed under this Act, have been required to be contained in the memorandum and are not authorised to be altered by this Act.

**9** None of the provisions of this Act (except section 461(3)) derogate from any power of altering the company's constitution or regulations which may, by virtue of any Act of Parliament or other instrument constituting or regulating it, be vested in the company.

## Schedule 21A – Branch Registration under the Eleventh Company Law Directive (89/666/EEC)

Section 690A

### DUTY TO REGISTER

**1(1)** A company shall, within one month of having opened a branch in a part of Great Britain, deliver to the registrar for registration a return in the prescribed form containing–

(a) such particulars about the company as are specified in paragraph 2,

(b) such particulars about the branch as are specified in paragraph 3, and

(c) if the company is one to which section 699AA applies, such particulars in relation to the registration of documents under Schedule 21D as are specified in paragraph 4.

**Note**

See note after para. 8(2).

**1(2)** The return shall, except where sub-paragraph (3) below applies, be accompanied by the documents specified in paragraph 5 and, if the company is one to which Part I of Schedule 21D applies, the documents specified in paragraph 6.

**1(3)** This sub-paragraph applies where–

(a) at the time the return is delivered, the company has another branch in the United Kingdom,

(b) the return contains a statement to the effect that the documents specified in paragraph 5, and, if the company is one to which Part I of Schedule 21D applies, paragraph 6, are included in the material registered in respect of the other branch, and

(c) the return states where the other branch is registered and what is its registered number.

**1(4)** In sub-paragraph (1) above, the reference to having opened a branch in a part of Great Britain includes a reference to a branch having become situated there on ceasing to be situated elsewhere.

**1(5)** If at the date on which the company opens the branch in Great Britain the company is subject to any proceedings referred to in section 703P(1) (winding up) or 703Q(1) (insolvency proceedings etc.), the company shall deliver a return under section 703P(1) or (as the case may be) 703Q(1) within one month of that date.

If on or before that date a person has been appointed to be liquidator of the company and continues in that office at that date, section 703P(3) and (4) (liquidator to make return within 14 days of appointment) shall have effect as if it required a return to be made under that section within one month of the date of the branch being opened.

## PARTICULARS REQUIRED

**2(1)** The particulars referred to in paragraph 1(1)(a) are–

(a) the corporate name of the company,

(b) its legal form,

(c) if it is registered in the country of its incorporation, the identity of the register in which it is registered and the number with which it is so registered,

(d) a list of its directors and secretary, containing–
  (i) with respect to each director, the particulars specified in sub-paragraph (3) below, and
  (ii) with respect to the secretary (or where there are joint secretaries, with respect to each of them) the particulars specified in sub-paragraph (4) below,

(e) the extent of the powers of the directors to represent the company in dealings with third parties and in legal proceedings, together with a statement as to whether they may act alone or must act jointly and, if jointly, the name of any other person concerned, and

(f) whether the company is an institution to which section 699A (or the equivalent provision in Northern Ireland) applies.

**2(2)** In the case of a company which is not incorporated in a Member State, those particulars also include–

(a) the law under which the company is incorporated,

(b) in the case of a company to which either paragraphs 2 and 3 of Part I of Schedule 21C or Schedule 21D applies) the period for which the company is required by the law under which it is incorporated to prepare accounts, together with the period allowed for the preparation and public disclosure of accounts for such a period, and

(c) unless disclosed by the documents specified in paragraph 5–
  (i) the address of its principal place of business in its country of incorporation,
  (ii) its objects, and
  (iii) the amount of its issued share capital.

**2(3)** The particulars referred to in sub-paragraph (1)(d)(i) above are–

(a) in the case of an individual–
  (i) his name,
  (ii) any former name,
  (iii) his usual residential address,

his nationality,
(v) his business occupation (if any),
(vi) particulars of any other directorships held by him, and
(vii) his date of birth;

(b) in the case of a corporation or Scottish firm, its corporate or firm name and registered or principal office.

**2(4)** The particulars referred to in sub-paragraph (1)(d)(ii) above are–

(a) in the case of an individual, his name, any former name and his usual residential address;

(b) in the case of a corporation or Scottish firm, its corporate or firm name and registered or principal office.

Where all the partners in a firm are joint secretaries of the company, the name and principal office of the firm may be stated instead of the particulars required by paragraph (a) above.

**2(5)** In sub-paragraphs (3)(a) and (4)(a) above–

(a) **"name"** means a person's forename and surname, except that in the case of a peer, or an individual usually known by a title, the title may be stated instead of his forename and surname, or in addition to either or both of them; and

(b) the reference to a former name does not include–
(i) in the case of a peer, or an individual normally known by a title, the name by which he was known previous to the adoption of or succession to the title;
(ii) in the case of any person, a former name which was changed or disused before he attained the age of 18 years or which has been changed or disused for 20 years or more;
(iii) in the case of a married woman, the name by which she was known previous to the marriage.

**2(6)** Where–

(a) at the time a return is delivered under paragraph 1(1) the company has another branch in the same part of Great Britain as the branch covered by the return; and

(b) the company has delivered the particulars required by sub-paragraphs (1)(b) to (f) and (2) to (5) to the registrar with respect to that branch (or to the extent it is required to do so by virtue of Schedule 21B to this Act) and has no outstanding obligation to make a return to the registrar in respect of that branch under paragraph 7 in relation to any alteration to those particulars,

the company may adopt the particulars so delivered as particulars which the registrar is to treat as having been filed by the return by referring in the return to the fact that the particulars have been filed in respect of that other branch and giving the number with which the other branch is registered.

**3** The particulars referred to in paragraph 1(1)(b) are–

(a) the address of the branch,

(b) the date on which it was opened,

(c) the business carried on at it,

(d) if different from the name of the company, the name in which that business is carried on,

(e) a list of the names and addresses of all persons resident in Great Britain authorised to accept on the company's behalf service of process in respect of the business of the branch and of any notices required to be served on the company in respect of the business of the branch,

(f) a list of the names and usual residential addresses of all persons authorised to represent the company as permanent representatives of the company for the business of the branch,

(g) the extent of the authority of any person falling within paragraph (f) above, including whether that person is authorised to act alone or jointly, and

(h) if a person falling within paragraph (f) above is not authorised to act alone, the name of any person with whom he is authorised to act.

**4** The particulars referred to in paragraph 1(1)(c) are–

(a) whether it is intended to register documents under paragraph 2(2) or, as the case may be, 10(1) of Schedule 21D in respect of the branch or in respect of some other branch in the United Kingdom, and

(b) if it is, where that other branch is registered and what is its registered number.

## DOCUMENTS REQUIRED

**5** The first documents referred to in paragraph 1(2) are–

(a) a certified copy of the charter, statutes or memorandum and articles of the company (or other instrument constituting or defining the company's constitution), and

(b) if any of the documents mentioned in paragraph (a) above is not written in the English language, a translation of it into English certified in the prescribed manner to be a correct translation.

**Note**

See note after para. 7(1).

**6(1)** The second documents referred to in paragraph 1(2) are–

(a) copies of the latest accounting documents prepared in relation to a financial period of the company to have been publicly disclosed in accordance with the law of the country in which it is incorporated before the end of the period allowed for compliance with paragraph 1 in respect of the branch or, if earlier, the date on which the company complies with paragraph 1 in respect of the branch, and

(b) if any of the documents mentioned in paragraph (a) above is not written in the English language, a translation of it into English certified in the prescribed manner to be a correct translation.

**Note**

See note after para. 7(1).

**6(2)** In sub-paragraph (1)(a) above, **"financial period"** and **"accounting documents"** shall be construed in accordance with paragraph 6 of Schedule 21D.

## ALTERATIONS

**7(1)** If, after a company has delivered a return under paragraph 1(1) above, any alteration is made in–

(a) its charter, statutes or memorandum and articles (or other instrument constituting or defining its constitution), or

(b) any of the particulars referred to in paragraph 1(1),

the company shall, within the time specified below, deliver to the registrar for registration a return in the prescribed form containing the prescribed particulars of the alteration.

In the case of an alteration in any of the documents referred to in paragraph (a), the return shall be accompanied by a certified copy of the document as altered, together with, if the document is not written in the English language, a translation of it into English certified in the prescribed manner to be a correct translation.

**Note**

For certification as a correct translation (and the prescribed form) see the Companies (Forms) (Amendment) Regulations 1992 (SI 1992/3006), reg. 3.

**7(2)** The time for the delivery of the return required by sub-paragraph (1) above is–

(a) in the case of an alteration in any of the particulars specified in paragraph 3, 21 days after the alteration is made; or

(b) in the case of any other alteration, 21 days after the date on which notice of the alteration in question could have been received in Great Britain in due course of post (if despatched with due diligence).

**7(3)** Where–

(a) a company has more than one branch in Great Britain, and

(b) an alteration relates to more than one of those branches, sub-paragraph (1) above shall have effect to require the company to deliver a return in respect of each of the branches to which the alteration relates.

**7(4)** For the purposes of sub-paragraph (3) above–

(a) an alteration in any of the particulars specified in paragraph 2 shall be treated as relating to every branch of the company (though where the company has more than one branch in a part of Great Britain a return in respect of an alteration in any of those particulars which gives the branch numbers of two or more such branches shall be treated as a return in respect of each branch whose number is given), but

(b) an alteration in the company's charter, statutes or memorandum and articles (or other instrument constituting or defining its constitution) shall only be treated as relating to a branch if the document altered is included in the material registered in respect of it.

**8(1)** Sub-paragraph (2) below applies where–

(a) a company's return under paragraph 1(1) includes a statement to the effect mentioned in paragraph 1(3)(b), and

(b) the statement ceases to be true so far as concerns the documents specified in paragraph 5.

**8(2)** The company shall, within the time specified below, deliver to the registrar of companies for registration in respect of the branch to which the return relates–

(a) the documents specified in paragraph 5, or

(b) a return in the prescribed form–

(i) containing a statement to the effect that those documents are included in the material which is registered in respect of another branch of the company in the United Kingdom, and

(ii) stating where the other branch is registered and what is its registered number.

**Note**

See the Companies (Forms) (Amendment) Regulations 1992 (SI 1992/3006).

**8(3)** The time for complying with sub-paragraph (2) above is 21 days after the date on which notice of the fact that the statement in the earlier return has ceased to be true could have been received in Great Britain in due course of post (if despatched with due diligence).

**8(4)** Sub-paragraph (2) above shall also apply where, after a company has made a return under sub-paragraph (2)(b) above, the statement to the effect mentioned in sub-paragraph (2)(b)(i) ceases to be true.

**8(5)** For the purposes of sub-paragraph (2)(b), where the company has more than one branch in a part of Great Britain a return which gives the branch numbers of two or more such branches shall be treated as a return in respect of each branch whose number is given.

**History**

Sch. 21A inserted by the Oversea Companies and Credit and Financial Institutions (Branch Disclosure) Regulations 1992 (SI 1992/3179), reg. 1(3), 3(1) and Sch. 2, para. 3 as from 1 January 1993, subject to transitional provisions (see reg. 5 and Sch. 4).

# Schedule 21B – Change in Registration Regime: Transitional Provisions

Section 692A

**1(1)** This paragraph applies where a company which becomes a company to which section 690A applies was, immediately before becoming such a company (referred to in this paragraph as the relevant time), a company to which section 691 applies.

**1(2)** The company need not include the particulars specified in paragraph 2(1)(d) of Schedule 21A in the first return to be delivered under paragraph 1(1) of that Schedule to the registrar for a part of Great Britain if at the relevant time–

(a) it had an established place of business in that part,

(b) it had complied with its obligations under section 691(1)(b)(i), and

(c) it had no outstanding obligation to make a return to the registrar for that part under subsection (1) of section 692, so far as concerns any alteration of the kind mentioned in subsection (1)(b) of that section,

and if it states in the return that the particulars have been previously filed in respect of a place of business of the company in that part, giving the company's registered number.

**1(3)** The company shall not be required to deliver the documents mentioned in paragraph 5 of Schedule 21A with the first return to be delivered under paragraph 1(1) of that Schedule to the registrar for a part of Great Britain if at the relevant time–

(a) it had an established place of business in that part,

(b) it had delivered the documents mentioned in section 691(1)(a) to the registrar for that part, and

(c) it had no outstanding obligation to make a return to that registrar under subsection (1) of section 692, so far as concerns any alteration in any of the documents mentioned in paragraph (a) of that subsection,

and if it states in the return that the documents have been previously filed in respect of a place of business of the company in that part, giving the company's registered number.

**2(1)** This paragraph applies where a company which becomes a company to which section 691 applies was, immediately before becoming such a company (referred to in this paragraph as the relevant time), a company to which section 690A applies.

**2(2)** The company shall not be required to deliver the documents mentioned in section 691(1)(a) to the registrar for a part of Great Britain if at the relevant time–

(a) it had a branch in that part,

(b) the documents mentioned in paragraph 5 of Schedule 21A were included in the material registered in respect of the branch, and

(c) it had no outstanding obligation to make a return to the registrar for that part under paragraph 7 of that Schedule, so far as concerns any alteration in any of the documents mentioned in sub-paragraph (1)(a) of that paragraph,

and if it states in the return that the documents have been previously filed in respect of a branch of the company, giving the branch's registered number.

**2(3)** The company need not include the particulars mentioned in section 691(1)(b)(i) in the return to be delivered under section 691(1)(b) to the registrar for a part of Great Britain if at the relevant time–

(a) it had a branch in that part,

(b) it had complied with its obligations under paragraph 1(1)(a) of Schedule 21A in respect of the branch so far as the particulars required by paragraph 2(1)(d) of that Schedule are concerned, and

(c) it had no outstanding obligation to make a return to the registrar for that part under paragraph 7 of that Schedule, so far as concerns any alteration in any of the particulars required by paragraph 2(1)(d) of that Schedule,

and if it states in the return that the particulars have been previously filed in respect of a branch of the company, giving the branch's registered number.

**2(4)** Where sub-paragraph (3) above applies, the reference in section 692(1)(b) to the list of the directors and secretary shall be construed as a reference to the list contained in the return under paragraph 1(1) of Schedule 21A with any alterations in respect of which a return under paragraph 7(1) of that Schedule has been made.

**History**
Sch. 21B inserted by the Oversea Companies and Credit and Financial Institutions (Branch Disclosure) Regulations 1992 (SI 1992/3179), reg. 1(3), 3(1) and Sch. 2, para. 5 as from 1 January 1993.

# Schedule 21C – Delivery of Reports and Accounts: Credit and Financial Institutions to which the Bank Branches Directive (89/117/EEC) Applies

Section 699A

## Part I – Institutions Required to Prepare Accounts under Parent Law

### SCOPE OF PART AND INTERPRETATION

**1(1)** This Part of this Schedule applies to any institution to which section 699A applies which is required by its parent law to prepare and have audited accounts for its financial periods and whose only or principal branch within the United Kingdom is in Great Britain.

**1(2)** In this Part of this Schedule, **"branch"** has the meaning given by section 699A.

### DUTY TO DELIVER COPIES IN GREAT BRITAIN

**2(1)** An institution to which this Part of this Schedule applies shall, within one month of becoming such an institution, deliver to the registrar for registration–

(a) copies of the latest accounting documents of the institution prepared in accordance with its parent law to have been disclosed before the end of the period allowed for compliance with this sub-paragraph or, if earlier, the date of compliance with it, and

(b) If any of the documents mentioned in paragraph (a) above is not written in the English language, a translation of it into English certified in the prescribed manner to be a correct translation.

Where an institution to which this Part of this Schedule applies had, immediately prior to becoming such an institution, a branch in Northern Ireland which was its only or principal branch within the United Kingdom it may, instead of delivering the documents mentioned in sub-paragraph (1)(a) under that paragraph, deliver thereunder a notice that it has become an institution to which this Part of this Schedule applies, provided that those documents have been delivered to the registrar for Northern Ireland pursuant to the Companies (Northern Ireland) Order 1986.

**Note**
See note after para. 12(2).

**3(1)** An institution to which this Part of this Schedule applies shall deliver to the registrar for registration–

(a) copies of all the accounting documents of the institution prepared in accordance with its parent law which are disclosed on or after the end of the period allowed for compliance with paragraph 2(1) or, if earlier, the date on which it complies with that paragraph, and

(b) if any of the documents mentioned in paragraph (a) above is not written in the English language, a translation of it into English, certified in the prescribed manner to be a correct translation.

**Note**
See note after para. 12(2).

**3(2)** The period allowed for delivery, in relation to a document required to be delivered under this paragraph, is 3 months from the date on which the document is first disclosed.

**4** Where an institution's parent law permits it to discharge an obligation with respect to the disclosure of accounting documents by disclosing documents in a modified form, it may discharge its obligation under paragraph 2 or 3 by delivering copies of documents modified as permitted by that law.

**5(1)** Neither paragraph 2 nor paragraph 3 shall require an institution to deliver documents to the registrar if at the end of the period allowed for compliance with that paragraph–

(a) it is not required by its parent law to register them,

(b) they are made available for inspection at each branch of the institution in Great Britain, and

(c) copies of them are available on request at a cost not exceeding the cost of supplying them.

**5(2)** Where by virtue of sub-paragraph (1) above an institution is not required to deliver documents under paragraph 2 or 3 and any of the conditions specified in that sub-paragraph ceases to be met, the institution shall deliver the documents to the registrar for registration within 7 days of the condition ceasing to be met.

### REGISTRAR TO WHOM DOCUMENTS TO BE DELIVERED

**6** The documents which an institution is required to deliver to the registrar under this Part of this Schedule shall be delivered–

(a) to the registrar for England and Wales if the institution's only branch, or (if it has more than one) its principal branch within the United Kingdom, is in England and Wales; or

(b) to the registrar for Scotland if the institution's only branch, or (if it has more than one) its principal branch within the United Kingdom, is in Scotland.

### PENALTY FOR NON-COMPLIANCE

**7(1)** If an institution fails to comply with paragraph 2, 3 or 5(2) before the end of the period allowed for compliance, the institution and every person who immediately before the end of that period was a director of the institution, or, in the case of an institution which does not have directors, a person occupying an equivalent office, is guilty of an offence and liable to a fine and, for continued contravention, to a daily default fine.

**7(2)** It is a defence for a person charged with an offence under this paragraph to prove that he took all reasonable steps for securing compliance with paragraph 2, 3 or 5(2), as the case may be.

### INTERPRETATION

**8(1)** In this Part of this Schedule–

**"financial period"** in relation to an institution, means a period for which the institution is required or permitted by its parent law to prepare accounts;

**"parent law"**, in relation to an institution, means the law of the country in which the institution has its head office;

and references to disclosure are to public disclosure, except where an institution is not required under its parent law, any enactment (including any subordinate legislation within the meaning of section 21 of the Interpretation Act 1978) having effect for Great Britain or its constitution to publicly disclose its accounts, in which case such references are to the disclosure of the accounts to the persons for whose information they have been prepared.

**8(2)** For the purposes of this Part of this Schedule, the following are accounting documents in relation to a financial period of an institution–

(a) the accounts of the institution for the period, including, if it has one or more subsidiaries, any consolidated accounts of the group,

(b) any annual report of the directors (or, in the case of an institution which does not have directors, the persons occupying equivalent offices) for the period,

(c) the report of the auditors on the accounts mentioned in paragraph (a) above, and

(d) any report of the auditors on the report mentioned in paragraph (b) above.

# Part II – Institutions not Required to Prepare Accounts under Parent Law

### SCOPE OF PART AND INTERPRETATION

**9(1)** This Part of this Schedule applies to any institution to which section 699A applies which–

(a) is incorporated, and

(b) is not required by the law of the country in which it has its head office to prepare and have audited accounts.

**9(2)** In this Part of this Schedule, **"branch"** has the meaning given by section 699A.

## PREPARATION OF ACCOUNTS AND REPORTS

**10** An institution to which this Part of this Schedule applies shall in respect of each financial year of the institution prepare the like accounts and directors' report, and cause to be prepared such an auditors' report, as would be required if the institution were a company to which section 700 applied.

**11** Sections 223 to 225 apply to an institution to which this Part of this Schedule applies subject to the following modifications–

(a) for the references to the incorporation of the company there shall be substituted references to the institution becoming an institution to which this Part of this Schedule applies; and

(b) section 225(4) shall be omitted.

## DUTY TO DELIVER ACCOUNTS AND REPORTS

**12(1)** An institution to which this Part of this Schedule applies shall in respect of each financial year of the institution deliver to the registrar copies of the accounts and reports prepared in accordance with paragraph 10.

**12(2)** If any document comprised in those accounts or reports is in a language other than English, the institution shall annex to the copy delivered a translation of it into English, certified in the prescribed manner to be a correct translation.

**Note**

For certification as a correct translation see the Companies (Forms) (Amendment) Regulations 1992 (SI 1992/3006), reg. 3.

## TIME FOR DELIVERY

**13(1)** The period allowed for delivering accounts and reports under paragraph 12 above is 13 months after the end of the relevant accounting reference period, subject to the following provisions of this paragraph.

**13(2)** If the relevant accounting reference period is the institution's first and is a period of more than 12 months, the period allowed is 13 months from the first anniversary of the institution's becoming an institution to which this Part of this Schedule applies.

**13(3)** If the relevant accounting reference period is treated as shortened by virtue of a notice given by the institution under section 225, the period allowed is that applicable in accordance with the above provisions or 3 months from the date of the notice under that section, whichever last expires.

**13(4)** If for any special reason the Secretary of State thinks fit he may, on an application made before the expiry of the period otherwise allowed, by notice in writing to an institution to which this Part of this Schedule applies, extend that period by such further period as may be specified in the notice.

**13(5)** In this paragraph **"the relevant accounting reference period"** means the accounting reference period by reference to which the financial year for the accounts in question was determined.

## REGISTRAR TO WHOM DOCUMENTS TO BE DELIVERED

**14** The documents which an institution is required to deliver to the registrar under this Part of the Schedule shall be delivered–

(a) to the registrar for England and Wales if the institution's only branch, or (if it has more than one) its principal branch within Great Britain, is in England and Wales; or

(b) to the registrar for Scotland if the institution's only branch, or (if it has more than one) its principal branch within Great Britain, is in Scotland.

### PENALTY FOR NON-COMPLIANCE

**15(1)** If the requirements of paragraph 12 are not complied with before the end of the period allowed for delivering accounts and reports, or if the accounts and reports delivered do not comply with the requirements of this Act, the institution and every person who immediately before the end of that period was a director of the institution, or, in the case of an institution which does not have directors, a person occupying an equivalent office, is guilty of an offence and liable to a fine and, for continued contravention, to a daily default fine.

**15(2)** It is a defence for a person charged with such an offence to prove that he took all reasonable steps for securing that the requirements in question would be complied with.

**15(3)** It is not a defence in relation to a failure to deliver copies to the registrar to prove that the documents in question were not in fact prepared as required by this Schedule.

**History**
Sch. 21C inserted by the Oversea Companies and Credit and Financial Institutions (Branch Disclosure) Regulations 1992 (SI 1992/3179), reg. 1(3), 2(2) and Sch. 1 as from 1 January 1993, subject to transitional provisions (see reg. 5 and Sch. 4).

# Schedule 21D – Delivery of Reports and Accounts: Companies to which the Eleventh Company Law Directive Applies

Section 699AA

## Part I – Companies Required to Make Disclosure under Parent Law

### SCOPE OF PART

**1** This Part of this Schedule applies to any company to which section 699AA applies which is required by its parent law to prepare, have audited and disclose accounts.

### DUTY TO DELIVER COPIES IN GREAT BRITAIN

**2(1)** This paragraph applies in respect of each branch which a company to which this Part of this Schedule applies has in Great Britain.

**2(2)** The company shall deliver to the registrar for registration in respect of the branch copies of all the accounting documents prepared in relation to a financial period of the company which are disclosed in accordance with its parent law on or after the end of the period allowed for compliance in respect of the branch with paragraph 1 of Schedule 21A or, if earlier, the date on which the company complies with that paragraph in respect of the branch.

**2(3)** Where the company's parent law permits it to discharge its obligation with respect to the disclosure of accounting documents by disclosing documents in a modified form, it may discharge its obligation under sub-paragaph (2) above by delivering copies of documents modified as permitted by that law.

**2(4)** If any document, a copy of which is delivered under sub-paragraph (2) above, is in a language other than English, the company shall annex to the copy delivered a translation of it into English, certified in the prescribed manner to be a correct translation.

**Note**
See note after para. 10(2).

**3** Paragraph 2 above shall not require documents to be delivered in respect of a branch if–

(a) before the end of the period allowed for compliance with that paragraph, they are delivered in respect of another branch in the United Kingdom, and

(b) the particulars registered under Schedule 21A in respect of the branch indicate an intention that they are to be registered in respect of that other branch and include the details of that other branch mentioned in paragraph 4(b) of that Schedule.

### TIME FOR DELIVERY

**4** The period allowed for delivery, in relation to a document required to be delivered under paragraph 2, is 3 months from the date on which the document is first disclosed in accordance with the company's parent law.

### PENALTY FOR NON-COMPLIANCE

**5(1)** If a company fails to comply with paragraph 2 before the end of the period allowed for compliance, it, and every person who immediately before the end of that period was a director of it, is guilty of an offence and liable to a fine and, for continued contravention, to a daily default fine.

**5(2)** It is a defence for a person charged with an offence under this paragraph to prove that he took all reasonable steps for securing compliance with paragraph 2.

### INTERPRETATION

**6(1)** In this Part of this Schedule–

**"financial period"** in relation to a company, means a period for which the company is required or permitted by its parent law to prepare accounts;

**"parent law"**, in relation to a company, means the law of the country in which the company is incorporated;

and references to disclosure are to public disclosure.

**6(2)** For the purposes of this Part of this Schedule, the following are accounting documents in relation to a financial period of a company–

(a) the accounts of the company for the period, including, if it has one or more subsidiaries, any consolidated accounts of the group,

(b) any annual report of the directors for the period,

(c) the report of the auditors on the accounts mentioned in paragraph (a) above, and

(d) any report of the auditors on the report mentioned in paragraph (b) above.

## Part II – Companies not Required to make Disclosure under Parent Law

### SCOPE OF PART

**7** This Part of this Schedule applies to any company to which section 699AA applies which is not required by the law of the country in which it is incorporated to prepare, have audited and publicly disclose accounts.

### PREPARATION OF ACCOUNTS AND REPORTS

**8** A company to which this Part of this Schedule applies shall in respect of each financial year of the company prepare the like accounts and directors' report, and cause to be prepared such an auditors' report, as would be required if the company were a company to which section 700 applied.

**9** Sections 223 to 225 apply to a company to which this Part of this Schedule applies subject to the following modifications–

(a) for the references to the incorporation of the company there shall be substituted references to the company becoming a company to which this Part of this Schedule applies, and

(b) section 225(4) shall be omitted.

### DUTY TO DELIVER ACCOUNTS AND REPORTS

**10(1)** A company to which this Part of this Schedule applies shall in respect of each financial year of the company deliver to the registrar copies of the accounts and reports prepared in accordance with paragraph 8.

**10(2)** If any document comprised in those accounts or reports is in a language other than English, the company shall annex to the copy delivered a translation of it into English, certified in the prescribed manner to be a correct translation.

**Note**
For certification as a correct translation see the Companies (Forms) (Amendment) Regulations 1992 (SI 1992/3006), reg. 3.

**10(3)** A company required to deliver documents under this paragraph in respect of a financial year shall deliver them in respect of each branch which it has in Great Britain at the end of that year.

**10(4)** Sub-paragraph (3) above is without prejudice to section 695A(3).

**11** Paragraph 10 shall not require documents to be delivered in respect of a branch if–

(a) before the end of the period allowed for compliance with that paragraph, they are delivered in respect of another branch in the United Kingdom, and

(b) the particulars registered under paragraph 1 of Schedule 21A in respect of the branch indicate an intention that they are to be registered in respect of that other branch and include the details of that other branch mentioned in paragraph 4(b) of that Schedule.

## TIME FOR DELIVERY

**12(1)** The period allowed for delivering accounts and reports under paragraph 10 is 13 months after the end of the relevant accounting reference period, subject to the following provisions of this paragraph.

**12(2)** If the relevant accounting reference period is the company's first and is a period of more than 12 months, the period allowed is 13 months from the first anniversary of the company's becoming a company to which this Part of this Schedule applies.

**12(3)** If the relevant accounting reference period is treated as shortened by virtue of a notice given by the company under section 225, the period allowed is that applicable in accordance with the above provisions or 3 months from the date of the notice under that section, whichever last expires.

**12(4)** If for any special reason the Secretary of State thinks fit he may, on an application made before the expiry of the period otherwise allowed, by notice in writing to a company to which this Part of this Schedule applies extend that period by such further period as may be specified in the notice.

**12(5)** In this paragraph **"the relevant accounting reference period"** means the accounting reference period by reference to which the financial year for the accounts in question was determined.

## PENALTY FOR NON-COMPLIANCE

**13(1)** If the requirements of paragraph 10 are not complied with before the end of the period allowed for delivering accounts and reports, or if the accounts and reports delivered do not comply with the requirements of this Act, the company and every person who immediately before the end of that period was a director of the company is guilty of an offence and liable to a fine and, for continued contravention, to a daily default fine.

**13(2)** It is a defence for a person charged with such an offence to prove that he took all reasonable steps for securing that the requirements in question would be complied with.

**13(3)** It is not a defence in relation to a failure to deliver copies to the registrar to prove that the documents in question were not in fact prepared as required by this Act.

**History**
Sch. 21D inserted by the Oversea Companies and Credit and Financial Institutions (Branch Disclosure) Regulations 1992 (SI 1992/3179), reg. 1(3), 3(1) and Sch. 2, para. 18 as from 1 January 1993.

# Schedule 22 — Provisions of this Act applying to Unregistered Companies

Section 718

| Provisions of this Act applied | Subject matter | Limitations and exceptions (if any) |
|---|---|---|
| In Part I — | | |
| section 18 ... ... ... ... ... | Statutory and other amendments of memorandum and articles to be registered. | Subject to section 718(3). |
| section 35 ... ... ... ... ... | Company's capacity; power of directors to bind it. | Subject to section 718(3). |
| section 36 ... ... ... ... ... | Company contracts. | Subject to section 718(3). |
| section 36A and 36B ... ... ... ... | Execution of documents. | Subject to section 718(3). |
| section 36C ... ... ... ... ... | Pre-incorporation contracts, deeds and obligations. | Subject to section 718(3). |
| section 40 ... ... ... ... ... | Official seal for share certificates, etc. | Subject to section 718(3). |
| section 42 ... ... ... ... ... | Events affecting a company's status to be officially notified. | Subject to section 718(3). |
| In Part IV, sections 82, 86 and 87 ... ... | Allotments. | Subject to section 718(3). |
| In Part V — | | |
| section 185(4) ... ... ... ... ... | Exemption from duty to prepare certificates where shares etc. issued to clearing house or nominee. | Subject to section 718(3). |
| section 186 ... ... ... ... ... | Certificate as evidence of title. | Subject to section 718(3). |
| Part VII, with — Schedules 4 to 9 ... ... ... ...; Schedule 9A and ... ... ... ...; Schedule 10 and 10A ... ... ... ... | Accounts and audit. | Subject to section 718(3). |
| In Part IX — | | |
| section 287 ... ... ... ... ... | Registered office. | Subject to section 718(3). |
| sections 288 to 290 ... ... ... ... | Register of directors and secretaries. | — |
| In Part X — | | |
| section 322A ... ... ... ... ... | Invalidity of certain transactions involving directors, etc. | Subject to section 718(3). |

| Provisions of this Act applied | Subject matter | Limitations and exceptions (if any) |
|---|---|---|
| sections 343 to 347 ... ... ... ... | Register to be kept of certain transactions not disclosed in accounts; other related matters. | Subject to section 718(3). |
| In Part XI — | | |
| section 351(1), (2) and (5)(a) ... ... ... | Particulars of company to be given in correspondence. | Subject to section 718(3). |
| sections 363 to 365 ... ... ... ... | Annual return. | Subject to section 718(3). |
| sections 384 to 394A ... ... ... ... | Appointment, etc., of auditors. | Subject to section 718(3). |
| Part XIV (except section 446) ... ... ... | Investigation of companies and their affairs; requisition of documents. | — |
| Part XV ... ... ... ... ... ... | Effect of order imposing restrictions on shares. | To apply so far only as relates to orders under section 445. |
| Part XVI ... ... ... ... ... ... | Fraudulent trading by a company. | — |
| In Part XXIV — | | |
| sections 706 to 710A, 713 and 715A ... ... | Miscellaneous provisions about registration. | — |
| section 711 ... ... ... ... ... | Public notice by registrar of companies with respect to certain documents. | Subject to section 718(3). |
| In Part XXV — | | |
| section 720 ... ... ... ... ... | Companies to publish periodical statement. | Subject to section 718(3). |
| section 721 ... ... ... ... ... | Production and inspection of company's books. | |
| section 722 ... ... ... ... ... | Form of company registers, etc. | To apply so far only as these provisions have effect in relation to provisions applying by virtue of the foregoing provisions of this Schedule. |
| section 723 ... ... ... ... ... | Use of computers for company records. | |
| section 723A ... ... ... ... ... | Rights of inspection and related matters. | |
| section 725 ... ... ... ... ... | Service of documents. | |
| section 730, with Schedule 24 ... ... ... | Punishment of offences; meaning of "officer in default". | |
| section 731 ... ... ... ... ... | Summary proceedings. | |
| section 732 ... ... ... ... ... | Prosecution by public authorities. | |

| Provisions of this Act applied | Subject matter | Limitations and exceptions (if any) |
|---|---|---|
| Part XXVI ... ... ... ... ... | Interpretation. | To apply so far as requisite for the interpretation of other provisions applied by section 718 and this Schedule. |

**History**
In Sch. 22 entry relating to Pt. III repealed by Financial Services Act 1986, s. 212(3) and Sch. 17, Pt. I and takes effect as follows:

- as from 12 January 1987 re any investment listed or the subject of a listing application under Financial Services Act 1986, Pt. IV for all purposes relating to the admission of securities offered by or on behalf of a Minister of the Crown or a body corporate controlled by a Minister of the Crown or a subsidiary of such a body corporate to the Official List in respect of which an application is made after that date (see SI 1986/2246 (C. 88));
- as from 16 February 1987 re any investment listed or the subject of a listing application under Financial Services Act 1986, Pt. IV for purposes relating to the admission of securities in respect of which an application is made after that date other than those referred to in the preceding paragraph and other wise for all purposes (see SI 1986/2246 (C. 88));
- as from 29 April 1988 as far as the entry would apply to a prospectus offering for subscription, or to any form of application for units in a body corporate which is a recognised scheme (see SI 1988/740 (C. 22));
- as from 19 June 1995 for all remaining purposes except CA 1985, s. 58, 59, 60, in so far as the entry is necessary for the purposes of CA 1985, s. 81, 83, 246, 248, 744; and CA 1985, Sch. 3, para. 2, in so far as it is necessary for the purposes of CA 1985, s. 83(1)(a); and CA 1985, s. 62, in so far as it is necessary for the purposes of CA 1985, s. 744 (see SI 1995/1538 (C. 33)).

The entry relating to Pt. III formerly read as follows:

| Provisions of this Act applied | Subject matter | Limitations and exceptions (if any) |
|---|---|---|
| "In Part III, Chapter I (with Schedule 3) | Prospectus and requirements in connection with it. | Subject to section 718(3)" |

In the second column of the entry in Sch. 22 relating to s. 185(4) the words "clearing house or" substituted for the former words "stock exchange" by Financial Services Act 1986, s. 212(2) and Sch. 16, para. 26 as from 29 April 1988 (see SI 1988/740 (C. 22)).
In Sch. 22 in the entry relating to Pt. VII, in column 1 the words "Schedule 4 to 9" and "Schedule 9A" substituted for the former words "Schedules 4 to 8" and "Schedule 9" respectively by the Companies Act 1985 (Bank Accounts) Regulations 1991 (SI 1991/2705), reg. 7 and Sch. 7, para. 2 as from 2 December 1991 (subject to transitional provisions in reg. 9); the words "(except sub-paragraphs (a) to (d) of paragraph 2, sub-paragraphs (c), (d) and (e) of paragraph 3 and sub-paragraph (1)(c) of paragraph 10)" formerly appearing after "Schedule 9A" omitted by the Companies Act 1985 (Insurance Companies Accounts) Regulations 1993 (SI 1993/3246), reg. 1, 5, Sch. 2, para. 9 as from 19 December 1993 subject to exemption in reg. 6 and transitional provisions in reg. 7 and the words "Schedules 10 and 10A" substituted for the former word "Schedule 10" by CA 1989, s. 23 and Sch. 10, para. 23 as from 1 April 1990 subject to transitional and saving provisions (see SI 1990/355 (C. 13), art. 3, Sch. 1 and also art. 6–9).
In Sch. 22 in the entry relating to Pt. X the reference to s. 322A inserted by CA 1989, s. 109(2) as from 4 February 1991 subject to transitional and saving provisions (see SI 1990/2569 (C. 68), art. 4(a), 7).
In Sch. 22 in the entry relating to Pt. XI, sections 384 to 394A in column 1 "394A" substituted for the former "393" and in column 2 the word "qualifications" formerly appearing after "Appointment" repealed by CA 1989, s. 123(5), 212 and Sch. 24 as from 1 April 1990 subject to transitional and saving provisions (see SI 1990/355 (C. 13), art. 4(a), 5(1)(b), (2) and also art. 6–10).
In Sch. 22 the entry relating to Pt. XIV substituted by CA 1989, s. 71 as from 21 February 1990 (see SI 1990/142 (C. 5), art. 4); the entry formerly read as follows:

| Provisions of this Act applied | Subject matter | Limitations and exceptions (if any) |
|---|---|---|
| "In Part XIV, sections 431 to 445 and 452(1) | Investigation of companies and their affairs. | —" |

In Sch. 22 the entry relating to Pt. XVI inserted by CA 1989, s. 145 and Sch. 19, para. 21 as from 1 March 1990 (see SI 1990/142 (C. 5), art. 5).
In Sch. 22 entries relating to s. 36, 36A, 36B and 36C inserted by CA 1989, s. 130(5) and former entry relating to s. 36(4) repealed by CA 1989, s. 212 and Sch. 24 as from 31 July 1990 (see SI 1990/1392 (C. 41), art. 2(b), 4(b)(i)); the former s. 36(4) entry read as follows:

| Provisions of this Act applied | Subject matter | Limitations and exceptions (if any) |
|---|---|---|
| "section 36(4) | Binding effect of contract made for company before its formation. | Subject to section 718(3)". |

In Sch. 22 in the entry relating to s. 363–365 the words "(with Schedule 15)" formerly appearing after "363" repealed by CA 1989, s. 212 and Sch. 24 as from 1 October 1990 subject to transitional and saving provisions (see SI 1990/1707 (C. 46), art. 3(a) and also art. 4, 5).
In Sch. 22 first entry in Pt. XXIV substituted by CA 1989, s. 127(7) as from 1 July 1991 (see SI 1991/488 (C. 11), art. 2(1)) — from 7 January 1991 until 1 July 1991 the resulting wording was "sections 706, 707, 708 to 710, 712, 713 and 715A" (see SI 1991/2569 (C. 68) art. 4(b)); the original wording was "sections 706, 708 to 710, 712 and 713".
In Sch. 22 the entry under Pt. XXV relating to s. 723A inserted by CA 1989, s. 143(11) as from 1 November 1991 (see SI 1991/1996 (C. 57), art. 2(2)(b)).

**Note**
Entry in Sch. 22 relating to Pt. IV repealed by Financial Services Act 1986, s. 212(3) and Sch. 17 to the extent to which those entries would apply re any investment listed or the subject of a listing application under Financial Services Act 1986, Pt. IV and commencing:

- on 12 January 1987 for all purposes relating to the admission of securities offered by or on behalf of a Minister of the Crown or a body corporate controlled by a Minister of the Crown or a subsidiary of such a body corporate to the Official List in respect of which an application is made after that date;

- on 16 February 1987 for purposes relating to the admission of securities in respect of which an applciation is made after that date other than those referred to in the preceding paragraph and otherwise for all purposes.

(See SI 1986/2246 (C. 88).)

The same entry repealed by Financial Services Act 1986, s. 212(3) and Sch. 17 as from 29 April 1988 as far as they would apply to a prospectus offering for subscription, or to any form of application for units in a body corporate which is a recognised scheme (see SI 1988/740 (C. 22)).

# Schedule 23 — Form of Statement to be Published by Certain Companies Under Section 720

Section 720

* The share capital of the company is , divided into shares of each.

The number of shares issued is

Calls to the amount of pounds per share have been made, under which the sum of pounds has been received.

The liabilities of the company on the first day of January (*or* July) were —

Debts owing to sundry persons by the company.

On judgment (in Scotland, in respect of which decree has been granted), £
On specialty, £
On notes or bills, £
On simple contracts, £
On estimated liabilities, £

The assets of the company on that day were —

Government securities [*stating them*]
Bills of exchange and promissory notes, £
Cash at the bankers, £
Other securities, £

---

* If the company has no share capital the portion of the statement relating to capital and shares must be omitted.

# Schedule 24 — Punishment of Offences Under this Act

Section 730

*Note:* In the fourth and fifth columns of this Schedule, **"the statutory maximum"** means —

(a) in England and Wales, the prescribed sum under section 32 of the Magistrates' Courts Act 1980 (c. 43), and

(b) in Scotland, the prescribed sum under section 289B of the Criminal Procedure (Scotland) Act 1975 (c. 21).

| Section of Act creating offence | General nature of offence | Mode of prosecution | Punishment | Daily default fine (where applicable) |
|---|---|---|---|---|
| 6(3) ... ... | Company failing to deliver to register notice or other document, following alteration of its objects. | Summary. | One-fifth of the statutory maximum. | One-fiftieth of the statutory maximum. |
| 18(3) ... ... | Company failing to register change in memorandum or articles. | Summary. | One-fifth of the statutory maximum. | One-fiftieth of the statutory maximum. |
| 19(2) ... ... | Company failing to send to one of its members a copy of the memorandum or articles, when so required by the member. | Summary. | One-fifth of the statutory maximum. | |
| 20(2) ... ... | Where company's memorandum altered, company issuing copy of the memorandum without the alteration. | Summary. | One-fifth of the statutory maximum for each occasion on which copies are so issued after the date of the alteration. | |
| 28(5) ... ... | Company failing to change name on direction of Secretary of State. | Summary. | One-fifth of the statutory maximum. | One-fiftieth of the statutory maximum. |
| 31(5) ... ... | Company altering its memorandum or articles, so ceasing to be exempt from having "limited" as part of its name. | Summary. | The statutory maximum. | One-tenth of the statutory maximum. |
| 31(6) ... ... | Company failing to change name, on Secretary of State's direction, so as to have "limited" (or Welsh equivalent) at the end. | Summary. | One-fifth of the statutory maximum. | One-fiftieth of the statutory maximum. |

| Section of Act creating offence | General nature of offence | Mode of prosecution | Punishment | Daily default fine (where applicable) |
|---|---|---|---|---|
| 32(4) ... ... | Company failing to comply with Secretary of State's direction to change its name, on grounds that the name is misleading. | Summary. | One-fifth of the statutory maximum. | One-fiftieth of the statutory maximum. |
| 33 ... ... | Trading under misleading name (use of "public limited company" or Welsh equivalent when not so entitled); purporting to be a private company. | Summary. | One-fifth of the statutory maximum. | One-fiftieth of the statutory maximum. |
| 34 ... ... | Trading or carrying on business with improper use of "limited" or "cyfyngedig". | Summary. | One-fifth of the statutory maximum. | One-fiftieth of the statutory maximum. |
| 54(10) ... ... | Public company failing to give notice, or copy of court order, to registrar, concerning application to re-register as private company. | Summary. | One-fifth of the statutory maximum. | One-fiftieth of the statutory maximum. |
| 80(9) ... ... | Directors exercising company's power of allotment without the authority required by section 80(1). | 1. On indictment.<br>2. Summary. | A fine.<br>The statutory maximum. | |
| 81(2) ... ... | Private limited company offering shares to the public, or allotting shares with a view to their being so offered. | 1. On indictment.<br>2. Summary. | A fine.<br>The statutory maximum. | |
| 82(5) ... ... | Allotting shares or debentures before third day after issue of prospectus. | 1. On indictment.<br>2. Summary. | A fine.<br>The statutory maximum. | |
| 86(6) ... ... | Company failing to keep money in separate bank account, where received in pursuance of prospectus stating that stock exchange listing is to be applied for. | 1. On indictment.<br>2. Summary. | A fine.<br>The statutory maximum. | |
| 87(4) ... ... | Offeror of shares for sale failing to keep proceeds in separate bank account. | 1. On indictment.<br>2. Summary. | A fine.<br>The statutory maximum. | |
| 88(5) ... ... | Officer of company failing to deliver return of allotments, etc., to registrar. | 1. On indictment.<br>2. Summary. | A fine.<br>The statutory maximum. | One-tenth of the statutory maximum. |



CCH.New Law
bbcl ca 1985d Mp 746—bcl24 170c

| Section of Act creating offence | General nature of offence | Mode of prosecution | Punishment | Daily default fine (where applicable) |
|---|---|---|---|---|
| 95(6) … … | Knowingly or recklessly authorising or permitting misleading, false or deceptive material in statement by directors under section 95(5). | 1. On indictment.<br>2. Summary. | 2 years or a fine; or both.<br>6 months or the statutory maximum; or both. | |
| 97(4) … … | Company failing to deliver to registrar the prescribed form disclosing amount or rate of share commission. | Summary. | One-fifth of the statutory maximum. | |
| 110(2) … … | Making misleading, false or deceptive statement in connection with valuation under section 103 or 104. | 1. On indictment.<br>2. Summary. | 2 years or a fine; or both.<br>6 months or the statutory maximum; or both. | |
| 111(3) … … | Officer of company failing to deliver copy of asset valuation report to registrar. | 1. On indictment.<br>2. Summary. | A fine.<br>The statutory maximum. | One-tenth of the statutory maximum. |
| 111(4) … … | Company failing to deliver to registrar copy of resolution under section 104(4), with respect to transfer of an asset as consideration for allotment. | Summary. | One-fifth of the statutory maximum. | One-fiftieth of the statutory maximum. |
| 114 … … | Contravention of any of the provisions of sections 99 to 104, 106. | 1. On indictment.<br>2. Summary. | A fine.<br>The statutory maximum. | |
| 117(7) … … | Company doing business or exercising borrowing powers contrary to section 117. | 1. On indictment.<br>2. Summary. | A fine.<br>The statutory maximum. | |
| 122(2) … … | Company failing to give notice to registrar of re-organisation of share capital. | Summary. | One-fifth of the statutory maximum. | One-fiftieth of the statutory maximum. |
| 123(4) … … | Company failing to give notice to registrar of increase of share capital. | Summary. | One-fifth of the statutory maximum. | One-fiftieth of the statutory maximum. |
| 127(5) … … | Company failing to forward to registrar copy of court order, when application made to cancel resolution varying shareholders' rights. | Summary. | One-fifth of the statutory maximum. | One-fiftieth of the statutory maximum. |

| Section of Act creating offence | General nature of offence | Mode of prosecution | Punishment | Daily default fine (where applicable) |
|---|---|---|---|---|
| 128(5) … … | Company failing to send to registrar statement or notice required by section 128 (particulars of shares carrying special rights). | Summary. | One-fifth of the statutory maximum. | One-fiftieth of the statutory maximum. |
| 129(4) … … | Company failing to deliver to registrar statement or notice required by section 129 (registration of newly created class rights). | Summary. | One-fifth of the statutory maximum. | One-fiftieth of the statutory maximum. |
| 141 … … | Officer of company concealing name of creditor entitled to object to reduction of capital, or wilfully misrepresenting nature or amount of debt or claim, etc. | 1. On indictment.<br>2. Summary. | A fine.<br>The statutory maximum. | |
| 142(2) … … | Director authorising or permitting non-compliance with section 142 (requirement to convene company meeting to consider serious loss of capital). | 1. On indictment.<br>2. Summary. | A fine.<br>The statutory maximum. | |
| 143(2) … … | Company acquiring its own shares in breach of section 143. | 1. On indictment. | In the case of the company, a fine.<br>In the case of an officer of the company who is in default, 2 years or a fine; or both. | |
| | | 2. Summary. | In the case of the company, the statutory maximum.<br>In the case of an officer of the company who is in default, 6 months or the statutory maximum; or both. | |

| Section of Act creating offence | General nature of offence | Mode of prosecution | Punishment | Daily default fine (where applicable) |
|---|---|---|---|---|
| 149(2) ... ... | Company failing to cancel its own shares, acquired by itself, as required by section 146(2); or failing to apply for re-registration as private company as so required in the case there mentioned. | Summary. | One-fifth of the statutory maximum. | One-fiftieth of the statutory maximum. |
| 151(3) ... ... | Company giving financial assistance towards acquisition of its own shares. | 1. On indictment. | Where the company is convicted, a fine. Where an officer of the company is convicted, 2 years or a fine; or both. | |
| | | 2. Summary. | Where the company is convicted, the statutory maximum. Where an officer of the company is convicted, 6 months or the statutory maximum; or both. | |
| 156(6) ... ... | Company failing to register statutory declaration under section 155. | Summary. | The statutory maximum. | One-fiftieth of the statutory maximum. |
| 156(7) ... ... | Director making statutory declaration under section 155, without having reasonable grounds for opinion expressed in it. | 1. On indictment.<br>2. Summary. | 2 years or a fine; or both.<br>6 months or the statutory maximum; or both. | |
| 169(6) ... ... | Default by company's officer in delivering to registrar the return required by section 169 (disclosure by company of purchase of own shares). | 1. On indictment.<br>2. Summary. | A fine.<br>The statutory maximum. | One-tenth of the statutory maximum. |
| 169(7) ... ... | Company failing to keep copy of contract, etc., at registered office; refusal of inspection to person demanding it. | Summary. | One-fifth of the statutory maximum. | One-fiftieth of the statutory maximum. |

| Section of Act creating offence | General nature of offence | Mode of prosecution | Punishment | Daily default fine (where applicable) |
|---|---|---|---|---|
| 173(6) ... ... | Director making statutory declaration under section 173 without having reasonable grounds for the opinion expressed in the declaration. | 1. On indictment.<br>2. Summary. | 2 years or a fine; or both.<br>6 months or the statutory maximum; or both. | |
| 175(7) ... ... | Refusal of inspection of statutory declaration and auditors' report under section 173, etc. | Summary. | One-fifth of the statutory maximum. | One-fiftieth of the statutory maximum. |
| 176(4) ... ... | Company failing to give notice to registrar of application to court under section 176, or to register court order. | Summary. | One-fifth of the statutory maximum. | One-fiftieth of the statutory maximum. |
| 183(6) ... ... | Company failing to send notice of refusal to register a transfer of shares or debentures. | Summary. | One-fifth of the statutory maximum. | One-fiftieth of the statutory maximum. |
| 185(5) ... ... | Company default in compliance with section 185(1) (certificates to be made ready following allotment or transfer of shares, etc.). | Summary. | One-fifth of the statutory maximum. | One-fiftieth of the statutory maximum. |
| 189(1) ... ... | Offences of fraud and forgery in connection with share warrants in Scotland. | 1. On indictment.<br>2. Summary. | 7 years or a fine; or both.<br>6 months or the statutory maximum; or both. | |
| 189(2) ... ... | Unauthorised making of, or using or possessing apparatus for making, share warrants in Scotland. | 1. On indictment.<br>2. Summary. | 7 years or a fine; or both.<br>6 months or the statutory maximum; or both. | |
| 191(4) ... ... | Refusal of inspection or copy of register of debenture-holders, etc. | Summary. | One-fifth of the statutory maximum. | One-fiftieth of the statutory maximum. |
| 210(3) ... ... | Failure to discharge obligation of disclosure under Part VI; other forms of non-compliance with that Part. | 1. On indictment.<br>2. Summary. | 2 years or a fine; or both.<br>6 months or the statutory maximum; or both. | |
| 211(10) ... | Company failing to keep register of interests disclosed under Part VI; other contraventions of section 211. | Summary. | One-fifth of the statutory maximum. | One-fiftieth of the statutory maximum. |

| Section of Act creating offence | General nature of offence | Mode of prosecution | Punishment | Daily default fine (where applicable) |
|---|---|---|---|---|
| 214(5) … … | Company failing to exercise powers under section 212, when so required by the members. | 1. On indictment.<br>2. Summary. | A fine.<br>The statutory maximum. | |
| 215(8) … … | Company default in compliance with section 215 (company report of investigation of shareholdings on members' requisition). | 1. On indictment.<br>2. Summary. | A fine.<br>The statutory maximum. | |
| 216(3) … … | Failure to comply with company notice under section 212; making false statement in response, etc. | 1. On indictment.<br>2. Summary. | 2 years or a fine; or both.<br>6 months or the statutory maximum; or both. | |
| 217(7) … … | Company failing to notify a person that he has been named as a shareholder; on removal of name from register, failing to alter associated index. | Summary. | One-fifth of the statutory maximum. | One-fiftieth of the statutory maximum. |
| 218(3) … … | Improper removal of entry from register of interests disclosed; company failing to restore entry improperly removed. | Summary. | One-fifth of the statutory maximum. | For continued contravention of section 218(2) one-fiftieth of the statutory maximum. |
| 219(3) … … | Refusal of inspection of register or report under Part VI; failure to send copy when required. | Summary. | One-fifth of the statutory maximum. | One-fiftieth of the statutory maximum. |
| 221(5) or 222(4) … | Company failing to keep accounting records (liability of officers). | 1. On indictment.<br>2. Summary. | 2 years or a fine; or both<br>6 months or the statutory maximum; or both. | |
| 222(6) … … | Officer of company failing to secure compliance with, or intentionally causing default under section 222(5) (preservation of accounting records for requisite number of years). | 1. On indictment.<br>2. Summary. | 2 years or a fine; or both.<br>6 months or the statutory maximum; or both. | |

| Section of Act creating offence | General nature of offence | Mode of prosecution | Punishment | Daily default fine (where applicable) |
|---|---|---|---|---|
| 231(6) ... ... | Company failing to annex to its annual return certain particulars required by Schedule 5 and not included in annual accounts. | Summary. | One-fifth of the statutory maximum. | One-fiftieth of the statutory maximum. |
| 232(4) ... ... | Default by director or officer of a company in giving notice of matters relating to himself for purposes of Schedule 6 Part I. | Summary. | One-fifth of the statutory maximum. | |
| 233(5) ... ... | Approving defective accounts. | 1. On indictment.<br>2. Summary. | A fine.<br>The statutory maximum. | |
| 233(6) ... ... | Laying or delivering of unsigned balance sheet; circulating copies of balance sheet without signatures. | Summary. | One-fifth of the statutory maximum. | |
| 234(5) ... ... | Non-compliance with Part VII, as to directors' report and its content; directors individually liable. | 1. On indictment.<br>2. Summary. | A fine.<br>The statutory maximum. | |
| 234A(4) ... | Laying, circulating or delivering directors' report without required signature. | Summary. | One-fifth of the statutory maximum. | |
| 236(4) ... ... | Laying, circulating or delivering auditors' report without required signature. | Summary. | One-fifth of the statutory maximum. | |
| 238(5) ... ... | Failing to send company's annual accounts, directors' report and auditors' report to those entitled to receive them. | 1. On indictment.<br>2. Summary. | A fine.<br>The statutory maximum. | |
| 239(3) ... ... | Company failing to supply copy of accounts and reports to shareholder on his demand. | Summary. | One-fifth of the statutory maximum. | One-fiftieth of the statutory maximum. |
| 240(6) ... ... | Failure to comply with requirements in connection with publication of accounts. | Summary. | One-fifth of the statutory maximum. | |
| 241(2) or 242(2) ... | Director in default as regards duty to lay and deliver company's annual accounts, directors' report and auditors' report. | Summary. | The statutory maximum. | One-tenth of the statutory maximum. |

| Section of Act creating offence | General nature of offence | Mode of prosecution | Punishment | Daily default fine (where applicable) |
|---|---|---|---|---|
| 251(6) ... ... | Failure to comply with requirements in relation to summary financial statements. | Summary. | One-fifth of the statutory maximum. | |
| 288(4) ... ... | Default in complying with section 288 (keeping register of directors and secretaries, refusal of inspection). | Summary. | The statutory maximum. | One-tenth of the statutory maximum. |
| 291(5) ... ... | Acting as director of a company without having the requisite share qualification. | Summary. | One-fifth of the statutory maximum. | One-fiftieth of the statutory maximum. |
| 294(4) ... ... | Director failing to give notice of his attaining retirement age; acting as director under appointment invalid due to his attaining it. | Summary. | One-fifth of the statutory maximum. | One-fiftieth of the statutory maximum. |
| 305(3) ... ... | Company default in complying with section 305 (directors' names to appear on company correspondence, etc.). | Summary. | One-fifth of the statutory maximum. | |
| 306(4) ... ... | Failure to state that liability of proposed director or manager is unlimited; failure to give notice of that fact to person accepting office. | 1. On indictment.<br>2. Summary. | A fine.<br>The statutory maximum. | |
| 314(3) ... ... | Director failing to comply with section 314 (duty to disclose compensation payable on takeover, etc.); a person's failure to include required particulars in a notice he has to give of such matters. | Summary. | One-fifth of the statutory maximum. | |
| 317(7) ... ... | Director failing to disclose interest in contract. | 1. On indictment.<br>2. Summary. | A fine.<br>The statutory maximum. | |

| Section of Act creating offence | General nature of offence | Mode of prosecution | Punishment | Daily default fine (where applicable) |
|---|---|---|---|---|
| 318(8) … … | Company default in complying with section 318(1) or (5) (directors' service contracts to be open to inspection); 14 days' default in complying with section 318(4) (notice to registrar as to where copies of contracts and memoranda are kept); refusal of inspection required under section 318(7). | Summary. | One-fifth of the statutory maximum. | One-fiftieth of the statutory maximum. |
| 322B(4) … | Terms of unwritten contract between sole member of a private company limited by shares or by guarantee and the company not set out in a written memorandum or recorded in minutes of a directors' meeting. | Summary. | Level 5 on the standard scale. | |
| 323(2) … … | Director dealing in options to buy or sell company's listed shares or debentures. | 1. On indictment.<br>2. Summary. | 2 years or a fine; or both.<br>6 months or the statutory maximum; or both. | |
| 324(7) … … | Director failing to notify interest in company's shares; making false statement in purported notification. | 1. On indictment.<br>2. Summary. | 2 years or a fine; or both.<br>6 months or the statutory maximum; or both. | |
| 326(2), (3), (4), (5) … | Various defaults in connection with company register of directors' interests. | Summary. | One-fifth of the statutory maximum. | Except in the case of section 326(5), one-fiftieth of the statutory maximum. |
| 328(6) … … | Director failing to notify company that members of his family have, or have exercised, options to buy shares or debentures; making false statement in purported notification. | 1. On indictment.<br>2. Summary. | 2 years or a fine; or both.<br>6 months or the statutory maximum; or both. | |
| 329(3) … … | Company failing to notify investment exchange of acquisition of its securities by a director. | Summary. | One-fifth of the statutory maximum. | One-fiftieth of the statutory maximum. |

| Section of Act creating offence | General nature of offence | Mode of prosecution | Punishment | Daily default fine (where applicable) |
|---|---|---|---|---|
| 342(1) … … | Director of relevant company authorising or permitting company to enter into transaction or arrangement, knowing or suspecting it to contravene section 330. | 1. On indictment.<br>2. Summary. | 2 years or a fine; or both.<br>6 months or the statutory maximum; or both. | |
| 342(2) … … | Relevant company entering into transaction or arrangement for a director in contravention of section 330. | 1. On indictment.<br>2. Summary. | 2 years or a fine; or both.<br>6 months or the statutory maximum; or both. | |
| 342(3) … … | Procuring a relevant company to enter into transaction or arrangement known to be contrary to section 330. | 1. On indictment.<br>2. Summary. | 2 years or a fine; or both.<br>6 months or the statutory maximum; or both. | |
| 343(8) … … | Company failing to maintain register of transactions, etc., made with and for directors and not disclosed in company accounts; failing to make register available at registered office or at company meeting. | 1. On indictment.<br>2. Summary. | A fine.<br>The statutory maximum. | |
| 348(2) … … | Company failing to paint or affix name; failing to keep it painted or affixed. | Summary. | One-fifth of the statutory maximum. | In the case of failure to keep the name painted or affixed, one-fiftieth of the statutory maximum. |
| 349(2) … … | Company failing to have name on business correspondence, invoices, etc. | Summary. | One-fifth of the statutory maximum. | |
| 349(3) … … | Officer of company issuing business letter or document not bearing company's name. | Summary. | One-fifth of the statutory maximum. | |
| 349(4) … … | Officer of company signing cheque, bill of exchange, etc. on which company's name not mentioned. | Summary. | One-fifth of the statutory maximum. | |
| 350(1) … … | Company failing to have its name engraved on company seal. | Summary. | One-fifth of the statutory maximum. | |

| Section of Act creating offence | General nature of offence | Mode of prosecution | Punishment | Daily default fine (where applicable) |
|---|---|---|---|---|
| 350(2) ... ... | Officer of company, etc., using company seal without name engraved on it. | Summary. | One-fifth of the statutory maximum. | |
| 351(5)(a) ... | Company failing to comply with section 351(1) or (2) (matters to be stated on business correspondence, etc.). | Summary. | One-fifth of the statutory maximum. | |
| 351(5)(b) ... | Officer or agent of company issuing or authorising issue of, business document not complying with those subsections. | Summary. | One-fifth of the statutory maximum. | |
| 351(5)(c) ... | Contravention of section 351(3) or (4) (information in English to be stated on Welsh Company's business correspondence, etc.). | Summary. | One-fifth of the statutory maximum. | For contravention of section 351(3), one-fiftieth of the statutory maximum. |
| 352(5) ... ... | Company default in complying with section 352 (requirement to keep register of members and their particulars). | Summary. | One-fifth of the statutory maximum. | One-fiftieth of the statutory maximum. |
| 352A(3) ... | Company default in complying with section 352A (statement that company has only one member). | Summary. | Level 2 on the standard scale. | One-tenth of level 2 on the standard scale. |
| 353(4) ... ... | Company failing to send notice to registrar as to place where register of members is kept. | Summary. | One-fifth of the statutory maximum. | One-fiftieth of the statutory maximum. |
| 354(4) ... ... | Company failing to keep index of members. | Summary. | One-fifth of the statutory maximum. | One-fiftieth of the statutory maximum. |
| 356(5) ... ... | Refusal of inspection of members' register; failure to send copy on requisition. | Summary. | One-fifth of the statutory maximum. | |
| 363(3) ... ... | Company with share capital failing to make annual return. | Summary. | The statutory maximum. | One-tenth of the statutory maximum. |
| 364(4) ... ... | Company without share capital failing to complete and register annual return in due time. | Summary. | The statutory maximum. | One-tenth of the statutory maximum. |

| Section of Act creating offence | General nature of offence | Mode of prosecution | Punishment | Daily default fine (where applicable) |
|---|---|---|---|---|
| 366(4) ... ... | Company default in holding annual general meeting. | 1. On indictment.<br>2. Summary. | A fine.<br>The statutory maximum. | |
| 367(3) ... ... | Company default in complying with Secretary of State's direction to hold company meeting. | 1. On indictment.<br>2. Summary. | A fine.<br>The statutory maximum. | |
| 367(5) ... ... | Company failing to register resolution that meeting held under section 367 is to be its annual general meeting. | Summary. | One-fifth of the statutory maximum. | One-fiftieth of the statutory maximum. |
| 372(4) ... ... | Failure to give notice, to member entitled to vote at company meeting, that he may do so by proxy. | Summary. | One-fifth of the statutory maximum. | |
| 372(6) ... ... | Officer of company authorising or permitting issue of irregular invitations to appoint proxies. | Summary. | One-fifth of the statutory maximum. | |
| 376(7) ... ... | Officer of company in default as to circulation of members' resolutions for company meeting. | 1. On indictment.<br>2. Summary. | A fine.<br>The statutory maximum. | |
| 380(5) ... ... | Company failing to comply with section 380 (copies of certain resolutions etc. to be sent to registrar of companies). | Summary. | One-fifth of the statutory maximum. | One-fiftieth of the statutory maximum. |
| 380(6) ... ... | Company failing to include copy of resolution to which section 380 applies in articles; failing to forward copy to member on request. | Summary. | One-fifth of the statutory maximum for each occasion on which copies are issued or, as the case may be, requested. | |
| 381B(2) ... | Director or secretary of company failing to notify auditors of proposed written resolution. | Summary. | Level 3 on the standard scale. | |
| 382(5) ... ... | Company failing to keep minutes of proceedings at company and board meetings, etc. | Summary. | One-fifth of the statutory maximum. | One-fiftieth of the statutory maximum. |

| Section of Act creating offence | General nature of offence | Mode of prosecution | Punishment | Daily default fine (where applicable) |
|---|---|---|---|---|
| 382B(2) ... | Failue of sole member to provide the company with a written record of decision. | Summary. | Level 2 on the standard scale. | |
| 383(4) ... ... | Refusal of inspection of minutes of general meeting; failure to send copy of minutes on member's request. | Summary. | One-fifth of the statutory maximum. | |
| 387(2) ... ... | Company failing to give Secretary of State notice of non-appointment of auditors. | Summary. | One-fifth of the statutory maximum. | One-fiftieth of the statutory maximum. |
| 389(10) ... | Person acting as company auditor knowing himself to be disqualified; failing to give notice vacating office when he becomes disqualified. | 1. On indictment.<br>2. Summary. | A fine.<br>The statutory maximum. | One-tenth of the statutory maximum. |
| 389A(2) ... | Officer of company making false, misleading or deceptive statement to auditors. | 1. On indictment.<br>2. Summary. | 2 years or a fine; or both.<br>6 months or the statutory maximum; or both. | |
| 389A(3) ... | Subsidiary undertaking or its auditor failing to give information to auditors of parent company. | Summary. | One-fifth of the statutory maximum. | |
| 389A(4) ... | Parent company failing to obtain from subsidiary undertaking information for purposes of audit. | Summary. | One-fifth of the statutory maximum. | |
| 391(2) ... ... | Failing to give notice to registrar of removal of auditor. | Summary. | One-fifth of the statutory maximum. | One-fiftieth of the statutory maximum. |
| 392(3) ... ... | Company failing to forward notice of auditor's resignation to registrar. | 1. On indictment.<br>2. Summary. | A fine.<br>The statutory maximum. | One-tenth of the statutory maximum. |
| 392A(5) ... | Directors failing to convene meeting requisitioned by resigning auditor. | 1. On indictment.<br>2. Summary. | A fine.<br>The statutory maximum. | |
| 394A(1) ... | Person ceasing to hold office as auditor failing to deposit statement as to circumstances. | 1. On indictment.<br>2. Summary. | A fine.<br>The statutory maximum. | |

| Section of Act creating offence | General nature of offence | Mode of prosecution | Punishment | Daily default fine (where applicable) |
|---|---|---|---|---|
| 394A(4) ... ... | Company failing to comply with requirements as to statement of person ceasing to hold office as auditor. | 1. On indictment.<br>2. Summary. | A fine.<br>The statutory maximum. | One-tenth of the statutory maximum. |
| 399(3) ... ... | Company failing to send to registrar particulars of charge created by it, or of issue of debentures which requires registration. | 1. On indictment.<br>2. Summary. | A fine.<br>The statutory maximum. | One-tenth of the statutory maximum. |
| 400(4) ... ... | Company failing to send to registrar particulars of charge on property acquired. | 1. On indictment.<br>2. Summary. | A fine.<br>The statutory maximum. | One-tenth of the statutory maximum. |
| 402(3) ... ... | Authorising or permitting delivery of debenture or certificate of debenture stock, without endorsement on it of certificate of registration of charge. | Summary. | One-fifth of the statutory maximum. | |
| 405(4) ... ... | Failure to give notice to registrar of appointment of receiver or manager, or of his ceasing to act. | Summary. | One-fifth of the statutory maximum. | One fiftieth of the statutory maximum. |
| 407(3) ... ... | Authorising or permitting omission from company register of charges. | 1. On indictment.<br>2. Summary | A fine.<br>The statutory maximum. | |
| 408(3) ... ... | Officer of company refusing inspection of charging instrument, or of register of charges. | Summary. | One-fifth of the statutory maximum. | One fiftieth of the statutory maximum. |
| 415(3) ... ... | Scottish company failing to send to registrar particulars of charge created by it, or of issue of debentures which requires registration. | 1. On indictment.<br>2. Summary. | A fine.<br>The statutory maximum. | One-tenth of the statutory maximum. |
| 416(3) ... ... | Scottish company failing to send to registrar particulars of charge on property acquired by it. | 1. On indictment.<br>2. Summary. | A fine.<br>The statutory maximum. | One-tenth of the statutory maximum. |
| 422(3) ... ... | Scottish company authorising or permitting omission from its register of charges. | 1. On indictment.<br>2. Summary. | A fine.<br>The statutory maximum. | |

| Section of Act creating offence | General nature of offence | Mode of prosecution | Punishment | Daily default fine (where applicable) |
|---|---|---|---|---|
| 423(3) ... ... | Officer of Scottish company refusing inspection of charging instrument, or of register of charges. | Summary. | One-fifth of the statutory maximum. | One-fiftieth of the statutory maximum. |
| 425(4) ... ... | Company failing to annex to memorandum court order sanctioning compromise or arrangement with creditors. | Summary. | One-fifth of the statutory maximum. | |
| 426(6) ... ... | Company failing to comply with requirements of section 426 (information to members and creditors about compromise or arrangement.) | 1. On indictment.<br>2. Summary. | A fine.<br>The statutory maximum. | |
| 426(7) ... ... | Director or trustee for debenture holders failing to give notice to company of matters necessary for purposes of section 426. | Summary. | One-fifth of the statutory maximum. | |
| 427(5) ... ... | Failure to deliver to registrar office copy of court order under section 427 (company reconstruction or amalgamation). | Summary. | One-fifth of the statutory maximum. | One-fiftieth of the statutory maximum. |
| 429(6) ... ... | Offeror failing to send copy of notice or making statutory declaration knowing it to be false, etc. | 1. On indictment.<br>2. Summary. | 2 years or a fine; or both.<br>6 months or the statutory maximum; or both. | One-fiftieth of the statutory maximum. |
| 430A(6) ... | Offeror failing to give notice of rights to minority shareholder. | 1. On indictment.<br>2. Summary. | A fine.<br>The statutory maximum. | One-fiftieth of the statutory maximum. |
| 444(3) ... ... | Failing to give Secretary of State, when required to do so, information about interests in shares, etc.; giving false information. | 1. On indictment.<br>2. Summary. | 2 years or a fine; or both.<br>6 months or the statutory maximum; or both. | |
| 447(6) ... ... | Failure to comply with requirement to produce documents imposed by Secretary of State under section 447. | 1. On indictment.<br>2. Summary. | A fine.<br>The statutory maximum. | |

| Section of Act creating offence | General nature of offence | Mode of prosecution | Punishment | Daily default fine (where applicable) |
|---|---|---|---|---|
| 448(7) ... ... | Obstructing the exercise of any rights conferred by a warrant or failing to comply with a requirement imposed under subsection (3)(d). | 1. On indictment.<br>2. Summary. | A fine.<br>The statutory maximum. | |
| 449(2) ... ... | Wrongful disclosure of information or document obtained under section 447 or 448. | 1. On indictment.<br>2. Summary. | 2 years or a fine; or both.<br>6 months or the statutory maximum; or both. | |
| 450 ... ... | Destroying or mutilating company documents; falsifying such documents or making false entries; parting with such documents or altering them or making omissions. | 1. On indictment.<br>2. Summary. | 7 years or a fine; or both.<br>6 months or the statutory maximum; or both. | |
| 451 ... ... | Making false statement or explanation in purported compliance with section 447. | 1. On indictment.<br>2. Summary. | 2 years or a fine; or both.<br>6 months or the statutory maximum; or both. | |
| 455(1) ... ... | Exercising a right to dispose of, or vote in respect of, shares which are subject to restrictions under Part XV; failing to give notice in respect of shares so subject; entering into agreement void under section 454(2), (3). | 1. On indictment.<br>2. Summary. | A fine.<br>The statutory maximum. | |
| 455(2) ... ... | Issuing shares in contravention of restrictions of Part XV. | 1. On indictment.<br>2. Summary. | A fine.<br>The statutory maximum. | |
| 458 ... ... | Being a party to carrying on company's business with intent to defraud creditors, or for any fraudulent purpose. | 1. On indictment.<br>2. Summary. | 7 years or a fine; or both.<br>6 months or the statutory maximum; or both. | |
| 461(5) ... ... | Failure to register office copy of court order under Part XVII altering, or giving leave to alter, company's memorandum. | Summary. | One-fifth of the statutory maximum. | One-fiftieth of the statutory maximum. |
| 652(3) ... ... | Person obtaining court order to declare company's dissolution void, then failing to register the order. | Summary. | One-fifth of the statutory maximum. | One-fiftieth of the statutory maximum. |

| Section of Act creating offence | General nature of offence | Mode of prosecution | Punishment | Daily default fine (where applicable) |
|---|---|---|---|---|
| 652E(1) ... | Person breaching or failing to perform duty imposed by section 652B or 652C. | 1. On indictment.<br>2. Summary. | A fine.<br>The statutory maximum. | |
| 652E(2) ... | Person failing to perform duty imposed by section 652B(6) or 652C(2) with intent to conceal the making of application under section 652A. | 1. On indictment.<br>2. Summary. | 7 years or a fine; or both.<br>6 months or the statutory maximum; or both. | |
| 652F(1) ... | Person furnishing false or misleading information in connection with application under section 652A. | 1. On indictment.<br>2. Summary. | A fine.<br>The statutory maximum. | |
| 652F(2) ... | Person making false application under section 652A. | 1. On indictment.<br>2. Summary. | A fine.<br>The statutory maximum. | |
| 697(1) ... ... | Oversea company failing to comply with any of sections 691 to 693 or 696. | Summary. | For an offence which is not a continuing offence, one-fifth of the statutory maximum.<br>For an offence which is a continuing offence, one-fifth of the statutory maximum. | <br>One-fiftieth of the statutory maximum. |
| 697(2) ... ... | Oversea company contravening section 694(6) (carrying on business under its corporate name after Secretary of State's direction). | 1. On indictment.<br>2. Summary. | A fine.<br>The statutory maximum. | <br>One-tenth of the statutory maximum. |
| 697(3) ... ... | Oversea company failing to comply with Section 695A or Schedule 21A. | Summary. | For an offence which is not a continuing offence, one fifth of level 5 of the standard scale.<br>For an offence which is a continuing offence one fifth of level 5 of the standard scale. | <br>£100. |



CCH.New Law
bbcl ca 1985d Mp 762—bcl24 170c

| Section of Act creating offence | General nature of offence | Mode of prosecution | Punishment | Daily default fine (where applicable) |
|---|---|---|---|---|
| 703(1) ... ... | Oversea company failing to comply with requirements as to accounts and reports. | 1. On indictment.<br>2. Summary. | A fine.<br>The statutory maximum. | One-tenth of the statutory maximum. |
| 703R(1) ... | Company failing to register winding up or commencement of insolvency proceedings etc. | 1. On indictment.<br>2. Summary. | A fine.<br>The statutory maximum. | £100. |
| 703R(2) ... | Liquidator failing to register appointment, termination of winding up or striking-off of company. | 1. On indictment.<br>2. Summary. | A fine.<br>The statutory maximum. | £100. |
| 720(4) ... ... | Insurance company etc. failing to send twice-yearly statement in form of Schedule 23. | Summary. | One-fifth of the statutory maximum. | One-fiftieth of the statutory maximum. |
| 722(3) ... ... | Company failing to comply with section 722(2), as regards the manner of keeping registers, minute books and accounting records. | Summary. | One-fifth of the statutory maximum. | One-fiftieth of the statutory maximum. |
| Sch. 14, Pt. II, para. 1(3) | Company failing to give notice of location of overseas branch register, etc. | Summary. | One-fifth of the statutory maximum. | One-fiftieth of the statutory maximum. |
| Sch. 14, Pt. II, para. 4(2) | Company failing to transmit to its registered office in Great Britain copies of entries in overseas branch register, or to keep a duplicate of overseas branch register. | Summary. | One-fifth of the statutory maximum. | One-fiftieth of the statutory maximum. |
| Sch. 21C, Pt. I, para. 7 ... | Credit or financial institution failing to deliver accounting documents. | 1. On indictment.<br>2. Summary. | A fine.<br>The statutory maximum. | £100. |
| Sch. 21C, Pt. II, para. 15 ... | Credit or financial institution failing to deliver accounts and reports. | 1. On indictment.<br>2. Summary. | A fine.<br>The statutory maximum. | £100. |
| Sch. 21D, Pt. I, para. 5 ... | Company failing to deliver accounting documents. | 1. On indictment.<br>2. Summary. | A fine.<br>The statutory maximum. | £100. |

| Section of Act creating offence | General nature of offence | Mode of prosecution | Punishment | Daily default fine (where applicable) |
|---|---|---|---|---|
| Sch. 21D, Pt. I, para. 13 … | Company failing to deliver accounts and reports. | 1. On indictment.<br>2. Summary. | A fine.<br>The statutory maximum. | £100. |

**Note**

The statutory maximum under Magistrates' Courts Act 1980, s. 32 and Criminal Procedure (Scotland) Act 1975, s. 289B is £5,000; in regard to references to levels on the standard scale see Criminal Justice Act 1982, s. 37 and Criminal Procedure (Scotland) Act 1975, s. 289G (all the above provisions as amended by Criminal Justice Act 1991, s. 17 as from 1 October 1992).

Entries in Sch. 24 relating to s. 81(2), 82(5), 86(6), 87(4) and 97(4) repealed by Financial Services Act 1986, s. 212(3) and Sch. 17 to the extent to which those entries would apply to any investment listed or the subject of a listing application under Financial Services Act 1986, Pt. IV and commencing:

- on 12 January 1987 for all purposes relating to the admission of securities offered by or on behalf of a Minister of the Crown or a body corporate controlled by a Minister of the Crown or a subsidiary of such a body corporate to the Official List in respect of which an application is made after that date;
- on 16 February 1987 for purposes relating to the admission of securities in respect of which an application is made after that date other than those referred to in the preceding paragraph and otherwise for all purposes.

(See SI 1986/2246 (C. 88).)

Those same entries repealed by Financial Services Act 1986, s. 212(3) and Sch. 17 as from 29 April 1988 as far as they would apply to a prospectus offering for subscription, or to any form of application for, units in a body corporate which is a recognised scheme (see SI 1988/740 (C. 22)).

The Companies (Single Member Private Limited Companies) Regulations 1992 (SI 1992/1699) (see below) implement the Twelfth EC Company Law Directive (89/667.)

**History**

(1) In Sch. 24 entries relating to s. 221(5)–251(6) amended as a result of CA 1989, s. 23, 212, Sch. 10, para. 24(1)–(3) and Sch. 24 as from 1 April 1990 subject to transitional and saving provisions (see SI 1990/355 (C. 13), art. 3, 5(1)(b), 2, and also art. 6–9) — see (11) below; prior to the amendments the entries read as follows:

| Section of Act creating offence | General nature of offence | Mode of prosecution | Punishment | Daily default fine (where applicable) |
|---|---|---|---|---|
| "223(1) … | Company failing to keep accounting records (liability of officers). | 1. On indictment.<br>2. Summary. | 2 years or a fine; or both<br>6 months or the statutory maximum; or both. | |
| 223(2) … … | Officer of company failing to secure compliance with, or intentionally causing default under section 222(4) (preservation of accounting records for requisite number of years). | 1. On indictment.<br>2. Summary. | 2 years or a fine; or both.<br>6 months or the statutory maximum; or both. | |
| 231(3) … … | Company failing to annex to its annual return certain particulars required by Schedule 5 and not included in annual accounts. | Summary. | One-fifth of the statutory maximum. | One-fiftieth of the statutory maximum. |

| Section of Act creating offence | General nature of offence | Mode of prosecution | Punishment | Daily default fine (where applicable) |
|---|---|---|---|---|
| 231(4) ... ... | Default by director or officer of a company in giving notice of matters relating to himself for purposes of Schedule 5 Part V. | Summary. | One-fifth of the statutory maximum. | |
| 235(7) ... ... | Non-compliance with the section, as to directors' report and its content; directors individually liable. | 1. On indictment.<br>2. Summary. | A fine.<br>The statutory maximum. | |
| 238(2) ... ... | Laying or delivery of unsigned balance sheet; circulating copies of balance sheet without signatures. | Summary. | One-fifth of the statutory maximum. | |
| 240(5) ... ... | Failing to send company balance sheet, directors' report and auditors' report to those entitled to receive them. | 1. On indictment.<br>2. Summary. | A fine.<br>The statutory maximum. | |
| 243(1) ... ... | Director in default as regards duty to lay and deliver company accounts. | Summary. | The statutory maximum. | One-tenth of the statutory maximum. |
| 245(1) ... ... | Company's individual accounts not in conformity with requirements of this Act; directors individually liable. | 1. On indictment.<br>2. Summary. | A fine.<br>The statutory maximum. | |
| 245(2) ... ... | Holding company's group accounts not in conformity with sections 229 and 230 and other requirements of this Act; directors individually liable. | 1. On indictment.<br>2. Summary. | A fine.<br>The statutory maximum. | |
| 246(2) ... ... | Company failing to supply copy of accounts to shareholder on his demand. | Summary. | One-fifth of the statutory maximum. | One-fiftieth of the statutory maximum. |
| 254(6) ... ... | Company or officer in default contravening section 254 as regards publication of full individual or group accounts. | Summary. | One-fifth of the statutory maximum. | |
| 255(5) ... ... | Company or officer in default contravening section 255 as regards publication of abridged accounts. | Summary. | One-fifth of the statutory maximum. | |
| 260(3) ... ... | Director of special category company failing to secure compliance with special disclosure provision. | 1. On indictment.<br>2. Summary. | A fine.<br>The statutory maximum." | |

(2) In Sch. 24 entries relating to s. 295(7) and 302(1) repealed by Company Directors Disqualification Act 1986, s. 23(2) and Sch. 4 as from 29 December 1986 (in regard to the date of the repeal, see CDDA 1986, s. 25, IA 1986, s. 443 and SI 1986/1924 (C. 71)); the former wording of those entries was as follows:

| Section of Act creating offence | General nature of offence | Mode of prosecution | Punishment | Daily default fine (where applicable) |
|---|---|---|---|---|
| "295(7) ... | Acting in contravention of a disqualification order under sections 295 to 300. | 1. On indictment.<br>2. Summary. | 2 years or a fine; or both.<br>6 months or the statutory maximum; or both. | |
| 302(1) ... ... | Undischarged bankrupt acting as director, etc. | 1. On indictment.<br>2. Summary. | 2 years or a fine; or both.<br>6 months or the statutory maximum; or both." | |

(3) Also in Sch. 24 entries relating to s. 467–641(2), and the entry relating to s. 710(4) repealed by Insolvency Act 1986, s. 438 and Sch. 12 as from 29 December 1986 (see IA 1986, s. 443 and SI 1986/1924 (C. 71)). The entries relating to s. 495(7), 496(6), 497(7), 528(7), 568(3), 583(2), 588(5) and 640(4) previously repealed by Insolvency Act 1985, s. 235 and Sch. 10, Pt. II immediately before that date (see SI 1986/1924 (C. 71)); the former wording of all the above entries was as follows:

| Section of Act creating offence | General nature of offence | Mode of prosecution | Punishment | Daily default fine (where applicable) |
|---|---|---|---|---|
| "467(4) ... | Body corporate or Scottish firm acting as receiver. | 1. On indictment.<br>2. Summary. | A fine.<br>The statutory maximum. | |
| 467(5) ... ... | Undischarged bankrupt acting as receiver. | 1. On indictment.<br>2. Summary. | 2 years or a fine; or both.<br>6 months or the statutory maximum; or both. | |
| 469(2) ... ... | Failing to deliver to registrar copy instrument of appointment of receiver. | Summary. | One-fifth of the statutory maximum. | One-fiftieth of the statutory maximum. |
| 470(3) ... ... | Failing to deliver to registrar the court's interlocuter making the appointment of a receiver. | Summary. | One-fifth of the statutory maximum. | One-fiftieth of the statutory maximum. |
| 478(5) ... ... | Failing to give notice to registrar of cessation or removal of receiver. | Summary. | One-fifth of the statutory maximum. | One-fiftieth of the statutory maximum. |
| 480(2) ... ... | Not stating on company documents that receiver has been appointed. | Summary. | One-fifth of the statutory maximum. | |
| 481(7) ... ... | Receiver making default in complying with provisions as to information where receiver appointed. | Summary. | One-fifth of the statutory maximum. | One-fiftieth of the statutory maximum. |
| 482(5) ... ... | Default in relation to provisions as to statement to be submitted to receiver. | Summary. | One-fifth of the statutory maximum. | One-fiftieth of the statutory maximum. |
| 489 ... ... | Body corporate acting as receiver. | 1. On indictment.<br>2. Summary. | A fine.<br>The statutory maximum. | |
| 490 ... ... | Undischarged bankrupt acting as receiver or manager. | 1. On indictment.<br>2. Summary. | 2 years or a fine; or both.<br>6 months or the statutory maximum; or both. | |
| 493(2) ... ... | Company failing to state in its correspondence, etc. that a receiver has been appointed. | Summary. | One-fifth of the statutory maximum. | |

| Section of Act creating offence | General nature of offence | Mode of prosecution | Punishment | Daily default fine (where applicable) |
|---|---|---|---|---|
| 495(7) ... ... | Receiver failing to notify his appointment to the company; failing to send company's statement of affairs to registrar and others concerned. | Summary. | One-fifth of the statutory maximum. | One-fiftieth of the statutory maximum. |
| 496(6) ... ... | Default in relation to statement of affairs to be given to receiver. | Summary. | One-fifth of the statutory maximum. | One-fiftieth of the statutory maximum. |
| 497(7) ... ... | Receiver failing to send accounts of his receipts and payments to registrar and others concerned. | Summary. | One-fifth of the statutory maximum. | One-fiftieth of the statutory maximum. |
| 498(4) ... ... | Receiver failing to send accounts to registrar for registration. | Summary. | One-fifth of the statutory maximum. | One-fiftieth of the statutory maximum. |
| 528(7) ... ... | Default in compliance with section 528 (submission of statement of company's affairs to official receiver). | 1. On indictment.<br>2. Summary. | A fine.<br>The statutory maximum. | One-tenth of the statutory maximum. |
| 568(3) ... ... | Liquidator failing to send to registrar of companies copy of court order dissolving company. | Summary. | One-fifth of the statutory maximum. | One-fiftieth of the statutory maximum. |
| 573(2) ... ... | Company failing to give notice in Gazette of resolution for voluntary winding up. | Summary. | One-fifth of the statutory maximum. | One-fiftieth of the statutory maximum. |
| 577(4) ... ... | Director making statutory declaration of company's solvency without reasonable grounds for his opinion. | 1. On indictment.<br>2. Summary. | 2 years or a fine; or both.<br>6 months or the statutory maximum; or both. | |
| 577(6) ... ... | Declaration under section 577 not delivered to registrar of companies within prescribed time. | Summary. | One-fifth of the statutory maximum. | One-fiftieth of the statutory maximum. |
| 583(2) ... ... | Liquidator failing to summon creditors' meeting in case of insolvency. | Summary. | One-fifth of the statutory maximum. | |
| 584(2) ... ... | Liquidator failing to summon general meeting of company at end of each year from commencement of winding up. | Summary. | One-fifth of the statutory maximum. | |
| 585(3) ... ... | Liquidator failing to send to registrar a copy of the account of a winding up and return of final general meeting. | Summary. | One-fifth of the statutory maximum. | One-fiftieth of the statutory maximum. |
| 585(6) ... ... | Failing to deliver to registrar office copy of court order for registration made under the section. | Summary. | One-fifth of the statutory maximum. | One-fiftieth of the statutory maximum. |
| 585(7) ... ... | Liquidator failing to summon final meeting of company prior to dissolution. | Summary. | One-fifth of the statutory maximum. | |
| 588(5) ... ... | Company or its directors or officers failing to comply with the section in relation to summoning or advertisement of creditors' meeting. | 1. On indictment.<br>2. Summary. | A fine.<br>The statutory maximum. | |

| Section of Act creating offence | General nature of offence | Mode of prosecution | Punishment | Daily default fine (where applicable) |
|---|---|---|---|---|
| 594(2) ... ... | Liquidator failing to summon general meeting of company, and meeting of creditors, at end of each year. | Summary. | One-fifth of the statutory maximum. | |
| 595(4) ... ... | Liquidator failing to send to registrar account of winding up and return of final company and creditors' meetings. | Summary. | One-fifth of the statutory maximum. | One-fiftieth of the statutory maximum. |
| 595(7) ... ... | Failing to deliver to registrar office copy of court order for registration made under the section. | Summary. | One-fifth of the statutory maximum. | One-fiftieth of the statutory maximum. |
| 595(8) ... ... | Liquidator failing to call final meeting of company or creditors. | Summary. | One-fifth of the statutory maximum. | |
| 600(2) ... ... | Liquidator failing to publish notice of his appointment. | Summary. | One-fifth of the statutory maximum. | One-fiftieth of the statutory maximum. |
| 624(2) ... ... | Fraud, etc., in anticipation of winding up (offence under subsection (1) or (2) of the section). | 1. On indictment.<br>2. Summary. | 7 years or a fine; or both.<br>6 months or the statutory maximum; or both. | |
| 624(5) ... ... | Knowingly taking in pawn or pledge, or otherwise receiving, company property. | 1. On indictment.<br>2. Summary. | 7 years or a fine; or both.<br>6 months or the statutory maximum; or both. | |
| 625 ... ... | Officer of company entering into transactions in fraud of company's creditors. | 1. On indictment.<br>2. Summary. | 2 years or a fine; or both.<br>6 months or the statutory maximum; or both. | |
| 626 ... ... | Officer of company misconducting himself in course of winding up. | 1. On indictment.<br>2. Summary. | 7 years or a fine; or both.<br>6 months or the statutory maximum; or both. | |
| 627 ... ... | Officer or contributory destroying, falsifying, etc., company's books. | 1. On indictment.<br>2. Summary. | 7 years or a fine; or both.<br>6 months or the statutory maximum; or both. | |
| 628 ... ... | Officer of company making material omission from statement relating to company's affairs. | 1. On indictment.<br>2. Summary. | 7 years or a fine; or both.<br>6 months or the statutory maximum; or both. | |
| 629 ... ... | False representation or fraud for purpose of obtaining creditors' consent to an agreement in connection with winding up. | 1. On indictment.<br>2. Summary. | 7 years or a fine; or both.<br>6 months or the statutory maximum; or both. | |
| 634 ... ... | Body corporate acting as liquidator. | 1. On indictment.<br>2. Summary. | A fine.<br>The statutory maximum. | |
| 635 ... ... | Giving, offering, etc., corrupt inducement affecting appointment of liquidator. | 1. On indictment.<br>2. Summary. | A fine.<br>The statutory maximum. | |
| 637(2) ... ... | Default in compliance with the section, as to notification that company is being wound up. | Summary. | One-fifth of the statutory maximum. | |

| Section of Act creating offence | General nature of offence | Mode of prosecution | Punishment | Daily default fine (where applicable) |
|---|---|---|---|---|
| 640(4) … … | Contravention of general rules as to disposal of company books and papers after winding up. | Summary. | One-fifth of the statutory maximum. | |
| 641(2) … … | Liquidator failing to notify registrar as to progress of winding up. | Summary. | One-fifth of the statutory maximum. | One-fiftieth of the statutory maximum. |
| 710(4) … … | Person untruthfully stating himself to be a member or creditor of company, for purpose of obtaining or inspecting company documents. | Summary. | One-fifth of the statutory maximum." | |

**(4)** Also in Sch. 24 in second column of entry relating to s. 329(3) the words "investment exchange" substituted for the former words "stock exchange" by Financial Services Act 1986, s. 212(2) and Sch. 16, para. 27(a) as from 29 April 1988 (see SI 1988/740 (C. 22)) and entries relating to s. 429(6) and s. 430A(6) inserted by Financial Services Act 1986, s. 212(2) and Sch. 16, para. 27(b) as from 4 June 1987 (see SI 1987/907 (C. 24)).

**(5)** Also in Sch. 24 former entries relating to s. 287(3), 384(5), 386(2), 390(7), 391(4), 392(2) and 393 repealed by CA 1989, s. 212 and Sch. 24 and entries relating to s. 387(2), 389A(2)–(4), 391(2), (3), 392A(5), 394A(1), (4) inserted by CA 1989, s. 119(2), 120(3), 122(2), 123(2) as from 1 April 1990 subject to transitional and saving provisions (see SI 1990/355 (C. 13), art. 4(a), 5(1)(b), (2) and also art. 6–10); the former entries read as follows:

| Section of Act creating offence | General nature of offence | Mode of prosecution | Punishment | Daily default fine (where applicable) |
|---|---|---|---|---|
| "287(3) … | Company failing to have registered office; failing to notify change in its situation. | Summary. | One-fifth of the statutory maximum. | One-fiftieth of the statutory maximum. |
| 384(5) … … | Company failing to give Secretary of State notice of non-appointment of auditors. | Summary. | One-fifth of the statutory maximum. | One-fiftieth of the statutory maximum. |
| 386(2) … … | Failing to give notice to registrar of removal of auditor. | Summary. | One-fifth of the statutory maximum. | One-fiftieth of the statutory maximum. |
| 390(7) … … | Company failing to forward notice of auditor's resignation to registrar or persons entitled under section 240 in Part VII; failing to send to persons so entitled statement as to effect of court order or, if no such order, the auditor's resignation statement. | 1. On indictment.<br>2. Summary. | A fine.<br>The statutory maximum. | One-tenth of the statutory maximum. |
| 391(4) … … | Directors failing to convene meeting requisitioned by resigning auditors. | 1. On indictment.<br>2. Summary. | A fine.<br>The statutory maximum. | |
| 392(2) … … | Failure of subsidiary to give its holding company, and failure of holding company to obtain from its subsidiary, information needed for purposes of audit; failure of subsidiary's auditors to give information and explanation to holding company's auditors. | Summary | One-fifth of the statutory maximum. | |

| Section of Act creating offence | General nature of offence | Mode of prosecution | Punishment | Daily default fine (where applicable) |
|---|---|---|---|---|
| 393 ... ... | Company officer making misleading, false or deceptive statement to auditors. | 1. On indictment.<br>2. Summary. | 2 years or a fine; or both.<br>6 months or the statutory maximum; or both." | |

**(6)** Also in Sch. 24 in entry relating to s. 447(6) the word "documents" substituted for the former words "books or papers" by CA 1989, s. 63(1), (8) as from 21 February 1990 (see SI 1990/142 (C. 5), art. 4).

**(7)** Also in Sch. 24 in entry relating to s. 448(7) in the first column "448(7)" substituted for "448(5)" and in the second column the words substituted by CA 1989, s. 64(2) as from 21 February 1990 (see SI 1990/142 (C. 5), art. 4); the words in the second column formerly read as follows:

"Obstructing the exercise of a right of entry or search, or a right to take possession of books or papers."

**(8)** Also in Sch. 24 in entry relating to s. 703(1) in column 2 the words "requirements as to accounts and reports" substituted for the former words "s. 700 as respects delivery of annual accounts" by CA 1989, s. 23 and Sch. 10, para. 24(1), (4) as from 1 April 1990 subject to transitional and saving provisions (see SI 1990/355 (C. 13), art. 3, Sch. 1 and also art. 6–9).

**(9)** Also in Sch. 24 in entry relating to s. 363(3) in first column "363(3)" substituted for the former "363(7)" by CA 1989, s. 139(3) as from 1 October 1990 subject to transitional and saving provisions (see SI 1990/1707 (C. 46), art. 2(a) and also art. 4, 5).

**(10)** Also in Sch. 24 former entry relating to s. 365(3) repealed by CA 1989, s. 212 and Sch. 24 as from 1 October 1990 subject to transitional and saving provisions (see SI 1990/1707 (C. 46), art. 3(a) and also art. 4, 5); the former entry read as follows:

| Section of Act creating offence | General nature of offence | Mode of prosecution | Punishment | Daily default fine (where applicable) |
|---|---|---|---|---|
| "365(3) ... | Company failing to complete and send annual return to registrar in due time. | Summary. | The statutory maximum. | One-tenth of the statutory maximum." |

**(11)** Also in Sch. 24 entry relating to s. 233(5) inserted by CA 1989, s. 23 and Sch. 10, para. 24(3) and former entries relating to s. 245(1) and 245(2) omitted and repealed by CA 1989, s. 23, 212, Sch. 10, para. 24(2) and Sch. 24 as from 7 January 1991 subject to transitional and saving provisions (see SI 1990/2569 (C. 68), art. 3, 5(c), 6) — see also (1) above; the former entries read as follows:

| Section of Act creating offence | General nature of offence | Mode of prosecution | Punishment | Daily default fine (where applicable) |
|---|---|---|---|---|
| "245(1) ... | Company's individual accounts not in conformity with requirements of this Act; directors individually liable. | 1. On indictment.<br>2. Summary. | A fine.<br>The statutory maximum. | |
| 245(2) ... ... | Holding company's group accounts not in conformity with sections 229 and 230 and other requirements of this Act; directors individually liable. | 1. On indictment.<br>2. Summary. | A fine.<br>The statutory maximum." | |

**(12)** Also in Sch. 24 entries relating to s. 322B(4), 352A(3) and 382B(2) inserted by the Companies (Single Member Private Limited Companies) Regulations 1992 (SI 1992/1699), reg. 2 and Sch., para. 3(3), 4(2) and 6(2) as from 15 July 1992.

**(13)** Also in Sch. 24 entries relating to s. 697(3), 703R(1), 703R(2), Sch. 21C, Pt. I, para. 7, Sch. 21C, Pt. II, para. 15, Sch. 21D, Pt. I, para. 5 and Sch. 21D, Pt. I, para. 13 inserted by the Oversea Companies and Credit and Financial Institutions (Branch Disclosure) Regulations 1992 (SI 1992/3179), reg. 1(3), 4 and Sch. 3, para. 9 as from 1 January 1993.

**(14)** Also in Sch. 24 entries relating to s. 56(4), 61, 64(5), 70(1), 78(1) repealed by Financial Services Act 1986, s. 212(3) and Sch. 17, Pt. I as follows:

- as from 12 January 1987 re any investment listed or the subject of a listing application under Financial Services Act 1986, Pt. IV for all purposes relating to the admission of securities offered by or on behalf of a Minister of the Crown or a body corporate controlled by a Minister of the Crown or a subsidiary of such a body corporate to the Official List in respect of which an application is made after that date (see SI 1986/2246 (C. 88));
- as from 16 February 1987 re any investment listed or the subject of a listing application under Financial Services Act 1986, Pt. IV for purposes relating to the admission of which an application is made after that date other than those referred to in the preceding paragraph and otherwise for all purposes (see SI 1986/2246 (C. 88));
- as from 29 April 1988 as far as the entries would apply to a prospectus offering for subscription, or to any form of application for units in a body corporate which is a recognised scheme (see SI 1988/740 (C. 22));
- as from 1 July 1988 as far as the entries would apply to a prospectus offering for subscription, or to any application form for, units in a body corporate which is an open-ended investment company (see SI 1988/740 (C. 22));
- as from 19 June 1995 for all remaining purposes except CA 1985, s. 58, 59, 60, in so far as the entries are necessary for the purposes of CA 1985, s. 81, 83, 246, 248, 744; and CA 1985, Sch. 3,para. 2, in so far as it is necessary for the purposes of CA 1985, s. 83(1)(a); and CA 1985, s. 62, in so far as it is necessary for the purposes of CA 1985, s. 744 (see SI 1995/1538 (C. 33)).

The entries formerly read as follows:

| Section of Act creating offence | General nature of offence | Mode of prosecution | Punishment | Daily default fine (where applicable) |
|---|---|---|---|---|
| "56(4) ... ... | Issuing form of application for shares or debentures without accompanying prospectus. | 1. On indictment.<br>2. Summary. | A fine.<br>The statutory maximum. | |
| 61 ... ... | Issuing prospectus with expert's statement in it, he not having given his consent; omission to state in prospectus that expert has consented. | 1. On indictment.<br>2. Summary. | A fine.<br>The statutory maximum. | |
| 64(5) ... ... | Issuing company prospectus without copy being delivered to registrar of companies, or without requisite documents endorsed or attached. | Summary. | One-fifth of the statutory maximum. | One-fiftieth of the statutory maximum. |
| 70(1) ... ... | Authorising issue of prospectus with untrue statement. | 1. On indictment.<br>2. Summary. | 2 years or a fine; or both.<br>6 months or the statutory maximum, or both. | |
| 78(1) ... ... | Being responsible for issue, circulation of prospectus, etc. contrary to Part III, Chapter II (oversea companies). | 1. On indictment.<br>2. Summary. | A fine.<br>The statutory maximum." | |

**(15)** Also in Sch. 24 entries relating to s. 652E–652F inserted by Deregulation and Contracting Out Act 1994, s. 13(1) and Sch. 5, para. 1, 4 as from 1 July 1995 (see SI 1995/1433 (C. 31), art. 2, 3(a)).

**(16)** Also in Sch. 24 entries relating to s. 381B inserted by the Deregulation (Resolutions of Private Companies) Order 1996 (SI 1996/1471), art. 1, 3(2)(c), as from 19 June 1996.

# Schedule 25 — Companies Act 1981, Section 38, as Originally Enacted

## 38 Relief from section 56 in respect of group reconstructions

**38(1)** This section applies where the issuing company—

(a) is a wholly-owned subsidiary of another company ("the holding company"); and

(b) allots shares to the holding company or to another wholly-owned subsidiary of the holding company in consideration for the transfer to it of shares in another subsidiary (whether wholly-owned or not) of the holding company.

**38(2)** Where the shares in the issuing company allotted in consideration for the transfer are issued at a premium, the issuing company shall not be required by section 56 of the 1948 Act to transfer any amount in excess of the minimum premium value to the share premium account.

**38(3)** In subsection (2) above **"the minimum premium value"** means the amount (if any) by which the base value of the shares transferred exceeds the aggregate nominal value of the shares allotted in consideration for the transfer.

**38(4)** For the purposes of subsection (3) above, the base value of the shares transferred shall be taken as—

(a) the cost of those shares to the company transferring them; or

(b) the amount at which those shares are stated in that company's accounting records immediately before the transfer; whichever is the less.

**38(5)** Section 37 of this Act shall not apply in a case to which this section applies.

**Note**

In Sch. 25 "subsidiary" has the meaning given by s. 736 as originally enacted (CA 1989, Sch. 18, para. 38).

# BUSINESS NAMES ACT 1985

## Table of Contents

# BUSINESS NAMES ACT 1985

(1985 Chapter 7)

## ARRANGEMENT OF SECTIONS

SECTION

# BUSINESS NAMES ACT 1985

(1985 Chapter 7)

An Act to consolidate certain enactments relating to the names under which persons may carry on business in Great Britain.

[*11th March 1985*]

## 1 Persons subject to this Act

**1(1) [Application]** This Act applies to any person who has a place of business in Great Britain and who carries on business in Great Britain under a name which–

(a) in the case of a partnership, does not consist of the surnames of all partners who are individuals and the corporate names of all partners who are bodies corporate without any addition other than an addition permitted by this Act;

(b) in the case of an individual, does not consist of his surname without any addition other than one so permitted;

(c) in the case of a company, being a company which is capable of being wound up under the Companies Act 1985, does not consist of its corporate name without any addition other than one so permitted.

**1(2) [Permitted additions for s. 1(1)]** The following are permitted additions for the purposes of subsection (1)–

(a) in the case of a partnership, the forenames of individual partners or the initials of those forenames or, where two or more individual partners have the same surname, the addition of "s" at the end of that surname; or

(b) in the case of an individual, his forename or its initial;

(c) in any case, any addition merely indicating that the business is carried on in succession to a former owner of the business.

## 2 Prohibition of use of certain business names

**2(1) [Exclusion of certain names]** Subject to the following subsections, a person to whom this Act applies shall not, without the written approval of the Secretary of State, carry on business in Great Britain under a name which–

(a) would be likely to give the impression that the business is connected with Her Majesty's Government, with any part of the Scottish Administration, or with any local authority; or

(b) includes any word or expression for the time being specified in regulations made under this Act.

**History**

In s. 2(1)(a) the words ", with any part of the Scottish Administration," inserted by the Scotland Act 1998 (Consequential Modifications) (No. 2) Order 1999 (SI 1999/1820), art. 1(2), 4, Sch. 2, Pt. I, para. 79 as from 1 July 1999.

**Note**

See the Company and Business Names Regulations 1981 (SI 1981/1685), as amended.

**2(2) [Non-application of s. 2(1)]** Subsection (1) does not apply to the carrying on of a business by a person–

(a) to whom the business has been transferred on or after 26th February 1982; and

(b) who carries on the business under the name which was its lawful business name immediately before that transfer,

during the period of 12 months beginning with the date of that transfer.

**2(3) [Further non-application of s. 2(1)]** Subsection (1) does not apply to the carrying on of a business by a person who–

(a) carried on that business immediately before 26th February 1982; and

(b) continues to carry it on under the name which immediately before that date was its lawful business name.

**2(4) [Offence]** A person who contravenes subsection (1) is guilty of an offence.

**Note**

See the Company and Business Names (Amendment) Regulations 1992 (SI 1992/1196), reg. 3.

## 3 Words and expressions requiring Secretary of State's approval

**3(1) [Regulations]** The Secretary of State may by regulations–

(a) specify words or expressions for the use of which as or as part of a business name his approval is required by section 2(1)(b); and

(b) in relation to any such word or expression, specify a Government department or other body as the relevant body for purposes of the following subsection.

**Note**

See the Company and Business Names Regulations 1981 (SI 1981/1685), as amended.

**3(2) [Request for use of certain names]** Where a person to whom this Act applies proposes to carry on a business under a name which is or includes any such word or expression, and a Government department or other body is specified under subsection (1)(b) in relation to that word or expression, that person shall–

(a) request (in writing) the relevant body to indicate whether (and if so why) it has any objections to the proposal; and

(b) submit to the Secretary of State a statement that such a request has been made and a copy of any response received from the relevant body.

**Note**

See the Company and Business Names (Amendment) Regulations 1992 (SI 1992/1196), reg. 3.

## 4 Disclosure required of persons using business names

**4(1) [Disclosure of names and addresses]** A person to whom this Act applies shall–

(a) subject to subsection (3), state in legible characters on all business letters, written orders for goods or services to be supplied to the business, invoices and receipts issued in the course of the business and written demands for payment of debts arising in the course of the business–

(i) in the case of a partnership, the name of each partner,

(ii) in the case of an individual, his name,

(iii) in the case of a company, its corporate name, and

(iv) in relation to each person so named, an address in Great Britain at which service of any document relating in any way to the business will be effective; and

(b) in any premises where the business is carried on and to which the customers of the business or suppliers of any goods or services to the business have access, display in a prominent position so that it may easily be read by such customers or suppliers a notice containing such names and addresses.

**4(2) [Names and addresses to be supplied on request]** A person to whom this Act applies shall secure that the names and addresses required by subsection (1)(a) to be stated on his business letters, or which would have been so required but for the subsection next following, are immediately given, by written notice to any person with whom anything is done or discussed in the course of the business and who asks for such names and addresses.

**4(3) [S. 4(1)(a) not to apply to certain partnerships]** Subsection (1)(a) does not apply in relation to any document issued by a partnership of more than 20 persons which maintains at its principal place of business a list of the names of all the partners if–

(a) none of the names of the partners appears in the document otherwise than in the text or as a signatory; and

(b) the document states in legible characters the address of the partnership's principal place of business and that the list of the partners' names is open to inspection at that place.

**4(4) [Inspection of list of partners' names]** Where a partnership maintains a list of the partners' names for purposes of subsection (3), any person may inspect the list during office hours.

**4(5) [Regulations]** The Secretary of State may by regulations require notices under subsection (1)(b) or (2) to be displayed or given in a specified form.

**4(6) [Offence]** A person who without reasonable excuse contravenes subsection (1) or (2), or any regulations made under subsection (5), is guilty of an offence.

**4(7) [Refusal of s. 4(4) inspection an offence]** Where an inspection required by a person in accordance with subsection (4) is refused, any partner of the partnership concerned who without reasonable excuse refused that inspection, or permitted it to be refused, is guilty of an offence.

## 5 Civil remedies for breach of s. 4

**5(1) [Dismissal of certain legal proceedings]** Any legal proceedings brought by a person to whom this Act applies to enforce a right arising out of a contract made in the course of a business in respect of which he was, at the time the contract was made, in breach of subsection (1) or (2) of section 4 shall be dismissed if the defendant (or, in Scotland, the defender) to the proceedings shows–

(a) that he has a claim against the plaintiff (pursuer) arising out of that contract which he has been unable to pursue by reason of the latter's breach of section 4(1) or (2), or

(b) that he has suffered some financial loss in connection with the contract by reason of the plaintiff's (pursuer's) breach of section 4(1) or (2),

unless the court before which the proceedings are brought is satisfied that it is just and equitable to permit the proceedings to continue.

**5(2) [Without prejudice]** This section is without prejudice to the right of any person to enforce such rights as he may have against another person in any proceedings brought by that person.

## 6 Regulations

**6(1) [Regulations by statutory instrument]** Regulations under this Act shall be made by statutory instrument and may contain such transitional provisions and savings as the Secretary of State thinks appropriate, and may make different provision for different cases or classes of case.

**6(2) [Regulations under s. 3]** In the case of regulations made under section 3, the statutory instrument containing them shall be laid before Parliament after the regulations are made and shall cease to have effect at the end of the period of 28 days beginning with the day on which they were made (but without prejudice to anything previously done by virtue of them or to the making of new regulations) unless during that period they are approved by a resolution of each House of Parliament.

In reckoning this period of 28 days, no account is to be taken of any time during which Parliament is dissolved or prorogued, or during which both Houses are adjourned for more than 4 days.

**6(3) [Regulations under s. 4]** In the case of regulations made under section 4, the statutory instrument containing them is subject to annulment in pursuance of a resolution of either House of Parliament.

**Note**

See the Company and Business Names Regulations 1981 (SI 1981/1685), as amended.

## 7 Offences

**7(1) [Summary conviction]** Offences under this Act are punishable on summary conviction.

**7(2) [Fine]** A person guilty of an offence under this Act is liable to a fine not exceeding one-fifth of the statutory maximum.

**7(3) [Fine for continued contravention]** If after a person has been convicted summarily of an offence under section 2 or 4(6) the original contravention is continued, he is liable on a second or subsequent summary conviction of the offence to a fine not exceeding one-fiftieth of the statutory maximum for each day on which the contravention is continued (instead of to the penalty which may be imposed on the first conviction of the offence).

**7(4) [Penalty relating to officers of body corporate]** Where an offence under section 2 or 4(6) or (7) committed by a body corporate is proved to have been committed with the consent or connivance of, or to be attributable to any neglect on the part of, any director, manager, secretary or other similar officer of the body corporate, or any person who was purporting to act in any such capacity, he as well as the body corporate is guilty of the offence and liable to be proceeded against and punished accordingly.

**7(5) [Where body corporate managed by members]** Where the affairs of a body corporate are managed by its members, subsection (4) applies in relation to the acts and defaults of a member in connection with his functions of management as if he were a director of the body corporate.

**7(6) [S. 731, 732(3) of Companies Act 1985]** For purposes of the following provisions of the Companies Act 1985–

(a) section 731 (summary proceedings under the Companies Acts), and

(b) section 732(3) (legal professional privilege),

this Act is to be treated as included in those Acts.

## 8 Interpretation

**8(1) [Definitions]** The following definitions apply for purposes of this Act–

**"business"** includes a profession;

**"initial"** includes any recognised abbreviation of a name;

**"lawful business name"**, in relation to a business, means a name under which the business was carried on without contravening section 2(1) of this Act or section 2 of the Registration of Business Names Act 1916;

**"local authority"** means any local authority within the meaning of the Local Government Act 1972 or the Local Government (Scotland) Act 1973, the Common Council of the City of London or the Council of the Isles of Scilly;

**"partnership"** includes a foreign partnership;

**"statutory maximum"** means–

(a) in England and Wales the prescribed sum under section 32 of the Magistrates' Courts Act 1980, and

(b) in Scotland, the prescribed sum under section 289B of the Criminal Procedure (Scotland) Act 1975;

and **"surname"**, in relation to a peer or person usually known by a British title different from his surname, means the title by which he is known.

**8(2) [Expressions also in Companies Act 1985]** Any expression used in this Act and also in the Companies Act 1985 has the same meaning in this Act as in that.

## 9 Northern Ireland

**9** This Act does not extend to Northern Ireland.

## 10 Commencement

**10** This Act comes into force on 1st July 1985.

## 11 Citation

**11** This Act may be cited as the Business Names Act 1985.

# COMPANIES CONSOLIDATION (CONSEQUENTIAL PROVISIONS) ACT 1985

Table of Contents

# COMPANIES CONSOLIDATION (CONSEQUENTIAL PROVISIONS) ACT 1985

(1985 Chapter 9)

## ARRANGEMENT OF SECTIONS

SCHEDULES

# COMPANIES CONSOLIDATION (CONSEQUENTIAL PROVISIONS) ACT 1985

(1985 Chapter 9)

An Act to make, in connection with the consolidation of the Companies Acts 1948 to 1983 and other enactments relating to companies, provision for transitional matters and savings, repeals (including the repeal, in accordance with recommendations of the Law Commission, of certain provisions of the Companies Act 1948 which are no longer of practical utility) and consequential amendments of other Acts.

*[11th March 1985]*

## OLD PUBLIC COMPANIES

### 1 Meaning of "old public company"

**1(1) [Definitions]** For the purposes of the Companies Act 1985 ("the principal Act") and this Act, an "old public company" is a company limited by shares or by guarantee and having a share capital in respect of which the following conditions are satisfied—

(a) the company either existed on 22nd December 1980 or was incorporated after that date pursuant to an application made before that date,

(b) on that date or, if later, on the day of the company's incorporation the company was not or (as the case may be) would not have been a private company within section 28 of the Companies Act 1948, and

(c) the company has not since that date or the day of the company's incorporation (as the case may be) either been re-registered as a public company or become a private company.

**1(2) [References to public company etc.]** References in the principal Act (other than so much of it as is derived from Part I of the Companies Act 1980, and other than section 33 (penalty for trading under misleading name)) to a public company or a company other than a private company are to be read as including (unless the context otherwise requires) references to an old public company, and references in that Act to a private company are to be read accordingly.

### 2 Re-registration as public company

**2(1) [Re-registration as public company]** An old public company may be re-registered as a public company if—

(a) the directors pass a resolution, complying with the following subsection, that it should be so re-registered, and

(b) an application for the purpose in the prescribed form and signed by a director or secretary of the company is delivered to the registrar of companies together with the documents mentioned in subsection (4) below; and

(c) at the time of the resolution, the conditions specified in section 3 below are satisfied.

**2(2) [Resolution in s. 2(1)]** The resolution must alter the company's memorandum so that it states that the company is to be a public company and make such other alterations in it as are necessary to bring it in substance and in form into conformity with the requirements of the principal Act with respect to the memorandum of a public company.

**2(3) [Copy of resolution to registrar]** A resolution of the directors under this section is subject to section 380 of the principal Act (copy of resolution to be forwarded to registrar of companies within 15 days).

**2(4) [Documents in s. 2(1)(b)]** The documents referred to in subsection (1)(b) are—

(a) a printed copy of the memorandum as altered in pursuance of the resolution, and

(b) a statutory declaration in the prescribed form by a director or secretary of the company that the resolution has been passed and that the conditions specified in section 3 of this Act were satisfied at the time of the resolution.

**2(5) [S. 2(4)(b) declaration sufficient evidence]** The registrar may accept a declaration under subsection (4)(b) as sufficient evidence that the resolution has been passed and the necessary conditions were satisfied.

**2(6) [Application of s. 47(1), (3)–(5) of principal Act]** Section 47(1) and (3) to (5) of the principal Act apply on an application for re-registration under this section as they apply on an application under section 43 of that Act.

## 3 Conditions for re-registering under s. 2

**3(1) [Conditions for s. 2(1)(c), 4]** The following are the conditions referred to in section 2(1)(c) (being conditions also relevant under section 4).

**3(2) [Nominal value of allotted share capital]** At the time concerned, the nominal value of the company's allotted share capital must not be less than the authorised minimum (defined in section 118 of the principal Act).

**3(3) [Shares — requirements]** In the case of all the shares of the company, or of all those of its shares which are comprised in a portion of the share capital which satisfies the condition in subsection (2)—

(a) each share must be paid up at least as to one-quarter of the nominal value of that share and the whole of any premium on it;

(b) where any of the shares in question or any premium payable on them has been fully or partly paid up by an undertaking given by any person that he or another should do work or perform services for the company or another, the undertaking must have been performed or otherwise discharged; and

(c) where any of the shares in question has been allotted as fully or partly paid up as to its nominal value or any premium payable on it otherwise than in cash, and the consideration for the allotment consists of or includes an undertaking (other than one to which paragraph (b) applies) to the company, then either—

(i) that undertaking must have been either performed or otherwise discharged, or

(ii) there must be a contract between the company and some person pursuant to which the undertaking is to be performed within 5 years from the time of the resolution.

## 4 Old public company becoming private

**4(1) [Non-registration as public company — resolution]** An old public company may pass a special resolution not to be re-registered under section 2 as a public company; and section 54 of the principal Act (litigated objection by shareholders) applies to the resolution as it would apply to a special resolution by a public company to be re-registered as private.

**4(2) [Certificate from registrar]** If either—

(a) 28 days from the passing of the resolution elapse without an application being made under section 54 of the principal Act (as applied), or

(b) such an application is made and proceedings are concluded on the application without the court making an order for the cancellation of the resolution,

the registrar of companies shall issue the company with a certificate stating that it is a private company; and the company then becomes a private company by virtue of the issue of the certificate.

**4(3) [Conclusion of proceedings on application]** For the purposes of subsection (2)(b), proceedings on the application are concluded—

(a) except in a case within the following paragraph, when the period mentioned in section 54(7) of the principal Act (as applied) for delivering an office copy of the court's order under that section to the registrar of companies has expired, or

(b) when the company has been notified that the application has been withdrawn.

**4(4) [Certificate from registrar]** If an old public company delivers to the registrar of companies a statutory declaration in the prescribed form by a director or secretary of the company that the company does not at the time of the declaration satisfy the conditions specified in section 3 for the company to be re-registered as public, the registrar shall issue the company with a certificate stating that it is a private company; and the company then becomes a private company by virtue of the issue of the certificate.

**4(5) [Certificate under s. 4(2), (4) conclusive evidence]** A certificate issued to a company under subsection (2) or (4) is conclusive evidence that the requirements of that subsection have been complied with and that the company is a private company.

# 5 Failure by old public company to obtain new classification

**5(1) [Offence]** If at any time a company which is an old public company has not delivered to the registrar of companies a declaration under section 4(4), the company and any officer of it who is in default is guilty of an offence unless at that time the company—

(a) has applied to be re-registered under section 2, and the application has not been refused or withdrawn, or

(b) has passed a special resolution not to be re-registered under that section, and the resolution has not been revoked, and has not been cancelled under section 54 of the principal Act as applied by section 4 above.

**5(2) [Penalty]** A person guilty of an offence under subsection (1) is liable on summary conviction to a fine not exceeding one-fifth of the statutory maximum or, on conviction after continued contravention, to a daily default fine not exceeding one-fiftieth of the statutory maximum for every day on which the subsection is contravened.

# 6 Shares of old public company held by itself; charges on own shares

**6(1) [Effect of section]** The following has effect notwithstanding section 1(2).

**6(2) [References in s. 146–149 of principal Act]** References to a public company in sections 146 to 149 of the principal Act (treatment of a company's shares when acquired by itself) do not include an old public company; and references in those sections to a private company are to be read accordingly.

**6(3) [Permitted charge]** In the case of a company which after 22nd March 1982 remained an old public company and did not before that date apply to be re-registered under section 8 of the Act of 1980 as a public company, any charge on its own shares which was in existence on or immediately before that date is a permitted charge for the purposes of Chapter V of Part V of the principal Act and accordingly not void under section 150 of that Act.

# 7 Offers of shares and debentures by old public company

7 (Repealed by Financial Services Act 1986, s. 212(3) and Sch. 17, Pt. I as from 29 April 1988.)

**History**

In regard to the date of the above repeal see SI 1988 740 (C. 22); s. 7 formerly read as follows:

"Section 81 of the principal Act applies to an old public company as if it were a private company such as is mentioned in subsection (1) of that section."

# 8 Trading under misleading name

**8(1) [Offence]** An old public company is guilty of an offence if it carries on any trade, profession or business under a name which includes, as its last part, the words "public limited company" or "cwmni cyfyngedig cyhoeddus".

**8(2) [Penalty]** A company guilty of an offence under this section, and any officer of the company who is in default, is liable on summary conviction as for an offence under section 33 of the principal Act.

## 9 Payment for share capital

**9(1) [Application of sections of principal Act]** Subject as follows, sections 99, 101 to 103, 106, 108 and 110 to 115 in Part IV of the principal Act apply to a company whose directors have passed and not revoked a resolution to be re-registered under section 2 of this Act, as those sections apply to a public company.

**9(2) [Non-application of sections of principal Act]** Sections 99, 101 to 103, 108 and 112 of the principal Act do not apply to the allotment of shares by a company, other than a public company registered as such on its original incorporation, where the contract for the allotment was entered into—

(a) except in a case falling within the following paragraph, on or before 22nd June 1982;

(b) in the case of a company re-registered or registered as a public company in pursuance of—

(i) a resolution to be re-registered under section 43 of the principal Act,

(ii) a resolution to be re-registered under section 2 of this Act, or

(iii) a resolution by a joint stock company that the company be a public company,

being a resolution that was passed on or before 22nd June 1982, before the date on which the resolution was passed.

MISCELLANEOUS SAVINGS

## 10 Pre-1901 companies limited by guarantee

**10** Section 15 of the principal Act does not apply in the case of companies registered before 1st January 1901.

## 11 Company official seal

**11(1) [Seal mentioned in s. 40 of principal Act]** A company which was incorporated before 12th February 1979 and which has such an official seal as is mentioned in section 40 of the principal Act may use the seal for sealing such securities and documents as are there mentioned, notwithstanding anything in any instrument constituting or regulating the company or in any instrument made before that date which relates to any securities issued by the company.

**11(2) [Application of instruments]** Any provision of such an instrument which requires any such securities or documents to be signed shall not apply to the securities or documents if they are sealed with that seal.

**11(3) [Requirements of Writing (Scotland) Act 1995]** The foregoing provisions of this section are without prejudice to the right of a company to subscribe such securities and documents in accordance with the Requirements of Writing (Scotland) Act 1995.

**History**

S. 11(3) inserted by Requirements of Writing (Scotland) Act 1995, s. 14(1), 15 and Sch. 4, para. 57 as from 1 August 1995.

## 12 Share premiums: retrospective relief

**12(1) [Application of section]** The relief given by this section (being a replacement of section 39 of the Companies Act 1981) applies only where a company has issued shares in circumstances to which this section applies before 4th February 1981.

**12(2) [Shares issued at a premium]** Subject as follows, this section applies where the issuing company (that is, the company issuing shares as mentioned in section 130 of the principal Act) has issued at a premium shares which were allotted in pursuance of any arrangement providing for the allotment of shares in the issuing company on terms that the consideration for the shares allotted was to be provided by the issue or transfer to the issuing company of shares in another company or by the cancellation of any shares in that other company not held by the issuing company.

**12(3) [Other company]** The other company in question must either have been at the time of the arrangement a subsidiary of the issuing company or of any company which was then the issuing company's holding company or have become such a subsidiary on the acquisition or cancellation of its shares in pursuance of the arrangement.

**12(4) [Premiums not transferred to account]** Any part of the premiums on the shares so issued which was not transferred to the company's share premium account in accordance with section 56 of the Act of 1948 shall be treated as if that section had never applied to those premiums (and may accordingly be disregarded in determining the sum to be included in the company's share premium account).

**12(5) [Interpretation]** Section 133(2) and (3) of the principal Act apply for the interpretation of this section; and for the purposes of this section—

(a) "company" (except in references to the issuing company) includes any body corporate, and

(b) the definition of "arrangement" in section 131(7) of the principal Act applies.

**12(6) [Regulations re relief from s. 130 of principal Act]** This section is deemed included in Chapter III of Part V of the principal Act for the purpose of the Secretary of State's power under section 134 of that Act to make regulations in respect of relief from the requirements of section 130 of that Act.

## 13 Saving, in case of re-issued debentures, of rights of certain mortgagees

**13** Whereas by section 104 of the Companies (Consolidation) Act 1908 it was provided that, upon the re-issue of redeemed debentures, the person entitled to the debentures should have the same rights and priorities as if the debentures had not previously been issued:

And whereas section 45 of the Companies Act 1928 amended section 104 of the Act of 1908 so as to provide (among other things) that the said person should have the same priorities as if the debentures had never been redeemed, but saved, in the case of debentures redeemed before, but re-issued after, 1st November 1929, the rights and priorities of persons under mortgages and charges created before that date:

Now, therefore, where any debentures which were redeemed before the date last mentioned have been re-issued after that date and before the commencement of the Act of 1948 (1st July 1948), or are or have been re-issued after that commencement, the re-issue of the debentures does not prejudice, and is deemed never to have prejudiced, any right or priority which any person would have had under or by virtue of any such mortgage or charge as above referred to if section 104 of the Act of 1908, as originally enacted, had been enacted in the Act of 1948 instead of section 90 of that Act, and in the principal Act instead of section 194 of that Act.

## 14 Removal of directors appointed for life pre-1945

**14** Section 303(1) of the principal Act does not, in the case of a private company, authorise the removal of a director holding office for life on 18th July 1945, whether or not subject to retirement under an age limit by virtue of the articles or otherwise.

## 15 Tax-free payments to directors

**15** Section 311(1) of the principal Act does not apply to remuneration under a contract which was in force on 18th July 1945 and provides expressly (and not by reference to the articles) for payment of remuneration as mentioned in that subsection; and section 311(2) does not apply to any provision contained in such a contract.

## 16 Statutory declaration of solvency in voluntary winding up

**16** In relation to a winding up commenced before 22nd December 1981, section 577 of the principal Act applies in the form of section 283 of the Act of 1948, without the amendment of that section made by section 105 of the Act of 1981.

## 17 Court's power to control proceedings

**17** Nothing in section 603 of the principal Act affects the practice or powers of the court as existing immediately before 1st November 1929, with respect to the staying of proceedings against a company registered in England and Wales and in course of being wound up.

## 18 Effect of floating charge in winding up

**18** In relation to a charge created before 31st December 1947, section 617(1) of the principal Act has effect with the substitution of "6 months" for "12 months".

## 19 Saving from s. 649 of principal Act

**19** Nothing in section 649 of the principal Act affects the practice or powers of the court as existing immediately before 1st November 1929, with respect to the costs of an application for leave to proceed with an action or proceeding against a company which is being wound up in England and Wales.

## 20 Continued application of certain provision of 1963 c. 16

**20** (Repealed by Banking Act 1987, s. 108(2) and Sch. 7, Pt. I as from 1 October 1987.)

**History**

In regard to the date of the above repeal see SI 1987/1664 (C. 50); s. 20 formerly read as follows:

"**20(1)** The repeal by the Banking Act 1979 (**the 1979 Act**) of the Protection of Depositors Act 1963 (**the 1963 Act**) shall not affect, and shall be deemed never to have affected, the application of the following provisions of the 1963 Act to unexempted companies on and after the commencement of Parts I and III of the 1979 Act, that is to say—

(a) sections 6 to 17, and

(b) so far as relevant to the operation of those sections, sections 5 and 22 to 27.

**(2)** In this section **'unexempted company'** means any company within the meaning of the 1963 Act which is not excepted by section 2(1) of the 1979 Act from the prohibition on the acceptance of deposits imposed by section 1 of the latter Act."

## 21 Priority of old debts in winding up

**21** Nothing in this Act affects the priority to which any person may have been entitled under section 319 of the 1948 Act in respect of a debt of any of the descriptions specified in paragraph (a)(ii) of subsection (1) of that section (which included references to profits tax and excess profits tax), or in paragraph (f) or (g) of that subsection (old workmen's compensation cases).

## 22 Saving as to certain old liquidations

**22(1) [Winding up provisions not to apply]** The provisions of the principal Act with respect to winding up (other than sections 635, 658 and 620 as applied for the purposes of section 620 and subsection (2) below) shall not apply to any company of which the winding up commenced before 1st November 1929; but every such company shall be wound up in the same manner and with the same incidents as if the Companies Act 1929, the Act of 1948 and the principal Act (apart from the sections above-mentioned) had not passed; and, for the purposes of the winding up, the Act or Acts under which the winding up commenced shall be deemed to remain in full force.

**22(2) [Copy of staying order to registrar]** A copy of every order staying or sisting the proceedings in a winding up commenced as above shall forthwith be forwarded by the company, or otherwise as may be prescribed, to the registrar of companies, who shall enter the order in his records relating to the company.

## 23 Restrictions on shares imposed pre-1982

**23** Where before 3rd December 1981 shares in a company were directed by order of the Secretary of State to be subject to the restrictions imposed by section 174 of the Act of 1948, and the order remains in force at the commencement date, nothing in this Act prevents the continued application of the order with such effect as it had immediately before the repeal of section 174 took effect.

## 24 Saving for conversion of winding up under 1981 s. 107

**24(1) [Effect of repeal of s. 107]** The repeal of section 107 of the 1981 Act (conversion of creditors' winding up into members' voluntary winding up, due to circumstances arising in the period April to August 1981) does not affect the enablement for such a conversion by means of a statutory declaration (complying with subsection (2) of the section) delivered to the registrar of companies after the commencement date.

**24(2) [For purposes of s. 577(4), 583 of principal Act]** For the purposes of sections 577(4) and 583 of the principal Act (consequences of actual or prospective failure to pay debts in full within the period stated by the directors in the declaration of solvency), the period stated in the declaration in the case of a winding up converted under section 107 is taken to have been 12 months from the commencement of the winding up, unless the contrary is shown.

MISCELLANEOUS AMENDMENTS

## 25 Security of information obtained for official purposes; privilege from disclosure

**25** In the Insurance Companies Act 1982, after section 47 the following sections are inserted—

"*Security of information*

**47A(1)** No information or document relating to a body which has been obtained under section 44(2) to (4) above shall, without the previous consent in writing of that body, be published or disclosed, except to a competent authority, unless the publication or disclosure is required for any of the purposes specified in section 449(1)(a) to (e) of the Companies Act.

**47A(2)** The competent authorities for the purposes of this section are the same as those specified in section 449 of that Act.

**47(A)3** This section does not extend to Northern Ireland.

*Privilege from disclosure*

**47B(1)** A requirement imposed under section 44(2) to (4) above shall not compel the production by any person of a document which he would in an action in the High Court or, in Scotland, in the Court of Session be entitled to refuse to produce on grounds of legal professional privilege or authorise the taking of possession of any such document which is in his possession.

**47B(2)** This section does not extend to Northern Ireland."

## 26 Industrial and Provident Societies Act 1967

**26(1) [Effect of section]** The following provisions of this section have effect with regard to the Industrial and Provident Societies Act 1967 (of which certain provisions were amended by section 10 of the Companies (Floating Charges and Receivers) (Scotland) Act 1972).

**26(2) [Substitution of s. 3 of 1967 Act]** For section 3 of the Act of 1967 the following shall be substituted—

"*Application to registered societies of provisions relating to floating charges*

**3(1)** Subject to the following provisions of this section, the following provisions of the Companies Act 1985 relating to floating charges, namely Chapter I of Part XVIII together with sections 517(2) and 617(3) (which provisions are in this Part referred to as 'the relevant provisions') shall apply to a registered society as they apply to an incorporated company.

**3(2)** Accordingly (subject as aforesaid) the relevant provisions shall, so far as applicable, apply as if—

(a) references to a company or an incorporated company were references to a registered society;

(b) references to the registrar and the registrar of companies were references to the registrar under this Act; and

(c) references, however expressed, to registration of a floating charge, or registration in accordance with Chapter II of Part XII of the Act of 1985, or delivery to or receipt by the registrar of particulars for registration, were references to the delivery to the registrar of any document required by section 4(1) of this Act to be so delivered.

**3(3)** Where, in the case of a registered society, there are in existence—

(a) a floating charge created by the society under the relevant provisions as applied by this section, and

(b) an agricultural charge created by the society under Part II of the Agricultural Credits (Scotland) Act 1929,

and any assets of the society are subject to both charges, sections 463(1)(c) and 464(4)(b) of the Act of 1985, shall have effect for the purpose of determining the ranking with one another of those charges as if the agricultural charge were a floating charge created under the relevant provisions and registered under that Act at the same time as it was registered under Part II of the Act of 1929.

3(4) In this section, and in the following provisions of this Part of this Act, 'registered society' does not include a registered society whose registered office is situated in England and Wales.

3(5) In their application to a registered society, the relevant provisions shall have effect with the following modifications—

(a) in sections 462(2) and 517(2), the references to the Court of Session shall be read as references to any sheriff court;

(b) section 462(5) shall be subject only to such provisions of the Act of 1985 as apply (by virtue of section 55 of the principal Act) to registered societies; and

(c) in section 466, subsections (4) and (5) and the words 'subsection (4) of' in subsection (6) shall be omitted."

**26(3) [Continuation of s. 4(1), (2)(a) of 1967 Act]** Subsections (1) and (2)(a) of section 4 of the Act of 1967 continue in force as amended by paragraph (iv) of section 10 of the Companies (Floating Charges and Receivers) (Scotland) Act 1972.

**26(4) [Substitution]** In sections 4 and 5 of the Act of 1967, for the words "Part I of the Act of 1972" there shall be substituted the words "the relevant provisions of the Companies Act 1985".

## 27 Amendment of Table A

27 In Table A scheduled to the Companies (Alteration of Table A etc.) Regulations 1984, for the words "the Acts", wherever they occur, there shall be substituted the words "the Act"; and in regulation 1 of the Table (definitions) for "Companies Acts 1948 to 1983" there shall be substituted "Companies Act 1985".

**Note**

Now see the Companies (Tables A to F) Regulations 1985 (SI 1985/805).

### REPEAL OF OBSOLETE PROVISIONS

## 28 Stannaries and cost-book companies

28 In the Act of 1948, the following enactments shall cease to have effect—

in section 218 (courts' winding-up jurisdiction), subsection (4) and, in subsection (5), the words from "An order made under this provision" to "1896";

section 357 (attachment of debt due to contributory in stannaries court winding-up);

section 358 (preferential payments in stannaries cases);

section 359 (provisions as to mine-club funds);

in section 382 (companies not formed under 1948 Act or its predecessors, but authorised to register), in subsection (1)(b), the words "or being a company within the stannaries";

in section 384(b) and section 385(b) (documents required for registration), the words "cost-book regulations" in each paragraph;

in section 394(7) (definition of "instrument"), the words "cost-book regulations";

in section 424 (registration offices), subsection (4);

in section 434 (prohibition of partnerships with more than 20 members), in subsection (1), the words from "or is a company" to the end of the subsection;

section 450 (jurisdiction of stannaries court); and

in section 455(1) (interpretation), the definition of "the court exercising the stannaries jurisdiction" and, in the definition of "the registrar of companies", the words "or in the stannaries".

# REPEALS, ETC. CONSEQUENTIAL ON COMPANIES ACTS CONSOLIDATION; CONTINUITY OF LAW

## 29 Repeals

**29** The enactments specified in the second column of Schedule 1 to this Act are repealed to the extent specified in the third column of the Schedule.

## 30 Amendment of post-1948 statutes

**30** The enactments specified in the first column of Schedule 2 to this Act (being enactments passed after the Act of 1948 and containing references to that Act or others of the Companies Acts 1948 to 1983) are amended as shown in the second column of the Schedule.

## 31 Continuity of law

**31(1) [Definitions]** In this section—

(a) **"the new Acts"** means the principal Act, the Company Securities (Insider Dealing) Act 1985, the Business Names Act 1985 and this Act;

(b) **"the old Acts"** means the Companies Acts 1948 to 1983 and any other enactment which is repealed by this Act and replaced by a corresponding provision in the new Acts; and

(c) **"the commencement date"** means 1st July 1985.

**31(2) [Anything done or treated as done under old Acts]** So far as anything done or treated as done under or for the purposes of any provision of the old Acts could have been done under or for the purposes of the corresponding provision of the new Acts, it is not invalidated by the repeal of that provision but has effect as if done under or for the purposes of the corresponding provision; and any order, regulation or other instrument made or having effect under any provision of the old Acts shall, in so far as its effect is preserved by this subsection, be treated for all purposes as made and having effect under the corresponding provision.

**31(3) [Periods of time in old Acts]** Where any period of time specified in a provision of the old Acts is current immediately before the commencement date, the new Acts have effect as if the corresponding provision had been in force when the period began to run; and (without prejudice to the foregoing) any period of time so specified and current is deemed for the purposes of the new Acts—

(a) to run from the date or event from which it was running immediately before the commencement date, and

(b) to expire (subject to any provision of the new Acts for its extension) whenever it would have expired if the new Acts had not been passed;

and any rights, priorities, liabilities, reliefs, obligations, requirements, powers, duties or exemptions dependent on the beginning, duration or end of such a period as above mentioned shall be under the new Acts as they were or would have been under the old.

**31(4) [References to provisions of new Acts]** Where in any provision of the new Acts there is a reference to another provision of those Acts, and the first-mentioned provision operates, or is capable of operating, in relation to things done or omitted, or events occurring or not occurring, in the past (including in particular past acts of compliance with any enactment, failures of compliance, contraventions, offences and convictions of offences), the reference to that other provision is to be read as including a reference to the corresponding provision of the old Acts.

**31(5) [Effect of contravention of old Acts before commencement date]** A contravention of any provision of the old Acts committed before the commencement date shall not be visited with any severer punishment under or by virtue of the new Acts than would have been applicable under that provision at the time of the contravention; but—

(a) where an offence for the continuance of which a penalty was provided has been committed under any provision of the old Acts, proceedings may be taken under the new Acts in respect of the continuance of the offence after the commencement date in the like manner as if the offence had been committed under the corresponding provision of the new Acts; and

(b) the repeal of any transitory provision of the old Acts (not replaced by any corresponding provision of the new Acts) requiring a thing to be done within a certain time does not affect a person's continued liability to be prosecuted and punished in respect of the failure, or continued failure, to do that thing.

**31(6) [Interpretation of references to old provisions]** A reference in any enactment, instrument or document (whether express or implied, and in whatever phraseology) to a provision (whether first in force before or after the Act of 1948 or contained in that Act) which is replaced by a corresponding provision of the new Acts is to be read, where necessary to retain for the enactment, instrument or document the same force and effect as it would have had but for the passing of the new Acts, as, or as including, a reference to that corresponding provision.

**31(7) [Effect of s. 31(6)]** The generality of subsection (6) is not affected by any specific conversion of references made by this Act, nor by the inclusion in any provision of the new Acts of a reference (whether express or implied, and in whatever phraseology) to the provision of the old Acts corresponding to that provision, or to a provision of the old Acts which is replaced by a corresponding provision of the new.

**31(8) [Effect of new Acts]** Nothing in the new Acts affects—

(a) the registration or re-registration of any company under the former Companies Acts, or the continued existence of any company by virtue of such registration or re-registration; or

(b) the application of—
  (i) Table B in the Joint Stock Companies Act 1856, or
  (ii) Table A in the Companies Act 1862, the Companies (Consolidation) Act 1908, the Companies Act 1929 or the Companies Act 1948,

to any company existing immediately before the commencement date; or

(c) the operation of any enactment providing for any partnership, association or company being wound up, or being wound up as a company or as an unregistered company under any of the former Companies Acts.

**31(9) [Savings from repeal of s. 459 of 1948 Act]** Anything saved from repeal by section 459 of the Act of 1948 and still in force immediately before the commencement date remains in force notwithstanding the repeal of the whole of that Act.

**31(10) [Provisions of new Acts previously in statutory instruments]** Where any provision of the new Acts was, immediately before the commencement date, contained in or given effect by a statutory instrument (whether or not made under a power in any of the old Acts), then—

(a) the foregoing provisions of this section have effect as if that provision was contained in the old Acts, and

(b) insofar as the provision was, immediately before that date, subject to a power (whether or not under the old Acts) of variation or revocation, nothing in the new Acts is to be taken as prejudicing any future exercise of the power.

**31(11) [Without prejudice]** The provisions of this section are without prejudice to the operation of sections 16 and 17 of the Interpretation Act 1978 (savings from, and effect of, repeals); and for the purposes of section 17(2) of that Act (construction of references to enactments repealed and replaced; continuity of powers preserved in repealing enactment), any provision of the old Acts which is replaced by a provision of the principal Act, the Company Securities (Insider Dealing) Act 1985 or the Business Names Act 1985 is deemed to have been repealed and re-enacted by that one of the new Acts and not by this Act.

GENERAL

## 32 Interpretation

**32** In this Act—

**"the Act of 1948"** means the Companies Act 1948,

**"the Act of 1980"** means the Companies Act 1980,

**"the Act of 1981"** means the Companies Act 1981, and
**"the principal Act"** means the Companies Act 1985;

and expressions used in this Act and also in the principal Act have the same meanings in this Act as in that (the provisions of Part XXVI of that Act to apply accordingly).

## 33 Northern Ireland

**33** Except in so far as it has effect for maintaining the continuity of the law, or—

(a) repeals any enactment which extends to Northern Ireland, or

(b) amends any enactment which extends to Northern Ireland (otherwise than by the insertion of provisions expressed not so to extend),

nothing in this Act extends to Northern Ireland.

## 34 Commencement

**34** This Act comes into force on 1st July 1985.

## 35 Citation

**35** This Act may be cited as the Companies Consolidation (Consequential Provisions) Act 1985.

# Schedule 1 — Enactments Repealed

Section 29

| Chapter | Short title | Extent of repeal |
|---|---|---|
| 1948 c. 38. | Companies Act 1948. | The whole Act. |
| 1952 c. 33. | Finance Act 1952. | In section 30, subsections (2) and (3); in subsection (5) the words "(2) or (3)"; and in subsection (6) the words from "and subsection (3)" to the end. |
| 1961 c. 46. | Companies (Floating Charges) (Scotland) Act 1961. | Section 7. |
| 1966 c. 18. | Finance Act 1966. | In Schedule 6, in paragraph 14, the words "section 319(1)(a)(ii) of the Companies Act 1948 and in". |
| 1966 c. 29. | Singapore Act 1966. | In the Schedule, paragraph 14. |
| 1967 c. 81. | Companies Act 1967. | The whole Act, except so much of Part II as remains unrepealed immediately before the commencement of this Act. |
| 1970 c. 8. | Insolvency Services (Accounting and Investment) Act 1970. | In section 1(3), paragraph (c) (with the "and" immediately preceding it). |
| 1972 c. 67. | Companies (Floating Charges and Receivers) (Scotland) Act 1972. | The whole Act. |
| 1972 c. 68. | European Communities Act 1972. | Section 9. |
| 1973 c. 38. | Social Security Act 1973. | In Schedule 27, paragraph 9. |
| 1973 c. 48. | Pakistan Act 1973. | In Schedule 3, paragraph 3(1) and (4). |
| 1973 c. 51. | Finance Act 1973. | In Schedule 19, paragraph 14. |
| 1974 c. 37. | Health and Safety at Work Etc. Act 1974. | Section 79. |
| 1975 c. 18. | Social Security (Consequential Provisions) Act 1975. | In Schedule 2, paragraph 7. |
| 1975 c. 45. | Finance (No. 2) Act 1975. | In Part IV of Schedule 12, paragraph 6(1)(e). |
| 1975 c. 60. | Social Security Pensions Act 1975. | In Schedule 4, paragraph 3. |
| 1976 c. 47. | Stock Exchange (Completion of Bargains) Act 1976. | Sections 1 to 4.<br>Section 7(3). |

| Chapter | Short title | Extent of repeal |
|---|---|---|
| 1976 c. 60. | Insolvency Act 1976. | In section 1(1), the words "the winding up of companies and".<br>Section 9.<br>Section 14(3).<br>In section 14(6), the word "9".<br>In Part I of Schedule 1, the heading "The Companies Act 1948" and the entries under that heading; and in Part II of that Schedule in paragraph 1, sub-paragraph (c), in paragraph 2, sub-paragraph (c), paragraph 6, and in paragraph 7, sub-paragraph (b).<br>In Schedule 2, paragraphs 3 and 4. |
| 1976 c. 69. | Companies Act 1976. | The whole Act. |
| 1979 c. 53. | Charging Orders Act 1979. | In section 4, the words "and in section 325 of the Companies Act 1948", and the words "in each case". |
| 1980 c. 22. | Companies Act 1980. | The whole Act. |
| 1981 c. 54. | Supreme Court Act 1981. | In Schedule 5, the entry relating to the Companies Act 1948. |
| 1981 c. 62. | Companies Act 1981. | The whole Act. |
| 1981 c. 63. | Betting and Gaming Duties Act 1981. | In section 30(1), the word "or" at the end of paragraph (b), and paragraph (c).<br>In section 30(2), paragraph (c). |
| 1981 c. 65. | Trustee Savings Banks Act 1981. | In Schedule 6, the entry under "COMPANIES ACT 1948". |
| 1982 c. 4. | Stock Transfer Act 1982. | In Schedule 2, paragraphs 4 and 5. |
| 1982 c. 46. | Employment Act 1982. | Section 1. |
| 1982 c. 48. | Criminal Justice Act 1982. | In section 46(4)(a) the words from "except" to "1981". |
| 1982 c. 50. | Insurance Companies Act 1982. | In Schedule 4, paragraph 14. |
| 1983 c. 50. | Companies (Beneficial Interests) Act 1983. | The whole Act. |
| 1983 c. 53. | Car Tax Act 1983. | In Schedule 1, in paragraph 4(1), the word "or" at the end of sub-paragraph (b), and sub-paragraph (c); and in that Schedule, in paragraph 4(2), sub-paragraph (c). |
| 1983 c. 55. | Value Added Tax Act 1983. | In Schedule 7, in paragraph 12(1), the word "or" at the end of sub-paragraph (b); and sub-paragraph (c), and in that Schedule, in paragraph 12(2), sub-paragraph (c). |

## Schedule 2 — Amendments of Enactments Consequential on Consolidation of Companies Acts

Section 30

| Enactment | Amendment |
|---|---|
| Landlord and Tenant Act 1954 (c. 56): | |
| Section 42(1) ... ... ... ... | For the words from "Companies Act 1948" to the end of the subsection substitute "Companies Act 1985 by section 736 of that Act". |
| Opticians Act 1958 (c. 32): | |
| Section 27(3) ... ... ... ... | For "paragraph (a) of subsection (1) of section one hundred and sixty-one of the Companies Act 1948 by the Board of Trade" substitute "section 389(1)(a) of the Companies Act 1985 by the Secretary of State". |
| Agricultural Marketing Act 1958 (c. 47): | |
| Schedule 2 ... ... ... ... ... | (a) In paragraph 4(1) for "Part IX of the Companies Act 1948" substitute "Part XXI of the Companies Act 1985".<br>(b) In paragraph 4(2), for "section three hundred and ninety-nine of the Companies Act 1948" substitute "sections 666 to 669 of the Companies Act 1985".<br>(c) For paragraph 4(3) substitute —<br>"(3) Section 668 shall not apply, and section 669 shall apply as if in paragraph (a) of that section the words "or any member of it as such" were omitted." |
| Horticultural Act 1960 (c. 22): | |
| Section 14(3) ... ... ... ... | For "paragraph (a) of subsection (1) of section one hundred and sixty-one of the Companies Act 1948 by the Board of Trade" substitute "section 389(1)(a) of the Companies Act 1985 by the Secretary of State". |
| Corporate Bodies' Contracts Act 1960 (c. 46): | |
| Section 2 ... ... ... ... ... | For "Companies Act 1948" substitute "Companies Act 1985". |
| Charities Act 1960 (c. 58): | |
| Section 8(3) ... ... ... ... ... | For "paragraph (a) of subsection (1) of section one hundred and sixty-one of the Companies Act 1948 by the Board of Trade" substitute "section 389(1)(a) of the Companies Act 1985 by the Secretary of State". |
| Professions Supplementary to Medicine Act 1960 (c. 66): | |

| Enactment | Amendment |
|---|---|
| Schedule 1, Part III ... ... ... | In paragraph 18(4), for "paragraph (a) of subsection (1) of section one hundred and sixty-one of the Companies Act 1948 by the Board of Trade" substitute "section 389(1)(a) of the Companies Act 1985 by the Secretary of State". |
| Transport Act 1962 (c. 46): | |
| Section 24(2) ... ... ... ... | For "paragraph (a) of subsection (1) of section one hundred and sixty-one of the Companies Act 1948 by the Board of Trade" substitute "section 389(1)(a) of the Companies Act 1985 by the Secretary of State". |
| Section 92 ... ... ... ... ... | In the definition of "subsidiary", for "section one hundred and fifty-four of the Companies Act 1948" substitute "section 736 of the Companies Act 1985". |
| Betting, Gaming and Lotteries Act 1963 (c. 2): | |
| Section 55(1) ... ... ... ... | In the definition of "qualified accountant", for "section 161(1)(a) of the Companies Act 1948 by the Board of Trade" substitute "section 389(1)(a) of the Companies Act 1985 by the Secretary of State". |
| Schedule 2 ... ... ... ... ... | (a) In paragraph 24(1), for "section 1 of the Companies Act 1976" substitute "section 241 of the Companies Act 1985".<br>(b) In paragraph 24(2), for "section 14(3), (4) and (6) of the Companies Act 1967" substitute —<br>"the following provisions of the Companies Act 1985 —<br>section 236(2), as read with section 262 (matters to be stated in auditors' report), and<br>section 237(1) and (4) (responsibilities of auditors in preparing their report)". |
| Stock Transfer Act 1963 (c. 18): | |
| Section 1(4) ... ... ... ... ... | In paragraph (a), for "Companies Act 1948" substitute "Companies Act 1985". |
| Section 2 ... ... ... ... ... | (a) In subsection (2), for "section 79(1) of the Companies Act 1948" substitute "section 184 of the Companies Act 1985".<br>(b) In subsection (3)(a), for "section 75 of the Companies Act 1948" substitute "section 183(1) and (2) of the Companies Act 1985". |
| Harbours Act 1964 (c. 40): | |
| Section 42 ... ... ... ... | (a) In subsection (6), for "Companies Act 1948 to 1981" substitute "Companies Act 1985"; and for "those Acts" substitute "that Act".<br>(b) In subsection (7)(a), for "Companies Acts 1948 to 1981" substitute "Companies Act 1985".<br>(c) In subsection (9), for "section 154 of the Companies Act 1948" substitute "section 736 of the Companies Act 1985". |

| Enactment | Amendment |
|---|---|
| Trading Stamps Act 1964 (c. 71): | |
| Section 1(4) ... ... ... ... ... | For "Companies Act 1948" substitute "Companies Act 1985". |
| Hairdressers (Registration) Act 1964 (c. 89): | |
| Section 13(2) ... ... ... ... | For "section 161(1)(a) of the Companies Act 1948 by the Board of Trade" substitute "section 389(1)(a) of the Companies Act 1985 by the Secretary of State". |
| Industrial and Provident Societies Act 1965 (c. 12): | |
| Section 1(2) ... ... ... ... ... | For "Companies Act 1948" substitute "Companies Act 1985". |
| Section 52(2) ... ... ... ... | The same amendment; and for "Act of 1948" substitute "Act of 1985". |
| Section 53 ... ... ... ... ... | (a) In subsection (1), for "section 141 of the Companies Act 1948" substitute "section 378 of the Companies Act 1985".<br>(b) In subsection (4), for "Companies Act 1948" substitute "Companies Act 1985". |
| Section 55 ... ... ... ... ... | For "Companies Act 1948" substitute "Companies Act 1985". |
| Section 74 ... ... ... ... ... | In the definition of "Companies Acts", the same amendment. |
| Cereals Marketing Act 1965 (c. 14): | |
| Section 21(5) ... ... ... ... | In paragraph (b), for "section 161(1)(a) of the Companies Act 1948 by the Board of Trade" substitute "section 389(1)(a) of the Companies Act 1985 by the Secretary of State". |
| Teaching Council (Scotland) Act 1965 (c. 19): | |
| Schedule 1 ... ... ... ... ... | In paragraph 13(3), for "section 161(1)(a) of the Companies Act 1948 by the Board of Trade" substitute "section 389(1)(a) of the Companies Act 1985 by the Secretary of State". |
| Coal Industry Act 1965 (c. 82): | |
| Section 1(2) ... ... ... ... ... | In paragraph (d), for "section 154 of the Companies Act 1948" substitute "section 736 of the Companies Act 1985". |
| National Health Service Act 1966 (c. 8): | |
| Section 8(2) ... ... ... ... ... | In paragraph (e), for "section 161(1)(a) of the Companies Act 1948 by the Board of Trade" substitute "section 389(1)(a) of the Companies Act 1985 by the Secretary of State". |
| Universities (Scotland) Act 1966 (c. 13): | |
| Section 12(2) ... ... ... ... | In paragraph (e), for "section 161(1)(a) of the Companies Act 1948 by the Board of Trade" substitute "section 389(1)(a) of the Companies Act 1985 by the Secretary of State". |
| General Rate Act 1967 (c. 9): | |
| Section 32A(6) ... ... ... ... | In the definition of "subsidiary", for "section 154 of the Companies Act 1948" substitute "section 736 of the Companies Act 1985". |

| Enactment | Amendment |
| --- | --- |
| Agriculture Act 1967 (c. 22): Section 19(3) ... ... ... ... | For "section 161(1)(a) of the Companies Act 1948 by the Board of Trade" substitute "section 389(1)(a) of the Companies Act 1985 by the Secretary of State". |
| Companies Act 1967 (c. 81): Section 90 ... ... ... ... ... | For this section substitute the following —<br>"*Summary proceedings*<br>**90(1)** Summary proceedings for an offence under this Part may (without prejudice to any jurisdiction exercisable apart from this subsection) be taken against a body corporate at any place at which the body has a place of business, and against any other person at any place at which he is for the time being.<br>**90(2)** Notwithstanding anything in section 127(1) of the Magistrates' Courts Act 1980, an information relating to an offence under this Part which is triable by a magistrates' court in England and Wales may be so tried if it is laid at any time within 3 years after the commission of the offence and within 12 months after the date on which evidence sufficient in the opinion of the Director of Public Prosecutions, the Secretary of State or the Industrial Assurance Commissioner (as the case may be) to justify the proceedings comes to his knowledge.<br>**90(3)** Summary proceedings in Scotland for an offence under this part shall not be commenced after the expiration of 3 years from the commission of the offence.<br>Subject to this (and notwithstanding anything in section 331 of the Criminal Procedure (Scotland) Act 1975), such proceedings may (in Scotland) be commenced at any time within 12 months after the date on which evidence sufficient in the Lord Advocate's opinion to justify the proceedings comes to his knowledge or, where such evidence was reported to him by the Secretary of State or the Industrial Assurance Commissioner, within 12 months after the date on which it came to the knowledge of the former or the latter (as the case may be); and subsection (3) of that section applies for the purpose of this subsection as it applies for the purposes of that section.<br>**90(4)** For purposes of this section, a certificate of the Director of Public Prosecutions, the Lord Advocate, the Secretary of State or the Industrial Assurance Commissioner (as the case may be) as to the date on which such evidence came to his knowledge is conclusive evidence." |

| Enactment | Amendment |
|---|---|
| Hearing Aid Council Act 1968 (c. 50): | |
| Section 12(3) ... ... ... ... | For "Board of Trade for the purposes of paragraph (a) of subsection (1) of section 161 of the Companies Act 1948" substitute "Secretary of State for the purposes of section 389(1)(a) of the Companies Act 1985". |
| Friendly and Industrial and Provident Societies Act 1968 (c. 55): | |
| Section 7(1) ... ... ... ... ... | For "section 161(1)(a) of the Companies Act 1948 by the Board of Trade" substitute "section 389(1)(a) of the Companies Act 1985 by the Secretary of State"; and for "by the Board of Trade under section 161(1)(b)" substitute "by the Secretary of State under section 389(1)(b)". |
| Section 8(2) ... ... ... ... ... | In paragraph (b), for "section 161(2) of the Companies Act 1948" substitute "section 389(6) of the Companies Act 1985". |
| Transport Act 1968 (c. 73): | |
| Section 14(2) ... ... ... ... | For "section 161(1)(a) of the Companies Act 1948 by the Board of Trade" substitute "section 389(1)(a) of the Companies Act 1985 by the Secretary of State". |
| Section 69(11) ... ... ... ... | For "section 154(5) of the Companies Act 1948" substitute "section 744 of the Companies Act 1985". |
| Section 92(1) ... ... ... ... | In the definition of "subsidiary", for "section 154 of the Companies Act 1948" substitute "section 736 of the Companies Act 1985". |
| Post Office Act 1969 (c. 48): | |
| Section 86(2) ... ... ... ... | For "section 154 of the Companies Act 1948" substitute "section 736 of the Companies Act 1985"; and for "section 150(4)" substitute "section 736(5)(b)". |
| Taxes Management Act 1970 (c. 9): | |
| Section 108(2) ... ... ... ... | For "Companies Act 1948" substitute "Companies Act 1985". |
| Income and Corporation Taxes Act 1970 (c. 10): | |
| Section 64A ... ... ... ... | For "proviso (b) to section 54(1) of the Companies Act 1948" substitute "section 153(4)(b) of the Companies Act 1985". |
| Section 242(1) ... ... ... ... | For "Companies Act 1948" substitute "Companies Act 1985". |
| Section 247(7) ... ... ... ... | The same amendment. |
| Section 265(5) ... ... ... ... | For "section 244 of the Companies Act 1948" substitute "section 538 of the Companies Act 1985". |
| Section 272(2) ... ... ... ... | For "Companies Act 1948" substitute "Companies Act 1985". |

| Enactment | Amendment |
|---|---|
| Section 280(3) … … … … | For "section 66 of the Companies Act 1948" substitute "section 135 of the Companies Act 1985". |
| Section 343(9) … … … … | For "Companies Act 1948" substitute "Companies Act 1985". |
| Section 482(10) … … … … | For "section 455 of the Companies Act 1948" substitute "Part XXVI of the Companies Act 1985". |
| Agriculture Act 1970 (c. 40): | |
| Section 20(2) … … … … | For "section 161(1)(a) of the Companies Act 1948 by the Board of Trade" substitute section 389(1)(a) of the Companies Act 1985 by the Secretary of State". |
| Section 24(3) … … … … | For "Companies Act 1948" substitute "Companies Act 1985". |
| Atomic Energy Authority Act 1971 (c. 11): | |
| Section 14 … … … … … | For "Companies Acts 1948 to 1967" substitute "Companies Act 1985". |
| Coal Industry Act 1971 (c. 16): | |
| Section 10(3) … … … … | For "section 154 of the Companies Act 1948" substitute "section 736 of the Companies Act 1985"; and for "subsection (4) of section 150 of that Act" substitute "subsection (5)(b) of that section". |
| Redemption of Standard Securities (Scotland) Act 1971 (c. 45): | |
| Section 2 … … … … … | For "section 89 of the Companies Act 1948" substitute "section 193 of the Companies Act 1985". |
| Prevention of Oil Pollution Act 1971 (c. 60): | |
| Section 15 … … … … … | (a) In subsection (1), for "section 412 or section 437 of the Companies Act 1948" substitute "section 695 or section 725 of the Companies Act 1985".<br>(b) In subsection (3), for "sections 412 and 437 of the Companies Act 1948" substitute "sections 695 and 725 of the Companies Act 1985". |
| Finance Act 1971 (c. 68): | |
| Section 31(4) … … … … | For "section 30 of the Finance Act 1952" substitute "section 614 of the Companies Act 1985 (with paragraph 3 of Schedule 19 to that Act)." |
| Finance Act 1972 (c. 41): | |
| Schedule 16 … … … … … | In paragraph 13(5), for "Companies Act 1948" substitute "Companies Act 1985". |
| Gas Act 1972 (c. 60): | |
| Section 23(7) … … … … | For "section 161(1)(a) of the Companies Act 1948" substitute "section 389(1)(a) of the Companies Act 1985". |

| Enactment | Amendment |
|---|---|
| Section 48(1) ... ... ... ... | (a) In the definition of "company", for "Companies Act 1948" substitute "Companies Act 1985".<br>(b) In the definition of "holding company", for "section 154 of the Companies Act 1948" substitute "section 736 of the Companies Act 1985".<br>(c) In the definition of "subsidiary", for "section 154 of the Companies Act 1948" substitute "section 736 of the Companies Act 1985"; and for "section 150(4) of that Act" substitute "subsection (5)(b) of that section". |
| Land Charges Act 1972 (c. 61):<br>Section 3(8) ... ... ... ... ... | Omit "and", and insert at the end of the subsection "and sections 395 to 398 of the Companies Act 1985". |
| Industry Act 1972 (c. 63):<br>Section 10 ... ... ... ... ... | For "Companies Act 1948 by section 154" substitute "Companies Act 1985 by section 736". |
| Coal Industy Act 1973 (c. 8):<br>Section 12(1) ... ... ... ... | For "section 154 of the Companies Act 1948" substitute "section 736 of the Companies Act 1985"; and for "subsection (4) of section 150 of that Act" substitute "subsection (5)(b) of that section". |
| Fair Trading Act 1973 (c. 41):<br>Section 92 ... ... ... ... ... | For subsections (2) and (3) substitute —<br>"(2) The matters which may be so specified or described are any matters which in the case of a company registered under the Companies Act 1985 (or the previous corresponding legislation) —<br>(a) could in accordance with sections 432 and 433 of that Act be investigated by an inspector appointed under section 432, or<br>(b) could in accordance with section 442 of that Act, or in accordance with any provisions as applied by section 443(1), be investigated by an inspector appointed under section 442.<br>(3) For purposes connected with any investigation made by an inspector appointed under this section —<br>(a) sections 434 to 436 of the Companies Act 1985 (or those sections as applied by section 443(1)) shall have effect as they do for the purposes of any investigation under section 432 or 442 of that Act, and |

| Enactment | Amendment |
| --- | --- |
| | (b) the provisions of that Act referred to in this and the last preceding subsection shall be taken to extend throughout the United Kingdom." |
| Section 137(5) ... ... ... ... | For "section 154 of the Companies Act 1948" substitute "section 736 of the Companies Act 1985". |
| Hallmarking Act 1973 (c. 43): Schedule 4 ... ... ... ... ... | In paragraph 19, sub-paragraph (2), for "section 161(1)(a) of the Companies Act 1948" substitute "section 389(1)(a) of the Companies Act 1985". |
| Merchant Shipping Act 1974 (c. 43): Section 2(9) ... ... ... ... ... | In the definition of "group", for "section 154 of the Companies Act 1948" substitute "section 736 of the Companies Act 1985". |
| Friendly Societies Act 1974 (c. 46): Section 36(1) ... ... ... ... | For "section 161(1)(a) of the Companies Act 1948" substitute "section 389(1)(a) of the Companies Act 1985"; and for "section 161(1)(b)" substitute "section 389(1)(b)". |
| Section 87(2) ... ... ... ... | For "Companies Act 1948" substitute "Companies Act 1985". |
| Section 111(1) ... ... ... ... | For "Companies Acts 1948 to 1967" substitute "Companies Act 1985". |
| Finance Act 1975 (c. 7): Section 48(5) ... ... ... ... | In paragaph (b), for "section 154 of the Companies Act 1948" substitute "section 736 of the Companies Act 1985". |
| Farriers Registration Act 1975 (c. 35): Schedule 1, Part I ... ... ... ... | In paragraph 12(2)(e) for "section 161(1)(a) of the Companies Act 1948" substitute "section 389(1)(a) of the Companies Act 1985". |
| Finance (No. 2) Act 1975 (c. 45): Section 36(4) ... ... ... ... | For "section 150(4) of the Companies Act 1948" substitute "section 736(5)(b) of the Companies Act 1985". |
| Schedule 12, Part IV ... ... ... | In paragraph 6(1), for "Companies Act 1948" substitute "Companies Act 1985"; and —<br>(a) in sub-paragraphs (a) to (d), for "107", "124", "125" and "126" substitute respectively "287", "363", "364" and "365";<br>(b) omit sub-paragraph (e);<br>(c) in sub-paragraphs (f) to (h), for "200(4)", "407" and "409" substitute respectively "288(2)", "691" and "692";<br>(d) in sub-paragraph (i), for "section 410" substitute "Chapter II of Part XXIII"; and<br>(e) in sub-paragraphs (j) and (k), for "411" and "416" substitute respectively "693" and "699". |

| Enactment | Amendment |
|---|---|
| Prescription and Limitation (Scotland) Act 1975 (c. 52): | |
| Section 9(1) ... ... ... ... ... | In paragraph (b), for "section 318 of the Companies Act 1948" substitute "section 613 of the Companies Act 1985". |
| Industry Act 1975 (c. 68): | |
| Section 37(1) ... ... ... ... | In the definitions of "holding company" and "subsidiary", for "section 154 of the Companies Act 1948" (twice) substitute "section 736 of the Companies Act 1985". |
| Welsh Development Agency Act 1975 (c. 70): | |
| Section 27(1) ... ... ... ... | In the definitions of "holding company" and "subsidiary", for "section 154 of the Companies Act 1948" (twice) substitute "section 736 of the Companies Act 1985"; and in the definition of "wholly-owned subsidiary", for "section 150(4) of the Companies Act 1948" substitute "section 736(5)(b) of the Companies Act 1985". |
| Petroleum and Submarine Pipe-lines Act 1975 (c. 74): | |
| Section 10(4) ... ... ... ... | For "section 161(1)(a) of the Companies Act 1948" substitute "section 389(1)(a) of the Companies Act 1985". |
| Section 48 ... ... ... ... ... | For "section 154 of the Companies Act 1948" substitute "section 736 of the Companies Act 1985"; and for "section 150(4) of the said Act of 1948" substitute "section 736(5)(b) of the said Act of 1985". |
| Policyholders Protection Act 1975 (c. 75): | |
| Section 5(1) ... ... ... ... ... | In paragraph (a), for "Companies Act 1948" substitute "Companies Act 1985". |
| Section 15(1) ... ... ... ... | For "section 238 of the Companies Act 1948" substitute "section 532 of the Companies Act 1985". |
| Section 16 ... ... ... ... ... | (a) In subsection (1)(b), for "Companies Act 1948" substitute "Companies Act 1985".<br>(b) In subsection (1)(c), for "section 206 of the Companies Act 1948" substitute "section 425 of the Companies Act 1985".<br>(c) In subsection (6), in paragaph (c) of the definition of "the relevant time", for "section 206 of the Companies Act 1948" substitute "section 425 of the Companies Act 1985". |
| Section 20 ... ... ... ... ... | For subsection (8) substitute —<br>"(8) In subsections (3) to (7) above, "company" includes any body corporate." |
| Section 27 ... ... ... ... ... | For "section 111 of the Companies Act 1967" substitute "section 449 of the Companies Act 1985". |
| Section 29 ... ... ... ... ... | The same amendment. |

| Enactment | Amendment |
|---|---|
| Schedule 1 ... ... ... ... ... | In paragraph 14(3), for "section 161(1)(a) of the Companies Act 1948" substitute "section 389(1)(a) of the Companies Act 1985". |
| Airports Authority Act 1975 (c. 78): | |
| Section 8(2) ... ... ... ... ... | For "section 161(1)(a) of the Companies Act 1948" substitute "section 389(1)(a) of the Companies Act 1985". |
| Development Land Tax Act 1976 (c. 24): | |
| Section 33(1) ... ... ... ... | For "section 244 of the Companies Act 1948" substitute "section 538 of the Companies Act 1985". |
| Section 42(4) ... ... ... ... | For paragraph (c) substitute —<br>"(c) section 614 of the Companies Act 1985, with paragraph 2 of Schedule 19 to that Act". |
| Theatres Trust Act 1976 (c. 27): | |
| Schedule ... ... ... ... ... | In paragraph 14, for "paragraph (a) of subsection (1) of section 161 of the Companies Act 1948" substitute "section 389(1)(a) of the Companies Act 1985". |
| Restrictive Trade Practices Act 1976 (c. 34): | |
| Section 33 ... ... ... ... ... | For "Companies Act 1948" (twice) substitute "Companies Act 1985". |
| Section 43(1) ... ... ... ... | For "section 154 of the Companies Act 1948" substitute "section 736 of the Companies Act 1985". |
| Resale Prices Act 1976 (c. 53): | |
| Section 27 ... ... ... ... ... | In the definition of "interconnected bodies corporate", for "section 154 of the Companies Act 1948" substitute "section 736 of the Companies Act 1985". |
| Insolvency Act 1976 (c. 60): | |
| Section 3(3) ... ... ... ... ... | In paragraph (b), for "Companies Act 1948" substitute "Companies Act 1985". |
| Industrial Common Ownership Act 1976 (c. 78): | |
| Section 2(5) ... ... ... ... ... | For "section 455(1) of the Companies Act 1948" substitute "section 735 of the Companies Act 1985"; and for "Companies Act 1948" (the second time) substitute "Companies Act 1985". |
| Dock Work Regulation Act 1976 (c. 79): | |
| Schedule 1 ... ... ... ... ... | In paragraph 11(1)(e), for "section 161(1)(a) of the Companies Act 1948" substitute "section 389(1)(a) of the Companies Act 1985". |

| Enactment | Amendment |
|---|---|
| Nuclear Industry (Finance) Act 1977 (c. 71): | |
| Section 3 ... ... ... ... ... | For "Companies Act 1948" substitute "Companies Act 1985". |
| Patents Act 1977 (c. 37): | |
| Section 88(3) ... ... ... ... | For "Companies Act 1948" substitute "Companies Act 1985". |
| Section 114(2) ... ... ... ... | In paragraph (a), the same amendment. |
| Section 131 ... ... ... ... ... | In paragraph (d), the same amendment. |
| Coal Industry Act 1977 (c. 39): | |
| Section 14(1) ... ... ... ... | For "section 150(4) of the Companies Act 1948" substitute "section 736(5)(b) of the Companies Act 1985". |
| Insurance Brokers (Registration) Act 1977 (c. 46): | |
| Section 11(4) ... ... ... ... | For "section 161(1)(b) of the Companies Act 1948" substitute "section 389(1)(b) of the Companies Act 1985". |
| Section 29(1) ... ... ... ... | In the definition of "recognised body of accountants", for "section 161(1)(a) of the Companies Act 1948" substitute "section 389(1)(a) of the Companies Act 1985". |
| Participation Agreements Act 1978 (c. 1): | |
| Section 1(4) ... ... ... ... ... | For "Sections 150(4) and 154 of the Companies Act 1948" substitute "Section 736 of the Companies Act 1985". |
| Commonwealth Development Corporation Act 1978 (c. 2): | |
| Section 9A(6)(b) ... ... ... ... | For "section 154 of the Companies Act 1948" substitute "section 736 of the Companies Act 1985". |
| Co-operative Development Agency Act 1978 (c. 21): | |
| Schedule 2 ... ... ... ... ... | In paragraph 1(2), for "section 161(1)(a) of the Companies Act 1948" substitute "section 389(21)(a) of the Companies Act 1985". |
| Capital Gains Tax Act 1979 (c. 14): | |
| Section 9(3) ... ... ... ... ... | In paragraph (b), for "section 154 of the Companies Act 1948" substitute "section 736 of the Companies Act 1985". |
| Section 149(7) ... ... ... ... | For "Companies Act 1948" substitute "Companies Act 1985". |

| Enactment | Amendment |
|---|---|
| Credit Unions Act 1979 (c. 34): | |
| Section 6(1) ... ... ... ... ... | For "section 222(d) of the Companies Act 1948" substitute "section 517(1)(e) of the Companies Act 1985"; and after the word "'seven'" insert "(or, in the case of section 517(1)(e) of the Act of 1985, for the word 'two')". |
| Nurses, Midwives and Health Visitors Act 1979 (c. 36): | |
| Schedule 4 ... ... ... ... ... | In paragraph 3, for "section 161(1)(a) of the Companies Act 1948" substitute "section 389(1)(a) of the Companies Act 1985". |
| Estate Agents Act 1979 (c. 38): | |
| Section 14 ... ... ... ... ... | (a) In subsection (6) —<br>(i) in paragraph (a), for "section 161(1)(a) of the Companies Act 1948" substitute "section 389(1)(a) of the Companies Act 1985";<br>(ii) in paragraph (b), for "section 161(1)(b) of the Companies Act 1948" substitute section 389(1)(b) of the Companies Act 1985"; and<br>(iii) in paragraph (c), for "section 13(1) of the Companies Act 1967" substitute "section 389(2) of the Companies Act 1985".<br>(b) In subsection (7), for "by subsection (2), subsection (3) or subsection (4) of either section 161 of the Companies Act 1948 or" substitute "either by subsection (6), subsection (7) or subsection (8) of section 389 of the Companies Act 1985 or by subsection (2), subsection (3) or subsection (4) of". |
| Crown Agents Act 1979 (c. 43): | |
| Section 22(6) ... ... ... ... | For "section 161(1)(a) of the Companies Act 1948" substitute "section 389(1)(a) of the Companies Act 1985". |
| Section 31 ... ... ... ... ... | In the definition of "subsidiary", for "section 154 of the Companies Act 1948" substitute "section 736 of the Companies Act 1985"; and in the definition of "wholly-owned subsidiary", for "section 150(4) of the Companies Act 1948" substitute "section 736(5)(b) of the Companies Act 1985". |
| Competition Act 1980 (c. 21): | |
| Section 11(3) ... ... ... ... | In paragraph (f), for "Companies Act 1948" substitute "Companies Act 1985". |
| Section 12(4) ... ... ... ... | The same amendment. |

| Enactment | Amendment |
|---|---|
| British Aerospace Act 1980 (c. 26): | |
| Section 3(3) ... ... ... ... ... | In paragraph (b), for "Companies Acts 1948 to 1980" substitute "Companies Act 1985". |
| Section 4 ... ... ... ... ... | (a) In subsection (3), for "section 40(2)(d) of the Companies Act 1980" substitute "section 264(3)(d) of the Companies Act 1985"; and for "section 40(2)(c)" substitute "section 264(3)(c)".<br>(b) In subsection (7), for "Companies Acts 1948 to 1980" substitute "Companies Act 1985". |
| Section 9(1) ... ... ... ... ... | In paragraph (a), for "Companies Act 1948" substitute "Companies Act 1985". |
| Industry Act 1980 (c. 33): | |
| Section 2(4) ... ... ... ... ... | For "section 154 of the Companies Act 1948" substitute "section 736 of the Companies Act 1985". |
| Section 3 ... ... ... ... ... | (a) In subsection (5), for "Companies Acts 1948 to 1980" substitute "Companies Act 1985".<br>(b) In subsection (7), for "Companies Act 1948"substitute "Companies Act 1985"; and for "section 154 of the said Act of 1948" substitute "section 736 of the said Act of 1985". |
| Transport Act 1980 (c. 34): | |
| Section 47 ... ... ... ... ... | (a) In subsection (2), for "section 56 of the Companies Act 1948" substitute "section 130 of the Companies Act 1985".<br>(b) In subsection (5), the same amendment. |
| Section 48(4) ... ... ... ... | For "section 161(1)(a) of the Companies Act 1948" substitute "section 389(1)(a) of the Companies Act 1985". |
| Education (Scotland) Act 1980 (c. 44): | |
| Section 111(3) ... ... ... ... | In paragraph (e), for "section 161(1)(a) of the Companies Act 1948" substitute "section 389(1)(a) of the Companies Act 1985". |
| Finance Act 1980 (c. 48): | |
| Schedule 10 ... ... ... ... ... | (a) In paragraph 10(1)(b), for "section 206 of the Companies Act 1948" substitute "section 425 of the Companies Act 1985".<br>(b) In paragraph 10(1)(c), for "section 209 of the said Act of 1948" substitute "sections 428 to 430 of the said Act of 1985". |
| Civil Aviation Act 1980 (c. 60): | |
| Section 4(3) ... ... ... ... ... | In paragraph (b), for "Companies Acts 1948 to 1980" substitute "Companies Act 1985". |
| Section 5(5) ... ... ... ... ... | The same amendment. |

| Enactment | Amendment |
|---|---|
| | (b) In paragraph (c), for "section 12 of the Companies Act 1976" substitute "sections 221 and 222 of the Companies Act". |
| Section 55 ... ... ... ... ... | (b) In subsection (6), for "333(1) of the said Act of 1948" substitute "631 of the Companies Act". |
| Section 56 ... ... ... ... ... | (b) In subsection (7), for "245(1) of the said Act of 1948" substitute "539(1) of the Companies Act". |
| Section 71 ... ... ... ... ... | After subsection (4), insert — "(4A) A person who publishes or discloses any information or document in contravention of section 47A above shall be guilty of an offence under section 449 of the Companies Act and liable accordingly." |
| Section 87 ... ... ... ... ... | (a) In subsection (1), for section 406 of the Companies Act 1948" substitute "the Companies Act".<br>(b) In subsection (2), for paragraphs (a) and (b) substitute — "(a) sections 691 to 693, 695 to 698, 700 to703 and 708 of the Companies Act". |
| Section 89 ... ... ... ... ... | (a) In subsection (1), for "434" substitute "716".<br>(b) In subsection (2), the same amendment. |
| Section 96(1) ... ... ... ... | (a) After the definition of "chief executive" insert — "'the Companies Act' means the Companies Act 1985".<br>(b) In the definition of "holding company", for "154" substitute "736".<br>(c) At the end of the definition of "former Companies Acts" add "and the Companies Acts 1948 to 1983".<br>(d) In the definition of "insolvent", for "222 and 223 or section 399" substitute "517 and 518 or section 666".<br>(e) In the definition of "registrar of companies", for "meaning given in section 455 of" substitute "the same meaning as in".<br>(f) In the definition of "subsidiary", for "154" substitute "736". |
| Section 100 ... ... ... ... ... | In subsection (3), after "Act" insert "except sections 47A, 47B and 71(4A)". |
| Pilotage Act 1983 (c. 21):<br>Section 4(4) ... ... ... ... ... | For "section 161(1)(a) of the Companies Act 1948" substitute "section 389(1)(a) of the Companies Act 1985". |
| Finance Act 1983 (c. 28):<br>Schedule 5 ... ... ... ... ... | (a) In paragraph 5(4), for "Companies Act 1948" substitute "Companies Act 1985".<br>(b) In paragraph 10(4)(a), for "Companies Act 1980" substitute "Companies Act 1985"; and for "section 4" (twice) substitute "section 117". |

| Enactment | Amendment |
|---|---|
| | (c) In paragraph 20(2), for "section 455 of the Companies Act 1948" substitute "section 735 of the Companies Act 1985". |
| National Heritage Act 1983 (c. 47): | |
| Schedule 3 ... ... ... ... ... | In paragraph 12(6)(a), for "section 161(1)(a) of the Companies Act 1948" substitute "section 389(1)(a) of the Companies Act 1985". |
| Car Tax Act 1983 (c. 53): | |
| Schedule 1 ... ... ... ... ... | In paragraph 4, in both sub-paragraphs (1)(c) and (2)(c), for "section 319 of the Companies Act 1948" substitute "section 614 of the Companies Act 1985, with Schedule 19 to that Act"; and for "section 94 of the Act of 1948" substitute "section 196 of the Act of 1985". |
| Medical Act 1983 (c. 54): | |
| Schedule 1 ... ... ... ... ... | In paragraph 18(3), for "section 161(1)(a) of the Companies Act 1948" substitute "section 389(1)(a) of the Companies Act 1985". |
| Value Added Tax Act 1983 (c. 55): | |
| Section 29(8) ... ... ... ... | For "Companies Act 1948" substitute "Companies Act 1985". |
| Schedule 7 ... ... ... ... ... | In paragraph 12, in both sub-paragraphs (1)(c) and (2)(c), for section 319 of the Companies Act 1948" substitute "section 614 of the Companies Act 1985, with Schedule 19 to that Act"; and for "section 94 of the Act of 1948" substitute "section 196 of the Act of 1985". |
| Telecommunications Act 1984 (c. 12): | |
| Section 60(3) ... ... ... ... | For "Companies Act 1948" substitute "Companies Act 1985 or the enactments thereby replaced". |
| Section 61(4) ... ... ... ... | In paragraph (b), for "Companies Acts 1948 to 1981" substitute "Companies Act 1985". |
| Section 66 ... ... ... ... ... | (a) In subsection (3), for "section 40(2)(d) of the Companies Act 1980" substitute "section 264(3)(d) of the Companies Act 1985"; and for "section 40(2)(c)" substitute "section 264(3)(c)".<br>(b) In subsection (6), for "Companies Acts 1948 to 1981" substitute "Companies Act 1985". |
| Section 68 ... ... ... ... ... | In subsection (1), for "Companies Act 1948" substitute "Companies Act 1985". |
| Section 70 ... ... ... ... ... | (a) In subsection (1), for "Schedule 4 to the Companies Act 1948" substitute "Schedule 3 to the Companies Act 1985".<br>(b) In subsection (3)(a), for "section 41 of the said Act of 1948" substitute "section 64(1) of the Companies Act 1985". |

| Enactment | Amendment |
|---|---|
| | (c) In subsection (5)(a), for "sections 37 to 46 of the said Act of 1948" substitute "Chapter I of Part III of the Companies Act 1985". |
| Section 73(1) … … … … | For "Companies Act 1948" substitute "Companies Act 1985". |
| Schedule 5 … … … … … | In paragraph 51, substitute the following for sub-paragraphs (1) and (2) —<br>"(1) Where a distribution is proposed to be declared during the accounting reference period of the successor company which includes the transfer date or before any accounts are laid or filed in respect of that period, sections 270 to 274 and 275(7) of the Companies Act 1985 (accounts relevant for determining whether a distribution may be made by a company without contravening Part VIII of that Act) shall have effect as if —<br>(a) the reference in section 270(2) to the company's accounts, and<br>(b) references in section 273 to initial accounts,<br>included references to such accounts as, on the assumptions stated in sub-paragraph (3) below, would have been prepared under Part VII of that Act in respect of the relevant year." |
| County Courts Act 1984 (c. 28): | |
| Section 98(3) … … … … | For "sections 325 and 326 of the Companies Act 1948" substitute "sections 621 and 622 of the Companies Act 1985". |
| Food Act 1984 (c. 30): | |
| Section 51(2) … … … … | In paragraph (a), for "1948" substitute "1985"; and for "Part IV" substitute "Part XI". |
| Capital Transfer Tax Act 1984 (c. 51): | |
| Section 13(5) … … … … | For "Companies Act 1948" substitute "Companies Act 1985". |
| Section 103(2) … … … … | The same amendment. |
| Section 234(3) … … … … | In paragraph (b), the same amendment. |

**History**

(1) In Sch. 2 entries relating to Insolvency Services (Accounting and Investment) Act 1970, s. 4; Employment Protection (Consolidation) Act 1978, s. 122(7); Banking Act 1979, s. 28(b), 31; and Insurance Companies Act 1982, s. 55(5), 56(4), 59 repealed by Insolvency Act 1985, s. 235 and Sch. 10, Pt. II. The repeals of provisions with reference to Companies Act 1985, s. 663 (Banking Act 1979, s. 31(7)(a); Insurance Companies Act 1982, s. 59), operate from 1 March 1986 (see SI 1986/185 (C. 7)) while the others operate from 29 December 1986 (see SI 1986/1924 (C. 71)).

(2) Also in Sch. 2 entries relating to Social Security Act 1975; Insolvency Act 1976, s. 2, 10(1), Sch. 1; Employment Protection (Consolidation) Act 1978; and Banking Act 1979, s. 18, 19(8)(a) repealed by Insolvency Act 1985, s. 235 and Sch. 10, Pt. IV. The repeal of Insolvency Act 1976, s. 10(1)(b) operates from 1 March 1986 (see SI 1986/185 (C. 7)) while the others operate from 29 December 1986 (see SI 1986/1924 (C. 71)). See Insolvency Act 1986, s. 437, Sch. 11, Pt. II for transitional provisions.

The former wording of all the above entries is as follows:

| Enactment | Amendment |
|---|---|
| "Insolvency Services (Accounting and Investment) Act 1970 (c. 8): | |
| Section 4 ... ... ... ... ... | For 'section 362(4) of the Companies Act 1948' substitute 'section 660(5) of the Companies Act 1985 (or the previous corresponding provision of the Companies Act 1948)'. |
| Social Security Act 1975 (c. 14): | |
| Schedule 18 ... ... ... ... ... | (a) In paragraph 2(1), for 'section 319 of the Companies Act 1948' substitute 'section 614 of the Companies Act 1985, taken with paragraph 8 of Schedule 19 to that Act'.<br>(b) In paragraph 3(1), for the words 'the following' and paragraphs (a) and (b) substitute 'sections 196 and 475 of the Companies Act 1985'. |
| [Insolvency Act 1976 (c. 60):] | |
| Section 2 ... ... ... ... ... | For this section substitute —<br>'**2(1)** The Secretary of State may cause any accounts sent to him under section 92 of the Bankruptcy Act of 1914 or section 543 of the Companies Act 1985 to be audited.<br>**2(2)** So much of section 92(3) of the Act of 1914 and section 543(4) of the Act of 1985 as enables the Secretary of State to call for vouchers and information and to require the production of and to inspect books and accounts applies whether or not he decides to cause an account to be audited and extends to production and inspection at the premises of the trustee or liquidator.<br>**2(3)** Where the Secretary of State decides not to cause an account to be audited, section 92(4) of the Act of 1914 and section 543(5) of the Act of 1985 apply as if the subsection in each case required copies of the accounts to be filed or delivered for filing forthwith; and the liquidator shall comply with section 543(5) when notified of the decision.<br>**2(4)** Only the copy filed with the court shall be open to inspection under section 92(4) of the Act of 1914 or section 543(5) of the Act of 1985.' |
| Section 10(1) ... ... ... ... ... | In paragraph (b), for 'section 365 of the Companies Act 1948' substitute 'section 663 of the Companies Act 1985'. |
| Schedule 1, Part II ... ... ... ... | In paragraph 1, for 'bankruptcy petition or winding-up' substitute 'or bankruptcy'. |
| Employment Protection (Consolidation) Act 1978 (c. 44): | |
| Section 121(1) ... ... ... ... ... | For paragraph (c) substitute —<br>'(c) section 614 of, and Schedule 19 to, the Companies Act 1985.'. |
| Section 122(7) ... ... ... ... ... | For 'section 317 of the Companies Act 1948' substitute 'section 612 of the Companies Act 1985'. |
| Section 125(2) ... ... ... ... ... | For paragraph (c) substitute —<br>'(c) section 614 of the Companies Act 1985, with Schedule 19 to that Act'. |
| [Banking Act 1979 (c. 37):] | |
| Section 18 ... ... ... ... ... | (a) In subsection (1), for 'Companies Act 1948' substitute 'Companies Act 1985'.<br>(b) For subsection (2) substitute —<br>'(2) If a petition is presented by the Bank by virtue of this section for the winding up of a recognised bank or licensed institution which, apart fom this subsection, would be excluded from being an unregistered company for the purposes of Part XXI of the Companies Act 1985 by virtue of —<br>(a) paragraph (c) of section 665 of that Act (partnerships with less than 8 members), or<br>(b) paragraph (d) of that section (limited partnerships),<br>the court has jurisdiction, and the Companies Act 1985 has effect, as if the institution concerned were an unregistered company within the meaning of Part XXI of that Act.' |
| [Section 19] | (b) In subsection (8)(a), for '165', '172' and '1948' substitute respectively '432', '442' and '1985'. |
| [Section 28] | (b) In subsection (6), in paragraph (b)(iv), for 'Part V or Part IX of the Companies Act 1948' substitute 'Part XX or Part XXI of the Companies Act 1985'. |
| Section 31 ... ... ... ... ... | In subsection (7), for 'section 365 of the Companies Act 1948' (twice) substitute 'section 663 of the Companies Act 1985'. |

| Enactment | Amendment |
|---|---|
| [Insurance Companies Act 1982 (c. 50):] | |
| [Section 55] ... ... ... ... ... | (a) In subsection (5), for '(1) and (2) of section 246' substitute '(1) to (3) of section 540'. |
| [Section 56] ... ... ... ... ... | (a) In subsection (4) —<br>(i) for 'Subsections (2) and (3) of section 263' substitute 'Section 556(3)', and<br>(ii) for 'section 263 of the said Act of 1948' substitute 'section 556 of the Companies Act'. |
| Section 59 ... ... ... ... ... | (a) In subsection (1), for '365'substitute '663'.<br>(b) In subsection (2), for '365 of the said Act of 1948' substitute '663 of the Companies Act'; and in paragraph (b) of the subsection, for '319 of the said Act of 1948' substitute '614 of, and Schedule 19 to, the Companies Act'." |

(3) In Sch. 2 the entry relating to the Banking Act 1979, s. 20 repealed by Financial Services Act 1986, s. 212(3) and Sch. 17 as from 27 November 1986 (see SI 1986/2031 (C. 76). The entry formerly read as follows:

"(a) In subsection (1)—

(i) in paragraph (a), for '109', '110', '1967' and '111' substitute respectively '447', '448', '1985' and '449'; and

(ii) in paragraph (b), for '164', '165', '172' and '1948' substitute respectively '431', '432', '442' and '1985'.

(b) in subsection (3)—

(i) in paragraph (a), for section 111 of the Companies Act 1967 substitute 'section 449 of the Companies Act 1985'; and

(ii) in paragraph (b), for '111' substitute '449'."

The remaining entries relating to the Banking Act 1979 repealed by Banking Act 1987, s. 108(2) and Sch. 7, Pt. I as from 1 October 1987 (see SI 1987/1664 (C. 50). The entries formerly read as follows:

| Enactment | Amendment |
|---|---|
| "Banking Act 1979 (c. 37): | |
| Section 6(3) ... ... ... ... ... | In paragraph (b), for 'Part IX of the Companies Act 1948' substitute 'Part XXI of the Companies Act 1985'. |
| Section 17(6) ... ... ... ... ... | In paragraph (a), for 'section 154 of the Companies Act 1948' substitute 'section 736 of the Companies Act 1985'. |
| Section 19 ... ... ... ... ... | (a) For subsection (5) substitute —<br>'(5) Nothing in subsection (1) above prohibits the disclosure to the Secretary of State of information relating to a body corporate to which section 432 or 442 of the Companies Act 1985 applies, if it appears to the bank that there may be circumstances relating to the body corporate in which the Secretary of State might wish to appoint inspectors under —<br>(a) any of paragraphs (a) to (c) of subsection (2) of the said section 432 (investigation of cases of fraud, etc.), or<br>(b) the said section 442 (investigation of ownership of companies, etc.).' |
| Section 28 ... ... ... ... ... | (a) In subsection (4), in paragraph (a), for 'Part IX of the Companies Act 1948' substitute 'Part XXI of the Companies Act 1985'. |
| Section 36 ... ... ... ... ... | In subsection (7)(a), for 'section 150(4) of the Companies Act 1948' substitute 'section 736 of the Companies Act 1985'. |
| Section 40 ... ... ... ... ... | (a) In subsection (4) —<br>(i) in paragraph (a), for 'section 407(1) of the Companies Act 1948' substitute 'section 691(1) of the Companies Act 1985'; and<br>(ii) in paragraph (b), for '407(1)' substitute '691(1)'.<br>(b) In subsection (5) —<br>(i) in paragraph (a), for 'section 409 of the Companies Act 1948' substitute 'section 692 of the Companies Act 1985'; and<br>(ii) in paragraph (b), for 'subsection (2) of section 413' substitute 'subsection (4) of section 696'.<br>(c) In subsection (6), for 'section 407, section 409 and subsection (2) of section 413 of the Companies Act 1948' substitute 'section 691, section 692 and subsection (4) of section 696 of the Companies Act 1985'. |

| Enactment | Amendment |
|---|---|
| Section 48(1) ... ... ... ... ... | For 'Companies Act 1948' substitute 'Companies Act 1985'. |
| Section 49(2) ... ... ... ... ... | The same amendment. |
| Section 50(1) ... ... ... ... ... | (a) In the definition of 'debenture', for Companies Act 1948 substitute 'Companies Act 1985'.<br>(b) In the definition of 'subsidiary', for 'section 154 of the Companies Act 1948' substitute 'section 736 of the Companies Act 1985'. |
| Schedule 3 ... ... ... ... ... | In paragraph 8, for sub-paragraph (a) substitute—<br>'(a) at the time of its application for recognition is either a company within the meaning of the Companies Act 1985 or any other body corporate having its place of central management and control in the United Kingdom (having in either case been such on 9th November 1978 and so continued since that date).' |
| Schedule 5 ... ... ... ... ... | In paragraph 4(4), for 'section 161(1)(a) of the Companies Act 1948' substitute 'section 389(1)(a) of the Companies Act 1985'; and for 'section 161(1)(b)' substitute 'section 389(1)(b)'." |

(4) In Sch. 2 the entry relating to the Baking Industry (Hours of Work) Act 1954, s. 11 repealed by the Sex Discrimination Act 1986 as from 27 February 1987 (see SI 1986/2313 (C. 95). The entry formerly read as follows:

"For 'Companies Act 1948' substitute 'Companies Act 1985'."

(5) In Sch. 2 the entries relating to the Housing Act 1964, Housing Subsidies Act 1967, Housing Act 1974, Housing Act 1980 and Housing and Building Control Act 1984 repealed by Housing (Consequential Provisions) Act 1985, s. 3 and Sch. 1, Pt. I. The entries formerly read as follows:

| Enactment | Amendment |
|---|---|
| "Housing Act 1964 (c. 56): | |
| Section 10 ... ... ... ... ... | For 'section 161(1)(a) of the Companies Act 1948 by the Board of Trade' substitute 'section 389(1)(a) of the Companies Act 1985 by the Secretary of State'. |
| Housing Subsidies Act 1967 (c. 29): | |
| Section 32(1) ... ... ... ... ... | In the definition of 'insurance company', for 'paragraph 24 of Schedule 8 to the Companies Act 1948' substitute 'paragraph 28 of Schedule 9 to the Companies Act 1985'. |
| Housing Act 1974 (c. 44): | |
| Section 12 ... ... ... ... ... | In the definition of 'subsidiary', for 'Companies Act 1948' substitute 'Companies Act 1985'. |
| Section 22(1) ... ... ... ... ... | The same amendment. |
| Section 24(4) ... ... ... ... ... | For 'section 141 of the Companies Act 1948' substitute 'section 378 of the Companies Act 1985'; and in paragraph (b) of the subsection, for 'section 143 of the Companies Act 1948' substitute 'section 380 of the Companies Act 1985'. |
| Section 25(1) ... ... ... ... ... | For 'Companies Act 1948' substitute 'Companies Act 1985'. |
| Housing Act 1980 (c. 51): | |
| Schedule 16 ... ... ... ... ... | In paragraph 3(2), for 'section 161(1)(a) of the Companies Act 1948' substitute 'section 389(1)(a) of the Companies Act 1985'; and for 'section 161(1)(b)' substitute 'section 389(1)(b)'. |
| Schedule 19 ... ... ... ... ... | In paragraph 17(2), for 'section 154 of the Companies Act 1948' substitute 'section 736 of the Companies Act 1985'. |
| Housing and Building Control Act 1984 (c. 29): | |
| Schedule 4 ... ... ... ... ... | (a) In paragraph 11(1), for 'section 161(1)(a) of the Companies Act 1948' substitute 'section 389(1)(a) of the Companies Act 1985'; and for 'section 161(1)(b)' substitute 'section 389(1)(b)'.<br>(b) In paragraph 11(2), for 'section 154 of the Companies Act 1948' substitute 'section 736 of the Companies Act 1985'." |

(6) In Sch. 2 the entry relating to the Weights and Measures Act 1979 repealed by Weights and Measures Act 1985, s. 98(1) and Sch. 13, Pt. I. The entry formerly read as follows:

| Enactment | Amendment |
|---|---|
| "Weights and Measures Act 1979 (c. 45): Section 10(3) ... ... ... ... ... | For 'section 161(1)(a) of the Companies Act 1948' substitute 'section 389(1)(a) of the Companies Act 1985'." |

(7) In Sch. 2 the entries relating to the Building Societies Act 1962 repealed by Building Societies Act 1986, s. 120(2) and Sch. 19, Pt. I as from 1 January 1987 (see SI 1986/1560 (C. 56). The entries formerly read as follows:

| Enactment | Amendment |
|---|---|
| "Building Societies Act 1962 (c. 37): | |
| Section 22(8) ... ... ... ... ... | For 'Companies Act 1948' substitute 'Companies Act 1985'. |
| Section 50(5) ... ... ... ... ... | The same amendment. |
| Section 55(5) ... ... ... ... ... | The same amendment. |
| Section 86(1)(e) ... ... ... ... ... | For 'paragraph (a) of subsection (1) of section one hundred and sixty-one of the Companies Act 1948 by the Board of Trade' substitute 'section 389(1)(a) of the Companies Act 1985 by the Secretary of State'. |
| Section 86(2) ... ... ... ... ... | For 'paragraph (b) of subsection (1) of section one hundred and sixty-one of the Companies Act 1948' substitute 'section 389(1)(b) of the Companies Act 1985'. |
| Section 92(4) ... ... ... ... ... | For 'Section four hundred and forty-eight of the Companies Act 1948' substitute 'Section 727 of the Companies Act 1985'. |
| Section 103 ... ... ... ... ... | For 'Companies Act 1948' substitute 'Companies Act 1985'. |
| Schedule 1 ... ... ... ... ... | In paragraphs 5 (twice) and 6(3), for 'Companies Act 1948' substitute 'Companies Act 1985'. |
| Schedule 3 ... ... ... ... ... | In paragraph 12(1)(b), for 'section 406 of the Companies Act 1948' substitute 'section 744 of the Companies Act 1985'." |

(8) In Sch. 2 the entry relating to the Finance Act 1973 repealed by Finance Act 1988, s. 148 and Sch. 14, Pt. XI as from 22 March 1988. The entry formerly read as follows:

| Enactment | Amendment |
|---|---|
| "Finance Act 1973 (c. 51): Section 47 ... ... ... ... ... | (a) In subsection (2)(a), for 'Companies Act 1948' substitute 'Companies Act 1985'.<br>(b) In subsection (3), for 'section 12 of Companies Act 1948' substitute 'section 10(1) of the Companies Act 1985'; and for 'the said section 12' substitute 'section 12 of the Companies Act 1985'. |
| Schedule 19 ... ... ... ... ... | In paragraph 11, for 'section 206 of the Companies Act 1948' substitute 'section 425 of the Companies Act 1985'." |

(9) In Sch. 2 entries relating to the Prevention of Fraud (Investments) Act 1958, the Scottish Development Agency Act 1975, Sch. 1, para. 19, the Welsh Development Agency Act 1975, Sch. 1, para. 22, the Stock Exchange (Completion of Bargains) Act 1976 and the Aircraft and Shipbuilding Industries Act 1977, s. 3(5) repealed by Financial Services Act 1986, s. 212(3) and Sch. 17, Pt. I as from 29 April 1988 (see SI 1988/740 (C. 22)). The entries formerly read as follows:

| Enactment | Amendment |
|---|---|
| "Prevention of Fraud (Investments) Act 1958 (c. 45): Section 2 ... ... ... ... ... | For subsection (2), to the end of sub-paragraph (d), substitute —<br>'(2) For the purpose of determining whether or not a person has contravened any of the restrictions imposed by section 1 of this Act, no account shall be taken of his having done any of the following things (whether as a principal or as an agent), that is to say —<br>(a) effecting transactions with, or through the agency of —<br>(i) such a person as is mentioned in paragraph (a), paragraph (b) or paragraph (c) of the preceding subsection, or a person acting on behalf of such a person as is so mentioned, or<br>(ii) the holder of a licence; |

| Enactment | Amendment |
|---|---|
| | (b) issuing any prospectus to which —<br>(i) section 56 of the Companies Act 1985 applies or would apply if not excluded by paragraph (b) of subsection (5) of that section, or<br>(ii) section 72 of that Act applies or would apply if not excluded by paragraph (b) of subsection (6) of that section or by section 76 of that Act;<br>(c) issuing any document relating to securities of a corporation incorporated in Great Britain which is not a registered company, being a document which —<br>(i) would, if the corporation were a registered company, be a prospectus to which section 56 of the Companies Act 1985 applies or would apply if not excluded by paragraph (b) of subsection (5) of that section, and<br>(ii) contains all the matters and is issued with the consents which, by virtue of sections 72 to 75 of that Act, it would have to contain and be issued with if the corporation were a company incorporated outside Great Britain and the document were a prospectus issued by that company; and<br>(d) issuing any form of application for shares in, or debentures of, a corporation together with —<br>(i) a prospectus which complies with the requirements of section 56 of the Companies Act 1985, or is not required to comply with it because excluded by paragraph (b) of subsection (5) of that section, or complies with the requirements of Chapter II of Part III of that Act relating to prospectuses and is not issued in contravention of sections 74 and 75 of that Act, or<br>(ii) in the case of a corporation incorporated in Great Britain which is not a registered company, a document containing all the matters and issued with the consents mentioned in paragraph (c)(ii) of this subsection'. |
| Section 12 ... ... ... ... ... | (a) For 'Board of Trade' (twice) substitute 'Secretary of State'.<br>(b) For 'the Board' substitute 'the Secretary of State'.<br>(c) In subsection (2) —<br>(i) for the words from the beginning to 'subsection (2)' substitute 'Sections 434 to 436 of the Companies Act 1985, subsection (1) of section 437 of that Act and so much of subsection (3)', and<br>(ii) for 'section one hundred and sixty-four' substitute 'section 431'. |
| Section 14 ... ... ... ... ... | (a) In subsection (2), for paragraphs (a) and (b) substitute —<br>'(a) in relation to any distribution of a prospectus to which section 56 of the Companies Act 1985 applies or would apply if not excluded by paragraph (b) of subsection (5) of that section or section 72 of that Act applies or would apply if not excluded by paragraph (b) of subsection (6) of that section or by section 76 of that Act, or in relation to any distribution of a document relating to securities of a corporation incorporated in Great Britain which is not a registered company, being a document which —<br>(i) would, if the corporation were a registered company, be a prospectus to which the said section 56 applies or would apply if not excluded as aforesaid, and<br>(ii) contains all the matters and is issued with the consents which, by virtue of sections 72 to 75 of that Act it would have to contain and be issued with if the corporation were a company incorporated outside Great Britain and the document were a prospectus issued by that company;<br>(b) in relation to any issue of a form of application for shares in, or debentures of, a corporation, together with —<br>(i) a prospectus which complies with the requirements of section 56 of the Companies Act 1985, or is not required to comply therewith because excluded by paragraph (b) of subsection (5) of that section, or complies with the requirements of Chapter II of Part III of that Act relating to prospectuses and is not issued in contravention of sections 74 and 75 of that Act, or<br>(ii) in the case of a corporation incorporated in Great Britain which is not a registered company, a document containing all the matters and issued with the consents mentioned in paragraph (a)(ii) of this subsection,<br>or in connection with a bona fide invitation to a person to enter into an underwriting agreement with respect to the shares or debentures, or'. |

| Enactment | Amendment |
|---|---|
| | (c) in subsection (3)(a)(iii), for 'section one hundred and fifty-four of the Companies Act 1948' substitute 'section 736 of the Companies Act 1985'. |
| Section 16 ... ... ... ... ... | In subsection (2)(a), for 'Companies Act 1948' substitute 'Companies Act 1985'. |
| Section 26 ... ... ... ... ... | In subsection (1) —<br>(a) in the definition of 'prospectus', for 'Companies Act 1948' substitute 'Companies Act 1985';<br>(b) in the definition of 'registered company', after the words 'registered under' insert 'the Companies Act 1985', and for 'section four hundred and fifty-five of the Companies Act 1948' substitute 'section 735(3) of the Companies Act 1985';<br>(c) in the definition of 'statutory corporation', for 'Companies Act 1948' substitute 'Companies Act 1985'. |
| Scottish Development Agency Act 1975 (c. 69):<br>Schedule 1 ... ... ... ... ... | In paragaph 19, for 'Section 209 of the Companies Act 1948' substitute 'Sections 428 to 430 of the Companies Act 1985'; and for 'that section' substitute 'those sections'. |
| Welsh Development Agency Act 1975 (c. 70):<br>Schedule 1 ... ... ... ... ... | In paragraph 22, for 'Section 209 of the Companies Act 1948' substitute 'Sections 428 to 430 of the Companies Act 1985'; and for 'that section' substitute 'those sections'." |
| Stock Exchange (Completion of Bargains) Act 1976 (c. 47):<br>Section 7 ... ... ... ... ... | For subsection (2) substitute —<br>'(2) In this Act 'stock exchange nominee' means the person designated by the Secretary of State by order under section 185(4) of the Companies Act 1985'. |
| Aircraft and Shipbuilding Industries Act 1977 (c. 3):<br>Section 3(5) ... ... ... ... ... | For 'Section 209 of the Companies Act 1948' substitute 'Sections 428 to 430 of the Companies Act 1985'. |
| Section 17(8) ... ... ... ... ... | For 'section 161(1)(a) of the Companies Act 1948' substitute 'section 389(1)(a) of the Companies Act 1985'. |
| Section 23(8) ... ... ... ... ... | For 'Companies Act 1948' substitute 'Companies Act 1985'. |
| Section 56(1) ... ... ... ... ... | (a) In the definition of 'equity share capital', for 'section 154 of the Companies Act 1948' substitute 'section 736 of the Companies Act 1985'.<br>(b) In the definition of 'holding company', for 'section 154 of the Companies Act 1948' substitute 'section 736 of the Companies Act 1985'.<br>(c) In the definition of 'subsidiary', for 'Companies Act 1948' substitute 'Companies Act 1985'.<br>(d) In the definition of 'wholly-owned subsidiary', for 'section 150 of the Companies Act 1948' substitute 'section 736(5)(b) of the Companies Act 1985'." |

**(10)** In Sch. 2 the entry relating to the Water Act 1973 repealed by Water Act 1989, s. 190(3) and Sch. 27, Pt. I as from 1 September 1989 (see Water Act 1989, s. 4, 194(3)(g) and SI 1989/1146 (C. 37) — see also SI 1989/1530 (C. 51)). The entry formerly read as follows:

| Enactment | Amendment |
|---|---|
| "Water Act 1973 (c. 37):<br>Schedule 3 ... ... ... ... ... | In paragraph 39(2)(a), for 'section 161(1)(a) of the Companies Act 1948' substitute 'section 389(1)(a) of the Companies Act 1985'." |

**(11)** In Sch. 2 the entry relating to the Scottish Development Agency Act 1975 repealed by Enterprise and New Towns (Scotland) Act 1990, s. 22, 38(2), 39(1), (3) and Sch. 5, Pt. I as from 1 April 1990 (see also SI 1990/1840 (C. 48) (S. 173), art. 4). The entry formerly read as follows:

| Enactment | Amendment |
|---|---|
| "Section 25(1) … … … … … | In the definitions of 'holding company' and 'subsidiary', for 'section 154 of the Companies Act 1948' substitute 'section 736 of the Companies Act 1985'; and in the definition of 'wholly-owned subsidiary' for 'section 150(4) of the Companies Act 1948' substitute 'section 736(5)(b) of the Companies Act 1985'." |

**(12)** In Sch. 2 the entries relating to the Broadcasting Act 1981 repealed by Broadcasting Act 1990, s. 203 and Sch. 21 as from 1 January 1991 subject to saving provisions (see SI 1990/2347 (C. 61), art. 3(1), (3), Sch. 2). The entries formerly read as follows:

| Enactment | Amendment |
|---|---|
| "Broadcasting Act 1981 (c. 68): | |
| Section 12(4) … … … … … | For 'section 154 of the Companies Act 1948' substitute 'section 736 of the Companies Act 1985'. |
| Section 42(2) … … … … … | For 'section 161(1)(a) of the Companies Act 1948' substitute 'section 389(1)(a) of the Companies Act 1985'. |
| Section 63(1) … … … … … | In the definition of 'associate', for 'section 154 of the Companies Act 1948' substitute 'section 736 of the Companies Act 1985'. |
| Schedule 7 … … … … … | In paragraph 8(2), for 'section 161(1)(a) of the Companies Act 1948' substitute 'section 389(1)(a) of the Companies Act 1985'." |

**Note**

See Insolvency Act 1986, s. 437 and Sch. 11, Pt. II re certain relevant transitional provisions.

**(13)** In Sch. 2, the entries relating to the Development of Inventions Act 1967, s. 12(3) and the Industry Act 1975 s. 37(1) (reference to definition of "wholly-owned subsidiary") and Sch. 1 and 2, repealed by British Technology Group Act 1991, s. 17(2), 18 and Sch. 2, Pt. I with effect from 6 January 1992 (see British Technology Group Act 1991 (Appointed Day) Order 1991 (SI 1991/2721), art. 2). The entries formerly read as follows:

| Enactment | Amendment |
|---|---|
| "Development of Inventions Act 1967 (c. 32): | |
| Section 12(3) … … … … … | For 'section 161(1)(a) of the Companies Act 1948 by the Board of Trade' substitute 'section 389(1)(a) of the Companies Act 1985 by the Secretary of State'." |
| "Industry Act 1975 (c. 68): | |
| Section 37(1) … … … … … | ; and in the definition of 'wholly-owned subsidiary', for 'section 150(4) of the Companies Act 1948' substitute 'section 736(5)(b) of the Companies Act 1985'. |
| Schedule 1 … … … … … | In paragraph 19, for 'Section 209 of the Companies Act 1948' substitute 'Sections 428 to 430 of the Companies Act 1985'; and for 'that section' substitute 'those sections'. |
| Schedule 2 … … … … … | In paragaph 7(2), for 'section 161(1)(a) of the Companies Act 1948' substitute 'Sections 389(1)(a) of the Companies Act 1985'." |

**(14)** In Sch. 2 the entry relating to the Charities Act 1960, s. 30(1) repealed by Charities Act 1992, s. 78(2) and Sch. 7 as from 1 September 1992 (see SI 1992/1900 (C. 64), art. 2 and Sch. 1). The entry formerly read as follows: "For 'Companies Act 1948' substitute 'Companies Act 1985'."

**(15)** In Sch. 2 the entries relating to the Trade Union and Labour Relations Act 1974 repealed by Trade Union and Labour Relations (Consolidation) Act 1992, s. 300(1) and Sch. 1 as from 16 October 1992 (see s. 302 of that Act). The entries formerly read as follows:

| Enactment | Amendment |
|---|---|
| "Trade Union and Labour Relations Act 1974 (c. 52): | |
| Section 2(2) … … … … … | For 'Companies Act 1948' substitute 'Companies Act 1985'. |
| Section 3(4) … … … … … | For 'section 434 of the Companies Act 1948' substitute 'section 716 of the Companies Act 1985'. |

# INSOLVENCY ACT 1986

(1986 Chapter 45)

## ARRANGEMENT OF SECTIONS

## THE FIRST GROUP OF PARTS COMPANY INSOLVENCY; COMPANIES WINDING UP

## PART I – COMPANY VOLUNTARY ARRANGEMENTS



## PART II – ADMINISTRATION ORDERS

## PART III – RECEIVERSHIP

### CHAPTER I – RECEIVERS AND MANAGERS (ENGLAND AND WALES)



### CHAPTER II – RECEIVERS (SCOTLAND)

SECTION

## CHAPTER IX – DISSOLUTION OF COMPANIES AFTER WINDING UP



## CHAPTER X – MALPRACTICE BEFORE AND DURING LIQUIDATION; PENALISATION OF COMPANIES AND COMPANY OFFICERS; INVESTIGATIONS AND PROSECUTIONS

*Offences of fraud, deception, etc.*



*Penalisation of directors and officers*



*Investigation and prosecution of malpractice*



## PART V – WINDING UP OF UNREGISTERED COMPANIES



## PART VI – MISCELLANEOUS PROVISIONS APPLYING TO COMPANIES WHICH ARE INSOLVENT OR IN LIQUIDATION

*Office-holders*



*Management by administrators, liquidators, etc.*

SECTION

*Creditor's petition*

267. Grounds of creditor's petition
268. Definition of "inability to pay", etc.; the statutory demand
269. Creditor with security
270. Expedited petition
271. Proceedings on creditor's petition

*Debtor's petition*

272. Grounds of debtor's petition
273. Appointment of insolvency practitioner by the court
274. Action on report of insolvency practitioner
275. Summary administration

*Other cases for special consideration*

276. Default in connection with voluntary arrangement
277. Petition based on criminal bankruptcy order

*Commencement and duration of bankruptcy; discharge*

278. Commencement and continuance
279. Duration
280. Discharge by order of the court
281. Effect of discharge
282. Court's power to annul bankruptcy order

## CHAPTER II – PROTECTION OF BANKRUPT'S ESTATE AND INVESTIGATION OF HIS AFFAIRS

283. Definition of bankrupt's estate
284. Restrictions on dispositions of property
285. Restriction on proceedings and remedies
286. Power to appoint interim receiver
287. Receivership pending appointment of trustee
288. Statement of affairs
289. Investigatory duties of official receiver
290. Public examination of bankrupt
291. Duties of bankrupt in relation to official receiver

## CHAPTER III – TRUSTEES IN BANKRUPTCY

*Tenure of office as trustee*

292. Power to make appointments
293. Summoning of meeting to appoint first trustee
294. Power of creditors to requisition meeting
295. Failure of meeting to appoint trustee
296. Appointment of trustee by Secretary of State
297. Special cases
298. Removal of trustee; vacation of office
299. Release of trustee
300. Vacancy in office of trustee

*Control of trustee*

301. Creditors' committee
302. Exercise by Secretary of State of functions of creditors' committee
303. General control of trustee by the court
304. Liability of trustee

SECTION

## CHAPTER IV – ADMINISTRATION BY TRUSTEE

*Preliminary*

305. General functions of trustee

*Acquisition, control and realisation of bankrupt's estate*

306. Vesting of bankrupt's estate in trustee
307. After-acquired property
308. Vesting in trustee of certain items of excess value
308A. Vesting in trustee of certain tenancies
309. Time-limit for notice under s. 307 or 308
310. Income payments orders
311. Acquisition by trustee of control
312. Obligation to surrender control to trustee
313. Charge on bankrupt's home
314. Powers of trustee

*Disclaimer of onerous property*

315. Disclaimer (general power)
316. Notice requiring trustee's decision
317. Disclaimer of leaseholds
318. Disclaimer of dwelling house
319. Disclaimer of land subject to rentcharge
320. Court order vesting disclaimed property
321. Order under s. 320 in respect of leaseholds

*Distribution of bankrupt's estate*

322. Proof of debts
323. Mutual credit and set-off
324. Distribution by means of dividend
325. Claims by unsatisfied creditors
326. Distribution of property in specie
327. Distribution in criminal bankruptcy
328. Priority of debts
329. Debts to spouse
330. Final distribution
331. Final meeting
332. Saving for bankrupt's home

*Supplemental*

333. Duties of bankrupt in relation to trustee
334. Stay of distribution in case of second bankruptcy
335. Adjustment between earlier and later bankruptcy estates

## CHAPTER V – EFFECT OF BANKRUPTCY ON CERTAIN RIGHTS, TRANSACTIONS, ETC.

*Rights under trusts of land*

335A. Rights under trusts of land

*Rights of occupation*

336. Rights of occupation etc. of bankrupt's spouse
337. Rights of occupation of bankrupt
338. Payments in respect of premises occupied by bankrupt

SECTION

*Adjustment of prior transactions, etc.*



## CHAPTER VI – BANKRUPTCY OFFENCES

*Preliminary*



*Wrongdoing by the bankrupt before and after bankruptcy*



## CHAPTER VII – POWERS OF COURT IN BANKRUPTCY



# PART X – INDIVIDUAL INSOLVENCY: GENERAL PROVISIONS



# PART XI – INTERPRETATION FOR SECOND GROUP OF PARTS

# THE THIRD GROUP OF PARTS MISCELLANEOUS MATTERS BEARING ON BOTH COMPANY AND INDIVIDUAL INSOLVENCY; GENERAL INTERPRETATION; FINAL PROVISIONS

## PART XII – PREFERENTIAL DEBTS IN COMPANY AND INDIVIDUAL INSOLVENCY



## PART XIII – INSOLVENCY PRACTITIONERS AND THEIR QUALIFICATION

*Restriction on unqualified persons acting as liquidator, trustee in bankruptcy, etc.*



*The requisite qualification, and the means of obtaining it*



## PART XIV – PUBLIC ADMINISTRATION (ENGLAND AND WALES)

*Official receivers*



*The Official Petitioner*



*Insolvency Service finance, accounting and investment*

# INSOLVENCY ACT 1986

(1986 Chapter 45)

An Act to consolidate the enactments relating to company insolvency and winding up (including the winding up of companies that are not insolvent, and of unregistered companies); enactments relating to the insolvency and bankruptcy of individuals; and other enactments bearing on those two subject matters, including the functions and qualification of insolvency practitioners, the public administration of insolvency, the penalisation and redress of malpractice and wrongdoing, and the avoidance of certain transactions at an undervalue.

[*25th July 1986*]

# THE FIRST GROUP OF PARTS COMPANY INSOLVENCY; COMPANIES WINDING UP

# PART I – COMPANY VOLUNTARY ARRANGEMENTS

**Note**
Re application of Pt. I to insolvent partnerships, see the Insolvent Partnerships Order 1994 (SI 1994/2421), especially reg. 4.5, Sch. 1.

THE PROPOSAL

## 1 Those who may propose an arrangement

**1(1) [Directors]** The directors of a company (other than one for which an administration order is in force, or which is being wound up) may make a proposal under this Part to the company and to its creditors for a composition in satisfaction of its debts or a scheme of arrangement of its affairs (from here on referred to, in either case, as a "voluntary arrangement").

**1(2) [Interpretation]** A proposal under this part is one which provides for some person ("the nominee") to act in relation to the voluntary arrangement either as trustee or otherwise for the purpose of supervising its implementation; and the nominee must be a person who is qualified to act as an insolvency practitioner in relation to the company.

**1(3) [Administrator, liquidator]** Such a proposal may also be made–

(a) where an administration order is in force in relation to the company, by the administrator, and

(b) where the company is being wound up, by the liquidator.

## 2 Procedure where nominee is not the liquidator or administrator

**2(1) [Application]** This section applies where the nominee under section 1 is not the liquidator or administrator of the company.

**2(2) [Report to court]** The nominee shall, within 28 days (or such longer period as the court may allow) after he is given notice of the proposal for a voluntary arrangement, submit a report to the court stating–

(a) whether, in his opinion, meetings of the company and of its creditors should be summoned to consider the proposal, and

(b) if in his opinion such meetings should be summoned, the date on which, and time and place at which, he proposes the meetings should be held.

**2(3) [Information to nominee]** For the purposes of enabling the nominee to prepare his report, the person intending to make the proposal shall submit to the nominee–

(a) a document setting out the terms of the proposed voluntary arrangement, and

(b) a statement of the company's affairs containing–

(i) such particulars of its creditors and of its debts and other liabilities and of its assets as may be prescribed, and

(ii) such other information as may be prescribed.

**2(4) [Replacement of nominee by court]** The court may, on an application made by the person intending to make the proposal, in a case where the nominee has failed to submit the report required by this section, direct that the nominee be replaced as such by another person qualified to act as an insolvency practitioner in relation to the company.

**Note**

For procedure and relevant forms prescribed for s. 2, see the Insolvency Rules 1986 (SI 1986/1925), r. 1.2–1.9.

## 3 Summoning of meetings

**3(1) [Meetings in accordance with report]** Where the nominee under section 1 is not the liquidator or administrator, and it has been reported to the court that such meetings as are mentioned in section 2(2) should be summoned, the person making the report shall (unless the court otherwise directs) summon those meetings for the time, date and place proposed in the report.

**3(2) [Where nominee liquidator or administrator]** Where the nominee is the liquidator or administrator, he shall summon meetings of the company and of its creditors to consider the proposal for such a time, date and place as he thinks fit.

**3(3) [Persons summoned]** The persons to be summoned to a creditors' meeting under this section are every creditor of the company of whose claim and address the person summoning the meeting is aware.

### CONSIDERATION AND IMPLEMENTATION OF PROPOSAL

## 4 Decisions of meetings

**4(1) [Decision]** The meetings summoned under section 3 shall decide whether to approve the proposed voluntary arrangement (with or without modifications).

**4(2) [Modifications]** The modifications may include one conferring the functions proposed to be conferred on the nominee on another person qualified to act as an insolvency practitioner in relation to the company.

But they shall not include any modification by virtue of which the proposal ceases to be a proposal such as is mentioned in section 1.

**4(3) [Limitation on approval]** A meeting so summoned shall not approve any proposal or modification which affects the right of a secured creditor of the company to enforce his security, except with the concurrence of the creditor concerned.

**4(4) [Further limitation]** Subject as follows, a meeting so summoned shall not approve any proposal or modification under which–

(a) any preferential debt of the company is to be paid otherwise than in priority to such of its debts as are not preferential debts, or

(b) a preferential creditor of the company is to be paid an amount in respect of a preferential debt that bears to that debt a smaller proportion than is borne to another preferential debt by the amount that is to be paid in respect of that other debt.

However, the meeting may approve such a proposal or modification with the concurrence of the preferential creditor concerned.



CCH.New Law
bbcl insa 1986aMp 1218—bcl98 1a

**4(5) [Meeting in accordance with rules]** Subject as above, each of the meetings shall be conducted in accordance with the rules.

**Note**
See the Insolvency Rules 1986 (SI 1986/1925), r. 1.13ff.

**4(6) [Report to court, notice]** After the conclusion of either meeting in accordance with the rules, the chairman of the meeting shall report the result of the meeting to the court, and, immediately after reporting to the court, shall give notice of the result of the meeting to such persons as may be prescribed.

**Note**
See the Insolvency Rules 1986 (SI 1986/1925), r. 1.14, 1.21.

**4(7) [Interpretation]** References in this section to preferential debts and preferential creditors are to be read in accordance with section 386 in Part XII of this Act.

# 5 Effect of approval

**5(1) [Operation]** This section has effect where each of the meetings summoned under section 3 approves the proposed voluntary arrangement either with the same modifications or without modifications.

**5(2) [Effect of composition or scheme]** The approved voluntary arrangement–

(a) takes effect as if made by the company at the creditors' meeting, and

(b) binds every person who in accordance with the rules had notice of, and was entitled to vote at, that meeting (whether or not he was present or represented at the meeting) as if he were a party to the voluntary arrangement.

**5(3) [Court powers]** Subject as follows, if the company is being wound up or an administration order is in force, the court may do one or both of the following, namely–

(a) by order stay or sist all proceedings in the winding up or discharge the administration order;

(b) give such directions with respect to the conduct of the winding up or the administration as it thinks appropriate for facilitating the implementation of the approved voluntary arrangement.

**5(4) [Limit on s. 5(3)(a)]** The court shall not make an order under subsection (3)(a)–

(a) at any time before the end of the period of 28 days beginning with the first day on which each of the reports required by section 4(6) has been made to the court, or

(b) at any time when an application under the next section or an appeal in respect of such an application is pending, or at any time in the period within which such an appeal may be brought.

# 6 Challenge of decisions

**6(1) [Application to court]** Subject to this section, an application to the court may be made, by any of the persons specified below, on one or both of the following grounds, namely–

(a) that a voluntary arrangement approved at the meetings summoned under section 3 unfairly prejudices the interests of a creditor, member or contributory of the company;

(b) that there has been some material irregularity at or in relation to either of the meetings.

**6(2) [Applicants]** The persons who may apply under this section are–

(a) a person entitled, in accordance with the rules, to vote at either of the meetings;

(b) the nominee or any person who has replaced him under section 2(4) or 4(2); and

(c) if the company is being wound up or an administration order is in force, the liquidator or administrator.

**6(3) [Time for application]** An application under this section shall not be made after the end of the period of 28 days beginning with the first day on which each of the reports required by section 4(6) has been made to the court.

**6(4) [Powers of court]** Where on such an application the court is satisfied as to either of the grounds mentioned in subsection (1), it may do one or both of the following, namely–

(a) revoke or suspend the approvals given by the meetings or, in a case falling within subsection (1)(b), any approval given by the meeting in question;

(b) give a direction to any person for the summoning of further meetings to consider any revised proposal the person who made the original proposal may make or, in a case falling within subsection (1)(b), a further company or (as the case may be) creditors' meeting to reconsider the original proposal.

**6(5) [Revocation or suspension of approval]** Where at any time after giving a direction under subsection (4)(b) for the summoning of meetings to consider a revised proposal the court is satisfied that the person who made the original proposal does not intend to submit a revised proposal, the court shall revoke the direction and revoke or suspend any approval given at the previous meetings.

**6(6) [Supplemental directions]** In a case where the court, on an application under this section with respect to any meeting–

(a) gives a direction under subsection (4)(b), or

(b) revokes or suspends an approval under subsection (4)(a) or (5),

the court may give such supplemental directions as it thinks fit and, in particular, directions with respect to things done since the meeting under any voluntary arrangement approved by the meeting.

**6(7) [Effect of irregularity]** Except in pursuance of the preceding provisions of this section, an approval given at a meeting summoned under section 3 is not invalidated by any irregularity at or in relation to the meeting.

**Note**

For procedure on making of s. 6 order, see the Insolvency Rules 1986 (SI 1986/1925), r. 1.25.

# 7 Implementation of proposal

**7(1) [Application]** This section applies where a voluntary arrangement approved by the meetings summoned under section 3 has taken effect.

**7(2) [Supervisor of composition or scheme]** The person who is for the time being carrying out in relation to the voluntary arrangement the functions conferred–

(a) by virtue of the approval on the nominee, or

(b) by virtue of section 2(4) or 4(2) on a person other than the nominee,

shall be known as the supervisor of the voluntary arrangement.

**7(3) [Application to court]** If any of the company's creditors or any other person is dissatisfied by any act, omission or decision of the supervisor, he may apply to the court; and on the application the court may–

(a) confirm, reverse or modify any act or decision of the supervisor,

(b) give him directions, or

(c) make such other order as it thinks fit.

**7(4) [Application for directions by supervisor]** The supervisor–

(a) may apply to the court for directions in relation to any particular matter arising under the voluntary arrangement, and

(b) is included among the persons who may apply to the court for the winding up of the company or for an administration order to be made in relation to it.

**7(5) [Court appointment powers]** The court may, whenever–

(a) it is expedient to appoint a person to carry out the functions of the supervisor, and

(b) it is inexpedient, difficult or impracticable for an appointment to be made without the assistance of the court,

make an order appointing a person who is qualified to act as an insolvency practitioner in relation to the company, either in substitution for the existing supervisor or to fill a vacancy.

**7(6) [Limit on s. 7(5) power]** The power conferred by subsection (5) is exercisable so as to increase the number of persons exercising the functions of supervisor or, where there is more than one person exercising those functions, so as to replace one or more of those persons.

# PART II – ADMINISTRATION ORDERS

**Note**
Re application of Pt. I to insolvent partnerships' see the Insolvent Partnerships Order 1994 (SI 1994/2421), especially reg. 6, Sch. 2.

## MAKING, ETC. OF ADMINISTRATION ORDER

## 8 Power of court to make order

**8(1) [Administration order]** Subject to this section, if the court–

(a) is satisfied that a company is or is likely to become unable to pay its debts (within the meaning given to that expression by section 123 of this Act), and

(b) considers that the making of an order under this section would be likely to achieve one or more of the purposes mentioned below,

the court may make an administration order in relation to the company.

**8(2) [Definition]** An administration order is an order directing that, during the period for which the order is in force, the affairs, business and property of the company shall be managed by a person ("the administrator") appointed for the purpose by the court.

**8(3) [Purposes for order]** The purposes for whose achievement an administration order may be made are–

(a) the survival of the company, and the whole or any part of its undertaking, as a going concern;

(b) the approval of a voluntary arrangement under Part I;

(c) the sanctioning under section 425 of the Companies Act of a compromise or arrangement between the company and any such persons as are mentioned in that section; and

(d) a more advantageous realisation of the company's assets than would be effected on a winding up;

and the order shall specify the purpose or purposes for which it is made.

**8(4) [Where order not to be made]** An administration order shall not be made in relation to a company after it has gone into liquidation, nor where it is–

(a) an insurance company within the meaning of the Insurance Companies Act 1982, or

(b) an authorised institution or former authorised institution within the meaning of the Banking Act 1987.

**History**
In s. 8(4), para. (b) substituted by Banking Act 1987, s. 108(1) and Sch. 6, para. 25(1) as from 1 October 1987 (see SI 1987/1664 (C 50)); the former para. (b) read as follows:
"(b) a recognised bank or licensed institution within the meaning of the Banking Act 1979, or an institution to which sections 16 and 18 of that Act apply as if it were a licensed institution."

**Note**
See Banks (Administration Proceedings) Order 1989 (SI 1989/1276) for modification of Pt. II for authorised institutions.

## 9 Application for order

**9(1) [Application to court]** An application to the court for an administration order shall be by petition presented either by the company or the directors, or by a creditor or creditors (including any contingent or prospective creditor or creditors), or by the clerk of a magistrates' court in the exercise of the power conferred by section 87A of the Magistrates' Courts Act 1980 (enforcement of fines imposed on companies) or by all or any of those parties, together or separately.

**History**
In s. 9(1) the words "or by the clerk of a magistrates' court in the exercise of the power conferred by section 87A of the Magistrates' Courts Act 1980 (enforcement of fines imposed on companies)" inserted by Criminal Justice Act 1988, s. 62(2)(a) as from 5 January 1989 (see SI 1988/2073 (C 78)).

**9(2) [On presentation of petition to court]** Where a petition is presented to the court–

(a) notice of the petition shall be given forthwith to any person who has appointed, or is or may be entitled to appoint, an administrative receiver of the company, and to such other persons as may be prescribed, and

(b) the petition shall not be withdrawn except with the leave of the court.

**Note**

For the "other persons" in s. 9(2)(a), see the Insolvency Rules 1986 (SI 1986/1925), r. 2.6.

**9(3) [Duties of court]** Where the court is satisfied that there is an administrative receiver of the company, the court shall dismiss the petition unless it is also satisfied either–

(a) that the person by whom or on whose behalf the receiver was appointed has consented to the making of the order, or

(b) that, if an administration order were made, any security by virtue of which the receiver was appointed would–

(i) be liable to be released or discharged under sections 238 to 240 in Part VI (transactions at an undervalue and preferences),

(ii) be avoided under section 245 in that Part (avoidance of floating charges), or

(iii) be challengeable under section 242 (gratuitous alienations) or 243 (unfair preferences) in that Part, or under any rule of law in Scotland.

**9(4) [Court powers on hearing petition]** Subject to subsection (3), on hearing a petition the court may dismiss it, or adjourn the hearing conditionally or unconditionally, or make an interim order or any other order that it thinks fit.

**9(5) [Extent of interim order]** Without prejudice to the generality of subsection (4), an interim order under that subsection may restrict the exercise of any powers of the directors or of the company (whether by reference to the consent of the court or of a person qualified to act as an insolvency practitioner in relation to the company, or otherwise).

## 10 Effect of application

**10(1) [Limitations]** During the period beginning with the presentation of a petition for an administration order and ending with the making of such an order or the dismissal of the petition–

(a) no resolution may be passed or order made for the winding up of the company;

(b) no steps may be taken to enforce any security over the company's property, or to repossess goods in the company's possession under any hire-purchase agreement, except with the leave of the court and subject to such terms as the court may impose; and

(c) no other proceedings and no execution or other legal process may be commenced or continued, and no distress may be levied, against the company or its property except with the leave of the court and subject to such terms as aforesaid.

**10(2) [Where leave not required]** Nothing in subsection (1) requires the leave of the court–

(a) for the presentation of a petition for the winding up of the company,

(b) for the appointment of an administrative receiver of the company, or

(c) for the carrying out by such a receiver (whenever appointed) of any of his functions.

**10(3) [Period in s. 10(1)]** Where–

(a) a petition for an administration order is presented at a time when there is an administrative receiver of the company, and

(b) the person by or on whose behalf the receiver was appointed has not consented to the making of the order,

the period mentioned in subsection (1) is deemed not to begin unless and until that person so consents.

**10(4) [Hire-purchase agreements]** References in this section and the next to hire-purchase agreements include conditional sale agreements, chattel leasing agreements and retention of title agreements.

**10(5) [Scotland]** In the application of this section and the next to Scotland, references to execution being commenced or continued include references to diligence being carried out or continued, and references to distress being levied shall be omitted.

## 11 Effect of order

**11(1) [On making of administration order]** On the making of an administration order–

(a) any petition for the winding up of the company shall be dismissed, and

(b) any administrative receiver of the company shall vacate office.

**11(2) [Vacation of office by receiver]** Where an administration order has been made, any receiver of part of the company's property shall vacate office on being required to do so by the administrator.

**11(3) [Limitations]** During the period for which an administration order is in force–

(a) no resolution may be passed or order made for the winding up of the company;

(b) no administrative receiver of the company may be appointed;

(c) no other steps may be taken to enforce any security over the company's property, or to repossess goods in the company's possession under any hire-purchase agreement, except with the consent of the administrator or the leave of the court and subject (where the court gives leave) to such terms as the court may impose; and

(d) no other proceedings and no execution or other legal process may be commenced or continued, and no distress may be levied, against the company or its property except with the consent of the administrator or the leave of the court and subject (where the court gives leave) to such terms as aforesaid.

**11(4) [Where vacation of office under s. 11(1)(b), (2)]** Where at any time an administrative receiver of the company has vacated office under subsection (1)(b), or a receiver of part of the company's property has vacated office under subsection (2)–

(a) his remuneration and any expenses properly incurred by him, and

(b) any indemnity to which he is entitled out of the assets of the company,

shall be charged on and (subject to subsection (3) above) paid out of any property of the company which was in his custody or under his control at that time in priority to any security held by the person by or on whose behalf he was appointed.

**11(5) [S. 40, 59]** Neither an administrative receiver who vacates office under subsection (1)(b) nor a receiver who vacates office under subsection (2) is required on or after so vacating office to take any steps for the purpose of complying with any duty imposed on him by section 40 or 59 of this Act (duty to pay preferential creditors).

## 12 Notification of order

**12(1) [Information in invoices etc.]** Every invoice, order for goods or business letter which, at a time when an administration order is in force in relation to a company, is issued by or on behalf of the company or the administrator, being a document on or in which the company's name appears, shall also contain the administrator's name and a statement that the affairs, business and property of the company are being managed by the administrator.

**12(2) [Penalty on default]** If default is made in complying with this section, the company and any of the following persons who without reasonable excuse authorises or permits the default, namely, the administrator and any officer of the company, is liable to a fine.

### ADMINISTRATORS

## 13 Appointment of administrator

**13(1) [Appointment]** The administrator of a company shall be appointed either by the administration order or by an order under the next subsection.

**13(2) [Court may fill vacancy]** If a vacancy occurs by death, resignation or otherwise in the office of the administrator, the court may by order fill the vacancy.

**13(3) [Application for s. 13(2) order]** An application for an order under subsection (2) may be made–

(a) by any continuing administrator of the company; or

(b) where there is no such administrator, by a creditors' committee established under section 26 below; or

(c) where there is no such administrator and no such committee, by the company or the directors or by any creditor or creditors of the company.

# 14 General powers

**14(1) [Powers of administrator]** The administrator of a company–

(a) may do all such things as may be necessary for the management of the affairs, business and property of the company, and

(b) without prejudice to the generality of paragraph (a), has the powers specified in Schedule 1 to this Act;

and in the application of that Schedule to the administrator of a company the words "he" and "him" refer to the administrator.

**14(2) [Extra powers]** The administrator also has power–

(a) to remove any director of the company and to appoint any person to be a director of it, whether to fill a vacancy or otherwise, and

(b) to call any meeting of the members or creditors of the company.

**14(3) [Application for directions]** The administrator may apply to the court for directions in relation to any particular matter arising in connection with the carrying out of his functions.

**14(4) [Conflict with other powers]** Any power conferred on the company or its officers, whether by this Act or the Companies Act or by the memorandum or articles of association, which could be exercised in such a way as to interfere with the exercise by the administrator of his powers is not exercisable except with the consent of the administrator, which may be given either generally or in relation to particular cases.

**14(5) [Administrator agent]** In exercising his powers the administrator is deemed to act as the company's agent.

**14(6) [Third party]** A person dealing with the administrator in good faith and for value is not concerned to inquire whether the administrator is acting within his powers.

# 15 Power to deal with charged property, etc.

**15(1) [Power of disposal etc.]** The administrator of a company may dispose of or otherwise exercise his powers in relation to any property of the company which is subject to a security to which this subsection applies as if the property were not subject to the security.

**15(2) [Court orders, on application by administrator]** Where, on an application by the administrator, the court is satisfied that the disposal (with or without other assets) of–

(a) any property of the company subject to a security to which this subsection applies, or

(b) any goods in the possession of the company under a hire-purchase agreement,

would be likely to promote the purpose or one or more of the purposes specified in the administration order, the court may by order authorise the administrator to dispose of the property as if it were not subject to the security or to dispose of the goods as if all rights of the owner under the hire-purchase agreement were vested in the company.

**15(3) [Application of s. 15(1), (2)]** Subsection (1) applies to any security which, as created, was a floating charge; and subsection (2) applies to any other security.

**15(4) [Effect of security where property disposed of]** Where property is disposed of under subsection (1), the holder of the security has the same priority in respect of any property of the company directly or indirectly representing the property disposed of as he would have had in respect of the property subject to the security.

**15(5) [Conditions for s. 15(2) order]** It shall be a condition of an order under subsection (2) that–

(a) the net proceeds of the disposal, and

(b) where those proceeds are less than such amount as may be determined by the court to be the net amount which would be realised on a sale of the property or goods in the open market by a willing vendor, such sums as may be required to make good the deficiency,

shall be applied towards discharging the sums secured by the security or payable under the hire-purchase agreement.

**15(6) [Where s. 15(5) condition re two or more securities]** Where a condition imposed in pursuance of subsection (5) relates to two or more securities, that condition requires the net proceeds of the disposal and, where paragraph (b) of that subsection applies, the sums mentioned in that paragraph to be applied towards discharging the sums secured by those securities in the order of their priorities.

**15(7) [Copy of s. 15(2) order to registrar]** An office copy of an order under subsection (2) shall, within 14 days after the making of the order, be sent by the administrator to the registrar of companies.

**15(8) [Non-compliance with s. 15(7)]** If the administrator without reasonable excuse fails to comply with subsection (7), he is liable to a fine and, for continued contravention, to a daily default fine.

**15(9) [Interpretation]** References in this section to hire-purchase agreements include conditional sale agreements, chattel leasing agreements and retention of title agreements.

## 16 Operation of s. 15 in Scotland

**16(1) [Administrator's duty]** Where property is disposed of under section 15 in its application to Scotland, the administrator shall grant to the disponee an appropriate document of transfer or conveyance of the property, and–

(a) that document, or

(b) where any recording, intimation or registration of the document is a legal requirement for completion of title to the property, that recording, intimation or registration,

has the effect of disencumbering the property of or, as the case may be, freeing the property from the security.

**16(2) [Disposal of goods on hire-purchase etc.]** Where goods in the possession of the company under a hire-purchase agreement, conditional sale agreement, chattel leasing agreement or retention of title agreement are disposed of under section 15 in its application to Scotland, the disposal has the effect of extinguishing, as against the disponee, all rights of the owner of the goods under the agreement.

## 17 General duties

**17(1) [Control of company property]** The administrator of a company shall, on his appointment, take into his custody or under his control all the property to which the company is or appears to be entitled.

**17(2) [Management of affairs etc.]** The administrator shall manage the affairs, business and property of the company–

(a) at any time before proposals have been approved (with or without modifications) under section 24 below, in accordance with any directions given by the court, and

(b) at any time after proposals have been so approved, in accordance with those proposals as from time to time revised, whether by him or a predecessor of his.

**17(3) [Summoning of creditors' meeting]** The administrator shall summon a meeting of the company's creditors if–

(a) he is requested, in accordance with the rules, to do so by one-tenth, in value, of the company's creditors, or

(b) he is directed to do so by the court.

**Note**

For the rules relevant for s. 17(3), see the Insolvency Rules 1986 (SI 1986/1925), r. 2.21ff.

## 18 Discharge or variation of administration order

**18(1) [Application to court by administrator]** The administrator of a company may at any time apply to the court for the administration order to be discharged, or to be varied so as to specify an additional purpose.

**18(2) [Duty to make application]** The administrator shall make an application under this section if–

(a) it appears to him that the purpose or each of the purposes specified in the order either has been achieved or is incapable of achievement, or

(b) he is required to do so by a meeting of the company's creditors summoned for the purpose in accordance with the rules.

**18(3) [Court order]** On the hearing of an application under this section, the court may by order discharge or vary the administration order and make such consequential provision as it thinks fit, or adjourn the hearing conditionally or unconditionally, or make an interim order or any other order it thinks fit.

**18(4) [Copy of order to registrar]** Where the administration order is discharged or varied the administrator shall, within 14 days after the making of the order effecting the discharge or variation, send an office copy of that order to the registrar of companies.

**18(5) [Non-compliance with s. 18(4)]** If the administrator without reasonable excuse fails to comply with subsection (4), he is liable to a fine and, for continued contravention, to a daily default fine.

## 19 Vacation of office

**19(1) [Removal or resignation]** The administrator of a company may at any time be removed from office by order of the court and may, in the prescribed circumstances, resign his office by giving notice of his resignation to the court.

**Note**

For the prescribed circumstances, see the Insolvency Rules 1986 (SI 1986/1925), r. 2.53.

**19(2) [Vacation of office etc.]** The administrator shall vacate office if–

(a) he ceases to be qualified to act as an insolvency practitioner in relation to the company, or

(b) the administration order is discharged.

**19(3) [Ceasing to be administrator]** Where at any time a person ceases to be administrator, the following subsections apply.

**History**

In s. 19(3) the word "following" substituted for the former words "next two" by Insolvency Act 1994, s. 1(1), (2), (7) with effect in relation to contracts of employment adopted on or after 15 March 1994.

**19(4) [Remuneration and expenses]** His remuneration and any expenses properly incurred by him shall be charged on and paid out of any property of the company which is in his custody or under his control at that time in priority to any security to which section 15(1) then applies.

**19(5) [Debts or liabilities re contracts entered into]** Any sums payable in respect of debts or liabilities incurred, while he was administrator, under contracts entered into by him or a predecessor of his in the carrying out of his or the predecessor's functions shall be charged on and paid out of any such property as is mentioned in subsection (4) in priority to any charge arising under that subsection.

**History**

In s. 19(5) the words "or contracts of employment adopted" formerly appearing after the words ", under contracts entered into" omitted and repealed by Insolvency Act 1994, s. 1(1), (3), (7), 5 and Sch. 2 with effect in relation to contracts of employment adopted on or after 15 March 1994. See also history note after s. 19(6).

**19(6) [Debts or liabilities re contracts of employment adopted]** Any sums payable in respect of liabilities incurred, while he was administrator, under contracts of employment adopted by him or a predecessor of his in the carrying out of his or the predecessor's functions shall, to the extent that the liabilities are qualifying liabilities, be charged on and paid out of any such property as is mentioned in subsection (4) and enjoy the same priority as any sums to which subsection (5) applies.

For this purpose, the administrator is not to be taken to have adopted a contract of employment by reason of anything done or omitted to be done within 14 days after his appointment.

**History**
First paragraph of s. 19(6) inserted by Insolvency Act 1994, s. 1(1), (4) and second paragraph moved from end of s. 19(5) by Insolvency Act 1994, s. 1(1), (5), (7) with effect in relation to contracts of employment adopted on or after 15 March 1994.

**19(7) [Interpretation of s. 19(6)]** For the purposes of subsection (6), a liability under a contract of employment is a qualifying liability if–

(a) it is a liability to pay a sum by way of wages or salary or contribution to an occupational pension scheme, and

(b) it is in respect of services rendered wholly or partly after the adoption of the contract.

**History**
See history note after s. 19(10).

**19(8) [Liability disregarded for s. 19(6)]** There shall be disregarded for the purposes of subsection (6) so much of any qualifying liability as represents payment in respect of services rendered before the adoption of the contract.

**History**
See history note after s. 19(10).

**19(9) [Interpretation of s. 19(7), (8)]** For the purposes of subsections (7) and (8)–

(a) wages or salary payable in respect of a period of holiday or absence from work through sickness or other good cause are deemed to be wages or (as the case may be) salary in respect of services rendered in that period, and

(b) a sum payable in lieu of holiday is deemed to be wages or (as the case may be) salary in respect of services rendered in the period by reference to which the holiday entitlement arose.

**History**
See history note after s. 19(10).

**19(10) [Interpretation of s. 19(9)(a)]** In subsection (9)(a), the reference to wages or salary payable in respect of a period of holiday includes any sums which, if they had been paid, would have been treated for the purposes of the enactments relating to social security as earnings in respect of that period.

**History**
S. 19(7)–(10) inserted by Insolvency Act 1994, s. 1(1), (6), (7) with effect in relation to contracts of employment adopted on or after 15 March 1994.

## 20 Release of administrator

**20(1) [Time of release]** A person who has ceased to be the administrator of a company has his release with effect from the following time, that is to say–

(a) in the case of a person who has died, the time at which notice is given to the court in accordance with the rules that he has ceased to hold office;

(b) in any other case, such time as the court may determine.

**Note**
The relevant rule for s. 20(1)(a) is the Insolvency Rules 1986 (SI 1986/1925), r. 2.54.

**20(2) [Discharge from liability, etc.]** Where a person has his release under this section, he is, with effect from the time specified above, discharged from all liability both in respect of acts or omissions of his in the administration and otherwise in relation to his conduct as administrator.

**20(3) [S. 212]** However, nothing in this section prevents the exercise, in relation to a person who has had his release as above, of the court's powers under section 212 in Chapter X of Part IV (summary remedy against delinquent directors, liquidators, etc.).

### ASCERTAINMENT AND INVESTIGATION OF COMPANY'S AFFAIRS

## 21 Information to be given by administrator

**21(1) [Duties of administrator]** Where an administration order has been made, the administrator shall–

(a) forthwith send to the company and publish in the prescribed manner a notice of the order, and

(b) within 28 days after the making of the order, unless the court otherwise directs, send such a notice to all creditors of the company (so far as he is aware of their addresses).

**21(2) [Copy of order to registrar]** Where an administration order has been made, the administrator shall also, within 14 days after the making of the order, send an office copy of the order to the registrar of companies and to such other persons as may be prescribed.

**Note**

See the Insolvency Rules 1986 (SI 1986/1925), r. 2.10.

**21(3) [Penalty for non-compliance]** If the administrator without reasonable excuse fails to comply with this section, he is liable to a fine and, for continued contravention, to a daily default fine.

## 22 Statement of affairs to be submitted to administrator

**22(1) [Duty of administrator]** Where an administration order has been made, the administrator shall forthwith require some or all of the persons mentioned below to make out and submit to him a statement in the prescribed form as to the affairs of the company.

**Note**

See the Insolvency Rules 1986 (SI 1986/1925), r. 2.11.

**22(2) [Contents of statement]** The statement shall be verified by affidavit by the persons required to submit it and shall show–

(a) particulars of the company's assets, debts and liabilities;

(b) the names and addresses of its creditors;

(c) the securities held by them respectively;

(d) the dates when the securities were respectively given; and

(e) such further or other information as may be prescribed.

**22(3) [Persons in s. 22(1)]** The persons referred to in subsection (1) are–

(a) those who are or have been officers of the company;

(b) those who have taken part in the company's formation at any time within one year before the date of the administration order;

(c) those who are in the company's employment or have been in its employment within that year, and are in the administrator's opinion capable of giving the information required;

(d) those who are or have been within that year officers of or in the employment of a company which is, or within that year was, an officer of the company.

In this subsection **"employment"** includes employment under a contract for services.

**22(4) [Time for submitting statement]** Where any persons are required under this section to submit a statement of affairs to the administrator, they shall do so (subject to the next subsection) before the end of the period of 21 days beginning with the day after that on which the prescribed notice of the requirement is given to them by the administrator.

**22(5) [Powers re release, extension of time]** The administrator, if he thinks fit, may–

(a) at any time release a person from an obligation imposed on him under subsection (1) or (2), or

(b) either when giving notice under subsection (4) or subsequently, extend the period so mentioned;

and where the administrator has refused to exercise a power conferred by this subsection, the court, if it thinks fit, may exercise it.

**22(6) [Penalty for non-compliance]** If a person without reasonable excuse fails to comply with any obligation imposed under this section, he is liable to a fine and, for continued contravention, to a daily default fine.

ADMINISTRATOR'S PROPOSALS

## 23 Statement of proposals

**23(1) [Duties of administrator]** Where an administration order has been made, the administrator shall, within 3 months (or such longer period as the court may allow) after the making of the order–

(a) send to the registrar of companies and (so far as he is aware of their addresses) to all creditors a statement of his proposals for achieving the purpose or purposes specified in the order, and

(b) lay a copy of the statement before a meeting of the company's creditors summoned for the purpose on not less than 14 days' notice.

**23(2) [Copies of statement]** The administrator shall also, within 3 months (or such longer period as the court may allow) after the making of the order, either–

(a) send a copy of the statement (so far as he is aware of their addresses) to all members of the company, or

(b) publish in the prescribed manner a notice stating an address to which members of the company should write for copies of the statement to be sent to them free of charge.

**Note**
See the Insolvency Rules 1986 (SI 1986/1925), r. 2.17.

**23(3) [Penalty for non-compliance]** If the administrator without reasonable excuse fails to comply with this section, he is liable to a fine and, for continued contravention, to a daily default fine.

## 24 Consideration of proposals by creditors' meeting

**24(1) [Creditors' meeting to decide]** A meeting of creditors summoned under section 23 shall decide whether to approve the administrator's proposals.

**24(2) [Approval, modifications]** The meeting may approve the proposals with modifications, but shall not do so unless the administrator consents to each modification.

**24(3) [Meeting in accordance with rules]** Subject as above, the meeting shall be conducted in accordance with the rules.

**Note**
See the Insolvency Rules 1986 (SI 1986/1925), r. 2.19ff.

**24(4) [Report and notice by administrator]** After the conclusion of the meeting in accordance with the rules, the administrator shall report the result of the meeting to the court and shall give notice of that result to the registrar of companies and to such persons as may be prescribed.

**Note**
See the Insolvency Rules 1986 (SI 1986/1925), r. 2.30.

**24(5) [If meeting does not approve]** If a report is given to the court under subsection (4) that the meeting has declined to approve the administrator's proposals (with or without modifications), the court may by order discharge the administration order and make such consequential provision as it thinks fit, or adjourn the hearing conditionally or unconditionally, or make an interim order or any other order that it thinks fit.

**24(6) [Where administration order discharged]** Where the administration order is discharged, the administrator shall, within 14 days after the making of the order effecting the discharge, send an office copy of that order to the registrar of companies.

**24(7) [Penalty for non-compliance]** If the administrator without reasonable excuse fails to comply with subsection (6), he is liable to a fine and, for continued contravention, to a daily default fine.

## 25 Approval of substantial revisions

**25(1) [Application]** This section applies where–

(a) proposals have been approved (with or without modifications) under section 24, and

(b) the administrator proposes to make revisions of those proposals which appear to him substantial.

**25(2) [Duties of administrator]** The administrator shall–

(a) send to all creditors of the company (so far as he is aware of their addresses) a statement in the prescribed form of his proposed revisions, and

(b) lay a copy of the statement before a meeting of the company's creditors summoned for the purpose on not less than 14 days' notice;

and he shall not make the proposed revisions unless they are approved by the meeting.

**25(3) [Copies of statement]** The administrator shall also either–

(a) send a copy of the statement (so far as he is aware of their addresses) to all members of the company, or

(b) publish in the prescribed manner a notice stating an address to which members of the company should write for copies of the statement to be sent to them free of charge.

**25(4) [Approval, modifications]** The meeting of creditors may approve the proposed revisions with modifications, but shall not do so unless the administrator consents to each modification.

**25(5) [Meeting in accordance with rules]** Subject as above, the meeting shall be conducted in accordance with the rules.

**25(6) [Notification to registrar, et al.]** After the conclusion of the meeting in accordance with the rules, the administrator shall give notice of the result of the meeting to the registrar of companies and to such persons as may be prescribed.

MISCELLANEOUS

## 26 Creditors' committee

**26(1) [Meeting may establish committee]** Where a meeting of creditors summoned under section 23 has approved the administrator's proposals (with or without modifications), the meeting may, if it thinks fit, establish a committee (**"the creditors' committee"**) to exercise the functions conferred on it by or under this Act.

**26(2) [Committee may summon administrator]** If such a committee is established, the committee may, on giving not less than 7 days' notice, require the administrator to attend before it at any reasonable time and furnish it with such information relating to the carrying out of his functions as it may reasonably require.

## 27 Protection of interests of creditors and members

**27(1) [Application by creditor or member]** At any time when an administration order is in force, a creditor or member of the company may apply to the court by petition for an order under this section on the ground–

(a) that the company's affairs, business and property are being or have been managed by the administrator in a manner which is unfairly prejudicial to the interests of its creditors or members generally, or of some part of its creditors or members (including at least himself), or

(b) that any actual or proposed act or omission of the administrator is or would be so prejudicial.

**27(2) [Court order]** On an application for an order under this section the court may, subject as follows, make such order as it thinks fit for giving relief in respect of the matters complained of, or adjourn the hearing conditionally or unconditionally, or make an interim order or any other order that it thinks fit.

**27(3) [Limits of order]** An order under this section shall not prejudice or prevent–

(a) the implementation of a voluntary arrangement approved under section 4 in Part I, or any compromise or arrangement sanctioned under section 425 of the Companies Act; or

(b) where the application for the order was made more than 28 days after the approval of any proposals or revised proposals under section 24 or 25, the implementation of those proposals or revised proposals.

**27(4) [Contents of order]** Subject as above, an order under this section may in particular–

(a) regulate the future management by the administrator of the company's affairs, business and property;

(b) require the administrator to refrain from doing or continuing an act complained of by the petitioner, or to do an act which the petitioner has complained he has omitted to do;

(c) require the summoning of a meeting of creditors or members for the purpose of considering such matters as the court may direct;

(d) discharge the administration order and make such consequential provision as the court thinks fit.

**27(5) [S. 15, 16]** Nothing in sections 15 or 16 is to be taken as prejudicing applications to the court under this section.

**27(6) [Copy of discharge order to registrar]** Where the administration order is discharged, the administrator shall, within 14 days after the making of the order effecting the discharge, send an office copy of that order to the registrar of companies; and if without reasonable excuse he fails to comply with this subsection, he is liable to a fine and, for continued contravention, to a daily default fine.

# PART III – RECEIVERSHIP

## Chapter I – Receivers and Managers (England and Wales)

### PRELIMINARY AND GENERAL PROVISIONS

### 28 Extent of this Chapter

**28** This Chapter does not apply to receivers appointed under Chapter II of this Part (Scotland).

### 29 Definitions

**29(1) [Interpretation]** It is hereby declared that, except where the context otherwise requires–

(a) any reference in the Companies Act or this Act to a receiver or manager of the property of a company, or to a receiver of it, includes a receiver or manager, or (as the case may be) a receiver of part only of that property and a receiver only of the income arising from the property or from part of it; and

(b) any reference in the Companies Act or this Act to the appointment of a receiver or manager under powers contained in an instrument includes an appointment made under powers which, by virtue of any enactment, are implied in and have effect as if contained in an instrument.

**29(2) ["Administrative receiver"]** In this Chapter **"administrative receiver"** means–

(a) a receiver or manager of the whole (or substantially the whole) of a company's property appointed by or on behalf of the holders of any debentures of the company secured by a charge which, as created, was a floating charge, or by such a charge and one or more other securities; or

(b) a person who would be such a receiver or manager but for the appointment of some other person as the receiver of part of the company's property.

### 30 Disqualification of body corporate from acting as receiver

**30** A body corporate is not qualified for appointment as receiver of the property of a company, and any body corporate which acts as such a receiver is liable to a fine.

### 31 Disqualification of undischarged bankrupt

**31** If a person being an undischarged bankrupt acts as receiver or manager of the property of a company on behalf of debenture holders, he is liable to imprisonment or a fine, or both.

This does not apply to a receiver or manager acting under an appointment made by the court.

## 32 Power for court to appoint official receiver

**32** Where application is made to the court to appoint a receiver on behalf of the debenture holders or other creditors of a company which is being wound up by the court, the official receiver may be appointed.

### RECEIVERS AND MANAGERS APPOINTED OUT OF COURT

## 33 Time from which appointment is effective

**33(1) [Effect of appointment]** The appointment of a person as a receiver or manager of a company's property under powers contained in an instrument–

(a) is of no effect unless it is accepted by that person before the end of the business day next following that on which the instrument of appointment is received by him or on his behalf, and

(b) subject to this, is deemed to be made at the time at which the instrument of appointment is so received.

**33(2) [Joint receivers or managers]** This section applies to the appointment of two or more persons as joint receivers or managers of a company's property under powers contained in an instrument, subject to such modifications as may be prescribed by the rules.

**Note**

See the Insolvency Rules 1986 (SI 1986/1925), r. 3.1.

## 34 Liability for invalid appointment

**34** Where the appointment of a person as the receiver or manager of a company's property under powers contained in an instrument is discovered to be invalid (whether by virtue of the invalidity of the instrument or otherwise), the court may order the person by whom or on whose behalf the appointment was made to indemnify the person appointed against any liability which arises solely by reason of the invalidity of the appointment.

## 35 Application to court for directions

**35(1) [Application]** A receiver or manager of the property of a company appointed under powers contained in an instrument, or the persons by whom or on whose behalf a receiver or manager has been so appointed, may apply to the court for directions in relation to any particular matter arising in connection with the performance of the functions of the receiver or manager.

**35(2) [Order, directions by court]** On such an application, the court may give such directions, or may make such order declaring the rights of persons before the court or otherwise, as it thinks just.

## 36 Court's power to fix remuneration

**36(1) [Remuneration]** The court may, on an application made by the liquidator of a company, by order fix the amount to be paid by way of remuneration to a person who, under powers contained in an instrument, has been appointed receiver or manager of the company's property.

**36(2) [Extent of court's power]** The court's power under subsection (1), where no previous order has been made with respect thereto under the subsection–

(a) extends to fixing the remuneration for any period before the making of the order or the application for it,

(b) is exercisable notwithstanding that the receiver or manager has died or ceased to act before the making of the order or the application, and

(c) where the receiver or manager has been paid or has retained for his remuneration for any period before the making of the order any amount in excess of that so fixed for that period, extends to requiring him or his personal representatives to account for the excess or such part of it as may be specified in the order.

But the power conferred by paragraph (c) shall not be exercised as respects any period before the making of the application for the order under this section, unless in the court's opinion there are special circumstances making it proper for the power to be exercised.

**36(3) [Variation, amendment of order]** The court may from time to time on an application made either by the liquidator or by the receiver or manager, vary or amend an order made under subsection (1).

## 37 Liability for contracts, etc.

**37(1) [Personal liability, indemnity]** A receiver or manager appointed under powers contained in an instrument (other than an administrative receiver) is, to the same extent as if he had been appointed by order of the court–

(a) personally liable on any contract entered into by him in the performance of his functions (except in so far as the contract otherwise provides) and on any contract of employment adopted by him in the performance of those functions, and

(b) entitled in respect of that liability to indemnity out of the assets.

**37(2) [Interpretation of s. 37(1)(a)]** For the purposes of subsection (1)(a), the receiver or manager is not to be taken to have adopted a contract of employment by reason of anything done or omitted to be done within 14 days after his appointment.

**37(3) [Extent of s. 37(1)]** Subsection (1) does not limit any right to indemnity which the receiver or manager would have apart from it, nor limit his liability on contracts entered into without authority, nor confer any right to indemnity in respect of that liability.

**37(4) [Vacation of office]** Where at any time the receiver or manager so appointed vacates office–

(a) his remuneration and any expenses properly incurred by him, and

(b) any indemnity to which he is entitled out of the assets of the company,

shall be charged on and paid out of any property of the company which is in his custody or under his control at that time in priority to any charge or other security held by the person by or on whose behalf he was appointed.

## 38 Receivership accounts to be delivered to registrar

**38(1) [Where appointment under powers in instrument]** Except in the case of an administrative receiver, every receiver or manager of a company's property who has been appointed under powers contained in an instrument shall deliver to the registrar of companies for registration the requisite accounts of his receipts and payments.

**38(2) [Time for delivering accounts]** The accounts shall be delivered within one month (or such longer period as the registrar may allow) after the expiration of 12 months from the date of his appointment and of every subsequent period of 6 months, and also within one month after he ceases to act as receiver or manager.

**38(3) [Form of accounts]** The requisite accounts shall be an abstract in the prescribed form showing–

(a) receipts and payments during the relevant period of 12 or 6 months, or

(b) where the receiver or manager ceases to act, receipts and payments during the period from the end of the period of 12 or 6 months to which the last preceding abstract related (or, if no preceding abstract has been delivered under this section, from the date of his appointment) up to the date of his so ceasing, and the aggregate amount of receipts and payments during all preceding periods since his appointment.

**38(4) ["Prescribed"]** In this section **"prescribed"** means prescribed by regulations made by statutory instrument by the Secretary of State.

**38(5) [Penalty on default]** A receiver or manager who makes default in complying with this section is liable to a fine and, for continued contravention, to a daily default fine.

PROVISIONS APPLICABLE TO EVERY RECEIVERSHIP

## 39 Notification that receiver or manager appointed

**39(1) [Statement in invoices etc.]** When a receiver or manager of the property of a company has been appointed, every invoice, order for goods or business letter issued by or on behalf of the company or the receiver or manager or the liquidator of the company, being a document on or in which the company's name appears, shall contain a statement that a receiver or manager has been appointed.

**39(2) [Penalty on default]** If default is made in complying with this section, the company and any of the following persons, who knowingly and wilfully authorises or permits the default, namely, any officer of the company, any liquidator of the company and any receiver or manager, is liable to a fine.

## 40 Payment of debts out of assets subject to floating charge

**40(1) [Application]** The following applies, in the case of a company, where a receiver is appointed on behalf of the holders of any debentures of the company secured by a charge which, as created, was a floating charge.

**40(2) [Payment of preferential debts]** If the company is not at the time in course of being wound up, its preferential debts (within the meaning given to that expression by section 386 in Part XII) shall be paid out of the assets coming to the hands of the receiver in priority to any claims for principal or interest in respect of the debentures.

**40(3) [Recoupment of payments]** Payments made under this section shall be recouped, as far as may be, out of the assets of the company available for payment of general creditors.

## 41 Enforcement of duty to make returns

**41(1) [Court order re defaults]** If a receiver or manager of a company's property–

(a) having made default in filing, delivering or making any return, account or other document, or in giving any notice, which a receiver or manager is by law required to file, deliver, make or give, fails to make good the default within 14 days after the service on him of a notice requiring him to do so, or

(b) having been appointed under powers contained in an instrument, has, after being required at any time by the liquidator of the company to do so, failed to render proper accounts of his receipts and payments and to vouch them and pay over to the liquidator the amount properly payable to him,

the court may, on an application made for the purpose, make an order directing the receiver or manager (as the case may be) to make good the default within such time as may be specified in the order.

**41(2) [Application for order]** In the case of the default mentioned in subsection (1)(a), application to the court may be made by any member or creditor of the company or by the registrar of companies; and in the case of the default mentioned in subsection (1)(b), the application shall be made by the liquidator.

In either case the court's order may provide that all costs of and incidental to the application shall be borne by the receiver or manager, as the case may be.

**41(3) [Other enactments]** Nothing in this section prejudices the operation of any enactment imposing penalties on receivers in respect of any such default as is mentioned in subsection (1).

ADMINISTRATIVE RECEIVERS: GENERAL

## 42 General powers

**42(1) [Powers in Sch. 1]** The powers conferred on the administrative receiver of a company by the debentures by virtue of which he was appointed are deemed to include (except in so far as they are inconsistent with any of the provisions of those debentures) the powers specified in Schedule 1 to this Act.

**42(2) [Interpretation of Sch. 1]** In the application of Schedule 1 to the administrative receiver of a company–

(a) the words "he" and "him" refer to the administrative receiver, and

(b) references to the property of the company are to the property of which he is or, but for the appointment of some other person as the receiver of part of the company's property, would be the receiver or manager.

**42(3) [Deemed capacity]** A person dealing with the administrative receiver in good faith and for value is not concerned to inquire whether the receiver is acting within his powers.

## 43 Power to dispose of charged property, etc.

**43(1) [Application to court]** Where, on an application by the administrative receiver, the court is satisfied that the disposal (with or without other assets) of any relevant property which is subject to a security would be likely to promote a more advantageous realisation of the company's assets than would otherwise be effected, the court may by order authorise the administrative receiver to dispose of the property as if it were not subject to the security.

**43(2) [Application of s. 43(1)]** Subsection (1) does not apply in the case of any security held by the person by or on whose behalf the administrative receiver was appointed, or of any security to which a security so held has priority.

**43(3) [Conditions for order]** It shall be a condition of an order under this section that–

(a) the net proceeds of the disposal, and

(b) where those proceeds are less than such amount as may be determined by the court to be the net amount which would be realised on the sale of the property in the open market by a willing vendor, such sums as may be required to make good the deficiency,

shall be applied towards discharging the sums secured by the security.

**43(4) [Where two or more securities]** Where a condition imposed in pursuance of subsection (3) relates to two or more securities, that condition shall require the net proceeds of the disposal and, where paragraph (b) of that subsection applies, the sums mentioned in that paragraph to be applied towards discharging the sums secured by those securities in the order of their priorities.

**43(5) [Copy of order to registrar]** An office copy of an order under this section shall, within 14 days of the making of the order, be sent by the administrative receiver to the registrar of companies.

**43(6) [Penalty for non-compliance]** If the administrative receiver without reasonable excuse fails to comply with subsection (5), he is liable to a fine and, for continued contravention, to a daily default fine.

**43(7) ["Relevant property"]** In this section **"relevant property"**, in relation to the administrative receiver, means the property of which he is or, but for the appointment of some other person as the receiver of part of the company's property, would be the receiver or manager.

## 44 Agency and liability for contracts

**44(1) [Position of administrative receiver]** The administrative receiver of a company–

(a) is deemed to be the company's agent, unless and until the company goes into liquidation;

(b) is personally liable on any contract entered into by him in the carrying out of his functions (except in so far as the contract otherwise provides) and, to the extent of any qualifying liability, on any contract of employment adopted by him in the carrying out of those functions; and

(c) is entitled in respect of that liability to an indemnity out of the assets of the company.

**History**

In s. 44(1)(b) the words ", to the extent of any qualifying liability," inserted by Insolvency Act 1994, s. 2(1), (2), (4) with effect in relation to contracts of employment adopted on or after 15 March 1994.

**44(2) [Interpretation]** For the purposes of subsection (1)(b) the administrative receiver is not to be taken to have adopted a contract of employment by reason of anything done or omitted to be done within 14 days after his appointment.

**44(2A) [Interpretation of s. 44(1)(b)]** For the purposes of subsection (1)(b), a liability under a contract of employment is a qualifying liability if–

(a) it is a liability to pay a sum by way of wages or salary or contribution to an occupational pension scheme,

(b) it is incurred while the administrative receiver is in office, and

(c) it is in respect of services rendered wholly or partly after the adoption of the contract.

**History**
See history note after s. 44(2D).

**44(2B) [Further interpretation of s. 44(1)(b)]** Where a sum payable in respect of a liability which is a qualifying liability for the purposes of subsection (1)(b) is payable in respect of services rendered partly before and partly after the adoption of the contract, liability under subsection (1)(b) shall only extend to so much of the sum as is payable in respect of services rendered after the adoption of the contract.

**History**
See history note after s. 44(2D).

**44(2C) [Interpretation of s. 44(2A), (2B)]** For the purposes of subsections (2A) and (2B)–

(a) wages or salary payable in respect of a period of holiday or absence from work through sickness or other good cause are deemed to be wages or (as the case may be) salary in respect of services rendered in that period, and

(b) a sum payable in lieu of holiday is deemed to be wages or (as the case may be) salary in respect of services rendered in the period by reference to which the holiday entitlement arose.

**History**
See history note after s. 44(2D).

**44(2D) [Interpretation of s. 44(2C)(a)]** In subsection (2C)(a), the reference to wages or salary payable in respect of a period of holiday includes any sums which, if they had been paid, would have been treated for the purposes of the enactments relating to social security as earnings in respect of that period.

**History**
S. 44(2A)–(2D) inserted by Insolvency Act 1994, s. 2(1), (3), (4) with effect in relation to contracts of employment adopted on or after 15 March 1994.

**44(3) [Effect on other rights]** This section does not limit any right to indemnity which the administrative receiver would have apart from it, nor limit his liability on contracts entered into or adopted without authority, nor confer any right to indemnity in respect of that liability.

## 45 Vacation of office

**45(1) [Removal by court, resignation]** An administrative receiver of a company may at any time be removed from office by order of the court (but not otherwise) and may resign his office by giving notice of his resignation in the prescribed manner to such persons as may be prescribed.

**45(2) [Vacation of office]** An administrative receiver shall vacate office if he ceases to be qualified to act as an insolvency practitioner in relation to the company.

**45(3) [Effect of vacation of office]** Where at any time an administrative receiver vacates office–

(a) his remuneration and any expenses properly incurred by him, and

(b) any indemnity to which he is entitled out of the assets of the company,

shall be charged on and paid out of any property of the company which is in his custody or under his control at that time in priority to any security held by the person by or on whose behalf he was appointed.

**45(4) [Notice to registrar]** Where an administrative receiver vacates office otherwise than by death, he shall, within 14 days after his vacation of office, send a notice to that effect to the registrar of companies.

**45(5) [Penalty for non-compliance]** If an administrative receiver without reasonable excuse fails to comply with subsection (4), he is liable to a fine and, for continued contravention, to a daily default fine.

## ADMINISTRATIVE RECEIVERS: ASCERTAINMENT AND INVESTIGATION OF COMPANY'S AFFAIRS

### 46 Information to be given by administrative receiver

**46(1) [Notices]** Where an administrative receiver is appointed, he shall–

(a) forthwith send to the company and publish in the prescribed manner a notice of his appointment, and

(b) within 28 days after his appointment, unless the court otherwise directs, send such a notice to all the creditors of the company (so far as he is aware of their addresses).

**46(2) [Non-application]** This section and the next do not apply in relation to the appointment of an administrative receiver to act–

(a) with an existing administrative receiver, or

(b) in place of an administrative receiver dying or ceasing to act,

except that, where they apply to an administrative receiver who dies or ceases to act before they have been fully complied with, the references in this section and the next to the administrative receiver include (subject to the next subsection) his successor and any continuing administrative receiver.

**46(3) [Where company being wound up]** If the company is being wound up, this section and the next apply notwithstanding that the administrative receiver and the liquidator are the same person, but with any necessary modifications arising from that fact.

**46(4) [Penalty for non-compliance]** If the administrative receiver without reasonable excuse fails to comply with this section, he is liable to a fine and, for continued contravention, to a daily default fine.

### 47 Statement of affairs to be submitted

**47(1) [Duty of administrative receiver]** Where an administrative receiver is appointed, he shall forthwith require some or all of the persons mentioned below to make out and submit to him a statement in the prescribed form as to the affairs of the company.

**47(2) [Contents of statement]** A statement submitted under this section shall be verified by affidavit by the persons required to submit it and shall show–

(a) particulars of the company's assets, debts and liabilities;

(b) the names and addresses of its creditors;

(c) the securities held by them respectively;

(d) the dates when the securities were respectively given; and

(e) such further or other information as may be prescribed.

**47(3) [Persons in s. 47(1)]** The persons referred to in subsection (1) are–

(a) those who are or have been officers of the company;

(b) those who have taken part in the company's formation at any time within one year before the date of the appointment of the administrative receiver;

(c) those who are in the company's employment, or have been in its employment within that year, and are in the administrative receiver's opinion capable of giving the information required;

(d) those who are or have been within that year officers of or in the employment of a company which is, or within that year was, an officer of the company.

In this subsection **"employment"** includes employment under a contract for services.

**47(4) [Time for statement]** Where any persons are required under this section to submit a statement of affairs to the administrative receiver, they shall do so (subject to the next subsection) before the end of the period of 21 days beginning with the day after that on which the prescribed notice of the requirement is given to them by the administrative receiver.

**47(5) [Release, extension of time]** The administrative receiver, if he thinks fit, may–

(a) at any time release a person from an obligation imposed on him under subsection (1) or (2), or

(b) either when giving notice under subsection (4) or subsequently, extend the period so mentioned;

and where the administrative receiver has refused to exercise a power conferred by this subsection, the court, if it thinks fit, may exercise it.

**47(6) [Penalty for non-compliance]** If a person without reasonable excuse fails to comply with any obligation imposed under this section, he is liable to a fine and, for continued contravention, to a daily default fine.

## 48 Report by administrative receiver

**48(1) [Duty of administrative receiver]** Where an administrative receiver is appointed, he shall, within 3 months (or such longer period as the court may allow) after his appointment, send to the registrar of companies, to any trustees for secured creditors of the company and (so far as he is aware of their addresses) to all such creditors a report as to the following matters, namely–

(a) the events leading up to his appointment, so far as he is aware of them;

(b) the disposal or proposed disposal by him of any property of the company and the carrying on or proposed carrying on by him of any business of the company;

(c) the amounts of principal and interest payable to the debenture holders by whom or on whose behalf he was appointed and the amounts payable to preferential creditors; and

(d) the amount (if any) likely to be available for the payment of other creditors.

**48(2) [Copies of report]** The administrative receiver shall also, within 3 months (or such longer period as the court may allow) after his appointment, either–

(a) send a copy of the report (so far as he is aware of their addresses) to all unsecured creditors of the company; or

(b) publish in the prescribed manner a notice stating an address to which unsecured creditors of the company should write for copies of the report to be sent to them free of charge,

and (in either case), unless the court otherwise directs, lay a copy of the report before a meeting of the company's unsecured creditors summoned for the purpose on not less than 14 days' notice.

**48(3) [Conditions for s. 48(2) direction]** The court shall not give a direction under subsection (2) unless–

(a) the report states the intention of the administrative receiver to apply for the direction, and

(b) a copy of the report is sent to the persons mentioned in paragraph (a) of that subsection, or a notice is published as mentioned in paragraph (b) of that subsection, not less than 14 days before the hearing of the application.

**48(4) [Where company in liquidation]** Where the company has gone or goes into liquidation, the administrative receiver–

(a) shall, within 7 days after his compliance with subsection (1) or, if later, the nomination or appointment of the liquidator, send a copy of the report to the liquidator, and

(b) where he does so within the time limited for compliance with subsection (2), is not required to comply with that subsection.

**48(5) [Report to include summary of statement]** A report under this section shall include a summary of the statement of affairs made out and submitted to the administrative receiver under section 47 and of his comments (if any) upon it.

**48(6) [Limit on report only]** Nothing in this section is to be taken as requiring any such report to include any information the disclosure of which would seriously prejudice the carrying out by the administrative receiver of his functions.

**48(7) [Application of s. 46(2)]** Section 46(2) applies for the purposes of this section also.

(a) any other receiver;
(b) the holder of a fixed security which is over property subject to the floating charge;
(c) the company or its liquidator, as the case may be.

**60(3) [Doubt as to person entitled]** Where any question arises as to the person entitled to a payment under this section, or where a receipt or a discharge of a security cannot be obtained in respect of any such payment, the receiver shall consign the amount of such payment in any joint stock bank of issue in Scotland in name of the Accountant of Court for behoof of the person or persons entitled thereto.

## 61 Disposal of interest in property

**61(1) [Application to court]** Where the receiver sells or disposes, or is desirous of selling or disposing, of any property or interest in property of the company which is subject to the floating charge by virtue of which the receiver was appointed and which is–

(a) subject to any security or interest of, or burden or encumbrance in favour of, a creditor the ranking of which is prior to, or pari passu with, or postponed to the floating charge, or
(b) property or an interest in property affected or attached by effectual diligence executed by any person,

and the receiver is unable to obtain the consent of such creditor or, as the case may be, such person to such a sale or disposal, the receiver may apply to the court for authority to sell or dispose of the property or interest in property free of such security, interest, burden, encumbrance or diligence.

**61(2) [Authorisation by court]** Subject to the next subsection, on such an application the court may, if it thinks fit, authorise the sale or disposal of the property or interest in question free of such security, interest, burden, encumbrance or diligence, and such authorisation may be on such terms or conditions as the court thinks fit.

**61(3) [Condition for authorisation]** In the case of an application where a fixed security over the property or interest in question which ranks prior to the floating charge has not been met or provided for in full, the court shall not authorise the sale or disposal of the property or interest in question unless it is satisifed that the sale or disposal would be likely to provide a more advantageous realisation of the company's assets than would otherwise be effected.

**61(4) [Condition for s. 61(3)]** It shall be a condition of an authorisation to which subsection (3) applies that–

(a) the net proceeds of the disposal, and
(b) where those proceeds are less than such amount as may be determined by the court to be the net amount which would be realised on a sale of the property or interest in the open market by a willing seller, such sums as may be required to make good the deficiency,

shall be applied towards discharging the sums secured by the fixed security.

**61(5) [Where s. 61(4) condition re several securities]** Where a condition imposed in pursuance of subsection (4) relates to two or more such fixed securities, that condition shall require the net proceeds of the disposal and, where paragraph (b) of that subsection applies, the sums mentioned in that paragraph to be applied towards discharging the sums secured by those fixed securities in the order of their priorities.

**61(6) [Copy of authorisation to registrar]** A copy of an authorisation under subsection (2) certified by the clerk of court shall, within 14 days of the granting of the authorisation, be sent by the receiver to the registrar of companies.

**Note**
S. 61(6) modified by Scotland Act 1998, s. 125(1) and Sch. 8, para. 23(1)–(3) so that anything done by the registrar of companies in Scotland or the assistant registrar of friendly societies for Scotland by virtue of s. 61(6) as applied in relation to friendly societies, industrial and provident societies or building societies may be done to or by the Accountant in Bankruptcy as from 1 July 1999 (see SI 1998/3178 (C 79), art. 2).

**61(7) [Penalty for non-compliance]** If the receiver without reasonable excuse fails to comply with subsection (6), he is liable to a fine and, for continued contravention, to a daily default fine.

**61(8) [Receiver to give document to disponee]** Where any sale or disposal is effected in accordance with the authorisation of the court under subsection (2), the receiver shall grant to the purchaser or disponee an appropriate document of transfer or conveyance of the property or interest in question, and that document has the effect, or, where recording, intimation or registration of that document is a legal requirement for completion of title to the property or interest, then that recording, intimation or registration (as the case may be) has the effect, of–

(a) disencumbering the property or interest of the security, interest, burden or encumbrance affecting it, and

(b) freeing the property or interest from the diligence executed upon it.

**61(9) [Ranking of creditor in winding up]** Nothing in this section prejudices the right of any creditor of the company to rank for his debt in the winding up of the company.

## 62 Cessation of appointment of receiver

**62(1) [Removal, resignation]** A receiver may be removed from office by the court under subsection (3) below and may resign his office by giving notice of his resignation in the prescribed manner to such persons as may be prescribed.

**62(2) [Cessation of qualification]** A receiver shall vacate office if he ceases to be qualified to act as an insolvency practitioner in relation to the company.

**62(3) [Removal on application]** Subject to the next subsection, a receiver may, on application to the court by the holder of the floating charge by virtue of which he was appointed, be removed by the court on cause shown.

**62(4) [On vacation of office]** Where at any time a receiver vacates office–

(a) his remuneration and any expenses properly incurred by him, and

(b) any indemnity to which he is entitled out of the property of the company,

shall be paid out of the property of the company which is subject to the floating charge and shall have priority as provided for in section 60(1).

**62(5) [Notice of cessation to registrar, penalty on default]** When a receiver ceases to act as such otherwise than by death he shall, and, when a receiver is removed by the court, the holder of the floating charge by virtue of which he was appointed shall, within 14 days of the cessation or removal (as the case may be) give the registrar of companies notice to that effect, and the registrar shall enter the notice in the register of charges.

If the receiver or the holder of the floating charge (as the case may require) makes default in complying with the requirements of this subsection, he is liable to a fine and, for continued contravention, to a daily default fine.

**Note**

See Form 3 (Scot) in regulations referred to in note to s. 50.

S. 62(5) modified by Scotland Act 1998, s. 125(1) and Sch. 8, para. 23(1)–(3) so that anything done by the registrar of companies in Scotland or the assistant registrar of friendly societies for Scotland by virtue of s. 62(5) as applied in relation to friendly societies, industrial and provident societies or building societies may be done to or by the Accountant in Bankruptcy as from 1 July 1999 (see SI 1998/3178 (C 79), art. 2).

**62(6) [Cessation of attachment of charge]** If by the expiry of a period of one month following upon the removal of the receiver or his ceasing to act as such no other receiver has been appointed, the floating charge by virtue of which the receiver was appointed–

(a) thereupon ceases to attach to the property then subject to the charge, and

(b) again subsists as a floating charge;

and for the purposes of calculating the period of one month under this subsection no account shall be taken of any period during which an administration order under Part II of this Act is in force.

## 63 Powers of court

**63(1) [Directions, on application]** The court on the application of–

(a) the holder of a floating charge by virtue of which a receiver was appointed, or

(b) a receiver appointed under section 51,

## 71 Prescription of forms, etc.; regulations

**71(1) [Prescribed forms]** The notice referred to in section 62(5), and the notice referred to in section 65(1)(a) shall be in such form as may be prescribed.

**71(2) [Regulations]** Any power conferred by this Chapter on the Secretary of State to make regulations is exercisable by statutory instrument; and a statutory instrument made in the exercise of the power so conferred to prescribe a fee is subject to annulment in pursuance of a resolution of either House of Parliament.

**Note**
See the note to s. 50.

# Chapter III – Receivers' Powers in Great Britain as a Whole

## 72 Cross-border operation of receivership provisions

**72(1) [Receivers' powers]** A receiver appointed under the law of either part of Great Britain in respect of the whole or any part of any property or undertaking of a company and in consequence of the company having created a charge which, as created, was a floating charge may exercise his powers in the other part of Great Britain so far as their exercise is not inconsistent with the law applicable there.

**72(2) ["Receiver"]** In subsection (1) **"receiver"** includes a manager and a person who is appointed both receiver and manager.

# PART IV – WINDING UP OF COMPANIES REGISTERED UNDER THE COMPANIES ACTS

**Note**
Re application of Pt. IV to insolvent partnerships, see the Insolvent Partnerships Order 1994 (SI 1994/2421), especially reg. 10.

# Chapter I – Preliminary

### MODES OF WINDING UP

## 73 Alternative modes of winding up

**73(1) [Voluntary, by court]** The winding up of a company, within the meaning given to that expression by section 735 of the Companies Act, may be either voluntary (Chapters II, III, IV and V in this Part) or by the court (Chapter VI).

**73(2) [Application of Ch. I, VII–X]** This Chapter, and Chapters VII to X, relate to winding up generally, except where otherwise stated.

### CONTRIBUTORIES

## 74 Liability as contributories of present and past members

**74(1) [Liability to contribute]** When a company is wound up, every present and past member is liable to contribute to its assets to any amount sufficient for payment of its debts and liabilities, and the expenses of the winding up, and for the adjustment of the rights of the contributories among themselves.

**74(2) [Qualifications to liability]** This is subject as follows–

(a) a past member is not liable to contribute if he has ceased to be a member for one year or more before the commencement of the winding up;

(b) a past member is not liable to contribute in respect of any debt or liability of the company contracted after he ceased to be a member;

(c) a past member is not liable to contribute, unless it appears to the court that the existing members are unable to satisfy the contributions required to be made by them in pursuance of the Companies Act and this Act;

(d) in the case of a company limited by shares, no contribution is required from any member exceeding the amount (if any) unpaid on the shares in respect of which he is liable as a present or past member;

(e) nothing in the Companies Act or this Act invalidates any provision contained in a policy of insurance or other contract whereby the liability of individual members on the policy or contract is restricted, or whereby the funds of the company are alone made liable in respect of the policy or contract;

(f) a sum due to any member of the company (in his character of a member) by way of dividends, profits or otherwise is not deemed to be a debt of the company, payable to that member in a case of competition between himself and any other creditor not a member of the company, but any such sum may be taken into account for the purpose of the final adjustment of the rights of the contributories among themselves.

**74(3) [Company limited by guarantee]** In the case of a company limited by guarantee, no contribution is required from any member exceeding the amount undertaken to be contributed by him to the company's assets in the event of its being wound up; but if it is a company with a share capital, every member of it is liable (in addition to the amount so undertaken to be contributed to the assets), to contribute to the extent of any sums unpaid on shares held by him.

## 75 Directors, etc. with unlimited liability

**75(1) [Liability in winding up]** In the winding up of a limited company, any director or manager (whether past or present) whose liability is under the Companies Act unlimited is liable, in addition to his liability (if any) to contribute as an ordinary member, to make a further contribution as if he were at the commencement of the winding up a member of an unlimited company.

**75(2) [Qualifications to liability]** However–

(a) a past director or manager is not liable to make such further contribution if he has ceased to hold office for a year or more before the commencement of the winding up;

(b) a past director or manager is not liable to make such further contribution in respect of any debt or liability of the company contracted after he ceased to hold office;

(c) subject to the company's articles, a director or manager is not liable to make such further contribution unless the court deems it necessary to require that contribution in order to satisfy the company's debts and liabilities, and the expenses of the winding up.

## 76 Liability of past directors and shareholders

**76(1) [Application]** This section applies where a company is being wound up and–

(a) it has under Chapter VII of Part V of the Companies Act (redeemable shares; purchase by a company of its own shares) made a payment out of capital in respect of the redemption or purchase of any of its own shares (the payment being referred to below as "the relevant payment"), and

(b) the aggregate amount of the company's assets and the amounts paid by way of contribution to its assets (apart from this section) is not sufficient for payment of its debts and liabilities, and the expenses of the winding up.

**76(2) [Contribution of past shareholders, directors]** If the winding up commenced within one year of the date on which the relevant payment was made, then–

(a) the person from whom the shares were redeemed or purchased, and

(b) the directors who signed the statutory declaration made in accordance with section 173(3) of the Companies Act for purposes of the redemption or purchase (except a director who shows that he had reasonable grounds for forming the opinion set out in the declaration),

are, so as to enable that insufficiency to be met, liable to contribute to the following extent to the company's assets.

**83(3)** **[Amounts liable to be contributed]** Every contributory is liable to contribute to the assets of the company, in the course of the winding up, all sums due from him in respect of any such liability.

**83(4)** **[Death etc. of contributory]** In the event of the death, bankruptcy or insolvency of any contributory, provisions of this Act, with respect to the personal representatives, to the heirs and legatees of the heritage of the heritable estate in Scotland of deceased contributories and to the trustees of bankrupt or insolvent contributories respectively, apply.

# Chapter II – Voluntary Winding Up (Introductory and General)

## RESOLUTIONS FOR, AND COMMENCEMENT OF, VOLUNTARY WINDING UP

## 84 Circumstances in which company may be wound up voluntarily

**84(1)** **[Circumstances]** A company may be wound up voluntarily–

(a) when the period (if any) fixed for the duration of the company by the articles expires, or the event (if any) occurs, on the occurence of which the articles provide that the company is to be dissolved, and the company in general meeting has passed a resolution requiring it to be wound up voluntarily;

(b) if the company resolves by special resolution that it be wound up voluntarily;

(c) if the company resolves by extraordinary resolution to the effect that it cannot by reason of its liabilities continue its business, and that it is advisable to wind up.

**84(2)** **[Definition]** In this Act the expression **"a resolution for voluntary winding up"** means a resolution passed under any of the paragraphs of subsection (1).

**84(3)** **[Copy of resolution to registrar]** A resolution passed under paragraph (a) of subsection (1), as well as a special resolution under paragraph (b) and an extraordinary resolution under paragraph (c), is subject to section 380 of the Companies Act (copy of resolution to be forwarded to registrar of companies within 15 days).

**Note**

S. 84(3) modified by Scotland Act 1998, s. 125(1) and Sch. 8, para. 23(1)–(3) so that anything done by the registrar of companies in Scotland or the assistant registrar of friendly societies for Scotland by virtue of s. 84(3) as applied in relation to friendly societies, industrial and provident societies or building societies may be done to or by the Accountant in Bankruptcy as from 1 July 1999 (see SI 1998/3178 (C 79), art. 2).

## 85 Notice of resolution to wind up

**85(1)** **[Notice in Gazette]** When a company has passed a resolution for voluntary winding up, it shall, within 14 days after the passing of the resolution, give notice of the resolution by advertisement in the Gazette.

**85(2)** **[Penalty on default]** If default is made in complying with this section, the company and every officer of it who is in default is liable to a fine and, for continued contravention, to a daily default fine.

For purposes of this subsection the liquidator is deemed an officer of the company.

## 86 Commencement of winding up

**86** A voluntary winding up is deemed to commence at the time of the passing of the resolution for voluntary winding up.

## CONSEQUENCES OF RESOLUTION TO WIND UP

## 87 Effect on business and status of company

**87(1)** **[Cessation of business]** In case of a voluntary winding up, the company shall from the commencement of the winding up cease to carry on its business, except so far as may be required for its beneficial winding up.

**87(2)** **[Continuation of corporate state etc.]** However, the corporate state and corporate powers of the company, notwithstanding anything to the contrary in its articles, continue until the company is dissolved.

## 88 Avoidance of share transfers, etc. after winding-up resolution

**88** Any transfer of shares, not being a transfer made to or with the sanction of the liquidator, and any alteration in the status of the company's members, made after the commencement of a voluntary winding up, is void.

DECLARATION OF SOLVENCY

## 89 Statutory declaration of solvency

**89(1)** **[Declaration by directors]** Where it is proposed to wind up a company voluntarily, the directors (or, in the case of a company having more than two directors, the majority of them) may at a directors' meeting make a statutory declaration to the effect that they have made a full inquiry into the company's affairs and that, having done so, they have formed the opinion that the company will be able to pay its debts in full, together with interest at the official rate (as defined in section 251), within such period, not exceeding 12 months from the commencement of the winding up, as may be specified in the declaration.

**89(2)** **[Requirements for declaration]** Such a declaration by the directors has no effect for purposes of this Act unless–

(a) it is made within the 5 weeks immediately preceding the date of the passing of the resolution for winding up, or on that date but before the passing of the resolution, and

(b) it embodies a statement of the company's assets and liabilities as at the latest practicable date before the making of the declaration.

**89(3)** **[Declaration to registrar]** The declaration shall be delivered to the registrar of companies before the expiration of 15 days immediately following the date on which the resolution for winding up is passed.

**Note**

S. 89(3) modified by Scotland Act 1998, s. 125(1) and Sch. 8, para. 23(1), (4), (5) so that anything directed to be done by the registrar of companies in Scotland or the assistant registrar of friendly societies for Scotland by virtue of s. 89(3) as applied in relation to friendly societies, industrial and provident societies or building societies shall be done to or by the Accountant in Bankruptcy as from 1 July 1999 (see SI 1998/3178 (C 79), art. 2).

**89(4)** **[Offence, penalty]** A director making a declaration under this section without having reasonable grounds for the opinion that the company will be able to pay its debts in full, together with interest at the official rate, within the period specified is liable to imprisonment or a fine, or both.

**89(5)** **[Presumption]** If the company is wound up in pursuance of a resolution passed within 5 weeks after the making of the declaration, and its debts (together with interest at the official rate) are not paid or provided for in full within the period specified, it is to be presumed (unless the contrary is shown) that the director did not have reasonable grounds for his opinion.

**89(6)** **[Penalty for non-compliance with s. 89(3)]** If a declaration required by subsection (3) to be delivered to the registrar is not so delivered within the time prescribed by that subsection, the company and every officer in default is liable to a fine and, for continued contravention, to a daily default fine.

## 90 Distinction between "members'" and "creditors'" voluntary winding up

**90** A winding up in the case of which a directors' statutory declaration under section 89 has been made is a "members' voluntary winding up"; and a winding up in the case of which such a declaration has not been made is a "creditors' voluntary winding up".

# Chapter III – Members' Voluntary Winding Up

## 91 Appointment of liquidator

**91(1) [Appointment by general meeting]** In a members' voluntary winding up, the company in general meeting shall appoint one or more liquidators for the purpose of winding up the company's affairs and distributing its assets.

**91(2) [Cessation of directors' powers]** On the appointment of a liquidator all the powers of the directors cease, except so far as the company in general meeting or the liquidator sanctions their continuance.

## 92 Power to fill vacancy in office of liquidator

**92(1) [Filling of vacancy]** If a vacancy occurs by death, resignation or otherwise in the office of liquidator appointed by the company, the company in general meeting may, subject to any arrangement with its creditors, fill the vacancy.

**92(2) [Convening of general meeting]** For that purpose a general meeting may be convened by any contributory or, if there were more liquidators than one, by the continuing liquidators.

**92(3) [Manner of holding meeting]** The meeting shall be held in manner provided by this Act or by the articles, or in such manner as may, on application by any contributory or by the continuing liquidators, be determined by the court.

## 93 General company meeting at each year's end

**93(1) [If winding up for more than one year]** Subject to sections 96 and 102, in the event of the winding up continuing for more than one year, the liquidator shall summon a general meeting of the company at the end of the first year from the commencement of the winding up, and of each succeeding year, or at the first convenient date within 3 months from the end of the year or such longer period as the Secretary of State may allow.

**93(2) [Account by liquidator]** The liquidator shall lay before the meeting an account of his acts and dealings, and of the conduct of the winding up, during the preceding year.

**93(3) [Penalty for non-compliance]** If the liquidator fails to comply with this section, he is liable to a fine.

## 94 Final meeting prior to dissolution

**94(1) [Account of winding up, final meeting]** As soon as the company's affairs are fully wound up, the liquidator shall make up an account of the winding up showing how it has been conducted and the company's property has been disposed of, and thereupon shall call a general meeting of the company for the purpose of laying before it the account and giving an explanation of it.

**94(2) [Advertisement in Gazette]** The meeting shall be called by advertisement in the Gazette, specifying its time, place and object and published at least one month before the meeting.

**94(3) [Copy of account etc. to registrar]** Within one week after the meeting, the liquidator shall send to the registrar of companies a copy of the account, and shall make a return to him of the holding of the meeting and of its date.

**Note**

S. 94(3) modified by Scotland Act 1998, s. 125(1) and Sch. 8, para. 23(1)–(3) so that anything done by the registrar of companies in Scotland or the assistant registrar of friendly societies for Scotland by virtue of s. 94(3) as applied in relation to friendly societies, industrial and provident societies or building societies may be done to or by the Accountant in Bankruptcy as from 1 July 1999 (see SI 1998/3178 (C 79), art. 2).

**94(4) [Penalty on default]** If the copy is not sent or the return is not made in accordance with subsection (3), the liquidator is liable to a fine and, for continued contravention, to a daily default fine.

**94(5) [If no quorum at meeting]** If a quorum is not present at the meeting, the liquidator shall, in lieu of the return mentioned above, make a return that the meeting was duly summoned and that no quorum was present; and upon such a return being made, the provisions of subsection (3) as to the making of the return are deemed complied with.

**94(6) [Penalty if no general meeting called]** If the liquidator fails to call a general meeting of the company as required by subsection (1), he is liable to a fine.

## 95 Effect of company's insolvency

**95(1) [Application]** This section applies where the liquidator is of the opinion that the company will be unable to pay its debts in full (together with interest at the official rate) within the period stated in the directors' declaration under section 89.

**95(2) [Duties of liquidator]** The liquidator shall–

(a) summon a meeting of creditors for a day not later than the 28th day after the day on which he formed that opinion;

(b) send notices of the creditors' meeting to the creditors by post not less than 7 days before the day on which that meeting is to be held;

(c) cause notice of the creditors' meeting to be advertised once in the Gazette and once at least in 2 newspapers circulating in the relevant locality (that is to say the locality in which the company's principal place of business in Great Britain was situated during the relevant period); and

(d) during the period before the day on which the creditors' meeting is to be held, furnish creditors free of charge with such information concerning the affairs of the company as they may reasonably require;

and the notice of the creditors' meeting shall state the duty imposed by paragraph (d) above.

**95(3) [Duties of liquidator re statement of affairs]** The liquidator shall also–

(a) make out a statement in the prescribed form as to the affairs of the company;

(b) lay that statement before the creditors' meeting; and

(c) attend and preside at that meeting.

**Note**

See the Insolvency Rules 1986 (SI 1986/1925), r. 4.34ff., 4.49.

**95(4) [Contents of statement of affairs]** The statement as to the affairs of the company shall be verified by affidavit by the liquidator and shall show–

(a) particulars of the company's assets, debts and liabilities;

(b) the names and addresses of the company's creditors;

(c) the securities held by them respectively;

(d) the dates when the securities were respectively given; and

(e) such further or other information as may be prescribed.

**95(5) [Where principal place of business in different places]** Where the company's principal place of business in Great Britain was situated in different localities at different times during the relevant period, the duty imposed by subsection (2)(c) applies separately in relation to each of those localities.

**95(6) [Where no place of business in Great Britain]** Where the company had no place of business in Great Britain during the relevant period, references in subsections (2)(c) and (5) to the company's principal place of business in Great Britain are replaced by references to its registered office.

**95(7) ["The relevant period"]** In this section **"the relevant period"** means the period of 6 months immediately preceding the day on which were sent the notices summoning the company meeting at which it was resolved that the company be wound up voluntarily.

**95(8) [Penalty for non-compliance]** If the liquidator without reasonable excuse fails to comply with this section, he is liable to a fine.

## 96 Conversion to creditors' voluntary winding up

**96** As from the day on which the creditors' meeting is held under section 95, this Act has effect as if–

(a) the directors' declaration under section 89 had not been made; and

(b) the creditors' meeting and the company meeting at which it was resolved that the company be wound up voluntarily were the meetings mentioned in section 98 in the next Chapter;

and accordingly the winding up becomes a creditors' voluntary winding up.

# Chapter IV – Creditors' Voluntary Winding Up

## 97 Application of this Chapter

**97(1) [Application]** Subject as follows, this Chapter applies in relation to a creditors' voluntary winding up.

**97(2) [Non-application of s. 98, 99]** Sections 98 and 99 do not apply where, under section 96 in Chapter III, a members' voluntary winding up has become a creditors' voluntary winding up.

## 98 Meeting of creditors

**98(1) [Duty of company]** The company shall–

(a) cause a meeting of its creditors to be summoned for a day not later than the 14th day after the day on which there is to be held the company meeting at which the resolution for voluntary winding up is to be proposed;

(b) cause the notices of the creditors' meeting to be sent by post to the creditors not less than 7 days before the day on which that meeting is to be held; and

(c) cause notice of the creditors' meeting to be advertised once in the Gazette and once at least in two newspapers circulating in the relevant locality (that is to say the locality in which the company's principal place of business in Great Britain was situated during the relevant period).

**98(2) [Contents of notice of meeting]** The notice of the creditors' meeting shall state either–

(a) the name and address of a person qualified to act as an insolvency practitioner in relation to the company who, during the period before the day on which that meeting is to be held, will furnish creditors free of charge with such information concerning the company's affairs as they may reasonably require; or

(b) a place in the relevant locality where, on the two business days falling next before the day on which that meeting is to be held, a list of the names and addresses of the company's creditors will be available for inspection free of charge.

**98(3) [Where principal place of business in different places, etc.]** Where the company's principal place of business in Great Britain was situated in different localities at different times during the relevant period, the duties imposed by subsections (1)(c) and (2)(b) above apply separately in relation to each of those localities.

**98(4) [Where no place of business in Great Britain]** Where the company had no place of business in Great Britain during the relevant period, references in subsections (1)(c) and (3) to the company's principal place of business in Great Britain are replaced by references to its registered office.

**98(5) ["The relevant period"]** In this section **"the relevant period"** means the period of 6 months immediately preceding the day on which were sent the notices summoning the company meeting at which it was resolved that the company be wound up voluntarily.

**98(6) [Penalty for non-compliance]** If the company without reasonable excuse fails to comply with subsection (1) or (2), it is guilty of an offence and liable to a fine.

**Note**
See the Insolvency Rules 1986 (SI 1986/1925), r. 4.49ff.

## 99 Directors to lay statement of affairs before creditors

**99(1) [Duty of directors]** The directors of the company shall–

(a) make out a statement in the prescribed form as to the affairs of the company;

(b) cause that statement to be laid before the creditors' meeting under section 98; and

(c) appoint one of their number to preside at that meeting;

and it is the duty of the director so appointed to attend the meeting and preside over it.

**99(2) [Contents of statement]** The statement as to the affairs of the company shall be verified by affidavit by some or all of the directors and shall show–

(a) particulars of the company's assets, debts and liabilities;

(b) the names and addresses of the company's creditors;

(c) the securities held by them respectively;

(d) the dates when the securities were respectively given; and

(e) such further or other information as may be prescribed.

**99(3) [Penalty for non-compliance]** If–

(a) the directors without reasonable excuse fail to comply with subsection (1) or (2); or

(b) any director without reasonable excuse fails to comply with subsection (1), so far as requiring him to attend and preside at the creditors' meeting,

the directors are or (as the case may be) the director is guilty of an offence and liable to a fine.

**Note**

See the Insolvency Rules 1986 (SI 1986/1925), r. 4.34ff.

## 100 Appointment of liquidator

**100(1) [Nomination of liquidator at meetings]** The creditors and the company at their respective meetings mentioned in section 98 may nominate a person to be liquidator for the purpose of winding up the company's affairs and distributing its assets.

**100(2) [Person who is liquidator]** The liquidator shall be the person nominated by the creditors or, where no person has been so nominated, the person (if any) nominated by the company.

**100(3) [Where different persons nominated]** In the case of different persons being nominated, any director, member or creditor of the company may, within 7 days after the date on which the nomination was made by the creditors, apply to the court for an order either–

(a) directing that the person nominated as liquidator by the company shall be liquidator instead of or jointly with the person nominated by the creditors, or

(b) appointing some other person to be liquidator instead of the person nominated by the creditors.

## 101 Appointment of liquidation committee

**101(1) [Creditors may appoint committee]** The creditors at the meeting to be held under section 98 or at any subsequent meeting may, if they think fit, appoint a committee ("the liquidation committee") of not more than 5 persons to exercise the functions conferred on it by or under this Act.

**101(2) [Members appointed by company]** If such a committee is appointed, the company may, either at the meeting at which the resolution for voluntary winding up is passed or at any time subsequently in general meeting, appoint such number of persons as they think fit to act as members of the committee, not exceeding 5.

**101(3) [Creditors may object to members appointed by company]** However, the creditors may, if they think fit, resolve that all or any of the persons so appointed by the company ought not to be members of the liquidation committee; and if the creditors so resolve–

(a) the persons mentioned in the resolution aré not then, unless the court otherwise directs, qualified to act as members of the committee; and

(b) on any application to the court under this provision the court may, if it thinks fit, appoint other persons to act as such members in place of the persons mentioned in the resolution.

**101(4) [Scotland]** In Scotland, the liquidation committee has, in addition to the powers and duties conferred and imposed on it by this Act, such of the powers and duties of commissioners on a bankrupt estate as may be conferred and imposed on liquidation committees by the rules.

## 102 Creditors' meeting where winding up converted under s. 96

**102** Where, in the case of a winding up which was, under section 96 in Chapter III, converted to a creditors' voluntary winding up, a creditors' meeting is held in accordance with section 95, any appointment made or committee established by that meeting is deemed to have been made or established by a meeting held in accordance with section 98 in this Chapter.

## 103 Cesser of directors' powers

**103** On the appointment of a liquidator, all the powers of the directors cease, except so far as the liquidation committee (or, if there is no such committee, the creditors) sanction their continuance.

## 104 Vacancy in office of liquidator

**104** If a vacancy occurs, by death, resignation or otherwise, in the office of a liquidator (other than a liquidator appointed by, or by the direction of, the court), the creditors may fill the vacancy.

## 105 Meetings of company and creditors at each year's end

**105(1) [Liquidator to summon meetings]** If the winding up continues for more than one year, the liquidator shall summon a general meeting of the company and a meeting of the creditors at the end of the first year from the commencement of the winding up, and of each succeeding year, or at the first convenient date within 3 months from the end of the year or such longer period as the Secretary of State may allow.

**105(2) [Liquidator to lay account]** The liquidator shall lay before each of the meetings an account of his acts and dealings and of the conduct of the winding up during the preceding year.

**105(3) [Penalty for non-compliance]** If the liquidator fails to comply with this section, he is liable to a fine.

**105(4) [Qualification to requirement]** Where under section 96 a members' voluntary winding up has become a creditors' voluntary winding up, and the creditors' meeting under section 95 is held 3 months or less before the end of the first year from the commencement of the winding up, the liquidator is not required by this section to summon a meeting of creditors at the end of that year.

## 106 Final meeting prior to dissolution

**106(1) [Account of winding up, meetings]** As soon as the company's affairs are fully wound up, the liquidator shall make up an account of the winding up, showing how it has been conducted and the company's property has been disposed of, and thereupon shall call a general meeting of the company and a meeting of the creditors for the purpose of laying the account before the meetings and giving an explanation of it.

**106(2) [Advertisement in Gazette]** Each such meeting shall be called by advertisement in the Gazette specifying the time, place and object of the meeting, and published at least one month before it.

**106(3) [Copy of account, return to registrar]** Within one week after the date of the meetings (or, if they are not held on the same date, after the date of the later one) the liquidator shall send to the registrar of companies a copy of the account, and shall make a return to him of the holding of the meetings and of their dates.

**Note**

S. 106(3) modified by Scotland Act 1998, s. 125(1) and Sch. 8, para. 23(1)–(3) so that anything done by the registrar of companies in Scotland or the assistant registrar of friendly societies for Scotland by virtue of s. 106(3) as applied in relation to friendly societies, industrial and provident societies or building societies may be done to or by the Accountant in Bankruptcy as from 1 July 1999 (see SI 1998/3178 (C 79), art. 2).

**106(4) [Penalty on default re s. 106(3)]** If the copy is not sent or the return is not made in accordance with subsection (3), the liquidator is liable to a fine and, for continued contravention, to a daily default fine.

**106(5) [If quorum not present at either meeting]** However, if a quorum is not present at either such meeting, the liquidator shall, in lieu of the return required by subsection (3), make a return that the meeting was duly summoned and that no quorum was present; and upon such return being made the provisions of that subsection as to the making of the return are, in respect of that meeting, deemed complied with.

**Note**

S. 106(5) modified by Scotland Act 1998, s. 125(1) and Sch. 8, para. 23(1)–(3) so that anything done by the registrar of companies in Scotland or the assistant registrar of friendly societies for Scotland by virtue of s. 106(5) as applied in relation to friendly societies, industrial and provident societies or building societies may be done to or by the Accountant in Bankruptcy as from 1 July 1999 (see SI 1998/3178 (C 79), art. 2).

**106(6) [Penalty if no meetings called]** If the liquidator fails to call a general meeting of the company or a meeting of the creditors as required by this section, he is liable to a fine.

# Chapter V – Provisions Applying to both kinds of Voluntary Winding Up

## 107 Distribution of company's property

**107** Subject to the provisions of this Act as to preferential payments, the company's property in a voluntary winding up shall on the winding up be applied in satisfaction of the company's liabilities pari passu and, subject to that application, shall (unless the articles otherwise provide) be distributed among the members according to their rights and interests in the company.

## 108 Appointment or removal of liquidator by the court

**108(1) [If no liquidator acting]** If from any cause whatever there is no liquidator acting, the court may appoint a liquidator.

**108(2) [Removal, replacement]** The court may, on cause shown, remove a liquidator and appoint another.

## 109 Notice by liquidator of his appointment

**109(1) [Notice in Gazette and to registrar]** The liquidator shall, within 14 days after his appointment, publish in the Gazette and deliver to the registrar of companies for registration a notice of his appointment in the form prescribed by statutory instrument made by the Secretary of State.

**Note**

S. 109(1) modified by Scotland Act 1998, s. 125(1) and Sch. 8, para. 23(1), (4), (5) so that anything directed to be done by the registrar of companies in Scotland or the assistant registrar of friendly societies for Scotland by virtue of s. 109(1) as applied in relation to friendly societies, industrial and provident societies or building societies shall be done to or by the Accountant in Bankruptcy as from 1 July 1999 (see SI 1998/3178 (C 79), art. 2).

**109(2) [Penalty on default]** If the liquidator fails to comply with this section, he is liable to a fine and, for continued contravention, to a daily default fine.

## 110 Acceptance of shares, etc., as consideration for sale of company property

**110(1) [Application]** This section applies, in the case of a company proposed to be, or being, wound up voluntarily, where the whole or part of the company's business or property is proposed to be transferred or sold to another company ("the transferee company"), whether or not the latter is a company within the meaning of the Companies Act.

**110(2) [Shares etc. in compensation for transfer]** With the requisite sanction, the liquidator of the company being, or proposed to be, wound up ("the transferor company") may receive, in compensation or part compensation for the transfer or sale, shares, policies or other like interests in the transferee company for distribution among the members of the transferor company.

**110(3) [Sanction for s. 110(2)]** The sanction requisite under subsection (2) is–

(a) in the case of a members' voluntary winding up, that of a special resolution of the company, conferring either a general authority on the liquidator or an authority in respect of any particular arrangement, and

(b) in the case of a creditors' voluntary winding up, that of either the court or the liquidation committee.

**110(4) [Alternative to s. 110(2)]** Alternatively to subsection (2), the liquidator may (with that sanction) enter into any other arrangement whereby the members of the transferor company may, in lieu of receiving cash, shares, policies or other like interests (or in addition thereto), participate in the profits of, or receive any other benefit from, the transferee company.

**110(5) [Sale binding on transferors]** A sale or arrangement in pursuance of this section is binding on members of the transferor company.

**110(6) [Special resolution]** A special resolution is not invalid for purposes of this section by reason that it is passed before or concurrently with a resolution for voluntary winding up or for appointing liquidators; but, if an order is made within a year for winding up the company by the court, the special resolution is not valid unless sanctioned by the court.

## 111 Dissent from arrangement under s. 110

**111(1) [Application]** This section applies in the case of a voluntary winding up where, for the purposes of section 110(2) or (4), there has been passed a special resolution of the transferor company providing the sanction requisite for the liquidator under that section.

**111(2) [Objections by members of transferor company]** If a member of the transferor company who did not vote in favour of the special resolution expresses his dissent from it in writing, addressed to the liquidator and left at the company's registered office within 7 days after the passing of the resolution, he may require the liquidator either to abstain from carrying the resolution into effect or to purchase his interest at a price to be determined by agreement or by arbitration under this section.

**111(3) [Where liquidator purchases member's interest]** If the liquidator elects to purchase the member's interest, the purchase money must be paid before the company is dissolved and be raised by the liquidator in such manner as may be determined by special resolution.

**111(4) [Arbitration]** For purposes of an arbitration under this section, the provisions of the Companies Clauses Consolidation Act 1845 or, in the case of a winding up in Scotland, the Companies Clauses Consolidation (Scotland) Act 1845 with respect to the settlement of disputes by arbitration are incorporated with this Act, and–

(a) in the construction of those provisions this Act is deemed the special Act and **"the company"** means the transferor company, and

(b) any appointment by the incorporated provisions directed to be made under the hand of the secretary or any two of the directors may be made in writing by the liquidator (or, if there is more than one liquidator, then any two or more of them).

## 112 Reference of questions to court

**112(1) [Application to court]** The liquidator or any contributory or creditor may apply to the court to determine any question arising in the winding up of a company, or to exercise, as respects the enforcing of calls or any other matter, all or any of the powers which the court might exercise if the company were being wound up by the court.

**112(2) [Court order]** The court, if satisfied that the determination of the question or the required exercise of power will be just and beneficial, may accede wholly or partially to the application on such terms and conditions as it thinks fit, or may make such other order on the application as it thinks just.

**112(3) [Copy of order to registrar]** A copy of an order made by virtue of this section staying the proceedings in the winding up shall forthwith be forwarded by the company, or otherwise as may be prescribed, to the registrar of companies, who shall enter it in his records relating to the company.

**Note**

S. 112(3) modified by Scotland Act 1998, s. 125(1) and Sch. 8, para. 23(1)–(3) so that anything done by the registrar of companies in Scotland or the assistant registrar of friendly societies for Scotland by virtue of s. 112(3) as applied in relation to friendly societies, industrial and provident societies or building societies may be done to or by the Accountant in Bankruptcy as from 1 July 1999 (see SI 1998/3178 (C 79), art. 2).

## 113 Court's power to control proceedings (Scotland)

**113** If the court, on the application of the liquidator in the winding up of a company registered in Scotland, so directs, no action or proceeding shall be proceeded with or commenced against the company except by leave of the court and subject to such terms as the court may impose.

## 114 No liquidator appointed or nominated by company

**114(1) [Application]** This section applies where, in the case of a voluntary winding up, no liquidator has been appointed or nominated by the company.

**114(2) [Limit on exercise of directors' powers]** The powers of the directors shall not be exercised, except with the sanction of the court or (in the case of a creditors' voluntary winding up) so far as may be necessary to secure compliance with sections 98 (creditors' meeting) and 99 (statement of affairs), during the period before the appointment or nomination of a liquidator of the company.

**114(3) [Non-application of s. 114(2)]** Subsection (2) does not apply in relation to the powers of the directors–

(a) to dispose of perishable goods and other goods the value of which is likely to diminish if they are not immediately disposed of, and

(b) to do all such other things as may be necessary for the protection of the company's assets.

**114(4) [Penalty for non-compliance]** If the directors of the company without reasonable excuse fail to comply with this section, they are liable to a fine.

## 115 Expenses of voluntary winding up

**115** All expenses properly incurred in the winding up, including the remuneration of the liquidator, are payable out of the company's assets in priority to all other claims.

## 116 Saving for certain rights

**116** The voluntary winding up of a company does not bar the right of any creditor or contributory to have it wound up by the court; but in the case of an application by a contributory the court must be satisfied that the rights of the contributories will be prejudiced by a voluntary winding up.

# Chapter VI – Winding Up by the Court

### JURISDICTION (ENGLAND AND WALES)

## 117 High Court and county court jurisdiction

**117(1) [High Court]** The High Court has jurisdiction to wind up any company registered in England and Wales.

**117(2) [County court]** Where the amount of a company's share capital paid up or credited as paid up does not exceed £120,000, then (subject to this section) the county court of the district in which the company's registered office is situated has concurrent jurisdiction with the High Court to wind up the company.

**117(3) [Increase, reduction of s. 117(2) sum]** The money sum for the time being specified in subsection (2) is subject to increase or reduction by order under section 416 in Part XV.

**117(4) [Exclusion of jurisdiction for county court]** The Lord Chancellor may by order in a statutory instrument exclude a county court from having winding-up jurisdiction, and for the purposes of that jurisdiction may attach its district, or any part thereof, to any other county court, and may by statutory instrument revoke or vary any such order.

application to stay, sist or restrain is by a creditor, this section extends to actions and proceedings against any contributory of the company.

## 127 Avoidance of property dispositions, etc.

**127** In a winding up by the court, any disposition of the company's property, and any transfer of shares, or alteration in the status of the company's members, made after the commencement of the winding up is, unless the court otherwise orders, void.

## 128 Avoidance of attachments, etc.

**128(1) [Attachments etc. void]** Where a company registered in England and Wales is being wound up by the court, any attachment, sequestration, distress or execution put in force against the estate or effects of the company after the commencement of the winding up is void.

**128(2) [Application to Scotland]** This section, so far as relates to any estate or effects of the company situated in England and Wales, applies in the case of a company registered in Scotland as it applies in the case of a company registered in England and Wales.

### COMMENCEMENT OF WINDING UP

## 129 Commencement of winding up by the court

**129(1) [Time of passing of resolution]** If, before the presentation of a petition for the winding up of a company by the court, a resolution has been passed by the company for voluntary winding up, the winding up of the company is deemed to have commenced at the time of the passing of the resolution; and unless the court, on proof of fraud or mistake, directs otherwise, all proceedings taken in the voluntary winding up are deemed to have been validly taken.

**129(2) [Time of presentation of petition]** In any other case, the winding up of a company by the court is deemed to commence at the time of the presentation of the petition for winding up.

## 130 Consequences of winding-up order

**130(1) [Copy of order to registrar]** On the making of a winding-up order, a copy of the order must forthwith be forwarded by the company (or otherwise as may be prescribed) to the registrar of companies, who shall enter it in his records relating to the company.

**Note**

S. 130(1) modified by Scotland Act 1998, s. 125(1) and Sch. 8, para. 23(1)–(3) so that anything done by the registrar of companies in Scotland or the assistant registrar of friendly societies for Scotland by virtue of s. 130(1) as applied in relation to friendly societies, industrial and provident societies or building societies may be done to or by the Accountant in Bankruptcy as from 1 July 1999 (see SI 1998/3178 (C 79), art. 2).

**130(2) [Actions stayed on winding-up order]** When a winding-up order has been made or a provisional liquidator has been appointed, no action or proceeding shall be proceeded with or commenced against the company or its property, except by leave of the court and subject to such terms as the court may impose.

**130(3) [Actions stayed re companies registered under CA 1985, s. 680]** When an order has been made for winding up a company registered under section 680 of the Companies Act, no action or proceeding shall be commenced or proceeded with against the company or its property or any contibutory of the company, in respect of any debt of the company, except by leave of the court, and subject to such terms as the court may impose.

**130(4) [Effect of order]** An order for winding up a company operates in favour of all the creditors and of all contributories of the company as if made on the joint petition of a creditor and of a contributory.

### INVESTIGATION PROCEDURES

## 131 Company's statement of affairs

**131(1) [Powers of official receiver]** Where the court has made a winding-up order or appointed a provisional liquidator, the official receiver may require some or all of the persons mentioned in subsection (3) below to make out and submit to him a statement in the prescribed form as to the affairs of the company.

**131(2) [Contents of statement]** The statement shall be verified by affidavit by the persons required to submit it and shall show–

(a) particulars of the company's assets, debts and liabilities;
(b) the names and addresses of the company's creditors;
(c) the securities held by them respectively;
(d) the dates when the securities were respectively given; and
(e) such further or other information as may be prescribed or as the official receiver may require.

**131(3) [Persons in s. 131(1)]** The persons referred to in subsection (1) are–

(a) those who are or have been officers of the company;
(b) those who have taken part in the formation of the company at any time within one year before the relevant date;
(c) those who are in the company's employment, or have been in its employment within that year, and are in the official receiver's opinion capable of giving the information required;
(d) those who are or have been within that year officers of, or in the employment of, a company which is, or within that year was, an officer of the company.

**131(4) [Time for submitting statement]** Where any persons are required under this section to submit a statement of affairs to the official receiver, they shall do so (subject to the next subsection) before the end of the period of 21 days beginning with the day after that on which the prescribed notice of the requirement is given to them by the official receiver.

**131(5) [Release, extension of time]** The official receiver, if he thinks fit, may–

(a) at any time release a person from an obligation imposed on him under subsection (1) or (2) above; or
(b) either when giving the notice mentioned in subsection (4) or subsequently, extend the period so mentioned;

and where the official receiver has refused to exercise a power conferred by this subsection, the court, if it thinks fit, may exercise it.

**131(6) [Definitions]** In this section–

**"employment"** includes employment under a contract for services; and

**"the relevant date"** means–

(a) in a case where a provisional liquidator is appointed, the date of his appointment; and
(b) in a case where no such appointment is made, the date of the winding-up order.

**131(7) [Penalty on default]** If a person without reasonable excuse fails to comply with any obligation imposed under this section, he is liable to a fine and, for continued contravention, to a daily default fine.

**131(8) [Scotland]** In the application of this section to Scotland references to the official receiver are to the liquidator or, in a case where a provisional liquidator is appointed, the provisional liquidator.

## 132 Investigation by official receiver

**132(1) [Duty of official receiver]** Where a winding-up order is made by the court in England and Wales, it is the duty of the official receiver to investigate–

(a) if the company has failed, the causes of the failure; and
(b) generally, the promotion, formation, business, dealings and affairs of the company,

and to make such report (if any) to the court as he thinks fit.

**132(2) [Report prima facie evidence]** The report is, in any proceedings, prima facie evidence of the facts stated in it.

## 133 Public examination of officers

**133(1) [Application to court]** Where a company is being wound up by the court, the official receiver or, in Scotland, the liquidator may at any time before the dissolution of the company apply to the court for the public examination of any person who–

(a) is or has been an officer of the company; or

(b) has acted as liquidator or administrator of the company or as receiver or manager or, in Scotland, receiver of its property; or

(c) not being a person falling within paragraph (a) or (b), is or has been concerned, or has taken part, in the promotion, formation or management of the company.

**133(2) [Request to make application]** Unless the court otherwise orders, the official receiver or, in Scotland, the liquidator shall make an application under subsection (1) if he is requested in accordance with the rules to do so by–

(a) one-half, in value, of the company's creditors; or

(b) three-quarters, in value, of the company's contributories.

**133(3) [Court's duties]** On an application under subsection (1), the court shall direct that a public examination of the person to whom the application relates shall be held on a day appointed by the court; and that person shall attend on that day and be publicly examined as to the promotion, formation or management of the company or as to the conduct of its business and affairs, or his conduct or dealings in relation to the company.

**133(4) [Persons taking part]** The following may take part in the public examination of a person under this section and may question that person concerning the matters mentioned in subsection (3), namely–

(a) the official receiver;

(b) the liquidator of the company;

(c) any person who has been appointed as special manager of the company's property or business;

(d) any creditor of the company who has tendered a proof or, in Scotland, submitted a claim in the winding up;

(e) any contributory of the company.

**Note**

See the Insolvency Rules 1986 (SI 1986/1925), r. 4.211ff.

## 134 Enforcement of s. 133

**134(1) [Non-attendance]** If a person without reasonable excuse fails at any time to attend his public examination under section 133, he is guilty of a contempt of court and liable to be punished accordingly.

**134(2) [Warrant etc. re non-attendance]** In a case where a person without reasonable excuse fails at any time to attend his examination under section 133 or there are reasonable grounds for believing that a person has absconded, or is about to abscond, with a view to avoiding or delaying his examination under that section, the court may cause a warrant to be issued to a constable or prescribed officer of the court–

(a) for the arrest of that person; and

(b) for the seizure of any books, papers, records, money or goods in that person's possession.

**134(3) [Consequences of warrant]** In such a case the court may authorise the person arrested under the warrant to be kept in custody, and anything seized under such a warrant to be held, in accordance with the rules, until such time as the court may order.

### APPOINTMENT OF LIQUIDATOR

## 135 Appointment and powers of provisional liquidator

**135(1) [Time of appointment]** Subject to the provisions of this section, the court may, at any time after the presentation of a winding-up petition, appoint a liquidator provisionally.

**135(2) [Appointment in England, Wales]** In England and Wales, the appointment of a provisional liquidator may be made at any time before the making of a winding-up order; and either the official receiver or any other fit person may be appointed.

**135(3) [Appointment in Scotland]** In Scotland, such an appointment may be made at any time before the first appointment of liquidators.

**135(4) [Provisional liquidator]** The provisional liquidator shall carry out such functions as the court may confer on him.

**135(5) [Powers of provisional liquidator]** When a liquidator is provisionally appointed by the court, his powers may be limited by the order appointing him.

## 136 Functions of official receiver in relation to office of liquidator

**136(1) [Application]** The following provisions of this section have effect, subject to section 140 below, on a winding-up order being made by the court in England and Wales.

**136(2) [Official receiver liquidator]** The official receiver, by virtue of his office, becomes the liquidator of the company and continues in office until another person becomes liquidator under the provisions of this Part.

**136(3) [Vacancy]** The official receiver is, by virtue of his office, the liquidator during any vacancy.

**136(4) [Powers of official receiver when liquidator]** At any time when he is the liquidator of the company, the official receiver may summon separate meetings of the company's creditors and contributories for the purpose of choosing a person to be liquidator of the company in place of the official receiver.

**136(5) [Duty of official receiver]** It is the duty of the official receiver–

(a) as soon as practicable in the period of 12 weeks beginning with the day on which the winding-up order was made, to decide whether to exercise his power under subsection (4) to summon meetings, and

(b) if in pursuance of paragraph (a) he decides not to exercise that power, to give notice of his decision, before the end of that period, to the court and to the company's creditors and contributories, and

(c) (whether or not he has decided to exercise that power) to exercise his power to summon meetings under subsection (4) if he is at any time requested, in accordance with the rules, to do so by one-quarter, in value, of the company's creditors;

and accordingly, where the duty imposed by paragraph (c) arises before the official receiver has performed a duty imposed by paragraph (a) or (b), he is not required to perform the latter duty.

**136(6) [Contents of s. 136(5)(b) notice]** A notice given under subsection (5)(b) to the company's creditors shall contain an explanation of the creditors' power under subsection (5)(c) to require the official receiver to summon meetings of the company's creditors and contributories.

## 137 Appointment by Secretary of State

**137(1) [Application by official receiver]** In a winding up by the court in England and Wales the official receiver may, at any time when he is the liquidator of the company, apply to the Secretary of State for the appointment of a person as liquidator in his place.

**137(2) [Decision by official receiver]** If meetings are held in pursuance of a decision under section 136(5)(a), but no person is chosen to be liquidator as a result of those meetings, it is the duty of the official receiver to decide whether to refer the need for an appointment to the Secretary of State.

**137(3) [Duty of Secretary of State]** On an application under subsection (1), or a reference made in pursuance of a decision under subsection (2), the Secretary of State shall either make an appointment or decline to make one.

**137(4) [Notice of appointment by liquidator]** Where a liquidator has been appointed by the Secretary of State under subsection (3), the liquidator shall give notice of his appointment to the company's creditors or, if the court so allows, shall advertise his appointment in accordance with the directions of the court.

**137(5) [Contents of notice or advertisement]** In that notice or advertisement the liquidator shall–

(a) state whether he proposes to summon a general meeting of the company's creditors under section 141 below for the purpose of determining (together with any meeting of contributories liable in payment of any calls, and of the amount due by each contributory, and of the date when that amount became due, to pronounce forthwith a decree against those contributories for payment of the sums so certified to be due, with interest from that date until payment (at 5 per cent per annum) in the same way and to the same effect as if they had severally consented to registration for execution, on a charge of 6 days, of a legal obligation to pay those calls and interest.

**161(2) [Extraction of decree]** The decree may be extracted immediately, and no suspension of it is competent, except on caution or consignation, unless with special leave of the court.

## 162 Appeals from orders in Scotland

**162(1) [Appeal from order on winding up]** Subject to the provisions of this section and to rules of court, an appeal from any order or decision made or given in the winding up of a company by the court in Scotland under this Act lies in the same manner and subject to the same conditions as an appeal from an order or decision of the court in cases within its ordinary jurisdiction.

**162(2) [Orders by judge acting as vacation judge]** In regard to orders or judgments pronounced by the judge acting as vacation judge–

(a) none of the orders specified in Part I of Schedule 3 to this Act are subject to review, reduction, suspension or stay of execution, and

(b) every other order or judgment (except as mentioned below) may be submitted to review by the Inner House by reclaiming motion enrolled within 14 days from the the date of the order or judgment.

**History**

In s. 162(2) the former words "in pursuance of section 4 of the Administration of Justice (Scotland) Act 1933" (which appeared after the words "vacation judge") repealed by Court of Session Act 1988, s. 52(2) and Sch. 2, Pt. I and III as from 29 September 1988.

**162(3) [Order in Sch. 3, Pt. II]** However, an order being one of those specified in Part II of that Schedule shall, from the date of the order and notwithstanding that it has been submitted to review as above, be carried out and receive effect until the Inner House have disposed of the matter.

**162(4) [Orders by Lord Ordinary]** In regard to orders of judgments pronounced in Scotland by a Lord Ordinary before whom proceedings in a winding up are being taken, any such order or judgment may be submitted to review by the Inner House by reclaiming motion enrolled within 14 days from its date; but should it not be so submitted to review during session, the provisions of this section in regard to orders or judgments pronounced by the judge acting as vacation judge apply.

**162(5) [Decrees for payment of calls in winding up]** Nothing in this section affects provisions of the Companies Act or this Act in reference to decrees in Scotland for payment of calls in the winding up of companies, whether voluntary or by the court.

# Chapter VII – Liquidators

### PRELIMINARY

## 163 Style and title of liquidators

**163** The liquidator of a company shall be described–

(a) where a person other than the official receiver is liquidator, by the style of "the liquidator" of the particular company, or

(b) where the official receiver is liquidator, by the style of "the official receiver and liquidator" of the particular company;

and in neither case shall he be described by an individual name.

## 164 Corrupt inducement affecting appointment

**164** A person who gives, or agrees or offers to give, to any member or creditor of a company any valuable consideration with a view to securing his own appointment or nomination, or to securing or preventing the appointment or nomination of some person other than himself, as the company's liquidator is liable to a fine.

## LIQUIDATOR'S POWERS AND DUTIES

## 165 Voluntary winding up

**165(1) [Application]** This section has effect where a company is being wound up voluntarily, but subject to section 166 below in the case of a creditors' voluntary winding up.

**165(2) [Powers in Sch. 4, Pt. I]** The liquidator may–

(a) in the case of a members' voluntary winding up, with the sanction of an extraordinary resolution of the company, and

(b) in the case of a creditors' voluntary winding up, with the sanction of the court or the liquidation committee (or, if there is no such committee, a meeting of the company's creditors),

exercise any of the powers specified in Part I of Schedule 4 to this Act (payment of debts, compromise of claims, etc.).

**165(3) [Powers in Sch. 4, Pt. II, III]** The liquidator may, without sanction, exercise either of the powers specified in Part II of that Schedule (institution and defence of proceedings; carrying on the business of the company) and any of the general powers specified in Part III of that Schedule.

**165(4) [Other powers]** The liquidator may–

(a) exercise the court's power of settling a list of contributories (which list is prima facie evidence of the liability of the persons named in it to be contributories),

(b) exercise the court's power of making calls,

(c) summon general meetings of the company for the purpose of obtaining its sanction by special or extraordinary resolution or for any other purpose he may think fit.

**165(5) [Duty re payment of debts]** The liquidator shall pay the company's debts and adjust the rights of the contributories among themselves.

**165(6) [Notice to committee re exercise of powers]** Where the liquidator in exercise of the powers conferred on him by this Act disposes of any property of the company to a person who is connected with the company (within the meaning of section 249 in Part VII), he shall, if there is for the time being a liquidation committee, give notice to the committee of that exercise of his powers.

## 166 Creditors' voluntary winding up

**166(1) [Application]** This section applies where, in the case of a creditors' voluntary winding up, a liquidator has been nominated by the company.

**166(2) [Non-exercise of s. 165 powers]** The powers conferred on the liquidator by section 165 shall not be exercised, except with the sanction of the court, during the period before the holding of the creditors' meeting under section 98 in Chapter IV.

**166(3) [Non-application of s. 166(2)]** Subsection (2) does not apply in relation to the power of the liquidator–

(a) to take into his custody or under his control all the property to which the company is or appears to be entitled;

(b) to dispose of perishable goods and other goods the value of which is likely to diminish if they are not immediately disposed of; and

(c) to do all such other things as may be necessary for the protection of the company's assets.

**166(4) [Liquidator to attend s. 98 meeting]** The liquidator shall attend the creditors' meeting held under section 98 and shall report to the meeting on any exercise by him of his powers (whether or not under this section or under section 112 or 165).

**166(5) [Where default re s. 98, 99]** If default is made–

(a) by the company in complying with subsection (1) or (2) of section 98, or

(b) by the directors in complying with subsection (1) or (2) of section 99,

the liquidator shall, within 7 days of the relevant day, apply to the court for directions as to the manner in which that default is to be remedied.

**166(6) ["The relevant day"] "The relevant day"** means the day on which the liquidator was nominated by the company or the day on which he first became aware of the default, whichever is the later.

**166(7) [Penalty for non-compliance]** If the liquidator without reasonable excuse fails to comply with this section, he is liable to a fine.

## 167 Winding up by the court

**167(1) [Powers of liquidator]** Where a company is being wound up by the court, the liquidator may–

(a) with the sanction of the court or the liquidation committee, exercise any of the powers specified in Parts I and II of Schedule 4 to this Act (payment of debts; compromise of claims, etc.; institution and defence of proceedings; carrying on of the business of the company), and

(b) with or without that sanction, exercise any of the general powers specified in Part III of that Schedule.

**167(2) [Duty of liquidator]** Where the liquidator (not being the official receiver), in exercise of the powers conferred on him by this Act–

(a) disposes of any property of the company to a person who is connected with the company (within the meaning of section 249 in Part VII), or

(b) employs a solicitor to assist him in the carrying out of his functions,

he shall, if there is for the time being a liquidation committee, give notice to the committee of that exercise of his powers.

**167(3) [Control of court]** The exercise by the liquidator in a winding up by the court of the powers conferred by this section is subject to the control of the court, and any creditor or contributory may apply to the court with respect to any exercise or proposed exercise of any of those powers.

## 168 Supplementary powers (England and Wales)

**168(1) [Application]** This section applies in the case of a company which is being wound up by the court in England and Wales.

**168(2) [Liquidator may summon general meetings]** The liquidator may summon general meetings of the creditors or contributories for the purpose of ascertaining their wishes; and it is his duty to summon meetings at such times as the creditors or contributories by resolution (either at the meeting appointing the liquidator or otherwise) may direct, or whenever requested in writing to do so by one-tenth in value of the creditors or contributories (as the case may be).

**168(3) [Liquidator may apply to court for directions]** The liquidator may apply to the court (in the prescribed manner) for directions in relation to any particular matter arising in the winding up.

**168(4) [Liquidator to use own discretion]** Subject to the provisions of this Act, the liquidator shall use his own discretion in the management of the assets and their distribution among the creditors.

**168(5) [Application to court re acts of liquidator]** If any person is aggrieved by an act or decision of the liquidator, that person may apply to the court; and the court may confirm, reverse or modify the act or decision complained of, and make such order in the case as it thinks just.

**Note**

Re insolvent partnerships, s. 168(5A)–(5C) inserted for the purposes of the Insolvent Partnerships Order 1994 (SI 1994/2421) as from 1 December 1994 (by art. 14(1)).

## 169 Supplementary powers (Scotland)

**169(1) [Where no liquidation committee]** In the case of a winding up in Scotland, the court may provide by order that the liquidator may, where there is no liquidation committee, exercise any of the following powers, namely–

(a) to bring or defend any action or other legal proceeding in the name and on behalf of the company, or

(b) to carry on the business of the company so far as may be necessary for its beneficial winding up,

without the sanction or intervention of the court.

**169(2) [Liquidator's powers]** In a winding up by the court in Scotland, the liquidator has (subject to the rules) the same powers as a trustee on a bankrupt estate.

**Note**

See the Insolvency (Scotland) Rules 1986 (SI 1986/1915 (S. 139)), r. 4.68.

## 170 Enforcement of liquidator's duty to make returns, etc.

**170(1) [Powers of court if liquidator fails to file returns etc.]** If a liquidator who has made any default–

(a) in filing, delivering or making any return, account or other document, or

(b) in giving any notice which he is by law required to file, deliver, make or give,

fails to make good the default within 14 days after the service on him of a notice requiring him to do so, the court has the following powers.

**170(2) [On application court may order to make good default]** On an application made by any creditor or contributory of the company, or by the registrar of companies, the court may make an order directing the liquidator to make good the default within such time as may be specified in the order.

**Note**

S. 170(2) modified by Scotland Act 1998, s. 125(1) and Sch. 8, para. 23(1)–(3) so that anything done by the registrar of companies in Scotland or the assistant registrar of friendly societies for Scotland by virtue of s. 170(2) as applied in relation to friendly societies, industrial and provident societies or building societies may be done to or by the Accountant in Bankruptcy as from 1 July 1999 (see SI 1998/3178 (C 79), art. 2).

**170(3) [Costs]** The court's order may provide that all costs of and incidental to the application shall be borne by the liquidator.

**170(4) [Penalties]** Nothing in this section prejudices the operation of any enactment imposing penalties on a liquidator in respect of any such default as is mentioned above.

### REMOVAL; VACATION OF OFFICE

## 171 Removal, etc. (voluntary winding up)

**171(1) [Application]** This section applies with respect to the removal from office and vacation of office of the liquidator of a company which is being wound up voluntarily.

**171(2) [Removal from office]** Subject to the next subsection, the liquidator may be removed from office only by an order of the court or–

(a) in the case of a members' voluntary winding up, by a general meeting of the company summoned specially for that purpose, or

(b) in the case of a creditors' voluntary winding up, by a general meeting of the company's creditors summoned specially for that purpose in accordance with the rules.

**171(3) [Where liquidator appointed by court under s. 108]** Where the liquidator was appointed by the court under section 108 in Chapter V, a meeting such as is mentioned in subsection (2) above shall be summoned for the purpose of replacing him only if he thinks fit or the court so directs or the meeting is requested, in accordance with the rules–

(a) in the case of a members' voluntary winding up, by members representing not less than one-half of the total voting rights of all the members having at the date of the request a right to vote at the meeting, or

(b) in the case of a creditors' voluntary winding up, by not less than one-half, in value, of the company's creditors.

**171(4) [Vacation of office]** A liquidator shall vacate office if he ceases to be a person who is qualified to act as an insolvency practitioner in relation to the company.

**171(5) [Resignation]** A liquidator may, in the prescribed circumstances, resign his office by giving notice of his resignation to the registrar of companies.

**Note**

S. 171(5) modified by Scotland Act 1998, s. 125(1) and Sch. 8, para. 23(1), (4), (5) so that anything directed to be done by the registrar of companies in Scotland or the assistant registrar of friendly societies for Scotland by virtue of s. 171(5) as applied in relation to friendly societies, industrial and provident societies or building societies shall be done to or by the Accountant in Bankruptcy as from 1 July 1999 (see SI 1998/3178 (C 79), art. 2).

**171(6) [Where final meetings held]** Where–

(a) in the case of a members' voluntary winding up, a final meeting of the company has been held under section 94 in Chapter III, or

(b) in the case of a creditors' voluntary winding up, final meetings of the company and of the creditors have been held under section 106 in Chapter IV,

the liquidator whose report was considered at the meeting or meetings shall vacate office as soon as he has complied with subsection (3) of that section and has given notice to the registrar of companies that the meeting or meetings have been held and of the decisions (if any) of the meeting or meetings.

**Note**

S. 171(6) modified by Scotland Act 1998, s. 125(1) and Sch. 8, para. 23(1), (4), (5) so that anything directed to be done by the registrar of companies in Scotland or the assistant registrar of friendly societies for Scotland by virtue of s. 171(6) as applied in relation to friendly societies, industrial and provident societies or building societies shall be done to or by the Accountant in Bankruptcy as from 1 July 1999 (see SI 1998/3178 (C 79), art. 2).

## 172 Removal, etc. (winding up by the court)

**172(1) [Application]** This section applies with respect to the removal from office and vacation of office of the liquidator of a company which is being wound up by the court, or of a provisional liquidator.

**172(2) [Removal from office]** Subject as follows, the liquidator may be removed from office only by an order of the court or by a general meeting of the company's creditors summoned specially for that purpose in accordance with the rules; and a provisional liquidator may be removed from office only by an order of the court.

**172(3) [Replacing certain types of liquidator]** Where–

(a) the official receiver is liquidator otherwise than in succession under section 136(3) to a person who held office as a result of a nomination by a meeting of the company's creditors or contributories, or

(b) the liquidator was appointed by the court otherwise than under section 139(4)(a) or 140(1), or was appointed by the Secretary of State,

a general meeting of the company's creditors shall be summoned for the purpose of replacing him only if he thinks fit, or the court so directs, or the meeting is requested, in accordance with the rules, by not less that one-quarter, in value, of the creditors.

**172(4) [If liquidator appointed by Secretary of State]** If appointed by the Secretary of State, the liquidator may be removed from office by a direction of the Secretary of State.

**172(5) [Vacation of office]** A liquidator or provisional liquidator, not being the official receiver, shall vacate office if he ceases to be a person who is qualified to act as an insolvency practitioner in relation to the company.

**172(6) [Resignation]** A liquidator may, in the prescribed circumstances, resign his office by giving notice of his resignation to the court.

**172(7) [Where s. 204 order]** Where an order is made under section 204 (early dissolution in Scotland) for the dissolution of the company, the liquidator shall vacate office when the dissolution of the company takes effect in accordance with that section.

**172(8) [Where final meeting under s. 146]** Where a final meeting has been held under section 146 (liquidator's report on completion of winding up), the liquidator whose report was considered at the meeting shall vacate office as soon as he has given notice to the court and the registrar of companies that the meeting has been held and of the decisions (if any) of the meeting.

**Note**

See the Insolvency Rules 1986 (SI 1986/1925), r. 4.119ff.

S. 172(8) modified by Scotland Act 1998, s. 125(1) and Sch. 8, para. 23(1)–(3) so that anything done by the registrar of companies in Scotland or the assistant registrar of friendly societies for Scotland by virtue of s. 172(8) as applied in relation to friendly societies, industrial and provident societies or building societies may be done to or by the Accountant in Bankruptcy as from 1 July 1999 (see SI 1998/3178 (C 79), art. 2).

## RELEASE OF LIQUIDATOR

# 173 Release (voluntary winding up)

**173(1) [Application]** This section applies with respect to the release of the liquidator of a company which is being wound up voluntarily.

**173(2) [Time of release]** A person who has ceased to be a liquidator shall have his release with effect from the following time, that is to say–

(a) in the case of a person who has been removed from office by a general meeting of the company or by a general meeting of the company's creditors that has not resolved against his release or who has died, the time at which notice is given to the registrar of companies in accordance with the rules that that person has ceased to hold office;

(b) in the case of a person who has been removed from office by a general meeting of the company's creditors that has resolved against his release, or by the court, or who has vacated office under section 171(4) above, such time as the Secretary of State may, on the application of that person, determine;

(c) in the case of a person who has resigned, such time as may be prescribed;

(d) in the case of a person who has vacated office under subsection (6)(a) of section 171, the time at which he vacated office;

(e) in the case of a person who has vacated office under subsection (6)(b) of that section–

 (i) if the final meeting of the creditors referred to in that subsection has resolved against that person's release, such time as the Secretary of State may, on an application by that person, determine, and

 (ii) if that meeting has not resolved against that person's release, the time at which he vacated office.

**Note**

S. 173(2) modified by Scotland Act 1998, s. 125(1) and Sch. 8, para. 23(1), (4), (5) so that anything directed to be done by the registrar of companies in Scotland or the assistant registrar of friendly societies for Scotland by virtue of s. 173(2) as applied in relation to friendly societies, industrial and provident societies or building societies shall be done to or by the Accountant in Bankruptcy as from 1 July 1999 (see SI 1998/3178 (C 79), art. 2).

**173(3) [Application to Scotland]** In the application of subsection (2) to the winding up of a company registered in Scotland, the references to a determination by the Secretary of State as to the time from which a person who has ceased to be liquidator shall have his release are to be read as references to such a determination by the Accountant of Court.

**173(4) [Effect of release]** Where a liquidator has his release under subsection (2), he is, with effect from the time specified in that subsection, discharged from all liability both in respect of acts or omissions of his in the winding up and otherwise in relation to his conduct as liquidator.

But nothing in this section prevents the exercise, in relation to a person who has had his release under subsection (2), of the court's powers under section 212 of this Act (summary remedy against delinquent directors, liquidators, etc.).

# 174 Release (winding up by the court)

**174(1) [Application]** This section applies with respect to the release of the liquidator of a company which is being wound up by the court, or of a provisional liquidator.

**174(2) [Where official receiver ceases to be liquidator]** Where the official receiver has ceased to be liquidator and a person becomes liquidator in his stead, the official receiver has his release with effect from the following time, that is to say–

(a) in a case where that person was nominated by a general meeting of creditors or contributories, or was appointed by the Secretary of State, the time at which the official receiver gives notice to the court that he has been replaced;

(b) in a case where that person is appointed by the court, such time as the court may determine.

**174(3) [Where official receiver gives notice to Secretary of State]** If the official receiver while he is a liquidator gives notice to the Secretary of State that the winding up is for practical purposes complete, he has his release with effect from such time as the Secretary of State may determine.

**174(4) [Person other than official receiver]** A person other than the official receiver who has ceased to be a liquidator has his release with effect from the following time, that is to say–

(a) in the case of a person who has been removed from office by a general meeting of creditors that has not resolved against his release or who has died, the time at which notice is given to the court in accordance with the rules that that person has ceased to hold office;

(b) in the case of a person who has been removed from office by a general meeting of creditors that has resolved against his release, or by the court or the Secretary of State, or who has vacated office under section 172(5) or (7), such time as the Secretary of State may, on an application by that person, determine;

(c) in the case of a person who has resigned, such time as may be prescribed;

(d) in the case of a person who has vacated office under section 172(8)–

(i) if the final meeting referred to in that subsection has resolved against that person's release, such time as the Secretary of State may, on an application by that person, determine, and

(ii) if that meeting has not so resolved, the time at which that person vacated office.

**Note**

See the Insolvency Rules 1986 (SI 1986/1925), r. 4.121, 4.132.

**174(5) [Provisional liquidator]** A person who has ceased to hold office as a provisional liquidator has his release with effect from such time as the court may, on an application by him, determine.

**174(6) [Effect of release]** Where the official receiver or a liquidator or provisional liquidator has his release under this section, he is, with effect from the time specified in the preceding provisions of this section, discharged from all liability both in respect of acts or omissions of his in the winding up and otherwise in relation to his conduct as liquidator or provisional liquidator.

But nothing in this section prevents the exercise, in relation to a person who has had his release under this section, of the court's powers under section 212 (summary remedy against delinquent directors, liquidators, etc.).

**174(7) [Application to Scotland]** In the application of this section to a case where the order for winding up has been made by the court in Scotland, the references to a determination by the Secretary of State as to the time from which a person who has ceased to be liquidator has his release are to such a determination by the Accountant of Court.

# Chapter VIII – Provisions of General Application in Winding Up

PREFERENTIAL DEBTS

## 175 Preferential debts (general provision)

**175(1) [Payment in priority]** In a winding up the company's preferential debts (within the meaning given by section 386 in Part XII) shall be paid in priority to all other debts.

**175(2) [Ranking and priority]** Preferential debts–

(a) rank equally among themselves after the expenses of the winding up and shall be paid in full, unless the assets are insufficient to meet them, in which case they abate in equal proportions; and

(b) so far as the assets of the company available for payment of general creditors are insufficient to meet them, have priority over the claims of holders of debentures secured by, or holders of, any floating charge created by the company, and shall be paid accordingly out of any property comprised in or subject to that charge.

## 176 Preferential charge on goods distrained

**176(1) [Application]** This section applies where a company is being wound up by the court in England and Wales, and is without prejudice to section 128 (avoidance of attachments, etc.).

**176(2) [Where distraining in previous 3 months]** Where any person (whether or not a landlord or person entitled to rent) has distrained upon the goods or effects of the company in the period of 3 months ending with the date of the winding-up order, those goods or effects, or the proceeds of their sale, shall be charged for the benefit of the company with the preferential debts of the company to the extent that the company's property is for the time being insufficient for meeting them.

**176(3) [Surrender of goods under s. 176(2)]** Where by virtue of a charge under subsection (2) any person surrenders any goods or effects to a company or makes a payment to a company, that person ranks, in respect of the amount of the proceeds of sale of those goods or effects by the liquidator or (as the case may be) the amount of the payment, as a preferential creditor of the company, except as against so much of the company's property as is available for the payment of preferential creditors by virtue of the surrender or payment.

SPECIAL MANAGERS

## 177 Power to appoint special manager

**177(1) [Power of court]** Where a company has gone into liquidation or a provisional liquidator has been appointed, the court may, on an application under this section, appoint any person to be the special manager of the business or property of the company.

**177(2) [Application to court]** The application may be made by the liquidator or provisional liquidator in any case where it appears to him that the nature of the business or property of the company, or the interests of the company's creditors or contributories or members generally, require the appointment of another person to manage the company's business or property.

**177(3) [Powers of special manager]** The special manager has such powers as may be entrusted to him by the court.

**177(4) [Extent of s. 177(3) powers]** The court's power to entrust powers to the special manager includes power to direct that any provision of this Act that has effect in relation to the provisional liquidator or liquidator of a company shall have the like effect in relation to the special manager for the purposes of the carrying out by him of any of the functions of the provisional liquidator or liquidator.

**177(5) [Duties of special manager]** The special manager shall–

(a) give such security or, in Scotland, caution as may be prescribed;

(b) prepare and keep such accounts as may be prescribed; and

(c) produce those accounts in accordance with the rules to the Secretary of State or to such other persons as may be prescribed.

DISCLAIMER (ENGLAND AND WALES ONLY)

## 178 Power to disclaim onerous property

**178(1) [Application]** This and the next two sections apply to a company that is being wound up in England and Wales.

**178(2) [Disclaimer by liquidator]** Subject as follows, the liquidator may, by the giving of the prescribed notice, disclaim any onerous property and may do so notwithstanding that he has taken possession of it, endeavoured to sell it, or otherwise exercised rights of ownership in relation to it.

**178(3) [Onerous property]** The following is onerous property for the purposes of this section–

(a) any unprofitable contract, and

(b) any other property of the company which is unsaleable or not readily saleable or is such that it may give rise to a liability to pay money or perform any other onerous act.

**178(4) [Effect of disclaimer]** A disclaimer under this section–

(a) operates so as to determine, as from the date of the disclaimer, the rights, interests and liabilities of the company in or in respect of the property disclaimed; but

(b) does not, except so far as is necessary for the purpose of releasing the company from any liability, affect the rights or liabilities of any other person.

**178(5) [Where notice of disclaimer not to be given]** A notice of disclaimer shall not be given under this section in respect of any property if–

(a) a person interested in the property has applied in writing to the liquidator or one of his predecessors as liquidator requiring the liquidator or that predecessor to decide whether he will disclaim or not, and

(b) the period of 28 days begining with the day on which that application was made, or such longer period as the court may allow, has expired without a notice of disclaimer having been given under this section in respect of that property.

**178(6) [Persons sustaining loss etc.]** Any person sustaining loss or damage in consequence of the operation of a disclaimer under this section is deemed a creditor of the company to the extent of the loss or damage and accordingly may prove for the loss or damage in the winding up.

## 179 Disclaimer of leaseholds

**179(1) [Requirement for disclaimer to take effect]** The disclaimer under section 178 of any property of a leasehold nature does not take effect unless a copy of the disclaimer has been served (so far as the liquidator is aware of their addresses) on every person claiming under the company as underlessee or mortgagee and either–

(a) no application under section 181 below is made with respect to that property before the end of the period of 14 days beginning with the day on which the last notice served under this subsection was served; or

(b) where such an application has been made, the court directs that the disclaimer shall take effect.

**179(2) [Court's directions or orders]** Where the court gives a direction under subsection (1)(b) it may also, instead of or in addition to any order it makes under section 181, make such orders with respect to fixtures, tenant's improvements and other matters arising out of the lease as it thinks fit.

## 180 Land subject to rentcharge

**180(1) [Application]** The following applies where, in consequence of the disclaimer under section 178 of any land subject to a rentcharge, that land vests by operation of law in the Crown or any other person (referred to in the next subsection as "the proprietor").

**180(2) [Liability of proprietor et al.]** The proprietor and the successors in title of the proprietor are not subject to any personal liability in repect of any sums becoming due under the rentcharge except sums becoming due after the proprietor, or some person claiming under or through the proprietor, has taken possession or control of the land or has entered into occupation of it.

## 181 Powers of court (general)

**181(1) [Application]** This section and the next apply where the liquidator has disclaimed property under section 178.

**181(2) [Application to court]** An application under this section may be made to the court by–

(a) any person who claims an interest in the disclaimed property, or

(b) any person who is under any liability in respect of the disclaimed property, not being a liability discharged by the disclaimer.

**181(3) [Powers of court]** Subject as follows, the court may on the application make an order, on such terms as it thinks fit, for the vesting of the disclaimed property in, or for its delivery to–

(a) a person entitled to it or a trustee for such a person, or

(b) a person subject to such a liability as is mentioned in subsection (2)(b) or a trustee for such a person.

**181(4) [Limit on court's powers]** The court shall not make an order under subsection (3)(b) except where it appears to the court that it would be just to do so for the purpose of compensating the person subject to the liability in respect of the disclaimer.

**181(5) [Relationship with s. 178(6)]** The effect of any order under this section shall be taken into account in assessing for the purpose of section 178(6) the extent of any loss or damage sustained by any person in consequence of the disclaimer.

**181(6) [Effect of vesting order]** An order under this section vesting property in any person need not be completed by conveyance, assignment or transfer.

## 182 Powers of court (leaseholds)

**182(1) [Limit on court's power]** The court shall not make an order under section 181 vesting property of a leasehold nature in any person claiming under the company as underlessee or mortgagee except on terms making that person–

(a) subject to the same liabilities and obligations as the company was subject to under the lease at the commencement of the winding up, or

(b) if the court thinks fit, subject to the same liabilities and obligations as that person would be subject to if the lease had been assigned to him at the commencement of the winding up.

**182(2) [Where order re part of property in lease]** For the purposes of an order under section 181 relating to only part of any property comprised in a lease, the requirements of subsection (1) apply as if the lease comprised only the property to which the order relates.

**182(3) [Court may vest estate in someone else]** Where subsection (1) applies and no person claiming under the company as underlessee or mortagee is willing to accept an order under section 181 on the terms required by virtue of that subsection, the court may, by order under that section, vest the company's estate or interest in the property in any person who is liable (whether personally or in a representative capacity, and whether alone or jointly with the company) to perform the lessee's covenants in the lease.

The court may vest that estate and interest in such a person freed and discharged from all estates, incumbrances and interests created by the company.

**182(4) [Where s. 182(1) applies]** Where subsection (1) applies and a person claiming under the company as underlessee or mortgagee declines to accept an order under section 181, that person is excluded from all interest in the property.

### EXECUTION, ATTACHMENT AND THE SCOTTISH EQUIVALENTS

## 183 Effect of execution or attachment (England and Wales)

**183(1) [Where creditor seeking benefit of execution or attachment]** Where a creditor has issued execution against the goods or land of a company or has attached any debt due to it, and the company is subsequently wound up, he is not entitled to retain the benefit of the execution or attachment against the liquidator unless he has completed the execution or attachment before the commencement of the winding up.

**183(2) [Qualifications]** However–

(a) if a creditor has had notice of a meeting having been called at which a resolution for voluntary winding up is to be proposed, the date on which he had notice is substituted, for the purpose of subsection (1), for the date of commencement of the winding up;

(b) a person who purchases in good faith under a sale by the sheriff any goods of a company on which execution has been levied in all cases acquires a good title to them against the liquidator; and

(c) the rights conferred by subsection (1) on the liquidator may be set aside by the court in favour of the creditor to such extent and subject to such terms as the court thinks fit.

**183(3) [Execution, attachment]** For the purposes of this Act–

(a) an execution against goods is completed by seizure and sale, or by the making of a charging order under section 1 of the Charging Orders Act 1979;

(b) an attachment of a debt is completed by receipt of the debt; and

(c) an execution against land is completed by seizure, by the appointment of a receiver, or by the making of a charging order under section 1 of the Act above mentioned.

**183(4) [Definitions]** In this section **"goods"** includes all chattels personal; and **"the sheriff"** includes any officer charged with the execution of a writ or other process.

**183(5) [Scotland]** This section does not apply in the case of a winding up in Scotland.

## 184 Duties of sheriff (England and Wales)

**184(1) [Application]** The following applies where a company's goods are taken in execution and, before their sale or the completion of the execution (by the receipt or recovery of the full amount of the levy), notice is served on the sheriff that a provisional liquidator has been appointed or that a winding-up order has been made, or that a resolution for voluntary winding up has been passed.

**184(2) [Sheriff to deliver goods and money to liquidator]** The sheriff shall, on being so required, deliver the goods and any money seized or received in part satisfaction of the execution to the liquidator; but the costs of execution are a first charge on the goods or money so delivered, and the liquidator may sell the goods, or a sufficient part of them, for the purpose of satisfying the charge.

**184(3) [Costs where goods sold etc.]** If under an execution in respect of a judgment for a sum exceeding £500 a company's goods are sold or money is paid in order to avoid sale, the sheriff shall deduct the costs of the execution from the proceeds of sale or the money paid and retain the balance for 14 days.

**Note**

The figure of £500 was increased from £250 by the Insolvency Proceedings (Monetary Limits) Order 1986 (SI 1986/1996) as from 29 December 1986.

**184(4) [If within time notice is served]** If within that time notice is served on the sheriff of a petition for the winding up of the company having been presented, or of a meeting having been called at which there is to be proposed a resolution for voluntary winding up, and an order is made or a resolution passed (as the case may be), the sheriff shall pay the balance to the liquidator who is entitled to retain it as against the execution creditor.

**184(5) [Liquidator's rights may be set aside by court]** The rights conferred by this section on the liquidator may be set aside by the court in favour of the creditor to such extent and subject to such terms as the court thinks fit.

**184(6) [Definitions]** In this section, **"goods"** includes all chattels personal; and **"the sheriff"** includes any officer charged with the execution of a writ or other process.

**184(7) [Increase, reduction of s. 184(3) sum]** The money sum for the time being specified in subsection (3) is subject to increase or reduction by order under section 416 in Part XV.

**184(8) [Scotland]** This section does not apply in the case of a winding up in Scotland.

## 185 Effect of diligence (Scotland)

**185(1) [Application of Bankruptcy (Scotland) Act]** In the winding up of a company registered in Scotland, the following provisions of the Bankruptcy (Scotland) Act 1985–

(a) subsections (1) to (6) of section 37 (effect of sequestration on diligence); and

(b) subsections (3), (4), (7) and (8) of section 39 (realisation of estate), apply, so far as consistent with this Act, in like manner as they apply in the sequestration of a debtor's estate, with the substitutions specified below and with any other necessary modifications.

**185(2) [Substitutions]** The substitutions to be made in those sections of the Act of 1985 are as follows–

(a) for references to the debtor, substitute references to the company;

(b) for references to the sequestration, substitute references to the winding up;

(c) for references to the date of sequestration, substitute references to the commencement of the winding up of the company; and

(d) for references to the permanent trustee, substitute references to the liquidator.

**185(3) [Definition]** In this section, **"the commencement of the winding up of the company"** means, where it is being wound up by the court, the day on which the winding-up order is made.

**185(4) [English company with estate in Scotland]** This section, so far as relating to any estate or effects of the company situated in Scotland, applies in the case of a company registered in England and Wales as in the case of one registered in Scotland.

## MISCELLANEOUS MATTERS

# 186 Rescission of contracts by the court

**186(1) [Power of court]** The court may, on the application of a person who is, as against the liquidator, entitled to the benefit or subject to the burden of a contract made with the company, make an order rescinding the contract on such terms as to payment by or to either party of damages for the non-performance of the contract, or otherwise as the court thinks just.

**186(2) [Damages]** Any damages payable under the order to such a person may be proved by him as a debt in the winding up.

# 187 Power to make over assets to employees

**187(1) [CA 1985, s. 719 payment on winding up]** On the winding up of a company (whether by the court or voluntarily), the liquidator may, subject to the following provisions of this section, make any payment which the company has, before the commencement of the winding up, decided to make under section 719 of the Companies Act (power to provide for employees or former employees on cessation or transfer of business).

**187(2) [Power exercisable by liquidator]** The power which a company may exercise by virtue only of that section may be exercised by the liquidator after the winding up has commenced if, after the company's liabilities have been fully satisfied and provision has been made for the expenses of the winding up, the exercise of that power has been sanctioned by such a resolution of the company as would be required of the company itself by section 719(3) before that commencement, if paragraph (b) of that subsection were omitted and any other requirement applicable to its exercise by the company had been met.

**187(3) [Source of payment]** Any payment which may be made by a company under this section (that is, a payment after the commencement of its winding up) may be made out of the company's assets which are available to the members on the winding up.

**187(4) [Control by court]** On a winding up by the court, the exercise by the liquidator of his powers under this section is subject to the court's control, and any creditor or contributory may apply to the court with respect to any exercise or proposed exercise of the power.

**187(5) [Effect]** Subsections (1) and (2) above have effect notwithstanding anything in any rule of law or in section 107 of this Act (property of company after satisfaction of liabilities to be distributed among members).

# 188 Notification that company is in liquidation

**188(1) [Statement in invoices etc.]** When a company is being wound up, whether by the court or voluntarily, every invoice, order for goods or business letter issued by or on behalf of the company, or a liquidator of the company, or a receiver or manager of the company's property, being a document on or in which the name of the company appears, shall contain a statement that the company is being wound up.

**188(2) [Penalty on default]** If default is made in complying with this section, the company and any of the following persons who knowingly and wilfully authorises or permits the default, namely, any officer of the company, any liquidator of the company and any receiver or manager, is liable to a fine.

## 189 Interest on debts

**189(1) [Payment of interest]** In a winding up interest is payable in accordance with this section on any debt proved in the winding up, including so much of any such debt as represents interest on the remainder.

**189(2) [Surplus after payment of debts]** Any surplus remaining after the payment of the debts proved in a winding up shall, before being applied for any other purpose, be applied in paying interest on those debts in respect of the periods during which they have been outstanding since the company went into liquidation.

**189(3) [Ranking of interest]** All interest under this section ranks equally, whether or not the debts on which it is payable rank equally.

**189(4) [Rate of interest]** The rate of interest payable under this section in respect of any debt ("the official rate" for the purposes of any provision of this Act in which that expression is used) is whichever is the greater of–

(a) the rate specified in section 17 of the Judgments Act 1838 on the day on which the company went into liquidation, and

(b) the rate applicable to that debt apart from the winding up.

**189(5) [Scotland]** In the application of this section to Scotland–

(a) references to a debt proved in a winding up have effect as references to a claim accepted in a winding up, and

(b) the reference to section 17 of the Judgments Act 1838 has effect as a reference to the rules.

**Note**

See the Insolvency (Scotland) Rules 1986 (SI 1986/1915 (S. 139)).

## 190 Documents exempt from stamp duty

**190(1) [Application]** In the case of a winding up by the court, or of a creditors' voluntary winding up, the following has effect as regards exemption from duties chargeable under the enactments relating to stamp duties.

**190(2) [Exempt documents of company registered in England and Wales]** If the company is registered in England and Wales, the following documents are exempt from stamp duty–

(a) every assurance relating solely to freehold or leasehold property, or to any estate, right or interest in, any real or personal property, which forms part of the company's assets and which, after the execution of the assurance, either at law or in equity, is or remains part of those assets, and

(b) every writ, order, certificate, or other instrument or writing relating solely to the property of any company which is being wound up as mentioned in subsection (1), or to any proceeding under such a winding up.

**"Assurance"** here includes deed, conveyance, assignment and surrender.

**190(3) [Exempt document of company registered in Scotland]** If the company is registered in Scotland, the following documents are exempt from stamp duty–

(a) every conveyance relating solely to property, which forms part of the company's assets and which, after the execution of the conveyance, is or remains the company's property for the benefit of its creditors,

(b) any articles of roup or sale, submission and every other instrument and writing whatsoever relating solely to the company's property, and

(c) every deed or writing forming part of the proceedings in the winding up.

"Conveyance" here includes assignation, instrument, discharge, writing and deed.

## 191 Company's books to be evidence

**191** Where a company is being wound up, all books and papers of the company and of the liquidators are, as between the contributories of the company, prima facie evidence of the truth of all matters purporting to be recorded in them.

## 192 Information as to pending liquidations

**192(1) [Statement to registrar]** If the winding up of a company is not concluded within one year after its commencment, the liquidator shall, at such intervals as may be prescribed, until the winding up is concluded, send to the registrar of companies a statement in the prescribed form and containing the prescribed particulars with respect to the proceedings in, and position of, the liquidation.

**Note**

S. 192(1) modified by Scotland Act 1998, s. 125(1) and Sch. 8, para. 23(1), (4), (5) so that anything directed to be done by the registrar of companies in Scotland or the assistant registrar of friendly societies for Scotland by virtue of s. 192(1) as applied in relation to friendly societies, industrial and provident societies or building societies shall be done to or by the Accountant in Bankruptcy as from 1 July 1999 (see SI 1998/3178 (C 79), art. 2).

**192(2) [Penalty on default]** If a liquidator fails to comply with this section, he is liable to a fine and, for continued contravention, to a daily default fine.

## 193 Unclaimed dividends (Scotland)

**193(1) [Application]** The following applies where a company registered in Scotland has been wound up, and is about to be dissolved.

**193(2) [Liquidator to lodge unclaimed money in bank]** The liquidator shall lodge in an appropriate bank or institution as defined in section 73(1) of the Bankruptcy (Scotland) Act 1985 (not being a bank or institution in or of which the liquidator is an acting partner, manager, agent or cashier) in the name of the Accountant of Court the whole unclaimed dividends and unapplied or undistributable balances, and the deposit receipts shall be transmitted to the Accountant of Court.

**193(3) [Application of Bankruptcy (Scotland) Act]** The provisions of section 58 of the Bankruptcy (Scotland) Act 1985 (so far as consistent with this Act and the Companies Act) apply with any necessary modifications to sums lodged in a bank or institution under this section as they apply to sums deposited under section 57 of the Act first mentioned.

## 194 Resolutions passed at adjourned meetings

**194** Where a resolution is passed at an adjourned meeting of a company's creditors or contributories, the resolution is treated for all purposes as having been passed on the date on which it was in fact passed, and not as having been passed on any earlier date.

## 195 Meetings to ascertain wishes of creditors or contributories

**195(1) [Power of court]** The court may–

(a) as to all matters relating to the winding up of a company, have regard to the wishes of the creditors or contributories (as proved to it by any sufficient evidence), and

(b) if it thinks fit, for the purpose of ascertaining those wishes, direct meetings of the creditors or contributories to be called, held and conducted in such manner as the court directs, and appoint a person to act as chairman of any such meeting and report the result of it to the court.

**195(2) [Creditors]** In the case of creditors, regard shall be had to the value of each creditor's debt.

**195(3) [Contributories]** In the case of contributories, regard shall be had to the number of votes conferred on each contributory by the Companies Act or the articles.

## 196 Judicial notice of court documents

**196** In all proceedings under this Part, all courts, judges and persons judicially acting, and all officers, judicial or ministerial, of any court, or employed in enforcing the process of any court shall take judicial notice–

(a) of the signature of any officer of the High Court or of a county court in England and Wales, or of the Court of Session or a sheriff court in Scotland, or of the High Court in Northern Ireland, and also

(b) of the official seal or stamp of the several offices of the High Court in England and Wales or Northern Ireland, or of the Court of Session, appended to or impressed on any document made, issued or signed under the provisions of this Act or the Companies Act, or any official copy of such a document.

## 197 Commission for receiving evidence

**197(1) [Courts for examination of witnesses]** When a company is wound up in England and Wales or in Scotland,the court may refer the whole or any part of the examination of witnesses–

(a) to a specified county court in England and Wales, or

(b) to the sheriff principal for a specified sheriffdom in Scotland, or

(c) to the High Court in Northern Ireland or a specified Northern Ireland County Court,

(**"specified"** meaning specified in the order of the winding-up court).

**197(2) [Commissioners for taking evidence]** Any person exercising jurisdiction as a judge of the court to which the reference is made (or, in Scotland, the sheriff principal to whom it is made) shall then, by virtue of this section, be a commissioner for the purpose of taking the evidence of those witnesses.

**197(3) [Power of judge or sheriff principal]** The judge or sheriff principal has in the matter referred the same power of summoning and examining witnesses, of requiring the production and delivery of documents, of punishing defaults by witnesses, and of allowing costs and expenses to witnesses, as the court which made the winding-up order.

These powers are in addition to any which the judge or sheriff principal might lawfully exercise apart from this section.

**197(4) [Return or report re examination]** The examination so taken shall be returned or reported to the court which made the order in such manner as that court requests.

**197(5) [Northern Ireland]** This section extends to Northern Ireland.

## 198 Court order for examination of persons in Scotland

**198(1) [Examination of any person on affairs of company]** The court may direct the examination in Scotland of any person for the time being in Scotland (whether a contributory of the company or not), in regard to the trade, dealings, affairs or property of any company in the course of being wound up, or of any person being a contributory of the company, so far as the company may be interested by reason of his being a contributory.

**198(2) [Directions to take examination]** The order or commission to take the examination shall be directed to the sheriff principal of the sheriffdom in which the person to be examined is residing or happens to be for the time; and the sheriff principal shall summon the person to appear before him at a time and place to be specified in the summons for examination on oath as a witness or as a haver, and to produce any books or papers called for which are in his possession or power.

**198(3) [Duties of sheriff principal re examination]** The sheriff principal may take the examination either orally or on written interrogatories, and shall report the same in writing in the usual form to the court, and shall transmit with the report the books and papers produced, if the originals are required and specified by the order or commission, or otherwise copies or extracts authenticated by the sheriff.

**198(4) [Where person fails to appear for examination]** If a person so summoned fails to appear at the time and place specified, or refuses to be examined or to make the production required, the sheriff principal shall proceed against him as a witness or haver duly cited; and failing to appear or refusing to give evidence or make production may be proceeded against by the law of Scotland.

**198(5) [Fees and allowances]** The sheriff principal is entitled to such fees, and the witness is entitled to such allowances, as sheriffs principal when acting as commissioners under appointment from the Court of Session and as witnesses and havers are entitled to in the like cases according to the law and practice of Scotland.

**198(6) [Objection by witness]** If any objection is stated to the sheriff principal by the witness, either on the ground of his incompetency as a witness, or as to the production required, or on any other ground, the sheriff principal may, if he thinks fit, report the objection to the court, and suspend the examination of the witness until it has been disposed of by the court.

## 199 Costs of application for leave to proceed (Scottish companies)

**199** Where a petition or application for leave to proceed with an action or proceeding against a company which is being wound up in Scotland is unopposed and is granted by the court, the costs of the petition or application shall, unless the court otherwise directs, be added to the amount of the petitioner's or applicant's claim against the company.

## 200 Affidavits etc. in United Kingdom and overseas

**200(1) [Swearing of affidavit]** An affidavit required to be sworn under or for the purposes of this Part may be sworn in the United Kingdom, or elsewhere in Her Majesty's dominions, before any court, judge or person lawfully authorised to take and receive affidavits, or before any of Her Majesty's consuls or vice-consuls in any place outside Her dominions.

**200(2) [Judicial notice of signatures etc.]** All courts, judges, justices, commissioners and persons acting judicially shall take judicial notice of the seal or stamp or signature (as the case may be) of any such court, judge, person, consul or vice-consul attached, appended or subscribed to any such affidavit, or to any other document to be used for the purposes of this Part.

# Chapter IX – Dissolution of Companies After Winding Up

## 201 Dissolution (voluntary winding up)

**201(1) [Application]** This section applies, in the case of a company wound up voluntarily, where the liquidator has sent to the registrar of companies his final account and return under section 94 (members' voluntary) or section 106 (creditors' voluntary).

**201(2) [Duty of registrar]** The registrar on receiving the account and return shall forthwith register them; and on the expiration of 3 months from the registration of the return the company is deemed to be dissolved.

**201(3) [Power of court re deferring date]** However, the court may, on the application of the liquidator or any other person who appears to the court to be interested, make an order deferring the date at which the dissolution of the company is to take effect for such time as the court thinks fit.

**201(4) [Copy of order to registrar]** It is the duty of the person on whose application an order of the court under this section is made within 7 days after the making of the order to deliver to the registrar an office copy of the order for registration; and if that person fails to do so he is liable to a fine and, for continued contravention, to a daily default fine.

## 202 Early dissolution (England and Wales)

**202(1) [Application]** This section applies where an order for the winding up of a company has been made by the court in England and Wales.

**202(2) [Official receiver may apply for dissolution]** The official receiver, if–

(a) he is the liquidator of the company, and

(b) it appears to him–
  (i) that the realisable assets of the company are insufficient to cover the expenses of the winding up, and
  (ii) that the affairs of the company do not require any further investigation,

may at any time apply to the registrar of companies for the early dissolution of the company.

**202(3) [Notice by official receiver]** Before making that application, the official receiver shall give not less than 28 days' notice of his intention to do so to the company's creditors and contributories and, if there is an administrative receiver of the company, to that receiver.

**202(4) [Effect of notice on official receiver]** With the giving of that notice the official receiver ceases (subject to any directions under the next section) to be required to perform any duties imposed on him in relation to the company, its creditors or contributories by virtue of any provision of this Act, apart from a duty to make an application under subsection (2) of this section.

**202(5) [Duty of registrar]** On the receipt of the official receiver's application under subsection (2) the registrar shall forthwith register it and, at the end of the period of 3 months beginning with the day of the registration of the application, the company shall be dissolved.

However, the Secretary of State may, on the application of the official receiver or any other person who appears to the Secretary of State to be interested, give directions under section 203 at any time before the end of that period.

## 203 Consequence of notice under s. 202

**203(1) [Application for directions]** Where a notice has been given under section 202(3), the official receiver or any creditor or contributory of the company, or the administrative receiver of the company (if there is one) may apply to the Secretary of State for directions under this section.

**203(2) [Grounds for application]** The grounds on which that application may be made are–

(a) that the realisable assets of the company are sufficient to cover the expenses of the winding up;

(b) that the affairs of the company do require further investigation; or

(c) that for any other reason the early dissolution of the company is inappropriate.

**203(3) [Scope of directions]** Directions under this section–

(a) are directions making such provision as the Secretary of State thinks fit for enabling the winding up of the company to proceed as if no notice had been given under section 202(3), and

(b) may, in the case of an application under section 202(5), include a direction deferring the date at which the dissolution of the company is to take effect for such period as the Secretary of State thinks fit.

**203(4) [Appeal to court]** An appeal to the court lies from any decision of the Secretary of State on an application for directions under this section.

**203(5) [Copy of directions etc. to registrar]** It is the duty of the person on whose application any directions are given under this section, or in whose favour an appeal with respect to an application for such directions is determined, within 7 days after the giving of the directions or the determination of the appeal, to deliver to the registrar of companies for registration such a copy of the directions or determination as is prescribed.

**203(6) [Penalty on default re s. 203(5)]** If a person without reasonable excuse fails to deliver a copy as required by subsection (5), he is liable to a fine and, for continued contravention, to a daily default fine.

## 204 Early dissolution (Scotland)

**204(1) [Application]** This section applies where a winding-up order has been made by the court in Scotland.

**204(2) [Application by liquidator]** If after a meeting or meetings under section 138 (appointment of liquidator in Scotland) it appears to the liquidator that the realisable assets of the company are insufficient to cover the expenses of the winding up, he may apply to the court for an order that the company be dissolved.

**204(3) [Court order]** Where the liquidator makes that application, if the court is satisfied that the realisable assets of the company are insufficient to cover the expenses of the winding up and it appears to the court appropriate to do so, the court shall make an order that the company be dissolved in accordance with this section.

**204(4) [Copy of order to registrar etc.]** A copy of the order shall within 14 days from its date be forwarded by the liquidator to the registrar of companies, who shall forthwith register it; and, at the end of the period of 3 months beginning with the day of the registration of the order, the company shall be dissolved.

**204(5) [Court may defer dissolution]** The court may, on an application by any person who appears to the court to have an interest, order that the date at which the dissolution of the company is to take effect shall be deferred for such period as the court thinks fit.

**204(6) [Copy of s. 204(5) order to registrar]** It is the duty of the person on whose application an order is made under subsection (5), within 7 days after the making of the order, to deliver to the registrar of companies such a copy of the order as is prescribed.

**204(7) [Penalty for non-compliance with s. 204(4)]** If the liquidator without reasonable excuse fails to comply with the requirements of subsection (4), he is liable to a fine and, for continued contravention, to a daily default fine.

**204(8) [Penalty for non-compliance with s. 204(6)]** If a person without reasonable excuse fails to deliver a copy as required by subsection (6), he is liable to a fine and, for continued contravention, to a daily default fine.

## 205 Dissolution otherwise than under s. 202–204

**205(1) [Application]** This section applies where the registrar of companies receives–

(a) a notice served for the purposes of section 172(8) (final meeting of creditors and vacation of office by liquidator), or

(b) a notice from the official receiver that the winding up of a company by the court is complete.

**205(2) [Duty of registrar etc.]** The registrar shall, on receipt of the notice, forthwith register it; and, subject as follows, at the end of the period of 3 months beginning with the day of the registration of the notice, the company shall be dissolved.

**205(3) [Deferral by Secretary of State]** The Secretary of State may, on the application of the official receiver or any other person who appears to the Secretary of State to be interested, give a direction deferring the date at which the dissolution of the company is to take effect for such period as the Secretary of State thinks fit.

**205(4) [Appeal to court]** An appeal to the court lies from any decision of the Secretary of State on an application for a direction under subsection (3).

**205(5) [Non-application of s. 205(3) in Scotland]** Subsection (3) does not apply in a case where the winding-up order was made by the court in Scotland, but in such a case the court may, on an application by any person appearing to the court to have an interest, order that the date at which the dissolution of the company is to take effect shall be deferred for such period as the court thinks fit.

**205(6) [Copy of direction etc. to registrar]** It is the duty of the person–

(a) on whose application a direction is given under subsection (3);

(b) in whose favour an appeal with respect to an application for such a direction is determined; or

(c) on whose application an order is made under subsection (5),

within 7 days after the giving of the direction, the determination of the appeal or the making of the order, to deliver to the registrar for registration such a copy of the direction, determination or order as is prescribed.

**205(7) [Penalty for non-compliance with s. 205(6)]** If a person without reasonable excuse fails to deliver a copy as required by subsection (6), he is liable to a fine and, for continued contravention, to a daily default fine.

# Chapter X – Malpractice before and during Liquidation; Penalisation of Companies and Company Officers; Investigations and Prosecutions

## OFFENCES OF FRAUD, DECEPTION, ETC.

## 206 Fraud, etc. in anticipation of winding up

**206(1) [Offences by officers]** When a company is ordered to be wound up by the court, or passes a resolution for voluntary winding up, any person, being a past or present officer of the company, is deemed to have committed an offence if, within the 12 months immediately preceding the commencement of the winding up, he has–

(a) concealed any part of the company's property to the value of £500 or more, or concealed any debt due to or from the company, or

(b) fraudulently removed any part of the company's property to the value of £500 or more, or

(c) concealed, destroyed, mutilated or falsified any book or paper affecting or relating to the company's property or affairs, or

(d) made any false entry in any book or paper affecting or relating to the company's property or affairs, or

(e) fraudulently parted with, altered or made any omission in any document affecting or relating to the company's property or affairs, or

(f) pawned, pledged or disposed of any property of the company which has been obtained on credit and has not been paid for (unless the pawning, pledging or disposal was in the ordinary way of the company's business).

**206(2) [Further offences]** Such a person is deemed to have committed an offence if within the period above mentioned he has been privy to the doing by others of any of the things mentioned in paragraphs (c), (d) and (e) of subsection (1); and he commits an offence if, at any time after the commencement of the winding up, he does any of the things mentioned in paragraphs (a) to (f) of that subsection, or is privy to the doing by others of any of the things mentioned in paragraphs (c) to (e) of it.

**206(3) ["Officer"]** For purposes of this section, **"officer"** includes a shadow director.

**206(4) [Defences]** It is a defence–

(a) for a person charged under paragraph (a) or (f) of subsection (1) (or under subsection (2) in respect of the things mentioned in either of those two paragraphs) to prove that he had no intent to defraud, and

(b) for a person charged under paragraph (c) or (d) of subsection (1) (or under subsection (2) in respect of the things mentioned in either of those two paragraphs) to prove that he had no intent to conceal the state of affairs of the company or to defeat the law.

**206(5) [Offence re person pawning property etc. as in s. 206(1)(f)]** Where a person pawns, pledges or disposes of any property in circumstances which amount to an offence under subsection (1)(f), every person who takes in pawn or pledge, or otherwise receives, the property knowing it to be pawned, pledged or disposed of in such circumstances, is guilty of an offence.

**206(6) [Penalty]** A person guilty of an offence under this section is liable to imprisonment or a fine, or both.

**206(7) [Increase, reduction of sums in s. 206(1)(a), (b)]** The money sums specified in paragraphs (a) and (b) of subsection (1) are subject to increase or reduction by order under section 416 in Part XV.

**Note**

The amount in s. 206(1)(a), (b) increased from £120 by the Insolvency Proceedings (Monetary Limits) Order 1986 (SI 1986/1996) as from 29 December 1986.

## 207 Transactions in fraud of creditors

**207(1) [Offences by officers]** When a company is ordered to be wound up by the court or passes a resolution for voluntary winding up, a person is deemed to have committed an offence if he, being at the time an officer of the company–

(a) has made or caused to be made any gift or transfer of, or charge on, or has caused or connived at the levying of any execution against, the company's property, or

(b) has concealed or removed any part of the company's property since, or within 2 months before, the date of any unsatisfied judgment or order for the payment of money obtained against the company.

**207(2) [Exception]** A person is not guilty of an offence under this section–

(a) by reason of conduct constituting an offence under subsection (1)(a) which occurred more than 5 years before the commencement of the winding up, or

(b) if he proves that, at the time of the conduct constituting the offence, he had no intent to defraud the company's creditors.

**207(3) [Penalty]** A person guilty of an offence under this section is liable to imprisonment or a fine, or both.

## 208 Misconduct in course of winding up

**208(1) [Offences by officers]** When a company is being wound up, whether by the court or voluntarily, any person, being a past or present officer of the company, commits an offence if he–

(a) does not to the best of his knowledge and belief fully and truly discover to the liquidator all the company's property, and how and to whom and for what consideration and when the company disposed of any part of that property (except such part as has been disposed of in the ordinary way of the company's business), or

(b) does not deliver up to the liquidator (or as he directs) all such part of the company's property as is in his custody or under his control, and which he is required by law to deliver up, or

(c) does not deliver up to the liquidator (or as he directs) all books and papers in his custody or under his control belonging to the company and which he is required by law to deliver up, or

(d) knowing or believing that a false debt has been proved by any person in the winding up, fails to inform the liquidator as soon as practicable, or

(e) after the commencement of the winding up, prevents the production of any book or paper affecting or relating to the company's property or affairs.

**208(2) [Further offences]** Such a person commits an offence if after the commencement of the winding up he attempts to account for any part of the company's property by fictitious losses or expenses; and he is deemed to have committed that offence if he has so attempted at any meeting of the company's creditors within the 12 months immediately preceding the commencement of the winding up.

**208(3) ["Officer"]** For purposes of this section, **"officer"** includes a shadow director.

**208(4) [Defences]** It is a defence–

(a) for a person charged under paragraph (a), (b) or (c) of subsection (1) to prove that he had no intent to defraud, and

(b) for a person charged under paragraph (e) of that subsection to prove that he had no intent to conceal the state of affairs of the company or to defeat the law.

**208(5) [Penalty]** A person guilty of an offence under this section is liable to imprisonment or a fine, or both.

## 209 Falsification of company's books

**209(1) [Offence by officer or contributory]** When a company is being wound up, an officer or contributory of the company commits an offence if he destroys, mutilates, alters or falsifies any books, papers or securities, or makes or is privy to the making of any false or fraudulent entry in any register, book of account or document belonging to the company with intent to defraud or deceive any person.

**209(2) [Penalty]** A person guilty of an offence under this section is liable to imprisonment or a fine, or both.

## 210 Material omissions from statement relating to company's affairs

**210(1) [Offence by past or present officer]** When a company is being wound up, whether by the court or voluntarily, any person, being a past or present officer of the company, commits an offence if he makes any material omission in any statement relating to the company's affairs.

**210(2) [Offence prior to winding up]** When a company has been ordered to be wound up by the court, or has passed a resolution for voluntary winding up, any such person is deemed to have committed that offence if, prior to the winding up, he has made any material omission in any such statement.

**210(3) ["Officer"]** For purposes of this section, **"officer"** includes a shadow director.

**210(4) [Defence]** It is a defence for a person charged under this section to prove that he had no intent to defraud.

**210(5) [Penalty]** A person guilty of an offence under this section is liable to imprisonment or a fine, or both.

## 211 False representations to creditors

**211(1) [Offences by past or present officer]** When a company is being wound up, whether by the court or voluntarily, any person, being a past or present officer of the company–

(a) commits an offence if he makes any false representation or commits any other fraud for the purpose of obtaining the consent of the company's creditors or any of them to an agreement with reference to the company's affairs or to the winding up, and

(b) is deemed to have committed that offence if, prior to the winding up, he has made any false representation, or committed any other fraud, for that purpose.

**211(2) ["Officer"]** For purposes of this section, **"officer"** includes a shadow director.

**211(3) [Penalty]** A person guilty of an offence under this section is liable to imprisonment or a fine, or both.

### PENALISATION OF DIRECTORS AND OFFICERS

## 212 Summary remedy against delinquent directors, liquidators, etc.

**212(1) [Application]** This section applies if in the course of the winding up of a company it appears that a person who–

(a) is or has been an officer of the company,

(b) has acted as liquidator, administrator or administrative receiver of the company, or

(c) not being a person falling within paragraph (a) or (b), is or has been concerned, or has taken part, in the promotion, formation or management of the company,

has misapplied or retained, or become accountable for, any money or other property of the company, or been guilty of any misfeasance or breach of any fiduciary or other duty in relation to the company.

**212(2) [Interpretation]** The reference in subsection (1) to any misfeasance or breach of any fiduciary or other duty in relation to the company includes, in the case of a person who has acted as liquidator or administrator of the company, any misfeasance or breach of any fiduciary or other duty in connection with the carrying out of his functions as liquidator or administrator of the company.

**212(3) [Examination, orders]** The court may, on the application of the official receiver or the liquidator, or of any creditor or contributory, examine into the conduct of the person falling within subsection (1) and compel him–

(a) to repay, restore or account for the money or property or any part of it, with interest at such rate as the court thinks just, or

(b) to contribute such sum to the company's assets by way of compensation in respect of the misfeasance or breach of fiduciary or other duty as the court thinks just.

**212(4) [Limit on s. 212(3) application]** The power to make an application under subsection (3) in relation to a person who has acted as liquidator or administrator of the company is not exercisable, except with the leave of the court, after that person has had his release.

**212(5) [Exercise of s. 212(3) power]** The power of a contributory to make an application under subsection (3) is not exercisable except with the leave of the court, but is exercisable notwithstanding that he will not benefit from any order the court may make on the application.

## 213 Fraudulent trading

**213(1) [Application]** If in the course of the winding up of a company it appears that any business of the company has been carried on with intent to defraud creditors of the company or creditors of any other person, or for any fraudulent purpose, the following has effect.

**213(2) [Court may hold persons liable]** The court, on the application of the liquidator may declare that any persons who were knowingly parties to the carrying on of the business in the manner above-mentioned are to be liable to make such contributions (if any) to the company's assets as the court thinks proper.

## 214 Wrongful trading

**214(1) [Declaration by court, on application]** Subject to subsection (3) below, if in the course of the winding up of a company it appears that subsection (2) of this section applies in relation to a person who is or has been a director of the company, the court, on the application of the liquidator, may declare that that person is to be liable to make such contribution (if any) to the company's assets as the court thinks proper.

**214(2) [Application]** This subsection applies in relation to a person if–

(a) the company has gone into insolvent liquidation,

(b) at some time before the commencement of the winding up of the company, that person knew or ought to have concluded that there was no reasonable prospect that the company would avoid going into insolvent liquidation, and

(c) that person was a director of the company at that time;

but the court shall not make a declaration under this section in any case where the time mentioned in paragraph (b) above was before 28th April 1986.

**214(3) [Limit on declaration]** The court shall not make a declaration under this section with respect to any person if it is satisfied that after the condition specified in subsection (2)(b) was first satisfied in relation to him that person took every step with a view to minimising the potential loss to the company's creditors as (assuming him to have known that there was no reasonable prospect that the company would avoid going into insolvent liquidation) he ought to have taken.

**214(4) [Interpretation of s. 214(2), (3)]** For the purposes of subsections (2) and (3), the facts which a director of a company ought to know or ascertain, the conclusions which he ought to reach and the steps which he ought to take are those which would be known or ascertained, or reached or taken, by a reasonably diligent person having both–

(a) the general knowledge, skill and experience that may reasonably be expected of a person carrying out the same functions as are carried out by that director in relation to the company, and

(b) the general knowledge, skill and experience that that director has.

**214(5) [Interpretation of s. 214(4)]** The reference in subsection (4) to the functions carried out in relation to a company by a director of the company includes any functions which he does not carry out but which have been entrusted to him.

**214(6) [Interpretation re insolvent liquidation]** For the purposes of this section a company goes into insolvent liquidation if it goes into liquidation at a time when its assets are insufficient for the payment of its debts and other liabilities and the expenses of the winding up.

**214(7) ["Director"]** In this section **"director"** includes a shadow director.

**214(8) [S. 213]** This section is without prejudice to section 213.

## 215 Proceedings under s. 213, 214

**215(1) [Evidence by liquidator]** On the hearing of an application under section 213 or 214, the liquidator may himself give evidence or call witnesses.

**215(2) [Further court directions]** Where under either section the court makes a declaration, it may give such further directions as it thinks proper for giving effect to the declaration; and in particular, the court may–

(a) provide for the liability of any person under the declaration to be a charge on any debt or obligation due from the company to him, or on any mortgage or charge or any interest in a mortgage or charge on assets of the company held by or vested in him, or any person on his behalf, or any person claiming as assignee from or through the person liable or any person acting on his behalf, and

(b) from time to time make such further order as may be necessary for enforcing any charge imposed under this subsection.

**215(3) ["Assignee"]** For the purposes of subsection (2), **"assignee"**–

(a) includes a person to whom or in whose favour, by the directions of the person made liable, the debt, obligation, mortgage or charge was created, issued or transferred or the interest created, but

(b) does not include an assignee for valuable consideration (not including consideration by way of marriage) given in good faith and without notice of any of the matters on the ground of which the declaration is made.

**215(4) [Directions re priority of debts]** Where the court makes a declaration under either section in relation to a person who is a creditor of the company, it may direct that the whole or any part of any debt owed by the company to that person and any interest thereon shall rank in priority after all other debts owed by the company and after any interest on those debts.

**215(5) [S. 213, 214]** Sections 213 and 214 have effect notwithstanding that the person concerned may be criminally liable in respect of matters on the ground of which the declaration under the section is to be made.

## 216 Restriction on re-use of company names

**216(1) [Application]** This section applies to a person where a company ("the liquidating company") has gone into insolvent liquidation on or after the appointed day and he was a director or shadow director of the company at any time in the period of 12 months ending with the day before it went into liquidation.

**216(2) [Prohibited name]** For the purposes of this section, a name is a prohibited name in relation to such a person if–

(a) it is a name by which the liquidating company was known at any time in that period of 12 months, or

(b) it is a name which is so similar to a name falling within paragraph (a) as to suggest an association with that company.

**216(3) [Restriction]** Except with leave of the court or in such circumstances as may be prescribed, a person to whom this section applies shall not at any time in the period of 5 years beginning with the day on which the liquidating company went into liquidation–

(a) be a director of any other company that is known by a prohibited name, or

(b) in any way, whether directly or indirectly, be concerned or take part in the promotion, formation or management of any such company, or

(c) in any way, whether directly or indirectly, be concerned or take part in the carrying on of a business carried on (otherwise than by a company) under a prohibited name.

**216(4) [Penalty]** If a person acts in contravention of this section, he is liable to imprisonment or a fine, or both.

**216(5) ["The court"]** In subsection (3) **"the court"** means any court having jurisdiction to wind up companies; and on an application for leave under that subsection, the Secretary of State or the official receiver may appear and call the attention of the court to any matters which seem to him to be relevant.

**216(6) [Interpretation re name]** References in this section, in relation to any time, to a name by which a company is known are to the name of the company at that time or to any name under which the company carries on business at that time.

**216(7) [Interpretation re insolvent liquidation]** For the purposes of this section a company goes into insolvent liquidation if it goes into liquidation at a time when its assets are insufficient for the payment of its debts and other liabilities and the expenses of the winding up.

**216(8) ["Company"]** In this section **"company"** includes a company which may be wound up under Part V of this Act.

## 217 Personal liability for debts, following contravention of s. 216

**217(1) [Personal liability]** A person is personally responsible for all the relevant debts of a company if at any time–

(a) in a contravention of section 216, he is involved in the management of the company, or

(b) as a person who is involved in the management of the company, he acts or is willing to act on instructions given (without the leave of the court) by a person whom he knows at that time to be in contravention in relation to the company of section 216.

**217(2) [Joint and several liability]** Where a person is personally responsible under this section for the relevant debts of a company, he is jointly and severally liable in respect of those debts with the company and any other person who, whether under this section or otherwise, is so liable.

**217(3) [Relevant debts of company]** For the purposes of this section the relevant debts of a company are–

(a) in relation to a person who is personally responsible under paragraph (a) of subsection (1), such debts and other liabilities of the company as are incurred at a time when that person was involved in the management of the company, and

(b) in relation to a person who is personally responsible under paragraph (b) of that subsection, such debts and other liabilities of the company as are incurred at a time when that person was acting or was willing to act on instructions given as mentioned in that paragraph.

**217(4) [Person involved in management]** For the purposes of this section, a person is involved in the management of a company if he is a director of the company or if he is concerned, whether directly or indirectly, or takes part, in the management of the company.

**217(5) [Interpretation]** For the purposes of this section a person who, as a person involved in the management of a company, has at any time acted on instructions given (without the leave of the court) by a person whom he knew at that time to be in contravention in relation to the company of section 216 is presumed, unless the contrary is shown, to have been willing at any time thereafter to act on any instructions given by that person.

**217(6) ["Company"]** In this section **"company"** includes a company which may be wound up under Part V.

INVESTIGATION AND PROSECUTION OF MALPRACTICE

## 218 Prosecution of delinquent officers and members of company

**218(1) [Court may direct matter to be referred for prosecution]** If it appears to the court in the course of a winding up by the court that any past or present officer, or any member, of the company has been guilty of any offence in relation to the company for which he is criminally liable, the court may (either on the application of a person interested in the winding up or of its own motion) direct the liquidator to refer the matter to the prosecuting authority.

**218(2) ["The prosecuting authority"]** **"The prosecuting authority"** means–

(a) in the case of a winding up in England and Wales, the Director of Public Prosecutions, and

(b) in the case of a winding up in Scotland, the Lord Advocate.

**218(3) [Report – winding up by court]** If in the case of a winding up by the court in England and Wales it appears to the liquidator, not being the official receiver, that any past or present officer of the company, or any member of it, has been guilty of an offence in relation to the company for which he is criminally liable, the liquidator shall report the matter to the official receiver.

**218(4) [Report – voluntary winding up]** If it appears to the liquidator in the course of a voluntary winding up that any past or present officer of the company, or any member of it, has been guilty of an offence in relation to the company for which he is criminally liable, he shall–

(a) forthwith report the matter to the prosecuting authority, and

(b) furnish to that authority such information and give to him such access to and facilities for inspecting and taking copies of documents (being information or documents in the possession or under the control of the liquidator and relating to the matter in question) as the authority requires.

**218(5) [Reference to Secretary of State]** Where a report is made to him under subsection (4), the prosecuting authority may, if he thinks fit, refer the matter to the Secretary of State for further enquiry; and the Secretary of State–

(a) shall thereupon investigate the matter reported to him and such other matters relating to the affairs of the company as appear to him to require investigation, and

(b) for the purpose of his investigation may exercise any of the powers which are exercisable by inspectors appointed under section 431 or 432 of the Companies Act to investigate a company's affairs.

**History**

In s. 218(5) para. (a) substituted by CA 1989, s. 78 as from 21 February 1990 (see SI 1990/142 (C 5), art. 4); para. (a) formerly read as follows:

"(a) shall thereupon investigate the matter, and"

**218(6) [Court may direct liquidator to make report]** If it appears to the court in the course of a voluntary winding up that–

(a) any past or present officer of the company, or any member of it, has been guilty as above-mentioned, and

(b) no report with respect to the matter has been made by the liquidator to the prosecuting authority under subsection (4),

the court may (on the application of any person interested in the winding up or of its own motion) direct the liquidator to make such a report.

On a report being made accordingly, this section has effect as though the report had been made in pursuance of subsection (4).

## 219 Obligations arising under s. 218

**219(1) [Assistance to investigation by Secretary of State]** For the purpose of an investigation by the Secretary of State under section 218(5), any obligation imposed on a person by any provision of the Companies Act to produce documents or give information to, or otherwise to assist, inspectors appointed as mentioned in that subsection is to be regarded as an obligation similarly to assist the Secretary of State in his investigation.

**219(2) [Answer may be used as evidence]** An answer given by a person to a question put to him in exercise of the powers conferred by section 218(5) may be used in evidence against him.

**219(3) [Liquidator and officer to assist, where criminal proceedings instituted]** Where criminal proceedings are instituted by the prosecuting authority or the Secretary of State following any report or reference under section 218, it is the duty of the liquidator and every officer and agent of the company past and present (other than the defendant or defender) to give to that authority or the Secretary of State (as the case may be) all assistance in connection with the prosecution which he is reasonably able to give.

For this purpose **"agent"** includes any banker or solicitor of the company and any person employed by the company as auditor, whether that person is or is not an officer of the company.

**219(4) [Direction by court re assistance]** If a person fails or neglects to give assistance in the manner required by subsection (3), the court may, on the application of the prosecuting authority or the Secretary of State (as the case may be) direct the person to comply with that subsection; and if the application is made with respect to a liquidator, the court may (unless it appears that the failure or neglect to comply was due to the liquidator not having in his hands sufficient assets of the company to enable him to do so) direct that the costs shall be borne by the liquidator personally.

# PART V – WINDING UP OF UNREGISTERED COMPANIES

**Note**

Re application of Pt. V to insolvent partnerships, see the Insolvent Partnerships Order (SI 1994/2421), especially reg. 7–9, 11, 12, 16, Sch. 3–6, 8.

## 220 Meaning of "unregistered company"

**220(1) ["Unregistered company"]** For the purposes of this Part, the expression **"unregistered company"** includes any association and any company, with the following exceptions–

(b) a company registered in any part of the United Kingdom under the Joint Stock Companies Acts or under the legislation (past or present) relating to companies in Great Britain.

**History**

In s. 220(1) the words "any trustee savings bank certified under the enactments relating to such banks" formerly appearing after the word "includes" ceased to have effect and repealed by virtue of s. 220(2).

In s. 220(1) para. (a) ceased to have effect and repealed by the Transport and Works Act 1992, s. 65(1)(f), 68(1), Sch. 4, Pt. I as from 1 January 1993 (see SI 1992/2784, art. 2); para. (a) formerly read as follows:

"(a) a railway company incorporated by Act of Parliament,"

**220(2) [Repeal of certain words]** On such day as the Treasury appoints by order under section 4(3) of the Trustee Savings Banks Act 1985, the words in subsection (1) from "any trustee" to "banks" cease to have effect and are hereby repealed.

**Note**

The relevant day is 5 July 1988 – see SI 1988/1168.

## 221 Winding up of unregistered companies

**221(1) [Application of winding-up provisions]** Subject to the provisions of this Part, any unregistered company may be wound up under this Act; and all the provisions of this Act and the Companies Act about winding up apply to an unregistered company with the exceptions and additions mentioned in the following subsections.

**221(2) [Principal place of business in Northern Ireland]** If an unregistered company has a principal place of business situated in Northern Ireland, it shall not be wound up under this Part unless it has a principal place of business situated in England and Wales or Scotland, or in both England and Wales and Scotland.

**221(3) [Deemed registration, registered office]** For the purpose of determining a court's winding-up jurisdiction, an unregistered company is deemed–

(a) to be registered in England and Wales or Scotland, according as its principal place of business is situated in England and Wales or Scotland, or

(b) if it has a principal place of business situated in both countries, to be registered in both countries;

and the principal place of business situated in that part of Great Britain in which proceedings are being instituted is, for all purposes of the winding up, deemed to be the registered office of the company.

**221(4) [No voluntary winding up]** No unregistered company shall be wound up under this Act voluntarily.

**221(5) [Circumstances for winding up]** The circumstances in which an unregistered company may be wound up are as follows–

(a) if the company is dissolved, or has ceased to carry on business, or is carrying on business only for the purpose of winding up its affairs;

(b) if the company is unable to pay its debts;

(c) if the court is of opinion that it is just and equitable that the company should be wound up.

**221(6)** (Repealed as from 21 July 1986 – see history note below)

**History**

The above date is appointed under Trustee Savings Bank Act 1985, s. 4(3) – see SI 1986/1223 (C 36); s. 221(6) formerly read as follows:

"A petition for winding up a trustee savings bank may be presented by the Trustee Savings Banks Central Board or by a commissioner appointed under section 35 of the Trustee Savings Banks Act 1981 as well as by any person authorised under Part IV of this Act to present a petition for the winding up of a company.

On such day as the Treasury appoints by order under section 4(3) of the Trustee Savings Bank Act 1985, this subsection ceases to have effect and is hereby repealed."

**221(7) [Scotland]** In Scotland, an unregistered company which the Court of Session has jurisdiction to wind up may be wound up by the court if there is subsisting a floating charge over property comprised in the company's property and undertaking, and the court is satisfied that the security of the creditor entitled to the benefit of the floating charge is in jeopardy.

For this purpose a creditor's security is deemed to be in jeopardy if the court is satisfied that events have occurred or are about to occur which render it unreasonable in the creditor's interest that the company should retain power to dispose of the property which is subject to the floating charge.

## 222 Inability to pay debts: unpaid creditor for £750 or more

**222(1) [Deemed inability to pay debts]** An unregistered company is deemed (for the purposes of section 221) unable to pay its debts if there is a creditor, by assignment or otherwise, to whom the company is indebted in a sum exceeding £750 then due and–

(a) the creditor has served on the company, by leaving at its principal place of business, or by delivering to the secretary or some director, manager or principal officer of the company, or by otherwise serving in such manner as the court may approve or direct, a written demand in the prescribed form requiring the company to pay the sum due, and

(b) the company has for 3 weeks after the service of the demand neglected to pay the sum or to secure or compound for it to the creditor's satisfaction.

**222(2) [Increase or reduction of s. 222(1) sum]** The money sum for the time being specified in subsection (1) is subject to increase or reduction by regulations under section 417 in Part XV; but no increase in the sum so specified affects any case in which the winding-up petition was presented before the coming into force of the increase.

## 223 Inability to pay debts: debt remaining unsatisfied after action brought

**223** An unregistered company is deemed (for the purposes of section 221) unable to pay its debts if an action or other proceeding has been instituted against any member for any debt or demand due, or claimed to be due, from the company, or from him in his character of member, and–

(a) notice in writing of the institution of the action or proceeding has been served on the company by leaving it at the company's principal place of business (or by delivering it to the secretary, or some director, manager or principal officer of the company, or by otherwise serving it in such manner as the court may approve or direct), and

(b) the company has not within 3 weeks after service of the notice paid, secured or compounded for the debt or demand, or procured the action or proceeding to be stayed or sisted, or indemnified the defendant or defender to his reasonable satisfaction against the action or proceeding, and against all costs, damages and expenses to be incurred by him because of it.

## 224 Inability to pay debts: other cases

**224(1) [Deemed inability to pay debts]** An unregistered company is deemed (for purposes of section 221) unable to pay its debts–

(a) if in England and Wales execution or other process issued on a judgment, decree or order obtained in any court in favour of a creditor against the company, or any member of it as such, or any person authorised to be sued as nominal defendant on behalf of the company, is returned unsatisfied;

(b) if in Scotland the induciae of a charge for payment on an extract decree, or an extract registered bond, or an extract registered protest, have expired without payment being made;

(c) if in Northern Ireland a certificate of unenforceability has been granted in respect of any judgment, decree or order obtained as mentioned in paragraph (a);

(d) it is otherwise proved to the satisfaction of the court that the company is unable to pay its debts as they fall due.

**224(2) [Deemed inability – another situation]** An unregistered company is also deemed unable to pay its debts if it is proved to the satisfaction of the court that the value of the company's assets is less than the amount of its liabilities, taking into account its contingent and prospective liabilities.

## 225 Oversea company may be wound up though dissolved

**225** Where a company incorporated outside Great Britain which has been carrying on business in Great Britain ceases to carry on business in Great Britain, it may be wound up as an unregistered company under this Act, notwithstanding that it has been dissolved or otherwise ceased to exist as a company under or by virtue of the laws of the country under which it was incorporated.

## 226 Contributories in winding up of unregistered company

**226(1) [Deemed contributory]** In the event of an unregistered company being wound up, every person is deemed a contributory who is liable to pay or contribute to the payment of any debt or liability of the company, or to pay or contribute to the payment of any sum for the adjustment of the rights of members among themselves, or to pay or contribute to the payment of the expenses of winding up the company.

**226(2) [Liability for contribution]** Every contributory is liable to contribute to the company's assets all sums due from him in respect of any such liability as is mentioned above.

**226(3) [Unregistered company re mines in stannaries]** In the case of an unregistered company engaged in or formed for working mines within the stannaries, a past member is not liable to contribute to the assets if he has ceased to be a member for 2 years or more either before the mine ceased to be worked or before the date of the winding-up order.

**226(4) [Death, bankruptcy, insolvency of contributory]** In the event of the death, bankruptcy or insolvency of any contributory, the provisions of this Act with respect to the personal representatives, to the heirs and legatees of heritage of the heritable estate in Scotland of deceased contributories, and to the trustees of bankrupt or insolvent contributories, respectively apply.

## 227 Power of court to stay, sist or restrain proceedings

**227** The provisions of this Part with respect to staying, sisting or restraining actions and proceedings against a company at any time after the presentation of a petition for winding up and before the making of a winding-up order extend, in the case of an unregistered company, where the application to stay, sist or restrain is presented by a creditor, to actions and proceedings against any contributory of the company.

## 228 Actions stayed on winding-up order

**228** Where an order has been made for winding up an unregistered company, no action or proceeding shall be proceeded with or commenced against any contributory of the company in respect of any debt of the company , except by leave of the court, and subject to such terms as the court may impose.

## 229 Provisions of this Part to be cumulative

**229(1) [Pt. V in addition to Pt. IV]** The provisions of this Part with respect to unregistered companies are in addition to and not in restriction of any provisions in Part IV with respect to winding up companies by the court; and the court or liquidator may exercise any powers or do any act in the case of unregistered companies which might be exercised or done by it or him in winding up companies formed and registered under the Companies Act.

**229(2) [Unregistered company not usually company under Companies Act]** However, an unregistered company is not, except in the event of its being wound up, deemed to be a company under the Companies Act, and then only to the extent provided by this Part of this Act.

# PART VI – MISCELLANEOUS PROVISIONS APPLYING TO COMPANIES WHICH ARE INSOLVENT OR IN LIQUIDATION

**Note**

Re application of Pt. VI to insolvent partnerships, see the Insolvent Partnerships Order 1994 (SI 1994/2421), especially reg. 6.

### OFFICE-HOLDERS

## 230 Holders of office to be qualified insolvency practitioners

**230(1) [Administrator]** Where an administration order is made in relation to a company, the administrator must be a person who is qualified to act as an insolvency practitioner in relation to the company.

**230(2) [Administrative receiver]** Where an administrative receiver of a company is appointed, he must be a person who is so qualified.

**230(3) [Liquidator]** Where a company goes into liquidation, the liquidator must be a person who is so qualified.

**230(4) [Provisional liquidator]** Where a provisional liquidator is appointed, he must be a person who is so qualified.

**230(5) [Official receiver]** Subsections (3) and (4) are without prejudice to any enactment under which the official receiver is to be, or may be, liquidator or provisional liquidator.

## 231 Appointment to office of two or more persons

**231(1) [Application]** This section applies if an appointment or nomination of any person to the office of administrator, administrative receiver, liquidator or provisional liquidator–

(a) relates to more than one person, or

(b) has the effect that the office is to be held by more than one person.

**231(2) [Declaration in appointment or nomination]** The appointment or nomination shall declare whether any act required or authorised under any enactment to be done by the administrator, administrative receiver, liquidator or provisional liquidator is to be done by all or any one or more of the persons for the time being holding the office in question.

## 232 Validity of office-holder's acts

**232** The acts of an individual as administrator, administrative receiver, liquidator or provisional liquidator of a company are valid notwithstanding any defect in his appointment, nomination or qualifications.

### MANAGEMENT BY ADMINISTRATORS, LIQUIDATORS, ETC.

## 233 Supplies of gas, water, electricity, etc.

**233(1) [Application]** This section applies in the case of a company where–

(a) an administration order is made in relation to the company, or

(b) an administrative receiver is appointed, or

(c) a voluntary arrangement under Part I, approved by meetings summoned under section 3, has taken effect, or

(d) the company goes into liquidation, or

(e) a provisional liquidator is appointed;

and **"the office-holder"** means the administrator, the administrative receiver, the supervisor of the voluntary arrangement, the liquidator or the provisional liquidator, as the case may be.

**233(2) [If request by office-holder]** If a request is made by or with the concurrence of the office-holder for the giving, after the effective date, of any of the supplies mentioned in the next subsection, the supplier–

(a) may make it a condition of the giving of the supply that the office-holder personally guarantees the payment of any charges in respect of the supply, but

(b) shall not make it a condition of the giving of the supply, or do anything which has the effect of making it a condition of the giving of the supply, that any outstanding charges in respect of a supply given to the company before the effective date are paid.

**233(3) [Supplies in s. 233(2)]** The supplies referred to in subsection (2) are–

(a) a public supply of gas,

(b) public supply of electricity,

(c) a supply of water by a water undertaker or, in Scotland, a water authority,

(d) a supply of telecommunication services by a public telecommunications operator.

**History**

In s. 233(3) para. (b) substituted by Electricity Act 1989, s. 112(1) and Sch. 16, para. 35(1), (2)(a) as from 31 March 1990 (see Electricity Act 1989, s. 113(2) and SI 1990/117 (C 4)); para. (b) formerly read as follows:

"(b) a supply of electricity by an Electricty Board;."

Also in s. 233(3)(c) the words "a water undertaker" substituted for the former words "statutory water undertakers" by Water Act 1989, s. 190(1) and Sch. 25, para. 78(1) as from 1 September 1989 (see Water Act 1989, s. 4, 194(4) and SI 1989/1146 (C 37) – see also SI 1989/1530 (C 51)).

**233(4) [Effective date]** "The effective date" for the purposes of this section is whichever is applicable of the following dates–

(a) the date on which the administration order was made,

(b) the date on which the administrative receiver was appointed (or, if he was appointed in succession to another administrative receiver, the date on which the first of his predecessors was appointed),

(c) the date on which the voluntary arrangement was approved by the meetings summoned under section 3,

(d) the date on which the company went into liquidation,

(e) the date on which the provisional liquidator was appointed.

**233(5) [Definitions]** The following applies to expressions used in subsection (3)–

(a) **"public supply of gas"** means a supply of gas by the British Gas Corporation or a public gas supplier within the meaning of Part I of the Gas Act 1986,

(b) **"public supply of electricty"** means a supply of electricity by a public electricity supplier within the meaning of Part I of the Electricity Act 1989,

(c) **"water authority"** means the same as in the Water (Scotland) Act 1980, and

(d) **"telecommunication services"** and **"public telecommunications operator"** mean the same as in the Telecommunications Act 1984, except that the former does not include local delivery services within the meaning of Part II of the Broadcasting Act 1990.

**History**

In s. 233(5) para. (b) substituted by Electricity Act 1989, s. 112(1) and Sch. 16, para. 35(1), (2)(b) as from 31 March 1990 (see Electricity Act 1989, s. 113(2) and SI 1990/117 (C 4), art. 3(a), Sch. 1); para. (b) formerly read as follows:

"(b) **"Electricity Board"** means the same as in the Energy Act 1983,"

Also in para. (d) the words "local delivery services within the meaning of Part II of the Broadcasting Act 1990" substituted by Broadcasting Act 1990, s. 203(1) and Sch. 20, para. 43 as from 1 January 1991 (see SI 1990/2347 (C 61), art. 3, Sch. 2); the former words read as follows:

"services consisting in the conveyance of programmes included in cable programme services (within the meaning of the Cable and Broadcasting Act 1984)."

## 234 Getting in the company's property

**234(1) [Application]** This section applies in the case of a company where–

(a) an administration order is made in relation to the company, or

(b) an administrative receiver is appointed, or

(c) the company goes into liquidation, or

(d) a provisional liquidator is appointed;

and **"the office-holder"** means the administrator, the administrative receiver, the liquidator or the provisional liquidator, as the case may be.

**234(2) [Court's powers]** Where any person has in his possession or control any property, books, papers or records to which the company appears to be entitled, the court may require that person forthwith (or within such period as the court may direct) to pay, deliver, convey, surrender or transfer the property, books, papers or records to the office-holder.

**234(3) [Application of s. 234(4)]** Where the office-holder–

(a) seizes or disposes of any property which is not property of the company, and

(b) at the time of seizure or disposal believes, and has reasonable grounds for believing, that he is entitled (whether in pursuance of an order of the court or otherwise) to seize or dispose of that property,

the next subsection has effect.

**234(4) [Liability of office-holder]** In that case the office-holder–

(a) is not liable to any person in respect of any loss or damage resulting from the seizure or disposal except in so far as that loss or damage is caused by the office-holder's own negligence, and

(b) has a lien on the property, or the proceeds of its sale, for such expenses as were incurred in connection with the seizure or disposal.

## 235 Duty to co-operate with office-holder

**235(1) [Application]** This section applies as does section 234; and it also applies, in the case of a company in respect of which a winding-up order has been made by the court in England and Wales, as if references to the office-holder included the official receiver, whether or not he is the liquidator.

**235(2) [Duty to give information etc.]** Each of the persons mentioned in the next subsection shall–

(a) give to the office-holder such information concerning the company and its promotion, formation, business, dealings, affairs or property as the office-holder may at any time after the effective date reasonably require, and

(b) attend on the office-holder at such times as the latter may reasonably require.

**235(3) [Persons in s. 235(2)]** The persons referred to above are–

(a) those who are or have at any time been officers of the company,

(b) those who have taken part in the formation of the company at any time within one year before the effective date,

(c) those who are in the employment of the company, or have been in its employment (including employment under a contract for services) within that year, and are in the office-holder's opinion capable of giving information which he requires,
(d) those who are, or have within that year been, officers of, or in the employment (including employment under a contract for services) of, another company which is, or within that year was, an officer of the company in question, and
(e) in the case of a company being wound up by the court, any person who has acted as administrator, administrative receiver or liquidator of the company.

**235(4) ["The effective date"]** For the purposes of subsections (2) and (3), **"the effective date"** is whichever is applicable of the following dates–
(a) the date on which the administration order was made,
(b) the date on which the administrative receiver was appointed or, if he was appointed in succession to another administrative receiver, the date on which the first of his predecessors was appointed,
(c) the date on which the provisional liquidator was appointed, and
(d) the date on which the company went into liquidation.

**235(5) [Penalty for non-compliance]** If a person without reasonable excuse fails to comply with any obligation imposed by this section, he is liable to a fine and, for continued contravention, to a daily default fine.

## 236 Inquiry into company's dealings, etc.

**236(1) [Application]** This section applies as does section 234; and it also applies in the case of a company in respect of which a winding-up order has been made by the court in England and Wales as if references to the office-holder included the official receiver, whether or not he is the liquidator.

**236(2) [Court's powers]** The court may, on the application of the office-holder, summon to appear before it–
(a) any officer of the company,
(b) any person known or suspected to have in his possession any property of the company or supposed to be indebted to the company, or
(c) any person whom the court thinks capable of giving information concerning the promotion, formation, business, dealings, affairs or property of the company.

**236(3) [Powers re account, production]** The court may require any such person as is mentioned in subsection (2)(a) to (c) to submit an affidavit to the court containing an account of his dealings with the company or to produce any books, papers or other records in his possession or under his control relating to the company or the matters mentioned in paragraph (c) of the subsection.

**236(4) [Application of s. 236(5)]** The following applies in a case where–
(a) a person without reasonable excuse fails to appear before the court when he is summoned to do so under this section, or
(b) there are reasonable grounds for believing that a person has absconded, or is about to abscond, with a view to avoiding his appearance before the court under this section.

**236(5) [Court's power re warrant]** The court may, for the purpose of bringing that person and anything in his possession before the court, cause a warrant to be issued to a constable or prescribed officer of the court–
(a) for the arrest of that person, and
(b) for the seizure of any books, papers, records, money or goods in that person's possession.

**236(6) [Court authorisation re custody]** The court may authorise a person arrested under such a warrant to be kept in custody, and anything seized under such a warrant to be held, in accordance with the rules, until that person is brought before the court under the warrant or until such other time as the court may order.

## 237 Court's enforcement powers under s. 236

**237(1) [Order to deliver property]** If it appears to the court, on consideration of any evidence obtained under section 236 or this section, that any person has in his possession any property of the company, the court may, on the application of the office-holder, order that person to deliver the whole or any part of the property to the officer-holder at such time, in such manner and on such terms as the court thinks fit.

**237(2) [Order to pay money due]** If it appears to the court, on consideration of any evidence so obtained, that any person is indebted to the company, the court may, on the application of the office-holder, order that person to pay to the office-holder, at such time and in such manner as the court may direct, the whole or any part of the amount due, whether in full discharge of the debt or otherwise, as the court thinks fit.

**237(3) [Order re examination of persons]** The court may, if it thinks fit, order that any person who if within the jurisdiction of the court would be liable to be summoned to appear before it under section 236 or this section shall be examined in any part of the United Kingdom where he may for the time being be, or in a place outside the United Kingdom.

**237(4) [Examination on oath etc.]** Any person who appears or is brought before the court under section 236 or this section may be examined on oath, either orally or (except in Scotland) by interrogatories, concerning the company or the matters mentioned in section 236(2)(c).

### ADJUSTMENT OF PRIOR TRANSACTIONS (ADMINISTRATION AND LIQUIDATION)

## 238 Transactions at an undervalue (England and Wales)

**238(1) [Application]** This section applies in the case of a company where–

(a) an administration order is made in relation to the company, or

(b) the company goes into liquidation;

and **"the office-holder"** means the administrator or the liquidator, as the case may be.

**238(2) [Application to court by office-holder]** Where the company has at a relevant time (defined in section 240) entered into a transaction with any person at an undervalue, the office-holder may apply to the court for an order under this section.

**238(3) [Court order]** Subject as follows, the court shall, on such an application, make such order as it thinks fit for restoring the position to what it would have been if the company had not entered into that transaction.

**238(4) [Interpretation]** For the purposes of this section and section 241, a company enters into a transaction with a person at an undervalue if–

(a) the company makes a gift to that person or otherwise enters into a transaction with that person on terms that provide for the company to receive no consideration, or

(b) the company enters into a transaction with that person for a consideration the value of which, in money or money's worth, is significantly less than the value, in money or money's worth, of the consideration provided by the company.

**238(5) [Restriction on court order]** The court shall not make an order under this section in respect of a transaction at an undervalue if it is satisfied–

(a) that the company which entered into the transaction did so in good faith and for the purpose of carrying on its business, and

(b) that at the time it did so there were reasonable grounds for believing that the transaction would benefit the company.

## 239 Preferences (England and Wales)

**239(1) [Application]** This section applies as does section 238.

**239(2) [Application to court by office-holder]** Where the company has at a relevant time (defined in the next section) given a preference to any person, the office-holder may apply to the court for an order under this section.

**239(3) [Court order]** Subject as follows, the court shall, on such an application, make such order as it thinks fit for restoring the position to what it would have been if the company had not given that preference.

**239(4) [Interpretation]** For the purposes of this section and section 241, a company gives a preference to a person if–

(a) that person is one of the company's creditors or a surety or guarantor for any of the company's debts or other liabilities, and

(b) the company does anything or suffers anything to be done which (in either case) has the effect of putting that person into a position which, in the event of the company going into insolvent liquidation, will be better than the position he would have been in if that thing had not been done.

**239(5) [Restriction on court order]** The court shall not make an order under this section in respect of a preference given to any person unless the company which gave the preference was influenced in deciding to give it by a desire to produce in relation to that person the effect mentioned in subsection (4)(b).

**239(6) [Presumption]** A company which has given a preference to a person connected with the company (otherwise than by reason only of being its employee) at the time the preference was given is presumed, unless the contrary is shown, to have been influenced in deciding to give it by such a desire as is mentioned in subsection (5).

**239(7) [Interpretation re preference]** The fact that something has been done in pursuance of the order of a court does not, without more, prevent the doing or suffering of that thing from constituting the giving of a preference.

## 240 "Relevant time" under s. 238, 239

**240(1) [Relevant time]** Subject to the next subsection, the time at which a company enters into a transaction at an undervalue or gives a preference is a relevant time if the transaction is entered into, or the preference given–

(a) in the case of a transaction at an undervalue or of a preference which is given to a person who is connected with the company (otherwise than by reason only of being its employee), at a time in the period of 2 years ending with the onset of insolvency (which expression is defined below),

(b) in the case of a preference which is not such a transaction and is not so given, at a time in the period of 6 months ending with the onset of insolvency, and

(c) in either case, at a time between the presentation of a petition for the making of an administration order in relation to the company and the making of such an order on that petition.

**240(2) [Where not relevant time]** Where a company enters into a transaction at an undervalue or gives a preference at a time mentioned in subsection (1)(a) or (b), that time is not a relevant time for the purposes of section 238 or 239 unless the company–

(a) is at that time unable to pay its debts within the meaning of section 123 in Chapter VI of Part IV, or

(b) becomes unable to pay its debts within the meaning of that section in consequence of the transaction or preference;

but the requirements of this subsection are presumed to be satisfied, unless the contrary is shown, in relation to any transaction at an undervalue which is entered into by a company with a person who is connected with the company.

**240(3) [Onset of insolvency]** For the purposes of subsection (1), the onset of insolvency is–

(a) in a case where section 238 or 239 applies by reason of the making of an administration order or of a company going into liquidation immediately upon the discharge of an administration order, the date of the presentation of the petition on which the administration order was made, and

(b) in a case where the section applies by reason of a company going into liquidation at any other time, the date of the commencement of the winding up.

## 241 Orders under s. 238, 239

**241(1) [Extent of orders]** Without prejudice to the generality of sections 238(3) and 239(3), an order under either of those sections with respect to a transaction or preference entered into or given by a company may (subject to the next subsection)–

(a) require any property transferred as part of the transaction, or in connection with the giving of the preference, to be vested in the company,

(b) require any property to be so vested if it represents in any person's hands the application either of the proceeds of sale of property so transferred or of money so transferred,

(c) release or discharge (in whole or in part) any security given by the company,

(d) require any person to pay, in respect of benefits received by him from the company, such sums to the office-holder as the court may direct,

(e) provide for any surety or guarantor whose obligations to any person were released or discharged (in whole or in part) under the transaction, or by the giving of the preference, to be under such new or revived obligations to that person as the court thinks appropriate,

(f) provide for security to be provided for the discharge of any obligation imposed by or arising under the order, for such an obligation to be charged on any property and for the security or charge to have the same priority as a security or charge released or discharged (in whole or in part) under the transaction or by the giving of the preference, and

(g) provide for the extent to which any person whose property is vested by the order in the company, or on whom obligations are imposed by the order, is to be able to prove in the winding up of the company for debts or other liabilities which arose from, or were released or discharged (in whole or in part) under or by, the transaction or the giving of the preference.

**241(2) [Restriction on orders]** An order under section 238 or 239 may affect the property of, or impose any obligation on, any person whether or not he is the person with whom the company in question entered into the transaction or (as the case may be) the person to whom the preference was given; but such an order–

(a) shall not prejudice any interest in property which was acquired from a person other than the company and was acquired in good faith and for value, or prejudice any interest deriving from such an interest, and

(b) shall not require a person who received a benefit from the transaction or preference in good faith and for value to pay a sum to the office-holder, except where that person was a party to the transaction or the payment is to be in respect of a preference given to that person at a time when he was a creditor of the company.

**History**
In s. 241(2) in both para. (a) and (b) the words "in good faith and for value" substituted for the former words "in good faith, for value and without notice of the relevant circumstances" by Insolvency (No. 2) Act 1994, s. 1(1), 6 as from 26 July 1994.

**241(2A) [Presumption re good faith in s. 241(2)]** Where a person has acquired an interest in property from a person other than the company in question, or has received a benefit from the transaction or preference, and at the time of that acquisition or receipt–

(a) he had notice of the relevant surrounding circumstances and of the relevant proceedings, or

(b) he was connected with, or was an associate of, either the company in question or the person with whom that company entered into the transaction or to whom that company gave the preference,

then, unless the contrary is shown, it shall be presumed for the purposes of paragraph (a) or (as the case may be) paragraph (b) of subsection (2) that the interest was acquired or the benefit was received otherwise than in good faith.

**History**
S. 241(2A) inserted by Insolvency (No. 2) Act 1994, s. 1(2), 6 as from 26 July 1994.

**241(3) [Relevant surrounding circumstances in s. 241(2A)(a)]** For the purposes of subsection (2A)(a), the relevant surrounding circumstances are (as the case may require)–

(a) the fact that the company in question entered into the transaction at an undervalue; or

(b) the circumstances which amounted to the giving of the preference by the company in question;

and subsections (3A) to (3C) have effect to determine whether, for those purposes, a person has notice of the relevant proceedings.

**History**

See history note after s. 241(3C).

**241(3A) [Notice where administration order made]** In a case where section 238 or 239 applies by reason of the making of an administration order, a person has notice of the relevant proceedings if he has notice–

(a) of the fact that the petition on which the administration order is made has been presented; or

(b) of the fact that the administration order has been made.

**History**

See history note after s. 241(3C).

**241(3B) [Notice where liquidation on discharge of administration order]** In a case where section 238 or 239 applies by reason of the company in question going into liquidation immediately upon the discharge of an administration order, a person has notice of the relevant proceedings if he has notice–

(a) of the fact that the petition on which the administration order is made has been presented;

(b) of the fact that the administration order has been made; or

(c) of the fact that the company has gone into liquidation.

**History**

See history note after s. 241(3C).

**241(3C) [Notice where liquidation at other times]** In a case where section 238 or 239 applies by reason of the company in question going into liquidation at any other time, a person has notice of the relevant proceedings if he has notice–

(a) where the company goes into liqudation on the making of a winding-up order, of the fact that the petition on which the winding-up order is made has been presented or of the fact that the company has gone into liquidation;

(b) in any other case, of the fact that the company has gone into liquidation.

**History**

S. 241(3)–(3C) substituted for the former s. 241(3) by Insolvency (No. 2) Act 1994, s. 1(3), 6 as from 26 July 1994; the former s. 241(3) read as follows:

"For the purposes of this section the relevant circumstances, in relation to a transaction or preference, are–

(a) the circumstances by virtue of which an order under section 238 or (as the case may be) 239 could be made in respect of the transaction or preference if the company were to go into liquidation, or an administration order were made in relation to the company, within a particular period after the transaction is entered into or the preference given, and

(b) if that period has expired, the fact that the company has gone into liquidation or that such an order has been made."

**241(4) [Application of s. 238–241]** The provisions of sections 238 to 241 apply without prejudice to the availability of any other remedy, even in relation to a transaction or preference which the company had no power to enter into or give.

# 242 Gratuitous alienations (Scotland)

**242(1) [Challenge to alienations]** Where this subsection applies and–

(a) the winding up of a company has commenced, an alienation by the company is challengeable by–

(i) any creditor who is a creditor by virtue of a debt incurred on or before the date of such commencement, or

(ii) the liquidator;

(b) an administration order is in force in relation to a company, an alienation by the company is challengeable by the administrator.

**242(2) [Application of s. 242(1)]** Subsection (1) applies where–

(a) by the alienation, whether before or after 1st April 1986 (the coming into force of section 75 of the Bankruptcy (Scotland) Act 1985), any part of the company's property is transferred or any claim or right of the company is discharged or renounced, and

(b) the alienation takes place on a relevant day.

**242(3) [Interpretation of s. 242(2)(b)]** For the purposes of subsection (2)(b), the day on which an alienation takes place is the day on which it becomes completely effectual; and in that subsection **"relevant day"** means, if the alienation has the effect of favouring–

(a) a person who is an associate (within the meaning of the Bankruptcy (Scotland) Act 1985) of the company, a day not earlier than 5 years before the date on which–
 (i) the winding up of the company commences, or
 (ii) as the case may be, the administration order is made; or

(b) any other person, a day not earlier than 2 years before that date.

**242(4) [Duties of court on challenge under s. 242(1)]** On a challenge being brought under subsection (1), the court shall grant decree of reduction or for such restoration of property to the company's assets or other redress as may be appropriate; but the court shall not grant such a decree if the person seeking to uphold the alienation establishes–

(a) that immediately, or at any other time, after the alienation the company's assets were greater than its liabilities, or

(b) that the alienation was made for adequate consideration, or

(c) that the alienation–
 (i) was a birthday, Christmas or other conventional gift, or
 (ii) was a gift made, for a charitable purpose, to a person who is not an associate of the company,

which, having regard to all the circumstances, it was reasonable for the company to make:

Provided that this subsection is without prejudice to any right or interest acquired in good faith and for value from or through the transferee in the alienation.

**242(5) ["Charitable purpose" in s. 242(4)]** In subsection (4) above, **"charitable purpose"** means any charitable, benevolent or philanthropic purpose, whether or not it is charitable within the meaning of any rule of law.

**242(6) [Interpretation]** For the purposes of the foregoing provisions of this section, an alienation in implementation of a prior obligation is deemed to be one for which there was no consideration or no adequate consideration to the extent that the prior obligation was undertaken for no consideration or no adequate consideration.

**242(7) [Rights of challenge]** A liquidator and an administrator have the same right as a creditor has under any rule of law to challenge an alienation of a company made for no consideration or no adequate consideration.

**242(8) [Scotland only]** This section applies to Scotland only.

## 243 Unfair preferences (Scotland)

**243(1) [Application of s. 243(4)]** Subject to subsection (2) below, subsection (4) below applies to a transaction entered into by a company, whether before or after 1st April 1986, which has the effect of creating a preference in favour of a creditor to the prejudice of the general body of creditors, being a preference created not earlier than 6 months before the commencement of the winding up of the company or the making of an administration order in relation to the company.

**243(2) [Non-application of s. 243(4)]** Subsection (4) below does not apply to any of the following transactions–

(a) a transaction in the ordinary course of trade or business;

(b) a payment in cash for a debt which when it was paid had become payable, unless the transaction was collusive with the purpose of prejudicing the general body of creditors;

(c) a transaction whereby the parties to it undertake reciprocal obligations (whether the performance by the parties of their respective obligations occurs at the same time or at different times) unless the transaction was collusive as aforesaid;

(d) the granting of a mandate by a company authorising an arrestee to pay over the arrested funds or part thereof to the arrester where–
  (i) there has been a decree for payment or a warrant for summary diligence, and
  (ii) the decree or warrant has been preceded by an arrestment on the dependence of the action or followed by an arrestment in execution.

**243(3) [Interpretation of s. 243(1)]** For the purposes of subsection (1) above, the day on which a preference was created is the day on which the preference became completely effectual.

**243(4) [Persons who may challenge]** A transaction to which this subsection applies is challengeable by–

(a) in the case of a winding up–
  (i) any creditor who is a creditor by virtue of a debt incurred on or before the date of commencement of the winding up, or
  (ii) the liquidator; and

(b) in the case of an administration order, the administrator.

**243(5) [Duties of court on s. 243(4) challenge]** On a challenge being brought under subsection (4) above, the court, if satisfied that the transaction challenged is a transaction to which this section applies, shall grant decree of reduction or for such restoration of property to the company's assets or other redress as may be appropriate:

Provided that this subsection is without prejudice to any right or interest acquired in good faith and for value from or through the creditor in whose favour the preference was created.

**243(6) [Rights of challenge]** A liquidator and an administrator have the same right as a creditor has under any rule of law to challenge a preference created by a debtor.

**243(7) [Scotland only]** This section applies to Scotland only.

## 244 Extortionate credit transactions

**244(1) [Application]** This section applies as does section 238, and where the company is, or has been, a party to a transaction for, or involving, the provision of credit to the company.

**244(2) [Court order re extortionate transaction]** The court may, on the application of the office-holder, make an order with respect to the transaction if the transaction is or was extortionate and was entered into in the period of 3 years ending with the day on which the administration order was made or (as the case may be) the company went into liquidation.

**244(3) [Extortionate transaction – interpretation]** For the purposes of this section a transaction is extortionate if, having regard to the risk accepted by the person providing the credit–

(a) the terms of it are or were such as to require grossly exorbitant payments to be made (whether unconditionally or in certain contingencies) in respect of the provision of the credit, or

(b) it otherwise grossly contravened ordinary principles of fair dealing;

and it shall be presumed, unless the contrary is proved, that a transaction with respect to which an application is made under this section is or, as the case may be, was extortionate.

**244(4) [Extent of court order]** An order under this section with respect to any transaction may contain such one or more of the following as the court thinks fit, that is to say–

(a) provision setting aside the whole or part of any obligation created by the transaction,

(b) provision otherwise varying the terms of the transaction or varying the terms on which any security for the purposes of the transaction is held,

(c) provision requiring any person who is or was a party to the transaction to pay to the office-holder any sums paid to that person, by virtue of the transaction, by the company,

(d) provision requiring any person to surrender to the office-holder any property held by him as security for the purposes of the transaction,

(e) provision directing accounts to be taken between any persons.

**244(5) [Exercise of powers]** The powers conferred by this section are exercisable in relation to any transaction concurrently with any powers exercisable in relation to that transaction as a transaction at an undervalue or under section 242 (gratuitous alienations in Scotland).

## 245 Avoidance of certain floating charges

**245(1) [Application]** This section applies as does section 238, but applies to Scotland as well as to England and Wales.

**245(2) [Invalidity of floating charge]** Subject as follows, a floating charge on the company's undertaking or property created at a relevant time is invalid except to the extent of the aggregate of–

(a) the value of so much of the consideration for the creation of the charge as consists of money paid, or goods or services supplied, to the company at the same time as, or after, the creation of the charge,

(b) the value of so much of that consideration as consists of the discharge or reduction, at the same time as, or after, the creation of the charge, of any debt of the company, and

(c) the amount of such interest (if any) as is payable on the amount falling within paragraph (a) or (b) in pursuance of any agreement under which the money was so paid, the goods or services were so supplied or the debt was so discharged or reduced.

**245(3) [Relevant time]** Subject to the next subsection, the time at which a floating charge is created by a company is a relevant time for the purposes of this section if the charge is created–

(a) in the case of a charge which is created in favour of a person who is connected with the company, at a time in the period of 2 years ending with the onset of insolvency,

(b) in the case of a charge which is created in favour of any other person, at a time in the period of 12 months ending with the onset of insolvency, or

(c) in either case, at a time between the presentation of a petition for the making of an administration order in relation to the company and the making of such an order on that petition.

**245(4) [Qualification to s. 245(3)(b)]** Where a company creates a floating charge at a time mentioned in subsection (3)(b) and the person in favour of whom the charge is created is not connected with the company, that time is not a relevant time for the purposes of this section unless the company–

(a) is at that time unable to pay its debts within the meaning of section 123 in Chapter VI of Part IV, or

(b) becomes unable to pay its debts within the meaning of that section in consequence of the transaction under which the charge is created.

**245(5) [Onset of insolvency in s. 245(3)]** For the purposes of subsection (3), the onset of insolvency is–

(a) in a case where this section applies by reason of the making of an administration order, the date of the presentation of the petition on which the order was made, and

(b) in a case where this section applies by reason of a company going into liquidation, the date of the commencement of the winding up.

**245(6) [Value of goods, services etc. in s. 245(2)(a)]** For the purposes of subsection (2)(a) the value of any goods or services supplied by way of consideration for a floating charge is the amount in money which at the time they were supplied could reasonably have been expected to be obtained for supplying the goods or services in the ordinary course of business and on the same terms (apart from the consideration) as those on which they were supplied to the company.

## 246 Unenforceability of liens on books, etc.

**246(1) [Application]** This section applies in the case of a company where–

(a) an administration order is made in relation to the company, or

(b) the company goes into liquidation, or

(c) a provisional liquidator is appointed;

and **"the office-holder"** means the administrator, the liquidator or the provisional liquidator, as the case may be.

**246(2) [Lien etc. unenforceable]** Subject as follows, a lien or other right to retain possession of any of the books, papers or other records of the company is unenforceable to the extent that its enforcement would deny possession of any books, papers or other records to the office-holder.

**246(3) [Non-application]** This does not apply to a lien on documents which give a title to property and are held as such.

# PART VII – INTERPRETATION FOR FIRST GROUP OF PARTS

**Note**

Re application of Pt. VII to insolvent partnerships, see the Insolvent Partnerships Order 1994 (SI 1994/2421), especially reg. 10.

## 247 "Insolvency" and "go into liquidation"

**247(1) ["Insolvency"]** In this Group of Parts, except in so far as the context otherwise requires, **"insolvency"**, in relation to a company, includes the approval of a voluntary arrangement under Part I, the making of an administration order or the appointment of an administrative receiver.

**247(2) [Company in liquidation]** For the purposes of any provision in this Group of Parts, a company goes into liquidation if it passes a resolution for voluntary winding up or an order for its winding up is made by the court at a time when it has not already gone into liquidation by passing such a resolution.

## 248 "Secured creditor", etc.

**248** In this Group of Parts, except in so far as the context otherwise requires–

(a) **"secured creditor"**, in relation to a company, means a creditor of the company who holds in respect of his debt a security over property of the company, and **"unsecured creditor"** is to be read accordingly; and

(b) **"security"** means–

(i) in relation to England and Wales, any mortgage, charge, lien or other security, and

(ii) in relation to Scotland, any security (whether heritable or moveable), any floating charge and any right of lien or preference and any right of retention (other than a right of compensation or set off).

## 249 "Connected" with a company

**249** For the purposes of any provision in this Group of Parts, a person is connected with a company if–

(a) he is a director or shadow director of the company or an associate of such a director or shadow director, or

(b) he is an associate of the company;

and **"associate"** has the meaning given by section 435 in Part XVIII of this Act.

## 250 "Member" of a company

**250** For the purposes of any provision in this Group of Parts, a person who is not a member of a company but to whom shares in the company have been transferred, or transmitted by operation of law, is to be regarded as a member of the company, and references to a member or members are to be read accordingly.

## 251 Expressions used generally

**251** In this Group of Parts, except in so far as the context otherwise requires–

**"administrative receiver"** means–

(a) an administrative receiver as defined by section 29(2) in Chapter I of Part III, or
(b) a receiver appointed under section 51 in Chapter II of that Part in a case where the whole (or substantially the whole) of the company's property is attached by the floating charge;

**"business day"** means any day other than a Saturday, a Sunday, Christmas Day, Good Friday or a day which is a bank holiday in any part of Great Britain;

**"chattel leasing agreement"** means an agreement for the bailment or, in Scotland, the hiring of goods which is capable of subsisting for more than 3 months;

**"contributory"** has the meaning given by section 79;

**"director"** includes any person occupying the position of director, by whatever name called;

**"floating charge"** means a charge which, as created, was a floating charge and includes a floating charge within section 462 of the Companies Act (Scottish floating charges);

**"office copy"**, in relation to Scotland, means a copy certified by the clerk of court;

**"the official rate"**, in relation to interest, means the rate payable under section 189(4);

**"prescribed"** means prescribed by the rules;

**"receiver"**, in the expression **"receiver or manager"**, does not include a receiver appointed under section 51 in Chapter II of Part III;

**"retention of title agreement"** means an agreement for the sale of goods to a company, being an agreement–

(a) which does not constitute a charge on the goods, but
(b) under which, if the seller is not paid and the company is wound up, the seller will have priority over all other creditors of the company as respects the goods or any property representing the goods;

**"the rules"** means rules under section 411 in Part XV; and

**"shadow director"**, in relation to a company, means a person in accordance with whose directions or instructions the directors of the company are accustomed to act (but so that a person is not deemed a shadow director by reason only that the directors act on advice given by him in a professional capacity);

and any expression for whose interpretation provision is made by Part XXVI of the Companies Act, other than an expression defined above in this section, is to be construed in accordance with that provision.

# THE SECOND GROUP OF PARTS INSOLVENCY OF INDIVIDUALS; BANKRUPTCY

# PART VIII – INDIVIDUAL VOLUNTARY ARRANGEMENTS

## MORATORIUM FOR INSOLVENT DEBTOR

### 252 Interim order of court

**252(1) [Power of court]** In the circumstances specified below, the court may in the case of a debtor (being an individual) make an interim order under this section.

**252(2) [Effect of interim order]** An interim order has the effect that, during the period for which it is in force–

(a) no bankruptcy petition relating to the debtor may be presented or proceeded with, and
(b) no other proceedings, and no execution or other legal process, may be commenced or continued against the debtor or his property except with the leave of the court.

# 253 Application for interim order

**253(1) [Where application made]** Application to the court for an interim order may be made where the debtor intends to make a proposal to his creditors for a composition in satisfaction of his debts or a scheme of arrangement of his affairs (from here on referred to, in either case, as a "voluntary arrangement").

**253(2) [Nominee]** The proposal must provide for some person ("the nominee") to act in relation to the voluntary arrangement either as trustee or otherwise for the purpose of supervising its implementation.

**253(3) [Applicants]** Subject as follows, the application may be made–

(a) if the debtor is an undischarged bankrupt, by the debtor, the trustee of his estate, or the official receiver, and

(b) in any other case, by the debtor.

**253(4) [Notice for s. 253(3)(a)]** An application shall not be made under subsection (3)(a) unless the debtor has given notice of his proposal (that is, the proposal to his creditors for a voluntary arrangement) to the official receiver and, if there is one, the trustee of his estate.

**253(5) [When application not to be made]** An application shall not be made while a bankruptcy petition presented by the debtor is pending, if the court has, under section 273 below, appointed an insolvency practitioner to inquire into the debtor's affairs and report.

# 254 Effect of application

**254(1) [Stay pending interim order]** At any time when an application under section 253 for an interim order is pending, the court may stay any action, execution or other legal process against the property or person of the debtor.

**254(2) [Stay or continuance]** Any court in which proceedings are pending against an individual may, on proof that an application under that section has been made in respect of that individual, either stay the proceedings or allow them to continue on such terms as it thinks fit.

# 255 Cases in which interim order can be made

**255(1) [Conditions for order]** The court shall not make an interim order on an application under section 253 unless it is satisfied–

(a) that the debtor intends to make such a proposal as is mentioned in that section;

(b) that on the day of the making of the application the debtor was an undischarged bankrupt or was able to petition for his own bankruptcy;

(c) that no previous application has been made by the debtor for an interim order in the period of 12 months ending with that day; and

(d) that the nominee under the debtor's proposal to his creditors is a person who is for the time being qualified to act as an insolvency practitioner in relation to the debtor, and is willing to act in relation to the proposal.

**255(2) [Order to facilitate consideration and implementation of proposal]** The court may make an order if it thinks that it would be appropriate to do so for the purpose of facilitating the consideration and implementation of the debtor's proposal.

**255(3) [Where debtor is undischarged bankrupt]** Where the debtor is an undischarged bankrupt, the interim order may contain provision as to the conduct of the bankruptcy, and the administration of the bankrupt's estate, during the period for which the order is in force.

**255(4) [Extent of s. 255(3) provision]** Subject as follows, the provision contained in an interim order by virtue of subsection (3) may include provision staying proceedings in the bankruptcy or modifying any provision in this Group of Parts, and any provision of the rules in their application to the debtor's bankruptcy.

**255(5) [Limit to interim order]** An interim order shall not, in relation to a bankrupt, make provision relaxing or removing any of the requirements of provisions in this Group of Parts, or of the rules, unless the court is satisfied that that provision is unlikely to result in any significant diminution in, or in the value of, the debtor's estate for the purposes of the bankruptcy.



CCH.New Law
bbcl insa 1986a Mp 1320—bcl98 1b

**255(6) [When order ceases to have effect]** Subject to the following provisions of this Part, an interim order made on an application under section 253 ceases to have effect at the end of the period of 14 days beginning with the day after the making of the order.

## 256 Nominee's report on debtor's proposal

**256(1) [Report to court]** Where an interim order has been made on an application under section 253, the nominee shall, before the order ceases to have effect, submit a report to the court stating–

(a) whether, in his opinion, a meeting of the debtor's creditors should be summoned to consider the debtor's proposal, and

(b) if in his opinion such a meeting should be summoned, the date on which, and time and place at which, he proposes the meeting should be held.

**256(2) [Information to nominee]** For the purpose of enabling a nominee to prepare his report the debtor shall submit to the nominee–

(a) a document setting out the terms of the voluntary arrangement which the debtor is proposing, and

(b) a statement of his affairs containing–

(i) such particulars of his creditors and of his debts and other liabilities and of his assets as may be prescribed, and

(ii) such other information as may be prescribed.

**256(3) [Directions by court]** The court may, on an application made by the debtor in a case where the nominee has failed to submit the report required by this section, do one or both of the following, namely–

(a) direct that the nominee shall be replaced as such by another person qualified to act as an insolvency practitioner in relation to the debtor;

(b) direct that the interim order shall continue, or (if it has ceased to have effect) be renewed, for such further period as the court may specify in the direction.

**256(4) [Extension of period of interim order]** The court may, on the application of the nominee, extend the period for which the interim order has effect so as to enable the nominee to have more time to prepare his report.

**256(5) [Extension for consideration by creditors]** If the court is satisfied on receiving the nominee's report that a meeting of the debtor's creditors should be summoned to consider the debtor's proposal, the court shall direct that the period for which the interim order has effect shall be extended, for such further period as it may specify in the direction, for the purpose of enabling the debtor's proposal to be considered by his creditors in accordance with the following provisions of this Part.

**256(6) [Discharge of interim order]** The court may discharge the interim order if it is satisfied, on the application of the nominee–

(a) that the debtor has failed to comply with his obligations under subsection (2), or

(b) that for any other reason it would be inappropriate for a meeting of the debtor's creditors to be summoned to consider the debtor's proposal.

## 257 Summoning of creditors' meeting

**257(1) [Meeting to be summoned]** Where it has been reported to the court under section 256 that a meeting of the debtor's creditors should be summoned, the nominee (or his replacement under section 256(3)(a)) shall, unless the court otherwise directs, summon that meeting for the time, date and place proposed in his report.

**257(2) [Persons summoned to meeting]** The persons to be summoned to the meeting are every creditor of the debtor of whose claim and address the person summoning the meeting is aware.

**257(3) [Creditors of debtor]** For this purpose the creditors of a debtor who is an undischarged bankrupt include–

(a) every person who is a creditor of the bankrupt in respect of a bankruptcy debt, and

(b) every person who would be such a creditor if the bankruptcy had commenced on the day on which notice of the meeting is given.

**Note**

Re s. 257 see the Companies Act 1985 (Audit Exemption) (Amendment) Regulations 1995 (SI 1995/589).

## CONSIDERATION AND IMPLEMENTATION OF DEBTOR'S PROPOSAL

## 258 Decisions of creditors' meeting

**258(1) [Decision re approval]** A creditors' meeting summoned under section 257 shall decide whether to approve the proposed voluntary arrangement.

**258(2) [Approval with modifications]** The meeting may approve the proposed voluntary arrangement with modifications, but shall not do so unless the debtor consents to each modification.

**258(3) [Extent of modifications]** The modifications subject to which the proposed voluntary arrangement may be approved may include one conferring the functions proposed to be conferred on the nominee on another person qualified to act as an insolvency practitioner in relation to the debtor.

But they shall not include any modification by virtue of which the proposal ceases to be a proposal such as is mentioned in section 253.

**258(4) [Certain modifications not to be approved]** The meeting shall not approve any proposal or modification which affects the right of a secured creditor of the debtor to enforce his security, except with the concurrence of the creditor concerned.

**258(5) [Other modifications not to be approved]** Subject as follows, the meeting shall not approve any proposal or modification under which–

(a) any preferential debt of the debtor is to be paid otherwise than in priority to such of his debts as are not preferential debts, or

(b) a preferential creditor of the debtor is to be paid an amount in respect of a preferential debt that bears to that debt a smaller proportion than is borne to another preferential debt by the amount that is to be paid in respect of that other debt.

However, the meeting may approve such a proposal or modification with the concurrence of the preferential creditor concerned.

**258(6) [Meeting in accordance with rules]** Subject as above, the meeting shall be conducted in accordance with the rules.

**258(7) [Definitions]** In this section **"preferential debt"** has the meaning given by section 386 in Part XII; and **"preferential creditor"** is to be construed accordingly.

## 259 Report of decisions to court

**259(1) [Report to court, notice]** After the conclusion in accordance with the rules of the meeting summoned under section 257, the chairman of the meeting shall report the result of it to the court and, immediately after so reporting, shall give notice of the result of the meeting to such persons as may be prescribed.

**259(2) [Discharge of interim order]** If the report is that the meeting has declined (with or without modifications) to approve the debtor's proposal, the court may discharge any interim order which is in force in relation to the debtor.

## 260 Effect of approval

**260(1) [Effect]** This section has effect where the meeting summoned under section 257 approves the proposed voluntary arrangement (with or without modifications).

**260(2) [Effect of approved composition or scheme]** The approved arrangement–

(a) takes effect as if made by the debtor at the meeting, and

(b) binds every person who in accordance with the rules had notice of, and was entitled to vote at, the meeting (whether or not he was present or represented at it) as if he were a party to the arrangement.

(b) if it thinks it would be inappropriate to make such an order, make a bankruptcy order.

**274(4) [Cessation of interim order]** An interim order by virtue of this section ceases to have effect at the end of such period as the court may specify for the purpose of enabling the debtor's proposal to be considered by his creditors in accordance with the applicable provisions of Part VIII.

**274(5) [Summoning of meeting]** Where it has been reported to the court under this section that a meeting of the debtor's creditors should be summoned, the person making the report shall, unless the court otherwise directs, summon that meeting for the time, date and place proposed in his report.

The meeting is then deemed to have been summoned under section 257 in Part VIII, and subsections (2) and (3) of that section, and sections 258 to 263 apply accordingly.

## 275 Summary administration

**275(1) [Issue of certificate]** Where on the hearing of a debtor's petition the court makes a bankruptcy order and the case is as specified in the next subsection, the court shall, if it appears to it appropriate to do so, issue a certificate for the summary administration of the bankrupt's estate.

**275(2) [Case for issue of certificate]** That case is where it appears to the court–

(a) that if a bankruptcy order were made the aggregate amount of the bankruptcy debts so far as unsecured would be less than the small bankruptcies level (within the meaning given by section 273), and

(b) that within the period of 5 years ending with the presentation of the petition the debtor has neither been adjudged bankrupt nor made a composition with his creditors in satisfaction of his debts or a scheme of arrangement of his affairs,

whether the bankruptcy order is made because it does not appear to the court as mentioned in section 273(1)(b) or (d), or it is made because the court thinks it would be inappropriate to make an interim order under section 252.

**275(3) [Revocation of certificate by court]** The court may at any time revoke a certificate issued under this section if it appears to it that, on any grounds existing at the time the certificate was issued, the certificate ought not to have been issued.

### OTHER CASES FOR SPECIAL CONSIDERATION

## 276 Default in connection with voluntary arrangement

**276(1) [Conditions for s. 264(1)(c) bankruptcy order]** The court shall not make a bankruptcy order on a petition under section 264(1)(c) (supervisor of, or person bound by, voluntary arrangement proposed and approved) unless it is satisfied–

(a) that the debtor has failed to comply with his obligations under the voluntary arrangement, or

(b) that information which was false or misleading in any material particular or which contained material omissions–

  (i) was contained in any statement of affairs or other document supplied by the debtor under Part VIII to any person, or

  (ii) was otherwise made available by the debtor to his creditors at or in connection with a meeting summoned under that Part, or

(c) that the debtor has failed to do all such things as may for the purposes of the voluntary arrangement have been reasonably required of him by the supervisor of the arrangement.

**276(2) [Expenses]** Where a bankruptcy order is made on a petition under section 264(1)(c), any expenses properly incurred as expenses of the administration of the voluntary arrangement in question shall be a first charge on the bankrupt's estate.

## 277 Petition based on criminal bankruptcy order

**277(1) [Duty of court]** Subject to section 266(3), the court shall make a bankruptcy order on a petition under section 264(1)(d) on production of a copy of the criminal bankruptcy order on which the petition is based.

This does not apply if it appears to the court that the criminal bankruptcy order has been rescinded on appeal.

**277(2) [Effect of appeal pending]** Subject to the provisions of this Part, the fact that an appeal is pending against any conviction by virtue of which a criminal bankruptcy order was made does not affect any proceedings on a petition under section 264(1)(d) based on that order.

**277(3) [When appeal is pending]** For the purposes of this section, an appeal against a conviction is pending–

(a) in any case, until the expiration of the period of 28 days beginning with the date of conviction;

(b) if notice of appeal to the Court of Appeal is given during that period and during that period the appellant notifies the official receiver of it, until the determination of the appeal and thereafter for so long as an appeal to the House of Lords is pending within the meaning of section 40(5) of the Powers of Criminal Courts Act 1973.

**Note**

S. 277 repealed by Criminal Justice Act 1988, s. 170(2) and Sch. 16 as from a day to be appointed.

## COMMENCEMENT AND DURATION OF BANKRUPTCY; DISCHARGE

## 278 Commencement and continuance

**278** The bankruptcy of an individual against whom a bankruptcy order has been made–

(a) commences with the day on which the order is made, and

(b) continues until the individual is discharged under the following provisions of this Chapter.

## 279 Duration

**279(1) [Discharge from bankruptcy]** Subject as follows, a bankrupt is discharged from bankruptcy–

(a) in the case of an individual who was adjudged bankrupt on a petition under section 264(1)(d) or who had been an undischarged bankrupt at any time in the period of 15 years ending with the commencement of the bankruptcy, by an order of the court under the section next following, and

(b) in any other case, by the expiration of the relevant period under this section.

**279(2) [Relevant period]** That period is as follows–

(a) where a certificate for the summary administration of the bankrupt's estate has been issued and is not revoked before the bankrupt's discharge, the period of 2 years beginning with the commencement of the bankruptcy, and

(b) in any other case, the period of 3 years beginning with the commencement of the bankruptcy.

**279(3) [Court order]** Where the court is satisfied on the application of the official receiver that an undischarged bankrupt in relation to whom subsection (1)(b) applies has failed or is failing to comply with any of his obligations under this Part, the court may order that the relevant period under this section shall cease to run for such period, or until the fulfilment of such conditions (including a condition requiring the court to be satisfied as to any matter), as may be specified in the order.

**279(4) [Power of annulment]** This section is without prejudice to any power of the court to annul a bankruptcy order.

## 280 Discharge by order of the court

**280(1) [Application to court]** An application for an order of the court discharging an individual from bankruptcy in a case falling within section 279(1)(a) may be made by the bankrupt at any time after the end of the period of 5 years beginning with the commencement of the bankruptcy.

**280(2) [Powers of court]** On an application under this section the court may–

(a) refuse to discharge the bankrupt from bankruptcy,

(a) all property belonging to or vested in the bankrupt at the commencement of the bankruptcy, and

(b) any property which by virtue of any of the following provisions of this Part is comprised in that estate or is treated as falling within the preceding paragraph.

**283(2) [Non-application of s. 283(1)]** Subsection (1) does not apply to–

(a) such tools, books, vehicles and other items of equipment as are necessary to the bankrupt for use personally by him in his employment, business or vocation;

(b) such clothing, bedding, furniture, household equipment and provisions as are necessary for satisfying the basic domestic needs of the bankrupt and his family.

This subsection is subject to section 308 in Chapter IV (certain excluded property reclaimable by trustee).

**283(3) [Further non-application of s. 283(1)]** Subsection (1) does not apply to–

(a) property held by the bankrupt on trust for any other person, or

(b) the right of nomination to a vacant ecclesiastical benefice.

**283(3A) [Further non-application of s. 283(1)]** Subject to section 308A in Chapter IV, subsection (1) does not apply to–

(a) a tenancy which is an assured tenancy or an assured agricultural occupancy, within the meaning of Part I of the Housing Act 1988, and the terms of which inhibit an assignment as mentioned in section 127(5) of the Rent Act 1977, or

(b) a protected tenancy, within the meaning of the Rent Act 1977, in respect of which, by virtue of any provision of Part IX of that Act, no premium can lawfully be required as a condition of assignment, or

(c) a tenancy of a dwelling-house by virtue of which the bankrupt is, within the meaning of the Rent (Agriculture) Act 1976, a protected occupier of the dwelling-house, and the terms of which inhibit an assignment as mentioned in section 127(5) of the Rent Act 1977, or

(d) a secure tenancy, within the meaning of Part IV of the Housing Act 1985, which is not capable of being assigned, except in the cases mentioned in section 91(3) of that Act.

**History**
S. 283(3A) inserted by Housing Act 1988, s. 117(1) and 141(3) as from 15 January 1989.

**283(4) [References to property]** References in any of this Group of Parts to property, in relation to a bankrupt, include references to any power exercisable by him over or in respect of property except in so far as the power is exercisable over or in respect of property not for the time being comprised in the bankrupt's estate and–

(a) is so exercisable at a time after either the official receiver has had his release in respect of that estate under section 299(2) in Chapter III or a meeting summoned by the trustee of that estate under section 331 in Chapter IV has been held, or

(b) cannot be so exercised for the benefit of the bankrupt;

and a power exercisable over or in respect of property is deemed for the purposes of any of this Group of Parts to vest in the person entitled to exercise it at the time of the transaction or event by virtue of which it is exercisable by that person (whether or not it becomes so exercisable at that time).

**283(5) [Property in bankrupt's estate]** For the purposes of any such provision in this Group of Parts, property comprised in a bankrupt's estate is so comprised subject to the rights of any person other than the bankrupt (whether as a secured creditor of the bankrupt or otherwise) in relation thereto, but disregarding–

(a) any rights in relation to which a statement such as is required by section 269(1)(a) was made in the petition on which the bankrupt was adjudged bankrupt, and

(b) any rights which have been otherwise given up in accordance with the rules.

**283(6) [Other enactments]** This section has effect subject to the provisions of any enactment not contained in this Act under which any property is to be excluded from a bankrupt's estate.

## 284 Restrictions on dispositions of property

**284(1) [Where person adjudged bankrupt]** Where a person is adjudged bankrupt, any disposition of property made by that person in the period to which this section applies is void except to the extent that it is or was made with the consent of the court, or is or was subsequently ratified by the court.

**284(2) [Application of s. 284(1) to payment]** Subsection (1) applies to a payment (whether in cash or otherwise) as it applies to a disposition of property and, accordingly, where any payment is void by virtue of that subsection, the person paid shall hold the sum paid for the bankrupt as part of his estate.

**284(3) [Relevant period]** This section applies to the period beginning with the day of the presentation of the petition for the bankruptcy order and ending with the vesting, under Chapter IV of this Part, of the bankrupt's estate in a trustee.

**284(4) [Limit to effect of s. 284(1)–(3)]** The preceding provisions of this section do not give a remedy against any person–

(a) in respect of any property or payment which he received before the commencement of the bankruptcy in good faith, for value and without notice that the petition had been presented, or

(b) in respect of any interest in property which derives from an interest in respect of which there is, by virtue of this subsection, no remedy.

**284(5) [Debt after commencement of bankruptcy]** Where after the commencement of his bankruptcy the bankrupt has incurred a debt to a banker or other person by reason of the making of a payment which is void under this section, that debt is deemed for the purposes of any of this Group of Parts to have been incurred before the commencement of the bankruptcy unless–

(a) that banker or person had notice of the bankruptcy before the debt was incurred, or

(b) it is not reasonably practicable for the amount of the payment to be recovered from the person to whom it was made.

**284(6) [Property not in bankrupt's estate]** A disposition of property is void under this section notwithstanding that the property is not or, as the case may be, would not be comprised in the bankrupt's estate; but nothing in this section affects any disposition made by a person of property held by him on trust for any other person.

## 285 Restriction on proceedings and remedies

**285(1) [Court's power to stay]** At any time when proceedings on a bankruptcy petition are pending or an individual has been adjudged bankrupt the court may stay any action, execution or other legal process against the property or person of the debtor or, as the case may be, of the bankrupt.

**285(2) [Where proceedings pending against individual]** Any court in which proceedings are pending against any individual may, on proof that a bankruptcy petition has been presented in respect of that individual or that he is an undischarged bankrupt, either stay the proceedings or allow them to continue on such terms as it thinks fit.

**285(3) [Limit on creditors' actions]** After the making of a bankruptcy order no person who is a creditor of the bankrupt in respect of a debt provable in the bankruptcy shall–

(a) have any remedy against the property or person of the bankrupt in respect of that debt, or

(b) before the discharge of the bankrupt, commence any action or other legal proceedings against the bankrupt except with leave of the court and on such terms as the court may impose.

This is subject to sections 346 (enforcement procedures) and 347 (limited right to distress).

**285(4) [Right of secured creditor]** Subject as follows, subsection (3) does not affect the right of a secured creditor of the bankrupt to enforce his security.

**285(5) [Where goods of undischarged bankrupt held by pledge etc.]** Where any goods of an undischarged bankrupt are held by any person by way of pledge, pawn or other security, the official receiver may, after giving notice in writing of his intention to do so, inspect the goods.

Where such a notice has been given to any person, that person is not entitled, without leave of the court, to realise his security unless he has given the trustee of the bankrupt's estate a reasonable opportunity of inspecting the goods and of exercising the bankrupt's right of redemption.

**285(6) [Interpretation]** References in this section to the property or goods of the bankrupt are to any of his property or goods, whether or not comprised in his estate.

## 286 Power to appoint interim receiver

**286(1) [Court's power]** The court may, if it is shown to be necessary for the protection of the debtor's property, at any time after the presentation of a bankruptcy petition and before making a bankruptcy order, appoint the official receiver to be interim receiver of the debtor's property.

**286(2) [Appointment of person instead of official receiver]** Where the court has, on a debtor's petition, appointed an insolvency practitioner under section 273 and it is shown to the court as mentioned in subsection (1) of this section, the court may, without making a bankruptcy order, appoint that practitioner, instead of the official receiver, to be interim receiver of the debtor's property.

**286(3) [Rights, powers etc. of interim receiver]** The court may by an order appointing any person to be an interim receiver direct that his powers shall be limited or restricted in any respect; but, save as so directed, an interim receiver has, in relation to the debtor's property, all the rights, powers, duties and immunities of a receiver and manager under the next section.

**286(4) [Contents of court order]** An order of the court appointing any person to be an interim receiver shall require that person to take immediate possession of the debtor's property or, as the case may be, the part of it to which his powers as interim receiver are limited.

**286(5) [Duties of debtor]** Where an interim receiver has been appointed, the debtor shall give him such inventory of his property and such other information, and shall attend on the interim receiver at such times, as the latter may for the purpose of carrying out his functions under this section reasonably require.

**286(6) [Application of s. 285(3)]** Where an interim receiver is appointed, section 285(3) applies for the period between the appointment and the making of a bankruptcy order on the petition, or the dismissal of the petition, as if the appointment were the making of such an order.

**286(7) [Ceasing to be interim receiver]** A person ceases to be interim receiver of a debtor's property if the bankruptcy petition relating to the debtor is dismissed, if a bankruptcy order is made on the petition or if the court by order otherwise terminates the appointment.

**286(8) [Interpretation]** References in this section to the debtor's property are to all his property, whether or not it would be comprised in his estate if he were adjudged bankrupt.

## 287 Receivership pending appointment of trustee

**287(1) [Official receiver, receiver and manager]** Between the making of a bankruptcy order and the time at which the bankrupt's estate vests in a trustee under Chapter IV of this Part, the official receiver is the receiver and (subject to section 370 (special manager)) the manager of the bankrupt's estate and is under a duty to act as such.

**287(2) [Function and powers of official receiver]** The function of the official receiver while acting as receiver or manager of the bankrupt's estate under this section is to protect the estate; and for this purpose–

(a) he has the same powers as if he were a receiver or manager appointed by the High Court, and

(b) he is entitled to sell or otherwise dispose of any perishable goods comprised in the estate and any other goods so comprised the value of which is likely to diminish if they are not disposed of.

**287(3) [Steps re protecting property]** The official receiver while acting as receiver or manager of the estate under this section–

(a) shall take all such steps as he thinks fit for protecting any property which may be claimed for the estate by the trustee of that estate,

(b) is not, except in pursuance of directions given by the Secretary of State, required to do anything that involves his incurring expenditure,

(c) may, if he thinks fit (and shall, if so directed by the court) at any time summon a general meeting of the bankrupt's creditors.

**287(4) [Liability of official receiver]** Where–

(a) the official receiver acting as receiver or manager of the estate under this section seizes or disposes of any property which is not comprised in the estate, and

(b) at the time of the seizure or disposal the official receiver believes, and has reasonable grounds for believing, that he is entitled (whether in pursuance of an order of the court or otherwise) to seize or dispose of that property,

the official receiver is not liable to any person in respect of any loss or damage resulting from the seizure or disposal except in so far as that loss or damage is caused by his negligence; and he has a lien on the property, or the proceeds of its sale, for such of the expenses of the bankruptcy as were incurred in connection with the seizure or disposal.

**287(5) [Non-application]** This section does not apply where by virtue of section 297 (appointment of trustee; special cases) the bankrupt's estate vests in a trustee immediately on the making of the bankruptcy order.

## 288 Statement of affairs

**288(1) [Submission of statement to official receiver]** Where a bankruptcy order has been made otherwise than on a debtor's petition, the bankrupt shall submit a statement of his affairs to the official receiver before the end of the period of 21 days beginning with the commencement of the bankruptcy.

**288(2) [Contents of statement]** The statement of affairs shall contain–

(a) such particulars of the bankrupt's creditors and of his debts and other liabilities and of his assets as may be prescribed, and

(b) such other information as may be prescribed.

**Note**

See also the Insolvency Rules 1986 (SI 1986/1925), r. 6.58–6.66.

**288(3) [Powers of official receiver]** The official receiver may, if he thinks fit–

(a) release the bankrupt from his duty under subsection (1), or

(b) extend the period specified in that subsection;

and where the official receiver has refused to exercise a power conferred by this section, the court, if it thinks fit, may exercise it.

**288(4) [Penalty for non-compliance]** A bankrupt who–

(a) without reasonable excuse fails to comply with the obligation imposed by this section, or

(b) without reasonable excuse submits a statement of affairs that does not comply with the prescribed requirements,

is guilty of a contempt of court and liable to be punished accordingly (in addition to any other punishment to which he may be subject).

## 289 Investigatory duties of official receiver

**289(1) [Investigation and report]** Subject to subsection (5) below, it is the duty of the official receiver to investigate the conduct and affairs of every bankrupt and to make such report (if any) to the court as he thinks fit.

**289(2) [Where application under s. 280]** Where an application is made by the bankrupt under section 280 for his discharge from bankruptcy, it is the duty of the official receiver to make a report to the court with respect to the prescribed matters; and the court shall consider that report before determining what order (if any) to make under that section.

**Note**

See also the Insolvency Rules 1986 (SI 1986/1925), r. 6.218.

**289(3) [Report prima facie evidence]** A report by the official receiver under this section shall, in any proceedings, be prima facie evidence of the facts stated in it.

**289(4) [Interpretation of s. 289(1)]** In subsection (1) the reference to the conduct and affairs of a bankrupt includes his conduct and affairs before the making of the order by which he was adjudged bankrupt.

**289(5) [Where certificate for administration]** Where a certificate for the summary administration of the bankrupt's estate is for the time being in force, the official receiver shall carry out an investigation under subsection (1) only if he thinks fit.

## 290 Public examination of bankrupt

**290(1) [Application to court]** Where a bankruptcy order has been made, the official receiver may at any time before the discharge of the bankrupt apply to the court for the public examination of the bankrupt.

**290(2) [Duty of official receiver to make application]** Unless the court otherwise orders, the official receiver shall make an application under subsection (1) if notice requiring him to do so is given to him, in accordance with the rules, by one of the bankrupt's creditors with the concurrence of not less than one-half, in value, of those creditors (including the creditor giving notice).

**290(3) [Direction re public examination]** On an application under subsection (1), the court shall direct that a public examination of the bankrupt shall be held on a day appointed by the court; and the bankrupt shall attend on that day and be publicly examined as to his affairs, dealings and property.

**290(4) [Persons taking part in examination]** The following may take part in the public examination of the bankrupt and may question him concerning his affairs, dealings and property and the causes of his failure, namely–

(a) the official receiver and, in the case of an individual adjudged bankrupt on a petition under section 264(1)(d), the Official Petitioner,

(b) the trustee of the bankrupt's estate, if his appointment has taken effect,

(c) any person who has been appointed as special manager of the bankrupt's estate or business,

(d) any creditor of the bankrupt who has tendered a proof in the bankruptcy.

**290(5) [Penalty re non-attendance]** If a bankrupt without reasonable excuse fails at any time to attend his public examination under this section he is guilty of a contempt of court and liable to be punished accordingly (in addition to any other punishment to which he may be subject).

## 291 Duties of bankrupt in relation to official receiver

**291(1) [Duties where bankruptcy order made]** Where a bankruptcy order has been made, the bankrupt is under a duty–

(a) to deliver possession of his estate to the official receiver, and

(b) to deliver up to the official receiver all books, papers and other records of which he has possession or control and which relate to his estate and affairs (including any which would be privileged from disclosure in any proceedings).

**291(2) [Property not capable of delivery to official receiver]** In the case of any part of the bankrupt's estate which consists of things possession of which cannot be delivered to the official receiver, and in the case of any property that may be claimed for the bankrupt's estate by the trustee, it is the bankrupt's duty to do all things as may reasonably be required by the official receiver for the protection of those things or that property.

**291(3) [Non-application of s. 291(1), (2)]** Subsections (1) and (2) do not apply where by virtue of section 297 below the bankrupt's estate vests in a trustee immediately on the making of the bankruptcy order.

**291(4) [Bankrupt to give information]** The bankrupt shall give the official receiver such inventory of his estate and such other information, and shall attend on the official receiver at such times, as the official receiver may for any of the purposes of this Chapter reasonably require.

**291(5) [Application of s. 291(4)]** Subsection (4) applies to a bankrupt after his discharge.

**291(6) [Penalty for non-compliance]** If the bankrupt without reasonable excuse fails to comply with any obligation imposed by this section, he is guilty of a contempt of court and liable to be punished accordingly (in addition to any other punishment to which he may be subject).

# Chapter III – Trustees In Bankruptcy

TENURE OF OFFICE AS TRUSTEE

## 292 Power to make appointments

**292(1) [Exercise of power]** The power to appoint a person as trustee of a bankrupt's estate (whether the first such trustee or a trustee appointed to fill any vacancy) is exercisable–

(a) except at a time when a certificate for the summary administration of the bankrupt's estate is in force, by a general meeting of the bankrupt's creditors;

(b) under section 295(2), 296(2) or 300(6) below in this Chapter, by the Secretary of State; or

(c) under section 297, by the court.

**292(2) [Qualification for trustee]** No person may be appointed as trustee of a bankrupt's estate unless he is, at the time of the appointment, qualified to act as an insolvency practitioner in relation to the bankrupt.

**292(3) [Joint trustees]** Any power to appoint a person as trustee of a bankrupt's estate includes power to appoint two or more persons as joint trustees; but such an appointment must make provision as to the circumstances in which the trustees must act together and the circumstances in which one or more of them may act for the others.

**292(4) [Requirement of acceptance of appointment]** The appointment of any person as trustee takes effect only if that person accepts the appointment in accordance with the rules. Subject to this, the appointment of any person as trustee takes effect at the time specified in his certificate of appointment.

**292(5) [Effect]** This section is without prejudice to the provisions of this Chapter under which the official receiver is, in certain circumstances, to be trustee of the estate.

## 293 Summoning of meeting to appoint first trustee

**293(1) [Duty of official receiver]** Where a bankruptcy order has been made and no certificate for the summary administration of the bankrupt's estate has been issued, it is the duty of the official receiver, as soon as practicable in the period of 12 weeks beginning with the day on which the order was made, to decide whether to summon a general meeting of the bankrupt's creditors for the purpose of appointing a trustee of the bankrupt's estate.

This section does not apply where the bankruptcy order was made on a petition under section 264(1)(d) (criminal bankruptcy); and it is subject to the provision made in sections 294(3) and 297(6) below.

**Note**

In s. 293(1) the words "does not apply where the bankruptcy order was made on a petition under section 264(1)(d) (criminal bankruptcy) and it" repealed by Criminal Justice Act 1988, s. 170(2) and Sch. 16 as from a day to be appointed.

**293(2) [Duty if no meeting summoned]** Subject to the next section, if the official receiver decides not to summon such a meeting, he shall, before the end of the period of 12 weeks above mentioned, give notice of his decision to the court and to every creditor of the bankrupt who is known to the official receiver or is identified in the bankrupt's statement of affairs.

**293(3) [Official receiver trustee from s. 293(2) notice]** As from the giving to the court of a notice under subsection (2), the official receiver is the trustee of the bankrupt's estate.

## 294 Power of creditors to requisition meeting

**294(1) [Request to official receiver]** Where in the case of any bankruptcy–

(a) the official receiver has not yet summoned, or has decided not to summon, a general meeting of the bankrupt's creditors for the purpose of appointing the trustee, and

(b) a certificate for the summary administration of the estate is not for the time being in force,

any creditor of the bankrupt may request the official receiver to summon such a meeting for that purpose.

**294(2) [Duty to summon meeting on request]** If such a request appears to the official receiver to be made with the concurrence of not less than one-quarter, in value, of the bankrupt's creditors (including the creditor making the request), it is the duty of the official receiver to summon the requested meeting.

**294(3) [Where s. 294(2) duty has arisen]** Accordingly, where the duty imposed by subsection (2) has arisen, the official receiver is required neither to reach a decision for the purposes of section 293(1) nor (if he has reached one) to serve any notice under section 293(2).

## 295 Failure of meeting to appoint trustee

**295(1) [Duty of official receiver]** If a meeting summoned under section 293 or 294 is held but no appointment of a person as trustee is made, it is the duty of the official receiver to decide whether to refer the need for an appointment to the Secretary of State.

**295(2) [Duty of Secretary of State]** On a reference made in pursuance of that decision, the Secretary of State shall either make an appointment or decline to make one.

**295(3) [Notice to court]** If–

(a) the official receiver decides not to refer the need for an appointment to the Secretary of State, or

(b) on such a reference the Secretary of State declines to make an appointment,

the official receiver shall give notice of his decision or, as the case may be, of the Secretary of State's decision to the court.

**295(4) [As from notice official receiver trustee]** As from the giving of notice under subsection (3) in a case in which no notice has been given under section 293(2), the official receiver shall be trustee of the bankrupt's estate.

## 296 Appointment of trustee by Secretary of State

**296(1) [Application for appointment instead of official receiver]** At any time when the official receiver is the trustee of a bankrupt's estate by virtue of any provision of this Chapter (other than section 297(1) below) he may apply to the Secretary of State for the appointment of a person as trustee instead of the official receiver.

**296(2) [Duty of Secretary of State]** On an application under subsection (1) the Secretary of State shall either make an appointment or decline to make one.

**296(3) [Making of application]** Such an application may be made notwithstanding that the Secretary of State has declined to make an appointment either on a previous application under subsection (1) or on a reference under section 295 or under section 300(4) below.

**296(4) [Notice etc., re appointment]** Where the trustee of a bankrupt's estate has been appointed by the Secretary of State (whether under this section or otherwise), the trustee shall give notice to the bankrupt's creditors of his appointment or, if the court so allows, shall advertise his appointment in accordance with the court's directions.

**296(5) [Contents of notice]** In that notice or advertisement the trustee shall–

(a) state whether he proposes to summon a general meeting of the bankrupt's creditors for the purpose of establishing a creditors' committee under section 301, and

(b) if he does not propose to summon such a meeting, set out the power of the creditors under this Part to require him to summon one.

## 297 Special cases

**297(1) [Where s. 264(1)(d) bankruptcy order]** Where a bankruptcy order is made on a petition under section 264(1)(d) (criminal bankruptcy), the official receiver shall be trustee of the bankrupt's estate.

**Note**

S. 297(1) repealed by Criminal Justice Act 1988, s. 170(2) and Sch. 16 as from a day to be appointed.

**297(2) [Where court issues certificate for summary administration]** Subject to the next subsection, where the court issues a certificate for the summary administration of a bankrupt's estate, the official receiver shall, as from the issue of that certificate, be the trustee.

**297(3) [Qualification to s. 297(2)]** Where such a certificate is issued or is in force, the court may, if it thinks fit, appoint a person other than the official receiver as trustee.

**297(4) [Where no certificate for summary administration]** Where a bankruptcy order is made in a case in which an insolvency practitioner's report has been submitted to the court under section 274 but no certificate for the summary administration of the estate is issued, the court, if it thinks fit, may on making the order appoint the person who made the report as trustee.

**297(5) [Where there is supervisor]** Where a bankruptcy order is made (whether or not on a petition under section 264(1)(c)) at a time when there is a supervisor of a voluntary arrangement approved in relation to the bankrupt under Part VIII, the court, if it thinks fit, may on making the order appoint the supervisor of the arrangement as trustee.

**297(6) [Exception re s. 293(1) duty]** Where an appointment is made under subsection (4) or (5) of this section, the official receiver is not under the duty imposed by section 293(1) (to decide whether or not to summon a meeting of creditors).

**297(7) [Notice where trustee appointed by court]** Where the trustee of a bankrupt's estate has been appointed by the court, the trustee shall give notice to the bankrupt's creditors of his appointment or, if the court so allows, shall advertise his appointment in accordance with the directions of the court.

**297(8) [Contents of notice]** In that notice or advertisement he shall–

(a) state whether he proposes to summon a general meeting of the bankrupt's creditors for the purpose of establishing a creditors' committee under section 301 below, and

(b) if he does not propose to summon such a meeting, set out the power of the creditors under this Part to require him to summon one.

## 298 Removal of trustee; vacation of office

**298(1) [Removal by court order or creditors' meeting]** Subject as follows, the trustee of a bankrupt's estate may be removed from office only by an order of the court or by a general meeting of the bankrupt's creditors summoned specially for that purpose in accordance with the rules.

**298(2) [Where official receiver trustee under s. 297(1)]** Where the official receiver is trustee by virtue of section 297(1), he shall not be removed from office under this section.

**298(3) [Where certificate for summary administration]** A general meeting of the bankrupt's creditors shall not be held for the purpose of removing the trustee at any time when a certificate for the summary administration of the estate is in force.

**298(4) [Where official receiver trustee under s. 293(3), 295(4)]** Where the official receiver is trustee by virtue of section 293(3) or 295(4) or a trustee is appointed by the Secretary of State or (otherwise than under section 297(5)) by the court, a general meeting of the bankrupt's creditors shall be summoned for the purpose of replacing the trustee only if–

(a) the trustee thinks fit, or

(b) the court so directs, or

(c) the meeting is requested by one of the bankrupt's creditors with the concurrence of not less than one-quarter, in value, of the creditors (including the creditor making the request).

**298(5) [Where trustee appointed by Secretary of State]** If the trustee was appointed by the Secretary of State, he may be removed by a direction of the Secretary of State.

**298(6) [Vacation of office]** The trustee (not being the official receiver) shall vacate office if he ceases to be a person who is for the time being qualified to act as an insolvency practitioner in relation to the bankrupt.

**298(7) [Resignation]** The trustee may, in the prescribed circumstances, resign his office by giving notice of his resignation to the court.

**298(8) [Vacation on s. 331 notice]** The trustee shall vacate office on giving notice to the court that a final meeting has been held under section 331 in Chapter IV and of the decision (if any) of that meeting.

**298(9) [When bankruptcy order annulled]** The trustee shall vacate office if the bankruptcy order is annulled.

## 299 Release of trustee

**299(1) [Time of release for official receiver]** Where the official receiver has ceased to be the trustee of a bankrupt's estate and a person is appointed in his stead, the official receiver shall have his release with effect from the following time, that is to say–

(a) where that person is appointed by a general meeting of the bankrupt's creditors or by the Secretary of State, the time at which the official receiver gives notice to the court that he has been replaced, and

(b) where that person is appointed by the court, such time as the court may determine.

**299(2) [Time of release if notice given by official receiver]** If the official receiver while he is the trustee gives notice to the Secretary of State that the administration of the bankrupt's estate in accordance with Chapter IV of this Part is for practical purposes complete, he shall have his release with effect from such time as the Secretary of State may determine.

**299(3) [Time of release for person not official receiver]** A person other than the official receiver who has ceased to be the trustee shall have his release with effect from the following time, that is to say–

(a) in the case of a person who has been removed from office by a general meeting of the bankrupt's creditors that has not resolved against his release or who has died, the time at which notice is given to the court in accordance with the rules that that person has ceased to hold office;

(b) in the case of a person who has been removed from office by a general meeting of the bankrupt's creditors that has resolved against his release, or by the court, or by the Secretary of State, or who has vacated office under section 298(6), such time as the Secretary of State may, on an application by that person, determine;

(c) in the case of a person who has resigned, such time as may be prescribed;

(d) in the case of a person who has vacated office under section 298(8)–

   (i) if the final meeting referred to in that subsection has resolved against that person's release, such time as the Secretary of State may, on an application by that person, determine; and

   (ii) if that meeting has not so resolved, the time at which the person vacated office.

**299(4) [Time of release where bankruptcy order annulled]** Where a bankruptcy order is annulled, the trustee at the time of the annulment has his release with effect from such time as the court may determine.

**299(5) [Effect of release]** Where the official receiver or the trustee has his release under this section, he shall, with effect from the time specified in the preceding provisions of this section, be discharged from all liability both in respect of acts or omissions of his in the administration of the estate and otherwise in relation to his conduct as trustee.

But nothing in this section prevents the exercise, in relation to a person who has had his release under this section, of the court's powers under section 304.

## 300 Vacancy in office of trustee

**300(1) [Application]** This section applies where the appointment of any person as trustee of a bankrupt's estate fails to take effect or, such an appointment having taken effect, there is otherwise a vacancy in the office of trustee.

**300(2) [Official receiver trustee]** The official receiver shall be trustee until the vacancy is filled.

**300(3) [Summoning creditors' meeting]** The official receiver may summon a general meeting of the bankrupt's creditors for the purpose of filling the vacancy and shall summon such a meeting if required to do so in pursuance of section 314(7) (creditors' requisition).

**300(4) [If no meeting summoned within 28 days]** If at the end of the period of 28 days beginning with the day on which the vacancy first came to the official receiver's attention he has not summoned, and is not proposing to summon, a general meeting of creditors for the purpose of filling the vacancy, he shall refer the need for an appointment to the Secretary of State.

**300(5) [Where certificate for summary administration]** Where a certificate for the summary administration of the estate is for the time being in force–

(a) the official receiver may refer the need to fill any vacancy to the court or, if the vacancy arises because a person appointed by the Secretary of State has ceased to hold office, to the court or the Secretary of State, and

(b) subsections (3) and (4) of this section do not apply.

**300(6) [Duty of Secretary of State re s. 300(4), (5)]** On a reference to the Secretary of State under subsection (4) or (5) the Secretary of State shall either make an appointment or decline to make one.

**300(7) [If no appointment on s. 300(4), (5) reference]** If on a reference under subsection (4) or (5) no appointment is made, the official receiver shall continue to be trustee of the bankrupt's estate, but without prejudice to his power to make a further reference.

**300(8) [Interpretation]** References in this section to a vacancy include a case where it is necessary, in relation to any property which is or may be comprised in a bankrupt's estate, to revive the trusteeship of that estate after holding of a final meeting summoned under section 331 or the giving by the official receiver of notice under section 299(2).

CONTROL OF TRUSTEE

## 301 Creditors' committee

**301(1) [Meeting may establish committee]** Subject as follows, a general meeting of a bankrupt's creditors (whether summoned under the preceding provisions of this Chapter or otherwise) may, in accordance with the rules, establish a committee (known as "the creditors' committee") to exercise the functions conferred on it by or under this Act.

**301(2) [Exception]** A general meeting of the bankrupt's creditors shall not establish such a committee, or confer any functions on such a committee, at any time when the official receiver is the trustee of the bankrupt's estate, except in connection with an appointment made by that meeting of a person to be trustee instead of the official receiver.

## 302 Exercise by Secretary of State of functions of creditors' committee

**302(1) [Where official receiver trustee]** The creditors' committee is not to be able or required to carry out its functions at any time when the official receiver is trustee of the bankrupt's estate; but at any such time the functions of the committee under this Act shall be vested in the Secretary of State, except to the extent that the rules otherwise provide.

**302(2) [Where no committee]** Where in the case of any bankruptcy there is for the time being no creditors' committee and the trustee of the bankrupt's estate is a person other than the official receiver, the functions of such a committee shall be vested in the Secretary of State, except to the extent that the rules otherwise provide.

## 303 General control of trustee by the court

**303(1) [Application to court]** If a bankrupt or any of his creditors or any other person is dissatisfied by any act, omission or decision of a trustee of the bankrupt's estate, he may apply to the court; and on such an application the court may confirm, reverse or modify any act or decision of the trustee, may give him directions or may make such other order as it thinks fit.

**303(2) [Application by trustee for directions]** The trustee of a bankrupt's estate may apply to the court for directions in relation to any particular matter arising under the bankruptcy.

## 304 Liability of trustee

**304(1) [Powers of court on application]** Where on an application under this section the court is satisfied–

(a) that the trustee of a bankrupt's estate has misapplied or retained, or become accountable for, any money or other property comprised in the bankrupt's estate, or

(b) that a bankrupt's estate has suffered any loss in consequence of any misfeasance or breach of fiduciary or other duty by a trustee of the estate in the carrying out of his functions,

the court may order the trustee, for the benefit of the estate, to repay, restore or account for money or other property (together with interest at such rate as the court thinks just) or, as the case may require, to pay such sum by way of compensation in respect of the misfeasance or breach of fiduciary or other duty as the court thinks just.

This is without prejudice to any liability arising apart from this section.

**304(2) [Applicants]** An application under this section may be made by the official receiver, the Secretary of State, a creditor of the bankrupt or (whether or not there is, or is likely to be, a surplus for the purposes of section 330(5) (final distribution)) the bankrupt himself.

But the leave of the court is required for the making of an application if it is to be made by the bankrupt or if it is to be made after the trustee has had his release under section 299.

**304(3) [Limit on liability]** Where–

(a) the trustee seizes or disposes of any property which is not comprised in the bankrupt's estate, and

(b) at the time of the seizure or disposal the trustee believes, and has reasonable grounds for believing, that he is entitled (whether in pursuance of an order of the court or otherwise) to seize or dispose of that property,

the trustee is not liable to any person (whether under this section or otherwise) in respect of any loss or damage resulting from the seizure or disposal except in so far as that loss or damage is caused by the negligence of the trustee; and he has a lien on the property, or the proceeds of its sale, for such of the expenses of the bankruptcy as were incurred in connection with the seizure or disposal.

# Chapter IV – Administration by Trustee

PRELIMINARY

## 305 General functions of trustee

**305(1) [Application of Ch. IV]** This Chapter applies in relation to any bankruptcy where either–

(a) the appointment of a person as trustee of a bankrupt's estate takes effect, or

(b) the official receiver becomes trustee of a bankrupt's estate.

**305(2) [Function of trustee]** The function of the trustee is to get in, realise and distribute the bankrupt's estate in accordance with the following provisions of this Chapter; and in the carrying out of that function and in the management of the bankrupt's estate the trustee is entitled, subject to those provisions, to use his own discretion.

**305(3) [Duties of trustee]** It is the duty of the trustee, if he is not the official receiver–

(a) to furnish the official receiver with such information,

(b) to produce to the official receiver, and permit inspection by the official receiver of, such books, papers and other records, and

(c) to give the official receiver such other assistance,

as the official receiver may reasonably require for the purpose of enabling him to carry out his functions in relation to the bankruptcy.

**305(4) [Official name of trustee]** The official name of the trustee shall be "the trustee of the estate of ............, a bankrupt" (inserting the name of the bankrupt); but he may be referred to as "the trustee in bankruptcy" of the particular bankrupt.

## ACQUISITION, CONTROL AND REALISATION OF BANKRUPT'S ESTATE

## 306 Vesting of bankrupt's estate in trustee

**306(1) [Time of vesting]** The bankrupt's estate shall vest in the trustee immediately on his appointment taking effect or, in the case of the official receiver, on his becoming trustee.

**306(2) [Mode of vesting]** Where any property which is, or is to be, comprised in the bankrupt's estate vests in the trustee (whether under this section or under any other provision of this Part), it shall so vest without any conveyance, assignment or transfer.

## 307 After-acquired property

**307(1) [Power of trustee]** Subject to this section and section 309, the trustee may by notice in writing claim for the bankrupt's estate any property which has been acquired by, or has devolved upon, the bankrupt since the commencement of the bankruptcy.

**307(2) [Limit on s. 307(1) notice]** A notice under this section shall not be served in respect of–

(a) any property falling within subsection (2) or (3) of section 283 in Chapter II,

(b) any property which by virtue of any other enactment is excluded from the bankrupt's estate, or

(c) without prejudice to section 280(2)(c) (order of court on application for discharge), any property which is acquired by, or devolves upon, the bankrupt after his discharge.

**307(3) [Vesting on service of notice]** Subject to the next subsection, upon the service on the bankrupt of a notice under this section the property to which the notice relates shall vest in the trustee as part of the bankrupt's estate; and the trustee's title to that property has relation back to the time at which the property was acquired by, or devolved upon, the bankrupt.

**307(4) [Outsiders]** Where, whether before or after service of a notice under this section–

(a) a person acquires property in good faith, for value and without notice of the bankruptcy, or

(b) a banker enters into a transaction in good faith and without such notice,

the trustee is not in respect of that property or transaction entitled by virtue of this section to any remedy against that person or banker, or any person whose title to any property derives from that person or banker.

**307(5) [Interpretation]** References in this section to property do not include any property which, as part of the bankrupt's income, may be the subject of an income payments order under section 310.

## 308 Vesting in trustee of certain items of excess value

**308(1) [Claim by trustee in writing]** Subject to section 309, where–

(a) property is excluded by virtue of section 283(2) (tools of trade, household effects, etc.) from the bankrupt's estate, and

(b) it appears to the trustee that the realisable value of the whole or any part of that property exceeds the cost of a reasonable replacement for that property or that part of it, the trustee may by notice in writing claim that property or, as the case may be, that part of it for the bankrupt's estate.

**History**
In s. 308(1) the words "section 309" substituted for the former words "the next section" by the Housing Act 1988, s. 140 and Sch. 17, para. 73 as from 15 January 1989 (SI 1991/828).

**308(2) [Vesting on service of s. 308(1) notice]** Upon the service on the bankrupt of a notice under this section, the property to which the notice relates vests in the trustee as part of the bankrupt's estate; and, except against a purchaser in good faith, for value and without notice of the bankruptcy, the trustee's title to that property has relation back to the commencement of the bankruptcy.

**308(3) [Application of funds by trustee]** The trustee shall apply funds comprised in the estate to the purchase by or on behalf of the bankrupt of a reasonable replacement for any property vested in the trustee under this section; and the duty imposed by this subsection has priority over the obligation of the trustee to distribute the estate.

**308(4) [Reasonable replacement]** For the purposes of this section property is a reasonable replacement for other property if it is reasonably adequate for meeting the needs met by the other property.

## 308A Vesting in trustee of certain tenancies

**308A** Upon the service on the bankrupt by the trustee of a notice in writing under this section, any tenancy–

(a) which is excluded by virtue of section 283(3A) from the bankrupt's estate, and

(b) to which the notice relates,

vests in the trustee as part of the bankrupt's estate; and, except against a purchaser in good faith, for value and without notice of the bankruptcy, the trustee's title to that tenancy has relation back to the commencement of the bankruptcy.

**History**
S. 308A inserted by Housing Act 1988, s. 117(2) and 141(3) as from 15 January 1989.

## 309 Time-limit for notice under s. 307 or 308

**309(1) [Timing of notice]** Except with the leave of the court, a notice shall not be served–

(a) under section 307, after the end of the period of 42 days beginning with the day on which it first came to the knowledge of the trustee that the property in question had been acquired by, or had devolved upon, the bankrupt;

(b) under section 308 or section 308A, after the end of the period of 42 days beginning with the day on which the property or tenancy in question first came to the knowledge of the trustee.

**History**
In s. 309(1) in para. (b) the words "or section 308A" and "or tenancy" inserted by Housing Act 1988, s. 117(3) and 141(3) as from 15 January 1989.

**309(2) [Deemed knowledge]** For the purposes of this section–

(a) anything which comes to the knowledge of the trustee is deemed in relation to any successor of his as trustee to have come to the knowledge of the successor at the same time; and

(b) anything which comes (otherwise than under paragraph (a)) to the knowledge of a person before he is the trustee is deemed to come to his knowledge on his appointment taking effect or, in the case of the official receiver, on his becoming trustee.

## 310 Income payments orders

**310(1) [Order by court]** The court may, on the application of the trustee, make an order ("an income payments order") claiming for the bankrupt's estate so much of the income of the bankrupt during the period for which the order is in force as may be specified in the order.

**310(2) [Limit on order]** The court shall not make an income payments order the effect of which would be to reduce the income of the bankrupt when taken together with any payments to which subsection (8) applies below what appears to the court to be necessary for meeting the reasonable domestic needs of the bankrupt and his family.

**History**

In s. 310(2) the words "when taken together with any payments to which subsection (8) applies" inserted after the words "income of the bankrupt" by the Pensions Act 1995, s. 122 and Sch. 3, para. 15(a) as from 6 April 1997 (see SI 1997/664 (C 23), art. 2(3), Sch., Pt. II).

**310(3) [Extent of order]** An income payments order shall, in respect of any payment of income to which it is to apply, either–

(a) require the bankrupt to pay the trustee an amount equal to so much of that payment as is claimed by the order, or

(b) require the person making the payment to pay so much of it as is so claimed to the trustee, instead of to the bankrupt.

**310(4) [Power to discharge or vary attachment of earnings]** Where the court makes an income payments order it may, if it thinks fit, discharge or vary any attachment of earnings order that is for the time being in force to secure payments by the bankrupt.

**310(5) [Sums part of estate]** Sums received by the trustee under an income payments order form part of the bankrupt's estate.

**310(6) [After discharge of bankrupt]** An income payments order shall not be made after the discharge of the bankrupt, and if made before, shall not have effect after his discharge except–

(a) in the case of a discharge under section 279(1)(a) (order of court), by virtue of a condition imposed by the court under section 280(2)(c) (income, etc. after discharge), or

(b) in the case of a discharge under section 279(1)(b) (expiration of relevant period), by virtue of a provision of the order requiring it to continue in force for a period ending after the discharge but no later than 3 years after the making of the order.

**310(7) [Income of the bankrupt]** For the purposes of this section the income of the bankrupt comprises every payment in the nature of income which is from time to time made to him or to which he from time to time becomes entitled, including any payment in respect of the carrying on of any business or in respect of any office or employment and (despite anything in section 11 or 12 of the Welfare Reform and Pensions Act 1999) any payment under a pension scheme but excluding any payment to which subsection (8) applies.

**History**

In s. 310(7):

- the words "(despite anything in section 11 or 12 of the Welfare Reform and Pensions Act 1999)" inserted by the Welfare Reform and Pensions Act 1999, s. 18, Sch. 2, para. 2 as from 29 May 2000 (see Welfare Reform and Pensions Act 1999 (Commencement No. 7) Order 2000 (SI 2000/1382 (C 41)), art. 2(c), (d));
- the words "and any payment" to the end inserted by the Pensions Act 1995, s. 122 and Sch. 3, para. 15(b) as from 6 April 1997 (see SI 1997/664 (C 23), art. 2(3), Sch., Pt. II).

**310(8) [Application]** This subsection applies to–

(a) payments by way of guaranteed minimum pension; and

(b) payments giving effect to the bankrupt's protected rights as a member of a pension scheme.

**History**

See history note after s. 310(9).

**310(9) [Definitions]** In this section, **"guaranteed minimum pension"** and **"protected rights"** have the same meaning as in the Pension Schemes Act 1993.

**History**

S. 310(8), (9) inserted by the Pensions Act 1995, s. 122 and Sch. 3, para. 15(b) as from 6 April 1997 (see SI 1997/664 (C 23), art. 2(3), Sch., Pt. II).

## 311 Acquisition by trustee of control

**311(1) [Trustee to take possession]** The trustee shall take possession of all books, papers and other records which relate to the bankrupt's estate or affairs and which belong to him or are in his possession or under his control (including any which would be privileged from disclosure in any proceedings).

**311(2) [Trustee like receiver]** In relation to, and for the purpose of acquiring or retaining possession of, the bankrupt's estate, the trustee is in the same position as if he were a receiver of property appointed by the High Court; and the court may, on his application, enforce such acquisition or retention accordingly.

**311(3) [Where estate includes transferable property]** Where any part of the bankrupt's estate consists of stock or shares in a company, shares in a ship or any other property transferable in the books of a company, office or person, the trustee may exercise the right to transfer the property to the same extent as the bankrupt might have exercised it if he had not become bankrupt.

**311(4) [Where estate includes things in action]** Where any part of the estate consists of things in action, they are deemed to have been assigned to the trustee; but notice of the deemed assignment need not be given except in so far as it is necessary, in a case where the deemed assignment is from the bankrupt himself, for protecting the priority of the trustee.

**311(5) [Where goods held by pledge]** Where any goods comprised in the estate are held by any person by way of pledge, pawn or other security and no notice has been served in respect of those goods by the official receiver under subsection (5) of section 285 (restriction on realising security), the trustee may serve such a notice in respect of the goods; and whether or not a notice has been served under this subsection or that subsection, the trustee may, if he thinks fit, exercise the bankrupt's right of redemption in respect of any such goods.

**311(6) [Effect of s. 311(5) notice]** A notice served by the trustee under subsection (5) has the same effect as a notice served by the official receiver under section 285(5).

## 312 Obligation to surrender control to trustee

**312(1) [Bankrupt to surrender property]** The bankrupt shall deliver up to the trustee possession of any property, books, papers or other records of which he has possession or control and of which the trustee is required to take possession.

This is without prejudice to the general duties of the bankrupt under section 333 in this Chapter.

**312(2) [Other persons in possession]** If any of the following is in possession of any property, books, papers or other records of which the trustee is required to take possession, namely–

(a) the official receiver,

(b) a person who has ceased to be trustee of the bankrupt's estate, or

(c) a person who has been the supervisor of a voluntary arrangement approved in relation to the bankrupt under Part VIII,

the official receiver or, as the case may be, that person shall deliver up possession of the property, books, papers or records to the trustee.

**312(3) [Bankers, agents et al. of bankrupt]** Any banker or agent of the bankrupt or any other person who holds any property to the account of, or for, the bankrupt shall pay or deliver to the trustee all property in his possession or under his control which forms part of the bankrupt's estate and which he is not by law entitled to retain as against the bankrupt or trustee.

**312(4) [Penalty for non-compliance]** If any person without reasonable excuse fails to comply with any obligation imposed by this section, he is guilty of a contempt of court and liable to be punished accordingly (in addition to any other punishment to which he may be subject).

## 313 Charge on bankrupt's home

**313(1) [Application to court by trustee]** Where any property consisting of an interest in a dwelling house which is occupied by the bankrupt or by his spouse or former spouse is comprised in the bankrupt's estate and the trustee is, for any reason, unable for the time being to realise that property, the trustee may apply to the court for an order imposing a charge on the property for the benefit of the bankrupt's estate.

**313(2) [Benefit of charge]** If on an application under this section the court imposes a charge on any property, the benefit of that charge shall be comprised in the bankrupt's estate and is enforceable, up to the value from time to time of the property secured, for the payment of any amount which is payable otherwise than to the bankrupt out of the estate and of interest on that amount at the prescribed rate.

**313(3) [Provision in order]** An order under this section made in respect of property vested in the trustee shall provide, in accordance with the rules, for the property to cease to be comprised in the bankrupt's estate and, subject to the charge (and any prior charge), to vest in the bankrupt.

**313(4) [Effect of Charging Orders Act]** Subsections (1) and (2) and (4) to (6) of section 3 of the Charging Orders Act 1979 (supplemental provisions with respect to charging orders) have effect in relation to orders under this section as in relation to charging orders under that Act.

## 314 Powers of trustee

**314(1) [Powers in Sch. 5, Pt. I and II]** The trustee may–

(a) with the permission of the creditors' committee or the court, exercise any of the powers specified in Part I of Schedule 5 to this Act, and

(b) without that permission, exercise any of the general powers specified in Part II of that Schedule.

**314(2) [Powers of appointment re bankrupt]** With the permission of the creditors' committee or the court, the trustee may appoint the bankrupt–

(a) to superintend the management of his estate or any part of it,

(b) to carry on his business (if any) for the benefit of his creditors, or

(c) in any other respect to assist in administering the estate in such manner and on such terms as the trustee may direct.

**314(3) [Permission in s. 314(1)(a), (2)]** A permission given for the purposes of subsection (1)(a) or (2) shall not be a general permission but shall relate to a particular proposed exercise of the power in question; and a person dealing with the trustee in good faith and for value is not to be concerned to enquire whether any permission required in either case has been given.

**314(4) [Where no permission under s. 314(1)(a), (2)]** Where the trustee has done anything without the permission required by subsection (1)(a) or (2), the court or the creditors' committee may, for the purpose of enabling him to meet his expenses out of the bankrupt's estate, ratify what the trustee has done.

But the committee shall not do so unless it is satisfied that the trustee has acted in a case of urgency and has sought its ratification without undue delay.

**314(5) [Powers in Sch. 5, Pt. III]** Part III of Schedule 5 to this Act has effect with respect to the things which the trustee is able to do for the purposes of, or in connection with, the exercise of any of his powers under any of this Group of Parts.

**314(6) [Notice to committee]** Where the trustee (not being the official receiver) in exercise of the powers conferred on him by any provision in this Group of Parts–

(a) disposes of any property comprised in the bankrupt's estate to an associate of the bankrupt, or

(b) employs a solicitor,

he shall, if there is for the time being a creditors' committee, give notice to the committee of that exercise of his powers.

**314(7) [Power to summon general meeting of creditors]** Without prejudice to the generality of subsection (5) and Part III of Schedule 5, the trustee may, if he thinks fit, at any time summon a general meeting of the bankrupt's creditors.

Subject to the preceding provisions in this Group of Parts, he shall summon such a meeting if he is requested to do so by a creditor of the bankrupt and the request is made with the concurrence of not less than one-tenth, in value, of the bankrupt's creditors (including the creditor making the request).

**314(8) [Capacity of trustee]** Nothing in this Act is to be construed as restricting the capacity of the trustee to exercise any of his powers outside England and Wales.

DISCLAIMER OF ONEROUS PROPERTY

## 315 Disclaimer (general power)

**315(1) [Power of trustee to disclaim]** Subject as follows, the trustee may, by the giving of the prescribed notice, disclaim any onerous property and may do so notwithstanding that he has taken possession of it, endeavoured to sell it or otherwise exercised rights of ownership in relation to it.

**315(2) [Onerous property]** The following is onerous property for the purposes of this section, that is to say–

(a) any unprofitable contract, and

(b) any other property comprised in the bankrupt's estate which is unsaleable or not readily saleable, or is such that it may give rise to a liability to pay money or perform any other onerous act.

**315(3) [Effect of disclaimer]** A disclaimer under this section–

(a) operates so as to determine, as from the date of the disclaimer, the rights, interests and liabilities of the bankrupt and his estate in or in respect of the property disclaimed, and

(b) discharges the trustee from all personal liability in respect of that property as from the commencement of his trusteeship,

but does not, except so far as is necessary for the purpose of releasing the bankrupt, the bankrupt's estate and the trustee from any liability, affect the rights or liabilities of any other person.

**315(4) [Where notice of disclaimer not to be given]** A notice of disclaimer shall not be given under this section in respect of any property that has been claimed for the estate under section 307 (after-acquired property) or 308 (personal property of bankrupt exceeding reasonable replacement value) or 308A, except with the leave of the court.

**History**

In s. 315(4) the words "or 308A" inserted by Housing Act 1988, s. 117(4) and 141(3) as from 15 January 1989.

**315(5) [Persons sustaining loss or damage]** Any person sustaining loss or damage in consequence of the operation of a disclaimer under this section is deemed to be a creditor of the bankrupt to the extent of the loss or damage and accordingly may prove for the loss or damage as a bankruptcy debt.

## 316 Notice requiring trustee's decision

**316(1) [Where notice not to be given]** Notice of disclaimer shall not be given under section 315 in respect of any property if–

(a) a person interested in the property has applied in writing to the trustee or one of his predecessors as trustee requiring the trustee or that predecessor to decide whether he will disclaim or not, and

(b) the period of 28 days beginning with the day on which that application was made has expired without a notice of disclaimer having been given under section 315 in respect of that property.

**316(2) [Deemed adoption]** The trustee is deemed to have adopted any contract which by virtue of this section he is not entitled to disclaim.

## 317 Disclaimer of leaseholds

**317(1) [Disclaimer of leasehold property]** The disclaimer of any property of a leasehold nature does not take effect unless a copy of the disclaimer has been served (so far as the trustee is aware of their addresses) on every person claiming under the bankrupt as underlessee or mortgagee and either–

(a) no application under section 320 below is made with respect to the property before the end of the period of 14 days beginning with the day on which the last notice served under this subsection was served, or

(b) where such an application has been made, the court directs that the disclaimer is to take effect.

**317(2) [Where court gives s. 317(1)(b) direction]** Where the court gives a direction under subsection (1)(b) it may also, instead of or in addition to any order it makes under section 320, make such orders with respect to fixtures, tenant's improvements and other matters arising out of the lease as it thinks fit.

## 318 Disclaimer of dwelling house

**318** Without prejudice to section 317, the disclaimer of any property in a dwelling house does not take effect unless a copy of the disclaimer has been served (so far as the trustee is aware of their addresses) on every person in occupation of or claiming a right to occupy the dwelling house and either–

(a) no application under section 320 is made with respect to the property before the end of the period of 14 days beginning with the day on which the last notice served under this section was served, or

(b) where such an application has been made, the court directs that the disclaimer is to take effect.

## 319 Disclaimer of land subject to rentcharge

**319(1) [Application]** The following applies where, in consequence of the disclaimer under section 315 of any land subject to a rentcharge, that land vests by operation of law in the Crown or any other person (referred to in the next subsection as "the proprietor").

**319(2) [Limit on liability]** The proprietor, and the successors in title of the proprietor, are not subject to any personal liability in respect of any sums becoming due under the rentcharge, except sums becoming due after the proprietor, or some person claiming under or through the proprietor, has taken possession or control of the land or has entered into occupation of it.

## 320 Court order vesting disclaimed property

**320(1) [Application]** This section and the next apply where the trustee has disclaimed property under section 315.

**320(2) [Application to court]** An application may be made to the court under this section by–

(a) any person who claims an interest in the disclaimed property,

(b) any person who is under any liability in respect of the disclaimed property, not being a liability discharged by the disclaimer, or

(c) where the disclaimed property is property in a dwelling house, any person who at the time when the bankruptcy petition was presented was in occupation of or entitled to occupy the dwelling house.

**320(3) [Order by court]** Subject as follows in this section and the next, the court may, on an application under this section, make an order on such terms as it thinks fit for the vesting of the disclaimed property in, or for its delivery to–

(a) a person entitled to it or a trustee for such a person,

(b) a person subject to such a liability as is mentioned in subsection (2)(b) or a trustee for such a person, or

(c) where the disclaimed property is property in a dwelling house, any person who at the time when the bankruptcy petition was presented was in occupation of or entitled to occupy the dwelling house.

**320(4) [Limit to s. 320(3)(b)]** The court shall not make an order by virtue of subsection (3)(b) except where it appears to the court that it would be just to do so for the purpose of compensating the person subject to the liability in respect of the disclaimer.

**320(5) [Effect of order in s. 315(5) assessment]** The effect of any order under this section shall be taken into account in assessing for the purposes of section 315(5) the extent of any loss or damage sustained by any person in consequence of the disclaimer.

**320(6) [Mode of vesting re order]** An order under this section vesting property in any person need not be completed by any conveyance, assignment or transfer.

## 321 Order under s. 320 in respect of leaseholds

**321(1) [Terms of order re leasehold property]** The court shall not make an order under section 320 vesting property of a leasehold nature in any person, except on terms making that person–

(a) subject to the same liabilities and obligations as the bankrupt was subject to under the lease on the day the bankruptcy petition was presented, or

(b) if the court thinks fit, subject to the same liabilities and obligations as that person would be subject to if the lease had been assigned to him on that day.

**321(2) [Where order re part of property in lease]** For the purposes of an order under section 320 relating to only part of any property comprised in a lease, the requirements of subsection (1) apply as if the lease comprised only the property to which the order relates.

**321(3) [Where no person accepts order in s. 162(5) case]** Where subsection (1) applies and no person is willing to accept an order under section 320 on the terms required by that subsection, the court may (by order under section 320) vest the estate or interest of the bankrupt in the property in any person who is liable (whether personally or in a representative capacity and whether alone or jointly with the bankrupt) to perform the lessee's covenants in the lease.

The court may by virtue of this subsection vest that estate and interest in such a person freed and discharged from all estates, incumbrances and interests created by the bankrupt.

**321(4) [Exclusion from interest in property]** Where subsection (1) applies and a person declines to accept any order under section 320, that person shall be excluded from all interest in the property.

DISTRIBUTION OF BANKRUPT'S ESTATE

## 322 Proof of debts

**322(1) [Proof in accordance with rules]** Subject to this section and the next, the proof of any bankruptcy debt by a secured or unsecured creditor of the bankrupt and the admission or rejection of any proof shall take place in accordance with the rules.

**322(2) [Where bankruptcy debt bears interest]** Where a bankruptcy debt bears interest, that interest is provable as part of the debt except in so far as it is payable in respect of any period after the commencement of the bankruptcy.

**322(3) [Estimation of debt]** The trustee shall estimate the value of any bankruptcy debt which, by reason of its being subject to any contingency or contingencies or for any other reason, does not bear a certain value.

**322(4) [Where estimate under s. 303, 322(3)]** Where the value of a bankruptcy debt is estimated by the trustee under subsection (3) or, by virtue of section 303 in Chapter III, by the court, the amount provable in the bankruptcy in respect of the debt is the amount of the estimate.

## 323 Mutual credit and set-off

**323(1) [Application]** This section applies where before the commencement of the bankruptcy there have been mutual credits, mutual debts or other mutual dealings between the bankrupt and any creditor of the bankrupt proving or claiming to prove for a bankruptcy debt.

**323(2) [Account to be taken]** An account shall be taken of what is due from each party to the other in respect of the mutual dealings and the sums due from one party shall be set off against the sums due from the other.

**323(3) [Qualification to s. 323(2)]** Sums due from the bankrupt to another party shall not be included in the account taken under subsection (2) if that other party had notice at the time they became due that a bankruptcy petition relating to the bankrupt was pending.

**323(4) [Balance to trustee]** Only the balance (if any) of the account taken under subsection (2) is provable as a bankruptcy debt or, as the case may be, to be paid to the trustee as part of the bankrupt's estate.

## 324 Distribution by means of dividend

**324(1) [Duty to declare and distribute]** Whenever the trustee has sufficient funds in hand for the purpose he shall, subject to the retention of such sums as may be necessary for the expenses of the bankruptcy, declare and distribute dividends among the creditors in respect of the bankruptcy debts which they have respectively proved.

**324(2) [Notice of intention to declare and distribute]** The trustee shall give notice of his intention to declare and distribute a dividend.

**324(3) [Notice of dividend etc.]** Where the trustee has declared a dividend, he shall give notice of the dividend and of how it is proposed to distribute it; and a notice given under this subsection shall contain the prescribed particulars of the bankrupt's estate.

**324(4) [Calculation and distribution of dividend]** In the calculation and distribution of a dividend the trustee shall make provision–

(a) for any bankruptcy debts which appear to him to be due to persons who, by reason of the distance of their place of residence, may not have had sufficient time to tender and establish their proofs,

(b) for any bankruptcy debts which are the subject of claims which have not yet been determined, and

(c) for disputed proofs and claims.

## 325 Claims by unsatisfied creditors

**325(1) [Entitlements of creditors]** A creditor who has not proved his debt before the declaration of any dividend is not entitled to disturb, by reason that he has not participated in it, the distribution of that dividend or any other dividend declared before his debt was proved, but–

(a) when he has proved that debt he is entitled to be paid, out of any money for the time being available for the payment of any further dividend, any dividend or dividends which he has failed to receive; and

(b) any dividend or dividends payable under paragraph (a) shall be paid before that money is applied to the payment of any such further dividend.

**325(2) [Order re payment of dividend]** No action lies against the trustee for a dividend, but if the trustee refuses to pay a dividend the court may, if it thinks fit, order him to pay it and also to pay, out of his own money–

(a) interest on the dividend, at the rate for the time being specified in section 17 of the Judgments Act 1838, from the time it was withheld, and

(b) the costs of the proceedings in which the order to pay is made.

## 326 Distribution of property in specie

**326(1) [Division of unsaleable property]** Without prejudice to sections 315 to 319 (disclaimer), the trustee may, with the permission of the creditors' committee, divide in its existing form amongst the bankrupt's creditors, according to its estimated value, any property which from its peculiar nature or other special circumstances cannot be readily or advantageously sold.

**326(2) [Permission under s. 326(1)]** A permission given for the purposes of subsection (1) shall not be a general permission but shall relate to a particular proposed exercise of the power in question; and a person dealing with the trustee in good faith and for value is not to be concerned to enquire whether any permission required by subsection (1) has been given.

**326(3) [Where no permission under s. 326(1)]** Where the trustee has done anything without the permission required by subsection (1), the court or the creditors' committee may, for the purpose of enabling him to meet his expenses out of the bankrupt's estate, ratify what the trustee has done.

But the committee shall not do so unless it is satisfied that the trustee acted in a case of urgency and has sought its ratification without undue delay.

## 327 Distribution in criminal bankruptcy

327 Where the bankruptcy order was made on a petition under section 264(1)(d) (criminal bankruptcy), no distribution shall be made under sections 324 to 326 so long as an appeal is pending (within the meaning of section 277) against the bankrupt's conviction of any offence by virtue of which the criminal bankruptcy order on which the petition was based was made.

**Note**
S. 327 repealed by Criminal Justice Act 1988, s. 170(2) and Sch. 16 as from a day to be appointed.

## 328 Priority of debts

**328(1) [Preferential debts to be paid first]** In the distribution of the bankrupt's estate, his preferential debts (within the meaning given by section 386 in Part XII) shall be paid in priority to other debts.

**328(2) [Ranking of preferential debts]** Preferential debts rank equally between themselves after the expenses of the bankruptcy and shall be paid in full unless the bankrupt's estate is insufficient for meeting them, in which case they abate in equal proportions between themselves.

**328(3) [Debts neither preferential nor under s. 329]** Debts which are neither preferential debts nor debts to which the next section applies also rank equally between themselves and, after the preferential debts, shall be paid in full unless the bankrupt's estate is insufficient for meeting them, in which case they abate in equal proportions between themselves.

**328(4) [Surplus after payment]** Any surplus remaining after the payment of the debts that are preferential or rank equally under subsection (3) shall be applied in paying interest on those debts in respect of the periods during which they have been outstanding since the commencement of the bankruptcy; and interest on preferential debts ranks equally with interest on debts other than preferential debts.

**328(5) [Rate of interest under s. 328(4)]** The rate of interest payable under subsection (4) in respect of any debt is whichever is the greater of the following–

(a) the rate specified in section 17 of the Judgments Act 1838 at the commencement of the bankruptcy, and

(b) the rate applicable to that debt apart from the bankruptcy.

**328(6) [Other enactments]** This section and the next are without prejudice to any provision of this Act or any other Act under which the payment of any debt or the making of any other payment is, in the event of bankruptcy, to have a particular priority or to be postponed.

## 329 Debts to spouse

**329(1) [Application]** This section applies to bankruptcy debts owed in respect of credit provided by a person who (whether or not the bankrupt's spouse at the time the credit was provided) was the bankrupt's spouse at the commencement of the bankruptcy.

**329(2) [Ranking, payment]** Such debts–

(a) rank in priority after the debts and interest required to be paid in pursuance of section 328(3) and (4), and

(b) are payable with interest at the rate specified in section 328(5) in respect of the period during which they have been outstanding since the commencement of the bankruptcy;

and the interest payable under paragraph (b) has the same priority as the debts on which it is payable.

## 330 Final distribution

**330(1) [Notice re dividend, etc.]** When the trustee has realised all the bankrupt's estate or so much of it as can, in the trustee's opinion, be realised without needlessly protracting the trusteeship, he shall give notice in the prescribed manner either–

(a) of his intention to declare a final dividend, or

(b) that no dividend, or further dividend, will be declared.

**330(2) [Contents of notice]** The notice under subsection (1) shall contain the prescribed particulars and shall require claims against the bankrupt's estate to be established by a date ("the final date") specified in the notice.

**330(3) [Postponement of final date]** The court may, on the application of any person, postpone the final date.

**330(4) [Trustee's duties after final date]** After the final date, the trustee shall–

(a) defray any outstanding expenses of the bankruptcy out of the bankrupt's estate, and

(b) if he intends to declare a final dividend, declare and distribute that dividend without regard to the claim of any person in respect of a debt not already proved in the bankruptcy.

**330(5) [Where surplus]** If a surplus remains after payment in full and with interest of all the bankrupt's creditors and the payment of the expenses of the bankruptcy, the bankrupt is entitled to the surplus.

## 331 Final meeting

**331(1) [Application]** Subject as follows in this section and the next, this section applies where–

(a) it appears to the trustee that the administration of the bankrupt's estate in accordance with this Chapter is for practical purposes complete, and

(b) the trustee is not the official receiver.

**331(2) [Duty of trustee]** The trustee shall summon a final general meeting of the bankrupt's creditors which–

(a) shall receive the trustee's report of his administration of the bankrupt's estate, and

(b) shall determine whether the trustee should have his release under section 299 in Chapter III.

**331(3) [Time for notice]** The trustee may, if he thinks fit, give the notice summoning the final general meeting at the same time as giving notice under section 330(1); but, if summoned for an earlier date, that meeting shall be adjourned (and, if necessary, further adjourned) until a date on which the trustee is able to report to the meeting that the administration of the bankrupt's estate is for practical purposes complete.

**331(4) [Expenses]** In the administration of the estate it is the trustee's duty to retain sufficient sums from the estate to cover the expenses of summoning and holding the meeting required by this section.

## 332 Saving for bankrupt's home

**332(1) [Application]** This section applies where–

(a) there is comprised in the bankrupt's estate property consisting of an interest in a dwelling house which is occupied by the bankrupt or by his spouse or former spouse, and

(b) the trustee has been unable for any reason to realise that property.

**332(2) [Conditions for s. 331 meeting]** The trustee shall not summon a meeting under section 331 unless either–

(a) the court has made an order under section 313 imposing a charge on that property for the benefit of the bankrupt's estate, or

(b) the court has declined, on an application under that section, to make such an order, or

(c) the Secretary of State has issued a certificate to the trustee stating that it would be inappropriate or inexpedient for such an application to be made in the case in question.

SUPPLEMENTAL

## 333 Duties of bankrupt in relation to trustee

**333(1) [Duties]** The bankrupt shall–

(a) give to the trustee such information as to his affairs,

(b) attend on the trustee at such times, and

(c) do all such other things,

as the trustee may for the purposes of carrying out his functions under any of this Group of Parts reasonably require.

**333(2) [Notice re after-acquired property]** Where at any time after the commencement of the bankruptcy any property is acquired by, or devolves upon, the bankrupt or there is an increase of the bankrupt's income, the bankrupt shall, within the prescribed period, give the trustee notice of the property or, as the case may be, of the increase.

**333(3) [Application of s. 333(1)]** Subsection (1) applies to a bankrupt after his discharge.

**333(4) [Penalty for non-compliance]** If the bankrupt without reasonable excuse fails to comply with any obligation imposed by this section, he is guilty of a contempt of court and liable to be punished accordingly (in addition to any other punishment to which he may be subject).

## 334 Stay of distribution in case of second bankruptcy

**334(1) [Application, definitions]** This section and the next apply where a bankruptcy order is made against an undischarged bankrupt; and in both sections–

(a) **"the later bankruptcy"** means the bankruptcy arising from that order,

(b) **"the earlier bankruptcy"** means the bankruptcy (or, as the case may be, most recent bankruptcy) from which the bankrupt has not been discharged at the commencement of the later bankruptcy, and

(c) **"the existing trustee"** means the trustee (if any) of the bankrupt's estate for the purposes of the earlier bankruptcy.

**334(2) [Certain distributions void]** Where the existing trustee has been given the prescribed notice of the presentation of the petition for the later bankruptcy, any distribution or other disposition by him of anything to which the next subsection applies, if made after the giving of the notice, is void except to the extent that it was made with the consent of the court or is or was subsequently ratified by the court.

This is without prejudice to section 284 (restrictions on dispositions of property following bankruptcy order).

**334(3) [Application of s. 334(2)]** This subsection applies to–

(a) any property which is vested in the existing trustee under section 307(3) (after-acquired property);

(b) any money paid to the existing trustee in pursuance of an income payments order under section 310; and

(c) any property or money which is, or in the hands of the existing trustee represents, the proceeds of sale or application of property or money falling within paragraph (a) or (b) of this subsection.

## 335 Adjustment between earlier and later bankruptcy estates

**335(1) [Matters in bankrupt's estate]** With effect from the commencement of the later bankruptcy anything to which section 334(3) applies which, immediately before the commencement of that bankruptcy, is comprised in the bankrupt's estate for the purposes of the earlier bankruptcy is to be treated as comprised in the bankrupt's estate for the purposes of the later bankruptcy and, until there is a trustee of that estate, is to be dealt with by the existing trustee in accordance with the rules.

**335(2) [Sums paid under s. 310]** Any sums which in pursuance of an income payments order under section 310 are payable after the commencement of the later bankruptcy to the existing trustee shall form part of the bankrupt's estate for the purposes of the later bankruptcy; and the court may give such consequential directions for the modification of the order as it thinks fit.

**335(3) [Charge re bankruptcy expenses]** Anything comprised in a bankrupt's estate by virtue of subsection (1) or (2) is so comprised subject to a first charge in favour of the existing trustee for any bankruptcy expenses incurred by him in relation thereto.

**335(4) [Property not in estate]** Except as provided above and in section 334, property which is, or by virtue of section 308 (personal property of bankrupt exceeding reasonable replacement value) or section 308A (vesting in trustee of certain tenancies) is capable of being, comprised in the bankrupt's estate for the purposes of the earlier bankruptcy, or of any bankruptcy prior to it, shall not be comprised in his estate for the purposes of the later bankruptcy.

**History**
In s. 335(4) the words "or section 308A (vesting in trustee of certain tenancies)" inserted by the Housing Act 1988, s. 140 and Sch. 17, para. 74 as from 15 January 1989 (SI 1988/2152).

**335(5) [Creditors of earlier bankruptcies]** The creditors of the bankrupt in the earlier bankruptcy and the creditors of the bankrupt in any bankruptcy prior to the earlier one, are not to be creditors of his in the later bankruptcy in respect of the same debts; but the existing trustee may prove in the later bankruptcy for–

(a) the unsatisfied balance of the debts (including any debt under this subsection) ovable against the bankrupt's estate in the earlier bankruptcy;

(b) any interest payable on that balance; and

(c) any unpaid expenses of the earlier bankruptcy.

**335(6) [Priority of amounts in s. 335(5)]** Any amount provable under subsection (5) ranks in priority after all the other debts provable in the later bankruptcy and after interest on those debts and, accordingly, shall not be paid unless those debts and that interest have first been paid in full.

# Chapter V – Effect of Bankruptcy on Certain Rights, Transactions, Etc.

RIGHTS UNDER TRUSTS OF LAND

## 335A Rights under trusts of land

**335A(1) [Application for order for sale of land]** Any application by a trustee of a bankrupt's estate under section 14 of the Trusts of Land and Appointment of Trustees Act 1996 (powers of court in relation to trusts of land) for an order under that section for the sale of land shall be made to the court having jurisdiction in relation to the bankruptcy.

**335A(2) [Interests considered before order]** On such an application the court shall make such order as it thinks just and reasonable having regard to–

(a) the interests of the bankrupt's creditors;

(b) where the application is made in respect of land which includes a dwelling house which is or has been the home of the bankrupt or the bankrupt's spouse or former spouse–

(i) the conduct of the spouse or former spouse, so far as contributing to the bankruptcy,

(ii) the needs and financial resources of the spouse or former spouse, and

(iii) the needs of any children; and

(c) all the circumstances of the case other than the needs of the bankrupt.

**335A(3) [Assumption by court re interests of creditors]** Where such an application is made after the end of the period of one year beginning with the first vesting under Chapter IV of this Part of the bankrupt's estate in a trustee, the court shall assume, unless the circumstances of the case are exceptional, that the interests of the bankrupt's creditors outweigh all other considerations.

**335A(4) [Exercise of powers conferred on court]** The powers conferred on the court by this section are exercisable on an application whether it is made before or after the commencement of this section.

**History**
S. 335A inserted by Trusts of Land and Appointment of Trustees Act 1996, Pt. III, s. 25(1), 27 and Sch. 3 as from 1 January 1997. (See the Trusts of Land and Appointment of Trustees Act 1996 (Commencement) Order 1996 (SI 1996/2974).

RIGHTS OF OCCUPATION

## 336 Rights of occupation etc. of bankrupt's spouse

**336(1) [Family Law Act 1996]** Nothing occurring in the initial period of the bankruptcy (that is to say, the period beginning with the day of the presentation of the petition for the bankruptcy order and ending with the vesting of the bankrupt's estate in a trustee) is to be taken as having given rise to any matrimonial home rights under Part IV of the Family Law Act 1996 in relation to a dwelling house comprised in the bankrupt's estate.

**History**
In s. 336(1) the words "matrimonial home rights under Part IV of the Family Law Act 1996" substituted for the former words "rights of occupation under the Matrimonial Homs Act 1983" by Family Law Act 1996, s. 66(1) and Sch. 8, Pt. III, para. 57(1), (2) as from 1 October 1997 (see SI 1997/1892 (C 76), art. 3(1)(b)).

**336(2) [Where spouse's rights of occupation charge on estate]** Where a spouse's matrimonial home rights under the Act of 1996 are a charge on the estate or interest of the other spouse, or of trustees for the other spouse, and the other spouse is adjudged bankrupt–

(a) the charge continues to subsist notwithstanding the bankruptcy and, subject to the provisions of that Act, binds the trustee of the bankrupt's estate and persons deriving title under that trustee, and

(b) any application for an order under section 33 of that Act shall be made to the court having jurisdiction in relation to the bankruptcy.

**History**
In s. 336(2) the words "matrimonial home rights under the Act of 1996" substituted for the former words "rights of occupation under the Act of 1983" and in s. 336(2)(b) the words "under section 33 of that Act" substituted for the former words "under section 1 of that Act" by Family Law Act 1996, s. 66(1) and Sch. 8, Pt. III, para. 57(1), (3) as from 1 October 1997 (see SI 1997/1982 (C 76), art. 3(1)(b)).

**336(3)** (Repealed by Trusts of Land and Appointment of Trustees Act 1996, Pt. III, s. 25(2), 27 and Sch. 4 as from 1 January 1997.)

**History**
In regard to the date of the above repeal, see the Trusts of Land and Appointment of Trustees Act 1996 (Commencement) Order 1996 (1996/2974). S. 336(3) formerly read as follows;

"Where a person and his spouse or former spouse are trustees for sale of a dwelling house and that person is adjudged bankrupt, any application by the trustee of the bankrupt's estate for an order under section 30 of the Law of Property Act 1925 (powers of court where trustees for sale refuse to act) shall be made to the court having jurisdiction in relation to the bankruptcy."

**336(4) [Court orders]** On such an application as is mentioned in subsection (2) the court shall make such order under section 33 of the Act of 1996 as it thinks just and reasonable having regard to–

(a) the interests of the bankrupt's creditors,

(b) the conduct of the spouse or former spouse, so far as contributing to the bankruptcy,

(c) the needs and financial resources of the spouse or former spouse,

(d) the needs of any children, and

(e) all the circumstances of the case other than the needs of the bankrupt.

**History**
In s. 336(4) the words "or (3)" formerly appearing after the words "subsection (2)" and the words "or section 30 of the Act of 1925" formerly appearing after the words "Act of 1983" repealed by Trusts of Land and Appointment of Trustees Act 1996, Pt. III, s. 25(2), 27 and Sch. 4 as from 1 January 1997. (See the Trusts of Land and Appointment of Trustees Act 1996 (Commencement) Order 1996 (SI 1996/2974).
Also in s. 336(4) the words "section 33 of the Act of 1996" substituted for the former words "section 1 of the Act of 1983" by Family Law Act 1996, s. 66(1) and Sch. 8, Pt. III, para. 57(1), (4) as from 1 October 1997 (see SI 1997/1892 (C 76), art. 3(1)(b)).

**336(5) [Assumption by court re interests of creditors]** Where such an application is made after the end of the period of one year beginning with the first vesting under Chapter IV of this Part of the bankrupt's estate in a trustee, the court shall assume, unless the circumstances of the case are exceptional, that the interests of the bankrupt's creditors outweigh all other considerations.

## 337 Rights of occupation of bankrupt

**337(1) [Application]** This section applies where–

(a) a person who is entitled to occupy a dwelling house by virtue of a beneficial estate or interest is adjudged bankrupt, and

(b) any persons under the age of 18 with whom that person had at some time occupied that dwelling house had their home with that person at the time when the bankruptcy petition was presented and at the commencment of the bankruptcy.

**337(2) [Rights of occupation, etc.]** Whether or not the bankrupt's spouse (if any) has matrimonial home rights under Part IV of the Family Law Act 1996–

(a) the bankrupt has the following rights as against the trustee of his estate–

(i) if in occupation, right not to be evicted or excluded from the dwelling house or any part of it, except with the leave of the court,

(ii) if not in occupation, a right with the leave of the court to enter into and occupy the dwelling house, and

(b) the bankrupt's rights are a charge, having the like priority as an equitable interest created immediately before the commencement of the bankruptcy, on so much of his estate or interest in the dwelling house as vests in the trustee.

**History**

In s. 337(2) the words "matrimonial home rights under Part IV of the Family Law Act 1996" substituted for the former words "rights of occupation under the Matrimonial Homes Act 1983" by Family Law Act 1996, s. 66(1) and Sch. 8, Pt. III, para. 58(1), (2) as from 1 October 1997 (see SI 1997/1892 (C 76), art. 3(1)(b)).

**337(3) [Application of Family Law Act]** The Act of 1996 has effect, with the necessary modifications, as if–

(a) the rights conferred by paragraph (a) of subsection (2) were matrimonial home rights under that Act,

(b) any application for leave such as is mentioned in that paragraph were an application for an order under section 33 of that Act, and

(c) any charge under paragraph (b) of that subsection on the estate or interest of the trustee were a charge under that Act on the estate or interest of a spouse.

**History**

S. 337(3) substituted by Family Law Act 1996, s. 66(1) and Sch. 8, Pt. III, para. 58(1), (3) as from 1 October 1997 (see SI 1997/1892 (C 76), art. 3(1)(b)). S. 337(3) formerly read as follows:

"The Act of 1983 has effect, with the necessary modifications, as if–

(a) the rights conferred by paragraph (a) of subsection (2) were rights of occupation under that Act,

(b) any application for leave such as is mentioned in that paragraph were an application for an order under section 1 of that Act, and

(c) any charge under paragraph (b) of that subsection on the estate or interest of the trustee were a charge under that Act on the estate or interest of a spouse."

**337(4) [Application to court]** Any application for leave such as is mentioned in subsection (2)(a) or otherwise by virtue of this section for an order under section 33 of the Act of 1996 shall be made to the court having jurisdiction in relation to the bankruptcy.

**History**

In s. 337(4) the words "section 33 of the Act of 1996" substituted for the former words "section 1 of the Act of 1983" by Family Law Act 1996, s. 66(1) and Sch. 8, Pt. III, para. 58(1), (4) as from 1 October 1997 (see SI 1997/1892 (C 76), art. 3(1)(b)).

**337(5) [Court order under s. 337(4)]** On such an application the court shall make such order under section 33 of the Act of 1996 as it thinks just and reasonable having regard to the interests of the creditors, to the bankrupt's financial resources, to the needs of the children and to all the circumstances of the case other than the needs of the bankrupt.

**History**

In s. 337(5) the words "section 33 of the Act of 1996" substituted for the former words "section 1 of the Act of 1983" by Family Law Act 1996, s. 66(1) and Sch. 8, Pt. III, para. 58(1), (4) as from 1 October 1997 (see SI 1997/1892 (C 76), art. 3(1)(b)).

**337(6) [Assumption re interests of creditors]** Where such an application is made after the end of the period of one year beginning with the first vesting (under Chapter IV of this Part) of the bankrupt's estate in a trustee, the court shall assume, unless the circumstances of the case are exceptional, that the interest of the bankrupt's creditors outweigh all other considerations.

## 338 Payments in respect of premises occupied by bankrupt

**338** Where any premises comprised in a bankrupt's estate are occupied by him (whether by virtue of the preceding section or otherwise) on condition that he makes payments towards satisfying any liability arising under a mortgage of the premises or otherwise towards the outgoings of the premises, the bankrupt does not, by virtue of those payments, acquire any interest in the premises.

### ADJUSTMENT OF PRIOR TRANSACTIONS, ETC.

## 339 Transactions at an undervalue

**339(1) [Application to court]** Subject as follows in this section and sections 341 and 342, where an individual is adjudged bankrupt and he has at a relevant time (defined in section 341) entered into a transaction with any person at an undervalue, the trustee of the bankrupt's estate may apply to the court for an order under this section.

**339(2) [Order by court]** The court shall, on such an application, make such order as it thinks fit for restoring the position to what it would have been if that individual had not entered into that transaction.

**339(3) [Where transaction is at undervalue]** For the purposes of this section and sections 341 and 342, an individual enters into a transaction with a person at an undervalue if–

(a) he makes a gift to that person or he otherwise enters into a transaction with that person on terms that provide for him to receive no consideration,

(b) he enters into a transaction with that person in consideration of marriage, or

(c) he enters into a transaction with that person for a consideration the value of which, in money or money's worth, is significantly less than the value, in money or money's worth, of the consideration provided by the individual.

## 340 Preferences

**340(1) [Application to court]** Subject as follows in this and the next two sections, where an individual is adjudged bankrupt and he has at a relevant time (defined in section 341) given a preference to any person, the trustee of the bankrupt's estate may apply to the court for an order under this section.

**340(2) [Order by court]** The court shall, on such an application, make such order as it thinks fit for restoring the position to what it would have been if that individual had not given that preference.

**340(3) [Where preference given]** For the purposes of this and the next two sections, an individual gives a preference to a person if–

(a) that person is one of the individual's creditors or a surety or guarantor for any of his debts or other liabilities, and

(b) the individual does anything or suffers anything to be done which (in either case) has the effect of putting that person into a position which, in the event of the individual's bankruptcy, will be better than the position he would have been in if that thing had not been done.

**340(4) [Where court not to make order]** The court shall not make an order under this section in respect of a preference given to any person unless the individual who gave the preference was influenced in deciding to give it by a desire to produce in relation to that person the effect mentioned in subsection (3)(b) above.

**340(5) [Preference to associate]** An individual who has given a preference to a person who, at the time the preference was given, was an associate of his (otherwise than by reason only of being his employee) is presumed, unless the contrary is shown, to have been influenced in deciding to give it by such a desire as is mentioned in subsection (4).

**340(6) [Things done under court order]** The fact that something has been done in pursuance of the order of a court does not, without more, prevent the doing or suffering of that thing from constituting the giving of a preference.

## 341 "Relevant time" under s. 339, 340

**341(1) [Where relevant time]** Subject as follows, the time at which an individual enters into a transaction at an undervalue or gives a preference is a relevant time if the transaction is entered into or the preference given–

(a) in the case of a transaction at an undervalue, at a time in the period of 5 years ending with the day of the presentation of the bankruptcy petition on which the individual is adjudged bankrupt,

(b) in the case of a preference which is not a transaction at an undervalue and is given to a person who is an associate of the individual (otherwise than by reason only of being his employee), at a time in the period of 2 years ending with that day, and

(c) in any other case of a preference which is not a transaction at an undervalue, at a time in the period of 6 months ending with that day.

**341(2) [Conditions for relevant time]** Where an individual enters into a transaction at an undervalue or gives a preference at a time mentioned in paragraph (a), (b) or (c) of subsection (1) (not being, in the case of a transaction at an undervalue, a time less than 2 years before the end of the period mentioned in paragraph (a)), that time is not a relevant time for the purposes of sections 339 and 340 unless the individual–

(a) is insolvent at that time, or

(b) becomes insolvent in consequence of the transaction or preference;

but the requirements of this subsection are presumed to be satisfied, unless the contrary is shown, in relation to any transaction at an undervalue which is entered into by an individual with a person who is an associate of his (otherwise than by reason only of being his employee).

**341(3) [Insolvent individual under s. 341(2)]** For the purposes of subsection (2), an individual is insolvent if–

(a) he is unable to pay his debts as they fall due, or

(b) the value of his assets is less than the amount of his liabilities, taking into account his contingent and prospective liabilities.

**341(4) [Where person later bankrupt under s. 264(1)(d)]** A transaction entered into or preference given by a person who is subsequently adjudged bankrupt on a petition under section 264(1)(d) (criminal bankruptcy) is to be treated as having been entered into or given at a relevant time for the purposes of sections 339 and 340 if it was entered into or given at any time on or after the date specified for the purposes of this subsection in the criminal bankruptcy order on which the petition was based.

**Note**

See note to s. 341(5).

**341(5) [Where appeal pending]** No order shall be made under section 339 or 340 by virtue of subsection (4) of this section where an appeal is pending (within the meaning of section 277) against the individual's conviction of any offence by virtue of which the criminal bankruptcy order was made.

**Note**

S. 341(4) and (5) repealed by Criminal Justice Act 1988, s. 170(2) and Sch. 16 as from a day to be appointed.

## 342 Orders under s. 339, 340

**342(1) [Extent of order]** Without prejudice to the generality of section 339(2) or 340(2), an order under either of those sections with respect to a transaction or preference entered into or given by an individual who is subsequently adjudged bankrupt may (subject as follows)–

(a) require any property transferred as part of the transaction, or in connection with the giving of the preference, to be vested in the trustee of the bankrupt's estate as part of that estate;

(b) require any property to be so vested if it represents in any person's hands the application either of the proceeds of sale of property so transferred or of money so transferred;

(c) release or discharge (in whole or in part) any security given by the individual;

(d) require any person to pay, in respect of benefits received by him from the individual, such sums to the trustee of his estate as the court may direct;

(e) provide for any surety or guarantor whose obligations to any person were released or discharged (in whole or in part) under the transaction or by the giving of the preference to be under such new or revived obligations to that person as the court thinks appropriate;

(f) provide for security to be provided for the discharge of any obligation imposed by or arising under the order, for such an obligation to be charged on any property and for the security or charge to have the same priority as a security or charge released or discharged (in whole or in part) under the transaction or by the giving of the preference; and

(g) provide for the extent to which any person whose property is vested by the order in the trustee of the bankrupt's estate, or on whom obligations are imposed by the order, is to be able to prove in the bankruptcy for debts or other liabilities which arose from, or were released or discharged (in whole or in part) under or by, the transaction or the giving of the preference.

**342(2) [Effect of order]** An order under section 339 or 340 may affect the property of, or impose any obligation on, any person whether or not he is the person with whom the individual in question entered into the transaction or, as the case may be, the person to whom the preference was given; but such an order–

(a) shall not prejudice any interest in property which was acquired from a person other than that individual and was acquired in good faith and for value, or prejudice any interest deriving from such an interest, and

(b) shall not require a person who received a benefit from the transaction or preference in good faith and for value to pay a sum to the trustee of the bankrupt's estate, except where he was a party to the transaction or the payment is to be in respect of a preference given to that person at a time when he was a creditor of that individual.

**History**
In s. 342(2) in both para. (a) and (b) the words "in good faith and for value" subsisted for the former words "in good faith, for value and without notice of the relevant circumstances" by Insolvency (No. 2) Act 1994, s. 2(1), 6 as from 26 July 1994.

**342(2A) [Presumption re good faith in s. 342(2)]** Where a person has acquired an interest in property from a person other than the individual in question, or has received a benefit from the transaction or preference, and at the time of that acquisition or receipt–

(a) he had notice of the relevant surrounding circumstances and of the relevant proceedings, or

(b) he was an associate of, or was connected with, either the individual in question or the person with whom that individual entered into the transaction or to whom that individual gave the preference,

then, unless the contrary is shown, it shall be presumed for the purposes of paragraph (a) or (as the case may be) paragraph (b) of subsection (2) that the interest was acquired or the benefit was received otherwise than in good faith.

**History**
S. 342(2A) inserted by Insolvency (No. 2) Act 1994, s. 2(2), 6 as from 26 July 1994.

**342(3) [Sums to be paid to trustee]** Any sums required to be paid to the trustee in accordance with an order under section 339 or 340 shall be comprised in the bankrupt's estate.

**342(4) [Relevant surrounding circumstances in s. 342(2A)(a)]** For the purposes of subsection (2A)(a), the relevant surrounding circumstances are (as the case may require)–

(a) the fact that the individual in question entered into the transaction at an undervalue; or

(b) the circumstances which amounted to the giving of the preference by the individual in question.

**History**
See history note after s. 342(6).

**342(5) [Notice of relevant proceedings in s. 342(2A)(a)]** For the purposes of subsection (2A)(a), a person has notice of the relevant proceedings if he has notice–

(a) of the fact that the petition on which the individual in question is adjudged bankrupt has been presented; or

(b) of the fact that the individual in question has been adjudged bankrupt.

**History**
See history note after s. 342(6).

**342(6) [Application of s. 249]** Section 249 in Part VII of this Act shall apply for the purposes of subsection (2A)(b) as it applies for the purposes of the first Group of Parts.

**History**
S. 342(4)–(6) substituted for the former s. 342(4) by Insolvency (No. 2) Act 1994, s. 2(3), 6 as from 26 July 1994; the former s. 342(4) read as follows:

"For the purposes of this section the relevant circumstances, in relation to a transaction or preference, are–

(a) the circumstances by virtue of which an order under section 339 or 340 could be made in respect of the transaction or preference if the individual in question were adjudged bankrupt within a particular period after the transaction is entered into or the preference given, and

(b) if that period has expired, the fact that that individual has been adjudged bankrupt within that period."

## 342A Recovery of excessive pension contributions

**342A(1) [Trustee to apply for order re pension scheme contributions]** Where an individual is adjudged bankrupt and–

(a) he has during the relevant period made contributions as a member of an occupational pension scheme, or

(b) contributions have during the relevant period been made to such a scheme on his behalf,

the trustee of the bankrupt's estate may apply to the court for an order under this section.

**342A(2) [Court order to restore position]** If, on an application for an order under this section, the court is satisfied that the making of any of the contributions ("the excessive contributions") has unfairly prejudiced the individual's creditors, the court may make such order as it thinks fit for restoring the position to what it would have been if the excessive contributions had not been made.

**342A(3) [Matters to determine for s. 342A(2)]** The court shall, in determining whether it is satisfied under subsection (2) , consider in particular–

(a) whether any of the contributions were made by or on behalf of the individual for the purpose of putting assets beyond the reach of his creditors or any of them,

(b) whether the total amount of contributions made by or on behalf of the individual (including contributions made to any other occupational pension scheme) during the relevant period was excessive in view of the individual's circumstances at the time when they were made, and

(c) whether the level of benefits under the scheme, together with benefits under any other occupational pension scheme, to which the individual is entitled, or is likely to become entitled, is excessive in all the circumstances of the case.

**History**
See history note after s. 342C.

## 342B Orders under section 342A

**342B(1) [Provision in s. 342A order]** Without prejudice to the generality of section 342A(2), an order under that section may include provision–

(a) requiring the trustees or managers of the scheme to pay an amount to the individual's trustee in bankruptcy,

(b) reducing the amount of any benefit to which the individual (or his spouse, widow, widower or dependant) is entitled, or to which he has an accrued right, under the scheme,

(c) reducing the amount of any benefit to which, by virtue of any assignment, commutation or surrender of the individual's entitlement (or that of his spouse, widow, widower or dependent) or accrued right under the scheme, another person is entitled or has an accrued right,

(d) otherwise, adjusting the liabilities of the scheme in respect of any such person as is mentioned in paragraph (b) or (c).

**342B(2) [Maximum reduction to scheme assets by s. 342A order]** The maximum amount by which an order under section 342A may require the assets of an occupational pension scheme to be reduced is the lesser of–

(a) the amount of the excessive contributions, and

(b) the value (determined in the prescribed manner) of the assets of the scheme which represent contributions made by or on behalf of the individual.

**342B(3) [Reduction of scheme liabilities to equal reduction of assets]** Subject to subsections (4) and (5), an order under section 342A must reduce the amount of the liabilities of the scheme by an amount equal to the amount of the reduction made in the value of the assets of the scheme.

**342B(4) [Forfeiture of excessive entitlement]** Subsection (3) does not apply where the individual's entitlement or accrued right to benefits under the scheme which he acquired by virtue of the excessive contributions (his "excessive entitlement") has been forfeited.

**342B(5) [Effect of forfeiture of excessive entitlement]** Where part of the individual's excessive entitlement has been forfeited, the amount of the reduction in the liabilities of the scheme required by subsection (3) is the value of the remaining part of his excessive entitlement.

**342B(6) [S. 342A order binding on scheme trustees or managers]** An order under section 342A in respect of an occupational pension scheme shall be binding on the trustees or managers of the scheme.

**History**
See history note after s. 342C.

## 342C Orders under section 342A: supplementary

**342C(1) [Disapplication of provisions in s. 342A order]** Nothing in–

(a) any provision of section 159 of the Pension Schemes Act 1993 or section 91 of the Pensions Act 1995 (which prevent assignment, or orders being made restraining a person from receiving anything which he is prevented from assigning, and make provision in relation to a person's pension on bankruptcy),

(b) any provision of any enactment (whether passed or made before or after the passing of the Pensions Act 1995) corresponding to any of the provisions mentioned in paragraph (a), or

(c) any provision of the scheme in question corresponding to any of those provisions,

applies to a court exercising its powers under section 342A.

**342C(2) [Payments to trustee of part of bankrupt's estate]** Where any sum is required by an order under section 342A to be paid to the trustee in bankruptcy, that sum shall be comprised in the bankrupt's estate.

**342C(3) [Effect of contributions to transferee scheme]** Where contributions have been made during the relevant period to any occupational pension scheme and the entitlement or accrued right to benefits acquired thereby has been transferred to a second or subsequent occupational pension scheme ("the transferee scheme"), sections 342A and 342B and this section shall apply as though the contributions had been made to the transferee scheme.

**342C(4) [Contributions and accrued rights]** For the purposes of this section and sections 342A and 342B–

(a) contributions are made during the relevant period if–

 (i) they are made by or on behalf of the individual at any time during the period of 5 years ending with the day of presentation of the bankruptcy petition on which the individual is adjudged bankrupt, or

 (ii) they are made on behalf of the individual at any time during the period between the presentation of the petition and the commencement of the bankruptcy, and

(b) the accrued rights of an individual under an occupational pension scheme at any time are the rights which have accrued to or in respect of him at that time to future benefits under the scheme.

**342C(5) [Definitions]** In this section and sections 342A and 342B–

**"occupational pension scheme"** has the meaning given by section 1 of the Pension Schemes Act 1993, and

**"trustees or managers"**, in relation to an occupational pension scheme, means–

(a) in the case of a scheme established under a trust, the trustees of the scheme, and

(b) in any other case, the managers of the scheme.

**History**
S. 342A–342C inserted for the purposes only of authorising the making of regulations, by Pensions Act 1995, s. 95 as from 6 April 1996 (see Pensions Act 1995 (Commencement No. 3) Order 1996 (SI 1996/778), art. 2(5)(a), Sch., Pt V). S. 342A–342C to be substituted by Welfare Reform and Pensions Act 1999, s. 15 and s. 342D–342F to be inserted by s. 84, Sch. 12, para. 70, 71 to that Act as from a day to be appointed.

## 343 Extortionate credit transactions

**343(1) [Application]** This section applies where a person is adjudged bankrupt who is or has been a party to a transaction for, or involving, the provision to him of credit.

**343(2) [Order by court]** The court may, on the application of the trustee of the bankrupt's estate, make an order with respect to the transaction if the transaction is or was extortionate and was not entered into more than 3 years before the commencement of the bankruptcy.

**343(3) [Extortionate transaction]** For the purposes of this section a transaction is extortionate if, having regard to the risk accepted by the person providing the credit–

(a) the terms of it are or were such as to require grossly exorbitant payments to be made (whether unconditionally or in certain contingencies) in respect of the provision of the credit, or

(b) it otherwise grossly contravened ordinary principles of fair dealing;

and it shall be presumed, unless the contrary is proved, that a transaction with respect to which an application is made under this section is or, as the case may be, was extortionate.

**343(4) [Extent of order]** An order under this section with respect to any transaction may contain such one or more of the following as the court thinks fit, that is to say–

(a) provision setting aside the whole or part of any obligation created by the transaction;

(b) provision otherwise varying the terms of the transaction or varying the terms on which any security for the purposes of the transaction is held;

(c) provision requiring any person who is or was party to the transaction to pay to the trustee any sums paid to that person, by virtue of the transaction, by the bankrupt;

(d) provision requiring any person to surrender to the trustee any property held by him as security for the purposes of the transaction;

(e) provision directing accounts to be taken between any persons.

**343(5) [Sums to trustee]** Any sums or property required to be paid or surrendered to the trustee in accordance with an order under this section shall be comprised in the bankrupt's estate.

**343(6) [Application under Consumer Credit Act]** Neither the trustee of a bankrupt's estate nor an undischarged bankrupt is entitled to make an application under section 139(1)(a) of the Consumer Credit Act 1974 (re-opening of extortionate credit agreements) for any agreement by which credit is or has been provided to the bankrupt to be re-opened.

But the powers conferred by this section are exercisable in relation to any transaction concurrently with any powers exercisable under this Act in relation to that transaction as a transaction at an undervalue.

## 344 Avoidance of general assignment of book debts

**344(1) [Application]** The following applies where a person engaged in any business makes a general assignment to another person of his existing or future book debts, or any class of them, and is subsequently adjudged bankrupt.

**344(2) [Certain assignments void against trustee]** The assignment is void against the trustee of the bankrupt's estate as regards book debts which were not paid before the presentation of the bankruptcy petition, unless the assignment has been registered under the Bills of Sale Act 1878.

**344(3) [Definitions]** For the purposes of subsections (1) and (2)–

(a) **"assignment"** includes an assignment by way of security or charge on book debts, and

(b) **"general assignment"** does not include–

(i) an assignment of book debts due at the date of the assignment from specified debtors or of debts becoming due under specified contracts, or

(ii) an assignment of book debts included either in a transfer of a business made in good faith and for value or in an assignment of assets for the benefit of creditors generally.

**344(4) [Registration under Bills of Sales Act]** For the purposes of registration under the Act of 1878 an assignment of book debts is to be treated as if it were a bill of sale given otherwise than by way of security for the payment of a sum of money; and the provisions of that Act with respect to the registration of bills of sale apply accordingly with such necessary modifications as may be made by rules under that Act.

## 345 Contracts to which bankrupt is a party

**345(1) [Application]** The following applies where a contract has been made with a person who is subsequently adjudged bankrupt.

**345(2) [Court order on application]** The court may, on the application of any other party to the contract, make an order discharging obligations under the contract on such terms as to payment by the applicant or the bankrupt of damages for non-performance or otherwise as appear to the court to be equitable.

**345(3) [Damages as bankruptcy debt]** Any damages payable by the bankrupt by virtue of an order of the court under this section are provable as a bankruptcy debt.

**345(4) [Where joint contract]** Where an undischarged bankrupt is a contractor in respect of any contract jointly with any person, that person may sue or be sued in respect of the contract without the joinder of the bankrupt.

## 346 Enforcement procedures

**346(1) [Creditor's execution against bankrupt]** Subject to section 285 in Chapter II (restrictions on proceedings and remedies) and to the following provisions of this section, where the creditor of any person who is adjudged bankrupt has, before the commencement of the bankruptcy–

(a) issued execution against the goods or land of that person, or

(b) attached a debt due to that person from another person,

that creditor is not entitled, as against the official receiver or trustee of the bankrupt's estate, to retain the benefit of the execution or attachment, or any sums paid to avoid it, unless the execution or attachment was completed, or the sums were paid, before the commencement of the bankruptcy.

**346(2) [Where goods taken in execution]** Subject as follows, where any goods of a person have been taken in execution, then, if before the completion of the execution notice is given to the sheriff or other officer charged with the execution that that person has been adjudged bankrupt–

(a) the sheriff or other officer shall on request deliver to the official receiver or trustee of the bankrupt's estate the goods and any money seized or recovered in part satisfaction of the execution, but

(b) the costs of the execution are a first charge on the goods or money so delivered and the official receiver or trustee may sell the goods or a sufficient part of them for the purpose of satisfying the charge.

**346(3) [Balance of sale proceeds]** Subject to subsection (6) below, where–

(a) under an execution in respect of a judgment for a sum exceeding such sum as may be prescribed for the purposes of this subsection, the goods of any person are sold or money is paid in order to avoid a sale, and

(b) before the end of the period of 14 days beginning with the day of the sale or payment the sheriff or other officer charged with the execution is given notice that a bankruptcy petition has been presented in relation to that person, and

(c) a bankruptcy order is or has been made on that petition,

the balance of the proceeds of sale or money paid, after deducting the costs of execution, shall (in priority to the claim of the execution creditor) be comprised in the bankrupt's estate.

**Note**
The minimum amount of judgment is £500 – see the Insolvency Proceedings (Monetary Limits) Order 1986 (SI 1986/1996).

**346(4) [Duty of sheriff re sum in s. 346(3)]** Accordingly, in the case of an execution in respect of a judgment for a sum exceeding the sum prescribed for the purposes of subsection (3), the sheriff or other officer charged with the execution–

(a) shall not dispose of the balance mentioned in subsection (3) at any time within the period of 14 days so mentioned or while there is pending a bankruptcy petition of which he has been given notice under that subsection, and

(b) shall pay that balance, where by virtue of that subsection it is comprised in the bankrupt's estate, to the official receiver or (if there is one) to the trustee of that estate.

**346(5) [Completion of execution or attachment]** For the purposes of this section–

(a) an execution against goods is completed by seizure and sale or by the making of a charging order under section 1 of the Charging Orders Act 1979;

(b) an execution against land is completed by seizure, by the appointment of a receiver or by the making of a charging order under that section;

(c) an attachment of a debt is completed by the receipt of the debt.

**346(6) [Setting aside of s. 346(1)–(3) rights by court]** The rights conferred by subsections (1) to (3) on the official receiver or the trustee may, to such extent and on such terms as it thinks fit, be set aside by the court in favour of the creditor who has issued the execution or attached the debt.

**346(7) [Acquisition in good faith]** Nothing in this section entitles the trustee of a bankrupt's estate to claim goods from a person who has acquired them in good faith under a sale by a sheriff or other officer charged with an execution.

**346(8) [Non-application of s. 346(2), (3)]** Neither subsection (2) nor subsection (3) applies in relation to any execution against property which has been acquired by or has devolved upon the bankrupt since the commencement of the bankruptcy, unless, at the time the execution is issued or before it is completed–

(a) the property has been or is claimed for the bankrupt's estate under section 307 (after-acquired property), and

(b) a copy of the notice given under that section has been or is served on the sheriff or other officer charged with the execution.

## 347 Distress, etc.

**347(1) [Limit on distraining goods]** The right of any landlord or other person to whom rent is payable to distrain upon the goods and effects of an undischarged bankrupt for rent due to him from the bankrupt is available (subject to subsection (5) below) against goods and effects comprised in the bankrupt's estate, but only for 6 months' rent accrued due before the commencement of the bankruptcy.

**347(2) [Distraining where order later made]** Where a landlord or other person to whom rent is payable has distrained for rent upon the goods and effects of an individual to whom a bankruptcy petition relates and a bankruptcy order is subsequently made on that petition, any amount recovered by way of that distress which–

(a) is in excess of the amount which by virtue of subsection (1) would have been recoverable after the commencement of the bankruptcy, or

(b) is in respect of rent for a period or part of a period after the distress was levied,

shall be held for the bankrupt as part of his estate.

**347(3) [Proceeds of sale re goods not held under s. 347(2)]** Where any person (whether or not a landlord or person entitled to rent) has distrained upon the goods or effects of an individual who is adjudged bankrupt before the end of the period of 3 months beginning with the distraint, so much of those goods or effects, or of the proceeds of their sale, as is not held for the bankrupt under subsection (2) shall be charged for the benefit of the bankrupt's estate with the preferential debts of the bankrupt to the extent that the bankrupt's estate is for the time being insufficient for meeting those debts.

**347(4) [Where surrender under s. 347(3)]** Where by virtue of any charge under subsection (3) any person surrenders any goods or effects to the trustee of a bankrupt's estate or makes a payment to such a trustee, that person ranks, in respect of the amount of the proceeds of the sale of those goods or effects by the trustee or, as the case may be, the amount of the payment, as a preferential creditor of the bankrupt, except as against so much of the bankrupt's estate as is available for the payment of preferential creditors by virtue of the surrender or payment.

**347(5) [Rights of landlord after discharge]** A landlord or other person to whom rent is payable is not at any time after the discharge of a bankrupt entitled to distrain upon any goods or effects comprised in the bankrupt's estate.

**347(6) [Restriction of landlord's rights]** Where in the case of any execution–

(a) a landlord is (apart from this section) entitled under section 1 of the Landlord and Tenant Act 1709 or section 102 of the County Courts Act 1984 (claims for rent where goods seized in execution) to claim for an amount not exceeding one year's rent, and

(b) the person against whom the execution is levied is adjudged bankrupt before the notice of claim is served on the sheriff or other officer charged with the execution,

the right of the landlord to claim under that section is restricted to a right to claim for an amount not exceeding 6 months' rent and does not extend to any rent payable in respect of a period after the notice of claim is so served.

**347(7) [Limit to s. 347(6)]** Nothing in subsection (6) imposes any liability on a sheriff or other officer charged with an execution to account to the official receiver or the trustee of a bankrupt's estate for any sums paid by him to a landlord at any time before the sheriff or other officer was served with notice of the bankruptcy order in question.

But this section is without prejudice to the liability of the landlord.

**347(8) [Rights to distrain other than for rent]** Nothing in this Group of Parts affects any right to distrain otherwise than for rent; and any such right is at any time exercisable without restriction against property comprised in a bankrupt's estate, even if that right is expressed by any enactment to be exercisable in like manner as a right to distrain for rent.

**347(9) [Exercise of right]** Any right to distrain against property comprised in a bankrupt's estate is exercisable notwithstanding that the property has vested in the trustee.

**347(10) [Landlord's right to prove]** The provisions of this section are without prejudice to a landlord's right in a bankruptcy to prove for any bankruptcy debt in respect of rent.

# 348 Apprenticeships, etc.

**348(1) [Application]** This section applies where–

(a) a bankruptcy order is made in respect of an individual to whom another individual was an apprentice or articled clerk at the time when the petition on which the order was made was presented, and

(b) the bankrupt or the apprentice or clerk gives notice to the trustee terminating the apprenticeship or articles.

**348(2) [Discharge etc.]** Subject to subsection (6) below, the indenture of apprenticeship or, as the case may be, the articles of agreement shall be discharged with effect from the commencement of the bankruptcy.

**348(3) [If money paid]** If any money has been paid by or on behalf of the apprentice or clerk to the bankrupt as a fee, the trustee may, on an application made by or on behalf of the apprentice or clerk pay such sum to the apprentice or clerk as the trustee thinks reasonable, having regard to–

(a) the amount of the fee,

(b) the proportion of the period in respect of which the fee was paid that has been served by the apprentice or clerk before the commencement of the bankruptcy, and

(c) the other circumstances of the case.

**348(4) [Priority of s. 348(3) power]** The power of the trustee to make a payment under subsection (3) has priority over his obligation to distribute the bankrupt's estate.

**348(5) [Instead of s. 348(3) payment]** Instead of making a payment under subsection (3), the trustee may, if it appears to him expedient to do so on an application made by or on behalf of the apprentice or clerk, transfer the indenture or articles to a person other than the bankrupt.

**348(6) [Where s. 348(5) transfer]** Where a transfer is made under subsection (5), subsection (2) has effect only as between the apprentice or clerk and the bankrupt.

# 349 Unenforceability of liens on books, etc.

**349(1) [Unenforceability]** Subject as follows, a lien or other right to retain possession of any of the books, papers or other records of a bankrupt is unenforceable to the extent that its enforcement would deny possession of any books, papers or other records to the official receiver or the trustee of the bankrupt's estate.

**349(2) [Non-application of s. 349(1)]** Subsection (1) does not apply to a lien on documents which give a title to property and are held as such.

# Chapter VI – Bankruptcy Offences

PRELIMINARY

## 350 Scheme of this Chapter

**350(1) [Application]** Subject to section 360(3) below, this Chapter applies where the court has made a bankruptcy order on a bankruptcy petition.

**350(2) [Effect of annulment of bankruptcy]** This Chapter applies whether or not the bankruptcy order is annulled, but proceedings for an offence under this Chapter shall not be instituted after the annulment.

**350(3) [Liability of bankrupt after discharge]** Without prejudice to his liability in respect of a subsequent bankruptcy, the bankrupt is not guilty of an offence under this Chapter in respect of anything done after his discharge; but nothing in this Group of Parts prevents the institution of proceedings against a discharged bankrupt for an offence committed before his discharge.

**350(4) [Where not defence]** It is not a defence in proceedings for an offence under this Chapter that anything relied on, in whole or in part, as constituting that offence was done outside England and Wales.

**350(5) [Institution of proceedings for offence]** Proceedings for an offence under this Chapter or under the rules shall not be instituted except by the Secretary of State or by or with the consent of the Director of Public Prosecutions.

**350(6) [Penalty]** A person guilty of any offence under this Chapter is liable to imprisonment or a fine, or both.

## 351 Definitions

**351** In the following provisions of this Chapter–

(a) references to property comprised in the bankrupt's estate or to property possession of which is required to be delivered up to the official receiver or the trustee of the bankrupt's estate include any property which would be such property if a notice in respect of it were given under section 307 (after-acquired property), section 308 (personal property and effects of bankrupt having more than replacement value) or section 308A (vesting in trustee of certain tenancies);

(b) **"the initial period"** means the period between the presentation of the bankruptcy petition and the commencement of the bankruptcy; and

(c) a reference to a number of months or years before petition is to that period ending with the presentation of the bankruptcy petition.

**History**

In s. 351 in para. (a) the words ", section 308" substituted for the former words "or 308" and the words "or section 308A (vesting in trustee of certain tenancies)" inserted by the Housing Act 1988, s. 140 and Sch. 17, para. 75 as from 15 January 1989 (see SI 1988/2152 (C 81)).

## 352 Defence of innocent intention

**352** Where in the case of an offence under any provision of this Chapter it is stated that this section applies, a person is not guilty of the offence if he proves that, at the time of the conduct constituting the offence, he had no intent to defraud or to conceal the state of his affairs.

WRONGDOING BY THE BANKRUPT BEFORE AND AFTER BANKRUPTCY

## 353 Non-disclosure

**353(1) [Offence]** The bankrupt is guilty of an offence if–

(a) he does not to the best of his knowledge and belief disclose all the property comprised in his estate to the official receiver or the trustee, or

(b) he does not inform the official receiver or the trustee of any disposal of any property which but for the disposal would be so comprised, stating how, when, to whom and for what consideration the property was disposed of.

**353(2) [Exception to s. 353(1)(b)]** Subsection (1)(b) does not apply to any disposal in the ordinary course of a business carried on by the bankrupt or to any payment of the ordinary expenses of the bankrupt or his family.

**353(3) [Application of s. 352]** Section 352 applies to this offence.

## 354 Concealment of property

**354(1) [Offence of concealment etc.]** The bankrupt is guilty of an offence if–

(a) he does not deliver up possession to the official receiver or trustee, or as the official receiver or trustee may direct, of such part of the property comprised in his estate as is in his possession or under his control and possession of which he is required by law so to deliver up,

(b) he conceals any debt due to or from him or conceals any property the value of which is not less than the prescribed amount and possession of which he is required to deliver up to the official receiver or trustee, or

(c) in the 12 months before petition, or in the initial period, he did anything which would have been an offence under paragraph (b) above if the bankruptcy order had been made immediately before he did it.

Section 352 applies to this offence.

**354(2) [Offence re removal of property]** The bankrupt is guilty of an offence if he removes, or in the initial period removed, any property the value of which was not less than the prescribed amount and possession of which he has or would have been required to deliver up to the official receiver or the trustee.

Section 352 applies to this offence.

**354(3) [Offence re failure to account for loss]** The bankrupt is guilty of an offence if he without reasonable excuse fails, on being required to do so by the official receiver or the court–

(a) to account for the loss of any substantial part of his property incurred in the 12 months before petition or in the initial period, or

(b) to give a satisfactory explanation of the manner in which such a loss was incurred.

## 355 Concealment of books and papers; falsification

**355(1) [Offence re non-delivery of books etc.]** The bankrupt is guilty of an offence if he does not deliver up possession to the official receiver or the trustee, or as the official receiver or trustee may direct, of all books, papers and other records of which he has possession or control and which relate to his estate or his affairs.

Section 352 applies to this offence.

**355(2) [Offence re destruction, concealment etc.]** The bankrupt is guilty of an offence if–

(a) he prevents, or in the initial period prevented, the production of any books, papers or records relating to his estate or affairs;

(b) he conceals, destroys, mutilates or falsifies, or causes or permits the concealment, destruction, mutilation or falsification of, any books, papers or other records relating to his estate or affairs;

(c) he makes, or causes or permits the making of, any false entries in any book, document or record relating to his estate or affairs; or

(d) in the 12 months before petition, or in the initial period, he did anything which would have been an offence under paragraph (b) or (c) above if the bankruptcy order had been made before he did it.

Section 352 applies to this offence.

**355(3) [Offence re disposal, alteration etc.]** The bankrupt is guilty of an offence if–

(a) he disposes of, or alters or makes any omission in, or causes or permits the disposal, altering or making of any omission in, any book, document or record relating to his estate or affairs, or

(b) in the 12 months before petition, or in the initial period, he did anything which would have been an offence under paragraph (a) if the bankruptcy order had been made before he did it.

Section 352 applies to this offence.

## 356 False statements

**356(1) [Offence re material omission]** The bankrupt is guilty of an offence if he makes or has made any material omission in any statement made under any provision in this Group of Parts and relating to his affairs.

Section 352 applies to this offence.

**356(2) [Offence re failing to inform etc.]** The bankrupt is guilty of an offence if–

(a) knowing or believing that a false debt has been proved by any person under the bankruptcy, he fails to inform the trustee as soon as practicable; or

(b) he attempts to account for any part of his property by fictitious losses or expenses; or

(c) at any meeting of his creditors in the 12 months before petition or (whether or not at such a meeting) at any time in the initial period, he did anything which would have been an offence under paragraph (b) if the bankruptcy order had been made before he did it; or

(d) he is, or at any time has been, guilty of any false representation or other fraud for the purpose of obtaining the consent of his creditors, or any of them, to an agreement with reference to his affairs or to his bankruptcy.

## 357 Fraudulent disposal of property

**357(1) [Offence re transfer]** The bankrupt is guilty of an offence if he makes or causes to be made, or has in the period of 5 years ending with the commencement of the bankruptcy made or caused to be made, any gift or transfer of, or any charge on, his property.

Section 352 applies to this offence.

**357(2) [Interpretation]** The reference to making a transfer of or charge on any property includes causing or conniving at the levying of any execution against that property.

**357(3) [Offence re concealment or removal of property]** The bankrupt is guilty of an offence if he conceals or removes, or has at any time before the commencement of the bankruptcy concealed or removed, any part of his property after, or within 2 months before, the date on which a judgment or order for the payment of money has been obtained against him, being a judgment or order which was not satisfied before the commencement of the bankruptcy.

Section 352 applies to this offence.

## 358 Absconding

**358** The bankrupt is guilty of an offence if–

(a) he leaves, or attempts or makes preparations to leave, England and Wales with any property the value of which is not less than the prescribed amount and possession of which he is required to deliver up to the official receiver or the trustee, or

(b) in the 6 months before petition, or in the initial period, he did anything which would have been an offence under paragraph (a) if the bankruptcy order had been made immediately before he did it.

Section 352 applies to this offence.

**Note**

The minimum value for para. (a) is £500 – see the Insolvency Proceedings (Monetary Limits) Order 1986 (SI 1986/1996).

## 359 Fraudulent dealing with property obtained on credit

**359(1) [Offence re disposal of property obtained on credit]** The bankrupt is guilty of an offence if, in the 12 months before petition, or in the initial period, he disposed of any property which he had obtained on credit and, at the time he disposed of it, had not paid for.

Section 352 applies to this offence.

**359(2) [Offence re knowingly dealing with bankrupt]** A person is guilty of an offence if, in the 12 months before petition or in the initial period, he acquired or received property from the bankrupt knowing or believing–

(a) that the bankrupt owed money in respect of the property, and

(b) that the bankrupt did not intend, or was unlikely to be able, to pay the money he so owed.

**359(3) [Disposals etc. in ordinary course of business]** A person is not guilty of an offence under subsection (1) or (2) if the disposal, acquisition or receipt of the property was in the ordinary course of a business carried on by the bankrupt at the time of the disposal, acquisition or receipt.

**359(4) [Ordinary course of business]** In determining for the purposes of this section whether any property is disposed of, acquired or received in the ordinary course of a business carried on by the bankrupt, regard may be had, in particular, to the price paid for the property.

**359(5) [Interpretation]** In this section references to disposing of property include pawning or pledging it; and references to acquiring or receiving property shall be read accordingly.

## 360 Obtaining credit; engaging in business

**360(1) [Offence re credit, non-disclosure of bankruptcy]** The bankrupt is guilty of an offence if–

(a) either alone or jointly with any other person, he obtains credit to the extent of the prescribed amount or more without giving the person from whom he obtains it the relevant information about his status; or

(b) he engages (whether directly or indirectly) in any business under a name other than that in which he was adjudged bankrupt without disclosing to all persons with whom he enters into any business transaction the name in which he was so adjudged.

**Note**
The figure from 29 December 1986 is £250 under the Insolvency Proceedings (Monetary Limits) Order 1986 (SI 1986/1996) made under s. 418.

**360(2) [Cases of bankrupt obtaining credit]** The reference to the bankrupt obtaining credit includes the following cases–

(a) where goods are bailed to him under a hire-purchase agreement, or agreed to be sold to him under a conditional sale agreement, and

(b) where he is paid in advance (whether in money or otherwise) for the supply of goods or services.

**360(3) [Scotland or Northern Ireland]** A person whose estate has been sequestrated in Scotland, or who has been adjudged bankrupt in Northern Ireland, is guilty of an offence if, before his discharge, he does anything in England and Wales which would be an offence under subsection (1) if he were an undischarged bankrupt and the sequestration of his estate or the adjudication in Northern Ireland were an adjudication under this Part.

**360(4) [Information for s. 360(1)(a)]** For the purposes of subsection (1)(a), the relevant information about the status of the person in question is the information that he is an undischarged bankrupt or, as the case may be, that his estate has been sequestrated in Scotland and that he has not been discharged.

## 361 Failure to keep proper accounts of business

**361(1) [Offence re no proper accounting records]** Where the bankrupt has been engaged in any business for any of the period of 2 years before petition, he is guilty of an offence if he–

(a) has not kept proper accounting records throughout that period and throughout any part of the initial period in which he was so engaged, or

(b) has not preserved all the accounting records which he has kept.

**361(2) [Exception to s. 361(1)]** The bankrupt is not guilty of an offence under subsection (1)–

(a) if his unsecured liabilities at the commencement of the bankruptcy did not exceed the prescribed amount, or

(b) if he proves that in the circumstances in which he carried on business the omission was honest and excusable.

**Note**

From 29 December 1986 the figure is £20,000 under the Insolvency Proceedings (Monetary Limits) Order 1986 (SI 1986/1996).

**361(3) [Interpretation]** For the purposes of this section a person is deemed not to have kept proper accounting records if he has not kept such records as are necessary to show or explain his transactions and financial position in his business, including–

(a) records containing entries from day to day, in sufficient detail, of all cash paid and received,

(b) where the business involved dealings in goods, statements of annual stock-takings, and

(c) except in the case of goods sold by way of retail trade to the actual customer, records of all goods sold and purchased showing the buyers and sellers in sufficient detail to enable the goods and the buyers and sellers to be identified.

**361(4) [Application of s. 355(2)(d), (3)(b)]** In relation to any such records as are mentioned in subsection (3), subsections (2)(d) and (3)(b) of section 355 apply with the substitution of 2 years for 12 months.

## 362 Gambling

**362(1) [Offence re gambling, rash and hazardous speculations]** The bankrupt is guilty of an offence if he has–

(a) in the 2 years before petition, materially contributed to, or increased the extent of, his insolvency by gambling or by rash and hazardous speculations, or

(b) in the initial period, lost any part of his property by gambling or by rash and hazardous speculations.

**362(2) [Rash and hazardous speculations]** In determining for the purposes of this section whether any speculations were rash and hazardous, the financial position of the bankrupt at the time when he entered into them shall be taken into consideration.

# Chapter VII – Powers of Court In Bankruptcy

## 363 General control of court

**363(1) [Power of court]** Every bankruptcy is under the general control of the court and, subject to the provisions in this Group of Parts, the court has full power to decide all questions of priorities and all other questions, whether of law or fact, arising in any bankruptcy.

**363(2) [Bankrupt to do as directed]** Without prejudice to any other provision in this Group of Parts, an undischarged bankrupt or a discharged bankrupt whose estate is still being administered under Chapter IV of this Part shall do all such things as he may be directed to do by the court for the purposes of his bankruptcy or, as the case may be, the administration of that estate.

**363(3) [Application for directions]** The official receiver or the trustee of a bankrupt's estate may at any time apply to the court for a direction under subsection (2).

**363(4) [Contempt of court]** If any person without reasonable excuse fails to comply with any obligation imposed on him by subsection (2), he is guilty of a contempt of court and liable to be punished accordingly (in addition to any other punishment to which he may be subject).

## 364 Power of arrest

**364(1) [Court's power re warrant]** In the cases specified in the next subsection the court may cause a warrant to be issued to a constable or prescribed officer of the court–

(a) for the arrest of a debtor to whom a bankruptcy petition relates or of an undischarged bankrupt, or of a discharged bankrupt whose estate is still being administered under Chapter IV of this Part, and

(b) for the seizure of any books, papers, records, money or goods in the possession of a person arrested under the warrant,

and may authorise a person arrested under such a warrant to be kept in custody, and anything seized under such a warrant to be held, in accordance with the rules, until such time as the court may order.

**364(2) [Where s. 364(1) powers exercisable]** The powers conferred by subsection (1) are exercisable in relation to a debtor or undischarged bankrupt if, at any time after the presentation of the bankruptcy petition relating to him or the making of the bankruptcy order against him, it appears to the court–

(a) that there are reasonable grounds for believing that he has absconded, or is about to abscond, with a view to avoiding or delaying the payment of any of his debts or his appearance to a bankruptcy petition or to avoiding, delaying or disrupting any proceedings in bankruptcy against him or any examination of his affairs, or

(b) that he is about to remove his goods with a view to preventing or delaying possession being taken of them by the official receiver or the trustee of his estate, or

(c) that there are reasonable grounds for believing that he has concealed or destroyed, or is about to conceal or destroy, any of his goods or any books, papers or records which might be of use to his creditors in the course of his bankruptcy or in connection with the administration of his estate, or

(d) that he has, without the leave of the official receiver or the trustee of his estate, removed any goods in his possession which exceed in value such sum as may be prescribed for the purposes of this paragraph, or

(e) that he has failed, without reasonable excuse, to attend any examination ordered by the court.

**Note**

From 29 December 1986 the figure is £500 under the Insolvency Proceedings (Monetary Limits) Order 1986 (SI 1986/1996).

## 365 Seizure of bankrupt's property

**365(1) [Court's power re warrant]** At any time after a bankruptcy order has been made, the court may, on the application of the official receiver or the trustee of the bankrupt's estate, issue a warrant authorising the person to whom it is directed to seize any property comprised in the bankrupt's estate which is, or any books, papers or records relating to the bankrupt's estate or affairs which are, in the possession or under the control of the bankrupt or any other person who is required to deliver the property, books, papers or records to the official receiver or trustee.

**365(2) [Power to break open premises etc.]** Any person executing a warrant under this section may, for the purpose of seizing any property comprised in the bankrupt's estate or any books, papers or records relating to the bankrupt's estate or affairs, break open any premises where the bankrupt or anything that may be seized under the warrant is or is believed to be and any receptacle of the bankrupt which contains or is believed to contain anything that may be so seized.

**365(3) [Power of court re search]** If, after a bankruptcy order has been made, the court is satisfied that any property comprised in the bankrupt's estate is, or any books, papers or records relating to the bankrupt's estate or affairs are, concealed in any premises not belonging to him, it may issue a warrant authorising any constable or prescribed officer of the court to search those premises for the property, books, papers or records.

**365(4) [Execution of s. 365(3) warrant]** A warrant under subsection (3) shall not be executed except in the prescribed manner and in accordance with its terms.

## 366 Inquiry into bankrupt's dealings and property

**366(1) [Power of court to summon bankrupt to appear]** At any time after a bankruptcy order has been made the court may, on the application of the official receiver or the trustee of the bankrupt's estate, summon to appear before it–

(a) the bankrupt or the bankrupt's spouse or former spouse,

(b) any person known or believed to have any property comprised in the bankrupt's estate in his possession or to be indebted to the bankrupt,

(c) any person appearing to the court to be able to give information concerning the bankrupt or the bankrupt's dealings, affairs or property.

The court may require any such person as is mentioned in paragraph (b) or (c) to submit an affidavit to the court containing an account of his dealings with the bankrupt or to produce any documents in his possession or under his control relating to the bankrupt or the bankrupt's dealings, affairs or property.

**366(2) [Application of s. 366(3)]** Without prejudice to section 364, the following applies in a case where–

(a) a person without reasonable excuse fails to appear before the court when he is summoned to do so under this section, or

(b) there are reasonable grounds for believing that a person has absconded, or is about to abscond, with a view to avoiding his appearance before the court under this section.

**366(3) [Issue of warrant re non-appearance]** The court may, for the purpose of bringing that person and anything in his possession before the court, cause a warrant to be issued to a constable or prescribed officer of the court–

(a) for the arrest of that person, and

(b) for the seizure of any books, papers, records, money or goods in that person's possession.

**366(4) [Power re custody etc.]** The court may authorise a person arrested under such a warrant to be kept in custody, and anything seized under such a warrant to be held, in accordance with the rules, until that person is brought before the court under the warrant or until such other time as the court may order.

## 367 Court's enforcement powers under s. 366

**367(1) [Power to order delivery]** If it appears to the court, on consideration of any evidence obtained under section 366 or this section, that any person has in his possession any property comprised in the bankrupt's estate, the court may, on the application of the official receiver or the trustee of the bankrupt's estate, order that person to deliver the whole or any part of the property to the official receiver or the trustee at such time, in such manner and on such terms as the court thinks fit.

**367(2) [Power to order payment from bankrupt debtor]** If it appears to the court, on consideration of any evidence obtained under section 366 or this section, that any person is indebted to the bankrupt, the court may, on the application of the official receiver or the trustee of the bankrupt's estate, order that person to pay to the official receiver or trustee, at such time and in such manner as the court may direct, the whole or part of the amount due, whether in full discharge of the debt or otherwise as the court thinks fit.

**367(3) [Place of examination]** The court may, if it thinks fit, order that any person who if within the jurisdiction of the court would be liable to be summoned to appear before it under section 366 shall be examined in any part of the United Kingdom where he may be for the time being, or in any place outside the United Kingdom.

**367(4) [Examination on oath]** Any person who appears or is brought before the court under section 366 or this section may be examined on oath, either orally or by interrogatories, concerning the bankrupt or the bankrupt's dealings, affairs and property.

## 368 Provision corresponding to s. 366, where interim receiver appointed

**368** Sections 366 and 367 apply where an interim receiver has been appointed under section 286 as they apply where a bankruptcy order has been made, as if–

(a) references to the official receiver or the trustee were to the interim receiver, and

(b) references to the bankrupt and to his estate were (respectively) to the debtor and his property.

## 369 Order for production of documents by inland revenue

**369(1) [Power of court]** For the purposes of an examination under section 290 (public examination of bankrupt) or proceedings under sections 366 to 368, the court may, on the application of the official receiver or the trustee of the bankrupt's estate, order an inland revenue official to produce to the court–

(a) any return, account or accounts submitted (whether before or after the commencement of the bankruptcy) by the bankrupt to any inland revenue official,

(b) any assessment or determination made (whether before or after the commencement of the bankruptcy) in relation to the bankrupt by any inland revenue official, or

(c) any correspondence (whether before or after the commencement of the bankruptcy) between the bankrupt and any inland revenue official.

**369(2) [Order re disclosure of document]** Where the court has made an order under subsection (1) for the purposes of any examination or proceedings, the court may, at any time after the document to which the order relates is produced to it, by order authorise the disclosure of the document, or of any part of its contents, to the official receiver, the trustee of the bankrupt's estate or the bankrupt's creditors.

**369(3) [Condition for s. 369(1) order]** The court shall not address an order under subsection (1) to an inland revenue official unless it is satisfied that that official is dealing, or has dealt, with the affairs of the bankrupt.

**369(4) [Where s. 369(1) document not in official's possession]** Where any document to which an order under subsection (1) relates is not in the possession of the official to whom the order is addressed, it is the duty of that official to take all reasonable steps to secure possession of it and, if he fails to do so, to report the reasons for his failure to the court.

**369(5) [Where document held by another official]** Where any document to which an order under subsection (1) relates is in the possession of an inland revenue official other than the one to whom the order is addressed, it is the duty of the official in possession of the document, at the request of the official to whom the order is addressed, to deliver it to the official making the request.

**369(6) ["Inland revenue official"]** In this section **"inland revenue official"** means any inspector or collector of taxes appointed by the Commissioners of Inland Revenue or any person appointed by the Commissioners to serve in any other capacity.

**369(7) [Non-application]** This section does not apply for the purposes of an examination under sections 366 and 367 which takes place by virtue of section 368 (interim receiver).

## 370 Power to appoint special manager

**370(1) [Power of court]** The court may, on an application under this section, appoint any person to be the special manager–

(a) of a bankrupt's estate, or

(b) of the business of an undischarged bankrupt, or

(c) of the property or business of a debtor in whose case the official receiver has been appointed interim receiver under section 286.

**370(2) [Application to court]** An application under this section may be made by the official receiver or the trustee of the bankrupt's estate in any case where it appears to the official receiver or trustee that the nature of the estate, property or business, or the interests of the creditors generally, require the appointment of another person to manage the estate, property or business.

**370(3) [Powers of special manager]** A special manager appointed under this section has such powers as may be entrusted to him by the court.

**370(4) [Powers included in s. 370(3)]** The power of the court under subsection (3) to entrust powers to a special manager include power to direct that any provision in this Group of Parts that has effect in relation to the official receiver, interim receiver or trustee shall have the like effect in relation to the special manager for the purposes of the carrying out by the special manager of any of the functions of the official receiver, interim receiver or trustee.

**370(5) [Duties of special manager]** A special manager appointed under this section shall–

(a) give such security as may be prescribed,

(b) prepare and keep such accounts as may be prescribed, and

(c) produce those accounts in accordance with the rules to the Secretary of State or to such other persons as may be prescribed.

## 371 Re-direction of bankrupt's letters, etc.

**371(1) [Power of court]** Where a bankruptcy order has been made, the court may from time to time, on the application of the official receiver or the trustee of the bankrupt's estate, order the Post Office to re-direct and send or deliver to the official receiver or trustee or otherwise any postal packet (within the meaning of the Post Office Act 1953) which would otherwise be sent or delivered by them to the bankrupt at such place or places as may be specified in the order.

**371(2) [Duration of court order]** An order under this section has effect for such period, not exceeding 3 months, as may be specified in the order.

# PART X – INDIVIDUAL INSOLVENCY: GENERAL PROVISIONS

**Note**

Re application of Pt. X to insolvent partnerships, see the Insolvent Partnerships Order 1994 (SI 1994/2421), especially reg. 10, 11, Sch. 7.

## 372 Supplies of gas, water, electricity, etc.

**372(1) [Application]** This section applies where on any day (**"the relevant day"**)–

(a) a bankruptcy order is made against an individual or an interim receiver of an individual's property is appointed, or

(b) a voluntary arrangement proposed by an individual is approved under Part VIII, or

(c) a deed of arrangement is made for the benefit of an individual's creditors;

and in this section **"the office-holder"** means the official receiver, the trustee in bankruptcy, the interim receiver, the supervisor of the voluntary arrangement or the trustee under the deed of arrangement, as the case may be.

**372(2) [Where s. 372(3) request]** If a request falling within the next subsection is made for the giving after the relevant day of any of the supplies mentioned in subsection (4), the supplier–

(a) may make it a condition of the giving of the supply that the office-holder personally guarantees the payment of any charges in respect of the supply, but

(b) shall not make it a condition of the giving of the supply, or do anything which has the effect of making it a condition of the giving of the supply, that any outstanding charges in respect of a supply given to the individual before the relevant day are paid.

**372(3) [Type of request]** A request falls within this subsection if it is made–

(a) by or with the concurrence of the office-holder, and

(b) for the purposes of any business which is or has been carried on by the individual, by a firm or partnership of which the individual is or was a member, or by an agent or manager for the individual or for such a firm or partnership.

**372(4) [Supplies in s. 372(2)]** The supplies referred to in subsection (2) are–

(a) a public supply of gas,

(b) public supply of electricity,

(c) a supply of water by a water undertaker,

(d) a supply of telecommunication services by a public telecommunications operator.

**History**

In s. 372(4) para. (b) substituted by Electricity Act 1989, s. 112(1) and Sch. 16, para. 35(1), (3)(a) as from 31 March 1990 (see Electricity Act 1989, s. 113(2) and SI 1990/117 (C 4)); para. (b) formerly read as follows:

"a supply of electricity by an Electricity Board,"

Also in para. (c) the words "a water undertaker" substituted for the former words "statutory water undertakers" by Water Act 1989, s. 190(1) and Sch. 25, para. 78(1) as from 1 September 1989 (see Water Act 1989, s. 4, 194(4) and SI 1989/1146 (C 37) – see also SI 1989/1530 (C 51)).

**372(5) [Definitions]** The following applies to expressions used in subsection (4)–

(a) **"public supply of gas"** means a supply of gas by the British Gas Corporation as a public gas supplier within the meaning of Part I of the Gas Act 1986,

(b) **"public supply of electricity"** means a supply of electricity by a public electricity supplier within the meaning of Part I of the Electricity Act 1989; and

(c) **"telecommunication services"** and **"public telecommunications operator"** mean the same as in the Telecommunications Act 1984, except that the former does not include local delivery services within the meaning of Part II of the Broadcasting Act 1990.

**History**

In s. 372(5) para. (b) substituted by Electricity Act 1989, s. 112(1) and Sch. 16, para. 35(1), (3)(b) as from 31 March 1990 (see Electricity Act 1989, s. 113(2) and SI 1990/117 (C 4), art. 3(b), Sch. 1); para. (b) formerly read as follows:

"(b) **"Electricity Board"** means the same as in the Energy Act 1983;"

Also in para. (c) the words "local delivery services within the meaning of Part II of the Broadcasting Act 1990" substituted by Broadcasting Act 1990, s. 203(1) and Sch. 20, para. 43 as from 1 January 1991 (see SI 1990/2347 (C 61), art. 3, Sch. 2); the former words read as follows:

"services consisting in the conveyance of programmes included in cable programme services (within the meaning of the Cable and Broadcasting Act 1984)".

## 373 Jurisdiction in relation to insolvent individuals

**373(1) [High Court and county courts]** The High Court and the county courts have jurisdiction throughout England and Wales for the purposes of the Parts in this Group.

**373(2) [Powers of county court]** For the purposes of those Parts, a county court has, in addition to its ordinary jurisdiction, all the powers and jurisdiction of the High Court; and the orders of the court may be enforced accordingly in the prescribed manner.

**373(3) [Exercise of jurisdiction]** Jurisdiction for the purposes of those Parts is exercised–

(a) by the High Court in relation to the proceedings which, in accordance with the rules, are allocated to the London insolvency district, and

(b) by each county court in relation to the proceedings which are so allocated to the insolvency district of that court.

**373(4) [Operation of s. 373(3)]** Subsection (3) is without prejudice to the transfer of proceedings from one court to another in the manner prescribed by the rules; and nothing in that subsection invalidates any proceedings on the grounds that they were initiated or continued in the wrong court.

## 374 Insolvency districts

**374(1) [Order by Lord Chancellor]** The Lord Chancellor may by order designate the areas which are for the time being to be comprised, for the purposes of the Parts in this Group, in the London insolvency district and the insolvency district of each county court; and an order under this section may–

(a) exclude any county court from having jurisdiction for the purposes of those Parts, or

(b) confer jurisdiction for those purposes on any county court which has not previously had that jurisdiction.

**374(2) [Incidental provisions etc.]** An order under this section may contain such incidental, supplemental and transitional provisions as may appear to the Lord Chancellor necessary or expedient.

**374(3) [Order by statutory instrument]** An order under this section shall be made by statutory instrument and, after being made, shall be laid before each House of Parliament.

**374(4) [Relevant districts]** Subject to any order under this section–

(a) the district which, immediately before the appointed day, is the London bankruptcy district becomes, on that day, the London insolvency district;

(b) any district which immediately before that day is the bankruptcy district of a county court becomes, on that day, the insolvency district of that court, and

(c) any county court which immediately before that day is excluded from having jurisdiction in bankruptcy is excluded, on and after that day, from having jurisdiction for the purposes of the Parts in this Group.

## 375 Appeals etc. from courts exercising insolvency jurisdiction

**375(1) [Review, rescission etc.]** Every court having jurisdiction for the purposes of the Parts in this Group may review, rescind or vary any order made by it in the exercise of that jurisdiction.

**375(2) [Appeals]** An appeal from a decision made in the exercise of jurisdiction for the purposes of those Parts by a county court or by a registrar in bankruptcy of the High Court lies to a single judge of the High Court; and an appeal from a decision of that judge on such an appeal lies to the Court of Appeal.

**History**

In s. 375(2) the words ", with the leave of the judge or of the Court of Appeal," formerly appearing after the words "on such an appeal lies" repealed by Access to Justice Act 1999, s. 106, 108(3)(f), Sch. 15, Pt. III as from 27 September 1999.

**375(3) [No other appeals]** A county court is not, in the exercise of its jurisdiction for the purposes of those Parts, to be subject to be restrained by the order of any other court, and no appeal lies from its decision in the exercise of that jurisdiction except as provided by this section.

## 376 Time-limits

**376** Where by any provision in this Group of Parts or by the rules the time for doing anything is limited, the court may extend the time, either before or after it has expired, on such terms, if any, as it thinks fit.

## 377 Formal defects

**377** The acts of a person as the trustee of a bankrupt's estate or as a special manager, and the acts of the creditors' committee established for any bankruptcy, are valid notwithstanding any defect in the appointment, election or qualifications of the trustee or manager or, as the case may be, of any member of the committee.

## 378 Exemption from stamp duty

**378** Stamp duty shall not be charged on–

(a) any document, being a deed, conveyance, assignment, surrender, admission or other assurance relating solely to property which is comprised in a bankrupt's estate and which, after the execution of that document, is or remains at law or in equity the property of the bankrupt or of the trustee of that estate,

(b) any writ, order, certificate or other instrument relating solely to the property of a bankrupt or to any bankruptcy proceedings.

## 379 Annual report

**379** As soon as practicable after the end of 1986 and each subsequent calendar year, the Secretary of State shall prepare and lay before each House of Parliament a report about the


bbcl insa 1986a Mp 1378—bcl98 1c

operation during that year of so much of this Act as is comprised in this Group of Parts, and about proceedings in the course of that year under the Deeds of Arrangement Act 1914.

# PART XI – INTERPRETATION FOR SECOND GROUP OF PARTS

**Note**

Re application of Pt. XI to insolvent partnerships, see the Insolvent Partnerships Order 1994 (SI 1994/2421), especially reg. 10, 11, Sch. 7.

## 380 Introductory

**380** The next five sections have effect for the interpretation of the provisions of this Act which are comprised in this Group of Parts; and where a definition is provided for a particular expression, it applies except so far as the context otherwise requires.

## 381 "Bankrupt" and associated terminology

**381(1) ["Bankrupt"] "Bankrupt"** means an individual who has been adjudged bankrupt and, in relation to a bankruptcy order, it means the individual adjudged bankrupt by that order.

**381(2) ["Bankruptcy order"] "Bankruptcy order"** means an order adjudging an individual bankrupt.

**381(3) ["Bankruptcy petition"] "Bankruptcy petition"** means a petition to the court for a bankruptcy order.

## 382 "Bankruptcy debt", etc.

**382(1) ["Bankruptcy debt"] "Bankruptcy debt"**, in relation to a bankrupt, means (subject to the next subsection) any of the following–

(a) any debt or liability to which he is subject at the commencement of the bankruptcy,

(b) any debt or liability to which he may become subject after the commencement of the bankruptcy (including after his discharge from bankruptcy) by reason of any obligation incurred before the commencement of the bankruptcy,

(c) any amount specified in pursuance of section 39(3)(c) of the Powers of Criminal Courts Act 1973 in any criminal bankruptcy order made against him before the commencement of the bankruptcy, and

(d) any interest provable as mentioned in section 322(2) in Chapter IV of Part IX.

**Note**

S. 382(1)(c) repealed by Criminal Justice Act 1988, s. 170(2) and Sch. 16 as from a day to be appointed.

**382(2) [Liability in tort]** In determining for the purposes of any provision in this Group of Parts whether any liability in tort is a bankruptcy debt, the bankrupt is deemed to become subject to that liability by reason of an obligation incurred at the time when the cause of action accrued.

**382(3) [References to debtor liability]** For the purposes of references in this Group of Parts to a debt or liability, it is immaterial whether the debt or liability is present or future, whether it is certain or contingent or whether its amount is fixed or liquidated, or is capable of being ascertained by fixed rules or as a matter of opinion; and references in this Group of Parts to owing a debt are to be read accordingly.

**382(4) ["Liability"]** In this Group of Parts, except in so far as the context otherwise requires, **"liability"** means (subject to subsection (3) above) a liability to pay money or money's worth, including any liability under an enactment, any liability for breach of trust, any liability in contract, tort or bailment and any liability arising out of an obligation to make restitution.

## 383 "Creditor", "security", etc.

**383(1) ["Creditor"] "Creditor"**–

(a) in relation to a bankrupt, means a person to whom any of the bankruptcy debts is owed (being, in the case of an amount falling within paragraph (c) of the definition in section 382(1) of **"bankruptcy debt"**, the person in respect of whom that amount is specified in the criminal bankruptcy order in question), and

(b) in relation to an individual to whom a bankruptcy petition relates, means a person who would be a creditor in the bankruptcy if a bankruptcy order were made on that petition.

**Note**

In s. 383(1), para. (a) the words from "(being," to "question)" repealed by Criminal Justice Act 1988, s. 170(2) and Sch. 16 as from a day to be appointed.

**383(2) [Securing of debt]** Subject to the next two subsections and any provision of the rules requiring a creditor to give up his security for the purposes of proving a debt, a debt is secured for the purposes of this Group of Parts to the extent that the person to whom the debt is owed holds any security for the debt (whether a mortgage, charge, lien or other security) over any property of the person by whom the debt is owed.

**383(3) [Where s. 269(1)(a) statement made]** Where a statement such as is mentioned in section 269(1)(a) in Chapter I of Part IX has been made by a secured creditor for the purposes of any bankruptcy petition and a bankruptcy order is subsequently made on that petition, the creditor is deemed for the purposes of the Parts in this Group to have given up the security specified in the statement.

**383(4) [Qualification to s. 383(2)]** In subsection (2) the reference to a security does not include a lien on books, papers or other records, except to the extent that they consist of documents which give a title to property and are held as such.

## 384 "Prescribed" and "the rules"

**384(1) [Definitions]** Subject to the next subsection, **"prescribed"** means prescribed by the rules; and **"the rules"** means rules made under section 412 in Part XV.

**384(2) [Interpretation]** References in this Group of Parts to the amount prescribed for the purposes of any of the following provisions–

section 273;
section 346(3);
section 354(1) and (2);
section 358;
section 360(1);
section 361(2); and
section 364(2)(d),

and references in those provisions to the prescribed amount are to be read in accordance with section 418 in Part XV and orders made under that section.

## 385 Miscellaneous definitions

**385(1) [Definitions]** The following definitions have effect–

**"the court"**, in relation to any matter, means the court to which, in accordance with section 373 in Part X and the rules, proceedings with respect to that matter are allocated or transferred;

**"creditor's petition"** means a bankruptcy petition under section 264(1)(a);

**"criminal bankruptcy order"** means an order under section 39(1) of the Powers of Criminal Courts Act 1973;

**"debt"** is to be construed in accordance with section 382(3);

**"the debtor"**–

(a) in relation to a proposal for the purposes of Part VIII, means the individual making or intending to make that proposal, and
(b) in relation to a bankruptcy petition, means the individual to whom the petition relates;

**"debtor's petition"** means a bankruptcy petition presented by the debtor himself under section 264(1)(b);

**"dwelling house"** includes any building or part of a building which is occupied as a dwelling and any yard, garden, garage or outhouse belonging to the dwelling house and occupied with it;

**"estate"**, in relation to a bankrupt is to be construed in accordance with section 283 in Chapter II of Part IX;

**"family"**, in relation to a bankrupt, means the persons (if any) who are living with him and are dependent on him;

**"secured"** and related expressions are to be construed in accordance with section 383; and

**"the trustee"**, in relation to a bankruptcy and the bankrupt, means the trustee of the bankrupt's estate.

**Note**

In s. 385(1) the definition of "criminal bankruptcy order" repealed by Criminal Justice Act 1988, s. 170(2) and Sch. 16 as from a day to be appointed.

**385(2) [Interpretation]** References in this Group of Parts to a person's affairs include his business, if any.

# THE THIRD GROUP OF PARTS MISCELLANEOUS MATTERS BEARING ON BOTH COMPANY AND INDIVIDUAL INSOLVENCY; GENERAL INTERPRETATION; FINAL PROVISIONS

# PART XII – PREFERENTIAL DEBTS IN COMPANY AND INDIVIDUAL INSOLVENCY

**Note**

Re application of Pt. XII to insolvent partnerships, see the Insolvent Partnerships Order 1994 (SI 1994/2421), especially reg. 10, 11, Sch. 7.

## 386 Categories of preferential debts

**386(1) [Debts listed in Sch. 6]** A reference in this Act to the preferential debts of a company or an individual is to the debts listed in Schedule 6 to this Act (money owed to the Inland Revenue for income tax deducted at source; VAT, insurance premium tax, landfill tax, climate change levy, car tax, betting and gaming duties, beer duty, lottery duty, air passenger duty; social security and pension scheme contributions; remuneration etc. of employees; levies on coal and steel production); and references to preferential creditors are to be read accordingly.

**History**

In s. 386(1) the words "climate change levy," inserted by the Finance Act 2000, s. 30(2) and Sch. 7, para. 3(1)(a) as from 28 July 2000. Previously in s. 386(1) the words "landfill tax" inserted by the Finance Act 1996, s. 60 and Sch. 5, para. 12(1) as from 29 April 1996. Previously to that in s. 386(1) the words ", insurance premium tax" inserted by Finance Act 1994, s. 64 and Sch. 7, para. 7(2) as from 3 May 1994; the words ", beer duty" inserted by Finance Act 1991, s. 7 and Sch. 2, para. 21A as inserted by Finance (No. 2) Act 1992, s. 9(1) as from 16 July 1992; the words ", lottery duty" inserted by Finance Act 1993, s. 36 as from 1 December 1993 (see SI 1993/2842 (C 61)); the words ", air passenger duty" inserted by Finance Act 1995, s. 17 as from 1 May 1995; and the words "; levies on coal and steel production" inserted by the Insolvency (ECSC Levy Debts) Regulations 1987 (SI 1987/2093), reg. 2(2) as from 1 January 1988.

**386(2) ["The debtor"]** In that Schedule **"the debtor"** means the company or the individual concerned.

**386(3) [Interpretation of Sch. 6]** Schedule 6 is to be read with Schedule 4 to the Pension Schemes Act 1993 (occupational pension scheme contributions).

**History**

In s. 386(3) the words "Schedule 4 to the Pension Schemes Act 1993" substituted for the former words "Schedule 3 to the Social Security Pensions Act 1975" by Pension Schemes Act 1993, s. 190 and Sch. 8, para. 18 as from 7 February 1994 (see SI 1994/86 (C 3), art. 2).

## 387 "The relevant date"

**387(1) [Explanation of Sch. 6]** This section explains references in Schedule 6 to the relevant date (being the date which determines the existence and amount of a preferential debt).

**387(2) [Pt. I, s. 4]** For the purposes of section 4 in Part I (meetings to consider company voluntary arrangement), the relevant date in relation to a company which is not being wound up is–

(a) where an administration order is in force in relation to the company, the date of the making of that order, and

(b) where no such order has been made, the date of the approval of the voluntary arrangement.

**387(3) [Company being wound up]** In relation to a company which is being wound up, the following applies–

(a) if the winding up is by the court, and the winding-up order was made immediately upon the discharge of an administration order, the relevant date is the date of the making of the administration order;

(b) if the case does not fall within paragraph (a) and the company–

(i) is being wound up by the court, and

(ii) had not commenced to be wound up voluntarily before the date of the making of the winding-up order,

the relevant date is the date of the appointment (or first appointment) of a provisional liquidator or, if no such appointment has been made, the date of the winding-up order;

(c) if the case does not fall within either paragraph (a) or (b), the relevant date is the date of the passing of the resolution for the winding up of the company.

**387(4) [Company in receivership]** In relation to a company in receivership (where section 40 or, as the case may be, section 59 applies), the relevant date is–

(a) in England and Wales, the date of the appointment of the receiver by debenture-holders, and

(b) in Scotland, the date of the appointment of the receiver under section 53(6) or (as the case may be) 54(5).

**387(5) [Pt. VIII, s. 258]** For the purposes of section 258 in Part VIII (individual voluntary arrangements), the relevant date is, in relation to a debtor who is not an undischarged bankrupt, the date of the interim order made under section 252 with respect to his proposal.

**387(6) [Bankrupt]** In relation to a bankrupt, the following applies–

(a) where at the time the bankruptcy order was made there was an interim receiver appointed under section 286, the relevant date is the date on which the interim receiver was first appointed after the presentation of the bankruptcy petition;

(b) otherwise, the relevant date is the date of the making of the bankruptcy order.

# PART XIII – INSOLVENCY PRACTITIONERS AND THEIR QUALIFICATION

**Note**

Re application of Pt. XIII to insolvent partnerships, see the Insolvent Partnerships Order 1994 (SI 1994/2421), especially reg. 10, 11, Sch. 7.

## RESTRICTIONS ON UNQUALIFIED PERSONS ACTING AS LIQUIDATOR, TRUSTEE IN BANKRUPTCY, ETC.

### 388 Meaning of "act as insolvency practitioner"

**388(1) [Acting as insolvency practitioner re company]** A person acts as an insolvency practitioner in relation to a company by acting–

(a) as its liquidator, provisional liquidator, administrator or administrative receiver, or

(b) as supervisor of a voluntary arrangement approved by it under Part I.

**388(2) [Acting as insolvency practitioner re individual]** A person acts as an insolvency practitioner in relation to an individual by acting–

(a) as his trustee in bankruptcy or interim receiver of his property or as permanent or interim trustee in the sequestration of his estate; or

(b) as trustee under a deed which is a deed of arrangement made for the benefit of his creditors or, in Scotland, a trust deed for his creditors; or

(c) as supervisor of a voluntary arrangement proposed by him and approved under Part VIII; or

(d) in the case of a deceased individual to the administration of whose estate this section applies by virtue of an order under section 421 (application of provisions of this Act to insolvent estates of deceased persons), as administrator of that estate.

**388(2A) [Acting as insolvency practitioner re insolvent partnership]** A person acts as an insolvency practitioner in relation to an insolvent partnership by acting–

(a) as its liquidator, provisional liquidator or administrator, or

(b) as trustee of the partnership under article 11 of the Insolvent Partnerships Order 1994, or

(c) as supervisor of a voluntary arrangement approved in relation to it under Part I of this Act.

**Note**
See note after s. 388(3).

**388(3) [Interpretation]** References in this section to an individual include, except in so far as the context otherwise requires, references to a partnership and to any debtor within the meaning of the Bankruptcy (Scotland) Act 1985.

**Note**
Re insolvent partnerships, s. 388(2A) inserted and in s. 388(3) the words "to a partnership and" omitted for the purposes of the Insolvent Partnerships Order 1994 (SI 1994/2421) as from 1 December 1994 (by art. 15).

**388(4) [Definitions]** In this section–

**"administrative receiver"** has the meaning given by section 251 in Part VII;

**"company"** means a company within the meaning given by section 735(1) of the Companies Act or a company which may be wound up under Part V of this Act (unregistered companies); and

**"interim trustee"** and **"permanent trustee"** mean the same as in the Bankruptcy (Scotland) Act 1985.

**Note**
In s. 388(4) purported substitution of definition of "company" by Building Societies Act 1986, s. 120 and Sch. 18, para. 17(2) as from 1 January 1987 (see SI 1986/1560 (C 56)) but to former provision, IA 1985, s. 1(5) – however Building Societies Act 1986, Sch. 18, para. 17(2) repealed by CA 1989, s. 212 and Sch. 24 as from 31 July 1990 (see SI 1990/1392 (C 41), art. 4(b)).

**388(5) [Application]** Nothing in this section applies to anything done by–

(a) the official receiver; or

(b) the Accountant in Bankruptcy (within the meaning of the Bankruptcy (Scotland) Act 1985).

**History**
S. 388(5) substituted by Bankruptcy (Scotland) Act 1993, s. 11(1), 12(3) and SI 1993/438 (C 9) (S 49), art. 3 as from 18 February and 1 April 1993; s. 388(5) formerly read as follows:
"Nothing in this section applies to anything done by the official receiver."

## 389 Acting without qualification an offence

**389(1) [Penalty]** A person who acts as an insolvency practitioner in relation to a company or an individual at a time when he is not qualified to do so is liable to imprisonment or a fine, or to both.

**389(2) [Non-application to official receiver]** This section does not apply to the official receiver or the Accountant in Bankruptcy (within the meaning of the Bankruptcy (Scotland) Act 1985).

**History**
In s. 389(2) the words "or the Accountant in Bankruptcy (within the meaning of the Bankruptcy (Scotland) Act 1985)" inserted by Bankruptcy (Scotland) Act 1993, s. 11(1), 12(3) and SI 1993/438 (C 9) (S 49), art. 3 as from 18 February and 1 April 1993.

THE REQUISITE QUALIFICATION,
AND THE MEANS OF OBTAINING IT

## 390 Persons not qualified to act as insolvency practitioners

**390(1) [Must be individual]** A person who is not an individual is not qualified to act as an insolvency practitioner.

**390(2) [Authorisation necessary]** A person is not qualified to act as an insolvency practitioner at any time unless at that time–

(a) he is authorised so to act by virtue of membership of a professional body recognised under section 391 below, being permitted so to act by or under the rules of that body, or

(b) he holds an authorisation granted by a competent authority under section 393.

**390(3) [Security as condition required]** A person is not qualified to act as an insolvency practitioner in relation to another person at any time unless–

(a) there is in force at that time security or, in Scotland, caution for the proper performance of his functions, and

(b) that security or caution meets the prescribed requirements with respect to his so acting in relation to that other person.

**390(4) [Disqualification]** A person is not qualified to act as an insolvency practitioner at any time if at that time–

(a) he has been adjudged bankrupt or sequestration of his estate has been awarded and (in either case) he has not been discharged,

(b) he is subject to a disqualification order made under the Company Directors Disqualification Act 1986, or

(c) he is a patient within the meaning of Part VII of the Mental Health Act 1983 or section 125(1) of the Mental Health (Scotland) Act 1984.

**Note**

Reference should be made to the Insolvency Practitioners Regulations 1990 (SI 1990/439), as amended.

## 391 Recognised professional bodies

**391(1) [Order by Secretary of State]** The Secretary of State may by order declare a body which appears to him to fall within subsection (2) below to be a recognised professional body for the purposes of this section.

**391(2) [Bodies recognised]** A body may be recognised if it regulates the practice of a profession and maintains and enforces rules for securing that such of its members as are permitted by or under the rules to act as insolvency practitioners–

(a) are fit and proper persons so to act, and

(b) meet acceptable requirements as to education and practical training and experience.

**391(3) [Interpretation]** References to members of a recognised professional body are to persons who, whether members of that body or not, are subject to its rules in the practice of the profession in question.

The reference in section 390(2) above to membership of a professional body recognised under this section is to be read accordingly.

**391(4) [Revocation of order]** An order made under subsection (1) in relation to a professional body may be revoked by a further order if it appears to the Secretary of State that the body no longer falls within subsection (2).

**391(5) [Effect of order]** An order of the Secretary of State under this section has effect from such date as is specified in the order; and any such order revoking a previous order may make provision whereby members of the body in question continue to be treated as authorised to act as insolvency practitioners for a specified period after the revocation takes effect.

**Note**

See the Insolvency Practitioners (Recognised Professional Bodies) Order 1986 (SI 1986/1764).

## 392 Authorisation by competent authority

**392(1) [Application]** Application may be made to a competent authority for authorisation to act as an insolvency practitioner.

**Note**
See the Insolvency Practitioners Regulations 1990 (SI 1990/439), as amended.

**392(2) [Competent authorities]** The competent authorities for this purpose are–

(a) in relation to a case of any description specified in directions given by the Secretary of State, the body or person so specified in relation to cases of that description, and

(b) in relation to a case not falling within paragraph (a), the Secretary of State.

**392(3) [Application]** The application–

(a) shall be made in such manner as the competent authority may direct,

(b) shall contain or be accompanied by such information as that authority may reasonably require for the purpose of determining the application, and

(c) shall be accompanied by the prescribed fee;

and the authority may direct that notice of the making of the application shall be published in such manner as may be specified in the direction.

**392(4) [Additional information]** At any time after receiving the application and before determining it the authority may require the applicant to furnish additional information.

**392(5) [Requirements may differ]** Directions and requirements given or imposed under subsection (3) or (4) may differ as between different applications.

**392(6) [Forms]** Any information to be furnished to the competent authority under this section shall, if it so requires, be in such form or verified in such manner as it may specify.

**392(7) [Withdrawal of application]** An application may be withdrawn before it is granted or refused.

**392(8) [Sums received]** Any sums received under this section by a competent authority other than the Secretary of State may be retained by the authority; and any sums so received by the Secretary of State shall be paid into the Consolidated Fund.

## 393 Grant, refusal and withdrawal of authorisation

**393(1) [Power to grant, refuse application]** The competent authority may, on an application duly made in accordance with section 392 and after being furnished with all such information as it may require under that section, grant or refuse the application.

**393(2) [Granting application]** The authority shall grant the application if it appears to it from the information furnished by the applicant and having regard to such other information, if any, as it may have–

(a) that the applicant is a fit and proper person to act as an insolvency practitioner, and

(b) that the applicant meets the prescribed requirements with respect to education and practical training and experience.

**393(3) [Duration of authorisation]** An authorisation granted under this section, if not previously withdrawn, continues in force for such period not exceeding the prescribed maximum as may be specified in the authorisation.

**393(4) [Withdrawal of authorisation]** An authorisation so granted may be withdrawn by the competent authority if it appears to it–

(a) that the holder of the authorisation is no longer a fit and proper person to act as an insolvency practitioner, or

(b) without prejudice to paragraph (a), that the holder–

(i) has failed to comply with any provision of this Part or of any regulations made under this Part or Part XV, or

(ii) in purported compliance with any such provision, has furnished the competent authority with false, inaccurate or misleading information.

**393(5) [Withdrawal on request]** An authorisation granted under this section may be withdrawn by the competent authority at the request or with the consent of the holder of the authorisation.

**Note**

See the regulations referred to in the note to s. 392(1).

## 394 Notices

**394(1) [Notice to applicant re grant]** Where a competent authority grants an authorisation under section 393, it shall give written notice of that fact to the applicant, specifying the date on which the authorisation takes effect.

**394(2) [Notice re proposed refusal, withdrawal]** Where the authority proposes to refuse an application, or to withdraw an authorisation under section 393(4), it shall give the applicant or holder of the authorisation written notice of its intention to do so, setting out particulars of the grounds on which is proposes to act.

**394(3) [Date to be stated re withdrawal]** In the case of a proposed withdrawal the notice shall state the date on which it is proposed that the withdrawal should take effect.

**394(4) [Notice to give details re rights]** A notice under subsection (2) shall give particulars of the rights exercisable under the next two sections by a person on whom the notice is served.

## 395 Right to make representations

**395(1) [Right exercisable within 14 days]** A person on whom a notice is served under section 394(2) may within 14 days after the date of service make written representations to the competent authority.

**395(2) [Representations to be considered]** The competent authority shall have regard to any representations so made in determining whether to refuse the application or withdraw the authorisation, as the case may be.

## 396 Reference to Tribunal

**396(1) [Application of Sch. 7]** The Insolvency Practitioners Tribunal (**"the Tribunal"**) continues in being; and the provisions of Schedule 7 apply to it.

**Note**

See the Insolvency Practitioners Tribunal (Conduct of Investigations) Rules 1986 (SI 1986/952).

**396(2) [Person served with notice]** Where a person is served with a notice under section 394(2), he may–

(a) at any time within 28 days after the date of service of the notice, or

(b) at any time after the making by him of representations under section 395 and before the end of the period of 28 days after the date of the service on him of a notice by the competent authority that the authority does not propose to alter its decision in consequence of the representations,

give written notice to the authority requiring the case to be referred to the Tribunal.

**396(3) [Reference]** Where a requirement is made under subsection (2), then, unless the competent authority–

(a) has decided or decides to grant the application or, as the case may be, not to withdraw the authorisation, and

(b) within 7 days after the date of the making of the requirement, gives written notice of that decision to the person by whom the requirement was made,

it shall refer the case to the Tribunal.

## 397 Action of Tribunal on reference

**397(1) [Duties of Tribunal]** On a reference under section 396 the Tribunal shall–

(a) investigate the case, and

(b) make a report to the competent authority stating what would in their opinion be the appropriate decision in the matter and the reasons for that opinion, and it is the duty of the competent authority to decide the matter accordingly.

**397(2) [Copy of report to applicant]** The Tribunal shall send a copy of the report to the applicant or, as the case may be, the holder of the authorisation; and the competent authority shall serve him with a written notice of the decision made by it in accordance with the report.

**397(3) [Publication of report]** The competent authority may, if he thinks fit, publish the report of the Tribunal.

## 398 Refusal or withdrawal without reference to Tribunal

**398** Where in the case of any proposed refusal or withdrawal of an authorisation either–

(a) the period mentioned in section 396(2)(a) has expired without the making of any requirement under that subsection or of any representations under section 395, or

(b) the competent authority has given a notice such as is mentioned in section 396(2)(b) and the period so mentioned has expired without the making of any such requirement,

the competent authority may give written notice of the refusal or withdrawal to the person concerned in accordance with the proposal in the notice given under section 394(2).

# PART XIV – PUBLIC ADMINISTRATION (ENGLAND AND WALES)

**Note**

Re application of Pt. XIV to insolvent partnerships, see the Insolvent Partnerships Order (SI 1994/2421), especially reg. 10, 11, Sch. 7.

### OFFICIAL RECEIVERS

## 399 Appointment, etc. of official receivers

**399(1) [Official receiver]** For the purposes of this Act the official receiver, in relation to any bankruptcy or winding up, is any person who by virtue of the following provisions of this section or section 401 below is authorised to act as the official receiver in relation to that bankruptcy or winding up.

**399(2) [Power of appointment by Secretary of State]** The Secretary of State may (subject to the approval of the Treasury as to numbers) appoint persons to the office of official receiver, and a person appointed to that office (whether under this section or section 70 of the Bankruptcy Act 1914)–

(a) shall be paid out of money provided by Parliament such salary as the Secretary of State may with the concurrence of the Treasury direct,

(b) shall hold office on such other terms and conditions as the Secretary of State may with the concurrence of the Treasury direct, and

(c) may be removed from office by a direction of the Secretary of State.

**399(3) [Attachment to particular court]** Where a person holds the office of official receiver, the Secretary of State shall from time to time attach him either to the High Court or to a county court having jurisdiction for the purposes of the second Group of Parts of this Act.

**399(4) [Person authorised to act as official receiver]** Subject to any directions under subsection (6) below, an official receiver attached to a particular court is the person authorised to act as the official receiver in relation to every bankruptcy or winding up falling within the jurisdiction of that court.

**399(5) [Each court to have official receiver]** The Secretary of State shall ensure that there is, at all times, at least one official receiver attached to the High Court and at least one attached to each county court having jurisdiction for the purposes of the second Group of Parts; but he may attach the same official receiver to two or more different courts.

**399(6) [Directions by Secretary of State]** The Secretary of State may give directions with respect to the disposal of the business of official receivers, and such directions may, in particular–

(a) authorise an official receiver attached to one court to act as the official receiver in relation to any case or description of cases falling within the jurisdiction of another court;

(b) provide, where there is more than one official receiver authorised to act as the official receiver in relation to cases falling within the jurisdiction of any court, for the distribution of their business between or among themselves.

**399(7) [Continuation of official receiver]** A person who at the coming into force of section 222 of the Insolvency Act 1985 (replaced by this section) is an official receiver attached to a court shall continue in office after the coming into force of that section as an official receiver attached to that court under this section.

## 400 Functions and status of official receivers

**400(1) [Functions]** In addition to any functions conferred on him by this Act, a person holding the office of official receiver shall carry out such other functions as may from time to time be conferred on him by the Secretary of State.

**400(2) [Status]** In the exercise of the functions of his office a person holding the office of official receiver shall act under the general directions of the Secretary of State and shall also be an officer of the court in relation to which he exercises those functions.

**400(3) [Death or ceasing to hold office]** Any property vested in his official capacity in a person holding the office of official receiver shall, on his dying, ceasing to hold office or being otherwise succeeded in relation to the bankruptcy or winding up in question by another official receiver, vest in his successor without any conveyance, assignment or transfer.

## 401 Deputy official receivers and staff

**401(1) [Deputy official receiver]** The Secretary of State may, if he thinks it expedient to do so in order to facilitate the disposal of the business of the official receiver attached to any court, appoint an officer of his department to act as deputy to that official receiver.

**401(2) [Same status and functions]** Subject to any directions given by the Secretary of State under section 399 or 400, a person appointed to act as deputy to an official receiver has, on such conditions and for such period as may be specified in the terms of his appointment, the same status and functions as the official receiver to whom he is appointed deputy.

Accordingly, references in this Act (except section 399(1) to (5)) to an official receiver include a person appointed to act as his deputy.

**401(3) [Termination of appointment]** An appointment made under subsection (1) may be terminated at any time by the Secretary of State.

**401(4) [Staff]** The Secretary of State may, subject to the approval of the Treasury as to numbers and remuneration and as to the other terms and conditions of the appointments, appoint officers of his department to assist official receivers in the carrying out of their functions.

### THE OFFICIAL PETITIONER

## 402 Official Petitioner

**402(1) [Continuation of officer]** There continues to be an officer known as the Official Petitioner for the purpose of discharging, in relation to cases in which a criminal bankruptcy order is made, the functions assigned to him by or under this Act; and the Director of Public Prosecutions continues, by virtue of his office, to be the Official Petitioner.

**402(2) [Functions]** The functions of the Official Petitioner include the following–

(a) to consider whether, in a case in which a criminal bankruptcy order is made, it is in the public interest that he should himself present a petition under section 264(1)(d) of this Act;

(b) to present such a petition in any case where he determines that it is in the public interest for him to do so;

(c) to make payments, in such cases as he may determine, towards expenses incurred by other persons in connection with proceedings in pursuance of such a petition; and

(d) to exercise, so far as he considers it in the public interest to do so, any of the powers conferred on him by or under this Act.

**402(3) [Discharge of functions on authority]** Any functions of the Official Petitioner may be discharged on his behalf by any person acting with his authority.

**402(4) [Inability]** Neither the Official Petitioner nor any person acting with his authority is liable to any action or proceeding in respect of anything done or omitted to be done in the discharge, or purported discharge, of the functions of the Official Petitioner.

**402(5) ["Criminal bankruptcy order"]** In this section **"criminal bankruptcy order"** means an order under section 39(1) of the Powers of Criminal Courts Act 1973.

**Note**

S. 402 repealed by Criminal Justice Act 1988, s. 170(2) and Sch. 16 as from a day to be appointed.

## INSOLVENCY SERVICE FINANCE, ACCOUNTING AND INVESTMENT

## 403 Insolvency Services Account

**403(1) [Payment into Account]** All money received by the Secretary of State in respect of proceedings under this Act as it applies to England and Wales shall be paid into the Insolvency Services Account kept by the Secretary of State with the Bank of England; and all payments out of money standing to the credit of the Secretary of State in that account shall be made by the Bank of England in such manner as he may direct.

**403(2) [Where excess amount]** Whenever the cash balance standing to the credit of the Insolvency Services Account is in excess of the amount which in the opinion of the Secretary of State is required for the time being to answer demands in respect of bankrupts' estates or companies' estates, the Secretary of State shall–

(a) notify the excess to the National Debt Commissioners, and

(b) pay into the Insolvency Services Investment Account (**"the Investment Account"**) kept by the Commissioners with the Bank of England the whole or any part of the excess as the Commissioners may require for investment in accordance with the following provisions of this Part.

**403(3) [Where invested money required]** Whenever any part of the money so invested is, in the opinion of the Secretary of State, required to answer any demand in respect of bankrupts' estates or companies' estates, he shall notify to the National Debt Commissioners the amount so required and the Commissioners–

(a) shall thereupon repay to the Secretary of State such sum as may be required to the credit of the Insolvency Services Account, and

(b) for that purpose may direct the sale of such part of the securities in which the money has been invested as may be necessary.

**Note**

See the Insolvency Regulations 1994 (SI 1994/2507).

## 404 Investment Account

**404** Any money standing to the credit of the Investment Account (including any money received by the National Debt Commissioners by way of interest on or proceeds of any investment under this section) may be invested by the Commissioners, in accordance with such directions as may be given by the Treasury, in any manner for the time being specified in Part II of Schedule 1 to the Trustee Investments Act 1961.

## 405 Application of income in Investment Account; adjustment of balances

**405(1) [Payment of excess into Consolidated Fund]** Where the annual account to be kept by the National Debt Commissioners under section 409 below shows that in the year for which it is made up the gross amount of the interest accrued from the securities standing to the credit of the Investment Account exceeded the aggregate of–

(a) a sum, to be determined by the Treasury, to provide against the depreciation in the value of the securities, and

(b) the sums paid into the Insolvency Services Account in pursuance of the next section together with the sums paid in pursuance of that section to the Commissioners of Inland Revenue,

the National Debt Commissioners shall, within 3 months after the account is laid before Parliament, cause the amount of the excess to be paid out of the Investment Account into the Consolidated Fund in such manner as may from time to time be agreed between the Treasury and the Commissioners.

**405(2) [Deficiency into Investment Account]** Where the said annual account shows that in the year for which it is made up the gross amount of interest accrued from the securities standing to the credit of the Investment Account was less than the aggregate mentioned in subsection (1), an amount equal to the deficiency shall, at such times as the Treasury direct, be paid out of the Consolidated Fund into the Investment Account.

**405(3) [If funds in Investment Account insufficient]** If the Investment Account is insufficient to meet its liabilities the Treasury may, on being informed of the insufficiency by the National Debt Commissioners, issue the amount of the deficiency out of the Consolidated Fund and the Treasury shall certify the deficiency to Parliament.

## 406 Interest on money received by liquidators and invested

**406** Where under rules made by virtue of paragraph 16 of Schedule 8 to this Act (investment of money received by company liquidators) a company has become entitled to any sum by way of interest, the Secretary of State shall certify that sum and the amount of tax payable on it to the National Debt Commissioners; and the Commissioners shall pay, out of the Investment Account–

(a) into the Insolvency Services Account, the sum so certified less the amount of tax so certified, and

(b) to the Commissioners of Inland Revenue, the amount of tax so certified.

## 407 Unclaimed dividends and undistributed balances

**407(1) [Duty of Secretary of State]** The Secretary of State shall from time to time pay into the Consolidated Fund out of the Insolvency Services Account so much of the sums standing to the credit of that Account as represents–

(a) dividends which were declared before such date as the Treasury may from time to time determine and have not been claimed, and

(b) balances ascertained before that date which are too small to be divided among the persons entitled to them.

**407(2) [Sums to credit of Insolvency Services Account]** For the purposes of this section the sums standing to the credit of the Insolvency Services Account are deemed to include any sums paid out of that Account and represented by any sums or securities standing to the credit of the Investment Account.

**407(3) [Power of Secretary of State]** The Secretary of State may require the National Debt Commissioners to pay out of the Investment Account into the Insolvency Services Account the whole or part of any sum which he is required to pay out of that account under subsection (1); and the Commissioners may direct the sale of such securities standing to the credit of the Investment Account as may be necessary for that purpose.

## 408 Recourse to Consolidated Fund

**408** If, after any repayment due to it from the Investment Account, the Insolvency Services Account is insufficient to meet its liabilities, the Treasury may, on being informed of it by the Secretary of State, issue the amount of the deficiency out of the Consolidated Fund, and the Treasury shall certify the deficiency to Parliament.

## 409 Annual financial statement and audit

**409(1) [Preparation of statement]** The National Debt Commissioners shall for each year ending on 31st March prepare a statement of the sums credited and debited to the Investment

Account in such form and manner as the Treasury may direct and shall transmit it to the Comptroller and Auditor General before the end of November next following the year.

**409(2) [Duty of Secretary of State]** The Secretary of State shall for each year ending 31st March prepare a statement of the sums received or paid by him under section 403 above in such form and manner as the Treasury may direct and shall transmit each statement to the Comptroller and Auditor General before the end of November next following the year.

**409(3) [Additional information]** Every such statement shall include such additional information as the Treasury may direct.

**409(4) [Examination etc. of statement]** The Comptroller and Auditor General shall examine, certify and report on every such statement and shall lay copies of it, and of his report, before Parliament.

SUPPLEMENTARY

## 410 Extent of this Part

**410** This Part of this Act extends to England and Wales only.

# PART XV – SUBORDINATE LEGISLATION

**Note**

Re application of Pt. XV to insolvent partnerships, see the Insolvent Partnerships Order 1994 (SI 1994/2421), especially reg. 10, 11, Sch. 7.

GENERAL INSOLVENCY RULES

## 411 Company insolvency rules

**411(1) [Rules]** Rules may be made–

(a) in relation to England and Wales, by the Lord Chancellor with the concurrence of the Secretary of State, or

(b) in relation to Scotland, by the Secretary of State,

for the purpose of giving effect to Parts I to VII of this Act.

**411(2) [Contents of rules]** Without prejudice to the generality of subsection (1), or to any provision of those Parts by virtue of which rules under this section may be made with respect to any matter, rules under this section may contain–

(a) any such provision as is specified in Schedule 8 to this Act or corresponds to provision contained immediately before the coming into force of section 106 of the Insolvency Act 1985 in rules made, or having effect as if made, under section 663(1) or (2) of the Companies Act (old winding-up rules), and

(b) such incidental, supplemental and transitional provisions as may appear to the Lord Chancellor or, as the case may be, the Secretary of State necessary or expedient.

**Note**

See the Insolvency Rules 1986 (SI 1986/1925), the Insolvency (Scotland) Rules 1986 (SI 1986/1915 (S. 139)), as amended.

For insurance companies see the Insurance Companies (Winding-up) (Amendment) Rules 1986 (SI 1986/2002) and the Insurance Companies (Winding Up) (Scotland) Rules 1986 (SI 1986/1918 (S. 142)). There are also the Companies (Unfair Prejudice Applications) Proceedings Rules 1986 (SI 1986/2000) and the two sets of rules on directors referred to in the note to Company Directors Disqualification Act 1986, s. 21(2) and the Insolvent Companies (Disqualification of Unfit Directors) Proceedings Rules 1987 (SI 1987/2023).

See also the Insolvent Companies (Reports on Conduct of Directors) Rules 1996 (SI 1996/1909) and the Insolvent Companies (Reports on Conduct of Directors) (Scotland) Rules 1996 (SI 1996/1910 (S. 154)).

**411(3) [Interpretation of Sch. 8]** In Schedule 8 to this Act "liquidator" includes a provisional liquidator; and references above in this section to Parts I to VII of this Act are to be read as including the Companies Act so far as relating to, and to matters connected with or arising out of, the insolvency or winding up of companies.

**411(4) [Rules by statutory instrument etc.]** Rules under this section shall be made by statutory instrument subject to annulment in pursuance of a resolution of either House of Parliament.

**411(5) [Regulations]** Regulations made by the Secretary of State under a power conferred by rules under this section shall be made by statutory instrument and, after being made, shall be laid before each House of Parliament.

**Note**
See the Insolvency Regulations 1994 (SI 1994/2507).

**411(6) [Rules of court]** Nothing in this section prejudices any power to make rules of court.

# 412 Individual insolvency rules (England and Wales)

**412(1) [Rules by Lord Chancellor]** The Lord Chancellor may, with the concurrence of the Secretary of State, make rules for the purpose of giving effect to Parts VIII to XI of this Act.

**Note**
See the Insolvency Rules 1986 (SI 1986/1925).

**412(2) [Contents of rules]** Without prejudice to the generality of subsection (1), or to any provision of those Parts by virtue of which rules under this section may be made with respect to any matter, rules under this section may contain–

(a) any such provision as is specified in Schedule 9 to this Act or corresponds to provision contained immediately before the appointed day in rules made under section 132 of the Bankruptcy Act 1914; and

(b) such incidental, supplemental and transitional provisions as may appear to the Lord Chancellor necessary or expedient.

**412(3) [Rules to be made by statutory instrument]** Rules under this section shall be made by statutory instrument subject to annulment in pursuance of a resolution of either House of Parliament.

**412(4) [Regulations]** Regulations made by the Secretary of State under a power conferred by rules under this section shall be made by statutory instrument and, after being made, shall be laid before each House of Parliament.

**Note**
See the Insolvency Regulations 1994 (SI 1994/2507).

**412(5) [Rules of court]** Nothing in this section prejudices any power to make rules of court.

# 413 Insolvency Rules Committee

**413(1) [Continuation of committee]** The committee established under section 10 of the Insolvency Act 1976 (advisory committee on bankruptcy and winding-up rules) continues to exist for the purpose of being consulted under this section.

**413(2) [Consultation by Lord Chancellor]** The Lord Chancellor shall consult the committee before making any rules under section 411 or 412 other than rules which contain a statement that the only provision made by the rules is provision applying rules made under section 411, with or without modifications, for the purposes of provision made by any of sections 23 to 26 of the Water Industry Act 1991 or Schedule 3 to that Act or by any of sections 59 to 65 of, or Schedule 6 or 7 to, the Railways Act 1993.

**History**
In s. 413(2):

- the words "any of sections 23 to 26 of the Water Industry Act 1991 or Schedule 3 to that Act" substituted for the former words "section 23 or 24 of or Schedule 6 to the Water Act 1989" by the Water Consolidation (Consequential Provisions) Act 1991, s. 2, 4(2) and Sch. 1, para. 16 as from 1 December 1991 and previously the words from "other than rules" to "Schedule 6 to the Water Act 1989" inserted by Water Act 1989, s. 190(1) and Sch. 25, para. 78(2) as from 1 September 1989 (see Water Act 1989, s. 4, 194(4) and SI 1989/1146 (C 37) – see also SI 1989/1530 (C 51));
- the words "or by any of sections 59 to 65 of, or Schedule 6 or 7 to, the Railways Act 1993" added by Railways Act 1993, s. 152 and Sch. 12, para. 25 as from 1 April 1994 (see SI 1994/571).

**Note**
See the Insolvent Companies (Reports on Conduct of Directors) Rules 1996 (SI 1996/1909).

**413(3) [Members of committee]** Subject to the next subsection, the committee shall consist of–

(a) a judge of the High Court attached to the Chancery Division;

(b) a circuit judge;

(c) a registrar in bankruptcy of the High Court;

(d) the registrar of a county court;

(e) a practising barrister;

(f) a practising solicitor; and

(g) a practising accountant;

and the appointment of any person as a member of the committee shall be made by the Lord Chancellor.

**413(4) [Additional members]** The Lord Chancellor may appoint as additional members of the committee any persons appearing to him to have qualifications or experience that would be of value to the committee in considering any matter with which it is concerned.

## FEES ORDERS

# 414 Fees orders (company insolvency proceedings)

**414(1) [Fees]** There shall be paid in respect of–

(a) proceedings under any of Parts I to VII of this Act, and

(b) the performance by the official receiver or the Secretary of State of functions under those Parts,

such fees as the competent authority may with the sanction of the Treasury by order direct.

**Note**

See the Insolvency Fees Order 1986 (SI 1986/2030) as amended, the Supreme Court Fees Order 1999 (SI 1999/687) and the County Court Fees Order 1999 (SI 1999/689).

**414(2) [Security for fees]** That authority is–

(a) in relation to England and Wales, the Lord Chancellor, and

(b) in relation to Scotland, the Secretary of State.

**414(3) [Order by Treasury]** The Treasury may by order direct by whom and in what manner the fees are to be collected and accounted for.

**414(4) [Security for fees]** The Lord Chancellor may, with the sanction of the Treasury, by order provide for sums to be deposited, by such persons, in such manner and in such circumstances as may be specified in the order, by way of security for fees payable by virtue of this section.

**414(5) [Incidental matter under order]** An order under this section may contain such incidental, supplemental and transitional provisions as may appear to the Lord Chancellor, the Secretary of State or (as the case may be) the Treasury necessary or expedient.

**414(6) [Order by statutory instrument etc.]** An order under this section shall be made by statutory instrument and, after being made, shall be laid before each House of Parliament.

**414(7) [Payment into Consolidated Fund]** Fees payable by virtue of this section shall be paid into the Consolidated Fund.

**414(8) [Interpretation]** References in subsection (1) to Parts I to VII of this Act are to be read as including the Companies Act so far as relating to, and to matters connected with or arising out of, the insolvency or winding up of companies.

**414(9) [Rules of court, Scotland]** Nothing in this section prejudices any power to make rules of court; and the application of this section to Scotland is without prejudice to section 2 of the Courts of Law Fees (Scotland) Act 1895.

# 415 Fees orders (individual insolvency proceedings in England and Wales)

**415(1) [Payment of fees]** There shall be paid in respect of–

(a) proceedings under Parts VIII to XI of this Act, and

(b) the performance by the official receiver or the Secretary of State of functions under those Parts,

such fees as the Lord Chancellor may with the sanction of the Treasury by order direct.

**415(2) [Order by Treasury]** The Treasury may by order direct by whom and in what manner the fees are to be collected and accounted for.

**415(3) [Security for fees]** The Lord Chancellor may, with the sanction of the Treasury, by order provide for sums to be deposited, by such persons, in such manner and in such circumstances as may be specified in the order, by way of security for–

(a) fees payable by virtue of this section, and

(b) fees payable to any person who has prepared an insolvency practitioner's report under section 274 in Chapter I of Part IX.

**415(4) [Incidental provisions etc. of order]** An order under this section may contain such incidental, supplemental and transitional provisions as may appear to the Lord Chancellor or, as the case may be, the Treasury, necessary or expedient.

**415(5) [Order by statutory instrument etc.]** An order under this section shall be made by statutory instrument and, after being made, shall be laid before each House of Parliament.

**415(6) [Payment into Consolidated Fund]** Fees payable by virtue of this section shall be paid into the Consolidated Fund.

**415(7) [Rules of court]** Nothing in this section prejudices any power to make rules of court.

**Note**

See note to s. 414(1).

### SPECIFICATION, INCREASE AND REDUCTION OF MONEY SUMS RELEVANT IN THE OPERATION OF THIS ACT

## 416 Monetary limits (companies winding up)

**416(1) [Increase or reduction of certain provisions]** The Secretary of State may by order in a statutory instrument increase or reduce any of the money sums for the time being specified in the following provisions in the first Group of Parts–

section 117(2) (amount of company's share capital determining whether county court has jurisdiction to wind it up);

section 120(3) (the equivalent as respects sheriff court jurisdiction in Scotland);

section 123(1)(a) (minimum debt for service of demand on company by unpaid creditor);

section 184(3) (minimum value of judgment, affecting sheriff's duties on levying execution);

section 206(1)(a) and (b) (minimum value of company property concealed or fraudulently removed, affecting criminal liability of company's officer).

**Note**

See the Insolvency Proceedings (Monetary Limits) Order 1986 (SI 1986/1996) in force from 29 December 1986 affecting s. 184(3) and 206(1)(a), (b).

**416(2) [Transitional provisions]** An order under this section may contain such transitional provisions as may appear to the Secretary of State necessary or expedient.

**416(3) [Approval by Parliament]** No order under this section increasing or reducing any of the money sums for the time being specified in section 117(2), 120(3) or 123(1)(a) shall be made unless a draft of the order has been laid before and approved by a resolution of each House of Parliament.

**416(4) [Annulment of statutory instrument]** A statutory instrument containing an order under this section, other than an order to which subsection (3) applies, is subject to annulment in pursuance of a resolution of either House of Parliament.

## 417 Money sum in s. 222

**417** The Secretary of State may by regulations in a statutory instrument increase or reduce the money sum for the time being specified in section 222(1) (minimum debt for service of demand on unregistered company by unpaid creditor); but such regulations shall not be made unless a draft of the statutory instrument containing them has been approved by resolution of each House of Parliament.

## 418 Monetary limits (bankruptcy)

**418(1) [Powers of Secretary of State]** The Secretary of State may by order prescribe amounts for the purposes of the following provisions in the second Group of Parts–

section 273 (minimum value of debtor's estate determining whether immediate bankruptcy order should be made; small bankruptcies level);

section 346(3) (minimum amount of judgment, determining whether amount recovered on sale of debtor's goods is to be treated as part of his estate in bankruptcy);

section 354(1) and (2) (minimum amount of concealed debt, or value of property concealed or removed, determining criminal liability under the section);

section 358 (minimum value of property taken by a bankrupt out of England and Wales, determining his criminal liability);

section 360(1) (maximum amount of credit which bankrupt may obtain without disclosure of his status);

section 361(2) (exemption of bankrupt from criminal liability for failure to keep proper accounts, if unsecured debts not more than the prescribed minimum);

section 364(2)(d) (minimum value of goods removed by the bankrupt, determining his liability to arrest);

and references in the second Group of Parts to the amount prescribed for the purposes of any of those provisions, and references in those provisions to the prescribed amount, are to be construed accordingly.

**418(2) [Transitional provisions]** An order under this section may contain such transitional provisions as may appear to the Secretary of State necessary or expedient.

**418(3) [Order by statutory instrument etc.]** An order under this section shall be made by statutory instrument subject to annulment in pursuance of a resolution of either House of Parliament.

**Note**

See the Insolvency Proceedings (Monetary Limits) Order 1986 (SI 1986/1996) in force from 29 December 1986.

## INSOLVENCY PRACTICE

# 419 Regulations for purposes of Part XIII

**419(1) [Power to make regulations]** The Secretary of State may make regulations for the purpose of giving effect to Part XIII of this Act; and **"prescribed"** in that Part means prescribed by regulations made by the Secretary of State.

**419(2) [Extent of regulations]** Without prejudice to the generality of subsection (1) or to any provision of that Part by virtue of which regulations may be made with respect to any matter, regulations under this section may contain–

(a) provision as to the matters to be taken into account in determining whether a person is a fit and proper person to act as an insolvency practitioner;

(b) provision prohibiting a person from so acting in prescribed cases, being cases in which a conflict of interest will or may arise;

(c) provision imposing requirements with respect to–
  (i) the preparation and keeping by a person who acts as an insolvency practitioner of prescribed books, accounts and other records, and
  (ii) the production of those books, accounts and records to prescribed persons;

(d) provision conferring power on prescribed persons–
  (i) to require any person who acts or has acted as an insolvency practitioner to answer any inquiry in relation to a case in which he is so acting or has so acted, and
  (ii) to apply to a court to examine such a person or any other person on oath concerning such a case;

(e) provision making non-compliance with any of the regulations a criminal offence; and

(f) such incidental, supplemental and transitional provisions as may appear to the Secretary of State necessary or expedient.

**419(3) [Power exercisable by statutory instrument etc.]** Any power conferred by Part XIII or this Part to make regulations, rules or orders is exercisable by statutory instrument subject to annulment by resolution of either House of Parliament.

**419(4) [Different provisions for different cases]** Any rule or regulation under Part XIII or this Part may make different provision with respect to different cases or descriptions of cases, including different provision for different areas.

**Note**
See the Insolvency Practitioners Regulations 1990 (SI 1990/439), as amended.

## OTHER ORDER-MAKING POWERS

## 420 Insolvent partnerships

**420(1) [Application to insolvent partnerships]** The Lord Chancellor may, by order made with the concurrence of the Secretary of State, provide that such provisions of this Act as may be specified in the order shall apply in relation to insolvent partnerships with such modifications as may be so specified.

**Note**
See note after s. 420(2).

**420(2) [Incidental provisions etc.]** An order under this section may make different provision for different cases and may contain such incidental, supplemental and transitional provisions as may appear to the Lord Chancellor necessary or expedient.

**Note**
See the Insolvent Partnerships (Amendment) Order 1996 (SI 1996/1308).

**420(3) [Order by statutory instrument etc.]** An order under this section shall be made by statutory instrument subject to annulment in pursuance of a resolution of either House of Parliament.

**Note**
See the Insolvent Partnerships Order 1994 (SI 1994/2421).

## 421 Insolvent estates of deceased persons

**421(1) [Order by Lord Chancellor]** The Lord Chancellor may, by order made with the concurrence of the Secretary of State, provide that such provisions of this Act as may be specified in the order shall apply to the administration of the insolvent estates of deceased persons with such modifications as may be so specified.

**421(2) [Incidental provisions etc.]** An order under this section may make different provision for different cases and may contain such incidental, supplemental and transitional provisions as may appear to the Lord Chancellor necessary or expedient.

**421(3) [Order by statutory instrument]** An order under this section shall be made by statutory instrument subject to annulment in pursuance of a resolution of either House of Parliament.

**421(4) [Interpretation]** For the purposes of this section the estate of a deceased person is insolvent if, when realised, it will be insufficient to meet in full all the debts and other liabilities to which it is subject.

**Note**
See the Administration of Insolvent Estates of Deceased Persons Order 1986 (SI 1986/1999).

## 422 Recognised banks, etc.

**422(1) [Order by Secretary of State]** The Secretary of State may, by order made with the concurrence of the Treasury and after consultation with the Financial Services Authority, provide that such provisions in the first Group of Parts as may be specified in the order shall apply in relation to authorised institutions and former authorised institutions within the meaning of the Banking Act 1987, with such modifications as may be so specified.

**History**
In s. 422(1) the words "Financial Services Authority" substituted for the former words "Bank of England" by the Bank of England Act 1998, s. 23(1), 45 and Sch. 5, para. 37 as from 1 June 1998 (see SI 1998/1120 (C25), art. 2).

Previously in s. 422(1) the words "authorised institutions and former authorised institutions within the meaning of the Banking Act 1987" substituted for the former para. (a) and (b) by Banking Act 1987, s. 108(1) and Sch. 6, para. 25(2) as from 1 October 1987 (see SI 1987/1664 (C 50)); the former para. (a) and (b) read as follows:

"(a) recognised banks and licensed institutions within the meaning of the Banking Act 1979, and
(b) institutions to which sections 16 and 18 of that Act apply as if they were licensed institutions,".

**422(2) [Incidental provisions etc.]** An order under this section may make different provision for different cases and may contain such incidental, supplemental and transitional provisions as may appear to the Secretary of State necessary or expedient.

**422(3) [Order by statutory instrument etc.]** An order under this section shall be made by statutory instrument subject to annulment in pursuance of a resolution of either House of Parliament.

**Note**
See the Banks (Administration Proceedings) Order 1989 (SI 1989/1276).

# PART XVI – PROVISIONS AGAINST DEBT AVOIDANCE (ENGLAND AND WALES ONLY)

**Note**
Re application of Pt. XVI to insolvent partnerships, see the Insolvent Partnerships Order 1994 (SI 1994/2421), especially reg. 10, 11, Sch. 7.

## 423 Transactions defrauding creditors

**423(1) [Transaction at undervalue]** This section relates to transactions entered into at an undervalue; and a person enters into such a transaction with another person if–

(a) he makes a gift to the other person or he otherwise enters into a transaction with the other on terms that provide for him to receive no consideration;

(b) he enters into a transaction with the other in consideration of marriage; or

(c) he enters into a transaction with the other for a consideration the value of which, in money or money's worth, is significantly less than the value, in money or money's worth, of the consideration provided by himself.

**423(2) [Order by court]** Where a person has entered into such a transaction, the court may, if satisfied under the next subsection, make such order as it thinks fit for–

(a) restoring the position to what it would have been if the transaction had not been entered into, and

(b) protecting the interests of persons who are victims of the transaction.

**423(3) [Conditions for court order]** In the case of a person entering into such a transaction, an order shall only be made if the court is satisfied that it was entered into by him for the purpose–

(a) of putting assets beyond the reach of a person who is making, or may at some time make, a claim against him, or

(b) of otherwise prejudicing the interests of such a person in relation to the claim which he is making or may make.

**423(4) ["The court"]** In this section **"the court"** means the High Court or–

(a) if the person entering into the transaction is an individual, any other court which would have jurisdiction in relation to a bankruptcy petition relating to him;

(b) if that person is a body capable of being wound up under Part IV or V of this Act, any other court having jurisdiction to wind it up.

**423(5) [Interpretation]** In relation to a transaction at an undervalue, references here and below to a victim of the transaction are to a person who is, or is capable of being, prejudiced by it; and in the following two sections the person entering into the transaction is referred to as **"the debtor"**.

## 424 Those who may apply for an order under s. 423

**424(1) [Conditions for s. 423 application]** An application for an order under section 423 shall not be made in relation to a transaction except–

(a) in a case where the debtor has been adjudged bankrupt or is a body corporate which is being wound up or in relation to which an administration order is in force, by the official receiver, by the trustee of the bankrupt's estate or the liquidator or administrator of the body corporate or (with the leave of the court) by a victim of the transaction;

(b) in a case where a victim of the transaction is bound by a voluntary arrangement approved under Part I or Part VIII of this Act, by the supervisor of the voluntary arrangement or by any person who (whether or not so bound) is such a victim; or

(c) in any other case, by a victim of the transaction.

**424(2) [Treatment of application]** An application made under any of the paragraphs of subsection (1) is to be treated as made on behalf of every victim of the transaction.

## 425 Provision which may be made by order under s. 423

**425(1) [Scope of order]** Without prejudice to the generality of section 423, an order made under that section with respect to a transaction may (subject as follows)–

(a) require any property transferred as part of the transaction to be vested in any person, either absolutely or for the benefit of all the persons on whose behalf the application for the order is treated as made;

(b) require any property to be so vested if it represents, in any person's hands, the application either of the proceeds of sale of property so transferred or of money so transferred;

(c) release or discharge (in whole or in part) any security given by the debtor;

(d) require any person to pay to any other person in respect of benefits received from the debtor such sums as the court may direct;

(e) provide for any surety or guarantor whose obligations to any person were released or discharged (in whole or in part) under the transaction to be under such new or revived obligations as the court thinks appropriate;

(f) provide for security to be provided for the discharge of any obligation imposed by or arising under the order, for such an obligation to be charged on any property and for such security or charge to have the same priority as a security or charge released or discharged (in whole or in part) under the transaction.

**425(2) [Limit to order]** An order under section 423 may affect the property of, or impose any obligation on, any person whether or not he is the person with whom the debtor entered into the transaction; but such an order–

(a) shall not prejudice any interest in property which was acquired from a person other than the debtor and was acquired in good faith, for value and without notice of the relevant circumstances, or prejudice any interest deriving from such an interest, and

(b) shall not require a person who received a benefit from the transaction in good faith, for value and without notice of the relevant circumstances to pay any sum unless he was a party to the transaction.

**425(3) [Relevant circumstances]** For the purposes of this section the relevant circumstances in relation to a transaction are the circumstances by virtue of which an order under section 423 may be made in respect of the transaction.

**425(4) ["Security"]** In this section **"security"** means any mortgage, charge, lien or other security.

# PART XVII – MISCELLANEOUS AND GENERAL

**Note**

Re application of Pt. XVII to insolvent partnerships, see the Insolvent Partnerships Order 1994 (SI 1994/2421), especially reg. 10, 11, Sch. 7.

## 426 Co-operation between courts exercising jurisdiction in relation to insolvency

**426(1) [Enforcement in other parts of UK]** An order made by a court in any part of the United Kingdom in the exercise of jurisdiction in relation to insolvency law shall be enforced in any other part of the United Kingdom as if it were made by a court exercising the corresponding jurisdiction in that other part.

**426(2) [Limit to s. 426(1)]** However, without prejudice to the following provisions of this section, nothing in subsection (1) requires a court in any part of the United Kingdom to enforce, in relation to property situated in that part, any order made by a court in any other part of the United Kingdom.

**426(3) [Order by Secretary of State]** The Secretary of State, with the concurrence in relation to property situated in England and Wales of the Lord Chancellor, may by order make provision for securing that a trustee or assignee under the insolvency law of any part of the United Kingdom has, with such modifications as may be specified in the order, the same rights in relation to any property situated in another part of the United Kingdom as he would have in the corresponding circumstances if he were a trustee or assignee under the insolvency law of that other part.

**426(4) [Assistance between courts]** The courts having jurisdiction in relation to insolvency law in any part of the United Kingdom shall assist the courts having the corresponding jurisdiction in any other part of the United Kingdom or any relevant country or territory.

**426(5) [Request under s. 426(4)]** For the purposes of subsection (4) a request made to a court in any part of the United Kingdom by a court in any other part of the United Kingdom or in a relevant country or territory is authority for the court to which the request is made to apply, in relation to any matters specified in the request, the insolvency law which is applicable by either court in relation to comparable matters falling within its jurisdiction.

In exercising its discretion under this subsection, a court shall have regard in particular to the rules of private international law.

**426(6) [Claim by trustee or assignee]** Where a person who is a trustee or assignee under the insolvency law of any part of the United Kingdom claims property situated in any other part of the United Kingdom (whether by virtue of an order under subsection (3) or otherwise), the submission of that claim to the court exercising jurisdiction in relation to insolvency law in that other part shall be treated in the same manner as a request made by a court for the purpose of subsection (4).

**426(7) [Application of Criminal Law Act]** Section 38 of the Criminal Law Act 1977 (execution of warrant of arrest throughout the United Kingdom) applies to a warrant which, in exercise of any jurisdiction in relation to insolvency law, is issued in any part of the United Kingdom for the arrest of a person as it applies to a warrant issued in that part of the United Kingdom for the arrest of a person charged with an offence.

**426(8) [Powers in subordinate legislation]** Without prejudice to any power to make rules of court, any power to make provision by subordinate legislation for the purpose of giving effect in relation to companies or individuals to the insolvency law of any part of the United Kingdom includes power to make provision for the purpose of giving effect in that part to any provision made by or under the preceding provisions of this section.

**426(9) [S. 426(3) order by statutory instrument etc.]** An order under subsection (3) shall be made by statutory instrument subject to annulment in pursuance of a resolution of either House of Parliament.

**426(10) ["Insolvency law"]** In this section **"insolvency law"** means–

(a) in relation to England and Wales, provision made by or under this Act or sections 6 to 10, 12, 15, 19(c) and 20 (with Schedule 1) of the Company Directors Disqualification Act 1986 and extending to England and Wales;

(b) in relation to Scotland, provision extending to Scotland and made by or under this Act, sections 6 to 10, 12, 15, 19(c) and 20 (with Schedule 1) of the Company Directors Disqualification Act 1986, Part XVIII of the Companies Act or the Bankrupty (Scotland) Act 1985;

(c) in relation to Northern Ireland, provision made by or under the Insolvency (Northern Ireland) Order 1989;

(d) in relation to any relevant country or territory, so much of the law of that country or territory as corresponds to provisions falling within any of the foregoing paragraphs;

and references in this subsection to any enactment include, in relation to any time before the coming into force of that enactment the corresponding enactment in force at that time.

**History**

In s. 426(10)(c) the words "the Insolvency (Northern Ireland) Order 1989" substituted for the former words "the Bankruptcy Acts (Northern Ireland) 1857 to 1980, Part V, VI or IX of the Companies Act (Northern Ireland) 1960 or Part

IV of the Companies (Northern Ireland) Order 1978" by the Insolvency (Northern Ireland) Order 1989 (SI 1989/2405 (N.I. 19)), art. 381 and Sch. 9, para. 41(a) as from 1 October 1991 (see SR 1991/411 (C 20), art. 2).

**426(11) ["Relevant country or territory"]** In this section **"relevant country or territory"** means–

(a) any of the Channel Islands or the Isle of Man, or

(b) any country or territory designated for the purposes of this section by the Secretary of State by order made by statutory instrument.

**Note**

See the Co-operation of Insolvency Courts (Designation of Relevant Countries and Territories) Order 1986 (SI 1986/2123), the Co-operation of Insolvency Courts (Designation of Relevant Countries) Order 1996 (SI 1996/253) and the Co-operation of Insolvency Courts (Designation of Relevant Country) Order 1998 (SI 1998/2766).

**426(12) [Application to Northern Ireland]** In the application of this section to Northern Ireland–

(a) for any reference to the Secretary of State there is substituted a reference to the Department of Economic Development in Northern Ireland;

(b) in subsection (3) for the words "another part of the United Kingdom" and the words "that other part" there is substituted the words "Northern Ireland";

(c) for subsection (9) there is substituted the following subsection–

"(9) An order made under subsection (3) by the Department of Economic Development in Northern Ireland shall be a statutory rule for the purposes of the Statutory Rules (Northern Ireland) Order 1979 and shall be subject to negative resolution within the meaning of section 41(6) of the Interpretation Act (Northern Ireland) 1954."

**History**

S. 426(12) inserted by the Insolvency (Northern Ireland) Order 1989 (SI 1989/2405 (N.I. 19)), art. 381 and Sch. 9, para. 41(b) as from 1 October 1991 (see SR 1991/411 (C 20), art. 2).

**Note**

For s. 426(4), (5), (10) and (11) see the Insolvency Act 1986 (Guernsey) Order 1989 (SI 1989/2409).

## 427 Parliamentary disqualification

**427(1) [Disqualification of bankrupt]** Where a court in England and Wales or Northern Ireland adjudges an individual bankrupt or a court in Scotland awards sequestration of an individual's estate, the individual is disqualified–

(a) for sitting or voting in the House of Lords,

(b) for being elected to, or sitting or voting in, the House of Commons, and

(c) for sitting or voting in a committee of either House.

**427(2) [When disqualification ceases]** Where an individual is disqualified under this section, the disqualification ceases–

(a) except where the adjudication is annulled or the award recalled or reduced without the individual having been first discharged, on the discharge of the individual, and

(b) in the excepted case, on the annulment, recall or reduction, as the case may be.

**427(3) [Disqualified peer]** No writ of summons shall be issued to any lord of Parliament who is for the time being disqualified under this section for sitting and voting in the House of Lords.

**427(4) [Disqualified MP]** Where a member of the House of Commons who is disqualified under this section continues to be so disqualified until the end of the period of 6 months beginning with the day of the adjudication or award, his seat shall be vacated at the end of that period.

**427(5) [Certification of s. 427(1) award etc.]** A court which makes an adjudication or award such as is mentioned in subsection (1) in relation to any lord of Parliament or member of the House of Commons shall forthwith certify the adjudication or award to the Speaker of the House of Lords or, as the case may be, to the Speaker of the House of Commons.

**427(6) [Further certification after s. 427(5)]** Where a court has certified an adjudication or award to the Speaker of the House of Commons under subsection (5), then immediately after it becomes apparent which of the following certificates is applicable, the court shall certify to the Speaker of the House of Commons–

(a) that the period of 6 months beginning with the day of the adjudication or award has expired without the adjudication or award having been annulled, recalled or reduced, or

(b) that the adjudication or award has been annulled, recalled or reduced before the end of that period.

**427(6A) [Effect re Scottish Parliament]** Subsections (4) to (6) have effect in relation to a member of the Scottish Parliament but as if–

(a) references to the House of Commons were to the Parliament and references to the Speaker were to the Presiding Officer, and

(b) in subsection (4), for "under this section" there were substituted "under section 15(1)(b) of the Scotland Act 1998 by virtue of this section".

**History**
S. 427(6A) inserted by the Scotland Act 1998, s. 125(1) and Sch. 8, para. 23 as from 19 November 1998.

**427(6B) [Effect re National Assembly for Wales]** Subsections (4) to (6) have effect in relation to a member of the National Assembly for Wales but as if–

(a) references to the House of Commons were to the Assembly and references to the Speaker were to the presiding officer, and

(b) in subsection (4), for "under this section" there were substituted "under section 12(2) of the Government of Wales Act 1998 by virtue of this section".

**History**
S. 427(6B) inserted by the Government of Wales Act 1998, s. 125, 158(1) and Sch. 12, para. 24 as from 1 April 1999 (see SI 1999/782).

**427(6C) [Members of the Northern Ireland Assembly]** Subsection (1), as applied to a member of the Northern Ireland Assembly by virtue of section 36(4) of the Northern Ireland Act 1998, has effect as if "or Northern Ireland" were omitted; and subsections (4) to (6) have effect in relation to such a member as if–

(a) references to the House of Commons were to the Assembly and references to the Speaker were to the Presiding Officer; and

(b) in subsection (4), for "under this section" there were substituted "under section 36(4) of the Northern Ireland Act 1998 by virtue of this section".

**History**
S. 427(6C) inserted by the Northern Ireland Act 1998, s. 99, 101 and Sch. 13, para. 6 with effect from 2 December 1999 (see Northern Ireland Act 1998 (Commencement No. 5) Order 1999 (SI 1999/3209 (C. 85)), art. 2 and Sch.).

**427(7) [Application of relevant law to peer or MP]** Subject to the preceding provisions of this section, so much of this Act and any other enactment (whenever passed) and of any subordinate legislation (whenever made) as–

(a) makes provision for or in connection with bankruptcy in one or more parts of the United Kingdom, or

(b) makes provision conferring a power of arrest in connection with the winding up or insolvency of companies in one or more parts of the United Kingdom,

applies in relation to persons having privilege of Parliament or peerage as it applies in relation to persons not having such privilege.

# 428 Exemptions from Restrictive Trade Practices Act

**428(1), (2)** (Repealed by Competition Act 1998 (Transitional, Consequential and Supplemental Provisions) Order 2000 (SI 2000/311), art. 1, 19(1), (2) as from 1 March 2000 subject to transitional provision in art. 4 of that order.)

**History**
Section 428(1), (2) formerly read as follows:

"**(1)** No restriction in respect of any of the matters specified in the next subsection shall, on or after the appointed day, be regarded as a restriction by virtue of which the Restrictive Trade Practices Act 1976 applies to any agreement (whenever made).

**(2)** Those matters are–

(a) the charges to be made, quoted or paid for insolvency services supplied, offered or obtained;
(b) the terms or conditions on or subject to which insolvency services are to be supplied or obtained;
(c) the extent (if any) to which, or the scale (if any) on which, insolvency services are to be made available, supplied or obtained;
(d) the form or manner in which insolvency services are to be made available, supplied or obtained;
(e) the persons or classes of persons for whom or from whom, or the areas or places in or from which, insolvency services are to be made available or supplied or are to be obtained."

**428(3) ["Insolvency services"]** In this section **"insolvency services"** means the services of persons acting as insolvency practitioners or carrying out under the law of Northern Ireland functions corresponding to those mentioned in section 388(1) or (2) in Part XIII, in their capacity as such.

**History**

In s. 428(3) the words "; and expressions which are also used in the Act of 1976 have the same meaning here as in that Act" formerly appearing at the end repealed by Competition Act 1998 (Transitional, Consequential and Supplemental Provisions) Order 2000 (SI 2000/311), art. 1, 19(1), (2) as from 1 March 2000 subject to transitional provision in art. 4 of that order.

## 429 Disabilities on revocation of administration order against an individual

**429(1) [Application]** The following applies where a person fails to make any payment which he is required to make by virtue of an administration order under Part VI of the County Courts Act 1984.

**429(2) [Power of court]** The court which is administering that person's estate under the order may, if it thinks fit–

(a) revoke the administration order, and

(b) make an order directing that this section and section 12 of the Company Directors Disqualification Act 1986 shall apply to the person for such period, not exceeding 2 years, as may be specified in the order.

**429(3) [Restrictions]** A person to whom this section so applies shall not–

(a) either alone or jointly with another person, obtain credit to the extent of the amount prescribed for the purposes of section 360(1)(a) or more, or

(b) enter into any transaction in the course of or for the purposes of any business in which he is directly or indirectly engaged,

without disclosing to the person from whom he obtains the credit, or (as the case may be) with whom the transaction is entered into, the fact that this section applies to him.

**429(4) [Person obtaining credit]** The reference in subsection (3) to a person obtaining credit includes–

(a) a case where goods are bailed or hired to him under a hire-purchase agreement or agreed to be sold to him under a conditional sale agreement, and

(b) a case where he is paid in advance (whether in money or otherwise) for the supply of goods or services.

**429(5) [Penalty]** A person who contravenes this section is guilty of an offence and liable to imprisonment or a fine, or both.

## 430 Provision introducing Schedule of punishments

**430(1) [Sch. 10]** Schedule 10 to this Act has effect with respect to the way in which offences under this Act are punishable on conviction.

**430(2) [First, second and third columns of Schedule]** In relation to an offence under a provision of this Act specified in the first column of the Schedule (the general nature of the offence being described in the second column), the third column shows whether the offence is punishable on conviction on indictment, or on summary conviction, or either in the one way or the other.

**430(3) [Fourth column]** The fourth column of the Schedule shows, in relation to an offence, the maximum punishment by way of fine or imprisonment under this Act which may be imposed on a person convicted of the offence in the way specified in relation to it in the third column (that is to say, on indictment or summarily), a reference to a period of years or months being to a term of imprisonment of that duration.

**430(4) [Fifth column]** The fifth column shows (in relation to an offence for which there is an entry in that column) that a person convicted of the offence after continued contravention is liable to a daily default fine; that is to say, he is liable on a second or subsequent conviction of the offence to the fine specified in that column for each day on which the contravention is continued (instead of the penalty specified for the offence in the fourth column of the Schedule).

**430(5)** **["Officer who is in default"]** For the purpose of any enactment in this Act whereby an officer of a company who is in default is liable to a fine or penalty, the expression **"officer who is in default"** means any officer of the company who knowingly and wilfully authorises or permits the default, refusal or contravention mentioned in the enactment.

## 431 Summary proceedings

**431(1)** **[Taking of summary proceedings]** Summary proceedings for any offence under any of Parts I to VII of this Act may (without prejudice to any jurisdiction exercisable apart from this subsection) be taken against a body corporate at any place at which the body has a place of business, and against any other person at any place at which he is for the time being.

**431(2)** **[Time for laying information]** Notwithstanding anything in section 127(1) of the Magistrates' Courts Act 1980, an information relating to such an offence which is triable by a magistrates' court in England and Wales may be so tried if it is laid at any time within 3 years after the commission of the offence and within 12 months after the date on which evidence sufficient in the opinion of the Director of Public Prosecutions or the Secretary of State (as the case may be) to justify the proceedings comes to his knowledge.

**431(3)** **[Time for commencement of summary proceedings in Scotland]** Summary proceedings in Scotland for such an offence shall not be commenced after the expiration of 3 years from the commission of the offence.

Subject to this (and notwithstanding anything in section 136 of the Criminal Procedure (Scotland) Act 1995), such proceedings may (in Scotland) be commenced at any time within 12 months after the date on which evidence sufficient in the Lord Advocate's opinion to justify the proceedings came to his knowledge or, where such evidence was reported to him by the Secretary of State, within 12 months after the date on which it came to the knowledge of the latter; and subsection (3) of that section applies for the purpose of this subsection as it applies for the purpose of that section.

**History**

In s. 431(3) the words "section 136 of the Criminal Procedure (Scotland) Act 1995" appearing after the words "anything in section" substituted for the former words "section 331 of the Criminal Procedure (Scotland) Act 1975" by the Criminal Procedure (Consequential Provisions) (Scotland) Act 1995, s. 5, Sch. 4, para. 61 as from 1 April 1996.

**431(4)** **[Certificate by DPP et al. conclusive evidence]** For the purposes of this section, a certificate of the Director of Public Prosecutions, the Lord Advocate or the Secretary of State (as the case may be) as to the date on which such evidence as is referred to above came to his knowledge is conclusive evidence.

## 432 Offences by bodies corporate

**432(1)** **[Application]** This section applies to offences under this Act other than those excepted by subsection (4).

**432(2)** **[Consent or connivance of various persons]** Where a body corporate is guilty of an offence to which this section applies and the offence is proved to have been committed with the consent or connivance of, or to be attributable to any neglect on the part of, any director, manager, secretary or other similar officer of the body corporate or any person who was purporting to act in any such capacity he, as well as the body corporate, is guilty of the offence and liable to be proceeded against and punished accordingly.

**432(3)** **[Where affairs managed by members]** Where the affairs of a body corporate are managed by its members, subsection (2) applies in relation to the acts and defaults of a member in connection with his functions of management as if he were a director of the body corporate.

**432(4)** **[Offences excepted]** The offences excepted from this section are those under sections 30, 39, 51, 53, 54, 62, 64, 66, 85, 89, 164, 188, 201, 206, 207, 208, 209, 210 and 211.

## 433 Admissibility in evidence of statements of affairs, etc.

**433(1)** **[General rule on admissibility of statements]** In any proceedings (whether or not under this Act)–

(a) a statement of affairs prepared for the purposes of any provision of this Act which is derived from the Insolvency Act 1985, and

(b) any other statement made in pursuance of a requirement imposed by or under any such provision or by or under rules made under this Act,

may be used in evidence against any person making or concurring in making the statement.

**History**

S. 433(1), formerly s. 433, was renumbered by Youth Justice and Criminal Evidence Act 1999, s. 59, 68(3) and Sch. 3, para. 7(2), with effect from 14 April 2000 (see Youth Justice and Criminal Evidence Act 1999 (Commencement No. 2) Order 2000 (SI 2000/1034 (C. 27)), art. 2(a)).

**433(2) [Limits on use of statement in criminal proceedings]** However, in criminal proceedings in which any such person is charged with an offence to which this subsection applies–

(a) no evidence relating to the statement may be adduced, and

(b) no question relating to it may be asked,

by or on behalf of the prosecution, unless evidence relating to it is adduced, or a question relating to it is asked, in the proceedings by or on behalf of that person.

**History**

S. 433(2) inserted by Youth Justice and Criminal Evidence Act 1999, s. 59, 68(3) and Sch. 3, para. 7(3), with effect from 14 April 2000 (see Youth Justice and Criminal Evidence Act 1999 (Commencement No. 2) Order 2000 (SI 2000/1034 (C. 27)), art. 2(a)).

**433(3) [Offences to which s. 433(2) applies]** Subsection (2) applies to any offence other than–

(a) an offence under section 22(6), 47(6), 48(8), 66(6), 67(8), 95(8), 98(6), 99(3)(a), 131(7), 192(2), 208(1)(a) or (d) or (2), 210, 235(5), 353(1), 354(1)(b) or (3) or 356(1) or 356(2)(a) or (b) or paragraph 4(3)(a) of Schedule 7;

(b) an offence which is–
  (i) created by rules made under this Act, and
  (ii) designated for the purposes of this subsection by such rules or by regulations made by the Secretary of State;

(c) an offence which is–
  (i) created by regulations made under any such rules, and
  (ii) designated for the purposes of this subsection by such regulations;

(d) an offence under section 1, 2 or 5 of the Perjury Act 1911 (false statements made on oath or made otherwise than on oath); or

(e) an offence under section 44(1) or (2) of the Criminal Law (Consolidation) (Scotland) Act 1995 (false statements made on oath or otherwise than on oath).

**History**

S. 433(3) inserted by Youth Justice and Criminal Evidence Act 1999, s. 59, 68(3) and Sch. 3, para. 7(3), with effect from 14 April 2000 (see Youth Justice and Criminal Evidence Act 1999 (Commencement No. 2) Order 2000 (SI 2000/1034 (C. 27)), art. 2(a)).

**433(4) [Procedure for making regulations]** Regulations under subsection (3)(b)(ii) shall be made by statutory instrument and, after being made, shall be laid before each House of Parliament.

**History**

S. 433(4) inserted by Youth Justice and Criminal Evidence Act 1999, s. 59, 68(3) and Sch. 3, para. 7(3), with effect from 14 April 2000 (see Youth Justice and Criminal Evidence Act 1999 (Commencement No. 2) Order 2000 (SI 2000/1034 (C. 27)), art. 2(a)).

## 434 Crown application

**434** For the avoidance of doubt it is hereby declared that provisions of this Act which derive from the Insolvency Act 1985 bind the Crown so far as affecting or relating to the following matters, namely–

(a) remedies against, or against the property of, companies or individuals;

(b) priorities of debts;

(c) transactions at an undervalue or preferences;

(d) voluntary arrangements approved under Part I or Part VIII, and

(e) discharge from bankruptcy.

# PART XVIII – INTERPRETATION

**Note**

Re application of Pt. XVIII to insolvent partnerships, see the Insolvent Partnerships Order 1994 (SI 1994/2421), especially reg. 10, 11, Sch. 7.

## 435 Meaning of "associate"

**435(1) [Determination of whether associate]** For the purposes of this Act any question whether a person is an associate of another person is to be determined in accordance with the following provisions of this section (any provision that a person is an associate of another person being taken to mean that they are associates of each other).

**435(2) [Associate of individual]** A person is an associate of an individual if that person is the individual's husband or wife, or is a relative, or the husband or wife of a relative, of the individual or of the individual's husband or wife.

**435(3) [Associate of partner]** A person is an associate of any person with whom he is in partership, and of the husband or wife or a relative of any individual with whom he is in partnership; and a Scottish firm is an associate of any person who is a member of the firm.

**435(4) [Associate of employee, employer]** A person is an associate of any person whom he employs or by whom he is employed.

**435(5) [Associate of trustee]** A person in his capacity as trustee of a trust other than–

(a) a trust arising under any of the second Group of Parts or the Bankruptcy (Scotland) Act 1985, or

(b) a pension scheme or an employees' share scheme (within the meaning of the Companies Act),

is an associate of another person if the beneficiaries of the trust include, or the terms of the trust confer a power that may be exercised for the benefit of, that other person or an associate of that other person.

**435(6) [Company associate of another company]** A company is an associate of another company–

(a) if the same person has control of both, or a person has control of one and persons who are his associates, or he and persons who are his associates, have control of the other, or

(b) if a group of two or more persons has control of each company, and the groups either consist of the same persons or could be regarded as consisting of the same persons by treating (in one or more cases) a member of either group as replaced by a person of whom he is an associate.

**435(7) [Company associate of another person]** A company is an associate of another person if that person has control of it or if that person and persons who are his associates together have control of it.

**435(8) [Person relative of individual]** For the purposes of this section a person is a relative of an individual if he is that individual's brother, sister, uncle, aunt, nephew, niece, lineal ancestor or lineal descendant, treating–

(a) any relationship of the half blood as a relationship of the whole blood and the stepchild or adopted child of any person as his child, and

(b) an illegitimate child as the legitimate child of his mother and reputed father;

and references in this section to a husband or wife include a former husband or wife and a reputed husband or wife.

**435(9) [Director employee]** For the purposes of this section any director or other officer of a company is to be treated as employed by that company.

**435(10) [Person with control]** For the purposes of this section a person is to be taken as having control of a company if–

(a) the directors of the company or of another company which has control of it (or any of them) are accustomed to act in accordance with his directions or instructions, or

(b) he is entitled to exercise, or control the exercise of, one third or more of the voting power at any general meeting of the company or of another company which has control of it;

and where two or more persons together satisfy either of the above conditions, they are to be taken as having control of the company.

**435(11) ["Company"]** In this section "**company**" includes any body corporate (whether incorporated in Great Britain or elsewhere); and references to directors and other officers of a company and to voting power at any general meeting of a company have effect with any necessary modifications.

## 436 Expressions used generally

**436** In this Act, except in so far as the context otherwise requires (and subject to Parts VII and XI)–

"**the appointed day**" means the day on which this Act comes into force under section 443;
"**associate**" has the meaning given by section 435;
"**business**" includes a trade or profession;
"**the Companies Act**" means the Companies Act 1985;
"**conditional sale agreement**" and "**hire-purchase agreement**" have the same meanings as in the Consumer Credit Act 1974;
"**modifications**" includes additions, alterations and omissions and cognate expressions shall be construed accordingly;
"**property**" includes money, goods, things in action, land and every description of property wherever situated and also obligations and every description of interest, whether present or future or vested or contingent, arising out of, or incidental to, property;
"**records**" includes computer records and other non-documentary records;
"**subordinate legislation**" has the same meaning as in the Interpretation Act 1978; and
"**transaction**" includes a gift, agreement or arrangement, and references to entering into a transaction shall be construed accordingly.

# PART XIX – FINAL PROVISIONS

**Note**
Re application of Pt. XIX to insolvent partnerships, see the Insolvent Partnerships Order 1994 (SI 1994/2421), especially reg. 10, 11, Sch. 7.

## 437 Transitional provisions and savings

**437** The transitional provisions and savings set out in Schedule 11 to this Act shall have effect, the Schedule comprising the following Parts–

Part I: company insolvency and winding up (matters arising before appointed day, and continuance of proceedings in certain cases as before that day);
Part II: individual insolvency (matters so arising, and continuance of bankruptcy proceedings in certain cases as before that day);
Part III: transactions entered into before the appointed day and capable of being affected by orders of the court under Part XVI of this Act;
Part IV: insolvency practitioners acting as such before the appointed day; and
Part V: general transitional provisions and savings required consequentially on, and in connection with, the repeal and replacement by this Act and the Company Directors Disqualification Act 1986 of provisions of the Companies Act, the greater part of the Insolvency Act 1985 and other enactments.

## 438 Repeals

**438** The enactments specified in the second column of Schedule 12 to this Act are repealed to the extent specified in the third column of that Schedule.

## 439 Amendment of enactments

**439(1) [Amendment of Companies Act]** The Companies Act is amended as shown in Parts I and II of Schedule 13 to this Act, being amendments consequential on this Act and the Company Directors Disqualification Act 1986.

**439(2) [Enactments in Sch. 14]** The enactments specified in the first column of Schedule 14 to this Act (being enactments which refer, or otherwise relate, to those which are repealed and replaced by this Act or the Company Directors Disqualification Act 1986) are amended as shown in the second column of that Schedule.

**439(3) [Consequential modifications of subordinate legislation]** The Lord Chancellor may by order make such consequential modifications of any provision contained in any subordinate legislation made before the appointed day and such transitional provisions in connection with those modifications as appear to him necessary or expedient in respect of–

(a) any reference in that subordinate legislation to the Bankruptcy Act 1914;

(b) any reference in that subordinate legislation to any enactment repealed by Part III or IV of Schedule 10 to the Insolvency Act 1985; or

(c) any reference in that subordinate legislation to any matter provided for under the Act of 1914 or under any enactment so repealed.

**439(4) [Order by statutory instrument etc.]** An order under this section shall be made by statutory instrument subject to annulment in pursuance of a resolution of either House of Parliament.

**Note**

See the Insolvency (Amendment of Subordinate Legislation) Order 1986 (SI 1986/2001) (and also the Insolvency (Land Registration Rules) Order 1986 (SI 1986/2245)).

## 440 Extent (Scotland)

**440(1) [Extension to Scotland except where stated]** Subject to the next subsection, provisions of this Act contained in the first Group of Parts extend to Scotland except where otherwise stated.

**440(2) [Provisions not extending to Scotland]** The following provisions of this Act do not extend to Scotland–

(a) in the first Groups of Parts–
section 43;
sections 238 to 241; and
section 246;

(b) the second Group of Parts;

(c) in the third Group of Parts–
sections 399 to 402,
sections 412, 413, 415, 418, 420 and 421,
sections 423 to 425, and
section 429(1) and (2); and

(d) in the Schedules–
Parts II and III of Schedule 11; and
Schedules 12 and 14 so far as they repeal or amend enactments which extend to England and Wales only.

## 441 Extent (Northern Ireland)

**441(1) [Provisions extending to Northern Ireland]** The following provisions of this Act extend to Northern Ireland–

(a) sections 197, 426, 427 and 428; and

(b) so much of section 439 and Schedule 14 as relates to enactments which extend to Northern Ireland.

**441(2) [Most of provisions not extending to Northern Ireland]** Subject as above, and to any provision expressly relating to companies incorporated elsewhere than in Great Britain, nothing in this Act extends to Northern Ireland or applies to or in relation to companies registered or incorporated in Northern Ireland.

## 442 Extent (other territories)

**442** Her Majesty may, by Order in Council, direct that such of the provisions of this Act as are specified in the Order, being provisions formerly contained in the Insolvency Act 1985, shall extend to any of the Channel Islands or any colony with such modifications as may be so specified.

**Note**
See the Insolvency Act 1986 (Guernsey) Order 1989 (SI 1989/2409).

## 443 Commencement

**443** This Act comes into force on the day appointed under section 236(2) of the Insolvency Act 1985 for the coming into force of Part III of that Act (individual insolvency and bankruptcy), immediately after that part of that Act comes into force for England and Wales.

**Note**
The relevant date is 29 December 1986: see SI 1986/1924 (C 71).

## 444 Citation

**444** This Act may be cited as the Insolvency Act 1986.

# SCHEDULES

## Schedule 1 – Powers of Administrator or Administrative Receiver

Sections 14, 42

**1** Power to take possession of, collect and get in the property of the company and, for that purpose, to take such proceedings as may seem to him expedient.

**2** Power to sell or otherwise dispose of the property of the company by public auction or private auction or private contract or, in Scotland, to sell, feu, hire out or otherwise dispose of the property of the company by public roup or private bargain.

**3** Power to raise or borrow money and grant security therefor over the property of the company.

**4** Power to appoint a solicitor or accountant or other professionally qualified person to assist him in the performance of his functions.

**5** Power to bring or defend any action or other legal proceedings in the name and on behalf of the company.

**6** Power to refer to arbitration any question affecting the company.

**7** Power to effect and maintain insurances in respect of the business and property of the company.

**8** Power to use the company's seal.

**9** Power to do all acts and to execute in the name and on behalf of the company any deed, receipt or other document.

**10** Power to draw, accept, make and endorse any bill of exchange or promissory note in the name and on behalf of the company.

**11** Power to appoint any agent to do any business which he is unable to do himself or which can more conveniently be done by an agent and power to employ and dismiss employees.

**12** Power to do all such things (including the carrying out of works) as may be necessary for the realisation of the property of the company.

**13** Power to make any payment which is necessary or incidental to the performance of his functions.

**14** Power to carry on the business of the company.

**15** Power to establish subsidiaries of the company.

**16** Power to transfer to subsidiaries of the company the whole or any part of the business and property of the company.

**17** Power to grant or accept a surrender of a lease or tenancy of any of the property of the company, and to take a lease or tenancy of any property required or convenient for the business of the company.

**18** Power to make any arrangement or compromise on behalf of the company.

**19** Power to call up any uncalled capital of the company.

**20** Power to rank and claim in the bankruptcy, insolvency, sequestration or liquidation of any person indebted to the company and to receive dividends, and to accede to trust deeds for the creditors of any such person.

**21** Power to present or defend a petition for the winding up of the company.

**22** Power to change the situation of the company's registered office.

**23** Power to do all other things incidental to the exercise of the foregoing powers.

# Schedule 2 – Powers of a Scottish Receiver (Additional to Those Conferred on him by the Instrument of Charge)

Section 55

**1** Power to take possession of, collect and get in the property from the company or a liquidator thereof or any other person, and for that purpose, to take such proceedings as may seem to him expedient.

**2** Power to sell, feu, hire out or otherwise dispose of the property by public roup or private bargain and with or without advertisement.

**3** Power to raise or borrow money and grant security therefor over the property.

**4** Power to appoint a solicitor or accountant or other professionally qualified person to assist him in the performance of his functions.

**5** Power to bring or defend any action or other legal proceedings in the name and on behalf of the company.

**6** Power to refer to arbitration all questions affecting the company.

**7** Power to effect and maintain insurances in respect of the business and property of the company.

**8** Power to use the company's seal.

**9** Power to do all acts and to execute in the name and on behalf of the company any deed, receipt or other document.

**10** Power to draw, accept, make and endorse any bill of exchange or promissory note in the name and on behalf of the company.

**11** Power to appoint any agent to do any business which he is unable to do himself or which can more conveniently be done by an agent, and power to employ and dismiss employees.

**12** Power to do all such things (including the carrying out of works), as may be necessary for the realisation of the property.

**13** Power to make any payment which is necessary or incidental to the performance of his functions.

**14** Power to carry on the business of the company or any part of it.

**15** Power to grant or accept a surrender of a lease or tenancy of any of the property, and to take a lease or tenancy of any property required or covenient for the business of the company.

**16** Power to make any arrangement or compromise on behalf of the company.

17 Power to call up any uncalled capital of the company.

18 Power to establish subsidiaries of the company.

19 Power to transfer to subsidiaries of the company the business of the company or any part of it and any of the property.

20 Power to rank and claim in the bankruptcy, insolvency, sequestrian or liquidation of any person or company indebted to the company and to receive dividends, and to accede to trust deeds for creditors of any such person.

21 Power to present or defend a petition for the winding up of the company.

22 Power to change the situation of the company's registered office.

23 Power to do all other things incidental to the exercise of the powers mentioned in section 55(1) of this Act or above in this Schedule.

# Schedule 3 – Orders in Course of Winding Up Pronounced in Vacation (Scotland)

Section 162

## Part I – Orders Which are to be Final

Orders under section 153, as to the time for proving debts and claims.

Orders under section 195 as to meetings for ascertaining wishes of creditors or contributories.

Orders under section 198, as to the examination of witnesses in regard to the property or affairs of a company.

## Part II – Orders Which are to take Effect until Matter Disposed of by Inner House

Orders under section 126(1), 130(2) or (3), 147, 227 or 228, restraining or permitting the commencement or the continuance of legal proceedings.

Orders under section 135(5), limiting the powers of provisional liquidators.

Orders under section 108, appointing a liquidator to fill a vacancy.

Orders under section 167 or 169, sanctioning the exercise of any powers by a liquidator, other than the powers specified in paragraphs 1, 2 and 3 of Schedule 4 to this Act.

Orders under section 158, as to the arrest and detention of an absconding contributory and his property.

# Schedule 4 – Powers of Liquidator in a Winding Up

Sections 165, 167

## Part I – Powers Exercisable with Sanction

1 Power to pay any class of creditors in full.

2 Power to make any compromise or arrangement with creditors or persons claiming to be creditors, or having or alleging themselves to have any claim (present or future, certain or contingent, ascertained or sounding only in damages) against the company, or whereby the company may be rendered liable.

**3** Power to compromise, on such terms as may be agreed–

(a) all calls and liabilities to calls, all debts and liabilities capable of resulting in debts, and all claims (present or future, certain or contingent, ascertained or sounding only in damages) subsisting or supposed to subsist between the company and a contributory or alleged contributory or other debtor or person apprehending liability to the company, and

(b) all questions in any way relating to or affecting the assets or the winding up of the company,

and take any security for the discharge of any such call, debt, liability or claim and give a complete discharge in respect of it.

## Part II – Powers Exercisable without Sanction in Voluntary Winding Up, with Sanction in Winding Up by the Court

**4** Power to bring or defend any action or other legal proceeding in the name and on behalf of the company.

**5** Power to carry on the business of the company so far as may be necessary for its beneficial winding up.

## Part III – Powers Exercisable Without Sanction in any Winding Up

**6** Power to sell any of the company's property by public auction or private contract, with power to transfer the whole of it to any person or to sell the same in parcels.

**7** Power to do all acts and execute, in the name and on behalf of the company, all deeds, receipts and other documents and for that purpose to use, when necessary, the company's seal.

**8** Power to prove, rank and claim in the bankruptcy, insolvency or sequestration of any contributory for any balance against his estate, and to receive dividends in the bankruptcy, insolvency or sequestration in respect of that balance, as a separate debt due from the bankrupt or insolvent, and rateably with the other separate creditors.

**9** Power to draw, accept, make and indorse any bill of exchange or promissory note in the name and on behalf of the company, with the same effect with respect to the company's liability as if the bill or note had been drawn, accepted, made or indorsed by or on behalf of the company in the course of its business.

**10** Power to raise on the security of the assets of the company any money requisite.

**11** Power to take out in his official name letters of administration to any deceased contributory, and to do in his official name any other act necessary for obtaining payment of any money due from a contributory or his estate which cannot conveniently be done in the name of the company.

In all such cases the money due is deemed, for the purpose of enabling the liquidator to take out the letters of administration or recover the money, to be due to the liquidator himself.

**12** Power to appoint an agent to do any business which the liquidator is unable to do himself.

**13** Power to do all such other things as may be necessary for winding up the company's affairs and distributing its assets.

# Schedule 5 – Powers of Trustee in Bankruptcy

Section 314

## Part I – Powers Exercisable with Sanction

**1** Power to carry on any business of the bankrupt so far as may be necessary for winding it up beneficially and so far as the trustee is able to do so without contravening any requirement imposed by or under any enactment.

2 Power to bring, institute or defend any action or legal proceedings relating to the property comprised in the bankrupt's estate.

3 Power to accept as the consideration for the sale of any property comprised in the bankrupt's estate a sum of money payable at a future time subject to such stipulations as to security or otherwise as the creditors' committee or the court thinks fit.

4 Power to mortgage or pledge any part of the property comprised in the bankrupt's estate for the purpose of raising money for the payment of his debts.

5 Power, where any right, option or other power forms part of the bankrupt's estate, to make payments or incur liabilities with a view to obtaining, for the benefit of the creditors, any property which is the subject of the right, option or power.

6 Power to refer to arbitration, or compromise on such terms as may be agreed on, any debts, claims or liabilities subsisting or supposed to subsist between the bankrupt and any person who may have incurred any liability to the bankrupt.

7 Power to make such compromise or other arrangement as may be thought expedient with creditors, or persons claiming to be creditors, in respect of bankruptcy debts.

8 Power to make such compromise or other arrangement as may be thought expedient with respect to any claim arising out of or incidental to the bankrupt's estate made or capable of being made on the trustee by any person or by the trustee on any person.

## Part II – General Powers

9 Power to sell any part of the property for the time being comprised in the bankrupt's estate, including the goodwill and book debts of any business.

10 Power to give receipts for any money received by him, being receipts which effectually discharge the person paying the money from all responsibility in respect of its application.

11 Power to prove, rank, claim and draw a dividend in respect of such debts due to the bankrupt as are comprised in his estate.

12 Power to exercise in relation to any property comprised in the bankrupt's estate any powers the capacity to exercise which is vested in him under Parts VIII to XI of this Act.

13 Power to deal with any property comprised in the estate to which the bankrupt is beneficially entitled as tenant in tail in the same manner as the bankrupt might have dealt with it.

## Part III – Ancillary Powers

14 For the purposes of, or in connection with, the exercise of any of his powers under Parts VIII to XI of this Act, the trustee may, by his official name–

(a) hold property of every description,

(b) make contracts,

(c) sue and be sued,

(d) enter into engagements binding on himself and, in respect of the bankrupt's estate, on his successors in office,

(e) employ an agent,

(f) execute any power of attorney, deed or other instrument;

and he may do any other act which is necessary or expedient for the purposes of or in connection with the exercise of those powers.

# Schedule 6 – The Categories of Preferential Debts

Section 386

### CATEGORY 1: DEBTS DUE TO INLAND REVENUE

1 Sums due at the relevant date from the debtor on account of deductions of income tax from emoluments paid during the period of 12 months next before that date.

The deductions here referred to are those which the debtor was liable to make under section 203 of the Income and Corporation Taxes Act 1988 (pay as you earn), less the amount of the repayments of income tax which the debtor was liable to make during that period.

**History**
In para. 1 the words "203 of the Income and Corporation Taxes Act 1988" substituted for the former words "204 of the Income and Corporation Taxes Act 1970" by Income and Corporation Taxes Act 1988, s. 844 and Sch. 29, para. 32 for companies' accounting periods ending after 5 April 1988 (see s. 843(1)).

**2** Sums due at the relevant date from the debtor in respect of such deductions as are required to be made by the debtor for that period under section 559 of the Income and Corporation Taxes Act 1988 (sub-contractors in the construction industry).

**History**
In para. 2 the words "559 of the Income and Corporation Taxes Act 1988" substituted for the former words "69 of the Finance (No. 2) Act 1975" by Income and Corporation Taxes Act 1988, s. 844 and Sch. 29, para. 32 for companies' accounting periods ending after 5 April 1988 (see s. 843(1)).

## CATEGORY 2: DEBTS DUE TO CUSTOMS AND EXCISE

**3** Any value added tax which is referable to the period of 6 months next before the relevant date (which period is referred to below as "the 6-month period").

For the purposes of this paragraph–

(a) where the whole of the prescribed accounting period to which any value added tax is attributable falls within the 6-month period, the whole amount of that tax is referable to that period; and

(b) in any other case the amount of any value added tax which is referable to the 6-month period is the proportion of the tax which is equal to such proportion (if any) of the accounting reference period in question as falls within the 6-month period;

and in sub-paragraph (a) **"prescribed"** means prescribed by regulations under the Value Added Tax Act 1994.

**History**
In para. 3 "1994" substituted for "1983" by Value Added Tax Act 1994, s. 100(1), 101(1) and Sch. 14, para. 8 as from 1 September 1994 subject to savings provisions in Sch. 13.

**3A** Any insurance premium tax which is referable to the period of 6 months next before the relevant date (which period is referred to below as "the 6-month period").

For the purposes of this paragraph–

(a) where the whole of the accounting period to which any insurance premium tax is attributable falls within the 6-month period, the whole amount of that tax is referable to that period; and

(b) in any other case the amount of any insurance premium tax which is referable to the 6-month period is the proportion of the tax which is equal to such proportion (if any) of the accounting period in question as falls within the 6-month period;

and references here to accounting periods shall be construed in accordance with Part III of the Finance Act 1994.

**History**
Para. 3A inserted by Finance Act 1994, Sch. 7, para. 7(2) as from 3 May 1994.

**3B** Any landfill tax which is referable to the period of 6 months next before the relevant date (which period is referred to below as "the 6-month period").

For the purposes of this paragraph–

(a) where the whole of the accounting period to which any landfill tax is attributable falls within the 6-month period, the whole amount of that tax is referable to that period; and

(b) in any other case the amount of any landfill tax which is referable to the 6-month period is the proportion of the tax which is equal to such proportion (if any) of the accounting period in question as falls within the 6-month period;

and references here to accounting periods shall be construed in accordance with Part III of the Finance Act 1996.

**History**
Para. 3B inserted by Finance Act 1996, s. 60 and Sch. 5, para. 12(1) as from 29 April 1996.

**3C** Any climate change levy which is referable to the period of 6 months next before the relevant date (which period is referred to below as "the 6-month period").

For the purposes of this paragraph–

(a) where the whole of the accounting period to which any climate change levy is attributable falls within the 6-month period, the whole amount of that levy is referable to that period; and

(b) in any other case the amount of any climate change levy which is referable to the 6-month period is the proportion of the levy which is equal to such proportion (if any) of the accounting period in question as falls within the 6-month period;

and references here to accounting periods shall be construed in accordance with Schedule 6 to the Finance Act 2000.

**History**
Para. 3C inserted by Finance Act 2000, s. 30(2) and Sch. 7, para. 3(1)(a), (2) as from 28 July 2000.

**4** The amount of any car tax which is due at the relevant date from the debtor and which became due within a period of 12 months next before that date.

**5** Any amount which is due–

(a) by way of general betting duty, bingo duty or gaming duty, or

(b) under section 12(1) of the Betting and Gaming Duties Act 1981 (general betting duty and pool betting duty recoverable from agent collecting stakes), or

(c) under section 14 of, or Schedule 2 to, that Act (gaming licence duty),

from the debtor at the relevant date and which became due within the period of 12 months next before that date.

**History**
In para. 5(a) the words ", bingo duty or gaming duty" substituted for the former words "or bingo duty" by Finance Act 1997, s. 13(2) and Sch. 2, para. 6 as from 19 March 1997.

**5A** The amount of any excise duty on beer which is due at the relevant date from the debtor and which became due within a period of 6 months next before that date.

**History**
Para. 5A inserted by Finance Act 1991, s. 7(4), (5), Sch. 2, para. 22 as from 1 May 1993 (see SI 1993/1152).

**5B** Any amount which is due by way of lottery duty from the debtor at the relevant date and which became due within the period of 12 months next before that date.

**History**
Para. 5B inserted by Finance Act 1993, s. 36(2) as from 1 December 1993 (see SI 1993/2842).

**5C** Any amount which is due by way of air passenger duty from the debtor at the relevant date and which became due within the period of six months next before that date.

**History**
Para. 5C inserted by Finance Act 1994, s. 40 and Sch. 6, para. 13 as from 31 October 1994 (see Finance Act 1994, s. 44).

## CATEGORY 3: SOCIAL SECURITY CONTRIBUTIONS

**6** All sums which on the relevant date are due from the debtor on account of Class 1 or Class 2 contributions under the Social Security Contributions and Benefits Act 1992 or the Social Security (Northern Ireland) Act 1975 and which became due from the debtor in the 12 months next before the relevant date.

**History**
In para. 6 the words "Social Security Contributions and Benefits Act 1992" substituted for the former words "Social Security Act 1975" by Social Security (Consequential Provisions) Act 1992, s. 4, 7(2) and Sch. 2, para. 73 as from 1 July 1992.

**7** All sums which on the relevant date have been assessed on and are due from the debtor on account of Class 4 contributions under either of those Acts of 1975, being sums which–

(a) are due to the Commissioners of Inland Revenue (rather than to the Secretary of State or a Northern Ireland department), and

(b) are assessed on the debtor up to 5th April next before the relevant date,

but not exceeding, in the whole, any one year's assessment.

## CATEGORY 4: CONTRIBUTIONS TO OCCUPATIONAL PENSION SCHEMES, ETC.

**8** Any sum which is owed by the debtor and is a sum to which Schedule 4 to the Pension Schemes Act 1993 applies (contributions to occupational pension schemes and state scheme premiums).

**History**

In para. 8 the words "Schedule 4 to the the Pension Schemes Act 1993" substituted for the former words "Schedule 3 to the Social Security Pensions Act 1975" by Pension Schemes Act 1993, s. 190 and Sch. 8, para. 18 as from 7 February 1994 (see SI 1994/86 (C 3), art. 2).

## CATEGORY 5: REMUNERATION, ETC., OF EMPLOYEES

**9** So much of any amount which–

(a) is owed by the debtor to a person who is or has been an employee of the debtor, and

(b) is payable by way of remuneration in respect of the whole or any part of the period of 4 months next before the relevant date,

as does not exceed so much as may be prescribed by order made by the Secretary of State.

**Note**

See Note after para. 12.

**10** An amount owed by way of accrued holiday remuneration, in respect of any period of employment before the relevant date, to a person whose employment by the debtor has been terminated, whether before, on or after that date.

**11** So much of any sum owed in respect of money advanced for the purpose as has been applied for the payment of a debt which, if it had not been paid, would have been a debt falling within paragraph 9 or 10.

**12** So much of any amount which–

(a) is ordered (whether before or after the relevant date) to be paid by the debtor under the Reserve Forces (Safeguard of Employment) Act 1985, and

(b) is so ordered in respect of a default made by the debtor before that date in the discharge of his obligations under that Act,

as does not exceed such amount as may be prescribed by order made by the Secretary of State.

**Note**

The amount for para. 9, 12 is £800 – see the Insolvency Proceedings (Monetary Limits) Order 1986 (SI 1986/1996), art. 4.

## INTERPRETATION FOR CATEGORY 5

**13(1)** For the purposes of paragraphs 9 to 12, a sum is payable by the debtor to a person by way of remuneration in respect of any period if–

(a) it is paid as wages or salary (whether payable for time or for piece work or earned wholly or partly by way of commission) in respect of services rendered to the debtor in that period, or

(b) it is an amount falling within the following sub-paragraph and is payable by the debtor in respect of that period.

**13(2)** An amount falls within this sub-paragraph if it is–

(a) a guarantee payment under Part III of the Employment Rights Act 1996 (employee without work to do);

(b) any payment for time off under section 53 (time off to look for work to arrange training) or section 56 (time off for ante-natal care) of that Act or under section 169 of the Trade Union and Labour Relations (Consolidation) Act 1992 (time off for carrying out trade union duties etc.);

(c) remuneration on suspension on medical grounds, or on maternity grounds, under Part VII of the Employment Rights Act 1996; or

(d) remuneration under a protective award under section 189 of the Trade Union and Labour Relations (Consolidation) Act 1992 (redundancy dismissal with compensation).



bbcl insa 1986a Mp 1415—bcl98 1c

**History**
Para. 13(2) substituted by the Employment Rights Act 1996, s. 240, 243 and Sch. 1, para. 24 as from 22 August 1996; para. 13(2) formerly read as follows:

"An amount falls within this sub-paragraph if it is–

(a) a guarantee payment under section 12(1) of the Employment Protection (Consolidation) Act 1978 (employee without work to do for a day or part of a day);

(b) remuneration on suspension on medical grounds under section 19 of that Act or remuneration on suspension on maternity grounds under section 47 of that Act;

(c) any payment for time off under section 31(3) or 31A(4) of that Act (looking for work, etc.; ante-natal care) or under section 169 of the Trade Union and Labour Relations (Consolidation) Act 1992 (trade union duties); or

(d) remuneration under a protective award made by an industrial tribunal under section 189 of the latter Act (redundancy dismissal with compensation)."

Previously in para. 13(2)(b) the words "or remuneration or suspension on maternity grounds under section 47 of that Act" inserted by Trade Union Reform and Employment Rights Act 1993, s. 49(2) and Sch. 8, para. 35 as from 10 June 1994 (see SI 1994/1365 but note art. 3(1)).

Previously in para. 13(2)(c) the words from "section 31(3)" to "(trade union duties)" substituted for the original words "section 27(3) (trade union duties), 31(3) (looking for work, etc.) or 31A(4) (ante-natal care) of that Act" and in para. 13(2)(d) the words "section 189 of the latter Act" substituted for the former words "section 101 of the Employment Protection Act 1975" by Trade Union and Labour Relations (Consolidation) Act 1992, s. 300(2) and Sch. 2, para. 33 as from 16 October 1992 (see s. 302 of the latter Act).

**14(1)** This paragraph relates to a case in which a person's employment has been terminated by or in consequence of his employer going into liquidation or being adjudged bankrupt or (his employer being a company not in liquidation) by or in consequence of–

(a) a receiver being appointed as mentioned in section 40 of this Act (debenture-holders secured by floating charge), or

(b) the appointment of a receiver under section 53(6) or 54(5) of this Act (Scottish company with property subject to floating charge), or

(c) the taking of possession by debenture-holders (so secured), as mentioned in section 196 of the Companies Act.

**14(2)** For the purposes of paragraphs 9 to 12, holiday remuneration is deemed to have accrued to that person in respect of any period of employment if, by virtue of his contract of employment or of any enactment, that remuneration would have accrued in respect of that period if his employment had continued until he became entitled to be allowed the holiday.

**14(3)** The reference in sub-paragraph (2) to any enactment includes an order or direction made under an enactment.

**15** Without prejudice to paragraphs 13 and 14–

(a) any remuneration payable by the debtor to a person in respect of a period of holiday or of absence from work through sickness or other good cause is deemed to be wages or (as the case may be) salary in respect of services rendered to the debtor in that period, and

(b) references here and in those paragraphs to remuneration in respect of a period of holiday include any sums which, if they had been paid, would have been treated for the purposes of the enactments relating to social security as earnings in repect of that period.

## CATEGORY 6: LEVIES ON COAL AND STEEL PRODUCTION

**15A** Any sums due at the relevant date from the debtor in respect of–

(a) the levies on the production of coal and steel referred to in Article 49 and 50 of the E.C.S.C. Treaty, or

(b) any surcharge for delay provided for in Article 50(3) of that Treaty and Article 6 of Decision 3/52 of the High Authority of the Coal and Steel Community.

**History**
Para. 15A inserted by the Insolvency (ECSC Levy Debts) Regulations 1987 (SI 1987/2093), reg. 2(1) as from 1 January 1988.

**Note**
See the Insolvency (ECSC Levy Debts) Regulations 1987 (SI 1987/2093), reg. 2(3) and 4 concerning the relevant date and preferential treatment under former law.

## ORDERS

**16** An order under paragraph 9 or 12–

(a) may contain such transitional provisions as may appear to the Secretary of State necessary or expedient;

(b) shall be made by statutory instrument subject to annulment in pursuance of a resolution of either House of Parliament.

# Schedule 7 – Insolvency Practitioners Tribunal

Section 396

## PANELS OF MEMBERS

**1(1)** The Secretary of State shall draw up and from time to time revise–

(a) a panel of persons who

(i) have a 7 year general qualification, within the meaning of s. 71 of the Courts and Legal Services Act 1990;

(ii) are advocates or solicitors in Scotland of at least 7 years' standing,

and are nominated for the purpose by the Lord Chancellor or the Lord President of the Court of Session, and

(b) a panel of persons who are experienced in insolvency matters;

and the members of the Tribunal shall be selected from those panels in accordance with this Schedule.

**History**
In para. 1(1)(a) the words from "(i) have a 7 year general qualification" to "at least 7 years' standing," substituted for the former words "are barristers, advocates or solicitors, in each case of at least 7 years' standing" by Courts and Legal Services Act 1990, s. 71(2), 124(3) and Sch. 10 as from 1 January 1991 (see SI 1990/2484, art. 2 and Sch.).

**1(2)** The power to revise the panels includes power to terminate a person's membership of either of them, and is accordingly to that extent subject to section 7 of the Tribunals and Inquiries Act 1992 (which makes it necessary to obtain the concurrence of the Lord Chancellor and the Lord President of the Court of Session to dismissals in certain cases).

**History**
In para. 1(2) the words "section 7 of the Tribunals and Inquiries Act 1992" substituted for the former words "section 8 of the Tribunals and Inquiries Act 1971" by Tribunals and Inquiries Act 1992, s. 18(1), 19 and Sch. 3, para. 19 as from 1 October 1992.

## REMUNERATION OF MEMBERS

**2** The Secretary of State may out of money provided by Parliament pay to members of the Tribunal such remuneration as he may with the approval of the Treasury determine; and such expenses of the Tribunal as the Secretary of State and the Treasury may approve shall be defrayed by the Secretary of State out of money so provided.

## SITTINGS OF TRIBUNAL

**3(1)** For the purposes of carrying out their functions in relation to any cases referred to them, the Tribunal may sit either as a single tribunal or in two or more divisions.

**3(2)** The functions of the Tribunal in relation to any case referred to them shall be exercised by three members consisting of–

(a) a chairman selected by the Secretary of State from the panel drawn up under paragraph 1(1)(a) above, and

(b) two other members selected by the Secretary of State from the panel drawn up under paragraph 1(1)(b).

## PROCEDURE OF TRIBUNAL

**4(1)** Any investigation by the Tribunal shall be so conducted as to afford a reasonable opportunity for representations to be made to the Tribunal by or on behalf of the person whose case is the subject of the investigation.

**4(2)** For the purposes of any such investigation, the Tribunal–

(a) may by summons require any person to attend, at such time and place as is specified in the summons, to give evidence or to produce any books, papers and other records in his possession or under his control which the Tribunal consider it necessary for the purposes of the investigation to examine, and

(b) may take evidence on oath, and for the purpose administer oaths, or may, instead of administering an oath, require the person examined to make and subscribe a declaration of the truth of the matter respecting which he is examined;

but no person shall be required, in obedience to such a summons, to go more than ten miles from his place of residence, unless the necessary expenses of his attendance are paid or tendered to him.

**4(3)** Every person who–

(a) without reasonable excuse fails to attend in obedience to a summons issued under this paragraph, or refuses to give evidence, or

(b) intentionally alters, suppresses, conceals or destroys or refuses to produce any document which he may be required to produce for the purpose of an investigation by the Tribunal,

is liable to a fine.

**4(4)** Subject to the provisions of this paragraph, the Secretary of State may make rules for regulating the procedure on any investigation by the Tribunal.

**4(5)** In their application to Scotland, sub-paragraphs (2) and (3) above have effect as if for any reference to a summons there where substituted a reference to a notice in writing.

**Note**

See the note to s. 396(1).

# Schedule 8 – Provisions Capable of Inclusion in Company Insolvency Rules

Section 411

## COURTS

**1** Provision for supplementing, in relation to the insolvency or winding up of companies, any provision made by or under section 117 of this Act (jurisdiction in relation to winding up).

**2** Provision for regulating the practice and procedure of any court exercising jurisdiction for the purposes of Parts I to VII of this Act or the Companies Act so far as relating to, and to matters connected with or arising out of, the insolvency or winding up of companies, being any provision that could be made by rules of court.

## NOTICES, ETC.

**3** Provision requiring notice of any proceedings in connection with or arising out of the insolvency or winding up of a company to be given or published in the manner prescribed by the rules.

**4** Provision with respect to the form, manner of serving, contents and proof of any petition, application, order, notice, statement or other document required to be presented, made, given, published or prepared under any enactment or subordinate legislation relating to, or to matters connected with or arising out of, the insolvency or winding up of companies.

**5** Provision specifying the persons to whom any notice is to be given.

## REGISTRATION OF VOLUNTARY ARRANGEMENTS

**6** Provision for the registration of voluntary arrangements approved under Part I of this Act, including provision for the keeping and inspection of a register.

## PROVISIONAL LIQUIDATOR

**7** Provision as to the manner in which a provisional liquidator appointed under section 135 is to carry out his functions.

## CONDUCT OF INSOLVENCY

**8** Provision with respect to the certification of any person as, and as to the proof that a person is, the liquidator, administrator or administrative receiver of a company.

**9** The following provision with respect to meetings of a company's creditors, contributories or members–

(a) provision as to the manner of summoning a meeting (including provision as to how any power to require a meeting is to be exercised, provision as to the manner of determining the value of any debt or contribution for the purposes of any such power and provision making the exercise of any such power subject to the deposit of a sum sufficient to cover the expenses likely to be incurred in summoning and holding a meeting);

(b) provision specifying the time and place at which a meeting may be held and the period of notice required for a meeting;

(c) provision as to the procedure to be followed at a meeting (including the manner in which decisions may be reached by a meeting and the manner in which the value of any vote at a meeting is to be determined);

(d) provision for requiring a person who is or has been an officer of the company to attend a meeting;

(e) provision creating, in the prescribed circumstances, a presumption that a meeting has been duly summoned and held;

(f) provision as to the manner of proving the decisions of a meeting.

**10(1)** Provision as to the functions, membership and proceedings of a committee established under section 26, 49, 68, 101, 141 or 142 of this Act.

**10(2)** The following provision with respect to the establishment of a committee under section 101, 141 or 142 of this Act, that is to say–

(a) provision for resolving differences between a meeting of the company's creditors and a meeting of its contributories or members;

(b) provision authorising the establishment of the committee without a meeting of contributories in a case where a company is being wound up on grounds including its inability to pay its debts; and

(c) provision modifying the requirements of this Act with respect to the establishment of the committee in a case where a winding-up order has been made immediately upon the discharge of an administration order.

**11** Provision as to the manner in which any requirement that may be imposed on a person under any Parts I to VII of this Act by the official receiver, the liquidator, administrator or administrative receiver of a company or a special manager appointed under section 177 is to be so imposed.

**12** Provision as to the debts that may be proved in a winding up, as to the manner and conditions of proving a debt and as to the manner and expenses of establishing the value of any debt or security.

**13** Provision with respect to the manner of the distribution of the property of a company that is being wound up, including provision with respect to unclaimed funds and dividends.

**14** Provision which, with or without modifications, applies in relation to the winding up of companies any enactment contained in Parts VIII to XI of this Act or in the Bankruptcy (Scotland) Act 1985.

## FINANCIAL PROVISIONS

**15** Provision as to the amount, or manner of determining the amount, payable to the liquidator, administrator or administrative receiver of a company or a special manager appointed under section 177, by way of remuneration for the carrying out of functions in connection with or arising out of the insolvency or winding up of a company.

**16** Provision with respect to the manner in which moneys received by the liquidator of a company in the course of carrying out his functions as such are to be invested or otherwise handled and with respect to the payment of interest on sums which, in pursuance of rules made by virtue of this paragraph, have been paid into the Insolvency Services Account.

**17** Provision as to the fees, costs, charges and other expenses that may be treated as the expenses of a winding up.

**18** Provisions as to the fees, costs, charges and other expenses that may be treated as properly incurred by the administrator or administrative receiver of a company.

**19** Provision as to the fees, costs, charges and other expenses that may be incurred for any of the purposes of Part I of this Act or in the administration of any voluntary arrangement approved under that Part.

## INFORMATION AND RECORDS

**20** Provision requiring registrars and other officers of courts having jurisdiction in England and Wales in relation to, or to matters connected with or arising out of, the insolvency or winding up of companies–

(a) to keep books and other records with respect to the exercise of that jurisdiction, and

(b) to make returns to the Secretary of State of the business of those courts.

**21** Provision requiring a creditor, member or contributory, or such a committee as is mentioned in paragraph 10 above, to be supplied (on payment in precribed cases of the prescribed fee) with such information and with copies of such documents as may be prescribed.

**22** Provision as to the manner in which public examinations under sections 133 and 134 of this Act and proceedings under sections 236 and 237 are to be conducted, as to the circumstances in which records of such examinations or proceedings are to be made available to prescribed persons and as to the costs of such examinations and proceedings.

**23** Provision imposing requirements with respect to–

(a) the preparation and keeping by the liquidator, administrator or administrative receiver of a company, or by the supervisor of a voluntary arrangement approved under Part I of this Act, of prescribed books, accounts and other records;

(b) the production of those books, accounts and records for inspection by prescribed persons;

(c) the auditing of accounts kept by the liquidator, administrator or administrative receiver of a company, or the supervisor of such a voluntary arrangement; and

(d) the issue by the administrator or administrative recever of a company of such a certificate as is mentioned in section 22(3)(b) of the Value Added Tax Act 1983 (refund of tax in cases of bad debts) and the supply of copies of the certificate to creditors of the company.

**24** Provision requiring the person who is the supervisor of a voluntary arrangement approved under Part I, when it appears to him that the voluntary arrangement has been fully implemented and nothing remains to be done by him under the arrangement–

(a) to give notice to that fact to persons bound by the voluntary arrangement, and

(b) to report to those persons on the carrying out of the functions conferred on the supervisor of the arrangement.

**25** Provision as to the manner in which the liquidator of a company is to act in relation to the books, papers and other records of the company, including provision authorising their disposal.

**26** Provision imposing requirements in connection with the carrying out of functions under section 7(3) of the Company Directors Disqualification Act 1986 (including, in particular, requirements with respect to the making of periodic returns).

**Note**

For para. 26, see the rules referred to in the notes to Company Directors Disqualification Act 1986, s. 7.

## GENERAL

**27** Provision conferring power on the Secretary of State to make regulations with respect to so much of any matter that may be provided for in the rules as relates to the carrying out of the functions of the liquidator, administrator or administrative receiver of a company.

**Note**

Re para. 27, see the Insolvency Regulations 1994 (SI 1994/2507).

**28** Provision conferring a discretion on the court.

**29** Provision conferring power on the court to make orders for the purpose of securing compliance with obligations imposed by or under section 22, 47, 66, 131, 143(2) or 235 of this Act or section 7(4) of the Company Directors Disqualification Act 1986.

**30** Provision making non-compliance with any of the rules a criminal offence.

**31** Provision making different provision for different cases or descriptions of cases, including different provisions for different areas.

# Schedule 9 – Provisions Capable of Inclusion in Individual Insolvency Rules

Section 412

## COURTS

**1** Provision with respect to the arrangement and disposition of the business under Parts VIII to XI of this Act of courts having jurisdiction for the purpose of those Parts, including provision for the allocation of proceedings under those Parts to particular courts and for the transfer of such proceedings from one court to another.

**2** Provision for enabling a registrar in bankruptcy of the High Court or a registrar of a county court having jurisdiction for the purposes of those Parts to exercise such of the jurisdiction conferred for those purposes on the High Court or, as the case may be, that county court as may be prescribed.

**3** Provision for regulating the practice and procedure of any court exercising jurisdiction for the purposes of those Parts, being any provision that could be made by rules of court.

**4** Provision conferring rights of audience, in courts exercising jurisdiction for the purposes of those Parts, on the official receiver and on solicitors.

## NOTICES ETC.

**5** Provision requiring notice of any proceedings under Parts VIII to XI of this Act or of any matter relating to or arising out of a proposal under Part VIII or a bankruptcy to be given or published in the prescribed manner.

**6** Provision with respect to the form, manner of serving, contents and proof of any petition, application, order, notice, statement or other document required to be presented, made, given, published or prepared under any enactment contained in Parts VIII to XI or subordinate legislation under those Parts or Part XV (including provision requiring prescribed matters to be verified by affidavit).

**7** Provision specifying the persons to whom any notice under Parts VIII to XI is to be given.

## REGISTRATION OF VOLUNTARY ARRANGEMENTS

**8** Provision for the registration of voluntary arrangements approved under Part VIII of this Act, including provision for the keeping and inspection of a register.

## INTERIM RECEIVER

**9** Provision as to the manner in which an interim receiver appointed under section 286 is to carry out his functions, including any such provision as is specified in relation to the trustee of a bankrupt's estate in paragraph 21 or 27 below.

## RECEIVER OR MANAGER

**10** Provision as to the manner in which the official receiver is to carry out his functions as receiver or manager of a bankrupt's estate under section 287, including any such provision as is specified in relation to the trustee of a bankrupt's estate in paragraph 21 or 27 below.

## ADMINISTRATION OF INDIVIDUAL INSOLVENCY

**11** Provision with respect to the certification of the appointment of any person as trustee of a bankrupt's estate and as to the proof of that appointment.

**12** The following provision with respect to meetings of creditors–

(a) provision as to the manner of summoning a meeting (including provision as to how any power to require a meeting is to be exercised, provision as to the manner of determining the value of any debt for the purposes of any such power and provision making the exercise of any such power subject to the deposit of a sum sufficient to cover the expenses likely to be incurred in summoning and holding a meeting);

(b) provision specifying the time and place at which a meeting may be held and the period of notice required for a meeting;

(c) provision as to the procedure to be followed at such a meeting (including the manner in which decisions may be reached by a meeting and the manner in which the value of any vote at a meeting is to be determined);

(d) provision for requiring a bankrupt or debtor to attend a meeting;

(e) provision creating, in the prescribed circumstances, a presumption that a meeting has been duly summoned and held; and

(f) provision as to the manner of proving the decisions of a meeting.

**13** Provision as to the functions, membership and proceedings of a credtors' committee established under section 301.

**14** Provision as to the manner in which any requirement that may be imposed on a person under Parts VIII to XI of this Act by the official receiver, the trustee of a bankrupt's estate or a special manager appointed under section 370 is to be imposed and, in the case of any requirement imposed under section 305(3) (information etc. to be given by the trustee to the official receiver), provision conferring power on the court to make orders for the purpose of securing compliance with that requirement.

**15** Provision as to the manner in which any requirement imposed by virtue of section 310(3) (compliance with income payments order) is to take effect.

**16** Provision as to the terms and conditions that may be included in a charge under section 313 (dwelling house forming part of bankrupt's estate).

**17** Provision as to the debts that may be proved in any bankruptcy, as to the manner and conditions of proving a debt and as to the manner and expenses of establishing the value of any debt or security.

**18** Provision with respect to the manner of the distribution of a bankrupt's estate, including provision with respect to unclaimed funds and dividends.

**19** Provision modifying the application of Parts VIII to XI of this Act in relation to a debtor or bankrupt who has died.

## FINANCIAL PROVISIONS

**20** Provision as to the amount, or manner of determining the amount, payable to an interim receiver, the trustee of a bankrupt's estate or a special manager appointed under section 370 by way of remuneration for the performance of functions in connection with or arising out of the bankruptcy of any person.

**21** Provision with respect to the manner in which moneys received by the trustee of a bankrupt's estate in the course of carrying out his functions as such are to be handled.

**22** Provision as to the fees, costs, charges and other expenses that may be treated as the expenses of a bankruptcy.

**23** Provision as to the fees, costs, charges and other expenses that may be incurred for any of the purposes of Part VIII of this Act or in the administration of any voluntary arrangement approved under that Part.

## INFORMATION AND RECORDS

**24** Provision requiring registrars and other officers of courts having jurisdiction for the purposes of Parts VIII to XI–

(a) to keep books and other records with respect to the exercise of that jurisdiction and of jurisdiction under the Deeds of Arrangement Act 1914, and

(b) to make returns to the Secretary of State of the business of those courts.

**25** Provision requiring a creditor or a committee established under section 301 to be supplied (on payment in prescribed cases of the prescribed fee) with such information and with copies of such documents as may be prescribed.

**26** Provision as to the manner in which public examinations under section 290 and proceedings under sections 366 to 368 are to be conducted, as to the circumstances in which records of such examinations and proceedings are to be made available to prescribed persons and as to the costs of such examinations and proceedings.

**27** Provision imposing requirements with respect to–

(a) the preparation and keeping by the trustee of a bankrupt's estate, or the supervisor of a voluntary arrangement approved under Part VIII, of prescribed books, accounts and other records;

(b) the production of those books, accounts and records for inspection by prescribed persons; and

(c) the auditing of accounts kept by the trustee of a bankrupt's estate or the supervisor of such a voluntary arrangement.

**28** Provision requiring the person who is the supervisor of a voluntary arrangement approved under Part VIII, when it appears to him that the voluntary arrangement has been fully implemented and that nothing remains to be done by him under it–

(a) to give notice of that fact to persons bound by the voluntary arrangement, and

(b) to report to those persons on the carrying out of the functions conferred on the supervisor of it.

**29** Provision as to the manner in which the trustee of a bankrupt's estate is to act in relation to the books, papers and other records of the bankrupt, including provision authorising their disposal.

## GENERAL

**30** Provision conferring power on the Secretary of State to make regulations with respect to so much of any matter that may be provided for in the rules as relates to the carrying out of the functions of an interim receiver appointed under section 286, of the official receiver while acting as a receiver or manager under section 287 or of a trustee of a bankrupt's estate.

**Note**

Re para. 30 see the Insolvency Regulations 1994 (SI 1994/2507).

**31** Provision conferring a discretion on the court.

**32** Provision making non-compliance with any of the rules a criminal offence.

**33** Provision making different provision for different cases, including different provision for different areas.

# Schedule 10 – Punishment of Offences under this Act

Section 430

*Note:* In the fourth and fifth columns of this Schedule, **"the statutory maximum"** means –

(a) in England and Wales, the prescribed sum under section 32 of the Magistrates' Courts Act 1980 (c. 43), and
(b) in Scotland, the prescribed sum under section 289B of the Criminal Procedure (Scotland) Act 1975 (c. 21).

| Section of Act creating offence | General nature of offence | Mode of prosecution | Punishment | Daily default fine (where applicable) |
|---|---|---|---|---|
| 12(2) | Company and others failing to state in correspondence etc. that administrator appointed. | Summary. | One-fifth of the statutory maximum. | |
| 15(8) | Failure of administrator to register office copy of court order permitting disposal of charged property. | Summary. | One-fifth of the statutory maximum. | One-fiftieth of the statutory maximum. |
| 18(5) | Failure of administrator to register office copy of court order varying or discharging administration order. | Summary. | One-fifth of the statutory maximum. | One fiftieth of the statutory maximum. |
| 21(3) | Administrator failing to register administration order and give notice of appointment. | Summary. | One-fifth of the statutory maximum. | One fiftieth of the statutory maximum. |
| 22(6) | Failure to comply with provisions relating to statement of affairs, where administrator appointed. | 1. On indictment.<br>2. Summary. | A fine.<br>The statutory maximum. | <br>One-tenth of the statutory maximum. |
| 23(3) | Administrator failing to send out, register and lay before creditors statement of his proposals. | Summary. | One-fifth of the statutory maximum. | One-fiftieth of the statutory maximum. |
| 24(7) | Administrator failing to file court order discharging administration order under s. 24. | Summary. | One-fifth of the statutory maximum. | One-fiftieth of the statutory maximum. |
| 27(6) | Administrator failing to file court order discharging administration order under s. 27. | Summary. | One-fifth of the statutory maximum. | One-fiftieth of the statutory maximum. |



CCH.New Law
bbcl insa 1986b Mp 1424—bcl98 2a

| Section of Act creating offence | General nature of offence | Mode of prosecution | Punishment | Daily default fine (where applicable) |
|---|---|---|---|---|
| 30 ... ... | Body corporate acting as receiver. | 1. On indictment.<br>2. Summary. | A fine.<br>The statutory maximum. | |
| 31 ... ... | Undischarged bankrupt acting as receiver or manager. | 1. On indictment.<br>2. Summary. | 2 years or a fine, or both.<br>6 months or the statutory maximum, or both. | |
| 38(5) | Receiver failing to deliver accounts to registrar. | Summary. | One-fifth of the statutory maximum. | One-fiftieth of the statutory maximum. |
| 39(2) | Company and others failing to state in correspondence that receiver appointed. | Summary. | One-fifth of the statutory maximum. | |
| 43(6) | Administrative receiver failing to file office copy of order permitting diposal of charged property. | Summary. | One-fifth of the statutory maximum. | One-fiftieth of the statutory maximum. |
| 45(5) | Administrative receiver failing to file notice of vacation of office. | Summary. | One-fifth of the statutory maximum. | One-fiftieth of the statutory maximum. |
| 46(4) | Administrative receiver failing to give notice of his appointment. | Summary. | One-fifth of the statutory maximum. | One-fiftieth of the statutory maximum. |
| 47(6) | Failure to comply with provisions relating to statement of affairs where administrative receiver appointed. | 1. On indictment.<br>2. Summary. | A fine.<br>The statutory maximum. | One-tenth of the statutory maximum. |
| 48(8) | Administrative receiver failing to comply with requirements as to his report. | Summary. | One-fifth of the statutory maximum. | One-fiftieth of the statutory maximum. |
| 51(4) | Body corporate or Scottish firm acting as receiver. | 1. On indictment.<br>2. Summary. | A fine.<br>The statutory maximum. | |
| 51(5) | Undischarged bankrupt acting as receiver (Scotland). | 1. On indictment.<br>2. Summary. | 2 years or a fine, or both.<br>6 months or the statutory maximum, or both. | |
| 53(2) | Failing to deliver to registrar copy of instrument of appointing of receiver. | Summary. | One-fifth of the statutory maximum. | One-fiftieth of the statutory maximum. |
| 54(3) | Failing to deliver to registrar the court's interlocutor appointing receiver. | Summary. | One-fifth of the statutory maximum. | One-fiftieth of the statutory maximum. |

| Section of Act creating offence | General nature of offence | Mode of prosecution | Punishment | Daily default fine (where applicable) |
|---|---|---|---|---|
| 61(7) | Receiver failing to send registrar certified copy of court order authorising disposal of charged property. | Summary. | One-fifth of the statutory maximum. | One-fiftieth of the statutory maximum. |
| 62(5) | Failing to give notice to registrar of cessation or removal of receiver. | Summary. | One-fifth of the statutory maximum. | One-fiftieth of the statutory maximum. |
| 64(2) | Company and others failing to state on correspondence etc. that receiver appointed. | Summary. | One-fifth of the statutory maximum. | |
| 65(4) | Receiver failing to send or publish notice of his appointment. | Summary. | One-fifth of the statutory maximum. | One-fiftieth of the statutory maximum. |
| 66(6) | Failing to comply with provisions concerning statement of affairs where receiver appointed. | 1. On indictment.<br>2. Summary. | A fine.<br>The statutory maximum. | One-tenth of the statutory maximum. |
| 67(8) | Receiver failing to comply with requirements as to his report. | Summary. | One-fifth of the statutory maximum. | One-fiftieth of the statutory maximum. |
| 85(2) | Company failing to give notice in Gazette of resolution for voluntary winding up. | Summary. | One-fifth of the statutory maximum. | One-fiftieth of the statutory maximum. |
| 89(4) | Director making statutory declaration of company's solvency without reasonable grounds for his opinion. | 1. On indictment.<br>2. Summary. | 2 years or a fine, or both.<br>6 months or the statutory maximum, or both. | |
| 89(6) | Declaration under s. 89 not delivered to registrar within prescribed time. | Summary. | One-fifth of the statutory maximum. | One-fiftieth of the statutory maximum. |
| 93(3) | Liquidator failing to summon general meeting of company at each year's end. | Summary. | One-fifth of the statutory maximum. | |
| 94(4) | Liquidator failing to send to registrar a copy of account of winding up and return of final meeting. | Summary. | One-fifth of the statutory maximum. | One-fiftieth of the statutory maximum. |
| 94(6) | Liquidator failing to call final meeting. | Summary. | One-fifth of the statutory maximum. | |
| 95(8) | Liquidator failing to comply with s. 95, where company insolvent | Summary. | The statutory maximum. | |



CCH.New Law
bbcl insa 1986b Mp 1426—bcl98 2a

| Section of Act creating offence | General nature of offence | Mode of prosecution | Punishment | Daily default fine (where applicable) |
|---|---|---|---|---|
| 98(6) | Company failing to comply with s. 98 in respect of summoning and giving notice of creditors' meeting. | 1. On indictment.<br>2. Summary. | A fine.<br>The statutory maximum. | |
| 99(3) | Directors failing to attend and lay statement in prescribed form before creditors' meeting. | 1. On indictment.<br>2. Summary. | A fine.<br>The statutory maximum. | |
| 105(3) | Liquidator failing to summon company general meeting and creditors' meeting at each year's end. | Summary. | One-fifth of the statutory maximum. | |
| 106(4) | Liquidator failing to send to registrar account of winding up and return of final meetings. | Summary. | One-fifth of the statutory maximum. | One-fiftieth of the statutory maximum. |
| 106(6) | Liquidator failing to call final meeting of company or creditors. | Summary. | One-fifth of the statutory maximum. | |
| 109(2) | Liquidator failing to publish notice of his appointment. | Summary. | One-fifth of the statutory maximum. | One-fiftieth of the statutory maximum. |
| 114(4) | Directors exercising powers in breach of s. 114, where no liquidator. | Summary. | The statutory maximum. | |
| 131(7) | Failing to comply with requirements as to statement of affairs, where liquidator appointed. | 1. On indictment.<br>2. Summary. | A fine.<br>The statutory maximum. | One-tenth of the statutory maximum. |
| 164 ... ... | Giving, offering etc. corrupt inducement affecting appointment of liquidator. | 1. On indictment.<br>2. Summary. | A fine.<br>The statutory maximum. | |
| 166(7) | Liquidator failing to comply with requirements of s. 166 in creditors' voluntary winding up. | Summary. | The statutory maximum. | |
| 188(2) | Default in compliance with s. 188 as to notification that company being wound up. | Summary. | One-fifth of the statutory maximum. | |
| 192(2) | Liquidator failing to notify registrar as to progress of winding up. | Summary. | One-fifth of the statutory maximum. | One-fiftieth of the statutory maximum. |
| 201(4) | Failing to deliver to registrar office copy of court order deferring dissolution. | Summary. | One-fifth of the statutory maximum. | One-fiftieth of the statutory maximum. |

| Section of Act creating offence | General nature of offence | Mode of prosecution | Punishment | Daily default fine (where applicable) |
|---|---|---|---|---|
| 203(6) | Failing to deliver to registrar copy of directions or result of appeal under s. 203. | Summary. | One-fifth of the statutory maximum. | One-fiftieth of the statutory maximum. |
| 204(7) | Liquidator failing to deliver to registrar copy of court order for early dissolution. | Summary. | One-fifth of the statutory maximum. | One-fiftieth of the statutory maximum. |
| 204(8) | Failing to deliver to registrar copy of court order deferring early dissolution. | Summary. | One-fifth of the statutory maximum. | One-fiftieth of the statutory maximum. |
| 205(7) | Failing to deliver to registrar copy of Secretary of State's directions or court order deferring dissolution. | Summary. | One-fifth of the statutory maximum. | One-fiftieth of the statutory maximum. |
| 206(1) | Fraud etc. in anticipation of winding up. | 1. On indictment.<br>2. Summary. | 7 years or a fine, or both.<br>6 months or the statutory maximum, or both. | |
| 206(2) | Privity to fraud in anticipation of winding up; fraud or privity to fraud, after commencement of winding up. | 1. On indictment.<br>2. Summary. | 7 years or a fine, or both.<br>6 months or the statutory maximum, or both. | |
| 206(5) | Knowingly taking in pawn or pledge, or otherwise receiving, company property. | 1. On indictment.<br>2. Summary. | 7 years or a fine, or both.<br>6 months or the statutory maximum, or both. | |
| 207 ... ... | Officer of company entering into transaction in fraud of company's creditors. | 1. On indictment.<br>2. Summary. | 2 years or a fine, or both.<br>6 months or the statutory maximum, or both. | |
| 208 ... ... | Officer of company misconducting himself in course of winding up. | 1. On indictment.<br>2. Summary. | 7 years or a fine, or both.<br>6 months or the statutory maximum, or both. | |
| 209 ... ... | Officer or contributory destroying, falsifying, etc. company's books. | 1. On indictment.<br>2. Summary. | 7 years or a fine, or both.<br>6 months or the statutory maximum, or both. | |
| 210 ... ... | Officer of company making material omission from statement relating to company's affairs. | 1. On indictment.<br>2. Summary. | 7 years or a fine, or both.<br>6 months or the statutory maximum, or both. | |

| Section of Act creating offence | General nature of offence | Mode of prosecution | Punishment | Daily default fine (where applicable) |
|---|---|---|---|---|
| 211 ... ... | False representation or fraud for purpose of obtaining creditors' consent to an agreement in connection with winding up. | 1. On indictment.<br>2. Summary. | 7 years or a fine, or both.<br>6 months or the statutory maximum, or both. | |
| 216(4) | Contravening restrictions on re-use of name of company in insolvent liquidation. | 1. On indictment.<br>2. Summary. | 2 years or a fine, or both.<br>6 months or the statutory maximum, or both. | |
| 235(5) | Failing to co-operate with office-holder. | 1. On indictment.<br>2. Summary. | A fine.<br>The statutory maximum. | One-tenth of the statutory maximum. |
| 353(1) | Bankrupt failing to disclose property or disposals to official receiver or trustee. | 1. On indictment.<br>2. Summary. | 7 years or a fine, or both.<br>6 months or the statutory maximum, or both. | |
| 354(1) | Bankrupt failing to deliver property to, or concealing property from, official receiver or trustee. | 1. On indictment.<br>2. Summary. | 7 years or a fine, or both.<br>6 months or the statutory maximum, or both. | |
| 354(2) | Bankrupt removing property which he is required to deliver to official receiver or trustee. | 1. On indictment.<br>2. Summary. | 7 years or a fine, or both.<br>6 months or the statutory maximum, or both. | |
| 354(3) | Bankrupt failing to account for loss of substantial part of property. | 1. On indictment.<br>2. Summary. | 2 years or a fine, or both.<br>6 months or the statutory maximum, or both. | |
| 355(1) | Bankrupt failing to deliver books, papers and records to official receiver or trustee. | 1. On indictment.<br>2. Summary. | 7 years or a fine, or both.<br>6 months or the statutory maximum, or both. | |
| 355(2) | Bankrupt concealing, destroying etc. books, papers or records, or making false entries in them. | 1. On indictment.<br>2. Summary. | 7 years or a fine, or both.<br>6 months or the statutory maximum, or both. | |
| 355(3) | Bankrupt disposing of, or altering, books, papers or records relating to his estate or affairs. | 1. On indictment.<br>2. Summary. | 7 years or a fine, or both.<br>6 months or the statutory maximum, or both. | |

| Section of Act creating offence | General nature of offence | Mode of prosecution | Punishment | Daily default fine (where applicable) |
|---|---|---|---|---|
| 356(1) | Bankrupt making material omission in statement relating to his affairs. | 1. On indictment.<br>2. Summary. | 7 years or a fine, or both.<br>6 months or the statutory maximum, or both. | |
| 356(2) | Bankrupt making false statement, or failing to inform trustee, where false debt proved. | 1. On indictment.<br>2. Summary. | 7 years or a fine, or both.<br>6 months or the statutory maximum, or both. | |
| 357 … … | Bankrupt fraudulently disposing of property. | 1. On indictment.<br>2. Summary. | 2 years or a fine, or both.<br>6 months or the statutory maximum, or both. | |
| 358 … … | Bankrupt absconding with property he is required to deliver to official receiver or trustee. | 1. On indictment.<br>2. Summary. | 2 years or a fine, or both.<br>6 months or the statutory maximum, or both. | |
| 359(1) | Bankrupt disposing of property obtained on credit and not paid for. | 1. On indictment.<br>2. Summary. | 7 years or a fine, or both.<br>6 months or the statutory maximum, or both. | |
| 359(2) | Obtaining property in respect of which money is owed by a bankrupt. | 1. On indictment.<br>2. Summary. | 7 years or a fine, or both.<br>6 months or the statutory maximum, or both. | |
| 360(1) | Bankrupt obtaining credit or engaging in business without disclosing his status or name in which he was made bankrupt. | 1. On indictment.<br>2. Summary. | 2 years or a fine, or both.<br>6 months or the statutory maximum, or both. | |
| 360(3) | Person made bankrupt in Scotland or Northern Ireland obtaining credit, etc. in England and Wales. | 1. On indictment.<br>2. Summary. | 2 years or a fine, or both.<br>6 months or the statutory maximum, or both. | |
| 361(1) | Bankrupt failing to keep proper accounting records. | 1. On indictment.<br>2. Summary. | 2 years or a fine, or both.<br>6 months or the statutory maximum, or both. | |
| 362 … … | Bankrupt increasing extent of insolvency by gambling. | 1. On indictment.<br>2. Summary. | 2 years or a fine, or both.<br>6 months or the statutory maximum, or both. | |





bbcl insa 1986b Mp 1430—bcl98 2a

| Section of Act creating offence | General nature of offence | Mode of prosecution | Punishment | Daily default fine (where applicable) |
|---|---|---|---|---|
| 389 … … | Acting as insolvency practitioner when not qualified. | 1. On indictment.<br>2. Summary. | 2 years or a fine, or both.<br>6 months or the statutory maximum, or both. | |
| 429(5) | Contravening s. 429 in respect of disabilities imposed by county court on revocation of administration order. | 1. On indictment.<br>2. Summary. | 2 years or a fine, or both.<br>6 months or the statutory maximum, or both. | |
| Sch. 7, para. 4(3) … … | Failure to attend and give evidence to Insolvency Practitioners Tribunal; suppressing, concealing, etc. relevant documents. | Summary. | Level 3 on the standard scale within the meaning given by section 75 of the Criminal Justice Act 1982. | |

**Note**
The current statutory maximum is £5,000 (CJA 1991, s. 17 and SI 1992/333, SI 1993/2118 effective 1 October 1992) – £2,000 in respect of offences committed before 1 October 1992.

# Schedule 11 – Transitional Provisions and Savings

Section 437

## Part I – Company Insolvency and Winding Up

### ADMINISTRATION ORDERS

**1(1)** Where any right to appoint an administrative receiver of a company is conferred by any debentures or floating charge created before the appointed day, the conditions precedent to the exercise of that right are deemed to include the presentation of a petition applying for an administration order to be made in relation to the company.

**1(2)** **"Administrative receiver"** here has the meaning assigned by section 251.

### RECEIVERS AND MANAGERS (ENGLAND AND WALES)

**2(1)** In relation to any receiver or manager of a company's property who was appointed before the appointed day, the new law does not apply; and the relevant provisions of the former law continue to have effect.

**2(2)** **"The new law"** here means Chapter I of Part III, and Part VI, of this Act; and **"the former law"** means the Companies Act and so much of this Act as replaces provisions of that Act (without the amendments in paragraphs 15 to 17 of Schedule 6 to the Insolvency Act 1985, or the associated repeals made by that Act), and any provision of the Insolvency Act 1985 which was in force before the appointed day.

**2(3)** This paragraph is without prejudice to the power conferred by the Act under which rules under section 411 may make transitional provision in connection with the coming into force of those rules; and such provision may apply those rules in relation to the receiver or manager of a company's property notwithstanding that he was appointed before the coming into force of the rules or section 411.

### RECEIVERS (SCOTLAND)

**3(1)** In relation to any receiver appointed under section 467 of the Companies Act before the appointed day, the new law does not apply and the relevant provisions of the former law continue to have effect.

**3(2)** **"The new law"** here means Chapter II of Part III, and Part VI, of this Act; and **"the former law"** means the Companies Act and so much of this Act as replaces provisions of that Act (without the amendments in paragraphs 18 to 22 of Schedule 6 to the Insolvency Act 1985 or the associated repeals made by that Act), and any provision of the Insolvency Act 1985 which was in force before the appointed day.

**3(3)** This paragraph is without prejudice to the power conferred by this Act under which rules under section 411 may make transitional provision in connection with the coming into force of those rules; and such provision may apply those rules in relation to a receiver appointed under section 467 notwithstanding that he was appointed before the coming into force of the rules or section 411.

### WINDING UP ALREADY IN PROGRESS

**4(1)** In relation to any winding up which has commenced, or is treated as having commenced, before the appointed day, the new law does not apply, and the former law continues to have effect, subject to the following paragraphs.

**4(2)** **"The new law"** here means any provisions in the first Group of Parts of this Act which replace sections 66 to 87 and 89 to 105 of the Insolvency Act 1985; and **"the former law"** means Parts XX and XXI of the Companies Act (without the amendments in paragraphs 23 to 52 of Schedule 6 to the Insolvency Act 1985, or the associated repeals made by that Act).

### STATEMENT OF AFFAIRS

**5(1)** Where a winding up by the court in England and Wales has commenced, or is treated as having commenced, before the appointed day, the official receiver or (on appeal from a refusal by him) the court may, at any time on or after that day–

(a) release a person from an obligation imposed on him by or under section 528 of the Companies Act (statement of affairs), or

(b) extend the period specified in subsection (6) of that section.

**5(2)** Accordingly, on and after the appointed day, section 528(6) has effect in relation to a winding up to which this paragraph applies with the omission of the words from "or within" onwards.

## PROVISIONS RELATING TO LIQUIDATOR

**6(1)** This paragraph applies as regards the liquidator in the case of a winding up by the court in England and Wales commenced, or treated as having commenced, before the appointed day.

**6(2)** The official receiver may, at any time when he is liquidator of the company, apply to the Secretary of State for the appointment of a liquidator in his (the official receiver's) place; and on any such application the Secretary of State shall either make an appointment or decline to make one.

**6(3)** Where immediately before the appointed day the liquidator of the company has not made an application under section 545 of the Companies Act (release of liquidators), then–

(a) except where the Secretary of State otherwise directs, sections 146(1) and (2) and 172(8) of this Act apply, and section 545 does not apply, in relation to any liquidator of that company who holds office on or at any time after the appointed day and is not the official receiver;

(b) section 146(3) applies in relation to the carrying out at any time after that day by any liquidator of the company of any of his functions; and

(c) a liquidator in relation to whom section 172(8) has effect by virtue of this paragraph has his release with effect from the time specified in section 174(4)(d) of this Act.

**6(4)** Subsection (6) of section 174 of this Act has effect for the purposes of sub-paragraph (3)(c) above as it has for the purposes of that section, but as if the reference to section 212 were to section 631 of the Companies Act.

**6(5)** The liquidator may employ a solicitor to assist him in the carrying out of his functions without the permission of the committee of inspection; but if he does so employ a solicitor he shall inform the committee of inspection that he has done so.

## WINDING UP UNDER SUPERVISION OF THE COURT

**7** The repeals in Part II of Schedule 10 to the Insolvency Act 1985 of references (in the Companies Act and elsewhere) to a winding up under the supervision of the court do not affect the operation of the enactments in which the references are contained in relation to any case in which an order under section 606 of the Companies Act (power to order winding up under supervision) was made before the appointed day.

## SAVING FOR POWER TO MAKE RULES

**8(1)** Paragraphs 4 to 7 are without prejudice to the power conferred by this Act under which rules made under section 411 may make transitional provision in connection with the coming into force of those rules.

**8(2)** Such provision may apply those rules in relation to a winding up notwithstanding that the winding up commenced, or is treated as having commenced, before the coming into force of the rules or section 411.

## SETTING ASIDE OF PREFERENCES AND OTHER TRANSACTIONS

**9(1)** Where a provision in Part VI of this Act applies in relation to a winding up or in relation to a case in which an administration order has been made, a preference given, floating charge created or other transaction entered into before the appointed day shall not be set aside under that provision except to the extent that it could have been set aside under the law in force immediately before that day, assuming for this purpose that any relevant administration order had been a winding-up order.

**9(2)** The references above to setting aside a preference, floating charge or other transaction include the making of an order which varies or reverses any effect of a preference, floating charge or other transaction.

# Part II – Individual Insolvency

## BANKRUPTCY (GENERAL)

**10(1)** Subject to the following provisions of this Part of this Schedule, so much of this Act as replaces Part III of the Insolvency Act 1985 does not apply in relation to any case in which a petition in bankruptcy was presented, or a receiving order or adjudication in bankruptcy was made, before the appointed day.

**10(2)** In relation to any such case as is mentioned above, the enactments specified in Schedule 8 to that Act, so far as they relate to bankruptcy, and those specified in Parts III and IV of Schedule 10 to that Act, so far as they so relate, have effect without the amendments and repeals specified in those Schedules.

**10(3)** Where any subordinate legislation made under an enactment referred to in sub-paragraph (2) is in force immediately before the appointed day, that subordinate legislation continues to have effect on and after that day in relation to any such case as is mentioned in sub-paragraph (1).

**11(1)** In relation to any such case as is mentioned in paragraph 10(1) the references in any enactment or subordinate legislation to a petition, order or other matter which is provided for under the Bankruptcy Act 1914 and corresponds to a petition, order or other matter provided for under provisions of this Act replacing Part III of the Insolvency Act 1985 continue on and after the appointed day to have effect as references to the petition, order or matter provided for by the Act of 1914; but otherwise those references have effect on and after that day as references to the petition, order or matter provided for by those provisions of this Act.

**11(2)** Without prejudice to sub-paragraph (1), in determining for the purposes of section 279 of this Act (period of bankruptcy) or paragraph 13 below whether any person was an undischarged bankrupt at a time before the appointed day, an adjudication in bankruptcy and an annulment of a bankruptcy under the Act of 1914 are to be taken into account in the same way, respectively, as a bankruptcy order under the provisions of this Act replacing Part III of the Insolvency Act 1985 and the annulment under section 282 of this Act of such an order.

**12** Transactions entered into before the appointed day have effect on and after that day as if references to acts of bankruptcy in the provisions for giving effect to those transactions continued to be references to acts of bankruptcy within the meaning of the Bankruptcy Act 1914, but as if such acts included failure to comply with a statutory demand served under section 268 of this Act.

## DISCHARGE FROM OLD BANKRUPTCY

**13(1)** Where a person–

(a) was adjudged bankrupt before the appointed day or is adjudged on or after that day on a petition presented before that day, and

(b) that person was not an undischarged bankrupt at any time in the period of 15 years ending with the adjudication,

that person is deemed (if not previously discharged) to be discharged from his bankruptcy for the purposes of the Bankruptcy Act 1914 at the end of the discharge period.

**13(2)** Subject to sub-paragraph (3) below, the discharge period for the purposes of this paragraph is–

(a) in the case of a person adjudged bankrupt before the appointed day, the period of 3 years beginning with that day, and

(b) in the case of a person who is adjudged bankrupt on or after that day on a petition presented before that day, the period of 3 years beginning with the date of the adjudication.

**13(3)** Where the court exercising jurisdiction in relation to a bankruptcy to which this paragraph applies is satisfied, on the application of the official receiver, that the bankrupt has failed, or is failing, to comply with any of his obligations under the Bankruptcy Act 1914, any rules made under that Act or any such rules as are mentioned in paragraph 19(1) below, the court may order that the discharge period shall cease to run for such period, or until the fulfilment of such conditions (including a condition requiring the court to be satisfied as to any matter) as may be specified in the order.

## PROVISIONS RELATING TO TRUSTEE

**14(1)** This paragraph applies as regards the trustee in the case of a person adjudged bankrupt before the appointed day, or adjudged bankrupt on or after that day on a petition presented before that day.

**14(2)** The official receiver may at any time when he is trustee of the bankrupt's estate apply to the Secretary of State for the appointment of a person as trustee instead of the official receiver; and on any such application the Secretary of State shall either make an appointment or decline to make one.

**14(3)** Where on the appointed day the trustee of a bankrupt's estate has not made an application under section 93 of the Bankruptcy Act 1914 (release of trustee), then–

(a) except where the Secretary of State otherwise directs, sections 298(8), 304 and 331(1) to (3) of this Act apply, and section 93 of the Act of 1914 does not apply, in relation to any trustee of the bankrupt's estate who holds office on or at any time after the appointed day and is not the official receiver;

(b) section 331(4) of this Act applies in relation to the carrying out at any time on or after the appointed day by the trustee of the bankrupt's estate of any of his functions; and

(c) a trustee in relation to whom section 298(8) of this Act has effect by virtue of this paragraph has his release with effect from the time specified in section 299(3)(d).

**14(4)** Subsection (5) of section 299 has effect for the purposes of sub-paragraph (3)(c) as it has for the purposes of that section.

**14(5)** In the application of subsection (3) of section 331 in relation to a case by virtue of this paragraph, the reference in that subsection to section 330(1) has effect as a reference to section 67 of the Bankruptcy Act 1914.

**14(6)** The trustee of the bankrupt's estate may employ a solicitor to assist him in the carrying out of his functions without the permission of the committee of inspection; but if he does so employ a solicitor, he shall inform the committee of inspection that he has done so.

## COPYRIGHT

**15** Where a person who is adjudged bankrupt on a petition presented on or after the appointed day is liable, by virtue of a transaction entered into before that day, to pay royalties or a share of the profits to any person in respect of any copyright or interest in copyright comprised in the bankrupt's estate, section 60 of the Bankruptcy Act 1914 (limitation on trustee's powers in relation to copyright) applies in relation to the trustee of that estate as it applies in relation to a trustee in bankruptcy under the Act of 1914.

## SECOND BANKRUPTCY

**16(1)** Sections 334 and 335 of this Act apply with the following modifications where the earlier bankruptcy (within the meaning of section 334) is a bankruptcy in relation to which the Act of 1914 applies instead of the second Group of Parts in this Act, that is to say–

(a) references to property vested in the existing trustee under section 307(3) of this Act have effect as references to such property vested in that trustee as was acquired by or devolved on the bankrupt after the commencement (within the meaning of the Act of 1914) of the earlier bankruptcy; and

(b) references to an order under section 310 of this Act have effect as references to an order under section 51 of the Act of 1914.

**16(2)** Section 39 of the Act of 1914 (second bankruptcy) does not apply where a person who is an undischarged bankrupt under that Act is adjudged bankrupt under this Act.

### SETTING ASIDE OF PREFERENCES AND OTHER TRANSACTIONS

**17(1)** A preference given, assignment made or other transaction entered into before the appointed day shall not be set aside under any of sections 339 to 344 of this Act except to the extent that it could have been set aside under the law in force immediately before that day.

**17(2)** References in sub-paragraph (1) to setting aside a preference assignment or other transaction include the making of any order which varies or reverses any effect of a preference, assignment or other transaction.

### BANKRUPTCY OFFENCES

**18(1)** Where a bankruptcy order is made under this Act on or after the appointed day, a person is not guilty of an offence under Chapter VI of Part IX in respect of anything done before that day; but, notwithstanding the repeal by the Insolvency Act 1985 of the Bankruptcy Act 1914, is guilty of an offence under the Act of 1914 in respect of anything done before the appointed day which would have been an offence under that Act if the making of the bankruptcy order had been the making of a receiving order under that Act.

**18(2)** Subsection (5) of section 350 of this Act applies (instead of sections 157(2), 158(2), 161 and 165 of the Act of 1914) in relation to proceedings for an offence under that Act which are instituted (whether by virtue of sub-paragraph (1) or otherwise) after the appointed day.

### POWER TO MAKE RULES

**19(1)** The preceding provisions of this Part of this Schedule are without prejudice to the power conferred by this Act under which rules under section 412 may make transitional provision in connection with the coming into force of those rules; and such provision may apply those rules in relation to a bankruptcy notwithstanding that it arose from a petition presented before either the coming into force of the rules or the appointed day.

**19(2)** Rules under section 412 may provide for such notices served before the appointed day as may be prescribed to be treated for the purposes of this Act as statutory demands served under section 268.

## Part III – Transitional Effect of Part XVI

**20(1)** A transaction entered into before the appointed day shall not be set aside under Part XVI of this Act except to the extent that it could have been set aside under the law in force immediately before that day.

**20(2)** References above to setting aside a transaction include the making of any order which varies or reverses any effect of a transaction.

## Part IV – Insolvency Practitioners

**21** Where an individual began to act as an insolvency practitioner in relation to any person before the appointed day, nothing in section 390(2) or (3) prevents that individual from being qualified to act as an insolvency practitioner in relation to that person.

## Part V – General Transitional Provisions and Savings

### INTERPRETATION FOR THIS PART

**22** In this Part of this Schedule, **"the former enactments"** means so much of the Companies Act as is repealed and replaced by this Act, the Insolvency Act 1985 and the other enactments repealed by this Act.

## GENERAL SAVING FOR PAST ACTS AND EVENTS

**23** So far as anything done or treated as done under or for the purposes of any provision of the former enactments could have been done under or for the purposes of the corresponding provision of this Act, it is not invalidated by the repeal of that provision but has effect as if done under or for the purposes of the corresponding provision; and any order, regulation, rule or other instrument made or having effect under any provision of the former enactments shall, insofar as its effect is preserved by this paragraph, be treated for all purposes as made and having effect under the corresponding provision.

## PERIODS OF TIME

**24** Where any period of time specified in a provision of the former enactments is current immediately before the appointed day, this Act has effect as if the corresponding provision had been in force when the period began to run; and (without prejudice to the foregoing) any period of time so specified and current is deemed for the purposes of this Act–

(a) to run from the date or event from which it was running immediately before the appointed day, and

(b) to expire (subject to any provision of this Act for its extension) whenever it would have expired if this Act had not been passed;

and any rights, priorities, liabilities, reliefs, obligations, requirements, powers, duties or exemptions dependent on the beginning, duration or end of such a period as above mentioned shall be under this Act as they were or would have been under the former enactments.

## INTERNAL CROSS-REFERENCES IN THIS ACT

**25** Where in any provision of this Act there is a reference to another such provision, and the first-mentioned provision operates, or is capable of operating, in relation to things done or omitted, or events occurring or not occurring, in the past (including in particular past acts of compliance with any enactment, failures of compliance, contraventions, offences and convictions of offences), the reference to the other provision is to be read as including a reference to the corresponding provision of the former enactments.

## PUNISHMENT OF OFFENCES

**26(1)** Offences committed before the appointed day under any provision of the former enactments may, notwithstanding any repeal by this Act, be prosecuted and punished after that day as if this Act had not passed.

**26(2)** A contravention of any provision of the former enactments committed before the appointed day shall not be visited with any severer punishment under or by virtue of this Act than would have been applicable under that provision at the time of the contravention; but where an offence for the continuance of which a penalty was provided has been committed under any provision of the former enactments, proceedings may be taken under this Act in respect of the continuance of the offence on and after the appointed day in the like manner as if the offence had been committed under the corresponding provision of this Act.

## REFERENCES ELSEWHERE TO THE FORMER ENACTMENTS

**27(1)** A reference in any enactment, instrument or document (whether express or implied, and in whatever phraseology) to a provision of the former enactments (including the corresponding provision of any yet earlier enactment) is to be read, where necessary to retain for the enactment, instrument or document the same force and effect as it would have had but for the passing of this Act, as, or as including, a reference to the corresponding provision by which it is replaced in this Act.

**27(2)** The generality of the preceding sub-paragraph is not affected by any specific conversion of references made by this Act, nor by the inclusion in any provision of this Act of a reference (whether express or implied, and in whatever phraseology) to the provision of the former enactments corresponding to that provision, or to a provision of the former enactments which is replaced by a corresponding provision of this Act.

## SAVING FOR POWER TO REPEAL PROVISIONS IN SECTION 51

**28** The Secretary of State may by order in a statutory instrument repeal subsections (3) to (5) of section 51 of this Act and the entries in Schedule 10 relating to subsections (4) and (5) of that section.

## SAVING FOR INTERPRETATION ACT 1978 SS. 16, 17

**29** Nothing in this Schedule is to be taken as prejudicing sections 16 and 17 of the Interpretation Act 1978 (savings from, and effect of, repeals); and for the purposes of section 17(2) of that Act (construction of references to enactments repealed and replaced, etc.), so much of section 18 of the Insolvency Act 1985 as is replaced by a provision of this Act is deemed to have been repealed by this Act and not by the Company Directors Disqualification Act 1986.

# Schedule 12 – Enactments Repealed

Section 438

| Chapter | Short title | Extent of repeal |
|---|---|---|
| 1970 c. 8. | The Insolvency Services (Accounting and Investment) Act 1970. | The whole Act. |
| 1976 c. 60. | The Insolvency Act 1976. | Section 3. |
| 1985 c. 6. | The Companies Act 1985. | In Section 463(4), the words "Subject to section 617". |
| | | Sections 467 to 485. |
| | | In section 486, in the definition of "company" the words "other than in Chapter II of this Part"; and the definitions of "instrument of appointment", "prescribed", "receiver" and "register of charges". |
| | | Sections 488 to 650. |
| | | Sections 659 to 664. |
| | | Sections 665 to 674. |
| | | Section 709(4). |
| | | Section 710(4). |
| | | Section 724. |
| | | Schedule 16. |
| | | In Schedule 24, the entries relating to the section 467; all entries thereafter up to and including section 641(2); and the entry relating to section 710(4). |
| 1985 c. 65. | The Insolvency Act 1985. | Sections 1 to 11. |
| | | Section 15. |
| | | Section 17. |
| | | Section 19. |
| | | Sections 20 to 107. |
| | | Section 108(1) and (3) to (7). |
| | | Sections 109 to 211. |
| | | Sections 212 to 214. |
| | | Section 216. |
| | | Section 217(1) to (3). |
| | | Sections 221 to 234. |
| | | In section 235, subsections (2) to (5). |
| | | In section 236, subsections (3) to (5). |
| | | In Schedule 1, paragraphs 1 to 4, and sub-paragraph (4) of paragraph 5. |
| | | Schedules 3 to 5. |
| | | In Schedule 6, paragraphs 5, 6, 9, 15 to 17, 20 to 22, 25 to 44 and 48 to 52. |
| | | Schedule 7. |

| Chapter | Short title | Extent of repeal |
|---|---|---|
| | | In Schedule 9, paragraphs 1 and 4 to 24.<br>Schedule 10. |
| 1985 c. 66. | The Bankruptcy (Scotland) Act 1985. | In Schedule 7, paragraphs 19 to 22. |
| 1986 c. 44. | The Gas Act 1986. | In Schedule 7, paragraph 31. |

# Schedule 13 – Consequential Amendments of Companies Act 1985

Section 439(1)

## Part I – Internal and Other Section References Amended or Re-amended

| Section of Act | Consequential amendment or re-amendment |
|---|---|
| Section 13(4) | After "this Act", add "and the Insolvency Act". |
| Section 44(7) | In paragraph (a), for "section 582" substitute "section 110 of the Insolvency Act". |
| Section 103(7) | In paragraph (a), the same amendment. |
| Section 131(7) | The same amendment. |
| Section 140(2) | In paragraph (b), for "section 518" substitute "section 123 of the Insolvency Act". |
| Section 153(3) | In paragraph (f), for "section 582" substitute "section 110 of the Insolvency Act".<br>In paragraph (g), for "Chapter II of Part II of the Insolvency Act 1985" substitute "Part I of the Insolvency Act". |
| Section 156(3) | For "section 517" substitute "section 122 of the Insolvency Act". |
| Section 173(4) | The same amendment. |
| Section 196 | For this section substitute–<br>"196.–(1) The following applies in the case of a company registered in England and Wales, where debentures of the company are secured by a charge which, as created, was a floating charge.<br>(2) If possession is taken, by or on behalf of the holders of any of the debentures, of any property comprised in or subject to the charge, and the company is not at that time in course of being wound up, the company's preferential debts shall be paid out of assets coming to the hands of the person taking possession in priority to any claims for principal or interest in respect of the debentures.<br>(3) "Preferential debts" means the categories of debts listed in Schedule 6 to the Insolvency Act; and for the purposes of that Schedule "the relevant date" is the date of possession being taken as above mentioned. |



CCH.New Law
bbcl insa 1986b Mp 1440—bcl98 2a

| Section of Act | Consequential amendment or re-amendment |
|---|---|
| | (4) Payments made under this section shall be recouped, as far as may be, out of the assets of the company available for payment of general creditors." |
| Section 380(4) | In paragraph (j), for "section 572(1)(a)" substitute "section 84(1)(a) of the Insolvency Act". |
| Section 441(1) | For "section 13 of the Insolvency Act 1985" substitute "section 8 of the Company Directors Disqualification Act 1986". |
| Section 449(1) | In paragraph (ba), for "section 12 or 13 of the Insolvency Act 1985" substitute "section 6, 7 or 8 of the Company Directors Disqualification Act 1986". |
| Section 461(6) | For "section 106 of the Insolvency Act 1985" substitute "section 411 of the Insolvency Act". |
| Section 462(5) | After "this Part" insert "and Part III of the Insolvency Act 1986". |
| Section 463(2) | For "Part XX (except section 623(4))" substitute "Part IV of the Insolvency Act (except section 185)". |
| Section 463(3) | For this subsection substitute–<br>"(3) Nothing in this section derogates from the provisions of sections 53(7) and 54(6) of the Insolvency Act (attachment of floating charge on appointment of receiver), or prejudices the operation of sections 175 and 176 of that Act (payment of preferential debts in winding up)". |
| Section 464(6) | For "section 89 of the Insolvency Act 1985" substitute "sections 175 and 176 of the Insolvency Act". |
| Section 657(2) | For "subsections (3) and (5) to (7) of section 91 of the Insolvency Act 1985 and section 92 of that Act" substitute "section 178(4) and sections 179 to 182 of the Insolvency Act". |
| Section 658(1) | For "Subsection (7) of section 91 of the Insolvency Act 1985" substitute "Section 180 of the Insolvency Act". |
| Section 711(2) | In paragraph (b), for "section 600" substitute "section 109 of the Insolvency Act". |
| Section 733 | In subsection (1), omit "295(7)".<br>In subsection (3), for "216(3) or 295(7)" substitute "or 216(3)". |

**History**
In Pt. I entries relating to s. 222(4) and 225 repealed by CA 1989, s. 212 and Sch. 24 as from 1 April 1990 (see SI 1990/355 (C 13), art. 5(1)(d)); the entries formerly read as follows:

| Section of Act | Consequential amendment or re-amendment |
|---|---|
| "Section 222(4) | For 'section 106 of the Insolvency Act 1985' substitute 'section 411 of the Insolvency Act'. |
| Section 225 | At the end of the section add–<br>'(8) At any time when an administration order under Part II of the Insolvency Act is in force, this section has effect as if subsections (3) and (5) to (7) were omitted'." |

# Part II – Amendment of Part XXVI (Interpretation)

In Part XXVI of the Companies Act, after section 735, insert the following section–

"*Relationship of this Act to Insolvency Act*

**735A(1)** In this Act **"the Insolvency Act"** means the Insolvency Act 1986; and in the following provisions of this Act, namely, sections 375(1)(b), 425(6)(a), 440, 449(1)(a) and (d), 460(2), 675, 676, 677, 699(1), 728 and Schedule 21, paragraph 6(1), the words "this Act" are to be read as including Parts I to VII of that Act, sections 411, 413, 414, 416 and 417 in Part XV of that Act, and also the Company Directors Disqualification Act 1986.

**735A(2)** In sections 704(5), 706(1), 707(1), 708(1)(a) and (4), 710(5), 713(1), 729 and 732(3) references to the Companies Acts include Parts I to VII of the Insolvency Act, sections 411, 413, 414, 416 and 417 in Part XV of that Act, and also the Company Directors Disqualification Act 1986.

**735A(3)** Subsections (1) and (2) apply unless the contrary intention appears."

# Schedule 14 – Consequential Amendments of other Enactments

Section 439(2)

| Enactment | Amendment |
|---|---|
| Deeds of Arrangement Act 1914 (c. 47): | |
| Section 3(1) | For "Part III of the Insolvency Act 1985" substitute "Parts VIII to XI of the Insolvency Act 1986". |
| Section 3(4) | The same amendment. |
| Section 11(1) and (2) | In each subsection, the same amendment. |
| Section 15(1) | For "section 207 of the Insolvency Act 1985" substitute "section 412 of the Insolvency Act 1986". |
| Section 16 | The same amendment as of section 3(1). |
| Section 23 | The same amendment. |
| Section 30(1) | For the definition of "property" substitute–<br>""property" has the meaning given by section 436 of the Insolvency Act 1986". |
| Law of Property Act 1925 (c. 20): | |
| Section 52(2)(b) | For "section 91 or 161 of the Insolvency Act 1985" substitute "sections 178 to 180 or sections 315 to 319 of the Insolvency Act 1986". |
| Land Registration Act 1925 (c. 21): | |
| Section 42(2) | For "section 161 of the Insolvency Act 1985" substitute "sections 315 to 319 of the Insolvency Act 1986". |
| Third Parties (Rights against Insurers) Act 1930 (c. 25): | |
| Section 1 | In subsection (1)(b), for the words from "a composition" to "that Chapter" substitute "a voluntary arrangement proposed for the purposes of Part I of the Insolvency Act 1986 being approved under that Part".<br>In subsection (2), for "228 of the Insolvency Act 1985" substitute "421 of the Insolvency Act 1986".<br>In subsection (3), the same amendment. |

| Enactment | Amendment |
|---|---|
| Section 2 | In subsection (1), the same amendment as of section 1(2).<br>In subsection (1A), for the words from "composition or scheme" to the end of the subsection substitute "voluntary arrangement proposed for the purposes of, and approved under, Part I or Part VIII of the Insolvency Act 1986". |
| Section 4 | In paragraph (b), the same amendment as of section 1(2). |
| Agricultural Marketing Act 1958 (c. 47): | |
| Schedule 2 | For paragraph 4 substitute—<br>"4.—(1) A scheme shall provide for the winding up of the board, and for that purpose may apply Part V of the Insolvency Act 1986 (winding up of unregistered companies), subject to the following modifications.<br>(2) For the purposes of sections 221, 222 and 224 of the Act of 1986, the principal place of business of the board is deemed to be the office of the board the address of which is registered by the Minister under paragraph 3 above.<br>(3) Section 223 does not apply.<br>(4) Section 224 applies as if the words "or any member of it as such" were omitted.<br>(5) A petition for winding up the board may be presented by the Minister as well as by any person authorised under Part IV of the Insolvency Act 1986 to present a petition for winding up a company". |
| Charities Act 1960 (c. 58): | |
| Section 30(1) | For "Companies Act 1985" substitute "Insolvency Act 1986". |
| Licensing Act 1964 (c. 26): | |
| Section 8(1) | In paragraph (c), for the words from "composition or scheme" to "Act 1985" substitute "voluntary arrangement proposed by the holder of the licence has been approved under Part VIII of the Insolvency Act 1986"; and for "composition or scheme" substitute "voluntary arrangement". |
| Section 10(5) | For the words from "composition or scheme" to "Act 1985" substitute "voluntary arrangement proposed by the holder of a justices' licence has been approved under Part VIII of the Insolvency Act 1986"; and for "composition or scheme" substitute "voluntary arrangement". |
| Industrial and Provident Societies Act 1965 (c. 12): | |
| Section 55 | For "Companies Act 1985" substitute "Insolvency Act 1986". |
| Medicine Act 1968 (c. 67): | |
| Section 72(4) | For the words from "composition or scheme" to the end of the subsection substitute "voluntary arrangement proposed for the purposes of, and approved under, Part VIII of the Insolvency Act 1986". |
| Conveyancing and Feudal Reform (Scotland) Act 1970 (c. 35): | |

| Enactment | Amendment |
|---|---|
| Schedule 3 | In Standard Condition 9(2)(b), for "228 of the Insolvency Act 1985" substitute "421 of the Insolvency Act 1986". |
| Superannuation Act 1972 (c. 11): | |
| Section 5(2) | For "156 of the Insolvency Act 1985" substitute "310 of the Insolvency Act 1986"; and for "the said section 156" substitute "the said section 310". |
| Land Charges Act 1972 (c. 61): | |
| Section 16(2) | For "207 of the Insolvency Act 1985" substitute "412 of the Insolvency Act 1986"; and for "Part III" substitute "Parts VIII to XI". |
| Matrimonial Causes Act 1973 (c. 18): | |
| Section 39 | For "section 174 of the Insolvency Act 1985" substitute "section 339 or 340 of the Insolvency Act 1986". |
| Powers of Criminal Courts Act 1973 (c. 62): | |
| Section 39(3): | In paragraph (d), for "174(10) of the Insolvency Act 1985" substitute "341(4) of the Insolvency Act 1986". |
| Friendly Societies Act 1974 (c. 46): | |
| Section 87(2) | For "Companies Act 1985" substitute "Insolvency Act 1986". |
| Recess Elections Act 1975 (c. 66): | |
| Section 1(2) | In the definition of "certificate of vacancy", for "214(6)(a) of the Insolvency Act 1985" substitute "427(6)(a) of the Insolvency Act 1986". |
| Policyholders Protection Act 1975 (c. 75): | |
| Section 5(1)(a) | For "Companies Act 1985" substitute "Insolvency Act 1986". |
| Section 15(1) | For "532 of the Companies Act 1985" substitute "135 of the Insolvency Act 1986". |
| Section 16(1)(b) | The same amendment as of section 5(1)(a). |
| Development Land Tax Act 1976 (c. 24): | |
| Section 33(1) | For "538 of the Companies Act 1985" substitute "145 of the Insolvency Act 1986". |
| Restrictive Trade Practices Act 1976 (c. 34): | |
| Schedule 1 | For paragraph 9A (inserted by Insolvency Act 1985, section 217(4)) substitute—<br>"9A. Insolvency services within the meaning of section 428 of the Insolvency Act 1986". |
| Credit Unions Act 1979 (c. 34): | |

| Enactment | Amendment |
|---|---|
| Section 6(1) | For "517(1)(e) of the Companies Act 1985" substitute "122(1)(e) of the Insolvency Act 1986"; and for "517(1)(e) of the Act of 1985" substitute "122(1)(e) of the Act of 1986". |
| Banking Act 1979 (c. 37): | |
| Section 6(3) | In paragraph (b), for "Part XXI of the Companies Act 1985" substitute "Part V of the Insolvency Act 1986". |
| Section 18 | In subsection (1), for "Companies Act 1985" substitute "Insolvency Act 1986"; and in paragraph (a) of the subsection for "518" substitute "123".<br>In subsection (2), for "Companies Act 1985" substitute "Insolvency Act 1986"; and for "Part XXI" substitute "Part V".<br>In subsection (4)—<br>in paragraph (a), for "Companies Act 1985" substitute "Insolvency Act 1986";<br>in paragraph (b), for "518 of the said Act of 1985" substitute "123 of the said Act of 1986"; and<br>in paragraph (c), for "Part XXI of the said Act of 1985" substitute "Part V of the said Act of 1986". |
| Section 19 | In subsection (2), for paragraph (ba) substitute—<br>"(ba) in connection with any proceedings under any provision of—<br>(i) Part XVIII or XX of the Companies Act 1985, or<br>(ii) Parts I to VII of the Insolvency Act 1986 (other than sections 236 and 237)".<br>In subsection (8), for paragraphs (a) and (aa) substitute—<br>"(a) for the references in subsection (2) to Part XVIII or XX of the Companies Act 1985 and Parts I to VII of the Insolvency Act 1986, there shall be substituted references to Parts V, VI and IX of the Companies Act (Northern Ireland) 1960 (the reference to sections 236 and 237 of the Act of 1986 being disregarded)". |
| Section 28 | In subsection (3), in paragraph (c), for "83 of the Insolvency Act 1985" substitute "95 of the Insolvency Act 1986".<br>In subsection (4), in paragraph (a), for "Part XXI of the Companies Act 1985" substitute "Part V of the Insolvency Act 1986".<br>In subsection (6)(b), for sub-paragraphs (ii) to (iv) substitute—<br>"(ii) to be a member of a liquidation committee established under Part IV or V of the Insolvency Act 1986;<br>(iii) to be a member of a creditors committee appointed under section 301 of that Act; and<br>(iv) to be a commissioner under section 30 of the Bankruptcy (Scotland) Act 1985";<br>(v) to be a member of a committee of inspection appointed for the purposes of Part V or Part IX of the Companies Act (Northern Ireland) 1960; |

| Enactment | Amendment |
|---|---|
| | and (in the passage following sub-paragraph (iv)) for "such a committee as is mentioned in paragraph (b)(ii) or (iv) above" substitute "a liquidation committee, creditors' committee or committee of inspection". |
| | In subsection (7), in paragraph (b), for the words from "section 116(4)" to the end of the paragraph substitute "section 261(1) of the Insolvency Act 1986 to any person in whom the property of the firm is vested under section 282(4) of that Act". |
| Section 31(7) | For paragraph (a) substitute— "(a) for England and Wales, under sections 411 and 412 of the Insolvency Act 1986"; and in paragraph (b) for "the said section 106" substitute "section 411 of that Act". |
| British Aerospace Act 1980 (c. 26): | |
| Section 9(1) | In paragraph (a), for "Companies Act 1985" substitute "Insolvency Act 1986". |
| Public Passenger Vehicles Act 1981 (c. 14): | |
| Section 19(3) | In paragraph (a), for "Chapter III of Part II of the Insolvency Act 1985" substitute "Part II of the Insolvency Act 1986". |
| Supreme Court Act 1981 (c. 54): | |
| Section 40A(2) | For "section 179 of the Insolvency Act 1985" substitute "section 346 of the Insolvency Act 1986"; and for "621 of the Companies Act 1985" substitute "183 of the Insolvency Act 1986". |
| Trustee Savings Banks Act 1981 (c. 65): | |
| Section 31 | In paragraph (b), for "666 to 669 of the Companies Act 1985" substitute "221 to 224 of the Insolvency Act 1986". |
| Section 54(2) | For "666(6) of the Companies Act 1985" substitute "221(6) of the Insolvency Act 1986". |
| Iron and Steel Act 1982 (c. 25): | |
| Schedule 4 | In paragraph 3(3) after "Companies Act 1985" insert "or the Insolvency Act 1986". |
| Civil Jurisdiction and Judgments Act 1982 (c. 27): | |
| Section 18(3) | In paragraph (ba), for "213 of the Insolvency Act 1985" substitute "426 of the Insolvency Act 1986". |
| Schedule 5 | In paragraph (1), for "Companies Act 1985" substitute "Insolvency Act 1986". |
| Insurance Companies Act 1982 (c. 50): | |
| Section 53 | For "Companies Act" (the first time) substitute "Insolvency Act 1986"; and for "Companies Act" (the second time) substitute "that Act of 1986". |

| Enactment | Amendment |
|---|---|
| Section 54 | In subsection (1), for "the Companies Act" (the first time) substitute "Part IV or V of the Insolvency Act 1986"; and in paragraph (a), for "518 or sections 667 to 669" substitute "123 or sections 222 to 224".<br>In subsection (4) for "Companies Act" (the first time) substitute "Insolvency Act 1986". |
| Section 55 | In subsection (5), for "subsection (3) of section 540 of the Companies Act" substitute "section 168(2) of the Insolvency Act 1986".<br>In subsection (6), for "631 of the Companies Act" substitute "212 of the Insolvency Act 1986". |
| Section 56 | In subsection (4), for "Section 90(5) of the Insolvency Act 1985" substitute "Section 177(5) of the Insolvency Act 1986"; and for "section 90 of the said Act of 1985" substitute "section 177 of the said Act of 1986".<br>In subsection (7), for "section 539(1) of the Companies Act" substitute "section 167 of, and Schedule 4 to, the Insolvency Act 1986". |
| Section 59 | In subsection (1), for "106 of the Insolvency Act 1985" substitute "411 of the Insolvency Act 1986".<br>In subsection (2), for "106 of the Insolvency Act 1985" substitute "411 of the Insolvency Act 1986"; and for "section 89 of, and Schedule 4 to, the Insolvency Act 1985" substitute "sections 175 and 176 of, and Schedule 6 to, the Insolvency Act 1986". |
| Section 96(1) | In the definition of "insolvent", for "517 and 518 or section 666 of the Companies Act" substitute "122 and 123 or section 221 of the Insolvency Act 1986". |
| Telecommunications Act 1984 (c. 12): | |
| Section 68(1) | In paragraph (a), for "Companies Act 1985" substitute "Insolvency Act 1986". |
| County Courts Act 1984 (c. 28): | |
| Section 98 | For subsection (3) substitute—<br>"(3) The provisions of this section have effect subject to those of sections 183, 184 and 346 of the Insolvency Act 1986". |
| Section 102 | For subsection (8) substitute—<br>"(8) Nothing in this section affects section 346 of the Insolvency Act 1986". |
| Section 109(2) | For "179 of the Insolvency Act 1985" substitute "346 of the Insolvency Act 1986". |
| Finance Act 1985 (c. 54): | |
| Section 79 | Omit the word "altogether"; and after "Companies Act 1985" insert "sections 110 and 111 of the Insolvency Act 1986". |
| Housing Act 1985 (c. 68): | |
| Schedule 18 | In paragraphs 3(4) and 5(3), for "228 of the Insolvency Act 1985" substitute "421 of the Insolvency Act 1986". |

**History**

**(1)** In Sch. 14 the entry relating to the Exchange Control Act 1947 repealed by the Finance Act 1987, s. 72(7) and Sch. 16 as from 15 May 1987; the entry formerly read as follows:

| Enactment | Amendment |
|---|---|
| "Exchange Control Act 1947 (c. 14): | |
| Schedule 4 | In paragraphs 6 and 8(4), for "section 120 of the Insolvency Act 1985" substitute "sections 267 to 270 of the Insolvency Act 1986"." |

**(2)** In Sch. 14 entries relating to the Income and Corporation Taxes Act 1970, the Finance Act 1972, the Finance Act 1981 and the Finance Act 1983 repealed by Income and Corporation Taxes Act 1988, s. 844 and Sch. 31 for companies' accounting periods ending after 5 April 1988 (see s. 843(1)): the entries formerly read as follows:

| Enactment | Amendment |
|---|---|
| "Income and Corporation Taxes Act 1970 (c. 10): | |
| Section 247(7) | For 'Companies Act 1985' substitute 'Insolvency Act 1986'. |
| Section 265(5) | For '538 of the Companies Act 1985' substitute '145 of the Insolvency Act 1986'. |
| Finance Act 1972 (c. 41): | |
| Schedule 16 | In paragraph 13(5), for 'Companies Act 1985' substitute 'Insolvency Act 1986'. |
| Finance Act 1981 (c. 35): | |
| Section 55(4) | For 'Companies Act 1985' substitute 'Insolvency Act 1986'. |
| Finance Act 1983 (c. 28): | |
| Schedule 5 | In paragraph 5(4), for 'Companies Act 1985' substitute 'Insolvency Act 1986'." |

**(3)** In Sch. 14 entry relating to Land Registration Act 1925, s. 112AA(3)(a) repealed by Land Registration Act 1988, s. 2: the entry formerly read as follows:

| Enactment | Amendment |
|---|---|
| "Section 112AA(3)(a) | For 'the Insolvency Act 1985 or the Companies Act 1985' substitute 'the Insolvency Act 1986'." |

**(4)** In Sch. 14 entry relating to Employment Protection (Consolidation) Act 1978, s. 125(2) repealed by Employment Act 1989, s. 29(4) and Sch. 7 as from 16 November 1989: the entry formerly read as follows:

| Enactment | Amendment |
|---|---|
| "Section 125(2) | For paragraph (a) substitute—<br>'(a) the following provisions of the Insolvency Act 1986—<br>(i) sections 175 and 176, 328 and 329, 348 and Schedule 6, and<br>(ii) any rules under that Act applying section 348 of it to the winding up of a company; and'" |

**(5)** In Sch. 14 the entry relating to the Road Traffic Act 1972 repealed by the Road Traffic (Consequential Provisions) Act 1988, s. 3 and Sch. 1 as from 15 May 1989; the entry formerly read as follows:

| Enactment | Amendment |
|---|---|
| "Road Traffic Act 1972 (c. 20): | |
| Section 150 | In subsection (1)(b), for "228 of the Insolvency Act 1985" substitute "421 of the Insolvency Act 1986".<br>In subsection (2), the same amendment." |

**(6)** In Sch. 14 entry relating to Tribunals and Inquiries Act 1971 repealed by Tribunals and Inquiries Act 1992, s. 18(2), 19 and Sch. 4, Pt. I as from 1 October 1992; the entry formerly read as follows:

| Enactment | Amendment |
|---|---|
| "Tribunals and Inquiries Act 1971 (c. 62): | |
| Schedule 1 | For paragraph 10A substitute—<br>'10A. The Insolvency Practitioners Tribunal referred to in section 396 of the Insolvency Act 1986'." |


bbcl insa 1986b Mp 1448—bcl98 2a

**(7)** In Sch. 14 the entries relating to the Social Security Pensions Act 1975 repealed by the Pension Schemes Act 1993, s. 188(1) and Sch. 5, as from 7 February 1994 (see SI 1994/86); the entry formerly read as follows:

| Enactment | Amendment |
|---|---|
| "Social Security Pensions Act 1975 (c. 60): | |
| Section 58 | The section is to have effect as originally enacted, and without the amendment made by paragraph 26(1) of Schedule 8 to the Insolvency Act 1985. |
| Schedule 3 | At the end of paragraph 3(1) add—<br>"or (in the case of a company not in liquidation)—<br>(a) the appointment of a receiver as mentioned in section 40 of the Insolvency Act 1986 (debenture-holders secured by floating charge), or<br>(b) the appointment of a receiver under section 53(6) or 54(5) of that Act (Scottish company with property subject to floating charge), or<br>(c) the taking of possession by debenture-holders (so secured) as mentioned in section 196 of the Companies Act 1985".<br>In paragraph 4, for the words from the beginning to "Act 1985" substitute "Section 196(3) of the Companies Act 1985 and section 387 of the Insolvency Act 1986 apply as regards the meaning in this Schedule of the expression 'the relevant date'."." |

**(8)** In Sch. 14 entries relating to the Employment Protection (Consolidation) Act 1978 repealed by Employment Rights Act 1996, s. 242, 243 and Sch. 3, Part I as from 22 August 1996; the entries formerly read as follows:

| Enactment | Amendment |
|---|---|
| "Employment Protection (Consolidation) Act 1978 (c. 44): | |
| Section 106(5) | In paragraph (b), for "228 of the Insolvency Act 1985" substitute "421 of the Insolvency Act 1986".<br>In paragraph (c), for the words from "a composition or" to the end of the paragraph substitute "a voluntary arrangement proposed for the purposes of Part I of the Insolvency Act 1986 is approved under that Part". |
| Section 106(6) | The same amendment as of section 106(5)(c). |
| Section 122 | In subsection (7), for "181 of the Insolvency Act 1985" substitute "348 of the Insolvency Act 1986"; and for "section 106" substitute "section 411".<br>In subsection (9), for the words from "composition or scheme" to "Act 1985" substitute "voluntary arrangement proposed for the purposes of, and approved under, Part I or VIII of the Insolvency Act 1986". |
| Section 123(6) | For the words from "composition or scheme" to "Act 1985" substitute "voluntary arrangement proposed for the purposes of, and approved under, Part I or VIII of the Insolvency Act 1986". |
| Section 127(1) | In paragraph (b), for "228 of the Insolvency Act 1985" substitute "421 of the Insolvency Act 1986".<br>In paragraph (c), for the words from "composition or" to the end of the paragraph substitute "voluntary arrangement proposed for the purposes of Part I of the Insolvency Act 1986 is approved under that Part". |
| Section 127(2) | In paragraph (c), the same amendment as of section 127(1)(c)." |

**(9)** In Sch. 14 the entry relating to the Arbitration Act 1950 repealed by the Arbitration Act 1996, s. 107(2) and Sch. 4 as from 31 January 1997 (see SI 1996/3146); the entry formerly read as follows:

| Enactment | Amendment |
|---|---|
| "Arbitration Act 1950 (c. 27: | |
| Section 3(2) | For "committee established under section 148 of the Insolvency Act 1985" substitute "creditors' committee established under section 301 of the Insolvency Act 1986"." |

# COMPANY DIRECTORS DISQUALIFICATION ACT 1986

---

Table of Contents

# COMPANY DIRECTORS DISQUALIFICATION ACT 1986

(1986 Chapter 46)

## ARRANGEMENT OF SECTIONS

## SCHEDULES

# COMPANY DIRECTORS DISQUALIFICATION ACT 1986

(1986 Chapter 46)

An Act to consolidate certain enactments relating to the disqualification of persons from being directors of companies, and from being otherwise concerned with a company's affairs.

*[25th July 1986]*

PRELIMINARY

## 1 Disqualification orders: general

**1(1) [Disqualification order]** In the circumstances specified below in this Act a court may, and under section 6 shall, make against a person a disqualification order, that is to say an order that he shall not, without leave of the court—

(a) be a director of a company, or

(b) be a liquidator or administrator of a company, or

(c) be a receiver or manager of a company's property, or

(d) in any way, whether directly or indirectly, be concerned or take part in the promotion, formation or management of a company,

for a specified period beginning with the date of the order.

**1(2) [Maximum, minimum periods]** In each section of this Act which gives to a court power or, as the case may be, imposes on it the duty to make a disqualification order there is specified the maximum (and, in section 6, the minimum) period of disqualification which may or (as the case may be) must be imposed by means of the order.

**1(3) [Where two orders]** Where a disqualification order is made against a person who is already subject to such an order, the periods specified in those orders shall run concurrently.

**1(4) [Criminal grounds]** A disqualification order may be made on grounds which are or include matters other than criminal convictions, notwithstanding that the person in respect of whom it is to be made may be criminally liable in respect of those matters.

DISQUALIFICATION FOR GENERAL MISCONDUCT IN CONNECTION WITH COMPANIES

## 2 Disqualification on conviction of indictable offence

**2(1) [Court's power]** The court may make a disqualification order against a person where he is convicted of an indictable offence (whether on indictment or summarily) in connection with the promotion, formation, management, liquidation or striking off of a company, or with the receivership or management of a company's property.

**History**
In s. 2(1) the words ", liquidation or striking off" substituted for the former words "or liquidation" by Deregulation and Contracting Out Act 1994, s. 39 and Sch. 11, para. 6 as from 1 July 1995 (see SI 1995/1433(C. 31), art. 1, 3(c), (d).

**2(2) ["The court"]** **"The court"** for this purpose means—

(a) any court having jurisdiction to wind up the company in relation to which the offence was committed, or

(b) the court by or before which the person is convicted of the offence, or

(c) in the case of a summary conviction in England and Wales, any other magistrates' court acting for the same petty sessions area;

and for the purposes of this section the definition of **"indictable offence"** in Schedule 1 to the Interpretation Act 1978 applies for Scotland as it does for England and Wales.

**2(3) [Maximum period]** The maximum period of disqualification under this section is—
(a) where the disqualification order is made by a court of summary jurisdiction, 5 years, and
(b) in any other case, 15 years.

## 3 Disqualification for persistent breaches of companies legislation

**3(1) [Court's power]** The court may make a disqualification order against a person where it appears to it that he has been persistently in default in relation to provisions of the companies legislation requiring any return, account or other document to be filed with, delivered or sent, or notice of any matter to be given, to the registrar of companies.

**3(2) [Conclusive proof of default]** On an application to the court for an order to be made under this section, the fact that a person has been persistently in default in relation to such provisions as are mentioned above may (without prejudice to its proof in any other manner) be conclusively proved by showing that in the 5 years ending with the date of the application he has been adjudged guilty (whether or not on the same occasion) of three or more defaults in relation to those provisions.

**3(3) [Guilty of default under s. 3(2)]** A person is to be treated under subsection (2) as being adjudged guilty of a default in relation to any provision of that legislation if—
(a) he is convicted (whether on indictment or summarily) of an offence consisting in a contravention of or failure to comply with that provision (whether on his own part or on the part of any company), or
(b) a default order is made against him, that is to say an order under any of the following provisions—
 (i) section 242(4) of the Companies Act (order requiring delivery of company accounts),
 (ia) section 245B of that Act (order requiring preparation of revised accounts),
 (ii) section 713 of that Act (enforcement of company's duty to make returns),
 (iii) section 41 of the Insolvency Act (enforcement of receiver's or manager's duty to make returns), or
 (iv) section 170 of that Act (corresponding provision for liquidator in winding up),
in respect of any such contravention of or failure to comply with that provision (whether on his own part or on the part of any company).

**History**
In s. 3(3)(b)(i) the words "section 242(4)" substituted for the former words "section 244" by CA 1989, s. 23 and Sch. 10, para. 35(1), (2)(a) as from 1 April 1990 subject to transitional and saving provisions (see SI 1990/355 (C.13), art. 3, Sch. 1 and also art. 6–9); s. 3(3)(b)(ia) inserted by CA 1989, s. 23 and Sch. 10, para. 35(1), (2)(b) as from 7 January 1991 (see SI 1990/2569 (C. 68), art. 3).

**3(4) ["The court"]** In this section **"the court"** means any court having jurisdiction to wind up any of the companies in relation to which the offence or other default has been or is alleged to have been committed.

**3(5) [Maximum period]** The maximum period of disqualification under this section is 5 years.

## 4 Disqualification for fraud, etc., in winding up

**4(1) [Court's power]** The court may make a disqualification order against a person if, in the course of the winding up of a company, it appears that he—
(a) has been guilty of an offence for which he is liable (whether he has been convicted or not) under section 458 of the Companies Act (fraudulent trading), or
(b) has otherwise been guilty, while an officer or liquidator of the company or receiver or manager of its property, of any fraud in relation to the company or of any breach of his duty as such officer, liquidator, receiver or manager.

**4(2) [Definitions]** In this section **"the court"** means any court having jurisdiction to wind up any of the companies in relation to which the offence or other default has been or is alleged to have been committed; and **"officer"** includes a shadow director.

**4(3) [Maximum period]** The maximum period of disqualification under this section is 15 years.

## 5 Disqualification on summary conviction

**5(1) [Relevant offences]** An offence counting for the purposes of this section is one of which a person is convicted (either on indictment or summarily) in consequence of a contravention of, or failure to comply with, any provision of the companies legislation requiring a return, account or other document to be filed with, delivered or sent, or notice of any matter to be given, to the registrar of companies (whether the contravention or failure is on the person's own part or on the part of any company).

**5(2) [Court's power]** Where a person is convicted of a summary offence counting for those purposes, the court by which he is convicted (or, in England and Wales, any other magistrates' court acting for the same petty sessions area) may make a disqualification order against him if the circumstances specified in the next subsection are present.

**5(3) [Circumstances in s. 5(2)]** Those circumstances are that, during the 5 years ending with the date of the conviction, the person has had made against him, or has been convicted of, in total not less than 3 default orders and offences counting for the purposes of this section; and those offences may include that of which he is convicted as mentioned in subsection (2) and any other offence of which he is convicted on the same occasion.

**5(4) [Definitions]** For the purposes of this section—

(a) the definition of **"summary offence"** in Schedule 1 to the Interpretation Act 1978 applies for Scotland as for England and Wales, and

(b) **"default order"** means the same as in section 3(3)(b).

**5(5) [Maximum period]** The maximum period of disqualification under this section is 5 years.

DISQUALIFICATION FOR UNFITNESS

## 6 Duty of court to disqualify unfit directors of insolvent companies

**6(1) [Court's duty]** The court shall make a disqualification order against a person in any case where, on an application under this section, it is satisfied—

(a) that he is or has been a director of a company which has at any time become insolvent (whether while he was a director or subsequently), and

(b) that his conduct as a director of that company (either taken alone or taken together with his conduct as a director of any other company or companies) makes him unfit to be concerned in the management of a company.

**6(2) [Interpretation]** For the purposes of this section and the next, a company becomes insolvent if—

(a) the company goes into liquidation at a time when its assets are insufficient for the payment of its debts and other liabilities and the expenses of the winding up,

(b) an administration order is made in relation to the company, or

(c) an administrative receiver of the company is appointed;

and references to a person's conduct as a director of any company or companies include, where that company or any of those companies has become insolvent, that person's conduct in relation to any matter connected with or arising out of the insolvency of that company.

**6(3) [Definitions]** In this section and the next **"the court"** means—

(a) in the case of a person who is or has been a director of a company which is being wound up by the court, the court by which the company is being wound up,

(b) in the case of a person who is or has been a director of a company which is being wound up voluntarily, any court having jurisdiction to wind up the company,

(c) in the case of a person who is or has been a director of a company in relation to which an administration order is in force, the court by which that order was made, and

(d) in any other case, the High Court or, in Scotland, the Court of Session;

and in both sections **"director"** includes a shadow director.

**6(4) [Minimum, maximum periods]** Under this section the minimum period of disqualification is 2 years, and the maximum period is 15 years.

**Note**

See note after s. 7; also for application re insolvent partnerships, see note after Sch. 1.

## 7 Applications to court under s. 6; reporting provisions

**7(1) [Application by Secretary of State, official receiver]** If it appears to the Secretary of State that it is expedient in the public interest that a disqualification order under section 6 should be made against any person, an application for the making of such an order against that person may be made—

(a) by the Secretary of State, or

(b) if the Secretary of State so directs in the case of a person who is or has been a director of a company which is being wound up by the court in England and Wales, by the official receiver.

**Note**

For details, see the Insolvent Companies (Disqualification of Unfit Directors) Proceedings Rules 1987 (SI 1987/2023).

**7(2) [Time for application]** Except with the leave of the court, an application for the making under that section of a disqualification order against any person shall not be made after the end of the period of 2 years beginning with the day on which the company of which that person is or has been a director became insolvent.

**7(3) [Report to Secretary of State]** If it appears to the office-holder responsible under this section, that is to say—

(a) in the case of a company which is being wound up by the court in England and Wales, the official receiver,

(b) in the case of a company which is being wound up otherwise, the liquidator,

(c) in the case of a company in relation to which an administration order is in force, the administrator, or

(d) in the case of a company of which there is an administrative receiver, that receiver,

that the conditions mentioned in section 6(1) are satisfied as respects a person who is or has been a director of that company, the office-holder shall forthwith report the matter to the Secretary of State.

**Note**

See sets of rules referred to in the note to s. 21(2).

**7(4) [Extra information etc.]** The Secretary of State or the official receiver may require the liquidator, administrator or administrative receiver of a company, or the former liquidator, administrator or administrative receiver of a company—

(a) to furnish him with such information with respect to any person's conduct as a director of the company, and

(b) to produce and permit inspection of such books, papers and other records relevant to that person's conduct as such a director,

as the Secretary of State or the official receiver may reasonably require for the purpose of determining whether to exercise, or of exercising, any function of his under this section.

**Note to s. 6, 7**

In s. 6, 7 purported insertion of a further subsection by Building Societies Act 1986, s. 120 and Sch. 18, para. 17(3) as from 1 January 1987 (see SI 1986/1560 (C. 56)) but to former provision, IA 1985, s. 12 — however Building Societies Act 1986, Sch. 18, para. 17(3) repealed by CA 1989, s. 212 and Sch. 24 as from 31 July 1990 (see SI 1990/1392 (C. 41), art. 4(b)); see also s. 22A below.

For application re insolvent partnerships, see note after Sch. 1.

## 8 Disqualification after investigation of company

**8(1) [Application by Secretary of State]** If it appears to the Secretary of State from a report made by inspectors under section 437 of the Companies Act or section 94 or 177 of the Financial Services Act 1986, or from information or documents obtained under section 447 or 448 of the Companies Act or section 105 of the Financial Services Act 1986 or section 2 of the Criminal Justice Act 1987 or section 28 of the Criminal Law (Consolidation) (Scotland) Act 1995 or section 83 of the Companies Act 1989, that it is expedient in the public interest that a disqualification order should be made against any person who is or has been a director or shadow director of any company, he may apply to the court for such an order to be made against that person.

**History**

In s. 8(1) the words "section 28 of the Criminal Law (Consolidation) (Scotland) Act 1995" substituted for the former words "section 52 of the Criminal Justice (Scotland) Act 1987" by the Criminal Procedure (Consequential Provisions) (Scotland) Act 1995, s. 5, Sch. 4, para. 62 as from 1 April 1996.

Previous to that in s. 8(1) the words "or section 94 or 177 of the Financial Services Act 1986" inserted by Financial Services Act 1986,s. 198(2)(a) as from 15 November 1986 (see SI 1986/1940 (C. 69)) and the words "the Companies Act or section 105 of the Financial Services Act 1986" substituted for the former words "that Act" by Financial Services Act 1986, s. 198(2)(b) as from 18 December 1986 (see SI 1986/2246 (C. 88)). In addition the words "or section 52 of the Criminal Justice (Scotland) Act 1987" inserted by Criminal Justice (Scotland) Act 1987, s. 55(b) as from 1 January 1988 (see SI 1987/2119 (C. 62) (S. 143)). Also inserted are the words "or section 2 of the Criminal Justice Act 1987" after the words "the Financial Services Act 1986" in the second place where they occur, by Criminal Justice Act 1988, s. 145(b) as from 12 October 1988 (see SI 1988/1676 (C.60)). The words "or section 83 of the Companies Act 1989" inserted by CA 1989, s. 79 as from 21 February 1990 (see SI 1990/142 (C.5), art. 4).

**8(2) [Court's power]** The court may make a disqualification order against a person where, on an application under this section, it is satisfied that his conduct in relation to the company makes him unfit to be concerned in the management of a company.

**8(3) ["The court"]** In this section **"the court"** means the High Court or, in Scotland, the Court of Session.

**8(4) [Maximum period]** The maximum period of disqualification under this section is 15 years.

**Note**

For application re insolvent partnerships, see note after Sch. 1.

## 9 Matters for determining unfitness of directors

**9(1) [Matters in Sch. 1]** Where it falls to a court to determine whether a person's conduct as a director or shadow director of any particular company or companies makes him unfit to be concerned in the management of a company, the court shall, as respects his conduct as a director of that company or, as the case may be, each of those companies, have regard in particular—

(a) to the matters mentioned in Part I of Schedule 1 to this Act, and

(b) where the company has become insolvent, to the matters mentioned in Part II of that Schedule;

and references in that Schedule to the director and the company are to be read accordingly.

**9(2) [Application of s. 6(2)]** Section 6(2) applies for the purposes of this section and Schedule 1 as it applies for the purposes of sections 6 and 7.

**9(3) [Interpretation of Sch. 1]** Subject to the next subsection, any reference in Schedule 1 to an enactment contained in the Companies Act or the Insolvency Act includes, in relation to any time before the coming into force of that enactment, the corresponding enactment in force at that time.

**9(4) [Modification of Sch. 1]** The Secretary of State may by order modify any of the provisions of Schedule 1; and such an order may contain such transitional provisions as may appear to the Secretary of State necessary or expedient.

**9(5) [Power exercisable by statutory instrument etc.]** The power to make orders under this section is exercisable by statutory instrument subject to annulment in pursuance of a resolution of either House of Parliament.

**Note**

For application re insolvent partnerships, see note after Sch. 1.

OTHER CASES OF DISQUALIFICATION

## 10 Participation in wrongful trading

**10(1) [Court's power]** Where the court makes a declaration under section 213 or 214 of the Insolvency Act that a person is liable to make a contribution to a company's assets, then, whether or not an application for such an order is made by any person, the court may, if it thinks fit, also make a disqualification order against the person to whom the declaration relates.

**10(2) [Maximum period]** The maximum period of disqualification under this section is 15 years.

**Note**

For application re insolvent partnerships, see note after Sch. 1.

## 11 Undischarged bankrupts

**11(1) [Offence]** It is an offence for a person who is an undischarged bankrupt to act as director of, or directly or indirectly to take part in or be concerned in the promotion, formation or management of, a company, except with the leave of the court.

**11(2) ["The court"]** "The court" for this purpose is the court by which the person was adjudged bankrupt or, in Scotland, sequestration of his estates was awarded.

**11(3) [Requirements for leave of court]** In England and Wales, the leave of the court shall not be given unless notice of intention to apply for it has been served on the official receiver; and it is the latter's duty, if he is of opinion that it is contrary to the public interest that the application should be granted, to attend on the hearing of the application and oppose it.

## 12 Failure to pay under county court administration order

**12(1) [Effect of s. 12(2)]** The following has effect where a court under section 429 of the Insolvency Act revokes an administration order under Part VI of the County Courts Act 1984.

**12(2) [Restriction on person]** A person to whom that section applies by virtue of the order under section 429(2)(b) shall not, except with the leave of the court which made the order, act as director or liquidator of, or directly or indirectly take part or be concerned in the promotion, formation or management of, a company.

### CONSEQUENCES OF CONTRAVENTION

## 13 Criminal penalties

**13** If a person acts in contravention of a disqualification order or of section 12(2), or is guilty of an offence under section 11, he is liable—

(a) on conviction on indictment, to imprisonment for not more than 2 years or a fine or both; and

(b) on summary conviction, to imprisonment for not more than 6 months or a fine not exceeding the statutory maximum, or both.

## 14 Offences by body corporate

**14(1) [Offence re officer]** Where a body corporate is guilty of an offence of acting in contravention of a disqualification order, and it is proved that the offence occurred with the consent or connivance of, or was attributable to any neglect on the part of any director, manager, secretary or other similar officer of the body corporate, or any person who was purporting to act in any such capacity he, as well as the body corporate, is guilty of the offence and liable to be proceeded against and punished accordingly.

**14(2) [Where managers are members]** Where the affairs of a body corporate are managed by its members, subsection (1) applies in relation to the acts and defaults of a member in connection with his functions of management as if he were a director of the body corporate.

## 15 Personal liability for company's debts where person acts while disqualified

**15(1) [Personal liability]** A person is personally responsible for all the relevant debts of a company if at any time—

(a) in contravention of a disqualification order or of section 11 of this Act he is involved in the management of the company, or

(b) as a person who is involved in the management of the company, he acts or is willing to act on instructions given without the leave of the court by a person whom he knows at that time to be the subject of a disqualification order or to be an undischarged bankrupt.

**15(2) [Joint and several liability]** Where a person is personally responsible under this section for the relevant debts of a company, he is jointly and severally liable in respect of those debts with the company and any other person who, whether under this section or otherwise, is so liable.

**15(3) [Relevant debts of company]** For the purposes of this section the relevant debts of a company are—

(a) in relation to a person who is personally responsible under paragraph (a) of subsection (1), such debts and other liabilities of the company as are incurred at a time when that person was involved in the management of the company, and

(b) in relation to a person who is personally responsible under paragraph (b) of that subsection, such debts and other liabilities of the company as are incurred at a time when that person was acting or was willing to act on instructions given as mentioned in that paragraph.

**15(4) [Person involved in management]** For the purposes of this section, a person is involved in the management of a company if he is a director of the company or if he is concerned, whether directly or indirectly, or takes part, in the management of the company.

**15(5) [Interpretation]** For the purposes of this section a person who, as a person involved in the management of a company, has at any time acted on instructions given without the leave of the court by a person whom he knew at that time to be the subject of a disqualification order or to be an undischarged bankrupt is presumed, unless the contrary is shown, to have been willing at any time thereafter to act on any instructions given by that person.

**Note**

For application re insolvent partnerships, see note after Sch. 1.

SUPPLEMENTARY PROVISIONS

# 16 Application for disqualification order

**16(1) [Notice, appearance, etc.]** A person intending to apply for the making of a disqualification order by the court having jurisdiction to wind up a company shall give not less than 10 days' notice of his intention to the person against whom the order is sought; and on the hearing of the application the last-mentioned person may appear and himself give evidence or call witnesses.

**16(2) [Applicants]** An application to a court with jurisdiction to wind up companies for the making against any person of a disqualification order under any of sections 2 to 5 may be made by the Secretary of State or the official receiver, or by the liquidator or any past or present member or creditor of any company in relation to which that person has committed or is alleged to have committed an offence or other default.

**16(3) [Appearance etc. of applicant]** On the hearing of any application under this Act made by the Secretary of State or the official receiver or the liquidator the applicant shall appear and call the attention of the court to any matters which seem to him to be relevant, and may himself give evidence or call witnesses.

# 17 Application for leave under an order

**17(1) [Court]** As regards the court to which application must be made for leave under a disqualification order, the following applies—

(a) where the application is for leave to promote or form a company, it is any court with jurisdiction to wind up companies, and

(b) where the application is for leave to be a liquidator, administrator or director of, or otherwise to take part in the management of a company, or to be a receiver or manager of a company's property, it is any court having jurisdiction to wind up that company.

**17(2) [Appearance etc. of Secretary of State et al.]** On the hearing of an application for leave made by a person against whom a disqualification order has been made on the application of the Secretary of State, the official receiver or the liquidator, the Secretary of State, official receiver or liquidator shall appear and call the attention of the court to any matters which seem to him to be relevant, and may himself give evidence or call witnesses.

# 18 Register of disqualification orders

**18(1) [Regulations re furnishing information]** The Secretary of State may make regulations requiring officers of courts to furnish him with such particulars as the regulations may specify of cases in which—

(a) a disqualification order is made, or
(b) any action is taken by a court in consequence of which such an order is varied or ceases to be in force, or
(c) leave is granted by a court for a person subject to such an order to do any thing which otherwise the order prohibits him from doing;

and the regulations may specify the time within which, and the form and manner in which, such particulars are to be furnished.

**Note**
See the Companies (Disqualification Orders) Regulations 1986 (SI 1986/2067) as amended.

**18(2) [Register of orders]** The Secretary of State shall, from the particulars so furnished, continue to maintain the register of orders, and of cases in which leave has been granted as mentioned in subsection (1)(c), which was set up by him under section 29 of the Companies Act 1976 and continued under section 301 of the Companies Act 1985.

**18(3) [Deletion of orders no longer in force]** When an order of which entry is made in the register ceases to be in force, the Secretary of State shall delete the entry from the register and all particulars relating to it which have been furnished to him under this section or any previous corresponding provision.

**18(4) [Inspection of register]** The register shall be open to inspection on payment of such fee as may be specified by the Secretary of State in regulations.

**18(5) [Regulations by statutory instrument etc.]** Regulations under this section shall be made by statutory instrument subject to annulment in pursuance of a resolution of either House of Parliament.

# 19 Special savings from repealed enactments

**19** Schedule 2 to this Act has effect—
(a) in connection with certain transitional cases arising under sections 93 and 94 of the Companies Act 1981, so as to limit the power to make a disqualification order, or to restrict the duration of an order, by reference to events occurring or things done before those sections came into force,
(b) to preserve orders made under section 28 of the Companies Act 1976 (repealed by the Act of 1981), and
(c) to preclude any applications for a disqualification order under section 6 or 8, where the relevant company went into liquidation before 28th April 1986.

**Note**
For application re insolvent partnerships, see note after Sch. 1.

## MISCELLANEOUS AND GENERAL

# 20 Admissibility in evidence of statements

**20(1) [General rule on admissibility of statements]** In any proceedings (whether or not under this Act), any statement made in pursuance of a requirement imposed by or under sections 6 to 10, 15 or 19(c) of, or Schedule 1 to, this Act, or by or under rules made for the purposes of this Act under the Insolvency Act, may be used in evidence against any person making or concurring in making the statement.

**History**
S. 20(1), formerly s. 20, was renumbered by Youth Justice and Criminal Evidence Act 1999, s. 59, 68(3) and Sch. 3, para. 8(2), with effect from 14 April 2000 (see Youth Justice and Criminal Evidence Act 1999 (Commencement No. 2) Order 2000 (SI 2000/1034 (C. 27)), art. 2(a)).

**20(2) [Limits on use of statement in criminal proceedings]** However, in criminal proceedings in which any such person is charged with an offence to which this subsection applies–
(a) no evidence relating to the statement may be adduced, and
(b) no question relating to it may be asked,

by or on behalf of the prosecution, unless evidence relating to it is adduced, or a question relating to it is asked, in the proceedings by or on behalf of that person.

**History**
S. 20(2) inserted by Youth Justice and Criminal Evidence Act 1999, s. 59, 68(3) and Sch. 3, para. 8(3), with effect from 14 April 2000 (see Youth Justice and Criminal Evidence Act 1999 (Commencement No. 2) Order 2000 (SI 2000/1034 (C. 27)), art. 2(a)).

**20(3) [Offences to which s. 20(2) applies]** Subsection (2) applies to any offence other than–

(a) an offence which is–
  (i) created by rules made for the purposes of this Act under the Insolvency Act, and
  (ii) designated for the purposes of this subsection by such rules or by regulations made by the Secretary of State;

(b) an offence which is–
  (i) created by regulations made under any such rules, and
  (ii) designated for the purposes of this subsection by such regulations;

(c) an offence under section 5 of the Perjury Act 1911 (false statements made otherwise than on oath); or

(d) an offence under section 44(2) of the Criminal Law (Consolidation) (Scotland) Act 1995 (false statements made otherwise than on oath).

**History**
S. 20(3) inserted by Youth Justice and Criminal Evidence Act 1999, s. 59, 68(3) and Sch. 3, para. 8(3), with effect from 14 April 2000 (see Youth Justice and Criminal Evidence Act 1999 (Commencement No. 2) Order 2000 (SI 2000/1034 (C. 27)), art. 2(a)).

**20(4) [Procedure for making regulations]** Regulations under subsection (3)(a)(ii) shall be made by statutory instrument and, after being made, shall be laid before each House of Parliament.

**History**
S. 20(4) inserted by Youth Justice and Criminal Evidence Act 1999, s. 59, 68(3) and Sch. 3, para. 8(3), with effect from 14 April 2000 (see Youth Justice and Criminal Evidence Act 1999 (Commencement No. 2) Order 2000 (SI 2000/1034 (C. 27)), art. 2(a)).

**Note**
For application of s. 20 re insolvent partnerships, see note after Sch. 1.

## 21 Interaction with Insolvency Act

**21(1) [Reference to official receiver]** References in this Act to the official receiver, in relation to the winding up of a company or the bankruptcy of an individual, are to any person who, by virtue of section 399 of the Insolvency Act, is authorised to act as the official receiver in relation to that winding up or bankruptcy; and, in accordance with section 401(2) of that Act, references in this Act to an official receiver includes a person appointed as his deputy.

**21(2) [Insolvency Act, Pt. I to VII]** Sections 6 to 10, 15, 19(c) and 20 of, and Schedule 1 to, this Act are deemed included in Parts I to VII of the Insolvency Act for the purposes of the following sections of that Act—

section 411 (power to make insolvency rules);
section 414 (fees orders);
section 420 (orders extending provisions about insolvent companies to insolvent partnerships);
section 422 (modification of such provisions in their application to recognised banks).

**History**
In s. 21(2) the words "and section 431 (summary proceedings)" formerly appearing at the end repealed by CA 1989, s. 212 and Sch. 24 as from 1 March 1990 (see SI 1990/142 (C.5), art. 7(d)).

**Note**
In regard to the entry for s. 411 see the Insolvent Companies (Reports on Conduct of Directors) No. 2 Rules 1986 (SI 1986/2134), the Insolvent Companies (Reports on Conduct of Directors) (No. 2) (Scotland) Rules 1986 (SI 1986/1916 (S. 140)) and the Insolvent Companies (Disqualification of Unfit Directors) Proceedings Rules 1987 (SI 1987/2023); the Insolvent Companies (Reports on Conduct of Directors) Rules 1996 (SI 1996/1909); and the Insolvent Companies (Reports on Conduct of Directors) (Scotland) Rules 1996 (SI 1996/1910) (s. 154).
In regard to the entry for s. 420 see the Insolvent Partnerships Order 1994 (SI 1994/2421) and the Insolvent Partnerships (Amendment) Order 1996 (SI 1996/1308).

**21(3) [Application of Insolvency Act, s. 434]** Section 434 of that Act (Crown application) applies to sections 6 to 10, 15, 19(c) and 20 of, and Schedule 1 to, this Act as it does to the provisions of that Act which are there mentioned.

**21(4) [Summary proceedings in Scotland]** For the purposes of summary proceedings in Scotland, section 431 of that Act applies to summary proceedings for an offence under section 11 or 13 of this Act as it applies to summary proceedings for an offence under Parts I to VII of that Act.

**History**
S. 21(4) added by CA 1989, s. 208 as from 1 March 1990 (see SI 1990/142 (C.5), art. 7(a)).

## 22 Interpretation

**22(1) [Effect]** This section has effect with respect to the meaning of expressions used in this Act, and applies unless the context otherwise requires.

**22(2) ["Company"]** The expression **"company"**—

(a) in section 11, includes an unregistered company and a company incorporated outside Great Britain which has an established place of business in Great Britain, and

(b) elsewhere, includes any company which may be wound up under Part V of the Insolvency Act.

**Note**
In s. 22(2)(a), (b) purported amendments by Building Societies Act 1986, s. 120 and Sch. 18, para. 16 as from 1 January 1987 (see SI 1986/1560 (C. 56)) but to former provisions, CA 1985, s. 295(3) and 302(4) — however Building Societies Act 1986, Sch. 18, para. 16 repealed by CA 1989, s. 212 and Sch. 24 as from 31 July 1990 (see SI 1990/1392 (C. 41), art. 4(b)); see also s. 22A below.

**22(3) [Application of Insolvency Act, s. 247, 251]** Section 247 in Part VII of the Insolvency Act (interpretation for the first Group of Parts of that Act) applies as regards references to a company's insolvency and to its going into liquidation; and **"administrative receiver"** has the meaning given by section 251 of that Act.

**22(4) ["Director"]** **"Director"** includes any person occupying the position of director, by whatever name called, and in sections 6 to 9 includes a shadow director.

**22(5) ["Shadow director"]** **"Shadow director"**, in relation to a company, means a person in accordance with whose directions or instructions the directors of the company are accustomed to act (but so that a person is not deemed a shadow director by reason only that the directors act on advice given by him in a professional capacity).

**22(6) [Application of CA, s. 740, 744]** Section 740 of the Companies Act applies as regards the meaning of **"body corporate"**; and **"officer"** has the meaning given by section 744 of that Act.

**22(7) [References to legislation]** In references to legislation other than this Act—

**"the Companies Act"** means the Companies Act 1985;

**"the Companies Acts"** has the meaning given by section 744 of that Act; and

**"the Insolvency Act"** means the Insolvency Act 1986;

and in sections 3(1) and 5(1) of this Act **"the companies legislation"** means the Companies Acts (except the Insider Dealing Act), Parts I to VII of the Insolvency Act and, in Part XV of that Act, sections 411, 413, 414, 416 and 417.

**22(8) [References to former legislation]** Any reference to provisions, or a particular provision, of the Companies Acts or the Insolvency Act includes the corresponding provisions or provision of the former Companies Acts (as defined by section 735(1)(c) of the Companies Act, but including also that Act itself) or, as the case may be, the Insolvency Act 1985.

**22(9) [Application of CA, Pt. XXVI]** Any expression for whose interpretation provision is made by Part XXVI of the Companies Act (and not by subsections (3) to (8) above) is to be construed in accordance with that provision.

## 22A Application of Act to building societies

**22A(1) [To building societies as to companies]** This Act applies to building societies as it applies to companies.

**22A(2) [Interpretation]** References in this Act to a company, or to a director or officer of a company include, respectively, references to a building society within the meaning of the Building Societies Act 1986 or to a director or officer, within the meaning of that Act, of a building society.

**22A(3) ["Shadow director"]** In relation to a building society the definition of "shadow director" in section 22(5) applies with the substitution of "building society" for "company".

**22A(4) [Sch. 1]** In the application of Schedule 1 to the directors of a building society, references to provisions of the Insolvency Act or the Companies Act include references to the corresponding provisions of the Building Societies Act 1986.

**History**
S. 22A inserted by CA 1989, s. 211(3) as from 31 July 1990 (see SI 1990/1392 (C. 41), art. 4(a)).

**Note**
See also notes to s. 6, 7, 22 and Sch. 1, para. 5.

## 22B Application of Act to incorporated friendly societies

**22B(1) [Application as to companies]** This Act applies to incorporated friendly societies as it applies to companies.

**22B(2) [Interpretation]** References in this Act to a company, or to a director or an officer of a company include, respectively, references to an incorporated friendly society within the meaning of the Friendly Societies Act 1992 or to a member of the committee of management or officer, within the meaning of that Act, of an incorporated friendly society.

**22B(3) [Shadow directors]** In relation to an incorporated friendly society every reference to a shadow director shall be omitted.

**22B(4) [Sch. 1]** In the application of Schedule 1 to the members of the committee of management of an incorporated friendly society, references to provisions of the Insolvency Act or the Companies Act include references to the corresponding provisions of the Friendly Societies Act 1992.

**History**
S. 22B inserted by Friendly Societies Act 1992, s. 120(1) and Sch. 21, para. 8 as from 1 February 1993 (see SI 1993/16 (C. 1), art. 2 and Sch. 3).

## 23 Transitional provisions, savings, repeals

**23(1) [Sch. 3]** The transitional provisions and savings in Schedule 3 to this Act have effect, and are without prejudice to anything in the Interpretation Act 1978 with regard to the effect of repeals.

**23(2) [Sch. 4]** The enactments specified in the second column of Schedule 4 to this Act are repealed to the extent specified in the third column of that Schedule.

## 24 Extent

**24(1) [England, Wales, Scotland]** This Act extends to England and Wales and to Scotland.

**24(2) [Northern Ireland]** Nothing in this Act extends to Northern Ireland.

## 25 Commencement

**25** This Act comes into force simultaneously with the Insolvency Act 1986.

**Note**
The relevant date is 29 December 1986 — see Insolvency Act 1986, s. 443 and SI 1986/1924 (C. 71).

## 26 Citation

**26** This Act may be cited as the Company Directors Disqualification Act 1986.

# SCHEDULES

# Schedule 1 — Matters for Determining Unfitness of Directors

Section 9

## Part I — Matters Applicable in all Cases

**1** Any misfeasance or breach of any fiduciary or other duty by the director in relation to the company.

**2** Any misapplication or retention by the director of, or any conduct by the director giving rise to an obligation to account for, any money or other property of the company.

**3** The extent of the director's responsibility for the company entering into any transaction liable to be set aside under Part XVI of the Insolvency Act (provisions against debt avoidance).

**4** The extent of the director's responsibility for any failure by the company to comply with any of the following provisions of the Companies Act, namely—

(a) section 221 (companies to keep accounting records);
(b) section 222 (where and for how long records to be kept);
(c) section 288 (register of directors and secretaries);
(d) section 352 (obligation to keep and enter up register of members);
(e) section 353 (location of register of members);
(f) section 363 (duty of company to make annual returns); and
(h) sections 399 and 415 (company's duty to register charges it creates).

**History**
In para. 4, para. (f) substituted for the former para. (f) and (g) by CA 1989, s. 139(4) as from 1 October 1990 subject to transitional and saving provisions (see SI 1990/1707 (C. 46), art. 2(a) and also art. 4, 5); former para. (f) and (g) read as follows:

"(f) sections 363 and 364 (company's duty to made annual return);
(g) section 365 (time for completion of annual return);".

**5** The extent of the director's responsibility for any failure by the directors of the company to comply with—

(a) section 226 or 227 of the Companies Act (duty to prepare annual accounts), or
(b) section 233 of that Act (approval and signature of accounts).

**History**
Para. 5 substituted by CA 1989, s. 23 and Sch. 10, para. 35(1), (3) as from 1 April 1990 subject to transitional and saving provisions (see SI 1990/355 (C.13), art. 3, Sch. 1 and also art. 6–9); para. 5 formerly read as follows:

"The extent of the director's responsibility for any failure by the directors of the company to comply with section 227 (directors' duty to prepare annual accounts) or section 238 (signing of balance sheet and documents to be annexed) of the Companies Act."

**Note**
In Sch. 1 purported insertion of para. 5A by Building Societies Act 1986, s. 120 and Sch. 18, para. 17(4) as from 1 January 1987 (see SI 1986/1560 (C. 56)) but to former provision, IA 1985, Sch. 2 — however Building Societies Act 1986, Sch. 18, para. 17(4) repealed by CA 1989, s. 212 and Sch. 24 as from 31 July 1990 (see SI 1990/1392 (C. 41), art. 4(b)); see also s. 22A above.

**5A** In the application of this Part of this Schedule in relation to any person who is a director of an investment company with variable capital, any reference to a provision of the Companies Act shall be taken to be a reference to the corresponding provision of the Open-Ended Investment Companies (Investment Companies with Variable Capital) Regulations 1996 or of any regulations made under regulation 6 of those Regulations (SIB regulations).

**History**
Para. 5A inserted by the Open-Ended Investment Companies (Investment Companies with Variable Capital) Regulations 1996 (SI 1996/2827), reg. 1, 75 and Sch. 8, para. 10 as from 6 January 1997.

# Part II — Matters Applicable Where Company Has Become Insolvent

**6** The extent of the director's responsibility for the causes of the company becoming insolvent.

**7** The extent of the director's responsibility for any failure by the company to supply any goods or services which have been paid for (in whole or in part).

**8** The extent of the director's responsibility for the company entering into any transaction or giving any preference, being a transaction or preference—

(a) liable to be set aside under section 127 or sections 238 to 240 of the Insolvency Act, or
(b) challengeable under section 242 or 243 of that Act or under any rule of law in Scotland.

**9** The extent of the director's responsibility for any failure by the directors of the company to comply with section 98 of the Insolvency Act (duty to call creditors' meeting in creditors' voluntary winding up).

**10** Any failure by the director to comply with any obligation imposed on him by or under any of the following provisions of the Insolvency Act—

(a) section 22 (company's statement of affairs in administration);
(b) section 47 (statement of affairs to administrative receiver);
(c) section 66 (statement of affairs in Scottish receivership);
(d) section 99 (directors' duty to attend meeting; statement of affairs in creditors' voluntary winding up);
(e) section 131 (statement of affairs in winding up by the court);
(f) section 234 (duty of any one with company property to deliver it up);
(g) section 235 (duty to co-operate with liquidator, etc.).

**Note**
Where an insolvent partnership is wound up as an unregistered company under Insolvency Act 1986, Pt. V, s. 6–10, 15, 19(c), 20 and Sch. 1 apply, as modified: see the Insolvent Partnerships Order 1994 (SI 1994/2421), art. 16 and Sch. 8.

# Schedule 2 — Savings from Companies Act 1981 s. 93, 94, and Insolvency Act 1985 Schedule 9

Section 19

**1** Sections 2 and 4(1)(b) do not apply in relation to anything done before 15th June 1982 by a person in his capacity as liquidator of a company or as receiver or manager of a company's property.

**2** Subject to paragraph 1—
(a) section 2 applies in a case where a person is convicted on indictment of an offence which he committed (and, in the case of a continuing offence, has ceased to commit) before 15th June 1982; but in such a case a disqualification order under that section shall not be made for a period in excess of 5 years;
(b) that section does not apply in a case where a person is convicted summarily—
(i) in England and Wales, if he had consented so to be tried before that date, or
(ii) in Scotland, if the summary proceedings commenced before that date.

**3** Subject to paragraph 1, section 4 applies in relation to an offence committed or other thing done before 15th June 1982; but a disqualification order made on the grounds of such an offence or other thing done shall not be made for a period in excess of 5 years.

**4** The powers of a court under section 5 are not exercisable in a case where a person is convicted of an offence which he committed (and, in the case of a continuing offence, had ceased to commit) before 15th June 1982.

**5** For purposes of section 3(1) and section 5, no account is to be taken of any offence which was committed, or any default order which was made, before 1st June 1977.

**6** An order made under section 28 of the Companies Act 1976 has effect as if made under section 3 of this Act; and an application made before 15th June 1982 for such an order is to be treated as an application for an order under the section last mentioned.

**7** Where—
(a) an application is made for a disqualification order under section 6 of this Act by virtue of paragraph (a) of subsection (2) of that section, and
(b) the company in question went into liquidation before 28th April 1986 (the coming into force of the provision replaced by section 6),

the court shall not make an order under that section unless it could have made a disqualification order under section 300 of the Companies Act as it had effect immediately before the date specified in sub-paragraph (b) above.

**8** An application shall not be made under section 8 of this Act in relation to a report made or information or documents obtained before 28th April 1986.

# Schedule 3 — Transitional Provisions and Savings

Section 23(1)

**1** In this Schedule, **"the former enactments"** means so much of the Companies Act, and so much of the Insolvency Act, as is repealed and replaced by this Act; and **"the appointed day"** means the day on which this Act comes into force.

**2** So far as anything done or treated as done under or for the purposes of any provision of the former enactments could have been done under or for the purposes of the corresponding provision of this Act, it is not invalidated by the repeal of that provision but has effect as if done under or for the purposes of the corresponding provision; and any order, regulation, rule or other instrument made or having effect under any provision of the former enactments shall, insofar as its effect is preserved by this paragraph, be treated for all purposes as made and having effect under the corresponding provision.

**3** Where any period of time specified in a provision of the former enactments is current immediately before the appointed day, this Act has effect as if the corresponding provision had been in force when the period began to run; and (without prejudice to the foregoing) any period of time so specified and current is deemed for the purposes of this Act—

(a) to run from the date or event from which it was running immediately before the appointed day, and

(b) to expire (subject to any provision of this Act for its extension) whenever it would have expired if this Act had not been passed;

and any rights, priorities, liabilities, reliefs, obligations, requirements, powers, duties or exemptions dependent on the beginning, duration or end of such a period as above mentioned shall be under this Act as they were or would have been under the former enactments.

**4** Where in any provision of this Act there is a reference to another such provision, and the first-mentioned provision operates, or is capable of operating, in relation to things done or omitted, or events occurring or not occurring, in the past (including in particular past acts of compliance with any enactment, failures of compliance, contraventions, offences and convictions of offences) the reference to the other provision is to be read as including a reference to the corresponding provision of the former enactments.

**5** Offences committed before the appointed day under any provision of the former enactments may, notwithstanding any repeal by this Act, be prosecuted and punished after that day as if this Act had not passed.

**6** A reference in any enactment, instrument or document (whether express or implied, and in whatever phraseology) to a provision of the former enactments (including the corresponding provision of any yet earlier enactment) is to be read, where necessary to retain for the enactment, instrument or document the same force and effect as it would have had but for the passing of this Act, as, or as including, a reference to the corresponding provision by which it is replaced in this Act.

# Schedule 4 — Repeals

Section 23(2)

| Chapter | Short title | Extent of repeal |
|---|---|---|
| 1985 c. 6. | The Companies Act 1985. | Sections 295 to 299.<br>Section 301.<br>Section 302.<br>Schedule 12.<br>In Schedule 24, the entries relating to sections 295(7) and 302(1). |
| 1985 c. 65. | The Insolvency Act 1985. | Sections 12 to 14.<br>Section 16.<br>Section 18.<br>Section 108(2).<br>Schedule 2.<br>In Schedule 6, paragraphs 1, 2, 7 and 14.<br>In Schedule 9, paragraphs 2 and 3. |

# FINANCIAL SERVICES ACT 1986

---

## Table of Contents

# FINANCIAL SERVICES ACT 1986

(1986 Chapter 60)

## ARRANGEMENT OF SECTIONS

## PART I – REGULATION OF INVESTMENT BUSINESS

### CHAPTER I – PRELIMINARY

SECTION

## CHAPTER XV – RELATIONS WITH OTHER REGULATORY AUTHORITIES



## PART II – INSURANCE BUSINESS



## PART III – FRIENDLY SOCIETIES



## PART IV – OFFICIAL LISTING OF SECURITIES



## PART V – OFFERS OF UNLISTED SECURITIES



## PART VI – TAKEOVER OFFERS

SECTION

## PART VII – INSIDER DEALING



## PART VIII – RESTRICTIONS ON DISCLOSURE OF INFORMATION



## PART IX – RECIPROCITY



## PART X – MISCELLANEOUS AND SUPPLEMENTARY

## SCHEDULES

# FINANCIAL SERVICES ACT 1986

(1986 Chapter 60)

An Act to regulate the carrying on of investment business; to make related provision with respect to insurance business and business carried on by friendly societies; to make new provision with respect to the official listing of securities, offers of unlisted securities, takeover offers and insider dealing; to make provision as to the disclosure of information obtained under enactments relating to fair trading, banking, companies and insurance; to make provision for securing reciprocity with other countries in respect of facilities for the provision of financial services; and for connected purposes.

[*7th November 1986*]

## PART I – REGULATION OF INVESTMENT BUSINESS

### Chapter I – Preliminary

#### 1 Investments and investment business

**1(1) ["Investment"]** In this Act, unless the context otherwise requires, **"investment"** means any asset, right or interest falling within any paragraph in Part I of Schedule 1 to this Act.

**1(2) ["Investment business"]** In this Act **"investment business"** means the business of engaging in one or more of the activities which fall within the paragraphs in Part II of that Schedule and are not excluded by Part III of that Schedule.

**1(3) [Carrying on investment business in the UK]** For the purposes of this Act a person carries on investment business in the United Kingdom if he–

(a) carries on investment business from a permanent place of business maintained by him in the United Kingdom; or

(b) engages in the United Kingdom in one or more of the activities which fall within the paragraphs in Part II of that Schedule and are not excluded by Part III or IV of that Schedule and his doing so constitutes the carrying on by him of a business in the United Kingdom.

**1(4) [Construction of Sch. 1]** Parts I to IV of that Schedule shall be construed in accordance with Part V.

#### 2 Power to extend or restrict scope of Act

**2(1) [Power of Secretary of State]** The Secretary of State may by order amend Schedule 1 to this Act so as–

(a) to extend or restrict the meaning of investment for the purposes of all or any provisions of this Act; or

(b) to extend or restrict for the purposes of all or any of those provisions the activities that are to constitute the carrying on of investment business or the carrying on of such business in the United Kingdom.

**2(2) [Amendments for s. 2(1)(b)]** The amendments that may be made for the purposes of subsection (1)(b) above include amendments conferring powers on the Secretary of State, whether by extending or modifying any provision of that Schedule which confers such powers or by adding further such provisions.

**2(3) [Approval of order by Parliament]** An order under this section which extends the meaning of investment or extends the activities that are to constitute the carrying on of investment business or the carrying on of such business in the United Kingdom shall be laid before Parliament after being made and shall cease to have effect at the end of the period of twenty-eight days beginning with the day on which it is made (but without prejudice to anything done under the order or to the making of a new order) unless before the end of that period the order is approved by a resolution of each House of Parliament.

**2(4) [Period in s. 2(3)]** In reckoning the period mentioned in subsection (3) above no account shall be taken of any time during which Parliament is dissolved or prorogued or during which both Houses are adjourned for more than four days.

**2(5) [Annulment of order by Parliament]** Any order under this section to which subsection (3) above does not apply shall be subject to annulment in pursuance of a resolution of either House of Parliament.

**2(6) [Transitional provisions]** An order under this section may contain such transitional provisions as the Secretary of State thinks necessary or expedient.

**Note**
See the Financial Services Act 1986 (Investment Services) (Extension of Scope of Act) Order 1995 (SI 1995/3271), the Financial Services Act 1986 (Uncertificated Securities) (Extension of Scope of Act) Order 1996 (SI 1996/1322), the Financial Services Act 1986 (Extension of Scope of Act) Order 1996 (SI 1996/2958) and the Financial Services Act 1986 (Restriction of Scope of Act and Meaning of Collective Investment Scheme) Order 1996 (SI 1996/2996).

# Chapter II – Restriction on Carrying on Business

## 3 Persons entitled to carry on investment business

3 No person shall carry on, or purport to carry on, investment business in the United Kingdom unless he is an authorised person under Chapter III or an exempted person under Chapter IV of this Part of this Act.

## 4 Offences

**4(1) [Offence, penalty]** Any person who carries on, or purports to carry on, investment business in contravention of section 3 above shall be guilty of an offence and liable–

(a) on conviction on indictment, to imprisonment for a term not exceeding two years or to a fine or to both;

(b) on summary conviction, to imprisonment for a term not exceeding six months or to a fine not exceeding the statutory maximum or to both.

**4(2) [Defence]** In proceedings brought against any person for an offence under this section it shall be a defence for him to prove that he took all reasonable precautions and exercised all due diligence to avoid the commission of the offence.

## 5 Agreements made by or through unauthorised persons

**5(1) [Unenforceable investment agreements]** Subject to subsection (3) below, any agreement to which this subsection applies–

(a) which is entered into by a person in the course of carrying on investment business in contravention of section 3 above; or

(b) which is entered into–

(i) by a person who is an authorised person or an exempted person in respect of the investment business in the course of which he enters into the agreement; but

(ii) in consequence of anything said or done by a person in the course of carrying on investment business in contravention of that section,

shall be unenforceable against the other party; and that party shall be entitled to recover any money or other property paid or transferred by him under the agreement, together with compensation for any loss sustained by him as a result of having parted with it.

**Note**
Concerning European investment firms, see the Investment Services Regulations 1995 (SI 1995/3275), reg. 32 and Sch. 7, para. 2.
Concerning European institutions see the Banking Coordination (Second Council Directive) Regulations 1992 (SI 1992/3218), reg. 55 and Sch. 9, para. 2.

**5(2) [Compensation under s. 5(1)]** The compensation recoverable under subsection (1) above shall be such as the parties may agree or as the court may, on the application of either party, determine.

**5(3) [Condition for court allowing agreement]** A court may allow an agreement to which subsection (1) above applies to be enforced or money and property paid or transferred under it to be retained if it is satisfied–

(a) in a case within paragraph (a) of that subsection, that the person mentioned in that paragraph reasonably believed that his entering into the agreement did not constitute a contravention of section 3 above;

(b) in a case within paragraph (b) of that subsection, that the person mentioned in sub-paragraph (i) of that paragraph did not know that the agreement was entered into as mentioned in sub-paragraph (ii) of that paragraph; and

(c) in either case, that it is just and equitable for the agreement to be enforced or, as the case may be, for the money or property paid or transferred under it to be retained.

**5(4) [Where agreement not performed]** Where a person elects not to perform an agreement which by virtue of this section is unenforceable against him or by virtue of this section recovers money paid or other property transferred by him under an agreement he shall repay any money and return any other property received by him under the agreement.

**5(5) [Where property has passed to third party]** Where any property transferred under an agreement to which this section applies has passed to a third party the references to that property in subsections (1), (3) and (4) above shall be construed as references to its value at the time of its transfer under the agreement.

**5(6) [Effect of contravention of s. 3]** A contravention of section 3 above shall not make an agreement illegal or invalid to any greater extent than is provided in this section.

**5(7) [Application of s. 5(1)]** Subsection (1) above applies to any agreement the making or performance of which by the person seeking to enforce it or from whom money or other property is recoverable under this section constitutes an activity which falls within any paragraph of Part II of Schedule 1 to this Act and is not excluded by Part III or IV of that Schedule.

## 6 Injunctions and restitution orders

**6(1) [Power of court]** If, on the application of the Secretary of State, the court is satisfied–

(a) that there is a reasonable likelihood that a person will contravene section 3 above; or

(b) that any person has contravened that section and that there is a reasonable likelihood that the contravention will continue or be repeated,

the court may grant an injunction restraining the contravention or, in Scotland, an interdict prohibiting the contravention.

**6(2) [Power of court where s. 3 contravened]** If, on the application of the Secretary of State, the court is satisfied that a person has entered into any transaction in contravention of section 3 above the court may order that person and any other person who appears to the court to have been knowingly concerned in the contravention to take such steps as the court may direct for restoring the parties to the position in which they were before the transaction was entered into.

**6(3) [Power of court to make s. 6(4), (5) order]** The court may, on the application of the Secretary of State, make an order under subsection (4) below or, in relation to Scotland, under subsection (5) below if satisfied that a person has been carrying on investment business in contravention of section 3 above and–

(a) that profits have accrued to that person as a result of carrying on that business; or

(b) that one or more investors have suffered loss or been otherwise adversely affected as a result of his contravention of section 47 or 56 below or failure to act substantially in accordance with any of the rules or regulations made under Chapter V of this Part of this Act.

**6(4) [Order re payment into court etc.]** The court may under this subsection order the person concerned to pay into court, or appoint a receiver to recover from him, such sum as appears to the court to be just having regard–

(a) in a case within paragraph (a) of subsection (3) above, to the profits appearing to the court to have accrued;

(b) in a case within paragraph (b) of that subsection, to the extent of the loss or other adverse effect; or

(c) in a case within both paragraphs (a) and (b) of that subsection, to the profits and to the extent of the loss or other adverse effect.

**6(5) [Order re payment to applicant]** The court may under this subsection order the person concerned to pay to the applicant such sum as appears to the court to be just having regard to the considerations mentioned in paragraphs (a) to (c) of subsection (4) above.

**6(6) [Payment of sums in s. 6(4), (5)]** Any amount paid into court by or recovered from a person in pursuance of an order under subsection (4) or (5) above shall be paid out to such person or distributed among such persons as the court may direct, being a person or persons appearing to the court to have entered into transactions with that person as a result of which the profits mentioned in paragraph (a) of subsection (3) above have accrued to him or the loss or other adverse effect mentioned in paragraph (b) of that subsection has been suffered.

**6(7) [Information on s. 6(3) application]** On an application under subsection (3) above the court may require the person concerned to furnish it with such accounts or other information as it may require for establishing whether any and, if so, what profits have accrued to him as mentioned in paragraph (a) of that subsection and for determining how any amounts are to be paid or distributed under subsection (6) above; and the court may require any such accounts or other information to be verified in such manner as it may direct.

**6(8) [Exercise of jurisdiction]** The jurisdiction conferred by this section shall be exercisable by the High Court and the Court of Session.

**6(9) [Other persons bringing proceedings]** Nothing in this section affects the right of any person other than the Secretary of State to bring proceedings in respect of any of the matters to which this section applies.

# Chapter III – Authorised Persons

MEMBERS OF RECOGNISED SELF-REGULATING ORGANISATIONS

## 7 Authorisation by membership of recognised self-regulating organisation

**7(1) [Authorised person if member]** Subject to subsection (2) below, a member of a recognised self-regulating organisation is an authorised person by virtue of his membership of that organisation.

**7(2) [Exception]** This section does not apply to a member who is an authorised person by virtue of section 22 or 23 below or an insurance company which is an authorised person by virtue of section 31 below.

**Note**

Concerning European investment firms, see the Investment Services Regulations 1995 (SI 1995/3275), reg. 1, 21(1).
Concerning European institutions, see the Banking Coordination (Second Council Directive) Regulations 1992 (SI 1992/3218), reg. 48(1).

## 8 Self-regulating organisations

**8(1) ["Self-regulating organisation"]** In this Act a **"self-regulating organisation"** means a body (whether a body corporate or an unincorporated association) which regulates the carrying on of investment business of any kind by enforcing rules which are binding on persons carrying on business of that kind either because they are members of that body or because they are otherwise subject to its control.

**8(2) [References to members]** In this Act references to the members of a self-regulating organisation are references to the persons who, whether or not members of the organisation, are subject to its rules in carrying on the business in question.

**8(3) [References to the rules]** In this Act references to the rules of a self-regulating organisation are references to the rules (whether or not laid down by the organisation itself) which the organisation has power to enforce in relation to the carrying on of the business in question or which relate to the admission and expulsion of members of the organisation or otherwise to its constitution.

**8(4) [References to guidance]** In this Act references to guidance issued by a self-regulating organisation are references to guidance issued or any recommendation made by it to all or any class of its members or persons seeking to become members which would, if it were a rule, fall within subsection (3) above.

## 9 Applications for recognition

**9(1) [Application to Secretary of State]** A self-regulating organisation may apply to the Secretary of State for an order declaring it to be a recognised self-regulating organisation for the purposes of this Act.

**9(2) [Requirements for application]** Any such application–

(a) shall be made in such manner as the Secretary of State may direct; and

(b) shall be accompanied by such information as the Secretary of State may reasonably require for the purpose of determining the application.

**9(3) [Further information to be furnished]** At any time after receiving an application and before determining it the Secretary of State may require the applicant to furnish additional information.

**9(4) [Directions, requirements under s. 9(2), (3)]** The directions and requirements given or imposed under subsections (2) and (3) above may differ as between different applications.

**9(5) [Form, verification of information]** Any information to be furnished to the Secretary of State under this section shall, if he so requires, be in such form or verified in such manner as he may specify.

**9(6) [Material to accompany application]** Every application shall be accompanied by a copy of the applicant's rules and of any guidance issued by the applicant which is intended to have continuing effect and is issued in writing or other legible form.

## 10 Grant and refusal of recognition

**10(1) [Power of Secretary of State]** The Secretary of State may, on an application duly made in accordance with section 9 above and after being furnished with all such information as he may require under that section, make or refuse to make an order ("a recognition order") declaring the applicant to be a recognised self-regulating organisation.

**10(2) [Duty of Secretary of State if s. 10(3), Sch. 2 requirements satisfied]** Subject to subsection (4) below and to Chapter XIV of this Part of this Act, the Secretary of State shall make a recognition order if it appears to him from the information furnished by the organisation making the application and having regard to any other information in his possession that the requirements of subsection (3) below and of Schedule 2 to this Act are satisfied as respects that organisation.

**10(3) [Where investment business with which s. 20 not concerned]** Where there is a kind of investment business with which the organisation is not concerned, its rules must preclude a member from carrying on investment business of that kind unless he is an authorised person otherwise than by virtue of his membership of the organisation or an exempted person in respect of that business.

**Note**
Concerning European investment firms, see the Investment Services Regulations 1995 (SI 1995/3275), reg. 32 and Sch. 7, para. 3.

**10(4) [Where Secretary of State may refuse to make order]** The Secretary of State may refuse to make a recognition order in respect of an organisation if he considers that its recognition is unnecessary having regard to the existence of one or more other organisations which are concerned with investment business of a kind with which the applicant is concerned and which have been or are likely to be recognised under this section.

**10(5) [Notice re refusal]** Where the Secretary of State refuses an application for a recognition order he shall give the applicant a written notice to that effect specifying a requirement which in the opinion of the Secretary of State is not satisfied, stating that the application is refused on the ground mentioned in subsection (4) above or stating that it is refused by virtue of Chapter XIV.

**10(6) [Order to include date]** A recognition order shall state the date on which it takes effect.

**Note**
Concerning European institutions, see the Banking Coordination (Second Council Directive) Regulations 1992 (SI 1992/3218), reg. 55 and Sch. 9, para. 3.

## 11 Revocation of recognition

**11(1) [Where recognition order may be revoked]** A recognition order may be revoked by a further order made by the Secretary of State if at any time it appears to him–

(a) that section 10(3) above or any requirement of Schedule 2 to this Act is not satisfied in the case of the organisation to which the recognition order relates ("the recognised organisation");

(b) that the recognised organisation has failed to comply with any obligation to which it is subject by virtue of this Act; or

(c) that the continued recognition of the organisation is undesirable having regard to the existence of one or more other organisations which have been or are to be recognised under section 10 above.

**11(2) [Revocation order to include date]** An order revoking a recognition order shall state the date on which it takes effect and that date shall not be earlier than three months after the day on which the revocation order is made.

**11(3) [Duties of Secretary of State before revocation]** Before revoking a recognition order the Secretary of State shall give written notice of his intention to do so to the recognised organisation, take such steps as he considers reasonably practicable for bringing the notice to the attention of members of the organisation and publish it in such manner as he thinks appropriate for bringing it to the attention of any other persons who are in his opinion likely to be affected.

**11(4) [Contents of s. 11(3) notice]** A notice under subsection (3) above shall state the reasons for which the Secretary of State proposes to act and give particulars of the rights conferred by subsection (5) below.

**11(5) [Where s. 11(3) notice written representations may be made]** An organisation on which a notice is served under subsection (3) above, any member of the organisation and any other person who appears to the Secretary of State to be affected may within three months after the date of service or publication, or within such longer time as the Secretary of State may allow, make written representations to the Secretary of State and, if desired, oral representations to a person appointed for that purpose by the Secretary of State; and the Secretary of State shall have regard to any representations made in accordance with this subsection in determining whether to revoke the recognition order.

**11(6) [Secretary of State may revoke recognition order in spite of s. 11(2), (3)]** If in any case the Secretary of State considers it essential to do so in the interests of investors he may revoke a recognition order without regard to the restriction imposed by subsection (2) above and notwithstanding that no notice has been given or published under subsection (3) above or that the time for making representations in pursuance of such a notice has not expired.

**11(7) [Transitional provisions in order]** An order revoking a recognition order may contain such transitional provisions as the Secretary of State thinks necessary or expedient.

**11(8) [Revocation on request]** A recognition order may be revoked at the request or with the consent of the recognised organisation and any such revocation shall not be subject to the restrictions imposed by subsections (1) and (2) or the requirements of subsections (3) to (5) above.

**11(9) [Written notice etc. re revocation order]** On making an order revoking a recognition order the Secretary of State shall give the organisation written notice of the making of the order, take such steps as he considers reasonably practicable for bringing the making of the order to the attention of members of the organisation and publish a notice of the making of the order in such manner as he thinks appropriate for bringing it to the attention of any other persons who are in his opinion likely to be affected.

## 12 Compliance orders

**12(1) [Application by Secretary of State]** If at any time it appears to the Secretary of State–

(a) that subsection (3) of section 10 above or any requirement of Schedule 2 to this Act is not satisfied in the case of a recognised organisation; or

(b) that a recognised organisation has failed to comply with any obligation to which it is subject by virtue of this Act,

he may, instead of revoking the recognition order under section 11 above, make an application to the court under this section.

**12(2) [Court may make compliance order]** If on any such application the court decides that subsection (3) of section 10 or the requirement in question is not satisfied or, as the case may be, that the organisation has failed to comply with the obligation in question it may order the organisation to take such steps as the court directs for securing that that subsection or requirement is satisfied or that that obligation is complied with.

**12(3) [Exercise of jurisdiction]** The jurisdiction conferred by this section shall be exercisable by the High Court and the Court of Session.

**Note**

For application of s. 12 to a listed person see the Financial Markets and Insolvency (Money Market) Regulations 1995 (SI 1995/2049), reg. 1, 6, 7.

## 13 Alteration of rules for protection of investors

**13(1)** (Omitted by Companies Act 1989, s. 206(1) and Sch. 23, para. 1(1), (2) as from 15 March 1990.)

**History**

In regard to the date of the above omission see SI 1990/354 (C 12), art. 3; s. 13(1) formerly read as follows:

"If at any time it appears to the Secretary of State that the rules of a recognised organisation do not satisfy the requirements of paragraph 3(1) of Schedule 2 to this Act he may, instead of revoking the recognition order or making an application under section 12 above, direct the organisation to alter, or himself alter, its rules in such manner as he considers necessary for securing that the rules satisfy those requirements."

**Note**

For transitional provisions in relation to the omission of s. 13(1) see SI 1990/354 (C 12), art. 6.

**13(2) [Direction to alter if Sch. 2, para. 3(1) not satisfied]** If at any time it appears to the Secretary of State that–

(a) a recognised self-regulating organisation is concerned with two or more kinds of investment business, and

(b) the requirement in paragraph 3(1) of Schedule 2 to this Act is not satisfied in respect of investment business of one or more but not all of those kinds,

he may, instead of revoking the recognition order or making an application under section 12 above, direct the organisation to alter, or himself alter, its rules so that they preclude a member from carrying on investment business of a kind in respect of which that requirement is not satisfied, unless he is an authorised person otherwise than by virtue of membership of the organisation or is an exempted person in respect of that business.

**History**
S. 13(2) substituted by CA 1989, s. 206(1) and Sch. 23, para. 1(1), (3) as from 15 March 1990 (see SI 1990/354 (C 12), art. 3); s. 13(2) formerly read as follows:

"If at any time it appears to the Secretary of State that the rules or practices of a recognised organisation which is concerned with two or more kinds of investment business do not satisfy any requirement of Schedule 2 to this Act in respect of investment business of any of those kinds he may, instead of revoking the recognition order or making an application under section 12 above, direct the organisation to alter, or himself alter, its rules so that they preclude a member from carrying on investment business of that kind unless he is an authorised person otherwise than by virtue of membership of the organisation or an exempted person in respect of that business."

**Note**
Concerning European investment firms, see the Investment Services Regulations 1995 (SI 1995/3275), reg. 32 and Sch. 7, para. 4.
Concerning European institutions, see the Banking Coordination (Second Council Directive) Regulations 1992 (SI 1992/3218), reg. 55 and Sch. 9, para. 4.
For transitional provisions in relation to the amendment to s. 13(2) see SI 1990/354(C 12), art. 6.

**13(3) [Enforcement of direction]** A direction under this section is enforceable on the application of the Secretary of State by injunction or, in Scotland, by an order under section 45 of the Court of Session Act 1988.

**History**
S. 13(3) substituted by CA 1989, s. 206(1) and Sch. 23, para. 1(1), (4) as from 15 March 1990 (see SI 1990/354 (C 12), art. 3); s. 13(3) formerly read as follows:

"Any direction given under this section shall, on the application of the Secretary of State, be enforceable by mandamus or, in Scotland, by an order for specific performance under section 91 of the Court of Session Act 1868."

**Note**
For transitional provisions in relation to the amendment to s. 13(3) see SI 1990/354 (C 12), art. 6.

**13(4)–(6)** (Omitted by Companies Act 1989, s. 206(1) and Sch. 23, para. 1(1), (5) as from 15 March 1990.)

**History**
In regard to the date of the above omission see SI 1990/354 (C 12), art. 3; s. 13(4)–(6) formerly read as follows:

"**13(4)** Before giving a direction or making any alteration under subsection (1) above the Secretary of State shall consult the organisation concerned.

**(5)** A recognised organisation whose rules have been altered by or pursuant to a direction given by the Secretary of State under subsection (1) above may apply to the court and if the court is satisfied–

(a) that the rules without the alteration satisfied the requirements mentioned in that subsection; or
(b) that other alterations proposed by the organisation would result in the rules satisfying those requirements

the court may set aside the alteration made by or pursuant to the direction given by the Secretary of State and, in a case within paragraph (b) above, order the organisation to make the alterations proposed by it; but the setting aside of an alteration under this subsection shall not affect its previous operation.

**(6)** The jurisdiction conferred by subsection (5) above shall be exercisable by the High Court and the Court of Session."

**13(7) [Application of s. 11(2)–(7), (9)]** Section 11(2) to (7) and (9) above shall, with the necessary modifications, have effect in relation to any direction given or alteration made by the Secretary of State under subsection (2) above as they have effect in relation to an order revoking a recognition order.

**13(8) [Subsequent alteration, revocation by organisation]** The fact that the rules of a recognised organisation have been altered by or pursuant to a direction given by the Secretary of State or pursuant to an order made by the court under this section shall not preclude their subsequent alteration or revocation by that organisation.

## 14 Notification requirements

**14(1) [Regulations re notification of certain events]** The Secretary of State may make regulations requiring a recognised organisation to give him forthwith notice of the occurrence of such events relating to the organisation or its members as are specified in the regulations and such information in respect of those events as is so specified.

**14(2) [Regulations re furnishing information]** The Secretary of State may make regulations requiring a recognised organisation to furnish him at such times or in respect of such periods as are specified in the regulations with such information relating to the organisation or its members as is so specified.

**14(3) [Extent of notices and information]** The notices and information required to be given or furnished under the foregoing provisions of this section shall be such as the Secretary of State may reasonably require for the exercise of his functions under this Act.

**14(4) [Regulations may require specified form, verification]** Regulations under the foregoing provisions of this section may require information to be given in a specified form and to be verified in a specified manner.

**14(5) [Manner of giving notice, information]** Any notice or information required to be given or furnished under the foregoing provisions of this section shall be given in writing or in such other manner as the Secretary of State may approve.

**14(6) [Notice where organisation amends rules etc.]** Where a recognised organisation amends, revokes or adds to its rules or guidance it shall within seven days give the Secretary of State written notice of the amendment, revocation or addition; but notice need not be given of the revocation of guidance other than such as is mentioned in section 9(6) above or of any amendment of or addition to guidance which does not result in or consist of such guidance as is there mentioned.

**14(7) [Offence]** Contravention of, or of regulations under, this section shall not be an offence.

## PERSONS AUTHORISED BY RECOGNISED PROFESSIONAL BODIES

## 15 Authorisation by certification by recognised professional body

**15(1) [Authorised person]** A person holding a certificate issued for the purposes of this Part of this Act by a recognised professional body is an authorised person.

**15(2) [Issue of certificate]** Such a certificate may be issued by a recognised professional body to an individual, a body corporate, a partnership or an unincorporated association.

**15(3) [Certificate issued to partnership]** A certificate issued to a partnership–

(a) shall be issued in the partnership name; and

(b) shall authorise the carrying on of investment business in that name by the partnership to which the certificate is issued, by any partnership which succeeds to that business or by any person who succeeds to that business having previously carried it on in partnership;

and, in relation to a certificate issued to a partnership constituted under the law of England and Wales or Northern Ireland or the law of any other country or territory under which a partnership is not a legal person, references in this Act to the person who holds the certificate or is certified shall be construed as references to persons or person for the time being authorised by the certificate to carry on investment business as mentioned in paragraph (b) above.

## 16 Professional bodies

**16(1) ["Professional body"]** In this Act a **"professional body"** means a body which regulates the practice of a profession and references to the practice of a profession do not include references to carrying on a business consisting wholly or mainly of investment business.

**16(2) [References to members]** In this Act references to the members of a professional body are references to individuals who, whether or not members of the body, are entitled to practice the profession in question and, in practising it, are subject to the rules of that body.

**16(3) [References to notes]** In this Act references to the rules of a professional body are references to the rules (whether or not laid down by the body itself) which the body has power to enforce in relation to the practice of the profession in question and the carrying on of investment business by persons practising that profession or which relate to the grant, suspension or withdrawal of certificates under section 15 above, the admission and expulsion of members or otherwise to the constitution of the body.

**16(4) [Reference to guidance]** In this Act references to guidance issued by a professional body are references to guidance issued or any recommendation made by it to all or any class of its members or persons seeking to become members, or to persons or any class of persons who are or are seeking to be certified by the body, and which would, if it were a rule, fall within subsection (3) above.

## 17 Applications for recognition

**17(1) [Application to Secretary of State]** A professional body may apply to the Secretary of State for an order declaring it to be a recognised professional body for the purposes of this Act.

**17(2) [Effect of s. 9(2)–(6)]** Subsections (2) to (6) of section 9 above shall have effect in relation to an application under subsection (1) above as they have effect in relation to an application under subsection (1) of that section.

For further effect of s. 27 see the Financial Institutions (Prudential Supervision) Regulations 1996 (SI 1996/1669), reg. 9.

## 28 Withdrawal and suspension of authorisation

**28(1) [Power of Secretary of State]** The Secretary of State may at any time withdraw or suspend any authorisation granted by him if it appears to him–

(a) that the holder of the authorisation is not a fit and proper person to carry on the investment business which he is carrying on or proposing to carry on; or

(b) without prejudice to paragraph (a) above, that the holder of the authorisation has contravened any provision of this Act or any rules or regulations made under it or, in purported compliance with any such provision, has furnished the Secretary of State with false, inaccurate or misleading information or has contravened any prohibition or requirement imposed under this Act.

**Note**

Concerning European investment firms, see the Investment Services Regulations 1995 (SI 1995/3275), reg. 32 and Sch. 7, para. 5.

Concerning European institutions, see the Banking Coordination (Second Council Directive) Regulations 1992 (SI 1992/3218), reg. 55 and Sch. 9, para. 5.

**28(2) [Matters in s. 27(3), (4)]** For the purposes of subsection (1)(a) above the Secretary of State may take into account any such matters as are mentioned in section 27(3) and (4) above.

**28(3) [Where holder of authorisation member of SRO]** Where the holder of the authorisation is a member of a recognised self-regulating organisation the rules, prohibitions and requirements referred to in paragraph (b) of subsection (1) above include the rules of that organisation and any prohibition or requirement imposed by virtue of those rules; and where he is a person certified by a recognised professional body the rules, prohibitions and requirements referred to in that paragraph include the rules of that body which regulate the carrying on by him of investment business and any prohibition or requirement imposed by virtue of those rules.

**28(4) [Suspension of authorisation]** The suspension of an authorisation shall be for a specified period or until the occurrence of a specified event or until specified conditions are complied with; and while an authorisation is suspended the holder shall not be an authorised person.

**28(5) [Variation of matters in s. 28(4)]** Any period, event or conditions specified under subsection (4) above in the case of an authorisation may be varied by the Secretary of State on the application of the holder.

## 29 Notice of proposed refusal, withdrawal or suspension

**29(1) [Written notice by Secretary of State]** Where the Secretary of State proposes–

(a) to refuse an application under section 26 or 28(5) above; or

(b) to withdraw or suspend an authorisation,

he shall give the applicant or the authorised person written notice of his intention to do so, stating the reasons for which he proposes to act.

**29(2) [Contents of notice]** In the case of a proposed withdrawal or suspension the notice shall state the date on which it is proposed that the withdrawal or suspension should take effect and, in the case of a proposed suspension, its proposed duration.

**29(3) [Copy of notice to other persons]** Where the reasons stated in a notice under this section relate specifically to matters which–

(a) refer to a person identified in the notice other than the applicant or the holder of the authorisation; and

(b) are in the opinion of the Secretary of State prejudicial to that person in any office or employment,

the Secretary of State shall, unless he considers it impracticable to do so, serve a copy of the notice on that person.

**29(4) [Notice to include reference to Tribunal]** A notice under this section shall give particulars of the right to require the case to be referred to the Tribunal under Chapter IX of this Part of this Act.

**29(5) [Where no right of reference to Tribunal]** Where a case is not required to be referred to the Tribunal by a person on whom a notice is served under this section the Secretary of State shall, at the expiration of the period within which such a requirement can be made–

(a) give that person written notice of the refusal, withdrawal or suspension; or

(b) give that person written notice of the grant of the application or, as the case may be, written notice that the authorisation is not to be withdrawn or suspended;

and the Secretary of State may give public notice of any decision notified by him under paragraph (a) or (b) above and the reasons for the decision except that he shall not do so in the case of a decision notified under paragraph (b) unless the person concerned consents to his doing so.

## 30 Withdrawal of applications and authorisations by consent

**30(1) [Power to withdraw application]** An application under section 26 above may be withdrawn before it is granted or refused; and, subject to subsections (2) and (3) below, an authorisation granted under section 27 above may be withdrawn by the Secretary of State at the request or with the consent of the authorised person.

**30(2) [Power of Secretary of State to refuse withdrawal]** The Secretary of State may refuse to withdraw any such authorisation if he considers that the public interest requires any matter affecting the authorised person to be investigated as a preliminary to a decision on the question whether the Secretary of State should in respect of that person exercise his powers under section 28 above or under any other provision of this Part of this Act.

**30(3) [Further power of Secretary of State]** The Secretary of State may also refuse to withdraw an authorisation where in his opinion it is desirable that a prohibition or restriction should be imposed on the authorised person under Chapter VI of this Part of this Act or that a prohibition or restriction imposed on that person under that Chapter should continue in force.

**30(4) [Public notice of s. 30(1) withdrawal]** The Secretary of State may give public notice of any withdrawal of authorisation under subsection (1) above.

### PERSONS AUTHORISED IN OTHER MEMBER STATES

## 31 Authorisation in other member State

**31(1) [Authorised person]** A person carrying on investment business in the United Kingdom is an authorised person if–

(a) he is established in a member State other than the United Kingdom;

(b) the law of that State recognises him as a national of that or another member State; and

(c) he is for the time being authorised under that law to carry on investment business or investment business of any particular kind.

**31(2) [Establishment in another member State]** For the purposes of this Act a person is established in a member State other than the United Kingdom if his head office is situated in that State and he does not transact investment business from a permanent place of business maintained by him in the United Kingdom.

**31(3) [Conditions for application to persons in other member States]** This section applies to a person only if the provisions of the law under which he is authorised to carry on the investment business in question–

(a) afford to investors in the United Kingdom protection, in relation to his carrying on of that business, which is at least equivalent to that provided for them by the provisions of this Chapter relating to members of recognised self-regulating organisations or to persons authorised by the Secretary of State; or

(b) satisfy the conditions laid down by a Community instrument for the co-ordination or approximation of the laws, regulations or administrative provisions of member States relating to the carrying on of investment business or investment business of the relevant kind.

**31(4) [Certificate re s. 31(3)(a)]** A certificate issued by the Secretary of State and for the time being in force to the effect that the provisions of the law of a member State comply with the requirements of subsection (3)(a) above, either as respects all investment business or as respects investment business of a particular kind, shall be conclusive evidence of that matter but the absence or revocation of such a certificate shall not be regarded as indicating that those requirements are not complied with.

**31(5) [Condition for s. 31(3)(b)]** This section shall not apply to a person by virtue of paragraph (b) of subsection (3) above unless the authority by which he is authorised to carry on the investment business in question certifies that he is authorised to do so under a law which complies with the requirements of that paragraph.

**Note**
Concerning European investment firms, see the Investment Services Regulations 1995 (SI 1995/3275), reg. 1, 24.
See also note after s. 32(1).

# 32 Notice of commencement of business

**32(1) [Written notice to be given offence]** A person who is an authorised person by virtue of section 31 above shall be guilty of an offence unless, not less than seven days before beginning to carry on investment business in the United Kingdom, he has given notice of his intention to do so to the Secretary of State either in writing or in such other manner as the Secretary of State may approve.

**Note**
Concerning European institutions, see the Banking Coordination (Second Council Directive) Regulations 1992 (SI 1992/3218), reg. 51, reg. 55 and Sch. 9, para. 6.

**32(2) [Contents of notice]** The notice shall contain–

(a) information as to the investment business which that person proposes to carry on in the United Kingdom and the services which he will hold himself out as able to provide in the carrying on of that business;

(b) information as to the authorisation of that person in the member State in question;

(c) the address of a place (whether in the United Kingdom or elsewhere) for the service on that person of any notice or other document required or authorised to be served on him under this Act;

(d) such other information as may be prescribed;

and the notice shall comply with such requirements as to the form in which any information is to be given and as to its verification as may be prescribed.

**32(3) [Certificate re s. 31]** A notice by a person claiming to be authorised by virtue of subsection (3)(b) of section 31 above shall be accompanied by a copy of the certificate required by subsection (5) of that section.

**32(4) [Penalty]** A person guilty of an offence under subsection (1) above shall be liable–

(a) on conviction on indictment, to a fine;

(b) on summary conviction, to a fine not exceeding the statutory maximum.

**32(5) [Defence]** In proceedings brought against any person for an offence under subsection (1) above it shall be a defence for him to prove that he took all reasonable precautions and exercised all due diligence to avoid the commission of the offence.

**Note**
Concerning European investment firms, see the Investment Services Regulations 1995 (SI 1995/3275), reg. 32 and Sch. 7, para. 6.

# 33 Termination and suspension of authorisation

**33(1) [Power of Secretary of State]** If it appears to the Secretary of State that a person who is an authorised person by virtue of section 31 above has contravened any provision of this Act or of any rules or regulations made under it or, in purported compliance with any such provision, has furnished the Secretary of State with false, inaccurate or misleading information or has contravened any prohibition or requirement imposed under this Act the Secretary of State may direct–

(a) that he shall cease to be an authorised person by virtue of that section; or

(b) that he shall not be an authorised person by virtue of that section for a specified period or until the occurrence of a specified event or until specified conditions are complied with.

**33(2) [Rules in s. 33(1) re member of SRO]** In the case of a person who is a member of a recognised self-regulating organisation the rules, prohibitions and requirements referred to in subsection (1) above include the rules of that organisation and any prohibition or requirement imposed by virtue of those rules; and in the case of a person who is certified by a recognised professional body the rules, prohibitions and requirements referred to in that subsection include the rules of that body which regulate the carrying on by him of investment business and any prohibition or requirement imposed by virtue of those rules.

**33(3) [Variation of matters in s. 33(1)(b)]** Any period, event or condition specified in a direction under subsection (1)(b) above may be varied by the Secretary of State on the application of the person to whom the direction relates.

**33(4) [Consultation with relevant authority before direction]** The Secretary of State shall consult the relevant supervisory authority before giving a direction under this section unless he considers it essential in the interests of investors that the direction should be given forthwith but in that case he shall consult the authority immediately after giving the direction and may then revoke or vary it if he considers it appropriate to do so.

**33(5) [Revocation of direction]** The Secretary of State shall revoke a direction under this section if he is satisfied, after consulting the relevant supervisory authority, that it will secure that the person concerned will comply with the provisions mentioned in subsection (1) above.

**33(6) ["The relevant supervisory authority"]** In this section **"the relevant supervisory authority"** means the authority of the member State where the person concerned is established which is responsible for supervising the carrying on of investment business of the kind which that person is or was carrying on.

## 34 Notice of proposed termination or suspension

**34(1) [Duty of Secretary of State to give written notice]** Where the Secretary of State proposes–

(a) to give a direction under section 33 above; or

(b) to refuse an application under subsection (3) of that section,

he shall give the authorised person written notice of his intention to do so, stating the reasons for which he proposes to act.

**34(2) [Where proposed direction under s. 33]** In the case of a proposed direction under section 33 above the notice shall state the date on which it is proposed that the direction should take effect and, in the case of a proposed direction under subsection (1)(b) of that section, its proposed duration.

**34(3) [Copy of notice to other persons]** Where the reasons stated in a notice under this section relate specifically to matters which–

(a) refer to a person identified in the notice other than the authorised person; and

(b) are in the opinion of the Secretary of State prejudicial to that person in any office or employment,

the Secretary of State shall, unless he considers it impracticable to do so, serve a copy of the notice on that other person.

**34(4) [Notice to include reference to Tribunal]** A notice under this section shall give particulars of the right to require the case to be referred to the Tribunal under Chapter IX of this Part of this Act.

**34(5) [Where case not required to be referred to Tribunal]** Where a case is not required to be referred to the Tribunal by a person on whom a notice is served under this section the Secretary of State shall, at the expiration of the period within which such a requirement can be made–

(a) give that person written notice of the direction or refusal; or

(b) give that person written notice that the direction is not to be given or, as the case may be, of the grant of the application;

and the Secretary of State may give public notice of any decision notified by him under paragraph (a) or (b) above and the reasons for the decision except that he shall not do so in the case of a decision within paragraph (b) unless the person concerned consents to his doing so.

# Chapter IV – Exempted Persons

THE BANK OF ENGLAND

## 35 The Bank of England

35 The Bank of England is an exempted person.

RECOGNISED INVESTMENT EXCHANGES AND CLEARING HOUSES

## 36 Investment exchanges

**36(1) [Recognised investment exchange]** A recognised investment exchange is an exempted person as respects anything done in its capacity as such which constitutes investment business.

**36(2) [References to rules of investment exchange]** In this Act references to the rules of an investment exchange are references to the rules made or conditions imposed by it with respect to the matters dealt with in Schedule 4 to this Act, with respect to the admission of persons to or their exclusion from the use of its facilities or otherwise relating to its constitution.

**36(3) [References to guidance issued by investment exchange]** In this Act references to guidance issued by an investment exchange are references to guidance issued or any recommendation made by it to all or any class of its members or users or persons seeking to become members of the exchange or to use its facilities and which would, if it were a rule, fall within subsection (2) above.

**Note**
Concerning the Investment Services Directive, see the Investment Services Regulations 1995 (SI 1995/3275), reg. 1, 25.

## 37 Grant and revocation of recognition

**37(1) [Application to Secretary of State]** Any body corporate or unincorporated association may apply to the Secretary of State for an order declaring it to be a recognised investment exchange for the purposes of this Act.

**37(2) [Effect of s. 9(2)–(5)]** Subsections (2) to (5) of section 9 above shall have effect in relation to an application under subsection (1) above as they have effect in relation to an application under subsection (1) of that section; and every application under subsection (1) above shall be accompanied by–

(a) a copy of the applicant's rules;

(b) a copy of any guidance issued by the applicant which is intended to have continuing effect and is issued in writing or other legible form; and

(c) particulars of any arrangements which the applicant has made or proposes to make for the provision of clearing services.

**37(3) [Power of Secretary of State to make order]** The Secretary of State may, on an application duly made in accordance with subsection (1) above and after being furnished with all such information as he may require in connection with the application, make or refuse to make an order ("a recognition order") declaring the applicant to be a recognised investment exchange for the purposes of this Act.

**37(4) [Where Sch. 4 requirements are satisfied]** Subject to Chapter XIV of this Part of this Act, the Secretary of State may make a recognition order if it appears to him from the information furnished by the exchange making the application and having regard to any other information in his possession that the requirements of Schedule 4 to this Act are satisfied as respects that exchange.

**37(5) [Notice to applicant re refusal]** Where the Secretary of State refuses an application for a recognition order he shall give the applicant a written notice to that effect stating the reasons for the refusal.

**37(6) [Date to be stated in order]** A recognition order shall state the date on which it takes effect.

**37(7) [Revocation of recognition order]** A recognition order may be revoked by a further order made by the Secretary of State if at any time it appears to him–

(a) that any requirement of Schedule 4 to this Act is not satisfied in the case of the exchange to which the recognition order relates; or

(b) that the exchange has failed to comply with any obligation to which it is subject by virtue of this Act;

and subsections (2) to (9) of section 11 above shall have effect in relation to the revocation of a recognition order under this subsection as they have effect in relation to the revocation of such an order under subsection (1) of that section.

**37(8) [Effect of s. 12]** Section 12 above shall have effect in relation to a recognised investment exchange and the requirements and obligations referred to in subsection (7) above as it has effect in relation to the requirements and obligations there mentioned.

## 38 Clearing houses

**38(1) [Recognised clearing house]** A recognised clearing house is an exempted person as respects anything done by it in its capacity as a person providing clearing services for the transaction of investment business.

**38(2) [References to rules of clearing house]** In this Act references to the rules of a clearing house are references to the rules made or conditions imposed by it with respect to the provision by it or its members of clearing services under clearing arrangements, that is to say, arrangements with a recognised investment exchange for the provision of clearing services in respect of transactions effected on the exchange.

**38(3) [References to guidance issued by clearing house]** In this Act references to guidance issued by a clearing house are references to guidance issued or any recommendation made by it to all or any class of its members or persons using or seeking to use its services and which would, if it were a rule, fall within subsection (2) above.

## 39 Grant and revocation of recognition

**39(1) [Application to Secretary of State]** Any body corporate or unincorporated association may apply to the Secretary of State for an order declaring it to be a recognised clearing house for the purposes of this Act.

**39(2) [Effect of s. 9(2)–(5)]** Subsections (2) to (5) of section 9 above shall have effect in relation to an application under subsection (1) above as they have effect in relation to an application under subsection (1) of that section; and any application under subsection (1) above shall be accompanied by–

(a) a copy of the applicant's rules;

(b) a copy of any guidance issued by the applicant which is intended to have continuing effect and is issued in writing or other legible form; and

(c) particulars of any recognised investment exchange with which the applicant proposes to make clearing arrangements and of any other person (whether or not such an exchange) for whom the applicant provides clearing services.

**39(3) [Power of Secretary of State to make order]** The Secretary of State may, on an application duly made in accordance with subsection (1) above and after being furnished with all such information as he may require in connection with the application, make or refuse to make an order ("a recognition order") declaring the applicant to be a recognised clearing house for the purposes of this Act.

**39(4) [Guidelines for making order]** Subject to Chapter XIV of this Part of this Act, the Secretary of State may make a recognition order if it appears to him from the information furnished by the clearing house making the application and having regard to any other information in his possession that the clearing house–

(a) has financial resources sufficient for the proper performance of its functions;

(b) has adequate arrangements and resources for the effective monitoring and enforcement of compliance with its rules or, as respects monitoring, arrangements providing for that function to be performed on behalf of the clearing house (and without affecting its responsibility) by another body or person who is able and willing to perform it;

(c) provides or is able to provide clearing services which would enable a recognised investment exchange to make arrangements with it that satisfy the requirements of Schedule 4 to this Act; and

(d) is able and willing to comply with duties corresponding to those imposed in the case of a recognised investment exchange by paragraph 5 of that Schedule.

**39(5) [Written notice to applicant re refusal]** Where the Secretary of State refuses an application for a recognition order he shall give the applicant a written notice to that effect stating the reasons for the refusal.

**39(6) [Order to state date]** A recognition order shall state the date on which it takes effect.

**39(7) [Revocation of recognition order]** A recognition order may be revoked by a further order made by the Secretary of State if at any time it appears to him–

(a) that any requirement of subsection (4) above is not satisfied in the case of the clearing house; or

(b) that the clearing house has failed to comply with any obligation to which it is subject by virtue of this Act;

and subsections (2) to (9) of section 11 above shall have effect in relation to the revocation of a recognition order under this subsection as they have effect in relation to the revocation of such an order under subsection (1) of that section.

**39(8) [Effect of s. 12]** Section 12 above shall have effect in relation to a recognised clearing house and the requirements and obligations referred to in subsection (7) above as it has effect in relation to the requirements and obligations there mentioned.

## 40 Overseas investment exchanges and clearing houses

**40(1) [Certain s. 37(1), 39(1) applications]** Any application under section 37(1) or 39(1) above by a body or association whose head office is situated in a country outside the United Kingdom shall contain the address of a place in the United Kingdom for the service on that body or association of notices or other documents required or authorised to be served on it under this Act.

**40(2) [Substitutions in s. 37(4), 39(4)]** In relation to any such body or association sections 37(4) and 39(4) above shall have effect with the substitution for the requirements there mentioned of the following requirements, that is to say–

(a) that the body or association is, in the country in which its head office is situated, subject to supervision which, together with the rules and practices of that body or association, is such that investors in the United Kingdom are afforded protection in relation to that body or association at least equivalent to that provided by the provisions of this Act in relation to investment exchanges and clearing houses in respect of which recognition orders and made otherwise than by virtue of this subsection; and

(b) that the body or association is able and willing to co-operate, by the sharing of information and otherwise, with the authorities, bodies and persons responsible in the United Kingdom for the supervision and regulation of investment business or other financial services; and

(c) that adequate arrangements exist for such co-operation between those responsible for the supervision of the body or association in the country mentioned in paragraph (a) above and the authorities, bodies and persons mentioned in paragraph (b) above.

**40(3) [Matter for determining whether to make s. 40(2) order]** In determining whether to make a recognition order by virtue of subsection (2) above the Secretary of State may have regard to the extent to which persons in the United Kingdom and persons in the country mentioned in that subsection have access to the financial markets in each others' countries.

**40(4) [Further matters re s. 40(2)]** In relation to a body or association declared to be a recognised investment exchange or recognised clearing house by a recognition order made by virtue of subsection (2) above–

(a) the reference in section 36(2) above to the matters dealt with in Schedule 4 to this Act shall be construed as a reference to corresponding matters;

(b) sections 37(7) and (8) and 39(7) and (8) above shall have effect as if the requirements mentioned in section 37(7)(a) and in section 39(7)(a) were those of subsection (2)(a) and (b) above; and

(c) the grounds on which the order may be revoked under section 37(7) or 39(7) above shall include the ground that it appears to the Secretary of State that revocation is desirable in the interests of investors and potential investors in the United Kingdom.

**40(5) ["Country"]** In this section **"country"** includes any territory or any part of a country or territory.

**40(6) ["Overseas investment exchange", "overseas clearing house"]** A body or association declared to be a recognised investment exchange or recognised clearing house by a recognition order made by virtue of subsection (2) above is in this Act referred to as an "overseas investment exchange" or an "overseas clearing house".

# 41 Notification requirements

**41(1) [Power of Secretary of State to make regulations re notice]** The Secretary of State may make regulations requiring a recognised investment exchange or recognised clearing house to give him forthwith notice of the occurrence of such events relating to the exchange or clearing house as are specified in the regulations and such information in respect of those events as is so specified.

**41(2) [Regulations re furnishing information]** The Secretary of State may make regulations requiring a recognised investment exchange or recognised clearing house to furnish him at such times or in respect of such periods as are specified in the regulations with such information relating to the exchange or clearing house as is so specified.

**41(3) [Extent of notices and information]** The notices and information required to be given or furnished under the foregoing provisions of this section shall be such as the Secretary of State may reasonably require for the exercise of his functions under this Act.

**41(4) [Form, verification of information]** Regulations under the foregoing provisions of this section may require information to be given in a specified form and to be verified in a specified manner.

**41(5) [Notice by recognised investment exchange]** Where a recognised investment exchange–

(a) amends, revokes or adds to its rules or guidance; or

(b) makes, terminates or varies any clearing arrangements,

it shall within seven days give written notice to the Secretary of State of the amendment, revocation or addition or, as the case may be, of the matters mentioned in paragraph (b) above.

**41(6) [Notice by recognised clearing house]** Where a recognised clearing house–

(a) amends, revokes or adds to its rules or guidance; or

(b) makes a change in the persons for whom it provides clearing services,

it shall within seven days give written notice to the Secretary of State of the amendment, revocation or addition or, as the case may be, of the change.

**41(7) [Limits on notice]** Notice need not be given under subsection (5) or (6) above of the revocation of guidance other than such as is mentioned in section 37(2)(b) or 39(2)(b) above or of any amendment of or addition to guidance which does not result in or consist of such guidance as is there mentioned.

OTHER EXEMPTIONS

# 42 Lloyd's

42 The Society of Lloyd's and persons permitted by the Council of Lloyd's to act as underwriting agents at Lloyd's are exempted persons as respects investment business carried on in connection with or for the purpose of insurance business at Lloyd's.

# 43 Listed money market institutions

**43(1) ["Listed institution"]** A person for the time being included in a list maintained by the Financial Services Authority ("the Authority") for the purposes of this section ("a listed institution") is an exempted person in respect of, and of anything done for the purposes of, any transaction to which Part I or Part II of Schedule 5 to this Act applies and in respect of any arrangements made by him with a view to other persons entering into a transaction to which Part III of that Schedule applies.

**History**
In s. 43(1) the words "Financial Services Authority ('the Authority')" substituted for the former words "Bank of England" by the Bank of England Act 1998, s. 23(1), 45 and Sch. 5, para. 44(1), (2) as from 1 June 1998 (see SI 1998/1120 (C 25), art. 2).

**43(2) [Admission to list etc.]** The conditions imposed by the Authority for admission to the list referred to in this section and the arrangements made by it for a person's admission to and removal from the list shall require the approval of the Treasury; and this section shall cease to have effect if that approval is withdrawn but without prejudice to its again having effect if approval is given for fresh conditions or arrangements.

**History**
In s. 43(2) the word "Authority" substituted for the former words "Bank of England" by the Bank of England Act 1998, s. 23(1), 45 and Sch. 5, para. 44(1), (3) as from 1 June 1998 (see SI 1998/1120 (C 25), art. 2).

**43(2A) [Conditions for admission]** Without prejudice to the generality of the Authority's power to impose conditions for admission to the list, the conditions for admission may include–

(a) a condition having the effect of requiring the payment of an application fee, and
(b) a condition having the effect of requiring the payment of periodic fees.

**History**
See history note after s. 43(2B).

**43(2B) [Condition referred to in s. 43(2A)]** A condition of the kind referred to in subsection (2A)(a) or (b) above–

(a) may provide for the amount payable to be such as is specified in, or determined under, the condition, and
(b) may make different provision for different cases.

**History**
S. 43(2A), (2B) inserted by the Bank of England Act 1998, s. 26(2), 45 as from 1 June 1998 (see SI 1998/1120 (C 25), art. 2).

**43(3) [Publication of list]** The Authority shall publish the list as for the time being in force and provide a certified copy of it at the request of any person wishing to refer to it in legal proceedings.

**History**
In s. 43(3) the word "Authority" substituted for the former words "Bank of England" by the Bank of England Act 1998, s. 23(1), 45 and Sch. 5, para. 44(1), (3) as from 1 June 1998 (see SI 1998/1120 (C 25), art. 2).

**43(4) [Certified copy of list]** Such a certified copy shall be evidence or, in Scotland, sufficient evidence of the contents of the list; and a copy purporting to be certified by or on behalf of the Authority shall be deemed to have been duly certified unless the contrary is shown.

**History**
In s. 43(4) the word "Authority" substituted for the former word "Bank" by the Bank of England Act 1998, s. 23(1), 45 and Sch. 5, para. 44(1), (4) as from 1 June 1998 (see SI 1998/1120 (C 25), art. 2).

**43(5) [Authority not liable]** Neither the Authority nor any person who is, or is acting as, an officer or servant of the Authority shall be liable in damages for anything done or omitted in the discharge or purported discharge of any of the Authority's functions under this section, unless it is shown that the act or omission was in bad faith.

**History**
S. 43(5) inserted by the Bank of England Act 1998, s. 25(1), 45 as from 1 June 1998 (see SI 1998/1120 (C 25), art. 2).

**Note**
The functions of the Bank of England relating to the listing of money market institutions transferred to the Financial Services Authority by the Bank of England Act 1998, s. 21(b)(i), 45 as from 1 June 1998 (see SI 1998/1120 (C 25), art. 2).
Concerning European investment firms, see the Investment Services Regulations 1995 (SI 1995/3275), reg. 1, 26.
Concerning European institutions, see the Banking (Second Council Directive) Regulations 1992 (SI 1992/3218), reg. 52.

## 44 Appointed representatives

**44(1) [Exempted person]** An appointed representative is an exempted person as respects investment business carried on by him as such a representative.

**44(2) [Definition]** For the purposes of this Act an appointed representative is a person–

(a) who is employed by an authorised person (his "principal") under a contract for services which–

  (i) requires or permits him to carry on investment business to which this section applies; and

  (ii) complies with subsections (4) and (5) below; and

(b) for whose activities in carrying on the whole or part of that investment business his principal has accepted responsibility in writing;

and the investment business carried on by an appointed representative as such is the investment business for which his principal has accepted responsibility.

**44(3) [Application of section]** This section applies to investment business carried on by an appointed representative which consists of–

(a) procuring or endeavouring to procure the persons with whom he deals to enter into investment agreements with his principal or (if not prohibited by his contract) with other persons;

(b) giving advice to the persons with whom he deals about entering into investment agreements with his principal or (if not prohibited by his contract) with other persons; or

(c) giving advice as to the sale of investments issued by his principal or as to the exercise of rights conferred by an investment whether or not issued as aforesaid.

**44(4) [Contract between appointed representative and principal]** If the contract between an appointed representative and his principal does not prohibit the representative from procuring or endeavouring to procure persons to enter into investment agreements with persons other than his principal it must make provision for enabling the principal either to impose such a prohibition or to restrict the kinds of investment to which those agreements may relate or the other persons with whom they may be entered into.

**44(5) [Further matter re s. 44(4) contract]** If the contract between an appointed representative and his principal does not prohibit the representative from giving advice about entering into investment agreements with persons other than his principal it must make provision for enabling the principal either to impose such a prohibition or to restrict the kinds of advice which the representative may give by reference to the kinds of investment in relation to which or the persons with whom the representative may advise that investment agreements should be made.

**44(6) [Responsibility of principal]** The principal of an appointed representative shall be responsible, to the same extent as if he had expressly authorised it, for anything said or done or omitted by the representative in carrying on the investment business for which he has accepted responsibility.

**44(7) [Determining compliance of authorised person]** In determining whether an authorised person has complied with–

(a) any provision contained in or made under this Act; or

(b) any rules of a recognised self-regulating organisation or recognised professional body,

anything which a person who at the material time is or was an appointed representative of the authorised person has said, done or omitted as respects investment business for which the authorised person has accepted responsibility shall be treated as having been said, done or omitted by the authorised person.

**44(8) [Limit on s. 44(7)]** Nothing in subsection (7) above shall cause the knowledge or intentions of an appointed representative to be attributed to his principal for the purpose of determining whether the principal has committed a criminal offence unless in all the circumstances it is reasonable for them to be attributed to him.

**44(9) ["Investment agreement"]** In this Act **"investment agreement"** means any agreement the making or performance of which by either party constitutes an activity which falls within any paragraph of Part II of Schedule 1 to this Act or would do so apart from Parts III and IV of that Schedule.

**Note**
Concerning the Investment Services Directive and European investment firms, see the Investment Services Regulations 1995 (SI 1995/3275), reg. 1, 27, 32 and Sch. 7, para. 7.
Concerning European institutions, see the Banking Coordination (Second Council Directive) Regulations 1992 (SI 1992/3218), reg. 55 and Sch. 9, para. 7.

## 45 Miscellaneous exemptions

**45(1) [Exempted persons]** Each of the following persons is an exempted person to the extent specified in relation to that person–

(a) the President of the Family Division of the High Court when acting in the exercise of his functions under section 9 of the Administration of Estates Act 1925;

(b) the Probate Judge of the High Court of Northern Ireland when acting in the exercise of his functions under section 3 of the Administration of Estates Act (Northern Ireland) 1955;

(c) the Accountant General of the Supreme Court when acting in the exercise of his functions under Part VI of the Administration of Justice Act 1982;

(d) the Accountant of Court when acting in the exercise of his functions in connection with the consignation or deposit of sums of money;

(e) the Public Trustee when acting in the exercise of his functions under the Public Trustee Act 1906;

(f) the Master of the Court of Protection when acting in the exercise of his functions under Part VII of the Mental Health Act 1983;

(g) the Official Solicitor to the Supreme Court when acting as judicial trustee under the Judicial Trustees Act 1896;

(h) a registrar of a county court when managing funds paid into court;

(i) a sheriff clerk when acting in the exercise of his functions in connection with the consignation or deposit of sums of money;

(j) a person acting in his capacity as manager of a fund established under section 22 or 22A of the Charities Act 1960, or section 24 or 25 of the Charities Act 1993, section 25 of the Charities Act (Northern Ireland) 1964, section 11 of the Trustee Investments Act 1961 or section 42 of the Administration of Justice Act 1982;

(k) the Central Board of Finance of the Church of England or a Diocesan Authority within the meaning of the Church Funds Investment Measure 1958 when acting in the exercise of its functions under that Measure;

(l) a person acting in his capacity as an official receiver within the meaning of section 399 of the Insolvency Act 1986 or in that capacity within the meaning of any corresponding provision in force in Northern Ireland.

**History**
In s. 45(1)(j) the words "or 22A" inserted by Charities Act 1992, s. 78(1) and Sch. 6, para. 14 as from 1 September 1992 (see SI 1992/1900 (C 64), art. 2 and Sch. 1) and the words ", or section 24 or 25 of the Charities Act 1993" inserted by Charities Act 1993, s. 98(1), 99(1) and Sch. 6, para. 22 as from 1 August 1993.

**45(2) [Where bankruptcy order re authorised person etc.]** Where a bankruptcy order is made in respect of an authorised person or of a person whose authorisation is suspended under section 28 above or who is the subject of a direction under section 33(1)(b) above or a winding-up order is made in respect of a partnership which is such a person, the trustee in bankruptcy or liquidator acting in his capacity as such is an exempted person but–

(a) sections 48 to 71 below and, so far as relevant to any of those provisions, Chapter IX of this Part of this Act; and

(b) sections 104, 105 and 106 below,

shall apply to him to the same extent as they applied to the bankrupt or partnership and, if the bankrupt or partnership was subject to the rules of a recognised self-regulating organisation or recognised professional body, he shall himself also be subject to those rules.

**Note**
Concerning European investment firms, see the Investment Services Regulations 1995 (SI 1995/3275), reg. 32 and Sch. 7, para. 8.

Concerning European institutions, see the Banking Coordination (Second Council Directive) Regulations 1992 (SI 1992/3218), reg. 55 and Sch. 9, para. 8.

**45(3) [Application of s. 45(2) to Scotland]** In the application of subsection (2) above to Scotland–

(a) for the reference to a bankruptcy order being made in respect of a person there shall be substituted a reference to the estate of that person being sequestrated;

(b) the reference to a winding-up order in respect of a partnership is a reference to such an order made under section 72 below;

(c) for the reference to the trustee in bankruptcy there shall be substituted a reference to the interim trustee or permanent trustee within the meaning of the Bankruptcy (Scotland) Act 1985; and

(d) for the references to the bankrupt there shall be substituted references to the debtor.

**45(4) [Application of s. 45(2) to Northern Ireland]** In the application of subsection (2) above to Northern Ireland for the reference to a bankruptcy order there shall be substituted a reference to an order of adjudication of bankruptcy and the reference to a trustee in bankruptcy shall include a reference to an assignee in bankruptcy.

SUPPLEMENTAL

## 46 Power to extend or restrict exemptions

**46(1) [Order by Secretary of State]** The Secretary of State may by order provide–

(a) for exemptions additional to those specified in the foregoing provisions of this Chapter; or

(b) for removing or restricting any exemption conferred by section 42, 43 or 45 above;

and any such order may contain such transitional provisions as the Secretary of State thinks necessary or expedient.

**46(2) [Approval etc. by Parliament]** An order making such provision as is mentioned in paragraph (a) of subsection (1) above shall be subject to annulment in pursuance of a resolution of either House of Parliament; and no order making such provision as is mentioned in paragraph (b) of that subsection shall be made unless a draft of it has been laid before and approved by a resolution of each House of Parliament.

**Note**

See the Financial Services Act 1986 (EEA Regulated Markets) (Exemption) Order 1995 (SI 1995/3273), the Financial Services Act 1986 (Exemption) Order 1996 (SI 1996/1587), the Financial Services Act 1986 (Corporate Debt Exemption) Order 1997 (SI 1997/816) and the Financial Services Act 1986 (Miscellaneous Exemptions) Order 1997 (SI 1997/3024).

# Chapter V – Conduct of Investment Business

## 47 Misleading statements and practices

**47(1) [Offence re statements]** Any person who–

(a) makes a statement, promise or forecast which he knows to be misleading, false or deceptive or dishonestly conceals any material facts; or

(b) recklessly makes (dishonestly or otherwise) a statement, promise or forecast which is misleading, false or deceptive,

is guilty of an offence if he makes the statement, promise or forecast or conceals the facts for the purpose of inducing, or is reckless as to whether it may induce, another person (whether or not the person to whom the statement, promise or forecast is made or from whom the facts are concealed) to enter or offer to enter into, or to refrain from entering or offering to enter into, an investment agreement or to exercise, or refrain from exercising, any rights conferred by an investment.

**47(2) [Offence re conduct]** Any person who does any act or engages in any course of conduct which creates a false or misleading impression as to the market in or the price or value of any investments is guilty of an offence if he does so for the purpose of creating that impression and of thereby inducing another person to acquire, dispose of, subscribe for or underwrite those investments or to refrain from doing so or to exercise, or refrain from exercising, any rights conferred by those investments.

**47(3) [Defence re s. 47(2)]** In proceedings brought against any person for an offence under subsection (2) above it shall be a defence for him to prove that he reasonably believed that his act or conduct would not create an impression that was false or misleading as to the matters mentioned in that subsection.

**47(4) [Non-application of s. 47(1)]** Subsection (1) above does not apply unless–

(a) the statement, promise or forecast is made in or from, or the facts are concealed in or from, the United Kingdom;

(b) the person on whom the inducement is intended to or may have effect is in the United Kingdom; or

(c) the agreement is or would be entered into or the rights are or would be exercised in the United Kingdom.

**47(5) [Non-application of s. 47(2)]** Subsection (2) above does not apply unless–

(a) the act is done or the course of conduct is engaged in in the United Kingdom; or

(b) the false or misleading impression is created there.

**47(6) [Penalty]** A person guilty of an offence under this section shall be liable–

(a) on conviction on indictment, to imprisonment for a term not exceeding seven years or to a fine or to both;

(b) on summary conviction, to imprisonment for a term not exceeding six months or to a fine not exceeding the statutory maximum or to both.

## 47A Statements of principle

**47A(1) [Power of Secretary of State to issue statements of principle]** The Secretary of State may issue statements of principle with respect to the conduct and financial standing expected of persons authorised to carry on investment business.

**47A(2) [Conduct expected]** The conduct expected may include compliance with a code or standard issued by another person, as for the time being in force, and may allow for the exercise of discretion by any person pursuant to any such code or standard.

**47A(3) [Consequence of failure to comply]** Failure to comply with a statement of principle under this section is a ground for the taking of disciplinary action or the exercise of powers of intervention, but it does not of itself give rise to any right of action by investors or other persons affected or affect the validity of any transaction.

**47A(4) [Extent of disciplinary action]** The disciplinary action which may be taken by virtue of subsection (3) is–

(a) the withdrawal or suspension of authorisation under section 28 or the termination or suspension of authorisation under section 33,

(b) the giving of a disqualification direction under section 59,

(c) the making of a public statement under section 60,

(d) the application by the Secretary of State for an injunction, interdict or other order under section 61(1), or

(e) the giving of a direction under regulation 18 of the Open-Ended Investment Companies (Investment Companies with Variable Capital) Regulations 1996 (directions) or the making of an application for an order under regulation 20 of those Regulations (application to court to remove director or depositary);

and the reference in that subsection to powers of intervention is to the powers conferred by Chapter VI of this Part.

**History**

In s. 47A(4)(c) the former word "or" appearing after the words "under section 60" omitted; in s. 47A(4)(d) the word "or" inserted after the words "section 61(1)"; and s. 47A(4)(e) inserted by the Open-Ended Investment Companies (Investment Companies with Variable Capital) Regulations 1996 (SI 1996/2827), reg. 1, 75 and Sch. 8, para. 12 as from 6 January 1997.

**47A(5) [Principles re compliance with code or standard]** Where a statement of principle relates to compliance with a code or standard issued by another person, the statement of principle may provide–

(a) that failure to comply with the code or standard shall be a ground for the taking of disciplinary action, or the exercise of powers of intervention, only in such cases and to such extent as may be specified; and

(b) that no such action shall be taken, or any such power exercised, except at the request of the person by whom the code or standard in question was issued.

**47A(6) [Manner of exercise of powers]** The Secretary of State shall exercise his powers in such manner as appears to him appropriate to secure compliance with statements of principle under this section.

**History**

S. 47A inserted by CA 1989, s. 192 as from 15 March 1990 (see SI 1990/354 (C 12), art. 3).

**Note**

Concerning European investment firms, see the Investment Services Regulations 1995 (SI 1995/3275), reg. 32 and Sch. 7, para. 9, and reg. 58 and Sch. 11, para. 4.

For transfer of the Secretary of State's functions under s. 47A see SI 1990/354 (C 12), art. 4(3)(a).

Concerning European institutions, see the Banking Coordination (Second Council Directive) Regulations 1992 (SI 1992/3218), reg. 55 and Sch. 9, para. 9; and reg. 83 and Sch. 11, para. 9.

## 48 Conduct of business rules

**48(1) [Power of Secretary of State to make rules]** The Secretary of State may make rules regulating the conduct of investment business by authorised persons but those rules shall not apply to persons certified by a recognised professional body in respect of investment business in the carrying on of which they are subject to the rules of the body.

**History**

In s. 48(1) the words "members of a recognised self-regulating organisation or" formerly appearing after the words "shall not apply to" and the words "organisation or" formerly appearing after the words "subject to the rules of the" omitted and repealed by CA 1989, s. 206(1), 212, Sch. 23, para. 2(1), (2), and Sch. 24 as from 15 March 1990 (see SI 1990/354 (C 12), art. 3).

**Note**

See note after s. 48(2).

**48(2) [Extent of rules]** Rules under this section may in particular make provision–

(a) prohibiting a person from carrying on, or holding himself out as carrying on–

(i) investment business of any kind specified in the rules; or

(ii) investment business of a kind or on a scale other than that notified by him to the Secretary of State in connection with an application for authorisation under Chapter III of this Part of this Act, in a notice under section 32 above or in accordance with any provision of the rules or regulations in that behalf;

(b) prohibiting a person from carrying on investment business in relation to persons other than those of a specified class or description;

(c) regulating the manner in which a person may hold himself out as carrying on investment business;

(d) regulating the manner in which a person makes a market in any investments;

(e) as to the form and content of advertisements in respect of investment business;

(f) requiring the principals of appointed representatives to impose restrictions on the investment business carried on by them;

(g) requiring the disclosure of the amount or value, or of arrangements for the payment or provision, of commissions or other inducements in connection with investment business and restricting the matters by reference to which or the manner in which their amount or value may be determined;

(h) enabling or requiring information obtained by an authorised person in the course of carrying on one part of his business to be withheld by him from persons with whom he deals in the course of carrying on another part and for that purpose enabling or requiring persons employed in one part of that business to withhold information from those employed in another part;

(i) as to the circumstances and manner in which and the time when or the period during which action may be taken for the purpose of stabilising the price of investments of any specified description;

(j) for arrangements for the settlement of disputes;

(k) requiring the keeping of accounts and other records, as to their form and content and for their inspection;

(l) requiring a person to whom the rules apply to make provision for the protection of investors in the event of the cessation of his investment business in consequence of his death, incapacity or otherwise.

**Note**

Concerning European investment firms, see the Investment Services Regulations 1995 (SI 1995/3275), reg. 32 and Sch. 7, para. 10.

**48(3) [Relationship between s. 48(1) and (2)]** Subsection (2) above is without prejudice to the generality of subsection (1) above and accordingly rules under this section may make provision for matters other than those mentioned in subsection (2) or further provision as to any of the matters there mentioned except that they shall not impose limits on the amount or value of commissions or other inducements paid or provided in connection with investment business.

**48(4) [Related business]** Rules under this section may also regulate or prohibit the carrying on in connection with investment business of any other business or the carrying on of any other business which is held out as being for the purposes of investment.

**48(5) ["Advertisement" in s. 48(2)(e)]** In paragraph (e) of subsection (2) above **"advertisement"** does not include any advertisement which is subject to section 154 below or which is required or permitted to be published by listing rules under Part IV of this Act and relates to securities which have been admitted to listing under that Part.

**History**

In s. 48(5) the words "and rules under that paragraph shall have effect subject to the provisions of Part V of this Act" formerly appearing at the end repealed by the Public Offers of Securities Regulations 1995 (SI 1995/1537), reg. 1, 17 and Sch. 2, para. 5(a) as from 19 June 1995.

**48(6) [Matters done in conformity with s. 48(2)(h)]** Nothing done in conformity with rules made under paragraph (h) of subsection (2) above shall be regarded as a contravention of section 47 above.

**48(7) [Contravention of s. 47(2)]** Section 47(2) above shall not be regarded as contravened by anything done for the purpose of stabilising the price of investments if it is done in conformity with rules made under this section and–

(a) (i) in respect of investments which fall within any of paragraphs 1 to 5 of Schedule 1 to this Act and are specified by the rules; and

(ii) during such period before or after the issue of those investments as is specified by the rules,

or

(b) (i) in respect of such investments as are mentioned in subparagraph (a)(i) above; and

(ii) during a period starting with the date of the first public announcement of an offer of those investments which states the price or the minimum price at which the investments are to be sold and ending on the 30th day after the closing date specified in the announcement for acceptances of such offer.

**History**

In s. 48(7), "(i)" inserted after "(a)", (ii) substituted for "(b)" formerly appearing before the words "during such period", and the word "or" and para. (b)(i) and (ii) added by the Financial Services Act 1986 (Stabilisation) Order 1988 (SI 1988/717), art. 2(a)–(c) as from 6 April 1988.

**48(7A) [Meaning of "an offer" in s. 48(7)(b)(ii)]** For the purposes of subparagraph (b)(ii) of subsection (7) above **"an offer"** means an offer for cash (other than in relation to the issue of the investments in question) where either–

(a) the investments have been admitted to dealing on a recognised investment exchange or any other exchange of repute outside the United Kingdom; or

(b) the offer is on the occasion of such admission or conditional on such admission;

and the total cost of the investments subject to the offer at the price stated in the first public announcement mentioned in subsection (7) above is at least £15,000,000 (or the equivalent in the currency or unit of account in which the price is stated on the date of the announcement).

**History**

S. 48(7A) added by the Financial Services Act 1986 (Stabilisation) Order 1988 (SI 1988/717), art. 2(d) as from 6 April 1988.

**48(8) [Power of Secretary of State to amend s. 48(7)]** The Secretary of State may by order amend subsection (7) above–

(a) by restricting or extending the kinds of investment to which it applies;

(b) by restricting it so as to apply only in relation to the issue of investments in specified circumstances or by extending it, in respect of investments of any kind specified in the order, so as to apply to things done during a specified period before or after events other than the issue of those investments.

**48(9) [Approval by Parliament of s. 48(8) order]** No order shall be made under subsection (8) above unless a draft of it has been laid before and approved by a resolution of each House of Parliament.

**48(10) [Incidental and transitional provisions]** Rules under this section may contain such incidental and transitional provisions as the Secretary of State thinks necessary or expedient.

**48(11) [Effect of s. 63A]** Section 63A below (application of designated rules) has effect as regards the application of rules under this section to members of recognised self-regulating organisations in respect of investment business in the carrying on of which they are subject to the rules of the organisation.

**History**

S. 48(11) inserted by CA 1989, s. 206(1) and Sch. 23, para. 2(1), (3) as from 15 March 1990 (see SI 1990/354 (C 12), art. 3).

**Note**

Concerning European investment firms, see the Investment Services Regulations 1995 (SI 1995/3275), reg. 58 and Sch. 11, para. 5.

Concerning European institutions, see the Banking Coordination (Second Council Directive) Regulations 1992 (SI 1992/3218), reg. 55 and Sch. 9, para. 10; and reg. 83 and Sch. 11, para. 10.

## 49 Financial resources rules

**49(1) [Power of Secretary of State to make rules]** The Secretary of State may make rules requiring–

(a) a person authorised to carry on investment business by virtue of section 25 or 31 above, or

(b) a member of a recognised self-regulating organisation carrying on investment business in the carrying on of which he is subject to the rules of the organisation,

to have and maintain in respect of that business such financial resources as are required by the rules.

**History**

S. 49(1) substituted by CA 1989, s. 206(1) and Sch. 23, para. 3(1), (2) as from 15 March 1990 (see SI 1990/354 (C 12), art. 3); s. 49(1) formerly read as follows:

"The Secretary of State may make rules requiring persons authorised to carry on investment business by virtue of section 25 or 31 above to have and maintain in respect of that business such financial resources as are required by the rules."

**49(2) [Extent of rules]** Without prejudice to the generality of subsection (1) above, rules under this section may–

(a) impose requirements which are absolute or which are to vary from time to time by reference to such factors as are specified in or determined in accordance with the rules;

(b) impose requirements which take account of any business (whether or not investment business) carried on by the person concerned in conjunction with or in addition to the business mentioned in subsection (1) above;

(c) make provision as to the assets, liabilities and other matters to be taken into account in determining a person's financial resources for the purposes of the rules and the extent to which and the manner in which they are to be taken into account for that purpose.

**49(3) [Effect of s. 63A]** Section 63A below (application of designated rules) has effect as regards the application of rules under this section to members of recognised self-regulating organisations in respect of investment business in the carrying on of which they are subject to the rules of the organisation.

**History**

S. 49(3) inserted by CA 1989, s. 206(1) and Sch. 23, para. 3(1), (3) as from 15 March 1990 (see SI 1990/354 (C 12), art. 3).

**Note**

Concerning European investment firms, see the Investment Services Regulations 1995 (SI 1995/3275), reg. 32 and Sch. 7, para. 11, and reg. 58 and Sch. 11, para. 6.

Concerning European institutions, see the Banking Coordination (Second Council Directive) Regulations 1992 (SI 1992/3218), reg. 55 and Sch. 9, para. 11; and reg. 83 and Sch. 11, para. 11.

## 50 Modification of conduct of business and financial resources rules for particular cases

**50(1) [Power of Secretary of State]** The Secretary of State may, on the application of any person to whom any rules made under section 48 or 49 above apply, alter the requirements of the rules so as to adapt them to the circumstances of that person or to any particular kind of business carried on or to be carried on by him.

**50(2) [Conditions for s. 50(1) power]** The Secretary of State shall not exercise the powers conferred by subsection (1) above in any case unless it appears to him that–

(a) compliance with the requirements in question would be unduly burdensome for the applicant having regard to the benefit which compliance would confer on investors; and

(b) the exercise of those powers will not result in any undue risk to investors.

**50(3) [Exercise of s. 50(1) powers]** The powers conferred by subsection (1) above may be exercised unconditionally or subject to conditions.

**50(4) [Effect of s. 63B powers exercisable]** The powers conferred by subsection (1) above shall not be exercised in a case where the powers conferred by section 63B below are exercisable (powers of recognised self-regulating organisation in relation to designated rules).

**History**

S. 50(4) inserted by CA 1989, s. 206(1) and Sch. 23, para. 4 as from 15 March 1990 (see SI 1990/354 (C 12), art. 3).

## 51 Cancellation rules

**51(1) [Power of Secretary of State]** The Secretary of State may make rules for enabling a person who has entered or offered to enter into an investment agreement with an authorised person to rescind the agreement or withdraw the offer within such period and in such manner as may be prescribed.

**51(2) [Extent of rules]** Without prejudice to the generality of subsection (1) above, rules under this section may make provision–

(a) for requiring the service of notices with respect to the rights exercisable under the rules;

(b) for the restitution of property and the making or recovery of payments where those rights are exercised; and

(c) for such other incidental matters as the Secretary of State thinks necessary or expedient.

**Note**

Concerning European investment firms, see the Investment Services Regulations 1995 (SI 1995/3275), reg. 32 and Sch. 7, para. 12, and reg. 58 and Sch. 11.

Concerning European institutions, see the Banking Coordination (Second Council Directive) Regulations 1992 (SI 1992/3218), reg. 55 and Sch. 9, para. 12; and reg. 83 and Sch. 11, para. 12.

## 52 Notification regulations

**52(1) [Regulations re notice of certain events]** The Secretary of State may make regulations requiring authorised persons to give him forthwith notice of the occurrence of such events as are specified in the regulations and such information in respect of those events as is so specified.

**52(2) [Regulations re furnishing information]** The Secretary of State may make regulations requiring authorised persons to furnish him at such times or in respect of such periods as are specified in the regulations with such information as is so specified.

**52(3) [Exceptions to application of regulations]** Regulations under this section shall not apply to a member of a recognised self-regulating organisation or a person certified by a recognised professional body unless he carries on investment business in the carrying on of which he is not subject to the rules of that organisation or body.

**History**

In s. 52(3) the words "not subject to the rules of that organisation or body" substituted for the words "subject to any of the rules made under section 48 above" by CA 1989, s. 206(1) and Sch. 23, para. 5 as from 15 March 1990 (see SI 1990/354 (C 12), art. 3).

**52(4) [Extent of regulations]** Without prejudice to the generality of subsections (1) and (2) above, regulations under this section may relate to–

(a) the nature of the investment business being carried on;

(b) the nature of any other business carried on with or for the purposes of the investment business;

(c) any proposal of an authorised person to alter the nature or extent of any business carried on by him;

(d) any person becoming or ceasing to be a person of the kind to whom regard could be had by the Secretary of State under subsection (3) of section 27 above in deciding an application for authorisation under that section;

(e) the financial position of an authorised person as respects his investment business or any other business carried on by him;

(f) any property managed, and any property or money held, by an authorised person on behalf of other persons.

**52(5) [Form, verification of information]** Regulations under this section may require information to be given in a specified form and to be verified in a specified manner.

**52(6) [Manner of giving notice of information]** Any notice or information required to be given or furnished under this section shall be given in writing or in such other manner as the Secretary of State may approve.

**Note**

Concerning European investment firms, see the Investment Services Regulations 1995 (SI 1995/3275), reg. 32 and Sch. 7, para. 13, and reg. 58 and Sch. 11, para. 8.

Concerning European institutions, see the Banking Coordination (Second Council Directive) Regulations 1992 (SI 1992/3218), reg. 55 and Sch. 9, para. 13; also reg. 83 and Sch. 11, para. 13.

## 53 Indemnity rules

**53(1) [Power of Secretary of State to make rules]** The Secretary of State may make rules concerning indemnity against any claim in respect of any description of civil liability incurred by an authorised person in connection with his investment business.

**Note**

Concerning European investment firms, see the Investment Services Regulations 1995 (SI 1995/3275), reg. 32 and Sch. 7, para. 14.

**53(2) [Exception to application of rules]** Rules under this section shall not apply to a member of a recognised self-regulating organisation or a person certified by a recognised professional body in respect of investment business in the carrying on of which he is subject to the rules of the organisation or body unless that organisation or body has requested that rules under this section should apply to him; and any such request shall not be capable of being withdrawn after rules giving effect to it have been made but without prejudice to the power of the Secretary of State to revoke the rules if he thinks fit.

**53(3) [Extent of rules providing indemnity]** For the purpose of providing indemnity the rules–

(a) may authorise the Secretary of State to establish and maintain a fund or funds;

(b) may authorise the Secretary of State to take out and maintain insurance with insurers authorised to carry on insurance business under the law of the United Kingdom or any other member State;

(c) may require any person to whom the rules apply to take out and maintain insurance with any such insurer.

**53(4) [Further extent of rules]** Without prejudice to the generality of the foregoing provisions, the rules may–

(a) specify the terms and conditions on which, and the extent to which, indemnity is to be available and any circumstances in which the right to it is to be excluded or modified;

(b) provide for the management, administration and protection of any fund maintained by virtue of subsection (3)(a) above and require persons to whom the rules apply to make payments to any such fund;

(c) require persons to whom the rules apply to make payments by way of premium on any insurance policy maintained by the Secretary of State by virtue of subsection (3)(b) above;

(d) prescribe the conditions which an insurance policy must satisfy for the purposes of subsection (3)(c) above;

(e) authorise the Secretary of State to determine the amount which the rules require to be paid to him or an insurer, subject to such limits or in accordance with such provisions as may be prescribed by the rules;

(f) specify circumstances in which, where sums are paid by the Secretary of State or an insurer in satisfaction of claims against a person subject to the rules, proceedings may be taken against that person by the Secretary of State or the insurer;

(g) specify circumstances in which persons are exempt from the rules;

(h) empower the Secretary of State to take such steps as he considers necessary or expedient to ascertain whether or not the rules are being complied with; and

(i) contain incidental or supplementary provisions.

**Note**
Concerning European institutions, see the Banking Coordination (Second Council Directive) Regulations 1992 (SI 1992/3218), reg. 55 and Sch. 9, para. 14.

## 54 Compensation fund

**54(1) [Power of Secretary of State]** The Secretary of State may by rules establish a scheme for compensating investors in cases where persons who are or have been authorised persons are unable, or likely to be unable, to satisfy claims in respect of any description of civil liability incurred by them in connection with their investment businesses.

**Note**
See note after s. 54(6).

**54(2) [Extent of rules]** Without prejudice to the generality of subsection (1) above, rules under this section may–

(a) provide for the administration of the scheme and, subject to the rules, the determination and regulation of any matter relating to its operation by a body appearing to the Secretary of State to be representative of, or of any class of, authorised persons;

(b) establish a fund out of which compensation is to be paid;

(c) provide for the levying of contributions from, or from any class of, authorised persons and otherwise for financing the scheme and for the payment of contributions and other money into the fund;

(d) specify the terms and conditions on which, and the extent to which, compensation is to be payable and any circumstances in which the right to compensation is to be excluded or modified;

(e) provide for treating compensation payable under the scheme in respect of a claim against any person as extinguishing or reducing the liability of that person in respect of the claim and for conferring on the body administering the scheme a right of recovery against that person, being, in the event of his insolvency, a right not exceeding such right, if any, as the claimant would have had in that event; and

(f) contain incidental and supplementary provisions.

**Note**
See note after s. 54(6).

**54(3) [Application of scheme to SRO members etc.]** A scheme under this section shall not be made so as to apply to persons who are members of a recognised self-regulating organisation except after consultation with that organisation or, except at the request of a recognised professionl body, to persons who are certified by it and subject to its rules in carrying on all the investment business carried on by them; and no scheme applying to such persons shall be made unless the Secretary of State is satisfied that the rules establishing it make sufficient provision–

(a) for the administration of the scheme by a body on which the interests of those persons are adequately represented; and

(b) for securing that the amounts which they are liable to contribute reflect, so far as practicable, the amount of the claims made or likely to be made or likely to be made in respect of those persons.

**54(4) [Where scheme applies to persons in s. 54(3)]** Where a scheme applies to such persons as are mentioned in subsection (3) above the rules under this section may–

(a) constitute the recognised self-regulating organisation or recognised professional body in question as the body administering the scheme in relation to those persons;

(b) provide for the levying of contributions from that organisation or body instead of from those persons; and

(c) establish a separate fund for the contributions and compensation payable in respect of those persons, with or without provision for payments and repayments in specified circumstances between that and any other fund established by the scheme.

**54(5) [Request under s. 54(3)]** A request by a recognised professional body under subsection (3) above shall not be capable of being withdrawn after rules giving effect to it have been made but without prejudice to the power of the Secretary of State to revoke the rules if he thinks fit.

**54(6) [Rules re procedure]** Rules may be made–

(a) for England and Wales, under sections 411 and 412 of the Insolvency Act 1986;

(b) for Scotland–

(i) under the said section 411; and

(ii) in relation to the application of this section where the persons who are or have been authorised persons are persons whose estates may be sequestrated under the Bankruptcy (Scotland) Act 1985, by the Secretary of State under this section; and

(c) for Northern Ireland, under Article 359 of the Insolvency (Northern Ireland) Order 1989 and section 65 of the Judicature (Northern Ireland) Act 1978,

for the purpose of integrating any procedure for which provision is made by virtue of subsection (2)(e) above into the general procedure on a winding-up, bankruptcy or sequestration.

• **History**

In s. 54(6)(c) the words "Article 359 of the Insolvency (Northern Ireland) Order 1989" substituted for the former words "Article 613 of the Companies (Northern Ireland) Order 1986" by Insolvency (Northern Ireland) Order 1989 (SI 1989/2405 (NI 19)), art. 381 and Sch. 9, para. 46 as from 1 October 1991 (see SR 1991/411 (C 20), art. 2).

**Note**

Concerning European investment firms, see the Investment Services Regulations 1995 (SI 1995/3275), reg. 32 and Sch. 7, para. 15, and reg. 58 and Sch. 11, para. 9.

Concerning European institutions, see the Banking Coordination (Second Council Directive) Regulations 1992 (SI 1992/3218), reg. 55 and Sch. 9, para. 15; also reg. 83 and Sch. 11, para. 14.

## 55 Clients' money

**55(1) [Power of Secretary of State to make regulations]** The Secretary of State may make regulations with respect to money (in this section referred to as "clients' money") which authorised persons, or authorised persons of any description, hold in such circumstances as are specified in the regulations.

**55(2) [Extent of regulations]** Without prejudice to the generality of subsection (1) above, regulations under this section may–

(a) provide that clients' money held by an authorised person is held on trust;

(b) require clients' money to be paid into an account the title of which contains the word "client" and which is with an institution of a kind specified in the regulations or, in the case of or a person certified by a recognised professional body, by the rules of that body;

(c) make provision with respect to the opening and keeping of clients' accounts, including

(ii) consists of or any part of listing particulars, supplementary listing particulars, a prospectus approved in accordance with listing rules made under section 144(2) or 156A(1) below, a supplementary prospectus approved in accordance with listing rules made for the purposes of section 147(1) below as applied by section 154A or 156A(3) below or any other document required or permitted to be published by listing rules under Part IV of this Act.

**History**
In s. 58(1)(d)(ii) the words ", a prospectus approved" to "section 154A or 156A(3) below" inserted and the words "or by an approved exchange under Part V of this Act" formerly appearing at the end repealed by the Public Offers of Securities Regulations 1995 (SI 1995/1537), reg. 1, 17 and Sch. 2, para. 5(b), 6(a) as from 19 June 1995.

**58(2)** (Repealed by the Public Offers of Securities Regulations 1995 (SI 1995/1537), reg. 1, 17 and Sch. 2, para. 5(c) as from 19 June 1995.)

**History**
S. 58(2) formerly read as follows:
"Section 57 above does not apply to an advertisement inviting persons to subscribe in cash for any investments to which Part V of this Act applies if the advertisement is issued or caused to be issued by the person by whom the investments are to be issued and either the advertisement consists of a prospectus registered in accordance with that Part or the following matters (and no others that would make it an investment advertisement) are contained in the advertisement–
(a) the name of that person and his address or particulars of other means of communicating with him;
(b) the nature of the investments, the number offered for subscription and their nominal value and price;
(c) a statement that a prospectus for the purposes of that Part of this Act is or will be available and, if it is not yet available, when it will be; and
(d) instructions for obtaining a copy of the prospectus."

**58(3) [Non-application of s. 57 re exempted advertisements]** Section 57 above does not apply to an advertisement issued in such circumstances as may be specified in an order made by the Secretary of State for the purpose of exempting from that section–

(a) advertisements appearing to him to have a private character, whether by reason of a connection between the person issuing them and those to whom they are issued or otherwise;
(b) advertisements appearing to him to deal with investment only incidentally;
(c) advertisements issued to persons appearing to him to be sufficiently expert to understand any risks involved; or
(d) such other classes of advertisement as he thinks fit.

**Note**
See note after s. 58(4).
See also SI 1988/716, SI 1992/813 and SI 1995/1266.

**58(4) [Extent of s. 58(3) order]** An order under subsection (3) above may require any person who by virtue of the order is authorised to issue an advertisement to comply with such requirements as are specified in the order.

**Note**
See the Financial Services Act 1986 (Investment Advertisements) (Exemptions) Order 1996 (SI 1996/1586) and the Financial Services Act 1986 (Investment Advertisements) (Exemptions) Order 1997 (SI 1997/963).

**58(5) [Parliament approval etc. re s. 58(3)]** An order made by virtue of paragraph (a), (b) or (c) of subsection (3) above shall be subject to annulment in pursuance of a resolution of either House of Parliament; and no order shall be made by virtue of paragraph (d) of that subsection unless a draft of it has been laid before and approved by a resolution of each House of Parliament.

**58(6) [Non-application of s. 58(1)(c), (2)]** Subsection (1)(c) above does not apply to any advertisement relating to an investment falling within paragraph 5 of Schedule 1 to this Act.

**History**
In s. 58(6) the words "Subsection (1)(c) above does" substituted for the former words "Subsections (1)(c) and (2) above do" by the Public Offers of Securities Regulations 1995 (SI 1995/1537), reg. 1, 17 and Sch. 2, para. 6(b) as from 19 June 1995.

## 59 Employment of prohibited persons

**59(1) [Power of direction by Secretary of State]** If it appears to the Secretary of State that any individual is not a fit and proper person to be employed in connection with investment business or investment business of a particular kind he may direct that he shall not, without the written consent of the Secretary of State, be employed in connection with investment business or, as the case may be, investment business of that kind–

(a) by authorised persons or exempted persons; or

(b) by any specified person or persons, or by persons of any specified description, falling within paragraph (a) above.

**59(2) ["A disqualification direction"]** A direction under this section ("a disqualification direction") shall specify the date on which it is to take effect and a copy of it shall be served on the person to whom it relates.

**59(3) [Consent by Secretary of State]** Any consent by the Secretary of State to the employment of a person who is the subject of a disqualification direction may relate to employment generally or to employment of a particular kind, may be given subject to conditions and restrictions and may be varied by him from time to time.

**59(4) [Notice by Secretary of State]** Where the Secretary of State proposes–

(a) to give a disqualification direction in respect of any person; or

(b) to refuse an application for his consent under this section or for the variation of such consent,

he shall give that person or the applicant written notice of his intention to do so, stating the reasons for which he proposes to act and giving particulars of the right to require the case to be referred to the Tribunal under Chapter IX of this Part of this Act.

**59(5) [Offence, penalty]** Any person who accepts or continues in any employment in contravention of a disqualification direction shall be guilty of an offence and liable on summary conviction to a fine not exceeding the fifth level on the standard scale.

**59(6) [Duty of authorised person, appointed representative]** It shall be the duty of an authorised person and an appointed representative to take reasonable care not to employ or continue to employ a person in contravention of a disqualification direction.

**59(7) [Revocation of disqualification direction]** The Secretary of State may revoke a disqualification direction.

**59(8) [Interpretation]** In this section references to employment include references to employment otherwise than under a contract of service.

**Note**

Concerning European investment firms, see the Investment Services Regulations 1995 (SI 1995/3275), reg. 32 and Sch. 7, para. 18.

Concerning European institutions, see the Banking Coordination (Second Council Directive) Regulations 1992 (SI 1992/3218), reg. 55 and Sch. 9, para. 18.

## 60 Public statement as to person's misconduct

**60(1) [Power of Secretary of State to publish statement]** If it appears to the Secretary of State that a person who is or was an authorised person by virtue of section 22, 24, 25 or 31 above has contravened–

(a) any provision of rules or regulations made under this Chapter or of section 56 or 59 above; or

(b) any condition imposed under section 50 above,

he may publish a statement to that effect.

**Note**

See note after s. 60(3).

**60(2) [Written notice to person concerned]** Before publishing a statement under subsection (1) above the Secretary of State shall give the person concerned written notice of the proposed statement and of the reasons for which he proposes to act.

**60(3) [Copy of notice to other persons]** Where the reasons stated in the notice relate specifically to matters which–

(a) refer to a person identified in the notice other than the person who is or was the authorised person; and

(b) are in the opinion of the Secretary of State prejudicial to that person in any office or employment,

the Secretary of State shall, unless he considers it impracticable to do so, serve a copy of the notice on that other person.

**Note**

Concerning European investment firms, see the Investment Services Regulations 1995 (SI 1995/3275), reg. 32 and Sch. 7, para. 19.

**60(4) [Notice to include reference to Tribunal]** A notice under this section shall give particulars of the right to have the case referred to the Tribunal under Chapter IX of this Part of this Act.

**60(5) [Where case not required to be referred to Tribunal]** Where a case is not required to be referred to the Tribunal by a person on whom a notice is served under this section the Secretary of State shall, at the expiration of the period within which such a requirement can be made, give that person written notice that the statement is or is not to be published; and if it is to be published the Secretary of State shall after publication send a copy of it to that person and to any person on whom a copy of the notice under subsection (2) above was served.

**Note**

Concerning European institutions, see the Banking Coordination (Second Council Directive) Regulations 1992 (SI 1992/3218), reg. 55 and Sch. 9, para. 19.

## 61 Injunctions and restitution orders

**61(1) [Power of court on application by Secretary of State]** If on the application of the Secretary of State the court is satisfied–

(a) that there is a reasonable likelihood that any person will contravene any provision of–
  (i) rules or regulations made under this Chapter;
  (ii) sections 47, 56, 57, or 59 above;
  (iii) any requirements imposed by an order under section 58(3) above; or
  (iv) the rules of a recognised self-regulating organisation, recognised professional body, recognised investment exchange or recognised clearing house to which that person is subject and which regulate the carrying on by him of investment business,

  or any condition imposed under section 50 above;

(b) that any person has contravened any such provision or condition and that there is a reasonable likelihood that the contravention will continue or be repeated; or

(c) that any person has contravened any such provision or condition and that there are steps that could be taken for remedying the contravention,

the court may grant an injunction restraining the contravention or, in Scotland, an interdict prohibiting the contravention or, as the case may be, make an order requiring that person and any other person who appears to the court to have been knowingly concerned in the contravention to take such steps as the court may direct to remedy it.

**61(2) [Restriction on s. 61(1) application]** No application shall be made by the Secretary of State under subsection (1) above in respect of any such rules as are mentioned in subsection (1)(a)(iv) above unless it appears to him that the organisation, body, exchange or clearing house is unable or unwilling to take appropriate steps to restrain the contravention or to require the person concerned to take such steps as are mentioned in subsection (1) above.

**61(3) [Power of court to make s. 61(4), (5) orders]** The court may, on the application of the Secretary of State, make an order under subsection (4) below or, in relation to Scotland, under subsection (5) below if satisfied–

(a) that profits have accrued to any person as a result of his contravention of any provision or condition mentioned in subsection (1)(a) above; or

(b) that one or more investors have suffered loss or been otherwise adversely affected as a result of that contravention.

**61(4) [Order re payment into court etc.]** The court may under this subsection order the person concerned to pay into court, or appoint a receiver to recover from him, such sum as appears to the court to be just having regard–

(a) in a case within paragraph (a) of subsection (3) above, to the profits appearing to the court to have accrued;

(b) in a case within paragraph (b) of that subsection, to the extent of the loss or other adverse effect; or

(c) in a case within both paragraphs (a) and (b) of that subsection, to the profits and to the extent of the loss or other adverse effect.

**61(5) [Order re payment of sum]** The court may under this subsection order the person concerned to pay to the applicant such sum as appears to the court to be just having regard to the considerations mentioned in paragraphs (a) to (c) of subsection (4) above.

**61(6) [Payment of sums in s. 61(4), (5)]** Any amount paid into court by or recovered from a person in pursuance of an order under subsection (4) or (5) above shall be paid out to such person or distributed among such persons as the court may direct, being a person or persons appearing to the court to have entered into transactions with that person as a result of which the profits mentioned in paragraph (a) of subsection (3) above have accrued to him or the loss or adverse effect mentioned in paragraph (b) of that subsection has been suffered.

**61(7) [Furnishing of accounts, etc. re s. 61(3)]** On an application under subsection (3) above the court may require the person concerned to furnish it with such accounts or other information as it may require for establishing whether any and, if so, what profits have accrued to him as mentioned in paragraph (a) of that subsection and for determining how any amounts are to be paid or distributed under subsection (6) above; and the court may require any such accounts or other information to be verified in such manner as it may direct.

**61(8) [Exercise of jurisdiction]** The jurisdiction conferred by this section shall be exercisable by the High Court and the Court of Session.

**61(9) [Effect on other rights]** Nothing in this section affects the right of any person other than the Secretary of State to bring proceedings in respect of the matters to which this section applies.

## 62 Actions for damages

**62(1) [Certain contraventions actionable]** Without prejudice to section 61 above, a contravention of–

(a) any rules or regulations made under this Chapter;

(b) any conditions imposed under section 50 above;

(c) any requirements imposed by an order under section 58(3) above;

(d) the duty imposed by section 59(6) above,

shall be actionable at the suit of a person who suffers loss as a result of the contravention subject to the defences and other incidents applying to actions for breach of statutory duty.

**62(2) [Additional application of s. 62(1)]** Subsection (1) applies also to a contravention by a member of a recognised self-regulating organisation or a person certified by a recognised professional body of any rules of the organisation or body relating to a matter in respect of which rules or regulations have been or could be made under this Chapter in relation to an authorised person who is not such a member or so certified.

**62(3) [Non-application of s. 62(1)]** Subsection (1) above does not apply–

(a) to a contravention of rules made under section 49 or conditions imposed under section 50 in connection with an alteration of the requirements of those rules; or

(b) by virtue of subsection (2) above to a contravention of rules relating to a matter in respect of which rules have been or could be made under section 49.

**62(4) [No offence re contraventions]** A person shall not be guilty of an offence by reason of any contravention to which subsection (1) above applies or of a contravention of rules made under section 49 above or such conditions as are mentioned in subsection (3)(a) above and no such contravention shall invalidate any transaction.

## 62A Restriction of right of action

**62A(1) [When s. 62 action not to lie]** No action in respect of a contravention to which section 62 above applies shall lie at the suit of a person other than a private investor, except in such circumstances as may be specified by regulations made by the Secretary of State.

prohibition or requirement if it appears to the Secretary of State that it is no longer necessary for the prohibition or requirement to take effect or continue in force or, as the case may be, that it should take effect or continue in force in a different form.

**Note**

See note after s. 70.

## 70 Notices

**70(1) [Power to impose prohibitions etc., by written notice]** The power to impose, rescind or vary a prohibition or requirement under this Chapter shall be exercisable by written notice served by the Secretary of State on the person concerned; and any such notice shall take effect on such date as is specified in the notice.

**70(2) [Written notice re refusal to rescind etc.]** If the Secretary of State refuses to rescind or vary a prohibition or requirement on the application of the person to whom it applies he shall serve that person with a written notice of the refusal.

**70(3) [Notice to state reasons]** A notice imposing a prohibition or requirement, or varying a prohibition or requirement otherwise than on the application of the person to whom it applies, and a notice under subsection (2) above shall state the reasons for which the prohibition or requirement was imposed or varied or, as the case may be, why the application was refused.

**70(4) [Service of copy of notice on other persons]** Where the reasons stated in a notice to which subsection (3) above applies relate specifically to matters which–

(a) refer to a person identified in the notice other than the person to whom the prohibition or requirement applies; and

(b) are in the opinion of the Secretary of State prejudicial to that person in any office or employment,

the Secretary of State shall, unless he considers it impracticable to do so, serve a copy of the notice on that person.

**70(5) [S. 70(3) notice to refer to Tribunal]** A notice to which subsection (3) above applies shall give particulars of the right to have the case referred to the Tribunal under Chapter IX of this Part of this Act.

**70(6) [Public notice by Secretary of State]** The Secretary of State may give public notice of any prohibition or requirement imposed by him under this Chapter and of the rescission and variation of any such prohibition or requirement; and any such notice may, if the Secretary of State thinks fit, include a statement of the reasons for which the prohibition or requirement was imposed, rescinded or varied.

**Note**

For application of s. 64, 65, 66, 68, 69, 70 to a listed person see the Financial Markets and Insolvency (Money Market) Regulations 1995 (SI 1995/2049), reg. 1, 6, 8–13.

## 71 Breach of prohibition or requirement

**71(1) [Effect of s. 60, 61, 62]** Sections 60, 61, and 62 above shall have effect in relation to a contravention of a prohibition or requirement imposed under this Chapter as they have effect in relation to any such contravention as is mentioned in those sections.

**71(2) [Application of s. 62(2)]** In its application by virtue of this section, section 62(2) shall have effect with the substitution–

(a) for the reference to the rules of a recognised self-regulating organisation of a reference to any prohibition or requirement imposed by it in the exercise of powers for purposes corresponding to those of this Chapter; and

(b) for the reference to the rules of a recognised professional body of a reference to any prohibition or requirement imposed in the exercise of powers for such purposes by that body or by any other body or person having functions in respect of the enforcement of the recognised professional body's rules relating to the carrying on of investment business.

**71(3) [Equitable remedies]** This section is without prejudice to any equitable remedy available in respect of property which by virtue of a requirement under section 67 above is subject to a trust.

# Chapter VII – Winding up and Administration Orders

## 72 Winding up orders

**72(1) [Power of court to wind up]** On a petition presented by the Secretary of State by virtue of this section, the court having jurisdiction under the Insolvency Act 1986 may wind up an authorised person or appointed representative to whom this subsection applies if–

(a) the person is unable to pay his debts within the meaning of section 123 or, as the case may be, section 221 of that Act; or

(b) the court is of the opinion that it is just and equitable that the person should be wound up.

**72(2) [Application of s. 72(1)]** Subsection (1) above applies to any authorised person, any person whose authorisation is suspended under section 28 above or who is the subject of a direction under section 33(1)(b) above or any appointed representative who is–

(a) a company within the meaning of section 735 of the Companies Act 1985;

(b) an unregistered company within the meaning of section 220 of the Insolvency Act 1986;

(c) an oversea company within the meaning of section 744 of the Companies Act 1985; or

(d) a partnership.

**72(3) [Person unable to pay debts]** For the purposes of a petition under subsection (1) above a person who defaults in an obligation to pay any sum due and payable under any investment agreement shall be deemed to be unable to pay his debts.

**72(4) [Winding up of partnerships etc.]** Where a petition is presented under subsection (1) above for the winding up of a partnership on the ground mentioned in paragraph (b) of subsection (1) above or, in Scotland, on a ground mentioned in paragraph (a) or (b) of that subsection, the court shall have jurisdiction and the Insolvency Act 1986 shall have effect as if the partnership were an unregistered company within the meaning of section 220 of that Act.

**72(5) [Winding up re SROs etc.]** The Secretary of State shall not present a petition under subsection (1) above for the winding up of any person who is an authorised person by virtue of membership of a recognised self-regulating organisation or certification by a recognised professional body and is subject to the rules of the organisation or body in the carrying on of all investment business carried on by him, unless that organisation or body has consented to his doing so.

**Note**

See note after s. 74.

**72(6) [Non-application of s. 72(5)]** Subsection (5) above does not apply to the presentation of a petition under subsection (1) above for the winding up of an investment company with variable capital.

**History**

S.72(6) inserted by the Open-Ended Investment Companies (Investment Companies with Variable Capital) Regulations 1996 (SI 1996/2827), reg. 1, 75 and Sch. 8, para. 13 as from 6 January 1997.

## 73 Winding up orders: Northern Ireland

**73(1) [Power of High Court in Northern Ireland to wind up]** On a petition presented by the Secretary of State by virtue of this section, the High Court in Northern Ireland may wind up an authorised person or appointed representative to whom this subsection applies if–

(a) the person is unable to pay his debts within the meaning of Article 103 or, as the case may be, Article 185 of the Insolvency (Northern Ireland) Order 1989; or

(b) the court is of the opinion that it is just and equitable that the person should be wound up.

**History**
In s. 73(1)(a) the words "Article 480 or," onwards substituted for the former words "Article 480 or, as the case may be, Article 616 of the Companies (Northern Ireland) Order 1986" by the Insolvency (Northern Ireland) Order 1989 (SI 1989/2405 (NI 19)), art. 381 and Sch. 9, para. 47(a) as from 1 October 1991 (see SR 1991/411 (C 20), art. 2).

**73(2) [Application of s. 73(1)]** Subsection (1) above applies to any authorised person, any person whose authorisation is suspended under section 28 above or who is the subject of a direction under section 33(1)(b) above or any appointed representative who is–

(a) a company within the meaning of Article 3 of the Companies (Northern Ireland) Order 1986;

(b) an unregistered company within the meaning of Article 184 of the Insolvency (Northern Ireland) Order 1989; or

(c) a Part XXIII company within the meaning of Article 2 of the Companies (Northern Ireland) Order 1986; or

(d) a partnership.

**History**
In s. 73(2)(b) the words "Article 184 of the Insolvency (Northern Ireland) Order 1989" substituted for the former words "Article 615 of that Order" and in s. 73(2)(c) the words "the Companies (Northern Ireland) Order 1986" substituted for the former words "that Order" by Insolvency (Northern Ireland) Order 1989 (SI 1989/2405 (NI 19)), art. 381 and Sch. 9, para. 47(b)(i) and (ii) respectively as from 1 October 1991 (see SR 1991/411 (C 20), art. 2).

**73(3) [Person unable to pay debts]** For the purposes of a petition under subsection (1) above a person who defaults in an obligation to pay any sum due and payable under any investment agreement shall be deemed to be unable to pay his debts.

**73(4) [Winding up of partnerships etc.]** Where a petition is presented under subsection (1) above for the winding up of a partnership on the ground mentioned in paragraph (b) of subsection (1) above, the High Court in Northern Ireland shall have jurisdiction and the Insolvency (Northern Ireland) Order 1989 shall have effect as if the partnership were an unregistered company within the meaning of Article 184 of that Order.

**History**
In s. 73(4) the words "Insolvency (Northern Ireland) Order 1989" substituted for the former words "Companies (Northern Ireland) Order 1986" and the words "Article 184" substituted for the former words "Article 615" by Insolvency (Northern Ireland) Order 1989 (SI 1989/2405 (NI 19)), art. 381 and Sch. 9, para. 47(c)(i) and (ii) respectively as from 1 October 1991 (see SR 1991/411 (C 20), art. 2).

**73(5) [Winding up re SROs etc.]** The Secretary of State shall not present a petition under subsection (1) above for the winding up of any person who is an authorised person by virtue of membership of a recognised self-regulating organisation or certification by a recognised professional body and is subject to the rules of the organisation or body in the carrying on of all investment business carried on by him, unless that organisation or body has consented to his doing so.

## 74 Administration orders

**74** A petition may be presented under section 9 of the Insolvency Act 1986 (applications for administration orders) in relation to a company to which section 8 of that Act applies, or under Article 22 of the Insolvency (Northern Ireland) Order 1989 (applications for administration orders) in relation to a company to which Article 21 of that Order applies, which is an authorised person, a person whose authorisation is suspended under section 28 above or who is the subject of a direction under section 33(1)(b) above or an appointed representative–

(a) in the case of an authorised person who is an authorised person by virtue of membership of a recognised self-regulating organisation or certification by a recognised professional body, by that organisation or body; and

(b) in the case of an appointed representative or an authorised person who is not authorised as mentioned in paragraph (a) above or is so authorised but is not subject to the rules of the organisation or body in question in the carrying on of all investment business carried on by him, by the Secretary of State.

**History**
In s. 74 the words ", or under Article 22" to "of that Order applies," inserted by Insolvency (Northern Ireland) Order 1989 (SI 1989/2405 (NI 19)), art. 381 and Sch. 9, para. 48 as from 1 October 1991 (see SR 1991/411 (C 20), art. 2).

**Note**
For application of s. 72 and 74 to a listed person see the Financial Markets and Insolvency (Money Market) Regulations 1995 (SI 1995/2049), reg. 1, 6, 14, 15.

# Chapter VIII – Collective Investment Schemes

PRELIMINARY

## 75 Interpretation

**75(1) ["A collective investment scheme"]** In this Act **"a collective investment scheme"** means, subject to the provisions of this section, any arrangements with respect to property of any description, including money, the purpose or effect of which is to enable persons taking part in the arrangements (whether by becoming owners of the property or any part of it or otherwise) to participate in or receive profits or income arising from the acquisition, holding, management or disposal of the property or sums paid out of such profits or income.

**75(2) [Arrangements for participants in s. 75(1)]** The arrangements must be such that the persons who are to participate as mentioned in subsection (1) above (in this Act referred to as **"participants"**) do not have day to day control over the management of the property in question, whether or not they have the right to be consulted or to give directions; and the arrangements must also have either or both of the characteristics mentioned in subsection (3) below.

**75(3) [Characteristics in s. 75(2)]** Those characteristics are–

(a) that the contributions of the participants and the profits or income out of which payments are to be made to them are pooled;

(b) that the property in question is managed as a whole by or on behalf of the operator of the scheme.

**75(4) [Where pooling as in s. 75(3)(a)]** Where any arrangements provide for such pooling as is mentioned in paragraph (a) of subsection (3) above in relation to separate parts of the property in question, the arrangements shall not be regarded as constituting a single collective investment scheme unless the participants are entitled to exchange rights in one part for rights in another.

**75(5) [Certain investments arrangements not a collective investment scheme]** Arrangements are not a collective investment scheme if–

(a) the property to which the arrangements relate (other than cash awaiting investment) consists of investments falling within any of paragraphs 1 to 5, 6 (so far as relating to units in authorised unit trust schemes and recognised schemes) and 10 of Schedule 1 to this Act;

(b) each participant is the owner of a part of that property and entitled to withdraw it at any time; and

(c) the arrangements do not have the characteristics mentioned in paragraph (a) of subsection (3) above and have those mentioned in paragraph (b) of that subsection only because the parts of the property belonging to different participants are not bought and sold separately except where a person becomes or ceases to be a participant.

**75(5A), (5B)** (Repealed by Financial Services Act 1986 (Restriction of Scope of Act and Meaning of Collective Investment Scheme) Order 1990 (SI 1990/349), art. 6(a) as from 26 March 1990.)

**History**
S. 75(5A), (5B) formerly read as follows:

"75(5A) Arrangements are not a collective investment scheme if–

(a) the property to which the arrangements relate (other than cash awaiting investment) consists of shares;

(b) they constitute a complying fund;

(c) each participant is the owner of a part of the property to which the arrangements relate and, to the extent that his part of that property–

(i) comprises relevant shares of a class which are admitted to the Official List of any member State or to dealings on a recognised investment exchange, he is entitled to withdraw it at any time after the end of the period of five years beginning with the date on which the shares in question were issued;

(ii) comprises relevant shares which do not fall within (i) above, he is entitled to withdraw it at any time after the end of the period of two years beginning with the date upon which the period referred to in (i) above expired;

(iii) comprises any other shares, he is entitled to withdraw it at any time after the end of the period of six months beginning with the date upon which the shares in question ceased to be relevant shares; and

(iv) comprises cash which the operator has not agreed (conditionally or unconditionally) to apply in subscribing for shares, he is entitled to withdraw it at any time; and

(d) the arrangements would meet the conditions described in paragraph (c) of subsection (5) above were it not for the fact that the operator is entitled to exercise all or any of the rights conferred by shares included within the property to which the arrangements relate.

**(5B)** For the purposes of subsection (5A) above–

(a) **"shares"** means investments falling within paragraph 1 of Schedule 1 to this Act;

(b) shares shall be regarded as being relevant shares if and so long as they are shares in respect of which neither–

(i) a claim for relief, made in accordance with section 306 of the Income and Corporation Taxes Act 1988 has been disallowed; nor

(ii) an assessment has been made pursuant to section 307 of that Act withdrawing or refusing relief by reason of the body corporate in which the shares are held having ceased to be a body corporate which is a qualifying company for the purposes of section 293 of that Act; and

(c) arrangements shall be regarded as constituting a complying fund if they provide that–

(i) the operator will, so far as practicable, make investments each of which, subject to each participant's individual circumstances, qualify for relief by virtue of Chapter III of Part VII of the Income and Corporation Taxes Act 1988; and

(ii) the minimum subscription to the arrangements made by each participant must be not less than £2000."

S. 75(5A) and (5B) formerly added by Financial Services Act 1986 (Restriction of Scope of Act and Meaning of Collective Investment Scheme) Order 1988 (SI 1988/803), art. 5(a) as from 29 April 1988; art. 5 revoked by Financial Services Act 1986 (Restriction of Scope of Act and Meaning of Collective Investment Scheme) Order 1990 (SI 1990/349), art. 8(c) as from 26 March 1990.

**75(6) [Further arrangements etc. not collective investment schemes]** The following are not collective investment schemes–

(a) arrangements operated by a person otherwise than by way of business;

(b) arrangements where each of the participants carries on a business other than investment business and enters into the arrangements for commercial purposes related to that business;

(c) arrangements where each of the participants is a body corporate in the same group as the operator;

(d) arrangements where–

(i) each of the participants is a bona fide employee or former employee (or the wife, husband, widow, widower, child or step-child under the age of eighteen of such an employee or former employee) of a body corporate in the same group as the operator; and

(ii) the property to which the arrangements relate consists of shares or debentures (as defined in paragraph 20(4) of Schedule 1 to this Act) in or of a member of that group;

(f) franchise arrangements, that is to say, arrangements under which a person earns profits or income by exploiting a right conferred by the arrangements to use a trade name or design or other intellectual property or the good-will attached to it;

(g) arrangements the predominant purpose of which is to enable persons participating in them to share in the use or enjoyment of a particular property or to make its use or enjoyment available gratuitously to other persons;

(h) arrangements under which the rights or interests of the participants are investments falling within paragraph 5 of Schedule 1 to this Act;

(i) arrangements the purpose of which is the provision of clearing services and which are operated by an authorised person, a recognised clearing house or a recognised investment exchange;

(j) contracts of insurance;

(k) occupational pension schemes;

(l) arrangements which by virtue of any of paragraphs 34 to 37 of Schedule 1 to this Act are not collective investment schemes for the purposes of that Schedule.

**History**

S. 75(6)(e) repealed by Financial Services Act 1986 (Restriction of Scope of Act and Meaning of Collective Investment Scheme) Order 1990 (SI 1990/349) art. 6(a) as from 26 March 1990; s. 75(6)(e) formerly read as follows:

"(e) arrangements where the entire contribution of each participant is a deposit within the meaning of section 5 of the Banking Act 1987 or a sum of a kind described in subsection (3) of that section."

Previously s. 75(6)(e) substituted by Financial Services Act 1986 (Extension of Scope of Act and Meaning of Collective Investment Scheme) Order 1988 (SI 1988/496), art. 4 as from 25 March 1988; art 4 revoked by Financial Services Act 1986 (Restriction of Scope of Act and Meaning of Collective Investment Scheme) Order 1990 (SI 1990/349), art. 8(b) as from 26 March 1990. The previous s. 75(6)(e) read as follows:

"(e) arrangements where the receipt of the participants' contributions constitutes the acceptance of deposits in the course of a business which is a deposit-taking business for the purposes of the Banking Act 1987 and does not constitute a transaction prescribed for the purposes of section 4(4) of that Act by regulations made by the Treasury;".

In the previous s. 75(6)(e) the words "Banking Act 1987", and "section 4(4)" previously substituted for the words "Banking Act 1979" and "section 2", respectively by Banking Act 1987, s. 108(1) and Sch. 6, para. 27(1) as from 1 October 1987 (see SI 1987/1664 (C 50)).

In s. 75(6)(l) the words "paragraphs 34 to 37" substituted for the former words "paragraphs 34 to 36" by the Financial Services Act 1986 (Restriction of Scope of Act and Meaning of Collective Investment Scheme) Order 1997 (SI 1997/32), art. 1, 2(1) as from 6 February 1997. Previously in s. 75(6)(l) the words "any of paragraphs 34 to 36" substituted for the words "paragraph 34 or 35" by the Financial Services Act 1986 (Restriction of Scope of Act and Meaning of Collective Investment Scheme) Order 1996 (SI 1996/2996) art.1, 3(1) as from 1 January 1997. Previously to that, s. 75(6)(l) substituted for former s. 75(6)(l)–(n) by Financial Services Act 1986 (Restriction of Scope of Act and Meaning of Collective Investment Scheme) Order 1990 (SI 1990/349), art. 6(b) as from 26 March 1990; s. 75(6)(l)–(n) formerly read as follows:

"(l) arrangements under which the rights or interests of the participants are represented by the following–
- (i) investments falling within paragraph 2 of Schedule 1 to this Act which are issued by a single body corporate which is not an open-ended investment company or which are issued by a single issuer which is not a body corporate and are guaranteed by the government of the United Kingdom, of Northern Ireland, or of any country or territory outside the United Kingdom; or
- (ii) investments falling within sub-paragraph (i) above which are convertible into or exchangeable for investments falling within paragraph 1 of Schedule 1 to this Act provided that those latter investments are issued by the same person as issued the investments falling within sub-paragraph (i) or are issued by a single other issuer; or
- (iii) investments falling within paragraph 3 of Schedule 1 to this Act issued by the same government, local authority or public authority; or
- (iv) investments falling within paragraph 4 of Schedule 1 to this Act which are issued otherwise than by an open-ended investment company and which confer rights in respect of investments, issued by the same issuer, falling within paragraph 1 of Schedule 1 to this Act or within sub-paragraph (i), (ii) or (iii) above;

(m) arrangements which would fall within paragraph (l) were it not for the fact that the rights or interests of a participant ("the counterparty") whose ordinary business involves him in engaging in activities which fall within Part II of Schedule 1 to this Act or would do so apart from Part III or Part IV of that Schedule are or include rights or interests under a swap arrangement, that is to say, an arrangement the purpose of which is to facilitate the making of payments to participants whether in a particular amount or currency or at a particular time or rate of interest or all or any combination of those things, being an arrangement under which–
- (i) the counterparty is entitled to receive amounts (whether representing principal or interest) payable in respect of any property subject to the scheme or sums determined by reference to such amounts; and
- (ii) the counterparty makes payments (whether or not of the same amount and whether or not in the same currency as those referred to in (i) above) which are calculated in accordance with an agreed formula by reference to the amounts or sums referred to in (i) above.

(n) arrangements under which the rights or interests of participants are rights to or interests in money held in a common account in circumstances in which the money so held is held on the understanding that an amount representing the contribution of each participant is to be applied either in making payments to him or in satisfaction of sums owed by him or in the acquisition of property or the provision of services for him."

S. 75(6)(l)–(n) originally added by Financial Services Act 1986 (Restriction of Scope of Act and Meaning of Collective Investment Scheme) Order 1988 (SI 1988/803), art. 5(b) as from 29 April 1988; art. 5 revoked by Financial Services Act 1986 (Restriction of Scope of Act and Meaning of Collective Investment Scheme) Order 1990 (SI 1990/349), art. 8(c) as from 26 March 1990.

**Note**

Concerning European investment firms, see the Investment Services Regulations 1995 (SI 1995/3275), reg. 32 and Sch. 7, para. 22.

Concerning European institutions, see the Banking Coordination (Second Council Directive) Regulations 1992 (SI 1992/3218), reg. 55 and Sch. 9, para. 24.

**75(7) [Certain bodies corporate not collective investment schemes]** No body incorporated under the law of, or of any part of, the United Kingdom relating to building societies or industrial and provident societies or registered under any such law relating to friendly societies, and no other body corporate other than an open-ended investment company, shall be regarded as constituting a collective investment scheme.

**75(8) [Definitions]** In this Act–

**"a unit trust scheme"** means a collective investment scheme under which the property in question is held on trust for the participants;

**"an open-ended investment company"** means a collective investment scheme under which–

(a) the property in question belongs beneficially to, and is managed by or on behalf of, a body corporate having as its purpose the investment of its funds with the aim of spreading investment risk and giving its members the benefit of the results of the management of those funds by or on behalf of that body; and

(b) the rights of the participants are represented by shares in or securities of that body which–
- (i) the participants are entitled to have redeemed or repurchased, or which (otherwise

than under Chapter VII of Part V of the Companies Act 1985 or the corresponding Northern Ireland provision) are redeemed or repurchased from them by, or out of funds provided by, that body; or

(ii) the body ensures can be sold by the participants on an investment exchange at a price related to the value of the property to which they relate;

**"trustee"**, in relation to a unit trust scheme, means the person holding the property in question on trust for the participants and, in relation to a collective investment scheme constituted under the law of a country or territory outside the United Kingdom, means any person who (whether or not under a trust) is entrusted with the custody of the property in question;

**"units"** means the rights or interests (however described) of the participants in a collective investment scheme;

**"the operator"**, in relation to a unit trust scheme with a separate trustee, means the manager and, in relation to an open-ended investment company, means that company.

**75(9) [Amendment of s. 2 order etc.]** If an order under section 2 above amends the references to a collective investment scheme in Schedule 1 to this Act it may also amend the provisions of this section.

**Note**
See the Financial Services Act 1986 (Restriction of Scope of Act and Meaning of Collective Investment Scheme) Order 1996 (SI 1996/2996).

## PROMOTION OF SCHEMES

### 76 Restrictions on promotion

**76(1) [Restriction on authorised person]** Subject to subsections (2), (3) and (4) below, an authorised person shall not–

(a) issue or cause to be issued in the United Kingdom any advertisement inviting persons to become or offer to become participants in a collective investment scheme or containing information calculated to lead directly or indirectly to persons becoming or offering to become participants in such a scheme; or

(b) advise or procure any person in the United Kingdom to become or offer to become a participant in such a scheme,

unless the scheme is an authorised unit trust scheme or an investment company with variable capital or a recognised scheme under the following provisions of this Chapter.

**History**
In s. 76(1) the words "or an investment company with variable capital" appearing after the words "authorised unit trust scheme" inserted by the Open-Ended Investment Companies (Investment Companies with Variable Capital) Regulations 1996 (SI 1996/2827), reg. 1, 75 and Sch. 8, para. 14 as from 6 January 1997.

**76(2) [Exception re advertisement to authorised person etc.]** Subsection (1) above shall not apply if the advertisement is issued to or the person mentioned in paragraph (b) of that subsection is–

(a) an authorised person; or

(b) a person whose ordinary business involves the acquisition and disposal of property of the same kind as the property, or a substantial part of the property, to which the scheme relates.

**76(3) [Exception re things done under regulations]** Subsection (1) above shall not apply to anything done in accordance with regulations made by the Secretary of State for the purpose of exempting from that subsection the promotion otherwise than to the general public of schemes of such descriptions as are specified in the regulations.

**76(4) [Exempting single property schemes under s. 76(1)]** The Secretary of State may by regulations make provision for exempting single property schemes from subsection (1) above.

**76(5) [Interpretation re s. 76(4)]** For the purposes of subsection (4) above a single property scheme is a scheme which has the characteristics mentioned in subsection (6) below and satisfies such other requirements as are specified in the regulations conferring the exemption.

**76(6) [Characteristics in s. 76(5)]** The characteristics referred to above are–

(a) that the property subject to the scheme (apart from cash or other assets held for management purposes) consists of–
   (i) a single building (or a single building with ancillary buildings) managed by or on behalf of the operator of the scheme; or
   (ii) a group of adjacent or contiguous buildings managed by him or on his behalf as a single enterprise,

with or without ancillary land and with or without furniture, fittings or other contents of the building or buildings in question; and

(b) that the units of the participants in the scheme are either dealt in on a recognised investment exchange or offered on terms such that any agreement for their acquisition is conditional on their admission to dealings on such an exchange.

**76(7) [Extent of s. 76(4) regulations]** Regulations under subsection (4) above may contain such supplementary and transitional provisions as the Secretary of State thinks necessary and may also contain provisions imposing obligations or liabilities on the operator and trustee (if any) of an exempted scheme, including, to such extent as he thinks appropriate, provisions for purposes corresponding to those for which provision can be made under section 85 below in relation to authorised unit trust schemes.

**Note**

Concerning European investment firms, see the Investment Services Regulations 1995 (SI 1995/3275), reg. 32 and Sch. 7, para. 23.

Concerning European institutions, see the Banking Coordination (Second Council Directive) Regulations 1992 (SI 1992/3218), reg. 55 and Sch. 9, para. 25.

## AUTHORISED UNIT TRUST SCHEMES

## 77 Applications for authorisation

**77(1) [Applicants for order]** Any application for an order declaring a unit trust scheme to be an authorised unit trust scheme shall be made by the manager and trustee, or proposed manager and trustee, of the scheme and the manager and trustee shall be different persons.

**77(2) [Manner of application, other information]** Any such application–

(a) shall be made in such manner as the Secretary of State may direct; and

(b) shall contain or be accompanied by such information as he may reasonably require for the purpose of determining the application.

**77(3) [Additional information]** At any time after receiving an application and before determining it the Secretary of State may require the applicant to furnish additional information.

**77(4) [Differing directions and requirements]** The directions and requirements given or imposed under subsections (2) and (3) above may differ as between different applications.

**77(5) [Form and verification of information]** Any information to be furnished to the Secretary of State under this section shall, if he so requires, be in such form or verified in such manner as he may specify.

## 78 Authorisation orders

**78(1) [Power of Secretary of State]** The Secretary of State may, on an application duly made in accordance with section 77 above and after being furnished with all such information as he may require under that section, make an order declaring a unit trust scheme to be an authorised unit trust scheme for the purposes of this Act if–

(a) it appears to him that the scheme complies with the requirements of the regulations made under section 81 below and that the following provisions of this section are satisfied; and

(b) he has been furnished with a copy of the trust deed and a certificate signed by a solicitor to the effect that it complies with such of those requirements as relate to its contents.

**78(2) [Manager and trustee independent]** The manager and the trustee must be persons who are independent of each other.

**78(3) [Manager and trustee member State bodies corporate]** The manager and the trustee must each be a body corporate incorporated in the United Kingdom or another member State, the affairs of each must be administered in the country in which it is incorporated, each must have a place of business in the United Kingdom and, if the manager is incorporated in another member State, the scheme must not be one which satisfies the requirements prescribed for the purposes of section 86 below.

**78(4) [Manager and trustee authorised persons]** The manager and the trustee must each be an authorised person and neither must be prohibited from acting as manager or trustee, as the case may be, by or under rules under section 48 above, by or under the rules of any recognised self-regulating organisation of which the manager or trustee is a member or by a prohibition imposed under section 65 above.

**78(5) [Name and purposes of scheme]** The name of the scheme must not be undesirable or misleading; and the purposes of the scheme must be reasonably capable of being successfully carried into effect.

**78(6) [Requirements re redemption of units etc.]** The participants must be entitled to have their units redeemed in accordance with the scheme at a price related to the net value of the property to which the units relate and determined in accordance with the scheme; but a scheme shall be treated as complying with this subsection if it requires the manager to ensure that a participant is able to sell his units on an investment exchange at a price not significantly different from that mentioned in this subsection.

**78(7) [Time for decision re application]** The Secretary of State shall inform the applicants of his decision on the application not later than six months after the date on which the application was received.

**78(8) [Certificate on making of order]** On making an order under this section the Secretary of State may issue a certificate to the effect that the scheme complies with the conditions necessary for it to enjoy the rights conferred by any relevant Community instrument.

## 79 Revocation of authorisation

**79(1) [Power of Secretary of State]** The Secretary of State may revoke an order declaring a unit trust scheme to be an authorised unit trust scheme if it appears to him–

(a) that any of the requirements for the making of the order are no longer satisfied;

(b) that it is undesirable in the interests of the participants or potential participants that the scheme should continue to be authorised; or

(c) without prejudice to paragraph (b) above, that the manager or trustee of the scheme has contravened any provision of this Act or any rules or regulations made under it or, in purported compliance with any such provision, has furnished the Secretary of State with false, inaccurate or misleading information or has contravened any prohibition or requirement imposed under this Act.

**79(2) [Matter for s. 79(1)(b)]** For the purposes of subsection (1)(b) above the Secretary of State may take into account any matter relating to the scheme, the manager or trustee, a director or controller of the manager or trustee or any person employed by or associated with the manager or trustee in connection with the scheme.

**79(3) [Rules in s. 79(1)(c)]** In the case of a manager or trustee who is a member of a recognised self-regulating organisation the rules, prohibitions and requirements referred to in subsection (1)(c) above include the rules of that organisation and any prohibition or requirement imposed by virtue of those rules.

**79(4) [Revocation at request of manager or trustee etc.]** The Secretary of State may revoke an order declaring a unit trust scheme to be an authorised unit trust scheme at the request of the manager or trustee of the scheme; but he may refuse to do so if he considers that any matter concerning the scheme should be investigated as a preliminary to a decision on the question whether the order should be revoked or that revocation would not be in the interests of the participants or would be incompatible with a Community obligation.

## 80 Representations against refusal or revocation

**80(1) [Written notice re refusal etc.]** Where the Secretary of State proposes–

(a) to refuse an application for an order under section 78 above; or

(b) to revoke such an order otherwise than at the request of the manager or trustee of the scheme,

he shall give the applicants or, as the case may be, the manager and trustee of the scheme written notice of his intention to do so, stating the reasons for which he proposes to act and giving particulars of the rights conferred by subsection (2) below.

**80(2) [Written representations to Secretary of State]** A person on whom a notice is served under subsection (1) above may, within twenty-one days of the date of service, make written representations to the Secretary of State and, if desired, oral representations to a person appointed for that purpose by the Secretary of State.

**80(3) [Secretary of State to have regard to representations]** The Secretary of State shall have regard to any representations made in accordance with subsection (2) above in determining whether to refuse the application or revoke the order, as the case may be.

## 81 Constitution and management

**81(1) [Power of Secretary of State to make regulations]** The Secretary of State may make regulations as to the constitution and management of authorised unit trust schemes, the powers and duties of the manager and trustee of any such scheme and the rights and obligations of the participants in any such scheme.

**81(2) [Extent of regulations]** Without prejudice to the generality of subsection (1) above, regulations under this section may make provision–

(a) as to the issue and redemption of the units under the scheme;

(b) as to the expenses of the scheme and the means of meeting them;

(c) for the appointment, removal, powers and duties of an auditor for the scheme;

(d) for restricting or regulating the investment and borrowing powers exercisable in relation to the scheme;

(e) requiring the keeping of records with respect to the transactions and financial position of the scheme and for the inspection of those records;

(f) requiring the preparation of periodical reports with respect to the scheme and the furnishing of those reports to the participants and to the Secretary of State; and

(g) with respect to the amendment of the scheme.

**81(3) [Contents of trust deed etc.]** Regulations under this section may make provision as to the contents of the trust deed, including provision requiring any of the matters mentioned in subsection (2) above to be dealt with in the deed; but regulations under this section shall be binding on the manager, trustee and participants independently of the contents of the deed and, in the case of the participants, shall have effect as if contained in it.

**81(4) [Remuneration to scheme manager]** Regulations under this section shall not impose limits on the remuneration payable to the manager of a scheme.

**81(5) [Incidental and transitional provisions]** Regulations under this section may contain such incidental and transitional provisions as the Secretary of State thinks necessary or expedient.

## 82 Alteration of schemes and changes of manager or trustee

**82(1) [Manager to give written notice re alteration etc.]** The manager of an authorised unit trust scheme shall give written notice to the Secretary of State of–

(a) any proposed alteration to the scheme; and

(b) any proposal to replace the trustee of the scheme;

and any notice given in respect of a proposed alteration involving a change in the trust deed shall be accompanied by a certificate signed by a solicitor to the effect that the change will not affect the compliance of the deed with the regulations made under section 81 above.

**82(2) [Trustee to give written notice re replacement]** The trustee of an authorised unit trust scheme shall give written notice to the Secretary of State of any proposal to replace the manager of the scheme.

**82(3) [Requirements for proposal to have effect]** Effect shall not be given to any such proposal unless–

(a) the Secretary of State has given his approval to the proposal; or

(b) one month has elapsed since the date on which the notice was given under subsection (1) or (2) above without the Secretary of State having notified the manager or trustee that the proposal is not approved.

**82(4) [Limit on replacements]** Neither the manager nor the trustee of an authorised unit trust scheme shall be replaced except by persons who satisfy the requirements of section 78(2) to (4) above.

# 83 Restrictions on activities of manager

**83(1) [Only certain activities]** The manager of an authorised unit trust scheme shall not engage in any activities other than those mentioned in subsection (2) below.

**83(2) [Activities in s. 83(1)]** Those activities are–

(a) acting as manager of–

(i) a unit trust scheme;

(ii) an open-ended investment company or any other body corporate whose business consists of investing its funds with the aim of spreading investment risk and giving its members the benefit of the results of the management of its funds by or on behalf of that body; or

(iii) any other collective investment scheme under which the contributions of the participants and the profits or income out of which payments are to be made to them are pooled;

(aa) acting as a director of an investment company with variable capital;

(b) activities for the purposes of or in connection with those mentioned in paragraph (a) or (aa) above.

**History**

S. 83(2)(aa) inserted and in s. 83(2)(b) the words "or (aa)" inserted by the Open-Ended Investment Companies (Investment Companies with Variable Capital) Regulations 1996 (SI 1996/2827), reg. 1, 75 and Sch. 8, para. 15 as from 6 January 1997.

**83(3) [S. 65 prohibition]** A prohibition under section 65 above may prohibit the manager of an authorised unit trust scheme from inviting persons in any specified country or territory outside the United Kingdom to become participants in the scheme.

# 84 Avoidance of exclusion clauses

**84** Any provision of the trust deed of an authorised unit trust scheme shall be void in so far as it would have the effect of exempting the manager or trustee from liability for any failure to exercise due care and diligence in the discharge of his functions in respect of the scheme.

# 85 Publication of scheme particulars

**85(1) [Power of Secretary of State to make regulations]** The Secretary of State may make regulations requiring the manager of an authorised unit trust scheme to submit to him and publish or make available to the public on request a document ("scheme particulars") containing information about the scheme and complying with such requirements as are specified in the regulations.

**85(2) [Revised or further scheme particulars]** Regulations under this section may require the manager of an authorised unit trust scheme to submit and publish or make available revised or further scheme particulars if–

(a) there is a significant change affecting any matter contained in such particulars previously published or made available whose inclusion was required by the regulations; or

(b) a significant new matter arises the inclusion of information in respect of which would have been required in previous particulars if it had arisen when those particulars were prepared.

**85(3) [Payment of compensation]** Regulations under this section may provide for the payment, by the person or persons who in accordance with the regulations are treated as responsible for any scheme particulars, of compensation to any person who has become or agreed to become a participant in the scheme and suffered loss as a result of any untrue or misleading statement in the particulars or the omission from them of any matter required by the regulations to be included.

**85(4) [Liability apart from regulations]** Regulations under this section shall not affect any liability which any person may incur apart from the regulations.

RECOGNITION OF OVERSEAS SCHEMES

## 86 Schemes constituted in other member States

**86(1) [Recognition on satisfying requirements]** Subject to subsection (2) below, a collective investment scheme constituted in a member State other than the United Kingdom is a recognised scheme if it satisfies such requirements as are prescribed for the purposes of this section.

**86(2) [Notice re invitation by scheme operator]** Not less than two months before inviting persons in the United Kingdom to become participants in the scheme the operator of the scheme shall give written notice to the Secretary of State of his intention to do so, specifying the manner in which the invitation is to be made; and the scheme shall not be a recognised scheme by virtue of this section if within two months of receiving the notice the Secretary of State notifies–

(a) the operator of the scheme; and

(b) the authorities of the State in question who are responsible for the authorisation of collective investment schemes,

that the manner in which the invitation is to be made does not comply with the law in force in the United Kingdom.

**86(3) [Requirements for s. 86(2) notice]** The notice to be given to the Secretary of State under subsection (2) above–

(a) shall be accompanied by a certificate from the authorities mentioned in subsection (2)(b) above to the effect that the scheme complies with the conditions necessary for it to enjoy the rights conferred by any relevant Community instrument;

(b) shall contain the address of a place in the United Kingdom for the service on the operator of notices or other documents required or authorised to be served on him under this Act; and

(c) shall contain or be accompanied by such other information and documents as may be prescribed.

**86(4) [Notice to contain reasons and s. 86(5) rights]** A notice given by the Secretary of State under subsection (2) above shall give the reasons for which he considers that the law in force in the United Kingdom will not be complied with and give particulars of the rights conferred by subsection (5) below.

**86(5) [Rights re representations]** A person on whom a notice is served by the Secretary of State under subsection (2) above may, within twenty-one days of the date of service, make written representations to the Secretary of State and, if desired, oral representations to a person appointed for that purpose by the Secretary of State.

**86(6) [Withdrawal of notice after representations]** The Secretary of State may in the light of any representations made in accordance with subsection (5) above withdraw his notice and in that event the scheme shall be a recognised scheme from the date on which the notice is withdrawn.

**86(7) [Application of s. 48 rules]** Rules under section 48 above shall not apply to investment business in respect of which the operator or trustee of a scheme recognised under this section is an authorised person by virtue of section 24 above except so far as they make provision as respects–

(a) procuring persons to become participants in the scheme and advising persons on the scheme and the exercise of the rights conferred by it;

(b) matters incidental to those mentioned in paragraph (a) above.

This subsection also applies to statements of principle under section 47A and codes of practice under section 63A so far as they relate to matters falling within the rule-making power in section 48.

**History**
In s. 86(7) the words "This subsection also applies" to the end added by CA 1989, s. 206(1) and Sch. 23, para. 8 as from 15 March 1990 (see SI 1990/354 (C 12), art. 3).

**86(8) [Interpretation]** For the purposes of this section a collective investment scheme is constituted in a member State if–

(a) it is constituted under the law of that State by a contract or under a trust and is managed by a body corporate incorporated under that law; or

(b) it takes the form of an open-ended investment company incorporated under that law.

**86(9) [Notice re cessation of recognition]** If the operator of a scheme recognised under this section gives written notice to the Secretary of State stating that he desires the scheme no longer to be recognised under this section it shall cease to be so recognised when the notice is given.

## 87 Schemes authorised in designated countries or territories

**87(1) [Recognised scheme other than under s. 86]** Subject to subsection (3) below, a collective investment scheme which is not a recognised scheme by virtue of section 86 above but is managed in and authorised under the law of a country or territory outside the United Kingdom is a recognised scheme if–

(a) that country or territory is designated for the purposes of this section by an order made by the Secretary of State; and

(b) the scheme is of a class specified by the order.

**87(2) [Requirements for Secretary of State's order]** Subject to subsection (2A) below, the Secretary of State shall not make an order designating any country or territory for the purposes of this section unless he is satisfied that the law under which collective investment schemes of the class to be specified by the order are authorised and supervised in that country or territory affords to investors in the United Kingdom protection at least equivalent to that provided for them by this Chapter in the case of an authorised unit trust scheme.

**History**
In s. 87(2) the words "Subject to subsection (2A) below," appearing at the beginning inserted by the Open-Ended Investment Companies (Investment Companies with Variable Capital) Regulations 1996 (SI 1996/2827), reg. 1, 75 and Sch. 8, para. 16 as from 6 January 1997.

**87(2A) [Where requirements of s. 87(2) not needed]** Nothing in subsection (2) above shall require the comparison set out in that subsection to be made where–

(a) the class of collective investment schemes to be specified in an order includes schemes having characteristics corresponding to those of an investment company with variable capital; and

(b) having regard to the characteristics of such schemes, it appears more appropriate to consider whether investors in the United Kingdom are afforded protection at least equivalent to that provided for them by the Open-Ended Investment Companies (Investment Companies with Variable Capital) Regulations 1996;

and, to the extent that the requirements of paragraph (b) above are met, the relevant comparison shall be between the protection afforded to investors in the United Kingdom by the law under which collective investment schemes of the class to be specified in the order are authorised and supervised in the country or territory concerned and the protection provided for such investors by the the Open-Ended Investment Companies (Investment Companies with Variable Capital) Regulations 1996.

**History**
S. 87(2A) inserted by the Open-Ended Investment Companies (Investment Companies with Variable Capital) Regulations 1996 (SI 1996/2827), reg. 1, 75 and Sch. 8, para. 16 as from 6 January 1997.

**87(3) [Written notice by scheme operator]** A scheme shall not be recognised by virtue of this section unless the operator of the scheme gives written notice to the Secretary of State that he wishes it to be recognised; and the scheme shall not be recognised if within such period from receiving the notice as may be prescribed the Secretary of State notifies the operator that the scheme is not to be recognised.

**87(4) [Contents of s. 87(3) notice]** The notice given by the operator under subsection (3) above–

(a) shall contain the address of a place in the United Kingdom for the service on the operator of notices or other documents required or authorised to be served on him under this Act; and

(b) shall contain or be accompanied by such information and documents as may be prescribed.

**87(5) [Effect of s. 85]** Section 85 above shall have effect in relation to a scheme recognised under this section as it has effect in relation to an authorised unit trust scheme, taking references to the manager as references to the operator and, in the case of an operator who is not an authorised person, references to publishing particulars as references to causing them to be published; and regulations made by virtue of this subsection may make provision whereby compliance with any requirements imposed by or under the law of a country or territory designated under this section is treated as compliance with any requirement of the regulations.

**87(6) [Transitional provisions in order]** An order under subsection (1) above may contain such transitional provisions as the Secretary of State thinks necessary or expedient and shall be subject to annulment in pursuance of a resolution of either House of Parliament.

**Note**

See the Financial Services Act 1986 (Investment Advertisements) (Exemptions) Order 1996 (SI 1996/1586).

## 88 Other overseas schemes

**88(1) [Power of Secretary of State to make order]** The Secretary of State may, on the application of the operator of a scheme which–

(a) is managed in a country or territory outside the United Kingdom; but

(b) does not satisfy the requirements mentioned in section 86(1) above and in relation to which there is no relevant order under section 87(1) above,

make an order declaring the scheme to be a recognised scheme if it appears to him that it affords adequate protection to the participants, makes adequate provision for the matters dealt with by regulations under section 81 above and satisfies the following provisions of this section.

**88(2) [General requirements]** The operator must be a body corporate or the scheme must take the form of an open-ended investment company.

**88(3) [Requirements re operator]** Subject to subsection (4) below, the operator and the trustee, if any, must be fit and proper persons to act as operator or, as the case may be, as trustee; and for that purpose the Secretary of State may take into account any matter relating to–

(a) any person who is or will be employed by or associated with the operator or trustee for the purposes of the scheme;

(b) any director or controller of the operator or trustee;

(c) any other body corporate in the same group as the operator or trustee and any director or controller of any such other body.

**88(4) [Non-application of s. 88(3)]** Subsection (3) above does not apply to an operator or trustee who is an authorised person and not prohibited from acting as operator or trustee, as the case may be, by or under rules under section 48 above, by or under the rules of any recognised self-regulating organisation of which he is a member or by any prohibition imposed under section 65 above.

**88(5) [Authorised person as representative in UK]** If the operator is not an authorised person he must have a representative in the United Kingdom who is an authorised person and has power to act generally for the operator and to accept service of notices and other documents on his behalf.

**88(6) [Name and purposes of scheme]** The name of the scheme must not be undesirable or misleading; and the purposes of the scheme must be reasonably capable of being successfully carried into effect.

**88(7) [Redemption of units by participants]** The participants must be entitled to have their units redeemed in accordance with the scheme at a price related to the net value of the property to which the units relate and determined in accordance with the scheme; but a scheme shall be treated as complying with this subsection if it requires the operator to ensure that a participant is able to sell his units on an investment exchange at a price not significantly different from that mentioned in this subsection.

**88(8) [Application of s. 77(2)–(5)]** Subsections (2) to (5) of section 77 above shall apply also to an application under this section.

**88(9) [Application of s. 82]** So much of section 82 above as applies to an alteration of the scheme shall apply also to a scheme recognised under this section, taking references to the manager as references to the operator and with the omission of the requirement relating to the solicitor's certificate; and if the operator or trustee of any such scheme is to be replaced the operator or, as the case may be, the trustee, or in either case the person who is to replace him, shall give at least one month's notice to the Secretary of State.

**88(10) [Effect of s. 85]** Section 85 above shall have effect in relation to a scheme recognised under this section as it has effect in relation to an authorised unit trust scheme, taking references to the manager as references to the operator and, in the case of an operator who is not an authorised person, references to publishing particulars as references to causing them to be published.

**Note**

See the Financial Services Act 1986 (Investment Advertisements) (Exemptions) Order 1996 (SI 1996/1586).

## 89 Refusal and revocation of recognition

**89(1) [Power of Secretary of State]** The Secretary of State may at any time direct that a scheme shall cease to be recognised by virtue of section 87 above or revoke an order under section 88 above if it appears to him–

(a) that it is undesirable in the interests of the participants or potential participants in the United Kingdom that the scheme should continue to be recognised;

(b) without prejudice to paragraph (a) above, that the operator or trustee of the scheme has contravened any provision of this Act or any rules or regulations made under it or, in purported compliance with any such provision, has furnished the Secretary of State with false, inaccurate or misleading information or has contravened any prohibition or requirement imposed under this Act; or

(c) in the case of an order under section 88 that any of the requirements for the making of the order are no longer satisfied.

**89(2) [Matters for s. 89(1)(a)]** For the purposes of subsection (1)(a) above the Secretary of State may take into account any matter relating to the scheme the operator or trustee, a director or controller of the operator or trustee or any person employed by or associated with the operator or trustee in connection with the scheme.

**89(3) [SRO member and s. 89(1)(b)]** In the case of an operator or trustee who is a member of a recognised self-regulating organisation the rules, prohibitions and requirements referred to in subsection (1)(b) above include the rules of that organisation and any prohibition or requirement imposed by virtue of those rules.

**89(4) [Revocation at request of operator]** The Secretary of State may give such a direction or revoke such an order as is mentioned in subsection (1) above at the request of the operator or trustee of the scheme; but he may refuse to do so if he considers that any matter concerning the scheme should be investigated as a preliminary to a decision on the question whether the direction should be given or the order revoked or that the direction or revocation would not be in the interests of the participants.

**89(5) [Written notice to operator re s. 87(3), 89(1)]** Where the Secretary of State proposes–

(a) to notify the operator of a scheme under section 87(3) above; or
(b) to give such a direction or to refuse to make or to revoke such an order as is mentioned in subsection (1) above,

he shall give the operator written notice of his intention to do so, stating the reasons for which he proposes to act and giving particulars of the rights conferred by subsection (6) below.

**89(6) [Written representations to Secretary of State]** A person on whom a notice is served under subsection (5) above may, within twenty-one days of the date of service, make written representations to the Secretary of State and, if desired, oral representations to a person appointed for that purpose by the Secretary of State.

**89(7) [Secretary of State to have regard to representations]** The Secretary of State shall have regard to any representations made in accordance with subsection (6) above in determining whether to notify the operator, give the direction or refuse to make or revoke the order, as the case may be.

# 90 Facilities and information in the United Kingdom

**90(1) [Regulations by Secretary of State]** The Secretary of State may make regulations requiring operators of recognised schemes to maintain in the United Kingdom, or in such part or parts of it as may be specified in the regulations, such facilities as he thinks desirable in the interests of participants and as are specified in the regulations.

**90(2) [Operator to include certain information]** The Secretary of State may by notice in writing require the operator of any recognised scheme to include such explanatory information as is specified in the notice in any investment advertisement issued or caused to be issued by him in the United Kingdom in which the scheme is named.

## POWERS OF INTERVENTION

# 91 Directions

**91(1) [Power of Secretary of State]** If it appears to the Secretary of State–

(a) that any of the requirements for the making of an order declaring a scheme to be an authorised unit trust scheme are no longer satisfied;
(b) that the exercise of the power conferred by this subsection is desirable in the interest of participants or potential participants in the scheme; or
(c) without prejudice to paragraph (b) above, that the manager or trustee of such a scheme has contravened any provision of this Act or any rules or regulations made under it or, in purported compliance with any such provision, has furnished the Secretary of State with false, inaccurate or misleading information or has contravened any prohibition or requirement imposed under this Act,

he may give a direction under subsection (2) below.

**91(2) [Scope of directions]** A direction under this subsection may–

(a) require the manager of the scheme to cease the issue or redemption, or both the issue and redemption, of units under the scheme on a date specified in the direction until such further date as is specified in that or another direction;
(b) require the manager and trustee of the scheme to wind it up by such date as is specified in the direction or, if no date is specified, as soon as practicable.

**91(3) [Effect of revocation of order]** The revocation of the order declaring an authorised unit trust scheme to be such a scheme shall not affect the operation of any direction under subsection (2) above which is then in force; and a direction may be given under that subsection in relation to a scheme in the case of which the order declaring it to be an authorised unit trust scheme has been revoked if a direction under that subsection was already in force at the time of revocation.

**91(4) [Effect of s. 60, 61, 62]** Sections 60, 61 and 62 above shall have effect in relation to a contravention of a direction under subsection (2) above as they have effect in relation to any such contravention as is mentioned in those sections.

**91(5) [Power to direct not to be scheme]** If it appears to the Secretary of State–

(a) that the exercise of the power conferred by this subsection is desirable in the interests of participants or potential participants in a scheme recognised under section 87 or 88 above who are in the United Kingdom;

(b) without prejudice to paragraph (a) above, that the operator of such a scheme has contravened any provision of this Act or any rules or regulations made under it or, in purported compliance with any such provision, has furnished the Secretary of State with false, inaccurate or misleading information or has contravened any prohibition or requirement imposed under this Act; or

(c) that any of the requirements for the recognition of a scheme under section 88 above are no longer satisfied,

he may direct that the scheme shall not be a recognised scheme for a specified period or until the occurrence of a specified event or until specified conditions are complied with.

**91(6) [Matter for s. 91(1)(b), (5)(a)]** For the purposes of subsections (1)(b) and (5)(a) above the Secretary of State may take into account any matter relating to the scheme, the manager, operator or trustee, a director or controller of the manager, operator or trustee or any person employed by or associated with the manager, operator or trustee in connection with the scheme.

**91(7) [Manager who is SRO member]** In the case of a manager, operator or trustee who is a member of a recognised self-regulating organisation the rules, prohibitions and requirements referred to in subsections (1)(c) and (5)(b) above include the rules of that organisation and any prohibition or requirement imposed by virtue of those rules.

**91(8) [Withdrawal or variation of directions]** The Secretary of State may, either of his own motion or on the application of the manager, trustee or operator of the scheme concerned, withdraw or vary a direction given under this section if it appears to the Secretary of State that it is no longer necessary for the direction to take effect or continue in force or, as the case may be, that it should take effect or continue in force in a different form.

## 92 Notice of directions

**92(1) [Exercise of power to give direction]** The power to give a direction under section 91 above in relation to a scheme shall be exercisable by written notice served by the Secretary of State on the manager and trustee or, as the case may be, on the operator of the scheme and any such notice shall take effect on such date as is specified in the notice.

**92(2) [Written notice of refusal]** If the Secretary of State refuses to withdraw or vary a direction on the application of the manager, trustee or operator of the scheme concerned he shall serve that person with a written notice of refusal.

**92(3) [Notice to state reasons for refusal etc.]** A notice giving a direction, or varying it otherwise than on the application of the manager, trustee or operator concerned, or refusing to withdraw or vary a direction on the application of such a person shall state the reasons for which the direction was given or varied or, as the case may be, why the application was refused.

**92(4) [Public notice of s. 91 direction]** The Secretary of State may give public notice of a direction given by him under section 91 above and of any withdrawal or variation of such a direction; and any such notice may, if the Secretary of State thinks fit, include a statement of the reasons for which the direction was given, withdrawn or varied.

## 93 Applications to the court

**93(1) [Application by Secretary of State]** In any case in which the Secretary of State has power to give a direction under section 91(2) above in relation to an authorised unit trust scheme or, by virtue of subsection (3) of that section, in relation to a scheme which has been such a scheme, he may apply to the court–

(a) for an order removing the manager or trustee, or both the manager and trustee, of the scheme and replacing either or both of them with a person or persons nominated by him and appearing to him to satisfy the requirements of section 78 above; or

(b) if it appears to the Secretary of State that no, or no suitable, person satisfying those requirements is available, for an order removing the manager or trustee, or both the manager and trustee, and appointing an authorised person to wind the scheme up.

**Note**

Concerning European investment firms, see the Investment Services Regulations 1995 (SI 1995/3275), reg. 32 and Sch. 7, para. 24.

Concerning European institutions, see the Banking Coordination (Second Council Directive) Regulations 1992 (SI 1992/3218), reg. 55 and Sch. 9, para. 26.

**93(2) [Power of court]** On an application under this section the court may make such order as it thinks fit; and the court may, on the application of the Secretary of State, rescind any such order as is mentioned in paragraph (b) of subsection (1) above and substitute such an order as is mentioned in paragraph (a) of that subsection.

**93(3) [Written notice to manager of making of application]** The Secretary of State shall give written notice of the making of an application under this section to the manager and trustee of the scheme concerned and take such steps as he considers appropriate for bringing the making of the application to the attention of the participants.

**93(4) [Exercise of jurisdiction]** The jurisdiction conferred by this section shall be exercisable by the High Court and the Court of Session.

**93(5) [Non-application of s. 83]** Section 83 above shall not apply to a manager appointed by an order made on an application under subsection (1)(b) above.

## SUPPLEMENTAL

# 94 Investigations

**94(1) [Power of Secretary of State to appoint inspectors]** The Secretary of State may appoint one or more competent inspectors to investigate and report on–

(a) the affairs of, or of the manager or trustee of, any authorised unit trust scheme;

(b) the affairs of, or of the operator or trustee of, any recognised scheme so far as relating to activities carried on in the United Kingdom; or

(c) the affairs of, or of the operator or trustee of, any other collective investment scheme,

if it appears to the Secretary of State that it is in the interests of the participants to do so or that the matter is of public concern.

**94(2) [Powers of inspector]** An inspector appointed under subsection (1) above to investigate the affairs of, or of the manager, trustee or operator of, any scheme may also, if he thinks it necessary for the purposes of that investigation, investigate the affairs of, or of the manager, trustee or operator of, any other such scheme as is mentioned in that subsection whose manager, trustee or operator is the same person as the manager, trustee or operator of the first mentioned scheme.

**94(3) [Application of Companies Act 1985]** Sections 434 to 436 of the Companies Act 1985 (production of documents and evidence to inspectors), shall apply in relation to an inspector appointed under this section as they apply to an inspector appointed under section 431 of that Act but with the modifications specified in subsection (4) below.

**History**

In s. 94(3) the words "except section 435(1)(a) and (b) and (2)" formerly appearing after the words "evidence to inspectors)," repealed by CA 1989, s. 212 and Sch. 24 as from 21 February 1990 (see SI 1990/142 (C 5), art. 7(d)).

**94(4) [Interpretation re s. 94(1)–(3)]** In the provisions applied by subsection (3) above for any reference to a company there shall be substituted a reference to the scheme under investigation by virtue of this section and any reference to an officer of the company shall include a reference to any director of the manager, trustee or operator of the scheme.

**History**

In s. 94(4) the words "or its affairs" formerly appearing after the words "reference to a company", the words "and the affairs mentioned in subsection (1) or (2) above" formerly appearing after the words "by virtue of this section" and the words "or director" formerly appearing after the words "reference to an officer" repealed by CA 1989, s. 212 and Sch. 24 as from 21 February 1990 (see SI 1990/142 (C 5), art. 7(d)).

**94(5) [Non-disclosure re legal professional privilege]** A person shall not under this section be required to disclose any information or produce any document which he would be entitled to refuse to disclose or produce on grounds of legal professional privilege in proceedings in the High Court or on grounds of confidentiality as between client and professional legal adviser in proceedings in the Court of Session except that a lawyer may be required to furnish the name and address of his client.

**94(6) [Where lien claimed]** Where a person claims a lien on a document its production under this section shall be without prejudice to the lien.

**94(7) [Disclosure re bankers]** Nothing in this section requires a person (except as mentioned in subsection (7A) below) to disclose any information or produce any document in respect of which he owes an obligation of confidence by virtue of carrying on the business of banking unless–

(a) the person to whom the obligation of confidence is owed consents to the disclosure or production, or

(b) the making of the requirement was authorised by the Secretary of State.

**History**

See history note after s. 94(7A).

**94(7A) [Non-application of s. 94(7)]** Subsection (7) does not apply where the person owing the obligation of confidence or the person to whom it is owed is–

(a) the manager, operator or trustee of the scheme under investigation, or

(b) a manager, operator or trustee whose own affairs are under investigation.

**History**

S. 94(7), (7A) substituted for the former s. 94(7) by CA 1989, s. 72(1), (2) as from 21 February 1990 (see SI 1990/142 (C 5), art. 4); the former s. 94(7) read as follows:

"Nothing in this section shall require a person carrying on the business of banking to disclose any information or produce any document relating to the affairs of a customer unless–

(a) the customer is a person who the inspector has reason to believe may be able to give information relevant to the investigation; and

(b) the Secretary of State is satisfied that the disclosure or production is necessary for the purposes of the investigation."

**94(8) [Reports by inspector]** An inspector appointed under this section may, and if so directed by the Secretary of State shall, make interim reports to the Secretary of State and on the conclusion of his investigation shall make a final report to him.

**94(8A) [Where suggestion re criminal offence]** If it appears to the Secretary of State that matters have come to light in the course of the inspectors' investigation which suggest that a criminal offence has been committed, and those matters have been referred to the appropriate prosecuting authority, he may direct the inspectors to take no further steps in the investigation or to take only such further steps as are specified in the direction.

**History**

See history note after s. 94(8B).

**94(8B) [Where s. 94(8A) direction]** Where an investigation is the subject of a direction under subsection (8A), the inspectors shall make a final report to the Secretary of State only where the Secretary of State directs them to do so.

**History**

S. 94(8A), (8B) inserted by CA 1989, s. 72(1), (3) as from 21 February 1990 (see SI 1990/142 (C 5), art. 4).

**94(9) [Form, publication of report]** Any such report shall be written or printed as the Secretary of State may direct and the Secretary of State may, if he thinks fit–

(a) furnish a copy, on request and on payment of the prescribed fee, to the manager, trustee or operator or any participant in a scheme under investigation or any other person whose conduct is referred to in the report; and

(b) cause the report to be published.

**94(10) [Order re expenses]** A person who is convicted on a prosecution instituted as a result of an investigation under this section may in the same proceedings be ordered to pay the expenses of the investigation to such extent as may be specified in the order.

There shall be treated as expenses of the investigation, in particular, such reasonable sums as the Secretary of State may determine in respect of general staff costs and overheads.

**History**
S. 94(10) added by CA 1989, s. 72(1), (4) as from 21 February 1990 (see SI 1990/142 (C 5), art. 4).

## 95 Contraventions

**95(1) [Effect of contravention of Ch. VIII]** A person who contravenes any provision of this Chapter, a manager or trustee of an authorised unit trust scheme who contravenes any regulations made under section 81 above and a person who contravenes any other regulations made under this Chapter shall be treated as having contravened rules made under Chapter V of this Part of this Act or, in the case of a person who is an authorised person by virtue of his membership of a recognised self-regulating organisation or certification by a recognised professional body, the rules of that organisation or body.

**95(2) [Additional application of s. 95(1)]** Subsection (1) above applies also to any contravention by the operator of a recognised scheme of a requirement imposed under section 90(2) above.

**95(3) [Action by virtue of s. 47A]** The disciplinary action which may be taken by virtue of section 47A(3) (failure to comply with statement of principle) includes–

(a) the giving of a direction under section 91(2), and

(b) the application by the Secretary of State for an order under section 93;

and subsection (6) of section 47A (duty of the Secretary of State as to exercise of powers) has effect accordingly.

**History**
S. 95(3) added by CA 1989, s. 206(1) and Sch. 23, para. 9 as from 15 March 1990 (see SI 1990/354 (C 12), art. 3).

# Chapter IX – The Tribunal

## 96 The Financial Services Tribunal

**96(1) ["The Tribunal"]** For the purposes of this Act there shall be a Tribunal known as the Financial Services Tribunal (in this Act referred to as **"the Tribunal"**).

**96(2) [Panel of members]** There shall be a panel of not less than ten persons to serve as members of the Tribunal when nominated to do so in accordance with subsection (3) below; and that panel shall consist of–

(a) persons with legal qualifications appointed by the Lord Chancellor after consultation with the Lord Advocate, including at least one person qualified in Scots law; and

(b) persons appointed by the Secretary of State who appear to him to be qualified by experience or otherwise to deal with the cases that may be referred to the Tribunal.

**96(3) [Where case referred to Tribunal]** Where a case is referred to the Tribunal the Secretary of State shall nominate three persons from the panel to serve as members of the Tribunal in respect of that case and nominate one of them to be chairman.

**96(4) [Requirements re members]** The person nominated to be chairman of the Tribunal in respect of any case shall be a person with legal qualifications and, so far as practicable, at least one of the other members shall be a person with recent practical experience in business relevant to the case.

**96(5) [Where member unable to act]** If while a case is being dealt with by the Tribunal one of the three persons serving as members in respect of that case becomes unable to act the case may, with the consent of the Secretary of State and of the person or persons at whose request the case was referred to the Tribunal, be dealt with by the other two members.

**96(6) [Sch. 6]** Schedule 6 to this Act shall have effect as respects the Tribunal and its proceedings.

## 97 References to the Tribunal

**97(1) [Requirement that Secretary of State make reference]** Any person–

(a) on whom a notice is served under section 29, 34, 59(4), 60(2) or 70 above; or

(b) on whom a copy of a notice under section 29, 34, 60(2) or 70 above is served or on whom the Secretary of State considers that a copy of such a notice would have been served if it had been practicable to do so,

may within twenty-eight days of the date of service of the notice require the Secretary of State to refer the matter to which the notice relates to the Tribunal and, subject to the provisions of this section, the Secretary of State shall refer that matter accordingly.

**97(2) [Where reference need not be made]** The Secretary of State need not refer a matter to the Tribunal at the request of the person on whom a notice was served under section 29, 34, 59(4) or 60(2) above if within the period mentioned in subsection (1) above he–

(a) decides to grant the application or, as the case may be, decides not to withdraw or suspend the authorisation, give the direction or publish the statement to which the notice relates; and

(b) gives written notice of his decision to that person.

**97(3) [Further non-reference situation]** The Secretary of State need not refer a matter to the Tribunal at the request of the person on whom a notice is served under section 70 above if–

(a) that matter is the refusal of an application for the rescission or variation of a prohibition or requirement and within the period mentioned in subsection (1) above he–
   (i) decides to grant the application; and
   (ii) gives written notice of his decision to that person; or

(b) that matter is the imposition or variation of a prohibition or requirement, being a prohibition, requirement or variation which has not yet taken effect, and within the period mentioned in subsection (1) above and before the prohibition, requirement or variation takes effect he–
   (i) decides to rescind the prohibition or requirement or decides not to make the variation; and
   (ii) gives written notice of his decision to that person.

**97(4) [Where new notice after suspension or withdrawal]** Where the notice served on a person under section 29 or 34 above–

(a) proposed the withdrawal of an authorisation or the giving of a direction under section 33(1)(a) above; or

(b) proposed the suspension of an authorisation or the giving of a direction under section 33(1)(b) above,

and at any time within the period mentioned in subsection (1) above the Secretary of State serves a new notice on that person in substitution for that previously served, then, if the substituted notice complies with subsection (5) below, subsection (1) above shall have effect in relation to the substituted notice instead of the original notice and as if the period there mentioned were twenty-eight days after the date of service of the original notice or fourteen days after the date of service of the substituted notice, whichever ends later.

**97(5) [Notices under s. 97(4)]** A notice served in substitution for a notice within subsection (4)(a) above complies with this subsection if it proposes–

(a) the suspension of an authorisation or the giving of a direction under section 33(1)(b) above; or

(b) the exercise of the power conferred by section 60 above;

and a notice served in substitution for a notice within subsection (4)(b) above complies with this subsection if it proposes a less severe suspension or direction under section 33(1)(b) or the exercise of the power conferred by section 60 above.

**97(6) [Effective date of notice]** The reference of the imposition or variation of a prohibition or requirement under Chapter VI of this Part of this Act to the Tribunal shall not affect the date on which it comes into effect.

**Note**

Concerning interpretation see the Investment Services Regulations 1995 (SI 1995/3275), reg. 9(5) and Sch. 4, para. 2.

## 98 Decisions on references by applicant or authorised person etc.

**98(1) [Where case referred to Tribunal]** Where a case is referred to the Tribunal at the request of a person within section 97(1)(a) above the Tribunal shall–

(a) investigate the case; and

(b) make a report to the Secretary of State stating what would in its opinion be the appropriate decision in the matter and the reasons for that opinion;

and it shall be the duty of the Secretary of State to decide the matter forthwith in accordance with the Tribunal's report.

**98(2) [Where matter referred is refusal of application]** Where the matter referred to the Tribunal is the refusal of an application the Tribunal may under this section report that the appropriate decision would be to grant or refuse the application or–

(a) in the case of an application for the variation of a suspension, direction, consent, prohibition or requirement, to vary it in a specified manner;

(b) in the case of an application for the rescission of a prohibition or requirement, to vary the prohibition or requirement in a specified manner.

**98(3) [Where matter referred is other action of Secretary of State]** Where the matter referred to the Tribunal is any action of the Secretary of State other than the refusal of an application the Tribunal may report that the appropriate decision would be–

(a) to take or not to take the action taken or proposed to be taken by the Secretary of State or to take any other action that he could take under the provision in question; or

(b) to take instead or in addition any action that he could take in the case of the person concerned under any one or more of the provisions mentioned in subsection (4) below other than that under which he was acting or proposing to act.

**98(4) [Provisions in s. 98(1)(b)]** Those provisions are sections 28, 33 and 60 above and Chapter VI of this Part of this Act; and sections 29, 34, 60(2) and (3) and 70(2) and (4) above shall not apply to any action taken by the Secretary of State in accordance with the Tribunal's report.

**98(5) [Copy of report, notice of decision]** The Tribunal shall send a copy of its report under this section to the person at whose request the case was referred to it; and the Secretary of State shall serve him with a written notice of the decision made by him in accordance with the report.

**Note**
Concerning interpretation see the Investment Services Regulations 1995 (SI 1995/3275), reg. 9(5) and Sch. 4, para. 3.

## 99 Decisions on references by third parties

**99** Where a case is referred to the Tribunal at the request of a person within section 97(1)(b) above the Tribunal shall report to the Secretary of State whether the reasons stated in the notice in question which relate to that person are substantiated; and the Tribunal shall send a copy of the report to that person and to the person on whom the notice was served.

## 100 Withdrawal of references

**100(1) [Person may withdraw reference]** A person who has required a case to be referred to the Tribunal may at any time before the conclusion of the proceedings before the Tribunal withdraw the reference.

**100(2) [Secretary of State may withdraw reference]** The Secretary of State may at any such time withdraw any reference made at the request of a person on whom a notice was served under any of the provisions mentioned in subsection (1)(a) of section 97 above if he–

(a) decides as mentioned in subsection (2)(a) or (3)(a)(i) or (b)(i) of that section; and

(b) gives such a notice as is mentioned in subsection (2)(b) or (3)(a)(ii) or (b)(ii) of that section;

but a reference shall not be withdrawn by virtue of such a decision and notice as are mentioned in paragraph (b) of subsection (3) unless the decision is made and the notice is given before the prohibition, requirement or variation has taken effect.

**Note**
See note after s. 100(5).

**100(3) [Where case withdrawn]** Where a case is withdrawn from the Tribunal under this section the Tribunal shall not further investigate the case or make a report under section 98 or 99 above; but where the reference is withdrawn otherwise than by the Secretary of State he may require the Tribunal to make a report to him on the results of its investigation up to the time when the reference was withdrawn.

**100(4) [Where withdrawal by one of two or more persons]** Where two or more persons have required a case to be referred to the Tribunal the withdrawal of the reference by one or more of them shall not affect the functions of the Tribunal as respects the case so far as relating to a person who has not withdrawn the reference.

**100(5) [Where withdrawal by persons served with s. 29, 34, 60 notice]** Where a person on whom a notice was served under section 29, 34 or 60 above withdraws a case from the Tribunal subsection (5) of each of those sections shall apply to him as if he had not required the case to be referred.

**Note**
Concerning interpretation see the Investment Services Regulations 1995 (SI 1995/3275), reg. 9(5) and Sch. 4, para. 4.

## 101 Reports

**101(1) [Exclusion re affairs of particular person]** In preparing its report on any case the Tribunal shall have regard to the need to exclude, so far as practicable, any matter which relates to the affairs of a particular person (not being a person who required or could have required the case to be referred to the Tribunal) where the publication of that matter would or might, in the opinion of the Tribunal, seriously and prejudicially affect the interests of that person.

**101(2) [Publication and sale of reports]** The Secretary of State may, in such cases as he thinks fit, publish the report of the Tribunal and offer copies of any such report for sale.

**101(3) [Copies to interested persons]** The Secretary of State may, on request and on payment of the prescribed fee, supply a copy of a report of the Tribunal to any person whose conduct is referred to in the report or whose interests as a client or creditor are affected by the conduct of a person to whom the proceedings before the Tribunal related.

**101(4) [Parts of report omitted from publication]** If the Secretary of State is of opinion that there is good reason for not disclosing any part of a report he may cause that part to be omitted from the report as published under subsection (2) or from the copy of it supplied under subsection (3) above.

**101(5) [Admissibility as evidence]** A copy of a report of the Tribunal endorsed with a certificate signed by or on behalf of the Secretary of State stating that it is a true copy shall be admissible as evidence of the opinion of the Tribunal as to any matter referred to in the report; and a certificate purporting to be signed as aforesaid shall be deemed to have been duly signed unless the contrary is shown.

# Chapter X – Information

## 102 Register of authorised persons and recognised organisations etc.

**102(1) [Secretary of State to keep register]** The Secretary of State shall keep a register containing an entry in respect of–

(a) each person who is an authorised person by virtue of an authorisation granted by the Secretary of State;

(b) each other person who appears to him to be an authorised person by virtue of any provision of this Part of this Act;

(c) each recognised self-regulating organisation, recognised professional body, recognised investment exchange and recognised clearing house;

(d) each authorised unit trust scheme and recognised scheme;

(e) each person in respect of whom a direction under section 59 above is in force.

**102(2) [Entry re each authorised person]** The entry in respect of each authorised person shall consist of–

(a) a statement of the provision by virtue of which he is an authorised person;

(b) in the case of a person who is an authorised person by virtue of membership of a recognised self-regulating organisation or certification by a recognised professional body, the name and address of the organisation or body;

(bb) in the case of an investment company with variable capital which is an authorised person by virtue of section 24A above, the name of the company, the address of the company's head office and the names and addresses of the directors and depositary of the company;

(c) in the case of a person who is an authorised person by virtue of section 25 or 31 above, information as to the services which that person holds himself out as able to provide;

(d) in the case of a person who is an authorised person by virtue of section 31 above, the address notified to the Secretary of State under section 32 above;

(e) in the case of a person who is an authorised person by virtue of any provision other than section 31 above, the date on which he became an authorised person by virtue of that provision; and

(f) such other information as the Secretary of State may determine.

**History**
S. 102(2)(bb) inserted by the Open-Ended Investment Companies (Investment Companies with Variable Capital) Regulations 1996 (SI 1996/2827), reg. 1, 75 and Sch. 8, para. 17 as from 6 January 1997.

**102(3) [Entry re s. 102(1)(c) organisations etc.]** The entry in respect of each such organisation, body, exchange or clearing house as is mentioned in subsection (1)(c) above shall consist of its name and address and such other information as the Secretary of State may determine.

**102(4) [Entry re s. 102(1)(d) schemes]** The entry in respect of each such scheme as is mentioned in subsection (1)(d) above shall consist of its name and, in the case of an authorised unit trust scheme, the name and address of the manager and trustee and, in the case of a recognised scheme, the name and address of the operator and of any representative of the operator in the United Kingdom and, in either case, such other information as the Secretary of State may determine.

**102(5) [Entry re s. 102(1)(e) persons]** The entry in respect of each such person as is mentioned in subsection (1)(e) above shall include particulars of any consent for that person's employment given by the Secretary of State.

**102(6) [Where s. 102 (1)(a), (b) person no longer authorised]** Where it appears to the Secretary of State that any person in respect of whom there is an entry in the register by virtue of subsection (1)(a), (b) or (bb) above has ceased to be an authorised person (whether by death, by withdrawal or other cessation of his authorisation, as a result of his ceasing to be a member of a recognised self-regulating organisation or otherwise) the Secretary of State shall make a note to that effect in the entry together with the reason why the person in question is no longer an authorised person.

[**CCH Note:** In the above section the words "(bb)" refer to s. 102(2)(bb).]

**History**
In s. 102(6) the words "or (b)" formerely appearing after the words "subsection (1)(a)" substituted by the words ", (b) or (bb)" by the Open-Ended Investment Companies (Investment Companies with Variable Capital) Regulations 1996 (SI 1996/2827), reg. 1, 75 and Sch. 8, para. 17 as from 6 January 1997.

**102(7) [Note re certain events]** Where–

(a) an organisation, body, exchange or clearing house in respect of which there is an entry in the register by virtue of paragraph (c) of subsection (1) above has ceased to be recognised or ceased to exist;

(b) an authorised unit trust scheme or recognised scheme in respect of which there is an entry in the register by virtue of paragraph (d) of that subsection has ceased to be authorised or recognised; or

(c) the direction applying to a person in respect of whom there is an entry in the register by virtue of paragraph (e) of that subsection has ceased to have effect, the Secretary of State shall make a note to that effect in the entry.

**102(8) [Removal of s. 102(6), (7) note]** An entry in respect of which a note is made under subsection (6) or (7) above may be removed from the register at the end of such period as the Secretary of State thinks appropriate.

**Note**

Concerning UK authorised investment firms which are authorised persons and European investment firms, see the Investment Services Regulations 1995 (SI 1995/3275), reg. 1, 28, 32 and Sch. 7, para. 25.

Concerning European institutions, see the Banking Coordination (Second Council Directive) Regulations 1992 (SI 1992/3218), reg. 55 and Sch. 9, para. 27.

## 103 Inspection of register

**103(1) [Inspection and publication of information]** The information contained in the entries included in the register otherwise than by virtue of section 102(1)(e) above shall be open to inspection; and the Secretary of State may publish the information contained in those entries in any form he thinks appropriate and may offer copies of any such information for sale.

**103(2) [Inspection re s. 102(1)(e) entries]** A person shall be entitled to ascertain whether there is an entry in the register by virtue of subsection (1)(e) of section 102 above (not being an entry in respect of which there is a note under subsection (7) of that section) in respect of a particular person specified by him and, if there is such an entry, to inspect it.

**103(3) [Limit on inspection re s. 102(1)(e) entries]** Except as provided by subsection (2) above the information contained in the register by virtue of section 102(1)(e) above shall not be open to inspection by any person unless he satisfies the Secretary of State that he has a good reason for seeking the information.

**103(4) [Limit on information available by s. 103(3)]** A person to whom information is made available by the Secretary of State under subsection (3) above shall not, without the consent of the Secretary of State or of the person to whom the information relates, make use of it except for the purpose for which it was made available.

**103(5) [Details re inspection]** Information which by virtue of this section is open to inspection shall be open to inspection free of charge but only at such times and places as the Secretary of State may appoint; and a person entitled to inspect any information may obtain a certified copy of it from the Secretary of State on payment of the prescribed fee.

**103(6) [Form of register]** The register may be kept by the Secretary of State in such form as he thinks appropriate with a view to facilitating inspection of the information which it contains.

## 104 Power to call for information

**104(1) [Information from s. 22, 24, 24A, 25, 31 persons]** The Secretary of State may by notice in writing require a person who is authorised to carry on investment business by virtue of section 22, 24, 24A, 25 or 31 above to furnish him with such information as he may reasonably require for the exercise of his functions under this Act.

**History**

In s. 104(1) the words "24A," appearing after the words "sections 22, 24," inserted by the Open-Ended Investment Companies (Investment Companies with Variable Capital) Regulations 1996 (SI 1996/2827), reg. 1, 75 and Sch. 8, para. 18 as from 6 January 1997.

**104(2) [Information from recognised bodies etc.]** The Secretary of State may by notice in writing require a recognised self-regulating organisation, recognised professional body, recognised investment exchange or recognised clearing house to furnish him with such information as he may reasonably require for the exercise of his functions under this Act.

**104(3) [Time, verification re information]** The Secretary of State may require any information which he requires under this section to be furnished within such reasonable time and verified in such manner as he may specify.

**104(4) [Effect of s. 60, 61, 62]** Sections 60, 61 and 62 above shall have effect in relation to a contravention of a requirement imposed under subsection (1) above as they have effect in relation to a contravention of the provisions to which those sections apply.

**Note**

Concerning European investment firms, see the Investment Services Regulations 1995 (SI 1995/3275), reg. 32 and Sch. 7, para. 26.

Concerning European institutions, see the Banking Coordination (Second Council Directive) Regulations 1992 (SI 1992/3218), reg. 55 and Sch. 9, para. 28.

## 105 Investigation powers

**105(1) [Where Secretary of State's powers to be exercised]** The powers of the Secretary of State under this section shall be exercisable in any case in which it appears to him that there is good reason to do so for the purpose of investigating the affairs, or any aspect of the affairs, of any person so far as relevant to any investment business which he is or was carrying on or appears to the Secretary of State to be or to have been carrying on.

**105(2) [Limit on exercise of powers]** Those powers shall not be exercisable for the purpose of investigating the affairs of any exempted person unless he is an appointed representative or the investigation is in respect of investment business in respect of which he is not an exempted person and shall not be exercisable for the purpose of investigating the affairs of a member of a recognised self-regulating organisation or a person certified by a recognised professional body in respect of investment business in the carrying on of which he is subject to its rules unless–

(a) that organisation or body has requested the Secretary of State to investigate those affairs; or

(b) it appears to him that the organisation or body is unable or unwilling to investigate them in a satisfactory manner.

**105(3) [Power re attendance before Secretary of State]** The Secretary of State may require the person whose affairs are to be investigated ("the person under investigation") or any connected person to attend before the Secretary of State at a specified time and place and answer questions or otherwise furnish information with respect to any matter relevant to the investigation.

**105(4) [Power re production of documents]** The Secretary of State may require the person under investigation or any other person to produce at a specified time and place any specified documents which appear to the Secretary of State to relate to any matter relevant to the investigation; and–

(a) if any such documents are produced, the Secretary of State may take copies or extracts from them or require the person producing them or any connected person to provide an explanation of any of them;

(b) if any such documents are not produced, the Secretary of State may require the person who was required to produce them to state, to the best of his knowledge and belief, where they are.

**105(5) [Statement admissible in evidence]** A statement by a person in compliance with a requirement imposed by virtue of this section may be used in evidence against him.

**105(5A) [Limits on use of statement in criminal proceedings]** However, in criminal proceedings in which that person is charged with an offence to which this subsection applies–

(a) no evidence relating to the statement may be adduced, and

(b) no question relating to it may be asked,

by or on behalf of the prosecution, unless evidence relating to it is adduced, or a question relating to it is asked, in the proceedings by or on behalf of that person.

**History**

S. 105(5A) inserted by Youth Justice and Criminal Evidence Act 1999, s. 59, 68(3) and Sch. 3, para. 11, with effect from 14 April 2000 (see Youth Justice and Criminal Evidence Act 1999 (Commencement No. 2) Order 2000 (SI 2000/1034 (C. 27)), art. 2(a)).

**105(5B) [Offences to which s. 105(5A) applies]** Subsection (5A) above applies to any offence other than–

(a) an offence under subsection (10) or section 200(1) below;

(b) an offence under section 5 of the Perjury Act 1911 (false statements made otherwise than on oath);

(c) an offence under section 44(2) of the Criminal Law (Consolidation) (Scotland) Act 1995 (false statements made otherwise than on oath); or

(d) an offence under Article 10 of the Perjury (Northern Ireland) Order 1979 (false statements made otherwise than on oath).

**History**
S. 105(5B) inserted by Youth Justice and Criminal Evidence Act 1999, s. 59, 68(3) and Sch. 3, para. 11, with effect from 14 April 2000 (see Youth Justice and Criminal Evidence Act 1999 (Commencement No. 2) Order 2000 (SI 2000/1034 (C. 27)), art. 2(a)).

**105(6) [Legal professional privilege, confidentiality]** A person shall not under this section be required to disclose any information or produce any document which he would be entitled to refuse to disclose or produce on grounds of legal professional privilege in proceedings in the High Court or on grounds of confidentiality as between client and professional legal adviser in proceedings in the Court of Session except that a lawyer may be required to furnish the name and address of his client.

**105(7)** (Omitted and repealed by Companies Act 1989, s. 73(1), (2), 212 and Sch. 24 as from 21 February 1990.)

**History**
In regard to the date of the above omission and repeal see SI 1990/142 (C 5), art. 4, 7(d); s. 105(7) formerly read as follows:
"The Secretary of State shall not require an institution authorised under the Banking Act 1987 to disclose any information or produce any document relating to the affairs of a customer unless the Secretary of State considers it necessary to do so for the purpose of investigating any investment business carried on, or appearing to the Secretary of State to be carried on or to have been carried on, by the institution or customer or, if the customer is a related company of the person under investigation, by that person."
In that former s. 105(7) the words, "an institution authorised under the Banking Act 1987", and, "institution", substituted for the original words, "a recognised or licensed institution within the meaning of the Banking Act 1979", and "bank, institution" respectively by Banking Act 1987, s. 108(1) and Sch. 6, para. 27(2) as from 1 October 1987 (see SI 1987/1664 (C 50)).

**105(8) [Where lien claimed]** Where a person claims a lien on a document its production under this section shall be without prejudice to the lien.

**105(9) [Definitions]** In this section–

**"connected person"**, in relation to any other person means–

(a) any person who is or was that other person's partner, employee, agent, appointed representative, banker, auditor or solicitor; and
(b) where the other person is a body corporate, any person who is or was a director, secretary or controller of that body corporate or of another body corporate of which it is or was a subsidiary; and
(c) where the other person is an unincorporated association, any person who is or was a member of the governing body or an officer or controller of the association; and
(d) where the other person is an appointed representative, any person who is or was his principal; and
(e) where the other person is the person under investigation (being a body corporate), any related company of that body corporate and any person who is a connected person in relation to that company;

**"documents"** includes information recorded in any form and, in relation to information recorded otherwise than in legible form, the power to require its production includes power to require the production of a copy of the information in legible form;

**"related company"**, in relation to a person under investigation (being a body corporate), means any other body corporate which is or at any material time was–

(a) a holding company or subsidiary of the person under investigation;
(b) a subsidiary of a holding company of that person; or
(c) a holding company of a subsidiary of that person,

and whose affairs it is in the Secretary of State's opinion necessary to investigate for the purpose of investigating the affairs of that person.

**History**
In s. 105(9) in the definition of "documents" the words "the power to require its productin includes power to require the production of" substituted for the former words "references to its production include references to producing" by CA 1989, s. 73(1), (3) as from 21 February 1990 (see SI 1990/142 (C 5), art. 4).

**105(10) [Offence, penalty]** Any person who without reasonable excuse fails to comply with a requirement imposed on him under this section shall be guilty of an offence and liable on summary conviction to imprisonment for a term not exceeding six months or to a fine not exceeding the fifth level on the standard scale or to both.

**105(11) [Order re expenses]** A person who is convicted on a prosecution instituted as a result of an investigation under this section may in the same proceedings be ordered to pay the expenses of the investigation to such extent as may be specified in the order.

There shall be treated as expenses of the investigation, in particular, such reasonable sums as the Secretary of State may determine in respect of general staff costs and overheads.

**History**
S. 105(11) added by CA 1989, s. 73(1), (4) as from 21 February 1990 (see SI 1990/142 (C 5), art. 4).

**Note**
See note after s. 106.

# 106 Exercise of investigation powers by officer etc.

**106(1) [Secretary of State may authorise officer]** The Secretary of State may authorise any officer of his or any other competent person to exercise on his behalf all or any of the powers conferred by section 105 above but no such authority shall be granted except for the purpose of investigating the affairs, or any aspects of the affairs, of a person specified in the authority.

**106(2) [Compliance, production of evidence re authority]** No person shall be bound to comply with any requirement imposed by a person exercising powers by virtue of an authority granted under this section unless he has, if required to do so, produced evidence of his authority.

**106(2A) [Disclosure by bankers]** A person shall not by virtue of an authority under this section be required to disclose any information or produce any documents in respect of which he owes an obligation of confidence by virtue of carrying on the business of banking unless–

(a) he is the person under investigation or a related company,

(b) the person to whom the obligation of confidence is owed is the person under investigation or a related company,

(c) the person to whom the obligation of confidence is owed consents to the disclosure or production, or

(d) the imposing on him of a requirement with respect to such information or documents has been specifically authorised by the Secretary of State.

In this subsection **"documents"**, **"person under investigation"** and **"related company"** have the same meaning as in section 105.

**History**
S. 106(2A) inserted by CA 1989, s. 73(5) as from 21 February 1990 (see SI 1990/142 (C 5), art. 4).

**106(3) [Report by officer re exercise of powers etc.]** Where the Secretary of State authorises a person other than one of his officers to exercise any powers by virtue of this section that person shall make a report to the Secretary of State in such manner as he may require on the exercise of those powers and the results of exercising them.

**Note**
Concerning European investment firms, see the Investment Services Regulations 1995 (SI 1995/3275), reg. 32 and Sch. 7, para. 27.
Concerning European institutions, see the Banking Coordination (Second Council Directive) Regulations 1992 (SI 1992/3218), reg. 55 and Sch. 9, para. 29.
For application s. 105 and 106 to a listed person see the Financial Markets and Insolvency (Money Market) Regulations 1995 (SI 1995/2049), reg. 1, 6, 16, 17.

# Chapter XI – Auditors

# 107 Appointment of auditors

**107(1) [Power of Secretary of State to make rules]** The Secretary of State may make rules requiring–

(a) a person authorised to carry on investment business by virtue of section 25 or 31 above, or

(b) a member of a recognised self-regulating organisation carrying on investment business in the carrying on of which he is subject to the rules of the organisation,

and who, apart from the rules, is not required by or under any enactment to appoint an auditor, to appoint as an auditor a person satisfying such conditions as to qualifications and otherwise as may be specified in or imposed under the rules.

**History**
S. 107(1) substituted by CA 1989, s. 206(1) and Sch. 23, para. 10(1), (2) as from 15 March 1990 (see SI 1990/354 (C 12), art. 3); s. 107(1) formerly read as follows:

"The Secretary of State may make rules requiring a person who is authorised to carry on investment business by virtue of section 25 or 31 above and who, apart from the rules, is not required by or under any enactment to appoint an auditor to appoint as an auditor a person satisfying such conditions as to qualifications and otherwise as may be specified in or imposed under the rules."

**107(2) [Extent of rules]** Rules under this section may make provision–

(a) specifying the manner in which and the time within which an auditor is to be appointed;

(b) requiring the Secretary of State to be notified of any such appointment and enabling the Secretary of State to make an appointment if no appointment is made or notified as required by the rules;

(c) with respect to the remuneration of an auditor appointed under the rules;

(d) with respect to the term of office, removal and resignation of any such auditor;

(e) requiring any such auditor who is removed, resigns or is not reappointed to notify the Secretary of State whether there are any circumstances connected with his ceasing to hold office which he considers should be brought to the Secretary of State's attention.

**107(3) [Duty of auditor]** An auditor appointed under the rules shall in accordance with the rules examine and report on the accounts of the authorised person in question and shall for that purpose have such duties and powers as are specified in the rules.

**Note**
Concerning European investment firms, see the Investment Services Regulations 1995 (SI 1995/3275), reg. 32 and Sch. 7, para. 28.
Concerning European institutions, see the Banking Coordination (Second Council Directive) Regulations 1992 (SI 1992/3218), reg. 55 and Sch. 9, para. 30.

**107(4) [Application to SRO members]** In its application to members of recognised self-regulating organisations, this section has effect subject to section 107A below.

**History**
S. 107(4) added by CA 1989, s.206(1) and Sch. 23, para. 10(1), (3) as from 15 March 1990 (see SI 1990/354 (C 12), art. 3).

## 107A Application of audit rules to members of self-regulating organisations

**107A(1) [Power of Secretary of State to make rules]** The Secretary of State may in rules under section 107 designate provisions which apply, to such extent as may be specified, to a member of a recognised self-regulating organisation in respect of investment business in the carrying on of which he is subject to the rules of the organisation.

**107A(2) [Extent of rules]** It may be provided that the designated rules have effect, generally or to such extent as may be specified, subject to the rules of the organisation.

**107A(3) [Contravention by SRO member]** A member of a recognised self-regulating organisation who contravenes a rule applying to him by virtue of that section shall be treated as having contravened the rules of the organisation.

**107A(4) [Application to SRO member]** Except as mentioned above, rules made under section 107 do not apply to members of recognised self-regulating organisations in respect of investment business in the carrying on of which they are subject to the rules of the organisation.

**107A(5) [Power of SRO to modify or dispense from rule]** A recognised self-regulating organisation may on the application of a member of the organisation–

(a) modify a rule designated under this section so as to adapt it to his circumstances or to any particular kind of business carried on by him, or

(b) dispense him from compliance with any such rule, generally or in relation to any particular kind of business carried on by him.

**107A(6) [Condition for s. 107A(5) power]** The powers conferred by subsection (5) shall not be exercised unless it appears to the organisation–

(a) that compliance with the rule in question would be unduly burdensome for the applicant having regard to the benefit which compliance would confer on investors, and

(b) that the exercise of those powers will not result in any undue risk to investors.

**107A(7) [Exercise of s. 107A(5) power may be conditional]** The powers conferred by subsection (5) may be exercised unconditionally or subject to conditions; and subsection (3) applies in the case of a contravention of a condition as in the case of contravention of a designated rule.

**107A(8) [Monitoring and enforcement of compliance]** The reference in paragraph 4(1) of Schedule 2 (requirements for recognition of self-regulating organisations) to monitoring and enforcement of compliance with rules includes monitoring and enforcement of compliance with conditions imposed by the organisation under subsection (7).

**History**
S. 107A inserted by CA 1989, s. 206(1) and Sch. 23, para. 11 as from 15 March 1990 (see SI 1990/354 (C 12), art. 3).

**Note**
For transfer of the Secretary of State's functions under s. 107A see SI 1990/354 (C 12), art. 4(5).

# 108 Power to require second audit

**108(1) [Power of Secretary of State]** If in any case it appears to the Secretary of State that there is good reason to do so he may direct any person who is authorised to carry on investment business by virtue of section 24A, 25 or 31 above to submit for further examination by a person approved by the Secretary of State–

(a) any accounts on which that person's auditor has reported or any information given under section 52 or 104 above which has been verified by that auditor; or

(b) such matters contained in any such accounts or information as are specified in the direction;

and the person making the further examination shall report his conclusions to the Secretary of State.

**History**
In s. 108(1) the words "24A," appearing after the words "by virtue of section" inserted by the Open-Ended Investment Companies (Investment Companies with Variable Capital) Regulations 1996 (SI 1996/2827), reg. 1, 75 and Sch. 8, para. 19 as from 6 January 1997.

**108(2) [Expense of further examination and report]** Any further examination and report required by a direction under this section shall be at the expense of the authorised person concerned and shall be carried out and made within such time as is specified in the direction or within such further time as the Secretary of State may allow.

**108(3) [Power of examiner]** The person carrying out an examination under this section shall have all the powers that were available to the auditor; and it shall be the duty of the auditor to afford him all such assistance as he may require.

**108(4) [Report being made available]** Where a report made under this section relates to accounts which under any enactment are required to be sent to or made available for inspection by any person or to be delivered for registration, the report, or any part of it (or a note that such a report has been made) may be similarly sent, made available or delivered by the Secretary of State.

# 109 Communication by auditor with supervisory authorities

**109(1) [Communication with Secretary of State]** No duty to which an auditor of an authorised person may be subject shall be regarded as contravened by reason of his communicating in good faith to the Secretary of State, whether or not in response to a request from him, any information or opinion on a matter of which the auditor has become aware in his capacity as auditor of that person and which is relevant to any functions of the Secretary of State under this Act.

**Note**
Concerning European investment firms, see the Investment Services Regulations 1995 (SI 1995/3275), reg. 32 and Sch. 7, para. 29.
Concerning European institutions, see the Banking Coordination (Second Council Directive) Regulations 1992 (SI 1992/3218), reg. 55 and Sch. 9, para. 31.

**109(2) [Power of Secretary of State to make rules]** If it appears to the Secretary of State that any auditor or class of auditor to whom subsection (1) above applies is not subject to satisfactory rules made or guidance issued by a professional body specifying circumstances in which matters are to be communicated to the Secretary of State as mentioned in that subsection the Secretary of State may himself make rules applying to that auditor or that class of auditor and specifying such circumstances; and it shall be the duty of an auditor to whom the rules made by the Secretary of State apply to communicate a matter to the Secretary of State in the circumstances specified by the rules.

**109(3) [Matters communicated]** The matters to be communicated to the Secretary of State in accordance with any such rules or guidance may include matters relating to persons other than the authorised person.

**109(4) [Approval etc. of s. 109(2) rules]** No such rules as are mentioned in subsection (2) above shall be made by the Secretary of State unless a draft of them has been laid before and approved by a resolution of each House of Parliament.

**109(5) [Application of section]** This section applies to–

(a) the communication by an auditor to a recognised self-regulating organisation or recognised professional body of matters relevant to its function of determining whether a person is a fit and proper person to carry on investment business; and

(b) the communication to such an organisation or body or any other authority or person of matters relevant to its or his function of determining whether a person is complying with the rules applicable to his conduct of investment business,

as it applies to the communication to the Secretary of State of matters relevant to his functions under this Act.

**Note**

For further effect of s. 109 see the Financial Institutions (Prudential Supervision) Regulations 1996 (SI 1996/1669), reg. 10.

## 110 Overseas business

**110(1) [Auditor of overseas person]** A person incorporated or having his head office outside the United Kingdom who is authorised as mentioned in subsection (1) of section 107 above may, whether or not he is required to appoint an auditor apart from the rules made under that subsection, appoint an auditor in accordance with those rules in respect of the investment business carried on by him in the United Kingdom and in that event that person shall be treated for the purposes of this Chapter as the auditor of that person.

**110(2) [Conditions as to qualifications]** In the case of a person to be appointed as auditor of a person incorporated or having his head office outside the United Kingdom the conditions as to qualifications imposed by or under the rules made under that section may be regarded as satisfied by qualifications obtained outside the United Kingdom which appear to the Secretary of State to be equivalent.

**110(3) [Conditions to be fit and proper person under s. 25]** A person incorporated or having his head office outside the United Kingdom shall not be regarded for the purposes of section 25 above as a fit and proper person to carry on investment business unless–

(a) he has appointed an auditor in accordance with rules made under section 107 above in respect of the investment business carried on by him in the United Kingdom; or

(b) he has an auditor having qualifications, powers and duties appearing to the Secretary of State to be equivalent to those applying to an auditor appointed in accordance with those rules,

and, in either case, the auditor is able and willing to communicate with the Secretary of State and other bodies and persons as mentioned in section 109 above.

**Note**

Concerning European investment firms, see the Investment Services Regulations 1995 (SI 1995/3275), reg. 32 and Sch. 7, para. 30.

Concerning European institutions, see the Banking Coordination (Second Council Directive) Regulations 1992 (SI 1992/3218), reg. 55 and Sch. 9, para. 32.

## 111 Offences and enforcement

**111(1) [Offence, penalty]** Any authorised person and any officer, controller or manager of an authorised person, who knowingly or recklessly furnishes an auditor appointed under the rules made under section 107 or a person carrying out an examination under section 108 above with information which the auditor or that person requires or is entitled to require and which is false or misleading in a material particular shall be guilty of an offence and liable–

(a) on conviction on indictment, to imprisonment for a term not exceeding two years or to a fine or to both;

(b) on summary conviction, to imprisonment for a term not exceeding six months or to a fine not exceeding the statutory maximum or to both.

**111(2) [Enforcement of auditor's duty]** The duty of an auditor under section 108(3) above shall be enforceable by mandamus or, in Scotland, by an order for specific performance under section 91 of the Court of Session Act 1868.

**111(3) [Secretary of State's disqualification power]** If it appears to the Secretary of State that an auditor has failed to comply with the duty mentioned in section 109(2) above, the Secretary of State may disqualify him from being the auditor of an authorised person or any class of authorised person; but the Secretary of State may remove any disqualification imposed under this subsection if satisfied that the person in question will in future comply with that duty.

**111(4) [Appointment of disqualified person]** An authorised person shall not appoint as auditor a person disqualified under subsection (3) above; and a person who is an authorised person by virtue of membership of a recognised self-regulating organisation or certification by a recognised professional body who contravenes this subsection shall be treated as having contravened the rules of the organisation or body.

# Chapter XII – Fees

## 112 Application fees

**112(1) [Applicant to pay required fees]** An applicant for a recognition order under Chapter III or IV of this Part of this Act shall pay such fees in respect of his application as may be required by a scheme made and published by the Secretary of State; and no application for such an order shall be regarded as duly made unless this subsection is complied with.

**112(2) [A scheme under s. 112(1)]** A scheme made for the purposes of subsection (1) above shall specify the time when the fees are to be paid and may–

(a) provide for the determination of the fees in accordance with a specified scale or other specified factors;

(b) provide for the return or abatement of any fees where an application is refused or withdrawn; and

(c) make different provision for different cases.

**112(3) [Date re s. 112(1) scheme]** Any scheme made for the purposes of subsection (1) above shall come into operation on such date as is specified in the scheme (not being earlier than the day on which it is first published) and shall apply to applications made on or after the date on which it comes into operation.

**112(4) [Power in s. 112(1) includes variation, revocation]** The power to make a scheme for the purposes of subsection (1) above includes power to vary or revoke a previous scheme made under those provisions.

**112(5) [Fee with application and notices]** Every application under section 26, 77 or 88 above shall be accompanied by the prescribed fee and every notice given to the Secretary of State under section 32, 86(2) or 87(3) above shall be accompanied by such fee as may be prescribed; and no such application or notice shall be regarded as duly made or given unless this subsection is complied with.

## 113 Periodical fees

**113(1) [Recognised bodies to pay]** Every recognised self-regulating organisation, recognised professional body, recognised investment exchange and recognised clearing house shall pay such periodical fees to the Secretary of State as may be prescribed.

**113(2) [Body authorised under s. 22]** So long as a body is authorised under section 22 above to carry on insurance business which is investment business it shall pay to the Secretary of State such periodical fees as may be prescribed.

**113(3) [Society authorised under s. 23]** So long as a friendly society is authorised under section 23 above to carry on investment business it shall pay to the Friendly Societies Commission such periodical fees as the Commission may by regulations specify.

**History**

S. 113(3) substituted by the Friendly Societies Act 1992, s. 98 and Sch. 18, para. 2 as from 1 February 1993 in regard to incorporated friendly societies (see SI 1993/16 (C 1), art. 2 and Sch. 4) and as from 1 January 1994 for all remaining purposes (see SI 1993/2213 (C 43), art. 2 and Sch. 5); s. 113(3) formerly read as follows:

"So long as a society is authorised under section 23 above to carry on investment business it shall–

(a) if it is authorised by virtue of subsection (1) of that section, pay to the Chief Registrar of friendly societies such periodical fees as he may by regulations specify; and

(b) if it is authorised by virtue of subsection (2) of that section, pay to the Registrar of Friendly Societies for Northern Ireland such periodical fees as he may by regulations specify."

**113(4) [Person authorised under s. 25, 31]** A person who is an authorised person by virtue of section 25 or 31 above shall pay such periodical fees to the Secretary of State as may be prescribed.

**113(5) [If person fails to pay s. 113(4) fee]** If a person fails to pay any fee which is payable by him under subsection (4) above the Secretary of State may serve on him a written notice requiring him to pay the fee within twenty-eight days of service of the notice; and if the fee is not paid within that period that person's authorisation shall cease to have effect unless the Secretary of State otherwise directs.

**113(6) [S. 113(5) direction may be retrospective]** A direction under subsection (5) above may be given so as to have retrospective effect; and the Secretary of State may under that subsection direct that the person in question shall continue to be an authorised person only for such period as is specified in the direction.

**113(7) [Fees as debts due to Crown]** Subsection (5) above is without prejudice to the recovery of any fee as a debt due to the Crown.

**113(8) [Manager, operator to pay periodical fees]** The manager of each authorised unit trust scheme and the operator of each recognised scheme shall pay such periodical fees to the Secretary of State as may be prescribed.

**Note**

Concerning European investment firms, see the Investment Services Regulations 1995 (SI 1995/3275), reg. 32 and Sch. 7, para. 31.

Concerning European institutions, see the Banking Coordination (Second Council Directive) Regulations 1992 (SI 1992/3218), reg. 55 and Sch. 9, para. 33.

# Chapter XIII – Transfer of Functions to Designated Agency

## 114 Power to transfer functions to designated agency

**114(1) [Power of Secretary of State]** If it appears to the Secretary of State–

(a) that a body corporate has been established which is able and willing to discharge all or any of the functions to which this section applies; and

(b) that the requirements of Schedule 7 to this Act are satisfied in the case of that body,

he may, subject to the provisions of this section and Chapter XIV of this Part of this Act, make an order transferring all or any of those functions to that body.

**114(2) [The Securities and Investments Board Limited]** The body to which functions are transferred by the first order made under subsection (1) above shall be the body known as The Securities and Investments Board Limited if it appears to the Secretary of State that it is able and willing to discharge them, that the requirements mentioned in paragraph (b) of that subsection are satisfied in the case of that body and that he is not precluded from making the order by the subsequent provisions of this section or Chapter XIV of this Part of this Act.

**114(3) ["A delegation order", "a designated agency"]** An order under subsection (1) above is in this Act referred to as "a delegation order" and a body to which functions are transferred by a delegation order is in this Act referred to as "a designated agency".

**114(4) [Application of section]** Subject to subsections (5) and (6) below, this section applies to any functions of the Secretary of State under Chapters II to XII of this Part of this Act and to his functions under paragraphs 23 and 25(2) of Schedule 1 and paragraphs 4, 5 and 15 of Schedule 15 to this Act.

**114(5) [Non-application of section]** This section does not apply to any functions under–

(a) section 31(4);

(b) section 46;

(c) section 48(8);

(d) section 58(3);

(dd) section 62A;

(e) section 86(1) or 87(1);

(f) section 96;

(g) section 109(2) above.

**History**

In s. 114(5) para. (dd) inserted by CA 1989, s. 193(2) as from 1 April 1991 (see SI 1991/488 (C 11), art. 3).

**114(6) [Overseas exchanges etc.]** This section does not apply to the making or revocation of a recognition order in respect of an overseas investment exchange or overseas clearing house or the making of an application to the court under section 12 above in respect of any such exchange or clearing house.

**114(7) [Transfer of functions]** Any function may be transferred by a delegation order either wholly or in part.

**114(8) [Functions under s. 6, 61, 72, 94, 105, 106]** In the case of a function under section 6 or 72 or a function under section 61 which is exercisable by virtue of subsection (1)(a)(ii) or (iii) of that section, the transfer may be subject to a reservation that it is to be exercisable by the Secretary of State concurrently with the designated agency and any transfer of a function under section 94, 105 or 106 shall be subject to such a reservation.

**114(9) [Conditions for transfer]** The Secretary of State shall not make a delegation order transferring any legislative functions unless–

(a) the agency has furnished him with a copy of the instruments it proposes to issue or make in the exercise of those functions, and

(b) he is satisfied that those instruments will afford investors an adequate level of protection and, in the case of such provisions as are mentioned in Schedule 8 to this Act, comply with the principles set out in that Schedule.

In this subsection **"legislative functions"** means the functions of issuing or making statements of principle, rules, regulations or codes of practice.

**History**

S. 114(9) substituted by CA 1989, s. 206(1) and Sch. 23, para. 12(1), (2) as from 15 March 1990 (see SI 1990/354 (C 12), art. 3); s. 114(9) formerly read as follows:

"The Secretary of State shall not make a delegation order transferring any function of making rules or regulations to a designated agency unless–

(a) the agency has furnished him with a copy of the rules and regulations which it proposes to make in the exercise of those functions; and

(b) he is satisfied that those rules and regulations will afford investors an adequate level of protection and, in the case of such rules and regulations as are mentioned in Schedule 8 to this Act, comply with the principles set out in that Schedule."

**114(10) [Guidance to be furnished]** The Secretary of State shall also before making a delegation order transferring any functions to a designated agency require it to furnish him with a copy of any guidance intended to have continuing effect which it proposes to issue in writing or other legible form and the Secretary of State may take any such guidance into account in determining whether he is satisfied as mentioned in subsection (9)(b) above.

**114(11) [Approval of delegation order]** No delegation order shall be made unless a draft of it has been laid before and approved by a resolution of each House of Parliament.

**114(12) [Interpretation re guidance]** In this Act references to guidance issued by a designated agency are references to guidance issued or any recommendation made by it which is issued or made to persons generally or to any class of persons, being, in either case, persons who are or may be subject to statements of principle, rules, regulations or codes of practice issued or made by it, or who are or may be recognised or authorised by it, in the exercise of its functions under a delegation order.

**History**
In s. 114(12) the words "statements of principle, rules, regulations or codes of practice issued or made" substituted for the former words "rules or regulations made" by CA 1989, s. 206(1) and Sch. 23, para. 12(1), (3) as from 15 March 1990 (see SI 1990/354 (C 12), art. 3).

# 115 Resumption of transferred functions

**115(1) [Power of Secretary of State]** The Secretary of State may at the request or with the consent of a designated agency make an order resuming all or any of the functions transferred to the agency by a delegation order.

**115(2) [Extent of resumption order]** The Secretary of State may, in the circumstances mentioned in subsection (3), (4) or (5) below, make an order resuming–

(a) all the functions transferred to a designated agency by a delegation order; or

(b) all, all legislative or all administrative functions transferred to a designated agency by a delegation order so far as relating to investments or investment business of any class.

**115(3) [S. 115(2) order if Sch. 7 not complied with]** An order may be made under subsection (2) above if at any time it appears to the Secretary of State that any of the requirements of Schedule 7 to this Act are not satisfied in the case of the agency.

**115(4) [S. 115(2) order if agency unable to discharge functions etc.]** An order may be made under subsection (2) above as respects functions relating to any class of investment or investment business if at any time it appears to the Secretary of State that the agency is unable or unwilling to discharge all or any of the transferred functions in respect of all or any investments or investment business falling within that class.

**115(5) [S. 115(2) order if agency rules do not satisfy s. 114(9)(b)]** Where the transferred functions consist of or include any legislative functions, an order may be made under subsection (2) above if at any time it appears to the Secretary of State that the instruments issued or made by the agency do not satisfy the requirements of section 114(9)(b) above.

**History**
S. 115(5) substituted by CA 1989, s. 206(1) and Sch. 23, para. 13(1), (2) as from 15 March 1990 (see SI 1990/354 (C 12), art. 3); s. 115(5) formerly read as follows:

"Where the transferred functions consist of or include any functions of making rules or regulations an order may be made under subsection (2) above if at any time it appears to the Secretary of State that the rules or regulations made by the agency do not satisfy the requirements of section 114(9)(b) above."

**115(6) [Approval of s. 115(1) order by Parliament]** An order under subsection (1) above shall be subject to annulment in pursuance of a resolution of either House of Parliament; and no other order shall be made under this section unless a draft of it has been laid before and approved by a resolution of each House of Parliament.

**115(7) [Definitions]** In this section –

(a) **"legislative functions"** means functions of issuing or making statements of principle, rules, regulations or codes of practice;

(b) **"administrative functions"** means functions other than legislative functions;

but the resumption of legislative functions shall not deprive a designated agency of any function of prescribing fees to be paid or information to be furnished in connection with administrative functions retained by the agency; and the resumption of administrative functions shall extend to the function of prescribing fees to be paid and information to be furnished in connection with those administrative functions.

**History**
In s. 115(7) in the opening words the words "this section" substituted for the former words "subsection (2)(b) above" and in para. (a) the words "functions of issuing or making statements of principle, rules, regulations or codes of practice" substituted for the former words "functions of making rules or regulations" by CA 1989, s. 206(1) and Sch. 23, para. 13(1), (3)(a) and (b) respectively as from 15 March 1990 (see SI 1990/354 (C 12), art. 3).

## 116 Status and exercise of transferred functions

**116** Schedule 9 to this Act shall have effect as respects the status of a designated agency and the exercise of the functions transferred to it by a delegation order.

## 117 Reports and accounts

**117(1) [Annual report by agency]** A designated agency shall at least once in each year for which the delegation order is in force make a report to the Secretary of State on the discharge of the functions transferred to it by the order and on such other matters as the order may require.

**117(2) [Copies of report before Parliament]** The Secretary of State shall lay before Parliament copies of each report received by him under this section.

**117(3) [Directions re accounts of agency]** The Secretary of State may give directions to a designated agency with respect to its accounts and the audit of its accounts; and it shall be the duty of the agency to comply with the directions.

**117(4) [Qualification to s. 117(3)]** Subsection (3) above shall not apply to a designated agency which is a company to which section 226 of the Companies Act 1985 applies; but the Secretary of State may require any designated agency (whether or not such a company) to comply with any provisions of that Act which would not otherwise apply to it or direct that any provision of that Act shall apply to the agency with such modifications as are specified in the direction; and it shall be the duty of the agency to comply with any such requirement or direction.

**History**
See history note after s. 117(5).

**117(5) [Northern Ireland]** In subsection (4) above the references to the Companies Act 1985 and section 226 of that Act include references to the corresponding Northern Ireland provisions.

**History**
In s. 117(4), (5) the words "section 226" substituted for the former words "section 227" by CA 1989, s. 23 and Sch. 10, para. 36(1), (2) as from 1 April 1990 subject to transitional and saving provisions (see SI 1990/355 (C 13), art. 3, Sch. 1 and also art. 6–9).

## 118 Transitional and supplementary provisions

**118(1) [Things previously done]** A delegation order shall not affect anything previously done in the exercise of a function which is transferred by the order; and any order resuming a function shall not affect anything previously done by the designated agency in the exercise of a function which is resumed.

**118(2) [Transitional, supplementary provisions in delegation order]** A delegation order and an order resuming any functions transferred by a delegation order may contain, or the Secretary of State may by a separate order under this section make, such transitional and other supplementary provisions as he thinks necessary or expedient in connection with the delegation order or the order resuming the functions in question.

**118(3) [Scope of provisions under s. 118(2)]** The provisions that may be made under subsection (2) above in connection with a delegation order include, in particular, provisions–

(a) for modifying or excluding any provision of this Act in its application to any function transferred by the order;

(b) for applying to a designated agency, in connection with any such function, any provision applying to the Secretary of State which is contained in or made under any other enactment;

(c) for the transfer of any property, rights or liabilities from the Secretary of State to a designated agency;

(d) for the carrying on and completion by a designated agency of anything in process of being done by the Secretary of State when the order takes effect; and

(e) for the substitution of a designated agency for the Secretary of State in any instrument, contract or legal proceedings.

**118(4) [Scope of provisions under s. 118(2) re resumption order]** The provisions that may be made under subsection (2) above in connection with an order resuming any functions include, in particular, provisions–

(a) for the transfer of any property, rights or liabilities from the agency to the Secretary of State;

(b) for the carrying on and completion by the Secretary of State of anything in process of being done by the agency when the order takes effect;

(c) for the substitution of the Secretary of State for the agency in any instrument, contract or legal proceedings; and

(d) in a case where some functions remain with the agency, for modifying or excluding any provision of this Act in its application to any such functions.

**118(5) [Scope of provisions under s. 118(2) re designated agency]** In a case where any function of a designated agency is resumed and is to be immediately transferred by a delegation order to another designated agency, the provisions that may be made under subsection (2) above may include provisions for any of the matters mentioned in paragraphs (a) to (c) of subsection (4) above, taking references to the Secretary of State as references to that other agency.

**118(6) [Order may be annulled by Parliament]** Any order under this section shall be subject to annulment in pursuance of a resolution of either House of Parliament.

# Chapter XIV – Prevention of Restrictive Practices

## EXAMINATION OF RULES AND PRACTICES

### 119 Recognised self-regulating organisations, investment exchanges and clearing houses

**119(1) [Conditions for making recognition order]** The Secretary of State shall not make a recognition order in respect of a self-regulating organisation, investment exchange or clearing house unless he is satisfied that–

(a) in the case of a self-regulating organisation, the rules and any guidance of which copies are furnished with the application for the order, together with any statements of principle, rules, regulations or codes of practice to which members of the organisation would be subject by virtue of Chapter V of this Part,

(b) in the case of an investment exchange, the rules and any guidance of which copies are furnished with the application for the order, together with any arrangements of which particulars are furnished with the application,

(c) in the case of a clearing house, the rules and any guidance of which copies are furnished with the application for the order,

do not have, and are not intended or likely to have, to any significant extent the effect of restricting, distorting or preventing competition or, if they have or are intended or likely to have that effect to any significant extent, that the effect is not greater than is necessary for the protection of investors.

**History**

S. 119(1)(a)–(c) substituted for former s. 119(1)(a), (b) by CA 1989, s. 206(1) and Sch. 23, para. 14(1), (2) as from 15 March 1990 (see SI 1990/354 (C 12), art. 3); former s. 119(1)(a), (b) read as follows:

"(a) the rules and any guidance of which copies are furnished with the application for the order; and
(b) in the case of an investment exchange, any arrangements of which particulars are furnished with the application,".

**Note**

See note after s. 119(2).

**119(2) [Where s. 119(3) powers to be exercised]** The powers conferred by subsection (3) below shall be exercisable by the Secretary of State if at any time it appears to him that–

(a) in the case of a self-regulating organisation–
 (i) any rules made or guidance issued by the organisation,
 (ii) any practices of the organisation, or
 (iii) any practices of persons who are members of, or otherwise subject to the rules made by, the organisation,

together with any statements of principle, rules, regulations or codes of practice to which members of the organisation are subject by virtue of Chapter V of this Part,

(b) in the case of a recognised investment exchange–
  (i) any rules made or guidance issued by the exchange,
  (ii) any practices of the exchange, or
  (iii) any practices of persons who are members of, or otherwise subject to the rules made by, the exchange,

(c) in the case of a recognised clearing house –
  (i) any rules made or guidance issued by the clearing house,
  (ii) any practices of the clearing house, or
  (iii) any practices of persons who are members of, or otherwise subject to the rules made by, the clearing house,

  or any clearing arrangements made by the clearing house,

have, or are intended or likely to have, to a significant extent the effect of restricting, distorting or preventing competition and that that effect is greater than is necessary for the protection of investors.

**History**
S. 119(2)(a)–(c) substituted by CA 1989, s. 206(1) and Sch. 23, para. 14(1), (3) as from 15 March 1990 (see SI 1990/354 (C 12), art. 3); s. 119(2) (a)–(c) formerly read as follows:
"(a) any rules made or guidance issued by a recognised self-regulating organisation, investment exchange or clearing house or any clearing arrangements made by a recognised clearing house;
(b) any practices of any such organisation, exchange or clearing house; or
(c) any practices of persons who are members of, or otherwise subject to the rules made by, any such organisation, exchange or clearing house,".

**Note**
Concerning the Investment Services Directive, see the Investment Services Regulations 1995 (SI 1995/3275), reg. 32 and Sch. 7, para. 32.
Concerning protection of investors, see the Banking Coordination (Second Council Directive) Regulations 1992 (SI 1992/3218), reg. 55 and Sch. 9, para. 34.

**119(3) [Powers re revocation etc.]** The powers exercisable under this subsection are–

(a) to revoke the recognition order of the organisation, exchange or clearing house;

(b) to direct it to take specified steps for the purpose of securing that its rules, or the guidance, arrangements or practices in question do not have the effect mentioned in subsection (2) above;

(c) to make alterations in its rules for that purpose;

and subsections (2) to (5), (7) and (9) of section 11 above shall have effect in relation to the revocation of a recognition order under this subsection as they have effect in relation to the revocation of such an order under subsection (1) of that section.

**History**
In s. 119(3)(b) the words "its rules, or the" substituted for the former words "the rules" and in s. 119(3)(c) the words "its rules" substituted for the former words "the rules" by CA 1989, s. 206(1) and Sch. 23, para. 14(1), (4)(a) and (b) respectively as from 15 March 1990 (see SI 1990/354 (C 12), art. 3).

**119(4) [Non-application of s. 119(3)(c)]** Subsection (3)(c) above does not apply to an overseas investment exchange or overseas clearing house.

**119(5) [Practices in s. 119(2)(b)]** The practices referred to in paragraph (a)(ii), (b)(ii) and (c)(ii) of subsection (2) above are practices of the organisation, exchange or clearing house in its capacity as such, being, in the case of a clearing house, practices in respect of its clearing arrangements.

**History**
In s. 119(5) the words "paragraph (a)(ii), (b)(ii) and (c)(ii)" substituted for the former words "paragraph (b)" and the words "and the practices referred to in paragraph (c) of that subsection are practices in relation to business in respect of which the persons in question are subject to the rules of the organisation, exchange or clearing house and which are required or contemplated by its rules or guidance or otherwise attributable to its conduct in its capacity as such." formerly appearing at the end omitted and repealed by CA 1989, s. 206(1) and Sch. 23, para 14(1), (5)(a) and (b) respectively and s. 212 and Sch. 24 as from 15 March 1990 (see SI 1990/354 (C 12), art. 3).

**119(6) [Practices in s. 119(2)]** The practices referred to in paragraph (a)(iii), (b)(iii) and (c)(iii) of subsection (2) above are–

(a) in relation to a recognised self-regulating organisation, practices in relation to business in respect of which the persons in question are subject to–
  (i) the rules of the organisation, or
  (ii) statements of principle, rules, regulations or codes of practice to which its members are subject by virtue of Chapter V of this Part,

and which are required or contemplated by the rules of the organisation or by those statements, rules, regulations or codes, or by guidance issued by the organisation,

(b) in relation to a recognised investment exchange or clearing house,practices in relation to business in respect of which the persons in question are subject to the rules of the exchange or clearing house, and which are required or contemplated by its rules or guidance,

or which are otherwise attributable to the conduct of the organisation, exchange or clearing house as such.

**History**
S. 119(6) inserted by CA 1989, s. 206(1) and Sch. 23, para. 14(1), (6) as from 15 March 1990 (see SI 1990/354 (C 12), art. 3).

**Note**
Re prevention of restrictive practices, see note after s. 120.

## 120 Modification of s. 119 where recognition function is transferred

**120(1) [Application]** This section applies instead of section 119 above where the function of making or revoking a recognition order in respect of a self-regulating organisation, investment exchange or clearing house is exercisable by a designated agency.

**120(2) [Duties of designated agency]** The designated agency–

(a) shall send to the Secretary of State a copy of the rules and of any guidance or arrangements of which copies or particulars are furnished with any application made to the agency for a recognition order together with any other information supplied with or in connection with the application; and

(b) shall not make the recognition order without the leave of the Secretary of State;

and he shall not give leave in any case in which he would (apart from the delegation order) have been precluded by section 119(1) above from making the recognition order.

**120(3) [Copy of notice to Secretary of State]** A designated agency shall send the Secretary of State a copy of any notice received by it under section 14(6) or 41(5) or (6) above.

**120(4) [Exercise of powers by Secretary of State]** If at any time it appears to the Secretary of State in the case of a recognised self-regulating organisation, recognised investment exchange or recognised clearing house that there are circumstances such that (apart from the delegation order) he would have been able to exercise any of the powers conferred by subsection (3) of section 119 above he may, notwithstanding the delegation order, himself exercise the power conferred by paragraph (a) of that subsection or direct the designated agency to exercise the power conferred by paragraph (b) or (c) of that subsection in such manner as he may specify.

**Note**
Concerning modifications to s. 119, 120 re prevention of restrictive practices, see the Uncertificated Securities Regulations 1995 (SI 1995/3272), reg. 13 and Sch. 2.

## 121 Designated agencies

**121(1) [Conditions re transferred functions]** The Secretary of State shall not make a delegation order transferring any function to a designated agency unless he is satisfied that any statements of principle, rules, regulations, codes of practice and guidance of which copies are furnished to him under section 114(9) or (10) above do not have, and are not intended or likely to have, to any significant extent the effect of restricting, distorting or preventing competition or, if they have or are intended or likely to have that effect to any significant extent, that the effect is not greater than is necessary for the protection of investors.

**History**
In s. 121(1) the words "statements of principle, rules, regulations, codes of practice" substituted for the former words "rules, regulations" by CA 1989, s. 206(1) and Sch. 23, para. 15(1), (2) as from 15 March 1990 (see SI 1990/354 (C 12), art. 3).

**Note**
See note after s. 121(2).

**121(2) [Exercise of s. 121(3) powers by Secretary of State]** The powers conferred by subsection (3) below shall be exercisable by the Secretary of State if at any time it appears to him that–

(a) any statements of principle, rules, regulations or codes of practice issued or made by a designated agency in the exercise of functions transferred to it by a delegation order or any guidance issued by a designated agency;

(b) any practices of a designated agency; or

(c) any practices of persons who are subject to statements of principle, rules, regulations or codes of practice issued or made by it in the exercise of those functions,

have, or are intended or are likely to have, to any significant extent the effect of restricting, distorting or preventing competition and that that effect is greater than is necessary for the protection of investors.

**History**

In s. 121(2)(a) and (c) the words "statements of principle, rules, regulations or codes of practice issued or made" substituted for the former words "rules or regulations made" by CA 1989, s. 206(1) and Sch. 23, para. 15(1), (3) as from 15 March 1990 (see SI 1990/354 (C 12), art. 3).

**Note**

Concerning effect of s. 121, see the Investment Services Regulations 1995 (SI 1995/3275), reg. 32 and Sch. 7, para. 33. Concerning protection of investors, see the Banking Coordination (Second Council Directive) Regulations 1992 (SI 1992/3218), reg. 55 and Sch. 9, para. 35.

**121(3) [Powers in s. 121(2)]** The powers exercisable under this subsection are–

(a) to make an order in respect of the agency under section 115(2) above as if the circumstances were such as are there mentioned; or

(b) to direct the agency to take specified steps for the purpose of securing that the statements of principle, rules, regulations, codes of practice, guidance or practices in question do not have the effect mentioned in subsection (2) above.

**History**

In s. 121(3)(b) the words "statements of principle, rules, regulations, codes of practice" substituted for the former words "rules, regulations" by CA 1989, s. 206(1) and Sch. 23, para. 15(1), (4) as from 15 March 1990 (see SI 1990/354 (C 12), art. 3).

**121(4) [Practices in s. 121(2)]** The practices referred to in paragraph (b) of subsection (2) above are practices of the designated agency in its capacity as such; and the practices referred to in paragraph (c) of that subsection are practices in relation to business in respect of which the persons in question are subject to any such statements of principle, rules, regulations or codes of practice as are mentioned in paragraph (a) of that subsection and which are required or contemplated by those statements of principle, rules, regulations or codes of practice or by any such guidance as is there mentioned or are otherwise attributable to the conduct of the agency in its capacity as such.

**History**

In s. 121(4) the words "statements of principle, rules, regulations or codes of practice" substituted (twice) for the former words "rules or regulations" by CA 1989, s. 206(1) and Sch. 23, para. 15(1), (5) as from 15 March 1990 (see SI 1990/354 (C 12), art. 3).

## CONSULTATION WITH DIRECTOR GENERAL OF FAIR TRADING

# 122 Reports by Director General of Fair Trading

**122(1) [Secretary of State to send copies of reports etc. to Director]** The Secretary of State shall before deciding–

(a) whether to refuse to make, or to refuse leave for the making of, a recognition order in pursuance of section 119(1) or 120(2) above; or

(b) whether he is precluded by section 121(1) above from making a delegation order,

send to the Director General of Fair Trading (in this Chapter referred to as "the Director") a copy of the rules, statements of principle, regulations and codes of practice and of any guidance or arrangements which the Secretary of State is required to consider in making that decision together with such other information as the Secretary of State considers will assist the Director in discharging his functions under subsection (2) below.

**History**

In s. 122(1) the words ", statements of principle, regulations and codes of practice" substituted for the former words "and regulations" by CA 1989, s. 206(1) and Sch. 23, para. 16(1), (2) as from 15 March 1990 (see SI 1990/354 (C 12), art. 3).

**122(2) [Report to Secretary of State by Director]** The Director shall report to the Secretary of State whether, in his opinion, the rules, statements of principle, regulations, codes of practice, guidance or arrangements of which copies are sent to him under subsection (1) above have, or are intended or likely to have, to any significant extent the effect of restricting, distorting, or preventing competition and, if so, what that effect is likely to be; and in making any such decision as is mentioned in that subsection the Secretary of State shall have regard to the Director's report.

**History**

In s. 122(2) the words "statements of principle, regulations, codes of practice," substituted for the former word "regulations," by CA 1989, s. 206(1) and Sch. 23, para. 16(1), (3) as from 15 March 1990 (see SI 1990/354 (C 12), art. 3).

**122(3) [Secretary of State to send copies of notices etc. to Director]** The Secretary of State shall send the Director copies of any notice received by him under section 14(6), 41(5) or (6) or 120(3) above or under paragraph 4 of Schedule 9 to this Act together with such other information as the Secretary of State considers will assist the Director in discharging his functions under subsections (4) and (5) below.

**122(4) [Review and report by Director re s. 119(2), 121(2), 122(3)]** The Director shall keep under review–

(a) the rules, statements of principle, regulations, codes of practice, guidance and arrangements mentioned in section 119(2) and 121(2) above; and

(b) the matters specified in the notices of which copies are sent to him under subsection (3) above;

and if at any time he is of the opinion that any such rules, statements of principle, regulations, codes of practice, guidance, arrangements or matters, or any such rules, statements of principle, regulations, codes of practice, guidance or arrangements taken together with any such matters, have, or are intended or likely to have, to any significant extent the effect mentioned in subsection (2) above, he shall make a report to the Secretary of State stating his opinion and what that effect is or is likely to be.

**History**

In s. 122(4):

- in para. (a) the words "rules, statements of principle, regulations, codes of practice, guidance and arrangements" substituted for the former words "rules, guidance, arrangements and regulations", and
- in the words following the paragraphs the words "rules, statements of principle, regulations, codes of practice, guidance, arrangements" substituted for the former words "rules, guidance, arrangements, regulations" and the words "rules, statements of principle, regulations, codes of practice, guidance or arrangements" substituted for the former words "rules, guidance, arrangements or regulations"

by CA 1989, s. 206(1) and Sch. 23, para. 16(1), (4)(a) and (b) respectively as from 15 March 1990 (see SI 1990/354 (C 12), art. 3).

**122(5) [Report re matter in s. 122(4)(b)]** The Director may report to the Secretary of State his opinion that any such matter as is mentioned in subsection (4)(b) above does not in his opinion have, and is not intended or likely to have, to any significant extent the effect mentioned in subsection (2) above.

**122(6) [Report etc. re s. 119(2), 121(2)]** The Director may from time to time consider whether any such practices as are mentioned in section 119(2) or 121(2) above have, or are intended or likely to have, to any significant extent the effect mentioned in subsection (2) above and, if so, what that effect is or is likely to be; and if he is of that opinion he shall make a report to the Secretary of State stating his opinion and what the effect is or is likely to be.

**122(7) [Limit on exercise of power in s. 119(3), 120(4), 121(3)]** The Secretary of State shall not exercise his powers under section 119(3), 120(4) or 121(3) above except after receiving and considering a report from the Director under subsection (4) or (6) above.

**122(8) [Publication of report by Director]** The Director may, if he thinks fit, publish any report made by him under this section but shall exclude from a published report, so far as practicable, any matter which relates to the affairs of a particular person (other than the self-regulating organisation, investment exchange, clearing house or designated agency concerned) the publication of which would or might in his opinion seriously and prejudicially affect the interests of that person.

**Note**

Concerning prevention of restrictive practices, see note after s. 125.

# 123 Investigations by Director General of Fair Trading

**123(1) [Powers of Director]** For the purpose of investigating any matter with a view to its consideration under section 122 above the Director may by a notice in writing–

(a) require any person to produce, at a time and place specified in the notice, to the Director or to any person appointed by him for the purpose, any documents which are specified or described in the notice and which are documents in his custody or under his control and relating to any matter relevant to the investigation; or

(b) require any person carrying on any business to furnish to the Director such information as may be specified or described in the notice, and specify the time within which, and the manner and form in which, any such information is to be furnished.

**123(2) [Legal professional privilege, confidentiality]** A person shall not under this section be required to produce any document or disclose any information which he would be entitled to refuse to produce or disclose on grounds of legal professional privilege in proceedings in the High Court or on grounds of confidentiality as between client and professional legal adviser in proceedings in the Court of Session.

**123(3) [Application of s. 85(6)–(8) of Fair Trading Act]** Subsections (6) to (8) of section 85 of the Fair Trading Act 1973 (enforcement provisions) shall apply in relation to a notice under this section as they apply in relation to a notice under subsection (1) of that section but as if, in subsection (7) of that section, for the words from "any one" to "the commission" there were substituted "the Director".

**History**
In s. 123(3) "(6)" substituted for the former "(5)" and the words from "but as if," to the end inserted by CA 1989, s. 153 and Sch. 20, para. 26 as from 1 April 1990 (see SI 1990/142 (C 5), art. 6(c)).

**Note**
Concerning prevention of restrictive practices, see note after s. 125.

## CONSEQUENTIAL EXEMPTIONS FROM COMPETITION LAW

# 124 The Fair Trading Act 1973

**124(1) [Consideration of whether monopoly situation]** For the purpose of determining whether a monopoly situation within the meaning of the Fair Trading Act 1973 exists by reason of the circumstances mentioned in section 7(1)(c) of that Act, no account shall be taken of–

(a) the rules made or guidance issued by a recognised self-regulating organisation, recognised investment exchange or recognised clearing house or any conduct constituting such a practice as is mentioned in section 119(2) above;

(b) any clearing arrangements or any conduct required or contemplated by any such arrangements; or

(c) the statements of principle, rules, regulations, codes of practice or guidance issued or made by a designated agency in the exercise of functions transferred to it by a delegation order or any conduct constituting such a practice as is mentioned in section 121(2) above.

**History**
In s. 124(1)(c) the words "statements of principle, rules, regulations, codes of practice or guidance issued or made" substituted for the former words "rules or regulations made or guidance issued" by CA 1989, s. 206(1) and Sch. 23, para. 17(1), (2) as from 15 March 1990 (see SI 1990/354 (C 12), art. 3).

**124(2) [Qualification to s. 124(1)]** Where a recognition order is revoked there shall be disregarded for the purpose mentioned in subsection (1) above any such conduct as is mentioned in that subsection which occurred while the order was in force.

**124(3) [Where monopoly situation found to exist]** Where on a monopoly reference under section 50 or 51 of the said Act of 1973 falling within section 49 of that Act the Competition Commission find that a monopoly situation within the meaning of that Act exists and–

(a) that the person (or, if more than one, any of the persons) in whose favour it exists is subject to the rules of a recognised self-regulating organisation, recognised investment exchange or recognised clearing house or to the statements of principle, rules, regulations or codes of practice issued or made by a designated agency in the exercise of functions transferred to it by a delegation order; or

**History**
S. 127 substituted by the Competition Act 1998, s. 3(1)(b), Sch. 2, para. 1(1),(4) as from 1 March 2000 (see the Competition Act 1998 (Commencement No. 5) Order 2000 (SI 2000/344 (C 9)), art. 2 and Sch.) subject to transitional provisions relating to s. 127(2), (3) in the Competition Act 1998, s. 74(2), Sch. 13, para. 26; s. 127 formerly read as follows:

"**127 Modification of Restrictive Trade Practices Act 1976 in relation to recognised professional bodies**

**127(1)** This section applies to–

(a) any agreement for the constitution of a recognised professional body, including any term deemed to be contained in it by virtue of section 16(3) of the Restrictive Trade Practices Act 1976; and

(b) any other agreement–

(i) the parties to which consist of or include such a body, a person certified by such a body or a member of such a body; and

(ii) to which that Act applies by virtue of any term the inclusion of which in the agreement is required or contemplated by rules or guidance of that body relating to the carrying on of investment business by persons certified by it.

**(2)** If it appears to the Secretary of State that the restrictions in an agreement to which this section applies–

(a) do not have, and are not intended or likely to have, to any significant extent the effect of restricting, distorting or preventing competition; or

(b) if all or any of them have, or are intended or likely to have, that effect to any significant extent, that the effect is not greater than is necessary for the protection of investors,

he may give a direction to the Director requiring him not to make an application to the Restrictive Practices Court under Part I of the said Act of 1976 in respect of the agreement.

**(3)** If it appears to the Secretary of State that one or more (but not all) of the restrictions in an agreement to which this section applies–

(a) do not have, and are not intended or likely to have, to any significant extent the effect mentioned in subsection (2) above; or

(b) if they have, or are intended or likely to have, that effect to any significant extent that the effect is not greater than is necessary for the protection of investors,

he may make a declaration to that effect and give notice of it to the Director and the Restrictive Practices Court.

**(4)** The Restrictive Practices Court shall not in any proceedings begun by an application made after notice has been given to it of a declaration under this section make any finding or exercise any power under Part I of the said Act of 1976 in relation to a restriction in respect of which the declaration has effect.

**(5)** The Director shall not make any application to the Restrictive Practices Court under Part I of the said Act of 1976 in respect of any agreement to which this section applies unless–

(a) he has notified the Secretary of State of his intention to do so; and

(b) the Secretary of State has either notified him that he does not intend to give a direction or make a declaration under this section or has given him notice of a declaration in respect of it;

and where the Director proposes to make any such application he shall furnish the Secretary of State with particulars of the agreement and the restrictions by virtue of which the said Act of 1976 applies to it and such other information as he considers will assist the Secretary of State in deciding whether to exercise his powers under this section or as the Secretary of State may request.

**(6)** The Secretary of State may–

(a) revoke a direction or declaration under this section;

(b) vary any such declaration; or

(c) give a direction or make a declaration notwithstanding a previous notification to the Director that he did not intend to give a direction or make a declaration;

if he is satisfied that there has been a material change of circumstances such that the grounds for the direction or declaration have ceased to exist, that there are grounds for a different declaration or that there are grounds for giving a direction or making a declaration, as the case may be.

**(7)** The Secretary of State shall give notice to the Director of the revocation of a direction and to the Director and the Restrictive Practices Court of the revocation or variation of a declaration; and no such variation shall have effect so as to restrict the powers of the Court in any proceedings begun by an application already made by the Director.

**(8)** A direction or declaration under this section shall cease to have effect if the agreement in question ceases to be one to which this section applies.

**(9)** This section applies to information provisions as it applies to restrictions."

## SUPPLEMENTAL

# 128 Supplementary provisions

**128(1) [Duty of Secretary of State before exercising power]** Before the Secretary of State exercises a power under section 119(3)(b) or (c) above, his power to refuse leave under section 120(2) above or his power to give a direction under section 120(4) above in respect of a self-regulating organisation, investment exchange or clearing house, or his power under section 121(3)(b) above in respect of a designated agency, he shall–

(a) give written notice of his intention to do so to the organisation, exchange, clearing house or agency and take such steps (whether by publication or otherwise) as he thinks appropriate for bringing the notice to the attention of any other person who in his opinion is likely to be affected by the exercise of the power; and

(b) have regard to any representation made within such time as he considers reasonable by the organisation, exchange, clearing house or agency or by any such other person.

**128(2) [Contents of s. 128(1) notice]** A notice under subsection (1) above shall give particulars of the manner in which the Secretary of State proposes to exercise the power in question and state the reasons for which he proposes to act; and the statement of reasons may include matters contained in any report received by him under section 122 above.

**128(3) [Enforcement of directions]** Any direction given under this Chapter shall, on the application of the person by whom it was given, be enforceable by mandamus or, in Scotland, by an order for specific performance under section 91 of the Court of Session Act 1868.

**128(4) [Alteration of altered rules etc.]** The fact that any rules or regulations made by a recognised self-regulating organisation, investment exchange or clearing house or by a designated agency have been altered by or pursuant to a direction given by the Secretary of State under this Chapter shall not preclude their subsequent alteration or revocation by that organisation, exchange, clearing house or agency.

**128(5) [Assumption re acting conforming to guidance]** In determining under this Chapter whether any guidance has, or is likely to have, any particular effect the Secretary of State and the Director may assume that the persons to whom it is addressed will act in conformity with it.

**Note**

Concerning modifications to s. 128 re prevention of restrictive practices, see the Uncertificated Securities Regulations 1995 (SI 1995/3272), reg. 13 and Sch. 2.

# Chapter XV – Relations with Other Regulatory Authorities

## 128A Relevance of other controls

**128A** In determining–

(a) in relation to a self-regulating organisation, whether the requirements of Schedule 2 are met, or

(b) in relation to a professional body, whether the requirements of Schedule 3 are met,

the Secretary of State shall take into account the effect of any other controls to which members of the organisation or body are subject.

**History**

See history note after s. 128C.

**Note**

For transfer of the Secretary of State's functions under s. 128A see SI 1990/354 (C 12), art. 4(2)(b).

## 128B Relevance of information given and action taken by other regulatory authorities

**128B(1) [Application]** The following provisions apply in the case of–

(a) a person whose principal place of business is in a country or territory outside the United Kingdom, or

(b) a person whose principal business is other than investment business;

and in relation to such a person **"the relevant regulatory authority"** means the appropriate regulatory authority in that country or territory or, as the case may be, in relation to his principal business.

**128B(2) [When Secretary of State satisfied]** The Secretary of State may regard himself as satisfied with respect to any matter relevant for the purposes of this Part if–

(a) the relevant regulatory authority informs him that it is satisfied with respect to that matter, and

(b) he is satisfied as to the nature and scope of the supervision exercised by that authority.

**128B(3) [Matters taken into account]** In making any decision with respect to the exercise of his powers under this Part in relation to any such person, the Secretary of State may take into account whether the relevant regulatory authority has exercised, or proposes to exercise, its powers in relation to that person.

**128B(4) [Power of Secretary of State to enter arrangements]** The Secretary of State may enter into such arrangements with other regulatory authorities as he thinks fit for the purposes of this section.

**128B(5) [Community and international obligations]** Where any functions under this Part have been transferred to a designated agency, nothing in this section shall be construed as affecting the responsibility of the Secretary of State for the discharge of Community obligations or other international obligations of the United Kingdom.

**History**
See history note after s. 128C.

**Note**
For transfer of the Secretary of State's functions under s. 128B(1)–(4) see SI 1990/354 (C 12), art. 4(3)(c).

## 128C Enforcement in support of overseas regulatory authority

**128C(1) [Powers of Secretary of State]** The Secretary of State may exercise his disciplinary powers or powers of intervention at the request of, or for the purpose of assisting, an overseas regulatory authority.

**Note**
See note after s. 128C(5).

**128C(2) [Description of disciplinary powers]** The disciplinary powers of the Secretary of State means his powers–

(a) to withdraw or suspend authorisation under section 28 or to terminate or suspend authorisation under section 33,
(b) to give a disqualification direction under section 59,
(c) to make a public statement under section 60, or
(d) to apply for an injunction, interdict or other order under section 61(1);

and the reference to his powers of intervention is to the powers conferred by Chapter VI of this Part.

**Note**
See notes after s. 128C(5), (6).

**128C(3) ["Overseas regulatory authority"]** An **"overseas regulatory authority"** means an authority in a country or territory outside the United Kingdom which exercises–

(a) any function corresponding to–
  (i) a function of the Secretary of State under this Act, the Insurance Companies Act 1982 or the Companies Act 1985,
  (ii) a function under this Act of a designated agency, transferee body or competent authority, or
  (iii) a function of the Financial Services Authority under the Banking Act 1987, or
(b) any functions in connection with the investigation of, or the enforcement of rules (whether or not having the force of law) relating to, conduct of the kind prohibited by Part V of the Criminal Justice Act 1993 (insider dealing), or
(c) any function prescribed for the purposes of this subsection, being a function which in the opinion of the Secretary of State relates to companies or financial services.

**History**
In s. 128C(3)(a)(iii) the words "Financial Services Authority" substituted for the former words "Bank of England" by the Bank of England Act 1998, s. 23(1), 45 and Sch. 5, para. 39 as from 1 June 1998 (see SI 1998/1120 (C 25), art. 1, 2).
Previously, in s. 128C(3) the words "Part V of the Criminal Justice Act 1993 (insider dealing)" substituted for the former words "the Company Securities (Insider Dealing) Act 1985" by Criminal Justice Act 1993, s. 79(3) and Sch. 5, para. 8 as from 1 March 1994 (see SI 1994/242 (C 7), art. 2 and Sch.).

**Note**
See note after s. 128C(6).

**128C(4) [Matters to be taken into account]** In deciding whether to exercise those powers the Secretary of State may take into account, in particular–

(a) whether corresponding assistance would be given in that country or territory to an authority exercising regulatory functions in the United Kingdom;
(b) whether the case concerns the breach of a law, or other requirement, which has no close parallel in the United Kingdom or involves the assertion of a jurisdiction not recognised by the United Kingdom;
(c) the seriousness of the case and its importance to persons in the United Kingdom;
(d) whether it is otherwise appropriate in the public interest to give the assistance sought.

**Note**
See notes after s. 128C(5), (6).

**128C(5) [Undertaking from overseas regulatory authority]** The Secretary of State may decline to exercise those powers unless the overseas regulatory authority undertakes to make such contribution towards the cost of their exercise as the Secretary of State considers appropriate.

**Note**
See the Banking Coordination (Second Council Directive) Regulations 1992 (SI 1992/3218), reg. 55 and Sch. 9, para. 36. See also note after s. 128C(6).

**128C(6) ["Financial services" in s. 128C(3)(c)]** The reference in subsection (3)(c) to financial services includes, in particular, investment business, insurance and banking.

**History**
S. 128A–128C inserted by CA 1989, s. 196 as from 15 March 1990 (see SI 1990/354 (C 12), art. 3).

**Note**
Concerning effect of s. 128C see the Investment Services Regulations 1995 (SI 1995/3275), reg. 32 and Sch. 7, para. 34. For transfer of the Secretary of State's functions under s. 128C see SI 1990/354 (C 12), art. 4(3)(d).

# PART II – INSURANCE BUSINESS

## 129 Application of investment business provisions to regulated insurance companies.

**129** Schedule 10 to this Act shall have effect with respect to the application of the foregoing provisions of this Act to regulated insurance companies, that is to say–

(a) insurance companies to which Part II of the Insurance Companies Act 1982 applies; and
(b) insurance companies which are authorised persons by virtue of section 31 above.

## 130 Restriction on promotion of contracts of insurance

**130(1) [Limit on advertisements]** Subject to subsections (2) and (3) below, no person shall–

(a) issue or cause to be issued in the United Kingdom an advertisement–
  (i) inviting any person to enter or offer to enter into a contract of insurance rights under which constitute an investment for the purposes of this Act, or
  (ii) containing information calculated to lead directly or indirectly to any person doing so; or
(b) in the course of a business, advise or procure any person in the United Kingdom to enter into such a contract.

**130(2) [Non-application of s. 130(1)]** Subsection (1) above does not apply where the contract of insurance referred to in that subsection is to be with–

(a) a body authorised under section 3 or 4 of the Insurance Companies Act 1982 to effect and carry out such contracts of insurance;
(b) a body registered under the enactments relating to friendly societies;
(c) an insurance company the head office of which is in a member State other than the United Kingdom and which is entitled to carry on there insurance business of the relevant class;
(d) an insurance company which has a branch or agency in such a member State and is entitled under the law of that State to carry on there insurance business of the relevant class;

and in this subsection **"the relevant class"** means the class of insurance business specified in Schedule 1 or 2 to the Insurance Companies Act 1982 into which the effecting and carrying out of the contract in question falls.

**130(3) [Additional non-application of s. 130(1)]** Subsection (1) above also does not apply where–

(a) the contract of insurance referred to in that subsection is to be with an insurance company authorised to effect or carry out such contracts of insurance in any country or territory which is for the time being designated for the purposes of this section by an order made by the Secretary of State; and

(b) any conditions imposed by the order designating the country or territory have been satisfied.

**Note**

For countries and territories designated under s. 130(3) see SI 1988/439 (Guernsey and Isle of Man), SI 1989/2380 (Pennsylvania) and SI 1993/1237 (Iowa).

**130(4) [Limit on Secretary of State's power]** The Secretary of State shall not make an order designating any country or territory for the purposes of this section unless he is satisfied that the law under which insurance companies are authorised and supervised in that country or territory affords adequate protection to policy holders and potential policy holders against the risk that the companies may be unable to meet their liabilities; and, if at any time it appears to him that the law of a country or territory which has been designated under this section does not satisfy that requirement, he may by a further order revoke the order designating that country or territory.

**130(5) [Annulment of order by Parliament]** An order under this section shall be subject to annulment in pursuance of a resolution of either House of Parliament.

**130(6) [Offence, penalty]** Subject to subsections (7) and (8) below, any person who contravenes this section shall be guilty of an offence and liable–

(a) on conviction on indictment, to imprisonment for a term not exceeding two years or to a fine or to both;

(b) on summary conviction, to imprisonment for a term not exceeding six months or to a fine not exceeding the statutory maximum or to both.

**130(7) [Defence]** A person who in the ordinary course of a business other than investment business issues an advertisement to the order of another person shall not be guilty of an offence under this section if he proves that the matters contained in the advertisement were not (wholly or in part) devised or selected by him or by any person under his direction or control and that he believed on reasonable grounds after due enquiry that the person to whose order the advertisement was issued was an authorised person.

**130(8) [Further defence]** A person other than the insurance company with which the contract of insurance is to be made shall not be guilty of an offence under this section if he proves that he believed on reasonable grounds after due enquiry that subsection (2) or (3) above applied in the case of the contravention in question.

## 131 Contracts made after contravention of s. 130

**131(1) [Effect of contravention of s. 130]** Where there has been a contravention of section 130 above, then, subject to subsections (3) and (4) below–

(a) the insurance company shall not be entitled to enforce any contract of insurance with which the advertisement, advice or procurement was concerned and which was entered into after the contravention occurred; and

(b) the other party shall be entitled to recover any money or other property paid or transferred by him under the contract, together with compensation for any loss sustained by him as a result of having parted with it.

**131(2) [Interest recoverable under s. 131(1)]** The compensation recoverable under subsection (1) above shall be such as the parties may agree or as a court may, on the application of either party, determine.

**131(3) [Where contravention by insurance company]** In a case where the contravention referred to in subsection (1) above was a contravention by the insurance company with which the contract was made, the court may allow the contract to be enforced or money or property paid or transferred under it to be retained if it is satisfied–

(a) that the person against whom enforcement is sought or who is seeking to recover the money or property was not influenced, or not influenced to any material extent, by the advertisement or, as the case may be, the advice in making his decision to enter into the contract; or

(b) that the advertisement or, as the case may be, the advice was not misleading as to the nature of the company with which the contract was to be made or the terms of the contract and fairly stated any risks involved in entering into it.

**131(4) [Where contravention by person other than insurance company]** In a case where the contravention of section 130 above referred to in subsection (1) above was a contravention by a person other than the insurance company with which the contract was made the court may allow the contract to be enforced or money or property paid or transferred under it to be retained if it is satisfied that at the time the contract was made the company had no reason to believe that any contravention of section 130 above had taken place in relation to the contract.

**131(5) [Where election not to perform contract unenforceable by s. 131(1)]** Where a person elects not to perform a contract which by virtue of subsection (1) above is unenforceable against him or by virtue of that subsection recovers money paid or other property transferred by him under a contract he shall not be entitled to any benefits under the contract and shall repay any money and return any other property received by him under the contract.

**131(6) [Where property has passed to third party]** Where any property transferred under a contract to which this section applies has passed to a third party the references to that property in this section shall be construed as references to its value at the time of its transfer under the contract.

**131(7) [Contravention of s. 130]** A contravention of section 130 above by an authorised person shall be actionable at the suit of any person who suffers loss as a result of the contravention.

**131(8) [Effect of s. 61 on s. 130 contravention]** Section 61 above shall have effect in relation to a contravention or proposed contravention of section 130 above as it has effect in relation to a contravention or proposed contravention of section 57 above.

## 132 Insurance contracts effected in contravention of s. 2 of Insurance Companies Act 1982

**132(1) [Contracts unenforceable against other party]** Subject to subsection (3) below, a contract of insurance (not being an agreement to which section 5(1) above applies) which is entered into by a person in the course of carrying on insurance business in contravention of section 2 of the Insurance Companies Act 1982 shall be unenforceable against the other party; and that party shall be entitled to recover any money or other property paid or transferred by him under the contract, together with compensation for any loss sustained by him as a result of having parted with it.

**132(2) [Compensation recoverable under s. 132(1)]** The compensation recoverable under subsection (1) above shall be such as the parties may agree or as a court may, on the application of either party, determine.

**132(3) [Court may allow enforcement of s. 132(1) contract]** A court may allow a contract to which subsection (1) above applies to be enforced or money or property paid or transferred under it to be retained if it is satisfied–

(a) that the person carrying on insurance business reasonably believed that his entering into the contract did not constitute a contravention of section 2 of the said Act of 1982; and

(b) that it is just and equitable for the contract to be enforced or, as the case may be, for the money or property paid or transferred under it to be retained.

**132(4) [Where election not to perform unenforceable contract]** Where a person elects not to perform a contract which by virtue of this section is unenforceable against him or by virtue of this section recovers money or property paid or transferred under a contract he shall not be entitled to any benefits under the contract and shall repay any money and return any other property received by him under the contract.

**132(5) [Where property has passed to third party]** Where any property transferred under a contract to which this section applies has passed to a third party the references to that property in this section shall be construed as references to its value at the time of its transfer under the contract.

**132(6) [Effect of contravention of s. 2 of 1982 Act]** A contravention of section 2 of the said Act of 1982 shall not make a contract of insurance illegal or invalid to any greater extent than is provided in this section; and a contravention of that section in respect of a contract of insurance shall not affect the validity of any re-insurance contract entered into in respect of that contract.

## 133 Misleading statements as to insurance contracts

**133(1) [Offence]** Any person who–

(a) makes a statement, promise or forecast which he knows to be misleading, false or deceptive or dishonestly conceals any material facts; or

(b) recklessly makes (dishonestly or otherwise) a statement, promise or forecast which is misleading, false or deceptive,

is guilty of an offence if he makes the statement, promise or forecast or conceals the facts for the purpose of inducing, or is reckless as to whether it may induce, another person (whether or not the person to whom the statement, promise or forecast is made or from whom the facts are concealed) to enter into or offer to enter into, or to refrain from entering or offering to enter into, a contract of insurance with an insurance company (not being an investment agreement) or to exercise, or refrain from exercising, any rights conferred by such a contract.

**133(2) [Conditions for s. 133(1)]** Subsection (1) above does not apply unless–

(a) the statement, promise or forecast is made in or from, or the facts are concealed in or from, the United Kingdom;

(b) the person on whom the inducement is intended to or may have effect is in the United Kingdom; or

(c) the contract is or would be entered into or the rights are or would be exercisable in the United Kingdom.

**133(3) [Penalty]** A person guilty of an offence under this section shall be liable–

(a) on conviction on indictment, to imprisonment for a term not exceeding seven years or to a fine or to both;

(b) on summary conviction, to imprisonment for a term not exceeding six months or to a fine not exceeding the statutory maximum or to both.

## 134 Controllers of insurance companies

**134** (Ceased to have effect as result of the Insurance Companies (Third Insurance Directives) Regulations 1994 (SI 1994/1696), reg. 1, 68, Sch. 8, para. 12 as from 1 July 1994).

**History**

S. 134 formerly read as follows:

"In section 7(4)(c) (ii) of the Insurance Companies Act 1982 (definition of controller by reference to exercise of not less than one-third of voting power) for the words "one-third" there shall be substituted the words "15 per cent"."

## 135 Communication by auditor with Secretary of State

**135(1) [Insertion of s. 21A of Insurance Companies Act 1982]** After section 21 of the Insurance Companies Act 1982 there shall be inserted–

"*Communication by auditor with Secretary of State*

**21A(1)** No duty to which an auditor of an insurance company to which this Part of this Act applies may be subject shall be regarded as contravened by reason of his communicating in good faith to the Secretary of State, whether or not in response to a request from him, any information or opinion on a matter of which the auditor has become aware in his capacity as auditor of that company and which is relevant to any functions of the Secretary of State under this Act.

**21A(2)** If it appears to the Secretary of State that any auditor or class of auditor to whom subsection (1) above applies is not subject to satisfactory rules made or guidance issued by a professional body specifying circumstances in which matters are to be communicated to the Secretary of State as mentioned in that subsection the Secretary of State may make regulations applying to that auditor or class of auditor and specifying such circumstances; and it shall be the duty of an auditor to whom the regulations made by the Secretary of State apply to communicate a matter to the Secretary of State in the circumstances specified by the regulations.

**21A(3)** The matters to be communicated to the Secretary of State in accordance with any such rules or guidance or regulations may include matters relating to persons other than the company.

**21A(4)** No regulations shall be made under subsection (2) above unless a draft of them has been laid before and approved by a resolution of each House of Parliament.

**21A(5)** If it appears to the Secretary of State that an auditor has failed to comply with duty mentioned in subsection (2) above, the Secretary of State may disqualify him from being the auditor of an insurance company or any class of insurance company to which Part II of this Act applies; but the Secretary of State may remove any disqualification imposed under this subsection if satisfied that the person in question will in future comply with that duty.

**21A(6)** An insurance company to which this Part of this Act applies shall not appoint as auditor a person disqualified under subsection (5) above."

**135(2)** **[Insertion in s. 71(7) of 1982 Act]** In section 71(7) of that Act (which lists the provisions of that Act default in complying with which is not an offence) after the words "section 16" there shall be inserted the word "21A", and in section 97(4) of that Act (which provides that regulations under that Act are to be subject to annulment) after the word "Act" there shall be inserted the words ", except regulations under section 21A(3),".

## 136 Arrangements to avoid unfairness between separate insurance funds etc.

**136(1)** **[Insertion of s. 31A of Insurance Companies Act 1982]** After section 31 of the Insurance Companies Act 1982 there shall be inserted–

"*Arrangements to avoid unfairness between separate insurance funds etc.*

**31A(1)** An insurance company to which this Part of this Act applies which carries on long term business in the United Kingdom shall secure that adequate arrangements are in force for securing that transactions affecting assets of the company (other than transactions outside its control) do not operate unfairly between the section 28 fund or funds and the other assets of the company or, in a case where the company has more than one identified fund, between those funds.

**31A(2)** In this section–

**"the section 28 fund or funds"** means the assets representing the fund or funds maintained by the company under section 28(1)(b) above; and

**"identified fund"**, in relation to a company, means assets representing the company's receipts from a particular part of its long term business which can be identified as such by virtue of accounting or other records maintained by the company."

**136(2)** **[Insertion in s. 71(7) of 1982 Act]** In section 71(7) of that Act (which lists the provisions of that Act default in complying with which is not an offence) before the word "or" there shall be inserted the word "31A".

## 137 Regulations in respect of linked long term policies

**137** In section 78(2) of the Insurance Companies Act 1982 (regulations in respect of linked long term policies) after paragraph (a) there shall be inserted–

"(aa) restricting the proportion of those benefits which may be determined by reference to property of a specified description or a specified index;".

## 138 Insurance brokers

**138(1)** **[Rules under s. 8 of Insurance Brokers (Registration) Act 1977]** Rules made under section 8 of the Insurance Brokers (Registration) Act 1977 may require an applicant for registration or enrolment to state whether he is an authorised person or exempted person under

**History**
In s. 142(1) the words "of The Stock Exchange" formerly appearing after the words "Official List" deleted by Official Listing of Securities (Change of Competent Authority) Regulations 1991 (SI 1991/2000), reg. 1(1) and 3(1)(a) as from 2 October 1991.

**Note**
See note after s. 142(9).

**142(2) [Application to Sch. 1 investments]** Subject to subsections (3) and (4) below, this section applies to any investment falling within paragraph 1, 2, 4 or 5 of Schedule 1 to this Act.

**Note**
See note after s. 142(9).

**142(3) [Application of paragraphs in s. 142(2)]** In the application of those paragraphs for the purposes of subsection (2) above–

(a) paragraphs 1, 4 and 5 shall have effect as if paragraph 1 did not contain the exclusion relating to building societies, industrial and provident societies or credit unions;

(b) paragraph 2 shall have effect as if it included any instrument falling within paragraph 3 issued otherwise than by the government of a member State or a local authority in a member State; and

(c) paragraphs 4 and 5 shall have effect as if they referred only to investments falling within paragraph 1.

**Note**
See note after s. 142(9).

**142(4) [Application to Sch. 1 para. 6 investments]** The Secretary of State may by order direct that this section shall apply also to investments falling within paragraph 6 of Schedule 1 to this Act or to such investments of any class or description.

**142(5) [Annulment of s. 142(4) order]** An order under subsection (4) above shall be subject to annulment in pursuance of a resolution of either House of Parliament.

**Note**
See note after s. 142(9).

**142(6) ["The competent authority"]** In this Part of this Act **"the competent authority"** means, subject to section 157 below, The Financial Services Authority; and that authority may make rules (in this Act referred to as "listing rules") for the purposes of any of the following provisions.

**History**
In s. 142(6)the words "The Financial Services Authority" substituted for the former words "The International Stock Exchange of the United Kingdom and the Republic of Ireland Limited" by the Official Listing of Securities (Change of Competent Authority) Regulations 2000 (SI 2000/968), reg. 1, 3 as from 1 May 2000. Previously in s. 142(6) the words "The International Stock Exchange of the United Kingdom and the Republic of Ireland Limited" substituted for the former words "the Council of The Stock Exchange" by the Official Listing of Securities (Change of Competent Authority) Regulations 1991 (SI 1991/2000), reg. 1(1) and 3(1)(b) as from 2 October 1991.

**Note**
See note after s. 142(9).

**142(7) [Other definitions]** In this Part of this Act–

**"approved exchange"** means, in relation to dealings in securities, a recognised investment exchange approved by the Treasury for the purposes of the Public Offers of Securities Regulations 1995 either generally or in relation to such dealings;

**"issuer"**, in relation to any securities, means the person by whom they have been or are to be issued except that in relation to a certificate or other instrument falling within paragraph 5 of Schedule 1 to this Act it means the person who issued or is to issue the securities to which the certificate or instrument relates;

**"the Official List"** means the list maintained by the competent authority for the purposes of this Part of this Act;

**"securities"** means investments to which this section applies;

and references to listing are references to inclusion in the Official List in pursuance of this Part of this Act.

**History**
In s. 142(7) the definition of "approved exchange" inserted by the Public Offers of Securities Regulations 1995 (SI 1995/1537), reg. 1, 17 and Sch. 2, para. 1(1), (2) as from 19 June 1995. Previously in s. 142(7) the definition of "the Official List" substituted by the Official Listing of Securities (Change of Competent Authority) Regulations 1991 (SI 1991/2000), reg. 1(1) and 3(1)(c) as from 2 October 1991; the former definition read as follows:

**"the Official List"** means the Official List of The Stock Exchange.

**Note**

See note after s. 142(9).

**142(7A) [What constitutes offer of securities]** For the purposes of this Act–

(a) a person offers securities if, as principal–

(i) he makes an offer which, if accepted, would give rise to a contract for their issue or sale (which for this purpose includes any disposal for valuable consideration) by him or by another person with whom he has made arrangements for their issue or sale; or

(ii) he invites a person to make such an offer,

but not otherwise; and, except where the context otherwise requires, "offer" and "offeror" shall be construed accordingly; and

(b) whether a person offers securities to the public in the United Kingdom shall be determined in accordance with Schedule 11A to this Act.

**History**

S. 142(7A) inserted by the Public Offers of Securities Regulations 1995 (SI 1995/1537), reg. 1, 17 and Sch. 2, para. 1(1), (3) as from 19 June 1995.

**Note**

See note after s. 142(9).

**142(8) [Exercise of functions of competent authority]** Any functions of the competent authority under this Part of this Act may be exercised by its governing body or by any committee or sub-committee of that body or by any officer or servant of the authority except that listing rules–

(a) shall be made only by the governing body of the authority or by a committee or sub-committee of that body; and

(b) if made by a committee or sub-committee, shall cease to have effect at the end of the period of twenty-eight days beginning with the day on which they are made (but without prejudice to anything done under them) unless before the end of that period they are confirmed by the governing body of the authority.

**History**

S. 142(8) substituted by the Official Listing of Securities (Change of Competent Authority) Regulations 1991 (SI 1991/2000), reg. 1(1) and 3(1)(d) as from 2 October 1991; s. 142(8) formerly read as follows:

"Any functions of the competent authority under this Part of this Act may be exercised by any committee, sub-committee, officer or servant of the authority except that listing rules–

(a) shall be made only by the authority itself or by a committee or sub-committee of the authority; and

(b) if made by a committee or sub-committee, shall cease to have effect at the end of the period of twenty-eight days beginning with the day on which they are made (but without prejudice to anything done under them) unless before the end of that period they are confirmed by the authority."

**Note**

See note after s. 142(9).

**142(9) [Effect on powers of competent authority]** Nothing in this Part of this Act affects the powers of the competent authority in respect of investments to which this section does not apply and such investments may be admitted to the Official List otherwise than in accordance with this Part of this Act.

**History**

In s. 142(9) the words "the competent authority" substituted for the former words "the Council of The Stock Exchange" by Official Listing of Securities (Change of Competent Authority) Regulations 1991 (SI 1991/2000), reg. 1(1) and 3(1)(e) as from 2 October 1991.

**Note**

Concerning effect of s. 142, see the Investment Services Regulations 1995 (SI 1995/3275), reg. 32 and Sch. 7, para. 35.

## 143 Applications for listing

**143(1) [Manner of making application]** An application for listing shall be made to the competent authority in such manner as the listing rules may require.

**143(2) [Consent of issuer of securities]** No application for the listing of any securities shall be made except by or with the consent of the issuer of the securities.

**143(3) [Private companies, old public companies]** No application for listing shall be made in respect of securities to be issued by a private company or by an old public company within the meaning of section 1 of the Companies Consolidation (Consequential Provisions) Act 1985 or the corresponding Northern Ireland provision.

instrument containing such an order shall be subject to annulment in pursuance of a resolution of either House of Parliament."

**174 Market makers, off-market dealers etc.**

**174(1)** In subsection (1) of section 3 of the Company Securities (Insider Dealing) Act 1985 (actions not prohibited by sections 1 and 2 of that Act) at the end of paragraph (c) there shall be inserted the words "; or

(d) doing any particular thing in relation to any particular securities if the information–

(i) was obtained by him in the course of a business of a market maker in those securities in which he was engaged or employed, and

(ii) was of a description which it would be reasonable to expect him to obtain in the ordinary course of that business,

and he does that thing in good faith in the course of that business."

**(2)** At the end of that subsection there shall be inserted–

""**Market maker**" means a person (whether an individual, partnership or company) who–

(a) holds himself out at all normal times in compliance with the rules of a recognised stock exchange as willing to buy and sell securities at prices specified by him; and

(b) is recognised as doing so by that recognised stock exchange.".

**(3)** The existing provisions of section 4 of that Act (off-market deals in advertised securities) shall become subsection (1) of that section and after that subsection there shall be inserted–

"**4(2)** In its application by virtue of this section the definition of "market maker" in section 3(1) shall have effect as if the references to a recognised stock exchange were references to a recognised investment exchange (other than an overseas investment exchange) within the meaning of the Financial Services Act 1986.".

**(4)** In section 13 of that Act–

(a) in subsection (1) (which defines dealing in securities and provides that references to dealing on a recognised stock exchange include dealing through an investment exchange) the words from "and references" onwards shall be omitted; and

(b) for subsection (3) (definition of off-market dealer) there shall be substituted–

"**13(3)** "**Off-market dealer**" means a person who is an authorised person within the meaning of the Financial Services Act 1986.".

**175 Price stabilisation**

**175** For section 6 of the Company Securities (Insider Dealing) Act 1985 (international bonds) there shall be substituted–

"*Price stabilisation*

**6(1)** No provision of section 1, 2, 4 or 5 prohibits an individual from doing anything for the purpose of stabilising the price of securities if it is done in conformity with rules made under section 48 of the Financial Services Act 1986 and–

(a) in respect of securities which fall within any of paragraphs 1 to 5 of Schedule 1 to that Act and are specified by the rules; and

(b) during such period before or after the issue of those securities as is specified by the rules.

**6(2)** Any order under subsection (8) of section 48 of that Act shall apply also in relation to subsection (1) of this section.".

**176 Contracts for differences by reference to securities**

**176** After subsection (1) of section 13 of the Company Securities (Insider Dealing) Act 1985 (definition of dealing in securities), there shall be inserted–

"**13(1A)** For the purposes of this Act a person who (whether as principal or agent) buys or sells or agrees to buy or sell investments within paragraph 9 of Schedule 1 to the Financial Services Act 1986 (contracts for differences etc.) where the purpose or pretended purpose mentioned in that paragraph is to secure a profit or avoid a loss wholly or partly by reference to fluctuations in the value or price of securities shall be treated as if he were dealing in those securities."."

## 177 Investigations into insider dealing

**177(1) [Power of Secretary of State to appoint inspectors]** If it appears to the Secretary of State that there are circumstances suggesting that an offence under Part V of the Criminal Justice Act 1993 (insider dealing) may have been committed, he may appoint one or more competent inspectors to carry out such investigations as are requisite to establish whether or not any such offence has been committed and to report the results of their investigations to him.

**History**

In s. 177(1) the words "an offence under Part V of the Criminal Justice Act 1993 (insider dealing) may have been committed" substituted for the former words "there may have been a contravention of section 1, 2, 4 or 5 of the Company Securities (Insider Dealing) Act 1985", and the words "offence has been committed" substituted for the former words "contravention has occurred" by Criminal Justice Act 1993, s. 79(3) and Sch. 5, para. 9(1) as from 1 March 1994 (see SI 1994/242 (C 7), art. 2 and Sch.).

**177(2) [Scope of appointment]** The appointment under this section of an inspector may limit the period during which he is to continue his investigation or confine it to particular matters.

**177(2A) [Variation of appointment]** At any time during the investigation the Secretary of State may vary the appointment by limiting or extending the period during which the inspector is to continue his investigation or by confining the investigation to particular matters.

**History**

S. 177(2A) inserted by CA 1989, s. 74(1), (2) as from 21 February 1990 (see SI 1990/142 (C 5), art. 4).

**177(3) [Power of inspectors re production, attendance etc.]** If the inspectors consider that any person is or may be able to give information concerning any such offence they may require that person–

(a) to produce to them any documents in his possession or under his control which appear to them to be relevant to the investigation;

(b) to attend before them; and

(c) otherwise to give them all assistance in connection with the investigation which he is reasonably able to give;

and it shall be the duty of that person to comply with that requirement.

**History**

In s. 177(3) the word "offence" substituted for the former word "contravention" and in subs. (a) the words "which appear to them to be relevant to the investigation" substituted for the former words "relating to the company in relation to whose securities the contravention is suspected to have occurred or to its securities" by Criminal Justice Act 1993, s. 79(3) and Sch. 5, para. 9(2) as from 1 March 1994 (see SI 1994/242 (C 7), art. 2 and Sch.).

**177(4) [Power re examination under oath]** An inspector may examine on oath any person who he considers is or may be able to give information concerning any such offence, and may administer an oath accordingly.

**History**

In s. 177(4) the word "offence" substituted for the former word "contravention" by Criminal Justice Act 1993, s. 79(3) and Sch. 5, para. 9(3) as from 1 March 1994 (see SI 1994/242 (C 7), art. 2 and Sch.).

**177(5) [Reports to Secretary of State]** The inspectors shall make such interim reports to the Secretary of State as they think fit or he may direct and on the conclusion of the investigation they shall make a final report to him.

**177(5A) [Direction by Secretary of State]** If the Secretary of State thinks fit, he may direct the inspector to take no further steps in the investigation or to take only such further steps as are specified in the direction; and where an investigation is the subject of such a direction, the inspectors shall make a final report to the Secretary of State only where the Secretary of State directs them to do so.

**History**

S. 177(5A) inserted by CA 1989, s. 74(1), (3) as from 21 February 1990 (see SI 1990/142 (C 5), art. 4).

**177(6) [Statement may be used in evidence]** A statement made by a person in compliance with a requirement imposed by virtue of this section may be used in evidence against him.

**177(6A) [Limits on use of statement in criminal proceedings]** However, in criminal proceedings in which that person is charged with an offence to which this subsection applies–

(a) no evidence relating to the statement may be adduced, and

(b) no question relating to it may be asked,

by or on behalf of the prosecution, unless evidence relating to it is adduced, or a question relating to it is asked, in the proceedings by or on behalf of that person.

**History**

S. 177(6A) inserted by Youth Justice and Criminal Evidence Act 1999, s. 59, 68(3) and Sch. 3, para. 12, with effect from 14 April 2000 (see Youth Justice and Criminal Evidence Act 1999 (Commencement No. 2) Order 2000 (SI 2000/1034 (C. 27)), art. 2(a)).

**177(6B) [Offences to which s. 177(6A) applies]** Subsection (6A) above applies to any offence other than–

(a) an offence under section 200(1) below;

(b) an offence under section 2 or 5 of the Perjury Act 1911 (false statements made on oath otherwise than in judicial proceedings or made otherwise than on oath);

(c) an offence under section 44(1) or (2) of the Criminal Law (Consolidation) (Scotland) Act 1995 (false statements made on oath or otherwise than on oath); or

(d) an offence under Article 7 or 10 of the Perjury (Northern Ireland) Order 1979 (false statements made on oath otherwise than in judicial proceedings or made otherwise than on oath).

**History**

S. 177(6B) inserted by Youth Justice and Criminal Evidence Act 1999, s. 59, 68(3) and Sch. 3, para. 12, with effect from 14 April 2000 (see Youth Justice and Criminal Evidence Act 1999 (Commencement No. 2) Order 2000 (SI 2000/1034 (C. 27)), art. 2(a)).

**177(7) [Legal professional privilege, confidentiality]** A person shall not under this section be required to disclose any information or produce any document which he would be entitled to refuse to disclose or produce on grounds of legal professional privilege in proceedings in the

High Court or on grounds of confidentiality as between client and professional legal adviser in proceedings in the Court of Session.

**177(8) [Disclosure by bankers]** A person shall not under this section be required to disclose any information or produce any document in respect of which he owes an obligation of confidence by virtue of carrying on the business of banking unless–

(a) the person to whom the obligation of confidence is owed consents to the disclosure or production, or

(b) the making of the requirement was authorised by the Secretary of State.

**History**
S. 177(8) substituted by CA 1989, s. 74(1), (4) as from 21 February 1990 (see SI 1990/142 (C 5), art. 4); s. 177(8) formerly read as follows:

"Nothing in this section shall require a person carrying on the business of banking to disclose any information or produce any document relating to the affairs of a customer unless–

(a) the customer is a person who the inspectors have reason to believe may be able to give information concerning a suspected contravention; and

(b) the Secretary of State is satisfied that the disclosure or production is necessary for the purposes of the investigation."

**177(9) [Where lien claimed]** Where a person claims a lien on a document its production under this section shall be without prejudice to his lien.

**177(10) ["Document"]** In this section **"document"** includes information recorded in any form; and in relation to information recorded otherwise than in legible form the power to require its production includes power to require the production of a copy of the information in legible form.

**History**
In s. 177(10) the words "the power to require its production includes power to require the production of" substituted for the former words "references to its production include references to producing" by CA 1989, s. 74(1), (5) as from 21 February 1990 (see SI 1990/142 (C 5), art. 4).

**177(11) [Expenses]** A person who is convicted on a prosecution instituted as a result of an investigation under this section may in the same proceedings be ordered to pay the expenses of the investigation to such extent as may be specified in the order.

There shall be treated as expenses of the investigation, in particular, such reasonable sums as the Secretary of State may determine in respect of general staff costs and overheads.

**History**
S. 177(11) added by CA 1989, s. 74(1), (6) as from 21 February 1990 (see SI 1990/142 (C 5), art. 4).

## 178 Penalties for failure to co-operate with s. 177 investigations

**178(1) [Certificate to court re refusal to co-operate]** If any person–

(a) refuses to comply with any request under subsection (3) of section 177 above; or

(b) refuses to answer any question put to him by the inspectors appointed under that section with respect to any matter relevant for establishing whether or not any suspected offence has been committed,

the inspectors may certify that fact in writing to the court and the court may inquire into the case.

**History**
In s. 178(1) the words "offence has been committed" substituted for the former words "contravention has occurred" by Criminal Justice Act 1993, s. 79(3) and Sch. 5, para. 10(1) as from 1 March 1994 (see SI 1994/242 (C 7), art. 2 and Sch.).

**178(2) [Power of court]** If, after hearing any witness who may be produced against or on behalf of the alleged offender and any statement which may be offered in defence, the court is satisfied that he did without reasonable excuse refuse to comply with such a request or answer any such question, the court may–

(a) punish him in like manner as if he had been guilty of contempt of the court; or

(b) direct that the Secretary of State may exercise his powers under this section in respect of him;

and the court may give a direction under paragraph (b) above notwithstanding that the offender is not within the jurisdiction of the court if the court is satisfied that he was notified of his right to appear before the court and of the powers available under this section.

**178(3) [Power of Secretary of State re authorised person on s. 178(2)(b) direction]** Where the court gives a direction under subsection (2)(b) above in respect of an authorised person the Secretary of State may serve a notice on him–

(a) cancelling any authorisation of his to carry on investment business after the expiry of a specified period after the service of the notice;

(b) disqualifying him from becoming authorised to carry on investment business after the expiry of a specified period;

(c) restricting any authorisation of his in respect of investment business during a specified period to the performance of contracts entered into before the notice comes into force;

(d) prohibiting him from entering into transactions of a specified kind or entering into them except in specified circumstances or to a specified extent;

(e) prohibiting him from soliciting business from persons of a specified kind or otherwise than from such persons; or

(f) prohibiting him from carrying on business in a specified manner or otherwise than in a specified manner.

**178(4) [Period in s. 178(3)(a)–(c)]** The period mentioned in paragraphs (a) and (c) of subsection (3) above shall be such period as appears to the Secretary of State reasonable to enable the person on whom the notice is served to complete the performance of any contracts entered into before the notice comes into force and to terminate such of them as are of a continuing nature.

**178(5) [Power of Secretary of State re unauthorised person on s. 178(2)(b) direction]** Where the court gives a direction under subsection (2)(b) above in the case of an unauthorised person the Secretary of State may direct that any authorised person who knowingly transacts investment business of a specified kind, or in specified circumstances or to a specified extent, with or on behalf of that unauthorised person shall be treated as having contravened rules made under Chapter V of Part I of this Act or, in the case of a person who is an authorised person by virtue of his membership of a recognised self-regulating organisation or certification by a recognised professional body, the rules of that organisation or body.

**178(6) [Interpretation re reasonable excuse in s. 178(2)]** A person shall not be treated for the purposes of subsection (2) above as having a reasonable excuse for refusing to comply with a request or answer a question in a case where the offence or suspected offence being investigated relates to dealing by him on the instructions or for the account of another person, by reason that at the time of the refusal–

(a) he did not know the identity of that other person; or

(b) he was subject to the law of a country or territory outside the United Kingdom which prohibited him from disclosing information relating to the dealing without the consent of that other person, if he might have obtained that consent or obtained exemption from that law.

**History**

In s. 178(6) the words "offence or suspected offence" substituted for the former words "contravention or suspected contravention" by Criminal Justice Act 1993, s. 79(3) and Sch. 5, para. 10(2) as from 1 March 1994 (see SI 1994/242 (C 7), art. 2 and Sch.).

**178(7) [Revocation of s. 178(3) above]** A notice served on a person under subsection (3) above may be revoked at any time by the Secretary of State by serving a revocation notice on him: and the Secretary of State shall revoke such a notice if it appears to him that he has agreed to comply with the relevant request or answer the relevant question.

**178(8) [Effect of revocation of s. 178(3)(a) above]** The revocation of such a notice as is mentioned in subsection (3)(a) above shall not have the effect of reviving the authorisation cancelled by the notice except where the person would (apart from the notice) at the time of the revocation be an authorised person by virtue of his membership of a recognised self-regulating organisation or certification by a recognised professional body; but nothing in this subsection shall be construed as preventing any person who has been subject to such a notice from again becoming authorised after the revocation of the notice.

**178(9) [Service of notice on designated agency, recognised body]** If it appears to the Secretary of State–

(a) that a person on whom he serves a notice under subsection (3) above is an authorised person by virtue of an authorisation granted by a designated agency or by virtue of membership of a recognised self-regulating organisation or certificate by a recognised professional body; or

(b) that a person on whom he serves a revocation notice under subsection (7) above was such an authorised person at the time that the notice which is being revoked was served,

he shall serve a copy of the notice on that agency, organisation or body.

**178(10) [Functions for s. 114]** The Functions to which section 114 above applies shall include the functions of the Secretary of State under this section but any transfer of those functions shall be subject to a reservation that they are to be exercisable by him concurrently with the designated agency and so as to be exercisable by the agency subject to such conditions or restrictions as the Treasury may from time to time impose.

**History**
In s. 178(10) the word "Treasury" substituted for the former words "Secretary of State" by the Transfer of Functions (Financial Services) Order 1992 (SI 1992/1315), art. 10(1) and Sch. 4, para. 3 as from 7 June 1992.

**Note**
Concerning effect of s. 178 re European investment firms, see the Investment Services Regulations 1995 (SI 1995/3275), reg. 32 and Sch. 7, para. 37.
Concerning European institutions, see the Banking Coordination (Second Council Directive) Regulations 1992 (SI 1992/3218), reg. 55 and Sch. 9, para. 39.

# PART VIII – RESTRICTIONS ON DISCLOSURE OF INFORMATION

## 179 Restrictions on disclosure of information

**179(1) [No disclosure without consent]** Subject to section 180 below, information which is restricted information for the purposes of this section and relates to the business or other affairs of any person shall not be disclosed by a person mentioned in subsection (3) below ("the primary recipient") or any person obtaining the information directly or indirectly from him without the consent of the person from whom the primary recipient obtained the information and if different, the person to whom it relates.

**179(2) [Restricted information]** Subject to subsection (4) below, information is restricted information for the purposes of this section if it was obtained by the primary recipient for the purposes of, or in the discharge of his functions under, this Act or any rules or regulations made under this Act (whether or not by virtue of any requirement to supply it made under those provisions).

**Note**
Concerning functions, see the Banking Coordination (Second Council Directive) Regulations 1992 (SI 1992/3218), reg. 55 and Sch. 9, para. 40.

**179(3) [Persons in s. 179(1)]** The persons mentioned in subsection (1) above are–

(aa) the Treasury;

(a) the Secretary of State;

(b) any designated agency, transferee body or body administering a scheme under section 54 above;

(ba) the Financial Services Authority, other than in its capacity as a designated agency;

(c) the Director General of Fair Trading;

(d) the Chief Registrar of friendly societies;

(e) the Friendly Societies Commission;

(g) any member of the Tribunal;

(h) any person appointed or authorised to exercise any powers under section 94, 106 or 177 above;

(i) any officer or servant of any such person as is mentioned in paragraphs (a) to (h) above;

(j) any constable or other person named in a warrant issued under this Act.

**History**
In s. 179(3), para. (ba) inserted by the Bank of England Act 1998, s. 23(1), 45 and Sch. 5, para. 65(1), (2) as from 1 June 1998 (see SI 1998/1120 (C 25), art. 2). Para. (f) omitted and repealed by the Bank of England Act 1998, s. 23(1), 43, 45 and Sch. 5, para. 65(1), (2) and Sch. 9, Pt. I as from 1 June 1998 (see SI 1998/1120 (C 25), art. 2). Para. (f) formerly read as follows: " the Bank of England;".
Previously in s. 179(3), para. (aa) inserted by the Transfer of Functions (Financial Services) Order 1992 (SI 1992/1315), art. 10(1) and Sch. 4, para. 4 as from 7 June 1992 and para. (e) substituted by Friendly Societies Act 1992, s. 98 and Sch. 18, para. 4 as from 1 February 1993 in regard to incorporated friendly societies (see SI 1993/16 (C 1) art. 2 and Sch. 4) and as from 1 January 1994 for all remaining purposes (see SI 1993/2213 (C 43), art. 2 and Sch. 5, app.); para. (e) formerly read "the Registrar of Friendly Societies for Northern Ireland".
Also in s. 179(3) the word "and" formerly preceding para. (i) omitted and repealed by CA 1989, s. 75(1)(a), 212 and Sch. 24 and in para. (i) the words "as is mentioned in paragraphs (a) to (h) above"; and para. (j) inserted by CA 1989, s. 75(1)(b), (c) as from 21 February 1990 (see SI 1990/142 (C 5), art. 4, 7(d)).

**179(4) [Information not to be treated as restricted]** Information shall not be treated as restricted information for the purposes of this section if it has been made available to the public by virtue of being disclosed in any circumstances in which or for any purpose for which disclosure is not precluded by this section.

**179(5) [Information obtained by competent authority]** Subject to section 180 below, information obtained by the competent authority in the exercise of its functions under Part IV of this Act or received by it pursuant to a Community obligation from any authority exercising corresponding functions in another member State shall not be disclosed without the consent of the person from whom the competent authority obtained the information and, if different, the person to whom it relates.

**179(6) [Offence, penalty]** Any person who contravenes this section shall be guilty of an offence and liable–

(a) on conviction on indictment, to imprisonment for a term not exceeding two years or to a fine or to both;

(b) on summary conviction, to imprisonment for a term not exceeding three months or to a fine not exceeding the statutory maximum or to both.

**Note**
See note after s. 180.
For non-application of s. 179 see the Financial Instutions (Prudential Supervision) Regulations (SI 1996/1669), reg. 12(2).

## 180 Exceptions from restrictions on disclosure

**180(1) [Disclosures not precluded by s. 179]** Section 179 above shall not preclude the disclosure of information–

(a) with a view to the institution of or otherwise for the purposes of criminal proceedings;

(b) with a view to the institution of or otherwise for the purposes of any civil proceedings arising under or by virtue of this Act or proceedings before the Tribunal;

(bb) for the purpose of enabling or assisting the Treasury to exercise any of their powers under the enactments relating to insurance companies, under this Act or under Part III or VII of the Companies Act 1989;

(c) for the purpose of enabling or assisting the Secretary of State to exercise any powers conferred on him by this Act or by the enactments relating to companies, insurance companies or insolvency or by Part II, III or VII of the Companies Act 1989 or for the purpose of enabling or assisting any inspector appointed by him under the enactments relating to companies to discharge his functions;

(d) for the purpose of enabling or assisting the Department of Economic Development for Northern Ireland to exercise any powers conferred on it by the enactments relating to companies or insolvency or for the purpose of enabling or assisting any inspector appointed by it under the enactments relating to companies to discharge his functions;

(e) for the purpose–
  (i) of enabling or assisting a designated agency to discharge its functions under this Act or Part VII of the Companies Act 1989,
  (ii) of enabling or assisting a transferee body or the competent authority to discharge its functions under this Act, or
  (iii) of enabling or assisting the body administering a scheme under section 54 above to discharge its functions under the scheme;

(ea) for the purpose of enabling or assisting the Financial Services Authority to discharge–

(i) its functions under this Act, other than as a designated agency,

(ii) its functions under the Banking Act 1987, or

(iii) its functions under section 171 of the Companies Act 1989;

(f) for the purpose of enabling or assisting the Bank of England to discharge any of its functions;

(g) for the purpose of enabling or assisting the Deposit Protection Board to discharge its functions under that Act;

(h) for the purpose of enabling or assisting the Friendly Societies Commission to discharge its functions under this Act, the enactments relating to friendly societies or the enactments relating to industrial assurance;

(hh) for the purpose of enabling or assisting a body established by order under section 46 of the Companies Act 1989 to discharge its functions under Part II of that Act, or of enabling or assisting a recognised supervisory or qualifying body within the meaning of that Part to discharge its functions as such;

(i) for the purpose of enabling or assisting the Industrial Assurance Commissioner or the Industrial Assurance Commissioner for Northern Ireland to discharge his functions under the enactments relating to industrial assurance;

(j) for the purpose of enabling or assisting the Insurance Brokers Registration Council to discharge its functions under the Insurance Brokers (Registration) Act 1977;

(k) for the purpose of enabling or assisting an official receiver to discharge his functions under the enactments relating to insolvency or for the purpose of enabling or assisting a body which is for the time being a recognised professional body for the purposes of section 391 of the Insolvency Act 1986 to discharge its functions as such;

(l) for the purpose of enabling or assisting the Building Societies Commission to discharge its functions under the Building Societies Act 1986;

(m) for the purpose of enabling or assisting the Director General of Fair Trading to discharge his functions under this Act;

(mm) for the purpose of enabling or assisting the Occupational Pensions Regulatory Authority or the Pensions Compensation Board to discharge their functions under the Pension Schemes Act 1993 or the Pensions Act 1995 or any enactment in force in Northern Ireland corresponding to either of them;

(n) for the purpose of enabling or assisting a recognised self-regulating organisation, recognised investment exhange, recognised professional body, or recognised clearing house to discharge its functions as such;

(nn) to an Operator approved under the Uncertificated Securities Regulations 1995 if the information is necessary to ensure the proper functioning of a relevant system within the meaning of those Regulations in relation to defaults and potential defaults by market-participants;

(o) with a view to the institution of, or otherwise for the purposes of, any disciplinary proceedings relating to the exercise by a solicitor, auditor, accountant, valuer or actuary of his professional duties;

(oo) with a view to the institution of, or otherwise for the purposes of, any disciplinary proceedings relating to the discharge by a public servant of his duties;

(p) for the purpose of enabling or assisting any person appointed or authorised to exercise any powers under section 43A or 44 of the Insurance Companies Act 1982, section 447 of the Companies Act 1985, section 94, 106 or 177 above or section 84 of the Companies act 1989 to discharge his functions;

(q) for the purpose of enabling or assisting an auditor of an authorised person or a person approved under section 108 above to discharge his functions;

(qq) for the purpose of enabling or assisting an overseas regulatory authority to exercise its regulatory functions;

(r) if the information is or has been available to the public from other sources;

(s) in a summary or collection of information framed in such a way as not to enable the identity of any person to whom the information relates to be ascertained; or

(t) in pursuance of any Community obligation.

**History**

In s. 180(1)(bb) the words " under the enactments relating to insurance companies," inserted by the Transfer of Functions (Insurance) Order (SI 1997/2781), art. 1, 8, Sch., para. 112 as from 5 January 1998.

Previously, s. 180(1)(bb) inserted by the Transfer of Functions (Financial Services) Order 1992 (SI 1992/1315), art. 10(1) and Sch. 4, para. 5 as from 7 June 1992.

In s. 180(1)(c) the words "or by Part II, III or VII of the Companies Act 1989" inserted by CA 1989, s. 75(2), (3)(a) as from 21 February 1990 except in regard to the reference to Pt. VII (see SI 1990/142 (C 5), art. 4(b)) which was inserted from 25 April 1991 (see SI 1991/878 (C 21), art. 2 and Sch.).

S. 180(1)(ea) inserted by the Banking Act 1998, s. 23(1), 45 and Sch. 5, para. 65(1), (3)(a) as from 1 June 1998 (see SI 1998/1120 (C 25), art. 2).

Previously, s. 180(1)(e) substituted by CA 1989, s. 75(2), (3)(b) as from 21 February 1990 except in regard to the reference to Pt. VII (see SI 1990/142 (C 5), art. 4(b)) which was substituted from 25 April 1991 (see SI 1991/878 (C 21), art. 2 and Sch.); s. 180(1)(e) formerly read as follows:

"(e) for the purpose of enabling or assisting a designated agency or transferee body or the competent authority to discharge its functions under this Act or of enabling or assisting the body administering a scheme under section 54 above to discharge its functions under the scheme".

In s. 180(1)(f) the words "any of its functions" substituted for the former words "its functions under the Banking Act 1987 or any other functions" by the Banking Act 1998, s. 23(1), 45 and Sch. 5, para. 65(1), (3)(b) as from 1 June 1998 (see SI 1998/1120 (C 25), art. 2).

In s. 180(1)(f) the words "Banking Act 1987" substituted for the former words "Banking Act 1979" by Banking Act 1987, s. 108(1) and Sch. 6, para. 27(3) as from 1 October 1987 (see SI 1987/1664 (C 50)).

S. 180(1)(h) substituted by Friendly Societies Act 1992, s. 98 and Sch. 18, para. 5 as from 1 February 1993 in regard to incorporated friendly societies (see SI 1993/16 (C 1) art. 2 and Sch. 4) and as from 1 January 1994 for all remaining purposes (see SI 1993/2213 (C 43), art. 2 and Sch. 5); s. 180(1)(h) previously read as follows:

"(h) for the purpose of enabling or assisting the Chief Registrar of friendly societies or the Registrar of Friendly Societies for Northern Ireland to discharge his functions under this Act or under the enactments relating to friendly societies or building societies;"

S. 180(1)(hh) inserted by CA 1989, s. 75(2), (3)(c) as from 21 February 1990 except in regard to the reference to a body established by an order under CA 1989, s. 46 (see SI 1990/142 (C 5), art. 4(a)).

S. 180(1)(mm) inserted by the Pensions Act 1995, s. 122, Sch. 3, para. 17 as from 6 April 1997 (see SI 1997/664 (C. 23), art. 2(3), Sch., Pt. II).

S. 180(1)(nn) inserted by the Uncertificated Securities Regulations 1995 (SI 1995/3272), reg. 1, 40(4) as from 19 December 1995.

S. 180(1)(oo) inserted by CA 1989, s. 75(2), (3)(d) as from 25 January 1990 (see SI 1990/98 (C 2), art. 2(a), (b)).

In s. 180(1)(p) the words "section 43A or 44" substituted for the former words " section 44" by the Insurance Companies (Third Insurance Directives) Regulations 1994 (SI 1994/1696), reg. 66(3) as from 1 July 1994; previously the words "section 44 of the Insurance Companies Act 1982, section 447 of the Companies Act 1985," and "or section 84 of the Companies Act 1989" inserted by CA 1989, s. 75(2), (3)(e) as from 21 February 1990 (see SI 1990/142 (C 5), art. 4).

S. 180(1)(qq) inserted by CA 1989, s. 75(2), (3)(f) as from 21 February 1990 (see SI 1990/142 (C 5), art. 4).

**Note**

Concerning effect of s. 180 re European investment firms, see the Investment Services Regulations 1995 (SI 1995/3275), reg. 32 and Sch. 7, para. 38.

Concerning functions under the Banking Act and the Building Societies Act, and European institutions, see the Banking Coordination (Second Council Directive) Regulations 1992 (SI 1992/3218), reg. 55 and Sch. 9, para. 41.

**180(1A)** **[Definitions]** In subsection (1)–

(a) in paragraph (oo) **"public servant"** means an officer or servant of the Crown or of any public or other authority for the time being designated for the purposes of that paragraph by order of the Secretary of State; and

(b) in paragraph (qq) **"overseas regulatory authority"** and **"regulatory functions"** have the same meaning as in section 82 of the Companies Act 1989.

**History**

S. 180(1A) inserted by CA 1989, s. 75(2), (4) as from 25 January 1990 in regard to the "public servant" definition (see SI 1990/98 (C 2), art. 2(a), (b)) and as from 21 February 1990 in regard to the other definitions (see SI 1990/142 (C 5), art. 4).

**180(2)** **[Disclosure to Secretary of State or Treasury]** Section 179 above shall not preclude the disclosure of information to the Secretary of State or to the Treasury if the disclosure is made in the interests of investors or in the public interest.

**180(3)** **[Disclosures assisting public authorities etc.]** Subject to subsection (4) below, section 179 above shall not preclude the disclosure of information for the purpose of enabling or assisting any public or other authority for the time being designated for the purposes of this subsection by an order made by the Secretary of State to discharge any functions which are specified in the order.

**History**
In s. 180(3) the words "designated for the purposes of this subsection" substituted for the former words "designated for the purposes of this section" by CA 1989, s. 75(2), (5) as from 21 February 1990 (see SI 1990/142 (C 5), art. 4).

**Note**
See note after s. 180(4).

**180(4) [Scope of s. 180(3) order]** An order under subsection (3) above designating an authority for the purposes of that subsection may–

(a) impose conditions subject to which the disclosure of information is permitted by that subsection; and

(b) otherwise restrict the circumstances in which that subsection permits disclosure.

**Note**
For orders made under s. 180(3), (4) see SI 1986/2031, SI 1987/859, SI 1987/1141, SI 1988/1058, SI 1989/940, SI 1989/2009, SI 1993/1826 and SI 1994/340.

**180(5) [Further disclosures not precluded by s. 179]** Section 179 above shall not preclude the disclosure–

(a) of any information contained in an unpublished report of the Tribunal which has been made available to any person under this Act, by the person to whom it was made available or by any person obtaining the information directly or indirectly from him;

(b) of any information contained in any notice or copy of a notice served under this Act, notice of the contents of which has not been given to the public, by the person on whom it was served or any person obtaining the information directly or indirectly from him;

(c) of any information contained in the register kept under section 102 above by virtue of subsection (1)(e) of that section, by a person who has inspected the register under section 103(2) or (3) above or any person obtaining the information directly or indirectly from him.

**180(6)** (Omitted and repealed by Companies Act 1989, s. 75(2), (6), 212 and Sch. 24 as from 21 February 1990.)

**History**
In regard to the date of the above omission and repeal see SI 1990/142 (C 5), art. 4, 7(d); s. 180(6) formerly read as follows:
"Section 179 above shall not preclude the disclosure of information for the purpose of enabling or assisting an authority in a country or territory outside the United Kingdom to exercise functions corresponding to those of the Secretary of State under this Act or the Insurance Companies Act 1982 or to those of the Bank of England under the Banking Act 1987 or to those of the competent authority under this Act or any other functions in connection with rules of law corresponding to the provisions of the Company Securities (Insider Dealing) Act 1985 or Part VII of this Act."
Previously the words "Banking Act 1987" substituted for the former words "Banking Act 1979" by Banking Act 1987, s. 108(1) and Sch. 6, para. 27(3) as from 1 October 1987 (see SI 1987/1664 (C 50)).

**180(7) [Disclosures by Director General of Fair Trading]** Section 179 above shall not preclude the disclosure of information by the Director General of Fair Trading or any officer or servant of his or any person obtaining the information directly or indirectly from the Director or any such officer or servant if the information was obtained by the Director or any such officer or servant for the purposes of or in the discharge of his functions under this Act (whether or not he was the primary recipient of the information within the meaning of section 179 above) and the disclosure is made–

(a) for the purpose of enabling or assisting the Director, the Secretary of State or any other Minister, the Competition Commission or any Northern Ireland department to discharge any function conferred on him or them by the Fair Trading Act 1973 (other than Part II or III of that Act), the Competition Act 1980 or the Competition Act 1998; or

(b) for the purposes of any civil proceedings under any of those provisions;

and information shall not be treated as restricted information for the purposes of section 179 above if it has been made available to the public by virtue of this subsection.

**History**
In s. 180(7)(a):

- the words "the Competition Commission" substituted for the former words "the Monopolies and Mergers Commission" by the Competition Act 1998 (Competition Commission) Transitional, Consequential and Supplemental Provisions Order 1999 (SI 1999/506), art. 1, 21 as from 1 April 1999; and
- the words "the Restrictive Trade Practices Act 1976 or" formerly appearing before the words "the Competition Act 1980" repealed, and the words "or the Competition Act 1998" inserted, by the Competition Act 1998 (Transitional, Consequential and Supplemental Provisions) Order 2000 (SI 2000/311), art. 1, 20, subject to transitional provision in art. 4 of that order.

**180(8) [Modification by Secretary of State]** The Secretary of State may by order modify the application of any provision of this section so as–

(a) to prevent the disclosure by virtue of that provision; or

(b) to restrict the extent to which disclosure is permitted by virtue of that provision,

of information received by a person specified in the order pursuant to a Community obligation from a person exercising functions in relation to a collective investment scheme who is also so specified.

**180(9) [Annulment of s. 180(1A)(a), (3), (8) order by Parliament]** An order under subsection (1A)(a), (3) or (8) above shall be subject to annulment in pursuance of a resolution of either House of Parliament.

**History**

In s. 180(9) the words "subsection (1A)(a), (3) or (8)" substituted for the former words "subsection (3) or (8)" by CA 1989, s. 75(2), (7) as from 25 January 1990 (see SI 1990/98 (C 2), art. 2(a), (b)).

# 181 Directions restricting disclosure of information overseas

**181(1) [Power of Secretary of State]** If it appears to the Secretary of State to be in the public interest to do so, he may give a direction prohibiting the disclosure to any person in a country or territory outside the United Kingdom which is specified in the direction, or to such persons in such a country or territory as may be so specified, of such information to which this section applies as may be so specified.

**181(2) [Extent of s. 181(1) direction]** A direction under subsection (1) above–

(a) may prohibit disclosure of the information to which it applies by all persons or only by such persons or classes of person as may be specified in it; and

(b) may prohibit such disclosure absolutely or in such cases or subject to such conditions as to consent or otherwise as may be specified in it;

and a direction prohibiting disclosure by all persons shall be published by the Secretary of State in such manner as appears to him to be appropriate.

**181(3) [Application of section]** This section applies to any information relating to the business or other affairs of any person which was obtained (whether or not by virtue of any requirement to supply it) directly or indirectly–

(a) by a designated agency, a transferee body, the competent authority or any person appointed or authorised to exercise any powers under section 94, 106 or 177 above (or any officer or servant of any such body or person) for the purposes or in the discharge of any functions of that body or person under this Act or any rules or regulations made under this Act or of any monitoring agency functions; or

(b) by a recognised self-regulating organisation, a recognised professional body, a recognised investment exchange or a recognised clearing house other than an overseas investment exchange or clearing house (or any officer or servant of such an organisation, body, investment exchange or clearing house) for the purposes or in the discharge of any of its functions as such or of any monitoring agency functions.

**181(4) ["Monitoring agency functions" in s. 181(3)]** In subsection (3) above **"monitoring agency functions"** means any functions exercisable on behalf of another body by virtue of arrangements made pursuant to paragraph 4(2) of Schedule 2, paragraph 4(6) of Schedule 3, paragraph 3(2) of Schedule 4 or paragraph 3(2) of Schedule 7 to this Act or of such arrangements as are mentioned in section 39(4)(b) above.

**181(5) [Disclosures not prohibited]** A direction under this section shall not prohibit the disclosure by any person other than a person mentioned in subsection (3) above of–

(a) information relating only to the affairs of that person; or

(b) information obtained by that person otherwise than directly or indirectly from a person mentioned in subsection (3) above.

**181(6) [Disclosures under Community obligations]** A direction under this section shall not prohibit the disclosure of information in pursuance of any Community obligation.

**181(7) [Offence, penalty]** A person who knowingly discloses information in contravention of a direction under this section shall be guilty of an offence and liable–

(a) on conviction on indictment, to imprisonment for a term not exceeding two years or to a fine or to both;

(b) on summary conviction, to imprisonment for a term not exceeding three months or to a fine not exceeding the statutory maximum or to both.

**181(8) [Exception re offence]** A person shall not be guilty of an offence under this section by virtue of anything done or omitted to be done by him outside the United Kingdom unless he is a British citizen, a British Dependent Territories citizen, a British Overseas citizen or a body corporate incorporated in the United Kingdom.

## 182 Disclosure of information under enactments relating to fair trading, banking, insurance and companies

**182** The enactments mentioned in Schedule 13 to this Act shall have effect with the amendments there specified (which relate to the circumstances in which information obtained under those enactments may be disclosed).

# PART IX – RECIPROCITY

## 183 Reciprocal facilities for financial business

**183(1) [Power of Secretary of State, Treasury to serve notice]** If it appears to the Secretary of State or the Treasury that by reason of–

(a) the law of any country outside the United Kingdom; or

(b) any action taken by or the practices of the government or any other authority or body in that country,

persons connected with the United Kingdom are unable to carry on investment, insurance or banking business in, or in relation to, that country on terms as favourable as those on which persons connected with that country are able to carry on any such business in, or in relation to, the United Kingdom, the Secretary of State or, as the case may be, the Treasury may serve a notice under this subsection on any person connected with that country who is carrying on or appears to them to intend to carry on any such business in, or in relation to, the United Kingdom.

**183(2) [Conditions for service of s. 183(1) notice]** No notice shall be served under subsection (1) above unless the Secretary of State or, as the case may be, the Treasury consider it in the national interest to serve it; and before doing so the Secretary of State or, as the case may be, the Treasury shall so far as they consider expedient consult such body or bodies as appear to them to represent the interests of persons likely to be affected.

**183(3) [Contents, date of notice]** A notice under subsection (1) above shall state the grounds on which it is given (identifying the country in relation to which those grounds are considered to exist); and any such notice shall come into force on such date as may be specified in it.

**183(4) [Connection with a country–interpretation]** For the purposes of this section a person is connected with a country if it appears to the Secretary of State or, as the case may be, the Treasury–

(a) in the case of an individual, that he is a national of or resident in that country or carries on investment, insurance or banking business from a principal place of business there;

(b) in the case of a body corporate, that it is incorporated or has a principal place of business in that country or is controlled by a person or persons connected with that country;

(c) in the case of a partnership, that it has a principal place of business in that country or that any partner is connected with that country;

(d) in the case of an unincorporated association which is not a partnership, that it is formed under the law of that country, has a principal place of business there or is controlled by a person or persons connected with that country.

**183(5) ["Country"]** In this section **"country"** includes any territory or part of a country or territory; and where it appears to the Secretary of State or, as the case may be, the Treasury that there are such grounds as are mentioned in subsection (1) above in the case of any part of a country or territory their powers under that subsection shall also be exercisable in respect of any person who is connected with that country or territory or any other part of it.

**Note**

For circumstances where a notice may not be served under s. 183, see the Insurance Companies (Amendment) Regulations 1993 (SI 1993/174), reg. 8 and the Banking Coordination (Second Council Directive) Regulations 1992 (SI 1992/3218), reg. 53.

See also the Investment Services Regulations 1995 (SI 1995/3275), reg. 1, 29.

## 184 Investment and insurance business

**184(1) [Extent of s. 183 notice]** A notice under section 183 above relating to the carrying on of investment business or insurance business shall be served by the Secretary of State and such a notice may be a disqualification notice, a restriction notice or a partial restriction notice and may relate to the carrying on of business of both kinds.

**184(2) [Effects of disqualification notice]** A disqualification notice as respects investment business or insurance business shall have the effect of–

(a) cancelling any authorisation of the person concerned to carry on that business after the expiry of such period after the service of the notice as may be specified in it;

(b) disqualifying him from becoming authorised to carry on that business after the expiry of that period; and

(c) restricting any authorisation of the person concerned in respect of that business during that period to the performance of contracts entered into before the notice comes into force;

and the period specified in such a notice shall be such period as appears to the Secretary of State to be reasonable to enable the person on whom it is served to complete the performance of those contracts and to terminate such of them as are of a continuing nature.

**184(3) [Effect of restriction notice]** A restriction notice as respects investment business or insurance business shall have the effect of restricting any authorisation of the person concerned in respect of that business to the performance of contracts entered into before the notice comes into force.

**184(4) [Effect of partial restriction notice]** A partial restriction notice as respects investment business may prohibit the person concerned from–

(a) entering into transactions of any specified kind or entering into them except in specified circumstances or to a specified extent;

(b) soliciting business from persons of a specified kind or otherwise than from such persons;

(c) carrying on business in a specified manner or otherwise than in a specified manner.

**184(5) [Effect of partial restriction notice re insurance business]** A partial restriction notice as respects insurance business may direct that the person concerned shall cease to be authorised under section 3 or 4 of the Insurance Companies Act 1982 to effect contracts of insurance of any description specified in the notice.

**184(6) [Copy of notice on designated agency, recognised body]** If it appears to the Secretary of State that a person on whom he serves a notice under section 183 above as respects investment business is an authorised person by virtue of an authorisation granted by a designated agency or by virtue of membership of a recognised self-regulating organisation or certification by a recognised professional body he shall serve a copy of the notice on that agency, organisation or body.

**184(7) [Power of Secretary of State re certain contraventions]** If it appears to the Secretary of State–

(a) that any person on whom a partial restriction notice has been served by him has contravened any provision of that notice or, in the case of a notice under subsection (5) above, effected a contract of insurance of a description specified in the notice; and

(b) that any such grounds as are mentioned in subsection (1) of section 183 above still exist in the case of the country concerned,

he may serve a disqualification notice or a restriction notice on him under that section.

**184(8) [Effect of s. 28, 33, 60, 61, 62 re s. 184(4) contravention]** Sections 28, 33, 60, 61 and 62 above shall have effect in relation to a contravention of such a notice as is mentioned in subsection (4) above as they have effect in relation to any such contravention as is mentioned in those sections.

## 185 Banking business

**185(1) [Service of s. 183 notice re banks]** A notice under section 183 above relating to the carrying on of a deposit-taking business as an authorised institution within the meaning of the Banking Act 1987 shall be served by the Treasury and may be either a disqualification notice or a partial restriction notice.

**History**

In s. 185(1) the words "an authorised institution within the meaning of the Banking Act 1987" substituted for the former words "a recognised bank or licensed institution within the meaning of the Banking Act 1979" by Banking Act 1987, s. 108(1) and Sch. 6, para. 27(4)(a) as from 1 October 1987 (see SI 1987/1664 (C 50)).

**185(2) [Effect of disqualification notice]** A disqualification notice relating to such business shall have the effect of–

(a) cancelling any authorisation granted to the person concerned under the Banking Act 1987; and

(b) disqualifying him from becoming an authorised institution within the meaning of that Act.

**History**

In s. 185(2) the words, "authorisation", "Banking Act 1987", and, "an authorised institution", substituted for the former words, "recognition or licence", "Banking Act 1979", and, "a recognised bank or licensed institution", by Banking Act 1987, s. 108(1) and Sch. 6, para. 27(4)(b) as from 1 October 1987 (see SI 1987/1664 (C 50)).

**185(3) [Effect of partial restriction notice]** A partial restriction notice relating to such business may–

(a) prohibit the person concerned from dealing with or disposing of his assets in any manner specified in the direction;

(b) impose limitations on the acceptance by him of deposits;

(c) prohibit him from soliciting deposits either generally or from persons who are not already depositors;

(d) prohibit him from entering into any other transaction or class of transactions;

(e) require him to take certain steps, to pursue or refrain from pursuing a particular course of activities or to restrict the scope of his business in a particular way.

**185(4) [Copy of s. 183 notice to Financial Services Authority]** The Treasury shall serve on the Financial Services Authority a copy of any notice served by them under section 183 above.

**History**

In s. 185(4) the words "Financial Services Authority" substituted for the former words "Bank of England" by the Bank of England Act 1998, s. 23(1), 45 and Sch. 5, para. 39 as from 1 June 1998 (see SI 1998/1120 (C 25), art. 2).

**185(5) [Offence, penalty re partial restriction notice]** Any person who contravenes any provision of a partial restriction notice served on him by the Treasury under this section shall be guilty of an offence and liable–

(a) on conviction on indictment, to a fine;

(b) on summary conviction, to a fine not exceeding the statutory maximum.

**185(6) [Persons who may sue]** Any such contravention shall be actionable at the suit of a person who suffers loss as a result of the contravention subject to the defences and other incidents applying to actions for breach of statutory duty, but no such contravention shall invalidate any transaction.

**185(7)** (Repealed by the Banking Act 1987, s. 108(2) and Sch. 7, Pt. I as from 1 October 1987.)

**History**
In regard to the date of the above repeal, see SI 1987/1664 (C 50), art. 2 and Sch.; s. 185(7) formerly read as follows:
"At the end of subsection (1) of section 8 of the Banking Act 1979 (power to give directions in connection with termination of deposit-taking authority) there shall be inserted–
"(d) at any time after a disqualification notice has been served on the institution by the Treasury under section 183 of the Financial Services Act 1986."."

## 186 Variation and revocation of notices

**186(1) [Power to vary restriction notice]** The Secretary of State or the Treasury may vary a partial restriction notice served under section 183 above by a notice in writing served on the person concerned; and any such notice shall come into force on such date as is specified in the notice.

**186(2) [Revocation of s. 183 notice]** A notice under section 183 above may be revoked at any time by the Secretary of State or, as the case may be, the Treasury by serving a revocation notice on the person concerned; and the Secretary of State or, as the case may be, the Treasury shall revoke a notice if it appears to them that there are no longer any such grounds as are mentioned in subsection (1) of that section in the case of the country concerned.

**186(3) [Effect of revocation of disqualification notice re investment, insurance business]** The revocation of a disqualification notice as respects investment business or insurance business shall not have the effect of reviving the authorisation which was cancelled by the notice except where the notice relates to investment business and the person concerned would (apart from the disqualification notice) at the time of the revocation be an authorised person as respects the investment business in question by virtue of his membership of a recognised self-regulating organisation or certification by a recognised professional body.

**186(4) [Effect of revocation of disqualification notice re banking business]** The revocation of a disqualification notice as respects banking business shall not have the effect of reviving the authorisation which was cancelled by the notice.

**History**
In s. 186(4) the word, "authorisation", substituted for the former words, "recognition or licence", by Banking Act 1987, s. 108(1) and Sch. 6, para. 27(5)(a) as from 1 October 1987 (see SI 1987/1664 (C 50)).

**186(5) [Limit on effect of s. 186(3), (4)]** Nothing in subsection (3) or (4) above shall be construed as preventing any person who has been subject to a disqualification notice as respects any business from again becoming authorised after the revocation of the notice.

**History**
In s. 186(5) the words, "or, as the case may be, becoming a recognised bank or licensed institution within the meaning of the Banking Act 1979", formerly appearing after the words, "from again becoming authorised", omitted and repealed by Banking Act 1987, s. 108(1) and Sch. 6, para. 27(5)(b) and s. 108(2) and Sch. 7, Pt. I as from 1 October 1987 (SI 1988/1664 (C 50), art. 2 and Sch.).

**186(6) [If person served notice is authorised designated agency, recognised body]** If it appears to the Secretary of State that a person on whom he serves a notice under this section as respects investment business was an authorised person by virtue of an authorisation granted by a designated agency or by virtue of membership of a recognised self-regulating organisation or certification by a recognised professional body at the time that the notice which is being varied or revoked was served, he shall serve a copy of the notice on that agency, organisation or body.

**186(7) [Copy of notice to Bank of England]** The Treasury shall serve on the Financial Services Authority a copy of any notice served by them under this section which varies or revokes a notice relating to the carrying on of a deposit-taking business as mentioned in section 185 above.

**History**
In s. 186(7) the words "Financial Services Authority" substituted for the former words "Bank of England" by the Bank of England Act 1998, s. 23(1), 45 and Sch. 5, para. 39 as from 1 June 1998 (see SI 1998/1120 (C 25), art. 2).
Previously in s. 186(7) the words from "which varies or revokes" to the end inserted by the Transfer of Functions (Financial Services) Order 1992 (SI 1992/1315), art. 10(1) and Sch. 4, para. 6 as from 7 June 1992.

# PART X – MISCELLANEOUS AND SUPPLEMENTARY

## 187 Exemption from liability for damages

**187(1) [Limit on liability re SROs and members]** Neither a recognised self-regulating organisation nor any of its officers or servants or members of its governing body shall be liable in damages for anything done or omitted in the discharge or purported discharge of any functions to which this subsection applies unless the act or omission is shown to have been in bad faith.

**187(2) [Functions for s. 187(1)]** The functions to which subsection (1) above applies are the functions of the organisation so far as relating to, or to matters arising out of–

(a) the rules, practices, powers and arrangements of the organisation to which the requirements in paragraphs 1 to 6 of Schedule 2 to this Act apply;

(b) the obligations with which paragraph 7 of that Schedule requires the organisation to comply;

(c) any guidance issued by the organisation;

(d) the powers of the organisation under section 53(2), 64(4), 72(5), 73(5) or 105(2)(a) above; or

(e) the obligations to which the organisation is subject by virtue of this Act.

**187(3) [Limit on liability of designated agency and members et al.]** No designated agency or transferee body nor any member, officer or servant of a designated agency or transferee body shall be liable in damages for anything done or omitted in the discharge or purported discharge of the functions exercisable by the agency by virtue of a delegation order or, as the case may be, the functions exercisable by the body by virtue of a transfer order unless the act or omission is shown to have been in bad faith.

**187(4) [Limit on liability of competent authority and members et al.]** Neither the competent authority nor any member, officer, or servant of that authority shall be liable in damages for anything done or omitted in the discharge or purported discharge of any functions of the authority under Part IV of this Act unless the act or omission is shown to have been in bad faith.

**187(5) [Functions included in s. 187(1), (3)]** The functions to which subsections (1) and (3) above apply also include any functions exercisable by a recognised self-regulating organisation, designated agency or transferee body on behalf of another body by virtue of arrangements made pursuant to paragraph 4(2) of Schedule 2, paragraph 4(6) of Schedule 3, paragraph 3(2) of Schedule 4 or paragraph 3(2) of Schedule 7 to this Act or of such arrangements as are mentioned in section 39(4)(b) above.

**187(6) [Condition in certificate by recognised professional body]** A recognised professional body may make it a condition of any certificate issued by it for the purposes of Part I of this Act that neither the body nor any of its officers or servants or members of its governing body is to be liable in damages for anything done or omitted in the discharge or purported discharge of any functions to which this subsection applies unless the act or omission is shown to have been in bad faith.

**187(7) [Functions for s. 187(6)]** The functions to which subsection (6) above applies are the functions of the body so far as relating to, or to matters arising out of–

(a) the rules, practices and arrangements of the body to which the requirements in paragraphs 2 to 5 of Schedule 3 to this Act apply;

(b) the obligations with which paragraph 6 of that Schedule requires the body to comply;

(c) any guidance issued by the body in respect of any matters dealt with by such rules as are mentioned in paragraph (a) above;

(d) the powers of the body under the provisions mentioned in subsection (2)(d) above or under section 54(3) above; or

(e) the obligations to which the body is subject by virtue of this Act.

## 188 Jurisdiction of High Court and Court of Session

**188(1) [Proceedings in High Court, Court of Session]** Proceedings arising out of any act or omission (or proposed act or omission) of–

(a) a recognised self-regulating organisation,

(b) a designated agency,

(c) a transferee body, or

(d) the competent authority,

in the discharge or purported discharge of any of its functions under this Act may be brought in the High Court or the Court of Session.

**188(2) [S. 188(1) jurisdiction additional]** The jurisdiction conferred by subsection (1) is in addition to any other jurisdiction exercisable by those courts.

**History**

S. 188 substituted by CA 1989, s. 200(1) as from 15 March 1990 (see SI 1990/354 (C 12), art. 3); s. 188 formerly read as follows:

"**188 Jurisdiction as respects actions concerning designated agency etc.**

**188(1)** Proceedings arising out of any act or omission (or proposed act or omission) of a designated agency, transferee body or the competent authority in the discharge or purported discharge of any of its functions under this Act may be brought in the High Court or the Court of Session.

**(2)** At the end of Schedule 5 to the Civil Jurisdiction and Judgments Act 1982 (exclusion of certain proceedings from the provisions of Schedule 4 to that Act which determine whether the courts in each part of the United Kingdom have jurisdiction in proceedings) there shall be inserted–

"*Proceedings concerning financial services agencies*

**10** Such proceedings as are mentioned in section 188 of the Financial Services Act 1986."."

## 189 Restriction of Rehabilitation of Offenders Act 1974

**189(1) [Effect of 1974 Act]** The Rehabilitation of Offenders Act 1974 shall have effect subject to the provisions of this section in cases where the spent conviction is for–

(a) an offence involving fraud or other dishonesty; or

(b) an offence under legislation (whether or not of the United Kingdom) relating to companies, building societies, industrial and provident societies, credit unions, friendly societies, insurance, banking or other financial services, insolvency, consumer credit or consumer protection or insider dealing.

**History**

In s. 189(1)(b) the words "(including insider dealing)", formerly appearing after the word "companies", omitted and repealed, and the words "or insider dealing" inserted by Criminal Justice Act 1993, s. 79(3), (14) and Sch. 5, para. 11, Sch. 6, Pt. 1 as from 1 March 1994 (see SI 1994/242 (C 7), art. 2 and Sch.).

**189(2) [Limit to s. 4(1) of 1974 Act]** Nothing in section 4(1) (restriction on evidence as to spent convictions in proceedings) shall prevent the determination in any proceedings specified in Part I of Schedule 14 to this Act of any issue, or prevent the admission or requirement in any such proceedings of any evidence, relating to a person's previous convictions for any such offence as is mentioned in subsection (1) above or to circumstances ancillary thereto.

**189(3) [Qualification re s. 4(2) of 1974 Act]** A conviction for any such offence as is mentioned in subsection (1) above shall not be regarded as spent for the purposes of section 4(2) (questions relating to an individual's previous convictions) if–

(a) the question is put by or on behalf of a person specified in the first column of Part II of that Schedule and relates to an individual (whether or not the person questioned) specified in relation to the person putting the question in the second column of that Part; and

(b) the person questioned is informed when the question is put that by virtue of this section convictions for any such offence are to be disclosed.

**189(4) [Limit on s. 4(3)(b) of 1974 Act]** Section 4(3)(b) (spent conviction not to be ground for excluding person from office, occupation etc.) shall not prevent a person specified in the first column of Part III of that Schedule from taking such action as is specified in relation to that person in the second column of that Part by reason, or partly by reason, of a spent conviction for any such offence as is mentioned in subsection (1) above of an individual who is–

(a) the person in respect of whom the action is taken;

(b) as respects action within paragraph 1 or 4 of that Part, an associate of that person; or

(c) as respects action within paragraph 1 of that Part consisting of a decision to refuse or revoke an order declaring a collective investment scheme to be an authorised unit trust scheme or a recognised scheme, the operator or trustee of the scheme or an associate of his, or of any circumstances ancillary to such a conviction or of a failure (whether or not by that individual) to disclose such a conviction or any such circumstances.

**189(5) [Sch. 14]** Parts I, II and III of that Schedule shall have effect subject to Part IV.

**189(6) ["Associate"]** In this section and that Schedule **"associate"** means–

(a) in relation to a body corporate, a director, manager or controller;

(b) in relation to a partnership, a partner or manager;

(c) in relation to a registered friendly society, a trustee, manager or member of the committee of the society;

(d) in relation to an unincorporated association, a member of its governing body or an officer, manager or controller;

(e) in relation to an individual, a manager.

**189(7) [Application to Northern Ireland]** This section and that Schedule shall apply to Northern Ireland with the substitution for the references to the said Act of 1974 and section 4(1), (2) and (3)(b) of that Act of references to the Rehabilitation of Offenders (Northern Ireland) Order 1978 and Articles 5(1), (2) and (3)(b) of that Order.

## 190 Data protection

**190** An order under section 30 of the Data Protection Act 1984 (exemption from subject access provisions of data held for the purpose of discharging designated functions conferred by or under enactments relating to the regulation of financial services etc.) may designate for the purposes of that section as if they were functions conferred by or under such an enactment as is there mentioned–

(a) any functions of a recognised self-regulating organisation in connection with the admission or expulsion of members, the suspension of a person's membership or the supervision or regulation of persons carrying on investment business by virtue of membership of the organisation;

(b) any functions of a recognised professional body in connection with the issue of certificates for the purposes of Part I of this Act, the withdrawal or suspension of such certificates or the supervision or regulation of persons carrying on investment business by virtue of certification by that body;

(c) any functions of a recognised self-regulating organisation for friendly societies in connection with the supervision or regulation of its member societies.

## 191 Occupational pension schemes

**191(1) [Person carrying on investment business]** Subject to the provisions of this section, a person who apart from this section would not be regarded as carrying on investment business shall be treated as doing so if he engages in the activity of management falling within paragraph 14 of Schedule 1 to this Act in a case where the assets referred to in that paragraph are held for the purposes of an occupational pension scheme.

**191(2) [Non-application of s. 191(1)]** Subsection (1) above does not apply where all decisions, or all day to day decisions, in the carrying on of that activity so far as relating to assets which are investments are taken on behalf of the person concerned by–

(a) an authorised person;

(b) an exempted person who in doing so is acting in the course of the business in respect of which he is exempt; or

(c) a person who does not require authorisation to manage the assets by virtue of Part IV of Schedule 1 to this Act.

**191(3) [Order by Secretary of State]** The Secretary of State may by order direct that a person of such description as is specified in the order shall not by virtue of this section be treated as carrying on investment business where the assets are held for the purposes of an occupational pension scheme of such description as is so specified, being a scheme in the case of which it appears to the Secretary of State that management by an authorised or exempted person is unnecessary having regard to the size of the scheme and the control exercisable over its affairs by the members.

**191(4) [Annulment of Order by Parliament]** An order under subsection (3) above shall be subject to annulment in pursuance of a resolution of either House of Parliament.

**191(5) [Sch. 1, para. 14]** For the purposes of subsection (1) above paragraph 14 of Schedule 1 to this Act shall be construed without reference to paragraph 22 of that Schedule.

**Note**

Concerning effect of s. 191 re European investment firms, see the Investment Services Regulations 1995 (SI 1995/3275), reg. 32 and Sch. 7, para. 39.

Concerning European institutions, see the Banking Coordination (Second Council Directive) Regulations 1992 (SI 1992/3218), reg. 55 and Sch. 9, para. 42.

## 192 International obligations

**192(1) [Power of direction by Secretary of State]** If it appears to the Secretary of State–

(a) that any action proposed to be taken by an authority or body to which this section applies would be incompatible with Community obligations or any other international obligations of the United Kingdom, or

(b) that any action which that authority or body has power to take is required for the purpose of implementing any such obligation,

he may direct the authority or body not to take or, as the case may be, to take the action in question.

**192(2) [Applicable authorities and bodies]** The authorities and bodies to which this section applies are the following–

(a) a recognised self-regulating organisation,

(b) a recognised investment exchange (other than an overseas investment exchange),

(c) a recognised clearing house (other than an overseas clearing house),

(d) a designated agency,

(e) a transferee body,

(f) a competent authority.

**192(3)** (Repealed by the Public Offers of Securities Regulations 1995 (SI 1995/1537), reg. 1, 17 and Sch. 2, para. 5(d) as from 19 June 1995.)

**History**

S. 192(3) formerly read as follows:

"This section also applies to an approved exchange within the meaning of Part V of this Act in respect of any action which it proposes to take or has power to take in respect of rules applying to a prospectus by virtue of a direction under section 162(3) above."

**192(4) [Supplementary or incidental requirements]** A direction under this section may include such supplementary or incidental requirements as the Secretary of State thinks necessary or expedient.

**192(5) [Where designated agency relevant]** Where the function of making or revoking a recognition order in respect of an authority or body to which this section applies is exercisable by a designated agency, any direction in respect of that authority or body shall be a direction requiring the agency to give the authority or body such a direction as is specified in the direction given by the Secretary of State.

**192(6) [Enforcement of direction]** A direction under this section is enforceable, on the application of the person who gave it, by injunction or, in Scotland, by an order under section 45 of the Court of Session Act 1988.

**History**

S. 192 substituted by CA 1989, s. 201 as from 25 April 1991 (see SI 1991/878 (C 21), art. 2 and Sch.); s. 192 formerly read as follows:

"**192(1)** If it appears to the Secretary of State–

(a) that any action proposed to be taken by a recognised self-regulating organisation, designated agency, transferee body or competent authority would be incompatible with Community obligations or any other international obligations of the United Kingdom; or

(b) that any action which that organisation, agency, body or authority has power to take is required for the purpose of implementing any such obligations,

he may direct the organisation, agency, body or authority not to take or, as the case may be, to take the action in question.

**(2)** Subsection (1) above applies also to an approved exchange within the meaning of Part V of this Act in respect of any action which it proposes to take or has power to take in respect of rules applying to a prospectus by virtue of a direction under section 162(3) above.

**(3)** A direction under this section may include such supplementary or incidental requirements as the Secretary of State thinks necessary or expedient.

**(4)** Where the function of making or revoking a recognition order in respect of a self-regulating organisation is exercisable by a designated agency any direction under subsection (1) above in respect of that organisation shall be a direction requiring the agency to give the organisation such a direction as is specified in the direction given by the Secretary of State.

**(5)** Any direction under this section shall, on the application of the person by whom it was given, be enforceable by mandamus or, in Scotland, by an order for specific performance under section 91 of the Court of Session Act 1868."

# 193 Exemption from Banking Act 1979

**193** (Repealed by Banking Act 1987, s. 108(2) and Sch. 7, Pt. I as from 29 April 1988.)

**History**

In regard to the date of the above repeal, see SI 1988/644 (C 20), art. 2; s. 193 formerly read as follows:

"**193(1)** Section 1(1) of the Banking Act 1979 (control of deposit-taking) shall not apply to the acceptance of a deposit by an authorised or exempted person in the course or for the purpose of engaging in any activity falling within paragraph 12 of Schedule 1 to this Act with or on behalf of the person by whom or on whose behalf the deposit is made or any activity falling within paragraph 13, 14 or 16 of that Schedule on behalf of that person.

**(2)** Subsection (1) above applies to an exempted person only if the activity is one in respect of which he is exempt; and for the purposes of that subsection the paragraphs of Schedule 1 there mentioned shall be construed without reference to Parts III and IV of that Schedule.

**(3)** This section is without prejudice to any exemption from the said Act of 1979 which applies to an authorised or exempted person apart from this section."

# 194 Transfers to or from recognised clearing houses

**194(1) [Amendments in s. 5 of Stock Exchange (Completion of Bargains) Act 1976]** In section 5 of the Stock Exchange (Completion of Bargains) Act 1976 (protection of trustees etc. in case of transfer of shares etc. to or from a stock exchange nominee)–

(a) for the words "a stock exchange nominee", in the first place where they occur, there shall be substituted the words "a recognised clearing house or a nominee of a recognised clearing house or of a recognised investment exchange";

(b) for those words in the second place where they occur there shall be substituted the words "such a clearing house or nominee";

(c) at the end there shall be added the words "; but no person shall be a nominee for the purposes of this section unless he is a person designated for the purposes of this section in the rules of the recognised investment exchange in question."

**194(2) [Insertion of s. 5(2) of 1976 Act]** The provisions of that section as amended by subsection (1) above shall become subsection (1) of that section and after that subsection there shall be inserted–

> "**5(2)** In this section **"a recognised clearing house"** means a recognised clearing house within the meaning of the Financial Services Act 1986 acting in relation to a recognised investment exchange within the meaning of that Act and **"a recognised investment exchange"** has the same meaning as in that Act."

**194(3) [Amendments in art. 7 of Stock Exchange (Completion of Bargains) (Northern Ireland) Order 1977]** In Article 7 of the Stock Exchange (Completion of Bargains) (Northern Ireland) Order 1977 (protection of trustees etc. in case of transfer of shares etc. to or from a stock exchange nominee)–

(a) for the words "a stock exchange nominee", in the first place where they occur, there shall be substituted the words "a recognised clearing house or a nominee of a recognised clearing house or of a recognised investment exchange";

(b) for those words in the second place where they occur there shall be substituted the words "such a clearing house or nominee";

(c) at the end there shall be added the words "; but no person shall be a nominee for the purposes of this Article unless he is a person designated for the purposes of this Article in the rules of the recognised investment exchange in question".

**194(4) [Insertion of art. 7(2) of 1977 Order]** The provisions of that Article as amended by subsection (3) above shall become paragraph (1) of that Article and after that paragraph there shall be inserted–

"**7(2)** In this Article **"a recognised clearing house"** means a recognised clearing house within the meaning of the Financial Services Act 1986 acting in relation to a recognised investment exchange within the meaning of that Act and "a recognised investment exchange" has the same meaning as in that Act."

**194(5) [Amendments in s. 185(4) of Companies Act 1985]** In subsection (4) of section 185 of the Companies Act 1985 (exemption from duty to issue certificates in respect of shares etc. in cases of allotment or transfer to a stock exchange nominee)–

(a) for the words "stock exchange nominee" in the first place where they occur there shall be substituted the words "a recognised clearing house or a nominee of a recognised clearing house or of a recognised investment exchange";

(b) for those words in the second place where they occur there shall be substituted the words "such a clearing house or nominee";

(c) at the end of the first paragraph in that subsection there shall be inserted the words "; but no person shall be a nominee for the purposes of this section unless he is a person designated for the purposes of this section in the rules of the recognised investment exchange in question"; and

(d) for the second paragraph in that subsection there shall be substituted–

""**Recognised clearing house"** means a recognised clearing house within the meaning of the Financial Services Act 1986 acting in relation to a recognised investment exchange and "recognised investment exchange" has the same meaning as in that Act".

**194(6) [Amendments in art. 195(4) of Companies (Northern Ireland) Order 1986]** In paragraph (4) of Article 195 of the Companies (Northern Ireland) Order 1986 (duty to issue certificates in respect of shares etc. in cases of allotment or transfer unless it is to a stock exchange nominee)–

(a) for the words "a stock exchange nominee" in the first place where they occur there shall be substituted the words "a recognised clearing house or a nominee of a recognised clearing house or of a recognised investment exchange";

(b) for those words in the second place where they occur there shall be substituted the words "such a clearing house or nominee";

(c) at the end of the first sub-paragraph in that paragraph there shall be inserted the words "; but no person shall be a nominee for the purposes of this Article unless he is a person designated for the purposes of this Article in the rules of the recognised investment exchange in question"; and

(d) for the second sub-paragraph in that paragraph there shall be substituted–

""**recognised clearing house"** means a recognised clearing house within the meaning of the Financial Services Act 1986 acting in relation to a recognised investment exchange and "recognised investment exchange" has the same meaning as in that Act.".

## 195 Offers of short-dated debentures

**195** As respects debentures which, under the terms of issue, must be repaid within five years of the date of issue–

(a) section 79(2) of the Companies Act 1985 (offer of debentures of oversea company deemed not to be an offer to the public if made to professional investor) shall apply for the purposes of Chapter I of Part III of that Act as well as for those of Chapter II of that Part; and

(b) Article 89(2) of the Companies (Northern Ireland) Order 1986 (corresponding provisions for Northern Ireland) shall apply for the purposes of Chapter I of Part IV of that Order as well as for those of Chapter II of that Part.

**History**
In s. 195 the words "repaid within five years of the date of issue" substituted for the former words "repaid within less than one year of the date of issue" by CA 1989, s. 202 as from 16 November 1989 (see CA 1989, s. 215(1)(c)).

# 196 Financial assistance for employees' share schemes

**196(1) [Amendment of s. 153 of Companies Act 1985]** Section 153 of the Companies Act 1985 (transactions not prohibited by section 151) shall be amended as follows.

**196(2) [Insertion of s. 153(4)(bb) of 1985 Act]** After subsection (4)(b) there shall be inserted–

"(bb) without prejudice to paragraph (b), the provision of financial assistance by a company or any of its subsidiaries for the purposes of or in connection with anything done by the company (or a company connected with it) for the purpose of enabling or facilitating transactions in shares in the first-mentioned company between, and involving the acquisition of beneficial ownership of those shares by, any of the following persons–

(i) the bona fide employees or former employees of that company or of another company in the same group; or

(ii) the wives, husbands, widows, widowers, children or step-children under the age of eighteen of any such employees or former employees."

**196(3)** (Repealed by Companies Act 1989, s. 212 and Sch. 24 as from 1 October 1991.)

**History**
In regard to the date of the above repeal see SI 1991/1996 (C 57), art. 2(1)(c)(iii); s. 196(3) formerly read as follows:

"After subsection (4) there shall be inserted–

"**153(5)** For the purposes of subsection (4)(bb) a company is connected with another company if–

(a) they are in the same group; or

(b) one is entitled, either alone or with any other company in the same group, to exercise or control the exercise of a majority of the voting rights attributable to the share capital which are exercisable in all circumstances at any general meeting of the other company or of its holding company;

and in this section **"group"**, in relation to a company, means that company, any other company which is its holding company or subsidiary and any other company which is a subsidiary of that holding company."."

**196(4) [Amendment of art. 163 of Companies (Northern Ireland) Order 1986]** Article 163 of the Companies (Northern Ireland) Order 1986 (transactions not prohibited by Article 161) shall be amended as follows.

**196(5) [Insertion of art. 163(4)(bb) of 1986 Order]** After paragraph (4)(b) there shall be inserted–

"(bb) without prejudice to sub-paragraph (b), the provision of financial assistance by a company or any of its subsidiaries for the purposes of or in connection with anything done by the company (or a company connected with it) for the purpose of enabling or facilitating transactions in shares in the first-mentioned company between, and involving the acquisition of beneficial ownership of those shares by, any of the following persons–

(i) the bona fide employees or former employees of that company or of another company in the same group; or

(ii) the wives, husbands, widows, widowers, children, step-children or adopted children under the age of eighteen of such employees of former employees."

**196(6)** (Repealed by Companies (No. 2) (Northern Ireland) Order 1990 (SI 1990/1504 (NI 10)), art. 113 and Sch. 6 as from 29 March 1993.)

**History**
In regard to the date of the above repeal see Companies (1990 No. 2 Order) (Commencement No. 6) Order (Northern Ireland) 1993 (SR 1993/64 (C 5)), art. 2(c)(ii); s. 196(6) formerly read as follows:

"After paragraph (4) there shall be inserted–

"**163(5)** For the purposes of paragraph (4)(bb) a company is connected with another company if–

(a) they are in the same group; or

(b) one is entitled, either alone or with any other company in the same group, to exercise or control the exercise of a majority of the voting rights attributable to the share capital which are exerciseable in all circumstances at any general meeting of the other company or of its holding company;

and in this Article **"group"**, in relation to a company, means that company, any other company which is its holding company or subsidiary and any other company which is a subsidiary of that holding company."."

# 197 Disclosure of interests in shares: interest held by market maker

**197(1) [Insertions in s. 209 of Companies Act 1985]** In section 209 of the Companies Act 1985 (interests to be disregarded for purposes of sections 198 to 202)–

(a) in subsection (1)(f) after the word "jobber" there shall be inserted the words "or market maker";

(b) after subsection (4) there shall be inserted–

"**209(4A)** A person is a market maker for the purposes of subsection (1)(f) if–

(a) he holds himself out at all normal times in compliance with the rules of a recognised investment exchange other than an overseas investment exchange (within the meaning of the Financial Services Act 1986) as willing to buy and sell securities at prices specified by him; and

(b) is recognised as doing so by that investment exchange;

and an interest of such a person in shares is an exempt interest if he carries on business as a market maker in the United Kingdom, is subject to such rules in the carrying on of that business and holds the interest for the purposes of that business.".

**197(2) [Insertions in art. 217 of Companies (Northern Ireland) Order 1986]** In Article 217 of the Companies (Northern Ireland) Order 1986 (interests to be disregarded for purposes of Articles 206 to 210 (disclosure of interests in shares))–

(a) in paragraph (1)(d) after the word "jobber" there shall be inserted the words "or market maker";

(b) after paragraph (4) there shall be inserted–

"**217(4A)** A person is a market maker for the purposes of paragraph (1)(d) if–

(a) he holds himself out at all normal times in compliance with the rules of a recognised investment exchange other than an overseas investment exchange (within the meaning of the Financial Services Act 1986) as willing to buy and sell securities at prices specified by him; and

(b) is recognised as doing so by that investment exchange,

and an interest of such a person in shares is an exempt interest if he carries on business as a market maker in the United Kingdom, is subject to such rules in the carrying on of that business and holds the interest for the purposes of that business.".

## 198 Power to petition for winding up etc. on information obtained under Act

**198(1)** (Repealed by Companies Act 1989, s. 212 and Sch. 24 as from 21 February 1990.)

**History**

In regard to the date of the above repeal see SI 1990/142 (C 5), art. 7(d); s. 198(1) formerly read as follows:

"In section 440 of the Companies Act 1985–

(a) after the words "section 437" there shall be inserted the words "above or section 94 of the Financial Services Act 1986"; and

(b) after the words "448 below" there shall be inserted the words "or section 105 of that Act"."

**198(2) [Amendments to s. 8 of Company Directors Disqualification Act 1986]** In section 8 of the Company Directors Disqualification Act 1986–

(a) after the words "the Companies Act" there shall be inserted the words "or section 94 or 177 of the Financial Services Act 1986"; and

(b) for the words "that Act" there shall be substituted the words "the Companies Act or section 105 of the Financial Services Act 1986".

**198(3)** (Repealed by Companies (No. 2) (Northern Ireland) Order 1990 (SI 1990/1504 (NI 10)), art. 113 and Sch. 6 as from 1 October 1991.)

**History**

In regard to the date of the above repeal see Companies (1990 No. 2 Order) (Commencement No. 5) Order (Northern Ireland) 1991 (SR 1991/438 (C 22)), art. 5(b); s. 198(3) formerly read as follows:

"In Article 433 of the Companies (Northern Ireland) Order 1986–

(a) after the words "Article 430" there shall be inserted the words "or section 94 of the Financial Services Act 1986"; and

(b) after the word "441" there shall be inserted the words "or section 105 of that Act"."

## 199 Powers of entry

**199(1) [Power of JP to issue warrant]** A justice of the peace may issue a warrant under this section if satisfied on information on oath given by or on behalf of the Secretary of State that there are reasonable grounds for believing that an offence has been committed–

(a) under section 4, 47, 57, 130 or 133 above, or

(b) under Part V of the Criminal Justice Act 1993 (insider dealing),

and that there are on any premises documents relevant to the question whether that offence has been committed.

**History**

In s. 199(1) para. (a) the words "or 133 above" substituted for "133 or 171(2) or (3)" by the Public Offers of Securities Regulations 1995 (SI 1995/1537), reg. 1, 17 and Sch. 2, para. 7 as from 19 June 1995; and para. (b) substituted by Criminal Justice Act 1993, s. 79(3) and Sch. 5, para. 12(1) as from 1 March 1994 (see SI 1994/242 (C 7), art. 2 and Sch.); para. (b) formerly read as follows:

"(b) section 1, 2, 4 or 5 of the Company Securities (Insider Dealing) Act 1985,".

See also history note after s. 199(2).

**199(2) [Further powers of JP]** A justice of the peace may also issue a warrant under this section if satisfied on information on oath given by or on behalf of the Secretary of State, or by a person appointed or authorised to exercise powers under section 94, 106 or 177 above, that there are reasonable grounds for believing that there are on any premises documents whose production has been required under section 94, 105 or 177 above and which have not been produced in compliance with the requirement.

**History**

S. 199(1), (2) substituted by CA 1989, s. 76(1), (2) as from 21 February 1990 (see SI 1990/142 (C 5), art. 4); s. 199(1), (2) formerly read as follows:

"**199(1)** A justice of the peace may issue a warrant under this section if satisfied on information on oath laid by or on behalf of the Secretary of State that there are reasonable grounds for believing–

(a) that an offence has been committed under section 4, 47, 57, 130, 133 or 171(2) or (3) above or section 1, 2, 4 or 5 of the Company Securities (Insider Dealing) Act 1985 and that there are on any premises documents relevant to the question whether that offence has been committed; or

(b) that there are on any premises owned or occupied by a person whose affairs, or any aspect of whose affairs, are being investigated under section 105 above documents whose production has been required under that section and which have not been produced in compliance with that requirement;

but paragraph (b) above applies only if the person there mentioned is an authorised person, a person whose authorisation has been suspended or who is the subject of a direction under section 33(1)(b) above or an appointed representative of an authorised person.

**(2)** A justice of the peace may issue a warrant under this section if satisfied on information on oath laid by an inspector appointed under section 94 above that there are reasonable grounds for believing that there are on any premises owned or occupied by–

(a) the manager, trustee or operator of any scheme the affairs of which are being investigated under subsection (1) of that section; or

(b) a manager, trustee or operator whose affairs are being investigated under that subsection,

any documents whose production has been required under that section and which have not been produced in compliance with that requirement."

**199(3) [Scope of warrant]** A warrant under this section shall authorise a constable, together with any other person named in it and any other constables–

(a) to enter the premises specified in the information, using such force as is reasonably necessary for the purpose;

(b) to search the premises and take possession of any documents appearing to be such documents as are mentioned in subsection (1) or, as the case may be, in subsection (2) above or to take, in relation to any such documents, any other steps which may appear to be necessary for preserving them or preventing interference with them;

(c) to take copies of any such documents; and

(d) to require any person named in the warrant to provide an explanation of them or to state where they may be found.

**History**

In s. 199(3)(b) the words "subsection (1)" substituted for the former words "subsection 1(a) or (b)" by CA 1989, s. 76(1), (3) as from 21 February 1990 (see SI 1990/142 (C 5), art. 4).

**199(4) [Duration of warrant]** A warrant under this section shall continue in force until the end of the period of one month beginning with the day on which it is issued.

**199(5) [Period for retention of documents]** Any documents of which possession is taken under this section may be retained–

(a) for a period of three months; or

(b) if within that period proceedings to which the documents are relevant are commenced against any person for any criminal offence, until the conclusion of those proceedings.

**History**

S. 199(5)(b) substituted by CA 1989, s. 76(1), (4) as from 21 February 1990 (see SI 1990/142 (C 5), art. 4); s. 199(5)(b) formerly read as follows:

"(b) if within that period proceedings to which the documents are relevant are commenced against any person for an offence under this Act or section 1, 2, 4 or 5 of the said Act of 1985, until the conclusion of those proceedings."

**199(6) [Offence, penalty]** Any person who intentionally obstructs the exercise of any rights conferred by a warrant issued under this section or fails without reasonable excuse to comply with any requirement imposed in accordance with subsection (3)(d) above shall be guilty of an offence and liable–

(a) on conviction on indictment, to a fine;

(b) on summary conviction, to a fine not exceeding the statutory maximum.

**History**

In s. 199(6) the word "intentionally" inserted by CA 1989, s. 76(1), (5) as from 21 February 1990 (see SI 1990/142 (C 5), art. 4).

**199(7) [Functions relevant for s. 114]** The functions to which section 114 above applies shall include the functions of the Secretary of State under this section; but if any of those functions are transferred under that section the transfer may be subject to a reservation that they are to be exercisable by the Secretary of State concurrently with the designated agency and, in the case of functions exercisable by virtue of subsection (1) above, so as to be exercisable by the agency subject to such conditions or restrictions as the Treasury may from time to time impose.

**History**

In s. 199(7) the words "subsection (1) above" substituted for the former words "subsection (1)(a) above" by CA 1989, s. 76(1), (6) as from 21 February 1990 (see SI 1990/142 (C 5), art. 4); and the word "Treasury" substituted for the former words "Secretary of State" by the Transfer of Functions (Financial Services) Order 1992 (SI 1992/1315), art. 10(1) and Sch. 4, para. 3 as from 7 June 1992.

**199(8) [Scotland]** In the application of this section to Scotland for the references to a justice of the peace substitute references to a justice of the peace or a sheriff, and for the references to information on oath substitute references to evidence on oath.

**History**

S. 199(8) substituted by CA 1989, s. 76(1), (7) as from 21 February 1990 (see SI 1990/142 (C 5), art. 4); s. 199(8) formerly read as follows:

"In the application of this section to Scotland the references to a justice of the peace shall include references to a sheriff and for references to the laying of information on oath there shall be substituted references to furnishing evidence on oath; and in the application of this section to Northern Ireland for references to the laying of information on oath there shall be substituted references to making a complaint on oath."

**199(8A) [Northern Ireland]** In the application of this section to Northern Ireland for the references to information on oath substitute references to complaint on oath.

**History**

S. 199(8A) inserted by Criminal Justice Act 1993, s. 79(3) and Sch. 5, para. 12(2) as from 1 March 1994 (see SI 1994/242 (C 7), art. 2 and Sch.).

**199(9) ["Documents"]** In this section **"documents"** includes information recorded in any form.

**History**

In s. 199(9) the words "and, in relation to information recorded otherwise than in legible form, references to its production include references to producing a copy of the information in legible form" formerly appearing at the end omitted by CA 1989, s. 76(1), (8) as from 21 February 1990 (see SI 1990/142 (C 5), art. 4) and repealed by CA 1989, s. 212 and Sch. 24 as from 1 March 1990 (see SI 1990/355 (C 13), art. 5(1)).

**CCH Note**

The above omission and repeal were obviously intended to coincide in SI 1990/142 (C 5), art. 7 purportedly attempting to effect a non-existent repeal in FSA 1986, s. 199(1) as from 21 February 1990; this clearly should have referred to s. 199(9) and the incorrect reference to s. 199(1) was revoked by SI 1990/355 (C 13), art. 16.

**Note**

For application of s. 199 to a listed person see the Financial Markets and Insolvency (Money Market) Regulations 1995 (SI 1995/2049), reg. 1, 6, 18.

## 200 False and misleading statements

**200(1) [Furnishing false information]** A person commits an offence if–

(a) for the purposes of or in connection with any application under this Act; or

(b) in purported compliance with any requirement imposed on him by or under this Act, he furnishes information which he knows to be false or misleading in a material particular or recklessly furnishes information which is false or misleading in a material particular.

**200(2) [False description of person]** A person commits an offence if, not being an authorised person or exempted person, he–

(a) describes himself as such a person; or

(b) so holds himself out as to indicate or be reasonably understood to indicate that he is such a person.

**200(3) [False description of status]** A person commits an offence if, not having a status to which this subsection applies, he–

(a) describes himself as having that status, or

(b) so holds himself out as to indicate or be reasonably understood to indicate that he has that status.

**200(4) [Application of s. 200(3)]** Subsection (3) above applies to the status of recognised self-regulating organisation, recognised professional body, recognised investment exchange or recognised clearing house.

**200(5) [Penalty for s. 200(1) offence]** A person guilty of an offence under subsection (1) above shall be liable–

(a) on conviction on indictment, to imprisonment for a term not exceeding two years or to a fine or to both;

(b) on summary conviction, to imprisonment for a term not exceeding six months or to a fine not exceeding the statutory maximum or to both.

**200(6) [Penalty for s. 200(2), (3) offences]** A person guilty of an offence under subsection (2) or (3) above shall be liable on summary conviction to imprisonment for a term not exceeding six months or to a fine not exceeding the fifth level on the standard scale or to both.

**200(7) [Maximum fine in s. 200(6) if public display]** Where a contravention of subsection (2) or (3) above involves a public display of the offending description or other matter the maximum fine that may be imposed under subsection (6) above shall be an amount equal to the fifth level on the standard scale multiplied by the number of days for which the display has continued.

**200(8) [Defence re s. 200(2), (3) offences]** In proceedings brought against any person for an offence under subsection (2) or (3) above it shall be a defence for him to prove that he took all reasonable precautions and exercised all due diligence to avoid the commission of the offence.

## 201 Prosecutions

**201(1) [Proceedings other than under s. 133, 185]** Proceedings in respect of an offence under any provision of this Act other than section 133 or 185 shall not be instituted–

(a) in England and Wales, except by or with the consent of the Secretary of State or the Director of Public Prosecutions; or

(b) in Northern Ireland, except by or with the consent of the Secretary of State or the Director of Public Prosecutions for Northern Ireland.

**201(2) [S. 133 proceedings]** Proceedings in respect of an offence under section 133 above shall not be instituted–

(a) in England and Wales, except by or with the consent of the Secretary of State, the Indusrial Assurance Commissioner or the Director of Public Prosecutions; or

(b) in Northern Ireland, except by or with the consent of the Secretary of State or the Director of Public Prosecutions for Northern Ireland.

**201(3) [S. 185 proceedings]** Proceedings in respect of an offence under section 185 above shall not be instituted–

(a) in England and Wales, except by or with the consent of the Treasury or the Director of Public Prosecutions; or

(b) in Northern Ireland, except by or with the consent of the Treasury or the Director of Public Prosecutions for Northern Ireland.

**201(4)** **[S. 114 functions]** The functions to which section 114 above applies shall include the function of the Secretary of State under subsection (1) above to institute proceedings but any transfer of that function shall be subject to a reservation that it is to be exercisable by him concurrently with the designated agency and so as to be exercisable by the agency subject to such conditions or restrictions as the Treasury may from time to time impose.

**History**

In s. 201(4) the word "Treasury" substituted for the former words "Secretary of State" by the Transfer of Functions (Financial Services) Order 1992 (SI 1992/1315), art. 10(1) and Sch. 4, para. 3 as from 7 June 1992.

## 202 Offences by bodies corporate, partnerships and unincorporated associations

**202(1)** **[Offences by body corporate with connivance of offices]** Where an offence under this Act committed by a body corporate is proved to have been committed with the consent or connivance of, or to be attributable to any neglect on the part of–

(a) any director, manager, secretary or other similar officer of the body corporate, or any person who was purporting to act in any such capacity; or

(b) a controller of the body corporate,

he, as well as the body corporate, shall be guilty of that offence and liable to be proceeded against and punished accordingly.

**202(2)** **[Where affairs of body corporate managed by members]** Where the affairs of a body corporate are managed by the members subsection (1) above shall apply in relation to the acts and defaults of a member in connection with his functions of management as if he were a director of the body corporate.

**202(3)** **[Offence by partnership]** Where a partnership is guilty of an offence under this Act every partner, other than a partner who is proved to have been ignorant of or to have attempted to prevent the commission of the offence, shall also be guilty of that offence and be liable to be proceeded against and punished accordingly.

**202(4)** **[Offence by unincorporated association]** Where an unincorporated association (other than a partnership) is guilty of an offence under this Act–

(a) every officer of the association who is bound to fulfil any duty of which the breach is the offence; or

(b) if there is no such officer, every member of the governing body other than a member who is proved to have been ignorant of or to have attempted to prevent the commission of the offence,

shall also be guilty of the offence and be liable to be proceeded against and punished accordingly.

## 203 Jurisdiction and procedure in respect of offences

**203(1)** **[Summary proceedings re place]** Summary proceedings for an offence under this Act may, without prejudice to any jurisdiction exercisable apart from this section, be taken against any body corporate or unincorporated association at any place at which it has a place of business and against an individual at any place where he is for the time being.

**203(2)** **[Proceedings against unincorporated association]** Proceedings for an offence alleged to have been committed under this Act by an unincorporated association shall be brought in the name of the association (and not in that of any of its members) and for the purposes of any such proceedings any rules of court relating to the service of documents shall have effect as if the association were a corporation.

**203(3)** **[Procedure re unincorporated associations]** Section 33 of the Criminal Justice Act 1925 and Schedule 3 to the Magistrates' Courts Act 1980 (procedure on charge of offence against a corporation) shall have effect in a case in which an unincorporated association is charged in England and Wales with an offence under this Act in like manner as they have effect in the case of a corporation.

**203(4) [Procedure in Scotland re unincorporated associations]** In relation to any proceedings on indictment in Scotland for an offence alleged to have been committed under this Act by an unincorporated association, section 74 of the Criminal Procedure (Scotland) Act 1975 (proceedings on indictment against bodies corporate) shall have effect as if the association were a body corporate.

**203(5) [Procedure in Northern Ireland re unincorporated associations]** Section 18 of the Criminal Justice Act (Northern Ireland) 1945 and Schedule 4 to the Magistrates' Courts (Northern Ireland) Order 1981 (procedure on charge of offence against a corporation) shall have effect in a case in which an unincorporated association is charged in Northern Ireland with an offence under this Act in like manner as they have effect in the case of a corporation.

**203(6) [Fine to be paid by unincorporated association]** A fine imposed on an unincorporated association on its conviction of an offence under this Act shall be paid out of the funds of the association.

## 204 Service of notices

**204(1) [Effect of section]** This section has effect in relation to any notice, direction or other document required or authorised by or under this Act to be given to or served on any person other than the Secretary of State or the Friendly Societies Commission.

**History**
In s. 204(1) the words "or the Friendly Societies Commission" substituted for the former words "the Chief Registrar of Friendly Societies or the Registrar of Friendly Societies for Northern Ireland" by Friendly Societies Act 1992, s. 98 and Sch. 18, para. 6 as from 1 February 1993 in regard to incorporated friendly societies (see SI 1993/16 (C 1), art. 2 and Sch. 4) and as from 1 January 1994 for all remaining purposes (see SI 1993/2213 (C 43), art. 2 and Sch. 5).

**204(2) [Service on person]** Any such document may be given to or served on the person in question–

(a) by delivering it to him;
(b) by leaving it at his proper address; or
(c) by sending it by post to him at that address.

**204(3) [Service on body corporate, partnership, unincorporated association, appointed representative]** Any such document may–

(a) in the case of a body corporate, be given to or served on the secretary or clerk of that body;
(b) in the case of a partnership, be given to or served on any partner;
(c) in the case of an unincorporated association other than a partnership, be given to or served on any member of the governing body of the association;
(d) in the case of an appointed representative, be given to or served on his principal.

**204(4) [Service by post]** For the purposes of this section and section 7 of the Interpretation Act 1978 (service of documents by post) in its application to this section, the proper address of any person is his last known address (whether of his residence or of a place where he carries on business or is employed) and also any address applicable in his case under the following provisions–

(a) in the case of a member of a recognised self-regulating organisation or a person certified by a recognised professional body who does not have a place of business in the United Kingdom, the address of that organisation or body;
(b) in the case of a body corporate, its secretary or its clerk, the address of its registered or principal office in the United Kingdom;
(c) in the case of an unincorporated association (other than a partnership) or a member of its governing body, its principal office in the United Kingdom.

**204(5) [Where new address notified re s. 204(4)]** Where a person has notified the Secretary of State of an address or a new address at which documents may be given to or served on him under this Act that address shall also be his proper address for the purposes mentioned in subsection (4) above or, as the case may be, his proper address for those purposes in substitution for that previously notified.

## 205 General power to make regulations

**205** The Secretary of State or the Treasury may make regulations prescribing anything which by this Act is authorised or required to be prescribed.

**History**
In s. 205 the words "or the Treasury" inserted by the Transfer of Functions (Financial Services) Order 1992 (SI 1992/1315), art. 10(1) and Sch. 4, para. 7 as from 7 June 1992.
See also history note after s. 205A.

**Note**
For transfer of the Secretary of State's functions under s. 205 see SI 1990/354 (C 12), art. 4(5) and SI 1992/1315.

## 205A Supplementary provisions with respect to subordinate legislation

**205A(1) [Application of power of Secretary of State]** Subsections (2) to (4) below apply to any power of the Secretary of State or the Treasury under this Act–

(a) to issue statements of principle,

(b) to make rules or regulations,

(c) to make orders (other than such orders as are expected by subsection (4) below), or

(d) to issue codes of practice.

**History**
In s. 205A(1) the words "The following provisions" formerly appearing at the beginning substituted by the words "Subsections (2) to (4) below" by the Open-Ended Investment Companies (Investment Companies with Variable Capital) Regulations 1996 (SI 1996/2827) reg.1, 75 and Sch. 8, para. 20 as from 6 January 1997. Also in s. 205A(1) the words "or the Treasury" inserted by the Transfer of Functions (Financial Services) Order 1992 (SI 1992/1315), art. 10(1) and Sch. 7, para. 8 as from 7 June 1992.

**205A(1A) [Application of s. 205A(2)-(4)]** Subsections (2) to (4) below apply to any power to make regulations by virtue of regulation 6 of the Open-Ended Investment Companies (Investment Companies with Variable Capital) Regulations 1996 in the event that that power becomes exercisable by the Treasury by virtue of an order under section 115 above.

**History**
S. 205A(1A) inserted by the Open-Ended Investment Companies (Investment Companies with Variable Capital) Regulations 1996 (SI 1996/2827) reg.1, 75 and Sch. 8, para. 20 as from 6 January 1997.

**205A(2) [Power exercisable by statutory instrument]** Any such power is exercisable by statutory instrument and includes power to make different provision for different cases.

**205A(3) [Annulment of statutory instrument]** Except as otherwise provided, a statutory instrument containing statements of principle, rules or regulations shall be subject to annulment in pursuance of a resolution of either House of Parliament.

**205A(4) [Non-application of s. 205A(1)–(3)]** The above provisions do not apply to a recognition order, an order declaring a collective investment scheme to be an authorised unit trust scheme or a recognised scheme or to an order revoking any such order.

**History**
S. 205, 205A substituted for former s. 205 by CA 1989, s. 206(1) and Sch. 23, para. 18 as from 15 March 1990 (see SI 1990/354 (C 12), art. 3); the former s. 205 read as follows:

"**205 Regulations, rules and orders**

**205(1)** The Secretary of State may make regulations prescribing anything which by this Act is authorised or required to be prescribed.

**(2)** Subject to subsection (5) below, any power of the Secretary of State to make regulations, rules or orders under this Act shall be exercisable by statutory instrument.

**(3)** Subject to subsection (5) below, any regulations, rules or orders made under this Act by the Secretary of State may make different provision for different cases.

**(4)** Except as otherwise provided, a statutory instrument containing regulations or rules under this Act shall be subject to annulment in pursuance of a resolution of either House of Parliament.

**(5)** Subsections (2) and (3) above do not apply to a recognition order, an order declaring a collective investment scheme to be an authorised unit trust scheme or a recognised scheme or to an order revoking any such order."

**Note**
See the Financial Services Act 1986 (Investment Advertisements) (Exemptions) Order 1995 (SI 1995/1266); the Financial Services Act 1986 (Investment Advertisements) (Exemptions) (No. 2) Order 1995 (SI 1995/1536); the Financial Services Act 1986 (Investment Services) (Extension of Scope Act) Order 1995 (SI 1995/3271); the Financial Services Act 1986 (Exemption) Order 1996 (SI 1996/1587); the Financial Services Act 1986 (Uncertificated Securities) (Extension of Scope of Act) Order 1996 (SI 1996/1322); the Financial Services Act 1986 (Investment Advertisements) (Exemptions) Order 1996 (SI 1996/1586), the Financial Services Act 1986 (Exemption) Order 1996 (SI 1996/1587), the Financial Services Act 1986 (Extension of Scope of Act) Order 1996 (SI 1996/2958) and the Financial Services Act 1986 (Investment Advertisements) (Exemptions) Order 1997 (SI 1997/963).

## 206 Publication of information and advice

**206(1) [Power of Secretary of State re information etc.]** The Secretary of State may publish information or give advice, or arrange for the publication of information or the giving of advice, in such form and manner as he considers appropriate with respect to–

(a) the operation of this Act and the statements of principle, rules, regulations and codes of practice issued or made under it, including in particular the rights of investors, the duties of authorised persons and the steps to be taken for enforcing those rights or complying with those duties;

(b) any matters relating to the functions of the Secretary of State under this Act or any such statements of principle, rules, regulations or codes of practice;

(bb) the operation of the Open-Ended Investment Companies (Investment Companies with Variable Capital) Regulations 1996 and any regulation made by virtue of regulation 6 of those Regulations;

(bc) any matters relating to the functions to which regulation 73 of those Regulations relates;

(c) any other matters about which it appears to him to be desirable to publish information or give advice for the protection of investors or any class of investors.

**History**

In s. 206(1)(a) the words "statements of principle, rules, regulations and codes of practice issued or made" substituted for the former words "rules and regulations made" and in s. 206(1)(b) the words "statements of principle, rules, regulations or codes of practice" substituted for the former words "rules or regulations" by CA 1989, s. 206(1) and Sch. 23, para. 19(a) and (b) respectively as from 15 March 1990 (see SI 1990/354 (C 12), art. 3).

S. 206(1)(bb), (bc) inserted by the Open-Ended Investment Companies (Investment Companies with Variable Capital) Regulations 1996 (SI 1996/2827) reg.1, 75 and Sch. 8, para. 21 as from 6 January 1997.

**Note**

Concerning effect of s. 206 re European investment firms, see the Investment Services Regulations 1995 (SI 1995/3275), reg. 32 and Sch. 7, para. 40.

Concerning European institutions, see the Banking Coordination (Second Council Directive) Regulations 1992 (SI 1992/3218), reg. 55 and Sch. 9, para. 43.

**206(2) [Sale of copies of information]** The Secretary of State may offer for sale copies of information published under this section and may, if he thinks fit, make a reasonable charge for advice given under this section at any person's request.

**206(3) [S. 179]** This section shall not be construed as authorising the disclosure of restricted information within the meaning of section 179 above in any case in which it could not be disclosed apart from the provisions of this section.

**206(4) [Functions under s. 114]** The functions to which section 114 above applies shall include the functions of the Secretary of State under this section.

## 207 Interpretation

**207(1) [Definitions]** In this Act, except where the context otherwise requires–

**"appointed representative"** has the meaning given in section 44 above;

**"authorised person"** means a person authorised under Chapter III of Part I of this Act;

**"authorised unit trust scheme"** means a unit trust scheme declared by an order of the Secretary of State for the time being in force to be an authorised unit trust scheme for the purposes of this Act;

**"body corporate"** includes a body corporate constituted under the law of a country or territory outside the United Kingdom;

**"certified"** and **"certification"** mean certified or certification by a recognised professional body for the purposes of Part I of this Act;

**"clearing arrangements"** has the meaning given in section 38(2) above;

**"competent authority"** means the competent authority for the purposes of Part IV of this Act;

**"collective investment scheme"** has the meaning given in section 75 above;

**"delegation order"** and **"designated agency"** have the meaning given in section 114(3) above;

**"director"**, in relation to a body corporate, includes a person occupying in relation to it the position of a director (by whatever name called) and any person in accordance with whose directions or instructions (not being advice given in a professional capacity) the directors of that body are accustomed to act;

**"ensure"** and **"ensuring"**, in relation to the performance of transactions on an investment exchange, have the meaning given in paragraph 6 of Schedule 4 to this Act;

**"exempted person"** means a person exempted under Chapter IV of Part I of this Act;

**"friendly society"**, **"incorporated friendly society"** and **"registered friendly society"** have the meaning given by section 116 of the Friendly Societies Act 1992;

**"group"**, in relation to a body corporate, means that body corporate, any other body corporate which is its holding company or subsidiary and any other body corporate which is a subsidiary of that holding company;

**"guidance"**, in relation to a self-regulating organisation, professional body, investment exchange, clearing house or designated agency, has the meaning given in section 8(4), 16(4), 36(3), 38(3) or 114(12) above;

**"investment advertisement"** has the meaning given in section 57(2) above;

**"investment agreement"** has the meaning given in section 44(9) above;

**"investment company with variable capital"** and, in relation to such a company, **"depositary"** have the same meaning as in the Open-Ended Investment Companies (Investment Companies with Variable Capital) Regulations 1996;

**"listing particulars"** has the meaning given in section 144(2A) above;

**"member"**, in relation to a self-regulating organisation or professional body, has the meaning given in section 8(2) or 16(2) above;

**"occupational pension scheme"** means any scheme or arrangement which is comprised in one or more instruments or agreements and which has, or is capable of having, effect in relation to one or more descriptions or categories of employment so as to provide benefits, in the form of pensions or otherwise, payable on termination of service, or on death or retirement, to or in respect of earners with qualifying service in an employment of any such description or category;

**"operator"**, in relation to a collective investment scheme, shall be construed in accordance with section 75(8) above;

**"open-ended investment company"** has the meaning given in section 75(8) above;

**"overseas investment exchange"** and **"overseas clearing house"** mean a recognised investment exchange or recognised clearing house in the case of which the recognition order was made by virtue of section 40 above;

**"participant"** has the meaning given in section 75(2) above;

**"partnership"** includes a partnership constituted under the law of a country or territory outside the United Kingdom;

**"prescribed"** means prescribed by regulations made by the Secretary of State or the Treasury;

**"principal"**, in relation to an appointed representative, has the meaning given in section 44 above;

**"private company"** has the meaning given in section 1(3) of the Companies Act 1985 or the corresponding Northern Ireland provision;

**"recognised clearing house"** means a body declared by an order of the Secretary of State for the time being in force to be a recognised clearing house for the purposes of this Act;

**"recognised investment exchange"** means a body declared by an order of the Secretary of State for the time being in force to be a recognised investment exchange for the purposes of this Act;

**"recognised professional body"** means a body declared by an order of the Secretary of State for the time being in force to be a recognised professional body for the purposes of this Act;

**"recognised scheme"** means a scheme recognised under section 86, 87 or 88 above;

**"recognised self-regulating organisation"** means a body declared by an order of the Secretary of State for the time being in force to be a recognised self-regulating organisation for the purposes of this Act;

**"recognised self-regulating organisation for friendly societies"** has the meaning given in paragraph 1 of Schedule 11 to this Act;

**"recognition order"** means an order declaring a body to be a recognised self-regulating organisation, self-regulating organisation for friendly societies, professional body, investment exchange or clearing house;

**"rules"**, in relation to a self-regulating organisation, professional body, investment exchange or clearing house, has the meaning given in section 8(3), 16(3), 36(2) or 38(2) above;

**"transfer order"** and **"transferee body"** have the meaning given in paragraph 28(4) of Schedule 11 to this Act;

**"the Tribunal"** means the Financial Services Tribunal;

**"trustee"**, in relation to a collective investment scheme, has the meaning given in section 75(8) above;

**"unit trust scheme"** and **"units"** have the meaning given in section 75(8) above.

**History**
In s. 207(1):

- the definitions of "ensure" and "ensuring" inserted by CA 1989, s. 205(3) as from 15 March 1990 (see SI 1990/354 (C 12), art. 3);
- the definition of "friendly society" inserted by Friendly Societies Act 1992, s. 98 and Sch. 18, para. 7 as from 1 February 1993 in regard to incorporated friendly societies (see SI 1993/16 (C 1), art. 2 and Sch. 4) and as from 1 January 1994 for all remaining purposes (see SI 1993/2213 (C 43), art. 2 and Sch. 5);
- the definition of "investment company with variable capital" inserted by the Open-Ended Investment Companies (Investment Companies with Variable Capital) Regulations 1996 (SI 1996/2827) reg.1, 75 and Sch. 8, para. 22 as from 6 January 1997.
- in the definition of "listing particulars", "144(2A)" substituted for "144(2)" by the Public Offers of Securities Regulations 1995 (SI 1995/1537), reg. 1, 17 and Sch. 2, para. 8 as from 8 June 1995;
- in the definition of "prescribed" the words "or the Treasury" inserted by the Transfer of Functions (Financial Services) Order 1992 (SI 1992/1315), art. 10(1) and Sch. 4, para. 9 as from 7 June 1992;
- the definition of "registered friendly society" repealed by Friendly Societies Act 1992, s. 120 and Sch. 22, Pt. I as from 28 April 1993 in regard to incorporated friendly societies (see SI 1993/1186 (C 23), art. 2(1), Sch. 1, app.) and as from 1 January 1994 for all remaining purposes (see SI 1993/2213 (C 43), art. 2 and Sch. 5, app.); the definition formerly read as follows:

"**"registered friendly society"** means–

(a) a society which is a friendly society within the meaning of section 7(1)(a) of the Friendly Societies Act 1974 and is registered within the meaning of that Act; or

(b) a society which is a friendly society within the meaning of section 1(1)(a) of the Friendly Societies Act (Northern Ireland) 1970 and is registered or deemed to be registered under that Act;."

**207(2) ["Advertisement"]** In this Act **"advertisement"** includes every form of advertising, whether in a publication, by the display of notices, signs, labels or showcards, by means of circulars, catalogues, price lists or other documents, by an exhibition of pictures or photographic or cinematographic films, by way of sound broadcasting or television or by inclusion in any programme service (within the meaning of the Broadcasting Act 1990) other than a sound or television broadcasting service, by the distribution of recordings, or in any other manner; and references to the issue of an advertisement shall be construed accordingly.

**History**
In s. 207(2) the words "or by inclusion in any programme service (within the meaning of the Broadcasting Act 1990) other than a sound or television broadcasting service" inserted by Broadcasting Act 1990, s. 203(1) and Sch. 20, para. 45(1)(a) as from 1 January 1991 (see SI 1990/2347 (C 61), art. 3, Sch. 2).

**207(3) [Issue of advertisement in UK]** For the purposes of this Act an advertisement or other information issued outside the United Kingdom shall be treated as issued in the United Kingdom if it is directed to persons in the United Kingdom or is made available to them otherwise than in a newspaper, journal, magazine or other periodical publication published and circulating principally outside the United Kingdom or in a sound or television broadcast transmitted principally for reception outside the United Kingdom.

**207(4)** (Repealed and omitted by Broadcasting Act 1990, s. 203(1), (3), Sch. 20, para. 45(1)(b) and Sch. 21 as from 1 January 1991.)

**History**
In regard to the date of the above omission and repeal see SI 1990/2347 (C 61), art. 3, Sch. 2; s. 207(4) formerly read as follows:

"The Independent Broadcasting Authority shall not be regarded as contravening any provision of this Act by reason of broadcasting an advertisement in accordance with the provisions of the Broadcasting Act 1981."

**207(5) ["Controller"]** In this Act **"controller"** means–

(a) in relation to a body corporate, a person who, either alone or with any associate or associates, is entitled to exercise, or control the exercise of, 15 per cent or more of the voting power at any general meeting of the body corporate or another body corporate of which it is a subsidiary; and

(b) in relation to an unincorporated association–

(i) any person in accordance with whose directions or instructions, either alone or with those of any associate or associates, the officers or members of the governing body of the association are accustomed to act (but disregarding advice given in a professional capacity); and

(ii) any person who, either alone or with any associate or associates, is entitled to exercise, or control the exercise of, 15 per cent or more of the voting power at any general meeting of the association;

and for the purposes of this subsection **"associate"**, in relation to any person, means that person's wife, husband or minor child or step-child, any body corporate of which that person is a director, any person who is an employee or partner of that person and, if that person is a body corporate, any subsidiary of that body corporate and any employee of any such subsidiary.

**Note**

Concerning effect of s. 207(5) see the Investment Services Regulations 1995 (SI 1995/3275), reg. 32 and Sch. 7, para. 41.

**207(6) ["Manager"]** In this Act, except in relation to a unit trust scheme or a registered friendly society, **"manager"** means an employee who–

(a) under the immediate authority of his employer is responsible, either alone or jointly with one or more other persons, for the conduct of his employer's business; or

(b) under the immediate authority of his employer or of a person who is a manager by virtue of paragraph (a) above exercises managerial functions or is responsible for maintaining accounts or other records of his employer;

and, where the employer is not an individual, references in this subsection to the authority of the employer are references to the authority, in the case of a body corporate, of the directors, in the case of a partnership, of the partners and, in the case of an unincorporated association, of its officers or the members of its governing body.

**207(7) ["Insurance business" etc.]** In this Act **"insurance business"**, **"insurance company"** and **"contract of insurance"** have the same meanings as in the Insurance Companies Act 1982.

**207(8) [Subsidiary, holding company]** Section 736 of the Companies Act 1985 (meaning of subsidiary and holding company) shall apply for the purposes of this Act.

**207(9) [Application to Scotland]** In the application of this Act to Scotland, references to a matter being actionable at the suit of a person shall be construed as references to the matter being actionable at the instance of that person.

**207(10) [Time limits]** For the purposes of any provision of this Act authorising or requiring a person to do anything within a specified number of days no account shall be taken of any day which is a public holiday in any part of the United Kingdom.

**207(11) [Investment business on behalf of Crown]** Nothing in Part I of this Act shall be construed as applying to investment business carried on by any person when acting as agent or otherwise on behalf of the Crown.

## 208 Gibraltar

**208(1) [Application to Gibraltar]** Subject to the provisions of this section, section 31, 58(1)(c), 86 and 130(2)(c) and (d) above shall apply as if Gibraltar were a member State.

**208(2) [References to national of member State]** References in those provisions to a national of a member State shall, in relation to Gibraltar, be construed as references to a British Dependent Territories citizen or a body incorporated in Gibraltar.

**208(3) [Reference in s. 86(3)(a) to relevant Community instrument]** In the case of a collective investment scheme constituted in Gibraltar the reference in subsection (3)(a) of section 86 above to a relevant Community instrument shall be taken as a reference to any Community instrument the object of which is the co-ordination or approximation of the laws, regulations or administrative provisions of member States relating to collective investment schemes of a kind which satisfy the requirements prescribed for the purposes of that section.

**208(4) [Power of Secretary of State to make regulations]** The Secretary of State may by regulations make such provision as appears to him to be necessary or expedient to secure–

(a) that he may give notice under subsection (2) of section 86 above on grounds relating to the law of Gibraltar; and

(b) that this Act applies as if a scheme which is constituted in a member State other than the United Kingdom and recognised in Gibraltar under provisions which appear to the Secretary of State to give effect to the provisions of a relevant Community instrument were a scheme recognised under that section.

## 209 Northern Ireland

**209(1) [Extent to Northern Ireland]** This Act extends to Northern Ireland.

**209(2) [Northern Ireland Constitution Act 1973]** Subject to any Order made after the passing of this Act by virtue of subsection (1)(a) of section 3 of the Northern Ireland Constitution Act 1973 the regulation of investment business, the official listing of securities and offers off unlisted securities shall not be transferred matters for the purposes of that Act but shall for the purposes of subsection (2) of that section be treated as specified in Schedule 3 to that Act.

## 210 Expenses and receipts

**210(1) [Defraying of expenses]** Any expenses incurred by the Secretary of State under this Act shall be defrayed out of moneys provided by Parliament.

**210(2) [Payment of fees etc.]** Any fees or other sums received by the Secretary of State under this Act shall be paid into the Consolidated Fund.

**210(3) [Expenses, fees re Friendly Societies Commission]** Subsections (1) and (2) above apply also to expenses incurred and fees received under this Act by the Friendly Societies Commission.

**History**
In s. 210(3) the words "the Friendly Societies Commission" substituted for the former words "the Chief Registrar of friendly societies; and any fees received under this Act by the Registrar of Friendly Societies for Northern Ireland shall be paid into the Consolidated Fund of Northern Ireland." by Friendly Societies Act 1992, s. 98 and Sch. 18, para. 8 as from 1 February 1993 in regard to incorporated friendly societies (see SI 1993/16 (C 1), art. 2 and Sch. 4) and as from 1 January 1994 for all remaining purposes (see SI 1993/2213 (C 43), art. 2 and Sch. 5).

## 211 Commencement and transitional provisions

**211(1) [Commencement days by Order]** This Act shall come into force on such day as the Secretary of State may by order appoint and different days may be appointed for different provisions or different purposes.

**211(2) [Commencement of s. 195]** Subsection (1) above does not apply to section 195 which shall come into force when this Act is passed.

**211(3) [Transitional matters]** Schedule 15 to this Act shall have effect with respect to the transitional matters there mentioned.

## 212 Short title, consequential amendments and repeals

**212(1) [Citation]** This Act may be cited as the Financial Services Act 1986.

**212(2) [Consequential amendments]** The enactments and instruments mentioned in Schedule 16 to this Act shall have effect with the amendments there specified, being amendments consequential on the provisions of this Act.

**212(3) [Repeals]** The enactments mentioned in Part I of Schedule 17 to this Act and the instruments mentioned in Part II of that Schedule are hereby repealed or revoked to the extent specified in the third column of those Parts.

# SCHEDULES

## Schedule 1 – Investments and Investment Business

Sections 1 and 2

## Part I – Investments

### SHARES ETC.

**1** Shares and stock in the share capital of a company.

*Note*

In this paragraph **"company"** includes any body corporate and also any unincorporated body constituted under the law of a country or territory outside the United Kingdom but does not, except in relation to any shares of a class defined as deferred shares for the purposes of section 119 of the Building Societies Act 1986, include a building society incorporated under the law of, or of any part of, the United Kingdom, nor does it include an open-ended investment company or any body incorporated under the law of, or of any part of, the United Kingdom relating to industrial and provident societies or credit unions.

**History**

In the Note to para. 1 the words "but does not," to the end substituted by Financial Services Act 1986 (Extension of Scope of Act) Order 1991 (SI 1991/1104), art. 2 as from 1 June 1991; the words formerly read as follows:

"but does not include an open-ended investment company or any body incorporated under the law of, or of any part of, the United Kingdom relating to building societies, industrial and provident societies or credit unions."

### DEBENTURES

**2** Debentures, including debenture stock, loan stock, bonds, certificates of deposit and other instruments creating or acknowledging indebtedness, not being instruments falling within paragraph 3 below.

*Note*

This paragraph shall not be construed as applying–

(a) to any instrument acknowledging or creating indebtedness for, or for money borrowed to defray, the consideration payable under a contract for the supply of goods or services;

(b) to a cheque or other bill of exchange, a banker's draft or a letter of credit; or

(c) to a banknote, a statement showing a balance in a current, deposit or savings account or (by reason of any financial obligation contained in it) to a lease or other disposition of property, a heritable security or an insurance policy.

### GOVERNMENT AND PUBLIC SECURITIES

**3** Loan stock, bonds and other instruments creating or acknowledging indebtedness issued by or on behalf of a government, local authority or public authority.

*Notes*

(1) In this paragraph **"government, local authority or public authority"** means–
   (a) the government of the United Kingdom, of Northern Ireland, or of any country or territory outside the United Kingdom;
   (b) a local authority in the United Kingdom or elsewhere;
   (c) any international organisation the members of which include the United Kingdom or another member State.

(2) The Note to paragraph 2 above shall, so far as applicable, apply also to this paragraph.

(3) This paragraph does not apply to any instrument creating or acknowledging indebtedness in respect of money received by the Director of Savings as deposits or otherwise in connection with the business of the National Savings Bank or in respect of money raised under the National Loans Act 1968 under the auspices of the Director of Savings or in respect of money treated as having been so raised by virtue of section 11(3) of the National Debt Act 1972.

**History**
In para. 3 Note (3) added by Financial Services Act 1986 (Restriction of Scope of Act and Meaning of Collective Investment Scheme) Order 1990 (SI 1990/349), art. 2(1) as from 26 March 1990.

## INSTRUMENTS ENTITLING TO SHARES OR SECURITIES

**4** Warrants or other instruments entitling the holder to subscribe for investments falling within paragraph 1, 2 or 3 above.

*Notes*

(1) It is immaterial whether the investments are for the time being in existence or identifiable.

(2) An investment falling within this paragraph shall not be regarded as falling within paragraph 7, 8 or 9 below.

## CERTIFICATES REPRESENTING SECURITIES

**5** Certificates or other instruments which confer–

(a) property rights in respect of any investment falling within paragraph 1, 2, 3 or 4 above;

(b) any right to acquire, dispose of, underwrite or convert an investment, being a right to which the holder would be entitled if he held any such investment to which the certificate or instrument relates; or

(c) a contractual right (other than an option) to acquire any such investment otherwise than by subscription.

*Note*

This paragraph does not apply to any instrument which confers rights in respect of two or more investments issued by different persons or in respect of two or more different investments falling within paragraph 3 above and issued by the same person.

## UNITS IN COLLECTIVE INVESTMENT SCHEME

**6** Units in a collective investment scheme, including shares in or securities of an open-ended investment company.

## OPTIONS

**7** Options to acquire or dispose of–

(a) an investment falling within any other paragraph of this Part of this Schedule;

(b) currency of the United Kingdom or of any other country or territory;

(c) gold, palladium, platinum or silver; or

(d) an option to acquire or dispose of an investment falling within this paragraph by virtue of (a), (b) or (c) above.

**History**
In para. 7(c) the words ", palladium, platinum" inserted after the word "gold" by the Financial Services Act 1986 (Extension of Scope of Act and Meaning of Collective Investment Scheme) Order 1988 (SI 1988/496), art. 2 as from 25 March 1988.

## FUTURES

**8** Rights under a contract for the sale of a commodity or property of any other description under which delivery is to be made at a future date and at a price agreed upon when the contract is made.

*Notes*

(1) This paragraph does not apply if the contract is made for commercial and not investment purposes.

(2) A contract shall be regarded as made for investment purposes if it is made or traded on a recognised investment exchange or made otherwise than on a recognised investment exchange but expressed to be as traded on such an exchange or on the same terms as those on which an equivalent contract would be made on such an exchange.

(3) A contract not falling within Note (2) above shall be regarded as made for commercial purposes if under the terms of the contract delivery is to be made within seven days.

(4) The following are indications that any other contract is made for a commercial purpose and the absence of any of them is an indication that it is made for investment purposes–

(a) either or each of the parties is a producer of the commodity or other property or uses it in his business;

(b) the seller delivers or intends to deliver the property or the purchaser takes or intends to take delivery of it.

(5) It is an indication that a contract is made for commercial purposes that the price, the lot, the delivery date or the other terms are determined by the parties for the purposes of the particular contract and not by reference to regularly published prices, to standard lots or delivery dates or to standard terms.

(6) The following are also indications that a contract is made for investment purposes–

(a) it is expressed to be as traded on a market or on an exchange;

(b) performance of the contract is ensured by an investment exchange or a clearing house;

(c) there are arrangements for the payment or provision of margin.

(7) A price shall be taken to have been agreed upon when a contract is made–

(a) notwithstanding that it is left to be determined by reference to the price at which a contract is to be entered into on a market or exchange or could be entered into at a time and place specified in the contract; or

(b) in a case where the contract is expressed to be by reference to a standard lot and quality, notwithstanding that provision is made for a variation in the price to take account of any variation in quantity or quality on delivery.

## CONTRACTS FOR DIFFERENCES ETC.

**9** Rights under a contract for differences or under any other contract the purpose or pretended purpose of which is to secure a profit or avoid a loss by reference to fluctuations in the value or price of property of any description or in an index or other factor designated for that purpose in the contract.

*Notes*

(1) This paragraph does not apply where the parties intend that the profit is to be obtained or the loss avoided by taking delivery of any property to which the contract relates.

(2) This paragraph does not apply to rights under any contract under which money is received by the Director of Savings as deposits or otherwise in connection with the business of the National Savings Bank or raised under the National Loans Act 1968 under the auspices of the Director of Savings or under which money raised is treated as having been so raised by virtue of section 11(3) of the National Debt Act 1972.

**History**

In para. 9 the word "Notes" substituted for the former word "Note", the previously unnumbered Note numbered (1) and Note (2) added by Financial Services Act 1986 (Restriction of Scope of Act and Meaning of Collective Investment Scheme) Order 1990 (SI 1990/349), art. 2(2) as from 26 March 1990.

## LONG TERM INSURANCE CONTRACTS

**10** Rights under a contract the effecting and carrying out of which constitutes long term business within the meaning of the Insurance Companies Act 1982.

*Notes*

(1) This paragraph does not apply to rights under a contract of insurance if–

(a) the benefits under the contract are payable only on death or in respect of incapacity due to injury, sickness or infirmity;

(b) no benefits are payable under the contract on a death (other than a death due to accident) unless it occurs within ten years of the date on which the life of the person in question was first insured under the contract or before that person attains a specified age not exceeding seventy years;

(c) the contract has no surrender value or the consideration consists of a single premium and the surrender value does not exceed that premium; and

(d) the contract does not make provision for its conversion or extension in a manner that would result in its ceasing to comply with paragraphs (a), (b) and (c) above.

(2) Where the provisions of a contract of insurance are such that the effecting and carrying out of the contract–

(a) constitutes both long term business within the meaning of the Insurance Companies Act 1982 and general business within the meaning of that Act; or

(b) by virtue of section 1(3) of that Act constitutes long term business notwithstanding the inclusion of subsidiary general business provisions,

references in this paragraph to rights and benefits under the contract are references only to such rights and benefits as are attributable to the provisions of the contract relating to long term business.

(3) This paragraph does not apply to rights under a reinsurance contract.

(4) Rights falling within this paragraph shall not be regarded as falling within paragraph 9 above.

## RIGHTS AND INTERESTS IN INVESTMENTS

**11** Rights to and interests in anything which is an investment falling within any other paragraph of this Part of this Schedule.

*Notes*

(1) This paragraph does not apply to interests under the trusts of an occupational pension scheme.

(2) This paragraph does not apply to rights or interests which are investments by virtue of any other paragraph of this Part of this Schedule.

# Part II – Activities Constituting Investment Business

## DEALING IN INVESTMENTS

**12** Buying, selling, subscribing for or underwriting investments or offering or agreeing to do so, either as principal or as an agent.

*Notes*

(1) This paragraph does not apply to a person by reason of his accepting, or offering or agreeing to accept, whether as principal or as agent, an instrument creating or acknowledging indebtedness in respect of any loan, credit, guarantee or other similar financial accommodation or assurance which he or his principal has made, granted or provided or which he or his principal has offered or agreed to make, grant or provide.

(2) The references in (1) above to a person accepting, or offering or agreeing to accept, an instrument include references to a person becoming, or offering or agreeing to become, a party to an instrument otherwise than as a debtor or a surety.

**History**

In para. 12 Notes (1) and (2) added by the Financial Services Act 1986 (Restriction of Scope of Act and Meaning of Collective Investment Scheme) Order 1988 (SI 1988/803), art. 2 as from 29 April 1988.

## ARRANGING DEALS IN INVESTMENTS

**13** Making, or offering or agreeing to make–

(a) arrangements with a view to another person buying, selling, subscribing for or underwriting a particular investment; or

(b) arrangements with a view to a person who participates in the arrangements buying, selling, subscribing for or underwriting investments.

*Notes*

(1) This paragraph does not apply to a person by reason of his making, or offering or agreeing to make, arrangements with a view to a transaction to which he will himself be a party as principal or which will be entered into by him as agent for one of the parties.

(2) The arrangements in (a) above are arrangements which bring about or would bring about the transaction in question.

(3) This paragraph does not apply to a person (**"the relevant person"**) who is either a money-lending company within the meaning of section 338 of the Companies Act 1985 or a body corporate incorporated under the law of, or of any part of, the United Kingdom relating to building societies or a person whose ordinary business includes the making of loans or the giving of guarantees in connection with loans by reason of the relevant person making, or offering or agreeing to make, arrangements with a view to a person ("the authorised person") who is either authorised under section 22 or 23 of this Act or who is authorised under section 31 of this Act and carries on insurance business which is investment business selling an investment which falls within paragraph 10 above or, so far as relevant to that paragraph, paragraph 11 above if the arrangements are either–

(a) that the authorised person or a person on his behalf will introduce persons to whom the authorised person has sold or proposes to sell an investment of the kind described above, or will advise such persons to approach, the relevant person with a view to the relevant person lending money on the security of that investment; or

(b) that the authorised person gives an assurance to the relevant person as to the amount which will or may be received by the relevant person, should that person lend money to a person to whom the authorised person has sold or proposes to sell an investment of the kind described above, on the surrender or maturity of that investment if it is taken as security for the loan.

(4) This paragraph does not apply to a person by reason of his making, or offering or agreeing to make, arrangements with a view to a person accepting, whether as principal or as agent, an instrument creating or acknowledging indebtedness in respect of any loan, credit, guarantee or other similar financial accommodation or assurance which he or his principal has made, granted or provided or which he or his principal has offered or agreed to make, grant or provide.

(5) Arrangements do not fall within (b) above by reason of their having as their purpose the provision of finance to enable a person to buy, sell, subscribe for or underwrite investments.

(6) This paragraph does not apply to arrangements for the introduction of persons to another person if–

(a) the person to whom the introduction is made is an authorised or exempted person or is a person whose ordinary business involves him in engaging in activities which fall within this Part of this Schedule or would do apart from the provisions of Part III or Part IV and who is not unlawfully carrying on investment business in the United Kingdom; and

(b) the introduction is made with a view to the provision of independent advice or the independent exercise of discretion either–

(i) in relation to investments generally; or

(ii) in relation to any class of investments if the transaction or advice is or is to be with respect to an investment within that class.

(7) The references in (4) above to a person accepting an instrument include references to a person becoming a party to an instrument otherwise than as a debtor or a surety.

**History**

In para. 13 Note (3) added by the Financial Services Act 1986 (Restriction of Scope of Act) Order 1988 (SI 1988/318), art. 2 as from 27 February 1988.

Notes (4)–(7) added by the Financial Services Act 1986 (Restriction of Scope of Act and Meaning of Collective Investment Scheme) Order 1988 (SI 1988/803), art. 3 as from 29 April 1988.

## CUSTODY OF INVESTMENTS

**13A(1)** Safeguarding and administering or arranging for the safeguarding and administration of assets belonging to another where–

(a) those assets consist of or include investments; or

(b) the arrangements for their safeguarding and administration are such that those assets may consist of or include investments and the arrangements have at any time been held out as being arrangements under which investments would be safeguarded and administered.

**13A(2)** Offering or agreeing to safeguard and administer, or to arrange for the safe guarding and administration of, assets belonging to another where the circumstances fall within sub-paragraph (1)(a) or (b) above.

*Notes*

(1) This paragraph does not apply to a person by reason of his safeguarding and administering assets, or offering or agreeing to do so, under arrangements–

(a) under which another person ("the primary custodian"), who is permitted to provide a service falling within this paragraph, undertakes to the person to whom the assets belong a responsibility in respect of the assets which is no less onerous than the responsibility which the primary custodian would undertake to that person if the primary custodian were safeguarding and administering the assets himself, and

(b) which are operated by the primary custodian in the course of carrying on in the United Kingdom investment business falling within this paragraph.

(2) None of the following activities constitutes the administration of assets–

(a) providing information as to the number of units or the value of any assets safeguarded;

(b) converting currency; and

(c) receiving documents relating to an investment solely for the purpose of onward transmission to, from or at the direction of the person to whom the investment belongs.

(3) For the purposes of this paragraph it is immaterial that the assets safeguarded and administered–

(a) constitute units of a security, title to which is recorded on the relevant register of securities as being held in uncertificated form; or

(b) may be transferred to another person, subject to a commitment by the person safeguarding and administering them, or arranging for their safeguarding and administration, that they will be replaced by equivalent assets at some future date or when so requested by the person to whom they belong.

(4) This paragraph does not apply to arrangements for the introduction of persons to another person if–

(a) the person to whom the introduction is made is permitted to provide a service falling within this paragraph; and

(b) the introduction is made with a view to the provision in the United Kingdom of a service falling within this paragraph or the making of arrangements operated in the United Kingdom for the provision of a service falling within this paragraph by a person who is not connected with the person by whom the introduction is made.

For the purposes of this Note, the person making the introduction shall be regarded as connected with the other person if he is either a body corporate in the same group as that other person or remunerated by that other person.

(5) For the purposes of Notes (1) and (4) above, a person is permitted to provide a service falling within this paragraph if–

(a) he is an authorised person who may provide that service–
   (i) without contravening any rules that apply to him under section 48 of this Act; or
   (ii) by virtue of his membership of a recognised self-regulating organisation or his certification by a recognised professional body; or

(b) he is an exempted person as respects any investment business which consists of or includes that service; or

(c) he is entitled to carry on investment business in the United Kingdom which consists of or includes that service pursuant either to regulation 5 of the Banking Coordination (Second Council Directive) Regulations 1992 or to regulation 5 of the Investment Services Regulations 1995.

**History**

Para. 13A inserted by the Financial Services Act 1986 (Extension of Scope of Act) Order 1996 (SI 1996/2958), art. 1, 3 as from 1 June 1997.

## MANAGING INVESTMENTS

**14** Managing, or offering or agreeing to manage, assets belonging to another person if–

(a) those assets consist of or include investments; or

(b) the arrangements for their management are such that those assets may consist of or include investments at the discretion of the person managing or offering or agreeing to manage them and either they have at any time since the date of the coming into force of section 3 of this Act done so or the arrangements have at any time (whether before or after that date) been held out as arrangements under which they would do so.

## INVESTMENT ADVICE

**15** Giving, or offering or agreeing to give, to persons in their capacity as investors or potential investors advice on the merits of their purchasing, selling, subscribing for or underwriting an investment, or exercising any right conferred by an investment to acquire, dispose of, underwrite or convert an investment.

## ESTABLISHING ETC. COLLECTIVE INVESTMENT SCHEMES

**16** Establishing, operating or winding up a collective investment scheme, including acting as trustee of an authorised unit trust scheme or as depositary or sole director of an investment company with variable capital.

**History**

In para. 16 the words beginning with "or as depositary" to the end inserted by the Financial Services Act 1986 (Extension of Scope of Act) Order1996 (SI 1996/2958), art. 1, 2 as from 6 January 1997.

## SENDING DEMATERIALISED INSTRUCTIONS ETC.

**16A** Sending on behalf of another person dematerialised instructions relating to an investment by means of–

(a) a relevant system in respect of which an Operator is approved under the Uncertificated Securities Regulations 1995; or

(b) a computer-based system, established by the Bank of England and the London Stock Exchange, through the medium of which specified securities may be transferred or allotted without the need for an instrument in writing,

or offering or agreeing to do so, or causing on behalf of another person such instructions to be sent by such means or offering or agreeing to do so.

*Notes*

(1) This paragraph does not apply to a person by reason of his sending, or causing the sending of, instructions by means of a system falling within (a) above on behalf of–

(a) a participating issuer or settlement bank acting in its capacity as such; or

(b) an offeror making a takeover offer,

or by reason of his offering or agreeing to do so.

(1A) This paragraph does not apply to a person–

(a) by reason of his sending, or causing the sending of, instructions by means of a system falling within (b) above on behalf of a settlement bank acting in its capacity as such, or by reason of his offering or agreeing to do so; or

(b) by reason of any activity in which he engages, or in which he offers or agrees to engage, at a time when he is accredited by the Bank of England as a provider of a network for the purposes of a system falling within (b) above and which is a necessary part of the provision of such a network.

(2) For the purposes of this paragraph a person shall be taken to cause, or to offer or agree to cause, the sending of a dematerialised instruction only if –

(a) in the case of a system falling within (a) above, he is a system-participant; and

(b) in the case of a system falling within (b) above, he is a person who, under an agreement with the Bank of England, is responsible for the operation of, and the maintenance of security over, a gateway.

(3) In this paragraph–

**"dematerialised instruction"**–

(a) in relation to a system falling within (a) above, has the meaning given by regulation 3 of the Uncertificated Securities Regulations 1995, and

(b) in relation to a system falling within (b) above, means an instruction sent by means of a gateway;

**"gateway"**, in relation to a system falling within (b) above, means computer hardware and software by means of which instructions are authenticated and encrypted for processing by the system;

**"offeror"** has the meaning given by section 428 of the Companies Act 1985;

**"Operator"**, **"participating issuer"** and **"relevant system"** have the meaning given by regulation 3 of the Uncertificated Securities Regulations 1995;

**"settlement bank"**–

(a) in relation to a system falling within (a) above, has the meaning given by regulation 3 of the Uncertificated Securities Regulations 1995, and

(b) in relation to a system falling within (b) above, means a person who has agreed to make payments in connection with the discharge of debts or liabilities arising from the transfer or allotment of specified securities made through the medium of that system;

**"specified securities"** has the meaning given by the Stock Transfer Act 1982;

**"system-participant"** has the meaning given by regulation 3 of the Uncertificated Securities Regulations 1995;

**"takeover offer"** has the meaning given by section 428 of the Companies Act 1985.

**History**

Para. 16A substituted by the Financial Services Act 1986 (Extension of Scope of Act) Order 1997 (SI 1997/2543), art. 1, art. 2(1), (2) as from 10 November 1997. Para. 16A formerly read as follows:

" Sending on behalf of another person dematerialised instructions relating to an investment by means of a relevant system in respect of which an Operator is approved under the Uncertificated Securities Regulations 1995, or offering or agreeing to do so, or causing on behalf of another person such instructions to be sent by such means or offering or agreeing to do so."

In Note (1) the words "by means of a system falling within (a) above" inserted by the Financial Services Act 1986 (Extension of Scope of Act) Order 1997 (SI 1997/2543), art. 1, art. 2(1), (3) as from 10 November 1997.

Note (1A) inserted by the Financial Services Act 1986 (Extension of Scope of Act) Order 1997 (SI 1997/2543), art. 1, art. 2(1), (4) as from 10 November 1997.

Notes (2) and (3) substituted by the Financial Services Act 1986 (Extension of Scope of Act) Order 1997 (SI 1997/2543), art. 1, art. 2(1), (5) as from 10 November 1997. Notes (2) and (3) formerly read as follows:

"**(2)** For the purposes of this paragraph a person shall be taken to cause, or to offer or agree to cause, the sending of a dematerialised instruction only if he is a system-participant.

**(3)** In this paragraph–

"**dematerialised instruction**", "**participating issuer**", "**relevant system**", "**settlement bank**", "**system-participant**" and "**Operator**" have the meanings given by regulation 3 of the Uncertificated Securities Regulations 1995; and "**offeror**" and "**takeover offer**" have the meanings given by section 428 of the Companies Act 1985."

Para. 16A originally added by the Financial Services Act 1986 (Uncertificated Securities) (Extension of Scope of Act) Order 1996 (SI 1996/1322), art. 1, 2, as from 15 July 1996.

**Note**

For exemption under Sch. 1, para. 16A, see the Financial Services Act 1986 (Exemption) Order 1996 (SI 1996/1587).

# Part III – Excluded Activities

## DEALINGS AS PRINCIPAL

**17(1)** Paragraph 12 above applies to a transaction which is or is to be entered into by a person as principal only if–

(a) he holds himself out as willing to enter into transactions of that kind at prices determined by him generally and continuously rather than in respect of each particular transaction; or

(b) he holds himself out as engaging in the business of buying investments with a view to selling them and those investments are or include investments of the kind to which the transaction relates; or

(c) he regularly solicits members of the public for the purpose of inducing them to enter as principals or agents into transactions to which that paragraph applies and the transaction is or is to be entered into as a result of his having solicited members of the public in that manner.

**17(2)** In sub-paragraph (1) above **"buying"** and **"selling"** means buying and selling by transactions to which paragraph 12 above applies and **"members of the public"**, in relation to the person soliciting them (**"the relevant person"**), means any other person except–

(a) authorised persons, exempted persons, or persons holding a permission under paragraph 23 below;

(b) members of the same group as the relevant person;

(c) persons who are, or propose to become, participators with the relevant person in a joint enterprise;

(d) any person who is solicited by the relevant person with a view to–

(i) the acquisition by the relevant person of 20 per cent, or more of the voting shares in a body corporate (that is to say, shares carrying not less than that percentage of the voting rights attributable to share capital which are exercisable in all circumstances at any general meeting of the body); or

(ii) if the relevant person (either alone or with other members of the same group as himself) holds 20 per cent, or more of the voting shares in a body corporate, the acquisition by him of further shares in the body or the disposal by him of shares in that body to the person solicited or to a member of the same group as that person; or

(iii) if the person solicited (either alone or with other members of the same group as himself) holds 20 per cent, or more of the voting shares in a body corporate, the disposal by the relevant person of further shares in that body to the person solicited or to a member of the same group as that person;

(e) any person whose head office is outside the United Kingdom, who is solicited by an approach made or directed to him at a place outside the United Kingdom and whose ordinary business involves him in engaging in activities which fall within Part II of this Schedule or would do so apart from this Part or Part IV.

**17(3)** Sub-paragraph (1) above applies only–

(a) if the investment to which the transaction relates or will relate falls within any of paragraphs 1 to 6 above or, so far as relevant to any of those paragraphs, paragraph 11 above; or

(b) if the transaction is the assignment (or, in Scotland, the assignation) of an investment falling within paragraph 10 above or is the assignment (or, in Scotland, the assignation) of an investment falling within paragraph 11 above which confers rights to or interests in an investment falling within paragraph 10 above.

**History**

Para. 17(3) substituted by the Financial Services Act 1986 (Restriction of Scope of Act) Order 1988 (SI 1988/318), art. 3(1) as from 27 February 1988; para. 17(3) formerly read as follows:

"Sub-paragraph (1) above applies only if the investment to which the transaction relates or will relate falls within any of paragraphs 1 to 6 above or, so far as relevant to any of those paragraphs, paragraph 11 above."

**17(4)** Paragraph 12 above does not apply to any transaction which relates or is to relate to an investment which falls within paragraph 10 above or, so far as relevant to that paragraph, paragraph 11 above nor does it apply to a transaction which relates or is to relate to an investment which falls within any of paragraphs 7 to 9 above or, so far as relevant to any of those paragraphs, paragraph 11 above being a transaction which, in either case, is or is to be entered into by a person as principal if he is not an authorised person and the transaction is or is to be entered into by him–

(a) with or through an authorised person, an exempted person or a person holding a permission under paragraph 23 below; or

(b) through an office outside the United Kingdom, maintained by a party to the transaction,



CCH.New Law

bbcl fsa 1986b Mp 1870—bcl98 3a

and with or through a person whose head office is situated outside the United Kingdom and whose ordinary business is such as is mentioned in sub-paragraph (2)(e) above.

**History**
In para. 17(4) the words ", other than a transaction of a kind described in paragraph 3(a) or (b) above," formerly appearing after the words "does not apply to any transaction" deleted by Financial Services Act 1986 (Restriction of Scope of Act and Meaning of Collective Investment Scheme) Order 1990 (SI 1990/349), art. 3 as from 26 March 1990.
Previously in para. 17(4) the words "any transaction, other than" to "in either case," substituted for the original words "a transaction which relates or is to relate to any other investment and which" by Financial Services Act 1986 (Restriction of Scope of Act) Order 1988 (SI 1988/318), art. 3(2) as from 27 February 1988.

**Note**
Concerning effect of para. 17 re European investment firms, see the Investment Services Regulations 1995 (SI 1995/3275), reg. 32 and Sch. 7, para. 42(1).
Concerning European institutions, see the Banking Coordination (Second Council Directive) Regulations 1992 (SI 1992/3218), reg. 55 and Sch. 9, para. 44(1).
Concerning effect of para. 17 re UK investment firms, see the Financial Services Act 1986 (Restriction of Scope of Act and Meaning of Collective Investment Scheme) Order 1996 (SI 1996/2996) art. 2.

## GROUPS AND JOINT ENTERPRISES

**18(1)** Paragraph 12 above does not apply to any transaction which is or is to be entered into by a person as principal with another person if–

(a) they are bodies corporate in the same group; or

(b) they are, or propose to become, participators in a joint enterprise and the transaction is or is to be entered into for the purposes of, or in connection with, that enterprise.

**18(2)** Paragraph 12 above does not apply to any transaction which is or is to be entered into by any person as agent for another person in the circumstances mentioned in sub-paragraph (1)(a) or (b) above if–

(a) where the investment falls within any of paragraphs 1 to 6 above or, so far as relevant to any of those paragraphs, paragraph 11 above, the agent does not–

  (i) hold himself out (otherwise than to other bodies corporate in the same group or persons who are or propose to become participators with him in a joint enterprise) as engaging in the business of buying investments with a view to selling them and those investments are or include investments of the kind to which the transaction relates; or

  (ii) regularly solicit members of the public for the purpose of inducing them to enter as principals or agents into transactions to which paragraph 12 above applies;

 and the transaction is not or is not to be entered into as a result of his having solicited members of the public in that manner;

(b) where the investment is not as mentioned in paragraph (a) above–

  (i) the agent enters into the transaction with or through an authorised person, an exempted person or a person holding a permission under paragraph 23 below; or

  (ii) the transaction is effected through an office outside the United Kingdom, maintained by a party to the transaction, and with or through a person whose head office is situated outside the United Kingdom and whose ordinary business involves him in engaging in activities which fall within Part II of this Schedule or would do so apart from this Part or Part IV.

**Note**
Concerning European institutions, see the Banking Coordination (Second Council Directive) Regulations 1992 (SI 1992/3218), reg. 55 and Sch. 9, para. 44(2).

**18(3)** Paragraph 13 above does not apply to arrangements which a person makes or offers or agrees to make if–

(a) that person is a body corporate and the arrangements are with a view to another body corporate in the same group entering into a transaction of the kind mentioned in that paragraph; or

(b) that person is or proposes to become a participator in a joint enterprise and the arrangements are with a view to another person who is or proposes to become a participator in the enterprise entering into such a transaction for the purposes of or in connection with that enterprise.

**18(3A)** Paragraph 13A above does not apply to a service which a person provides or offers or agrees to provide or to arrangements which a person makes or offers or agrees to make for the provision of a service if–

(a) that person is a body corporate and the service is or is to be provided to a body corporate in the same group and relates or will relate to assets which belong to that other body corporate; or

(b) that person is or proposes to become a participator in a joint enterprise and the assets to which the service relates or will relate are or are to be held on behalf of another person who is or proposes to become a participator in the enterprise and are or are to be held for the purposes of or in connection with the enterprise.

**History**

Para. 3A inserted by the Financial Services Act 1986 (Extension of Scope of Act) Order 1996 SI 1996/2958), art. 1, 4 as from 1 June 1997.

**18(4)** Paragraph 14 above does not apply to a person by reason of his managing or offering or agreeing to manage the investments of another person if–

(a) they are bodies corporate in the same group; or

(b) they are, or propose to become, participators in a joint enterprise and the investments are or are to be managed for the purposes of, or in connection with, that enterprise.

**18(5)** Paragraph 15 above does not apply to advice given by a person to another person if–

(a) they are bodies corporate in the same group; or

(b) they are, or propose to become, participators in a joint enterprise and the advice is given for the purposes of, or in connection with, that enterprise.

**18(5A)** Paragraph 16A does not apply to a body corporate by reason of its sending, or causing the sending of, dematerialised instructions relating to an investment or offering or agreeing to do so if–

(a) the person on whose behalf the instructions are, or are to be, sent or caused to be sent is a body corporate in the same group; and

(b) the investment to which the instructions relate, or will relate, is one in respect of which a body corporate in the same group is registered as the holder on the appropriate register of securities, or will be so registered as a result of the instructions.

**History**

See history note after para. 18(5B).

**18(5B)** In sub-paragraph (5A) **"register of securities"**–

(a) in relation to a system falling within paragraph 16A(a) above, has the meaning given by regulation 3 of the Uncertificated Securities Regulations 1995; and

(b) in relation to a system falling within paragraph 16A(b) above, means a register of holders of specified securities (within the meaning of the Stock Transfer Act 1982) which is kept by the Bank of England.

**History**

Para. 18(5B) substituted by the Financial Services Act 1986 (Extension of Scope of Act) Order 1997 (SI 1997/2543), art. 1, art. 3 as from 10 November 1997. Para. 18(5B) formerly read as follows:

"In sub-paragraph (5A) **"register of securities"** has the meaning given by regulation 3 of the Uncertificated Securities Regulations 1995."

Para. 18(5A) and (5B) originally added by the Financial Services Act 1986 (Uncertificated Securities) (Extension of Scope of Act) Order 1996 (SI 1996/1322), art. 1, 2 as from 15 July 1996.

**18(6)** The definitions in paragraph 17(2) above shall apply also for the purposes of sub-paragraph (2)(a) above except that the relevant person referred to in paragraph 17(2)(d) shall be the person for whom the agent is acting.

**Note**

Concerning effect of para. 18 re European investment firms, see the Investment Services Regulations 1995 (SI 1995/3275), reg. 32 and Sch. 7, para. 42(2).

Concerning effect of para. 18 re UK investment firms, see the Financial Services Act 1986 (Restriction of Scope of Act and Meaning of Collective Investment Scheme) Order 1996 (SI 1996/2996) art. 2.

## SALE OF GOODS AND SUPPLY OF SERVICES

**19(1)** Subject to sub-paragraph (9) below, this paragraph has effect where a person ("the supplier") sells or offers or agrees to sell goods to another person ("the customer") or supplies or offers or agrees to supply him with services and the supplier's main business is to supply goods or services and not to engage in activities falling within Part II of this Schedule.

**History**
In para. 19(1) the words "Subject to sub-paragraph (9) below," inserted by the Financial Services Act 1986 (Extension of Scope of Act and Meaning of Collective Investment Scheme) Order 1988 (SI 1988/496), art. 3(a) as from 25 March 1988.

**19(2)** Paragraph 12 above does not apply to any transaction which is or is to be entered into by the supplier as principal if it is or is to be entered into by him with the customer for the purposes of or in connection with the sale or supply or a related sale or supply (that is to say, a sale or supply to the customer otherwise than by the supplier but for or in connection with the same purpose as the first-mentioned sale or supply).

**19(3)** Paragraph 12 above does not apply to any transaction which is or is to be entered into by the supplier as agent for the customer if it is or is to be entered into for the purposes of or in connection with the sale or supply or a related sale or supply and–

(a) where the investment falls within any of paragraphs 1 to 5 above or, so far as relevant to any of those paragraphs, paragraph 11 above, the supplier does not–
   (i) hold himself out (otherwise than to the customer) as engaging in the business of buying investments with a view to selling them and those investments are or include investments of the kind to which the transaction relates; or
   (ii) regularly solicit members of the public for the purpose of inducing them to enter as principals or agents into transactions to which paragraph 12 above applies; and the transaction is not or is not to be entered into as a result of his having solicited members of the public in that manner;

(b) where the investment is not as mentioned in paragraph (a) above, the supplier enters into the transaction–
   (i) with or through an authorised person, an exempted person or a person holding a permission under paragraph 23 below; or
   (ii) through an office outside the United Kingdom, maintained by a party to the transaction, and with or through a person whose head office is situated outside the United Kingdom and whose ordinary business involves him in engaging in activities which fall within Part II of this Schedule or would do so apart from this Part or Part IV.

**History**
In para. 19(3)(a) the figure "5" substituted for the figure "6" by Financial Services Act 1986 (Restriction of Scope of Act and Meaning of Collective Investment Scheme) (No. 2) Order 1990 (SI 1990/1493), art. 3 as from 25 July 1990.

**19(4)** Paragraph 13 above does not apply to arrangements which the supplier makes or offers or agrees to make with a view to the customer entering into a transaction for the purposes of or in connection with the sale or supply or a related sale or supply.

**19(4A)** Paragraph 13A above does not apply to a service which the supplier provides or offers or agrees to provide or to arrangements which the supplier makes or offers or agrees to make for the provision of a service where the assets to which the service relates or will relate are or are to be held for the purposes of or in connection with the sale or supply or a related sale or supply.

**History**
Para 19(4A) inserted by the Financial Services Act 1986 (Extension of Scope of Act) Order 1996 SI 1996/2958), art. 1, 5 as from 1 June 1997.

**19(5)** Paragraph 14 above does not apply to the supplier by reason of his managing or offering or agreeing to manage the investments of the customer if they are or are to be managed for the purposes of or in connection with the sale or supply or a related sale or supply.

**19(6)** Paragraph 15 above does not apply to advice given by the supplier to the customer for the purposes of or in connection with the sale or supply or a related sale or supply or to a person with whom the customer proposes to enter into a transaction for the purposes of or in connection with the sale or supply or a related sale or supply.

**19(7)** Where the supplier is a body corporate and a member of a group sub-paragraphs (2) to (6) above shall apply to any other member of the group as they apply to the supplier; and where the customer is a body corporate and a member of a group references in those sub-paragraphs to the customer include references to any other member of the group.

**19(8)** The definitions in paragraph 17(2) above shall apply also for the purposes of sub-paragraph (3)(a) above.

**19(9)** This paragraph does not have effect where either–

(a) the customer is an individual; or

(b) the transaction in question is the purchase or sale of an investment which falls within paragraph 6 or 10 above or, so far as relevant to either of those paragraphs, paragraph 11 above; or

(c) the investments which the supplier manages or offers or agrees to manage consist of investments falling within paragraph 6 or 10 above or, so far as relevant to either of those paragraphs, paragraph 11 above; or

(d) the advice which the supplier gives is advice on an investment falling within the paragraph 6 or 10 above or, so far as relevant to either of those paragraphs, paragraph 11 above.

**History**
Para. 19(9) added by the Financial Services Act 1986 (Extension of Scope of Act and Meaning of Collective Investment Scheme) Order 1988 (SI 1988/496), art. 3 as from 25 March 1988.

**Note**
Concerning effect of para. 19 re UK investment firms, see the Financial Services Act 1986 (Restriction of Scope of Act and Meaning of Collective Investment Scheme) Order 1996 (SI 1996/2996) art. 2.

## EMPLOYEES' SHARE SCHEMES

**20(1)** Paragraphs 12, 13 and 13A above do not apply to anything done by a body corporate, a body corporate connected with it or a relevant trustee for the purpose of enabling or facilitating transactions in shares in or debentures of the first-mentioned body between or for the benefit of any of the persons mentioned in sub-paragraph (2) below or the holding of such shares or debentures by or for the benefit of any such persons.

**History**
In para. 20(1) the words ", 13 and 13A" substituted for the former words "and 13" by the Financial Services Act 1986 (Extension of Scope of Act) Order 1996 SI 1996/2958), art. 1, 6 as from 1 June 1997.

**20(2)** The persons referred to in sub-paragraph (1) above are–

(a) the bona fide employees or former employees of the body corporate or of another body corporate in the same group; or

(b) the wives, husbands, widows, widowers, or children or step-children under the age of eighteen of such employees or former employees.

**20(3)** In this paragraph **"a relevant trustee"** means a person holding shares in or debentures of a body corporate as trustee in pursuance of arrangements made for the purpose mentioned in sub-paragraph (1) above by, or by a body corporate connected with, that body corporate.

**20(4)** In this paragraph "shares" and "debentures" include any investment falling within paragraph 1 or 2 above and also include any investment falling within paragraph 4 or 5 above so far as relating to those paragraphs or any investment falling within paragraph 11 above so far as relating to paragraph 1, 2, 4 or 5.

**20(5)** For the purposes of this paragraph a body corporate is connected with another body corporate if–

(a) they are in the same group; or

(b) one is entitled, either alone or with any other body corporate in the same group, to exercise or control the exercise of a majority of the voting rights attributable to the share capital which are exercisable in all circumstances at any general meeting of the other body corporate or of its holding company.

## SALE OF BODY CORPORATE

**21(1)** Paragraphs 12 and 13 above do not apply to the acquisition or disposal of, or to anything done for the purposes of the acquisition or disposal of, shares in a body corporate other than an open-ended investment company, and paragraph 15 above does not apply to advice given in connection with the acquisition or disposal of such shares, if–

(a) the shares consist of or include shares carrying 75 per cent or more of the voting rights attributable to share capital which are exercisable in all circumstances at any general meeting of the body corporate; or

(b) the shares, together with any already held by the person acquiring them, carry not less than that percentage of those voting rights; and

(c) in either case, the acquisition and disposal is, or is to be between parties each of whom is a body corporate, a partnership, a single individual or a group of connected individuals.

**History**
The heading to para. 21 substituted by the Financial Services Act 1986 (Restriction of Scope of Act) Order 1988 (SI 1988/318), art. 4(a) as from 27 February 1988. The former heading read: "SALE OF PRIVATE COMPANY".
In para. 21(1) the words "body corporate other than an open-ended investment company" substituted for the former words "private company" by the Financial Services Act 1986 (Restriction of Scope of Act) Order 1988 (SI 1988/318), art. 4(b) as from 27 February 1988.
In para. 21(1)(a) the words "body corporate" substituted for the former word "company" by the Financial Services Act 1986 (Restriction of Scope of Act) Order 1988 (SI 1988/318), art. 4(d) as from 27 February 1988.

**21(2)** For the purposes of subsection (1)(c) above **"a group of connected individuals"**, in relation to the party disposing of the shares, means persons each of whom is, or is a close relative of, a director or manager of the body corporate and, in relation to the party acquiring the shares, means persons each of whom is, or is a close relative of, a person who is to be a director or manager of the body corporate.

**History**
In para. 21(2) the words "body corporate" substituted for the former word "company" where it appeared by the Financial Services Act 1986 (Restriction of Scope of Act) Order 1988 (SI 1988/318), art. 4(d) as from 27 February 1988.

**21(3)** In this paragraph **"close relative"** means a person's spouse, his children and step-children, his parents and step-parents, his brothers and sisters and his step-brothers and step-sisters.

**History**
In para. 21(3) the words ""private company" means a private company within the meaning of section 1(3) of the Companies Act 1985 or the corresponding Northern Ireland provision and", formerly appearing after the words, "In this paragraph", deleted by the Financial Services Act 1986 (Restriction of Scope of Act) Order 1988 (SI 1988/318), art. 4(c) as from 27 February 1988.

**Note**
Concerning effect of para. 21 re UK investment firms, see the Financial Services Act 1986 (Restriction of Scope of Act and Meaning of Collective Investment Scheme) Order 1996 SI 1996/2996), art. 2.

## TRUSTEES AND PERSONAL REPRESENTATIVES

**22(1)** Paragraph 12 above does not apply to a person by reason of his buying, selling or subscribing for an investment or offering or agreeing to do so if–

(a) the investment is or, as the case may be, is to be held by him as bare trustee or, in Scotland, as nominee for another person;

(b) he is acting on that person's instructions; and

(c) he does not hold himself out as providing a service of buying and selling investments.

**22(2)** Paragraph 13 above does not apply to anything done by a person as trustee or personal representative with a view to–

(a) a fellow trustee or personal representative and himself engaging in their capacity as such in an activity falling within paragraph 12 above; or

(b) a beneficiary under the trust, will or intestacy engaging in any such activity,

unless that person is remunerated for what he does in addition to any remuneration he receives for discharging his duties as trustee or personal representative.

**22(2A)** Paragraph 13A above does not apply to anything done by a person as a trustee or personal representative unless–

(a) he holds himself out as providing a service falling within paragraph 13A above; or

(b) he is remunerated for providing such a service in addition to any remuneration he receives for discharging his duties as trustee or personal representative.

**History**
Para. 22(2A) inserted by the Financial Services Act 1986 (Extension of Scope of Act) Order 1996 SI 1996/2958), art. 1, 7 as from 1 June 1997.

**22(3)** Paragraph 14 above does not apply to anything done by a person as trustee or personal representative unless he holds himself out as offering investment management services or is remunerated for providing such services in addition to any remuneration he receives for discharging his duties as trustee or personal representative.

**22(4)** Paragraph 15 above does not apply to advice given by a person as trustee or personal representative to–

(a) a fellow trustee or personal representative for the purposes of the trust or estate; or

(b) a beneficiary under the trust, will or intestacy concerning his interest in the trust fund or estate,

unless that person is remunerated for doing so in addition to any remuneration he receives for discharging his duties as trustee or personal representative.

**22(4A)** Paragraph 16A does not apply to a person by reason of his sending, or causing the sending of, dematerialised instructions relating to an investment held by him as trustee or as personal representative, or by reason of his offering or agreeing to do so.

**History**

Para. 22(4A) added by the Financial Services Act 1986 (Uncertificated Securities) (Extension of Scope of Act) Order 1996 SI 1996/1322), art. 1, 3 as from 15 July 1996.

**22(5)** Sub-paragraph (1) above has effect to the exclusion of paragraph 17 above as respects any transaction in respect of which the conditions in sub-paragraph (1)(a) and (b) are satisfied.

## DEALINGS IN COURSE OF NON-INVESTMENT BUSINESS

**23(1)** Paragraph 12 above does not apply to anything done by a person–

(a) as principal;

(b) if that person is a body corporate in a group, as agent for another member of the group; or

(c) as agent for a person who is or proposes to become a participator with him in a joint enterprise and for the purposes of or in connection with that enterprise,

if it is done in accordance with the terms and conditions of a permission granted to him by the Secretary of State under this paragraph.

**23(2)** Any application for permission under this paragraph shall be accompanied or supported by such information as the Secretary of State may require and shall not be regarded as duly made unless accompanied by the prescribed fee.

**23(3)** The Secretary of State may grant a permission under this paragraph if it appears to him–

(a) that the applicant's main business, or if he is a member of a group the main business of the group, does not consist of activities for which a person is required to be authorised under this Act;

(b) that the applicant's business is likely to involve such activities which fall within paragraph 12 above; and

(c) that, having regard to the nature of the applicant's main business and, if he is a member of a group, the main business of the group taken as a whole, the manner in which, the persons with whom and the purposes for which the applicant proposes to engage in activities that would require him to be an authorised person and to any other relevant matters, it is inappropriate to require him to be subject to regulation as an authorised person.

**23(4)** Any permission under this paragraph shall be granted by a notice in writing; and the Secretary of State may by a further notice in writing withdraw any such permission if for any reason it appears to him that it is not appropriate for it to continue in force.

**23(5)** The Secretary of State may make regulations requiring persons holding permissions under this paragraph to furnish him with information for the purpose of enabling him to determine whether those permissions should continue in force; and such regulations may, in particular, require such persons–

(a) to give him notice forthwith of the occurrence of such events as are specified in the regulations and such information in respect of those events as is so specified;

(b) to furnish him at such times or in respect of such periods as are specified in the regulations with such information as is so specified.

**23(6)** Section 61 of this Act shall have effect in relation to a contravention of any condition imposed by a permission under this paragraph as it has effect in relation to any such contravention as is mentioned in subsection (1)(a) of that section.

**23(7)** Section 104 of this Act shall apply to a person holding a permission under this paragraph as if he were authorised to carry on investment business as there mentioned; and sections 105 and 106 of this Act shall have effect as if anything done by him in accordance with such permission constituted the carrying on of investment business.

## ADVICE GIVEN OR ARRANGEMENTS MADE IN COURSE OF PROFESSION OR NON-INVESTMENT BUSINESS

**24(1)** Paragraph 15 above does not apply to advice–

(a) which is given in the course of the carrying on of any profession or of a business not otherwise constituting investment business; and

(b) the giving of which is a necessary part of other advice or services given in the course of carrying on that profession or business.

**24(2)** Paragraph 13 above does not apply to arrangements–

(a) which are made in the course of the carrying on of any profession or of a business not otherwise constituting investment business; and

(b) the making of which is a necessary part of other services provided in the course of carrying on that profession or business.

**24(2A)** Paragraph 13A above does not apply to the provision of a service or to arrangements made for the provision of a service where–

(a) the service is provided or the arrangements are made in the course of the carrying on of any profession or of a business not otherwise constituting investment business; and

(b) the provision of the service or the making of the arrangements is a necessary part of other services provided in the course of carrying on that profession or business.

**History**

Para. 24(2A) inserted by the Financial Services Act 1986 (Extension of Scope of Act) Order 1996 SI 1996/2958), art. 1, 8(1) as from 1 June 1997.

**24(3)** Advice shall not be regarded as falling within sub-paragraph (1)(b) above, the making of arrangements shall not be regarded as falling within sub-paragraph (2)(b) above and the provision of a service or the arranging for the provision of a service shall not be regarded as falling within sub-paragraph (2A)(b) above if the giving of the advice, the making of the arrangements or the provision, or the arranging for the provision, of the service is remunerated separately from the other advice or services.

**History**

Para. 24(3) substituted for the former para. 24(3) by the Financial Services Act 1986 (Extension of Scope of Act) Order 1996 SI 1996/2958), art. 1, 8(2) as from 1 June 1997. The former para. 24(3) read as follows:

"Advice shall not be regarded as falling within sub-paragraph (1)(b) above and the making of arrangements shall not be regarded as falling within sub-paragraph (2)(b) above if the giving of the advice or the making of the arrangements is remunerated separately from the other advice or services."

Previously, the words "OR ARRANGEMENTS MADE" in the heading to para. 24 inserted by the Financial Services Act 1986 (Restriction of Scope of Act and Meaning of Collective Investment Scheme) Order 1988 (SI 1988/803), art. 4(1) as from 29 April 1988.

Also previously, para. 24(2) and (3) substituted for the former para. 24(2) by the Financial Services Act 1986 (Restriction of Scope of Act and Meaning of Collective Investment Scheme) Order 1988 (SI 1988/803), art. 4(2) as from 29 April 1988; the original para. 24(2) read as follows:

"Advice shall not be regarded as falling within sub-paragraph (1)(b) above if it is remunerated separately from the other advice or services."

## CUSTODY OF GROUP PENSION FUNDS BY CERTAIN INSURANCE COMPANIES

**24A(1)** Paragraph 13A above does not apply to anything done by a relevant insurance company in relation to the investments of any pension fund which is established solely for the benefit of the officers or employees and their dependants of that company or of any other body corporate in the same group as that company.

**24A(2)** In sub-paragraph (1) above **"relevant insurance company"** means an insurance company to which Part II of the Insurance Companies Act 1982 applies but to which section 22 of this Act does not apply.

**History**
Para. 24A inserted by the Financial Services Act 1986 (Extension of Scope of Act) Order 1996 (SI 1996/2958), art. 1, 9 as from 1 June 1997.

## NEWSPAPERS

**25(1)** Paragraph 15 above does not apply to advice given in a newspaper, journal, magazine or other periodical publication if the principal purpose of the publication, taken as a whole and including any advertisements contained in it, is not to lead persons to invest in any particular investment.

**25(2)** The Secretary of State may, on the application of the proprietor of any periodical publication, certify that it is of the nature described in sub-paragraph (1) above and revoke any such certificate if he considers that it is no longer justified.

**25(3)** A certificate given under sub-paragraph (2) above and not revoked shall be conclusive evidence of the matters certified.

## ADVICE GIVEN IN TELEVISION, SOUND OR TELETEXT SERVICES

**25A(1)** Paragraph 15 above does not apply to any advice given in any programme included, or made for inclusion, in –

(a) any television broadcasting service or other programme service (within the meaning of Part I of the Broadcasting Act 1990); or

(b) any sound broadcasting service or licensable sound programme service (within the meaning of Part III of that Act); or

(c) any teletext service.

**History**
See history note after para. 25A(2).

**25A(2)** For the purposes of this paragraph, **"programme"**, in relation to a service mentioned in sub-paragraph (1) above, includes an advertisement and any other item included in the service.

**History**
Para. 25A and the heading preceding it substituted by the Financial Services Act 1986 (Extension of Scope of Act) Order 1992 (SI 1992/273), art. 2 as from 1 June 1992; para. 25A formerly read as follows:

"ADVICE GIVEN IN SOUND, TELEVISION OR CABLE PROGRAMMES

**25A(1)** Paragraph 15 above does not apply in respect of any advice given in any programme included, or made for inclusion, in a programme service.

**(2)** In this paragraph–

(a) **"programme"**, in relation to a programme service, includes an advertisement and any other item included in that service; and

(b) **"programme service"** has the same meaning as in the Broadcasting Act 1990."

Previously in para. 25A(1) the words "included, or made for inclusion, in a programme service" substituted by Broadcasting Act 1990, s. 203(1) and Sch. 20, para. 45(2)(a) as from 1 January 1991 (see SI 1990/2347 (C 61), art. 3, Sch. 2); the former words read as follows:

"or teletext transmission–

(a) broadcast, or made for broadcasting, by the British Broadcasting Corporation or by the Independent Broadcasting Authority in accordance with the provisions of the Broadcasting Act 1981; or

(b) included, or made for inclusion, in a cable programme service which is, or does not require to be, licensed under the Cable and Broadcasting Act 1984; or

(c) broadcast, or made for broadcasting, by the Independent Broadcasting Authority in a DBS service."

Also previously para. 25A(2) substituted by Broadcasting Act 1990, s. 203(1) and Sch. 20, para. 45(2)(b) as from 1 January 1991 (see SI 1990/2347 (C 61), art. 3, Sch. 2); para. 25A(2) formerly read as follows:

"In this paragraph–

(a) **"DBS service"** has the same meaning as in section 37(3) of the Cable and Broadcasting Act 1984;

(b) **"programme"**, in relation to a television or sound broadcasting service or a cable programme service, includes an advertisement and any other item included in that service; and

(c) **"teletext transmission"** has the same meaning as in section 14(6) of the Broadcasting Act 1981 and includes any such transmission broadcast in a DBS service or in a service which is an additional teletext service within the meaning of section 47(2) of the Cable and Broadcasting Act 1984."

Previously to that all of para. 25A substituted by Financial Services Act 1986 (Restriction of Scope of Act and Meaning of Collective Investment Scheme) Order 1990 (SI 1990/349), art. 5 as from 26 March 1990; prior to that substitution para. 25A read as follows:

"**25A(1)** Paragraph 15 above does not apply to any advice given in any programme or teletext transmission–

(a) broadcast, or made for broadcasting, by the British Broadcasting Corporation or by the Independent Broadcasting Authority in accordance with the provisions of the Broadcasting Act 1981; or
(b) included, or made for inclusion, in a cable programme service which is, or does not require to be, licensed under the Cable and Broadcasting Act 1984.

**(2)** In this paragraph–

**"programme"**, in relation to a television or sound broadcasting service or a cable programme service, includes an advertisement and any other item included in that service; and

**"teletext transmission"** has the same meaning as in section 14(6) of the Broadcasting Act 1981 and includes any such transmission broadcast by a service which is an additional teletext service within the meaning of section 47(2) of the Cable and Broadcasting Act 1984."

Originally para. 25A inserted by Financial Services Act 1986 (Restriction of Scope of Act) Order 1988 (SI 1988/318), art. 5 as from 27 February 1988; art. 5 revoked by Financial Services Act 1986 (Restriction of Scope of Act and Meaning of Collective Investment Scheme) Order 1990 (SI 1990/349), art. 8(a) as from 26 March 1990.

## INTERNATIONAL SECURITIES SELF-REGULATING ORGANISATIONS

**25B(1)** An activity within paragraph 13 above engaged in for the purposes of carrying out the functions of a body or association which is approved under this paragraph as an international securities self-regulating organisation, whether by the organisation or by any person acting on its behalf, shall not constitute the carrying on of investment business in the United Kingdom for the purposes of Chapter II of Part I of this Act.

**25B(2)** In this paragraph–

**"international securities business"** means the business of buying, selling, subscribing for or underwriting investments (or offering or agreeing to do so, either as principal or agent) which fall within any of the paragraphs in Part I above other than paragraph 10 and, so far as relevant to paragraph 10, paragraph 11 and which, by their nature, and the manner in which the business is conducted, may be expected normally to be bought or dealt in by persons sufficiently expert to understand any risks involved, where either the transaction is international or each of the parties may be expected to be indifferent to the location of the other, and, for the purposes of this definition, the fact that the investments may ultimately be bought otherwise than in the course of international securities business by persons not so expert shall be disregarded; and

**"international securities self-regulating organisation"** means a body corporate or unincorporated association which

(a) does not have its head office in the United Kingdom;
(b) is not eligible for recognition under section 37 or section 39 of this Act on the ground that (whether or not it has applied, and whether or not it would be eligible on other grounds) it is unable to satisfy the requirements of section 40(2)(a) or (c) of this Act;
(c) has a membership composed of persons falling within any of the following categories, that is to say, authorised persons, exempted persons, persons holding a permission under paragraph 23 above and persons whose head offices are outside the United Kingdom and whose ordinary business is such as is mentioned in paragraph 17(2)(e) above; and
(d) which facilitates and regulates the activity of its members in the conduct of international securities business.

**25B(3)** The Secretary of State may approve as an international securities self-regulating organisation any body or association appearing to him to fall within sub-paragraph (2) above if, having regard to such matters affecting international trade, overseas earnings and the balance of payments or otherwise as he considers relevant, it appears to him that to do so would be desirable and not result in any undue risk to investors.

**25B(4)** Any approval under this paragraph shall be given by notice in writing; and the Secretary of State may by a further notice in writing withdraw any such approval if for any reason it appears to him that it is not appropriate for it to continue in force.

**History**

Para. 25B inserted by the Financial Services Act 1986 (Restriction of Scope of Act) Order 1988 (SI 1988/318), art. 6 as from 27 February 1988.

# Part IV – Additional Exclusions for Persons Without Permanent Place of Business in United Kingdom

## TRANSACTIONS WITH OR THROUGH AUTHORISED OR EXEMPTED PERSONS

**26(1)** Paragraph 12 above does not apply to any transaction by a person not falling within section 1(3)(a) of this Act ("an overseas person") with or through–

(a) an authorised person; or

(b) an exempted person acting in the course of business in respect of which he is exempt.

**26(2)** Paragraph 13 above does not apply if–

(a) the arrangements are made by an overseas person with, or the offer or agreement to make them is made by him to or with, an authorised person or an exempted person and, in the case of an exempted person, the arrangements are with a view to his entering into a transaction in respect of which he is exempt; or

(b) the transactions with a view to which the arrangements are made are, as respects transactions in the United Kingdom, confined to transactions by authorised persons and transactions by exempted persons in respect of which they are exempt.

**Note**

Concerning effect of para. 26 re European investment firms, see the Investment Services Regulations 1995 (SI 1995/3275), reg. 32 and Sch. 7, para. 42(3).

Concerning European institutions, see the Banking Coordination (Second Council Directive) Regulations 1992 (SI 1992/3218), reg. 55 and Sch. 9, para. 44(3).

## UNSOLICITED OR LEGITIMATELY SOLICITED TRANSACTIONS ETC. WITH OR FOR OTHER PERSONS

**27(1)** Paragraph 12 above does not apply to any transaction entered into by an overseas person as principal with, or as agent for, a person in the United Kingdom, paragraphs 13, 13A, 14 and 15 above do not apply to any offer made by an overseas person to or agreement made by him with a person in the United Kingdom and paragraph 15 above does not apply to any advice given by an overseas person to a person in the United Kingdom if the transaction, offer, agreement or advice is the result of–

(a) an approach made to the overseas person by or on behalf of the person in the United Kingdom which either has not been in any way solicited by the overseas person or has been solicited by him in a way which has not contravened section 56 or 57 of this Act; or

(b) an approach made by the overseas person which has not contravened either of those sections.

**History**

In para. 27(1) the words "13A," appearing after the words "paragraphs 13" inserted by the Financial Services Act 1986 (Extension of Scope of Act) Order 1996 (SI 1996/2958), art. 1, 10 as from 1 June 1997.

**27(2)** Where the transaction is entered into by the overseas person as agent for a person in the United Kingdom, sub-paragraph (1) above applies only if–

(a) the other party is outside the United Kingdom; or

(b) the other party is in the United Kingdom and the transaction is the result of such an approach by the other party as is mentioned in sub-paragraph (1)(a) above or of such an approach as is mentioned in sub-paragraph (1)(b) above.

**27(3)** Paragraph 16A does not apply to any offer made by an overseas person to or agreement made by him with a person in the United Kingdom if the offer or agreement is the result of–

(a) an approach made to the overseas person by or on behalf of the person in the United Kingdom which either has not been in any way solicited by the overseas person, or has been solicited by him in a way which has not contravened section 56 or 57 of this Act; or

(b) an approach made by the overseas person which has not contravened either of those sections.

**History**
Para. 27(3) added by the Financial Services Act 1986 (Uncertificated Securities) (Extension of Scope of Act) Order 1996 (SI 1996/1322), art. 1, 4 as from 15 July 1996.

# Part V – Interpretation

**28(1)** In this Schedule–
(a) **"property"** includes currency of the United Kingdom or any other country or territory;
(b) references to an instrument include references to any record whether or not in the form of a document;
(c) references to an offer include references to an invitation to treat;
(d) references to buying and selling include references to any acquisition or disposal for valuable consideration.

**28(2)** In sub-paragraph (1)(d) above **"disposal"** includes–
(a) in the case of an investment consisting of rights under a contract or other arrangements, assuming the corresponding liabilities under the contract or arrangements;
(b) in the case of any other investment, issuing or creating the investment or granting the rights or interests of which it consists;
(c) in the case of an investment consisting of rights under a contract, surrendering, assigning or converting those rights.

**28(3)** A company shall not by reason of issuing its own shares or share warrants, and a person shall not by reason of issuing his own debentures or debenture warrants, be regarded for the purpose of this Schedule as disposing of them or, by reason of anything done for the purpose of issuing them, be regarded as making arrangements with a view to a person subscribing for or otherwise acquiring them or underwriting them.

**28(4)** In sub-paragraph (3) above **"company"** has the same meaning as in paragraph 1 above, "shares" and "debentures" include any investments falling within paragraph 1 or 2 above and **"share warrants"** and **"debenture warrants"** means any investment which falls within paragraph 4 above and relates to shares in the company concerned or, as the case may be, to debentures issued by the person concerned.

**29** For the purposes of this Schedule a transaction is entered into through a person if he enters into it as agent or arranges for it to be entered into by another person as principal or agent.

**30(1)** For the purposes of this Schedule a group shall be treated as including any body corporate in which a member of the group holds a qualifying capital interest.

**30(2)** A qualifying capital interest means an interest in relevant shares of the body corporate which the member holds on a long-term basis for the purpose of securing a contribution to its own activities by the exercise of control or influence arising from that interest.

**30(3)** Relevant shares means shares comprised in the equity share capital of the body corporate of a class carrying rights to vote in all circumstances at general meetings of the body.

**30(4)** A holding of 20 per cent or more of the nominal value of the relevant shares of a body corporate shall be presumed to be a qualifying capital interest unless the contrary is shown.

**30(5)** In this paragraph "equity share capital" has the same meaning as in the Companies Act 1985 and the Companies (Northern Ireland) Order 1986.

**History**
Para. 30 substituted by CA 1989, s. 23 and Sch. 10, para. 36(1), (3) as from 1 April 1990 subject to transitional and savings provisions (see SI 1990/355 (C 13), art. 3, Sch. 1 and also art. 6–9); para. 30 formerly read as follows:

"For the purposes of this Schedule a group shall be treated as including any body corporate which is a related company within the meaning of paragraph 92 of Schedule 4 to the Companies Act 1985 of any member of the group or would be such a related company if the member of the group were a company within the meaning of that Act."

**31** In this Schedule **"a joint enterprise"** means an enterprise into which two or more persons (**"the participators"**) enter for commercial reasons related to a business or businesses (other than investment business) carried on by them; and where a participator is a body corporate and a member of a group each other member of the group shall also be regarded as a participator in the enterprise.

32 Where a person is an exempted person as respects only part of the investment business carried on by him anything done by him in carrying on that part shall be disregarded in determining whether any paragraph of Part III or IV of this Schedule applies to anything done by him in the course of business in respect of which he is not exempt.

33 In determining for the purposes of this Schedule whether anything constitutes an investment or the carrying on of investment business section 18 of the Gaming Act 1845, section 1 of the Gaming Act 1892, any corresponding provision in force in Northern Ireland and any rule of the law of Scotland whereby a contract by way of gaming or wagering is not legally enforceable shall be disregarded.

34(1) For the purposes of this Schedule arrangements are not a collective investment scheme if–

(a) the property to which the arrangements relate (other than cash awaiting investment) consists of shares;

(b) they constitute a complying fund;

(c) each participant is the owner of a part of the property to which the arrangements relate and, to the extent that his part of that property–

(i) comprises relevant shares of a class which are admitted to the Official List of any member State or to dealings on a recognised investment exchange, he is entitled to withdraw it at any time after the end of the period of five years beginning with the date on which the shares in question were issued;

(ii) comprises relevant shares which do not fall within sub-paragraph (i) above, he is entitled to withdraw it at any time after the end of the period of two years beginning with the date upon which the period referred to in sub-paragraph (i) above expired;

(iii) comprises any other shares, he is entitled to withdraw it at any time after the end of the period of six months beginning with the date upon which the shares in question ceased to be relevant shares; and

(iv) comprises cash which the operator has not agreed (conditionally or unconditionally) to apply in subscribing for shares, he is entitled to withdraw it at any time; and

(d) the arrangements would meet the conditions described in section 75(5)(c) of this Act were it not for the fact that the operator is entitled to exercise all or any of the rights conferred by shares included in the property to which the arrangements relate.

34(2) For the purposes of this paragraph–

(a) **"shares"** means investments falling within paragraph 1 of this Schedule;

(b) shares shall be regarded as being relevant shares if and so long as they are shares in respect of which neither–

(i) a claim for relief made in accordance with section 306 of the Income and Corporation Taxes Act 1988 has been disallowed; nor

(ii) an assessment has been made pursuant to section 307 of that Act withdrawing or refusing relief by reason of the body corporate in which the shares are held having ceased to be a body corporate which is a qualifying company for the purposes of section 293 of that Act; and

(c) arrangements shall be regarded as constituting a complying fund if they provide that–

(i) the operator will, so far as practicable, make investments each of which, subject to each participant's individual circumstances, qualify for relief by virtue of Chapter III of Part VII of the Income and Corporation Taxes Act 1988; and

(ii) the minimum subscription to the arrangements made by each participant must be not less than £2,000.

**History**

See history note after para. 35.

35 For the purposes of this Schedule the following are not collective investment schemes–

(a) arrangements where the entire contribution of each participant is a deposit within the meaning of section 5 of the Banking Act 1987 or a sum of a kind described in subsection (3) of that section;

(b) arrangements under which the rights or interests of the participants are represented by the following–
   (i) investments falling within paragraph 2 of this Schedule which are issued by a single body corporate which is not an open-ended investment company or which are issued by a single issuer which is not a body corporate and are guaranteed by the government of the United Kingdom, of Northern Ireland, or of any country or territory outside the United Kingdom; or
   (ii) investments falling within sub-paragraph (i) above which are convertible into or exchangeable for investments falling within paragraph 1 of this Schedule provided that those latter investments are issued by the same person as issued the investments falling within sub-paragraph (i) above or are issued by a single other issuer; or
   (iii) investments falling within paragraph 3 of this Schedule issued by the same government, local authority or public authority; or
   (iv) investments falling within paragraph 4 of this Schedule which are issued otherwise than by an open-ended investment company and which confer rights in respect of investments, issued by the same issuer, falling within paragraph 1 of this Schedule or within sub-paragraph (i), (ii) or (iii) above;

(c) arrangements which would fall within paragraph (b) above were it not for the fact that the rights or interests of a participant ("the counterparty") whose ordinary business involves him in engaging in activities which fall within Part II of this Schedule or would do so apart from Part III or IV are or include rights or interests under a swap arrangement, that is to say, an arrangement the purpose of which is to facilitate the making of payments to participants whether in a particular amount or currency or at a particular time or rate of interest or all or any combination of those things, being an arrangement under which–
   (i) the counterparty is entitled to receive amounts (whether representing principal or interest) payable in respect of any property subject to the scheme or sums determined by reference to such amounts; and
   (ii) the counterparty makes payments (whether or not of the same amount and whether or not in the same currency as those referred to in sub-paragraph (i) above) which are calculated in accordance with an agreed formula by reference to the amounts or sums referred to in sub-paragraph (i) above;

(d) arrangements under which the rights or interests of participants are rights to or interests in money held in a common account in circumstances in which the money so held is held on the understanding that an amount representing the contribution of each participant is to be applied either in making payments to him or in satisfaction of sums owed by him or in the acquisition of property or the provision of services for him;

(e) arrangements under which the rights and interests of participants are rights and interests in a fund which is a trust fund within the meaning of section 42(1) of the Landlord and Tenant Act 1987.

(f) arrangements where–
   (i) each of the participants is a bona fide employee or former employee (or the wife, husband, widow, widower, or child (including, in Northern Ireland, adopted child) or step-child under the age of eighteen of such an employee or former employee) of any of the following bodies corporate, that is to say, The National Grid Company plc, Electricity Association Services Limited or any other body corporate in the same group as either of them being arrangements which are operated by any of those bodies corporate; and
   (ii) the property to which the arrangements relate consists of shares or debentures (as defined in paragraph 20(4) above) in or of a body corporate which is an electricity successor company for the purposes of Part II of the Electricity Act 1989 or a body corporate which would be regarded as connected with such an electricity successor company for the purposes of paragraph 20 above,

and for the purposes of this paragraph references to former employees shall have the same meaning as in the Financial Services Act 1986 (Electricity Industry Exemptions) Order 1990.

**History**

In para. 35(f)(i) the words "being arrangements which are" substituted for the former words "and which is" by Financial Services Act 1986 (Schedule 1 (Amendment) and Miscellaneous Exemption) Order 1991 (SI 1991/1516), art. 2 as from 1 August 1991.

Previously para. 35(f) added by Financial Services Act 1986 (Restriction of Scope of Act and Meaning of Collective Investment Scheme) (No. 2) Order 1990 (SI 1990/1493), art. 2 as from 25 July 1990.

Para. 34 and 35 originally added by Financial Services Act 1986 (Restriction of Scope of Act and Meaning of Collective Investment Scheme) Order 1990 (SI 1990/349), art. 7 as from 26 March 1990.

**36(1)** For the purposes of this Schedule, arrangements are not a collective investment scheme if they are operated by a body corporate, a body corporate connected with it or a relevant trustee, for the purpose of enabling or facilitating transactions in shares in or debentures of the first-mentioned body between or for the benefit of any of the persons mentioned in sub-paragraph (2) below or the holding of such shares or debentures by or for the benefit of any such persons.

**36(2)** The persons referred to in sub-paragraph (1) above are–

(a) the bona fide employees or former employees of the body corporate or of another body corporate in the same group; or

(b) the wives, husbands, widows, widowers, or children or step-children under the age of eighteen of such employees or former employees.

**36(3)** In this paragraph, **"a relevant trustee"** means a person holding shares in or debentures of a body corporate as trustee in pursuance of arrangements mentioned in sub-paragraph (1) above which were made by, or by a body corporate connected with, that body corporate.

**36(4)** In this paragraph **"shares"** and **"debentures"** include any investment falling within paragraph 1 or 2 above and also include any investment falling within paragraph 4 or 5 above so far as relating to those paragraphs or any investment falling within paragraph 11 above so far as relating to paragraphs 1, 2, 4 or 5.

**36(5)** For the purposes of this paragraph a body corporate is connected with another body corporate if–

(a) they are in the same group; or

(b) one is entitled, either alone or with any other body corporate in the same group, to exercise or control the exercise of a majority of the voting rights attributable to the share capital which are exercisable in all circumstances at any general meeting of the other body corporate or its holding company.

**History**

Para. 36 inserted by the Financial Services Act 1986 (Restriction of Scope of Act and Meaning of Collective Investment Scheme) Order 1996 (SI 1996/2996), art. 1 and 3(2) as from 1 January 1997.

**37** For the purposes of this Schedule, arrangements are not a collective investment scheme if–

(a) the purpose of the arrangements is that participants should receive, by way of reward, payments or other benefits in respect of the introduction by any person of other persons who become participants;

(b) the arrangements are such that the payments or other benefits referred to in paragraph (a) above are to be wholly or mainly funded out of the contributions of other participants; and

(c) the only reason why the arrangements have either or both of the characteristics mentioned in section 75(3) of this Act is because, pending their being used to fund those payments or other benefits, contributions of participants are managed as a whole by or on behalf of the operator of the scheme.

**History**

Para. 37 inserted by the Financial Services Act 1986 (Restriction of Scope of Act and Meaning of Collective Investment Scheme) Order 1997 (SI 1997/32), art. 1, 2(2) as from 6 February 1997.

# Schedule 2 – Requirements for Recognition of Self-Regulating Organisation

Section 10

## MEMBERS TO BE FIT AND PROPER PERSONS

**1(1)** The rules and practices of the organisation must be such as to secure that its members are fit and proper persons to carry on investment business of the kind with which the organisation is concerned.

**1(2)** Where the organisation is concerned with investment business of different kinds its rules and practices must be such as to secure that a member carrying on investment business of any of those kinds is a fit and proper person to carry on investment business of that kind.

**1(3)** The matters which may be taken into account under the rules in determining whether a person is a fit and proper person must include those that the Secretary of State may take into account under section 27 above.

**1(4)** This paragraph does not apply to a person who is not an authorised person by virtue of being a member of the organisation.

**Note**
Concerning effect of para. 1 see the Investment Services Regulations 1995 (SI 1995/3275), reg. 1, 21(2)–(4).

## ADMISSION, EXPULSION AND DISCIPLINE

**2** The rules and practices of the organisation relating to–

(a) the admission and expulsion of members; and

(b) the discipline it exercises over its members,

must be fair and reasonable and include adequate provision for appeals.

**Note**
Concerning effect of para. 2 see the Investment Services Regulations 1995 (SI 1995/3275), reg. 1, 21(5).
Concerning effect of para. 2 re European investment firms, see the Investment Services Regulations 1995 (SI 1995/3275), reg. 32 and Sch. 7, para. 43(1).
See the Banking Coordination (Second Council Directive) Regulations 1992 (SI 1992/3218), reg. 48(2)–(3), reg. 55 and Sch. 9, para. 45.

## SAFEGUARDS FOR INVESTORS

**3(1)** The organisation must have rules governing the carrying on of investment business by its members which, together with the statements of principle, rules, regulations and codes of practice to which its members are subject under Chapter V of Part I of this Act, are such as to afford an adequate level of protection for investors.

**3(2)** In determining in any case whether an adequate level of protection is afforded for investors of any description, regard shall be had to the nature of the investment business carried on by members of the organisation, the kinds of investors involved and the effectiveness of the organisation's arrangements for enforcing compliance.

**History**
Para. 3(1), (2) substituted by CA 1989, s. 203(1) as from 15 March 1990 (see SI 1990/354 (C 12), art. 3); para. 3(1), (2) formerly read as follows:

"**3(1)** The rules of the organisation governing the carrying on of investment business of any kind by its members must afford investors protection at least equivalent to that afforded in respect of investment business of that kind by the rules and regulations for the time being in force under Chapter V of Part I of this Act.
**(2)** The rules under that Chapter to be taken into account for the purposes of sub-paragraph (1) above include the rules made under section 49 and under sections 53 and 54 so far as not themselves applying to the members of the organisation."

**Note**
For transitional provisions in relation to para. 3(1), (2) see CA 1989, s. 203(3) and SI 1990/354 (C 2), art. 6.

**3(3)** The organisation must, so far as practicable, have powers for purposes corresponding to those of Chapter VI of Part I of this Act.

**3(4)** The rules of the organisation must enable it to prevent a member resigning from the organisation if the organisation considers that any matter affecting him should be investigated as a preliminary to a decision on the question whether he should be expelled or otherwise disciplined or if it considers that it is desirable that a prohibition or requirement should be imposed on him under the powers mentioned in sub-paragraph (3) above or that any prohibition or requirement imposed on him under those powers should continue in force.

**Note**

Concerning effect of para. 3 re European investment firms, see the Investment Services Regulations 1995 (SI 1995/3275), reg. 32 and Sch. 7, para. 43(2), (3).

Concerning European institutions, see the Banking Coordination (Second Council Directive) Regulations 1992 (SI 1992/3218), reg. 55 and Sch. 9, para. 45(2)–(3).

## TAKING ACCOUNT OF COSTS OF COMPLIANCE

**3A** The organisation must have satisfactory arrangements for taking account, in framing its rules, of the cost to those to whom the rules would apply of complying with those rules and any other controls to which they are subject.

**History**

Para. 3A inserted by CA 1989, s. 204(1) as from 15 March 1990 (see SI 1990/354 (C 12), art. 3).

**Note**

See CA 1989, s. 204(2), (3).

## MONITORING AND ENFORCEMENT

**4(1)** The organisation must have adequate arrangements and resources for the effective monitoring and enforcement of compliance with its rules and with any statements of principle, rules, regulations or codes of practice to which its members are subject under Chapter V of Part I of this Act in respect of investment business of a kind regulated by the organisation.

**History**

In para. 4(1) the words "statements of principle, rules, regulations or codes of practice" substituted for the former words "rules or regulations" by CA 1989, s. 206(1) and Sch. 23, para. 20 as from 15 March 1990 (see SI 1990/354 (C 12), art. 3).

**4(2)** The arrangements for monitoring may make provision for that function to be performed on behalf of the organisation (and without affecting its responsibility) by any other body or person who is able and willing to perform it.

## THE GOVERNING BODY

**5(1)** The arrangements of the organisation with respect to the appointment, removal from office and functions of the persons responsible for making or enforcing the rules of the organisation must be such as to secure a proper balance–

(a) between the interests of the different members of the organisation; and

(b) between the interests of the organisation or its members and the interests of the public.

**5(2)** The arrangements shall not be regarded as satisfying the requirements of this paragraph unless the persons responsible for those matters include a number of persons independent of the organisation and its members sufficient to secure the balance referred to in sub-paragraph (1)(b) above.

## INVESTIGATION OF COMPLAINTS

**6(1)** The organisation must have effective arrangements for the investigation of complaints against the organisation or its members.

**6(2)** The arrangements may make provision for the whole or part of that function to be performed by and to be the responsibility of a body or person independent of the organisation.

## PROMOTION AND MAINTENANCE OF STANDARDS

**7** The organisation must be able and willing to promote and maintain high standards of integrity and fair dealing in the carrying on of investment business and to co-operate, by the sharing of information and otherwise, with the Secretary of State and any other authority, body or person having responsibility for the supervision or regulation of investment business or other financial services.

**Note**

Concerning effect of para. 7 see the Investment Services Regulations 1995 (SI 1995/3275), reg. 32 and Sch. 7, para. 43(4).

Concerning European co-operation, see the Banking Coordination (Second Council Directive) Regulations 1992 (SI 1992/3218), reg. 55 and Sch. 9, para. 45(4).

# Schedule 3 – Requirements for Recognition of Professional Body

Section 18

## STATUTORY STATUS

**1** The body must–

(a) regulate the practice of a profession in the exercise of statutory powers; or

(b) be recognised (otherwise than under this Act) for a statutory purpose by a Minister of the Crown or by, or by the head of, a Northern Ireland department; or

(c) be specified in a provision contained in or made under an enactment as a body whose members are qualified to exercise functions or hold offices specified in that provision.

## CERTIFICATION

**2(1)** The body must have rules, practices and arrangements for securing that no person can be certified by the body for the purposes of Part I of this Act unless the following conditions are satisfied.

**2(2)** The certified person must be either–

(a) an individual who is a member of the body; or

(b) a person managed and controlled by one or more individuals each of whom is a member of a recognised professional body and at least one of whom is a member of the certifying body.

**2(3)** Where the certified person is an individual his main business must be the practice of the profession regulated by the certifying body and he must be practising that profession otherwise than in partnership; and where the certified person is not an individual that person's main business must be the practice of the profession or professions regulated by the recognised professional body or bodies of which the individual or individuals mentioned in sub-paragraph (2)(b) above are members.

**2(4)** In the application of sub-paragraphs (2) and (3) above to a certificate which is to be or has been issued to a partnership constituted under the law of England and Wales or Northern Ireland or the law of any other country or territory under which a partnership is not a legal person, references to the certified person shall be construed as references to the partnership.

**Note**

Concerning effect of para. 2 see the Investment Services Regulations 1995 (SI 1995/3275), reg. 1, 31.

## SAFEGUARDS FOR INVESTORS

**3(1)** The body must have rules regulating the carrying on of investment business by persons certified by it which, together with the statements of principle, rules, regulations and codes of practice to which those persons are subject under Chapter V of Part I of this Act, afford an adequate level of protection for investors.

**3(2)** In determining in any case whether an adequate level of protection is afforded for investors of any description, regard shall be had to the nature of the investment business carried on by persons certified by the body, the kinds of investors involved and the effectiveness of the body's arrangements for enforcing compliance.

**History**

Para. 3 substituted by CA 1989, s. 203(2) as from 15 March 1990 (see SI 1990/354 (C 12), art. 3); para. 3 formerly read as follows:

"**3(1)** The body must have rules regulating the carrying on of investment business by persons certified by it; and those rules must in respect of investment business of any kind regulated by them afford to investors protection at least equivalent to that afforded in respect of investment business of that kind by the rules and regulations for the time being in force under Chapter V of Part I of this Act.

**(2)** The rules under that Chapter to be taken into account for the purposes of this paragraph include the rules made under section 49 and under sections 53 and 54 so far as not themselves applying to persons certified by the body."

**Note**

For transitional provisions in relation to para. 3 see CA 1989, s. 203(3) and SI 1990/354 (C 12), art. 6.

## TAKING ACCOUNT OF COSTS OF COMPLIANCE

**3A** The organisation must have satisfactory arrangements for taking account, in framing its rules, of the cost to those to whom the rules would apply of complying with those rules and any other controls to which they are subject.

**History**
Para. 3A inserted by CA 1989, s. 204(1) as from 15 March 1990 (see SI 1990/354 (C 12), art. 3).

**Note**
See CA 1989, s. 204(2), (3).

## MONITORING AND ENFORCEMENT

**4(1)** The body must have adequate arrangements and resources for the effective monitoring of the continued compliance by persons certified by it with the conditions mentioned in paragraph 2 above and rules, practices and arrangements for the withdrawal or suspension of certification (subject to appropriate transitional provisions) in the event of any of those conditions ceasing to be satisfied.

**4(2)** The body must have adequate arrangements and resources for the effective monitoring and enforcement of compliance by persons certified by it with the rules of the body relating to the carrying on of investment business and with any statements of principle, rules, regulations or codes of practice to which those persons are subject under Chapter V of Part I of this Act in respect of business of a kind regulated by the body.

**History**
In para. 4(2) the words "statements of principle, rules, regulations or codes of practice" substituted for the former words "rules or regulations" by CA 1989, s. 206(1) and Sch. 23, para. 21 as from 15 March 1990 (see SI 1990/354 (C 12), art. 3).

**4(3)** The arrangements for enforcement must include provision for the withdrawal or suspension of certification and may include provision for disciplining members of the body who manage or control a certified person.

**4(4)** The arrangements for enforcement may make provision for the whole or part of that function to be performed by and to be the responsibility of a body or person independent of the professional body.

**4(5)** The arrangements for enforcement must be such as to secure a proper balance between the interests of persons certified by the body and the interests of the public; and the arrangements shall not be regarded as satisfying that requirement unless the persons responsible for enforcement include a sufficient number of persons who are independent of the body and its members and of persons certified by it.

**4(6)** The arrangements for monitoring may make provision for that function to be performed on behalf of the body (and without affecting its responsibility) by any other body or person who is able and willing to perform it.

## INVESTIGATION OF COMPLAINTS

**5(1)** The body must have effective arrangements for the investigation of complaints relating to–

(a) the carrying on by persons certified by it of investment business in respect of which they are subject to its rules; and

(b) its regulation of investment business.

**5(2)** Paragraph 4(4) above applies also to arrangements made pursuant to this paragraph.

## PROMOTION AND MAINTENANCE OF STANDARDS

**6** The body must be able and willing to promote and maintain high standards of integrity and fair dealing in the carrying on of investment business and to co-operate, by the sharing of information and otherwise, with the Secretary of State and any other authority, body or person having responsibility for the supervision or regulation of investment business or other financial services.

# Schedule 4 – Requirements for Recognition of Investment Exchange

Sections 36 and 37

## FINANCIAL RESOURCES

**1** The exchange must have financial resources sufficient for the proper performance of its functions.

## SAFEGUARDS FOR INVESTORS

**2(1)** The rules and practices of the exchange must ensure that business conducted by means of its facilities is conducted in an orderly manner and so as to afford proper protection to investors.

**2(2)** The exchange must–

(a) limit dealings on the exchange to investments in which there is a proper market; and

(b) where relevant, require issuers of investments dealt in on the exchange to comply with such obligations as will, so far as possible, afford to persons dealing in the investments proper information for determining their current value.

**2(3)** (Repealed by the Official Listing of Securities (Change of Competent Authority) Regulations 2000 (SI 2000/968), reg. 1, 9 as from 1 May 2000.)

**History**

Para. 2(3) formerly read as follows:

"In the case of securities to which Part IV of this Act applies compliance by The London Stock Exchange with the provisions of that Part shall be treated as compliance by it with sub-paragraph (2) above."

**2(4)** The exchange must either have its own arrangements for ensuring the performance of transactions effected on the exchange or ensure their performance by means of services provided under clearing arrangements made by it with a recognised clearing house.

**2(5)** The exchange must either itself have or secure the provision on its behalf of satisfactory arrangements for recording the transactions effected on the exchange.

**2(6)** Sub-paragraphs (2), (4) and (5) above are without prejudice to the generality of sub-paragraph (1) above.

## MONITORING AND ENFORCEMENT

**3(1)** The exchange must have adequate arrangements and resources for the effective monitoring and enforcement of compliance with its rules and any clearing arrangements made by it.

**3(2)** The arrangements for monitoring may make provision for that function to be performed on behalf of the exchange (and without affecting its responsibility) by any other body or person who is able and willing to perform it.

## INVESTIGATION OF COMPLAINTS

**4** The exchange must have effective arrangements for the investigation of complaints in respect of business transacted by means of its facilities.

## PROMOTION AND MAINTENANCE OF STANDARDS

**5** The exchange must be able and willing to promote and maintain high standards of integrity and fair dealing in the carrying on of investement business and to co-operate, by the sharing of information and otherwise, with the Secretary of State and any other authority, body or person having responsibility for the supervision or regulation of investment business or other financial services.

## SUPPLEMENTARY

**6(1)** The provisions of this Schedule relate to an exchange only so far as it provides facilities for the carrying on of investment business; and nothing in this Schedule shall be construed as requiring an exchange to limit dealings on the exchange to dealings in investments.

**6(2)** The references in this Schedule, and elsewhere in this Act, to ensuring the performance of transactions on an exchange are to providing satisfactory procedures (including default procedures) for the settlement of transactions on the exchange.

**History**

Para. 6 inserted by CA 1989, s. 205(1) as from 15 March 1990 (see SI 1990/354 (C 12), art. 3) but the amendment is deemed always to have had effect (see CA 1989, s. 205(2)).

# Schedule 5 – Listed Money Market Institutions

Section 43

## Part I – Transactions not Subject to Monetary Limit

**1** This Part of this Schedule applies to any transaction entered into by the listed institution as principal (or as agent for another listed institution) with another listed institution, the Treasury or the Bank of England (whether acting as principal or agent) if the transaction falls within paragraph 2 or 3 below.

**History**

In para. 1 the words ", the Treasury" inserted by the Bank of England Act 1998, s. 32(a), 45 as from 1 June 1998 (see SI 1998/1120 (C 25), art. 2).

**2(1)** A transaction falls within this paragraph if it is in respect of an investment specified in sub-paragraph (2) below and–

(a) in the case of an investment within any of paragraphs (a) to (d) of that sub-paragraph, the transaction is not regulated by the rules of a recognised investment exchange; and

(b) in the case of any other investment specified in that sub-paragraph, the transaction is not made on such an exchange or expressed to be as so made.

**2(2)** The investments referred to above are–

(a) a debenture or other instrument falling within paragraph 2 of Schedule 1 to this Act which is issued on terms requiring payment not later than five years from the date of the issue;

(c) loan stock, or any other instrument, falling within paragraph 3 of Schedule 1 to this Act which is issued on terms requiring repayment not later than one year or, if issued by a local authority in the United Kingdom, five years from the date of issue;

(d) a warrant or other instrument falling within paragraph 4 of Schedule 1 to this Act which entitles the holder to subscribe for an investment within paragraph (a) or (c) above;

(e) any certificate or other instrument falling within paragraph 5 or 11 of Schedule 1 to this Act and relating to an investment within paragraph (a) or (c) above;

(f) an option falling within paragraph 7 of Schedule 1 to this Act and relating to–

  (i) an investment within paragraph (a) or (c) above;

  (ii) currency of the United Kingdom or of any other country or territory; or

  (iii) gold or silver;

(g) rights under a contract falling within paragraph 8 of Schedule 1 to this Act for the sale of–

  (i) an investment within paragraph (a) or (c) above;

  (ii) currency of the United Kingdom or of any other country or territory; or

  (iii) gold or silver;

(h) rights under a contract falling within paragraph 9 of Schedule 1 to this Act by reference to fluctuations in–

  (i) the value or price of any investment falling within any of the foregoing paragraphs; or

  (ii) currency of the United Kingdom or of any other country or territory; or

  (iii) the rate of interest on loans in any such currency or any index of such rates;

(i) an option to acquire or dispose of an investment within paragraph (f), (g) or (h) above.

**History**
Para. 2(2)(a) substituted for the former para. 2(2)(a) and (b) by the Financial Services Act 1986 (Corporate Debt Exemption) Order 1997 (SI 1997/816), art. 1 and 2(a) as from 3 April 1997. The former para. 2(2)(a) and (b) read as follows:

"(a) a debenture or other instrument falling within paragraph 2 of Schedule 1 to this Act which is issued–
- (i) by an authorised institution within the meaning of the Banking Act 1987 or a building society incorporated in, or in any part of, the United Kingdom; and
- (ii) on terms requiring repayment not later than five years from the date of issue;

(b) any other debenture or instrument falling within paragraph 2 of Schedule 1 to this Act which is issued on terms requiring repayment not later than one year from the date of issue;"

In para. 2(2)(d), (e), (f)(i) and (g)(i) the words "paragraph (a) or (c)" substituted for the former words "paragraph (a), (b) or (c)" by the Financial Services Act 1986 (Corporate Debt Exemption) Order 1997 (SI 1997/816), art. 1 and 2(b) as from 3 April 1997.

Previously in para. 2(2) the words, "an authorised institution within the meaning of the Banking Act 1987", substituted for the former words "a recognised bank or licensed institution within the meaning of the Banking Act 1979" by Banking Act 1987, s. 108(1) and Sch. 6, para. 27(6) as from 1 October 1987 (see SI 1987/1664 (C 50)).

**Note**
Concerning European institutions, see the Banking Coordination (Second Council Directive) Regulations 1992 (SI 1992/3218), reg. 82 and Sch. 10, para. 23.

**3(1)** A transaction falls within this paragraph if it is a transaction by which one of the parties agrees to sell or transfer an investment falling within paragraph 2 or 3 of Schedule 1 to this Act and by the same or a collateral agreement that party agrees, or acquires an option, to buy back or re-acquire that investment or an equivalent amount of a similar investment within twelve months of the sale or transfer.

**3(2)** For the purposes of this paragraph investments shall be regarded as similar if they entitle their holders to the same rights against the same persons as to capital and interest and the same remedies for the enforcement of those rights.

# Part II – Transactions Subject to Monetary Limit

**4(1)** This Part of the Schedule applies to any transaction entered into by the listed institution–

(a) as principal (or as agent for another listed institution) with an unlisted person (whether acting as principal or agent);

(b) as agent for an unlisted person with a listed institution, the Treasury or the Bank of England (whether acting as principal or agent); or

(c) as agent for an unlisted person with another unlisted person (whether acting as principal or agent),

if the transaction falls within paragraph 2 or 3 above and the conditions in paragraph 5 or, as the case may be, paragraph 7 below are satisfied.

**History**
In para. 4(1)(b) the words ", the Treasury" inserted by the Bank of England Act 1998, s. 32(b), 45 as from 1 June 1998 (see SI 1998/1120 (C 25), art. 2).

**4(2)** In this Part of this Schedule and in Part III below **"unlisted person"** means a person who is neither a listed institution, the Treasury nor the Bank of England.

**History**
In para. 4(2) the words ", the Treasury" inserted by the Bank of England Act 1998, s. 32(b), 45 as from 1 June 1998 (see SI 1998/1120 (C 25), art. 2).

**5(1)** In the case of a transaction falling within paragraph 2 above the conditions referred to above are as follows but subject to paragraph 6 below.

**5(2)** The consideration for a transaction in respect of an investment falling within paragraph 2(2)(a), (c) or (e) above must be not less than £100,000.

**History**
In para. 5(2) the words "paragraph (2)(a), (c) or (e) above" substituted for the former words "paragraph 2(2)(a), (b), (c) or (e)" by the Financial Services Act 1986 (Corporate Debt Exemption) Order 1997 (SI 1997/816), art. 1 and 3 as from 3 April 1997.

**Note**
In para 5(2) the words "paragraph (2)(a), (b), (c) or (e) above" were originally "paragraph 2(2)(a), (b), (c) or (e)" in the Financial Services Act 1986, Sch. 5, Pt. II, para 5(2). The Financial Services Act 1986 (Corporate Debt Exemption) Order 1997 (SI 1997/816) failed to mention "2".]

**5(3)** The consideration payable on subscription in the case of an investment falling within paragraph 2(2)(d) must not be less than £500,000.

**5(4)** The value or price of the property in respect of which an option within paragraph 2(2)(f) above is granted must not be less than £500,000.

**5(5)** The price payable under a contract within paragraph 2(2)(g) above must be not less than £500,000.

**5(6)** The value or price the fluctuation in which, or the amount the fluctuation in the interest on which, is relevant for the purposes of a contract within paragraph 2(2)(h) above must not be less than £500,000.

**5(7)** In the case of an option falling within paragraph 2(2)(i) above the condition in sub-paragraph (4), (5) or (6) above, as the case may be, must be satisfied in respect of the investment to which the option relates.

**6** The conditions in paragraph 5 above do not apply to a transaction entered into by the listed institution as mentioned in paragraph (a), (b) or (c) of paragraph 4(1) above if–

(a) the unlisted person mentioned in paragraph (a) or (b) or, as the case may be, each of the unlisted persons mentioned in paragraph (c) has in the previous eighteen months entered into another transaction in respect of an investment specified in paragraph 2(2) above;

(b) those conditions were satisfied in the case of that other transaction; and

(c) that other transaction was entered into by that person (whether acting as principal or agent) with the listed institution (whether acting as principal or agent) or was entered into by that person through the agency of that institution or was entered into by him (whether acting as principal or agent) as a result of arrangements made by that institution.

**7** In the case of a transaction falling within paragraph 3 above the condition referred to in paragraph 4 above is that the consideration for the sale or transfer must be not less than £100,000.

**8** The monetary limits mentioned in this Part of this Schedule refer to the time when the transaction is entered into; and where the consideration, value, price or amount referred to above is not in sterling it shall be converted at the rate of exchange prevailing at that time.

## Part III – Transactions Arranged by Listed Institutions

**9** Subject to paragraphs 10 and 11 below, this Part of this Schedule applies to any transaction arranged by the listed institution which–

(a) is entered into by another listed institution as principal (or as agent for another listed institution) with another listed institution, the Treasury or the Bank of England (whether acting as principal or agent);

(b) is entered into by another listed institution (whether acting as principal or agent) with an unlisted person (whether acting as principal or agent); or

(c) is entered into between unlisted persons (whether acting as principal or agent),

if the transaction falls within paragraph 2 or 3 above.

**History**

In para. 9(a) the words ", the Treasury" inserted by the Bank of England Act 1998, s. 32(c), 45 as from 1 June 1998 (see SI 1998/1120 (C 25), art. 2).

**10** In the case of a transaction falling within paragraph 2 above paragraph 9(b) and (c) above do not apply unless either the conditions in paragraph 5 above are satisfied or–

(a) the unlisted person mentioned in paragraph (b) or, as the case may be, each of the unlisted persons mentioned in paragraph (c) has in the previous eighteen months entered into another transaction in respect of an investment specified in paragraph 2(2) above;

(b) those conditions were satisfied in the case of that other transaction; and

(c) that other transaction was entered into by that person (whether acting as principal or agent) with the listed institution making the arrangements (whether acting as principal or agent) or through the agency of that institution or was entered into by that person (whether acting as principal or agent) as a result of arrangments made by that institution.

**11** In the case of a transaction falling within paragraph 3 above paragraph 9(b) and (c) above do not apply unless the condition in paragraph 7 above is satisfied.

# Schedule 6 – The Financial Services Tribunal

Section 96(6)

## TERM OF OFFICE OF MEMBERS

**1(1)** A person appointed to the panel mentioned in section 96(2) of this Act shall hold and vacate his office in accordance with the terms of his appointment and on ceasing to hold office shall be eligible for re-appointment.

**1(2)** A member of the panel appointed by the Lord Chancellor may resign his office by notice in writing to the Lord Chancellor; and a member of the panel appointed by the Secretary of State may resign his office by notice in writing to the Secretary of State.

## EXPENSES

**2** The Secretary of State shall pay to the persons serving as members of the Tribunal such remuneration and allowances as he may determine and shall defray such other expenses of the Tribunal as he may approve.

## STAFF

**3** The Secretary of State may provide the Tribunal with such officers and servants as he thinks necessary for the proper discharge of its functions.

## PROCEDURE

**4(1)** The Secretary of State may make rules for regulating the procedure of the Tribunal, including provision for the holding of any proceedings in private, for the awarding of costs (or, in Scotland, expenses) and for the payment of expenses to persons required to attend before the Tribunal.

**4(2)** The Tribunal may appoint counsel or a solicitor to assist it in proceedings before the Tribunal.

## EVIDENCE

**5(1)** The Tribunal may by summons require any person to attend, at such time and place as is specified in the summons, to give evidence or to produce any document in his custody or under his control which the Tribunal considers it necessary to examine.

**5(2)** The Tribunal may take evidence on oath and for that purpose administer oaths or may, instead of administering an oath, require the person examined to make and subscribe a declaration of the truth of the matters in respect of which he is examined.

**5(3)** Any person who without reasonable excuse–

(a) refuses or fails to attend in obedience to a summons issued by the Tribunal or to give evidence; or

(b) alters, suppresses, conceals or destroys or refuses to produce a document which he may be required to produce for the purposes of proceedings before the Tribunal,

shall be guilty of an offence.

**5(4)** A person guilty of an offence under paragraph (a) of sub-paragraph (3) above shall be liable on summary conviction to a fine not exceeding the fifth level on the standard scale; and a person guilty of an offence under paragraph (b) of that sub-paragraph shall be liable–

(a) on conviction on indictment, to imprisonment for a term not exceeding two years or to a fine or to both;

(b) on summary conviction, to a fine not exceeding the statutory maximum.

**5(5)** A person shall not under this paragraph be required to disclose any information or produce any document which he would be entitled to refuse to disclose or produce on grounds of legal professional privilege in proceedings in the High Court or on grounds of confidentiality as between client and professional legal adviser in proceedings in the Court of Session except that a lawyer may be required to furnish the name and address of his client.

**5(6)** Any reference in this paragraph to the production of a document includes a reference to the production of a legible copy of information recorded otherwise than in legible form; and the reference to suppressing a document includes a reference to destroying the means of reproducing information recorded otherwise than in legible form.

### APPEALS AND SUPERVISION BY COUNCIL ON TRIBUNALS

**6** (Repealed by Tribunals and Inquiries Act 1992, s. 18(2), 19(2) and Sch. 4, Pt. I as from 1 October 1992.)

**History**
Para. 6 formerly read as follows:
"The Tribunals and Inquiries Act 1971 shall be amended as follows–
(a) in section 8(2) after "6A" there shall be inserted "6B";
(b) in section 13(1) after "6" there shall be inserted "6B";
(c) in Schedule 1, after paragraph 6A there shall be inserted–
"*Financial services*
**6B** The Financial Services Tribunal established by section 96 of the Financial Services Act 1986.""

### PARLIAMENTARY DISQUALIFICATION

**7(1)** In Part III of Schedule 1 to the House of Commons Disqualification Act 1975 (disqualifying offices) there shall be inserted at the appropriate place "Any member of the Financial Services Tribunal in receipt of remuneration".

**7(2)** A corresponding amendment shall be made in Part III of Schedule 1 to the Northern Ireland Assembly Disqualification Act 1975.

## Schedule 7 – Qualifications of Designated Agency

Section 114

### CONSTITUTION

**1(1)** The constitution of the agency must provide for it to have–
(a) a chairman; and
(b) a governing body consisting of the chairman and other members;
and the provisions of the constitution relating to the chairman and the other members of the governing body must comply with the following provisions of this paragraph.

**1(2)** The chairman and other members of the governing body must be persons appointed and liable to removal from office by the Treasury.

**History**
In para. 1(2) the words "and the Governor of the Bank of England acting jointly" appearing after the words "by the Treasury" omitted and repealed by the Bank of England Act 1998, s. 31, 43, 45 and Sch. 9, Pt. I as from 1 June 1998 (see SI 1998/1120, art. 2).
Previously in para. 1(2) the word "Treasury" substituted for the former words "Secretary of State" by the Transfer of Functions (Financial Services) Order 1992 (SI 1992/1315), para. 10(1) and Sch. 4, para. 10 as from 7 June 1992.

**1(3)** The members of the governing body must include–
(a) persons with experience of investment business of a kind relevant to the functions or proposed functions of the agency; and
(b) other persons, including regular users on their own account or on behalf of others of services provided by persons carrying on investment business of any such kind;
and the composition of that body must be such as to secure a proper balance between the interests of persons carrying on investment business and the interests of the public.

### ARRANGEMENTS FOR DISCHARGE OF FUNCTIONS

**2(1)** The agency's arrangements for the discharge of its functions must comply with the following provisions of this paragraph.

**2(2)** Any statements of principle, rules, regulations and codes of practice must be issued or made by the governing body of the agency.

**History**
In para. 2(2) the words "statements of principle, rules, regulations and codes of practice must be issued or made" substituted for the former words "rules or regulations must be made" by CA 1989, s. 206(1) and Sch. 23, para. 22 as from 15 March 1990 (see SI 1990/354 (C 12), art. 3).

**2(3)** Any decision taken in the exercise of other functions must be taken at a level appropriate to the importance of the decision.

**2(4)** In the case of functions to be discharged by the governing body, the members falling respectively within paragraphs (a) and (b) of paragraph 1(3) above must, so far as practicable, have an opportunity to express their opinions.

**2(5)** Subject to sub-paragraphs (2) to (4) above, the arrangements may enable any functions to be discharged by a committee, sub-committee, officer or servant of the agency.

## TAKING ACCOUNT OF COSTS OF COMPLIANCE

**2A(1)** The agency must have satisfactory arrangements for taking account, in framing any provisions which it proposes to make in the exercise of its legislative functions, of the cost to those to whom the provisions would apply of complying with those provisions and any other controls to which they are subject.

**2A(2)** In this paragraph **"legislative functions"** means the functions of issuing or making statements of principle, rules, regulations or codes of practice.

**History**
Para. 2A inserted by CA 1989, s. 204(4) as from 15 March 1990 (see SI 1990/354 (C 12), art. 3).

**Note**
See CA 1989, s. 204(5), (6).

## MONITORING AND ENFORCEMENT

**3(1)** The agency must have a satisfactory system–

(a) for enabling it to determine whether persons regulated by it are complying with the obligations which it is the responsibility of the agency to enforce; and

(b) for the discharge of the agency's responsibility for the enforcement of those obligations.

**3(2)** The system may provide for the functions mentioned in sub-paragraph (1)(a) to be performed on its behalf (and without affecting its responsiblity) by any other body or person who is able and willing to perform them.

## INVESTIGATION OF COMPLAINTS

**4(1)** The agency must have effective arrangements for the investigation of complaints arising out of the conduct of investment business by authorised persons or against any recognised self-regulating organisation, professional body, investment exchange or clearing house.

**4(2)** The arrangements must make provision for the investigation of complaints in respect of authorised persons to be carried out in appropriate cases independently of the agency and those persons.

**Note**
See note after para. 5.
Concerning effect of para. 4 re European investment firms, see the Investment Services Regulations 1995 (SI 1995/3275), reg. 32 and Sch. 7, para. 44(1).

## PROMOTION AND MAINTENANCE OF STANDARDS

**5** The agency must be able and willing to promote and maintain high standards of integrity and fair dealing in the carrying on of investment business and to co-operate, by the sharing of information and otherwise, with the Secretary of State and any other authority, body or person having responsibility for the supervision or regulation of investment business or other financial services.

**Note**
Concerning effect of para. 5, see the Investment Services Regulations 1995 (SI 1995/3275), reg. 32 and Sch. 7, para. 44(2).
Concerning European institutions and co-operation, see the Banking Coordination (Second Council Directive) Regulations 1992 (SI 1992/3218), reg. 55 and Sch. 9, para. 46.

RECORDS

6 The agency must have satisfactory arrangements for recording decisions made in the exercise of its functions and for the safe-keeping of those records which ought to be preserved.

# Schedule 8 – Principles Applicable to Designated Agency's Legislative Provisions

Section 114

**History**

In the heading to Sch. 8 the words "Legislative Provisions" substituted for the former words "Rules and Regulations" by CA 1989, s. 206(1) and Sch. 23, para. 23(1), (2) as from 15 March 1990 (see SI 1990/354 (C 12), art. 3).

INTRODUCTION

**1(1)** In this Schedule **"legislative provisions"** means the provisions of statements of principle, rules, regulations and codes of practice issued or made under Part I of this Act and the provisions of regulations made under regulation 6 of the Open-Ended Investment Companies (Investment Companies with Variable Capital) Regulations 1996.

**1(2)** References in this Schedule to "conduct of business provisions" are to rules made under section 48 of this Act and statements of principle and codes of practice so far as they relate to matters falling within that rule-making power.

**1(3)** References in this Schedule to provisions made for the purposes of a specified section or Chapter are to rules or regulations made under that section or Chapter and statements of principle and codes of practice so far as they relate to matters falling within that power to make rules or regulations.

**History**

In para. 1(1) the words "regulations made under regulation 6" to the end inserted by the Open-Ended Investment Companies (Investment Companies with Variable Capital) Regulations 1996 (SI 1996/2827) reg.1, 75 and Sch. 8, para. 23 as from 6 January 1997.

See history note after para. 1A.

STANDARDS

**1A** The conduct of business provisions and the other legislative provisions must promote high standards of integrity and fair dealing in the conduct of investment business.

**History**

Para. 1, 1A substituted for the former para. 1 and the cross-heading preceding it by CA 1989, s. 206(1) and Sch. 23, para. 23(1), (3) as from 15 March 1990 (see SI 1990/354 (C 12), art. 3); the former para. 1 read as follows:

"STANDARDS

The rules made under section 48 of this Act (in this Schedule referred to as "conduct of business rules") and the other rules and regulations made under Part I of this Act must promote high standards of integrity and fair dealing in the conduct of investment business."

**2** The conduct of business provisions must make proper provision for requiring an authorised person to act with due skill, care and diligence in providing any service which he provides or holds himself out as willing to provide.

**History**

See history note after para. 6.

**3** The conduct of business provisions must make proper provision for requiring an authorised person to subordinate his own interests to those of his clients and to act fairly between his clients.

**History**

See history note after para. 6.

**4** The conduct of business provisions must make proper provision for requiring an authorised person to ensure that, in anything done by him for the persons with whom he deals, due regard is had to their circumstances.

**History**

See history note after para. 6.

DISCLOSURE

**5** The conduct of business provisions must make proper provision for the disclosure by an authorised person of interests in, and facts material to, transactions which are entered into by him in the course of carrying on investment business or in respect of which he gives advice in the course of carrying on such business, including information as to any commissions or other inducements received or receivable from a third party in connection with any such transaction.

**History**

See history note after para. 6.

**6** The conduct of business provisions must make proper provision for the disclosure by an authorised person of the capacity in which and the terms on which he enters into any such transaction.

**History**

In para. 2–6 the words "conduct of business provisions" substituted for the former words "conduct of business rules" by CA 1989, s. 206(1) and Sch. 23, para. 23(1), (4) as from 15 March 1990 (see SI 1990/354 (C 12), art. 3).

**7** The conduct of business provisions, or those provisions and provisions made for the purposes of section 51 of this Act, must make proper provision for requiring an authorised person who in the course of carrying on investment business enters or offers to enter into a transaction in respect of an investment with any person, or gives any person advice about such a transaction, to give that person such information as to the nature of the investment and the financial implications of the transaction as will enable him to make an informed decision.

**History**

In para. 7 the words "conduct of business provisions" substituted for the former words "conduct of business rules" and the words "those provisions and provisions made for the purposes of" substituted for the former words "those rules and rules under" by CA 1989, s. 206(1) and Sch. 23, para. 23(1), (4), (5) as from 15 March 1990 (see SI 1990/354 (C 12), art. 3).

**8** Provisions made for the purposes of section 48 of this Act regulating action for the purpose of stabilising the price of investments must make proper provision for ensuring that where action is or is to be taken in conformity with the rules adequate arrangements exist for making known that the price of the investments in respect of which the action is or is to be taken (and, where relevant, of any other investments) may be affected by that action and the period during which it may be affected; and where a transaction is or is to be entered into during a period when it is known that the price of the investment to which it relates may be affected by any such action the information referred to in paragraph 7 above includes information to that effect.

**History**

In para. 8 the words "Provisions made for the purposes of" substituted for the former words "Rules made under" by CA 1989, s. 206(1) and Sch. 23, para. 23(1), (6) as from 15 March 1990 (see SI 1990/354 (C 12), art. 3).

## PROTECTION

**9** The conduct of business provisions and any provisions made for the purposes of section 55 of this Act must make proper provision for the protection of property for which an authorised person is liable to account to another person.

**History**

In para. 9 the words "conduct of business provisions" substituted for the former words "conduct of business rules" and the words "provisions made for the purposes of" substituted for the former words "regulations made under" by CA 1989, s. 206(1) and Sch. 23, para. 23(1), (4), (7) as from 15 March 1990 (see SI 1990/354 (C 12), art. 3).

**10** Provisions made for the purposes of section 53 and 54 of this Act must make the best provision that can reasonably be made for the purposes of those sections.

**History**

In para. 10 the words "Provisions made for the purposes of" substituted for the former words "Rules made under" and the words "for the purposes of those sections" substituted for the former words "under those sections" by CA 1989, s. 206(1) and Sch. 23, para. 23(1), (8) as from 15 March 1990 (see SI 1990/354 (C 12), art. 3).

## RECORDS

**11** The conduct of business provisions must require the keeping of proper records and make provision for their inspection in appropriate cases.

**History**

In para. 11 the words "conduct of business provisions" substituted for the words "conduct of business rule" by CA 1989, s. 206(1) and Sch. 23, para. 23(1), (4) as from 15 March 1990 (see SI 1990/354 (C 12), art. 3).

## CLASSES OF INVESTORS

**12** The conduct of business provisions and the other provisions made for the purposes of Chapter V of Part I of this Act must take proper account of the fact that provisions that are appropriate for regulating the conduct of business in relation to some classes of investors may not (by reason of their knowledge, experience or otherwise) be appropriate in relation to others.

**History**
In para. 12 the words "conduct of business provisions" substituted for the former words "conduct of business rules" and the words "provisions made for the purposes of" substituted for the former words "rules and regulations made under" by CA 1989, s. 206(1), (4), (9) as from 15 March 1990 (see SI 1990/354 (C 12), art. 3).
**Note**
Concerning European investment firms, see the Investment Services Regulations 1995 (SI 1995/3275), reg. 32 and Sch. 7, para. 45.
Concerning European institutions, see the Banking Coordination (Second Council Directive) Regulations 1992 (SI 1992/3218), reg. 55 and Sch. 9, para. 47.

# Schedule 9 – Designated Agencies: Status and Exercise of Transferred Functions

Section 16

## STATUS

**1(1)** A designated agency shall not be regarded as acting on behalf of the Crown and its members, officers and servants shall not be regarded as Crown servants.

**1(2)** In Part III of Schedule 1 to the House of Commons Disqualification Act 1975 (disqualifying offices) there shall be inserted at the appropriate place–

"Chairman of a designated agency within the meaning of the Financial Services Act 1986 if he is in receipt of remuneration."

**1(3)** An amendment corresponding to that in sub-paragraph (2) above shall be made in Part III of Schedule 1 to the Northern Ireland Assembly Disqualification Act 1975.

## EXEMPTION FROM REQUIREMENT OF "LIMITED" IN NAME OF DESIGNATED AGENCY

**2(1)** A company is exempt from the requirements of the Companies Act 1985 relating to the use of "limited" as part of the company name if–

(a) it is a designated agency; and

(b) its memorandum or articles comply with the requirements specified in paragraph (b) of subsection (3) of section 30 of that Act.

**2(2)** In subsection (4) of that section (statutory declaration of compliance with requirements entitling company to exemption) the reference to the requirements of subsection (3) of that section shall include a reference to the requirements of sub-paragraph (1) above.

**2(3)** In section 31 of that Act (provisions applicable to exempted companies) the reference to a company which is exempt under section 30 of that Act shall include a reference to a company that is exempt under this paragraph and, in relation to such a company, the power conferred by subsection (2) of that section (direction to include "limited" in company name) shall be exercisable on the ground that the company has ceased to be a designated agency instead of the ground mentioned in paragraph (a) of that subsection.

**2(4)** In this paragraph references to the said Act of 1985 and sections 30 and 31 of that Act include references to the corresponding provisions in force in Northern Ireland.

## THE TRIBUNAL

**3(1)** Where a case is referred to the Tribunal by a designated agency the Tribunal shall send the Secretary of State a copy of any report made by it to the agency in respect of that case.

**3(2)** Where the powers which the Tribunal could, apart from any delegation order, require the Secretary of State to exercise are by virtue of such an order or of an order resuming any function transferred by it, exercisable partly by the Secretary of State and partly by a designated agency or designated agencies the Tribunal may require any of them to exercise such of those powers as are exercisable by them respectively.

## LEGISLATIVE FUNCTIONS

**4(1)** A designated agency shall send the Secretary of State a copy of any statements of principle, rules, regulations or codes of practice issued or made by it by virtue of functions transferred to it by a delegation order and give him written notice of any amendment or revocation of or addition to any such rules or regulations.

**History**

In para. 4(1) the words "any statements of principle, rules, regulations or codes of practice issued or made" substituted for the former words "any rules or regulations made" by CA 1989, s. 206(1) and Sch. 23, para. 24(1), (2) as from 15 March 1990 (see SI 1990/354 (C 12), art. 3).

**4(2)** A designated agency shall–

(a) send the Secretary of State a copy of any guidance issued by the agency which is intended to have continuing effect and is issued in writing or other legible form; and

(b) give him written notice of any amendment, revocation of or addition to guidance issued by it;

but notice need not be given of the revocation of guidance other than such as is mentioned in paragraph (a) above or of any amendment or addition which does not result in or consist of such guidance as is there mentioned.

**5** Paragraphs 6 to 9 below have effect instead of section 205A of this Act in relation to statements of principle, rules, regulations and codes of practice issued or made by a designated agency in the exercise of powers transferred to it by a delegation order.

**History**

See history note after para. 6.

**6** Any such power is exercisable by instrument in writing and includes power to make different provision for different cases.

**History**

Para. 5 and 6 substituted by CA 1989, s. 206(1) and Sch. 23, para. 24(1), (3) as from 15 March 1990 (see SI 1990/354 (C 12), art. 3); former para. 5 and 6 read as follows:

"**5** Paragraphs 6 to 9 below shall have effect instead of section 205(2) and (4) of this Act in relation to rules and regulations made by a designated agency in the exercise of functions transferred to it by a delegation order.
**6** The rules and regulations shall be made by an instrument in writing."

**7** The instrument shall specify the provision of this Act or, as the case may be, the provision of the Open-Ended Investment Companies (Investment Companies with Variable Capital) Regulations 1996, under which it is made.

**History**

In para. 7, the words beginning with "or, as the case may be," and ending with "Variable Capital) Regulations 1996," inserted by the Open-Ended Investment Companies (Investment Companies with Variable Capital) Regulations 1996 (SI 1996/2827) reg.1, 75 and Sch. 8, para. 24 as from 6 January 1997.

**8(1)** Immediately after an instrument is issued or made it shall be printed and made available to the public with or without payment.

**History**

In para. 8(1) the words "is issued or made" substituted for the former words "is made" by CA 1989, s. 206(1) and Sch. 23, para. 24(1), (4)(a) as from 15 March 1990 (see SI 1990/354 (C 12), art. 3).

**8(2)** A person shall not be taken to have contravened any statement of principle, rule, regulation or code of practice if he shows that at the time of the alleged contravention the instrument containing the statement of principle, rule, regulation or code of practice had not been made available as required by this paragraph.

**History**

In para. 8(2) the words "statement of principle, rule, regulation or code of practice" substituted (twice) for the words "rule or regulation" by CA 1989, s. 206(1) and Sch. 23, para. 24(1), (4)(b) as from 15 March 1990 (see SI 1990/354 (C 12), art. 3).

**9(1)** The production of a printed copy of an instrument purporting to be made or issued by the agency on which is endorsed a certificate signed by an officer of the agency authorised by it for that purpose and stating–

(a) that the instrument was made or issued by the agency;

(b) that the copy is a true copy of the instrument; and

(c) that on a specified date the instrument was made available to the public as required by paragraph 8 above,

shall be prima facie evidence or, in Scotland, sufficient evidence of the facts stated in the certificate.

**History**
See history note after para. 9(3).

**9(2)** Any certificate purporting to be signed as mentioned in sub-paragraph (1) above shall be deemed to have been duly signed unless the contrary is shown.

**9(3)** Any person wishing in any legal proceedings to cite an instrument made or issued by the agency may require the agency to cause a copy of it to be endorsed with such a certificate as is mentioned in this paragraph.

**History**
In para. 9 the words "made or issued by the agency" substituted for the former words "made by the agency" by CA 1989, s. 206(1) and Sch. 23, para. 24(1), (5) as from 15 March 1990 (see SI 1990/354 (C 12), art. 3).

## FEES

**10(1)** A designated agency may retain any fees payable to it by virtue of the delegation order.

**10(2)** Any such fees shall be applicable for meeting the expenses of the agency in discharging its functions under the order and for any purposes incidental thereto.

**10(3)** Any fees payable to a designated agency by virtue of a delegation order made before the coming into force of section 3 of this Act may also be applied for repaying the principal of, and paying interest on, any money borrowed by the agency (or by any other person whose liabilities in respect of the money are assumed by the agency) which has been used for the purpose of defraying expenses incurred before the making of the order (whether before or after the passing of this Act) in making preparations for the agency becoming a designated agency.

**11** If the function of prescribing the amount of any fee, or of making a scheme under section 112 above, is exercisable by a designated agency it may prescribe or make provision for such fees as will enable it to defray any such expenses as are mentioned in paragraph 10 above.

## CONSULTATION

**12(1)** Where a designated agency proposes, in the exercise of powers transferred to it by a delegation order, to issue or make any statements of principle, rules, regulations or codes of practice, it shall publish the proposed instrument in such manner as appears to it best calculated to bring the proposals to the attention of the public, together with a statement that representations about the proposals (and, in particular, representations as to the cost of complying with the proposed provisions) can be made to the agency within a specified time.

**12(2)** Before issuing or making the instrument the agency shall have regard to any representations duly made in accordance with that statement.

**12(3)** The above requirements do not apply–

(a) where the agency considers that the delay involved in complying with them would be prejudicial to the interests of investors;

(b) to the issuing or making of an instrument in the same, or substantially the same, terms as a proposed instrument which was furnished by the agency to the Secretary of State for the purposes of section 114(9) of this Act.

**History**
Para. 12 substituted by CA 1989, s. 206(1) and Sch. 23, para. 24(1), (6) as from 15 March 1990 (see SI 1990/354 (C 12), art. 3); para. 12 formerly read as follows:

"**12(1)** Before making any rules or regulations by virtue of functions transferred to it by a delegation order a designated agency shall, subject to sub-paragraphs (2) and (3) below, publish the proposed rules and regulations in such manner as appears to the agency to be best calculated to bring them to the attention of the public, together with a statement that representations in respect of the proposals can be made to the agency within a specified period; and before making the rules or regulations the agency shall have regard to any representations duly made in accordance with that statement.

**(2)** Sub-paragraph (1) above does not apply in any case in which the agency considers that the delay involved in complying with that sub-paragraph would be prejudicial to the interests of investors.

**(3)** Sub-paragraph (1) above does not apply to the making of any rule or regulation if it is in the same terms (or substantially the same terms) as a proposed rule or regulation which was furnished by the agency to the Secretary of State for the purposes of section 114(9) of this Act."

## EXCHANGE OF INFORMATION

**13(1)** The Secretary of State may communicate to a designated agency any information in his possession of which he could have availed himself for the purpose of exercising any function which by virtue of a delegation order is for the time being exercisable by the agency.

**13(2)** A designated agency may in the exercise of any function which by virtue of a delegation order is for the time being exercisable by it communicate to any other person any information which has been communicated to the agency by the Secretary of State and which the Secretary of State could have communicated to that person in the exercise of that function.

**13(3)** No communication of information under sub-paragraph (1) above shall constitute publication for the purposes of the law of defamation.

# Schedule 10 – Regulated Insurance Companies

Section 129

## PRELIMINARY

**1** In this Part of this Schedule **"a regulated insurance company"** means any such company as is mentioned in section 129 of this Act.

## AUTHORISATIONS FOR INVESTMENT BUSINESS AND INSURANCE BUSINESS

**2(1)** An insurance company to which section 22 of this Act applies shall not be an authorised person except by virtue of that section.

**2(2)** If an insurance company to which Part II of the Insurance Companies Act 1982 applies but to which section 22 of this Act does not apply becomes an authorised person by virtue of any other provision of this Act it shall be an authorised person only as respects the management of the investments of any pension fund which is established solely for the benefit of the officers or employees and their dependants of that company or of any other body corporate in the same group as that company.

**2(3)** An insurance company to which section 31 of this Act applies shall not, so long as it is an authorised person by virtue of that section, be an authorised person by virtue of any other provision of this Act.

**2(3A)** An insurance company–

(a) to which section 31 of this Act applies; and

(b) which has complied with the requirements of section 81B of the Insurance Companies Act 1982 (documents to be furnished to the Secretary of State) in relation to the provision of long term insurance in the United Kingdom,

shall be deemed to have complied with section 32 of this Act in relation to any investment business consisting in the covering of commitments for the time being mentioned in the statement given by it in accordance with subsection (1)(c) of the said section 81B.

**History**
See history note after para. 2(3B).

**2(3B)** In sub-paragraph (3A) above **"commitment"** and **"provision of long term insurance"** have respectively the same meanings as in the Insurance Companies Act 1982.

**History**
Para. 2(3A) and (3B) inserted by Insurance Companies (Amendment) Regulations 1993 (SI 1993/174), reg. 7 as from 20 May 1993.

**2(4)** None of the provisions of Part I of this Act shall be construed as authorising any person to carry on insurance business in any case in which he could not lawfully do so apart from those provisions.

## RECOGNITION OF SELF-REGULATING ORGANISATION WITH INSURANCE COMPANY MEMBERS

**3(1)** In the case of a self-regulating organisation whose members include or may include regulated insurance companies the requirements of Schedule 2 to this Act shall include a requirement that the rules of the organisation must take proper account of Part II of the Insurance Companies Act 1982 or, as the case may be, of the provisions for corresponding purposes in the law of any member State in which such companies are established.

**3(2)** Where the function of making or revoking a recognition order in respect of such a self-regulating organisation is exercisable by a designated agency it shall not regard that requirement as satisfied unless the Secretary of State has certified that he also regards it as satisfied.

**3(3)** A delegation order–

(a) may reserve to the Secretary of State the function of revoking a recognition order in respect of such a self-regulating organisation as is mentioned in sub-paragraph (1) above on the ground that the requirement there mentioned is not satisfied; and

(b) shall not transfer to a designated agency the function of revoking any such recognition order on the ground that the organisation has contravened sub-paragraphs (3) or (4) of paragraph 6 below as applied by sub-paragraph (5) of that paragraph.

**3(4)** In the case of such a self-regulating organisation as is mentioned in sub-paragraph (1) above the requirements of Schedule 2 to this Act referred to in section 187(2)(a) of this Act shall include the requirement mentioned in that sub-paragraph.

## MODIFICATION OF PROVISIONS AS TO CONDUCT OF INVESTMENT BUSINESS

**4(1)** The rules under section 48 of this Act shall not apply to a regulated insurance company except so far as they make provision as respects the matters mentioned in sub-paragraph (2) below.

**4(2)** The matters referred to in sub-paragraph (1) above are–

(a) procuring proposals for policies the rights under which constitute an investment for the purposes of this Act and advising persons on such policies and the exercise of the rights conferred by them;

(b) managing the investments of pension funds, procuring persons to enter into contracts for the management of such investments and advising persons on such contracts and the exercise of the rights conferred by them;

(c) matters incidental to those mentioned in paragraph (a) and (b) above.

**4(2A)** Sub-paragraphs (1) and (2) also apply to statements of principle under section 47A and codes of practice under section 63A so far as they relate to matters falling within the rule-making power in section 48.

**History**
Para. 4(2A) inserted by CA 1989, s. 206(1) and Sch. 23, para. 25(1), (2) as from 15 March 1990 (see SI 1990/354 (C 12), art. 3).

**4(3)** The rules under section 49 of this Act shall not apply to an insurance company which is an authorised person by virtue of section 31 of this Act.

**4(4)** The rules under sections 53 and 54 of this Act shall not apply to loss arising as a result of a regulated insurance company being unable to meet its liabilities under a contract of insurance.

**4(5)** A direction under section 59 of this Act shall not prohibit the employment of a person by a regulated insurance company except in connection with–

(a) the matters mentioned in sub-paragraph (2) above; or

(b) investment business carried on in connection with or for the purposes of those matters.

**4(6)** The Secretary of State shall not make a delegation order transferring any functions of making rules or regulations under Chapter V of Part I of this Act in relation to a regulated insurance company unless he is satisfied that those rules and regulations will take proper account of Part II of the Insurance Companies Act 1982 or, as the case may be, of the provisions for corresponding purposes in the law of the member State in which the company is established; and in section 115(5) of this Act the reference to the requirements of section 114(9)(b) shall include a reference to the requirements of this sub-paragraph.

## RESTRICTION OF PROVISIONS AS TO CONDUCT OF INSURANCE BUSINESS

**5(1)** Regulations under section 72 of the Insurance Companies Act 1982 (insurance advertisements) shall not apply to so much of any advertisement issued by an authorised person as relates to a contract of insurance the rights under which constitute an investment for the purposes of this Act.

**5(2)** No requirement imposed under section 74 of that Act (intermediaries in insurance transactions) shall apply in respect of an invitation issued by, or by an appointed representative of, an authorised person in relation to a contract of insurance the rights under which constitute an investment for the purposes of this Act.

**5(3)** Subject to sub-paragraph (4) below, sections 75 to 77 of that Act (right to withdraw from long-term policies) shall not apply to a regulated insurance company in respect of a contract of insurance the rights under which constitute an investment for the purposes of this Act.

**5(4)** Sub-paragraph (3) above does not affect the operation of the said sections 75 to 77 in a case in which the statutory notice required by those sections has been or ought to have been served before the coming into force of that sub-paragraph.

## EXERCISE OF POWERS OF INTERVENTION ETC.

**6(1)** The powers conferred by Chapter VI of Part I of this Act shall not be exercisable in relation to a regulated insurance company on the ground specified in section 64(1)(a) of this Act for reasons relating to the ability of the company to meet its liabilities to policy holders or potential policy holders.

**6(2)** The powers conferred by sections 66 and 68 of this Act, and those conferred by section 67 of this Act so far as applicable to assets belonging to the authorised person, shall not be exercisable in relation to a regulated insurance company.

**6(3)** A designated agency shall not in the case of a regulated insurance company impose any prohibition or requirement under section 65 or 67 of this Act, or vary any such prohibition or requirement, unless it has given reasonable notice of its intention to do so to the Secretary of State and informed him–

(a) of the manner in which and the date on or after which it intends to exercise that power; and

(b) in the case of a proposal to impose a prohibition or requirement, on which of the grounds specified in section 64(1) of this Act it proposes to act and its reasons for considering that the ground in question exists and that it is necessary to impose the prohibition or requirement.

**6(4)** A designated agency shall not exercise any power to which sub-paragraph (3) above applies if the Secretary of State has before the date specified in accordance with sub-paragraph (3), above served on it a notice in writing directing it not to do so; and the Secretary of State may serve such a notice if he considers it desirable for protecting policy holders or potential policy holders of the company against the risk that it may be unable to meet its liabilities or to fulfil the reasonable expectations of its policy holders or potential policy holders.

**6(5)** Sub-paragraphs (3) and (4) above shall, with the necessary modifications, apply also where a recognised self-regulating organisation proposes to exercise, in the case of a member who is a regulated insurance company, any powers of the organisation for purposes corresponding to those of Chapter VI of Part I of this Act.

**6(6)** The powers conferred by sections 72 and 73 of this Act shall not be exercisable in relation to a regulated insurance company.

## WITHDRAWAL OF INSURANCE BUSINESS AUTHORISATION

**7(1)** At the end of section 11(2)(a) of the Insurance Companies Act 1982 (withdrawal of authorisation in respect of new business where insurance company has failed to satisfy an obligation to which it is subject by virtue of that Act) there shall be inserted the words "or the Financial Services Act 1986 or, if it is a member of a recognised self-regulating organisation within the meaning of that Act, an obligation to which it is subject by virtue of the rules of that organisation".

**7(2)** After subsection (2) of section 13 of that Act (final withdrawal of authorisation) there shall be inserted–

> "**(2A)** The Secretary of State may direct that an insurance company shall cease to be authorised to carry on business which is insurance business by virtue of section 95 (c)(ii) of this Act if it appears to him that the company has failed to satisfy an obligation to which it is subject by virtue of the Financial Services Act 1986 or, if it is a member of a

recognised self-regulating organisation within the meaning of that Act, an obligation to which it is subject by virtue of the rules of that organisation.

**(2B)** Subsections (3), (5) and (6) of section 11 and subsections (1) and (5) to (8) of section 12 above shall apply to a direction under subsection (2A) above as they apply to a direction under section 11."

**7(3)** The disciplinary action which may be taken by virtue of section 47A(3) of this Act (failure to comply with statement of principle) includes–

(a) the withdrawal of authorisation under section 11(2)(a) of the Insurance Companies Act 1982, and

(b) the giving of a direction under section 13(2A) of that Act; and subsection (6) of section 47A (duty of the Secretary of State as to exercise of powers) has effect accordingly.

**History**

Para. 7(3) inserted by CA 1989, s. 206(1) and Sch. 23, para. 25(1), (3) as from 15 March 1990 (see SI 1990/354 (C 12), art. 3).

## TERMINATION OF INVESTMENT BUSINESS AUTHORISATION OF INSURER ESTABLISHED IN OTHER MEMBER STATE

**8(1)** Sections 33(1)(b) and 34 of this Act shall not apply to a regulated insurance company.

**8(2)** A direction under section 33(1)(a) of this Act in respect of such an insurance company may provide that the company shall cease to be an authorised person except as respects investment business of a kind specified in the direction and shall not make it unlawful for the company to effect a contract of insurance in pursuance of a subsisting contract of insurance.

**8(3)** Where the Secretary of State proposes to give a direction under section 33(1)(a) of this Act in respect of such an insurance company he shall give it written notice of his intention to do so, giving particulars of the grounds on which he proposes to act and of the rights exercisable under sub-paragraph (4) below.

**8(4)** An insurance company on which a notice is served under sub-paragraph (3) above may within fourteen days after the date of service make written representations to the Secretary of State and, if desired, oral representations to a person appointed for that purpose by the Secretary of State; and the Secretary of State shall have regard to any representations made in accordance with this sub-paragraph in determining whether to give the direction.

**8(5)** After giving a direction under section 33(1)(a) of this Act in respect of a regulated insurance company the Secretary of State shall inform the company in writing of the reasons for giving the direction.

**8(6)** A delegation order shall not transfer to a designated agency the function of giving a direction under section 33(1)(a) of this Act in respect of a regulated insurance company.

## POWERS OF TRIBUNAL

**9** In the case of a regulated insurance company the provisions mentioned in section 98(4) of this Act shall include sections 11 and 13(2A) of the Insurance Companies Act 1982 but where the Tribunal reports that the appropriate decision would be to take action under either of those sections or under section 33(1)(a) of this Act the Secretary of State shall take the report into consideration but shall not be bound to act upon it.

## CONSULTATION WITH DESIGNATED AGENCIES

**10(1)** Where any functions under this Act are for the time being exercisable by a designated agency in relation to regulated insurance companies the Secretary of State shall, before issuing an authorisation under section 3 of the Insurance Companies Act 1982 to a applicant who proposes to carry on in the United Kingdom insurance business which is investment business–

(a) seek the advice of the designated agency with respect to any matters which are relevant to those functions of the agency and relate to the applicant, his proposed business or persons who will be associated with him in, or in connection with, that business; and

(b) take into account any advice on those matters given to him by the agency before the end of the period within which the application is required to be decided.

**10(2)** The Secretary of State may for the purpose of obtaining the advice of a designated agency under sub-paragraph (1) above furnish it with any information obtained by him in connection with the application.

**10(3)** If a designated agency by which any functions under this Act are for the time being exercisable in relation to regulated insurance companies has reasonable grounds for believing that any such insurance company has failed to comply with an obligation to which it is subject by virtue of this Act it shall forthwith give notice of that fact to the Secretary of State so that he can take it into consideration in deciding whether to give a direction in respect of the company under section 11 or 13(2A) of the said Act of 1982 or section 33 of this Act.

**10(4)** A notice under sub-paragraph (3) above shall contain particulars of the obligation in question and of the agency's reasons for considering that the company has failed to satisfy that obligation.

**10(5)** A designated agency need not give a notice under sub-paragraph (3) above in respect of any matter unless it considers that that matter (either alone or in conjunction with other matters) would justify the withdrawal of authorisation under section 28 of this Act in the case of a person to whom that section applies.

# Schedule 11 – Friendly Societies

Section 140

## Part I – Preliminary

**1** In this Schedule–

**"a regulated friendly society"** means a society which is an authorised person by virtue of section 23 of this Act as respects such investment business as is mentioned in that section;

**"regulated business"** in relation to a regulated friendly society, means investment business as respects which the society is authorised by virtue of that section;

**"a self-regulating organisation for friendly societies"** means a self-regulating organisation which is permitted under its rules to admit regulated friendly societies as members and to regulate the carrying on by such societies of regulated business;

**"a recognised self-regulating organisation for friendly societies"** means a body declared by a recognition order for the time being in force to be a recognised self-regulating organisation for friendly societies for the purposes of this Schedule;

**"a member society"** means a regulated friendly society which is a member of a recognised self-regulating organisation for friendly societies and is subject to its rules in carrying on all its regulated business;

**"recognition order"** means –

(a) an order made by the Chief Registrar of friendly societies or the Registrar of Friendly Societies for Northern Ireland before Schedule 18 to the Friendly Societies Act 1992 came into force; or

(b) an order made by the Commission after that Schedule came into force;

**"the Commission"** means the Friendly Societies Commission.

**History**

In para. 1 –

- in the definition of "a recognised self-regulating organisation for friendly societies" the words "a recognition order" substituted for the former words "an order of the Registrar";
- in the definition of "a member society" the word "a" (on its third occurrence) substituted for the former words "an appropriate" and the words

  "and, for the purposes of this definition, **"an appropriate recognised self-regulating organisation for friendly societies"** means–

  (a) in the case of any such society as is mentioned in section 23(1) of this Act, an organisation declared by an order of the Chief Registrar of friendly societies for the time being in force to be a recognised self-regulating organisation for friendly societies for the purposes of this Schedule; and

  (b) in the case of any such society as is mentioned in section 23(2) of this Act, an organisation declared by an order of the Registrar of Friendly Societies for Northern Ireland for the time being in force to be such an organisation;"

formerly appearing at the end omitted and repealed; and

- the definitions of "recognition order" and "the Commission" substituted for the former definition of "the Registrar";

by Friendly Societies Act 1992, s. 120 and Sch. 18, para. 11 as from 1 February 1993 in regard to incorporated friendly societies (see SI 1993/16 (C 1), art. 2 and Sch. 4). The amendments to the definition of "a member society" came into force from 28 April 1993 for all remaining purposes (see SI 1993/1186 (C 23)), reg. 2(1), Sch. 1, app.). The other amendments made by Sch. 18, para. 11 came into force as from 1 January 1994 for all remaining purposes (see SI 1993/2213 (C 43), art. 2 and Sch. 5). The former definition of "the Registrar" read as follows:

"**"the Registrar"** means–

(a) in relation to any such society as is mentioned in section 23(1) of this Act, or to any self-regulating organisation for friendly societies which has applied for or been granted a recognition order made by him, the Chief Registrar of friendly societies; and

(b) in relation to any such society as is mentioned in section 23(2) of this Act, or to any self-regulating organisation for friendly societies which has applied for or been granted a recognition order made by him, the Registrar of Friendly Societies for Northern Ireland."

# Part II – Self-Regulating Organisations for Friendly Societies

**Note**
See history note at end of Sch. 11.

## RECOGNITION

**2(1)** A self-regulating organisation for friendly societies may apply to the Commission for an order declaring it to be a recognised self-regulating organisation for friendly societies for the purposes of this Schedule.

**History**
In para. 2(1) the words "the Commission" substituted for the former words "the Chief Registrar of friendly societies or the Registrar of Friendly Societies for Northern Ireland" by Friendly Societies Act 1992, s. 98 and Sch. 18, para. 10 as from 1 February 1993 in regard to incorporated friendly societies (see SI 1993/16 (C 1), art. 2 and Sch. 4) and as from 1 January 1994 for all remaining purposes (see SI 1993/2213 (C 43), art. 2 and Sch. 5).

**2(2)** An application under sub-paragraph (1) above–

(a) shall be made in such manner as the Commission may direct; and

(b) shall be accompanied by such information as the Commission may reasonably require for the purpose of determining the application.

**2(3)** At any time after receiving an application and before determining it the Commission may require the applicant to furnish additional information.

**2(4)** The directions and requirements given or imposed under sub-paragraphs (2) and (3) above may differ as between different applications.

**2(5)** Any information to be furnished to the Commission under this paragraph shall, if the Commission so requires, be in such form or verified in such manner as the Commission may specify.

**2(6)** Every application shall be accompanied by a copy of the applicant's rules and of any guidance issued by the applicant which is intended to have continuing effect and is issued in writing or other legible form.

**3(1)** If, on an application duly made in accordance with paragraph 2 above and after being furnished with all such information as the Commission may require under that paragraph, it appears to the Commission from that information and having regard to any other information in the Commission's possession that the requirements mentioned in paragraph 4 below are satisfied as respects that organisation, the Commission may, with the consent of the Secretary of State and subject to sub-paragraph (2) below, make a recognition order in respect of the organisation declaring the applicant to be a recognised self-regulating organisation for friendly societies.

**History**
In para. 3(1) the words "a recognition order" to the end substituted for the former words "an order ("a recognition order") declaring the applicant to be a recognised self-regulating organisation for friendly societies" by Friendly Societies Act 1992, s. 98 and Sch. 18, para. 12 as from 1 February 1993 in regard to incorporated friendly societies (see SI 1993/16 (C 1), art. 2 and Sch. 4) and as from 1 January 1994 for all remaining purposes (see SI 1993/2213 (C 43), art. 2 and Sch. 5).

**3(2)** Where the Commission proposes to grant an application for a recognition order the Commission shall send to the Secretary of State a copy of the application together with a copy of the rules and any guidance accompanying the application and the Secretary of State shall not consent to the making of the recognition order unless he is satisfied that the rules and guidance of which copies have been sent to him under this sub-paragraph, together with any statements of principle, rules, regulations or codes of practice to which members of the organisation would be subject by virtue of this Schedule, do not have, and are not intended or likely to have, to any significant extent the effect of restricting, distorting or preventing competition or, if they have or are intended or likely to have that effect to any significant extent, that the effect is not greater than is necessary for the protection of investors.

**History**
In para. 3(2) the words ", together with any statements of principle," to "by virtue of this Schedule," inserted by CA 1989, s. 206(1) and Sch. 23, para. 26, 27 as from 15 March 1990 (see SI 1990/354 (C 12), art. 3).

**3(3)** Section 122 of this Act shall apply in relation to the decision whether to consent to the making of a recognition order under this paragraph as it applies to the decisions mentioned in subsection (1) of that section.

**3(4)** Subsections (1) and (2) of section 128 of this Act shall apply for the purposes of this paragraph as if the powers there mentioned included the power of refusing consent to the making of a recognition order under this paragraph and subsection (5) of that section shall apply for that purpose as if the reference to Chapter XIV of Part I included a reference to this paragraph.

**3(5)** The Commission may refuse to make a recognition order in respect of an organisation if the Commission considers that its recognition is unnecessary having regard to the existence of one or more other organisations which are concerned with such investment business as is mentioned in section 23 of this Act and which have been or are likely to be recognised under this paragraph.

**3(6)** Where the Commission refuses an application for a recognition order the Commission shall give the applicant a written notice to that effect specifying a requirement which in the opinion of the Commission is not satisfied, stating that the application is refused on the ground mentioned in sub-paragraph (5) above or stating that the Secretary of State has refused to consent to the making of the order.

**3(7)** A recognition order shall state the date on which it takes effect.

**4(1)** The requirements referred to in paragraph 3 above are that mentioned in sub-paragraph (2) below and those set out in paragraphs 2 to 7 of Schedule 2 to this Act as modified in sub-paragraphs (3) to (5) below.

**4(2)** The rules of the organisation must take proper account of Parts V and VIII of the Friendly Societies Act 1992.

**History**
In para. 4(2) the words "Part V and VIII of the Friendly Societies Act 1992" substituted for the former words "the Friendly Societies Act 1974, or as the case may be, the Friendly Societies Act (Northern Ireland) 1970" by Friendly Societies Act 1992, s. 98 and Sch. 18, para. 13 as from 1 February 1993 in regard to incorporated friendly societies (see SI 1993/16 (C 1), art. 2 and Sch. 4) and as from 1 January 1994 for all remaining purposes (see SI 1993/3226 (C 65), art. 2 and Sch. 1).

**4(3)** References in paragraphs 2, 3, 4 and 6 of Schedule 2 to members who are regulated friendly societies.

**4(4)** In paragraph 3 of that Schedule–

(a) in sub-paragraph (1) for the reference to Chapter V of Part I of this Act there shall be substituted a reference to paragraphs 14 to 22D below; and

(c) in sub-paragraph (3) for the reference to Chapter VI of that Part there shall be substituted a reference to the powers exercisable by the Commission by virtue of paragraph 23 below.

**History**
In para. 4(4):

- in para. (a) "22D" substituted for "22", and
- para. (b) omitted and repealed

by CA 1989, s. 206(1), 212, Sch. 23, para. 26, 28(1), (2) and Sch. 24 as from 15 March 1990 (see SI 1990/354 (C 12), art. 3); former para. 4(4)(b) read as follows:

"in sub-paragraph (2) the reference to section 49 of this Act shall be omitted and for the reference to sections 53 and 54 there shall be substituted a reference to paragraphs 17 and 18 below; and."

**4(5)** In paragraph 4 of that Schedule for the reference to Chapter V of Part I of this Act there shall be substituted references to paragraphs 14 to 22D below.

**History**

In para. 4(5) "22D" substituted for "22" by CA 1989, s. 206(1) and Sch. 23, para. 26, 28(1), (3) as from 15 March 1990 (see SI 1990/354 (C 12), art. 3).

## REVOCATION OF RECOGNITION

**5(1)** A recognition order may be revoked by a further order made by the Commission if at any time it appears to the Commission–

(a) that any requirement mentioned in paragraph 4(1) above is not satisfied in the case of the organisation to which the recognition order relates ("the recognised organisation");

(b) that the recognised organisation has failed to comply with any obligation to which it is subject by virtue of this Act; or

(c) that the continued recognition of the organisation is undesirable having regard to the existence of one or more other organisations which have been or are to be recognised under paragraph 3 above.

**5(2)** Subsections (2) to (9) of section 11 of this Act shall have effect in relation to the revocation of a recognition order under this paragraph as they have effect in relation to the revocation of a recognition order under subsection (1) of that section but with the substitution–

(a) for references to the Secretary of State of references to the Commission;

(b) for the reference in subsection (3) to members of a reference to members of the organisation which are member societies in relation to it; and

(c) for the reference in subsection (6) to investors of a reference to members of the societies which are member societies in relation to the organisation.

## COMPLIANCE ORDERS

**6(1)** If at any time it appears to the Commission–

(a) that any requirement mentioned in paragraph 3 above is not satisfied in the case of a recognised self-regulating organisation for friendly societies; or

(b) that such an organisation has failed to comply with any obligation to which it is subject by virtue of this Act,

the Commission may, instead of revoking the recognition order under paragraph 5 above, make an application to the court under this paragraph.

**6(2)** If on any such application the court decides that the requirement in question is not satisfied or, as the case may be, that the organisation has failed to comply with the obligation in question it may order the organisation concerned to take such steps as the court directs for securing that that requirement is satisfied or that that obligation is complied with.

**6(3)** The jurisdiction conferred by this paragraph shall be exercisable by the High Court and the Court of Session.

**7** (Omitted by Companies Act 1989, s. 206(1) and Sch. 23, para. 26, 29 as from 15 March 1990 subject to transitional provisions.)

**History**

In relation to the above see SI 1990/354 (C 12), art. 3 and also art. 6; para. 7 formerly read as follows:

"**7(1)** If at any time it appears to the Registrar that the rules of a recognised self-regulating organisation for friendly societies do not satisfy the requirements of paragraph 3(1) of Schedule 2 to this Act as modified by paragraph 4(4) above he may, instead of revoking the recognition order or making an application under paragraph 6 above, direct the organisation to alter, or himself alter, its rules in such manner as he considers necessary for securing that the rules satisfy those requirements.

**(2)** Before giving a direction or making any alteration under this paragraph the Registrar shall consult the organisation concerned.

**(3)** Any direction given under sub-paragraph (1) above shall, on the application of the Registrar, be enforceable by mandamus or, in Scotland, by an order for specific performance under section 91 of the Court of Session Act 1868.

**(4)** A recognised self-regulating organisation for friendly societies whose rules have been altered by or pursuant to a direction given by the Registrar under sub-paragraph (1) above may apply to the court and if the court is satisfied–

(a) that the rules without the alteration satisfied the requirements mentioned in that sub-paragraph; or

(b) that other alterations proposed by the organisation would result in the rules satisfying those requirements,

the court may set aside the alteration made by or pursuant to the direction given by the Registrar and, in a case within paragraph (b) above, order the organisation to make the alterations proposed by it; but the setting aside of an alteration under this sub-paragraph shall not affect its previous operation.

**(5)** The jurisdiction conferred by sub-paragraph (4) above shall be exercisable by the High Court and the Court of Session.
**(6)** Subsections (2) to (7) and (9) of section 11 of this Act shall, with the modifications mentioned in paragraph 5(2) above and any other necessary modifications, have effect in relation to any direction given or alteration made by the Registrar under sub-paragraph (1) above as they have effect in relation to an order revoking a recognition order.
**(7)** The fact that the rules of an organisation have been altered by or pursuant to a direction given by the Registrar, or pursuant to an order made by the court, under this paragraph shall not preclude their subsequent alteration or revocation by that organisation."

**Note**
In para. 7(1) (if still in force in accordance with transitional provisions in SI 1990/354 (C 12), art. 6) the words "itself alter, the rules of the organisation" substituted for the words "himself alter, its rules" by Friendly Societies Act 1992, s. 98 and Sch. 18, para. 13 as from 1 February 1993 in regard to incorporated friendly societies (see SI 1993/16 (C 1), art. 2 and Sch. 4) and as from 1 January 1994 for all remaining purposes (see SI 1993/2213 (C 43), art. 2 and Sch. 5).

**8(1)** The Commission or the Secretary of State may make regulations requiring a recognised self-regulating organisation for friendly societies to give the Commission or, as the case may be, the Secretary of State forthwith notice of the occurrence of such events relating to the organisation or its members as are specified in the regulations and such information in respect of those events as is so specified.

**8(2)** The Commission or the Secretary of State may make regulations requiring a recognised self-regulating organisation for friendly societies to furnish the Commission or, as the case may be, the Secretary of State at such times or in respect of such periods as are specified in the regulations with such information relating to the organisation or its members as is so specified.

**8(3)** The notices and information required to be given or furnished under the foregoing provisions of this paragraph shall be such as the Commission or, as the case may be, the Secretary of State may reasonably require for the exercise of his functions under this Act.

**8(4)** Regulations under the foregoing provisions of this paragraph may require information to be given in a specified form and to be verified in a specified manner.

**8(5)** A notice or information required to be given or furnished under the foregoing provisions of this paragraph shall be given in writing or such other manner as the Commission or, as the case may be, the Secretary of State may approve.

**8(6)** Where a recognised self-regulating organisation for friendly societies amends, revokes or adds to its rules or guidance it shall within seven days give the Commission written notice of the amendment, revocation or addition; but notice need not be given of the revocation of guidance other than such as is mentioned in paragraph 2(6) above or of any amendment of or addition to guidance which does not result in or consist of such guidance as is there mentioned.

**8(7)** The Commission shall send the Secretary of State a copy of any notice given to the Commission under sub-paragraph (6) above.

**8(8)** Contravention of or of regulations under this paragraph shall not be an offence.

**9(1)** A recognised self-regulating organisation for friendly societies shall not exercise any powers for purposes corresponding to those of the powers exercisable by the Commission by virtue of paragraph 23 below in relation to a regulated friendly society unless it has given reasonable notice of its intention to do so to the Commission and informed the Commission–

(a) of the manner in which and the date on or after which it intends to exercise the power; and

(b) in the case of a proposal to impose a prohibition or requirement, of the reason why it proposes to act and its reasons for considering that that reason exists and that it is necessary to impose the prohibition or requirement.

**9(2)** A recognised self-regulating organisation for friendly societies shall not exercise any power to which sub-paragraph (1)(a) above applies if before the date given in the notice in pursuance of that sub-paragraph the Commission has served on it a notice in writing directing it not to do so; and the Commission may serve such a notice if the Commission considers it is desirable for protecting members or potential members of the society against the risk that it may be unable to meet its liabilities or to fulfil the reasonable expectations of its members or potential members.

## PREVENTION OF RESTRICTIVE PRACTICES

**10(1)** The powers conferred by sub-paragraph (2) below shall be exercisable by the Secretary of State if at any time it appears to him that–

(a) any rules made or guidance issued by a recognised self-regulating organisation for friendly societies;

(b) any practices of any such organisation; or

(c) any practices of persons who are members of, or otherwise subject to the rules made by, any such organisation,

together with any statements of principle, rules, regulations or codes of practice to which members of the organisation are subject by virtue of this Schedule, have, or are intended or likely to have, to a significant extent the effect of restricting, distorting or preventing competition and that that effect is greater than is necessary for the protection of investors.

**History**

In para. 10(1) the words "together with any statements" to "by virtue of this Schedule" inserted by CA 1989, s. 206(1) and Sch. 23, para. 26, 30(1), (2) as from 15 March 1990 (see SI 1990/354 (C 12), art. 3).

**10(2)** The powers exercisable under this sub-paragraph are to direct the Commission–

(a) to revoke the recognition order of the organisation;

(b) to direct the organisation to take specified steps for the purpose of securing that its rules, or the guidance or practices in question do not have the effect mentioned in sub-paragraph (1) above;

(c) to make alterations in its rules for that purpose;

and subsections (2) to (5), (7) and (9) of section 11 of this Act, as applied by sub-paragraph (2) of paragraph 5 above, shall have effect in relation to the revocation of a recognition order by virtue of a direction under this sub-paragraph as they have effect in relation to the revocation of such an order under sub-paragraph (1) of that paragraph.

**History**

In para. 10(2)(b) the words "its rules, or the" substituted for the former words "the rules" and in para. 10(2)(c) the words "its rules" substituted for the former words "the rules" by CA 1989, s. 206(1) and Sch. 23, para. 26, 30(1), (3) as from 15 March 1990 (see SI 1990/354 (C 12), art. 3).

**10(3)** The practices referred to in paragraph (b) of sub-paragraph (1) above are practices of the organisation in its capacity as such.

**History**

In para. 10(3) the words "and the practices referred to in paragraph (c) of that sub-paragraph are practices in relation to business in respect of which the persons in question are subject to the rules of the organisation and which are required or contemplated by its rules or guidance or otherwise attributable to its conduct in its capacity as such" formerly appearing after the words "in its capacity as such" omitted and repealed by CA 1989, s. 206(1), 212, Sch. 23, para. 26, 30(1), (4) and Sch. 24 as from 15 March 1990 (see SI 1990/354 (C 12), art. 3).

**10(3A)** The practices referred to in paragraph (c) of sub-paragraph (1) above are practices in relation to business in respect of which the persons in question are subject to–

(a) the rules of the organisation, or

(b) statements of principle, rules, regulations or codes of practice to which its members are subject by virtue of this Schedule,

and which are required or contemplated by the rules of the organisation or by those statements, rules, regulations or codes, or by guidance issued by the organisation, or which are otherwise attributable to the conduct of the organisation as such.

**History**

Para. 10(3A) inserted by CA 1989, s. 206(1) and Sch. 23, para. 26, 30(1), (4) as from 15 March 1990 (see SI 1990/354 (C 12), art. 3).

**10(4)** Subsections (3) to (8) of section 122 of this Act shall apply for the purposes of this paragraph as if–

(a) the reference to a notice in subsection (3) included a notice received under paragraph 8(7) above or 33(4) below;

(b) the references to rules and guidance in subsection (4) included such rules and guidance as are mentioned in sub-paragraph (1) above;

(c) the reference to practices in subsection (6) included such practices as are mentioned in sub-paragraph (1) above; and

(d) the reference to the Secretary of State's powers in subsection (7) included his powers under sub-paragraph (2) above.

**10(5)** Section 128 of this Act shall apply for the purposes of this paragraph as if–

(a) the powers referred to in subsection (1) of that section included the powers conferred by sub-paragraph (2)(b) and (c) above;

(b) the references to Chapter XIV of Part I included references to this paragraph; and

(c) the reference to a recognised self-regulating organisation included a reference to a recognised self-regulating organisation for friendly societies.

### FEES

**11(1)** An applicant for a recognition order under paragraph 3 above shall pay such fees in respect of his application as may be required by a scheme made and published by the Commission; and no application for such an order shall be regarded as duly made unless this sub-paragraph is complied with.

**11(2)** Subsections (2) to (4) of section 112 of this Act apply to a scheme under sub-paragraph (1) above as they apply to a scheme under subsection (1) of that section.

**11(3)** Every recognised self-regulating organisation for friendly societies shall pay such periodical fees to the the Commission as the Commission may by regulations prescribe.

### APPLICATION OF PROVISIONS OF THIS ACT

**12(1)** Subject to the following provisions of this paragraph, sections 44(7), 102(1)(c), 124, 125, 180(1)(n), 181, 187, 192 and 200(4) of this Act shall apply in relation to recognised self-regulating organisations for friendly societies as they apply in relation to recognised self-regulating organisations.

**History**
In para. 12(1) "126" omitted by the Competition Act 1998, s. 74(1), Sch. 12, para. 8(a) as from 1 March 2000 (see the Competition Act 1998 (Commencement No. 5) Order 2000 (SI 2000/344 (C 9), art. 2, Sch).

**12(2)** (Omitted by the Competition Act 1998, s. 74(1), Sch. 12, para. 8(b) as from 1 March 2000.

**History**
In relation to the date of the omission see the Competition Act 1998 (Commencement No. 5) Order 2000 (SI 2000/344 (C 9), art. 2, Sch; para. 12(2) formerly read as follows:

"In its application by virtue of sub-paragraph (1) above section 126(1) of this Act shall have effect as it the reference to section 119(2) were a reference to paragraph 10(1) above."

**12(3)** In its application by virtue of sub-paragraph (1) above subsection (2) of section 187 of this Act shall have effect as if–

(a) the reference in paragraph (a) to paragraphs 1 to 6 of Schedule 2 were to paragraphs 2 to 6 of that Schedule (as they apply by virtue of paragraph 4 above) and to sub-paragraph (2) of paragraph 4 above; and

(b) paragraph (d) referred to the powers of the organisation under paragraph 23(4) below.

**12(4)** A direction under subsection (1) of section 192 of this Act as it applies by virtue of sub-paragraph (1) above shall direct the Commission to direct the organisation not to take or, as the case may be, to take the action in question; and where the function of making or revoking a recognition order in respect of a self-regulating organisation for friendly societies is exercisable by a transferee body any direction under that subsection as it applies as aforesaid shall be a direction requiring the Commission to direct the transferee body to give the organisation such a direction as is specified in the direction given by the Secretary of State.

**12(5)** Subsection (5) of that section shall not apply to a direction given to the Commission by virtue of this paragraph.

## Part III – Commission's Powers in Relation to Regulated Friendly Societies

**Note**
See history note at end of Sch. 11.

### SPECIAL PROVISIONS FOR REGULATED FRIENDLY SOCIETIES

**13** Paragraphs 13A to 25 below shall have effect in connection with the exercise of powers for the regulation of regulated friendly societies in relation to regulated business, but nothing in this Part of this Schedule shall affect the exercise of any power conferred by this Act in relation to a regulated friendly society which is an authorised person by virtue of section 25 of this Act to the extent that the power relates to other investment business.

**History**

In para. 13 the words "Paragraph 13A to 25" substituted for the former words "Paragraphs 14 to 25" by CA 1989, s. 206(1) and Sch. 23, para. 26, 31 as from 15 March 1990 (see SI 1990/354 (C 12), art. 3).

## CONDUCT OF INVESTMENT BUSINESS

**13A(1)** The Commission may issue statements of principle with respect to the conduct expected of regulated friendly societies.

**13A(2)** The conduct expected may include compliance with a code or standard issued by another person, as for the time being in force, and may allow for the exercise of discretion by any person pursuant to any such code or standard.

**13A(3)** Failure to comply with a statement of principle under this paragraph is a ground for the taking of disciplinary action or the exercise of powers of intervention, but it does not give rise to any right of action by investors or other persons affected or affect the validity of any transaction.

**13A(4)** The disciplinary action which may be taken by virtue of sub-paragraph (3) is–

(a) the making of a public statement under paragraph 21, or

(b) the application by the Commission for an injunction, interdict or other order under paragraph 22(1), or

(c) any action under paragraph 26 or 27 of this Schedule;

and the reference in that sub-paragraph to powers of intervention is to the powers conferred by Chapter VI of Part I of this Act.

**13A(5)** Where a statement of principle relates to compliance with a code or standard issued by another person, the statement of principle may provide–

(a) that failure to comply with the code or standard shall be a ground for the taking of disciplinary action, or the exercise of powers of intervention, only in such cases and to such extent as may be specified; and

(b) that no such action shall be taken, or any such power exercised, except at the request of the person by whom the code or standard in question was issued.

**13A(6)** The Commission shall exercise its powers in such manner as appears to the Commission appropriate to secure compliance with statements of principle under this paragraph.

**History**

Para. 13A inserted by CA 1989, s. 206(1) and Sch. 23, para. 26, 32 as from 15 March 1990 (see SI 1990/354 (C 12), art. 3).

**Note**

For transfer of the Registrar's functions under para. 13A see SI 1990/354 (C 12), art. 5(1).

**14(1)** The rules under section 48 of this Act shall not apply to a regulated friendly society but the Commission may, with the consent of the Secretary of State, make such rules as may be made under that section regulating the conduct of any such society as respects the matters mentioned in sub-paragraph (2) below.

**History**

In para. 14(1) the words "other than a member society" formerly appearing after the words "the conduct of any such society" omitted and repealed by CA 1989, s. 206(1), 212, Sch. 23, para. 26, 33(1), (2) and Sch. 24 as from 15 March 1990 (see SI 1990/354 (C 12), art. 3).

**14(2)** The matters referred to in sub-paragraph (1) above are–

(a) procuring persons to transact regulated business with it and advising persons as to the exercise of rights conferred by investments acquired from the society in the course of such business;

(b) managing the investments of pension funds, procuring persons to enter into contracts for the management of such investments and advising persons on such contracts and the exercise of the rights conferred by them;

(c) matters incidental to those mentioned in paragraphs (a) and (b) above.

**14(2A)** Paragraph 22B below has effect as regards the application of rules under this paragraph to member societies in respect of investment business in the carrying on of which they are subject to the rules of a recognised self-regulating organisation for friendly societies.

**History**
Para. 14(2A) inserted by CA 1989, s. 206(1) and Sch. 23, para. 26, 33(1), (3) as from 15 March 1990 (see SI 1990/354 (C 12), art. 3).

**14(3)** Section 50 of this Act shall apply in relation to rules under this paragraph as it applies in relation to rules under section 48 except that–

(a) for the reference to the Secretary of State there shall be substituted a reference to the Commission;

(b) the Commission shall not exercise the power under subsection (1) to alter the requirement of rules made under this paragraph without the consent of the Secretary of State; and

(c) for the references in subsection (4) to section 63B and a recognised self-regulating organisation there shall be substituted references to paragraph 13B and a recognised self-regulating organisation for friendly societies.

**History**
In para. 14(3)(a) the word "and" formerly appearing at the end omitted and repealed and after para. 14(3)(b) the word "; and" and para. 14(3)(c) inserted by CA 1989, s. 206(1), 212, Sch. 23, para. 26, 33(1), (4), Sch. 24 as from 15 March 1990 (see SI 1990/354 (C 12), art. 3).

**15(1)** The rules under section 51 of this Act shall not apply to any investment agreement which a person has entered or offered to enter into with a regulated friendly society if, as respects the society, entering into the agreement constitutes the carrying on of regulated business but the Commission may, with the consent of the Secretary of State, make rules for enabling a person who has entered or offered to enter into such an agreement to rescind the agreement or withdraw the offer within such period and in such manner as may be specified in the rules.

**15(2)** Subsection (2) of section 51 of this Act shall apply in relation to rules under this paragraph as it applies in relation to rules under that section but with the substitution for the reference to the Secretary of State of a reference to the Commission.

**16(1)** Regulations under section 52 of this Act shall not apply to any regulated friendly society but the Commission may, with the consent of the Secretary of State, make such regulations as may be made under that section imposing requirements on regulated friendly societies other than member societies.

**16(2)** Any notice or information required to be given or furnished under this paragraph shall be given in writing or in such other manner as the Commission may approve.

**17(1)** Rules under section 53 of this Act shall not apply to any regulated friendly society but the Commission may, with the consent of the Secretary of State make rules concerning indemnity against any claim in respect of any description of civil liability incurred by a regulated friendly society in connection with any regulated business.

**17(2)** Such rules shall not apply to a member society of a recognised self-regulating organisation for friendly societies unless that organisation has requested that such rules should apply to it; and any such request shall not be capable of being withdrawn after rules giving effect to it have been made but without prejudice to the power of the Commission to revoke the rules if the Commission and the Secretary of State think fit.

**17(3)** Subsections (3) and (4) of section 53 of this Act shall apply in relation to such rules as they apply to rules under that section but with the substitution for references to the Secretary of State of references to the Commission.

**18(1)** No scheme established by rules under section 54 shall apply in cases where persons who are or have been regulated friendly societies are unable, or likely to be unable, to satisfy claims in respect of any description of civil liability incurred by them in connection with any regulated business but the Commission may, with the consent of the Secretary of State, by rules establish a scheme for compensating investors in such cases.

**18(2)** Subject to sub-paragraph (3) below, subsections (2) to (4) and (6) of that section shall apply in relation to such rules as they apply to rules under that section but with the substitution for the references to the Secretary of State, authorised persons, members and a recognised self-regulating organisation of references respectively to the Commission, regulated friendly societies, member societies and a recognised self-regulating organisation for friendly societies.

**18(3)** Subsection (3) of that section shall have effect with the substitution for the words "the Secretary of State is satisfied" of the words "the Commission and the Secretary of State are satisfied".

**18(4)** The references in section 179(3)(b) and 180(1)(e) of this Act to the body administering a scheme established under section 54 of this Act shall include the body administering a scheme established under this paragraph.

**19(1)** Regulations under section 55 of this Act shall not apply to money held by regulated friendly societies but the Commission may, with the consent of the Secretary of State, make regulations with respect to money held by a regulated friendly society in such circumstances as may be specified in the regulations.

**19(2)** Regulations under this paragraph shall not provide that money held by a regulated friendly society shall be held as mentioned in paragraph (a) of subsection (2) of that section but paragraphs (b) to (f) of that subsection and subsections (3) and (4) of that section shall apply in relation to regulations made under this paragraph as they apply in relation to regulations under that section (but with the substitution for the reference in paragraph (e) of subsection (2) to the Secretary of State of a reference to the Commission).

**History**

In para. 19(2) the words "(but with the substitution for the reference in paragraph (e)" to the end substituted for the former words "(but with the substitution for the reference in paragraphs (b) and (e) of subsection (2) to a member of a recognised self-regulating organisation of a reference to a member society of a recognised self-regulating organisation for friendly societies and for the reference in paragraph (e) of that subsection to the Secretary of State of a reference to the Registrar)." by CA 1989, s. 206(1) and Sch. 23, para. 26, 34(1), (2) as from 15 March 1990 (see SI 1990/354 (C 12), art. 3).

**19(3)** Paragraph 22B below has effect as regards the application of regulations under this paragraph to member societies in respect of investment business in the carrying on of which they are subject to the rules of a recognised self-regulating organisation for friendly societies.

**History**

Para. 19(3) inserted by CA 1989, s. 206(1) and Sch. 23, para. 26, 34(1), (3) as from 15 March 1990 (see SI 1990/354 (C 12), art. 3).

**20(1)** Regulations under section 56(1) of this Act shall not permit anything to be done by a regulated friendly society but that section shall not apply to anything done by such a society in the course of or in consequence of an unsolicited call which, as respects the society, constitutes the carrying on of regulated business, if it is permitted to be done by the society by regulations made by the Commission with the consent of the Secretary of State.

**20(2)** Paragraph 22B below has effect as regards the application of regulations under this paragraph to member societies in respect of investment business in the carrying on of which they are subject to the rules of a recognised self-regulating organisation for friendly societies.

**20(3)** As it applies to such persons in respect of such business, the reference in sub-paragraph (1) above to conduct permitted by regulations made by the Commission with the consent of the Secretary of State shall be construed–

(a) where or to the extent that the regulations do not apply, as a reference to conduct permitted by the rules of the organisation; and

(b) where or to the extent that the regulations do not apply but are expressed to have effect subject to the rules of the organisation, as a reference to conduct permitted by the regulations together with the rules of the organisation.

**History**

Para. 20 substituted by CA 1989, s. 206(1) and Sch. 23, para. 26, 35 as from 15 March 1990 (see SI 1990/354 (C 12), art. 3); para. 20 formerly read as follows:

"**20** Regulations under section 56(1) of this Act shall not permit anything to be done by a regulated friendly society but that section shall not apply to anything done by such a society in the course of or in consequence of an unsolicited call which, as respects the society constitutes the carrying on of regulated business, if it is permitted to be done by the society in those circumstances–

(a) in the case of a member society, by the rules of the recognised self-regulating organisation for friendly societies of which it is a member; and

(b) in any other case, by regulations made by the Registrar with the consent of the Secretary of State."

**21(1)** If it appears to the Commission that a regulated friendly society other than a member society has contravened–

(a) any provision of rules or regulations made under this Schedule or of section 56 or 59 of this Act;

(b) any condition imposed under section 50 of this Act as it applies by virtue of paragraph 14(3) above;

(c) any prohibition or requirement imposed under Chapter VI of Part I of this Act as it applies by virtue of paragraph 23 below; or

(d) any requirement imposed under paragraph 24 below;

the Commission may publish a statement to that effect.

**21(2)** Subsections (2) to (5) of section 60 above shall apply in relation to the power under sub-paragraph (1) above as they apply in relation to the power in subsection (1) of that section but with the substitution for the references to the Secretary of State of references to the Commission.

**22(1)** If on the application of the Commission the court is satisfied–

(a) that there is a reasonable likelihood that any regulated friendly society will contravene any provision of–

(i) any prohibition or requirement imposed under Chapter VI of Part I of this Act as it applies by virtue of paragraph 23 below;

(ii) the rules or regulations made under this Schedule;

(iii) any requirement imposed under paragraph 24 below;

(iv) section 47, 56 or 59 of this Act;

(v) the rules of a recognised self-regulating organisation for friendly societies in relation to which it is a member society,

or any condition imposed under section 50 of this Act as it applies by virtue of paragraph 14(3) above;

(b) that any regulated friendly society has contravened any such provision or condition and that there is a reasonable likelihood that the contravention will continue or be repeated; or

(c) that any person has contravened any such provision or condition and that there are steps that could be taken for remedying the contravention,

the court may grant an injunction restraining the contravention or, in Scotland, an interdict prohibiting the contravention or, as the case may be, make an order requiring the society and any other person who appears to the court to have been knowingly concerned in the contravention to take steps to remedy it.

**22(2)** No application shall be made by the Commission under sub-paragraph (1) above in respect of any such rules as are mentioned in paragraph (a)(v) of that sub-paragraph unless it appears to the Commission that the organisation is unable or unwilling to take appropriate steps to restrain the contravention or to require the society concerned to take such steps as are mentioned in sub-paragraph (1) above.

**22(3)** Subsections (3) to (9) of section 61 of this Act apply to such a contravention as is mentioned in sub-paragraph (1)(a) above as they apply to such a contravention as is mentioned in subsection (3) of that section, but with the substitution for the references to the Secretary of State of references to the Commission.

**22(4)** Without prejudice to the preceding provisions of this paragraph–

(a) a contravention of any rules or regulations made under this Schedule;

(b) a contravention of any prohibition or requirement imposed under Chapter VI of Part I of this Act as it applies by virtue of paragraph 23 below;

(c) a contravention of any requirement imposed under paragraph 24 below;

(d) a contravention by a member society of any rules of the recognised self-regulating organisation for friendly societies of which it is a member relating to a matter in respect of which rules or regulations have been or could be made under this Schedule or of any requirement or prohibition imposed by the organisation in the exercise of powers for purposes corresponding to those of the said Chapter VI or paragraph 24;

shall be actionable at the suit of a person who suffers loss as a result of the contravention subject to the defences and other incidents applying to actions for breach of statutory duty, but no person shall be guilty of an offence by reason of any such contravention and no such contravention shall invalidate any transaction.

**22(5)** This paragraph is without prejudice to any equitable remedy available in respect of property which by virtue of a requirement under section 67 of this Act as it applies by virtue of paragraph 23 below is subject to a trust.

**22A(1)** No action in respect of a contravention to which paragraph 22(4) above applies shall lie at the suit of a person other than a private investor, except in such circumstances as may be specified by regulations made by the Commission.

**22A(2)** The meaning of the expression **"private investor"** for the purposes of sub-paragraph (1) shall be defined by regulations made by the Commission.

**22A(3)** Regulations under sub-paragraph (1) may make different provision with respect to different cases.

**22A(4)** The Commission shall, before making any regulations affecting the right to bring an action in respect of a contravention of any rules or regulations made by a person other than the Commission, consult that person.

**History**
Para. 22A inserted by CA 1989, s. 193(3) as from 15 March 1990 (see SI 1990/354 (C 12), art. 3) in so far as is necessary in order to enable regulations to be made under that paragraph and from 1 April 1991 subject to saving provision in so far as not previously in force (see SI 1991/488 (C 11), art. 3 and 4).

**Note**
See the Financial Services Act 1986 (Restriction of Right of Action) (Friendly Societies) Regulations 1991 (SI 1991/538).

**22B(1)** The Commission may in rules and regulations under–

(a) paragraph 14 (conduct of business rules),
(b) paragraph 19 (clients' money regulations), or
(c) paragraph 20 (regulations as to unsolicited calls),

designate provisions which apply, to such extent as may be specified, to a member society in respect of investment business in the carrying on of which it is subject to the rules of a recognised self-regulating organisation for friendly societies.

**22B(2)** It may be provided that the designated rules or regulations have effect, generally or to such extent as may be specified, subject to the rules of the organisation.

**22B(3)** A member society which contravenes a rule or regulation applying to it by virtue of this paragraph shall be treated as having contravened the rules of the relevant recognised self-regulating organisation for friendly societies.

**22B(4)** It may be provided that, to such extent as may be specified, the designated rules or regulations may not be modified or waived (under paragraph 22C below or section 50) in relation to a member society.

Where such provision is made any modification or waiver previously granted shall cease to have effect, subject to any transitional provision or saving contained in the rules or regulations.

**22B(5)** Except as mentioned in sub-paragraph (1), the rules and regulations referred to in that sub-paragraph do not apply to a member society in respect of investment business in the carrying on of which it is subject to the rules of a recognised self-regulating organisation for friendly societies.

**History**
See history note after para. 22D.

**Note**
See note after para. 22D.

**22C(1)** A recognised self-regulating organisation for friendly societies may on the application of a society which is a member of the organisation–

(a) modify a rule or regulation designated under paragraph 22B so as to adapt it to the circumstances of the society or to any particular kind of business carried on by it, or
(b) dispense the society from compliance with any such rule or regulation, generally or in relation to any particular kind of business carried on by it.

**33(1)** This paragraph applies where the function of making or revoking a recognition order in respect of a self-regulating organisation for friendly societies is exercisable by a transferee body.

**33(2)** Paragraph 3(2) above shall have effect as if the first reference to the Secretary of State included a reference to the Commission.

**33(3)** The transferee body shall not regard the requirement mentioned in paragraph 4(2) as satisfied unless the Commission has certified that the Commission also regards it as satisfied.

**33(4)** A transferee body shall send the Commission and the Secretary of State a copy of any notice received by it under paragraph 8(6) above.

**33(5)** Where the Secretary of State exercises any of the powers conferred by paragraph 10(2) above in relation to an organisation the Commission shall direct the transferee body to take the appropriate action in relation to that organisation and such a direction shall, on the application of the Commission, be enforceable by mandamus or, in Scotland, by an order for specific performance under section 91 of the Court of Session Act 1868.

**34(1)** A transferee body to which the Commission has transferred any legislative functions may exercise those functions without the consent of the Secretary of State.

**34(2)** In this paragraph **"legislative functions"** means the functions of issuing or making statements of principle, rules, regulations or codes of practice.

**History**
Para. 34 substituted by CA 1989, s. 206(1) and Sch. 23, para. 26, 40 as from 15 March 1990 (see SI 1990/354 (C 12), art. 3); para. 34 formerly read as follows:
"A transferee body to which the Registrar has transferred any function of making rules or regulations may make those rules or regulations without the consent of the Secretary of State."

**35(1)** A transferee body shall not impose any prohibition or requirement under section 65 or 67 of this Act on a regulated friendly society or vary any such prohibition or requirement unless it has given reasonable notice of its intention to do so to the Commission and informed the Commission–

(a) of the manner in which and the date on or after which it intends to exercise the power; and

(b) in the case of a proposal to impose a prohibition or requirement, on which of the grounds specified in paragraph 23(2) above it proposes to act and its reasons for considering that the ground in question exists and that it is necessary to impose the prohibition or requirement.

**35(2)** A transferee body shall not exercise any power to which sub-paragraph (1) above applies if before the date given in the notice in pursuance of sub-paragraph (1)(a) above the Commission has served on it a notice in writing directing it not to do so; and the Commission may serve such a notice if the Commission considers it is desirable for protecting members or potential members of the regulated friendly society against the risk that it may be unable to meet its liabilities or to fulfil the reasonable expectations of its members or potential members.

**36(1)** The Secretary of State shall not consent to the making of an order by the Commission under paragraph 28 above transferring any functions to a transferee body unless he is satisfied that any statements of principle, rules, regulations, codes of practice, guidance and recommendations of which copies are furnished to him under paragraphs 29(a) and 30(1) above do not have, and are not intended or likely to have, to any significant extent the effect of restricting, distorting or preventing competition or, if they have or are intended or likely to have that effect to any significant extent, that the effect is not greater than is necessary for the protection of investors.

**History**
See history note after para. 36(3).

**36(2)** Section 121(2) and (4) and sections 122 to 128 above shall have effect in relation to transferee bodies and transfer orders as they have effect in relation to designated agencies and designation orders but subject to the following modifications.

**36(3)** Those provisions shall have effect as if the powers exercisable under section 121(3) were–

(a) to make an order transferring back to the Commission all or any of the functions transferred to the transferee body by a transfer order; or

(b) to direct the Commission to direct the transferee body to take specified steps for the purpose of securing that the statements of principle, rules, regulations, codes of practice, guidance or practices in question do not have the effect mentioned in sub-paragraph (1) above.

**History**
In para. 36(1) and (3)(b) the words "statements of principle, rules, regulations, codes of practice" substituted for the former words "rules, regulations" by CA 1989, s. 206(1) and Sch. 23, para. 26, 41 as from 15 March 1990 (see SI 1990/354 (C 12), art. 3).

**36(4)** No order shall be made by virtue of sub-paragraph (3) above unless a draft of it has been laid before and approved by a resolution of each House of Parliament.

**36(5)** For the decisions referred to in section 122(1) there shall be substituted a reference to the Secretary of State's decision whether he is precluded by sub-paragraph (1) above from giving his consent to the making of a transfer order.

**36(6)** Section 128 shall apply as if–

(a) the powers referred to in subsection (1) of that section included the power conferred by sub-paragraph (3)(b) above; and

(b) the references to Chapter XIV of Part I included references to this paragraph.

**37(1)** If a transferee body has reasonable grounds for believing that any regulated friendly society has failed to comply with an obligation to which it is subject by virtue of this Act it shall forthwith give notice of that fact to the Commission so that the Commission can take it into consideration in deciding whether to exercise in relation to the society any of the relevant powers.

**History**
See history note after para. 37(1A).

**37(1A)** In sub-paragraph (1) above **"the relevant powers"** means those powers specified in paragraph 26(2).

**History**
In para. 37(1) the words "relevant powers" substituted for the former words "powers conferred on him by sections 87 to 89 and 91 of the Friendly Societies Act 1974 or, as the case may be, sections 77 to 80 of the Friendly Societies Act (Northern Ireland) 1970 (inspection, winding up, suspension of business and cancellation and suspension of registration)" and para. 37(1A) inserted by Friendly Societies Act 1992, s. 98 and Sch. 18, para. 20 as from 1 February 1993 in regard to incorporated friendly societies (see SI 1993/16 (C 1), art. 2 and Sch. 4) and as from 1 January 1994 for all remaining purposes (see SI 1993/2213 (C 43), art. 2 and Sch. 5).

**37(2)** A notice under sub-paragraph (1) above shall contain particulars of the obligation in question and of the transferee body's reasons for considering that the society has failed to satisfy that obligation.

**37(3)** A transferee body need not give a notice under sub-paragraph (1) above in respect of any matter unless it considers that that matter (either alone or in conjunction with other matters) would justify the withdrawal of authorisation under section 28 of this Act in the case of a person to whom that provision applies.

# Part V – Miscellaneous and Supplemental

**Note**
See history note at end of Sch. 11.

**38(1)** The Commission may publish information or give advice, or arrange for the publication of information or the giving of advice, in such form and manner as the Commission considers appropriate with respect to–

(a) the operation of this Schedule and the statements of principle, rules, regulations and codes of practice issued or made under it in relation to friendly societies, including in particular the rights of their members, the duties of such societies and the steps to be taken for enforcing those rights or complying with those duties;

(b) any matters relating to the functions of the Commission under this Schedule or any such statements of principle, rules, regulations or codes of practice;

(c) any other matters about which it appears to the Commission to be desirable to publish information or give advice for the protection of those members or any class of them.

**History**
In para. 38(1)(a) the word "registered" formerly appearing before the words "friendly societies" repealed by Friendly Societies Act 1992, s. 120 and Sch. 22, Pt. I as from 28 April 1993 in regard to incorporated friendly societies (see SI 1993/1186 (C 23), art. 2(1), Sch. 1, app.) and as from 1 January 1994 for all remaining purposes (see SI 1993/2213 (C 43), art. 2 and Sch. 5, app.).
Previously in para. 38(1)(a) the words "statements of principle, rules, regulations and codes of practice issued or made" substituted for the former words "rules and regulations made", and in para. 38(1)(b) the words "statements of principle, rules, regulations or codes of practice" substituted for the former words "rules or regulations" by CA 1989, s. 206(1) and Sch. 23, para. 26, 42(a), (b) as from 15 March 1990 (see SI 1990/354 (C 12), art. 3).

**38(2)** The Commission may offer for sale copies of information published under this paragraph and may, if the Commission thinks fit, make reasonable charges for advice given under this paragraph at any person's request.

**38(3)** This paragraph shall not be construed as authorising the disclosure of restricted information within the meaning of section 179 of this Act in any case in which it could not be disclosed apart from the provisions of this paragraph.

**39** In the case of an application for authorisation under section 26 of this Act made by a society which is registered under the Friendly Societies Act 1974 within the meaning of that Act or is registered or deemed to be registered under the Friendly Societies Act (Northern Ireland) 1970 ("a registered society"), section 27(3)(c) of this Act shall have effect as if it referred only to any person who is a trustee manager or member of the committee of the society.

**40** Where the other person mentioned in paragraph (c) of the definition of "connected person" in section 105(9) of this Act is a registered society that paragraph shall have effect with the substitution for the words from "member" onwards of the words "trustee, manager or member of the committee of the society".

**40A(1)** In the case of an application for authorisation under section 26 of this Act made by an incorporated friendly society section 27(3) shall have effect as if the following paragraph were substituted for paragraph (a)–

"(a) to any member of the committee of management or any director or controller of a subsidiary of the society or of a body jointly controlled by the society."

**40A(2)** Where the other person mentioned in paragraph (b) of the definition of "connected person" in section 105(9) of this Act is an incorporated friendly society that paragraph shall have effect with the substitution for the words from "director" onwards of the words "member of the committee of management of the society or any director, secretary or controller of a subsidiary of the society or a body jointly controlled by the society".

**History**
Para. 40A inserted by Friendly Societies Act 1992, s. 98 and Sch. 18, para. 21 as from 1 February 1993 in regard to incorporated friendly societies (see SI 1993/16 (C 1), art. 2 and Sch. 4) and as from 1 January 1994 for all remaining purposes (see SI 1993/2213 (C 43), art. 2 and Sch. 5).

**41** In relation to any such document as is mentioned in subsection (1) of section 204 of this Act which is required or authorised to be given to or served on a registered society–

(a) subsection (3)(c) of that section shall have effect with the substitution for the words from "member" onwards of the words "trustee, manager or member of the committee of the society"; and

(b) subsection (4)(c) of that section shall have effect as if for the words from "member" onwards there were substituted the words "trustee, manager or member of the committee of the society, the office which is its registered office in accordance with its rules".

**42** Rules under paragraphs 14, 15, 17 and 18 above and regulations under paragraphs 16, 19 and 20 above shall apply notwithstanding any provision to the contrary in the rules of any regulated friendly society to which they apply.

**43** (Repealed by Friendly Societies Act 1992, s. 120 and Sch. 22, Pt. I as from 28 April 1993 in regard to incorporated friendly societies and as from 1 January 1994 for all remaining purposes.)

**History**
In regard to the above repeal see SI 1993/1186 (C 23), art. 2(1), Sch. 1, app. and SI 1993/2213 (C 43), art. 2 and Sch. 5, app.; para. 43 formerly read as follows:

"**43(1)** Where it appears to the Commission, the assistant registrar for Scotland, the Industrial Assurance Commissioner or the Industrial Assurance Commissioner for Northern Ireland that any such rules as are mentioned in section 48(2)(j) of this Act which are made by virtue of paragraph 14 above (or any corresponding rules made by a self-regulating organisation for friendly societies) make arrangements for the settlement of a dispute referred to him under section 77 of the Friendly Societies Act 1974, section 65 of the Friendly Societies Act (Northern Ireland) 1970, section 32 of the Industrial Assurance Act 1923 or Article 36 of the Industrial Assurance (Northern Ireland) Order 1979 or that such rules relate to some of the matters in dispute he may, if he thinks fit, delegate his functions in respect of the dispute so as to enable it to be settled in accordance with the rules.

**(2)** If such rules provide that any dispute may be referred to such a person, that person may deal with any dispute referred to him in pursuance of those rules as if it were a dispute referred to him as aforesaid and may delegate his functions in respect of any such dispute to any other person."

**44(1)** In Part III of Schedule 1 to the House of Commons Disqualification Act 1975 (disqualifying offices) there shall be inserted at the appropriate place–

"Chairman of a transferee body within the meaning of Schedule 11 to the Financial Services Act 1986 if he is in receipt of remuneration."

**44(2)** A corresponding amendment shall be made in Part III of Schedule 1 to the Northern Ireland Assembly Disqualification Act 1975.

**45(1)** Any power of the Commission to make regulations, rules or orders which is exercisable by virtue of this Act shall be exercisable by statutory instrument and the Statutory Instruments Act 1946 shall apply to any such power as if the Commission were a Minister of the Crown.

**45(2)** Any regulations, rules or orders made under this Schedule by the Commission may make different provision for different cases.

**History**

Para. 45 substituted by Friendly Societies Act 1992, s. 98 and Sch. 18, para. 22 as from 1 February 1993 in regard to incorporated friendly societies (see SI 1993/16 (C 1), art. 2 and Sch. 4) and as from 1 January 1994 for all remaining purposes (see SI 1993/2213 (C 43), art. 2 and Sch. 5); para. 45 formerly read as follows:

"**45(1)** Any power of the Chief Registrar of friendly societies to issue or make statements of principle, rules, regulations, orders or codes of practice which is exercisable by virtue of this Act shall be exercisable by statutory instrument and the Statutory Instruments Act 1946 shall apply to any such power as if the Chief Registrar of friendly societies were a Minister of the Crown.

**(2)** Any such power of the Registrar of Friendly Societies for Northern Ireland shall be exercisable by statutory rule for the purposes of the Statutory Rules (Northern Ireland) Order 1979.

**(3)** Any statements of principle, rules, regulations, orders or codes of practice made under this Schedule by the Registrar may make different provision for different cases."

Previously in para. 45(1) the words "issue or make statements of principle, rules, regulations, orders or codes of practice" substituted for the former words "make regulations, rules or orders" by CA 1989, s. 206(1) and Sch. 23, para. 26, 43(a) as from 15 March 1990 (see SI 1990/354 (C 12), art. 3).

Previously in para. 45(3) the words "statements of principle, rules, regulations, orders or codes of practice" substituted for the former words "regulations, rules or orders" by CA 1989, s. 206(1) and Sch. 23, para. 26, 43(b) as from 15 March 1990 (see SI 1990/354 (C 12), art. 3).

**History to Sch. 11**

In Sch. 11 the words "the Commission" substituted for the former words "the Registrar" wherever appearing, and for the former words "he" or "him" where referring to the Registrar previously mentioned in the same subparagraph, by the Friendly Societies Act 1992, s. 98 and Sch. 18, para. 10 as from 1 February 1993 in regard to incorporated friendly societies (see SI 1993/16 (C 1), art. 2 and Sch. 4) and as from 1 January 1994 for all remaining purposes (see SI 1993/2213 (C 43), art. 2 and Sch. 5).

# Schedule 11A – Offers of Securities to the Public in the United Kingdom

**1** A person offers securities to the public in the United Kingdom if–

(a) to the extent that the offer is made to persons in the United Kingdom, it is made to the public; and

(b) paragraph 2 below does not apply in relation to the offer;

and, for this purpose, an offer which is made to any section of the public, whether selected as members or debenture holders of a body corpoate, or as clients of the person making the offer, or in any other manner, is to be regarded as made to the public.

**2** This paragraph applies in relation to an offer of securities where, to the extent that the offer is made to persons in the United Kingdom–

(a) the condition specified in any one of the paragraphs of sub-paragraph (1) of paragraph 3 below is satisfied in relation to the offer; or

(b) paragraph 4 below applies in relation to the offer.

**3(1)** The following are the conditions specified in this sub-paragraph–

(a) the securities are offered to persons–

(i) whose ordinary activities involve them in acquiring, holding, managing or disposing of investments (as principal or agent) for the purposes of their businesses; or

(ii) who it is reasonable to expect will acquire, hold, manage or dispose of investments (as principal or agent) for the purposes of their businesses;

or are otherwise offered to persons in the context of their trades, professions or occupations;

(b) the securities are offered to no more than fifty persons;

(c) the securities are offered to the members of a club or association (whether or not incorporated) and the members can reasonably be regarded as having a common interest with each other and with the club or association in the affairs of the club or association and in what is to be done with the proceeds of the offer;

(d) the securities are offered to a restricted circle of persons whom the offerer reasonably believes to be sufficiently knowledgeable to understand the risks involved in accepting the offer;

(e) the securities are offered in connection with a bona fide invitation to enter into an underwriting agreement with respect to them;

(f) the securities are offered to a government, local authority or public authority, as defined in paragraph 3 of Schedule 1 to this Act;

(g) the total consideration payable for the securities cannot exceed ecu 40,000 (or an equivalent amount);

(h) the minimum consideration which may be paid by any person for securities acquired by him pursuant to the offer is at least ecu 40,000 (or an equivalent amount);

(i) the securities are denominated in amounts of at least ecu 40,000 (or an equivalent amount);

(j) the securities are offered in connection with a takeover offer;

(k) the securities are offered in connection with a merger within the meaning of Council Directive No. 78/855/EEC;

(l) the securities are shares and are offered free of charge to any or all of the holders of shares in the issuer;

(m) the securities are shares, or investments falling within paragraph 4 or 5 of Schedule 1 to this Act relating to shares, in a body corporate and are offered in exchange for shares in the same body corporate, and the offer cannot result in any increase in the issued share capital of the body corporate;

(n) the securities are issued by a body corporate and offered–

(i) by the issuer, by a body corporate connected with the issuer or by a relevant trustee;

(ii) only to qualifying persons; and

(iii) on terms that a contract to acquire any such securities may be entered into only by the qualifying person to whom they were offered or, if the terms of the offer so permit, any qualifying person;

(o) the securities result from the conversion of convertible securities and listing particulars or a prospectus relating to the convertible securities were or was published in the United Kingdom under or by virtue of Part IV of this Act, Part III of the Companies Act 1985 or the Public Offers of Securities Regulations 1995;

(p) the securities are issued by–

(i) a charity within the meaning of section 96(1) of the Charities Act 1993;

(ii) a housing association within the meaning of section 5(1) of the Housing Act 1985;

(iii) an industrial or provident society registered in accordance with section 1(2)(b) of the Industrial and Provident Societies Act 1965; or

(iv) a non-profit making association or body, recognised by the country or territory in which it is established, with objectives similar to those of a body falling within any of sub-paragraphs (i) to (iii) above;

and the proceeds of the offer will be used for the purposes of the issuer's objectives;

(q) the securities offered are shares which are issued by, or ownership of which entitles the holder to membership of or to obtain the benefit of services provided by,–

(i) a building society incorporated under the law of, or of any part of, the United Kingdom;

(ii) any body incorporated under the law of, or any part of, the United Kingdom relating to industrial and provident societies or credit unions; or

(iii) a body of a similar nature established in a Member State;

(r) the securities offered are Euro-securities, and no advertisement relating to the offer is issued in the United Kingdom, or is caused to be so issued, by the issuer of the Euro-securities or by any credit institution or other financial institution through which the Euro-securities may be acquired pursuant to the offer, or by any body corporate which is a member of the same group as that issuer or any of those institutions, other than–

(i) an advertisement falling within article 8 of the Financial Services Act 1986 (Investment Advertisements) (Exemptions) (No. 2) Order 1995; or

(ii) an advertisement which would fall within article 11 of the Financial Services Act 1986 (Investment Advertisements) (Exemptions) Order 1996 if the person issuing the advertisement were a relevant person within the meaning of that article and there were added to the list of persons in paragraph (3) of that article a person with or for whom any credit institution or other financial institution through which the Euro-securities may be acquired pursuant to the offer has effected or arranged for the effecting of a transaction within the period of twelve months ending with the date on which the offer is first made;

(s) the securities are of the same class, and were issued at the same time, as securities in respect of which a prospectus has been published under or by virtue of Part IV of this Act, Part III of the Companies Act 1985 or the Public Offers of Securities Regulations 1995;

(t) the securities are investments falling within paragraph 2 of Schedule 1 to this Act with a maturity of less than one year from their date of issue;

(u) the securities are investments falling within paragraph 3 of Schedule 1 to this Act;

(v) the securities are not transferable.

**History**

In para. 3(1):

- in para. (h) the words "paid by any person for securities acquired by him" substituted for the former words "paid for securities acquired" by the Public Offers of Securities (Amendment) Regulations 1999 (SI 1999/734), reg. 1, 4(a) as from 10 May 1999.
- in para. (n) the words from ", body corporate" to the end inserted by the Public Offers of Securities (Amendment) Regulations 1999 (SI 1999/734), reg. 1, 4(b) as from 10 May 1999.
- para. (r) substituted by the Public Offers of Securities (Amendment) (No. 2) Regulations 1999 (SI 1999/1146), reg. 1, 3 as from 10 May 1999. The former para. (r) read as follows:

"(r) the securities offered are Euro-securities and are not the subject of advertising likely to come to the attention of persons who are not professionally experienced in matters relating to investment;"

There was a previous substitution of reg. 3(1)(r) by the Public Offers of Securities (Amendment) Regulations 1999 (SI 1999/734), reg. 4(c) as from 10 May 1999 which in fact never came into force because the Regulations were revoked by the Public Offers of Securities (Amendment) (No. 2) Regulations 1999 (SI 1999/1146), reg. 1, 4 as from 10 May 1999.

**3(2)** For the purposes of this paragraph–

**"convertible securities"** means–

(a) securities falling within paragraph 2 of Schedule 1 to this Act which can be converted into, or exchanged for, or which confer rights to acquire, securities; or

(b) securities falling within paragraph 4 or 5 of that Schedule (as applied for the purposes of section 142(2) of this Act);

and **"conversion"** in relation to convertible securities means their conversion into or exchange for, or the exercise of rights conferred by them to acquire, other securities;

**"credit institution"** means a credit institution as defined in Article 1 of Council Directive No. 77/780/EEC;

**"ecu"** means the European currency unit as defined in Article 1 of Council Regulation No. 3320/94/EC or any Council regulation replacing the same, in either case as amended from time to time;

**"Euro-securities"** means investments which–

(a) are to be underwritten (by whatever means, including acquisition or subscription, with a view to resale) and distributed by a syndicate at least two if the members of which have their registered offices in different countries or territories;

(b) are to be offered on a significant scale in one or more countries or territories other than the country or territory in which the issuer has its registered office; and

(c) may be acquired pursuant to the offer only through a credit institution or other financial institution;

**"financial institution"** means a financial institution as defined in Article 1 of Council Directive No. 89/646/EEC; and

**"shares"**, except in relation to a takeover offer, means investments which are securities by virtue of falling within paragraph 1 of Schedule 1 to this Act (as applied for the purposes of section 142(3) of this Act).

**History**
In para. 3(2), in para. (a) of the definition of "Euro-securities" the words "(by whatever means, including acquisition or subscription, with a view to resale)" appearing after the word "underwritten" inserted by the Public Offers of Securities (Amendment) Regulations 1999 (SI 1999/734), reg. 1, 4(d) as from 10 May 1999.

**3(3)** For the purposes of determining whether the condition specified in paragraph (b) or (g) of sub-paragraph (1) above is satisfied in relation to an offer, the offer shall be taken together with any other offer of the same securities which was–

(a) made by the same person;

(b) open at any time within the period of 12 months ending with the date on which the offer is first made; and

(c) not an offer to the public in the United Kingdopm by virtue of that condition being satisfied.

**3(3A)** For the purposes of paragraph (b) of sub-paragraph (1) above, the making of an offer of securities to trustees of a trust or members of a partnership in their capacity as such, or the making of such an offer to any other two or more persons jointly, shall be treated as the making of an offer to a single person.

**History**
Para. 3(3A) inserted by the Public Offers of Securities (Amendment) Regulations 1999 (SI 1999/734), reg. 1, 4(e) as from 10 May 1999.

**3(4)** In determining for the purposes of paragraph (d) of sub-paragraph (1) above whether a person is sufficiently knowledgeable to understand the risks involved in accepting an offer of securities, any information supplied by the person making the offer shall be disregarded, apart from information about–

(a) the issuer of the securities; or

(b) if the securities confer the right to acquire other securities, the issuer of those other securities.

**3(5)** For the purposes of determining whether the condition specified in paragraph (g), (h) or (i) of sub-paragraph (1) above is satisfied in relation to an offer, an amount, in relation to an amount denominated in ecu, is an "equivalent amount" if it is an amount of equal value, calculated at the latest practicable date before (but in any event not more than 3 days before) the date on which the offer is first made, denominated wholly or partly in another currency or unit of account.

**3(6)** For the purposes of paragraph (j) of sub-paragraph (1) above, "**takeover offer**" means–

(a) an offer to acquire shares in a body corporate incorporated in the United Kingdom which is a takeover offer within the meaning of Part XIIIA of the Companies Act 1985 (or would be such an offer if that Part of that Act applied in relation to any body corporate);

(b) an offer to acquire all or substantially all the shares, or the shares of a particular class, in a body corporate incorporated outside the United Kingdom; or

(c) an offer made to all the holders of shares, or of shares of a particular class, in a body corporate to acquire a specified proportion of those shares;

but in determining whether an offer falls within paragraph (b) above there shall be disregarded any shares which the offeror or any associate of his holds or has contracted to acquire; and in determining whether an offer falls within paragraph (c) above the offeror, any associate of his and any person whose shares the offeror or any such associate has contracted to acquire shall not be regarded as holders of the shares.

**History**

See history note below para. 3(6A).

**3(6A)** In sub-paragraph (6) above–

**"associate"** has the same meaning as in section 430E of the Companies Act 1985; and

**"share"** has the same meaning as in section 428(1) of that Act.

**History**

Para. 3(6), (6A) substituted for the former para. 3(6) by the Public Offers of Securities (Amendment) Regulations 1999 (SI 1999/734), reg. 1, 4(f) as from 10 May 1999. Para. 3(6) formerly read as follows:

"**3(6)** For the purposes of paragraph (j) of sub-paragraph (1) above, "**takeover offer**" means–

(a) an offer which is a takeover offer within the meaning of Part XIIIA of the Companies Act 1985 (or would be such an offer if that Part of that Act applied in relation to any body corporate); or

(b) an offer made to all the holders of shares, or of shares of a particular class, in a body corporate to acquire a specified proportion of those shares ("**holders**" and "**shares**" being construed in accordance with that Part);

but in determining for the purposes of paragraph (b) above whether an offer is made to all the holders of shares, or of shares of any class, the offeror, any associate of his (within the meaning of section 430E of that Act) and any person whose shares the offeror or any such associate has contracted to acquire shall not be regarded as holders of the shares."

**3(7)** For the purposes of paragraph (1) of sub-paragraph (1) above, "**holders of shares**" means the persons who, at the close of business on a date specified in the offer and falling within the period of 60 days ending with the date on which the offer is first made, were the holders of such shares.

**History**

In para. 3(7) the words "60 days" substituted for the former words "28 days" by the Public Offers of Securities (Amendment) Regulations 1999 (SI 1999/734), reg. 1, 4(g) as from 10 May 1999.

**3(8)** For the purposes of paragraph (n) of sub-paragraph (1) above–

(a) a person is a "**qualifying person**", in relation to an issuer, if he is a bona fide employee or former employee of the issuer or of another body corporate in the same group (within the meaning of Schedule 1 to this Act) or the wife, husband, widow, widower or child or stepchild under the age of eighteen of such an employee or former employee;

(b) the definition of "**issuer**" in section 142(7) applies with the omission of the words from "except that" to the end of the definition; and

(c) the references to "a body corporate connected with the issuer" and to "a relevant trustee" shall be construed in accordance with paragraph 20 of Schedule 1 to this Act.

**History**

In para. 3(8):

- in para. (a) the words "(within the meaning of Schedule 1 to this Act)" appearing after the words "same group" inserted and the word "and" formerly appearing at the end omitted by the Public Offers of Securities (Amendment) Regulations 1999 (SI 1999/734), reg. 1, 4(h)(i) and (ii) respectively, as from 10 May 1999;
- after para. (b) the word "and" and para. (c) inserted by the Public Offers of Securities (Amendment) Regulations 1999 (SI 1999/734), reg. 1, 4(h)(iii) as from 10 May 1999.

**4(1)** This paragraph applies in relation to an offer where the condition specified in one relevant paragraph is satisfied in relation to part, but not the whole, of the offer and, in relation to each other part of the offer, the condition specified in a different relevant paragraph is satisfied.

**4(2)** For the purposes of this paragraph, "**relevant paragraph**" means any of paragraph (a) to (f), (j) to (p) and (s) of paragraph 3(1) above.

**History**

In para. 4(2) the words "paragraphs (a) to (f), (j) to (p) and (s)" appearing after the words "any of paragraph" substituted for the former words " (a) to (f), (j) to (m), (o), (p) and (s)" by the Public Offers of Securities (Amendment) Regulations 1999 (SI 1999/734), reg. 1, 4(i) as from 10 May 1999.

Sch. 11A inserted by the Public Offers of Securities Regulations 1995 (SI 1995/1537), reg. 1, 17 and Sch. 2, para. 3(2), Sch. 3 as from 19 June 1995.

# Schedule 12 – Takeover Offers: Provisions Substituted for Sections 428, 429 and 430 of Companies Act 1985

**Note**
S. 428 – 430F (Pt. XIIIA) inserted into Companies Act 1985 as from 30 April 1987 (see SI 1986/2246 (C 88)). They are not reproduced here.

# Schedule 13 – Disclosure of Information

Section 182

**1** In section 133(2)(a) of the Fair Trading Act 1973 after the words "the Telecommunications Act 1984" there shall be inserted the words "or Chapter XIV of Part I of the Financial Services Act 1986".

**2** In section 41(1)(a) of the Restrictive Trade Practices Act 1976 after the words "the Telecommunications Act 1984" there shall be inserted the words "or Chapter XIV of Part I of the Financial Services Act 1986".

**3** (Repealed by Banking Act 1987, s. 108(2) and Sch. 7, Pt. I as from 1 October 1987.)

**History**
In regard to the above date see SI 1987/1664 (C 50), art. 2 and Sch.; para. 3 formerly read as follows:

"**3(1)** In section 19 of the Banking Act 1979 after subsection (2) there shall be inserted–

"**(2A)** Nothing in subsection (1) above prohibits the disclosure of information by the Bank to any person specified in the first column of the following Table if the Bank considers–

(a) that the disclosure would enable or assist the Bank to discharge its functions under this Act; or
(b) that it would enable or assist that person to discharge the functions specified in relation to him in the second column of that Table.

TABLE

| *Person* | *Functions* |
|---|---|
| The Secretary of State. | Functions under the Insurance Companies Act 1982 or the Financial Services Act 1986. |
| The Chief Registrar of friendly societies or the Registrar of Friendly Societies for Northern Ireland. | Functions under the Financial Services Act 1986 or under the enactments relating to friendly societies. |
| A designated agency or transferee body or the competent authority (within the meaning of the Financial Services Act 1986). | Functions under the Financial Services Act 1986. |
| A recognised self-regulating organisation, recognised professional body, recognised investment exchange, recognised clearing house or recognised self-regulating organisation for friendly societies (within the meaning of the Financial Services Act 1986). | Functions in its capacity as an organisation, body, exchange or clearing house recognised under the Financial Services Act 1986. |
| A person appointed or authorised to exercise any powers under section 94, 106 or 177 of the Financial Services Act 1986. | Functions arising from his appointment or authorisation under that section. |
| The body administering a scheme under section 54 of paragraph 18 of Schedule 11 to the Financial Services Act 1986. | Functions under the scheme. |

**(2B)** Nothing in subsection (1) above prohibits the disclosure by a person specified in the first column of the Table in subsection (2A) above of information obtained by him by virtue of a disclosure authorised by that subsection if he makes the disclosure with the consent of the Bank and for the purpose of enabling or assisting himself to discharge any functions specified in relation to him in the second column of that Table; and before deciding whether to give its consent to such a disclosure by any person the Bank shall take account of any representations made by him as to the desirability of or the necessity for the disclosure".

**3(2)** For subsection (6) of that section there shall be substituted–

"**(6)** Nothing in subsection (1) above prohibits the disclosure of information by or with the consent of the Bank for the purpose of enabling or assisting an authority in a country or territory outside the United Kingdom to exercise functions corresponding to those of the Bank under this Act, or to those of the Secretary of State under the Insurance Companies Act 1982 or the Financial Services Act 1986 or to those of the competent authority under the said Act of 1986 or any other functions in connection with rules of law corresponding to the provisions of the Company Securities (Insider Dealing) Act 1985 or Part VII of the said Act of 1986.""

**4** (Repealed by Banking Act 1987, s. 108(2) and Sch. 7, Pt. I as from 15 July 1987.)

**History**
In regard to the above date see SI 1987/1189 (C 32); art. 2 and Sch.; para. 4 formerly read as follows:

"**4** In section 20(4) of that Act–

(a) for the words "in a country or territory outside the United Kingdom" there shall be substituted the words "in a member State other than the United Kingdom"; and

(b) in paragraph (b) for the words "subsections (4) to (6)" there shall be substituted the words "subsections (2A), (2B) and (4) to (6)"."

5 At the end of section 19(3) of the Competition Act 1980 there shall be inserted–

"(h) Chapter XIV of Part I of the Financial Services Act 1986."

6 For subsections (1) and (2) of section 47A of the Insurance Companies Act 1982 there shall be substituted–

"**(1)** Subject to the following provisions of this section, no information relating to the business or other affairs of any person which has been obtained under section 44(2) to (4) above shall be disclosed without the consent of the person from whom the information was obtained and, if different, the person to whom it relates.

**(2)** Subsection (1) above shall not preclude the disclosure of information to any person who is a competent authority for the purposes of section 449 of the Companies Act 1985.

**(2A)** Subsection (1) above shall not preclude the disclosure of information as mentioned in any of the paragraphs except (m) of subsection (1) of section 180 of the Financial Services Act 1986 or in subsection (3) or (4) of that section or as mentioned in section 449(1) of the Companies Act 1985.

**(2B)** Subsection (1) above shall not preclude the disclosure of any such information as is mentioned in section 180(5) of the Financial Services Act 1986 by any person who by virtue of that section is not precluded by section 179 of that Act from disclosing it."

7 After subsection (1) of section 437 of the Companies Act 1985 there shall be inserted–

"**437(1A)** Any persons who have been appointed under section 431 or 432 may at any time and, if the Secretary of State directs them to do so, shall inform him of any matters coming to their knowledge as a result of their investigations.;"

and subsection (2) of section 433 of that Act shall be omitted.

8 In section 446 of that Act–

(a) in subsection (3) for the words "to 436" there shall be substituted the words "to 437"; and

(b) subsection (5) shall be omitted.

9(1) In subsection (1) of section 449 of that Act–

(a) for paragraphs (a) and (b) there shall be substituted–

"(a) with a view to the institution of or otherwise for the purposes of criminal proceedings;"

(b) for paragraph (d) there shall be substituted–

"(d) for the purpose of enabling or assisting the Secretary of State to exercise any of his functions under this Act, the Insider Dealing Act, the Prevention of Fraud (Investments) Act 1958, the Insurance Companies Act 1982, the Insolvency Act 1986, the Company Directors Disqualification Act 1986 or the Financial Services Act 1986.

(dd) for the purpose of enabling or assisting the Department of Economic Development for Northern Ireland to exercise any powers conferred on it by the enactments relating to companies or insolvency or for the purpose of enabling or assisting any inspector appointed by it under the enactments relating to companies to discharge his functions;"

(c) after paragraph (e) there shall be inserted–

"(f) for the purpose of enabling or assisting the Bank of England to discharge its functions under the Banking Act 1979 or any other functions,

(g) for the purpose of enabling or assisting the Deposit Protection Board to discharge its functions under that Act,

(h) for any purpose mentioned in section 180(1)(b), (e), (h), (n) or (p) of the Financial Services Act 1986,

(i) for the purpose of enabling or assisting the Industrial Assurance Commissioner or the Industrial Assurance Commissioner for Northern Ireland to discharge his functions under the enactments relating to industrial assurance,

(j) for the purpose of enabling or assisting the Insurance Brokers Registration Council to discharge its functions under the Insurance Brokers (Registration) Act 1977,

(k) for the purpose of enabling or assisting an official receiver to discharge his functions under the enactments relating to insolvency or for the purpose of enabling or assisting a body which is for the time being a recognised professional body for the purposes of section 391 of the Insolvency Act 1986 to discharge its functions as such,

(l) with a view to the institution of, or otherwise for the purposes of, any disciplinary proceedings relating to the exercise by a solicitor, auditor, accountant, valuer or actuary of his professional duties,

(m) for the purpose of enabling or assisting an authority in a country or territory outside the United Kingdom to exercise corresponding supervisory functions."

**9(2)** After subsection (1) of that section there shall be inserted–

"**(1A)** In subsection (1) above **"corresponding supervisory functions"** means functions corresponding to those of the Secretary of State or the competent authority under the Financial Services Act 1986 or to those of the Secretary of State under the Insurance Companies Act 1982 or to those of the Bank of England under the Banking Act 1979 or any other functions in connection with rules of law corresponding to the provisions of the Insider Dealing Act or Part VII of the Financial Services Act 1986.

**(1B)** Subject to subsection (1C), subsection (1) shall not preclude publication or disclosure for the purpose of enabling or assisting any publicor other authority for the time being designated for the purposes of this section by the Secretary of State by an order in a statutory instrument to discharge any functions which are specified in the order.

**(1C)** An order under subsection (1B) designating an authority for the purpose of that subsection may–

(a) impose conditions subject to which the publication or disclosure of any information or document is permitted by that subsection; and

(b) otherwise restrict the circumstances in which that subsection permits publication or disclosure.

**(1D)** Subsection (1) shall not preclude the publication or disclosure of any such information as is mentioned in section 180(5) of the Financial Services Act 1986 by any person who by virtue of that section is not precluded by section 179 of that Act from disclosing it."

**9(3)** For subsection (3) of that section (competent authorities) there shall be substituted–

"**(3)** For the purposes of this section each of the following is a competent authority–

(a) the Secretary of State,

(b) the Department of Economic Development for Northern Ireland and any officer of that Department,

(c) an inspector appointed under this Part by the Secretary of State,

(d) the Treasury and any officer of the Treasury,

(e) the Bank of England and any officer or servant of the Bank,

(f) the Lord Advocate,

(g) the Director of Public Prosecutions, and the Director of Public Prosecutions for Northern Ireland,

(h) any designated agency or transferee body within the meaning of the Financial Services Act 1986 and any officer or servant of such an agency or body,

(i) any person appointed or authorised to exercise any powers under section 94, 106 or 177 of the Financial Services Act 1986 and any officer or servant of such a person,

(j) the body administering a scheme under section 54 of or paragraph 18 of Schedule 11 to that Act and any officer or servant of such a body,

(k) the chief Registrar of friendly societies and the Registrar of Friendly Societies for Northern Ireland and any officer or servant of either of them,

(l) the Industrial Assurance Commissioner and the Industrial Assurance Commissioner for Northern Ireland and any officer of either of them,

(m) any constable,

(n) any procurator fiscal.

**(4)** A statutory instrument containing an order under subsection (1B) is subject to annulment in pursuance of a resolution of either House of Parliament."

**10** After section 451 of that Act there shall be inserted–

"*Disclosure of information by Secretary of State*

**451A** The Secretary of State may, if he thinks fit, disclose any information obtained under this Part of this Act–

(a) to any person who is a competent authority for the purposes of section 449, or

(b) in any circumstances in which or for any purpose for which that section does not preclude the disclosure of the information to which it applies."

**11** After Article 430(1) of the Companies (Northern Ireland) Order 1986 there shall be inserted–

"**(1A)** Any persons who have been appointed under Article 424 or 425 may at any time and, if the Department directs them to do so shall, inform it of any matters coming to their knowledge as a result of their investigation.;"

and Article 426(2) of that Order shall be omitted.

**12** In Article 439 of that Order–

(a) in paragraph (3) for the words "to 429" there shall be substituted the words "to 430"; and

(b) paragraph (5) shall be omitted.

**13(1)** In paragraph (1) of Article 442 of that Order–

(a) for sub-paragraphs (a) and (b) there shall be substituted–

"(a) with a view to the institution of or otherwise for the purposes of criminal proceedings;"

(b) for sub-paragraph (d) there shall be substituted–

"(d) for the purpose of enabling or assisting the Department to exercise any of its functions under this Order, the Insider Dealing Order or the Prevention of Fraud (Investments) Act (Northern Ireland) 1940;

(dd) for the purpose of enabling or assisting the Secretary of State to exercise any functions conferred on him by the enactments relating to companies or insolvency, the Prevention of Fraud (Investments) Act 1958, the Insurance Companies Act 1982, or the Financial Services Act 1986, or for the purpose of enabling or assisting any inspector appointed by him under the enactments relating to companies to discharge his functions;"

(c) after sub-paragraph (e) there shall be inserted–

"(f) for the purposes of enabling or assisting the Bank of England to discharge its functions under the Banking Act 1979 or any other functions;

(g) for the purposes of enabling or assisting the Deposit Protection Board to discharge its functions under that Act;

(h) for any purpose mentioned in section 180(1)(b), (e), (h), (n) or (p) of the Financial Services Act 1986;

(i) for the purpose of enabling or assisting the Industrial Assurance Commissioner for Northern Ireland or the Industrial Assurance Commissioner in Great Britain to discharge his functions under the enactments relating to industrial assurance;

(j) for the purpose of enabling or assisting the Insurance Brokers Registration Council to discharge its functions under the Insurance Brokers (Registration) Act 1977;

(k) for the purpose of enabling or assisting the official assignee to discharge his functions under the enactments relating to companies or bankruptcy;

(l) with a view to the institution of, or otherwise for the purposes of, any disciplinary proceedings relating to the exercise by a solicitor, auditor, accountant, valuer or actuary of his professional duties;

(m) for the purpose of enabling or assisting an authority in a country or territory outside the United Kingdom to exercise corresponding supervisory functions.".

**13(2)** After paragraph (1) of that Article there shall be inserted–

"**(1A)** In paragraph (1) **"corresponding supervisory functions"** means functions corresponding to those of the Secretary of State or the competent authority under the Financial Services Act 1986 or to those of the Secretary of State under the Insurance Companies Act 1982 or to those of the Bank of England under the Banking Act 1979 or any other functions in connection with rules of law corresponding to the provisions of the Insider Dealing Order or Part VII of the Financial Services Act 1986.

**(1B)** Subject to paragraph (1C), paragraph (1) shall not preclude publication or disclosure for the purpose of enabling or assisting any public or other authority for the time being designated for the purposes of this Article by an order made by the Department to discharge any functions which are specified in the order.

**(1C)** An order under paragraph (1B) designating an authority for the purpose of that paragraph may–

(a) impose conditions subject to which the publication or disclosure of any information or document is permitted by that paragraph; and

(b) otherwise restrict the circumstances in which that paragraph permits publication or disclosure.

**(1D)** Paragraph (1) shall not preclude the publication or disclosure of any such information as is mentioned in section 180(5) of the Financial Services Act 1986 by any person who by virtue of that section is not precluded by section 179 of that Act from disclosing it."

**13(3)** For paragraph (3) of that Article (competent authorities) there shall be substituted–

"**(3)** For the purposes of this Article each of the following is a competent authority–

(a) the Department and any officer of the Department,

(b) the Secretary of State,

(c) an inspector appointed under this Part by the Department,

(d) the Department of Finance and Personnel and any officer of that Department;

(e) the Treasury and any officer of the Treasury,

(f) the Bank of England and any officer or servant of the Bank,

(g) the Lord Advocate,

(h) the Director of Public Prosecutions for Northern Ireland and the Director of Public Prosecutions in England and Wales,

(i) any designated agency or transferee body within the meaning of the Financial Services Act 1986 and any officer or servant of such an agency or body,

(j) any person appointed or authorised to exercise any powers under section 94, 106 or 177 of the Financial Services Act 1986 and any officer or servant of such a person,

(k) the body administering a scheme under section 54 of or paragraph 18 of Schedule 11 to that Act and any officer or servant of such a body,

(l) the Registrar of Friendly Societies and the Chief Registrar of friendly societies in Great Britain and any officer or servant of either of them,

(m) the Industrial Assurance Commissioner for Northern Ireland and the Industrial Assurance Commissioner in Great Britain and any officer of either of them,

(n) any constable,

(o) any procurator fiscal.

**(4)** An order under paragraph (1B) is subject to negative resolution."

**14** After Article 444 of that order there shall be inserted–

"*Disclosure of information by Department*

**444A** The Department may, if it thinks fit, disclose any information obtained under this Part–

(a) to any person who is a competent authority for the purposes of Article 442, or

(b) in any circumstances in which or for any purpose for which that Article does not preclude the disclosure of the information to which it applies."

# Schedule 14 – Restriction of Rehabilitation of Offenders Act 1974

Section 189

## Part I – Exempted Proceedings

**1** Any proceedings with respect to a decision or proposed decision of the Secretary of State or a designated agency–

(a) refusing, withdrawing or suspending an authorisation;

(b) refusing an application under section 28(5) of this Act;

(c) giving a direction under section 59 of this Act or refusing an application for consent or for the variation of a consent under that section;

(d) exercising a power under Chapter VI of Part I of this Act or refusing an application for the rescission or variation of a prohibition or requirement imposed under that Chapter;

(e) refusing to make or revoking an order declaring a collective investment scheme to be an authorised unit trust scheme or a recognised scheme.

**2** Any proceedings with respect to a decision or proposed decision of a recognised self-regulating organisation–

(a) refusing or suspending a person's membership of the organisation;

(b) expelling a member of the organisation;

(c) exercising a power of the organisation for purposes corresponding to those of Chapter VI of Part I of this Act.

**3(1)** Any proceedings with respect to a decision or proposed decision of a recognised professional body–

(a) refusing or suspending a person's membership of the body;

(b) expelling a member of the body.

**3(2)** Any proceedings with respect to a decision or proposed decision of a recognised professional body or of any other body or person having functions in respect of the enforcement of the recognised professional body's rules relating to the carrying on of investment business–

(a) exercising a power for purposes corresponding to those of Chapter VI of Part I of this Act;

(b) refusing, suspending or withdrawing a certificate issued for the purposes of Part I of this Act.

**4** Any proceedings with respect to a decision or proposed decision of the competent authority under Part IV of this Act refusing an application for listing or to discontinue or suspend the listing of any securities.

**5** Any proceedings with respect to a decision or proposed decision of the Friendly Societies Commission or a transferee body, exercising a power exercisable by virtue of paragraph 23 of Schedule 11 to this Act or refusing an application for the rescission or variation of a prohibition or requirement imposed in the exercise of such a power.

**History**

See history note after Pt. III, para. 4.

**6** Any proceedings with respect to a decision or proposed decision of a recognised self-regulating organisation for friendly societies–

(a) refusing or suspending a society's membership of the organisation;

(b) expelling a member of the organisation;

(c) exercising a power of the organisation for purposes corresponding to those for which powers are exercisable by the Friendly Societies Commission by virtue of paragraph 23 of Schedule 11 to this Act.

**History**

In para. 6 of Pt. I the words "Friendly Societies Commission" substituted for the former word "Registrar" by Friendly Societies Act 1992, s. 98 and Sch. 18, para. 9(2) as from 1 February 1993 in regard to incorporated friendly societies (see SI 1993/16 (C 1), art. 2 and Sch. 4) and as from 1 January 1994 for all remaining purposes (see SI 1993/2213 (C 43), art. 2 and Sch. 5).

# Part II – Exempted Questions

| *Person putting question* | *Individual to whom question relates* |
|---|---|
| **1** The Secretary of State or a designated agency. | (a) An authorised person.<br>(b) An applicant for authorisation under section 26 of this Act.<br>(c) A person whose authorisation is suspended.<br>(d) The operator or trustee of a recognised scheme or a collective investment scheme in respect of which a notice has been given by the operator under section 87(3) or an application made under section 88 of this Act.<br>(e) An individual who is an associate of a person (whether or not an individual) described in paragraph (a), (b), (c) or (d) above. |
| **2** A recognised self-regulating organisation or recognised professional body. | (a) A member of the organisation or body.<br>(b) An applicant for membership of the organisation or body.<br>(c) A person whose membership of the organisation or body is suspended.<br>(d) An individual who is an associate of a person (whether or not an individual) described in paragraph (a), (b) or (c) above. |
| **3** A recognised professional body. | (a) A person certified by the body.<br>(b) An applicant for certification by the body.<br>(c) A person whose certification by the body is suspended.<br>(d) An individual who is an associate of a person (whether or not an individual) described in paragraph (a), (b) or (c) above. |
| **4** A person (whether or not an individual) described in paragraph 1(a), (b), (c) or (d), paragraph 2(a), (b) or (c) or paragraph 3(a), (b) or (c) above. | An individual who is or is seeking to become an associate of the person in column 1. |
| **5** The competent authority or any other person. | An individual from or in respect of whom information is sought in connection with an application for listing under Part IV of this Act. |

| Person putting question | Individual to whom question relates |
|---|---|
| 6 The competent authority. | An individual who is or is seeking to become an associate of the issuer of securities listed under Part IV of this Act and from or in respect of whom information is sought which the issuer of the securities is required to furnish under listing rules. |
| 7 The Friendly Societies Commission or a transferee body. | An individual who is an associate of a society which is authorised under section 23 of this Act. |

**History**
See history note after Pt. III, para. 4.

| | |
|---|---|
| 8 A recognised self-regulating organisation for friendly societies. | An individual who is an associate of a member or an applicant for membership of the organisation or of a society whose membership of the organisation is suspended. |

# Part III – Exempted Actions

| Person taking action | Exempted action |
|---|---|
| 1 The Secretary of State, a designated agency, a recognised self-regulating organisation, a recognised professional body, any other body or person mentioned in paragraph 3(2) of Part I of this Schedule or the competent authority. | Any such decision or proposed decision as is mentioned in Part I of this Schedule. |
| 2 A person (whether or not an individual) described in paragraph 1(a), (b), (c) or (d), paragraph 2(a), (b) or (c) or paragraph 3(a), (b) or (c) of Part II of this Schedule. | Dismissing or excluding an individual from being or becoming an associate or the person in column 1. |
| 3 The issuer of securities listed or subject to an application for listing under Part IV of this Act. | Dismissing or excluding an individual from being or becoming an associate of the issuer. |
| 4 The Friendly Societies Commission, a transferee body or a recognised self-regulating organisation for friendly societies. | Any such decision or proposed decision as is mentioned in Part I of this Schedule. |

**History**
In para. 5 of Pt. I, para. 7 of Pt. II and para. 4 of Pt. III the words "Friendly Societies Commission" substituted for the former words "Chief Registrar of friendly societies or the Registrar of Friendly Societies for Northern Ireland" by Friendly Societies Act 1992, s. 98 and Sch. 18, para. 9(1) as from 1 February 1993 in regard to incorporated friendly societies (see SI 1993/16 (C 1), art. 2 and Sch. 4) and as from 1 January 1994 for all remaining purposes (see SI 1993/2213 (C 43), art. 2 and Sch. 5).

# Part IV – Supplemental

**1** In Part I of this Schedule **"proceedings"** includes any proceedings within the meaning of section 4 of the Rehabilitation of Offenders Act 1974.

**2** In Parts II and III of this Schedule–

(a) references to an applicant for authorisation, membership or certification are references to an applicant who has not yet been informed of the decision on his application;

(b) references to an application for listing under Part IV of this Act are references to an application the decision on which has not yet been communicated to the applicant and which is not taken by virtue of section 144(5) of this Act to have been refused.

**3** Paragraph 1(d) of Part II of this Schedule and so much of paragraph 1(e) as relates to it–

(a) apply only if the question is put to elicit information for the purpose of determining whether the operator or trustee is a fit and proper person to act as operator or trustee of the scheme in question;

(b) apply in the case of a scheme in respect of which a notice has been given under subsection (3) of section 87 only until the end of the period within which the operator may receive a notification from the Secretary of State under that subsection or, if earlier, the receipt by him of such a notification;

(c) apply in the case of a scheme in respect of which an application has been made under section 88 only until the applicant has been informed of the decision on the application.

# Schedule 15 – Transitional Provisions

Section 211(3)

## INTERIM AUTHORISATION

**1(1)** If before such day as is appointed for the purposes of this paragraph by an order made by the Secretary of State a person has applied–

(a) for membership of any body which on that day is a recognised self-regulating organisation; or

(b) for authorisation by the Secretary of State,

and the application has not been determined before the day on which section 3 of this Act comes into force, that person shall, subject to sub-paragraphs (2), (3) and (4) below, be treated until the determination of the application as if he had been granted an authorisation by the Secretary of State.

**1(2)** Sub-paragraph (1) above does not apply to a person who immediately before the day on which section 3 of this Act comes into force is prohibited by the Prevention of Fraud (Investments) Act 1958 (in this Schedule referred to as "the previous Act") from carrying on the business of dealing in securities–

(a) by reason of the refusal or revocation at any time before that day of a licence under that Act; or

(b) by reason of the revocation at any time before that day of an order declaring him to be an exempted dealer.

**1(3)** If a person who has made any such application as is mentioned in sub-paragraph (1) above has before the day on which section 3 of this Act comes into force been served with a notice under section 6 or 16(3) of the previous Act (proposed refusal or revocation of licence or proposed revocation of exemption order) but the refusal or revocation to which the notice relates has not taken place before that day–

(a) the provisions of that Act with respect to the refusal or revocation of a licence or the revocation of an order under section 16 of that Act shall continue to apply to him until the application mentioned in sub-paragraph (1) above is determined; and

(b) that sub-paragraph shall cease to apply to him if before the determination of the application mentioned in that sub-paragraph his application for a licence under that Act is refused, his licence under that Act is revoked or the order declaring him to be an exempted dealer under that Act is revoked.

**1(4)** Notwithstanding sub-paragraph (1) above section 102(1)(a) of this Act shall not apply to a person entitled to carry on investment business by virtue of that sub-paragraph but the Secretary of State may make available for public inspection the information with respect to the holders of principal's licences mentioned in section 9 of the previous Act, any information in his possession by virtue of section 15(3) or (4) of that Act and the information mentioned in section 16(4) of that Act.

**1(5)** Notwithstanding subsection (2) of section 3 of the previous Act a licence granted under that section before the day on which section 3 of this Act comes into force shall, unless revoked under section 6 of that Act, continue in force until that day.

## RETURN OF FEES ON PENDING APPLICATIONS

**2** Any fee paid in respect of an application under section 3 of the previous Act which is pending on the day on which that Act is repealed shall be repaid to the applicant.

## DEPOSITS AND UNDERTAKINGS

**3** The repeal of section 4 of the previous Act shall not affect the operation of that section in a case where–

(a) a sum deposited in accordance with that section has become payable as provided in subsection (2) of that section before the date on which the repeal takes effect; or

(b) a sum has become payable before that date in pursuance of an undertaking given under subsection (4) of that section,

but, subject as aforesaid, any sum deposited under that section may be withdrawn by the depositor on application to the Accountant General of the Supreme Court and any undertaking given under that section shall be discharged.

## INTERIM RECOGNITION OF PROFESSIONAL BODIES

**4(1)** If on an application made under section 17 of this Act it appears to the Secretary of State that any of the requirements of section 18(3) of this Act or paragraphs 2 to 6 of Schedule 3 to this Act are not satisfied he may in accordance with this paragraph make a recognition order under section 18 of this Act ("an interim recognition order") notwithstanding that all or any of those requirements are not satisfied.

**4(2)** The Secretary of State may, subject to sub-paragraphs (3) and (4) below, make an interim recognition order if he is satisfied–

(a) that the applicant proposes to adopt rules and practices and to make arrangements which will satisfy such of the requirements mentioned in sub-paragraph (1) above as are not satisfied;

(b) that it is not practicable for those rules, practices and arrangements to be brought into effect before the date on which section 3 of this Act comes into force but that they will be brought into effect within a reasonable time thereafter; and

(c) that in the meantime the applicant will enforce its existing rules in such a way, and issue such guidance, as will in respect of investment business of any kind carried on by persons certified by it (or by virtue of paragraph 5 below treated as certified by it) afford to investors protection as nearly as may be equivalent to that provided as respects investment business of that kind by the rules and regulations under Chapter V of Part I of this Act.

**4(3)** Where the requirements which are not satisfied consist of or include those mentioned in paragraph 2 of Schedule 3 to this Act an application for an interim recognition order shall be accompanied by–

(a) a list of the persons to whom the applicant proposes to issue certificates for the purposes of Part I of this Act; and

(b) particulars of the criteria adopted for determining the persons included in the list;

and the Secretary of State shall not make the order unless it appears to him that those criteria conform as nearly as may be to the conditions mentioned in that paragraph and that the applicant will, until the requirements of that paragraph are satisfied, have arrangements for securing that no person is certified by it (or by virtue of paragraph 5 below treated as certified by it) except in accordance with those criteria and for the effective monitoring of continued compliance by those persons with those criteria.

**4(4)** Where the requirements which are not satisfied consist of or include that mentioned in paragraph 6 of Schedule 3 to this Act, the Secretary of State shall not make an interim recognition order unless it appears to him that the applicant will, until that requirement is satisfied, take such steps for complying with it as are reasonably practicable.

**4(5)** An application for an interim recognition order shall be accompanied by a copy of the rules and by particulars of the practices and arrangements referred to in sub-paragraph (2)(a) above.

**4(6)** An interim recognition order shall not be revocable but shall cease to be in force at the end of such period as is specified in it; and that period shall be such as will in the opinion of the Secretary of State allow a reasonable time for the rules, practices and arrangements mentioned in sub-paragraph (5) above to be brought into effect.

**4(7)** The Secretary of State may on the application of the body to which an interim recognition order relates extend the period specified in it if that body satisfies him–

(a) that there are sufficient reasons why the rules, practices and arrangements mentioned in sub-paragraph (5) above cannot be brought into effect by the end of that period; and

(b) that those rules, practices and arrangements, or other rules, practices and arrangements which satisfy the requirements mentioned in sub-paragraph (2)(a) above and of which copies or particulars are furnished to the Secretary of State, will be brought into effect within a reasonable time thereafter;

but not more than one application shall be made by a body under this sub-paragraph.

**4(8)** A recognition order under section 18 of this Act shall cease to be an interim recognition order if before it ceases to be in force–

(a) the rules, practices and arrangements of which copies or particulars were furnished to the Secretary of State under sub-paragraph (5) or (7)(b) above are brought into effect; or

(b) the Secretary of State certifies that other rules, practices and arrangements which have been brought into effect comply with the requirements mentioned in sub-paragraph (1) above.

**4(9)** In this paragraph references to the adoption of rules or the making of arrangements include references to taking such other steps as may be necessary for bringing them into effect.

## INTERIM AUTHORISATION BY RECOGNISED PROFESSIONAL BODIES

**5(1)** If at the time when an interim recognition order is made in respect of a professional body that body is unable to issue certificates for the purposes of this Act, any person who at that time is included in the list furnished by that body to the Secretary of State in accordance with paragraph 4(3)(a) above shall be treated for the purposes of this Act as a person certified by that body.

**5(2)** If at any time while an interim recognition order is in force in respect of a professional body and before the body is able to issue certificates as mentioned in sub-paragraph (1) above the body notifies the Secretary of State that a person not included in that list satisfies the criteria of which particulars were furnished by the body in accordance with paragraph 4(3)(b) above, that person shall, on receipt of the notification by the Secretary of State, be treated for the purposes of this Act as a person certified by that body.

**5(3)** If at any time while an interim recognition order is in force in respect of a professional body it appears to the body–

(a) that a person treated by virtue of sub-paragraph (1) or (2) above as certified by it has ceased (after the expiration of such transitional period, if any, as appears to the body to be appropriate) to satisfy the criteria mentioned in sub-paragraph (2) above; or

(b) that any such person should for any other reason cease to be treated as certified by it,

it shall forthwith give notice of that fact to the Secretary of State and the person in question shall, on receipt of that notification by the Secretary of State, cease to be treated as certified by that body.

**5(4)** Where by virtue of this paragraph a partnership is treated as certified by a recognised professional body section 15(3) of this Act shall apply as it applies where a certificate has in fact been issued to a partnership.

**5(5)** Where by virtue of this paragraph any persons are treated as certified by a recognised professional body the requirements of paragraph 2 of Schedule 3 to this Act so far as relating to the retention by a person of a certificate issued by that body and the requirements of paragraph 4 of that Schedule shall apply to the body as if the references to persons certified by it included references to persons treated as certified.

## POWER OF RECOGNISED PROFESSIONAL BODY TO MAKE RULES REQUIRED BY THIS ACT

**6(1)** Where a recognised professional body regulates the practice of a profession in the exercise of statutory powers the matters in respect of which rules can be made in the exercise of those powers shall, if they would not otherwise do so, include any matter in respect of which rules are required to be made–

(a) so that the recognition order in respect of that body can cease to be an interim recognition order; or

(b) where the recognition order was not, or has ceased to be, an interim recognition order, so that the body can continue to be a recognised professional body.

**6(2)** Rules made by virtue of this paragraph may in particular make provision for the issue, withdrawal and suspension of certificates for the purposes of this Act and the making of charges in respect of their issue and may accordingly apply to persons who are, or are to be, certified or treated as certified by the body in question whether or not they are persons in relation to whom rules could be made apart from this paragraph.

**6(3)** Rules made by virtue of this paragraph may make different provision for different cases.

**6(4)** The Secretary of State may at the request of a recognised professional body by order extend, modify or exclude any statutory provision relating to the regulation of the conduct, practice, or discipline of members of that body to such extent as he thinks necessary or expedient in consequence of the provisions of this paragraph; and any order made by virtue of this sub-paragraph shall be subject to annulment in pursuance of a resolution of either House of Parliament.

## NOTICE OF COMMENCEMENT OF BUSINESS

**7** In the case of a person who is carrying on investment business in the United Kingdom on the day on which section 31 of this Act comes into force, section 32 of this Act shall have effect as if it required him to give the notice referred to in that section forthwith.

## ADVERTISEMENTS

**8** (Repealed by the Public Offers of Securities Regulations 1995 (SI 1995/1537), reg. 1, 17 and Sch. 2, para. 9 as from 19 June 1995.)

**History**

Para. 8 formerly read as follows:

"**8(1)** So long as Part III of the Companies Act 1985 remains in force section 57 of this Act shall not apply–

(a) in relation to any distribution of a prospectus to which section 56 of that Act applies or would apply if not excluded by subsection (5)(b) of that section or to which section 72 of that Act applies or would apply if not excluded by subsection (6)(b) of that section or by section 76 of that Act, or in relation to any distribution of a document relating to securities of a corporation incorporated in Great Britain which is not a registered company, being a document which–

(i) would, if the corporation were a registered company, be a prospectus to which section 56 of that Act applies or would apply if not excluded as aforesaid, and

(ii) contains all the matters and is issued with the consents which, by virtue of sections 72 to 75 of that Act, it would have to contain and be issued with if the corporation were a company incorporated outside Great Britain and the document were a prospectus issued by that company;

(b) in relation to any issue of a form of application for shares in, or debentures of, a corporation, together with–

(i) a prospectus which complies with the requirements of section 56 of that Act or is not required to comply with them because excluded by subsection (5)(b) of that section, or complies with the requirements of Chapter II of Part III of that Act relating to prospectuses and is not issued in contravention of sections 74 and 75 of that Act, or

(ii) in the case of a corporation incorporated in Great Britain which is not a registered company, a document containing all the matters and issued with the consents mentioned in sub-paragraph (a)(ii) of this paragraph, or in connection with a bona fide invitation to a person to enter into an underwriting agreement with respect to the shares or debentures.

**(2)** The provisions of this paragraph shall apply to Northern Ireland with the substitution for the references to Part III and Chapter II of Part III of the Companies Act 1985 of references to Part IV and Chapter II of Part IV of the Companies (Northern Ireland) Order 1986, for the references to sections 56, 56(5)(b), 72, 72(6)(b), 74, 76 and 72 to 75 of the Companies Act 1985 of references to Articles 66, 66(5)(b), 82, 82(6)(b), 84, 86 and 82 to 85 of the Companies (Northern Ireland) Order 1986, for the references to a corporation incorporated in Great Britain of references to a corporation incorporated in Northern Ireland and for the reference to a company incorporated outside Great Britain of a reference to a company incorporated outside the United Kingdom."

## AUTHORISED UNIT TRUST SCHEMES

**9(1)** Where an order under section 17 of the previous Act (authorisation of unit trust schemes) is in force in respect of a unit trust scheme immediately before the coming into force of Chapter

VIII of Part I of this Act the scheme shall be treated as an authorised unit trust scheme under that Part and the order as an order under section 78 of this Act.

**9(2)** In relation to any such authorised unit trust scheme the reference in section 79(1)(a) of this Act to the requirements for the making of the order shall be construed as a reference to the requirements for the making of an order under section 78, but the scheme shall not be regarded as failing to comply with those requirements by reason of the manager or trustee not being an authorised person if he is treated as such a person by virtue of paragraph 1 above.

**9(3)** If before the day on which Chapter VIII of Part I comes into force a notice in respect of a scheme has been served under subsection (2) of section 17 of the previous Act (proposed revocation of authorisation of unit trust scheme) but the revocation has not taken place before that day, the provisions of that subsection shall continue to apply in relation to the scheme and sub-paragraph (1) above shall cease to apply to it if the authorisation is revoked under that subsection.

## RECOGNISED COLLECTIVE INVESTMENT SCHEMES

**10(1)** If at any time before the coming into force of section 86 of this Act it appears to the Secretary of State that the law of a member State other than the United Kingdom confers rights on the managers and trustees of authorised unit trust schemes entitling them to carry on in that State on terms equivalent to those of that section–

(a) investment business which consists in operating or acting as trustee in relation to such schemes; and

(b) any investment business which is carried on by them in connection with or for the purposes of such schemes,

he may by order direct that schemes constituted in that State which satisfy such requirements as are specified in the order shall be recognised schemes for the purposes of this Act.

**10(2)** Subsections (2) to (9) of section 86 of this Act shall have effect in relation to any scheme recognised by virtue of this paragraph; and the references in section 24 and 207(1) of this Act to a scheme recognised under section 86, and in section 76(1) of this Act to a scheme recognised under Chapter VIII of Part I of this Act, shall include references to any scheme recognised by virtue of this paragraph.

**10(3)** In section 86(3)(a) as applied by sub-paragraph (2) above the reference to the rights conferred by any relevant Community instrument shall be construed as a reference to the rights conferred by virtue of an order made under this paragraph.

**11(1)** Subsection (7) of section 88 of this Act shall not apply to a scheme which is in existence on the date on which this Act is passed if–

(a) the units under the scheme are included in the Official List of The Stock Exchange and have been so included throughout the period of five years ending on the date on which this paragraph comes into force;

(b) the law of the country or territory in which the scheme is established precludes the participants being entitled or the operator being required as mentioned in that subsection; and

(c) throughout the period of five years ending on the date on which the application is made under that section, units under the scheme have in fact been regularly redeemed as mentioned in that subsection or the operator has in fact regularly ensured that participants were able to sell their units as there mentioned.

**11(2)** The grounds for revoking an order made under section 88 of this Act by virtue of this paragraph shall include the ground that it appears to the Secretary of State that since the making of the order units under the scheme have ceased to be regularly redeemed or the operator has ceased regularly to ensure their sale as mentioned in sub-paragraph (1)(c) above.

## DELEGATION ORDERS

**12(1)** A delegation order may transfer a function notwithstanding that the provision conferring it has not yet come into force but no such function shall be exercisable by virtue of the order until the coming into force of that provision.

**12(2)** Sub-paragraph (1) above applies also to a transfer order under paragraph 28(1) of Schedule 11 to this Act.

## DISCLOSURE OF INFORMATION

**13** In determining for the purposes of section 180(6) of this Act and the enactments amended by paragraphs 3(2), 9(2) and 13(2) of Schedule 13 to this Act whether the functions of an authority in a country or territory outside the United Kingdom correspond to functions conferred by any of the provisions of this Act regard shall be had to those provisions whether or not they have already come into force.

## TEMPORARY EXEMPTIONS FOR FRIENDLY SOCIETIES

**14(1)** A friendly society which transacts no investment business after the date on which section 3 of this Act comes into force except for the purpose of making or carrying out relevant existing members' contracts shall be treated for the purposes of that section as if it were an exempted person under Chapter IV of Part I of this Act.

**History**

In para. 14(1) the word "registered" formerly appearing before the words "friendly society" repealed by Friendly Societies Act 1992, s. 120 and Sch. 22, Pt. I as from 28 April 1993 in regard to incorporated friendly societies (see SI 1993/1186 (C 23), art. 2(1), Sch. 1, app.) and as from 1 January 1994 for all remaining purposes (see SI 1993/2213 (C 43), art. 2 and Sch. 5, app.).

**14(2)** Subject to sub-paragraph (3) below, for the purposes of this paragraph **"relevant existing members' contracts"**, in relation to any society, means–

(a) contracts made by the society before that date; and

(b) in the case of a small income society–

  (i) during the period of three years beginning with that date, tax exempt investment agreements made by it with persons who were members of the society before that date; and

  (ii) after the expiry of that period, tax exempt investment agreements made by it with such persons before the expiry of that period.

**14(3)** Paragraph (b) of sub-paragraph (2) above shall not apply to a friendly society after the expiry of the period of two years beginning with that date unless before the expiry of that period it has by special resolution (within the meaning of the Friendly Societies Act 1974) determined–

(a) to transact no further investment business except for the purpose of carrying out contracts entered into before the expiry of the said period of three years; or

(b) to take such action as is necessary to procure the transfer of its engagements to another such society or a company or the amalgamation of the society with another such society under section 82 of the said Act of 1974,

and a copy of that resolution has been registered in accordance with section 86 of the said Act of 1974.

**History**

In para. 14(3) the word "registered" formerly appearing before the words "friendly society", the words "or, as the case may be, the Friendly Societies Act (Northern Ireland) 1970" formerly appearing after the words "Friendly Societies Act 1974", the words "or, as the case may be, section 70 of the said Act of 1970" formerly appearing after the words "section 82 of the said Act of 1974" and the words "or, as the case may be, section 75 of the said Act of 1970" formerly appearing after the words "section 86 of the said Act of 1974" repealed by Friendly Societies Act 1992, s. 120 and Sch. 22, Pt. I as from 28 April 1993 in regard to incorporated friendly societies (see SI 1993/1186 (C 23), art. 2(1), Sch. 1, app.) and as from 1 January 1994 for all remaining purposes (see SI 1993/2213 (C 43), art. 2 and Sch. 5, app.).

**14(4)** For the purpose of sub-paragraph (2) above a society is a small income society if its income in 1985 from members' contributions did not exceed £50,000.

**14(5)** For the purposes of sub-paragraph (2) above an investment agreement is a tax exempt investment agreement if the society by which it is made may obtain exemption from income and corporation tax on the profits from it under section 460(1) or 461(1) of the Income and Corporation Taxes Act 1988.

**History**

In para. 14(5) the words "460(1) or 461(1) of the Income and Corporation Taxes Act 1988" substituted for the former words "332 of the Income and Corporation Taxes Act 1970" by Income and Corporation Taxes Act 1988, s. 844 and Sch. 29, para. 32, Table for accounting periods ending after 5 April 1988 (see s. 843(1)).

**14(6)** A society to which sub-paragraph (1) or (2) above applies shall not be an authorised person for the purposes of this Act nor a regulated friendly society for the purposes of the provisions of Schedule 11 to this Act.

DEALINGS IN COURSE OF NON-INVESTMENT BUSINESS

**15** If before the day on which section 3 of this Act comes into force a person has applied for permission under paragraph 23 of Schedule 1 to this Act and the application has not been determined before that day, that person shall, until the determination of the application and subject to his complying with such requirements as the Secretary of State may impose, be treated as if he had been granted a permission under that paragraph.

NORTHERN IRELAND

**16** The foregoing provisions shall apply to Northern Ireland with the substitution for references to the previous Act or any provision of that Act of references to the Prevention of Fraud (Investments) Act (Northern Ireland) 1940 and the corresponding provision of that Act.

# Schedule 16 – Consequential Amendments

Section 212(2)

**1** (Repealed by Charities Act 1993, s. 98(2), 99(1) and Sch. 7 as from 1 August 1993.)

**History**

Para. 1 formerly read as follows:

"In section 22 of the Charities Act 1960–

(a) subsection (10) shall be omitted; and

(b) in subsection (11) for the words "Subsections (9) and (10)" there shall be substituted the words "Subsection (9)"."

**2** In the Trustee Investments Act 1961–

(a) in section 11(3) for the words "the Prevention of Fraud (Investments) Act 1958 or the Prevention of Fraud (Investments) Act (Northern Ireland) 1940" there shall be substituted the words "the Financial Services Act 1986";

(b) for paragraph 3 of Part III of Schedule 1 there shall be substituted–

"**3.** In any units of an authorised unit trust scheme within the meaning of the Financial Services Act 1986;"

(c) in paragraph 2(a) of Part IV of Schedule 1 for the words from "a recognised stock exchange" onwards there shall be substituted the words "a recognised investment exchange within the meaning of the Financial Services Act 1986";

(d) in the definition of "securities" in paragraph 4 of Part IV of that Schedule after the word "debentures" there shall be inserted the words "units within paragraph 3 of Part III of this Schedule".

**3** In section 32 of the Clergy Pensions Measure 1961 No. 3–

(a) for paragraph (t) of subsection (1) there shall be substituted–

"(t) in any units in any authorised unit trust scheme or a recognised scheme within the meaning of the Financial Services Act 1986"; and

(b) in subsection (5)(a) for the words from "a recognised stock exchange" onwards there shall be substituted the words "a recognised investment exchange within the meaning of the Financial Services Act 1986.".

**4** In the Stock Transfer Act 1963–

(a) for paragraph (e) of section 1(4) there shall be substituted–

"(e) units of an authorised unit trust scheme or a recognised scheme within the meaning of the Financial Services Act 1986"; and

(b) in the definition of "securities" in section 4(1) for the words from "unit trust scheme" to "scheme" there shall be substituted the words "collective investment scheme within the meaning of the Financial Services Act 1986".

**5** In the Stock Transfer Act (Northern Ireland) 1963–

(a) for paragraph (e) of section 1(4) there shall be substituted–

"(e) units of an authorised unit trust scheme or a recognised scheme within the meaning of the Financial Services Act 1986"; and

(b) in the definition of "securities" in section 4(1) for the words from "unit trust scheme" to "scheme" there shall be substituted the words "collective investment scheme within the meaning of the Financial Services Act 1986".

**6** In section 25 of the Charities Act (Northern Ireland) 1964–

(a) subsection (16) shall be omitted; and

(b) in subsection (17) for the words "Subsections (15) and (16)" there shall be substituted the words "Subsection (15)".

**7** In the Local Authorities' Mutual Investment Trust Act 1968–

(a) in section 1(2) for the words "recognised stock exchange within the meaning of the Prevention of Fraud (Investments) Act 1958" there shall be substituted the words "recognised investment exchange within the meaning of the Financial Services Act 1986"; and

(b) in the definition of "unit trust scheme" in section 2 for the words "Prevention of Fraud (Investments) Act 1958" there shall be substituted the words "Financial Services Act 1986".

**8** In the Local Government Act 1972–

(a) in section 98(1) for the words from "and" onwards there shall be substituted the words "means–

(a) investments falling within any of paragraphs 1 to 6 of Schedule 1 to the Financial Services Act 1986 or, so far as relevant to any of those paragraphs, paragraph 11 of that Schedule; or

(b) rights (whether actual or contingent) in respect of money lent to, or deposited with, any society registered under the Industrial and Provident Societies Act 1965 or any building society within the meaning of the Building Societies Act 1986."; and

(b) for the definition of "securities" in section 146(2) there shall be substituted–

"**"securities"** has the meaning given in section 98(1) above."

**9** For subsection (1) of section 42 of the Local Government (Scotland) Act 1973 there shall be substituted–

"**(1)** In sections 39 and 41 of this Act **"securities"** means–

(a) investments falling within any of paragraphs 1 to 6 of Schedule 1 to the Financial Services Act 1986 or, so far as relevant to any of those paragraphs, paragraph 11 of that Schedule; or

(b) rights (whether actual or contingent) in respect of money lent to, or deposited with, any society registered under the Industrial and Provident Societies Act 1965 or any building society within the meaning of the Building Societies Act 1986."

**10** (Repealed by British Technology Group Act 1991, s. 17(2), 18 and Sch. 2, Pt. I with effect from 6 January 1992.)

**History**

Para. 10 repealed by British Technology Group Act 1991, s. 17(2), 18 and Sch. 2, Pt. I with effect from 6 January 1992 (see British Technology Group Act 1991 (Appointed Day) Order 1991 (SI 1991/2721), art. 2). The paragraph formerly read as follows:

"**10** For paragraph 20 of Schedule 1 to the Industry Act 1975 there shall be substituted–

"**20** Section 57 of the Financial Services Act 1986 (restrictions on advertising) shall not apply to any investment advertisement within the meaning of that section which the Board issue or cause to be issued in the discharge of their functions.""

**11** (Repealed by Enterprise and New Towns (Scotland) Act 1990, s. 38(2), 39(1), (3) and Sch. 5, Pt. I as from 1 April 1991.)

**History**

In relation to the above date see Enterprise and New Towns (Scotland) Act 1990, s. 22(1)(a) and SI 1990/1840 (C 48) (S 173); para. 11 formerly read as follows:

"**11** For paragraph 20 of Schedule 1 to the Scottish Development Agency Act 1975 there shall be substituted–

"**20** Section 57 of the Financial Services Act 1986 (restrictions on advertising) shall not apply to any investment advertisement within the meaning of that section which the Agency issue or cause to be issued in the discharge of their functions.""

**12** For paragraph 21 of Schedule 1 to the Welsh Development Agency Act 1975 there shall be substituted–

> "**21** Section 57 of the Financial Services Act 1986 (restrictions on advertising) shall not apply to any investment advertisement within the meaning of that section which the Agency issue or cause to be issued in the discharge of their functions."

**13** In section 3(5) of the Aircraft and Shipbuilding Industries Act 1977 the words "Sections 428 to 430 of the Companies Act 1985 and" shall be omitted and for the words "those sections" there shall be substituted the words "that section".

**14** In paragraph 10(1)(c) of Part II of Schedule 10 to the Finance Act 1980 for the words "sections 428 to 430" there shall be substituted the words "sections 428 to 430F".

**15** For the definition of "securities" in section 3(6) of the Licensing (Alcohol Education and Research) Act 1981 there shall be substituted–

> ""**securities**" means any investments falling within any of paragraphs 1 to 6 of Schedule 1 to the Financial Services Act 1986 or, so far as relevant to any of those paragraphs, paragraph 11 of that Schedule."

**16** (Repealed by the Public Offers of Securities Regulations 1995 (SI 1995/1537), reg. 1, 17 and Sch. 2, para. 5(e) as from 19 June 1995.)

**History**

Para. 16 formerly read as follows:

"In section 97 of the Companies Act 1985–

(a) in subsection (1) after the word "conditions" there shall be inserted the words "and any conditions which apply in respect of any such payment by virtue of rules made under section 169(2) of the Financial Services Act 1986"; and

(b) in subsection (2)(a) for the words from "10 per cent" onwards there shall be substituted the words–

> "(i) any limit imposed on it by those rules or, if none is so imposed, 10 per cent, of the price at which the shares are issued; or
>
> (ii) the amount or rate authorised by the articles, whichever is the less.""

**17** In section 163 of the Companies Act 1985–

(a) for the words "a recognised stock exchange" in each place where they occur there shall be substituted the words "a recognised investment exchange";

(b) for the words "that stock exchange" in subsection (1) there shall be substituted the words "that investment exchange";

(c) in subsection (2) in paragraph (a) for the words "on that stock exchange" there shall be substituted the words "under Part IV of the Financial Services Act 1986" and in paragraph (b) for the words "that stock exchange" in both places where they occur there shall be substituted the words "that investment exchange";

(d) after subsection (3) of that section there shall be inserted–

> "**(4)** In this section "recognised investment exchange" means a recognised investment exchange other than an overseas investment exchange within the meaning of the Financial Services Act 1986."

**18** In section 209(1)(c) of the Companies Act 1985 for the words "the Prevention of Fraud (Investments) Act 1958" there shall be substituted the words "the Financial Services Act 1986".

**19** In section 265(4)(a) of the Companies Act 1985 for the words "recognised stock exchange" there shall be substituted the words "recognised investment exchange other than an overseas investment exchange within the meaning of the Financial Services Act 1986".

**20** In section 329(1) of the Companies Act 1985 for the words "recognised stock exchange", "that stock exchange" and "the stock exchange" there shall be substituted respectively the words "recognised investment exchange other than an overseas investment exchange within the meaning of the Financial Services Act 1986", "that investment exchange" and "the investment exchange".

**21** For paragraphs (a) to (c) of section 446(4) of the Companies Act 1985 there shall be substituted–

"(a) to any individual who is an authorised person within the meaning of the Financial Services Act 1986;

(b) to any individual who holds a permission granted under paragraph 23 of Schedule 1 to that Act;

(c) to any officer (whether past or present) of a body corporate which is such an authorised person or holds such a permission;

(d) to any partner (whether past or present) in a partnership which is such an authorised person or holds such a permission;

(e) to any member of the governing body or officer (in either case whether past or present) of an unincorporated association which is such an authorised person or holds such a permission."

**22** (Repealed by Companies Act 1989, s. 212 and Sch. 24 as from 1 April 1990.)

**History**

In relation to the above date see SI 1990/355 (C 13), art. 5(1); para. 22 formerly read as follows:

"At the end of sections 716(2) and 717(1) of the Companies Act 1985 there shall be inserted the words–

"and in this subsection **"recognised stock exchange"** means The Stock Exchange and any other stock exchange which is declared to be a recognised stock exchange for the purposes of this section by an order in a statutory instrument made by the Secretary of State which is for the time being in force;"."

**23** In Schedule 4 to the Companies Act 1985–

(a) in paragraph 45 for the words "recognised stock exchange" there shall be substituted the words "recognised investment exchange other than an overseas investment exchange within the meaning of the Financial Services Act 1986"; and

(b) in paragraph 84 for the words from "on a recognised stock exchange" onwards there shall be substituted the words "on a recognised investment exchange other than an overseas investment exchange within the meaning of the Financial Services Act 1986 or on any stock exchange of repute outside Great Britain".

**24** In Schedule 9 to the Companies Act 1985 in paragraphs 10(3) and 33 for the words "recognised stock exchange" there shall be substituted the words "recognised investment exchange other than an overseas investment exchange within the meaning of the Financial Services Act 1986".

**25** In paragraph 11 of Schedule 13 to the Companies Act 1985 for paragraph (a) there shall be substituted–

"(a) any unit trust scheme which is an authorised unit trust scheme within the meaning of the Financial Services Act 1986."

**26** In Schedule 22 to the Companies Act 1985, in the second column of the entry relating to section 185(4) for the words "stock exchange" there shall be substituted the words "clearing house or".

**27** In Schedule 24 to the Companies Act 1985–

(a) in the second column of the entry relating to section 329(3) for the words "stock exchange" there shall be substituted the words "investment exchange"; and

(b) after the entry relating to section 427(5) there shall be inserted–

| | | | | |
|---|---|---|---|---|
| "429(6) | Offeror failing to send copy of notice or making statutory declaration knowing it to be false, etc. | 1. On indictment.<br>2. Summary. | 2 years or a fine; or both.<br>6 months or the statutory maximum; or both. | One-fiftieth of the statutory maximum. |
| 430A(6) | Offeror failing to give notice of rights to minority shareholder. | 1. On indictment.<br>2. Summary. | A fine.<br>The statutory maximum. | One-fiftieth of the statutory maximum." |

**28** (Repealed by Criminal Justice Act 1993, s. 79(14) and Sch. 6, Pt. I as from 1 March 1994.)

**History**

In regard to the date of the above repeal see SI 1994/242 (C 7), art. 2 and Sch.; para. 28 formerly read as follows:

"In section 16 of the Company Securities (Insider Dealing) Act 1985–

(a) in subsection (1) for the definition of "recognised stock exchange" there shall be substituted–

""**recognised stock exchange**" means The Stock Exchange and any other investment exchange which is declared by an order of the Secretary of State for the time being in force to be a recognised stock exchange for the purposes of this Act;";

(b) after that subsection there shall be inserted–

"**(1A)** The power to make an order under subsection (1) above shall be exercisable by statutory instrument."; and

(c) in subsection (2) for the word "15" there shall be substituted the word "14"."

**29** For paragraph (c) of section 10(1) of the Bankruptcy (Scotland) Act 1985 there shall be substituted–

"(c) a petition is before a court for the winding up of the debtor under Part IV or V of the Insolvency Act 1986 or section 72 of the Financial Services Act 1986;"

**30** In section 101 of the Building Societies Act 1986–

(a) for paragraph (1)(a) there shall be substituted–

"(a) offer for sale or invite subscription for any shares in or debentures of the company or allot or agree to allot any such shares or debentures with a view to their being offered for sale;";

(b) in subsection (1) after the words "the effect of the offer" there shall be inserted the words "the invitation"; and

(c) in subsection (2) for the words "the public" there shall be substituted the words ", invite subscription for,".

**31** In Article 107 of the Companies (Northern Ireland) Order 1986–

(a) in paragraph (1) after the word "conditions" there shall be inserted the words "and any conditions which apply in respect of any such payment by virtue of rules made under section 169(2) of the Financial Services Act 1986"

(b) in sub-paragraph (2)(a) for the words from "10 per cent" onwards there shall be substituted the words–

"(i) any limit imposed on it by those rules or, if none is so imposed, 10 per cent of the price at which the shares are issued; or

(ii) the amount or rate authorised by the articles, whichever is the less."

**32** In Article 173 of the Companies (Northern Ireland) Order 1986–

(a) for the words "a recognised stock exchange", in each place where they occur, there shall be substituted the words "a recognised investment exchange";

(b) for the words "that stock exchange" in paragraph (1) there shall be substituted the words "that investment exchange";

(c) in paragraph (2), in sub-paragraph (a) for the words "on that stock exchange" there shall be substituted the words "under Part IV of the Financial Services Act 1986" and in sub-paragraph (b) for the words "that stock exchange" in both places where they occur there shall be substituted the words "that investment exchange";

(d) after paragraph (3) there shall be inserted–

"**(4)** In this Article **"recognised investment exchange"** means a recognised investment exchange other than an overseas investment exchange within the meaning of the Financial Services Act 1986."

**33** In Article 217(1)(b) of the Companies (Northern Ireland) Order 1986 for the words "the Prevention of Fraud (Investments) Act (Northern Ireland) 1940 or of the Prevention of Fraud (Investments) Act 1958" there shall be substituted the words "the Financial Services Act 1986".

**34** In Article 273(4)(a) of the Companies (Northern Ireland) Order 1986 for the words "recognised stock exchange" there shall be substituted the words "recognised investment exchange other than an overseas investment exchange within the meaning of the Financial Services Act 1986".

**35** In Article 337(1) of the Companies (Northern Ireland) Order 1986 for the words "recognised stock exchange", "that stock exchange" and "the stock exchange" there shall be substituted respectively the words "recognised investment exchange", "that investment exchange" and "the investment exchange".

**36** For sub-paragraphs (a) to (c) of Article 439(4) of the Companies (Northern Ireland) Order 1986 there shall be substituted–

"(a) to any individual who is an authorised person within the meaning of the Financial Services Act 1986;

(b) to any individual who holds a permission granted under paragraph 23 of Schedule 1 to that Act;

(c) to an officer (whether past or present) of a body corporate which is such an authorised person or holds such a permission;

(d) to any partner (whether past or present) in a partnership which is such an authorised person or holds such a permission;

(e) to any member of the governing body or officer (in either case whether past or present) of an unincorporated association which is such an authorised person or holds such a permission."

**37** (Repealed by Companies (No. 2) (Northern Ireland) Order 1990 (SI 1990/1504 (NI 10)), art. 113 and Sch. 6 as from 11 March 1991.)

**History**

In regard to the date of the above repeal see Companies (1990 No. 2 Order) (Commencement No. 1) Order (Northern Ireland) 1991 (SR 1991/26 (C 2)), art. 10(1)(b); para. 37 formerly read as follows:

"At the end of Articles 665(2) and 666(1) of the Companies (Northern Ireland) Order 1986 there shall be inserted the words–

"and in this paragraph **"recognised stock exchange"** means The Stock Exchange and any other stock exchange which is declared by an order of the Department for the time being in force to be a recognised stock exchange for the purposes of this Article;"."

**38** In Schedule 4 to the Companies (Northern Ireland) Order 1986–

(a) in paragraph 45 for the words "recognised stock exchange" there shall be substituted the words "recognised investment exchange other than an overseas investment exchange within the meaning of the Financial Services Act 1986"

(b) in paragraph 83 for the words from "on a recognised stock exchange" onwards there shall be substituted the words "on a recognised investment exchange other than an overseas investment exchange within the meaning of the Financial Services Act 1986 or on any stock exchange of repute outside Northern Ireland".

**39** In Schedule 9 to the Companies (Northern Ireland) Order 1986, in paragraph 10(3) and 33 for the words "recognised stock exchange" there shall be substituted the words "recognised investment exchange other than an overseas investment exchange within the meaning of the Financial Services Act 1986."

**40** In paragraph 11 of Schedule 13 to the Companies (Northern Ireland) Order 1986 for paragraph (a) there shall be substituted–

"(a) any unit trust scheme which is an authorised unit trust scheme within the meaning of the Financial Services Act 1986."

**41** In Schedule 21 to the Companies (Northern Ireland) Order 1986 in the second column of the entry relating to Article 195(4) for the words "stock exchange" there shall be substituted the words "clearing house or".

**42** In Schedule 23 to the Companies (Northern Ireland) Order 1986 in the second column of the entry relating to Article 337(3) for the words "stock exchange" there shall be substituted the words "investment exchange".

**43** (Repealed by Criminal Justice Act 1993, s. 79(14) and Sch. 6, Pt. I as from 1 March 1994.)

**History**

In regard to the date of the above repeal see SI 1994/242 (C 7), art. 2 and Sch.); para. 43 formerly read as follows:

"In Article 2(1) of the Company Securities (Insider Dealing) (Northern Ireland) Order 1986, for the definition of "recognised stock exchange" there shall be substituted–

""**recognised stock exchange"** means The Stock Exchange and any other investment exchange which is declared by an order of the Department for the time being in force to be a recognised stock exchange for the purposes of this Order;"."

# Schedule 17 – Repeals and Revocations

Section 212(3)

## Part I – Enactments

| Chapter | Short title | Extent of repeal |
|---|---|---|
| 4 & 5 Geo. 6. c. 9 (N.I.). | The Prevention of Fraud (Investments) Act (Northern Ireland) 1940. | The whole Act. |
| 6 & 7 Eliz. 2. c. 45. | The Prevention of Fraud (Investments) Act 1958. | The whole Act. |
| 8 & 9 Eliz. 2. c. 58. | The Charities Act 1960. | Section 22(10). |
| 10 & 11 Eliz. 2. c. 23. | The South Africa Act 1962. | In Schedule 4, the entry relating to the Prevention of Fraud (Investments) Act 1958. |
| 1964 c. 33 (N.I.). | The Charities Act (Northern Ireland) 1964. | Section 25(16). |
| 1965 c. 2. | The Administration of Justice Act 1965. | Section 14(1)(e) and 5(e).<br>In Schedule 1, the entry relating to the Prevention of Fraud (Investments) Act 1958. |
| 1971 c. 62. | The Tribunals and Inquiries Act 1971. | In Part I of Schedule 1, the entry relating to the tribunal constituted under section 6 of the Prevention of Fraud (Investments) Act 1958. |
| 1972 c. 71. | The Criminal Justice Act 1972. | In Schedule 5, the entry relating to the Prevention of Fraud (Investments) Act 1958. |
| 1975 c. 24. | The House of Commons Disqualification Act 1975. | In Part II of Schedule 1 the words "The Tribunal established under the Prevention of Fraud (Investments) Act 1958." |
| 1975 c. 68. | The Industry Act 1975. | In Schedule 1, paragraph 19. |
| 1975 c. 70. | The Welsh Development Agency Act 1975. | In Schedule 1, paragraph 22. |
| 1976 c. 47. | The Stock Exchange (Completion of Bargains) Act 1976. | Section 7(2). |
| 1977 c. 3. | The Aircraft and Shipbuilding Industries Act 1977. | In section 3(5), the words "Sections 428 to 430 of the Companies Act 1985 and". |
| 1978 c. 23. | The Judicature (Northern Ireland) Act 1978. | Section 84(3)(c). |
| 1979 c. 37. | The Banking Act 1979. | Section 20(1) to (3).<br>In Schedule 1, paragraph 9.<br>In Schedule 6, paragraphs 4 and 5. |
| 1982 c. 50. | The Insurance Companies Act 1982. | Section 73.<br>Section 79. |

| Chapter | Short title | Extent of repeal |
|---|---|---|
| 1982 c. 53. | The Administration of Justice Act 1982. | Section 42(8). |
| 1984 c. 2. | The Restrictive Trade Practices (Stock Exchange) Act 1984. | The whole Act. |
| 1985 c. 6. | The Companies Act 1985. | Part III.<br>Sections 81 to 83.<br>In section 84(1) the words from "This" onwards. In section 85(1) the words "83 or".<br>Sections 86 and 87.<br>In section 97, subsection (2)(b) together with the word "and" immediately preceding it and subsections (3) and (4).<br>Section 433(2).<br>Section 446(5) and (6).<br>In section 449(1)(d), the words "the Prevention of Fraud (Investments) Act 1958".<br>In section 693, paragraph (a) and in paragraph (d) the words "in every such prospectus as above-mentioned and".<br>Section 709(2) and (3).<br>In section 744, the definitions of "recognised stock exchange" and "prospectus issued generally".<br>Schedule 3.<br>In Schedule 22, the entries relating to Parts III and IV.<br>In Schedule 24, the entries relating to sections 56(4), 61, 64(5), 70(1), 78(1), 81(2), 82(5), 86(6), 87(4) and 97(4). |
| 1985 c. 8. | The Company Securities (Insider Dealing) Act 1985. | In section 3(1), the word "or" immediately preceding paragraph (c).<br>In section 13, in subsection (1), the words from "and references" onwards and subsection (2).<br>Section 15. |

| Chapter | Short title | Extent of repeal |
|---|---|---|
| 1985 c. 9. | The Companies Consolidation (Consequential Provisions) Act 1985. | Section 7.<br>In Schedule 2, the entries relating to the Prevention of Fraud (Investments) Act 1958, paragraph 19 of Schedule 1 to the Scottish Development Agency Act 1975, paragraph 22 of Schedule 1 to the Welsh Development Agency Act 1975, the Stock Exchange (Completion of Bargains) Act 1976, section 3(5) of the Aircraft and Shipbuilding Industries Act 1977 and section 20 of the Banking Act 1979. |
| 1986 c. 31. | The Airports Act 1986. | Section 10. |
| 1986 c. 44. | The Gas Act 1986. | Section 58. |
| 1986 c. 60. | The Financial Services Act 1986. | Section 195. |

## Part II – Instruments

| Number | Title | Extent of revocation |
|---|---|---|
| SI 1977/1254 (6 N.I. 21). | The Stock Exchange (Completion of Bargains) (Northern Ireland) Order 1977. | Article 2(2). |
| SI 1986/1032 (N.I. 6). | The Companies (Northern Ireland) Order 1986. | Article 2(1), the definitions of "prospectus issued generally" and "recognised stock exchange".<br>Part IV.<br>Articles 91 to 93.<br>In Article 94(1) the words from "This" onwards.<br>In Article 95(1) the words "93 or".<br>Articles 96 and 97.<br>In Article 107, paragraph (2)(b) together with the word "and" immediately preceding it and paragraphs (3) and (4).<br>Article 426(2).<br>Article 439(5) and (6).<br>In Article 442(1)(d), the words "the Prevention of Fraud (Investments) Act (Northern Ireland) 1940". |

| Number | Title | Extent of revocation |
|---|---|---|
| | | In Article 643(1), sub-paragraph (a) and in sub-paragraph (d) the words "in every such prospectus as is mentioned in sub-paragraph (a) and". Article 658(2) and (3). Schedule 3. In Schedule 21, the entries relating to Parts IV and V. In Schedule 23, the entries relating to Articles 66(4), 71, 74(5), 80(1), 88(1), 91(2), 92(5), 96(6), 97(4) and 107(4). |
| SI 1986/1035 (N.I. 9). | The Companies (Consequential Provisions) (Northern Ireland) Order 1986. | In Schedule 2, the entries relating to the Prevention of Fraud (Investments) Act (Northern Ireland) 1940 and section 20 of the Banking Act 1979. |
| SI 1984/716. | The Stock Exchange (Listing) Regulations 1984. | The whole Regulations. |

**History**
In Sch. 17, Pt. I entry relating to the Scottish Development Agency Act 1975 repealed by Enterprise and New Towns (Scotland) Act 1990, s. 38(2), 39(1), (2) and Sch. 5, Pt. I as from 1 April 1991 (see s. 22(1)(a) and SI 1990/1840 (C 48) (S 173); the former entry read as follows:

| Chapter | Short title | Extent of repeal |
|---|---|---|
| "1975 c. 69. | The Scottish Development Agency Act 1975. | In Schedule 1, paragraph 19." |

# THE FINANCIAL SERVICES ACT 1986 (COMMENCEMENT) (NO. 13) ORDER 1995

(SI 1995/1538 (C 33))

*Made on 14 June 1995 by the Treasury under s. 211(1) of the Financial Services Act 1986.*

[**CCH Note**: A note providing relevant details of previous commencements appears at the end of this Order.]

## CITATION AND INTERPRETATION

**1(1)** This Order may be cited as the Financial Services Act 1986 (Commencement) (No. 13) Order 1995.

**1(2)** In this Order "**the Act**" means the Financial Services Act 1986.

## PROVISIONS BROUGHT INTO FORCE

**2** Section 212(3) of and Schedule 17 to the Act shall come into force on 19th June 1995 to the extent necessary to repeal–

(a) Part III of and Schedule 3 to the Companies Act 1985, and in Schedule 22 to that Act the entry relating to Part III, and in Schedule 24 to that Act the entries relating to sections 56(4), 61, 64(5), 70(1) and 78(1), for all remaining purposes except–

(i) sections 58, 59 and 60 of the Companies Act 1985, in so far as it is necessary for the purposes of sections 81, 83, 246, 248 and 744 of that Act; and
(ii) paragraph 2 of Schedule 3 to the Companies Act 1985, in so far as it is necessary for the purposes of section 83(1)(a) of that Act; and
(iii) section 62 of the Companies Act 1985, in so far as it is necessary for purposes of section 744 of that Act; and

(b) the corresponding provisions of the Companies (Northern Ireland) Order 1986, for corresponding purposes.

## EXPLANATORY NOTE

*(This Note is not part of the Order)*

This Order brings into force on 19th June 1995 section 212(3) of and Schedule 17 to the Financial Services Act 1986, to the extent necessary to repeal Part III of and Schedule 3 to the Companies Act 1985 for all purposes except the interpretation of certain other provisions of the latter Act.

## NOTE AS TO EARLIER COMMENCEMENT ORDERS

*(This Note is not part of the Order)*

The following provisions of the Financial Services Act 1986 have been brought into force by commencement orders made before the date of this Order.

| Provisions of the Act | SI No. |
|---|---|
| s. 1 | 1986/2246<br>1987/1997<br>1987/2158 |
| s. 2 | 1986/2246 |
| ss. 3 and 4 | 1988/740 |
| s. 5 | 1986/2246<br>1988/740 |
| ss. 6 and 7 | 1988/740 |
| ss. 8 to 11 | 1987/907 |
| s. 12 | 1987/1997 |
| ss. 13 and 14 | 1987/907 |
| s. 15 | 1987/907<br>1988/740 |
| ss. 16 to 19 | 1987/907 |
| s. 20 | 1987/1997 |
| s. 21 | 1987/907 |
| ss. 22 and 23 | 1988/740 |
| s. 24 (partially) | 1988/740 |
| s. 25 | 1988/740 |
| ss. 26 to 30 | 1987/2158 |
| s. 31 | 1987/2158<br>1988/740 |
| ss. 32 to 34 | 1988/740 |
| s. 35 | 1986/2246<br>1988/740 |
| s. 36 | 1987/907<br>1988/740 |

| Provisions of the Act | SI No. |
|---|---|
| s. 37 | 1987/907<br>1987/1997 |
| s. 38 | 1987/907<br>1988/740 |
| s. 39 | 1987/907<br>1987/1997 |
| s. 40 | 1987/1997 |
| s. 41 | 1987/907 |
| s. 42 | 1986/2246<br>1988/740 |
| s. 43 | 1987/2158 |
| s. 44 | 1988/740 |
| s. 45 | 1986/2246<br>1988/740 |
| s. 46 | 1987/907 |
| s. 47 | 1988/740 |
| ss. 48 to 52 | 1987/907 |
| s. 54 and 55 | 1987/907 |
| s. 56 | 1987/907<br>1988/740 |
| s. 57 | 1988/740 |
| s. 58 (partially) | 1988/740 |
| ss. 59 to 61 | 1988/740 |
| s. 62 | 1987/1997 |
| s. 63 | 1987/623 |
| ss. 64 to 75 | 1988/740 |
| s. 76 | 1988/740<br>1988/995<br>1988/1960<br>1988/2285<br>Articles 6(2) and 7 of SI 1988/740 were amended by SI 1988/995 and revoked by SI 1988/1960. Articles 3 and 4 of SI 1988/1960 were amended by SI 1988/2285 |
| ss. 77 to 85 | 1988/740 |
| s. 86 (partially) | 1988/740 |
| ss. 87 to 95 | 1988/740 |
| s. 96 | 1987/1997 |
| ss. 97 to 101 | 1988/740 |
| ss. 102 and 103 | 1987/907 |
| s. 104 | 1987/907<br>1988/740 |
| ss. 105 and 106 | 1986/2246 |
| s. 107 | 1987/907 |
| ss. 108 and 109 | 1988/740 |
| s. 110 | 1987/907 |

| Provisions of the Act | SI No. |
|---|---|
| s. 111 | 1988/740 |
| s. 112 | 1987/907 |
| | 1987/2158 |
| | 1988/740 |
| s. 113 | 1987/907 |
| | 1988/740 |
| ss. 114 to 118 | 1986/2246 |
| ss. 119 to 120 | 1987/907 |
| s. 121 | 1986/2246 |
| ss. 122 and 123 | 1986/2246 |
| | 1987/907 |
| s. 124 | 1986/2246 |
| s. 125 | 1987/907 |
| | 1988/995 |
| s. 126 | 1986/2246 |
| s. 127 | 1987/907 |
| s. 128 | 1986/2246 |
| s. 129 | 1986/2246 |
| | 1987/907 |
| | 1988/740 |
| | 1988/995 |
| ss. 130 and 131 | 1988/740 |
| s. 132 | 1986/2246 |
| | 1988/740 |
| s. 133 | 1988/740 |
| s. 134 (partially) | 1986/2246 |
| ss. 135 and 136 | 1988/740 |
| s. 137 | 1986/2246 |
| s. 138 | 1986/2246 |
| | 1987/907 |
| | 1988/740 |
| s. 139 | 1986/2246 |
| | 1988/740 |
| s. 140 (partially) | 1986/2246 |
| | 1987/907 |
| | 1987/1997 |
| | 1987/2158 |
| | 1988/740 |
| ss. 141 to 153 | 1986/2246 |
| s. 154 | 1986/2246 |
| | 1988/740 |
| ss. 155 to 157 | 1986/2246 |
| s. 160 (partially) | 1988/740 |
| s. 162 (partially) | 1988/740 |
| s. 169 | 1988/740 |
| s. 170 (partially) | 1988/740 |
| s. 172 and 173 | 1986/2246 |

| Provisions of the Act | SI No. |
|---|---|
| s. 174 | 1986/2246 |
| | 1988/740 |
| s. 175 | 1988/740 |
| s. 176 | 1986/2246 |
| s. 177 | 1986/1940 |
| s. 178 | 1986/1940 |
| | 1988/740 |
| | 1986/2246 |
| s. 179 | 1986/1940 |
| | 1986/2246 |
| s. 180 | 1986/1940 |
| s. 181 | 1986/2246 |
| s. 182 | 1986/1940 |
| | 1986/2031 |
| | 1986/2246 |
| ss. 183 and 184 | 1987/623 |
| | 1988/740 |
| s. 185 | 1987/623 |
| s. 186 | 1987/623 |
| | 1988/740 |
| s. 187 | 1986/2246 |
| | 1987/907 |
| s. 188 | 1986/2246 |
| s. 189 (partially) | 1986/2246 |
| | 1987/1997 |
| | 1987/2158 |
| ss. 190 and 191 | 1987/907 |
| s. 192 | 1986/2246 |
| s. 194 | 1988/740 |
| s. 195 | s. 211(2) |
| s. 196 | 1987/1997 |
| s. 197 | 1988/740 |
| s. 198 | 1986/1940 |
| | 1986/2246 |
| | 1987/907 |
| | 1988/740 |
| s. 199 | 1986/1940 |
| | 1986/2246 |
| | 1988/740 |
| s. 200 | 1986/1940 |
| | 1986/2246 |
| | 1987/907 |
| | 1987/2158 |
| | 1988/740 |
| s. 201 | 1986/1940 |
| | 1986/2246 |
| | 1987/623 |
| | 1988/740 |

| Provisions of the Act | SI No. |
|---|---|
| ss. 202 and 203 | 1986/1940<br>1986/2246 |
| s. 204 | 1986/2246 |
| s. 205 | 1986/1940<br>1986/2246 |
| s. 206 | 1987/907 |
| s. 207 | 1986/1940<br>1986/2246 |
| s. 208 (partially) | 1988/740 |
| s. 209 and 210 | 1986/1940<br>1986/2246 |
| s. 211 | 1986/2031<br>1986/2246<br>1987/907<br>1987/2158<br>1988/740 |
| s. 212 (partially) | 1986/2031<br>1986/2246<br>1987/907<br>1988/740<br>1988/995<br>1988/1960<br>1988/2285 |
| Schedule 1 | 1986/2246<br>1987/1997<br>1987/2158 |
| Schedules 2 to 4 | 1987/907 |
| Schedule 5 | 1987/2158 |
| Schedule 6 | 1987/1997 |
| Schedule 7 to 9 | 1986/2246 |
| Schedule 10 | 1986/2246<br>1987/907<br>1988/740<br>1988/995 |
| Schedule 11 | 1986/2246<br>1987/907<br>1987/1997<br>1987/2158<br>1987/740 |
| Schedule 12 | 1986/2246 |
| Schedule 13 | 1986/1940<br>1986/2031<br>1986/2246 |
| Schedule 14 (partially) | 1986/2246<br>1987/1997<br>1987/2158 |

| Provisions of the Act | SI No. |
|---|---|
| Schedule 15 | 1986/2031<br>1986/2246<br>1987/907<br>1987/2158<br>1988/740 |
| Schedule 16 (partially) | 1986/2246<br>1987/907<br>1988/740 |
| Schedule 17 (partially) | 1986/2031<br>1986/2246<br>1988/740<br>1988/995<br>1988/1960<br>1988/2285 |

# THE FINANCIAL SERVICES ACT 1986 (COMMENCEMENT) (NO. 14) ORDER 1999

(SI 1999/727)

*Made on 9 March 1999 by the Treasury under s. 211(1) of the Financial Services Act 1986. Operative from 10 May 1999.*

**1** This Order may be cited as the Financial Services Act 1986 (Commencement) (No. 14) Order 1999.

**2** Section 212(3) of, and Schedule 17 to, the Financial Services Act 1986 shall come into force on 10th May 1999 to the extent necessary to repeal–

(a) sections 82 and 83 of the Companies Act 1985, and the corresponding provisions of the Companies (Northern Ireland) Order 1986, for all remaining purposes except for the purposes of prospectuses to which regulation 8 of the Public Offers of Securities Regulations 1995 applies; and

(b) sections 86 and 87 of the Companies Act 1985, and the corresponding provisions of the Companies (Northern Ireland) Order 1986, for all remaining purposes.

## EXPLANATORY NOTE

(*This Note is not part of the Regulations*)

This Order brings into force, on 10th May 1999, section 212(3) of, and Schedule 17 to, the Financial Services Act 1986 to the extent necessary to repeal certain provisions of the Companies Act 1985. The repeals are of–

(a) sections 82 and 83 of the 1985 Act (which concern the timing of the allotment of a company's shares or debentures in pursuance of a prospectus issued generally, and provide that no allotment is to be made unless a minimum subscription is received), except for the purposes of prospectuses to which regulation 8 of the Public Offers of Securities Regulations 1995 applies; and

(b) sections 86 and 87 of the 1985 Act (which concern the situation where a prospectus states that an application has been or will be made for permission for the shares or debentures to be listed on a stock exchange, but no such application is made or the application is refused), for all remaining purposes.

The corresponding provisions of the Companies (Northern Ireland) Order 1986 are repealed to the corresponding extent.

Section 212(3) of, and Schedule 17 to, the 1986 Act have been brought into force for the purposes of repealing the above provisions, for certain purposes, by the following commencement orders made before the date of this Order, namely SI 1986/2246 and SI 1988/740. A full note as to earlier commencement orders under the 1986 Act accompanies SI 1995/1538.

# COMPANIES ACT 1989

## Table of Contents

# COMPANIES ACT 1989

(1986 Chapter 40)

## ARRANGEMENT OF SECTIONS

[**CCH Note:** operative provisions amending other provisions in *British Companies Legislation* not reproduced — see table at p. 2,317ff.]

## PART II – ELIGIBILITY FOR APPOINTMENT AS COMPANY AUDITOR

## PART III – INVESTIGATIONS AND POWERS TO OBTAIN INFORMATION

*Amendments of other enactments*



*Powers exercisable to assist overseas regulatory authorities*



## PART IV – REGISTRATION OF COMPANY CHARGES

*Introduction*



*Registration in the companies charges register*



*Copies of instruments and register to be kept by company*



*Supplementary provisions*



## PART V – OTHER AMENDMENTS OF COMPANY LAW

*A company's capacity and related matters*

## PART VIII – AMENDMENTS OF THE FINANCIAL SERVICES ACT 1986



## PART IX – TRANSFER OF SECURITIES



## PART X – MISCELLANEOUS AND GENERAL PROVISIONS



## SCHEDULES

**SCHEDULE**

# COMPANIES ACT 1989

(1989 Chapter 40)

An Act to amend the law relating to company accounts; to make new provision with respect to the persons eligible for appointment as company auditors; to amend the Companies Act 1985 and certain other enactments with respect to investigations and powers to obtain information and to confer new powers exercisable to assist overseas regulatory authorities; to make new provision with respect to the registration of company charges and otherwise to amend the law relating to companies; to amend the Fair Trading Act 1973; to enable provision to be made for the payment of fees in connection with the exercise by the Secretary of State, the Director General of Fair Trading and the Monopolies and Mergers Commission of their functions under Part V of that Act; to make provision for safeguarding the operation of certain financial markets; to amend the Financial Services Act 1986; to enable provision to be made for the recording and transfer of title to securities without a written instrument; to amend the Company Directors Disqualification Act 1986, the Company Securities (Insider Dealing) Act 1985, the Policyholders Protection Act 1975 and the law relating to building societies; and for connected purposes.

[*16th November 1989*]

**[CCH Note:** operative provisions amending other provisions in *British Companies Legislation* not reproduced — see table at p. 2,317ff.]

# PART II – ELIGIBILITY FOR APPOINTMENT AS COMPANY AUDITOR

**Note**

Pt. II implements the Eighth EC Company Law Directive (84/253).

Part II in force from 1 March 1990 and 1 October 1991 (with the exception of s. 46, 47(2)–(6), 48(3) and Sch. 13) (see SI 1990/142 (C 5) and SI 1991/1996 (C 57)).

## INTRODUCTION

### 24 Introduction

**24(1) [Purposes of Pt. II]** The main purposes of this Part are to secure that only persons who are properly supervised and appropriately qualified are appointed company auditors, and that audits by persons so appointed are carried out properly and with integrity and with a proper degree of independence.

**24(2) ["Company auditor"]** A **"company auditor"** means a person appointed as auditor under Chapter V of Part XI of the Companies Act 1985; and the expressions "company audit" and "company audit work" shall be construed accordingly.

## ELIGIBILITY FOR APPOINTMENT

### 25 Eligibility for appointment

**25(1) [Limits on eligibility]** A person is eligible for appointment as a company auditor only if he–

(a) is a member of a recognised supervisory body, and

(b) is eligible for the appointment under the rules of that body.

**25(2) [Who may be appointed]** An individual or a firm may be appointed a company auditor.

**25(3) [Restriction on eligibility]** In the cases to which section 34 applies (individuals retaining only 1967 Act authorisation) a person's eligibility for appointment as a company auditor is restricted as mentioned in that section.

## 26 Effect of appointment of partnership

**26(1) [Application]** The following provisions apply to the appointment as company auditor of a partnership constituted under the law of England and Wales or Northern Ireland, or under the law of any other country or territory in which a partnership is not a legal person.

**26(2) [Not appointment of partners]** The appointment is (unless a contrary intention appears) an appointment of the partnership as such and not of the partners.

**26(3) [Where partnership ceases]** Where the partnership ceases, the appointment shall be treated as extending to–

(a) any partnership which succeeds to the practice of that partnership and is eligible for the appointment, and

(b) any person who succeeds to that practice having previously carried it on in partnership and is eligible for the appointment.

**26(4) [Successor partnerships]** For this purpose a partnership shall be regarded as succeeding to the practice of another partnership only if the members of the successor partnership are substantially the same as those of the former partnership; and a partnership or other person shall be regarded as succeeding to the practice of a partnership only if it or he succeeds to the whole or substantially the whole of the business of the former partnership.

**26(5) [Extension of appointment by consent]** Where the partnership ceases and no person succeeds to the appointment under subsection (3), the appointment may with the consent of the company be treated as extending to a partnership or other person eligible for the appointment who succeeds to the business of the former partnership or to such part of it as is agreed by the company shall be treated as comprising the appointment.

## 27 Ineligibility on ground of lack of independence

**27(1) [Meaning of lack of independence]** A person is ineligible for appointment as company auditor of a company if he is–

(a) an officer or employee of the company, or

(b) a partner or employee of such a person, or a partnership of which such a person is a partner,

or if he is ineligible by virtue of paragraph (a) or (b) for appointment as company auditor of any associated undertaking of the company.

For this purpose an auditor of a company shall not be regarded as an officer or employee of the company.

**27(2) [Regulations]** A person is also ineligible for appointment as company auditor of a company if there exists between him or any associate of his and the company or any associated undertaking a connection of any such description as may be specified by regulations made by the Secretary of State.

The regulations may make different provisions for different cases.

**27(3) ["Associated undertaking"]** In this section **"associated undertaking"**, in relation to a company, means–

(a) a parent undertaking or subsidiary undertaking of the company, or

(b) a subsidiary undertaking of any parent undertaking of the company.

**27(4) [Regulations by statutory instrument]** Regulations under this section shall be made by statutory instrument which shall be subject to annulment in pursuance of a resolution of either House of Parliament.

## 28 Effect of ineligibility

**28(1) [Ineligibility bars appointment]** No person shall act as a company auditor if he is ineligible for appointment to the office.

**28(2)** **[Becoming ineligible]** If during his term of office a company auditor becomes ineligible for appointment to the office, he shall thereupon vacate office and shall forthwith give notice in writing to the company concerned that he has vacated it by reason of ineligibility.

**28(3)** **[Offence]** A person who acts as company auditor in contravention of subsection (1), or fails to give notice of vacating his office as required by subsection (2), is guilty of an offence and liable–

(a) on conviction on indictment, to a fine, and

(b) on summary conviction, to a fine not exceeding the statutory maximum.

**28(4)** **[Continued contravention]** In the case of continued contravention he is liable on a second or subsequent summary conviction (instead of the fine mentioned in subsection (3)(b)) to a fine not exceeding one-tenth of the statutory maximum in respect of each day on which the contravention is continued.

**28(5)** **[Defence]** In proceedings against a person for an offence under this section it is a defence for him to show that he did not know and had no reason to believe that he was, or had become, ineligible for appointment.

## 29 Power of Secretary of State to require second audit

**29(1)** **[Effect of ineligible appointment]** Where a person appointed company auditor was, for any part of the period during which the audit was conducted, ineligible for appointment to that office, the Secretary of State may direct the company concerned to retain a person eligible for appointment as auditor of the company–

(a) to audit the relevant accounts again, or

(b) to review the first audit and to report (giving his reasons) whether a second audit is needed;

and the company shall comply with such a direction within 21 days of its being given.

**29(2)** **[Second audit recommended]** If a second audit is recommended the company shall forthwith take such steps as are necessary to comply with the recommendation.

**29(3)** **[Copy direction to registrar]** Where a direction is given under this section, the Secretary of State shall send a copy of the direction to the registrar of companies; and the company shall within 21 days of receiving any report under subsection (1)(b) send a copy of it to the registrar of companies.

The provisions of the Companies Act 1985 relating to the delivery of documents to the registrar apply for the purposes of this subsection.

**29(4)** **[Application of first audit provisions]** Any statutory or other provisions applying in relation to the first audit shall apply, so far as practicable, in relation to a second audit under this section.

**29(5)** **[Offence]** If a company fails to comply with the requirements of this section, it is guilty of an offence and liable on summary conviction to a fine not exceeding the statutory maximum; and in the case of continued contravention it is liable on a second or subsequent summary conviction (instead of the fine mentioned above) to a fine not exceeding one-tenth of the statutory maximum in respect of each day on which the contravention is continued.

**29(6)** **[Enforcement]** A direction under this section is, on the application of the Secretary of State, enforceable by injunction or, in Scotland, by an order under section 45 of the Court of Session Act 1988.

**29(7)** **[Costs payable by ineligible auditor]** If a person accepts an appointment, or continues to act, as company auditor at a time when he knows he is ineligible, the company concerned may recover from him any costs incurred by it in complying with the requirements of this section.

### RECOGNITION OF SUPERVISORY BODIES AND PROFESSIONAL QUALIFICATIONS

## 30 Supervisory bodies

**30(1)** **["Supervisory body"]** In this Part a **"supervisory body"** means a body established in the United Kingdom (whether a body corporate or an unincorporated association) which maintains and enforces rules as to–

(a) the eligibility of persons to seek appointment as company auditors, and

(b) the conduct of company audit work,

which are binding on persons seeking appointment or acting as company auditors either because they are members of that body or because they are otherwise subject to its control.

**30(2) [Membership]** In this Part references to the members of a supervisory body are to the persons who, whether or not members of the body, are subject to its rules in seeking appointment or acting as company auditors.

**30(3) [Rules]** In this Part references to the rules of a supervisory body are to the rules (whether or not laid down by the body itself) which the body has power to enforce and which are relevant for the purposes of this Part.

This includes rules relating to the admission and expulsion of members of the body, so far as relevant for the purposes of this Part.

**30(4) [Guidance]** In this Part references to guidance issued by a supervisory body are to guidance issued or any recommendation made by it to all or any class of its members or persons seeking to become members which would, if it were a rule, fall within subsection (3).

**30(5) [Application of Sch. 11]** The provisions of Parts I and II of Schedule 11 have effect with respect to the recognition of supervisory bodies for the purposes of this Part.

## 31 Meaning of "appropriate qualification"

**31(1) [Person holding appropriate qualification]** A person holds an appropriate qualification for the purposes of this Part if–

(a) he was, by virtue of membership of a body recognised for the purposes of section 389(1)(a) of the Companies Act 1985, qualified for appointment as auditor of a company under that section immediately before 1st January 1990 and immediately before the commencement of section 25 above,

(b) he holds a recognised professional qualification obtained in the United Kingdom, or

(c) he holds an approved overseas qualification and satisfies any additional educational requirements applicable in accordance with section 33(4).

**31(2) [Notice to retain qualification]** A person who, immediately before 1st January 1990 and immediately before the commencement of section 25 above, was qualified for appointment as auditor of a company under section 389 of the Companies Act 1985 otherwise than by virtue of membership of a body recognised for the purposes of section 389(1)(a)–

(a) shall be treated as holding an appropriate qualification for twelve months from the day on which section 25 comes into force, and

(b) shall continue to be so treated if within that period he notifies the Secretary of State that he wishes to retain the benefit of his qualification.

The notice shall be in writing and shall contain such information as the Secretary of State may require.

**31(3) [Application out of time]** If a person fails to give such notice within the time allowed he may apply to the Secretary of State, giving such information as would have been required in connection with a notice, and the Secretary of State may, if he is satisfied–

(a) that there was good reason why the applicant did not give notice in time, and

(b) that the applicant genuinely intends to practise as an auditor in Great Britain,

direct that he shall be treated as holding an appropriate qualification for the purposes of this Part.

**31(4) [Approval by Secretary of State]** A person who–

(a) began before 1st January 1990 a course of study or practical training leading to a professional qualification in accountancy offered by a body established in the United Kingdom, and

(b) obtained that qualification on or after that date and before 1st January 1996, shall be treated as holding an appropriate qualification if the qualification is approved by the Secretary of State for the purposes of this subsection.

**31(5) [Limit on approving professional qualification]** Approval shall not be given unless the Secretary of State is satisfied that the body concerned has or, as the case may be, had at the relevant time adequate arrangements to ensure that the qualification is, or was, awarded only to persons educated and trained to a standard equivalent to that required in the case of a recognised professional qualification.

**31(6) [No qualification except as above]** A person shall not be regarded as holding an appropriate qualification for the purposes of this Part except in the above cases.

## 32 Qualifying bodies and recognised professional qualifications

**32(1) ["Qualifying body"]** In this Part a **"qualifying body"** means a body established in the United Kingdom (whether a body corporate or an unincorporated association) which offers a professional qualification in accountancy.

**32(2) [Rules]** In this Part references to the rules of a qualifying body are to the rules (whether or not laid down by the body itself) which the body has power to enforce and which are relevant for the purposes of this Part.

This includes rules relating to–

(a) admission to or expulsion from a course of study leading to a qualification,

(b) the award or deprivation of a qualification, or

(c) the approval of a person for the purposes of giving practical training or the withdrawal of such approval,

so far as relevant for the purposes of this Part.

**32(3) [Guidance]** In this Part references to guidance issued by any such body are to any guidance which the body issues, or any recommendation it makes to all or any class of persons holding or seeking to hold a qualification, or approved or seeking to be approved by the body for the purpose of giving practical training, which would, if it were a rule, fall within subsection (2).

**32(4) [Application of Sch. 12]** The provisions of Parts I and II of Schedule 12 have effect with respect to the recognition for the purposes of this Part of a professional qualification offered by a qualifying body.

## 33 Approval of overseas qualifications

**33(1) [Declaration by Secretary of State]** The Secretary of State may declare that persons who–

(a) are qualified to audit accounts under the law of a specified country or territory outside the United Kingdom, or

(b) hold a specified professional qualification in accountancy recognised under the law of a country or territory outside the United Kingdom,

shall be regarded for the purposes of this Part as holding an approved overseas qualification.

**33(2) [Equivalence]** A qualification shall not be so approved by the Secretary of State unless he is satisfied that it affords an assurance of professional competence equivalent to that afforded by a recognised professional qualification.

**33(3) [Reciprocity]** In exercising the power conferred by subsection (1) the Secretary of State may have regard to the extent to which persons–

(a) eligible under this Part for appointment as a company auditor, or

(b) holding a professional qualification recognised under this Part,

are recognised by the law of the country or territory in question as qualified to audit accounts there.

**33(4) [Additional educational qualification]** The Secretary of State may direct that a person holding an approved overseas qualification shall not be treated as holding an appropriate qualification for the purposes of this Part unless he holds such additional educational qualifications as the Secretary of State may specify for the purpose of ensuring that such persons have an adequate knowledge of the law and practice in the United Kingdom relevant to the audit of accounts.

**33(5) [Directions]** Different directions may be given in relation to different qualifications.

**33(6) [Withdrawal of approval]** The Secretary of State may if he thinks fit, having regard to the considerations mentioned in subsections (2) and (3), withdraw his approval of an overseas qualification in relation to persons becoming qualified as mentioned in subsection (1)(a), or obtaining such a qualification as is mentioned in subsection (1)(b), after such date as he may specify.

## 34 Eligibility of individuals retaining only 1967 Act authorisation

**34(1) [Auditor of unquoted company]** A person whose only appropriate qualification is that he retains an authorisation granted by the Board of Trade or the Secretary of State under section 13(1) of the Companies Act 1967 is eligible only for appointment as auditor of an unquoted company.

**34(2) ["Unquoted" company]** A company is "unquoted" if, at the time of the person's appointment, no shares or debentures of the company, or of a parent undertaking of which it is a subsidiary undertaking, have been quoted on a stock exchange (in Great Britain or elsewhere) or offered (whether in Great Britain or elsewhere) to the public for subscription or purchase.

**34(3) [Excluding certain companies]** This section does not authorise the appointment of such a person as auditor of a company that carries on business as the promoter of a trading stamp scheme within the meaning of the Trading Stamps Act 1964.

**34(4) [Excluding other bodies]** References to a person eligible for appointment as company auditor under section 25 in enactments relating to eligibility for appointment as auditor of a body other than a company do not include a person to whom this section applies.

DUTIES OF RECOGNISED BODIES

## 35 The register of auditors

**35(1) [Regulations]** The Secretary of State shall make regulations requiring the keeping of a register of–

(a) the individuals and firms eligible for appointment as company auditor, and

(b) the individuals holding an appropriate qualification who are responsible for company audit work on behalf of such firms.

**Note**
See the Companies Act 1989 (Register of Auditors and Information about Audit Firms) Regulations 1991 (SI 1991/1566).

**35(2) [Contents of register entry]** The regulations shall provide that each person's entry in the register shall give–

(a) his name and address, and

(b) in the case of a person eligible as mentioned in subsection (1)(a), the name of the relevant supervisory body,

together with such other information as may be specified by the regulations.

**35(3) [Obligations]** The regulations may impose such obligations as the Secretary of State thinks fit–

(a) on recognised supervisory bodies,

(b) on persons eligible for appointment as company auditor, and

(c) on any person with whom arrangements are made by one or more recognised supervisory bodies with respect to the keeping of the register.

**35(4) [Supplementary provisions]** The regulations may include provision–

(a) requiring the register to be open to inspection at such times and places as may be specified in the regulations or determined in accordance with them,

(b) enabling a person to require a certified copy of an entry in the register, and
(c) authorising the charging of fees for inspection, or the provision of copies, of such reasonable amount as may be specified in the regulations or determined in accordance with them;

and may contain such other supplementary and incidental provisions as the Secretary of State thinks fit.

**35(5) [Regulations by statutory instrument]** Regulations under this section shall be made by statutory instrument which shall be subject to annulment in pursuance of a resolution of either House of Parliament.

**35(6) [Enforcement by injunction]** The obligations imposed by regulations under this section on such persons as are mentioned in subsection (3)(a) or (c) are enforceable on the application of the Secretary of State by injunction or, in Scotland, by an order under section 45 of the Court of Session Act 1988.

## 36 Information about firms to be available to public

**36(1) [Regulations]** The Secretary of State shall make regulations requiring recognised supervisory bodies to keep and make available to the public the following information with respect to the firms eligible under their rules for appointment as a company auditor–
(a) in relation to a body corporate, the name and address of each person who is a director of the body or holds any shares in it,
(b) in relation to a partnership, the name and address of each partner,

and such other information as may be specified in the regulations.

**Note**
See the Companies Act 1989 (Register of Auditors and Information about Audit Firms) Regulations 1991 (SI 1991/1566).

**36(2) [Obligations]** The regulations may impose such obligations as the Secretary of State thinks fit–
(a) on recognised supervisory bodies,
(b) on persons eligible for appointment as company auditor, and
(c) on any person with whom arrangements are made by one or more recognised supervisory bodies with respect to the keeping of the information.

**36(3) [Supplementary provisions]** The regulations may include provision–
(a) requiring that the information be open to inspection at such times and places as may be specified in the regulations or determined in accordance with them,
(b) enabling a person to require a certified copy of the information or any part of it, and
(c) authorising the charging of fees for inspection, or the provision of copies, of such reasonable amount as may be specified in the regulations or determined in accordance with them;

and may contain such other supplementary and incidental provisions as the Secretary of State thinks fit.

**36(4) [Supplementary provisions]** The regulations may make different provision in relation to different descriptions of information and may contain such other supplementary and incidental provisions as the Secretary of State thinks fit.

**36(5) [Regulations by statutory instrument]** Regulations under this section shall be made by statutory instrument which shall be subject to annulment in pursuance of a resolution of either House of Parliament.

**36(6) [Enforcement]** The obligations imposed by regulations under this section on such persons as are mentioned in subsection (2)(a) or (c) are enforceable on the application of the Secretary of State by injunction or, in Scotland, by an order under section 45 of the Court of Session Act 1988.

## 37 Matters to be notified to the Secretary of State

**37(1) [Secretary of State's requirements]** The Secretary of State may require a recognised supervisory or qualifying body–

(a) to notify him forthwith of the occurrence of such events as he may specify in writing and to give him such information in respect of those events as is so specified;

(b) to give him, at such times or in respect of such periods as he may specify in writing, such information as is so specified.

**37(2) [Reasonable requirements]** The notices and information required to be given shall be such as the Secretary of State may reasonably require for the exercise of his functions under this Part.

**37(3) [Form of notification]** The Secretary of State may require information given under this section to be given in a specified form or verified in a specified manner.

**37(4) [Notice in writing]** Any notice or information required to be given under this section shall be given in writing unless the Secretary of State specifies or approves some other manner.

## 38 Power to call for information

**38(1) [Information reasonably required]** The Secretary of State may by notice in writing require a recognised supervisory or qualifying body to give him such information as he may reasonably require for the exercise of his functions under this Part.

**38(2) [Time for giving information]** The Secretary of State may require that any information which he requires under this section shall be given within such reasonable time and verified in such manner as he may specify.

## 39 Compliance orders

**39(1) [Application to court]** If at any time it appears to the Secretary of State–

(a) in the case of a recognised supervisory body, that any requirement of Schedule 11 is not satisfied,

(b) in the case of a recognised professional qualification, that any requirement of Schedule 12 is not satisfied, or

(c) that a recognised supervisory or qualifying body has failed to comply with an obligation to which it is subject by virtue of this Part,

he may, instead of revoking the relevant recognition order, make an application to the court under this section.

**39(2) [Court order]** If on such application the court decides that the subsection or requirement in question is not satisfied or, as the case may be, that the body has failed to comply with the obligation in question it may order the supervisory or qualifying body in question to take such steps as the court directs for securing that the subsection or requirement is satisfied or that the obligation is complied with.

**39(3) [Jurisdiction]** The jurisdiction conferred by this section is exercisable by the High Court and the Court of Session.

## 40 Directions to comply with international obligations

**40(1) [Secretary of State's direction]** If it appears to the Secretary of State–

(a) that any action proposed to be taken by a recognised supervisory or qualifying body, or a body established by order under section 46, would be incompatible with Community obligations or any other international obligations of the United Kingdom, or

(b) that any action which that body has power to take is required for the purpose of implementing any such obligations,

he may direct the body not to take or, as the case may be, to take the action in question.

**40(2) [Supplementary requirements]** A direction may include such supplementary or incidental requirements as the Secretary of State thinks necessary or expedient.

**40(3) [Enforcement]** A direction under this section is enforceable on the application of the Secretary of State by injunction or, in Scotland, by an order under section 45 of the Court of Session Act 1988.

OFFENCES

## 41 False and misleading statements

**41(1) [Offence]** A person commits an offence if–

(a) for the purposes of or in connection with any application under this Part, or

(b) in purported compliance with any requirement imposed on him by or under this Part,

he furnishes information which he knows to be false or misleading in a material particular or recklessly furnishes information which is false or misleading in a material particular.

**41(2) [Person not on register]** It is an offence for a person whose name does not appear on the register of auditors kept under regulations under section 35 to describe himself as a registered auditor or so to hold himself out as to indicate, or be reasonably understood to indicate, that he is a registered auditor.

**41(3) [Body which is not recognised]** It is an offence for a body which is not a recognised supervisory or qualifying body to describe itself as so recognised or so to describe itself or hold itself out as to indicate, or be reasonably understood to indicate, that it is so recognised.

**41(4) [S. 41(1) penalties]** A person guilty of an offence under subsection (1) is liable–

(a) on conviction on indictment, to imprisonment for a term not exceeding two years or to a fine or both;

(b) on summary conviction, to imprisonment for a term not exceeding six months or to a fine not exceeding the statutory maximum or both.

**41(5) [S. 41(2), (3) penalties]** A person guilty of an offence under subsection (2) or (3) is liable on summary conviction to imprisonment for a term not exceeding six months or to a fine not exceeding level 5 on the standard scale or both.

Where a contravention of subsection (2) or (3) involves a public display of the offending description, the maximum fine that may be imposed is (in place of that mentioned above) an amount equal to level 5 on the standard scale multiplied by the number of days for which the display has continued.

**41(6) [S. 41(2), (3) defence]** It is a defence for a person charged with an offence under subsection (2) or (3) to show that he took all reasonable precautions and exercised all due diligence to avoid the commission of the offence.

## 42 Offences by bodies corporate, partnerships and unincorporated associations

**42(1) [Officer liable]** Where an offence under this Part committed by a body corporate is proved to have been committed with the consent or connivance of, or to be attributable to any neglect on the part of, a director, manager, secretary or other similar officer of the body, or a person purporting to act in any such capacity, he as well as the body corporate is guilty of the offence and liable to be proceeded against and punished accordingly.

**42(2) [Member liable as manager]** Where the affairs of a body corporate are managed by its members, subsection (1) applies in relation to the acts and defaults of a member in connection with his functions of management as to a director of a body corporate.

**42(3) [Partner liable]** Where an offence under this Part committed by a partnership is proved to have been committed with the consent or connivance of, or to be attributable to any neglect on the part of, a partner, he as well as the partnership is guilty of the offence and liable to be proceeded against and punished accordingly.

**42(4) [Unincorporated association]** Where an offence under this Part committed by an unincorporated association (other than a partnership) is proved to have been committed with the consent or connivance of, or to be attributable to any neglect on the part of, any officer of the association or any member of its governing body, he as well as the association is guilty of the offence and liable to be proceeded against and punished accordingly.

## 43 Time limits for prosecution of offences

**43(1) [Offence triable by magistrates' court]** An information relating to an offence under this Part which is triable by a magistrates' court in England and Wales may be so tried on an information laid at any time within twelve months after the date on which evidence sufficient in the opinion of the Director of Public Prosecutions or the Secretary of State to justify the proceedings comes to his knowledge.

**43(2) [Scotland]** Proceedings in Scotland for an offence under this Part may be commenced at any time within twelve months after the date on which evidence sufficient in the Lord Advocate's opinion to justify the proceedings came to his knowledge or, where such evidence was reported to him by the Secretary of State, within twelve months after the date on which it came to the knowledge of the latter.

For the purposes of this subsection proceedings shall be deemed to be commenced on the date on which a warrant to apprehend or to cite the accused is granted, if the warrant is executed without undue delay.

**43(3) [Time limit]** Subsection (1) does not authorise the trial of an information laid, and subsection (2) does not authorise the commencement of proceedings, more than three years after the commission of the offence.

**43(4) [Certificate as evidence]** For the purposes of this section a certificate of the Director of Public Prosecutions, the Lord Advocate or the Secretary of State as to the date on which such evidence as is referred to above came to his knowledge is conclusive evidence.

**43(5) [Usual time limits not affected]** Nothing in this section affects proceedings within the time limits prescribed by section 127(1) of the Magistrates' Courts Act 1980 or section 331 of the Criminal Procedure (Scotland) Act 1975 (the usual time limits for criminal proceedings).

## 44 Jurisdiction and procedure in respect of offences

**44(1) [Summary proceedings]** Summary proceedings for an offence under this Part may, without prejudice to any jurisdiction exercisable apart from this section, be taken against a body corporate or unincorporated association at any place at which it has a place of business and against an individual at any place where he is for the time being.

**44(2) [Unincorporated association]** Proceedings for an offence alleged to have been committed under this Part by an unincorporated association shall be brought in the name of the association (and not in that of any of its members), and for the purposes of any such proceedings any rules of court relating to the service of documents apply as in relation to a body corporate.

**44(3) [Procedure where unincorporated association charged]** Section 33 of the Criminal Justice Act 1925 and Schedule 3 to the Magistrates' Courts Act 1980 (procedure on charge of offence against a corporation) apply in a case in which an unincorporated association is charged in England and Wales with an offence under this Part as they apply in the case of a corporation.

**44(4) [Scotland]** In relation to proceedings on indictment in Scotland for an offence alleged to have been committed under this Part by an unincorporated association, section 70 of the Criminal Procedure (Scotland) Act 1995 (proceedings on indictment against bodies corporate) applies as if the association were a body corporate.

**History**
In s. 44(4) the words "section 70 of the Criminal Procedure (Scotland) Act 1995" appearing after the words "unincorporated association" substituted for the former words "section 74 of the Criminal Procedure (Scotland) Act 1975" by the Criminal Procedure (Consequential Provisions) (Scotland) Act 1995, s. 5, Sch. 4, para. 74(2) as from 1 April 1996.

**44(5) [Fine]** A fine imposed on an unincorporated association on its conviction of such an offence shall be paid out of the funds of the association.

SUPPLEMENTARY PROVISIONS

## 45 Fees

**45(1) [Application fee]** An applicant for a recognition order under this Part shall pay such fee in respect of his application as may be prescribed; and no application shall be regarded as duly made unless this subsection is complied with.

**45(2) [Periodical fees]** Every recognised supervisory or qualifying body shall pay such periodical fees to the Secretary of State as may be prescribed.

**Note**

See note after s. 45(4).

**45(3) ["Prescribed"]** In this section **"prescribed"** means prescribed by regulations made by the Secretary of State, which may make different provision for different cases or classes of case.

**45(4) [Regulations]** Regulations under this section shall be made by statutory instrument which shall be subject to annulment in pursuance of a resolution of either House of Parliament.

**Note**

See the Company Auditors (Recognition Orders) (Application Fees) Regulations 1990 (SI 1990/1206) and the Companies Act 1989 (Recognised Supervisory Bodies) (Periodical Fees) Regulations 1993 (SI 1993/1881).

**45(5) [Destination of fees]** Fees received by the Secretary of State by virtue of this Part shall be paid into the Consolidated Fund.

# 46 Delegation of functions of Secretary of State

**46(1) [Delegation order]** The Secretary of State may by order (a "delegation order") establish a body corporate to exercise his functions under this Part.

**46(2) [Effect of order]** A delegation order has the effect of transferring to the body established by it, subject to such exceptions and reservations as may be specified in the order, all the functions of the Secretary of State under this Part except–

(a) such functions under Part I of Schedule 14 (prevention of restrictive practices) as are excepted by regulations under section 47, and

(b) his functions in relation to the body itself;

and the order may also confer on the body such other functions supplementary or incidental to those transferred as appear to the Secretary of State to be appropriate.

**46(3) [Reservation of functions]** Any transfer of the functions under the following provisions shall be subject to the reservation that they remain exercisable concurrently by the Secretary of State–

(a) section 38 (power to call for information), and

(b) section 40 (directions to comply with international obligations);

and any transfer of the function of refusing to approve an overseas qualification, or withdrawing such approval, on the grounds referred to in section 33(3) (lack of reciprocity) shall be subject to the reservation that the function is exercisable only with the consent of the Secretary of State.

**46(4) [Amendment of order]** A delegation order may be amended or, if it appears to the Secretary of State that it is no longer in the public interest that the order should remain in force, revoked by a further order under this section.

**46(5) [Supplementary order]** Where functions are transferred or resumed, the Secretary of State may by order confer or, as the case may be, take away such other functions supplementary or incidental to those transferred or resumed as appear to him to be appropriate.

**46(6) [Application of Sch. 13]** The provisions of Schedule 13 have effect with respect to the status, constitution and proceedings of a body established by a delegation order, the exercise by it of certain functions transferred to it and other supplementary matters.

**46(7) [Order by statutory instrument]** An order under this section shall be made by statutory instrument.

**46(8) [Approval by Parliament]** An order which has the effect of transferring or resuming any functions shall not be made unless a draft of it has been laid before and approved by resolution of each House of Parliament; and any other description of order shall be subject to annulment in pursuance of a resolution of either House of Parliament.

# 47 Restrictive practices

**47(1) [Application of Sch. 14]** The provisions of Schedule 14 have effect with respect to certain matters relating to restrictive practices and competition law.

**47(2) [Regulations]** The Secretary of State may make provision by regulations as to the discharge of the functions under paragraphs 1 to 7 of that Schedule when a delegation order is in force.

**47(3) [Scope of regulations]** The regulations may–

(a) except any function from the effect of the delegation order,

(b) modify any of the provisions mentioned in subsection (2), and

(c) impose such duties on the body established by the delegation order, the Secretary of State and Director General of Fair Trading as appear to the Secretary of State to be appropriate.

**47(4) [Reservations]** The regulations shall contain such provision as appears to the Secretary of State to be necessary or expedient for reserving to him the decision–

(a) to refuse recognition on the ground mentioned in paragraph 1(3) of that Schedule, or

(b) to exercise the powers conferred by paragraph 6 of that Schedule.

**47(5) [Prohibitions]** For that purpose the regulations may–

(a) prohibit the body from granting a recognition order without the leave of the Secretary of State, and

(b) empower the Secretary of State to direct the body to exercise its powers in such manner as may be specified in the direction.

**47(6) [Regulations by statutory instrument]** Regulations under this section shall be made by statutory instrument which shall be subject to annulment in pursuance of a resolution of either House of Parliament.

**Note**
S. 47(1) in force from 1 March 1990 (see SI 1990/142 (C 5)).

## 48 Exemption from liability for damages

**48(1) [Discharge of functions]** Neither a recognised supervisory body, nor any of its officers or employees or members of its governing body, shall be liable in damages for anything done or omitted in the discharge or purported discharge of functions to which this subsection applies, unless the act or omission is shown to have been in bad faith.

**48(2) [Relevant functions]** Subsection (1) applies to the functions of the body so far as relating to, or to matters arising out of–

(a) such rules, practices, powers and arrangements of the body to which the requirements of Part II of Schedule 11 apply, or

(b) the obligations with which paragraph 16 of that Schedule requires the body to comply,

(c) any guidance issued by the body, or

(d) the obligations to which the body is subject by virtue of this Part.

**48(3) [Body established by delegation order]** Neither a body established by a delegation order, nor any of its members, officers or employees, shall be liable in damages for anything done or omitted in the discharge or purported discharge of the functions exercisable by virtue of an order under section 46, unless the act or omission is shown to have been in bad faith.

**Note**
S. 48(1), (2) in force from 1 March 1990 (see SI 1990/142 (C 5)).

## 49 Service of notices

**49(1) [Application]** This section has effect in relation to any notice, direction or other document required or authorised by or under this Part to be given to or served on any person other than the Secretary of State.

**49(2) [Service]** Any such document may be given to or served on the person in question–

(a) by delivering it to him,

(b) by leaving it at his proper address, or

(c) by sending it by post to him at that address.

**49(3) [Relevant persons]** Any such document may–

(a) in the case of a body corporate, be given to or served on the secretary or clerk of that body;

(b) in the case of a partnership, be given to or served on any partner;

(c) in the case of an unincorporated association other than a partnership, be given to or served on any member of the governing body of the association.

**49(4) [Addresses]** For the purposes of this section and section 7 of the Interpretation Act 1978 (service of documents by post) in its application to this section, the proper address of any person is his last known address (whether of his residence or of a place where he carries on business or is employed) and also–

(a) in the case of a person who is eligible under the rules of a recognised supervisory body for appointment as company auditor and who does not have a place of business in the United Kingdom, the address of that body;

(b) in the case of a body corporate, its secretary or its clerk, the address of its registered or principal office in the United Kingdom;

(c) in the case of an unincorporated association (other than a partnership) or a member of its governing body, its principal office in the United Kingdom.

## 50 Power to make consequential amendments

**50(1) [Regulations]** The Secretary of State may by regulations make such amendments of enactments as appear to him to be necessary or expedient in consequence of the provisions of this Part having effect in place of section 389 of the Companies Act 1985.

**50(2) [Scope of power]** That power extends to making such amendments as appear to the Secretary of State necessary or expedient of–

(a) enactments referring by name to the bodies of accountants recognised for the purposes of section 389(1)(a) of the Companies Act 1985, and

(b) enactments making with respect to other statutory auditors provision as to the matters dealt with in relation to company auditors by section 389 of the Companies Act 1985.

**50(3) [Provision for other statutory auditors]** The provision which may be made with respect to other statutory auditors includes provision as to–

(a) eligibility for the appointment,

(b) the effect of appointing a partnership which is not a legal person and the manner of exercise of the auditor's rights in such a case, and

(c) ineligibility on the ground of lack of independence or any other ground.

**50(4) [Supplementary provisions]** The regulations may contain such supplementary, incidental and transitional provision as appears to the Secretary of State to be necessary or expedient.

**50(5) [Consent of minister required]** The Secretary of State shall not make regulations under this section with respect to any statutory auditors without the consent of–

(a) the Minister responsible for their appointment or responsible for the body or person by, or in relation to whom, they are appointed, or

(b) if there is no such Minister, the person by whom they are appointed.

**50(6) ["Statutory auditor"]** In this section a **"statutory auditor"** means a person appointed auditor in pursuance of any enactment authorising or requiring the appointment of an auditor or auditors.

**50(7) [Regulations by statutory instrument]** Regulations under this section shall be made by statutory instrument which shall be subject to annulment in pursuance of a resolution of either House of Parliament.

**Note**

See the Companies Act 1989 (Eligibility for Appointment as Company Auditor) (Consequential Amendments) Regulations 1991 (SI 1991/1997); the Companies Act 1989 Part II (Consequential Amendments) Regulations 1995 (SI 1995/1163) and the Companies Act 1989 Part II (Consequential Amendments) Regulations 1995 (SI 1995/2723).

## 51 Power to make provision in consequence of changes affecting accountancy bodies

**51(1) [Power to amend enactment]** The Secretary of State may by regulations make such amendments of enactments as appear to him to be necessary or expedient in consequence of any change of name, merger or transfer of engagements affecting–

(a) a recognised supervisory or qualifying body under this Part, or

(b) a body of accountants referred to in, or approved, authorised or otherwise recognised for the purposes of, any other enactment.

**51(2) [Regulations by statutory instrument]** Regulations under this section shall be made by statutory instrument which shall be subject to annulment in pursuance of a resolution of either House of Parliament.

## 52 Meaning of "associate"

**52(1) ["Associate"]** In this Part **"associate"**, in relation to a person, shall be construed as follows.

**52(2) [Individual]** In relation to an individual **"associate"** means–

(a) that individual's spouse or minor child or step-child,

(b) any body corporate of which that individual is a director, and

(c) any employee or partner of that individual.

**52(3) [Body corporate]** In relation to a body corporate **"associate"** means–

(a) any body corporate of which that body is a director,

(b) any body corporate in the same group as that body, and

(c) any employee or partner of that body or of any body corporate in the same group.

**52(4) [Scottish firm, partnership]** In relation to a Scottish firm, or a partnership constituted under the law of any other country or territory in which a partnership is a legal person, **"associate"** means–

(a) any body corporate of which the firm is a director,

(b) any employee of or partner in the firm, and

(c) any person who is an associate of a partner in the firm.

**52(5) [Partnership]** In relation to a partnership constituted under the law of England and Wales or Northern Ireland, or the law of any other country or territory in which a partnership is not a legal person, **"associate"** means any person who is an associate of any of the partners.

## 53 Minor definitions

**53(1) [Definitions]** In this Part–

**"address"** means–

(a) in relation to an individual, his usual residential or business address, and

(b) in relation to a firm, its registered or principal office in Great Britain;

**"company"** means any company or other body to which section 384 of the Companies Act 1985 (duty to appoint auditors) applies;

**"director"**, in relation to a body corporate, includes any person occupying in relation to it the position of a director (by whatever name called) and any person in accordance with whose directions or instructions (not being advice given in a professional capacity) the directors of the body are accustomed to act;

**"enactment"** includes an enactment contained in subordinate legislation within the meaning of the Interpretation Act 1978;

**"firm"** means a body corporate or a partnership;

**"group"**, in relation to a body corporate, means the body corporate, any other body corporate which is its holding company or subsidiary and any other body corporate which is a subsidiary of that holding company; and

**"holding company"** and **"subsidiary"** have the meaning given by section 736 of the Companies Act 1985;

**"parent undertaking"** and **"subsidiary undertaking"** have the same meaning as in Part VII of the Companies Act 1985.

**53(2) ["Established in the UK"]** For the purposes of this Part a body shall be regarded as "established in the United Kingdom" if and only if–

(a) it is incorporated or formed under the law of the United Kingdom or a part of the United Kingdom, or
(b) its central management and control is exercised in the United Kingdom;

and any reference to a qualification "obtained in the United Kingdom" is to a qualification obtained from such a body.

## 54 Index of defined expressions

**54** The following Table shows provisions defining or otherwise explaining expressions used in this Part (other than provisions defining or explaining an expression used only in the same section)–

| | |
|---|---|
| address | section 53(1) |
| appropriate qualification | section 31 |
| associate | section 52 |
| company | section 53(1) |
| company auditor, company audit and company audit work | section 24(2) |
| delegation order | section 46 |
| director (of a body corporate) | section 53(1) |
| Director (in Schedule 14) | paragraph 1(1) of that Schedule |
| enactment | section 53(1) |
| established in the United Kingdom | section 53(2) |
| firm | section 53(1) |
| group (in relation to a body corporate) | section 53(1) |
| guidance | |
| —of a qualifying body | section 32(3) |
| —of a supervisory body | section 30(4) |
| holding company | section 53(1) |
| member (of a supervisory body) | section 30(2) |
| obtained in the United Kingdom | section 53(2) |
| parent undertaking | section 53(1) |
| purposes of this Part | section 24(1) |
| qualifying body | section 32(1) |
| recognised | |
| —in relation to a professional qualification | section 32(4) and Schedule 12 |
| —in relation to a qualifying body | paragraph 2(1) of Schedule 12 |
| —in relation to a supervisory body | section 30(5) and Schedule 11 |
| rules | |
| —of a qualifying body | section 32(2) |
| —of a supervisory body | section 30(3) |
| subsidiary and subsidiary undertaking | section 53(1) |
| supervisory body | section 30(1) |

# PART III – INVESTIGATIONS AND POWERS TO OBTAIN INFORMATION

AMENDMENTS OF OTHER ENACTMENTS

## 77 Amendments of the Insurance Companies Act 1982

**77(1) [Amendment of Insurance Companies Act 1982, Pt. II]** Part II of the Insurance Companies Act 1982 is amended as follows.

**77(2) [Substitutions in s. 44]** In section 44 (power to obtain information and require production of documents), for "books or papers" (wherever occurring) substitute "documents", and for subsection (6) substitute–

"(6) In this section "document" includes information recorded in any form; and, in relation to information recorded otherwise than in legible form, the power to require its production includes power to require the production of a copy of the information in legible form.".

**77(3) [Insertion of s. 44A]** After that section insert–

"*Entry and search of premises*

**44A(1)** A justice of the peace may issue a warrant under this section if satisfied on information on oath given by or on behalf of the Secretary of State, or by a person authorised to exercise powers under section 44 above, that there are reasonable grounds for believing that there are on any premises documents whose production has been required under section 44(2) to (4) above and which have not been produced in compliance with the requirement.

**44A(2)** A justice of the peace may also issue a warrant under this section if satisfied on information on oath given by or on behalf of the Secretary of State, or by a person authorised to exercise powers under section 44 above–

(a) that there are reasonable grounds for believing that an offence has been committed for which the penalty on conviction on indictment is imprisonment for a term of not less than two years and that there are on any premises documents relating to whether the offence has been committed,

(b) that the Secretary of State or, as the case may be, the authorised person has power to require the production of the documents under section 44(2) to (4) above, and

(c) that there are reasonable grounds for believing that if production was so required the documents would not be produced but would be removed from the premises, hidden, tampered with or destroyed.

**44A(3)** A warrant under this section shall authorise a constable, together with any other person named in it and any other constables–

(a) to enter the premises specified in the information, using such force as is reasonably necessary for the purpose;

(b) to search the premises and take possession of any documents appearing to be such documents as are mentioned in subsection (1) or (2), as the case may be, or to take, in relation to any such documents, any other steps which may appear to be necessary for preserving them or preventing interference with them;

(c) to take copies of any such documents; and

(d) to require any person named in the warrant to provide an explanation of them or to state where they may be found.

**44A(4)** If in the case of a warrant under subsection (2) the justice of the peace is satisfied on information on oath that there are reasonable grounds for believing that there are also on the premises other documents relevant to the investigation, the warrant shall also authorise the actions mentioned in subsection (3) to be taken in relation to such documents.

**44A(5)** A warrant under this section shall continue in force until the end of the period of one month beginning with the day on which it is issued.

**44A(6)** Any documents of which possession is taken under this section may be retained–

(a) for a period of three months; or

(b) if within that period proceedings to which the documents are relevant are commenced against any person for any criminal offence, until the conclusion of those proceedings.

**44A(7)** In the application of this section to Scotland for the references to a justice of the peace substitute references to a justice of the peace or a sheriff, and for the references to information on oath substitute references to evidence on oath.

44A(8) In this section "document" includes information recorded in any form.".

**77(4) [Insertion in s. 47A]** In section 47A(1) (restriction on disclosure of information), after "section 44(2) to (4)" insert "or 44A".

**77(5) [Insertion of s. 71(2A)]** In section 71 (offences and penalties), after subsection (2) insert–

"**(2A)** A person who intentionally obstructs the exercise of any rights conferred by a warrant issued under section 44A above or fails without reasonable excuse to comply with any requirement imposed in accordance with subsection (3)(d) of that section is guilty of an offence and liable–

(a) on conviction on indictment, to a fine, and

(b) on summary conviction, to a fine not exceeding the statutory maximum.".

**77(6) [Substitution in s. 71(6)]** In section 71(6) (defence to failure to comply with requirement to produce books or papers) for "books or papers" substitute "documents".

**Note**

S. 77 in force from 21 February 1990 (see SI 1990/142 (C 5)).

## POWERS EXERCISABLE TO ASSIST OVERSEAS REGULATORY AUTHORITIES

# 82 Request for assistance by overseas regulatory authority

**82(1) [Purpose of s. 83 powers]** The powers conferred by section 83 are exercisable by the Secretary of State for the purpose of assisting an overseas regulatory authority which has requested his assistance in connection with inquiries being carried out by it or on its behalf.

**82(2) ["Overseas regulatory authority"]** An **"overseas regulatory authority"** means an authority which in a country or territory outside the United Kingdom exercises–

(a) any function corresponding to–

(i) a function under the Financial Services Act 1986 of a designated agency, transferee body or competent authority (within the meaning of that Act),

(ii) a function of the Secretary of State under the Insurance Companies Act 1982, the Companies Act 1985 or the Financial Services Act 1986, or

(iii) a function of the Financial Services Authority under the Banking Act 1987, or

(b) any function in connection with the investigation of, or the enforcement of rules (whether or not having the force of law) relating to, conduct of the kind prohibited by Part V of the Criminal Justice Act 1993 (insider dealing), or

(c) any function prescribed for the purposes of this subsection by order of the Secretary of State, being a function which in the opinion of the Secretary of State relates to companies or financial services.

An order under paragraph (c) shall be made by statutory instrument which shall be subject to annulment in pursuance of a resolution of either House of Parliament.

**History**

In s. 82(2)(a)(iii) the words "Financial Services Authority" substituted for the former words "Bank of England" by the Bank of England Act 1998, s. 23(1), 45 and Sch. 5, para. 66(1), (2)(a) as from 1 June 1998 (see SI 1998/1120 (C 25), art. 2).
Previously in s. 82(2)(b) the words "Part V of the Criminal Justice Act 1993 (insider dealing)" substituted for the former words "Company Securities (Insider Dealing) Act 1985" by Criminal Justice Act 1993, s. 79(13) and Sch. 5, para. 16 as from 1 March 1994 (see SI 1994/242 (C 7)).

**82(3) [Restriction on exercise of powers]** The Secretary of State shall not exercise the powers conferred by section 83 unless he is satisfied that the assistance requested by the overseas regulatory authority is for the purposes of its regulatory functions.

An authority's **"regulatory functions"** means any functions falling within subsection (2) and any other functions relating to companies or financial services.

**82(4) [Matters to be taken into account]** In deciding whether to exercise those powers the Secretary of State may take into account, in particular–

(a) whether corresponding assistance would be given in that country or territory to an authority exercising regulatory functions in the United Kingdom;

(b) whether the inquiries relate to the possible breach of a law, or other requirement, which has no close parallel in the United Kingdom or involves the assertion of a jurisdiction not recognised by the United Kingdom;

(c) the seriousness of the matter to which the inquiries relate, the importance to the inquiries of the information sought in the United Kingdom and whether the assistance could be obtained by other means;

(d) whether it is otherwise appropriate in the public interest to give the assistance sought.

**82(5) ["Banking supervisor"]** Before deciding whether to exercise those powers in a case where the overseas regulatory authority is a banking supervisor, the Secretary of State shall consult the Financial Services Authority.

A **"banking supervisor"** means an overseas regulatory authority with respect to which the Financial Services Authority has notified the Secretary of State, for the purposes of this subsection, that it exercises functions corresponding to those of the Authority under the Banking Act 1987.

**History**

In s. 82(5) the words "Financial Services Authority" substituted for the former words "Bank of England" in both places and the word "Authority" substituted for the former word "Bank" by the Bank of England Act 1998, s. 23(1), 45 and Sch. 5, para. 66(1), (2)(b)(i) and (ii), respectively as from 1 June 1998 (see SI 1998/1120 (C 25), art. 2).

**82(6) [Contribution towards costs]** The Secretary of State may decline to exercise those powers unless the overseas regulatory authority undertakes to make such contribution towards the costs of their exercise as the Secretary of State considers appropriate.

**82(7) [Meaning of financial services]** References in this section to financial services include, in particular, investment business, insurance and banking.

**Note**

See note after s. 86.

# 83 Power to require information, documents or other assistance

**83(1) [Powers exercisable for good reason]** The following powers may be exercised in accordance with section 82, if the Secretary of State considers there is good reason for their exercise.

**83(2) [Requirements]** The Secretary of State may require any person–

(a) to attend before him at a specified time and place and answer questions or otherwise furnish information with respect to any matter relevant to the inquiries,

(b) to produce at a specified time and place any specified documents which appear to the Secretary of State to relate to any matter relevant to the inquiries, and

(c) otherwise to give him such assistance in connection with the inquiries as he is reasonably able to give.

**83(3) [Examination on oath]** The Secretary of State may examine a person on oath and may administer an oath accordingly.

**83(4) [Copying documents]** Where documents are produced the Secretary of State may take copies or extracts from them.

**83(5) [Legal professional privilege]** A person shall not under this section be required to disclose information or produce a document which he would be entitled to refuse to disclose or produce on grounds of legal professional privilege in proceedings in the High Court or on grounds of confidentiality as between client and professional legal adviser in proceedings in the Court of Session, except that a lawyer may be required to furnish the name and address of his client.

**83(6) [Statement as evidence]** A statement by a person in compliance with a requirement imposed under this section may be used in evidence against him.

**83(6A) [Limits on use of statement in criminal proceedings]** However, in criminal proceedings in which that person is charged with an offence to which this subsection applies–

(a) no evidence relating to the statement may be adduced, and

(b) no question relating to it may be asked,

by or on behalf of the prosecution, unless evidence relating to it is adduced, or a question relating to it is asked, in the proceedings by or on behalf of that person.

**History**
S. 83(6A) inserted by Youth Justice and Criminal Evidence Act 1999, s. 59, 68(3) and Sch. 3, para. 21, with effect from 14 April 2000 (see Youth Justice and Criminal Evidence Act 1999 (Commencement No. 2) Order 2000 (SI 2000/1034 (C. 27)); art. 2(a)).

**83(6B) [Offences to which s. 83(6A) applies]** Subsection (6A)above applies to any offence other than–

(a) an offence under section 85;

(b) an offence under section 2 or 5 of the Perjury Act 1911 (false statements made on oath otherwise than in judicial proceedings or made otherwise than on oath);

(c) an offence under section 44(1) or (2) of the Criminal Law (Consolidation) (Scotland) Act 1995 (false statements made on oath or otherwise than on oath); or

(d) an offence under Article 7 or 10 of the Perjury (Northern Ireland) Order 1979 (false statements made on oath otherwise than in judicial proceedings or made otherwise than on oath).

**History**
S. 83(6B) inserted by Youth Justice and Criminal Evidence Act 1999, s. 59, 68(3) and Sch. 3, para. 21, with effect from 14 April 2000 (see Youth Justice and Criminal Evidence Act 1999 (Commencement No. 2) Order 2000 (SI 2000/1034 (C. 27)), art. 2(a)).

**83(7) [Lien on document]** Where a person claims a lien on a document, its production under this section is without prejudice to his lien.

**83(8) ["Documents"]** In this section "documents" includes information recorded in any form; and, in relation to information recorded otherwise than in legible form, the power to require its production includes power to require the production of a copy of it in legible form.

**Note**
See note after s. 86.

# 84 Exercise of powers by officer, etc.

**84(1) [Authority from Secretary of State]** The Secretary of State may authorise an officer of his or any other competent person to exercise on his behalf all or any of the powers conferred by section 83.

**84(2) [Purpose of authority]** No such authority shall be granted except for the purpose of investigating–

(a) the affairs, or any aspects of the affairs, of a person specified in the authority, or

(b) a subject-matter so specified,

being a person who, or subject-matter which, is the subject of the inquiries being carried out by or on behalf of the overseas regulatory authority.

**84(3) [Evidence of authority]** No person shall be bound to comply with a requirement imposed by a person exercising powers by virtue of an authority granted under this section unless he has, if required, produced evidence of his authority.

**84(4) [Banking confidentiality]** A person shall not by virtue of an authority under this section be required to disclose any information or produce any documents in respect of which he owes an obligation of confidence by virtue of carrying on the business of banking unless–

(a) the imposing on him of a requirement with respect to such information or documents has been specifically authorised by the Secretary of State, or

(b) the person to whom the obligation of confidence is owed consents to the disclosure or production.

In this subsection **"documents"** has the same meaning as in section 83.

**84(5) [Report to Secretary of State]** Where the Secretary of State authorises a person other than one of his officers to exercise any powers by virtue of this section, that person shall make a report to the Secretary of State in such manner as he may require on the exercise of those powers and the results of exercising them.

**Note**
See note after s. 86.

## 85 Penalty for failure to comply with requirement, etc.

**85(1) [Failure to comply]** A person who without reasonable excuse fails to comply with a requirement imposed on him under section 83 commits an offence and is liable on summary conviction to imprisonment for a term not exceeding six months or to a fine not exceeding level 5 on the standard scale, or both.

**85(2) [Purported compliance]** A person who in purported compliance with any such requirement furnishes information which he knows to be false or misleading in a material particular, or recklessly furnishes information which is false or misleading in a material particular, commits an offence and is liable–

(a) on conviction on indictment, to imprisonment for a term not exceeding two years or to a fine, or both;

(b) on summary conviction, to imprisonment for a term not exceeding six months or to a fine not exceeding the statutory maximum, or both.

**Note**
See note after s. 86.

## 86 Restrictions on disclosure of information

**86(1) [Application]** This section applies to information relating to the business or other affairs of a person which–

(a) is supplied by an overseas regulatory authority in connection with a request for assistance, or

(b) is obtained by virtue of the powers conferred by section 83, whether or not any requirement to supply it is made under that section.

**86(2) [Consent]** Except as permitted by section 87 below, such information shall not be disclosed for any purpose–

(a) by the primary recipient, or

(b) by any person obtaining the information directly or indirectly from him,

without the consent of the person from whom the primary recipient obtained the information and, if different, the person to whom it relates.

**86(3) ["Primary recipient"]** The **"primary recipient"** means, as the case may be–

(a) the Secretary of State,

(b) any person authorised under section 84 to exercise powers on his behalf, and

(c) any officer or servant of any such person.

**86(4) [Information available to public]** Information shall not be treated as information to which this section applies if it has been made available to the public by virtue of being disclosed in any circumstances in which, or for any purpose for which, disclosure is not precluded by this section.

**86(5) [Offence]** A person who contravenes this section commits an offence and is liable–

(a) on conviction on indictment, to imprisonment for a term not exceeding two years or to a fine, or both;

(b) on summary conviction, to imprisonment for a term not exceeding three months or to a fine not exceeding the statutory maximum, or both.

**Note**
S. 82–86 in force from 21 February 1990 (see SI 1990/142 (C 5)).

## 87 Exceptions from restrictions on disclosure

**87(1) [Permitted disclosure]** Information to which section 86 applies may be disclosed–

(a) to any person with a view to the institution of, or otherwise for the purposes of, relevant proceedings,

(b) for the purpose of enabling or assisting a relevant authority to discharge any relevant function (including functions in relation to proceedings),

(c) to the Treasury, if the disclosure is made in the interests of investors or in the public interest,

(d) if the information is or has been available to the public from other sources,

(e) in a summary or collection of information framed in such a way as not to enable the identity of any person to whom the information relates to be ascertained, or

(f) in pursuance of any Community obligation.

**87(2) [Meaning of relevant proceedings]** The relevant proceedings referred to in subsection (1)(a) are–

(a) any criminal proceedings,

(b) civil proceedings arising under or by virtue of the Financial Services Act 1986 and proceedings before the Financial Services Tribunal, and

(c) disciplinary proceedings relating to–

(i) the exercise by a solicitor, auditor, accountant, valuer or actuary of his professional duties, or

(ii) the discharge by a public servant of his duties.

**87(3) ["Public servant" in s. 87(2)(c)(ii)]** In subsection (2)(c)(ii) **"public servant"** means an officer or servant of the Crown or of any public or other authority for the time being designated for the purposes of that provision by order of the Secretary of State.

**87(4) [Relevant authorities, functions]** The relevant authorities referred to in subsection (1)(b), and the relevant functions in relation to each such authority, are as follows–

| *Authority* | *Functions* |
|---|---|
| The Secretary of State. | Functions under the enactments relating to companies, insurance companies or insolvency, or under the Financial Services Act 1986 or Part II, this Part or Part VII of this Act. |
| The Treasury. | Functions under the enactments relating to insurance companies, under the Financial Services Act 1986 or under this Part or Part VII of this Act. |
| An inspector appointed under Part XIV of the Companies Act 1985 or section 94 or 177 of the Financial Services Act 1986. | Functions under that Part or that section. |
| A person authorised to exercise powers or appointed under section 43A or 44 of the Insurance Companies Act 1982, section 447 of the Companies Act 1985, section 106 of the Financial Services Act 1986 or section 84 of this Act. | Functions under that section. |
| An overseas regulatory authority. | Its regulatory functions (within the meaning of section 82 of this Act). |
| The Department of Economic Development in Northern Ireland or a person appointed or authorised by that Department. | Functions conferred on it or him by the enactments relating to companies or insolvency. |
| A designated agency within the meaning of the Financial Services Act 1986. | Functions under that Act or Part VII of this Act. |
| A transferee body or the competent authority within the meaning of the Financial Services Act 1986. | Functions under that Act. |
| The body administering a scheme under section 54 of the Financial Services Act 1986. | Functions under the scheme. |

| *Authority* | *Functions* |
|---|---|
| A recognised self-regulating organisation, recognised professional body, recognised investment exchange, recognised clearing house or recognised self-regulating organisation for friendly societies (within the meaning of the Financial Services Act 1986). | Functions in its capacity as an organisation, body, exchange or clearing house recognised under that Act. |
| The Chief Registrar of friendly societies, the Registrar of Friendly Societies for Northern Ireland and the Assistant Registrar of Friendly Societies for Scotland. | Functions under the Financial Services Act 1986 or the enactments relating to friendly societies or building societies. |
| The Friendly Societies Commission. | Functions under the enactments relating to friendly societies or under the Financial Services Act 1986. |
| The Bank of England. | Any of its functions. |
| The Financial Services Authority. | Functions under the Financial Services Act 1986 (other than as a designated agency within the meaning of that Act), the Banking Act 1987 or section 171 of the Companies Act 1989. |
| The Deposit Protection Board. | Functions under the Banking Act 1987. |
| A body established by order under section 46 of this Act. | Functions under Part II of this Act. |
| A recognised supervisory or qualifying body within the meaning of Part II of this Act. | Functions as such a body. |
| The Industrial Assurance Commissioner and the Industrial Assurance Commissioner for Northern Ireland. | Functions under the enactments relating to industrial assurance. |
| The Insurance Brokers Registration Council. | Functions under the Insurance Brokers (Registration) Act 1977. |
| The Official Receiver or, in Northern Ireland, the Official Assignee for company liquidations or for bankruptcy. | Functions under the enactments relating to insolvency. |
| A recognised professional body (within the meaning of section 391 of the Insolvency Act 1986). | Functions in its capacity as such a body under the Insolvency Act 1986. |
| The Building Societies Commission. | Functions under the Building Societies Act 1986. |
| The Occupational Pensions Regulatory Authority. | Functions under the Pension Schemes Act 1993 or the Pensions Act 1995 or any enactment in force in Northern Ireland corresponding to either of them. |
| The Director General of Fair Trading. | Functions under the Financial Services Act 1986. |
| A person authorised by the Secretary of State under sections 245C of the Companies Act 1985. | Functions relating to the securing of compliance by companies with the accounting requirements of that Act. |
| The Director General of the National Lottery. | Functions under sections 5 to 10 inclusive and section 15 of the National Lottery etc. Act 1993. |

| *Authority* | *Functions* |
|---|---|
| The Scottish Ministers. | Functions under the enactments relating to Insolvency. |
| The Accountant in Bankruptcy. | Functions he has under the enactments relating to Insolvency. |

**History**

In the table in s. 87(4) the entries in relation to The Scottish Ministers and to The Accountant in Bankruptcy inserted by the Scotland Act 1998 (Consequential Modifications) (No. 2) Order 1999 (SI 1999/1820), art. 1(2), 4, Sch. 2, Pt. I, para. 96 as from 1 July 1999.

Previously in s. 87(4) in the entry relating to the Bank of England, the words "Any of its functions" substituted for the former words "Functions under the Banking 1987 and any other functions" and the entry relating to the Financial Services Authority inserted by the Bank of England Act 1998, s. 23(1), 45 and Sch. 5, para. 66(1), (3) as from 1 June 1998 (see SI 1998/1120 (C 25), art. 2).

Previously to that in s. 87(4) the entry relating to the Occupational Pensions Regulatory Authority inserted by the Pensions Act 1995, s. 122, Sch. 3, para. 19 as from 6 April 1997 (see SI 1997/664 (C 23), art. 2(3), Sch., Pt. II).

Previously to that in s. 87(4) in the entry relating to the Treasury the words "under the enactments relating to insurance companies," inserted by the Transfer of Functions (Insurance) Order 1997 (SI 1997/2781), art 1, 8 and Sch., para. 116 as from 5 January 1998; the entry in relation to the Treasury originally inserted by the Transfer of Functions (Financial Services) Order 1992 (SI 1992/1315), art. 10(1) and Sch. 4, para. 12 as from 7 June 1992; in the fourth entry the words "or appointed under section 43A or 44" substituted for the former words "under section 44" by the Insurance Companies (Third Insurance Directives) Regulations 1994 (SI 1994/1696), reg. 1, 68, Sch. 8, para. 18 as from 1 July 1994; the entry relating to the Friendly Societies Commission inserted by Friendly Societies Act 1992, s. 120(1) and Sch. 21, para. 11 as from 1 February 1993 (see SI 1993/16 (C 1), art. 2 and Sch. 3); the entry relating to the person authorised under s. 245C of Companies Act 1985 inserted by the Financial Services (Disclosure of Information) (Designated Authorities) (No. 7) Order 1993 (SI 1993/1826), art. 1, 3 as from 16 August 1993; and the entry relating to the Director General of the National Lottery inserted by the Financial Services (Disclosure of Information) (Designated Authorities) (No. 8) Order 1994 (SI 1994/340), art. 1, 3 as from 10 March 1994.

**87(5) [Amending s. 87(4) Table]** The Secretary of State may by order amend the Table in subsection (4) so as to–

(a) add any public or other authority to the Table and specify the relevant functions of that authority,

(b) remove any authority from the Table, or

(c) add functions to, or remove functions from, those which are relevant functions in relation to an authority specified in the Table;

and the order may impose conditions subject to which, or otherwise restrict the circumstances in which, disclosure is permitted.

**Note**

See the Financial Services (Disclosure of Information) (Designated Authorities) (No. 7) Order 1993 (SI 1993/1826) and the Financial Services (Disclosure of Information) (Designated Authorities) (No. 8) Order 1994 (SI 1994/340).

**87(6) [Order by statutory instrument]** An order under this section shall be made by statutory instrument which shall be subject to annulment in pursuance of a resolution of either House of Parliament.

**Note**

S. 87(1), (2), (3), (5), (6) in force from 21 February 1990 (see SI 1990/142 (C 5)); s. 87(4) in force from 25 April 1990 (see SI 1991/878 (C 121)).

## 88 Exercise of powers in relation to Northern Ireland

**88(1) [Application]** The following provisions apply where it appears to the Secretary of State that a request for assistance by an overseas regulatory authority may involve the powers conferred by section 83 being exercised in Northern Ireland in relation to matters which are transferred matters within the meaning of the Northern Ireland Constitution Act 1973.

**88(2) [Authorisation]** The Secretary of State shall before deciding whether to accede to the request consult the Department of Economic Development in Northern Ireland, and if he decides to accede to the request and it appears to him–

(a) that the powers should be exercised in Northern Ireland, and

(b) that the purposes for which they should be so exercised relate wholly or primarily to transferred matters,

he shall by instrument in writing authorise the Department to exercise in Northern Ireland his powers under section 83.

**88(3) [Applicable provisions]** The following provisions have effect in relation to the exercise of powers by virtue of such an authority with the substitution for references to the Secretary of State of references to the Department of Economic Development in Northern Ireland–

(a) section 84 (exercise of powers by officer, etc.),

(b) section 449 of the Companies Act 1985, section 53 or 54 of the Building Societies Act 1986, sections 179 and 180 of the Financial Services Act 1986, section 84 of the Banking Act 1987 and sections 86 and 87 above (restrictions on disclosure of information), and

(c) section 89 (authority for institution of criminal proceedings);

and references to the Secretary of State in other enactments which proceed by reference to those provisions shall be construed accordingly as being or including references to the Department.

**88(4) [Revocation of authority]** The Secretary of State may after consultation with the Department of Economic Development in Northern Ireland revoke an authority given to the Department under this section.

**88(5) [Non-application of s. 88(3)(b)]** In that case nothing in the provisions referred to in subsection (3)(b) shall apply so as to prevent the Department from giving the Secretary of State any information obtained by virtue of the authority; and (without prejudice to their application in relation to disclosure by the Department) those provisions shall apply to the disclosure of such information by the Secretary of State as if it had been obtained by him in the first place.

**88(6) [Secretary of State's powers]** Nothing in this section affects the exercise by the Secretary of State of any powers in Northern Ireland–

(a) in a case where at the time of acceding to the request it did not appear to him that the circumstances were such as to require him to authorise the Department of Economic Development in Northern Ireland to exercise those powers, or

(b) after the revocation by him of any such authority;

and no objection shall be taken to anything done by or in relation to the Secretary of State or the Department on the ground that it should have been done by or in relation to the other.

**Note**
S. 88 in force from 21 February 1990 (see SI 1990/142 (C 5)).

## 89 Prosecutions

**89** Proceedings for an offence under section 85 or 86 shall not be instituted–

(a) in England and Wales, except by or with the consent of the Secretary of State or the Director of Public Prosecutions;

(b) in Northern Ireland, except by or with the consent of the Secretary of State or the Director of Public Prosecutions for Northern Ireland.

**Note**
S. 89 in force from 21 February 1990 (see SI 1990/142 (C 5)).

## 90 Offences by bodies corporate, partnerships and unincorporated associations

**90(1) [Officer liable]** Where an offence under section 85 or 86 committed by a body corporate is proved to have been committed with the consent or connivance of, or to be attributable to any neglect on the part of, a director, manager, secretary or other similar officer of the body, or a person purporting to act in any such capacity, he as well as the body corporate is guilty of the offence and liable to be proceeded against and punished accordingly.

**90(2) [Member liable as manager]** Where the affairs of a body corporate are managed by its members, subsection (1) applies in relation to the acts and defaults of a member in connection with his functions of management as to a director of a body corporate.

**90(3) [Partner liable]** Where an offence under section 85 or 86 committed by a partnership is proved to have been committed with the consent or connivance of, or to be attributable to any neglect on the part of, a partner, he as well as the partnership is guilty of the offence and liable to be proceeded against and punished accordingly.

**90(4) [Unincorporated association]** Where an offence under section 85 or 86 committed by an unincorporated association (other than a partnership) is proved to have been committed with the consent or connivance of, or to be attributable to any neglect on the part of, any officer of the association or any member of its governing body, he as well as the association is guilty of the offence and liable to be proceeded against and punished accordingly.

**Note**

S. 90 in force from 21 February 1990 (see SI 1990/142 (C 5)).

## 91 Jurisdiction and procedure in respect of offences

**91(1) [Summary proceedings]** Summary proceedings for an offence under section 85 may, without prejudice to any jurisdiction exercisable apart from this section, be taken against a body corporate or unincorporated association at any place at which it has a place of business and against an individual at any place where he is for the time being.

**91(2) [Unincorporated association]** Proceedings for an offence alleged to have been committed under section 85 or 86 by an unincorporated association shall be brought in the name of the association (and not in that of any of its members), and for the purposes of any such proceedings any rules of court relating to the service of documents apply as in relation to a body corporate.

**91(3) [Procedure where unincorporated association charged]** Section 33 of the Criminal Justice Act 1925 and Schedule 3 to the Magistrates' Courts Act 1980 (procedure on charge of offence against a corporation) apply in a case in which an unincorporated association is charged in England and Wales with an offence under section 85 or 86 as they apply in the case of a corporation.

**91(4) [Scotland]** In relation to proceedings on indictment in Scotland for an offence alleged to have been committed under section 85 or 86 by an unincorporated association, section 70 of the Criminal Procedure (Scotland) Act 1995 (proceedings on indictment against bodies corporate) applies as if the association were a body corporate.

**History**

In s. 91(4) the words "section 70 of the Criminal Procedure (Scotland) Act 1995" appearing after the words "unincorporated association" substituted for the former words "section 74 of the Criminal Procedure (Scotland) Act 1975" by the Criminal Procedure (Consequential Provisions) (Scotland) Act 1995, Sch. 4 as from 1 April 1996.

**91(5) [Northern Ireland]** Section 18 of the Criminal Justice Act (Northern Ireland) 1945 and Schedule 4 to the Magistrates' Courts (Northern Ireland) Order 1981 (procedure on charge of offence against a corporation) apply in a case in which an unincorporated association is charged in Northern Ireland with an offence under section 85 or 86 as they apply in the case of a corporation.

**91(6) [Fine]** A fine imposed on an unincorporated association on its conviction of such an offence shall be paid out of the funds of the association.

**Note**

S. 91 in force from 21 February 1990 (see SI 1990/142 (C 5)).

# PART IV – REGISTRATION OF COMPANY CHARGES

**Note**

Part IV unlikely to be brought into force in that form.

### INTRODUCTION

## 92 Introduction

**92** The provisions of this Part amend the provisions of the Companies Act 1985 relating to the registration of company charges–

(a) by inserting in Part XII of that Act (in place of sections 395 to 408 and 410 to 423) new provisions with respect to companies registered in Great Britain, and

(b) by inserting as Chapter III of Part XXIII of that Act (in place of sections 409 and 424) new provisions with respect to oversea companies.

REGISTRATION IN THE COMPANIES CHARGES REGISTER

## 93 Charges requiring registration

**93** The following sections are inserted in Part XII of the Companies Act 1985–

"REGISTRATION IN THE COMPANY CHARGES REGISTER

*Introductory provisions*

**395(1)** The purpose of this Part is to secure the registration of charges on a company's property.

**395(2)** In this Part–

**"charge"** means any form of security interest (fixed or floating) over property, other than an interest arising by operation of law; and

**"property"**, in the context of what is the subject of a charge, includes future property.

**395(3)** It is immaterial for the purposes of this Part where the property subject to a charge is situated.

**395(4)** References in this Part to "the registrar" are–

(a) in relation to a company registered in England and Wales, to the registrar of companies for England and Wales, and

(b) in relation to a company registered in Scotland, to the registrar of companies for Scotland;

and references to registration, in relation to a charge, are to registration in the register kept by him under this Part.

*Charges requiring registration*

**396(1)** The charges requiring registration under this Part are–

(a) a charge on land or any interest in land, other than–

(i) in England and Wales, a charge for rent or any other periodical sum issuing out of the land,

(ii) in Scotland, a charge for any rent, ground annual or other periodical sum payable in respect of the land;

(b) a charge on goods or any interest in goods, other than a charge under which the chargee is entitled to possession either of the goods or of a document of title to them;

(c) a charge on intangible movable property (in Scotland, incorporeal moveable property) of any of the following descriptions–

(i) goodwill,

(ii) intellectual property,

(iii) book debts (whether book debts of the company or assigned to the company),

(iv) uncalled share capital of the company or calls made but not paid;

(d) a charge for securing an issue of debentures; or

(e) a floating charge on the whole or part of the company's property.

**396(2)** The descriptions of charge mentioned in subsection (1) shall be construed as follows–

(a) a charge on a debenture forming part of an issue or series shall not be treated as falling within paragraph (a) or (b) by reason of the fact that the debenture is secured by a charge on land or goods (or on an interest in land or goods);

(b) in paragraph (b) **"goods"** means any tangible movable property (in Scotland, corporeal moveable property) other than money;

(c) a charge is not excluded from paragraph (b) because the chargee is entitled to take possession in case of default or on the occurrence of some other event;

(d) in paragraph (c)(ii) **"intellectual property"** means–

(i) any patent, trade mark, service mark, registered design, copyright or design right, or

(ii) any licence under or in respect of any such right;

(e) a debenture which is part of an issue or series shall not be treated as a book debt for the purposes of paragraph (c)(iii);

(f) the deposit by way of security of a negotiable instrument given to secure the payment of book debts shall not be treated for the purposes of paragraph (c)(iii) as a charge on book debts;

(g) a shipowner's lien on subfreights shall not be treated as a charge on book debts for the purposes of paragraph (c)(iii) or as a floating charge for the purposes of paragraph (e).

**396(3)** Whether a charge is one requiring registration under this Part shall be determined–

(a) in the case of a charge created by a company, as at the date the charge is created, and

(b) in the case of a charge over property acquired by a company, as at the date of the acquisition.

**396(4)** The Secretary of State may by regulations amend subsections (1) and (2) so as to add any description of charge to, or remove any description of charge from, the charges requiring registration under this Part.

**396(5)** Regulations under this section shall be made by statutory instrument which shall be subject to annulment in pursuance of a resolution of either House of Parliament.

**396(6)** In the following provisions of this Part references to a charge are, unless the context otherwise requires, to a charge requiring registration under this Part.

Where a charge not otherwise requiring registration relates to property by virtue of which it requires to be registered and to other property, the references are to the charge so far as it relates to property of the former description.".

## 94 The companies charges register

**94** The following section is inserted in Part XII of the Companies Act 1985–

"*The companies charges register*

**397(1)** The registrar shall keep for each company a register, in such form as he thinks fit, of charges on property of the company.

**397(2)** The register shall consist of a file containing with respect to each charge the particulars and other information delivered to the registrar under the provisions of this Part.

**397(3)** Any person may require the registrar to provide a certificate stating the date on which any specified particulars of, or other information relating to, a charge were delivered to him.

**397(4)** The certificate shall be signed by the registrar or authenticated by his official seal.

**397(5)** The certificate shall be conclusive evidence that the specified particulars or other information were delivered to the registrar no later than the date stated in the certificate; and it shall be presumed unless the contrary is proved that they were not delivered earlier than that date.".

## 95 Delivery of particulars for registration

**95** The following sections are inserted in Part XII of the Companies Act 1985–

"*Company's duty to deliver particulars of charge for registration*

**398(1)** It is the duty of a company which creates a charge, or acquires property subject to a charge–

(a) to deliver the prescribed particulars of the charge, in the prescribed form, to the registrar for registration, and

(b) to do so within 21 days after the date of the charge's creation or, as the case may be, the date of the acquisition;

but particulars of a charge may be delivered for registration by any person interested in the charge.

**398(2)** Where the particulars are delivered for registration by a person other than the company concerned, that person is entitled to recover from the company the amount of any fees paid by him to the registrar in connection with the registration.

**398(3)** If a company fails to comply with subsection (1), then, unless particulars of the charge have been delivered for registration by another person, the company and every officer of it who is in default is liable to a fine.

**398(4)** Where prescribed particulars in the prescribed form are delivered to the registrar for registration, he shall file the particulars in the register and shall note, in such form as he thinks fit, the date on which they were delivered to him.

**398(5)** The registrar shall send to the company and any person appearing from the particulars to be the chargee, and if the particulars were delivered by another person interested in the charge to that person, a copy of the particulars filed by him and of the note made by him as to the date on which they were delivered.

*Effect of failure to deliver particulars for registration*

**399(1)** Where a charge is created by a company and no prescribed particulars in the prescribed form are delivered for registration within the period of 21 days after the date of the charge's creation, the charge is void against–

(a) an administrator or liquidator of the company, and

(b) any person who for value acquires an interest in or right over property subject to the charge,

where the relevant event occurs after the creation of the charge, whether before or after the end of the 21 day period.

This is subject to section 400 (late delivery of particulars).

**399(2)** In this Part **"the relevant event"** means–

(a) in relation to the voidness of a charge as against an administrator or liquidator, the beginning of the insolvency proceedings, and

(b) in relation to the voidness of a charge as against a person acquiring an interest in or right over property subject to a charge, the acquisition of that interest or right;

and references to "a relevant event" shall be construed accordingly.

**399(3)** Where a relevant event occurs on the same day as the charge is created, it shall be presumed to have occurred after the charge is created unless the contrary is proved.

*Late delivery of particulars*

**400(1)** Where prescribed particulars of a charge created by a company, in the prescribed form, are delivered for registration more than 21 days after the date of the charge's creation, section 399(1) does not apply in relation to relevant events occurring after the particulars are delivered.

**400(2)** However, where in such a case–

(a) the company is at the date of delivery of the particulars unable to pay its debts, or subsequently becomes unable to pay its debts in consequence of the transaction under which the charge is created, and

(b) insolvency proceedings begin before the end of the relevant period beginning with the date of delivery of the particulars,

the charge is void as against the administrator or liquidator.

**400(3)** For this purpose–

(a) the company is "unable to pay its debts" in the circumstances specified in section 123 of the Insolvency Act 1986; and

(b) the "relevant period" is–

  (i) two years in the case of a floating charge created in favour of a person connected with the company (within the meaning of section 249 of that Act),

(ii) one year in the case of a floating charge created in favour of a person not so connected, and

(iii) six months in any other case.

**400(4)** Where a relevant event occurs on the same day as the particulars are delivered, it shall be presumed to have occurred before the particulars are delivered unless the contrary is proved.".

## 96 Delivery of further particulars

**96** The following section is inserted in Part XII of the Companies Act 1985–

"*Delivery of further particulars*

**401(1)** Further particulars of a charge, supplementing or varying the registered particulars, may be delivered to the registrar for registration at any time.

**401(2)** Further particulars must be in the prescribed form signed by or on behalf of both the company and the chargee.

**401(3)** Where further particulars are delivered to the registrar for registration and appear to him to be duly signed, he shall file the particulars in the register and shall note, in such form as he thinks fit, the date on which they were delivered to him.

**401(4)** The registrar shall send to the company and any person appearing from the particulars to be the chargee, and if the particulars were delivered by another person interested in the charge to that other person, a copy of the further particulars filed by him and of the note made by him as to the date on which they were delivered.".

## 97 Effect of omissions and errors in registered particulars

**97** The following section is inserted in Part XII of the Companies Act 1985–

"*Effect of omissions and errors in registered particulars*

**402(1)** Where the registered particulars of a charge created by a company are not complete and accurate, the charge is void, as mentioned below to the extent that rights are not disclosed by the registered particulars which would be disclosed if they were complete and accurate.

**402(2)** The charge is void to that extent, unless the court on the application of the chargee orders otherwise, as against–

(a) an administrator or liquidator of the company, and

(b) any person who for value acquires an interest in or right over property subject to the charge,

where the relevant event occurs at a time when the particulars are incomplete or inaccurate in a relevant respect.

**402(3)** Where a relevant event occurs on the same day as particulars or further particulars are delivered, it shall be presumed to have occurred before those particulars are delivered unless the contrary is proved.

**402(4)** The court may order that the charge is effective as against an administrator or liquidator of the company if it is satisfied–

(a) that the omission or error is not likely to have misled materially to his prejudice any unsecured creditor of the company, or

(b) that no person became an unsecured creditor of the company at a time when the registered particulars of the charge were incomplete or inaccurate in a relevant respect.

**402(5)** The court may order that the charge is effective as against a person acquiring an interest in or right over property subject to the charge if it is satisfied that he did not rely, in connection with the acquisition, on registered particulars which were incomplete or inaccurate in a relevant respect.

**402(6)** For the purposes of this section an omission or inaccuracy with respect to the name of the chargee shall not be regarded as a failure to disclose the rights of the chargee.".

## 98 Memorandum of charge ceasing to affect company's property

**98** The following section is inserted in Part XII of the Companies Act 1985–

"*Memorandum of charge ceasing to affect company's property*

**403(1)** Where a charge of which particulars have been delivered ceases to affect the company's property, a memorandum to that effect may be delivered to the registrar for registration.

**403(2)** The memorandum must be in the prescribed form signed by or on behalf of both the company and the chargee.

**403(3)** Where a memorandum is delivered to the registrar for registration and appears to him to be duly signed, he shall file it in the register, and shall note, in such form as he thinks fit, the date on which it was delivered to him.

**403(4)** The registrar shall send to the company and any person appearing from the memorandum to be the chargee, and if the memorandum was delivered by another person interested in the charge to that person, a copy of the memorandum filed by him and of the note made by him as to the date on which it was delivered.

**403(5)** If a duly signed memorandum is delivered in a case where the charge in fact continues to affect the company's property, the charge is void as against–

(a) an administrator or liquidator of the company, and

(b) any person who for value acquires an interest in or right over property subject to the charge,

where the relevant event occurs after the delivery of the memorandum.

**403(6)** Where a relevant event occurs on the same day as the memorandum is delivered, it shall be presumed to have occurred before the memorandum is delivered unless the contrary is proved.".

## 99 Further provisions with respect to voidness of charges

**99** The following sections are inserted in Part XII of the Companies Act 1985–

"FURTHER PROVISIONS WITH RESPECT TO VOIDNESS OF CHARGES

*Exclusion of voidness as against unregistered charges*

**404(1)** A charge is not void by virtue of this Part as against a subsequent charge unless some or all of the relevant particulars of that charge are duly delivered for registration–

(a) within 21 days after the date of its creation, or

(b) before complete and accurate relevant particulars of the earlier charge are duly delivered for registration.

**404(2)** Where relevant particulars of the subsequent charge so delivered are incomplete or inaccurate, the earlier charge is void as against that charge only to the extent that rights are disclosed by registered particulars of the subsequent charge duly delivered for registration before the corresponding relevant particulars of the earlier charge.

**404(3)** The relevant particulars of a charge for the purposes of this section are those prescribed particulars relating to rights inconsistent with those conferred by or in relation to the other charge.

*Restrictions on voidness by virtue of this Part*

**405(1)** A charge is not void by virtue of this Part as against a person acquiring an interest in or right over property where the acquisition is expressly subject to the charge.

**405(2)** Nor is a charge void by virtue of this Part in relation to any property by reason of a relevant event occurring after the company which created the charge has disposed of the whole of its interest in that property.

*Effect of exercise of power of sale*

**406(1)** A chargee exercising a power of sale may dispose of property to a purchaser freed from any interest or right arising from the charge having become void to any extent by virtue of this Part–

(a) against an administrator or liquidator of the company, or

(b) against a person acquiring a security interest over property subject to the charge;

and a purchaser is not concerned to see or inquire whether the charge has become so void.

**406(2)** The proceeds of the sale shall be held by the chargee in trust to be applied–

First, in discharge of any sum effectively secured by prior incumbrances to which the sale is not made subject;

Second, in payment of all costs, charges and expenses properly incurred by him in connection with the sale, or any previous attempted sale, of the property;

Third, in discharge of any sum effectively secured by the charge and incumbrances ranking *pari passu* with the charge;

Fourth, in discharge of any sum effectively secured by incumbrances ranking after the charge;

and any residue is payable to the company or to a person authorised to give a receipt for the proceeds of the sale of the property.

**406(3)** For the purposes of subsection (2)–

(a) prior incumbrances include any incumbrance to the extent that the charge is void as against it by virtue of this Part; and

(b) no sum is effectively secured by a charge to the extent that it is void as against an administrator or liquidator of the company.

**406(4)** In this section–

(a) references to things done by a chargee include things done by a receiver appointed by him, whether or not the receiver acts as his agent;

(b) **"power of sale"** includes any power to dispose of, or grant an interest out of, property for the purpose of enforcing a charge (but in relation to Scotland does not include the power to grant a lease), and references to **"sale"** shall be construed accordingly; and

(c) **"purchaser"** means a person who in good faith and for valuable consideration acquires an interest in property.

**406(5)** The provisions of this section as to the order of application of the proceeds of sale have effect subject to any other statutory provision (in Scotland, any other statutory provision or rule of law) applicable in any case.

**406(6)** Where a chargee exercising a power of sale purports to dispose of property freed from any such interest or right as is mentioned in subsection (1) to a person other than a purchaser, the above provisions apply, with any necessary modifications, in relation to a disposition to a purchaser by that person or any successor in title of his.

**406(7)** In Scotland, subsections (2) and (7) of section 27 of the Conveyancing and Feudal Reform (Scotland) Act 1970 apply to a chargee unable to obtain a discharge for any payment which he is required to make under subsection (2) above as they apply to a creditor in the circumstances mentioned in those subsections.

*Effect of voidness on obligation secured*

**407(1)** Where a charge becomes void to any extent by virtue of this Part, the whole of the sum secured by the charge is payable forthwith on demand; and this applies notwithstanding that the sum secured by the charge is also the subject of other security.

**407(2)** Where the charge is to secure the repayment of money, the references in subsection (1) to the sum secured include any interest payable.".

## 100 Additional information to be registered

**100** The following sections are inserted in Part XII of the Companies Act 1985–

"ADDITIONAL INFORMATION TO BE REGISTERED

*Particulars of taking up of issue of debentures*

**408(1)** Where particulars of a charge for securing an issue of debentures have been delivered for registration, it is the duty of the company–

(a) to deliver to the registrar for registration particulars in the prescribed form of the date on which any debentures of the issue are taken up, and of the amount taken up, and

(b) to do so before the end of the period of 21 days after the date on which they are taken up.

**408(2)** Where particulars in the prescribed form are delivered to the registrar for registration under this section, he shall file them in the register.

**408(3)** If a company fails to comply with subsection (1), the company and every officer of it who is in default is liable to a fine.

*Notice of appointment of receiver or manager, etc.*

**409(1)** If a person obtains an order for the appointment of a receiver or manager of a company's property, or appoints such a receiver or manager under powers contained in an instrument, he shall within seven days of the order or of the appointment under those powers, give notice of that fact in the prescribed form to the registrar for registration.

**409(2)** Where a person appointed receiver or manager of a company's property under powers contained in an instrument ceases to act as such receiver or manager, he shall, on so ceasing, give notice of that fact in the prescribed form to the registrar for registration.

**409(3)** Where a notice under this section in the prescribed form is delivered to the registrar for registration, he shall file it in the register.

**409(4)** If a person makes default in complying with the requirements of subsection (1) or (2), he is liable to a fine.

**409(5)** This section does not apply in relation to companies registered in Scotland (for which corresponding provision is made by sections 53, 54 and 62 of the Insolvency Act 1986).

*Notice of crystallisation of floating charge, etc.*

**410(1)** The Secretary of State may by regulations require notice in the prescribed form to be given to the registrar of–

(a) the occurrence of such events as may be prescribed affecting the nature of the security under a floating charge of which particulars have been delivered for registration, and

(b) the taking of such action in exercise of powers conferred by a fixed or floating charge of which particulars have been delivered for registration, or conferred in relation to such a charge by an order of the court, as may be prescribed.

**410(2)** The regulations may make provision as to–

(a) the persons by whom notice is required to be, or may be, given, and the period within which notice is required to be given;

(b) the filing in the register of the particulars contained in the notice and the noting of the date on which the notice was given; and

(c) the consequences of failure to give notice.

**410(3)** As regards the consequences of failure to give notice of an event causing a floating charge to crystallise, the regulations may include provision to the effect that the crystallisation–

(a) shall be treated as ineffective until the prescribed particulars are delivered, and

(b) if the prescribed particulars are delivered after the expiry of the prescribed period, shall continue to be ineffective against such persons as may be prescribed,

subject to the exercise of such powers as may be conferred by the regulations on the court.

**410(4)** The regulations may provide that if there is a failure to comply with such of the requirements of the regulations as may be prescribed, such persons as may be prescribed are liable to a fine.

**410(5)** Regulations under this section shall be made by statutory instrument which shall be subject to annulment in pursuance of a resolution of either House of Parliament.

**410(6)** Regulations under this section shall not apply in relation to a floating charge created under the law of Scotland by a company registered in Scotland.".

COPIES OF INSTRUMENTS AND REGISTER TO BE KEPT BY COMPANY

## 101 Copies of instruments and register to be kept by company

**101** The following sections are inserted in Part XII of the Companies Act 1985–

"COPIES OF INSTRUMENTS AND REGISTER TO BE KEPT BY COMPANY

*Duty to keep copies of instruments and register*

**411(1)** Every company shall keep at its registered office a copy of every instrument creating or evidencing a charge over the company's property.

In the case of a series of uniform debentures, a copy of one debenture of the series is sufficient.

**411(2)** Every company shall also keep at its registered office a register of all such charges, containing entries for each charge giving a short description of the property charged, the amount of the charge and (except in the case of securities to bearer) the names of the persons entitled to it.

**411(3)** This section applies to any charge, whether or not particulars are required to be delivered to the registrar for registration.

**411(4)** If a company fails to comply with any requirement of this section, the company and every officer of if who is in default is liable to a fine.

*Inspection of copies and register*

**412(1)** The copies and the register referred to in section 411 shall be open to the inspection of any creditor or member of the company without fee; and to the inspection of any other person on payment of such fee as may be prescribed.

**412(2)** Any person may request the company to provide him with a copy of–

(a) any instrument creating or evidencing a charge over the company's property, or

(b) any entry in the register of charges kept by the company, on payment of such fee as may be prescribed.

This subsection applies to any charge, whether or not particulars are required to be delivered to the registrar for registration.

**412(3)** The company shall send the copy to him not later than ten days after the day on which the request is received or, if later, on which payment is received.

**412(4)** If inspection of the copies or register is refused, or a copy requested is not sent within the time specified above–

(a) the company and every officer of it who is in default is liable to a fine, and

(b) the court may by order compel an immediate inspection of the copies or register or, as the case may be, direct that the copy be sent immediately.".

SUPPLEMENTARY PROVISIONS

## 102 Power to make further provision by regulations

**102** The following section is inserted in Part XII of the Companies Act 1985–

"SUPPLEMENTARY PROVISIONS

*Power to make further provision by regulations*

**413(1)** The Secretary of State may by regulations make further provision as to the application of the provisions of this Part in relation to charges of any description specified in the regulations.

Nothing in the following provisions shall be construed as restricting the generality of that power.

**413(2)** The regulations may require that where the charge is contained in or evidenced or varied by a written instrument there shall be delivered to the registrar for registration, instead of particulars or further particulars of the charge, the instrument itself or a certified copy of it together with such particulars as may be prescribed.

**413(3)** The regulations may provide that a memorandum of a charge ceasing to affect property of the company shall not be accepted by the registrar unless supported by such evidence as may be prescribed, and that a memorandum not so supported shall be treated as not having been delivered.

**413(4)** The regulations may also provide that where the instrument creating the charge is delivered to the registrar in support of such a memorandum, the registrar may mark the instrument as cancelled before returning it and shall send copies of the instrument cancelled to such persons as may be prescribed.

**413(5)** The regulations may exclude or modify, in such circumstances and to such extent as may be prescribed, the operation of the provisions of this Part relating to the voidness of a charge.

**413(6)** The regulations may require, in connection with the delivery of particulars, further particulars or a memorandum of the charge's ceasing to affect property of the company, the delivery of such supplementary information as may be prescribed, and may–

(a) apply in relation to such supplementary information any provisions of this Part relating to particulars, further particulars or such a memorandum, and

(b) provide that the particulars, further particulars or memorandum shall be treated as not having been delivered until the required supplementary information is delivered.

**413(7)** Regulations under this section shall be made by statutory instrument which shall be subject to annulment in pursuance of a resolution of either House of Parliament.".

## 103 Other supplementary provisions

**103** The following sections are inserted in Part XII of the Companies Act 1985–

"*Date of creation of charge*

**414(1)** References in this Part to the date of creation of a charge by a company shall be construed as follows.

**414(2)** A charge created under the law of England and Wales shall be taken to be created–

(a) in the case of a charge created by an instrument in writing, when the instrument is executed by the company or, if its execution by the company is conditional, upon the conditions being fulfilled, and

(b) in any other case, when an enforceable agreement is entered into by the company conferring a security interest intended to take effect forthwith or upon the company acquiring an interest in property subject to the charge.

**414(3)** A charge created under the law of Scotland shall be taken to be created–

(a) in the case of a floating charge, when the instrument creating the floating charge is executed by the company, and

(b) in any other case, when the right of the person entitled to the benefit of the charge is constituted as a real right.

**414(4)** Where a charge is created in the United Kingdom but comprises property outside the United Kingdom, any further proceedings necessary to make the charge valid or effectual under the law of the country where the property is situated shall be disregarded in ascertaining the date on which the charge is to be taken to be created.

*Prescribed particulars and related expressions*

**415(1)** References in this Part to the prescribed particulars of a charge are to such particulars of, or relating to, the charge as may be prescribed.

**415(2)** The prescribed particulars may, without prejudice to the generality of subsection (1), include–

(a) whether the company has undertaken not to create other charges ranking in priority to or *pari passu* with the charge, and

(b) whether the charge is a market charge within the meaning of Part VII of the Companies Act 1989 or a charge to which the provisions of that Part apply as they apply to a market charge.

**415(3)** References in this Part to the registered particulars of a charge at any time are to such particulars and further particulars of the charge as have at that time been duly delivered for registration.

**415(4)** References in this Part to the registered particulars of a charge being complete and accurate at any time are to their including all the prescribed particulars which would be required to be delivered if the charge were then newly created.

*Notice of matters disclosed on register*

**416(1)** A person taking a charge over a company's property shall be taken to have notice of any matter requiring registration and disclosed on the register at the time the charge is created.

**416(2)** Otherwise, a person shall not be taken to have notice of any matter by reason of its being disclosed on the register or by reason of his having failed to search the register in the course of making such inquiries as ought reasonably to be made.

**416(3)** The above provisions have effect subject to any other statutory provision as to whether a person is to be taken to have notice of any matter disclosed on the register.

*Power of court to dispense with signature*

**417(1)** Where it is proposed to deliver further particulars of a charge, or to deliver a memorandum of a charge ceasing to affect the company's property, and–

(a) the chargee refuses to sign or authorise a person to sign on his behalf, or cannot be found, or

(b) the company refuses to authorise a person to sign on its behalf,

the court may on the application of the company or the chargee, or of any other person having a sufficient interest in the matter, authorise the delivery of the particulars or memorandum without that signature.

**417(2)** The order may be made on such terms as appear to the court to be appropriate.

**417(3)** Where particulars or a memorandum are delivered to the registrar for registration in reliance on an order under this section, they must be accompanied by an office copy of the order.

In such a case the references in sections 401 and 403 to the particulars or memorandum being duly signed are to their being otherwise duly signed.

**417(4)** The registrar shall file the office copy of the court order along with the particulars or memorandum.".

# 104 Interpretation, etc.

**104** The following sections are inserted in Part XII of the Companies Act 1985–

Britain, subject to such exceptions, adaptations or modifications as may be specified in the regulations.

Regulations under this subsection shall be made by statutory instrument which shall be subject to annulment in pursuance of a resolution of either House of Parliament.

**Note**
See the Foreign Companies (Execution of Documents) Regulations 1994 (SI 1994/950), as amended.

**130(7) [Consequential amendments]** Schedule 17 contains further minor and consequential amendments relating to company contracts, the execution of documents by companies and related matters.

## 133 Issue of redeemable shares

**133(1) [Amendment of Pt. V, Ch. III of 1985 Act]** In Part V of the Companies Act 1985 (share capital, its increase, maintenance and reduction), Chapter III (redeemable shares, purchase by a company of its own shares) is amended as follows.

**133(2) [Insertion of s. 159A]** After section 159 (power to issue redeemable shares) insert–

"*Terms and manner of redemption*

> **159A(1)** Redeemable shares may not be issued unless the following conditions are satisfied as regards the terms and manner of redemption.
>
> **159A(2)** The date on or by which, or dates between which, the shares are to be or may be redeemed must be specified in the company's articles or, if the articles so provide, fixed by the directors, and in the latter case the date or dates must be fixed before the shares are issued.
>
> **159A(3)** Any other circumstances in which the shares are to be or may be redeemed must be specified in the company's articles.
>
> **159A(4)** The amount payable on redemption must be specified in, or determined in accordance with, the company's articles, and in the latter case the articles must not provide for the amount to be determined by reference to any person's discretion or opinion.
>
> **159A(5)** Any other terms and conditions of redemption shall be specified in the company's articles.
>
> **159A(6)** Nothing in this section shall be construed as requiring a company to provide in its articles for any matter for which provision is made by this Act.".

**133(3) [Amendment of s. 160]** In section 160 (financing, etc. of redemption)–

(a) omit subsection (3) (which is superseded by the new section 159A), and

(b) in subsection (4) (cancellation of shares on redemption) for "redeemed under this section" substitute "redeemed under this Chapter".

**133(4) [Substitution of s. 162(2)]** In section 162 (power of company to purchase own shares), for subsection (2) (application of provisions relating to redeemable shares) substitute–

> "(2) Sections 159, 160 and 161 apply to the purchase by a company under this section of its own shares as they apply to the redemption of redeemable shares.".

**Note**
S. 133 unlikely to be brought into force.

## 134 Disclosure of interests in shares

**134(1)–(5)** (Amendment of Companies Act 1985, Part VI.)

**134(6) [Regulations]** Any regulations made under section 209(1)(j) which are in force immediately before the repeal of that paragraph by this Act shall have effect as if made under section 210A(1)(d) as inserted by subsection (5) above.

**Note**
See note to CA 1985, s. 210A(1).

## 135 Orders imposing restrictions on shares

**135(1) [Regulations]** The Secretary of State may by regulations made by statutory instrument make such amendments of the provisions of the Companies Act 1985 relating to orders imposing restrictions on shares as appear to him necessary or expedient–

(a) for enabling orders to be made in a form protecting the rights of third parties;

(b) with respect to the circumstances in which restrictions may be relaxed or removed;

(c) with respect to the making of interim orders by a court.

**135(2) [Relevant provisions]** The provisions referred to in subsection (1) are section 210(5), section 216(1) and (2), section 445 and Part XV of the Companies Act 1985.

**135(3) [Supplementary provisions]** The regulations may make different provision for different cases and may contain such transitional and other supplementary and incidental provisions as appear to the Secretary of State to be appropriate.

**135(4) [Approval by Parliament]** Regulations under this section shall not be made unless a draft of the regulations has been laid before Parliament and approved by resolution of each House of Parliament.

**Note**

S. 135 in force from 7 January 1991 (see SI 1990/2569 (C 68)).

See the Companies (Disclosure of Interests in Shares) (Orders imposing restrictions on shares) Regulations 1991 (SI 1991/1646).

## 140 Floating charges (Scotland)

**140(1)–(6)** (Amendments in Companies Act 1985, s. 463(1), 464(1)(b), (1A), (3), (5)).

**140(7) [Insertion in s. 464(6)]** In subsection (6) after the words "subject to" there shall be inserted the words "Part XII and to".

**140(8) [Amendment of s. 466]** In section 466 of the Companies Act 1985 (alteration of floating charges), subsections (4) and (5) and in subsection (6) the words "falling under subsection (4) of this section" shall cease to have effect.

## 142 Abolition of doctrine of deemed notice

**142(1) [Insertion of s. 711A of 1985 Act]** In Part XXIV of the Companies Act 1985 (the registrar of companies, his functions and offices), after section 711 insert–

"*Exclusion of deemed notice*

**711A(1)** A person shall not be taken to have notice of any matter merely because of its being disclosed in any document kept by the registrar of companies (and thus available for inspection) or made available by the company for inspection.

**711A(2)** This does not affect the question whether a person is affected by notice of any matter by reason of a failure to make such inquiries as ought reasonably to be made.

**711A(3)** In this section "document" includes any material which contains information.

**711A(4)** Nothing in this section affects the operation of–

(a) section 416 of this Act (under which a person taking a charge over a company's property is deemed to have notice of matters disclosed on the companies charges register), or

(b) section 198 of the Law of Property Act 1925 as it applies by virtue of section 3(7) of the Land Charges Act 1972 (under which the registration of certain land charges under Part XII, or Chapter III of Part XXIII, of this Act is deemed to constitute actual notice for all purposes connected with the land affected).".

**142(2) [Insertion in Sch. 22]** In Schedule 22 to the Companies Act 1985 (unregistered companies), in the entry for Part XXIV at the appropriate place insert–

| | | |
|---|---|---|
| "Section 711A | Abolition of doctrine of deemed notice. | Subject to section 718(3).". |

**Note**

See note to Part IV.

## 144 "Subsidiary", "holding company" and "wholly-owned subsidiary"

**144(1)** (Substitution of Companies Act 1985, s. 736, 736A.)

**144(2) [Reference in other enactment]** Any reference in any enactment (including any enactment contained in subordinate legislation within the meaning of the Interpretation Act 1978) to a "subsidiary" or "holding company" within the meaning of section 736 of the Companies Act 1985 shall, subject to any express amendment or saving made by or under this Act, be read as referring to a subsidiary or holding company as defined in section 736 as substituted by subsection (1) above.

This applies whether the reference is specific or general, or express or implied.

**Note**
See note after s. 144(6).

**144(3)** (Insertion of Companies Act 1985, s. 736B.)

**144(4) [Consequential amendments]** Schedule 18 contains amendments and savings consequential on the amendments made by this section; and the Secretary of State may by regulations make such further amendments or savings as appear to him to be necessary or expedient.

**Note**
In regard to Electricity Act 1989 see the Definition of Subsidiary (Consequential Amendments) Regulations 1990 (SI 1990/1395).

**144(5) [Regulations by statutory instrument]** Regulations under this section shall be made by statutory instrument which shall be subject to annulment in pursuance of a resolution of either House of Parliament.

**Note**
See note after s. 144(6).

**144(6) [Non-application of Interpretation Act 1978, s. 23(3)]** So much of section 23(3) of the Interpretation Act 1978 as applies section 17(2)(a) of that Act (presumption as to meaning of references to enactments repealed and re-enacted) to deeds or other instruments or documents does not apply in relation to the repeal and re-enactment by this section of section 736 of the Companies Act 1985.

**Note**
S. 144(2), (5) and (6) in force from 1 November 1990 subject to transitional provisions (see SI 1990/1392 (C 41)).

# PART VI – MERGERS AND RELATED MATTERS

## 152 Fees

**152(1) [Regulations]** The Secretary of State may by regulations made by statutory instrument require the payment to him or to the Director of such fees as may be prescribed by the regulations in connection with the exercise by the Secretary of State, the Director and the Commission of their functions under Part V of the Fair Trading Act 1973.

**Note**
See the Merger (Fees) Regulations 1990 (SI 1990/1660).

**152(2) [Scope of regulations]** The regulations may provide for fees to be payable–

(a) in respect of–
  (i) an application for the consent of the Secretary of State under section 58(1) of the Fair Trading Act 1973 to the transfer of a newspaper or of newspaper assets, and
  (ii) a notice under section 75A(1) of that Act, and

(b) on the occurrence of any event specified in the regulations.

**152(3) [S. 152(2)(b) events]** The events that may be specified in the regulations by virtue of subsection (2)(b) above include–

(a) the making by the Secretary of State of a merger reference to the Commission under section 64 or 75 of the Fair Trading Act 1973,

(b) the announcement by the Secretary of State of his decision not to make a merger reference in any case where, at the time the announcement is made, he would under one of those sections have power to make such a reference.

**152(4) [Further provisions]** The regulations may also contain provision–

(a) for ascertaining the persons by whom fees are payable,

(b) specifying whether any fee is payable to the Secretary of State or to the Director,

(c) for the amount of any fee to be calculated by reference to matters which may include–

(i) in a case involving functions of the Secretary of State under sections 57 to 61 of the Fair Trading Act 1973, the number of newspapers concerned, the number of separate editions (determined in accordance with the regulations) of each newspaper and the average circulation per day of publication (within the meaning of Part V of that Act) of each newspaper, and

(ii) in any other case, the value (determined in accordance with the regulations) of any assets concerned,

(d) as to the time when any fee is to be paid, and

(e) for the repayment by the Secretary of State or the Director of the whole or part of any fee in specified circumstances.

**152(5) [Different provision for different cases]** The regulations may make different provision for different cases.

**152(6) [Without prejudice to s. 152(1)]** Subsections (2) to (5) above do not prejudice the generality of subsection (1) above.

**152(7) [Costs taken into account]** In determining the amount of any fees to be prescribed by the regulations, the Secretary of State may take into account all costs incurred by him and by the Director in respect of the exercise by him, by the Commission and by the Director of their respective functions–

(a) under Part V of the Fair Trading Act 1973, and

(b) under Parts I, VII and VIII of that Act in relation to merger references or other matters arising under Part V.

**152(8) [Annulment by Parliament]** A statutory instrument containing regulations under this section shall be subject to annulment in pursuance of a resolution of either House of Parliament.

**152(9) [Destination of fees]** Fees paid to the Secretary of State or the Director under this section shall be paid into the Consolidated Fund.

**152(10) [Definitions]** In this section–

**"the Commission"**,
**"the Director"**, and
**"merger reference"**,

have the same meaning as in the Fair Trading Act 1973, and **"newspaper"** has the same meaning as in Part V of that Act.

**152(11) [Water Act 1989]** References in this section to Part V of the Fair Trading Act 1973 and to merger references under section 64 or 75 of that Act or under that Part include sections 32 and 34 of the Water Industry Act 1991 and any reference under section 32 of that Act.

**Notes**

In s. 152(11) the words "include sections 32 and 34 of the Water Industry Act 1991 and any reference under section 32 of that Act" appearing after the words "under that Part" substituted for the former words "include sections 29 and 30 of the Water Act 1989 and any reference under section 29 of that Act" by the Water Consolidation (Consequential Provisions) Act 1991, s. 2(1), Sch. 1, para. 52 as from 1 December 1991.
S. 152 in force from 1 March 1990 (see SI 1990/142 (C 5)).

# PART VII – FINANCIAL MARKETS AND INSOLVENCY

**Note**

Pt. VII, Sch. 21 and 22 are in force from 25 April 1991, except where stated otherwise, as a result of SI 1991/878 (C 21), art. 2 and Sch. subject to saving provisions in art. 3 relating to s. 157, 160, 166, 174(1), 175, 177, 179 and 180. Regulations making powers in s. 155(4), (5), 158(4), (5), 160(5), 173(4), (5), 174(2)–(4), 185, 186, 187(3) and Sch. 21, para. 2(3) are in force from 25 March 1991 as a result of SI 1991/488 (C 11), art. 2(2). The regulations are the Financial Markets and Insolvency Regulations 1991 (SI 1991/880).

## INTRODUCTION

## 154 Introduction

**154** This Part has effect for the purposes of safeguarding the operation of certain financial markets by provisions with respect to–

(a) the insolvency, winding up or default of a person party to transactions in the market (sections 155 to 172),

(b) the effectiveness or enforcement of certain charges given to secure obligations in connection with such transactions (sections 173 to 176), and

(c) rights and remedies in relation to certain property provided as cover for margin in relation to such transactions or subject to such a charge (sections 177 to 181).

## RECOGNISED INVESTMENT EXCHANGES AND CLEARING HOUSES

## 155 Market contracts

**155(1) ["Market contracts"]** This Part applies to the following descriptions of contract connected with a recognised investment exchange or recognised clearing house.

The contracts are referred to in this Part as "market contracts".

**155(2) [Recognised investment exchange]** Except as provided in subsection (2A), in relation to a recognised investment exchange this Part applies to–

(a) contracts entered into by a member or designated non-member of the exchange with a person other than the exchange which are either

(i) contracts made on the exchange or on an exchange to whose undertaking the exchange has succeeded whether by amalgamation, merger or otherwise; or

(ii) contracts in the making of which the member or designated non-member was subject to the rules of the exchange or of an exchange to whose undertaking the exchange has succeeded whether by amalgamation, merger or otherwise; and

(b) contracts entered into by the exchange with its members for the purpose of enabling the rights and liabilities of that member under transactions in investments to be settled.

A **"designated non-member"** means a person in respect of whom action may be taken under the default rules of the exchange but who is not a member of the exchange.

**History**

In s. 155(2)(a) the words "with a person other than the exchange" inserted after the word "exchange" where it first appears and s. 155(2)(b) replaced by the Financial Markets and Insolvency Regulations 1998 (SI 1998/1748), reg. 1, 2, 3(a) and (b) respectively as from 11 August 1998. S. 155(2)(b) formerly read as follows:

"contracts subject to the rules of the exchange entered into by the exchange for the purposes of or in connection with the provision of clearing services."

See history note after s. 155(2A).

**155(2A) [Recognised overseas investment exchange]** This Part does not apply to contracts falling within paragraph (a) of subsection (2) above where the exchange in question is a recognised overseas investment exchange.

**History**

S. 155(2) and 155(2A) substituted for former s. 155(2) by the Financial Markets and Insolvency Regulations 1991 (SI 1991/880), reg. 1 and 3 as from 25 April 1991; s. 155(2) formerly read as follows:

"In relation to a recognised investment exchange, this Part applies to–

(a) contracts entered into by a member or designated non-member of the exchange which are made on or otherwise subject to the rules of the exchange; and

(b) contracts subject to the rules of the exchange entered into by the exchange for the purposes of or in connection with the provision of clearing services.

A **"designated non-member"** means a person in respect of whom action may be taken under the default rules of the exchange but who is not a member of the exchange."

**155(3) [Recognised clearing house]** In relation to a recognised clearing house, this Part applies to contracts entered into by the clearing house with a member of the clearing house for the purpose of enabling the rights and liabilities of that member under transactions in investments to be settled.

**History**

S. 155(3) replaced by the Financial Markets and Insolvency Regulations 1998 (SI 1998/1748), reg. 1, 2, 4 as from 11 August 1998. S. 155(3) formerly read as follows:

"In relation to a recognised clearing house, this Part applies to contracts subject to the rules of the clearing house entered into by the clearing house for the purposes of or in connection with the provision of clearing services for a recognised investment exchange."

**155(4) [Regulations]** The Secretary of State may by regulations make further provision as to the contracts to be treated as "market contracts", for the purposes of this Part, in relation to a recognised investment exchange or recognised clearing house.

**Note**

See the Financial Markets and Insolvency Regulations 1991 (SI 1991/880).

**155(5) [Scope of regulations]** The regulations may add to, amend or repeal the provisions of subsections (2) and (3) above.

**Note**

See the Financial Markets and Insolvency Regulations 1998 (SI 1998/1748).

## 156 Additional requirements for recognition: default rules, etc.

**156(1) [Sch. 21]** The Financial Services Act 1986 shall have effect as if the requirements set out in Schedule 21 to this Act (the "additional requirements") were among those specified in that Act for recognition of an investment exchange or clearing house.

**156(2) [Contents of Schedule]** In particular, that Act shall have effect–

(a) as if the requirements set out in Part I of that Schedule were among those specified in Schedule 4 to that Act (requirements for recognition of UK investment exchange),

(b) as if the requirements set out in Part II of that Schedule were among those specified in section 39(4) of that Act (requirements for recognition of UK clearing house), and

(c) as if the requirement set out in Part III of that Schedule was among those specified in section 40(2) of that Act (requirements for recognition of overseas investment exchange or clearing house).

**156(3) [Notice by Secretary of State]** The additional requirements do not affect the status of an investment exchange or clearing house recognised before the commencement of this section, but if the Secretary of State is of the opinion that any of those requirements is not met in the case of such a body, he shall within one month of commencement give notice to the body stating his opinion.

**156(3A) [Default rules]** Nothing in subsection (2)(a) or (b) shall be taken as requiring a UK investment exchange or a UK clearing house which does not enter into such contracts as are mentioned in section 155(2)(b) or (3) to have default rules relating to such contracts.

**History**

S. 156(3A) inserted by the Financial Markets and Insolvency Regulations 1996 (SI 1996/1469), reg. 1, 9 as from 15 July 1996.

**156(4) [Six month notice period]** Where the Secretary of State gives such a notice, he shall not–

(a) take action to revoke the recognition of such a body on the ground that any of the additional requirements is not met, unless he considers it essential to do so in the interests of investors, or

(b) apply on any such ground for a compliance order under section 12 of the Financial Services Act 1986,

until after the end of the period of six months beginning with the date on which the notice was given.

**156(5) [Extension of period]** The Secretary of State may extend, or further extend, that period if he considers there is good reason to do so.

(b) shall be taken into account for the purposes of any rule of law relating to set-off applicable in sequestration or winding up,

in the same way as a debt due before the date of sequestration (within the meaning of section 73(1) of the Bankruptcy (Scotland) Act 1985) or the commencement of the winding up (within the meaning of section 129 of the Insolvency Act 1986).

**163(4) [Notice]** However, where (or to the extent that) a sum is taken into account by virtue of subsection (2)(b) or (3)(b) which arises from a contract entered into at a time when the creditor had notice–

(a) that a bankruptcy petition or, in Scotland, a petition for sequestration was pending, or

(b) that a meeting of creditors had been summoned under section 98 of the Insolvency Act 1986 or that a winding-up petition was pending,

the value of any profit to him arising from the sum being so taken into account (or being so taken into account to that extent) is recoverable from him by the relevant office-holder unless the court directs otherwise.

**Note**
See Act of Sederunt (Applications under Part VII of the Companies Act 1989) 1991 (SI 1991/145 (S 10)).

**163(5) [Non-application of s. 163(4)]** Subsection (4) does not apply in relation to a sum arising from a contract effected under the default rules of a recognised investment exchange or recognised clearing house.

**163(6) [Priority]** Any sum recoverable by virtue of subsection (4) ranks for priority, in the event of the insolvency of the person from whom it is due, immediately before preferential or, in Scotland, preferred debts.

**Note**
See note after s. 182.

## 164 Disclaimer of property, rescission of contracts, etc.

**164(1) [Disapplication of Insolvency Act 1986, s. 178, 186, 315, 345]** Sections 178, 186, 315 and 345 of the Insolvency Act 1986 (power to disclaim onerous property and court's power to order rescission of contracts, etc.) do not apply in relation to–

(a) a market contract, or

(b) a contract effected by the exchange or clearing house for the purpose of realising property provided as margin in relation to market contracts.

In the application of this subsection in Scotland, the reference to sections 178, 315 and 345 shall be construed as a reference to any rule of law having the like effect as those sections.

**164(2) [Scotland]** In Scotland, a permanent trustee on the sequestrated estate of a defaulter or a liquidator is bound by any market contract to which that defaulter is a party and by any contract as is mentioned in subsection (1 )(b) above notwithstanding section 42 of the Bankruptcy (Scotland) Act 1985 or any rule of law to the like effect applying in liquidations.

**164(3) [Disapplication of Insolvency Act 1986, s. 127, 284]** Sections 127 and 284 of the Insolvency Act 1986 (avoidance of property dispositions effected after commencement of winding up or presentation of bankruptcy petition), and section 32(8) of the Bankruptcy (Scotland) Act 1985 (effect of dealing with debtor relating to estate vested in permanent trustee), do not apply to–

(a) a market contract, or any disposition of property in pursuance of such a contract,

(b) the provision of margin in relation to market contracts,

(c) a contract effected by the exchange or clearing house for the purpose of realising property provided as margin in relation to a market contract, or any disposition of property in pursuance of such a contract, or

(d) any disposition of property in accordance with the rules of the exchange or clearing house as to the application of property provided as margin.

**164(4) [Notice]** However, where–

(a) a market contract is entered into by a person who has notice that a petition has been presented for the winding up or bankruptcy or sequestration of the estate of the other party to the contract, or

(b) margin in relation to a market contract is accepted by a person who has notice that such a petition has been presented in relation to the person by whom or on whose behalf the margin is provided,

the value of any profit to him arising from the contract or, as the case may be, the amount or value of the margin is recoverable from him by the relevant office-holder unless the court directs otherwise.

**Note**

See Act of Sederunt (Applications under Part VII of the Companies Act 1989) 1991 (SI 1991/145 (S 10)).

**164(5) [Non-application of s. 164(4)]** Subsection (4)(a) does not apply where the person entering into the contract is a recognised investment exchange or recognised clearing house acting in accordance with its rules, or where the contract is effected under the default rules of such an exchange or clearing house; but subsection (4)(b) applies in relation to the provision of margin in relation to such a contract.

**164(6) [Priority]** Any sum recoverable by virtue of subsection (4) ranks for priority, in the event of the insolvency of the person from whom it is due, immediately before preferential or, in Scotland, preferred debts.

**Note**

See note after s. 182.

## 165 Adjustment of prior transactions

**165(1) [Disapplication of Insolvency Act 1986 provisions]** No order shall be made in relation to a transaction to which this section applies under–

(a) section 238 or 339 of the Insolvency Act 1986 (transactions at an under-value),

(b) section 239 or 340 of that Act (preferences), or

(c) section 423 of that Act (transactions defrauding creditors).

**165(2) [Scotland]** As respects Scotland, no decree shall be granted in relation to any such transaction–

(a) under section 34 or 36 of the Bankruptcy (Scotland) Act 1985 or section 242 or 243 of the Insolvency Act 1986 (gratuitous alienations and unfair preferences), or

(b) at common law on grounds of gratuitous alienations or fraudulent preferences.

**165(3) [Application]** This section applies to–

(a) a market contract to which a recognised investment exchange or recognised clearing house is a party or which is entered into under its default rules, and

(b) a disposition of property in pursuance of such a market contract.

**165(4) [Margin]** Where margin is provided in relation to a market contract and (by virtue of subsection (3)(a) or otherwise) no such order or decree as is mentioned in subsection (1) or (2) has been, or could be, made in relation to that contract, this section applies to–

(a) the provision of the margin,

(b) any contract effected by the exchange or clearing house in question for the purpose of realising the property provided as margin, and

(c) any disposition of property in accordance with the rules of the exchange or clearing house as to the application of property provided as margin.

## 166 Powers of Secretary of State to give directions

**166(1) [Application]** The powers conferred by this section are exercisable in relation to a recognised UK investment exchange or recognised UK clearing house.

**166(2) [No action under default rules]** Where in any case an exchange or clearing house has not taken action under its default rules–

(a) if it appears to the Secretary of State that it could take action, he may direct it to do so, and

(b) if it appears to the Secretary of State that it is proposing to take or may take action, he may direct it not to do so.

**166(3) [Consultation]** Before giving such a direction the Secretary of State shall consult the exchange or clearing house in question; and he shall not give a direction unless he is satisfied, in the light of that consultation–

(a) in the case of a direction to take action, that failure to take action would involve undue risk to investors or other participants in the market, or

(b) in the case of a direction not to take action, that the taking of action would be premature or otherwise undesirable in the interests of investors or other participants in the market.

**166(4) [Direction]** A direction shall specify the grounds on which it is given.

**166(5) [Duration of direction]** A direction not to take action may be expressed to have effect until the giving of a further direction (which may be a direction to take action or simply revoking the earlier direction).

**166(6) [Effect of insolvency]** No direction shall be given not to take action if, in relation to the person in question–

(a) a bankruptcy order or an award of sequestration of his estate has been made, or an interim receiver or interim trustee has been appointed, or

(b) a winding up order has been made, a resolution for voluntary winding up has been passed or an administrator, administrative receiver or provisional liquidator has been appointed;

and any previous direction not to take action shall cease to have effect on the making or passing of any such order, award or appointment.

**166(7) [Action under default rules]** Where an exchange or clearing house has taken or been directed to take action under its default rules, the Secretary of State may direct it to do or not to do such things (being things which it has power to do under its default rules) as are specified in the direction.

The Secretary of State shall not give such a direction unless he is satisfied that it will not impede or frustrate the proper and efficient conduct of the default proceedings.

**166(8) [Enforcement]** A direction under this section is enforceable, on the application of the Secretary of State, by injunction or, in Scotland, by an order under section 45 of the Court of Session Act 1988; and where an exchange or clearing house has not complied with a direction, the court may make such order as it thinks fit for restoring the position to what it would have been if the direction had been complied with.

**Note**

See note after s. 167.

## 167 Application to determine whether default proceedings to be taken

**167(1) [Application by office-holder]** Where there has been made or passed in relation to a member or designated non-member of a recognised investment exchange or a member of a recognised clearing house–

(a) a bankruptcy order or an award of sequestration of his estate, or an order appointing an interim receiver of his property, or

(b) an administration or winding up order, a resolution for voluntary winding up or an order appointing a provisional liquidator,

and the exchange or clearing house has not taken action under its default rules in consequence of the order, award or resolution or the matters giving rise to it, a relevant office-holder appointed by, or in consequence of or in connection with, the order, award or resolution may apply to the Secretary of State.

**167(2) [Contents of application]** The application shall specify the exchange or clearing house concerned and the grounds on which it is made.

**167(3) [Secretary of State's duty]** On receipt of the application the Secretary of State shall notify the exchange or clearing house, and unless within three business days after the day on which the notice is received the exchange or clearing house–

(a) takes action under its default rules, or

(b) notifies the Secretary of State that it proposes to do so forthwith,

then, subject as follows, the provisions of sections 158 to 165 above do not apply in relation to market contracts to which the member or designated non-member in question is a party or to anything done by the exchange or clearing house for the purposes of, or in connection with, the settlement of any such contract.

For this purpose a **"business day"** means any day which is not a Saturday or Sunday, Christmas Day, Good Friday or a bank holiday in any part of the United Kingdom under the Banking and Financial Dealings Act 1971.

**167(4) [Application of s. 158–165]** The provisions of sections 158 to 165 are not disapplied if before the end of the period mentioned in subsection (3) the Secretary of State gives the exchange or clearing house a direction under section 166(2)(a) (direction to take action under default rules).

No such direction may be given after the end of that period.

**167(5) [Enforcement]** If the exchange or clearing house notifies the Secretary of State that it proposes to take action under its default rules forthwith, it shall do so; and that duty is enforceable, on the application of the Secretary of State, by injunction or, in Scotland, by an order under section 45 of the Court of Session Act 1988.

**Note**

For application of s. 166 to a listed person see the Financial Markets and Insolvency (Money Market) Regulations 1995 (995/2049), reg. 1, 19.

## 168 Delegation of functions to designated agency

**168(1) [Application of Financial Services Act 1986, s. 114]** Section 114 of the Financial Services Act 1986 (power to transfer functions to designated agency) applies to the functions of the Secretary of State under this Part in relation to a UK investment exchange or clearing house, with the exception of his functions with respect to the making of orders and regulations.

**168(2) [Designated agency]** If immediately before the commencement of this section–

(a) a designated agency is exercising all functions in relation to such bodies which are capable of being transferred under that section, and

(b) no draft order is lying before Parliament resuming any of those functions,

the order bringing this section into force shall have effect as a delegation order made under that section transferring to that agency all the functions which may be transferred by virtue of this section.

**168(3) [Secretary of State's powers]** The Secretary of State may–

(a) in the circumstances mentioned in subsection (3), (4) or (5) of section 115 of the Financial Services Act 1986, or

(b) if it appears to him that a designated agency is unable or unwilling to discharge all or any of the functions under this Part which have been transferred to it,

make an order under that section resuming all functions under this Part which have been transferred to the agency.

This does not affect his power to make an order under subsection (1) or (2) of that section with respect to such functions.

## 169 Supplementary provisions

**169(1) [Application of Financial Services Act 1986, s. 61]** Section 61 of the Financial Services Act 1986 (injunctions and restitution orders) applies in relation to a contravention of any provision of the rules of a recognised investment exchange or recognised clearing house relating to the matters mentioned in Schedule 21 to this Act as it applies in relation to a contravention of any provision of such rules relating to the carrying on of investment business.

**169(2) [Application of s. 12, 37(7)(b), 39(7)(b)]** The following provisions of the Financial Services Act 1986–

section 12 (compliance orders), as it applies by virtue of section 37(8) or 39(8),
section 37(7)(b) (revocation of recognition of UK investment exchange), and
section 39(7)(b) (revocation of recognition of UK clearing house),

apply in relation to a failure by a recognised investment exchange or recognised clearing house to comply with an obligation under this Part as to a failure to comply with an obligation under that Act.

**169(3) [Revocation of recognition]** Where the recognition of an investment exchange or clearing house is revoked under the Financial Services Act 1986, the Secretary of State may, before or after the revocation order, give such directions as he thinks fit with respect to the continued application of the provisions of this Part, with such exceptions, additions and adaptations as may be specified in the direction, in relation to cases where a relevant event of any description specified in the directions occurred before the revocation order takes effect.

**169(4) [Investor protection]** The references in sections 119 and 121 of the Financial Services Act 1986 (competition) to what is necessary for the protection of investors shall be construed as including references to what is necessary for the purposes of this Part.

**Note**
S. 169(4) not in force with rest of section.

**169(5) [Application of s. 204]** Section 204 of the Financial Services Act 1986 (service of notices) applies in relation to a notice, direction or other document required or authorised by or under this Part to be given to or served on any person other than the Secretary of State.

## OTHER EXCHANGES AND CLEARING HOUSES

## 170 Certain overseas exchanges and clearing houses

**170(1) [Regulations]** The Secretary of State may by regulations provide that this Part applies in relation to contracts connected with an overseas investment exchange or clearing house which is approved by him in accordance with such procedures as may be specified in the regulations, as satisfying such requirements as may be so specified, as it applies in relation to contracts connected with a recognised investment exchange or clearing house.

**170(2) [Approval by Secretary of State]** The Secretary of State shall not approve an overseas investment exchange or clearing house unless he is satisfied–

(a) that the rules and practices of the body, together with the law of the country in which the body's head office is situated, provide adequate procedures for dealing with the default of persons party to contracts connected with the body, and

(b) that it is otherwise appropriate to approve the body.

**170(3) [S. 170(2)(a) default]** The reference in subsection (2)(a) to default is to a person being unable to meet his obligations.

**170(4) [Application of Financial Services Act 1986]** The regulations may apply in relation to the approval of a body under this section such of the provisions of the Financial Services Act 1986 as the Secretary of State considers appropriate.

**170(5) [Scope of regulations]** The Secretary of State may make regulations which, in relation to a body which is so approved–

(a) apply such of the provisions of the Financial Services Act 1986 as the Secretary of State considers appropriate, and

(b) provide that the provisions of this Part apply with such exceptions, additions and adaptations as appear to the Secretary of State to be necessary or expedient;

and different provision may be made with respect to different bodies or descriptions of body.

**170(6) [Modification of Financial Services Act 1986 provisions]** Where the regulations apply any provisions of the Financial Services Act 1986, they may provide that those provisions apply with such exceptions, additions and adaptations as appear to the Secretary of State to be necessary or expedient.

**Note**
S. 170 not in force with rest of Part.

# 171 Certain money market institutions

**171(1) [Regulations]** The Secretary of State may by regulations provide that this Part applies to contracts of any specified description in relation to which settlement arrangements are provided by a person for the time being included in a list maintained by the Financial Services Authority ("the Authority") for the purposes of this section, as it applies to contracts connected with a recognised investment exchange or recognised clearing house.

**History**

S. 171(1) the words "Financial Services Authority ('the Authority')" substituted for the former words "Bank of England" by the Bank of England Act 1998, s. 23(1), 45 and Sch. 5, para. 46, 47(1), (2) as from 1 June 1998 (see SI 1998/1120 (C 25), art. 2).

**171(2) [Bank of England supervision]** The Secretary of State shall not make any such regulations unless he is satisfied, having regard to the extent to which the contracts in question–

(a) involve, or are likely to involve, investments falling within paragraph 2 of Schedule 5 to the Financial Services Act 1986 (money market investments), or

(b) are otherwise of a kind dealt in by persons supervised by the Authority,

that it is appropriate that the arrangements should be subject to the supervision of the Authority.

**History**

In s. 171(2) the word "Authority" substituted for the former words "Bank of England" in both places by the Bank of England Act 1998, s. 23(1), 45 and Sch. 5, para. 46, 47(1), (3) as from 1 June 1998 (see SI 1998/1120 (C 25), art. 2).

**171(2A) [References to supervision in s. 171(2)]** In subsection (2), references to supervision by the Authority are to supervision otherwise than in its capacity as a designated agency within the meaning of the Financial Services Act 1986.

**History**

S. 171(2A) inserted by the Bank of England Act 1998, s. 23(1), 45 and Sch. 5, para. 46, 47(1), (4) as from 1 June 1998 (see SI 1998/1120 (C 25), art. 2).

**171(3) [Treasury approval]** The approval of the Treasury is required for–

(a) the conditions imposed by the Authority for admission to the list maintained by it for the purposes of this section, and

(b) the arrangements for a person's admission to and removal from the list;

and any regulations made under this section shall cease to have effect if the approval of the Treasury is withdrawn, but without prejudice to their having effect again if approval is given for fresh conditions or arrangements.

**History**

In s. 171(3)(a) the word "Authority" substituted for the former words "Bank of England" by the Bank of England Act 1998, s. 23(1), 45 and Sch. 5, para. 46, 47(1), (5) as from 1 June 1998 (see SI 1998/1120 (C 25), art. 2).

**171(3A) [Conditions for admission]** Without prejudice to the generality of the Authority's power to impose conditions for admission to the list, the conditions for admission may include–

(a) a condition having the effect of requiring the payment of an application fee, and

(b) a condition having the effect of requiring the payment of periodic fees.

**History**

See history note after s. 171(3B).

**171(3B) [Condition referred to in s. 171(3A)]** A condition of the kind referred to in subsection (3A)(a) or (b)–

(a) may provide for the amount payable to be such as is specified in, or determined under, the condition, and

(b) may make different provision for different cases.

**History**

S. 171(3A), (3B) inserted by the Bank of England Act 1998, s. 26(3), 45 as from 1 June 1998 (see SI 1998/1120 (C 25), art. 2).

**171(3C) [The Authority to consult the Bank of England]** The Authority shall consult the Bank of England before it submits to the Treasury for approval under subsection (3) its proposals for conditions or arrangements of the kind referred to in that subsection.

**History**

S. 171(3C) inserted by the Bank of England Act 1998, s. 23(1), 45 and Sch. 5, para. 46, 47(1), (6) as from 1 June 1998 (see SI 1998/1120 (C 25), art. 2).

**171(4) [Publication of list]** The Authority shall publish the list as for the time being in force and provide a certified copy of it at the request of any person wishing to refer to it in legal proceedings.

A certified copy shall be evidence (in Scotland, sufficient evidence) of the contents of the list; and a copy purporting to be certified by or on behalf of the Bank shall be deemed to have been duly certified unless the contrary is shown.

**History**
In s. 171(4) the word "Authority" substituted for the former words "Bank of England" by the Bank of England Act 1998, s. 23(1), 45 and Sch. 5, para. 46, 47(1), (7) as from 1 June 1998 (see SI 1998/1120 (C 25), art. 2).

**171(5) [Application of Financial Services Act 1986]** Regulations under this section may, in relation to a person included in the list–

(a) apply, with such exceptions, additions and adaptations as appear to the Secretary of State to be necessary or expedient, such of the provisions of the Financial Services Act 1986 as he considers appropriate, and

(b) provide that the provisions of this Part apply with such exceptions, additions and adaptations as appear to the Secretary of State to be necessary or expedient.

**171(6) [Consultation]** Before making any regulations under this section, the Secretary of State and the Treasury shall consult the Bank of England and the Authority.

**History**
In s. 171(6) the words "and the Authority" inserted after the words "Bank of England" by the Bank of England Act 1998, s. 23(1), 45 and Sch. 5, para. 46, 47(1), (8) as from 1 June 1998 (see SI 1998/1120 (C 25), art. 2).
Previously in s. 171(6) the words "and the Treasury shall consult" substituted for the former words "shall consult the Treasury and" by the Transfer of Functions (Financial Services) Order 1992 (SI 1992/1315), art. 10(1) and Sch. 4, para. 13(a) as from 7 June 1992.

**171(6A) [Authority not liable]** Neither the Authority nor any person who is, or is acting as, an officer or servant of the Authority shall be liable in damages for anything done or omitted in the discharge or purported discharge of any of the Authority's functions under this section, unless it is shown that the act or omission was in bad faith.

**History**
S. 171(6A) inserted by the Bank of England Act 1998 s. 25(3), 45 as from 1 June 1998 (see SI 1998/1120 (C 25), art. 2).

**171(7) [Addition to Banking Act 1987, s. 84(1) Table]** In section 84(1) of the Banking Act 1987 (disclosure of information obtained under that Act), in the Table showing the authorities to which, and functions for the purposes of which, disclosure may be made, at the end add–

"A person included in the list maintained by the Bank for the purposes of section 171 of the Companies Act 1989.

Functions under settlement arrangements to which regulations under that section relate.".

**Note**
The functions of the Bank of England under s. 171 (relating to the listing of persons providing settlement arrangements) transferred to the Financial Services Authority by the Bank of England Act 1998, s. 21(c), 45 as from 1 June 1998 (see SI 1998/1120 (C 25), art. 2).
S. 171 brought into force by SI 1995/1591 (C 34), art. 1, 2 as from 4 July 1995. See also the Financial Markets and Insolvency (Money Market) Regulations (995/2049).

## 172 Settlement arrangements provided by the Bank of England

**172(1) [Regulations]** The Secretary of State may by regulations provide that this Part applies to contracts of any specified description in relation to which settlement arrangements are provided by the Bank of England, as it applies to contracts connected with a recognised investment exchange or recognised clearing house.

**172(2) [Modification of provisions]** Regulations under this section may provide that the provisions of this Part apply with such exceptions, additions and adaptations as appear to the Secretary of State to be necessary or expedient.

**172(3) [Consultation]** Before making any regulations under this section, the Secretary of State and the Treasury shall consult the Bank of England.

**History**
In s. 172(3) the words "and the Treasury shall consult" substituted for the former words "shall consult the Treasury and" by the Transfer of Functions (Financial Services) Order 1992 (SI 1992/1315), art. 10(1) and Sch. 4, para. 13(b) as from 7 June 1992.

**Note**
S. 172 not in force with rest of Part.

## MARKET CHARGES

# 173 Market charges

**173(1) ["Market charge"]** In this Part **"market charge"** means a charge, whether fixed or floating, granted–

(a) in favour of a recognised investment exchange, for the purpose of securing debts or liabilities arising in connection with the settlement of market contracts;

(aa) in favour of The Stock Exchange, for the purpose of securing debts or liabilities arising in connection with short term certificates;

(b) in favour of a recognised clearing house, for the purpose of securing debts or liabilities arising in connection with their ensuring the performance of market contracts; or

(c) in favour of a person who agrees to make payments as a result of the transfer or allotment of specified securities made through the medium of a computer-based system established by the Bank of England and The Stock Exchange, for the purpose of securing debts or liabilities of the transferee or allottee arising in connection therewith.

**History**
In s. 173(1), para. (aa) inserted, and in para. (c) the words "or allotment" and "or allottee" inserted, by the Financial Markets and Insolvency Regulations 1991 (SI 1991/880), reg. 1 and 9(a), (b) as from 25 April 1991.

**173(2) [Specified purposes]** Where a charge is granted partly for purposes specified in subsection (1)(a), (aa), (b) or (c) and partly for other purposes, it is a "market charge" so far as it has effect for the specified purposes.

**History**
In s. 173(2) "(aa)," inserted by the Financial Markets and Insolvency Regulations 1991 (SI 1991/880), reg. 1 and 9(c) as from 25 April 1991.

**Note**
See the Financial Markets and Insolvency Regulations 1996 (SI 1996/1469), reg. 3(3).

**173(3) [Definitions]** In subsection (1)–

**"short term certificate"** means an instrument issued by The Stock Exchange undertaking to procure the transfer of property of a value and description specified in the instrument to or to the order of the person to whom the instrument is issued or his endorsee or to a person acting on behalf of either of them and also undertaking to make appropriate payments in cash, in the event that the obligation to procure the transfer of property cannot be discharged in whole or in part;

**"specified securities"** means securities for the time being specified in the list in Schedule 1 to the Stock Transfer Act 1982, and includes any right to such securities; and

**"transfer"**, in relation to any such securities or right, means a transfer of the beneficial interest.

**History**
In s. 173(3) the words "In subsection (1)–" to "in whole or in part;" substituted for the former words "In subsection (1)(c)–" by the Financial Markets and Insolvency Regulations 1991 (SI 1991/880), reg. 1 and 9(d) as from 25 April 1991.

**173(4) [Regulations]** The Secretary of State may by regulations make further provision as to the charges granted in favour of any such person as is mentioned in subsection (1)(a), (b) or (c) which are to be treated as "market charges" for the purposes of this Part; and the regulations may add to, amend or repeal the provisions of subsections (1) to (3) above.

**Note**
See the Financial Markets and Insolvency Regulations 1991 (SI 1991/880).

**173(5) [Scope of regulations]** The regulations may provide that a charge shall or shall not be treated as a market charge if or to the extent that it secures obligations of a specified description, is a charge over property of a specified description or contains provisions of a specified description.

**173(6) [Consultation]** Before making regulations under this section in relation to charges granted in favour of a person within subsection (1)(c), the Secretary of State and the Treasury shall consult the Bank of England.

**History**
In s. 173(6) the words "and the Treasury shall consult" substituted for the former words "shall consult the Treasury and" by the Transfer of Functions (Financial Services) Order 1992 (SI 1992/1315) art. 10(1) and Sch. 4, para. 13(c) as from 7 June 1992.

(b) apply any of those provisions with such exceptions, additions or adaptations as are specified in the regulations.

**176(6) [Consultation]** Before making regulations under this section relating to a description of charges defined by reference to their being granted in favour of a person included in the list maintained by the Financial Services Authority for the purposes of section 171, or in connection with exchange facilities or clearing services provided by a person included in that list, the Secretary of State and the Treasury shall consult the Authority and the Bank of England.

**176(6A) [Consultation]** Before making regulations under this section relating to a description of charges defined by reference to their being granted in favour of the Bank of England, or in connection with settlement arrangements provided by the Bank, the Secretary of State and the Treasury shall consult the Bank.

**History**
S. 176(6), (6A) substituted for the former s. 176(6) by the Bank of England Act 1998, s. 23(1), 45 and Sch. 5, para. 46, 48(1), (3) as from 1 June 1998 (see SI 1998/1120 (C 25), art. 2). The former s. 176(6) read as follows:
"Before making regulations under this section relating to a description of charges defined by reference to their being granted–
(a) in favour of a person included in the list maintained by the Bank of England for the purposes of section 171, or in connection with exchange facilities or clearing services provided by a person included in that list, or
(b) in favour of the Bank of England, or in connection with settlement arrangements provided by the Bank,
the Secretary of State and the Treasury shall consult the Bank of England."

**176(7) [Further provisions]** Regulations under this section may provide that they apply or do not apply to a charge if or to the extent that it secures obligations of a specified description, is a charge over property of a specified description or contains provisions of a specified description.

**Note**
S. 176 brought into force by SI 1995/1591 (C 34), art. 1, 2 as from 4 July 1995. See also the Financial Markets and Insolvency (Money Market) Regulations 1995 (995/2049).

## MARKET PROPERTY

## 177 Application of margin not affected by certain other interests

**177(1) [Property held as margin]** The following provisions have effect with respect to the application by a recognised investment exchange or recognised clearing house of property (other than land) held by the exchange or clearing house as margin in relation to a market contract.

**177(2) [Prior interest]** So far as necessary to enable the property to be applied in accordance with the rules of the exchange or clearing house, it may be so applied notwithstanding any prior equitable interest or right, or any right or remedy arising from a breach of fiduciary duty, unless the exchange or clearing house had notice of the interest, right or breach of duty at the time the property was provided as margin.

**177(3) [Subsequent right]** No right or remedy arising subsequently to the property being provided as margin may be enforced so as to prevent or interfere with the application of the property by the exchange or clearing house in accordance with its rules.

**177(4) [Disponee]** Where an exchange or clearing house has power by virtue of the above provisions to apply property notwithstanding an interest, right or remedy, a person to whom the exchange or clearing house disposes of the property in accordance with its rules takes free from that interest, right or remedy.

## 178 Priority of floating market charge over subsequent charges

**178(1) [Regulations]** The Secretary of State may by regulations provide that a market charge which is a floating charge has priority over a charge subsequently created or arising, including a fixed charge.

**178(2) [Different provision for different cases]** The regulations may make different provision for cases defined, as regards the market charge or the subsequent charge, by reference to the description of charge, its terms, the circumstances in which it is created or arises, the nature of the charge, the person in favour of whom it is granted or arises or any other relevant factor.

**Note**
S. 178 not in force with rest of Part.

## 179 Priority of market charge over unpaid vendor's lien

**179** Where property subject to an unpaid vendor's lien becomes subject to a market charge, the charge has priority over the lien unless the chargee had actual notice of the lien at the time the property became subject to the charge.

## 180 Proceedings against market property by unsecured creditors

**180(1) [No legal proceedings]** Where property (other than land) is held by a recognised investment exchange or recognised clearing house as margin in relation to market contracts or is subject to a market charge, no execution or other legal process for the enforcement of a judgment or order may be commenced or continued, and no distress may be levied, against the property by a person not seeking to enforce any interest in or security over the property, except with the consent of–

(a) in the case of property provided as cover for margin, the investment exchange or clearing house in question, or

(b) in the case of property subject to a market charge, the person in whose favour the charge was granted.

**180(2) [Consent]** Where consent is given the proceedings may be commenced or continued notwithstanding any provision of the Insolvency Act 1986 or the Bankruptcy (Scotland) Act 1985.

**180(3) [Limit on ancillary relief]** Where by virtue of this section a person would not be entitled to enforce a judgment or order against any property, any injunction or other remedy granted with a view to facilitating the enforcement of any such judgment or order shall not extend to that property.

**180(4) [Scotland]** In the application of this section to Scotland, the reference to execution being commenced or continued includes a reference to diligence being carried out or continued, and the reference to distress being levied shall be omitted.

## 181 Power to apply provisions to other cases

**181(1) [Power to apply s. 177–180]** The power of the Secretary of State to make provision by regulations under–

(a) section 170, 171 or 172 (power to extend provisions relating to market contracts), or

(b) section 176 (power to extend provisions relating to market charges),

includes power to apply sections 177 to 180 to any description of property provided as cover for margin in relation to contracts in relation to which the power is exercised or, as the case may be, property subject to charges in relation to which the power is exercised.

**181(2) [Modification of s. 177–180 by regulations]** The regulations may provide that those sections apply with such exceptions, additions and adaptations as may be specified in the regulations.

**Note**

S. 181 brought into force by SI 1995/1591 (C 34), art. 1, 2 as from 4 July 1995. See also the Financial Markets and Insolvency (Money Market) Regulations 1995 (995/2049).

### SUPPLEMENTARY PROVISIONS

## 182 Powers of court in relation to certain proceedings begun before commencement

**182(1) [Relevant persons]** The powers conferred by this section are exercisable by the court where insolvency proceedings in respect of–

(a) a member of a recognised investment exchange or a recognised clearing house, or

(b) a person by whom a market charge has been granted,

are begun on or after 22nd December 1988 and before the commencement of this section.

That person is referred to in this section as "the relevant person".

**182(2) ["Insolvency proceedings"]** For the purposes of this section **"insolvency proceedings"** means proceedings under Part II, IV, V or IX of the Insolvency Act 1986 (administration,

the Insolvency Act 1986 are to that law or provision as modified by the Building Societies Act 1986.

**190(7)** **[Scotland]** In relation to Scotland, references in this Part–

(a) to sequestration include references to the administration by a judicial factor of the insolvent estate of a deceased person, and

(b) to an interim or permanent trustee include references to a judicial factor on the insolvent estate of a deceased person,

unless the context otherwise requires.

## 191 Index of defined expressions

**191** The following Table shows provisions defining or otherwise explaining expressions used in this Part (other than provisions defining or explaining an expression used only in the same section or paragraph)–

| | |
|---|---|
| administrative receiver | section 190(1) |
| charge | section 190(1) |
| clearing house | section 190(1) |
| cover for margin | section 190(3) |
| default rules (and related expressions) | section 188 |
| designated non-member | section 155(2) |
| ensuring the performance of a transaction | section 190(4) |
| insolvency law (and similar expressions) | section 190(6) |
| interim trustee | section 190(1) and (7)(b) |
| investment | section 190(1) |
| investment exchange | section 190(1) |
| margin | section 190(3) |
| market charge | section 173 |
| market contract | section 155 |
| notice | section 190(5) |
| overseas (in relation to an investment exchange or clearing house) | section 190(1) |
| party (in relation to a market contract) | section 187 |
| permanent trustee | section 190(1) and (7)(b) |
| recognised | section 190(1) |
| relevant office-holder | section 189 |
| sequestration | section 190(7)(a) |
| set off (in relation to Scotland) | section 190(1) |
| settlement and related expressions (in relation to a market contract) | section 190(2) |
| The Stock Exchange | section 190(1) |
| trustee, interim or permanent (in relation to Scotland) | section 190(7)(b) |
| UK (in relation to an investment exchange or clearing house) | section 190(1) |

# PART VIII – AMENDMENTS OF THE FINANCIAL SERVICES ACT 1986

## 206 Consequential amendments and delegation of functions on commencement

**206(1)** **[Sch. 23]** The Financial Services Act 1986 has effect with the amendments specified in Schedule 23 which are consequential on the amendments made by sections 192, 194 and 195.

**206(2)** **[Designated agency]** If immediately before the commencement of any provision of this Part which amends Part I of the Financial Services Act 1986–

(a) a designated agency is exercising by virtue of a delegation order under section 114 of that Act any functions of the Secretary of State under that Part, and

(b) no draft order is lying before Parliament resuming any of those functions,

the order bringing that provision into force may make, in relation to any functions conferred on the Secretary of State by the amendment, any such provision as may be made by an order under that section.

**206(3) [Registrar]** If immediately before the commencement of any provision of Schedule 23 which amends Part III of the Financial Services Act 1986–

(a) a transferee body (within the meaning of that Act) is exercising by virtue of a transfer order under paragraph 28 of Schedule 11 to that Act any functions of the Registrar under that Part, and

(b) no draft order is lying before Parliament resuming any of those functions,

the order bringing that provision into force may make, in relation to any functions conferred on the Registrar by the amendment, any such provision as may be made by an order under that paragraph.

**206(4) [Financial Services Act 1986 references]** References in the Financial Services Act 1986 to a delegation order made under section 114 of that Act or to a transfer order made under paragraph 28 of Schedule 11 to that Act include an order made containing any such provision as is authorised by subsection (2) or (3).

**Note**

S. 206 in force from 15 March 1990 (see SI 1990/354 (C 12)).

# PART IX – TRANSFER OF SECURITIES

## 207 Transfer of securities

**207(1) [Regulations]** The Secretary of State may make provision by regulations for enabling title to securities to be evidenced and transferred without a written instrument.

In this section–

(a) **"securities"** means shares, stock, debentures, debenture stock, loan stock, bonds, units of a collective investment scheme within the meaning of the Financial Services Act 1986 and other securities of any description;

(b) references to title to securities include any legal or equitable interest in securities; and

(c) references to a transfer of title include a transfer by way of security.

**207(2) [Scope of regulations]** The regulations may make provision–

(a) for procedures for recording and transferring title to securities, and

(b) for the regulation of those procedures and the persons responsible for or involved in their operation.

**207(3) [Safeguards]** The regulations shall contain such safeguards as appear to the Secretary of State appropriate for the protection of investors and for ensuring that competition is not restricted, distorted or prevented.

**207(4) [Preservation of rights, obligations]** The regulations may for the purpose of enabling or facilitating the operation of the new procedures make provision with respect to the rights and obligations of persons in relation to securities dealt with under the procedures.

But the regulations shall be framed so as to secure that the rights and obligations in relation to securities dealt with under the new procedures correspond, so far as practicable, with those which would arise apart from any regulations under this section.

**207(5) [Supplementary provisions]** The regulations may include such supplementary, incidental and transitional provisions as appear to the Secretary of State to be necessary or expedient.

In particular, provision may be made for the purpose of giving effect to–

(a) the transmission of title to securities by operation of law;

(b) any restriction on the transfer of title to securities arising by virtue of the provisions of any enactment or instrument, court order or agreement;

(c) any power conferred by any such provision on a person to deal with securities on behalf of the person entitled.

**207(6) [Responsible persons]** The regulations may make provision with respect to the persons responsible for the operation of the new procedures–

(a) as to the consequences of their insolvency or incapacity, or

(b) as to the transfer from them to other persons of their functions in relation to the new procedures.

**207(7) [Effecting s. 207(5) purposes]** The regulations may for the purposes mentioned above–

(a) modify or exclude any provision of any enactment or instrument, or any rule of law;

(b) apply, with such modifications as may be appropriate, the provisions of any enactment or instrument (including provisions creating criminal offences);

(c) require the payment of fees, or enable persons to require the payment of fees, of such amounts as may be specified in the regulations or determined in accordance with them;

(d) empower the Secretary of State to delegate to any person willing and able to discharge them any functions of his under the regulations.

**207(8) [Different provision for different cases]** The regulations may make different provision for different cases.

**207(9) [Regulations by statutory instrument]** Regulations under this section shall be made by statutory instrument; and no such regulations shall be made unless a draft of the instrument has been laid before and approved by resolution of each House of Parliament.

**207(10) [Transfer without a written instrument in s. 207(1)]** In subsection (1), the reference to transfer without a written instrument includes, in relation to bearer securities, transfer without delivery.

**History**
S. 207(10) inserted by the Bank of England Act 1998, s. 35, 45 as from 1 June 1998 (see SI 1998/1120 (C 25), art. 2).

**Note**
S. 207 in force from 1 November 1990 (see SI 1990/1392 (C 41)).
See the Uncertificated Securities Reguations 1995 (SI 1995/3272).

# PART X – MISCELLANEOUS AND GENERAL PROVISIONS

## MISCELLANEOUS

## 209 Prosecutions in connection with insider dealing

**209** (Repealed by Criminal Justice Act 1993, s. 79(14) and Sch. 6 as from 1 March 1994.)

**History**
In regard to the date of the above repeal, see SI 1994/242 (C 7), art. 2, Sch., App.; s. 209 formerly read as follows:
"In section 8 of the Company Securities (Insider Dealing) Act 1985 (punishment of contraventions), in subsection (2) (institution of proceedings in England and Wales), for "by the Secretary of State or by, or with the consent of, the Director of Public Prosecutions" substitute "by, or with the consent of, the Secretary of State or the Director of Public Prosecutions"."

## 210 Restriction of duty to supply statements of premium income

**210(1) [Amendment of Policyholders Protection Act 1975, Sch. 3]** Schedule 3 to the Policyholders Protection Act 1975 (provisions with respect to levies on authorised insurance companies) is amended as follows.

**210(2) [Substitution of para. 4]** For paragraph 4 (statements of premium income to be sent to Secretary of State) substitute–

"4(1) The Secretary of State may by notice in writing require an authorised insurance company to send him a statement of–

(a) any income of the company for the year preceding that in which the notice is received by the company which is income liable to the general business levy, and

(b) any income of the company for that year which is income liable to the long term business levy.

**4(2)** An authorised insurance company which receives a notice under this paragraph shall send the statement required by the notice to the Secretary of State within three months of receiving the notice.

**4(3)** Where an authorised insurance company is required under this paragraph to send a statement to the Secretary of State in respect of income of both descriptions mentioned in sub-paragraph (1)(a) and (b) above it shall send a separate statement in respect of income of each description.".

**210(3) [Substitution in para. 5(3)]** In paragraph 5(3) (application of provisions of the Insurance Companies Act 1982 to failure to meet obligation imposed by paragraph 4) for "the obligation imposed on an insurance company by paragraph 4" substitute "an obligation imposed on an insurance company under paragraph 4".

**210(4) [Omission in para. 6]** In paragraph 6 (declaration and enforcement of levies) omit sub-paragraph (4) (provision about notices).

**210(5) [Insertion of para. 8]** After paragraph 7 insert–

"NOTICES UNDER PARAGRAPHS 4 AND 6

**8** A notice under paragraph 4 or 6 above may be sent by post, and a letter containing such a notice shall be deemed to be properly addressed if it is addressed to the insurance company to which it is sent at its last known place of business in the United Kingdom.".

**Note**
S. 210 in force from 1 April 1990 (see SI 1990/142 (C 5)).

# 211 Building societies: miscellaneous amendments

**211(1) [Amendment of Building Societies Act 1986, s. 104(2)]** In section 104 of the Building Societies Act 1986 (power to assimilate law relating to building societies and law relating to companies), in subsection (2) (relevant provisions of that Act), omit the word "and" before paragraph (d) and after that paragraph add–

"; and

(e) section 110 (provisions exempting officers and auditors from liability).".

**Note**
S. 211(1) in force from 1 October 1991 (see SI 1991/1996 (C 57)).

**211(2) [Amendment of Sch.15, para. 1(a), 3(2)(b)]** In Schedule 15 to the Building Societies Act 1986 (application of companies winding-up legislation)–

(a) in paragraph 1(a) (provisions of Insolvency Act 1986 applied) for "and XII" substitute ", XII and XIII";

(b) in paragraph 3(2)(b) (adaptations: references to be omitted), omit ", a shadow director".

**Note**
S. 211(2) in force from 31 July 1990 (see SI 1990/1392 (C 41)).

**211(3)** (Insertion of Company Directors Disqualification Act 1986, s. 22A.)

GENERAL

# 213 Provisions extending to Northern Ireland

**213(1) [Amending applicable enactment]** The provisions of this Act extend to Northern Ireland so far as they amend, or provide for the amendment of, an enactment which so extends.

**213(2) [Application of Companies Act 1985, s. 745(1), Insolvency Act 1986, s. 441(2)]** So far as any provision of this Act amends the Companies Act 1985 or the Insolvency Act 1986, its application to companies registered or incorporated in Northern Ireland is subject to section 745(1) of the Companies Act 1985 or section 441(2) of the Insolvency Act 1986, as the case may be.

**213(3) [S. 82–91]** In Part III (investigations and powers to obtain information), sections 82 to 91, (powers exercisable to assist overseas regulatory authorities) extend to Northern Ireland.

**213(4) [Pt. VI]** Part VI (mergers and related matters) extends to Northern Ireland.

**213(5) [Pt. VII]** In Part VII (financial markets and insolvency) the following provisions extend to Northern Ireland–

(a) sections 154 and 155 (introductory provisions and definition of "market contract"),

(b) section 156 and Schedule 21 (additional requirements for recognition of investment exchange or clearing house),

(c) sections 157, 160, 162, and 166 to 169 (provisions relating to recognised investment exchanges and clearing houses),

(d) sections 170 to 172 (power to extend provisions to other financial markets),

(e) section 184 (indemnity for certain acts), and

(f) sections 185 to 191 (supplementary provisions).

**213(6) [Pt. VIII]** Part VIII (amendments of Financial Services Act 1986) extends to Northern Ireland.

**213(7) [Pt. IX]** Part IX (transfer of securities) extends to Northern Ireland.

Subject to any Order made after the passing of this Act by virtue of section 3(1)(a) of the Northern Ireland Constitution Act 1973, the transfer of securities shall not be a transferred matter for the purposes of that Act but shall for the purposes of section 3(2) be treated as specified in Schedule 3 to that Act.

**213(8) [Pt. X]** In Part X (miscellaneous and general provisions), this section and sections 214 to 216 (general provisions) extend to Northern Ireland.

**213(9) [Application]** Except as mentioned above, the provisions of this Act do not extend to Northern Ireland.

**Note**
S. 213 in force from 2 February 1990 (see SI 1990/142 (C 5)).

## 214 Making of corresponding provision for Northern Ireland

**214(1) [Order in Council]** An Order in Council under paragraph 1(1)(b) of Schedule 1 to the Northern Ireland Act 1974 (legislation for Northern Ireland in the interim period) which contains a statement that it is only made for purposes corresponding to the purposes of provisions of this Act to which this section applies–

(a) shall not be subject to paragraph 1(4) and (5) of that Schedule (affirmative resolution of both Houses of Parliament), but

(b) shall be subject to annulment in pursuance of a resolution of either House of Parliament.

**214(2) [Application]** The provisions of this Act to which this section applies are–

(a) Parts I to V, and

(b) Part VII, except sections 156, 157, 169 and Schedule 21.

**Note**
S. 214 in force from 2 February 1990 (see SI 1990/142 (C 5)).

## 215 Commencement and transitional provisions

**215(1) [Royal Assent]** The following provisions of this Act come into force on Royal Assent–

(a) in Part V (amendments of company law), section 141 (application to declare dissolution of company void);

(b) in Part VI (mergers)–
   (i) sections 147 to 150, and
   (ii) paragraphs 2 to 12, 14 to 16, 18 to 20, 22 to 25 of Schedule 20, and section 153 so far as relating to those paragraphs;

(c) in Part VIII (amendments of the Financial Services Act 1986), section 202 (offers of short-dated debentures);

(d) in Part X (miscellaneous and general provisions), the repeals made by Schedule 24 in sections 71, 74, 88 and 89 of, and Schedule 9 to, the Fair Trading Act 1973, and section 212 so far as relating to those repeals.

**215(2)** **[Days to be appointed]** The other provisions of this Act come into force on such day as the Secretary of State may appoint by order made by statutory instrument; and different days may be appointed for different provisions and different purposes.

**Note**

See the Companies Act 1989 (Commencement No. 17) Order 1998 (SI 1998/1747) (C. 34)).

**215(3)** **[Further provisions]** An order bringing into force any provision may contain such transitional provisions and savings as appear to the Secretary of State to be necessary or expedient.

**215(4)** **[Amendment of other enactments]** The Secretary of State may also by order under this section amend any enactment which refers to the commencement of a provision brought into force by the order so as to substitute a reference to the actual date on which it comes into force.

## 216 Short title

**216** This Act may be cited as the Companies Act 1989.

# SCHEDULES

# Schedule 10 – Amendments Consequential on Part I

Section 23

**Note**

Sch. 10 in force from 1 March 1990 (except para. 19 in force from 1 August 1990) (see SI 1990/355 (C 13)).

## Part II – Amendments of Other Enactments

### BETTING, GAMING AND LOTTERIES ACT 1963 (c. 2)

**25** In Schedule 2 to the Betting, Gaming and Lotteries Act 1963 (registered pool promoters), in paragraph 24(2) (duties with respect to delivery of accounts and audit) for the words from "and the following provisions" to "their report)" substitute "and sections 235(2) and 237(1) and (3) of the Companies Act 1985 (matters to be stated in auditors' report and responsibility of auditors in preparing their report)".

### HARBOURS ACT 1964 (c. 40)

**26(1)** Section 42 of the Harbours Act 1964 (accounts and reports of statutory harbour undertakers) is amended as follows.

**26(2)** For subsection (2) substitute–

"(2) Where a statutory harbour undertaker is a parent undertaking with subsidiary undertakings which carry on harbour activities or any associated activities, then, it shall be the duty of the company also to prepare group accounts relating to the harbour activities and associated activities carried on by it and its subsidiary undertakings."

**26(3)** In subsection (6) (application of provisions of the Companies Act 1985)–

(a) in paragraph (a) for "company accounts" substitute "individual company accounts";

(b) in paragraph (c) omit the words "required to be attached to a company's balance sheet".

**26(4)** In subsection (9), for the definition of "holding company" and "subsidiary" substitute–

"**"parent undertaking"** and **"subsidiary undertaking"** have the same meaning as in Part VII of the Companies Act 1985;".

### COAL INDUSTRY ACT 1971 (c. 16)

**27(1)** Section 8 of the Coal Industry Act 1971 (further provisions as to accounts of British Coal Corporation) is amended as follows.

**27(2)** In subsections (1) and (2) for "subsidiaries" (three times) substitute "subsidiary undertakings".

**27(3)** After subsection (2) insert–

"(3) In this section **"subsidiary undertaking"** has the same meaning as in Part VII of the Companies Act 1985.".

## AIRCRAFT AND SHIPBUILDING INDUSTRIES ACT 1977 (c. 3)

**28(1)** Section 17 of the Aircraft and Shipbuilding Industries Act 1977 (British Shipbuilders: accounts and audit) is amended as follows.

**28(2)** In subsection (1)(c) (duty to prepare consolidated accounts) for "subsidiaries" substitute "subsidiary undertakings".

**28(3)** In subsection (9) (copies of accounts to be sent to the Secretary of State) for "subsidiaries" substitute "subsidiary undertakings" and for "subsidiary" substitute "subsidiary undertaking".

**28(4)** After subsection (9) add–

"(10) In this section **"subsidiary undertaking"** has the same meaning as in Part VII of the Companies Act 1985.".

## CROWN AGENTS ACT 1979 (c. 43)

**29** In section 22 of the Crown Agents Act 1979 (accounts and audit), in subsection (2) (duty to prepare consolidated accounts) for "subsidiaries" (three times) substitute "subsidiary undertakings", and at the end of that subsection add –

"In this subsection **"subsidiary undertaking"** has the same meaning as in Part VII of the Companies Act 1985.".

## BRITISH TELECOMMUNICATIONS ACT 1981 (c. 38)

**30** In section 75 of the British Telecommunications Act 1981 (accounts of the Post Office), in subsection (1)(c)(i) for "subsidiaries" substitute "subsidiary undertakings within the meaning of Part VII of the Companies Act 1985".

## TRANSPORT ACT 1981 (c. 56)

**31** In section 11(4) of the Transport Act 1981, for "section 235" substitute "section 234".

## IRON AND STEEL ACT 1982 (c. 25)

**32** In section 24(5) of the Iron and Steel Act 1982 (meaning of "directors' report") for the words from "which, under section 235" to the end substitute "which is required to be prepared under section 234 of the Companies Act 1985".

## OIL AND PIPELINES ACT 1985 (c. 62)

**33** In Schedule 3 to the Oil and Pipelines Act 1985 (Oil and Pipelines Agency: financial and other provisions), in paragraph 9(2) (duty to prepare consolidated accounts) for "subsidiaries" (three times) substitute "subsidiary undertakings", and at the end of that sub-paragraph add –

"In this sub-paragraph **"subsidiary undertaking"** has the same meaning as in Part VII of the Companies Act 1985.".

## PATENTS, DESIGNS AND MARKS ACT 1986 (c. 39)

**34** In Schedule 2 to the Patents, Designs and Marks Act 1986 (service marks), in paragraph 1(2) (provisions in which reference to trade mark includes service mark) for sub-paragraph (ii) substitute–

"(ii) Part I of Schedule 4 and paragraphs 5(2)(d) and 10(1)(b) and (2) of Schedule 9 (form of company balance sheets); and".

## BANKING ACT 1987 (c. 22)

**37(1)** The Banking Act 1987 is amended as follows.

**37(2)** In section 46(2) (duties of auditor of authorised institution), in paragraph (c) for "section 236" substitute "section 235(2)" and for "section 237" substitute "section 235(3) or section 237"; and in section 46(4) (adaptation of references for Northern Ireland) for "236 and 237" substitute "235(2) and 235(3) and 237".

**37(3)** After section 105 insert–

"*Meaning of "related company"*

**105A(1)** In this Act a "related company", in relation to an institution or the holding company of an institution, means a body corporate (other than a subsidiary) in which the institution or holding company holds a qualifying capital interest.

**105A(2)** A qualifying capital interest means an interest in relevant shares of the body corporate which the institution or holding company holds on a long-term basis for the purpose of securing a contribution to its own activities by the exercise of control or influence arising from that interest.

**105A(3)** Relevant shares means shares comprised in the equity share capital of the body corporate of a class carrying rights to vote in all circumstances at general meetings of the body.

**105A(4)** A holding of 20 per cent or more of the nominal value of the relevant shares of a body corporate shall be presumed to be a qualifying capital interest unless the contrary is shown.

**105A(5)** In this paragraph "equity share capital" has the same meaning as in the Companies Act 1985 and the Companies (Northern Ireland) Order 1986.".

**37(4)** In section 106(1) (interpretation), for the definition of "related company" substitute–

""**related company"** has the meaning given by section 105A above;".

### INCOME AND CORPORATION TAXES ACT 1988 (c. 1)

**38(1)** The Income and Corporation Taxes Act 1988 is amended as follows.

**38(2)** In section 180 (annual return of registered profit-related pay scheme), in subsection (3) for "section 242(3)" substitute "section 244(3)".

**38(3)** In section 565(6) (conditions for exemption from provisions relating to sub- contractors in construction industry: compliance with requirements of Companies Act 1985), in paragraph (a) for "section 227 and 241" substitute "sections 226, 241 and 242".

### DARTFORD–THURROCK CROSSING ACT 1988 (c. 20)

**39** In section 33 of the Dartford-Thurrock Crossing Act 1988 (duty to lay before Parliament copies of accounts of persons appointed to levy tolls), for subsection (2) substitute–

"(2) In relation to a company **"accounts"** in subsection (1) means the company's annual accounts for a financial year, together with the relevant directors' report and the auditors' report on those accounts.

Expressions used in this subsection have the same meaning as in Part VII of the Companies Act 1985.".

# Schedule 11 – Recognition of Supervisory Body

Section 30(5)

**Note**

Sch. 11 in force from 1 March 1990 (see SI 1990/142(C 5)).

## Part I – Grant and Revocation of Recognition

### APPLICATION FOR RECOGNITION OF SUPERVISORY BODY

**1(1)** A supervisory body may apply to the Secretary of State for an order declaring it to be a recognised supervisory body for the purposes of this Part of this Act.

**1(2)** Any such application–

(a) shall be made in such manner as the Secretary of State may direct, and

(b) shall be accompanied by such information as the Secretary of State may reasonably require for the purpose of determining the application.

**1(3)** At any time after receiving an application and before determining it the Secretary of State may require the applicant to furnish additional information.

**1(4)** The directions and requirements given or imposed under sub-paragraphs (2) and (3) may differ as between different applications.

**1(5)** Any information to be furnished to the Secretary of State under this paragraph shall, if he so requires, be in such form or verified in such manner as he may specify.

**1(6)** Every application shall be accompanied by a copy of the applicant's rules and of any guidance issued by the applicant which is intended to have continuing effect and is issued in writing or other legible form.

## GRANT AND REFUSAL OF RECOGNITION

**2(1)** The Secretary of State may, on an application duly made in accordance with paragraph 1 and after being furnished with all such information as he may require under that paragraph, make or refuse to make an order (a "recognition order") declaring the applicant to be a recognised supervisory body for the purposes of this Part of this Act.

**2(2)** The Secretary of State shall not make a recognition order unless it appears to him, from the information furnished by the body and having regard to any other information in his possession, that the requirements of Part II of this Schedule are satisfied as respects that body.

**2(3)** The Secretary of State may refuse to make a recognition order in respect of a body if he considers that its recognition is unnecessary having regard to the existence of one or more other bodies which maintain and enforce rules as to the appointment and conduct of company auditors and which have been or are likely to be recognised.

**2(4)** Where the Secretary of State refuses an application for a recognition order he shall give the applicant a written notice to that effect specifying which requirements in the opinion of the Secretary of State are not satisfied or stating that the application is refused on the ground mentioned in sub-paragraph (3).

**2(5)** A recognition order shall state the date on which it takes effect.

## REVOCATION OF RECOGNITION

**3(1)** A recognition order may be revoked by a further order made by the Secretary of State if at any time it appears to him–

(a) that any requirement of Part II of this Schedule is not satisfied in the case of the body to which the recognition order relates ("the recognised body"),

(b) that the recognised body has failed to comply with any obligation to which it is subject by virtue of this Part of this Act, or

(c) that the continued recognition of the body is undesirable having regard to the existence of one or more other bodies which have been or are to be recognised.

**3(2)** An order revoking a recognition order shall state the date on which it takes effect and that date shall not be earlier than three months after the day on which the revocation order is made.

**3(3)** Before revoking a recognition order the Secretary of State shall give written notice of his intention to do so to the recognised body, take such steps as he considers reasonably practicable for bringing the notice to the attention of members of the body and publish it in such manner as he thinks appropriate for bringing it to the attention of any other persons who are in his opinion likely to be affected.

**3(4)** A notice under sub-paragraph (3) shall state the reasons for which the Secretary of State proposes to act and give particulars of the rights conferred by sub-paragraph (5).

**3(5)** A body on which a notice is served under sub-paragraph (3), any member of the body and any other person who appears to the Secretary of State to be affected may within three months after the date of service or publication, or within such longer time as the Secretary of State may allow, make written representations to the Secretary of State and, if desired, oral representations to a person appointed for that purpose by the Secretary of State; and the

Secretary of State shall have regard to any representations made in accordance with this sub-paragraph in determining whether to revoke the recognition order.

3(6) If in any case the Secretary of State considers it essential to do so in the public interest he may revoke a recognition order without regard to the restriction imposed by sub-paragraph (2) and notwithstanding that no notice has been given or published under sub-paragraph (3) or that the time for making representations in pursuance of such a notice has not expired.

3(7) An order revoking a recognition order may contain such transitional provisions as the Secretary of State thinks necessary or expedient.

3(8) A recognition order may be revoked at the request or with the consent of the recognised body and any such revocation shall not be subject to the restrictions imposed by sub-paragraphs (1) and (2) or the requirements of sub-paragraphs (3) to (5).

3(9) On making an order revoking a recognition order the Secretary of State shall give the body written notice of the making of the order, take such steps as he considers reasonably practicable for bringing the making of the order to the attention of members of the body and publish a notice of the making of the order in such manner as he thinks appropriate for bringing it to the attention of any other persons who are in his opinion likely to be affected.

# Part II – Requirements for Recognition

## HOLDING OF APPROPRIATE QUALIFICATION

4(1) The body must have rules to the effect that a person is not eligible for appointment as a company auditor unless–

(a) in the case of an individual, he holds an appropriate qualification;

(b) in the case of a firm–

(i) the individuals responsible for company audit work on behalf of the firm hold an appropriate qualification, and

(ii) the firm is controlled by qualified persons (see paragraph 5 below).

4(2) This does not prevent the body from imposing more stringent requirements.

4(3) A firm which has ceased to comply with the conditions mentioned in sub-paragraph (1)(b) may be permitted to remain eligible for appointment as a company auditor for a period of not more than three months.

5(1) The following provisions explain what is meant in paragraph 4(1)(b)(ii) by a firm being "controlled by qualified persons".

5(2) For this purpose references to a person being qualified are, in relation to an individual, to his holding an appropriate qualification, and in relation to a firm, to its being eligible for appointment as a company auditor.

5(3) A firm shall be treated as controlled by qualified persons if, and only if–

(a) a majority of the members of the firm are qualified persons, and

(b) where the firm's affairs are managed by a board of directors, committee or other management body, a majority of the members of that body are qualified persons or, if the body consists of two persons only, at least one of them is a qualified person.

5(4) A majority of the members of a firm means–

(a) where under the firm's constitution matters are decided upon by the exercise of voting rights, members holding a majority of the rights to vote on all, or substantially all, matters;

(b) in any other case, members having such rights under the constitution of the firm as enable them to direct its overall policy or alter its constitution.

5(5) A majority of the members of the management body of a firm means–

(a) where matters are decided at meetings of the management body by the exercise of voting rights, members holding a majority of the rights to vote on all, or substantially all, matters at such meetings;

(a) lasted at least one year, and

(b) is attested by an examination recognised by the Secretary of State for the purposes of this paragraph;

but the period of professional experience may not be so reduced by more than four years.

**6(3)** The period of professional experience together with the practical training required in the case of persons satisfying the requirement in paragraph 5 by virtue of having a sufficient period of professional experience must not be shorter than the course of theoretical instruction referred to in that paragraph and the practical training required in the case of persons satisfying the requirement of that paragraph by virtue of having completed such a course.

## EXAMINATION

**7(1)** The qualification must be restricted to persons who have passed an examination (at least part of which is in writing) testing–

(a) theoretical knowledge of the subjects prescribed for the purposes of this paragraph by regulations made by the Secretary of State, and

(b) ability to apply that knowledge in practice,

and requiring a standard of attainment at least equivalent to that required to obtain a degree from a university or similar establishment in the United Kingdom.

**7(2)** The qualification may be awarded to a person without his theoretical knowledge of a subject being tested by examination if he has passed a university or other examination of equivalent standard in that subject or holds a university degree or equivalent qualification in it.

**7(3)** The qualification may be awarded to a person without his ability to apply his theoretical knowledge of a subject in practice being tested by examination if he has received practical training in that subject which is attested by an examination or diploma recognised by the Secretary of State for the purposes of this paragraph.

**7(4)** Regulations under this paragraph shall be made by statutory instrument which shall be subject to annulment in pursuance of a resolution of either House of Parliament.

**Note**
See the Company Auditors (Examinations) Regulations 1990 (SI 1990/1146).

## PRACTICAL TRAINING

**8(1)** The qualification must be restricted to persons who have completed at least three years' practical training of which–

(a) part was spent being trained in company audit work, and

(b) a substantial part was spent being trained in company audit work or other audit work of a description approved by the Secretary of State as being similar to company audit work.

For this purpose **"company audit work"** includes the work of a person appointed as auditor under the Companies (Northern Ireland) Order 1986 or under the law of a country or territory outside the United Kingdom where it appears to the Secretary of State that the law and practice with respect to the audit of company accounts is similar to that in the United Kingdom.

**8(2)** The training must be given by persons approved by the body offering the qualification as persons as to whom the body is satisfied, in the light of undertakings given by them and the supervision to which they are subject (whether by the body itself or some other body or organisation), that they will provide adequate training.

**8(3)** At least two-thirds of the training must be given by a fully-qualified auditor, that is, a person–

(a) eligible in accordance with this Part of this Act to be appointed as a company auditor, or

(b) satisfying the corresponding requirements of the law of Northern Ireland or another member State of the European Economic Community.

## THE BODY OFFERING THE QUALIFICATION

**9(1)** The body offering the qualification must have–

(a) rules and arrangements adequate to ensure compliance with the requirements of paragraphs 4 to 8, and

(b) adequate arrangements for the effective monitoring of its continued compliance with those requirements.

9(2) The arrangements must include arrangements for monitoring the standard of its examinations and the adequacy of the practical training given by the persons approved by it for that purpose.

# Schedule 13 – Supplementary Provisions with Respect to Delegation Order

Section 46(6)

## INTRODUCTORY

1 The following provisions have effect in relation to a body established by a delegation order under section 46; and any power to make provision by order is to make provision by order under that section.

## STATUS

2 The body shall not be regarded as acting on behalf of the Crown and its members, officers and employees shall not be regarded as Crown servants.

## NAME, MEMBERS AND CHAIRMAN

3(1) The body shall be known by such name as may be specified in the delegation order.

3(2) The body shall consist of such persons (not being less than eight) as the Secretary of State may appoint after such consultation as he thinks appropriate; and the chairman of the body shall be such person as the Secretary of State may appoint from amongst its members.

3(3) The Secretary of State may make provision by order as to the terms on which the members of the body are to hold and vacate office and as to the terms on which a person appointed as chairman is to hold and vacate the office of chairman.

## FINANCIAL PROVISIONS

4(1) The body shall pay to its chairman and members such remuneration, and such allowances in respect of expenses properly incurred by them in the performance of their duties, as the Secretary of State may determine.

4(2) As regards any chairman or member in whose case the Secretary of State so determines, the body shall pay or make provision for the payment of–

(a) such pension, allowance or gratuity to or in respect of that person on his retirement or death, or

(b) such contributions or other payment towards the provision of such a pension, allowance or gratuity,

as the Secretary of State may determine.

4(3) Where a person ceases to be a member of the body otherwise than on the expiry of his term of office and it appears to the Secretary of State that there are special circumstances which make it right for him to receive compensation, the body shall make a payment to him by way of compensation of such amount as the Secretary of State may determine.

## PROCEEDINGS

5(1) The delegation order may contain such provision as the Secretary of State considers appropriate with respect to the proceedings of the body.

5(2) The order may, in particular–

(a) authorise the body to discharge any functions by means of committees consisting wholly or partly of members of the body;

(b) provide that the validity of proceedings of the body, or of any such committee, is not affected by any vacancy among the members or any defect in the appointment of any member.

## FEES

**6(1)** The body may retain fees payable to it.

**6(2)** The fees shall be applied for meeting the expenses of the body in discharging its functions and for any purposes incidental to those functions.

**6(3)** Those expenses include any expenses incurred by the body on such staff, accommodation, services and other facilities as appear to it to be necessary or expedient for the proper performance of its functions.

**6(4)** In prescribing the amount of fees in the exercise of the functions transferred to it the body shall prescribe such fees as appear to it sufficient to defray those expenses, taking one year with another.

**6(5)** Any exercise by the body of the power to prescribe fees requires the approval of the Secretary of State; and the Secretary of State may, after consultation with the body, by order vary or revoke any regulations made by it prescribing fees.

## LEGISLATIVE FUNCTIONS

**7(1)** Regulations made by the body in the exercise of the functions transferred to it shall be made by instrument in writing, but not by statutory instrument.

**7(2)** The instrument shall specify the provision of this Part of this Act under which it is made.

**7(3)** The Secretary of State may by order impose such requirements as he thinks necessary or expedient as to the circumstances and manner in which the body must consult on any regulations it proposes to make.

**8(1)** Immediately after an instrument is made it shall be printed and made available to the public with or without payment.

**8(2)** A person shall not be taken to have contravened any regulation if he shows that at the time of the alleged contravention the instrument containing the regulation had not been made available as required by this paragraph.

**9(1)** The production of a printed copy of an instrument purporting to be made by the body on which is endorsed a certificate signed by an officer of the body authorised by it for the purpose and stating–

(a) that the instrument was made by the body,

(b) that the copy is a true copy of the instrument, and

(c) that on a specified date the instrument was made available to the public as required by paragraph 8,

is prima facie evidence or, in Scotland, sufficient evidence of the facts stated in the certificate.

**9(2)** A certificate purporting to be signed as mentioned in sub-paragraph (1) shall be deemed to have been duly signed unless the contrary is shown.

**9(3)** Any person wishing in any legal proceedings to cite an instrument made by the body may require the body to cause a copy of it to be endorsed with such a certificate as is mentioned in this paragraph.

## REPORT AND ACCOUNTS

**10(1)** The body shall at least once in each year for which the delegation order is in force make a report to the Secretary of State on the discharge of the functions transferred to it and on such other matters as the Secretary of State may by order require.

**10(2)** The Secretary of State shall lay before Parliament copies of each report received by him under this paragraph.

**10(3)** The Secretary of State may, with the consent of the Treasury, give directions to the body with respect to its accounts and the audit of its accounts and it is the duty of the body to comply with the directions.

**10(4)** A person shall not be appointed auditor of the body unless he is eligible for appointment as a company auditor under section 25.

### OTHER SUPPLEMENTARY PROVISIONS

**11(1)** The transfer of a function to a body established by a delegation order does not affect anything previously done in the exercise of the function transferred; and the resumption of a function so transferred does not affect anything previously done in exercise of the function resumed.

**11(2)** The Secretary of State may by order make such transitional and other supplementary provision as he thinks necessary or expedient in relation to the transfer or resumption of a function.

**11(3)** The provision that may be made in connection with the transfer of a function includes, in particular, provision–

(a) for modifying or excluding any provision of this Part of this Act in its application to the function transferred;

(b) for applying to the body established by the delegation order, in connection with the function transferred, any provision applying to the Secretary of State which is contained in or made under any other enactment;

(c) for the transfer of any property, rights or liabilities from the Secretary of State to that body;

(d) for the carrying on and completion by that body of anything in process of being done by the Secretary of State when the order takes effect;

(e) for the substitution of that body for the Secretary of State in any instrument, contract or legal proceedings.

**11(4)** The provision that may be made in connection with the resumption of a function includes, in particular, provision–

(a) for the transfer of any property, rights or liabilities from that body to the Secretary of State;

(b) for the carrying on and completion by the Secretary of State of anything in process of being done by that body when the order takes effect;

(c) for the substitution of the Secretary of State for that body in any instrument, contract or legal proceedings.

**12** Where a delegation order is revoked, the Secretary of State may by order make provision–

(a) for the payment of compensation to persons ceasing to be employed by the body established by the delegation order; and

(b) as to the winding up and dissolution of the body.

# Schedule 14 – Supervisory and Qualifying Bodies: Restrictive Practices

Section 47(1)

**Note**

Sch. 14 in force from 1 March 1990 (see SI 1990/142 (C 5)).

## Part I – Prevention of Restrictive Practices

### REFUSAL OF RECOGNITION ON GROUNDS RELATED TO COMPETITION

**1(1)** The Secretary of State shall before deciding whether to make a recognition order in respect of a supervisory body or professional qualification send to the Director General of Fair Trading (in this Schedule referred to as "the Director") a copy of the rules and of any guidance

**History**
Para. 10 formerly read as follows:
"**10(1)** No course of conduct constituting any such practice as is mentioned in paragraph 3(4) above shall constitute an anti-competitive practice for the purposes of the Competition Act 1980.
**(2)** Where a recognition order is revoked there shall not be treated as an anti- competitive practice for the purposes of that Act any such course of conduct as is mentioned in sub-paragraph (1) which occurred while the order was in force."

# Schedule 15 – Charges on Property of Oversea Companies

[Section 105]

**Note**
See note to Part IV.

The following provisions are inserted in Part XXIII of the Companies Act 1985–

**"Chapter III – Registration of Charges**

*Introductory provisions*

**703A(1)** The provisions of this Chapter have effect for securing the registration in Great Britain of charges on the property of a registered oversea company.

**703A(2)** Section 395(2) and (3) (meaning of "charge" and "property") have effect for the purposes of this Chapter.

**703A(3)** A **"registered oversea company"**, in relation to England and Wales or Scotland, means an oversea company which

(a) has duly delivered documents under paragraph 1 of Schedule 21A to the registrar for that part of Great Britain and has not subsequently given notice to him under section 695A(3) that it has closed the branch in respect of which the documents were registered, or

(b) has duly delivered documents to the registrar for that part of Great Britain under section 691 and has not subsequently given notice to him under section 696(4) that it has ceased to have an established place of business in that part.

**703A(4)** References in this Chapter to the registrar shall be construed in accordance with section 703E below and references to registration in relation to a charge, are to registration in the register kept by him under this Chapter.

*Charges requiring registration*

**703B(1)** The charges requiring registration under this Chapter are those which if created by a company registered in Great Britain would require registration under Part XII of this Act.

**703B(2)** Whether a charge is one requiring registration under this Chapter shall be determined–

(a) in the case of a charge over property of a company at the date when it becomes a registered oversea company, as at that date,

(b) in the case of a charge created by a registered oversea company, as at the date the charge is created, and

(c) in the case of a charge over property acquired by a registered oversea company, as at the date of the acquisition.

**703B(3)** In the following provisions of this Chapter references to a charge are, unless the context otherwise requires, to a charge requiring registration under this Chapter.

Where a charge not otherwise requiring registration relates to property by virtue of which it requires to be registered and to other property, the references are to the charge so far as it relates to property of the former description.

*The register*

**703C(1)** The registrar shall keep for each registered oversea company a register, in such form as he thinks fit, of charges on property of the company.

**703C(2)** The register shall consist of a file containing with respect to each such charge the particulars and other information delivered to the registrar under or by virtue of the following provisions of this Chapter.

**703C(3)** Section 397(3) to (5) (registrar's certificate as to date of delivery of particulars) applies in relation to the delivery of any particulars or other information under this Chapter.

*Company's duty to deliver particulars of charges for registration*

**703D(1)** If when an oversea company

(a) delivers documents for registration under paragraph 1 of Schedule 21A–

(i) in respect of a branch in England and Wales, or

(ii) in respect of a branch in Scotland,

for the first time since becoming a company to which section 690A applies, or

(b) delivers documents for registration under section 691,

any of its property is situated in Great Britain and subject to a charge, it is the company's duty at the same time to deliver the prescribed particulars of the charge, in the prescribed form, to the registrar for registration.

**703D(1A)** Subsection (1) above does not apply in relation to a charge if–

(a) the particulars of it required to be delivered under that subsection have already been so delivered to the registrar to whom the documents mentioned in subsection (1) above are delivered, and

(b) the company has at all times since they were so delivered to him been a registered oversea company in relation to the part of Great Britain for which he is registrar.

**703D(2)** Where a registered oversea company–

(a) creates a charge on property situated in Great Britain, or

(b) acquires property which is situated in Great Britain and subject to a charge,

it is the company's duty to deliver the prescribed particulars of the charge, in the prescribed form, to the registrar for registration within 21 days after the date of the charge's creation or, as the case may be, the date of the acquisition.

This subsection does not apply if the property subject to the charge is at the end of that period no longer situated in Great Britain.

**703D(3)** Where the preceding subsections do not apply and property of a registered oversea company is for a continuous period of four months situated in Great Britain and subject to a charge, it is the company's duty before the end of that period to deliver the prescribed particulars of the charge, in the prescribed form, to the registrar for registration.

**703D(4)** Particulars of a charge required to be delivered under subsections (1), (2) or (3) may be delivered for registration by any person interested in the charge.

**703D(5)** If a company fails to comply with subsection (1), (2) or (3), then, unless particulars of the charge have been delivered for registration by another person, the company and every officer of it who is in default is liable to a fine.

**703D(6)** Section 398(2), (4) and (5) (recovery of fees paid in connection with registration, filing of particulars in register and sending of copy of particulars filed and note as to date) apply in relation to particulars delivered under this Chapter.

*Registrar to whom particulars, etc. to be delivered*

**703E(1)** The particulars required to be delivered by section 703D(1) (charges over property of oversea company becoming registered in a part of Great Britain) shall be delivered to the registrar to whom the documents are delivered under paragraph 1 of Schedule 21A or, as the case may be, section 691.

**703E(2)** The particulars required to be delivered by section 703D(2) or (3) (charges over property of registered oversea company) shall be, delivered–

(a) where the company is a company to which section 690A applies–

(i) if it has registered a branch in one part of Great Britain but has not registered a branch in the other, to the registrar for the part in which it has registered a branch,

(ii) if it has registered a branch in both parts of Great Britain but the property subject to the charge is situated in one part of Great Britain only, to the registrar for that part, and

(iii) in any other case, to the registrars for both parts of Great Britain; and

(b) where the company is a company to which section 691 applies–

(i) if it is registered in one part of Great Britain and not in the other, to the registrar for the part in which it is registered,

(ii) if it is registered in both parts of Great Britain but the property subject to the charge is situated in one part of Great Britain only, to the registrar for that part, and

(iii) in any other case, to the registrar for both parts of Great Britain.

**703E(3)** Other documents required or authorised by virtue of this Chapter to be delivered to the registrar shall be delivered to the registrar or registrars to whom particulars of the charge to which they relate have been, or ought to have been, delivered.

**703E(4)** If a company ceases to be a registered oversea company in relation to either part of Great Britain, charges over property of the company shall cease to be subject to the provisions of this Chapter, as regards registration in that part of Great Britain, as from the date on which the notice under section 695A(3) or, as the case may be, 696(3) is given.

This is without prejudice to rights arising by reason of events occurring before that date.

*Effect of failure to deliver particulars, late delivery and effect of errors and omissions*

**703F(1)** The following provisions of Part XII–

(a) section 399 (effect of failure to deliver particulars),

(b) section 400 (late delivery of particulars), and

(c) section 402 (effect of errors and omissions in particulars delivered),

apply, with the following modifications, in relation to a charge created by a registered oversea company of which particulars are required to be delivered under this Chapter.

**703F(2)** Those provisions do not apply to a charge of which particulars are required to be delivered under section 703D(1) (charges existing when company delivers documents under section 691).

**703F(3)** In relation to a charge of which particulars are required to be delivered under section 703D(3) (charges registrable by virtue of property being within Great Britain for requisite period), the references to the period of 21 days after the charge's creation shall be construed as references to the period of four months referred to in that subsection.

*Delivery of further particulars or memorandum*

**703G** Sections 401 and 403 (delivery of further particulars and memorandum of charge ceasing to affect company's property) apply in relation to a charge of which particulars have been delivered under this Chapter.

*Further provisions with respect to voidness of charges*

**703H(1)** The following provisions of Part XII apply in relation to the voidness of a charge by virtue of this Chapter–

(a) section 404 (exclusion of voidness as against unregistered charges),

(b) section 405 (restrictions on cases in which charge is void),

(c) section 406 (effect of exercise of power of sale), and

(d) section 407 (effect of voidness on obligation secured).

**703H(2)** In relation to a charge of which particulars are required to be delivered under section 703D(3) (charges registrable by virtue of property being within Great Britain for requisite period), the reference in section 404 to the period of 21 days after the charge's creation shall be construed as a reference to the period of four months referred to in that subsection.

*Additional information to be registered*

**703I(1)** Section 408 (particulars of taking up of issue of debentures) applies in relation to a charge of which particulars have been delivered under this Chapter.

**703I(2)** Section 409 (notice of appointment of receiver or manager) applies in relation to the appointment of a receiver or manager of property of a registered oversea company.

**703I(3)** Regulations under section 410 (notice of crystallisation of floating charge, etc.) may apply in relation to a charge of which particulars have been delivered under this Chapter; but subject to such exceptions, adaptations and modifications as may be specified in the regulations.

*Copies of instruments and register to be kept by company*

**703J(1)** Sections 411 and 412 (copies of instruments and register to be kept by company) apply in relation to a registered oversea company and any charge over property of the company situated in Great Britain.

**703J(2)** They apply to any charge, whether or not particulars are required to be delivered to the registrar.

**703J(3)** In relation to such a company the references to the company's registered office shall be construed as references to its principal place of business in Great Britain.

*Power to make further provision by regulations*

**703K(1)** The Secretary of State may by regulations make further provision as to the application of the provisions of this Chapter, or the provisions of Part XII applied by this Chapter, in relation to charges of any description specified in the regulations.

**703K(2)** The regulations may apply any provisions of regulations made under section 413 (power to make further provision with respect to application of Part XII) or make any provision which may be made under that section with respect to the application of provisions of Part XII.

*Provisions as to situation of property*

**703L(1)** The following provisions apply for determining for the purposes of this Chapter whether a vehicle which is the property of an oversea company is situated in Great Britain–

(a) a ship, aircraft or hovercraft shall be regarded as situated in Great Britain if, and only if, it is registered in Great Britain;

(b) any other description of vehicle shall be regarded as situated in Great Britain on a day if, and only if, at any time on that day the management of the vehicle is directed from a place of business of the company in Great Britain;

and for the purposes of this Chapter a vehicle shall not be regarded as situated in one part of Great Britain only.

**703L(2)** For the purposes of this Chapter as it applies to a charge on future property, the subject-matter of the charge shall be treated as situated in Great Britain unless it relates exclusively to property of a kind which cannot, after being acquired or coming into existence, be situated in Great Britain; and references to property situated in a part of Great Britain shall be similarly construed.

*Other supplementary provisions*

**703M** The following provisions of Part XII apply for the purposes of this Chapter–

(a) section 414 (construction of references to date of creation of charge),
(b) section 415 (prescribed particulars and related expressions),
(c) section 416 (notice of matters disclosed on the register),
(d) section 417 (power of court to dispense with signature),
(e) section 418 (regulations) and
(f) section 419 (minor definitions).

*Index of defined expressions*

**703N** The following Table shows the provisions of this Chapter and Part XII defining or otherwise explaining expressions used in this Chapter (other than expressions used only in the same section)–

| | |
|---|---|
| charge | sections 703A(2), 703B(3) and 395(2) |
| charge requiring registration | sections 703B(1) and 396 |
| creation of charge | sections 703M(f) and 419(2) |
| date of acquisition (of property by a company) | sections 703M(f) and 419(3) |
| date of creation of charge | sections 703M(a) and 414 |
| property | sections 703A(2) and 395(2) |
| registered oversea company | section 703A(3) |
| registrar and registration in relation to a charge | sections 703A(4) and 703E |
| situated in Great Britain in relation to vehicles | section 703L(1) |
| in relation to future property | section 703L(2)". |

**History**
Prospective Ch. III amended by the Oversea Companies and Credit and Financial Institutions (Branch Disclosure) Regulations 1992 (SI 1992/3179), reg. 4 and Sch. 3, para. 11–15 as from 1 January 1993 as follows:

- s. 703A(3)(a) inserted and remainder renumbered (b);
- s. 703B(2)(a) substituted; s. 703B(2)(a) previously read as follows:

"(a) in the case of a charge over property of a company at the date it delivers documents for registration under section 691, as at that date."

- s. 703D(1)(a)–(b) substituted for the former words "delivers documents for registration under section 691" and s. 703D(1A) inserted;
- in s. 703E(1) the words "paragraph 1 of Schedule 21A or, as the case may be," inserted; and s. 703E(2)(a)–(b) substituted; s. 703E(2)(a)–(b) previously read as follows:

"(a) if the company is registered in one part of Great Britain and not in the other, to the registrar for the part in which it is registered, and

(b) if the company is registered in both parts of Great Britain but the property subject to the charge is situated in one part of Great Britain only, to the registrar for that part;

and in any other case the particulars shall be delivered to the registrars for both parts of Great Britain."

- in s. 703E(4) first sentence substituted; the first sentence previously read as follows:

"If a company gives notice under section 696(4) that it has ceased to have an established place of business in either part of Great Britain, charges over property of the company shall cease to be subject to the provisions of this Chapter, as regards registration in that part of Great Britain, as from the date on which notice is so given."

# Schedule 16 – Amendments Consequential on Part IV

Section 107

**Note**
See note to Pt. IV.

## LAND CHARGES ACT 1972 (c. 61)

**1(1)** Section 3 of the Land Charges Act 1972 (registration of land charges) is amended as follows.

**1(2)** In subsection (7) (registration in companies charges register to have same effect as registration under that Act), for "any of the enactments mentioned in subsection (8) below" substitute "Part XII, or Chapter III of Part XXIII, of the Companies Act 1985 (or corresponding earlier enactments)".

**1(3)** In subsection (8) for "The enactments" substitute "The corresponding earlier enactments" and at the end insert "as originally enacted".

## COMPANIES ACT 1985 (c. 6)

**1A** Section 695A(1) is amended by the insertion of the words "or Chapter III of this Part" after "Schedule 21C".

**History**
Para. 1A inserted by the Oversea Companies and Credit and Financial Institutions (Branch Disclosure) Regulations 1992 (SI 1992/3179), reg. 4 and Sch. 3, para. 16 as from 1 January 1993.

**2(1)** Schedule 24 to the Companies Act 1985 (punishment of offences) is amended as follows.

**2(2)** For the entries relating to sections 399(3) to 423(3) (offences under Part XII: registration of charges) substitute–

| | | | |
|---|---|---|---|
| "398(3) | Company failing to deliver particulars of charge to registrar. | 1. On indictment.<br>2. Summary. | A fine.<br>The statutory maximum. |
| 408(3) | Company failing to deliver particulars of taking up of issue of debentures. | Summary. | One-fifth of the statutory maximum. |
| 409(4) | Failure to give notice to registrar of appointment of receiver or manager, or of his ceasing to act. | Summary. | One-fifth of the statutory maximum. |
| 410(4) | Failure to comply with requirements of regulations under s. 410. | Summary. | One-fifth of the statutory maximum. |
| 411(4) | Failure to keep copies of charging instruments or register at registered office. | 1. On indictment.<br>2. Summary. | A fine.<br>The statutory maximum. |
| 412(4) | Refusing inspection of charging instrument or register or failing to supply copies. | Summary. | One-fifth of the statutory maximum.". |

**2(3)** After the entry relating to section 703(1) insert–

| | | | |
|---|---|---|---|
| "703D(5) | Oversea company failing to deliver particulars of charge to registrar. | 1. On indictment.<br>2. Summary. | A fine.<br>The statutory maximum.". |

## INSOLVENCY ACT 1986 (c. 45)

**3(1)** The Insolvency Act 1986 is amended as follows.

**3(2)** In section 9(3) (restrictions on making administration order where administrative receiver has been appointed), in paragraph (b) (exceptions) insert–

"(i) be void against the administrator to any extent by virtue of the provisions of Part XII of the Companies Act 1985 (registration of company charges),";

and renumber the existing sub-paragraphs as (ii) to (iv).

**3(3)** In sections 45(5), 53(2), 54(3) and 62(5) (offences of failing to deliver documents relating to appointment or cessation of appointment of receiver) omit the words "and, for continued contravention, to a daily default fine".

## COMPANY DIRECTORS DISQUALIFICATION ACT 1986 (c. 46)

**4** In Schedule 1 to the Company Directors Disqualification Act 1986 (matters relevant to determining unfitness of directors), in paragraph 4 (failure of company to comply with certain provisions), for sub-paragraph (h) substitute–

"(h) sections 398 and 703D (duty of company to deliver particulars of charges on its property).".

## ATOMIC ENERGY AUTHORITY ACT 1986 (c. 3)

**42** In section 9 of the Atomic Energy Authority Act 1986 (interpretation), in the definition of "subsidiary" and "wholly-owned subsidiary" for "have the same meaning as in" substitute "have the meaning given by section 736 of".

## AIRPORTS ACT 1986 (c. 31)

**43** In section 82 of the Airports Act 1986 (general interpretation), in the definition of "subsidiary" for "has the same meaning as in" substitute "has the meaning given by section 736 of".

## GAS ACT 1986 (c. 44)

**44** In the Gas Act 1986–

(a) in section 48(1) (interpretation of Part I), in the definitions of "holding company" and "subsidiary", and

(b) in section 61(1) (interpretation of Part II), in the definition of "subsidiary",

for "has the same meaning as in" substitute "has the meaning given by section 736 of".

## BUILDING SOCIETIES ACT 1986 (c. 53)

**45** In section 119 of the Building Societies Act 1986 (interpretation), in the definition of "subsidiary" for "has the same meaning as in" substitute "has the meaning given by section 736 of".

## INCOME AND CORPORATION TAXES ACT 1988 (c. 1)

**46** In section 141 of the Income and Corporation Taxes Act 1988 (benefits in kind: non-cash vouchers), in the definition of "subsidiary" in subsection (7) for "section 736(5)(b)" substitute "section 736".

## BRITISH STEEL ACT 1988 (c. 35)

**47** In section 15(1) of the British Steel Act 1988 (interpretation), in the definition of "subsidiary" for "has the same meaning as in" substitute "has the meaning given by section 736 of".

# Schedule 20 – Amendments about Mergers and Related Matters

Section 153

**Note**
Sch. 20, para. 1,17,21 in force from 1 April 1990 (see SI 1990/142 (C 5)); para. 2,12,14-16,19,20, 22-25 in force from 16 November 1989 (see CA 1989, s. 215(1)(b)(ii)).

## FAIR TRADING ACT 1973 (c. 41)

**1** In section 46 of the Fair Trading Act 1973, subsection (3) is omitted.

**2(1)** In section 60 of that Act–

(a) in subsection (1) for "the period of three months beginning with the date of the" there is substituted "such period (not being longer than three months beginning with the date of the reference) as may be specified in the",

(b) in subsection (2) for "original period of three months" there is substituted "period specified in the newspaper merger reference", and

(c) in subsection (3) for "subsection (1)" there is substituted "the newspaper merger reference".

**2(2)** This paragraph does not apply in relation to any newspaper merger reference made before the passing of this Act.

**12(1)** In section 83 of that Act, after subsection (3) there is inserted–

"(3A) Without prejudice to subsection (3) above, if the Minister or Ministers to whom any such report is made consider that it would not be in the public interest to disclose–

(a) any matter contained in the report relating to the private affairs of an individual whose interests would, in the opinion of the Minister or Ministers, be seriously and prejudicially affected by the publication of that matter, or

(b) any matter contained in the report relating specifically to the affairs of a particular person whose interests would, in the opinion of the Minister or Ministers, be seriously and prejudicially affected by the publication of that matter,

the Minister or Ministers shall exclude that matter from the copies of the report as laid before Parliament and from the report as published under this section.".

**12(2)** This paragraph does not apply in relation to any report made before the passing of this Act.

**14(1)** In section 88 of that Act, in subsection (1) for the words from "if requested" to "the relevant parties" there is substituted "to comply with any request of the appropriate Minister or Ministers to consult with any persons mentioned in the request (referred to below in this section as "the relevant parties")".

**14(2)** After subsection (2) of that section there is inserted–

"(2A) Where–

(a) an undertaking is given under this section after the commencement of this subsection, or

(b) an undertaking given under this section is varied or released after that time,

the Minister to whom the undertaking is or was given shall cause the undertaking or, as the case may be, the variation or release to be published in such manner as the Minister may consider appropriate.".

**14(3)** In subsection (4) of that section–

(a) in paragraph (a) for "it" there is substituted "the undertaking is no longer appropriate and either the relevant parties (or any of them) can be released from the undertaking or the undertaking", and

(b) in paragraph (b) for "that it" there is substituted "that any person can be so released or that an undertaking",

and in subsection (5), after "varied" (in both places) there is inserted "or revoked".

**14(4)** In subsection (6) of that section the words from ""the relevant parties"" to the "and" immediately following paragraph (c) are omitted.

**14(5)** Sub-paragraphs (1) and (4) (and the repeal in Schedule 24 corresponding to sub-paragraph (4)) do not apply in relation to any report made before the passing of this Act.

**15(1)** In section 89 of that Act, in subsection (1), for paragraphs (a) and (b) there is substituted–

"(a) in the circumstances specified in subsection (1) of any of the following sections–

(i) sections 56, 73 and 75K of this Act, and

(ii) section 10 of the Competition Act 1980,

the Secretary of State makes, has made, or has under consideration the making or, an order under the section in question exercising any of the powers specified in Schedule 8 to this Act, or

(b) in the circumstances specified in subsection (1) or section 12 of the Competition Act 1980 the Secretary of State makes, has made, or has under consideration the making of, an order under subsection (5) of that section exercising any of those powers.".

**15(2)** In subsection (2) of that section, "Part II of" is omitted.

**15(3)** In subsection (3) of that section, after paragraph (b) there is inserted–

"(bb) require any person to furnish any such information to the Director as may be specified or described in the order;".

**15(4)** The amendments made by sub-paragraphs (1) to (3) have effect in relation to the making of any order under section 89 of the Fair Trading Act 1973 after the passing of this Act, whether the principal order (within the meaning of that section) was made before or after that time.

**16(1)** Section 90 of that Act is amended as follows.

**16(2)** In subsection (1) after "section 74" there is inserted ", section 75K".

**16(3)** For subsection (5) there is substituted–

"(5) Nothing in any order to which this section applies shall have effect so as to–

(a) cancel or modify conditions in licences granted–

(i) under a patent granted under the Patents Act 1949 or the Patents Act 1977 or a European patent (UK) (within the meaning of the Patents Act 1977), or

(ii) in respect of a design registered under the Registered Designs Act 1949,

by the proprietor of the patent or design, or

(b) require an entry to be made in the register of patents or the register of designs to the effect that licences under such a patent or such a design are to be available as of right.".

**17** In section 132(1) of that Act, after "85(6)" there is inserted "section 93B".

**19(1)** Schedule 8 to that Act is amended as follows.

**19(2)** [Insertion of Sch. 8, para. 9A.]

**19(3)** [Insertion of Sch. 8, para. 12A–12C.]

**20(1)** In Schedule 9 to that Act, in paragraph 4 the words from "either" to the end are omitted.

**20(2)** This paragraph has effect in relation to the laying of any draft order under paragraph 4 of Schedule 9 to the Fair Trading Act 1973 after the passing of this Act, whether the notice under that Schedule was published before or after that time.

## COMPETITION ACT 1980 (C. 21)

**21–24** (Omitted and repealed by Competition Act 1998, s. 74(1), Sch. 12, para. 13 and s. 74(3), Sch. 14 as from 1 March 2000.)

**History**
In relation to the date of omission and repeal of para. 21–24 see Competition Act (Commencement No. 5) Order 2000 (SI 2000/344 (C 9)), art. 2, Sch.; para. 21–24 formerly read as follows:

"**21** In section 3(8) of the Competition Act 1980–

(a) for "(5)" there is substituted "(6)", and

(b) at the end there is inserted "but as if, in subsection (7) of that section, for the words from "any one" to "the Commission" there were substituted "the Director"".

**22** In section 4(4) of that Act for paragraph (a) there is substituted–

"(a) to arrange for–

(i) any undertaking accepted by him under this section, and

(ii) any variation or release of such an undertaking after the passing of the Companies Act 1989,to be published in such manner as appears to him to be appropriate,".

**23** In section 9(4) of that Act–

(a) in paragraph (a), after "undertaking" there is inserted "and of any variation of it after the passing of the Companies Act 1989", and

(b) in paragraph (b), after "undertaking" there is inserted "and any variation or release of it after that time".

**24** In section 29(1)(a) of that Act after "section" there is inserted "75G or"."

## TELECOMMUNICATIONS ACT 1984 (c. 12)

**25(1)** In section 13(9) of the Telecommunications Act 1984, after "Commission)" there is inserted "together with section 24 of the Competition Act 1980 (modification of provisions about performance of Commission's functions)".

**25(2)** The Monopolies and Mergers Commission (Performance of Functions) Order 1989 shall have effect as if sub-paragraph (1) above had come into force immediately before the making of the Order.

# Schedule 21 – Additional Requirements for Recognition

Section 156(1)

**Note**
See note at beginning of Pt. VII.

## Part I – UK Investment Exchanges

### DEFAULT RULES

**1(1)** The exchange must have default rules which, in the event of a member of the exchange appearing to be unable to meet his obligations in respect of one or more market contracts, enable action to be taken in respect of unsettled market contracts to which he is party.

**1(2)** The rules may authorise the taking of the same or similar action in relation to a member who appears to be likely to become unable to meet his obligations in respect of one or more market contracts.

**1(3)** The rules must enable action to be taken in respect of all unsettled market contracts, other than those entered into by a recognised clearing house for the purposes of or in connection with the provision of clearing services for the exchange.

**1(4)** As regards contracts falling within section 155(2)(b) above, the rules must contain provision corresponding to that required by paragraphs 9 to 11 below in the case of a UK clearing house.

**History**
In para. 1(4) the former words "entered into by the exchange for the purposes of or in connection with the provision of its own clearing services" appearing after the words "As regards contracts" replaced by the words "falling within section 155(2)(b) above" by the Financial Markets and Insolvency Regulations 1998 (SI 1998/1748), reg. 1, 2 and 5(1) as from 11 August 1998.

**1(5)** As regards contracts falling within section 155(2)(a) above the rules must contain provision complying with paragraphs 2 and 3 below.

**History**
In para. 1(4) the former words "other contracts" appearing after the words "As regards" replaced by the words "contracts falling within section 155(2)(a) above" by the Financial Markets and Insolvency Regulations 1998 (SI 1998/1748), reg. 1, 2 and 5(2) as from 11 August 1998.

### CONTENT OF RULES

**2(1)** The rules must provide for all rights and liabilities between those party as principal to unsettled market contracts to which the defaulter is party as principal to be discharged and for there to be paid by one party to the other such sum of money (if any) as may be determined in accordance with the rules.

**2(2)** The rules must further provide–

(a) for the sums so payable in respect of different contracts between the same parties to be aggregated or set off so as to produce a net sum, and

(b) for the certification by or on behalf of the exchange of the net sum payable or, as the case may be, of the fact that no sum is payable.

**2(3)** The rules may make special provision with respect to, or exclude from the provisions required by sub-paragraphs (1) and (2), contracts of any description prescribed for the purposes of this sub-paragraph by regulations made by the Secretary of State.

**Note**
See the Financial Markets and Insolvency Regulations 1991 (SI 1991/880).

**2(4)** The reference in sub-paragraph (1) to rights and liabilities between those party as principal to unsettled market contracts does not include rights and liabilities–

(a) in respect of margin; or

(b) arising out of a failure to perform a market contract.

**History**
Para. 2(4) added by the Financial Markets and Insolvency Regulations 1991 (SI 1991/880), reg. 1 and 17 as from 25 April 1991.

(a) may be claimed in the sequestration or winding up or, as the case may be, is payable to the relevant office-holder, and

(b) shall be taken into account for the purposes of any rule of law relating to compensation or set-off applicable in sequestration or winding up,

in the same way as a debt due before the date of sequestration (within the meaning of section 73(1) of the Bankruptcy (Scotland) Act 1985) or the commencement of the winding up.

**7(1)** Sections 178, 186, 315 and 345 of the Insolvency Act 1986 (power to disclaim onerous property and court's power to order rescission of contracts, etc.) do not apply in relation to–

(a) a market contract, or

(b) a contract effected by the exchange or clearing house for the purpose of realising property provided as margin in relation to market contracts.

In the application of this sub-paragraph in Scotland, the reference to sections 178 and 315 shall be construed as a reference to any rule of law having the like effect as those sections.

**7(2)** Sections 127 and 284 of the Insolvency Act 1986 (avoidance of property dispositions effected after commencement of winding up or presentation of bankruptcy petition) do not apply to–

(a) a market contract, or any disposition of property in pursuance of such a contract,

(b) the provision of margin in relation to market contracts,

(c) a contract effected by the exchange or clearing house for the purpose of realising property provided as margin in relation to a market contract, or any disposition of property in pursuance of such a contract, or

(d) any disposition of property in accordance with the rules of the exchange or clearing house as to the application of property provided as margin.

**7(3)** However, if a person enters into a market contract knowing that a petition has been presented for the winding up or bankruptcy of the other party to the contract, the value of any profit or benefit to him arising from the contract is recoverable from him by the relevant office-holder unless the court directs otherwise.

**7(4)** Any sum recoverable by virtue of sub-paragraph (3) has the same priority, in the event of the insolvency of the person from whom it is due, as if it were secured by a fixed charge.

**8(1)** No order shall be made in relation to a market contract under–

(a) section 238 or 339 of the Insolvency Act 1986 (transactions at an under- value),

(b) section 239 or 340 of that Act (preferences), or

(c) section 423 of that Act (transactions defrauding creditors),

unless the court is satisfied that the person in favour of whom the contract was made knew at the time he entered into it that it was at an under-value (within the meaning of the relevant provision) or, as the case may be, that a preference was being given.

**8(2)** As respects Scotland, no decree shall be granted in relation to a market contract–

(a) under section 34 or 36 of the Bankruptcy (Scotland) Act 1985 or section 242 or 243 of the Insolvency Act 1986 (gratuitous alienations and unfair preferences), or

(b) at common law,

unless the court is satisfied that the person with whom the contract was made knew at the time he entered into it that it was challengeable under any of the provisions mentioned in paragraph (a) or at common law.

**8(3)** Sub-paragraphs (1) and (2) apply in relation to–

(a) a disposition of property in pursuance of a market contract,

(b) the provision of margin in relation to market contracts,

(c) a contract effected by a recognised investment exchange or recognised clearing house for the purpose of realising property provided as margin, or

(d) a disposition of property in accordance with the rules of the exchange or clearing house as to the application of property provided as margin, as they apply in relation to the making of a market contract.

## MARKET CHARGES

**9(1)** The charges to which paragraphs 10 to 12 apply are charges, whether fixed or floating, granted–

(a) in favour of a recognised investment exchange, for the purpose of securing debts or liabilities arising in connection with the settlement of market contracts,

(b) in favour of a recognised clearing house, for the purpose of securing debts or liabilities arising in connection with their ensuring the performance of market contracts, or

(c) in favour of a person who agrees to make payments as a result of the transfer of specified securities made through the medium of a computer-based system established by the Bank of England and The Stock Exchange, for the purpose of securing debts or liabilities of the transferee arising in connection with the payments.

Those charges are referred to in this Schedule as "market charges".

**9(2)** Where a charge is granted partly for purposes specified in sub-paragraph (1)(a), (b) or (c) and partly for other purposes, paragraphs 10 to 12 apply to it so far as it has effect for the specified purposes; and the expression "market charge" shall be construed accordingly.

**9(3)** In this paragraph and paragraphs 10 to 12–

**"charge"** means any form of security, including a mortgage and, in Scotland, a heritable security; and

**"specified securities"** means securities for the time being specified in the list in Schedule 1 to the Stock Transfer Act 1982, and includes any right to such securities.

**10** The general law of insolvency has effect in relation to market charges and action taken in enforcing them subject to the following provisions of this Schedule.

**11(1)** Sections 10(1)(b) and 11(3)(c) of the Insolvency Act 1986 (no enforcement of security while petition for administration order pending or order in force) do not apply to a market charge.

**11(2)** Section 11(2) of that Act (receiver to vacate office when so required by administrator) does not apply to a receiver appointed under a market charge.

**11(3)** Section 15(1) and (2) of that Act (administrator's power to deal with charged property) do not apply to a market charge.

**11(4)** Sections 127 and 284 of that Act (avoidance of property dispositions effected after commencement of winding up or presentation of bankruptcy petition) do not apply to–

(a) a disposition of property as a result of which the property becomes subject to a market charge, or any transaction pursuant to which that disposition is made, or

(b) any disposition of property made in enforcing a market charge.

**11(5)** However, if a person (other than the chargee under the market charge) who is a party to a disposition mentioned in sub-paragraph (4)(a) knows at the time of the disposition that a petition has been presented for the winding up or bankruptcy of the party making the disposition, the value of any profit or benefit to him arising from the disposition is recoverable from him by the relevant office-holder unless the court directs otherwise.

**11(6)** Any sum recoverable by virtue of sub-paragraph (5) has the same priority, in the event of the insolvency of the person from whom it is due, as if it were secured by a fixed charge.

**12(1)** No legal proceedings, execution or other legal process may be commenced or continued, and no distress may be levied against property which is, or becomes, subject to a market charge except with the consent of the person in whose favour the charge was granted or the leave of the court.

**12(2)** The court may give leave subject to such terms as it thinks fit.

**12(3)** Sub-paragraph (1) does not apply to proceedings to enforce any security over, or any equitable interest in, the property.

**12(4)** Sections 10(1)(c), 11(3)(d), 130(3) and 285(3) of the Insolvency Act 1986 (which restrict the taking of certain legal proceedings and other steps) have effect accordingly.

| Companies Act 1989 provision | Main effect | Affected provision |
|---|---|---|
| | substitution | |
| 19 | insertion | CA 1985, s. 256 |
| 20 | insertion | s. 257 |
| 21 | insertion | s. 258, Sch. 10A |
| 22 | insertion | s. 259, 260, 261, 262, 262A |
| 23 | | |
| 24–54 | | See CA 1985, Ch. V |
| 55 | insertion | s. 432 |
| 56 | amendment; substitution; insertion | s. 434, 436 |
| 57 | insertion | s. 437 |
| 58 | substitution | s. 438 |
| 59 | amendment; substitution | s. 439 |
| 60 | repeal; substitution; insertion | s. 440<br>IA 1986, s. 124(4)(b)<br>s. 124A |
| 61 | substitution | CA 1985, s. 441 |
| 62 | substitution | s. 442 |
| 63(1) | amendment | s. 447 |
| 63(2) | omission; substitution | s. 447(1)<br>s. 447(2)–(6) |
| 63(3) | substitution | s. 447 |
| 63(4) | substitution | s. 447(3) |
| 63(5) | insertion | s. 447(4) |
| 63(6) | substitution | s. 447(6) |
| 63(7) | insertion | s. 447(9) |
| 63(8) | substitution | Sch. 24 |
| 64(1) | substitution | s. 448 |
| 64(2) | substitution | Sch. 24 |
| 65(1) | amendment | s. 449 |
| 65(2) | amendment | s. 449(1) |
| 65(3) | substitution | s. 449(1A) |
| 65(4) | substitution | s. 449(1B) |
| 65(5) | substitution | s. 449(2) |
| 65(6) | substitution | s. 449(3) |
| 65(7) | substitution | s. 449(4) |
| 66(1) | amendment | s. 450 |
| 66(2) | substitution | s. 450(1) |
| 66(3) | substitution | s. 450(4) |
| 66(4) | insertion | s. 450(5) |
| 67 | substitution | s. 451 |
| 68 | substitution | s. 451A |
| 69(1) | amendment | s. 452 |
| 69(2) | omission | s. 452(1)(b) |
| 69(3) | insertion | s. 452(1A), (1B) |
| 69(4) | insertion | s. 452(3) |
| 70 | substitution | s. 453 |
| 71 | substitution | Sch. 22 |
| 72(1) | amendment | FSA 1986, s. 94 |
| 72(2) | substitution | s. 94(7), (7A) |

| Companies Act 1989 provision | Main effect | Affected provision |
|---|---|---|
| 72(3) | insertion | FSA 1986, s. 94(8A), (8B) |
| 72(4) | addition | s. 94(10) |
| 73(1) | amendment | s. 105 |
| 73(2) | omission | s. 105(7) |
| 73(3) | substitution | s. 105(9) |
| 73(4) | addition | s. 105(11) |
| 73(5) | insertion | s. 106(2A) |
| 74(1) | amendment | s. 177 |
| 74(2) | insertion | s. 177(2A) |
| 74(3) | insertion | s. 177(5A) |
| 74(4) | substitution | s. 177(8) |
| 74(5) | substitution | s. 177(10) |
| 74(6) | addition | s. 177(11) |
| 75(1) | amendment | s. 179(3) |
| 75(2) | amendment | s. 180 |
| 75(3) | amendment | s. 180(1) |
| 75(4) | insertion | s. 180(1A) |
| 75(5) | substitution | s. 180(3) |
| 75(6) | omission | s. 180(6) |
| 75(7) | substitution | s. 180(9) |
| 76(1) | amendment | s. 199 |
| 76(2) | substitution | s. 199(1), (2) |
| 76(3) | substitution | s. 199(3)(b) |
| 76(4) | substitution | s. 199(5)(b) |
| 76(5) | insertion | s. 199(6) |
| 76(6) | insertion | s. 199(7) |
| 76(7) | substitution | s. 199(8) |
| 76(8) | omission | s. 199(9) |
| 77(1) | amendment | ICA 1982, Part II |
| 77(2) | substitution | s. 44 |
| 77(3) | insertion | s. 44A |
| 77(4) | insertion | s. 47A |
| 77(5) | insertion | s. 71(2A) |
| 77(6) | substitution | s. 71(6) |
| 78 | amendment | IA 1986, s. 218(5) |
| 79 | amendment | CDDA 1986, s. 8 |
| 80 | amendment | BSA 1987, s. 53 |
| 81(1)–(5) | amendment | s. 84(1) |
| 92–107 | insertion | CA 1985, Pt.XII |
| 108(1) | substitution | s. 35–35B |
| 108(2) | insertion | s. 322A |
| 108(3) | substitution | Sch. 22 |
| 109(1) | insertion | s. 322A |
| 109(2) | insertion | Sch. 22 |
| 110(1) | insertion | s. 3A |
| 110(2) | substitution | s. 4 |
| 111 | repealed | ChA 1960, s. 30 |
| 112(3) | non–application | CA 1985, s. 35, 35A |
| 112(8) | application | s. 349(2)–(4) |
| 113(2) | insertion | s. 381A–381C |
| 113(3) | insertion | s. 382A |
| 114(1) | insertion | Sch. 15A |

| Companies Act 1989 provision | Main effect | Affected provision |
|---|---|---|
| 115(1) | insertion | CA 1985, Pt.IV |
| 115(2) | insertion | s. 366A |
| 115(3) | insertion | s. 369(4), 378(3) |
| 116(1) | | |
| 116(2) | insertion | s. 379A |
| 116(3) | insertion | s. 380(4)(bb) |
| 118(1) | replacement | Sch.V, Pt. XI |
| 118(2) | exception | s. 389 |
| 119(1) | insertion | s. 384–388A |
| 119(2) | insertion | Sch. 24 |
| 119(3) | substitution | BA 1987, s. 46(2), (4) |
| 120(1) | insertion | CA 1985, s. 389A–390 |
| 120(2) | insertion | s. 734 |
| 120(3) | insertion | Sch. 24 |
| 120(4) | substitution | ISA 1982, Sch. 4, para 3(6) |
| 121 | insertion | CA 1985, s. 390A, 390B |
| 122(1) | insertion | s. 391–393 |
| 122(2) | insertion | Sch. 24 |
| 123(1) | insertion | s. 394–394A |
| 123(2) | insertion | Sch. 24 |
| 123(3) | insertion | s. 733 |
| 124 | repeal | TULR(C)A 1992, s. 300(1), Sch. 1 |
| 125(1) | substitution | CA 1985, s. 706 |
| 125(2) | substitution | s. 707 |
| 126(1) | insertion | s. 707A |
| 126(2) | substitution | s. 709–710A |
| 127(1) | insertion | s. 715A |
| 127(2) | amendment | s. 708 |
| 127(3) | omission | s. 712, 715 |
| 127(4) | substitution | s. 713(1) |
| 127(5) | amendment | s. 735A(2) |
| 127(6) | insertion | s. 735B |
| 127(7) | substitution | Sch. 22 |
| 128 | insertion | s. 8A |
| 129(1) | substitution | s. 23 |
| 129(2) | substitution | Sch. 2 |
| 130(1) | substitution | s. 36 |
| 130(2) | insertion | s. 36A |
| 130(3) | repealed | |
| 130(4) | insertion | s. 36C |
| 130(5) | insertion | Sch. 22 |
| 130(6) | | |
| 130(7) | | |
| 131(1) | insertion | s. 111A |
| 131(2) | substitution | s. 116 |
| 132 | substitution | s. 153 |
| 133(2) | insertion | s. 159 |
| 133(3) | amendment | s. 160 |
| 133(4) | substitution | s. 162(2) |
| 134(2) | substitution | s. 199(2) |
| 134(3) | substitution | s. 202(1), (4), 206(8) |

| Companies Act 1989 provision | Main effect | Affected provision |
|---|---|---|
| 134(4) | substitution | CA 1985, s. 202(3) |
| 134(5) | insertion | s. 210A |
| 134(6) | | |
| 135 | | |
| 136 | substitution | s. 287 |
| 137(1) | substitution | s. 310(3) |
| 137(2) | insertion | Sch. 7 |
| 138 | amendment | Pt.X |
| 139(1) | substitution | s. 363–365 |
| 139(3) | substitution | Sch. 24 |
| 139(4) | substitution | CDDA 1986, Sch. 1 |
| 139(5) | substitution | ICTA 1988, s. 565(6) |
| 140(1) | substitution | CA 1985, s. 463(1) |
| 140(2) | amendment | s. 464 |
| 140(3) | insertion | s. 464(1)(b) |
| 140(4) | insertion | s. 464(1A) |
| 140(5) | substitution | s. 464(3) |
| 140(6) | addition | s. 464(5)(e) |
| 140(7) | insertion | s. 464(6) |
| 140(8) | amendment | s. 466 |
| 141(1) | amendment | s. 651 |
| 141(2) | omission | s. 651(1) |
| 141(3) | addition | s. 651(4)–(7) |
| 141(4) | application | s. 651(5) |
| 141(5) | | |
| 142(1) | insertion | s. 711A |
| 142(2) | insertion | Sch. 22 |
| 143(1) | insertion | s. 723A |
| 143(2) | omission | s. 169(5) |
| 143(3) | omission | s. 175(6)(b) |
| 143(4) | amendment | s. 191(1)–(3) |
| 143(5) | amendment | s. 219(1), (2) |
| 143(6) | omission | s. 288(3) |
| 143(7) | omission | s. 318(7) |
| 143(8) | amendment | s. 356(1)–(4) |
| 143(9) | amendment | s. 383(1)–(3) |
| 143(10) | amendment | Sch. 13 |
| 143(11) | insertion | Sch. 22 |
| 144(1) | substitution | s. 736, 736A |
| 144(2) | | |
| 144(3) | insertion | s. 736B |
| 145 | | |
| 146 | insertion | FTA 1973, s. 75A–75F |
| 147 | insertion | s. 75G–75K |
| 148 | insertion | s. 93A |
| 149(1) | insertion | s. 75(4A)– (4M) |
| 150(1) | insertion | s. 66A |
| 151 | insertion | s. 93B |
| 168(1) | application | FSA 1986, s. 114 |
| 168(3) | reference | s. 115 |
| 169(1) | application | s. 61 |
| 169(2) | application | s. 12, 37(7)(b), 39(7)(b) |

| Provisions of relevant Acts | Companies Act 1989 provision |
|---|---|
| *Companies Act 1985* | |
| 287 | 136 |
| 288(3) | 143(6), Sch. 24 |
| 289 | Sch. 19, para. 2 |
| 289(4) | Sch. 10, para. 9 |
| 290 | Sch. 19, para. 3 |
| 305 | Sch. 19, para. 4 |
| 310(3) | 137(1) |
| 318(7) | 143(7), Sch. 24 |
| 321 | Sch. 19, para. 8 |
| *322A* | *109(1)* |
| 332(1)(b) | 138(a) |
| 334 | 138(b) |
| 338(4) | Sch. 10, para. 10 |
| 338(4), (6) | 138(c) |
| 339(4) | Sch. 10, para. 10 |
| 343(1)(a) | Sch. 10, para.10 |
| 343(2), (4) | Sch. 10, para. 11 |
| 344(2) | Sch. 10, para. 10 |
| 350(1) | Sch. 17, para. 7 |
| 356(1)–(4) | 143(8) |
| 356(1), (2), (4) | Sch. 24 |
| *363–365* | *139(1)* |
| 363–365 | 139(1) |
| *366A* | *115(2)* |
| 368 | Sch. 19, para. 9 |
| 369(4) | 115(3) |
| 378(3) | 115(3) |
| *379A* | *116(2)* |
| 380(4) | 116(3) |
| *381A–381C* | *113(2)* |
| *382A* | *113(3)* |
| 383(1)–(3) | 143(9), Sch. 24 |
| 384 | 119(1) |
| 384–394 | 118–124 |
| *384–394A* | *119–123* |
| 385 | 121 |
| 386–388 | 122(1) |
| 387 | 120(1) |
| 389 | 24–54, Sch. 24 |
| 390, 391 | 122(1), 123(1) |
| 395 | 99 |
| 395, 396 | 93 |
| 395–408 | 92(a) |

| Provisions of relevant Acts | Companies Act 1989 provision |
|---|---|
| *Companies Act 1985* | |
| *395–420* | *93–104* |
| 397 | 100 |
| 399, 400, 404 | 95–97 |
| 401 | 94 |
| 403 | 98 |
| 405 | 100 |
| 406–408 | 101 |
| 409 | 92(b), 105, Sch. 15 |
| 410 | 93, 99 |
| 410–423 | 92(a) |
| 413 | 100 |
| 415, 416 | 95 |
| 417, 418 | 94 |
| 419 | 98 |
| 420 | 95–97 |
| 421–423 | 101 |
| 424 | 92(b), 105, Sch. 15 |
| 427A(1), (8) | 114(2) |
| 432 | 55 |
| *432(2A)* | *55* |
| 434 | 56 |
| *434(6)* | *56(5)* |
| 435 | Sch. 24 |
| 437 | 57 |
| *437(1B), (1C)* | *57* |
| 438 | 58 |
| 439 | 59 |
| 440 | 60, Sch. 24 |
| 441 | 61 |
| 442 | 62 |
| 443(4) | Sch. 24 |
| 445 | 135 |
| 446(3), (7) | Sch. 24 |
| 447 | 63 |
| 447(1) | Sch. 24 |
| *447(9)* | *63(7)* |
| 448 | 64(1) |
| 449 | 65 |
| 449(1) | Sch. 24 |
| 450 | 66 |
| *450(5)* | *66(4)* |
| 451 | 67 |
| 451A | 68 |

| Provisions of relevant Acts | Companies Act 1989 provision |
|---|---|
| *Companies Act 1985* | |
| 452 | 69 |
| 452(1)(b) | Sch. 24 |
| *452(1A), (1B)* | *69(3)* |
| 453 | 70 |
| 454(2), (3) | Sch. 19, para. 10(2) |
| 454–457 | 135 |
| 456(3) | Sch. 19, para. 10(1) |
| 459(1) | Sch. 19, para. 11 |
| 460(1) | Sch. 24 |
| 460(1)(b) | Sch. 19, para. 11 |
| 462(2), (3) | Sch. 17, para. 8 |
| 463(1) | 140(1) |
| *463(1A)* | *140(4)* |
| 464 | 140(2)–(7) |
| 464(5) | Sch. 24 |
| 466(2) | Sch. 17, para. 9, Sch. 24 |
| 466(4)–(6) | 140(8), Sch. 24 |
| 651 | 141 |
| 651(1) | Sch. 24 |
| 651(4)–(7) | 141(3) |
| 684(1) | Sch. 19, para. 12 |
| 686 | Sch. 19, para. 5 |
| 691 | Sch. 19, para. 6 |
| 696 | Sch. 19, para. 13 |
| 699(3) | Sch. 10, para. 12 |
| 700–703 | Sch. 10, para. 13 |
| *703A–703N* | *105, Sch. 15* |
| 705 | Sch. 19, para. 14 |
| 706 | 125(1) |
| 707 | 125(2) |
| *707A* | *126(1)* |
| 708(1) | 127(2) |
| 709, 710 | 126(2) |
| 711(1)(k) | Sch. 10, para. 14 |
| *711A* | *142(1)* |
| 712 | 127(3), Sch. 24 |
| 713(1) | 127(4) |
| 715 | 127(3), Sch. 24 |
| *715A* | *127(1)* |
| 716 | Sch. 19, para. 15 |
| 716(2) | Sch. 24 |
| 717 | Sch. 19, para. 16 |
| 717(1) | Sch. 24 |

| Provisions of relevant Acts | Companies Act 1989 provision |
|---|---|
| *Companies Act 1985* | |
| *723A* | *143(1)* |
| 730 | Sch. 19, para. 17 |
| 733(1) | 123(3) |
| 733(3) | Sch. 24 |
| 734 | Sch. 19, para. 18 |
| 734(1) | 120(2), 123(4) |
| 735A(1) | Sch. 24 |
| 735A(2) | 127(5) |
| *735B* | *127(6)* |
| 736 | 21, 144(1) |
| *736B* | *144(3)* |
| 742 | 22, Sch. 10, para. 15 |
| *743A* | *Sch. 19, para. 19* |
| 744 | Sch. 10, para. 16, Sch. 24 |
| *744A* | *Sch. 19, para. 20* |
| 746 | Sch. 24 |
| Sch. 1, para. 1, 3, 4 | Sch. 19, para. 7 |
| Sch. 1, para. 2(2)(a) | Sch. 10, para. 17 |
| Sch. 2 | Sch. 10, para. 18 |
| Sch. 2, para. 1 | Sch. 24 |
| Sch. 2, para. 1(1), 3(1), 4(2) | 129(2) |
| Sch. 2, para. 2–4 | Sch. 24 |
| Sch. 3, Pt. II | Sch. 10, para. 19 |
| Sch. 4 | 4(2), Sch. 1 |
| Sch. 4–10 | 1(b) (and Pt. I) |
| Sch. 4, para. 12(b) | Sch. 10, para. 20 |
| Sch. 4, para. 50(6), 53(7), 60–70, 74, 75, 77–81, 87, 90–92, 95 | Sch. 24 |
| *Sch. 4A* | *Sch. 2* |
| Sch. 5 | Sch. 3 |
| Sch. 5 (and 231) | 6(2), Sch. 3 |
| Sch. 6 | Sch. 4 |
| Sch. 6 (and 232–234) | 6(4), Sch. 4 |
| Sch. 7 | 8(2), Sch. 5 |
| *Sch. 7, para. 5A* | *137(2)* |
| Sch. 8 | 13(2), 18(5), Sch. 6, Sch. 8 |
| Sch. 9 | 18(3), (4), Sch. 7 |
| Sch. 9, para. 1, 13(3), (18), 16, 18(5), 19(3)–(7), 21–26 | Sch. 24 |
| Sch. 9, para. 27(4) | Sch. 24 |
| Sch. 9, para. 28–31 | Sch. 24 |
| Sch. 10 | Sch. 8 |
| *Sch. 10A* | *Sch. 9* |

| Provisions of relevant Acts | Companies Act 1989 provision |
|---|---|
| *Companies Act 1985* | |
| Sch. 11 | Sch. 10, para. 21 |
| Sch. 11, para. 4(b), (c), 5(b) | Sch. 24 |
| Sch. 13, para. 25, 26(1) | 143(10) |
| Sch. 13, para. 25 | Sch. 24 |
| Sch. 15 | Sch. 24 |
| Sch. 15A | 114(2), Sch. 10, para. 22 |
| Sch. 21, para. 6 | 108(2) |
| *Sch. 21, para. 6(6)* | *108(2)* |
| Sch. 22 | 106, 129(5), 142(2), 143(11), Sch. 19, para. 21, Sch. 24 |
| *Sch. 22* | *130(5), 142(2), 143(11), Sch. 19, para. 21* |
| Sch. 22 | |
| entry re 35 | 108(3) |
| entry re Pt. VII | Sch. 10, para. 23 |
| entry re 384–393 | 123(5) |
| entry re Pt. XIV | 71 |
| entry re Pt. XXIV | 127(7) |
| *Sch. 22* | |
| *entry re 322A* | *109(2)* |
| *entry re Pt. XII* | *106* |
| Sch. 24 | 119(2), 120(3), 122(2), 123(2), Sch. 16, para. 2, Sch. 24 |
| *Sch. 24* | *120(3), 122(2), 123(2)* |
| Sch. 24 | |
| entry re Pt. VII | Sch. 10, para. 24(1)–(3) |
| entry re 363(7) | 139(1) |
| entry re 448(5) | 64(2) |
| entry re 703(1) | Sch. 10, para. 24(4) |
| *Sch. 24* | |
| *entry re 387(2)* | *119(2)* |
| **Insolvency Act 1986** | |
| generally | 159–165 |
| 9(3) | Sch. 16, para. 3(2) |
| 10(1)(b) | 175(1)(a), Sch. 22, para. 11(1) |
| 11(2) | 175, Sch. 22, para. 11(2) |
| 11(3)(c) | 175(1)(a), Sch. 22, para. 11(1) |
| 15(1), (2) | 175(1)(b), Sch. 22, para. 11(2) |
| 43 | 175(3)(a) |
| 45(5) | Sch. 16, para. 3(3), Sch. 24 |
| 53(2) | Sch. 16, para. 3(3), Sch. 24 |
| 53(3) | Sch. 17, para. 10 |
| 54(3) | Sch. 16, para. 3(3), Sch. 24 |
| 61 | 169(1), 175(3)(b) |
| 62(5) | Sch. 16, para. 3(3), Sch. 24 |

| Provisions of relevant Acts | Companies Act 1989 provision |
|---|---|
| *Insolvency Act 1986* | |
| 124 | 60(2), (3) |
| 127 | 164(3), 175(4), Sch. 22, para. 7(2), 11(4) |
| 178 | 164(1), Sch. 22, para. 7(1) |
| 186 | 164(1), Sch. 22, para. 7(1) |
| 218(5) | 78 |
| 238 | 165(1)(a) |
| 239 | 165(1)(b) |
| 242, 243 | 165(2)(a) |
| 284 | 164(3), 175(4), Sch. 22, para. 7(2), 11(4) |
| 315 | 164(1), Sch. 22, para. 7(1) |
| 323 | 163(2)(b) |
| 339 | 165(1)(a) |
| 340 | 165(1)(b) |
| 345 | 764(1), Sch. 22, para. 7(1) |
| 423 | 165(1)(c) |
| 426 | 183(1) |
| Sch. 10 | Sch. 24 |
| Sch. 13, Pt. I | Sch. 24 |
| **Company Directors Disqualification Act 1986** | |
| 3(3)(b) | Sch. 10, para. 35(2) |
| 8 | 79 |
| 8(2) | 209 |
| 21 | 208 |
| 21(2) | Sch. 24 |
| *21(4)* | *208* |
| *22A* | *211(3)* |
| Sch. 1, para. 4(f), (g) | 139(4) |
| Sch. 1, para. 4(h) | Sch. 16, para. 4 |
| Sch. 1, para. 5 | Sch. 10, para. 35(3) |
| **Financial Services Act 1986** | |
| generally | 154–191, Sch. 21 |
| 12 | 156(4)(b), 169(2) |
| 13 | Sch. 23, para. 1 |
| 13(1), (4)–(6) | Sch. 24 |
| *22A* | *193(3)* |
| 37(7)(b) | 169(2) |
| 39(4) | Sch. 21, Pt. II |
| 39(7)(b) | 169(2) |
| 40(2) | Sch. 21, Pt. III |
| *47A* | *192* |
| 48 | Sch. 23, para. 2 |

| Provisions of relevant Acts | Companies Act 1989 provision |
|---|---|
| *Financial Services Act 1986* | |
| 48(1) | Sch. 24 |
| *48(11)* | *Sch. 23, para. 2(3)* |
| 49 | Sch. 23, para. 3 |
| *49(3)* | *Sch. 23, para. 3(3)* |
| 50 | Sch. 23, para. 4 |
| *50(4)* | *Sch. 23, para. 4* |
| 52 | Sch. 23, para. 5 |
| 55 | Sch. 23, para. 6 |
| 55(2)(b), (e), (3) | Sch. 24 |
| *55(6)* | *Sch. 23, para. 6(4)* |
| 56(7) | Sch. 23, para. 7 |
| *62A* | *193(1)* |
| *63A, 63B* | *194* |
| *63C* | *195* |
| 86(7) | Sch. 23, para. 8 |
| 94 | 72 |
| 94(3), (4) | Sch. 24 |
| *94(8A), (8B)* | *72(3)* |
| *94(10)* | *72(4)* |
| 95 | Sch. para. 9 |
| *95(3)* | *Sch. 23, para. 9* |
| 105 | 73(1)–(4) |
| 105(7) | Sch. 24 |
| *105(11)* | *73(4)* |
| 106 | 73(5) |
| *106(2A)* | *73(5)* |
| 107 | Sch. 23, para. 10 |
| *107(4)* | *Sch. 23, para. 10(4)* |
| *107A* | *Sch. 23, para. 11* |
| 114, 115 | 168 |
| 114 | Sch. 23, para. 12 |
| 114(5) | 193(2) |
| 115 | Sch. 23, para. 13 |
| 115(2) | 204(6) |
| 117(4), (5) | Sch. 10, para. 36(2) |
| 119 | 169(4), Sch. 23, para. 14 |
| 119(5) | Sch. 24 |
| *119(6)* | *Sch. 23, para. 14(6)* |
| 121 | 169(4), Sch. 23, para. 15 |
| 122 | Sch. 23, para. 16 |
| 124 | Sch. 23, para. 17 |
| *128A–128C* | *196* |
| 150(6) | 197(1) |

| Provisions of relevant Acts | Companies Act 1989 provision |
|---|---|
| *Financial Services Act 1986* | |
| 154(5) | 197(2) |
| 159 | 198(3) |
| 159(1) | Sch. 24 |
| 160(1) | Sch. 24 |
| 160(6)–(9) | 198(4) |
| *160A* | *198(1)* |
| 170(2)–(4) | 199 |
| 171(1)(b), (3) | 198(5) |
| 177 | 74 |
| *177(2A)* | *74(2)* |
| *177(5A)* | *74(3)* |
| *177(11)* | *74(6)* |
| 179(3) | 75(1), Sch. 24 |
| 180 | 75(2)–(7) |
| 180(1) | 75(2) |
| *180(1A)* | *75(4)* |
| 180(6) | Sch. 24 |
| 188 | 200(1) |
| 192 | 201 |
| 195 | 202 |
| 196(3) | Sch. 24 |
| 198(1) | Sch. 24 |
| 199 | 76 |
| 199(9) | Sch. 24 |
| 204 | 169(5) |
| 205 | Sch. 23, para. 18 |
| 206(1) | Sch. 23, para. 19 |
| 207(1) | 205(3) |
| Sch. 1, para. 30 | Sch. 10, para. 36(3) |
| Sch. 2, para. 3(1), (2) | 203(1) |
| *Sch. 2, para. 3A* | *204(1)* |
| Sch. 2, para. 4 | Sch. 23, para. 20 |
| Sch. 3, para. 3 | 203(2) |
| *Sch. 3, para. 3A* | *204(1)* |
| Sch. 3, para. 4(2) | Sch. 23, para. 21 |
| Sch. 4 | Sch. 21, Pt. I |
| *Sch. 4, para. 6* | *205(1)* |
| Sch. 7, para. 2(2) | Sch. 23, para. 22 |
| *Sch. 7, para. 2A* | *204(4)* |
| Sch. 8 | Sch. 23, para. 23 |
| Sch. 9 | Sch. 23, para. 24 |
| Sch. 10 | Sch. 23, para. 25 |
| *Sch. 10, para. 4(2A)* | *Sch. 23, para. 25(2)* |

| Provisions of relevant Acts | Companies Act 1989 provision |
|---|---|
| *Financial Services Act 1986* | |
| *Sch. 10, para. 7(3)* | *Sch. 23, para. 25(3)* |
| Sch. 11 | Sch. 23, para. 26–43 |
| Sch. 11, para. 4(4)(b) | Sch. 24 |
| Sch. 11, para. 7 | Sch. 24 |
| Sch. 11, para. 10(3) | Sch. 24 |
| *Sch. 11, para. 10(3A)* | *Sch. 23, para. 30(4)* |
| *Sch. 11, para. 13A, 13B* | *Sch. 23, para. 32* |
| Sch. 11, para. 14(1) | Sch. 24 |
| *Sch. 11, para. 14(2A)* | *Sch. 23, para. 33(3)* |
| Sch. 11, para. 14(3) | Sch. 24 |
| *Sch. 11, para. 19(3)* | *Sch. 23, para. 34(3)* |
| Sch. 11, para. 28(5) | 193(4) |
| *Sch. 11, para. 22B–22D* | *Sch. 23, para. 36* |
| Sch. 16, para. 22 | Sch. 24 |
| **Fair Trading Act 1973** | |
| 63(1) | Sch. 20, para. 3 |
| 66 | Sch. 20, para. 4 |
| *66A* | *150(1)* |
| 67 | Sch. 20, para. 5 |
| 68(4) | Sch. 20, para. 6 |
| 71 | Sch. 20, para. 7 |
| 71(1), (2) | Sch. 24 |
| 74(1) | Sch. 24 |
| 74(1) | Sch. 20, para. 8 |
| 75(4) | Sch. 20, para. 9 |
| *75A–75K* | *146–147* |
| 123(3) | Sch. 20, para. 26 |
| Sch. 8 | Sch. 20, para. 19 |
| **Industry Act 1975** | |
| 37(1) | Sch. 18, para. 11 |

# FINANCIAL SERVICES AND MARKETS ACT 2000

Table of Contents

**12(7) ["Independent"] "Independent"** means appearing to the Treasury to be independent of the Authority.

# 13 Right to obtain documents and information

**13(1) [Rights of person conducting s. 12 review]** A person conducting a review under section 12–

(a) has a right of access at any reasonable time to all such documents as he may reasonably require for purposes of the review; and

(b) may require any person holding or accountable for any such document to provide such information and explanation as are reasonably necessary for that purpose.

**13(2) [Application of s. 13(1)]** Subsection (1) applies only to documents in the custody or under the control of the Authority.

**13(3) [Injunction]** An obligation imposed on a person as a result of the exercise of powers conferred by subsection (1) is enforceable by injunction or, in Scotland, by an order for specific performance under section 45 of the Court of Session Act 1988.

INQUIRIES

# 14 Cases in which the Treasury may arrange independent inquiries

**14(1) [Application of section]** This section applies in two cases.

**14(2) [Events relating to collective investment scheme or regulated activity]** The first is where it appears to the Treasury that–

(a) events have occurred in relation to–
   (i) a collective investment scheme, or
   (ii) a person who is, or was at the time of the events, carrying on a regulated activity (whether or not as an authorised person),

which posed or could have posed a grave risk to the financial system or caused or risked causing significant damage to the interests of consumers; and

(b) those events might not have occurred, or the risk or damage might have been reduced, but for a serious failure in–
   (i) the system established by this Act for the regulation of such schemes or of such persons and their activities; or
   (ii) the operation of that system.

**14(3) [Events relating to listed securities]** The second is where it appears to the Treasury that–

(a) events have occurred in relation to listed securities or an issuer of listed securities which caused or could have caused significant damage to holders of listed securities; and

(b) those events might not have occurred but for a serious failure in the regulatory system established by Part VI or in its operation.

**14(4) [Power of Treasury to arrange inquiry under s. 15]** If the Treasury consider that it is in the public interest that there should be an independent inquiry into the events and the circumstances surrounding them, they may arrange for an inquiry to be held under section 15.

**14(5) ["Consumers"] "Consumers"** means persons–

(a) who are consumers for the purposes of section 138; or

(b) who, in relation to regulated activities carried on otherwise than by authorised persons, would be consumers for those purposes if the activities were carried on by authorised persons.

**14(6) ["The financial system"] "The financial system"** has the same meaning as in section 3.

**14(7) ["Listed securities"] "Listed securities"** means anything which has been admitted to the official list under Part VI.

# 15 Power to appoint person to hold an inquiry

**15(1) [Power of Treasury]** If the Treasury decide to arrange for an inquiry to be held under this section, they may appoint such person as they consider appropriate to hold the inquiry.

**15(2) [Control of inquiry by direction]** The Treasury may, by a direction to the appointed person, control–

(a) the scope of the inquiry;

(b) the period during which the inquiry is to be held;

(c) the conduct of the inquiry; and

(d) the making of reports.

**15(3) [Extent of direction]** A direction may, in particular–

(a) confine the inquiry to particular matters;

(b) extend the inquiry to additional matters;

(c) require the appointed person to discontinue the inquiry or to take only such steps as are specified in the direction;

(d) require the appointed person to make such interim reports as are so specified.

## 16 Powers of appointed person and procedure

**16(1) [Powers of person appointed under s. 15]** The person appointed to hold an inquiry under section 15 may–

(a) obtain such information from such persons and in such manner as he thinks fit;

(b) make such inquiries as he thinks fit; and

(c) determine the procedure to be followed in connection with the inquiry.

**16(2) [Provision of relevant documentation, etc.]** The appointed person may require any person who, in his opinion, is able to provide any information, or produce any document, which is relevant to the inquiry to provide any such information or produce any such document.

**16(3) [Witnesses]** For the purposes of an inquiry, the appointed person has the same powers as the court in respect of the attendance and examination of witnesses (including the examination of witnesses abroad) and in respect of the production of documents.

**16(4) ["Court"] "Court"** means–

(a) the High Court; or

(b) in Scotland, the Court of Session.

## 17 Conclusion of inquiry

**17(1) [Written report upon conclusion of s. 15 inquiry]** On completion of an inquiry under section 15, the person holding the inquiry must make a written report to the Treasury–

(a) setting out the result of the inquiry; and

(b) making such recommendations (if any) as he considers appropriate.

**17(2) [Publication of report]** The Treasury may publish the whole, or any part, of the report and may do so in such manner as they consider appropriate.

**17(3) [Application of s. 17(4)]** Subsection (4) applies if the Treasury propose to publish a report but consider that it contains material–

(a) which relates to the affairs of a particular person whose interests would, in the opinion of the Treasury, be seriously prejudiced by publication of the material; or

(b) the disclosure of which would be incompatible with an international obligation of the United Kingdom.

**17(4) [Removal of s. 17(3) material]** The Treasury must ensure that the material is removed before publication.

**17(5) [S. 17(2) report to be laid before Parliament]** The Treasury must lay before each House of Parliament a copy of any report or part of a report published under subsection (2).

**17(6) [Expenses]** Any expenses reasonably incurred in holding an inquiry are to be met by the Treasury out of money provided by Parliament.

## 18 Obstruction and contempt

**18(1) [Obstruction, etc. of s. 15 inquiry]** If a person ("A")–

(a) fails to comply with a requirement imposed on him by a person holding an inquiry under section 15, or

(b) otherwise obstructs such an inquiry,

the person holding the inquiry may certify the matter to the High Court (or, in Scotland, the Court of Session).

**18(2) [Power of court]** The court may enquire into the matter.

**18(3) [Contempt of court]** If, after hearing–

(a) any witnesses who may be produced against or on behalf of A, and

(b) any statement made by or on behalf of A,

the court is satisfied that A would have been in contempt of court if the inquiry had been proceedings before the court, it may deal with him as if he were in contempt.

# PART II – REGULATED AND PROHIBITED ACTIVITIES

THE GENERAL PROHIBITION

## 19 The general prohibition

**19(1) [Requirement of authorisation or exemption]** No person may carry on a regulated activity in the United Kingdom, or purport to do so, unless he is–

(a) an authorised person; or

(b) an exempt person.

**19(2) [The general prohibition]** The prohibition is referred to in this Act as the general prohibition.

REQUIREMENT FOR PERMISSION

## 20 Authorised persons acting without permission

**20(1) [Authorised person acting without permission]** If an authorised person carries on a regulated activity in the United Kingdom, or purports to do so, otherwise than in accordance with permission–

(a) given to him by the Authority under Part IV, or

(b) resulting from any other provision of this Act,

he is to be taken to have contravened a requirement imposed on him by the Authority under this Act.

**20(2) [Contravention of s. 20(1)]** The contravention does not–

(a) make a person guilty of an offence;

(b) make any transaction void or unenforceable; or

(c) (subject to subsection (3)) give rise to any right of action for breach of statutory duty.

**20(3) [Contravention actionable]** In prescribed cases the contravention is actionable at the suit of a person who suffers loss as a result of the contravention, subject to the defences and other incidents applying to actions for breach of statutory duty.

FINANCIAL PROMOTION

## 21 Restrictions on financial promotion

**21(1) [Restriction on invitations, etc. to engage in investment activity]** A person ("A") must not, in the course of business, communicate an invitation or inducement to engage in investment activity.

**21(2) [Non-application of s. 21(1)]** But subsection (1) does not apply if–

(a) A is an authorised person; or

(b) the content of the communication is approved for the purposes of this section by an authorised person.

**21(3) [Communications from outside UK]** In the case of a communication originating outside the United Kingdom, subsection (1) applies only if the communication is capable of having an effect in the United Kingdom.

**21(4) [Power of Treasury to make order]** The Treasury may by order specify circumstances in which a person is to be regarded for the purposes of subsection (1) as–

(a) acting in the course of business;

(b) not acting in the course of business.

**21(5) [Power of Treasury to make order – s. 21(1) not applicable]** The Treasury may by order specify circumstances (which may include compliance with financial promotion rules) in which subsection (1) does not apply.

**21(6) [S. 21(5) orders – non-application of s. 21(1)]** An order under subsection (5) may, in particular, provide that subsection (1) does not apply in relation to communications–

(a) of a specified description;

(b) originating in a specified country or territory outside the United Kingdom;

(c) originating in a country or territory which falls within a specified description of country or territory outside the United Kingdom; or

(d) originating outside the United Kingdom.

**21(7) [Power of Treasury to make order]** The Treasury may by order repeal subsection (3).

**21(8) ["Engaging in investment activity"] "Engaging in investment activity"** means–

(a) entering or offering to enter into an agreement the making or performance of which by either party constitutes a controlled activity; or

(b) exercising any rights conferred by a controlled investment to acquire, dispose of, underwrite or convert a controlled investment.

**21(9) [Controlled activity]** An activity is a controlled activity if–

(a) it is an activity of a specified kind or one which falls within a specified class of activity; and

(b) it relates to an investment of a specified kind, or to one which falls within a specified class of investment.

**21(10) [Controlled investment]** An investment is a controlled investment if it is an investment of a specified kind or one which falls within a specified class of investment.

**21(11) [Application of Sch. 2]** Schedule 2 (except paragraph 26) applies for the purposes of subsections (9) and (10) with references to section 22 being read as references to each of those subsections.

**21(12) [Non-limitation of s. 21(9) or (10)]** Nothing in Schedule 2, as applied by subsection (11), limits the powers conferred by subsection (9) or (10).

**21(13) ["Communicate"] "Communicate"** includes causing a communication to be made.

**21(14) ["Investment"] "Investment"** includes any asset, right or interest.

**21(15) ["Specified"] "Specified"** means specified in an order made by the Treasury.

REGULATED ACTIVITIES

## 22 The classes of activity and categories of investment

**22(1) [Regulated activity]** An activity is a regulated activity for the purposes of this Act if it is an activity of a specified kind which is carried on by way of business and–

(a) relates to an investment of a specified kind; or

(b) in the case of an activity of a kind which is also specified for the purposes of this paragraph, is carried on in relation to property of any kind.

**22(2) [Sch. 2 supplements s. 22]** Schedule 2 makes provision supplementing this section.

**22(3) [Non-limitation of s. 22(1)]** Nothing in Schedule 2 limits the powers conferred by subsection (1).

**22(4) ["Investment"] "Investment"** includes any asset, right or interest.

**22(5) ["Specified"] "Specified"** means specified in an order made by the Treasury.

OFFENCES

# 23 Contravention of the general prohibition

**23(1) [Offence, penalty]** A person who contravenes the general prohibition is guilty of an offence and liable–

(a) on summary conviction, to imprisonment for a term not exceeding six months or a fine not exceeding the statutory maximum, or both;

(b) on conviction on indictment, to imprisonment for a term not exceeding two years or a fine, or both.

**23(2) ["An authorisation offence"]** In this Act **"an authorisation offence"** means an offence under this section.

**23(3) [Defence]** In proceedings for an authorisation offence it is a defence for the accused to show that he took all reasonable precautions and exercised all due diligence to avoid committing the offence.

# 24 False claims to be authorised or exempt

**24(1) [Offence]** A person who is neither an authorised person nor, in relation to the regulated activity in question, an exempt person is guilty of an offence if he–

(a) describes himself (in whatever terms) as an authorised person;

(b) describes himself (in whatever terms) as an exempt person in relation to the regulated activity; or

(c) behaves, or otherwise holds himself out, in a manner which indicates (or which is reasonably likely to be understood as indicating) that he is–

(i) an authorised person; or

(ii) an exempt person in relation to the regulated activity.

**24(2) [Defence]** In proceedings for an offence under this section it is a defence for the accused to show that he took all reasonable precautions and exercised all due diligence to avoid committing the offence.

**24(3) [Penalty]** A person guilty of an offence under this section is liable on summary conviction to imprisonment for a term not exceeding six months or a fine not exceeding level 5 on the standard scale, or both.

**24(4) [Penalty – public display of material]** But where the conduct constituting the offence involved or included the public display of any material, the maximum fine for the offence is level 5 on the standard scale multiplied by the number of days for which the display continued.

# 25 Contravention of section 21

**25(1) [Offence, penalty]** A person who contravenes section 21(1) is guilty of an offence and liable–

(a) on summary conviction, to imprisonment for a term not exceeding six months or a fine not exceeding the statutory maximum, or both;

(b) on conviction on indictment, to imprisonment for a term not exceeding two years or a fine, or both.

**25(2) [Defence]** In proceedings for an offence under this section it is a defence for the accused to show–

(a) that he believed on reasonable grounds that the content of the communication was prepared, or approved for the purposes of section 21, by an authorised person; or

(b) that he took all reasonable precautions and exercised all due diligence to avoid committing the offence.

ENFORCEABILITY OF AGREEMENTS

## 26 Agreements made by unauthorised persons

**26(1) [Agreements in contravention of general prohibition]** An agreement made by a person in the course of carrying on a regulated activity in contravention of the general prohibition is unenforceable against the other party.

**26(2) [Recovery, compensation]** The other party is entitled to recover–

(a) any money or other property paid or transferred by him under the agreement; and

(b) compensation for any loss sustained by him as a result of having parted with it.

**26(3) ["Agreement"] "Agreement"** means an agreement–

(a) made after this section comes into force; and

(b) the making or performance of which constitutes, or is part of, the regulated activity in question.

**26(4) [Non-application of section]** This section does not apply if the regulated activity is accepting deposits.

## 27 Agreements made through unauthorised persons

**27(1) [Unenforceable agreement]** An agreement made by an authorised person ("the provider")–

(a) in the course of carrying on a regulated activity (not in contravention of the general prohibition), but

(b) in consequence of something said or done by another person ("the third party") in the course of a regulated activity carried on by the third party in contravention of the general prohibition,

is unenforceable against the other party.

**27(2) [Recovery, compensation]** The other party is entitled to recover–

(a) any money or other property paid or transferred by him under the agreement; and

(b) compensation for any loss sustained by him as a result of having parted with it.

**27(3) ["Agreement"] "Agreement"** means an agreement–

(a) made after this section comes into force; and

(b) the making or performance of which constitutes, or is part of, the regulated activity in question carried on by the provider.

**27(4) [Non-application of section]** This section does not apply if the regulated activity is accepting deposits.

## 28 Agreements made unenforceable by section 26 or 27

**28(1) [Application of section]** This section applies to an agreement which is unenforceable because of section 26 or 27.

**28(2) [Compensation]** The amount of compensation recoverable as a result of that section is–

(a) the amount agreed by the parties; or

(b) on the application of either party, the amount determined by the court.

**28(3) [Power of court]** If the court is satisfied that it is just and equitable in the circumstances of the case, it may allow–

(a) the agreement to be enforced; or

(b) money and property paid or transferred under the agreement to be retained.

**28(4) [Enforcement conditions]** In considering whether to allow the agreement to be enforced or (as the case may be) the money or property paid or transferred under the agreement to be retained the court must–

(a) if the case arises as a result of section 26, have regard to the issue mentioned in subsection (5); or

(b) if the case arises as a result of section 27, have regard to the issue mentioned in subsection (6).

**28(5) [Reasonable belief of non-contravention]** The issue is whether the person carrying on the regulated activity concerned reasonably believed that he was not contravening the general prohibition by making the agreement.

**28(6) [Third party]** The issue is whether the provider knew that the third party was (in carrying on the regulated activity) contravening the general prohibition.

**28(7) [Repayment]** If the person against whom the agreement is unenforceable–

(a) elects not to perform the agreement, or

(b) as a result of this section, recovers money paid or other property transferred by him under the agreement,

he must repay any money and return any other property received by him under the agreement.

**28(8) [Property transferred to third party]** If property transferred under the agreement has passed to a third party, a reference in section 26 or 27 or this section to that property is to be read as a reference to its value at the time of its transfer under the agreement.

**28(9) [Effect of authorisation offence]** The commission of an authorisation offence does not make the agreement concerned illegal or invalid to any greater extent than is provided by section 26 or 27.

# 29 Accepting deposits in breach of general prohibition

**29(1) [Application of section]** This section applies to an agreement between a person ("the depositor") and another person ("the deposit-taker") made in the course of the carrying on by the deposit-taker of accepting deposits in contravention of the general prohibition.

**29(2) [Recovery – application to court]** If the depositor is not entitled under the agreement to recover without delay any money deposited by him, he may apply to the court for an order directing the deposit-taker to return the money to him.

**29(3) [Recovery – power of court]** The court need not make such an order if it is satisfied that it would not be just and equitable for the money deposited to be returned, having regard to the issue mentioned in subsection (4).

**29(4) [Deposit-taker's belief]** The issue is whether the deposit-taker reasonably believed that he was not contravening the general prohibition by making the agreement.

**29(5) ["Agreement"] "Agreement"** means an agreement–

(a) made after this section comes into force; and

(b) the making or performance of which constitutes, or is part of, accepting deposits.

# 30 Enforceability of agreements resulting from unlawful communications

**30(1) [Definitions]** In this section–

**"unlawful communication"** means a communication in relation to which there has been a contravention of section 21(1);

**"controlled agreement"** means an agreement the making or performance of which by either party constitutes a controlled activity for the purposes of that section; and

**"controlled investment"** has the same meaning as in section 21.

**30(2) [Controlled agreement]** If in consequence of an unlawful communication a person enters as a customer into a controlled agreement, it is unenforceable against him and he is entitled to recover–

(a) any money or other property paid or transferred by him under the agreement; and

(b) compensation for any loss sustained by him as a result of having parted with it.

**30(3) [Exercise of rights conferred by investment]** If in consequence of an unlawful communication a person exercises any rights conferred by a controlled investment, no obligation to which he is subject as a result of exercising them is enforceable against him and he is entitled to recover–

(a) any money or other property paid or transferred by him under the obligation; and

(b) compensation for any loss sustained by him as a result of having parted with it.

**30(4) [Power of court]** But the court may allow–

(a) the agreement or obligation to be enforced, or

(b) money or property paid or transferred under the agreement or obligation to be retained,

if it is satisfied that it is just and equitable in the circumstances of the case.

**30(5) [Enforcement conditions]** In considering whether to allow the agreement or obligation to be enforced or (as the case may be) the money or property paid or transferred under the agreement to be retained the court must have regard to the issues mentioned in subsections (6) and (7).

**30(6) [Applicant's belief – communication made]** If the applicant made the unlawful communication, the issue is whether he reasonably believed that he was not making such a communication.

**30(7) [Applicant's knowledge – communication not made]** If the applicant did not make the unlawful communication, the issue is whether he knew that the agreement was entered into in consequence of such a communication.

**30(8) ["Applicant"] "Applicant"** means the person seeking to enforce the agreement or obligation or retain the money or property paid or transferred.

**30(9) [Causing communication]** Any reference to making a communication includes causing a communication to be made.

**30(10) [Compensation]** The amount of compensation recoverable as a result of subsection (2) or (3) is–

(a) the amount agreed between the parties; or

(b) on the application of either party, the amount determined by the court.

**30(11) [Repayment – election not to perform agreement]** If a person elects not to perform an agreement or an obligation which (by virtue of subsection (2) or (3)) is unenforceable against him, he must repay any money and return any other property received by him under the agreement.

**30(12) [Repayment – money recovered by s. 30(2) or (3)]** If (by virtue of subsection (2) or (3)) a person recovers money paid or property transferred by him under an agreement or obligation, he must repay any money and return any other property received by him as a result of exercising the rights in question.

**30(13) [Returned property – valuation]** If any property required to be returned under this section has passed to a third party, references to that property are to be read as references to its value at the time of its receipt by the person required to return it.

# PART III – AUTHORISATION AND EXEMPTION

## AUTHORISATION

## 31 Authorised persons

**31(1) [Categories of authorised person]** The following persons are authorised for the purposes of this Act–

(a) a person who has a Part IV permission to carry on one or more regulated activities;

(b) an EEA firm qualifying for authorisation under Schedule 3;

(c) a Treaty firm qualifying for authorisation under Schedule 4;

(d) a person who is otherwise authorised by a provision of, or made under, this Act.

**31(2) ["Authorised person"]** In this Act **"authorised person"** means a person who is authorised for the purposes of this Act.

# 32 Partnerships and unincorporated associations

**32(1) [Authorised firm – change of membership]** If a firm is authorised–

(a) it is authorised to carry on the regulated activities concerned in the name of the firm; and

(b) its authorisation is not affected by any change in its membership.

**32(2) [Dissolution of firm]** If an authorised firm is dissolved, its authorisation continues to have effect in relation to any firm which succeeds to the business of the dissolved firm.

**32(3) [Succeeding firm]** For the purposes of this section, a firm is to be regarded as succeeding to the business of another firm only if–

(a) the members of the resulting firm are substantially the same as those of the former firm; and

(b) succession is to the whole or substantially the whole of the business of the former firm.

**32(4) ["Firm"] "Firm"** means–

(a) a partnership; or

(b) an unincorporated association of persons.

**32(5) ["Partnership"] "Partnership"** does not include a partnership which is constituted under the law of any place outside the United Kingdom and is a body corporate.

## ENDING OF AUTHORISATION

# 33 Withdrawal of authorisation by the Authority

**33(1) [Application of section]** This section applies if–

(a) an authorised person's Part IV permission is cancelled; and

(b) as a result, there is no regulated activity for which he has permission.

**33(2) [Direction]** The Authority must give a direction withdrawing that person's status as an authorised person.

# 34 EEA firms

**34(1) [Cessation of Sch. 3 qualification for authorisation]** An EEA firm ceases to qualify for authorisation under Part II of Schedule 3 if it ceases to be an EEA firm as a result of–

(a) having its EEA authorisation withdrawn; or

(b) ceasing to have an EEA right in circumstances in which EEA authorisation is not required.

**34(2) [Cancellation of Sch. 3 authorisation]** At the request of an EEA firm, the Authority may give a direction cancelling its authorisation under Part II of Schedule 3.

**34(3) [Pt. IV permission]** If an EEA firm has a Part IV permission, it does not cease to be an authorised person merely because it ceases to qualify for authorisation under Part II of Schedule 3.

# 35 Treaty firms

**35(1) [Cessation of Sch. 4 qualification for authorisation]** A Treaty firm ceases to qualify for authorisation under Schedule 4 if its home State authorisation is withdrawn.

**35(2) [Cancellation of Sch. 4 authorisation]** At the request of a Treaty firm, the Authority may give a direction cancelling its Schedule 4 authorisation.

**35(3) [Pt. IV permission]** If a Treaty firm has a Part IV permission, it does not cease to be an authorised person merely because it ceases to qualify for authorisation under Schedule 4.

## 36 Persons authorised as a result of paragraph 1(1) of Schedule 5

**36(1) [Cancellation of authorisation]** At the request of a person authorised as a result of paragraph 1(1) of Schedule 5, the Authority may give a direction cancelling his authorisation as such a person.

**36(2) [Pt. IV permission]** If a person authorised as a result of paragraph 1(1) of Schedule 5 has a Part IV permission, he does not cease to be an authorised person merely because he ceases to be a person so authorised.

EXERCISE OF EEA RIGHTS BY UK FIRMS

## 37 Exercise of EEA rights by UK firms

37 Part III of Schedule 3 makes provision in relation to the exercise outside the United Kingdom of EEA rights by UK firms.

EXEMPTION

## 38 Exemption orders

**38(1) [Power of Treasury to make order]** The Treasury may by order ("an exemption order") provide for–

(a) specified persons, or

(b) persons falling within a specified class,

to be exempt from the general prohibition.

**38(2) [Pt. IV permission]** But a person cannot be an exempt person as a result of an exemption order if he has a Part IV permission.

**38(3) [Effect of order]** An exemption order may provide for an exemption to have effect–

(a) in respect of all regulated activities;

(b) in respect of one or more specified regulated activities;

(c) only in specified circumstances;

(d) only in relation to specified functions;

(e) subject to conditions.

**38(4) ["Specified"] "Specified"** means specified by the exemption order.

## 39 Exemption of appointed representatives

**39(1) [Exemption where principal accepts responsibility]** If a person (other than an authorised person)–

(a) is a party to a contract with an authorised person ("his principal") which–
  (i) permits or requires him to carry on business of a prescribed description, and
  (ii) complies with such requirements as may be prescribed, and

(b) is someone for whose activities in carrying on the whole or part of that business his principal has accepted responsibility in writing,

he is exempt from the general prohibition in relation to any regulated activity comprised in the carrying on of that business for which his principal has accepted responsibility.

**39(2) [Appointed representative]** A person who is exempt as a result of subsection (1) is referred to in this Act as an appointed representative.

**39(3) [Appointed representative – principal]** The principal of an appointed representative is responsible, to the same extent as if he had expressly permitted it, for anything done or omitted by the representative in carrying on the business for which he has accepted responsibility.

**39(4) [Acts, etc. of relevant person]** In determining whether an authorised person has complied with a provision contained in or made under this Act, anything which a relevant person has done or omitted as respects business for which the authorised person has accepted responsibility is to be treated as having been done or omitted by the authorised person.

**52(5) [Effective date of permission]** The notice must state the date from which the permission, or the variation, has effect.

**52(6) [Warning notice – Pt. IV permission]** If the Authority proposes–

(a) to give a Part IV permission but to exercise its power under section 42(7)(a) or (b) or 43(1), or

(b) to vary a Part IV permission on the application of an authorised person but to exercise its power under any of those provisions (as a result of section 44(5)),

it must give the applicant a warning notice.

**52(7) [Warning notice – refusal of application]** If the Authority proposes to refuse an application made under this Part, it must (unless subsection (8) applies) give the applicant a warning notice.

**52(8) [Application of subsection]** This subsection applies if it appears to the Authority that–

(a) the applicant is an EEA firm; and

(b) the application is made with a view to carrying on a regulated activity in a manner in which the applicant is, or would be, entitled to carry on that activity in the exercise of an EEA right whether through a United Kingdom branch or by providing services in the United Kingdom.

**52(9) [Decision notice]** If the Authority decides–

(a) to give a Part IV permission but to exercise its power under section 42(7)(a) or (b) or 43(1),

(b) to vary a Part IV permission on the application of an authorised person but to exercise its power under any of those provisions (as a result of section 44(5)), or

(c) to refuse an application under this Part,

it must give the applicant a decision notice.

## 53 Exercise of own-initiative power: procedure

**53(1) [Application of section]** This section applies to an exercise of the Authority's own-initiative power to vary an authorised person's Part IV permission.

**53(2) [Effective date of variation]** A variation takes effect–

(a) immediately, if the notice given under subsection (4) states that that is the case;

(b) on such date as may be specified in the notice; or

(c) if no date is specified in the notice, when the matter to which the notice relates is no longer open to review.

**53(3) [Variations immediately effective]** A variation may be expressed to take effect immediately (or on a specified date) only if the Authority, having regard to the ground on which it is exercising its own-initiative power, reasonably considers that it is necessary for the variation to take effect immediately (or on that date).

**53(4) [Written notice – variation of Pt. IV permission]** If the Authority proposes to vary the Part IV permission, or varies it with immediate effect, it must give the authorised person written notice.

**53(5) [Contents of notice]** The notice must–

(a) give details of the variation;

(b) state the Authority's reasons for the variation and for its determination as to when the variation takes effect;

(c) inform the authorised person that he may make representations to the Authority within such period as may be specified in the notice (whether or not he has referred the matter to the Tribunal);

(d) inform him of when the variation takes effect; and

(e) inform him of his right to refer the matter to the Tribunal.

**53(6) [Extension of period for representations]** The Authority may extend the period allowed under the notice for making representations.

**53(7) [Written notice – variation of permission as proposed]** If, having considered any representations made by the authorised person, the Authority decides–

(a) to vary the permission in the way proposed, or

(b) if the permission has been varied, not to rescind the variation,

it must give him written notice.

**53(8) [Written notice – variation of permission, etc.]** If, having considered any representations made by the authorised person, the Authority decides–

(a) not to vary the permission in the way proposed,

(b) to vary the permission in a different way, or

(c) to rescind a variation which has effect,

it must give him written notice.

**53(9) [Right of referral to Tribunal]** A notice given under subsection (7) must inform the authorised person of his right to refer the matter to the Tribunal.

**53(10) [S. 53(8)(b) notice]** A notice under subsection (8)(b) must comply with subsection (5).

**53(11) [Procedure upon referral to Tribunal]** If a notice informs a person of his right to refer a matter to the Tribunal, it must give an indication of the procedure on such a reference.

**53(12) [S. 53(2)(c) – determination of review]** For the purposes of subsection (2)(c), whether a matter is open to review is to be determined in accordance with section 391(8).

## 54 Cancellation of Part IV permission: procedure

**54(1) [Warning notice – cancellation of permission]** If the Authority proposes to cancel an authorised person's Part IV permission otherwise than at his request, it must give him a warning notice.

**54(2) [Decision notice – cancellation of permission]** If the Authority decides to cancel an authorised person's Part IV permission otherwise than at his request, it must give him a decision notice.

### REFERENCES TO THE TRIBUNAL

## 55 Right to refer matters to the Tribunal

**55(1) [Aggrieved applicant]** An applicant who is aggrieved by the determination of an application made under this Part may refer the matter to the Tribunal.

**55(2) [Aggrieved authorised person]** An authorised person who is aggrieved by the exercise of the Authority's own-initiative power may refer the matter to the Tribunal.

# PART V – PERFORMANCE OF REGULATED ACTIVITIES

### PROHIBITION ORDERS

## 56 Prohibition orders

**56(1) [Application of s. 56(2)]** Subsection (2) applies if it appears to the Authority that an individual is not a fit and proper person to perform functions in relation to a regulated activity carried on by an authorised person.

**56(2) ["Prohibition order"]** The Authority may make an order ("a prohibition order") prohibiting the individual from performing a specified function, any function falling within a specified description or any function.

**56(3) [Scope of prohibition order]** A prohibition order may relate to–

THE OFFICIAL LIST

## 74 The official list

**74(1) [Duty of competent authority]** The competent authority must maintain the official list.

**74(2) [Admission to listing]** The competent authority may admit to the official list such securities and other things as it considers appropriate.

**74(3) [Power of Treasury to make order]** But–

(a) nothing may be admitted to the official list except in accordance with this Part; and

(b) the Treasury may by order provide that anything which falls within a description or category specified in the order may not be admitted to the official list.

**74(4) ["Listing rules"]** The competent authority may make rules ("listing rules") for the purposes of this Part.

**74(5) ["Security", "listing"]** In the following provisions of this Part–

**"security"** means anything which has been, or may be, admitted to the official list; and

**"listing"** means being included in the official list in accordance with this Part.

LISTING

## 75 Applications for listing

**75(1) [Admission to official list]** Admission to the official list may be granted only on an application made to the competent authority in such manner as may be required by listing rules.

**75(2) [Consent of issuer of securities]** No application for listing may be entertained by the competent authority unless it is made by, or with the consent of, the issuer of the securities concerned.

**75(3) [Prescribed bodies]** No application for listing may be entertained by the competent authority in respect of securities which are to be issued by a body of a prescribed kind.

**75(4) [Compliance with listing rules]** The competent authority may not grant an application for listing unless it is satisfied that–

(a) the requirements of listing rules (so far as they apply to the application), and

(b) any other requirements imposed by the authority in relation to the application,

are complied with.

**75(5) [Refusal of application – detrimental to investors]** An application for listing may be refused if, for a reason relating to the issuer, the competent authority considers that granting it would be detrimental to the interests of investors.

**75(6) [Refusal of application – failure to comply with EEA obligations]** An application for listing securities which are already officially listed in another EEA State may be refused if the issuer has failed to comply with any obligations to which he is subject as a result of that listing.

## 76 Decision on application

**76(1) [Notification of decision]** The competent authority must notify the applicant of its decision on an application for listing–

(a) before the end of the period of six months beginning with the date on which the application is received; or

(b) if within that period the authority has required the applicant to provide further information in connection with the application, before the end of the period of six months beginning with the date on which that information is provided.

**76(2) [Failure to comply with s. 76(1)]** If the competent authority fails to comply with subsection (1), it is to be taken to have decided to refuse the application.

**76(3) [Written notice – grant of application]** If the competent authority decides to grant an application for listing, it must give the applicant written notice.

**76(4) [Warning notice – proposal to refuse application]** If the competent authority proposes to refuse an application for listing, it must give the applicant a warning notice.

**76(5) [Decision notice – decision to refuse application]** If the competent authority decides to refuse an application for listing, it must give the applicant a decision notice.

**76(6) [Right of referral to Tribunal]** If the competent authority decides to refuse an application for listing, the applicant may refer the matter to the Tribunal.

**76(7) [Effect of admission to official list]** If securities are admitted to the official list, their admission may not be called in question on the ground that any requirement or condition for their admission has not been complied with.

## 77 Discontinuance and suspension of listing

**77(1) [Discontinuance of listing]** The competent authority may, in accordance with listing rules, discontinue the listing of any securities if satisfied that there are special circumstances which preclude normal regular dealings in them.

**77(2) [Suspension of listing]** The competent authority may, in accordance with listing rules, suspend the listing of any securities.

**77(3) [Effect of s. 77(2) suspension]** If securities are suspended under subsection (2) they are to be treated, for the purposes of sections 96 and 99, as still being listed.

**77(4) [Application of section]** This section applies to securities whenever they were admitted to the official list.

**77(5) [Right of referral to Tribunal]** If the competent authority discontinues or suspends the listing of any securities, the issuer may refer the matter to the Tribunal.

## 78 Discontinuance or suspension: procedure

**78(1) [Effective date]** A discontinuance or suspension takes effect–

(a) immediately, if the notice under subsection (2) states that that is the case;

(b) in any other case, on such date as may be specified in that notice.

**78(2) [Written notice – proposal to suspend, etc. listing]** If the competent authority–

(a) proposes to discontinue or suspend the listing of securities, or

(b) discontinues or suspends the listing of securities with immediate effect,

it must give the issuer of the securities written notice.

**78(3) [Contents of notice]** The notice must–

(a) give details of the discontinuance or suspension;

(b) state the competent authority's reasons for the discontinuance or suspension and for choosing the date on which it took effect or takes effect;

(c) inform the issuer of the securities that he may make representations to the competent authority within such period as may be specified in the notice (whether or not he has referred the matter to the Tribunal);

(d) inform him of the date on which the discontinuance or suspension took effect or will take effect; and

(e) inform him of his right to refer the matter to the Tribunal.

**78(4) [Extension of period for representations]** The competent authority may extend the period within which representations may be made to it.

**78(5) [Written notice – decision to suspend, etc. listing]** If, having considered any representations made by the issuer of the securities, the competent authority decides–

(a) to discontinue or suspend the listing of the securities, or

(b) if the discontinuance or suspension has taken effect, not to cancel it,

the competent authority must give the issuer of the securities written notice.

**78(6) [Right of referral to Tribunal]** A notice given under subsection (5) must inform the issuer of the securities of his right to refer the matter to the Tribunal.

**78(7) [Procedure upon referral]** If a notice informs a person of his right to refer a matter to the Tribunal, it must give an indication of the procedure on such a reference.

**78(8) [Written notice – decision not to suspend, etc. listing]** If the competent authority decides–

(a) not to discontinue or suspend the listing of the securities, or

(b) if the discontinuance or suspension has taken effect, to cancel it,

the competent authority must give the issuer of the securities written notice.

**78(9) [Effect of cancelling a discontinuance]** The effect of cancelling a discontinuance is that the securities concerned are to be readmitted, without more, to the official list.

**78(10) [Warning notice – proposal to refuse application for cancellation]** If the competent authority has suspended the listing of securities and proposes to refuse an application by the issuer of the securities for the cancellation of the suspension, it must give him a warning notice.

**78(11) [Duty of competent authority following representations]** The competent authority must, having considered any representations made in response to the warning notice–

(a) if it decides to refuse the application, give the issuer of the securities a decision notice;

(b) if it grants the application, give him written notice of its decision.

**78(12) [Right of referral to Tribunal]** If the competent authority decides to refuse an application for the cancellation of the suspension of listed securities, the applicant may refer the matter to the Tribunal.

**78(13) ["Discontinuance"] "Discontinuance"** means a discontinuance of listing under section 77(1).

**78(14) ["Suspension"] "Suspension"** means a suspension of listing under section 77(2).

## LISTING PARTICULARS

# 79 Listing particulars and other documents

**79(1) [Submission of listing particulars to competent authority]** Listing rules may provide that securities (other than new securities) of a kind specified in the rules may not be admitted to the official list unless–

(a) listing particulars have been submitted to, and approved by, the competent authority and published; or

(b) in such cases as may be specified by listing rules, such document (other than listing particulars or a prospectus of a kind required by listing rules) as may be so specified has been published.

**79(2) ["Listing particulars"] "Listing particulars"** means a document in such form and containing such information as may be specified in listing rules.

**79(3) [Determination of responsibility for listing particulars]** For the purposes of this Part, the persons responsible for listing particulars are to be determined in accordance with regulations made by the Treasury.

**79(4) [Non-application of section]** Nothing in this section affects the competent authority's general power to make listing rules.

# 80 General duty of disclosure in listing particulars

**80(1) [Content of s. 79 listing particulars]** Listing particulars submitted to the competent authority under section 79 must contain all such information as investors and their professional advisers would reasonably require, and reasonably expect to find there, for the purpose of making an informed assessment of–

(a) the assets and liabilities, financial position, profits and losses, and prospects of the issuer of the securities; and

(b) the rights attaching to the securities.

**80(2) [Additional information for admission to official list]** That information is required in addition to any information required by–

(a) listing rules, or

(b) the competent authority,

as a condition of the admission of the securities to the official list.

**80(3) [Application of s. 80(1)]** Subsection (1) applies only to information–

(a) within the knowledge of any person responsible for the listing particulars; or

(b) which it would be reasonable for him to obtain by making enquiries.

**80(4) [S. 80(1) – determination of information required]** In determining what information subsection (1) requires to be included in listing particulars, regard must be had (in particular) to–

(a) the nature of the securities and their issuer;

(b) the nature of the persons likely to consider acquiring them;

(c) the fact that certain matters may reasonably be expected to be within the knowledge of professional advisers of a kind which persons likely to acquire the securities may reasonably be expected to consult; and

(d) any information available to investors or their professional advisers as a result of requirements imposed on the issuer of the securities by a recognised investment exchange, by listing rules or by or under any other enactment.

## 81 Supplementary listing particulars

**81(1) [Duty of issuer]** If at any time after the preparation of listing particulars which have been submitted to the competent authority under section 79 and before the commencement of dealings in the securities concerned following their admission to the official list–

(a) there is a significant change affecting any matter contained in those particulars the inclusion of which was required by–

(i) section 80,

(ii) listing rules, or

(iii) the competent authority, or

(b) a significant new matter arises, the inclusion of information in respect of which would have been so required if it had arisen when the particulars were prepared,

the issuer must, in accordance with listing rules, submit supplementary listing particulars of the change or new matter to the competent authority, for its approval and, if they are approved, publish them.

**81(2) ["Significant"] "Significant"** means significant for the purpose of making an informed assessment of the kind mentioned in section 80(1).

**81(3) [Non-application of s. 81(1) where issuer lacks notification]** If the issuer of the securities is not aware of the change or new matter in question, he is not under a duty to comply with subsection (1) unless he is notified of the change or new matter by a person responsible for the listing particulars.

**81(4) [Duty of person responsible for listing particulars]** But it is the duty of any person responsible for those particulars who is aware of such a change or new matter to give notice of it to the issuer.

**81(5) [Application of s. 81(1)]** Subsection (1) applies also as respects matters contained in any supplementary listing particulars previously published under this section in respect of the securities in question.

## 82 Exemptions from disclosure

**82(1) [Power of competent authority]** The competent authority may authorise the omission from listing particulars of any information, the inclusion of which would otherwise be required by section 80 or 81, on the ground–

(a) that its disclosure would be contrary to the public interest;

(b) that its disclosure would be seriously detrimental to the issuer; or

(c) in the case of securities of a kind specified in listing rules, that its disclosure is unnecessary for persons of the kind who may be expected normally to buy or deal in securities of that kind.

**82(2) [Scope of s. 82(1)(b)]** But–

(a) no authority may be granted under subsection (1)(b) in respect of essential information; and

(b) no authority granted under subsection (1)(b) extends to any such information.

**82(3) [Power of Secretary of State, etc.]** The Secretary of State or the Treasury may issue a certificate to the effect that the disclosure of any information (including information that would otherwise have to be included in listing particulars for which they are themselves responsible) would be contrary to the public interest.

**82(4) [Entitlement to act on certificate]** The competent authority is entitled to act on any such certificate in exercising its powers under subsection (1)(a).

**82(5) [Powers of competent authority unaffected]** This section does not affect any powers of the competent authority under listing rules made as a result of section 101(2).

**82(6) ["Essential information"] "Essential information"** means information which a person considering acquiring securities of the kind in question would be likely to need in order not to be misled about any facts which it is essential for him to know in order to make an informed assessment.

**82(7) ["Listing particulars"] "Listing particulars"** includes supplementary listing particulars.

## 83 Registration of listing particulars

**83(1) [Delivery to registrar of companies]** On or before the date on which listing particulars are published as required by listing rules, a copy of the particulars must be delivered for registration to the registrar of companies.

**83(2) [Statement of delivery]** A statement that a copy has been delivered to the registrar must be included in the listing particulars when they are published.

**83(3) [Offence]** If there has been a failure to comply with subsection (1) in relation to listing particulars which have been published–

(a) the issuer of the securities in question, and

(b) any person who is a party to the publication and aware of the failure,

is guilty of an offence.

**83(4) [Penalty]** A person guilty of an offence under subsection (3) is liable–

(a) on summary conviction, to a fine not exceeding the statutory maximum;

(b) on conviction on indictment, to a fine.

**83(5) ["Listing particulars"] "Listing particulars"** includes supplementary listing particulars.

**83(6) ["Registrar of companies"] "The registrar of companies"** means–

(a) if the securities are, or are to be, issued by a company incorporated in Great Britain whose registered office is in England and Wales, the registrar of companies in England and Wales;

(b) if the securities are, or are to be, issued by a company incorporated in Great Britain whose registered office is in Scotland, the registrar of companies in Scotland;

(c) if the securities are, or are to be, issued by a company incorporated in Northern Ireland, the registrar of companies for Northern Ireland; and

(d) in any other case, any of those registrars.

PROSPECTUSES

## 84 Prospectuses

**84(1) [Approval by competent authority]** Listing rules must provide that no new securities for which an application for listing has been made may be admitted to the official list unless a prospectus has been submitted to, and approved by, the competent authority and published.

**84(2) ["New securities"] "New securities"** means securities which are to be offered to the public in the United Kingdom for the first time before admission to the official list.

**84(3) ["Prospectus"] "Prospectus"** means a prospectus in such form and containing such information as may be specified in listing rules.

**84(4) [Non-limitation of power to make listing rules]** Nothing in this section affects the competent authority's general power to make listing rules.

## 85 Publication of prospectus

**85(1) [Offers before publication of prospectus]** If listing rules made under section 84 require a prospectus to be published before particular new securities are admitted to the official list, it is unlawful for any of those securities to be offered to the public in the United Kingdom before the required prospectus is published.

**85(2) [Offence, penalty]** A person who contravenes subsection (1) is guilty of an offence and liable–

(a) on summary conviction, to imprisonment for a term not exceeding three months or a fine not exceeding level 5 on the standard scale;

(b) on conviction on indictment, to imprisonment for a term not exceeding two years or a fine, or both.

**85(3) [Prospectus not fully in compliance with listing rules]** A person is not to be regarded as contravening subsection (1) merely because a prospectus does not fully comply with the requirements of listing rules as to its form or content.

**85(4) [Compensation]** But subsection (3) does not affect the question whether any person is liable to pay compensation under section 90.

**85(5) [Contravention of s. 85(1)]** Any contravention of subsection (1) is actionable, at the suit of a person who suffers loss as a result of the contravention, subject to the defences and other incidents applying to actions for breach of statutory duty.

## 86 Application of this Part to prospectuses

**86(1) [Application of provisions of Pt. VI]** The provisions of this Part apply in relation to a prospectus required by listing rules as they apply in relation to listing particulars.

**86(2) [Interpretation]** In this Part–

(a) any reference to listing particulars is to be read as including a reference to a prospectus; and

(b) any reference to supplementary listing particulars is to be read as including a reference to a supplementary prospectus.

## 87 Approval of prospectus where no application for listing

**87(1) [Approval of prospectus]** Listing rules may provide for a prospectus to be submitted to and approved by the competent authority if–

(a) securities are to be offered to the public in the United Kingdom for the first time;

(b) no application for listing of the securities has been made under this Part; and

(c) the prospectus is submitted by, or with the consent of, the issuer of the securities.

**87(2) ["Non-listing prospectus"] "Non-listing prospectus"** means a prospectus submitted to the competent authority as a result of any listing rules made under subsection (1).

**87(3) [Content of listing rules made under s. 87(1)]** Listing rules made under subsection (1) may make provision–

(a) as to the information to be contained in, and the form of, a non-listing prospectus; and

(b) as to the timing and manner of publication of a non-listing prospectus.

**87(4) [S. 87(3)(b) subject to Treasury order]** The power conferred by subsection (3)(b) is subject to such provision made by or under any other enactment as the Treasury may by order specify.

**87(5) [Modification of Pt. VI by Sch. 9]** Schedule 9 modifies provisions of this Part as they apply in relation to non-listing prospectuses.

SPONSORS

## 88 Sponsors

**88(1) [Requirements of listing rules]** Listing rules may require a person to make arrangements with a sponsor for the performance by the sponsor of such services in relation to him as may be specified in the rules.

**88(2) ["Sponsor"]** **"Sponsor"** means a person approved by the competent authority for the purposes of the rules.

**88(3) [Content of listing rules]** Listing rules made by virtue of subsection (1) may–

(a) provide for the competent authority to maintain a list of sponsors;

(b) specify services which must be performed by a sponsor;

(c) impose requirements on a sponsor in relation to the provision of services or specified services;

(d) specify the circumstances in which a person is qualified for being approved as a sponsor.

**88(4) [Warning notice]** If the competent authority proposes–

(a) to refuse a person's application for approval as a sponsor, or

(b) to cancel a person's approval as a sponsor,

it must give him a warning notice.

**88(5) [Written notice]** If, after considering any representations made in response to the warning notice, the competent authority decides–

(a) to grant the application for approval, or

(b) not to cancel the approval,

it must give the person concerned, and any person to whom a copy of the warning notice was given, written notice of its decision.

**88(6) [Decision notice]** If, after considering any representations made in response to the warning notice, the competent authority decides–

(a) to refuse to grant the application for approval, or

(b) to cancel the approval,

it must give the person concerned a decision notice.

**88(7) [Right of referral to Tribunal]** A person to whom a decision notice is given under this section may refer the matter to the Tribunal.

## 89 Public censure of sponsor

**89(1) [Listing rules – publication of statement]** Listing rules may make provision for the competent authority, if it considers that a sponsor has contravened a requirement imposed on him by rules made as a result of section 88(3)(c), to publish a statement to that effect.

**89(2) [Warning notice]** If the competent authority proposes to publish a statement it must give the sponsor a warning notice setting out the terms of the proposed statement.

**89(3) [Decision notice]** If, after considering any representations made in response to the warning notice, the competent authority decides to make the proposed statement, it must give the sponsor a decision notice setting out the terms of the statement.

**89(4) [Right of referral to Tribunal]** A sponsor to whom a decision notice is given under this section may refer the matter to the Tribunal.

COMPENSATION

## 90 Compensation for false or misleading particulars

**90(1) [Compensation – misleading, etc. particulars]** Any person responsible for listing particulars is liable to pay compensation to a person who has–

(a) acquired securities to which the particulars apply; and

(b) suffered loss in respect of them as a result of–

(i) any untrue or misleading statement in the particulars; or

(ii) the omission from the particulars of any matter required to be included by section 80 or 81.

**90(2) [S. 90(1) subject to Sch. 10 exemptions]** Subsection (1) is subject to exemptions provided by Schedule 10.

**90(3) [Omission of information in listing particulars]** If listing particulars are required to include information about the absence of a particular matter, the omission from the particulars of that information is to be treated as a statement in the listing particulars that there is no such matter.

**90(4) [Compensation – non-compliance with s. 81]** Any person who fails to comply with section 81 is liable to pay compensation to any person who has–

(a) acquired securities of the kind in question; and

(b) suffered loss in respect of them as a result of the failure.

**90(5) [S. 90(4) subject to Sch. 10 exemptions]** Subsection (4) is subject to exemptions provided by Schedule 10.

**90(6) [Liability]** This section does not affect any liability which may be incurred apart from this section.

**90(7) [Acquisition of securities]** References in this section to the acquisition by a person of securities include references to his contracting to acquire them or any interest in them.

**90(8) [Promoters of companies failing to disclose information]** No person shall, by reason of being a promoter of a company or otherwise, incur any liability for failing to disclose information which he would not be required to disclose in listing particulars in respect of a company's securities–

(a) if he were responsible for those particulars; or

(b) if he is responsible for them, which he is entitled to omit by virtue of section 82.

**90(9) [Interpretation]** The reference in subsection (8) to a person incurring liability includes a reference to any other person being entitled as against that person to be granted any civil remedy or to rescind or repudiate an agreement.

**90(10) ["Listing particulars"] "Listing particulars"**, in subsection (1) and Schedule 10, includes supplementary listing particulars.

PENALTIES

## 91 Penalties for breach of listing rules

**91(1) [Penalty]** If the competent authority considers that–

(a) an issuer of listed securities, or

(b) an applicant for listing,

has contravened any provision of listing rules, it may impose on him a penalty of such amount as it considers appropriate.

**91(2) [Penalty – director of issuer, etc.]** If, in such a case, the competent authority considers that a person who was at the material time a director of the issuer or applicant was knowingly concerned in the contravention, it may impose on him a penalty of such amount as it considers appropriate.

**99(3) [Non-inclusion of Pt. VI penalties]** In fixing the amount of any fee which is to be payable to the competent authority, no account is to be taken of any sums which it receives, or expects to receive, by way of penalties imposed by it under this Part.

**99(4) [Application of s. 99(2)(c)]** Subsection (2)(c) applies whether expenses were incurred before or after the coming into force of this Part.

**99(5) [Fees recoverable as debt]** Any fee which is owed to the competent authority under any provision made by or under this Part may be recovered as a debt due to it.

## 100 Penalties

**100(1) [Duty of competent authority re penalty policy]** In determining its policy with respect to the amount of penalties to be imposed by it under this Part, the competent authority must take no account of the expenses which it incurs, or expects to incur, in discharging its functions under this Part.

**100(2) [Duty of competent authority re scheme]** The competent authority must prepare and operate a scheme for ensuring that the amounts paid to it by way of penalties imposed under this Part are applied for the benefit of issuers of securities admitted to the official list.

**100(3) [Variability of scheme]** The scheme may, in particular, make different provision with respect to different classes of issuer.

**100(4) [Scheme details]** Up to date details of the scheme must be set out in a document ("the scheme details").

**100(5) [Publication of scheme details]** The scheme details must be published by the competent authority in the way appearing to it to be best calculated to bring them to the attention of the public.

**100(6) [Publication of draft scheme]** Before making the scheme, the competent authority must publish a draft of the proposed scheme in the way appearing to it to be best calculated to bring it to the attention of the public.

**100(7) [Representations]** The draft must be accompanied by notice that representations about the proposals may be made to the competent authority within a specified time.

**100(8) [Regard to representations]** Before making the scheme, the competent authority must have regard to any representations made to it under subsection (7).

**100(9) [Publication of representations, etc.]** If the competent authority makes the proposed scheme, it must publish an account, in general terms, of–

(a) the representations made to it in accordance with subsection (7); and

(b) its response to them.

**100(10) [Publication of differences]** If the scheme differs from the draft published under subsection (6) in a way which is, in the opinion of the competent authority, significant the competent authority must (in addition to complying with subsection (9)) publish details of the difference.

**100(11) [Copy to Treasury]** The competent authority must, without delay, give the Treasury a copy of any scheme details published by it.

**100(12) [Fees]** The competent authority may charge a reasonable fee for providing a person with a copy of–

(a) a draft published under subsection (6);

(b) scheme details.

**100(13) [Application of s. 100(6)–(10), (12)]** Subsections (6) to (10) and (12) apply also to a proposal to alter or replace the scheme.

## 101 Listing rules: general provisions

**101(1) [Variability of listing rules]** Listing rules may make different provision for different cases.

**101(2) [Modification, etc. of applicability of rules]** Listing rules may authorise the competent authority to dispense with or modify the application of the rules in particular cases and by reference to any circumstances.

**101(3) [Instrument in writing]** Listing rules must be made by an instrument in writing.

**101(4) [Distribution of instrument]** Immediately after an instrument containing listing rules is made, it must be printed and made available to the public with or without payment.

**101(5) [Defence where s. 101(4) not complied with]** A person is not to be taken to have contravened any listing rule if he shows that at the time of the alleged contravention the instrument containing the rule had not been made available as required by subsection (4).

**101(6) [Endorsement of copy]** The production of a printed copy of an instrument purporting to be made by the competent authority on which is endorsed a certificate signed by an officer of the authority authorised by it for that purpose and stating–

(a) that the instrument was made by the authority,

(b) that the copy is a true copy of the instrument, and

(c) that on a specified date the instrument was made available to the public as required by subsection (4),

is evidence (or in Scotland sufficient evidence) of the facts stated in the certificate.

**101(7) [Presumption of proper signing]** A certificate purporting to be signed as mentioned in subsection (6) is to be treated as having been properly signed unless the contrary is shown.

**101(8) [Endorsement for purposes of legal proceedings]** A person who wishes in any legal proceedings to rely on a rule-making instrument may require the Authority to endorse a copy of the instrument with a certificate of the kind mentioned in subsection (6).

## 102 Exemption from liability in damages

**102(1) [Competent authority, officers, etc.]** Neither the competent authority nor any person who is, or is acting as, a member, officer or member of staff of the competent authority is to be liable in damages for anything done or omitted in the discharge, or purported discharge, of the authority's functions.

**102(2) [Non-application of s. 102(1)]** Subsection (1) does not apply–

(a) if the act or omission is shown to have been in bad faith; or

(b) so as to prevent an award of damages made in respect of an act or omission on the ground that the act or omission was unlawful as a result of section 6(1) of the Human Rights Act 1998.

## 103 Interpretation of this Part

**103(1) [Definitions]** In this Part–

**"application"** means an application made under section 75;

**"issuer"**, in relation to anything which is or may be admitted to the official list, has such meaning as may be prescribed by the Treasury;

**"listing"** has the meaning given in section 74(5);

**"listing particulars"** has the meaning given in section 79(2);

**"listing rules"** has the meaning given in section 74(4);

**"new securities"** has the meaning given in section 84(2);

**"the official list"** means the list maintained as the official list by the Authority immediately before the coming into force of section 74, as that list has effect for the time being;

**"security"** (except in section 74(2)) has the meaning given in section 74(5).

**103(2) [Interpretation]** In relation to any function conferred on the competent authority by this Part, any reference in this Part to the competent authority is to be read as a reference to the person by whom that function is for the time being exercisable.

**103(3) [S. 91 powers where functions exercisable by different persons]** If, as a result of an order under Schedule 8, different functions conferred on the competent authority by this Part are exercisable by different persons, the powers conferred by section 91 are exercisable by such person as may be determined in accordance with the provisions of the order.

**103(4) [Offering of securities]** For the purposes of this Part, a person offers securities if, and only if, as principal–

(a) he makes an offer which, if accepted, would give rise to a contract for their issue or sale by him or by another person with whom he has made arrangements for their issue or sale; or

(b) he invites a person to make such an offer.

**103(5) ["Offer", "offeror"]** "Offer" and "offeror" are to be read accordingly.

**103(6) [Offering of securities in UK]** For the purposes of this Part, the question whether a person offers securities to the public in the United Kingdom is to be determined in accordance with Schedule 11.

**103(7) ["Sale"]** For the purposes of subsection (4) "sale" includes any disposal for valuable consideration.

# PART VII – CONTROL OF BUSINESS TRANSFERS

## 104 Control of business transfers

**104** No insurance business transfer scheme or banking business transfer scheme is to have effect unless an order has been made in relation to it under section 111(1).

## 105 Insurance business transfer schemes

**105(1) [Characteristics of scheme]** A scheme is an insurance business transfer scheme if it–

(a) satisfies one of the conditions set out in subsection (2);

(b) results in the business transferred being carried on from an establishment of the transferee in an EEA State; and

(c) is not an excluded scheme.

**105(2) [Conditions]** The conditions are that–

(a) the whole or part of the business carried on in one or more member States by a UK authorised person who has permission to effect or carry out contracts of insurance ("the authorised person concerned") is to be transferred to another body ("the transferee");

(b) the whole or part of the business, so far as it consists of reinsurance, carried on in the United Kingdom through an establishment there by an EEA firm qualifying for authorisation under Schedule 3 which has permission to effect or carry out contracts of insurance ("the authorised person concerned") is to be transferred to another body ("the transferee");

(c) the whole or part of the business carried on in the United Kingdom by an authorised person who is neither a UK authorised person nor an EEA firm but who has permission to effect or carry out contracts of insurance ("the authorised person concerned") is to be transferred to another body ("the transferee").

**105(3) [Excluded scheme]** A scheme is an excluded scheme for the purposes of this section if it falls within any of the following cases:

**CASE 1**

Where the authorised person concerned is a friendly society.

**CASE 2**

Where–

(a) the authorised person concerned is a UK authorised person;

(b) the business to be transferred under the scheme is business which consists of the effecting or carrying out of contracts of reinsurance in one or more EEA States other than the United Kingdom; and

(c) the scheme has been approved by a court in an EEA State other than the United Kingdom or by the host state regulator.

CASE 3

Where–

(a) the authorised person concerned is a UK authorised person;

(b) the business to be transferred under the scheme is carried on in one or more countries or territories (none of which is an EEA State) and does not include policies of insurance (other than reinsurance) against risks arising in an EEA State; and

(c) the scheme has been approved by a court in a country or territory other than an EEA State or by the authority responsible for the supervision of that business in a country or territory in which it is carried on.

CASE 4

Where the business to be transferred under the scheme is the whole of the business of the authorised person concerned and–

(a) consists solely of the effecting or carrying out of contracts of reinsurance, or

(b) all the policyholders are controllers of the firm or of firms within the same group as the firm which is the transferee,

and, in either case, all of the policyholders who will be affected by the transfer have consented to it.

**105(4) [Court order sanctioning scheme]** The parties to a scheme which falls within Case 2, 3 or 4 may apply to the court for an order sanctioning the scheme as if it were an insurance business transfer scheme.

**105(5) [Application of s. 105(6)]** Subsection (6) applies if the scheme involves a compromise or arrangement falling within section 427A of the Companies Act 1985 (or Article 420A of the Companies (Northern Ireland) Order 1986).

**105(6) [Companies Act 1985, s. 425–427]** Sections 425 to 427 of that Act (or Articles 418 to 420 of that Order) have effect as modified by section 427A of that Act (or Article 420A of that Order) in relation to that compromise or arrangement.

**105(7) [Limitation of s. 105(6)]** But subsection (6) does not affect the operation of this Part in relation to the scheme.

**105(8) ["UK authorised person"] "UK authorised person"** means a body which is an authorised person and which–

(a) is incorporated in the United Kingdom; or

(b) is an unincorporated association formed under the law of any part of the United Kingdom.

**105(9) ["Establishment"] "Establishment"** means, in relation to a person, his head office or a branch of his.

## 106 Banking business transfer schemes

**106(1) [Characteristics of scheme]** A scheme is a banking business transfer scheme if it–

(a) satisfies one of the conditions set out in subsection (2);

(b) is one under which the whole or part of the business to be transferred includes the accepting of deposits; and

(c) is not an excluded scheme.

**106(2) [Conditions]** The conditions are that–

(a) the whole or part of the business carried on by a UK authorised person who has

27 of the first life insurance directive, or Article 23 of the first non-life insurance directive, transfers to another body all its rights and obligations under any UK policies.

**116(3) [Effect of instrument in law]** If appropriate notice of the execution of an instrument giving effect to the transfer is published, the instrument has the effect in law–

(a) of transferring to the transferee all the transferor's rights and obligations under the UK policies to which the instrument applies, and

(b) if the instrument so provides, of securing the continuation by or against the transferee of any legal proceedings by or against the transferor which relate to those rights and obligations.

**116(4) [Agreement, etc. not required]** No agreement or consent is required before subsection (3) has the effects mentioned.

**116(5) ["Authorised transfer"] "Authorised transfer"** means–

(a) in subsection (1), a transfer authorised in the home State of the EEA firm in accordance with–
  (i) Article 11 of the third life directive; or
  (ii) Article 12 of the third non-life directive; and

(b) in subsection (2), a transfer authorised in an EEA State other than the United Kingdom in accordance with–
  (i) Article 31a of the first life directive; or
  (ii) Article 28a of the first non-life directive.

**116(6) ["UK policy"] "UK policy"** means a policy evidencing a contract of insurance (other than a contract of reinsurance) to which the applicable law is the law of any part of the United Kingdom.

**116(7) ["Appropriate notice"] "Appropriate notice"** means–

(a) if the UK policy evidences a contract of insurance in relation to which an EEA State other than the United Kingdom is the State of the commitment, notice given in accordance with the law of that State;

(b) if the UK policy evidences a contract of insurance where the risk is situated in an EEA State other than the United Kingdom, notice given in accordance with the law of that EEA State;

(c) in any other case, notice given in accordance with the applicable law.

**116(8) [Application of para. 6, Sch. 12]** Paragraph 6 of Schedule 12 applies for the purposes of this section as it applies for the purposes of that Schedule.

MODIFICATIONS

## 117 Power to modify this Part

**117** The Treasury may by regulations–

(a) provide for prescribed provisions of this Part to have effect in relation to prescribed cases with such modifications as may be prescribed;

(b) make such amendments to any provision of this Part as they consider appropriate for the more effective operation of that or any other provision of this Part.

# PART VIII – PENALTIES FOR MARKET ABUSE

MARKET ABUSE

## 118 Market abuse

**118(1) [Behaviour amounting to market abuse]** For the purposes of this Act, market abuse is behaviour (whether by one person alone or by two or more persons jointly or in concert)–

(a) which occurs in relation to qualifying investments traded on a market to which this section applies;

(b) which satisfies any one or more of the conditions set out in subsection (2); and

(c) which is likely to be regarded by a regular user of that market who is aware of the behaviour as a failure on the part of the person or persons concerned to observe the standard of behaviour reasonably expected of a person in his or their position in relation to the market.

**118(2) [Conditions]** The conditions are that–

(a) the behaviour is based on information which is not generally available to those using the market but which, if available to a regular user of the market, would or would be likely to be regarded by him as relevant when deciding the terms on which transactions in investments of the kind in question should be effected;

(b) the behaviour is likely to give a regular user of the market a false or misleading impression as to the supply of, or demand for, or as to the price or value of, investments of the kind in question;

(c) a regular user of the market would, or would be likely to, regard the behaviour as behaviour which would, or would be likely to, distort the market in investments of the kind in question.

**118(3) [Power of Treasury to make order]** The Treasury may by order prescribe (whether by name or by description)–

(a) the markets to which this section applies; and

(b) the investments which are qualifying investments in relation to those markets.

**118(4) [Variability of order]** The order may prescribe different investments or descriptions of investment in relation to different markets or descriptions of market.

**118(5) [Behaviour to occur within UK, etc.]** Behaviour is to be disregarded for the purposes of subsection (1) unless it occurs–

(a) in the United Kingdom; or

(b) in relation to qualifying investments traded on a market to which this section applies which is situated in the United Kingdom or which is accessible electronically in the United Kingdom.

**118(6) [Behaviour occurring in relation to qualifying investments]** For the purposes of this section, the behaviour which is to be regarded as occurring in relation to qualifying investments includes behaviour which–

(a) occurs in relation to anything which is the subject matter, or whose price or value is expressed by reference to the price or value, of those qualifying investments; or

(b) occurs in relation to investments (whether qualifying or not) whose subject matter is those qualifying investments.

**118(7) [Available information]** Information which can be obtained by research or analysis conducted by, or on behalf of, users of a market is to be regarded for the purposes of this section as being generally available to them.

**118(8) [Conformity with rules]** Behaviour does not amount to market abuse if it conforms with a rule which includes a provision to the effect that behaviour conforming with the rule does not amount to market abuse.

**118(9) [Interpretation]** Any reference in this Act to a person engaged in market abuse is a reference to a person engaged in market abuse whether alone or with one or more other persons.

**118(10) [Definitions]** In this section–

**"behaviour"** includes action or inaction;

**"investment"** is to be read with section 22 and Schedule 2;

**"regular user"**, in relation to a particular market, means a reasonable person who regularly deals on that market in investments of the kind in question.

THE CODE

## 119 The code

**119(1) [Duty of Authority]** The Authority must prepare and issue a code containing such provisions as the Authority considers will give appropriate guidance to those determining whether or not behaviour amounts to market abuse.

**119(2) [Contents of code]** The code may among other things specify–

(a) descriptions of behaviour that, in the opinion of the Authority, amount to market abuse;

(b) descriptions of behaviour that, in the opinion of the Authority, do not amount to market abuse;

(c) factors that, in the opinion of the Authority, are to be taken into account in determining whether or not behaviour amounts to market abuse.

**119(3) [Variability of code]** The code may make different provision in relation to persons, cases or circumstances of different descriptions.

**119(4) [Alteration, etc. of code]** The Authority may at any time alter or replace the code.

**119(5) [Issue of altered, etc. code]** If the code is altered or replaced, the altered or replacement code must be issued by the Authority.

**119(6) [Effective publication]** A code issued under this section must be published by the Authority in the way appearing to the Authority to be best calculated to bring it to the attention of the public.

**119(7) [Copy to Treasury]** The Authority must, without delay, give the Treasury a copy of any code published under this section.

**119(8) [Fees]** The Authority may charge a reasonable fee for providing a person with a copy of the code.

## 120 Provisions included in the Authority's code by reference to the City Code

**120(1) [Behaviour not amounting to market abuse]** The Authority may include in a code issued by it under section 119 ("the Authority's code") provision to the effect that in its opinion behaviour conforming with the City Code–

(a) does not amount to market abuse;

(b) does not amount to market abuse in specified circumstances; or

(c) does not amount to market abuse if engaged in by a specified description of person.

**120(2) [Treasury approval]** But the Treasury's approval is required before any such provision may be included in the Authority's code.

**120(3) [Duty of Authority]** If the Authority's code includes provision of a kind authorised by subsection (1), the Authority must keep itself informed of the way in which the Panel on Takeovers and Mergers interprets and administers the relevant provisions of the City Code.

**120(4) ["City Code"] "City Code"** means the City Code on Takeovers and Mergers issued by the Panel as it has effect at the time when the behaviour occurs.

**120(5) ["Specified"] "Specified"** means specified in the Authority's code.

## 121 Codes: procedure

**121(1) [Publication of draft proposed code]** Before issuing a code under section 119, the Authority must publish a draft of the proposed code in the way appearing to the Authority to be best calculated to bring it to the attention of the public.

**121(2) [Matters to accompany draft]** The draft must be accompanied by–

(a) a cost benefit analysis; and

(b) notice that representations about the proposal may be made to the Authority within a specified time.

**121(3) [Regard to representations]** Before issuing the proposed code, the Authority must have regard to any representations made to it in accordance with subsection (2)(b).

**121(4) [Publication of representations, etc.]** If the Authority issues the proposed code it must publish an account, in general terms, of–

(a) the representations made to it in accordance with subsection (2)(b); and

(b) its response to them.

**121(5) [Publication of differences]** If the code differs from the draft published under subsection (1) in a way which is, in the opinion of the Authority, significant–

(a) the Authority must (in addition to complying with subsection (4)) publish details of the difference; and

(b) those details must be accompanied by a cost benefit analysis.

**121(6) [Non-application of s. 121(1)–(5)]** Subsections (1) to (5) do not apply if the Authority considers that there is an urgent need to publish the code.

**121(7) [Non-application of s. 121(2)(a), (5)(b)]** Neither subsection (2)(a) nor subsection (5)(b) applies if the Authority considers–

(a) that, making the appropriate comparison, there will be no increase in costs; or

(b) that, making that comparison, there will be an increase in costs but the increase will be of minimal significance.

**121(8) [Fees]** The Authority may charge a reasonable fee for providing a person with a copy of a draft published under subsection (1).

**121(9) [Application of section]** This section also applies to a proposal to alter or replace a code.

**121(10) ["Cost benefit analysis"] "Cost benefit analysis"** means an estimate of the costs together with an analysis of the benefits that will arise–

(a) if the proposed code is issued; or

(b) if subsection (5)(b) applies, from the code that has been issued.

**121(11) ["The appropriate comparison"] "The appropriate comparison"** means–

(a) in relation to subsection (2)(a), a comparison between the overall position if the code is issued and the overall position if it is not issued;

(b) in relation to subsection (5)(b), a comparison between the overall position after the issuing of the code and the overall position before it was issued.

## 122 Effect of the code

**122(1) [Compliance with s. 119 code]** If a person behaves in a way which is described (in the code in force under section 119 at the time of the behaviour) as behaviour that, in the Authority's opinion, does not amount to market abuse that behaviour of his is to be taken, for the purposes of this Act, as not amounting to market abuse.

**122(2) [S. 119 code definitive of market abuse]** Otherwise, the code in force under section 119 at the time when particular behaviour occurs may be relied on so far as it indicates whether or not that behaviour should be taken to amount to market abuse.

### POWER TO IMPOSE PENALTIES

## 123 Power to impose penalties in cases of market abuse

**123(1) [Penalty]** If the Authority is satisfied that a person ("A")–

(a) is or has engaged in market abuse, or

(b) by taking or refraining from taking any action has required or encouraged another person or persons to engage in behaviour which, if engaged in by A, would amount to market abuse,

it may impose on him a penalty of such amount as it considers appropriate.

**123(2) [Limitation on power to impose penalty]** But the Authority may not impose a penalty on a person if, having considered any representations made to it in response to a warning notice, there are reasonable grounds for it to be satisfied that–

(a) he believed, on reasonable grounds, that his behaviour did not fall within paragraph (a) or (b) of subsection (1), or

(b) he took all reasonable precautions and exercised all due diligence to avoid behaving in a way which fell within paragraph (a) or (b) of that subsection.

**123(3) [Publication of statement]** If the Authority is entitled to impose a penalty on a person under this section it may, instead of imposing a penalty on him, publish a statement to the effect that he has engaged in market abuse.

STATEMENT OF POLICY

## 124 Statement of policy

**124(1) [Duty of Authority]** The Authority must prepare and issue a statement of its policy with respect to–

(a) the imposition of penalties under section 123; and

(b) the amount of penalties under that section.

**124(2) [Determination of amount of penalty]** The Authority's policy in determining what the amount of a penalty should be must include having regard to–

(a) whether the behaviour in respect of which the penalty is to be imposed had an adverse effect on the market in question and, if it did, how serious that effect was;

(b) the extent to which that behaviour was deliberate or reckless; and

(c) whether the person on whom the penalty is to be imposed is an individual.

**124(3) [Contents of statement]** A statement issued under this section must include an indication of the circumstances in which the Authority is to be expected to regard a person as–

(a) having a reasonable belief that his behaviour did not amount to market abuse; or

(b) having taken reasonable precautions and exercised due diligence to avoid engaging in market abuse.

**124(4) [Alteration, etc. of policy]** The Authority may at any time alter or replace a statement issued under this section.

**124(5) [Issue of alterations, etc.]** If a statement issued under this section is altered or replaced, the Authority must issue the altered or replacement statement.

**124(6) [Regard to s. 124 statement]** In exercising, or deciding whether to exercise, its power under section 123 in the case of any particular behaviour, the Authority must have regard to any statement published under this section and in force at the time when the behaviour concerned occurred.

**124(7) [Effective publication]** A statement issued under this section must be published by the Authority in the way appearing to the Authority to be best calculated to bring it to the attention of the public.

**124(8) [Fees]** The Authority may charge a reasonable fee for providing a person with a copy of a statement published under this section.

**124(9) [Copy to Treasury]** The Authority must, without delay, give the Treasury a copy of any statement which it publishes under this section.

## 125 Statement of policy: procedure

**125(1) [Publication of draft proposed statement]** Before issuing a statement of policy under section 124, the Authority must publish a draft of the proposed statement in the way appearing to the Authority to be best calculated to bring it to the attention of the public.

**125(2) [Matters to accompany draft]** The draft must be accompanied by notice that representations about the proposal may be made to the Authority within a specified time.

**125(3) [Regard to representations]** Before issuing the proposed statement, the Authority must have regard to any representations made to it in accordance with subsection (2).

**125(4) [Publication of representations, etc.]** If the Authority issues the proposed statement it must publish an account, in general terms, of–

(a) the representations made to it in accordance with subsection (2); and

(b) its response to them.

**125(5) [Publication of differences]** If the statement differs from the draft published under subsection (1) in a way which is, in the opinion of the Authority, significant, the Authority must (in addition to complying with subsection (4)) publish details of the difference.

**125(6) [Fees]** The Authority may charge a reasonable fee for providing a person with a copy of a draft published under subsection (1).

**125(7) [Application of section]** This section also applies to a proposal to alter or replace a statement.

PROCEDURE

# 126 Warning notices

**126(1) [S. 123 action]** If the Authority proposes to take action against a person under section 123, it must give him a warning notice.

**126(2) [Amount of proposed penalty]** A warning notice about a proposal to impose a penalty must state the amount of the proposed penalty.

**126(3) [Terms of proposed statement]** A warning notice about a proposal to publish a statement must set out the terms of the proposed statement.

# 127 Decision notices and right to refer to Tribunal

**127(1) [S. 123 action]** If the Authority decides to take action against a person under section 123, it must give him a decision notice.

**127(2) [Amount of penalty]** A decision notice about the imposition of a penalty must state the amount of the penalty.

**127(3) [Terms of statement]** A decision notice about the publication of a statement must set out the terms of the statement.

**127(4) [Right of referral to Tribunal]** If the Authority decides to take action against a person under section 123, that person may refer the matter to the Tribunal.

MISCELLANEOUS

# 128 Suspension of investigations

**128(1) [Power of Authority]** If the Authority considers it desirable or expedient because of the exercise or possible exercise of a power relating to market abuse, it may direct a recognised investment exchange or recognised clearing house–

(a) to terminate, suspend or limit the scope of any inquiry which the exchange or clearing house is conducting under its rules; or

(b) not to conduct an inquiry which the exchange or clearing house proposes to conduct under its rules.

**128(2) [Form, enforceability of direction]** A direction under this section–

(a) must be given to the exchange or clearing house concerned by notice in writing; and

(b) is enforceable, on the application of the Authority, by injunction or, in Scotland, by an order under section 45 of the Court of Session Act 1988.

**128(3) [Power of Authority re market abuse]** The Authority's powers relating to market abuse are its powers–

(a) to impose penalties under section 123; or

(b) to appoint a person to conduct an investigation under section 168 in a case falling within subsection (2)(d) of that section.

## 129 Power of court to impose penalty in cases of market abuse

**129(1) [S. 381, s. 383 applications]** The Authority may on an application to the court under section 381 or 383 request the court to consider whether the circumstances are such that a penalty should be imposed on the person to whom the application relates.

**129(2) [Power of court]** The court may, if it considers it appropriate, make an order requiring the person concerned to pay to the Authority a penalty of such amount as it considers appropriate.

## 130 Guidance

**130(1) [Power of Treasury]** The Treasury may from time to time issue written guidance for the purpose of helping relevant authorities to determine the action to be taken in cases where behaviour occurs which is behaviour–

(a) with respect to which the power in section 123 appears to be exercisable; and

(b) which appears to involve the commission of an offence under section 397 of this Act or Part V of the Criminal Justice Act 1993 (insider dealing).

**130(2) [Consent of Attorney General and Secretary of State]** The Treasury must obtain the consent of the Attorney General and the Secretary of State before issuing any guidance under this section.

**130(3) ["Relevant authorities"]** In this section **"relevant authorities"**–

(a) in relation to England and Wales, means the Secretary of State, the Authority, the Director of the Serious Fraud Office and the Director of Public Prosecutions;

(b) in relation to Northern Ireland, means the Secretary of State, the Authority, the Director of the Serious Fraud Office and the Director of Public Prosecutions for Northern Ireland.

**130(4) [Non-application of s. 130(1)–(3)]** Subsections (1) to (3) do not apply to Scotland.

**130(5) [Scotland]** In relation to Scotland, the Lord Advocate may from time to time, after consultation with the Treasury, issue written guidance for the purpose of helping the Authority to determine the action to be taken in cases where behaviour mentioned in subsection (1) occurs.

## 131 Effect on transactions

**131** The imposition of a penalty under this Part does not make any transaction void or unenforceable.

# PART IX – HEARINGS AND APPEALS

## 132 The Financial Services and Markets Tribunal

**132(1) ["The Tribunal"]** For the purposes of this Act, there is to be a tribunal known as the Financial Services and Markets Tribunal (but referred to in this Act as "the Tribunal").

**132(2) [Functions of Tribunal]** The Tribunal is to have the functions conferred on it by or under this Act.

**132(3) [Power of Lord Chancellor to make rules]** The Lord Chancellor may by rules make such provision as appears to him to be necessary or expedient in respect of the conduct of proceedings before the Tribunal.

**132(4) [Application of Sch. 13]** Schedule 13 is to have effect as respects the Tribunal and its proceedings (but does not limit the Lord Chancellor's powers under this section).

## 133 Proceedings: general provision

**133(1) [Referral period]** A reference to the Tribunal under this Act must be made before the end of–

(a) the period of 28 days beginning with the date on which the decision notice or supervisory notice in question is given; or
(b) such other period as may be specified in rules made under section 132.

**133(2) [Extension of referral period]** Subject to rules made under section 132, the Tribunal may allow a reference to be made after the end of that period.

**133(3) [Consideration of new evidence]** On a reference the Tribunal may consider any evidence relating to the subject-matter of the reference, whether or not it was available to the Authority at the material time.

**133(4) [Determination of appropriate Authority action]** On a reference the Tribunal must determine what (if any) is the appropriate action for the Authority to take in relation to the matter referred to it.

**133(5) [Remittance to Authority with directions]** On determining a reference, the Tribunal must remit the matter to the Authority with such directions (if any) as the Tribunal considers appropriate for giving effect to its determination.

**133(6) [Limitation of power of Tribunal – decision notice]** In determining a reference made as a result of a decision notice, the Tribunal may not direct the Authority to take action which the Authority would not, as a result of section 388(2), have had power to take when giving the decision notice.

**133(7) [Limitation of power of Tribunal – supervisory notice]** In determining a reference made as a result of a supervisory notice, the Tribunal may not direct the Authority to take action which would have otherwise required the giving of a decision notice.

**133(8) [Power of Tribunal – recommendations]** The Tribunal may, on determining a reference, make recommendations as to the Authority's regulating provisions or its procedures.

**133(9) [Duty not to take action specified in decision notice]** The Authority must not take the action specified in a decision notice–
(a) during the period within which the matter to which the decision notice relates may be referred to the Tribunal; and
(b) if the matter is so referred, until the reference, and any appeal against the Tribunal's determination, has been finally disposed of.

**133(10) [Duty to act in accordance with determination of Tribunal]** The Authority must act in accordance with the determination of, and any direction given by, the Tribunal.

**133(11) [Enforcement of order of Tribunal]** An order of the Tribunal may be enforced–
(a) as if it were an order of a county court; or
(b) in Scotland, as if it were an order of the Court of Session.

**133(12) ["Supervisory notice"] "Supervisory notice"** has the same meaning as in section 395.

LEGAL ASSISTANCE BEFORE THE TRIBUNAL

# 134 Legal assistance scheme

**134(1) [Power of Lord Chancellor to make regulations]** The Lord Chancellor may by regulations establish a scheme governing the provision of legal assistance in connection with proceedings before the Tribunal.

**134(2) [Criteria for eligibility]** If the Lord Chancellor establishes a scheme under subsection (1), it must provide that a person is eligible for assistance only if–
(a) he falls within subsection (3); and
(b) he fulfils such other criteria (if any) as may be prescribed as a result of section 135(1)(d).

**134(3) [Referral under s. 127(4)]** A person falls within this subsection if he is an individual who has referred a matter to the Tribunal under section 127(4).

**134(4) ["The legal assistance scheme"]** In this Part of this Act **"the legal assistance scheme"** means any scheme in force under subsection (1).

## 135 Provisions of the legal assistance scheme

**135(1) [Scope of scheme]** The legal assistance scheme may, in particular, make provision as to–

(a) the kinds of legal assistance that may be provided;

(b) the persons by whom legal assistance may be provided;

(c) the manner in which applications for legal assistance are to be made;

(d) the criteria on which eligibility for legal assistance is to be determined;

(e) the persons or bodies by whom applications are to be determined;

(f) appeals against refusals of applications;

(g) the revocation or variation of decisions;

(h) its administration and the enforcement of its provisions.

**135(2) [Conditions, etc. re legal assistance]** Legal assistance under the legal assistance scheme may be provided subject to conditions or restrictions, including conditions as to the making of contributions by the person to whom it is provided.

## 136 Funding of the legal assistance scheme

**136(1) [Duty of Authority ]** The Authority must pay to the Lord Chancellor such sums at such times as he may, from time to time, determine in respect of the anticipated or actual cost of legal assistance provided in connection with proceedings before the Tribunal under the legal assistance scheme.

**136(2) [Duty of Authority to make rules]** In order to enable it to pay any sum which it is obliged to pay under subsection (1), the Authority must make rules requiring the payment to it by authorised persons or any class of authorised person of specified amounts or amounts calculated in a specified way.

**136(3) [Consolidated Fund]** Sums received by the Lord Chancellor under subsection (1) must be paid into the Consolidated Fund.

**136(4) [Duty of Lord Chancellor]** The Lord Chancellor must, out of money provided by Parliament fund the cost of legal assistance provided in connection with proceedings before the Tribunal under the legal assistance scheme.

**136(5) [Application of s. 136(6)]** Subsection (6) applies if, as respects a period determined by the Lord Chancellor, the amount paid to him under subsection (1) as respects that period exceeds the amount he has expended in that period under subsection (4).

**136(6) [Repayment of excess monies]** The Lord Chancellor must–

(a) repay, out of money provided by Parliament, the excess to the Authority; or

(b) take the excess into account on the next occasion on which he makes a determination under subsection (1).

**136(7) [Distribution, etc. of sums repaid under s. 136(6)(a)]** The Authority must make provision for any sum repaid to it under subsection (6)(a)–

(a) to be distributed among–
  (i) the authorised persons on whom a levy was imposed in the period in question as a result of rules made under subsection (2); or
  (ii) such of those persons as it may determine;

(b) to be applied in order to reduce any amounts which those persons, or such of them as it may determine, are or will be liable to pay to the Authority, whether under rules made under subsection (2) or otherwise; or

(c) to be partly so distributed and partly so applied.

**136(8) [Disposal where compliance with s. 136(7) not practical]** If the Authority considers that it is not practicable to deal with any part of a sum repaid to it under subsection (6)(a) in accordance with provision made by it as a result of subsection (7), it may, with the consent [of] the Lord Chancellor, apply or dispose of that part of that sum in such manner as it considers appropriate.

**Note**

In s. 136(8) the word [of] inserted by CCH.New Law.

**136(9) ["Specified"]** "Specified" means specified in the rules.

APPEALS

# 137 Appeal on a point of law

**137(1) [Appeal from Tribunal]** A party to a reference to the Tribunal may with permission appeal–

(a) to the Court of Appeal, or

(b) in Scotland, to the Court of Session,

on a point of law arising from a decision of the Tribunal disposing of the reference.

**137(2) ["Permission"]** "Permission" means permission given by the Tribunal or by the Court of Appeal or (in Scotland) the Court of Session.

**137(3) [Power of court]** If, on an appeal under subsection (1), the court considers that the decision of the Tribunal was wrong in law, it may–

(a) remit the matter to the Tribunal for rehearing and determination by it; or

(b) itself make a determination.

**137(4) [Appeal from Court of Appeal]** An appeal may not be brought from a decision of the Court of Appeal under subsection (3) except with the leave of–

(a) the Court of Appeal; or

(b) the House of Lords.

**137(5) [Appeal from Court of Session]** An appeal lies, with the leave of the Court of Session or the House of Lords, from any decision of the Court of Session under this section, and such leave may be given on such terms as to costs, expenses or otherwise as the Court of Session or the House of Lords may determine.

**137(6) [Applicability of s. 132 rules]** Rules made under section 132 may make provision for regulating or prescribing any matters incidental to or consequential on an appeal under this section.

# PART X – RULES AND GUIDANCE

## Chapter I – Rule-making Powers

# 138 General rule-making power

**138(1) [Power of Authority to make rules]** The Authority may make such rules applying to authorised persons–

(a) with respect to the carrying on by them of regulated activities, or

(b) with respect to the carrying on by them of activities which are not regulated activities,

as appear to it to be necessary or expedient for the purpose of protecting the interests of consumers.

**138(2) [General rules]** Rules made under this section are referred to in this Act as the Authority's general rules.

**138(3) [Non-limitation of powers]** The Authority's power to make general rules is not limited by any other power which it has to make regulating provisions.

**138(4) [Scope of general rules]** The Authority's general rules may make provision applying to authorised persons even though there is no relationship between the authorised persons to whom the rules will apply and the persons whose interests will be protected by the rules.

**138(5) [Group activity]** General rules may contain requirements which take into account, in the case of an authorised person who is a member of a group, any activity of another member of the group.

**138(6) [EEA firms]** General rules may not–

(a) make provision prohibiting an EEA firm from carrying on, or holding itself out as carrying on, any activity which it has permission conferred by Part II of Schedule 3 to carry on in the United Kingdom;

(b) make provision, as respects an EEA firm, about any matter responsibility for which is, under any of the single market directives, reserved to the firm's home state regulator.

**138(7) ["Consumers"] "Consumers"** means persons–

(a) who use, have used, or are or may be contemplating using, any of the services provided by–
  (i) authorised persons in carrying on regulated activities; or
  (ii) persons acting as appointed representatives;

(b) who have rights or interests which are derived from, or are otherwise attributable to, the use of any such services by other persons; or

(c) who have rights or interests which may be adversely affected by the use of any such services by persons acting on their behalf or in a fiduciary capacity in relation to them.

**138(8) [Beneficiaries of trust]** If an authorised person is carrying on a regulated activity in his capacity as a trustee, the persons who are, have been or may be beneficiaries of the trust are to be treated as persons who use, have used or are or may be contemplating using services provided by the authorised person in his carrying on of that activity.

**138(9) [Persons dealing with authorised persons]** For the purposes of subsection (7) a person who deals with an authorised person in the course of the authorised person's carrying on of a regulated activity is to be treated as using services provided by the authorised person in carrying on those activities.

## 139 Miscellaneous ancillary matters

**139(1) [Rules re clients' money]** Rules relating to the handling of money held by an authorised person in specified circumstances ("clients' money") may–

(a) make provision which results in that clients' money being held on trust in accordance with the rules;

(b) treat two or more accounts as a single account for specified purposes (which may include the distribution of money held in the accounts);

(c) authorise the retention by the authorised person of interest accruing on the clients' money; and

(d) make provision as to the distribution of such interest which is not to be retained by him.

**139(2) [Limitation of liability – institutions]** An institution with which an account is kept in pursuance of rules relating to the handling of clients' money does not incur any liability as constructive trustee if money is wrongfully paid from the account, unless the institution permits the payment–

(a) with knowledge that it is wrongful; or

(b) having deliberately failed to make enquiries in circumstances in which a reasonable and honest person would have done so.

**139(3) [Application of s. 139(1) to Scotland]** In the application of subsection (1) to Scotland, the reference to money being held on trust is to be read as a reference to its being held as agent for the person who is entitled to call for it to be paid over to him or to be paid on his direction or to have it otherwise credited to him.

**139(4) [Rules re rescission, etc.]** Rules may–

(a) confer rights on persons to rescind agreements with, or withdraw offers to, authorised persons within a specified period; and

(b) make provision, in respect of authorised persons and persons exercising those rights, for the restitution of property and the making or recovery of payments where those rights are exercised.

**139(5) ["Rules"]** "Rules" means general rules.

**139(6) ["Specified"]** "Specified" means specified in the rules.

## 140 Restriction on managers of authorised unit trust schemes

**140(1) [Power of Authority to make rules]** The Authority may make rules prohibiting an authorised person who has permission to act as the manager of an authorised unit trust scheme from carrying on a specified activity.

**140(2) [Non-regulated activities]** Such rules may specify an activity which is not a regulated activity.

## 141 Insurance business rules

**141(1) [Power of Authority to make rules]** The Authority may make rules prohibiting an authorised person who has permission to effect or carry out contracts of insurance from carrying on a specified activity.

**141(2) [Non-regulated activities]** Such rules may specify an activity which is not a regulated activity.

**141(3) [Rules re long-term insurance business]** The Authority may make rules in relation to contracts entered into by an authorised person in the course of carrying on business which consists of the effecting or carrying out of contracts of long-term insurance.

**141(4) [Rules re description of property]** Such rules may, in particular–

(a) restrict the descriptions of property or indices of the value of property by reference to which the benefits under such contracts may be determined;

(b) make provision, in the interests of the protection of policyholders, for the substitution of one description of property, or index of value, by reference to which the benefits under a contract are to be determined for another such description of property or index.

**141(5) [Insurance business rules]** Rules made under this section are referred to in this Act as insurance business rules.

## 142 Insurance business: regulations supplementing Authority's rules

**142(1) [Power of Treasury to make regulations]** The Treasury may make regulations for the purpose of preventing a person who is not an authorised person but who–

(a) is a parent undertaking of an authorised person who has permission to effect or carry out contracts of insurance, and

(b) falls within a prescribed class,

from doing anything to lessen the effectiveness of asset identification rules.

**142(2) ["Asset identification rules"]** "Asset identification rules" means rules made by the Authority which require an authorised person who has permission to effect or carry out contracts of insurance to identify assets which belong to him and which are maintained in respect of a particular aspect of his business.

**142(3) [Scope of regulations]** The regulations may, in particular, include provision–

(a) prohibiting the payment of dividends;

(b) prohibiting the creation of charges;

(c) making charges created in contravention of the regulations void.

**142(4) [Further scope of regulations]** The Treasury may by regulations provide that, in prescribed circumstances, charges created in contravention of asset identification rules are void.

**142(5) [Offence, penalty]** A person who contravenes regulations under subsection (1) is guilty of an offence and liable on summary conviction to a fine not exceeding level 5 on the standard scale.

**142(6) ["Charges"]** "Charges" includes mortgages (or in Scotland securities over property).

## 143 Endorsement of codes etc.

**143(1) [Power of Authority to make rules]** The Authority may make rules ("endorsing rules")–

(a) endorsing the City Code on Takeovers and Mergers issued by the Panel on Takeovers and Mergers;

(b) endorsing the Rules Governing Substantial Acquisitions of Shares issued by the Panel.

**143(2) [Scope of endorsement]** Endorsement may be–

(a) as respects all authorised persons; or

(b) only as respects a specified kind of authorised person.

**143(3) [Exercise of powers at request of Panel]** At any time when endorsing rules are in force, and if asked to do so by the Panel, the Authority may exercise its powers under Part IV or section 66 as if failure to comply with an endorsed provision was a ground entitling the Authority to exercise those powers.

**143(4) [Exercise of Pt. XIII, XIV or XXV powers]** At any time when endorsing rules are in force and if asked to do so by the Panel, the Authority may exercise its powers under Part XIII, XIV or XXV as if the endorsed provisions were rules applying to the persons in respect of whom they are endorsed.

**143(5) [Failure to comply with imposed requirement]** For the purposes of subsections (3) and (4), a failure to comply with a requirement imposed, or ruling given, under an endorsed provision is to be treated as a failure to comply with the endorsed provision under which that requirement was imposed or ruling was given.

**143(6) [Alteration of endorsed provisions]** If endorsed provisions are altered, subsections (3) and (4) apply to them as altered, but only if before the alteration the Authority has notified the Panel (and has not withdrawn its notification) that it is satisfied with the Panel's consultation procedures.

**143(7) ["Consultation procedures"] "Consultation procedures"** means procedures designed to provide an opportunity for persons likely to be affected by alterations to those provisions to make representations about proposed alterations to any of those provisions.

**143(8) [Application of s. 155(1), (2)(d), (4), (5), (6)(a) and (12)]** Subsections (1), (2)(d), (4), (5), (6)(a) and (12) of section 155 apply (with the necessary modifications) to a proposal to give notification of the kind mentioned in subsection (6) as they apply to a proposal to make endorsing rules.

**143(9) [Application of section]** This section applies in relation to particular provisions of the code or rules mentioned in subsection (1) as it applies to the code or the rules.

### SPECIFIC RULES

## 144 Price stabilising rules

**144(1) [Power of Authority to make rules]** The Authority may make rules ("price stabilising rules") as to–

(a) the circumstances and manner in which,

(b) the conditions subject to which, and

(c) the time when or the period during which,

action may be taken for the purpose of stabilising the price of investments of specified kinds.

**144(2) [Application of rules to authorised persons, etc.]** Price stabilising rules–

(a) are to be made so as to apply only to authorised persons;

(b) may make different provision in relation to different kinds of investment.

**144(3) [Conformity with price stabalising rules]** The Authority may make rules which, for the purposes of section 397(5)(b), treat a person who acts or engages in conduct–

(a) for the purpose of stabilising the price of investments, and

(b) in conformity with such provisions corresponding to price stabilising rules and made by a body or authority outside the United Kingdom as may be specified in the rules under this subsection,

as acting, or engaging in that conduct, for that purpose and in conformity with price stabilising rules.

**144(4) [Power of Treasury to make order]** The Treasury may by order impose limitations on the power to make rules under this section.

**144(5) [Scope of order]** Such an order may, in particular–

(a) specify the kinds of investment in relation to which price stabilising rules may make provision;

(b) specify the kinds of investment in relation to which rules made under subsection (3) may make provision;

(c) provide for price stabilising rules to make provision for action to be taken for the purpose of stabilising the price of investments only in such circumstances as the order may specify;

(d) provide for price stabilising rules to make provision for action to be taken for that purpose only at such times or during such periods as the order may specify.

**144(6) [Notification of alteration to s. 144(3) rules]** If provisions specified in rules made under subsection (3) are altered, the rules continue to apply to those provisions as altered, but only if before the alteration the Authority has notified the body or authority concerned (and has not withdrawn its notification) that it is satisfied with its consultation procedures.

**144(7) ["Consultation procedures"] "Consultation procedures"** has the same meaning as in section 143.

## 145 Financial promotion rules

**145(1) [Power of Authority to make rules]** The Authority may make rules applying to authorised persons about the communication by them, or their approval of the communication by others, of invitations or inducements–

(a) to engage in investment activity; or

(b) to participate in a collective investment scheme.

**145(2) [Scope of rules]** Rules under this section may, in particular, make provision about the form and content of communications.

**145(3) [Application of s. 145(1)]** Subsection (1) applies only to communications which–

(a) if made by a person other than an authorised person, without the approval of an authorised person, would contravene section 21(1);

(b) may be made by an authorised person without contravening section 238(1).

**145(4) ["Engage in investment activity"] "Engage in investment activity"** has the same meaning as in section 21.

**145(5) [Power of Treasury to make order]** The Treasury may by order impose limitations on the power to make rules under this section.

## 146 Money laundering rules

**146** The Authority may make rules in relation to the prevention and detection of money laundering in connection with the carrying on of regulated activities by authorised persons.

## 147 Control of information rules

**147(1) [Power of Authority to make rules]** The Authority may make rules ("control of information rules") about the disclosure and use of information held by an authorised person ("A").

**147(2) [Content of rules]** Control of information rules may–

(a) require the withholding of information which A would otherwise have to disclose to a person ("B") for or with whom A does business in the course of carrying on any regulated or other activity;

(b) specify circumstances in which A may withhold information which he would otherwise have to disclose to B;

(c) require A not to use for the benefit of B information A holds which A would otherwise have to use in that way;

(d) specify circumstances in which A may decide not to use for the benefit of B information A holds which A would otherwise have to use in that way.

MODIFICATION OR WAIVER

## 148 Modification or waiver of rules

**148(1) [Application of section]** This section applies in relation to the following–

(a) auditors and actuaries rules;

(b) control of information rules;

(c) financial promotion rules;

(d) general rules;

(e) insurance business rules;

(f) money laundering rules; and

(g) price stabilising rules.

**148(2) [Power of Authority]** The Authority may, on the application or with the consent of an authorised person, direct that all or any of the rules to which this section applies–

(a) are not to apply to the authorised person; or

(b) are to apply to him with such modifications as may be specified in the direction.

**148(3) [Manner of application]** An application must be made in such manner as the Authority may direct.

**148(4) [Limitation on Authority's powers to give direction]** The Authority may not give a direction unless it is satisfied that–

(a) compliance by the authorised person with the rules, or with the rules as unmodified, would be unduly burdensome or would not achieve the purpose for which the rules were made; and

(b) the direction would not result in undue risk to persons whose interests the rules are intended to protect.

**148(5) [Conditions]** A direction may be given subject to conditions.

**148(6) [Effective publication]** Unless it is satisfied that it is inappropriate or unnecessary to do so, a direction must be published by the Authority in such a way as it thinks most suitable for bringing the direction to the attention of–

(a) those likely to be affected by it; and

(b) others who may be likely to make an application for a similar direction.

**148(7) [Matters to consider re publication]** In deciding whether it is satisfied as mentioned in subsection (6), the Authority must–

(a) take into account whether the direction relates to a rule contravention of which is actionable in accordance with section 150;

(b) consider whether its publication would prejudice, to an unreasonable degree, the commercial interests of the authorised person concerned or any other member of his immediate group; and

(c) consider whether its publication would be contrary to an international obligation of the United Kingdom.

**148(8) [S. 148(7)(b),(c) – non-disclosure of identity]** For the purposes of paragraphs (b) and (c) of subsection (7), the Authority must consider whether it would be possible to publish the direction without either of the consequences mentioned in those paragraphs by publishing it without disclosing the identity of the authorised person concerned.

**148(9) [Revocation, etc. of direction]** The Authority may–

(a) revoke a direction; or

(b) vary it on the application, or with the consent, of the authorised person to whom it relates.

**148(10) ["Direction"] "Direction"** means a direction under subsection (2).

**148(11) ["Immediate group"] "Immediate group"**, in relation to an authorised person ("A"), means–

(a) A;
(b) a parent undertaking of A;
(c) a subsidiary undertaking of A;
(d) a subsidiary undertaking of a parent undertaking of A;
(e) a parent undertaking of a subsidiary undertaking of A.

CONTRAVENTION OF RULES

# 149 Evidential provisions

**149(1) [Consequences of contravention of rule]** If a particular rule so provides, contravention of the rule does not give rise to any of the consequences provided for by other provisions of this Act.

**149(2) [Scope of rule]** A rule which so provides must also provide–

(a) that contravention may be relied on as tending to establish contravention of such other rule as may be specified; or

(b) that compliance may be relied on as tending to establish compliance with such other rule as may be specified.

**149(3) [S. 149(1) provision]** A rule may include the provision mentioned in subsection (1) only if the Authority considers that it is appropriate for it also to include the provision required by subsection (2).

# 150 Actions for damages

**150(1) [Contravention of rules – private persons]** A contravention by an authorised person of a rule is actionable at the suit of a private person who suffers loss as a result of the contravention, subject to the defences and other incidents applying to actions for breach of statutory duty.

**150(2) [Non-application of s. 150(1)]** If rules so provide, subsection (1) does not apply to contravention of a specified provision of those rules.

**150(3) [Contravention of rules – non-private persons]** In prescribed cases, a contravention of a rule which would be actionable at the suit of a private person is actionable at the suit of person who is not a private person, subject to the defences and other incidents applying to actions for breach of statutory duty.

**150(4) [Interpretation]** In subsections (1) and (3) "rule" does not include–

(a) listing rules; or

(b) a rule requiring an authorised person to have or maintain financial resources.

**150(5) ["Private person"] "Private person"** has such meaning as may be prescribed.

# 151 Limits on effect of contravening rules

**151(1) [No offence]** A person is not guilty of an offence by reason of a contravention of a rule made by the Authority.

**151(2) [Transaction enforceable]** No such contravention makes any transaction void or unenforceable.

PROCEDURAL PROVISIONS

## 152 Notification of rules to the Treasury

**152(1) [Copy to Treasury]** If the Authority makes any rules, it must give a copy to the Treasury without delay.

**152(2) [Written notice – alteration, etc. of rules]** If the Authority alters or revokes any rules, it must give written notice to the Treasury without delay.

**152(3) [Details of alteration]** Notice of an alteration must include details of the alteration.

## 153 Rule-making instruments

**153(1) [Power of Authority exercisable in writing]** Any power conferred on the Authority to make rules is exercisable in writing.

**153(2) [Specification of rule making provision]** An instrument by which rules are made by the Authority ("a rule-making instrument") must specify the provision under which the rules are made.

**153(3) [Effect of non-compliance with 153(2)]** To the extent to which a rule-making instrument does not comply with subsection (2), it is void.

**153(4) [Effective publication]** A rule-making instrument must be published by the Authority in the way appearing to the Authority to be best calculated to bring it to the attention of the public.

**153(5) [Fees]** The Authority may charge a reasonable fee for providing a person with a copy of a rule-making instrument.

**153(6) [Defence]** A person is not to be taken to have contravened any rule made by the Authority if he shows that at the time of the alleged contravention the rule-making instrument concerned had not been made available in accordance with this section.

## 154 Verification of rules

**154(1) [Certification of instrument]** The production of a printed copy of a rule-making instrument purporting to be made by the Authority–

(a) on which is endorsed a certificate signed by a member of the Authority's staff authorised by it for that purpose, and

(b) which contains the required statements,

is evidence (or in Scotland sufficient evidence) of the facts stated in the certificate.

**154(2) [Required statements]** The required statements are–

(a) that the instrument was made by the Authority;

(b) that the copy is a true copy of the instrument; and

(c) that on a specified date the instrument was made available to the public in accordance with section 153(4).

**154(3) [Presumption of proper signing]** A certificate purporting to be signed as mentioned in subsection (1) is to be taken to have been properly signed unless the contrary is shown.

**154(4) [Power to require certification]** A person who wishes in any legal proceedings to rely on a rule-making instrument may require the Authority to endorse a copy of the instrument with a certificate of the kind mentioned in subsection (1).

## 155 Consultation

**155(1) [Publication of draft proposed rules]** If the Authority proposes to make any rules, it must publish a draft of the proposed rules in the way appearing to it to be best calculated to bring them to the attention of the public.

**155(2) [Matters to accompany draft]** The draft must be accompanied by–

(a) a cost benefit analysis;

(b) an explanation of the purpose of the proposed rules;

(c) an explanation of the Authority's reasons for believing that making the proposed rules is compatible with its general duties under section 2; and

(d) notice that representations about the proposals may be made to the Authority within a specified time.

**155(3) [S. 155(9) – expenditure details]** In the case of a proposal to make rules under a provision mentioned in subsection (9), the draft must also be accompanied by details of the expected expenditure by reference to which the proposal is made.

**155(4) [Representations]** Before making the proposed rules, the Authority must have regard to any representations made to it in accordance with subsection (2)(d).

**155(5) [Publication of representations, etc.]** If the Authority makes the proposed rules, it must publish an account, in general terms, of–

(a) the representations made to it in accordance with subsection (2)(d); and

(b) its response to them.

**155(6) [Publication of differences]** If the rules differ from the draft published under subsection (1) in a way which is, in the opinion of the Authority, significant–

(a) the Authority must (in addition to complying with subsection (5)) publish details of the difference; and

(b) those details must be accompanied by a cost benefit analysis.

**155(7) [Non-application of s. 155(1)–(6)]** Subsections (1) to (6) do not apply if the Authority considers that the delay involved in complying with them would be prejudicial to the interests of consumers.

**155(8) [Non-application of s. 155(2)(a), 6(b)]** Neither subsection (2)(a) nor subsection (6)(b) applies if the Authority considers–

(a) that, making the appropriate comparison, there will be no increase in costs; or

(b) that, making that comparison, there will be an increase in costs but the increase will be of minimal significance.

**155(9) [S. 155(2)(a), (6)(b) – cost benefit analysis]** Neither subsection (2)(a) nor subsection (6)(b) requires a cost benefit analysis to be carried out in relation to rules made under–

(a) section 136(2);

(b) subsection (1) of section 213 as a result of subsection (4) of that section;

(c) section 234;

(d) paragraph 17 of Schedule 1.

**155(10) ["Cost benefit analysis"] "Cost benefit analysis"** means an estimate of the costs together with an analysis of the benefits that will arise–

(a) if the proposed rules are made; or

(b) if subsection (6) applies, from the rules that have been made.

**155(11) ["The appropriate comparison"] "The appropriate comparison"** means–

(a) in relation to subsection (2)(a), a comparison between the overall position if the rules are made and the overall position if they are not made;

(b) in relation to subsection (6)(b), a comparison between the overall position after the making of the rules and the overall position before they were made.

**155(12) [Fees]** The Authority may charge a reasonable fee for providing a person with a copy of a draft published under subsection (1).

## 156 General supplementary powers

**156(1) [Variability of rules]** Rules made by the Authority may make different provision for different cases and may, in particular, make different provision in respect of different descriptions of authorised person, activity or investment.

**156(2) [Incidental, etc. provisions]** Rules made by the Authority may contain such incidental, supplemental, consequential and transitional provision as the Authority considers appropriate.

# Chapter II – Guidance

## 157 Guidance

**157(1) [Power of Authority]** The Authority may give guidance consisting of such information and advice as it considers appropriate–

(a) with respect to the operation of this Act and of any rules made under it;

(b) with respect to any matters relating to functions of the Authority;

(c) for the purpose of meeting the regulatory objectives;

(d) with respect to any other matters about which it appears to the Authority to be desirable to give information or advice.

**157(2) [Financial, etc. assistance]** The Authority may give financial or other assistance to persons giving information or advice of a kind which the Authority could give under this section.

**157(3) [Application of s. 155(1),(2),(4)–(10)]** If the Authority proposes to give guidance to regulated persons generally, or to a class of regulated person, in relation to rules to which those persons are subject, subsections (1), (2) and (4) to (10) of section 155 apply to the proposed guidance as they apply to proposed rules.

**157(4) [Publication, etc.]** The Authority may–

(a) publish its guidance;

(b) offer copies of its published guidance for sale at a reasonable price; and

(c) if it gives guidance in response to a request made by any person, make a reasonable charge for that guidance.

**157(5) [Interpretation]** In this Chapter, references to guidance given by the Authority include references to any recommendation made by the Authority to persons generally, to regulated persons generally or to any class of regulated person.

**157(6) ["Regulated persons"] "Regulated person"** means any–

(a) authorised person;

(b) person who is otherwise subject to rules made by the Authority.

## 158 Notification of guidance to the Treasury

**158(1) [Copy to Treasury]** On giving any general guidance, the Authority must give the Treasury a copy of the guidance without delay.

**158(2) [Written notice – alteration]** If the Authority alters any of its general guidance, it must give written notice to the Treasury without delay.

**158(3) [Details of alteration]** The notice must include details of the alteration.

**158(4) [Written notice – revocation]** If the Authority revokes any of its general guidance, it must give written notice to the Treasury without delay.

**158(5) ["General guidance"] "General guidance"** means guidance given by the Authority under section 157 which is–

(a) given to persons generally, to regulated persons generally or to a class of regulated person;

(b) intended to have continuing effect; and

(c) given in writing or other legible form.

**158(6) ["Regulated person"] "Regulated person"** has the same meaning as in section 157.

# Chapter III – Competition Scrutiny

## 159 Interpretation

**159(1) [Definitions]** In this Chapter–

**"Director"** means the Director General of Fair Trading;

**"practices"**, in relation to the Authority, means practices adopted by the Authority in the exercise of functions under this Act;

**"regulating provisions"** means any–

(a) rules;

(b) general guidance (as defined by section 158(5));

(c) statement issued by the Authority under section 64;

(d) code issued by the Authority under section 64 or 119.

**159(2) [Adverse effect on competition]** For the purposes of this Chapter, regulating provisions or practices have a significantly adverse effect on competition if–

(a) they have, or are intended or likely to have, that effect; or

(b) the effect that they have, or are intended or likely to have, is to require or encourage behaviour which has, or is intended or likely to have, a significantly adverse effect on competition.

**159(3) [Practices, etc. having adverse effect on competition]** If regulating provisions or practices have, or are intended or likely to have, the effect of requiring or encouraging exploitation of the strength of a market position they are to be taken, for the purposes of this Chapter, to have an adverse effect on competition.

**159(4) [Presumption of acting in accordance with provisions]** In determining under this Chapter whether any of the regulating provisions have, or are likely to have, a particular effect, it may be assumed that the persons to whom the provisions concerned are addressed will act in accordance with them.

## 160 Reports by Director General of Fair Trading

**160(1) [Duty of Director]** The Director must keep the regulating provisions and the Authority's practices under review.

**160(2) [Report – significantly adverse effect on competition]** If at any time the Director considers that–

(a) a regulating provision or practice has a significantly adverse effect on competition, or

(b) two or more regulating provisions or practices taken together, or a particular combination of regulating provisions and practices, have such an effect,

he must make a report to that effect.

**160(3) [Report – no significantly adverse effect on competition]** If at any time the Director considers that–

(a) a regulating provision or practice does not have a significantly adverse effect on competition, or

(b) two or more regulating provisions or practices taken together, or a particular combination of regulating provisions and practices, do not have any such effect,

he may make a report to that effect.

**160(4) [Details of adverse effect]** A report under subsection (2) must include details of the adverse effect on competition.

**160(5) [S. 160(2) – copies, publication]** If the Director makes a report under subsection (2) he must–

(a) send a copy of it to the Treasury, the Competition Commission and the Authority; and

(b) publish it in the way appearing to him to be best calculated to bring it to the attention of the public.

(b) a controller of A;
(c) any other member of a partnership of which A is a member; or
(d) in relation to A, a person mentioned in Part I of Schedule 15.

## 166 Reports by skilled persons

**166(1) [Power of Authority]** The Authority may, by notice in writing given to a person to whom subsection (2) applies, require him to provide the Authority with a report on any matter about which the Authority has required or could require the provision of information or production of documents under section 165.

**166(2) [Application of subsection]** This subsection applies to–
(a) an authorised person ("A"),
(b) any other member of A's group,
(c) a partnership of which A is a member, or
(d) a person who has at any relevant time been a person falling within paragraph (a), (b) or (c),

who is, or was at the relevant time, carrying on a business.

**166(3) [Form of report]** The Authority may require the report to be in such form as may be specified in the notice.

**166(4) [Person to be sufficiently skilled, etc.]** The person appointed to make a report required by subsection (1) must be a person–
(a) nominated or approved by the Authority; and
(b) appearing to the Authority to have the skills necessary to make a report on the matter concerned.

**166(5) [Duty to provide assistance]** It is the duty of any person who is providing (or who at any time has provided) services to a person to whom subsection (2) applies in relation to a matter on which a report is required under subsection (1) to give a person appointed to provide such a report all such assistance as the appointed person may reasonably require.

**166(6) [Injunction]** The obligation imposed by subsection (5) is enforceable, on the application of the Authority, by an injunction or, in Scotland, by an order for specific performance under section 45 of the Court of Session Act 1988.

### APPOINTMENT OF INVESTIGATORS

## 167 Appointment of persons to carry out general investigations

**167(1) [Power of investigating authority]** If it appears to the Authority or the Secretary of State ("the investigating authority") that there is good reason for doing so, the investigating authority may appoint one or more competent persons to conduct an investigation on its behalf into–
(a) the nature, conduct or state of the business of an authorised person or of an appointed representative;
(b) a particular aspect of that business; or
(c) the ownership or control of an authorised person.

**167(2) [Investigation of group members, etc.]** If a person appointed under subsection (1) thinks it necessary for the purposes of his investigation, he may also investigate the business of a person who is or has at any relevant time been–
(a) a member of the group of which the person under investigation ("A") is part; or
(b) a partnership of which A is a member.

**167(3) [Written notice – decision to investigate]** If a person appointed under subsection (1) decides to investigate the business of any person under subsection (2) he must give that person written notice of his decision.

**167(4) [Investigation of former authorised persons]** The power conferred by this section may be exercised in relation to a former authorised person (or appointed representative) but only in relation to–

(a) business carried on at any time when he was an authorised person (or appointed representative); or

(b) the ownership or control of a former authorised person at any time when he was an authorised person.

**167(5) ["Business"] "Business"** includes any part of a business even if it does not consist of carrying on regulated activities.

# 168 Appointment of persons to carry out investigations in particular cases

**168(1) [Application of s. 168(3)]** Subsection (3) applies if it appears to an investigating authority that there are circumstances suggesting that–

(a) a person may have contravened any regulation made under section 142; or

(b) a person may be guilty of an offence under section 177, 191, 346 or 398(1) or under Schedule 4.

**168(2) [Further application of s. 168(3)]** Subsection (3) also applies if it appears to an investigating authority that there are circumstances suggesting that–

(a) an offence under section 24(1) or 397 or under Part V of the Criminal Justice Act 1993 may have been committed;

(b) there may have been a breach of the general prohibition;

(c) there may have been a contravention of section 21 or 238; or

(d) market abuse may have taken place.

**168(3) [Appointment of investigators]** The investigating authority may appoint one or more competent persons to conduct an investigation on its behalf.

**168(4) [Application of s. 168(5)]** Subsection (5) applies if it appears to the Authority that there are circumstances suggesting that–

(a) a person may have contravened section 20;

(b) a person may be guilty of an offence under prescribed regulations relating to money laundering;

(c) an authorised person may have contravened a rule made by the Authority;

(d) an individual may not be a fit and proper person to perform functions in relation to a regulated activity carried on by an authorised or exempt person;

(e) an individual may have performed or agreed to perform a function in breach of a prohibition order;

(f) an authorised or exempt person may have failed to comply with section 56(6);

(g) an authorised person may have failed to comply with section 59(1) or (2);

(h) a person in relation to whom the Authority has given its approval under section 59 may not be a fit and proper person to perform the function to which that approval relates; or

(i) a person may be guilty of misconduct for the purposes of section 66.

**168(5) [Power of Authority re appointment of investigators]** The Authority may appoint one or more competent persons to conduct an investigation on its behalf.

**168(6) ["Investigating authority"] "Investigating authority"** means the Authority or the Secretary of State.

ASSISTANCE TO OVERSEAS REGULATORS

# 169 Investigations etc. in support of overseas regulator

**169(1) [Power of Authority]** At the request of an overseas regulator, the Authority may–

(a) exercise the power conferred by section 165; or

(b) appoint one or more competent persons to investigate any matter.

**169(2) [Powers of investigator]** An investigator has the same powers as an investigator appointed under section 168(3) (as a result of subsection (1) of that section).

**169(3) [Request by competent authority]** If the request has been made by a competent authority in pursuance of any Community obligation the Authority must, in deciding whether or not to exercise its investigative power, consider whether its exercise is necessary to comply with any such obligation.

**169(4) [Investigative powers – matters to be considered]** In deciding whether or not to exercise its investigative power, the Authority may take into account in particular–

(a) whether in the country or territory of the overseas regulator concerned, corresponding assistance would be given to a United Kingdom regulatory authority;

(b) whether the case concerns the breach of a law, or other requirement, which has no close parallel in the United Kingdom or involves the assertion of a jurisdiction not recognised by the United Kingdom;

(c) the seriousness of the case and its importance to persons in the United Kingdom;

(d) whether it is otherwise appropriate in the public interest to give the assistance sought.

**169(5) [Contribution to costs]** The Authority may decide that it will not exercise its investigative power unless the overseas regulator undertakes to make such contribution towards the cost of its exercise as the Authority considers appropriate.

**169(6) [Non-application of s. 169(4),(5)]** Subsections (4) and (5) do not apply if the Authority considers that the exercise of its investigative power is necessary to comply with a Community obligation.

**169(7) [Representative of competent authority]** If the Authority has appointed an investigator in response to a request from an overseas regulator, it may direct the investigator to permit a representative of that regulator to attend, and take part in, any interview conducted for the purposes of the investigation.

**169(8) [Limitation of s. 169(7) direction]** A direction under subsection (7) is not to be given unless the Authority is satisfied that any information obtained by an overseas regulator as a result of the interview will be subject to safeguards equivalent to those contained in Part XXIII.

**169(9) [Statement of policy re s. 169(7) interviews]** The Authority must prepare a statement of its policy with respect to the conduct of interviews in relation to which a direction under subsection (7) has been given.

**169(10) [Treasury approval]** The statement requires the approval of the Treasury.

**169(11) [Publication of approval]** If the Treasury approve the statement, the Authority must publish it.

**169(12) [Publication to precede s. 169(7) direction]** No direction may be given under subsection (7) before the statement has been published.

**169(13) ["Overseas regulator"] "Overseas regulator"** has the same meaning as in section 195.

**169(14) ["Investigative power"] "Investigative power"** means one of the powers mentioned in subsection (1).

**169(15) ["Investigator"] "Investigator"** means a person appointed under subsection (1)(b).

## CONDUCT OF INVESTIGATIONS

## 170 Investigations: general

**170(1) [Application of section]** This section applies if an investigating authority appoints one or more competent persons ("investigators") under section 167 or 168(3) or (5) to conduct an investigation on its behalf.

**170(2) [Written notice to person under investigation]** The investigating authority must give written notice of the appointment of an investigator to the person who is the subject of the investigation ("the person under investigation").

**170(3) [Non-application of s. 170(2) and (9)]** Subsections (2) and (9) do not apply if –

(a) the investigator is appointed as a result of section 168(1) or (4) and the investigating authority believes that the notice required by subsection (2) or (9) would be likely to result in the investigation being frustrated; or

(b) the investigator is appointed as a result of subsection (2) of section 168.

**170(4) [Contents of notice]** A notice under subsection (2) must–

(a) specify the provisions under which, and as a result of which, the investigator was appointed; and

(b) state the reason for his appointment.

**170(5) [Power of investigating authority]** Nothing prevents the investigating authority from appointing a person who is a member of its staff as an investigator.

**170(6) [Duty of investigator to report]** An investigator must make a report of his investigation to the investigating authority.

**170(7) [Control of investigation by direction]** The investigating authority may, by a direction to an investigator, control–

(a) the scope of the investigation;

(b) the period during which the investigation is to be conducted;

(c) the conduct of the investigation; and

(d) the reporting of the investigation.

**170(8) [Scope of direction]** A direction may, in particular–

(a) confine the investigation to particular matters;

(b) extend the investigation to additional matters;

(c) require the investigator to discontinue the investigation or to take only such steps as are specified in the direction;

(d) require the investigator to make such interim reports as are so specified.

**170(9) [Written notice – investigation prejudicial]** If there is a change in the scope or conduct of the investigation and, in the opinion of the investigating authority, the person subject to investigation is likely to be significantly prejudiced by not being made aware of it, that person must be given written notice of the change.

**170(10) ["Investigating authority"] "Investigating authority"**, in relation to an investigator, means–

(a) the Authority, if the Authority appointed him;

(b) the Secretary of State, if the Secretary of State appointed him.

## 171 Powers of persons appointed under section 167

**171(1) [Power of investigator]** An investigator may require the person who is the subject of the investigation ("the person under investigation") or any person connected with the person under investigation–

(a) to attend before the investigator at a specified time and place and answer questions; or

(b) otherwise to provide such information as the investigator may require.

**171(2) [Production of documents]** An investigator may also require any person to produce at a specified time and place any specified documents or documents of a specified description.

**171(3) [Scope of s. 171(1) and (2) powers]** A requirement under subsection (1) or (2) may be imposed only so far as the investigator concerned reasonably considers the question, provision of information or production of the document to be relevant to the purposes of the investigation.

**171(4) [Connected persons]** For the purposes of this section and section 172, a person is connected with the person under investigation ("A") if he is or has at any relevant time been–

(a) a member of A's group;

(b) a controller of A;

# PART XII – CONTROL OVER AUTHORISED PERSONS

## NOTICE OF CONTROL

### 178 Obligation to notify the Authority

**178(1) [Control over authorised persons]** If a step which a person proposes to take would result in his acquiring–

(a) control over a UK authorised person,

(b) an additional kind of control over a UK authorised person, or

(c) an increase in a relevant kind of control which he already has over a UK authorised person,

he must notify the Authority of his proposal.

**178(2) [Control over authorised person acquired passively]** A person who, without himself taking any such step, acquires any such control or additional or increased control must notify the Authority before the end of the period of 14 days beginning with the day on which he first becomes aware that he has acquired it.

**178(3) [Further requirements re notification]** A person who is under the duty to notify the Authority imposed by subsection (1) must also give notice to the Authority on acquiring, or increasing, the control in question.

**178(4) ["UK authorised person"]** In this Part **"UK authorised person"** means an authorised person who–

(a) is a body incorporated in, or an unincorporated association formed under the law of, any part of the United Kingdom; and

(b) is not a person authorised as a result of paragraph 1 of Schedule 5.

**178(5) ["A notice of control"]** A notice under subsection (1) or (2) is referred to in this Part as **"a notice of control"**.

## ACQUIRING, INCREASING AND REDUCING CONTROL

### 179 Acquiring control

**179(1) [Acquisition of control]** For the purposes of this Part, a person ("the acquirer") acquires control over a UK authorised person ("A") on first falling within any of the cases in subsection (2).

**179(2) [Cases where person acquires control]** The cases are where the acquirer–

(a) holds 10% or more of the shares in A;

(b) is able to exercise significant influence over the management of A by virtue of his shareholding in A;

(c) holds 10% or more of the shares in a parent undertaking ("P") of A;

(d) is able to exercise significant influence over the management of P by virtue of his shareholding in P;

(e) is entitled to exercise, or control the exercise of, 10% or more of the voting power in A;

(f) is able to exercise significant influence over the management of A by virtue of his voting power in A;

(g) is entitled to exercise, or control the exercise of, 10% or more of the voting power in P; or

(h) is able to exercise significant influence over the management of P by virtue of his voting power in P.

**179(3) ["The acquirer"]** In subsection (2) **"the acquirer"** means–

(a) the acquirer;

(b) any of the acquirer's associates; or

(c) the acquirer and any of his associates.

**179(4) [Control for the purposes of Pt. XII]** For the purposes of this Part, each of the following is to be regarded as a kind of control–

(a) control arising as a result of the holding of shares in A;

(b) control arising as a result of the holding of shares in P;

(c) control arising as a result of the entitlement to exercise, or control the exercise of, voting power in A;

(d) control arising as a result of the entitlement to exercise, or control the exercise of, voting power in P.

**179(5) [Definitions]** For the purposes of this section and sections 180 and 181, **"associate"**, **"shares"** and **"voting power"** have the same meaning as in section 422.

## 180 Increasing control

**180(1) [Increase in control for purposes of Pt. XII]** For the purposes of this Part, a controller of a person ("A") who is a UK authorised person increases his control over A if–

(a) the percentage of shares held by the controller in A increases by any of the steps mentioned in subsection (2);

(b) the percentage of shares held by the controller in a parent undertaking ("P") of A increases by any of the steps mentioned in subsection (2);

(c) the percentage of voting power which the controller is entitled to exercise, or control the exercise of, in A increases by any of the steps mentioned in subsection (2);

(d) the percentage of voting power which the controller is entitled to exercise, or control the exercise of, in P increases by any of the steps mentioned in subsection (2); or

(e) the controller becomes a parent undertaking of A.

**180(2) [Steps]** The steps are–

(a) from below 10% to 10% or more but less than 20%;

(b) from below 20% to 20% or more but less than 33%;

(c) from below 33% to 33% or more but less than 50%;

(d) from below 50% to 50% or more.

**180(3) ["The controller"]** In paragraphs (a) to (d) of subsection (1) **"the controller"** means–

(a) the controller;

(b) any of the controller's associates; or

(c) the controller and any of his associates.

**180(4) ["Acquiring control", "having control"]** In the rest of this Part **"acquiring control"** or **"having control"** includes–

(a) acquiring or having an additional kind of control; or

(b) acquiring an increase in a relevant kind of control, or having increased control of a relevant kind.

## 181 Reducing control

**181(1) [Decrease in control for purposes of Pt. XII]** For the purposes of this Part, a controller of a person ("A") who is a UK authorised person reduces his control over A if–

(a) the percentage of shares held by the controller in A decreases by any of the steps mentioned in subsection (2),

(b) the percentage of shares held by the controller in a parent undertaking ("P") of A decreases by any of the steps mentioned in subsection (2),

(c) the percentage of voting power which the controller is entitled to exercise, or control the exercise of, in A decreases by any of the steps mentioned in subsection (2),

(d) the percentage of voting power which the controller is entitled to exercise, or control the exercise of, in P decreases by any of the steps mentioned in subsection (2), or

(e) the controller ceases to be a parent undertaking of A,

unless the controller ceases to have the kind of control concerned over A as a result.

**181(2) [Steps]** The steps are–

(a) from 50% or more to 33% or more but less than 50%;

(b) from 33% or more to 20% or more but less than 33%;

(c) from 20% or more to 10% or more but less than 20%;

(d) from 10% or more to less than 10%.

**181(3) ["The controller "]** In paragraphs (a) to (d) of subsection (1) **"the controller"** means–

(a) the controller;

(b) any of the controller's associates; or

(c) the controller and any of his associates.

ACQUIRING OR INCREASING CONTROL: PROCEDURE

## 182 Notification

**182(1) [Notice of control]** A notice of control must–

(a) be given to the Authority in writing; and

(b) include such information and be accompanied by such documents as the Authority may reasonably require.

**182(2) [Additional information, etc.]** The Authority may require the person giving a notice of control to provide such additional information or documents as it reasonably considers necessary in order to enable it to determine what action it is to take in response to the notice.

**182(3) [Variability of requirements]** Different requirements may be imposed in different circumstances.

## 183 Duty of Authority in relation to notice of control

**183(1) [Consideration period]** The Authority must, before the end of the period of three months beginning with the date on which it receives a notice of control ("the period for consideration"), determine whether–

(a) to approve of the person concerned having the control to which the notice relates; or

(b) to serve a warning notice under subsection (3) or section 185(3).

**183(2) [Consultation with overseas regulators]** Before doing so, the Authority must comply with such requirements as to consultation with competent authorities outside the United Kingdom as may be prescribed.

**183(3) [Warning notice – s. 186(1) objection]** If the Authority proposes to give the person concerned a notice of objection under section 186(1), it must give him a warning notice.

## 184 Approval of acquisition of control

**184(1) [Notice of approval]** If the Authority decides to approve of the person concerned having the control to which the notice relates it must notify that person of its approval in writing without delay.

**184(2) [Approval where s. 183(1) not complied with]** If the Authority fails to comply with subsection (1) of section 183 it is to be treated as having given its approval and notified the person concerned at the end of the period fixed by that subsection.

**184(3) [Period in which control must be acquired]** The Authority's approval remains effective only if the person to whom it relates acquires the control in question–

(a) before the end of such period as may be specified in the notice; or

(b) if no period is specified, before the end of the period of one year beginning with the date–

(i) of the notice of approval;
(ii) on which the Authority is treated as having given approval under subsection (2); or
(iii) of a decision on a reference to the Tribunal which results in the person concerned receiving approval.

## 185 Conditions attached to approval

**185(1) [S. 184 approval]** The Authority's approval under section 184 may be given unconditionally or subject to such conditions as the Authority considers appropriate.

**185(2) [Duty of Authority – s. 41 duty]** In imposing any conditions, the Authority must have regard to its duty under section 41.

**185(3) [Warning notice – conditions]** If the Authority proposes to impose conditions on a person it must give him a warning notice.

**185(4) [Decision notice – conditions]** If the Authority decides to impose conditions on a person it must give him a decision notice.

**185(5) [Variation, etc. of condition]** A person who is subject to a condition imposed under this section may apply to the Authority–

(a) for the condition to be varied; or
(b) for the condition to be cancelled.

**185(6) [Cancellation of condition]** The Authority may, on its own initiative, cancel a condition imposed under this section.

**185(7) [Right of referral to Tribunal]** If the Authority has given its approval to a person subject to a condition, he may refer to the Tribunal–

(a) the imposition of the condition; or
(b) the Authority's decision to refuse an application made by him under subsection (5).

## 186 Objection to acquisition of control

**186(1) [Power of Authority]** On considering a notice of control, the Authority may give a decision notice under this section to the person acquiring control ("the acquirer") unless it is satisfied that the approval requirements are met.

**186(2) [Approval requirements]** The approval requirements are that–

(a) the acquirer is a fit and proper person to have the control over the authorised person that he has or would have if he acquired the control in question; and
(b) the interests of consumers would not be threatened by the acquirer's control or by his acquiring that control.

**186(3) [Approval requirements – duty of Authority]** In deciding whether the approval requirements are met, the Authority must have regard, in relation to the control that the acquirer–

(a) has over the authorised person concerned ("A"), or
(b) will have over A if the proposal to which the notice of control relates is carried into effect,

to its duty under section 41 in relation to each regulated activity carried on by A.

**186(4) [Decision notice – steps to satisfy approval requirements]** If the Authority gives a notice under this section but considers that the approval requirements would be met if the person to whom a notice is given were to take, or refrain from taking, a particular step, the notice must identify that step.

**186(5) [Right of referral to Tribunal]** A person to whom a notice under this section is given may refer the matter to the Tribunal.

**186(6) ["Consumers"] "Consumers"** means persons who are consumers for the purposes of section 138.

## 187 Objection to existing control

**187(1) [Decision notice – failure to comply with s. 178]** If the Authority is not satisfied that the approval requirements are met, it may give a decision notice under this section to a person if he has failed to comply with a duty to notify imposed by section 178.

**187(2) [Failure to comply with s. 178(1), (2) – approval of control]** If the failure relates to subsection (1) or (2) of that section, the Authority may (instead of giving a notice under subsection (1)) approve the acquisition of the control in question by the person concerned as if he had given it a notice of control.

**187(3) [Decision notice – controllers]** The Authority may also give a decision notice under this section to a person who is a controller of a UK authorised person if the Authority becomes aware of matters as a result of which it is satisfied that–

(a) the approval requirements are not met with respect to the controller; or

(b) a condition imposed under section 185 required that person to do (or refrain from doing) a particular thing and the condition has been breached as a result of his failing to do (or doing) that thing.

**187(4) [Right of referral to Tribunal]** A person to whom a notice under this section is given may refer the matter to the Tribunal.

**187(5) ["Approval requirements"] "Approval requirements"** has the same meaning as in section 186.

## 188 Notices of objection under section 187: procedure

**188(1) [Warning notice]** If the Authority proposes to give a notice of objection to a person under section 187, it must give him a warning notice.

**188(2) [Consultation]** Before doing so, the Authority must comply with such requirements as to consultation with competent authorities outside the United Kingdom as may be prescribed.

**188(3) [Warning notice – time period]** If the Authority decides to give a warning notice under this section, it must do so before the end of the period of three months beginning–

(a) in the case of a notice to be given under section 187(1), with the date on which it became aware of the failure to comply with the duty in question;

(b) in the case of a notice to be given under section 187(3), with the date on which it became aware of the matters in question.

**188(4) [Additional information, etc.]** The Authority may require the person concerned to provide such additional information or documents as it considers reasonable.

**188(5) [Variability of requirements]** Different requirements may be imposed in different circumstances.

**188(6) ["Notice of objection"]** In this Part **"notice of objection"** means a notice under section 186 or 187.

### IMPROPERLY ACQUIRED SHARES

## 189 Improperly acquired shares

**189(1) [Holding of shares in contravention of notice of objection]** The powers conferred by this section are exercisable if a person has acquired, or has continued to hold, any shares in contravention of–

(a) a notice of objection; or

(b) a condition imposed on the Authority's approval.

**189(2) [Restriction notice]** The Authority may by notice in writing served on the person concerned ("a restriction notice") direct that any such shares which are specified in the notice are, until further notice, subject to one or more of the following restrictions–

(a) a transfer of (or agreement to transfer) those shares, or in the case of unissued shares any transfer of (or agreement to transfer) the right to be issued with them, is void;

(b) no voting rights are to be exercisable in respect of the shares;

(c) no further shares are to be issued in right of them or in pursuance of any offer made to their holder;

(d) except in a liquidation, no payment is to be made of any sums due from the body corporate on the shares, whether in respect of capital or otherwise.

**189(3) [Power of court – order for sale of shares]** The court may, on the application of the Authority, order the sale of any shares to which this section applies and, if they are for the time being subject to any restriction under subsection (2), that they are to cease to be subject to that restriction.

**189(4) [S. 189(3) – time restriction]** No order may be made under subsection (3)–

(a) until the end of the period within which a reference may be made to the Tribunal in respect of the notice of objection; and

(b) if a reference is made, until the matter has been determined or the reference withdrawn.

**189(5) [Power of court – further order for sale of shares]** If an order has been made under subsection (3), the court may, on the application of the Authority, make such further order relating to the sale or transfer of the shares as it thinks fit.

**189(6) [Proceeds to be paid into court]** If shares are sold in pursuance of an order under this section, the proceeds of sale, less the costs of the sale, must be paid into court for the benefit of the persons beneficially interested in them; and any such person may apply to the court for the whole or part of the proceeds to be paid to him.

**189(7) [Application of section]** This section applies–

(a) in the case of an acquirer falling within section 178(1), to all the shares–

  (i) in the authorised person which the acquirer has acquired;

  (ii) which are held by him or an associate of his; and

  (iii) which were not so held immediately before he became a person with control over the authorised person;

(b) in the case of an acquirer falling within section 178(2), to all the shares held by him or an associate of his at the time when he first became aware that he had acquired control over the authorised person; and

(c) to all the shares in an undertaking ("C")–

  (i) which are held by the acquirer or an associate of his, and

  (ii) which were not so held before he became a person with control in relation to the authorised person,

where C is the undertaking in which shares were acquired by the acquirer (or an associate of his) and, as a result, he became a person with control in relation to that authorised person.

**189(8) [Service of restriction notice]** A copy of the restriction notice must be served on–

(a) the authorised person to whose shares it relates; and

(b) if it relates to shares held by an associate of that authorised person, on that associate.

**189(9) [High Court, Court of Session]** The jurisdiction conferred by this section may be exercised by the High Court and the Court of Session.

## REDUCING CONTROL: PROCEDURE

# 190 Notification

**190(1) [Proposal for reduction, etc. of control]** If a step which a controller of a UK authorised person proposes to take would result in his–

(a) ceasing to have control of a relevant kind over the authorised person, or

(b) reducing a relevant kind of control over that person,

he must notify the Authority of his proposal.

**190(2) [Notification]** A controller of a UK authorised person who, without himself taking any such step, ceases to have that control or reduces that control must notify the Authority before the end of the period of 14 days beginning with the day on which he first becomes aware that–

it must give it written notice.

**197(8) [Right of referral to Tribunal]** A notice given under subsection (6) must inform the firm of its right to refer the matter to the Tribunal.

**197(9) [S. 197(7)(b) notice – requirements]** A notice under subsection (7)(b) must comply with subsection (4).

**197(10) [Procedure upon referral]** If a notice informs a person of his right to refer a matter to the Tribunal, it must give an indication of the procedure on such a reference.

# 198 Power to apply to court for injunction in respect of certain overseas insurance companies

**198(1) [Application of section]** This section applies if the Authority has received a request made in respect of an incoming EEA firm in accordance with–

(a) Article 20.5 of the first non-life insurance directive; or

(b) Article 24.5 of the first life insurance directive.

**198(2) [Power of court to grant injunction]** The court may, on an application made to it by the Authority with respect to the firm, grant an injunction restraining (or in Scotland an interdict prohibiting) the firm disposing of or otherwise dealing with any of its assets.

**198(3) [Injunction – subsequent orders of court]** If the court grants an injunction, it may by subsequent orders make provision for such incidental, consequential and supplementary matters as it considers necessary to enable the Authority to perform any of its functions under this Act.

**198(4) ["The court"] "The court"** means–

(a) the High Court; or

(b) in Scotland, the Court of Session.

# 199 Additional procedure for EEA firms in certain cases

**199(1) [Application of section]** This section applies if it appears to the Authority that its power of intervention is exercisable in relation to an EEA firm exercising EEA rights in the United Kingdom ("an incoming EEA firm") in respect of the contravention of a relevant requirement.

**199(2) [Relevant requirements]** A requirement is relevant if–

(a) it is imposed by the Authority under this Act; and

(b) as respects its contravention, any of the single market directives provides that a procedure of the kind set out in the following provisions of this section is to apply.

**199(3) [Duty of Authority]** The Authority must, in writing, require the firm to remedy the situation.

**199(4) [Duty of Authority – failure to comply with s. 199(3) requirement]** If the firm fails to comply with the requirement under subsection (3) within a reasonable time, the Authority must give a notice to that effect to the firm's home state regulator requesting it–

(a) to take all appropriate measures for the purpose of ensuring that the firm remedies the situation which has given rise to the notice; and

(b) to inform the Authority of the measures it proposes to take or has taken or the reasons for not taking such measures.

**199(5) [Limitation on power of intervention]** Except as mentioned in subsection (6), the Authority may not exercise its power of intervention unless satisfied–

(a) that the firm's home state regulator has failed or refused to take measures for the purpose mentioned in subsection (4)(a); or

(b) that the measures taken by the home state regulator have proved inadequate for that purpose.

**199(6) [Urgent intervention]** If the Authority decides that it should exercise its power of intervention in respect of the incoming EEA firm as a matter of urgency in order to protect the interests of consumers, it may exercise that power–

(a) before complying with subsections (3) and (4); or

(b) where it has complied with those subsections, before it is satisfied as mentioned in subsection (5).

**199(7) [Duty of Authority where s. 199(6) power exercised]** In such a case the Authority must at the earliest opportunity inform the firm's home state regulator and the Commission.

**199(8) [Duty of Authority to comply with Commission decision]** If–

(a) the Authority has (by virtue of subsection (6)) exercised its power of intervention before complying with subsections (3) and (4) or before it is satisfied as mentioned in subsection (5), and

(b) the Commission decides under any of the single market directives that the Authority must rescind or vary any requirement imposed in the exercise of its power of intervention,

the Authority must in accordance with the decision rescind or vary the requirement.

SUPPLEMENTAL

## 200 Rescission and variation of requirements

**200(1) [Power of Authority]** The Authority may rescind or vary a requirement imposed in exercise of its power of intervention on its own initiative or on the application of the person subject to the requirement.

**200(2) [Written notice]** The power of the Authority on its own initiative to rescind a requirement is exercisable by written notice given by the Authority to the person concerned, which takes effect on the date specified in the notice.

**200(3) [Application of s. 197]** Section 197 applies to the exercise of the power of the Authority on its own initiative to vary a requirement as it applies to the imposition of a requirement.

**200(4) [Warning notice – refusal]** If the Authority proposes to refuse an application for the variation or rescission of a requirement, it must give the applicant a warning notice.

**200(5) [Right of referral to Tribunal]** If the Authority decides to refuse an application for the variation or rescission of a requirement–

(a) the Authority must give the applicant a decision notice; and

(b) that person may refer the matter to the Tribunal.

## 201 Effect of certain requirements on other persons

**201** If the Authority, in exercising its power of intervention, imposes on an incoming firm a requirement of a kind mentioned in subsection (3) of section 48, the requirement has the same effect in relation to the firm as it would have in relation to an authorised person if it had been imposed on the authorised person by the Authority acting under section 45.

## 202 Contravention of requirement imposed under this Part

**202(1) [Contravention of Pt. XIII requirement]** Contravention of a requirement imposed by the Authority under this Part does not–

(a) make a person guilty of an offence;

(b) make any transaction void or unenforceable; or

(c) (subject to subsection (2)) give rise to any right of action for breach of statutory duty.

**202(2) [Contravention actionable]** In prescribed cases the contravention is actionable at the suit of a person who suffers loss as a result of the contravention, subject to the defences and other incidents applying to actions for breach of statutory duty.

POWERS OF DIRECTOR GENERAL OF FAIR TRADING

## 203 Power to prohibit the carrying on of Consumer Credit Act business

**203(1) [Power of Director General]** If it appears to the Director General of Fair Trading ("the Director") that subsection (4) has been, or is likely to be, contravened as respects a consumer credit EEA firm, he may by written notice given to the firm impose on the firm a consumer credit prohibition.

**203(2) [Power of Director General re s. 204 restriction]** If it appears to the Director that a restriction imposed under section 204 on an EEA consumer credit firm has not been complied with, he may by written notice given to the firm impose a consumer credit prohibition.

**203(3) ["Consumer credit prohibition"] "Consumer credit prohibition"** means a prohibition on carrying on, or purporting to carry on, in the United Kingdom any Consumer Credit Act business which consists of or includes carrying on one or more listed activities.

**203(4) [Contravention of subsection]** This subsection is contravened as respects a firm if–

(a) the firm or any of its employees, agents or associates (whether past or present), or

(b) if the firm is a body corporate, any controller of the firm or an associate of any such controller,

does any of the things specified in paragraphs (a) to (d) of section 25(2) of the Consumer Credit Act 1974.

**203(5) [Scope of prohibition]** A consumer credit prohibition may be absolute or may be imposed–

(a) for such period,

(b) until the occurrence of such event, or

(c) until such conditions are complied with,

as may be specified in the notice given under subsection (1) or (2).

**203(6) [Variation of period, etc.]** Any period, event or condition so specified may be varied by the Director on the application of the firm concerned.

**203(7) [Withdrawal of prohibition]** A consumer credit prohibition may be withdrawn by written notice served by the Director on the firm concerned, and any such notice takes effect on such date as is specified in the notice.

**203(8) [Sch. 16]** Schedule 16 has effect as respects consumer credit prohibitions and restrictions under section 204.

**203(9) [Offence, penalty]** A firm contravening a prohibition under this section is guilty of an offence and liable–

(a) on summary conviction, to a fine not exceeding the statutory maximum;

(b) on conviction on indictment, to a fine.

**203(10) [Definitions]** In this section and section 204–

**"a consumer credit EEA firm"** means an EEA firm falling within any of paragraphs (a) to (c) of paragraph 5 of Schedule 3 whose EEA authorisation covers any Consumer Credit Act business;

**"Consumer Credit Act business"** means consumer credit business, consumer hire business or ancillary credit business;

**"consumer credit business"**, **"consumer hire business"** and **"ancillary credit business"** have the same meaning as in the Consumer Credit Act 1974;

**"listed activity"** means an activity listed in the Annex to the second banking co-ordination directive or the Annex to the investment services directive;

**"associate"** has the same meaning as in section 25(2) of the Consumer Credit Act 1974;

**"controller"** has the meaning given by section 189(1) of that Act.

## 204 Power to restrict the carrying on of Consumer Credit Act business

**204(1) ["Restriction"]** In this section **"restriction"** means a direction that a consumer credit EEA firm may not carry on in the United Kingdom, otherwise than in accordance with such condition or conditions as may be specified in the direction, any Consumer Credit Act business which–

(a) consists of or includes carrying on any listed activity; and
(b) is specified in the direction.

**204(2) [Power of Director to impose restrictions]** If it appears to the Director that the situation as respects a consumer credit EEA firm is such that the powers conferred by section 203(1) are exercisable, the Director may, instead of imposing a prohibition, impose such restriction as appears to him desirable.

**204(3) [Written notice – withdrawal, etc. of restriction]** A restriction–
(a) may be withdrawn, or
(b) may be varied with the agreement of the firm concerned,

by written notice served by the Director on the firm, and any such notice takes effect on such date as is specified in the notice.

**204(4) [Offence, penalty]** A firm contravening a restriction is guilty of an offence and liable–
(a) on summary conviction, to a fine not exceeding the statutory maximum;
(b) on conviction on indictment, to a fine.

# PART XIV – DISCIPLINARY MEASURES

## 205 Public censure

**205** If the Authority considers that an authorised person has contravened a requirement imposed on him by or under this Act, the Authority may publish a statement to that effect.

## 206 Financial penalties

**206(1) [Power of Authority]** If the Authority considers that an authorised person has contravened a requirement imposed on him by or under this Act, it may impose on him a penalty, in respect of the contravention, of such amount as it considers appropriate.

**206(2) [Limitation of Authority's power]** The Authority may not in respect of any contravention both require a person to pay a penalty under this section and withdraw his authorisation under section 33.

**206(3) [Penalty payable to Authority]** A penalty under this section is payable to the Authority.

## 207 Proposal to take disciplinary measures

**207(1) [Warning notice]** If the Authority proposes–
(a) to publish a statement in respect of an authorised person (under section 205), or
(b) to impose a penalty on an authorised person (under section 206),

it must give the authorised person a warning notice.

**207(2) [Terms of statement]** A warning notice about a proposal to publish a statement must set out the terms of the statement.

**207(3) [Statement re amount of penalty]** A warning notice about a proposal to impose a penalty, must state the amount of the penalty.

## 208 Decision notice

**208(1) [Duty of Authority]** If the Authority decides–
(a) to publish a statement under section 205 (whether or not in the terms proposed), or
(b) to impose a penalty under section 206 (whether or not of the amount proposed),

it must without delay give the authorised person concerned a decision notice.

**208(2) [Terms of statement]** In the case of a statement, the decision notice must set out the terms of the statement.

**208(3) [Statement re amount of penalty]** In the case of a penalty, the decision notice must state the amount of the penalty.

**208(4) [Right of referral to Tribunal]** If the Authority decides to–

(a) publish a statement in respect of an authorised person under section 205, or

(b) impose a penalty on an authorised person under section 206,

the authorised person may refer the matter to the Tribunal.

# 209 Publication

**209** After a statement under section 205 is published, the Authority must send a copy of it to the authorised person and to any person on whom a copy of the decision notice was given under section 393(4).

# 210 Statements of policy

**210(1) [Duty of Authority]** The Authority must prepare and issue a statement of its policy with respect to–

(a) the imposition of penalties under this Part; and

(b) the amount of penalties under this Part.

**210(2) [Matters to be considered re penalty policy]** The Authority's policy in determining what the amount of a penalty should be must include having regard to–

(a) the seriousness of the contravention in question in relation to the nature of the requirement contravened;

(b) the extent to which that contravention was deliberate or reckless; and

(c) whether the person on whom the penalty is to be imposed is an individual.

**210(3) [Alteration, etc. of material]** The Authority may at any time alter or replace a statement issued under this section.

**210(4) [Publication of altered, etc. material]** If a statement issued under this section is altered or replaced, the Authority must issue the altered or replacement statement.

**210(5) [Copy to Treasury]** The Authority must, without delay, give the Treasury a copy of any statement which it publishes under this section.

**210(6) [Effective publication]** A statement issued under this section must be published by the Authority in the way appearing to the Authority to be best calculated to bring it to the attention of the public.

**210(7) [Matters to be considered re s. 206 power]** In exercising, or deciding whether to exercise, its power under section 206 in the case of any particular contravention, the Authority must have regard to any statement published under this section and in force at the time when the contravention in question occurred.

**210(8) [Fees]** The Authority may charge a reasonable fee for providing a person with a copy of the statement.

# 211 Statements of policy: procedure

**211(1) [Publication of draft proposed statement]** Before issuing a statement under section 210, the Authority must publish a draft of the proposed statement in the way appearing to the Authority to be best calculated to bring it to the attention of the public.

**211(2) [Notice re representations]** The draft must be accompanied by notice that representations about the proposal may be made to the Authority within a specified time.

**211(3) [Regard to representations]** Before issuing the proposed statement, the Authority must have regard to any representations made to it in accordance with subsection (2).

**211(4) [Publication of representations, etc.]** If the Authority issues the proposed statement it must publish an account, in general terms, of–

(a) the representations made to it in accordance with subsection (2); and

(b) its response to them.

**211(5) [Publication of differences]** If the statement differs from the draft published under subsection (1) in a way which is, in the opinion of the Authority, significant, the Authority must (in addition to complying with subsection (4)) publish details of the difference.

**211(6) [Fees]** The Authority may charge a reasonable fee for providing a person with a copy of a draft published under subsection (1).

**211(7) [Application of section]** This section also applies to a proposal to alter or replace a statement.

# PART XV – THE FINANCIAL SERVICES COMPENSATION SCHEME

## THE SCHEME MANAGER

## 212 The scheme manager

**212(1) [Duty of Authority]** The Authority must establish a body corporate ("the scheme manager") to exercise the functions conferred on the scheme manager by or under this Part.

**212(2) [Manager capable of exercising Part XV functions]** The Authority must take such steps as are necessary to ensure that the scheme manager is, at all times, capable of exercising those functions.

**212(3) [Constitution]** The constitution of the scheme manager must provide for it to have–

(a) a chairman; and

(b) a board (which must include the chairman) whose members are the scheme manager's directors.

**212(4) [Membership of board]** The chairman and other members of the board must be persons appointed, and liable to removal from office, by the Authority (acting, in the case of the chairman, with the approval of the Treasury).

**212(5) [Independence of board members]** But the terms of their appointment (and in particular those governing removal from office) must be such as to secure their independence from the Authority in the operation of the compensation scheme.

**212(6) [Manager not exercising functions for Crown]** The scheme manager is not to be regarded as exercising functions on behalf of the Crown.

**212(7) [Manager's staff, etc. not Crown servants]** The scheme manager's board members, officers and staff are not to be regarded as Crown servants.

## THE SCHEME

## 213 The compensation scheme

**213(1) [Establishment of scheme]** The Authority must by rules establish a scheme for compensating persons in cases where relevant persons are unable, or are likely to be unable, to satisfy claims against them.

**213(2) [The compensation scheme]** The rules are to be known as the Financial Services Compensation Scheme (but are referred to in this Act as "the compensation scheme").

**213(3) [Provision for scheme manager to assess compensation, etc.]** The compensation scheme must, in particular, provide for the scheme manager–

(a) to assess and pay compensation, in accordance with the scheme, to claimants in respect of claims made in connection with regulated activities carried on (whether or not with permission) by relevant persons; and

(b) to have power to impose levies on authorised persons, or any class of authorised person, for the purpose of meeting its expenses (including in particular expenses incurred, or expected to be incurred, in paying compensation, borrowing or insuring risks).

**213(4) [Power of scheme manager to impose levies]** The compensation scheme may provide for the scheme manager to have power to impose levies on authorised persons, or any class of authorised person, for the purpose of recovering the cost (whenever incurred) of establishing the scheme.

**213(5) [Duty of Authority re s. 213(3)(b)]** In making any provision of the scheme by virtue of subsection (3)(b), the Authority must take account of the desirability of ensuring that the amount of the levies imposed on a particular class of authorised person reflects, so far as practicable, the amount of the claims made, or likely to be made, in respect of that class of person.

**213(6) [Recovery of levies as debts due]** An amount payable to the scheme manager as a result of any provision of the scheme made by virtue of subsection (3)(b) or (4) may be recovered as a debt due to the scheme manager.

**213(7) [Application of s. 214–217]** Sections 214 to 217 make further provision about the scheme but are not to be taken as limiting the power conferred on the Authority by subsection (1).

**213(8) ["Specified"]** In those sections **"specified"** means specified in the scheme.

**213(9) ["Relevant person"]** In this Part (except in sections 219, 220 or 224) **"relevant person"** means a person who was–

(a) an authorised person at the time the act or omission giving rise to the claim against him took place; or

(b) an appointed representative at that time.

**213(10) [Qualification for authorisation under Sch. 3]** But a person who, at that time–

(a) qualified for authorisation under Schedule 3, and

(b) fell within a prescribed category,

is not to be regarded as a relevant person in relation to any activities for which he had permission as a result of any provision of, or made under, that Schedule unless he had elected to participate in the scheme in relation to those activities at that time.

## PROVISIONS OF THE SCHEME

## 214 General

**214(1) [Provisions of the scheme]** The compensation scheme may, in particular, make provision–

(a) as to the circumstances in which a relevant person is to be taken (for the purposes of the scheme) to be unable, or likely to be unable, to satisfy claims made against him;

(b) for the establishment of different funds for meeting different kinds of claim;

(c) for the imposition of different levies in different cases;

(d) limiting the levy payable by a person in respect of a specified period;

(e) for repayment of the whole or part of a levy in specified circumstances;

(f) for a claim to be entertained only if it is made by a specified kind of claimant;

(g) for a claim to be entertained only if it falls within a specified kind of claim;

(h) as to the procedure to be followed in making a claim;

(i) for the making of interim payments before a claim is finally determined;

(j) limiting the amount payable on a claim to a specified maximum amount or a maximum amount calculated in a specified manner;

(k) for payment to be made, in specified circumstances, to a person other than the claimant.

**214(2) [Variability of provisions]** Different provision may be made with respect to different kinds of claim.

**214(3) [Provision for manager to determine, etc. scheme matters]** The scheme may provide for the determination and regulation of matters relating to the scheme by the scheme manager.

**214(4) [Scope of scheme]** The scheme, or particular provisions of the scheme, may be made so as to apply only in relation to–

(a) activities carried on,

(b) claimants,

(c) matters arising, or

(d) events occurring,

in specified territories, areas or localities.

**214(5) [Persons qualified for authorisation under Sch. 3]** The scheme may provide for a person who–

(a) qualifies for authorisation under Schedule 3, and

(b) falls within a prescribed category,

to elect to participate in the scheme in relation to some or all of the activities for which he has permission as a result of any provision of, or made under, that Schedule.

**214(6) [Power of scheme manager where entitlement to payment under other scheme, etc.]** The scheme may provide for the scheme manager to have power–

(a) in specified circumstances,

(b) but only if the scheme manager is satisfied that the claimant is entitled to receive a payment in respect of his claim–

(i) under a scheme which is comparable to the compensation scheme, or

(ii) as the result of a guarantee given by a government or other authority,

to make a full payment of compensation to the claimant and recover the whole or part of the amount of that payment from the other scheme or under that guarantee.

## 215 Rights of the scheme in relevant person's insolvency

**215(1) [Provisions of the scheme]** The compensation scheme may, in particular, make provision–

(a) as to the effect of a payment of compensation under the scheme in relation to rights or obligations arising out of the claim against a relevant person in respect of which the payment was made;

(b) for conferring on the scheme manager a right of recovery against that person.

**215(2) [Right of recovery in event of insolvency]** Such a right of recovery conferred by the scheme does not, in the event of the relevant person's insolvency, exceed such right (if any) as the claimant would have had in that event.

**215(3) [Manager's rights equivalent to Authority's under s. 362]** If a person other than the scheme manager presents a petition under section 9 of the 1986 Act or Article 22 of the 1989 Order in relation to a company or partnership which is a relevant person, the scheme manager has the same rights as are conferred on the Authority by section 362.

**215(4) [Manager's rights equivalent to Authority's under s. 371]** If a person other than the scheme manager presents a petition for the winding up of a body which is a relevant person, the scheme manager has the same rights as are conferred on the Authority by section 371.

**215(5) [Manager's rights equivalent to Authority's under s. 374]** If a person other than the scheme manager presents a bankruptcy petition to the court in relation to an individual who, or an entity which, is a relevant person, the scheme manager has the same rights as are conferred on the Authority by section 374.

**215(6) [Power to make insolvency rules]** Insolvency rules may be made for the purpose of integrating any procedure for which provision is made as a result of subsection (1) into the general procedure on the administration of a company or partnership or on a winding-up, bankruptcy or sequestration.

**215(7) ["Bankruptcy petition"] "Bankruptcy petition"** means a petition to the court–

(a) under section 264 of the 1986 Act or Article 238 of the 1989 Order for a bankruptcy order to be made against an individual;
(b) under section 5 of the 1985 Act for the sequestration of the estate of an individual; or
(c) under section 6 of the 1985 Act for the sequestration of the estate belonging to or held for or jointly by the members of an entity mentioned in subsection (1) of that section.

**215(8) ["Insolvency rules"] "Insolvency rules"** are–
(a) for England and Wales, rules made under sections 411 and 412 of the 1986 Act;
(b) for Scotland, rules made by order by the Treasury, after consultation with the Scottish Ministers, for the purposes of this section; and
(c) for Northern Ireland, rules made under Article 359 of the 1989 Order and section 55 of the Judicature (Northern Ireland) Act 1978.

**215(9) [Interpretation] "The 1985 Act", "the 1986 Act", "the 1989 Order"** and **"court"** have the same meaning as in Part XXIV.

## 216 Continuity of long-term insurance policies

**216(1) [Duty of scheme manager]** The compensation scheme may, in particular, include provision requiring the scheme manager to make arrangements for securing continuity of insurance for policyholders, or policyholders of a specified class, of relevant long-term insurers.

**216(2) ["Relevant long-term insurers"] "Relevant long-term insurers"** means relevant persons who–
(a) have permission to effect or carry out contracts of long-term insurance; and
(b) are unable, or likely to be unable, to satisfy claims made against them.

**216(3) [Transfer of policies to another authorised person, etc.]** The scheme may provide for the scheme manager to take such measures as appear to him to be appropriate–
(a) for securing or facilitating the transfer of a relevant long-term insurer's business so far as it consists of the carrying out of contracts of long-term insurance, or of any part of that business, to another authorised person;
(b) for securing the issue by another authorised person to the policyholders concerned of policies in substitution for their existing policies.

**216(4) [Payments to policyholders]** The scheme may also provide for the scheme manager to make payments to the policyholders concerned–
(a) during any period while he is seeking to make arrangements mentioned in subsection (1);
(b) if it appears to him that it is not reasonably practicable to make such arrangements.

**216(5) [S. 213(3)(b) – further powers]** A provision of the scheme made by virtue of section 213(3)(b) may include power to impose levies for the purpose of meeting expenses of the scheme manager incurred in–
(a) taking measures as a result of any provision of the scheme made by virtue of subsection (3);
(b) making payments as a result of any such provision made by virtue of subsection (4).

## 217 Insurers in financial difficulties

**217(1) [Measures to safeguard policyholders]** The compensation scheme may, in particular, include provision for the scheme manager to have power to take measures for safeguarding policyholders, or policyholders of a specified class, of relevant insurers.

**217(2) ["Relevant insurers"] "Relevant insurers"** means relevant persons who–
(a) have permission to effect or carry out contracts of insurance; and
(b) are in financial difficulties.

**217(3) [Measures to transfer insurance business, etc.]** The measures may include such measures as the scheme manager considers appropriate for–
(a) securing or facilitating the transfer of a relevant insurer's business so far as it consists of

the carrying out of contracts of insurance, or of any part of that business, to another authorised person;

(b) giving assistance to the relevant insurer to enable it to continue to effect or carry out contracts of insurance.

**217(4) [Further provisions re s. 217(3) measures, etc.]** The scheme may provide–

(a) that if measures of a kind mentioned in subsection (3)(a) are to be taken, they should be on terms appearing to the scheme manager to be appropriate, including terms reducing, or deferring payment of, any of the things to which any of those who are eligible policyholders in relation to the relevant insurer are entitled in their capacity as such;

(b) that if measures of a kind mentioned in subsection (3)(b) are to be taken, they should be conditional on the reduction of, or the deferment of the payment of, the things to which any of those who are eligible policyholders in relation to the relevant insurer are entitled in their capacity as such;

(c) for ensuring that measures of a kind mentioned in subsection (3)(b) do not benefit to any material extent persons who were members of a relevant insurer when it began to be in financial difficulties or who had any responsibility for, or who may have profited from, the circumstances giving rise to its financial difficulties, except in specified circumstances;

(d) for requiring the scheme manager to be satisfied that any measures he proposes to take are likely to cost less than it would cost to pay compensation under the scheme if the relevant insurer became unable, or likely to be unable, to satisfy claims made against him.

**217(5) [Provision for power of Authority]** The scheme may provide for the Authority to have power–

(a) to give such assistance to the scheme manager as it considers appropriate for assisting the scheme manager to determine what measures are practicable or desirable in the case of a particular relevant insurer;

(b) to impose constraints on the taking of measures by the scheme manager in the case of a particular relevant insurer;

(c) to require the scheme manager to provide it with information about any particular measures which the scheme manager is proposing to take.

**217(6) [Provision to make interim payments, etc.]** The scheme may include provision for the scheme manager to have power–

(a) to make interim payments in respect of eligible policyholders of a relevant insurer;

(b) to indemnify any person making payments to eligible policyholders of a relevant insurer.

**217(7) [Imposition of levies to meet expenses]** A provision of the scheme made by virtue of section 213(3)(b) may include power to impose levies for the purpose of meeting expenses of the scheme manager incurred in–

(a) taking measures as a result of any provision of the scheme made by virtue of subsection (1);

(b) making payments or giving indemnities as a result of any such provision made by virtue of subsection (6).

**217(8) [Interpretation] "Financial difficulties"** and **"eligible policyholders"** have such meanings as may be specified.

ANNUAL REPORT

## 218 Annual report

**218(1) [Duty of scheme manager]** At least once a year, the scheme manager must make a report to the Authority on the discharge of its functions.

**218(2) [Content, etc. of report]** The report must–

(a) include a statement setting out the value of each of the funds established by the compensation scheme; and

(b) comply with any requirements specified in rules made by the Authority.

**218(3) [Publication]** The scheme manager must publish each report in the way it considers appropriate.

## INFORMATION AND DOCUMENTS

# 219 Scheme manager's power to require information

**219(1) [Power of scheme manager]** The scheme manager may, by notice in writing given to the relevant person in respect of whom a claim is made under the scheme or to a person otherwise involved, require that person–

(a) to provide specified information or information of a specified description; or

(b) to produce specified documents or documents of a specified description.

**219(2) [Form, etc. of information]** The information or documents must be provided or produced–

(a) before the end of such reasonable period as may be specified; and

(b) in the case of information, in such manner or form as may be specified.

**219(3) [Application of section]** This section applies only to information and documents the provision or production of which the scheme manager considers–

(a) to be necessary for the fair determination of the claim; or

(b) to be necessary (or likely to be necessary) for the fair determination of other claims made (or which it expects may be made) in respect of the relevant person concerned.

**219(4) [Power to take copies, etc. of documents]** If a document is produced in response to a requirement imposed under this section, the scheme manager may–

(a) take copies or extracts from the document; or

(b) require the person producing the document to provide an explanation of the document.

**219(5) [Failure to produce documents]** If a person who is required under this section to produce a document fails to do so, the scheme manager may require the person to state, to the best of his knowledge and belief, where the document is.

**219(6) [Limitation of section in case of insolvency]** If the relevant person is insolvent, no requirement may be imposed under this section on a person to whom section 220 or 224 applies.

**219(7) [Lien claimed]** If a person claims a lien on a document, its production under this Part does not affect the lien.

**219(8) ["Relevant person"] "Relevant person"** has the same meaning as in section 224.

**219(9) ["Specified"] "Specified"** means specified in the notice given under subsection (1).

**219(10) [Involvement in claim]** A person is involved in a claim made under the scheme if he was knowingly involved in the act or omission giving rise to the claim.

# 220 Scheme manager's power to inspect information held by liquidator etc.

**220(1) [Inspection of relevant documents]** For the purpose of assisting the scheme manager to discharge its functions in relation to a claim made in respect of an insolvent relevant person, a person to whom this section applies must permit a person authorised by the scheme manager to inspect relevant documents.

**220(2) [Extracts, etc. from documents]** A person inspecting a document under this section may take copies of, or extracts from, the document.

**220(3) [Application to section]** This section applies to–

(a) the administrative receiver, administrator, liquidator or trustee in bankruptcy of an insolvent relevant person;

(b) the permanent trustee, within the meaning of the Bankruptcy (Scotland) Act 1985, on the estate of an insolvent relevant person.

**220(4) [Scope of section]** This section does not apply to a liquidator, administrator or trustee in bankruptcy who is–

(a) the Official Receiver;

(b) the Official Receiver for Northern Ireland; or

(c) the Accountant in Bankruptcy.

**220(5) ["Relevant person"] "Relevant person"** has the same meaning as in section 224.

## 221 Powers of court where information required

**221(1) [Power of court]** If a person ("the defaulter")–

(a) fails to comply with a requirement imposed under section 219, or

(b) fails to permit documents to be inspected under section 220,

the scheme manager may certify that fact in writing to the court and the court may enquire into the case.

**221(2) [Penalty]** If the court is satisfied that the defaulter failed without reasonable excuse to comply with the requirement (or to permit the documents to be inspected), it may deal with the defaulter (and, in the case of a body corporate, any director or officer) as if he were in contempt.

**221(3) ["Court"] "Court"** means–

(a) the High Court;

(b) in Scotland, the Court of Session.

MISCELLANEOUS

## 222 Statutory immunity

**222(1) [Immunity of scheme manager, etc.]** Neither the scheme manager nor any person who is, or is acting as, its board member, officer or member of staff is to be liable in damages for anything done or omitted in the discharge, or purported discharge, of the scheme manager's functions.

**222(2) [Non-application of s. 222(1)]** Subsection (1) does not apply–

(a) if the act or omission is shown to have been in bad faith; or

(b) so as to prevent an award of damages made in respect of an act or omission on the ground that the act or omission was unlawful as a result of section 6(1) of the Human Rights Act 1998.

## 223 Management expenses

**223(1) [Limit on expenses]** The amount which the scheme manager may recover, from the sums levied under the scheme, as management expenses attributable to a particular period may not exceed such amount as may be fixed by the scheme as the limit applicable to that period.

**223(2) [Calculation of levy]** In calculating the amount of any levy to be imposed by the scheme manager, no amount may be included to reflect management expenses unless the limit mentioned in subsection (1) has been fixed by the scheme.

**223(3) ["Management expenses"] "Management expenses"** means expenses incurred, or expected to be incurred, by the scheme manager in connection with its functions under this Act other than those incurred–

(a) in paying compensation;

(b) as a result of any provision of the scheme made by virtue of section 216(3) or (4) or 217(1) or (6).

## 224 Scheme manager's power to inspect documents held by Official Receiver etc.

**224(1) [Duty of Official Receiver, etc. re inspection of documents]** If, as a result of the insolvency or bankruptcy of a relevant person, any documents have come into the possession of a person to whom this section applies, he must permit any person authorised by the scheme manager to inspect the documents for the purpose of establishing–

(a) the identity of persons to whom the scheme manager may be liable to make a payment in accordance with the compensation scheme; or

(b) the amount of any payment which the scheme manager may be liable to make.

**224(2) [Extracts, etc. from documents]** A person inspecting a document under this section may take copies or extracts from the document.

**224(3) ["Relevant person"]** In this section **"relevant person"** means a person who was–

(a) an authorised person at the time the act or omission which may give rise to the liability mentioned in subsection (1)(a) took place; or

(b) an appointed representative at that time.

**224(4) [Persons qualified for authorisation under Sch. 3]** But a person who, at that time–

(a) qualified for authorisation under Schedule 3, and

(b) fell within a prescribed category,

is not to be regarded as a relevant person for the purposes of this section in relation to any activities for which he had permission as a result of any provision of, or made under, that Schedule unless he had elected to participate in the scheme in relation to those activities at that time.

**224(5) [Application of section]** This section applies to–

(a) the Official Receiver;

(b) the Official Receiver for Northern Ireland; and

(c) the Accountant in Bankruptcy.

# PART XVI – THE OMBUDSMAN SCHEME

## THE SCHEME

## 225 The scheme and the scheme operator

**225(1) [The scheme]** This Part provides for a scheme under which certain disputes may be resolved quickly and with minimum formality by an independent person.

**225(2) ["The scheme operator"]** The scheme is to be administered by a body corporate ("the scheme operator").

**225(3) ["The ombudsman scheme"]** The scheme is to be operated under a name chosen by the scheme operator but is referred to in this Act as "the ombudsman scheme".

**225(4) [Sch. 17]** Schedule 17 makes provision in connection with the ombudsman scheme and the scheme operator.

## 226 Compulsory jurisdiction

**226(1) [Scheme – compulsory jurisdiction]** A complaint which relates to an act or omission of a person ("the respondent") in carrying on an activity to which compulsory jurisdiction rules apply is to be dealt with under the ombudsman scheme if the conditions mentioned in subsection (2) are satisfied.

**226(2) [Conditions re jurisdiction of scheme]** The conditions are that–

(a) the complainant is eligible and wishes to have the complaint dealt with under the scheme;

(b) the respondent was an authorised person at the time of the act or omission to which the complaint relates; and

(c) the act or omission to which the complaint relates occurred at a time when compulsory jurisdiction rules were in force in relation to the activity in question.

**226(3) ["Compulsory jurisdiction rules"] "Compulsory jurisdiction rules"** means rules–

(a) made by the Authority for the purposes of this section; and
(b) specifying the activities to which they apply.

**226(4) [Regulated activities]** Only activities which are regulated activities, or which could be made regulated activities by an order under section 22, may be specified.

**226(5) [Specification by category]** Activities may be specified by reference to specified categories (however described).

**226(6) [Eligibility of complainant]** A complainant is eligible, in relation to the compulsory jurisdiction of the ombudsman scheme, if he falls within a class of person specified in the rules as eligible.

**226(7) [Scope of rules]** The rules–

(a) may include provision for persons other than individuals to be eligible; but
(b) may not provide for authorised persons to be eligible except in specified circumstances or in relation to complaints of a specified kind.

**226(8) [Compulsory jurisdiction]** The jurisdiction of the scheme which results from this section is referred to in this Act as the "compulsory jurisdiction".

# 227 Voluntary jurisdiction

**227(1) [Scheme – voluntary jurisdiction rules]** A complaint which relates to an act or omission of a person ("the respondent") in carrying on an activity to which voluntary jurisdiction rules apply is to be dealt with under the ombudsman scheme if the conditions mentioned in subsection (2) are satisfied.

**227(2) [Conditions re jurisdiction of scheme]** The conditions are that–

(a) the complainant is eligible and wishes to have the complaint dealt with under the scheme;
(b) at the time of the act or omission to which the complaint relates, the respondent was participating in the scheme;
(c) at the time when the complaint is referred under the scheme, the respondent has not withdrawn from the scheme in accordance with its provisions;
(d) the act or omission to which the complaint relates occurred at a time when voluntary jurisdiction rules were in force in relation to the activity in question; and
(e) the complaint cannot be dealt with under the compulsory jurisdiction.

**227(3) ["Voluntary jurisdiction rules"] "Voluntary jurisdiction rules"** means rules–

(a) made by the scheme operator for the purposes of this section; and
(b) specifying the activities to which they apply.

**227(4) [Specification of activities]** The only activities which may be specified in the rules are activities which are, or could be, specified in compulsory jurisdiction rules.

**227(5) [Specification by category]** Activities may be specified by reference to specified categories (however described).

**227(6) [Authority approval]** The rules require the Authority's approval.

**227(7) [Eligibility of complainant]** A complainant is eligible, in relation to the voluntary jurisdiction of the ombudsman scheme, if he falls within a class of person specified in the rules as eligible.

**227(8) [Further provisions re eligibility]** The rules may include provision for persons other than individuals to be eligible.

**227(9) [Ombudsman scheme – qualification]** A person qualifies for participation in the ombudsman scheme if he falls within a class of person specified in the rules in relation to the activity in question.

**227(10) [Ombudsman scheme – persons other those authorised]** Provision may be made in the rules for persons other than authorised persons to participate in the ombudsman scheme.

**227(11) [Variability of rules]** The rules may make different provision in relation to complaints arising from different activities.

**227(12) [Voluntary jurisdiction]** The jurisdiction of the scheme which results from this section is referred to in this Act as the "voluntary jurisdiction".

**227(13) [Non-application of s. 227(2)(b) or (d)]** In such circumstances as may be specified in voluntary jurisdiction rules, a complaint–

(a) which relates to an act or omission occurring at a time before the rules came into force, and

(b) which could have been dealt with under a scheme which has to any extent been replaced by the voluntary jurisdiction,

is to be dealt with under the ombudsman scheme even though paragraph (b) or (d) of subsection (2) would otherwise prevent that.

**227(14) [Ombudsman scheme – respondent's agreement]** In such circumstances as may be specified in voluntary jurisdiction rules, a complaint is to be dealt with under the ombudsman scheme even though–

(a) paragraph (b) or (d) of subsection (2) would otherwise prevent that, and

(b) the complaint is not brought within the scheme as a result of subsection (13),

but only if the respondent has agreed that complaints of that kind were to be dealt with under the scheme.

## DETERMINATION OF COMPLAINTS

## 228 Determination under the compulsory jurisdiction

**228(1) [Application of section]** This section applies only in relation to the compulsory jurisdiction.

**228(2) [Determination of complaints]** A complaint is to be determined by reference to what is, in the opinion of the ombudsman, fair and reasonable in all the circumstances of the case.

**228(3) [Written statement – determination]** When the ombudsman has determined a complaint he must give a written statement of his determination to the respondent and to the complainant.

**228(4) [Form and content of written statement]** The statement must–

(a) give the ombudsman's reasons for his determination;

(b) be signed by him; and

(c) require the complainant to notify him in writing, before a date specified in the statement, whether he accepts or rejects the determination.

**228(5) [Acceptance of determination]** If the complainant notifies the ombudsman that he accepts the determination, it is binding on the respondent and the complainant and final.

**228(6) [Rejection of determination]** If, by the specified date, the complainant has not notified the ombudsman of his acceptance or rejection of the determination he is to be treated as having rejected it.

**228(7) [Notification to respondent]** The ombudsman must notify the respondent of the outcome.

**228(8) [Evidence]** A copy of the determination on which appears a certificate signed by an ombudsman is evidence (or in Scotland sufficient evidence) that the determination was made under the scheme.

**228(9) [Presumption certificate duly signed]** Such a certificate purporting to be signed by an ombudsman is to be taken to have been duly signed unless the contrary is shown.

## 229 Awards

**229(1) [Application of section]** This section applies only in relation to the compulsory jurisdiction.

**229(2) [Determination in favour of complainant]** If a complaint which has been dealt with under the scheme is determined in favour of the complainant, the determination may include–

(a) an award against the respondent of such amount as the ombudsman considers fair compensation for loss or damage (of a kind falling within subsection (3)) suffered by the complainant ("a money award");

(b) a direction that the respondent take such steps in relation to the complainant as the ombudsman considers just and appropriate (whether or not a court could order those steps to be taken).

**229(3) [Money awards]** A money award may compensate for –

(a) financial loss; or

(b) any other loss, or any damage, of a specified kind.

**229(4) [Maximum award]** The Authority may specify the maximum amount which may be regarded as fair compensation for a particular kind of loss or damage specified under subsection (3)(b).

**229(5) [Awards not to exceed monetary limit]** A money award may not exceed the monetary limit; but the ombudsman may, if he considers that fair compensation requires payment of a larger amount, recommend that the respondent pay the complainant the balance.

**229(6) [Monetary limit]** The monetary limit is such amount as may be specified.

**229(7) [Variability of amounts awarded]** Different amounts may be specified in relation to different kinds of complaint.

**229(8) [Money awards – further considerations]** A money award–

(a) may provide for the amount payable under the award to bear interest at a rate and as from a date specified in the award; and

(b) is enforceable by the complainant in accordance with Part III of Schedule 17.

**229(9) [Injunction]** Compliance with a direction under subsection (2)(b)–

(a) is enforceable by an injunction; or

(b) in Scotland, is enforceable by an order under section 45 of the Court of Session Act 1988.

**229(10) [Proceedings at instance of complainant]** Only the complainant may bring proceedings for an injunction or proceedings for an order.

**229(11) ["Specified"]** "Specified" means specified in compulsory jurisdiction rules.

## 230 Costs

**230(1) [Costs rules]** The scheme operator may by rules ("costs rules") provide for an ombudsman to have power, on determining a complaint under the compulsory jurisdiction, to award costs in accordance with the provisions of the rules.

**230(2) [Approval of Authority]** Costs rules require the approval of the Authority.

**230(3) [Respondent's costs]** Costs rules may not provide for the making of an award against the complainant in respect of the respondent's costs.

**230(4) [Provision for awards against the complainant]** But they may provide for the making of an award against the complainant in favour of the scheme operator, for the purpose of providing a contribution to resources deployed in dealing with the complaint, if in the opinion of the ombudsman–

(a) the complainant's conduct was improper or unreasonable; or

(b) the complainant was responsible for an unreasonable delay.

**230(5) [Awards – interest]** Costs rules may authorise an ombudsman making an award in accordance with the rules to order that the amount payable under the award bears interest at a rate and as from a date specified in the order.

**230(6) [Recovery as debt due]** An amount due under an award made in favour of the scheme operator is recoverable as a debt due to the scheme operator.

**230(7) [Awards for purposes of para. 16, Sch. 17]** Any other award made against the respondent is to be treated as a money award for the purposes of paragraph 16 of Schedule 17.

INFORMATION

## 231 Ombudsman's power to require information

**231(1) [Power of ombudsman]** An ombudsman may, by notice in writing given to a party to a complaint, require that party–

(a) to provide specified information or information of a specified description; or

(b) to produce specified documents or documents of a specified description.

**231(2) [Form, etc. of information]** The information or documents must be provided or produced–

(a) before the end of such reasonable period as may be specified; and

(b) in the case of information, in such manner or form as may be specified.

**231(3) [Application of section]** This section applies only to information and documents the production of which the ombudsman considers necessary for the determination of the complaint.

**231(4) [Extracts, etc. from documents]** If a document is produced in response to a requirement imposed under this section, the ombudsman may–

(a) take copies or extracts from the document; or

(b) require the person producing the document to provide an explanation of the document.

**231(5) [Failure to produce document]** If a person who is required under this section to produce a document fails to do so, the ombudsman may require him to state, to the best of his knowledge and belief, where the document is.

**231(6) [Lien claimed]** If a person claims a lien on a document, its production under this Part does not affect the lien.

**231(7) ["Specified"] "Specified"** means specified in the notice given under subsection (1).

## 232 Powers of court where information required

**232(1) [Failure to comply with s. 231]** If a person ("the defaulter") fails to comply with a requirement imposed under section 231, the ombudsman may certify that fact in writing to the court and the court may enquire into the case.

**232(2) [Contempt of court]** If the court is satisfied that the defaulter failed without reasonable excuse to comply with the requirement, it may deal with the defaulter (and, in the case of a body corporate, any director or officer) as if he were in contempt.

**232(3) ["Court"] "Court"** means–

(a) the High Court;

(b) in Scotland, the Court of Session.

## 233 Data protection

**233** In section 31 of the Data Protection Act 1998 (regulatory activity), after subsection (4), insert–

> "**(4A)** Personal data processed for the purpose of discharging any function which is conferred by or under Part XVI of the Financial Services and Markets Act 2000 on the body established by the Financial Services Authority for the purposes of that Part are exempt from the subject information provisions in any case to the extent to which the application of those provisions to the data would be likely to prejudice the proper discharge of the function."

FUNDING

## 234 Industry funding

**234(1) [Power of Authority]** For the purpose of funding–

(a) the establishment of the ombudsman scheme (whenever any relevant expense is incurred), and

(b) its operation in relation to the compulsory jurisdiction,

the Authority may make rules requiring the payment to it or to the scheme operator, by authorised persons or any class of authorised person of specified amounts (or amounts calculated in a specified way).

**234(2) ["Specified"]** "**Specified**" means specified in the rules.

# PART XVII – COLLECTIVE INVESTMENT SCHEMES

## Chapter I – Interpretation

### 235 Collective investment schemes

**235(1) ["Collective investment scheme"]** In this Part "**collective investment scheme**" means any arrangements with respect to property of any description, including money, the purpose or effect of which is to enable persons taking part in the arrangements (whether by becoming owners of the property or any part of it or otherwise) to participate in or receive profits or income arising from the acquisition, holding, management or disposal of the property or sums paid out of such profits or income.

**235(2) [Nature of arrangements]** The arrangements must be such that the persons who are to participate ("participants") do not have day-to-day control over the management of the property, whether or not they have the right to be consulted or to give directions.

**235(3) [Characteristics of arrangements]** The arrangements must also have either or both of the following characteristics–

(a) the contributions of the participants and the profits or income out of which payments are to be made to them are pooled;

(b) the property is managed as a whole by or on behalf of the operator of the scheme.

**235(4) [Pooled arrangements]** If arrangements provide for such pooling as is mentioned in subsection (3)(a) in relation to separate parts of the property, the arrangements are not to be regarded as constituting a single collective investment scheme unless the participants are entitled to exchange rights in one part for rights in another.

**235(5) [Power of Treasury to make order]** The Treasury may by order provide that arrangements do not amount to a collective investment scheme–

(a) in specified circumstances; or

(b) if the arrangements fall within a specified category of arrangement.

### 236 Open-ended investment companies

**236(1) ["An open-ended investment company"]** In this Part "**an open-ended investment company**" means a collective investment scheme which satisfies both the property condition and the investment condition.

**236(2) [The property condition]** The property condition is that the property belongs beneficially to, and is managed by or on behalf of, a body corporate ("BC") having as its purpose the investment of its funds with the aim of–

(a) spreading investment risk; and

(b) giving its members the benefit of the results of the management of those funds by or on behalf of that body.

**236(3) [The investment condition]** The investment condition is that, in relation to BC, a reasonable investor would, if he were to participate in the scheme–

(a) expect that he would be able to realize, within a period appearing to him to be reasonable, his investment in the scheme (represented, at any given time, by the value of shares in, or securities of, BC held by him as a participant in the scheme); and

(b) be satisfied that his investment would be realized on a basis calculated wholly or mainly by reference to the value of property in respect of which the scheme makes arrangements.

**236(4) [Determination of investment condition]** In determining whether the investment condition is satisfied, no account is to be taken of any actual or potential redemption or repurchase of shares or securities under–

(a) Chapter VII of Part V of the Companies Act 1985;

(b) Chapter VII of Part VI of the Companies (Northern Ireland) Order 1986;

(c) corresponding provisions in force in another EEA State; or

(d) provisions in force in a country or territory other than an EEA state which the Treasury have, by order, designated as corresponding provisions.

**236(5) [Power of Treasury to make order]** The Treasury may by order amend the definition of "an open-ended investment company" for the purposes of this Part.

## 237 Other definitions

**237(1) ["Unit trust scheme"]** In this Part **"unit trust scheme"** means a collective investment scheme under which the property is held on trust for the participants.

**237(2) [Definitions]** In this Part–

**"trustee"**, in relation to a unit trust scheme, means the person holding the property in question on trust for the participants;

**"depositary"**, in relation to–

(a) a collective investment scheme which is constituted by a body incorporated by virtue of regulations under section 262, or

(b) any other collective investment scheme which is not a unit trust scheme,

means any person to whom the property subject to the scheme is entrusted for safekeeping;

**"the operator"**, in relation to a unit trust scheme with a separate trustee, means the manager and in relation to an open-ended investment company, means that company;

**"units"** means the rights or interests (however described) of the participants in a collective investment scheme.

**237(3) [Further definitions]** In this Part–

**"an authorised unit trust scheme"** means a unit trust scheme which is authorised for the purposes of this Act by an authorisation order in force under section 243;

**"an authorised open-ended investment company"** means a body incorporated by virtue of regulations under section 262 in respect of which an authorisation order is in force under any provision made in such regulations by virtue of subsection (2)(l) of that section;

**"a recognised scheme"** means a scheme recognised under section 264, 270 or 272.

# Chapter II – Restrictions on Promotion

## 238 Restrictions on promotion

**238(1) [General restriction]** An authorised person must not communicate an invitation or inducement to participate in a collective investment scheme.

**238(2) [General restriction – limitation]** But that is subject to the following provisions of this section and to section 239.

**238(3) [Application of s. 238(1)]** Subsection (1) applies in the case of a communication originating outside the United Kingdom only if the communication is capable of having an effect in the United Kingdom.

**238(4) [Non-application of s. 238(1)]** Subsection (1) does not apply in relation to–

(a) an authorised unit trust scheme;

(b) a scheme constituted by an authorised open-ended investment company; or

(c) a recognised scheme.

**238(5) [Further non-application of s. 238(1)]** Subsection (1) does not apply to anything done in accordance with rules made by the Authority for the purpose of exempting from that subsection the promotion otherwise than to the general public of schemes of specified descriptions.

**238(6) [Power of Treasury to make order]** The Treasury may by order specify circumstances in which subsection (1) does not apply.

**238(7) [S. 238(6) orders – non-application of s. 238(1)]** An order under subsection (6) may, in particular, provide that subsection (1) does not apply in relation to communications–

(a) of a specified description;

(b) originating in a specified country or territory outside the United Kingdom;

(c) originating in a country or territory which falls within a specified description of country or territory outside the United Kingdom; or

(d) originating outside the United Kingdom.

**238(8) [Treasury power to make order]** The Treasury may by order repeal subsection (3).

**238(9) ["Communicate"] "Communicate"** includes causing a communication to be made.

**238(10) ["Promotion otherwise than to the general public"] "Promotion otherwise than to the general public"** includes promotion in a way designed to reduce, so far as possible, the risk of participation by persons for whom participation would be unsuitable.

**238(11) ["Participate"] "Participate"**, in relation to a collective investment scheme, means become a participant (within the meaning given by section 235(2)) in the scheme.

## 239 Single property schemes

**239(1) [Power of Treasury to make regulations]** The Treasury may by regulations make provision for exempting single property schemes from section 238(1).

**239(2) [Nature of scheme]** For the purposes of subsection (1) a single property scheme is a scheme which has the characteristics mentioned in subsection (3) and satisfies such other requirements as are prescribed by the regulations conferring the exemption.

**239(3) [Characteristics of scheme]** The characteristics are–

(a) that the property subject to the scheme (apart from cash or other assets held for management purposes) consists of–

  (i) a single building (or a single building with ancillary buildings) managed by or on behalf of the operator of the scheme, or

  (ii) a group of adjacent or contiguous buildings managed by him or on his behalf as a single enterprise,

with or without ancillary land and with or without furniture, fittings or other contents of the building or buildings in question; and

(b) that the units of the participants in the scheme are either dealt in on a recognised investment exchange or offered on terms such that any agreement for their acquisition is conditional on their admission to dealings on such an exchange.

**239(4) [Power of Authority to make rules]** If regulations are made under subsection (1), the Authority may make rules imposing duties or liabilities on the operator and (if any) the trustee or depositary of a scheme exempted by the regulations.

**239(5) [Content of rules]** The rules may include, to such extent as the Authority thinks appropriate, provision for purposes corresponding to those for which provision can be made under section 248 in relation to authorised unit trust schemes.

## 240 Restriction on approval of promotion

**240(1) [Restriction on s. 21 approval]** An authorised person may not approve for the purposes of section 21 the content of a communication relating to a collective investment scheme if he would be prohibited by section 238(1) from effecting the communication himself or from causing it to be communicated.

**240(2) [Determination of contravention of s. 21(1)]** For the purposes of determining in any case whether there has been a contravention of section 21(1), an approval given in contravention of subsection (1) is to be regarded as not having been given.

## 241 Actions for damages

**241** If an authorised person contravenes a requirement imposed on him by section 238 or 240, section 150 applies to the contravention as it applies to a contravention mentioned in that section.

# Chapter III – Authorised Unit Trust Schemes

APPLICATIONS FOR AUTHORISATION

## 242 Applications for authorisation of unit trust schemes

**242(1) [Manager or trustee to make application]** Any application for an order declaring a unit trust scheme to be an authorised unit trust scheme must be made to the Authority by the manager and trustee, or proposed manager and trustee, of the scheme.

**242(2) [Manager and trustee to be separate]** The manager and trustee (or proposed manager and trustee) must be different persons.

**242(3) [Form and content of application]** The application–

(a) must be made in such manner as the Authority may direct; and

(b) must contain or be accompanied by such information as the Authority may reasonably require for the purpose of determining the application.

**242(4) [Provision of further information]** At any time after receiving an application and before determining it, the Authority may require the applicants to provide it with such further information as it reasonably considers necessary to enable it to determine the application.

**242(5) [Variability of directions]** Different directions may be given, and different requirements imposed, in relation to different applications.

**242(6) [Presentation of information]** The Authority may require applicants to present information which they are required to give under this section in such form, or to verify it in such a way, as the Authority may direct.

## 243 Authorisation orders

**243(1) [Power of Authority]** If, on an application under section 242 in respect of a unit trust scheme, the Authority–

(a) is satisfied that the scheme complies with the requirements set out in this section,

(b) is satisfied that the scheme complies with the requirements of the trust scheme rules, and

(c) has been provided with a copy of the trust deed and a certificate signed by a solicitor to the effect that it complies with such of the requirements of this section or those rules as relate to its contents,

the Authority may make an order declaring the scheme to be an authorised unit trust scheme.

**243(2) [Written notice]** If the Authority makes an order under subsection (1), it must give written notice of the order to the applicant.

**243(3) ["Authorisation order"]** In this Chapter **"authorisation order"** means an order under subsection (1).

**243(4) [Manager and trustee to be separate]** The manager and the trustee must be persons who are independent of each other.

**243(5) [Corporate status, etc. of manager, trustee]** The manager and the trustee must each–

(a) be a body corporate incorporated in the United Kingdom or another EEA State, and

(b) have a place of business in the United Kingdom,

and the affairs of each must be administered in the country in which it is incorporated.

**243(6) [Managers incorporated in other EEA state]** If the manager is incorporated in another EEA State, the scheme must not be one which satisfies the requirements prescribed for the purposes of section 264.

**243(7) [Authorisation and permission]** The manager and the trustee must each be an authorised person and the manager must have permission to act as manager and the trustee must have permission to act as trustee.

**243(8) [Name of scheme]** The name of the scheme must not be undesirable or misleading.

**243(9) [Purposes of scheme]** The purposes of the scheme must be reasonably capable of being successfully carried into effect.

**243(10) [Redemption of units]** The participants must be entitled to have their units redeemed in accordance with the scheme at a price–

(a) related to the net value of the property to which the units relate; and

(b) determined in accordance with the scheme.

**243(11) [Sale of units on investment exchange]** But a scheme is to be treated as complying with subsection (10) if it requires the manager to ensure that a participant is able to sell his units on an investment exchange at a price not significantly different from that mentioned in that subsection.

## 244 Determination of applications

**244(1) [Duty of Authority]** An application under section 242 must be determined by the Authority before the end of the period of six months beginning with the date on which it receives the completed application.

**244(2) [Incomplete applications]** The Authority may determine an incomplete application if it considers it appropriate to do so; and it must in any event determine such an application within twelve months beginning with the date on which it first receives the application.

**244(3) [Withdrawal of applications]** The applicant may withdraw his application, by giving the Authority written notice, at any time before the Authority determines it.

APPLICATIONS REFUSED

## 245 Procedure when refusing an application

**245(1) [Warning notice]** If the Authority proposes to refuse an application made under section 242 it must give each of the applicants a warning notice.

**245(2) [Decision notice, right of referral to Tribunal]** If the Authority decides to refuse the application–

(a) it must give each of the applicants a decision notice; and

(b) either applicant may refer the matter to the Tribunal.

CERTIFICATES

## 246 Certificates

**246(1) [Power of Authority]** If the manager or trustee of a unit trust scheme which complies with the conditions necessary for it to enjoy the rights conferred by any relevant Community instrument so requests, the Authority may issue a certificate to the effect that the scheme complies with those conditions.

**246(2) [When certificate can be issued]** Such a certificate may be issued on the making of an authorisation order in respect of the scheme or at any subsequent time.

RULES

## 247 Trust scheme rules

**247(1) [Power of Authority to make rules]** The Authority may make rules ("trust scheme rules") as to–

(a) the constitution, management and operation of authorised unit trust schemes;

(b) the powers, duties, rights and liabilities of the manager and trustee of any such scheme;

(c) the rights and duties of the participants in any such scheme; and

(d) the winding up of any such scheme.

**247(2) [Content of trust scheme rules]** Trust scheme rules may, in particular, make provision–

(a) as to the issue and redemption of the units under the scheme;

(b) as to the expenses of the scheme and the means of meeting them;

(c) for the appointment, removal, powers and duties of an auditor for the scheme;

(d) for restricting or regulating the investment and borrowing powers exercisable in relation to the scheme;

(e) requiring the keeping of records with respect to the transactions and financial position of the scheme and for the inspection of those records;

(f) requiring the preparation of periodical reports with respect to the scheme and the provision of those reports to the participants and to the Authority; and

(g) with respect to the amendment of the scheme.

**247(3) [Content of trust deed]** Trust scheme rules may make provision as to the contents of the trust deed, including provision requiring any of the matters mentioned in subsection (2) to be dealt with in the deed.

**247(4) [Status of trust scheme rules]** But trust scheme rules are binding on the manager, trustee and participants independently of the contents of the trust deed and, in the case of the participants, have effect as if contained in it.

**247(5) [Power of Treasury to make order]** If–

(a) a modification is made of the statutory provisions in force in Great Britain or Northern Ireland relating to companies,

(b) the modification relates to the rights and duties of persons who hold the beneficial title to any shares in a company without also holding the legal title, and

(c) it appears to the Treasury that, for the purpose of assimilating the law relating to authorised unit trust schemes to the law relating to companies as so modified, it is expedient to modify the rule-making powers conferred on the Authority by this section,

the Treasury may by order make such modifications of those powers as they consider appropriate.

## 248 Scheme particulars rules

**248(1) [Power of Authority to make rules]** The Authority may make rules ("scheme particulars rules") requiring the manager of an authorised unit trust scheme–

(a) to submit scheme particulars to the Authority; and

(b) to publish scheme particulars or make them available to the public on request.

**248(2) ["Scheme particulars"]** "**Scheme particulars**" means particulars in such form, containing such information about the scheme and complying with such requirements, as are specified in scheme particulars rules.

**248(3) [Changes to previously published scheme particulars]** Scheme particulars rules may require the manager of an authorised unit trust scheme to submit, and to publish or make available, revised or further scheme particulars if there is a significant change affecting any matter–

(a) which is contained in scheme particulars previously published or made available; and

(b) whose inclusion in those particulars was required by the rules.

**248(4) [Publication of revised, etc. scheme particulars]** Scheme particulars rules may require the manager of an authorised unit trust scheme to submit, and to publish or make available, revised or further scheme particulars if–

(a) a significant new matter arises; and

(b) the inclusion of information in respect of that matter would have been required in previous particulars if it had arisen when those particulars were prepared.

**248(5) [Compensation]** Scheme particulars rules may provide for the payment, by the person or persons who in accordance with the rules are treated as responsible for any scheme particulars, of compensation to any qualifying person who has suffered loss as a result of–

(a) any untrue or misleading statement in the particulars; or

(b) the omission from them of any matter required by the rules to be included.

**248(6) ["Qualifying person"] "Qualifying person"** means a person who–

(a) has become or agreed to become a participant in the scheme; or

(b) although not being a participant, has a beneficial interest in units in the scheme.

**248(7) [Other liabilities]** Scheme particulars rules do not affect any liability which any person may incur apart from the rules.

## 249 Disqualification of auditor for breach of trust scheme rules

**249(1) [Power of Authority]** If it appears to the Authority that an auditor has failed to comply with a duty imposed on him by trust scheme rules, it may disqualify him from being the auditor for any authorised unit trust scheme or authorised open-ended investment company.

**249(2) [Application of s. 345(2)–(5)]** Subsections (2) to (5) of section 345 have effect in relation to disqualification under subsection (1) as they have effect in relation to disqualification under subsection (1) of that section.

## 250 Modification or waiver of rules

**250(1) ["Rules"]** In this section **"rules"** means–

(a) trust scheme rules; or

(b) scheme particulars rules.

**250(2) [Power of Authority – persons to whom rules apply]** The Authority may, on the application or with the consent of any person to whom any rules apply, direct that all or any of the rules–

(a) are not to apply to him as respects a particular scheme; or

(b) are to apply to him, as respects a particular scheme, with such modifications as may be specified in the direction.

**250(3) [Power of Authority – manager, trustee]** The Authority may, on the application or with the consent of the manager and trustee of a particular scheme acting jointly, direct that all or any of the rules–

(a) are not to apply to the scheme; or

(b) are to apply to the scheme with such modifications as may be specified in the direction.

**250(4) [Directions under s. 250(2) – application of s. 148(3)–(9), (11)]** Subsections (3) to (9) and (11) of section 148 have effect in relation to a direction under subsection (2) as they have effect in relation to a direction under section 148(2) but with the following modifications–

(a) subsection (4)(a) is to be read as if the words "by the authorised person" were omitted;

(b) any reference to the authorised person (except in subsection (4)(a)) is to be read as a reference to the person mentioned in subsection (2); and

(c) subsection (7)(b) is to be read, in relation to a participant of the scheme, as if the word "commercial" were omitted.

**250(5) [Directions under s. 250(3) – application of s. 148(3)–(9), (11)]** Subsections (3) to (9) and (11) of section 148 have effect in relation to a direction under subsection (3) as they have effect in relation to a direction under section 148(2) but with the following modifications–

(a) subsection (4)(a) is to be read as if the words "by the authorised person" were omitted;

(b) subsections (7)(b) and (11) are to be read as if references to the authorised person were references to each of the manager and the trustee of the scheme;

(c) subsection (7)(b) is to be read, in relation to a participant of the scheme, as if the word "commercial" were omitted;

(d) subsection (8) is to be read as if the reference to the authorised person concerned were a reference to the scheme concerned and to its manager and trustee; and

(e) subsection (9) is to be read as if the reference to the authorised person were a reference to the manager and trustee of the scheme acting jointly.

ALTERATIONS

# 251 Alteration of schemes and changes of manager or trustee

**251(1) [Duty of manager re alterations]** The manager of an authorised unit trust scheme must give written notice to the Authority of any proposal to alter the scheme or to replace its trustee.

**251(2) [Requirements where proposed change to trust deed]** Any notice given in respect of a proposal to alter the scheme involving a change in the trust deed must be accompanied by a certificate signed by a solicitor to the effect that the change will not affect the compliance of the deed with the trust scheme rules.

**251(3) [Duty of trustee re manager]** The trustee of an authorised unit trust scheme must give written notice to the Authority of any proposal to replace the manager of the scheme.

**251(4) [When effect can be given to s. 251(1) or (3) notice]** Effect is not to be given to any proposal of which notice has been given under subsection (1) or (3) unless–

(a) the Authority, by written notice, has given its approval to the proposal; or

(b) one month, beginning with the date on which the notice was given, has expired without the manager or trustee having received from the Authority a warning notice under section 252 in respect of the proposal.

**251(5) [Duty of Authority re approval]** The Authority must not approve a proposal to replace the manager or the trustee of an authorised unit trust scheme unless it is satisfied that, if the proposed replacement is made, the scheme will continue to comply with the requirements of section 243(4) to (7).

# 252 Procedure when refusing approval of change of manager or trustee

**252(1) [Warning notice]** If the Authority proposes to refuse approval of a proposal to replace the trustee or manager of an authorised unit trust scheme, it must give a warning notice to the person by whom notice of the proposal was given under section 251(1) or (3).

**252(2) [Separate warning notice to manager and trustee]** If the Authority proposes to refuse approval of a proposal to alter an authorised unit trust scheme it must give separate warning notices to the manager and the trustee of the scheme.

**252(3) [Validity of warning notice]** To be valid the warning notice must be received by that person before the end of one month beginning with the date on which notice of the proposal was given.

**252(4) [Decision notice, right of referral to Tribunal]** If, having given a warning notice to a person, the Authority decides to refuse approval–

(a) it must give him a decision notice; and

(b) he may refer the matter to the Tribunal.

EXCLUSION CLAUSES

## 253 Avoidance of exclusion clauses

**253** Any provision of the trust deed of an authorised unit trust scheme is void in so far as it would have the effect of exempting the manager or trustee from liability for any failure to exercise due care and diligence in the discharge of his functions in respect of the scheme.

ENDING OF AUTHORISATION

## 254 Revocation of authorisation order otherwise than by consent

**254(1) [Power of Authority to make order]** An authorisation order may be revoked by an order made by the Authority if it appears to the Authority that–

(a) one or more of the requirements for the making of the order are no longer satisfied;

(b) the manager or trustee of the scheme concerned has contravened a requirement imposed on him by or under this Act;

(c) the manager or trustee of the scheme has, in purported compliance with any such requirement, knowingly or recklessly given the Authority information which is false or misleading in a material particular;

(d) no regulated activity is being carried on in relation to the scheme and the period of that inactivity began at least twelve months earlier; or

(e) none of paragraphs (a) to (d) applies, but it is desirable to revoke the authorisation order in order to protect the interests of participants or potential participants in the scheme.

**254(2) [S. 254(1)(e) – matters to be considered]** For the purposes of subsection (1)(e), the Authority may take into account any matter relating to–

(a) the scheme;

(b) the manager or trustee;

(c) any person employed by or associated with the manager or trustee in connection with the scheme;

(d) any director of the manager or trustee;

(e) any person exercising influence over the manager or trustee;

(f) any body corporate in the same group as the manager or trustee;

(g) any director of any such body corporate;

(h) any person exercising influence over any such body corporate.

## 255 Procedure

**255(1) [Duty of Authority]** If the Authority proposes to make an order under section 254 revoking an authorisation order ("a revoking order"), it must give separate warning notices to the manager and the trustee of the scheme.

**255(2) [Decision notice, right of referral to Tribunal]** If the Authority decides to make a revoking order, it must without delay give each of them a decision notice and either of them may refer the matter to the Tribunal.

## 256 Requests for revocation of authorisation order

**256(1) [Power of Authority to make order]** An authorisation order may be revoked by an order made by the Authority at the request of the manager or trustee of the scheme concerned.

**256(2) [Written notice of order]** If the Authority makes an order under subsection (1), it must give written notice of the order to the manager and trustee of the scheme concerned.

**256(3) [Refusal to make order]** The Authority may refuse a request to make an order under this section if it considers that–

(a) the public interest requires that any matter concerning the scheme should be investigated before a decision is taken as to whether the authorisation order should be revoked; or

(a) revoke the Open-Ended Investment Companies (Investment Companies with Variable Capital) Regulations 1996; and

(b) provide for things done under or in accordance with those regulations to be treated as if they had been done under or in accordance with regulations under this section.

## 263 Amendment of section 716 Companies Act 1985

**263** In section 716(1) of the Companies Act 1985 (prohibition on formation of companies with more than 20 members unless registered under the Act etc.), after "this Act," insert "is incorporated by virtue of regulations made under section 262 of the Financial Services and Markets Act 2000".

# Chapter V – Recognised Overseas Schemes

### SCHEMES CONSTITUTED IN OTHER EEA STATES

## 264 Schemes constituted in other EEA States

**264(1) [Overseas schemes – recognition requirements]** A collective investment scheme constituted in another EEA State is a recognised scheme if–

(a) it satisfies such requirements as are prescribed for the purposes of this section; and

(b) not less than two months before inviting persons in the United Kingdom to become participants in the scheme, the operator of the scheme gives notice to the Authority of his intention to do so, specifying the way in which the invitation is to be made.

**264(2) [Limitation of s. 264(1)]** But this section does not make the scheme a recognised scheme if within two months of receiving the notice under subsection (1) the Authority notifies–

(a) the operator of the scheme, and

(b) the authorities of the State in question who are responsible for the authorisation of collective investment schemes,

that the way in which the invitation is to be made does not comply with the law in force in the United Kingdom.

**264(3) [Notice to Authority – contents]** The notice to be given to the Authority under subsection (1)–

(a) must be accompanied by a certificate from the authorities mentioned in subsection (2)(b) to the effect that the scheme complies with the conditions necessary for it to enjoy the rights conferred by any relevant Community instrument;

(b) must contain the address of a place in the United Kingdom for the service on the operator of notices or other documents required or authorised to be served on him under this Act; and

(c) must contain or be accompanied by such other information and documents as may be prescribed.

**264(4) [Notice given by Authority – contents]** A notice given by the Authority under subsection (2) must–

(a) give the reasons for which the Authority considers that the law in force in the United Kingdom will not be complied with; and

(b) specify a reasonable period (which may not be less than 28 days) within which any person to whom it is given may make representations to the Authority.

**264(5) [Schemes constituted in EEA states – requirements]** For the purposes of this section a collective investment scheme is constituted in another EEA State if–

(a) it is constituted under the law of that State by a contract or under a trust and is managed by a body corporate incorporated under that law; or

(b) it takes the form of an open-ended investment company incorporated under that law.

**264(6) [De-recognition of scheme]** The operator of a recognised scheme may give written notice to the Authority that he desires the scheme to be no longer recognised by virtue of this section.

**264(7) [Effect of s. 264(6) notice]** On the giving of notice under subsection (6), the scheme ceases to be a recognised scheme.

## 265 Representations and references to the Tribunal

**265(1) [Application of section]** This section applies if any representations are made to the Authority, before the period for making representations has ended, by a person to whom a notice was given by the Authority under section 264(2).

**265(2) [Withdrawal of notice]** The Authority must, within a reasonable period, decide in the light of those representations whether or not to withdraw its notice.

**265(3) [Effect of withdrawal of notice]** If the Authority withdraws its notice the scheme is a recognised scheme from the date on which the notice is withdrawn.

**265(4) [Decision not to withdraw notice]** If the Authority decides not to withdraw its notice, it must give a decision notice to each person to whom the notice under section 264(2) was given.

**265(5) [Right of referral to Tribunal]** The operator of the scheme to whom the decision notice is given may refer the matter to the Tribunal.

## 266 Disapplication of rules

**266(1) [Non-application of rules]** Apart from–

(a) financial promotion rules, and

(b) rules under section 283(1),

rules made by the Authority under this Act do not apply to the operator, trustee or depositary of a scheme in relation to the carrying on by him of regulated activities for which he has permission in that capacity.

**266(2) ["Scheme"]** "Scheme" means a scheme which is a recognised scheme by virtue of section 264.

## 267 Power of Authority to suspend promotion of scheme

**267(1) [Application of s. 267(2)]** Subsection (2) applies if it appears to the Authority that the operator of a scheme has communicated an invitation or inducement in relation to the scheme in a manner contrary to financial promotion rules.

**267(2) [Non-application of s. 238(1)]** The Authority may direct that–

(a) the exemption from subsection (1) of section 238 provided by subsection (4)(c) of that section is not to apply in relation to the scheme; and

(b) subsection (5) of that section does not apply with respect to things done in relation to the scheme.

**267(3) [Effect of s. 267(2) direction]** A direction under subsection (2) has effect–

(a) for a specified period;

(b) until the occurrence of a specified event; or

(c) until specified conditions are complied with.

**267(4) [Variation of direction]** The Authority may, either on its own initiative or on the application of the operator of the scheme concerned, vary a direction given under subsection (2) if it appears to the Authority that the direction should take effect or continue in force in a different form.

**267(5) [Revocation of direction]** The Authority may, either on its own initiative or on the application of the operator of the recognised scheme concerned, revoke a direction given under subsection (2) if it appears to the Authority–

(a) that the conditions specified in the direction have been complied with; or

(b) that it is no longer necessary for the direction to take effect or continue in force.

**267(6) [Specified events]** If an event is specified, the direction ceases to have effect (unless revoked earlier) on the occurrence of that event.

**267(7) [Interpretation]** For the purposes of this section and sections 268 and 269–

(a) the scheme's home State is the EEA State in which the scheme is constituted (within the meaning given by section 264);

(b) the competent authorities in the scheme's home State are the authorities in that State who are responsible for the authorisation of collective investment schemes.

**267(8) ["Scheme"]** "Scheme" means a scheme which is a recognised scheme by virtue of section 264.

**267(9) ["Specified"]** "Specified", in relation to a direction, means specified in it.

## 268 Procedure on giving directions under section 267 and varying them on Authority's own initiative

**268(1) [Effective date of direction]** A direction under section 267 takes effect–

(a) immediately, if the notice given under subsection (3)(a) states that that is the case;

(b) on such date as may be specified in the notice; or

(c) if no date is specified in the notice, when the matter to which it relates is no longer open to review.

**268(2) [Directions taking effect immediately]** A direction may be expressed to take effect immediately (or on a specified date) only if the Authority, having regard to its reasons for exercising its power under section 267, considers that it is necessary for the direction to take effect immediately (or on that date).

**268(3) [Written notice, etc.]** If the Authority proposes to give a direction under section 267, or gives such a direction with immediate effect, it must–

(a) give the operator of the scheme concerned written notice; and

(b) inform the competent authorities in the scheme's home State of its proposal or (as the case may be) of the direction.

**268(4) [Contents of notice]** The notice must–

(a) give details of the direction;

(b) inform the operator of when the direction takes effect;

(c) state the Authority's reasons for giving the direction and for its determination as to when the direction takes effect;

(d) inform the operator that he may make representations to the Authority within such period as may be specified in it (whether or not he has referred the matter to the Tribunal); and

(e) inform him of his right to refer the matter to the Tribunal.

**268(5) [Extension of representation period]** The Authority may extend the period allowed under the notice for making representations.

**268(6) [Application of s. 268(7)]** Subsection (7) applies if, having considered any representations made by the operator, the Authority decides–

(a) to give the direction in the way proposed, or

(b) if it has been given, not to revoke the direction.

**268(7) [Written notice, etc.]** The Authority must–

(a) give the operator of the scheme concerned written notice; and

(b) inform the competent authorities in the scheme's home State of the direction.

**268(8) [Application of s. 268(9)]** Subsection (9) applies if, having considered any representations made by a person to whom the notice was given, the Authority decides–

(a) not to give the direction in the way proposed,

(b) to give the direction in a way other than that proposed, or

(c) to revoke a direction which has effect.

**268(9) [Duty of Authority]** The Authority must–

(a) give the operator of the scheme concerned written notice; and

(b) inform the competent authorities in the scheme's home State of its decision.

**268(10) [Right of referral to Tribunal]** A notice given under subsection (7)(a) must inform the operator of his right to refer the matter to the Tribunal.

**268(11) [S. 268(9)(a) notice to comply with s. 268(4)]** A notice under subsection (9)(a) given as a result of subsection (8)(b) must comply with subsection (4).

**268(12) [Procedure upon referral]** If a notice informs a person of his right to refer a matter to the Tribunal, it must give an indication of the procedure on such a reference.

**268(13) [Application of section]** This section applies to the variation of a direction on the Authority's own initiative as it applies to the giving of a direction.

**268(14) [Matters open to review]** For the purposes of subsection (1)(c), whether a matter is open to review is to be determined in accordance with section 391(8).

## 269 Procedure on application for variation or revocation of direction

**269(1) [Warning notice]** If, on an application under subsection (4) or (5) of section 267, the Authority proposes–

(a) to vary a direction otherwise than in accordance with the application, or

(b) to refuse the application,

it must give the operator of the scheme concerned a warning notice.

**269(2) [Decision notice]** If, on such an application, the Authority decides–

(a) to vary a direction otherwise than in accordance with the application, or

(b) to refuse the application,

it must give the operator of the scheme concerned a decision notice.

**269(3) [Right of referral to Tribunal]** If the application is refused, the operator of the scheme may refer the matter to the Tribunal.

**269(4) [Written notice]** If, on such an application, the Authority decides to grant the application it must give the operator of the scheme concerned written notice.

**269(5) [Revocation of s. 267 direction]** If the Authority decides on its own initiative to revoke a direction given under section 267 it must give the operator of the scheme concerned written notice.

**269(6) [Duty of Authority re competent authority]** The Authority must inform the competent authorities in the scheme's home State of any notice given under this section.

### SCHEMES AUTHORISED IN DESIGNATED COUNTRIES OR TERRITORIES

## 270 Schemes authorised in designated countries or territories

**270(1) [Scheme not recognised by virtue of s. 264]** A collective investment scheme which is not a recognised scheme by virtue of section 264 but is managed in, and authorised under the law of, a country or territory outside the United Kingdom is a recognised scheme if–

(a) that country or territory is designated for the purposes of this section by an order made by the Treasury;

(b) the scheme is of a class specified by the order;

(c) the operator of the scheme has given written notice to the Authority that he wishes it to be recognised; and

(d) either–

(i) the Authority, by written notice, has given its approval to the scheme's being recognised; or

**284(3) [Power of investigator to require information]** If the person appointed to conduct an investigation under this section ("B") considers that a person ("C") is or may be able to give information which is relevant to the investigation, B may require C–

(a) to produce to B any documents in C's possession or under his control which appear to B to be relevant to the investigation,

(b) to attend before B, and

(c) otherwise to give B all assistance in connection with the investigation which C is reasonably able to give,

and it is C's duty to comply with that requirement.

**284(4) [Application of s. 170(5)–(9)]** Subsections (5) to (9) of section 170 apply if an investigating authority appoints a person under this section to conduct an investigation on its behalf as they apply in the case mentioned in subsection (1) of that section.

**284(5) [Application of s. 174]** Section 174 applies to a statement made by a person in compliance with a requirement imposed under this section as it applies to a statement mentioned in that section.

**284(6) [S. 175(2)–(4), (6) and 177 – interpretation]** Subsections (2) to (4) and (6) of section 175 and section 177 have effect as if this section were contained in Part XI.

**284(7) [Application of s. 176(1)–(9)]** Subsections (1) to (9) of section 176 apply in relation to a person appointed under subsection (1) as if–

(a) references to an investigator were references to a person so appointed;

(b) references to an information requirement were references to a requirement imposed under section 175 or under subsection (3) by a person so appointed;

(c) the premises mentioned in subsection (3)(a) were the premises of a person whose affairs are the subject of an investigation under this section or of an appointed representative of such a person.

**284(8) [Confidential information]** No person may be required under this section to disclose information or produce a document in respect of which he owes an obligation of confidence by virtue of carrying on the business of banking unless subsection (9) or (10) applies.

**284(9) [Application of subsection]** This subsection applies if–

(a) the person to whom the obligation of confidence is owed consents to the disclosure or production; or

(b) the imposing on the person concerned of a requirement with respect to information or a document of a kind mentioned in subsection (8) has been specifically authorised by the investigating authority.

**284(10) [Application of subsection]** This subsection applies if the person owing the obligation of confidence or the person to whom it is owed is–

(a) the manager, trustee, operator or depositary of any collective investment scheme which is under investigation;

(b) the director of a body incorporated by virtue of regulations under section 262 which is under investigation;

(c) any other person whose own affairs are under investigation.

**284(11) ["Investigating authority"] "Investigating authority"** means the Authority or the Secretary of State.

# PART XVIII – RECOGNISED INVESTMENT EXCHANGES AND CLEARING HOUSES

## Chapter I – Exemption

GENERAL

### 285 Exemption for recognised investment exchanges and clearing houses

**285(1) [Definitions]** In this Act–

(a) **"recognised investment exchange"** means an investment exchange in relation to which a recognition order is in force; and

(b) **"recognised clearing house"** means a clearing house in relation to which a recognition order is in force.

**285(2) [RIEs – exemption from general prohibition]** A recognised investment exchange is exempt from the general prohibition as respects any regulated activity–

(a) which is carried on as a part of the exchange's business as an investment exchange; or

(b) which is carried on for the purposes of, or in connection with, the provision of clearing services by the exchange.

**285(3) [RCHs – exemption from general prohibition]** A recognised clearing house is exempt from the general prohibition as respects any regulated activity which is carried on for the purposes of, or in connection with, the provision of clearing services by the clearing house.

### 286 Qualification for recognition

**286(1) [Power of Treasury to make regulations]** The Treasury may make regulations setting out the requirements–

(a) which must be satisfied by an investment exchange or clearing house if it is to qualify as a body in respect of which the Authority may make a recognition order under this Part; and

(b) which, if a recognition order is made, it must continue to satisfy if it is to remain a recognised body.

**286(2) [Approval of Secretary of State]** But if regulations contain provision as to the default rules of an investment exchange or clearing house, or as to proceedings taken under such rules by such a body, they require the approval of the Secretary of State.

**286(3) ["Default rules"] "Default rules"** means rules of an investment exchange or clearing house which provide for the taking of action in the event of a person's appearing to be unable, or likely to become unable, to meet his obligations in respect of one or more market contracts connected with the exchange or clearing house.

**286(4) ["Market contract"] "Market contract"** means–

(a) a contract to which Part VII of the Companies Act 1989 applies as a result of section 155 of that Act or a contract to which Part V of the Companies (No. 2)(Northern Ireland) Order 1990 applies as a result of Article 80 of that Order; and

(b) such other kind of contract as may be prescribed.

**286(5) [Recognition requirements]** Requirements resulting from this section are referred to in this Part as "recognition requirements".

APPLICATIONS FOR RECOGNITION

### 287 Application by an investment exchange

**287(1) [Application]** Any body corporate or unincorporated association may apply to the Authority for an order declaring it to be a recognised investment exchange for the purposes of this Act.

**287(2) [Manner and contents of application]** The application must be made in such manner as the Authority may direct and must be accompanied by–
(a) a copy of the applicant's rules;
(b) a copy of any guidance issued by the applicant;
(c) the required particulars; and
(d) such other information as the Authority may reasonably require for the purpose of determining the application.

**287(3) [Required particulars]** The required particulars are–
(a) particulars of any arrangements which the applicant has made, or proposes to make, for the provision of clearing services in respect of transactions effected on the exchange;
(b) if the applicant proposes to provide clearing services in respect of transactions other than those effected on the exchange, particulars of the criteria which the applicant will apply when determining to whom it will provide those services.

## 288 Application by a clearing house

**288(1) [Application]** Any body corporate or unincorporated association may apply to the Authority for an order declaring it to be a recognised clearing house for the purposes of this Act.

**288(2) [Manner and contents of application]** The application must be made in such manner as the Authority may direct and must be accompanied by–
(a) a copy of the applicant's rules;
(b) a copy of any guidance issued by the applicant;
(c) the required particulars; and
(d) such other information as the Authority may reasonably require for the purpose of determining the application.

**288(3) [Required particulars]** The required particulars are–
(a) if the applicant makes, or proposes to make, clearing arrangements with a recognised investment exchange, particulars of those arrangements;
(b) if the applicant proposes to provide clearing services for persons other than recognised investment exchanges, particulars of the criteria which it will apply when determining to whom it will provide those services.

## 289 Applications: supplementary

**289(1) [Further information]** At any time after receiving an application and before determining it, the Authority may require the applicant to provide such further information as it reasonably considers necessary to enable it to determine the application.

**289(2) [Verification, etc. of information]** Information which the Authority requires in connection with an application must be provided in such form, or verified in such manner, as the Authority may direct.

**289(3) [Variability of directions]** Different directions may be given, or requirements imposed, by the Authority with respect to different applications.

## 290 Recognition orders

**290(1) [Power of Authority]** If it appears to the Authority that the applicant satisfies the recognition requirements applicable in its case, the Authority may make a recognition order declaring the applicant to be–
(a) a recognised investment exchange, if the application is made under section 287;
(b) a recognised clearing house, if it is made under section 288.

**290(2) [Treasury approval]** The Treasury's approval of the making of a recognition order is required under section 307.

**290(3) [Relevant information]** In considering an application, the Authority may have regard to any information which it considers is relevant to the application.

**290(4) [Effective date of order]** A recognition order must specify a date on which it is to take effect.

**290(5) [Effect of s. 298]** Section 298 has effect in relation to a decision to refuse to make a recognition order–

(a) as it has effect in relation to a decision to revoke such an order; and

(b) as if references to a recognised body were references to the applicant.

**290(6) [Non-application of s. 290(5)]** Subsection (5) does not apply in a case in which the Treasury have failed to give their approval under section 307.

## 291 Liability in relation to recognised body's regulatory functions

**291(1) [Statutory immunity]** A recognised body and its officers and staff are not to be liable in damages for anything done or omitted in the discharge of the recognised body's regulatory functions unless it is shown that the act or omission was in bad faith.

**291(2) [Human Rights Act 1998, s. 6(1)]** But subsection (1) does not prevent an award of damages made in respect of an act or omission on the ground that the act or omission was unlawful as a result of section 6(1) of the Human Rights Act 1998.

**291(3) ["Regulatory functions"] "Regulatory functions"** means the functions of the recognised body so far as relating to, or to matters arising out of, the obligations to which the body is subject under or by virtue of this Act.

## 292 Overseas investment exchanges and overseas clearing houses

**292(1) [Service of notices, etc.]** An application under section 287 or 288 by an overseas applicant must contain the address of a place in the United Kingdom for the service on the applicant of notices or other documents required or authorised to be served on it under this Act.

**292(2) [Power of Authority]** If it appears to the Authority that an overseas applicant satisfies the requirements of subsection (3) it may make a recognition order declaring the applicant to be–

(a) a recognised investment exchange;

(b) a recognised clearing house.

**292(3) [Requirements to be satisfied]** The requirements are that–

(a) investors are afforded protection equivalent to that which they would be afforded if the body concerned were required to comply with recognition requirements;

(b) there are adequate procedures for dealing with a person who is unable, or likely to become unable, to meet his obligations in respect of one or more market contracts connected with the investment exchange or clearing house;

(c) the applicant is able and willing to co-operate with the Authority by the sharing of information and in other ways;

(d) adequate arrangements exist for co-operation between the Authority and those responsible for the supervision of the applicant in the country or territory in which the applicant's head office is situated.

**292(4) [Matters to be considered by Authority]** In considering whether it is satisfied as to the requirements mentioned in subsection (3)(a) and (b), the Authority is to have regard to–

(a) the relevant law and practice of the country or territory in which the applicant's head office is situated;

(b) the rules and practices of the applicant.

**292(5) [Interpretation]** In relation to an overseas applicant and a body or association declared to be a recognised investment exchange or recognised clearing house by a recognition order made by virtue of subsection (2)–

Authority, that it is appropriate for the arrangements mentioned in subsection (2) to be supervised by the Authority.

**301(4) [Treasury approval]** The approval of the Treasury is required for–

(a) the conditions set by the Authority for admission to the list; and

(b) the arrangements for admission to, and removal from, the list.

**301(5) [Suspension of regulations]** If the Treasury withdraw an approval given by them under subsection (4), all regulations made under this section and then in force are to be treated as suspended.

**301(6) [End of suspension of regulations]** But if–

(a) the Authority changes the conditions or arrangements (or both), and

(b) the Treasury give a fresh approval under subsection (4),

the suspension of the regulations ends on such date as the Treasury may, in giving the fresh approval, specify.

**301(7) [Publication, etc. of list]** The Authority must–

(a) publish the list as for the time being in force; and

(b) provide a certified copy of it to any person who wishes to refer to it in legal proceedings.

**301(8) [Certified copies of list]** A certified copy of the list is evidence (or in Scotland sufficient evidence) of the contents of the list.

**301(9) [Presumption of duly certified copy]** A copy of the list which purports to be certified by or on behalf of the Authority is to be taken to have been duly certified unless the contrary is shown.

**301(10) [Application, etc. of regulations]** Regulations under this section may, in relation to a person included in the list–

(a) apply (with such exceptions, additions and modifications as appear to the Secretary of State and the Treasury to be necessary or expedient) such provisions of, or made under, this Act as they consider appropriate;

(b) provide for the provisions of Part VII of the Companies Act 1989 and Part V of the Companies (No. 2)(Northern Ireland) Order 1990 to apply (with such exceptions, additions or modifications as appear to the Secretary of State and the Treasury to be necessary or expedient).

# Chapter II – Competition Scrutiny

## 302 Interpretation

**302(1) [Definitions]** In this Chapter and Chapter III–

**"practices"** means–

(a) in relation to a recognised investment exchange, the practices of the exchange in its capacity as such; and

(b) in relation to a recognised clearing house, the practices of the clearing house in respect of its clearing arrangements;

**"regulatory provisions"** means–

(a) the rules of an investment exchange or a clearing house;

(b) any guidance issued by an investment exchange or clearing house;

(c) in the case of an investment exchange, the arrangements and criteria mentioned in section 287(3);

(d) in the case of a clearing house, the arrangements and criteria mentioned in section 288(3).

**302(2) [Anti-competitive practices]** For the purposes of this Chapter, regulatory provisions or practices have a significantly adverse effect on competition if–

(a) they have, or are intended or likely to have, that effect; or

(b) the effect that they have, or are intended or likely to have, is to require or encourage behaviour which has, or is intended or likely to have, a significantly adverse effect on competition.

**302(3) [Provisions, etc. encouraging exploitation of market position]** If regulatory provisions or practices have, or are intended or likely to have, the effect of requiring or encouraging exploitation of the strength of a market position they are to be taken, for the purposes of this Chapter, to have an adverse effect on competition.

**302(4) [Presumption of compliance with provisions]** In determining under this Chapter whether any regulatory provisions have, or are intended or likely to have, a particular effect, it may be assumed that persons to whom the provisions concerned are addressed will act in accordance with them.

### ROLE OF DIRECTOR GENERAL OF FAIR TRADING

## 303 Initial report by Director

**303(1) [Duty of Authority re Treasury]** The Authority must send to the Treasury and to the Director a copy of any regulatory provisions with which it is provided on an application for recognition under section 287 or 288.

**303(2) [Duty of Authority re Director]** The Authority must send to the Director such information in its possession as a result of the application for recognition as it considers will assist him in discharging his functions in connection with the application.

**303(3) [Significant anti-competitive effect]** The Director must issue a report as to whether–

(a) a regulatory provision of which a copy has been sent to him under subsection (1) has a significantly adverse effect on competition; or

(b) a combination of regulatory provisions so copied to him have such an effect.

**303(4) [Statement of reasons]** If the Director's conclusion is that one or more provisions have a significantly adverse effect on competition, he must state his reasons for that conclusion.

**303(5) [Copy to Authority, etc.]** When the Director issues a report under subsection (3), he must send a copy of it to the Authority, the Competition Commission and the Treasury.

## 304 Further reports by Director

**304(1) [Duty of Director]** The Director must keep under review the regulatory provisions and practices of recognised bodies.

**304(2) [Significant anti-competitive effect – duty to report]** If at any time the Director considers that–

(a) a regulatory provision or practice has a significantly adverse effect on competition, or

(b) regulatory provisions or practices, or a combination of regulating provisions and practices have such an effect,

he must make a report.

**304(3) [Significant anti-competitive effect – power to report]** If at any time the Director considers that–

(a) a regulatory provision or practice does not have a significantly adverse effect on competition, or

(b) regulatory provisions or practices, or a combination of regulatory provisions and practices do not have any such effect,

he may make a report to that effect.

**304(4) [S. 304(2) report – contents]** A report under subsection (2) must contain details of the adverse effect on competition.

**304(5) [S. 304(2) report – copies to Treasury, etc.]** If the Director makes a report under subsection (2), he must–

(a) send a copy of it to the Treasury, to the Competition Commission and to the Authority; and

(b) publish it in the way appearing to him to be best calculated to bring it to the attention of the public.

**304(6) [S. 304(3) report – copies to Treasury, etc.]** If the Director makes a report under subsection (3)–

(a) he must send a copy of it to the Treasury, to the Competition Commission and to the Authority; and

(b) he may publish it.

**304(7) [Exclusion of prejudicial matters – individuals]** Before publishing a report under this section, the Director must, so far as practicable, exclude any matter which relates to the private affairs of a particular individual the publication of which, in the opinion of the Director, would or might seriously and prejudicially affect his interests.

**304(8) [Exclusion of prejudicial matters – bodies]** Before publishing such a report, the Director must exclude any matter which relates to the affairs of a particular body the publication of which, in the opinion of the Director, would or might seriously and prejudicially affect its interests.

**304(9) [Non-application of s. 304(7) and (8)]** Subsections (7) and (8) do not apply to the copy of a report which the Director is required to send to the Treasury, the Competition Commission and the Authority under subsection (5)(a) or (6)(a).

**304(10) [Defamation – absolute privilege]** For the purposes of the law of defamation, absolute privilege attaches to any report of the Director under this section.

## 305 Investigations by Director

**305(1) [Power of Director]** For the purpose of investigating any matter with a view to its consideration under section 303 or 304, the Director may exercise the powers conferred on him by this section.

**305(2) [Production of documents]** The Director may by notice in writing require any person to produce to him or to a person appointed by him for the purpose, at a time and place specified in the notice, any document which–

(a) is specified or described in the notice; and

(b) is a document in that person's custody or under his control.

**305(3) [Provision of information]** The Director may by notice in writing–

(a) require any person carrying on any business to provide him with such information as may be specified or described in the notice; and

(b) specify the time within which, and the manner and form in which, any such information is to be provided.

**305(4) [Documents, etc. to be relevant]** A requirement may be imposed under subsection (2) or (3)(a) only in respect of documents or information which relate to any matter relevant to the investigation.

**305(5) [Non-compliance with s. 305 notice – power of court]** If a person ("the defaulter") refuses, or otherwise fails, to comply with a notice under this section, the Director may certify that fact in writing to the court and the court may enquire into the case.

**305(6) [Contempt of court]** If, after hearing any witness who may be produced against or on behalf of the defaulter and any statement which may be offered in defence, the court is satisfied that the defaulter did not have a reasonable excuse for refusing or otherwise failing to comply with the notice, the court may deal with the defaulter as if he were in contempt.

**305(7) ["The court"]** In this section, **"the court"** means–

(a) the High Court; or

(b) in Scotland, the Court of Session.

ROLE OF COMPETITION COMMISSION

## 306 Consideration by Competition Commission

**306(1) [Duty of Commission]** If subsection (2) or (3) applies, the Commission must investigate the matter which is the subject of the Director's report.

**306(2) [Application of subsection]** This subsection applies if the Director sends to the Competition Commission a report–

(a) issued by him under section 303(3) which concludes that one or more regulatory provisions have a significantly adverse effect on competition, or

(b) made by him under section 304(2).

**306(3) [Application of subsection]** This subsection applies if the Director asks the Commission to consider a report–

(a) issued by him under section 303(3) which concludes that one or more regulatory provisions do not have a significantly adverse effect on competition, or

(b) made by him under section 304(3).

**306(4) [Report]** The Commission must then make its own report on the matter unless it considers that, as a result of a change of circumstances, no useful purpose would be served by a report.

**306(5) [Decision not to report]** If the Commission decides in accordance with subsection (4) not to make a report, it must make a statement setting out the change of circumstances which resulted in that decision.

**306(6) [Contents of report]** A report made under this section must state the Commission's conclusion as to whether–

(a) the regulatory provision or practice which is the subject of the report has a significantly adverse effect on competition, or

(b) the regulatory provisions or practices or combination of regulatory provisions and practices which are the subject of the report have such an effect.

**306(7) [Further contents of report]** A report under this section stating the Commission's conclusion that there is a significantly adverse effect on competition must also–

(a) state whether the Commission considers that that effect is justified; and

(b) if it states that the Commission considers that it is not justified, state its conclusion as to what action, if any, the Treasury ought to direct the Authority to take.

**306(8) [Application of s. 306(9)]** Subsection (9) applies whenever the Commission is considering, for the purposes of this section, whether a particular adverse effect on competition is justified.

**306(9) [Compatibility with obligations imposed by Act]** The Commission must ensure, so far as that is reasonably possible, that the conclusion it reaches is compatible with the obligations imposed on the recognised body concerned by or under this Act.

**306(10) [Contents of report – conclusion]** A report under this section must contain such an account of the Commission's reasons for its conclusions as is expedient, in the opinion of the Commission, for facilitating proper understanding of them.

**306(11) [Sch. 14]** The provisions of Schedule 14 (except paragraph 2(b)) apply for the purposes of this section as they apply for the purposes of section 162.

**306(12) [Copies to Treasury, etc]** If the Commission makes a report under this section it must send a copy to the Treasury, the Authority and the Director.

ROLE OF THE TREASURY

## 307 Recognition orders: role of the Treasury

**307(1) [Application of s. 307(2)]** Subsection (2) applies if, on an application for a recognition order–

(a) the Director makes a report under section 303 but does not ask the Competition Commission to consider it under section 306;

(b) the Competition Commission concludes–

(i) that the applicant's regulatory provisions do not have a significantly adverse effect on competition; or

(ii) that if those provisions do have that effect, the effect is justified.

**307(2) [Power of Treasury to refuse recognition order]** The Treasury may refuse to approve the making of the recognition order only if they consider that the exceptional circumstances of the case make it inappropriate for them to give their approval.

**307(3) [Application of s. 307(4)]** Subsection (4) applies if, on an application for a recognition order, the Competition Commission concludes–

(a) that the applicant's regulatory provisions have a significantly adverse effect on competition; and

(b) that that effect is not justified.

**307(4) [Duty of Treasury to refuse recognition order]** The Treasury must refuse to approve the making of the recognition order unless they consider that the exceptional circumstances of the case make it inappropriate for them to refuse their approval.

# 308 Directions by the Treasury

**308(1) [Application of section]** This section applies if the Competition Commission makes a report under section 306(4) (other than a report on an application for a recognition order) which states the Commission's conclusion that there is a significantly adverse effect on competition.

**308(2) [Remedial direction to Authority]** If the Commission's conclusion, as stated in the report, is that the adverse effect on competition is not justified, the Treasury must give a remedial direction to the Authority.

**308(3) [Non-application of s. 308(2)]** But subsection (2) does not apply if the Treasury consider–

(a) that, as a result of action taken by the Authority or the recognised body concerned in response to the Commission's report, it is unnecessary for them to give a direction; or

(b) that the exceptional circumstances of the case make it inappropriate or unnecessary for them to do so.

**308(4) [Duty to have regard to s. 306(7)(b) conclusion]** In considering the action to be specified in a remedial direction, the Treasury must have regard to any conclusion of the Commission included in the report because of section 306(7)(b).

**308(5) [Application of s. 308(6)]** Subsection (6) applies if–

(a) the Commission's conclusion, as stated in its report, is that the adverse effect on competition is justified; but

(b) the Treasury consider that the exceptional circumstances of the case require them to act.

**308(6) [Direction to Authority]** The Treasury may give a direction to the Authority requiring it to take such action–

(a) as they consider to be necessary in the light of the exceptional circumstances of the case; and

(b) as may be specified in the direction.

**308(7) [Remedial direction specifying Authority direction]** If the action specified in a remedial direction is the giving by the Authority of a direction–

(a) the direction to be given must be compatible with the recognition requirements applicable to the recognised body in relation to which it is given; and

(b) subsections (3) and (4) of section 296 apply to it as if it were a direction given under that section.

**308(8) ["Remedial direction"]** "**Remedial direction**" means a direction requiring the Authority–
(a) to revoke the recognition order for the body concerned; or
(b) to give such directions to the body concerned as may be specified in it.

## 309 Statements by the Treasury

**309(1) [Treasury declining to act under s. 308(2)]** If, in reliance on subsection (3)(a) or (b) of section 308, the Treasury decline to act under subsection (2) of that section, they must make a statement to that effect, giving their reasons.

**309(2) [S. 308 direction – statement]** If the Treasury give a direction under section 308 they must make a statement giving–
(a) details of the direction; and
(b) if the direction is given under subsection (6) of that section, their reasons for giving it.

**309(3) [Publication, etc. of statement]** The Treasury must–
(a) publish any statement made under this section in the way appearing to them best calculated to bring it to the attention of the public; and
(b) lay a copy of it before Parliament.

## 310 Procedure on exercise of certain powers by the Treasury

**310(1) [Application of s. 310(2)]** Subsection (2) applies if the Treasury are considering–
(a) whether to refuse their approval under section 307;
(b) whether section 308(2) applies; or
(c) whether to give a direction under section 308(6).

**310(2) [Duty of Treasury]** The Treasury must–
(a) take such steps as they consider appropriate to allow the exchange or clearing house concerned, and any other person appearing to the Treasury to be affected, an opportunity to make representations–
  (i) about any report made by the Director under section 303 or 304 or by the Competition Commission under section 306;
  (ii) as to whether, and if so how, the Treasury should exercise their powers under section 307 or 308; and
(b) have regard to any such representations.

# Chapter III – Exclusion from the Competition Act 1998

## 311 The Chapter I prohibition

**311(1) [Non-application – constitution of recognised body]** The Chapter I prohibition does not apply to an agreement for the constitution of a recognised body to the extent to which the agreement relates to the regulatory provisions of that body.

**311(2) [Non-application – constitution of investment exchanges, etc.]** If the conditions set out in subsection (3) are satisfied, the Chapter I prohibition does not apply to an agreement for the constitution of–
(a) an investment exchange which is not a recognised investment exchange, or
(b) a clearing house which is not a recognised clearing house,
to the extent to which the agreement relates to the regulatory provisions of that body.

**311(3) [Conditions]** The conditions are that–
(a) the body has applied for a recognition order in accordance with the provisions of this Act; and
(b) the application has not been determined.

**311(4) [Non-application – regulatory provisions of recognised body]** The Chapter I prohibition does not apply to a recognised body's regulatory provisions.

**311(5) [Non-application – decisions made by recognised body]** The Chapter I prohibition does not apply to a decision made by a recognised body to the extent to which the decision relates to any of that body's regulatory provisions or practices.

**311(6) [Non-application – trading practices]** The Chapter I prohibition does not apply to practices of a recognised body.

**311(7) [Non-application – agreements between recognised bodies, etc.]** The Chapter I prohibition does not apply to an agreement the parties to which consist of or include–

(a) a recognised body, or

(b) a person who is subject to the rules of a recognised body,

to the extent to which the agreement consists of provisions the inclusion of which is required or encouraged by any of the body's regulatory provisions or practices.

**311(8) [Revocation of recognition order]** If a recognised body's recognition order is revoked, this section is to have effect as if that body had continued to be recognised until the end of the period of six months beginning with the day on which the revocation took effect.

**311(9) ["The Ch. I prohibition"] "The Chapter I prohibition"** means the prohibition imposed by section 2(1) of the Competition Act 1998.

**311(10) [Interpretation]** Expressions used in this section which are also used in Part I of the Competition Act 1998 are to be interpreted in the same way as for the purposes of that Part of that Act.

## 312 The Chapter II prohibition

**312(1) [Non-application of Ch. II prohibition]** The Chapter II prohibition does not apply to–

(a) practices of a recognised body;

(b) the adoption or enforcement of such a body's regulatory provisions;

(c) any conduct which is engaged in by such a body or by a person who is subject to the rules of such a body to the extent to which it is encouraged or required by the regulatory provisions of the body.

**312(2) [Meaning of Ch. II prohibition]** The Chapter II prohibition means the prohibition imposed by section 18(1) of the Competition Act 1998.

# Chapter IV – Interpretation

## 313 Interpretation of Part XVIII

**313(1) [Definitions]** In this Part–

**"application"** means an application for a recognition order made under section 287 or 288;

**"applicant"** means a body corporate or unincorporated association which has applied for a recognition order;

**"Director"** means the Director General of Fair Trading;

**"overseas applicant"** means a body corporate or association which has neither its head office nor its registered office in the United Kingdom and which has applied for a recognition order;

**"overseas investment exchange"** means a body corporate or association which has neither its head office nor its registered office in the United Kingdom and in relation to which a recognition order is in force;

**"overseas clearing house"** means a body corporate or association which has neither its head office nor its registered office in the United Kingdom and in relation to which a recognition order is in force;

"**recognised body**" means a recognised investment exchange or a recognised clearing house;
"**recognised clearing house**" has the meaning given in section 285;
"**recognised investment exchange**" has the meaning given in section 285;
"**recognition order**" means an order made under section 290 or 292;
"**recognition requirements**" has the meaning given by section 281;
"**remedial direction**" has the meaning given in section 308(8);
"**revocation order**" has the meaning given in section 297.

**313(2) [References to rules of investment exchange, etc.]** References in this Part to rules of an investment exchange (or a clearing house) are to rules made, or conditions imposed, by the investment exchange (or the clearing house) with respect to–

(a) recognition requirements;
(b) admission of persons to, or their exclusion from the use of, its facilities; or
(c) matters relating to its constitution.

**313(3) [References to guidance issued by investment exchange]** References in this Part to guidance issued by an investment exchange are references to guidance issued, or any recommendation made, in writing or other legible form and intended to have continuing effect, by the investment exchange to–

(a) all or any class of its members or users, or
(b) persons seeking to become members of the investment exchange or to use its facilities,

with respect to any of the matters mentioned in subsection (2)(a) to (c).

**313(4) [References to guidance issued by clearing house]** References in this Part to guidance issued by a clearing house are to guidance issued, or any recommendation made, in writing or other legible form and intended to have continuing effect, by the clearing house to–

(a) all or any class of its members, or
(b) persons using or seeking to use its services,

with respect to the provision by it or its members of clearing services.

# PART XIX – LLOYD'S

## GENERAL

## 314 Authority's general duty

**314(1) [Matters Authority must remain informed about]** The Authority must keep itself informed about–

(a) the way in which the Council supervises and regulates the market at Lloyd's; and
(b) the way in which regulated activities are being carried on in that market.

**314(2) [Desirability of exercising Pt. XIX, etc. powers]** The Authority must keep under review the desirability of exercising–

(a) any of its powers under this Part;
(b) any powers which it has in relation to the Society as a result of section 315.

## THE SOCIETY

## 315 The Society: authorisation and permission

**315(1) [Status of Society]** The Society is an authorised person.

**315(2) [Permitted regulated activities, etc.]** The Society has permission to carry on a regulated activity of any of the following kinds–

(a) arranging deals in contracts of insurance written at Lloyd's ("the basic market activity");
(b) arranging deals in participation in Lloyd's syndicates ("the secondary market activity"); and

(c) an activity carried on in connection with, or for the purposes of, the basic or secondary market activity.

**315(3) [Permission for purposes of Pt. IV]** For the purposes of Part IV, the Society's permission is to be treated as if it had been given on an application for permission under that Part.

**315(4) [Exercise of s. 45 power]** The power conferred on the Authority by section 45 may be exercised in anticipation of the coming into force of the Society's permission (or at any other time).

**315(5) [Exclusion of society from certain requirements of Act]** The Society is not subject to any requirement of this Act concerning the registered office of a body corporate.

## POWER TO APPLY ACT TO LLOYD'S UNDERWRITING

## 316 Direction by Authority

**316(1) [Application of general prohibition]** The general prohibition or (if the general prohibition is not applied under this section) a core provision applies to the carrying on of an insurance market activity by–

(a) a member of the Society, or

(b) the members of the Society taken together,

only if the Authority so directs.

**316(2) ["Insurance market direction"]** A direction given under subsection (1) which applies a core provision is referred to in this Part as "an insurance market direction".

**316(3) [Definitions]** In subsection (1)–

**"core provision"** means a provision of this Act mentioned in section 317; and

**"insurance market activity"** means a regulated activity relating to contracts of insurance written at Lloyd's.

**316(4) [Matters to be considered by Authority]** In deciding whether to give a direction under subsection (1), the Authority must have particular regard to–

(a) the interests of policyholders and potential policyholders;

(b) any failure by the Society to satisfy an obligation to which it is subject as a result of a provision of the law of another EEA State which–

(i) gives effect to any of the insurance directives; and

(ii) is applicable to an activity carried on in that State by a person to whom this section applies;

(c) the need to ensure the effective exercise of the functions which the Authority has in relation to the Society as a result of section 315.

**316(5) [Form of s. 316(1) direction]** A direction under subsection (1) must be in writing.

**316(6) [Application of s. 316(1) direction]** A direction under subsection (1) applying the general prohibition may apply it in relation to different classes of person.

**316(7) [Content of insurance market direction]** An insurance market direction–

(a) must specify each core provision, class of person and kind of activity to which it applies;

(b) may apply different provisions in relation to different classes of person and different kinds of activity.

**316(8) [Effective date of s. 316(1) direction]** A direction under subsection (1) has effect from the date specified in it, which may not be earlier than the date on which it is made.

**316(9) [Publication]** A direction under subsection (1) must be published in the way appearing to the Authority to be best calculated to bring it to the attention of the public.

**316(10) [Fees]** The Authority may charge a reasonable fee for providing a person with a copy of the direction.

**316(11) [Copy to Treasury]** The Authority must, without delay, give the Treasury a copy of any direction which it gives under this section.

## 317 The core provisions

**317(1) [Core provisions]** The core provisions are Parts V, X, XI, XII, XIV, XV, XVI, XXII and XXIV, sections 384 to 386 and Part XXVI.

**317(2) [References in applied core provision]** References in an applied core provision to an authorised person are (where necessary) to be read as references to a person in the class to which the insurance market direction applies.

**317(3) [Insurance market direction]** An insurance market direction may provide that a core provision is to have effect, in relation to persons to whom the provision is applied by the direction, with modifications.

## 318 Exercise of powers through Council

**318(1) [Power of Authority]** The Authority may give a direction under this subsection to the Council or to the Society (acting through the Council) or to both.

**318(2) [S. 318(1) direction]** A direction under subsection (1) is one given to the body concerned–

(a) in relation to the exercise of its powers generally with a view to achieving, or in support of, a specified objective; or

(b) in relation to the exercise of a specified power which it has, whether in a specified manner or with a view to achieving, or in support of, a specified objective.

**318(3) ["Specified"]** "Specified" means specified in the direction.

**318(4) [S. 318(1) direction – further considerations]** A direction under subsection (1) may be given–

(a) instead of giving a direction under section 316(1); or

(b) if the Authority considers it necessary or expedient to do so, at the same time as, or following, the giving of such a direction.

**318(5) [Underwriting agents]** A direction may also be given under subsection (1) in respect of underwriting agents as if they were among the persons mentioned in section 316(1).

**318(6) [Form of direction]** A direction under this section–

(a) does not, at any time, prevent the exercise by the Authority of any of its powers;

(b) must be in writing.

**318(7) [Effective publication]** A direction under subsection (1) must be published in the way appearing to the Authority to be best calculated to bring it to the attention of the public.

**318(8) [Fees]** The Authority may charge a reasonable fee for providing a person with a copy of the direction.

**318(9) [Copy to Treasury]** The Authority must, without delay, give the Treasury a copy of any direction which it gives under this section.

## 319 Consultation

**319(1) [Publication of draft proposed direction]** Before giving a direction under section 316 or 318, the Authority must publish a draft of the proposed direction.

**319(2) [Matters to accompany draft]** The draft must be accompanied by–

(a) a cost benefit analysis; and

(b) notice that representations about the proposed direction may be made to the Authority within a specified time.

**319(3) [Regard to representations]** Before giving the proposed direction, the Authority must have regard to any representations made to it in accordance with subsection (2)(b).

**319(4) [Publication of representations, etc.]** If the Authority gives the proposed direction it must publish an account, in general terms, of–

(a) the representations made to it in accordance with subsection (2)(b); and

**327(7) [Regulated activities]** The activities must be the only regulated activities carried on by P (other than regulated activities in relation to which he is an exempt person).

**327(8) ["Professional services"] "Professional services"** means services–

(a) which do not constitute carrying on a regulated activity, and
(b) the provision of which is supervised and regulated by a designated professional body.

# 328 Directions in relation to the general prohibition

**328(1) [Non-application of s. 327(1)]** The Authority may direct that section 327(1) is not to apply to the extent specified in the direction.

**328(2) [Form, etc. of s. 328(1) direction]** A direction under subsection (1)–

(a) must be in writing;
(b) may be given in relation to different classes of person or different descriptions of regulated activity.

**328(3) [Effective publication]** A direction under subsection (1) must be published in the way appearing to the Authority to be best calculated to bring it to the attention of the public.

**328(4) [Fees]** The Authority may charge a reasonable fee for providing a person with a copy of the direction.

**328(5) [Copy to Treasury]** The Authority must, without delay, give the Treasury a copy of any direction which it gives under this section.

**328(6) [Exercise of s. 328(1) power]** The Authority may exercise the power conferred by subsection (1) only if it is satisfied that it is desirable in order to protect the interests of clients.

**328(7) [S. 328(1) power – matters to be considered]** In considering whether it is so satisfied, the Authority must have regard amongst other things to the effectiveness of any arrangements made by any designated professional body–

(a) for securing compliance with rules made under section 332(1);
(b) for dealing with complaints against its members in relation to the carrying on by them of exempt regulated activities;
(c) in order to offer redress to clients who suffer, or claim to have suffered, loss as a result of misconduct by its members in their carrying on of exempt regulated activities;
(d) for co-operating with the Authority under section 325(4).

**328(8) ["Clients"]** In this Part **"clients"** means–

(a) persons who use, have used or are or may be contemplating using, any of the services provided by a member of a profession in the course of carrying on exempt regulated activities;
(b) persons who have rights or interests which are derived from, or otherwise attributable to, the use of any such services by other persons; or
(c) persons who have rights or interests which may be adversely affected by the use of any such services by persons acting on their behalf or in a fiduciary capacity in relation to them.

**328(9) [Beneficiaries of trust]** If a member of a profession is carrying on an exempt regulated activity in his capacity as a trustee, the persons who are, have been or may be beneficiaries of the trust are to be treated as persons who use, have used or are or may be contemplating using services provided by that person in his carrying on of that activity.

# 329 Orders in relation to the general prohibition

**329(1) [Application of s. 329(2)]** Subsection (2) applies if it appears to the Authority that a person to whom, as a result of section 327(1), the general prohibition does not apply is not a fit and proper person to carry on regulated activities in accordance with that section.

**329(2) [Non-application of s. 327(1)]** The Authority may make an order disapplying section 327(1) in relation to that person to the extent specified in the order.

**329(3) [Variation, etc. of order]** The Authority may, on the application of the person named in an order under subsection (1), vary or revoke it.

**329(4) ["Specified"] "Specified"** means specified in the order.

**329(5) [Partnerships]** If a partnership is named in an order under this section, the order is not affected by any change in its membership.

**329(6) [Dissolution of partnership]** If a partnership named in an order under this section is dissolved, the order continues to have effect in relation to any partnership which succeeds to the business of the dissolved partnership.

**329(7) [Succeeding partnership]** For the purposes of subsection (6), a partnership is to be regarded as succeeding to the business of another partnership only if–

(a) the members of the resulting partnership are substantially the same as those of the former partnership; and

(b) succession is to the whole or substantially the whole of the business of the former partnership.

## 330 Consultation

**330(1) [Publication of draft proposed direction]** Before giving a direction under section 328(1), the Authority must publish a draft of the proposed direction.

**330(2) [Matters to accompany draft]** The draft must be accompanied by–

(a) a cost benefit analysis; and

(b) notice that representations about the proposed direction may be made to the Authority within a specified time.

**330(3) [Representations]** Before giving the proposed direction, the Authority must have regard to any representations made to it in accordance with subsection (2)(b).

**330(4) [Publication of representations, etc.]** If the Authority gives the proposed direction it must publish an account, in general terms, of–

(a) the representations made to it in accordance with subsection (2)(b); and

(b) its response to them.

**330(5) [Significant differences between draft and direction]** If the direction differs from the draft published under subsection (1) in a way which is, in the opinion of the Authority, significant–

(a) the Authority must (in addition to complying with subsection (4)) publish details of the difference; and

(b) those details must be accompanied by a cost benefit analysis.

**330(6) [Non-application of s. 330(1)–(5)]** Subsections (1) to (5) do not apply if the Authority considers that the delay involved in complying with them would prejudice the interests of consumers.

**330(7) [Non-application of s. 330(2)(a), (5)(b)]** Neither subsection (2)(a) nor subsection (5)(b) applies if the Authority considers–

(a) that, making the appropriate comparison, there will be no increase in costs; or

(b) that, making that comparison, there will be an increase in costs but the increase will be of minimal significance.

**330(8) [Fees]** The Authority may charge a reasonable fee for providing a person with a copy of a draft published under subsection (1).

**330(9) [Effective publication]** When the Authority is required to publish a document under this section it must do so in the way appearing to it to be best calculated to bring it to the attention of the public.

**330(10) ["Cost benefit analysis"] "Cost benefit analysis"** means an estimate of the costs together with an analysis of the benefits that will arise–

(a) if the proposed direction is given; or

(b) if subsection (5)(b) applies, from the direction that has been given.

**330(11) ["The appropriate comparison"] "The appropriate comparison"** means–

(a) in relation to subsection (2)(a), a comparison between the overall position if the direction is given and the overall position if it is not given;

(b) in relation to subsection (5)(b), a comparison between the overall position after the giving of the direction and the overall position before it was given.

# 331 Procedure on making or varying orders under section 329

**331(1) [Warning notice]** If the Authority proposes to make an order under section 329, it must give the person concerned a warning notice.

**331(2) [Contents of warning notice]** The warning notice must set out the terms of the proposed order.

**331(3) [Decision notice]** If the Authority decides to make an order under section 329, it must give the person concerned a decision notice.

**331(4) [Contents of decision notice]** The decision notice must–

(a) name the person to whom the order applies;

(b) set out the terms of the order; and

(c) be given to the person named in the order.

**331(5) [Application of s. 331(6)–(8)]** Subsections (6) to (8) apply to an application for the variation or revocation of an order under section 329.

**331(6) [Written notice – decision to grant application]** If the Authority decides to grant the application, it must give the applicant written notice of its decision.

**331(7) [Written notice – proposal to refuse application]** If the Authority proposes to refuse the application, it must give the applicant a warning notice.

**331(8) [Decision notice – refusal of application]** If the Authority decides to refuse the application, it must give the applicant a decision notice.

**331(9) [Right of referral to Tribunal]** A person–

(a) against whom the Authority have decided to make an order under section 329, or

(b) whose application for the variation or revocation of such an order the Authority had decided to refuse,

may refer the matter to the Tribunal.

**331(10) [Limitation of s. 329 power]** The Authority may not make an order under section 329 unless–

(a) the period within which the decision to make to the order may be referred to the Tribunal has expired and no such reference has been made; or

(b) if such a reference has been made, the reference has been determined.

# 332 Rules in relation to persons to whom the general prohibition does not apply

**332(1) [Power of Authority to make rules]** The Authority may make rules applicable to persons to whom, as a result of section 327(1), the general prohibition does not apply.

**332(2) [Exercise of s. 332(1) power]** The power conferred by subsection (1) is to be exercised for the purpose of ensuring that clients are aware that such persons are not authorised persons.

**332(3) [Duty of designated professional body]** A designated professional body must make rules–

(a) applicable to members of the profession in relation to which it is established who are not authorised persons; and

(b) governing the carrying on by those members of regulated activities (other than regulated activities in relation to which they are exempt persons).

**332(4) [Design of s. 332(3) rules]** Rules made in compliance with subsection (3) must be designed to secure that, in providing a particular professional service to a particular client, the member carries on only regulated activities which arise out of, or are complementary to, the provision by him of that service to that client.

**332(5) [Approval of Authority]** Rules made by a designated professional body under subsection (3) require the approval of the Authority.

## 333 False claims to be a person to whom the general prohibition does not apply

**333(1) [Offence]** A person who–

(a) describes himself (in whatever terms) as a person to whom the general prohibition does not apply, in relation to a particular regulated activity, as a result of this Part, or

(b) behaves, or otherwise holds himself out, in a manner which indicates (or which is reasonably likely to be understood as indicating) that he is such a person,

is guilty of an offence if he is not such a person.

**333(2) [Defence]** In proceedings for an offence under this section it is a defence for the accused to show that he took all reasonable precautions and exercised all due diligence to avoid committing the offence.

**333(3) [Penalty]** A person guilty of an offence under this section is liable on summary conviction to imprisonment for a term not exceeding six months or a fine not exceeding level 5 on the standard scale, or both.

**333(4) [Penalty re public display of material]** But where the conduct constituting the offence involved or included the public display of any material, the maximum fine for the offence is level 5 on the standard scale multiplied by the number of days for which the display continued.

# PART XXI – MUTUAL SOCIETIES

### FRIENDLY SOCIETIES

## 334 The Friendly Societies Commission

**334(1) [Power of Treasury re transfer of functions]** The Treasury may by order provide–

(a) for any functions of the Friendly Societies Commission to be transferred to the Authority;

(b) for any functions of the Friendly Societies Commission which have not been, or are not being, transferred to the Authority to be transferred to the Treasury.

**334(2) [Power of Treasury re cessation]** If the Treasury consider it appropriate to do so, they may by order provide for the Friendly Societies Commission to cease to exist on a day specified in or determined in accordance with the order.

**334(3) [Amendment of Pt. I of Sch. 18]** The enactments relating to friendly societies which are mentioned in Part I of Schedule 18 are amended as set out in that Part.

**334(4) [Function of Pt. II of Sch. 18]** Part II of Schedule 18–

(a) removes certain restrictions on the ability of incorporated friendly societies to form subsidiaries and control corporate bodies; and

(b) makes connected amendments.

## 335 The Registry of Friendly Societies

**335(1) [Power of Treasury re Registrar]** The Treasury may by order provide–

(a) for any functions of the Chief Registrar of Friendly Societies, or of an assistant registrar of friendly societies for the central registration area, to be transferred to the Authority;

(b) for any of their functions which have not been, or are not being, transferred to the Authority to be transferred to the Treasury.

**335(2) [Power of Treasury re central office of registry]** The Treasury may by order provide–

(a) for any functions of the central office of the registry of friendly societies to be transferred to the Authority;

(b) for any functions of that office which have not been, or are not being, transferred to the Authority to be transferred to the Treasury.

**335(3) [Power of Treasury re assistant registrar]** The Treasury may by order provide–

(a) for any functions of the assistant registrar of friendly societies for Scotland to be transferred to the Authority;

(b) for any functions of the assistant registrar which have not been, or are not being, transferred to the Authority to be transferred to the Treasury.

**335(4) [Power of Treasury re cessation]** If the Treasury consider it appropriate to do so, they may by order provide for–

(a) the office of Chief Registrar of Friendly Societies,

(b) the office of assistant registrar of friendly societies for the central registration area,

(c) the central office, or

(d) the office of assistant registrar of friendly societies for Scotland,

to cease to exist on a day specified in or determined in accordance with the order.

BUILDING SOCIETIES

## 336 The Building Societies Commission

**336(1) [Power of Treasury re transfer of functions]** The Treasury may by order provide–

(a) for any functions of the Building Societies Commission to be transferred to the Authority;

(b) for any functions of the Building Societies Commission which have not been, or are not being, transferred to the Authority to be transferred to the Treasury.

**336(2) [Power of Treasury re cessation]** If the Treasury consider it appropriate to do so, they may by order provide for the Building Societies Commission to cease to exist on a day specified in or determined in accordance with the order.

**336(3) [Amendment of Pt. II of Sch. 18]** The enactments relating to building societies which are mentioned in Part III of Schedule 18 are amended as set out in that Part.

## 337 The Building Societies Investor Protection Board

337 The Treasury may by order provide for the Building Societies Investor Protection Board to cease to exist on a day specified in or determined in accordance with the order.

INDUSTRIAL AND PROVIDENT SOCIETIES AND CREDIT UNIONS

## 338 Industrial and provident societies and credit unions

**338(1) [Power of Treasury re transfer of functions]** The Treasury may by order provide for the transfer to the Authority of any functions conferred by–

(a) the Industrial and Provident Societies Act 1965;

(b) the Industrial and Provident Societies Act 1967;

(c) the Friendly and Industrial and Provident Societies Act 1968;

(d) the Industrial and Provident Societies Act 1975;

(e) the Industrial and Provident Societies Act 1978;

(f) the Credit Unions Act 1979.

**338(2) [Transfer to Treasury]** The Treasury may by order provide for the transfer to the Treasury of any functions under those enactments which have not been, or are not being, transferred to the Authority.

**338(3) [Amendment of Pt. IV of Sch. 18]** The enactments relating to industrial and provident societies which are mentioned in Part IV of Schedule 18 are amended as set out in that Part.

**338(4) [Amendment of Pt. V of Sch. 18]** The enactments relating to credit unions which are mentioned in Part V of Schedule 18 are amended as set out in that Part.

SUPPLEMENTAL

## 339 Supplemental provisions

**339(1) [Power of Treasury – s. 334, s. 335, s. 336 and s. 338 orders]** The additional powers conferred by section 428 on a person making an order under this Act include power for the Treasury, when making an order under section 334, 335, 336 or 338 which transfers functions, to include provision–

(a) for the transfer of any functions of a member of the body, or servant or agent of the body or person, whose functions are transferred by the order;

(b) for the transfer of any property, rights or liabilities held, enjoyed or incurred by any person in connection with transferred functions;

(c) for the carrying on and completion by or under the authority of the person to whom functions are transferred of any proceedings, investigations or other matters commenced, before the order takes effect, by or under the authority of the person from whom the functions are transferred;

(d) amending any enactment relating to transferred functions in connection with their exercise by, or under the authority of, the person to whom they are transferred;

(e) for the substitution of the person to whom functions are transferred for the person from whom they are transferred, in any instrument, contract or legal proceedings made or begun before the order takes effect.

**339(2) [Power of Treasury – s. 334(2), s. 335(4), s. 336(2) and s. 337 orders]** The additional powers conferred by section 428 on a person making an order under this Act include power for the Treasury, when making an order under section 334(2), 335(4), 336(2) or 337, to include provision–

(a) for the transfer of any property, rights or liabilities held, enjoyed or incurred by any person in connection with the office or body which ceases to have effect as a result of the order;

(b) for the carrying on and completion by or under the authority of such person as may be specified in the order of any proceedings, investigations or other matters commenced, before the order takes effect, by or under the authority of the person whose office, or the body which, ceases to exist as a result of the order;

(c) amending any enactment which makes provision with respect to that office or body;

(d) for the substitution of the Authority the Treasury or such other body as may be specified in the order in any instrument, contract or legal proceedings made or begun before the order takes effect.

**339(3) [Power of Treasury – incidental, etc. provisions]** On or after the making of an order under any of sections 334 to 338 ("the original order"), the Treasury may by order make any incidental, supplemental, consequential or transitional provision which they had power to include in the original order.

**339(4) [Certificate conclusive evidence of transfer]** A certificate issued by the Treasury that property vested in a person immediately before an order under this Part takes effect has been transferred as a result of the order is conclusive evidence of the transfer.

**339(5) [Interpretation]** Subsections (1) and (2) are not to be read as affecting in any way the powers conferred by section 428.

# PART XXII – AUDITORS AND ACTUARIES

APPOINTMENT

## 340 Appointment

**340(1) [Rules concerning appointment of auditor, etc.]** Rules may require an authorised person, or an authorised person falling within a specified class–

(a) to appoint an auditor, or
(b) to appoint an actuary,

if he is not already under an obligation to do so imposed by another enactment.

**340(2) [Rules concerning periodic financial reports, etc.]** Rules may require an authorised person, or an authorised person falling within a specified class–

(a) to produce periodic financial reports; and
(b) to have them reported on by an auditor or an actuary.

**340(3) [Rules concerning duties of auditors, etc.]** Rules may impose such other duties on auditors of, or actuaries acting for, authorised persons as may be specified.

**340(4) [S. 340(1) rules]** Rules under subsection (1) may make provision–

(a) specifying the manner in which and time within which an auditor or actuary is to be appointed;
(b) requiring the Authority to be notified of an appointment;
(c) enabling the Authority to make an appointment if no appointment has been made or notified;
(d) as to remuneration;
(e) as to the term of office, removal and resignation of an auditor or actuary.

**340(5) [Duties and powers of auditors, etc.]** An auditor or actuary appointed as a result of rules under subsection (1), or on whom duties are imposed by rules under subsection (3)–

(a) must act in accordance with such provision as may be made by rules; and
(b) is to have such powers in connection with the discharge of his functions as may be provided by rules.

**340(6) ["Auditor", "actuary"]** In subsections (1) to (3) **"auditor"** or **"actuary"** means an auditor, or actuary, who satisfies such requirements as to qualifications, experience and other matters (if any) as may be specified.

**340(7) ["Specified"] "Specified"** means specified in rules.

## INFORMATION

## 341 Access to books etc

**341(1) [Power of appointed auditor, etc.]** An appointed auditor of, or an appointed actuary acting for, an authorised person–

(a) has a right of access at all times to the authorised person's books, accounts and vouchers; and
(b) is entitled to require from the authorised person's officers such information and explanations as he reasonably considers necessary for the performance of his duties as auditor or actuary.

**341(2) ["Appointed"] "Appointed"** means appointed under or as a result of this Act.

## 342 Information given by auditor or actuary to the Authority

**342(1) [Application of section]** This section applies to a person who is, or has been, an auditor of an authorised person appointed under or as a result of a statutory provision.

**342(2) [Further application of section]** This section also applies to a person who is, or has been, an actuary acting for an authorised person and appointed under or as a result of a statutory provision.

**342(3) [Auditor, etc. – non-contravention of duty]** An auditor or actuary does not contravene any duty to which he is subject merely because he gives to the Authority–

(a) information on a matter of which he has, or had, become aware in his capacity as auditor of, or actuary acting for, the authorised person, or
(b) his opinion on such a matter,

if he is acting in good faith and he reasonably believes that the information or opinion is relevant to any functions of the Authority.

**342(4) [Application of s. 342(3)]** Subsection (3) applies whether or not the auditor or actuary is responding to a request from the Authority.

**342(5) [Power of Treasury to make regulations]** The Treasury may make regulations prescribing circumstances in which an auditor or actuary must communicate matters to the Authority as mentioned in subsection (3).

**342(6) [Auditor's, etc. duty to communicate]** It is the duty of an auditor or actuary to whom any such regulations apply to communicate a matter to the Authority in the circumstances prescribed by the regulations.

**342(7) [Matters to be communicated]** The matters to be communicated to the Authority in accordance with the regulations may include matters relating to persons other than the authorised person concerned.

## 343 Information given by auditor or actuary to the Authority: persons with close links

**343(1) [Application of section]** This section applies to a person who–

(a) is, or has been, an auditor of an authorised person appointed under or as a result of a statutory provision; and

(b) is, or has been, an auditor of a person ("CL") who has close links with the authorised person.

**343(2) [Further application of section]** This section also applies to a person who–

(a) is, or has been, an actuary acting for an authorised person and appointed under or as a result of a statutory provision; and

(b) is, or has been, an actuary acting for a person ("CL") who has close links with the authorised person.

**343(3) [Auditor, etc. communicating information in good faith]** An auditor or actuary does not contravene any duty to which he is subject merely because he gives to the Authority–

(a) information on a matter concerning the authorised person of which he has, or had, become aware in his capacity as auditor of, or actuary acting for, CL, or

(b) his opinion on such a matter,

if he is acting in good faith and he reasonably believes that the information or opinion is relevant to any functions of the Authority.

**343(4) [Application of s. 343(3)]** Subsection (3) applies whether or not the auditor or actuary is responding to a request from the Authority.

**343(5) [Power of Treasury to make regulations]** The Treasury may make regulations prescribing circumstances in which an auditor or actuary must communicate matters to the Authority as mentioned in subsection (3).

**343(6) [Auditor's, etc. duty to communicate]** It is the duty of an auditor or actuary to whom any such regulations apply to communicate a matter to the Authority in the circumstances prescribed by the regulations.

**343(7) [Matters to be communicated]** The matters to be communicated to the Authority in accordance with the regulations may include matters relating to persons other than the authorised person concerned.

**343(8) [Interpretation]** CL has close links with the authorised person concerned ("A") if CL is–

(a) a parent undertaking of A;

(b) a subsidiary undertaking of A;

(c) a parent undertaking of a subsidiary undertaking of A; or

(d) a subsidiary undertaking of a parent undertaking of A.

**343(9) ["Subsidiary undertaking"]** **"Subsidiary undertaking"** includes all the instances mentioned in Article 1(1) and (2) of the Seventh Company Law Directive in which an entity may be a subsidiary of an undertaking.

## 344 Duty of auditor or actuary resigning etc. to give notice

**344(1) [Application of section]** This section applies to an auditor or actuary to whom section 342 applies.

**344(2) [Notification – removal from office, etc.]** He must without delay notify the Authority if he–

(a) is removed from office by an authorised person;

(b) resigns before the expiry of his term of office with such a person; or

(c) is not re-appointed by such a person.

**344(3) [Notification – cessation of office]** If he ceases to be an auditor of, or actuary acting for, such a person, he must without delay notify the Authority–

(a) of any matter connected with his so ceasing which he thinks ought to be drawn to the Authority's attention; or

(b) that there is no such matter.

DISQUALIFICATION

## 345 Disqualification

**345(1) [Failure to comply with duty imposed by Act]** If it appears to the Authority that an auditor or actuary to whom section 342 applies has failed to comply with a duty imposed on him under this Act, it may disqualify him from being the auditor of, or (as the case may be) from acting as an actuary for, any authorised person or any particular class of authorised person.

**345(2) [Warning notice]** If the Authority proposes to disqualify a person under this section it must give him a warning notice.

**345(3) [Decision notice]** If it decides to disqualify him it must give him a decision notice.

**345(4) [Removal of disqualification]** The Authority may remove any disqualification imposed under this section if satisfied that the disqualified person will in future comply with the duty in question.

**345(5) [Right of referral to Tribunal]** A person who has been disqualified under this section may refer the matter to the Tribunal.

OFFENCE

## 346 Provision of false or misleading information to auditor or actuary

**346(1) [Offence, penalty]** An authorised person who knowingly or recklessly gives an appointed auditor or actuary information which is false or misleading in a material particular is guilty of an offence and liable–

(a) on summary conviction, to imprisonment for a term not exceeding six months or a fine not exceeding the statutory maximum, or both;

(b) on conviction on indictment, to imprisonment for a term not exceeding two years or a fine, or both.

**346(2) [Application of s. 346(1)]** Subsection (1) applies equally to an officer, controller or manager of an authorised person.

**346(3) ["Appointed"]** **"Appointed"** means appointed under or as a result of this Act.

# PART XXIII – PUBLIC RECORD, DISCLOSURE OF INFORMATION AND CO-OPERATION

## THE PUBLIC RECORD

### 347 The record of authorised persons etc

**347(1) [Duty of Authority]** The Authority must maintain a record of every–

(a) person who appears to the Authority to be an authorised person;
(b) authorised unit trust scheme;
(c) authorised open-ended investment company;
(d) recognised scheme;
(e) recognised investment exchange;
(f) recognised clearing house;
(g) individual to whom a prohibition order relates;
(h) approved person; and
(i) person falling within such other class (if any) as the Authority may determine.

**347(2) [Contents of record]** The record must include such information as the Authority considers appropriate and at least the following information–

(a) in the case of a person appearing to the Authority to be an authorised person–
   (i) information as to the services which he holds himself out as able to provide; and
   (ii) any address of which the Authority is aware at which a notice or other document may be served on him;
(b) in the case of an authorised unit trust scheme, the name and address of the manager and trustee of the scheme;
(c) in the case of an authorised open-ended investment company, the name and address of–
   (i) the company;
   (ii) if it has only one director, the director; and
   (iii) its depositary (if any);
(d) in the case of a recognised scheme, the name and address of–
   (i) the operator of the scheme; and
   (ii) any representative of the operator in the United Kingdom;
(e) in the case of a recognised investment exchange or recognised clearing house, the name and address of the exchange or clearing house;
(f) in the case of an individual to whom a prohibition order relates–
   (i) his name; and
   (ii) details of the effect of the order;
(g) in the case of a person who is an approved person–
   (i) his name;
   (ii) the name of the relevant authorised person;
   (iii) if the approved person is performing a controlled function under an arrangement with a contractor of the relevant authorised person, the name of the contractor.

**347(3) [Removal of entry from record]** If it appears to the Authority that a person in respect of whom there is an entry in the record as a result of one of the paragraphs of subsection (1) has ceased to be a person to whom that paragraph applies, the Authority may remove the entry from the record.

**347(4) [Decision not to remove entry from record]** But if the Authority decides not to remove the entry, it must–

(a) make a note to that effect in the record; and
(b) state why it considers that the person has ceased to be a person to whom that paragraph applies.

**347(5) [Availability of record for public inspection]** The Authority must–

(a) make the record available for inspection by members of the public in a legible form at such times and in such place or places as the Authority may determine; and

(b) provide a certified copy of the record, or any part of it, to any person who asks for it–
  (i) on payment of the fee (if any) fixed by the Authority; and
  (ii) in a form (either written or electronic) in which it is legible to the person asking for it.

**347(6) [Publication, etc. of record]** The Authority may–

(a) publish the record, or any part of it;

(b) exploit commercially the information contained in the record, or any part of that information.

**347(7) [Interpretation]** **"Authorised unit trust scheme"**, **"authorised open-ended investment company"** and **"recognised scheme"** have the same meaning as in Part XVII, and associated expressions are to be read accordingly.

**347(8) ["Approved person"]** **"Approved person"** means a person in relation to whom the Authority has given its approval under section 59 and **"controlled function"** and **"arrangement"** have the same meaning as in that section.

**347(9) ["Relevant authorised person"]** **"Relevant authorised person"** has the meaning given in section 66.

## DISCLOSURE OF INFORMATION

## 348 Restrictions on disclosure of confidential information by Authority etc

**348(1) [Duty not to disclose confidential information]** Confidential information must not be disclosed by a primary recipient, or by any person obtaining the information directly or indirectly from a primary recipient, without the consent of–

(a) the person from whom the primary recipient obtained the information; and

(b) if different, the person to whom it relates.

**348(2) ["Confidential information"]** In this Part **"confidential information"** means information which–

(a) relates to the business or other affairs of any person;

(b) was received by the primary recipient for the purposes of, or in the discharge of, any functions of the Authority, the competent authority for the purposes of Part VI or the Secretary of State under any provision made by or under this Act; and

(c) is not prevented from being confidential information by subsection (4).

**348(3) [Manner of receipt of information]** It is immaterial for the purposes of subsection (2) whether or not the information was received–

(a) by virtue of a requirement to provide it imposed by or under this Act;

(b) for other purposes as well as purposes mentioned in that subsection.

**348(4) [Non-confidential information]** Information is not confidential information if–

(a) it has been made available to the public by virtue of being disclosed in any circumstances in which, or for any purposes for which, disclosure is not precluded by this section; or

(b) it is in the form of a summary or collection of information so framed that it is not possible to ascertain from it information relating to any particular person.

**348(5) [Primary recipients]** Each of the following is a primary recipient for the purposes of this Part–

(a) the Authority;

(b) any person exercising functions conferred by Part VI on the competent authority;

(c) the Secretary of State;

(d) a person appointed to make a report under section 166;
(e) any person who is or has been employed by a person mentioned in paragraphs (a) to (c);
(f) any auditor or expert instructed by a person mentioned in those paragraphs.

**348(6) ["Expert"]** In subsection (5)(f) **"expert"** includes–
(a) a competent person appointed by the competent authority under section 97;
(b) a competent person appointed by the Authority or the Secretary of State to conduct an investigation under Part XI;
(c) any body or person appointed under paragraph 6 of Schedule 1 to perform a function on behalf of the Authority.

## 349 Exceptions from section 348

**349(1) [Disclosure of confidential information]** Section 348 does not prevent a disclosure of confidential information which is–
(a) made for the purpose of facilitating the carrying out of a public function; and
(b) permitted by regulations made by the Treasury under this section.

**349(2) [Regulations permitting disclosure of confidential information]** The regulations may, in particular, make provision permitting the disclosure of confidential information or of confidential information of a prescribed kind–
(a) by prescribed recipients, or recipients of a prescribed description, to any person for the purpose of enabling or assisting the recipient to discharge prescribed public functions;
(b) by prescribed recipients, or recipients of a prescribed description, to prescribed persons, or persons of prescribed descriptions, for the purpose of enabling or assisting those persons to discharge prescribed public functions;
(c) by the Authority to the Treasury or the Secretary of State for any purpose;
(d) by any recipient if the disclosure is with a view to or in connection with prescribed proceedings.

**349(3) [Regulations – further provisions]** The regulations may also include provision–
(a) making any permission to disclose confidential information subject to conditions (which may relate to the obtaining of consents or any other matter);
(b) restricting the uses to which confidential information disclosed under the regulations may be put.

**349(4) ["Recipient"]** In relation to confidential information, each of the following is a "recipient"–
(a) a primary recipient;
(b) a person obtaining the information directly or indirectly from a primary recipient.

**349(5) ["Public functions"] "Public functions"** includes–
(a) functions conferred by or in accordance with any provision contained in any enactment or subordinate legislation;
(b) functions conferred by or in accordance with any provision contained in the Community Treaties or any Community instrument;
(c) similar functions conferred on persons by or under provisions having effect as part of the law of a country or territory outside the United Kingdom;
(d) functions exercisable in relation to prescribed disciplinary proceedings.

**349(6) ["Enactment"] "Enactment"** includes–
(a) an Act of the Scottish Parliament;
(b) Northern Ireland legislation.

**349(7) ["Subordinate legislation"] "Subordinate legislation"** has the meaning given in the Interpretation Act 1978 and also includes an instrument made under an Act of the Scottish Parliament or under Northern Ireland legislation.

## 350 Disclosure of information by the Inland Revenue

**350(1) [Disclosure of information for s. 168 purposes]** No obligation as to secrecy imposed by statute or otherwise prevents the disclosure of Revenue information to–

(a) the Authority, or

(b) the Secretary of State,

if the disclosure is made for the purpose of assisting in the investigation of a matter under section 168 or with a view to the appointment of an investigator under that section.

**350(2) [Disclosure with authority of Commissioners]** A disclosure may only be made under subsection (1) by or under the authority of the Commissioners of Inland Revenue.

**350(3) [Non-application of s. 348]** Section 348 does not apply to Revenue information.

**350(4) [Use of information obtained via s. 350(1)]** Information obtained as a result of subsection (1) may not be used except–

(a) for the purpose of deciding whether to appoint an investigator under section 168;

(b) in the conduct of an investigation under section 168;

(c) in criminal proceedings brought against a person under this Act or the Criminal Justice Act 1993 as a result of an investigation under section 168;

(d) for the purpose of taking action under this Act against a person as a result of an investigation under section 168;

(e) in proceedings before the Tribunal as a result of action taken as mentioned in paragraph (d).

**350(5) [Disclosure of information obtained via s. 350(1)]** Information obtained as a result of subsection (1) may not be disclosed except–

(a) by or under the authority of the Commissioners of Inland Revenue;

(b) in proceedings mentioned in subsection (4)(c) or (e) or with a view to their institution.

**350(6) [Limitation of s. 350(5)]** Subsection (5) does not prevent the disclosure of information obtained as a result of subsection (1) to a person to whom it could have been disclosed under subsection (1).

**350(7) ["Revenue information"]** **"Revenue information"** means information held by a person which it would be an offence under section 182 of the Finance Act 1989 for him to disclose.

## 351 Competition information

**351(1) [Offence]** A person is guilty of an offence if he has competition information (whether or not it was obtained by him) and improperly discloses it–

(a) if it relates to the affairs of an individual, during that individual's lifetime;

(b) if it relates to any particular business of a body, while that business continues to be carried on.

**351(2) [Improper disclosure]** For the purposes of subsection (1) a disclosure is improper unless it is made–

(a) with the consent of the person from whom it was obtained and, if different–
  (i) the individual to whose affairs the information relates, or
  (ii) the person for the time being carrying on the business to which the information relates;

(b) to facilitate the performance by a person mentioned in the first column of the table set out in Part I of Schedule 19 of a function mentioned in the second column of that table;

(c) in pursuance of a Community obligation;

(d) for the purpose of criminal proceedings in any part of the United Kingdom;

(e) in connection with the investigation of any criminal offence triable in the United Kingdom or any part of the United Kingdom;

(f) with a view to the institution of, or otherwise for the purposes of, civil proceedings brought under or in connection with–
  (i) a competition provision; or
  (ii) a specified enactment.

**351(3) [Penalty]** A person guilty of an offence under this section is liable–

(a) on summary conviction, to a fine not exceeding the statutory maximum;

(b) on conviction on indictment, to imprisonment for a term not exceeding two years or to a fine or to both.

**351(4) [Non-application of s. 348]** Section 348 does not apply to competition information.

**351(5) ["Competition information"] "Competition information"** means information which–

(a) relates to the affairs of a particular individual or body;

(b) is not otherwise in the public domain; and

(c) was obtained under or by virtue of a competition provision.

**351(6) ["Competition provision"] "Competition provision"** means any provision of–

(a) an order made under section 95;

(b) Chapter III of Part X; or

(c) Chapter II of Part XVIII.

**351(7) ["Specified enactment"] "Specified enactment"** means an enactment specified in Part II of Schedule 19.

## 352 Offences

**352(1) [Offence – contravention of s. 348 or s. 350(5)]** A person who discloses information in contravention of section 348 or 350(5) is guilty of an offence.

**352(2) [Penalty]** A person guilty of an offence under subsection (1) is liable–

(a) on summary conviction, to imprisonment for a term not exceeding three months or a fine not exceeding the statutory maximum, or both;

(b) on conviction on indictment, to imprisonment for a term not exceeding two years or a fine, or both.

**352(3) [Offence – contravention of s. 349]** A person is guilty of an offence if, in contravention of any provision of regulations made under section 349, he uses information which has been disclosed to him in accordance with the regulations.

**352(4) [Offence – contravention of s. 350(4)]** A person is guilty of an offence if, in contravention of subsection (4) of section 350, he uses information which has been disclosed to him in accordance with that section.

**352(5) [Penalty]** A person guilty of an offence under subsection (3) or (4) is liable on summary conviction to imprisonment for a term not exceeding three months or a fine not exceeding level 5 on the standard scale, or both.

**352(6) [Defence]** In proceedings for an offence under this section it is a defence for the accused to prove–

(a) that he did not know and had no reason to suspect that the information was confidential information or that it had been disclosed in accordance with section 350;

(b) that he took all reasonable precautions and exercised all due diligence to avoid committing the offence.

## 353 Removal of other restrictions on disclosure

**353(1) [Power of Treasury to make regulations]** The Treasury may make regulations permitting the disclosure of any information, or of information of a prescribed kind–

(a) by prescribed persons for the purpose of assisting or enabling them to discharge prescribed functions under this Act or any rules or regulations made under it;

(b) by prescribed persons, or persons of a prescribed description, to the Authority for the purpose of assisting or enabling the Authority to discharge prescribed functions.

**353(2) [Scope of regulations]** Regulations under this section may not make any provision in relation to the disclosure of confidential information by primary recipients or by any person obtaining confidential information directly or indirectly from a primary recipient.

**353(3) [Disclosure of information permitted by regulations]** If a person discloses any information as permitted by regulations under this section the disclosure is not to be taken as a contravention of any duty to which he is subject.

CO-OPERATION

## 354 Authority's duty to co-operate with others

**354(1) [Duty of Authority]** The Authority must take such steps as it considers appropriate to co-operate with other persons (whether in the United Kingdom or elsewhere) who have functions–

(a) similar to those of the Authority; or

(b) in relation to the prevention or detection of financial crime.

**354(2) [Sharing of information]** Co-operation may include the sharing of information which the Authority is not prevented from disclosing.

**354(3) ["Financial crime"] "Financial crime"** has the same meaning as in section 6.

# PART XXIV – INSOLVENCY

INTERPRETATION

## 355 Interpretation of this Part

**355(1) [Interpretation]** In this Part–

**"the 1985 Act"** means the Bankruptcy (Scotland) Act 1985;

**"the 1986 Act"** means the Insolvency Act 1986;

**"the 1989 Order"** means the Insolvency (Northern Ireland) Order 1989;

**"body"** means a body of persons–

(a) over which the court has jurisdiction under any provision of, or made under, the 1986 Act (or the 1989 Order); but

(b) which is not a building society, a friendly society or an industrial and provident society; and

**"court"** means–

(a) the court having jurisdiction for the purposes of the 1985 Act or the 1986 Act; or

(b) in Northern Ireland, the High Court.

**355(2) ["Insurer"]** In this Part **"insurer"** has such meaning as may be specified in an order made by the Treasury.

VOLUNTARY ARRANGEMENTS

## 356 Authority's powers to participate in proceedings: company voluntary arrangements

**356(1) [Application of section]** This section applies if a voluntary arrangement has been approved under Part I of the 1986 Act (or Part II of the 1989 Order) in respect of a company or insolvent partnership which is an authorised person.

**356(2) [Insolvency Act 1986, s. 6, etc. – applications to court]** The Authority may make an application to the court in relation to the company or insolvent partnership under section 6 of the 1986 Act (or Article 19 of the 1989 Order).

**356(3) [Authority's right of audience]** If a person other than the Authority makes an application to the court in relation to the company or insolvent partnership under either of those provisions, the Authority is entitled to be heard at any hearing relating to the application.

# 357 Authority's powers to participate in proceedings: individual voluntary arrangements

**357(1) [Authority's right of audience]** The Authority is entitled to be heard on an application by an individual who is an authorised person under section 253 of the 1986 Act (or Article 227 of the 1989 Order).

**357(2) [Application of s. 357(3)–(6)]** Subsections (3) to (6) apply if such an order is made on the application of such a person.

**357(3) [Meetings of creditors]** A person appointed for the purpose by the Authority is entitled to attend any meeting of creditors of the debtor summoned under section 257 of the 1986 Act (or Article 231 of the 1989 Order).

**357(4) [Duty of chairman of meeting]** Notice of the result of a meeting so summoned is to be given to the Authority by the chairman of the meeting.

**357(5) [Application to court]** The Authority may apply to the court–

(a) under section 262 of the 1986 Act (or Article 236 of the 1989 Order); or

(b) under section 263 of the 1986 Act (or Article 237 of the 1989 Order).

**357(6) [Authority's right of audience]** If a person other than the Authority makes an application to the court under any provision mentioned in subsection (5), the Authority is entitled to be heard at any hearing relating to the application.

# 358 Authority's powers to participate in proceedings: trust deeds for creditors in Scotland

**358(1) [Application of section]** This section applies where a trust deed has been granted by or on behalf of a debtor who is an authorised person.

**358(2) [Duty of trustee]** The trustee must, as soon as practicable after he becomes aware that the debtor is an authorised person, send to the Authority–

(a) in every case, a copy of the trust deed;

(b) where any other document or information is sent to every creditor known to the trustee in pursuance of paragraph 5(1)(c) of Schedule 5 to the 1985 Act, a copy of such document or information.

**358(3) [Application of Bankruptcy (Scotland) Act 1985, Sch. 5, para. 7]** Paragraph 7 of that Schedule applies to the Authority as if it were a qualified creditor who has not been sent a copy of the notice as mentioned in paragraph 5(1)(c) of the Schedule.

**358(4) [Notice to be given to Authority]** The Authority must be given the same notice as the creditors of any meeting of creditors held in relation to the trust deed.

**358(5) [Authority's right to attend, etc. meeting]** A person appointed for the purpose by the Authority is entitled to attend and participate in (but not to vote at) any such meeting of creditors as if the Authority were a creditor under the deed.

**358(6) [Rights of Authority as creditor unaffected]** This section does not affect any right the Authority has as a creditor of a debtor who is an authorised person.

**358(7) [Interpretation]** Expressions used in this section and in the 1985 Act have the same meaning in this section as in that Act.

## ADMINISTRATION ORDERS

# 359 Petitions

**359(1) [Petition under Insolvency Act 1986, s. 9, etc.]** The Authority may present a petition to the court under section 9 of the 1986 Act (or Article 22 of the 1989 Order) in relation to a company or insolvent partnership which–

(a) is, or has been, an authorised person;
(b) is, or has been, an appointed representative; or
(c) is carrying on, or has carried on, a regulated activity in contravention of the general prohibition.

**359(2) [Application of s. 359(3)]** Subsection (3) applies in relation to a petition presented by the Authority by virtue of this section.

**359(3) [Companies in default of obligation under agreement]** If the company or partnership is in default on an obligation to pay a sum due and payable under an agreement, it is to be treated for the purpose of section 8(1)(a) of the 1986 Act (or Article 21(1)(a) of the 1989 Order) as unable to pay its debts.

**359(4) ["Agreement"] "Agreement"** means an agreement the making or performance of which constitutes or is part of a regulated activity carried on by the company or partnership.

**359(5) ["Company"] "Company"** means–
(a) a company to which section 8 of the 1986 Act applies; or
(b) in relation to Northern Ireland, a company to which Article 21 of the 1989 Order applies.

## 360 Insurers

**360(1) [Power of Treasury to make order]** The Treasury may by order provide that such provisions of Part II of the 1986 Act (or Part III of the 1989 Order) as may be specified are to apply in relation to insurers with such modifications as may be specified.

**360(2) [Provisions, etc. of s. 360 order]** An order under this section–
(a) may provide that such provisions of this Part as may be specified are to apply in relation to the administration of insurers in accordance with the order with such modifications as may be specified; and
(b) requires the consent of the Secretary of State.

**360(3) ["Specified"] "Specified"** means specified in the order.

## 361 Administrator's duty to report to Authority

**361(1) [Duty of Administrator]** If–
(a) an administration order is in force in relation to a company or partnership by virtue of a petition presented by a person other than the Authority, and
(b) it appears to the administrator that the company or partnership is carrying on, or has carried on, a regulated activity in contravention of the general prohibition,

the administrator must report the matter to the Authority without delay.

**361(2) ["An administration order"] "An administration order"** means an administration order under Part II of the 1986 Act (or Part III of the 1989 Order).

## 362 Authority's powers to participate in proceedings

**362(1) [Application of section]** This section applies if a person other than the Authority presents a petition to the court under section 9 of the 1986 Act (or Article 22 of the 1989 Order) in relation to a company or partnership which–
(a) is, or has been, an authorised person;
(b) is, or has been, an appointed representative; or
(c) is carrying on, or has carried on, a regulated activity in contravention of the general prohibition.

**362(2) [Authority's right of audience]** The Authority is entitled to be heard–
(a) at the hearing of the petition; and
(b) at any other hearing of the court in relation to the company or partnership under Part II of the 1986 Act (or Part III of the 1989 Order).

**362(3) [Notices, etc.]** Any notice or other document required to be sent to a creditor of the company or partnership must also be sent to the Authority.

**362(4) [Applications under Insolvency Act 1986, s. 27, etc.]** The Authority may apply to the court under section 27 of the 1986 Act (or Article 39 of the 1989 Order); and on such an application, section 27(1)(a) (or Article 39(1)(a)) has effect with the omission of the words "(including at least himself)".

**362(5) [Attendance at meetings]** A person appointed for the purpose by the Authority is entitled–

(a) to attend any meeting of creditors of the company or partnership summoned under any enactment;

(b) to attend any meeting of a committee established under section 26 of the 1986 Act (or Article 38 of the 1989 Order); and

(c) to make representations as to any matter for decision at such a meeting.

**362(6) [Applications under Companies Act 1985, s. 425, etc.]** If, during the course of the administration of a company, a compromise or arrangement is proposed between the company and its creditors, or any class of them, the Authority may apply to the court under section 425 of the Companies Act 1985 (or Article 418 of the Companies (Northern Ireland) Order 1986).

RECEIVERSHIP

# 363 Authority's powers to participate in proceedings

**363(1) [Application of section]** This section applies if a receiver has been appointed in relation to a company which–

(a) is, or has been, an authorised person;

(b) is, or has been, an appointed representative; or

(c) is carrying on, or has carried on, a regulated activity in contravention of the general prohibition.

**363(2) [Authority's right of audience]** The Authority is entitled to be heard on an application made under section 35 or 63 of the 1986 Act (or Article 45 of the 1989 Order).

**363(3) [Applications to court]** The Authority is entitled to make an application under section 41(1)(a) or 69(1)(a) of the 1986 Act (or Article 51(1)(a) of the 1989 Order).

**363(4) [Reports]** A report under section 48(1) or 67(1) of the 1986 Act (or Article 58(1) of the 1989 Order) must be sent by the person making it to the Authority.

**363(5) [Attendance at meetings]** A person appointed for the purpose by the Authority is entitled–

(a) to attend any meeting of creditors of the company summoned under any enactment;

(b) to attend any meeting of a committee established under section 49 or 68 of the 1986 Act (or Article 59 of the 1989 Order); and

(c) to make representations as to any matter for decision at such a meeting.

# 364 Receiver's duty to report to Authority

**364** If–

(a) a receiver has been appointed in relation to a company, and

(b) it appears to the receiver that the company is carrying on, or has carried on, a regulated activity in contravention of the general prohibition,

the receiver must report the matter to the Authority without delay.

VOLUNTARY WINDING UP

# 365 Authority's powers to participate in proceedings

**365(1) [Application of section]** This section applies in relation to a company which–

(a) is being wound up voluntarily;

(b) is an authorised person; and

(c) is not an insurer effecting or carrying out contracts of long-term insurance.

**365(2) [Applications to court under Insolvency Act 1986, s. 112]** The Authority may apply to the court under section 112 of the 1986 Act (or Article 98 of the 1989 Order) in respect of the company.

**365(3) [Authority's right of audience]** The Authority is entitled to be heard at any hearing of the court in relation to the voluntary winding up of the company.

**365(4) [Notices, etc.]** Any notice or other document required to be sent to a creditor of the company must also be sent to the Authority.

**365(5) [Attendance at meetings]** A person appointed for the purpose by the Authority is entitled–

(a) to attend any meeting of creditors of the company summoned under any enactment;

(b) to attend any meeting of a committee established under section 101 of the 1986 Act (or Article 87 of the 1989 Order); and

(c) to make representations as to any matter for decision at such a meeting.

**365(6) [Voluntary winding-up of company]** The voluntary winding up of the company does not bar the right of the Authority to have it wound up by the court.

**365(7) [Applications under Companies Act 1985, s. 425, etc.]** If, during the course of the winding up of the company, a compromise or arrangement is proposed between the company and its creditors, or any class of them, the Authority may apply to the court under section 425 of the Companies Act 1985 (or Article 418 of the Companies (Northern Ireland) Order 1986).

## 366 Insurers effecting or carrying out long-term contracts or insurance

**366(1) [Voluntary winding-up]** An insurer effecting or carrying out contracts of long-term insurance may not be be wound up voluntarily without the consent of the Authority.

**366(2) [Notice of general meeting]** If notice of a general meeting of such an insurer is given, specifying the intention to propose a resolution for voluntary winding up of the insurer, a director of the insurer must notify the Authority as soon as practicable after he becomes aware of it.

**366(3) [Offence, penalty]** A person who fails to comply with subsection (2) is guilty of an offence and liable on summary conviction to a fine not exceeding level 5 on the standard scale.

**366(4) [Non-application of provisions]** The following provisions do not apply in relation to a winding-up resolution–

(a) sections 378(3) and 381A of the Companies Act 1985 ("the 1985 Act"); and

(b) Articles 386(3) and 389A of the Companies (Northern Ireland) Order 1986 ("the 1986 Order").

**366(5) [Copies of winding-up resolutions]** A copy of a winding-up resolution forwarded to the registrar of companies in accordance with section 380 of the 1985 Act (or Article 388 of the 1986 Order) must be accompanied by a certificate issued by the Authority stating that it consents to the voluntary winding up of the insurer.

**366(6) [Compliance with s. 366(5)]** If subsection (5) is complied with, the voluntary winding up is to be treated as having commenced at the time the resolution was passed.

**366(7) [Non-compliance with s. 366(5)]** If subsection (5) is not complied with, the resolution has no effect.

**366(8) ["Winding-up resolution"] "Winding-up resolution"** means a resolution for voluntary winding up of an insurer effecting or carrying out contracts of long-term insurance.

WINDING UP BY THE COURT

## 367 Winding-up petitions

**367(1) [Power of Authority re petition for winding-up]** The Authority may present a petition to the court for the winding up of a body which–

(a) is, or has been, an authorised person;

(b) is, or has been, an appointed representative; or

(c) is carrying on, or has carried on, a regulated activity in contravention of the general prohibition.

**367(2) ["Body"]** In subsection (1) **"body"** includes any partnership.

**367(3) [Power of court]** On such a petition, the court may wind up the body if–

(a) the body is unable to pay its debts within the meaning of section 123 or 221 of the 1986 Act (or Article 103 or 185 of the 1989 Order); or

(b) the court is of the opinion that it is just and equitable that it should be wound up.

**367(4) [Body in default of obligation under agreement]** If a body is in default on an obligation to pay a sum due and payable under an agreement, it is to be treated for the purpose of subsection (3)(a) as unable to pay its debts.

**367(5) ["Agreement"] "Agreement"** means an agreement the making or performance of which constitutes or is part of a regulated activity carried on by the body concerned.

**367(6) [Application of s. 367(7)]** Subsection (7) applies if a petition is presented under subsection (1) for the winding up of a partnership–

(a) on the ground mentioned in subsection (3)(b); or

(b) in Scotland, on a ground mentioned in subsection (3)(a) or (b).

**367(7) [Jurisdiction of court]** The court has jurisdiction, and the 1986 Act (or the 1989 Order) has effect, as if the partnership were an unregistered company as defined by section 220 of that Act (or Article 184 of that Order).

## 368 Winding-up petitions: EEA and Treaty firms

**368** The Authority may not present a petition to the court under section 367 for the winding up of–

(a) an EEA firm which qualifies for authorisation under Schedule 3, or

(b) a Treaty firm which qualifies for authorisation under Schedule 4,

unless it has been asked to do so by the home state regulator of the firm concerned.

## 369 Insurers: service of petition etc. on Authority

**369(1) [Petition for winding-up – persons other than Authority]** If a person other than the Authority presents a petition for the winding up of an authorised person with permission to effect or carry out contracts of insurance, the petitioner must serve a copy of the petition on the Authority.

**369(2) [Appointment of liquidator – persons other than Authority]** If a person other than the Authority applies to have a provisional liquidator appointed under section 135 of the 1986 Act (or Article 115 of the 1989 Order) in respect of an authorised person with permission to effect or carry out contracts of insurance, the applicant must serve a copy of the application on the Authority.

## 370 Liquidator's duty to report to Authority

**370** If–

(a) a company is being wound up voluntarily or a body is being wound up on a petition presented by a person other than the Authority, and

(b) it appears to the liquidator that the company or body is carrying on, or has carried on, a regulated activity in contravention of the general prohibition, the liquidator must report the matter to the Authority without delay.

# 371 Authority's powers to participate in proceedings

**371(1) [Application of section]** This section applies if a person other than the Authority presents a petition for the winding up of a body which–

(a) is, or has been, an authorised person;

(b) is, or has been, an appointed representative; or

(c) is carrying on, or has carried on, a regulated activity in contravention of the general prohibition.

**371(2) [Authority's right of audience]** The Authority is entitled to be heard–

(a) at the hearing of the petition; and

(b) at any other hearing of the court in relation to the body under or by virtue of Part IV or V of the 1986 Act (or Part V or VI of the 1989 Order).

**371(3) [Notice, etc.]** Any notice or other document required to be sent to a creditor of the body must also be sent to the Authority.

**371(4) [Attendance at meetings]** A person appointed for the purpose by the Authority is entitled–

(a) to attend any meeting of creditors of the body;

(b) to attend any meeting of a committee established for the purposes of Part IV or V of the 1986 Act under section 101 of that Act or under section 141 or 142 of that Act;

(c) to attend any meeting of a committee established for the purposes of Part V or VI of the 1989 Order under Article 87 of that Order or under Article 120 of that Order; and

(d) to make representations as to any matter for decision at such a meeting.

**371(5) [Applications under Companies Act 1985, s. 425, etc.]** If, during the course of the winding up of a company, a compromise or arrangement is proposed between the company and its creditors, or any class of them, the Authority may apply to the court under section 425 of the Companies Act 1985 (or Article 418 of the Companies (Northern Ireland) Order 1986).

## BANKRUPTCY

# 372 Petitions

**372(1) [Power of Authority]** The Authority may present a petition to the court–

(a) under section 264 of the 1986 Act (or Article 238 of the 1989 Order) for a bankruptcy order to be made against an individual; or

(b) under section 5 of the 1985 Act for the sequestration of the estate of an individual.

**372(2) [Grounds for presentation of petition]** But such a petition may be presented only on the ground that–

(a) the individual appears to be unable to pay a regulated activity debt; or

(b) the individual appears to have no reasonable prospect of being able to pay a regulated activity debt.

**372(3) [Companies in default of obligation under agreement]** An individual appears to be unable to pay a regulated activity debt if he is in default on an obligation to pay a sum due and payable under an agreement.

**372(4) [Ability to pay regulated activity debt]** An individual appears to have no reasonable prospect of being able to pay a regulated activity debt if–

(a) the Authority has served on him a demand requiring him to establish to the satisfaction of the Authority that there is a reasonable prospect that he will be able to pay a sum payable under an agreement when it falls due;

(b) at least three weeks have elapsed since the demand was served; and

(c) the demand has been neither complied with nor set aside in accordance with rules.

**372(5) [Demands made under s. 372(4)(a)]** A demand made under subsection (4)(a) is to be treated for the purposes of the 1986 Act (or the 1989 Order) as if it were a statutory demand under section 268 of that Act (or Article 242 of that Order).

**372(6) [S. 372(1)(b) petitions]** For the purposes of a petition presented in accordance with subsection (1)(b)–

(a) the Authority is to be treated as a qualified creditor; and

(b) a ground mentioned in subsection (2) constitutes apparent insolvency.

**372(7) ["Individual"] "Individual"** means an individual–

(a) who is, or has been, an authorised person; or

(b) who is carrying on, or has carried on, a regulated activity in contravention of the general prohibition.

**372(8) ["Agreement"] "Agreement"** means an agreement the making or performance of which constitutes or is part of a regulated activity carried on by the individual concerned.

**372(9) ["Rules"] "Rules"** means–

(a) in England and Wales, rules made under section 412 of the 1986 Act;

(b) in Scotland, rules made by order by the Treasury, after consultation with the Scottish Ministers, for the purposes of this section; and

(c) in Northern Ireland, rules made under Article 359 of the 1989 Order.

# 373 Insolvency practitioner's duty to report to Authority

**373(1) [Duty of insolvency practitioner]** If–

(a) a bankruptcy order or sequestration award is in force in relation to an individual by virtue of a petition presented by a person other than the Authority, and

(b) it appears to the insolvency practitioner that the individual is carrying on, or has carried on, a regulated activity in contravention of the general prohibition,

the insolvency practitioner must report the matter to the Authority without delay.

**373(2) ["Bankruptcy order"] "Bankruptcy order"** means a bankruptcy order under Part IX of the 1986 Act (or Part IX of the 1989 Order).

**373(3) ["Sequestration award"] "Sequestration award"** means an award of sequestration under section 12 of the 1985 Act.

**373(4) ["Individual"] "Individual"** includes an entity mentioned in section 374(1)(c).

# 374 Authority's powers to participate in proceedings

**374(1) [Application of section]** This section applies if a person other than the Authority presents a petition to the court–

(a) under section 264 of the 1986 Act (or Article 238 of the 1989 Order) for a bankruptcy order to be made against an individual;

(b) under section 5 of the 1985 Act for the sequestration of the estate of an individual; or

(c) under section 6 of the 1985 Act for the sequestration of the estate belonging to or held for or jointly by the members of an entity mentioned in subsection (1) of that section.

**374(2) [Authority's right of audience]** The Authority is entitled to be heard–

(a) at the hearing of the petition; and

(b) at any other hearing in relation to the individual or entity under–
 (i) Part IX of the 1986 Act;
 (ii) Part IX of the 1989 Order; or
 (iii) the 1985 Act.

**374(3) [Insolvency Act 1986, s. 274, etc. report – copy to Authority]** A copy of the report prepared under section 274 of the 1986 Act (or Article 248 of the 1989 Order) must also be sent to the Authority.

**374(4) [Attendance at meetings]** A person appointed for the purpose by the Authority is entitled–

(a) to attend any meeting of creditors of the individual or entity;

(b) to attend any meeting of a committee established under section 301 of the 1986 Act (or Article 274 of the 1989 Order);

(c) to attend any meeting of commissioners held under paragraph 17 or 18 of Schedule 6 to the 1985 Act; and

(d) to make representations as to any matter for decision at such a meeting.

**374(5) ["Individual"] "Individual"** means an individual who–

(a) is, or has been, an authorised person; or

(b) is carrying on, or has carried on, a regulated activity in contravention of the general prohibition.

**374(6) ["Entity"] "Entity"** means an entity which–

(a) is, or has been, an authorised person; or

(b) is carrying on, or has carried on, a regulated activity in contravention of the general prohibition.

PROVISIONS AGAINST DEBT AVOIDANCE

## 375 Authority's right to apply for an order

**375(1) [Insolvency Act 1986, s. 423, etc. – application]** The Authority may apply for an order under section 423 of the 1986 Act (or Article 367 of the 1989 Order) in relation to a debtor if–

(a) at the time the transaction at an undervalue was entered into, the debtor was carrying on a regulated activity (whether or not in contravention of the general prohibition); and

(b) a victim of the transaction is or was party to an agreement entered into with the debtor, the making or performance of which constituted or was part of a regulated activity carried on by the debtor.

**375(2) [Treatment of s. 375(1)(b) applications]** An application made under this section is to be treated as made on behalf of every victim of the transaction to whom subsection (1)(b) applies.

**375(3) [Interpretation]** Expressions which are given a meaning in Part XVI of the 1986 Act (or Article 367, 368 or 369 of the 1989 Order) have the same meaning when used in this section.

SUPPLEMENTAL PROVISIONS CONCERNING INSURERS

## 376 Continuation of contracts of long-term insurance where insurer in liquidation

**376(1) [Application of section]** This section applies in relation to the winding up of an insurer which effects or carries out contracts of long-term insurance.

**376(2) [Duty of liquidator]** Unless the court otherwise orders, the liquidator must carry on the insurer's business so far as it consists of carrying out the insurer's contracts of long-term insurance with a view to its being transferred as a going concern to a person who may lawfully carry out those contracts.

**376(3) [Duty of liquidator – carrying on the business]** In carrying on the business, the liquidator–

(a) may agree to the variation of any contracts of insurance in existence when the winding up order is made; but

(b) must not effect any new contracts of insurance.

**376(4) [Appointment of special manager]** If the liquidator is satisfied that the interests of the creditors in respect of liabilities of the insurer attributable to contracts of long-term insurance effected by it require the appointment of a special manager, he may apply to the court.

**376(5) [Power of court]** On such an application, the court may appoint a special manager to act during such time as the court may direct.

**376(6) [Powers of special manager]** The special manager is to have such powers, including any of the powers of a receiver or manager, as the court may direct.

**376(7) [Application of Insolvency Act 1986, s. 177(5), etc.]** Section 177(5) of the 1986 Act (or Article 151(5) of the 1989 Order) applies to a special manager appointed under subsection (5) as it applies to a special manager appointed under section 177 of the 1986 Act (or Article 151 of the 1989 Order).

**376(8) [Company contracts – reduction of value]** If the court thinks fit, it may reduce the value of one or more of the contracts of long-term insurance effected by the insurer.

**376(9) [Terms, etc. of reduction]** Any reduction is to be on such terms and subject to such conditions (if any) as the court thinks fit.

**376(10) [Appointment of independent actuary]** The court may, on the application of an official, appoint an independent actuary to investigate the insurer's business so far as it consists of carrying out its contracts of long-term insurance and to report to the official–

(a) on the desirability or otherwise of that part of the insurer's business being continued; and

(b) on any reduction in the contracts of long-term insurance effected by the insurer that may be necessary for successful continuation of that part of the insurer's business.

**376(11) ["Official"] "Official"** means–

(a) the liquidator;

(b) a special manager appointed under subsection (5); or

(c) the Authority.

**376(12) [Applications by liquidator]** The liquidator may make an application in the name of the insurer and on its behalf under Part VII without obtaining the permission that would otherwise be required by section 167 of, and Schedule 4 to, the 1986 Act (or Article 142 of, and Schedule 2 to, the 1989 Order).

## 377 Reducing the value of contracts instead of winding up

**377(1) [Application of section]** This section applies in relation to an insurer which has been proved to be unable to pay its debts.

**377(2) [Power of court]** If the court thinks fit, it may reduce the value of one or more of the insurer's contracts instead of making a winding up order.

**377(3) [Terms, etc. of reduction]** Any reduction is to be on such terms and subject to such conditions (if any) as the court thinks fit.

## 378 Treatment of assets on winding up

**378(1) [Power of Treasury to make regulations]** The Treasury may by regulations provide for the treatment of the assets of an insurer on its winding up.

**378(2) [Content of regulations]** The regulations may, in particular, provide for–

(a) assets representing a particular part of the insurer's business to be available only for meeting liabilities attributable to that part of the insurer's business;

(b) separate general meetings of the creditors to be held in respect of liabilities attributable to a particular part of the insurer's business.

## 379 Winding-up rules

**379(1) [Content]** Winding-up rules may include provision–

(a) for determining the amount of the liabilities of an insurer to policyholders of any class or description for the purpose of proof in a winding up; and

(b) generally for carrying into effect the provisions of this Part with respect to the winding up of insurers.

**379(2) [Further contents]** Winding-up rules may, in particular, make provision for all or any of the following matters–

(a) the identification of assets and liabilities;

(b) the apportionment, between assets of different classes or descriptions, of–

(i) the costs, charges and expenses of the winding up; and

(ii) any debts of the insurer of a specified class or description;

(c) the determination of the amount of liabilities of a specified description;

(d) the application of assets for meeting liabilities of a specified description;

(e) the application of assets representing any excess of a specified description.

**379(3) ["Specified"] "Specified"** means specified in winding-up rules.

**379(4) ["Winding-up rules"] "Winding-up rules"** means rules made under section 411 of the 1986 Act (or Article 359 of the 1989 Order).

**379(5) [Winding-up rules under Insolvency Act 1986, etc.]** Nothing in this section affects the power to make winding-up rules under the 1986 Act or the 1989 Order.

# PART XXV – INJUNCTIONS AND RESTITUTION

## INJUNCTIONS

### 380 Injunctions

**380(1) [Restraining order]** If, on the application of the Authority or the Secretary of State, the court is satisfied–

(a) that there is a reasonable likelihood that any person will contravene a relevant requirement, or

(b) that any person has contravened a relevant requirement and that there is a reasonable likelihood that the contravention will continue or be repeated,

the court may make an order restraining (or in Scotland an interdict prohibiting) the contravention.

**380(2) [Remedying contravention]** If on the application of the Authority or the Secretary of State the court is satisfied–

(a) that any person has contravened a relevant requirement, and

(b) that there are steps which could be taken for remedying the contravention,

the court may make an order requiring that person, and any other person who appears to have been knowingly concerned in the contravention, to take such steps as the court may direct to remedy it.

**380(3) [Disposal, etc. of assets]** If, on the application of the Authority or the Secretary of State, the court is satisfied that any person may have–

(a) contravened a relevant requirement, or

(b) been knowingly concerned in the contravention of such a requirement,

it may make an order restraining (or in Scotland an interdict prohibiting) him from disposing of, or otherwise dealing with, any assets of his which it is satisfied he is reasonably likely to dispose of or otherwise deal with.

**380(4) [Jurisdiction]** The jurisdiction conferred by this section is exercisable by the High Court and the Court of Session.

**380(5) [Mitigating effect of contravention]** In subsection (2), references to remedying a contravention include references to mitigating its effect.

**380(6) ["Relevant requirement"] "Relevant requirement"**–

(a) in relation to an application by the Authority, means a requirement–

(i) which is imposed by or under this Act; or

(ii) which is imposed by or under any other Act and whose contravention constitutes an offence which the Authority has power to prosecute under this Act;

(b) in relation to an application by the Secretary of State, means a requirement which is imposed by or under this Act and whose contravention constitutes an offence which the Secretary of State has power to prosecute under this Act.

**380(7) [Application of s. 380(6) to Scotland]** In the application of subsection (6) to Scotland–

(a) in paragraph (a)(ii) for "which the Authority has power to prosecute under this Act" substitute "mentioned in paragraph (a) or (b) of section 402(1)"; and

(b) in paragraph (b) omit "which the Secretary of State has power to prosecute under this Act".

## 381 Injunctions in cases of market abuse

**381(1) [Restraining order]** If, on the application of the Authority, the court is satisfied–

(a) that there is a reasonable likelihood that any person will engage in market abuse, or

(b) that any person is or has engaged in market abuse and that there is a reasonable likelihood that the market abuse will continue or be repeated,

the court may make an order restraining (or in Scotland an interdict prohibiting) the market abuse.

**381(2) [Remedying market abuse]** If on the application of the Authority the court is satisfied–

(a) that any person is or has engaged in market abuse, and

(b) that there are steps which could be taken for remedying the market abuse,

the court may make an order requiring him to take such steps as the court may direct to remedy it.

**381(3) [Application of s. 381(4)]** Subsection (4) applies if, on the application of the Authority, the court is satisfied that any person–

(a) may be engaged in market abuse; or

(b) may have been engaged in market abuse.

**381(4) [Disposal, etc. of assets]** The court make an order restraining (or in Scotland an interdict prohibiting) the person concerned from disposing of, or otherwise dealing with, any assets of his which it is satisfied that he is reasonably likely to dispose of, or otherwise deal with.

**381(5) [Jurisdiction]** The jurisdiction conferred by this section is exercisable by the High Court and the Court of Session.

**381(6) [Mitigating effect of market abuse]** In subsection (2), references to remedying any market abuse include references to mitigating its effect.

### RESTITUTION ORDERS

## 382 Restitution orders

**382(1) [Power of court]** The court may, on the application of the Authority or the Secretary of State, make an order under subsection (2) if it is satisfied that a person has contravened a relevant requirement, or been knowingly concerned in the contravention of such a requirement, and–

(a) that profits have accrued to him as a result of the contravention; or

(b) that one or more persons have suffered loss or been otherwise adversely affected as a result of the contravention.

**382(2) [Payments to Authority]** The court may order the person concerned to pay to the Authority such sum as appears to the court to be just having regard–

(a) in a case within paragraph (a) of subsection (1), to the profits appearing to the court to have accrued;

(b) in a case within paragraph (b) of that subsection, to the extent of the loss or other adverse effect;

(c) in a case within both of those paragraphs, to the profits appearing to the court to have accrued and to the extent of the loss or other adverse effect.

 [The next page is 106,351] 

**382(3) [Duty of Authority to distribute payment]** Any amount paid to the Authority in pursuance of an order under subsection (2) must be paid by it to such qualifying person or distributed by it among such qualifying persons as the court may direct.

**382(4) [Supply of accounts, etc.]** On an application under subsection (1) the court may require the person concerned to supply it with such accounts or other information as it may require for any one or more of the following purposes–

(a) establishing whether any and, if so, what profits have accrued to him as mentioned in paragraph (a) of that subsection;

(b) establishing whether any person or persons have suffered any loss or adverse effect as mentioned in paragraph (b) of that subsection and, if so, the extent of that loss or adverse effect; and

(c) determining how any amounts are to be paid or distributed under subsection (3).

**382(5) [Verification of accounts, etc.]** The court may require any accounts or other information supplied under subsection (4) to be verified in such manner as it may direct.

**382(6) [Jurisdiction]** The jurisdiction conferred by this section is exercisable by the High Court and the Court of Session.

**382(7) [Rights of others to bring proceedings]** Nothing in this section affects the right of any person other than the Authority or the Secretary of State to bring proceedings in respect of the matters to which this section applies.

**382(8) ["Qualifying person"] "Qualifying person"** means a person appearing to the court to be someone–

(a) to whom the profits mentioned in subsection (1)(a) are attributable; or

(b) who has suffered the loss or adverse effect mentioned in subsection (1)(b).

**382(9) ["Relevant requirement"] "Relevant requirement"**–

(a) in relation to an application by the Authority, means a requirement–

(i) which is imposed by or under this Act; or

(ii) which is imposed by or under any other Act and whose contravention constitutes an offence which the Authority has power to prosecute under this Act;

(b) in relation to an application by the Secretary of State, means a requirement which is imposed by or under this Act and whose contravention constitutes an offence which the Secretary of State has power to prosecute under this Act.

**382(10) [Application of s. 382(9) to Scotland]** In the application of subsection (9) to Scotland–

(a) in paragraph (a)(ii) for "which the Authority has power to prosecute under this Act" substitute "mentioned in paragraph (a) or (b) of section 402(1)"; and

(b) in paragraph (b) omit "which the Secretary of State has power to prosecute under this Act".

## 383 Restitution orders in cases of market abuse

**383(1) [Power of court]** The court may, on the application of the Authority, make an order under subsection (4) if it is satisfied that a person ("the person concerned")–

(a) has engaged in market abuse, or

(b) by taking or refraining from taking any action has required or encouraged another person or persons to engage in behaviour which, if engaged in by the person concerned, would amount to market abuse,

and the condition mentioned in subsection (2) is fulfilled.

**383(2) [Condition]** The condition is–

(a) that profits have accrued to the person concerned as a result; or

(b) that one or more persons have suffered loss or been otherwise adversely affected as a result.

**383(3) [Defence]** But the court may not make an order under subsection (4) if it is satisfied that–

(a) the person concerned believed, on reasonable grounds, that his behaviour did not fall within paragraph (a) or (b) of subsection (1); or

(b) he took all reasonable precautions and exercised all due diligence to avoid behaving in a way which fell within paragraph (a) or (b) of subsection (1).

**383(4) [Order to make payment to Authority]** The court may order the person concerned to pay to the Authority such sum as appears to the court to be just having regard–

(a) in a case within paragraph (a) of subsection (2), to the profits appearing to the court to have accrued;

(b) in a case within paragraph (b) of that subsection, to the extent of the loss or other adverse effect;

(c) in a case within both of those paragraphs, to the profits appearing to the court to have accrued and to the extent of the loss or other adverse effect.

**383(5) [Duty of Authority to distribute payment]** Any amount paid to the Authority in pursuance of an order under subsection (4) must be paid by it to such qualifying person or distributed by it among such qualifying persons as the court may direct.

**383(6) [Supply of accounts, etc.]** On an application under subsection (1) the court may require the person concerned to supply it with such accounts or other information as it may require for any one or more of the following purposes–

(a) establishing whether any and, if so, what profits have accrued to him as mentioned in subsection (2)(a);

(b) establishing whether any person or persons have suffered any loss or adverse effect as mentioned in subsection (2)(b) and, if so, the extent of that loss or adverse effect; and

(c) determining how any amounts are to be paid or distributed under subsection (5).

**383(7) [Verification of accounts, etc.]** The court may require any accounts or other information supplied under subsection (6) to be verified in such manner as it may direct.

**383(8) [Jurisdiction]** The jurisdiction conferred by this section is exercisable by the High Court and the Court of Session.

**383(9) [Rights of others to bring proceedings]** Nothing in this section affects the right of any person other than the Authority to bring proceedings in respect of the matters to which this section applies.

**383(10) ["Qualifying person"] "Qualifying person"** means a person appearing to the court to be someone–

(a) to whom the profits mentioned in paragraph (a) of subsection (2) are attributable; or
(b) who has suffered the loss or adverse effect mentioned in paragraph (b) of that subsection.

RESTITUTION REQUIRED BY AUTHORITY

## 384 Power of Authority to require restitution

**384(1) [Power of Authority]** The Authority may exercise the power in subsection (5) if it is satisfied that an authorised person ("the person concerned") has contravened a relevant requirement, or been knowingly concerned in the contravention of such a requirement, and–

(a) that profits have accrued to him as a result of the contravention; or

(b) that one or more persons have suffered loss or been otherwise adversely affected as a result of the contravention.

**384(2) [Power of Authority – market abuse]** The Authority may exercise the power in subsection (5) if it is satisfied that a person ("the person concerned")–

(a) has engaged in market abuse, or

(b) by taking or refraining from taking any action has required or encouraged another person or persons to engage in behaviour which, if engaged in by the person concerned, would amount to market abuse,

and the condition mentioned in subsection (3) is fulfilled,

**384(3) [Condition]** The condition is–

(a) that profits have accrued to the person concerned as a result of the market abuse; or

(b) that one or more persons have suffered loss or been otherwise adversely affected as a result of the market abuse.

**384(4) [Limitation of Authority's power]** But the Authority may not exercise that power as a result of subsection (2) if, having considered any representations made to it in response to a warning notice, there are reasonable grounds for it to be satisfied that–

(a) the person concerned believed, on reasonable grounds, that his behaviour did not fall within paragraph (a) or (b) of that subsection; or

(b) he took all reasonable precautions and exercised all due diligence to avoid behaving in a way which fell within paragraph (a) or (b) of that subsection.

**384(5) [S. 384(1) and (2) – power to require payment]** The power referred to in subsections (1) and (2) is a power to require the person concerned, in accordance with such arrangements as the Authority considers appropriate, to pay to the appropriate person or distribute among the appropriate persons such amount as appears to the Authority to be just having regard–

(a) in a case within paragraph (a) of subsection (1) or (3), to the profits appearing to the Authority to have accrued;

(b) in a case within paragraph (b) of subsection (1) or (3), to the extent of the loss or other adverse effect;

(c) in a case within paragraphs (a) and (b) of subsection (1) or (3), to the profits appearing to the Authority to have accrued and to the extent of the loss or other adverse effect.

**384(6) ["Appropriate person"] "Appropriate person"** means a person appearing to the Authority to be someone–

(a) to whom the profits mentioned in paragraph (a) of subsection (1) or (3) are attributable; or

(b) who has suffered the loss or adverse effect mentioned in paragraph (b) of subsection (1) or (3).

**384(7) ["Relevant requirement"] "Relevant requirement"** means–

(a) a requirement imposed by or under this Act; and

(b) a requirement which is imposed by or under any other Act and whose contravention constitutes an offence in relation to which this Act confers power to prosecute on the Authority.

**384(8) [Application of s. 384(7) to Scotland]** In the application of subsection (7) to Scotland, in paragraph (b) for "in relation to which this Act confers power to prosecute on the Authority" substitute "mentioned in paragraph (a) or (b) of section 402(1)".

## 385 Warning notices

**385(1) [Exercise of s. 384(5) power]** If the Authority proposes to exercise the power under section 384(5) in relation to a person, it must give him a warning notice.

**385(2) [Specification of amount]** A warning notice under this section must specify the amount which the Authority proposes to require the person concerned to pay or distribute as mentioned in section 384(5).

## 386 Decision notices

**386(1) [Exercise of s. 384(5) power]** If the Authority decides to exercise the power under section 384(5), it must give a decision notice to the person in relation to whom the power is exercised.

**386(2) [Contents of notice]** The decision notice must–

(a) state the amount that he is to pay or distribute as mentioned in section 384(5);

(b) identify the person or persons to whom that amount is to be paid or among whom that amount is to be distributed; and

(c) state the arrangements in accordance with which the payment or distribution is to be made.

**386(3) [Right of referral to Tribunal]** If the Authority decides to exercise the power under section 384(5), the person in relation to whom it is exercised may refer the matter to the Tribunal.

# PART XXVI – NOTICES

## WARNING NOTICES

## 387 Warning notices

**387(1) [Form, content of notice]** A warning notice must–

(a) state the action which the Authority proposes to take;

(b) be in writing;

(c) give reasons for the proposed action;

(d) state whether section 394 applies; and

(e) if that section applies, describe its effect and state whether any secondary material exists to which the person concerned must be allowed access under it.

**387(2) [Period for representations]** The warning notice must specify a reasonable period (which may not be less than 28 days) within which the person to whom it is given may make representations to the Authority.

**387(3) [Extension of representation period]** The Authority may extend the period specified in the notice.

**387(4) [Decision notice]** The Authority must then decide, within a reasonable period, whether to give the person concerned a decision notice.

## DECISION NOTICES

## 388 Decision notices

**388(1) [Form, content of notice]** A decision notice must–

(a) be in writing;

(b) give the Authority's reasons for the decision to take the action to which the notice relates;

(c) state whether section 394 applies;

(d) if that section applies, describe its effect and state whether any secondary material exists to which the person concerned must be allowed access under it; and

(e) give an indication of–

(i) any right to have the matter referred to the Tribunal which is given by this Act; and

(ii) the procedure on such a reference.

**388(2) [Decision notice preceded by warning notice]** If the decision notice was preceded by a warning notice, the action to which the decision notice relates must be action under the same Part as the action proposed in the warning notice.

**388(3) [Further decision notice]** The Authority may, before it takes the action to which a decision notice ("the original notice") relates, give the person concerned a further decision notice which relates to different action in respect of the same matter.

**388(4) [Further decision notice – consent]** The Authority may give a further decision notice as a result of subsection (3) only if the person to whom the original notice was given consents.

**388(5) [Right of referral to Tribunal]** If the person to whom a decision notice is given under subsection (3) had the right to refer the matter to which the original decision notice related to the Tribunal, he has that right as respects the decision notice under subsection (3).

CONCLUSION OF PROCEEDINGS

# 389 Notices of discontinuance

**389(1) [Duty of Authority]** If the Authority decides not to take–

(a) the action proposed in a warning notice, or

(b) the action to which a decision notice relates,

it must give a notice of discontinuance to the person to whom the warning notice or decision notice was given.

**389(2) [Non-application s. 389(1)]** But subsection (1) does not apply if the discontinuance of the proceedings concerned results in the granting of an application made by the person to whom the warning or decision notice was given.

**389(3) [Identification of proceedings]** A notice of discontinuance must identify the proceedings which are being discontinued.

# 390 Final notices

**390(1) [Duty of Authority – matter not referred to Tribunal]** If the Authority has given a person a decision notice and the matter was not referred to the Tribunal within the period mentioned in section 133(1), the Authority must, on taking the action to which the decision notice relates, give the person concerned and any person to whom the decision notice was copied a final notice.

**390(2) [Duty of Authority – matter referred to Tribunal]** If the Authority has given a person a decision notice and the matter was referred to the Tribunal, the Authority must, on taking action in accordance with any directions given by–

(a) the Tribunal, or

(b) the court under section 137,

give that person and any person to whom the decision notice was copied a final notice.

**390(3) [Content of final notice about statement]** A final notice about a statement must–

(a) set out the terms of the statement;

(b) give details of the manner in which, and the date on which, the statement will be published.

**390(4) [Content of final notice about order]** A final notice about an order must–

(a) set out the terms of the order;

(b) state the date from which the order has effect.

**390(5) [Content of final notice about penalty]** A final notice about a penalty must–

(a) state the amount of the penalty;

(b) state the manner in which, and the period within which, the penalty is to be paid;

(c) give details of the way in which the penalty will be recovered if it is not paid by the date stated in the notice.

**390(6) [Content of final notice about requirement]** A final notice about a requirement to make a payment or distribution in accordance with section 384(5) must state–

(a) the persons to whom,

(b) the manner in which, and

(c) the period within which,

it must be made.

**390(7) [Content of final notice in other cases]** In any other case, the final notice must–

(a) give details of the action being taken;

(b) state the date on which the action is to be taken.

**390(8) [S. 390(5)(b), (6)(c) time period]** The period stated under subsection (5)(b) or (6)(c) may not be less than 14 days beginning with the date on which the final notice is given.

**390(9) [Recovery as debt]** If all or any of the amount of a penalty payable under a final notice is outstanding at the end of the period stated under subsection (5)(b), the Authority may recover the outstanding amount as a debt due to it.

**390(10) [Injunction]** If all or any of a required payment or distribution has not been made at the end of a period stated in a final notice under subsection (6)(c), the obligation to make the payment is enforceable, on the application of the Authority, by injunction or, in Scotland, by an order under section 45 of the Court of Session Act 1988.

PUBLICATION

## 391 Publication

**391(1) [Prohibition against publication]** Neither the Authority nor a person to whom a warning notice or decision notice is given or copied may publish the notice or any details concerning it.

**391(2) [Notice of discontinuance – publication with consent]** A notice of discontinuance must state that, if the person to whom the notice is given consents, the Authority may publish such information as it considers appropriate about the matter to which the discontinued proceedings related.

**391(3) [Copy of notice of discontinuance]** A copy of a notice of discontinuance must be accompanied by a statement that, if the person to whom the notice is copied consents, the Authority may publish such information as it considers appropriate about the matter to which the discontinued proceedings related, so far as relevant to that person.

**391(4) [Final notice]** The Authority must publish such information about the matter to which a final notice relates as it considers appropriate.

**391(5) [Supervisory notice]** When a supervisory notice takes effect, the Authority must publish such information about the matter to which the notice relates as it considers appropriate.

**391(6) [Publication prejudicial]** But the Authority may not publish information under this section if publication of it would, in its opinion, be unfair to the person with respect to whom the action was taken or prejudicial to the interests of consumers.

**391(7) [Manner of publication]** Information is to be published under this section in such manner as the Authority considers appropriate.

**391(8) [Effective date of supervisory notice]** For the purposes of determining when a supervisory notice takes effect, a matter to which the notice relates is open to review if–

(a) the period during which any person may refer the matter to the Tribunal is still running;

(b) the matter has been referred to the Tribunal but has not been dealt with;

(c) the matter has been referred to the Tribunal and dealt with but the period during which an appeal may be brought against the Tribunal's decision is still running; or

(d) such an appeal has been brought but has not been determined.

**391(9) ["Notice of discontinuance"] "Notice of discontinuance"** means a notice given under section 389.

**391(10) ["Supervisory notice"] "Supervisory notice"** has the same meaning as in section 395.

**391(11) ["Consumers"] "Consumers"** means persons who are consumers for the purposes of section 138.

THIRD PARTY RIGHTS AND ACCESS TO EVIDENCE

## 392 Application of sections 393 and 394

**392** Sections 393 and 394 apply to–

(a) a warning notice given in accordance with section 54(1), 57(1), 63(3), 67(1), 88(4)(b), 89(2), 92(1), 126(1), 207(1), 255(1), 280(1), 331(1), 345(2) (whether as a result of subsection (1) of that section or section 249(1)) or 385(1);

(b) a decision notice given in accordance with section 54(2), 57(3), 63(4), 67(4), 88(6)(b), 89(3), 92(4), 127(1), 208(1), 255(2), 280(2), 331(3), 345(3) (whether as a result of subsection (1) of that section or section 249(1)) or 386(1).

## 393 Third party rights

**393(1) [Copy of warning notice]** If any of the reasons contained in a warning notice to which this section applies relates to a matter which–

(a) identifies a person ("the third party") other than the person to whom the notice is given, and

(b) in the opinion of the Authority, is prejudicial to the third party,

a copy of the notice must be given to the third party.

**393(2) [Exceptions to s. 393(1)]** Subsection (1) does not require a copy to be given to the third party if the Authority–

(a) has given him a separate warning notice in relation to the same matter; or

(b) gives him such a notice at the same time as it gives the warning notice which identifies him.

**393(3) [Period for representations]** The notice copied to a third party under subsection (1) must specify a reasonable period (which may not be less than 28 days) within which he may make representations to the Authority.

**393(4) [Copy of decision notice to third party]** If any of the reasons contained in a decision notice to which this section applies relates to a matter which–

(a) identifies a person ("the third party") other than the person to whom the decision notice is given, and

(b) in the opinion of the Authority, is prejudicial to the third party,

a copy of the notice must be given to the third party.

**393(5) [Decision notice preceded by warning notice]** If the decision notice was preceded by a warning notice, a copy of the decision notice must (unless it has been given under subsection (4)) be given to each person to whom the warning notice was copied.

**393(6) [S. 393(4) – exceptions]** Subsection (4) does not require a copy to be given to the third party if the Authority–

(a) has given him a separate decision notice in relation to the same matter; or

(b) gives him such a notice at the same time as it gives the decision notice which identifies him.

**393(7) [Copy of notice impracticable]** Neither subsection (1) nor subsection (4) requires a copy of a notice to be given to a third party if the Authority considers it impracticable to do so.

**393(8) [Application of s. 393(9)–(11)]** Subsections (9) to (11) apply if the person to whom a decision notice is given has a right to refer the matter to the Tribunal.

**393(9) [Right of referral to Tribunal]** A person to whom a copy of the notice is given under this section may refer to the Tribunal–

(a) the decision in question, so far as it is based on a reason of the kind mentioned in subsection (4); or

(b) any opinion expressed by the Authority in relation to him.

**393(10) [Procedure upon referral, etc.]** The copy must be accompanied by an indication of the third party's right to make a reference under subsection (9) and of the procedure on such a reference.

**393(11) [Right of referral to Tribunal – non-receipt of copy]** A person who alleges that a copy of the notice should have been given to him, but was not, may refer to the Tribunal the alleged failure and–

(a) the decision in question, so far as it is based on a reason of the kind mentioned in subsection (4); or

(b) any opinion expressed by the Authority in relation to him.

**393(12) [Application of s. 394]** Section 394 applies to a third party as it applies to the person to whom the notice to which this section applies was given, in so far as the material which the Authority must disclose under that section relates to the matter which identifies the third party.

**393(13) [Content of copy – effect of s. 394]** A copy of a notice given to a third party under this section must be accompanied by a description of the effect of section 394 as it applies to him.

**393(14) [Copy of notice of discontinuance]** Any person to whom a warning notice or decision notice was copied under this section must be given a copy of a notice of discontinuance applicable to the proceedings to which the warning notice or decision notice related.

## 394 Access to Authority material

**394(1) [Duty of Authority]** If the Authority gives a person ("A") a notice to which this section applies, it must–

(a) allow him access to the material on which it relied in taking the decision which gave rise to the obligation to give the notice;

(b) allow him access to any secondary material which, in the opinion of the Authority, might undermine that decision.

**394(2) [Excluded material, etc.]** But the Authority does not have to allow A access to material under subsection (1) if the material is excluded material or it–

(a) relates to a case involving a person other than A; and

(b) was taken into account by the Authority in A's case only for purposes of comparison with other cases.

**394(3) [Access not in public interest, etc.]** The Authority may refuse A access to particular material which it would otherwise have to allow him access to if, in its opinion, allowing him access to the material–

(a) would not be in the public interest; or

(b) would not be fair, having regard to–

   (i) the likely significance of the material to A in relation to the matter in respect of which he has been given a notice to which this section applies; and

   (ii) the potential prejudice to the commercial interests of a person other than A which would be caused by the material's disclosure.

**394(4) [Written notice – excluded material]** If the Authority does not allow A access to material because it is excluded material consisting of a protected item, it must give A written notice of–

(a) the existence of the protected item; and

(b) the Authority's decision not to allow him access to it.

**394(5) [Written notice – s. 394(3) refusal]** If the Authority refuses under subsection (3) to allow A access to material, it must give him written notice of–

(a) the refusal; and

(b) the reasons for it.

**394(6) ["Secondary material"] "Secondary material"** means material, other than material falling within paragraph (a) of subsection (1) which–

(a) was considered by the Authority in reaching the decision mentioned in that paragraph; or

(b) was obtained by the Authority in connection with the matter to which the notice to which this section applies relates but which was not considered by it in reaching that decision.

**394(7) ["Excluded material"] "Excluded material"** means material which–

(a) has been intercepted in obedience to a warrant issued under any enactment relating to the interception of communications;

(b) indicates that such a warrant has been issued or that material has been intercepted in obedience to such a warrant; or

(c) is a protected item (as defined in section 413).

THE AUTHORITY'S PROCEDURES

## 395 The Authority's procedures

**395(1) [Duty of Authority]** The Authority must determine the procedure that it proposes to follow in relation to the giving of–

(a) supervisory notices; and

(b) warning notices and decision notices.

**395(2) [Avoidance of conflict of duty]** That procedure must be designed to secure, among other things, that the decision which gives rise to the obligation to give any such notice is taken by a person not directly involved in establishing the evidence on which that decision is based.

**395(3) [S. 395(2) – exception]** But the procedure may permit a decision which gives rise to an obligation to give a supervisory notice to be taken by a person other than a person mentioned in subsection (2) if–

(a) the Authority considers that, in the particular case, it is necessary in order to protect the interests of consumers; and

(b) the person taking the decision is of a level of seniority laid down by the procedure.

**395(4) [S. 395(3)(b) – level of seniority]** A level of seniority laid down by the procedure for the purposes of subsection (3)(b) must be appropriate to the importance of the decision.

**395(5) [Statement of procedure]** The Authority must issue a statement of the procedure.

**395(6) [Effective publication]** The statement must be published in the way appearing to the Authority to be best calculated to bring it to the attention of the public.

**395(7) [Fees]** The Authority may charge a reasonable fee for providing a person with a copy of the statement.

**395(8) [Copy to Treasury]** The Authority must, without delay, give the Treasury a copy of any statement which it issues under this section.

**395(9) [Duty to follow stated procedure]** When giving a supervisory notice, or a warning notice or a decision notice, the Authority must follow its stated procedure.

**395(10) [Publication where procedure revised]** If the Authority changes the procedure in a material way, it must publish a revised statement.

**395(11) [Authority's failure to follow procedure]** The Authority's failure in a particular case to follow its procedure as set out in the latest published statement does not affect the validity of a notice given in that case.

**395(12) [Tribunal may take account of failure]** But subsection (11) does not prevent the Tribunal from taking into account any such failure in considering a matter referred to it.

**395(13) ["Supervisory notice"]** "Supervisory notice" means a notice given in accordance with section–

(a) 53(4), (7) or (8)(b);
(b) 78(2) or (5);
(c) 197(3), (6) or (7)(b);
(d) 259(3), (8) or (9)(b);
(e) 268(3), (7)(a) or (9)(a) (as a result of subsection (8)(b));
(f) 282(3), (6) or (7)(b);
(g) 321(2) or (5).

## 396 Statements under section 395: consultation

**396(1) [Duty of Authority – publication of draft]** Before issuing a statement of procedure under section 395, the Authority must publish a draft of the proposed statement in the way appearing to the Authority to be best calculated to bring it to the attention of the public.

**396(2) [Notice re representations]** The draft must be accompanied by notice that representations about the proposal may be made to the Authority within a specified time.

**396(3) [Regard to representations]** Before issuing the proposed statement of procedure, the Authority must have regard to any representations made to it in accordance with subsection (2).

**396(4) [Publication of representations, etc.]** If the Authority issues the proposed statement of procedure it must publish an account, in general terms, of–

(a) the representations made to it in accordance with subsection (2); and

(b) its response to them.

**396(5) [Publication of altered statement]** If the statement of procedure differs from the draft published under subsection (1) in a way which is, in the opinion of the Authority, significant, the Authority must (in addition to complying with subsection (4)) publish details of the difference.

**396(6) [Fees]** The Authority may charge a reasonable fee for providing a person with a copy of a draft published under subsection (1).

**396(7) [Application of section]** This section also applies to a proposal to revise a statement of policy.

# PART XXVII – OFFENCES

## MISCELLANEOUS OFFENCES

## 397 Misleading statements and practices

**397(1) [Application of subsection]** This subsection applies to a person who–

(a) makes a statement, promise or forecast which he knows to be misleading, false or deceptive in a material particular;

(b) dishonestly conceals any material facts whether in connection with a statement, promise or forecast made by him or otherwise; or

(c) recklessly makes (dishonestly or otherwise) a statement, promise or forecast which is misleading, false or deceptive in a material particular.

**397(2) [Offence]** A person to whom subsection (1) applies is guilty of an offence if he makes the statement, promise or forecast or conceals the facts for the purpose of inducing, or is reckless as to whether it may induce, another person (whether or not the person to whom the statement, promise or forecast is made)–

(a) to enter or offer to enter into, or to refrain from entering or offering to enter into, a relevant agreement; or

(b) to exercise, or refrain from exercising, any rights conferred by a relevant investment.

**397(3) [Offence]** Any person who does any act or engages in any course of conduct which creates a false or misleading impression as to the market in or the price or value of any relevant investments is guilty of an offence if he does so for the purpose of creating that impression and of thereby inducing another person to acquire, dispose of, subscribe for or underwrite those investments or to refrain from doing so or to exercise, or refrain from exercising, any rights conferred by those investments.

**397(4) [Defence – s. 397(2)]** In proceedings for an offence under subsection (2) brought against a person to whom subsection (1) applies as a result of paragraph (a) of that subsection, it is a defence for him to show that the statement, promise or forecast was made in conformity with price stabilising rules or control of information rules.

**397(5) [Defence – s. 397(3)]** In proceedings brought against any person for an offence under subsection (3) it is a defence for him to show–

(a) that he reasonably believed that his act or conduct would not create an impression that was false or misleading as to the matters mentioned in that subsection;

(b) that he acted or engaged in the conduct–

(i) for the purpose of stabilising the price of investments; and
(ii) in conformity with price stabilising rules; or

(c) that he acted or engaged in the conduct in conformity with control of information rules.

**397(6) [Non-application of s. 397(1), (2)]** Subsections (1) and (2) do not apply unless–

(a) the statement, promise or forecast is made in or from, or the facts are concealed in or from, the United Kingdom or arrangements are made in or from the United Kingdom for the statement, promise or forecast to be made or the facts to be concealed;

(b) the person on whom the inducement is intended to or may have effect is in the United Kingdom; or

(c) the agreement is or would be entered into or the rights are or would be exercised in the United Kingdom.

**397(7) [Non-application of s. 397(3)]** Subsection (3) does not apply unless–

(a) the act is done, or the course of conduct is engaged in, in the United Kingdom; or

(b) the false or misleading impression is created there.

**397(8) [Penalty]** A person guilty of an offence under this section is liable–

(a) on summary conviction, to imprisonment for a term not exceeding six months or a fine not exceeding the statutory maximum, or both;

(b) on conviction on indictment, to imprisonment for a term not exceeding seven years or a fine, or both.

**397(9) ["Relevant agreement"] "Relevant agreement"** means an agreement–

(a) the entering into or performance of which by either party constitutes an activity of a specified kind or one which falls within a specified class of activity; and

(b) which relates to a relevant investment.

**397(10) ["Relevant investment"] "Relevant investment"** means an investment of a specified kind or one which falls within a prescribed class of investment.

**397(11) [Application of Sch. 2]** Schedule 2 (except paragraphs 25 and 26) applies for the purposes of subsections (9) and (10) with references to section 22 being read as references to each of those subsections.

**397(12) [Non-limitation of s. 397(9) or (10) by Sch. 2]** Nothing in Schedule 2, as applied by subsection (11), limits the power conferred by subsection (9) or (10).

**397(13) ["Investment"] "Investment"** includes any asset, right or interest.

**397(14) ["Specified"] "Specified"** means specified in an order made by the Treasury.

## 398 Misleading the Authority: residual cases

**398(1) [Offence]** A person who, in purported compliance with any requirement imposed by or under this Act, knowingly or recklessly gives the Authority information which is false or misleading in a material particular is guilty of an offence.

**398(2) [Application of s. 398(1)]** Subsection (1) applies only to a requirement in relation to which no other provision of this Act creates an offence in connection with the giving of information.

**398(3) [Penalty]** A person guilty of an offence under this section is liable–

(a) on summary conviction, to a fine not exceeding the statutory maximum;

(b) on conviction on indictment, to a fine.

## 399 Misleading the Director General of Fair Trading

**399** Section 44 of the Competition Act 1998 (offences connected with the provision of false or misleading information) applies in relation to any function of the Director General of Fair Trading under this Act as if it were a function under Part I of that Act.

BODIES CORPORATE AND PARTNERSHIPS

## 400 Offences by bodies corporate etc

**400(1) [Offence – officer of body corporate]** If an offence under this Act committed by a body corporate is shown–

(a) to have been committed with the consent or connivance of an officer, or

(b) to be attributable to any neglect on his part,

the officer as well as the body corporate is guilty of the offence and liable to be proceeded against and punished accordingly.

**400(2) [Application of s. 400(1)]** If the affairs of a body corporate are managed by its members, subsection (1) applies in relation to the acts and defaults of a member in connection with his functions of management as if he were a director of the body.

**400(3) [Offence – partnerships]** If an offence under this Act committed by a partnership is shown–

(a) to have been committed with the consent or connivance of a partner, or

(b) to be attributable to any neglect on his part,

the partner as well as the partnership is guilty of the offence and liable to be proceeded against and punished accordingly.

**400(4) ["Partner"]** In subsection (3) **"partner"** includes a person purporting to act as a partner.

**400(5) ["Officer"] "Officer"**, in relation to a body corporate, means–

(a) a director, member of the committee of management, chief executive, manager, secretary or other similar officer of the body, or a person purporting to act in any such capacity; and

(b) an individual who is a controller of the body.

**400(6) [Offence – unincorporated association]** If an offence under this Act committed by an unincorporated association (other than a partnership) is shown–

(a) to have been committed with the consent or connivance of an officer of the association or a member of its governing body, or

(b) to be attributable to any neglect on the part of such an officer or member,

that officer or member as well as the association is guilty of the offence and liable to be proceeded against and punished accordingly.

**400(7) [Regulations re overseas corporations, etc.]** Regulations may provide for the application of any provision of this section, with such modifications as the Treasury consider appropriate, to a body corporate or unincorporated association formed or recognised under the law of a territory outside the United Kingdom.

INSTITUTION OF PROCEEDINGS

## 401 Proceedings for offences

**401(1) ["Offence"]** In this section **"offence"** means an offence under this Act or subordinate legislation made under this Act.

**401(2) [England and Wales]** Proceedings for an offence may be instituted in England and Wales only–

(a) by the Authority or the Secretary of State; or

(b) by or with the consent of the Director of Public Prosecutions.

**401(3) [Northern Ireland]** Proceedings for an offence may be instituted in Northern Ireland only–

(a) by the Authority or the Secretary of State; or

(b) by or with the consent of the Director of Public Prosecutions for Northern Ireland.

**401(4) [Proceedings for offences under s. 203]** Except in Scotland, proceedings for an offence under section 203 may also be instituted by the Director General of Fair Trading.

**401(5) [Conditions, etc. imposed by Treasury]** In exercising its power to institute proceedings for an offence, the Authority must comply with any conditions or restrictions imposed in writing by the Treasury.

**401(6) [Conditions, etc. imposed under s. 401(5)]** Conditions or restrictions may be imposed under subsection (5) in relation to–

(a) proceedings generally; or

(b) such proceedings, or categories of proceedings, as the Treasury may direct.

## 402 Power of the Authority to institute proceedings for certain other offences

**402(1) [Insider dealing, money laundering]** Except in Scotland, the Authority may institute proceedings for an offence under–

(a) Part V of the Criminal Justice Act 1993 (insider dealing); or

(b) prescribed regulations relating to money laundering.

**402(2) [Conditions, etc. imposed by Treasury]** In exercising its power to institute proceedings for any such offence, the Authority must comply with any conditions or restrictions imposed in writing by the Treasury.

**402(3) [Conditions, etc. imposed under s. 402(2)]** Conditions or restrictions may be imposed under subsection (2) in relation to–

(a) proceedings generally; or

(b) such proceedings, or categories of proceedings, as the Treasury may direct.

## 403 Jurisdiction and procedure in respect of offences

**403(1) [Unincorporated associations – fines]** A fine imposed on an unincorporated association on its conviction of an offence is to be paid out of the funds of the association.

**403(2) [Proceedings in name of association]** Proceedings for an offence alleged to have been committed by an unincorporated association must be brought in the name of the association (and not in that of any of its members).

**403(3) [Service of documents]** Rules of court relating to the service of documents are to have effect as if the association were a body corporate.

**403(4) [Proceedings]** In proceedings for an offence brought against an unincorporated association–

(a) section 33 of the Criminal Justice Act 1925 and Schedule 3 to the Magistrates' Courts Act 1980 (procedure) apply as they do in relation to a body corporate;

(b) section 70 of the Criminal Procedure (Scotland) Act 1995 (procedure) applies as if the association were a body corporate;

(c) section 18 of the Criminal Justice (Northern Ireland) Act 1945 and Schedule 4 to the Magistrates' (Courts Northern Ireland) Order 1981 (procedure) apply as they do in relation to a body corporate.

**403(5) [Summary proceedings]** Summary proceedings for an offence may be taken–

(a) against a body corporate or unincorporated association at any place at which it has a place of business;

(b) against an individual at any place where he is for the time being.

**403(6) [S. 403(5) – effect on other jurisdiction]** Subsection (5) does not affect any jurisdiction exercisable apart from this section.

**403(7) ["Offence"] "Offence"** means an offence under this Act.

# PART XXVIII – MISCELLANEOUS

SCHEMES FOR REVIEWING PAST BUSINESS

## 404 Schemes for reviewing past business

**404(1) [Application of s. 404(2)]** Subsection (2) applies if the Treasury are satisfied that there is evidence suggesting–

(a) that there has been a widespread or regular failure on the part of authorised persons to comply with rules relating to a particular kind of activity; and

(b) that, as a result, private persons have suffered (or will suffer) loss in respect of which authorised persons are (or will be) liable to make payments ("compensation payments").

**404(2) [Power of Treasury to make order]** The Treasury may by order ("a scheme order") authorise the Authority to establish and operate a scheme for–

(a) determining the nature and extent of the failure;

(b) establishing the liability of authorised persons to make compensation payments; and

(c) determining the amounts payable by way of compensation payments.

**404(3) [Compliance with specified requirements]** An authorised scheme must be made so as to comply with specified requirements.

**404(4) [Scheme order]** A scheme order may be made only if–

(a) the Authority has given the Treasury a report about the alleged failure and asked them to make a scheme order;

(b) the report contains details of the scheme which the Authority propose to make; and

(c) the Treasury are satisfied that the proposed scheme is an appropriate way of dealing with the failure.

**404(5) [Provisions of scheme order]** A scheme order may provide for specified provisions of or made under this Act to apply in relation to any provision of, or determination made under, the resulting authorised scheme subject to such modifications (if any) as may be specified.

**404(6) [Failure to comply with provision of authorised scheme]** For the purposes of this Act, failure on the part of an authorised person to comply with any provision of an authorised scheme is to be treated (subject to any provision made by the scheme order concerned) as a failure on his part to comply with rules.

**404(7) [Power of Treasury]** The Treasury may prescribe circumstances in which loss suffered by a person ("A") acting in a fiduciary or other prescribed capacity is to be treated, for the purposes of an authorised scheme, as suffered by a private person in relation to whom A was acting in that capacity.

**404(8) [Application of section]** This section applies whenever the failure in question occurred.

**404(9) ["Authorised scheme"] "Authorised scheme"** means a scheme authorised by a scheme order.

**404(10) ["Private person"] "Private person"** has such meaning as may be prescribed.

**404(11) ["Specified"] "Specified"** means specified in a scheme order.

THIRD COUNTRIES

## 405 Directions

**405(1) [Power of Treasury]** For the purpose of implementing a third country decision, the Treasury may direct the Authority to–

(a) refuse an application for permission under Part IV made by a body incorporated in, or formed under the law of, any part of the United Kingdom;

(b) defer its decision on such an application either indefinitely or for such period as may be specified in the direction;

(c) give a notice of objection to a person who has served a notice of control to the effect that he proposes to acquire a 50% stake in a UK authorised person; or

(d) give a notice of objection to a person who has acquired a 50% stake in a UK authorised person without having served the required notice of control.

**405(2) [Directions]** A direction may also be given in relation to–

(a) any person falling within a class specified in the direction;

(b) future applications, notices of control or acquisitions.

**405(3) [Revocation]** The Treasury may revoke a direction at any time.

**405(4) [Effect of revocation]** But revocation does not affect anything done in accordance with the direction before it was revoked.

**405(5) ["Third country decision"] "Third country decision"** means a decision of the Council or the Commission under–

(a) Article 7(5) of the investment services directive;

(b) Article 9(4) of the second banking coordination directive;

(c) Article 29b(4) of the first non-life insurance directive; or

(d) Article 32b(4) of the first life insurance directive.

## 406 Interpretation of section 405

**406(1) [Acquisition of 50 per cent stake]** For the purposes of section 405, a person ("the acquirer") acquires a 50% stake in a UK authorised person ("A") on first falling within any of the cases set out in subsection (2).

**406(2) [Cases]** The cases are where the acquirer–

(a) holds 50% or more of the shares in A;

(b) holds 50% or more of the shares in a parent undertaking ("P") of A;

(c) is entitled to exercise, or control the exercise of, 50% or more of the voting power in A; or

(d) is entitled to exercise, or control the exercise of, 50% or more of the voting power in P.

**406(3) ["The acquirer"]** In subsection (2) **"the acquirer"** means–

(a) the acquirer;

(b) any of the acquirer's associates; or

(c) the acquirer and any of his associates.

**406(4) [Definitions] "Associate", "shares"** and **"voting power"** have the same meaning as in section 422.

## 407 Consequences of a direction under section 405

**407(1) [Refusal of application for permission]** If the Authority refuses an application for permission as a result of a direction under section 405(1)(a)–

(a) subsections (7) to (9) of section 52 do not apply in relation to the refusal; but

(b) the Authority must notify the applicant of the refusal and the reasons for it.

**407(2) [Deferral of decision]** If the Authority defers its decision on an application for permission as a result of a direction under section 405(1)(b)–

(a) the time limit for determining the application mentioned in section 52(1) or (2) stops running on the day of the deferral and starts running again (if at all) on the day the period specified in the direction (if any) ends or the day the direction is revoked; and

(b) the Authority must notify the applicant of the deferral and the reasons for it.

**407(3) [Notice of objection]** If the Authority gives a notice of objection to a person as a result of a direction under section 405(1)(c) or (d)–

(a) sections 189 and 191 have effect as if the notice was a notice of objection within the meaning of Part XII; and

(b) the Authority must state in the notice the reasons for it.

## 408 EFTA firms

**408(1) [Power of Treasury]** If a third country decision has been taken, the Treasury may make a determination in relation to an EFTA firm which is a subsidiary undertaking of a parent undertaking which is governed by the law of the country to which the decision relates.

**408(2) ["Determination"] "Determination"** means a determination that the firm concerned does not qualify for authorisation under Schedule 3 even if it satisfies the conditions in paragraph 13 or 14 of that Schedule.

**408(3) [Determination in relation to firms]** A determination may also be made in relation to any firm falling within a class specified in the determination.

**408(4) [Withdrawal of determination]** The Treasury may withdraw a determination at any time.

**408(5) [Effect of withdrawal]** But withdrawal does not affect anything done in accordance with the determination before it was withdrawn.

**408(6) [Written notice]** If the Treasury make a determination in respect of a particular firm, or withdraw such a determination, they must give written notice to that firm.

**408(7) [Publication of determination, etc.]** The Treasury must publish notice of any determination (or the withdrawal of any determination)–

(a) in such a way as they think most suitable for bringing the determination (or withdrawal) to the attention of those likely to be affected by it; and

(b) on, or as soon as practicable after, the date of the determination (or withdrawal).

**408(8) ["EFTA firm"] "EFTA firm"** means a firm, institution or undertaking which–

(a) is an EEA firm as a result of paragraph 5(a), (b) or (d) of Schedule 3; and

(b) is incorporated in, or formed under the law of, an EEA State which is not a member State.

**408(9) ["Third country decision"] "Third country decision"** has the same meaning as in section 405.

## 409 Gibraltar

**409(1) [Power of Treasury to make order]** The Treasury may by order–

(a) modify Schedule 3 so as to provide for Gibraltar firms of a specified description to qualify for authorisation under that Schedule in specified circumstances;

(b) modify Schedule 3 so as to make provision in relation to the exercise by UK firms of rights under the law of Gibraltar which correspond to EEA rights;

(c) modify Schedule 4 so as to provide for Gibraltar firms of a specified description to qualify for authorisation under that Schedule in specified circumstances;

(d) modify section 264 so as to make provision in relation to collective investment schemes constituted under the law of Gibraltar;

(e) provide for the Authority to be able to give notice under section 264(2) on grounds relating to the law of Gibraltar;

(f) provide for this Act to apply to a Gibraltar recognised scheme as if the scheme were a scheme recognised under section 264.

**409(2) [Application for Pt. IV permission]** The fact that a firm may qualify for authorisation under Schedule 3 as a result of an order under subsection (1) does not prevent it from applying for a Part IV permission.

**409(3) ["Gibraltar firm"] "Gibraltar firm"** means a firm which has its head office in Gibraltar or is otherwise connected with Gibraltar.

**409(4) ["Gibraltar recognised scheme"] "Gibraltar recognised scheme"** means a collective investment scheme–

(a) constituted in an EEA State other than the United Kingdom, and
(b) recognised in Gibraltar under provisions which appear to the Treasury to give effect to the provisions of a relevant Community instrument.

**409(5) ["Specified"]** "Specified" means specified in the order.

**409(6) ["UK firm", "EEA right"]** "UK firm" and "EEA right" have the same meaning as in Schedule 3.

INTERNATIONAL OBLIGATIONS

## 410 International obligations

**410(1) [Power of Treasury – direction not to take action]** If it appears to the Treasury that any action proposed to be taken by a relevant person would be incompatible with Community obligations or any other international obligations of the United Kingdom, they may direct that person not to take that action.

**410(2) [Power of Treasury – direction to take action]** If it appears to the Treasury that any action which a relevant person has power to take is required for the purpose of implementing any such obligations, they may direct that person to take that action.

**410(3) [S. 410 direction – supplemental, etc. requirements]** A direction under this section–

(a) may include such supplemental or incidental requirements as the Treasury consider necessary or expedient; and
(b) is enforceable, on an application made by the Treasury, by injunction or, in Scotland, by an order for specific performance under section 45 of the Court of Session Act 1988.

**410(4) ["Relevant person"]** "Relevant person" means–

(a) the Authority;
(b) any person exercising functions conferred by Part VI on the competent authority;
(c) any recognised investment exchange (other than one which is an overseas investment exchange);
(d) any recognised clearing house (other than one which is an overseas clearing house);
(e) a person included in the list maintained under section 301; or
(f) the scheme operator of the ombudsman scheme.

TAX TREATMENT OF LEVIES AND REPAYMENTS

## 411 Tax treatment of levies and repayments

**411(1) [Substitution]** In the Income and Corporation Taxes Act 1988 ("the 1988 Act"), in section 76 (expenses of management: insurance companies), for subsections (7) and (7A) substitute–

"**(7)** For the purposes of this section any sums paid by a company by way of a levy shall be treated as part of its expenses of management.

**(7A)** "**Levy**" means–

(a) a payment required under rules made under section 136(2) of the Financial Services and Markets Act 2000 ("the Act of 2000");
(b) a levy imposed under the Financial Services Compensation Scheme;
(c) a payment required under rules made under section 234 of the Act of 2000;
(d) a payment required in accordance with the standard terms fixed under paragraph 18 of Schedule 17 to the Act of 2000."

**411(2) [Insertion]** After section 76 of the 1988 Act insert–

"*Levies and repayments under the Financial Services and Markets Act 2000*

**76A(1)** In computing the amount of the profits to be charged under Case I of Schedule D arising from a trade carried on by an authorised person (other than an investment company)–

(a) to the extent that it would not be deductible apart from this section, any sum expended by the authorised person in paying a levy may be deducted as an allowable expense;

(b) any payment which is made to the authorised person as a result of a repayment provision is to be treated as a trading receipt.

**76A(2)** **"Levy"** has the meaning given in section 76(7A).

**76A(3)** **"Repayment provision"** means any provision made by virtue of–

(a) section 136(7) of the Financial Services and Markets Act 2000 ("the Act of 2000");

(b) section 214(1)(e) of the Act of 2000.

**76A(4)** **"Authorised person"** has the same meaning as in the Act of 2000.

*Levies and repayments under the Financial Services and Markets Act 2000: investment companies*

**76B(1)** For the purposes of section 75 any sums paid by an investment company–

(a) by way of a levy, or

(b) as a result of an award of costs under costs rules,

shall be treated as part of its expenses of management.

**76B(2)** If a payment is made to an investment company as a result of a repayment provision, the company shall be charged to tax under Case VI of Schedule D on the amount of that payment.

**76B(3)** **"Levy"** has the meaning given in section 76(7A).

**76B(4)** **"Costs rules"** means–

(a) rules made under section 230 of the Financial Services and Markets Act 2000;

(b) provision relating to costs contained in the standard terms fixed under paragraph 18 of Schedule 17 to that Act.

**76B(5)** **"Repayment provision"** has the meaning given in section 76A(3)."

GAMING CONTRACTS

## 412 Gaming contracts

**412(1)** **[Enforceability of s. 412 contracts]** No contract to which this section applies is void or unenforceable because of–

(a) section 18 of the Gaming Act 1845, section 1 of the Gaming Act 1892 or Article 170 of the Betting, Gaming, Lotteries and Amusements (Northern Ireland) Order 1985; or

(b) any rule of the law of Scotland under which a contract by way of gaming or wagering is not legally enforceable.

**412(2)** **[Application of section]** This section applies to a contract if–

(a) it is entered into by either or each party by way of business;

(b) the entering into or performance of it by either party constitutes an activity of a specified kind or one which falls within a specified class of activity; and

(c) it relates to an investment of a specified kind or one which falls within a specified class of investment.

**412(3)** **[Application of Pt. II of Sch. 2]** Part II of Schedule 2 applies for the purposes of subsection (2)(c), with the references to section 22 being read as references to that subsection.

**412(4)** **[Non-limitation of s. 412(2)(c)]** Nothing in Part II of Schedule 2, as applied by subsection (3), limits the power conferred by subsection (2)(c).

**412(5)** **["Investment"]** **"Investment"** includes any asset, right or interest.

**412(6)** **["Specified"]** **"Specified"** means specified in an order made by the Treasury.

LIMITATION ON POWERS TO REQUIRE DOCUMENTS

## 413 Protected items

**413(1)** **[Disclosure, etc. of protected items]** A person may not be required under this Act to produce, disclose or permit the inspection of protected items.

**413(2) ["Protected items"] "Protected items"** means–

(a) communications between a professional legal adviser and his client or any person representing his client which fall within subsection (3);

(b) communications between a professional legal adviser, his client or any person representing his client and any other person which fall within subsection (3) (as a result of paragraph (b) of that subsection);

(c) items which–

(i) are enclosed with, or referred to in, such communications;

(ii) fall within subsection (3); and

(iii) are in the possession of a person entitled to possession of them.

**413(3) [Communications in connection with legal advice, etc.]** A communication or item falls within this subsection if it is made–

(a) in connection with the giving of legal advice to the client; or

(b) in connection with, or in contemplation of, legal proceedings and for the purposes of those proceedings.

**413(4) [Criminal purpose]** A communication or item is not a protected item if it is held with the intention of furthering a criminal purpose.

SERVICE OF NOTICES

## 414 Service of notices

**414(1) [Power of Treasury to make regulations]** The Treasury may by regulations make provision with respect to the procedure to be followed, or rules to be applied, when a provision of or made under this Act requires a notice, direction or document of any kind to be given or authorises the imposition of a requirement.

**414(2) [Regulations – provisions]** The regulations may, in particular, make provision–

(a) as to the manner in which a document must be given;

(b) as to the address to which a document must be sent;

(c) requiring, or allowing, a document to be sent electronically;

(d) for treating a document as having been given, or as having been received, on a date or at a time determined in accordance with the regulations;

(e) as to what must, or may, be done if the person to whom a document is required to be given is not an individual;

(f) as to what must, or may, be done if the intended recipient of a document is outside the United Kingdom.

**414(3) [Application of s. 414(1)]** Subsection (1) applies however the obligation to give a document is expressed (and so, in particular, includes a provision which requires a document to be served or sent).

**414(4) [Interpretation Act 1978, s. 7]** Section 7 of the Interpretation Act 1978 (service of notice by post) has effect in relation to provisions made by or under this Act subject to any provision made by regulations under this section.

JURISDICTION

## 415 Jurisdiction in civil proceedings

**415(1) [High Court proceedings]** Proceedings arising out of any act or omission (or proposed act or omission) of–

(a) the Authority,

(b) the competent authority for the purposes of Part VI,

(c) the scheme manager, or

(d) the scheme operator,

in the discharge or purported discharge of any of its functions under this Act may be brought before the High Court or the Court of Session.

**415(2) [S. 415(1) – jurisdiction]** The jurisdiction conferred by subsection (1) is in addition to any other jurisdiction exercisable by those courts.

REMOVAL OF CERTAIN UNNECESSARY PROVISIONS

## 416 Provisions relating to industrial assurance and certain other enactments

**416(1) [Cessation of enactments]** The following enactments are to cease to have effect–

(a) the Industrial Assurance Act 1923;

(b) the Industrial Assurance and Friendly Societies Act 1948;

(c) the Insurance Brokers (Registration) Act 1977.

**416(2) [Revocation]** The Industrial Assurance (Northern Ireland) Order 1979 is revoked.

**416(3) [Cessation of bodies]** The following bodies are to cease to exist–

(a) the Insurance Brokers Registration Council;

(b) the Policyholders Protection Board;

(c) the Deposit Protection Board;

(d) the Board of Banking Supervision.

**416(4) [Power of Treasury to make order]** If the Treasury consider that, as a consequence of any provision of this section, it is appropriate to do so, they may by order make any provision of a kind that they could make under this Act (and in particular any provision of a kind mentioned in section 339) with respect to anything done by or under any provision of Part XXI.

**416(5) [Interpretation of s. 416(4)]** Subsection (4) is not to be read as affecting in any way any other power conferred on the Treasury by this Act.

# PART XXIX – INTERPRETATION

## 417 Definitions

**417(1) [Definitions]** In this Act–

**"appointed representative"** has the meaning given in section 39(2);

**"auditors and actuaries rules"** means rules made under section 340;

**"authorisation offence"** has the meaning given in section 23(2);

**"authorised open-ended investment company"** has the meaning given in section 237(3);

**"authorised person"** has the meaning given in section 31(2);

**"the Authority"** means the Financial Services Authority;

**"body corporate"** includes a body corporate constituted under the law of a country or territory outside the United Kingdom;

**"chief executive"**–

(a) in relation to a body corporate whose principal place of business is within the United Kingdom, means an employee of that body who, alone or jointly with one or more others, is responsible under the immediate authority of the directors, for the conduct of the whole of the business of that body; and

(b) in relation to a body corporate whose principal place of business is outside the United Kingdom, means the person who, alone or jointly with one or more others, is responsible for the conduct of its business within the United Kingdom;

**"collective investment scheme"** has the meaning given in section 235;

**"the Commission"** means the European Commission (except in provisions relating to the Competition Commission);

**"the compensation scheme"** has the meaning given in section 213(2);

**"control of information rules"** has the meaning given in section 147(1);
**"director,"** in relation to a body corporate, includes–

(a) a person occupying in relation to it the position of a director (by whatever name called); and
(b) a person in accordance with whose directions or instructions (not being advice given in a professional capacity) the directors of that body are accustomed to act;

**"documents"** includes information recorded in any form and, in relation to information recorded otherwise than in legible form, references to its production include references to producing a copy of the information in legible form;
**"exempt person,"** in relation to a regulated activity, means a person who is exempt from the general prohibition in relation to that activity as a result of an exemption order made under section 38(1) or as a result of section 39(1) or 285(2) or (3);
**"financial promotion rules"** means rules made under section 145;
**"friendly society"** means an incorporated or registered friendly society;
**"general prohibition"** has the meaning given in section 19(2);
**"general rules"** has the meaning given in section 138(2);
**"incorporated friendly society"** means a society incorporated under the Friendly Societies Act 1992;
**"industrial and provident society"** means a society registered or deemed to be registered under the Industrial and Provident Societies Act 1965 or the Industrial and Provident Societies Act (Northern Ireland) 1969;
**"market abuse"** has the meaning given in section 118;
**"Minister of the Crown"** has the same meaning as in the Ministers of the Crown Act 1975;
**"money laundering rules"** means rules made under section 146;
**"notice of control"** has the meaning given in section 178(5);
**"the ombudsman scheme"** has the meaning given in section 225(3);
**"open-ended investment company"** has the meaning given in section 236;
**"Part IV permission"** has the meaning given in section 40(4);
**"partnership"** includes a partnership constituted under the law of a country or territory outside the United Kingdom;
**"prescribed"** (where not otherwise defined) means prescribed in regulations made by the Treasury;
**"price stabilising rules"** means rules made under section 144;
**"private company"** has the meaning given in section 1(3) of the Companies Act 1985 or in Article 12(3) of the Companies (Northern Ireland) Order 1986;
**"prohibition order"** has the meaning given in section 56(2);
**"recognised clearing house"** and **"recognised investment exchange"** have the meaning given in section 285;
**"registered friendly society"** means a society which is–

(a) a friendly society within the meaning of section 7(1)(a) of the Friendly Societies Act 1974; and
(b) registered within the meaning of that Act;

**"regulated activity"** has the meaning given in section 22;
**"regulating provisions"** has the meaning given in section 159(1);
**"regulatory objectives"** means the objectives mentioned in section 2;
**"regulatory provisions"** has the meaning given in section 302;
**"rule"** means a rule made by the Authority under this Act;
**"rule-making instrument"** has the meaning given in section 153;
**"the scheme manager"** has the meaning given in section 212(1);
**"the scheme operator"** has the meaning given in section 225(2);
**"scheme particulars rules"** has the meaning given in section 248(1);
**"Seventh Company Law Directive"** means the European Council Seventh Company Law Directive of 13 June 1983 on consolidated accounts (No. 83/349/EEC);

**"threshold conditions,"** in relation to a regulated activity, has the meaning given in section 41;

**"the Treaty"** means the treaty establishing the European Community;

**"trust scheme rules"** has the meaning given in section 247(1);

**"UK authorised person"** has the meaning given in section 178(4); and

**"unit trust scheme"** has the meaning given in section 237.

**417(2) [Application of Act to Scotland]** In the application of this Act to Scotland, references to a matter being actionable at the suit of a person are to be read as references to the matter being actionable at the instance of that person.

**417(3) [Public holidays]** For the purposes of any provision of this Act authorising or requiring a person to do anything within a specified number of days no account is to be taken of any day which is a public holiday in any part of the United Kingdom.

# 418 Carrying on regulated activities in the United Kingdom

**418(1) [Person carrying on regulated activity in UK]** In the four cases described in this section, a person who–

(a) is carrying on a regulated activity, but

(b) would not otherwise be regarded as carrying it on in the United Kingdom,

is, for the purposes of this Act, to be regarded as carrying it on in the United Kingdom.

**418(2) [First case]** The first case is where–

(a) his registered office (or if he does not have a registered office his head office) is in the United Kingdom;

(b) he is entitled to exercise rights under a single market directive as a UK firm; and

(c) he is carrying on in another EEA State a regulated activity to which that directive applies.

**418(3) [Second case]** The second case is where–

(a) his registered office (or if he does not have a registered office his head office) is in the United Kingdom;

(b) he is the manager of a scheme which is entitled to enjoy the rights conferred by an instrument which is a relevant Community instrument for the purposes of section 264; and

(c) persons in another EEA State are invited to become participants in the scheme.

**418(4) [Third case]** The third case is where–

(a) his registered office (or if he does not have a registered office his head office) is in the United Kingdom;

(b) the day-to-day management of the carrying on of the regulated activity is the responsibility of–

  (i) his registered office (or head office); or

  (ii) another establishment maintained by him in the United Kingdom.

**418(5) [Fourth case]** The fourth case is where–

(a) his head office is not in the United Kingdom; but

(b) the activity is carried on from an establishment maintained by him in the United Kingdom.

**418(6) [Location of person carrying on regulated activity]** For the purposes of subsections (2) to (5) it is irrelevant where the person with whom the activity is carried on is situated.

# 419 Carrying on regulated activities by way of business

**419(1) [Power of Treasury to make order]** The Treasury may by order make provision–

(a) as to the circumstances in which a person who would otherwise not be regarded as carrying on a regulated activity by way of business is to be regarded as doing so;

(b) as to the circumstances in which a person who would otherwise be regarded as carrying on a regulated activity by way of business is to be regarded as not doing so.

**419(2) [Application of s. 419(1) order]** An order under subsection (1) may be made so as to apply–

(a) generally in relation to all regulated activities;

(b) in relation to a specified category of regulated activity; or

(c) in relation to a particular regulated activity.

**419(3) [Further application of s. 419(1) order]** An order under subsection (1) may be made so as to apply–

(a) for the purposes of all provisions;

(b) for a specified group of provisions; or

(c) for a specified provision.

**419(4) ["Provision"] "Provision"** means a provision of, or made under, this Act.

**419(5) [S. 428(3) unaffected by section]** Nothing in this section is to be read as affecting the provisions of section 428(3).

## 420 Parent and subsidiary undertaking

**420(1) [Interpretation]** In this Act, except in relation to an incorporated friendly society, **"parent undertaking"** and **"subsidiary undertaking"** have the same meaning as in Part VII of the Companies Act 1985 (or Part VIII of the Companies (Northern Ireland) Order 1986).

**420(2) ["Parent undertaking", "subsidiary undertaking"]** But–

(a) **"parent undertaking"** also includes an individual who would be a parent undertaking for the purposes of those provisions if he were taken to be an undertaking (and "subsidiary undertaking" is to be read accordingly);

(b) **"subsidiary undertaking"** also includes, in relation to a body incorporated in or formed under the law of an EEA State other than the United Kingdom, an undertaking which is a subsidiary undertaking within the meaning of any rule of law in force in that State for purposes connected with implementation of the Seventh Company Law Directive (and "parent undertaking" is to be read accordingly).

**420(3) ["Subsidiary undertaking"]** In this Act **"subsidiary undertaking"**, in relation to an incorporated friendly society, means a body corporate of which the society has control within the meaning of section 13(9)(a) or (aa) of the Friendly Societies Act 1992 (and "parent undertaking" is to be read accordingly).

## 421 Group

**421(1) ["Group"]** In this Act **"group"**, in relation to a person ("A"), means A and any person who is–

(a) a parent undertaking of A;

(b) a subsidiary undertaking of A;

(c) a subsidiary undertaking of a parent undertaking of A;

(d) a parent undertaking of a subsidiary undertaking of A;

(e) an undertaking in which A or an undertaking mentioned in paragraph (a), (b), (c) or (d) has a participating interest;

(f) if A or an undertaking mentioned in paragraph (a) or (d) is a building society, an associated undertaking of the society; or

(g) if A or an undertaking mentioned in paragraph (a) or (d) is an incorporated friendly society, a body corporate of which the society has joint control (within the meaning of section 13(9)(c) or (cc) of the Friendly Societies Act 1992).

**421(2) ["Participating interest"] "Participating interest"** has the same meaning as in Part VII of the Companies Act 1985 or Part VIII of the Companies (Northern Ireland) Order 1986; but also includes an interest held by an individual which would be a participating interest for the purposes of those provisions if he were taken to be an undertaking.

**421(3) ["Associated undertaking"] "Associated undertaking"** has the meaning given in section 119(1) of the Building Societies Act 1986.

## 422 Controller

**422(1) ["Controller"]** In this Act **"controller"**, in relation to an undertaking ("A"), means a person who falls within any of the cases in subsection (2).

**422(2) [Cases where person regarded as controller]** The cases are where the person–

(a) holds 10% or more of the shares in A;

(b) is able to exercise significant influence over the management of A by virtue of his shareholding in A;

(c) holds 10% or more of the shares in a parent undertaking ("P") of A;

(d) is able to exercise significant influence over the management of P by virtue of his shareholding in P;

(e) is entitled to exercise, or control the exercise of, 10% or more of the voting power in A;

(f) is able to exercise significant influence over the management of A by virtue of his voting power in A;

(g) is entitled to exercise, or control the exercise of, 10% or more of the voting power in P; or

(h) is able to exercise significant influence over the management of P by virtue of his voting power in P.

**422(3) ["The person"]** In subsection (2) **"the person"** means–

(a) the person;

(b) any of the person's associates; or

(c) the person and any of his associates.

**422(4) ["Associate"] "Associate"**, in relation to a person ("H") holding shares in an undertaking ("C") or entitled to exercise or control the exercise of voting power in relation to another undertaking ("D"), means–

(a) the spouse of H;

(b) a child or stepchild of H (if under 18);

(c) the trustee of any settlement under which H has a life interest in possession (or in Scotland a life interest);

(d) an undertaking of which H is a director;

(e) a person who is an employee or partner of H;

(f) if H is an undertaking–

(i) a director of H;

(ii) a subsidiary undertaking of H;

(iii) a director or employee of such a subsidiary undertaking; and

(g) if H has with any other person an agreement or arrangement with respect to the acquisition, holding or disposal of shares or other interests in C or D or under which they undertake to act together in exercising their voting power in relation to C or D, that other person.

**422(5) ["Settlement"] "Settlement"**, in subsection (4)(c), includes any disposition or arrangement under which property is held on trust (or subject to a comparable obligation).

**422(6) ["Shares"] "Shares"**–

(a) in relation to an undertaking with a share capital, means allotted shares;

(b) in relation to an undertaking with capital but no share capital, means rights to share in the capital of the undertaking;

(c) in relation to an undertaking without capital, means interests–

(i) conferring any right to share in the profits, or liability to contribute to the losses, of the undertaking; or

(ii) giving rise to an obligation to contribute to the debts or expenses of the undertaking in the event of a winding up.

**422(7) ["Voting power"] "Voting power"**, in relation to an undertaking which does not have general meetings at which matters are decided by the exercise of voting rights, means the right under the constitution of the undertaking to direct the overall policy of the undertaking or alter the terms of its constitution.

## 423 Manager

**423(1) ["Manager"]** In this Act, except in relation to a unit trust scheme or a registered friendly society, **"manager"** means an employee who–

(a) under the immediate authority of his employer is responsible, either alone or jointly with one or more other persons, for the conduct of his employer's business; or

(b) under the immediate authority of his employer or of a person who is a manager by virtue of paragraph (a) exercises managerial functions or is responsible for maintaining accounts or other records of his employer.

**423(2) [Authority of employer where not an individual]** If the employer is not an individual, references in subsection (1) to the authority of the employer are references to the authority–

(a) in the case of a body corporate, of the directors;

(b) in the case of a partnership, of the partners; and

(c) in the case of an unincorporated association, of its officers or the members of its governing body.

**423(3) ["Manager" – further defined] "Manager"**, in relation to a body corporate, means a person (other than an employee of the body) who is appointed by the body to manage any part of its business and includes an employee of the body corporate (other than the chief executive) who, under the immediate authority of a director or chief executive of the body corporate, exercises managerial functions or is responsible for maintaining accounts or other records of the body corporate.

## 424 Insurance

**424(1) [Interpretation]** In this Act, references to–

(a) contracts of insurance,

(b) reinsurance,

(c) contracts of long-term insurance,

(d) contracts of general insurance,

are to be read with section 22 and Schedule 2.

**424(2) ["policy", "policyholder"]** In this Act "policy" and "policyholder", in relation to a contract of insurance, have such meaning as the Treasury may by order specify.

**424(3) [Contracts of insurance]** The law applicable to a contract of insurance, the effecting of which constitutes the carrying on of a regulated activity, is to be determined, if it is of a prescribed description, in accordance with regulations made by the Treasury.

## 425 Expressions relating to authorisation elsewhere in the single market

**425(1) [Interpretation]** In this Act–

(a) **"EEA authorisation"**, **"EEA firm"**, **"EEA right"**, **"EEA State"**, **"first life insurance directive"**, **"first non-life insurance directive"**, **"insurance directives"**, **"investment services directive"**, **"single market directives"** and **"second banking coordination directive"** have the meaning given in Schedule 3; and

(b) "home state regulator", in relation to an EEA firm, has the meaning given in Schedule 3.

**425(2) [Interpretation]** In this Act–

(a) "home state authorisation" has the meaning given in Schedule 4;

(a) **"Treaty firm"** has the meaning given in Schedule 4; and

(c) **"home state regulator"**, in relation to a Treaty firm, has the meaning given in Schedule 4.

# PART XXX – SUPPLEMENTAL

## 426 Consequential and supplementary provision

**426(1) [Power of Minister of Crown to make order]** A Minister of the Crown may by order make such incidental, consequential, transitional or supplemental provision as he considers necessary or expedient for the general purposes, or any particular purpose, of this Act or in consequence of any provision made by or under this Act or for giving full effect to this Act or any such provision.

**426(2) [Scope of s. 426(1) order]** An order under subsection (1) may, in particular, make provision–

(a) for enabling any person by whom any powers will become exercisable, on a date set by or under this Act, by virtue of any provision made by or under this Act to take before that date any steps which are necessary as a preliminary to the exercise of those powers;

(b) for applying (with or without modifications) or amending, repealing or revoking any provision of or made under an Act passed before this Act or in the same Session;

(c) dissolving any body corporate established by any Act passed, or instrument made, before the passing of this Act;

(d) for making savings, or additional savings, from the effect of any repeal or revocation made by or under this Act.

**426(3) [S. 426 amendments]** Amendments made under this section are additional, and without prejudice, to those made by or under any other provision of this Act.

**426(4) [Non-limitation of s. 426 powers]** No other provision of this Act restricts the powers conferred by this section.

## 427 Transitional provisions

**427(1) [Application of s. 427(2), (3)]** Subsections (2) and (3) apply to an order under section 426 which makes transitional provisions or savings.

**427(2) [Scope of s. 426 order]** The order may, in particular–

(a) if it makes provision about the authorisation and permission of persons who before commencement were entitled to carry on any activities, also include provision for such persons not to be treated as having any authorisation or permission (whether on an application to the Authority or otherwise);

(b) make provision enabling the Authority to require persons of such descriptions as it may direct to re-apply for permissions having effect by virtue of the order;

(c) make provision for the continuation as rules of such provisions (including primary and subordinate legislation) as may be designated in accordance with the order by the Authority, including provision for the modification by the Authority of provisions designated;

(d) make provision about the effect of requirements imposed, liabilities incurred and any other things done before commencement, including provision for and about investigations, penalties and the taking or continuing of any other action in respect of contraventions;

(e) make provision for the continuation of disciplinary and other proceedings begun before commencement, including provision about the decisions available to bodies before which such proceedings take place and the effect of their decisions;

(f) make provision as regards the Authority's obligation to maintain a record under section 347 as respects persons in relation to whom provision is made by the order.

**427(3) [S. 426 order – further provisions]** The order may–

(a) confer functions on the Treasury, the Secretary of State, the Authority, the scheme manager, the scheme operator, members of the panel established under paragraph 4 of Schedule 17, the Competition Commission or the Director General of Fair Trading;

(b) confer jurisdiction on the Tribunal;

(c) provide for fees to be charged in connection with the carrying out of functions conferred under the order;

(d) modify, exclude or apply (with or without modifications) any primary or subordinate legislation (including any provision of, or made under, this Act).

**427(4) ["Commencement"]** In subsection (2) **"commencement"** means the commencement of such provisions of this Act as may be specified by the order.

## 428 Regulations and orders

**428(1) [Power exercisable by statutory instrument]** Any power to make an order which is conferred on a Minister of the Crown by this Act and any power to make regulations which is conferred by this Act is exercisable by statutory instrument.

**428(2) [Lord Chancellor's power]** The Lord Chancellor's power to make rules under section 132 is exercisable by statutory instrument.

**428(3) [Contents, etc. of statutory instruments]** Any statutory instrument made under this Act may–

(a) contain such incidental, supplemental, consequential and transitional provision as the person making it considers appropriate; and

(b) make different provision for different cases.

**Commencement**

S. 428 in force as from 14 June 2000 (see s. 431(1)(b) FSMA 2000)

## 429 Parliamentary control of statutory instruments

**429(1) [Draft orders to be laid before Parliament]** No order is to be made under–

(a) section 144(4), 192(b) or (e), 236(5), 404 or 419, or

(b) paragraph 1 of Schedule 8,

unless a draft of the order has been laid before Parliament and approved by a resolution of each House.

**429(2) [Draft regulations to be laid before Parliament]** No regulations are to be made under section 262 unless a draft of the regulations has been laid before Parliament and approved by a resolution of each House.

**429(3) [Orders to which s. 429(4) or (5) applicable]** An order to which, if it is made, subsection (4) or (5) will apply is not to be made unless a draft of the order has been laid before Parliament and approved by a resolution of each House.

**429(4) [Application of subsection to s. 21 orders]** This subsection applies to an order under section 21 if–

(a) it is the first order to be made, or to contain provisions made, under section 21(4);

(b) it varies an order made under section 21(4) so as to make section 21(1) apply in circumstances in which it did not previously apply;

(c) it is the first order to be made, or to contain provision made, under section 21(5);

(d) it varies a previous order made under section 21(5) so as to make section 21(1) apply in circumstances in which it did not, as a result of that previous order, apply;

(e) it is the first order to be made, or to contain provisions made, under section 21(9) or (10);

(f) it adds one or more activities to those that are controlled activities for the purposes of section 21; or

(g) it adds one or more investments to those which are controlled investments for the purposes of section 21.

**429(5) [Application of subsection to s. 38 orders]** This subsection applies to an order under section 38 if–

(a) it is the first order to be made, or to contain provisions made, under that section; or

(b) it contains provisions restricting or removing an exemption provided by an earlier order made under that section.

**429(6) [Orders to which s. 429(7) provisions apply]** An order containing a provision to which, if the order is made, subsection (7) will apply is not to be made unless a draft of the order has been laid before Parliament and approved by a resolution of each House.

**429(7) [Application of subsection – exercise of s. 326(1) or s. 327(6) powers]** This subsection applies to a provision contained in an order if–

(a) it is the first to be made in the exercise of the power conferred by subsection (1) of section 326 or it removes a body from those for the time being designated under that subsection; or

(b) it is the first to be made in the exercise of the power conferred by subsection (6) of section 327 or it adds a description of regulated activity or investment to those for the time being specified for the purposes of that subsection.

**429(8) [Annulment of statutory instruments]** Any other statutory instrument made under this Act, apart from one made under section 431(2) or to which paragraph 26 of Schedule 2 applies, shall be subject to annulment in pursuance of a resolution of either House of Parliament.

## 430 Extent

**430(1) [Extension of Act to Northern Ireland ]** This Act, except Chapter IV of Part XVII, extends to Northern Ireland.

**430(2) [Extent of amendments, etc.]** Except where Her Majesty by Order in Council provides otherwise, the extent of any amendment or repeal made by or under this Act is the same as the extent of the provision amended or repealed.

**430(3) [Extension of Act to Channel Islands, etc.]** Her Majesty may by Order in Council provide for any provision of or made under this Act relating to a matter which is the subject of other legislation which extends to any of the Channel Islands or the Isle of Man to extend there with such modifications (if any) as may be specified in the Order.

**Commencement**

S. 430 in force as from 14 June 2000 (see s. 431(1)(b) FSMA 2000)

## 431 Commencement

**431(1) [Commencement]** The following provisions come into force on the passing of this Act–

(a) this section;

(b) sections 428, 430 and 433;

(c) paragraphs 1 and 2 of Schedule 21.

**431(2) [Commencement by order]** The other provisions of this Act come into force on such day as the Treasury may by order appoint; and different days may be appointed for different purposes.

**Commencement**

S. 431 in force as from 14 June 2000 (see s. 431(1)(a) FSMA 2000)

## 432 Minor and consequential amendments, transitional provisions and repeals

**432(1)** **[Minor and consequential amendments]** Schedule 20 makes minor and consequential amendments.

**432(2)** **[Transitional provisions]** Schedule 21 makes transitional provisions.

**432(3)** **[Repeals]** The enactments set out in Schedule 22 are repealed.

## 433 Short title

**433** This Act may be cited as the Financial Services and Markets Act 2000.

**Commencement**

S. 433 in force as from 14 June 2000 (see s. 431(1)(b) FSMA 2000)

# SCHEDULES

# SCHEDULE 1 – THE FINANCIAL SERVICES AUTHORITY

## Part I – General

### INTERPRETATION

**1(1)** In this Schedule–

**"the 1985 Act"** means the Companies Act 1985;

**"non-executive committee"** means the committee maintained under paragraph 3;

**"functions"**, in relation to the Authority, means functions conferred on the Authority by or under any provision of this Act.

**1(2)** For the purposes of this Schedule, the following are the Authority's legislative functions–

(a) making rules;

(b) issuing codes under section 64 or 119;

(c) issuing statements under section 64, 69, 124 or 210;

(d) giving directions under section 316, 318 or 328;

(e) issuing general guidance (as defined by section 158(5)).

### CONSTITUTION

**2(1)** The constitution of the Authority must continue to provide for the Authority to have–

(a) a chairman; and

(b) a governing body.

**2(2)** The governing body must include the chairman.

**2(3)** The chairman and other members of the governing body must be appointed, and be liable to removal from office, by the Treasury.

**2(4)** The validity of any act of the Authority is not affected–

(a) by a vacancy in the office of chairman; or

(b) by a defect in the appointment of a person as a member of the governing body or as chairman.

### NON-EXECUTIVE MEMBERS OF THE GOVERNING BODY

**3(1)** The Authority must secure–

(a) that the majority of the members of its governing body are non-executive members; and

(b) that a committee of its governing body, consisting solely of the non-executive members, is set up and maintained for the purposes of discharging the functions conferred on the committee by this Schedule.

**3(2)** The members of the non-executive committee are to be appointed by the Authority.

**3(3)** The non-executive committee is to have a chairman appointed by the Treasury from among its members.

## FUNCTIONS OF THE NON-EXECUTIVE COMMITTEE

**4(1)** In this paragraph **"the committee"** means the non-executive committee.

**4(2)** The non-executive functions are functions of the Authority but must be discharged by the committee.

**4(3)** The non-executive functions are–

(a) keeping under review the question whether the Authority is, in discharging its functions in accordance with decisions of its governing body, using its resources in the most efficient and economic way;

(b) keeping under review the question whether the Authority's internal financial controls secure the proper conduct of its financial affairs; and

(c) determining the remuneration of–

(i) the chairman of the Authority's governing body; and

(ii) the executive members of that body.

**4(4)** The function mentioned in sub-paragraph (3)(b) and those mentioned in sub-paragraph (3)(c) may be discharged on behalf of the committee by a sub-committee.

**4(5)** Any sub-committee of the committee–

(a) must have as its chairman the chairman of the committee; but

(b) may include persons other than members of the committee.

**4(6)** The committee must prepare a report on the discharge of its functions for inclusion in the Authority's annual report to the Treasury under paragraph 10.

**4(7)** The committee's report must relate to the same period as that covered by the Authority's report.

## ARRANGEMENTS FOR DISCHARGING FUNCTIONS

**5(1)** The Authority may make arrangements for any of its functions to be discharged by a committee, sub-committee, officer or member of staff of the Authority.

**5(2)** But in exercising its legislative functions, the Authority must act through its governing body.

**5(3)** Sub-paragraph (1) does not apply to the non-executive functions.

## MONITORING AND ENFORCEMENT

**6(1)** The Authority must maintain arrangements designed to enable it to determine whether persons on whom requirements are imposed by or under this Act are complying with them.

**6(2)** Those arrangements may provide for functions to be performed on behalf of the Authority by any body or person who, in its opinion, is competent to perform them.

**6(3)** The Authority must also maintain arrangements for enforcing the provisions of, or made under, this Act.

**6(4)** Sub-paragraph (2) does not affect the Authority's duty under sub-paragraph (1).

## ARRANGEMENTS FOR THE INVESTIGATION OF COMPLAINTS

**7(1)** The Authority must–

(a) make arrangements ("the complaints scheme") for the investigation of complaints arising in connection with the exercise of, or failure to exercise, any of its functions (other than its legislative functions); and

(b) appoint an independent person ("the investigator") to be responsible for the conduct of investigations in accordance with the complaints scheme.

**7(2)** The complaints scheme must be designed so that, as far as reasonably practicable, complaints are investigated quickly.

**7(3)** The Treasury's approval is required for the appointment or dismissal of the investigator.

**7(4)** The terms and conditions on which the investigator is appointed must be such as, in the opinion of the Authority, are reasonably designed to secure–

(a) that he will be free at all times to act independently of the Authority; and

(b) that complaints will be investigated under the complaints scheme without favouring the Authority.

**7(5)** Before making the complaints scheme, the Authority must publish a draft of the proposed scheme in the way appearing to the Authority best calculated to bring it to the attention of the public.

**7(6)** The draft must be accompanied by notice that representations about it may be made to the Authority within a specified time.

**7(7)** Before making the proposed complaints scheme, the Authority must have regard to any representations made to it in accordance with sub-paragraph (6).

**7(8)** If the Authority makes the proposed complaints scheme, it must publish an account, in general terms, of–

(a) the representations made to it in accordance with sub-paragraph (6); and

(b) its response to them.

**7(9)** If the complaints scheme differs from the draft published under sub-paragraph (5) in a way which is, in the opinion of the Authority, significant the Authority must (in addition to complying with sub-paragraph (8)) publish details of the difference.

**7(10)** The Authority must publish up-to-date details of the complaints scheme including, in particular, details of–

(a) the provision made under paragraph 8(5); and

(b) the powers which the investigator has to investigate a complaint.

**7(11)** Those details must be published in the way appearing to the Authority to be best calculated to bring them to the attention of the public.

**7(12)** The Authority must, without delay, give the Treasury a copy of any details published by it under this paragraph.

**7(13)** The Authority may charge a reasonable fee for providing a person with a copy of–

(a) a draft published under sub-paragraph (5);

(b) details published under sub-paragraph (10).

**7(14)** Sub-paragraphs (5) to (9) and (13)(a) also apply to a proposal to alter or replace the complaints scheme.

## INVESTIGATION OF COMPLAINTS

**8(1)** The Authority is not obliged to investigate a complaint in accordance with the complaints scheme which it reasonably considers would be more appropriately dealt with in another way (for example by referring the matter to the Tribunal or by the institution of other legal proceedings).

**8(2)** The complaints scheme must provide–

(a) for reference to the investigator of any complaint which the Authority is investigating; and

(b) for him–

(i) to have the means to conduct a full investigation of the complaint;

(ii) to report on the result of his investigation to the Authority and the complainant; and

(iii) to be able to publish his report (or any part of it) if he considers that it (or the part) ought to be brought to the attention of the public.

**8(3)** If the Authority has decided not to investigate a complaint, it must notify the investigator.

**8(4)** If the investigator considers that a complaint of which he has been notified under sub-paragraph (3) ought to be investigated, he may proceed as if the complaint had been referred to him under the complaints scheme.

**8(5)** The complaints scheme must confer on the investigator the power to recommend, if he thinks it appropriate, that the Authority–

(a) makes a compensatory payment to the complainant,

(b) remedies the matter complained of,

or takes both of those steps.

**8(6)** The complaints scheme must require the Authority, in a case where the investigator–

(a) has reported that a complaint is well-founded, or

(b) has criticised the Authority in his report,

to inform the investigator and the complainant of the steps which it proposes to take in response to the report.

**8(7)** The investigator may require the Authority to publish the whole or a specified part of the response.

**8(8)** The investigator may appoint a person to conduct the investigation on his behalf but subject to his direction.

**8(9)** Neither an officer nor an employee of the Authority may be appointed under sub-paragraph (8).

**8(10)** Sub-paragraph (2) is not to be taken as preventing the Authority from making arrangements for the initial investigation of a complaint to be conducted by the Authority.

## RECORDS

**9** The Authority must maintain satisfactory arrangements for–

(a) recording decisions made in the exercise of its functions; and

(b) the safe-keeping of those records which it considers ought to be preserved.

## ANNUAL REPORT

**10(1)** At least once a year the Authority must make a report to the Treasury on–

(a) the discharge of its functions;

(b) the extent to which, in its opinion, the regulatory objectives have been met;

(c) its consideration of the matters mentioned in section 2(3); and

(d) such other matters as the Treasury may from time to time direct.

**10(2)** The report must be accompanied by–

(a) the report prepared by the non-executive committee under paragraph 4(6); and

(b) such other reports or information, prepared by such persons, as the Treasury may from time to time direct.

**10(3)** The Treasury must lay before Parliament a copy of each report received by them under this paragraph.

**10(4)** The Treasury may–

(a) require the Authority to comply with any provisions of the 1985 Act about accounts and their audit which would not otherwise apply to it; or

(b) direct that any such provision of that Act is to apply to the Authority with such modifications as are specified in the direction.

**10(5)** Compliance with any requirement imposed under sub-paragraph (4)(a) or (b) is enforceable by injunction or, in Scotland, an order under section 45(b) of the Court of Session Act 1988.

**10(6)** Proceedings under sub-paragraph (5) may be brought only by the Treasury.

### ANNUAL PUBLIC MEETING

**11(1)** Not later than three months after making a report under paragraph 10, the Authority must hold a public meeting ("the annual meeting") for the purposes of enabling that report to be considered.

**11(2)** The Authority must organise the annual meeting so as to allow–

(a) a general discussion of the contents of the report which is being considered; and

(b) a reasonable opportunity for those attending the meeting to put questions to the Authority about the way in which it discharged, or failed to discharge, its functions during the period to which the report relates.

**11(3)** But otherwise the annual meeting is to be organised and conducted in such a way as the Authority considers appropriate.

**11(4)** The Authority must give reasonable notice of its annual meeting.

**11(5)** That notice must–

(a) give details of the time and place at which the meeting is to be held;

(b) set out the proposed agenda for the meeting;

(c) indicate the proposed duration of the meeting;

(d) give details of the Authority's arrangements for enabling persons to attend; and

(e) be published by the Authority in the way appearing to it to be most suitable for bringing the notice to the attention of the public.

**11(6)** If the Authority proposes to alter any of the arrangements which have been included in the notice given under sub-paragraph (4) it must–

(a) give reasonable notice of the alteration; and

(b) publish that notice in the way appearing to the Authority to be best calculated to bring it to the attention of the public.

### REPORT OF ANNUAL MEETING

**12** Not later than one month after its annual meeting, the Authority must publish a report of the proceedings of the meeting.

## Part II – Status

**13** In relation to any of its functions–

(a) the Authority is not to be regarded as acting on behalf of the Crown; and

(b) its members, officers and staff are not to be regarded as Crown servants.

### EXEMPTION FROM REQUIREMENT OF "LIMITED" IN AUTHORITY'S NAME

**14** The Authority is to continue to be exempt from the requirements of the 1985 Act relating to the use of "limited" as part of its name.

**15** If the Secretary of State is satisfied that any action taken by the Authority makes it inappropriate for the exemption given by paragraph 14 to continue he may, after consulting the Treasury, give a direction removing it.

## Part III – Penalties and fees

### PENALTIES

**16(1)** In determining its policy with respect to the amounts of penalties to be imposed by it under this Act, the Authority must take no account of the expenses which it incurs, or expects to incur, in discharging its functions.

**16(2)** The Authority must prepare and operate a scheme for ensuring that the amounts paid to the Authority by way of penalties imposed under this Act are applied for the benefit of authorised persons.

**16(3)** The scheme may, in particular, make different provision with respect to different classes of authorised person.

**16(4)** Up to date details of the scheme must be set out in a document ("the scheme details").

**16(5)** The scheme details must be published by the Authority in the way appearing to it to be best calculated to bring them to the attention of the public.

**16(6)** Before making the scheme, the Authority must publish a draft of the proposed scheme in the way appearing to the Authority to be best calculated to bring it to the attention of the public.

**16(7)** The draft must be accompanied by notice that representations about the proposals may be made to the Authority within a specified time.

**16(8)** Before making the scheme, the Authority must have regard to any representations made to it in accordance with sub-paragraph (7).

**16(9)** If the Authority makes the proposed scheme, it must publish an account, in general terms, of–

(a) the representations made to it in accordance with sub-paragraph (7); and

(b) its response to them.

**16(10)** If the scheme differs from the draft published under sub-paragraph (6) in a way which is, in the opinion of the Authority, significant the Authority must (in addition to complying with sub-paragraph (9)) publish details of the difference.

**16(11)** The Authority must, without delay, give the Treasury a copy of any scheme details published by it.

**16(12)** The Authority may charge a reasonable fee for providing a person with a copy of–

(a) a draft published under sub-paragraph (6);

(b) scheme details.

**16(13)** Sub-paragraphs (6) to (10) and (12)(a) also apply to a proposal to alter or replace the complaints scheme.

## FEES

**17(1)** The Authority may make rules providing for the payment to it of such fees, in connection with the discharge of any of its functions under or as a result of this Act, as it considers will (taking account of its expected income from fees and charges provided for by any other provision of this Act) enable it–

(a) to meet expenses incurred in carrying out its functions or for any incidental purpose;

(b) to repay the principal of, and pay any interest on, any money which it has borrowed and which has been used for the purpose of meeting expenses incurred in relation to its assumption of functions under this Act or the Bank of England Act 1998; and

(c) to maintain adequate reserves.

**17(2)** In fixing the amount of any fee which is to be payable to the Authority, no account is to be taken of any sums which the Authority receives, or expects to receive, by way of penalties imposed by it under this Act.

**17(3)** Sub-paragraph (1)(b) applies whether expenses were incurred before or after the coming into force of this Act or the Bank of England Act 1998.

**17(4)** Any fee which is owed to the Authority under any provision made by or under this Act may be recovered as a debt due to the Authority.

## SERVICES FOR WHICH FEES MAY NOT BE CHARGED

**18** The power conferred by paragraph 17 may not be used to require–

(a) a fee to be paid in respect of the discharge of any of the Authority's functions under paragraphs 13, 14, 19 or 20 of Schedule 3; or

(b) a fee to be paid by any person whose application for approval under section 59 has been granted.

# Part IV – Miscellaneous

### EXEMPTION FROM LIABILITY IN DAMAGES

**19(1)** Neither the Authority nor any person who is, or is acting as, a member, officer or member of staff of the Authority is to be liable in damages for anything done or omitted in the discharge, or purported discharge, of the Authority's functions.

**19(2)** Neither the investigator appointed under paragraph 7 nor a person appointed to conduct an investigation on his behalf under paragraph 8(8) is to be liable in damages for anything done or omitted in the discharge, or purported discharge, of his functions in relation to the investigation of a complaint.

**19(3)** Neither sub-paragraph (1) nor sub-paragraph (2) applies–

(a) if the act or omission is shown to have been in bad faith; or

(b) so as to prevent an award of damages made in respect of an act or omission on the ground that the act or omission was unlawful as a result of section 6(1) of the Human Rights Act 1998.

### DISQUALIFICATION FOR MEMBERSHIP OF HOUSE OF COMMONS

**20** In Part III of Schedule 1 to the House of Commons Disqualification Act 1975 (disqualifying offices), insert at the appropriate place–

"Member of the governing body of the Financial Services Authority".

### DISQUALIFICATION FOR MEMBERSHIP OF NORTHERN IRELAND ASSEMBLY

**21** In Part III of Schedule 1 to the Northern Ireland Assembly Disqualification Act 1975 (disqualifying offices), insert at the appropriate place–

"Member of the governing body of the Financial Services Authority".

# SCHEDULE 2 – REGULATED ACTIVITIES

## Part I – Regulated activities

### GENERAL

**1** The matters with respect to which provision may be made under section 22(1) in respect of activities include, in particular, those described in general terms in this Part of this Schedule.

### DEALING IN INVESTMENTS

**2(1)** Buying, selling, subscribing for or underwriting investments or offering or agreeing to do so, either as a principal or as an agent.

**2(2)** In the case of an investment which is a contract of insurance, that includes carrying out the contract.

### ARRANGING DEALS IN INVESTMENTS

**3** Making, or offering or agreeing to make–

(a) arrangements with a view to another person buying, selling, subscribing for or underwriting a particular investment;

(b) arrangements with a view to a person who participates in the arrangements buying, selling, subscribing for or underwriting investments.

## DEPOSIT TAKING

**4** Accepting deposits.

## SAFEKEEPING AND ADMINISTRATION OF ASSETS

**5(1)** Safeguarding and administering assets belonging to another which consist of or include investments or offering or agreeing to do so.

**5(2)** Arranging for the safeguarding and administration of assets belonging to another, or offering or agreeing to do so.

## MANAGING INVESTMENTS

**6** Managing, or offering or agreeing to manage, assets belonging to another person where–

(a) the assets consist of or include investments; or

(b) the arrangements for their management are such that the assets may consist of or include investments at the discretion of the person managing or offering or agreeing to manage them.

## INVESTMENT ADVICE

**7** Giving or offering or agreeing to give advice to persons on–

(a) buying, selling, subscribing for or underwriting an investment; or

(b) exercising any right conferred by an investment to acquire, dispose of, underwrite or convert an investment.

## ESTABLISHING COLLECTIVE INVESTMENT SCHEMES

**8** Establishing, operating or winding up a collective investment scheme, including acting as–

(a) trustee of a unit trust scheme;

(b) depositary of a collective investment scheme other than a unit trust scheme; or

(c) sole director of a body incorporated by virtue of regulations under section 262.

## USING COMPUTER-BASED SYSTEMS FOR GIVING INVESTMENT INSTRUCTIONS

**9(1)** Sending on behalf of another person instructions relating to an investment by means of a computer-based system which enables investments to be transferred without a written instrument.

**9(2)** Offering or agreeing to send such instructions by such means on behalf of another person.

**9(3)** Causing such instructions to be sent by such means on behalf of another person.

**9(4)** Offering or agreeing to cause such instructions to be sent by such means on behalf of another person.

# Part II – Investments

## GENERAL

**10** The matters with respect to which provision may be made under section 22(1) in respect of investments include, in particular, those described in general terms in this Part of this Schedule.

## SECURITIES

**11(1)** Shares or stock in the share capital of a company.

**11(2)** "Company" includes–

(a) any body corporate (wherever incorporated), and

(b) any unincorporated body constituted under the law of a country or territory outside the United Kingdom,

other than an open-ended investment company.

## INSTRUMENTS CREATING OR ACKNOWLEDGING INDEBTEDNESS

**12** Any of the following–

(a) debentures;

(b) debenture stock;

(c) loan stock;

(d) bonds;

(e) certificates of deposit;

(f) any other instruments creating or acknowledging a present or future indebtedness.

## GOVERNMENT AND PUBLIC SECURITIES

**13(1)** Loan stock, bonds and other instruments–

(a) creating or acknowledging indebtedness; and

(b) issued by or on behalf of a government, local authority or public authority.

**13(2)** **"Government, local authority or public authority"** means–

(a) the government of the United Kingdom, of Northern Ireland, or of any country or territory outside the United Kingdom;

(b) a local authority in the United Kingdom or elsewhere;

(c) any international organisation the members of which include the United Kingdom or another member State.

## INSTRUMENTS GIVING ENTITLEMENT TO INVESTMENTS

**14(1)** Warrants or other instruments entitling the holder to subscribe for any investment.

**14(2)** It is immaterial whether the investment is in existence or identifiable.

## CERTIFICATES REPRESENTING SECURITIES

**15** Certificates or other instruments which confer contractual or property rights–

(a) in respect of any investment held by someone other than the person on whom the rights are conferred by the certificate or other instrument; and

(b) the transfer of which may be effected without requiring the consent of that person.

## UNITS IN COLLECTIVE INVESTMENT SCHEMES

**16(1)** Shares in or securities of an open-ended investment company.

**16(2)** Any right to participate in a collective investment scheme.

## OPTIONS

**17** Options to acquire or dispose of property.

## FUTURES

**18** Rights under a contract for the sale of a commodity or property of any other description under which delivery is to be made at a future date.

## CONTRACTS FOR DIFFERENCES

**19** Rights under–

(a) a contract for differences; or

(b) any other contract the purpose or pretended purpose of which is to secure a profit or avoid a loss by reference to fluctuations in–

(i) the value or price of property of any description; or

(ii) an index or other factor designated for that purpose in the contract.

## CONTRACTS OF INSURANCE

**20** Rights under a contract of insurance, including rights under contracts falling within head C of Schedule 2 to the Friendly Societies Act 1992.

### PARTICIPATION IN LLOYD'S SYNDICATES

**21(1)** The underwriting capacity of a Lloyd's syndicate.

**21(2)** A person's membership (or prospective membership) of a Lloyd's syndicate.

### DEPOSITS

**22** Rights under any contract under which a sum of money (whether or not denominated in a currency) is paid on terms under which it will be repaid, with or without interest or a premium, and either on demand or at a time or in circumstances agreed by or on behalf of the person making the payment and the person receiving it.

### LOANS SECURED ON LAND

**23(1)** Rights under any contract under which–

(a) one person provides another with credit; and

(b) the obligation of the borrower to repay is secured on land.

**23(2)** **"Credit"** includes any cash loan or other financial accommodation.

**23(3)** **"Cash"** includes money in any form.

### RIGHTS IN INVESTMENTS

**24** Any right or interest in anything which is an investment as a result of any other provision made under section 22(1).

# Part III – Supplemental provisions

### THE ORDER-MAKING POWER

**25(1)** An order under section 22(1) may–

(a) provide for exemptions;

(b) confer powers on the Treasury or the Authority;

(c) authorise the making of regulations or other instruments by the Treasury for purposes of, or connected with, any relevant provision;

(d) authorise the making of rules or other instruments by the Authority for purposes of, or connected with, any relevant provision;

(e) make provision in respect of any information or document which, in the opinion of the Treasury or the Authority, is relevant for purposes of, or connected with, any relevant provision;

(f) make such consequential, transitional or supplemental provision as the Treasury consider appropriate for purposes of, or connected with, any relevant provision.

**25(2)** Provision made as a result of sub-paragraph (1)(f) may amend any primary or subordinate legislation, including any provision of, or made under, this Act.

**25(3)** **"Relevant provision"** means any provision–

(a) of section 22 or this Schedule; or

(b) made under that section or this Schedule.

### PARLIAMENTARY CONTROL

**26(1)** This paragraph applies to the first order made under section 22(1).

**26(2)** This paragraph also applies to any subsequent order made under section 22(1) which contains a statement by the Treasury that, in their opinion, the effect (or one of the effects) of the proposed order would be that an activity which is not a regulated activity would become a regulated activity.

**26(3)** An order to which this paragraph applies–

(a) must be laid before Parliament after being made; and

(b) ceases to have effect at the end of the relevant period unless before the end of that period the order is approved by a resolution of each House of Parliament (but without that affecting anything done under the order or the power to make a new order).

**26(4)** **"Relevant period"** means a period of twenty-eight days beginning with the day on which the order is made.

**26(5)** In calculating the relevant period no account is to be taken of any time during which Parliament is dissolved or prorogued or during which both Houses are adjourned for more than four days.

### INTERPRETATION

**27(1)** In this Schedule–

**"buying"** includes acquiring for valuable consideration;
**"offering"** includes inviting to treat;
**"property"** includes currency of the United Kingdom or any other country or territory; and
**"selling"** includes disposing for valuable consideration.

**27(2)** In sub-paragraph (1) **"disposing"** includes–

(a) in the case of an investment consisting of rights under a contract–
(i) surrendering, assigning or converting those rights; or
(ii) assuming the corresponding liabilities under the contract;

(b) in the case of an investment consisting of rights under other arrangements, assuming the corresponding liabilities under the contract or arrangements;

(c) in the case of any other investment, issuing or creating the investment or granting the rights or interests of which it consists.

**27(3)** In this Schedule references to an instrument include references to any record (whether or not in the form of a document).

# SCHEDULE 3 – EEA PASSPORT RIGHTS

## Part I – Defined terms

### THE SINGLE MARKET DIRECTIVES

**1** **"The single market directives"** means–

(a) the first banking co-ordination directive;

(b) the second banking co-ordination directive;

(c) the insurance directives; and

(d) the investment services directive.

### THE BANKING CO-ORDINATION DIRECTIVES

**2(1)** **"The first banking co-ordination directive"** means the Council Directive of 12 December 1977 on the co-ordination of laws, regulations and administrative provisions relating to the taking up and pursuit of the business of credit institutions (No. 77/780/EEC).

**2(2)** **"The second banking co-ordination directive"** means the Council Directive of 15 December 1989 on the co-ordination of laws, etc, relating to the taking up and pursuit of the business of credit institutions and amending Directive 77/780/EEC (No. 89/646/EEC).

### THE INSURANCE DIRECTIVES

**3(1)** **"The insurance directives"** means the first, second and third non-life insurance directives and the first, second and third life insurance directives.

**3(2) "First non-life insurance directive"** means the Council Directive of 24 July 1973 on the co-ordination of laws, regulations and administrative provisions relating to the taking up and pursuit of the business of direct insurance other than life assurance (No. 73/239/EEC).

**3(3) "Second non-life insurance directive"** means the Council Directive of 22 June 1988 on the co-ordination of laws, etc, and laying down provisions to facilitate the effective exercise of freedom to provide services and amending Directive 73/239/EEC (No. 88/357/EEC).

**3(4) "Third non-life insurance directive"** means the Council Directive of 18 June 1992 on the co-ordination of laws, etc, and amending Directives 73/239/EEC and 88/357/EEC (No. 92/49/EEC).

**3(5) "First life insurance directive"** means the Council Directive of 5 March 1979 on the co-ordination of laws, regulations and administrative provisions relating to the taking up and pursuit of the business of direct life assurance (No. 79/267/EEC).

**3(6) "Second life insurance directive"** means the Council Directive of 8 November 1990 on the co-ordination of laws, etc, and laying down provisions to facilitate the effective exercise of freedom to provide services and amending Directive 79/267/EEC (No. 90/619/EEC).

**3(7) "Third life insurance directive"** means the Council Directive of 10 November 1992 on the co-ordination of laws, etc, and amending Directives 79/267/EEC and 90/619/EEC (No. 92/96/EEC).

## THE INVESTMENT SERVICES DIRECTIVE

**4 "The investment services directive"** means the Council Directive of 10 May 1993 on investment services in the securities field (No. 93/22/EEC).

## EEA FIRM

**5 "EEA firm"** means any of the following if it does not have its head office in the United Kingdom–

(a) an investment firm (as defined in Article 1.2 of the investment services directive) which is authorised (within the meaning of Article 3) by its home state regulator;

(b) a credit institution (as defined in Article 1 of the first banking co-ordination directive) which is authorised (within the meaning of Article 1) by its home state regulator;

(c) a financial institution (as defined in Article 1 of the second banking co-ordination directive) which is a subsidiary of the kind mentioned in Article 18.2 and which fulfils the conditions in Article 18; or

(d) an undertaking pursuing the activity of direct insurance (within the meaning of Article 1 of the first life insurance directive or of the first non-life insurance directive) which has received authorisation under Article 6 from its home state regulator.

## EEA AUTHORISATION

**6 "EEA authorisation"** means authorisation granted to an EEA firm by its home state regulator for the purpose of the relevant single market directive.

## EEA RIGHT

**7 "EEA right"** means the entitlement of a person to establish a branch, or provide services, in an EEA State other than that in which he has his head office–

(a) in accordance with the Treaty as applied in the EEA; and

(b) subject to the conditions of the relevant single market directive.

## EEA STATE

**8 "EEA State"** means a State which is a contracting party to the agreement on the European Economic Area signed at Oporto on 2 May 1992 as it has effect for the time being.

## HOME STATE REGULATOR

**9 "Home state regulator"** means the competent authority (within the meaning of the relevant single market directive) of an EEA State (other than the United Kingdom) in relation to the EEA firm concerned.

### UK FIRM

**10** **"UK firm"** means a person whose head office is in the UK and who has an EEA right to carry on activity in an EEA State other than the United Kingdom.

### HOST STATE REGULATOR

**11** **"Host state regulator"** means the competent authority (within the meaning of the relevant single market directive) of an EEA State (other than the United Kingdom) in relation to a UK firm's exercise of EEA rights there.

## Part II – Exercise of passport rights by EEA firms

### FIRMS QUALIFYING FOR AUTHORISATION

**12(1)** Once an EEA firm which is seeking to establish a branch in the United Kingdom in exercise of an EEA right satisfies the establishment conditions, it qualifies for authorisation.

**12(2)** Once an EEA firm which is seeking to provide services in the United Kingdom in exercise of an EEA right satisfies the service conditions, it qualifies for authorisation.

### ESTABLISHMENT

**13(1)** The establishment conditions are that–

(a) the Authority has received notice ("a consent notice") from the firm's home state regulator that it has given the firm consent to establish a branch in the United Kingdom;

(b) the consent notice–

(i) is given in accordance with the relevant single market directive;
(ii) identifies the activities to which consent relates; and
(iii) includes such other information as may be prescribed; and

(c) the firm has been informed of the applicable provisions or two months have elapsed beginning with the date when the Authority received the consent notice.

**13(2)** If the Authority has received a consent notice, it must–

(a) prepare for the firm's supervision;

(b) notify the firm of the applicable provisions (if any); and

(c) if the firm falls within paragraph 5(d), notify its home state regulator of the applicable provisions (if any).

**13(3)** A notice under sub-paragraph (2)(b) or (c) must be given before the end of the period of two months beginning with the day on which the Authority received the consent notice.

**13(4)** For the purposes of this paragraph–

**"applicable provisions"** means the host state rules with which the firm is required to comply when carrying on a permitted activity through a branch in the United Kingdom;

**"host state rules"** means rules–

(a) made in accordance with the relevant single market directive; and
(b) which are the responsibility of the United Kingdom (both as to implementation and as to supervision of compliance) in accordance with that directive; and

**"permitted activity"** means an activity identified in the consent notice.

### SERVICES

**14(1)** The service conditions are that–

(a) the firm has given its home state regulator notice of its intention to provide services in the United Kingdom ("a notice of intention");

(b) if the firm falls within paragraph 5(a) or (d), the Authority has received notice ("a regulator's notice") from the firm's home state regulator containing such information as may be prescribed; and

(c) if the firm falls within paragraph 5(d), its home state regulator has informed it that the regulator's notice has been sent to the Authority.

**14(2)** If the Authority has received a regulator's notice or, where none is required by sub-paragraph (1), has been informed of the firm's intention to provide services in the United Kingdom, it must–

(a) prepare for the firm's supervision; and

(b) notify the firm of the applicable provisions (if any).

**14(3)** A notice under sub-paragraph (2)(b) must be given before the end of the period of two months beginning on the day on which the Authority received the regulator's notice, or was informed of the firm's intention.

**14(4)** For the purposes of this paragraph–

**"applicable provisions"** means the host state rules with which the firm is required to comply when carrying on a permitted activity by providing services in the United Kingdom;

**"host state rules"** means rules–

(a) made in accordance with the relevant single market directive; and

(b) which are the responsibility of the United Kingdom (both as to implementation and as to supervision of compliance) in accordance with that directive; and

**"permitted activity"** means an activity identified in–

(a) the regulator's notice; or

(b) where none is required by sub-paragraph (1), the notice of intention.

## GRANT OF PERMISSION

**15(1)** On qualifying for authorisation as a result of paragraph 12, a firm has, in respect of each permitted activity which is a regulated activity, permission to carry it on through its United Kingdom branch (if it satisfies the establishment conditions) or by providing services in the United Kingdom (if it satisfies the service conditions).

**15(2)** The permission is to be treated as being on terms equivalent to those appearing from the consent notice, regulator's notice or notice of intention.

**15(3)** Sections 21, 39(1) and 147(1) of the Consumer Credit Act 1974 (business requiring a licence under that Act) do not apply in relation to the carrying on of a permitted activity which is Consumer Credit Act business by a firm which qualifies for authorisation as a result of paragraph 12, unless the Director General of Fair Trading has exercised the power conferred on him by section 203 in relation to the firm.

**15(4)** **"Consumer Credit Act business"** has the same meaning as in section 203.

## EFFECT OF CARRYING ON REGULATED ACTIVITY WHEN NOT QUALIFIED FOR AUTHORISATION

**16(1)** This paragraph applies to an EEA firm which is not qualified for authorisation under paragraph 12.

**16(2)** Section 26 does not apply to an agreement entered into by the firm.

**16(3)** Section 27 does not apply to an agreement in relation to which the firm is a third party for the purposes of that section.

**16(4)** Section 29 does not apply to an agreement in relation to which the firm is the deposit-taker.

## CONTINUING REGULATION OF EEA FIRMS

**17** Regulations may–

(a) modify any provision of this Act which is an applicable provision (within the meaning of paragraph 13 or 14) in its application to an EEA firm qualifying for authorisation;

(b) make provision as to any change (or proposed change) of a prescribed kind relating to an EEA firm or to an activity that it carries on in the United Kingdom and as to the procedure to be followed in relation to such cases;

(c) provide that the Authority may treat an EEA firm's notification that it is to cease to carry on regulated activity in the United Kingdom as a request for cancellation of its qualification for authorisation under this Schedule.

### GIVING UP RIGHT TO AUTHORISATION

**18** Regulations may provide that in prescribed circumstances an EEA firm falling within paragraph 5(c) may, on following the prescribed procedure–

(a) have its qualification for authorisation under this Schedule cancelled; and

(b) seek to become an authorised person by applying for a Part IV permission.

## Part III – Exercise of passport rights by UK firms

### ESTABLISHMENT

**19(1)** A UK firm may not exercise an EEA right to establish a branch unless three conditions are satisfied.

**19(2)** The first is that the firm has given the Authority, in the specified way, notice of its intention to establish a branch ("a notice of intention") which–

(a) identifies the activities which it seeks to carry on through the branch; and

(b) includes such other information as may be specified.

**19(3)** The activities identified in a notice of intention may include activities which are not regulated activities.

**19(4)** The second is that the Authority has given notice in specified terms ("a consent notice") to the host state regulator.

**19(5)** The third is that–

(a) the host state regulator has notified the firm (or, where the EEA right in question derives from any of the insurance directives, the Authority) of the applicable provisions; or

(b) two months have elapsed beginning with the date on which the Authority gave the consent notice.

**19(6)** If the firm's EEA right derives from the investment services directive or the second banking coordination directive and the first condition is satisfied, the Authority must give a consent notice to the host state regulator unless it has reason to doubt the adequacy of the firm's resources or its administrative structure.

**19(7)** If the firm's EEA right derives from any of the insurance directives and the first condition is satisfied, the Authority must give a consent notice unless it has reason–

(a) to doubt the adequacy of the firm's resources or its administrative structure, or

(b) to question the reputation, qualifications or experience of the directors or managers of the firm or the person proposed as the branch's authorised agent for the purposes of those directives,

in relation to the business to be conducted through the proposed branch.

**19(8)** If the Authority proposes to refuse to give a consent notice it must give the firm concerned a warning notice.

**19(9)** If the firm's EEA right derives from any of the insurance directives and the host state regulator has notified it of the applicable provisions, the Authority must inform the firm of those provisions.

**19(10)** Rules may specify the procedure to be followed by the Authority in exercising its functions under this paragraph.

**19(11)** If the Authority gives a consent notice it must give written notice that it has done so to the firm concerned.

**19(12)** If the Authority decides to refuse to give a consent notice–

(a) it must, within three months beginning with the date when it received the notice of intention, give the person who gave that notice a decision notice to that effect; and

(b) that person may refer the matter to the Tribunal.

**19(13)** In this paragraph, **"applicable provisions"** means the host state rules with which the firm will be required to comply when conducting business through the proposed branch in the EEA State concerned.

**19(14)** In sub-paragraph (13), **"host state rules"** means rules–

(a) made in accordance with the relevant single market directive; and

(b) which are the responsibility of the EEA State concerned (both as to implementation and as to supervision of compliance) in accordance with that directive.

**19(15)** **"Specified"** means specified in rules.

## SERVICES

**20(1)** A UK firm may not exercise an EEA right to provide services unless the firm has given the Authority, in the specified way, notice of its intention to provide services ("a notice of intention") which–

(a) identifies the activities which it seeks to carry out by way of provision of services; and

(b) includes such other information as may be specified.

**20(2)** The activities identified in a notice of intention may include activities which are not regulated activities.

**20(3)** If the firm's EEA right derives from the investment services directive or a banking coordination directive, the Authority must, within one month of receiving a notice of intention, send a copy of it to the host state regulator.

**20(4)** When the Authority sends the copy under sub-paragraph (3), it must give written notice to the firm concerned.

**20(5)** If the firm concerned's EEA right derives from the investment services directive, it must not provide the services to which its notice of intention relates until it has received written notice from the Authority under sub-paragraph (4).

**20(6)** **"Specified"** means specified in rules.

## OFFENCE RELATING TO EXERCISE OF PASSPORT RIGHTS

**21(1)** If a UK firm which is not an authorised person contravenes the prohibition imposed by–

(a) sub-paragraph (1) of paragraph 19, or

(b) sub-paragraph (1) or (5) of paragraph 20,

it is guilty of an offence.

**21(2)** A firm guilty of an offence under sub-paragraph (1) is liable–

(a) on summary conviction, to a fine not exceeding the statutory maximum; or

(b) on conviction on indictment, to a fine.

**21(3)** In proceedings for an offence under sub-paragraph (1), it is a defence for the firm to show that it took all reasonable precautions and exercised all due diligence to avoid committing the offence.

## CONTINUING REGULATION OF UK FIRMS

**22(1)** Regulations may make such provision as the Treasury consider appropriate in relation to a UK firm's exercise of EEA rights, and may in particular provide for the application (with or without modification) of any provision of, or made under, this Act in relation to an activity of a UK firm.

**22(2)** Regulations may–

(a) make provision as to any change (or proposed change) of a prescribed kind relating to a

UK firm or to an activity that it carries on and as to the procedure to be followed in relation to such cases;

(b) make provision with respect to the consequences of the firm's failure to comply with a provision of the regulations.

**22(3)** Where a provision of the kind mentioned in sub-paragraph (2) requires the Authority's consent to a change (or proposed change)–

(a) consent may be refused only on prescribed grounds; and

(b) if the Authority decides to refuse consent, the firm concerned may refer the matter to the Tribunal.

**23(1)** Sub-paragraph (2) applies if a UK firm–

(a) has a Part IV permission; and

(b) is exercising an EEA right to carry on any Consumer Credit Act business in an EEA State other than the United Kingdom.

**23(2)** The Authority may exercise its power under section 45 in respect of the firm if the Director of Fair Trading has informed the Authority that–

(a) the firm,

(b) any of the firm's employees, agents or associates (whether past or present), or

(c) if the firm is a body corporate, a controller of the firm or an associate of such a controller,

has done any of the things specified in paragraphs (a) to (d) of section 25(2) of the Consumer Credit Act 1974.

**23(3)** **"Associate"**, **"Consumer Credit Act business"** and **"controller"** have the same meaning as in section 203.

**24(1)** Sub-paragraph (2) applies if a UK firm–

(a) is not required to have a Part IV permission in relation to the business which it is carrying on; and

(b) is exercising the right conferred by Article 18.2 of the second banking co-ordination directive to carry on that business in an EEA State other than the United Kingdom.

**24(2)** If requested to do so by the host state regulator in the EEA State in which the UK firm's business is being carried on, the Authority may impose any requirement in relation to the firm which it could impose if–

(a) the firm had a Part IV permission in relation to the business which it is carrying on; and

(b) the Authority was entitled to exercise its power under that Part to vary that permission.

# SCHEDULE 4 – TREATY RIGHTS

## DEFINITIONS

**1** In this Schedule–

**"consumers"** means persons who are consumers for the purposes of section 138;

**"Treaty firm"** means a person–

(a) whose head office is situated in an EEA State (its "home state") other than the United Kingdom; and

(b) which is recognised under the law of that State as its national; and

**"home state regulator"**, in relation to a Treaty firm, means the competent authority of the firm's home state for the purpose of its home state authorisation (as to which see paragraph 3(1)(a)).

## FIRMS QUALIFYING FOR AUTHORISATION

**2** Once a Treaty firm which is seeking to carry on a regulated activity satisfies the conditions set out in paragraph 3(1), it qualifies for authorisation.

## EXERCISE OF TREATY RIGHTS

**3(1)** The conditions are that–

(a) the firm has received authorisation ("home state authorisation") under the law of its home state to carry on the regulated activity in question ("the permitted activity");

(b) the relevant provisions of the law of the firm's home state–
  (i) afford equivalent protection; or
  (ii) satisfy the conditions laid down by a Community instrument for the co-ordination or approximation of laws, regulations or administrative provisions of member States relating to the carrying on of that activity; and

(c) the firm has no EEA right to carry on that activity in the manner in which it is seeking to carry it on.

**3(2)** A firm is not to be regarded as having home state authorisation unless its home state regulator has so informed the Authority in writing.

**3(3)** Provisions afford equivalent protection if, in relation to the firm's carrying on of the permitted activity, they afford consumers protection which is at least equivalent to that afforded by or under this Act in relation to that activity.

**3(4)** A certificate issued by the Treasury that the provisions of the law of a particular EEA State afford equivalent protection in relation to the activities specified in the certificate is conclusive evidence of that fact.

## PERMISSION

**4(1)** On qualifying for authorisation under this Schedule, a Treaty firm has permission to carry on each permitted activity through its United Kingdom branch or by providing services in the United Kingdom.

**4(2)** The permission is to be treated as being on terms equivalent to those to which the firm's home state authorisation is subject.

**4(3)** If, on qualifying for authorisation under this Schedule, a firm has a Part IV permission which includes permission to carry on a permitted activity, the Authority must give a direction cancelling the permission so far as it relates to that activity.

**4(4)** The Authority need not give a direction under sub-paragraph (3) if it considers that there are good reasons for not doing so.

## NOTICE TO AUTHORITY

**5(1)** Sub-paragraph (2) applies to a Treaty firm which–

(a) qualifies for authorisation under this Schedule, but

(b) is not carrying on in the United Kingdom the regulated activity, or any of the regulated activities, which it has permission to carry on there.

**5(2)** At least seven days before it begins to carry on such a regulated activity, the firm must give the Authority written notice of its intention to do so.

**5(3)** If a Treaty firm to which sub-paragraph (2) applies has given notice under that sub-paragraph, it need not give such a notice if it again becomes a firm to which that sub-paragraph applies.

**5(4)** Subsections (1), (3) and (6) of section 51 apply to a notice under sub-paragraph (2) as they apply to an application for a Part IV permission.

## OFFENCES

**6(1)** A person who contravenes paragraph 5(2) is guilty of an offence.

**6(2)** In proceedings against a person for an offence under sub-paragraph (1) it is a defence for him to show that he took all reasonable precautions and exercised all due diligence to avoid committing the offence.

**6(3)** A person is guilty of an offence if in, or in connection with, a notice given by him under paragraph 5(2) he–

(a) provides information which he knows to be false or misleading in a material particular; or

(b) recklessly provides information which is false or misleading in a material particular.

**6(4)** A person guilty of an offence under this paragraph is liable–

(a) on summary conviction, to a fine not exceeding the statutory maximum;

(b) on conviction on indictment, to a fine.

# SCHEDULE 5 – PERSONS CONCERNED IN COLLECTIVE INVESTMENT SCHEMES

### AUTHORISATION

**1(1)** A person who for the time being is an operator, trustee or depositary of a recognised collective investment scheme is an authorised person.

**1(2)** **"Recognised"** means recognised by virtue of section 264.

**1(3)** An authorised open-ended investment company is an authorised person.

### PERMISSION

**2(1)** A person authorised as a result of paragraph 1(1) has permission to carry on, so far as it is a regulated activity–

(a) any activity, appropriate to the capacity in which he acts in relation to the scheme, of the kind described in paragraph 8 of Schedule 2;

(b) any activity in connection with, or for the purposes of, the scheme.

**2(2)** A person authorised as a result of paragraph 1(3) has permission to carry on, so far as it is a regulated activity–

(a) the operation of the scheme;

(b) any activity in connection with, or for the purposes of, the operation of the scheme.

# SCHEDULE 6 – THRESHOLD CONDITIONS

## Part I – Part IV permission

### LEGAL STATUS

**1(1)** If the regulated activity concerned is the effecting or carrying out of contracts of insurance, the authorised person must be a body corporate, a registered friendly society or a member of Lloyd's.

**1(2)** If the person concerned appears to the Authority to be seeking to carry on, or to be carrying on, a regulated activity constituting accepting deposits, it must be–

(a) a body corporate; or

(b) a partnership.

### LOCATION OF OFFICES

**2(1)** If the person concerned is a body corporate constituted under the law of any part of the United Kingdom–

(a) its head office, and

(b) if it has a registered office, that office,

must be in the United Kingdom.

**2(2)** If the person concerned has its head office in the United Kingdom but is not a body corporate, it must carry on business in the United Kingdom.

### CLOSE LINKS

**3(1)** If the person concerned ("A") has close links with another person ("CL") the Authority must be satisfied–

(a) that those links are not likely to prevent the Authority's effective supervision of A; and

(b) if it appears to the Authority that CL is subject to the laws, regulations or administrative provisions of a territory which is not an EEA State ("the foreign provisions"), that neither the foreign provisions, nor any deficiency in their enforcement, would prevent the Authority's effective supervision of A.

**3(2)** A has close links with CL if–

(a) CL is a parent undertaking of A;

(b) CL is a subsidiary undertaking of A;

(c) CL is a parent undertaking of a subsidiary undertaking of A;

(d) CL is a subsidiary undertaking of a parent undertaking of A;

(e) CL owns or controls 20% or more of the voting rights or capital of A; or

(f) A owns or controls 20% or more of the voting rights or capital of CL.

**3(3)** **"Subsidiary undertaking"** includes all the instances mentioned in Article 1(1) and (2) of the Seventh Company Law Directive in which an entity may be a subsidiary of an undertaking.

### ADEQUATE RESOURCES

**4(1)** The resources of the person concerned must, in the opinion of the Authority, be adequate in relation to the regulated activities that he seeks to carry on, or carries on.

**4(2)** In reaching that opinion, the Authority may–

(a) take into account the person's membership of a group and any effect which that membership may have; and

(b) have regard to–

(i) the provision he makes and, if he is a member of a group, which other members of the group make in respect of liabilities (including contingent and future liabilities); and

(ii) the means by which he manages and, if he is a member of a group, which other members of the group manage the incidence of risk in connection with his business.

### SUITABILITY

**5** The person concerned must satisfy the Authority that he is a fit and proper person having regard to all the circumstances, including–

(a) his connection with any person;

(b) the nature of any regulated activity that he carries on or seeks to carry on; and

(c) the need to ensure that his affairs are conducted soundly and prudently.

## Part II – Authorisation

### AUTHORISATION UNDER SCHEDULE 3

**6** In relation to an EEA firm qualifying for authorisation under Schedule 3, the conditions set out in paragraphs 1 and 3 to 5 apply, so far as relevant, to–

(a) an application for permission under Part IV;

(b) exercise of the Authority's own-initiative power under section 45 in relation to a Part IV permission.

AUTHORISATION UNDER SCHEDULE 4

7 In relation to a person who qualifies for authorisation under Schedule 4, the conditions set out in paragraphs 1 and 3 to 5 apply, so far as relevant, to–

(a) an application for an additional permission;

(b) the exercise of the Authority's own-initiative power under section 45 in relation to additional permission.

## Part III – Additional conditions

**8(1)** If this paragraph applies to the person concerned, he must, for the purposes of such provisions of this Act as may be specified, satisfy specified additional conditions.

**8(2)** This paragraph applies to a person who–

(a) has his head office outside the EEA; and

(b) appears to the Authority to be seeking to carry on a regulated activity relating to insurance business.

**8(3)** **"Specified"** means specified in, or in accordance with, an order made by the Treasury.

**9** The Treasury may by order–

(a) vary or remove any of the conditions set out in Parts I and II;

(b) add to those conditions.

# SCHEDULE 7 – THE AUTHORITY AS COMPETENT AUTHORITY FOR PART VI

GENERAL

**1** This Act applies in relation to the Authority when it is exercising functions under Part VI as the competent authority subject to the following modifications.

THE AUTHORITY'S GENERAL FUNCTIONS

**2** In section 2–

(a) subsection (4)(a) does not apply to listing rules;

(b) subsection (4)(c) does not apply to general guidance given in relation to Part VI; and

(c) subsection (4)(d) does not apply to functions under Part VI.

DUTY TO CONSULT

**3** Section 8 does not apply.

RULES

**4(1)** Sections 149, 153, 154 and 156 do not apply.

**4(2)** Section 155 has effect as if–

(a) the reference in subsection (2)(c) to the general duties of the Authority under section 2 were a reference to its duty under section 73; and

(b) section 99 were included in the provisions referred to in subsection (9).

STATEMENTS OF POLICY

**5(1)** Paragraph 5 of Schedule 1 has effect as if the requirement to act through the Authority's governing body applied also to the exercise of its functions of publishing statements under section 93.

**5(2)** Paragraph 1 of Schedule 1 has effect as if section 93 were included in the provisions referred to in sub-paragraph (2)(d).

### PENALTIES

**6** Paragraph 16 of Schedule 1 does not apply in relation to penalties under Part VI (for which separate provision is made by section 100).

### FEES

**7** Paragraph 17 of Schedule 1 does not apply in relation to fees payable under Part VI (for which separate provision is made by section 99).

### EXEMPTION FROM LIABILITY IN DAMAGES

**8** Schedule 1 has effect as if–

(a) sub-paragraph (1) of paragraph 19 were omitted (similar provision being made in relation to the competent authority by section 102) and

(b) for the words from the beginning to "(a)" in sub-paragraph (3) of that paragraph, there were substituted "Sub-paragraph (2) does not apply".

# SCHEDULE 8 – TRANSFER OF FUNCTIONS UNDER PART VI

### THE POWER TO TRANSFER

**1(1)** The Treasury may by order provide for any function conferred on the competent authority which is exercisable for the time being by a particular person to be transferred so as to be exercisable by another person.

**1(2)** An order may be made under this paragraph only if–

(a) the person from whom the relevant functions are to be transferred has agreed in writing that the order should be made;

(b) the Treasury are satisfied that the manner in which, or efficiency with which, the functions are discharged would be significantly improved if they were transferred to the transferee; or

(c) the Treasury are satisfied that it is otherwise in the public interest that the order should be made.

### SUPPLEMENTAL

**2(1)** An order under this Schedule does not affect anything previously done by any person ("the previous authority") in the exercise of functions which are transferred by the order to another person ("the new authority").

**2(2)** Such an order may, in particular, include provision–

(a) modifying or excluding any provision of Part VI, IX or XXVI in its application to any such functions;

(b) for reviews similar to that made, in relation to the Authority, by section 12;

(c) imposing on the new authority requirements similar to those imposed, in relation to the Authority, by sections 152, 155 and 354;

(d) as to the giving of guidance by the new authority;

(e) for the delegation by the new authority of the exercise of functions under Part VI and as to the consequences of delegation;

(f) for the transfer of any property, rights or liabilities relating to any such functions from the previous authority to the new authority;

(g) for the carrying on and completion by the new authority of anything in the process of being done by the previous authority when the order takes effect;

(h) for the substitution of the new authority for the previous authority in any instrument, contract or legal proceedings;

(i) for the transfer of persons employed by the previous authority to the new authority and as to the terms on which they are to transfer;

(j) making such amendments to any primary or subordinate legislation (including any provision of, or made under, this Act) as the Treasury consider appropriate in consequence of the transfer of functions effected by the order.

**2(3)** Nothing in this paragraph is to be taken as restricting the powers conferred by section 428.

**3** If the Treasury have made an order under paragraph 1 ("the transfer order") they may, by a separate order made under this paragraph, make any provision of a kind that could have been included in the transfer order.

# SCHEDULE 9 – NON-LISTING PROSPECTUSES

## GENERAL APPLICATION OF PART VI

**1** The provisions of Part VI apply in relation to a non-listing prospectus as they apply in relation to listing particulars but with the modifications made by this Schedule.

## REFERENCES TO LISTING PARTICULARS

**2(1)** Any reference to listing particulars is to be read as a reference to a prospectus.

**2(2)** Any reference to supplementary listing particulars is to be read as a reference to a supplementary prospectus.

## GENERAL DUTY OF DISCLOSURE

**3(1)** In section 80(1), for "section 79" substitute "section 87".

**3(2)** In section 80(2), omit "as a condition of the admission of the securities to the official list".

## SUPPLEMENTARY PROSPECTUSES

**4** In section 81(1), for "section 79 and before the commencement of dealings in the securities concerned following their admission to the official list" substitute "section 87 and before the end of the period during which the offer to which the prospectus relates remains open".

## EXEMPTION FROM LIABILITY FOR COMPENSATION

**5(1)** In paragraphs 1(3) and 2(3) of Schedule 10, for paragraph (d) substitute–

"(d) the securities were acquired after such a lapse of time that he ought in the circumstances to be reasonably excused and, if the securities are dealt in on an approved exchange, he continued in that belief until after the commencement of dealings in the securities on that exchange."

**5(2)** After paragraph 8 of that Schedule, insert–

"MEANING OF "APPROVED EXCHANGE"

9 **"Approved exchange"** has such meaning as may be prescribed."

## ADVERTISEMENTS

**6** In section 98(1), for "If listing particulars are, or are to be, published in connection with an application for listing," substitute "If a prospectus is, or is to be, published in connection with an application for approval, then, until the end of the period during which the offer to which the prospectus relates remains open,".

## FEES

**7** Listing rules made under section 99 may require the payment of fees to the competent authority in respect of a prospectus submitted for approval under section 87.

# SCHEDULE 10 – COMPENSATION: EXEMPTIONS

## STATEMENTS BELIEVED TO BE TRUE

**1(1)** In this paragraph **"statement"** means–

(a) any untrue or misleading statement in listing particulars; or

(b) the omission from listing particulars of any matter required to be included by section 80 or 81.

**1(2)** A person does not incur any liability under section 90(1) for loss caused by a statement if he satisfies the court that, at the time when the listing particulars were submitted to the competent authority, he reasonably believed (having made such enquiries, if any, as were reasonable) that–

(a) the statement was true and not misleading, or

(b) the matter whose omission caused the loss was properly omitted,

and that one or more of the conditions set out in sub-paragraph (3) are satisfied.

**1(3)** The conditions are that–

(a) he continued in his belief until the time when the securities in question were acquired;

(b) they were acquired before it was reasonably practicable to bring a correction to the attention of persons likely to acquire them;

(c) before the securities were acquired, he had taken all such steps as it was reasonable for him to have taken to secure that a correction was brought to the attention of those persons;

(d) he continued in his belief until after the commencement of dealings in the securities following their admission to the official list and they were acquired after such a lapse of time that he ought in the circumstances to be reasonably excused.

## STATEMENTS BY EXPERTS

**2(1)** In this paragraph **"statement"** means a statement included in listing particulars which–

(a) purports to be made by, or on the authority of, another person as an expert; and

(b) is stated to be included in the listing particulars with that other person's consent.

**2(2)** A person does not incur any liability under section 90(1) for loss in respect of any securities caused by a statement if he satisfies the court that, at the time when the listing particulars were submitted to the competent authority, he reasonably believed that the other person–

(a) was competent to make or authorise the statement, and

(b) had consented to its inclusion in the form and context in which it was included,

and that one or more of the conditions set out in sub-paragraph (3) are satisfied.

**2(3)** The conditions are that–

(a) he continued in his belief until the time when the securities were acquired;

(b) they were acquired before it was reasonably practicable to bring the fact that the expert was not competent, or had not consented, to the attention of persons likely to acquire the securities in question;

(c) before the securities were acquired he had taken all such steps as it was reasonable for him to have taken to secure that that fact was brought to the attention of those persons;

(d) he continued in his belief until after the commencement of dealings in the securities following their admission to the official list and they were acquired after such a lapse of time that he ought in the circumstances to be reasonably excused.

## CORRECTIONS OF STATEMENTS

**3(1)** In this paragraph **"statement"** has the same meaning as in paragraph 1.

**3(2)** A person does not incur liability under section 90(1) for loss caused by a statement if he satisfies the court–

(a) that before the securities in question were acquired, a correction had been published in a manner calculated to bring it to the attention of persons likely to acquire the securities; or

(b) that he took all such steps as it was reasonable for him to take to secure such publication and reasonably believed that it had taken place before the securities were acquired.

**3(3)** Nothing in this paragraph is to be taken as affecting paragraph 1.

### CORRECTIONS OF STATEMENTS BY EXPERTS

**4(1)** In this paragraph **"statement"** has the same meaning as in paragraph 2.

**4(2)** A person does not incur liability under section 90(1) for loss caused by a statement if he satisfies the court–

(a) that before the securities in question were acquired, the fact that the expert was not competent or had not consented had been published in a manner calculated to bring it to the attention of persons likely to acquire the securities; or

(b) that he took all such steps as it was reasonable for him to take to secure such publication and reasonably believed that it had taken place before the securities were acquired.

**4(3)** Nothing in this paragraph is to be taken as affecting paragraph 2.

### OFFICIAL STATEMENTS

**5** A person does not incur any liability under section 90(1) for loss resulting from–

(a) a statement made by an official person which is included in the listing particulars, or

(b) a statement contained in a public official document which is included in the listing particulars,

if he satisfies the court that the statement is accurately and fairly reproduced.

### FALSE OR MISLEADING INFORMATION KNOWN ABOUT

**6** A person does not incur any liability under section 90(1) or (4) if he satisfies the court that the person suffering the loss acquired the securities in question with knowledge–

(a) that the statement was false or misleading,

(b) of the omitted matter, or

(c) of the change or new matter,

as the case may be.

### BELIEF THAT SUPPLEMENTARY LISTING PARTICULARS NOT CALLED FOR

**7** A person does not incur any liability under section 90(4) if he satisfies the court that he reasonably believed that the change or new matter in question was not such as to call for supplementary listing particulars.

### MEANING OF "EXPERT"

**8** **"Expert"** includes any engineer, valuer, accountant or other person whose profession, qualifications or experience give authority to a statement made by him.

# SCHEDULE 11 – OFFERS OF SECURITIES

### THE GENERAL RULE

**1(1)** A person offers securities to the public in the United Kingdom if–

(a) to the extent that the offer is made to persons in the United Kingdom, it is made to the public; and

(b) the offer is not an exempt offer.

**1(2)** For this purpose, an offer which is made to any section of the public, whether selected–

(a) as members or debenture holders of a body corporate,

(b) as clients of the person making the offer, or

(c) in any other manner,

is to be regarded as made to the public.

## EXEMPT OFFERS

**2(1)** For the purposes of this Schedule, an offer of securities is an "exempt offer" if, to the extent that the offer is made to persons in the United Kingdom–

(a) the condition specified in any of paragraphs 3 to 24 is satisfied in relation to the offer; or

(b) the condition specified in one relevant paragraph is satisfied in relation to part, but not the whole, of the offer and, in relation to each other part of the offer, the condition specified in a different relevant paragraph is satisfied.

**2(2)** The relevant paragraphs are 3 to 8, 12 to 18 and 21.

## OFFERS FOR BUSINESS PURPOSES

**3** The securities are offered to persons–

(a) whose ordinary activities involve them in acquiring, holding, managing or disposing of investments (as principal or agent) for the purposes of their businesses, or

(b) who it is reasonable to expect will acquire, hold, manage or dispose of investments (as principal or agent) for the purposes of their businesses,

or are otherwise offered to persons in the context of their trades, professions or occupations.

## OFFERS TO LIMITED NUMBERS

**4(1)** The securities are offered to no more than fifty persons.

**4(2)** In determining whether this condition is satisfied, the offer is to be taken together with any other offer of the same securities which was–

(a) made by the same person;

(b) open at any time within the period of 12 months ending with the date on which the offer is first made; and

(c) not an offer to the public in the United Kingdom by virtue of this condition being satisfied.

**4(3)** For the purposes of this paragraph–

(a) the making of an offer of securities to trustees or members of a partnership in their capacity as such, or

(b) the making of such an offer to any other two or more persons jointly,

**4** is to be treated as the making of an offer to a single person.

## CLUBS AND ASSOCIATIONS

**5** The securities are offered to the members of a club or association (whether or not incorporated) and the members can reasonably be regarded as having a common interest with each other and with the club or association in the affairs of the club or association and in what is to be done with the proceeds of the offer.

## RESTRICTED CIRCLES

**6(1)** The securities are offered to a restricted circle of persons whom the offeror reasonably believes to be sufficiently knowledgeable to understand the risks involved in accepting the offer.

**6(2)** In determining whether a person is sufficiently knowledgeable to understand the risks involved in accepting an offer of securities, any information supplied by the person making the offer is to be disregarded, apart from information about–

(a) the issuer of the securities; or

(b) if the securities confer the right to acquire other securities, the issuer of those other securities.

## UNDERWRITING AGREEMENTS

**7** The securities are offered in connection with a genuine invitation to enter into an underwriting agreement with respect to them.

## OFFERS TO PUBLIC AUTHORITIES

**8(1)** The securities are offered to a public authority.

**8(2)** **"Public authority"** means–

(a) the government of the United Kingdom;

(b) the government of any country or territory outside the United Kingdom;

(c) a local authority in the United Kingdom or elsewhere;

(d) any international organisation the members of which include the United Kingdom or another EEA State; and

(e) such other bodies, if any, as may be specified.

## MAXIMUM CONSIDERATION

**9(1)** The total consideration payable for the securities cannot exceed 40,000 euros (or an equivalent amount).

**9(2)** In determining whether this condition is satisfied, the offer is to be taken together with any other offer of the same securities which was–

(a) made by the same person;

(b) open at any time within the period of 12 months ending with the date on which the offer is first made; and

(c) not an offer to the public in the United Kingdom by virtue of this condition being satisfied.

**9(3)** An amount (in relation to an amount denominated in euros) is an "equivalent amount" if it is an amount of equal value, calculated at the latest practicable date before (but in any event not more than 3 days before) the date on which the offer is first made, denominated wholly or partly in another currency or unit of account.

## MINIMUM CONSIDERATION

**10(1)** The minimum consideration which may be paid by any person for securities acquired by him pursuant to the offer is at least 40,000 euros (or an equivalent amount).

**10(2)** Paragraph 9(3) also applies for the purposes of this paragraph.

## SECURITIES DENOMINATED IN EUROS

**11(1)** The securities are denominated in amounts of at least 40,000 euros (or an equivalent amount).

**11(2)** Paragraph 9(3) also applies for the purposes of this paragraph.

## TAKEOVERS

**12(1)** The securities are offered in connection with a takeover offer.

**12(2)** **"Takeover offer"** means–

(a) an offer to acquire shares in a body incorporated in the United Kingdom which is a takeover offer within the meaning of the takeover provisions (or would be such an offer if those provisions applied in relation to any body corporate);

(b) an offer to acquire all or substantially all of the shares, or of the shares of a particular class, in a body incorporated outside the United Kingdom; or

(c) an offer made to all the holders of shares, or of shares of a particular class, in a body corporate to acquire a specified proportion of those shares.

**12(3)** "The takeover provisions" means–

(a) Part XIIIA of the Companies Act 1985; or

(b) in relation to Northern Ireland, Part XIVA of the Companies (Northern Ireland) Order 1986.

**12(4)** For the purposes of sub-paragraph (2)(b), any shares which the offeror or any associate of his holds or has contracted to acquire are to be disregarded.

**12(5)** For the purposes of sub-paragraph (2)(c), the following are not to be regarded as holders of the shares in question–

(a) the offeror;

(b) any associate of the offeror; and

(c) any person whose shares the offeror or any associate of the offeror has contracted to acquire.

**12(6)** **"Associate"** has the same meaning as in–

(a) section 430E of the Companies Act 1985; or

(b) in relation to Northern Ireland, Article 423E of the Companies (Northern Ireland) Order 1986.

## MERGERS

**13** The securities are offered in connection with a merger (within the meaning of Council Directive No. 78/855/EEC).

## FREE SHARES

**14(1)** The securities are shares and are offered free of charge to any or all of the holders of shares in the issuer.

**14(2)** **"Holders of shares"** means the persons who at the close of business on a date–

(a) specified in the offer, and

(b) falling within the period of 60 days ending with the date on which the offer is first made,

**14** were holders of such shares.

## EXCHANGE OF SHARES

**15** The securities–

(a) are shares, or investments of a specified kind relating to shares, in a body corporate, and

(b) are offered in exchange for shares in the same body corporate,

and the offer cannot result in any increase in the issued share capital of the body corporate.

## QUALIFYING PERSONS

**16(1)** The securities are issued by a body corporate and are offered–

(a) by the issuer, by a body corporate connected with the issuer or by a relevant trustee;

(b) only to qualifying persons; and

(c) on terms that a contract to acquire any such securities may be entered into only by the qualifying person to whom they were offered or, if the terms of the offer so permit, any qualifying person.

**16(2)** A person is a "qualifying person", in relation to an issuer, if he is a genuine employee or former employee of the issuer or of another body corporate in the same group or the wife, husband, widow, widower or child or stepchild under the age of eighteen of such an employee or former employee.

**16(3)** In relation to an issuer of securities, **"connected with"** has such meaning as may be prescribed.

**16(4)** **"Group"** and **"relevant trustee"** have such meaning as may be prescribed.

## CONVERTIBLE SECURITIES

**17(1)** The securities result from the conversion of convertible securities and listing particulars (or a prospectus) relating to the convertible securities were (or was) published in the United

Kingdom under or by virtue of Part VI or such other provisions applying in the United Kingdom as may be specified.

**17(2)** **"Convertible securities"** means securities of a specified kind which can be converted into, or exchanged for, or which confer rights to acquire, other securities.

**17(3)** **"Conversion"** means conversion into or exchange for, or the exercise of rights conferred by the securities to acquire, other securities.

## CHARITIES

**18** The securities are issued by–

(a) a charity within the meaning of–
  (i) section 96(1) of the Charities Act 1993, or
  (ii) section 35 of the Charities Act (Northern Ireland) 1964,

(b) a recognised body within the meaning of section 1(7) of the Law Reform (Miscellaneous Provisions) (Scotland) Act 1990,

(c) a housing association within the meaning of–
  (i) section 5(1) of the Housing Act 1985,
  (ii) section 1 of the Housing Associations Act 1985, or
  (iii) Article 3 of the Housing (Northern Ireland) Order 1992,

(d) an industrial or provident society registered in accordance with–
  (i) section 1(2)(b) of the Industrial and Provident Societies Act 1965, or
  (ii) section 1(2)(b) of the Industrial and Provident Societies Act 1969, or

(e) a non-profit making association or body, recognised by the country or territory in which it is established, with objectives similar to those of a body falling within any of paragraphs (a) to (c),

and the proceeds of the offer will be used for the purposes of the issuer's objectives.

## BUILDING SOCIETIES ETC.

**19** The securities offered are shares which are issued by, or ownership of which entitles the holder to membership of or to obtain the benefit of services provided by–

(a) a building society incorporated under the law of, or of any part of, the United Kingdom;

(b) any body incorporated under the law of, or of any part of, the United Kingdom relating to industrial and provident societies or credit unions; or

(c) a body of a similar nature established in another EEA State.

## EURO-SECURITIES

**20(1)** The securities offered are Euro-securities and no advertisement relating to the offer is issued in the United Kingdom, or is caused to be so issued–

(a) by the issuer of the Euro-securities;

(b) by any credit institution or other financial institution through which the Euro-securities may be acquired pursuant to the offer; or

(c) by any body corporate which is a member of the same group as the issuer or any of those institutions.

**20(2)** But sub-paragraph (1) does not apply to an advertisement of a prescribed kind.

**20(3)** **"Euro-securities"** means investments which–

(a) are to be underwritten and distributed by a syndicate at least two of the members of which have their registered offices in different countries or territories;

(b) are to be offered on a significant scale in one or more countries or territories, other than the country or territory in which the issuer has its registered office; and

(c) may be acquired pursuant to the offer only through a credit institution or other financial institution.

**20(4)** **"Credit institution"** means a credit institution as defined in Article 1 of Council Directive No 77/780/EEC.

**20(5)** **"Financial institution"** means a financial institution as defined in Article 1 of Council Directive No 89/646/EEC.

**20(6)** **"Underwritten"** means underwritten by whatever means, including by acquisition or subscription, with a view to resale.

SAME CLASS SECURITIES

**21** The securities are of the same class, and were issued at the same time, as securities in respect of which a prospectus has been published under or by virtue of–

(a) Part VI;

(b) Part III of the Companies Act 1985; or

(c) such other provisions applying in the United Kingdom as may be specified.

SHORT DATE SECURITIES

**22** The securities are investments of a specified kind with a maturity of less than one year from their date of issue.

GOVERNMENT AND PUBLIC SECURITIES

**23(1)** The securities are investments of a specified kind creating or acknowledging indebtedness issued by or on behalf of a public authority.

**23(2)** **"Public authority"** means–

(a) the government of the United Kingdom;

(b) the government of any country or territory outside the United Kingdom;

(c) a local authority in the United Kingdom or elsewhere;

(d) any international organisation the members of which include the United Kingdom or another EEA State; and

(e) such other bodies, if any, as may be specified.

NON-TRANSFERABLE SECURITIES

**24** The securities are not transferable.

GENERAL DEFINITIONS

**25** For the purposes of this Schedule–

**"shares"** has such meaning as may be specified; and

**"specified"** means specified in an order made by the Treasury.

# SCHEDULE 12 – TRANSFER SCHEMES: CERTIFICATES

## Part I – Insurance business transfer schemes

**1(1)** For the purposes of section 111(2) the appropriate certificates, in relation to an insurance business transfer scheme, are–

(a) a certificate under paragraph 2;

(b) if sub-paragraph (2) applies, a certificate under paragraph 3;

(c) if sub-paragraph (3) applies, a certificate under paragraph 4;

(d) if sub-paragraph (4) applies, a certificate under paragraph 5.

**1(2)** This sub-paragraph applies if–

(a) the authorised person concerned is a UK authorised person which has received authorisation under Article 6 of the first life insurance directive or of the first non-life insurance directive from the Authority; and

(b) the establishment from which the business is to be transferred under the proposed insurance business transfer scheme is in an EEA State other than the United Kingdom.

**1(3)** This sub-paragraph applies if–

(a) the authorised person concerned has received authorisation under Article 6 of the first life insurance directive from the Authority;

(b) the proposed transfer relates to business which consists of the effecting or carrying out of contracts of long-term insurance; and

(c) as regards any policy which is included in the proposed transfer and which evidences a contract of insurance (other than reinsurance), an EEA State other than the United Kingdom is the State of the commitment.

**1(4)** This sub-paragraph applies if–

(a) the authorised person concerned has received authorisation under Article 6 of the first non-life insurance directive from the Authority;

(b) the business to which the proposed insurance business transfer scheme relates is business which consists of the effecting or carrying out of contracts of general insurance; and

(c) as regards any policy which is included in the proposed transfer and which evidences a contract of insurance (other than reinsurance), the risk is situated in an EEA State other than the United Kingdom.

## CERTIFICATES AS TO MARGIN OF SOLVENCY

**2(1)** A certificate under this paragraph is to be given–

(a) by the relevant authority; or

(b) in a case in which there is no relevant authority, by the Authority.

**2(2)** A certificate given under sub-paragraph (1)(a) is one certifying that, taking the proposed transfer into account–

(a) the transferee possesses, or will possess before the scheme takes effect, the necessary margin of solvency; or

(b) there is no necessary margin of solvency applicable to the transferee.

**2(3)** A certificate under sub-paragraph (1)(b) is one certifying that the Authority has received from the authority which it considers to be the authority responsible for supervising persons who effect or carry out contracts of insurance in the place to which the business is to be transferred that, taking the proposed transfer into account–

(a) the transferee possesses or will possess before the scheme takes effect the margin of solvency required under the law applicable in that place; or

(b) there is no such margin of solvency applicable to the transferee .

**2(4)** **"Necessary margin of solvency"** means the margin of solvency required in relation to the transferee, taking the proposed transfer into account, under the law which it is the responsibility of the relevant authority to apply.

**2(5)** **"Margin of solvency"** means the excess of the value of the assets of the transferee over the amount of its liabilities.

**2(6)** **"Relevant authority"** means–

(a) if the transferee is an EEA firm falling within paragraph 5(d) of Schedule 3, its home state regulator;

(b) if the transferee is a Swiss general insurer, the authority responsible in Switzerland for supervising persons who effect or carry out contracts of insurance;

(c) if the transferee is an authorised person not falling within paragraph (a) or (b), the Authority.

**2(7)** In sub-paragraph (6), any reference to a transferee of a particular description includes a reference to a transferee who will be of that description if the proposed scheme takes effect.

**2(8)** **"Swiss general insurer"** means a body–

(a) whose head office is in Switzerland;

(b) which has permission to carry on regulated activities consisting of the effecting and carrying out of contracts of general insurance; and

(c) whose permission is not restricted to the effecting or carrying out of contracts of reinsurance.

## CERTIFICATES AS TO CONSENT

**3** A certificate under this paragraph is one given by the Authority and certifying that the host State regulator has been notified of the proposed scheme and that–

(a) that regulator has responded to the notification; or

(b) that it has not responded but the period of three months beginning with the notification has elapsed.

## CERTIFICATES AS TO LONG-TERM BUSINESS

**4** A certificate under this paragraph is one given by the Authority and certifying that the authority responsible for supervising persons who effect or carry out contracts of insurance in the State of the commitment has been notified of the proposed scheme and that–

(a) that authority has consented to the proposed scheme; or

(b) the period of three months beginning with the notification has elapsed and that authority has not refused its consent.

## CERTIFICATES AS TO GENERAL BUSINESS

**5** A certificate under this paragraph is one given by the Authority and certifying that the authority responsible for supervising persons who effect or carry out contracts of insurance in the EEA State in which the risk is situated has been notified of the proposed scheme and that–

(a) that authority has consented to the proposed scheme; or

(b) the period of three months beginning with the notification has elapsed and that authority has not refused its consent.

## INTERPRETATION OF PART I

**6(1)** **"State of the commitment"**, in relation to a commitment entered into at any date, means–

(a) if the policyholder is an individual, the State in which he had his habitual residence at that date;

(b) if the policyholder is not an individual, the State in which the establishment of the policyholder to which the commitment relates was situated at that date.

**6(2)** **"Commitment"** means a commitment represented by contracts of insurance of a prescribed class.

**6(3)** References to the EEA State in which a risk is situated are–

(a) if the insurance relates to a building or to a building and its contents (so far as the contents are covered by the same policy), to the EEA State in which the building is situated;

(b) if the insurance relates to a vehicle of any type, to the EEA State of registration;

(c) in the case of policies of a duration of four months or less covering travel or holiday risks (whatever the class concerned), to the EEA State in which the policyholder took out the policy;

(d) in a case not covered by paragraphs (a) to (c)–

   (i) if the policyholder is an individual, to the EEA State in which he has his habitual residence at the date when the contract is entered into; and

   (ii) otherwise, to the EEA State in which the establishment of the policyholder to which the policy relates is situated at that date.

# Part II – Banking business transfer schemes

**7(1)** For the purposes of section 111(2) the appropriate certificates, in relation to a banking business transfer scheme, are–

(a) a certificate under paragraph 8; and

(b) if sub-paragraph (2) applies, a certificate under paragraph 9.

**7(2)** This sub-paragraph applies if the authorised person concerned or the transferee is an EEA firm falling within paragraph 5(b) of Schedule 3.

CERTIFICATES AS TO FINANCIAL RESOURCES

**8(1)** A certificate under this paragraph is one given by the relevant authority and certifying that, taking the proposed transfer into account, the transferee possesses, or will possess before the scheme takes effect, adequate financial resources.

**8(2)** **"Relevant authority"** means–

(a) if the transferee is a person with a Part IV permission or with permission under Schedule 4, the Authority;

(b) if the transferee is an EEA firm falling within paragraph 5(b) of Schedule 3, its home state regulator;

(c) if the transferee does not fall within paragraph (a) or (b), the authority responsible for the supervision of the transferee's business in the place in which the transferee has its head office.

**8(3)** In sub-paragraph (2), any reference to a transferee of a particular description of person includes a reference to a transferee who will be of that description if the proposed banking business transfer scheme takes effect.

CERTIFICATES AS TO CONSENT OF HOME STATE REGULATOR

**9** A certificate under this paragraph is one given by the Authority and certifying that the home State regulator of the authorised person concerned or of the transferee has been notified of the proposed scheme and that–

(a) the home State regulator has responded to the notification; or

(b) the period of three months beginning with the notification has elapsed.

# Part III – Insurance business transfers effected outside the United Kingdom

**10(1)** This paragraph applies to a proposal to execute under provisions corresponding to Part VII in a country or territory other than the United Kingdom an instrument transferring all the rights and obligations of the transferor under general or long-term insurance policies, or under such descriptions of such policies as may be specified in the instrument, to the transferee if any of the conditions in sub-paragraphs (2), (3) or (4) is met in relation to it.

**10(2)** The transferor is an EEA firm falling within paragraph 5(d) of Schedule 3 and the transferee is an authorised person whose margin of solvency is supervised by the Authority.

**10(3)** The transferor is a company authorised in an EEA State other than the United Kingdom under Article 27 of the first life insurance directive, or Article 23 of the first non-life insurance directive and the transferee is a UK authorised person which has received authorisation under Article 6 of either of those directives.

**10(4)** The transferor is a Swiss general insurer and the transferee is a UK authorised person which has received authorisation under Article 6 of the first life insurance directive or the first non-life insurance directive.

**10(5)** In relation to a proposed transfer to which this paragraph applies, the Authority may, if it is satisfied that the transferee possesses the necessary margin of solvency, issue a certificate to that effect.

**10(6) "Necessary margin of solvency"** means the margin of solvency which the transferee, taking the proposed transfer into account, is required by the Authority to maintain.

**10(7) "Swiss general insurer"** has the same meaning as in paragraph 2.

**10(8) "General policy"** means a policy evidencing a contract which, if it had been effected by the transferee, would have constituted the carrying on of a regulated activity consisting of the effecting of contracts of general insurance.

**10(9) "Long-term policy"** means a policy evidencing a contract which, if it had been effected by the transferee, would have constituted the carrying on of a regulated activity consisting of the effecting of contracts of long-term insurance.

# SCHEDULE 13 – THE FINANCIAL SERVICES AND MARKETS TRIBUNAL

## Part I – General

### INTERPRETATION

**1** In this Schedule–

**"panel of chairmen"** means the panel established under paragraph 3(1);
**"lay panel"** means the panel established under paragraph 3(4);
**"rules"** means rules made by the Lord Chancellor under section 132.

## Part II – The Tribunal

### PRESIDENT

**2(1)** The Lord Chancellor must appoint one of the members of the panel of chairmen to preside over the discharge of the Tribunal's functions.

**2(2)** The member so appointed is to be known as the President of the Financial Services and Markets Tribunal (but is referred to in this Act as "the President").

**2(3)** The Lord Chancellor may appoint one of the members of the panel of chairmen to be Deputy President.

**2(4)** The Deputy President is to have such functions in relation to the Tribunal as the President may assign to him.

**2(5)** The Lord Chancellor may not appoint a person to be the President or Deputy President unless that person–

(a) has a ten year general qualification within the meaning of section 71 of the Courts and Legal Services Act 1990;

(b) is an advocate or solicitor in Scotland of at least ten years' standing; or

(c) is–
   (i) a member of the Bar of Northern Ireland of at least ten years' standing; or
   (ii) a solicitor of the Supreme Court of Northern Ireland of at least ten years' standing.

**2(6)** If the President (or Deputy President) ceases to be a member of the panel of chairmen, he also ceases to be the President (or Deputy President).

**2(7)** The functions of the President may, if he is absent or is otherwise unable to act, be discharged–

(a) by the Deputy President; or

(b) if there is no Deputy President or he too is absent or otherwise unable to act, by a person appointed for that purpose from the panel of chairmen by the Lord Chancellor.

## PANELS

**3(1)** The Lord Chancellor must appoint a panel of persons for the purposes of serving as chairmen of the Tribunal.

**3(2)** A person is qualified for membership of the panel of chairmen if–

(a) he has a seven year general qualification within the meaning of section 71 of the Courts and Legal Services Act 1990;

(b) he is an advocate or solicitor in Scotland of at least seven years' standing; or

(c) he is–
   (i) a member of the Bar of Northern Ireland of at least seven years' standing; or
   (ii) a solicitor of the Supreme Court of Northern Ireland of at least seven years' standing.

**3(3)** The panel of chairmen must include at least one member who is a person of the kind mentioned in sub-paragraph (2)(b).

**3(4)** The Lord Chancellor must also appoint a panel of persons who appear to him to be qualified by experience or otherwise to deal with matters of the kind that may be referred to the Tribunal.

## TERMS OF OFFICE ETC

**4(1)** Subject to the provisions of this Schedule, each member of the panel of chairmen and the lay panel is to hold and vacate office in accordance with the terms of his appointment.

**4(2)** The Lord Chancellor may remove a member of either panel (including the President) on the ground of incapacity or misbehaviour.

**4(3)** A member of either panel–

(a) may at any time resign office by notice in writing to the Lord Chancellor;

(b) is eligible for re-appointment if he ceases to hold office.

## REMUNERATION AND EXPENSES

**5** The Lord Chancellor may pay to any person, in respect of his service–

(a) as a member of the Tribunal (including service as the President or Deputy President), or

(b) as a person appointed under paragraph 7(4),

such remuneration and allowances as he may determine.

## STAFF

**6(1)** The Lord Chancellor may appoint such staff for the Tribunal as he may determine.

**6(2)** The remuneration of the Tribunal's staff is to be defrayed by the Lord Chancellor.

**6(3)** Such expenses of the Tribunal as the Lord Chancellor may determine are to be defrayed by the Lord Chancellor.

# Part III – Constitution of Tribunal

**7(1)** On a reference to the Tribunal, the persons to act as members of the Tribunal for the purposes of the reference are to be selected from the panel of chairmen or the lay panel in accordance with arrangements made by the President for the purposes of this paragraph ("the standing arrangements").

**7(2)** The standing arrangements must provide for at least one member to be selected from the panel of chairmen.

**7(3)** If while a reference is being dealt with, a person serving as member of the Tribunal in respect of the reference becomes unable to act, the reference may be dealt with by–

(a) the other members selected in respect of that reference; or

(b) if it is being dealt with by a single member, such other member of the panel of chairmen as may be selected in accordance with the standing arrangements for the purposes of the reference.

**7(4)** If it appears to the Tribunal that a matter before it involves a question of fact of special difficulty, it may appoint one or more experts to provide assistance.

# Part IV – Tribunal procedure

**8** For the purpose of dealing with references, or any matter preliminary or incidental to a reference, the Tribunal must sit at such times and in such place or places as the Lord Chancellor may direct.

**9** Rules made by the Lord Chancellor under section 132 may, in particular, include provision–

(a) as to the manner in which references are to be instituted;

(b) for the holding of hearings in private in such circumstances as may be specified in the rules;

(c) as to the persons who may appear on behalf of the parties;

(d) for a member of the panel of chairmen to hear and determine interlocutory matters arising on a reference;

(e) for the suspension of decisions of the Authority which have taken effect;

(f) as to the withdrawal of references;

(g) as to the registration, publication and proof of decisions and orders.

## PRACTICE DIRECTIONS

**10** The President of the Tribunal may give directions as to the practice and procedure to be followed by the Tribunal in relation to references to it.

## EVIDENCE

**11(1)** The Tribunal may by summons require any person to attend, at such time and place as is specified in the summons, to give evidence or to produce any document in his custody or under his control which the Tribunal considers it necessary to examine.

**11(2)** The Tribunal may–

(a) take evidence on oath and for that purpose administer oaths; or

(b) instead of administering an oath, require the person examined to make and subscribe a declaration of the truth of the matters in respect of which he is examined.

**11(3)** A person who without reasonable excuse–

(a) refuses or fails–

(i) to attend following the issue of a summons by the Tribunal, or

(ii) to give evidence, or

(b) alters, suppresses, conceals or destroys, or refuses to produce a document which he may be required to produce for the purposes of proceedings before the Tribunal,

is guilty of an offence.

**11(4)** A person guilty of an offence under sub-paragraph (3)(a) is liable on summary conviction to a fine not exceeding the statutory maximum.

**11(5)** A person guilty of an offence under sub-paragraph (3)(b) is liable–

(a) on summary conviction, to a fine not exceeding the statutory maximum;

(b) on conviction on indictment, to imprisonment for a term not exceeding two years or a fine or both.

## DECISIONS OF TRIBUNAL

**12(1)** A decision of the Tribunal may be taken by a majority.

**12(2)** The decision must–

(a) state whether it was unanimous or taken by a majority;

(b) be recorded in a document which–

(i) contains a statement of the reasons for the decision; and

(ii) is signed and dated by the member of the panel of chairmen dealing with the reference.

**12(3)** The Tribunal must–

(a) inform each party of its decision; and

(b) as soon as reasonably practicable, send to each party and, if different, to any authorised person concerned, a copy of the document mentioned in sub-paragraph (2).

**12(4)** The Tribunal must send the Treasury a copy of its decision.

### COSTS

**13(1)** If the Tribunal considers that a party to any proceedings on a reference has acted vexatiously, frivolously or unreasonably it may order that party to pay to another party to the proceedings the whole or part of the costs or expenses incurred by the other party in connection with the proceedings.

**13(2)** If, in any proceedings on a reference, the Tribunal considers that a decision of the Authority which is the subject of the reference was unreasonable it may order the Authority to pay to another party to the proceedings the whole or part of the costs or expenses incurred by the other party in connection with the proceedings.

# SCHEDULE 14 – ROLE OF THE COMPETITION COMMISSION

### PROVISION OF INFORMATION BY TREASURY

**1(1)** The Treasury's powers under this paragraph are to be exercised only for the purpose of assisting the Commission in carrying out an investigation under section 162.

**1(2)** The Treasury may give to the Commission–

(a) any information in their possession which relates to matters falling within the scope of the investigation; and

(b) other assistance in relation to any such matters.

**1(3)** In carrying out an investigation under section 162, the Commission must have regard to any information given to it under this paragraph.

### CONSIDERATION OF MATTERS ARISING ON A REPORT

**2** In considering any matter arising from a report made by the Director under section 160, the Commission must have regard to–

(a) any representations made to it in connection with the matter by any person appearing to the Commission to have a substantial interest in the matter; and

(b) any cost benefit analysis prepared by the Authority (at any time) in connection with the regulatory provision or practice, or any of the regulatory provisions or practices, which are the subject of the report.

### APPLIED PROVISIONS

**3(1)** The provisions mentioned in sub-paragraph (2) are to apply in relation to the functions of the Commission under section 162 as they apply in relation to the functions of the Commission in relation to a reference to the Commission under the Fair Trading Act 1973.

**3(2)** The provisions are–

(a) section 82(2), (3) and (4) of the Fair Trading Act 1973 (general provisions about reports);

(b) section 85 of that Act (attendance of witnesses and production of documents);

(c) section 93B of that Act (false or misleading information);

(d) section 24 of the Competition Act 1980 (modifications of provisions about the performance of the Commission's functions);

(d) Part II of Schedule 7 to the Competition Act 1998 (performance by the Commission of its general functions).

**3(3)** But the reference in paragraph 15(7)(b) in Schedule 7 to the 1998 Act to section 75(5) of that Act is to be read as a reference to the power of the Commission to decide not to make a report in accordance with section 162(2).

### PUBLICATION OF REPORTS

**4(1)** If the Commission makes a report under section 162, it must publish it in such a way as appears to it to be best calculated to bring it to the attention of the public.

**4(2)** Before publishing the report the Commission must, so far as practicable, exclude any matter which relates to the private affairs of a particular individual the publication of which, in the opinion of the Commission, would or might seriously and prejudicially affect his interests.

**4(3)** Before publishing the report the Commission must, so far as practicable, also exclude any matter which relates to the affairs of a particular body the publication of which, in the opinion of the Commission, would or might seriously and prejudicially affect its interests.

**4(4)** Sub-paragraphs (2) and (3) do not apply in relation to copies of a report which the Commission is required to send under section 162(10).

# SCHEDULE 15 – INFORMATION AND INVESTIGATIONS: CONNECTED PERSONS

## Part I – Rules for specific bodies

### CORPORATE BODIES

**1** If the authorised person ("BC") is a body corporate, a person who is or has been–

(a) an officer or manager of BC or of a parent undertaking of BC;

(b) an employee of BC;

(c) an agent of BC or of a parent undertaking of BC.

### PARTNERSHIPS

**2** If the authorised person ("PP") is a partnership, a person who is or has been a member, manager, employee or agent of PP.

### UNINCORPORATED ASSOCIATIONS

**3** If the authorised person ("UA") is an unincorporated association of persons which is neither a partnership nor an unincorporated friendly society, a person who is or has been an officer, manager, employee or agent of UA.

### FRIENDLY SOCIETIES

**4(1)** If the authorised person ("FS") is a friendly society, a person who is or has been an officer, manager or employee of FS.

**4(2)** In relation to FS, **"officer"** and **"manager"** have the same meaning as in section 119(1) of the Friendly Societies Act 1992.

### BUILDING SOCIETIES

**5(1)** If the authorised person ("BS") is a building society, a person who is or has been an officer or employee of BS.

**5(2)** In relation to BS, **"officer"** has the same meaning as it has in section 119(1) of the Building Societies Act 1986.

INDIVIDUALS

**6** If the authorised person ("IP") is an individual, a person who is or has been an employee or agent of IP.

APPLICATION TO SECTIONS 171 AND 172

**7** For the purposes of sections 171 and 172, if the person under investigation is not an authorised person the references in this Part of this Schedule to an authorised person are to be taken to be references to the person under investigation.

## Part II – Additional rules

**8** A person who is, or at the relevant time was, the partner, manager, employee, agent, appointed representative, banker, auditor, actuary or solicitor of–

(a) the person under investigation ("A");

(b) a parent undertaking of A;

(c) a subsidiary undertaking of A;

(d) a subsidiary undertaking of a parent undertaking of A; or

(e) a parent undertaking of a subsidiary undertaking of A.

# SCHEDULE 16 – PROHIBITIONS AND RESTRICTIONS IMPOSED BY DIRECTOR GENERAL OF FAIR TRADING

PRELIMINARY

**1** In this Schedule–

**"appeal period"** has the same meaning as in the Consumer Credit Act 1974;

**"prohibition"** means a consumer credit prohibition under section 203;

**"restriction"** means a restriction under section 204.

NOTICE OF PROHIBITION OR RESTRICTION

**2(1)** This paragraph applies if the Director proposes, in relation to a firm–

(a) to impose a prohibition;

(b) to impose a restriction; or

(c) to vary a restriction otherwise than with the agreement of the firm.

**2(2)** The Director must by notice–

(a) inform the firm of his proposal, stating his reasons; and

(b) invite the firm to submit representations in accordance with paragraph 4.

**2(3)** If he imposes the prohibition or restriction or varies the restriction, the Director may give directions authorising the firm to carry into effect agreements made before the coming into force of the prohibition, restriction or variation.

**2(4)** A prohibition, restriction or variation is not to come into force before the end of the appeal period.

**2(5)** If the Director imposes a prohibition or restriction or varies a restriction, he must serve a copy of the prohibition, restriction or variation–

(a) on the Authority; and

(b) on the firm's home state regulator.

### APPLICATION TO REVOKE PROHIBITION OR RESTRICTION

**3(1)** This paragraph applies if the Director proposes to refuse an application made by a firm for the revocation of a prohibition or restriction.

**3(2)** The Director must by notice–

(a) inform the firm of the proposed refusal, stating his reasons; and

(b) invite the firm to submit representations in accordance with paragraph 4.

### REPRESENTATIONS TO DIRECTOR

**4(1)** If this paragraph applies to an invitation to submit representations, the Director must invite the firm, within 21 days after the notice containing the invitation is given to it or such longer period as he may allow–

(a) to submit its representations in writing to him; and

(b) to give notice to him, if the firm thinks fit, that it wishes to make representations orally.

**4(2)** If notice is given under sub-paragraph (1)(b), the Director must arrange for the oral representations to be heard.

**4(3)** The Director must give the firm notice of his determination.

### APPEALS

**5** Section 41 of the Consumer Credit Act 1974 (appeals to the Secretary of State) has effect as if–

(a) the following determinations were mentioned in column 1 of the table set out at the end of that section–
   (i) imposition of a prohibition or restriction or the variation of a restriction; and
   (ii) refusal of an application for the revocation of a prohibition or restriction; and

(b) the firm concerned were mentioned in column 2 of that table in relation to those determinations.

# SCHEDULE 17 – THE OMBUDSMAN SCHEME

## Part I – General

### INTERPRETATION

**1** In this Schedule–

**"ombudsman"** means a person who is a member of the panel; and
**"the panel"** means the panel established under paragraph 4.

## Part II – The Scheme Operator

### ESTABLISHMENT BY THE AUTHORITY

**2(1)** The Authority must establish a body corporate to exercise the functions conferred on the scheme operator by or under this Act.

**2(2)** The Authority must take such steps as are necessary to ensure that the scheme operator is, at all times, capable of exercising those functions.

### CONSTITUTION

**3(1)** The constitution of the scheme operator must provide for it to have–

(a) a chairman; and

(b) a board (which must include the chairman) whose members are the scheme operator's directors.

**3(2)** The chairman and other members of the board must be persons appointed, and liable to removal from office, by the Authority (acting, in the case of the chairman, with the approval of the Treasury).

**3(3)** But the terms of their appointment (and in particular those governing removal from office) must be such as to secure their independence from the Authority in the operation of the scheme.

**3(4)** The function of making voluntary jurisdiction rules under section 227 and the functions conferred by paragraphs 4, 5, 7, 9 or 14 may be exercised only by the board.

**3(5)** The validity of any act of the scheme operator is unaffected by–

(a) a vacancy in the office of chairman; or

(b) a defect in the appointment of a person as chairman or as a member of the board.

## THE PANEL OF OMBUDSMEN

**4(1)** The scheme operator must appoint and maintain a panel of persons, appearing to it to have appropriate qualifications and experience, to act as ombudsmen for the purposes of the scheme.

**4(2)** A person's appointment to the panel is to be on such terms (including terms as to the duration and termination of his appointment and as to remuneration) as the scheme operator considers–

(a) consistent with the independence of the person appointed; and

(b) otherwise appropriate.

## THE CHIEF OMBUDSMAN

**5(1)** The scheme operator must appoint one member of the panel to act as Chief Ombudsman.

**5(2)** The Chief Ombudsman is to be appointed on such terms (including terms as to the duration and termination of his appointment) as the scheme operator considers appropriate.

## STATUS

**6(1)** The scheme operator is not to be regarded as exercising functions on behalf of the Crown.

**6(2)** The scheme operator's board members, officers and staff are not to be regarded as Crown servants.

**6(3)** Appointment as Chief Ombudsman or to the panel or as a deputy ombudsman does not confer the status of Crown servant.

## ANNUAL REPORTS

**7(1)** At least once a year–

(a) the scheme operator must make a report to the Authority on the discharge of its functions; and

(b) the Chief Ombudsman must make a report to the Authority on the discharge of his functions.

**7(2)** Each report must distinguish between functions in relation to the scheme's compulsory jurisdiction and functions in relation to its voluntary jurisdiction.

**7(3)** Each report must also comply with any requirements specified in rules made by the Authority.

**7(4)** The scheme operator must publish each report in the way it considers appropriate.

## GUIDANCE

**8** The scheme operator may publish guidance consisting of such information and advice as it considers appropriate and may charge for it or distribute it free of charge.

### BUDGET

**9(1)** The scheme operator must, before the start of each of its financial years, adopt an annual budget which has been approved by the Authority.

**9(2)** The scheme operator may, with the approval of the Authority, vary the budget for a financial year at any time after its adoption.

**9(3)** The annual budget must include an indication of–

(a) the distribution of resources deployed in the operation of the scheme, and

(b) the amounts of income of the scheme operator arising or expected to arise from the operation of the scheme,

distinguishing between the scheme's compulsory and voluntary jurisdiction.

### EXEMPTION FROM LIABILITY IN DAMAGES

**10(1)** No person is to be liable in damages for anything done or omitted in the discharge, or purported discharge, of any functions under this Act in relation to the compulsory jurisdiction.

**10(2)** Sub-paragraph (1) does not apply–

(a) if the act or omission is shown to have been in bad faith; or

(b) so as to prevent an award of damages made in respect of an act or omission on the ground that the act or omission was unlawful as a result of section 6(1) of the Human Rights Act 1998.

### PRIVILEGE

**11** For the purposes of the law relating to defamation, proceedings in relation to a complaint which is subject to the compulsory jurisdiction are to be treated as if they were proceedings before a court.

# Part III – The compulsory jurisdiction

### INTRODUCTION

**12** This Part of this Schedule applies only in relation to the compulsory jurisdiction.

### AUTHORITY'S PROCEDURAL RULES

**13(1)** The Authority must make rules providing that a complaint is not to be entertained unless the complainant has referred it under the ombudsman scheme before the applicable time limit (determined in accordance with the rules) has expired.

**13(2)** The rules may provide that an ombudsman may extend that time limit in specified circumstances.

**13(3)** The Authority may make rules providing that a complaint is not to be entertained (except in specified circumstances) if the complainant has not previously communicated its substance to the respondent and given him a reasonable opportunity to deal with it.

**13(4)** The Authority may make rules requiring an authorised person who may become subject to the compulsory jurisdiction as a respondent to establish such procedures as the Authority considers appropriate for the resolution of complaints which–

(a) may be referred to the scheme; and

(b) arise out of activity to which the Authority's powers under Part X do not apply.

### THE SCHEME OPERATOR'S RULES

**14(1)** The scheme operator must make rules, to be known as "scheme rules", which are to set out the procedure for reference of complaints and for their investigation, consideration and determination by an ombudsman.

**14(2)** Scheme rules may, among other things–

(a) specify matters which are to be taken into account in determining whether an act or omission was fair and reasonable;

(b) provide that a complaint may, in specified circumstances, be dismissed without consideration of its merits;

(c) provide for the reference of a complaint, in specified circumstances and with the consent of the complainant, to another body with a view to its being determined by that body instead of by an ombudsman;

(d) make provision as to the evidence which may be required or admitted, the extent to which it should be oral or written and the consequences of a person's failure to produce any information or document which he has been required (under section 231 or otherwise) to produce;

(e) allow an ombudsman to fix time limits for any aspect of the proceedings and to extend a time limit;

(f) provide for certain things in relation to the reference, investigation or consideration (but not determination) of a complaint to be done by a member of the scheme operator's staff instead of by an ombudsman;

(g) make different provision in relation to different kinds of complaint.

**14(3)** The circumstances specified under sub-paragraph (2)(b) may include the following–

(a) the ombudsman considers the complaint frivolous or vexatious;

(b) legal proceedings have been brought concerning the subject-matter of the complaint and the ombudsman considers that the complaint is best dealt with in those proceedings; or

(c) the ombudsman is satisfied that there are other compelling reasons why it is inappropriate for the complaint to be dealt with under the ombudsman scheme.

**14(4)** If the scheme operator proposes to make any scheme rules it must publish a draft of the proposed rules in the way appearing to it to be best calculated to bring them to the attention of persons appearing to it to be likely to be affected.

**14(5)** The draft must be accompanied by a statement that representations about the proposals may be made to the scheme operator within a time specified in the statement.

**14(6)** Before making the proposed scheme rules, the scheme operator must have regard to any representations made to it under sub-paragraph (5).

**14(7)** The consent of the Authority is required before any scheme rules may be made.

## FEES

**15(1)** Scheme rules may require a respondent to pay to the scheme operator such fees as may be specified in the rules.

**15(2)** The rules may, among other things–

(a) provide for the scheme operator to reduce or waive a fee in a particular case;

(b) set different fees for different stages of the proceedings on a complaint;

(c) provide for fees to be refunded in specified circumstances;

(d) make different provision for different kinds of complaint.

## ENFORCEMENT OF MONEY AWARDS

**16** A money award, including interest, which has been registered in accordance with scheme rules may–

(a) if a county court so orders in England and Wales, be recovered by execution issued from the county court (or otherwise) as if it were payable under an order of that court;

(b) be enforced in Northern Ireland as a money judgment under the Judgments Enforcement (Northern Ireland) Order 1981;

(c) be enforced in Scotland by the sheriff, as if it were a judgment or order of the sheriff and whether or not the sheriff could himself have granted such judgment or order.

# Part IV – The voluntary jurisdiction

## INTRODUCTION

**17** This Part of this Schedule applies only in relation to the voluntary jurisdiction.

## TERMS OF REFERENCE TO THE SCHEME

**18(1)** Complaints are to be dealt with and determined under the voluntary jurisdiction on standard terms fixed by the scheme operator with the approval of the Authority.

**18(2)** Different standard terms may be fixed with respect to different matters or in relation to different cases.

**18(3)** The standard terms may, in particular–

(a) require the making of payments to the scheme operator by participants in the scheme of such amounts, and at such times, as may be determined by the scheme operator;

(b) make provision as to the award of costs on the determination of a complaint.

**18(4)** The scheme operator may not vary any of the standard terms or add or remove terms without the approval of the Authority.

**18(5)** The standard terms may include provision to the effect that (unless acting in bad faith) none of the following is to be liable in damages for anything done or omitted in the discharge or purported discharge of functions in connection with the voluntary jurisdiction–

(a) the scheme operator;

(b) any member of its governing body;

(c) any member of its staff;

(d) any person acting as an ombudsman for the purposes of the scheme.

## DELEGATION BY AND TO OTHER SCHEMES

**19(1)** The scheme operator may make arrangements with a relevant body–

(a) for the exercise by that body of any part of the voluntary jurisdiction of the ombudsman scheme on behalf of the scheme; or

(b) for the exercise by the scheme of any function of that body as if it were part of the voluntary jurisdiction of the scheme.

**19(2)** A "relevant body" is one which the scheme operator is satisfied–

(a) is responsible for the operation of a broadly comparable scheme (whether or not established by statute) for the resolution of disputes; and

(b) in the case of arrangements under sub-paragraph (1)(a), will exercise the jurisdiction in question in a way compatible with the requirements imposed by or under this Act in relation to complaints of the kind concerned.

**19(3)** Such arrangements require the approval of the Authority.

## VOLUNTARY JURISDICTION RULES: PROCEDURE

**20(1)** If the scheme operator makes voluntary jurisdiction rules, it must give a copy to the Authority without delay.

**20(2)** If the scheme operator revokes any such rules, it must give written notice to the Authority without delay.

**20(3)** The power to make voluntary jurisdiction rules is exercisable in writing.

**20(4)** Immediately after making voluntary jurisdiction rules, the scheme operator must arrange for them to be printed and made available to the public.

**20(5)** The scheme operator may charge a reasonable fee for providing a person with a copy of any voluntary jurisdiction rules.

## VERIFICATION OF THE RULES

**21(1)** The production of a printed copy of voluntary jurisdiction rules purporting to be made by the scheme operator–

(a) on which is endorsed a certificate signed by a member of the scheme operator's staff authorised by the scheme operator for that purpose, and

(b) which contains the required statements,

is evidence (or in Scotland sufficient evidence) of the facts stated in the certificate.

**21(2)** The required statements are–

(a) that the rules were made by the scheme operator;

(b) that the copy is a true copy of the rules; and

(c) that on a specified date the rules were made available to the public in accordance with paragraph 20(4).

**21(3)** A certificate purporting to be signed as mentioned in sub-paragraph (1) is to be taken to have been duly signed unless the contrary is shown.

### CONSULTATION

**22(1)** If the scheme operator proposes to make voluntary jurisdiction rules, it must publish a draft of the proposed rules in the way appearing to it to be best calculated to bring them to the attention of the public.

**22(2)** The draft must be accompanied by–

(a) an explanation of the proposed rules; and

(b) a statement that representations about the proposals may be made to the scheme operator within a specified time.

**22(3)** Before making any voluntary jurisdiction rules, the scheme operator must have regard to any representations made to it in accordance with sub-paragraph (2)(b).

**22(4)** If voluntary jurisdiction rules made by the scheme operator differ from the draft published under sub-paragraph (1) in a way which the scheme operator considers significant, the scheme operator must publish a statement of the difference.

# SCHEDULE 18 – MUTUALS

## Part I – Friendly Societies

### THE FRIENDLY SOCIETIES ACT 1974 (C.46)

**1** Omit sections 4 (provision for separate registration areas) and 10 (societies registered in one registration area carrying on business in another).

**2** In section 7 (societies which may be registered), in subsection (2)(b), for "in the central registration area or in Scotland" substitute "in the United Kingdom, the Channel Islands or the Isle of Man".

**3** In section 11 (additional registration requirements for societies with branches), omit "and where any such society has branches in more than one registration area, section 10 above shall apply to that society".

**4** In section 99(4) (punishment of fraud etc and recovery of property misapplied), omit "in the central registration area".

### THE FRIENDLY SOCIETIES ACT 1992 (C.40)

**5** Omit sections 31 to 36A (authorisation of friendly societies business).

**6** In section 37 (restrictions on combinations of business), omit subsections (1), (1A) and (7A) to (9).

**7** Omit sections 38 to 43 (restrictions on business of certain authorised societies).

**8** Omit sections 44 to 50 (regulation of friendly societies business).

# Part II – Friendly Societies: Subsidiaries and Controlled Bodies

## INTERPRETATION

**9** In this Part of this Schedule–

**"the 1992 Act"** means the Friendly Societies Act 1992; and

**"section 13"** means section 13 of that Act.

## QUALIFYING BODIES

**10(1)** Subsections (2) to (5) of section 13 (incorporated friendly societies allowed to form or acquire control or joint control only of qualifying bodies) cease to have effect.

**10(2)** As a result, omit–

(a) subsections (8) and (11) of that section, and

(b) Schedule 7 to the 1992 Act (activities which may be carried on by a subsidiary of, or body jointly controlled by, an incorporated friendly society).

## BODIES CONTROLLED BY SOCIETIES

**11** In section 13(9) (defined terms), after paragraph (a) insert–

**(aa)** an incorporated friendly society also has control of a body corporate if the body corporate is itself a body controlled in one of the ways mentioned in paragraph (a)(i), (ii) or (iii) by a body corporate of which the society has control;".

## JOINT CONTROL BY SOCIETIES

**12** In section 13(9), after paragraph (c) insert–

**(cc)** an incorporated friendly society also has joint control of a body corporate if–

"(i) a subsidiary of the society has joint control of the body corporate in a way mentioned in paragraph (c)(i), (ii) or (iii);

(ii) a body corporate of which the society has joint control has joint control of the body corporate in such a way; or

(iii) the body corporate is controlled in a way mentioned in paragraph (a)(i), (ii) or (iii) by a body corporate of which the society has joint control;."

## ACQUISITION OF JOINT CONTROL

**13** In section 13(9), in the words following paragraph (d), after "paragraph (c)" insert "or (cc)".

## AMENDMENT OF SCHEDULE 8 TO THE 1992 ACT

**14(1)** Schedule 8 to the 1992 Act (provisions supplementing section 13) is amended as follows.

**14(2)** Omit paragraph 3(2).

**14(3)** After paragraph 3 insert–

"**3A(1)** A body is to be treated for the purposes of section 13(9) as having the right to appoint to a directorship if–

(a) a person's appointment to the directorship follows necessarily from his appointment as an officer of that body; or

(b) the directorship is held by the body itself.

**(2)** A body ("B") and some other person ("P") together are to be treated, for the purposes of section 13(9), as having the right to appoint to a directorship if–

(a) P is a body corporate which has directors and a person's appointment to the directorship follows necessarily from his appointment both as an officer of B and a director of P;

(b) P is a body corporate which does not have directors and a person's appointment to the directorship follows necessarily from his appointment both as an officer of B and as a member of P's managing body; or

(c) the directorship is held jointly by B and P.

**(3)** For the purposes of section 13(9), a right to appoint (or remove) which is exercisable only with the consent or agreement of another person must be left out of account unless no other person has a right to appoint (or remove) in relation to that directorship.

**(4)** Nothing in this paragraph is to be read as restricting the effect of section 13(9)."

**14(4)** In paragraph 9 (exercise of certain rights under instruction by, or in the interests of, incorporated friendly society) insert at the end "or in the interests of any body over which the society has joint control".

CONSEQUENTIAL AMENDMENTS

**15(1)** Section 52 of the 1992 Act is amended as follows.

**15(2)** In subsection (2), omit paragraph (d).

**15(3)** In subsection (3), for "(4) below" substitute "(2)".

**15(4)** For subsection (4) substitute–

"(4) A court may not make an order under subsection (5) unless it is satisfied that one or more of the conditions mentioned in subsection (2) are satisfied."

**15(5)** In subsection (5), omit the words from "or, where" to the end.

REFERENCES IN OTHER ENACTMENTS

**16** References in any provision of, or made under, any enactment to subsidiaries of, or bodies jointly controlled by, an incorporated friendly society are to be read as including references to bodies which are such subsidiaries or bodies as a result of any provision of this Part of this Schedule.

## Part III – Building Societies

THE BUILDING SOCIETIES ACT 1986 (C.53)

**17** Omit section 9 (initial authorisation to raise funds and borrow money).

**18** Omit Schedule 3 (supplementary provisions about authorisation).

## Part IV – Industrial and Provident Societies

THE INDUSTRIAL AND PROVIDENT SOCIETIES ACT 1965 (C.12)

**19** Omit section 8 (provision for separate registration areas for Scotland and for England, Wales and the Channel Islands).

**20** Omit section 70 (scale of fees to be paid in respect of transactions and inspection of documents).

## Part V – Credit Unions

THE CREDIT UNIONS ACT 1979 (C.34)

**21** In section 6 (minimum and maximum number of members), omit subsections (2) to (6).

**22** In section 11 (loans), omit subsections (2) and (6).

**23** Omit sections 11B (loans approved by credit unions), 11C (grant of certificates of approval) and 11D (withdrawal of certificates of approval).

**24** In section 12, omit subsections (4) and (5).

**25** In section 14, omit subsections (2), (3), (5) and (6).

**26** In section 28 (offences), omit subsection (2).

# SCHEDULE 19 – COMPETITION INFORMATION

## Part I – Persons and functions for the purposes of section 351

**1** The Table set out after this paragraph has effect for the purposes of section 351(3)(b).

TABLE

| *Person* | *Function* |
|---|---|
| 1. The Commission. | Any function of the Commission under Community law relating to competition. |
| 2. The Comptroller and Auditor General. | Any function of his. |
| 3. A Minister of the Crown. | Any function of his under a specified enactment. |
| 4. Director General of Telecommunications. | Any function of his under a specified enactment. |
| 5. Director General of Gas Supply | Any function of his under a specified enactment. |
| 6. The Director General of Gas for Northern Ireland. | Any function of his under a specified enactment. |
| 7. The Director General of Electricity Supply. | Any function of his under a specified anactment. |
| 8. The Director General of Electricity Supply for Northern Ireland. | Any function of his under a specified enactment. |
| 9. The Director General of Water Services. | Any function of his under a specified enactment. |
| 10. The Civil Aviation Authority. | Any function of that authority under a specified enactment. |
| 11. The Rail Regulator. | Any function of his under a specified enactment. |
| 12. The Director General of Fair Trading. | Any function of his under a specified enactment. |
| 13. The Competition Commission. | Any function of the Competition Commission under a specified enactment. |
| 14. The Authority. | Any function of the Authority under a specified enactment. |
| 15. A person of a description specified in an order made by the Treasury. | Any function of his which is specified in the order. |

## Part II – The Enactments

**1** The Fair Trading Act 1973

**2** The Consumer Credit Act 1974

**3** The Estate Agents Act 1979

**4** The Competition Act 1980

**5** The Telecommunications Act 1984

**6** The Airports Act 1986

**7** The Gas Act 1986

**8** The Control of Misleading Advertisements Regulations 1988

**9** The Electricity Act 1989

**10** The Broadcasting Act 1990

**11** The Water Industry Act 1991

**12** The Electricity (Northern Ireland) Order 1992

**13** The Railways Act 1993

**14** Part IV of the Airports (Northern Ireland) Order 1994

**15** The Gas (Northern Ireland) Order 1996

**16** The EC Competition (Articles 88 and 89) Enforcement Regulations 1996

**17** The Unfair Terms in Consumer Contracts Regulations 1999

**18** This Act.

**19** An enactment specified for the purposes of this paragraph in an order made by the Treasury.

# SCHEDULE 20 – MINOR AND CONSEQUENTIAL AMENDMENTS

## THE HOUSE OF COMMONS DISQUALIFICATION ACT 1975 (C. 24)

**1** In Part III of Schedule 1 to the House of Commons Disqualification Act 1975 (disqualifying offices)–

(a) omit–
"Any member of the Financial Services Tribunal in receipt of remuneration"; and

(b) at the appropriate place, insert–
"Any member, in receipt of remuneration, of a panel of persons who may be selected to act as members of the Financial Services and Markets Tribunal".

## THE NORTHERN IRELAND ASSEMBLY DISQUALIFICATION ACT 1975 (C. 25)

**2** In Part III of Schedule 1 to the Northern Ireland Assembly Disqualification Act 1975 (disqualifying offices)–

(a) omit–
"Any member of the Financial Services Tribunal in receipt of remuneration"; and

(b) at the appropriate place, insert–
"Any member, in receipt of remuneration, of a panel of persons who may be selected to act as members of the Financial Services and Markets Tribunal".

## THE CIVIL JURISDICTION AND JUDGMENTS ACT 1982 (C. 27)

**3** In paragraph 10 of Schedule 5 to the Civil Jurisdiction and Judgments Act 1982 (proceedings excluded from the operation of Schedule 4 to that Act), for "section 188 of the Financial Services Act 1986" substitute "section 415 of the Financial Services and Markets Act 2000".

## THE INCOME AND CORPORATION TAXES ACT 1988 (C. 1)

**4(1)** The Income and Corporation Taxes Act 1988 is amended as follows.

**4(2)** In section 76 (expenses of management: insurance companies), in subsection (8), omit the definitions of–

**"the 1986 Act; "**
**"authorised person; "**
**"investment business;"**
**"investor;"**
**"investor protection scheme;"**
**"prescribed and"**
**"recognised self-regulating organisation."**

**4(3)** In section 468 (authorised unit trusts), in subsections (6) and (8), for "78 of the Financial Services Act 1986" substitute "243 of the Financial Services and Markets Act 2000".

**4(4)** In section 469(7) (other unit trust schemes), for "Financial Services Act 1986" substitute "Financial Services and Markets Act 2000".

**4(5)** In section 728 (information in relation to transfers of securities), in subsection (7)(a), for "Financial Services Act 1986" substitute "Financial Services and Markets Act 2000".

**4(6)** In section 841(3) (power to apply certain provisions of the Tax Acts to recognised investment exchange), for "Financial Services Act 1986" substitute "Financial Services and Markets Act 2000".

### THE FINANCE ACT 1991 (C. 31)

**5(1)** The Finance Act 1991 is amended as follows.

**5(2)** In section 47 (investor protection schemes), omit subsections (1), (2) and (4).

**5(3)** In section 116 (investment exchanges and clearing houses: stamp duty), in subsection (4)(b), for "Financial Services Act 1986" substitute "Financial Services and Markets Act 2000".

### THE TRIBUNALS AND INQUIRIES ACT 1992 (C. 53)

**6(1)** The Tribunals and Inquiries Act 1992 is amended as follows.

**6(2)** In Schedule 1 (tribunals under supervision of the Council on Tribunals), for the entry relating to financial services and paragraph 18, substitute–
"Financial services and markets
18. The Financial Services and Markets Tribunal."

### THE JUDICIAL PENSIONS AND RETIREMENT ACT 1993 (C. 8)

**7(1)** The Judicial Pensions and Retirement Act 1993 is amended as follows.

**7(2)** In Schedule 1 (offices which may be qualifying offices), in Part II, after the entry relating to the President or chairman of the Transport Tribunal insert–

"President or Deputy President of the Financial Services and Markets Tribunal"

**7(3)** In Schedule 5 (relevant offices in relation to retirement provisions)–

(a) omit the entry–
"Member of the Financial Services Tribunal appointed by the Lord Chancellor"; and

(b) at the end insert–
"Member of the Financial Services and Markets Tribunal".

# SCHEDULE 21 – TRANSITIONAL PROVISIONS AND SAVINGS

## SELF-REGULATING ORGANISATIONS

**1(1)** No new application under section 9 of the 1986 Act (application for recognition) may be entertained.

**1(2)** No outstanding application made under that section before the passing of this Act may continue to be entertained.

**1(3)** After the date which is the designated date for a recognised self-regulating organisation–

(a) the recognition order for that organisation may not be revoked under section 11 of the 1986 Act (revocation of recognition);

(b) no application may be made to the court under section 12 of the 1986 Act (compliance orders) with respect to that organisation.

**Note**

The Financial Services and Markets (Transitional Provisions) (Designated Date for Certain Self-Regulating Organisations) Order 2000 (SI 2000/1734), art. 1, 2 designates 25 July 2000 for the Personal Investment Authority Limited and the Investment Management Regulatory Organisation Limited.

**1(4)** The powers conferred by section 13 of the 1986 Act (alteration of rules for protection of investors) may not be exercised.

**1(5)** **"Designated date"** means such date as the Treasury may by order designate.

**Note**
The Financial Services and Markets (Transitional Provisions) (Designated Date for Certain Self-Regulating Organisations) Order 2000 (SI 2000/1734), art. 1, 2 designates 25 July 2000 for the Personal Investment Authority Limited and the Investment Management Regulatory Organisation Limited.

**1(6)** Sub-paragraph (3) does not apply to a recognised self-regulating organisation in respect of which a notice of intention to revoke its recognition order was given under section 11(3) of the 1986 Act before the passing of this Act if that notice has not been withdrawn.

**1(7)** Expenditure incurred by the Authority in connection with the winding up of any body which was, immediately before the passing of this Act, a recognised self-regulating organisation is to be treated as having been incurred in connection with the discharge by the Authority of functions under this Act.

**1(8)** **"Recognised self-regulating organisation"** means an organisation which, immediately before the passing of this Act, was such an organisation for the purposes of the 1986 Act.

**1(9)** **"The 1986 Act"** means the Financial Services Act 1986.

**Commencement**
Para. 1 in force as from 14 June 2000 (see s. 431(1)(c) FSMA 2000)

## SELF-REGULATING ORGANISATIONS FOR FRIENDLY SOCIETIES

**2(1)** No new application under paragraph 2 of Schedule 11 to the 1986 Act (application for recognition) may be entertained.

**2(2)** No outstanding application made under that paragraph before the passing of this Act may continue to be entertained.

**2(3)** After the date which is the designated date for a recognised self-regulating organisation for friendly societies–

(a) the recognition order for that organisation may not be revoked under paragraph 5 of Schedule 11 to the 1986 Act (revocation of recognition);

(b) no application may be made to the court under paragraph 6 of that Schedule (compliance orders) with respect to that organisation.

**Note**
The Financial Services and Markets (Transitional Provisions) (Designated Date for Certain Self-Regulating Organisations) Order 2000 (SI 2000/1734), art. 1, 2 designates 25 July 2000 for the Personal Investment Authority Limited and the Investment Management Regulatory Organisation Limited.

**2(4)** **"Designated date"** means such date as the Treasury may by order designate.

**Note**
The Financial Services and Markets (Transitional Provisions) (Designated Date for Certain Self-Regulating Organisations) Order 2000 (SI 2000/1734), art. 1, 2 designates 25 July 2000 for the Personal Investment Authority Limited and the Investment Management Regulatory Organisation Limited.

**2(5)** Sub-paragraph (3) does not apply to a recognised self-regulating organisation for friendly societies in respect of which a notice of intention to revoke its recognition order was given under section 11(3) of the 1986 Act (as applied by paragraph 5(2) of that Schedule) before the passing of this Act if that notice has not been withdrawn.

**2(6)** Expenditure incurred by the Authority in connection with the winding up of any body which was, immediately before the passing of this Act, a recognised self-regulating organisation for friendly societies is to be treated as having been incurred in connection with the discharge by the Authority of functions under this Act.

**2(7)** **"Recognised self-regulating organisation for friendly societies"** means an organisation which, immediately before the passing of this Act, was such an organisation for the purposes of the 1986 Act.

**2(8)** **"The 1986 Act"** means the Financial Services Act 1986.

**Commencement**
Para. 2 in force as from 14 June 2000 (see s. 431(1)(c) FSMA 2000)

# SCHEDULE 22 – REPEALS

REPEALS

| Chapter | Short title | Extent of repeal |
|---|---|---|
| 1923 c. 8. | The Industrial Assurance Act 1923. | The whole Act. |
| 1948 c. 39. | The Industrial Assurance and Friendly Societies Act 1948. | The whole Act. |
| 1965 c. 12. | The Industrial and Provident Societies Act 1965. | Section 8.<br>Section 70. |
| 1974 c. 46. | The Friendly Societies Act 1974. | Section 4.<br>Section 10.<br>In section 11, from "and where" to "that society".<br>In section 99(4), "in the central registration area". |
| 1975 c. 24. | The House of Commons Disqualification Act 1975. | In Schedule 1, in Part III, "Any member of the Financial Services Tribunal in receipt of remuneration". |
| 1975 c. 25. | The Northern Ireland Assembly Disqualification Act 1975. | In Schedule 1, in Part III, "Any member of the Financial Services Tribunal in receipt of remuneration". |
| 1977 c. 46. | The Insurance Brokers (Registration) Act 1977. | The whole Act. |
| 1979 c. 34. | The Credit Unions Act 1979. | Section 6(2) to (6).<br>Section 11(2) and (6).<br>Sections 11B, 11C and 11D.<br>Section 12(4) and (5).<br>In section 14, subsections (2), (3), (5) and (6).<br>Section 28(2). |
| 1986 c. 53. | The Building Societies Act 1986. | Section 9.<br>Schedule 3. |
| 1988 c. 1. | The Income and Corporation Taxes Act 1988. | In section 76, in subsection (8), the definitions of "the 1986 Act", "authorised person", "investment business", "investor", "investor protection scheme", "prescribed" and "recognised self-regulating organisation". |
| 1991 c. 31. | The Finance Act 1991. | In section 47, subsections (1), (2) and (4). |

| Chapter | Short title | Extent of repeal |
|---|---|---|
| 1992 c. 40 | The Friendly Societies Act 1992. | In section 13, subsections (2) to (5), (8) and (11).<br>Sections 31 to 36.<br>In section 37, subsections (1), (1A) and (7A) to (9).<br>Sections 38 to 50.<br>In section 52, subsection (2)(d) and, in subsection (5), the words from "or where" to the end.<br>Schedule 7.<br>In Schedule 8, paragraph 3(2). |
| 1993 c. 8. | The Judicial Pensions and Retirement Act 1993. | In Schedule 5, "Member of the Financial Services Tribunal appointed by the Lord Chancellor". |

# ANCILLARY ACTS

## Table of Contents

**Stamp Duty and Stamp Duty Reserve Tax**

The following provisions relating to Stamp Duty and Stamp Duty Reserve Tax are reproduced only in the CD-ROM edition of this volume: Finance Act 1930, s. 42; Finance Act 1976, s. 127; Finance Act 1985, s. 81; Finance Act 1986, s. 66, 75–77, 79–82, 84, 86–92 and 99; Finance Act 1987, s. 50; Finance Act 1988, s. 143; Finance Act 1989, s. 175, 176; Finance Act 1990, s. 107–113; Finance Act 1993, s. 204; Finance Act 1997, s. 95–98, 100–103; Finance Act 1998, s. 150; Finance Act 1999, s. 112 and Sch. 13, para. 1–3, 16, 17, 24 and 26; and Finance Act 2000, s. 122.



**continued over**

# PARTNERSHIP ACT 1890

(53 & 54 Vict. c. 39)

## ARRANGEMENT OF SECTIONS

# PARTNERSHIP ACT 1890

(53 & 54 Vict. c. 39)

An Act to declare and amend the Law of Partnership.

[*14th August 1890*

NATURE OF PARTNERSHIP

## 1 Definition of partnership

**1(1) [Definition]** Partnership is the relation which subsists between persons carrying on a business in common with a view of profit.

**1(2) [Exclusion]** But the relation between members of any company or association which is–

(a) Registered as a company under the Companies Act 1862, or any other Act of Parliament for the time being in force and relating to the registration of joint stock companies; or

(b) Formed or incorporated by or in pursuance of any other Act of Parliament or letters patent, or Royal Charter:

is not a partnership within the meaning of this Act.

**History**

In s. 1(2) the word "; or" formerly appearing after the words "Royal Charter" and s. 1(2)(c) repealed and revoked by the Statute Law (Repeals) Act 1998, s. 1 and Sch. 1 as from 19 November 1998. S. 1(2)(c) formerly read as follows:
"A company engaged in working mines within and subject to the jurisdiction of the Stannaries".

## 2 Rules for determining existence of partnership

**2** In determining whether a partnership does or does not exist, regard shall be had to the following rules:

(1) Joint tenancy, tenancy in common, joint property, common property, or part ownership does not of itself create a partnership as to anything so held or owned, whether the tenants or owners do or do not share any profits made by the use thereof.

(2) The sharing of gross returns does not of itself create a partership, whether the persons sharing such returns have or have not a joint or common right or interest in any property from which or from the use of which the returns are derived.

(3) The receipt by a person of a share of the profits of a business is *primâ facie* evidence that he is a partner in the business, but the receipt of such a share, or of a payment contingent on or varying with the profits of a business, does not of itself make him a partner in the business; and in particular–

(a) The receipt by a person of a debt or other liquidated amount by instalments or otherwise out of the accruing profits of a business does not of itself make him a partner in the business or liable as such:

(b) A contract for the remuneration of a servant of agent of a person engaged in a business by a share of the profits of the business does not of itself make the servant or agent a partner in the business or liable as such:

(c) A person being the widow or child of a deceased partner, and receiving by way of annuity a portion of the profits made in the business in which the deceased person was a partner, is not by reason only of such receipt a partner in the business or liable as such:

(d) The advance of money by way of loan to a person engaged or about to engage in any business on a contract with that person that the lender shall receive a rate of interest varying with the profits, or shall receive a share of the profits arising from carrying on the business, does not of itself make the lender a partner with the person or persons carrying on the business or liable as such. Provided that the contract is in writing, and signed by or on behalf of all the parties thereto:

(e) A person receiving by way of annuity or otherwise a portion of the profits of a business in consideration of the sale by him of the goodwill of the business is not by reason only of such receipt a partner in the business or liable as such.

## 3 Postponement of rights of person lending or selling in consideration of share of profits in case of insolvency

**3** In the event of any person to whom money has been advanced by way of loan upon such a contract as is mentioned in the last foregoing section, or of any buyer of a goodwill in consideration of a share of the profits of the business, being adjudged a bankrupt, entering into an arrangement to pay his creditors less than 100p in the pound, or dying in insolvent circumstances, the lender of the loan shall not be entitled to recover anything in respect of his loan, and the seller of the goodwill shall not be entitled to recover anything in respect of the share of profits contracted for, until the claims of the other creditors of the borrower or buyer for valuable consideration in money or money's worth have been satisfied.

**History**
S. 3 amended by Decimal Currency Act 1969, s. 10(1).

## 4 Meaning of firm

**4(1) [Firm, firm-name]** Persons who have entered into partnership with one another are for the purposes of this Act called collectively a firm, and the name under which their business is carried on is called the firm-name.

**4(2) [Scotland]** In Scotland a firm is a legal person distinct from the partners of whom it is composed, but an individual partner may be charged on a decree or diligence directed against the firm, and on payment of the debts is entitled to relief *pro ratâ* from the firm and its other members.

**Note**
For the purposes of inheritance tax, occupation of any property by a Scottish partnership is treated as occupation by the partners, notwithstanding s. 4(2) (see Inheritance Tax Act 1984, s. 119(2)).

RELATIONS OF PARTNERS TO PERSONS DEALING WITH THEM

## 5 Power of partner to bind the firm

**5** Every partner is an agent of the firm and his other partners for the purpose of the business of the partnership; and the acts of every partner who does any act for carrying on in the usual way business of the kind carried on by the firm of which he is a member bind the firm and his partners, unless the partner so acting has in fact no authority to act for the firm in the particular matter, and the person with whom he is dealing either knows that he has no authority, or does not know or believe him to be a partner.

## 6 Partners bound by acts on behalf of firm

**6** An act or instrument relating to the business of the firm done or executed in the firm-name, or in any other manner showing an intention to bind the firm, by any person thereto authorised, whether a partner or not, is binding on the firm and all the partners.

Provided that this section shall not affect any general rule of law relating to the execution of deeds or negotiable instruments.

## 7 Partner using credit of firm for private purposes

**7** Where one partner pledges the credit of the firm for a purpose apparently not connected with the firm's ordinary course of business, the firm is not bound, unless he is in fact specially authorised by the other partners; but this section does not affect any personal liability incurred by an individual partner.

## 8 Effect of notice that firm will not be bound by acts of partner

**8** If it has been agreed between the partners that any restriction shall be placed on the power of any one or more of them to bind the firm, no act done in contravention of the agreement is binding on the firm with respect to persons having notice of the agreement.

## 9 Liability of partners

**9** Every partner in a firm is liable jointly with the other partners, and in Scotland severally also, for all debts and obligations of the firm incurred while he is a partner; and after his death his estate is also severally liable in a due course of administration for such debts and obligations, so far as they remain unsatisfied, but subject in England or Ireland to the prior payment of his separate debts.

## 10 Liability of the firm for wrongs

**10** Where, by any wrongful act or omission of any partner acting in the ordinary course of the business of the firm, or with the authority of his co-partners, loss or injury is caused to any person not being a partner in the firm, or any penalty is incurred, the firm is liable therefor to the same extent as the partner so acting or omitting to act.

## 11 Misapplication of money or property received for or in custody of the firm

**11** In the following cases; namely–

(a) Where one partner acting within the scope of his apparent authority receives the money or property of a third person and misapplies it; and

(b) Where a firm in the course of its business receives money or property of a third person, and the money or property so received is misapplied by one or more of the partners while it is in the custody of the firm;

the firm is liable to make good the loss.

## 12 Liability for wrongs joint and several

**12** Every partner is liable jointly with his co-partners and also severally for everything for which the firm while he is a partner therein becomes liable under either of the two last preceding sections.

## 13 Improper employment of trust-property for partnership purposes

**13** If a partner, being a trustee, improperly employs trust-property in the business or on the account of the partnership, no other partner is liable for the trust property to the persons beneficially interested therein:

Provided as follows:–

(1) This section shall not affect any liability incurred by any partner by reason of his having notice of a breach of trust; and

(2) Nothing in this section shall prevent trust money from being followed and recovered from the firm if still in its possession or under its control.

## 14 Persons liable by "holding out"

**14(1) [Liability as partner]** Every one who by words spoken or written or by conduct represents himself, or who knowingly suffers himself to be represented, as a partner in a particular firm, is liable as a partner to any one who has on the faith of any such representation given credit to the firm, whether the representation has or has not been made or communicated to the person so giving credit by or with the knowledge of the apparent partner making the representation or suffering it to be made.

**14(2) [Exception for estate etc. after death]** Provided that where after a partner's death the partnership business is continued in the old firm's name, the continued use of that name or of the deceased partner's name as part thereof shall not of itself make his executors or administrators estate or effects liable for any partnership debts contracted after his death.

## 15 Admissions and representations of partners

**15** An admission or representation made by any partner concerning the partnership affairs, and in the ordinary course of its business, is evidence against the firm.

## 16 Notice to acting partner to be notice to the firm

**16** Notice to any partner who habitually acts in the partnership business of any matter relating to partnership affairs operates as notice to the firm, except in the case of a fraud on the firm committed by or with the consent of that partner.

## 17 Liabilities of incoming and outgoing partners

**17(1) [Admitted partner]** A person who is admitted as a partner into an existing firm does not thereby become liable to the creditors of the firm for anything done before he became a partner.

**17(2) [Retiring partner]** A partner who retires from a firm does not thereby cease to be liable for partnership debts or obligations incurred before his retirement.

**17(3) [Discharge agreement re retiring partner]** A retiring partner may be discharged from any existing liabilities, by an agreement to that effect between himself and the members of the firm as newly constituted and the creditors, and this agreement may be either expressed or inferred as a fact from the course of dealing between the creditors and the firm as newly constituted.

## 18 Revocation of continuing guaranty by change in firm

**18** A continuing guaranty or cautionary obligation given either to a firm or to a third person in respect of the transactions of a firm is, in the absence of agreement to the contrary, revoked as to future transactions by any change in the constitution of the firm to which, or of the firm in respect of the transactions of which, the guaranty or obligation was given.

### RELATIONS OF PARTNERS TO ONE ANOTHER

## 19 Variation by consent of terms of partnership

**19** The mutual rights and duties of partners, whether ascertained by agreement or defined by this Act, may be varied by the consent of all the partners, and such consent may be either express or inferred from a course of dealing.

## 20 Partnership property

**20(1) [Property in partnership]** All property and rights and interests in property originally brought into the partnership stock or acquired, whether by purchase or otherwise, on account of the firm, or for the purposes and in the course of the partnership business, are called in this Act partnership property, and must be held and applied by the partners exclusively for the purposes of the partnership and in accordance with the partnership agreement.

**20(2) [Devolution of legal estate etc.]** Provided that the legal estate or interest in any land, or in Scotland the title to and interest in any heritable estate, which belongs to the partnership shall devolve according to the nature and tenure thereof, and the general rules of law thereto applicable, but in trust so far as necessary, for the persons beneficially interested in the land under this section.

**20(3) [Co-owners of land]** Where co-owners of an estate or interest in any land, or in Scotland of any heritable estate, not being itself partnership property, are partners as to profits made by the use of that land or estate, and purchase other land or estate out of the profits to be used in like manner, the land or estate so purchased belongs to them, in the absence of an agreement to the contrary, not as partners, but as co-owners for the same respective estates and interests as are held by them in the land or estate first mentioned at the date of the purchase.

# 21 Property bought with partnership money

**21** Unless the contrary intention appears, property bought with money belonging to the firm is deemed to have been bought on account of the firm.

# 22 Conversion into personal estate of land held as partnership property

**22** (Repealed by Trusts of Land and Appointment of Trustees Act 1996, s. 25(2), 27 and Sch. 4 as from 1 January 1997.)

**History**
In regard to the date of the above repeal, see the Trusts of Land and Appointment of Trustees Act 1996 (Commencement) Order 1996 (SI 1996/2974). S. 22 formerly read as follows:
"Where land or any heritable interest therein has become partnership property, it shall, unless the contrary intention appears, be treated as between the partners (including the representatives of a deceased partner), and also as between the heirs of a deceased partner and his executors or administrators, as personal or moveable and not real or heritable estate."

# 23 Procedure against partnership property for a partner's separate judgment debt

**23(1) [Executions must be against firm]** A writ of execution shall not issue against any partnership property except on a judgment against the firm.

**23(2) [Order by court etc.]** The High Court, or a judge thereof, a county court, may, on the application by summons of any judgment creditor of a partner, make an order charging that partner's interest in the partnership property and profits with payment of the amount of the judgment debt and interest thereon, and may by the same or a subsequent order appoint a receiver of that partner's share of profits (whether already declared or accruing), and of any other money which may be coming to him in respect of the partnership, and direct all accounts and inquiries, and give all other orders and directions which might have been directed or given if the charge had been made in favour of the judgment creditor by the partner, or which the circumstances of the case may require.

**History**
S. 23(2) amended by Courts Act 1971, Sch. 11, Pt. II.

**23(3) [Right of redemption, purchase by other partner]** The other partner or partners shall be at liberty at any time to redeem the interest charged, or in case of a sale being directed, to purchase the same.

**23(4)** (Repealed by the Statute Law (Repeals) Act 1998, s. 1 and Sch. 1 as from 19 November 1998.)

**23(5) [Scotland]** This section shall not apply to Scotland.

**History**
S. 23(4) formerly read as follows:
"This section shall apply in the case of a cost-book company as if the company were a partnership within the meaning of this Act."

# 24 Rules as to interests and duties of partners subject to special agreement

**24** The interests of partners in the partnership property and their rights and duties in relation to the partnership shall be determined, subject to any agreement express or implied between the partners, by the following rules:–

(1) All the partners are entitled to share equally in the capital and profits of the business, and must contribute equally towards the losses whether of capital or otherwise sustained by the firm.

(2) The firm must indemnify every partner in respect of payments made and personal liabilities incurred by him–

(a) In the ordinary and proper conduct of the business of the firm; or

(b) In or about anything necessarily done for the preservation of the business or property of the firm.

(3) A partner making, for the purpose of the partnership, any actual payment or advance beyond the amount of capital which he has agreed to subscribe, is entitled to interest at the rate of five per cent per annum from the date of the payment or advance.

(4) A partner is not entitled, before the ascertainment of profits, to interest on the capital subscribed by him.

(5) Every partner may take part in the management of the partnership business.

(6) No partner shall be entitled to remuneration for acting in the partnership business.

(7) No person may be introduced as a partner without the consent of all existing partners.

(8) Any difference arising as to ordinary matters connected with the partnership business may be decided by a majority of the partners, but no change may be made in the nature of the partnership business without the consent of all existing partners.

(9) The partnership books are to be kept at the place of business of the partnership (or the principal place, if there is more than one), and every partner may, when he thinks fit, have access to and inspect and copy any of them.

## 25 Expulsion of partner

**25** No majority of the partners can expel any partner unless a power to do so has been conferred by express agreement between the partners.

## 26 Retirement from partnership at will

**26(1) [Notice to all other partners]** Where no fixed term has been agreed upon for the duration of the partnership, any partner may determine the partnership at any time on giving notice of his intention so to do to all the other partners.

**26(2) [Partnership constituted by deed]** Where the partnership has originally been constituted by deed, a notice in writing, signed by the partner giving it, shall be sufficient for this purpose.

## 27 Where partnership for term is continued over, continuance on old terms presumed

**27(1) [Where continuance]** Where a partnership entered into for a fixed term is continued after the term has expired, and without any express new agreement, the rights and duties of the partners remain the same as they were at the expiration of the term, so far as is consistent with the incidents of a partnership at will.

**27(2) [Presumed continuance]** A continuance of the business by the partners or such of them as habitually acted therein during the term, without any settlement or liquidation of the partnership affairs, is presumed to be a continuance of the partnership.

## 28 Duty of partners to render accounts, &c.

**28** Partners are bound to render true accounts and full information of all things affecting the partnership to any partner or his legal representatives.

## 29 Accountability of partners for private profits

**29(1) [Every partner to account]** Every partner must account to the firm for any benefit derived by him without the consent of the other partners from any transaction concerning the partnership, or from any use by him of the partnership property name or business connexion.

**29(2) [Where partnership dissolved by death]** This section applies also to transactions undertaken after a partnership has been dissolved by the death of a partner, and before the affairs thereof have been completely wound up, either by any surviving partner or by the representatives of the deceased partner.

## 30 Duty of partner not to compete with firm

**30** If a partner, without the consent of the other partners, carries on any business of the same nature as and competing with that of the firm, he must account for and pay over to the firm all profits made by him in that business.

## 31 Rights of assignee of share in partnership

**31(1) [Effect of assignment]** An assignment by any partner of his share in the partnership, either absolute or by way of mortgage or redeemable charge, does not, as against the other partners, entitle the assignee, during the continuance of the partnership, to interfere in the management or administration of the partnership business or affairs, or to require any accounts of the partnership transactions, or to inspect the partnership books, but entitles the assignee only to receive the share of profits to which the assigning partner would otherwise be entitled, and the assignee must accept the account of profits agreed to by the partners.

**31(2) [Where partnership dissolved]** In case of a dissolution of the partnership, whether as respects all the partners or as respects the assigning partner, the assignee is entitled to receive the share of the partnership assets to which the assigning partner is entitled as between himself and the other partners, and, for the purpose of ascertaining that share, to an account as from the date of the dissolution.

### DISSOLUTION OF PARTNERSHIP, AND ITS CONSEQUENCES

## 32 Dissolution by expiration or notice

**32** Subject to any agreement between the partners, a partnership is dissolved–

(a) If entered into for a fixed term, by the expiration of that term:

(b) If entered into for a single adventure or undertaking, by the termination of that adventure or undertaking:

(c) If entered into for an undefined time, by any partner giving notice to the other or others of his intention to dissolve the partnership.

In the last-mentioned case the partnership is dissolved as from the date mentioned in the notice as the date of dissolution, or, if no date is so mentioned, as from the date of the communication of the notice.

## 33 Dissolution by bankruptcy, death or charge

**33(1) [Bankruptcy, death]** Subject to any agreement between the partners, every partnership is dissolved as regards all the partners by the death or bankruptcy of any partner.

**33(2) [Charge]** A partnership may, at the option of the other partners, be dissolved if any partner suffers his share of the partnership property to be charged under this Act for his separate debt.

## 34 Dissolution by illegality of partnership

**34** A partnership is in every case dissolved by the happening of any event which makes it unlawful for the business of the firm to be carried on or for the members of the firm to carry it on in partnership.

## 35 Dissolution by the Court

**35** On application by a partner the Court may decree a dissolution of the partnership in any of the following cases:

(a) When a partner is found lunatic by inquisition, or in Scotland by cognition, or is shown to the satisfaction of the Court to be of permanently unsound mind, in either of which cases the application may be made as well on behalf of that partner by his committee or next friend or person having title to intervene as by any other partner:

(b) When a partner, other than the partner suing, becomes in any other way permanently incapable of performing his part of the partnership contract:

(c) When a partner, other than the partner suing, has been guilty of such conduct as, in the opinion of the Court, regard being had to the nature of the business, is calculated to prejudicially affect the carrying on of the business:

(d) When a partner, other than the partner suing, wilfully or persistently commits a breach of the partnership agreement, or otherwise so conducts himself in matters relating to the partnership business that it is not reasonably practicable for the other partner or partners to carry on the business in partnership with him:

(e) When the business of the partnership can only be carried on at a loss:

(f) Whenever in any case circumstances have arisen which, in the opinion of the Court, render it just and equitable that the partnership be dissolved.

**History**
S. 35(f) amended by National Health Service (Amendment) Act 1949, s. 714.

**Note**
S. 35(a) repealed for England and Wales by Mental Health Act 1959, Sch. 8, Pt. I.

## 36 Rights of persons dealing with firm against apparent members of firm

**36(1) [After change]** Where a person deals with a firm after a change in its constitution he is entitled to treat all apparent members of the old firm as still being members of the firm until he has notice of the change.

**36(2) [Advertisement in Gazette]** An advertisement in the London Gazette as to a firm whose principal place of business is in England or Wales, in the Edinburgh Gazette as to a firm whose principal place of business is in Scotland, and in the Belfast Gazette as to a firm whose principal place of business is in Ireland, shall be notice as to persons who had not dealings with the firm before the date of the dissolution or change so advertised.

**History**
S. 36(2) amended by SR & O 1921/1804, art. 7(a).

**Note**
Reference to Ireland to be construed as exclusive of Republic of Ireland: SR & O 1923/405, art. 2.

**36(3) [Estate etc. not liable]** The estate of a partner who dies, or who becomes bankrupt, or of a partner who, not having been known to the person dealing with the firm to be a partner, retires from the firm, is not liable for partnership debts contracted after the date of the death, bankruptcy, or retirement respectively.

## 37 Right of partners to notify dissolution

**37** On the dissolution of a partnership or retirement of a partner any partner may publicly notify the same, and may require the other partner or partners to concur for that purpose in all necessary or proper acts, if any, which cannot be done without his or their concurrence.

## 38 Continuing authority of partners for purposes of winding up

**38** After the dissolution of a partnership the authority of each partner to bind the firm, and the other rights and obligations of the partners, continue notwithstanding the dissolution so far as may be necessary to wind up the affairs of the partnership, and to complete transactions begun but unfinished at the time of the dissolution, but not otherwise.

Provided that the firm is in no case bound by the acts of a partner who has become bankrupt; but this proviso does not affect the liability of any person who has after the bankruptcy represented himself or knowingly suffered himself to be represented as a partner of the bankrupt.

## 39 Rights of partners as to application of partnership property

**39** On the dissolution of a partnership every partner is entitled, as against the other partners in the firm, and all persons claiming through them in respect of their interests as partners, to have the property of the partnership applied in payment of the debts and liabilities of the firm, and to have the surplus assets after such payment applied in payment of what may be due to the partner respectively after deducting what may be due from them as partners to the firm; and for that purpose any partner or his representatives may on the termination of the partnership apply to the Court to wind up the business and affairs of the firm.

## 40 Apportionment of premium where partnership prematurely dissolved

**40** Where one partner has paid a premium to another on entering into a partnership for a fixed term, and the partnership is dissolved before the expiration of that term otherwise than by the death of a partner, the Court may order the repayment of the premium, or of such part thereof as it thinks just, having regard to the terms of the partnership contract and to the length of time during which the partnership has continued; unless

(a) the dissolution is, in the judgment of the Court, wholly or chiefly due to the misconduct of the partner who paid the premium, or

(b) the partnership has been dissolved by an agreement containing no provision for a return of any part of the premium.

## 41 Rights where partnership dissolved for fraud or misrepresentation

**41** Where a partnership contract is rescinded on the ground of the fraud or misrepresentation of one of the parties thereto, the party entitled to rescind is, without prejudice to any other right, entitled–

(a) to a lien on, or right of retention of, the surplus of the partnership assets, after satisfying the partnership liabilities, for any sum of money paid by him for the purchase of a share in the partnership and for any capital contributed by him, and is

(b) to stand in the place of the creditors of the firm for any payments made by him in respect of the partnership liabilities, and

(c) to be indemnified by the person guilty of the fraud or making the representation against all the debts and liabilities of the firm.

## 42 Right of outgoing partner in certain cases to share profits made after dissolution

**42(1) [Amount for outgoing partner or estate]** Where any member of a firm has died or otherwise ceased to be a partner, and the surviving or continuing partners carry on the business of the firm with its capital or assets without any final settlement of accounts as between the firm and the outgoing partner or his estate, then, in the absence of any agreement to the contrary, the outgoing partner or his estate is entitled at the option of himself or his repesentatives to such share of the profits made since the dissolution as the Court may find to be attributable to the use of his share of the partnership assets, or to interest at the rate of five per cent per annum on the amount of his share of the partnership assets.

**42(2) [Where option in partnership contract]** Provided that where by the partnership contract an option is given to surviving or continuing partners to purchase the interest of a deceased or outgoing partner, and that option is duly exercised, the estate of the deceased partner, or the outgoing partner or his estate, as the case may be, is not entitled to any further or other share of profits; but if any partner assuming to act in exercise of the option does not in all material respects comply with the terms thereof, he is liable to account under the foregoing provisions of this section.

## 43 Retiring or deceased partner's share to be a debt

**43** Subject to any agreement between the partners, the amount due from surviving or continuing partners to an outgoing partner or the representatives of a deceased partner in respect of the outgoing or deceased partner's share is a debt accruing at the date of the dissolution or death.

## 44 Rule for distribution of assets on final settlement of accounts

**44** In settling accounts between the partners after a dissolution of partnership, the following rules shall, subject to any agreement, be observed:

(a) Losses, including losses and deficiencies of capital, shall be paid first out of profits, next out of capital, and lastly, if necessary, by the partners individually in the proportion in which they were entitled to share profits:

(b) The assets of the firm including the sums, if any, contributed by the partners to make up losses or deficiencies of capital, shall be applied in the following manner and order:

(1) In paying the debts and liabilities of the firm to persons who are not partners therein:

(2) In paying to each partner rateably what is due from the firm to him for advances as distinguished from capital:

(3) In paying to each partner rateably what is due from the firm to him in respect of capital:

(4) The ultimate residue, if any, shall be divided among the partners in the proportion in which profits are divisible.

SUPPLEMENTAL

## 45 Definitions of "court" and "business"

**45** In this Act, unless the contrary intention appears,–

The expression **"court"** includes every court and judge having jurisdiction in the case:

The expression **"business"** includes every trade, occupation, or profession.

## 46 Saving for rules of equity and common law

**46** The rules of equity and of common law applicable to partnership shall continue in force except so far as they are inconsistent with the express provisions of this Act.

## 47 Provision as to bankruptcy in Scotland

**47(1) [Bankruptcy to mean sequestration]** In the application of this Act to Scotland the bankruptcy of a firm or of an individual shall mean sequestration under the Bankruptcy (Scotland) Acts, and also in the case of an individual the issue against him of a decree of cessio bonorum.

**47(2) [Rules of law of Scotland]** Nothing in this Act shall alter the rules of the law of Scotland relating to the bankruptcy of a firm or of the individual partners thereof.

**48,49** (Repealed by Statute Law Revision Law Act 1908.)

## 50 Short title

**50** This Act may be cited as the Partnership Act 1890.

# SCHEDULE

(Repealed by Statute Law Revision Act 1908.)

# FORGED TRANSFERS ACT 1891

(54 & 55 Vict. c. 43)

An Act for preserving Purchasers of Stock from Losses by Forged Transfers

[*5th August 1891*]

## 1 Power to make compensation for losses from forged transfer

**1(1) [Cash compensation]** Where a company or local authority issue or have issued shares, stock, or securities transferable by an instrument in writing or an exempt transfer, within the meaning of the Stock Transfer Act 1982 or by an entry, in any books or register kept by or on behalf of the company or local authority, they shall have power to make compensation by a cash payment out of their funds for any loss arising from a transfer of any such shares, stock, or securities, in pursuance of a forged instrument or of a transfer under a forged power of attorney, whether such loss arises, and whether the instrument or power of attorney was forged before or after the passing of this Act, and whether the person receiving such compensation, or any person through whom he claims, has or has not paid any fee or otherwise contributed to any fund out of which the compensation is paid.

**1(1A) ["Instrument" in s. 1(1)]** In subsection (1) above **"instrument"** has the same meaning as in Part I of the Forgery and Counterfeiting Act 1981.

**History**
S. 1(1) amended and s. 1(1A) added by Stock Transfer Act 1982, Sch. 2.

**1(2) [Fees for compensation fund]** Any company or local authority may, if they think fit, provide, either by fees not exceeding the rate of 5p on every one hundred pounds transferred with a minimum charge equal to that for twenty-five pounds to be paid by the transferee upon the entry of the transfer in the books of the company or local authority, or by insurance, reservation of capital, accumulation of income, or in any other manner which they may resolve upon, a fund to meet claims for such compensation.

**History**
S. 1(2) amended by Decimal Currency Act 1969, s. 10(1).

**1(3) [Borrowings to meet compensation]** For the purpose of providing such compensation any company may borrow on the security of their property, and any local authority may borrow with the like consent and on the like security and subject to the like conditions as to repayment by means of instalments or the provision of a sinking fund and otherwise as in the case of the securities in respect of which compensation is to be provided, but any money so borrowed by a local authority shall be repaid within a term not longer than five years. Any expenses incurred by a local authority in making compensation, or in the repayment of, or the payment of interest on, or otherwise in connexion with, any loan raised as aforesaid, shall, except so far as they may be met by such fees as aforesaid, be paid out of the revenues on which the security in respect of which compensation is to be made is charged.

**History**
In s. 1(3) the word "revenues" substituted for the former words "fund or rate" by Local Government Finance (Miscellaneous Amendments and Repeal) Order 1990 (SI 1990/1285), art. 2, Sch., Pt. I, para. 1 with effect from 19 July 1990.

**1(4) [Restrictions on transfers]** Any such company or local authority may impose such reasonable restrictions on the transfer of their shares, stock, or securities, or with respect to powers of attorney for the transfer thereof, as they may consider requisite for guarding against losses arising from forgery.

**1(5) [Remedies]** Where a company or local authority compensate a person under this Act for any loss arising from forgery, the company or local authority shall, without prejudice to any other rights or remedies, have the same rights and remedies against the person liable for the loss as the person compensated would have had.

## 2 Definitions

**2** For the purposes of this Act–

The expression **"company"** shall mean any company incorporated by or in pursuance of any Act of Parliament, or by royal charter.

The expression **"local authority"** shall mean –

(a) a billing authority or a precepting authority, as defined in section 69 of the Local Government Finance Act 1992;

(aa) a council constituted under section 2 of the Local Government etc. (Scotland) Act 1994;

(ab) a combined finance authority, as defined in section 144 of the Local Government Finance Act 1988;

(b) a levying body within the meaning of section 74 of that Act;

(c) a body as regards which section 75 of that Act applies.

**History**
In s. 2, in the definition of "local authority", para (aa) substituted by Local Government (Translations Amendments) (Scotland) Order 1996 (SI 1996/974), art. 2(1) and Sch. 1, Pt. I, para. 1 with effect from 1 April 1996. Para. (aa) previously read as follows:

"(aa) a regional, islands or district council within the meaning of the Local Government (Scotland) Act 1973;"

In para. (ab) of that definition, the words "a combined police authority or" repealed by Police and Magistrates' Courts Act 1994, s. 93 and Sch. 9, Pt. I with effect from 1 April 1995 (see Police and Magistrates' Courts Act 1994 (Commencement No. 5 and Transitional Provisions) Order 1994 (SI 1994/3262), art. 2 and Sch.).

Previous para. (a) of the definition of "local authority" substituted by para. (a), (aa) and (ab) by Local Government Finance Act 1992, s. 117(1) and Sch. 13, para. 1 with effect from 1 April 1993. Previous para. (a) read as follows:

"(a) a charging authority, a precepting authority, a combined police authority or a combined fire authority, as defined in section 144 of the Local Government Finance Act 1988;".

Before that, the whole definition was substituted by Local Government Finance Act (Miscellaneous Amendments and Repeal) Order 1990 (SI 1990/1285), art. 2 and Sch., Pt. I, para 2. Prior to 19 July 1990, the definition read as follows:

"The expression "local authority" shall mean the council of any county or municipal borough, and any authority having power to levy or require the levy of a rate the proceeds of which are applicable to public local purposes."

## 3 Application to industrial societies, etc.

**3** This Act shall apply to any industrial provident, friendly benefit, building, or loan society incorporated by or in pursuance of any Act of Parliament as if the society were a company.

## 4 Application to harbour and conservancy authorities

**4(1) [Application]** This act shall apply to any harbour authority or conservancy authority as if the authority were a company.

**4(2) ["Harbour authority"]** For the purposes of this act the expression **"harbour authority"** includes all persons, being proprietors of, or entrusted with the duty or invested with power of constructing, improving, managing, regulating, maintaining, or lighting any harbour otherwise than for profit, and not being a joint stock company.

**4(3) ["Conservancy authority"]** For the purposes of this Act the expression **"conservancy authority"** includes all persons entrusted with the duty or invested with the power of conserving, maintaining, or improving the navigation of any tidal water otherwise than for profit, and not being a joint stock company.

## 5 Application to colonial stock

**5** (Repealed by the Statute Law (Repeals) Act 1998, s. 1 and Sch. 1 as from 19 November 1998.)

**History**
S. 5 formerly read as follows:

"In the case of any colonial stock to which the Colonial Stock Act, 1877, applies, the Government of the colony of which the stock forms the whole or part of the public debt may, if they think fit, by declaration under their seal or under the signature of a person authorised by them in that behalf, and in either case deposited with the Commissioners of Inland Revenue, adopt this Act, and thereupon this Act shall apply to the colonial stock as if the registrar of the Government were a company and the stock were issued by him."

## 6 Short title

**6** This Act may be cited as the Forged Transfers Act, 1891.

# FORGED TRANSFERS ACT 1892

(55 & 56 Vict., Chapter 36)

An Act to remove doubts as to the meaning of the Forged Transfers Act, 1891

[*27th June 1892*]

[**Note:** Only extant, non-amending provisions of this Act are reproduced here.]

## 1 Short title

**1** This Act may be cited as the Forged Transfers Act, 1892, and this Act and the Forged Transfers Act, 1891, may be cited together as the Forged Transfers Acts, 1891 and 1892.

## 4 Provision where one company takes over shares, etc., of another company

**4** Where the shares, stock, or securities of a company or local authority have by amalgamation or otherwise become the shares, stock, or securities of another company or local authority, the last-mentioned company and authority shall have the same power under the Forged Transfers Act, 1891, and this Act, as the original company or authority would have had if it had continued.

# LIMITED PARTNERSHIPS ACT 1907

(7 Edw. 7 c. 24)

## ARRANGEMENT OF SECTIONS

SECTION

# LIMITED PARTNERSHIPS ACT 1907

(7 Edw. 7 c. 24)

An Act to establish Limited Partnerships.

[*28th August 1907*]

## 1 Short title

**1** This Act may be cited for all purposes as the Limited Partnerships Act 1907.

**2** (Repealed by Statute Law Revision Act 1927.)

## 3 Interpretation of terms

**3** In the construction of this Act the following words and expressions shall have the meanings respectively assigned to them in this section, unless there be something in the subject or context repugnant to such construction:–

> **"Firm"**, **"firm name"** and **"business"** have the same meanings as in the Partnership Act 1890:
>
> **"General partner"** shall mean any partner who is not a limited partner as defined by this Act.

## 4 Definition and constitution of limited partnership

**4(1) [Formation]** Limited partnerships may be formed in the manner and subject to the conditions by this Act provided.

**History**
S. 4(1) amended by Statute Law Revision Act 1927.

**4(2) [Constitution]** A limited partnership shall not consist of more than twenty persons, and must consist of one or more persons called general partners, who shall be liable for all debts and obligations of the firm, and one or more persons to be called limited partners, who shall at the time of entering into such partnership contribute thereto a sum or sums as capital or property valued at a stated amount, and who shall not be liable for the debts or obligations of the firm beyond the amount so contributed.

**History**
S. 4(2) amended by Banking Act 1979, Sch. 7.

**Note**
S. 4(2) excluded by CA 1985, s. 717(1), (2) and SI 1971/782.

**4(3) [Limitations]** A limited partner shall not during the continuance of the partnership, either directly or indirectly, draw out or receive back any part of his contribution, and if he does so draw out or receive back any such part shall be liable for the debts and obligations of the firm up to the amount so drawn out or received back.

**4(4) [Body corporate]** A body corporate may be a limited partner.

## 5 Registration of limited partnership required

**5** Every limited partnership must be registered as such in accordance with the provisions of this Act, or in default thereof it shall be deemed to be a general partnership, and every limited partner shall be deemed to be a general partner.

## 6 Modifications of general law in case of limited partnerships

**6(1) [Management, binding the firm]** A limited partner shall not take part in the management of the partnership business, and shall not have power to bind the firm:

Provided that a limited partner may by himself or his agent at any time inspect the books of the firm and examine into the state and prospects of the partnership business, and may advise with the partners thereon.

If a limited partner takes part in the management of the partnership business he shall be liable for all debts and obligations of the firm incurred while he so takes part in the management as though he were a general partner.

**6(2) [Limits on dissolution]** A limited partnership shall not be dissolved by the death or bankruptcy of a limited partner, and the lunacy of a limited partner shall not be a ground for dissolution of the partnership by the court unless the lunatic's share cannot be otherwise ascertained and realised.

**Note**

In s. 6(2) reference to "lunatic" to be substituted by reference to "person of unsound mind" by virtue of Mental Treatment Act 1930, s. 20(5). Mental Treatment Act repealed but effect preserved by Mental Health Act 1983, Sch. 5, para. 29. For power of the judge of the Court of Protection to make orders or give directions for the dissolution of a partnership of which a patient (a person suffering or appearing to suffer from mental disorder) is a member, see the Mental Health Act 1983, s. 96(1)(g).

**6(3) [Winding up of affairs]** In the event of the dissolution of a limited partnership its affairs shall be wound up by the general partners unless the court otherwise orders.

**6(4)** (Repealed by Companies (Consolidation) Act 1908, s. 286, Sch 6, Pt. I.)

**6(5) [General]** Subject to any agreement expressed or implied between the partners–

(a) Any difference arising as to ordinary matters connected with the partnership business may be decided by a majority of the general partners;

(b) A limited partner may, with the consent of the general partners, assign his share in the partnership, and upon such an assignment the assignee shall become a limited partner with all the rights of the assignor;

(c) The other partners shall not be entitled to dissolve the partnership by reason of any limited partner suffering his share to be charged for his separate debt;

(d) A person may be introduced as a partner without the consent of the existing limited partners;

(e) A limited partner shall not be entitled to dissolve the partnership by notice.

## 7 Law as to private partnerships to apply where not excluded by this Act

7 Subject to the provisions of this Act, the Partnership Act 1890, and the rules of equity and of common law applicable to partnerships, except so far as they are inconsistent with the express provisions of the last-mentioned Act, shall apply to limited partnerships.

## 8 Manner and particulars of registration

8 The registration of a limited partnership shall be effected by sending by post or delivering to the registrar at the register office in that part of the United Kingdom in which the principal place of business of the limited partnership is situated or proposed to be situated a statement signed by the partners containing the following particulars:–

(a) The firm name;

(b) The general nature of the business;

(c) The principal place of business;

(d) The full name of each of the partners;

(e) The term, if any, for which the partnership is entered into, and the date of its commencement;

(f) A statement that the partnership is limited, and the description of every limited partner as such;

(g) The sum contributed by each limited partner, and whether paid in cash or how otherwise.

## 9 Registration of changes in partnerships

**9(1) [Statement re changes to registrar]** If during the continuance of a limited partnership any change is made or occurs in–

(a) the firm name,
(b) the general nature of the business,
(c) the principal place of business,
(d) the partners or the name of any partner,
(e) the term of character of the partnership,
(f) the sum contributed by any limited partner,
(g) the liability of any partner by reason of his becoming a limited instead of a general partner or a general instead of a limited partner,

a statement, signed by the firm, specifying the nature of the change, shall within seven days be sent by post or delivered to the registrar at the register office in that part of the United Kingdom in which the partnership is registered.

**9(2) [Penalty on default]** If default is made in compliance with the requirements of this section each of the general partners shall, on conviction under the Magistrates' Courts Act 1952, be liable to a fine not exceeding one pound for each day during which the default continues.

**History**
S. 9(2) amended by Interpretation Act 1978, s. 17(2)(a).

## 10 Advertisement in Gazette of statement of general partner becoming a limited partner and of assignment of share of limited partner

**10(1) [Notice]** Notice of any arrangement or transaction under which any person will cease to be a general partner in any firm, and will become a limited partner in that firm, or under which the share of a limited partner in a firm will be assigned to any person, shall be forthwith advertised in the Gazette, and until notice of the arrangement or transaction is so advertised the arrangement or transaction shall, for the purposes of this Act, be deemed to be of no effect.

**10(2) ["The Gazette"]** For the purposes of this section, the expression **"the Gazette"** means–

In the case of a limited partnership registered in England, the London Gazette;
In the case of a limited partnership registered in Scotland, the Edinburgh Gazette;
In the case of a limited partnership registered in Ireland, the Belfast Gazette.

**History**
S. 10(2) amended by SR & O 1921/1804, art. 7(a).

**Note**
Reference to Ireland to be construed as exclusive of Republic of Ireland: SR & O 1923/405, art. 2.

**11** (Repealed by Finance Act 1973, Sch. 22, Pt. V.)

**12** (Repealed by Perjury Act 1911, Schedule and False Oaths (Scotland) Act 1933, Schedule.)

## 13 Registrar to file statement and issue certificate of registration

**13** On receiving any statement made in pursuance of this Act the registrar shall cause the same to be filed, and he shall send by post to the firm from whom such statement shall have been received a certificate of the registration thereof.

## 14 Register and index to be kept

**14** At each of the register offices herein-after referred to the registrar shall keep, in proper books to be provided for the purpose, a register and an index of all the limited partnerships registered as aforesaid, and of all the statements registered in relation to such partnerships.

## 15 Registrar of joint stock companies to be registrar under Act

**15** The registrar of joint stock companies shall be the registrar of limited partnerships, and the several offices for the registration of joint stock companies in London, Edinburgh, and Belfast shall be the offices for the registration of limited partnerships carrying on business within those parts of the United Kingdom in which they are respectively situated.

**History**
S. 15 amended by SR & O 1921/1804, art. 7(b).

## 16 Inspection of statements registered

**16(1) [Inspection, certificates etc.]** Any person may inspect the statements filed by the registrar in the register offices aforesaid, and there shall be paid for such inspection such fees as may be appointed by the Board of Trade, not exceeding 5p for each inspection; and any person may require a certificate of the registration of any limited partnership, or a copy of or extract from any registered statement, to be certified by the registrar, and there shall be paid for such certificate of registration, certified copy, or extract such fees as the Board of Trade may appoint, not exceeding 10p for the certificate of registration, and not exceeding $2^1/_2$p for each folio of seventy-two words, or in Scotland for each sheet of two hundred words.

**History**
S. 16(1) amended by Decimal Currency Act 1969, s. 10(1).

**Note**
Re exercise of Functions by Secretary of State, see SI 1970/1537, art. 2(1)(a).
The halfpenny was abolished by Royal proclamation with effect from 12 December 1984.

**16(2) [Certificate to be received in evidence]** A certificate of registration, or a copy of or extract from any statement registered under this Act, if duly certified to be a true copy under the hand of the registrar or one of the assistant registrars (whom it shall not be necessary to prove to be the registrar or assistant registrar) shall, in all legal proceedings, civil or criminal, and in all cases whatsoever be received in evidence.

## 17 Power to Board of Trade to make rules

17 The Board of Trade may make rules (but as to fees with the concurrence of the Treasury) concerning any of the following matters:–

(a) The fees to be paid to the registrar under this Act, so that they do not exceed in the case of the original registration of a limited partnership the sum of two pounds, and in any other case the sum of 25p;

(b) The duties or additional duties to be performed by the registrar for the purposes of this Act;

(c) The performance by assistant registrars and other officers of acts by this Act required to be done by the registrar;

(d) The forms to be used for the purposes of this Act;

(e) Generally the conduct and regulation of registration under this Act and any matters incidental thereto.

**History**
S. 17 amended by Decimal Currency Act 1969, s. 10(1).

**Note**
Re exercise of Functions by Secretary of State, see SI 1970/1537, art. 2(1)(a).

# STOCK TRANSFER ACT 1963

(1963 c. 18)

An Act to amend the law with respect to the transfer of securities.

*[10th July 1963]*

## TABLE OF SECTIONS

SECTION

SCHEDULES



# 1 Simplified transfer of securities

**1(1) [Transfer of certain securities]** Registered securities to which this section applies may be transferred by means of an instrument under hand in the form set out in Schedule 1 to this Act (in this Act referred to as a stock transfer), executed by the transferor only and specifying (in addition to the particulars of the consideration, of the description and number or amount of the securities, and of the person by whom the transfer is made) the full name and address of the transferee.

**Note**
See note after s. 1(3).

**1(2) [Execution, other particulars]** The execution of a stock transfer need not be attested; and where such a transfer has been executed for the purpose of a stock exchange transaction, the particulars of the consideration and of the transferee may either be inserted in that transfer or, as the case may require, supplied by means of separate instruments in the form set out in Schedule 2 to this Act (in this Act referred to as brokers transfers), identifying the stock transfer and specifying the securities to which each such instrument relates and the consideration paid for those securities.

**1(3) [Transfers apart from Act]** Nothing in this section shall be construed as affecting the validity of any instrument which would be effective to transfer securities apart from this section; and any instrument purporting to be made in any form which was common or usual before the commencement of this Act, or in any other form authorised or required for that purpose apart from this section, shall be sufficient, whether or not it is completed in accordance with the form, if it complies with the requirements as to execution and contents which apply to a stock transfer.

**History**
In s. 1(3) the words "for which the form set out in Schedule 2 to the Stock Transfer (Addition and Substitution of Forms) Order 1996 is substituted" substituted for the former words "for which the form set out in the Schedule to the Stock Transfer (Substitution of Forms) Order 1990 is substituted" by the Stock Transfer (Addition and Substitution of Forms) Order 1996 (SI 1996/1571), art. 1, 3(3) as from 15 July 1996. Previous to that, the words "for which the form set out in the Schedule to the Stock Transfer (Substitution of Forms) Order 1990 is substituted" substituted for the original words "which was common or usual before the commencement of this Act" by the Stock Transfer (Substitution of Forms) Order 1990 (SI 1990/18) art. 1, 3 as from 31 January 1990.

**Note**
See the Stock Transfer (Substitution of Forms) Order 1990 (SI 1990/18), art. 3, 4 and the Stock Transfer (Addition and Substitution of Forms) Order 1996 (SI 1996/1571), art. 2, 3.

**1(4) [Application]** This section applies to fully paid up registered securities of any description, being–

(a) securities issued by any company within the meaning of the Companies Act 1985 except a company limited by guarantee or an unlimited company;

(b) securities issued by any body (other than a company within the meaning of the said Act) incorporated in Great Britain by or under any enactment or by Royal Charter except a building society within the meaning of the Building Societies Act 1986 or a society registered under the Industrial and Provident Societies Act 1893;

(c) securities issued by the Government of the United Kingdom, except stock or bonds in the National Savings Stock Register and except national savings certificates;

(d) securities issued by any local authority;

(e) units of an authorised unit trust scheme or a recognised scheme within the meaning of the Financial Services Act 1986.

(f) shares issued by an investment company with variable capital within the meaning of the Open-Ended Investment Companies (Investment Companies with Variable Capital) Regulations 1996.

**History**

- S. 1 amended to facilitate the "Talisman" settlement system for transactions in securities on the Stock Exchange by the Stock Transfer (Addition of Forms) Order 1979, SI 1979/277, effective from 4 April 1979. Rules 3 and 4 of that Order read as follows:

"**3(1)** Section 1 of the Stock Transfer Act 1963 shall have effect subject to the amendment that a sold transfer form, and a stock transfer form used to transfer securities to a stock exchange nominee, need not specify–

(a) particulars of the consideration;
(b) the address of the transferee.

**(2)** Section 1 of that Act shall have effect subject to the further amendment that a bought transfer form, and a stock transfer form used to transfer securities from a stock exchange nominee, need not, in the case of a transferor which is a body corporate, be executed under hand but shall be sufficiently executed by or on behalf of such transferor if they bear a facsimile of the corporate seal of the transferor, authenticated by the signature (whether actual or facsimile) of a director or the secretary of the transferor.

**4** In this Order "stock exchange nominee" has the same meaning as that given to it by section 7(2) of the Stock Exchange (Completion of Bargains) Act 1976."

- S. 1(4)(a) amended as from 1 July 1985 by Companies Consolidation (Consequential Provisions) Act 1985, Sch. 2.
- S. 1(4)(b) amended by Building Societies Act 1986, s. 120(1) and Sch. 18, Pt. I, para. 5 as from 1 January 1987 (see SI 1986/1560 (C.56)).
- S. 1(4)(c) amended by Finance Act 1964, s. 24, 26(7), Sch. 8, para. 10, Sch. 10; Post Office Act 1969, s. 108(1)(f).
- S. 1(4)(e) substituted by Financial Services Act 1986, s. 212(2) and Sch. 16, para. 4(a) as from 29 April 1988 (see SI 1988/740 (C. 22)); s. 1(4)(e) formerly read as follows:

"(e) units of a unit trust scheme, or other shares of the investments subject to the trusts of such a scheme, being a scheme in the case of which there is in force an order of the Board of Trade under section 17 of the Prevention of Fraud (Investments) Act 1958."

- S. 1(4)(f) inserted by the Open-Ended Investment Companies (Investment Companies with Variable Capital) Regulations 1996 (SI 1996/2827), reg. 1, 75 and Sch. 8, para. 2 as from 6 January 1997.

## 2 Supplementary provisions as to simplified transfer

**2(1) [Application of s. 1]** Section 1 of this Act shall have effect in relation to the transfer of any securities to which that section applies notwithstanding anything to the contrary in any enactment or instrument relating to the transfer of those securities; but nothing in that section affects–

(a) any right to refuse to register a person as the holder of any securities on any ground other than the form in which those securities purport to be transferred to him: or

(b) any enactment or rule of law regulating the execution of documents by companies or other bodies corporate, or any articles of association or other instrument regulating the execution of documents by any particular company or body corporate.

**2(2) [Application of other enactments and instruments]** Subject to the provisions of this section, any enactment or instrument relating to the transfer of securities to which section 1 of this Act applies shall, with any necessary modifications, apply in relation to an instrument of transfer authorised by that section as it applies in relation to an instrument of transfer to which it applies apart from this subsection; and without prejudice to the generality of the foregoing provision, the reference in section 184 of the Companies Act 1985 (certification of transfers) to any instrument of transfer shall be construed as including a reference to a brokers transfer.

**History**

S. 2(2) amended as from 1 July 1985 by Companies Consolidation (Consequential Provisions) Act 1985, Sch. 2.

**2(3) [Interpretation]** In relation to the transfer of securities by means of a stock transfer and a brokers transfer–

(a) any reference in any enactment or instrument (including in particular section 183(1) and (2) of the Companies Act 1985) to the delivery or lodging of an instrument (or proper instrument) of transfer shall be construed as a reference to the delivery or lodging of the stock transfer and the brokers transfer;

(b) any such reference to the date on which an instrument of transfer is delivered or lodged shall be construed as a reference to the date by which the later of those transfers to be delivered or lodged has been delivered or lodged; and

(c) subject to the foregoing provisions of this subsection, the brokers transfer (and not the stock transfer) shall be deemed to be the conveyance or transfer for the purposes of the enactments relating to stamp duty.

**History**
In s. 2(3)(a) the words "and section 56(4) of the Finance Act 1946" repealed by Finance Act 1999, s. 139 and Sch. 20, Pt. V(5) in respect of instruments executed on or after 6 February 2000. S. 2(3)(a) previously amended as from 1 July 1985 by Companies Consolidation (Consequential Provisions) Act 1985, Sch. 2.

**Note**
S. 2(3)(c) to be repealed from the appointed day in accordance with Finance Act 1990, s. 107–111 (Finance Act 1990, s. 132 and Sch. 19, Pt. VI).

**2(4)** (Repealed by Requirements of Writing (Scotland) Act 1995, s. 14(2), 15 and Sch. 5 as from 1 August 1995.)

**History**
S. 2(4) formerly read as follows:

"Without prejudice to subsection (1) of this section, section 1 of this Act shall have effect, in its application to Scotland, notwithstanding anything to the contrary in any enactment relating to the execution of instruments or the validity of instruments delivered with particulars left blank; but so much of subsection (2) of that section as provides that the execution of a stock transfer need not be attested shall not apply to a transfer executed in accordance with section 18 of the Conveyancing (Scotland) Act 1924 on behalf of a person who is blind or unable to write."

# 3 Additional provisions as to transfer forms

**3(1) [Forms in schedules]** References in this Act to the forms set out in Schedule 1 and Schedule 2 include references to forms substantially corresponding to those forms respectively.

**3(2) [Amendments to schedules by order]** The Treasury may by order amend the said Schedules either by altering the forms set out therein or by substituting different forms for those forms or by the addition of forms for use as alternatives to those forms; and references in this Act to the forms set out in those Schedules (including references in this section) shall be construed accordingly.

**Note**
See Stock Transfer (Substitution of Forms) Order 1990 (SI 1990/18) – also SI 1974/1214 and SI 1979/277 – amendments included in Schedules.

**3(3) [Direction in s. 3(2) order]** Any order under subsection (2) of this section which substitutes a different form for a form set out in Schedule 1 to this Act may direct that subsection (3) of section 1 of this Act shall apply, with any necessary modifications, in relation to the form for which that form is substituted as it applies to any form which was common or usual before the commencement of this Act.

**3(4) [Order by statutory instrument]** Any order of the Treasury under this section shall be made by statutory instrument, and may be varied or revoked by a subsequent order; and any statutory instrument made by virtue of this section shall be subject to annulment in pursuance of a resolution of either House of Parliament.

**3(5) [Contents of s. 3(2) order]** An order under subsection (2) of this section may–

(a) provide for forms on which some of the particulars mentioned in subsection (1) of section 1 of this Act are not required to be specified;

(b) provide for that section to have effect, in relation to such forms as are mentioned in the preceding paragraph or other forms specified in the order, subject to such amendments as are so specified (which may include an amendment of the reference in subsection (1) of that section to an instrument under hand);

(c) provide for all or any of the provisions of the order to have effect in such cases only as are specified in the order.

**History**
S. 3(5) inserted by Stock Exchange (Completion of Bargains) Act 1976, s. 6.

**Note**
See the Stock Transfer (Addition and Substitution of Forms) Order 1996 (SI 1996/1571).

# 4 Interpretation

**4(1) [Definitions]** In this Act the following expressions have the meanings hereby respectively assigned to them, that is to say–

**"local authority"** means, in relation to England and Wales–

(a) a billing authority or a precepting authority as defined in section 69 of the Local Government Finance Act 1992;

(aa) a combined fire authority, as defined in section 144 of the Local Government Finance Act 1988;

(b) a levying body within the meaning of section 74 of that Act; and

(c) a body as regards which section 75 of that Act applies,

and, in relation to Scotland, a county council, a town council and any statutory authority, commissioners or trustees to whom section 270 of the Local Government (Scotland) Act 1947 applies;

**"registered securities"** means transferable securities the holders of which are entered in a register (whether maintained in Great Britain or not);

**"securities"** means shares, stock, debentures, debenture stock, loan stock, bonds, units of a collective investment scheme within the meaning of the Financial Services Act 1986, and other securities of any description;

**"stock exchange transaction"** means a sale and purchase of securities in which each of the parties is a member of a stock exchange acting in the ordinary course of his business as such or is acting through the agency of such a member;

**"stock exchange"** means the Stock Exchange, London, and any other stock exchange (whether in Great Britain or not) which is declared by order of the Treasury to be a recognised stock exchange for the purposes of this Act.

**History**

In s. 4(1) in the definition of "local authority" the words "a combined police authority or" formerly appearing before the words "a combined fire authority" in para. (aa) repealed by the Police and Magistrates' Courts Act 1994, s. 93; Sch. 9 as from 1 April 1995 (see SI 1994/3262).

Previously in s. 4(1) in the definition of "local authority" para. (a), (aa) substituted for the former para. (a) by the Local Government Finance Act 1992, s. 117(1); Sch. 13, para. 12, as from 2 November 1992 (see SI 1992/2454). Para. (a) formerly read as follows:

"a charging authority, a precepting authority, a combined police authority or a combined fire authority, as defined in section 144 of the Local Government Finance Act 1988;"

Previously to that in s. 4(1) in the definition of "local authority" para. (a)–(c) substituted for the former words "any authority being, within the meaning of the Local Loans Act 1875, an authority having power to levy a rate" by the Local Government Finance (Repeals, Savings and Consequential Amendments) Order 1990 (SI 1990/776), art. 8; Sch. 3, para. 8, as from 1 April 1990.

In s. 4(1) in the definition of "securities" the words "collective investment scheme within the meaning of the Financial Services Act 1986" substituted for the former words "unit trust scheme, or other shares of the investments subject to the trusts of such a scheme" by Financial Services Act 1986, s. 212(2) and Sch. 16, para. 4(b) as from 29 April 1988 (see SI 1988/740 (C. 22)).

**4(2) [Order under section]** Any order of the Treasury under this section shall be made by statutory instrument, and may be varied or revoked by a subsequent order.

## 5 Application to Northern Ireland

**5(1) [Limited application to Northern Ireland]** This Act, so far as it applies to things done outside Great Britain, extends to Northern Ireland.

**5(2) [Application of Act to securities in Northern Ireland register]** Without prejudice to subsection (1) of this section, the provisions of this Act affecting securities issued by the Government of the United Kingdom shall apply to any such securities entered in a register maintained in Northern Ireland.

**5(3)** (Repealed by Northern Ireland Constitution Act 1973, s. 41(1), Sch. 6, Part I.)

**5(4) [Extent]** Except as provided by this section, this Act shall not extend to Northern Ireland.

## 6 Short title and commencement

**6(1) [Citation]** This Act may be cited as the Stock Transfer Act 1963.

**6(2) [Commencement]** Subsection (3) of section 5 of this Act shall come into force on the passing of this Act, and the remaining provisions of this Act shall come into force on such date as the Treasury may by order made by statutory instrument direct.

# SCHEDULES

## Schedule 1 – Stock Transfer Form

| | | Certificate lodged with the Registrar<br>(For completion by the Registrar/Stock Exchange |
|---|---|---|
| Consideration Money | £ ............... | |
| Name of Undertaking. | | |
| Description of security. | | |
| Number or amount of Shares, Stock or other security and, in figures column only, number and denomination of units, if any. | Words | Figures<br>( units of ) |
| Name(s) of registered holder(s) should be given in full: the address should be given where there is only one holder.<br>If the transfer is not made by the registered holder(s) insert also the name(s) and capacity (eg, Executor(s)), of the person(s) making the transfer. | in the name(s) of | |

| | | |
|---|---|---|
| Delete words in italics except for stock exchange transactions. | I/We hereby transfer the above security out of the name(s) aforesaid to the person(s) named below *or to the several persons named in Parts 2 of Brokers Transfer forms relating to the above security*:<br>Signature(s) of transferor(s)<br>1 ........................................ 3 ........................................<br>2 ........................................ 4 ........................................<br>A body corporate should execute this transfer under its common seal or otherwise in accordance with applicable statutory requirements | Stamp of Selling Broker(s) or, for transactions which are not stock exchange transactions, of Agent(s), if any, acting for the Transferor(s).<br><br>Date ...................... |

| | |
|---|---|
| Full name(s), full postal address(es) (including County or, if applicable, Postal District number) of the person(s) to whom the security is transferred.<br>Please state title, if any, or whether Mr, Mrs, or Miss.<br>Please complete in type or in Block Capitals. | |

I/We request that such entries be made in the register as are necessary to give effect to this transfer.

| Stamp of Buying Broker(s) (if any). | Stamp or name and address of person lodging this form (if other than the Buying Broker(s)). |
|---|---|
| | |

Reference to the Registrar in this form means the registrar or registration agent of the undertaking, not the Registrar of Companies at Companies House.

*(Endorsement for use only in stock exchange transactions)*

*The security represented by the transfer overleaf has been sold as follows:–*

| | |
|---|---|
| .................................. *Shares/Stock* | .................................. *Shares/Stock* |
| .................................. *Shares/Stock* | .................................. *Shares/Stock* |
| .................................. *Shares/Stock* | .................................. *Shares/Stock* |
| .................................. *Shares/Stock* | .................................. *Shares/Stock* |
| .................................. *Shares/Stock* | .................................. *Shares/Stock* |
| .................................. *Shares/Stock* | .................................. *Shares/Stock* |

..................................................

*Balance (if any) due to Selling Broker(s)*

*Amount of Certificate(s)*

*Brokers Transfer Forms for above amount certified*

*Stamp of certifying Stock Exchange* *Stamp of Selling Broker(s)*

**History**

The above stock transfer form substituted for the former stock transfer form in Sch. 1 by the Stock Transfer (Addition and Substitution of Forms) Order 1996 (SI 1996/1571), art. 1, 3(1) as from 15 July 1996.

**Note**

For exemption of stock transfers from stamp duty, see the Stamp Duty (Exempt Instruments) Regulations 1987 (SI 1987/516), reg. 2(1) and Sch.

TALISMAN
SOLD
TRANSFER

This transfer is exempt from Transfer Stamp Duty

Above this line for Registrar's use only

Bargain Reference No

Certificate lodged with Registrar

Name of Undertaking

Description of Security

(for completion by the Registrars/ Stock Exchange)

Amount of Stock or number of Stock units or shares or other security in words

Figures

In the name(s) of

Account Designation (if any)

Name(s) of registered holder(s) should be given in full; the address should be given where there is only one holder.

If the transfer is not made by the registered holder(s) insert also the name(s) and capacity (e.g. Executor(s)) of the person(s) making the transfer.

I/We hereby transfer the above security out of the name(s) aforesaid into the name of and request the necessary entries to be made in the register.

Balance Certificate Required for (amount or number in figures)

Bodies corporate should affix their common seal and each signatory should state his/her representative capacity (e.g. 'Company Secretary' 'Director') against his/her signature.

Stamp of Lodging Agent

PLEASE SIGN HERE ⇨

1 ______

2 ______

3 ______

4 ______

Date

is lodging this transfer at the direction and on behalf of the Lodging Agent whose stamp appears herein ("the Original Lodging Agent") and does not in any manner or to any extent warrant or represent the validity, genuineness or correctness of the transfer instructions contained herein or the genuineness of the signature(s) of the transferor(s). The Original Lodging Agent by delivering this transfer to authorises to lodge this transfer for registration and agrees to be deemed for all purposes to be the person(s) actually lodging this transfer for registration

INSP Code (if applicable)

**History**

The above sold transfer form substituted in Sch. 1 from 31 January 1990 by Stock Transfer (Substitution of Forms) Order 1990 (SI 1990/18), reg. 2 and Sch.: the former form was itself inserted from 4 April 1979, as an alternative to the stock transfer form preceding it, by Stock Transfer (Addition of Forms) Order 1979 (SI 1979/277): for previous form see that 1979 Order set out in this tab division.

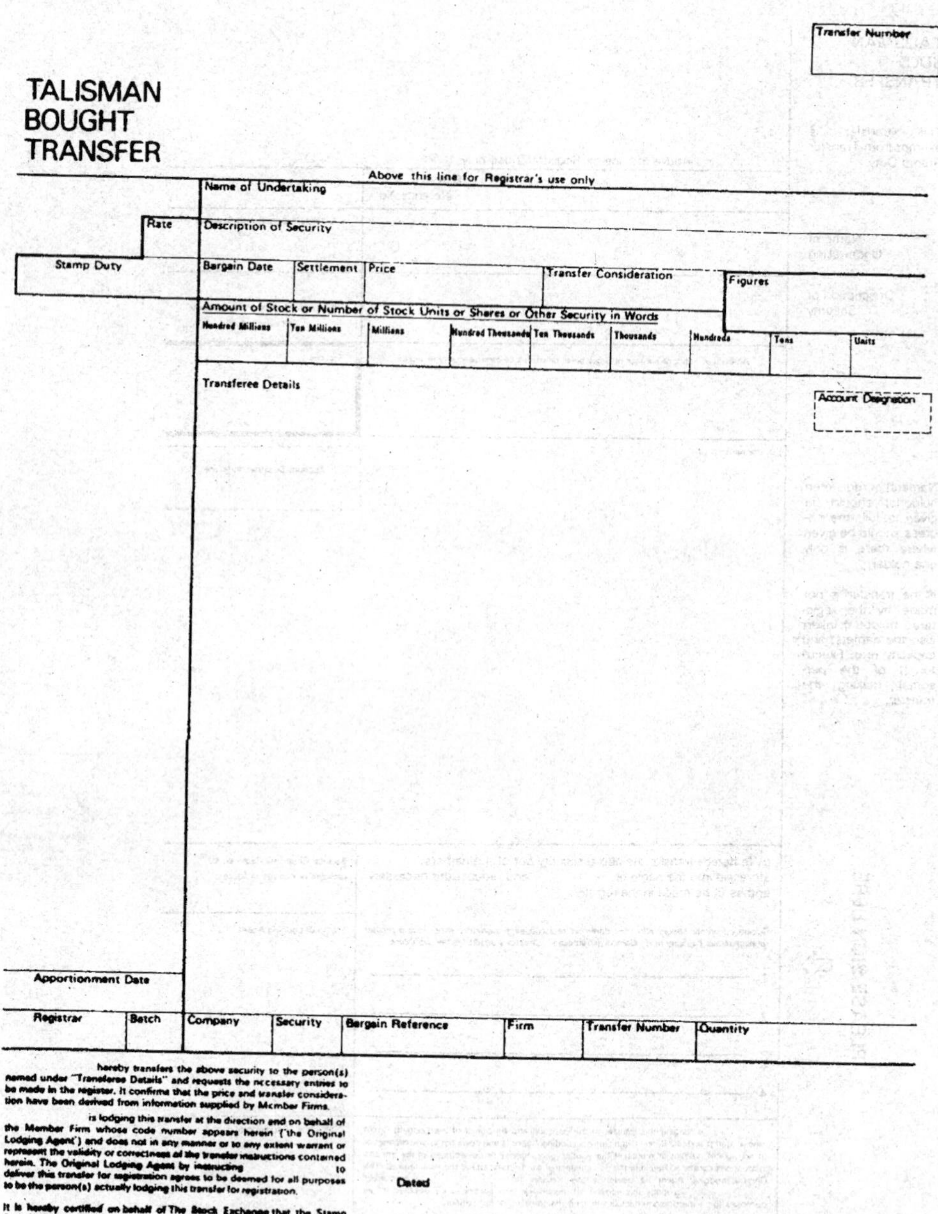

Transfer Number

TALISMAN
BOUGHT
TRANSFER

Above this line for Registrar's use only

Name of Undertaking

Rate

Description of Security

Stamp Duty

| Bargain Date | Settlement | Price | Transfer Consideration | Figures |
|---|---|---|---|---|
| | | | | |

Amount of Stock or Number of Stock Units or Shares or Other Security in Words

| Hundred Millions | Ten Millions | Millions | Hundred Thousands | Ten Thousands | Thousands | Hundreds | Tens | Units |
|---|---|---|---|---|---|---|---|---|
| | | | | | | | | |

Transferee Details

Account Designation

Apportionment Date

| Registrar | Batch | Company | Security | Bargain Reference | Firm | Transfer Number | Quantity |
|---|---|---|---|---|---|---|---|
| | | | | | | | |

hereby transfers the above security to the person(s) named under "Transferee Details" and requests the necessary entries to be made in the register. It confirms that the price and transfer consideration have been derived from information supplied by Member Firms.

is lodging this transfer at the direction and on behalf of the Member Firm whose code number appears herein ('the Original Lodging Agent') and does not in any manner or to any extent warrant or represent the validity or correctness of the transfer instructions contained herein. The Original Lodging Agent by instructing to deliver this transfer for registration agrees to be deemed for all purposes to be the person(s) actually lodging this transfer for registration.

Dated

It is hereby certified on behalf of The Stock Exchange that the Stamp Duty indicated hereon has been or will be accounted for to the Commissioners of Inland Revenue pursuant to an agreement under Section 33 of the Finance Act 1970 as amended.

**History**

The above bought transfer form, for use where registered securities to which s. 1 applies are transferred from a stock exchange nominee, inserted in Sch. 1 from 4 April 1979, as an alternative to the stock transfer form set out at the commencement of Sch. 1, by Stock Transfer (Addition of Forms) Order 1979 (SI 1979/277).

Above this line for Registrar's use

**TRANSFER**

| Counter Location Stamp | Barcode or reference RN |
|---|---|

Above this line for completion by the depositing system-user only.

| | | |
|---|---|---|
| | Consideration Money | Certificate(s) lodged with Registrar (To be completed by Registrar) |
| Name of Undertaking. | | |
| Description of Security | | |
| Please complete form in type or in block capitals. | Amount of shares or other security in words | Figures |
| Name(s) of registered holder(s) should be given in full; the address should be given where there is only one holder. If the transfer is not made by the registered holder(s) insert also the name(s) and capacity (e.g. executor(s)) of the person(s) making the transfer. | In the name(s) of | Designation (if any) Balance certificate(s) required |
| | I/We hereby transfer the above security out of the name(s) aforesaid into the name(s) of the system-member set out below and request that the necessary entries be made in the undertaking's own register of members. Signature(s) of tranferor(s) 1. 2. 3. 4. A body corporate should execute this transfer under its common seal or otherwise in accordance with applicable statutory requirements. | Stamp of depositing system-user Date |
| Full name(s) of the person(s) to whom the security is transferred Such person(s) must be a system-member. | | Participant ID Member Account ID |
| Reference to the Registrar in this form means the registrar or registration agent of the undertaking, not the Registrar of Companies at Companies House. | is delivering this transfer at the direction and on behalf of the depositing system-user whose stamp appears herein and does not in any manner or to any extent warrant or represent the validity, genuineness or correctness of the transfer instructions contained herein or the genuineness of the signature(s) of the transferor(s). The depositing system-user by delivering this transfer to authorises to deliver this transfer for registration and agrees to be deemed for all purposes to be the person(s) actually so delivering this transfer for registration. | |

**History**

The transfer form above, for use where units of a registered security to which s. 1 applies are transferred to a system-member to be held by him as uncertificated units of that security, added to Sch. 1 by the Stock Transfer (Addition and Substitution of Forms) Order 1996 (SI 1996/1571), art. 1, 2, Sch. 1, as from 15 July 1996.

# Schedule 2 — Brokers Transfer Form

Section 1

| Consideration Money | £...................... | Certificate lodged with the Registrar<br>(For completion by the Registrar/Stock Exchange) |
|---|---|---|
| Part 1<br>Name of Undertaking. | | |
| Description of security. | | |
| Number of amount of Shares, Stock or other security and, in figures column only, number and denomination of units, if any. | Words | Figures<br><br>( units of ) |
| Name(s) of registered holder(s) should be given in full: the address should be given where this is only one holder.<br>If the transfer is not made by the registered holder(s) insert also the name(s) and capacity (e.g., Executor(s)), of the person(s) making the transfer. | in the name(s) of | |

I/We confirm that the Stock Transfer Form relating to the security set out above has been lodged with the Registrar, and that the said security has been sold by me/us by a stock exchange transaction within the meaning of the Stock Transfer Act 1963.

*Date and Stamp of Selling Broker(s)*

Part 2

Full name(s), full postal address(es) (including County or, if applicable, Postal District number) of the person(s) to whom the security is transferred.

Please state title, if any, or whether Mr., Mrs. or Miss.

Please complete in typewriting or in Block Capitals.

I/We confirm that the security set out in Part 1 above has been purchased by a stock exchange transaction within the meaning of the Stock Transfer Act 1963, and I/we request that such entries be made in the register as are necessary to give effect to this transfer.

| Stamp of Buying Broker(s). | Stamp of Lodging Agent (if other than the Buying Broker(s)). |
|---|---|

(Endorsement for use only in stock exchange transactions)

The security represented by the transfer overleaf has been sold as follows:

| | |
|---|---|
| ............................ Shares/Stock | ............................ Shares/Stock |
| ............................ Shares/Stock | ............................ Shares/Stock |
| ............................ Shares/Stock | ............................ Shares/Stock |
| ............................ Shares/Stock | ............................ Shares/Stock |
| ............................ Shares/Stock | ............................ Shares/Stock |
| ............................ Shares/Stock | ............................ Shares/Stock |
| ............................ Shares/Stock | ............................ Shares/Stock |

Balance (if any) due to Selling Broker(s) ................................

Amount of Certificate(s)

Brokers Transfer forms for above amounts certified

*Stamp of certifying Stock Exchange* *Stamp of Selling Broker(s)*

**History**
Brokers transfer from amended by SI 1974/1214.

# THEFT ACT 1968

(1968 Chapter 60)

[*26th July 1968*]

[**Note:** Only extant, non-amending provisions relevant to companies are reproduced here.]

## 17 False accounting

**17(1) [Penalty]** Where a person dishonestly, with a view to gain for himself or another or with intent to cause loss to another,–

(a) destroys, defaces, conceals or falsifies any account or any record or document made or required for any accounting purpose; or

(b) in furnishing information for any purpose produces or makes use of any account, or any such record or document as aforesaid, which to his knowledge is or may be misleading, false or deceptive in a material particular;

he shall, on conviction on indictment, be liable to imprisonment for a term not exceeding seven years.

**17(2) [Interpretation]** For purposes of this section a person who makes or concurs in making in an account or other document an entry which is or may be misleading, false or deceptive in a material particular, or who omits or concurs in omitting a material particular from an account or other document, is to be treated as falsifying the account or document.

## 18 Liability of company officers for certain offences by company

**18(1) [Officers liable]** Where an offence committed by a body corporate under section 15, 16 or 17 of this Act is proved to have been committed with the consent or connivance of any director, manager, secretary or other similar officer of the body corporate, or any person who was purporting to act in any such capacity, he as well as the body corporate shall be guilty of that offence, and shall be liable to be proceeded against and punished accordingly.

**18(2) [Members liable]** Where the affairs of a body corporate are managed by its members, this section shall apply in relation to the acts and defaults of a member in connection with his functions of management as if he were a director of the body corporate.

## 19 False statements by company directors, etc.

**19(1) [Offence, penalty]** Where an officer of a body corporate or unincorporated association (or person purporting to act as such), with intent to deceive members or creditors of the body corporate or association about its affairs, publishes or concurs in publishing a written statement or account which to his knowledge is or may be misleading, false or deceptive in a material particular, he shall on conviction on indictment be liable to imprisonment for a term not exceeding seven years.

**19(2) [Interpretation]** For purposes of this section a person who has entered into a security for the benefit of a body corporate or association is to be treated as a creditor of it.

**19(3) [Application]** Where the affairs of a body corporate or association are managed by its members, this section shall apply to any statement which a member publishes or concurs in publishing in connection with his functions of management as if he were an officer of the body corporate or association.

## 20 Suppression, etc. of documents

**20(1) [Penalty for destruction]** A person who dishonestly, with a view to gain for himself or another or with intent to cause loss to another, destroys, defaces or conceals any valuable security, any will or other testamentary document or any original document of or belonging to, or filed or deposited in, any court of justice or any government department shall on conviction on indictment be liable to imprisonment for a term not exceeding seven years.

**20(2) [Penalty for procuring execution of securities etc.]** A person who dishonestly, with a view to gain for himself or another or with intent to cause loss to another, by any deception procures the execution of a valuable security shall on conviction on indictment be liable to imprisonment for a term not exceeding seven years; and this subsection shall apply in relation to the making, acceptance, indorsement, alteration, cancellation or destruction in whole or in part of a valuable security, and in relation to the signing or sealing of any paper or other material in order that it may be made or converted into, or used or dealt with as, a valuable security, as if that were the execution of a valuable security.

**20(3) [Definitions]** For purposes of this section **"deception"** has the same meaning as in section 15 of this Act, and **"valuable security"** means any document creating, transferring, surrendering or releasing any right to, in or over property, or authorising the payment of money or delivery of any property, or evidencing the creation, transfer, surrender or release of any such right, or the payment of money or delivery of any property, or the satisfaction of any obligation.

# FAIR TRADING ACT 1973

(1973 Chapter 41)

*[25th July 1973]*

[**Note:** Only certain provisions relating to merger control (other than that of newspapers) included.]

# PART V – MERGERS

OTHER MERGER REFERENCES

## 63 Mergers references to which s. 64 to 75 apply

**63(1) [Construction]** Sections 64 to 75K of this Act shall not have effect in relation to newspaper merger references; and accordingly in those sections **"merger reference"** shall be construed–

(a) as not including a reference made under section 59 of this Act, but

(b) as including any merger reference relating to a transfer of a newspaper or of newspaper assets, if the reference is made under section 64 or section 75 of this Act in a case falling within section 59(2) of this Act.

**History**

In s. 63(1) the words "to 75K of this Act shall not have effect in relation to" substituted for the former words "to 75 of this Act shall have effect in relation to merger references other than" by CA 1989, s. 153 and Sch. 20, para. 3 as from 16 November 1989 (see CA 1989, s. 215(1)(b)(ii)).

**63(2) [Definition]** In the following provisions of this Part of this Act **"enterprise"** means the activities, or part of the activities, of a business.

# 64 Merger situation qualifying for investigation

**64(1) [Merger references]** A merger reference may be made to the Commission by the Secretary of State where it appears to him that it is or may be the fact that two or more enterprises (in this section referred to as "the relevant enterprises"), of which one at least was carried on in the United Kingdom or by or under the control of a body corporate incorporated in the United Kingdom, have, at a time or in circumstances falling within subsection (4) of this section, ceased to be distinct enterprises, and that either–

(a) as a result, the condition specified in subsection (2) or in subsection (3) of this section prevails, or does so to a greater extent, with respect to the supply of goods or services of any description, or

(b) the value of the assets taken over exceeds £70 million.

**History**

In s. 64(1)(b) the sum "£70 million" substituted for the former sum "£30 million" by the Merger References (Increase in Value of Assets) Order 1994 (SI 1994/72) as from 9 February 1994 subject to proviso that the variation not have effect in relation to any merger reference made to Monopolies and Mergers Commission before commencement of the order; the former sum was substituted by the Merger References (Increase in Value of Assets) Order 1984 (SI 1984/932).

**Note**

See the EEC Merger Control (Consequential Provisions) Regulations 1990 (SI 1990/1563), reg. 3 – a merger reference may be made under s. 64 in a case in which the relevant enterprises ceased to be distinct enterprises at a time and in circumstances not falling within s. 64(4) if by reason of the EEC Merger Control Regulation or anything done under it or in accordance with it the reference could have been made earlier than six months before the date on which it is to be made.

**64(2) [Supply of goods]** The condition referred to in subsection (1)(a) of this section, in relation to the supply of goods of any description, is that at least one-quarter of all the goods of that description which are supplied in the United Kingdom, or in a substantial part of the United Kingdom, either–

(a) are supplied by one and the same person or are supplied to one and the same person, or

(b) are supplied by the persons by whom the relevant enterprises (so far as they continue to be carried on) are carried on, or are supplied to those persons.

**64(3) [Supply of services]** The condition referred to in subsection (1)(a) of this section, in relation to the supply of services of any description, is that the supply of services of that description in the United Kingdom, or in a substantial part of the United Kingdom, is, to the extent of at least one-quarter, either–

(a) supply by one and the same person, or supply for one and the same person, or

(b) supply by the persons by whom the relevant enterprises (so far as they continue to be carried on) are carried on, or supply for those persons.

**64(4) [Cessation of distinct enterprises]** For the purposes of subsection (1) of this section enterprises shall be taken to have ceased to be distinct enterprises at a time or in circumstances falling within this subsection if either–

(a) they did so not earlier than four months before the date on which the merger reference relating to them is to be made, or

(b) they did so under or in consequence of arrangements or transactions which were entered into without prior notice being given to the Secretary of State or to the Director of material facts about the proposed arrangements or transactions and in circumstances in which those facts had not been made public, and notice of those facts was not given to the Secretary of State or to the Director or made public more than four months before the date mentioned in the preceding paragraph.

**History**
In s. 64(4)(a), (b) the words "four months" substituted for the former words "six months" by the Deregulation (Fair Trading Act 1973) (Amendment) (Merger Reference Time Limits) Order 1996 (SI 1996/345), art. 1, 2 as from 19 March 1996.

**64(5) [Determination as soon as practicable]** In determining whether to make a merger reference to the Commission the Secretary of State shall have regard, with a view to the prevention or removal of uncertainty, to the need for making a determination as soon as is reasonably practicable.

**64(6) [Publication of reference]** On making a merger reference, the Secretary of State shall arrange for it to be published in such manner as he thinks most suitable for bringing it to the attention of persons who in his opinion would be affected by it.

**64(7) [Statutory instrument]** The Secretary of State may by order made by statutory instrument provide, subject to any transitional provisons contained in the order, that for the sum specified in subsection (1)(b) of this section (whether as originally enacted or as previously varied by an order under this subsection) there shall be substituted such other sum (not being less than £5 million) as is specified in the order.

**64(8) [Creation of merger situation]** The fact that two or more enterprises have ceased to be distinct enterprises in the circumstances described in subsection (1) of this section (including in those circumstances the result specified in paragraph (a), or fulfilment of the condition specified in paragraph (b), of that subsection) shall, for the purposes of this act, be regarded as creating a merger situation qualifying for investigation; and in this Act **"merger situation qualifying for investigation"** and any reference to the creation of such a situation shall be construed accordingly.

**64(9) [Definition]** In this section **"made public"** means so publicised as to be generally known or readily ascertainable.

# 65 Enterprises ceasing to be distinct enterprises

**65(1) [Distinct enterprises]** For the purposes of this Part of this Act any two enterprises shall be regarded as ceasing to be distinct enterprises if either–

(a) they are brought under common ownership or common control (whether or not the business to which either of them formerly belonged continues to be carried on under the same or different ownership or control), or

(b) either of the enterprises ceases to be carried on at all and does so in consequence of any arrangements or transaction entered into to prevent competition between the enterprises.

**65(2) [Common control]** For the purposes of the preceding subsection enterprises shall (without prejudice to the generality of the words "common control" in that subsection) be regarded as being under common control if they are–

(a) enterprises of interconnected bodies corporate, or

(b) enterprises carried on by two or more bodies corporate of which one and the same person or group of persons has control, or

(c) an enterprise carried on by a body corporate and an enterprise carried on by a person or group of persons having control of that body corporate.

**65(3) [Persons able to control policy]** A person or group of persons able, directly or indirectly, to control or materially to influence the policy of a body corporate, or the policy of any person in carrying on an enterprise, but without having a controlling interest in that body corporate or in that enterprise, may for the purposes of subsections (1) and (2) of this section be treated as having control of it.

**Note**
For modified application of s. 65(3) in the exclusion of merger agreements from the Chapter I and II prohibitions in the Competition Act 1998, see Competition Act 1998, Sch. 1, para. 1(4) and 2.

**65(4) [Control of person carrying on enterprise]** For the purposes of subsection (1)(a) of this section, in so far as it relates to bringing two or more enterprises under common control, a person or group of persons may be treated as bringing an enterprise under his or their control if–

(a) being already able to control or materially to influence the policy of the person carrying on the enterprise, that person or group of persons acquires a controlling interest in the enterprise, or, in the case of an enterprise carried on by a body corporate, acquires a controlling interest in that body corporate, or

(b) being already able materially to influence the policy of the person carrying on the enterprise, that person or group of persons becomes able to control that policy.

**Note**
For modified application of s. 65(4) in the exclusion of merger agreements from the Chapter I and II prohibitions in the Competition Act, see Competition Act 1998, Sch. 1, para. 1(4) and 2.

## 66 Time when enterprises cease to be distinct

**66(1) [Events treated as simultaneous]** Where under or in consequence of the same arrangements or transaction, or under or in consequence of successive arrangements or transactions between the same parties or interests, successive events to which this subsection applies occur within a period of two years, then for the purposes of a merger reference those events may, if the Secretary of State or the Commission thinks fit, be treated as having occurred simultaneously on the date on which the latest of them occurred.

**History**
In s. 66(1) the words "or the Commission" inserted by CA 1989, s. 153 and Sch. 20, para. 4(a) as from 16 November 1989 (see CA 1989, s. 215(1)(b)(ii)).

**66(2) [Applicable events]** The preceding subsection applies to any event whereby, under or in consequence of the arrangements or the transaction or transactions in question, any enterprises cease as between themselves to be distinct enterprises.

**66(3) [Arrangements between same interests]** For the purposes of subsection (1) of this section any arrangements or transactions may be treated by the Secretary of State or the Commission as arrangements or transactions between the same interests if it appears to him to be appropriate that they should be so treated, having regard to the persons who are substantially concerned in them.

**History**
In s. 66(3) the words "or the Commission" inserted by CA 1989, s. 153 and Sch. 20, para. 4(a) as from 16 November 1989 (see CA 1989, s. 215(1)(b)(ii)).

**66(4) [Time when enterprises cease to be distinct]** Subject to the preceding provisions of this section and to section 66A of this Act, the time at which any two enterprises cease to be distinct enterprises, where they do so under or in consequence of any arrangements or transaction not having immediate effect, or having immediate effect in part only, shall be taken to be the time when the parties to the arrangements or transaction become bound to such extent as will result, on effect being given to their obligations, in the enterprises ceasing to be distinct enterprises.

**History**
In s. 66(4) the words "and to section 66A of this Act" inserted by CA 1989, s. 153 and Sch. 20, para. 4(b) as from 16 November 1989 (see CA 1989, s. 215(1)(b)(ii)).

**66(5) [Options or conditional rights]** In accordance with subsection (4) of this section (but without prejudice to the generality of that subsection) for the purpose of determining the time at which any two enterprises cease to be distinct enterprises no account shall be taken of any option or other conditional right until the option is exercised or the condition is satisfied.

## 66A Obtaining control by stages

**66A(1) [Two s. 66A(2) transactions on same day]** Where an enterprise is brought under the control of a person or group of persons in the course of two or more transactions (referred to in this section as a "series of transactions") falling within subsection (2) of this section, those transactions may, if the Secretary of State or, as the case may be, the Commission thinks fit, be treated for the purposes of a merger reference as having occurred simultaneously on the date on which the latest of them occurred.

**66A(2) ["Series of transactions" by which control attained]** The transactions falling within this subsection are–

(a) any transaction which–
  (i) enables that person or group of persons directly or indirectly to control or materially to influence the policy of any person carrying on the enterprise,
  (ii) enables that person or group of persons to do so to a greater degree, or
  (iii) is a step (whether direct or indirect) towards enabling that person or group of persons to do so, and

(b) any transaction whereby that person or group of persons acquires a controlling interest in the enterprise or, where the enterprise is carried on by a body corporate, in that body corporate.

**66A(3) [Any transaction after s. 66A(2)(b) transaction]** Where a series of transactions includes a transaction falling within subsection (2)(b) of this section, any transaction occurring after the occurrence of that transaction is to be diregarded for the purposes of subsection (1) of this section.

**66A(4) [Where relevant period exceeds two years]** Where the period within which a series of transactions occurs exceeds two years, the transactions that may be treated as mentioned in subsection (1) of this section are any of those transactions that occur within a period of two years.

**66A(5) [Application of s. 65(2)–(4), 77(1), (4)–(6)]** Sections 65(2) to (4) and 77(1) and (4) to (6) of this Act apply for the purposes of this section to determine whether an enterprise is brought under the control of a person or group of persons and whether a transaction falls within subsection (2) of this section as they apply for the purposes of section 65 of this Act to determine whether enterprises are brought under common control.

**66A(6) [Determination of time of transaction]** In determining for the purposes of this section the time at which any transaction occurs, no account shall be taken of any option or other conditional right until the option is exercised or the condition is satisfied.

**History**

S. 66A inserted by CA 1989, s. 150(1) as from 16 November 1989 (see CA 1989, s. 215(1)(b)(i)).

**Note**

S. 66A does not apply in relation to any merger reference made before 16 November 1989 (see CA 1989, s. 150(2)).

## 67 Valuation of assets taken over

**67(1) [Effect]** The provisions of this section shall have effect for the purposes of section 64(1)(b) of this Act.

**67(2) [Value of assets]** Subject to subsection (4) of this section, the value of the assets taken over–

(a) shall be determined by taking the total value of the assets employed in, or appropriated to, the enterprises which cease to be distinct enterprises, except
  (i) any enterprise which remains under the same ownership and control, or
  (ii) if none of the enterprises remains under the same ownership and control, the enterprise having the assets with the highest value, and

(b) shall be so determined by reference to the values at which, on the enterprises ceasing to be distinct enterprises or (if they have not then done so) on the making of the merger reference to the Commission, the assets stand in the books of the relevant business, less any relevant provisions for depreciation, renewals or diminution in value.

**History**

In s. 67(2)(a) para. (i) and (ii) substituted by CA 1989, s. 153 and Sch. 20, para. 5(1) as from 16 November 1989 (see CA 1989, s. 215(1)(b)(ii)); the former words read as follows:

"any enterprise which remains under the same ownership and control, or if none of the enterprises remains under the same ownership and control, then that one of the enterprises having the assets with the highest value, and".

**67(3) [Appropriation of assets]** For the purposes of subsection (2) of this section any assets of a body corporate which, on a change in the control of the body corporate or of any enterprise of it, are dealt with in the same way as assets appropriated to any such enterprise shall be treated as appropriated to that enterprise.

**67(4) [Events treated as simultaneous]** Where in accordance with subsection (1) of section 66 or subsection (1) of section 66A of this Act events to which either of those subsections applies are treated as having occurred simultaneously, subsection (2) of this section shall apply with such adjustments as appear to the Secretary of State or to the Commission to be appropriate.

**History**
In s. 67(4) the words "or subsection (1) of section 66A" inserted and the words "either of those subsections" substituted for the former words "that subsection" by CA 1989, s. 153 and Sch. 20, para. 5(2) as from 16 November 1989 (see CA 1989, s. 215(1)(b)(ii)).

# 68 Supplementary provisions as to merger situations qualifying for investigation

**68(1) [Appropriate construction]** In relation to goods or services of any description which are the subject of different forms of supply–

(a) references in subsection (2) of section 64 of this Act to the supply of goods, or

(b) references in subsection (3) of that section to the supply of services,

shall be construed in whichever of the following ways appears to the Secretary of State or the Commission, as the case may be, to be appropriate in all the circumstances, that is to say, as references to any of those forms of supply taken separately, to all those forms of supply taken together, or to any of those forms of supply taken in groups.

**68(2) [Material differences]** For the purposes of the preceding subsection the Secretary of State or the Commission may treat goods or services as being the subject of different forms of supply whenever the transactions in question differ as to their nature, their parties, their terms or their surrounding circumstances, and the difference is one which, in the opinion of the Secretary of State or of the Commission, as the case may be, ought for the purposes of that subsection to be treated as a material difference.

**68(3) [Applicable criteria]** For the purpose of determining whether the proportion of one-quarter mentioned in subsection (2) or subsection (3) of section 64 of this Act is fulfilled with respect to goods or services of any description, the Secretary of State or the Commission, as the case may be, shall apply such criterion (whether it be value or cost or price or quantity or capacity or number of workers employed or some other criterion, of whatever nature) or such combination of criteria as may appear to the Secretary of State or the commission to be most suitable in all the circumstances.

**68(4) [Goods and services]** The criteria for determining when goods or services can be treated, for the purposes of section 64 of this Act, as goods or services of a separate description shall be such as in any particular case the Secretary of State or, as the case may be, the Commission thinks most suitable in the circumstances of that case.

**History**
In s. 68(4) the words "or, as the case may be, the Commission" inserted by CA 1989, s. 153 and Sch. 20, para. 6 as from 16 November 1989 (see CA 1989, s. 215(1)(b)(ii)).

# 69 Different kinds of merger references

**69(1) [Investigation and report]** Subject to the following provisions of this Part of this Act, on a merger reference the Commission shall investigate and report on the questions–

(a) whether a merger situation qualifying for investigation has been created, and

(b) if so, whether the creation of that situation operates, or may be expected to operate, against the public interest.

**69(2) [Exclusions from consideration]** A merger reference may be so framed as to require the Commission, in relation to the question whether a merger situation qualifying for investigation has been created, to exclude from consideration paragraph (a) of subsection (1) of section 64 of this Act, or to exclude from consideration paragraph (b) of that subsection, or to exclude one of those paragraphs if the Commission find the other satisfied.

**69(3) [Confinement of investigation]** In relation to the question whether any such result as is mentioned in section 64(1)(a) of this Act has arisen, a merger reference may be so framed as to require the Commission to confine their investigation to the supply of goods or services in a specified part of the United Kingdom.

**69(4) [Limitation of investigation]** A merger reference may require the Commission, if they find that a merger situation qualifying for investigation has been created, to limit their consideration thereafter to such elements in, or possible consequences of, the creation of that situation as may be specified in the reference, and to consider whether, in respect only of those elements or possible consequences, the situation operates, or may be expected to operate, against the public interest.

## 70 Time-limit for report on merger reference

**70(1) [Period for report to be made]** Every merger reference shall specify a period (not being longer than six months beginning with the date of the reference) within which a report on the reference is to be made; and a report of the Commission on a merger reference shall not have effect, and no action shall be taken in relation to it under this Act, unless the report is made before the end of that period or of such further period (if any) as may be allowed by the Secretary of State in accordance with the next following subsection.

**70(2) [Extension of time limit]** The Secretary of State shall not allow any further period for a report on a merger reference except on representations made by the Commission and on being satisfied that there are special reasons why the report cannot be made within the period specified in the reference; and the Secretary of State shall allow only one such further period on any one reference, and no such further period shall be longer than three months.

## 71 Variation of certain merger references

**71(1) [Variation]** Subject to the following provisions of this section, the Secretary of State may at any time vary a merger reference.

**History**
In s. 71(1) the words "made under section 69(4) of this Act" formerly appearing at the end omitted by CA 1989, s. 153 and Sch. 20, para. 7(a) and repealed by CA 1989, s. 212 and Sch. 24 as from 16 November 1989 (see CA 1989, s. 215(1)(b)(ii), (d)).

**71(2)** (Omitted by Companies Act 1989, s. 153 and Sch. 20, para. 7(b) and repealed by Companies Act 1989, s. 212 and Sch. 24 as from 16 November 1989.)

**History**
In regard to the omission and repeal of s. 71(2), see CA 1989, s. 215(1)(b)(ii), (d); s. 71(2) formerly read as follows:
"A merger reference made under section 69(4) of this Act shall not be so varied that it ceases to be a reference limited in accordance with that subsection."

**71(3) [Further restriction]** Without prejudice to the powers of the Secretary of State under section 70 of this Act, a merger reference shall not be varied so as to specify a period within which a report on the reference is to be made which is different from the period specified in the reference in accordance with that section.

## 72 Report of Commission on merger reference

**72(1) [Matters to be in report]** In making their report on a merger reference, the Commission shall include in it definite conclusions on the questions comprised in the reference, together with–

(a) such an account of their reasons for those conclusions, and

(b) such a survey of the general position with respect to the subject-matter of the reference, and of the developments which have led to that position,

as in their opinion are expedient for facilitating a proper understanding of those questions and of their conclusions.

**72(2) [Effects adverse to public interest]** Where on a merger reference the Commission find that a merger situation qualifying for investigation has been created and that the creation of that situation operates or may be expected to operate against the public interest (or, in a case falling within subsection (4) of section 69 of this Act, find that one or more elements in or consequences of that situation which were specified in the reference in accordance with that subsection so operate or may be expected so to operate) the Commission shall specify in their report the particular effects, adverse to the public interest, which in their opinion the creation of that situation (or, as the case may be, those elements in or consequences of it) have or may be expected to have; and the Commission–

(a) shall, as part of their investigations, consider what action (if any) should be taken for the purpose of remedying or preventing those adverse effects, and

(b) may, if they think fit, include in their report recommendations as to such action.

**72(3) [Action to remedy adverse effect]** In paragraph (a) of subsection (2) of this section the reference to action to be taken for the purpose mentioned in that paragraph is a reference to action to be taken for that purpose either–

(a) by one or more Ministers (including Ministers or departments of the Government of Northern Ireland) or other public authorities, or

(b) by one or more persons specified in the report as being persons carrying on, owning or controlling any of the enterprises which, in accordance with the conclusions of the Commission, have ceased to be distinct enterprises.

## 73 Order of Secretary of State on report on merger reference

**73(1) [Application]** The provisions of this section shall have effect where a report of the commission on a merger reference has been laid before Parliament in accordance with the provisions of Part VII of this act, and the conclusions of the commission set out in the report, as so laid,–

(a) include conclusions to the effect that a merger situation qualifying for investigation has been created and that its creation, or particular elements in or consequences of it specified in the report, operate or may be expected to operate against the public interest, and

(b) specify particular effects, adverse to the public interest, which in the opinion of the Commission the creation of that situation, or (as the case may be) those elements in or consequences of it, have or may be expected to have.

**73(2) [Schedule 8 powers]** In the circumstances mentioned in the preceding subsection the Secretary of State may by order made by statutory instrument exercise such one or more of the powers specified in Parts I and II of Schedule 8 to this Act as he may consider it requisite to exercise for the purpose of remedying or preventing the adverse effects specified in the report as mentioned in the preceding subsection; and those powers may be so exercised to such extent and in such manner as the Secretary of State considers requisite for that purpose.

**73(3) [Recommendations of Commission]** In determining whether, or to what extent or in what manner, to exercise any of those powers, the Secretary of State shall take into account any recommendations included in the report of the Commission in pursuance of section 72(2)(b) of this Act and any advice given by the Director under section 88 of this Act.

## 74 Interim order in respect of merger reference

**74(1) [Content of orders]** Where a merger reference has been made to the Commission, then, with a view to preventing action to which this subsection applies, the Secretary of State, subject to subsection (3) of this section, may by order made by statutory instrument–

(a) prohibit or restrict the doing of things which in his opinion would constitute action to which this subsection applies, or

(b) impose on any person concerned obligations as to the carrying on of any activities or the safeguarding of any assets, or

(c) provide for the carrying on of any activities or the safeguarding of any assets either by the appointment of a person to conduct or supervise the conduct of any activities (on such terms and with such powers as may be specified or described in the order) or in any other manner, or

(d) exercise any of the powers which, by virtue of paragraphs 12 and 12A of Schedule 8 to this Act, are exercisable by an order under section 73 of this Act.

**History**
In s. 74(1) the words "and does not impose on the Commission a limitation under section 69(4) of this Act" omitted by CA 1989, s. 153 and Sch. 20, para. 8(a) and repealed by CA 1989, s. 212 and Sch. 24; and in para. (d) the words "paragraphs 12 and 12A" substituted for the former words "paragraph 12" by CA 1989, s. 153 and Sch. 20, para. 8(b) as from 16 November 1989 (see CA 1989, s. 215(1)(b)(ii), (d)).

**74(2) [Application of s. 74(1)]** In relation to a merger reference the preceding subsection applies to any action which might prejudice the reference or impede the taking of any action under this Act which may be warranted by the Commission's report on the reference.

**74(3) [Restriction on orders]** No order shall be made under this section in respect of a merger reference after whichever of the following events first occurs, that is to say–

(a) the time (including any further period) allowed to the Commission for making a report on the reference expires without their having made such a report;

(b) the period for forty days beginning with the day on which a report of the Commission on the reference is laid before Parliament expires.

**74(4) [Cessation of orders]** An order under this section made in respect of a merger reference (if it has not previously ceased to have effect) shall cease to have effect on the occurrence of whichever of those events first occurs, but without prejudice to anything previously done under the order.

**74(5) [Restricted application of s. 74(4)]** Subsection (4) of this section shall have effect without prejudice–

(a) to the operation, in relation to any such order, of section 134(1) of this Act, or

(b) to the operation of any order made under section 73 of this Act which exercises the same or similar powers to those exercised by the order under this section.

## 75 Reference in anticipation of merger

**75(1) [Merger references]** A merger reference may be made to the Commission by the Secretary of State where it appears to him that it is or may be the fact that arrangements are in progress or in contemplation which, if carried into effect, will result in the creation of a merger situation qualifying for investigation.

**75(2) [Procedure on reference]** Subject to the following provisions of this section, on a merger reference under this section the Commission shall proceed in relation to the prospective and (if events so require) the actual results of the arrangements proposed or made as, in accordance with the preceding provisions of this Part of this Act, they could proceed if the arrangements in question had actually been made, and the results in question had followed immediately before the date of the reference under this section.

**75(3) [Limitation of Commission's consideration]** A merger reference under this section may require the Commission, if they find that a merger situation qualifying for investigation has been created, or will be created if the arrangements in question are carried into effect, to limit their consideration thereafter to such elements in, or possible consequences of, the creation of that situation as may be specified in the reference, and to consider whether, in respect only of those elements or possible consequences, the situation might be expected to operate against the public interest.

**75(4) [Application of other provisions]** In relation to a merger reference under this section, sections 66, 66A, 67, 69, 71, 72, 73 and 74 of this Act shall apply subject to the following modifications, that is to say–

(a) section 66 shall apply, where an event by which any enterprises cease as between themselves to be distinct enterprises will occur if the arrangements are carried into effect, as if the event had occurred immediately before the date of the reference;

(aa) section 66A shall apply, where a transaction falling within subsection (2) of that section will occur if the arrangements are carried into effect, as if the transaction had occurred immediately before the date of the reference;

(b) in section 67(4) the references to subsection (1) of section 66 and subsection (1) of section 66A shall be construed as references to those subsections as modified in accordance with paragraph (a) or (aa) of this subsection;

(c) in section 69, subsection (1) shall be construed as modified by subsection (2) of this section; in subsections (2) and (3) any reference to the question whether a merger situation qualifying for investigation has been created, or whether a result mentioned in section

64(1)(a) of this Act has arisen, shall be construed as including a reference to the question whether such a situation will be created or such a result will arise if the arrangements in question are carried into effect; and subsection (4) of that section shall not apply;

(d) in section 71, in section 72(2) and in section 74(1), the references to section 69(4) of this Act shall be construed as references to subsection (3) of this section; and

(e) in section 73(1), the reference to conclusions to the effect that a merger situation qualifying for investigation has been created shall be construed as including a reference to conclusions to the effect that such a situation will be created if the arrangements in question are carried into effect.

**History**
In s. 75(4) "66A" inserted and para. (a), (aa) and (b) substituted for the former para. (a) and (b) by CA 1989, s. 153 and Sch. 20, para. 9 as from 16 November 1989 (see CA 1989, s. 215(1)(b)(ii)); the former para. (a) and (b) read as follows:

"(a) section 66 shall apply with the necessary adaptations in relation to enterprises which will or may cease to be distinct enterprises under or in consequence of arrangements not yet carried into effect or not yet fully carried into effect;

(b) in section 67(4) the reference to subsection (1) of section 66 shall be construed as a reference to that subsection as modified in accordance with the preceding paragraph;".

**75(4A) [Effect of merger reference]** Where a merger reference is made under this section, it shall be unlawful, except with the consent of the Secretary of State under subsection (4C) of this section–

(a) for any person carrying on any enterprise to which the reference relates or having control of any such enterprise or for any subsidiary of his, or

(b) for any person associated with him or for any subsidiary of such a person,

directly or indirectly to acquire, at any time during the period mentioned in subsection (4B) of this section, an interest in shares in a company if any enterprise to which the reference relates is carried on by or under the control of that company.

**History**
See history note after s. 75(4M).

**75(4B) [Period in s. 75(4A)]** The period referred to in subsection (4A) of this section is the period beginning with the announcement by the Secretary of State of the making of the merger reference concerned and ending–

(a) where the reference is laid aside at any time, at that time,

(b) where the time (including any further period) allowed to the Commission for making a report on the reference expires without their having made such a report, on the expiration of that time,

(c) where a report of the Commission on the reference not including such conclusions as are referred to in section 73(1)(b) of this Act is laid before Parliament, at the end of the day on which the report is so laid,

(d) where a report of the Commission on the reference including such conclusions is laid before Parliament, at the end of the period of forty days beginning with the day on which the report is so laid,

and where such a report is laid before each House on different days, it is to be treated for the purposes of this subsection as laid on the earlier day.

**History**
See history note after s. 75(4M).

**75(4C) [Secretary of State's consent]** The consent of the Secretary of State–

(a) may be either general or special,

(b) may be revoked by the Secretary of State, and

(c) shall be published in such way as, in the opinion of the Secretary of State, to give any person entitled to the benefit of it an adequate opportunity of getting to know of it, unless in the Secretary of State's opinion publication is not necessary for that purpose.

**History**
See history note after s. 75(4M).

**75(4D) [Application of s. 93]** Section 93 of this Act applies to any contravention or apprehended contravention of subsection (4A) of this section as it applies to a contravention or apprehended contravention of an order to which section 90 of this Act applies.

**History**
See history note after s. 75(4M).

**75(4E) [Interpretation of s. 75(4A)]** Subsections (4F) to (4K) of this section apply for the interpretation of subsection (4A).

**History**
See history note after s. 75(4M).

**75(4F) [Circumstances where person acquires interest in shares]** The circumstances in which a person acquires an interest in shares include those where–

(a) he enters into a contract to acquire the shares (whether or not for cash),

(b) not being the registered holder, he acquires a right to exercise, or to control the exercise of, any right conferred by the holding of the shares, or

(c) he acquires a right to call for delivery of the shares to himself or to his order or to acquire an interest in the shares or assumes an obligation to acquire such an interest,

but does not include those where he acquires an interest in pursuance of an obligation assumed before the announcement by the Secretary of State of the making of the merger reference concerned.

**History**
See history note after s. 75(4M).

**75(4G) [Circumstances where s. 75(4F) right acquired]** The circumstances in which a person acquires a right mentioned in subsection (4F) of this section–

(a) include those where he acquires a right or asumes an obligation the exercise or fulfilment of which would give him that right, but

(b) does not include those where he is appointed as proxy to vote at a specified meeting of a company or of any class of its members or at any adjournment of the meeting or he is appointed by a corporation to act as its representative at any meeting of the company or of any class of its members,

and references to rights and obligations in this subsection and subsection (4F) of this section include conditional rights and conditional obligations.

**History**
See history note after s. 75(4M).

**75(4H) [Person carrying on or having control of enterprise]** Any reference to a person carrying on or having control of any enterprise includes a group of persons carrying on or having control of an enterprise and any member of such a group.

**History**
See history note after s. 75(4M).

**75(4J) [Application of s. 65(2)–(4), 77(1), (4)–(6)]** Sections 65(2) to (4) and 77(1) and (4) to (6) of this Act apply to determine whether any person or group of persons has control of any enterprise and whether persons are associated as they apply for the purposes of section 65 of this Act to determine whether enterprises are brought under common control.

**History**
See history note after s. 75(4M).

**75(4K) ["Subsidiary"] "Subsidiary"** has the meaning given by section 736 of the Companies Act 1985, but that section and section 736A of that Act also apply to determine whether a company is a subsidiary of an individual or of a group of persons as they apply to determine whether it is a subsidiary of a company and references to a subsidiary in subsections (8) and (9) of section 736A as so applied are to be read accordingly.

**History**
See history note after s. 75(4M).

**75(4L) ["Company", "share"]** In this section–

**"company"** includes any body corporate, and

**"share"** means share in the capital of a company, and includes stock.

**History**
See history note after s. 75(4M).

**75(4M) [Acts outside UK]** Nothing in subsection (4A) of this section makes anything done by a person outside the United Kingdom unlawful unless he is–

(a) a British citizen, a British Dependent Territories citizen, a British Overseas citizen or a British National (Overseas),

(b) a body corporate incorporated under the law of the United Kingdom or of a part of the United Kingdom, or

(c) a person carrying on business in the United Kingdom, either alone or in partnership with one or more other persons.

**History**
S. 75(4A)–(4M) inserted by CA 1989, s. 149(1) as from 16 November 1989 (see CA 1989, s. 215(1)(b)(i)).

**Note**
S. 75(4A)–(4M) do not apply to any merger reference made before 16 November 1989 (see CA 1989, s. 149(2)).

**75(5) [Abandonment of proposals]** If, in the course of their investigations on a merger reference under this section, it appears to the Commission that the proposal to make arrangements such as are mentioned in the reference has been abandoned, the Commission–

(a) shall, if the Secretary of State consents, lay the reference aside, but

(b) shall in that case furnish to the Secretary of State such information as he may require as to the results until then of the investigations.

## RESTRICTION ON POWER TO MAKE MERGER REFERENCE WHERE PRIOR NOTICE HAS BEEN GIVEN

# 75A General rule where notice given by acquirer and no reference made within period for considering notice

**75A(1) [Notice]** Notice may be given to the Director by a person authorised by regulations to do so of proposed arrangements which might result in the creation of a merger situation qualifying for investigation.

**Note**
See the Merger (Prenotification) Regulations 1990 (SI 1990/501) (as amended).

**75A(2) [Form of notice]** The notice must be in the prescribed form and state that the existence of the proposal has been made public.

**75A(3) [If period expires]** If the period for considering the notice expires without any reference being made to the Commission with respect to the notified arrangements, no reference may be made under this Part of this Act to the Commission with respect to those arrangements or to the creation or possible creation of any merger situation qualifying for investigation which is created in consequence of carrying those arrangements into effect.

**75A(4) [Qualification to s. 75A(3)]** Subsection (3) of this section is subject to sections 75B(5) and 75C of this Act.

**75A(5) ["Merger notice"]** A notice under subsection (1) of this section is referred to in sections 75B to 75F of this Act as a "merger notice".

**History**
See history note after s. 75F.

# 75B The role of the Director

**75B(1) [Duty of Director]** The Director shall, when the period for considering any merger notice begins, take such action as he considers appropriate to bring the existence of the proposal, the fact that the merger notice has been given and the date on which the period for considering the notice may expire to the attention of those who in his opinion would be affected if the arrangements were carried into effect.

**75B(2) [Period for considering merger notice]** The period for considering a merger notice is the period of twenty days, determined in accordance with subsection (9) of this section, beginning with the first day after–

(a) the notice has been received by the Director, and

(b) any fee payable to the Director in respect of the notice has been paid.

**75B(3) [Extension of s. 75B(2) period]** The Director may, and shall if required to do so by the Secretary of State, by notice to the person who gave the merger notice extend the period mentioned in subsection (2) of this section by a further fifteen days.

**History**

In s. 75B(3) the words from "extend the period" to the end substituted by the Fair Trading Act (Amendment) (Merger Prenotification) Regulations 1994 (SI 1994/1934), reg. 1, 2 as from 18 August 1994; the former words read as follows:

"(a) extend the period mentioned in subsection (2) of this section by a further ten days, and
(b) extend that period as extended under paragraph (a) of this subsection by a further fifteen days."

**75B(4) [Request for information]** The Director may by notice to the person who gave the merger notice request him to provide the Director within such period as may be specified in the notice with such information as may be so specified.

**75B(5) [Where s. 75G undertakings]** If the Director gives to the person who gave the merger notice (in this subsection referred to as "the relevant person") a notice stating that the Secretary of State is seeking undertakings under section 75G of this Act, section 75A(3) of this Act does not prevent a reference being made to the Commission unless–

(a) after the Director has given that notice, the relevant person has given a notice to the Director stating that he does not intend to give such undertakings, and

(b) the period of ten days beginning with the first day after the notice under paragraph (a) of this subsection was received by the Director has expired.

**75B(6) [S. 75B(3), (4), (5) notice]** A notice by the Director under subsection (3), (4) or (5) of this section must either be given to the person who gave the merger notice before the period for considering the merger notice expires or be sent in a properly addressed and pre-paid letter posted to him at such time that, in the ordinary course of post, it would be delivered to him before that period expires.

**75B(7) [Rejection of notice]** The Director may, at any time before the period for considering any merger notice expires, reject the notice if–

(a) he suspects that any information given in respect of the notified arrangements, whether in the merger notice or otherwise, by the person who gave the notice or any connected person is in any material respect false or misleading,

(b) he suspects that it is not proposed to carry the notified arrangements into effect,

(c) any prescribed information is not given in the merger notice or any information requested by notice under subsection (4) of this section is not provided within the period specified in the notice, or

(d) it appears to him that the notified arrangements are, or if carried into effect would result in, a concentration with a Community dimension within the meaning of Council Regulation (EEC) No. 4064/89 of 21st December 1989 on the control of concentrations between undertakings.

**History**

In s. 75B(7) the word "or" formerly appearing at the end of para. (b) omitted and the word "or," and para. (d) added at the end of para. (c) by the EEC Merger Control (Consequential Provisions) Regulations 1990 (SI 1990/1563), reg. 2 as from 21 September 1990.

**75B(8) [Where s. 75B(3)(b) extension but no recommendation]** If–

(a) under subsection (3) of this section the period for considering a merger notice has been extended by a further fifteen days, but

(b) the Director has not made any recommendation to the Secretary of State under section 76(b) of this Act as to whether or not it would in the Director's opinion be expedient for the Secretary of State to make a reference to the Commission with respect to the notified arrangements,

then, during the last five of those fifteen days, the power of the Secretary of State to make a reference to the Commission with respect to the notified arrangements is not affected by the absence of any such recommendation.

**History**

In s.75B(8) in para. (a) "(3)" substituted for the former "(3)(b)" by the Fair Trading Act (Amendment) (Merger Prenotification) Regulations 1994 (SI 1994/1934), reg. 1, 3 as from 18 August 1994.

**75B(9) [Determining period for s. 75B(2), (3), (5)]** In determining any period for the purposes of subsections (2), (3) and (5) of this section no account shall be taken of–

(a) Saturday, Sunday, Good Friday and Christmas Day, and

(b) any day which is a bank holiday in England and Wales.

**History**
See history note after s. 75F.

## 75C Cases where power to refer unaffected

**75C(1) [Effect of s. 75A(3)]** Section 75A(3) of this Act does not prevent any reference being made to the Commission if–

(a) before the end of the period for considering the merger notice, it is rejected by the Director under section 75B(7) of this Act,

(b) before the end of that period, any of the enterprises to which the notified arrangements relate cease to be distinct from each other,

(c) any information (whether prescribed information or not) that–
 (i) is, or ought to be, known to the person who gave the merger notice or any connected person, and
 (ii) is material to the notified arrangements;

is not disclosed to the Secretary of State or the Director by such time before the end of that period as may be specified in regulations,

(d) at any time after the merger notice is given but before the enterprises to which the notified arrangements relate cease to be distinct from each other, any of those enterprises ceases to be distinct from any enterprise other than an enterprise to which those arrangements relate,

(e) the six months beginning with the end of the period for considering the merger notice expires without the enterprises to which the notified arrangements relate ceasing to be distinct from each other,

(f) the merger notice is withdrawn, or

(g) any information given in respect of the notified arrangements, whether in the merger notice or otherwise, by the person who gave the notice or any connected person is in any material respect false or misleading.

**Note**
Re s. 75C(1)(C) see the Merger (Prenotification) Regulations 1990 (SI 1990/501) (as amended).

**75C(2) [Further restriction re effect of s. 75A(3)]** Where–

(a) two or more transactions which have occurred or, if any arrangements are carried into effect, will occur may be treated for the purposes of a merger reference as having occurred simultaneously on a particular date, and

(b) subsection (3) of section 75A of this Act does not prevent such a reference with respect to the last of those transactions,

that subsection does not prevent such a reference with respect to any of those transactions which actually occurred less than six months before–

(i) that date, or

(ii) the actual occurrence of another of those transactions with respect to which such a reference may be made (whether or not by virtue of this subsection).

**75C(3) [Determining time of transaction for s. 75C(2)]** In determining for the purposes of subsection (2) of this section the time at which any transaction actually occurred, no account shall be taken of any option or other conditional right until the option is exercised or the condition is satisfied.

**History**
See history note after s. 75F.

## 75D Regulations

**75D(1) [Power of Secretary of State]** The Secretary of State may make regulations for the purposes of sections 75A to 75C of this Act.

**75D(2) [Scope of regulations]** The regulations may, in particular–

(a) provide for section 75B(2) or (3) or section 75C(1)(e) of this Act to apply as if any reference to a period of days or months were a reference to a period specified in the regulations for the purposes of the provision in question,

(b) provide for the manner in which any merger notice is authorised or required to be given, rejected or withdrawn, and the time at which any merger notice is to be treated as received or rejected,

(c) provide for the manner in which any information requested by the Director or any other material information is authorised or required to be provided or disclosed, and the time at which such information is to be treated as provided or disclosed,

(d) provide for the manner in which any notice under section 75B of this Act is authorised or required to be given,

(e) provide for the time at which any notice under section 75B(5)(a) of this Act is to be treated as received,

(f) provide for the address which is to be treated for the purposes of section 75B(6) of this Act and of the regulations as a person's proper address,

(g) provide for the time at which any fee is to be treated as paid, and

(h) provide that a person is, or is not, to be treated, in such circumstances as may be specified in the regulations, as acting on behalf of a person authorised by regulations to give a merger notice or a person who has given such a notice.

**75D(3) [Different provisions]** The regulations may make different provision for different cases.

**75D(4) [By statutory instrument]** Regulations under this section shall be made by statutory instrument.

**History**
See history note after s. 75F.

**Note**
See the Merger (Prenotification) Regulations 1990 (SI 1990/501) (as amended).

## 75E Interpretation of s. 75A to 75D

**75E** In this section and sections 75A to 75D of this Act–

**"connected person"**, in relation to the person who gave a merger notice, means–

(a) any person who, for the purposes of section 77 of this Act, is associated with him, or

(b) any subsidiary of the person who gave the merger notice or of any person so associated with him,

**"merger notice"** is to be interpreted in accordance with section 75A(5) of this Act,

**"notified arrangements"** means the arrangements mentioned in the merger notice or arrangements not differing from them in any material respect,

**"prescribed"** means prescribed by the Director by notice having effect for the time being and published in the London, Edinburgh and Belfast Gazettes,

**"regulations"** means regulations under section 75D of this Act, and

**"subsidiary"** has the meaning given by section 75(4K) of this Act,

and references to the enterprises to which the notified arrangements relate are references to those enterprises that would have ceased to be distinct from one another if the arrangements mentioned in the merger notice in question had been carried into effect at the time when the notice was given.

**History**
See history note after s. 75F.

## 75F Power to amend s. 75B to 75D

**75F(1) [Power of Secretary of State]** The Secretary of State may, for the purpose of determining the effect of giving a merger notice and the steps which may be or are to be taken by any person in connection with such a notice, by regulations made by statutory instrument amend sections 75B to 75D of this Act.

**75F(2) [Different provisions]** The regulations may make different provision for different cases and may contain such incidental and supplementary provisions as the Secretary of State thinks fit.

**Note**

Re s. 75F(1), (2) see the EEC Merger Control (Consequential Provisions) Regulations 1990 (SI 1990/1563).

**75F(3) [Approval by Parliament]** No regulations shall be made under this section unless a draft of the regulations has been laid before and approved by resolution of each House of Parliament.

**History**

S. 75A–75F inserted by CA 1989, s. 146 as from 1 April 1990 (see SI 1990/142 (C. 5), art. 6(b)).

## UNDERTAKINGS AS ALTERNATIVE TO MERGER REFERENCE

# 75G Acceptance of undertakings

**75G(1) [Powers of Secretary of State]** Where–

(a) the Secretary of State has power to make a merger reference to the Commission under section 64 or 75 of this Act,

(b) the Director has made a recommendation to the Secretary of State under section 76 of this Act that such a reference should be made, and

(c) the Director has (in making that recommendation or subsequently) given advice to the Secretary of State specifying particular effects adverse to the public interest which in his opinion the creation of the merger situation qualifying for investigation may have or might be expected to have,

the Secretary of State may, instead of making a merger reference to the Commission, accept from such of the parties concerned as he considers appropriate undertakings to take specified action which the Secretary of State considers appropriate to remedy or prevent the effects adverse to the public interest specified in the advice.

**History**

In s. 75G(1), the words "complying with subsections (2) and (3) of this section" appearing after "undertakings" repealed by Deregulation and Contracting Out Act 1994, s. 81, 82(2)(g) and Sch. 17, with effect from 3 January 1995.

**75G(2), (3)** (Ceased to have effect and repealed by Deregulation and Contracting Out Act 1994, s. 9(1), 81, 82(2)(a), (g) and Sch. 17 with effect from 3 January 1995.)

**History**

Section 75G(2) and (3) formerly read as follows:

"**(2)** The undertakings must provide for one or more of the following–

(a) the division of a business by the sale of any part of the undertaking or assets or otherwise (for which purpose all the activities carried on by way of business by any one person or by any two or more interconnected bodies corporate may be treated as a single business),

(b) the division of a group of interconnected bodies corporate, and

(c) the separation, by the sale of any part of the undertaking or assets concerned or other means, of enterprises which are under common control otherwise than by reason of their being enterprises of interconnected bodies corporate.

**(3)** The undertakings may also contain provision–

(a) preventing or restricting the doing of things which might prevent or impede the division or separation,

(b) as to the carrying on of any activities or the safeguarding of any assets until the division or separation is effected,

(c) for any matters necessary to effect or take account of the division or separation, and

(d) for enabling the Secretary of State to ascertain whether the undertakings are being fulfilled."

**75G(4) [Effect of acceptance of undertakings]** If the Secretary of State has accepted one or more undertakings under this section, no reference may be made to the Commission with respect to the creation or possible creation of the merger situation qualifying for investigation by reference to which the undertakings were accepted, except in a case falling within subsection (5) of this section.

**75G(5) [Qualification to s. 75G(4)]** Subsection (4) of this section does not prevent a reference being made to the Commission if material facts about the arrangements or transactions, or proposed arrangements or transactions, in consequence of which the enterprises concerned ceased or may cease to be distinct enterprises were not–

(a) notified to the Secretary of State or the Director, or

(b) made public,

before the undertakings were accepted.

**75G(6) ["Made public" in s. 75G(5)]** In subsection (5) of this section **"made public"** has the same meaning as in section 64 of this Act.

**History**
S. 75G inserted by CA 1989, s. 147 as from 16 November 1989 (see CA 1989, s. 215(1)(b)(i)).

## 75H Publication of undertakings

**75H(1) [Duty of Secretary of State]** The Secretary of State shall arrange for–

(a) any undertaking accepted by him under section 75G of this Act,

(b) the advice given by the Director for the purposes of subsection (1)(c) of that section in any case where such an undertaking has been accepted, and

(c) any variation or release of such an undertaking,

to be published in such manner as he may consider appropriate.

**75H(2) [Giving advice for s. 75G(1)(c) purposes]** In giving advice for the purposes of section 75G(1)(c) of this Act the Director shall have regard to the need for excluding, so far as practicable, any matter to which subsection (4) of this section applies.

**75H(3) [Duty of Secretary of State re exclusion]** The Secretary of State shall exclude from any such advice as published under this section–

(a) any matter to which subsection (4) of this section applies and in relation to which he is satisfied that its publication in the advice would not be in the public interest, and

(b) any other matter in relation to which he is satisfied that its publication in the advice would be against the public interest.

**75H(4) [Matters excluded from publication]** This subsection applies to–

(a) any matter which relates to the private affairs of an individual, where publication of that matter would or might, in the opinion of the Director or the Secretary of State, as the case may be, seriously and prejudicially affect the interests of that individual, and

(b) any matter which relates specifically to the affairs of a particular body of persons, whether corporate or incorporate, where publication of that matter would or might, in the opinion of the Director or the Secretary of State, as the case may be, seriously and prejudicially affect the interests of that body, unless in his opinion the inclusion of that matter relating specifically to that body is necesary for the purposes of the advice.

**75H(5) [Absolute privilege re s. 75G(1)(c) matters]** For the purposes of the law relating to defamation, absolute privilege shall attach to any advice given by the Director for the purposes of section 75G(1)(c) of this Act.

**History**
S. 75H inserted by CA 1989, s. 147 as from 16 November 1989 (see CA 1989, s. 215(1)(b)(i)).

## 75J Review of undertakings

**75J** Where an undertaking has been accepted by the Secretary of State under section 75G of this Act, it shall be the duty of the Director–

(a) to keep under review the carrying out of that undertaking, and from time to time consider whether, by reason of any change of circumstances, the undertaking is no longer appropriate and either–

  (i) one or more of the parties to it can be released from it, or

  (ii) it needs to be varied or to be superseded by a new undertaking, and

(b) if it appears to him that the undertaking has not been or is not being fulfilled, that any person can be so released or that the undertaking needs to be varied or superseded, to give such advice to the Secretary of State as he may think proper in the circumstances.

**History**
S. 75J inserted by CA 1989, s. 147 as from 16 November 1989 (see CA 1989, s. 215(1)(b)(i)).

## 75K Order of Secretary of State where undertaking not fulfilled

**75K(1) [Application]** The provisions of this section shall have effect where it appears to the Secretary of State that an undertaking accepted by him under section 75G of this Act has not been, is not being or will not be fulfilled.

**75K(2) [Powers of Secretary of State]** The Secretary of State may by order made by statutory instrument exercise such one or more of the relevant powers as he may consider it requisite to exercise for the purpose of remedying or preventing the adverse effects specified in the advice given by the Director for the purposes of section 75G(1)(c) of this Act; and those powers may be so exercised to such extent and in such manner as the Secretary of State considers requisite for that purpose.

**History**
In s. 75K(2), the words "relevant powers" substituted for the words "powers specified in paragraphs 9A and 12 to 12C and Part II of Schedule 8 to this Act" by Deregulation and Contracting Out Act 1994, s. 9(2), 82(2)(a), with effect from 3 January 1995.

**75K(3) [S. 75J(b) advice to be considered]** In determining whether, or to what extent or in what manner, to exercise any of those powers, the Secretary of State shall take into account any advice given by the Director under section 75J(b) of this Act.

**75K(4) [Order may differ from undertaking]** The provision contained in an order under this section may be different from that contained in the undertaking.

**75K(5) [Effect of order]** On the making of an order under this section, the undertaking and any other undertaking accepted under section 75G of this Act by reference to the same merger situation qualifying for investigation are released by virtue of this section.

**75K(6) [Relevant powers]** In subsection (2) of this section, **"the relevant powers"** means–

(a) in relation to an undertaking to which subsection (7) of this section applies ("a divestment undertaking"), the powers specified in paragraphs 9A and 12 to 12Cand Part II of Schedule 8 to this Act, and

(b) in relation to an undertaking which is not a divestment undertaking, the powers specified in that Schedule.

**History**
S. 75K(6) inserted by Deregulation and Contracting Out Act 1994, s. 9(3), 82(2)(a), with effect from 3 January 1995.

**75K(7) [Divestment undertaking]** This subsection applies to an undertaking which provides for–

(a) the division of a business by the sale of any part of the undertaking or assets or otherwise (for which purpose all the activities carried on by way of business by any one person or by any two or more interconnected bodies corporate may be treated as a single business),

(b) the division of a group of interconnected bodies corporate, or

(c) the separation, by the sale of any part of the undertaking or assets concerned or other means, of enterprises which are under common control otherwise than by reason of their being enterprises of interconnected bodies corporate.

**History**
S. 75K(7) inserted by Deregulation and Contracting Out Act 1994, s. 9(3), 82(2)(a), with effect from 3 January 1995.

**75K(8) [Modification to Sch. 8, para. 1]** Schedule 8 to this Act shall, to such extent as is necessary for the purpose of giving effect to subsection (2) of this section, have effect as if, in paragraph 1 of that Schedule, after "section 73" there were inserted "or section 75K".

**History**
S. 75K(8) inserted by Deregulation and Contracting Out Act 1994, s. 9(3), 82(2)(a), with effect from 3 January 1995.
S. 75K originally inserted by CA 1989, s. 147 as from 16 November 1989 (see CA 1989, s. 215(1)(b)(i)).

## SUPPLEMENTARY

# 76 Functions of Director in relation to merger situations

**76(1) [Duty of Director]** It shall be the duty of the Director–

(a) to take all such steps as are reasonably practicable for keeping himself informed about actual or prospective arrangements or transactions which may constitute or result in the creation of merger situations qualifying for investigation, and

(b) to make recommendations to the Secretary of State as to any action under this Part of this Act which in the opinion of the Director it would be expedient for the Secretary of State to take in relation to any such arrangements or transactions.

**76(2) [Matters to be considered]** In exercising his duty under this section the Director shall take into consideration any representations made to him by persons appearing to him to have a substantial interest in any such arrangements or transactions or by bodies appearing to him to represent substantial numbers of persons who have such an interest.

**History**
S. 76(2) added by CA 1989, s. 153 and Sch. 20, para. 11 as from 16 November 1989 (see CA 1989, s. 215(1)(b)(ii)).

## 77 Associated persons

**77(1) [Persons treated as one person]** For the following purposes, that is to say–

(a) for the purpose of determining under section 57(1) or (1A) of this Act whether a person is a newspaper proprietor and, if so, which newspapers are his newspapers;

(b) for the purpose of determining under section 65 of this Act whether any two enterprises have been brought under common ownership or common control; and

(c) for the purpose of determining what activities are carried on by way of business by any one person, in so far as that question arises in the application, by virtue of an order under section 73 of this Act, of paragraph 14 of Schedule 8 to this Act,

associated persons, and any bodies corporate which they or any of them control, shall (subject to the next following subsection) be treated as one person.

**History**
In s. 77(1)(a), the words "or (1A)" inserted by Deregulation and Contracting Out Act 1994, s. 39 and Sch. 11, para. 2(2)(a) with effect from 3 January 1995 (Deregulation and Contracting Out Act 1994 (Commencement No. 2) Order 1994 (SI 1994/3188 (C. 76)), art. 2, 3(f), (q)).

**77(2) [Restriction on s. 77(1)]** The preceding subsection shall not have effect–

(a) for the purpose mentioned in paragraph (a) of that subsection so as to exclude from section 58 of this Act any case which would otherwise fall within that section, or

(b) for the purpose mentioned in paragraph (b) of the preceding subsection so as to exclude from section 65 of this Act any case which would otherwise fall within that section.

**77(3) [Excluded matters]** A merger reference other than a newspaper merger reference (whether apart from this section the reference could be made or not) may be so framed as to exclude from consideration, either altogether or for any specified purpose or to any specified extent, any matter which, apart from this section, would not have been taken into account on that reference.

**77(4) [Associates]** For the purposes of this section the following persons shall be regarded as associated with one another, that is to say–

(a) any individual and that individual's husband or wife and any relative, or husband or wife of a relative, of that individual or of that individual's husband or wife;

(b) any person in his capacity as trustee of a settlement and the settlor or grantor and any person associated with the settlor or grantor;

(c) persons carrying on business in partnership and the husband or wife and relatives of any of them;

(d) any two or more persons acting together to secure or exercise control of a body corporate or other association or to secure control of any enterprise or assets.

**77(5) ["Control"]** The reference in subsection (1) of this section to bodies corporate which associated persons control shall be construed as follows, that is to say–

(a) in its application for the purpose mentioned in paragraph (a) of that subsection, **"control"** in that reference means having a primary controlling interest within the meaning of section 57(4) of this Act, and

(b) in its application for any other purpose mentioned in subsection (1) of this section, **"control"** in that reference shall be construed in accordance with section 65(3) and (4) of this Act.

**History**
In s. 77(5)(a), the word "primary" inserted by Deregulation and Contracting Out Act 1994, s. 39 and Sch. 11, para. 2(2)(a) with effect from 3 January 1995 (Deregulation and Contracting Out Act 1994 (Commencement No. 2) Order 1994 (SI 1994/3188 (C. 76)), art. 2, 3(f), (q)).

**77(6) [Interpretation]** In this section **"relative"** means a brother, sister, uncle, aunt, nephew, niece, lineal ancestor or descendant (the stepchild or illegitimate child of any person, or anyone adopted by a person, whether legally or otherwise, as his child, being taken into account as a relative or to trace a relationship in the same way as that person's child); and references to a wife or husband shall include a former wife or husband and a reputed wife or husband.

# PART VIII – ADDITIONAL PROVISIONS RELATING TO REFERENCES TO COMMISSION

## 84 Public interest

**84(1) [Matters to be considered]** In determining for any purposes to which this section applies whether any particular matter operates, or may be expected to operate, against the public interest, the Commission shall take into account all matters which appear to them in the particular circumstances to be relevant and, among other things, shall have regard to the desirability–

(a) of maintaining and promoting effective competition between persons supplying goods and services in the United Kingdom;

(b) of promoting the interests of consumers, purchasers and other users of goods and services in the United Kingdom in respect of the prices charged for them and in respect of their quality and the variety of goods and services supplied;

(c) of promoting, through competition, the reduction of costs and the development and use of new techniques and new products, and of facilitating the entry of new competitors into existing markets;

(d) of maintaining and promoting the balanced distribution of industry and employment in the United Kingdom; and

(e) of maintaining and promoting competitive activity in markets outside the United Kingdom on the part of producers of goods, and of suppliers of goods and services, in the United Kingdom.

**84(2) [Application]** This section applies to the purposes of any functions of the Commission under this Act other than functions to which section 59(3) of this Act applies.

## 85 Attendance of witnesses and production of documents

**85(1) [Power of Commission]** For the purposes of any investigation or a reference made to them under this Act the Commission may, by notice in writing signed on their behalf by any of their members or by their secretary–

(a) require any person to attend at a time and place specified in the notice, and to give evidence to the Commission or a member of the Commission nominated by them for the purpose, or

(b) require any person to produce, at a time and place specified in the notice, to the Commission or to any person nominated by the Commission for the purpose,

(i) any documents which are specified or described in the notice, or

(ii) any document which falls within a category of document which is specified, or described, in the notice,

and which are documents in his custody or under his control and relating to any matter relevant to the investigation, or

(c) require any person carrying on any business to furnish to the Commission such estimates, forecasts, returns or other information as may be specified or described in the notice, and specify the time, the manner and the form in which any such estimates, forecasts, returns or information are to be furnished.

**History**

In s. 85(1)(b) after the word "purpose" the word "(i)" inserted and after the words "described in the notice" the word "or" and s. 85(1)(b)(ii) inserted by the Competition Act 1998, s. 74(1), 76, Sch. 12, para. 1(10)(a) and (b) respectively as from 1 April 1999 (see SI 1999/505 (C. 9), art. 1, 2 and Sch.).

In s. 85(1)(c) after the word "estimates", in both places, the word "forecasts" inserted by the Competition Act 1998, s. 74(1), 76, Sch. 12, para. 1(11) as from 1 April 1999 (see SI 1999/505 (C. 9), art. 1, 2 and Sch.).

**85(1A) [Powers covered by s. 85(1)]** For the purposes of subsection (1) above–

(a) **"document"** includes information recorded in any form;

(b) the power to require the production of documents includes power to take copies of, or extracts from, any document produced; and

(c) in relation to information recorded otherwise than in legible form, the power to require it to be produced includes power to require it to be produced in legible form, so far as the means to do so are within the custody or under the control of the person on whom the requirement is imposed.

**History**

S. 85(1A) inserted by the Competition Act 1998, s. 74(1), 76, Sch. 12, para. 1(12) as from 1 April 1999 (see SI 1999/505 (C. 9), art. 1, 2 and Sch.).

**85(2) [Power to take evidence]** For the purposes of an investigation of the kind mentioned in subsection (1) the Commission, or a member of the Commission nominated by them for that purpose, may take evidence on oath, and for that purpose may administer oaths.

**History**

S. 85(2) the words "an investigation of the kind mentioned in subsection (1)" substituted for the former words "any such investigation" by the Competition Act 1998, s. 74(1), 76, Sch. 12, para. 1(13) as from 1 April 1999 (see SI 1999/505 (C. 9), art. 1, 2 and Sch.).

**85(3) [Limit on powers of evidence, production]** No person shall be compelled for the purpose of any such investigation to give any evidence or produce any document which he could not be compelled to give or produce in civil proceedings before the court or, in complying with any requirement for the furnishing of information, to give any information which he could not be compelled to give in evidence in such proceedings.

**85(4) [Expenses of attendance]** No person shall be required, in obedience to a notice under subsection (1) of this section, to go more than ten miles from his place of residence unless the necessary expenses of his attendance are paid or tendered to him.

**85(5)** (Omitted and repealed by Companies Act 1989, s. 153, 212, Sch. 20, para. 13(2) and Sch. 24 as from 1 April 1990.)

**History**

In regard to the above omission and repeal see SI 1990/142 (C. 5), art. 6(c), 7(d); s. 85(5) formerly read as follows:

"Any person who refuses or, without reasonable excuse, fails to do anything duly required of him by a notice under subsection (1) of this section shall be guilty of an offence and liable on summary conviction to a fine not exceeding level 5 on the standard scale."

**85(6) [Offence, penalty]** Any person who–

(a) wilfully alters, suppresses or destroys any document which he has been required by any such notice to produce,

shall be guilty of an offence and liable on summary conviction to a fine not exceeding the prescribed sum or, on conviction on indictment, to imprisonment for a term not exceeding two years or to a fine or to both.

**History**

In s. 85(6) para. (b) omitted and repealed (together with the word "or" formerly preceding it) by CA 1989, s. 153, 212, Sch. 20, para. 13(2) and Sch. 24 as from 1 April 1990 (see SI 1990/142 (C. 5), art. 6(c), 7(d)); para (b) formerly read as follows:

"in furnishing any estimate, return or other information required of him under any such notice, makes any statement which he knows to be false in a material particular or recklessly makes any statement which is false in a material particular,".

**85(7) [Certification re non-compliance with notice]** If any person (referred to in subsection (7A) of this section as "the defaulter") refuses or otherwise fails to comply with any notice under subsection (1) of this section, any one of those who, in relation to the investigation in question, are performing the functions of the Commission may certify that fact in writing to the court and the court may enquire into the case.

**History**

See history note after s. 85(7A).

**85(7A) [Punishment of defaulter]** If, after hearing any witness who may be produced against or on behalf of the defaulter and any statement which may be offered in defence, the court is satisfied that the defaulter did without reasonable excuse refuse or otherwise fail to comply with the notice, the court may punish the defaulter (and, in the case of a body corporate, any director or officer) in like manner as if the defaulter had been guilty of contempt of court.

**History**
S. 85(7), (7A) substituted for the former s. 85(7) by CA 1989, s. 153 and Sch. 20, para. 13(2) as from 1 April 1990 (see SI 1990/142 (C. 5), art. 6(c)); the former s. 85(7) read as follows:
"If a person makes default in complying with a notice under subsection (1) of this section, the court may, on the application of the Secretary of State, make such order as the court thinks fit for requiring the default to be made good; and any such order may provide that all the costs or expenses of and incidental to the application shall be borne by the person in default or by any officers of a company or other association who are responsible for its default."

**85(8) ["The court"]** In this section **"the court"** –

(a) in relation to England and Wales, means the High Court;

(b) in relation to Scotland, means the Court of Session; and

(c) in relation to Northern Ireland, means the High Court or a judge of the High Court.

**Note**
Re s. 85(6)–(8) see the EEC Merger Control (Distinct Market Investigations) Regulations 1990 (SI 1990/1715), art. 3.

**Note**
Re s. 85(6)–(8) see the EEC Merger Control (Distinct Market Investigations) Regulations 1990 (SI 1990/1715), art. 3.
For application of s. 85 in relation to the functions of the Competition Commission in assessing the impact on competition of regulating provisions or practices adopted by the Financial Services Authority under the Financial Services and Markets Act 2000, see Sch. 14, para. 3 to that Act.

## 93A Enforcement of undertakings

**93A(1) [Application]** This section applies where a person (in this section referred to as "the responsible person") has given an undertaking which–

(a) has been accepted by the Secretary of State pursuant to a proposal under section 56A of this Act or under section 56F or section 75G of this Act,

(b) has been accepted by the appropriate Minister or Ministers under section 88 of this Act after the commencement of this section.

**History**
In s. 93A(1)(a) the words "pursuant to a proposal under section 56A of this Act or under section 56F or" substituted for "under section" by Deregulation and Contracting Out Act 1994, s. 39, 82(2)(e) and Sch. 11, para. 2(3) with effect from 3 January 1995.
In s. 93A(1), the word ", or" formerly appearing at the end of para. (b), and para. (c) repealed by the Competition Act 1998 (Transitional, Consequential and Supplemental Provisions) Order 2000 (SI 2000/311), art. 1, 9(4) as from 1 March 2000, subject to transitional provision in art. 4 of that order; s. 93A(1)(c) formerly read as follows:
"(c) has been accepted by the Director under section 4 or 9 of the Competition Act 1980 after that time."

**93A(2) [Right to bring civil proceedings]** Any person may bring civil proceedings in respect of any failure, or apprehended failure, of the responsible person to fulfil the undertaking, as if the obligations imposed by the undertaking on the responsible person had been imposed by an order to which section 90 of this Act applies.

**History**
S. 93A inserted by CA 1989, s. 148 as from 16 November 1989 (see CA 1989, s. 215(1)(b)(i)).

## 93B False or misleading information

**93B(1) [Offence]** If a person furnishes any information–

(a) to the Secretary of State, the Director or the Commission in connection with any of their functions under Parts IV, V, VI or this Part of this Act or under the Competition Act 1980, or

(b) to the Commission in connection with functions of the Commission under the Telecommunications Act 1984 or the Airports Act 1986,

and either he knows the information to be false or misleading in a material particular, or he furnishes the information recklessly and it is false or misleading in a material particular, he is guilty of an offence.

**93B(2) [Further offence]** A person who–

(a) furnishes any information to another which he knows to be false or misleading in a material particular, or

(b) recklessly furnishes any information to another which is false or misleading in a material particular,

knowing that the information is to be used for the purpose of furnishing information as mentioned in subsection (1)(a) or (b) of this section, is guilty of an offence.

**93B(3) [Penalties]** A person guilty of an offence under subsection (1) or (2) of this section is liable–

(a) on summary conviction, to a fine not exceeding the statutory maximum, or
(b) on conviction on indictment, to imprisonment for a term not exceeding two years or to a fine or to both.

**Note**
Re s. 93B(3)(a) see the EEC Merger Control (Distinct Market Investigations) Regulations 1990 (SI 1990/1715), reg. 4

**93B(4) [Non-application of s. 129(1)]** Section 129(1) of this Act does not apply to an offence under this section.

**History**
S. 93B inserted by CA 1989, s. 151 as from 1 April 1990 (see SI 1990/142 (C. 5), art. 6(b)).
For application of s. 93B in relation to the functions of the Competition Commission in assessing the impact on competition of regulating provisions or practices adopted by the Financial Services Authority under the Financial Services and Markets Act 2000, see Sch. 14, para. 3 to that Act.

# Schedule 8 – Powers Exercisable by Orders Under Sections 56 and 73

Sections 56, 73, 74, 77, 89, and 91

## Part I – Powers Exercisable in All Cases

**1** Subject to paragraph 3 of this Schedule, an order under section 56 or section 73 of this Act (in this Schedule referred to as an "order") may declare it to be unlawful, except to such extent and in such circumstances as may be provided by or under the order, to make or to carry out any such agreement as may be specified or described in the order.

**Note**
Sch. 8 to have effect as if in para. 1 "or s. 75K" were inserted after "section 73", to the extent necessary to give effect to s. 75K(2)) (powers of Secretary of State to exercise powers in Sch. 8 ("relevant powers") (see s. 75K(8)).

**2** Subject to the next following paragraph, an order may require any party to any such agreement as may be specified or described in the order to terminate the agreement within such time as may be so specified, either wholly or to such extent as may be so specified.

**3(1), (2)** (Omitted and repealed by the Competition Act 1998, s. 74(1), Sch. 12, para. 1(1), (3)(d) and s. 74(3), Sch. 14 as from 10 November 1999.)

**History**
In regard to the date of the omission of Sch. 8, para. 3(1), (2) see the Competition Act 1998 (Commencement No. 4) Order 1999 (SI 1999/2859 (C 74)), art. 2(a); ommission subject to transitional provisions in the Competition Act 1998, s. 74(2), Sch. 13, para. 40, 41; Sch. 8, para. 3(1), (2) formerly read as follows:
"**(1)** An order shall not by virtue of paragraph 1 of this Schedule declare it to be unlawful to make any agreement in so far as, if made, it would be an agreement to which the Act of 1976 would apply.
**(2)** An order shall not by virtue of paragraph 1 or paragraph 2 of this Schedule declare it to be unlawful to carry out, or require any person to terminate, an agreement in so far as it is an agreement to which the Act of 1976 applies."

**3(3)** An order shall not by virtue of either of those paragraphs declare it to be unlawful to make or to carry out, or require any person to terminate, an agreement in so far as, if made, it would relate, (or as the case may be) in so far as it relates, to the terms and conditions of employment of any workers, or to the physical conditions in which any workers are required to work.

**3(4)** In this paragraph **"terms and conditions of employment"** has the meaning assigned to it by section 167(1) of the Industrial Relations Act 1971.

**4** An order may declare it to be unlawful, except to such extent and in such circumstances as may be provided by or under the order, to withhold or to agree to withhold or to threaten to withhold, or to procure others to withhold or to agree to withhold or threaten to withhold, from any such persons as may be specified or described in the order, any supplies or services so specified or described or any orders for such supplies or services (whether the withholding is absolute or is to be effectual only in particular circumstances).

**5** An order may declare it to be unlawful, except to such extent and in such circumstances as may be provided by or under the order, to require, as a condition of the supplying of goods or services to any person,–

(a) the buying of any goods, or

(b) the making of any payment in respect of services other than the goods or services supplied, or

(c) the doing of any other such matter as may be specified or described in the order.

**6** An order may declare it to be unlawful, except to such extent and in such circumstances as may be provided by or under the order,–

(a) to discriminate in any manner specified or described in the order between any persons in the prices charged for goods or services so specified or described, or

(b) to do anything so specified or described which appears to the appropriate Minister to amount to such discrimination,

or to procure others to do any of the things mentioned in sub-paragraph (a) or sub-paragraph (b) of this paragraph.

**7** An order may declare it to be unlawful, except to such extent and in such circumstances as may be provided by or under the order,–

(a) to give or agree to give in other ways any such preference in respect of the supply of goods or services, or the giving of orders for goods or services, as may be specified or described in the order, or

(b) to do anything so specified or described which appears to the appropriate Minister to amount to giving such preference,

or to procure others to do any of the things mentioned in sub-paragraph (a) or sub-paragraph (b) of this paragraph.

**8** An order may declare it to be unlawful, except to such extent and in such circumstances as may be provided by or under the order, to charge for goods or services supplied prices differing from those in any published list or notification, or to do anything specified or described in the order which appears to the appropriate Minister to amount to charging such prices.

**9** An order may require a person supplying goods or services to publish a list of or otherwise notify prices, with or without such further information as may be specified or described in the order.

**9A(1)** An order may require a person supplying goods or services to publish–

(a) any such accounting information in relation to the supply of the goods or services, and

(b) any such information in relation to–

(i) the quantities of goods or services supplied, or

(ii) the geographical areas in which they are supplied,

as may be specified or described in the order.

**9A(2)** In this paragraph **"accounting information"**, in relation to a supply of goods or service, means information as to–

(a) the costs of the supply, including fixed costs and overheads,

(b) the manner in which fixed costs and overheads are calculated and apportioned for accounting purposes of the supplier, and

(c) the income attributable to the supply.

**History**
Para. 9A inserted by CA 1989, s. 153 and Sch. 20, para. 19(2) as from 16 November 1989 (see CA 1989, s. 215(1)(b)(ii)).

**10(1)** Subject to the following provisions of this paragraph, an order may, to such extent and in such circumstances as may be provided by or under the order, regulate the prices to be charged for any goods or services specified or described in the order.

**10(2)** An order shall not exercise the power conferred by the preceding sub-paragraph in respect of goods or services of any description unless the matters specified in the relevant report as being those which in the opinion of the Commission operate, or may be expected to operate, against the public interest relate, or include matters relating, to the prices charged for goods or services of that description.

**10(3)** In this paragraph **"the relevant report"**, in relation to an order, means the report of the Commission in consequence of which the order is made, in the form in which that report is laid before Parliament.

**11** An order may declare it to be unlawful, except to such extent and in such circumstances as may be provided by or under the order, for any person, by publication or otherwise, to notify, to persons supplying goods or services, prices recommended or suggested as appropriate to be charged by those persons for those goods or services.

**12(1)** An order may prohibit or restrict the acquisition by any person of the whole or part of the undertaking or assets of another person's business, or the doing of anything which will or may have a result to which this paragraph applies, or may require that, if such an acquisition is made or anything is done which has such a result, the persons concerned or any of them shall thereafter observe any prohibitions or restrictions imposed by or under the order.

**12(2)** This paragraph applies to any result which consists in two or more bodies corporate becoming interconnected bodies corporate.

**12(3)** Where an order is made in consequence of a report of the Commission under section 72 of this Act, or is made under section 74 of this Act, this paragraph also applies to any result (other than that specified in sub-paragraph (2) of this paragraph) which, in accordance with section 65 of this Act, consists in two or more enterprises ceasing to be distinct enterprises.

**12A** An order may require any person to furnish any such information to the Director as may be specified or described in the order.

**History**
See history note after para. 12C.

**12B** An order may require any activities to be carried on separately from any other activities.

**History**
See history note after para. 12C.

**12C** An order may prohibit or restrict the exercise of any right to vote exercisable by virtue of the holding of any shares, stock or securities.

**History**
Para. 12A–12C inserted by CA 1989, s. 153 and Sch. 20, para. 19(3) as from 16 November 1989 (see CA 1989, s. 215(1)(b)(ii)).

**13** In this Part of this schedule **"the appropriate Minister"**, in relation to an order, means the Minister by whom the order is made.

# Part II – Powers Exercisable Except in Cases Falling Within Section 56(6)

**14** An order may provide for the division of any business by the sale of any part of the undertaking or assets or otherwise (for which purpose all the activities carried on by way of business by any one person or by any two or more interconnected bodies corporate may be treated as a single business), or for the division of any group of interconnected bodies corporate, and for all such matters as may be necessary to effect or take account of the division, including–

(a) the transfer or vesting of property, rights, liabilities or obligations;

(b) the adjustment of contracts, whether by discharge or reduction of any liability or obligation or otherwise;

(c) the creation, allotment, surrender or cancellation of any shares, stock or securities;

(d) the formation or winding up of a company or other association, corporate or unincorporate, or the amendment of the memorandum and articles or other instruments regulating any company or association;

(e) the extent to which, and the circumstances in which, provisions of the order affecting a company or association in its share, constitution or other matters may be altered by the company or association, and the registration under any enactment of the order by companies or associations so affected;

(f) the continuation, with any necessary change of parties, of any legal proceedings.

**15** In relation to an order under section 73 of this Act, the reference in paragraph 14 of this Schedule to the division of a business as mentioned in that paragraph shall be construed as including a reference to the separation, by the sale of any part of any undertaking or assets concerned or other means, of enterprises which are under common control otherwise than by reason of their being enterprises of interconnected bodies corporate.

# INDUSTRY ACT 1975

(1975 Chapter 68)

*[12 November 1975]*

[Note: The Industry Act 1975 came fully into force on 20 November 1975 (see Industry Act 1975 (Commencement) Order 1975 (SI 1975/1881).]

## PART II – POWERS IN RELATION TO TRANSFERS OF CONTROL OF IMPORTANT MANUFACTURING UNDERTAKINGS TO NON-RESIDENTS

### 11 General extent of powers in relation to control of important manufacturing undertakings

**11(1) [Effect]** The powers conferred by this Part of this Act shall have effect in relation to changes of control of important manufacturing undertakings.

**11(2) [Definition]** In this Part of this Act–

"**"important manufacturing undertaking**" means an undertaking which, in so far as it is carried on in the United Kingdom, is wholly or mainly engaged in manufacturing industry and appears to the Secretary of State to be of special importance to the United Kingdom or to any substantial part of the United Kingdom."

### 12 Meaning of "change of control"

**12(1) [Change on relevant event]** There is a change of control of an important manufacturing undertaking for the purposes of this Part of this Act only upon the happening of a relevant event.

**12(2) ["Relevant event"]** In subsection (1) above **"relevant event"** means any event as a result of which–

(a) the person carrying on the whole or part of the undertaking ceases to be resident in the United Kingdom;

(b) a person not resident in the United Kingdom acquires the whole or part of the undertaking;

(c) a body corporate resident in the United Kingdom but controlled by a person not so resident acquires the whole or part of the undertaking;

(d) a person not resident in the United Kingdom becomes able to exercise or control the exercise of the first, second or third qualifying percentage of votes in a body corporate carrying on the whole or part of the undertaking or in any other body corporate which is in control of such a body; or

(e) a person resident in the United Kingdom and able to exercise or control the exercise of the first, second or third qualifying percentage of votes in a body corporate carrying on the whole or part of the undertaking or in any other body corporate which is in control of such a body ceases to be resident in the United Kingdom.

**12(3) [Control]** For the purposes of subsection (2) above–

(a) a body corporate or individual entitled to cast 30 per cent or more of the votes that may be cast at any general meeting of a body corporate, is in control of that body; and

(b) control of a body corporate which has control of another body corporate gives control of the latter body.

**12(4) [Power to direct shareholders]** Any power to direct the holder of shares or stock in a body corporate as to the exercise of his votes at a general meeting of that body corporate is to be treated as entitlement to cast the votes in respect of the shares or stock in question.

**12(5) [Persons acting together]** Two or more persons acting together in concert may be treated as a single person for the purposes of any provision of this Part of this Act relating to change of control.

**12(6) [Qualifying percentages]** For the purposes of this Part of this Act–

(a) the first qualifying percentage of votes is 30 per cent;

(b) the second qualifying percentage is 40 per cent; and

(c) the third qualifying percentage is 50 per cent;

and the references to votes in this subsection are references to votes that may be cast at a general meeting.

## 13 Power to make orders

**13(1) [Conditions for making orders]** If it appears to the Secretary of State–

(a) that there is a serious and immediate probability of a change of control of an important manufacturing undertaking; and

(b) that that change of control would be contrary to the interests of the United Kingdom, or contrary to the interest of any substantial part of the United Kingdom,

he may by order (in this Part of this Act referred to as a "prohibition order") specify the undertaking and

(i) prohibit that change of control; and

(ii) prohibit or restrict the doing of things which in his opinion would constitute or lead to it;

and may make such incidental or supplementary provision in the order as appears to him to be necessary or expedient.

**13(2) [Vesting orders]** Subject to subsection (3) below, if–

(a) the conditions specified in paragraphs (a) and (b) of subsection (1) above are satisfied, or

(b) a prohibition order has been made in relation to an important manufacturing undertaking, or

(c) the Secretary of State has learnt of circumstances which appear to him to constitute a change of control of an important manufacturing undertaking, occurring on or after 1st February 1975, and is satisfied that that change is contrary to the interests of the United Kingdom, or contrary to the interests of any substantial part of the United Kingdom,

the Secretary of State may by order made with the approval of the Treasury (in this Part of this Act referred to as a "vesting order") direct that on a day specified in the order–

(i) share capital and loan capital to which this subsection applies, or

(ii) any assets which are employed in the undertaking,

shall vest [in] in himself or in nominees for himself and may make such incidental or supplementary provision in the order as appears to him to be necessary or expedient.

**History**

In s. 13(2), the words "the Board or", which appeared after the words "shall vest in" and "in nominees for", repealed by British Technology Group Act 1991, s. 17(2), 18 and Sch. 2, Pt. I with effect from 6 January 1992 (see British Technology Group Act 1991 (Appointed Day) Order 1991 (SI 1991/2721 (C. 83)), art. 2).

**Note**
Presumably the word "in" identified above in square parentheses should also have been repealed.

**13(3) [Vesting orders]** A vesting order may only be made if the Secretary of State is satisfied that the order is necessary in the national interest and that, having regard to all the circumstances, that interest cannot, or cannot appropriately, be protected in any other way.

**13(4) [Applicable share and loan capital]** The share capital and loan capital to which subsection (2) above applies are–

(a) in any case where the Secretary of State considers that the interests mentioned in subsection (2) (c) above cannot, or cannot appropriately, be protected unless all the share capital of any relevant body corporate vests by virtue of the order, the share capital of that body corporate, together with so much (if any) of the loan capital of that body as may be specified in the order,

(b) in any other case, that part of the share capital of any relevant body corporate which, at the time that the draft of the order is laid before Parliament under section 15 (3) below, appears to the Secretary of State to be involved in the change of control.

**13(5) [Definition]** In this section **"relevant body corporate"** means–

(a) a body corporate incorporated in the United Kingdom carrying on in the United Kingdom as the whole or the major part of its business there the whole or part of an important manufacturing undertaking, or

(b) a body corporate incorporated in the United Kingdom–
  (i) which is the holding company of a group of companies carrying on in the United Kingdom as the whole or the major part of their business there the whole or part of an important manufacturing undertaking, and
  (ii) as to which one of the conditions specified in subsection (6) below is satisfied.

**13(6) [Conditions]** The conditions mentioned in subsection (5) above are–

(a) that it appears to the Secretary of State that there is a serious and immediate probability of the happening of an event in relation to the company which would constitute a change of control of the undertaking, or

(b) that the Secretary of State has learnt of circumstances relating to the company which appear to him to constitute a change of control of the undertaking on or after 1st February 1975.

**13(7) [Interests of the UK]** In sections (1)(b) and (2)(c) **"interests"** means interests which relate to public policy, public security or public health.

**History**
S. 13(7) added by Industry Act 1975 (Prohibition and Vesting Order) Regulations 1998 (SI 1998/3035), reg. 2, with effect from 31 December 1998.

**13(8) [The national interest]** In subsection (3) **"the national interest"** means the national interest in relation to public policy, public security or public health.

**History**
S. 13(8) added by Industry Act 1975 (Prohibition and Vesting Order) Regulations 1998 (SI 1998/3035), reg. 2, with effect from 31 December 1998.

# 14 Notices to extend vesting orders to other holdings

**14(1) [Notice to be served by Secretary of State]** Where 30 per cent or more of the share capital of the body corporate vests in the Secretary of State by virtue of a vesting order, the Secretary of State shall serve on the holders of all the share capital that does not so vest, and on any other persons who to his knowledge have a present or prospective right to subscribe for share capital of the body corporate, within 28 days of the making of the order, a notice informing them of the making of the order and of the right of each of them to require the order to extend to the share capital or rights held by him.

**History**
In s. 14(1), the words "or the Board", which appeared after the words "in the Secretary of State", repealed by British Technology Group Act 1991, s. 17(2), 18 and Sch. 2, Pt. I with effect from 6 January 1992 (see British Technology Group Act 1991 (Appointed Day) Order 1991 (SI 1991/2721 (C. 83)), art. 2).

**14(2) [Service of counter-notice]** The recipient of a notice under subsection (1) above may, within three months of the date of the notice, serve on the Secretary of State a counter-notice requiring the order to extend to the share capital or rights held by the recipient in the body corporate.

**14(3) [Vesting orders]** A vesting order shall have effect, from the date of a counter-notice, as if the share capital or rights specified in the notice had been specified in the vesting order.

**14(4) [Share capital vesting in nominees]** Subsections (1) to (3) above shall have the same effect in relation to share capital vesting in nominees for the Secretary of State as in relation to share capital vesting as mentioned in those subsections.

**History**

In s. 14(4), the words "or the Board", which appeared after the words "the Secretary of State", repealed by British Technology Group Act 1991, s. 17(2), 18 and Sch. 2, Pt. I with effect from 6 January 1992 (see British Technology Group Act 1991 (Appointed Day) Order 1991 (SI 1991/2721 (C. 83)), art. 2).

## 15 Parliamentary control of orders

**15(1) [Approval of prohibition orders]** A prohibition order shall be laid before Parliament after being made, and the order shall cease to have effect at the end of the period of 28 days beginning on the day on which it was made (but without prejudice to anything previously done by virtue of the order or to the making of a new order) unless during that period it is approved by resolution of each House of Parliament.

**15(2) [Parliamentary term]** In reckoning the period mentioned in subsection (1) above no account shall be taken of any time during which Parliament is dissolved or prorogued or during which both Houses are adjourned for more than four days.

**15(3) [Draft orders]** A vesting order shall not be made unless a draft of the order has been laid before and approved by resolution of each House of Parliament.

**15(4) [Restriction on draft orders]** A draft of a vesting order shall not be laid before Parliament–

(a) in a case such as is mentioned in paragraph (a) of section 13 (2) above, after the end of a period of three months from the service of a notice under section 16 (7) below of the Secretary of State's intention to lay the draft before Parliament;

(b) in a case such as is mentioned in paragraph (b) of that subsection (2), after the end of a period of three months from the making of the prohibition order unless such circumstances as are mentioned in paragraph (a) or (c) of that subsection exist at the time when the draft of the order is laid before Parliament under subsection (3) above; and

(c) in a case such as is mentioned in paragraph (c) of that subsection, after the end of a period of three months from the date on which the Secretary of State learnt of circumstances such as are mentioned in that paragraph.

**15(5) [Parliamentary treatment of draft order]** On the expiry of 28 days from the laying of the draft of a vesting order in a House of Parliament the order shall proceed in that House, whether or not it has been referred to a committee under Standing Orders of that House relating to Private Bills, as if its provisions would require to be enacted by a Public Bill which cannot be referred to such a Committee.

**15(6) [Parliamentary term]** In reckoning, for purposes of proceedings in either House of Parliament, the period mentioned in subsection (5) above, no account shall be taken of any time during which Parliament is dissolved or prorogued or during which that House is adjourned for more than four days.

## 16 Contents of vesting order

**16(1) [Provisions of orders]** Without prejudice to the generality of section 13(2) above, a vesting order may contain provisions by virtue of which rights, liabilities or incumbrances to which assets or capital which will vest by virtue of the order are subject–

(a) will be extinguished in consideration of the payment of compensation as provided under section 19 below, or

(b) will be transferred to the Secretary of State, or

(c) will be charged on the compensation under section 19 below.

**History**
In s. 16(1)(b), the words "or the Board", which appeared after the words "the Secretary of State", repealed by British Technology Group Act 1991, s. 17(2), 18 and Sch. 2, Pt. I with effect from 6 January 1992 (see British Technology Group Act 1991 (Appointed Day) Order 1991 (SI 1991/2721 (C. 83)), art. 2).

**16(2) [Prohibitions in orders]** A vesting order which provides for the vesting of assets employed in an undertaking may prohibit or set aside any transfer of assets so employed or of any right in respect of such assets.

**16(3) [Safeguarding provisions]** A vesting order may include such provisions as the Secretary of State considers necessary or expedient to safeguard–

(a) any capital which will vest by virtue of the order; and

(b) any assets–
 (i) of a body corporate whose capital will so vest, or
 (ii) of any subsidiary of such a body corporate;

and may in particular, but without prejudice to the generality of this subsection, prohibit or set aside the transfer of any such capital or assets or any right in respect of such capital or assets.

**16(4) [Recovery of capital and assets]** A vesting order setting aside a transfer of capital or a transfer of assets such as are mentioned in subsection (2) above shall entitle the Secretary of State to recover the capital or assets transferred.

**History**
In s. 16(4), the words "or the Board", which appeared after the words "the Secretary of State", repealed by British Technology Group Act 1991, s. 17(2), 18 and Sch. 2, Pt. I with effect from 6 January 1992 (see British Technology Group Act 1991 (Appointed Day) Order 1991 (SI 1991/2721 (C. 83)), art. 2).

**16(5) [Recovery by body corporate]** A vesting order setting aside a transfer of assets such as are mentioned in subsection (3) (b) above shall entitle the body corporate or subsidiary to recover the assets transferred.

**16(6) [Compensation]** Any vesting order setting aside a transfer shall give the person entitled to recover the capital or assets a right to be compensated in respect of the transfer.

**16(7) [Transfers affected]** The transfers to which this section applies include transfers made before the draft of the order is laid before Parliament but after the Secretary of State has served notice on the person concerned of his intention to lay a draft order.

**16(8) [Definition]** In subsection (7) above **"the person concerned"** means–

(a) in the case of an order such as is mentioned in paragraph (i) of section 13(2) above, the relevant body corporate, and

(b) in the case of an order such as is mentioned in paragraph (ii) of that subsection, the person carrying on the undertaking.

**16(9) [Publication in Gazette]** The Secretary of State shall publish a copy of any such notice in the London Gazette, the Edinburgh Gazette and the Belfast Gazette as soon as practicable after he has served it.

## 17 Remedies for contravention of prohibition orders

**17(1) [No criminal proceedings]** No criminal proceedings shall lie against any person on the ground that he has committed, or aided, abetted, counselled or procured the commission of, or conspired or attempted to commit, or incited others to commit, any contravention of a prohibition order.

**17(2) [Civil proceedings]** Nothing in subsection (1) above shall limit any right of any person to bring civil proceedings in respect of any contravention or apprehended contravention of a prohibition order, and (without prejudice to the generality of the preceding words) compliance with any such order shall be enforceable by civil proceedings by the Crown for an injunction or interdict or for any other appropriate relief.

## 18 Territorial scope of orders

**18(1) [Acts outside UK]** Nothing in a prohibition order shall have effect so as to apply to any person in relation to his conduct outside the United Kingdom unless he is–

(a) a citizen of the United Kingdom and Colonies or,

(b) a body corporate incorporated in the United Kingdom or,
(c) a person carrying on business in the United Kingdom either alone or in partnership with one or more other persons,

but in a case falling within paragraph (a), (b) or (c) above, any such order may extend to acts or omissions outside the United Kingdom.

**18(2) [Corporate residence]** For the purposes of this Part of this Act a body corporate shall be deemed not to be resident in the United Kingdom if it is not incorporated in the United Kingdom.

## 19 Compensation orders

**19(1) [Order to be laid before Parliament]** No vesting order shall be made until there has also been laid before both Houses of Parliament an order (in this Part of this Act referred to as a "compensation order") providing for the payment of compensation for the acquisition of the capital or assets and for any extinguishment or transfer of rights, liabilities or encumbrances in question.

**19(2) [Special parliamentary procedure]** A compensation order shall be subject to special parliamentary procedure.

**19(3) [Contents of orders]** A compensation order–

(a) shall identify the persons or descriptions of persons to be paid compensation and determine their rights and duties in relation to any compensation paid to them;
(b) shall specify the manner in which compensation is to be paid;
(c) shall provide for the payment of interest on compensation in respect of the relevant period;
(d) may make different provision in relation to different descriptions of capital or assets and different rights, liabilities or incumbrances; and
(e) may contain incidental and supplementary provisions;

and in paragraph (c) above **"the relevant period"** means–

(i) in relation to capital or assets, the period commencing with the date on which the capital or assets vest in the Secretary of State or [their or] his nominees and ending with the date of payment of compensation; and
(ii) in relation to rights, liabilities and incumbrances, the period commencing with the date on which they are extinguished and ending on the date of payment.

**History**

In s. 19(3)(i), the words "the Board or", which appeared before the words "the Secretary of State", repealed by British Technology Group Act 1991, s. 17(2), 18 and Sch. 2, Pt. I with effect from 6 January 1992 (see British Technology Group Act 1991 (Appointed Day) Order 1991 (SI 1991/2721 (C. 83)), art. 2). Presumably the words "their or" in para. (i) (in square parentheses) should also have been repealed.

**19(4) [Funding of compensation]** Compensation may be paid out–

(a) out of moneys provided by Parliament, or
(b) by the issue of government stock (that is to say, stock the principal whereof and the interest whereon is charged on the National Loans Fund with recourse to the Consolidated Fund),

and the power conferred by subsection (3) (b) above is a power to provide for compensation by one or both of the means specified in this subsection.

**19(5) [Withdrawal or further consideration]** The proviso to section 6(2) of the Statutory Orders (Special Procedure Act 1945 (power to withdraw an order or submit it to Parliament for further consideration by means of a Bill for its confirmation) shall have effect in relation to compensation orders as if for the words "may by notice given in the prescribed manner, withdraw the order or may" there were substituted the word "shall".

## 20 Arbitration of disputes relating to vesting and compensation orders

**20(1) [Determination of disputes]** Any dispute to which this section applies shall be determined under Schedule 3 to this Act.

**20(2)** **[Tribunal]** Where any such dispute has been submitted to a tribunal constituted under that Schedule, any other dispute to which this section applies shall be determined by the same tribunal.

**20(3)** **[Applicable disputes]** This section applies to a dispute which arises out of a vesting order or a compensation order and to which one of the parties is the Secretary of State or a body corporate the whole or part of whose share capital has vested by virtue of the order in either of them or in nominees for either of them–

(a) if the provisions of the order require it to be submitted to arbitration; or

(b) if one of the parties wishes it to be so submitted;

and where this section applies to a dispute which arises out of an order, it also applies to any dispute which arises out of a related order.

**History**

In s. 20(3), the words ", the Board", which appeared after the words "the Secretary of State", repealed by British Technology Group Act 1991, s. 17(2), 18 and Sch. 2, Pt. I with effect from 6 January 1992 (see British Technology Group Act 1991 (Appointed Day) Order 1991 (SI 1991/2721 (C. 83)), art. 2).

**20(4)** **[Related orders]** A vesting order and a compensation order are related for the purposes of this section if they relate to the same capital or assets.

# PART V – GENERAL AND SUPPLEMENTARY

## 35 Expenses

**35** Any expenses of the Secretary of State or Minister of Agriculture, Fisheries and Food incurred in consequence of the provisions of this Act, including any increase attributable to those provisions in sums payable under any other Act, shall be defrayed out of money provided by Parliament.

## 36 Service of documents

**36(1)** **[Method of service]** Any notice or other document required or authorised by or by virtue of this Act to be served on any person may be served on him either by delivering it to him or by leaving it at his proper address or by sending it by post.

**36(2)** **[Service on firm's officer]** Any notice or other document so required or authorised to be served on a body corporate or a firm shall be duly served if it is served on the secretary or clerk of that body or a partner of that firm.

**36(3)** **["Proper address"]** For the purposes of this section, and of section 26 of the Interpretation Act 1889 in its application to this section, the proper address of a person, in the case of a secretary or clerk of a body corporate, shall be that of the registered or principal office of that body, in the case of a partner of a firm shall be that of the principal office of the firm, and in any other case shall be the last known address of the person to be served.

## 37 Interpretation

**37(1)** **[Definitions]** In this Act, unless the context otherwise requires–

**"enactment"** includes an enactment of the Parliament of Northern Ireland or the Northern Ireland Assembly;

**"holding company"** means a holding company as defined by section 736 of the Companies Act 1985 or Article 4 of the Companies (Northern Ireland) Order 1986;

**"industry"** includes any description of commercial activity, and any section of an industry, and "industrial" has a corresponding meaning;

**"manufacturing industry"** means, subject to subsection (3) below, activities which are described in any of the minimum list headings in Orders III to XIX (inclusive) of the Standard Industrial Classification;

**"Standard Industrial Classification"** means the revised edition published by Her Majesty's Stationery Office in 1968 of the publication of that name prepared by the Central Statistical Office of the Chancellor of the Exchequer;

**"subsidiary"** means a subsidiary as defined by section 736 of the Companies Act 1985 or Article 4 of the Companies (Northern Ireland) Order 1986.

**History**

S. 37(1) amended by Industry Act 1980, Sch. 2 and as from 1 July 1985 by Companies Consolidation (Consequential Provisions) Act 1985, Sch. 2.

Definition of "accounting year" repealed by British Technology Group Act 1991, s. 17(2), 18 and Sch. 2, Pt. I with effect from 6 January 1992 (see British Technology Group Act 1991 (Appointed Day) Order 1991 (SI 1991/2721 (C.83)), art. 2). The definition previously read as follows:

"**"accounting year"**, in relation to the Board, means, subject to subsection (2) below, the period of twelve months ending with the 31st December in any year, except that the Board's first accounting year shall end on 31st December 1976;"

In definition of "Standard Industrial Classification" the words " of the Chancellor of the Exchequer" inserted by Transfer of Functions (Economic Statistics) Order 1989 (SI 1989/992), art. 6(4) and Sch. 2, para. 2 with effect from 31 July 1989.

Definition of "wholly owned subsidiary" repealed by British Technology Group Act 1991, s. 17(2), 18 and Sch. 2, Pt. I with effect from 6 January 1992 (see British Technology Group Act 1991 (Appointed Day) Order 1991 (SI 1991/2721 (C. 83)), art. 2). The definition previously read as follows:

"**"wholly-owned subsidiary"** has the meaning assigned to it by section 736 of the Companies Act 1985 or Article 4(5)(b) of the Companies (Northern Ireland) Order 1986."

Previously in that definition, the words "section 736" substituted for the former words "section 736(5)(b)" by CA 1989, s. 144(4) and Sch. 18, para. 11 as from 1 November 1990 subject to transitional provisions (see SI 1990/1392 (C. 41), art. 2(d) and also art. 6).

Also amendments by Co-operative Development Agency and Industrial Development Act 1984, s. 5, Sch. 1 and the Companies Consolidation (Consequential Provisions) (Northern Ireland) Order 1986 (SI 1986/1035).

**37(2)** (Repealed by British Technology Group Act 1991, s. 17(2), 18 and Sch. 2, Pt. I with effect from 6 January 1992 (see British Technology Group Act 1991 (Appointed Day) Order 1991 (SI 1991/2721 (C. 83)), art. 2)).

**History**

S. 37(2) formerly read as follows:

"**(2)** The Secretary of State may direct that any accounting year of the Board shall end on a date before or after that on which it would otherwise end."

**37(3)** **[Manufacturing industry]** In determining the extent to which an undertaking is engaged in manufacturing industry, the following activities shall be treated as manufacturing industry so far as they relate to products manufactured or to be manufactured by the undertaking–

research,
transport,
distribution,
repair and maintenance of machinery,
sales and marketing,
storage,
mining and quarrying,
production and distribution of energy and heating,
administration,
training of staff,
packaging.

**37(4)** (Repealed by British Technology Group Act 1991, s. 17(2), 18 and Sch. 2, Pt. I with effect from 6 January 1992 (see British Technology Group Act 1991 (Appointed Day) Order 1991 (SI 1991/2721 (C. 83)), art. 2)).

**History**

S. 37(4) formerly read as follows:

"**(4)** Securities and other property are publicly owned for the purposes of this Act if they are held–

(a) by or on behalf of the Crown;
(b) by a company all of whose shares are held by or on behalf of the Crown or by a wholly owned subsidiary of such a company;
(c) by any corporation constituted by or under any enactment under which an industry or part of an industry is carried on by that corporation under national ownership or control; or
(d) by a wholly owned subsidiary of any such corporation."

**37(5)** **[Interpretation]** Except in so far as the context otherwise requires, any reference in this Act to an enactment shall be construed as a reference to that enactment as amended, applied or extended by or under any other enactment, including this Act.

## 38 Orders

**38(1)** **[Power exercisable by statutory instrument]** Any power to make an order conferred by this Act shall be exercisable by statutory instrument.

**38(2) [Power of variation, revocation]** Any power to make an order conferred by any provision of this Act shall include power to make an order varying or revoking any order previously made under that provision.

**38(3) [Scope of power]** It is hereby declared that any power of giving directions or making determinations conferred on the Secretary of State by any provision of this Act includes power to vary or revoke directions or determinations given or made under that provision.

## 39 Citation etc.

**39(1) [Citation]** This Act may be cited as the Industry Act 1975.

**39(2), (3)** (Provisions not relevant to this service, and not reproduced here.)

**39(4) [Northern Ireland]** It is hereby declared that this Act extends to Northern Ireland.

**39(5) [Application to compensation order]** Notwithstanding the provisions–

(a) of section 12(3) of the Statutory Orders (Special Procedure) Act 1945,

the former Act shall apply to any compensation order which extends to Northern Ireland.

**History**
S. 39(5) amended by Industry Act 1980, s. 21 and Sch. 2.

**39(6) [Commencement]** This Act shall come into force on such day as the Secretary of State may by order made by statutory instrument appoint.

**39(7) [Varying dates]** An order under subsection (6) above may appoint different days for different provisions and for different purposes.

# ADMINISTRATION OF JUSTICE ACT 1977

(1977 Chapter 38)

*[29th July 1977]*

# PART I – GENERAL

## 7 Extent of powers of receivers and managers in respect of companies

**7(1) [Receivers' powers]** A receiver appointed under the law of any part of the United Kingdom in respect of the whole or part of any property or undertaking of a company and in consequence of the company having created a charge which, as created, was a floating charge may exercise his powers in any other part of the United Kingdom so far as their exercise is not inconsistent with the law applicable there.

**7(2) [Definition]** In subsection (1) above **"receiver"** includes a manager and a person who is appointed both receiver and manager.

**Note**
S. 7 effective from 29 August 1977.

# CRIMINAL JUSTICE ACT 1987

(1987 Chapter 38)

*[15th May 1987]*

[**Note:** Reproduced below are s. 1–3, 12 and Sch. 1. Section 1 and Sch. 1 came into force on 20 July 1987 for the purpose of various appointments and the establishment of the Serious Fraud Office and s. 12 on the same date (see SI 1987/1061 (C. 27)); s. 1 and Sch. 1 (as far as not already in force) and s. 2 and 3 came into force on 6 April 1988 (see SI 1988/397 (C. 10)).]

## SERIOUS FRAUD OFFICE

## 1 The Serious Fraud Office

**1(1) [Constitution]** A Serious Fraud Office shall be constituted for England and Wales and Northern Ireland.

**1(2) [Appointment of Director]** The Attorney General shall appoint a person to be the Director of the Serious Fraud Office (referred to in this Part of this Act as "the Director"), and he shall discharge his functions under the superintendence of the Attorney General.

**1(3) [Power of investigation]** The Director may investigate any suspected offence which appears to him on reasonable grounds to involve serious or complex fraud.

**1(4) [Power re proper persons to join investigation]** The Director may, if he thinks fit, conduct any such investigation in conjunction either with the police or with any other person who is, in the opinion of the Director, a proper person to be concerned in it.

**1(5) [Power re criminal proceedings]** The Director may–

(a) institute and have the conduct of any criminal proceedings which appear to him to relate to such fraud; and

(b) take over the conduct of any such proceedings at any stage.

**1(6) [Discharge of functions]** The Director shall discharge such other functions in relation to fraud as may from time to time be assigned to him by the Attorney General.

**1(7) [Proper persons for s. 1(5)]** The Director may designate for the purposes of subsection (5) above any member of the Serious Fraud Office who is–

(a) a barrister in England and Wales or Northern Ireland;

(b) a solicitor of the Supreme Court; or

(c) a solicitor of the Supreme Court of Judicature of Northern Ireland.

**1(8) [Power of proper persons]** Any member so designated shall, without prejudice to any functions which may have been assigned to him in his capacity as a member of that Office, have all the powers of the Director as to the institution and conduct of proceedings but shall exercise those powers under the direction of the Director.

**1(9)–(11)** (Repealed by Access to Justice Act 1999, s, 106 and Sch. 15, Pt. II, with effect from 31 July 2000 (see Access to Justice Act 1999 (Commencement No. 4 and Transitional Provisions) Order 2000 (SI 2000/1920 (C. 4), art. 2).)

**History**

S. 1(9)–(11) formerly read as follows:

"**(9)** Any member so designated who is a barrister in England and Wales or a solicitor of the Supreme Court shall have, in any court, the rights of audience enjoyed by solicitors holding practising certificates and shall have such additional rights of audience in the Crown Court in England and Wales as may be given by virtue of subsection (11) below.

**(10)** The reference in subsection (9) above to rights of audience enjoyed in any court by solicitors includes a reference to rights enjoyed in the Crown Court by virtue of any direction given by the Lord Chancellor under section 83 of the Supreme Court Act 1981.

**(11)** For the purpose of giving members so designated who are barristers in England and Wales or solicitors of the Supreme Court additional rights of audience in the Crown Court in England and Wales, the Lord Chancellor may give any such direction as respects such members as he could give under the said section 83."

**1(12) [Rights of audience – Northern Ireland]** Any member so designated who is a barrister in Northern Ireland or a solicitor of the Supreme Court of Judicature of Northern Ireland shall have–

(a) in any court the rights of audience enjoyed by solicitors of the Supreme Court of Judicature of Northern Ireland and, in the Crown Court in Northern Ireland, such additional rights of audience as may be given by virtue of subsection (14) below; and

(b) in the Crown Court in Northern Ireland, the rights of audience enjoyed by barristers employed by the Director of Public Prosecutions for Northern Ireland.

**1(13) [Interpretation re s. 1(12)(a)]** Subject to subsection (14) below, the reference in subsection (12)(a) above to rights of audience enjoyed by solicitors of the Supreme Court of Judicature of Northern Ireland is a reference to such rights enjoyed in the Crown Court in Northern Ireland as restricted by any direction given by the Lord Chief Justice of Northern Ireland under section 50 of the Judicature (Northern Ireland) Act 1978.

**1(14) [Direction re s. 1(13)]** For the purpose of giving any member so designated who is a barrister in Northern Ireland or a solicitor of the Supreme Court of Judicature of Northern Ireland additional rights of audience in the Crown Court in Northern Ireland, the Lord Chief Justice of Northern Ireland may direct that any direction given by him under the said section 50 shall not apply to such members.

**1(15) [Sch. 1]** Schedule 1 to this Act shall have effect.

**1(16) [References to conduct of proceedings]** For the purposes of this section (including that Schedule) references to the conduct of any proceedings include references to the proceedings being discontinued and to the taking of any steps (including the bringing of appeals and making of representations in respect of applications for bail) which may be taken in relation to them.

**1(17) [Application to Northern Ireland]** In the application of this section (including that Schedule) to Northern Ireland references to the Attorney General are to be construed as references to him in his capacity as Attorney General for Northern Ireland.

## 2 Director's investigation powers

**2(1) [Exercise of Director's powers]** The powers of the Director under this section shall be exercisable, but only for the purposes of an investigation under section 1 above or, on a request made by an authority entitled to make such a request, in any case in which it appears to him that there is good reason to do so for the purpose of investigating the affairs, or any aspect of the affairs, of any person.

**History**

In s. 2(1) the words "an authority entitled to make such a request" substituted for the former words "the Attorney General of the Isle of Man, Jersey or Guernsey, under legislation corresponding to that section and having effect in the Island whose Attorney General makes the request" by the Criminal Justice and Public Order Act 1994, s. 164(2)(a), 172(2) as from 3 February 1995 (see SI 1995/127).

Previously in s. 2(1) the words from "or, on a request made" to "whose Attorney General makes the request," inserted by Criminal Justice Act 1988, s. 143 and 171(5) as from 29 July 1988.

**2(1A) [Authorities]** The authorities entitled to request the Director to exercise his powers under this section are–

(a) the Attorney-General of the Isle of Man, Jersey or Guernsey, acting under legislation corresponding to section 1 of this Act and having effect in the island whose Attorney-General makes the request; and

(b) the Secretary of State acting under section 4(2A) of the Criminal Justice (International Co-operation) Act 1990, in response to a request received by him from an overseas court, tribunal or authority (an "overseas authority").

**2(1B) [Director not to exercise power]** The Director shall not exercise his powers on a request from the Secretary of State acting in response to a request received from an overseas authority within subsection (1A)(b) above unless it appears to the Director on reasonable grounds that the offence in respect of which he has been requested to obtain evidence involves serious or complex fraud.

**History**
S. 2(1A), (1B) inserted by the Criminal Justice and Public Order Act 1994, s. 164(2)(a), 172(2)(b) as from 3 February 1995 (see SI 1995/127).

**2(2) [Notice to attend]** The Director may by notice in writing require the person whose affairs are to be investigated ("the person under investigation") or any other person whom he has reason to believe has relevant information to answer questions or otherwise furnish information with respect to any matter relevant to the investigation at a specified place and either at a specified time or forthwith.

**History**
In s. 2(2) the words from "answer questions" to the end substituted for the former words "attend before the Director at a specified time and place and answer questions or otherwise furnish information with respect to any matter relevant to the investigation" by Criminal Justice Act 1988, s. 170(1), Sch. 15, para. 113(1) and s. 171(5) as from 29 July 1988.

**2(3) [Notice to produce etc.]** The Director may by notice in writing require the person under investigation or any other person to produce at such place as may be specified in the notice and either forthwith or at such time as may be so specified, any specified documents which appear to the Director to relate to any matter relevant to the investigation or any documents of a specified description which appear to him so to relate; and–

(a) if any such documents are produced, the Director may–
  (i) take copies or extracts from them;
  (ii) require the person producing them to provide an explanation of any of them;

(b) if any such documents are not produced, the Director may require the person who was required to produce them to state, to the best of his knowledge and belief, where they are.

**History**
In s. 2(3) the words from "such place" to "as may be so specified" substituted for the former words "a specified time and place" and the word "description" substituted for the former word "class" by Criminal Justice Act 1988, s. 170(1), Sch. 15, para. 113(2) and s. 171(5) as from 29 July 1988.

**2(4) [Issue of warrant]** Where, on information on oath laid by a member of the Serious Fraud Office, a justice of the peace is satisfied, in relation to any documents, that there are reasonable grounds for believing–

(a) that–
  (i) a person has failed to comply with an obligation under this section to produce them;
  (ii) it is not practicable to serve a notice under subsection (3) above in relation to them; or
  (iii) the service of such a notice in relation to them might seriously prejudice the investigation; and

(b) that they are on premises specified in the information,

he may issue such a warrant as is mentioned in subsection (5) below.

**2(5) [Scope of warrant in s. 2(4)]** The warrant referred to above is a warrant authorising any constable–

(a) to enter (using such force as is reasonably necessary for the purpose) and search the premises, and

(b) to take possession of any documents appearing to be documents of the description specified in the information or to take in relation to any documents so appearing any other steps which may appear to be necessary for preserving them and preventing interference with them.

**2(6) [Constable to be accompanied]** Unless it is not practicable in the circumstances, a constable executing a warrant issued under subsection (4) above shall be accompanied by an appropriate person.

**2(7) ["Appropriate person" in s. 2(6)]** In subsection (6) above **"appropriate person"** means–

(a) a member of the Serious Fraud Office; or

(b) some person who is not a member of that Office but whom the Director has authorised to accompany the constable.

**2(8) [Use of statement in evidence]** A statement by a person in response to a requirement imposed by virtue of this section may only be used in evidence against him–

(a) on a prosecution for an offence under subsection (14) below; or

(b) on a prosecution for some other offence where in giving evidence he makes a statement inconsistent with it.

**2(8AA) [Limits on use of statement in criminal proceedings]** However, the statement may not be used against that person by virtue of paragraph (b) of subsection (8) unless evidence relating to it is adduced, or a question relating to it asked, by or on behalf of that person in the proceedings arising out of the prosecution.

**History**
S. 2(8AA) inserted by Youth Justice and Criminal Evidence Act 1999, s. 59 and Sch. 3, para. 20 with effect from 14 April 2000 (see Youth Justice and Criminal Evidence Act 1999 (Commencement No. 2) Order 2000 (SI 2000/1034 (C. 27)), art. 2).

**2(8A) [Director to provide Secretary of State with evidence]** Any evidence obtained by the Director for use by an overseas authority shall be furnished by him to the Secretary of State for transmission to the overseas authority which requested it.

**History**
S. 2(8A) inserted by the Criminal Justice and Public Order Act 1994, s. 164(2)(a), 172(2)(c) as from 3 February 1995 (see SI 1995/127).

**2(8B) [Director to provide Secretary of State with documents relating to evidence]** If in order to comply with the request of the overseas authority it is necessary for any evidence obtained by the Director to be accompanied by any certificate, affidavit or other verifying document, the Director shall also furnish for transmission such document of that nature as may be specified by the Secretary of State when asking the Director to obtain the evidence.

**History**
S. 2(8B) inserted by the Criminal Justice and Public Order Act 1994, s. 164(2)(a), 172(2)(c) as from 3 February 1995 (see SI 1995/127).

**2(8C) [Transmission of evidence]** Where any evidence obtained by the Director for use by an overseas authority consists of a document the original or a copy shall be transmitted, and where it consists of any other article the article itself or a description, photograph or other representation of it shall be transmitted, as may be necessary in order to comply with the request of the overseas authority.

**History**
S. 2(8C) inserted by the Criminal Justice and Public Order Act 1994, s. 164(2)(a), 172(2)(c) as from 3 February 1995 (see SI 1995/127).

**2(9) [Legal professional privilege]** A person shall not under this section be required to disclose any information or produce any document which he would be entitled to refuse to disclose or produce on grounds of legal professional privilege in proceedings in the High Court except that a lawyer may be required to furnish the name and address of his client.

**2(10) [Obligation of confidence re banking business]** A person shall not under this section be required to disclose information or produce a document in respect of which he owes an obligation of confidence by virtue of carrying on any banking business unless–

(a) the person to whom the obligation of confidence is owed consents to the disclosure or production; or

(b) the Director has authorised the making of the requirement or, if it is impracticable for him to act personally, a member of the Serious Fraud Office designated by him for the purposes of this subsection has done so.

**2(11) [Power to appoint outside investigator]** Without prejudice to the powers of the Director to assign functions to members of the Serious Fraud Office, the Director may authorise any competent investigator (other than a constable) who is not a member of that Office to exercise on his behalf all or any of the powers conferred by this section, but no such authority shall be granted except for the purpose of investigating the affairs, or any aspect of the affairs, of a person specified in the authority.

**2(12) [Compliance with requirement of person in s. 2(11)]** No person shall be bound to comply with any requirement imposed by a person exercising powers by virtue of any authority granted under subsection (11) above unless he has, if required to do so, produced evidence of his authority.

**2(13) [Offence, penalty]** Any person who without reasonable excuse fails to comply with a requirement imposed on him under this section shall be guilty of an offence and liable on summary conviction to imprisonment for a term not exceeding six months or to a fine not exceeding level 5 on the standard scale or to both.

**2(14) [Offence re false or misleading statement]** A person who, in purported compliance with a requirement under this section–

(a) makes a statement which he knows to be false or misleading in a material particular; or

(b) recklessly makes a statement which is false or misleading in a material particular,

shall be guilty of an offence.

**2(15) [Penalty re s. 2(14)]** A person guilty of an offence under subsection (14) above shall–

(a) on conviction on indictment, be liable to imprisonment for a term not exceeding two years or a fine or to both; and

(b) on summary conviction, be liable to imprisonment for a term not exceeding six months or to a fine not exceeding the statutory maximum, or to both.

**2(16) [Offence re falsifying documents etc.]** Where any person–

(a) knows or suspects that an investigation by the police or the Serious Fraud Office into serious or complex fraud is being or is likely to be carried out; and

(b) falsifies, conceals, destroys or otherwise disposes of, or causes or permits the falsification, concealment, destruction or disposal of documents which he knows or suspects are or would be relevant to such an investigation,

he shall be guilty of an offence unless he proves that he had no intention of concealing the facts disclosed by the documents from persons carrying out such an investigation.

**2(17) [Penalty re s. 2(16)]** A person guilty of an offence under subsection (16) above shall–

(a) on conviction on indictment, be liable to imprisonment for a term not exceeding 7 years or to a fine or to both; and

(b) on summary conviction, be liable to imprisonment for a term not exceeding 6 months or to a fine not exceeding the statutory maximum or to both.

**2(18) ["Documents"]** In this section, **"documents"** includes information recorded in any form and, in relation to information recorded otherwise than in legible form, references to its production include references to producing a copy of the information in legible form; and "evidence" (in relation to subsections (1A)(b), (8A), (8B) and (8C) above) includes documents and other articles.

**History**

In s. 2(18) the words from "; and" to the end inserted by the Criminal Justice and Public Order Act 1994, s. 164(2)(a), 172(2)(d) as from 3 February 1995 (see SI 1995/127).

**2(19) [Application to Scotland]** In the application of this section to Scotland, the reference to a justice of the peace is to be construed as a reference to the sheriff; and in the application of this section to Northern Ireland, subsection (4) above shall have effect as if for the references to information there were substituted references to a complaint.

**Note**

See CA 1989, s. 124A for petition for winding up on grounds of public interest on basis of information obtained under s. 2.

## 3 Disclosure of information

**3(1) [Disclosure of information protected under Taxes Management Act]** Where any information subject to an obligation of secrecy under the Taxes Management Act 1970 had been disclosed by the Commissioners of Inland Revenue or an officer of those Commissioners to any member of the Serious Fraud Office for the purposes of any prosecution of an offence relating to inland revenue, that information may be disclosed by any member of the Serious Fraud Office–

(a) for the purposes of any prosecution of which that Office has the conduct;

(b) to any member of the Crown Prosecution Service for the purposes of any prosecution of an offence relating to inland revenue; and

(c) to the Director of Public Prosecutions for Northern Ireland for the purposes of any prosecution of an offence relating to inland revenue, but not otherwise.

**3(2) [Police and Criminal Evidence Act]** Where the Serious Fraud Office has the conduct of any prosecution of an offence which does not relate to inland revenue, the court may not prevent the prosecution from relying on any evidence under section 78 of the Police and Criminal Evidence Act 1984 (discretion to exclude unfair evidence) by reason only of the fact that the information concerned was disclosed by the Commissioners of Inland Revenue or an officer of those Commissioners for the purposes of any prosecution of an offence relating to inland revenue.

**3(3) [Disclosure of information protected under other legislation]** Where any information is subject to an obligation of secrecy imposed by or under any enactment other than an enactment contained in the Taxes Management Act 1970, the obligation shall not have effect to prohibit the disclosure of that information to any person in his capacity as a member of the Serious Fraud Office but any information disclosed by virtue of this subsection may only be disclosed by a member of the Serious Fraud Office for the purposes of any prosecution in England and Wales, Northern Ireland or elsewhere and may only be disclosed by such a member if he is designated by the Director for the purposes of this subsection.

**3(4) [Agreement re non-disclosure]** Without prejudice to his power to enter into agreements apart from this subsection, the Director may enter into a written agreement for the supply of information to or by him subject, in either case, to an obligation not to disclose the information concerned otherwise than for a specified purpose.

**3(5) [Disclosure of information–general]** Subject to subsections (1) and (3) above and to any provision of an agreement for the supply of information which restricts the disclosure of the information supplied, information obtained by any person in his capacity as a member of the Serious Fraud Office may be disclosed by any member of that office designated by the Director for the purposes of this subsection–

(a) to any government department or Northern Ireland department or other authority or body discharging its functions on behalf of the Crown (including the Crown in right of Her Majesty's Government in Northern Ireland);

(b) to any competent authority;

(c) for the purposes of any prosecution in England and Wales, Northern Ireland or elsewhere; and

(d) for the purposes of assisting any public or other authority for the time being designated for the purposes of this paragraph by an order made by the Secretary of State to discharge any functions which are specified in the order.

**3(6) [Competent authorities for s. 3(5)]** The following are competent authorities for the purposes of subsection (5) above–

(a) an inspector appointed under Part XIV of the Companies Act 1985 or Part XV of the Companies (Northern Ireland) Order 1986;

(b) an Official Receiver;

(c) the Accountant in Bankruptcy;

(d) the official receiver for Northern Ireland;

(e) a person appointed to carry out an investigation under section 55 of the Building Societies Act 1986;

(f) a body administering a compensation scheme under section 54 of the Financial Services Act 1986;

(g) an inspector appointed under section 94 of that Act;

(h) a person exercising powers by virtue of section 106 of that Act;

(i) an inspector appointed under section 177 of that Act;

(j) a person appointed by the Bank of England under section 41 of the Banking Act 1987 to carry out an investigation and make a report;

(k) a person exercising powers by virtue of section 44(2) of the Insurance Companies Act 1982;

(l) any body having supervisory, regulatory or disciplinary functions in relation to any profession or any area of commercial activity; and

(m) any person or body having, under the law of any country or territory outside the United Kingdom, functions corresponding to any of the functions of any person or body mentioned in any of the foregoing paragraphs.

**History**

S. 3(6)(d) substituted by the Insolvency (Northern Ireland) Order 1989 (SI 1989/2405 (N.I. 19)), art. 381 and Sch. 9, para. 56 as from 1 October 1991 (see SR 1991/411 (C. 20), art. 2); s. 3(6)(d) formerly read as follows:

"(d) an Official Assignee;"

In s. 3(6)(i), the words "or any corresponding enactment having effect in Northern Ireland" repealed by Criminal Justice Act 1993, s. 79(14) and Sch. 6, Pt. I, with effect from 1 March 1994 (see Criminal Justice Act 1993 (Commencement No. 5) 1994 (SI 1994/242), art. 2 and Sch.).

S. 3(6)(j) substituted by Criminal Justice Act 1988, s. 170(1), Sch. 15, para. 111 and s. 171(5) as from 29 July 1988; s. 3(6)(j) formerly read as follows:

"(j) an inspector appointed under section 38 of the Banking Act 1987;"

**3(7) [Extent of s. 3(5)(d) order]** An order under subsection (5)(d) above may impose conditions subject to which, and otherwise restrict the circumstances in which, information may be disclosed under that paragraph.

### CONSPIRACY TO DEFRAUD

## 12 Charges of and penalty for conspiracy to defraud

**12(1) [Possibility of charge being brought]** If–

(a) a person agrees with any other person or persons that a course of conduct shall be pursued; and

(b) that course of conduct will necessarily amount to or involve the commission of any offence or offences by one or more of the parties to the agreement if the agreement is carried out in accordance with their intentions,

the fact that it will do so shall not preclude a charge of conspiracy to defraud being brought against any of them in respect of the agreement.

**12(2)** (Amends Criminal Law Act 1977, s. 5(2).)

**12(3) [Penalty]** A person guilty of conspiracy to defraud is liable on conviction on indictment to imprisonment for a term not exceeding 10 years or a fine or both.

# Schedule 1 – The Serious Fraud Office

Section 1

### GENERAL

**1** There shall be paid to the Director of the Serious Fraud Office such remuneration as the Attorney General may, with the approval of the Treasury, determine.

**2** The Director shall appoint such staff for the Serious Fraud Office as, with the approval of the Treasury as to numbers, remuneration and other terms and conditions of service, he considers necessary for the discharge of his functions.

**3(1)** As soon as practicable after 4th April in any year the Director shall make to the Attorney General a report on the discharge of his functions during the year ending with that date.

**3(2)** The Attorney General shall lay before Parliament a copy of every report received by him under sub-paragraph (1) above and shall cause every such report to be published.

### PROCEDURE

**4(1)** Where any enactment (whenever passed) prohibits the taking of any step–

(a) except by the Director of Public Prosecutions or except by him or another; or

(b) without the consent of the Director of Public Prosecutions or without his consent or the consent of another,

it shall not prohibit the taking of any such step by the Director of the Serious Fraud Office.

**4(2)** In this paragraph references to the Director of Public Prosecutions include references to the Director of Public Prosecutions for Northern Ireland.

**5(1)** Where the Director has the conduct of any criminal proceedings in England and Wales, the Director of Public Prosecutions shall not in relation to those proceedings be subject to any duty by virtue of section 3(2) of the Prosecution of Offences Act 1985.

**5(2)** Where the Director has the conduct of any criminal proceedings in Northern Ireland, the Director of Public Prosecutions for Northern Ireland shall not in relation to those proceedings be required to exercise any function under Article 5 of the Prosecution of Offences (Northern Ireland) Order 1972.

**6(1)** Where the Director or any member of the Serious Fraud Office designated for the purposes of section 1(5) above ("designated official") gives notice to any justice of the peace that he has instituted, or is conducting, any criminal proceedings in England and Wales, the justice shall–

(a) at the prescribed time and in the prescribed manner; or

(b) in a particular case, at the time and in the manner directed by the Attorney General;

send him every recognizance, information, certificate, deposition, document and thing connected with those proceedings which the justice is required by law to deliver to the appropriate officer of the Crown Court.

**History**
In para. 6(1) in the reference to s. 1, "(5)" substituted for the former "(4)" by Criminal Justice Act 1988, s. 170(1), (5) and Sch. 15, para. 116 as from 29 July 1988.

**6(2)** Where the Director of any designated official gives notice that he has instituted, or is conducting, any criminal proceedings in Northern Ireland–

(a) to a resident magistrate or a justice of the peace in Northern Ireland;

(b) to a clerk of petty sessions in Northern Ireland,

the person to whom the notice is given shall–

(i) at the prescribed time and in the prescribed manner; or

(ii) in a particular case, at the time and in the manner directed by the Attorney General,

send him every recognizance, complaint, certificate, deposition, document and thing connected with those proceedings which that person is required by law to deliver to the appropriate officer of the Crown Court.

**6(3)** The Attorney General may make regulations for the purpose of supplementing this paragraph; and in this paragraph "prescribed" means prescribed by the regulations.

**6(4)** The Director or, as the case may be, designated official shall–

(a) subject to the regulations, cause anything which is sent to him under this paragraph to be delivered to the appropriate officer of the Crown Court; and

(b) to be under the same obligation (on the same payment) to deliver to an applicant copies of anything so sent as that officer.

**7(1)** The Attorney General may make regulations requiring the chief officer of any police force to which the regulations are expressed to apply to give to the Director information with respect to every offence of a kind prescribed by the regulations which is alleged to have been committed in his area and in respect of which it appears to him that there is a prima facie case for proceedings.

**7(2)** The regulations may also require every such chief officer to give to the Director such information as the Director may require with respect to such cases or classes of case as he may from time to time specify.

**8(1)** The Attorney General may, with the approval of the Treasury, by regulations make such provision as he considers appropriate in relation to–

(a) the fees of counsel briefed to appear on behalf of the Serious Fraud Office in any criminal proceedings; and

(b) the costs and expenses of witnesses attending to give evidence at the instance of the

Serious Fraud Office and, subject to sub-paragraph (2) below, of any other person who in the opinion of that Office necessarily attends for the purpose of the case otherwise than to give evidence.

**History**
In para. 8(1)(b) the word "of" before the words "any other person" substituted for the former word "to" by Criminal Justice Act 1988, s. 166(5)(a) and 171(5) as from 29 July 1988.

**8(2)** The power conferred on the Attorney General by sub-paragraph (1)(b) above only relates to the costs and expenses of an interpreter if he is required because of the lack of English of a person attending to give evidence at the instance of the Serious Fraud Office.

**8(3)** The regulations may, in particular–

(a) prescribe scales or rates of fees, costs or expenses; and

(b) specify conditions for the payment of fees, costs or expenses.

**8(4)** Regulations made under sub-paragraph (1)(b) above may provide that scales or rates of costs and expenses shall be determined by the Attorney General with the consent of the Treasury.

**8(5)** In sub-paragraph (1)(b) above **"attends"** means attends at the court or elsewhere.

**History**
Para. 8(5) inserted by Criminal Justice Act 1988, s. 166(5)(b) and 171(5) as from 29 July 1988.

**9(1)** Any power to make regulations under this Schedule shall be exercisable by statutory instrument subject to annulment in pursuance of a resolution of either House of Parliament.

**9(2)** Any such regulations may make different provision with respect to different cases or classes of case.

# FOREIGN CORPORATIONS ACT 1991

(1991 Chapter 44)

An Act to make provision about the status in the United Kingdom of bodies incorporated or formerly incorporated under the laws of certain territories outside the United Kingdom.

[*25th July 1991*]

## 1 Recognition of corporate status of certain foreign corporations

**1(1)** **[Determination of questions]** If at any time–

(a) any question arises whether a body which purports to have or, as the case may be, which appears to have lost corporate status under the laws of a territory which is not at that time a recognised State should or should not be regarded as having legal personality as a body corporate under the law of any part of the United Kingdom, and

(b) it appears that the laws of that territory are at that time applied by a settled court system in that territory,

that question and any other material question relating to the body shall be determined (and account shall be taken of those laws) as if that territory were a recognised State.

**1(2)** **[Interpretation of s. 1(1)]** For the purposes of subsection (1) above–

(a) **"a recognised State"** is a territory which is recognised by Her Majesty's Government in the United Kingdom as a State;

(b) the laws of a territory which is so recognised shall be taken to include the laws of any part of the territory which are acknowledged by the federal or other central government of the territory as a whole; and

(c) a material question is a question (whether as to capacity, constitution or otherwise) which, in the case of a body corporate, falls to be determined by reference to the laws of the territory under which the body is incorporated.

**1(3) [Validity of previous registrations]** Any registration or other thing done at a time before the coming into force of this section shall be regarded as valid if it would have been valid at that time, had subsections (1) and (2) above then been in force.

## 2 Citation, extent and commencement

**2(1) [Citation]** This Act may be cited as the Foreign Corporations Act 1991.

**2(2) [Extent]** This Act extends to Northern Ireland.

**2(3) [Commencement]** This Act shall come into force at the end of the period of two months beginning with the day on which it is passed.

# CHARITIES ACT 1993

(1993 Chapter 10)

[**Note:** the provisions below (s. 63–69) replace the former provisions (s. 30–30C) of the Charities Act 1960. Sections 30–30C were substituted by the Companies Act 1989, s. 111(1) and repealed by the Charities Act 1993, s. 98(2) and Sch. 7. The provisions below came into force (except s. 69) on 1 August 1993 (see Charities Act 1993, s. 99).]

# PART VIII – CHARITABLE COMPANIES

## 63 Winding up

**63(1) [Petition by Attorney-General or others authorised]** Where a charity may be wound up by the High Court under the Insolvency Act 1986, a petition for it to be wound up under that Act by any court in England and Wales having jurisdiction may be presented by the Attorney General, as well as by any person authorised by that Act.

**63(2) [Petition by Commissioners]** Where a charity may be so wound up by the High Court, such a petition may also be presented by the Commissioners if, at any time after they have instituted an inquiry under section 8 above with respect to the charity, they are satisfied as mentioned in section 18(1)(a) or (b) above.

**63(3) [Where charitable company dissolved]** Where a charitable company is dissolved, the Commissioners may make an application under section 651 of the Companies Act 1985 (power of court to declare dissolution of company void) for an order to be made under that section with respect to the company; and for this purpose subsection (1) of that section shall have effect in relation to a charitable company as if the reference to the liquidator of the company included a reference to the Commissioners.

**63(4) [Where name struck off register of companies]** Where a charitable company's name has been struck off the register of companies under section 652 of the Companies Act 1985 (power of registrar to strike defunct company off register), the Commissioners may make an application under section 653(2) of that Act (objection to striking off by person aggrieved) for an order restoring the company's name to that register; and for this purpose section 653(2) shall have effect in relation to a charitable company as if the reference to any such person aggrieved as is there mentioned included a reference to the Commissioners.

**63(5) [Exercise of Commissioners' powers]** The powers exercisable by the Commissioners by virtue of this section shall be exercisable by them of their own motion, but shall be exercisable only with the agreement of the Attorney General on each occasion.

**63(6) ["Charitable company"]** In this section **"charitable company"** means a company which is a charity.

## 64 Alteration of objects clause

**64(1) [Limit on exercise of power]** Where a charity is a company or other body corporate having power to alter the instruments establishing or regulating it as a body corporate, no exercise of that power which has the effect of the body ceasing to be a charity shall be valid so as to affect the application of–

(a) any property acquired under any disposition or agreement previously made otherwise than for full consideration in money or money's worth, or any property representing property so acquired,

(b) any property representing income which has accrued before the alteration is made, or

(c) the income from any such property as aforesaid.

**64(2) [Prior written consent of Commissioners]** Where a charity is a company, any alteration by it–

(a) of the objects clause in its memorandum of association, or

(b) of any other provision in its memorandum of association, or any provision in its articles of association, which is a provision directing or restricting the manner in which property of the company may be used or applied,

is ineffective without the prior written consent of the Commissioners.

**64(3) [Copy of consent to accompany certain documents]** Where a company has made any such alteration in accordance with subsection (2) above and–

(a) in connection with the alteration is required by virtue of–

(i) section 6(1) of the Companies Act 1985 (delivery of documents following alteration of objects), or

(ii) that provision as applied by section 17(3) of that Act (alteration of condition in memorandum which could have been contained in articles),

to deliver to the registrar of companies a printed copy of its memorandum, as altered, or

(b) is required by virtue of section 380(1) of that Act (registration etc. of resolutions and agreements) to forward to the registrar a printed or other copy of the special resolution effecting the alteration,

the copy so delivered or forwarded by the company shall be accompanied by a copy of the Commissioner's consent.

**64(4) [Application of Companies Act 1985, s. 6(3)]** Section 6(3) of that Act (offences) shall apply to any default by a company in complying with subsection (3) above as it applies to any such default as is mentioned in that provision.

## 65 Invalidity of certain transactions

**65(1) [Application of Companies Act 1985, s. 35, 35A]** Sections 35 and 35A of the Companies Act 1985 (capacity of company not limited by its memorandum; power of directors to bind company) do not apply to the acts of a company which is a charity except in favour of a person who–

(a) gives full consideration in money or money's worth in relation to the act in question, and

(b) does not know that the act is not permitted by the company's memorandum or, as the case may be, is beyond the powers of the directors,

or who does not know at the time the act is done that the company is a charity.

**65(2) [Effect of exceeding powers or title of acquirer]** However, where such a company purports to transfer or grant an interest in property, the fact that the act was not permitted by the company's memorandum or, as the case may be, that the directors in connection with the act exceeded any limitation on their powers under the company's constitution, does not affect the title of a person who subsequently acquires the property or any interest in it for full consideration without actual notice of any such circumstances affecting the validity of the company's act.

**65(3) [Burden of proof in s. 65(1) proceedings]** In any proceedings arising out of subsection (1) above the burden of proving–

(a) that a person knew that an act was not permitted by the company's memorandum or was beyond the powers of the directors, or

(b) that a person knew that the company was a charity,

lies on the person making that allegation.

**65(4) [Ratification ineffective without Commissioners' consent]** Where a company is a charity, the ratification of an act under section 35(3) of the Companies Act 1985, or the ratification of a transaction to which section 322A of that Act applies (invalidity of certain transactions to which directors or their associates are parties), is ineffective without the prior written consent of the Commissioners.

## 66 Requirement of consent of Commissioners to certain acts

**66(1) [Consent for certain Companies Act approvals or affirmations]** Where a company is a charity–

(a) any approval given by the company for the purposes of any of the provisions of the Companies Act 1985 specified in subsection (2) below, and

(b) any affirmation by it for the purposes of section 322(2)(c) of that Act (affirmation of voidable arrangements under which assets are acquired by or from a director or person connected with him),

is ineffective without the prior written consent of the Commissioners.

**66(2) [Provisions referred to in s. 66(1)]** The provisions of the Companies Act 1985 referred to in subsection (1)(a) above are–

(a) section 312 (payment to director in respect of loss of office or retirement);

(b) section 313(1) (payment to director in respect of loss of office or retirement made in connection with transfer of undertaking or property of company);

(c) section 319(3) (incorporation in director's service contract of term whereby his employment will or may continue for a period of more than five years);

(d) section 320(1) (arrangement whereby assets are acquired by or from director or person connected with him);

(e) section 337(3)(a) (provision of funds to meet certain expenses incurred by director).

## 67 Name to appear on correspondence etc.

**67** Section 30(7) of the Companies Act 1985 (exemption from requirements relating to publication of name etc.) shall not, in its application to any company which is a charity, have the effect of exempting the company from the requirements of section 349(1) of that Act (company's name to appear in its correspondence etc.).

## 68 Status to appear on correspondence etc.

**68(1) [Where status to be indicated if not in name]** Where a company is a charity and its name does not include the word "charity" or the word "charitable" then, subject to subsection (1A), the fact that the company is a charity shall be stated in legible characters–

(a) in all business letters of the company,

(b) in all its notices and other official publications,

(c) in all bills of exchange, promissory notes, endorsements, cheques and orders for money or goods purporting to be signed on behalf of the company,

(d) in all conveyances purporting to be executed by the company, and

(e) in all bills rendered by it and in all its invoices, receipts, and letters of credit.

**History**

In s. 68(1) the words "then, subject to subsection (1A)" inserted and the words "in English", which appeared after "shall be stated", omitted and repealed by Welsh Language Act 1993, s. 33(2), 35(1), 36(1) and Sch. 2 with effect from 21 December 1993.

**68(1A) [Documents entirely in Welsh]** Where a company's name includes the word "elusen" or the word "elusennol" (the Welsh equivalents of the words "charity" and "charitable"), subsection (1) above shall not apply in relation in relation to any document which is wholly in Welsh.

**History**
S. 68(1A) inserted by Welsh Language Act 1993, s. 33(3) and 36(1) with effect from 21 December 1993.

**68(1B) [Statement of charitable status in English or Welsh]** The statement required by subsection (1) above shall be in English, except that, in the case of a document which is otherwise wholly in Welsh, the statement may be in Welsh if it consists of or includes the word "elusen" or the word "elusennol".

**History**
S. 68(1B) inserted by Welsh Language Act 1993, s. 33(3) and 36(1) with effect from 21 December 1993.

**68(2) [Conveyance]** In subsection (1)(d) above **"conveyance"** means any instrument creating, transferring, varying or extinguishing an interest in land.

**68(3) [Application of Companies Act 1985, s. 349(2)–(4)]** Subsections (2) to (4) of section 349 of the Companies Act 1985 (offences in connection with failure to include required particulars in business letters etc.) shall apply in relation to a contravention of subsection (1) above, taking the reference in subsection (3)(b) of that section to a bill of parcels as a reference to any such bill as is mentioned in subsection (1)(e) above.

## 69 Investigation of accounts

**69(1) [Powers of Commissioners by order]** In the case of a charity which is a company the Commissioners may by order require that the condition and accounts of the charity for such period as they think fit shall be investigated and audited by an auditor appointed by them, being a person eligible for appointment as a company auditor under section 25 of the Companies Act 1989.

**69(2) [Powers of auditor under s. 69(1)]** An auditor acting under subsection (1) above–

(a) shall have a right of access to all books, accounts and documents relating to the charity which are in the possession or control of the charity trustees or to which the charity trustees have access;

(b) shall be entitled to require from any charity trustee, past or present, and from any past or present officer or employee of the charity such information and explanation as he thinks necessary for the performance of his duties;

(c) shall at the conclusion or during the progress of the audit make such reports to the Commissioners about the audit or about the accounts or affairs of the charity as he thinks the case requires, and shall send a copy of any such report to the charity trustees.

**69(3) [Payment of expenses of audit]** The expenses of any audit under subsection (1) above, including the remuneration of the auditor, shall be paid by the Commissioners.

**69(4) [Directions re default]** If any person fails to afford an auditor any facility to which he is entitled under subsection (2) above the Commissioners may by order give to that person or to the charity trustees for the time being such directions as the Commissioners think appropriate for securing that the default is made good.

**Note**
In the above provisions under Charities Act 1993, s. 97 **"company"** means a company formed and registered under the Companies Act 1985 or to which the provisions of that Act apply as they apply to such a company.
For Scottish charities, see Charities Act 1993, s. 80.

# CRIMINAL JUSTICE ACT 1993

(1993 Chapter 36)

[*27th July 1993*]

[**Note:** Reproduced below are Pt. V, Sch. 1, 2, and relevant parts of Sch. 5 and 6 brought into force from 1 March 1994 by the Criminal Justice Act 1993 (Commencement No. 5) Order 1994 (SI 1994/242 (C. 7)). The provisions of Pt. V and of Sch. 1 and 2 extend to the whole of the UK (s. 79(2)). The 1993 Act repealed the Company Securities (Insider Dealing) Act 1985 which is reproduced thereafter.]

# PART V – INSIDER DEALING

## THE OFFENCE OF INSIDER DEALING

### 52 The offence

**52(1) [Primary offence]** An individual who has information as an insider is guilty of insider dealing if, in the circumstances mentioned in subsection (3), he deals in securities that are price-affected securities in relation to the information.

**52(2) [Additional offence]** An individual who has information as an insider is also guilty of insider dealing if–

(a) he encourages another person to deal in securities that are (whether or not that other knows it) price-affected securities in relation to the information, knowing or having reasonable cause to believe that the dealing would take place in the circumstances mentioned in subsection (3); or

(b) he discloses the information, otherwise than in the proper performance of the functions of his employment, office or profession, to another person.

**52(3) [Circumstances in s. 52(1), (2)]** The circumstances referred to above are that the acquisition or disposal in question occurs on a regulated market, or that the person dealing relies on a professional intermediary or is himself acting as a professional intermediary.

**52(4) [Effect]** This section has effect subject to section 53.

### 53 Defences

**53(1) [Defence to s. 52(1) offence]** An individual is not guilty of insider dealing by virtue of dealing in securities if he shows–

(a) that he did not at the time expect the dealing to result in a profit attributable to the fact that the information in question was price-sensitive information in relation to the securities, or

(b) that at the time he believed on reasonable grounds that the information had been disclosed widely enough to ensure that none of those taking part in the dealing would be prejudiced by not having the information, or

(c) that he would have done what he did even if he had not had the information.

**53(2) [Defence to s. 52(2)(a) offence]** An individual is not guilty of insider dealing by virtue of encouraging another person to deal in securities if he shows–

(a) that he did not at the time expect the dealing to result in a profit attributable to the fact that the information in question was price-sensitive information in relation to the securities, or

(b) that at the time he believed on reasonable grounds that the information had been or would be disclosed widely enough to ensure that none of those taking part in the dealing would be prejudiced by not having the information, or

(c) that he would have done what he did even if he had not had the information.

**53(3) [Defence to s. 52(2)(b) offence]** An individual is not guilty of insider dealing by virtue of a disclosure of information if he shows–

(a) that he did not at the time expect any person, because of the disclosure, to deal in securities in the circumstances mentioned in subsection (3) of section 52; or

(b) that, although he had such an expectation at the time, he did not expect the dealing to result in a profit attributable to the fact that the information was price-sensitive information in relation to the securities.

**53(4) [Sch. 1]** Schedule 1 (special defences) shall have effect.

**53(5) [Amendment of Sch. 1]** The Treasury may by order amend Schedule 1.

**53(6) [Interpretation]** In this section references to a profit include references to the avoidance of a loss.

INTERPRETATION

# 54 Securities to which Part V applies

**54(1) [Application]** This Part applies to any security which–

(a) falls within any paragraph of Schedule 2; and

(b) satisfies any conditions applying to it under an order made by the Treasury for the purposes of this subsection;

and in the provisions of this Part (other than that Schedule) any reference to a security is a reference to a security to which this Part applies.

**Note**

See the Insider Dealing (Securities and Regulated Markets) Order 1994 (SI 1994/187) (as amended).

**54(2) [Amendment of Sch. 2]** The Treasury may by order amend Schedule 2.

# 55 "Dealing" in securities

**55(1) [Where person deals in securities]** For the purposes of this Part, a person deals in securities if–

(a) he acquires or disposes of the securities (whether as principal or agent); or

(b) he procures, directly or indirectly, an acquisition or disposal of the securities by any other person.

**55(2) ["Acquire"]** For the purposes of this Part, **"acquire"**, in relation to a security, includes–

(a) agreeing to acquire the security; and

(b) entering into a contract which creates the security.

**55(3) ["Dispose"]** For the purposes of this Part, **"dispose"**, in relation to a security, includes–

(a) agreeing to dispose of the security; and

(b) bringing to an end a contract which created the security.

**55(4) [Interpretation of s. 55(1)]** For the purposes of subsection (1), a person procures an acquisition or disposal of a security if the security is acquired or disposed of by a person who is–

(a) his agent,

(b) his nominee, or

(c) a person who is acting at his direction,

in relation to the acquisition or disposal.

**55(5) [Extent of s. 55(4)]** Subsection (4) is not exhaustive as to the circumstances in which one person may be regarded as procuring an acquisition or disposal of securities by another.

# 56 "Inside information", etc.

**56(1) ["Inside information"]** For the purposes of this section and section 57, **"inside information"** means information which–

(a) relates to particular securities or to a particular issuer of securities or to particular issuers of securities and not to securities generally or to issuers of securities generally;

(b) is specific or precise;

(c) has not been made public; and

(d) if it were made public would be likely to have a significant effect on the price of any securities.

**56(2) ["Price-affected securities", "price-sensitive information"]** For the purposes of this Part, securities are **"price-affected securities"** in relation to inside information, and inside information is **"price-sensitive information"** in relation to securities, if and only if the information would, if made public, be likely to have a significant effect on the price of the securities.

**56(3) ["Price"]** For the purposes of this section **"price"** includes value.

## 57 "Insiders"

**57(1) [Where person has information as insider]** For the purposes of this Part, a person has information as an insider if and only if–

(a) it is, and he knows that it is, inside information, and

(b) he has it, and knows that he has it, from an inside source.

**57(2) [Interpretation of s. 57(1)]** For the purposes of subsection (1), a person has information from an inside source if and only if–

(a) he has it through–

(i) being a director, employee or shareholder of an issuer of securities; or

(ii) having access to the information by virtue of his employment, office or profession; or

(b) the direct or indirect source of his information is a person within paragraph (a).

## 58 Information "made public"

**58(1) ["Made public"]** For the purposes of section 56, **"made public"**, in relation to information, shall be construed in accordance with the following provisions of this section; but those provisions are not exhaustive as to the meaning of that expression.

**58(2) [Where information made public]** Information is made public if–

(a) it is published in accordance with the rules of a regulated market for the purpose of informing investors and their professional advisers;

(b) it is contained in records which by virtue of any enactment are open to inspection by the public;

(c) it can be readily acquired by those likely to deal in any securities–

(i) to which the information relates, or

(ii) of an issuer to which the information relates; or

(d) it is derived from information which has been made public.

**58(3) [Information treated as made public]** Information may be treated as made public even though–

(a) it can be acquired only by persons exercising diligence or expertise;

(b) it is communicated to a section of the public and not to the public at large;

(c) it can be acquired only by observation;

(d) it is communicated only on payment of a fee; or

(e) it is published only outside the United Kingdom.

## 59 "Professional intermediary"

**59(1) ["Professional intermediary"]** For the purposes of this Part, a **"professional intermediary"** is a person–

(a) who carries on a business consisting of an activity mentioned in subsection (2) and who holds himself out to the public or any section of the public (including a section of the public constituted by persons such as himself) as willing to engage in any such business; or

(b) who is employed by a person falling within paragraph (a) to carry out any such activity.

**59(2) [Activities in s. 59(1)]** The activities referred to in subsection (1) are–

(a) acquiring or disposing of securities (whether as principal or agent); or

(b) acting as an intermediary between persons taking part in any dealing in securities.

**59(3) [Interpretation re s. 59(2)]** A person is not to be treated as carrying on a business consisting of an activity mentioned in subsection (2)–

(a) if the activity in question is merely incidental to some other activity not falling within subsection (2); or

(b) merely because he occasionally conducts one of those activities.

**59(4) [Purposes of s. 52]** For the purposes of section 52, a person dealing in securities relies on a professional intermediary if and only if a person who is acting as a professional intermediary carries out an activity mentioned in subsection (2) in relation to that dealing.

## 60 Other interpretation provisions

**60(1) ["Regulated market"]** For the purposes of this Part, **"regulated market"** means any market, however operated, which, by an order made by the Treasury, is identified (whether by name or by reference to criteria prescribed by the order) as a regulated market for the purposes of this Part.

**Note**

See the Insider Dealing (Securities and Regulated Markets) Order 1994 (SI 1994/187) (as amended).

**60(2) ["Issuer"]** For the purposes of this Part an **"issuer"**, in relation to any securities, means any company, public sector body or individual by which or by whom the securities have been or are to be issued.

**60(3) ["Company", "public sector body"]** For the purposes of this Part–

(a) **"company"** means any body (whether or not incorporated and wherever incorporated or constituted) which is not a public sector body; and

(b) **"public sector body"** means–

  (i) the government of the United Kingdom, of Northern Ireland or of any country or territory outside the United Kingdom;

  (ii) a local authority in the United Kingdom or elsewhere;

  (iii) any international organisation the members of which include the United Kingdom or another member state;

  (iv) the Bank of England; or

  (v) the central bank of any sovereign State.

**60(4) [Further interpretation]** For the purposes of this Part, information shall be treated as relating to an issuer of securities which is a company not only where it is about the company but also where it may affect the company's business prospects.

## 61 Penalties and prosecution

**61(1) [Penalties]** An individual guilty of insider dealing shall be liable–

(a) on summary conviction, to a fine not exceeding the statutory maximum or imprisonment for a term not exceeding six months or to both; or

(b) on conviction on indictment, to a fine or imprisonment for a term not exceeding seven years or to both.

**61(2) [Institution of proceedings]** Proceedings for offences under this Part shall not be instituted in England and Wales except by or with the consent of–

(a) the Secretary of State; or

(b) the Director of Public Prosecutions.

**61(3) [Northern Ireland]** In relation to proceedings in Northern Ireland for offences under this Part, subsection (2) shall have effect as if the reference to the Director of Public Prosecutions were a reference to the Director of Public Prosecutions for Northern Ireland.

## 62 Territorial scope of offence of insider dealing

**62(1) [Conditions for s. 52(1) offence]** An individual is not guilty of an offence falling within subsection (1) of section 52 unless–

(a) he was within the United Kingdom at the time when he is alleged to have done any act constituting or forming part of the alleged dealing;

(b) the regulated market on which the dealing is alleged to have occurred is one which, by an order made by the Treasury, is identified (whether by name or by reference to criteria prescribed by the order) as being, for the purposes of this Part, regulated in the United Kingdom; or

(c) the professional intermediary was within the United Kingdom at the time when he is alleged to have done anything by means of which the offence is alleged to have been committed.

**Note**
See the Insider Dealing (Securities and Regulated Markets) Order 1994 (SI 1994/187) (as amended).

**62(2) [Conditions for s. 52(2) offence]** An individual is not guilty of an offence falling within subsection (2) of section 52 unless–

(a) he was within the United Kingdom at the time when he is alleged to have disclosed the information or encouraged the dealing; or

(b) the alleged recipient of the information or encouragement was within the United Kingdom at the time when he is alleged to have received the information or encouragement.

## 63 Limits on section 52

**63(1) [Non-application of s. 52]** Section 52 does not apply to anything done by an individual acting on behalf of a public sector body in pursuit of monetary policies or policies with respect to exchange rates or the management of public debt or foreign exchange reserves.

**63(2) [Effect on contracts]** No contract shall be void or unenforceable by reason only of section 52.

## 64 Orders

**64(1) [Orders by statutory instrument]** Any power under this Part to make an order shall be exercisable by statutory instrument.

**Note**
See the Insider Dealing (Securities and Regulated Markets) Order 1994 (SI 1994/187) (as amended).

**64(2) [Approval by Parliament]** No order shall be made under this Part unless a draft of it has been laid before and approved by a resolution of each House of Parliament.

**64(3) [Provisions in orders]** An order under this Part–

(a) may make different provision for different cases; and

(b) may contain such incidental, supplemental and transitional provisions as the Treasury consider expedient.

**Note**
See the Insider Dealing (Securities and Regulated Markets) Order 1994 (SI 1994/187) (as amended).

# SCHEDULES

## Schedule 1 – Special Defences

Section 53(4)

### MARKET MAKERS

**1(1)** An individual is not guilty of insider dealing by virtue of dealing in securities or encouraging another person to deal if he shows that he acted in good faith in the course of–

(a) his business as a market maker, or

(b) his employment in the business of a market maker.

**1(2)** A market maker is a person who–

(a) holds himself out at all normal times in compliance with the rules of a regulated market or an approved organisation as willing to acquire or dispose of securities; and

(b) is recognised as doing so under those rules.

**1(3)** In this paragraph **"approved organisation"** means an international securities self-regulating organisation approved under paragraph 25B of Schedule 1 to the Financial Services Act 1986.

## MARKET INFORMATION

**2(1)** An individual is not guilty of insider dealing by virtue of dealing in securities or encouraging another person to deal if he shows that–

(a) the information which he had as an insider was market information; and

(b) it was reasonable for an individual in his position to have acted as he did despite having that information as an insider at the time.

**2(2)** In determining whether it is reasonable for an individual to do any act despite having market information at the time, there shall, in particular, be taken into account–

(a) the content of the information;

(b) the circumstances in which he first had the information and in what capacity; and

(c) the capacity in which he now acts.

**3** An individual is not guilty of insider dealing by virtue of dealing in securities or encouraging another person to deal if he shows–

(a) that he acted–

  (i) in connection with an acquisition or disposal which was under consideration or the subject of negotiation, or in the course of a series of such acquisitions or disposals; and

  (ii) with a view to facilitating the accomplishment of the acquisition or disposal or the series of acquisitions or disposals; and

(b) that the information which he had as an insider was market information arising directly out of his involvement in the acquisition or disposal or series of acquisitions or disposals.

**4** For the purposes of paragraphs 2 and 3 market information is information consisting of one or more of the following facts–

(a) that securities of a particular kind have been or are to be acquired or disposed of, or that their acquisition or disposal is under consideration or the subject of negotiation;

(b) that securities of a particular kind have not been or are not to be acquired or disposed of;

(c) the number of securities acquired or disposed of or to be acquired or disposed of or whose acquisition or disposal is under consideration or the subject of negotiation;

(d) the price (or range of prices) at which securities have been or are to be acquired or disposed of or the price (or range of prices) at which securities whose acquisition or disposal is under consideration or the subject of negotiation may be acquired or disposed of;

(e) the identity of the persons involved or likely to be involved in any capacity in an acquisition or disposal.

## PRICE STABILISATION

**5(1)** An individual is not guilty of insider dealing by virtue of dealing in securities or encouraging another person to deal if he shows that he acted in conformity with the price stabilisation rules.

**5(2)** In this paragraph **"the price stabilisation rules"** means rules which–

(a) are made under section 48 of the Financial Services Act 1986 (conduct of business rules); and

(b) make provision of a description mentioned in paragraph (i) of subsection (2) of that section (price stabilisation rules).

# Schedule 2 – Securities

Section 54

## SHARES

**1** Shares and stock in the share capital of a company (**"shares"**).

## DEBT SECURITIES

**2** Any instrument creating or acknowledging indebtedness which is issued by a company or public sector body, including, in particular, debentures, debenture stock, loan stock, bonds and certificates of deposit (**"debt securities"**).

## WARRANTS

**3** Any right (whether conferred by warrant or otherwise) to subscribe for shares or debt securities (**"warrants"**).

## DEPOSITARY RECEIPTS

**4(1)** The rights under any depositary receipt.

**4(2)** For the purposes of sub-paragraph (1) a **"depositary receipt"** means a certificate or other record (whether or not in the form of a document)–

(a) which is issued by or on behalf of a person who holds any relevant securities of a particular issuer; and

(b) which acknowledges that another person is entitled to rights in relation to the relevant securities or relevant securities of the same kind.

**4(3)** In sub-paragraph (2) **"relevant securities"** means shares, debt securities and warrants.

## OPTIONS

**5** Any option to acquire or dispose of any security falling within any other paragraph of this Schedule.

## FUTURES

**6(1)** Rights under a contract for the acquisition or disposal of relevant securities under which delivery is to be made at a future date and at a price agreed when the contract is made.

**6(2)** In sub-paragraph (1)–

(a) the references to a future date and to a price agreed when the contract is made include references to a date and a price determined in accordance with terms of the contract; and

(b) **"relevant securities"** means any security falling within any other paragraph of this Schedule.

## CONTRACTS FOR DIFFERENCES

**7(1)** Rights under a contract which does not provide for the delivery of securities but whose purpose or pretended purpose is to secure a profit or avoid a loss by reference to fluctuations in–

(a) a share index or other similar factor connected with relevant securities;

(b) the price of particular relevant securities; or

(c) the interest rate offered on money placed on deposit.

**7(2)** In sub-paragraph (1) **"relevant securities"** means any security falling within any other paragraph of this Schedule.

# Schedule 5 – Consequential Amendments

Section 79(13)

[**Note:** reproduced below are only those paragraphs relevant to this publication.]

## THE COMPANIES ACT 1985 (C. 6)

**4(1)** In section 744 of the Companies Act 1985 (interpretation), for the definition of "the Insider Dealing Act", there shall be substituted–

> "**"the insider dealing legislation"** means Part V of the Criminal Justice Act 1993 (insider dealing)."

**4(2)** In the 1985 Act for "Insider Dealing Act", wherever it occurs, there shall be substituted "insider dealing legislation".

## THE FINANCIAL SERVICES ACT 1986 (C. 60)

**7** The Financial Services Act 1986 shall be amended as follows.

**8** In section 128C(3)(b) (enforcement in support of overseas regulatory authority) for "the Company Securities (Insider Dealing) Act 1985" there shall be substituted "Part V of the Criminal Justice Act 1993 (insider dealing)".

**9(1)** In section 177 (investigations into insider dealing), in subsection (1)–

(a) for the words "there may have been a contravention of section 1, 2, 4 or 5 of the Company Securities (Insider Dealing) Act 1985" there shall be substituted "an offence under Part V of the Criminal Justice Act 1993 (insider dealing) may have been committed"; and

(b) for the words "contravention has occurred" there shall be substituted "offence has been committed".

**9(2)** In subsection (3) of that section–

(a) for the word "contravention" there shall be substituted "offence"; and

(b) in paragraph (a) for the words from "relating to" to the end there shall be substituted "which appear to them to be relevant to the investigation".

**9(3)** In subsection (4) of that section for the word "contravention" there shall be substituted "offence"

**10(1)** In 'section 178 (penalties for failure to co-operate with section 177 investigations), in subsection (1) for the words "contravention has occurred" there shall be substituted "offence has been committed".

**10(2)** In subsection (6) of that section for the words "contravention or suspected contravention" there shall be substituted "offence or suspected offence".

**11** In subsection (1) of section 189 (restriction of Rehabilitation of Offenders Act 1974), in paragraph (b) "(including insider dealing)" shall be omitted and at the end there shall be inserted "or insider dealing".

**12(1)** In section 199 (powers of entry), in subsection (1) for paragraph (b) there shall be substituted–

> "(b) under Part V of the Criminal Justice Act 1993 (insider dealing).".

**12(2)** After subsection (8) of that section there shall be inserted–

> "(8A) In the application of this section to Northern Ireland for the references to information on oath substitute references to complaint on oath.".

## THE COMPANIES ACT 1989 (C. 40)

**16** In section 82(2)(b) of the Companies Act 1989 (request for assistance by overseas regulatory authority) for "the Company Securities (Insider Dealing) Act 1985" there shall be substituted "Part V of the Criminal Justice Act 1993 (insider dealing)".

# Schedule 6 – Repeals and Revocations

Section 79(14)

[**Note:** reproduced below are only those entries relevant to this publication.]

## Part I – Repeals

| Chapter | Short title | Extent of repeal |
|---|---|---|
| 1985 c. 8. | The Company Securities (Insider Dealing) Act 1985. | The whole Act. |
| 1986 c. 60. | The Financial Services Act 1986. | Sections 173 to 176. In section 189(1)(b), the words "(including insider dealing)". In Schedule 16, paragraphs 28 and 43. |
| 1987 c. 38. | The Criminal Justice Act 1987. | In section 3(6)(i), the words "or any corresponding enactment having effect in Northern Ireland". |
| 1989 c. 40. | The Companies Act 1989. | Section 209. |

## Part II – Revocations

| Number | Title | Extent of revocation |
|---|---|---|
| SI 1992/3218. | The Banking Coordination (Second Council Directive) Regulations 1992. | In Schedule 8, paragraphs 8(3), 9(2) and 10(3). In Schedule 10, paragraphs 17 and 25. |

**Note**

Reproduced below is the text of the Company Securities (Insider Dealing) Act 1985 which was repealed by the Criminal Justice Act 1993, s. 79(14) and Sch. 6, Pt. I as from 1 March 1994 (see SI 1994/242 (C. 7), art. 2 and Sch.).

**"COMPANY SECURITIES (INSIDER DEALING) ACT 1985**

(1985 Chapter 8)

**Arrangement of Sections**

An Act to consolidate the enactments relating to insider dealing in company securities.

[*11th March 1985*]

REGULATION OF INSIDER DEALING

**1 Prohibition on stock exchange deals by insiders, etc.**

**1(1)** Subject to section 3, an individual who is, or at any time in the preceding 6 months has been, knowingly connected with a company shall not deal on a recognised stock exchange in securities of that company if he has information which–

(a) he holds by virtue of being connected with the company,
(b) it would be reasonable to expect a person so connected, and in the position by virtue of which he is so connected, not to disclose except for the proper performance of the functions attaching to that position, and
(c) he knows is unpublished price sensitive information in relation to those securities.

**(2)** Subject to section 3, an individual who is, or at any time in the preceding 6 months has been, knowingly connected with a company shall not deal on a recognised stock exchange in securities of any other company if he has information which–

(a) he holds by virtue of being connected with the first company,
(b) it would be reasonable to expect a person so connected, and in the position by virtue of which he is so connected, not to disclose except for the proper performance of the functions attaching to that position,
(c) he knows is unpublished price sensitive information in relation to those securities of that other company, and
(d) relates to any transaction (actual or contemplated) involving both the first company and that other company, or involving one of them and securities of the other, or to the fact that any such transaction is no longer contemplated.

**(3)** The next subsection applies where–

(a) an individual has information which he knowingly obtained (directly or indirectly) from another individual who–
  (i) is connected with a particular company, or was at any time in the 6 months preceding the obtaining of the information so connected, and
  (ii) the former individual knows or has reasonable cause to believe held the information by virtue of being so connected, and
(b) the former individual knows or has reasonable cause to believe that, because of the latter's connection and position, it would be reasonable to expect him not to disclose the information except for the proper performance of the functions attaching to that position.

**(4)** Subject to section 3, the former individual in that case–

(a) shall not himself deal on a recognised stock exchange in securities of that company if he knows that the information is unpublished price sensitive information in relation to those securities, and
(b) shall not himself deal on a recognised stock exchange in securities of any other company if he knows that the information is unpublished price sensitive information in relation to those securities and it relates to any transaction (actual or contemplated) involving the first company and the other company, or involving one of them and securities of the other, or to the fact that any such transaction is no longer contemplated.

**(5)** Subject to section 3, where an individual is contemplating, or has contemplated, making (whether with or without another person) a take-over offer for a company in a particular capacity, that individual shall not deal on a recognised stock exchange in securities of that company in another capacity if he knows that information that the offer is contemplated, or is no longer contemplated, is unpublished price sensitive information in relation to those securities.

**(6)** Subject to section 3, where an individual has knowingly obtained (directly or indirectly), from an individual to whom subsection (5) applies, information that the offer referred to in that subsection is being contemplated or is no longer contemplated, the former individual shall not himself deal on a recognised stock exchange in securities of that company if he knows that the information is unpublished price sensitive information in relation to those securities.

**(7)** Subject to section 3, an individual who is for the time being prohibited by any provision of this section from dealing on a recognised stock exchange in any securities shall not counsel or procure any other person to deal in those securities, knowing or having reasonable cause to believe that that person would deal in them on a recognised stock exchange.

**(8)** Subject to section 3, an individual who is for the time being prohibited as above mentioned from dealing on a recognised stock exchange in any securities by reason of his having any information, shall not communicate that information to any other person if he knows or has reasonable cause to believe that that or some other person will make use of the information for the purpose of dealing, or of counselling or procuring any other person to deal, on a recognised stock exchange in those securities.

**2 Abuse of information obtained in official capacity**

**2(1)** This section applies to any information which–

(a) is held by a public servant or former public servant by virtue of his position or former position as a public servant, or is knowingly obtained by an individual (directly or indirectly) from a public servant or former public servant who he knows or has reasonable cause to believe held the information by virtue of any such position,
(b) it would be reasonable to expect an individual in the position of the public servant or former position of the former public servant not to disclose except for the proper performance of the functions attaching to that position, and
(c) the individual holding it knows is unpublished price sensitive information in relation to securities of a particular company (**"relevant securities"**).

**(2)** This section applies to a public servant or former public servant holding information to which this section applies and to any individual who knowingly obtained any such information (directly or indirectly) from a public servant or former public servant who that individual knows or has reasonable cause to believe held the information by virtue of his position or former position as a public servant."

(Previously in s. 2(1), (2) the word "public" wherever appearing substituted for the former word "Crown" by Financial Services Act 1986, s. 173(1) as from 12 January 1987 (see SI 1986/2246 (C. 88)).)

"**(3)** Subject to section 3, an individual to whom this section applies–

(a) shall not deal on a recognised stock exchange in any relevant securities,
(b) shall not counsel or procure any other person to deal in any such securities, knowing or having reasonable cause to believe that that other person would deal in them on a recognised stock exchange, and

(c) shall not communicate to any other person the information held or (as the case may be) obtained by him as mentioned in subsection (2) if he knows or has reasonable cause to believe that that or some other person will make use of the information for the purpose of dealing, or of counselling or procuring any other person to deal, on a recognised stock exchange in any such securities.

**(4) "Public servant"** means–

(a) a Crown servant;

(b) a member, officer or servant of a designated agency, competent authority or transferee body (within the meaning of the Financial Services Act 1986);

(c) an officer or servant of a recognised self-regulating organisation, recognised investment exchange or recognised clearing house (within the meaning of that Act);

(d) any person declared by an order for the time being in force under subsection (5) to be a public servant for the purposes of this section.

**(5)** If it appears to the Secretary of State that the members, officers or employees of or persons otherwise connected with any body appearing to him to exercise public functions may have access to unpublished price sensitive information relating to securities, he may by order declare that those persons are to be public servants for the purposes of this section."

(See the Insider Dealing (Public Servants) Order 1989 (SI 1989/2164).

"**(6)** The power to make an order under subsection (5) shall be exercisable by statutory instrument and an instrument containing such an order shall be subject to annulment in pursuance of a resolution of either House of Parliament."

(S. 2(4)–(6) added by Financial Services Act 1986, s. 173(2) as from 12 January 1987 (see SI 1986/2246 (C. 88)).)

**"3 Actions not prohibited by s. 1, 2**

**3(1)** Sections 1 and 2 do not prohibit an individual by reason of his having any information from–

(a) doing any particular thing otherwise than with a view to the making of a profit or the avoidance of a loss (whether for himself or another person) by the use of that information;

(b) entering into a transaction in the course of the exercise in good faith of his functions as liquidator, receiver or trustee in bankruptcy;

(c) doing any particular thing if the information–

(i) was obtained by him in the course of a business of a jobber in which he was engaged or employed, and

(ii) was of a description which it would be reasonable to expect him to obtain in the ordinary course of that business,

and he does that thing in good faith in the course of that business; or

(d) doing any particular thing in relation to any particular securities if the information–

(i) was obtained by him in the course of a business of a market maker in those securities in which he was engaged or employed, and

(ii) was of a description which it would be reasonable to expect him to obtain in the ordinary course of that business,

and he does that thing in good faith in the course of that business.

**"Jobber"** means an individual, partnership or company dealing in securities on a recognised stock exchange and recognised by the Council of The Stock Exchange as carrying on the business of a jobber.

**"Market maker"** means a person (whether an individual, partnership or company) who–

(a) holds himself out at all normal times in compliance with the rules of a recognised stock exchange as willing to buy and sell securities at prices specified by him; and

(b) is recognised as doing so by that recognised stock exchange."

(Previously in s. 3(1) the word "; or", para. (d) and the definition of "market maker" inserted by Financial Services Act 1986, s. 174(1), (2) as from 18 December 1986 (see SI 1986/2246 (C. 88)). The word "or" formerly appearing immediately preceding para. (c) repealed by Financial Services Act 1986, s. 212(3) and Sch. 17 as from 12 January 1987 (see SI 1986/2246 (C. 88)).)

"**(2)** An individual is not, by reason only of his having information relating to any particular transaction, prohibited–

(a) by section 1(2), (4)(b), (5) or (6) from dealing on a recognised stock exchange in any securities, or

(b) by section 1(7) or (8) from doing any other thing in relation to securities which he is prohibited from dealing in by any of the provisions mentioned in paragraph (a), or

(c) by section 2 from doing anything,

if he does that thing in order to facilitate the completion or carrying out of the transaction.

**4 Off-market deals in advertised securities**

**4(1)** Subject to section 6, sections 1 to 3 apply in relation to–

(a) dealing otherwise than on a recognised stock exchange in the advertised securities of any company–

(i) through an off-market dealer who is making a market in those securities, in the knowledge that he is an off-market dealer, that he is making a market in those securities and that the securities are advertised securities, or

(ii) as an off-market dealer who is making a market in those securities or as an officer, employee or agent of such a dealer acting in the course of the dealer's business;

(b) counselling or procuring a person to deal in advertised securities in the knowledge or with reasonable cause to believe that he would deal in them as mentioned in paragraph (a);

(c) communicating any information in the knowledge or with reasonable cause to believe that it would be used for such dealing or for such counselling or procuring,

as they apply in relation to dealing in securities on a recognised stock exchange and to counselling or procuring or communicating any information in connection with such dealing.

**(2)** In its application by virtue of this section the definition of "market maker" in section 3(1) shall have effect as if the references to a recognised stock exchange were references to a recognised investment exchange (other than an overseas investment exchange) within the meaning of the Financial Services Act 1986."

(Previously s. 4(1) renumbered as such and s. 4(2) inserted by Financial Services Act, s. 174(3) as from 29 April 1988 (see SI 1988/740 (C. 22)).)

**"5 Restriction on promoting off-market deals abroad**

**5(1)** An individual who, by reason of his having information, is for the time being prohibited by any provision of section 1 or 2 from dealing in any securities shall not–

(a) counsel or procure any other person to deal in those securities in the knowledge or with reasonable cause to believe that that person would deal in the securities outside Great Britain on any stock exchange other than a recognised stock exchange, or

(b) communicate that information to any other person in the knowledge or with reasonable cause to believe that that or some other person will make use of the information for the purpose of dealing or of counselling or procuring any other person to deal in the securities outside Great Britain on any stock exchange other than a recognised stock exchange.

**(2)** Subsection (1) does not prohibit an individual by reason of his having any information from acting as mentioned in any of paragraphs (a) to (c) of section 3(1).

**(3)** An individual is not, by reason only of having information relating to a particular transaction, prohibited by any provision of this section from doing anything if he does that thing in order to facilitate the completion or carrying out of the transaction.

**6 Price stabilisation**

**6(1)** No provision of section 1, 2, 4 or 5 prohibits an individual from doing anything for the purpose of stabilising the price of securities if it is done in conformity with rules made under section 48 of the Financial Services Act 1986 and–

(a) in respect of securities which fall within any of paragraphs 1 to 5 of Schedule 1 to that Act and are specified by the rules; and

(b) during such period before or after the issue of those securities as is specified by the rules.

**(2)** Any order under subsection (8) of section 48 of that Act shall apply also in relation to subsection (1) of this section."

(Previously s. 6 substituted by Financial Services Act 1986, s. 175 as from 29 April 1988 (see SI 1988/740 (C. 22)): s. 6 formerly read as follows:

**"6 International bonds**

**6(1)** Section 1 does not by virtue of section 4 or 5 prohibit an individual from doing anything in relation to a debenture, or a right to subscribe for, call for or make delivery of a debenture, if–

(a) that thing is done by him in good faith in connection with an international bond issue–

(i) not later than 3 months after the issue date, or

(ii) in a case where the international bond issue is not proceeded with, before the decision is taken not to proceed with the issue,

and he is an issue manager for that issue or is an officer, employee or agent of an issue manager for that issue, or

(b) he is or was an issue manager for an international bond issue who is making a market in that debenture or right, or is an officer, employee or agent of such an issue manager, and that thing is done by him in good faith as a person making a market in that debenture or right or as an officer, employee or agent of such a person,

and in either case the unpublished price sensitive information by virtue of which section 1 would (but for this section) apply in relation to that thing is information which he holds by virtue of his being (or having been) such an issue manager or an officer, employee or agent of such an issue manager, and is information which it would be reasonable to expect him to have obtained as an issue manager, or as such officer, employee or agent.

**(2)** Where an individual holds unpublished price sensitive information in relation to any securities but by virtue of subsection (1) of this section he is not prohibited by section 1 from doing anything in relation to those securities, he is also not prohibited (by virtue of his holding that information) by section 5 from doing any other thing in relation to those securities.

**(3)** The Secretary of State may by regulations made by statutory instrument make provision–

(a) extending the exemptions conferred by subsection (1) or (2) (or both) for things done in relation to other advertised securities or other advertised securities of any specified class;

(b) amending or disapplying sub-paragraph (i) or (ii) (or both) of subsection (1)(a) in relation to an international bond issue or an international bond issue of a specified class.

**(4)** Regulations under subsection (3)–

(a) may make different provision for different cases or classes of case and may contain such incidental and supplementary provisions as the Secretary of State may think fit,

(b) shall not be made unless a draft of the instrument containing them has been laid before Parliament and approved by a resolution of each House.")

**"7 Trustees and personal representatives**

**7(1)** Where a trustee or personal representative or, where a trustee or personal representative is a body corporate, an individual acting on behalf of that trustee or personal representative who, apart from paragraph (a) of section 3(1) or, as the case may be, subsection (2) of section 5, would be prohibited by any of sections 1 to 5 from dealing, or counselling or procuring any other person to deal, in any securities deals in those securities or counsels or procures any other person to deal in them, he is presumed to have acted with propriety if he acted on the advice of a person who–

(a) appeared to him to be an appropriate person from whom to seek such advice, and

(b) did not appear to him to be prohibited by section 1, 2, 4 or 5 from dealing in those securities.

**(2) "With propriety"** means otherwise than with a view to the making of a profit or the avoidance of a loss (whether for himself or another person) by the use of the information in question.

**8 Punishment of contraventions**

**8(1)** An individual who contravenes section 1, 2, 4 or 5 is liable–

(a) on conviction on indictment to imprisonment for a term not exceeding 7 years or a fine, or both, and

(b) on summary conviction to imprisonment for a term not exceeding 6 months or a fine not exceeding the statutory maximum, or both."

(Previously in s. 8(1)(a) the figure "7" substituted for the former figure "2" by Criminal Justice Act 1988, s. 48(1) and 171(6) as from 29 September 1988.)

"**(2)** Proceedings for an offence under this section shall not be instituted in England and Wales except by, or with the consent of, the Secretary of State or the Director of Public Prosecutions."

(Previously in s. 8(2) the words "by, or with the consent of, the Secretary of State or the Director of Public Prosecutions" substituted for the former words "by the Secretary or by, or with the consent of, the Director of Public Prosecutions" by CA 1989, s. 209 as from 21 February 1990 (see SI 1990/142 (C. 5), art. 7(b)).)

"**(3)** No transaction is void or voidable by reason only that it was entered into in contravention of section 1, 2, 4 or 5.

INTERPRETATION FOR S. 1–8

**9 "Connected with a company"**

**9** For purposes of this Act, an individual is connected with a company if, but only if–

(a) he is a director of that company or a related company, or

(b) he occupies a position as an officer (other than a director) or employee of that company or a related company or a position involving a professional or business relationship between himself (or his employer or a company of which he is a director) and the first company or a related company which in either case may reasonably be expected to give him access to information which, in relation to securities of either company, is unpublished price sensitive information, and which it would be reasonable to expect a person in his position not to disclose except for the proper performance of his functions.

**10 "Unpublished price sensitive information"**

10 Any reference in this Act to unpublished price sensitive information in relation to any securities of a company is a reference to information which–

(a) relates to specific matters relating or of concern (directly or indirectly) to that company, that is to say, is not of a general nature relating or of concern to that company, and

(b) is not generally known to those persons who are accustomed or would be likely to deal in those securities but which would if it were generally known to them be likely materially to affect the price of those securities.

**11 "Company"; "related company"**

11 In this Act–

(a) **"company"** means any company, whether or not a company within the meaning of the Companies Act 1985, and

(b) **"related company"**, in relation to a company, means any body corporate which is that company's subsidiary or holding company, or a subsidiary of that company's holding company.

**12 "Securities", etc.**

12 In this Act–

(a) **"securities"** means listed securities and, in the case of a company within the meaning of the Companies Act 1985, or a company registered under Chapter II of Part XXII of that Act or an unregistered company, the following securities (whether or not listed), that is to say, any shares, any debentures, or any right to subscribe for, call for or make delivery of a share or debenture;

(b) **"listed securities"**, in relation to a company, means any securities of the company listed on a recognised stock exchange; and

(c) **"advertised securities"**, in relation to a particular occurrence, means listed securities or securities in respect of which, not more than 6 months before that occurrence, information indicating the prices at which persons have dealt or were willing to deal in those securities has been published for the purpose of facilitating deals in those securities.

**13 "Deal in securities"; "off-market dealer", etc.**

**13(1)** For purposes of this Act, a person deals in securities if (whether as principal or agent) he buys or sells or agrees to buy or sell any securities; and references to dealing in securities on a recognised stock exchange include dealing in securities through an investment exchange.

**(1A)** For the purposes of this Act a person who (whether as principal or agent) buys or sells or agrees to buy or sell investments within paragraph 9 of Schedule 1 to the Financial Services Act 1986 (contracts for differences etc.) where the purpose or pretended purpose mentioned in that paragraph is to secure a profit or avoid a loss wholly or partly by reference to fluctuations in the value or price of securities shall be treated as if he were dealing in those securities."

(Previously s. 13(1A) inserted by Financial Services Act 1986, s. 176 as from 12 January 1987 (see SI 1986/2246 (C. 88)).)

"**(2) "Investment exchange"** means an organisation maintaining a system whereby an offer to deal in securities made by a subscriber to the organisation is communicated, without his identity being revealed, to other subscribers to the organisation, and whereby any acceptance of that offer by any of those other subscribers is recorded and confirmed.

**(3) "Off-market dealer"** means a person who is an authorised person within the meaning of the Financial Services Act 1986."

(Previously s. 13(3) substituted by Financial Services Act 1986, s. 174(4)(b) as from 29 April 1988 (see SI 1988/740 (C. 22)): s. 13(3) formerly read as follows:

"**(3) "Off-market dealer"** means a person who–

(a) holds a licence under section 3 of the Prevention of Fraud (Investments) Act 1958 (principals' and representatives' licences for dealers in securities), or

(b) is a member of a recognised stock exchange or recognised association of dealers in securities within the meaning of that Act, or

(c) is an exempted dealer within the meaning of that Act.)"

"**(4)** An off-market dealer is taken–

(a) to deal in advertised securities, if he deals in such securities or acts as an intermediary in connection with deals made by other persons in such securities (references to such a dealer's officer, employee or agent dealing in such securities to be construed accordingly), and

(b) to make a market in any securities, if in the course of his business as an off-market dealer he holds himself out both to prospective buyers and to prospective sellers of those securities (other than particular buyers or sellers) as willing to deal in them otherwise than on a recognised stock exchange.

**(5)** For purposes of section 4, an individual is taken to deal through an off-market dealer if the latter is a party to the transaction, is an agent for either party to the transaction or is acting as an intermediary in connection with the transaction.

**14 "Take-over offer"**

14 In this Act, **"take-over offer for a company"** means an offer made to all the holders (or all the holders other than the person making the offer and his nominees) of the shares in the company to acquire those shares or a specified proportion of them, or to all the holders (or all the holders other than the person making the offer and his nominees) of a particular class of those shares to acquire the shares of that class or a specified proportion of them."

**15 Expressions used in s. 6**

15 (Repealed by Financial Services Act 1986, s. 212(3) and Sch. 17, Pt. I as from 29 April 1988)

(In regard to the date of the above repeal see SI 1988/740 (C. 22): s. 15 formerly read as follows (in s. 15(3) the words ", British National (Overseas)," having been inserted by SI 1986/948):

"**15(1)** For purposes of section 6, the following definitions apply–

(a) **"international bond issue"** means an issue of debentures of a company ("the issuing company")–

(i) all of which are offered or to be offered by an off-market dealer to persons (whether principals or agents) whose ordinary business includes the buying or selling of debentures, and

(ii) where the debentures are denominated in sterling, not less than 50 per cent in nominal value of the debentures are or are to be so offered to persons who have not the requisite connection with the United Kingdom;

(b) **"issue date"** means the date on which the first of those debentures is issued by the issuing company; and
(c) **"issue manager"** means–
(i) an off-market dealer acting as an agent of the issuing company for the purposes of an international bond issue, or
(ii) where the issuing company issues or proposes to issue the debentures to an off-market dealer under an arrangement in pursuance of which he is to sell them to other persons, that off-market dealer.

**(2)** The Secretary of State may by regulations in a statutory instrument provide–
(a) for permitting persons of any specified class to be treated as issue managers for purposes of subsection (1) or (2) (or both) of section 6,
(b) for permitting persons of any specified class to be treated as off-market dealers for those purposes,
(c) for permitting an issue of international securities of any specified class to be treated as an international bond issue for those purposes.

**(3)** The reference in subsection (1)(a)(ii) of this section to persons who have not the requisite connection with the United Kingdom is to persons who are neither–
(a) British citizens, British Dependent Territories citizens, British National (Overseas), or British Overseas citizens, nor
(b) companies incorporated or otherwise formed under the law of any part of the United Kingdom.

**(4)** The reference in subsection (2)(c) to international securities is to any securities (whether listed, advertised or other) which are in any way connected with a country outside Great Britain for example–
(a) securities issued by a body incorporated or resident outside Great Britain, or
(b) securities which are denominated in a currency other than sterling, or dealt in by bodies incorporated or resident outside Great Britain or by individuals so resident.)"

**"16 General interpretation provisions**

**16(1)** In this Act–

**"Crown servant"** means an individual who holds office under, or is employed by, the Crown;

**"debenture"** has the same meaning in relation to companies not incorporated under the Companies Act 1985 as it has in relation to companies so incorporated;

**"recognised stock exchange"** means The Stock Exchange and any other investment exchange which is declared by an order of the Secretary of State for the time being in force to be a recognised stock exchange for the purposes of this Act;

**"share"** has the same meaning in relation to companies not incorporated under the Companies Act 1985 as it has in relation to companies so incorporated;

**"statutory maximum"** means–
(a) in England and Wales, the prescribed sum within section 32 of the Magistrates' Courts Act 1980, and
(b) in Scotland, the prescribed sum within section 289B of the Criminal Procedure (Scotland) Act 1975;

**"unregistered company"** means any body corporate to which the provisions of the Companies Act 1985 specified in Schedule 22 to that Act apply by virtue of section 718 of that Act."

(Previously in s. 16(1) the definition of "recognised stock exchange" substituted by Financial Services Act 1986, s. 212(2) and Sch. 16, para. 28(a) as from 12 January 1987 (see SI 1986/2246 (C. 88); the former definition read as follows:

""**recognised stock exchange"** means any body of persons which is for the time being a recognised stock exchange for the purposes of the Prevention of Fraud (Investments) Act 1958;")

**"16(1A)** The power to make an order under subsection (1) above shall be exercisable by statutory instrument."

(Previously s. 16(1A) inserted by Financial Services Act 1986, s. 212(2) and Sch. 16, para. 28(b) as from 12 January 1987 (see SI 1986/2246 (C. 88)).)

"**16(2)** Subject to sections 9 to 14 and this section, expressions used in this Act and the Companies Act 1985 have the same meaning in this Act as in that."

(Previously in s. 16(2) the word "14" substituted for the former word "15" by Financial Services Act 1986, s. 212(2) and Sch. 16, para. 28(c) as from 29 April 1988 (see SI 1988/740 (C. 22)).

See Insider Dealing (Recognised Stock Exchange) Order 1989 (SI 1989/2165), Insider Dealing (Recognised Stock Exchange) (No. 2 Order) 1990 (SI 1990/47) and Insider Dealing (Recognised Stock Exchange) Order 1992 (SI 1992/451) made under s. 16(1) and (1A).)

"**16(3)** The definitions in sections 11, 12(a) and (b), 13(2) and 14, and in subsection (1) above, apply except where the context otherwise requires.

## GENERAL

**17 Northern Ireland**

**17** This Act does not extend to Northern Ireland.

**18 Commencement**

**18** This Act comes into force on 1st July 1985.

**19 Citation**

**19** This Act may be cited as the Company Securities (Insider Dealing) Act 1985.

## TABLE OF DERIVATIONS

[This table has no official status]

The following abbreviations are used in this Table:—

'1948' = Companies Act 1948 (c. 38).
'1980' = Companies Act 1980 (c. 22).
'1981' = Companies Act 1981 (c. 62).

| Provision | Derivation |
|---|---|
| 1 | 1980 s. 68(1)–(7). |
| 2 | 1980 s. 69(1)–(3). |
| 3 | 1980 ss. 68(8), (10), 69(4) (in part), (5). |
| 4 | 1980 s. 70(1). |

| | |
|---|---|
| 5 | 1980 s. 70(2). |
| 6 | 1980 s. 71(1), (1A), (3), (d), (e), (5); 1981 s. 112. |
| 7 | 1980 ss. 68(11), 69(4), 70(2) (end piece). |
| 8 | 1980 s. 72; 1981 Sch. 3, para. 59. |
| 9 | 1980 s. 73(1). |
| 10 | 1980 s. 73(2). |
| 11 | 1980 s. 73(5). |
| 12 | 1980 ss. 70(3), 73(5). |
| 13 | 1980 ss. 70(3)–(5), 73(3), (5). |
| 14 | 1980 s. 73(5). |
| 15 | 1980 s. 71(2), (3)(a)–(c), (4). |
| 16 | 1948 s. 455(1); 1980 ss. 68(9), 73(5), 87(1). |
| 17 | (Northern Ireland). |
| 18 | (Commencement). |
| 19 | (Citation)." |

# PENSION SCHEMES ACT 1993

(1993 Chapter 48)

[*5 November 1993*]

# PART VII – INSOLVENCY OF EMPLOYERS

## Chapter II – Payment by Secretary of State of Unpaid Contributions

### 123 Interpretation of Chapter II

**123(1) [Insolvency of employer for purposes of Ch. II]** For the purposes of this Chapter, an employer shall be taken to be insolvent if, but only if, in England and Wales–

(a) he has been adjudged bankrupt or has made a composition or arrangement with his creditors;

(b) he has died and his estate falls to be administered in accordance with an order under section 421 of the Insolvency Act 1986; or

(c) where the employer is a company–

(i) a winding-up order or an administration order is made or a resolution for voluntary winding up is passed with respect to it,

(ii) a receiver or manager of its undertaking is duly appointed,

(iii) possession is taken, by or on behalf of the holders of any debentures secured by a floating charge, of any property of the company comprised in or subject to the charge, or

(iv) a voluntary arrangement proposed for the purpose of Part I of the Insolvency Act 1986 is approved under that Part.

**123(2) [Insolvency of employer in Scotland for purposes of Ch. II]** For the purposes of this Chapter, an employer shall be taken to be insolvent if, but only if, in Scotland–

(a) sequestration of his estate is awarded or he executes a trust deed for his creditors or enters into a composition contract;

(b) he has died and a judicial factor appointed under section 11A of the Judicial Factors (Scotland) Act 1889 is required by that section to divide his insolvent estate among his creditors; or

(c) where the employer is a company–
   (i) a winding-up order or an administration order is made or a resolution for voluntary winding up is passed with respect to it,
   (ii) a receiver of its undertaking is duly appointed, or
   (iii) a voluntary arrangement proposed for the purpose of Part I of the Insolvency Act 1986 is approved under that Part.

**123(3) [Definitions]** In this Chapter–

**"contract of employment"**, **"employee"**, **"employer"** and **"employment"** and other expressions which are defined in the Employment Rights Act 1996 have the same meaning as in that Act;

**"holiday pay"**means–

(a) pay in respect of holiday actually taken; or
(b) any accrued holiday pay which under the employee's contract of employment would in the ordinary course have become payable to him in respect of the period of a holiday if his employment with the employer had continued until he became entitled to a holiday;

**"occupational pension scheme"**means any scheme or arrangement which provides or is capable of providing, in relation to employees in any description of employment, benefits, in the form of pensions or otherwise, payable to or in respect of any such employees on the termination of their employment or on their death or retirement.

**History**

In s. 123(3), the words "the Employment Rights Act 1996" substituted for the former words "the Employment Protection (Consolidation) Act 1978" by the Employment Rights Act 1996, s. 240, 243 and Sch. 1, para. 61(2) with effect from 22 August 1996.

**123(4) [Definitions]** For the purposes of this Chapter, the definition of **"personal pension scheme"** in section 1 has effect with the substitution for the words **"employed earners"** of the word **"employees"**.

**123(5) [Resources of a scheme]** Any reference in this Chapter to the resources of a scheme is a reference to the funds out of which the benefits provided by the scheme are from time to time payable.

## 124 Duty of Secretary of State to pay unpaid contributions to schemes

**124(1) [Duty of Secretary of State]** If, on an application made to him in writing by the persons competent to act in respect of an occupational pension scheme or a personal pension scheme, the Secretary of State is satisfied–

(a) that an employer has become insolvent; and
(b) that at the time he did so there remained unpaid relevant contributions falling to be paid by him to the scheme,

then, subject to the provisions of this section and section 125, the Secretary of State shall pay into the resources of the scheme the sum which in his opinion is payable in respect of the unpaid relevant contributions.

**124(2) [Relevant contributions]** In this section and section 125 **"relevant contributions"** means contributions falling to be paid by an employer to an occupational pension scheme or a personal pension scheme, either on his own account or on behalf of an employee. and for the purposes of this section a contribution shall not he treated as falling to be paid on behalf of an employee unless a sum equal to that amount has been deducted from the pay of the employee by way of a contribution from him.

**124(3) [Sum payable by employer re unpaid contributions]** Subject to subsection (3A), the sum payable under this section in respect of unpaid contributions of an employer on his own account to an occupational pension scheme or a personal pension scheme shall be the least of the following amounts–

(a) the balance of relevant contributions remaining unpaid on the date when he became insolvent and payable by the employer on his own account to the scheme in respect of the 12 months immediately preceding that date;

(b) the amount certified by an actuary to be necessary for the purpose of meeting the liability of the scheme on dissolution to pay the benefits provided by the scheme to or in respect of the employees of the employer;

(c) an amount equal to 10 per cent of the total amount of remuneration paid or payable to those employees in respect of the 12 months immediately preceding the date on which the employer became insolvent.

**History**
In s. 124(3), the words "Subject to subsection (3A)," inserted by the Pensions Act 1995, s. 90 with effect from 2 October 1995 (see Pensions Act 1995 (Commencement No. 1) Order 1995 (SI 1995/2548 (C. 51)), art. 2.

**124(3A) [Sum payable into money purchase scheme]** Where the scheme in question is a money purchase scheme, the sum payable under this section by virtue of subsection (3) shall be the lesser of the amounts mentioned in paragraphs (a) and (c) of that subsection.

**History**
S. 124(3A) inserted by the Pensions Act 1995, s. 90 with effect from 2 October 1995 (see Pensions Act 1995 (Commencement No. 1) Order 1995 (SI 1995/2548 (C. 51)), art. 2.

**124(4) [Remuneration]** For the purposes of subsection (3)(c), **"remuneration"** includes holiday pay, statutory sick pay, statutory maternity pay under Part V of the Social Security Act 1986 or Part XII of the Social Security Contributions and Benefits Act 1992, and any payment such as is referred to in section 184(2) of the Employment Rights Act 1996 .

**History**
In s. 124(4), the words "and any payment such as is referred to in section 184(2) of the Employment Rights Act 1996" substituted for the former words "maternity pay under Part III of the Employment Protection (Consolidation) Act 1978 and any such payment as is referred to in section 122(4) of that Act (guarantee payments etc.)" by the Employment Rights Act 1996, s. 240, 243 and Sch. 1, para. 61(3) with effect from 22 August 1996.

**124(5) [Limit on payment of unpaid contributions]** Any sum payable under this section in respect of unpaid contributions on behalf of an employee shall not exceed the amount deducted from the pay of the employee in respect of the employee's contributions to the scheme during the 12 months immediately preceding the date on which the employer became insolvent.

## 125 Certification of amounts payable under s. 124 by insolvency officers

**125(1) [Application of s. 125(1)]** This section applies where one of the officers mentioned in subsection (2) (**"the relevant officer"**) has been or is required to be appointed in connection with an employer's insolvency.

**125(2) [Officers referred to in s. 125(1)]** The officers referred to in subsection (1) are–

(a) a trustee in bankruptcy;

(b) a liquidator;

(c) an administrator;

(d) a receiver or manager; or

(e) a trustee under a composition or arrangement between the employer and his creditors or under a trust deed for his creditors executed by the employer;

and in this subsection **"trustee"**, in relation to a composition or arrangement, includes the supervisor of a voluntary arrangement proposed for the purposes of and approved under Part I or VIII of the Insolvency Act 1986.

**125(3) [Payment under s. 124 on receipt of statement by relevant officer]** Subject to subsection (5), where this section applies the Secretary of State shall not make any payment under section 124 in respect of unpaid relevant contributions until he has received a statement from the relevant officer of the amount of relevant contributions which appear to have been unpaid on the date on which the employer became insolvent and to remain unpaid; and the relevant officer shall on request by the Secretary of State provide him as soon as reasonably practicable with such a statement.

**125(4) [Amount payable]** Subject to subsection (5), an amount shall be taken to be payable, paid or deducted as mentioned in subsection (3)(a) or (c) or (5) of section 124 only if it is so certified by the relevant officer.

**125(5) [Power of secretary of State to make payment]** If the Secretary of State is satisfied–

(a) that he does not require a statement under subsection (3) in order to determine the amount of relevant contributions that was unpaid on the date on which the employer became insolvent and remains unpaid, or

(b) that he does not require a certificate under subsection (4) in order to determine the amounts payable, paid or deducted as mentioned in subsection (3)(a) or (c) or (5) of section 124,

he may make a payment under that section in respect of the contributions in question without having received such a statement or, as the case may be, such a certificate.

## 126 Complaint to industrial tribunal

**126(1) [Persons acting re pension schemes]** Any persons who are competent to act in respect of an occupational pension scheme or a personal pension scheme and who have applied for a payment to be made under section 124 into the resources of the scheme may present a complaint to an industrial tribunal that–

(a) the Secretary of State has failed to make any such payment; or

(b) any such payment made by him is less than the amount which should have been paid.

**126(2) [Entitlement to complain]** Such a complaint must be presented within the period of three months beginning with the date on which the decision of the Secretary of State on that application was communicated to the persons presenting it or, if that is not reasonably practicable, within such further period as is reasonable.

**126(3) [Declaration by tribunal]** Where an industrial tribunal finds that the Secretary of State ought to make a payment under section 124, it shall make a declaration to that effect and shall also declare the amount of any such payment which it finds that the Secretary of State ought to make.

## 127 Transfer to Secretary of State of rights and remedies

**127(1) [Where Secretary of State makes s. 124 payment]** Where in pursuance of section 124 the Secretary of State makes any payment into the resources of an occupational pension scheme or a personal pension scheme in respect of any contributions to the scheme, any rights and remedies in respect of those contributions belonging to the persons competent to act in respect of the scheme shall, on the making of the payment, become rights and remedies of the Secretary of State.

**127(2) [Extent of rights and remedies re s. 127(1)]** Where the Secretary of State makes any such payment as is mentioned in subsection (1) and the sum (or any part of the sum) falling to be paid by the employer on account of the contributions in respect of which the payment is made constitutes–

(a) a preferential debt within the meaning of the Insolvency Act 1986 for the purposes of any provision of that Act (including any such provision as applied by an order made under that Act) or any provision of the Companies Act 1985; or

(b) a preferred debt within the meaning of the Bankruptcy (Scotland) Act 1985 for the purposes of any provision of that Act (including any such provision as applied by section 11A of the Judicial Factors (Scotland) Act 1889),

then, without prejudice to the generality of subsection (1), there shall be included among the rights and remedies which become rights and remedies of the Secretary of State in accordance with that subsection any right arising under any such provision by reason of the status of that sum (or that part of it) as a preferential or preferred debt.

**127(3) [Computation of claims in s. 127(2)(a)]** In computing for the purposes of any provision referred to in subsection (2)(a) or (b) the aggregate amount payable in priority to other creditors of the employer in respect of–

(a) any claim of the Secretary of State to be so paid by virtue of subsection (2); and

(b) any claim by the persons competent to act in respect of the scheme, any claim falling within paragraph (a) shall be treated as if it were a claim of those persons; but the Secretary of State shall be entitled, as against those persons, to be so paid in respect of any such claim of his (up to the full amount of the claim) before any payment is made to them in respect of any claim falling within paragraph (b).

# Chapter III – Priority in Bankruptcy

## 128 Priority in bankruptcy etc.

**128** Schedule 4 shall have effect for the purposes of paragraph 8 of Schedule 6 to the Insolvency Act 1986 and paragraph 4 of Schedule 3 to the Bankruptcy (Scotland) Act 1985 (by virtue of which sums to which Schedule 4 to this Act applies are preferential or, as the case may be, preferred debts in cases of insolvency).

# Schedule 4 – Priority In Bankruptcy etc

Section 128

### EARNER'S CONTRIBUTIONS TO OCCUPATIONAL PENSION SCHEME

**1** This Schedule applies to any sum owed on account of an earner's contributions to an occupational pension scheme being contributions deducted from earnings paid in the period of four months immediately preceding the relevant date or otherwise due in respect of earnings paid or payable in that period.

### EMPLOYER'S CONTRIBUTIONS TO OCCUPATIONAL PENSION SCHEME

**2(1)** This Schedule applies to any sum owed on account of an employer's contributions to a salary related contracted-out scheme which were payable in the period of 12 months immediately preceding the relevant date.

**History**
Para. 2(1)–(3A) substituted for former para. 2(1)–(3) by Welfare Reform and Pensions Act 1999, s. 18 and Sch. 2, para. 8(2) with effect from 25 April 2000 (see Welfare Reform and Pensions Act 1999 (Commencement No. 4) Order 2000 (SI 2000/1047 (C. 29)), art. 2(2) and Sch., Pt. II). For former wording of para. 2(1), see history note to para. 2(3A) below.

**2(1A)** The amount of the debt having priority by virtue of sub-paragraph (1) shall be taken to be an amount equal to the appropriate amount.

**History**
Para. 2(1)–(3A) substituted for former para. 2(1)–(3) by Welfare Reform and Pensions Act 1999, s. 18 and Sch. 2, para. 8(2) with effect from 25 April 2000 (see Welfare Reform and Pensions Act 1999 (Commencement No. 4) Order 2000 (SI 2000/1047 (C. 29)), art. 2(2) and Sch., Pt. II).

**2(2)** This Schedule applies to any sum owed on account of an employer's minimum payments to a money purchase contracted-out scheme falling to be made in the period of 12 months immediately preceding the relevant date.

**History**
Para. 2(1)–(3A) substituted for former para. 2(1)–(3) by Welfare Reform and Pensions Act 1999, s. 18 and Sch. 2, para. 8(2) with effect from 25 April 2000 (see Welfare Reform and Pensions Act 1999 (Commencement No. 4) Order 2000 (SI 2000/1047 (C. 29)), art. 2(2) and Sch., Pt. II). For former wording of para. 2(2), see history note to para. 2(3A) below.

**2(3)** In so far as payments cannot from the terms of the scheme be identified as falling within sub-paragraph (2), the amount of the debt having priority by virtue of that sub-paragraph shall be taken to be an amount equal to the appropriate amount.

**History**
Para. 2(1)–(3A) substituted for former para. 2(1)–(3) by Welfare Reform and Pensions Act 1999, s. 18 and Sch. 2, para. 8(2) with effect from 25 April 2000 (see Welfare Reform and Pensions Act 1999 (Commencement No. 4) Order 2000 (SI 2000/1047 (C. 29)), art. 2(2) and Sch., Pt. II). For former wording of para. 2(3), see history note to para. 2(3A) below.

**2(3A)** In sub-paragraph (1A) or (3) **"the appropriate amount"** means the aggregate of–

(a) the percentage for non-contributing earners of the total reckonable earnings paid or payable, in the period of 12 months referred to in sub-paragraph (1) or (2) (as the case may be), to or for the benefit of non-contributing earners; and

(b) the percentage for contributing earners of the total reckonable earnings paid or payable, in that period, to or for the benefit of contributing earners.

**History**

Para. 2(1)–(3A) substituted for former para. 2(1)–(3) by Welfare Reform and Pensions Act 1999, s. 18 and Sch. 2, para. 8(2) with effect from 25 April 2000 (see Welfare Reform and Pensions Act 1999 (Commencement No. 4) Order 2000 (SI 2000/1047 (C. 29)), art. 2(2) and Sch., Pt. II). Para 2(1)–(3) formerly read as follows:

"**2(1)** This Schedule applies to any sum owed on account of an employer's contributions to a contracted-out scheme, being contributions payable–

(a) in the period of 12 months immediately preceding the relevant date; and

(b) in respect of earners in employment which is contracted-out by reference to the scheme towards the provision for those earners of guaranteed minimum pensions under the scheme.

**(2)** This Schedule applies to any sum owed on account of an employer's minimum payments to a contracted-out scheme falling to be made in the period of 12 months immediately preceding the relevant date.

**(3)** In so far as contributions or payments cannot from the terms of the scheme be identified as falling within sub-paragraph (1) or (2), the amount of the debt having priority by virtue of that sub-paragraph shall be deemed to be an amount equal to–

(a) 4. 8 per cent of the total reckonable earnings paid or payable, in the period of 12 months referred to in that sub-paragraph, to or for the benefit of non-contributing earners; and

(b) 3 per cent of the total reckonable earnings paid or payable in that period to or for the benefit of contributing earners. "

**2(4)** For the purposes of sub-paragraph (3A)–

(a) the earnings to be taken into account as reckonable earnings are those paid or payable to or for the benefit of earners in employment which is contracted-out by reference to the scheme in the whole or any part of the period of 12 months there mentioned; and

(b) earners are to be identified as contributing or non-contributing in relation to service of theirs in employment which is contracted-out by reference to the scheme according to whether or not in the period in question they were liable under the terms of the scheme to contribute in respect of that service towards the provision of pensions under the scheme.

**History**

In para. 2(4), the words "sub-paragraph (3A)" substituted for the former words "sub-paragraph (3)" by Welfare Reform and Pensions Act 1999, s. 18 and Sch. 2, para. 8(3) with effect from 25 April 2000 (see Welfare Reform and Pensions Act 1999 (Commencement No. 4) Order 2000 (SI 2000/1047 (C. 29)), art. 2(2) and Sch., Pt. II).

**2(5)** In this paragraph–

**"employer"** shall be construed in accordance with regulations made under section 181(2); and

**"reckonable earnings"**, in relation to any employment, means the earner's earnings from that employment so far as those earnings–

(a) were comprised in any payment of earnings made to him or for his benefit at a time when the employment was contracted-out employment; and

(b) exceeded the current lower earnings limit but not the current upper earnings limit.

## STATE SCHEME PREMIUMS

**3(1)** This Schedule applies to any sum owed on account of a state scheme premium payable at any time before, or in consequence of; a person going into liquidation or beings adjudged bankrupt, or in Scotland, the sequestration of a debtor's estate, or (in the case a company not in liquidation)–

(a) the appointment of a receiver as mentioned in section 40 of the Insolvency Act 1986 (debenture-holders secured by floating charge), or

(b) the appointment of a receiver under section 53(6) or 54(5) of that Act (Scottish company with property subject to floating charge), or

(c) the taking of possession by debenture-holders (so secured) as mentioned section 196 of the Companies Act 1985.

**3(2)** Where any such premium is payable in respect of a period of service of more than 12 months (taking into account any previous linked qualifying service), the amount to be paid in priority by virtue of this paragraph shall be limited to the amount of the premium that would have been payable if the service had been confined to the last 12 months taken into account in fixing the actual amount of the premium.

**3(3)** Where–

(a) by virtue of this paragraph the whole or part of a premium is required to be paid in priority to other debts of the debtor or his estate; and

(b) the person liable for the payment would be entitled to recover the whole or part of any sum paid on account of it from another person either under section 61 or under any provision made by the relevant scheme for the purposes of that section or otherwise,

then, subject to sub-paragraph (4), that other person shall be liable for any part of the premium for the time being unpaid.

**3(4)** No person shall be liable by virtue of sub-paragraph (3) for an amount in excess of the sum which might be so recovered from him if the premium had been paid in full by the person liable for it, after deducting from that sum any amount which has been or may be recovered from him in respect of any part of that payment paid otherwise than under that sub-paragraph.

**3(5)** The payment under sub-paragraph (3) of any amount in respect of a premium shall have the same effect on the rights and liabilities of the person making it (other than his liabilities under that sub-paragraph) as if it had been a payment of that amount on account of the sum recoverable from him in respect of a premium as mentioned in sub-paragraph (3)(b).

### INTERPRETATION

**4(1)** In this Schedule–

(a) in its application in England and Wales, section 196(3) of the Companies Act 1985 and section 387 of the Insolvency Act 1986 apply as regards the meaning of the expression "the relevant date"; and

(b) in its application in Scotland, that expression has the same meaning as in Part I of Schedule 3 to the Bankruptcy (Scotland) Act 1985.

**4(2)** In this Schedule references to a contracted-out scheme, contracted-out employment and a state scheme premium include references to a contracted-out scheme, contracted out employment and a state scheme premium (other than a personal pension protected rights premium) within the meaning of any provisions in force in Northern Ireland and corresponding to the provisions of this Act.

# INSOLVENCY ACT 1994

(1994 Chapter 7)

An Act to amend the Insolvency Act 1986 in relation to contracts of employment adopted by administrators, administrative receivers and certain other receivers; and to make corresponding provision for Northern Ireland.

[*24th March 1994*]

## 1 Administrators: priority of liabilities under adopted contracts of employment

**1(1)–(6)** [Amendments to s. 19 of Insolvency Act 1986]

**1(7)** **[Effective date]** This section shall have effect in relation to contracts of employment adopted on or after 15th March 1994.

## 2 Administrative receivers: extent of personal liability on adopted contracts of employment

**2(1)–(3)** [Amendments to s. 44 of Insolvency Act 1986]

**2(4) [Effective date]** This section shall have effect in relation to contracts of employment adopted on or after 15th March 1994.

## 3 Receivers (Scotland): extent of personal liability on, and agency in relation to, adopted contracts of employment

**3(1)–(4)** [Amendments to s. 57 of Insolvency Act 1986]

**3(5) [Effective date]** This section shall have effect in relation to contracts of employment adopted on or after 15th March 1994.

## 4 Corresponding provision for Northern Ireland

**4** Schedule 1 to this Act (which makes provision for Northern Ireland corresponding to that made by sections 1 and 2 above) shall have effect.

## 5 Short title, repeals and extent

**5(1) [Citation]** This Act may be cited as the Insolvency Act 1994.

**5(2) [Sch. 2]** The enactments mentioned in Schedule 2 to this Act are hereby repealed to the extent specified in the third column of that Schedule.

**5(3) [Extent of amendments, repeals]** The extent of any amendment or repeal of an enactment made by this Act is the same as that of the enactment amended or repealed.

# SCHEDULES

## Schedule 1 – Corresponding Provision for Northern Ireland

Section 4

**1(1)** Article 31 of the Insolvency (Northern Ireland) Order 1989 (vacation of office) shall be amended as follows.

**1(2)** In paragraph (3) (which provides for paragraphs (4) and (5) to apply where a person ceases to be administrator) for "paragraphs (4) and (5)" there shall be substituted "the following paragraphs".

**1(3)** In paragraph (5) (which provides for certain debts and liabilities incurred during administration, including those incurred under contracts of employment adopted by the administrator, to be charged on the company's property in priority to his remuneration and expenses) the words "or contracts of employment adopted" and the words from "and for the purpose" to the end shall be omitted.

**1(4)** At the end there shall be inserted–

"(6) Any sums payable in respect of liabilities incurred, while he was administrator, under contracts of employment adopted by him or a predecessor of his in the carrying out of his or the predecessor's functions shall, to the extent that the liabilities are qualifying liabilities, be charged on and paid out of any such property as is mentioned in paragraph (4) and enjoy the same priority as any sums to which paragraph (5) applies; and for the purpose of this paragraph the administrator is not to be taken to have adopted a contract of employment by reason of anything done or omitted to be done within 14 days from his appointment.

(7) For the purposes of paragraph (6), a liability under a contract of employment is a qualifying liability if–

(a) it is a liability to pay a sum by way of wages or salary or contribution to an occupational pension scheme, and
(b) it is in respect of services rendered wholly or partly after the adoption of the contract.

(8) There shall be disregarded for the purposes of paragraph (6) so much of any qualifying liability as represents payment in respect of services rendered before the adoption of the contract.

(9) For the purposes of paragraphs (7) and (8)–
(a) wages or salary payable in respect of a period of holiday or absence from work through sickness or other good cause are deemed to be wages or (as the case may be) salary in respect of services rendered in that period, and
(b) a sum payable in lieu of holiday is deemed to be wages or (as the case may be) salary in respect of services rendered in the period by reference to which the holiday entitlement arose.

(10) In paragraph (9)(a), the reference to wages or salary payable in respect of a period of holiday includes any sums which, if they had been paid, would have been treated for the purposes of the statutory provisions relating to social security as earnings in respect of that period."

**2(1)** Article 54 of the Insolvency (Northern Ireland) Order 1989 (personal liability of administrative receiver for certain contracts) shall be amended as follows.

**2(2)** In paragraph (1)(b) (liability for contracts of employment adopted in carrying out his functions) after "provides) and " there shall be inserted ", to the extent of any qualifying liability,".

**2(3)** After paragraph (2) there shall be inserted–

"(2A) For the purposes of paragraph (1)(b), a liability under a contract of employment is a qualifying liability if–
(a) it is liability to pay a sum by way of wages or salary or contribution to an occupational pension scheme,
(b) it is incurred while the administrative receiver is in office, and
(c) it is in respect of services rendered wholly or partly after the adoption of the contract.

(2B) Where a sum payable in respect of a liability which is a qualifying liability for the purposes of paragraph (1)(b) is payable in respect of services rendered partly before and partly after the adoption of the contract, liability under paragraph (1)(b) shall only extend to so much of the sum as is payable in respect of services rendered after the adoption of the contract.

(2C) For the purposes of paragraphs (2A) and (2B)–
(a) wages or salary payable in respect of a period of holiday or absence from work through sickness or other good cause are deemed to be wages or (as the case may be) salary in respect of services rendered in that period, and
(b) a sum payable in lieu of holiday is deemed to be wages or (as the case may be) salary in respect of services rendered in the period by reference to which the holiday entitlement arose.

(2D) In paragraph (2C)(a), the reference to wages or salary payable in respect of a period of holiday includes any sums which, if they had been paid, would have been treated for the purposes of the statutory provisions relating to social security as earnings in respect of that period."

**3** The preceding provisions shall have effect in relation to contracts of employment adopted on or after 15th March 1994.

## Schedule 2 – Repeals

Section 5

| Chapter | Short title | Extent of repeal |
|---|---|---|
| 1986 c. 45 | The Insolvency Act 1986. | In section 19(5), the words "or contracts of employment adopted". |
| SI 1989/2405 (N.I. 19) | The Insolvency (Northern Ireland) Order 1989. | In Article 31(5), the words "or contracts of employment adopted" and the words from "and for the purpose" to the end. |

# INSOLVENCY (No. 2) ACT 1994

(1994 Chapter 12)

An Act to amend the law relating to company insolvency and winding up, and the insolvency and bankruptcy of individuals, so far as it concerns the adjustment of certain transactions; and for connected purposes.

[*26th May 1994*]

## 1 Adjustment of certain transactions in case of liquidation etc: England and Wales

**1(1)–(3)** [Amendments to s. 241 of Insolvency Act 1986]

## 2 Adjustment of certain transactions in case of bankruptcy: England and Wales

**2(1)–(3)** [Amendments to s. 342 of Insolvency Act 1986]

## 3 Adjustment of certain transactions in case of liquidation etc: Northern Ireland

**3(1) [Amendment of art. 205(2) of Insolvency Order]** In paragraph (2) of Article 205 of the Insolvency (Northern Ireland) Order 1989 (which relates to orders under Article 202 or 203 and, in sub-paragraphs (a) and (b), protects certain interests and certain persons who received benefits) in each of sub-paragraphs (a) and (b), for the words "in good faith, for value and without notice of the relevant circumstances" there shall be substituted "in good faith and for value".

**3(2) [Insertion of art. 205(2A)]** After that paragraph there shall be inserted the following paragraph–

"(2A) Where a person has acquired an interest in property from a person other than the company in question, or has received a benefit from the transaction or preference, and at the time of that acquisition or receipt–

(a) he had notice of the relevant surrounding circumstances and of the relevant proceedings, or

(b) he was connected with, or was an associate of, either the company in question or the person with whom that company entered into the transaction or to whom that company gave the preference, then, unless the contrary is shown, it shall be presumed for the purposes of sub-paragraph (a) or (as the case may be) sub-paragraph (b) of paragraph (2) that the interest was acquired or the benefit was received otherwise than in good faith."

**3(3) [Substitution of new art. 205(3)–(3C)]** For paragraph (3) of that Article there shall be substituted the following paragraphs–

"(3) For the purposes of paragraph (2A)(a), the relevant surrounding circumstances are (as the case may require)–

(a) the fact that the company in question entered into the transaction at an undervalue; or

(b) the circumstances which amounted to the giving of the preference by the company in question;

and paragraphs (3A) to (3C) have effect to determine whether, for those purposes, a person has notice of the relevant proceedings.

(3A) In a case where Article 202 or 203 applies by reason of the making of an administration order, a person has notice of the relevant proceedings if he has notice–

(a) of the fact that the petition on which the administration order is made has been presented; or

(b) of the fact that the administration order has been made.

(3B) In a case where Article 202 or 203 applies by reason of the company in question going into liquidation immediately upon the discharge of an administration order, a person has notice of the relevant proceedings if he has notice–

(a) of the fact that the petition on which the administration order is made has been presented;

(b) of the fact that the administration order has been made; or

(c) of the fact that the company has gone into liquidation.

(3C) In a case where Article 202 or 203 applies by reason of the company in question going into liquidation at any other time, a person has notice of the relevant proceedings if he has notice–

(a) where the company goes into liquidation on the making of a winding-up order, of the fact that the petition on which the winding-up order is made has been presented or of the fact that the company has gone into liquidation;

(b) in any other case, of the fact that the company has gone into liquidation."

## 4 Adjustment of certain transactions in case of bankruptcy: Northern Ireland

**4(1) [Amendment of art. 315(2) of Insolvency Order]** In paragraph (2) of Article 315 of the Insolvency (Northern Ireland) Order 1989 (which relates to orders under Article 312 or 313 and, in sub-paragraphs (a) and (b), protects certain interests and certain persons who received benefits) in each of sub-paragraphs (a) and (b), for the words "in good faith, for value and without notice of the relevant circumstances" there shall be substituted "in good faith and for value".

**4(2) [Insertion of art. 315(2A)]** After that paragraph there shall be inserted the following paragraph–

"(2A) Where a person has acquired an interest in property from a person other than the individual in question, or has received a benefit from the transaction or preference, and at the time of that acquisition or receipt–

(a) he had notice of the relevant surrounding circumstances and of the relevant proceedings, or

(b) he was an associate of, or was connected with, either the individual in question or the person with whom that individual entered into the transaction or to whom that individual gave the preference, then, unless the contrary is shown, it shall be presumed for the purposes of sub-paragraph (a) or (as the case may be) sub-paragraph (b) of paragraph (2) that the interest was acquired or the benefit was received otherwise than in good faith."

**4(3) [Substitution of new art. 315(4)–(6)]** For paragraph (4) of that Article there shall be substituted the following paragraphs–

"(4) For the purposes of paragraph (2A)(a), the relevant surrounding circumstances are (as the case may require)–

(a) the fact that the individual in question entered into the transaction at an undervalue; or

(b) the circumstances which amounted to the giving of the preference by the individual in question.

(5) For the purposes of paragraph (2A)(a), a person has notice of the relevant proceedings if he has notice–

(a) of the fact that the petition on which the individual in question is adjudged bankrupt has been presented; or

(b) of the fact that the individual in question has been adjudged bankrupt.

(6) Article 7 shall apply for the purposes of paragraph (2A)(b) as it applies for the purposes of Parts II to VII."

## 5 Application to the Crown

**5(1) [Amendments bind Crown]** The amendments of the Insolvency Act 1986 made by this Act bind the Crown.

**5(2) [Amendments in Insolvency Order bind Crown]** The amendments of the Insolvency (Northern Ireland) Order 1989 made by this Act bind the Crown in accordance with Article 378 of that Order.

## 6 Short title, commencement and extent

**6(1) [Citation]** This Act may be cited as the Insolvency (No. 2) Act 1994.

**6(2) [Commencement]** This Act shall come into force at the end of the period of two months beginning with the day on which it is passed.

**6(3) [Interest and benefits after commencement]** This Act has effect in relation to interests acquired and benefits received after this Act comes into force.

**6(4) [Extent of s. 1, 2, 5(1)]** Sections 1, 2 and 5(1) above extend to England and Wales only.

**6(5) [Extent of s. 3, 4, 5(2)]** Sections 3, 4 and 5(2) above extend to Northern Ireland only.

**6(6) [Extent of s. 6]** This section extends to England and Wales and Northern Ireland only.

# EMPLOYMENT RIGHTS ACT 1996

(1996 Chapter 18)

*[22nd May 1996]*

[**Note:** Reproduced below are the provisions of Pt. XII, that is s. 182–190. Under s. 243 of the Act, they came into force on 22 August 1996. They replace s. 122, 124–127 of the Employment Protection (Consolidation) Act 1978 which were repealed by s. 242 and Sch. 3, Pt. I of the 1996 Act.]

# PART XII – INSOLVENCY OF EMPLOYERS

## 182 Employee's rights on insolvency of employer

**182** If, on an application made to him in writing by an employee, the Secretary of State is satisfied that–

(a) the employee's employer has become insolvent,

(b) the employee's employment has been terminated, and

(c) on the appropriate date the employee was entitled to be paid the whole or part of any debt to which this Part applies,

the Secretary of State shall, subject to section 186, pay the employee out of the National Insurance Fund the amount to which, in the opinion of the Secretary of State, the employee is entitled in respect of the debt.

## 183 Insolvency

**183(1) [Insolvency of employer]** An employer has become insolvent for the purposes of this Part–

(a) where the employer is an individual, if (but only if) subsection (2) is satisfied, and

(b) where the employer is a company, if (but only if) subsection (3) is satisfied.

**183(2) [Insolvent individual employer]** This subsection is satisfied in the case of an employer who is an individual–

(a) in England and Wales if–
  (i) he has been adjudged bankrupt or has made a composition or arrangement with his creditors, or
  (ii) he has died and his estate falls to be administered in accordance with an order under section 421 of the Insolvency Act 1986, and

(b) in Scotland if–
  (i) sequestration of his estate has been awarded or he has executed a trust deed for his creditors or has entered into a composition contract, or
  (ii) he has died and a judicial factor appointed under section 11A of the Judicial Factors (Scotland) Act 1889 is required by that section to divide his insolvent estate among his creditors.

**183(3) [Insolvent company employer]** This subsection is satisfied in the case of an employer which is a company–

(a) if a winding up order or an administration order has been made, or a resolution for voluntary winding up has been passed, with respect to the company,

(b) if a receiver or (in England and Wales only) a manager of the company's undertaking has been duly appointed, or (in England and Wales only) possession has been taken, by or on behalf of the holders of any debentures secured by a floating charge, of any property of the company comprised in or subject to the charge, or

(c) if a voluntary arrangement proposed in the case of the company for the purposes of Part I of the Insolvency Act 1986 has been approved under that Part of that Act.

## 184 Debts to which Part applies

**184(1) [Application of Pt. XII]** This Part applies to the following debts–

(a) any arrears of pay in respect of one or more (but not more than eight) weeks,

(b) any amount which the employer is liable to pay the employee for the period of notice required by section 86(1) or (2) or for any failure of the employer to give the period of notice required by section 86(1),

(c) any holiday pay–
  (i) in respect of a period or periods of holiday not exceeding six weeks in all, and
  (ii) to which the employee became entitled during the twelve months ending with the appropriate date,

(d) any basic award of compensation for unfair dismissal or so much of an award under a designated dismissal procedures agreement as does not exceed any basic award of compensation for unfair dismissal to which the employee would be entitled but for the agreement, and

(e) any reasonable sum by way of reimbursement of the whole or part of any fee or premium paid by an apprentice or articled clerk.

**History**

In s. 184(1)(d), the words "or so much of an award under a designated dismissal procedures agreement as does not exceed any basic award of compensation for unfair dismissal to which the employee would be entitled but for the agreement" inserted by Employment Rights (Dispute Resolution) Act 1998, s. 12(4) with effect from 1 August 1998 (see Employment Rights (Dispute Resolution) Act 1998 (Commencement and Transitional and Savings) Order 1998 (SI 1998/1658) (C. 53)), art. 2(1) and Sch 1.

**184(2) [Arrears of pay for s. 184(1)(a)]** For the purposes of subsection (1)(a) the following amounts shall be treated as arrears of pay–

(a) a guarantee payment,

(b) any payment for time off under Part VI of this Act or section 169 of the Trade Union and Labour Relations (Consolidation) Act 1992 (payment for time off for carrying out trade union duties etc.),

(c) remuneration on suspension on medical grounds under section 64 of this Act and remuneration on suspension on maternity grounds under section 68 of this Act, and

(d) remuneration under a protective award under section 189 of the Trade Union and Labour Relations (Consolidation) Act 1992.

**184(3) ["Holiday pay" in s. 184(1)(c)]** In subsection (1)(c) **"holiday pay"**, in relation to an employee, means–

(a) pay in respect of a holiday actually taken by the employee, or

(b) any accrued holiday pay which, under the employee's contract of employment, would in the ordinary course have become payable to him in respect of the period of a holiday if his employment with the employer had continued until he became entitled to a holiday.

**184(4) [Reasonable sum under s. 184(1)(e)]** A sum shall be taken to be reasonable for the purposes of subsection (1)(e) in a case where a trustee in bankruptcy, or (in Scotland) a permanent or interim trustee (within the meaning of the Bankruptcy (Scotland) Act 1985), or liquidator has been or is required to be appointed–

(a) as respects England and Wales, if it is admitted to be reasonable by the trustee in bankruptcy or liquidator under section 348 of the Insolvency Act 1986 (effect of bankruptcy on apprenticeships etc.), whether as originally enacted or as applied to the winding up of a company by rules under section 411 of that Act, and

(b) as respects Scotland, if it is accepted by the permanent or interim trustee or liquidator for the purposes of the sequestration or winding up.

## 185 The appropriate date

**185** In this Part **"the appropriate date"**–

(a) in relation to arrears of pay (not being remuneration under a protective award made under section 189 of the Trade Union and Labour Relations (Consolidation) Act 1992) and to holiday pay, means the date on which the employer became insolvent,

(b) in relation to a basic award of compensation for unfair dismissal and to remuneration under a protective award so made, means whichever is the latest of–

(i) the date on which the employer became insolvent,

(ii) the date of the termination of the employee's employment, and

(iii) the date on which the award was made, and

(c) in relation to any other debt to which this Part applies, means whichever is the later of–

(i) the date on which the employer became insolvent, and

(ii) the date of the termination of the employee's employment.

## 186 Limit on amount payable under s. 182

**186(1) [Maximum amount for Pt. XII]** The total amount payable to an employee in respect of any debt to which this Part applies, where the amount of the debt is referable to a period of time, shall not exceed–

(a) £230 in respect of any one week, or

(b) in respect of a shorter period, an amount bearing the same proportion to £230 as that shorter period bears to a week.

**History**
In s. 186(1), the figure "£230" substituted for the former figure of "£220" by Employment Rights (Increase of Limits) Order 1999 (SI 1999/3375), art. 3 where the appropriate day (art. 4) falls on or after 1 February 2000. The figure "£220" previously substituted for the former figure "£210" by the Employment Rights (Increase of Limits) Order 1998 (SI 1998/924), art. 1, 3 and Sch. as from 1 April 1998.

**Note**
The figures in s. 186(1)(a) and (b) may be varied by the Secretary of State (see Employment Relations Act 1999, s. 34(1)(d)).

**186(2)** (Repealed by Employment Relations Act 1999, s. 36(1)(a), 44 and Sch 9, Pt. 10 with effect from 17 December 1999 (see Employment Relations Act 1999 (Commencement No. 3 and Transitional Provision) Order 1999 (SI 1999/3374 (C. 90), art. 2 and Sch.).)

**History**
S. 186(2) formerly read as follows:
"**186(2)** The Secretary of State may vary the limit specified in subsection (1), after a review under section 208, by order made in accordance with that section."

## 187 Role of relevant officer

**187(1) [No payment until statement received]** Where a relevant officer has been, or is required to be, appointed in connection with an employer's insolvency, the Secretary of State shall not make a payment under section 182 in respect of a debt until he has received a statement from the relevant officer of the amount of that debt which appears to have been owed to the employee on the appropriate date and to remain unpaid.

**187(2) [Power of Secretary of State to make payment]** If the Secretary of State is satisfied that he does not require a statement under subsection (1) in order to determine the amount of a debt which was owed to the employee on the appropriate date and remains unpaid, he may make a payment under section 182 in respect of the debt without having received such a statement.

**187(3) [Duty of relevant officer to provide statement]** A relevant officer shall, on request by the Secretary of State, provide him with a statement for the purposes of subsection (1) as soon as is reasonably practicable.

**187(4) [Relevant officers for purposes of s. 187]** The following are relevant officers for the purposes of this section–

(a) a trustee in bankruptcy or a permanent or interim trustee (within the meaning of the Bankruptcy (Scotland) Act 1985),

(b) a liquidator,

(c) an administrator,

(d) a receiver or manager,

(e) a trustee under a composition or arrangement between the employer and his creditors, and

(f) a trustee under a trust deed for his creditors executed by the employer.

**187(5) ["Trustee" in s. 187(4)(e)]** In subsection (4)(e) **"trustee"** includes the supervisor of a voluntary arrangement proposed for the purposes of, and approved under, Part I or VIII of the Insolvency Act 1986.

## 188 Complaints to industrial tribunals

**188(1) [Entitlement to present complaint]** A person who has applied for a payment under section 182 may present a complaint to an industrial tribunal–

(a) that the Secretary of State has failed to make any such payment, or

(b) that any such payment made by him is less than the amount which should have been paid.

**188(2) [Time-limit for presentation of complaint]** An industrial tribunal shall not consider a complaint under subsection (1) unless it is presented–

(a) before the end of the period of three months beginning with the date on which the decision of the Secretary of State on the application was communicated to the applicant, or

(b) within such further period as the tribunal considers reasonable in a case where it is not reasonably practicable for the complaint to be presented before the end of that period of three months.

**188(3) [Declaration by tribunal]** Where an industrial tribunal finds that the Secretary of State ought to make a payment under section 182, the tribunal shall–

(a) make a declaration to that effect, and

(b) declare the amount of any such payment which it finds the Secretary of State ought to make.

## 189 Transfer to Secretary of State of rights and remedies

**189(1) [Where s. 182 payment made to employee]** Where, in pursuance of section 182, the Secretary of State makes a payment to an employee in respect of a debt to which this Part applies–

(a) on the making of the payment any rights and remedies of the employee in respect of the debt (or, if the Secretary of State has paid only part of it, in respect of that part) become rights and remedies of the Secretary of State, and

(b) any decision of an industrial tribunal requiring an employer to pay that debt to the employee has the effect that the debt (or the part of it which the Secretary of State has paid) is to be paid to the Secretary of State.

**189(2) [Extent of rights and remedies re s. 182]** Where a debt (or any part of a debt) in respect of which the Secretary of State has made a payment in pursuance of section 182 constitutes–

(a) a preferential debt within the meaning of the Insolvency Act 1986 for the purposes of any provision of that Act (including any such provision as applied by any order made under that Act) or any provision of the Companies Act 1985, or–

(b) a preferred debt within the meaning of the Bankruptcy (Scotland) Act 1985 for the purposes of any provision of that Act (including any such provision as applied by section 11A of the Judicial Factors (Scotland) Act 1889),

the rights which become rights of the Secretary of State in accordance with subsection (1) include any right arising under any such provision by reason of the status of the debt (or that part of it) as a preferential or preferred debt.

**189(3) [Computation of debts in s. 189(2)]** In computing for the purposes of any provision mentioned in subsection (2)(a) or (b) the aggregate amount payable in priority to other creditors of the employer in respect of–

(a) any claim of the Secretary of State to be paid in priority to other creditors of the employer by virtue of subsection (2), and

(b) any claim by the employee to be so paid made in his own right,

any claim of the Secretary of State to be so paid by virtue of subsection (2) shall be treated as if it were a claim of the employee.

**189(4) [Secretary of State to be paid before employee]** But the Secretary of State shall be entitled, as against the employee, to be so paid in respect of any such claim of his (up to the full amount of the claim) before any payment is made to the employee in respect of any claim by the employee to be so paid made in his own right.

**189(5) [Sum recovered to be paid into National Insurance Fund]** Any sum recovered by the Secretary of State in exercising any right, or pursuing any remedy, which is his by virtue of this section shall be paid into the National Insurance Fund.

## 190 Power to obtain information

**190(1) [Power of Secretary of State on application]** Where an application is made to the Secretary of State under section 182 in respect of a debt owed by an employer, the Secretary of State may require–

(a) the employer to provide him with such information as he may reasonably require for the purpose of determining whether the application is well-founded, and

(b) any person having the custody or control of any relevant records or other documents to produce for examination on behalf of the Secretary of State any such document in that person's custody or under his control which is of such a description as the Secretary of State may require.

**190(2) [Requirement by notice, etc.]** Any such requirement–

(a) shall be made by notice in writing given to the person on whom the requirement is imposed, and

(b) may be varied or revoked by a subsequent notice so given.

**190(3) [Penalty for refusal, etc.]** If a person refuses or wilfully neglects to furnish any information or produce any document which he has been required to furnish or produce by a notice under this section he is guilty of an offence and liable on summary conviction to a fine not exceeding level 3 on the standard scale.

**190(4) [Penalty for false statement]** If a person, in purporting to comply with a requirement of a notice under this section, knowingly or recklessly makes any false statement he is guilty of an offence and liable on summary conviction to a fine not exceeding level 5 on the standard scale.

**190(5) [Offence by body corporate and officers under s. 190]** Where an offence under this section committed by a body corporate is proved–

(a) to have been committed with the consent or connivance of, or

(b) to be attributable to any neglect on the part of,

any director, manager, secretary or other similar officer of the body corporate, or any person who was purporting to act in any such capacity, he (as well as the body corporate) is guilty of the offence and liable to be proceeded against and punished accordingly.

**190(6) [Application of s. 190(5)]** Where the affairs of a body corporate are managed by its members, subsection (5) applies in relation to the acts and defaults of a member in connection with his functions of management as if he were a director of the body corporate.

# BANK OF ENGLAND ACT 1998

(1998 Chapter 11)

[*23rd April 1998*]

[**Note:** Only provisions relating to banking supervision included. The Act entered into force on 1 June 1998 (see s. 2 and the Bank of England Act 1998 (Commencement) Order 1998 (SI 1998/1120 (C. 25)), art. 2).]

## PART III – TRANSFER OF SUPERVISORY FUNCTIONS OF THE BANK TO THE FINANCIAL SERVICES AUTHORITY

TRANSFER OF FUNCTIONS TO THE AUTHORITY

### 21 Transfer

**21** The following functions of the Bank are hereby transferred to the Authority–

(a) its functions under–

(i) the Banking Act 1987,

(ii) the Banking Coordination (Second Council Directive) Regulations 1992, and

(iii) section 101(4) of the Building Societies Act 1986,
(banking supervision functions),

(b) its functions under–
(i) section 43 of the Financial Services Act 1986, and
(ii) Investment Services Regulations 1995,
(functions relating to the listing of money market institutions), and

(c) its functions under section 171 of the Companies Act 1989 (functions relating to the listing of persons providing settlement arrangements).

## 22 Supplementary provisions

**22** Schedule 4 (transfer of functions: supplementary provisions) shall have effect.

## 23 Consequential amendments

**23(1) [Sch. 5 to have effect]** Schedule 5 (amendments of primary, and other principal, legislation consequential on the transfer of functions by section 21) shall have effect.

**23(2) [Amendment or revocation in consequence of Pt. III]** The Treasury may by order make such amendments or revocations of any instrument made under an Act as they think necessary or expedient in consequence of the transfer of functions by this Part.

**23(3) [Reference to the Bank]** If a reference in a relevant provision to the Bank is predicated on the continuing exercise by the Bank of any of the transferred functions, it shall, in relation to any time after the coming into force of this Act, have effect as a reference to the Authority.

**23(4) ["Relevant provision"]** In subsection (3), **"Relevant provision"** means a provision which–

(a) has effect before, as well as after, the coming into force of this Act, and

(b) is contained in a document other than an Act or an instrument made under an Act.

AUTHORITY'S POSITION IN RELATION TO TRANSFERRED FUNCTIONS

## 24 Status

**24** In relation to the carrying out of any of the transferred functions–

(a) the Authority shall not be regarded as acting on behalf of the Crown, and

(b) its members, officers and servants shall not be regarded as Crown servants.

## 25 Liability

**25(1)** [Insertion of s. 43(5) into the Financial Services Act 1986.]

**25(2)** [Insertion of reg. 26(6) into the Investment Services Regulations 1995 (SI 1995/3275).]

**25(3)** [Insertion of s. 171(6A) into the Companies Act 1989.]

## 26 Power to charge fees

**26(1) [Sch. 6 to have effect]** Schedule 6 (banking supervision fees) shall have effect.

**26(2)** [Insertion of s. 43(2A), (2B) into the Financial Services Act 1986.]

**26(3)** [Insertion of s. 171(3A), (3B) into the Companies Act 1989.]

## 27 Power to channel information through agent

**27 [Amendment to s. 39(1)(a)]** In section 39(1)(a) of the Banking Act 1987 (power to require the provision of information)–

(a) after "provide the Bank," there is inserted "or such person acting on behalf of the Authority as may be specified in the notice,", and

(b) for "specified in the notice" there is substituted "so specified".

CONSEQUENTIAL CHANGES TO BANKING BODIES

## 28 Board of Banking Supervision

**28(1) [Substitution of s. 2(1), (2)]** In section 2 of the Banking Act 1987 (Board of Banking Supervision), for subsections (1) and (2) there is substituted–

"(1) There shall continue to be a committee known as the Board of Banking Supervision.

(2) The Board shall consist of–

(a) two ex officio members, namely, the Chairman of the Authority and the holder of such other office within the Authority as the Chairman of the Authority may designate for the purposes of this provision; and

(b) six independent members, that is to say, members appointed jointly by the Chancellor of the Exchequer and the Chairman of the Authority, being persons having no executive responsibility in the Authority.

(2A) The independent members shall elect one of their number to chair the Board."

**28(2) [Amendments to s. 2]** In that section, in subsections (3), (4), (6) and (7), for "Bank", wherever occurring, there is substituted "Authority".

**28(3) [Amendment to Sch. 1]** In Schedule 1 to that Act (Board of Banking Supervision), for "Bank", wherever occurring, there is substituted "Authority".

## 29 Deposit Protection Board

**29(1) [Amendments to Sch. 4]** Schedule 4 to the Banking Act 1987 (Deposit Protection Board) paragraph 1 (constitution) is amended as follows.

**29(2) [Substitution of para. 1(1)(a) to (c)]** In sub-paragraph (1), for paragraphs (a) to (c) (ex officio members of the Board) there is substituted–

"(a) the Chairman of the Authority, who shall chair the Board;

(b) the holder of such other office within the Authority as the Chairman of the Authority may designate for the purposes of this provision; and

(c) the Deputy Governor of the Bank of England responsible for financial stability;"

**29(3) [Substitution of para. 1(2)]** For sub-paragraph (2) there is substituted–

"(2) The Chairman of the Authority shall appoint as ordinary members of the Board–

(a) three persons who are directors, controllers or managers of contributory institutions; and

(b) persons who are officers or employees of the Authority."

**29(4) [Substitution of para. 1(3)]** For sub-paragraph (3) there is substituted–

"(3) An ex officio member of the Board may appoint an alternate member to perform his duties as a member in his absence as follows–

(a) the Chairman of the Authority or the holder of a designated office within the Authority may appoint an officer or employee of the Authority, and

(b) the Deputy Governor of the Bank of England may appoint an officer or employee of the Bank."

**29(5) [Amendment to para. 1(4)]** In sub-paragraph (4) (appointment of alternates for ordinary members), in paragraph (b), for "Bank" there is substituted "Authority".

SUPPLEMENTARY

## 30 Interpretation of Part III

**30** In this Part–

**"the Authority"** means the Financial Services Authority;

**"transferred functions"** means the functions transferred to the Authority by this Part.

# PART IV – MISCELLANEOUS AND GENERAL

## MISCELLANEOUS

## 31 Qualifications of a designated agency.

31 [Amendments to Sch. 7, para. 1 to the Financial Services Act 1986.]

## 32 Listed institutions: exemption of transactions with Treasury

32 In Schedule 5 to the Financial Services Act 1986 (transactions in relation to which institutions listed under section 43 are exempt from authorisation)–

(a) in paragraph 1, after "with another listed institution", there is inserted ", the Treasury",

(b) in paragraph 4(1)(b) and (2), after "listed institution" there is inserted ", the Treasury", and

(c) in paragraph 9(a), after "with another listed institution" there is inserted ", the Treasury".

## 33 Closure of National Savings Stock Register to gilts

**33(1) [Closure of National Savings Stock Register to gilts]** The Treasury may by order–

(a) make provision excluding gilts from registration in the Register on and after a day specified in the order,

(b) make provision for the transfer to the books of the Bank of the entries in the Register at the beginning of the day specified under paragraph (a) which relate to gilts, and

(c) make provision for the transfer to the Bank of rights and liabilities of the Director of Savings in relation to the registration of gilts in the Register or any transaction associated therewith.

**Note**

Power conferred by s. 33(1) exercised in National Savings Stock Register (Closure of Register to Gilts) Order 1998 (SI 1998/1446) which closed the register to the registration of gilts on or after 20 July 1998.

**33(2) [Power conferred by s. 33(1)(b)]** The power conferred by paragraph (b) of subsection (1) includes power to make provision in relation to gilts which were not registered in the Register at the beginning of the day specified under paragraph (a) of that subsection, but which should have been.

**33(3) [Order under s. 33(1) to contain necessary or expedient provisions]** An order under subsection (1) may contain such consequential, incidental, supplementary and transitional provisions as appear to the Treasury to be necessary or expedient.

**33(4) [Provisions re Director of Savings, Register]** Without prejudice to subsection (3), an order under subsection (1) may contain–

(a) provision requiring things done by, or in relation to, the Director of Savings, to be treated as done by, or in relation to, the Bank,

(b) provision requiring references in documents to the Register to be construed as references to the books of the Bank, and

(c) provision requiring certificates issued by the Director of Savings in relation to registration in the Register to be treated as issued by the Bank in relation to registration in the books of the Bank.

**33(5) [Provisions re different cases, amending enactments]** An order under subsection (1) may–

(a) make different provision for different cases, and

(b) contain provision amending, or repealing or revoking, an enactment contained in–

   (i) an Act, whenever passed, or

   (ii) an instrument, whenever made, under an Act, whenever passed.

**33(6) [Definitions]** In this section–

**"gilts"** means stock or bonds of any of the descriptions included in Part I of Schedule 11 to the Finance Act 1942 (whether on or after the passing of this Act); and

**"the Register"** means the National Savings Stock Register.

## 34 Provision of brokerage service in connection with gilt registration.

34 **[Insertion of s. 47(1ZA) into the Finance Act 1942]** In section 47 of the Finance Act 1942 (transfer and registration of Government stock), after subsection (1) there is inserted–

"(1ZA) Regulations under subsection (1) of this section may make provision with respect to the purchase and sale of such stock and bonds by any person, or any description of person, through the Bank of England and, in relation to purchase or sale under the regulations, may–

(a) make provision with respect to the commission and fees payable, and

(b) make provision limiting the amount which any person, or any description of person, may purchase or sell on any day."

## 35 Section 207 of the Companies Act 1989: bearer securities

35 [Insertion of s. 207(10) into the Companies Act 1989.]

## 36 Disclosure of information: minor amendments

36(1) **[Amendment of s. 86(2)(a)]** In the Banking Act 1987, in section 86(2)(a), after "functions" there is inserted "or any functions in its capacity as a designated agency within the meaning of the Financial Services Act 1986".

36(2) **[Amendment of s. 86(5)]** Section 86(5) of that Act as applied by paragraph 57(1) of Schedule 5 shall have effect with the following modifications–

(a) in the definition of "relevant functions", at the end there is inserted "and its functions as a supervisor of systems for the transfer of funds between credit institutions and their customers", and

(b) in the definition of "relevant recipient", for "1 to 8" there is substituted "1 to 9".

36(3) **[Amendment of s. 87(3A)]** Section 87(3A) of that Act as applied by paragraph 59(1) of Schedule 5 shall have effect with the following modifications–

(a) in the definition of "relevant functions", at the end there is inserted "and its functions as a supervisor of systems for the transfer of funds between credit institutions and their customers", and

(b) in the definition of "relevant recipient", for "1 to 8" there is substituted "1 to 9".

36(4) **[Amendments to Pt. V]** Part V of that Act shall have effect, in relation to information relating to the business or other affairs of institutions which are authorised institutions, but not credit institutions, within the meaning of that Act, with the amendments made by the following regulations–

(a) regulations 38, 39(2) to (4) and 40 to 42 of the Banking Coordination (Second Council Directive) Regulations 1992, and

(b) regulation 5 of the Financial Institutions (Prudential Supervision) Regulations 1996.

GENERAL

## 37 Restriction on disclosure of information

37 Schedule 7 (which restricts the disclosure of information obtained for monetary policy or cash ratio deposit purposes) shall have effect.

## 38 Offences in relation to supplying information to the Bank

38(1) **[Penalty]** A person who fails without reasonable excuse to comply with any requirement imposed on him under section 17(1) or paragraph 9 of Schedule 2 shall be guilty of an offence and liable on summary conviction to a fine not exceeding level 4 on the standard scale.

38(2) **[Penalty for continuing failure]** If after conviction of an offence under subsection (1) a person continues the failure for which he was convicted, he shall be guilty of a further offence under that subsection and liable on summary conviction to be punished accordingly.

**38(3) [Penalty for false or misleading information]** A person who in purported compliance with a requirement imposed on him under section 17(1) or paragraph 9 of Schedule 2 provides information which he knows to be false or misleading in a material particular, or recklessly provides information which is false or misleading in a material particular, shall be guilty of an offence and liable–

(a) on conviction on indictment, to imprisonment for a term not exceeding 2 years, or to a fine, or to both, or

(b) on summary conviction, to imprisonment for a term not exceeding 3 months, or to a fine not exceeding the statutory maximum, or to both.

## 39 Offences by bodies corporate

**39(1) [Offence by body corporate]** Where an offence under this Part committed by a body corporate is proved to have been committed with the consent or connivance of, or to be attributable to any neglect on the part of, any director, manager, secretary or other similar officer of the body corporate, or any person who was purporting to act in any such capacity, he, as well as the body corporate, shall be guilty of that offence and be liable to be proceeded against and punished accordingly.

**39(2) [Application of s. 39(1)]** Where the affairs of a body corporate are managed by its members, subsection (1) shall apply in relation to the acts and defaults of a member in connection with his functions of management as if he were a director of the body corporate.

## 40 Orders

**40(1) [Power of Treasury to make order]** Any power of the Treasury to make an order under this Act shall be exercisable by statutory instrument.

**40(2) [Approval of Houses of Parliament]** An order under–

section 17(4) or (5),
paragraph 1(2) or 5 of Schedule 2, or
paragraph 3(2) of Schedule 7,

shall not be made unless a draft of the order has been laid before and approved by resolution of each House of Parliament.

**40(3) [Statutory instrument subject to annulment]** A statutory instrument containing an order under–

section 23(2),
paragraph 2(2) or 8 of Schedule 2,
paragraph 1(5) of Schedule 4, or
paragraph 3(3) of Schedule 7,

shall be subject to annulment in pursuance of a resolution of either House of Parliament.

**40(4) [Statutory instrument containing order under s. 33]** A statutory instrument containing an order under section 33 shall be subject to annulment in pursuance of a resolution of the House of Commons.

**40(5) [Parliamentary procedure re order under s. 19]** Section 19 contains its own provisions about parliamentary procedure in relation to an order under that section.

## 41 General interpretation

**41** In this Act, "the Bank" means the Bank of England.

## 42 Transitional provisions and savings

**42** Schedule 8 (transitional provisions and savings) shall have effect.

## 43 Repeals

**43** The enactments and instruments specified in Schedule 9 are hereby repealed or revoked to the extent specified in the final column of that Schedule.

FINAL PROVISIONS

## 44 Extent

**44(1) [Northern Ireland]** This Act extends to Northern Ireland.

**44(2) [Channel Islands, Isle of Man]** Section 33 extends to the Channel Islands and the Isle of Man.

**44(3) [Extent of amendment, repeal or revocation]** The extent of any amendment, repeal or revocation by this Act is the same as that of the enactment amended, repealed or revoked.

## 45 Commencement

**45** This Act shall come into force on such day as the Treasury may by order appoint.

## 46 Short title

**46** This Act may be cited as the Bank of England Act 1998.

# SCHEDULES

## Schedule 4 – Transfer of Functions: Supplementary Provisions

Section 22

CONTINUITY OF EXERCISE OF FUNCTIONS

**1(1)** The transfer of functions by this Part shall not affect the validity of anything done (or having effect as if done) by or in relation to the Bank before the day on which this Act comes into force ("the transfer day").

**1(2)** Anything which, immediately before the transfer day, is in the process of being done by or in relation to the Bank may, if it relates to any of the transferred functions, be continued by or in relation to the Authority.

**1(3)** Anything done (or having effect as if done) by, or in relation to, the Bank before the transfer day for the purpose of, or in connection with, any of the transferred functions, shall, so far as is required for continuing its effect on and after that day, have effect as if done by, or in relation to, the Authority.

**1(4)** Any reference to the Bank in any document constituting or relating to anything to which the foregoing provisions of this paragraph apply shall, so far as is required for giving effect to those provisions, be construed as a reference to the Authority.

**1(5)** The Treasury may, in relation to any of the transferred functions, by order exclude, modify or supplement any of the foregoing provisions of this paragraph or make such other transitional provisions as they think necessary or expedient.

TRANSFER OF STAFF

**2** The transfer of functions by this Part shall be regarded for the purposes of the Transfer of Undertakings (Protection of Employment) Regulations 1981 as the transfer of part of an undertaking, whether or not it would be so regarded apart from this provision.

TRANSFER OF PROPERTY, RIGHTS AND LIABILITIES

**3(1)** The Bank shall make a scheme under this paragraph for the transfer to the Authority of such of the Bank's property, rights and liabilities as appear to the Bank appropriate to be so transferred in consequence of the transfer of functions by this Part.

**3(2)** A scheme under this paragraph made by the Bank shall not be capable of coming into force unless it is approved by the Treasury.

**Note**

See note after para. 3(7).

**3(3)** The Bank may not submit a scheme under this paragraph to the Treasury for their approval without the consent of the Authority.

**3(4)** Where a scheme under this paragraph is submitted to the Treasury for their approval, they may, before approving it, make such modifications to it as appear to them to be appropriate.

**3(5)** Where this sub-paragraph applies, the Treasury may, after consultation with the Bank and the Authority, make a scheme under this paragraph for the transfer to the Authority of such of the Bank's property, rights and liabilities as appear to them appropriate to be so transferred in consequence of the transfer of functions by this Part.

**3(6)** Sub-paragraph (5) applies if–

(a) the Bank fails, before such time as may be notified to it by the Treasury as the latest time for submission of a scheme under this paragraph, to submit such a scheme to them for their approval, or

(b) the Treasury decide not to approve a scheme that has been submitted to them by the Bank (either with or without modifications).

**3(7)** A scheme under this paragraph shall come into force on such day as the Treasury may by order appoint.

**Note**

The appointed day for the transfer scheme is 1 October 1998. See the Bank of England Act 1998 (Transfer Scheme Appointed Day) Order 1998 (SI 1998/2372).

**3(8)** When a scheme under this paragraph comes into force, the property, rights and liabilities of the Bank to which the scheme relates shall, by virtue of this paragraph and without further assurance, be transferred to and vested in the Authority in accordance with the provisions of the scheme.

**3(9)** The Bank shall provide the Treasury with all such information and other assistance as they may reasonably require for the purposes of, or otherwise in connection with, the exercise of any power conferred on them by this paragraph.

**4(1)** The property, rights and liabilities capable of being transferred in accordance with a scheme under paragraph 3 shall include property, rights and liabilities that would not otherwise be capable of being transferred or assigned by the Bank.

**4(2)** The transfers authorised by sub-paragraph (1) include transfers which are to take effect as if there were–

(a) no such requirement to obtain any person's consent or concurrence,

(b) no such liability in respect of a contravention of any other requirement, and

(c) no such interference with any interest or right,

as there would be, in the case of any transaction apart from this Act, by reason of provisions having effect (whether under any enactment or agreement or otherwise) in relation to the terms on which the Bank is entitled or subject in relation to any property, right or liability.

**5(1)** A scheme under paragraph 3 may also contain provision–

(a) for rights and liabilities to be transferred so as to be enforceable by or against both the Bank and the Authority,

(b) for the creation in favour of the Bank of an interest or right in or in relation to property transferred in accordance with the scheme,

(c) for giving effect to a transfer to the Authority in accordance with the scheme by the creation in favour of the Authority of an interest or right in or in relation to property retained by the Bank,

(d) for imposing on the Bank and the Authority obligations to enter into such written agreements with each other as may be specified in the scheme, and

(e) for imposing on either one of them obligations to execute such instruments in favour of the other as may be so specified.

**5(2)** An obligation imposed by a provision included in a scheme by virtue of sub-paragraph (1)(d) or (e) shall be enforceable by civil proceedings by the Bank or the Authority for an injunction or for any other appropriate relief.

**5(3)** A transaction of any description effected in pursuance of a provision included in a scheme by virtue of sub-paragraph (1)(d) or (e)–

(a) shall have effect subject to the provisions of any enactment which provides for transactions of that description to be registered in any statutory register, but

(b) subject to that, shall be binding on all other persons, notwithstanding that it would, apart from this provision, have required the consent or concurrence of any other person.

**6(1)** A scheme under paragraph 3 may make such supplemental, consequential and transitional provision for the purposes of, or in connection with, any transfer of property, rights or liabilities for which the scheme provides or in connection with any other provisions contained in the scheme as the Bank may consider appropriate.

**6(2)** In particular, such a scheme may provide–

(a) that for purposes connected with any transfer made in accordance with the scheme (including the transfer of rights and liabilities under an enactment) the Authority is to be treated as the same person in law as the Bank,

(b) that, so far as may be necessary for the purposes of or in connection with any such transfer, agreements made, transactions effected and other things done by or in relation to the Bank are to be treated as made, effected or done by or in relation to the Authority,

(c) that, so far as may be necessary for the purposes of or in connection with any such transfer, references to the Bank in any agreement (whether or not in writing), deed, bond, instrument or other document are to have effect with such modifications as are specified in the scheme,

(d) that proceedings commenced by or against the Bank are to be continued by or against the Authority, and

(e) that the Bank and the Authority are to co-operate with each other for the purposes of and in connection with the scheme.

# Schedule 5 – Transfer of Functions: Consequential Amendments

## Part I – Banking Supervision

### Chapter I – Banking Act 1987

1 The Banking Act 1987 is amended as follows.

2 In section 1–

(a) in subsection (1), for the words from the beginning to "Bank"); there is substituted "The Financial Services Authority (in this Act referred to as "the Authority")",

(b) in subsections (2) and (3), for "Bank" there is substituted "Authority", and

(c) in subsection (4)–

(i) for the words from the beginning to "Bank", in the second place where it occurs, there is substituted "Neither the Authority nor any person who is, or is acting as, an officer or servant of the Authority", and

(ii) for "Bank", in the third place where it occurs, there is substituted "Authority".

3 In sections 3(1) and 4(3), for "Bank" there is substituted "Authority".

4 In sections 7 to 10, for "Bank", wherever occurring, there is substituted "Authority".

5 In section 11–

(a) for "Bank", wherever occurring, except subsection (1A)(c), there is substituted "Authority", and

(b) in subsection (1A)(c)–

(i) for "the Bank is informed by The Securities and Investments Board, or" there is substituted "it appears to the Authority, or the Authority is informed by", and
(ii) in paragraph (ii), for "that Board or" there is substituted "the Authority or that".

**6** In section 12–
(a) for "Bank", wherever occurring, there is substituted "Authority", and
(b) in subsection (1)(a), for "Bank's" there is substituted "Authority's".

**7** In sections 12A to 17, for "Bank", wherever occurring, there is substituted "Authority".

**8** In section 19–
(a) for "Bank", wherever occurring, there is substituted "Authority", and
(b) in subsection (3), for "Bank's" there is substituted "Authority's".

**9** In sections 20 to 27, for "Bank", wherever occurring, there is substituted "Authority".

**10** In section 29–
(a) for "Bank", wherever occurring, there is substituted "Authority", and
(b) in subsection (3), for "Bank's", in both places, there is substituted "Authority's".

**11** In sections 30 to 34 and 36 to 42, for "Bank", wherever occurring, there is substituted "Authority".

**12** In section 43(1)–
(a) for "Bank" there is substituted "Authority", and
(b) for "Bank's" there is substituted "Authority's".

**13** In sections 46 to 49, for "Bank", wherever occurring, there is substituted "Authority".

**14** In sections 52(2A), 58(2A)(b), 59(1)(a) and (4), 65(1), 67(6), 68(7) and 69(7), for "Bank" there is substituted "Authority".

**15** In sections 70 to 72 and 75, for "Bank", wherever occurring, there is substituted "Authority".

**16** In section 76–
(a) for "Bank", wherever occurring, there is substituted "Authority", and
(b) in subsection (3)(b), for "Bank's" there is substituted "Authority's".

**17** In sections 77 to 80, for "Bank", wherever occurring, there is substituted "Authority".

**18** In sections 92 to 96, 99 to 101 and 105, for "Bank", wherever occurring, there is substituted "Authority".

**19** In section 106(1)–
(a) in the definition of "authorisation", for "Bank" there is substituted "Authority",
(b) after that definition there is inserted–
""the Authority" means the Financial Services Authority;", and
(c) in the definition of "relevant supervisory authority", in paragraph (b), for "Bank" there is substituted "Authority".

**20** In Schedule 3, for "Bank", wherever occurring, there is substituted "Authority".

## Chapter II – Banking Coordination (Second Council Directive) Regulations 1992

**21** The Banking Coordination (Second Council Directive) Regulations 1992 are amended as follows.

**22** [Amendment of reg. 2(1).]

**23** In regulations 8 to 10, for "Bank", wherever occurring, there is substituted "Authority".

**24** In regulation 11–
(a) for "Bank", wherever occurring, there is substituted "Authority", and
(b) in paragraph (1), for "Bank's" there is substituted "Authority's".

25 In regulations 12 to 13A, for "Bank", wherever occurring, there is substituted "Authority".

26 [Substitution of reg. 14.]

27 In regulations 20, 23, 38 and 58, for "Bank", wherever occurring, there is substituted "Authority".

28 In regulation 62(a), for "Bank's" there is substituted "Authority's".

29 In Schedules 2 and 3, for "Bank", wherever occurring, there is substituted "Authority".

30 [Omission of Sch. 4, para. 1(6)(a).]

31 In Schedules 5 to 7, for "Bank", wherever occurring, there is substituted "Authority".

32 In Schedule 8–

(a) for "Bank", wherever occurring, there is substituted "Authority", and

(b) for "Bank's" there is substituted "Authority's".

33 In Schedule 9, in paragraph 19(c), for "Bank" there is substituted "Authority".

34 In Schedule 10–

(a) in paragraph 33, for "Bank" there is substituted "Authority", and

(b) in paragraph 40(2), for "Bank of England" there is substituted "Financial Services Authority".

35 In Schedule 11, in paragraphs 4(6) and 5(2), for "Bank" there is substituted "Authority".

## Chapter III – Other Enactments

### CONSUMER CREDIT ACT 1974 (C. 39)

36 In the Consumer Credit Act 1974, in section 16(3)(f), for "Bank of England" there is substituted "Financial Services Authority".

### INSOLVENCY ACT 1986 (C. 45)

37 In the Insolvency Act 1986, in section 422(1), for "Bank of England" there is substituted "Financial Services Authority".

### BUILDING SOCIETIES ACT 1986 (C. 53)

38(1) Section 101 of the Building Societies Act 1986 is amended as follows.

38(2) In subsection (4), for "Bank", in both places, there is substituted "Authority".

38(3) In subsection (6)–

(a) for the definition of "the Bank" there is substituted–

""the Authority" means the Financial Services Authority", and

(b) in paragraph (c) of the definition of "financial institution", for "Bank" there is substituted "Authority".

### FINANCIAL SERVICES ACT 1986 (C. 60)

39 In the Financial Services Act 1986, in sections 128C(3)(a)(iii), 185(4) and 186(7), for "Bank of England" there is substituted "Financial Services Authority".

### INSOLVENCY (NORTHERN IRELAND) ORDER 1989 S.I. 1989/2405 (N.I. 19)

40 In the Insolvency (Northern Ireland) Order 1989, in Article 366, for "Bank of England" there is substituted "Financial Services Authority".

### COURTS AND LEGAL SERVICES ACT 1990 (C. 41)

41(1) The Courts and Legal Services Act 1990 is amended as follows.

41(2) In sections 37(8)(a) and 48(4)(a), the words "by the Bank of England" are omitted.

41(3) In section 52(6)–

(a) in paragraph (a), the words "by the Bank of England" are omitted, and

(b) for "with the Bank of England" there is substituted "with the Financial Services Authority".

**41(4)** In section 54(1), in the inserted subsection (2)(e)(i), the words "by the Bank of England," are omitted.

### CHARITIES ACT 1993 (C. 10)

**42** In the Charities Act 1993, in section 28(8)(b)(ii), for "Bank of England" there is substituted "Financial Services Authority".

### BUILDING SOCIETIES ACT 1997 (C. 32)

**43(1)** Section 32 of the Building Societies Act 1997 is amended as follows.

**43(2)** In subsection (1), for "Bank" there is substituted "Authority".

**43(3)** In subsection (3)(a), for "Governor of the Bank" there is substituted "Chairman of the Authority".

**43(4)** In subsection (7), for the definition of "the Bank" there is substituted–

""the Authority" means the Financial Services Authority."

# Part II – Supervision Under Section 43 of the Financial Services Act 1986

### FINANCIAL SERVICES ACT 1986 (C. 60)

**44(1)** Section 43 of the Financial Services Act 1986 is amended as follows.

**44(2)** In subsection (1), for "Bank of England" there is substituted "Financial Services Authority ("the Authority")".

**44(3)** In subsections (2) and (3), for "Bank of England" there is substituted "Authority".

**44(4)** In subsection (4), for "Bank" there is substituted "Authority".

### INVESTMENT SERVICES REGULATIONS 1995 (S.I. 1995/3275)

**45(1)** The Investment Services Regulations 1995 are amended as follows.

**45(2)** In regulation 2(1)–

(a) [Insertion of the definition of "the Authority".]

(b) [Amendment to the definition of "the Board".]

**45(3)** In regulations 17(4) and 18(2), for "Bank" there is substituted "Authority".

**45(4)** In regulation 26–

(a) in paragraph (2)–

(i) in sub-paragraph (b), for "Bank", in the first place where it occurs, there is substituted "Authority", and the words "by the Bank" are omitted, and

(ii) in sub-paragraph (c), for "Bank" there is substituted "Authority" and for "Bank's" there is substituted "Authority's", and

(b) in paragraphs (3) and (4), for "Bank", wherever occurring, there is substituted "Authority".

**45(5)** In regulation 42(10), at the end there is inserted "in a case in which it is the relevant regulator by virtue of regulation 46(5)(b)(i) below".

**45(6)** In regulation 44(2), for the words from the beginning to "person, the Bank," there is substituted "The Authority".

**45(7)** In regulation 46(5), for paragraphs (b) and (c) there is substituted

"and

(b) the Authority, in a case in which the firm in question–

(i) is subject, in providing core services, to rules made by the Authority, or

(ii) is not an authorised person and is an exempted person by virtue of being admitted to the list maintained for the purposes of section 43 of the Financial Services Act."

**45(8)** In regulation 54(1), for "Bank", wherever occurring, there is substituted "Authority".

**45(9)** In regulation 56, at the end there is inserted–

"(3) Paragraph (1) above does not have effect in relation to–

(a) any function acquired by virtue of the Bank of England Act 1998, or

(b) so much of any function as is exercisable by virtue of that Act."

**45(10)** In Schedule 6, in paragraphs 4(6)(b) and 7(5)(b), for "the Bank" there is substituted "it".

**45(11)** In that Schedule, in paragraph 8, the existing provision becomes sub-paragraph (1) and after that sub-paragraph there is inserted–

"(2) Sub-paragraph (1) above shall not apply where the decision is in relation to a UK authorised investment firm which is an exempted person by virtue of its inclusion in the list maintained for the purposes of section 43 of the Financial Services Act and which is not an authorised person."

# Part III – Supervision Under Section 171 of the Companies Act 1989

## COMPANIES ACT 1989 (C. 40)

**46** The Companies Act 1989 is amended as follows.

**47(1)** Section 171 is amended as follows.

**47(2)** In subsection (1), for "Bank of England" there is substituted

"Financial Services Authority ("the Authority")".

**47(3)** In subsection (2), for "Bank of England", in both places, there is substituted "Authority".

**47(4)** [Insertion of s. 171(2A).]

**47(5)** In subsection (3)(a), for "Bank of England" there is substituted "Authority".

**47(6)** [Insertion of s. 171(3C).]

**47(7)** In subsection (4), for "Bank of England" and "Bank" there is substituted "Authority".

**47(8)** In subsection (6), after "Bank of England" there is inserted "and the Authority".

**48(1)** Section 176 is amended as follows.

**48(2)** In subsection (2)(b), for "Bank of England" there is substituted "Financial Services Authority".

**48(3)** [Substitution of s. 176(6).]

## COMPANIES (NO. 2) (NORTHERN IRELAND) ORDER 1990 (S.I. 1990/1504 (N.I. 10))

**49(1)** The Companies (No. 2) (Northern Ireland) Order 1990 is amended as follows.

**50** In article 93(3), for "and the Bank of England" there is substituted ", the Bank of England and the Financial Services Authority".

**51(1)** Article 98 is amended as follows.

**51(2)** In paragraph (2)(b), for "Bank of England" there is substituted "Financial Services Authority".

**51(3)** For paragraph (6) there is substituted–

"(6) Before making regulations under this Article relating to a description of charges defined by reference to their being granted in favour of a person included in the list maintained by the Financial Services Authority for the purposes of section 171 of the Companies Act 1989, or in connection with exchange facilities or clearing services provided by a person included in that list, the Department shall consult the Treasury, the Authority and the Bank of England.

(6A) Before making regulations under this Article relating to a description of charges defined by reference to their being granted in favour of the Bank of England, or in connection with settlement arrangements provided by the Bank, the Department shall consult the Treasury and the Bank."

# Part IV – General: Disclosure of Information

## Chapter I – Banking Act 1987

**52** The Banking Act 1987 is amended as follows.

**53(1)** Section 83 is amended as follows.

**53(2)** In subsection (1)–

(a) for "Bank" there is substituted "Authority",

(b) after paragraph (a) there is inserted–

"(aa) its functions in its capacity as a designated agency within the meaning of the Financial Services Act 1986; or",

(c) paragraph (b) is omitted,

(d) in paragraph (c), the words "and gilt market" are omitted, and

(e) paragraph (d), and the word "or" immediately preceding it, are omitted.

**53(3)** In subsections (2) and (3), for "Bank", wherever occurring, there is substituted "Authority".

**54(1)** Section 84 is amended as follows.

**54(2)** In subsection (1), for "Bank", in both places, there is substituted "Authority".

**54(3)** In the Table in that subsection, after entry 4 there is inserted–

| | |
|---|---|
| "4A The Bank of England. | Functions in its capacity as a monetary authority or supervisor of systems for the transfer of funds between credit institutions and their customers." |

**54(4)** In that Table, in entry 18, for "Bank" there is substituted "Authority".

**54(5)** In subsections (2), (4), (5), (5A), (6) and (7), for "Bank", wherever occurring, there is substituted "Authority".

**55** In section 85(1) and (2), for "Bank", wherever occurring, there is substituted "Authority".

**56(1)** Section 86 is amended as follows.

**56(2)** In subsections (1), (2)(a), (3) and (4A), for "Bank", wherever occurring, there is substituted "Authority".

**56(3)** In subsection (5), for the definition of "relevant functions" there is substituted–

""relevant functions", in relation to the Authority, means its functions under this Act and its functions as a supervisor of money market institutions;".

**57(1)** Section 86 shall also have effect without the amendments made by paragraph 56 above or section 36(1) above, but with the substitution of the following for the definition of "relevant functions" in subsection (5)–

""relevant functions", in relation to the Bank, means its functions as a monetary authority;".

**57(2)** In its application by virtue of sub-paragraph (1), section 86 shall have effect as if the provisions of Part V of the Banking Act 1987 were not amended by the preceding paragraphs of this Part of this Schedule, but were amended as follows.

**57(3)** In section 84, in subsection (1), in the Table, after entry 1 there is inserted–

| | |
|---|---|
| "1A The Authority. | Functions under the Financial Services Act 1986 (other than as a designated agency within the meaning of that Act), the Banking Act 1987 or section 171 of the Companies Act 1989." |

**57(4)** In that section, for subsections (5) and (5A) there is substituted–

"(5) Section 82 above does not preclude the disclosure by the Bank of information to the Treasury if disclosure appears to the Bank to be in the public interest and in accordance with article 12(7) of the First Council Directive.

(5A) Section 82 above does not preclude the disclosure by the Bank of information to the Secretary of State for purposes other than those specified in relation to him in subsection (1) above if–

(a) the disclosure is made with the consent of the Treasury,

(b) the information relates to an authorised institution or former authorised institution and does not enable the financial affairs of any other identifiable person to be ascertained, and

(c) disclosure appears to the Bank to be–

(i) in the public interest, and

(ii) in accordance with article 12(7) of the First Council Directive."

**58(1)** Section 87 is amended as follows.

**58(2)** In subsection (2)–

(a) for "Bank" there is substituted "Authority", and

(b) for "subsection (3)" there is substituted "subsection (3)(ha)".

**58(3)** In subsection (3)–

(a) for "Bank" there is substituted "Authority", and

(b) for "paragraph (3)" there is substituted "paragraph (3)(ha)".

**58(4)** In subsections (3A) and (4), for "Bank" there is substituted "Authority"..

**59(1)** Section 87(2), (3) and (3A) shall also have effect without the amendments made by paragraph 58, but with the following modifications.

**59(2)** In subsections (2) and (3), the words "for the purpose of enabling or assisting it to discharge its functions under this Act or" are omitted.

**59(3)** In subsection (3A)–

(a) in paragraph (b), for "section 84(5)(a) or (5A)" there is substituted "section 84(5A)", and

(b) for """relevant functions" has the same meaning as in section 86 above" there is substituted """relevant functions", in relation to the Bank, means its functions as a monetary authority;".

**59(4)** In their application by virtue of sub-paragraph (1), section 87(2), (3) and (3A) shall have effect as if the provisions of Part V of the Banking Act 1987 were not amended by the preceding paragraphs of this Part of this Schedule, but were amended as follows.

**59(5)** In section 84, in subsection (1), in the Table, after entry 1 there is inserted–

| | |
|---|---|
| "1A The Authority. | Functions under the Financial Services Act 1986 (other than as a designated agency within the meaning of that Act), the Banking Act 1987 or section 171 of the Companies Act 1989." |

**59(6)** In that section, for subsection (5A) there is substituted–

"(5A) Section 82 above does not preclude the disclosure by the Bank of information to the Secretary of State for purposes other than those specified in relation to him in subsection (1) above if–

(a) the disclosure is made with the consent of the Treasury, and
(b) the information relates to an authorised institution or former authorised institution and does not enable the financial affairs of any other identifiable person to be ascertained, and
(c) disclosure appears to the Bank to be–
   (i) in the public interest, and
   (ii) in accordance with article 12(7) of the First Council Directive."

## Chapter II – Other Enactments

### CONSUMER CREDIT ACT 1974 (C. 39)

**60** In section 174(3A) of the Consumer Credit Act 1974–

(a) for "Bank of England" there is substituted "Financial Services Authority", and

(b) for "Bank" there is substituted "Authority".

### INSURANCE COMPANIES ACT 1982 (C. 50)

**61(1)** Paragraph 3 of Schedule 2B to the Insurance Companies Act 1982 is amended as follows.

**61(2)** In sub-paragraph (1), in the Table, after entry 1 there is inserted–

| "1A The Financial Services Authority. | Functions under the Financial Services Act 1986 (other than as a designated agency within the meaning of that Act), the Banking Act 1987 or section 171 of the Companies Act 1989." |
|---|---|

**61(3)** In sub-paragraph (5), at the end there is inserted

", or

(e) the Financial Services Authority under that Act (other than in its capacity as a designated agency) or the Banking Act 1987;".

### COMPANIES ACT 1985 (C. 6)

**62(1)** Section 449 of the Companies Act 1985 is amended as follows.

**62(2)** [Substitution of s. 449(1)(f).]

**62(3)** [Insertion of s. 449(3)(ha).]

### COMPANIES (NORTHERN IRELAND) ORDER 1986 (S.I. 1986/1032 (N.I. 6))

**63(1)** Article 442 of the Companies (Northern Ireland) Order 1986 is amended as follows.

**63(2)** In paragraph (1), for sub-paragraph (f) there is substituted–

"(f) for the purpose of enabling or assisting the Bank of England to discharge its functions;
(fa) for the purpose of enabling or assisting the Financial Services Authority to discharge–
   (i) any functions under the Financial Services Act 1986, other than as a designated agency within the meaning of that Act,
   (ii) its functions under the Banking Act 1987, or
   (iii) its functions under section 171 of the Companies Act 1989;"

**63(3)** In subsection (3), after paragraph (h) there is inserted–

"(ha) the Financial Services Authority, other than in its capacity as a designated agency within the meaning of the Financial Services Act 1986,".

### BUILDING SOCIETIES ACT 1986 (C. 53)

**64(1)** The Building Societies Act 1986 is amended as follows.

**64(2)** In section 53, in subsection (5)–

(a) for "Bank of England", in the first place where it occurs, there is substituted "Financial Services Authority",

(b) for paragraph (b) there is substituted

"(b) by the Authority of any of its functions under the Banking Act 1987 or as a supervisor of money market institutions;", and

(c) for "Bank of England", in the second place where it occurs, there is substituted "Authority".

**64(3)** In that section, after subsection (5) there is inserted–

"(5A) Nothing in subsection (1) above prohibits the disclosure of information to the Bank of England where, in the opinion of the Commission, it is desirable or expedient that the information should be disclosed with a view to facilitating the discharge–

(a) by the Commission of any of its functions under this Act; or

(b) by the Bank of any of its functions;

nor does subsection (1) above prohibit further disclosure of the information by the Bank of England with the consent of the Commission."

**64(4)** In section 54(3A)–

(a) for "Bank of England", in the first place where it occurs, there is substituted "Financial Services Authority, other than in its capacity as a designated agency within the meaning of the Financial Services Act 1986,", and

(b) for "Bank of England", in the second place where it occurs, there is substituted "Financial Services Authority".

## FINANCIAL SERVICES ACT 1986 (C. 60)

**65(1)** The Financial Services Act 1986 is amended as follows.

**65(2)** In section 179(3)–

(a) after paragraph (b) there is inserted–

"(ba) the Financial Services Authority, other than in its capacity as a designated agency;", and

(b) paragraph (f) is omitted.

**65(3)** In section 180(1)–

(a) after paragraph (e) there is inserted–

"(ea) for the purpose of enabling or assisting the Financial Services Authority to discharge–

(i) its functions under this Act, other than as a designated agency,

(ii) its functions under the Banking Act 1987, or

(iii) its functions under section 171 of the Companies Act 1989;", and

(b) in paragraph (f), for the words from "its" to the end there is substituted "any of its functions".

## COMPANIES ACT 1989 (C. 40)

**66(1)** The Companies Act 1989 is amended as follows.

**66(2)** In section 82–

(a) in subsection (2)(a)(iii) for "Bank of England" there is substituted "Financial Services Authority", and

(b) in subsection (5)–

(i) for "Bank of England", in both places, there is substituted "Financial Services Authority", and

(ii) for "Bank" there is substituted "Authority".

**66(3)** In section 87(4), in the Table, in the entry relating to the Bank of England, for the words in the second column there is substituted "Any of its functions", and after that entry there is inserted–

"The Financial Services Authority. | Functions under the Financial Services Act 1986 (other than as a designated agency within the meaning of that Act), the Banking Act 1987 or section 171 of the Companies Act 1989."

## COURTS AND LEGAL SERVICES ACT 1990 (C. 41)

**67** In section 50(2) of the Courts and Legal Services Act 1990–

(a) after paragraph (f) there is inserted–

"(fa) the Financial Services Authority to discharge any of its functions under the Financial Services Act 1986 (other than as a designated agency within the meaning of that Act), the Banking Act 1987 or section 171 of the Companies Act 1989;", and

(b) in paragraph (p)(i), for "Bank of England" there is substituted "Financial Services Authority".

## FRIENDLY SOCIETIES ACT 1992 (C. 40)

**68** In section 64(5) of the Friendly Societies Act 1992, in the Table, in the entry relating to the Bank of England, for the words in the second column there is substituted "Any of its functions", and after that entry there is inserted–

"The Financial Services Authority. | Functions under the Financial Services Act 1986 (other than as a designated agency within the meaning of that Act), the Banking Act 1987 or section 171 of the Companies Act 1989."

## PENSION SCHEMES ACT 1993 (C. 48)

**69(1)** The Pension Schemes Act 1993 is amended as follows.

**69(2)** In section 149(6)(e), for "Bank of England" there is substituted "Financial Services Authority".

**68(3)** In section 158A(1), in the Table, in the entry relating to the Bank of England, for the words in the second column there is substituted "Any of its functions", and after that entry there is inserted–

"The Financial Services Authority. | Functions under the Financial Services Act 1986 (other than as a designated agency within the meaning of that Act), the Banking Act 1987 or section 171 of the Companies Act 1989."

## PENSION SCHEMES (NORTHERN IRELAND) ACT 1993 (C.49)

**70(1)** The Pension Schemes (Northern Ireland) Act 1993 is amended as follows.

**70(2)** In section 145(6)(e), for "Bank of England" there is substituted "Financial Services Authority".

**70(3)** In section 154A(1), in the Table, in the entry relating to the Bank of England, for the words in the second column there is substituted "Any of its functions", and after that entry there is inserted–

"The Financial Services Authority. | Functions under the Financial Services Act 1986 (other than as a designated agency within the meaning of that Act), the Banking Act 1987 or section 171 of the Companies Act 1989."

## PENSIONS ACT 1995 (C. 26)

**71** In section 107(1) of the Pensions Act 1995, in the Table, in the entry relating to the Bank of England, for the words in the second column there is substituted "Any of its functions", and after that entry there is inserted–

"The Financial Services Authority. Functions under the Financial Services Act 1986 (other than as a designated agency within the meaning of that Act), the Banking Act 1987 or section 171 of the Companies Act 1989."

## PENSIONS (NORTHERN IRELAND) ORDER 1995 (S.I. 1995/3213 (N.I. 22))

**72** In Article 105(1) of the Pensions (Northern Ireland) Order 1995, in the Table, in the entry relating to the Bank of England, for the words in the second column there is substituted "Any of its functions", and after that entry there is inserted–

"The Financial Services Authority. Functions under the Financial Services Act 1986 (other than as a designated agency within the meaning of that Act), the Banking Act 1987 or section 171 of the Companies Act 1989."

# Schedule 6 – Banking Supervision Fees

Section 26

## POWERS

**1(1)** Every application for authorisation under the Banking Act 1987 and every notice given to the Authority under section 75 of that Act (notice by overseas institution of establishment of representative office in the United Kingdom) shall be accompanied by such fee as the Authority may by regulations prescribe; and no such application or notice shall be regarded as duly made or given unless this sub-paragraph is complied with.

**1(2)** Every authorised institution and every European authorised institution which has lawfully established a branch in the United Kingdom for the purpose of accepting deposits or other repayable funds from the public shall pay such periodical fees to the Authority as it may by regulations prescribe.

**1(3)** The powers conferred by this paragraph may be used to prescribe such fees as will enable the Authority–

(a) to meet the expenses which it incurs in carrying out the transferred functions or for any incidental purposes, and

(b) to repay the principal of, and pay any interest on, any money which it has borrowed and which has been used for the purpose of meeting expenses which it has incurred in relation to the transfer to it of the transferred functions.

**1(4)** Regulations under this paragraph shall specify the time when the fees are to be paid and may–

(a) provide for the determination of the fees in accordance with a specified scale or other specified factors,

(b) provide for the return or abatement of any fees, and

(c) make different provision for different cases.

**1(5)** In this paragraph–

**"authorised"** has the same meaning as in the Banking Act 1987;

**"European authorised institution"** has the same meaning as in the Banking Coordination (Second Council Directive) Regulations 1992;

**"institution"** has the same meaning as in the Banking Act 1987.

## CONSULTATION

**2(1)** Before making regulations under paragraph 1, the Authority shall–

(a) publish the proposed regulations in such manner as appears to it best calculated to bring the proposals to the attention of those likely to be affected by them, together with a statement that representations about the proposals can be made to the Authority within a specified time, and

(b) have regard to any representations duly made in accordance with the statement.

**2(2)** Sub-paragraph (1) does not apply where the Authority considers that the delay involved in complying with it would be prejudicial to the interests of depositors.

### MODE OF EXERCISE

**3** Power to make regulations under paragraph 1 is exercisable by instrument in writing which shall state that it is made under that paragraph.

### PUBLICATION

**4(1)** Immediately after regulations under paragraph 1 are made they shall be printed and made available to the public with or without payment.

**4(2)** A person shall not be liable to pay a fee under regulations under paragraph 1 if he shows that, at the time the fee became payable, the regulations had not been made available as required by this paragraph.

### PROOF OF REGULATIONS

**5(1)** The production of a printed copy of regulations purporting to be made by the Authority under paragraph 1 on which is endorsed a certificate signed by an officer of the Authority authorised by it for that purpose and stating–

(a) that the regulations were made by the Authority,

(b) that the copy is a true copy of the regulations, and

(c) that on a specified date the regulations were made available to the public as required by paragraph 4,

shall be prima facie evidence or, in Scotland, sufficient evidence of the facts stated in the certificate.

**5(2)** Any certificate purporting to be signed as mentioned in sub-paragraph (1) shall be deemed to have been duly signed unless the contrary is shown.

**5(3)** Any person wishing in any legal proceedings to cite regulations under paragraph 1 may require the Authority to cause a copy of them to be endorsed with such a certificate as is mentioned in this paragraph.

## Schedule 7 – Restriction on Disclosure of Information

Section 37

### RESTRICTED INFORMATION

**1(1)** Subject to sub-paragraph (2), information is restricted information for the purposes of this paragraph if–

(a) it is obtained by the Bank by virtue of the power conferred by section 17(1) or paragraph 9 of Schedule 2 (whether or not it was obtained pursuant to a notice under that provision), and

(b) it relates to the business or other affairs of any person.

**1(2)** Information is not restricted information for the purposes of this paragraph if–

(a) it has been made available to the public from other sources, or

(b) it is in the form of a summary or collection of information so framed as not to enable information relating to any particular person to be ascertained from it.

**1(3)** Except as permitted by the following provisions of this Schedule, restricted information shall not be disclosed by–

(a) the Bank or any officer or servant of the Bank, or

(b) any person obtaining the information directly or indirectly from the Bank,

without the consent of the person from whom the Bank obtained the information and, if different, the person to whom the information relates.

**1(4)** Any person who discloses information in contravention of this paragraph shall be guilty of an offence and liable–

(a) on conviction on indictment, to imprisonment for a term not exceeding 2 years, or to a fine, or to both;

(b) on summary conviction, to imprisonment for a term not exceeding 3 months, or to a fine not exceeding the statutory maximum, or to both.

## DISCLOSURE FOR THE PURPOSES OF THE BANK'S FUNCTIONS

**2(1)** Paragraph 1 does not preclude the disclosure of information in any case in which disclosure is for the purpose of enabling or assisting the Bank to discharge–

(a) its functions as a monetary authority,

(b) its functions as a supervisor of systems for the transfer of funds between credit institutions and their customers, or

(c) its functions under Schedule 2.

**2(2)** In sub-paragraph (1)(b), "credit institution" has the same meaning as in the Banking Coordination (Second Council Directive) Regulations 1992.

## DISCLOSURE BY THE BANK TO OTHER AUTHORITIES

**3(1)** Paragraph 1 does not preclude the disclosure by the Bank of information to any authority specified in the first column of the following Table if the Bank considers that the disclosure would enable or assist that authority to discharge any of the functions specified in relation to it in the second column of that Table.

TABLE

| *Authority* | *Functions* |
|---|---|
| The Treasury. | Functions under the Insurance Companies Act 1982 or the Financial Services Act 1986. |
| An inspector appointed under Part XIV of the Companies Act 1985, section 94 or 177 of the Financial Services Act 1986 or Part XV of the Companies (Northern Ireland) Order 1986. | Functions under that Part or section. |
| A person authorised to exercise powers or appointed under section 43A or 44 of the Insurance Companies Act 1982, section 447 of the Companies Act 1985, section 106 of the Financial Services Act 1986, article 440 of the Companies (Northern Ireland) Order 1986 or section 84 of the Companies Act 1989. | Functions under that section or article. |
| A designated agency within the meaning of the Financial Services Act 1986. | Functions under that Act or Part VII of the Companies Act 1989. |
| The Financial Services Authority. | Functions under the Financial Services Act 1986 (other than as a designated agency within the meaning of that Act), the Banking Act 1987 or section 171 of the Companies Act 1989. |

| *Authority* | *Functions* |
|---|---|
| The Office for National Statistics. | Functions under the Statistics of Trade Act 1947. |
| The Friendly Societies Commission. | Functions under the enactments relating to friendly societies or under the Financial Services Act 1986. |
| The Building Societies Commission. | Functions under the Building Societies Act 1986 and protecting the interests of the shareholders and depositors of building societies. |
| The Occupational Pensions Regulatory Authority. | Functions under the Pension Schemes Act 1993 or the Pensions Act 1995 or any enactment in force in Northern Ireland corresponding to either of them. |

**3(2)** The Treasury may by order amend the Table in sub-paragraph (1) by–

(a) adding any public or other authority and specifying functions in relation to it,

(b) removing any authority for the time being specified in the Table, or

(c) altering the functions for the time being specified in the Table in relation to any authority.

**3(3)** The Treasury may by order restrict the circumstances in which, or impose conditions subject to which, disclosure is permitted in the case of any authority for the time being specified in the Table.

**3(4)** Before making an order under this paragraph, the Treasury shall consult the Bank.

### ONWARD DISCLOSURE

**4(1)** Paragraph 1 does not preclude the disclosure by any authority specified in the first column of the Table in paragraph 3(1) of information obtained by it by virtue of that provision if it makes the disclosure–

(a) with the consent of the Bank, and

(b) for the purpose of enabling or assisting it to discharge any functions specified in relation to it in the second column of that Table.

**4(2)** Before deciding whether to give its consent to disclosure under this paragraph, the Bank shall take account of such representations as the authority proposing to make the disclosure may make about the desirability of or necessity for the disclosure.

### OTHER PERMITTED DISCLOSURES

**5** Paragraph 1 does not preclude the disclosure of information–

(a) with a view to the institution of, or otherwise for the purposes of, any proceedings in connection with a payment due under Schedule 2 (payment in lieu of cash ratio deposit),

(b) with a view to the institution of, or otherwise for the purposes of, any criminal proceedings, whether under this Act or otherwise, or

(c) in pursuance of any Community obligation.

## Schedule 8 – Transitional Provisions and Savings

Section 42

### BANK'S IMMUNITY FROM SUIT

**1** Section 1(4) of the Banking Act 1987 (immunity in relation to things done or omitted in discharge of functions under the Act) shall continue to have effect without the amendments made by paragraph 2(c) of Schedule 5–

(a) in relation to things done or omitted before the day on which this Act comes into force, and

(b) in relation to anything done on or after that day for the purposes of, or in connection with, any proceedings arising from anything done or omitted before that day.

## DISCLOSURE OF INFORMATION

**2** Sections 83 to 85 of the Banking Act 1987 (exceptions to restriction on disclosure of information received under or for the purposes of the Act) shall, in relation to information received before the day on which this Act comes into force, continue to have effect without the amendments made by paragraphs 53 to 55 of Schedule 5, but with the modifications mentioned in paragraphs 3 to 5 below.

**3(1)** Section 83 is amended as follows.

**3(2)** In subsection (1), paragraphs (a) and (c) are omitted.

**3(3)** Subsections (2) and (3) are omitted.

**4(1)** Section 84 is amended as follows.

**4(2)** In subsection (1), in the Table, after entry 1 there is inserted–

| | |
|---|---|
| "1A The Financial Services Authority. | Functions under the Financial Services Act 1986 (other than as a designated agency within the meaning of that Act), the Banking Act 1987 or section 171 of the Companies Act 1989."; |

and in entry 18, for "Bank" there is substituted "Financial Services Authority".

**4(3)** Subsections (2) and (3) are omitted.

**4(4)** In subsection (6)(a)(i), for "Bank" there is substituted "Financial Services Authority".

**5** In section 85(1)(f), for "Bank" there is substituted "Financial Services Authority".

## PRE-COMMENCEMENT CONSULTATION

**6** If, before the day on which this Act comes into force, anything is done which, had it been done after that day, would to any extent have satisfied–

(a) any requirement to consult before making an order under this Act, or

(b) any requirement of paragraph 2(1) of Schedule 6,

that requirement shall to that extent be taken to have been satisfied.

## MEMBERSHIP OF THE DEPOSIT PROTECTION BOARD

**7** The terms of a person's appointment as an ordinary member of the Deposit Protection Board shall, if he holds office as such immediately before the coming into force of this Act, have effect after the coming into force of this Act as if any reference to the Bank were a reference to the Financial Services Authority and any reference to the Governor of the Bank were a reference to the Chairman of the Financial Services Authority.

# Schedule 9 – Repeals and Revocations

Section 43

## Part I – Repeals

| Chapter | Short title | Extent of repeal |
|---|---|---|
| 1946 c. 27. | The Bank of England Act 1946. | Sections 2 and 4(2). Schedule 2. |
| 1986 c. 60. | The Financial Services Act 1986. | Section 179(3)(f). In Schedule 7, in paragraph 1(2), the words "and the Governor of the Bank of England acting jointly". |
| 1987 c. 22. | The Banking Act 1987. | In section 83(1), paragraph (b), in paragraph (c), the words "and gilt market", and paragraph (d) and the word "or" immediately preceding it. |
| 1990 c. 41. | The Courts and Legal Services Act 1990. | In sections 37(8)(a), 48(4)(a) and 52(6), the words "by the Bank of England". In section 54(1), in the inserted subsection (2)(e)(i), the words "by the Bank of England,". |

## Part II – Revocations

| Number | Title | Extent of revocation |
|---|---|---|
| S.I. 1992/3218. | The Banking Coordination (Second Council Directive) Regulations 1992. | Regulation 76(4). In Schedule 4, paragraph 1(6)(a). In Schedule 10, in paragraphs 8(1) and 31, the words "by the Bank,". |

| Number | Title | Extent of revocation |
|---|---|---|
| S.I. 1995/3275. | The Investment Services Regulations 1995. | Regulations 8(3), 13 and 14.<br>In regulation 26(2)(b), the words "by the Bank".<br>In Schedule 3, in paragraph 1, in sub-paragraph (1)(b), the words ", or in the case of a listed firm, the Bank,", in sub-paragraph (2), in paragraph (b), the words ", or in the case of a listed firm, the Bank," and, in paragraph (c), in both places, the words "or, as the case may be, the Bank", in paragraph 3(2), the words "or, as the case may be, the Bank", in paragraph 4, in sub-paragraph (1), the words ", or, in the case of a listed firm, to the Bank,", in sub-paragraph (2), the words "or, as the case may be, to the Bank", and, in sub-paragraph (3), the words "or, as the case may be, the Bank", in paragraph 5, in sub-paragraph (1), in paragraph (a), the words ", or, in the case of a listed firm, to the Bank," and, in paragraphs (b) and (c), the words "or, as the case may be, the Bank", wherever occurring, in sub-paragraph (2), the words "or, as the case may be, to the Bank", in sub-paragraph (3), the words "or, as the case may be, the Bank", and paragraph 6. |

| Number | Title | Extent of revocation |
|---|---|---|
| | | In Schedule 6, in paragraph 1, in sub-paragraph (1), the words ", or in the case of a listed person, to the Bank," and, in sub-paragraph (2), in paragraph (a), the words ", or, in the case of a listed firm, to the Bank,", and, in paragraphs (b) and (c)(ii), the words "or, as the case may be, the Bank", in paragraph 2, the words "or, as the case may be, to the Bank", in paragraphs 3 and 4, the words "or, as the case may be, the Bank", wherever occurring, in paragraph 5, in sub-paragraph (1), the words "or, in a case in which a firm is a listed person, to the Bank" and, in sub-paragraph (2), the words "or, in the case of a firm which is a listed person, the Bank", in paragraph 6, in sub-paragraph (1), in paragraph (a), the words "or, in the case of a firm which is a listed person, to the Bank" and, in paragraph (b), the words "or, as the case may be, the Bank", and in sub-paragraph (2), the words "or, in the case of a firm which is a listed person, to the Bank", in paragraph 7, the words "or, as the case may be, the Bank", wherever occurring, and paragraph 9. |

# COMPETITION ACT 1998

(1998 Chapter 41)

[*9th November 1998*]

[**Note:** Only certain provisions relating to merger control included. The provisions are fully in force from 1 March 2000 (see SI 2000/344 (C 9) although some were brought into force for certain purposes on 11 January 1999 (see SI 1998/3166).)]

# PART I – COMPETITION

## Chapter I – Agreements

THE PROHIBITION

### 2 Agreements etc. preventing, restricting or distorting competition

**2(1) [Prohibited agreements]** Subject to section 3, agreements between undertakings, decisions by associations of undertakings or concerted practices which–

(a) may affect trade within the United Kingdom, and

(b) have as their object or effect the prevention, restriction or distortion of competition within the United Kingdom,

are prohibited unless they are exempt in accordance with the provisions of this Part.

**2(2) [Agreements to which s. 2(1) applicable]** Subsection (1) applies, in particular, to agreements, decisions or practices which–

(a) directly or indirectly fix purchase or selling prices or any other trading conditions;

(b) limit or control production, markets, technical development or investment;

(c) share markets or sources of supply;

(d) apply dissimilar conditions to equivalent transactions with other trading parties, thereby placing them at a competitive disadvantage;

(e) make the conclusion of contracts subject to acceptance by the other parties of supplementary obligations which, by their nature or according to commercial usage, have no connection with the subject of such contracts.

**2(3) [Implementation of agreement in UK only]** Subsection (1) applies only if the agreement, decision or practice is, or is intended to be, implemented in the United Kingdom.

**2(4) [Prohibited agreement void]** Any agreement or decision which is prohibited by subsection (1) is void.

**2(5) [Application to decision of associated undertakings or concerted practice]** A provision of this Part which is expressed to apply to, or in relation to, an agreement is to be read as applying equally to, or in relation to, a decision by an association of undertakings or a concerted practice (but with any necessary modifications).

**2(6) [Non-application of s. 2(5)]** Subsection (5) does not apply where the context otherwise requires.

**2(7) ["The United Kingdom"]** In this section "the United Kingdom" means, in relation to an agreement which operates or is intended to operate only in a part of the United Kingdom, that part.

**2(8) ["The Chapter I prohibition"]** The prohibition imposed by subsection (1) is referred to in this Act as the "Chapter I prohibition".

EXCLUDED AGREEMENTS

## 3 Excluded agreements

**3(1) [Exclusions from Chapter I prohibtion]** The Chapter I prohibition does not apply in any of the cases in which it is excluded by or as a result of–

(a) Schedule 1 (mergers and concentrations) . . .

# Chapter II – Abuse of Dominant Position

THE PROHIBITION

## 18 Abuse of dominant position

**18(1) [Prohibited conduct]** Subject to section 19, any conduct on the part of one or more undertakings which amounts to the abuse of a dominant position in a market is prohibited if it may affect trade within the United Kingdom.

**18(2) [Conduct constituting abuse of dominant position]** Conduct may, in particular, constitute such an abuse if it consists in–

(a) directly or indirectly imposing unfair purchase or selling prices or other unfair trading conditions;

(b) limiting production, markets or technical development to the prejudice of consumers;

(c) applying dissimilar conditions to equivalent transactions with other trading parties, thereby placing them at a competitive disadvantage;

(d) making the conclusion of contracts subject to acceptance by the other parties of supplementary obligations which, by their nature or according to commercial usage, have no connection with the subject of the contracts.

**18(3) ["Dominant position", "United Kingdom"]** In this section–

**"dominant position"** means a dominant position within the United Kingdom; and
**"the United Kingdom"** means the United Kingdom or any part of it.

**18(4) ["The Chapter II prohibition"]** The prohibition imposed by subsection (1) is referred to in this Act as "the Chapter II prohibition".

EXCLUDED CASES

## 19 Excluded cases

**19(1) [Exclusions from Chapter II prohibition]** The Chapter II prohibition does not apply in any of the cases in which it is excluded by or as a result of–

(a) Schedule 1 (mergers and concentrations) . . .

# SCHEDULES

# Schedule 1 – Exclusions: Mergers and Concentrations

## Part I – Mergers

ENTERPRISES CEASING TO BE DISTINCT: THE CHAPTER I PROHIBITION

**1(1)** To the extent to which an agreement (either on its own or when taken together with another agreement) results, or if carried out would result, in any two enterprises ceasing to be distinct enterprises for the purposes of Part V of the Fair Trading Act 1973 ("the 1973 Act"), the Chapter I prohibition does not apply to the agreement.

**1(2)** The exclusion provided by sub-paragraph (1) extends to any provision directly related and necessary to the implementation of the merger provisions.

**1(3)** In sub-paragraph (2) "merger provisions" means the provisions of the agreement which cause, or if carried out would cause, the agreement to have the result mentioned in sub-paragraph (1).

**1(4)** Section 65 of the 1973 Act applies for the purposes of this paragraph as if–

(a) in subsection (3) (circumstances in which a person or group of persons may be treated as having control of an enterprise), and

(b) in subsection (4) (circumstances in which a person or group of persons may be treated as bringing an enterprise under their control),

for "may" there were substituted "must".

## ENTERPRISES CEASING TO BE DISTINCT: THE CHAPTER II PROHIBITION

**2(1)** To the extent to which conduct (either on its own or when taken together with other conduct)–

(a) results in any two enterprises ceasing to be distinct enterprises for the purposes of Part V of the 1973 Act), or

(b) is directly related and necessary to the attainment of the result mentioned in paragraph (a),

the Chapter II prohibition does not apply to that conduct.

**2(2)** Section 65 of the 1973 Act applies for the purposes of this paragraph as it applies for the purposes of paragraph 1.

## WITHDRAWAL OF THE PARAGRAPH 1 EXCLUSION

**4(1)** The exclusion provided by paragraph 1 does not apply to a particular agreement if the Director gives a direction under this paragraph to that effect.

**4(2)** If the Director is considering whether to give a direction under this paragraph, he may by notice in writing require any party to the agreement in question to give him such information in connection with the agreement as he may require.

**4(3)** The Director may give a direction under this paragraph only as provided in sub-paragraph (4) or (5).

**4(4)** If at the end of such period as may be specified in rules under section 51 a person has failed, without reasonable excuse, to comply with a requirement imposed under sub-paragraph (2), the Director may give a direction under this paragraph.

**4(5)** The Director may also give a direction under this paragraph if–

(a) he considers–

(i) that the agreement will, if not excluded, infringe the Chapter I prohibition; and

(ii) that he is not likely to grant it an unconditional individual exemption; and

(b) the agreement is not a protected agreement.

**4(6)** For the purposes of sub-paragraph (5), an individual exemption is unconditional if no conditions or obligations are imposed in respect of it under section 4(3)(a).

**4(7)** A direction under this paragraph–

(a) must be in writing;

(b) may be made so as to have effect from a date specified in the direction (which may not be earlier than the date on which it is given).

## PROTECTED AGREEMENTS

**5** An agreement is a protected agreement for the purposes of paragraph 4 if–

(a) the Secretary of State has announced his decision not to make a merger reference to the

Competition Commission under section 64 of the 1973 Act in connection with the agreement;

(b) the Secretary of State has made a merger reference to the Competition Commission under section 64 of the 1973 Act in connection with the agreement and the Commission has found that the agreement has given rise to, or would if carried out give rise to, a merger situation qualifying for investigation;

(c) the agreement does not fall within sub-paragraph (a) or (b) but has given rise to, or would if carried out give rise to, enterprises to which it relates being regarded under section 65 of the 1973 Act as ceasing to be distinct enterprises (otherwise than as the result of subsection (3) or (4)(b) of that section); or

(d) the Secretary of State has made a merger reference to the Competition Commission under section 32 of the Water Industry Act 1991 in connection with the agreement and the Commission has found that the agreement has given rise to, or would if carried out give rise to, a merger of the kind to which that section applies.

## Part II – Concentrations Subject to EC Controls

**6(1)** To the extent to which an agreement (either on its own or when taken together with another agreement) gives rise to, or would if carried out give rise to, a concentration, the Chapter I prohibition does not apply to the agreement if the Merger Regulation gives the Commission exclusive jurisdiction in the matter.

**6(2)** To the extent to which conduct (either on its own or when taken together with other conduct) gives rise to, or would if pursued give rise to, a concentration, the Chapter II prohibition does not apply to the conduct if the Merger Regulation gives the Commission exclusive jurisdiction in the matter.

**6(3)** In this paragraph–

**"concentration"** means a concentration with a Community dimension within the meaning of Articles 1 and 3 of the Merger Regulation; and

**"Merger Regulation"** means Council Regulation (EEC) No. 4064/89 of 21st December 1989 on the control of concentrations between undertakings as amended by Council Regulation (EC) No. 1310/97 of 30th June 1997.

# COMPANY AND BUSINESS NAMES (CHAMBER OF COMMERCE, ETC.) ACT 1999

(1999 Chapter 19)

An Act to make provision concerning the approval of company or business names containing the expression "chamber of commerce" or any related expression; and for connected purposes.

[27th July 1999]

## 1 Approval to be required for company or business names including the expression "chamber of commerce".

1 It is the duty of the Secretary of State to secure that the expression "chamber of commerce" and its Welsh equivalent ("siambr fasnach") is specified–

(a) in regulations under section 29(1)(a) of the Companies Act 1985, and

(b) in regulations under section 3(1)(a) of the Business Names Act 1985,

as an expression for the registration of which as or as part of a company's name, or for the use of which as or part of a business name, the approval of the Secretary of State is required.

## 2 Approval of certain company names

**2(1) [Consultation before approval decision]** Before determining under section 26(2) of the Companies Act 1985 whether to approve the registration of a company under a name which includes–

(a) the expression "chamber of commerce" or "siambr fasnach", or

(b) any other expression for the time being specified in regulations under section 29(1)(a) of the Companies Act 1985 which begins with the words "chamber of" or "chambers of" (or the Welsh equivalents),

the Secretary of State must consult at least one relevant representative body.

**2(2) [Guidance re approval]** The Secretary of State may publish guidance with respect to factors which may be taken into account in determining whether to approve the registration of a name to which this section applies.

## 3 Approval of certain business names

**3(1) [Consultation before approval decision]** Before determining under section 2(1) of the Business Names Act 1985 whether to approve the carrying on of a business under a name which includes–

(a) the expression "chamber of commerce" or "siambr fasnach", or

(b) any other expression for the time being specified in regulations under section 3(1)(a) of the Business Names Act 1985 which begins with the words "chamber of" or "chambers of" (or the Welsh equivalents),

the Secretary of State must consult at least one relevant representative body.

**3(2) [Guidance re approval]** The Secretary of State may publish guidance with respect to factors which may be taken into account in determining whether to approve the use of a business name to which this section applies.

## 4 Relevant representative bodies

**4(1) [Interpretation of s. 2(1), 3(1)]** The relevant representative bodies for the purposes of this Act are–

(a) British Chambers of Commerce;

(b) the body known as Scottish Chambers of Commerce.

**4(2) [Amendment of s. 4(1)]** The Secretary of State may by order amend subsection (1) by adding to or deleting from it the name of any body (whether corporate or unincorporated).

**4(3) [Orders under section]** The power to make an order under this section is exercisable by statutory instrument which shall be liable to annulment in pursuance of a resolution of either House of Parliament.

## 5 Citation, commencement and extent

**5(1) [Citation]** This Act may be cited as the Company and Business Names (Chamber of Commerce, Etc.) Act 1999.

**5(2) [Commencement]** This Act shall come into force on such day as the Secretary of State may by order made by statutory instrument appoint.

**5(3) [Northern Ireland]** This Act does not extend to Northern Ireland.

# LIMITED LIABILITY PARTNERSHIPS ACT 2000

(2000 Chapter 12)

## ARRANGEMENT OF SECTIONS



## SCHEDULES

# LIMITED LIABILITY PARTNERSHIPS ACT 2000

(2000 Chapter 12)

An Act to make provision for limited liability partnerships.

*[20th July 2000]*

INTRODUCTORY

## 1 Limited liability partnerships

**1(1) [Legal entity]** There shall be a new form of legal entity to be known as a limited liability partnership.

**1(2) [Body corporate]** A limited liability partnership is a body corporate (with legal personality separate from that of its members) which is formed by being incorporated under this Act; and–

(a) in the following provisions of this Act (except in the phrase "oversea limited liability partnership"), and

(b) in any other enactment (except where provision is made to the contrary or the context otherwise requires),

references to a limited liability partnership are to such a body corporate.

**1(3) [Unlimited capacity]** A limited liability partnership has unlimited capacity.

**1(4) [Liability of members]** The members of a limited liability partnership have such liability to contribute to its assets in the event of its being wound up as is provided for by virtue of this Act.

**1(5) [Application of partnership law]** Accordingly, except as far as otherwise provided by this Act or any other enactment, the law relating to partnerships does not apply to a limited liability partnership.

**1(6) [Names and registered offices]** The Schedule (which makes provision about the names and registered offices of limited liability partnerships) has effect.

INCORPORATION

## 2 Incorporation document etc.

**2(1) [Requirements for incorporation]** For a limited liability partnership to be incorporated–

(a) two or more persons associated for carrying on a lawful business with a view to profit must have subscribed their names to an incorporation document,

(b) there must have been delivered to the registrar either the incorporation document or a copy authenticated in a manner approved by him, and

(c) there must have been so delivered a statement in a form approved by the registrar, made by either a solicitor engaged in the formation of the limited liability partnership or anyone who subscribed his name to the incorporation document, that the requirement imposed by paragraph (a) has been complied with.

**2(2) [Incorporation document]** The incorporation document must–

(a) be in a form approved by the registrar (or as near to such a form as circumstances allow),

(b) state the name of the limited liability partnership,

(c) state whether the registered office of the limited liability partnership is to be situated in England and Wales, in Wales or in Scotland,

(d) state the address of that registered office,

(e) state the name and address of each of the persons who are to be members of the limited liability partnership on incorporation, and

(f) either specify which of those persons are to be designated members or state that every person who from time to time is a member of the limited liability partnership is a designated member.

**2(3) [False statement under s. 2(1)(c) an offence]** If a person makes a false statement under subsection (1)(c) which he–

(a) knows to be false, or

(b) does not believe to be true,

he commits an offence.

**2(4) [Penalty for s. 2(3) offence]** A person guilty of an offence under subsection (3) is liable–

(a) on summary conviction, to imprisonment for a period not exceeding six months or a fine not exceeding the statutory maximum, or to both, or

(b) on conviction on indictment, to imprisonment for a period not exceeding two years or a fine, or to both.

## 3 Incorporation by registration

**3(1) [Act of registration]** When the requirements imposed by paragraphs (b) and (c) of subsection (1) of section 2 have been complied with, the registrar shall retain the incorporation document or copy delivered to him and, unless the requirement imposed by paragraph (a) of that subsection has not been complied with, he shall–

(a) register the incorporation document or copy, and

(b) give a certificate that the limited liability partnership is incorporated by the name specified in the incorporation document.

**3(2) [Section 2(1)(c) statement effectual]** The registrar may accept the statement delivered under paragraph (c) of subsection (1) of section 2 as sufficient evidence that the requirement imposed by paragraph (a) of that subsection has been complied with.

**3(3) [Authentication of certificate]** The certificate shall either be signed by the registrar or be authenticated by his official seal.

**3(4) [Certificate conclusive evidence of incorporation]** The certificate is conclusive evidence that the requirements of section 2 are complied with and that the limited liability partnership is incorporated by the name specified in the incorporation document.

MEMBERSHIP

## 4 Members

**4(1) [Members on incorporation]** On the incorporation of a limited liability partnership its members are the persons who subscribed their names to the incorporation document (other than any who have died or been dissolved).

**4(2) [Subsequent members]** Any other person may become a member of a limited liability partnership by and in accordance with an agreement with the existing members.

**4(3) [Cessation of membership]** A person may cease to be a member of a limited liability partnership (as well as by death or dissolution) in accordance with an agreement with the other members or, in the absence of agreement with the other members as to cessation of membership, by giving reasonable notice to the other members.

**4(4) [Member not employee]** A member of a limited liability partnership shall not be regarded for any purpose as employed by the limited liability partnership unless, if he and the other members were partners in a partnership, he would be regarded for that purpose as employed by the partnership.

## 5 Relationship of members etc.

**5(1) [Rights and duties of LLP and members]** Except as far as otherwise provided by this Act or any other enactment, the mutual rights and duties of the members of a limited liability partnership, and the mutual rights and duties of a limited liability partnership and its members, shall be governed–

(a) by agreement between the members, or between the limited liability partnership and its members, or

(b) in the absence of agreement as to any matter, by any provision made in relation to that matter by regulations under section 15(c).

**5(2) [Pre-incorporation agreement]** An agreement made before the incorporation of a limited liability partnership between the persons who subscribe their names to the incorporation document may impose obligations on the limited liability partnership (to take effect at any time after its incorporation).

## 6 Members as agents

**6(1) [Every member an agent]** Every member of a limited liability partnership is the agent of the limited liability partnership.

**6(2) [Effect of lack of authority]** But a limited liability partnership is not bound by anything done by a member in dealing with a person if–

(a) the member in fact has no authority to act for the limited liability partnership by doing that thing, and

(b) the person knows that he has no authority or does not know or believe him to be a member of the limited liability partnership.

**6(3) [Liability of former members]** Where a person has ceased to be a member of a limited liability partnership, the former member is to be regarded (in relation to any person dealing with the limited liability partnership) as still being a member of the limited liability partnership unless–

(a) the person has notice that the former member has ceased to be a member of the limited liability partnership, or

(b) notice that the former member has ceased to be a member of the limited liability partnership has been delivered to the registrar.

**6(4) [Liability for members' wrongful acts]** Where a member of a limited liability partnership is liable to any person (other than another member of the limited liability partnership) as a result of a wrongful act or omission of his in the course of the business of the limited liability partnership or with its authority, the limited liability partnership is liable to the same extent as the member.

## 7 Ex-members

**7(1) [Application of section]** This section applies where a member of a limited liability partnership has either ceased to be a member or–

(a) has died,

(b) has become bankrupt or had his estate sequestrated or has been wound up,

(c) has granted a trust deed for the benefit of his creditors, or

(d) has assigned the whole or any part of his share in the limited liability partnership (absolutely or by way of charge or security).

**7(2) [Non-interference by former members etc.]** In such an event the former member or–

(a) his personal representative,

(b) his trustee in bankruptcy or permanent or interim trustee (within the meaning of the Bankruptcy (Scotland) Act 1985) or liquidator,

(c) his trustee under the trust deed for the benefit of his creditors, or

(d) his assignee,

may not interfere in the management or administration of any business or affairs of the limited liability partnership.

**7(3) [Right to receive amount from LLP]** But subsection (2) does not affect any right to receive an amount from the limited liability partnership in that event.

# 8 Designated members

**8(1) [Incorporation document may specify]** If the incorporation document specifies who are to be designated members–

(a) they are designated members on incorporation, and

(b) any member may become a designated member by and in accordance with an agreement with the other members,

and a member may cease to be a designated member in accordance with an agreement with the other members.

**8(2) [Otherwise every member designated member]** But if there would otherwise be no designated members, or only one, every member is a designated member.

**8(3) [Where every member designated member]** If the incorporation document states that every person who from time to time is a member of the limited liability partnership is a designated member, every member is a designated member.

**8(4) [Effect of notice to registrar]** A limited liability partnership may at any time deliver to the registrar–

(a) notice that specified members are to be designated members, or

(b) notice that every person who from time to time is a member of the limited liability partnership is a designated member,

and, once it is delivered, subsection (1) (apart from paragraph (a)) and subsection (2), or subsection (3), shall have effect as if that were stated in the incorporation document.

**8(5) [Formalities for s. 8(4) notice]** A notice delivered under subsection (4)–

(a) shall be in a form approved by the registrar, and

(a) shall be signed by a designated member of the limited liability partnership or authenticated in a manner approved by the registrar.

**8(6) [Cessation as designated member]** A person ceases to be a designated member if he ceases to be a member.

# 9 Registration of membership changes

**9(1) [Notice of membership changes]** A limited liability partnership must ensure that–

(a) where a person becomes or ceases to be a member or designated member, notice is delivered to the registrar within fourteen days, and

(b) where there is any change in the name or address of a member, notice is delivered to the registrar within 28 days.

**9(2) [When notice not required]** Where all the members from time to time of a limited liability partnership are designated members, subsection (1)(a) does not require notice that a person has become or ceased to be a designated member as well as a member.

**9(3) [Formalities for s. 9(1) notice]** A notice delivered under subsection (1)–

(a) shall be in a form approved by the registrar, and

(b) shall be signed by a designated member of the limited liability partnership or authenticated in a manner approved by the registrar,

and, if it relates to a person becoming a member or designated member, shall contain a statement that he consents to becoming a member or designated member signed by him or authenticated in a manner approved by the registrar.

**9(4) [Failure to give notice an offence]** If a limited liability partnership fails to comply with subsection (1), the partnership and every designated member commits an offence.

**9(5) [Defence to s. 9(4) offence]** But it is a defence for a designated member charged with an offence under subsection (4) to prove that he took all reasonable steps for securing that subsection (1) was complied with.

**9(6) [Penalty for s. 9(4) offence]** A person guilty of an offence under subsection (4) is liable on summary conviction to a fine not exceeding level 5 on the standard scale.

TAXATION

## 10 Income tax and chargeable gains

**10(1) [Insertion of ICTA 1988, s. 118ZA–118ZD]** In the Income and Corporation Taxes Act 1988, after section 118 insert–

"LIMITED LIABILITY PARTNERSHIPS

*Treatment of limited liability partnerships*

**118ZA** For the purposes of the Tax Acts, a trade, profession or business carried on by a limited liability partnership with a view to profit shall be treated as carried on in partnership by its members (and not by the limited liability partnership as such); and, accordingly, the property of the limited liability partnership shall be treated for those purposes as partnership property.

*Restriction on relief*

**118ZB** Sections 117 and 118 have effect in relation to a member of a limited liability partnership as in relation to a limited partner, but subject to sections 118ZC and 118ZD.

*Member's contribution to trade*

**118ZC(1)** Subsection (3) of section 117 does not have effect in relation to a member of a limited liability partnership.

**118ZC(2)** But, for the purposes of that section and section 118, such a member's contribution to a trade at any time ("the relevant time") is the greater of–

(a) the amount subscribed by him, and
(b) the amount of his liability on a winding up.

**118ZC(3)** The amount subscribed by a member of a limited liability partnership is the amount which he has contributed to the limited liability partnership as capital, less so much of that amount (if any) as–

(a) he has previously, directly or indirectly, drawn out or received back,
(b) he so draws out or receives back during the period of five years beginning with the relevant time,
(c) he is or may be entitled so to draw out or receive back at any time when he is a member of the limited liability partnership, or
(d) he is or may be entitled to require another person to reimburse to him.

**118ZC(4)** The amount of the liability of a member of a limited liability partnership on a winding up is the amount which–

(a) he is liable to contribute to the assets of the limited liability partnership in the event of its being wound up, and
(b) he remains liable so to contribute for the period of at least five years beginning with the relevant time (or until it is wound up, if that happens before the end of that period).

*Carry forward of unrelieved losses*

**118ZD(1)** Where amounts relating to a trade carried on by a member of a limited liability partnership are, in any one or more chargeable periods, prevented from being given or allowed by section 117 or 118 as it applies otherwise than by virtue of this section (his "total unrelieved loss"), subsection (2) applies in each subsequent chargeable period in which–

(a) he carries on the trade as a member of the limited liability partnership, and
(b) any of his total unrelieved loss remains outstanding.

**118ZD(2)** Sections 380, 381, 393A(1) and 403 (and sections 117 and 118 as they apply in relation to those sections) shall have effect in the subsequent chargeable period as if–

(a) any loss sustained or incurred by the member in the trade in that chargeable period were increased by an amount equal to so much of his total unrelieved loss as remains outstanding in that period, or

(b) (if no loss is so sustained or incurred) a loss of that amount were so sustained or incurred.

**118ZD(3)** To ascertain whether any (and, if so, how much) of a member's total unrelieved loss remains outstanding in the subsequent chargeable period, deduct from the amount of his total unrelieved loss the aggregate of–

(a) any relief given under any provision of the Tax Acts (otherwise than as a result of subsection (2)) in respect of his total unrelieved loss in that or any previous chargeable period, and

(b) any amount given or allowed in respect of his total unrelieved loss as a result of subsection (2) in any previous chargeable period (or which would have been so given or allowed had a claim been made).".

**10(2) [Insertion into ICTA 1988, s. 362(2)(a)]** In section 362(2)(a) of that Act (loan to buy into partnership), after "partner" insert "in a limited partnership registered under the Limited Partnerships Act 1907".

**10(3) [Insertion of TCGA 1992, s. 59A]** In the Taxation of Chargeable Gains Act 1992, after section 59 insert–

"*Limited liability partnerships*

**59A(1)** Where a limited liability partnership carries on a trade or business with a view to profit–

(a) assets held by the limited liability partnership shall be treated for the purposes of tax in respect of chargeable gains as held by its members as partners, and

(b) any dealings by the limited liability partnership shall be treated for those purposes as dealings by its members in partnership (and not by the limited liability partnership as such),

and tax in respect of chargeable gains accruing to the members of the limited liability partnership on the disposal of any of its assets shall be assessed and charged on them separately.

**59A(2)** Where subsection (1) ceases to apply in relation to a limited liability partnership with the effect that tax is assessed and charged–

(a) on the limited liability partnership (as a company) in respect of chargeable gains accruing on the disposal of any of its assets, and

(b) on the members in respect of chargeable gains accruing on the disposal of any of their capital interests in the limited liability partnership,

it shall be assessed and charged on the limited liability partnership as if subsection (1) had never applied in relation to it.

**59A(3)** Neither the commencement of the application of subsection (1) nor the cessation of its application in relation to a limited liability partnership is to be taken as giving rise to the disposal of any assets by it or any of its members."

**10(4) [Insertion of TCGA 1992, s. 156A]** After section 156 of that Act insert–

"*Cessation of trade by limited liability partnership*

**156A(1)** Where, immediately before the time of cessation of trade, a member of a limited liability partnership holds an asset, or an interest in an asset, acquired by him for a consideration treated as reduced under section 152 or 153, he shall be treated as if a chargeable gain equal to the amount of the reduction accrued to him immediately before that time.

**156A(2)** Where, as a result of section 154(2), a chargeable gain on the disposal of an asset, or an interest in an asset, by a member of a limited liability partnership has not accrued before the time of cessation of trade, the member shall be treated as if the chargeable gain accrued immediately before that time.

**156A(3)** In this section "the time of cessation of trade", in relation to a limited liability partnership, means the time when section 59A(1) ceases to apply in relation to the limited liability partnership."

## 11 Inheritance tax

**11** In the Inheritance Tax Act 1984, after section 267 insert–

"*Limited liability partnerships*

**267A** For the purposes of this Act and any other enactments relating to inheritance tax–

(a) property to which a limited liability partnership is entitled, or which it occupies or uses, shall be treated as property to which its members are entitled, or which they occupy or use, as partners,

(b) any business carried on by a limited liability partnership shall be treated as carried on in partnership by its members,

(c) incorporation, change in membership or dissolution of a limited liability partnership shall be treated as formation, alteration or dissolution of a partnership, and

(d) any transfer of value made by or to a limited liability partnership shall be treated as made by or to its members in partnership (and not by or to the limited liability partnership as such)."

## 12 Stamp duty

**12(1) [No duty on transfer of property to partnership on incorporation]** Stamp duty shall not be chargeable on an instrument by which property is conveyed or transferred by a person to a limited liability partnership in connection with its incorporation within the period of one year beginning with the date of incorporation if the following two conditions are satisfied.

**12(2) [First condition]** The first condition is that at the relevant time the person–

(a) is a partner in a partnership comprised of all the persons who are or are to be members of the limited liability partnership (and no-one else), or

(b) holds the property conveyed or transferred as nominee or bare trustee for one or more of the partners in such a partnership.

**12(3) [Second condition]** The second condition is that–

(a) the proportions of the property conveyed or transferred to which the persons mentioned in subsection (2)(a) are entitled immediately after the conveyance or transfer are the same as those to which they were entitled at the relevant time, or

(b) none of the differences in those proportions has arisen as part of a scheme or arrangement of which the main purpose, or one of the main purposes, is avoidance of liability to any duty or tax.

**12(4) [Holding property as bare trustee]** For the purposes of subsection (2) a person holds property as bare trustee for a partner if the partner has the exclusive right (subject only to satisfying any outstanding charge, lien or other right of the trustee to resort to the property for payment of duty, taxes, costs or other outgoings) to direct how the property shall be dealt with.

**12(5) ["The relevant time"]** In this section **"the relevant time"** means–

(a) if the person who conveyed or transferred the property to the limited liability partnership acquired the property after its incorporation, immediately after he acquired the property, and

(b) in any other case, immediately before its incorporation.

**12(6) [Instrument to be stamped]** An instrument in respect of which stamp duty is not chargeable by virtue of subsection (1) shall not be taken to be duly stamped unless–

(a) it has, in accordance with section 12 of the Stamp Act 1891, been stamped with a particular stamp denoting that it is not chargeable with any duty or that it is duly stamped, or

(b) it is stamped with the duty to which it would be liable apart from that subsection.

## 13 Class 4 national insurance contributions

**13** In section 15 of the Social Security Contributions and Benefits Act 1992 and section 15 of the Social Security Contributions and Benefits (Northern Ireland) Act 1992 (Class 4 contributions), after subsection (3) insert–

"(3A) Where income tax is (or would be) charged on a member of a limited liability partnership in respect of profits or gains arising from the carrying on of a trade or profession by the limited liability partnership, Class 4 contributions shall be payable by him if they would be payable were the trade or profession carried on in partnership by the members."

REGULATIONS

## 14 Insolvency and winding up

**14(1) [Regulations to apply or incorporate Parts of Insolvency Act 1986]** Regulations shall make provision about the insolvency and winding up of limited liability partnerships by applying or incorporating, with such modifications as appear appropriate, Parts I to IV, VI and VII of the Insolvency Act 1986.

**14(2) [Other regulations]** Regulations may make other provision about the insolvency and winding up of limited liability partnerships, and provision about the insolvency and winding up of oversea limited liability partnerships, by–

(a) applying or incorporating, with such modifications as appear appropriate, any law relating to the insolvency or winding up of companies or other corporations which would not otherwise have effect in relation to them, or

(b) providing for any law relating to the insolvency or winding up of companies or other corporations which would otherwise have effect in relation to them not to apply to them or to apply to them with such modifications as appear appropriate.

**14(3) ["Oversea limited liability partnership"]** In this Act **"oversea limited liability partnership"** means a body incorporated or otherwise established outside Great Britain and having such connection with Great Britain, and such other features, as regulations may prescribe.

## 15 Application of company law etc.

**15** Regulations may make provision about limited liability partnerships and oversea limited liability partnerships (not being provision about insolvency or winding up) by–

(a) applying or incorporating, with such modifications as appear appropriate, any law relating to companies or other corporations which would not otherwise have effect in relation to them,

(b) providing for any law relating to companies or other corporations which would otherwise have effect in relation to them not to apply to them or to apply to them with such modifications as appear appropriate, or

(c) applying or incorporating, with such modifications as appear appropriate, any law relating to partnerships.

## 16 Consequential amendments

**16(1) [Regulation-making power]** Regulations may make in any enactment such amendments or repeals as appear appropriate in consequence of this Act or regulations made under it.

**16(2) [Regulations affecting companies, corporations or partnerships]** The regulations may, in particular, make amendments and repeals affecting companies or other corporations or partnerships.

## 17 General

**17(1) ["Regulations"]** In this Act **"regulations"** means regulations made by the Secretary of State by statutory instrument.

**17(2) [Particular purpose of regulations]** Regulations under this Act may in particular–

(a) make provision for dealing with non-compliance with any of the regulations (including the creation of criminal offences),

(b) impose fees (which shall be paid into the Consolidated Fund), and

(c) provide for the exercise of functions by persons prescribed by the regulations.

**17(3) [Further provision of regulations]** Regulations under this Act may–

(a) contain any appropriate consequential, incidental, supplementary or transitional provisions or savings, and

(b) make different provision for different purposes.

**17(4) [Parliamentary approval]** No regulations to which this subsection applies shall be made unless a draft of the statutory instrument containing the regulations (whether or not together with other provisions) has been laid before, and approved by a resolution of, each House of Parliament.

**17(5) [Regulations to which Parliamentary approval applies]** Subsection (4) applies to–

(a) regulations under section 14(2) not consisting entirely of the application or incorporation (with or without modifications) of provisions contained in or made under the Insolvency Act 1986,

(b) regulations under section 15 not consisting entirely of the application or incorporation (with or without modifications) of provisions contained in or made under Part I, Chapter VIII of Part V, Part VII, Parts XI to XIII, Parts XVI to XVIII, Part XX or Parts XXIV to XXVI of the Companies Act 1985,

(c) regulations under section 14 or 15 making provision about oversea limited liability partnerships, and

(d) regulations under section 16.

**17(6) [Regulations subject to annulment]** A statutory instrument containing regulations under this Act shall (unless a draft of it has been approved by a resolution of each House of Parliament) be subject to annulment in pursuance of a resolution of either House of Parliament.

SUPPLEMENTARY

# 18 Interpretation

**18** In this Act–

**"address"**, in relation to a member of a limited liability partnership, means–

(a) if an individual, his usual residential address, and

(b) if a corporation or Scottish firm, its registered or principal office,

**"business"** includes every trade, profession and occupation,

**"designated member"** shall be construed in accordance with section 8,

**"enactment"** includes subordinate legislation (within the meaning of the Interpretation Act 1978),

**"incorporation document"** shall be construed in accordance with section 2,

**"limited liability partnership"** has the meaning given by section 1(2),

**"member"** shall be construed in accordance with section 4,

**"modifications"** includes additions and omissions,

**"name"**, in relation to a member of a limited liability partnership, means–

(a) if an individual, his forename and surname (or, in the case of a peer or other person usually known by a title, his title instead of or in addition to either or both his forename and surname), and

(b) if a corporation or Scottish firm, its corporate or firm name,

**"oversea limited liability partnership"** has the meaning given by section 14(3),

**"the registrar"** means–

(a) if the registered office of the limited liability partnership is, or is to be, situated in England and Wales or in Wales, the registrar or other officer performing under the Companies Act 1985 the duty of registration of companies in England and Wales, and

(b) if its registered office is, or is to be, situated in Scotland, the registrar or other officer performing under that Act the duty of registration of companies in Scotland, and

**"regulations"** has the meaning given by section 17(1).

## 19 Commencement, extent and short title

**19(1) [Commencement]** The preceding provisions of this Act shall come into force on such day as the Secretary of State may by order made by statutory instrument appoint; and different days may be appointed for different purposes.

**19(2) [Transitional provisions and savings]** The Secretary of State may by order made by statutory instrument make any transitional provisions and savings which appear appropriate in connection with the coming into force of any provision of this Act.

**19(3) [Pre-commencement enactment for Scotland Act 1998]** For the purposes of the Scotland Act 1998 this Act shall be taken to be a pre-commencement enactment within the meaning of that Act.

**19(4) [Northern Ireland]** Apart from sections 10 to 13 (and this section), this Act does not extend to Northern Ireland.

**19(5) [Citation]** This Act may be cited as the Limited Liability Partnerships Act 2000.

# SCHEDULE – NAMES AND REGISTERED OFFICES

Section 1

## Part I – Names

### INDEX OF NAMES

1 In section 714(1) of the Companies Act 1985 (index of names), after paragraph (d) insert–

"(da) limited liability partnerships incorporated under the Limited Liability Partnerships Act 2000,".

### NAME TO INDICATE STATUS

2(1) The name of a limited liability partnership must end with–

(a) the expression "limited liability partnership", or

(b) the abbreviation "llp" or "LLP".

2(2) But if the incorporation document for a limited liability partnership states that the registered office is to be situated in Wales, its name must end with–

(a) one of the expressions "limited liability partnership" and "partneriaeth atebolrwydd cyfyngedig", or

(b) one of the abbreviations "llp", "LLP", "pac" and "PAC".

### REGISTRATION OF NAMES

3(1) A limited liability partnership shall not be registered by a name–

(a) which includes, otherwise than at the end of the name, either of the expressions "limited liability partnership" and "partneriaeth atebolrwydd cyfyngedig" or any of the abbreviations "llp", "LLP", "pac" and "PAC",

(b) which is the same as a name appearing in the index kept under section 714(1) of the Companies Act 1985,

(c) the use of which by the limited liability partnership would in the opinion of the Secretary of State constitute a criminal offence, or

(d) which in the opinion of the Secretary of State is offensive.

3(2) Except with the approval of the Secretary of State, a limited liability partnership shall not be registered by a name which–

(a) in the opinion of the Secretary of State would be likely to give the impression that it is connected in any way with Her Majesty's Government or with any local authority, or

(b) includes any word or expression for the time being specified in regulations under section 29 of the Companies Act 1985 (names needing approval),

and in paragraph (a) **"local authority"** means any local authority within the meaning of the Local Government Act 1972 or the Local Government etc. (Scotland) Act 1994, the Common Council of the City of London or the Council of the Isles of Scilly.

## CHANGE OF NAME

**4(1)** A limited liability partnership may change its name at any time.

**4(2)** Where a limited liability partnership has been registered by a name which–

(a) is the same as or, in the opinion of the Secretary of State, too like a name appearing at the time of registration in the index kept under section 714(1) of the Companies Act 1985, or

(b) is the same as or, in the opinion of the Secretary of State, too like a name which should have appeared in the index at that time,

the Secretary of State may within twelve months of that time in writing direct the limited liability partnership to change its name within such period as he may specify.

**4(3)** If it appears to the Secretary of State–

(a) that misleading information has been given for the purpose of the registration of a limited liability partnership by a particular name, or

(b) that undertakings or assurances have been given for that purpose and have not been fulfilled,

he may, within five years of the date of its registration by that name, in writing direct the limited liability partnership to change its name within such period as he may specify.

**4(4)** If in the Secretary of State's opinion the name by which a limited liability partnership is registered gives so misleading an indication of the nature of its activities as to be likely to cause harm to the public, he may in writing direct the limited liability partnership to change its name within such period as he may specify.

**4(5)** But the limited liability partnership may, within three weeks from the date of the direction apply to the court to set it aside and the court may set the direction aside or confirm it and, if it confirms it, shall specify the period within which it must be complied with.

**4(6)** In sub-paragraph (5) **"the court"**means–

(a) if the registered office of the limited liability partnership is situated in England and Wales or in Wales, the High Court, and

(b) if it is situated in Scotland, the Court of Session.

**4(7)** Where a direction has been given under sub-paragraph (2), (3) or (4) specifying a period within which a limited liability partnership is to change its name, the Secretary of State may at any time before that period ends extend it by a further direction in writing.

**4(8)** If a limited liability partnership fails to comply with a direction under this paragraph–

(a) the limited liability partnership, and

(b) any designated member in default,

commits an offence.

**4(9)** A person guilty of an offence under sub-paragraph (8) is liable on summary conviction to a fine not exceeding level 3 on the standard scale.

## NOTIFICATION OF CHANGE OF NAME

**5(1)** Where a limited liability partnership changes its name it shall deliver notice of the change to the registrar.

**5(2)** A notice delivered under sub-paragraph (1)–

(a) shall be in a form approved by the registrar, and

(b) shall be signed by a designated member of the limited liability partnership or authenticated in a manner approved by the registrar.

**5(3)** Where the registrar receives a notice under sub-paragraph (2) he shall (unless the new name is one by which a limited liability partnership may not be registered)–

(a) enter the new name in the index kept under section 714(1) of the Companies Act 1985, and

(b) issue a certificate of the change of name.

**5(4)** The change of name has effect from the date on which the certificate is issued.

### EFFECT OF CHANGE OF NAME

**6** A change of name by a limited liability partnership does not–

(a) affect any of its rights or duties,

(b) render defective any legal proceedings by or against it,

and any legal proceedings that might have been commenced or continued against it by its former name may be commenced or continued against it by its new name.

### IMPROPER USE OF "LIMITED LIABILITY PARTNERSHIP" ETC.

**7(1)** If any person carries on a business under a name or title which includes as the last words–

(a) the expression "limited liability partnership" or "partneriaeth atebolrwydd cyfyngedig", or

(b) any contraction or imitation of either of those expressions,

that person, unless a limited liability partnership or oversea limited liability partnership, commits an offence.

**7(2)** A person guilty of an offence under sub-paragraph (1) is liable on summary conviction to a fine not exceeding level 3 on the standard scale.

### SIMILARITY OF NAMES

**8** In determining for the purposes of this Part whether one name is the same as another there are to be disregarded–

(1) the definite article as the first word of the name,

(2) any of the following (or their Welsh equivalents or abbreviations of them or their Welsh equivalents) at the end of the name–
"limited liability partnership",
"company",
"and company",
"company limited",
"and company limited",
"limited",
"unlimited",
"public limited company", and
"investment company with variable capital", and

(3) type and case of letters, accents, spaces between letters and punctuation marks,

and "and" and "&"are to be taken as the same.

## Part II – Registered Offices

### SITUATION OF REGISTERED OFFICE

**9(1)** A limited liability partnership shall–

(a) at all times have a registered office situated in England and Wales or in Wales, or

(b) at all times have a registered office situated in Scotland,

to which communications and notices may be addressed.

**9(2)** On the incorporation of a limited liability partnership the situation of its registered office shall be that stated in the incorporation document.

**9(3)** Where the registered office of a limited liability partnership is situated in Wales, but the incorporation document does not state that it is to be situated in Wales (as opposed to England and Wales), the limited liability partnership may deliver notice to the registrar stating that its registered office is to be situated in Wales.

**9(4)** A notice delivered under sub-paragraph (3)–

(a) shall be in a form approved by the registrar, and

(b) shall be signed by a designated member of the limited liability partnership or authenticated in a manner approved by the registrar.

CHANGE OF REGISTERED OFFICE

**10(1)** A limited liability partnership may change its registered office by delivering notice of the change to the registrar.

**10(2)** A notice delivered under sub-paragraph (1)–

(a) shall be in a form approved by the registrar, and

(b) shall be signed by a designated member of the limited liability partnership or authenticated in a manner approved by the registrar.

# INSOLVENCY RULES 1986

## Table of Contents

# THE INSOLVENCY RULES 1986

(SI 1986/1925)

*Made on 10 November 1986 by the Lord Chancellor under s. 411 and 412 of the Insolvency Act 1986. Operative from 29 December 1986.*

[**CCH Note:** These Rules are amended by the Insolvency (Amendment) Rules 1987 (SI 1987/1919) as from 11 January 1988, by the Insolvency (Amendment) Rules 1989 (SI 1989/397) as from 3 April 1989, by the Insolvency (Amendment) Rules 1991 (SI 1991/495) as from 2 April 1991, the Insolvency (Amendment) Rules 1993 (SI 1993/602) as from 5 April 1993 and the Insolvency (Amendment) Rules 1995 (SI 1995/586) as from 1 April 1995, the Insolvency (Amendment) Rules 1999 (SI 1999/359) as from 22 March 1999, Insolvency (Amendment) (No. 2) Rules 1999 (SI 1999/1022) as from 22 March 1999.]

## ARRANGEMENT OF RULES

RULE

2.13. Limited disclosure.
2.14. Release from duty to submit statement of affairs; extension of time.
2.15. Expenses of statement of affairs.
2.16. Statement to be annexed to proposals.
2.17. Notice of proposals to creditors.

## CHAPTER 3 — CREDITORS' AND COMPANY MEETINGS

*Section A: creditors' meetings*

2.18. Meeting to consider administrator's proposals.
2.19. Creditors' meetings generally.
2.20. The chairman at meetings.
2.21. Meeting requisitioned by creditors.
2.22. Entitlement to vote.
2.23. Admission and rejection of claims.
2.24. Secured creditors.
2.25. Holders of negotiable instruments.
2.26. Retention of title creditors.
2.27. Hire-purchase, conditional sale and chattel leasing agreements.
2.28. Resolutions and minutes.
2.29. Reports and notices under s. 23 and 25.
2.30. Notices to creditors.

*Section B: company meetings*

2.31. Venue and conduct of company meeting.

## CHAPTER 4 — THE CREDITORS' COMMITTEE

2.32. Constitution of committee.
2.33. Formalities of establishment.
2.34. Functions and meetings of the committee.
2.35. The chairman at meetings.
2.36. Quorum.
2.37. Committee-members' representatives.
2.38. Resignation.
2.39. Termination of membership.
2.40. Removal.
2.41. Vacancies.
2.42. Procedure at meetings.
2.43. Resolutions by post.
2.44. Information from administrator.
2.45. Expenses of members.
2.46. Members' dealings with the company.
2.46A. Formal defects.

## CHAPTER 5 — THE ADMINISTRATOR

2.47. Fixing of remuneration.
2.48. Recourse to meeting of creditors.
2.49. Recourse to the court.
2.50. Creditors' claim that remuneration is excessive.
2.51. Disposal of charged property, etc.
2.52. Abstract of receipts and payments.
2.53. Resignation.
2.54. Administrator deceased.

## CHAPTER 6 — VAT BAD DEBT RELIEF



# PART 3 — ADMINISTRATIVE RECEIVERSHIP

## CHAPTER 1 — APPOINTMENT OF ADMINISTRATIVE RECEIVER



## CHAPTER 2 — STATEMENT OF AFFAIRS AND REPORT TO CREDITORS



## CHAPTER 3 — CREDITORS' MEETING



## CHAPTER 4 — THE CREDITORS' COMMITTEE



## CHAPTER 5 — THE ADMINISTRATIVE RECEIVER (MISCELLANEOUS)

## CHAPTER 15 — DISCLAIMER



## CHAPTER 16 — SETTLEMENT OF LIST OF CONTRIBUTORIES (NO CVL APPLICATION)



## CHAPTER 17 — CALLS (NO CVL APPLICATION)



## CHAPTER 18 — SPECIAL MANAGER



## CHAPTER 19 — PUBLIC EXAMINATION OF COMPANY OFFICERS AND OTHERS



## CHAPTER 20 — ORDER OF PAYMENT OF COSTS, ETC., OUT OF ASSETS

## PART 8 — PROXIES AND COMPANY REPRESENTATION



## PART 9 — EXAMINATION OF PERSONS CONCERNED IN COMPANY AND INDIVIDUAL INSOLVENCY



## PART 10 — OFFICIAL RECEIVERS



## PART 11 — DECLARATION AND PAYMENT OF DIVIDEND (WINDING UP AND BANKRUPTCY)

## PART 12 — MISCELLANEOUS AND GENERAL



## PART 13 — INTERPRETATION AND APPLICATION



## SCHEDULES

**SCHEDULE**
4. Forms.
5. Punishment of Offences under the Rules.

# THE INSOLVENCY RULES 1986

(SI 1986/1925)

*Made on 10 November 1986 by the Lord Chancellor under s. 411 and 412 of the Insolvency Act 1986. Operative from 29 December 1986.*

[**CCH Note:** These Rules are amended by the Insolvency (Amendment) Rules 1987 (SI 1987/1919) as from 11 January 1988, by the Insolvency (Amendment) Rules 1989 (SI 1989/397) as from 3 April 1989, by the Insolvency (Amendment) Rules 1991 (SI 1991/495) as from 2 April 1991, the Insolvency (Amendment) Rules 1993 (SI 1993/602) as from 5 April 1993 and the Insolvency (Amendment) Rules 1995 (SI 1995/586) as from 1 April 1995, the Insolvency (Amendment) Rules 1999 (SI 1999/359) as from 22 March 1999 and the Insolvency (Amendment) (No. 2) Rules 1999 (SI 1999/1022) as from 22 March 1999.]

## INTRODUCTORY PROVISIONS

## 0.1 Citation and commencement

**0.1** These Rules may be cited as the Insolvency Rules 1986 and shall come into force on 29th December 1986.

**Note**

The relevant day is the same as for the Insolvency Act 1986 and Company Directors Disqualification Act 1986 and for a number of other statutory instruments (some since amended).

The Insolvency (Scotland) Rules 1986 (SI 1986/1915 (S 139))
The Insolvent Companies (Reports on Conduct of Directors) (No. 2) (Scotland) Rules 1986 (SI 1986/1916 (S 140) – revoked and replaced by SI 1996/1910)
The Receivers (Scotland) Regulations 1986 (SI 1986/1917 (S 141))
The Insurance Companies (Winding Up) (Scotland) Rules 1986 (SI 1986/1918 (S 142))
The Insolvency Regulations 1986 (SI 1986/1994 – revoked and replaced by SI 1994/2507)
The Insolvency Proceedings (Monetary Limits) Order 1986 (SI 1986/1996)
The Administration of Insolvent Estates of Deceased Persons Order 1986 (SI 1986/1999)
The Companies (Unfair Prejudice Applications) Rules 1986 (SI 1986/2000)
The Insolvency (Amendments of Subordinate Legislation) Order 1986 (SI 1986/2001)
The Insurance Companies (Winding-up) (Amendments) Rules 1986 (SI 1986/2002)
The Insolvency Fees Order 1986 (SI 1986/2030)
The Companies (Disqualification Orders) Regulations 1986 (SI 1986/2067)
The Co-operation of Insolvency Courts (Designation of Relevant Countries and Territories) Order 1986 (SI 1986/2123)
The Insolvent Companies (Reports on Conduct of Directors) No. 2 Rules 1986 (SI 1986/2134 – revoked and replaced by SI 1996/1909)
The Insolvent Partnerships Order 1986 (SI 1986/2142 – revoked and replaced by SI 1994/2421)
The Insolvency Practitioners Regulations 1986 (SI 1986/1995 – revoked and replaced by SI 1990/439)

## 0.2 Construction and interpretation

**0.2(1) [Definitions]** In these Rules–

**"the Act"**means the Insolvency Act 1986 (any reference to a numbered section being to a section of that Act);

**"the Companies Act"**means the Companies Act 1985;

**"CPR"**means the Civil Procedure Rules 1998 and **"CPR"** followed by a Part or rule by number means the Part or rule with that number in those Rules;

**"RSC"**followed by an Order by number means the Order with that number set out in Schedule 1 to the CPR; and

**"the Rules"**means the Insolvency Rules 1986.

**0.2(2) [Ex parte hearings]** References in the Rules to *ex parte* hearings shall be construed to as references to hearings without notice being served on any other party; references to applications made *ex parte* as references to applications made without notice being served on any other party and other references which include the expression "*ex parte*" shall be similarly construed.

**0.2(3) [Part 13]** Subject to paragraphs (1) and (2), Part 13 of the Rules has effect for their interpretation and application.

**History**
R. 0.2 substituted by the Insolvency (Amendment) (No.2) Rules 1999 (SI 1999/1022), r. 3, Sch., para. 1 as from 26 April 1999; r. 0.2 formerly read as follows:

"**0.2(1)** In these Rules–
**"the Act"** means the Insolvency Act 1986 (any reference to a numbered section being to a section of that Act);
**"the Companies Act"** means the Companies Act 1985;
**"the Rules"** means the Insolvency Rules 1986.
**0.2(2)** Subject to paragraph (1), Part 13 of the Rules has effect for their interpretation and application."

Originally r. 0.2 substituted by the Insolvency (Amendment) Rules 1987 (SI 1987/1919), r. 3(1), Sch., Pt. 1, para. 1 as from 11 January 1988; r. 0.2 originally read as follows:

**"Construction of principal references**
**0.2** In these Rules–
**"the Act"** means the Insolvency Act 1986 (any reference to a numbered section being to a section of that Act);
**"the Companies Act"** means the Companies Act 1985; and
**"the Rules"** means the Insolvency Rules 1986."

## 0.3 Extent

**0.3(1) [Pt. 1, 2 and 4]** Parts 1, 2, and 4 of the Rules, and Parts 7 to 13 as they relate to company insolvency, apply in relation to companies which the courts in England and Wales have jurisdiction to wind up.

**0.3(2) [Pt. 3]** Rule 3.1 applies to all receivers to whom Part III of the Act applies and the remainder of Part 3 of the Rules applies to administrative receivers appointed otherwise than under section 51 (Scottish Receivership).

**History**
In r. 0.3(2) the words from the beginning to "the remainder of" inserted by the Insolvency (Amendment) Rules 1987 (SI 1987/1919), r. 3(1), Sch., Pt. 1, para. 2 as from 11 January 1988.

**0.3(3) [Pt. 5 and 6]** Parts 5 and 6 of the Rules, and Parts 7 to 13 as they relate to individual insolvency, extend to England and Wales only.

# THE FIRST GROUP OF PARTS COMPANY INSOLVENCY; COMPANIES WINDING UP

# PART 1 – COMPANY VOLUNTARY ARRANGEMENTS

## Chapter 1 – Preliminary

### 1.1 Scope of this Part; interpretation

**1.1(1) [Application of Pt. 1 Rules]** The Rules in this Part apply where, pursuant to Part I of the Act, it is intended to make, and there is made, a proposal to a company and its creditors for a voluntary arrangement, that is to say, a composition in satisfaction of its debts or a scheme of arrangement of its affairs.

**1.1(2) [Application of Ch. 2–6]** In this Part–

(a) Chapter 2 applies where the proposal for a voluntary arrangement is made by the directors of the company, and neither is the company in liquidation, nor is an administration order (under Part II of the Act) in force in relation to it;

(b) Chapter 3 applies where the company is in liquidation or an administration order is in force, and the proposal is made by the liquidator or (as the case may be) the administrator, he in either case being the nominee for the purposes of the proposal;

(c) Chapter 4 applies in the same case as Chapter 3, but where the nominee is an insolvency practitioner other than the liquidator or the administrator; and

(d) Chapters 5 and 6 apply in all the three cases mentioned in sub-paragraphs (a) to (c) above.

**1.1(3) ["The responsible insolvency practitioner" in Ch. 3–5]** In Chapters 3, 4 and 5, the liquidator or the administrator is referred to as "the responsible insolvency practitioner".

# Chapter 2 – Proposal by Directors

## 1.2 Preparation of proposal

**1.2** The directors shall prepare for the intended nominee a proposal on which (with or without amendments to be made under Rule 1.3 below) to make his report to the court under section 2.

## 1.3 Contents of proposal

**1.3(1) [Explanation why voluntary arrangement desirable]** The directors' proposal shall provide a short explanation why, in their opinion, a voluntary arrangement under Part I of the Act is desirable, and give reasons why the company's creditors may be expected to concur with such an arrangement.

**1.3(2) [Other matters]** The following matters shall be stated, or otherwise dealt with, in the directors' proposal–

(a) the following matters, so far as within the directors' immediate knowledge–
  (i) the company's assets, with an estimate of their respective values,
  (ii) the extent (if any) to which the assets are charged in favour of creditors,
  (iii) the extent (if any) to which particular assets are to be excluded from the voluntary arrangement;

(b) particulars of any property, other than assets of the company itself, which is proposed to be included in the arrangement, the source of such property and the terms on which it is to be made available for inclusion;

(c) the nature and amount of the company's liabilities (so far as within the directors' immediate knowledge), the manner in which they are proposed to be met, modified, postponed or otherwise dealt with by means of the arrangement, and (in particular)–
  (i) how it is proposed to deal with preferential creditors (defined in section 4(7)) and creditors who are, or claim to be, secured,
  (ii) how persons connected with the company (being creditors) are proposed to be treated under the arrangement, and
  (iii) whether there are, to the directors' knowledge, any circumstances giving rise to the possibility, in the event that the company should go into liquidation, of claims under–

  section 238 (transactions at an undervalue),
  section 239 (preferences),
  section 244 (extortionate credit transactions), or
  section 245 (floating charges invalid);

  and, where any such circumstances are present, whether, and if so how, it is proposed under the voluntary arrangement to make provision for wholly or partly indemnifying the company in respect of such claims;

(d) whether any, and if so what, guarantees have been given of the company's debts by other persons, specifying which (if any) of the guarantors are persons connected with the company;

(e) the proposed duration of the voluntary arrangement;

(f) the proposed dates of distributions to creditors, with estimates of their amounts;

(g) the amount proposed to be paid to the nominee (as such) by way of remuneration and expenses;

(h) the manner in which it is proposed that the supervisor of the arrangement should be remunerated, and his expenses defrayed;

(j) whether, for the purposes of the arrangement, any guarantees are to be offered by directors, or other persons, and whether (if so) any security is to be given or sought;

(k) the manner in which funds held for the purposes of the arrangement are to be banked, invested or otherwise dealt with pending distribution to creditors;

(l) the manner in which funds held for the purpose of payment to creditors, and not so paid on the termination of the arrangement, are to be dealt with;

(m) the manner in which the business of the company is proposed to be conducted during the course of the arrangement;

(n) details of any further credit facilities which it is intended to arrange for the company, and how the debts so arising are to be paid;

(o) the functions which are to be undertaken by the supervisor of the arrangement; and

(p) the name, address and qualification of the person proposed as supervisor of the voluntary arrangement, and confirmation that he is (so far as the directors are aware) qualified to act as an insolvency practitioner in relation to the company.

**1.3(3) [Amendment of proposal]** With the agreement in writing of the nominee, the directors' proposal may be amended at any time up to delivery of the former's report to the court under section 2(2).

## 1.4 Notice to intended nominee

**1.4(1) [Written notice]** The directors shall give to the intended nominee written notice of their proposal.

**1.4(2) [Delivery of notice]** The notice, accompanied by a copy of the proposal, shall be delivered either to the nominee himself, or to a person authorised to take delivery of documents on his behalf.

**1.4(3) [Endorsement of receipt]** If the intended nominee agrees to act, he shall cause a copy of the notice to be endorsed to the effect that it has been received by him on a specified date; and the period of 28 days referred to in section 2(2) then runs from that date.

**1.4(4) [Return of endorsed notice]** The copy of the notice so endorsed shall be returned by the nominee forthwith to the directors at an address specified by them in the notice for that purpose.

## 1.5 Statement of affairs

**1.5(1) [Delivery of statement]** The directors shall, within 7 days after their proposal is delivered to the nominee, or within such longer time as he may allow, deliver to him a statement of the company's affairs.

**1.5(2) [Particulars in statement]** The statement shall comprise the following particulars (supplementing or amplifying, so far as is necessary for clarifying the state of the company's affairs, those already given in the directors' proposal)–

(a) a list of the company's assets, divided into such categories as are appropriate for easy identification, with estimated values assigned to each category;

(b) in the case of any property on which a claim against the company is wholly or partly secured, particulars of the claim and its amount, and of how and when the security was created;

(c) the names and addresses of the company's preferential creditors (defined in section 4(7)), with the amounts of their respective claims;

(d) the names and addresses of the company's unsecured creditors, with the amounts of their respective claims;

(e) particulars of any debts owed by or to the company to or by persons connected with it;

(f) the names and addresses of the company's members, with details of their respective shareholdings;

(g) such other particulars (if any) as the nominee may in writing require to be furnished for the purposes of making his report to the court on the directors' proposal.

**1.5(3) [Relevant date]** The statement of affairs shall be made up to a date not earlier than 2 weeks before the date of the notice to the nominee under Rule 1.4.

However, the nominee may allow an extension of that period to the nearest practicable date (not earlier than 2 months before the date of the notice under Rule 1.4); and if he does so, he shall give his reasons in his report to the court on the directors' proposal.

**1.5(4) [Certification of statement]** The statement shall be certified as correct, to the best of their knowledge and belief, by two or more directors of the company, or by the company secretary and at least one director (other than the secretary himself).

## 1.6 Additional disclosure for assistance of nominee

**1.6(1) [Nominee may request further information]** If it appears to the nominee that he cannot properly prepare his report on the basis of information in the directors' proposal and statement of affairs, he may call on the directors to provide him with–

(a) further and better particulars as to the circumstances in which, and the reasons why, the company is insolvent or (as the case may be) threatened with insolvency;

(b) particulars of any previous proposals which have been made in respect of the company under Part I of the Act;

(c) any further information with respect to the company's affairs which the nominee thinks necessary for the purposes of his report.

**1.6(2) [Information about directors etc.]** The nominee may call on the directors to inform him, with respect to any person who is, or at any time in the 2 years preceding the notice under Rule 1.4 had been, a director or officer of the company, whether and in what circumstances (in those 2 years or previously) that person–

(a) has been concerned in the affairs of any other company (whether or not incorporated in England and Wales) which has become insolvent, or

(b) has himself been adjudged bankrupt or entered into an arrangement with his creditors.

**1.6(3) [Access to accounts and records]** For the purpose of enabling the nominee to consider their proposal and prepare his report on it, the directors must give him access to the company's accounts and records.

## 1.7 Nominee's report on the proposal

**1.7(1) [Accompanying documents]** With his report to the court under section 2 the nominee shall deliver–

(a) a copy of the directors' proposal (with amendments, if any, authorised under Rule 1.3(3)); and

(b) a copy or summary of the company's statement of affairs.

**1.7(2) [Nominee's opinion re meetings]** If the nominee makes known his opinion that meetings of the company and its creditors should be summoned under section 3, his report shall have annexed to it his comments on the proposal.

If his opinion is otherwise, he shall give his reasons for that opinion.

**1.7(3) [Endorsement of date of filing, and right to inspect]** The court shall cause the nominee's report to be endorsed with the date on which it is filed in court. Any director, member or creditor of the company is entitled, at all reasonable times on any business day, to inspect the file.

**1.7(4) [Copy to company]** The nominee shall send a copy of his report, and of his comments (if any), to the company.

## 1.8 Replacement of nominee

**1.8** Where any person intends to apply to the court under section 2(4) for the nominee to be replaced, he shall give to the nominee at least 7 days' notice of his application.

## 1.9 Summoning of meetings under s. 3

**1.9(1) [Date for meetings]** If in his report the nominee states that in his opinion meetings of the company and its creditors should be summoned to consider the directors' proposal, the date on which the meetings are to be held shall be not less than 14, nor more than 28, days from that on which the nominee's report is filed in court under Rule 1.7.

**1.9(2) [Notices of meetings]** Notices calling the meetings shall be sent by the nominee, at least 14 days before the day fixed for them to be held–

(a) in the case of the creditors' meeting, to all the creditors specified in the statement of affairs, and any other creditors of the company of whom he is otherwise aware; and

(b) in the case of the meeting of members of the company, to all persons who are, to the best of the nominee's belief, members of it.

**1.9(3) [Contents etc. of notice]** Each notice sent under this Rule shall specify the court to which the nominee's report under section 2 has been delivered and shall state the effect of Rule 1.19(1), (3) and (4) (requisite majorities (creditors)); and with each notice there shall be sent–

(a) a copy of the directors' proposal;

(b) a copy of the statement of affairs or, if the nominee thinks fit, a summary of it (the summary to include a list of creditors and the amount of their debts); and

(c) the nominee's comments on the proposal.

# Chapter 3 – Proposal by Administrator or Liquidator (Himself the Nominee)

## 1.10 Preparation of proposal

**1.10(1) [Matters to be specified]** The responsible insolvency practitioner's proposal shall specify–

(a) all such matters as under Rule 1.3 in Chapter 2 the directors of the company would be required to include in a proposal by them, with the addition, where the company is subject to an administration order, of the names and addresses of the company's preferential creditors (defined in section 4(7)), with the amounts of their respective claims, and

(b) such other matters (if any) as the insolvency practitioner considers appropriate for ensuring that members and creditors of the company are enabled to reach an informed decision on the proposal.

**History**
In r. 1.10(1)(a) the words ", with the addition," to "amounts of their respective claims" inserted by the Insolvency (Amendment) Rules 1987 (SI 1987/1919), r. 3(1), Sch., Pt. 1, para. 3 as from 11 January 1988.

**1.10(2) [Notice to official receiver]** Where the company is being wound up by the court, the insolvency practitioner shall give notice of the proposal to the official receiver.

## 1.11 Summoning of meetings under s. 3

**1.11(1) [Venues and notice of meetings]** The responsible insolvency practitioner shall fix a venue for the creditors' meeting and the company meeting, and give at least 14 days' notice of the meetings–

(a) in the case of the creditors' meeting, to all the creditors specified in the company's statement of affairs, and to any other creditors of whom the insolvency practitioner is aware; and

(b) in the case of the company meeting, to all persons who are, to the best of his belief, members of the company.

**1.11(2) [Contents etc. of notice]** Each notice sent out under this Rule shall state the effect of Rule 1.19(1), (3) and (4) (requisite majorities (creditors)); and with it there shall be sent–

(a) a copy of the responsible insolvency practitioner's proposal, and

(b) a copy of the statement of affairs or, if he thinks fit, a summary of it (the summary to include a list of creditors and the amounts of their debts).

# Chapter 4 – Proposal by Administrator or Liquidator (Another Insolvency Practitioner the Nominee)

## 1.12 Preparation of proposal and notice to nominee

**1.12(1) [Manner of giving notice etc.]** The responsible insolvency practitioner shall give notice to the intended nominee, and prepare his proposal for a voluntary arrangement, in the same manner as is required of the directors, in the case of a proposal by them, under Chapter 2.

**1.12(2) [Application of r. 1.2 and 1.4]** Rule 1.2 applies to the responsible insolvency practitioner as it applies to the directors; and Rule 1.4 applies as regards the action to be taken by the nominee.

**1.12(3) [Content of proposal]** The content of the proposal shall be as required by Rule 1.3 (and, where relevant, Rule 1.10), reading references to the directors as referring to the responsible insolvency practitioner.

**History**

In r. 1.12(3) the words "(and, where relevant, Rule 1.10)" inserted by the Insolvency (Amendment) Rules 1987 (SI 1987/1919), r. 3(1), Sch., Pt. 1, para. 4 as from 11 January 1988.

**1.12(4) [Application of r. 1.6]** Rule 1.6 applies in respect of the information to be furnished to the nominee, reading references to the directors as referring to the responsible insolvency practitioner.

**1.12(5) [Copy statement of affairs]** With the proposal the responsible insolvency practitioner shall provide a copy of the company's statement of affairs.

**1.12(6) [Copy proposal to official receiver]** Where the company is being wound up by the court, the responsible insolvency practitioner shall send a copy of the proposal to the official receiver, accompanied by the name and address of the insolvency practitioner who has agreed to act as nominee.

**1.12(7) [Application of r. 1.7–1.9]** Rules 1.7 to 1.9 apply as regards a proposal under this Chapter as they apply to a proposal under Chapter 2.

# Chapter 5 – Proceedings on a Proposal made by the Directors, or by the Administrator, or by the Liquidator

### SECTION A: MEETINGS OF COMPANY'S CREDITORS AND MEMBERS

## 1.13 Summoning of meetings

**1.13(1) [Convenience of venue]** Subject as follows, in fixing the venue for the creditors' meeting and the company meeting, the person summoning the meeting ("the convener") shall have regard primarily to the convenience of the creditors.

**1.13(2) [Time of meetings]** Meetings shall in each case be summoned for commencement between 10.00 and 16.00 hours on a business day.

**1.13(3) [Creditors' meeting in advance]** The meetings shall be held on the same day and in the same place, but the creditors' meeting shall be fixed for a time in advance of the company meeting.

**1.13(4) [Forms of proxy]** With every notice summoning either meeting there shall be sent out forms of proxy.

[FORM 8.1]

## 1.14 The chairman at meetings

**1.14(1) [Convener to be chairman]** Subject as follows, at both the creditors' meeting and the company meeting, and at any combined meeting, the convener shall be chairman.

**1.14(2) [Other nominated chairman]** If for any reason he is unable to attend, he may nominate another person to act as chairman in his place; but a person so nominated must be either–

(a) a person qualified to act as an insolvency practitioner in relation to the company, or

(b) an employee of the convener or his firm who is experienced in insolvency matters.

## 1.15 The chairman as proxy-holder

**1.15** The chairman shall not by virtue of any proxy held by him vote to increase or reduce the amount of the remuneration or expenses of the nominee or the supervisor of the proposed arrangement, unless the proxy specifically directs him to vote in that way.

## 1.16 Attendance by company officers

**1.16(1) [Notice to directors and officers]** At least 14 days' notice to attend the meetings shall be given by the convener–

(a) to all directors of the company, and

(b) to any persons in whose case the convener thinks that their presence is required as being officers of the company, or as having been directors or officers of it at any time in the 2 years immediately preceding the date of the notice.

**1.16(2) [Exclusion of director etc.]** The chairman may, if he thinks fit, exclude any present or former director or officer from attendance at a meeting, either completely or for any part of it; and this applies whether or not a notice under this Rule has been sent to the person excluded.

### SECTION B: VOTING RIGHTS AND MAJORITIES

## 1.17 Voting rights (creditors)

**1.17(1) [Entitlement to vote]** Subject as follows, every creditor who was given notice of the creditors' meeting is entitled to vote at the meeting or any adjournment of it.

**1.17(2) [Calculation of votes]** Votes are calculated according to the amount of the creditor's debt as at the date of the meeting or, where the company is being wound up or is subject to an administration order, the date of its going into liquidation or (as the case may be) of the administration order.

**1.17(3) [Limitation on voting]** A creditor shall not vote in respect of a debt for an unliquidated amount, or any debt whose value is not ascertained, except where the chairman agrees to put upon the debt an estimated minimum value for the purpose of entitlement to vote.

**1.17(4) [Chairman's discretion]** At any creditors' meeting the chairman has power to admit or reject a creditor's claim for the purpose of his entitlement to vote, and the power is exercisable with respect to the whole or any part of the claim.

**1.17(5) [Appeal from chairman's decision]** The chairman's decision on a creditor's entitlement to vote is subject to appeal to the court by any creditor or member of the company.

**1.17(6) [Voting subject to objection]** If the chairman is in doubt whether a claim should be admitted or rejected, he shall mark it as objected to and allow the creditor to vote, subject to his vote being subsequently declared invalid if the objection to the claim is sustained.

**1.17(7) [Where chairman's decision reversed etc.]** If on an appeal the chairman's decision is reversed or varied, or a creditor's vote is declared invalid, the court may order another meeting to be summoned, or make such other order as it thinks just.

The court's power to make an order under this paragraph is exercisable only if it considers that the matter is such as gives rise to unfair prejudice or material irregularity.

**1.17(8) [Time for appeal]** An application to the court by way of appeal against the chairman's decision shall not be made after the end of the period of 28 days beginning with the first day on which each of the reports required by section 4(6) has been made to the court.

**1.17(9) [Costs of appeal]** The chairman is not personally liable for any costs incurred by any person in respect of an appeal under this Rule.

## 1.18 Voting rights (members)

**1.18(1) [Voting rights in accordance with articles]** Subject as follows, members of the company at their meeting vote according to the rights attaching to their shares respectively in accordance with the articles.

**1.18(2) [Where no voting rights]** Where no voting rights attach to a member's shares, he is nevertheless entitled to vote either for or against the proposal or any modification of it.

**1.18(3) [Interpretation]** References in this Rule to a person's shares include any other interest which he may have as a member of the company.

## 1.19 Requisite majorities (creditors)

**1.19(1) [Three-quarters majority]** Subject as follows, at the creditors' meeting for any resolution to pass approving any proposal or modification there must be a majority in excess of three-quarters in value of the creditors present in person or by proxy and voting on the resolution.

**1.19(2) [One-half majority]** The same applies in respect of any other resolution proposed at the meeting, but substituting one-half for three-quarters.

**1.19(3) [Votes to be left out of account]** In the following cases there is to be left out of account a creditor's vote in respect of any claim or part of a claim–

(a) where written notice of the claim was not given, either at the meeting or before it, to the chairman or convener of the meeting;

(b) where the claim or part is secured;

(c) where the claim is in respect of a debt wholly or partly on, or secured by, a current bill of exchange or promissory note, unless the creditor is willing–

(i) to treat the liability to him on the bill or note of every person who is liable on it antecedently to the company, and against whom a bankruptcy order has not been made (or in the case of a company, which has not gone into liquidation), as a security in his hands, and

(ii) to estimate the value of the security and (for the purpose of entitlement to vote, but not of any distribution under the arrangement) to deduct it from his claim.

**1.19(4) [Voting rendering resolution invalid]** Any resolution is invalid if those voting against it include more than half in value of the creditors, counting in these latter only those–

(a) to whom notice of the meeting was sent;

(b) whose votes are not to be left out of account under paragraph (3); and

(c) who are not, to the best of the chairman's belief, persons connected with the company.

**1.19(5) [Chairman's powers]** It is for the chairman of the meeting to decide whether under this Rule–

(a) a vote is to be left out of account in accordance with paragraph (3), or

(b) a person is a connected person for the purposes of paragraph (4)(c);

and in relation to the second of these two cases the chairman is entitled to rely on the information provided by the company's statement of affairs or otherwise in accordance with this Part of the Rules.

**1.19(6) [Use of proxy contrary to r. 1.15]** If the chairman uses a proxy contrary to Rule 1.15, his vote with that proxy does not count towards any majority under this Rule.

**1.19(7) [Application of r. 1.17]** Paragraphs (5) to (9) of Rule 1.17 apply as regards an appeal against the decision of the chairman under this Rule.

## 1.20 Requisite majorities (members)

**1.20(1) [One-half majority]** Subject as follows, and to any express provision made in the articles, at a company meeting any resolution is to be regarded as passed if voted for by more than one-half in value of the members present in person or by proxy and voting on the resolution.

**SI 1986/1925, r. 1.18(1)**

The value of members is determined by reference to the number of votes conferred on each member by the company's articles.

**History**
In r. 1.20(1) the words "in value" after the words "one-half" inserted and the second subparagraph added by the Insolvency (Amendment) Rules 1987 (SI 1987/1919), r. 3(1), Sch., Pt. 1, para. 5 as from 11 January 1988.

**1.20(2) [Rule 1.18(2) votes to be left out]** In determining whether a majority for any resolution has been obtained, there is to be left out of account any vote cast in accordance with Rule 1.18(2).

**1.20(3) [Use of proxy contrary to r. 1.15]** If the chairman uses a proxy contrary to Rule 1.15, his vote with that proxy does not count towards any majority under this Rule.

## 1.21 Proceedings to obtain agreement on the proposal

**1.21(1) [Meetings may be adjourned, and held together]** On the day on which the meetings are held, they may from time to time be adjourned; and, if the chairman thinks fit for the purpose of obtaining the simultaneous agreement of the meetings to the proposal (with the same modifications, if any), the meetings may be held together.

**1.21(2) [Adjournment]** If on that day the requisite majority for the approval of the voluntary arrangement (with the same modifications, if any) has not been obtained from both creditors and members of the company, the chairman may, and shall if it is so resolved, adjourn the meetings for not more than 14 days.

**1.21(3) [Final adjournment]** If there are subsequently further adjournments, the final adjournment shall not be to a day later than 14 days after the date on which the meetings were originally held.

**1.21(4) [Meetings must be adjourned to same day]** There shall be no adjournment of either meeting unless the other is also adjourned to the same business day.

**1.21(5) [Notice of adjournment]** In the case of a proposal by the directors, if the meetings are adjourned under paragraph (2), notice of the fact shall be given by the nominee forthwith to the court.

**1.21(6) [Deemed rejection of proposal]** If following any final adjournment of the meetings the proposal (with the same modifications, if any) is not agreed by both meetings, it is deemed rejected.

### SECTION C: IMPLEMENTATION OF THE ARRANGEMENT

## 1.22 Resolutions to follow approval

**1.22(1) [Resolution re supervisory acts]** If the voluntary arrangement is approved (with or without modifications) by the two meetings, a resolution may be taken by the creditors, where two or more insolvency practitioners are appointed to act as supervisor, on the question whether acts to be done in connection with the arrangement may be done by any one of them, or must be done by both or all.

**1.22(2) [Resolution in anticipation of approval]** A resolution under paragraph (1) may be passed in anticipation of the approval of the voluntary arrangement by the company meeting if that meeting has not then been concluded.

**1.22(3) [Other than nominee to be supervisor]** If at either meeting a resolution is moved for the appointment of some person other than the nominee to be supervisor of the arrangement, there must be produced to the chairman, at or before the meeting–

(a) that person's written consent to act (unless he is present and then and there signifies his consent), and

(b) his written confirmation that he is qualified to act as an insolvency practitioner in relation to the company.

## 1.23 Hand-over of property etc. to supervisor

**1.23(1) [Putting supervisor into possession of assets]** After the approval of the voluntary arrangement–

(a) the directors, or

(b) where the company is in liquidation or is subject to an administration order, and a person other than the responsible insolvency practitioner is appointed as supervisor of the voluntary arrangement, the insolvency practitioner,

shall forthwith do all that is required for putting the supervisor into possession of the assets included in the arrangement.

**1.23(2) [Discharge of insolvency practitioner's remuneration etc.]** Where the company is in liquidation or is subject to an administration order, the supervisor shall on taking possession of the assets discharge any balance due to the insolvency practitioner by way of remuneration or on account of–

(a) fees, costs, charges and expenses properly incurred and payable under the Act or the Rules, and

(b) any advances made in respect of the company, together with interest on such advances at the rate specified in section 17 of the Judgments Act 1838 at the date on which the company went into liquidation or (as the case may be) became subject to the administration order.

**1.23(3) [Undertaking to discharge]** Alternatively, the supervisor must, before taking possession, give the responsible insolvency practitioner a written undertaking to discharge any such balance out of the first realisation of assets.

**1.23(4) [Charge on assets]** The insolvency practitioner has a charge on the assets included in the voluntary arrangement in respect of any sums due as above until they have been discharged, subject only to the deduction from realisations by the supervisor of the proper costs and expenses of such realisations.

**1.23(5) [Discharge of guarantees etc.]** The supervisor shall from time to time out of the realisation of assets discharge all guarantees properly given by the responsible insolvency practitioner for the benefit of the company, and shall pay all the insolvency practitioner's expenses.

**1.23(6) [Interpretation]** References in this Rule to the responsible insolvency practitioner include, where a company is being wound up by the court, the official receiver, whether or not in his capacity as liquidator; and any sums due to the official receiver take priority over those due to a liquidator.

## 1.24 Report of meetings

**1.24(1) [Chairman to prepare report]** A report of the meetings shall be prepared by the person who was chairman of them.

**1.24(2) [Contents of report]** The report shall–

(a) state whether the proposal for a voluntary arrangement was approved or rejected and, if approved, with what (if any) modifications;

(b) set out the resolutions which were taken at each meeting, and the decision on each one;

(c) list the creditors and members of the company (with their respective values) who were present or represented at the meetings, and how they voted on each resolution; and

(d) include such further information (if any) as the chairman thinks it appropriate to make known to the court.

**1.24(3) [Copy report to be filed in court]** A copy of the chairman's report shall, within 4 days of the meetings being held, be filed in court; and the court shall cause that copy to be endorsed with the date of filing.

**1.24(4) [Notice of result]** In respect of each of the meetings, the persons to whom notice of its result is to be sent by the chairman under section 4(6) are all those who were sent notice of the meeting under this Part of the Rules.

The notice shall be sent immediately after a copy of the chairman's report is filed in court under paragraph (3).

**1.24(5) [Copy report to registrar of companies]** If the voluntary arrangement has been approved by the meetings (whether or not in the form proposed), the supervisor shall forthwith send a copy of the chairman's report to the registrar of companies. [FORM 1.1]

# 1.25 Revocation or suspension of the arrangement

**1.25(1) [Application of Rule]** This Rule applies where the court makes an order of revocation or suspension under section 6.

**1.25(2) [Service of copy orders]** The person who applied for the order shall serve sealed copies of it–

(a) on the supervisor of the voluntary arrangement, and

(b) on the directors of the company or the administrator or liquidator (according to who made the proposal for the arrangement).

Service on the directors may be effected by service of a single copy of the order on the company at its registered office.

**1.25(3) [Notice re further meetings]** If the order includes a direction by the court under section 6(4)(b) for any further meetings to be summoned, notice shall also be given (by the person who applied for the order) to whoever is, in accordance with the direction, required to summon the meetings.

**1.25(4) [Notice of order, and of intention re proposal]** The directors or (as the case may be) the administrator or liquidator shall–

(a) forthwith after receiving a copy of the court's order, give notice of it to all persons who were sent notice of the creditors' and company meetings or who, not having been sent that notice, appear to be affected by the order;

(b) within 7 days of their receiving a copy of the order (or within such longer period as the court may allow), give notice to the court whether it is intended to make a revised proposal to the company and its creditors, or to invite re-consideration of the original proposal.

**1.25(5) [Copy order to registrar of companies]** The person on whose application the order of revocation or suspension was made shall, within 7 days after the making of the order, deliver a copy of the order to the registrar of companies. [FORM 1.2]

# 1.26 Supervisor's accounts and reports

**1.26(1) [Obligation to keep accounts etc.]** Where the voluntary arrangement authorises or requires the supervisor–

(a) to carry on the business of the company or trade on its behalf or in its name, or

(b) to realise assets of the company, or

(c) otherwise to administer or dispose of any of its funds,

he shall keep accounts and records of his acts and dealings in and in connection with the arrangement, including in particular records of all receipts and payments of money.

**1.26(2) [Abstract of receipts and payments]** The supervisor shall, not less often than once in every 12 months beginning with the date of his appointment, prepare an abstract of such receipts and payments, and send copies of it, accompanied by his comments on the progress and efficacy of the arrangement, to–

(a) the court,

(b) the registrar of companies,

(c) the company, [FORM 1.3]

(d) all those of the company's creditors who are bound by the arrangement,

(e) subject to paragraph (5) below, the members of the company who are so bound, and

(f) if the company is not in liquidation, the company's auditors for the time being.

If in any period of 12 months he has made no payments and had no receipts, he shall at the end of that period send a statement to that effect to all those specified in sub-paragraphs (a) to (f) above.

**1.26(3) [Abstract under r. 1.26(2)]** An abstract provided under paragraph (2) shall relate to a period beginning with the date of the supervisor's appointment or (as the case may be) the day following the end of the last period for which an abstract was prepared under this Rule; and copies of the abstract shall be sent out, as required by paragraph (2), within the 2 months following the end of the period to which the abstract relates.

**1.26(4) [If supervisor not authorised as in r. 1.26(1)]** If the supervisor is not authorised as mentioned in paragraph (1), he shall, not less often than once in every 12 months beginning with the date of his appointment, send to all those specified in paragraph (2)(a) to (f) a report on the progress and efficacy of the voluntary arrangement.

**1.26(5) [Powers of court]** The court may, on application by the supervisor–

(a) dispense with the sending under this Rule of abstracts or reports to members of the company, either altogether or on the basis that the availability of the abstract or report to members is to be advertised by the supervisor in a specified manner;

(b) vary the dates on which the obligation to send abstracts or reports arises.

# 1.27 Production of accounts and records to Secretary of State

**1.27(1) [Powers of Secretary of State]** The Secretary of State may at any time during the course of the voluntary arrangement or after its completion require the supervisor to produce for inspection–

(a) his records and accounts in respect of the arrangement, and

(b) copies of abstracts and reports prepared in compliance with Rule 1.26.

**1.27(2) [Production and duty to comply]** The Secretary of State may require production either at the premises of the supervisor or elsewhere; and it is the duty of the supervisor to comply with any requirement imposed on him under this Rule.

**1.27(3) [Audit of accounts and records]** The Secretary of State may cause any accounts and records produced to him under this Rule to be audited; and the supervisor shall give to the Secretary of State such further information and assistance as he needs for the purposes of his audit.

# 1.28 Fees, costs, charges and expenses

**1.28** The fees, costs, charges and expenses that may be incurred for any of the purposes of the voluntary arrangement are –

(a) any disbursements made by the nominee prior to the approval of the arrangement, and any remuneration for his services as such agreed between himself and the company (or, as the case may be, the administrator or liquidator);

(b) any fees, costs, charges or expenses which–
   (i) are sanctioned by the terms of the arrangement, or
   (ii) would be payable, or correspond to those which would be payable, in an administration or winding up.

# 1.29 Completion of the arrangement

**1.29(1) [Supervisor to send notice]** Not more than 28 days after the final completion of the voluntary arrangement, the supervisor shall send to all the creditors and members of the company who are bound by it a notice that the voluntary arrangement has been fully implemented.

**1.29(2) [Supervisor's report]** With the notice there shall be sent to each creditor and member a copy of a report by the supervisor summarising all receipts and payments made by him in pursuance of the arrangement, and explaining any difference in the actual implementation of it as compared with the proposal as approved by the creditors' and company meetings.

**1.29(3) [Copy notice and report to registrar]** The supervisor shall, within the 28 days mentioned above, send to the registrar of companies and to the court a copy of the notice to creditors and members under paragraph (1), together with a copy of the report under paragraph (2).

[FORM 1.4]

**1.29(4) [Extension of time]** The court may, on application by the supervisor, extend the period of 28 days under paragraphs (1) and (3).

## Chapter 6 – General

### 1.30 False representations, etc.

**1.30(1) [Offence]** A person being a past or present officer of a company commits an offence if he makes any false representation or commits any other fraud for the purpose of obtaining the approval of the company's members or creditors to a proposal for a voluntary arrangement under Part I of the Act.

**1.30(2) ["Officer"]** For this purpose "officer" includes a shadow director.

**1.30(3) [Penalties]** A person guilty of an offence under this Rule is liable to imprisonment or a fine, or both.

# PART 2 – ADMINISTRATION PROCEDURE

## Chapter 1 – Application for, and Making of, the Order

### 2.1 Affidavit to support petition

**2.1(1) [Affidavit required]** Where it is proposed to apply to the court by petition for an administration order to be made in relation to a company, an affidavit complying with Rule 2.3 below must be prepared and sworn, with a view to its being filed in court in support of the petition. [FORM 2.1]

**2.1(2) [Petition presented by company or directors]** If the petition is to be presented by the company or by the directors, the affidavit must be made by one of the directors, or the secretary of the company, stating himself to make it on behalf of the company or, as the case may be, on behalf of the directors.

**2.1(3) [Creditor's petition]** If the petition is to be presented by creditors, the affidavit must be made by a person acting under the authority of them all, whether or not himself one of their number. In any case there must be stated in the affidavit the nature of his authority and the means of his knowledge of the matters to which the affidavit relates.

**2.1(4) [Supervisor's petition]** If the petition is to be presented by the supervisor of a voluntary arrangement under Part I of the Act, it is to be treated as if it were a petition by the company.

### 2.2 Independent report on company's affairs

**2.2(1) [Report that administrator's appointment expedient]** There may be prepared, with a view to its being exhibited to the affidavit in support of the petition, a report by an independent person to the effect that the appointment of an administrator for the company is expedient.

**2.2(2) [Who may report]** The report may be by the person proposed as administrator, or by any other person having adequate knowledge of the company's affairs, not being a director, secretary, manager, member, or employee of the company.

**2.2(3) [Report to specify purpose of order]** The report shall specify the purposes which, in the opinion of the person preparing it, may be achieved for the company by the making of an administration order, being purposes particularly specified in section 8(3).

### 2.3 Contents of affidavit

**2.3(1) [Statements in affidavit]** The affidavit shall state–

(a) the deponent's belief that the company is, or is likely to become, unable to pay its debts and the grounds of that belief; and

(b) which of the purposes specified in section 8(3) is expected to be achieved by the making of an administration order.

**2.3(2) [Company's financial position]** There shall in the affidavit be provided a statement of the company's financial position, specifying (to the best of the deponent's knowledge and belief) assets and liabilities, including contingent and prospective liabilities.

**2.3(3) [Details of creditors' security]** Details shall be given of any security known or believed to be held by creditors of the company, and whether in any case the security is such as to confer power on the holder to appoint an administrative receiver. If an administrative receiver has been appointed, that fact shall be stated.

**2.3(4) [Details of winding-up petition]** If any petition has been presented for the winding up of the company, details of it shall be given in the affidavit, so far as within the immediate knowledge of the deponent.

**2.3(5) [Other matters]** If there are other matters which, in the opinion of those intending to present the petition for an administration order, will assist the court in deciding whether to make such an order, those matters (so far as lying within the knowledge or belief of the deponent) shall also be stated.

**2.3(6) [Rule 2.2 report]** If a report has been prepared for the company under Rule 2.2, that fact shall be stated. If not, an explanation shall be provided why not.

## 2.4 Form of petition

**2.4(1) [Petition presented by company or directors]** If presented by the company or by the directors, the petition shall state the name of the company and its address for service, which (in the absence of special reasons to the contrary) is that of the company's registered office.

**2.4(2) [Single creditor's petition]** If presented by a single creditor, the petition shall state his name and address for service.

**2.4(3) [Director's petition]** If the petition is presented by the directors, it shall state that it is so presented under section 9; but from and after presentation it is to be treated for all purposes as the petition of the company.

**2.4(4) [Creditors' petition]** If the petition is presented by two or more creditors, it shall state that it is so presented (naming them); but from and after presentation it is to be treated for all purposes as the petition of one only of them, named in the petition as petitioning on behalf of himself and other creditors. An address for service for that one shall be specified.

**2.4(5) [Specification of proposed administrator]** The petition shall specify the name and address of the person proposed to be appointed as administrator; and it shall be stated that, to the best of the petitioner's knowledge and belief, the person is qualified to act as an insolvency practitioner in relation to the company.

**2.4(6) [Documents to be exhibited]** There shall be exhibited to the affidavit in support of the petition–

(a) a copy of the petition;

(b) a written consent by the proposed administrator to accept appointment, if an administration order is made; and [FORM 2.2]

(c) if a report has been prepared under Rule 2.2, a copy of it.

## 2.5 Filing of petition

**2.5(1) [Filing in court]** The petition and affidavit shall be filed in court, with a sufficient number of copies for service and use as provided by Rule 2.6.

**2.5(2) [Sealed copies]** Each of the copies delivered shall have applied to it the seal of the court and be issued to the petitioner; and on each copy there shall be endorsed the date and time of filing.

**2.5(3) [Venue for hearing]** The court shall fix a venue for the hearing of the petition and this also shall be endorsed on each copy of the petition issued under paragraph (2).

**2.5(4) [After petition filed]** After the petition is filed, it is the duty of the petitioner to notify the court in writing of any winding-up petition presented against the company, as soon as he becomes aware of it.

## 2.6 Service of petition

**2.6(1) [Interpretation]** In the following paragraphs of this Rule, references to the petition are to a copy of the petition issued by the court under Rule 2.5(2) together with the affidavit in support of it and the documents (other than the copy petition) exhibited to the affidavit.

**2.6(2) [Persons to be served]** The petition shall be served–

(a) on any person who has appointed, or is or may be entitled to appoint, an administrative receiver for the company;

(b) if an administrative receiver has been appointed, on him;

(c) if there is pending a petition for the winding up of the company, on the petitioner (and also on the provisional liquidator, if any); and

(d) on the person proposed as administrator.

**History**
In r. 2.6(2) para. (a) substituted by the Insolvency (Amendment) Rules 1987 (SI 1987/1919), r. 3(1), Sch., Pt. 1, para. 6 as from 11 January 1988; para. (a) formerly read as follows:

"(a) on any person who has appointed an administrative receiver for the company, or has the power to do so;"

**2.6(3) [Creditors' petition]** If the petition for the making of an administration order is presented by creditors of the company, the petition shall be served on the company.

## 2.6A Notice to sheriff, etc.

**2.6A** The petitioner shall forthwith after filing the petition give notice of its presentation to–

(a) any sheriff or other officer who to his knowledge is charged with an execution or other legal process against the company or its property, and

(b) any person who to his knowledge has distrained against the company or its property.

**History**
R. 2.6A inserted by the Insolvency (Amendment) Rules 1987 (SI 1987/1919), r. 3(1), Sch., Pt. 1, para. 7 as from 11 January 1988.

## 2.7 Manner in which service to be effected

**2.7(1) [Person to effect service]** Service of the petition in accordance with Rule 2.6 shall be effected by the petitioner, or his solicitor, or by a person instructed by him or his solicitor, not less than 5 days before the date fixed for the hearing.

**2.7(2) [How effected]** Service shall be effected as follows–

(a) on the company (subject to paragraph (3) below), by delivering the documents to its registered office;

(b) on any other person (subject to paragraph (4)), by delivering the documents to his proper address;

(c) in either case, in such other manner as the court may direct.

**2.7(3) [Service to registered office not practicable]** If delivery to the company's registered office is not practicable, service may be effected by delivery to its last known principal place of business in England and Wales.

**2.7(4) [Proper address under r. 2.7(2)(b)]** Subject to paragraph (4A), for the purposes of paragraph (2)(b), a person's proper address is any which he has previously notified as his address for service; but if he has not notified any such address, service may be effected by delivery to his usual or last known address.

**History**
In r. 2.7(4) the words "Subject to paragraph (4A)," inserted by the Insolvency (Amendments) Rules 1987 (SI 1987/1919), r. 3(1), Sch., Pt. 1, para. 8(1) as from 11 January 1988.

**2.7(4A) [Other person re r. 2.7(2)(b), 2.7(4)]** In the case of a person who–

(a) is an authorised institution or former authorised institution within the meaning of the Banking Act 1987,

(b) has appointed, or is or may be entitled to appoint, an administrative receiver of the company, and

(c) has not notified an address for service,

the proper address is the address of an office of that person where, to the knowledge of the petitioner, the company maintains a bank account or, where no such office is known to the petitioner, the registered office of that person, or, if there is no such office, his usual or last known address.

**History**

R. 2.7(4A) inserted by the Insolvency (Amendment) Rules 1987 (SI 1987/1919), r. 3(1), Sch., Pt. 1, para. 8(2) as from 11 January 1988.

**2.7(5) [What constitutes delivery]** Delivery of documents to any place or address may be made by leaving them there, or sending them by first class post.

## 2.8 Proof of service

**2.8(1) [Verifying affidavit]** Service of the petition shall be verified by affidavit, specifying the date on which, and the manner in which, service was effected. [FORM 2.3]

**2.8(2) [Filing in court]** The affidavit, with a sealed copy of the petition exhibited to it, shall be filed in court forthwith after service, and in any event not less than one day before the hearing of the petition.

## 2.9 The hearing

**2.9(1) [Appearances]** At the hearing of the petition, any of the following may appear or be represented–

(a) the petitioner;

(b) the company;

(c) any person who has appointed, or is or may be entitled to appoint, an administrative receiver of the company;

(d) if an administrative receiver has been appointed, he;

(e) any person who has presented a petition for the winding up of the company;

(f) the person proposed for appointment as administrator; and

(g) with the leave of the court, any other person who appears to have an interest justifying his appearance.

**History**

In r. 2.9(1) para. (c) substituted by the Insolvency (Amendment) Rules 1987 (SI 1987/1919), r. 3(1), Sch., Pt. 1, para. 9 as from 11 January 1988; para. (c) formerly read as follows:

"(c) any person who has appointed an administrative receiver, or has the power to do so;".

**2.9(2) [Costs]** If the court makes an administration order, the costs of the petitioner, and of any person appearing whose costs are allowed by the court, are payable as an expense of the administration. [FORM 2.4]

## 2.10 Notice and advertisement of administration order

**2.10(1) [Court to give notice]** If the court makes an administration order, it shall forthwith give notice to the person appointed as administrator. [FORM 2.4A]

**History**

Against r. 2.10(1) the words "[FORM 2.4A]" inserted by the Insolvency (Amendment) Rules 1987 (SI 1987/1919), r. 3(1), Sch., Pt. 2, para. 156(1) as from 11 January 1988.

**2.10(2) [Advertisement]** Forthwith after the order is made, the administrator shall advertise its making once in the Gazette, and once in such newspaper as he thinks most appropriate for ensuring that the order comes to the notice of the company's creditors. [FORM 2.5]

**2.10(3) [Administrator to give notice]** The administrator shall also forthwith give notice of the making of the order–

(a) to any person who has appointed, or is or may be entitled to appoint, an administrative receiver of the company;

(b) if an administrative receiver has been appointed, to him;

(c) if there is pending a petition for the winding up of the company, to the petitioner (and also to the provisional liquidator, if any); and

(d) to the registrar of companies. [FORM 2.6]

**History**

In r. 2.10(3) para. (a) substituted by the Insolvency (Amendment) Rules 1987 (SI 1987/1919), r. 3(1), Sch., Pt. 1, para. 10 as from 11 January 1988; para. (a) formerly read as follows:

"(a) to any person who has appointed an administrative receiver, or has power to do so;".

**2.10(4) [Sealed copies]** Two sealed copies of the order shall be sent by the court to the administrator, one of which shall be sent by him to the registrar of companies in accordance with section 21(2). [FORM 2.7]

**2.10(5) [Directions under s. 9(4)]** If under section 9(4) the court makes any other order, it shall give directions as to the persons to whom, and how, notice of it is to be given.

# Chapter 2 – Statement of Affairs and Proposals to Creditors

## 2.11 Notice requiring statement of affairs

**2.11(1) [Notice]** Where the administrator determines to require a statement of the company's affairs to be made out and submitted to him in accordance with section 22, he shall send notice to each of the persons whom he considers should be made responsible under that section, requiring them to prepare and submit the statement. [FORM 2.8]

**History**

In r. 2.11(1) the first word "Where" substituted for the former word "If" by the Insolvency (Amendment) Rules 1987 (SI 1987/1919), r. 3(1), Sch., Pt. 1, para. 11 as from 11 January 1988.

**2.11(2) ["The deponents"]** The persons to whom the notice is sent are referred to in this Chapter as "the deponents".

**2.11(3) [Contents of notice]** The notice shall inform each of the deponents–

(a) of the names and addresses of all others (if any) to whom the same notice has been sent;

(b) of the time within which the statement must be delivered;

(c) of the effect of section 22(6) (penalty for non-compliance); and

(d) of the application to him, and to each of the other deponents, of section 235 (duty to provide information, and to attend on the administrator if required).

**2.11(4) [Instructions for preparation of statement]** The administrator shall, on request, furnish each deponent with the forms required for the preparation of the statement of affairs.

**History**

In r. 2.11(4) the words "the forms required" to the end substituted by the Insolvency (Amendment) Rules 1987 (SI 1987/1919), r. 3(1), Sch., Pt. 1, para. 12 as from 11 January 1988: the former words read as follows:

"instructions for the preparation of the statement and with the forms required for that purpose".

## 2.12 Verification and filing

**2.12(1) [Form and verification]** The statement of affairs shall be in Form 2.9, shall contain all the particulars required by that form and shall be verified by affidavit by the deponents (using the same form). [FORM 2.9]

**2.12(2) [Affidavits of concurrence]** The administrator may require any of the persons mentioned in section 22(3) to submit an affidavit of concurrence, stating that he concurs in the statement of affairs.

**2.12(3) [Affidavit may be qualified]** An affidavit of concurrence may be qualified in respect of matters dealt with in the statement of affairs, where the maker of the affidavit is not in agreement with the deponents, or he considers the statement to be erroneous or misleading, or he is without the direct knowledge necessary for concurring with it.

**2.12(4) [Delivery of statement to administrator]** The statement of affairs shall be delivered to the administrator by the deponent making the affidavit of verification (or by one of them, if more than one), together with a copy of the verified statement.

**2.12(5) [Delivery of affidavit of concurrence]** Every affidavit of concurrence shall be delivered by the person who makes it, together with a copy.

**2.12(6) [Filing in court]** The administrator shall file the verified copy of the statement, and the affidavits of concurrence (if any) in court.

## 2.13 Limited disclosure

**2.13(1) [Administrator may apply to court]** Where the administrator thinks that it would prejudice the conduct of the administration for the whole or part of the statement of affairs to be disclosed, he may apply to the court for an order of limited disclosure in respect of the statement, or any specified part of it.

**2.13(2) [Powers of court]** The court may on the application order that the statement or, as the case may be, the specified part of it, be not filed in court, or that it is to be filed separately and not be open to inspection otherwise than with leave of the court.

**2.13(3) [Directions]** The court's order may include directions as to the delivery of documents to the registrar of companies and the disclosure of relevant information to other persons.

## 2.14 Release from duty to submit statement of affairs; extension of time

**2.14(1) [Exercise of s. 22(5) power]** The power of the administrator under section 22(5) to give a release from the obligation imposed by that section, or to grant an extension of time, may be exercised at the administrator's own discretion, or at the request of any deponent.

**2.14(2) [Deponent may apply to court]** A deponent may, if he requests a release or extension of time and it is refused by the administrator, apply to the court for it.

**2.14(3) [Court may dismiss application etc.]** The court may, if it thinks that no sufficient cause is shown for the application, dismiss it; but it shall not do so unless the applicant has had an opportunity to attend the court for an *ex parte* hearing, of which he has been given at least 7 days' notice.

If the application is not dismissed under this paragraph, the court shall fix a venue for it to be heard, and give notice to the deponent accordingly.

**2.14(4) [Deponent to send notice to administrator]** The deponent shall, at least 14 days before the hearing, send to the administrator a notice stating the venue and accompanied by a copy of the application, and of any evidence which he (the deponent) intends to adduce in support of it.

**2.14(5) [Appearance etc. by administrator]** The administrator may appear and be heard on the application; and, whether or not he appears, he may file a written report of any matters which he considers ought to be drawn to the court's attention.

If such a report is filed, a copy of it shall be sent by the administrator to the deponent, not later than 5 days before the hearing.

**2.14(6) [Sealed copies of order]** Sealed copies of any order made on the application shall be sent by the court to the deponent and the administrator.

**2.14(7) [Applicant's costs]** On any application under this Rule the applicant's costs shall be paid in any event by him and, unless the court otherwise orders, no allowance towards them shall be made out of the assets.

## 2.15 Expenses of statement of affairs

**2.15(1) [Payment of expenses]** A deponent making the statement of affairs and affidavit shall be allowed, and paid by the administrator out of his receipts, any expenses incurred by the deponent in so doing which the administrator considers reasonable.

**2.15(2) [Appeal to court]** Any decision by the administrator under this Rule is subject to appeal to the court.

**2.15(3) [Effect of Rule]** Nothing in this Rule relieves a deponent from any obligation with respect to the preparation, verification and submission of the statement of affairs, or to the provision of information to the administrator.

## 2.16 Statement to be annexed to proposals

**2.16(1) [Contents of statement]** There shall be annexed to the administrator's proposals, when sent to the registrar of companies under section 23 and laid before the creditors' meeting to be summoned under that section, a statement by him showing–

(a) details relating to his appointment as administrator, the purposes for which an administration order was applied for and made, and any subsequent variation of those purposes;

(b) the names of the directors and secretary of the company;

(c) an account of the circumstances giving rise to the application for an administration order;

(d) if a statement of affairs has been submitted, a copy or summary of it, with the administrator's comments, if any;

(e) if no statement of affairs has been submitted, details of the financial position of the company at the latest practicable date (which must, unless the court otherwise orders, be a date not earlier than that of the administration order);

(f) the manner in which the affairs and business of the company–
   (i) have, since the date of the administrator's appointment, been managed and financed, and
   (ii) will, if the administrator's proposals are approved, continue to be managed and financed; and

(g) such other information (if any) as the administrator thinks necessary to enable creditors to decide whether or not to vote for the adoption of the proposals.

**History**
R. 2.16(1) renumbered as such and para. (f) substituted by the Insolvency (Amendment) Rules 1987 (SI 1987/1919), r. 3(1), Sch., Pt. 1, para. 12(1) as from 11 January 1988; para. (f) formerly read as follows:
"(f) the manner in which the affairs of the company will be managed and its business financed, if the administrator's proposals are approved; and".

**2.16(2) [Where s. 18 application]** Where the administrator intends to apply to the court under section 18 for the administration order to be discharged at a time before he has sent a statement of his proposals to creditors in accordance with section 23(1), he shall, at least 10 days before he makes such an application, send to all creditors of the company (so far as he is aware of their addresses) a report containing the information required by paragraph (1)(a)–(f)(i) of this Rule.

**History**
R. 2.16(2) added by the Insolvency (Amendment) Rules 1987 (SI 1987/1919), r. 3(1), Sch., Pt. 1, para. 12(2) as from 11 January 1988.

## 2.17 Notice to members of proposals to creditors

**2.17** The manner of publishing–

(a) under section 23(2)(b), notice to members of the administrator's proposals to creditors, and

(b) under section 25(3)(b), notice to members of substantial revisions of the proposals,

shall be by gazetting; and the notice shall also in either case be advertised once in the newspaper in which the administration order was advertised.

# Chapter 3 – Creditors' and Company Meetings

### SECTION A: CREDITORS' MEETINGS

## 2.18 Meeting to consider administrator's proposals

**2.18(1) [Notice of s. 23(1) meeting]** Notice of the creditors' meeting to be summoned under section 23(1) shall be given to all the creditors of the company who are identified in the statement of affairs, or are known to the administrator and had claims against the company at the date of the administration order.

**2.18(2) [Newspaper advertisement]** Notice of the meeting shall also (unless the court otherwise directs) be given by advertisement in the newspaper in which the administration order was advertised.

**2.18(3) [Notice to directors etc.]** Notice to attend the meeting shall be sent out at the same time to any directors or officers of the company (including persons who have been directors or officers in the past) whose presence at the meeting is, in the administrator's opinion, required.

[FORM 2.10]

**2.18(4) [Adjournment of meeting]** If at the meeting there is not the requisite majority for approval of the administrator's proposals (with modifications, if any), the chairman may, and shall if a resolution is passed to that effect, adjourn the meeting for not more than 14 days.

## 2.19 Creditors' meetings generally

**2.19(1) [Application of Rule]** This Rule applies to creditors' meetings summoned by the administrator under–

(a) section 14(2)(b) (general power to summon meetings of creditors);

(b) section 17(3) (requisition by creditors; direction by the court);

(c) section 23(1) (to consider administrator's proposals); or

(d) section 25(2)(b) (to consider substantial revisions).

**2.19(2) [Convenience of venue]** In fixing the venue for the meeting, the administrator shall have regard to the convenience of creditors.

**2.19(3) [Time of meeting]** The meeting shall be summoned for commencement between 10.00 and 16.00 hours on a business day, unless the court otherwise directs.

**2.19(4) [Notice]** Notice of the meeting shall be given to all creditors who are known to the administrator and had claims against the company at the date of the administration order; and the notice shall specify the purpose of the meeting and contain a statement of the effect of Rule 2.22(1) (entitlement to vote).

[FORM 2.11]
[FORM 2.22]

**History**

In r. 2.19(4) the words "At least 21 days" formerly appearing at the beginning omitted by the Insolvency (Amendment) Rules 1987 (SI 1987/1919), r. 3(1), Sch., Pt. 1, para. 13(1) as from 11 January 1988. Also against r. 2.19(4) the words "[FORM 2.22]" inserted by the Insolvency (Amendment) Rules 1987 (SI 1987/1919), r. 3(1), Sch., Pt. 2, para. 156(1) as from the same date.

**2.19(4A) [Period of notice]** Except in relation to a meeting summoned under section 23(1) or 25(2), at least 21 days' notice of the meeting shall be given.

**History**

R. 2.19(4A) inserted by the Insolvency (Amendment) Rules 1987 (SI 1987/1919), r. 3(1), Sch., Pt. 1, para. 13(2) as from 11 January 1988.

**2.19(5) [Forms of proxy]** With the notice summoning the meeting there shall be sent out forms of proxy.

[FORM 8.2]

**2.19(6) [Adjournment if no chairman]** If within 30 minutes from the time fixed for commencement of the meeting there is no person present to act as chairman, the meeting stands adjourned to the same time and place in the following week or, if that is not a business day, to the business day immediately following.

**2.19(7) [Further adjournments]** The meeting may from time to time be adjourned, if the chairman thinks fit, but not for more than 14 days from the date on which it was fixed to commence.

## 2.20 The chairman at meetings

**2.20(1) [Administrator or his nominee to be chairman]** At any meeting of creditors summoned by the administrator, either he shall be chairman, or a person nominated by him in writing to act in his place.

**2.20(2) [Nominee chairman]** A person so nominated must be either–

(a) one who is qualified to act as an insolvency practitioner in relation to the company, or

(b) an employee of the administrator or his firm who is experienced in insolvency matters.

## 2.21 Meeting requisitioned by creditors

**2.21(1) [Documents to accompany request]** Any request by creditors to the administrator for a meeting of creditors to be summoned shall be accompanied by–

(a) a list of the creditors concurring with the request, showing the amounts of their respective claims in the administration;

(b) from each creditor concurring, written confirmation of his concurrence; and

(c) a statement of the purpose of the proposed meeting.

This paragraph does not apply if the requisitioning creditor's debt is alone sufficient, without the concurrence of other creditors.

**2.21(2) [Fixing of venue]** The administrator shall, if he considers the request to be properly made in accordance with section 17(3), fix a venue for the meeting, not more than 35 days from his receipt of the request, and give at least 21 days' notice of the meeting to creditors.

**2.21(3) [Expenses]** The expenses of summoning and holding a meeting at the instance of any person other than the administrator shall be paid by that person, who shall deposit with the administrator security for their payment.

**2.21(4) [Deposit under r. 2.21(3)]** The sum to be deposited shall be such as the administrator may determine, and he shall not act without the deposit having been made.

**2.21(5) [Resolution of meeting re expenses]** The meeting may resolve that the expenses of summoning and holding it are to be payable out of the assets of the company, as an expense of the administration.

**2.21(6) [Repayment of deposit]** To the extent that any deposit made under this Rule is not required for the payment of expenses of summoning and holding the meeting, it shall be repaid to the person who made it.

## 2.22 Entitlement to vote

**2.22(1) [Conditions for voting]** Subject as follows, at a meeting of creditors in administration proceedings a person is entitled to vote only if–

(a) he has given to the administrator, not later than 12.00 hours on the business day before the day fixed for the meeting, details in writing of the debt which he claims to be due to him from the company, and the claim has been duly admitted under the following provisions of this Rule, and

(b) there has been lodged with the administrator any proxy which he intends to be used on his behalf.

Details of the debt must include any calculation for the purposes of Rules 2.24 to 2.27.

**2.22(2) [Failure to comply with r. 2.22(1)(a)]** The chairman of the meeting may allow a creditor to vote, notwithstanding that he has failed to comply with paragraph (1)(a), if satisfied that the failure was due to circumstances beyond the creditor's control.

**2.22(3) [Production of documents]** The administrator or, if other, the chairman of the meeting may call for any document or other evidence to be produced to him, where he thinks it necessary for the purpose of substantiating the whole or any part of the claim.

**2.22(4) [Calculation of votes]** Votes are calculated according to the amount of a creditor's debt as at the date of the administration order, deducting any amounts paid in respect of the debt after that date.

**2.22(5) [Limitation on voting]** A creditor shall not vote in respect of a debt for an unliquidated amount, or any debt whose value is not ascertained, except where the chairman agrees to put upon the debt an estimated minimum value for the purpose of entitlement to vote and admits the claim for that purpose.

## 2.23 Admission and rejection of claims

**2.23(1) [Power of chairman]** At any creditors' meeting the chairman has power to admit or reject a creditor's claim for the purpose of his entitlement to vote; and the power is exercisable with respect to the whole or any part of the claim.

**2.23(2) [Appeal from chairman's decision]** The chairman's decision under this Rule, or in respect of any matter arising under Rule 2.22, is subject to appeal to the court by any creditor.

**2.23(3) [Voting subject to objection]** If the chairman is in doubt whether a claim should be admitted or rejected, he shall mark it as objected to and allow the creditor to vote, subject to his vote being subsequently declared invalid if the objection to the claim is sustained.

**2.23(4) [If chairman's decision reversed etc.]** If on an appeal the chairman's decision is reversed or varied, or a creditor's vote is declared invalid, the court may order that another meeting be summoned, or make such other order as it thinks just.

**2.23(5) [In case of s. 23 meeting]** In the case of the meeting summoned under section 23 to consider the administrator's proposals, an application to the court by way of appeal under this Rule against a decision of the chairman shall not be made later than 28 days after the delivery of the administrator's report in accordance with section 24(4).

**2.23(6) [Costs of appeal]** Neither the administrator nor any person nominated by him to be chairman is personally liable for costs incurred by any person in respect of an appeal to the court under this Rule, unless the court makes an order to that effect.

## 2.24 Secured creditors

**2.24** At a meeting of creditors a secured creditor is entitled to vote only in respect of the balance (if any) of his debt after deducting the value of his security as estimated by him.

## 2.25 Holders of negotiable instruments

**2.25** A creditor shall not vote in respect of a debt on, or secured by, a current bill of exchange or promissory note, unless he is willing–

(a) to treat the liability to him on the bill or note of every person who is liable on it antecedently to the company, and against whom a bankruptcy order has not been made (or, in the case of a company, which has not gone into liquidation), as a security in his hands, and

(b) to estimate the value of the security and, for the purpose of his entitlement to vote, to deduct it from his claim.

## 2.26 Retention of title creditors

**2.26** For the purpose of entitlement to vote at a creditors' meeting in administration proceedings, a seller of goods to the company under a retention of title agreement shall deduct from his claim the value, as estimated by him, of any rights arising under that agreement in respect of goods in possession of the company.

## 2.27 Hire-purchase, conditional sale and chattel leasing agreements

**2.27(1) [Entitlement to vote]** Subject as follows, an owner of goods under a hire-purchase or chattel leasing agreement, or a seller of goods under a conditional sale agreement, is entitled to vote in respect of the amount of the debt due and payable to him by the company as at the date of the administration order.

**2.27(2) [Calculating amount of debt]** In calculating the amount of any debt for this purpose, no account shall be taken of any amount attributable to the exercise of any right under the relevant agreement, so far as the right has become exercisable solely by virtue of the presentation of the petition for an administration order or any matter arising in consequence of that, or of the making of the order.

## 2.28 Resolutions and minutes

**2.28(1) [Resolution passed by majority in value]** Subject to paragraph (1A), at a creditors' meeting in administration proceedings, a resolution is passed when a majority (in value) of those present and voting, in person or by proxy, have voted in favour of it.

**History**
In r. 2.28(1) the words "Subject to paragraph (1A)", at the beginning inserted by the Insolvency (Amendment) Rules 1987 (SI 1987/1919), r. 3(1), Sch., Pt. 1, para. 14(1) as from 11 January 1988.

**2.28(1A) [Resolution invalid]** Any resolution is invalid if those voting against it include more than half in value of the creditors to whom notice of the meeting was sent and who are not, to the best of the chairman's belief, persons connected with the company.

**History**
R. 2.28(1A) inserted by the Insolvency (Amendment) Rules 1987 (SI 1987/1919), r. 3(1), Sch., Pt. 1, para. 14(2) as from 11 January 1988.

**2.28(2) [Minute book]** The chairman of the meeting shall cause minutes of its proceedings to be entered in the company's minute book.

**2.28(3) [Contents of minutes]** The minutes shall include a list of the creditors who attended (personally or by proxy) and, if a creditors' committee has been established, the names and addresses of those elected to be members of the committee.

## 2.29 Reports and notices under s. 23 and 25

**2.29** Any report or notice by the administrator of the result of a creditors' meeting held under section 23 or 25 shall have annexed to it details of the proposals which were considered by the meeting and of the revisions and modifications to the proposals which were so considered.

**History**
R. 2.29 substituted by the Insolvency (Amendment) Rules 1987 (SI 1987/1919), r. 3(1), Sch., Pt. 1, para. 15 as from 11 January 1988; r. 2.29 formerly read as follows:

**"2.29 Administrator's report**
2.29 Any report by the administrator of the result of creditors' meetings held under section 23 or 25 shall have annexed to it details of the proposals which were considered by the meeting in question and of the modifications which were so considered."

## 2.30 Notices to creditors

**2.30(1) [Notice of result of meeting]** Within 14 days of the conclusion of a meeting of creditors to consider the administrator's proposals or revised proposals, the administrator shall send notice of the result of the meeting (including, where appropriate, details of the proposals as approved) to every creditor who received notice of the meeting under the Rules, and to any other creditor of whom the administrator has since become aware. [FORM 2.12]

**2.30(2) [Administrator's report]** Within 14 days of the end of every period of 6 months beginning with the date of approval of the administrator's proposals or revised proposals, the administrator shall send to all creditors of the company a report on the progress of the administration.

**2.30(3) [Administrator vacating office]** On vacating office the administrator shall send to creditors a report on the administration up to that time.

This does not apply where the administration is immediately followed by the company going into liquidation, nor when the administrator is removed from office by the court or ceases to be qualified as an insolvency practitioner.

### SECTION B: COMPANY MEETINGS

## 2.31 Venue and conduct of company meeting

**2.31(1) [Fixing of venue]** Where the administrator summons a meeting of members of the company, he shall fix a venue for it having regard to their convenience.

**2.31(2) [Chairman]** The chairman of the meeting shall be the administrator or a person nominated by him in writing to act in his place.

**2.31(3) [Nominee chairman]** A person so nominated must be either–

(a) one who is qualified to act as an insolvency practitioner in relation to the company, or

(b) an employee of the administrator or his firm who is experienced in insolvency matters.

**2.31(4) [Adjournment if no chairman]** If within 30 minutes from the time fixed for commencement of the meeting there is no person present to act as chairman, the meeting stands adjourned to the same time and place in the following week or, if that is not a business day, to the business day immediately following.

**2.31(5) [Summoning and conduct of meeting]** Subject as above, the meeting shall be summoned and conducted as if it were a general meeting of the company summoned under the company's articles of association, and in accordance with the applicable provisions of the Companies Act.

**2.31(6) [Minutes]** The chairman of the meeting shall cause minutes of its proceedings to be entered in the company's minute book.

# Chapter 4 – The Creditors' Committee

## 2.32 Constitution of committee

**2.32(1) [Three–five creditors]** Where it is resolved by a creditors' meeting to establish a creditors' committee for the purposes of the administration, the committee shall consist of at least 3 and not more than 5 creditors of the company elected at the meeting.

**2.32(2) [Eligibility of creditors]** Any creditor of the company is eligible to be a member of the committee, so long as his claim has not been rejected for the purpose of his entitlement to vote.

**2.32(3) [Body corporate as member]** A body corporate may be a member of the committee, but it cannot act as such otherwise than by a representative appointed under Rule 2.37 below.

## 2.33 Formalities of establishment

**2.33(1) [Certificate of due constitution]** The creditors' committee does not come into being, and accordingly cannot act, until the administrator has issued a certificate of its due consitution.

**2.33(2) [Agreement to act]** No person may act as a member of the committee unless and until he has agreed to do so and, unless the relevant proxy or authorisation contains a statement to the contrary, such agreement may be given by his proxy-holder or representative under section 375 of the Companies Act present at the meeting establishing the committee.

**2.33(2A) [Issue of administrator's certificate]** The administrator's certificate of the committee's due constitution shall not issue unless and until at least 3 of the persons who are to be members of the committee have agreed to act.

**History**

R. 2.33(2) and (2A) substituted for the former r. 2.33(2) by the Insolvency (Amendment) Rules 1987 (SI 1987/1919), r. 3(1), Sch., Pt. 1, para. 16 as from 11 January 1988; the former r. 2.33(2) read as follows:

"No person may act as a member of the committee unless and until he has agreed to do so; and the administrator's certificate of the committee's due constitution shall not issue unless and until at least 3 of the persons who are to be members of it have agreed to act."

**2.33(3) [Amended certificate]** As and when the others (if any) agree to act, the administrator shall issue an amended certificate.

**2.33(4) [Filing of certificates]** The certificate, and any amended certificate, shall be filed in court by the administrator. [FORM 2.13]

**2.33(5) [Change in membership]** If after the first establishment of the committee there is any change in its membership, the administrator shall report the change to the court. [FORM 2.14]

## 2.34 Functions and meetings of the committee

**2.34(1) [Functions]** The creditors' committee shall assist the administrator in discharging his functions, and act in relation to him in such manner as may be agreed from time to time.

**2.34(2) [Holding of meetings]** Subject as follows, meetings of the committee shall be held when and where determined by the administrator.

**2.34(3) [First and subsequent meetings]** The administrator shall call a first meeting of the committee not later than 3 months after its first establishment; and thereafter he shall call a meeting–

(a) if so requested by a member of the committee or his representative (the meeting then to be held within 21 days of the request being received by the administrator), and

(b) for a specified date, if the committee has previously resolved that a meeting be held on that date.

**2.34(4) [Notice of venue]** The administrator shall give 7 days' written notice of the venue of any meeting to every member of the committee (or his representative designated for that purpose), unless in any case the requirement of notice has been waived by or on behalf of any member.

Waiver may be signified either at or or before the meeting.

## 2.35 The chairman at meetings

**2.35(1) [Administrator to be chairman]** Subject to Rule 2.44(3), the chairman at any meeting of the creditors' committee shall be the administrator or a person nominated by him in writing to act.

**2.35(2) [Other nominated chairman]** A person so nominated must be either–

(a) one who is qualified to act as an insolvency practitioner in relation to the company, or

(b) an employee of the administrator or his firm who is experienced in insolvency matters.

## 2.36 Quorum

**2.36** A meeting of the committee is duly constituted if due notice of it has been given to all the members, and at least 2 members are present or represented.

## 2.37 Committee-members' representatives

**2.37(1) [Representation]** A member of the committee may, in relation to the business of the committee, be represented by another person duly authorised by him for that purpose.

**2.37(2) [Letter of authority]** A person acting as a committee-member's representative must hold a letter of authority entitling him so to act (either generally or specially) and signed by or on behalf of the committee-member, and for this purpose any proxy or any authorisation under section 375 of the Companies Act in relation to any meeting of creditors of the company shall, unless it contains a statement to the contrary, be treated as a letter of authority to act generally signed by or on behalf of the committee-member.

**History**

In r. 2.37(2) the words ", and for this purpose" to the end added by the Insolvency (Amendment) Rules 1987 (SI 1987/1919), r. 3(1), Sch., Pt. 1, para. 17 as from 11 January 1988.

**2.37(3) [Production of letter of authority]** The chairman at any meeting of the committee may call on a person claiming to act as a committee-member's representative to produce his letter of authority, and may exclude him if it appears that his authority is deficient.

**2.37(4) [Who may not be a representative]** No member may be represented by a body corporate, or by a person who is an undischarged bankrupt, or is subject to a composition or arrangement with his creditors.

**2.37(5) [No dual representation]** No person shall–

(a) on the same committee, act at one and the same time as representative of more than one committee-member, or

(b) act both as a member of the committee and as representative of another member.

**2.37(6) [Signing as representative]** Where a member's representative signs any document on the member's behalf, the fact that he so signs must be stated below his signature.

## 2.38 Resignation

**2.38** A member of the committee may resign by notice in writing delivered to the administrator.

## 2.39 Termination of membership

**2.39(1) [Automatic termination]** Membership of the creditors' committee is automatically terminated if the member–

(a) becomes bankrupt, or compounds or arranges with his creditors, or

(b) at 3 consecutive meetings of the committee is neither present nor represented (unless at the third of those meetings it is resolved that this Rule is not to apply in his case), or

(c) ceases to be, or is found never to have been, a creditor.

**2.39(2) [Termination on bankruptcy]** However, if the cause of termination is the member's bankruptcy, his trustee in bankruptcy replaces him as a member of the committee.

## 2.40 Removal

**2.40** A member of the committee may be removed by resolution at a meeting of creditors, at least 14 days' notice having been given of the intention to move that resolution.

## 2.41 Vacancies

**2.41(1) [Application of Rule]** The following applies if there is a vacancy in the membership of the creditors' committee.

**2.41(2) [Agreement not to fill vacancy]** The vacancy need not be filled if the administrator and a majority of the remaining members of the committee so agree, provided that the total number of members does not fall below the minimum required under Rule 2.32.

**2.41(3) [Filling vacancy]** The administrator may appoint any creditor (being qualified under the Rules to be a member of the committee) to fill the vacancy, if a majority of the other members of the committee agree to the appointment, and the creditor concerned consents to act.

## 2.42 Procedure at meetings

**2.42(1) [Votes and passing of resolutions]** At any meeting of the creditors' committee, each member of it (whether present himself, or by his representative) has one vote; and a resolution is passed when a majority of the members present or represented have voted in favour of it.

**2.42(2) [Record of resolutions]** Every resolution passed shall be recorded in writing, either separately or as part of the minutes of the meeting.

**2.42(3) [Signing of records etc.]** A record of each resolution shall be signed by the chairman and placed in the company's minute book.

## 2.43 Resolutions by post

**2.43(1) [Proposed resolution sent to members]** In accordance with this Rule, the administrator may seek to obtain the agreement of members of the creditors' committee to a resolution by sending to every member (or his representative designated for the purpose) a copy of the proposed resolution.

**2.43(2) [Copy of proposed resolution]** Where the administrator makes use of the procedure allowed by this Rule, he shall send out to members of the committee or their representatives (as the case may be) a copy of any proposed resolution on which a decision is sought, which shall be set out in such a way that agreement with or dissent from each separate resolution may be indicated by the recipient on the copy so sent.

**History**

In r. 2.43(2) the words "a copy of any proposed resolution" to the end substituted by the Insolvency (Amendment) Rules 1987 (SI 1987/1919), r. 3(1), Sch. Pt. 1, para. 18 as from 11 January 1988; the former words were as follows:

"a statement incorporating the resolution to which their agreement is sought, each resolution (if more than one) being sent out in a separate document."

**2.43(3) [Member may require meeting]** Any member of the committee may, within 7 business days from the date of the administrator sending out a resolution, require him to summon a meeting of the committee to consider the matters raised by the resolution.

## 2.57 Notice to creditors

**2.57(1) [Time for giving notice]** Notice of the issue of the certificate shall be given by the administrator within 3 months of his appointment or within 2 months of issuing the certificate, whichever is the later, to all of the company's unsecured creditors of whose address he is then aware and who have, to his knowledge, made supplies to the company, with a charge to value added tax, at any time before his appointment.

**2.57(2) [Later notice]** Thereafter, he shall give the notice to any such creditor of whose address and supplies to the company he becomes aware.

**2.57(3) [No obligation re certificate]** He is not under obligation to provide any creditor with a copy of the certificate.

## 2.58 Preservation of certificate with company's records

**2.58(1) [Retention of certificate]** The certificate shall be retained with the company's accounting records, and section 222 of the Companies Act (where and for how long records are to be kept) shall apply to the certificate as it applies to those records.

**2.58(2) [Duty of administrator]** It is the duty of the administrator, on vacating office, to bring this Rule to the attention of the directors or (as the case may be) any successor of his as administrator.

# PART 3 – ADMINISTRATIVE RECEIVERSHIP

## Chapter 1 – Appointment of Administrative Receiver

## 3.1 Acceptance and confirmation of acceptance of appointment

**3.1(1) [Two or more persons appointed jointly]** Where two or more persons are appointed as joint receivers or managers of a company's property under powers contained in an instrument, the acceptance of such an appointment shall be made by each of them in accordance with section 33 as if that person were a sole appointee, but the joint appointment takes effect only when all such persons have so accepted and is then deemed to have been made at the time at which the instrument of appointment was received by or on behalf of all such persons.

**3.1(2) [Sole or joint receiver]** Subject to the next paragraph, where a person is appointed as the sole or joint receiver of a company's property under powers contained in an instrument, the appointee shall, if he accepts the appointment, within 7 days confirm his acceptance in writing to the person appointing him.

**3.1(3) [Non-application of r. 3.1(2)]** Paragraph (2) does not apply where an appointment is accepted in writing. [FORM 3.1]

**3.1(4) [Who may accept or confirm]** Any acceptance or confirmation of acceptance of appointment as a receiver or manager of a company's property, whether under the Act or the Rules, may be given by any person (including, in the case of a joint appointment, any joint appointee) duly authorised for that purpose on behalf of the receiver or manager.

**3.1(5) [Statements in confirmation]** In confirming acceptance the appointee or person authorised for that purpose shall state–

(a) the time and date of receipt of the instrument of appointment, and

(b) the time and date of acceptance.

**History**
R. 3.1 substituted by the Insolvency (Amendment) Rules 1987 (SI 1987/1919), r. 3(1), Sch., Pt. 1, para. 23 as from 11 January 1988; r. 3.1 formerly read as follows:

"**3.1 Acceptance of appointment**
**3.1(1)** Where a person is appointed as the sole or joint administrative receiver of a company's property under powers contained in an instrument, the appointee, if he accepts the appointment, shall within 7 days confirm his acceptance in writing to the appointer.
**(2)** If two or more persons are appointed jointly as administrative receivers, each of them shall confirm acceptance on his own behalf; but the appointment is effective only when all those jointly appointed have complied with this Rule."

**(3)** Confirmation under this Rule may be given on the appointee's behalf by a person whom he has duly authorised to give it.

**(4)** In confirming his acceptance, the appointee shall state–

(a) the time and date of his receipt of notice of the appointment, and

(b) the time and date of his acceptance."

Also against r. 3.1(3) the words "[FORM 3.1]" inserted by the Insolvency (Amendment) Rules 1987 (SI 1987/1919), r. 3(1), Sch., Pt. 2, para. 156(1) as from 11 January 1988.

## 3.2 Notice and advertisement of appointment

**3.2(1) [Notice required by s. 46(1)]** This Rule relates to the notice which a person is required by section 46(1) to send and publish, when appointed as administrative receiver.

**3.2(2) [Matters to be stated in notice]** The following matters shall be stated in the notices sent to the company and the creditors–

(a) the registered name of the company, as at the date of the appointment, and its registered number;

(b) any other name with which the company has been registered in the 12 months preceding that date;

(c) any name under which the company has traded at any time in those 12 months, if substantially different from its then registered name;

(d) the name and address of the administrative receiver, and the date of his appointment;

(e) the name of the person by whom the appointment was made;

(f) the date of the instrument conferring the power under which the appointment was made, and a brief description of the instrument;

(g) a brief description of the assets of the company (if any) in respect of which the person appointed is not made the receiver.

**History**

In r. 3.2(2) the words "notices sent to the company and the creditors" substituted for the former word "notice" by the Insolvency (Amendment) Rules 1987 (SI 1987/1919), r. 3(1), Sch., Pt. 1, para. 24 as from 11 January 1988.

**3.2(3) [Advertisement]** The administrative receiver shall cause notice of his appointment to be advertised once in the Gazette, and once in such newspaper as he thinks most appropriate for ensuring that it comes to the notice of the company's creditors. [FORM 3.1A]

**History**

Against r. 3.2(3) the words "[FORM 3.1A]" inserted by the Insolvency (Amendment) Rules 1987 (SI 1987/1919), r. 3(1), Sch., Pt. 2, para. 156(1) as from 11 January 1988.

**3.2(4) [Contents of advertisement]** The advertisment shall state all the matters specified in sub-paragraphs (a) to (e) of paragraph (2) above.

# Chapter 2 – Statement of Affairs and Report to Creditors

## 3.3 Notice requiring statement of affairs

**3.3(1) [Notice re s. 47 statement]** Where the administrative receiver determines to require a statement of the company's affairs to be made out and submitted to him in accordance with section 47, he shall send notice to each of the persons whom he considers should be made responsible under that section, requiring them to prepare and submit the statement. [FORM 3.1B]

**History**

In r. 3.3(1) the word "Where" substituted for the former word "If" by the Insolvency (Amendment) Rules 1987 (SI 1987/1919), r. 3(1), Sch., Pt. 1, para. 25(1) as from 11 January 1988. Also against r. 3.3(1) the words "[FORM 3.1B]" substituted for the former words "[FORM 3.1]" by the Insolvency (Amendment) Rules 1987 (SI 1987/1919), r. 3(1), Sch., Pt. 2, para. 156(2) as from the same date.

**3.3(2) ["The deponents"]** The persons to whom the notice is sent are referred to in this Chapter as "the deponents".

**3.3(3) [Contents of notice]** The notice shall inform each of the deponents–

(a) of the names and addresses of all others (if any) to whom the same notice has been sent;

(b) of the time within which the statement must be delivered;

(c) of the effect of section 47(6) (penalty for non-compliance); and

(d) of the application to him, and to each of the other deponents, of section 235 (duty to provide information, and to attend on the administrative receiver if required).

**3.3(4) [Instructions for preparation of statement]** The administrative receiver shall, on request, furnish each deponent with the forms required for the preparation of the statement of affairs.

**History**
In r. 3.3(4) the words "the forms required for the preparation of the statement of affairs" substituted by the Insolvency (Amendment) Rules 1987 (SI 1987/1919), r. 3(1), Sch., Pt. 1, para. 25(2) as from 11 January 1988; the former words were as follows:
"instructions for the preparation of the statement and with the forms required for that purpose."

## 3.4 Verification and filing

**3.4(1) [Form of statement and verification]** The statement of affairs shall be in Form 3.2, shall contain all the particulars required by that form and shall be verified by affidavit by the deponents (using the same form). [FORM 3.2]

**3.4(2) [Affidavits of concurrence]** The administrative receiver may require any of the persons mentioned in section 47(3) to submit an affidavit of concurrence, stating that he concurs in the statement of affairs.

**3.4(3) [Affidavit may be qualified]** An affidavit of concurrence may be qualified in respect of matters dealt with in the statement of affairs, where the maker of the affidavit is not in agreement with the deponents, or he considers the statement to be erroneous or misleading, or he is without the direct knowledge necessary for concurring with it.

**3.4(4) [Delivery of statement to receiver]** The statement of affairs shall be delivered to the receiver by the deponent making the affidavit of verification (or by one of them, if more than one), together with a copy of the verified statement.

**3.4(5) [Delivery of affidavit of concurrence]** Every affidavit of concurrence shall be delivered by the person who makes it, together with a copy.

**3.4(6) [Retention of copy statement etc.]** The administrative receiver shall retain the verified copy of the statement and the affidavits of concurrence (if any) as part of the records of the receivership.

## 3.5 Limited disclosure

**3.5(1) [Application to court]** Where the administrative receiver thinks that it would prejudice the conduct of the receivership for the whole or part of the statement of affairs to be disclosed, he may apply to the court for an order of limited disclosure in respect of the statement or a specified part of it.

**3.5(2) [Powers of court]** The court may on the application order that the statement, or, as the case may be, the specified part of it, be not open to inspection otherwise than with leave of the court.

**3.5(3) [Directions]** The court's order may include directions as to the delivery of documents to the registrar of companies and the disclosure of relevant information to other persons.

## 3.6 Release from duty to submit statement of affairs; extension of time

**3.6(1) [Exercise of s. 47(5) power]** The power of the administrative receiver under section 47(5) to give a release from the obligation imposed by that section, or to grant an extension of time, may be exercised at the receiver's own discretion, or at the request of any deponent.

**3.6(2) [Application to court]** A deponent may, if he requests a release or extension of time and it is refused by the receiver, apply to the court for it.

**3.6(3) [Court may dismiss application etc.]** The court may, if it thinks that no sufficient cause is shown for the application, dismiss it; but it shall not do so unless the applicant has had an opportunity to attend the court for an *ex parte* hearing, of which he has been given at least 7 days' notice.

If the application is not dismissed under this paragraph, the court shall fix a venue for it to be heard, and give notice to the deponent accordingly.

**3.6(4) [Deponent to send notice to receiver]** The deponent shall, at least 14 days before the hearing, send to the receiver a notice stating the venue and accompanied by a copy of the application, and of any evidence which he (the deponent) intends to adduce in support of it.

**3.6(5) [Appearance etc. by receiver]** The receiver may appear and be heard on the application; and, whether or not he appears, he may file a written report of any matters which he considers ought to be drawn to the court's attention.

If such a report is filed, a copy of it shall be sent by the receiver to the deponent, not later than 5 days before the hearing.

**3.6(6) [Sealed copies of order]** Sealed copies of any order made on the application shall be sent by the court to the deponent and the receiver.

**3.6(7) [Costs]** On any application under this Rule the applicant's costs shall be paid in any event by him and, unless the court otherwise orders, no allowance towards them shall be made out of the assets under the administrative receiver's control.

## 3.7 Expenses of statement of affairs

**3.7(1) [Payment of expenses]** A deponent making the statement of affairs and affidavit shall be allowed, and paid by the administrative receiver out of his receipts, any expenses incurred by the deponent in so doing which the receiver thinks reasonable.

**3.7(2) [Appeal to court]** Any decision by the receiver under this Rule is subject to appeal to the court.

**3.7(3) [Effect of Rule]** Nothing in this Rule relieves a deponent from any obligation with respect to the preparation, verification and submission of the statement of affairs, or to the provision of information to the receiver.

## 3.8 Report to creditors

**3.8(1) [Notice under s. 48(2)]** If under section 48(2) the administrative receiver determines not to send a copy of his report to creditors, but to publish notice under paragraph (b) of that subsection, the notice shall be published in the newspaper in which the receiver's appointment was advertised.

**3.8(2) [No s. 48(2) meeting proposed]** If he proposes to apply to the court to dispense with the holding of the meeting of unsecured creditors (otherwise required by section 48(2)), he shall in his report to creditors or (as the case may be) in the notice published as above, state the venue fixed by the court for the hearing of the application.

**3.8(3) [Documents to be attached to report]** Subject to any order of the court under Rule 3.5, the copy of the receiver's report which under section 48(1) is to be sent to the registrar of companies shall have attached to it a copy of any statement of affairs under section 47, and copies of any affidavits of concurrence.

**3.8(4) [Late submission of documents]** If the statement of affairs or affidavits of concurrence, if any, have not been submitted to the receiver by the time he sends a copy of his report to the registrar of companies, he shall send a copy of the statement and any affidavits of concurrence as soon thereafter as he receives them.

[FORM 3.3]

# Chapter 3 – Creditors' Meeting

## 3.9 Procedure for summoning meeting under s. 48(2)

**3.9(1) [Convenience of venue]** In fixing the venue for a meeting of creditors summoned under section 48(2), the administrative receiver shall have regard to the convenience of the persons who are invited to attend.

**3.9(2) [Time of meeting]** The meeting shall be summoned for commencement between 10.00 and 16.00 hours on a business day, unless the court otherwise directs.

**3.9(3) [Notice of venue]** At least 14 days' notice of the venue shall be given to all creditors of the company who are identified in the statement of affairs, or are known to the receiver and had claims against the company at the date of his appointment.

**3.9(4) [Forms of proxy]** With the notice summoning the meeting there shall be sent out forms of proxy. [FORM 8.3]

**3.9(5) [Statement in notice]** The notice shall include a statement to the effect that creditors whose claims are wholly secured are not entitled to attend or be represented at the meeting.

**3.9(6) [Publication of notice]** Notice of the venue shall also be published in the newspaper in which the receiver's appointment was advertised.

**3.9(7) [R. 3.11(1) statement]** The notice to creditors and the newspaper advertisement shall contain a statement of the effect of Rule 3.11(1) below (voting rights).

## 3.10 The chairman at the meeting

**3.10(1) [Receiver or his nominee to be chairman]** The chairman at the creditors' meeting shall be the receiver, or a person nominated by him in writing to act in his place.

**3.10(2) [Nominee chairman]** A person so nominated must be either–

(a) one who is qualified to act as an insolvency practitioner in relation to the company, or

(b) an employee of the receiver or his firm who is experienced in insolvency matters.

## 3.11 Voting rights

**3.11(1) [Entitlement to vote]** Subject as follows, at the creditors' meeting a person is entitled to vote only if–

(a) he has given to the receiver, not later than 12.00 hours on the business day before the day fixed for the meeting, details in writing of the debt that he claims to be due to him from the company, and the claim has been duly admitted under the following provisions of this Rule, and

(b) there has been lodged with the administrative receiver any proxy which the creditor intends to be used on his behalf.

**3.11(2) [Failure to comply with r. 3.11(1)(a)]** The chairman of the meeting may allow a creditor to vote, notwithstanding that he has failed to comply with paragraph (1)(a), if satisifed that the failure was due to circumstances beyond the creditor's control.

**3.11(3) [Production of documents]** The receiver or (if other) the chairman of the meeting may call for any document or other evidence to be produced to him where he thinks it necessary for the purpose of substantiating the whole or any part of the claim.

**3.11(4) [Calculation of votes]** Votes are calculated according to the amount of a creditor's debt as at the date of the appointment of the receiver, after deducting any amounts paid in respect of that debt after that date.

**3.11(5) [Limitation on voting]** A creditor shall not vote in respect of a debt for an unliquidated amount, or any debt whose value is not ascertained, except where the chairman agrees to put upon the debt an estimated minimum value for the purpose of entitlement to vote and admits the claim for that purpose.

**3.11(6) [Secured creditors]** A secured creditor is entitled to vote only in respect of the balance (if any) of his debt after deducting the value of his security as estimated by him.

**3.11(7) [Further limitation on voting]** A creditor shall not vote in respect of a debt on, or secured by, a current bill of exchange or promissory note, unless he is willing–

(a) to treat the liability to him on the bill or note of every person who is liable on it antecedently to the company, and against whom a bankruptcy order has not been made (or, in the case of a company, which has not gone into liquidation), as a security in his hands, and

(b) to estimate the value of the security and, for the purpose of his entitlement to vote, to deduct it from his claim.

## 3.12 Admission and rejection of claim

**3.12(1) [Power of chairman]** At the creditors' meeting the chairman has power to admit or reject a creditor's claim for the purpose of his entitlement to vote; and the power is exercisable with respect to the whole or any part of the claim.

**3.12(2) [Appeal from chairman's decision]** The chairman's decision under this Rule, or in respect of any matter arising under Rule. 3.11, is subject to appeal to the court by any creditor.

**3.12(3) [Voting subject to objection]** If the chairman is in doubt whether a claim should be admitted or rejected, he shall mark it as objected to and allow the creditor to vote, subject to his vote being subsequently declared invalid if the objection to the claim is sustained.

**3.12(4) [If chairman's decision reversed etc.]** If on an appeal the chairman's decision is reversed or varied, or a creditor's vote is declared invalid, the court may order that another meeting be summoned, or make such other order as it thinks just.

**3.12(5) [Costs of appeal]** Neither the receiver nor any person nominated by him to be chairman is personally liable for costs incurred by any person in respect of an appeal to the court under this Rule, unless the court makes an order to that effect.

## 3.13 Quorum

3.13 (Omitted by the Insolvency (Amendment) Rules 1987 (SI 1987/1919), r. 3(1), Sch. Pt. 1, para. 26 as from 11 January 1988.)

**History**

R. 3.13 formerly read as follows:

"**3.13(1)** The creditors' meeting is not competent to act unless there are present in person or by proxy at least 3 creditors (or all of the creditors, if their number does not exceed 3), being in either case entitled to vote.

**(2)** One person constitutes a quorum if–

(a) he is himself a creditor or representative under section 375 of the Companies Act, with entitlement to vote, and he holds a number of proxies sufficient to ensure that, with his own vote, paragraph (1) is complied with, or

(b) being the chairman or any other person, he holds that number of proxies."

## 3.14 Adjournment

**3.14(1) [Chairman's decision]** The creditors' meeting shall not be adjourned, even if no quorum is present, unless the chairman decides that it is desirable; and in that case he shall adjourn it to such date, time and place as he thinks fit.

**3.14(2) [Application of r. 3.9]** Rule 3.9(1) and (2) applies, with necessary modifications, to any adjourned meeting.

**3.14(3) [If no quorum or adjournment]** If there is no quorum, and the meeting is not adjourned, it is deemed to have been duly summoned and held.

## 3.15 Resolutions and minutes

**3.15(1) [Resolution passed by majority in value]** At the creditors' meeting, a resolution is passed when a majority (in value) of those present and voting in person or by proxy have voted in favour of it.

**3.15(2) [Record of proceedings]** The chairman of the meeting shall cause a record to be made of the proceedings and kept as part of the records of the receivership.

**3.15(3) [Contents of record]** The record shall include a list of the creditors who attended (personally or by proxy) and, if a creditors' committee has been established, the names and addresses of those elected to be members of the committee.

# Chapter 4 – The Creditors' Committee

## 3.16 Constitution of committee

**3.16(1) [Three–five creditors]** Where it is resolved by the creditors' meeting to establish a creditors' committee, the committee shall consist of at least 3 and not more than 5 creditors of the company elected at the meeting.

**3.16(2) [Eligibility]** Any creditor of the company is eligible to be a member of the committee, so long as his claim has not been rejected for the purpose of his entitlement to vote.

**3.16(3) [Body corporate as member]** A body corporate may be a member of the committee, but it cannot act as such otherwise than by a representative appointed under Rule 3.21 below.

## 3.17 Formalities of establishment

**3.17(1) [Certificate of due constitution]** The creditors' committee does not come into being, and accordingly cannot act, until the administrative receiver has issued a certificate of its due constitution.

**3.17(2) [Agreement to act]** No person may act as a member of the committee unless and until he has agreed to do so and, unless the relevant proxy or authorisation contains a statement to the contrary, such agreement may be given by his proxy-holder or representative under section 375 of the Companies Act present at the meeting establishing the committee.

**3.17(2A) [Issue of certificate]** The receiver's certificate of the committee's due constitution shall not issue unless and until at least 3 of the persons who are to be members of the committee have agreed to act.

**History**
R. 3.17(2) and (2A) substituted for the former r. 3.17(2) by the Insolvency (Amendment) Rules 1987 (SI 1987/1919), r. 3(1), Sch., Pt. 1, para. 27 as from 11 January 1988; the former r. 3.17(2) read as follows:

"No person may act as a member of the committee unless and until he has agreed to do so; and the receiver's certificate of the committee's due constitution shall not issue unless and until at least 3 of the persons who are to be members of it have agreed to act."

**3.17(3) [Amended certificate]** As and when the others (if any) agree to act, the receiver shall issue an amended certificate.

**3.17(4) [Certificates to be sent to registrar]** The certificate, and any amended certificate, shall be sent by the receiver to the registrar of companies. [FORM 3.4]

**3.17(5) [Change in membership]** If, after the first establishment of the committee, there is any change in its membership, the receiver shall report the change to the registrar of companies. [FORM 3.5]

## 3.18 Functions and meetings of the committee

**3.18(1) [Functions]** The creditors' committee shall assist the administrative receiver in discharging his functions, and act in relation to him in such manner as may be agreed from time to time.

**3.18(2) [Holding of meetings]** Subject as follows, meetings of the committee shall be held when and where determined by the receiver.

**3.18(3) [First and subsequent meetings]** The receiver shall call a first meeting of the committee not later than 3 months after its establishment; and thereafter he shall call a meeting–

(a) if requested by a member of the committee or his representative (the meeting then to be held within 21 days of the request being received by the receiver), and

(b) for a specified date, if the committee has previously resolved that a meeting be held on that date.

**3.18(4) [Notice of venue]** The receiver shall give 7 days' written notice of the venue of any meeting to every member (or his representative designated for that purpose), unless in any case the requirement of notice has been waived by or on behalf of any member.

Waiver may be signified either at or before the meeting.

## 3.19 The chairman at meetings

**3.19(1) [Chairman]** Subject to Rule 3.28(3), the chairman at any meeting of the creditors' committee shall be the administrative receiver, or a person nominated by him in writing to act.

**3.19(2) [Nominated chairman]** A person so nominated must be either–

(a) one who is qualified to act as an insolvency practitioner in relation to the company, or

(b) an employee of the receiver or his firm who is experienced in insolvency matters.

## 3.20 Quorum

**3.20** A meeting of the committee is duly constituted if due notice has been given to all the members, and at least 2 members are present or represented.

## 3.21 Committee-members' representatives

**3.21(1) [Representation]** A member of the committee may, in relation to the business of the committee, be represented by another person duly authorised by him for that purpose.

**3.21(2) [Letter of authority]** A person acting as a committee-member's representative must hold a letter of authority entitling him so to act (either generally or specially) and signed by or on behalf of the committee-member, and for this purpose any proxy or any authorisation under section 375 of the Companies Act in relation to any meeting of creditors of the company shall, unless it contains a statement to the contrary, be treated as a letter of authority to act generally signed by or on behalf of the committee-member.

**History**
In r. 3.21(2) the words from ", and for this purpose any proxy" to the end added by the Insolvency (Amendment) Rules 1987 (SI 1987/1919) r. 3(1), Sch., Pt. 1, para. 27 as from 11 January 1988.

**3.21(3) [Production of letter of authority]** The chairman at any meeting of the committee may call on a person claiming to act as a committee-member's representative to produce his letter of authority, and may exclude him if it appears that his authority is deficient.

**3.21(4) [Who may not be a representative]** No member may be represented by a body corporate, or by a person who is an undischarged bankrupt, or is subject to a composition or arrangement with his creditors.

**3.21(5) [No dual representation]** No person shall–

(a) on the same committee, act at one and the same time as representative of more than one committee-member, or

(b) act both as a member of the committee and as representative of another member.

**3.21(6) [Signing as representative]** Where a member's representative signs any document on the member's behalf, the fact that he so signs must be stated below his signature.

## 3.22 Resignation

**3.22** A member of the committee may resign by notice in writing delivered to the administrative receiver.

## 3.23 Termination of membership

**3.23(1) [Automatic termination]** Membership of the creditors' committee is automatically terminated if the member–

(a) becomes bankrupt, or compounds or arranges with his creditors, or

(b) at 3 consecutive meetings of the committee is neither present nor represented (unless at the third of those meetings it is resolved that this Rule is not to apply in his case), or

(c) ceases to be, or is found never to have been, a creditor.

**3.23(2) [Termination on bankruptcy]** However, if the cause of termination is the member's bankruptcy, his trustee in bankruptcy replaces him as a member of the committee.

## 3.24 Removal

**3.24** A member of the committee may be removed by resolution at a meeting of creditors, at least 14 days' notice having been given of the intention to move that resolution.

## 3.25 Vacancies

**3.25(1) [Application of Rule]** The following applies if there is a vacancy in the membership of the creditors' committee.

**3.25(2) [Agreement not to fill vacancy]** The vacancy need not be filled if the administrative receiver and a majority of the remaining members of the committee so agree, provided that the total number of members does not fall below the minimum required under Rule 3.16.

**3.25(3) [Filling vacancy]** The receiver may appoint any creditor (being qualified under the Rules to be a member of the committee) to fill the vacancy, if a majority of the other members of the committee agree to the appointment and the creditor concerned consents to act.

the amount or rate of the charge must be separately identified, and the grounds on which payment of it is claimed must be stated.

In either case the amount claimed must be limited to that which has accrued due at the date of the demand.

## 4.6 Information to be given in statutory demand

**4.6(1) [Explanation of demand generally]** The statutory demand must include an explanation to the company of the following matters–

(a) the purpose of the demand, and the fact that, if the demand is not complied with, proceedings may be instituted for the winding up of the company;

(b) the time within which it must be complied with, if that consequence is to be avoided; and

(c) the methods of compliance which are open to the company.

**4.6(2) [Information re named individuals]** Information must be provided for the company as to how an officer or representative of it may enter into communication with one or more named individuals, with a view to securing or compounding for the debt to the creditor's satisfaction.

In the case of any individual so named in the demand, his address and telephone number (if any) must be given.

# Chapter 3 – Petition to Winding-up Order

### (NO CVL APPLICATION)

### (No Application to Petition by Contributories)

## 4.7 Presentation and filing of petition

**4.7(1) [Filing with verifying affidavit]** The petition, verified by affidavit in accordance with Rule 4.12 below, shall be filed in court. [FORM 4.2]
[FORM 4.3]

**4.7(2) [Receipt for deposit payable on presentation]** No petition shall be filed unless there is produced with it the receipt for the deposit payable on presentation.

**4.7(3) [Petitioner other than company]** If the petitioner is other than the company itself, there shall be delivered with the petition–

(a) one copy for service on the company, and

(b) one copy to be exhibited to the affidavit verifying service.

**4.7(4) [Accompanying documents]** There shall in any case be delivered with the petition–

(a) if the company is in course of being wound up voluntarily, and a liquidator has been appointed, one copy of the petition to be sent to him;

(b) if an administration order is in force in relation to the company, one copy to be sent to the administrator;

(c) if an administrative receiver has been appointed in relation to the company, one copy to be sent to him;

(d) if there is in force for the company a voluntary arrangement under Part I of the Act, one copy for the supervisor of the arrangement; and

(e) if the company is an authorised institution or former authorised institution within the meaning of the Banking Act 1987 and the petitioner is not the Financial Services Authority, one copy to be sent to the Authority.

**History**
In r. 4.7(4)(e) the words "Financial Services Authority" and "Authority" substituted for the former words "Bank of England" and "Bank", respectively by the Bank of England Act 1998 (Consequential Amendments of Subordinate Legislation) Order 1998 (SI 1998/1129), art. 1, 2 and Sch. 1, para. 4(1), (3) as from 1 June 1998.

Previously in r. 4.7(4)(e) the words "an authorised institution" to "Banking Act 1987" substituted by the Insolvency (Amendment) Rules 1987 (SI 1987/1919), r. 3(1), Sch., Pt. 1, para. 36(1) as from 11 January 1988; the former words were as follows:

"(i) a recognised bank or licensed institution within the meaning of the Banking Act 1979, or
(ii) an institution to which sections 16 and 18 of that Act apply as if it were licensed."

**4.7(5) [Sealed copies issued to petitioner]** Each of the copies delivered shall have applied to it the seal of the court, and shall be issued to the petitioner.

**4.7(6) [Venue for hearing]** The court shall fix a venue for the hearing of the petition; and this shall be endorsed on any copy issued to the petitioner under paragraph (5).

**4.7(7) [Petition by administrator]** Where a petition is filed at the instance of a company's administrator the petition shall–

(a) be expressed to be the petition of the company by its administrator,

(b) state the name of the administrator, the number of the petition on which the administration order was made and the date of that order, and

(c) contain an application under section 18 requesting that the administration order be discharged and that the court make any such order consequential upon that discharge as it thinks fit.

**4.7(8) [Filing if in administration or voluntary arrangement]** Any petition filed in relation to a company in respect of which there is in force an administration order or a voluntary arrangement under Part I of the Act shall be presented to the court which made the administration order or, as the case may be, to which the nominee's report under section 2 was submitted.

**4.7(9) [Treatment of petition of administrator or supervisor]** Any petition such as is mentioned in paragraph (7) above or presented by the supervisor of a voluntary arrangement under Part I of the Act in force for the company shall be treated as if it were a petition filed by contributories, and Chapter 4 in this Part of the Rules shall apply accordingly.

**4.7(10) [Request for appointment under s. 140]** Where a petition contains a request for the appointment of a person as liquidator in accordance with section 140 (appointment of former administrator or supervisor as liquidator) the person whose appointment is sought shall, not less than 2 days before the return day for the petition, file in court a report including particulars of–

(a) a date on which he notified creditors of the company, either in writing or at a meeting of creditors, of the intention to seek his appointment as liquidator, such date to be at least 10 days before the day on which the report under this paragraph is filed, and

(b) details of any response from creditors to that notification, including any objections to his appointment.

**History**
R. 4.7(7) to (10) added by the Insolvency (Amendment) Rules 1987 (SI 1987/1919), r. 3(1), Sch., Pt. 1, para. 36(2) as from 11 January 1988.

## 4.8 Service of petition

**4.8(1) [Application of Rule]** The following paragraphs apply as regards service of the petition on the company (where the petitioner is other than the company itself); and references to the petition are to a copy of the petition bearing the seal of the court in which it is presented.

**4.8(2) [Service]** Subject as follows, the petition shall be served at the company's registered office, that is to say–

(a) the place which is specified, in the company's statement delivered under section 10 of the Companies Act as the intended situation of its registered office on incorporation, or

(b) if notice has been given by the company to the registrar of companies under section 287 of that Act (change of registered office), the place specified in that notice or, as the case may be, in the last such notice.

**4.8(3) [Means of service]** Service of the petition at the registered office may be effected in any of the following ways–

(a) it may be handed to a person who there and then acknowledges himself to be, or to the best of the server's knowledge, information and belief is, a director or other officer, or employee, of the company; or

(b) it may be handed to a person who there and then acknowledges himself to be authorised to accept service of documents on the company's behalf; or

(c) in the absence of any such person as is mentioned in sub-paragraph (a) or (b), it may be deposited at or about the registered office in such a way that it is likely to come to the notice of a person attending at the office.

**4.8(4) [Service at registered office not practicable etc.]** If for any reason service at the registered office is not practicable, or the company has no registered office or is an unregistered company, the petition may be served on the company by leaving it at the company's last known principal place of business in such a way that it is likely to come to the attention of a person attending there, or by delivering it to the secretary or some director, manager or principal officer of the company, wherever that person may be found.

**History**
R. 4.8(4) substituted by the Insolvency (Amendment) Rules 1987 (SI 1987/1919), r. 3(1), Sch., Pt. 1, para. 37(1) as from 11 January 1988; r. 4.8(4) formerly read as follows:
"If for any reason service at the registered office is not practicable, or the company has no registered office, or it is an unregistered company, the petition may be served at the company's last known principal place of business in England and Wales, or at some place in England and Wales at which it has carried on business, by handing it to such a person as is mentioned in paragraph (3)(a) or (b) above."

**4.8(5) [Oversea company]** In the case of an oversea company, service may be effected in any manner provided for by section 695 of the Companies Act.

**4.8(6) [Service in another manner]** If for any reason it is impracticable to effect service as provided by paragraphs (2) to (5), the petition may be served in such other manner as the court may approve or direct.

**History**
The words "approve or" after the words "the court may" inserted by the Insolvency (Amendment) Rules 1987 (SI 1987/1919), r. 3(1), Sch., Pt. 1, para. 37(2) as from 11 January 1988.

**Note**
See practice direction [1987] 1 All ER 107.

**4.8(7) [Application under r. 4.8(6)]** Application for leave of the court under paragraph (6) may be made *ex parte*, on affidavit stating what steps have been taken to comply with paragraphs (2) to (5), and the reasons why it is impracticable to effect service as there provided.

## 4.9 Proof of service

**4.9(1) [Affidavit of service]** Service of the petition shall be proved by affidavit, specifying the manner of service.
[FORM 4.4]
[FORM 4.5]

**4.9(2) [Exhibits]** The affidavit shall have exhibited to it–

(a) a sealed copy of the petition, and

(b) if substituted service has been ordered, a sealed copy of the order;

and it shall be filed in court immediately after service.

## 4.10 Other persons to receive copies of petition

**4.10(1) [Company being wound up voluntarily]** If to the petitioner's knowledge the company is in course of being wound up voluntarily, a copy of the petition shall be sent by him to the liquidator.

**4.10(2) [Administrative receiver appointed etc.]** If to the petitioner's knowledge an administrative receiver has been appointed in relation to the company, or an administration order is in force in relation to it, a copy of the petition shall be sent by him to the receiver or, as the case may be, the administrator.

**4.10(3) [Voluntary arrangement in force]** If to the petitioner's knowledge there is in force for the company a voluntary arrangement under Part I of the Act, a copy of the petition shall be sent by him to the supervisor of the voluntary arrangement.

**4.10(4) [If company is authorised institution under Banking Act]** If the company is an authorised institution or former authorised institution within the meaning of the Banking Act 1987, a copy of the petition shall be sent by the petitioner to the Financial Services Authority.

This does not apply if the petitioner is the Financial Services Authority itself.

**History**

In r. 4.10(4) the words "Financial Services Authority" substituted for the former words "Bank of England" in both places by the Bank of England Act 1998 (Consequential Amendments of Subordinate Legislation) Order 1998 (SI 1998/1129), art. 1, 2 and Sch. 1, para. 4(1), (4) as from 1 June 1998.

Previously in r. 4.10(4) the words "an authorised institution" to "Banking Act 1987" substituted by the Insolvency (Amendment) Rules 1987 (SI 1987/1919), r. 3(1), Sch., Pt. 1, para. 38 as from 11 January 1988; the former words read as follows:

"a recognised bank or a licensed institution within the meaning of the Banking Act 1979, or an institution to which sections 16 and 18 of that Act apply as if it were a licensed institution".

**4.10(5) [Time for sending copy of petition]** A copy of the petition which is required by this Rule to be sent shall be despatched on the next business day after the day on which the petition is served on the company.

# 4.11 Advertisement of petition

**4.11(1) [Advertisement in Gazette]** Unless the court otherwise directs, the petition shall be advertised once in the Gazette. [FORM 4.6]

**4.11(2) [Time for advertisement]** The advertisement must be made to appear–

(a) if the petitioner is the company itself, not less than 7 business days before the day appointed for the hearing, and

(b) otherwise, not less than 7 business days after service of the petition on the company, nor less than 7 business days before the day so appointed.

**4.11(3) [Newspaper instead of Gazette]** The court may, if compliance with paragraph (2) is not reasonably practicable, direct that advertisement of the petition be made to appear in a specified newspaper, instead of in the Gazette.

**History**

In r. 4.11(3) the words "London morning newspaper, or other" formerly appearing before the word "newspaper" omitted by the Insolvency (Amendment) Rules 1991 (SI 1991/495), r. 3, Sch., para. 1 as from 2 April 1991.

**4.11(4) [Contents of advertisement]** The advertisement of the petition must state–

(a) the name of the company and the address of its registered office, or–
  (i) in the case of an unregistered company, the address of its principal place of business;
  (ii) in the case of an oversea company, the address at which service of the petition was effected;

(b) the name and address of the petitioner;

(c) where the petitioner is the company itself, the address of its registered office or, in the case of an unregistered company, of its principal place of business;

(d) the date on which the petition was presented;

(e) the venue fixed for the hearing of the petition;

(f) the name and address of the petitioner's solicitor (if any); and

(g) that any person intending to appear at the hearing (whether to support or oppose the petition) must give notice of his intention in accordance with Rule 4.16.

**4.11(5) [Court may dismiss petition]** If the petition is not duly advertised in accordance with this Rule, the court may dismiss it.

# 4.12 Verification of petition

**4.12(1) [Verifying affidavit]** The petition shall be verified by an affidavit that the statements in the petition are true, or are true to the best of the deponent's knowledge, information and belief.

[FORM 4.2]
[FORM 4.3]

**4.12(2) [Debts due to different creditors]** If the petition is in respect of debts due to different creditors, the debts to each creditor must be separately verified.

**4.12(3) [Petition to be exhibited]** The petition shall be exhibited to the affidavit verifying it.

**4.12(4) [Who shall make affidavit]** The affidavit shall be made–

(a) by the petitioner (or if there are two or more petitioners, any one of them), or

(b) by some person such as a director, company secretary or similar company officer, or a solicitor, who has been concerned in the matters giving rise to the presentation of the petition, or

(c) by some responsible person who is duly authorised to make the affidavit and has the requisite knowledge of those matters.

**4.12(5) [Where deponent not petitioner]** Where the deponent is not the petitioner himself, or one of the petitioners, he must in the affidavit identify himself and state–

(a) the capacity in which, and the authority by which, he makes it, and

(b) the means of his knowledge of the matters sworn to in the affidavit.

**4.12(6) [Affidavit as prima facie evidence]** The affidavit is prima facie evidence of the statements in the petition to which it relates.

**4.12(7) [Affidavit verifying more than one petition]** An affidavit verifying more than one petition shall include in its title the names of the companies to which it relates and shall set out, in respect of each company, the statements relied on by the petitioner; and a clear and legible photocopy of the affidavit shall be filed with each petition which it verifies.

# 4.13 Persons entitled to copy of petition

**4.13** Every director, contributory or creditor of the company is entitled to be furnished by the solicitor for the petitioner (or by the petitioner himself, if acting in person) with a copy of the petition within 2 days after requiring it, on payment of the appropriate fee.

# 4.14 Certificate of compliance

**4.14(1) [Filing in court]** The petitioner or his solicitor shall, at least 5 days before the hearing of the petition, file in court a certificate of compliance with the Rules relating to service and advertisement. [FORM 4.7]

**4.14(2) [Contents of certificate]** The certificate shall show–

(a) the date of presentation of the petition,

(b) the date fixed for the hearing, and

(c) the date or dates on which the petition was served and advertised in compliance with the Rules.

A copy of the advertisement of the petition shall be filed in court with the certificate.

**4.14(3) [Effect of non-compliance]** Non-compliance with this Rule is a ground on which the court may, if it thinks fit, dismiss the petition.

# 4.15 Leave for petitioner to withdraw

**4.15** If at least 5 days before the hearing the petitioner, on an *ex parte* application, satisfies the court that–

(a) the petition has not been advertised, and

(b) no notices (whether in support or in opposition) have been received by him with reference to the petition, and

(c) the company consents to an order being made under this Rule,

the court may order that the petitioner has leave to withdraw the petition on such terms as to costs as the parties may agree. [FORM 4.8]

**Note**
See practice direction [1987] 1 All ER 107.

# 4.16 Notice of appearance

**4.16(1) [Notice of intention]** Every person who intends to appear on the hearing of the petition shall give to the petitioner notice of his intention in accordance with this Rule. [FORM 4.9]

**4.16(2) [Contents of notice]** The notice shall specify–

(a) the name and address of the person giving it, and any telephone number and reference which may be required for communication with him or with any other person (to be also specified in the notice) authorised to speak or act on his behalf;
(b) whether his intention is to support or oppose the petition; and
(c) the amount and nature of his debt.

**4.16(3) [Address for sending notice]** The notice shall be sent to the petitioner at the address shown for him in the court records, or in the advertisement of the petition required by Rule 4.11; or it may be sent to his solicitor.

**4.16(4) [Time for sending notice]** The notice shall be sent so as to reach the addressee not later than 16.00 hours on the business day before that which is appointed for the hearing (or, where the hearing has been adjourned, for the adjourned hearing).

**4.16(5) [Effect of non-compliance]** A person failing to comply with this Rule may appear on the hearing of the petition only with the leave of the court.

## 4.17 List of appearances

**4.17(1) [Petitioner to prepare list]** The petitioner shall prepare for the court a list of the persons (if any) who have given notice under Rule 4.16, specifying their names and addresses and (if known to him) their respective solicitors.

[FORM 4.10]

**4.17(2) [Whether creditors support or oppose]** Against the name of each creditor in the list it shall be stated whether his intention is to support the petition, or to oppose it.

**4.17(3) [Copy of list handed to court]** On the day appointed for the hearing of the petition, a copy of the list shall be handed to the court before the commencement of the hearing.

**4.17(4) [Leave under r. 4.16(5)]** If any leave is given under Rule 4.16(5), the petitioner shall add to the list the same particulars in respect of the person to whom leave has been given.

## 4.18 Affidavit in opposition

**4.18(1) [Filing in court]** If the company intends to oppose the petition, its affidavit in opposition shall be filed in court not less than 7 days before the date fixed for the hearing.

**4.18(2) [Copy to petitioner]** A copy of the affidavit shall be sent by the company to the petitioner, forthwith after filing.

## 4.19 Substitution of creditor or contributory for petitioner

**4.19(1) [Application of Rule]** This Rule applies where a person petitions and is subsequently found not entitled to do so, or where the petitioner–
(a) fails to advertise his petition within the time prescribed by the Rules or such extended time as the court may allow, or
(b) consents to withdraw his petition, or to allow it to be dismissed, consents to an adjournment, or fails to appear in support of his petition when it is called on in court on the day originally fixed for the hearing, or on a day to which it is adjourned, or
(c) appears, but does not apply for an order in the terms of the prayer of his petition.

**4.19(2) [Power of court]** The court may, on such terms as it thinks just, substitute as petitioner any creditor or contributory who in its opinion would have a right to present a petition, and who is desirous of prosecuting it.

**4.19(3) [Making of order]** An order of the court under this Rule may, where a petitioner fails to advertise his petition within the time prescribed by these Rules, or consents to withdraw his petition, be made at any time.

**Note**
See practice direction [1987] 1 All ER 107.

## 4.20 Notice and settling of winding-up order

**4.20(1) [Notice to official receiver]** When a winding-up order has been made, the court shall forthwith give notice of the fact to the official receiver.

[FORM 4.11]
[FORM 4.12]
[FORM 4.13]

**4.20(2) [Documents to be left at court]** The petitioner and every other person who has appeared on the hearing of the petition shall, not later than the business day following that on which the order is made, leave at the court all the documents required for enabling the order to be completed forthwith.

**4.20(3) [Appointment of venue]** It is not necessary for the court to appoint a venue for any person to attend to settle the order, unless in any particular case the special circumstances make an appointment necessary.

## 4.21 Transmission and advertisement of order

**4.21(1) [Copy of orders to official receiver]** When the winding-up order has been made, 3 copies of it, sealed with the seal of the court, shall be sent forthwith by the court to the official receiver.

**4.21(2) [Service on company etc.]** The official receiver shall cause a sealed copy of the order to be served on the company by prepaid letter addressed to it at its registered office (if any) or, if there is no registered office, at its principal or last known principal place of business.

Alternatively, the order may be served on such other person or persons, or in such other manner, as the court directs.

**4.21(3) [Copy of order to registrar]** The official receiver shall forward to the registrar of companies the copy of the order which by section 130(1) is directed to be so forwarded by the company.

**4.21(4) [Advertisement]** The official receiver shall forthwith–

(a) cause the order to be gazetted, and

(b) advertise the order in such newspaper as the official receiver may select.

**History**

In r. 4.21(4) the word "local" formerly appearing before the word "newspaper" omitted by the Insolvency (Amendment) Rules 1991 (SI 1991/495), r. 3, Sch., para. 2 as from 2 April 1991.

## 4.21A Expenses of voluntary arrangement

**4.21A** Where a winding-up order is made and there is at the time of the presentation of the petition in force for the company a voluntary arrangement under Part I of the Act, any expenses properly incurred as expenses of the administration of the arrangement in question shall be a first charge on the company's assets.

**History**

R. 4.21A inserted by the Insolvency (Amendment) Rules 1987 (SI 1987/1919), r. 3(1), Sch., Pt. 1, para. 39 as from 11 January 1988.

# Chapter 4 – Petition by Contributories

### (NO CVL APPLICATION)

## 4.22 Presentation and service of petition

**4.22(1) [Form of petition and filing in court]** The petition shall specify the grounds on which it is presented and shall be filed in court with one copy for service under this Rule. [FORM 4.14]

**History**

In r. 4.22(1) the words "and the nature of the relief which is sought by the petitioner," formerly appearing after the words "on which it is presented" omitted by the Insolvency (Amendment) Rules 1987 (SI 1987/1919), r. 3(1), Sch., Pt. 1, para. 40(1) as from 11 January 1988.

**4.22(1A) [Deposit receipt to be produced]** No petition shall be filed unless there is produced with it the receipt for the deposit payable on presentation.

**History**

R. 4.22(1A) inserted by the Insolvency (Amendment) Rules 1987 (SI 1987/1919), r. 3(1), Sch., Pt. 1, para. 40(2) as from 11 January 1988.

**4.22(2) [Fixing return day]** The court shall fix a hearing for a day ("the return day") on which, unless the court otherwise directs, the petitioner and the company shall attend before the registrar in chambers for directions to be given in relation to the procedure on the petition.

**4.22(3) [Copy of petition for service]** On fixing the return day, the court shall return to the petitioner a sealed copy of the petition for service, endorsed with the return day and time of hearing.

**4.22(4) [Service on company]** The petitioner shall, at least 14 days before the return day, serve a sealed copy of the petition on the company.

**Note**
See practice direction [1987] 1 All ER 107.

## 4.23 Return of petition

**4.23(1) [Directions]** On the return day, or at any time after it, the court shall give such directions as it thinks appropriate with respect to the following matters–

(a) service of the petition, whether in connection with the venue for a further hearing, or for any other purpose;

(b) whether particulars of claim and defence are to be delivered, and generally as to the procedure on the petition;

(c) whether, and if so by what means, the petition is to be advertised;

(d) the manner in which any evidence is to be adduced at any hearing before the judge and in particular (but without prejudice to the generality of the above) as to–
   (i) the taking of evidence wholly or in part by affidavit or orally;
   (ii) the cross-examination of any deponents to affidavits;
   (iii) the matters to be dealt with in evidence;

(e) any other matter affecting the procedure on the petition or in connection with the hearing and disposal of the petition.

**4.23(2) [Directions under r. 4.23(1)(a)]** In giving directions under paragraph (1)(a), the court shall have regard to whether any of the persons specified in Rule 4.10 should be served with a copy of the petition.

## 4.24 Application of Rules in Chapter 3

**4.24** The following Rules in Chapter 3 apply, with the necessary modifications–

Rule 4.16 (notice of appearance);
Rule 4.17 (list of appearances);
Rule 4.20 (notice and settling of winding-up order);
Rule 4.21 (transmission and advertisement of order); and
Rule 4.21A (expenses of voluntary arrangement)

**History**
In r. 4.24 the word "and" at the end of the line beginning "Rule 4.20" omitted and the words "; and" and the line beginning "Rule 4.21A" added by the Insolvency (Amendment) Rules 1987 (SI 1987/1919), r. 3(1), Sch., Pt. 1, para. 41 as from 11 January 1988.

# Chapter 5 – Provisional Liquidator

**(NO CVL APPLICATION)**

## 4.25 Appointment of provisional liquidator

**4.25(1) [Who may apply to court]** An application to the court for the appointment of a provisional liquidator under section 135 may be made by the petitioner, or by a creditor of the company, or by a contributory, or by the company itself, or by the Secretary of State, or by any person who under any enactment would be entitled to present a petition for the winding up of the company.

**4.25(2) [Supporting affidavit]** The application must be supported by an affidavit stating–

(a) the grounds on which it is proposed that a provisional liquidator should be appointed;

(b) if some person other than the official receiver is proposed to be appointed, that the person has consented to act and, to the best of the applicant's belief, is qualified to act as an insolvency practitioner in relation to the company;

(c) whether or not the official receiver has been informed of the application and, if so, has been furnished with a copy of it;

(d) whether to the applicant's knowledge–
  (i) there has been proposed or is in force for the company a voluntary arrangement under Part I of the Act, or
  (ii) an administrator or administrative receiver is acting in relation to the company, or
  (iii) a liquidator has been appointed for its voluntary winding up; and

(e) the applicant's estimate of the value of the assets in respect of which the provisional liquidator is to be appointed.

**4.25(3) [Copies to official receiver etc.]** The applicant shall send copies of the application and of the affidavit in support to the official receiver, who may attend the hearing and make any representations which he thinks appropriate.

If for any reason it is not practicable to comply with this paragraph, the official receiver must be informed of the application in sufficient time for him to be able to attend.

**4.25(4) [Powers of court]** The court may on the application, if satisfied that sufficient grounds are shown for the appointment, make it on such terms as it thinks fit.

## 4.25A Notice of appointment

**4.25A(1) [Notice to official receiver]** Where a provisional liquidator has been appointed the court shall forthwith give notice of the fact to the official receiver.

**4.25A(2) [Copy to provisional liquidator]** A copy of that notice shall at the same time be sent by the court to the provisional liquidator where he is not the official receiver. [FORM 4.14A]

**History**
R. 4.25A inserted by the Insolvency (Amendment) Rules 1987 (SI 1987/1919), r. 3(1), Sch., Pt. 1, para. 42 as from 11 January 1988. Also against r. 4.25A the words "[FORM 4.14A]" inserted by the Insolvency (Amendment) Rules 1987 (SI 1987/1919), r. 3(1), Sch., Pt. 2, para. 156(1) as from the same date.

## 4.26 Order of appointment

**4.26(1) [Form of order]** The order appointing the provisional liquidator shall specify the functions to be carried out by him in relation to the company's affairs. [FORM 4.15]

**4.26(2) [Sealed copies]** The court shall, forthwith after the order is made, send sealed copies of the order as follows–

(a) if the official receiver is appointed, two copies to him;

(b) if a person other than the official receiver is appointed–
  (i) two copies to that person, and
  (ii) one copy to the official receiver;

(c) if there is an administrative receiver acting in relation to the company, one copy to him.

**4.26(3) [One r. 4.26(2) copy sent to company or liquidator]** Of the two copies of the order sent to the official receiver under paragraph (2)(a), or to another person under paragraph (2)(b)(i), one shall in each case be sent by the recipient to the company or, if a liquidator has been appointed for the company's voluntary winding up, to him.

## 4.27 Deposit

**4.27(1) [Security for official receiver's remuneration etc.]** Before an order appointing the official receiver as provisional liquidator is issued, the applicant for it shall deposit with him, or otherwise secure to his satisfaction, such sum as the court directs to cover the official receiver's remuneration and expenses.

**4.27(2) [Insufficiency of deposit etc.]** If the sum deposited or secured subsequently proves to be insufficient, the court may, on application by the official receiver, order that an additional sum be deposited or secured. If the order is not complied with within 2 days after service of it on the person to whom it is directed, the court may discharge the order appointing the provisional liquidator.

**4.27(3) [Repayment of deposit etc.]** If a winding-up order is made after a provisional liquidator has been appointed, any money deposited under this Rule shall (unless it is required by reason of insufficiency of assets for payment of remuneration and expenses of the provisional liquidator) be repaid to the person depositing it (or as that person may direct) out of the assets, in the prescribed order of priority.

## 4.28 Security

**4.28(1) [Application of Rule]** The following applies where an insolvency practitioner is appointed to be provisional liquidator under section 135.

**4.28(2) [Cost of providing security]** The cost of providing the security required under the Act shall be paid in the first instance by the provisional liquidator; but–

(a) if a winding-up order is not made, the person so appointed is entitled to be reimbursed out of the property of the company, and the court may make an order on the company accordingly, and

(b) if a winding-up order is made, he is entitled to be reimbursed out of the assets in the prescribed order of priority.

## 4.29 Failure to give or keep up security

**4.29(1) [Powers of court]** If the provisional liquidator fails to give or keep up his security, the court may remove him, and make such order as it thinks fit as to costs.

**4.29(2) [Directions for replacement]** If an order is made under this Rule removing the provisional liquidator, or discharging the order appointing him, the court shall give directions as to whether any, and if so what, steps should be taken for the appointment of another person in his place.

## 4.30 Remuneration

**4.30(1) [To be fixed by court]** The remuneration of the provisional liquidator (other than the official receiver) shall be fixed by the court from time to time on his application.

**4.30(2) [Matters to be taken into account]** In fixing his remuneration, the court shall take into account–

(a) the time properly given by him (as provisional liquidator) and his staff in attending to the company's affairs;

(b) the complexity (or otherwise) of the case;

(c) any respects in which, in connection with the company's affairs, there falls on the provisional liquidator any responsibility of an exceptional kind or degree;

(d) the effectiveness with which the provisional liquidator appears to be carrying out, or to have carried out, his duties; and

(e) the value and nature of the property with which he has to deal.

**4.30(3) [Source of payment of remuneration etc.]** Without prejudice to any order the court may make as to costs, the provisional liquidator's remuneration (whether the official receiver or another) shall be paid to him, and the amount of any expenses incurred by him (including the remuneration and expenses of any special manager appointed under section 177) reimbursed–

(a) if a winding-up order is not made, out of the property of the company; and

(b) if a winding-up order is made, out of the assets, in the prescribed order of priority,

or, in either case (the relevant funds being insufficient), out of the deposit under Rule 4.27.

**History**

In r. 4.30(3) the words from the beginning to "out of the property of the company" in para. (a) substituted by the Insolvency (Amendment) Rules 1987 (SI 1987/1919), r. 3(1), Sch., Pt. 1, para. 43(1) as from 11 January 1988; the former words read as follows:

"The provisional liquidator's remuneration (whether the official receiver or another) shall be paid to him, and the amount of any expenses incurred by him reimbursed–

(a) if a winding-up order is not made, out of the property of the company (and the court may make an order on the company accordingly)".

**4.30(3A) [Power of retention]** Unless the court otherwise directs, in a case falling within paragraph (3)(a) above the provisional liquidator may retain out of the company's property such sums or property as are or may be required for meeting his remuneration and expenses.

**History**

R. 4.30(3A) inserted by the Insolvency (Amendment) Rules 1987 (SI 1987/1919), r. 3(1), Sch., Pt. 1, para. 43(2) as from 11 January 1988.

**4.30(4) [Provisional liquidator other than official receiver]** Where a person other than the official receiver has been appointed provisional liquidator, and the official receiver has taken any steps for the purpose of obtaining a statement of affairs or has performed any other duty under the Rules, he shall pay the official receiver such sum (if any) as the court may direct.

## 4.31 Termination of appointment

**4.31(1) [Termination by court]** The appointment of the provisional liquidator may be terminated by the court on his application, or on that of any of the persons specified in Rule 4.25(1).

**4.31(2) [Directions on termination]** If the provisional liquidator's appointment terminates, in consequence of the dismissal of the winding-up petition or otherwise, the court may give such directions as it thinks fit with respect to the accounts of his administration or any other matters which it thinks appropriate.

**4.31(3)** (Omitted by the Insolvency (Amendment) Rules 1987 (SI 1987/1919), r. 3(1), Sch., Pt. 1, para. 44 as from 11 January 1988.)

**History**

R. 4.31(3) formerly read as follows:

"The court may under paragraph (2)–

(a) direct that any expenses properly incurred by the provisional liquidator during the period of his appointment, including any remuneration to which he is entitled, be paid out of the property of the company, and

(b) authorise him to retain out of that property such sums as are required for meeting those expenses.

Alternatively, the court may make such order as it thinks fit with respect to those matters."

# Chapter 6 – Statement of Affairs and Other Information

## 4.32 Notice requiring statement of affairs

(NO CVL APPLICATION)

**4.32(1) [Application of Rule]** The following applies where the official receiver determines to require a statement of the company's affairs to be made out and submitted to him in accordance with section 131. [FORM 4.16]

**4.32(2) [Notice]** He shall send notice to each of the persons whom he considers should be made responsible under that section, requiring them to prepare and submit the statement.

**4.32(3) ["The deponents"]** The persons to whom that notice is sent are referred to in this Chapter as "the deponents".

**4.32(4) [Contents of notice]** The notice shall inform each of the deponents–

(a) of the names and addresses of all others (if any) to whom the same notice has been sent;

(b) of the time within which the statement must be delivered;

(c) of the effect of section 131(7) (penalty for non-compliance); and

(d) of the application to him, and to each of the other deponents, of section 235 (duty to provide information, and to attend on the official receiver if required).

**4.32(5) [Instructions for preparation of statement]** The official receiver shall, on request, furnish a deponent with instructions for the preparation of the statement and with the forms required for that purpose.

## 4.33 Verification and filing

(NO CVL APPLICATION)

**4.33(1) [Form and verification]** The statement of affairs shall be in Form 4.17, shall contain all the particulars required by that form and shall be verified by affidavit by the deponents (using the same form). [FORM 4.17]

**4.33(2) [Affidavits of concurrence]** The official receiver may require any of the persons mentioned in section 131(3) to submit an affidavit of concurrence, stating that he concurs in the statement of affairs.

**4.33(3) [Affidavit may be qualified]** An affidavit of concurrence made under paragraph (2) may be qualified in respect of matters dealt with in the statement of affairs, where the maker of the affidavit is not in agreement with the deponents, or he considers the statement to be erroneous or misleading, or he is without the direct knowledge necessary for concurring in the statement.

**4.33(4) [Delivery of statement to official receiver]** The statement of affairs shall be delivered to the official receiver by the deponent making the affidavit of verification (or by one of them, if more than one), together with a copy of the verified statement.

**4.33(5) [Delivery of affidavit of concurrence]** Every affidavit of concurrence shall be delivered to the official receiver by the person who makes it, together with a copy.

**4.33(6) [Filing in court]** The official receiver shall file the verified copy of the statement and the affidavits of concurrence (if any) in court.

**4.33(7) [Swearing of affidavit]** The affidavit may be sworn before an official receiver or a deputy official receiver, or before an officer of the Department or the court duly authorised in that behalf.

## 4.34–CVL Statement of affairs

**4.34–CVL(1) [Application of Rule]** This Rule applies with respect to the statement of affairs made out by the liquidator under section 95(3) or (as the case may be) by the directors under section 99(1).
[FORM 4.18]
[FORM 4.19]

**4.34–CVL(2) [Made out by liquidator]** Where it is made out by the liquidator, the statement of affairs shall be delivered by him to the registrar of companies within 7 days after the creditors' meeting summoned under section 95(2). [FORM 4.20]

**4.34–CVL(3) [Made out by directors]** Where it is made out by the directors under section 99(1) the statement of affairs shall be delivered by them to the liquidator in office following the creditors' meeting summoned under section 98 forthwith after that meeting has been held; and he shall, within 7 days, deliver it to the registrar of companies. [FORM 4.20]

**4.34–CVL(4) [Date where made out by directors]** A statement of affairs under section 99(1) may be made up to a date not more than 14 days before that on which the resolution for voluntary winding up is passed by the company.

**History**
R. 4.34(3) and (4) substituted for the former r. 4.34(3) by the Insolvency (Amendment) Rules 1987 (SI 1987/1919), r. 3(1), Sch., Pt. 1, para. 45 as from 11 January 1988; the former r. 4.34(3) read as follows:

"Where it is made out by the directors under section 99(1), the statement of affairs shall be delivered by them to the liquidator, when appointed; and he shall, within 7 days, deliver it to the registrar of companies."

## 4.34A–CVL Copy statement of affairs

**4.34A–CVL** Where a liquidator is nominated by the company at a general meeting held on a day prior to that on which the creditors' meeting summoned under section 98 is held, the directors shall forthwith after his nomination or the making of the statement of affairs, whichever is the later, deliver to him a copy of the statement of affairs.

**History**
R. 4.34A–CVL inserted by the Insolvency (Amendment) Rules 1987 (SI 1987/1919) r. 3(1), Sch., Pt. 1, para. 46 as from 11 January 1988.

## 4.35 Limited disclosure

(NO CVL APPLICATION)

**4.35(1) [Official receiver may apply to court]** Where the official receiver thinks that it would prejudice the conduct of the liquidation for the whole or part of the statement of affairs to be disclosed, he may apply to the court for an order of limited disclosure in respect of the statement, or any specified part of it.

**History**
R. 4.49A inserted by the Insolvency (Amendment) Rules 1987 (SI 1987/1919), r. 3(1), Sch., Pt. 1, para. 49 as from 11 January 1988.

# Chapter 8 – Meetings of Creditors and Contributories

## SECTION A: RULES OF GENERAL APPLICATION

## 4.50 First meetings

(NO CVL APPLICATION)

**4.50(1) [Venue for meetings etc.]** If under section 136(5) the official receiver decides to summon meetings of the company's creditors and contributories for the purpose of nominating a person to be liquidator in place of himself, he shall fix a venue for each meeting, in neither case more than 4 months from the date of the winding-up order.

**4.50(2) [Notice of meetings]** When for each meeting a venue has been fixed, notice of the meetings shall be given to the court and–

(a) in the case of the creditors' meeting, to every creditor who is known to the official receiver or is identified in the company's statement of affairs; and

(b) in the case of the contributories' meeting, to every person appearing (by the company's books or otherwise) to be a contributory of the company.

**4.50(3) [Time for giving notice]** Notice to the court shall be given forthwith, and the other notices shall be given at least 21 days before the date fixed for each meeting respectively.

**4.50(4) [Contents of notice]** The notice to creditors shall specify a time and date, not more than 4 days before the date fixed for the meeting, by which they must lodge proofs and (if applicable) proxies, in order to be entitled to vote at the meeting; and the same applies in respect of contributories and their proxies.

**4.50(5) [Public advertisement]** Notice of the meetings shall also be given by public advertisement.

**4.50(6) [Request by creditors under s. 136(5)(c)]** Where the official receiver receives a request by creditors under section 136(5)(c) for meetings of creditors and contributories to be summoned, and it appears to him that the request is properly made in accordance with the Act, he shall–

(a) withdraw any notices previously given by him under section 136(5)(b) (that he has decided not to summon such meetings),

(b) fix the venue of each meeting for not more than 3 months from his receipt of the creditors' request, and

(c) act in accordance with paragraphs (2) to (5) above, as if he had decided under section 136 to summon the meetings. [FORM 4.21]

**4.50(7) [Names of meetings]** Meetings summoned by the official receiver under this Rule are known respectively as "the first meeting of creditors" and "the first meeting of contributories", and jointly as "the first meetings in the liquidation".

**4.50(8) [Where company is authorised institution under Banking Act]** Where the company is an authorised institution or former authorised institution within the meaning of the Banking Act 1987, additional notices are required by Rule 4.72.

**History**
In r. 4.50(8) the words from "an authorised institution" to "Banking Act 1987" substituted by the Insolvency (Amendment) Rules 1987 (SI 1987/1919), r. 3(1), Sch., Pt. 1, para. 50 as from 11 January 1988; the former words read as follows:

"a recognised bank or licensed institution under the Banking Act 1979, or an institution to which sections 16 and 18 of that Act apply as if it were a licensed institution".

## 4.51–CVL First meeting of creditors

**4.51–CVL(1) [Application of Rule]** This Rule applies in the case of a meeting of creditors summoned by the liquidator under section 95 (where, in what starts as a members' voluntary winding up, he forms the opinion that the company will be unable to pay its debts) or a meeting under section 98 (first meeting of creditors in a creditors' voluntary winding up).

**4.51–CVL(2) [Contents of notice]** The notice summoning the meeting shall specify a venue for the meeting and the time (not earlier than 12.00 hours on the business day before the day fixed for the meeting) by which, and the place at which, creditors must lodge any proxies necessary to entitle them to vote at the meeting.

**History**
In r. 4.51(2) the words from "any proxies necessary" to the end substituted for the former words "proofs and (if applicable) proxies" by the Insolvency (Amendment) Rules 1987 (SI 1987/1919), r. 3(1), Sch., Pt. 1, para. 51(1) as from 11 January 1988.

**4.51–CVL(3) [Where company is authorised institution under Banking Act]** Where the company is an authorised institution or former authorised institution within the meaning of the Banking Act 1987, additional notices are required by Rule 4.72.

**History**
In r. 4.51(3) the words from "an authorised institution" to "Banking Act 1987" substituted by the Insolvency (Amendment) Rules 1987 (SI 1987/1919), r. 3(1), Sch., Pt. 1, para. 51(2) as from 11 January 1988; the former words read as follows: "a recognised bank or licensed institution under the Banking Act 1979, or an institution to which sections 16 and 18 of that Act apply as if it were a licensed institution".

## 4.52 Business at first meetings in the liquidation

(NO CVL APPLICATION)

**4.52(1) [Limitation on resolutions at first meeting of creditors]** At the first meeting of creditors, no resolutions shall be taken other than the following–

(a) a resolution to appoint a named insolvency practitioner to be liquidator, or two or more insolvency practitioners as joint liquidators;

(b) a resolution to establish a liquidation committee;

(c) (unless it has been resolved to establish a liquidation committee) a resolution specifying the terms on which the liquidator is to be remunerated, or to defer consideration of that matter;

(d) (if, and only if, two or more persons are appointed to act jointly as liquidator) a resolution specifying whether acts are to be done by both or all of them, or by only one;

(e) (where the meeting has been requisitioned under section 136), a resolution authorising payment out of the assets, as an expense of the liquidation, of the cost of summoning and holding the meeting and any meeting of contributories so requisitioned and held;

(f) a resolution to adjourn the meeting for not more than 3 weeks;

(g) any other resolution which the chairman thinks it right to allow for special reasons.

**4.52(2) [At first meeting of contributories]** The same applies as regards the first meeting of contributories, but that meeting shall not pass any resolution to the effect of paragraph (1)(c) or (e).

**4.52(3) [Limitation at either meeting]** At neither meeting shall any resolution be proposed which has for its object the appointment of the official receiver as liquidator.

## 4.53–CVL Business at meeting under s. 95 or 98

**4.53–CVL** Rule 4.52(1), except sub-paragraph (e), applies to a creditors' meeting under section 95 or 98.

## 4.53A–CVL Effect of adjournment of company meeting

**4.53A–CVL** Where a company meeting at which a resolution for voluntary winding up is to be proposed is adjourned, any resolution passed at a meeting under section 98 held before the holding of the adjourned company meeting only has effect on and from the passing by the company of a resolution for winding up.

**History**
See note after r. 4.53B.

## 4.53B–CVL Report by director, etc.

**4.53B–CVL(1) [State of company's affairs]** At any meeting held under section 98 where the statement of affairs laid before the meeting does not state the company's affairs as at the date of the meeting, the directors of the company shall cause to be made to the meeting, either by the director presiding at the meeting or by another person with knowledge of the relevant matters, a report (written or oral) on any material transactions relating to the company occurring between the date of the making of the statement of affairs and that of the meeting.

**4.53B–CVL(2) [Recorded in minutes]** Any such report shall be recorded in the minutes of the meeting kept under Rule 4.71.

**History**
R. 4.53A and 4.53B inserted by the Insolvency (Amendment) Rules 1987 (SI 1987/1919), r. 3(1), Sch., Pt. 1, para. 52 as from 11 January 1988.

## 4.54 General power to call meetings

**4.54(1) [General power, "the convener"]** The official receiver or the liquidator may at any time summon and conduct meetings of creditors or of contributories for the purpose of ascertaining their wishes in all matters relating to the liquidation; and in relation to any meeting summoned under the Act or the Rules, the person summoning it is referred to as "the convener".

**4.54(2) [Notice of venue]** When (in either case) a venue for the meeting has been fixed, notice of it shall be given by the convener–

(a) in the case of a creditors' meeting, to every creditor who is known to him or is identified in the company's statement of affairs; and [FORM 4.22]

(b) in the case of a meeting of contributories, to every person appearing (by the company's books or otherwise) to be a contributory of the company. [FORM 4.23]

**4.54(3) [Time for giving notice etc.]** Notice of the meeting shall be given at least 21 days before the date fixed for it, and shall specify the purpose of the meeting.

**4.54(4) [Contents of notice]** The notice shall specify a time and date, not more than 4 days before the date fixed for the meeting, by which, and the place at which, creditors must lodge proofs and proxies, in order to be entitled to vote at the meeting; and the same applies in respect of contributories and their proxies.
(NO CVL APPLICATION)

**4.54(5–CVL) [Contents of notice]** The notice shall specify a time and date, not more than 4 days before that fixed for the meeting, by which, and the place at which, creditors (if not individuals attending in person) must lodge proxies, in order to be entitled to vote at the meeting.

**4.54(6) [Additional notice by public advertisement]** Additional notice of the meeting may be given by public advertisement if the convener thinks fit, and shall be so given if the court orders.

## 4.55 The chairman at meetings

(NO CVL APPLICATION)

**4.55(1) [Application of Rule]** This Rule applies both to a meeting of creditors and to a meeting of contributories.

**4.55(2) [Where convener official receiver]** Where the convener of the meeting is the official receiver, he, or a person nominated by him, shall be chairman.

A nomination under this paragraph shall be in writing, unless the nominee is another official receiver or a deputy official receiver.

**4.55(3) [Where convener not official receiver]** Where the convener is other than the official receiver, the chairman shall be he, or a person nominated in writing by him.

A person nominated under this paragraph must be either–

(a) one who is qualified to act as an insolvency practitioner in relation to the company, or

(b) an employee of the liquidator or his firm who is experienced in insolvency matters.

## 4.56–CVL The chairman at meetings

**4.56–CVL(1) [Application of Rule]** This Rule applies both to a meeting of creditors (except a meeting under section 95 or 98) and to a meeting of contributories.

**History**

In r. 4.56–CVL(1) the words "section 95 or 98" substituted for the former words "section 98" by the Insolvency (Amendment) Rules 1987 (SI 1987/1919), r. 3(1), Sch., Pt. 1, para. 53 as from 11 January 1988.

**4.56–CVL(2) [Liquidator or his nominee to be chairman]** The liquidator, or a person nominated by him in writing to act, shall be chairman of the meeting.

A person nominated under this paragraph must be either–

(a) one who is qualified to act as an insolvency practitioner in relation to the company, or
(b) an employee of the liquidator or his firm who is experienced in insolvency matters.

## 4.57 Requisitioned meetings

**4.57(1) [Documents to accompany creditors' request]** Any request by creditors to the liquidator (whether or not the official receiver) for a meeting of creditors or contributories, or meetings of both, to be summoned shall be accompanied by–

(a) a list of the creditors concurring with the request and the amount of their respective claims in the winding up;
(b) from each creditor concurring, written confirmation of his concurrence; and
(c) a statement of the purpose of the proposed meeting.

Sub-paragraphs (a) and (b) do not apply if the requisitioning creditor's debt is alone sufficient, without the concurrence of other creditors.

[FORM 4.21]

**4.57(2) [Liquidator to fix venue]** The liquidator shall, if he considers the request to be properly made in accordance with the Act, fix a venue for the meeting, not more than 35 days from his receipt of the request.

**4.57(3) [Notice of meeting]** The liquidator shall give 21 days' notice of the meeting, and the venue for it, to creditors.

**4.57(4) [Application of r. 4.57(1)–(3) to contributories' meetings]** Paragraphs (1) to (3) above apply to the requisitioning by contributories of contributories' meetings, with the following modifications–

(a) for the reference in paragraph (1)(a) to the creditors' respective claims substitute the contributories' respective values (being the amounts for which they may vote at any meeting); and
(b) the persons to be given notice under paragraph (3) are those appearing (by the company's books or otherwise) to be contributories of the company. [FORM 4.24]

(NO CVL APPLICATION)

## 4.58 Attendance at meetings of company's personnel

**4.58(1) [Application of Rule]** This Rule applies to meetings of creditors and to meetings of contributories.

**4.58(2) [Notice to company's personnel]** Whenever a meeting is summoned, the convener shall give at least 21 days' notice to such of the company's personnel as he thinks should be told of, or be present at, the meeting.

"The company's personnel" means the persons referred to in paragraphs (a) to (d) of section 235(3) (present and past officers, employees, etc.).

**4.58(3) [Notice of adjournment]** If the meeting is adjourned, the chairman of the meeting shall, unless for any reason he thinks it unnecessary or impracticable, give notice of the adjournment to such (if any) of the company's personnel as he considers appropriate, being persons who were not themselves present at the meeting.

**4.58(4) [Notice that presence required]** The convener may, if he thinks fit, give notice to any one or more of the company's personnel that he is, or they are, required to be present at the meeting, or to be in attendance.

**4.58(5) [Admission to meetings]** In the case of any meeting, any one or more of the company's personnel, and any other persons, may be admitted, but–

(a) they must have given reasonable notice of their wish to be present, and

(b) it is a matter for the chairman's discretion whether they are to be admitted or not, and his decision is final as to what (if any) intervention may be made by any of them.

**4.58(6) [Adjournment for obtaining attendance]** If it is desired to put questions to any one of the company's personnel who is not present, the chairman may adjourn the meeting with a view to obtaining his attendance.

**4.58(7) [Chairman's discretion re questions]** Where one of the company's personnel is present at a meeting, only such questions may be put to him as the chairman may in his discretion allow.

## 4.59 Notice of meetings by advertisement only

**4.59(1) [Power of court]** In the case of any meeting of creditors or contributories to be held under the Act or the Rules, the court may order that notice of the meeting be given by public advertisement, and not by individual notice to the persons concerned.

**4.59(2) [Matters for court to consider]** In considering whether to act under this Rule, the court shall have regard to the cost of public advertisement, to the amount of the assets available, and to the extent of the interest of creditors or of contributories, or any particular class of either of them.

## 4.60 Venue

**4.60(1) [Convenience of venue]** In fixing the venue for a meeting of creditors or contributories, the convener shall have regard to the convenience of the persons (other than whoever is to be chairman) who are invited to attend.

**4.60(2) [Time of meetings]** Meetings shall in all cases be summoned for commencement between the hours of 10.00 and 16.00 hours on a business day, unless the court otherwise directs.

**4.60(3) [Forms of proxy]** With every notice summoning a meeting of creditors or contributories there shall be sent out forms of proxy. [FORM 8.4] or [FORM 8.5]

## 4.61 Expenses of summoning meetings

**4.61(1) [Deposit for payment of expenses]** Subject as follows, the expenses of summoning and holding a meeting of creditors or contributories at the instance of any person other than the official receiver or the liquidator shall be paid by that person, who shall deposit with the liquidator security for their payment.

**4.61(2) [Appropriate security]** The sum to be deposited shall be such as the official receiver or liquidator (as the case may be) determines to be appropriate; and neither shall act without the deposit having been made.

**4.61(3) [Vote for expenses to be paid out of assets]** Where a meeting of creditors is so summoned, it may vote that the expenses of summoning and holding it, and of summoning and holding any meeting of contributories requisitioned at the same time, shall be payable out of the assets, as an expense of the liquidation.

**4.61(4) [Contributories' meeting]** Where a meeting of contributories is summoned on the requisition of contributories, it may vote that the expenses of summoning and holding it shall be payable out of the assets, but subject to the right of creditors to be paid in full, with interest.

**4.61(5) [Repayment of deposit]** To the extent that any deposit made under this Rule is not required for the payment of expenses of summoning and holding a meeting, it shall be repaid to the person who made it.

## 4.62–CVL Expenses of meeting under s. 98

**4.62–CVL(1) [Payment out of assets]** Payment may be made out of the company's assets, either before or after the commencement of the winding up, of any reasonable and necessary expenses incurred in connection with the summoning, advertisement and holding of a creditors' meeting under section 98.

Any such payment is an expense of the liquidation.

**4.62–CVL(2) [Payment before commencement of winding up]** Where such payments are made before the commencement of the winding up, the director presiding at the creditors' meeting shall inform the meeting of their amount and the identity of the persons to whom they were made.

**4.62–CVL(3) [Payment by s. 100 liquidator]** The liquidator appointed under section 100 may make such a payment (subject to the next paragraph); but if there is a liquidation committee, he must give the committee at least 7 days' notice of his intention to make the payment.

**4.62–CVL(4) [No payment by liquidator to himself]** Such a payment shall not be made by the liquidator to himself, or to any associate of his, otherwise than with the approval of the liquidation committee, the creditors, or the court.

**4.62–CVL(5) [Powers of court under r. 4.219]** This Rule is without prejudice to the powers of the court under Rule 4.219 (voluntary winding up superseded by winding up by the court).

## 4.63 Resolutions

**4.63(1) [Resolution passed by majority in value]** Subject as follows, at a meeting of creditors or contributories, a resolution is passed when a majority (in value) of those present and voting, in person or by proxy, have voted in favour of the resolution.

The value of contributories is determined by reference to the number of votes conferred on each contributory by the company's articles.

**History**
In r. 4.63(1) the words "Subject as follows," at the beginning inserted by the Insolvency (Amendment) Rules 1987 (SI 1987/1919), r. 3(1), Sch., Pt. 1, para. 54(1) as from 11 January 1988.

**4.63(2) [Resolution for appointment of liquidator]** In the case of a resolution for the appointment of a liquidator–

(a) subject to paragraph (2A), if on any vote there are two nominees for appointment, the person who obtains the most support is appointed;

(b) if there are three or more nominees, and one of them has a clear majority over both or all the others together, that one is appointed; and

(c) in any other case, the chairman of the meeting shall continue to take votes (disregarding at each vote any nominee who has withdrawn and, if no nominee has withdrawn, the nominee who obtained the least support last time), until a clear majority is obtained for any one nominee.

**History**
In r. 4.63(2), para. (a) the words "Subject to paragraph (2A)," at the beginning inserted by the Insolvency (Amendment) Rules 1987 (SI 1987/1919), r. 3(1), Sch., Pt. 1, para. 54(2) as from 11 January 1988.

**4.63(2A) [Majority in value]** In a winding up by the court the support referred to in paragraph (2)(a) must represent a majority in value of all those present (in person or by proxy) at the meeting and entitled to vote. (NO CVL APPLICATION).

**History**
R. 4.63(2A) inserted by the Insolvency (Amendment) Rules 1987 (SI 1981/1919), r. 3(1), Sch., Pt. 1 para. 54(3) as from 11 January 1988.

**4.63(3) [Resolution for joint appointment]** The chairman may at any time put to the meeting a resolution for the joint appointment of any two or more nominees.

**4.63(4) [Resolution affecting liquidator etc.]** Where a resolution is proposed which affects a person in respect of his remuneration or conduct as liquidator, or as proposed or former liquidator, the vote of that person, and of any partner or employee of his, shall not be reckoned in the majority required for passing the resolution.

This paragraph applies with respect to a vote given by a person (whether personally or on his behalf by a proxy-holder) either as creditor or contributory or as proxy-holder for a creditor or a contributory (but subject to Rule 8.6 in Part 8 of the Rules).

**History**
In the second paragraph of r. 4.63(4) the words "whether personally or on his behalf by a proxy-holder)" inserted and the word "proxy-holder" substituted for the former word "proxy" by the Insolvency (Amendment) Rules 1987 (SI 1987/1919), r. 3(1), Sch., Pt. 1, para. 54(4) as from 11 January 1988.

# 4.64 Chairman of meeting as proxy-holder

**4.64** Where the chairman at a meeting of creditors or contributories holds a proxy which requires him to vote for a particular resolution, and no other person proposes that resolution–

(a) he shall himself propose it, unless he considers that there is good reason for not doing so, and

(b) if he does not propose it, he shall forthwith after the meeting notify his principal of the reason why not.

# 4.65 Suspension and adjournment

**4.65(1) [Application of Rule]** This Rule applies to meetings of creditors and to meetings of contributories.

**4.65(2) [Suspension at chairman's discretion]** Once only in the course of any meeting, the chairman may, in his discretion and without an adjournment, declare the meeting suspended for any period up to one hour.

**4.65(3) [Adjournment]** The chairman at any meeting may in his discretion, and shall if the meeting so resolves, adjourn it to such time and place as seems to him to be appropriate in the circumstances.

This is subject to Rule 4.113(3) or, as the case may be, 4.114–CVL(3), in a case where the liquidator or his nominee is chairman, and a resolution has been proposed for the liquidator's removal.

**History**
In r. 4.65(3) the words "or, as the case may be, 4.114–CVL(3)," inserted by the Insolvency (Amendment) Rules 1987 (SI 1987/1919), r. 3(1), Sch., Pt. 1, para. 55(1) as from 11 January 1988.

**4.65(4) [Adjourned if inquorate]** If within a period of 30 minutes from the time appointed for the commencement of a meeting a quorum is not present, then the chairman may, at his discretion, adjourn the meeting to such time and place as he may appoint.

**History**
In r. 4.65(4) the words from "the chairman may, at his discretion," to the end substituted by the Insolvency (Amendment) Rules 1987 (SI 1987/1919), r. 3(1), Sch., Pt. 1, para. 55(2) as from 11 January 1988; the former words read as follows:
"by virtue of this Rule the meeting stands adjourned to such time and place as may be appointed by the chairman."

**4.65(5) [Period of adjournment]** An adjournment under this Rule shall not be for a period of more than 21 days; and Rule 4.60(1) and (2) applies.

**4.65(6) [If no chairman]** If there is no person present to act as chairman, some other person present (being entitled to vote) may make the appointment under paragraph (4), with the agreement of others present (being persons so entitled).

Failing agreement, the adjournment shall be to the same time and place in the next following week or, if that is not a business day, to the business day immediately following.

**4.65(7) [Use of proofs and proxies at adjourned meeting]** Where a meeting is adjourned under this Rule, proofs and proxies may be used if lodged at any time up to midday on the business day immediately before the adjourned meeting.

# 4.66 Quorum

**4.66** (Omitted by the Insolvency (Amendment) Rules 1987 (SI 1987/1919), r. 3(1), Sch., Pt. 1, para. 56 as from 11 January 1988).

**History**
R. 4.66 formerly read as follows:
"**4.66(1)** A meeting is not competent to act, in the absence of a quorum, for any purpose except–

(a) the election of a chairman,
(b) in the case of a creditors' meeting, the admission by the chairman of proofs for the purpose of entitlement of creditors to vote, and
(c) the adjournment of the meeting.
(NO CVL APPLICATION)

**(2–CVL)** A meeting is not competent to act, in the absence of a quorum, for any purpose except the election of a chairman, or the adjournment of the meeting.

**(3)** Subject to paragraph (4), a quorum is–
(a) in the case of a creditors' meeting, at least 3 creditors entitled to vote, or all the creditors so entitled, if their number does not exceed 3;
(b) in the case of a meeting of contributories, at least 2 contributories so entitled, or all the contributories, if their number does not exceed 2.

The references to creditors and contributories are to those present in person or by proxy, or duly represented under section 375 of the Companies Act.

**(4)** One person present constitutes a quorum if–
(a) he is himself a creditor or representative under section 375 of the Companies Act or (as the case may be) a contributory with entitlement to vote and he holds a number of proxies sufficient to ensure that, with his own vote, paragraph (3) is complied with, or
(b) being the chairman or any other person, he holds that number of proxies."

# 4.67 Entitlement to vote (creditors)

**4.67(1) [Conditions for voting]** Subject as follows in this Rule and the next, at a meeting of creditors a person is entitled to vote as a creditor only if–
(a) there has been duly lodged (in a winding up by the court by the time and date stated in the notice of the meeting) a proof of the debt claimed to be due to him from the company, and the claim has been admitted under Rule 4.70 for the purpose of entitlement to vote, and
(b) there has been lodged, by the time and date stated in the notice of the meeting, any proxy requisite for that entitlement.

**4.67(2) [Powers of court]** The court may, in exceptional circumstances, by order declare the creditors, or any class of them, entitled to vote at creditors' meetings, without being required to prove their debts.

Where a creditor is so entitled, the court may, on the application of the liquidator, make such consequential orders as it thinks fit (as for example an order treating a creditor as having proved his debt for the purpose of permitting payment of dividend).

**4.67(3) [Limitation on voting]** A creditor shall not vote in respect of a debt for an unliquidated amount, or any debt whose value is not ascertained, except where the chairman agrees to put upon the debt an estimated minimum value for the purpose of entitlement to vote and admits his proof for that purpose.

**4.67(4) [Secured creditor]** A secured creditor is entitled to vote only in respect of the balance (if any) of his debt after deducting the value of his security as estimated by him.

**4.67(5) [Further limitation on voting]** A creditor shall not vote in respect of a debt on, or secured by, a current bill of exchange or promissory note, unless he is willing–
(a) to treat the liability to him on the bill or note of every person who is liable on it antecedently to the company, and against whom a bankruptcy order has not been made (or, in the case of a company, which has not gone into liquidation), as a security in his hands, and
(b) to estimate the value of the security and (for the purpose of entitlement to vote, but not for dividend) to deduct it from his proof.

# 4.68–CVL Chairman's discretion to allow vote

**4.68–CVL** At a creditors' meeting, the chairman may allow a creditor to vote, notwithstanding that he has failed to comply with Rule 4.67(1)(a), if satisfied that the failure was due to circumstances beyond the creditor's control.

# 4.69 Entitlement to vote (contributories)

**4.69** At a meeting of contributories, voting rights are as at a general meeting of the company, subject to any provision in the articles affecting entitlement to vote, either generally or at a time when the company is in liquidation.

## 4.70 Admission and rejection of proof (creditors' meeting)

**4.70(1) [Power of chairman]** At any creditors' meeting the chairman has power to admit or reject a creditor's proof for the purpose of his entitlement to vote; and the power is exercisable with respect to the whole or any part of the proof.

**4.70(2) [Appeal from chairman's decision]** The chairman's decision under this Rule, or in respect of any matter arising under Rule 4.67, is subject to appeal to the court by any creditor or contributory.

**4.70(3) [Voting subject to objection]** If the chairman is in doubt whether a proof should be admitted or rejected, he shall mark it as objected to and allow the creditor to vote, subject to his vote being subsequently declared invalid if the objection to the proof is sustained.

**4.70(4) [If chairman's decision reversed etc.]** If on an appeal the chairman's decision is reversed or varied, or a creditor's vote is declared invalid, the court may order that another meeting be summoned, or make such other order as it thinks just.

**4.70(5) [Costs re application]** Neither the official receiver, nor any person nominated by him to be chairman, is personally liable for costs incurred by any person in respect of an application under this Rule; and the chairman (if other than the official receiver or a person so nominated) is not so liable unless the court makes an order to that effect.
(NO CVL APPLICATION)

**4.70–CVL(6) [Costs re application]** The liquidator or his nominee as chairman is not personally liable for costs incurred by any person in respect of an application under this Rule, unless the court makes an order to that effect.

## 4.71 Record of proceedings

**4.71(1) [Minutes of proceedings]** At any meeting, the chairman shall cause minutes of the proceedings to be kept. The minutes shall be signed by him, and retained as part of the records of the liquidation.

**4.71(2) [List of creditors or contributories attending]** The chairman shall also cause to be made up and kept a list of all the creditors or, as the case may be, contributories who attended the meeting.

**4.71(3) [Record of resolutions]** The minutes of the meeting shall include a record of every resolution passed.

**4.71(4) [Chairman's duty to deliver particulars]** It is the chairman's duty to see to it that particulars of all such resolutions, certified by him, are filed in court not more than 21 days after the date of the meeting.
(NO CVL APPLICATION)

### SECTION B: WINDING UP OF RECOGNISED BANKS, ETC.

## 4.72 Additional provisions as regards certain meetings

**4.72(1) [Application of Rule]** This Rule applies where a company goes, or proposes to go, into liquidation and it is an authorised institution or former authorised institution within the meaning of the Banking Act 1987.

**History**
In r. 4.72(1) the words from "an authorised institution" to the end substituted by the Insolvency (Amendment) Rules 1987 (SI 1987/1919), r. 3(1), Sch., Pt. 1, para. 57 as from 11 January 1988; the former words read as follows:
"(a) a recognised bank or licensed institution within the meaning of the Banking Act 1979, or
(b) an institution to which sections 16 and 18 of that Act apply as if it were a licensed institution."

**4.72(2) [Notice re proposed winding up]** Notice of any meeting of the company at which it is intended to propose a resolution for its winding up shall be given by the directors to the Financial Services Authority and to the Deposit Protection Board.

**History**
In r. 4.72(2) the words "Financial Services Authority" substituted for the former words "Bank of England" by the Bank of England Act 1998 (Consequential Amendments of Subordinate Legislation) Order 1998 (SI 1998/1129), art. 1, 2 and Sch. 1, para. 4(1), (5) (a) as from 1 June 1998.

**4.72(3) [Form of notice]** Notice to the Authority and the Board shall be the same as given to members of the company.

**History**
See history note after r. 4.72(6).

**4.72(4) [Where creditors' meeting summoned under s. 95 or 98]** Where a creditors' meeting is summoned by the liquidator under section 95 or, in a creditors' voluntary winding up, is summoned under section 98, the same notice of the meeting must be given to the Authority and the Board as is given to creditors under Rule 4.51–CVL.

**History**
See history note after r. 4.72(6).

**4.72(5) [Where company being wound up by court]** Where the company is being wound up by the court, notice of the first meetings of creditors and contributories shall be given to the Authority and the Board by the official receiver.

**History**
See history note after r. 4.72(6).

**4.72(6) [Where meeting to receive liquidator's resignation etc.]** Where in the winding up (whether voluntary or by the court) a meeting of creditors or contributories or of the company is summoned for the purpose of–

(a) receiving the liquidator's resignation, or
(b) removing the liquidator, or
(c) appointing a new liquidator,

the person summoning the meeting and giving notice of it shall also give notice to the Authority and the Board.

**History**
In r. 4.72(3), (4), (5), (6), the word "Authority" substituted for the word "Bank" by the Bank of England Act 1998 (Consequential Amendments of Subordinate Legislation) Order 1998 (SI 1998/1129), art. 1, 2 and Sch. 1, para. 4(1), (5)(b) as from 1 June 1998.

**4.72(7) [Representation of Deposit Protection Board]** The Board is entitled to be represented at any meeting of which it is required by this Rule to be given notice; and Schedule 1 to the Rules has effect with respect to the voting rights of the Board at such a meeting.

# Chapter 9 – Proof of Debts in a Liquidation

## SECTION A: PROCEDURE FOR PROVING

## 4.73 Meaning of "prove"

**4.73(1) [Winding up by court]** Where a company is being wound up by the court, a person claiming to be a creditor of the company and wishing to recover his debt in whole or in part must (subject to any order of the court under Rule 4.67(2)) submit his claim in writing to the liquidator. (NO CVL APPLICATION)

**4.73–CVL(2) [Voluntary winding up]** In a voluntary winding up (whether members' or creditors') the liquidator may require a person claiming to be a creditor of the company and wishing to recover his debt in whole or in part, to submit the claim in writing to him.

**4.73(3) ["Proving" and "proof"]** A creditor who claims (whether or not in writing) is referred to as "proving" for his debt; and a document by which he seeks to establish his claim is his "proof".

**4.73(4) ["Proof of debt"]** Subject to the next paragraph, a proof must be in the form known as "proof of debt" (whether the form prescribed by the Rules, or a substantially similar form), which shall be made out by or under the directions of the creditor, and signed by him or a person authorised in that behalf. (NO CVL APPLICATION) [FORM 4.25]

**4.73(5) [Debt due to Crown etc.]** Where a debt is due to a Minister of the Crown or a Government Department, the proof need not be in that form, provided that there are shown all such particulars of the debt as are required in the form used by other creditors, and as are relevant in the circumstances. (NO CVL APPLICATION)

**4.73–CVL(6) [Creditor's proof]** The creditor's proof may be in any form.

**4.73(7) [Proof in form of affidavit]** In certain circumstances, specified below in this Chapter, the proof must be in the form of an affidavit.

## 4.74 Supply of forms

(NO CVL APPLICATION)

**4.74(1) [Forms to be sent to every creditor]** Forms of proof shall be sent out by the liquidator to every creditor of the company who is known to him, or is identified in the company's statement of affairs.

**4.74(2) [Forms to accompany first notice]** The forms shall accompany (whichever is first)–

(a) the notice to creditors under section 136(5)(b) (official receiver's decision not to call meetings of creditors and contributories), or

(b) the first notice calling a meeting of creditors, or

(c) where a liquidator is appointed by the court, the notice of his appointment sent by him to creditors.

**4.74(3) [Where liquidator advertises his appointment]** Where, with the leave of the court under Rule 4.102(5), the liquidator advertises his appointment, he shall send proofs to the creditors within 4 months after the date of the winding-up order.

**4.74(4) [Rule subject to order of court]** The above paragraphs of this Rule are subject to any order of the court dispensing with the requirement to send out forms of proof, or altering the time at which the forms are to be sent.

**Note**
See practice direction [1987] 1 All ER 1707.

## 4.75 Contents of proof

(NO CVL APPLICATION)

**4.75(1) [Matters to be stated in creditor's proof]** Subject to Rule 4.73(5), the following matters shall be stated in a creditor's proof of debt–

(a) the creditor's name and address;

(b) the total amount of his claim as at the date on which the company went into liquidation;

(c) whether or not that amount includes outstanding uncapitalised interest;

(d) whether or not the claim includes value added tax;

(e) whether the whole or any part of the debt falls within any (and if so which) of the categories of preferential debts under section 386 of, and Schedule 6 to, the Act (as read with Schedule 3 to the Social Security Pensions Act 1975);

(f) particulars of how and when the debt was incurred by the company;

(g) particulars of any security held, the date when it was given and the value which the creditor puts upon it; and

(h) the name, address and authority of the person signing the proof (if other than the creditor himself).

**History**
In r. 4.75(1) the words "Subject to Rule 4.73(5)," at the beginning inserted by the Insolvency (Amendment) Rules 1987 (SI 1987/1919), r. 3(1), Sch., Pt. 1, para. 58 as from 11 January 1988.

**4.75(2) [Specified documents]** There shall be specified in the proof any documents by reference to which the debts can be substantiated; but (subject as follows) it is not essential that such documents be attached to the proof or submitted with it.

**4.75(3) [Production of documents etc.]** The liquidator, or the chairman or convener of any meeting, may call for any document or other evidence to be produced to him, where he thinks it necessary for the purpose of substantiating the whole or any part of the claim made in the proof.

## 4.76–CVL Particulars of creditor's claim

**4.76–CVL** The liquidator, or the convenor or chairman of any meeting, may, if he thinks it necessary for the purpose of clarifying or substantiating the whole or any part of a creditor's claim made in his proof, call for details of any matter specified in paragraphs (a) to (h) of Rule 4.75(1), or for the production to him of such documentary or other evidence as he may require.

## 4.77 Claim established by affidavit

**4.77(1) [Liquidator may require "affidavit of debt"]** The liquidator may, if he thinks it necessary, require a claim of debt to be verified by means of an affidavit, for which purpose there shall be used the form known as "affidavit of debt", or a substantially similar form.

[FORM 4.26]

**4.77(2) [In addition to proof]** An affidavit may be required notwithstanding that a proof of debt has already been lodged.

**4.77(3) [Swearing of affidavit]** The affidavit may be sworn before an official receiver or deputy official receiver, or before an officer of the Department or of the court duly authorised in that behalf. (NO CVL APPLICATION)

## 4.78 Cost of proving

**4.78(1) [Creditor bears cost of proving own debt]** Subject as follows, every creditor bears the cost of proving his own debt, including such as may be incurred in providing documents or evidence under Rule 4.75(3) or 4.76–CVL.

**4.78(2) [Liquidator's costs]** Costs incurred by the liquidator in estimating the quantum of a debt under Rule 4.86 (debts not bearing a certain value) are payable out of the assets, as an expense of the liquidation.

**4.78(3) [Application of r. 4.78(1), (2)]** Paragraphs (1) and (2) apply unless the court otherwise orders.

## 4.79 Liquidator to allow inspection of proofs

**4.79** The liquidator shall, so long as proofs lodged with him are in his hands, allow them to be inspected, at all reasonable times on any business day, by any of the following persons–

(a) any creditor who has submitted his proof of debt (unless his proof has been wholly rejected for purposes of dividend or otherwise);

(b) any contributory of the company;

(c) any person acting on behalf of either of the above.

## 4.80 Transmission of proofs to liquidator

(NO CVL APPLICATION)

**4.80(1) [On liquidator's appointment]** Where a liquidator is appointed, the official receiver shall forthwith transmit to him all the proofs which he has so far received, together with an itemised list of them.

**4.80(2) [Receipt for proofs]** The liquidator shall sign the list by way of receipt for the proofs, and return it to the official receiver.

**4.80(3) [All later proofs to liquidator]** From then on, all proofs of debt shall be sent to the liquidator, and retained by him.

## 4.81 New liquidator appointed

**4.81(1) [On appointment]** If a new liquidator is appointed in place of another, the former liquidator shall transmit to him all proofs which he has received, together with an itemised list of them.

**4.81(2) [Receipt for proofs]** The new liquidator shall sign the list by way of receipt for the proofs, and return it to his predecessor.

## 4.82 Admission and rejection of proofs for dividend

**4.82(1) [Admission]** A proof may be admitted for dividend either for the whole amount claimed by the creditor, or for part of that amount.

**4.82(2) [Rejection]** If the liquidator rejects a proof in whole or in part, he shall prepare a written statement of his reasons for doing so, and send it forthwith to the creditor.

## 4.83 Appeal against decision on proof

**4.83(1) [Application by creditor]** If a creditor is dissatisifed with the liquidator's decision with respect to his proof (including any decision on the question of preference), he may apply to the court for the decision to be reversed or varied.

The application must be made within 21 days of his receiving the statement sent under Rule 4.82(2).

**4.83(2) [Application by contributory etc.]** A contributory or any other creditor may, if dissatisfied with the liquidator's decision admitting or rejecting the whole or any part of a proof, make such an application within 21 days of becoming aware of the liquidator's decision.

**4.83(3) [Venue and notice]** Where application is made to the court under this Rule, the court shall fix a venue for the application to be heard, notice of which shall be sent by the applicant to the creditor who lodged the proof in question (if it is not himself) and to the liquidator.

**4.83(4) [Relevant proof etc. to be filed in court]** The liquidator shall, on receipt of the notice, file in court the relevant proof, together (if appropriate) with a copy of the statement sent under Rule 4.82(2).

**4.83(5) [Return of proof]** After the application has been heard and determined, the proof shall, unless it has been wholly disallowed, be returned by the court to the liquidator.

**4.83(6) [Costs re application]** The official receiver is not personally liable for costs incurred by any person in respect of an application under this Rule; and the liquidator (if other than the official receiver) is not so liable unless the court makes an order to that effect.

## 4.84 Withdrawal or variation of proof

**4.84** A creditor's proof may at any time, by agreement between himself and the liquidator, be withdrawn or varied as to the amount claimed.

## 4.85 Expunging of proof by the court

**4.85(1) [Expunging or reduction of amount]** The court may expunge a proof or reduce the amount claimed–

(a) on the liquidator's application, where he thinks that the proof has been improperly admitted, or ought to be reduced; or

(b) on the application of a creditor, if the liquidator declines to interfere in the matter.

**4.85(2) [Venue and notice]** Where application is made to the court under this Rule, the court shall fix a venue for the application to be heard, notice of which shall be sent by the applicant–

(a) in the case of an application by the liquidator, to the creditor who made the proof, and

(b) in the case of an application by a creditor, to the liquidator and to the creditor who made the proof (if not himself).

**Note**
See practice direction [1987] 1 All ER 107.

### SECTION B: QUANTIFICATION OF CLAIM

## 4.86 Estimate of quantum

**4.86(1) [Estimating value of debts etc.]** The liquidator shall estimate the value of any debt which, by reason of its being subject to any contingency or for any other reason, does not bear a certain value; and he may revise any estimate previously made, if he thinks fit by reference to any change of circumstances or to information becoming available to him.

He shall inform the creditor as to his estimate and any revision of it.

**4.86(2) [Amount provable in winding up]** Where the value of a debt is estimated under this Rule, or by the court under section 168(3) or (5), the amount provable in the winding up in the case of that debt is that of the estimate for the time being.

## 4.87 Negotiable instruments, etc.

**4.87** Unless the liquidator allows, a proof in respect of money owed on a bill of exchange, promissory note, cheque or other negotiable instrument or security cannot be admitted unless there is produced the instrument or security itself or a copy of it, certified by the creditor or his authorised representative to be a true copy.

## 4.88 Secured creditors

**4.88(1) [Proving for balance of debt]** If a secured creditor realises his security, he may prove for the balance of his debt, after deducting the amount realised.

**4.88(2) [Proving for whole debt]** If a secured creditor voluntarily surrenders his security for the general benefit of creditors, he may prove for his whole debt, as if it were unsecured.

## 4.89 Discounts

**4.89** There shall in every case be deducted from the claim all trade and other discounts which would have been available to the company but for its liquidation, except any discount for immediate, early or cash settlement.

## 4.90 Mutual credit and set-off

**4.90(1) [Application of Rule]** This Rule applies where, before the company goes into liquidation there have been mutual credits, mutual debts or other mutual dealings between the company and any creditor of the company proving or claiming to prove for a debt in the liquidation.

**4.90(2) [Account of mutual dealings and set-off]** An account shall be taken of what is due from each party to the other in respect of the mutual dealings, and the sums due from one party shall be set off against the sums due from the other.

**4.90(3) [Sums not to be included in account]** Sums due from the company to another party shall not be included in the account taken under paragraph (2) if that other party had notice at the time they became due that a meeting of creditors had been summoned under section 98 or (as the case may be) a petition for the winding up of the company was pending.

**4.90(4) [Only balance (if any) provable etc.]** Only the balance (if any) of the account is provable in the liquidation. Alternatively (as the case may be) the amount shall be paid to the liquidator as part of the assets.

## 4.91 Debt in foreign currency

**4.91(1) [Conversion into sterling]** For the purpose of proving a debt incurred or payable in a currency other than sterling, the amount of the debt shall be converted into sterling at the official exchange rate prevailing on the date when the company went into liquidation.

**4.91(2) ["The official exchange rate"]** "The official exchange rate" is the middle market rate at the Bank of England, as published for the date in question. In the absence of any such published rate, it is such rate as the court determines.

## 4.92 Payments of a periodical nature

**4.92(1) [Rent etc.]** In the case of rent and other payments of a periodical nature, the creditor may prove for any amounts due and unpaid up to the date when the company went into liquidation.

**4.92(2) [If accruing from day to day]** Where at that date any payment was accruing due, the creditor may prove for so much as would have fallen due at that date, if accruing from day to day.

## 4.93 Interest

**4.93(1) [Where debt bears interest]** Where a debt proved in the liquidation bears interest, that interest is provable as part of the debt except in so far as it is payable in respect of any period after the company went into liquidation.

**4.93(2) [Where claim may include interest]** In the following circumstances the creditor's claim may include interest on the debt for periods before the company went into liquidation, although not previously reserved or agreed.

**History**
The words "(NO CVL APPLICATION)" at the end of r. 4.106 inserted by the Insolvency (Amendment) Rules 1987 (SI 1987/1919), r. 3(1), Sch., Pt. 1, para. 63 as from 11 January 1988.

## 4.107 Hand-over of assets to liquidator

(NO CVL APPLICATION)

**4.107(1) [Application of Rule]** This Rule applies only where the liquidator is appointed in succession to the official receiver acting as liquidator.

**4.107(2) [On liquidator's appointment]** When the liquidator's appointment takes effect, the official receiver shall forthwith do all that is required for putting him into possession of the assets.

**4.107(3) [Discharge of balance due to official receiver]** On taking possession of the assets, the liquidator shall discharge any balance due to the official receiver on account of–

(a) expenses properly incurred by him and payable under the Act or the Rules, and

(b) any advances made by him in respect of the assets, together with interest on such advances at the rate specified in section 17 of the Judgments Act 1838 at the date of the winding-up order.

**4.107(4) [Undertaking to discharge]** Alternatively, the liquidator may (before taking office) give to the official receiver a written undertaking to discharge any such balance out of the first realisation of assets.

**4.107(5) [Official receiver's charge]** The official receiver has a charge on the assets in respect of any sums due to him under paragraph (3). But, where the liquidator has realised assets with a view to making those payments, the official receiver's charge does not extend in respect of sums deductible by the liquidator from the proceeds of realisation, as being expenses properly incurred therein.

**4.107(6) [Discharge of guarantees etc.]** The liquidator shall from time to time out of the realisation of assets discharge all guarantees properly given by the official receiver for the benefit of the estate, and shall pay all the official receiver's expenses.

**4.107(7) [Official receiver to give liquidator information]** The official receiver shall give to the liquidator all such information relating to the affairs of the company and the course of the winding up as he (the official receiver) considers to be reasonably required for the effective discharge by the liquidator of his duties as such.

**4.107(8) [Copy of Ch. 7 report]** The liquidator shall also be furnished with a copy of any report made by the official receiver under Chapter 7 of this Part of the Rules.

### SECTION B: RESIGNATION AND REMOVAL; VACATION OF OFFICE

## 4.108 Creditors' meeting to receive liquidator's resignation

**4.108(1) [Liquidator must call meeting etc.]** Before resigning his office, the liquidator must call a meeting of creditors for the purpose of receiving his resignation. The notice summoning the meeting shall indicate that this is the purpose, or one of the purposes, of it, and shall draw the attention of creditors to Rule 4.121 or, as the case may be, Rule 4.122–CVL with respect to the liquidator's release. [FORM 4.22]

**4.108(2) [Copy of notice to official receiver]** A copy of the notice shall at the same time also be sent to the official receiver. (NO CVL APPLICATION)

**4.108(3) [Account of liquidator's administration]** The notice to creditors under paragraph (1) must be accompanied by an account of the liquidator's administration of the winding up, including–

(a) a summary of his receipts and payments, and

(b) a statement by him that he has reconciled his account with that which is held by the Secretary of State in respect of the winding up.

**4.108(4) [Grounds for proceeding under Rule]** Subject as follows, the liquidator may only proceed under this Rule on grounds of ill health or because–

(a) he intends ceasing to be in practice as an insolvency practitioner, or

(b) there is some conflict of interest or change of personal circumstances which precludes or makes impracticable the further discharge by him of the duties of liquidator.

**4.108(5) [Where joint liquidators]** Where two or more persons are acting as liquidator jointly, any one of them may proceed under this Rule (without prejudice to the continuation in office of the other or others) on the ground that, in his opinion and that of the other or others, it is no longer expedient that there should continue to be the present number of joint liquidators.

**4.108(6) [If no quorum]** If there is no quorum present at the meeting summoned to receive the liquidator's resignation, the meeting is deemed to have been held, a resolution is deemed to have been passed that the liquidator's resignation be accepted and the creditors are deemed not to have resolved against the liquidator having his release.

**4.108(7) [Application of r. 4.108(6)]** Where paragraph (6) applies any reference in the Rules to a resolution that the liquidator's resignation be accepted is replaced by a reference to the making of a written statement, signed by the person who, had there been a quorum present, would have been chairman of the meeting, that no quorum was present and that the liquidator may resign.

**History**

R. 4.108(6) and (7) added by the Insolvency (Amendment) Rules 1987 (SI 1987/1919), r. 3(1), Sch., Pt. 1, para. 64 as from 11 January 1988.

# 4.109 Action following acceptance of resignation

(NO CVL APPLICATION)

**4.109(1) [Application of Rule]** This Rule applies where a meeting is summoned to receive the liquidator's resignation.

**4.109(2) [Copy of resolutions to official receiver etc.]** If the chairman of the meeting is other than the official receiver, and there is passed at the meeting any of the following resolutions–

(a) that the liquidator's resignation be accepted,

(b) that a new liquidator be appointed,

(c) that the resigning liquidator be not given his release,

the chairman shall, within 3 days, send to the official receiver a copy of the resolution.

If it has been resolved to accept the liquidator's resignation, the chairman shall send to the official receiver a certificate to that effect.

**4.109(3) [If creditors resolve to appoint new liquidator]** If the creditors have resolved to appoint a new liquidator, the certificate of his appointment shall also be sent to the official receiver within that time; and Rule 4.100 shall be complied with in respect of it.

**4.109(4) [If liquidator's resignation accepted]** If the liquidator's resignation is accepted, the notice of it required by section 172(6) shall be given by him forthwith after the meeting; and he shall send a copy of the notice to the official receiver.

The notice shall be accompanied by a copy of the account sent to creditors under Rule 4.108(3). [FORM 4.32]

**4.109(5) [Copy notice]** The official receiver shall file a copy of the notice in court.

**4.109(6) [Effective date of resignation]** The liquidator's resignation is effective as from the date on which the official receiver files the copy notice in court, that date to be endorsed on the copy notice.

# 4.110–CVL Action following acceptance of resignation

**4.110–CVL(1) [Application of Rule]** This Rule applies where a meeting is summoned to receive the liquidator's resignation.

**4.110–CVL(2) [S. 171(5) notice]** If his resignation is accepted, the notice of it required by section 171(5) shall be given by him forthwith after the meeting. [FORM 4.33]

**4.110–CVL(3) [Certificate of new liquidator's appointment]** Where a new liquidator is appointed in place of the one who has resigned, the certificate of his appointment shall be delivered forthwith by the chairman of the meeting to the new liquidator.

## 4.111 Leave to resign granted by the court

**4.111(1) [If liquidator's resignation not accepted]** If at a creditors' meeting summoned to accept the liquidator's resignation it is resolved that it be not accepted, the court may, on the liquidator's application, make an order giving him leave to resign. [FORM 4.34]

**4.111(2) [Extent of order under r. 4.111(1)]** The court's order may include such provision as it thinks fit with respect to matters arising in connection with the resignation, and shall determine the date from which the liquidator's release is effective.

**4.111(3) [Sealed copies of order]** The court shall send two sealed copies of the order to the liquidator, who shall send one of the copies forthwith to the official receiver. (NO CVL APPLICATION)

**4.111–CVL(4) [Sealed copies]** The court shall send two sealed copies of the order to the liquidator, who shall forthwith send one of them to the registrar of companies. [FORM 4.35]

**4.111(5) [Copy notice to court and official receiver]** On sending notice of his resignation to the court, the liquidator shall send a copy of it to the official receiver. (NO CVL APPLICATION) [FORM 4.36]

**Note**
See practice direction [1987] 1 All ER 107.

## 4.112 Advertisement of resignation

**4.112** Where a new liquidator is appointed in place of one who has resigned, the former shall, in giving notice of his appointment, state that his predecessor has resigned and (if it be the case) that he has been given his release.

## 4.113 Meeting of creditors to remove liquidator

(NO CVL APPLICATION)

**4.113(1) [Notice]** Where a meeting of creditors is summoned for the purpose of removing the liquidator, the notice summoning it shall indicate that this is the purpose, or one of the purposes, of the meeting; and the notice shall draw the attention of creditors to section 174(4) with respect to the liquidator's release. [FORM 4.22]

**4.113(2) [Copy notice to official receiver]** A copy of the notice shall at the same time also be sent to the official receiver.

**4.113(3) [Chairman; if liquidator chairman etc.]** At the meeting, a person other than the liquidator or his nominee may be elected to act as chairman; but if the liquidator or his nominee is chairman and a resolution has been proposed for the liquidator's removal, the chairman shall not adjourn the meeting without the consent of at least one-half (in value) of the creditors present (in person or by proxy) and entitled to vote.

**4.113(4) [Copy resolutions to official receiver]** Where the chairman of the meeting is other than the official receiver, and there is passed at the meeting any of the following resolutions–

(a) that the liquidator be removed,

(b) that a new liquidator be appointed,

(c) that the removed liquidator be not given his release,

the chairman shall, within 3 days, send to the official receiver a copy of the resolution.

If it has been resolved to remove the liquidator, the chairman shall send to the official receiver a certificate to that effect. [FORM 4.37]

**4.113(5) [If creditors resolve to appoint new liquidator]** If the creditors have resolved to appoint a new liquidator, the certificate of his appointment shall also be sent to the official receiver within that time; and Rule 4.100 above shall be complied with in respect of it.

## 4.114–CVL Meeting of creditors to remove liquidator

**4.114–CVL(1) [S. 171(2)(b) meeting requested]** A meeting held under section 171(2)(b) for the removal of the liquidator shall be summoned by him if requested by 25 per cent in value of the company's creditors, excluding those who are connected with it.

**4.114–CVL(2) [Notice]** The notice summoning the meeting shall indicate that the removal of the liquidator is the purpose, or one of the purposes, of the meeting; and the notice shall draw the attention of creditors to section 173(2) with respect to the liquidator's release. [FORM 4.22]

**4.114–CVL(3) [Chairman; if liquidator chairman etc.]** At the meeting, a person other than the liquidator or his nominee may be elected to act as chairman, but if the liquidator or his nominee is chairman and a resolution has been proposed for the liquidator's removal, the chairman shall not adjourn the meeting without the consent of at least one-half (in value) of the creditors present (in person or by proxy) and entitled to vote.

## 4.115 Court's power to regulate meetings under Rules 4.113, 4.114–CVL

**4.115** Where a meeting under Rule 4.113 or 4.114–CVL is to be held, or is proposed to be summoned, the court may, on the application of any creditor, give directions as to the mode of summoning it, the sending out and return of forms of proxy, the conduct of the meeting, and any other matter which appears to the court to require regulation or control under this Rule.

## 4.116 Procedure on removal

(NO CVL APPLICATION)

**4.116(1) [Certificate of removal to be filed]** Where the creditors have resolved that the liquidator be removed, the official receiver shall file in court the certificate of removal.

**4.116(2) [Effective date of removal resolution]** The resolution is effective as from the date on which the official receiver files the certificate of removal in court, and that date shall be endorsed on the certificate.

**4.116(3) [Copy of certificate]** A copy of the certificate, so endorsed, shall be sent by the official receiver to the liquidator who has been removed and, if a new liquidator has been appointed, to him.

**4.116(4) [Reconciliation of accounts]** The official receiver shall not file the certificate in court unless and until the Secretary of State has certified to him that the removed liquidator has reconciled his account with that held by the Secretary of State in respect of the winding up.

## 4.117–CVL Procedure on removal

**4.117–CVL** Where the creditors have resolved that the liquidator be removed, the chairman of the creditors' meeting shall forthwith–

(a) if at the meeting another liquidator was not appointed, send the certificate of the liquidator's removal to the registrar of companies, and

(b) otherwise, deliver the certificate to the new liquidator, who shall send it to the registrar.

[FORM 4.38]

## 4.118 Advertisement of removal

**4.118** Where a new liquidator is appointed in place of one removed, the former shall, in giving notice of his appointment, state that his predecessor has been removed and (if it be the case) that he has been given his release.

## 4.119 Removal of liquidator by the court

(NO CVL APPLICATION)

**4.119(1) [Application of Rule]** This Rule applies where application is made to the court for the removal of the liquidator, or for an order directing the liquidator to summon a meeting of creditors for the purpose of removing him. [FORM 4.39]

**4.119(2) [Court may dismiss application etc.]** The court may, if it thinks that no sufficient cause is shown for the application, dismiss it; but it shall not do so unless the applicant has had an opportunity to attend the court for an *ex parte* hearing, of which he has been given at least 7 days' notice.

If the application is not dismissed under this paragraph, the court shall fix a venue for it to be heard.

**4.119(3) [Deposit or security for costs]** The court may require the applicant to make a deposit or give security for the costs to be incurred by the liquidator on the application.

**4.119(4) [Notice etc.]** The applicant shall, at least 14 days before the hearing, send to the liquidator and the official receiver a notice stating the venue and accompanied by a copy of the application, and of any evidence which he intends to adduce in support of it.

**4.119(5) [Costs]** Subject to any contrary order of the court, the costs of the application are not payable out of the assets.

**4.119(6) [Where court removes liquidator]** Where the court removes the liquidator–

(a) it shall send copies of the order of removal to him and to the official receiver;

(b) the order may include such provision as the court thinks fit with respect to matters arising in connection with the removal; and

(c) if the court appoints a new liquidator, Rule 4.102 applies.

## 4.120–CVL Removal of liquidator by the court

**4.120–CVL(1) [Application of Rule]** This Rule applies where application is made to the court for the removal of the liquidator, or for an order directing the liquidator to summon a creditors' meeting for the purpose of removing him. [FORM 4.39]

**4.120–CVL(2) [Court may dismiss application etc.]** The court may, if it thinks that no sufficient cause is shown for the application, dismiss it; but it shall not do so unless the applicant has had an opportunity to attend the court for an *ex parte* hearing, of which he has been given at least 7 days' notice.

If the application is not dismissed under this paragraph, the court shall fix a venue for it to be heard.

**4.120–CVL(3) [Deposit or security for costs]** The court may require the applicant to make a deposit or give security for the costs to be incurred by the liquidator on the application.

**4.120–CVL(4) [Notice etc.]** The applicant shall, at least 14 days before the hearing, send to the liquidator a notice stating the venue and accompanied by a copy of the application, and of any evidence which he intends to adduce in support of it.

**4.120–CVL(5) [Costs]** Subject to any contrary order of the court, the costs of the application are not payable out of the assets.

**4.120–CVL(6) [Where court removes liquidator]** Where the court removes the liquidator–

(a) it shall send 2 copies of the order of removal to him, one to be sent by him forthwith to the registrar of companies, with notice of his ceasing to act;

(b) the order may include such provision as the court thinks fit with respect to matters arising in connection with the removal; and

(c) if the court appoints a new liquidator, Rule 4.103–CVL applies. [FORM 4.40]

## 4.121 Release of resigning or removed liquidator

(NO CVL APPLICATION)

**4.121(1) [Where liquidator's resignation accepted]** Where the liquidator's resignation is accepted by a meeting of creditors which has not resolved against his release, he has his release from when his resignation is effective under Rule 4.109.

**4.121(2) [Where liquidator removed by meeting]** Where the liquidator is removed by a meeting of creditors which has not resolved against his release, the fact of his release shall be stated in the certificate of removal.

**4.121(3) [Application to Secretary of State]** Where–

(a) the liquidator resigns, and the creditors' meeting called to receive his resignation has resolved against his release, or

(b) he is removed by a creditors' meeting which has so resolved, or is removed by the court,

he must apply to the Secretary of State for his release. [FORM 4.41]

**4.121(4) [Certificate of release]** When the Secretary of State gives the release, he shall certify it accordingly, and send the certificate to the official receiver, to be filed in court.

**4.121(5) [Copy of certificate]** A copy of the certificate shall be sent by the Secretary of State to the former liquidator, whose release is effective from the date of the certificate.

## 4.122–CVL Release of resigning or removed liquidator

**4.122–CVL(1) [Where liquidator's resignation accepted]** Where the liquidator's resignation is accepted by a meeting of creditors which has not resolved against his release, he has his release from when he gives notice of his resignation to the registrar of companies. [FORM 4.40]

**4.122–CVL(2) [Where liquidator removed by meeting]** Where the liquidator is removed by a creditors' meeting which has not resolved against his release, the fact of his release shall be stated in the certificate of removal.

**4.122–CVL(3) [Application to Secretary of State]** Where–

(a) the liquidator resigns, and the creditors' meeting called to receive his resignation has resolved against his release, or

(b) he is removed by a creditors' meeting which has so resolved, or is removed by the court,

he must apply to the Secretary of State for his release. [FORM 4.41]

**4.122–CVL(4) [Certificate of release]** When the Secretary of State gives the release, he shall certify it accordingly, and send the certificate to the registrar of companies.

**4.122–CVL(5) [Copy of certificate]** A copy of the certificate shall be sent by the Secretary of State to the former liquidator, whose release is effective from the date of the certificate.

## 4.123 Removal of liquidator by Secretary of State

(NO CVL APPLICATION)

**4.123(1) [Notice to liquidator etc.]** If the Secretary of State decides to remove the liquidator, he shall before doing so notify the liquidator and the official receiver of his decision and the grounds of it, and specify a period within which the liquidator may make representations against implementation of the decision.

**4.123(2) [On removal]** If the Secretary of State directs the removal of the liquidator, he shall forthwith–

(a) file notice of his decision in court, and

(b) send notice to the liquidator and the official receiver.

**4.123(3) [If liquidator removed]** If the liquidator is removed by direction of the Secretary of State–

(a) Rule 4.121 applies as regards the liquidator obtaining his release, as if he had been removed by the court, and

(b) the court may make any such order in his case as it would have power to make if he had been so removed.

SECTION C: RELEASE ON COMPLETION OF ADMINISTRATION

## 4.124 Release of official receiver

(NO CVL APPLICATION)

**4.124(1) [Notice of intention]** The official receiver shall, before giving notice to the Secretary of State under section 174(3) (that the winding up is for practical purposes complete), send out notice of his intention to do so to all creditors who have proved their debts.

**4.124(2) [Accompanying summary]** The notice shall in each case be accompanied by a summary of the official receiver's receipts and payments as liquidator.

**4.124(3) [Notice to court of date of release]** The Secretary of State, when he has determined the date from which the official receiver is to have his release, shall give notice to the court that he has done so. The notice shall be accompanied by the summary referred to in paragraph (2).

## 4.125 Final meeting

(NO CVL APPLICATION)

**4.125(1) [Notice to creditors etc.]** Where the liquidator is other than the official receiver, he shall give at least 28 days' notice of the final meeting of creditors to be held under section 146. The notice shall be sent to all creditors who have proved their debts; and the liquidator shall cause it to be gazetted at least one month before the meeting is to be held. [FORM 4.22]

**4.125(2) [Liquidator's report]** The liquidator's report laid before the meeting under that section shall contain an account of the liquidator's administration of the winding up, including–

(a) a summary of his receipts and payments, and

(b) a statement by him that he has reconciled his account with that which is held by the Secretary of State in respect of the winding up.

**4.125(3) [Questioning of liquidator]** At the final meeting, the creditors may question the liquidator with respect to any matter contained in his report, and may resolve against him having his release.

**4.125(4) [Notice to court]** The liquidator shall give notice to the court that the final meeting has been held; and the notice shall state whether or not he has been given his release, and be accompanied by a copy of the report laid before the final meeting. A copy of the notice shall be sent by the liquidator to the official receiver. [FORM 4.42]

**4.125(5) [No quorum at final meeting]** If there is no quorum present at the final meeting, the liquidator shall report to the court that a final meeting was summoned in accordance with the Rules, but there was no quorum present; and the final meeting is then deemed to have been held, and the creditors not to have resolved against the liquidator having his release.

**4.125(6) [Release of liquidator]** If the creditors at the final meeting have not so resolved, the liquidator is released when the notice under paragraph (4) is filed in court. If they have so resolved, the liquidator must obtain his release from the Secretary of State and Rule 4.121 applies accordingly.

## 4.126–CVL Final meeting

**4.126–CVL(1) [Notice to creditors]** The liquidator shall give at least 28 days' notice of the final meeting of creditors to be held under section 106. The notice shall be sent to all creditors who have proved their debts. [FORM 4.22]

**4.126–CVL(2) [Questioning of liquidator]** At the final meeting, the creditors may question the liquidator with respect to any matter contained in the account required under the section, and may resolve against the liquidator having his release.

**4.126–CVL(3) [Release of liquidator]** Where the creditors have so resolved, he must obtain his release from the Secretary of State; and Rule 4.122–CVL applies accordingly.

### SECTION D: REMUNERATION

## 4.127 Fixing of remuneration

**4.127(1) [Entitlement to remuneration]** The liquidator is entitled to receive remuneration for his services as such.

**4.127(2) [How fixed]** The remuneration shall be fixed either–

(a) as a percentage of the value of the assets which are realised or distributed, or of the one value and the other in combination, or

(b) by reference to the time properly given by the insolvency practitioner (as liquidator) and his staff in attending to matters arising in the winding up.

**4.127(3) [Determination under r. 4.127(2)]** Where the liquidator is other than the official receiver, it is for the liquidation committee (if there is one) to determine whether the remuneration is to be fixed under paragraph (2)(a) or (b) and, if under paragraph (2)(a), to determine any percentage to be applied as there mentioned.

**4.127(4) [Matters relevant r. 4.127(3) determination]** In arriving at that determination, the committee shall have regard to the following matters–

(a) the complexity (or otherwise) of the case,

(b) any respects in which, in connection with the winding up, there falls on the insolvency practitioner (as liquidator) any responsibility of an exceptional kind or degree,

(c) the effectiveness with which the insolvency practitioner appears to be carrying out, or to have carried out, his duties as liquidator, and

(d) the value and nature of the assets with which the liquidator has to deal.

**4.127(5) [If no committee or no determination]** If there is no liquidation committee, or the committee does not make the requisite determination, the liquidator's remuneration may be fixed (in accordance with paragraph (2)) by a resolution of a meeting of creditors; and paragraph (4) applies to them as it does to the liquidation committee.

**4.127(6) [Otherwise fixed]** If not fixed as above, the liquidator's remuneration shall be in accordance with the scale laid down for the official receiver by general regulations.

## 4.128 Other matters affecting remuneration

**4.128(1) [Where liquidator sells for secured creditor]** Where the liquidator sells assets on behalf of a secured creditor, he is entitled to take for himself, out of the proceeds of sale, a sum by way of remuneration equivalent to that which is chargeable in corresponding circumstances by the official receiver under general regulations.

**4.128(2) [Where joint liquidators]** Where there are joint liquidators, it is for them to agree between themselves as to how the remuneration payable should be apportioned. Any dispute arising between them may be referred–

(a) to the court, for settlement by order, or

(b) to the liquidation committee or a meeting of creditors, for settlement by resolution.

**4.128(3) [If liquidator is a solicitor]** If the liquidator is a solicitor and employs his own firm, or any partner in it, to act on behalf of the company, profit costs shall not be paid unless this is authorised by the liquidation committee, the creditors or the court.

## 4.129 Recourse of liquidator to meeting of creditors

**4.129** If the liquidator's remuneration has been fixed by the liquidation committee, and he considers the rate or amount to be insufficient, he may request that it be increased by resolution of the creditors.

## 4.130 Recourse to the court

**4.130(1) [Liquidator may apply to court]** If the liquidator considers that the remuneration fixed for him by the liquidation committee, or by resolution of the creditors, or as under Rule 4.127(6), is insufficient, he may apply to the court for an order increasing its amount or rate.

**4.130(2) [Notice to committee etc.]** The liquidator shall give at least 14 days' notice of his application to the members of the liquidation committee; and the committee may nominate one or more members to appear or be represented, and to be heard, on the application.

**4.130(3) [Where no committee]** If there is no liquidation committee, the liquidator's notice of his application shall be sent to such one or more of the company's creditors as the court may direct, which creditors may nominate one or more of their number to appear or be represented.

**4.130(4) [Costs of application]** The court may, if it appears to be a proper case, order the costs of the liquidator's application, including the costs of any member of the liquidation committee appearing or being represented on it, or any creditor so appearing or being represented, to be paid out of the assets.

**History**

In r. 4.130(4) the words "or being represented" in both places where they occur inserted by the Insolvency (Amendment) Rules 1987 (SI 1987/1919), r. 3(1), Sch., Pt. 1, para. 65 as from 11 January 1988.

# 4.131 Creditors' claim that remuneration is excessive

**4.131(1) [Creditor may apply to court]** Any creditor of the company may, with the concurrence of at least 25 per cent. in value of the creditors (including himself), apply to the court for an order that the liquidator's remuneration be reduced, on the grounds that it is, in all the circumstances, excessive.

**4.131(2) [Power of court to dismiss etc.]** The court may, if it thinks that no sufficient cause is shown for a reduction, dismiss the application; but it shall not do so unless the applicant has had an opportunity to attend the court for an *ex parte* hearing, of which he has been given at least 7 days' notice.

If the application is not dismissed under this paragraph, the court shall fix a venue for it to be heard, and give notice to the applicant accordingly.

**4.131(3) [Notice to liquidator]** The applicant shall, at least 14 days before the hearing, send to the liquidator a notice stating the venue and accompanied by a copy of the application, and of any evidence which the applicant intends to adduce in support of it.

**4.131(4) [Court order]** If the court considers the application to be well-founded, it shall make an order fixing the remuneration at a reduced amount or rate.

**4.131(5) [Costs of application]** Unless the court orders otherwise, the costs of the application shall be paid by the applicant, and are not payable out of the assets.

SECTION E: SUPPLEMENTARY PROVISIONS

# 4.132 Liquidator deceased

(NO CVL APPLICATION)

**4.132(1) [Notice to official receiver]** Subject as follows, where the liquidator (other than the official receiver) has died, it is the duty of his personal representatives to give notice of the fact to the official receiver, specifying the date of the death.

This does not apply if notice has been given under any of the following paragraphs of this Rule.

**4.132(2) [Notice by partner etc.]** If the deceased liquidator was a partner in a firm, notice may be given to the official receiver by a partner in the firm who is qualified to act as an insolvency practitioner, or is a member of any body recognised by the Secretary of State for the authorisation of insolvency practitioners.

**4.132(3) [Notice by others]** Notice of the death may be given by any person producing to the official receiver the relevant death certificate or a copy of it.

**4.132(4) [Notice by official receiver]** The official receiver shall give notice to the court, for the purpose of fixing the date of the deceased liquidator's release.

# 4.133–CVL Liquidator deceased

**4.133–CVL(1) [Notice to registrar and committee]** Subject as follows, where the liquidator has died, it is the duty of his personal representatives to give notice of the fact, and of the date of death, to the registrar of companies and to the liquidation committee (if any) or a member of that committee. [FORM 4.44]

**4.133–CVL(2) [Notice by others]** In the alternative, notice of the death may be given–

(a) if the deceased liquidator was a partner in a firm, by a partner qualified to act as an insolvency practitioner or who is a member of any body approved by the Secretary of State for the authorisation of insolvency practitioners, or

(b) by any person, if he delivers with the notice a copy of the relevant death certificate.

# 4.134 Loss of qualification as insolvency practitioner

(NO CVL APPLICATION)

**4.134(1) [Application of Rule]** This Rule applies where the liquidator vacates office on ceasing to be qualified to act as an insolvency practitioner in relation to the company.

**4.134(2) [Notice to official receiver etc.]** He shall forthwith give notice of his doing so to the official receiver, who shall give notice to the Secretary of State.

The official receiver shall file in court a copy of his notice under this paragraph.

[FORM 4.45]

**4.134(3) [Application of r. 4.121]** Rule 4.121 applies as regards the liquidator obtaining his release, as if he had been removed by the court.

# 4.135–CVL Loss of qualification as insolvency practitioner

**4.135–CVL(1) [Application of Rule]** This Rule applies where the liquidator vacates office on ceasing to be qualified to act as an insolvency practitioner in relation to the company.

**4.135–CVL(2) [Notice]** He shall forthwith give notice of his doing so to the registrar of companies and the Secretary of State. [FORM 4.45]

[FORM 4.46]

**4.135–CVL(3) [Application of r. 4.122–CVL]** Rule 4.122–CVL applies as regards the liquidator obtaining his release, as if he had been removed by the court.

# 4.136–CVL Vacation of office on making of winding-up order

**4.136–CVL** Where the liquidator vacates office in consequence of the court making a winding-up order against the company, Rule 4.122–CVL applies as regards his obtaining his release, as if he had been removed by the court.

# 4.137 Notice to official receiver of intention to vacate office

(NO CVL APPLICATION)

**4.137(1) [Notice to official receiver]** Where the liquidator intends to vacate office, whether by resignation or otherwise, he shall give notice of his intention to the official receiver together with notice of any creditors' meeting to be held in respect of his vacation of office, including any meeting to receive his resignation.

**4.137(2) [Time limit for notice]** The notice to the official receiver must be given at least 21 days before any such creditors' meeting.

**4.137(3) [Details of property]** Where there remains any property of the company which has not been realised, applied, distributed or otherwise fully dealt with in the winding up, the liquidator shall include in his notice to the official receiver details of the nature of that property, its value (or the fact that it has no value), its location, any action taken by the liquidator to deal with that property or any reason for his not dealing with it, and the current position in relation to it.

**History**

R. 4.137 substituted by the Insolvency (Amendment) Rules 1987 (SI 1987/1919), r. 3(1), Sch., Pt. 1, para. 66 as from 11 January 1988; r. 4.137 formerly read as follows:

"**4.137(1)** Where the liquidator intends to vacate office, whether by resignation or otherwise, and there remain any unrealised assets, he shall give notice of his intention to the official reciever, informing him of the nature, value and whereabouts of the assets in question.

**(2)** Where there is to be a creditors' meeting to receive the liquidator's resignation, or otherwise in respect of his vacation of office, the notice to the official receiver must be given at least 21 days before the meeting."

# 4.138 Liquidator's duties on vacating office

**4.138(1) [Obligation to deliver up assets etc.]** Where the liquidator ceases to be in office as such, in consequence of removal, resignation or cesser of qualification as an insolvency practitioner, he is under obligation forthwith to deliver up to the person succeeding him as liquidator the assets (after deduction of any expenses properly incurred, and distributions made, by him) and further to deliver up to that person–

(a) the records of the liquidation, including correspondence, proofs and other related papers appertaining to the administration while it was within his responsibility, and

(b) the company's books, papers and other records.

**4.138(2) [When winding up complete]** When the winding up is for practical purposes complete, the liquidator shall forthwith file in court all proofs remaining with him in the proceedings. (NO CVL APPLICATION)

**4.138(3) [Vacation following creditors' final meeting]** Where the liquidator vacates office under section 172(8) (final meeting of creditors), he shall deliver up to the official receiver the company's books, papers and other records which have not already been disposed of in accordance with general regulations in the course of the liquidation. (NO CVL APPLICATION).

**History**
R. 4.138(3) added by the Insolvency (Amendment) Rules 1987 (SI 1987/1919), r. 3(1), Sch., Pt. 1, para. 67 as from 11 January 1988.

## SECTION F: THE LIQUIDATOR IN A MEMBERS' VOLUNTARY WINDING UP

## 4.139 Appointment by the company

**4.139(1) [Application of Rule]** This Rule applies where the liquidator is appointed by a meeting of the company.

**4.139(2) [Certifying appointment etc.]** Subject as follows, the chairman of the meeting shall certify the appointment, but not unless and until the person appointed has provided him with a written statement to the effect that he is an insolvency practitioner, duly qualified under the Act to be the liquidator, and that he consents so to act. [FORM 4.27]
[FORM 4.28]

**4.139(3) [Certificate to liquidator]** The chairman shall send the certificate forthwith to the liquidator, who shall keep it as part of the records of the liquidation.

**4.139(4) [Notice to creditors]** Not later than 28 days from his appointment, the liquidator shall give notice of it to all creditors of the company of whom he is aware in that period.

## 4.140 Appointment by the court

**4.140(1) [Application of Rule]** This Rule applies where the liquidator is appointed by the court under section 108.

**4.140(2) [Issue of court order]** The court's order shall not issue unless and until the person appointed has filed in court a statement to the effect that he is an insolvency practitioner, duly qualified under the Act to be the liquidator, and that he consents so to act. [FORM 4.29]
[FORM 4.30]

**4.140(3) [Copy of order to liquidator]** Thereafter, the court shall send a sealed copy of the order to the liquidator, whose appointment takes effect from the date of the order.

**4.140(4) [Notice to creditors]** Not later than 28 days from his appointment, the liquidator shall give notice of it all creditors of the company of whom he is aware in that period.

## 4.141 Authentication of liquidator's appointment

**4.141** A copy of the certificate of the liquidator's appointment or (as the case may be) a sealed copy of the court's order appointing him may in any proceedings be adduced as proof that the person appointed is duly authorised to exercise the powers and perform the duties of liquidator in the company's winding up.

## 4.142 Company meeting to receive liquidator's resignation

**4.142(1) [Liquidator must call meeting etc.]** Before resigning his office, the liquidator must call a meeting of the company for the purpose of receiving his resignation. The notice summoning the meeting shall indicate that this is the purpose, or one of the purposes, of it.

**4.142(2) [Account of liquidator's administration]** The notice under paragraph (1) must be accompanied by an account of the liquidator's administration of the winding up, including–

(a) a summary of his receipts and payments, and

(b) a statement by him that he has reconciled his account with that which is held by the Secretary of State in respect of the winding up.

**4.142(3) [Grounds for proceeding under Rule]** Subject as follows, the liquidator may only proceed under this Rule on grounds of ill health or because–

(a) he intends ceasing to be in practice as an insolvency practitioner, or

(b) there is some conflict of interest or change of personal circumstances which precludes or makes impracticable the further discharge by him of the duties of liquidator.

**4.142(4) [Where joint liquidators]** Where two or more persons are acting as liquidator jointly, any one of them may proceed under this Rule (without prejudice to the continuation in office of the other or others) on the ground that, in his opinion or that of the other or others, it is no longer expedient that there should continue to be the present number of joint liquidators.

**4.142(4A) [If no quorum]** If there is no quorum present at the meeting summoned to receive the liquidator's resignation, the meeting is deemed to have been held.

**History**

R. 4.142(4A) inserted by the Insolvency (Amendment) Rules 1987 (SI 1987/1919), r. 3(1), Sch., Pt. 1, para. 68 as from 11 January 1988.

**4.142(5) [S. 171(5) notice]** The notice of the liquidator's resignation required by section 171(5) shall be given by him forthwith after the meeting. [FORM 4.33]

**4.142(6) [Where new liquidator appointed]** Where a new liquidator is appointed in place of one who has resigned, the former shall, in giving notice of his appointment, state that his predecessor has resigned.

## 4.143 Removal of liquidator by the court

**4.143(1) [Application of Rule]** This Rule applies where application is made to the court for the removal of the liquidator, or for an order directing the liquidator to summon a company meeting for the purpose of removing him.

**4.143(2) [Court may dismiss application etc.]** The court may, if it thinks that no sufficient cause is shown for the application, dismiss it; but it shall not do so unless the applicant has had an opportunity to attend the court for an *ex parte* hearing, of which he has been given at least 7 days' notice.

If the application is not dismissed under this paragraph, the court shall fix a venue for it to be heard.

**4.143(3) [Deposit or security for costs]** The court may require the applicant to make a deposit or give security for the costs to be incurred by the liquidator on the application.

**4.143(4) [Notice etc.]** The applicant shall, at least 14 days before the hearing, send to the liquidator a notice stating the venue and accompanied by a copy of the application, and of any evidence which he intends to adduce in support of it.

Subject to any contrary order of the court, the costs of the application are not payable out of the assets.

**4.143(5) [Where court removes liquidator]** Where the court removes the liquidator–

(a) it shall send 2 copies of the order of removal to him, one to be sent by him forthwith to the registrar of companies, with notice of his ceasing to act;

(b) the order may include such provision as the court thinks fit with respect to matters arising in connection with the removal; and

(c) if the court appoints a new liquidator, Rule 4.140 applies. [FORM 4.39]
[FORM 4.40]

## 4.144 Release of resigning or removed liquidator

**4.144(1) [Where liquidator resigns]** Where the liquidator resigns, he has his release from the date on which he gives notice of his resignation to the registrar of companies. [FORM 4.40]

**4.144(2) [Where removed by meeting]** Where the liquidator is removed by a meeting of the company, he shall forthwith give notice to the registrar of companies of his ceasing to act. [FORM 4.40]

**4.144(3) [Where removed by court]** Where the liquidator is removed by the court, he must apply to the Secretary of State for his release. [FORM 4.41]

**4.144(4) [Certifying release etc.]** When the Secretary of State gives the release, he shall certify it accordingly, and send the certificate to the registrar of companies.

**4.144(5) [Copy of certificate]** A copy of the certificate shall be sent by the Secretary of State to the former liquidator, whose release is effective from the date of the certificate.

## 4.145 Liquidator deceased

**4.145(1) [Duty to give notice]** Subject as follows, where the liquidator has died, it is the duty of his personal representatives to give notice of the fact, and of the date of death, to the company's directors, or any one of them, and to the registrar of companies. [FORM 4.44]

**4.145(2) [Notice by partner or others]** In the alternative, notice of the death may be given–

(a) if the deceased liquidator was a partner in a firm, by a partner qualified to act as an insolvency practitioner or who is a member of any body approved by the Secretary of State for the authorisation of insolvency practitioners, or

(b) by any person, if he delivers with the notice a copy of the relevant death certificate.

## 4.146 Loss of qualification as insolvency practitioner

**4.146(1) [Application of Rule]** This Rule applies where the liquidator vacates office on ceasing to be qualified to act as an insolvency practitioner in relation to the company.

**4.146(2) [Notice]** He shall forthwith give notice of his doing so to the registrar of companies and the Secretary of State. [FORM 4.45] [FORM 4.46]

**4.146(3) [Application of r. 4.144]** Rule 4.144 applies as regards the liquidator obtaining his release, as if he had been removed by the court.

## 4.147 Vacation of office on making of winding-up order

**4.147** Where the liquidator vacates office in consequence of the court making a winding-up order against the company. Rule 4.144 applies as regards his obtaining his release, as if he had been removed by the court.

## 4.148 Liquidator's duties on vacating office

**4.148** Where the liquidator ceases to be in office as such, in consequence of removal, resignation or cesser of qualification as an insolvency practitioner, he is under obligation forthwith to deliver up to the person succeeding him as liquidator the assets (after deduction of any expenses properly incurred, and distributions made, by him) and further to deliver up to that person–

(a) the records of the liquidation, including correspondence, proofs and other related papers appertaining to the administration while it was within his responsibility, and

(b) the company's books, papers and other records.

## 4.148A Remuneration of liquidator in members' voluntary winding up

**4.148A(1) [Entitlement]** The liquidator is entitled to receive remuneration for his services as such.

**4.148A(2) [How fixed]** The remuneration shall be fixed either –

(a) as a percentage of the value of the assets which are realised or distributed, or of the one value and the other in combination, or

(b) by reference to the time properly given by the insolvency practitioner (as liquidator) and his staff in attending to matters arising in the winding up;

and the company in general meeting shall determine whether the remuneration is to be fixed under subparagraph (a) or (b) and, if under subparagraph (a), the percentage to be applied as there mentioned.

**4.148A(3) [Matters in determination]** In arriving at that determination the company in general meeting shall have regard to the matters set out in paragraph (4) of Rule 4.127.

**4.148A(4) [Otherwise fixed]** If not fixed as above, the liquidator's remuneration shall be in accordance with the scale laid down for the official receiver by general regulations.

**4.148A(5) [Application of r. 4.128]** Rule 4.128 shall apply in relation to the remuneration of the liquidator in respect of the matters there mentioned and for this purpose references in that Rule to "the liquidation committee" and "a meeting of creditors" shall be read as references to the company in general meeting.

**4.148A(6) [Liquidator may apply to court]** If the liquidator considers that the remuneration fixed for him by the company in general meeting, or as under paragraph (4), is insufficient, he may apply to the court for an order increasing its amount or rate.

**4.148A(7) [Notice to contributories]** The liquidator shall give at least 14 days' notice of an application under paragraph (6) to the company's contributories, or such one or more of them as the court may direct, and the contributories may nominate any one or more of their number to appear or be represented.

**4.148A(8) [Costs of application]** The court may, if it appears to be a proper case, order the costs of the liquidator's application, including the costs of any contributory appearing or being represented on it, to be paid out of the assets.

**History**

R. 4.148A inserted by the Insolvency (Amendment) Rules 1987 (SI 1987/1919), r. 3(1), Sch., Pt. 1, para. 69 as from 11 January 1988.

## SECTION G: RULES APPLYING IN EVERY WINDING UP, WHETHER VOLUNTARY OR BY THE COURT

### 4.149 Power of court to set aside certain transactions

**4.149(1) [Liquidator's transaction with associate]** If in the administration of the estate the liquidator enters into any transaction with a person who is an associate of his, the court may, on the application of any person interested, set the transaction aside and order the liquidator to compensate the company for any loss suffered in consequence of it.

**4.149(2) [Where r. 4.149(1) does not apply]** This does not apply if either–

(a) the transaction was entered into with the prior consent of the court, or

(b) it is shown to the court's satisfaction that the transaction was for value, and that it was entered into by the liquidator without knowing, or having any reason to suppose, that the person concerned was an associate.

**4.149(3) [Effect of Rule]** Nothing in this Rule is to be taken as prejudicing the operation of any rule of law or equity with respect to a liquidator's dealings with trust property, or the fiduciary obligations of any person.

### 4.150 Rule against solicitation

**4.150(1) [Power of court]** Where the court is satisfied that any improper solicitation has been used by or on behalf of the liquidator in obtaining proxies or procuring his appointment, it may order that no remuneration out of the assets be allowed to any person by whom, or on whose behalf, the solicitation was exercised.

**4.150(2) [Effect of court order]** An order of the court under this Rule overrides any resolution of the liquidation committee or the creditors, or any other provision of the Rules relating to the liquidator's remuneration.

# Chapter 12 – The Liquidation Committee

## 4.151 Preliminary

(NO CVL APPLICATION)

**4.151** For the purposes of this Chapter–

(a) an "insolvent winding up" is where the company is being wound up on grounds which include inability to pay its debts, and

(b) a "solvent winding up" is where the company is being wound up on grounds which do not include that one.

## 4.152 Membership of committee

**4.152(1) [Numbers to be elected]** Subject to Rule 4.154 below, the liquidation committee shall consist as follows–

(a) in any case of at least 3, and not more than 5, creditors of the company, elected by the meeting of creditors held under section 141 of the Act, and

(b) also, in the case of a solvent winding up, where the contributories' meeting held under that section so decides, of up to 3 contributories, elected by that meeting.

(NO CVL APPLICATION)

**4.152–CVL(2) [At least three members]** The committee must have at least 3 members before it can be established.

**4.152(3) [Eligibility]** Any creditor of the company (other than one whose debt is fully secured) is eligible to be a member of the committee, so long as–

(a) he has lodged a proof of his debt, and

(b) his proof has netiher been wholly disallowed for voting purposes, nor wholly rejected for purposes of distribution or dividend.

**4.152(4) [No dual membership]** No person can be a member as both a creditor and a contributory.

**4.152(5) [Representation of body corporate]** A body corporate may be a member of the committee, but it cannot act as such otherwise than by a representative appointed under Rule 4.159.

**4.152(6) ["Creditor members", "contributory members"]** Members of the committee elected or appointed to represent the creditors are called "creditor members"; and those elected or appointed to represent the contributories are called "contributory members".

**4.152(7) [Deposit Protection Board as creditor member]** Where a representative of the Deposit Protection Board exercises the right (under section 58 of the Banking Act 1987) to be a member of the committee, he is to be regarded as an additional creditor member.

**History**

In r. 4.152(7) the words "58 of the Banking Act 1987" substituted for the former words "28 of the Banking Act 1979" by the Insolvency (Amendment) Rules 1987 (SI 1987/1919), r. 3(1), Sch., Pt. 1, para. 70 as from 11 January 1988.

## 4.153 Formalities of establishment

**4.153(1) [Liquidator's certificate]** The liquidation committee does not come into being, and accordingly cannot act, until the liquidator has issued a certificate of its due constitution.

[FORM 4.47]

**4.153(2) [If chairman of meeting not liquidator]** If the chairman of the meeting which resolves to establish the committee is not the liquidator, he shall forthwith give notice of the resolution to the liquidator (or, as the case may be, the person appointed as liquidator by that same meeting), and inform him of the names and addresses of the persons elected to be members of the committee.

**4.153(3) [Agreement to act]** No person may act as a member of the committee unless and until he has agreed to do so and, unless the relevant proxy or authorisation contains a statement to the contrary, such agreement may be given by his proxy-holder or representative under section 375 of the Companies Act present at the meeting establishing the committee.

**4.153(3A) [No certificate without agreement]** The liquidator's certificate of the committee's due constitution shall not issue before the minimum number of persons (in accordance with Rule 4.152) who are to be members of the committee have agreed to act.

**History**

R. 4.153(3) and (3A) substituted for the former r. 4.153(3) by the Insolvency (Amendment) Rules 1987 (SI 1987/1919), r. 3(1), Sch., Pt. 1, para. 71 as from 11 January 1988; the former r. 4.153(3) read as follows:

"No person may act as a member of the committee unless and until he has agreed to do so; and the liquidator's certificate of the committee's due constitution shall not issue before the minimum number of persons (in accordance with Rule 4.152) who are to be members of it have agreed to act."

**4.153(4) [Amended certificate]** As and when the others (if any) agree to act, the liquidator shall issue an amended certificate.

**4.153(5) [Certificate to be filed in court]** The certificate, and any amended certificate, shall be filed in court by the liquidator. (NO CVL APPLICATION)

**4.153–CVL(6) [Certificate to registrar]** The certificate, and any amended certificate, shall be sent by the liquidator to the registrar of companies. [FORM 4.47]
[FORM 4.48]

**4.153(7) [Change in membership]** It after the first establishment of the committee there is any change in its membership, the liquidator shall report the change to the court.
(NO CVL APPLICATION) [FORM 4.49]

**4.153–CVL(8) [Change in membership]** If after the first establishment of the committee there is any change in its membership, the liquidator shall report the change to the registrar of companies. [FORM 4.49]
[FORM 4.48]

## 4.154 Committee established by contributories

(NO CVL APPLICATION)

**4.154(1) [Application of Rule]** The following applies where the creditors' meeting under section 141 does not decide that a liquidation committee should be established, or decides that a committee should not be established.

**4.154(2) [Further creditors' meeting]** The meeting of contributories under that section may appoint one of their number to make application to the court for an order to the liquidator that a further creditors' meeting be summoned for the purpose of establishing a liquidation committee; and–

(a) the court may, if it thinks that there are special circumstances to justify it, make that order, and

(b) the creditors' meeting summoned by the liquidator in compliance with the order is deemed to have been summoned under section 141.

**4.154(3) [Meeting of contributories]** If the creditors' meeting so summoned does not establish a liquidation committee, a meeting of contributories may do so.

**4.154(4) [Constitution of committee]** The committee shall then consist of at least 3, and not more than 5, contributories elected by that meeting; and Rule 4.153 applies, substituting for the reference in paragraph (3A) of that Rule to Rule 4.152 a reference to this paragraph.

**History**

In r. 4.154(4) the words from "substituting" to the end substituted for the former words "substituting references to contributories for references to creditors" by the Insolvency (Amendment) Rules 1987 (SI 1987/1919), r. 3(1), Sch., Pt. 1, para. 72 as from 11 January 1988.

## 4.155 Obligations of liquidator to committee

**4.155(1) [Liquidator's duty to report]** Subject as follows, it is the duty of the liquidator to report to the members of the liquidation committee all such matters as appear to him to be, or as they have indicated to him as being, of concern to them with respect to the winding up.

their representatives in respect of their attendance at the committee's meetings, or otherwise on the committee's business.

## 4.170 Dealings by committee-members and others

**4.170(1) [Application of Rule]** This Rule applies to–

(a) any member of the liquidation committee,
(b) any committee-member's representative,
(c) any person who is an associate of a member of the committee or a committee-member's representative, and
(d) any person who has been a member of the committee at any time in the last 12 months.

**4.170(2) [Prohibited transactions]** Subject as follows, a person to whom this Rule applies shall not enter into any transaction whereby he–

(a) receives out of the company's assets any payment for services given or goods supplied in connection with the administration, or
(b) obtains any profit from the administration, or
(c) acquires any asset forming part of the estate.

**4.170(3) [Leave or sanction for r. 4.170(2) transaction]** Such a transaction may be entered into by a person to whom this Rule applies–

(a) with the prior leave of the court, or
(b) if he does so as a matter of urgency, or by way of performance of a contract in force before the date on which the company went into liquidation, and obtains the court's leave for the transaction, having applied for it without undue delay, or
(c) with the prior sanction of the liquidation committee, where it it satisfied (after full disclosure of the circumstances) that the person will be giving full value in the transaction.

**4.170(4) [Resolution to sanction transaction]** Where in the committee a resolution is proposed that sanction be accorded for a transaction to be entered into which, without that sanction or the leave of the court, would be in contravention of this Rule, no member of the committee, and no representative of a member, shall vote if he is to participate directly or indirectly in the transaction.

**4.170(5) [Powers of court]** The court may, on the application of any person interested–

(a) set aside a transaction on the ground that it has been entered into in contravention of this Rule, and
(b) make with respect to it such other order as it thinks fit, including (subject to the following paragraph) an order requiring a person to whom this Rule applies to account for any profit obtained from the transaction and compensate the estate for any resultant loss.

**4.170(6) [Member's or representative's associate]** In the case of a person to whom this Rule applies as an associate of a member of the committee or of a committee-member's representative, the court shall not make any order under paragraph (5), if satisfied that he entered into the relevant transaction without having any reason to suppose that in doing so he would contravene this Rule.

**4.170(7) [Costs of application]** The costs of an application to the court for leave under this Rule are not payable out of the assets, unless the court so orders.

## 4.171 Composition of committee when creditors paid in full

**4.171(1) [Application of Rule]** This Rule applies if the liquidator issues a certificate that the creditors have been paid in full, with interest in accordance with section 189.

**4.171(2) [Liquidator to file certificate in court]** The liquidator shall forthwith file the certificate in court. (NO CVL APPLICATION) [FORM 4.50]

**4.171–CVL(3) [Copy of certificate to registrar]** The liquidator shall forthwith send a copy of the certificate to the registrar of companies. [FORM 4.51]
[FORM 4.50]

**History**
Against r. 4.171(3–CVL) the words "[FORM 4.50]" inserted by the Insolvency (Amendment) Rules 1987 (SI 1987/1919), r. 3(1), Sch., Pt. 2, para. 156(1) as from 11 January 1988.

**4.171(4) [Creditor members]** The creditor members of the liquidation committee cease to be members of the committee.

**4.171(5) [Contributory members]** The committee continues in being unless and until abolished by decision of a meeting of contributories, and (subject to the next paragraph) so long as it consists of at least 3 contributory members.

**4.171(6) [Cessation or suspension]** The committee does not cease to exist on account of the number of contributory members falling below 3, unless and until 28 days have elapsed since the issue of the liquidator's certificate under paragraph (1).

But at any time when the committee consists of less than 3 contributory members, it is suspended and cannot act.

**4.171(7) [Co-opting etc. of contributories]** Contributories may be co-opted by the liquidator, or appointed by a contributories' meeting, to be members of the committee; but the maximum number of members is 5.

**4.171(8) [Application of Rules]** The foregoing Rules in this Chapter continue to apply to the liquidation committee (with any necessary modifications) as if all the members of the committee were creditor members.

## 4.172 Committee's functions vested in Secretary of State

(NO CVL APPLICATION)

**4.172(1) [Liquidator's notices and reports]** At any time when the functions of the liquidation committee are vested in the Secretary of State under section 141(4) or (5), requirements of the Act or the Rules about notices to be given, or reports to be made, to the committee by the liquidator do not apply, otherwise than as enabling the committee to require a report as to any matter.

**4.172(2) [Exercise by official receiver]** Where the committee's functions are so vested under section 141(5), they may be exercised by the official receiver.

## 4.172A Formal defects

**4.172A** The acts of the liquidation committee established for any winding up are valid notwithstanding any defect in the appointment, election or qualifications of any member of the committee or any committee-member's representative or in the formalities of its establishment.

**History**
R. 4.172A inserted by the Insolvency (Amendment) Rules 1987 (SI 1987/1919), r. 3(1), Sch., Pt. 1, para. 75 as from 11 January 1988.

# Chapter 13 – The Liquidation Committee Where Winding Up Follows Immediately on Administration (NO CVL APPLICATION)

## 4.173 Preliminary

**4.173(1) [Application of Rules]** The Rules in this Chapter apply where–

(a) the winding-up order has been made immediately upon the discharge of an administration order under Part II of the Act, and

(b) the court makes an order under section 140(1) of the Act appointing as liquidator the person who was previously the administrator.

**4.173(2) [Definitions]** In this Chapter, **"insolvent winding up"**, **"solvent winding up"**, **"creditor member"** and **"contributory member"** mean the same as in Chapter 12.

## 4.174 Continuation of creditors' committee

**4.174(1) [Creditors' committee as liquidation committee]** If under section 26 a creditors' committee has been established for the purposes of the administration, then (subject as follows in this Chapter) that committee continues in being as the liquidation committee for the purposes of the winding up, and–

(a) it is deemed to be a committee established as such under section 141, and

(b) no action shall be taken under subsections (1) to (3) of that section to establish any other.

**4.174(2) [Non-application of Rule]** This Rule does not apply if, at the time when the court's order under section 140(1) is made, the committee under section 26 consists of less than 3 members; and a creditor who was, immediately before that date, a member of it, ceases to be a member on the making of the order if his debt is fully secured.

## 4.175 Membership of committee

**4.175(1) [Three–five creditors]** Subject as follows, the liquidation committee shall consist of at least 3, and not more than 5, creditors of the company, elected by the creditors' meeting held under section 26 or (in order to make up numbers or fill vacancies) by a creditors' meeting summoned by the liquidator after the company goes into liquidation.

**4.175(2) [In a solvent winding up]** In the case of a solvent winding up, the liquidator shall, on not less than 21 days' notice, summon a meeting of contributories, in order to elect (if it so wishes) contributory members of the liquidation committee, up to 3 in number.

## 4.176 Liquidator's certificate

**4.176(1) [Certificate of continuance]** The liquidator shall issue a certificate of the liquidation committee's continuance, specifying the persons who are, or are to be, members of it.
[FORM 4.52]

**4.176(2) [Contents of certificate]** It shall be stated in the certificate whether or not the liquidator has summoned a meeting of contributories under Rule 4.175(2), and whether (if so) the meeting has elected contributories to be members of the committee.

**4.176(3) [Effect of certificate]** Pending the issue of the liquidator's certificate, the committee is suspended and cannot act.

**4.176(4) [Agreement to act]** No person may act, or continue to act, as a member of the committee unless and until he has agreed to do so; and the liquidator's certificate shall not issue until at least the minimum number of persons required under Rule 4.175 to form a committee have signified their agreement.

**4.176(5) [Amended certificate]** As and when the others signify their agreement, the liquidator shall issue an amended certificate.
[FORM 4.52]

**4.176(6) [Certificate to be filed in court]** The liquidator's certificate (or, as the case may be, the amended certificate) shall be filed by him in court.

**4.176(7) [Change in membership]** If subsequently there is any change in the committee's membership, the liquidator shall report the change to the court.
[FORM 4.49]

## 4.177 Obligations of liquidator to committee

**4.177(1) [Liquidator's report]** As soon as may be after the issue of the liquidator's certificate under Rule 4.176, the liquidator shall report to the liquidation committee what actions he has taken since the date on which the company went into liquidation.

**4.177(2) [Summary report]** A person who becomes a member of the committee after that date is not entitled to require a report to him by the liquidator, otherwise than in a summary form, of any matters previously arising.

**4.177(3) [Access to records etc.]** Nothing in this Rule disentitles the committee, or any member of it, from having access to the records of the liquidation (whether relating to the period when he was administrator, or to any subsequent period), or from seeking an explanation of any matter within the committee's responsibility.

## 4.178 Application of Chapter 12

**4.178** Except as provided above in this Chapter, Rules 4.155 to 4.172A in Chapter 12 apply to the liquidation committee following the issue of the liquidator's certificate under Rule 4.176, as if it had been established under section 141.

**History**
In r. 4.178 "4.172A" substituted for the former "4.172" by the Insolvency (Amendment) Rules 1987 (SI 1987/1919), r. 3(1), Sch., Pt. 1, para. 76 as from 11 January 1988.

# Chapter 14 – Collection and Distribution of Company's Assets by Liquidator

## 4.179 General duties of liquidator

(NO CVL APPLICATION)

**4.179(1) [Officer of the court]** The duties imposed on the court by the Act with regard to the collection of the company's assets and their application in discharge of its liabilities are discharged by the liquidator as an officer of the court subject to its control.

**4.179(2) [Same powers as a receiver]** In the discharge of his duties the liquidator, for the purposes of acquiring and retaining possession of the company's property, has the same powers as a receiver appointed by the High Court, and the court may on his application enforce such acquisition or retention accordingly.

## 4.180 Manner of distributing assets

**4.180(1) [Dividends]** Whenever the liquidator has sufficient funds in hand for the purpose he shall, subject to the retention of such sums as may be necessary for the expenses of the winding up, declare and distribute dividends among the creditors in respect of the debts which they have respectively proved.

**4.180(2) [Notice of intention]** The liquidator shall give notice of his intention to declare and distribute a dividend.

**4.180(3) [Notice of dividend]** Where the liquidator has declared a dividend, he shall give notice of it to the creditors, stating how the dividend is proposed to be distributed. The notice shall contain such particulars with respect to the company, and to its assets and affairs, as will enable the creditors to comprehend the calculation of the amount of the dividend and the manner of its distribution.

## 4.181 Debts of insolvent company to rank equally

(NO CVL APPLICATION)

**4.181(1) [Ranking and priority]** Debts other than preferential debts rank equally between themselves in the winding up and, after the preferential debts, shall be paid in full unless the assets are insufficient for meeting them, in which case they abate in equal proportions between themselves.

**4.181(2) [Application of r. 4.181(1)]** Paragraph (1) applies whether or not the company is unable to pay its debts.

**History**
R. 4.181(1) renumbered as such and r. 4.181(2) added by the Insolvency (Amendment) Rules 1987 (SI 1987/1919), r. 3(1), Sch., Pt. 1, para. 77 as from 11 January 1988.

## 4.182 Supplementary provisions as to dividend

**4.182(1) [Calculation and distribution]** In the calculation and distribution of a dividend the liquidator shall make provision–

(a) for any debts which appear to him to be due to persons who, by reason of the distance of their place of residence, may not have had sufficient time to tender and establish their proofs,

(b) for any debts which are the subject of claims which have not yet been determined, and

(c) for disputed proofs and claims.

**4.182(2) [Proof after dividend declared]** A creditor who has not proved his debt before the declaration of any dividend is not entitled to disturb, by reason that he has not participated in it, the distribution of that dividend or any other dividend declared before his debt was proved, but–

(a) when he has proved that debt he is entitled to be paid, out of any money for the time being available for the payment of any further dividend, any dividend or dividends which he has failed to receive, and

(b) any dividend or dividends payable under sub-paragraph (a) shall be paid before that money is applied to the payment of any such further dividend.

**4.182(3) [Order for payment etc.]** No action lies against the liquidator for a dividend; but if he refuses to pay a dividend the court may, if it thinks fit, order him to pay it and also to pay, out of his own money–

(a) interest on the dividend, at the rate for the time being specified in section 17 of the Judgments Act 1838, from the time when it was withheld, and

(b) the costs of the proceedings in which the order to pay is made.

# 4.182A Distribution in members' voluntary winding up

(NO CVL APPLICATION)

**4.182A(1) [Notice of intention]** In a members' voluntary winding up the liquidator may give notice in such newspaper as he considers most appropriate for the purpose of drawing the matter to the attention of the company's creditors that he intends to make a distribution to creditors.

**4.182A(2) ["The last date for proving"]** The notice shall specify a date ("the last date for proving") up to which proofs may be lodged. The date shall be the same for all creditors and not less than 21 days from that of the notice.

**4.182A(3) [Proofs lodged out of time]** The liquidator is not obliged to deal with proofs lodged after the last date for proving; but he may do so, if he thinks fit.

**4.182A(4) [Distribution not to be disturbed]** A creditor who has not proved his debt before the last date for proving or after that date increases the claim in his proof is not entitled to disturb, by reason that he has not participated in it, either at all or, as the case may be, to the extent that his increased claim would allow, that distribution or any other distribution made before his debt was proved or his claim increased; but when he has proved his debt or, as the case may be, increased his claim, he is entitled to be paid, out of any money for the time being available for the payment of any further distribution, any distribution or distributions which he has failed to receive.

**4.182A(5) [Only or final distribution]** Where the distribution proposed to be made is to be the only or the final distribution in that winding up, the liquidator may, subject to paragraph (6), make that distribution without regard to the claim of any person in respect of a debt not already proved.

**4.182A(6) [Notice in r. 4.182A(5)]** Where the distribution proposed to be made is one specified in paragraph (5), the notice given under paragraph (1) shall state the effect of paragraph (5).

**History**

R. 4.182A inserted by the Insolvency (Amendment) Rules 1987 (SI 1987/1919), r. 3(1), Sch., Pt. 1, para. 78 as from 11 January 1988.

# 4.183 Division of unsold assets

**4.183** Without prejudice to provisions of the Act about disclaimer, the liquidator may, with the permission of the liquidation committee, divide in its existing form amongst the company's creditors, according to its estimated value, any property which from its peculiar nature or other special circumstances cannot be readily or advantageously sold.

## 4.184 General powers of liquidator

**4.184(1) [Particular permission]** Any permission given by the liquidation committee or the court under section 167(1)(a), or under the Rules, shall not be a general permission but shall relate to a particular proposed exercise of the liquidator's power in question; and a person dealing with the liquidator in good faith and for value is not concerned to enquire whether any such permission has been given.

**4.184(2) [Ratification]** Where the liquidator has done anything without that permission, the court or the liquidation committee may, for the purpose of enabling him to meet his expenses out of the assets, ratify what he has done; but neither shall do so unless it is satisfied that the liquidator has acted in a case of urgency and has sought ratification without undue delay.

## 4.185 Enforced delivery up of company's property

(NO CVL APPLICATION)

**4.185(1) [Powers under s. 234]** The powers conferred on the court by section 234 (enforced delivery of company property) are exercisable by the liquidator or, where a provisional liquidator has been appointed, by him.

**4.185(2) [Duty to comply]** Any person on whom a requirement under section 234(2) is imposed by the liquidator or provisional liquidator shall, without avoidable delay, comply with it.

## 4.186 Final distribution

**4.186(1) [Notice under Pt. 11]** When the liquidator has realised all the company's assets or so much of them as can, in his opinion, be realised without needlessly protracting the liquidation, he shall give notice, under Part 11 of the Rules, either–

(a) of his intention to declare a final dividend, or

(b) that no dividend, or further dividend, will be declared.

**4.186(2) [Contents of notice]** The notice shall contain all such particulars as are required by Part 11 of the Rules and shall require claims against the assets to be established by a date specified in the notice.

**4.186(3) [Final dividend]** After that date, the liquidator shall–

(a) defray any outstanding expenses of the winding up out of the assets, and

(b) if he intends to declare a final dividend, declare and distribute that dividend without regard to the claim of any person in respect of a debt not already proved.

**4.186(4) [Postponement]** The court may, on the application of any person, postpone the date specified in the notice.

# Chapter 15 – Disclaimer

## 4.187 Liquidator's notice of disclaimer

**4.187(1) [Contents of notice]** Where the liquidator disclaims property under section 178, the notice of disclaimer shall contain such particulars of the property disclaimed as enable it to be easily identified.

[FORM 4.53]

**4.187(2) [Notice to be signed etc.]** The notice shall be signed by the liquidator and filed in court, with a copy. The court shall secure that both the notice and the copy are sealed and endorsed with the date of filing.

**4.187(3) [Copy of notice returned to liquidator]** The copy notice, so sealed and endorsed, shall be returned by the court to the liquidator as follows–

(a) if the notice has been delivered at the offices of the court by the liquidator in person, it shall be handed to him,

(b) if it has been delivered by some person acting on the liquidator's behalf, it shall be handed to that person, for immediate transmission to the liquidator, and

**5.4(2) [Delivery of notice]** The notice, accompanied by a copy of the proposal, shall be delivered either to the nominee himself, or to a person authorised to take delivery of documents on his behalf.

**5.4(3) [Endorsement of receipt]** If the intended nominee agrees to act, he shall cause a copy of the notice to be endorsed to the effect that it has been received by him on a specified date.

**5.4(4) [Return of endorsed notice]** The copy of the notice so endorsed shall be returned by the nominee forthwith to the debtor at an address specified by him in the notice for that purpose.

**5.4(5) [Notice in Case 1]** Where (in Case 1) the debtor gives notice of his proposal to the official receiver and (if any) the trustee, the notice must contain the name and address of the insolvency practitioner who has agreed to act as nominee.

## 5.5 Application for interim order

**5.5(1) [Accompanying affidavit]** An application to the court for an interim order under Part VIII of the Act shall be accompanied by an affidavit of the following matters–

(a) the reasons for making the application;

(b) particulars of any execution or other legal process which, to the debtor's knowledge, has been commenced against him;

(c) that he is an undischarged bankrupt or (as the case may be) that he is able to petition for his own bankruptcy;

(d) that no previous application for an interim order has been made by or in respect of the debtor in the period of 12 months ending with the date of the affidavit; and

(e) that the nominee under the proposal (naming him) is a person who is qualified to act as an insolvency practitioner in relation to the debtor, and is willing to act in relation to the proposal.

**5.5(2) [Rule 5.4 notice to be exhibited]** A copy of the notice to the intended nominee under Rule 5.4, endorsed to the effect that he agrees so to act, and a copy of the debtor's proposal given to the nominee under that Rule shall be exhibited to the affidavit.

**History**
In r. 5.5(2) the words "and a copy of the debtor's proposal given to the nominee under that Rule" inserted by the Insolvency (Amendment) Rules 1987 (SI 1987/1919), r. 3(1), Sch., Pt. 1, para. 84 as from 11 January 1988.

**5.5(3) [Court to fix venue]** On receiving the application and affidavit, the court shall fix a venue for the hearing of the application.

**5.5(4) [Notice of hearing]** The applicant shall give at least 2 days' notice of the hearing–

(a) in Case 1, to the bankrupt, the official receiver and the trustee (whichever of those three is not himself the applicant),

(b) in Case 2, to any creditor who (to the debtor's knowledge) has presented a bankruptcy petition against him, and

(c) in either case, to the nominee who has agreed to act in relation to the debtor's proposal.

## 5.5A Court in which application to be made

**5.5A(1) [Debtor not bankrupt]** Except in the case of a bankrupt, an application to the court under Part VIII of the Act shall be made to a court in which the debtor would be entitled to present his own petition in bankruptcy under Rule 6.40.

**5.5A(2) [Information in application]** The application shall contain sufficient information to establish that it is brought in the appropriate court.

**5.5A(3) [Debtor bankrupt]** In the case of a bankrupt such an application shall be made to the court having the conduct of his bankruptcy and shall be filed with those bankruptcy proceedings.

**History**
R. 5.5A inserted by the Insolvency (Amendment) Rules 1987 (SI 1987/1919), r. 3(1), Sch., Pt. 1, para. 85 as from 11 January 1988.

## 5.6 Hearing of the application

**5.6(1) [Appearances etc.]** Any of the persons who have been given notice under Rule 5.5(4) may appear or be represented at the hearing of the application.

**5.6(2) [Representations re order]** The court, in deciding whether to make an interim order on the application, shall take into account any representations made by or on behalf of any of those persons (in particular, whether an order should be made containing such provision as is referred to in section 255(3) and (4)).

**5.6(3) [Consideration of nominee's report]** If the court makes an interim order, it shall fix a venue for consideration of the nominee's report. Subject to the following paragraph, the date for that consideration shall be not later than that on which the interim order ceases to have effect under section 255(6).

**5.6(4) [Extension of time under s. 256(4)]** If under section 256(4) an extension of time is granted for filing the nominee's report, the court shall, unless there appear to be good reasons against it, correspondingly extend the period for which the interim order has effect.

## 5.7 Action to follow making of order

**5.7(1) [Sealed copies]** Where an interim order is made, at least 2 sealed copies of the order shall be sent by the court forthwith to the person who applied for it; and that person shall serve one of the copies on the nominee under the debtor's proposal. [FORM 5.2]

**History**

Against r. 5.7(1) the words "[FORM 5.2]" inserted by the Insolvency (Amendment) Rules 1987 (SI 1987/1919), r. 3(1), Sch., Pt. 2, para. 156(1) as from 11 January 1988.

**5.7(2) [Notice of order]** The applicant shall also forthwith give notice of the making of the order to any person who was given notice of the hearing pursuant to Rule 5.5(4) and was not present or represented at it.

## 5.8 Statement of affairs

**5.8(1) [In Case 1]** In Case 1, if the debtor has already delivered a statement of affairs under section 272 (debtor's petition) or 288 (creditor's petition), he need not deliver a further statement unless so required by the nominee, with a view to supplementing or amplifying the former one.

**5.8(2) [In Case 2]** In Case 2, the debtor shall, within 7 days after his proposal is delivered to the nominee, or within such longer time as the latter may allow, deliver to the nominee a statement of his (the debtor's) affairs.

**5.8(3) [Particulars in statement]** The statement shall comprise the following particulars (supplementing or amplifying, so far as is necessary for clarifying the state of the debtor's affairs, those already given in his proposal)–

(a) a list of his assets, divided into such categories as are appropriate for easy indentification, with estimated values assigned to each category;

(b) in the case of any property on which a claim against the debtor is wholly or partly secured, particulars of the claim and its amount, and of how and when the security was created;

(c) the names and addresses of the debtor's preferential creditors (defined in section 258(7)), with the amounts of their respective claims;

(d) the names and addresses of the debtor's unsecured creditors, with the amounts of their respective claims;

(e) particulars of any debts owed by or to the debtor to or by persons who are associates of his;

(f) such other particulars (if any) as the nominee may in writing require to be furnished for the purposes of making his report to the court on the debtor's proposal.

**5.8(4) [Relevant date]** The statement of affairs shall be made up to a date not earlier than 2 weeks before the date of the notice to the nominee under Rule. 5.4.

However, the nominee may allow an extension of that period to the nearest practicable date (not earlier than 2 months before the date of the notice under Rule 5.4); and if he does so, he shall give his reasons in his report to the court on the debtor's proposal.

**5.8(5) [Certification of statement]** The statement shall be certified by the debtor as correct, to the best of his knowledge and belief.

## 5.9 Additional disclosure for assistance of nominee

**5.9(1) [Nominee may request further information]** If it appears to the nominee that he cannot properly prepare his report on the basis of information in the debtor's proposal and statement of affairs, he may call on the debtor to provide him with–

(a) further and better particulars as to the circumstances in which, and the reasons why, he is insolvent or (as the case may be) threatened with insolvency;

(b) particulars of any previous proposals which have been made by him under Part VIII of the Act;

(c) any further information with respect to his affairs which the nominee thinks necessary for the purposes of his report.

**5.9(2) [Whether debtor concerned with insolvent company, bankrupt etc.]** The nominee may call on the debtor to inform him whether and in what circumstances he has at any time–

(a) been concerned in the affairs of any company (whether or not incorporated in England and Wales) which has become insolvent, or

(b) been adjudged bankrupt, or entered into an arrangement with his creditors.

**5.9(3) [Access to accounts and records]** For the purpose of enabling the nominee to consider the debtor's proposal and prepare his report on it, the latter must give him access to his accounts and records.

## 5.10 Nominee's report on the proposal

**5.10(1) [Time for delivery]** The nominee's report shall be delivered by him to the court not less than 2 days before the interim order ceases to have effect.

**5.10(2) [Accompanying documents]** With his report the nominee shall deliver–

(a) a copy of the debtor's proposal (with amendments, if any, authorised under Rule 5.3(3)); and

(b) a copy or summary of any statement of affairs provided by the debtor.

**5.10(3) [Nominee's opinion re meeting]** If the nominee makes known his opinion that a meeting of the debtor's creditors should be summoned under section 257, his report shall have annexed to it his comments on the debtor's proposal.

If his opinion is otherwise, he shall give his reasons for that opinion.

**5.10(4) [Endorsement of date of filing and right to inspect]** The court shall cause the nominee's report to be endorsed with the date on which it is filed in court. Any creditor of the debtor is entitled, at all reasonable times on any business day, to inspect the file.

**5.10(5) [Directions in Cases 1 and 2]** In Case 1, the nominee shall send to the official receiver and (if any) the trustee–

(a) a copy of the debtor's proposal,

(b) a copy of his (the nominee's) report and his comments accompanying it (if any), and

(c) a copy or summary of the debtor's statement of affairs.

In Case 2, the nominee shall send a copy of each of those documents to any person who has presented a bankruptcy petition against the debtor.

**History**
In r. 5.10(5) the words "and (if any) the trustee" inserted by the Insolvency (Amendment) Rules 1987 (SI 1987/1919), r. 3(1), Sch., Pt. 1, para. 86 as from 11 January 1988.

## 5.11 Replacement of nominee

**5.11** Where the debtor intends to apply to the court under section 256(3) for the nominee to be replaced, he shall give to the nominee at least 7 days' notice of his application.

## SECTION B: ACTION ON THE PROPOSAL; CREDITORS' MEETING

# 5.12 Consideration of nominee's report

**5.12(1) [Appearances etc.]** At the hearing by the court to consider the nominee's report, any of the persons who have been given notice under Rule 5.5(4) may appear or be represented.

**5.12(2) [Application of r. 5.7]** Rule 5.7 applies to any order made by the court at the hearing.

# 5.13 Summoning of creditors' meeting

**5.13(1) [Date for meeting]** If in his report the nominee states that in his opinion a meeting of creditors should be summoned to consider the debtor's proposal, the date on which the meeting is to be held shall be not less than 14 days from that on which the nominee's report is filed in court under Rule 5.10, nor more than 28 days from that on which that report is considered by the court under Rule 5.12.

**History**
In r. 5.13(1) the words ", nor more than 28," formerly appearing after "14" omitted and the words ", no more than 28 days from that" to the end added by the Insolvency (Amendment) Rules 1987 (SI 1987/1919), r. 3(1), Sch., Pt. 1, para. 87 as from 11 January 1988.

**5.13(2) [Notices of meeting]** Notices calling the meeting shall be sent by the nominee, at least 14 days before the day fixed for it to be held, to all the creditors specified in the debtor's statement of affairs, and any other creditors of whom the nominee is otherwise aware.

**5.13(3) [Contents etc. of notice]** Each notice sent under this Rule shall specify the court to which the nominee's report on the debtor's proposal has been delivered and shall state the effect of Rule 5.18(1), (3) and (4) (requisite majorities); and with it there shall be sent–

(a) a copy of the proposal,

(b) a copy of the statement of affairs or, if the nominee thinks fit, a summary of it (the summary to include a list of the creditors and the amounts of their debts), and

(c) the nominee's comments on the proposal.

# 5.14 Creditors' meeting: supplementary

**5.14(1) [Convenience of venue]** Subject as follows, in fixing the venue for the creditors' meeting, the nominee shall have regard to the convenience of creditors.

**5.14(2) [Time of meeting]** The meeting shall be summoned for commencement between 10.00 and 16.00 hours on a business day.

**5.14(3) [Forms of proxy]** With every notice summoning the meeting there shall be sent out forms of proxy.

[FORM 8.1]

# 5.15 The chairman at the meeting

**5.15(1) [Nominee to be chairman]** Subject as follows, the nominee shall be chairman of the creditors' meeting.

**5.15(2) [Other nominated chairman]** If for any reason the nominee is unable to attend, he may nominate another person to act as chairman in his place; but a person so nominated must be either–

(a) a person qualified to act as an insolvency practitioner in relation to the debtor, or

(b) an employee of the nominee or his firm who is experienced in insolvency matters.

# 5.16 The chairman as proxy-holder

**5.16** The chairman shall not by virtue of any proxy held by him vote to increase or reduce the amount of the remuneration or expenses of the nominee or the supervisor of the proposed arrangement, unless the proxy specifically directs him to vote in that way.

# 5.17 Voting rights

**5.17(1) [Entitlement to vote]** Subject as follows, every creditor who was given notice of the creditors' meeting is entitled to vote at the meeting or any adjournment of it.

**5.17(2) [Calculation of votes]** In Case 1, votes are calculated according to the amount of the creditor's debt as at the date of the bankruptcy order, and in Case 2 according to the amount of the debt as at the date of the meeting.

**5.17(3) [Limitation on voting]** A creditor shall not vote in respect of a debt for an unliquidated amount, or any debt whose value is not ascertained, except where the chairman agrees to put upon the debt an estimated minimum value for the purpose of entitlement to vote.

**5.17(4) [Chairman's discretion]** The chairman has power to admit or reject a creditor's claim for the purpose of his entitlement to vote, and the power is exercisable with respect to the whole or any part of the claim.

**5.17(5) [Appeal from chairman's decision]** The chairman's decision on entitlement to vote is subject to appeal to the court by any creditor, or by the debtor.

**5.17(6) [Voting subject to objection]** If the chairman is in doubt whether a claim should be admitted or rejected, he shall mark it as objected to and allow the creditor to vote, subject to his vote being subsequently declared invalid if the objection to the claim is sustained.

**5.17(7) [Where chairman's decision reversed etc.]** If on an appeal the chairman's decision is reversed or varied, or a creditor's vote is declared invalid, the court may order another meeting to be summoned, or make such other order as it thinks just.

The court's power to make an order under this paragraph is exercisable only if it considers that the matter is such as to give rise to unfair prejudice or a material irregularity.

**5.17(8) [Time for appeal]** An application to the court by way of appeal under this Rule against the chairman's decision shall not be made after the end of the period of 28 days beginning with the day on which the chairman's report to the court is made under section 259.

**5.17(9) [Costs of appeal]** The chairman is not personally liable for any costs incurred by any person in respect of an appeal under this Rule.

## 5.18 Requisite majorities

**5.18(1) [Three-quarters majority]** Subject as follows, at the creditors' meeting for any resolution to pass approving any proposal or modification there must be a majority in excess of three-quarters in value of the creditors present in person or by proxy and voting on the resolution.

**5.18(2) [One-half majority]** The same applies in respect of any other resolution proposed at the meeting, but substituting one-half for three-quarters.

**5.18(3) [Votes to be left out of account]** In the following cases there is to be left out of account a creditor's vote in respect of any claim or part of a claim–

(a) where written notice of the claim was not given, either at the meeting or before it, to the chairman or the nominee;

(b) where the claim or part is secured;

(c) where the claim is in respect of a debt wholly or partly on, or secured by, a current bill of exchange or promissory note, unless the creditor is willing–

 (i) to treat the liability to him on the bill or note of every person who is liable on it antecendently to the debtor, and against whom a bankruptcy order has not been made (or, in the case of a company, which has not gone into liquidation), as a security in his hands, and

 (ii) to estimate the value of the security and (for the purpose of entitlement to vote, but not of any distribution under the arrangement) to deduct it from his claim.

**5.18(4) [Votes rendering resolution invalid]** Any resolution is invalid if those voting against it include more than half in value of the creditors, counting in these latter only those–

(a) to whom notice of the meeting was sent;

(b) whose votes are not to be left out of account under paragraph (3); and

(c) who are not, to the best of the chairman's belief, associates of the debtor.

**5.18(5) [Chairman's powers]** It is for the chairman of the meeting to decide whether under this Rule–

(a) a vote is to be left out of account in accordance with paragraph (3), or

(b) a person is an associate of the debtor for the purposes of paragraph (4)(c);

and in relation to the second of these two cases the chairman is entitled to rely on the information provided by the debtor's statement of affairs or otherwise in accordance with this Part of the Rules.

**5.18(6) [Chairman's use of proxy]** If the chairman uses a proxy contrary to Rule 5.16, his vote with that proxy does not count towards any majority under this Rule.

**5.18(7) [Application of r. 5.17]** Paragraphs (5) to (9) of Rule 5.17 apply as regards an appeal against the decision of the chairman under this Rule.

## 5.19 Proceedings to obtain agreement on the proposal

**5.19(1) [Adjournments]** On the day on which the creditors' meeting is held, it may from time to time be adjourned.

**5.19(2) [Failure to obtain requisite majority]** If on that day the requisite majority for the approval of the voluntary arrangement (with or without modifications) has not been obtained, the chairman may, and shall if it is so resolved, adjourn the meeting for not more than 14 days.

**5.19(3) [Final adjournment]** If there are subsequently further adjournments, the final adjournment shall not be to a day later than 14 days after that on which the meeting was originally held.

**5.19(4) [Notice of adjournment]** If the meeting is adjourned under paragraph (2), notice of the fact shall be given by the chairman forthwith to the court.

**5.19(5) [Deemed rejection of proposal]** If following any final adjournment of the meeting the proposal (with or without modifications) is not agreed to, it is deemed rejected.

### SECTION C: IMPLEMENTATION OF THE ARRANGEMENT

## 5.20 Resolutions to follow approval

**5.20(1) [Resolution re supervisory acts]** If the voluntary arrangement is approved (with or without modifications), a resolution may be taken by the creditors, where two or more insolvency practitioners are appointed to act as supervisor, on the question whether acts to be done in connection with the arrangement may be done by any one of them, or must be done by both or all.

**5.20(2) [Other than nominee to be supervisor]** If at the creditors' meeting a resolution is moved for the appointment of some person other than the nominee to be supervisor of the arrangement, there must be produced to the chairman, at or before the meeting–

(a) that person's written consent to act (unless he is present and then and there signifies his consent), and

(b) his written confirmation that he is qualified to act as an insolvency practitioner in relation to the debtor.

## 5.21 Hand-over of property, etc. to supervisor

**5.21(1) [Putting supervisor into possession of assets]** Forthwith after the approval of the voluntary arrangement, the debtor in Case 2, and the official receiver or trustee in Case 1, shall do all that is required for putting the supervisor into possession of the assets included in the arrangement.

**5.21(2) [Discharge of official receiver's remuneration etc.]** On taking possession of the assets in Case 1, the supervisor shall discharge any balance due to the official receiver and (if other) the trustee by way of remuneration or on account of–

(a) fees, costs, charges and expenses properly incurred and payable under the Act or the Rules, and

(b) any advances made in respect of the insolvent estate, together with interest on such advances at the rate specified in section 17 of the Judgments Act 1838 at the date of the bankruptcy order.

**5.21(3) [Undertaking to discharge etc.]** Alternatively in Case 1, the supervisor must, before taking possession, give the official receiver or the trustee a written undertaking to discharge any such balance out of the first realisation of assets.

**5.21(4) [Charge on assets]** The official receiver and (if other) the trustee has in Case 1 a charge on the assets included in the voluntary arrangement in respect of any sums due as above until they have been discharged, subject only to the deduction from realisations by the supervisor of the proper costs and expenses of realisation.

Any sums due to the official receiver take priority over those due to a trustee.

**5.21(5) [Discharge of guarantees etc.]** The supervisor shall from time to time out of the realisation of assets discharge all guarantees properly given by the official receiver or the trustee for the benefit of the estate, and shall pay all their expenses.

## 5.22 Report of creditors' meeting

**5.22(1) [Chairman to prepare report]** A report of the creditors' meeting shall be prepared by the chairman of the meeting.

**5.22(2) [Contents of report]** The report shall–

(a) state whether the proposal for a voluntary arrangement was approved or rejected and, if approved, with what (if any) modifications;

(b) set out the resolutions which were taken at the meeting, and the decision on each one;

(c) list the creditors (with their respective values) who were present or represented at the meeting, and how they voted on each resolution; and

(d) include such further information (if any) as the chairman thinks it appropriate to make known to the court.

**5.22(3) [Copy of report to be filed in court]** A copy of the chairman's report shall, within 4 days of the meeting being held, be filed in court; and the court shall cause that copy to be endorsed with the date of filing.

**5.22(4) [Notice of result]** The persons to whom notice of the result is to be given, under section 259(1), are all those who were sent notice of the meeting under this Part of the Rules and, in Case 1, the official receiver and (if any) the trustee.

The notice shall be sent immediately after a copy of the chairman's report is filed in court under paragraph (3).

**History**

In r. 5.22(4) the words "and, in Case 1, the official receiver and (if any) the trustee" inserted by the Insolvency (Amendment) Rules 1987 (SI 1987/1919), r. 3(1), Sch., Pt. 1, para. 88 as from 11 January 1988.

## 5.23 Register of voluntary arrangements

**5.23(1) [Register maintained by Secretary of State]** The Secretary of State shall maintain a register of individual voluntary arrangements, and shall enter in it all such matters as are reported to him in pursuance of Rules 5.24 and 5.29 and orders of suspension made under section 262 reported to him in pursuance of Rule 5.25.

**History**

In r. 5.23(1) the words ", 5.25" formerly appearing after the words "5.24" deleted and the words from "and orders of suspension made under section" to the end added by the Insolvency (Amendment) Rules 1999 (SI 1999/359), r. 1, Sch., para. 1(1) as from 22 March 1999.

Previously in r. 5.23(1) the words "Rules 5.24, 5.25 and 5.29" substituted for the former words "this Part of the Rules" by the Insolvency (Amendment) Rules 1987 (SI 1987/1919), r. 3(1), Sch., Pt. 1, para. 89 as from 11 January 1988.

**5.23(1A) [Deletion from register upon notice of revocation]** Where the Secretary of State has received notice of the making of a revocation order or that an arrangement has been fully implemented in pursuance of Rules 5.25 or 5.29 or has otherwise received written notice of the termination of an arrangement from the supervisor and–

(a) the revocation order under section 262 was made prior to 22nd March 1999, or

(b) the final completion or termination of the arrangement occurred more than two years prior to 22nd March 1999,

the Secretary of State shall delete from the register all matters entered in it relating to such arrangement.

**History**

See history note after r. 5.23(1C).

**5.23(1B) [Notice under r. 5.25(5)]** Where the Secretary of State receives notice under Rule 5.25(5) of the making of a revocation order in respect of an individual voluntary arrangement of which entry is made in the register the Secretary of State shall delete from the register all matters entered in it relating to that arrangement.

**History**

See history note after r. 5.23(1C).

**5.23(1C) [Notice under r. 5.29(3)]** Where the Secretary of State receives notice under Rule 5.29(3) of the full implementation or termination of an individual voluntary arrangement of which entry is made in the register the Secretary of State shall, on the expiry of two years after the final completion or termination of such individual voluntary arrangement, delete from the register all matters entered in it relating to that arrangement.

**History**

R. 5.23(1A), (1B) and 1(C) inserted by the Insolvency (Amendment) Rules 1999 (SI 1999/359), r. 1, Sch., para. 1(2) as from 22 March 1999.

**5.23(2) [Open to public inspection]** The register shall be open to public inspection.

**5.23(2) [Open to public inspection]** The register shall be open to public inspection.

## 5.24 Reports to Secretary of State

**5.24(1) [Details of arrangement]** Immediately after the chairman of the creditors' meeting has filed in court a report that the meeting has approved the voluntary arrangement, he shall report to the Secretary of State the following details of the arrangement–

(a) the name and address of the debtor;

(b) the date on which the arrangement was approved by the creditors;

(c) the name and address of the supervisor; and

(d) the court in which the chairman's report has been filed.

**5.24(2) [Notice of appointment as supervisor etc.]** A person who is appointed to act as supervisor of an individual voluntary arrangement (whether in the first instance or by way of replacement of another person previously appointed) shall forthwith give written notice to the Secretary of State of his appointment.

If he vacates office as supervisor, he shall forthwith give written notice of that fact also to the Secretary of State.

## 5.25 Revocation or suspension of the arrangement

**5.25(1) [Application of Rule]** This Rule applies where the court makes an order of revocation or suspension under section 262.

**5.25(2) [Service of copies of orders]** The person who applied for the order shall serve sealed copies of it–

(a) in Case 1, on the debtor, the official receiver and the trustee;

(b) in Case 2, on the debtor; and

(c) in either case on the supervisor of the voluntary arrangement.

**5.25(3) [Notice re further creditors' meeting]** If the order includes a direction by the court under section 262(4)(b) for any further creditors' meeting to be summoned, notice shall also be given (by the person who applied for the order) to whoever is, in accordance with the direction, required to summon the meeting.

**5.25(4) [Notice of order and of intention re proposal]** The debtor (in Case 2) and trustee, or if there is no trustee, the official receiver (in Case 1) shall–

(a) forthwith after receiving a copy of the court's order, give notice of it to all persons who were sent notice of the creditors' meeting which approved the voluntary arrangement or who, not having been sent that notice, appear to be affected by the order;

(b) within 7 days of their receiving a copy of the order (or within such longer period as the court may allow), give notice to the court whether it is intended to make a revised proposal to creditors, or to invite re-consideration of the original proposal.

**History**
In r. 5.25(4) the words "trustee or if there is no trustee, the official receiver" substituted for the former words "the official receiver or the trustee" by the Insolvency (Amendment) Rules 1987 (SI 1987/1919), r. 3(1), Sch., Pt. 1, para. 90 as from 11 January 1988.

**5.25(5) [Notice to Secretary of State]** The person on whose application the order of revocation or suspension was made shall, within 7 days after the making of the order, give written notice of it to the Secretary of State and shall, in the case of an order of suspension, within 7 days of the expiry of any suspension order, give written notice of such expiry to the Secretary of State.

**History**
In r. 5.25(5) the words from "and shall, in the case" to the end added by the Insolvency (Amendment) Rules 1999 (SI 1999/359), r. 1, Sch., para. 2 as from 22 March 1999.

## 5.26 Supervisor's accounts and reports

**5.26(1) [Obligation to keep accounts etc.]** Where the voluntary arrangement authorises or requires the supervisor–

(a) to carry on the debtor's business or to trade on his behalf or in his name, or

(b) to realise assets of the debtor or (in Case 1) belonging to the estate, or

(c) otherwise to administer or dispose of any funds of the debtor or the estate,

he shall keep accounts and records of his acts and dealings in and in connection with the arrangement, including in particular records of all receipts and payments of money.

**5.26(2) [Abstract of receipts and payments]** The supervisor shall, not less often than once in every 12 months beginning with the date of his appointment, prepare an abstract of such receipts and payments, and send copies of it, accompanied by his comments on the progress and efficacy of the arrangement, to–

(a) the court,

(b) the debtor, and

(c) all those of the debtor's creditors who are bound by the arrangement.

If in any period of 12 months he has made no payments and had no receipts, he shall at the end of that period send a statement to that effect to all who are specified in sub-paragraphs (a) to (c) above.

**5.26(3) [Abstract under r. 5.26(2)]** An abstract provided under paragraph (2) shall relate to a period beginning with the date of the supervisor's appointment or (as the case may be) the day following the end of the last period for which an abstract was prepared under this Rule; and copies of the abstract shall be sent out, as required by paragraph (2), within the 2 months following the end of the period to which the abstract relates.

**5.26(4) [If supervisor not authorised as in r. 5.26(1)]** If the supervisor is not authorised as mentioned in paragraph (1), he shall, not less often than once in every 12 months beginning with the date of his appointment, send to all those specified in paragraph (2)(a) to (c) a report on the progress and efficacy of the voluntary arrangement.

**5.26(5) [Powers of court]** The court may, on application by the supervisor, vary the dates on which the obligation to send abstracts or reports arises.

## 5.27 Production of accounts and records to Secretary of State

**5.27(1) [Powers of Secretary of State]** The Secretary of State may at any time during the course of the voluntary arrangement or after its completion require the supervisor to produce for inspection–

(a) his records and accounts in respect of the arrangement, and

(b) copies of abstracts and reports prepared in compliance with Rule 5.26.

**5.27(2) [Production and duty to comply]** The Secretary of State may require production either at the premises of the supervisor or elsewhere; and it is the duty of the supervisor to comply with any requirement imposed on him under this Rule.

**5.27(3) [Audit of accounts and records]** The Secretary of State may cause any accounts and records produced to him under this Rule to be audited; and the supervisor shall give to the Secretary of State such further information and assistance as he needs for the purposes of his audit.

## 5.28 Fees, costs, charges and expenses

**5.28** The fees, costs, charges and expenses that may be incurred for any purposes of the voluntary arrangement are–

(a) any disbursements made by the nominee prior to the approval of the arrangement, and any remuneration for his services as such agreed between himself and the debtor, the official receiver or the trustee;

(b) any fees, costs, charges or expenses which–
  (i) are sanctioned by the terms of the arrangement, or
  (ii) would be payable, or correspond to those which would be payable, in the debtor's bankruptcy.

## 5.29 Completion or termination of the arrangement

**History**
The title to r. 5.29 substituted for the former title "Completion of the arrangement" by the Insolvency (Amendment) Rules 1999 (SI 1999/359), r. 1, Sch., para. 3(1) as from 22 March 1999.

**5.29(1) [Supervisor to send notice]** Not more than 28 days after the final completion or termination of the voluntary arrangement, the supervisor shall send to all creditors of the debtor who are bound by the arrangement, and to the debtor, a notice that the arrangement has been fully implemented or (as the case may be) terminated.

**History**
In r. 5.29(1) the words "or termination" appearing after the words "final completion" inserted and the words "or (as the case may be) terminated" added by the Insolvency (Amendment) Rules 1999 (SI 1999/359), r. 1, Sch., para. 3(2) as from 22 March 1999.

**5.29(2) [Supervisor's report]** With the notice there shall be sent to each of those persons a copy of a report by the supervisor summarising all receipts and payments made by him in pursuance of the arrangement, and explaining any difference in the actual implementation of it as compared with the proposal as approved by the creditors' meeting or (in the case of termination of the arrangement) explaining the reasons why the arrangement has not been implemented in accordance with the proposal as approved by the creditors' meeting.

**History**
In r. 5.29(2) the words from "or (in the case of" to the end added by the Insolvency (Amendment) Rules 1999 (SI 1999/359), r. 1, Sch., para. 3(3) as from 22 March 1999.

**5.29(3) [Copies of notices and reports]** The supervisor shall, within the 28 days mentioned above, send to the Secretary of State and to the court a copy of the notice under paragraph (1), together with a copy of the report under paragraph (2) and he shall not vacate office until after such copies have been sent.

**History**
In r. 5.29(3) the words from "and he shall not" to the end added by the Insolvency (Amendment) Rules 1999 (SI 1999/359), r. 1, Sch., para. 3(4) as from 22 March 1999.

**5.29(4) [Extension of time]** The court may, on application by the supervisor, extend the period of 28 days under paragraphs (1) and (3).

SECTION D: GENERAL

## 5.30 False representations, etc.

**5.30(1) [Offence]** The debtor commits an offence if he makes any false representation or commits any other fraud for the purpose of obtaining the approval of his creditors to a proposal for a voluntary arrangement under Part VIII of the Act.

**5.30(2) [Penalties]** A person guilty of an offence under this Rule is liable to imprisonment or a fine, or both.

# PART 6 – BANKRUPTCY

## Chapter 1 – The Statutory Demand

### 6.1 Form and content of statutory demand

**6.1(1) [Must be dated and signed]** A statutory demand under section 268 must be dated, and be signed either by the creditor himself or by a person stating himself to be authorised to make the demand on the creditor's behalf.

[FORM 6.1]
or [FORM 6.2]
or [FORM 6.3]

**6.1(2) [Whether s. 268(1) or (2)]** The statutory demand must specify whether it is made under section 268(1) (debt payable immediately) or section 268(2) (debt not so payable).

**6.1(3) [Further contents]** The demand must state the amount of the debt, and the consideration for it (or, if there is no consideration, the way in which it arises) and–

(a) if made under section 268(1) and founded on a judgment or order of a court, it must give details of the judgment or order, and

(b) if made under section 268(2), it must state the grounds on which it is alleged that the debtor appears to have no reasonable prospect of paying the debt.

**6.1(4) [Interest and accruing charges]** If the amount claimed in the demand includes–

(a) any charge by way of interest not previously notified to the debtor as a liability of his, or

(b) any other charge accruing from time to time,

the amount or rate of the charge must be separately identified, and the grounds on which payment of it is claimed must be stated.

In either case the amount claimed must be limited to that which has accrued due at the date of the demand.

**6.1(5) [If creditor holds security]** If the creditor holds any security in respect of the debt, the full amount of the debt shall be specified, but–

(a) there shall in the demand be specified the nature of the security, and the value which the creditor puts upon it as at the date of the demand, and

(b) the amount of which payment is claimed by the demand shall be the full amount of the debt, less the amount specified as the value of the security.

### 6.2 Information to be given in statutory demand

**6.2(1) [Explanation of demand generally]** The statutory demand must include an explanation to the debtor of the following matters–

(a) the purpose of the demand, and the fact that, if the debtor does not comply with the demand, bankruptcy proceedings may be commenced against him;

(b) the time within which the demand must be complied with, if that consequence is to be avoided;

(c) the methods of compliance which are open to the debtor; and

(d) his right to apply to the court for the statutory demand to be set aside.

**6.2(2) [Information re named individuals]** The demand must specify one or more named individuals with whom the debtor may, if he wishes, enter into communication with a view to securing or compounding for the debt to the satisfaction of the creditor or (as the case may be) establishing to the creditor's satisfaction that there is a reasonable prospect that the debt will be paid when it falls due.

In the case of any individual so named in the demand, his address and telephone number (if any) must be given.

## 6.3 Requirements as to service

**6.3(1) [Effect of r. 6.11]** Rule 6.11 in Chapter 2 below has effect as regards service of the statutory demand, and proof of that service by affidavit to be filed with a bankruptcy petition.

**6.3(2) [Creditor's obligation to effect personal service etc.]** The creditor is, by virtue of the Rules, under an obligation to do all that is reasonable for the purpose of bringing the statutory demand to the debtor's attention and, if practicable in the particular circumstances, to cause personal service of the demand to be effected.

**6.3(3) [Advertisement of demand for sum due under judgment etc.]** Where the statutory demand is for payment of a sum due under a judgment or order of any court and the creditor knows, or believes with reasonable cause–

(a) that the debtor has absconded or is keeping out of the way with a view to avoiding service, and

(b) there is no real prospect of the sum due being recovered by execution or other process,

the demand may be advertised in one or more newspapers; and the time limited for compliance with the demand runs from the date of the advertisement's appearance or (as the case may be) its first appearance.

## 6.4 Application to set aside statutory demand

**6.4(1) [Time for application]** The debtor may, within the period allowed by this Rule, apply to the appropriate court for an order setting the statutory demand aside. [FORM 6.4]

That period is 18 days from the date of the service on him of the statutory demand or, where the demand is advertised in a newspaper pursuant to Rule 6.3, from the date of the advertisement's appearance or (as the case may be) its first appearance.

**6.4(2) [Appropriate court where creditor is Minister etc.]** Where the creditor issuing the statutory demand is a Minister of the Crown or a Government Department, and–

(a) the debt in respect of which the demand is made, or a part of it equal to or exceeding the bankruptcy level (within the meaning of section 267), is the subject of a judgment or order of any court, and

(b) the statutory demand specifies the date of the judgment or order and the court in which it was obtained, but indicates the creditor's intention to present a bankruptcy petition against the debtor in the High Court,

the appropriate court under this Rule is the High Court; and in any other case it is that to which the debtor would, in accordance with paragraphs (1) and (2) of Rule 6.40 in Chapter 3 below, present his own bankruptcy petition.

**6.4(3) [Effect of filing application in court]** As from (inclusive) the date on which the application is filed in court, the time limited for compliance with the statutory demand ceases to run, subject to any order of the court under Rule 6.5(6).

**6.4(4) [Supporting affidavit]** The debtor's application shall be supported by an affidavit–

(a) specifying the date on which the statutory demand came into his hands, and

(b) stating the grounds on which he claims that is should be set aside.

The affidavit shall have exhibited to it a copy of the statutory demand. [FORM 6.5]

**Note**

See practice note [1987] 1 WLR 119.

## 6.5 Hearing of application to set aside

**6.5(1) [Court may dismiss application etc.]** On receipt of an application under Rule 6.4, the court may, if satisfied that no sufficient cause is shown for it, dismiss it without giving notice to the creditor. As from (inclusive) the date on which the application is dismissed, the time limited for compliance with the statutory demand runs again.

**6.5(2) [Application not dismissed under r. 6.5(1)]** If the application is not dismissed under paragraph (1), the court shall fix a venue for it to be heard, and shall give at least 7 days' notice of it to–

(a) the debtor or, if the debtor's application was made by a solicitor acting for him, to the solicitor,

(b) the creditor, and

(c) whoever is named in the statutory demand as the person with whom the debtor may enter into communication with reference to the demand (or, if more than one person is so named, the first of them).

**6.5(3) [Summary determination or adjournment]** On the hearing of the application, the court shall consider the evidence then available to it, and may either summarily determine the application or adjourn it, giving such directions as it thinks appropriate.

**6.5(4) [Setting aside demand]** The court may grant the application if–

(a) the debtor appears to have a counterclaim, set-off or cross demand which equals or exceeds the amount of the debt or debts specified in the statutory demand; or

(b) the debt is disputed on grounds which appear to the court to be substantial; or

(c) it appears that the creditor holds some security in respect of the debt claimed by the demand, and either Rule 6.1(5) is not complied with in respect of it, or the court is satisfied that the value of the security equals or exceeds the full amount of the debt; or

(d) the court is satisfied, on other grounds, that the demand ought to be set aside.

[FORM 6.6]

**6.5(5) [Under-valued security]** Where the creditor holds some security in respect of his debt, and Rule 6.1(5) is complied with in respect of it but the court is satisfied that the security is under-valued in the statutory demand, the creditor may be required to amend the demand accordingly (but without prejudice to his right to present a bankruptcy petition by reference to the original demand).

**6.5(6) [On dismissal of application]** If the court dismisses the application, it shall make an order authorising the creditor to present a bankruptcy petition either forthwith, or on or after a date specified in the order.

A copy of the order shall be sent by the court forthwith to the creditor.

# Chapter 2 – Bankruptcy Petition (Creditor's)

## 6.6 Preliminary

**6.6** The Rules in this Chapter relate to a creditor's petition, and the making of a bankruptcy order thereon; and in those Rules **"the debt"** means, except where the context otherwise requires, the debt (or debts) in respect of which the petition is presented.

Those Rules also apply to a petition under section 264(1)(c) (supervisor of, or person bound by, voluntary arrangement), with any necessary modifications. [FORM 6.7]
or [FORM 6.8]
or [FORM 6.9]
or [FORM 6.10]

**Note**

See practice note [1987] 1 WLR 81.

## 6.7 Identification of debtor

**6.7(1) [Contents of petition]** The petition shall state the following matters with respect to the debtor, so far as they are within the petitioner's knowledge–

(a) his name, place of residence and occupation (if any);

(b) the name or names in which he carries on business, if other than his true name, and whether, in the case of any business of a specified nature, he carries it on alone or with others;

(c) the nature of his business, and the address or addresses at which he carries it on;

(d) any name or names, other than his true name, in which he has carried on business at or after the time when the debt was incurred, and whether he has done so alone or with others;

(e) any address or addresses at which he has resided or carried on business at or after that time, and the nature of that business.

**6.7(2) [Title of proceedings]** The particulars of the debtor given under this Rule determine the full title of the proceedings.

**6.7(3) [Debtor's other names]** If to the petitioner's personal knowledge the debtor has used any name other than the one specified under paragraph (1)(a), that fact shall be stated in the petition.

## 6.8 Identification of debt

**6.8(1) [Contents of petition]** There shall be stated in the petition, with reference to every debt in respect of which it is presented–

(a) the amount of the debt, the consideration for it (or, if there is no consideration, the way in which it arises) and the fact that it is owed to the petitioner;

(b) when the debt was incurred or became due;

(c) if the amount of the debt includes–

(i) any charge by way of interest not previously notified to the debtor as a liability of his, or

(ii) any other charge accruing from time to time,

the amount or rate of the charge (separately identified) and the grounds on which it is claimed to form part of the debt, provided that such amount or rate must, in the case of a petition based on a statutory demand, be limited to that claimed in that demand;

(d) either–

(i) that the debt is for a liquidated sum payable immediately, and the debtor appears to be unable to pay it, or

(ii) that the debt is for a liquidated sum payable at some certain, future time (that time to be specified), and the debtor appears to have no reasonable prospect of being able to pay it,

and, in either case (subject to section 269) that the debt is unsecured.

**History**

In r. 6.8(1)(c) the words from ", provided that such amount" to the end added by the Insolvency (Amendment) Rules 1987 (SI 1987/1919), r.3(1), Sch., Pt. 1, para. 91 as from 11 January 1988.

**6.8(2) [Where statutory demand served]** Where the debt is one for which, under section 268, a statutory demand must have been served on the debtor–

(a) there shall be specified the date and manner of service of the statutory demand, and

(b) it shall be stated that, to the best of the creditor's knowledge and belief–

(i) the demand has been neither complied with nor set aside in accordance with the Rules, and

(ii) no application to set it aside is outstanding.

**6.8(3) [If case within s. 268(1)(b)]** If the case is within section 268(1)(b) (debt arising under judgment or order of court; execution returned unsatisfied), the court from which the execution or other process issued shall be specified, and particulars shall be given relating to the return.

## 6.9 Court in which petition to be presented

**6.9(1) [Presentation to High Court]** In the following cases, the petition shall be presented to the High Court–

(a) if the petition is presented by a Minister of the Crown or a Government Department, and either in any statutory demand on which the petition is based the creditor has indicated the intention to present a bankruptcy petition to that Court, or the petition is presented under section 268(1)(b), or

(b) if the debtor has resided or carried on business within the London insolvency district for the greater part of the 6 months immediately preceding the presentation of the petition, or for a longer period in those 6 months than in any other insolvency district, or

(c) if the debtor is not resident in England and Wales, or

(d) if the petitioner is unable to ascertain the residence of the debtor, or his place of business.

**6.9(2) [County court]** In any other case the petition shall be presented to the county court for the insolvency district in which the debtor has resided or carried on business for the longest period during those 6 months.

**6.9(3) [Insolvency districts]** If the debtor has for the greater part of those 6 months carried on business in one insolvency district and resided in another, the petition shall be presented to the court for the insolvency district in which he has carried on business.

**6.9(4) [Principal place of business]** If the debtor has during those 6 months carried on business in more than one insolvency district, the petition shall be presented to the court for the insolvency district in which is, or has been for the longest period in those 6 months, his principal place of business.

**6.9(4A) [Voluntary arrangement in force]** Notwithstanding any other provision of this Rule, where there is in force for the debtor a voluntary arrangement under Part VIII of the Act, the petition shall be presented to the court to which the nominee's report under section 256 was submitted.

**History**

R. 6.9(4A) inserted by the Insolvency (Amendment) Rules 1987 (SI 1987/1919), r. 3(1), Sch., Pt. 1, para. 92 as from 11 January 1988.

**6.9(5) [Establishing appropriate court]** The petition shall contain sufficient information to establish that it is brought in the appropriate court.

## 6.10 Procedure for presentation and filing

**6.10(1) [Filing with verifying affidavit]** The petition, verified by affidavit in accordance with Rule 6.12(1) below, shall be filed in court.

**6.10(2) [Receipt for deposit payable on presentation]** No petition shall be filed unless there is produced with it the receipt for the deposit payable on presentation.

**6.10(3) [Copies of petition]** The following copies of the petition shall also be delivered to the court with the petition–

(a) one for service on the debtor,

(b) one to be exhibited to the affidavit verifying that service, and

(c) if there is in force for the debtor a voluntary arrangement under Part VIII of the Act, and the petitioner is not the supervisor of the arrangement, one copy for him.

Each of these copies shall have applied to it the seal of the court, and shall be issued to the petitioner.

**History**

In r. 6.10(3) the word "and" formerly at the end of para. (a) omitted and the word ", and" and para. (c) added at the end of para. (b) by the Insolvency (Amendment) Rules 1987 (SI 1987/1919), r. 3(1), Sch., Pt. 1, para. 93(1) as from 11 January 1988.

**6.10(4) [Endorsing of r. 6.10(3) copies]** The date and time of filing the petition shall be endorsed on the petition and on any copy issued under paragraph (3).

**6.10(5) [Venue for hearing]** The court shall fix a venue for hearing the petition, and this also shall be endorsed on the petition and on any copy so issued.

**6.10(6) [Former supervisor requested as trustee]** Where a petition contains a request for the appointment of a person as trustee in accordance with section 297(5) (appointment of former supervisor as trustee) the person whose appointment is sought shall, not less than 2 days before the day appointed for hearing the petition, file in court a report including particulars of–

(a) a date on which he gave written notification to creditors bound by the arrangement of the intention to seek his appointment as trustee, such date to be at least 10 days before the day on which the report under this paragraph is filed, and

(b) details of any response from creditors to that notice, including any objections to his appointment.

**History**

R. 6.10(6) added by the Insolvency (Amendment) Rules 1987 (SI 1987/1919), r. 3(1), Sch., Pt. 1, para. 93(2) as from 11 January 1988.

# 6.11 Proof of service of statutory demand

**6.11(1) [Affidavit of service]** Where under section 268 the petition must have been preceded by a statutory demand, there must be filed in court, with the petition, an affidavit or affidavits proving service of the demand.

**History**

In r. 6.11(1) the words "or affidavits" inserted by the Insolvency (Amendment) Rules 1987 (SI 1987/1919), r. 3(1), Sch., Pt. 1, para. 94(1) as from 11 January 1988.

**6.11(2) [Copy of demand to be exhibited]** Every affidavit must have exhibited to it a copy of the demand as served.

**History**

In r. 6.11(2) the words "Every affidavit" substituted for the former words "The affidavit" by the Insolvency (Amendment) Rules 1987 (SI 1987/1919), r. 3(1), Sch., Pt. 1, para. 94(2) as from 11 January 1988.

**6.11(3) [Affidavit of personal service]** Subject to the next paragraph, if the demand has been served personally on the debtor, the affidavit must be made by the person who effected that service. [FORM 6.11]

**6.11(4) [If service of demand acknowledged]** If service of the demand (however effected) has been acknowledged in writing either by the debtor himself, or by some person stating himself in the acknowledgement to be authorised to accept service on the debtor's behalf, the affidavit must be made either by the creditor or by a person acting on his behalf, and the acknowledgement of service must be exhibited to the affidavit.

**6.11(5) [If neither r. 6.11(3) or (4) applies]** If neither paragraph (3) nor paragraph (4) applies, the affidavit or affidavits must be made by a person or persons having direct personal knowledge of the means adopted for serving the statutory demand, and must–

(a) give particulars of the steps which have been taken with a view to serving the demand personally, and

(b) state the means whereby (those steps having been ineffective) it was sought to bring the demand to the debtor's attention, and

(c) specify a date by which, to the best of the knowledge, information and belief of the person making the affidavit, the demand will have come to the debtor's attention.

[FORM 6.12]

**History**

In r. 6.11(5) the words "or affidavits", "or persons" and "personally" (in para. (a)) inserted by the Insolvency (Amendment) Rules 1987 (SI 1987/1919), r. 3(1), Sch., Pt. 1, para. 94(3) as from 11 January 1988.

**6.11(6) [Sufficiency of r. 6.11(5)(a) particulars]** The steps of which particulars are given for the purposes of paragraph (5)(a) must be such as would have sufficed to justify an order for substituted service of a petition.

**6.11(7) [Deemed date of service]** If the affidavit specifies a date for the purposes of compliance with paragraph (5)(c), then unless the court otherwise orders, that date is deemed for the purposes of the Rules to have been the date on which the statutory demand was served on the debtor.

**6.11(8) [Newspaper advertisement]** Where the creditor has taken advantage of Rule 6.3(3) (newspaper advertisement), the affidavit must be made either by the creditor himself or by a person having direct personal knowledge of the circumstances; and there must be specified in the affidavit–

(a) the means of the creditor's knowledge or (as the case may be) belief required for the purposes of that Rule, and

(b) the date or dates on which, and the newspaper in which, the statutory demand was advertised under that Rule;

and there shall be exhibited to the affidavit a copy of any advertisement of the statutory demand.

**6.11(9) [Discharge of r. 6.3(2) obligation]** The court may decline to file the petition if not satisfied that the creditor has discharged the obligation imposed on him by Rule 6.3(2).

**Note**

See practice note [1987] 1 WLR 85.

## 6.12 Verification of petition

**6.12(1) [Verifying affidavit]** The petition shall be verified by an affidavit that the statements in the petition are true, or are true to the best of the deponent's knowledge, information and belief.
[FORM 6.13]

**6.12(2) [Debts due to different creditors]** If the petition is in respect of debts to different creditors, the debts to each creditor must be separately verified.

**6.12(3) [Petition to be exhibited]** The petition shall be exhibited to the affidavit verifying it.

**6.12(4) [Who shall make the affidavit]** The affidavit shall be made–

(a) by the petitioner (or if there are two or more petitioners, any one of them), or

(b) by some person such as a director, company secretary or similar company officer, or a solicitor, who has been concerned in the matters giving rise to the presentation of the petition, or

(c) by some responsible person who is duly authorised to make the affidavit and has the requisite knowledge of those matters.

**6.12(5) [Where deponent not petitioner]** Where the maker of the affidavit is not the petitioner himself, or one of the petitioners, he must in the affidavit identify himself and state–

(a) the capacity in which, and the authority by which, he makes it, and

(b) the means of his knowledge of the matters sworn to in the affidavit.

**6.12(6) [Affidavit as prima facie evidence]** The affidavit is prima facie evidence of the truth of the statements in the petition to which it relates.

**6.12(7) [Delay between demand and petition]** If the petition is based upon a statutory demand, and more than 4 months have elapsed between the service of the demand and the presentation of the petition, the affidavit must also state the reasons for the delay.

## 6.13 Notice to Chief Land Registrar

**6.13** When the petition is filed, the court shall forthwith send to the Chief Land Registrar notice of the petition together with a request that it may be registered in the register of pending actions.
[FORM 6.14]

## 6.14 Service of petition

**6.14(1) [Personal service]** Subject as follows, the petition shall be served personally on the debtor by an officer of the court, or by the petitioning creditor or his solicitor, or by a person instructed by the creditor or his solicitor for that purpose; and service shall be effected by delivering to him a sealed copy of the petition.

**6.14(2) [Substituted service]** If the court is satisfied by affidavit or other evidence on oath that prompt personal service cannot be effected because the debtor is keeping out of the way to avoid service of the petition or other legal process, or for any other cause, it may order substituted service to be effected in such manner as it thinks fit.

**6.14(3) [Deemed service]** Where an order for substituted service has been carried out, the petition is deemed duly served on the debtor.
[FORM 6.15]
[FORM 6.16]

**6.14(4) [If voluntary arrangement in force]** If to the petitioner's knowledge there is in force for the debtor a voluntary arrangement under Part VIII of the Act, and the petitioner is not himself the supervisor of the arrangement, a copy of the petition shall be sent by him to the supervisor.

**History**

R. 6.14(4) added by the Insolvency (Amendment) Rules 1987 (SI 1987/1919), r. 3(1), Sch., Pt. 1, para. 95 as from 11 January 1988.

## 6.15 Proof of service

**6.15(1) [Affidavit of service]** Service of the petition shall be proved by affidavit.

**6.15(2) [Exhibits]** The affidavit shall have exhibited to it–

(a) a sealed copy of the petition, and

(b) if substituted service has been ordered, a sealed copy of the order;

and it shall be filed in court immediately after service. [FORM 6.17] or [FORM 6.18]

## 6.16 Death of debtor before service

**6.16** If the debtor dies before service of the petition, the court may order service to be effected on his personal representatives or on such other persons as it thinks fit.

## 6.17 Security for costs (s. 268(2) only)

**6.17(1) [Application of Rule]** This Rule applies where the debt in respect of which the petition is presented is for a liquidated sum payable at some future time, it being claimed in the petition that the debtor appears to have no reasonable prospect of being able to pay it.

**6.17(2) [Debtor's application for security]** The petitioning creditor may, on the debtor's application, be ordered to give security for the debtor's costs.

**6.17(3) [Court's discretion]** The nature and amount of the security to be ordered is in the court's discretion.

**6.17(4) [If order made]** If an order is made under this Rule, there shall be no hearing of the petition until the whole amount of the security has been given.

## 6.18 Hearing of petition

**6.18(1) [Time for hearing]** Subject as follows, the petition shall not be heard until at least 14 days have elapsed since it was served on the debtor.

**6.18(2) [Expedited hearing]** The court may, on such terms as it thinks fit, hear the petition at an earlier date, if it appears that the debtor has absconded, or the court is satisfied that is is a proper case for an expedited hearing, or the debtor consents to a hearing within the 14 days.

**6.18(3) [Appearances]** Any of the following may appear and be heard, that is to say, the petitioning creditor, the debtor, the supervisor of any voluntary arrangement under Part VIII of the Act in force for the debtor and any creditor who has given notice under Rule 6.23 below.

**History**

In r. 6.18(3) the words from ", the supervisor" to "in force for the debtor" inserted by the Insolvency (Amendment) Rules 1987 (SI 1987/1919), r. 3(1), Sch., Pt. 1, para. 96 as from 11 January 1988.

## 6.19 Petition against two or more debtors

**6.19** (Omitted by the Insolvency (Amendment) Rules 1987 (SI 1987/1919), r. 3(1), Sch., Pt. 1, para. 97 as from 11 January 1988).

**History**

R. 6.19 formerly read as follows:

"Where two or more debtors are named in the petition, and the petition has not been served on both or all of them, the petition may be heard separately or collectively as regards any of those who have been served, and may subsequently be heard (separately or collectively) as regards the others, as and when service on them is effected."

## 6.20 Petition by moneylender

**6.20** A petition in respect of a moneylending transaction made before 27th January 1980 of a creditor who at the time of the transaction was a licensed moneylender shall at the hearing of the petition be supported by an affidavit incorporating a statement setting out in detail the particulars mentioned in section 9(2) of the Moneylenders Act 1927.

## 6.21 Petition opposed by debtor

**6.21** Where the debtor intends to oppose the petition, he shall not later than 7 days before the day fixed for the hearing–

(a) file in court a notice specifying the grounds on which he will object to the making of a bankruptcy order, and

(b) send a copy of the notice to the petitioning creditor or his solicitor. [FORM 6.19]

## 6.22 Amendment of petition

**6.22** With the leave of the court (given on such terms, if any, as the court thinks fit to impose), the petition may be amended at any time after presentation by the omission of any creditor or any debt.

## 6.23 Notice by persons intending to appear

**6.23(1) [Notice of intention]** Every creditor who intends to appear on the hearing of the petition shall give to the petitioning creditor notice of his intention in accordance with this Rule. [FORM 6.20]

**6.23(2) [Contents of notice]** The notice shall specify–

(a) the name and address of the person giving it, and any telephone number and reference which may be required for communication with him or with any other person (to be also specified in the notice) authorised to speak or act on his behalf;

(b) whether his intention is to support or oppose the petition; and

(c) the amount and nature of his debt.

**6.23(3) [Time for sending notice]** The notice shall be sent so as to reach the addressee not later than 16.00 hours on the business day before that which is appointed for the hearing (or, where the hearing has been adjourned, for the adjourned hearing).

**6.23(4) [Effect of non-compliance]** A person failing to comply with this Rule may appear on the hearing of the petition only with the leave of the court.

## 6.24 List of appearances

**6.24(1) [Petitioning creditor to prepare list]** The petitioning creditor shall prepare for the court a list of the creditors (if any) who have given notice under Rule 6.23, specifying their names and addresses and (if known to him) their respective solicitors. [FORM 6.21]

**6.24(2) [Whether creditors support or oppose]** Against the name of each creditor in the list it shall be stated whether his intention is to support the petition, or to oppose it.

**6.24(3) [Copy list handed to court]** On the day appointed for the hearing of the petition, a copy of the list shall be handed to the court before the commencement of the hearing.

**6.24(4) [Leave under r. 6.23(4)]** If any leave is given under Rule 6.23(4), the petitioner shall add to the list the same particulars in respect of the person to whom leave has been given.

## 6.25 Decision on the hearing

**6.25(1) [Bankruptcy order]** On the hearing of the petition, the court may make a bankruptcy order if satisfied that the statements in the petition are true, and that the debt on which it is founded has not been paid, or secured or compounded for.

**6.25(2) [Stay or dismissal]** If the petition is brought in respect of a judgment debt, or a sum ordered by any court to be paid, the court may stay or dismiss the petition on the ground that an appeal is pending from the judgment or order, or that execution of the judgment has been stayed. [FORM 6.22]

**6.25(3) [Debt over-stated in demand]** A petition preceded by a statutory demand shall not be dismissed on the ground only that the amount of the debt was over-stated in the demand, unless the debtor, within the time allowed for complying with the demand, gave notice to the creditor disputing the validity of the demand on that ground; but, in the absence of such notice, the debtor is deemed to have complied with the demand if he has, within the time allowed, paid the correct amount.

**Note**

See practice note [1987] 1 WLR 120.

## 6.26 Non-appearance of creditor

**6.26** If the petitioning creditor fails to appear on the hearing of the petition, no subsequent petition against the same debtor, either alone or jointly with any other person, shall be presented by the same creditor in respect of the same debt, without the leave of the court to which the previous petition was presented.

## 6.27 Vacating registration on dismissal of petition

**6.27** If the petition is dismissed or withdrawn by leave of the court, an order shall be made at the same time permitting vacation of the registration of the petition as a pending action; and the court shall send to the debtor two sealed copies of the order. [FORM 6.22]

## 6.28 Extension of time for hearing

**6.28(1) [If petition not served]** The petitioning creditor may, if the petition has not been served, apply to the court to appoint another venue for the hearing.

**6.28(2) [Why petition not served]** The application shall state the reasons why the petition has not been served.

**6.28(3) [Costs]** No costs occasioned by the application shall be allowed in the proceedings except by order of the court.

**6.28(4) [Notification of creditors]** If the court appoints another day for the hearing, the petitioning creditor shall forthwith notify any creditor who has given notice under Rule 6.23.

## 6.29 Adjournment

**6.29(1) [Application of Rule]** If the court adjourns the hearing of the petition, the following applies. [FORM 6.23]

**6.29(2) [Notice of adjournment]** Unless the court otherwise directs, the petitioning creditor shall forthwith send–

(a) to the debtor, and

(b) where any creditor has given notice under Rule 6.23 but was not present at the hearing, to him,

notice of the making of the order of adjournment. The notice shall state the venue for the adjourned hearing. [FORM 6.24]

## 6.30 Substitution of petitioner

**6.30(1) [Application of Rule]** This Rule applies where a creditor petitions and is subsequently found not entitled to do so, or where the petitioner–

(a) consents to withdraw his petition or to allow it to be dismissed, or consents to an adjournment, or fails to appear in support of his petition when it is called on in court on the day originally fixed for the hearing, or on a day to which it is adjourned, or

(b) appears, but does not apply for an order in terms of the prayer of his petition.

**6.30(2) [Substitution]** The court may, on such terms as it thinks just, order that there be substituted as petitioner any creditor who–

(a) has under Rule 6.23 given notice of his intention to appear at the hearing,

(b) is desirous of prosecuting the petition, and

(c) was, at the date on which the petition was presented, in such a position in relation to the debtor as would have enabled him (the creditor) on that date to present a bankruptcy petition in respect of a debt or debts owed to him by the debtor, paragraphs (a) to (d) of section 267(2) being satisfied in respect of that debt or those debts. [FORM 6.24A]

**History**

Against r. 6.30(2) the words "[FORM 6.24A]" inserted by the Insolvency (Amendment) Rules 1987 (SI 1987/1919), r. 3(1), Sch., Pt. 2, para. 156(1) as from 11 January 1988.

## 6.31 Change of carriage of petition

**6.31(1) [Application by creditor]** On the hearing of the petition, any person who claims to be a creditor of the debtor, and who has given notice under Rule 6.23 of his intention to appear at the hearing, may apply to the court for an order giving him carriage of the petition in place of the petitioning creditor, but without requiring any amendment of the petition.

**6.31(2) [Powers of court]** The court may, on such terms as it thinks just, make a change of carriage order if satisfied that–

(a) the applicant is an unpaid and unsecured creditor of the debtor, and

(b) the petitioning creditor either–

(i) intends by any means to secure the postponement, adjournment or withdrawal of the petition, or

(ii) does not intend to prosecute the petition, either diligently or at all. [FORM 6.24B]

**History**

Against r. 6.31(2) the words "[FORM 6.24B]" inserted by the Insolvency (Amendment) Rules 1987 (SI 1987/1919), r. 3(1), Sch., Pt. 2, para. 156(1) as from 11 January 1988.

**6.31(3) [Where court not to make order]** The court shall not make the order if satisfied that the petitioning creditor's debt has been paid, secured or compounded for by means of–

(a) a disposition of property made by some person other than the debtor, or

(b) a disposition of the debtor's own property made with the approval of, or ratified by, the court.

**6.31(4) [Appearance by petitioning creditor]** A change of carriage order may be made whether or not the petitioning creditor appears at the hearing.

**6.31(5) [If order made]** If the order is made, the person given the carriage of the petition is entitled to rely on all evidence previously adduced in the proceedings (whether by affidavit or otherwise).

# 6.32 Petitioner seeking dismissal or leave to withdraw

**6.32(1) [Affidavit specifying grounds of application etc.]** Where the petitioner applies to the court for the petition to be dismissed, or for leave to withdraw it, he must, unless the court otherwise orders, file in court an affidavit specifying the grounds of the application and the circumstances in which it is made.

**6.32(2) [If payment made since petition filed]** If, since the petition was filed, any payment has been made to the petitioner by way of settlement (in whole or in part) of the debt or debts in respect of which the petition was brought, or any arrangement has been entered into for securing or compounding it or them, the affidavit must state–

(a) what dispositions of property have been made for the purposes of the settlement or arrangement, and

(b) whether, in the case of any disposition, it was property of the debtor himself, or of some other person, and

(c) whether, if it was property of the debtor, the disposition was made with the approval of, or has been ratified by, the court (if so, specifying the relevant court order).

**6.32(3) [No order before hearing]** No order giving leave to withdraw a petition shall be given before the petition is heard. [FORM 6.22]

# 6.33 Settlement and content of bankruptcy order

**6.33(1) [Order to be settled by court]** The bankruptcy order shall be settled by the court. [FORM 6.25]

**6.33(2) [Contents of order]** The order shall–

(a) state the date of the presentation of the petition on which the order is made, and the date and time of the making of the order, and

(b) contain a notice requiring the bankrupt, forthwith after service of the order on him, to attend on the official receiver at the place stated in the order.

**6.33(3) [Order staying proceedings]** Subject to section 346 (effect of bankruptcy on enforcement procedures), the order may include provision staying any action or proceeding against the bankrupt.

**6.33(4) [Where petitioning creditor represented by solicitor]** Where the petitioning creditor is represented by a solicitor, the order shall be endorsed with the latter's name, address, telephone number and reference (if any).

## 6.34 Action to follow making of order

**6.34(1) [Copies of order to official receiver etc.]** At least two sealed copies of the bankruptcy order shall be sent forthwith by the court to the official receiver, who shall forthwith send one of them to the bankrupt.

**6.34(2) [Official receiver to send notice etc.]** Subject to the next paragraph, the official receiver shall–

(a) send notice of the making of the order to the Chief Land Registrar, for registration in the register of writs and orders affecting land,

(b) cause the order to be advertised in such newspaper as the official receiver thinks fit, and

(c) cause the order to be gazetted. [FORM 6.26]

**History**

In r. 6.34(2) the word "newspaper" substituted for the former words "local paper" by the Insolvency (Amendment) Rules 1991 (SI 1991/495), r. 3, Sch., para. 3 as from 2 April 1991.

**6.34(3) [Suspension of action under r. 6.34(2)]** The court may, on the application of the bankrupt or a creditor, order the official receiver to suspend action under paragraph (2) and Rule 6.223(B)(1), pending a further order of the court.

An application under this paragraph shall be supported by an affidavit stating the grounds on which it is made.

**History**

In r. 6.34(3) the words "and Rule 6.223(B)(1)" inserted by the Insolvency (Amendment) Rules 1999 (SI 1999/359), r. 1, Sch., para. 4 as from 22 March 1999.

**6.34(4) [Where order made under r.6.34(3)]** Where an order is made under paragraph (3), the applicant for the order shall forthwith deliver a copy of it to the official receiver.

## 6.35 Amendment of title of proceedings

**6.35(1) [Application for amendment]** At any time after the making of a bankruptcy order, the official receiver or the trustee may apply to the court for an order amending the full title of the proceedings.

**6.35(2) [Where amendment order made]** Where such an order is made, the official receiver shall forthwith send notice of it to the Chief Land Registrar, for corresponding amendment of the register; and, if the court so directs he shall also cause notice of the order to be gazetted, and to be advertised in such newspaper as the official receiver thinks fit.

**History**

In r. 6.35(2) the word "local" formerly appearing before the word "newspaper" omitted by the Insolvency (Amendment) Rules 1991 (SI 1991/495), r. 3, Sch., para. 3 as from 2 April 1991.

## 6.36 Old bankruptcy notices

**6.36(1) [Proceeding on old notice]** Subject as follows, a person who has before the appointed day for the purposes of the Act served a bankruptcy notice under the Bankruptcy Act 1914 may, on or after that day, proceed on the notice as if it were a statutory demand duly served under Chapter 1 of this Part of the Rules.

**6.36(2) [Conditions of application of Rule]** The conditions of the application of this Rule are that–

(a) the debt in respect of which the bankruptcy notice was served has not been paid, secured or compounded for in the terms of the notice and the Act of 1914;

(b) the date by which compliance with the notice was required was not more than 3 months before the date of presentation of the petition; and

(c) there has not, before the appointed day, been presented any bankruptcy petition with reference to an act of bankruptcy arising from non-compliance with the bankruptcy notice.

**6.36(3) [Application to set old notice aside]** If before, on or after the appointed day, application is made (under the Act of 1914) to set the bankruptcy notice aside, that application is to be treated, on and after that day, as an application duly made (on the date on which it was in fact made) to set aside a statutory demand duly served on the date on which the bankruptcy notice was in fact served.

# Chapter 3 – Bankruptcy Petition (Debtor's)

## 6.37 Preliminary

**6.37** The Rules in this Chapter relate to a debtor's petition, and the making of a bankruptcy order thereon. [FORM 6.27]

## 6.38 Identification of debtor

**6.38(1) [Contents of petition]** The petition shall state the following matters with respect to the debtor–

(a) his name, place of residence and occupation (if any);

(b) the name or names in which he carries on business, if other than his true name, and whether, in the case of any business of a specified nature, he carries it on alone or with others;

(c) the nature of his business, and the address or addresses at which he carries it on;

(d) any name or names, other than his true name, in which he has carried on business in the period in which any of his bankruptcy debts were incurred and, in the case of any such business, whether he had carried it on alone or with others; and

(e) any address or addresses at which he has resided or carried on business during that period, and the nature of that business.

**6.38(2) [Title of proceedings]** The particulars of the debtor given under this Rule determine the full title of the proceedings.

**6.38(3) [Debtor's other names]** If the debtor has at any time used a name other than the one given under paragraph (1)(a), that fact shall be stated in the petition.

## 6.39 Admission of insolvency

**6.39(1) [Contents of petition]** The petition shall contain the statement that the petitioner is unable to pay his debts, and a request that a bankruptcy order be made against him.

**6.39(2) [Particulars in preceding five-year period]** If within the period of 5 years ending with the date of the petition the petitioner has been adjudged bankrupt, or has made a composition with his creditors in satisfaction of his debts or a scheme of arrangement of his affairs, or he has entered into any voluntary arrangement or been subject to an administration order under Part VI of the County Courts Act 1984, particulars of these matters shall be given in the petition.

**6.39(3) [If voluntary arrangement in force]** If there is at the date of the petition in force for the debtor a voluntary arrangement under Part VIII of the Act, the particulars required by paragraph (2) above shall contain a statement to that effect and the name and address of the supervisor of the arrangement.

**History**
R. 6.39(3) added by the Insolvency (Amendment) Rules 1987 (SI 1987/1919), r. 3(1), Sch., Pt. 1, para. 98 as from 11 January 1988.

## 6.40 Court in which petition to be filed

**6.40(1) [Presentation to High Court]** In the following cases, the petition shall be presented to the High Court–

(a) if the debtor has resided or carried on business in the London insolvency district for the greater part of the 6 months immediately preceding the presentation of the petition, or for a longer period in those 6 months than in any other insolvency district, or

(b) if the debtor is not resident in England and Wales.

**6.40(2) [County court]** In any other case, the petition shall (subject to paragraph (3) below), be presented to the debtor's own county court, which is–

(a) the county court for the insolvency district in which he has resided or carried on business for the longest period in those 6 months, or

(b) if he has for the greater part of those 6 months carried on business in one insolvency district and resided in another, the county court for that in which he has carried on business, or

(c) if he has during those 6 months carried on business in more than one insolvency district, the county court for that in which is, or has been for the longest period in those 6 months, his principal place of business.

**6.40(3) [Case not falling within r. 6.40(1)]** If, in a case not falling within paragraph (1), it is more expedient for the debtor with a view to expediting his petition–

(a) it may in any case be presented to whichever court is specified by Schedule 2 to the Rules as being, in relation to the debtor's own court, the nearest full-time court, and

(b) it may alternatively, in a case falling within paragraph (2)(b), be presented to the court for the insolvency district in which he has resided for the greater part of the 6 months there referred to.

**6.40(3A) [Where voluntary arrangement in force]** Notwithstanding any other provision of this Rule, where there is in force for the debtor a voluntary arrangement under Part VIII of the Act the petition shall be presented to the court to which the nominee's report under section 256 was submitted.

**History**

R. 6.40(3) and (3A) substituted for the former r. 6.40(3) by the Insolvency (Amendment) Rules 1987 (SI 1987/1919), r. 3(1), Sch., Pt. 1, para. 99 as from 11 January 1988; the former r. 6.40(3) read as follows:

"If, in a case not falling within paragraph (1), it is more expedient for the debtor with a view to expediting his petition, it may be presented to whichever county court is specified by Schedule 2 to the Rules as being, in relation to the debtor's own county court, the nearest full-time court."

**6.40(4) [Establishing appropriateness of court]** The petition shall contain sufficient information to establish that it is brought in the appropriate court.

## 6.41 Statement of affairs

**6.41(1) [Accompanying statement etc.]** The petition shall be accompanied by a statement of the debtor's affairs, verified by affidavit.
[FORM 6.28]

**6.41(2) [Application of Section B of Ch. 5]** Section B of Chapter 5 below applies with respect to the statement of affairs.

## 6.42 Procedure for presentation and filing

**6.42(1) [Filing in court]** The petition and the statement of affairs shall be filed in court, together with three copies of the petition, and two copies of the statement. No petition shall be filed unless there is produced with it the receipt for the deposit payable on presentation.

**6.42(2) [Powers of court]** Subject to paragraph (2A), the court may hear the petition forthwith. If it does not do so, it shall fix a venue for the hearing.

**History**

In r. 6.42(2) the words "Subject to paragraph (2A)," inserted by the Insolvency (Amendment) Rules 1987 (SI 1987/1919), r. 3(1), Sch., Pt. 1, para. 100(1) as from 11 January 1988.

**6.42(2A) [If petition refers to voluntary arrangement]** If the petition contains particulars of a voluntary arrangement under Part VIII of the Act in force for the debtor, the court shall fix a venue for the hearing and give at least 14 days' notice of it to the supervisor of the arrangement; the supervisor may appear and be heard on the petition.

**History**

R. 6.42(2A) inserted by the Insolvency (Amendment) Rules 1987 (SI 1987/1919), r. 3(1), Sch., Pt. 1, para. 100(2) as from 11 January 1988.

**6.42(3) [Copies of petition]** Of the three copies of the petition delivered–

(a) one shall be returned to the petitioner, endorsed with any venue fixed;
(b) another, so endorsed, shall be sent by the court to the official receiver; and
(c) the remaining copy shall be retained by the court, to be sent to an insolvency practitioner (if appointed under section 273(2)).

**History**
In r. 6.42(3)(b) the words "sent by the court to the official receiver; and" substituted by the Insolvency (Amendment) Rules 1987 (SI 1987/1919), r. 3(1), Sch., Pt. 1, para. 100(3) as from 11 January 1988; the former words read as follows: "retained by the court, to be sent to the official receiver if he is appointed interim receiver or a bankruptcy order is made; and".

**6.42(4) [Copies of statement of affairs]** Of the two copies of the statement of affairs–
(a) one shall be sent by the court to the official receiver; and
(b) the other shall be retained by the court to be sent to the insolvency practitioner (if appointed).

**History**
R. 6.42(4)(a) substituted by the Insolvency (Amendment) Rules 1987 (SI 1987/1919), r. 3(1), Sch., Pt. 1, para. 100(4) as from 11 January 1988; the former words read as follows:
"(a) one shall be retained by the court, to be sent to the official receiver if he is appointed interim receiver or a bankruptcy order is made; and".

**6.42(5) [Swearing verifying affidavit]** The affidavit verifying the debtor's statement of affairs may be sworn before an officer of the court duly authorised in that behalf.

**6.42(6) [Documents to official receiver]** Where the court hears a petition forthwith, or it will in the opinion of the court otherwise expedite the delivery of any document to the official receiver, the court may, instead of sending that document to the official receiver, direct the bankrupt forthwith to deliver it to him.

**6.42(7) [Former supervisor requested as trustee]** Where a petition contains a request for the appointment of a person as trustee in accordance with section 297(5) (appointment of former supervisor as trustee) the person whose appointment is sought shall, not less than 2 days before the day appointed for hearing the petition, file in court a report including particulars of–
(a) a date on which he gave written notification to creditors bound by the arrangement of the intention to seek his appointment as trustee, such date to be at least 10 days before the day on which the report under this paragraph is filed, and
(b) details of any response from creditors to that notice, including any objections to his appointment.

**History**
R. 6.42(6) and (7) added by the Insolvency (Amendment) Rules 1987 (SI 1987/1919), r. 3(1), Sch., Pt. 1, para. 100(5) as from 11 January 1988.

# 6.43 Notice to Chief Land Registrar

**6.43** When the petition is filed, the court shall forthwith send to the Chief Land Registrar notice of the petition, for registration in the register of pending actions. [FORM 6.14]

# 6.44 Report of insolvency practitioner

**6.44(1) [If court appoints insolvency practitioner]** If the court under section 273(2) appoints an insolvency practitioner to act in the debtor's case, it shall forthwith–
(a) send to the person appointed–
  (i) a sealed copy of the order of appointment, and
  (ii) copies of the petition and statement of affairs,
(b) fix a venue for the insolvency practitioner's report to be considered, and
(c) send notice of the venue to the insolvency practitioner and the debtor. [FORM 6.29]

**6.44(2) [Insolvency practitioner's report]** The insolvency practitioner shall file his report in court and send one copy of it to the debtor, so as to be in his hands not less than 3 days before the date fixed for consideration of the report, and a further copy to the official receiver.

**History**
In r. 6.44(2) the words "with one copy," formerly appearing after the words "report in court" omitted and the words ", and a further copy to the official receiver" added by the Insolvency (Amendment) Rules 1987 (SI 1987/1919), r. 3(1), Sch., Pt. 1, para. 101(1) as from 11 January 1988.

**6.44(3) [Debtor's attendance etc.]** The debtor is entitled to attend when the report is considered, and shall attend if so directed by the court. If he attends, the court shall hear any representations which he makes with respect to any of the matters dealt with in the report.

**6.44(4)** (Omitted by the Insolvency (Amendment) Rules 1987 (SI 1987/1919), r. 3(1), Sch., Pt. 1, para. 101(2) as from 11 January 1988).

**History**
R. 6.44(4) formerly read as follows:
"If the official receiver is appointed interim receiver or a bankruptcy order is made, a copy of the insolvency practitioner's report, the debtor's petition and his statement of affairs shall be sent by the court to the official receiver."

## 6.45 Settlement and content of bankruptcy order

**6.45(1) [Order to be settled by court]** The bankruptcy order shall be settled by the court.

[FORM 6.30]

**6.45(2) [Contents of order]** The order shall–

(a) state the date of the presentation of the petition on which the order is made, and the date and time of the making of the order, and

(b) contain a notice requiring the bankrupt, forthwith after the service of the order on him, to attend on the official receiver at the place stated in the order.

**6.45(3) [Order staying proceedings]** Subject to section 346 (effect of bankruptcy on enforcement procedures), the order may include provision staying any action or proceeding against the bankrupt.

**6.45(4) [Where bankrupt represented by solicitor]** Where the bankrupt is represented by a solicitor, the order shall be endorsed with the latter's name, address, telephone number and reference.

## 6.46 Action to follow making of order

**6.46(1) [Copy orders to official receiver etc.]** At least two sealed copies of the bankruptcy order shall be sent forthwith by the court to the official receiver, who shall forthwith send one of them to the bankrupt.

**6.46(2) [Official receiver to send notice etc.]** Subject to the next paragraph, the official receiver shall–

(a) send notice of the making of the order to the Chief Land Registrar, for registration in the register of writs and orders affecting land,

(b) cause the order to be advertised in such newspaper as the official receiver thinks fit, and

(c) cause notice of the order to be gazetted. [FORM 6.26]

**History**
In r. 6.46(2) the word "newspaper" substituted for the former words "local paper" by the Insolvency (Amendment) Rules 1991 (SI 1991/495), r. 3, Sch., para. 3 as from 2 April 1991.

**6.46(3) [Suspension of action under r. 6.46(2)]** The court may, on the application of the bankrupt or a creditor, order the official receiver to suspend action under paragraph (2) and Rule 6.223(B)(1), pending a further order of the court.

An application under this paragraph shall be supported by an affidavit stating the grounds on which it is made.

**History**
In r. 6.46(3) the words "and Rule 6.223(B)(1)" inserted by the Insolvency (Amendment) Rules 1999 (SI 1999/359), r. 1, Sch., para. 5 as from 22 March 1999.

**6.46(4) [Where order made under r. 6.46(3)]** Where an order is made under paragraph (3), the applicant shall forthwith deliver a copy of it to the official receiver.

## 6.46A Expenses of voluntary arrangement

**6.46A** Where a bankruptcy order is made on a debtor's petition and there is at the time of the petition in force for the debtor a voluntary arrangement under Part VIII of the Act, any expenses properly incurred as expenses of the administration of the arrangement in question shall be a first charge on the bankrupt's estate.

**History**
R. 6.46A inserted by the Insolvency (Amendment) Rules 1987 (SI 1987/1919), r. 3(1), Sch., Pt. 1, para. 102 as from 11 January 1988.

## 6.47 Amendment of title of proceedings

**6.47(1) [Application for amendment]** At any time after the making of the bankruptcy order, the official receiver or the trustee may apply to the court for an order amending the full title of the proceedings.

**6.47(2) [Where amendment order made]** Where such an order is made, the official receiver shall forthwith send notice of it to the Chief Land Registrar, for corresponding amendment of the register; and, if the court so directs, he shall also–

(a) cause notice of the order to be gazetted, and

(b) cause notice of the order to be advertised in such newspaper as the official receiver thinks appropriate.

**History**
In r. 6.47(2) the word "newspaper" substituted for the former words "local paper" by the Insolvency (Amendment) Rules 1991 (SI 1991/495), r. 3, Sch., para. 3 as from 2 April 1991.

## 6.48 Certificate of summary administration

**6.48(1) [S. 275 certificate]** If the court under section 275 issues a certificate for the summary administration of the bankrupt's estate, the certificate may be included in the bankruptcy order.
[FORM 6.30]

**6.48(2) [Copy of certificate]** If the certificate is not so included, the court shall forthwith send copies of it to the official receiver and the bankrupt.

## 6.49 Duty of official receiver in summary administration

**6.49(1) [Where trustee appointed]** Where a trustee has been appointed, the official receiver shall send a copy of the certificate of summary administration (whether or not included in the bankruptcy order) to him.

**6.49(2) [Notice to creditors]** Within 12 weeks after the issue of the certificate the official receiver shall (insofar as he has not already done so) give notice to creditors of the making of the bankruptcy order.

## 6.50 Revocation of certificate of summary administration

**6.50(1) [Powers of court]** The court may under section 275(3) revoke a certificate for summary administration, either of its own motion or on the application of the official receiver.
[FORM 6.31]

**6.50(2) [Notice to bankrupt]** If the official receiver applies for the certificate to be revoked, he shall give at least 14 days' notice of the application to the bankrupt.

**6.50(3) [Notice of revocation]** If the court revokes the certificate, it shall forthwith give notice to the official receiver and the bankrupt.

**6.50(4) [Copy of notice to trustee]** If at the time of revocation there is a trustee other than the official receiver, the official receiver shall send a copy of the court's notice to him.

# Chapter 4 – The Interim Receiver

## 6.51 Application for appointment of interim receiver

**6.51(1) [Who may apply]** An application to the court for the appointment of an interim receiver under section 286 may be made by a creditor or by the debtor, or by an insolvency practitioner appointed under section 273(2).

**6.51(2) [Supporting affidavit]** The application must be supported by an affidavit stating–

(a) the grounds on which it is proposed that the interim receiver should be appointed,

(b) whether or not the official receiver has been informed of the application and, if so, has been furnished with a copy of it,

(c) whether to the applicant's knowledge there has been proposed or is in force a voluntary arrangement under Part VIII of the Act, and

(d) the applicant's estimate of the value of the property or business in respect of which the interim receiver is to be appointed.

**6.51(3) [If insolvency practitioner to be interim receiver]** If an insolvency practitioner has been appointed under section 273, and it is proposed that he (and not the official receiver) should be appointed interim receiver, and it is not the insolvency practitioner himself who is the applicant under this Rule, the affidavit under paragraph (2) must state that he has consented to act.

**6.51(4) [Copies of application and affidavit]** The applicant shall send copies of the application and the affidavit to the person proposed to be appointed interim receiver. If that person is the official receiver and an insolvency practitioner has been appointed under section 273 (and he is not himself the applicant), copies of the application and affidavit shall be sent by the applicant to the insolvency practitioner.

If, in any case where a copy of the application is to be sent to a person under this paragraph, it is for any reason not practicable to send a copy, that person must be informed of the application in sufficient time to enable him to be present at the hearing.

**6.51(5) [Appearances]** The official receiver and (if appointed) the insolvency practitioner may attend the hearing of the application and make representations.

**6.51(6) [Powers of court]** The court may on the application, if satisfied that sufficient grounds are shown for the appointment, make it on such terms as it thinks fit.

## 6.52 Order of appointment

**6.52(1) [Contents of order]** The order appointing the interim receiver shall state the nature and a short description of the property of which the person appointed is to take possession, and the duties to be performed by him in relation to the debtor's affairs. [FORM 6.32]

**6.52(2) [Sealed copies]** The court shall, forthwith after the order is made, send 2 sealed copies of it to the person appointed interim receiver (one of which shall be sent by him forthwith to the debtor).

## 6.53 Deposit

**6.53(1) [Security for official receiver's remuneration etc.]** Before an order appointing the official receiver as interim receiver is issued, the applicant for it shall deposit with him, or otherwise secure to his satisfaction, such sum as the court directs to cover his remuneration and expenses.

**6.53(2) [Sufficiency of deposit etc.]** If the sum deposited or secured subsequently proves to be insufficient, the court may, on application by the official receiver, order that an additional sum be deposited or secured. If the order is not complied with within 2 days after service on the person to whom the order is directed, the court may discharge the order appointing the interim receiver.

**6.53(3) [Repayment etc. of deposit]** If a bankruptcy order is made after an interim receiver has been appointed, any money deposited under this Rule shall (unless it is required by reason of insufficiency of assets for payment of remuneration and expenses of the interim receiver, or the deposit was made by the debtor out of his own property) be repaid to the person depositing it (or as that person may direct) out of the bankrupt's estate, in the prescribed order of priority.

## 6.54 Security

**6.54(1) [Application of Rule]** The following applies where an insolvency practitioner is appointed to be interim receiver under section 286(2).

**6.54(2) [Cost of providing security]** The cost of providing the security required under the Act shall be paid in the first instance by the interim receiver; but–

(a) if a bankruptcy order is not made, the person so appointed is entitled to be reimbursed out of the property of the debtor, and the court may make an order on the debtor accordingly, and

(b) if a bankruptcy order is made, he is entitled to be reimbursed out of the estate in the prescribed order of priority.

# 6.55 Failure to give or keep up security

**6.55(1) [Powers of court]** If the interim receiver fails to give or keep up his security, the court may remove him, and make such order as it thinks fit as to costs.

**6.55(2) [Directions on removal etc.]** If an order is made under this Rule removing the interim receiver, or discharging the order appointing him, the court shall give directions as to whether any, and if so what, steps should be taken for the appointment of another person in his place.

# 6.56 Remuneration

**6.56(1) [To be fixed by court]** The remuneration of the interim receiver (other than the official receiver) shall be fixed by the court from time to time on his application.

**6.56(2) [Matters to be taken into account]** In fixing the interim receiver's remuneration, the court shall take into account–

(a) the time properly given by him (as interim receiver) and his staff in attending to the debtor's affairs,

(b) the complexity (or otherwise) of the case,

(c) any respects in which, in connection with the debtor's affairs, there falls on the interim receiver any responsibility of an exceptional kind or degree,

(d) the effectiveness with which the interim receiver appears to be carrying out, or to have carried out, his duties as such, and

(e) the value and nature of the property with which he has to deal.

**6.56(3) [Source of payment of remuneration etc.]** Without prejudice to any order the court may make as to costs, the interim receiver's remuneration (whether the official receiver or another) shall be paid to him, and the amount of any expenses incurred by him (including the remuneration and expenses of any special manager appointed under section 370) reimbursed–

(a) if a bankruptcy order is not made, out of the property of the debtor, and

(b) if a bankruptcy order is made, out of the estate in the prescribed order of priority,

or, in either case (the relevant funds being insufficient), out of the deposit under Rule 6.53.

**History**

In r. 6.56(3) the words from the beginning to "out of the property of the debtor" substituted by the Insolvency (Amendment) Rules 1987 (SI 1987/1919), r. 3(1), Sch., Pt. 1, para. 103(1) as from 11 January 1988; the former words read as follows:

"The interim receiver's remuneration (whether the official receiver or another) shall be paid to him, and the amount of any expenses incurred by him reimbursed–

(a) if a bankruptcy order is not made, out of the property of the debtor (and the court may make an order on the debtor accordingly)".

**6.56(4) [Power of retention]** Unless the court otherwise directs, in a case falling within paragraph (3)(a) above the interim receiver may retain out of the debtor's property such sums or property as are or may be required for meeting his remuneration and expenses.

**History**

R. 6.56(4) added by the Insolvency (Amendment) Rules 1987 (SI 1987/1919), r. 3(1), Sch., Pt. 1, para. 103(2) as from 11 January 1988.

# 6.57 Termination of appointment

**6.57(1) [Termination by court]** The appointment of the interim receiver may be terminated by the court on his application, or on that of the official receiver, the debtor or any creditor.

**6.57(2) [Directions on termination]** If the interim receiver's appointment terminates, in consequence of the dismissal of the bankruptcy petition or otherwise, the court may give such directions as it thinks fit with respect to the accounts of his administration and any other matters which it thinks appropriate.

**6.57(3)** (Omitted by the Insolvency (Amendment) Rules 1987 (SI 1987/1919), r. 3(1), Sch., Pt. 1, para. 104 as from 11 January 1988).

**History**
R. 6.57(3) formerly read as follows:
"The court may under paragraph (2)–
(a) direct that any expenses properly incurred by the interim receiver during the period of his appointment, and any remuneration to which he is entitled, be paid out of property of the debtor, and
(b) authorise him to retain out of that property such sums as are required for meeting his expenses and remuneration.
Alternatively, the court may make such order as it thinks fit with respect to those matters."

# Chapter 5 – Disclosure by Bankrupt with Respect to the State of his Affairs

SECTION A: CREDITOR'S PETITION

## 6.58 Preliminary

**6.58** The Rules in this Section apply with respect to the statement of affairs required by section 288(1) to be submitted by the bankrupt, following a bankruptcy order made on a creditor's petition, and the further and other disclosure which is required of him in that case.

## 6.59 The statement of affairs

**6.59** The bankrupt's statement of affairs shall be in Form 6.33, and contain all the particulars required by that form. [FORM 6.33]

## 6.60 Verification and filing

**6.60(1) [Instructions for preparation of statement]** The bankrupt shall be furnished by the official receiver with instructions for the preparation of his statement of affairs, and the forms required for that purpose.

**6.60(2) [Verification and delivery]** The statement of affairs shall be verified by affidavit and delivered to the official receiver, together with one copy.

**6.60(3) [Filing in court]** The official receiver shall file the verified statement in court.

**6.60(4) [Swearing verifying affidavit]** The affidavit may be sworn before an official receiver or a deputy official receiver, or before an officer of the Department or the court duly authorised in that behalf.

## 6.61 Limited disclosure

**6.61(1) [Official receiver may apply to court]** Where the official receiver thinks that it would prejudice the conduct of the bankruptcy for the whole or part of the statement of affairs to be disclosed, he may apply to the court for an order of limited disclosure in respect of the statement, or any specified part of it.

**6.61(2) [Powers of court]** The court may on the application order that the statement or, as the case may be, the specified part of it be not filed in court, or that it is to be filed separately and not be open to inspection otherwise than with leave of the court.

## 6.62 Release from duty to submit statement of affairs; extension of time

**6.62(1) [Exercise of s. 288(3) power]** The power of the official receiver under section 288(3) to release the bankrupt from his duty to submit a statement of affairs, or to grant an extension of time, may be exercised at the official receiver's own discretion, or at the bankrupt's request.

**6.62(2) [Bankrupt may apply to court]** The bankrupt may, if he requests a release or extension of time and it is refused by the official receiver, apply to the court for it.

**6.62(3) [Court may dismiss application etc.]** The court may, if it thinks that no sufficient cause is shown for the application, dismiss it; but it shall not do so unless the bankrupt has had an opportunity to attend the court for an *ex parte* hearing, of which he has been given at least 7 days' notice.

If the application is not dismissed under this paragraph, the court shall fix a venue for it to be heard, and give notice to the bankrupt accordingly.

**6.62(4) [Bankrupt to send notice to official receiver]** The bankrupt shall, at least 14 days before the hearing, send to the official receiver a notice stating the venue and accompanied by a copy of the application, and of any evidence which he (the bankrupt) intends to adduce in support of it.

**6.62(5) [Appearance etc. by official receiver]** The official receiver may appear and be heard on the application; and, whether or not he appears, he may file a written report of any matters which he considers ought to be drawn to the court's attention.

If such a report is filed, a copy of it shall be sent by the official receiver to the bankrupt, not later than 5 days before the hearing.

**6.62(6) [Sealed copies of order]** Sealed copies of any order made on the application shall be sent by the court to the bankrupt and the official receiver.

**6.62(7) [Bankrupt's costs]** On any application under this Rule the bankrupt's costs shall be paid in any event by him and, unless the court otherwise orders, no allowance towards them shall be made out of the estate.

## 6.63 Expenses of statement of affairs

**6.63(1) [Persons assisting in preparation of statement]** If the bankrupt cannot himself prepare a proper statement of affairs, the official receiver may, at the expense of the estate, employ some person or persons to assist in the preparation of the statement.

**6.63(2) [Allowance towards expenses]** At the request of the bankrupt, made on the grounds that he cannot himself prepare a proper statement, the official receiver may authorise an allowance payable out of the estate (in accordance with the prescribed order of priority) towards expenses to be incurred by the bankrupt in employing some person or persons to assist him in preparing it.

**6.63(3) [Estimate of expenses]** Any such request by the bankrupt shall be accompanied by an estimate of the expenses involved; and the official receiver shall only authorise the employment of a named person or a named firm, being in either case approved by him.

**6.63(4) [Authorisation subject to conditions]** An authorisation given by the official receiver under this Rule shall be subject to such conditions (if any) as he thinks fit to impose with respect to the manner in which any person may obtain access to relevant books and papers.

**6.63(5) [Effect of Rule]** Nothing in this Rule relieves the bankrupt from any obligation with respect to the preparation, verification and submission of his statement of affairs, or to the provision of information to the official receiver or the trustee.

## 6.64 Requirement to submit accounts

**6.64(1) [At request of official receiver]** The bankrupt shall, at the request of the official receiver, furnish him with accounts relating to his affairs of such nature, as at such date and for such period as he may specify.

**6.64(2) [Beginning of specified period]** The period specified may begin from a date up to 3 years preceding the date of the presentation of the bankruptcy petition.

**6.64(3) [Accounts for earlier period]** The court may, on the official receiver's application, require accounts in respect of any earlier period.

**6.64(4) [Application of r. 6.63]** Rule 6.63 applies (with the necessary modifications) in relation to accounts to be furnished under this Rule as it applies in relation to the statement of affairs.

## 6.65 Submission and filing of accounts

**6.65(1) [Verification and delivery]** The accounts to be furnished under Rule 6.64 shall, if the official receiver so requires, be verified by affidavit, and (whether or not so verified) delivered to him within 21 days of the request under Rule 6.64(1), or such longer period as he may allow.

**6.65(2) [Copies of accounts etc. to official receiver]** Two copies of the accounts and (where required) the affidavit shall be delivered by the bankrupt to the official receiver, who shall file one copy in court (with the affidavit, if any).

## 6.66 Further disclosure

**6.66(1) [Official receiver may require further information]** The official receiver may at any time require the bankrupt to submit (in writing) further information amplifying, modifying or explaining any matter contained in his statement of affairs, or in accounts submitted in pursuance of the Act or the Rules.

**6.66(2) [Verification and delivery]** The information shall, if the official receiver so directs, be verified by affidavit, and (whether or not so verified) delivered to him within 21 days of the requirement under this Rule, or such longer period as he may allow.

**6.66(3) [Copies to official receiver etc.]** Two copies of the documents containing the information and (where verification is directed) the affidavit shall be delivered by the bankrupt to the official receiver, who shall file one copy in court (with the affidavit, if any).

### SECTION B: DEBTOR'S PETITION

## 6.67 Preliminary

**6.67** The Rules in this Section apply with respect to the statement of affairs required in the case of a person petitioning for a bankruptcy order to be made against him, and the further disclosure which is required of him in that case.

## 6.68 Contents of statement

**6.68** The statement of affairs required by Rule 6.41 to accompany the debtor's petition shall be in Form 6.28, and contain all the particulars required by that form. [FORM 6.28]

## 6.69 Requirement to submit accounts

**6.69(1) [At request of official receiver]** The bankrupt shall, at the request of the official receiver, furnish him with accounts relating to his affairs of such nature, as at such date and for such period as he may specify.

**6.69(2) [Beginning of specified period]** The period specified may begin from a date up to 3 years preceding the date of the presentation of the bankruptcy petition.

**6.69(3) [Accounts for earlier period]** The court may, on the official receiver's application, require accounts in respect of any earlier period.

## 6.70 Submission and filing of accounts

**6.70(1) [Verification and delivery]** The accounts to be furnished under Rule 6.69 shall, if the official receiver so requires, be verified by affidavit, and (whether or not so verified) delivered to him within 21 days of the request under Rule 6.69, or such longer period as he may allow.

**6.70(2) [Copies of accounts etc. to official receiver]** Two copies of the accounts and (where required) the affidavit shall be delivered by the bankrupt to the official receiver, who shall file one copy in court (with the affidavit, if any).

## 6.71 Expenses of preparing accounts

**6.71(1) [Persons assisting in preparation of accounts]** If the bankrupt cannot himself prepare proper accounts under Rule 6.69, the official receiver may, at the expense of the estate, employ some person or persons to assist in their preparation.

**6.71(2) [Allowance towards expenses]** At the request of the bankrupt, made on the grounds that he cannot himself prepare the accounts, the official receiver may authorise an allowance payable out of the estate (in accordance with the prescribed order of priority) towards expenses to be incurred by the bankrupt in employing some person or persons to assist him in their preparation.

(b) there has been lodged, by that time and date, any proxy requisite for that entitlement.

**6.93(2) [Powers of court]** The court may, in exceptional circumstances, by order declare the creditors, or any class of them, entitled to vote at creditors' meetings, without being required to prove their debts.

Where a creditor is so entitled, the court may, on the application of the trustee, make such consequential orders as it thinks fit (as for example an order treating a creditor as having proved his debt for the purpose of permitting payment of dividend).

**6.93(3) [Limitation on voting]** A creditor shall not vote in respect of a debt for an unliquidated amount, or any debt whose value is not ascertained, expect where the chairman agrees to put upon the debt an estimated minimum value for the purpose of entitlement to vote and admits his proof for that purpose.

**6.93(4) [Secured creditor]** A secured creditor is entitled to vote only in respect of the balance (if any) of his debt after deducting the value of his security as estimated by him.

**6.93(5) [Further limitation on voting]** A creditor shall not vote in respect of a debt on, or secured by, a current bill of exchange or promissory note, unless he is willing–

(a) to treat the liability to him on the bill or note of every person who is liable on it antecedently to the bankrupt, and against whom a bankruptcy order has not been made (or, in the case of a company, which has not gone into liquidation), as a security in his hands, and

(b) to estimate the value of the security and (for the purpose of entitlement to vote, but not for dividend) to deduct it from his proof.

# 6.94 Admission and rejection of proof

**6.94(1) [Power of chairman]** At any creditors' meeting the chairman has power to admit or reject a creditor's proof for the purpose of his entitlement to vote; and the power is exercisable with respect to the whole or any part of the proof.

**6.94(2) [Appeal from chairman's decision]** The chairman's decision under this Rule, or in respect of any matter arising under Rule 6.93, is subject to appeal to the court by any creditor, or by the bankrupt.

**6.94(3) [Voting subject to objection]** If the chairman is in doubt whether a proof should be admitted or rejected, he shall mark it as objected to and allow the creditor to vote, subject to his vote being subsequently declared invalid if the objection to the proof is sustained.

**6.94(4) [If chairman's decision reversed etc.]** If on an appeal the chairman's decision is reversed or varied, or a creditor's vote is declared invalid, the court may order that another meeting be summoned, or make such other order as it thinks just.

**6.94(5) [Costs re application]** Neither the official receiver nor any person nominated by him to be chairman is personally liable for costs incurred by any person in respect of an application to the court under this Rule; and the chairman (if other than the official receiver or a person so nominated) is not so liable unless the court makes an order to that effect.

# 6.95 Record of proceedings

**6.95(1) [Minutes of proceedings]** The chairman at any creditors' meeting shall cause minutes of the proceedings at the meeting, signed by him, to be retained by him as part of the records of the bankruptcy.

**6.95(2) [List of creditors attending]** He shall also cause to be made up and kept a list of all the creditors who attended the meeting.

**6.95(3) [Record of resolutions]** The minutes of the meeting shall include a record of every resolution passed; and it is the chairman's duty to see to it that particulars of all such resolutions, certified by him, are filed in court not more than 21 days after the date of the meeting.

# Chapter 8 – Proof of Bankruptcy Debts

## SECTION A: PROCEDURE FOR PROVING

## 6.96 Meaning of "prove"

**6.96(1) [Claim to be submitted in writing etc.]** A person claiming to be a creditor of the bankrupt and wishing to recover his debt in whole or in part must (subject to any order of the court under Rule 6.93(2)) submit his claim in writing to the official receiver, where acting as receiver and manager, or to the trustee.

**6.96(2) ["Proving" and "proof"]** The creditor is referred to as **"proving"** for his debt; and the document by which he seeks to establish his claim is his **"proof"**.

**6.96(3) ["Proof of debt"]** Subject to the next two paragraphs, the proof must be in the form known as **"proof of debt"** (whether the form prescribed by the Rules, or a substantially similar form), which shall be made out by or under the directions of the creditor, and signed by him or a person authorised in that behalf. [FORM 6.37]

**6.96(4) [Debt due to Crown etc.]** Where a debt is due to a Minister of the Crown or a Government Department, the proof need not be in that form, provided that there are shown all such particulars of the debt as are required in the form used by other creditors, and as are relevant in the circumstances.

**6.96(5) [Proof under s. 335(5)]** Where an existing trustee proves in a later bankruptcy under section 335(5), the proof must be in Form 6.38. [FORM 6.38]

**6.96(6) [Proof in form of affidavit]** In certain circumstances, specified below in this Chapter, the proof must be in the form of an affidavit. [FORM 6.39]

## 6.97 Supply of forms

**6.97(1) [Forms to be sent to every creditor]** Forms of proof shall be sent out by the official receiver or the trustee to every creditor of the bankrupt who is known to the sender, or is identified in the bankrupt's statement of affairs.

**History**

In r. 6.97(1) the words "of proof" substituted for the former words "to be used for the purpose of proving bankruptcy debts" by the Insolvency (Amendment) Rules 1987 (SI 1987/1919), r. 3(1), Sch., Pt. 1, para. 110 as from 11 January 1988.

**6.97(2) [Forms to accompany first notice]** The forms shall accompany (whichever is first)–

(a) the notice to creditors under section 293(2) (official receiver's decision not to call meeting of creditors), or

(b) the first notice calling a meeting of creditors, or

(c) where a certificate of summary administration has been issued by the court, the notice sent by the official receiver under Rule 6.49(2), or

(d) where a trustee is appointed by the court, the notice of his appointment sent by him to creditors.

**6.97(3) [Where trustee advertises his appointment]** Where, with leave of the court under section 297(7), the trustee advertises his appointment, he shall send proofs to the creditors within 4 months after the date of the bankruptcy order.

**6.97(4) [Rule subject to order of court]** The above paragraphs of this Rule are subject to any order of the court dispensing with the requirement to send out forms of proof, or altering the time at which the forms are to be sent.

## 6.98 Contents of proof

**6.98(1) [Matters to be stated]** Subject to Rule 6.96(4), the following matters shall be stated in a creditor's proof of debt–

(a) the creditor's name and address;

(b) the total amount of his claim as at the date of the bankruptcy order;

(c) whether or not that amount includes outstanding uncapitalised interest;

(d) whether or not the claim includes value added tax;

(e) whether the whole or any part of the debt falls within any (and if so which) of the categories of preferential debts under section 386 of, and Schedule 6 to, the Act (as read with Schedule 3 to the Social Security Pensions Act 1975);

(f) particulars of how and when the debt was incurred by the debtor;

(g) particulars of any security held, the date when it was given and the value which the creditor puts upon it; and

(h) the name, address and authority of the person signing the proof (if other than the creditor himself).

**History**

In r. 6.98(1) the words "Subject to Rule 6.96(4)," inserted by the Insolvency (Amendment) Rules 1987 (SI 1987/1919), r. 3(1), Sch., Pt. 1, para. 111 as from 11 January 1988.

**6.98(2) [Specified documents]** There shall be specified in the proof any documents by reference to which the debt can be substantiated; but (subject as follows) it is not essential that such documents be attached to the proof or submitted with it.

**6.98(3) [Production of documents etc.]** The trustee, or the convener or chairman of any meeting, may call for any document or other evidence to be produced to him, where he thinks it necessary for the purpose of substantiating the whole or any part of the claim made in the proof.

## 6.99 Claim established by affidavit

**6.99(1) [Trustee may require "affidavit of debt"]** The trustee may, if he thinks it necessary, require a claim of debt to be verified by affidavit, for which purpose there shall be used the form known as **"affidavit of debt"**. [FORM 6.39]

**6.99(2) [In addition to proof]** An affidavit may be required notwithstanding that a proof of debt has already been lodged.

**6.99(3) [Swearing of affidavit]** The affidavit may be sworn before an official receiver or a deputy official receiver, or before an officer of the Department or of the court duly authorised in that behalf.

## 6.100 Cost of proving

**6.100(1) [Creditor bears cost of proving own debt]** Subject as follows, every creditor bears the cost of proving his own debt, including such as may be incurred in providing documents or evidence under Rule 6.98(3).

**6.100(2) [Trustee's costs]** Costs incurred by the trustee in estimating the value of a bankruptcy debt under section 322(3) (debts not bearing a certain value) fall on the estate, as an expense of the bankruptcy.

**6.100(3) [Application of r. 6.100(1), (2)]** Paragraphs (1) and (2) apply unless the court otherwise orders.

## 6.101 Trustee to allow inspection of proofs

**6.101** The trustee shall, so long as proofs lodged with him are in his hands, allow them to be inspected, at all reasonable times on any business day, by any of the following persons–

(a) any creditor who has submitted his proof of debt (unless his proof has been wholly rejected for purposes of dividend or otherwise),

(b) the bankrupt, and

(c) any person acting on behalf of either of the above.

## 6.102 Proof of licensed moneylender

**6.102** A proof of debt in respect of a moneylending transaction made before 27th January 1980, where the creditor was at the time of the transaction a licensed moneylender, shall have endorsed on or annexed to it a statement setting out in detail the particulars mentioned in section 9(2) of the Moneylenders Act 1927.

## 6.103 Transmissions of proofs to trustee

**6.103(1) [On trustee's appointment]** Where a trustee is appointed, the official receiver shall forthwith transmit to him all the proofs which he has so far received, together with an itemised list of them.

**6.103(2) [Receipt for proofs]** The trustee shall sign the list by way of receipt for the proofs, and return it to the official receiver.

**6.103(3) [All later proofs to trustee]** From then on, all proofs of debt shall be sent to the trustee and retained by him.

## 6.104 Admission and rejection of proofs for dividend

**6.104(1) [Admission]** A proof may be admitted for dividend either for the whole amount claimed by the creditor, or for part of that amount.

**6.104(2) [Rejection]** If the trustee rejects a proof in whole or in part, he shall prepare a written statement of his reasons for doing so, and send it forthwith to the creditor.

## 6.105 Appeal against decision on proof

**6.105(1) [Application by creditor]** If a creditor is dissatisfied with the trustee's decision with respect to his proof (including any decision on the question of preference), he may apply to the court for the decision to be reversed or varied.

The application must be made within 21 days of his receiving the statement sent under Rule 6.104(2).

**6.105(2) [Application by bankrupt etc.]** The bankrupt or any other creditor may, if dissatisfied with the trustee's decision admitting or rejecting the whole or any part of a proof, make such an application within 21 days of becoming aware of the trustee's decision.

**6.105(3) [Venue and notice]** Where application is made to the court under this Rule, the court shall fix a venue for the application to be heard, notice of which shall be sent by the applicant to the creditor who lodged the proof in question (if it is not himself) and to the trustee.

**6.105(4) [Relevant proof etc. to be filed in court]** The trustee shall, on receipt of the notice, file in court the relevant proof, together (if appropriate) with a copy of the statement sent under Rule 6.104(2).

**6.105(5) [Return of proof]** After the application has been heard and determined, the proof shall, unless it has been wholly disallowed, be returned by the court to the trustee.

**6.105(6) [Costs re application]** The official receiver is not personally liable for costs incurred by any person in respect of an application under this Rule; and the trustee (if other than the official receiver) is not so liable unless the court makes an order to that effect.

## 6.106 Withdrawal or variation of proof

**6.106** A creditor's proof may at any time, by agreement between himself and the trustee, be withdrawn or varied as to the amount claimed.

## 6.107 Expunging of proof by the court

**6.107(1) [Expunging or reduction of amount]** The court may expunge a proof or reduce the amount claimed–

(a) on the trustee's application, where he thinks that the proof has been improperly admitted, or ought to be reduced; or

(b) on the application of a creditor, if the trustee declines to interfere in the matter.

**6.107(2) [Venue and notice]** Where application is made to the court under this Rule, the court shall fix a venue for the application to be heard, notice of which shall be sent by the applicant–

(a) in the case of an application by the trustee, to the creditor who made the proof, and

(b) in the case of an application by a creditor, to the trustee and to the creditor who made the proof (if not himself).

SECTION B: QUANTIFICATION OF CLAIM

## 6.108 Negotiable instruments, etc.

**6.108** Unless the trustee allows, a proof in respect of money owed on a bill of exchange, promissory note, cheque or other negotiable instrument or security cannot be admitted unless there is produced the instrument or security itself or a copy of it, certified by the creditor or his authorised representative to be a true copy.

## 6.109 Secured creditors

**6.109(1) [Proving for balance of debt]** If a secured creditor realises his security, he may prove for the balance of his debt, after deducting the amount realised.

**6.109(2) [Proving for whole debt]** If a secured creditor voluntarily surrenders his security for the general benefit of creditors, he may prove for his whole debt, as if it were unsecured.

## 6.110 Discounts

**6.110** There shall in every case be deducted from the claim all trade and other discounts which would have been available to the bankrupt but for his bankruptcy, except any discount for immediate, early or cash settlement.

## 6.111 Debt in foreign currency

**6.111(1) [Conversion into sterling]** For the purpose of proving a debt incurred or payable in a currency other than sterling, the amount of the debt shall be converted into sterling at the official exchange rate prevailing on the date of the bankruptcy order.

**6.111(2) ["The official exchange rate"] "The official exchange rate"** is the middle market rate at the Bank of England, as published for the date in question. In the absence of any such published rate, it is such rate as the court determines.

## 6.112 Payments of a periodical nature

**6.112(1) [Rent etc.]** In the case of rent and other payments of a periodical nature, the creditor may prove for any amounts due and unpaid up to the date of the bankruptcy order.

**6.112(2) [If accruing from day to day]** Where at that date any payment was accruing due, the creditor may prove for so much as would have fallen due at that date, if accruing from day to day.

## 6.113 Interest

**6.113(1) [Where claim may include interest]** In the following circumstances the creditor's claim may include interest on the debt for periods before the bankruptcy order, although not previously reserved or agreed.

**6.113(2) [Debt due by written instrument]** If the debt is due by virtue of a written instrument and payable at a certain time, interest may be claimed for the period from that time to the date of the bankruptcy order.

**6.113(3) [Debt due otherwise]** If the debt is due otherwise, interest may only be claimed if, before the presentation of the bankruptcy petition, a demand for payment was made in writing by or on behalf of the creditor, and notice given that interest would be payable from the date of the demand to the date of payment and for all the purposes of the Act and the Rules shall be chargeable at a rate not exceeding that mentioned in paragraph (5).

**History**

In r. 6.113(3) the words from "and for all the purposes" to the end added by the Insolvency (Amendment) Rules 1987 (SI 1987/1919), r. 3(1), Sch., Pt. 1, para. 112(1) as from 11 January 1988.

**6.113(4) [Period of claim]** Interest under paragraph (3) may only be claimed for the period from the date of the demand to that of the bankruptcy order.

**6.113(5) [Rate of interest]** The rate of interest to be claimed under paragraphs (2) and (3) is the rate specified in section 17 of the Judgments Act 1838 on the date of the bankruptcy order.

**History**
R. 6.113(4) and (5) substituted for the former second paragraph of r. 6.113(3) and the former r. 6.113(4) by the Insolvency (Amendment) Rules 1987 (SI 1987/1919), r. 3(1), Sch., Pt. 1, para. 112(2) as from 11 January 1988; the former second paragraph of r. 6.113(3) and r. 6.113(4) read as follows:

"In that case interest may be claimed under this Rule for the period from the date of the demand to that of the bankruptcy order.

**6.113(4)** The rate of interest to be claimed under this Rule is the rate specified in section 17 of the Judgments Act 1838 on the date of the bankruptcy order; except that, where the case falls within paragraph (3), the rate is that specified in the notice there referred to, not exceeding the rate under the Judgments Act as mentioned above."

## 6.114 Debt payable at future time

**6.114** A creditor may prove for a debt of which payment was not yet due at the date of the bankruptcy order, but subject to Rule 11.13 in Part 11 of the Rules (adjustment of dividend where payment made before time).

# Chapter 9 – Secured Creditors

## 6.115 Value of security

**6.115(1) [Altering value]** A secured creditor may, with the agreement of the trustee or the leave of the court, at any time alter the value which he has, in his proof of debt, put upon his security.

**6.115(2) [Limitation on re-valuation]** However, if a secured creditor–

(a) being the petitioner, has in the petition put a value on his security, or

(b) has voted in respect of the unsecured balance of his debt,

he may re-value his security only with leave of the court.

## 6.116 Surrender for non-disclosure

**6.116(1) [Omission to disclose security]** If a secured creditor omits to disclose his security in his proof of debt, he shall surrender his security for the general benefit of creditors, unless the court, on application by him, relieves him from the effect of this Rule on the ground that the omission was inadvertent or the result of honest mistake.

**6.116(2) [Relief from effect of r. 6.116(1)]** If the court grants that relief, it may require or allow the creditor's proof of debt to be amended, on such terms as may be just.

## 6.117 Redemption by trustee

**6.117(1) [Notice of proposed redemption]** The trustee may at any time give notice to a creditor whose debt is secured that he proposes, at the expiration of 28 days from the date of the notice, to redeem the security at the value put upon it in the creditor's proof.

**6.117(2) [Time for re-valuation]** The creditor then has 21 days (or such longer period as the trustee may allow) in which, if he so wishes, to exercise his right to re-value his security (with the leave of the court, where Rule 6.115(2) applies).

If the creditor re-values his security, the trustee may only redeem at the new value.

**6.117(3) [If trustee redeems]** If the trustee redeems the security, the cost of transferring it is borne by the estate.

**6.117(4) [Notice to trustee to elect etc.]** A secured creditor may at any time, by a notice in writing, call on the trustee to elect whether he will or will not exercise his power to redeem the security at the value then placed on it; and the trustee then has 6 months in which to exercise the power or determine not to exercise it.

## 6.118 Test of security's value

**6.118(1) [Offer for sale]** Subject as follows, the trustee, if he is dissatisfied with the value which a secured creditor puts on his security (whether in his proof or by way of re-valuation under Rule 6.117), may require any property comprised in the security to be offered for sale.

**6.118(2) [Terms of sale]** The terms of sale shall be such as may be agreed, or as the court may direct; and if the sale is by auction, the trustee on behalf of the estate, and the creditor on his own behalf, may appear and bid.

**6.118(3) [Non-application of Rule]** This Rule does not apply if the security has been re-valued and the re-valuation has been approved by the court.

## 6.119 Realisation of security by creditor

**6.119** If a creditor who has valued his security subsequently realises it (whether or not at the instance of the trustee)–

(a) the net amount realised shall be substituted for the value previously put by the creditor on the security, and

(b) that amount shall be treated in all respects as an amended valuation made by him.

# Chapter 10 – The Trustee in Bankruptcy

SECTION A: APPOINTMENT AND ASSOCIATED FORMALITIES

## 6.120 Appointment by creditors' meeting

**6.120(1) [Application of Rule]** This Rule applies where a person has been appointed trustee by resolution of a creditors' meeting.

**6.120(2) [Certification of appointment]** The chairman of the meeting shall certify the appointment, but not unless and until the person to be appointed has provided him with a written statement to the effect that he is an insolvency practitioner, duly qualified under the Act to act as trustee in relation to the bankrupt, and that he consents so to act. [FORM 6.40] or [FORM 6.41]

**6.120(3) [Date when appointment effective]** The trustee's appointment is effective from the date on which the appointment is certified, that date to be endorsed on the certificate.

**6.120(4) [Certificate to official receiver]** The chairman of the meeting (if not himself the official receiver) shall send the certificate to the official receiver.

**6.120(5) [Certificate to trustee, copy to be filed]** The official receiver shall in any case send the certificate to the trustee and file a copy of it in court.

**History**

R. 6.120(3), (4) and (5) substituted for the former r. 6.120(3) and (4) by the Insolvency (Amendment) Rules 1987 (SI 1987/1919), r. 3(1), Sch., Pt. 1, para. 113 as from 11 January 1988; the former r. 6.120(3) and (4) read as follows:

"**6.120(3)** The chairman (if not himself the official receiver) shall send the certificate to the official receiver.

**(4)** The official receiver shall in any case file a copy of the certificate in court; and the trustee's appointment is effective as from the date on which the official receiver files the copy certificate in court, that date to be endorsed on the copy certificate. The certificate, so endorsed, shall be sent by the official receiver to the trustee."

## 6.121 Appointment by the court

**6.121(1) [Application of Rule]** This Rule applies where the court under section 297(3), (4) or (5) appoints the trustee. [FORM 6.42] or [FORM 6.43]

**6.121(2) [Issue of court order]** The court's order shall not issue unless and until the person appointed has filed in court a statement to the effect that he is an insolvency practitioner, duly qualified under the Act to be the trustee, and that he consents so to act.

**6.121(3) [Copies of orders to official receiver etc.]** Thereafter, the court shall send 2 copies of the order to the official receiver. One of the copies shall be sealed, and this shall be sent by him to the person appointed as trustee.

**6.121(4) [Commencement of appointment]** The trustee's appointment takes effect from the date of the order.

## 6.122 Appointment by Secretary of State

**6.122(1) [Application of Rule]** This Rule applies where the official receiver–

(a) under section 295 or 300, refers to the Secretary of State the need for an appointment of a trustee, or

(b) under section 296, applies to the Secretary of State to make the appointment.

**6.122(2) [Copies of certificate to official receiver etc.]** If the Secretary of State makes an appointment he shall send two copies of the certificate of appointment to the official receiver, who shall transmit one such copy to the person appointed, and file the other copy in court.

The certificate shall specify the date which the trustee's appointment is to be effective.

## 6.123 Authentication of trustee's appointment

**6.123** Where a trustee is appointed under any of the 3 preceding Rules, a sealed copy of the order of appointment or (as the case may be) a copy of the certificate of his appointment may in any proceedings be adduced as proof that he is duly authorised to exercise the powers and perform the duties of trustee of the bankrupt's estate.

## 6.124 Advertisement of appointment

**6.124(1) [Where trustee appointed by meeting]** Where the trustee is appointed by a creditors' meeting, he shall, forthwith after receiving his certificate of appointment, give notice of his appointment in such newspaper as he thinks most appropriate for ensuring that it comes to the notice of the bankrupt's creditors.

**6.124(2) [Expense of giving notice]** The expense of giving the notice shall be borne in the first instance by the trustee; but he is entitled to be reimbursed by the estate, as an expense of the bankruptcy.

The same applies also in the case of the notice or advertisement under section 296(4) (appointment of trustee by Secretary of State), and of the notice or advertisement under section 297(7) (appointment by the court).

## 6.125 Hand-over of estate to trustee

**6.125(1) [Application of Rule]** This Rule applies only where–

(a) the bankrupt's estate vests in the trustee under Chapter IV of Part IX of the Act, following a period in which the official receiver is the receiver and manager of the estate according to section 287, or

(b) the trustee is appointed in succession to the official receiver acting as trustee.

**6.125(2) [On trustee's appointment]** When the trustee's appointment takes effect, the official receiver shall forthwith do all that is required for putting him into possession of the estate.

**6.125(3) [Discharge of balance due to official receiver]** On taking possession of the estate, the trustee shall discharge any balance due to the official receiver on account of–

(a) expenses properly incurred by him and payable under the Act or the Rules, and

(b) any advances made by him in respect of the estate, together with interest on such advances at the rate specified in section 17 of the Judgments Act 1838 on the date of the bankruptcy order.

**6.125(4) [Undertaking to discharge]** Alternatively, the trustee may (before taking office) give to the official receiver a written undertaking to discharge any such balance out of the first realisation of assets.

**6.125(5) [Official receiver's charge]** The official receiver has a charge on the estate in respect of any sums due to him under paragraph (3). But, where the trustee has realised assets with a view to making those payments, the official receiver's charge does not extend in respect of sums deductible by the trustee from the proceeds of realisation, as being expenses properly incurred therein.

**6.125(6) [Discharge of guarantees etc.]** The trustee shall from time to time out of the realisation of assets discharge all guarantees properly given by the official receiver for the benefit of the estate, and shall pay all the official receiver's expenses.

**6.125(7) [Official receiver to give trustee information]** The official receiver shall give to the trustee all such information, relating to the affairs of the bankrupt and the course of the bankruptcy, as he (the official receiver) considers to be reasonably required for the effective discharge by the trustee of his duties in relation to the estate.

**6.125(8) [Ch. 6 report]** The trustee shall also be furnished with any report of the official receiver under Chapter 6 of this Part of the Rules.

## SECTION B: RESIGNATION AND REMOVAL; VACATION OF OFFICE

# 6.126 Creditors' meeting to receive trustee's resignation

**6.126(1) [Trustee must call meeting etc.]** Before resigning his office, the trustee must call a meeting of creditors for the purpose of receiving his resignation. Notice of the meeting shall be sent to the official receiver at the same time as it is sent to creditors.

**6.126(2) [Account of trustee's administration]** The notice to creditors must be accompanied by an account of the trustee's administration of the bankrupt's estate, including–

(a) a summary of his receipts and payments and

(b) a statement by him that he has reconciled his accounts with that which is held by the Secretary of State in respect of the bankruptcy.

**6.126(3) [Grounds for proceedings under Rule]** Subject as follows, the trustee may only proceed under this Rule on grounds of ill health or because–

(a) he intends ceasing to be in practice as an insolvency practitioner, or

(b) there is some conflict of interest or change of personal circumstances which precludes or makes impracticable the further discharge by him of the duties of trustee.

**6.126(4) [Where joint trustees]** Where two or more persons are acting as trustee jointly, any one of them may proceed under this Rule (without prejudice to the continuation in office of the other or others) on the ground that, in his opinion and that of the other or others, it is no longer expedient that there should continue to be the present number of joint trustees.

**6.126(5) [If no quorum]** If there is no quorum present at the meeting summoned to receive the trustee's resignation, the meeting is deemed to have been held, a resolution is deemed to have been passed that the trustee's resignation be accepted and the creditors are deemed not to have resolved against the trustee having his release.

**6.126(6) [Application of r. 6.126(5)]** Where paragraph (5) applies any reference in the Rules to a resolution that the trustee's resignation be accepted is replaced by a reference to the making of a written statement, signed by the person who, had there been a quorum present, would have been chairman of the meeting, that no quorum was present and that the trustee may resign.

**History**

R. 6.126(5) and (6) added by the Insolvency (Amendment) Rules 1987 (SI 1987/1919), r. 3(1), Sch., Pt. 1, para. 114 as from 11 January 1988.

# 6.127 Action following acceptance of resignation

**6.127(1) [Notice of meeting to indicate purpose etc.]** Where a meeting of creditors is summoned for the purpose of receiving the trustee's resignation, the notice summoning it shall indicate that this is the purpose, or one of the purposes, of the meeting; and the notice shall draw the attention of creditors to Rule 6.135 with respect to the trustee's release. [FORM 6.35]

**6.127(2) [Copy of notice to official receiver]** A copy of the notice shall at the same time also be sent to the official receiver.

**6.127(3) [Where chairman other than official receiver]** Where the chairman of the meeting is other than the official receiver, and there is passed at the meeting any of the following resolutions–

(a) that the trustee's resignation be accepted,

(b) that a new trustee be appointed,

(c) that the resigning trustee be not given his release,

the chairman shall, within 3 days, send to the official receiver a copy of the resolution.

If it has been resolved to accept the trustee's resignation, the chairman shall send to the official receiver a certificate to that effect. [FORM 6.44]

**6.127(4) [If creditors resolve to appoint new trustee]** If the creditors have resolved to appoint a new trustee, the certificate of his appointment shall also be sent to the official receiver within that time; and Rule 6.120 above shall be complied with in respect of it.

**6.127(5) [If trustee's resignation accepted]** If the trustee's resignation is accepted, the notice of it required by section 298(7) shall be given by him forthwith after the meeting; and he shall send a copy of the notice to the official receiver.

The notice shall be accompanied by a copy of the account sent to creditors under Rule 6.126(2).

**6.127(6) [Copy of notice]** The official receiver shall file a copy of the notice in court.

**6.127(7) [Effective date of resignation]** The trustee's resignation is effective as from the date on which the official receiver files the copy notice in court, that date to be endorsed on the copy notice.

## 6.128 Leave to resign granted by the court

**6.128(1) [If creditors resolve not to accept resignation]** If at a creditors' meeting summoned to accept the trustee's resignation it is resolved that it be not accepted, the court may, on the trustee's application, make an order giving him leave to resign. [FORM 6.45]

**6.128(2) [Extent of order under r. 6.128(1)]** The court's order under this Rule may include such provision as it thinks fit with respect to matters arising in connection with the resignation, and shall determine the date from which the trustee's release is effective.

**6.128(3) [Sealed copies of order]** The court shall send two sealed copies of the order to the trustee, who shall send one of the copies forthwith to the official receiver.

**6.128(4) [Copy notice to court and official receiver]** On sending notice of his resignation to the court, as required by section 298(7), the trustee shall send a copy of it to the official receiver. [FORM 6.46]

## 6.129 Meeting of creditors to remove trustee

**6.129(1) [Notice]** Where a meeting of creditors is summoned for the purpose of removing the trustee, the notice summoning it shall indicate that this is the purpose, or one of the purposes, of the meeting; and the notice shall draw the attention of creditors to section 299(3) with respect to the trustee's release. [FORM 6.35]

**6.129(2) [Copy of notice to official receiver]** A copy of the notice shall at the same time also be sent to the official receiver.

**6.129(3) [Chairman, if trustee chairman etc.]** At the meeting, a person other than the trustee or his nominee may be elected to act as chairman; but if the trustee or his nominee is chairman and a resolution has been proposed for the trustee's removal, the chairman shall not adjourn the meeting without the consent of at least one-half (in value) of the creditors present (in person or by proxy) and entitled to vote.

**6.129(4) [Where chairman other than official receiver]** Where the chairman of the meeting is other than the official receiver, and there is passed at the meeting any of the following resolutions–

(a) that the trustee be removed,

(b) that a new trustee be appointed,

(c) that the removed trustee be not given his release,

the chairman shall, within 3 days, send to the official receiver a copy of the resolution.

If it has been resolved to remove the trustee, the chairman shall send to the official receiver a certificate to that effect. [FORM 6.47]

**6.129(5) [If creditors resolve to appoint new trustee]** If the creditors have resolved to appoint a new trustee, the certificate of his appointment shall also be sent to the official receiver within that time; and Rule 6.120 shall be complied with in respect of it.

## 6.130 Court's power to regulate meeting under Rule 6.129

**6.130** Where a meeting under Rule 6.129 is to be held, or is proposed to be summoned, the court may on the application of any creditor give directions as to the mode of summoning it, the sending out and return of forms of proxy, the conduct of the meeting, and any other matter which appears to the court to require regulation or control.

## 6.131 Procedure on removal

**6.131(1) [Certificate of removal to be filed]** Where the creditors have resolved that the trustee be removed, the official receiver shall file the certificate of removal in court.

**6.131(2) [Effective date]** The resolution is effective as from the date on which the official receiver files the certificate of removal in court, and that date shall be endorsed on the certificate.

**6.131(3) [Copy of certificate]** A copy of the certificate, so endorsed, shall be sent by the official receiver to the trustee who has been removed and, if a new trustee has been appointed, to him.

**6.131(4) [Reconciliation of accounts]** The official receiver shall not file the certificate in court until the Secretary of State has certified to him that the removed trustee has reconciled his account with that held by the Secretary of State in respect of the bankruptcy.

## 6.132 Removal of trustee by the court

**6.132(1) [Application of Rule]** This Rule applies where application is made to the court for the removal of the trustee, or for an order directing the trustee to summon a meeting of creditors for the purpose of removing him. [FORM 6.48]

**6.132(2) [Court may dismiss application etc.]** The court may, if it thinks that no sufficient cause is shown for the application, dismiss it; but it shall not do so unless the applicant has had an opportunity to attend the court for an *ex parte* hearing, of which he has been given at least 7 days' notice.

If the application is not dismissed under this paragraph, the court shall fix a venue for it to be heard.

**6.132(3) [Notice etc.]** The applicant shall, at least 14 days before the hearing, send to the trustee and the official receiver notice stating the venue so fixed; and the notice shall be accompanied by a copy of the application, and of any evidence which the applicant intends to adduce in support of it.

**6.132(4) [Costs]** Subject to any contrary order of the court, the costs of the application do not fall on the estate.

**6.132(5) [Where court removes trustee]** Where the court removes the trustee–

(a) it shall send copies of the order of removal to him and to the official receiver;

(b) the order may include such provision as the court thinks fit with respect to matters arising in connection with the removal; and

(c) if the court appoints a new trustee, Rule 6.121 applies.

## 6.133 Removal of trustee by Secretary of State

**6.133(1) [Notice to trustee etc.]** If the Secretary of State decides to remove the trustee, he shall before doing so notify the trustee and the official receiver of his decision and the grounds of it, and specify a period within which the trustee may make representations against implementation of the decision.

**6.133(2) [On removal]** If the Secretary of State directs the removal of the trustee, he shall forthwith–

(a) file notice of his decision in court, and

(b) send notice to the trustee and the official receiver.

**6.133(3) [If trustee removed]** If the trustee is removed by direction of the Secretary of State, the court may make any such order in his case as it would have power to make if he had been removed by itself.

## 6.134 Advertisement of resignation or removal

**6.134** Where a new trustee is appointed in place of one who has resigned or been removed, the new trustee shall, in the advertisement of his appointment, state that his predecessor has resigned or, as the case may be, been removed and (if it be the case) that he has been given his release.

## 6.135 Release of resigning or removed trustee

**6.135(1) [Where trustee's resignation accepted]** Where the trustee's resignation is accepted by a meeting of creditors which has not resolved against his release, he has his release from when his resignation is effective under Rule 6.127.

**6.135(2) [Where trustee removed by meeting]** Where the trustee is removed by a meeting of creditors which has not resolved against his release, the fact of his release shall be stated in the certificate of removal.

**6.135(3) [Application to Secretary of State]** Where–

(a) the trustee resigns, and the creditor's meeting called to receive his resignation has resolved against his release, or

(b) he is removed by a creditors' meeting which has so resolved, or is removed by the court,

he must apply to the Secretary of State for his release. [FORM 6.49]

**6.135(4) [Certificate of release]** When the Secretary of State gives the release, he shall certify it accordingly, and send the certificate to the official receiver, to be filed in court.

**6.135(5) [Copy of certificate]** A copy of the certificate shall be sent by the Secretary of State to the former trustee, whose release is effective from the date of the certificate.

SECTION C: RELEASE ON COMPLETION OF ADMINISTRATION

## 6.136 Release of official receiver

**6.136(1) [Notice of intention]** The official receiver shall, before giving notice to the Secretary of State under section 299(2) (that the administration of the estate is for practical purposes complete), send out notice of his intention to do so to all creditors who have proved their debts, and to the bankrupt.

**6.136(2) [Accompanying summary]** The notice shall in each case be accompanied by a summary of the official receiver's receipts and payments as trustee.

**6.136(3) [Notice to court of date of release]** The Secretary of State, when he has under section 299(2) determined the date from which the official receiver is to have his release, shall give notice to the court that he has done so. The notice shall be accompanied by the summary referred to in paragraph (2).

## 6.137 Final meeting of creditors

**6.137(1) [Notice to creditors etc.]** Where the trustee is other than the official receiver, he shall give at least 28 days' notice of the final meeting of creditors to be held under section 331. The notice shall be sent to all creditors who have proved their debts, and to the bankrupt.

[FORM 6.35]

**6.137(2) [Trustee's report]** The trustee's report laid before the meeting under that section shall include–

(a) a summary of his receipts and payments, and

(b) a statement by him that he has reconciled his account with that which is held by the Secretary of State in respect of the bankruptcy.

**6.137(3) [Questioning of trustee]** At the final meeting, the creditors may question the trustee with respect to any matter contained in his report, and may resolve against him having his release.

**6.137(4) [Notice to court]** The trustee shall give notice to the court that the final meeting has been held; and the notice shall state whether or not he has given his release, and be accompanied by a copy of the report laid before the final meeting. A copy of the notice shall be sent by the trustee to the official receiver. [FORM 6.50]

**6.137(5) [No quorum at final meeting]** If there is no quorum present at the final meeting, the trustee shall report to the court that a final meeting was summoned in accordance with the Rules, but there was no quorum present; and the final meeting is then deemed to have been held, and the creditors not to have resolved against the trustee having his release.

**6.137(6) [Release of trustee]** If the creditors at the final meeting have not so resolved, the trustee is released when the notice under paragraph (4) is filed in court. If they have so resolved, the trustee must obtain his release from the Secretary of State, as provided by Rule 6.135.

## SECTION D: REMUNERATION

# 6.138 Fixing of remuneration

**6.138(1) [Entitlement to remuneration]** The trustee is entitled to receive remuneration for his services as such.

**6.138(2) [How fixed]** The remuneration shall be fixed either–

(a) as a percentage of the value of the assets in the bankrupt's estate which are realised or distributed, or of the one value and the other in combination, or

(b) by reference to the time properly given by the insolvency practitioner (as trustee) and his staff in attending to matters arising in the bankruptcy.

**6.138(3) [Determination under r. 6.138(2)]** Where the trustee is other than the official receiver, it is for the creditors' committee (if there is one) to determine whether his remuneration is to be fixed under paragraph (2)(a) or (b) and, if under paragraph (2)(a), to determine any percentage to be applied as there mentioned.

**6.138(4) [Matters relevant to r. 6.138(3) determination]** In arriving at that determination, the committee shall have regard to the following matters–

(a) the complexity (or otherwise) of the case,

(b) any respects in which, in connection with the administration of the estate, there falls on the insolvency practitioner (as trustee) any responsibility of an exceptional kind or degree,

(c) the effectiveness with which the insolvency practitioner appears to be carrying out, or to have carried out, his duties as trustee, and

(d) the value and nature of the assets in the estate with which the trustee has to deal.

**6.138(5) [If no committee or no determination]** If there is no creditors' committee, or the committee does not make the requisite determination, the trustee's remuneration may be fixed (in accordance with paragraph (2)) by a resolution of a meeting of creditors; and paragraph (4) applies to them as it does to the creditors' committee.

**6.138(6) [Otherwise fixed]** If not fixed as above, the trustee's remuneration shall be on the scale laid down for the official receiver by general regulations.

# 6.139 Other matters affecting remuneration

**6.139(1) [Where trustee sells for secured creditor]** Where the trustee sells assets on behalf of a secured creditor, he is entitled to take for himself, out of the proceeds of sale, a sum by way of remuneration equivalent to the remuneration chargeable in corresponding circumstances by the official receiver under general regulations.

**6.139(2) [Where joint trustees]** Where there are joint trustees, it is for them to agree between themselves as to how the remuneration payable should be apportioned. Any dispute arising between them may be referred–

(a) to the court, for settlement by order, or

(b) to the creditors' committee or a meeting of creditors, for settlement by resolution.

**6.139(3) [If trustee is a solicitor]** If the trustee is a solicitor and employs his own firm, or any partner in it, to act on behalf of the estate, profit costs shall not be paid unless this is authorised by the creditors' committee, the creditors or the court.

## 6.140 Recourse of trustee to meeting of creditors

**6.140** If the trustee's remuneration has been fixed by the creditors' committee, and he considers the rate or amount to be insufficient, he may request that it be increased by resolution of the creditors.

## 6.141 Recourse to the court

**6.141(1) [Trustee may apply to court]** If the trustee considers that the remuneration fixed for him by the creditors' committee, or by resolution of the creditors, or as under Rule 6.138(6), is insufficient, he may apply to the court for an order increasing its amount or rate.

**6.141(2) [Notice to committee etc.]** The trustee shall give at least 14 days' notice of his application to the members of the creditors' committee; and the committee may nominate one or more members to appear or be represented, and to be heard, on the application.

**6.141(3) [If no committee]** If there is no creditors' committee, the trustee's notice of his application shall be sent to such one or more of the bankrupt's creditors as the court may direct, which creditors may nominate one or more of their number to appear or be represented.

**6.141(4) [Costs of application]** The court may, if it appears to be a proper case, order the costs of the trustee's application, including the costs of any member of the creditors' committee appearing or being represented on it, or any creditor so appearing or being represented, to be paid out of the estate.

**History**
In r. 6.141(4) the words "or being represented" in both places where they occur inserted by the Insolvency (Amendment) Rules 1987 (SI 1987/1919), r. 3(1), Sch., Pt. 1, para. 115 as from 11 January 1988.

## 6.142 Creditor's claim that remuneration is excessive

**6.142(1) [Creditor may apply to court]** Any creditor of the bankrupt may, with the concurrence of at least 25 per cent. in value of the creditors (including himself), apply to the court for an order that the trustee's remuneration be reduced, on the grounds that it is, in all the circumstances, excessive.

**6.142(2) [Court may dismiss application etc.]** The court may, if it thinks that no sufficient cause is shown for the application, dismiss it; but it shall not do so unless the applicant has had an opportunity to attend the court for an *ex parte* hearing, of which he has been given at least 7 days' notice.

If the application is not dismissed under this paragraph, the court shall fix a venue for it to be heard.

**6.142(3) [Notice to trustee]** The applicant shall, at least 14 days before the hearing, send to the trustee a notice stating the venue so fixed; and the notice shall be accompanied by a copy of the application, and of any evidence which the applicant intends to adduce in support of it.

**6.142(4) [Court order]** If the court considers the application to be well-founded, it shall make an order fixing the remuneration at a reduced amount or rate.

**6.142(5) [Costs of application]** Unless the court orders otherwise, the costs of the application shall be paid by the applicant, and do not fall on the estate.

### SECTION E: SUPPLEMENTARY PROVISIONS

## 6.143 Trustee deceased

**6.143(1) [Notice to official receiver]** Subject as follows, where the trustee (other than the official receiver) has died, it is the duty of his personal representatives to give notice of the fact to the official receiver, specifying the date of the death.

This does not apply if notice has been given under any of the following paragraphs of this Rule.

**6.143(2) [Notice by partner etc.]** If the deceased trustee was a partner in a firm, which may be given to the official receiver by a partner in the firm who is qualified to act as an insolvency practitioner, or is a member of any body recognised by the Secretary of State for the authorisation of insolvency practitioners.

**6.143(3) [Notice by others]** Notice of the death may be giver by any person producing to the official receiver the relevant death certificate or a copy of it.

**6.143(4) [Notice to court by official receiver]** The official receiver shall give notice to the court, for the purpose of fixing the date of the deceased trustee's release in accordance with section 299(3)(a).

## 6.144 Loss of qualification as insolvency practitioner

**6.144(1) [Application of Rule]** This Rule applies where the trustee vacates office, under section 298(6), on his ceasing to be qualified to act as an insolvency practitioner in relation to the bankrupt.

**6.144(2) [Notice to official receiver etc.]** The trustee vacating office shall forthwith give notice of his doing so to the official receiver, who shall give notice to the Secretary of State.

The official receiver shall file in court a copy of his notice under this paragraph.

[FORM 6.51]

**6.144(3) [Application of r. 6.135]** Rule 6.135 applies as regards the trustee obtaining his release, as if he had been removed by the court.

## 6.145 Notice to official receiver of intention to vacate office

**6.145(1) [Notice of official receiver]** Where the trustee intends to vacate office, whether by resignation or otherwise, he shall give notice of his intention to the official receiver together with notice of any creditors' meeting to be held in respect of his vacation of office, including any meeting to receive his resignation.

**6.145(2) [Time limit for notice]** The notice to the official receiver must be given at least 21 days before any such creditors' meeting.

**6.145(3) [Details of property]** Where there remains in the bankrupt's estate any property which has not been realised, applied, distributed or otherwise fully dealt with in the bankruptcy, the trustee shall include in his notice to the official receiver details of the nature of that property, its value (or the fact that it has no value), its location, any action taken by the trustee to deal with that property or any reason for his not dealing with it, and the current position in relation to it.

**History**

R. 6.145 substituted by the Insolvency (Amendment) Rules 1987 (SI 1987/1919), r. 3(1), Sch., Pt. 1. para. 116 as from 11 January 1988; r. 6.145 formerly read as follows:

"**6.145(1)** Where the trustee intends to vacate office, whether by resignation or otherwise, and there remain in the estate any unrealised assets, he shall give notice of his intention to the official receiver. Informing him of the nature, value and whereabouts of the assets in question.

**(2)** Where there is to be a creditors' meeting so receive the trustee's resignation, or otherwise in respect of his vacation of office, the notice to the official receiver must be given at least 21 days before the meeting."

## 6.146 Trustee's duties on vacating office

**6.146(1) [Obligation to deliver any assets etc.]** Where the trustee ceases to be in office as such, in consequence of removal, resignation or lesser of qualification as an insolvency practitioner, he is under obligation forthwith to deliver up to the person succeeding him as trustee the assets of the estate (after deduction of any expenses properly incurred, and distributions made, by him) and further to deliver up to that person–

(a) the records of the bankruptcy, including correspondence, proofs and other related papers appertaining to the bankruptcy while it was within his responsibility, and

(b) the bankrupt's books, papers and other records.

**6.146(2) [When administration complete]** When the administration of the bankrupt's estate is for practical purposes complete, the trustee shall forthwith file in court all proofs remaining with him in the proceedings.

## 6.147 Power of court to set aside certain transactions

**6.147(1) [Trustee's transaction with associate]** If in the administration of the estate the trustee enters into any transaction with a person who is an associate of his, the court may, on the application of any person interested, set the transaction aside and order the trustee to compensate the estate for any loss suffered in consequence of it.

**6.147(2) [Where r. 6.147(1) does not apply]** This does not apply if either–

(a) the transaction was entered into with the prior consent of the court, or

(b) it is shown to the court's satisfaction that the transaction was for value, and that it was entered into by the trustee without knowing, or having any reason to suppose, that the person concerned was an associate.

**6.147(3) [Effect of Rule]** Nothing in this Rule is to be taken as prejudicing the operation of any rule of law or equity with respect to a trustee's dealings with trust property, or the fiduciary obligations of any person.

## 6.148 Rule against solicitation

**6.148(1) [Power of court]** Where the court is satisfied that any improper solicitation has been used by or on behalf of the trustee in obtaining proxies or procuring his appointment, it may order that no remuneration out of the estate be allowed to any person by whom, or on whose behalf, the solicitation was exercised.

**6.148(2) [Effect of court order]** An order of the court under this Rule overrides any resolution of the creditors' committee or the creditors, or any other provision of the Rules relating to the trustee's remuneration.

## 6.149 Enforcement of trustee's obligations to official receiver

**6.149(1) [Powers of court]** The court may, on the application of the official receiver, make such orders as it thinks necessary for enforcement of the duties of the trustee under section 305(3) (information and assistance to be given; production and inspection of books and records relating to the bankruptcy).

**6.149(2) [Extent of order]** An order of the court under this Rule may provide that all costs of and incidental to the official receiver's application shall be borne by the trustee.

# Chapter 11 – The Creditors' Committee

## 6.150 Membership of creditors' committee

**6.150(1) [Three-five members]** The creditors' committee shall consist of at least 3, and not more than 5, members.

**6.150(2) [Eligibility]** All the members of the committee must be creditors of the bankrupt; and any creditor (other than one who is fully secured) may be a member, so long as–

(a) he has lodged a proof of his debt, and

(b) his proof has neither been wholly disallowed for voting purposes, nor wholly rejected for the purposes of distribution or dividend.

**6.150(3) [Representation of body corporate]** A body corporate may be a member of the committee, but it cannot act as such otherwise than by a representative appointed under Rule 6.156.

## 6.151 Formalities of establishment

**6.151(1) [Trustee's certificate of due constitution]** The creditors' committee does not come into being, and accordingly cannot act, until the trustee has issued a certificate of its due constitution. [FORM 6.52]

**6.151(2) [If chairman of meeting not trustee]** If the chairman of the creditors' meeting which resolves to establish the committee is not the trustee, he shall forthwith give notice of the resolution to the trustee (or, as the case may be, the person appointed as trustee by that same meeting), and inform him of the names and addresses of the persons elected to be members of the committee.

**6.151(3) [Agreement to act]** No person may act as a member of the committee unless and until he has agreed to do so and, unless the relevant proxy contains a statement to the contrary, such agreement may be given by his proxy-holder present at the meeting establishing the committee.

**6.151(3A) [No certificate without agreement]** The trustee's certificate of the committee's due constitution shall not issue before at least 3 persons elected to be members of the committee have agreed to act.

**History**
R. 6.151(3) and (3A) substituted for the former r. 6.151(3) by the Insolvency (Amendment) Rules 1987 (SI 1987/1919), r. 3(1), Sch., Pt. 1, para. 117 as from 11 January 1988; the former r. 6.151(3) read as follows:
"No person may act as a member of the committee unless and until he has agreed so do so; and the trustee's certificate of the committee's due constitution shall not issue before at least 3 persons elected to be members of it have agreed to act."

**6.151(4) [Amended certificate]** As and when the others (if any) agree to act, the trustee shall issue an amended certificate. [FORM 6.52]

**6.151(5) [Certificate to be filed]** The certificate, and any amended certificate, shall be filed in court by the trustee.

**6.151(6) [Change in membership]** If after the first establishment of the committee there is any change in its membership, the trustee shall report the change to the court. [FORM 6.53]

## 6.152 Obligations of trustee to committee

**6.152(1) [Trustee's duty to report]** Subject as follows, it is the duty of the trustee to report to the members of the creditors' committee all such matters as appear to him to be, or as they have indicated to him as being, of concern to them with respect to the bankruptcy.

**6.152(2) [Non-compliance with request for information]** In the case of matters so indicated to him by the committee, the trustee need not comply with any request for information where it appears to him that–

(a) the request is frivolous or unreasonable, or

(b) the cost of complying would be excessive, having regard to the relative importance of the information, or

(c) the estate is without funds sufficient for enabling him to comply.

**6.152(3) [Report in summary form]** Where the committee has come into being more than 28 days after the appointment of the trustee, the latter shall report to them, in summary form, what actions he has taken since his appointment, and shall answer such questions as they may put to him regarding his conduct of the bankruptcy hitherto.

**6.152(4) [Summary report for subsequent member]** A person who becomes a member of the committee at any time after its first establishment is not entitled to require a report to him by the trustee, otherwise than in summary form, of any matters previously arising.

**6.152(5) [Access to trustee's records]** Nothing in this Rule disentitles the committee, or any member of it, from having access to the trustee's records of the bankruptcy, or from seeking an explanation of any matter within the committee's responsibility.

## 6.153 Meetings of the committee

**6.153(1) [Holding of meetings]** Subject as follows, meetings of the creditors' committee shall be held when and where determined by the trustee.

**6.153(2) [First and subsequent meetings]** The trustee shall call a first meeting of the committee to take place within 3 months of his appointment or of the committee's establishment (whichever is the later); and thereafter he shall call a meeting–

(a) if so requested by a member of the committee or his representative (the meeting then to be held within 21 days of the request being received by the trustee), and

(b) for a specified date, if the committee has previously resolved that a meeting be held on that date.

**6.153(3) [Notice of venue]** The trustee shall give 7 days' notice in writing of the venue of any meeting to every member of the committee (or his representative, if designated for that purpose), unless in any ease the requirement of the notice has been waived by or on behalf of any member.

Waiver may be signified either at or before the meeting.

## 6.154 The chairman at meetings

**6.154(1) [Trustee or his nominee]** The chairman at any meeting of the creditors committee shall be the trustee, or a person appointed by him in writing to act.

**6.154(2) [Nominated chairman]** A person so nominated must be either–

(a) one who is qualified to act as an insolvency practitioner in relation to the bankrupt, or

(b) an employee of the trustee or his firm who is experienced in insolvency matters.

## 6.155 Quorum

**6.155** A meeting of the committee is duly constituted if due notice of it has been given to all the members and at least 2 of the members are present or represented.

## 6.156 Committee-members' representatives

**6.156(1) [Representation]** A member of the creditors' committee may, in relation to the business of the committee, be represented by another person duly authorised by him for that purpose.

**6.156(2) [Letter of authority]** A person acting as a committee-member's representative must hold a letter of authority entitling him so to act (either generally or specially) and signed by or on behalf of the committee-member, and for this purpose any proxy in relation to any meeting of creditors of the bankrupt shall, unless it contains a statement to the contrary, be treated as such a letter of authority to act generally signed by or on behalf of the committee-member.

**History**

In r. 6.156(2) the words from "specially)" to the end substituted by the Insolvency (Amendment) Rules 1987 (SI 1987/1919), r. 3(1), Sch., Pt. 1, para. 118(1) as from 11 January 1988; the former words read as follows:

"specially). The letter must be signed by or on behalf of the committee-member."

**6.156(3) [Production of letter of authority]** The chairman at any meeting of the committee may call on a person claiming to act as a committee-member's representative to produce his letter of authority, and may exclude him if it appears that his authority is deficient.

**6.156(4) [Who may not be a representative]** No member may be represented by a body corporate, or by a person who is an undischarged bankrupt or is subject to a composition or arrangement with his creditors.

**6.156(5) [No dual representation]** No person shall–

(a) on the same committee, act at one and the same time as representative of more than one committee-member, or

(b) act both as a member of the committee and as representative of another member.

**6.156(6) [Signing as representative]** Where the representative of a committee-member signs any document on the latter's behalf, the fact that he so signs must be stated below his signature.

**6.156(7) [Validity of acts]** The acts of the committee are valid notwithstanding any defect in the appointment or qualifications of any committee-member's representative.

**History**

R. 6.156(7) added by the Insolvency (Amendment) Rules 1987 (SI 1987/1919), r. 3(1), Sch., Pt. 1. para. 115(2) as from 11 January 1988.

## 6.157 Resignation

**6.157** A member of the creditors' committee may resign by notice in writing delivered to the trustee.

## 6.158 Termination of membership

**6.158(1) [Automatic termination]** A person's membership of the creditors committee is automatically terminated if–

(a) he becomes bankrupt or compounds or arranges with his creditors, or

(b) at 3 consecutive meetings of the committee he is neither present nor represented (unless at the third of those meetings it is resolved that this Rule is not to apply in his case), or

(c) he ceases to be, or is found never to have been, a creditor.

**6.158(2) [Termination on bankruptcy]** However, if the cause of termination is the member's bankruptcy, his trustee in bankruptcy replaces him as a member of the committee.

# 6.159 Removal

**6.159** A member of the creditors' committee may be removed by resolution at a meeting of creditors, at least 14 days' notice having been given of the intention to move that resolution.

# 6.160 Vacancies

**6.160(1) [Application of Rule]** The following applies if there is a vacancy in the membership of the creditors' committee.

**6.160(2) [Agreement not to fill vacancy]** The vacancy need not be filled if the trustee and a majority of the remaining committee-members so agree, provided that the number of members does not fall below the minimum required by Rule 6.150(1).

**6.160(3) [Appointment by trustee]** The trustee may appoint any creditor (being qualified under the Rules to be a member of the committee) to fill the vacancy, if a majority of the other members of the committee agree to the appointment and the creditor concerned consents to act.

**6.160(4) [Appointment by resolution]** Alternatively, a meeting of creditors may resolve that a creditor be appointed (with his consent) to fill the vacancy. In this case at least 14 days' notice must have been given of a resolution to make such an appointment (whether or not of a person named in the notice).

**6.160(5) [Report to trustee]** Where the vacancy is filled by an appointment made by a creditors' meeting at which the trustee is not present, the chairman of the meeting shall report to the trustee the appointment which has been made.

# 6.161 Voting rights and resolutions

**6.161(1) [Votes etc.]** At any meeting of the committee, each member (whether present himself, or by his representative) has one vote; and a resolution is passed when a majority of the members present or represented have voted in favour of it.

**6.161(2) [Record of resolutions]** Every resolution passed shall be recorded in writing, either separately or as part of the minutes of the meeting. The record shall be signed by the chairman and kept with the records of the bankruptcy.

# 6.162 Resolutions by post

**6.162(1) [Sending proposed resolution]** In accordance with this Rule, the trustee may seek to obtain the agreement of members of the creditors' committee to a resolution by sending to every member (or his representative designated for the purpose) a copy of the proposed resolution.

**6.162(2) [Copy of proposed resolution]** Where the trustee makes use of the procedure allowed by this Rule, he shall send out to members of the committee or their representatives (as the case may be) a copy of any proposed resolution on which a decision is sought, which shall be set out in such a way that agreement with or dissent from each separate resolution may be indicated by the recipient on the copy so sent.

**History**

In r. 6.162(2) the words from "a copy of any proposed resolution" to the end substituted by the Insolvency (Amendment) Rules 1987 (SI 1987/1919), r. 3(1), Sch., Pt. 1, para. 119(1) as from 11 January 1988; the former words read as follows:

"a statement incorporating the resolution to which their agreement is sought, each resolution (if more than one) being set out in a separate document."

**6.162(3) [Member requiring meeting]** Any member of the committee may, within 7 business days from the date of the trustee sending out a resolution, require the trustee to summon a meeting of the committee to consider the matters raised by the resolution.

**History**
In r. 6.162(3) the word "business" inserted by the Insolvency (Amendment) Rules 1987 (SI 1987/1919), r. 3(1), Sch., Pt. 1, para. 119(2) as from 11 January 1988.

**6.162(4) [Deemed passing of resolution]** In the absence of such a request, the resolution is deemed to have been carried in the committee if and when the trustee is notified in writing by a majority of the members that they concur with it.

**6.162(5) [Copy resolutions]** A copy of every resolution passed under this Rule, and a note that the concurrence of the committee was obtained, shall be kept with the records of the bankruptcy.

## 6.163 Trustee's reports

**6.163(1) [(Trustee directed to report]** The trustee shall, as and when directed by the creditors' committee (but not more often than once in any period of 2 months), send a written report to every member of the committee setting out the position generally as regards the progress of the bankruptcy and matters arising in connection with it, to which he (the trustee) considers the committee's attention should be drawn.

**6.163(2) [If no directions to report]** In the absence of any such directions by the committee, the trustee shall send such a report not less often than once in every period of 6 months.

**6.163(3) [Effect of Rule]** The obligations of the trustee under this Rule are without prejudice to those imposed by Rule 6.152.

## 6.164 Expenses of members etc.

**6.164** The trustee shall defray out of the estate, in the prescribed order of priority, any reasonable travelling expenses directly incurred by members of the creditors' committee or their representatives in respect of their attendance at the committee's meetings, or otherwise on the committee's business.

## 6.165 Dealings by committee-members and others

**6.165(1) [Application of Rule]** This Rule applies to–

(a) any member of the creditors' committee,
(b) any committee-member's representative,
(c) any person who is an associate of a member of the committee or a committee-member's representative, and
(d) any person who has been a member of the committee at any time in the last 12 months.

**6.165(2) [Prohibited transactions]** Subject as follows, a person to whom this Rule applies shall not enter into any transaction whereby he–

(a) receives out of the estate any payment for services given or goods supplied in connection with the estate's administration, or
(b) obtains any profit from the administration, or
(c) acquires any asset forming part of the estate.

**6.165(3) [Leave or sanction for r. 6.165(2) transaction]** Such a transaction may be entered into by a person to whom this Rule applies–

(a) with the prior leave of the court, or
(b) if he does so as a matter of urgency , or by way of performance of a contract in force before the commencement of the bankruptcy, and obtains the court's leave for the transaction, having applied for it without undue delay, or
(c) with the prior sanction of the creditors' committee, where it is satisfied (after full disclosure of the circumstances) that the person will be giving full value in the transaction.

**6.165(4) [Resolution to sanction transaction]** Where in the committee a resolution is proposed that sanction be accorded for a transaction to be entered into which, without the sanction or the leave of the court, would be in contravention of this Rule, no member of the committee, and no representative of a member, shall vote if he is to participate directly or indirectly in the transaction.

**6.165(5) [Powers of court]** The court may, on application of any person interested–

(a) set aside a transaction on the ground that it has been entered into in contravention of this Rule, and

(b) make with respect to it such other order as it thinks fit, including (subject to the following paragraph) an order requiring a person to whom this Rule applies to account for any profit obtained from the transaction and compensate the estate for any resultant loss.

**6.165(6) [Member's or representative's associate]** In the case of a person to whom this Rule applies as an associate of a member of the committee or of a committee-member's representative the court shall not make any order under paragraph (5), if satisfied that he entered into the relevant transaction without having any reason to suppose that in doing so he would contravene this Rule.

**6.165(7) [Costs of application]** The costs of an application to the court for leave under this Rule do not fall on the estate, unless the court so orders.

## 6.166 Committee's functions vested in Secretary of State

**6.166(1) [Trustee's notices and reports]** At any time when the functions of the creditors' committee are bested in the Secretary of State under section 302(1) or (2), requirements of the Act or the Rules about notices to be given, or reports to be made, to the committee by the trustee do not apply, otherwise than as enabling the committee to require a report as to any matter.

**6.166(2) [Exercise by official receiver]** Where the committee's functions are so vested under section 302(2), they may be exercised by the official receiver.

# Chapter 12 – Special Manager

## 6.167 Appointment and remuneration

**6.167(1) [Application under s. 370 to be supported by report]** An application made by the official receiver or trustee under section 370 for the appointment of a person to be special manager shall be supported by a report setting out the reasons for the application.

The report shall include the applicant's estimate of the value of the estate, property or business in respect of which the special manager is to be appointed.

**6.167(2) [Duration of appointment]** The court's order appointing the special manager shall specify the duration of his appointment, which may be for a period of time, or until the occurrence of a specified event. Alternatively, the order may specify that the duration of the appointment is to be subject to a further order of the court. [FORM 6.54]

**6.167(3) [Renewal]** The appointment of a special manager may be renewed by order of the court.

**6.167(4) [Remuneration]** The special manager's remuneration shall be fixed from time to time by the court.

## 6.168 Security

**6.168(1) [Effect of giving security]** The appointment of the special manager does not take effect until the person appointed has given (or, being allowed by the court to do so, undertaken to give) security to the person who applies for him to be appointed.

**6.168(2) [Special or general security]** It is not necessary that security shall be given for each separate bankruptcy; but it may be given either specially for a particular bankruptcy, or generally for any bankruptcy in relation to which the special manager may be employed as such.

**6.168(3) [Amount of security]** The amount of the security shall be not less than the value of the estate, property or business in respect of which he is appointed, as estimated by the applicant in his report under Rule 6.167(1).

**6.168(4) [Certificate of adequacy]** When the special manager has given security to the person applying for his appointment, that person's certificate as to the adequacy of the security shall be filed in court.

**6.168(5) [Cost of providing security]** The cost of providing the security shall be paid in the first instance by the special manager; but–

(a) where a bankruptcy order is not made, he is entitled to be reimbursed out of the property of the debtor, and the court may make an order on the debtor accordingly, and

(b) where a bankruptcy order is made, he is entitled to be reimbursed out of the estate in the prescribed order of priority.

## 6.169 Failure to give or keep up security

**6.169(1) [Failure to give security]** If the special manager fails to give the required security within the time stated for that purpose by the order appointing him, or any extension of that time may be allowed, the official receiver or trustee (as the case may be) shall report the failure to the court, which may thereupon discharge the order appointing the special manager.

**6.169(2) [Failure to keep up security]** If the special manager fails to keep up his security, the official receiver or trustee shall report his failure to the court, which may thereupon remove the special manager, and make such order as it thinks fit as to costs.

**6.169(3) [Directions on removal]** If an order is made under this Rule removing the special manager, or discharging the order appointing him, the court shall give directions as to whether any, and if so what, steps should be taken for the appointment of another special manager in his place.

## 6.170 Accounting

**6.170(1) [Contents of accounts]** The special manager shall produce accounts, containing details of his receipts and payments, for the approval of the trustee.

**6.170(2) [Period of accounts]** The accounts shall be in respect of 3-month periods for the duration of the.special manager's appointment (or for a lesser period, if his appointment terminates less than 3 months from its date, or from the date to which the last accounts were made up).

**6.170(3) [When accounts approved]** When the accounts have been approved, the special manager's receipts and payments shall be added to those of the trustee.

## 6.171 Termination of appointment

**6.171(1) [Automatic termination]** The special manager's appointment terminates if the bankruptcy petition is dismissed or if, an interim receiver having been appointed, the latter is discharged without a bankruptcy order having been made.

**6.171(2) [Application to court]** If the official receiver or the trustee is of opinion that the employment of the special manager is no longer necessary or profitable for the estate, he shall apply to the court for directions, and the court may order the special manager's appointment to be terminated.

**6.171(3) [Resolution of creditors]** The official receiver or the trustee shall make the same application if a resolution of the creditors is passed, requesting that the appointment be terminated.

# Chapter 13 – Public Examination of Bankrupt

## 6.172 Order for public examination

**6.172(1) [Copy of order to bankrupt]** If the official receiver applies to the court, under section 290, for the public examination of the bankrupt, a copy of the court's order shall, forthwith after its making, be sent by the official receiver to the bankrupt. [FORM 6.55]

**6.172(2) [Venue and bankrupt's attendance]** The order shall appoint a venue for the hearing, and direct the bankrupt's attendance thereat.

**6.172(3) [Notice of hearing]** The official receiver shall give at least 14 days' notice of the hearing–

(a) if a trustee has been nominated or appointed, to him;

(b) if a special manager has been appointed, to him; and

(c) subject to any contrary direction of the court, to every creditor of the bankrupt who is known to the official receiver or is identified in the bankrupt's statement of affairs.

**6.172(4) [Advertisement]** The official receiver may, if he thinks fit, cause notice of the order to be given, by public advertisement in one or more newspapers, at least 14 days before the day fixed for the hearing.

## 6.173 Order on request by creditors

**6.173(1) [Form of request etc.]** A request by a creditor to the official receiver, under section 290(2), for the bankrupt to be publicly examined shall be made in writing and be accompanied by–

(a) a list of the creditors concurring with the request and the amount of their respective claims in the bankruptcy,

(b) from each creditor concurring, written confirmation of his concurrence, and

(c) a statement of the reasons why the examination is requested.

Sub-paragraphs (a) and (b) do not apply if the requisitioning creditor's debt is alone sufficient, without the concurrence of others. [FORM 6.56]

**6.173(2) [Security for expenses of hearing]** Before an application to the court is made on the request, the requisitionist shall deposit with the official receiver such sum as the latter may determine to be appropriate by way of security for the expenses of the hearing of a public examination, if ordered.

**6.173(3) [Time for application]** Subject as follows, the official receiver shall, within 28 days of receiving the request, make the application to the court required by section 290(2).

**6.173(4) [Relief from unreasonable request]** If the official receiver is of opinion that the request is an unreasonable one in the circumstances, he may apply to the court for an order relieving him from the obligation to make the application otherwise required by that subsection.

**6.173(5) [Notice of relief order etc.]** If the court so orders, and the application for the order was made *ex parte*, notice of the order shall be given forthwith by the official receiver to the requisitionist. If the application for an order is dismissed, the official receiver's application under section 290(2) shall be made forthwith on conclusion of the hearing of the application first mentioned.

## 6.174 Bankrupt unfit for examination

**6.174(1) [Application for stay etc.]** Where the bankrupt is suffering from any mental disorder or physical affliction or disability rendering him unfit to undergo or attend for public examination, the court may, on application in that behalf, either stay the order for his public examination or direct that it shall be conducted in such manner and at such place as it thinks fit. [FORM 6.57]

**6.174(2) [Who may apply]** Application under this Rule shall be made–

(a) by a person who has been appointed by a court in the United Kingdom or elsewhere to manage the affairs of, or to represent, the bankrupt, or

(b) by a relative or friend of the bankrupt whom the court considers to be a proper person to make the application, or

(c) by the official receiver.

**6.174(3) [Application not by official receiver]** Where the application is made by a person other than the official receiver, then–

(a) it shall, unless the bankrupt is a patient within the meaning of the Mental Health Act 1983, be supported by the affidavit of a registered medical practitioner as to the bankrupt's mental and physical condition;
(b) at least 7 days' notice of the application shall be given to the official receiver and the trustee (if any); and
(c) before any order is made on the application, the applicant shall deposit with the official receiver such sum as the latter certifies to be necessary for the additional expenses of any examination that may be ordered on the application.

An order made on the application may provide that the expenses of the examination are to be payable, as to a specified proportion, out of the deposit under sub-paragraph (c), instead of out of the estate.

**6.174(4) [Application by official receiver]** Where the application is made by the official receiver, it may be made *ex parte*, and may be supported by evidence in the form of a report by the official receiver to the court.

## 6.175 Procedure at hearing

**6.175(1) [Examination on oath]** The bankrupt shall at the hearing be examined on oath; and he shall answer all such questions as the court may put, or allow to be put, to him.

**6.175(2) [Appearances etc.]** Any of the persons allowed by section 290(4) to question the bankrupt may, with the approval of the court (made known either at the hearing or in advance of it), appear by solicitor or counsel; or he may in writing authorise another person to question the bankrupt on his behalf.

**6.175(3) [Representation of bankrupt]** The bankrupt may at his own expense employ a solicitor with or without counsel, who may put to him such questions as the court may allow for the purpose of enabling him to explain or qualify any answers given by him, and may make representations on his behalf.

**6.175(4) [Record of examination]** There shall be made in writing such record of the examination as the court thinks proper. The record shall be read over either to or by the bankrupt, signed by him, and verified by affidavit at a venue fixed by the court. [FORM 6.58]

**6.175(5) [Record as evidence]** The written record may, in any proceedings (whether under the Act or otherwise) be used as evidence against the bankrupt of any statement made by him in the course of his public examination.

**6.175(6) [Criminal proceedings etc.]** If criminal proceedings have been instituted against the bankrupt, and the court is of opinion that the continuance of the hearing would be calculated to prejudice a fair trial of those proceedings, the hearing may be adjourned.

## 6.176 Adjournment

**6.176(1) [Adjourned by court]** The public examination may be adjourned by the court from time to time, either to a fixed date or generally. [FORM 6.59]

**6.176(2) [Resumption]** Where the examination has been adjourned generally, the court may at any time on the application of the official receiver or of the bankrupt–
(a) fix a venue for the resumption of the examination, and
(b) give directions as to the manner in which, and the time within which, notice of the resumed public examination is to be given to persons entitled to take part in it.

[FORM 6.60]

**6.176(3) [Deposit for expenses re application]** Where application under paragraph (2) is made by the bankrupt, the court may grant it on terms that the expenses of giving the notices required by that paragraph shall be paid by him and that, before a venue for the resumed public examination is fixed, he shall deposit with the official receiver such sum as the latter considers necessary to cover those expenses.

**6.176(4) [Official receiver's application under s. 279(3)]** Where the examination is adjourned generally, the official receiver may, there and then, make application under section 279(3) (suspension of automatic discharge).

**6.176(5) [Copies of order to be sent by court]** If, on the hearing of an application pursuant to paragraph (4), the court makes an order suspending the bankrupt's discharge, copies of such order shall be sent by the court to the official receiver, the trustee and the bankrupt.

**History**

R. 6.176(5) inserted by the Insolvency (Amendment) Rules 1999 (SI 1999/359), r. 1, Sch., para. 6 as from 22 March 1999.

## 6.177 Expenses of examination

**6.177(1) [Expenses paid out of r. 6.173(2) deposit]** Where a public examination of the bankrupt has been ordered by the court on a creditors' requisition under Rule 6.173, the court may order that the expenses of the examination are to be paid, as to a specified proportion, out of the deposit under Rule 6.173(2), instead of out of the estate.

**6.177(2) [Official receiver not liable for costs]** In no case do the costs and expenses of a public examination fall on the official receiver personally.

# Chapter 14 – Disclaimer

## 6.178 Trustee's notice of disclaimer

**6.178(1) [Contents of notice]** Where the trustee disclaims property under section 315, the notice of disclaimer shall contain such particulars of the property disclaimed as enable it to be easily identified. [FORM 6.61]

**6.178(2) [Notice to be signed etc.]** The notice shall be signed by the trustee and filed in court, with a copy. The court shall secure that both the notice and the copy are sealed and endorsed with the date of filing.

**6.178(3) [Copy notice returned to trustee]** The copy notice, so sealed and endorsed, shall be returned by the court to the trustee as follows–

(a) if the notice has been delivered at the offices of the court by the trustee in person, it shall be handed to him,

(b) if it has been delivered by some person acting on the trustee's behalf, it shall be handed to that person, for immediate transmission to the trustee, and

(c) otherwise, it shall be sent to the trustee by first class post.

The court shall cause to be endorsed on the original notice, or otherwise recorded on the file, the manner in which the copy notice was returned to the trustee.

**6.178(4) [Date of notice]** For the purposes of section 315 the date of the prescribed notice is that which is endorsed on it, and on the copy, in accordance with this Rule.

## 6.179 Communication of disclaimer to persons interested

**6.179(1) [Copy notices]** Within 7 days after the day on which a copy of the notice of disclaimer is returned to him, the trustee shall send or give copies of the notice (showing the date endorsed as required by Rule 6.178) to the persons mentioned in paragraphs (2) to (5) below.

**6.179(2) [Leasehold property]** Where the property disclaimed is of a leasehold nature, he shall send or give a copy to every person who (to his knowledge) claims under the bankrupt as underlessee or mortgagee.

**6.179(3) [Property in a dwelling-house]** Where the disclaimer is of property in a dwelling-house, he shall send or give a copy to every person who (to his knowledge) is in occupation of, or claims a right to occupy, the house.

**6.179(4) [Giving notice]** He shall in any case send or give a copy of the notice to every person who (to his knowledge)–

(a) claims an interest in the disclaimed property, or

(b) is under any liability in respect of the property, not being a liability discharged by the disclaimer.

**6.179(5) [Unprofitable contract]** If the disclaimer is of an unprofitable contract, he shall send or give copies of the notice to all such persons as, to his knowledge, are parties to the contract or have interests under it.

**6.179(6) [Late communication]** If subsequently it comes to the trustee's knowledge, in the case of any person, that he has such an interest in the disclaimed property as would have entitled him to receive a copy of the notice of disclaimer in pursuance of paragraphs (2) to (5), the trustee shall then forthwith send or give to that person a copy of the notice.

But compliance with this paragraph is not required if–

(a) the trustee is satisfied that the person has already been made aware of the disclaimer and its date, or

(b) the court, on the trustee's application, orders that compliance is not required in that particular case.

**6.179(7) [Notice to minor re dwelling-house]** A notice or copy notice to be served on any person under the age of 18 in relation to the disclaimer of property in a dwelling-house is sufficiently served if sent or given to the parent or guardian of that person.

**History**

R. 6.179(7) added by the Insolvency (Amendment) Rules 1987 (SI 1987/1919), r. 3(1), Sch., Pt. 1, para. 120 as from 11 January 1988.

## 6.180 Additional notices

**6.180** The trustee disclaiming property may, without prejudice to his obligations under sections 315 to 319 and Rules 6.178 and 6.179, at any time give notice of the disclaimer to any persons who in his opinion ought, in the public interest or otherwise, to be informed of it.

## 6.181 Duty to keep court informed

**6.181** The trustee shall notify the court from time to time as to the persons to whom he has sent or given copies of the notice of disclaimer under the two preceding Rules, giving their names and addresses, and the nature of their respective interests.

## 6.182 Application for leave to disclaim

**6.182(1) [Applying ex parte]** Where under section 315(4) the trustee requires the leave of the court to disclaim property claimed for the bankrupt's estate under section 307 or 308, he may apply for that leave *ex parte*.

**6.182(2) [Accompanying report]** The application must be accompanied by a report–

(a) giving such particulars of the property proposed to be disclaimed as enable it to be easily identified,

(b) setting out the reasons why, the property having been claimed for the estate, the court's leave to disclaim is now applied for, and

(c) specifying the persons (if any) who have been informed of the trustee's intention to make the application.

**6.182(3) [Copy of consent to disclaimer]** If it is stated in the report that any person's consent to the disclaimer has been signified, a copy of that consent must be annexed to the report.

**6.182(4) [Court may grant leave etc.]** The court may, on consideration of the application, grant the leave applied for; and it may, before granting leave–

(a) order that notice of the application be given to all such persons who, if the property is disclaimed, will be entitled to apply for a vesting or other order under section 320, and

(b) fix a venue for the hearing of the application under section 315(4).

## 6.183 Application by interested party under s. 316

**6.183(1) [Application of Rule]** The following applies where, in the case of any property, application is made to the trustee by an interested party under section 316 (request for decision whether the property is to be disclaimed or not).

**6.183(2) [Delivery and form of application]** The application–

(a) shall be delivered to the trustee personally or by registered post, and

(b) shall be made in the form known as "notice to elect", or a substantially similar form. [FORM 6.62]

**6.183(3) [Where property cannot be disclaimed without leave of court]** This paragraph applies in a case where the property concerned cannot be disclaimed by the trustee without the leave of the court.

If within the period of 28 days mentioned in section 316(1) the trustee applies to the court for leave to disclaim, the court shall extend the time allowed by that section for giving notice of disclaimer to a date not earlier than the date fixed for the hearing of the application.

## 6.184 Interest in property to be declared on request

**6.184(1) [Notice to declare interest]** If, in the case of property which the trustee has the right to disclaim, it appears to him that there is some person who claims, or may claim, to have an interest in the property, he may give notice to that person calling on him to declare within 14 days whether he claims any such interest and, if so, the nature and extent of it. [FORM 6.63]

**6.184(2) [Failing compliance with notice]** Failing compliance with the notice, the trustee is entitled to assume that the person concerned has no such interest in the property as will prevent or impede its disclaimer.

## 6.185 Disclaimer presumed valid and effective

**6.185** Any disclaimer of property by the trustee is presumed valid and effective, unless it is proved that he has been in breach of his duty with respect to the giving of notice of disclaimer, or otherwise under sections 315 to 319, or under this Chapter of the Rules.

## 6.186 Application for exercise of court's powers under s. 320

**6.186(1) [Application of Rule]** This Rule applies with respect to an application by any person under section 320 for an order of the court to vest or deliver disclaimed property.

**6.186(2) [Time for application]** The application must be made within 3 months of the applicant becoming aware of the disclaimer, or of his receiving a copy of the trustee's notice of disclaimer sent under Rule 6.179, whichever is the earlier.

**6.186(3) [Contents of affidavit]** The applicant shall with his application file an affidavit–

(a) stating whether he applies under paragraph (a) of section 320(2) (claim of interest in the property), under paragraph (b) (liability not discharged) or under paragraph (c) (occupation of dwelling-house);

(b) specifying the date on which he received a copy of the trustee's notice of disclaimer, or otherwise became aware of the disclaimer; and

(c) specifying the grounds of his application and the order which he desires the court to make under section 320.

**6.186(4) [Venue for hearing]** The court shall fix a venue for the hearing of the application; and the applicant shall, not later than 7 days before the date fixed, give to the trustee notice of the venue, accompanied by copies of the application and the affidavit under paragraph (3).

**6.186(5) [Directions for notice etc.]** On the hearing of the application, the court may give directions as to other persons (if any) who should be sent or given notice of the application and the grounds on which it is made.

**6.186(6) [Sealed copies of order]** Sealed copies of any order made on the application shall be sent by the court to the applicant and the trustee.

**6.186(7) [Leasehold property or property in a dwelling-house]** In a case where the property disclaimed is of a leasehold nature, or is property in a dwelling-house, and section 317 or (as the case may be) section 318 applies to suspend the effect of the disclaimer, there shall be included in the court's order a direction giving effect to the disclaimer.

This paragraph does not apply if, at the time when the order is issued, other applications under section 320 are pending in respect of the same property.

# Chapter 15 – Replacement of Exempt Property

## 6.187 Purchase of replacement property

**6.187(1) [Time for purchase]** A purchase of replacement property under section 308(3) may be made either before or after the realisation by the trustee of the value of the property vesting in him under the section.

**6.187(2) [Sufficiency of funds in estate]** The trustee is under no obligation, by virtue of the section, to apply funds to the purchase of a replacement for property vested in him, unless and until he has sufficient funds in the estate for that purpose.

## 6.188 Money provided in lieu of sale

**6.188(1) [Application of Rule]** The following applies where a third party proposes to the trustee that he (the former) should provide the estate with a sum of money enabling the bankrupt to be left in possession of property which would otherwise be made to vest in the trustee under section 308.

**6.188(2) [Reasonableness of proposal]** The trustee may accept that proposal, if satisfied that it is a reasonable one, and that the estate will benefit to the extent of the value of the property in question less the cost of a reasonable replacement.

# Chapter 16 – Income Payments Orders

## 6.189 Application for order

**6.189(1) [Court to fix venue]** Where the trustee applies for an income payments order under section 310, the court shall fix a venue for the hearing of the application.

**6.189(2) [Notice etc. to bankrupt]** Notice of the application, and of the venue, shall be sent by the trustee to the bankrupt at least 28 days before the day fixed for the hearing, together with a copy of the trustee's application and a short statement of the grounds on which it is made.

[FORM 6.64]

**6.189(3) [Contents of notice]** The notice shall inform the bankrupt that–

(a) unless at least 7 days before the date fixed for the hearing he sends to the court and to the trustee written consent to an order being made in the terms of the application, he is required to attend the hearing, and

(b) if he attends, he will be given an opportunity to show cause why the order should not be made, or an order should be made otherwise than as applied for by the trustee.

## 6.190 Action to follow making of order

**6.190(1) [Copy of order to bankrupt]** Where the court makes an income payments order, a sealed copy of the order shall, forthwith after it is made, be sent by the trustee to the bankrupt.

[FORM 6.65]
or [FORM 6.66]

**6.190(2) [Copy of order under s. 310(3)(b)]** If the order is made under section 310(3)(b), a sealed copy of the order shall also be sent by the trustee to the person to whom the order is directed.

## 6.191 Variation of order

**6.191(1) [Non-compliance with s. 310(3)(a) order]** If an income payments order is made under section 310(3)(a), and the bankrupt does not comply with it, the trustee may apply to the court for the order to be varied, so as to take effect under section 310(3)(b) as an order to the payor of the relevant income. [FORM 6.67]

**6.191(2) [Ex parte application]** The trustee's application under this Rule may be made *ex parte*.

**6.191(3) [Copy order to trustee and bankrupt]** Sealed copies of any order made on the application shall, forthwith after it is made, be sent by the court to the trustee and the bankrupt.

**6.191(4) [Variation etc. of s. 310(3)(b) order]** In the case of an order varying or discharging an income payments order made under section 310(3)(b), an additional sealed copy shall be sent to the trustee, for transmission forthwith to the payor of the relevant income.

## 6.192 Order to payor of income: administration

**6.192(1) [Compliance by payer]** Where a person receives notice of an income payments order under section 310(3)(b), with reference to income otherwise payable by him to the bankrupt, he shall make the arrangements requisite for immediate compliance with the order.

**6.192(2) [Costs of compliance]** When making any payment to the trustee, he may deduct the appropriate fee towards the clerical and administrative costs of compliance with the income payments order.

He shall give to the bankrupt a written statement of any amount deducted by him under this paragraph.

**6.192(3) [Where payer no longer liable etc.]** Where a person receives notice of an income payments order imposing on him a requirement under section 310(3)(b), and either–

(a) he is then no longer liable to make to the bankrupt any payment of income, or

(b) having made payments in compliance with the order, he ceases to be so liable,

he shall forthwith give notice of that fact to the trustee.

## 6.193 Review of order

**6.193(1) [Application to court]** Where an income payments order is in force, either the trustee or the bankrupt may apply to the court for the order to be varied or discharged.

**6.193(2) [Application by trustee]** If the application is made by the trustee, Rule 6.189 applies (with any necessary modification) as in the case of an application for an income payments order.

**6.193(3) [Application by bankrupt]** If the application is made by the bankrupt, it shall be accompanied by a short statement of the grounds on which it is made.

**6.193(4) [Court may dismiss application etc.]** The court may, if it thinks that no sufficient cause is shown for the application, dismiss it; but it shall not do so unless the applicant has had an opportunity to attend the court for an *ex parte* hearing, of which he has been given at least 7 days' notice.

If the application is not dismissed under this paragraph, the court shall fix a venue for it to be heard.

**6.193(5) [Notice of venue etc.]** At least 28 days before the date fixed for the hearing, the applicant shall send to the trustee or the bankrupt (whichever of them is not himself the applicant) notice of the venue, accompanied by a copy of the application.

Where the applicant is the bankrupt, the notice shall be accompanied by a copy of the statement of grounds under paragraph (3).

**6.193(6) [Appearance etc. by trustee]** The trustee may, if he thinks fit, appear and be heard on the application; and, whether or not he intends to appear, he may, not less than 7 days before the date fixed for the hearing, file a written report of any matters which he considers ought to be drawn to the court's attention.

If such a report is filed, a copy of it shall be sent by the trustee to the bankrupt.

**6.193(7) [Sealed copies of order]** Sealed copies of any order made on the application shall, forthwith after the order is made, be sent by the court to the trustee, the bankrupt and the payor (if other than the bankrupt). [FORM 6.66]

# Chapter 17 – Action by Court Under Section 369 Order to Inland Revenue Official

## 6.194 Application for order

**6.194(1) [Application to specify documents etc.]** An application by the official receiver or the trustee for an order under section 369 (order to inland revenue official to produce documents) shall specify (with such particularity as will enable the order, if made, to be most easily complied with) the documents whose production to the court is desired, naming the official to whom the order is to be addressed.

**6.194(2) [Court to fix venue]** The court shall fix a venue for the hearing of the application.

**6.194(3) [Notice of venue etc. to Commissioners]** Notice of the venue, accompanied by a copy of the application, shall be sent by the applicant to the Commissioners of Inland Revenue ("the Commissioners") at least 28 days before the hearing.

**6.194(4) [Whether Commissioners consent or object]** The notice shall require the Commissioners, not later than 7 days before the date fixed for the hearing of the application, to inform the court whether they consent or object to the making of an order under the section.

**6.194(5) [If Commissioners consent]** If the Commissioners consent to the making of an order, they shall inform the court of the name of the official to whom it should be addressed, if other than the one named in the application.

**6.194(6) [If Commissioners object]** If the Commissioners object to the making of an order, they shall secure that an officer of theirs attends the hearing of the application and, not less than 7 days before it, deliver to the court a statement in writing of their grounds of objection.

A copy of the statement shall be sent forthwith to the applicant.

## 6.195 Making and service of the order

**6.195(1) [Powers of court]** If on the hearing of the application it appears to the court to be a proper case, the court may make the order applied for, with such modifications (if any) as appear appropriate having regard to any representations made on behalf of the Commissioners. [FORM 6.69]

**6.195(2) [Form and contents of order]** The order–

(a) may be addressed to an inland revenue official other than the one named in the application,

(b) shall specify a time, not less than 28 days after service on the official to whom the order is addressed, within which compliance is required, and

(c) may include requirements as to the manner in which documents to which the order relates are to be produced.

**6.195(3) [Service of copy of order]** A sealed copy of the order shall be served by the applicant on the official to whom it is addressed.

**6.195(4) [If official unable to comply]** If the official is unable to comply with the order because he has not the relevant documents in his possession, and has been unable to obtain possession of them, he shall deliver to the court a statement in writing as to the reasons for his non-compliance.

A copy of the statement shall be sent forthwith by the official to the applicant.

## 6.196 Custody of documents

**6.196** Where in compliance with an order under section 369 original documents are produced, and not copies, any person who, by order of the court under section 369(2) (authorised disclosure to persons with right of inspection), has them in his possession or custody is responsible to the court for their safe keeping and return as and when directed.

# Chapter 18 – Mortgaged Property

## 6.197 Claim by mortgagee of land

**6.197(1) [Application for order for sale, "land"]** Any person claiming to be the legal or equitable mortgagee of land belonging to the bankrupt may apply to the court for an order directing that the land be sold.

"Land" includes any interest in, or right over, land.

**6.197(2) [Court may direct accounts to be taken etc.]** The court, if satisfied as to the applicant's title, may direct accounts to be taken and enquiries made to ascertain–

(a) the principal, interest and costs due under the mortgage, and

(b) where the mortgagee has been in possession of the land or any part of it, the rents and profits, dividends, interest, or other proceeds received by him or on his behalf.

Directions may be given by the court under this paragraph with respect to any mortgage (whether prior or subsequent) on the same property, other than that of the applicant.

**6.197(3) [Powers of court]** For the purpose of those accounts and enquiries, and of making title to the purchaser, any of the parties may be examined by the court, and shall produce on oath before the court all such documents in their custody or under their control relating to the estate of the bankrupt as the court may direct.

**History**

In r. 6.197 the words from "The court may" to the end substituted for the former words "The court may under this paragraph authorise the service of interrogatories on any party." by the Insolvency (Amendment) (No.2) Rules 1999 (SI 1999/1022), r. 3, Sch., para. 2 as from 26 April 1999.

**6.197(4) [In like manner as in High Court]** In any proceedings between a mortgagor and mortgagee, or the trustee of either of them, the court may order accounts to be taken and enquiries made in like manner as in the Chancery Division of the High Court.

## 6.198 Power of court to order sale

**6.198(1) [Order for sale etc.]** The court may order that the land, or any specified part of it, be sold; and any party bound by the order and in possession of the land or part, or in receipt of the rents and profits from it, may be ordered to deliver up possession or receipt to the purchaser or to such other person as the court may direct.

**6.198(2) [Directions re sale]** The court may permit the person having the conduct of the sale to sell the land in such manner as he thinks fit. Alternatively, the court may direct that the land be sold as directed by the order.

**6.198(3) [Contents of order]** The court's order may contain directions–

(a) appointing the persons to have the conduct of the sale;

(b) fixing the manner of sale (whether by contract conditional on the court's approval, private treaty, public auction, or otherwise);

(c) settling the particulars and conditions of sale;

(d) obtaining evidence of the value of the property, and fixing a reserve or minimum price;

(e) requiring particular persons to join in the sale and conveyance;

(f) requiring the payment of the purchase money into court, or to trustees or others;

(g) if the sale is to be by public auction, fixing the security (if any) to be given by the auctioneer, and his remuneration.

**6.198(4) [Sale by auction]** The court may direct that, if the sale is to be by public auction, the mortgagee may appear and bid on his own behalf.

## 6.199 Proceeds of sale

**6.199(1) [Application of proceeds]** The proceeds of sale shall be applied–

(a) first, in payment of the expenses of the trustee, of and occasioned by the application to the court, of the sale and attendance thereat, and of any costs arising from the taking of accounts, and making of enquiries, as directed by the court under Rule 6.197; and

(b) secondly, in payment of the amount found due to any mortgagee, for principal, interest and costs;

and the balance (if any) shall be retained by or paid to the trustee.

**6.199(2) [Where proceeds insufficient]** Where the proceeds of the sale are insufficient to pay in full the amount found due to any mortgagee, he is entitled to prove as a creditor for any deficiency, and to receive dividends rateably with other creditors, but not so as to disturb any dividend already declared.

# Chapter 19 – After-Acquired Property

## 6.200 Duties of bankrupt in respect of after-acquired property

**6.200(1) [Time for bankrupt to give notice]** The notice to be given by the bankrupt to the trustee, under section 333(2), of property acquired by, or devolving upon, him, or of any increase of his income, shall be given within 21 days of his becoming aware of the relevant facts.

**6.200(2) [Not to dispose of property]** Having served notice in respect of property acquired by or devolving upon him, the bankrupt shall not, without the trustee's consent in writing, dispose of it within the period of 42 days beginning with the date of the notice.

**6.200(3) [To identify etc. disponee]** If the bankrupt disposes of property before giving the notice required by this Rule or in contravention of paragraph (2), it is his duty forthwith to disclose to the trustee the name and address of the disponee, and to provide any other information which may be necessary to enable the trustee to trace the property and recover it for the estate.

**6.200(4) [Property to which r. 6.200 (1)–(3) do not apply]** Subject as follows, paragraphs (1) to (3) do not apply to property acquired by the bankrupt in the ordinary course of a business carried on by him.

**6.200(5) [If bankrupt carries on business]** If the bankrupt carries on a business, he shall, not less often than 6-monthly, furnish to the trustee information with respect to it, showing the total of goods bought and sold (or, as the case may be, services supplied) and the profit or loss arising from the business.

The trustee may require the bankrupt to furnish fuller details (including accounts) of the business carried on by him.

## 6.201 Trustee's recourse to disponee of property

**6.201(1) [Trustee may serve notice on disponee]** Where property has been disposed of by the bankrupt before giving the notice required by Rule 6.200 or otherwise in contravention of that Rule, the trustee may serve notice on the disponee, claiming the property as part of the estate by virtue of section 307(3).

**6.201(2) [Time for serving notice]** The trustee's notice under this rule must be served within 28 days of his becoming aware of the disponee's identity and an address at which he can be served.

## 6.202 Expenses of getting in property for the estate

**6.202** Any expenses incurred by the trustee in acquiring title to after-acquired property shall be paid out of the estate, in the prescribed order of priority.

# Chapter 20 – Leave to Act as Director, Etc.

## 6.203 Application for leave

**6.203(1) [Application supported by affidavit]** An application by the bankrupt for leave, under section 11 of the Company Directors Disqualification Act 1986, to act as director of, or to take part or be concerned in the promotion, formation or management of a company, shall be supported by an affidavit complying with this Rule.

**6.203(2) [Contents of affidavit]** The affidavit must identify the company and specify–

(a) the nature of its business or intended business, and the place or places where that business is, or is to be, carried on,

(b) whether it is, or is to be, a private or a public company,

(c) the persons who are, or are to be, principally responsible for the conduct of its affairs (whether as directors, shadow directors, managers or otherwise),

(d) the manner and capacity in which the applicant proposes to take part or be concerned in the promotion or formation of the company or, as the case may be, its management, and

(e) the emoluments and other benefits to be obtained from the directorship.

**6.203(3) [If company in existence]** If the company is already in existence, the affidavit must specify the date of its incorporation and the amount of its nominal and issued share capital; and if not, it must specify the amount, or approximate amount, of its proposed commencing share capital, and the sources from which that capital is to be obtained.

**6.203(4) [Taking part in promotion etc.]** Where the bankrupt intends to take part or be concerned in the promotion or formation of a company, the affidavit must contain an undertaking by him that he will, within not less than 7 days of the company being incorporated, file in court a copy of its memorandum of association and certificate of incorporation under section 13 of the Companies Act.

**6.203(5) [Venue and notice]** The court shall fix a venue for the hearing of the bankrupt's application, and give notice to him accordingly.

## 6.204 Report of official receiver

**6.204(1) [Notice of venue etc.]** The bankrupt shall, not less than 28 days before the date fixed for the hearing, give to the official receiver and the trustee notice of the venue, accompanied by copies of the application and the affidavit under Rule 6.203.

**6.204(2) [Official receiver's report]** The official receiver may, not less than 14 days before the date fixed for the hearing, file in court a report of any matters which he considers ought to be drawn to the court's attention. A copy of the report shall be sent by him, forthwith after it is filed, to the bankrupt and to the trustee.

**6.204(3) [Where bankrupt disputes report]** The bankrupt may, not later than 7 days before the date of the hearing, file in court a notice specifying any statements in the official receiver's report which he intends to deny or dispute.

If he gives notice under this paragraph, he shall send copies of it, not less than 4 days before the date of the hearing, to the official receiver and the trustee.

**6.204(4) [Appearances]** The official receiver and the trustee may appear on the hearing of the application, and may make representations and put to the bankrupt such questions as the court may allow.

## 6.205 Court's order on application

**6.205(1) [If court grants application]** If the court grants the bankrupt's application for leave under section 11 of the Company Directors Disqualification Act 1986, its order shall specify that which by virtue of the order the bankrupt has leave to do.

**6.205(2) [Powers of court]** The court may at the same time, having regard to any representations made by the trustee on the hearing of the application–

(a) include in the order provision varying an income payments order already in force in respect of the bankrupt, or

(b) if no income payments order is in force, make one.

**6.205(3) [Copies of order]** Whether or not the application is granted, copies of the order shall be sent by the court to the bankrupt, the trustee and the official receiver.

# Chapter 21 – Annulment of Bankruptcy Order

## 6.206 Application for annulment

**6.206(1) [Form of application]** An application to the court under section 282(1) for the annulment of a bankruptcy order shall specify whether it is made–

(a) under subsection (1)(a) of the section (claim that the order ought not to have been made), or

(b) under subsection (1)(b) (debts and expenses of the bankruptcy all paid or secured).

**6.206(2) [Supporting affidavit]** The application shall, in either case, be supported by an affidavit stating the grounds on which it is made; and, where it is made under section 282(1)(b), there shall be set out in the affidavit all the facts by reference to which the court is, under the Act and the Rules, required to be satisfied before annulling the bankruptcy order.

**6.206(3) [Copy of application etc.]** A copy of the application and supporting affidavit shall be filed in court; and the court shall give to the applicant notice of the venue fixed for the hearing.

**6.206(4) [Notice of venue]** The applicant shall give to the official receiver and (if other) the trustee notice of the venue, accompanied by copies of the application and the affidavit under paragraph (2)–

(a) where the application is made under section 282(1)(a), in sufficient time to enable them to be present at the hearing, and

(b) where the application is made under section 282(1)(b), not less than 28 days before the hearing.

**History**

In r. 6.206(4) the words ", not less than 28 days before the hearing," formerly appearing after the words "The applicant shall" omitted and para. (a) and (b) added by the Insolvency (Amendment) Rules 1987 (SI 1987/1919), r. 3(1), Sch., Pt. 1, para. 121(1) as from 11 January 1988.

**6.206(5) [Where application under s. 282(1)(a)]** Where the application is made under section 282(1)(a), paragraph (4) shall additionally be complied with in relation to the person on whose petition the bankruptcy order was made.

**History**

R. 6.206(5) added by the Insolvency (Amendment) Rules 1987 (SI 1987/1919), r. 3(1), Sch., Pt. 1, para. 121(2) as from 11 January 1988.

## 6.207 Report by trustee

**6.207(1) [Application of Rule]** The following applies where the application is made under section 282(1)(b) (debts and expenses of the bankruptcy all paid or secured).

**6.207(2) [Contents of report]** Not less than 21 days before the date fixed for the hearing, the trustee or, if no trustee has been appointed, the official receiver shall file in court a report with respect to the following matters–

(a) the circumstances leading to the bankruptcy;

(b) (in summarised form) the extent of the bankrupt's assets and liabilities at the date of the bankruptcy order and at the date of the present application;

(c) details of creditors (if any) who are known to him to have claims, but have not proved; and

(d) such other matters as the person making the report considers to be, in the circumstances, necessary for the information of the court.

**6.207(3) [Particulars of debts etc.]** The report shall include particulars of the extent (if any) to which, and the manner in which, the debts and expenses of the bankruptcy have been paid or secured.

In so far as debts and expenses are unpaid but secured, the person making the report shall state in it whether and to what extent he considers the security to be satisfactory.

**6.207(4) [Copy of report to applicant]** A copy of the report shall be sent to the applicant at least 14 days before the date fixed for the hearing; and he may, if he wishes, file further affidavits in answer to statements made in the report.

Copies of any such affidavits shall be sent by the applicant to the official receiver and (if other) the trustee.

**6.207(5) [If trustee not official receiver]** If the trustee is other than the official receiver, a copy of his report shall be sent to the official receiver at least 21 days before the hearing. The official receiver may then file an additional report, a copy of which shall be sent to the applicant at least 7 days before the hearing.

## 6.208 Power of court to stay proceedings

**6.208(1) [Interim order]** The court may, in advance of the hearing, make an interim order staying any proceedings which it thinks ought, in the circumstances of the application, to be stayed.

**6.208(2) [Ex parte application]** Except in relation to an application for an order staying all or any part of the proceedings in the bankruptcy, application for an order under this Rule may be made *ex parte*.

**6.208(3) [Copies of application]** Where application is made under this Rule for an order staying all or any part of the proceedings in the bankruptcy, the applicant shall send copies of the application to the official receiver and (if other) the trustee in sufficient time to enable them to be present at the hearing and (if they wish to do so) make representations.

**6.208(4) [Effect of staying order on annulment]** Where the court makes an order under this Rule staying all or any part of the proceedings in the bankruptcy, the rules in this Chapter nevertheless continue to apply to any application for, or other matters in connection with, the annulment of the bankruptcy order.

**6.208(5) [Copies of staying order]** If the court makes an order under this Rule, it shall send copies of the order to the applicant, the official receiver and (if other) the trustee.

**History**
R. 6.208(2) to (5) substituted for the former r. 6.208(2) by the Insolvency (Amendment) Rules 1987 (SI 1987/1919), r. 3(1), Sch., Pt. 1, para. 122 as from 11 January 1988; the former r. 6.208(2) read as follows:
"Application for an interim order under this Rule may be made *ex parte*".

## 6.209 Notice to creditors who have not proved

**6.209** Where the application for annulment is made under section 282(1)(b) and it has been reported to the court Rule 6.207 that there are known creditors of the bankrupt who have not proved, the court may–

(a) direct the trustee or, if no trustee has been appointed, the official receiver to send notice of the application to such of those creditors as the court thinks ought to be informed of it, with a view to their proving their debts (if they so wish) within 21 days, and

(b) direct the trustee or, if no trustee has been appointed, the official receiver to advertise the fact that the application has been made, so that creditors who have not proved may do so within a specified time, and

(c) adjourn the application meanwhile, for any period not less than 35 days.

**History**
In r. 6.209(a) and (b) the words "or, if no trustee has been appointed, the official receiver" in both places where they occur inserted by the Insolvency (Amendment) Rules 1987 (SI 1987/1919), r. 3(1), Sch., Pt. 1, para. 123 as from 11 January 1988.

## 6.210 The hearing

**6.210(1) [Trustee to attend]** The trustee shall attend the hearing of the application.

**6.210(2) [Attendance of official receiver]** The official receiver, if he is not the trustee, may attend, but is not required to do so unless he has filed a report under Rule 6.207.

**6.210(3) [Copies of order]** If the court makes an order on the application, it shall send copies of the order to the applicant, the official receiver and (if other) the trustee. [FORM 6.71]

## 6.211 Matters to be proved under s. 282(1)(b)

**6.211(1) [Application of Rule]** This rule applies with regard to the matters which must, in an application under section 282(1)(b), be proved to the satisfaction of the court.

**6.211(2) [Debts paid in full]** Subject to the following paragraph, all bankruptcy debts which have been proved must have been paid in full.

**6.211(3) [If debt disputed etc.]** If a debt is disputed, or a creditor who has proved can no longer be traced, the bankrupt must have given such security (in the form of money paid into court, or a bond entered into with approved sureties) as the court considers adequate to satisfy any sum that may subsequently be proved to be due to the creditor concerned and (if the court thinks fit) costs.

**6.211(4) [Advertisement in case of untraced creditor]** Where under paragraph (3) security has been given in the case of an untraced creditor, the court may direct that particulars of the alleged debt, and the security, be advertised in such manner as it thinks fit.

If advertisement is ordered under this paragraph, and no claim on the security is made within 12 months from the date of the advertisement (or the first advertisement, if more than one), the court shall, on application in that behalf, order the security to be released.

## 6.212 Notice to creditors

**6.212(1) [Notice of annulment]** Where the official receiver has notified creditors of the debtor's bankruptcy, and the bankruptcy order is annulled, he shall forthwith notify them of the annulment.

**6.212(2) [Expenses of giving notice]** Expenses incurred by the official receiver in giving notice under this Rule are a charge in his favour on the property of the former bankrupt, whether or not actually in his hands.

**6.212(3) [Property in hands of trustee etc.]** Where any property is in the hands of a trustee or any person other than the former bankrupt himself, the official receiver's charge is valid subject only to any costs that may be incurred by the trustee or that other person in effecting realisation of the property for the purpose of satisfying the charge.

## 6.212A Annulment under s. 261

**6.212A** Rules 6.206 to 6.212 apply to an application for annulment under section 261 as they apply to such an application under section 282(1)(a).

**History**

R. 6.212A inserted by the Insolvency (Amendment) Rules 1987 (SI 1987/1919), r. 3(1), Sch., Pt. 1, para. 124 as from 11 January 1988.

## 6.213 Other matters arising on annulment

**6.213(1) [Contents of s. 261 or 282 order]** In an order under section 261 or 282 the court shall include provision permitting vacation of the registration of the bankruptcy petition as a pending action, and of the bankruptcy order, in the register of writs and orders affecting land.

**History**

In r. 6.213(1) the words "261 or" inserted by the Insolvency (Amendment) Rules 1987 (SI 1987/1919), r. 3(1), Sch., Pt. 1, para. 125 as from 11 January 1988.

**6.213(2) [Notice of order]** The court shall forthwith give notice of the making of the order to the Secretary of State.

**6.213(3) [Requiring advertisement of order]** The former bankrupt may require the Secretary of State to give notice of the making of the order–

(a) in the Gazette, or

(b) in any newspaper in which the bankruptcy order was advertised, or

(c) in both.

**6.213(4) [Requirement under r. 6.213(3), cost of advertisement]** Any requirement by the former bankrupt under paragraph (3) shall be addressed to the Secretary of State in writing. The Secretary of State shall notify him forthwith as to the cost of the advertisement, and is under no obligation to advertise until that sum has been paid.

**6.213(5) [Former bankrupt deceased etc.]** Where the former bankrupt has died, or is a person incapable of managing his affairs (within the meaning of Chapter 7 in Part 7 of the Rules), the references to him in paragraphs (3) and (4) are to be read as referring to his personal representative or, as the case may be, a person appointed by the court to represent or act for him.

## 6.214 Trustee's final account

**6.214(1) [Duty to account for all transactions]** Where a bankruptcy order is annulled under section 261 or 282, this does not of itself release the trustee from any duty or obligation, imposed on him by or under the Act or the Rules, to account for all his transactions in connection with the former bankrupt's estate.

**History**
In r. 6.214(1) the words "261 or" inserted by the Insolvency (Amendment) Rules 1987 (SI 1987/1919), r. 3(1), Sch., Pt. 1, para. 126 as from 11 January 1988.

**6.214(2) [Final account to Secretary of State etc.]** The trustee shall submit a copy of his final account to the Secretary of State, as soon as practicable after the court's order annulling the bankruptcy order; and he shall file a copy of the final account in court.

**6.214(3) [Contents of final account]** The final account must include a summary of the trustee's receipts and payments in the administration, and contain a statement to the effect that he has reconciled his account with that which is held by the Secretary of State in respect of the bankruptcy.

**6.214(4) [Release of trustee]** The trustee is released from such time as the court may determine, having regard to whether–

(a) paragraph (2) of this Rule has been complied with, and

(b) any security given under Rule 6.211(3) has been, or will be, released.

# Chapter 22 – Discharge

## 6.215 Application for suspension of discharge

**6.215(1) [Application of Rule]** The following applies where the official receiver applies to the court for an order under section 279(3) (suspension of automatic discharge), but not where he makes that application, pursuant to Rule 6.176(4), on the adjournment of the bankrupt's public examination.

**6.215(2) [Official receiver's report]** The official receiver shall with his application file a report setting out the reasons why it appears to him that such an order should be made.

**6.215(3) [Venue and notice]** The court shall fix a venue for the hearing of the application, and give notice of it to the official receiver, the trustee and the bankrupt.

**6.215(4) [Copies of report to trustee and bankrupt]** Copies of the official receiver's report under this Rule shall be sent by him to the trustee and the bankrupt, so as to reach them at least 21 days before the date fixed for the hearing.

**6.215(5) [Where bankrupt disputes report]** The bankrupt may, not later than 7 days before the date of the hearing, file in court a notice specifying any statements in the official receiver's report which he intends to deny or dispute.

If he gives notice under this paragraph, he shall send copies of it, not less than 4 days before the date of the hearing, to the official receiver and the trustee.

**6.215(6) [Copies of order]** If on the hearing the court makes an order suspending the bankrupt's discharge, copies of the order shall be sent by the court to the official receiver, the trustee and the bankrupt. [FORM 6.72]

## 6.216 Lifting of suspension of discharge

**6.216(1) [Bankrupt may apply to court]** Where the court has made an order under section 279(3) that the relevant period (that is to say, the period after which the bankrupt may under that section have his discharge) shall cease to run, the bankrupt may apply to it for the order to be discharged.

**6.216(2) [Venue and notice]** The court shall fix a venue for the hearing of the application; and the bankrupt shall, not less than 28 days before the date fixed for hearing, give notice of the venue to the official receiver and the trustee, accompanied in each case by a copy of the application.

**6.216(3) [Appearances etc.]** The official receiver and the trustee may appear and be heard on the bankrupt's application; and, whether or not he appears, the official receiver may file in court a report of any matters which he considers ought to be drawn to the court's attention.

**6.216(4) [If conditions specified in order]** If the court's order under section 279(3) was for the relevant period to cease to run until the fulfilment of specified conditions, the court may request a report from the official receiver as to whether those conditions have or have not been fulfilled.

**6.216(5) [Copies of r. 6.216(3), (4) report]** If a report is filed under paragraph (3) or (4), copies of it shall be sent by the official receiver to the bankrupt and the trustee, not later than 14 days before the hearing.

**6.216(6) [Where bankrupt disputes report]** The bankrupt may, not later than 7 days before the date of the hearing, file in court a notice specifying any statements in the official receiver's report which he intends to deny or dispute.

If he gives notice under this paragraph, he shall send copies of it, not less than 4 days before the date of the hearing, to the official receiver and the trustee.

**6.216(7) [If court discharges s. 279(3) order]** If on the bankrupt's application the court discharges the order under section 279(3) (being satisfied that the relevant period should begin to run again), it shall issue to the bankrupt a certificate that it has done so, with effect from a specified date and shall send copies of the certificate to the official receiver and the trustee.

[FORM 6.73] [FORM 6.74]

**History**

In r. 6.216(7) the words from "and shall send copies" to the end added by the Insolvency (Amendment) Rules 1999 (SI 1999/359), r. 1, Sch., para. 7 as from 22 March 1999.

## 6.217 Application by bankrupt for discharge

**6.217(1) [If bankrupt makes s. 280 application]** If the bankrupt applies under section 280 for an order discharging him from bankruptcy, he shall give to the official receiver notice of the application, and deposit with him such sum as the latter may require to cover his costs of the application.

**6.217(2) [Venue and notice]** The court, if satisfied that paragraph (1) has been complied with, shall fix a venue for the hearing of the application, and give at least 42 days' notice of it to the official receiver and the bankrupt.

**6.217(3) [Notice by official receiver]** The official receiver shall give notice accordingly–

(a) to the trustee, and

(b) to every creditor who, to the official receiver's knowledge, has a claim outstanding against the estate which has not been satisfied.

**6.217(4) [Time for r. 6.217(3) notice]** Notices under paragraph (3) shall be given not later than 14 days before the date fixed for the hearing of the bankrupt's application.

## 6.218 Report of official receiver

**6.218(1) [Contents etc. of report]** Where the bankrupt makes an application under section 280, the official receiver shall, at least 21 days before the date fixed for the hearing of the application, file in court a report containing the following information with respect to the bankrupt–

(a) any failure by him to comply with his obligations under Parts VIII to XI of the Act;

(b) the circumstances surrounding the present bankruptcy, and those surrounding any previous bankruptcy of his;

(c) the extent to which, in the present and in any previous bankruptcy, his liabilities have exceeded his assets; and

(d) particulars of any distribution which has been, or is expected to be, made to creditors in the present bankruptcy or, if such is the case, that there has been and is to be no distribution;

and the official receiver shall include in his report any other matters which in his opinion ought to be brought to the court's attention.

**6.218(2) [Copies of reports]** The official receiver shall send a copy of the report to the bankrupt and the trustee, so as to reach them at least 14 days before the date of the hearing of the application under section 280.

**6.218(3) [Where bankrupt disputes report]** The bankrupt may, not later than 7 days before the date of the hearing, file in court a notice specifying any statements in the official receiver's report which he intends to deny or dispute.

If he gives notice under this paragraph, he shall send copies of it, not less than 4 days before the date of the hearing, to the official receiver and the trustee. [FORM 6.75]

**6.218(4) [Appearances]** The official receiver, the trustee and any creditor may appear on the hearing of the bankrupt's application, and may make representations and put to the bankrupt such questions as the court may allow.

## 6.219 Order of discharge on application

**6.219(1) [Order to take effect when drawn up by court]** An order of the court under section 280(2)(b) (discharge absolutely) or (c) (discharge subject to conditions with respect to income or property) shall bear the date on which it is made, but does not take effect until such time as it is drawn up by the court. [FORM 6.76]

**6.219(2) [Retrospective effect]** The order then has effect retrospectively to the date on which it was made.

**6.219(3) [Copies of order]** Copies of any order made by the court on an application by the bankrupt for discharge under section 280 shall be sent by the court to the bankrupt, the trustee and the official receiver.

## 6.220 Certificate of discharge

**6.220(1) [Where bankrupt is discharged]** Where it appears to the court that a bankrupt is discharged, whether by expiration of time or otherwise, the court shall, on his application, issue to him a certificate of his discharge, and the date from which it is effective. [FORM 6.77]

**6.220(2) [Requiring advertisement of discharge]** The discharged bankrupt may require the Secretary of State to give notice of the discharge–

(a) in the Gazette, or

(b) in any newspaper in which the bankruptcy was advertised, or

(c) in both.

**6.220(3) [Requirement in r. 6.220(2), cost of advertisement]** Any requirement by the former bankrupt under paragraph (2) shall be addressed to the Secretary of State in writing. The Secretary of State shall notify him forthwith as to the cost of the advertisement, and is under no obligation to advertise until that sum has been paid.

**6.220(4) [Former bankrupt deceased etc.]** Where the former bankrupt has died, or is a person incapable of managing his affairs (within the meaning of Chapter 7 in Part 7 of the Rules), the references to him in paragraphs (2) and (3) are to be read as referring to his personal representative or, as the case may be, a person appointed by the court to represent or act for him.

## 6.221 Deferment of issue of order pending appeal

**6.221** An order made by the court on an application by the bankrupt for discharge under section 280 shall not be issued or gazetted until the time allowed for appealing has expired or, if an appeal is entered, until the appeal has been determined.

## 6.222 Costs under this Chapter

**6.222** In no case do any costs or expenses arising under this Chapter fall on the official receiver personally.

## 6.223 Bankrupt's debts surviving discharge

**6.223** Discharge does not release the bankrupt from any obligation arising under a confiscation order made under section 1 of the Drug Trafficking Offences Act 1986 or section 1 of the Criminal Justice (Scotland) Act 1987 or section 71 of the Criminal Justice Act 1988.

**History**

In r. 6.223 the words "or section 71 of the Criminal Justice Act 1988" added by the Insolvency (Amendment) Rules 1989 (SI 1989/397), r. 3(1), Sch. as from 3 April 1989.

Previously the words "or section 1 of the Criminal Justice (Scotland) Act 1987" added by the Insolvency (Amendment) Rules 1987 (SI 1987/1919), r. 3(1), Sch., Pt. 1, para. 127 as from 11 January 1988.

# Chapter 22A – Register of Bankruptcy Orders

## 6.223(A) Register of bankruptcy orders

**6.223(A)(1) [Secretary of State to maintain register]** The Secretary of State shall maintain a register of bankruptcy orders ("the register") which shall contain the specified bankruptcy information entered in it by the official receiver in pursuance of Rule 6.223(B), any information entered in it by the official receiver in pursuance of Rule 6.223(C) and the information set out in paragraphs (2) and (3).

**6.223(A)(2) [Notice of annulment order]** The Secretary of State shall cause to be entered in the register notice of the making of an annulment order under section 261(1)(a) or 282(1)(b) given to him in pursuance of Rule 6.213(2).

**6.223(A)(3) [Information to be entered in the register, etc.]** The Secretary of State shall cause to be entered in the register such of the specified bankruptcy information and notice of the making of any annulment order under section 261(1)(a) or 282(1)(b) relating to any bankruptcy order where such bankruptcy order was made in the period of five years prior to 22nd March 1999 as is in the possession of the Secretary of State on that date but excluding information relating to–

(a) any bankruptcy order which has been annulled under section 282(1)(a) or which has been rescinded under section 375,

(b) any bankruptcy order which has been annulled under section 261(1)(a) or 282(1)(b) more than two years prior to 22nd March 1999, and

(c) any bankruptcy order in respect of which an order made under Rule 6.34(3) or 6.46(3) is in force on that date and a copy of which has been delivered to the official receiver under Rule 6.34(4) or 6.46(4), provided that where after that date the order under Rule 6.34(3) or 6.46(3) expires, the Secretary of State shall enter in the register such of the specified bankruptcy information relating to the bankruptcy order previously the subject of the order under Rule 6.34(3) or 6.46(3) as is in his possession as at the date of expiry of such order, except where the official receiver receives a copy of any further order of the court under Rule 6.34(3) or 6.46(3) in respect of such bankruptcy order, in which event the Secretary of State shall not enter such specified bankruptcy information in the register until the expiry of such further order.

**6.223(A)(4) [Deletion of bankruptcy information from register]** Where a bankrupt in respect of whom specified bankruptcy information has been entered in the register is discharged from the bankruptcy or obtains an annulment order under section 261(1)(a) or 282(1)(b) in respect of the bankruptcy order, the Secretary of State shall, on the expiry of two years after the date of such discharge or annulment order (or where a certificate for the summary administration of the bankrupt's estate has been issued under section 275(1), on the expiry of three years after the date on which the bankrupt is discharged from the bankruptcy) delete from the register the specified bankruptcy information and any other information entered in the register in respect of such bankruptcy order.

**6.223(A)(5) [Deletion from register upon annulment]** If a bankruptcy order in respect of which specified bankruptcy information has been entered in the register is annulled by the court under section 282(1)(a), the Secretary of State shall delete from the register the specified bankruptcy information and any other information entered in the register in respect of such bankruptcy order upon receiving notice of such annulment under Rule 6.213(2).

**6.223(A)(6) [Deletion from register upon rescission]** If a bankruptcy order in respect of which specified bankruptcy information has been entered in the register is rescinded by the court under section 375 the Secretary of State shall delete from the register the specified bankruptcy information and any other information entered in the register in respect of such bankruptcy order upon receiving a copy of the order of the court rescinding the bankruptcy order.

**6.223(A)(7) [Public inspection]** The register shall be open to public inspection.

**History**
See history note after r. 6.223(C).

# 6.223(B) Specified bankruptcy information

**6.223(B)(1) [Entry in register by official receiver]** Following the receipt by the official receiver pursuant to Rule 6.34 or 6.46 of a copy of the bankruptcy order from the court, the official receiver shall cause to be entered in the register the information listed in paragraph (5)(a) and shall cause to be entered in the register the information listed in paragraph 5(b) upon receipt by him of such information.

**6.223(B)(2) [Entry of r. 6.223(B)(5)(c) information in register]** Following the receipt by the official receiver–

(a) pursuant to Rule 6.50(3), of notice of the revocation of a certificate for summary administration,

(b) pursuant to Rule 6.176(5), of a copy of an order suspending the bankrupt's discharge,

(c) pursuant to Rule 6.215(6), of a copy of an order suspending the bankrupt's discharge,

(d) pursuant to Rule 6.216(7), of a copy of a certificate certifying the discharge of an order under section 279(3), or

(e) pursuant to Rule 6.219(3), of a copy of an order discharging the bankrupt absolutely or subject to conditions,

the official receiver shall cause the information listed in paragraph (5)(c) to be entered in the register.

**6.223(B)(3) [Amendments to register on rescission of s. 279(3) order]** Where an order referred to in paragraph 2(d) is subsequently rescinded by the court the official receiver shall cause the specified bankruptcy information relating to such bankruptcy to be amended to record the fact that the bankrupt is not discharged and, where the information in respect of such bankruptcy has been deleted from the register pursuant to paragraph (4) of Rule 6.223(A), shall cause such information to be restored to the register.

**6.223(B)(4) [Discharge from bankruptcy noted in register]** Where a bankrupt is discharged from bankruptcy under section 279(1)(b) the official receiver shall cause the fact and date of such discharge to be entered in the register.

**6.223(B)(5) ["Specified bankruptcy information"]** In this Chapter **"specified bankruptcy information"** means the following information–

(a) (i) the matters listed in Rules 6.7 and 6.38 with respect to the debtor as stated in the bankruptcy petition;
  (ii) the bankruptcy order date, the court and court reference number;

(b) (i) the name, gender, occupation (if any) and date of birth of the bankrupt;
  (ii) the bankrupt's last known address;
  (iii) where the bankrupt has been an undischarged bankrupt at any time in the period of 15 years ending with the date of the bankruptcy order in question, the date of the most recent of any previous bankruptcy orders (but excluding an order annulled under section 282(1)(a) or rescinded under section 375);

(iv) any name by which the bankrupt is known other than his true name;
(v) the name or names in which he carries on business if other than his true name and any address at which he carries on business;
(vi) the contact address of the official receiver's office;
(vii) the name and address of the insolvency practitioner (where appointed);
(viii) the automatic discharge date under section 279(1)(b) or, where section 279(1)(a) applies, a statement that there is no automatic discharge date;
(ix) where a certificate for summary administration has been issued, a statement to that effect; and

(c) (i) the revised automatic discharge date where– (aa) the court has revoked a certificate for the summary administration of a bankrupt's estate under section 275(3), (bb) the court has made an order under section 279(3) that the relevant period under that section shall cease to run for the period specified in the order, or (cc) the court has discharged an order under section 279(3) being satisfied that the relevant period should begin to run again;
(ii) a statement that discharge has been suspended where the court has made an order under section 279(3) that the relevant period under that section shall cease to run until the fulfilment of such conditions as may be specified in the order;
(iii) the fact that and date on which the bankrupt is discharged.

**History**
See history note after r. 6.223(C).

## 6.223(C) Notification of changes

**6.223(C)(1) [Rectification of incorrect information on register]** If the official receiver becomes aware that the information which has been entered in the register is inaccurate he shall rectify the information entered in the register.

**6.223(C)(2) [Death of bankrupt to be entered in the register]** If the official receiver receives notice of the date of death of a bankrupt in respect of whom specified bankruptcy information has been entered in the register he shall cause such date to be entered in the register.

**History**
Ch. 22A (r. 6.223(A), (B), (C)) inserted by the Insolvency (Amendment) Rules 1999 (SI 1999/359), r. 1, Sch., para. 8 as from 22 March 1999.

# Chapter 23 – Order of Payment of Costs, Etc., out of Estate

## 6.224 General rule as to priority

**6.224(1) [Priority of expenses]** The expenses of the bankruptcy are payable out of the estate in the following order of priority–

(a) expenses properly chargeable or incurred by the official receiver or the trustee in preserving, realising or getting in any of the assets of the bankrupt, including those incurred in acquiring title to after-acquired property;

(b) any other expenses incurred or disbursements made by the official receiver or under his authority, including those incurred or made in carrying on the business of a debtor or bankrupt;

(c) the fees payable under any order made under section 415, including those payable to the official receiver (other than the fee referred to in sub-paragraph (d)(i) below), and any remuneration payable to him under general regulations;

(d)
(i) the fee payable under any order made under section 415 for the performance by the official receiver of his general duties as official receiver;
(ii) any repayable deposit lodged under any such order as security for the fee mentioned in sub-paragraph (i) (except where the deposit is applied to the payment of the remuneration of an insolvency practitioner appointed under section 273 (debtor's petition));

(e) the cost of any security provided by an interim receiver, trustee or special manager in accordance with the Act or the Rules;
(f) the remuneration of the interim receiver (if any);
(g) any deposit lodged on an application for the appointment of an interim receiver;
(h) the costs of the petitioner, and of any person appearing on the petition whose costs are allowed by the court;
(j) the remuneration of the special manager (if any);
(k) any amount payable to a person employed or authorised, under Chapter 5 of this Part of the Rules, to assist in the preparation of a statement of affairs or of accounts;
(l) any allowance made, by order of the court, towards costs on an application for release from the obligation to submit a statement of affairs, or for an extension of time for submitting such a statement;
(m) any necessary disbursements by the trustee in the course of his administration (including any expenses incurred by members of the creditors' committee or their representatives and allowed by the trustee under Rule 6.164, but not including any payment of capital gains tax in circumstances referred to in sub-paragraph (p) below);
(n) the remuneration or emoluments of any person (including the bankrupt) who has been employed by the trustee to perform any services for the estate, as required or authorised by or under the Act or the Rules;
(o) the remuneration of the trustee, up to any amount not exceeding that which is payable to the official receiver under general regulations;
(p) the amount of any capital gains tax on chargeable gains accruing on the realisation of any asset of the bankrupt (without regard to whether the realisation is effected by the trustee, a secured creditor, or a receiver or manager appointed to deal with a security);
(q) the balance, after payment of any sums due under sub-paragraph (o) above, of any remuneration due to the trustee.

**History**
In r. 6.224(1) para. (c) and (d) substituted by the Insolvency (Amendment) Rules 1995 (SI 1995/586), r. 3, Sch., para. 2 as from 1 April 1995; para. (c) and (d) formerly read as follows:

"(c) (i) the fee payable under any order made under section 415 for the performance by the official receiver of his general duties as official receiver;
(ii) any repayable deposit lodged by the petitioner under any such order as security for the fee mentioned in subparagraph (i) (except where the deposit is applied to the payment of the remuneration of an insolvency practitioner appointed under section 273 (debtor's petition));
(d) any other fees payable under any order made under section 415, including those payable to the official receiver, and any remuneration payable to him under general regulations;"

**6.224(2) [Costs of shorthand writer]** The costs of employing a shorthand writer, if appointed by an order of the court made at the instance of the official receiver in connection with an examination, rank in priority with those specified in paragraph (1)(a). The costs of employing a shorthand writer so appointed in any other case rank after the allowance mentioned in paragraph (1)(l) and before the disbursements mentioned in paragraph (1)(m).

**6.224(3) [Expenses of r. 6.174 examination]** Any expenses incurred in holding an examination under Rule 6.174 (examinee unfit), where the application for it is made by the official receiver, rank in priority with those specified in paragraph (1)(a).

# Chapter 24 – Second Bankruptcy

## 6.225 Scope of this Chapter

**6.225(1) [Application of Ch. 24 Rules]** The Rules in this Chapter relate to the manner in which, in the case of a second bankruptcy, the trustee in the earlier bankruptcy is to deal with property and money to which section 334(3) applies, until there is a trustee of the estate in the later bankruptcy.

**6.225(2) [Definitions] "The earlier bankruptcy", "the later bankruptcy"** and **"the existing trustee"** have the meanings given by section 334(1).

## 6.226 General duty of existing trustee

**6.226(1) [Duty to get in property etc.]** Subject as follows, the existing trustee shall take into his custody or under his control all such property and money, in so far as he has not already done so as part of his duties as trustee in the earlier bankruptcy.

**6.226(2) [Power to sell perishable goods etc.]** Where any of that property consists of perishable goods, or goods the value of which is likely to diminish if they are not disposed of, the existing trustee has power to sell or otherwise dispose of those goods.

**6.226(3) [Proceeds of sale]** The proceeds of any such sale or disposal shall be held, under the existing trustee's control, with the other property and money comprised in the bankrupt's estate.

## 6.227 Delivery up to later trustee

**6.227** The existing trustee shall, as and when requested by the trustee for the purposes of the later bankruptcy, deliver up to the latter all such property and money as is in his custody or under his control in pursuance of Rule 6.226.

## 6.228 Existing trustee's expenses

**6.228** Any expenses incurred by the existing trustee in compliance with section 335(1) and this Chapter of the Rules shall be defrayed out of, and are a charge on, all such property and money as is referred to in section 334(3), whether in the hands of the existing trustee or of the trustee for the purposes of the later bankruptcy.

# Chapter 25 – Criminal Bankruptcy

## 6.229 Presentation of petition

**6.229(1) [Presentation to High Court]** In criminal bankruptcy, the petition under section 264(1)(d) shall be presented to the High Court, and accordingly Rule 6.9 in Chapter 2 (court in which other petitions to be presented) does not apply. [FORM 6.79]

**6.229(2) [Effect of Rule]** This does not affect the High Court's power to order that the proceedings be transferred.

## 6.230 Status and functions of Official Petitioner

**6.230(1) [Official Petitioner as a creditor]** Subject as follows, the Official Petitioner is to be regarded for all purposes of the Act and the Rules as a creditor of the bankrupt.

**6.230(2) [Attendance, representation etc.]** He may attend or be represented at any meeting of creditors, and is to be given any notice under the Act or the Rules which is required or authorised to be given to creditors; and the requirements of the Rules as to the lodging or use of proxies do not apply.

## 6.231 Interim receivership

**6.231** Chapter 4 of this Part of the Rules applies in criminal bankruptcy only in so far as it provides for the appointment of the official receiver as interim receiver.

## 6.232 Proof of bankruptcy debts and notice of order

**6.232(1) [Effect of order]** The making of a bankruptcy order on a criminal bankruptcy petition does not affect the right of creditors to prove for their debts arising otherwise than in consequence of the criminal proceedings.

**6.232(2) [Person suffering loss etc.]** A person specified in a criminal bankruptcy order as having suffered loss or damage shall be treated as a creditor of the bankrupt; and a copy of the order is sufficient evidence of his claim, subject to its being shown by any party to the bankruptcy proceedings that the loss or damage actually suffered was more or (as the case may be) less than the amount specified in the order.

**6.232(3) [Non-application of Rules]** The requirements of the Rules with respect to the proof of debts do not apply to the Official Petitioner.

**6.232(4) [Forms of proof]** In criminal bankruptcy, forms of proof shall be sent out by the official receiver within 12 weeks from the making of the bankruptcy order, to every creditor who is known to him, or is identified in the bankrupt's statements of affairs.

**History**
R. 6.232(4) substituted by the Insolvency (Amendment) Rules 1987 (SI 1987/1919), r. 3(1), Sch., Pt. 1, para. 128 as from 11 January 1988; r. 6.232(4) formerly read as follows:

"In criminal bankruptcy, the forms to be used by any person for the purpose of proving bankruptcy debts shall be sent out by the official receiver, not less than 12 weeks from the making of the bankruptcy order, to every creditor who is known to him, or is identified in the bankrupt's statement of affairs."

**6.232(5) [Notice to creditors]** The official receiver shall, within those 12 weeks, send to every such creditor notice of the making of the bankruptcy order.

## 6.233 Meetings under the Rules

**6.233(1) [Non-application of Ch. 6 Rules]** The following Rules in Chapter 6 of this Part do not apply in criminal bankruptcy–

Rules 6.79 and 6.80 (first meeting of creditors, and business thereat);
Rule 6.82(2) (the chairman, if other than the official receiver);
Rule 6.88(2) and (3) (resolution for appointment of trustee).

**6.233(2) [Non-application of r. 6.97]** Rule 6.97 (supply of forms for proof of debts) does not apply.

## 6.234 Trustee in bankruptcy; creditors' committee; annulment of bankruptcy order

**6.234(1) [Non-application of Ch. 10 Rules]** Chapter 10 of this Part of the Rules does not apply in criminal bankruptcy, except Rules 6.136 (release of official receiver) and 6.147 (power of court to set aside transactions).

**History**
In r. 6.234(1) the words "Chapter 10" substituted for the former words "Chapter 11" by the Insolvency (Amendment) Rules 1987 (SI 1987/1919), r. 3(1), Sch., Pt. 1, para. 129(1) as from 11 January 1988.

**6.234(2) [Non-application of Ch. 11 Rules]** Chapter 11 (creditors' committee) does not apply.

**History**
In r. 6.234(2) the words "Chapter 11" substituted for the former words "Chapter 12" by the Insolvency (Amendment) Rules 1987 (SI 1987/1919), r. 3(1), Sch., Pt. 1, para. 129(2) as from 11 January 1988.

**6.234(3) [Application of Ch. 21 Rules]** Chapter 21 (annulment of bankruptcy order) applies to an application to the court under section 282(2) as it applies to an application under section 282(1), with any necessary modifications.

# Chapter 26 – Miscellaneous Rules in Bankruptcy

## 6.235 Bankruptcy of solicitors

**6.235** Where a bankruptcy order is made against a solicitor, or such an order made against a solicitor is rescinded or annulled, the court shall forthwith give notice to the Secretary of the Law Society of the order that it has made.

## 6.236 Consolidation of petitions

**6.236** Where two or more bankruptcy petitions are presented against the same debtor, the court may order the consolidation of the proceedings, on such terms as it thinks fit.

## 6.237 Bankrupt's dwelling-house and home

**6.237(1) [Application of Rule]** This Rule applies where the trustee applies to the court under section 313 for an order imposing a charge on property consisting of an interest in a dwelling-house.

[FORM 6.79A]

**History**
Against r. 6.237(1) the words "[FORM 6.79A]" inserted by the Insolvency (Amendment) Rules 1987 (SI 1987/1919), r. 3(1), Sch., Pt. 2, para. 156(1) as from 11 January 1988.

**6.237(2) [Respondents to application]** The bankrupt's spouse or former spouse shall be made respondent to the application; and the court may, if it thinks fit, direct other persons to be made respondents also, in respect of any interest which they may have in the property.

**6.237(3) [Contents of trustee's report]** The trustee shall make a report to the court, containing the following particulars–

(a) the extent of the bankrupt's interest in the property which is the subject of the application; and

(b) the amount which, at the date of the application, remains owing to unsecured creditors of the bankrupt.

**6.237(4) [Terms of charge]** The terms of the charge to be imposed shall be agreed between the trustee and the bankrupt or, failing agreement, shall be settled by the court.

**6.237(5) [Rate of interest]** The rate of interest applicable under section 313(2) is the rate specified in section 17 of the Judgments Act 1838 on the day on which the charge is imposed, and the rate so applicable shall be stated in the court's order imposing the charge.

**6.237(6) [Contents of order]** The court's order shall also–

(a) describe the property to be charged;

(b) state whether the title to the property is registered and, if it is, specify the title number;

(c) set out the extent of the bankrupt's interest in the property which has vested in the trustee;

(d) indicate, by reference to any, or the total, amount which is payable otherwise than to the bankrupt out of the estate and of interest on that amount, how the amount of the charge to be imposed is to be ascertained;

(e) set out the conditions (if any) imposed by the court under section 3(1) of the Charging Orders Act 1979;

(f) identify when any property charged under section 313 shall cease to be comprised in the bankrupt's estate and, subject to the charge (and any prior charge), to vest in the bankrupt.

**History**
In r. 6.237(6) para. (d) and (f) substituted by the Insolvency (Amendment) Rules 1987 (SI 1987/1919), r. 3(1), Sch., Pt. 1, para. 130 as from 11 January 1988; para. (d) and (f) formerly read as follows:

"(d) indicate, by reference to the amount which remains owing to unsecured creditors of the bankrupt, the amount of the charge to be imposed;

(f) provide for any property comprised in the charge to vest again in the bankrupt as from a specified date."

**6.237(7) [Date under r. 6.237(6)(f)]** Unless the court is of the opinion that a different date is appropriate, the date under paragraph (6)(f) shall be that of the registration of the charge in accordance with section 3(2) of the Charging Orders Act 1979.

**6.237(8) [Notice to Chief Land Registrar]** The trustee shall, forthwith after the making of the court's order, send notice of it and its effect to the Chief Land Registrar.

# THE THIRD GROUP OF PARTS

# PART 7 – COURT PROCEDURE AND PRACTICE

## Chapter 1 – Applications

### 7.1 Preliminary

**7.1** This Chapter applies to any application made to the court under the Act or Rules except a petition for–

(a) an administration order under Part II,
(b) a winding-up order under Part IV, or
(c) a bankruptcy order under Part IX

of the Act.

## 7.2 Interpretation

**7.2(1) [Definitions]** In this Chapter, except in so far as the context otherwise requires–

**"originating application"** means an application to the court which is not an application in pending proceedings before the court; and [FORM 7.1]

**"ordinary application"** means any other application to the court. [FORM 7.2]

**7.2(2) [Form of application]** Every application shall be in the form appropriate to the application concerned.

## 7.3 Form and contents of application

**7.3(1) [Contents etc. of application]** Each application shall be in writing and shall state–

(a) the names of the parties;
(b) the nature of the relief or order applied for or the directions sought from the court;
(c) the names and addresses of the persons (if any) on whom it is intended to serve the application or that no person is intended to be served;
(d) where the Act or Rules require that notice of the application is to be given to specified persons, the names and addresses of all those persons (so far as known to the applicant); and
(e) the applicant's address for service.

**7.3(2) [Grounds for application]** An originating application shall set out the grounds on which the applicant claims to be entitled to the relief or order sought.

**7.3(3) [Application must be signed etc.]** The application must be signed by the applicant if he is acting in person or, when he is not so acting, by or on behalf of his solicitor.

## 7.4 Filing and service of application

**7.4(1) [Filing etc.]** The application shall be filed in court, accompanied by one copy and a number of additional copies equal to the number of persons who are to be served with the application.

**7.4(2) [Venue]** Subject as follows in this Rule and the next, or unless the Rule under which the application is brought provides otherwise, or the court otherwise orders, upon the presentation of the documents mentioned in paragraph (1) above, the court shall fix a venue for the application to be heard.

**7.4(3) [Service]** Unless the court otherwise directs, the applicant shall serve a sealed copy of the application, endorsed with the venue for the hearing, on the respondent named in the application (or on each respondent if more than one).

**7.4(4) [Directions]** The court may give any of the following directions–

(a) that the application be served upon persons other than those specified by the relevant provision of the Act or Rules;
(b) that the giving of notice to any person may be dispensed with;
(c) that notice be given in some way other than that specified in paragraph (3).

**7.4(5) [Time for service]** Unless the provision of the Act or Rules under which the application is made provides otherwise, and subject to the next paragraph, the application must be served at least 14 days before the date fixed for the hearing.

**7.4(6) [In case of urgency]** Where the case is one of urgency, the court may (without prejudice to its general power to extend or abridge time limits)–

(a) hear the application immediately, either with or without notice to, or the attendance of, other parties, or

(b) authorise a shorter period of service than that provided for by paragraph (5);

and any such application may be heard on terms providing for the filing or service of documents, or the carrying out of other formalities, as the court thinks fit.

## 7.5 Other hearings *ex parte*

**7.5(1) [Ex parte applications]** Where the relevant provisions of the Act or Rules do not require service of the application on, or notice of it to be given to, any person, the court may hear the application *ex parte*.

**7.5(2) [Power of court]** Where the application is properly made *ex parte*, the court may hear it forthwith, without fixing a venue as required by Rule 7.4(2).

**7.5(3) [Alternative power]** Alternatively, the court may fix a venue for the application to be heard, in which case Rule 7.4 applies (so far as relevant).

## 7.6 Hearing of application

**7.6(1) [Hearing in chambers]** Unless allowed or authorised to be made otherwise, every application before the registrar shall, and every application before the judge may, be heard in chambers.

**7.6(2) [Registrar's jurisdiction]** Unless either–

(a) the judge has given a general or special direction to the contrary, or

(b) it is not within the registrar's power to make the order required,

the jurisdiction of the court to hear and determine the application may be exercised by the registrar, and the application shall be made to the registrar in the first instance.

**7.6(3) [Reference to judge]** Where the application is made to the registrar he may refer to the judge any matter which he thinks should properly be decided by the judge, and the judge may either dispose of the matter or refer it back to the registrar with such directions as he thinks fit.

**7.6(4) [Effect of Rule]** Nothing in this Rule precludes an application being made directly to the judge in a proper case.

## 7.7 Use of affidavit evidence

**7.7(1) [Affidavit evidence, attendance for cross-examination]** In any proceedings evidence may be given by affidavit unless by any provision of the Rules it is otherwise provided or the court otherwise directs; but the court may, on the application of any party, order the attendance for cross-examination of the person making the affidavit.

**7.7(2) [Where attendance for cross-examination ordered]** Where, after such an order has been made, the person in question does not attend, his affidavit shall not be used in evidence without the leave of the court.

## 7.8 Filing and service of affidavits

**7.8(1) [Filing in court etc.]** Unless the provision of the Act or Rules under which the application is made provides otherwise, or the court otherwise allows–

(a) if the applicant intends to rely at the first hearing on affidavit evidence, he shall file the affidavit or affidavits (if more than one) in court and serve a copy or copies on the respondent, not less than 14 days before the date fixed for the hearing, and

(b) where a respondent to an application intends to oppose it and to rely for that purpose on affidavit evidence, he shall file the affidavit or affidavits (if more than one) in court and serve a copy or copies on the applicant, not less than 7 days before the date fixed for the hearing.

**7.8(2) [Swearing of affidavits]** Any affidavit may be sworn by the applicant or by the respondent or by some other person possessing direct knowledge of the subject matter of the application.

## 7.9 Use of reports

**7.9(1) [Filing report instead of affidavit]** A report may be filed in court instead of an affidavit–

(a) in any case, by the official receiver (whether or not he is acting in any capacity mentioned in sub-paragraph (b)), or a deputy official receiver, or

(b) unless the application involves other parties or the court otherwise orders, by–
   (i) an administrator, a liquidator or a trustee in bankruptcy,
   (ii) a provisional liquidator or an interim receiver,
   (iii) a special manager, or
   (iv) an insolvency practitioner appointed under section 273(2).

**7.9(2) [Report to be treated as affidavit]** In any case where a report is filed instead of an affidavit, the report shall be treated for the purposes of Rule 7.8(1) and any hearing before the court as if it were an affidavit.

**7.9(3) [Official receiver's report as prima facie evidence]** Any report filed by the official receiver in accordance with the Act or the Rules is prima facie evidence of any matter contained in it.

## 7.10 Adjournment of hearing; directions

**7.10(1) [Powers of court]** The court may adjourn the hearing of an application on such terms (if any) as it thinks fit.

**7.10(2) [Directions]** The court may at any time give such directions as it thinks fit as to–

(a) service or notice of the application on or to any person, whether in connection with the venue of a resumed hearing or for any other purpose;

(b) whether particulars of claim and defence are to be delivered and generally as to the procedure on the applications;

(c) the manner in which any evidence is to be adduced at a resumed hearing and in particular (but without prejudice to the generality of this sub-paragraph) as to–
   (i) the taking of evidence wholly or in part by affidavit or orally;
   (ii) the cross-examination either before the judge or registrar on the hearing in court or in chambers, of any deponents to affidavits;
   (iii) any report to be given by the official receiver or any person mentioned in Rule 7.9(1)(b);

(d) the matters to be dealt with in evidence.

# Chapter 2 – Transfer of Proceedings Between Courts

## 7.11 General power of transfer

**7.11(1) [Transfer to county court]** Where winding-up or bankruptcy proceedings are pending in the High Court, the court may order them to be transferred to a specified county court.

**7.11(2) [Transfer to High Court etc.]** Where winding-up or bankruptcy proceedings are pending in a county court, the court may order them to be transferred either to the High Court or to another county court.

**7.11(3) [Transfer to county court with jurisdiction]** In any case where proceedings are transferred to a county court, the transfer must be to a court which has jurisdiction to wind up companies or, as the case may be, jurisdiction in bankruptcy.

**7.11(4) [Power of High Court judge]** Where winding-up or bankruptcy proceedings are pending in a county court, a judge of the High Court may order them to be transferred to that Court.

**7.11(5) [Order for transfer]** A transfer of proceedings under this Rule may be ordered–

(a) by the court of its own motion, or

(b) on the application of the official receiver, or

(c) on the application of a person appearing to the court to have an interest in the proceedings.

**7.11(6) [Proceedings commenced before coming into force of Rules]** A transfer of proceedings under this Rule may be ordered notwithstanding that the proceedings commenced before the coming into force of the Rules.

**Note**

See practice direction [1987] 1 All ER 107.

## 7.12 Proceedings commenced in wrong court

7.12 Where winding-up or bankruptcy proceedings are commenced in a court which is, in relation to those proceedings, the wrong court, that court may–

(a) order the transfer of the proceedings to the court in which they ought to have been commenced;

(b) order that the proceedings be continued in the court in which they have been commenced; or

(c) order the proceedings to be struck out.

## 7.13 Applications for transfer

**7.13(1) [Official receiver's report]** An application by the official receiver for proceedings to be transferred shall be made with a report by him–

(a) setting out the reasons for the transfer, and

(b) including a statement either that the petitioner consents to the transfer, or that he has been given at least 14 days' notice of the official receiver's application.

**7.13(2) [More convenient conduct of proceedings]** If the court is satisfied from the official receiver's report that the proceedings can be conducted more conveniently in another court, the proceedings shall be transferred to that court.

**7.13(3) [Application not made by official receiver]** Where an application for the transfer of proceedings is made otherwise than by the official receiver, at least 14 days' notice of the application shall be given by the applicant–

(a) to the official receiver attached to the court in which the proceedings are pending, and

(b) to the official receiver attached to the court to which it is proposed that they should be transferred.

## 7.14 Procedure following order for transfer

**7.14(1) [Copy of order etc. to transferee court]** Subject as follows, the court making an order under Rule 7.11 shall forthwith send to the transferee court a sealed copy of the order, and the file of the proceedings.

**7.14(2) [On receipt]** On receipt of these, the transferee court shall forthwith send notice of the transfer to the official receivers attached to that court and the transferor court respectively.

**7.14(3) [Non-application of r. 7.14(1)]** Paragraph (1) does not apply where the order is made by the High Court under Rule 7.11(4). In that case–

(a) the High Court shall send sealed copies of the order to the county court from which the proceedings are to be transferred, and to the official receivers attached to that court and the High Court respectively, and

(b) that county court shall send the file of the proceedings to the High Court.

**7.14(4) [Following compliance with Rule]** Following compliance with this Rule, if the official receiver attached to the court to which the proceedings are ordered to be transferred is not already, by virtue of directions given by the Secretary of State under section 399(6)(a), the official receiver in relation to those proceedings, he becomes, in relation to those proceedings, the official receiver in place of the official receiver attached to the other court concerned.

## 7.15 Consequential transfer of other proceedings

**7.15(1) [Application of Rule]** This Rule applies where–

(a) an order for the winding up of a company, or a bankruptcy order in the case of an individual, has been made by the High Court, or

(b) in either such case, a provisional liquidator or (as the case may be) an interim receiver has been appointed, or

(c) winding-up or bankruptcy proceedings have been transferred to that Court from a county court.

**7.15(2) [Power of High Court judge]** A judge of any Division of the High Court may, of his own motion, order the transfer to that Division of any such proceedings as are mentioned below and are pending against the company or individual concerned ("the insolvent") either in another Division of the High Court or in a court in England and Wales other than the High Court.

**7.15(3) [Proceedings which may be transferred]** Proceedings which may be so transferred are those brought by or against the insolvent for the purpose of enforcing a claim against the insolvent estate, or brought by a person other than the insolvent for the purpose of enforcing any such claim (including in either case proceedings of any description by a debenture-holder or mortgagee).

**7.15(4) [Where proceedings are transferred]** Where proceedings are transferred under this Rule, the registrar may (subject to general or special directions of the judge) dispose of any matter arising in the proceedings which would, but for the transfer, have been disposed of in chambers or, in the case of proceedings transferred from a county court, by the registrar of that court.

# Chapter 3 – Shorthand Writers

## 7.16 Nomination and appointment of shorthand writers

**7.16(1) [Nomination]** In the High Court the judge and, in a county court, the registrar may in writing nominate one or more persons to be official shorthand writers to the court.

[FORM 7.3]

**7.16(2) [Appointment]** The court may, at any time in the course of insolvency proceedings, appoint a shorthand writer to take down the evidence of a person examined under section 133, 236, 290 or 366.

[FORM 7.4]

**7.16(3) [Application by official receiver etc.]** Where the official receiver applies to the court for an order appointing a shorthand writer, he shall name the person he proposes for appointment; and that appointment shall be made, unless the court otherwise orders.

## 7.17 Remuneration

**7.17(1) [Payment]** The remuneration of a shorthand writer appointed in insolvency proceedings shall be paid by the party at whose instance the appointment was made, or out of the insolvent estate, or otherwise, as the court may direct.

**7.17(2) [Court's discretion]** Any question arising as to the rates of remuneration payable under this Rule shall be determined by the court in its discretion.

**History**

R. 7.17(2) substituted by the Insolvency (Amendment) Rules 1993 (SI 1993/602), r. 3, Sch., para. 1 as from 5 April 1993; r. 7.17(2) formerly read as follows:

"The remuneration payable shall be calculated in accordance with Schedule 3 to the Rules."

## 7.18 Cost of shorthand note

**7.18** Where in insolvency proceedings the court appoints a shorthand writer on the application of the official receiver, in order that a written record may be taken of the evidence of a person to be examined, the cost of the written record is deemed an expense of the official receiver in the proceedings.

# Chapter 4 – Enforcement Procedures

## 7.19 Enforcement of court orders

**7.19(1) [Orders enforced as judgments]** In any insolvency proceedings, orders of the court may be enforced in the same manner as a judgment to the same effect.

**7.19(2) [Enforcement etc. by any county court]** Where an order in insolvency proceedings is made, or any process is issued, by a county court ("the primary court"), the order or process may be enforced, executed and dealt with by any other county court ("the secondary court"), as if it had been made or issued for the enforcement of a judgment or order to the same effect made by the secondary court.

This applies whether or not the secondary court has jurisdiction to take insolvency proceedings.

## 7.20 Orders enforcing compliance with the Rules

**7.20(1) [Application by competent person]** The court may, on application by the competent person, make such orders as it thinks necessary for the enforcement of obligations falling on any person in accordance with–

(a) section 22, 47 or 131 (duty to submit statement of affairs in administration, administrative receivership or winding up),

(b) section 143(2) (liquidator to furnish information, books, papers, etc.), or

(c) section 235 (duty of various persons to co-operate with office-holder).

**7.20(2) [Who is competent person]** The competent person for this purpose is–

(a) under section 22, the administrator,

(b) under section 47, the administrative receiver,

(c) under section 131 or 143(2), the official receiver, and

(d) under section 235, the official receiver, the administrator, the administrative receiver, the liquidator or the provisional liquidator, as the case may be.

**7.20(3) [Costs]** An order of the court under this Rule may provide that all costs of and incidental to the application for it shall be borne by the person against whom the order is made.

## 7.21 Warrants (general provisions)

**7.21(1) [Address for warrant]** A warrant issued by the court under any provision of the Act shall be addressed to such officer of the High Court or of a county court (whether or not having jurisdiction in insolvency proceedings) as the warrant specifies, or to any constable.

**7.21(2) [Prescribed officer of the court]** The persons referred to in sections 134(2), 236(5), 364(1), 365(3) and 366(3) (court's powers of enforcement) as the prescribed officer of the court are–

(a) in the case of the High Court, the tipstaff and his assistants of the court, and

(b) in the case of a county court, the registrar and the bailiffs.

**7.21(3) [Definition]** In this Chapter references to property include books, papers and records.

## 7.22 Warrants under s. 134, 364

**7.22** When a person is arrested under a warrant issued by the court under section 134 (officer of company failing to attend for public examination), or section 364 (arrest of debtor or bankrupt)–

(a) the officer apprehending him shall give him into the custody of the governor of the prison named in the warrant, who shall keep him in custody until such time as the court otherwise orders and shall produce him before the court as it may from time to time direct; and [FORM 7.9]

(b) any property in the arrested person's possession which may be seized shall be–
   (i) lodged with, or otherwise dealt with as instructed by, whoever is specified in the warrant as authorised to receive it, or
   (ii) kept by the officer seizing it pending the receipt of written orders from the court as to its disposal,

as may be directed by the court in the warrant. [FORM 7.6]
[FORM 7.7]

**History**
Against r. 7.22(a) the words "[FORM 7.9]" inserted by the Insolvency (Amendment) Rules 1987 (SI 1987/1919), r. 3(1), Sch., Pt. 2, para. 156(1) as from 11 January 1988.

## 7.23 Warrants under s. 236, 366

**7.23(1) [When person arrrested]** When a person is arrested under a warrant issued under section 236 (inquiry into insolvent company's dealings) or 366 (the equivalent in bankruptcy), the officer arresting him shall forthwith bring him before the court issuing the warrant in order that he may be examined. [FORM 7.8]

**7.23(2) [If not brought before court immediately]** If he cannot immediately be brought up for examination, the officer shall deliver him into the custody of the governor of the prison named in the warrant, who shall keep him in custody and produce him before the court as it may from time to time direct. [FORM 7.9]

**7.23(3) [Report of arrest etc.]** After arresting the person named in the warrant, the officer shall forthwith report to the court the arrest or delivery into custody (as the case may be) and apply to the court to fix a venue for the person's examination.

**7.23(4) [Time for examination etc.]** The court shall appoint the earliest practicable time for the examination, and shall–

(a) direct the governor of the prison to produce the person for examination at the time and place appointed, and

(b) forthwith give notice of the venue to the person who applied for the warrant.

[FORM 7.9]

**7.23(5) [Property in arrested person's possession]** Any property in the arrested person's possession which may be seized shall be–

(a) lodged with, or otherwise dealt with as instructed by, whoever is specified in the warrant as authorised to receive it, or

(b) kept by the officer seizing it pending the receipt of written orders from the court as to its disposal,

as may be directed by the court.

## 7.24 Execution of warrants outside court's district

**7.24(1) [Application of Rule]** This Rule applies where a warrant for a person's arrest has been issued in insolvency proceedings by a county court ("the primary court") and is addressed to another county court ("the secondary court") for execution in its district. [FORM 7.10]

**7.24(2) [Power of secondary court]** The secondary court may send the warrant to the registrar of any other county court (whether or not having jurisdiction to take insolvency proceedings) in whose district the person to be arrested is or is believed to be, with a notice to the effect that the warrant is transmitted to that court under this Rule for execution in its district at the request of the primary court.

**7.24(3) [Court receiving warrant]** The court receiving a warrant transmitted by the secondary court under this Rule shall apply its seal to the warrant, and secure that all such steps are taken for its execution as would be appropriate in the case of a warrant issued by itself.

## 7.25 Warrants under s. 365

**7.25(1) [Seizure]** A warrant issued under section 365(3) (search of premises not belonging to the bankrupt) shall authorise any person executing it to seize any property of the bankrupt found as a result of the execution of the warrant.

**7.25(2) [Seized property]** Any property seized under a warrant issued under section 365(2) or (3) shall be–

(a) lodged with, or otherwise dealt with as instructed by, whoever is specified in the warrant as authorised to receive it, or

(b) kept by the officer seizing it pending the receipt of written orders from the court as to its disposal,

as may be directed by the warrant.

[FORM 7.12]
[FORM 7.13]

# Chapter 5 – Court Records and Returns

## 7.26 Title of proceedings

**7.26(1) [Proceedings under Pt. I–VII]** Every proceeding under Parts I to VII of the Act shall, with any necessary additions, be intituled "IN THE MATTER OF . . . (naming the company to which the proceedings relate) AND IN THE MATTER OF THE INSOLVENCY ACT 1986".

**7.26(2) [Proceedings under Pt. IX–XI]** Every proceeding under Parts IX to XI of the Act shall be intituled "IN BANKRUPTCY".

## 7.27 Court records

**7.27** The court shall keep records of all insolvency proceedings, and shall cause to be entered in the records the taking of any step in the proceedings, and such decisions of the court in relation thereto, as the court thinks fit.

## 7.28 Inspection of records

**7.28(1) [Open to inspection by any person]** Subject as follows, the court's records of insolvency proceedings shall be open to inspection by any person.

**7.28(2) [Application to inspect etc.]** If in the case of a person applying to inspect the records the registrar is not satisfied as to the propriety of the purpose for which inspection is required, he may refuse to allow it. The person may then apply forthwith and *ex parte* to the judge, who may refuse the inspection, or allow it on such terms as he thinks fit.

**7.28(3) [Judge's decision final]** The judge's decision under paragraph (2) is final.

## 7.29 Returns to Secretary of State

**7.29(1) [Particulars of proceedings]** The court shall from time to time send to the Secretary of State the following particulars relating to winding-up and bankruptcy proceedings–

(a) the full title of the proceedings, including the number assigned to each case;

(b) where a winding-up or bankruptcy order has been made, the date of the order.

**7.29(2) [Request for particulars etc.]** The Secretary of State may, on the request of any person, furnish him with particulars sent by the court under this Rule.

## 7.30 File of court proceedings

**7.30(1) [Court file]** In respect of all insolvency proceedings, the court shall open and maintain a file for each case; and (subject to directions of the registrar) all documents relating to such proceedings shall be placed on the relevant file.

**7.30(2) [No filing in Central Office]** No proceedings shall be filed in the Central Office of the High Court.

## 7.31 Right to inspect the file

**7.31(1) [Who has right to inspect]** In the case of any insolvency proceedings, the following have the right, at all reasonable times, to inspect the court's file of the proceedings–

(a) the person who, in relation to those proceedings, is the responsible insolvency practitioner;

(b) any duly authorised officer of the Department; and

(c) any person stating himself in writing to be a creditor of the company to which, or the individual to whom, the proceedings relate.

**7.31(2) [Exercise of right]** The same right of inspection is exercisable–

(a) in proceedings under Parts I to VII of the Act, by every person who is, or at any time has been, a director or officer of the company to which the proceedings relate, or who is a member of the company or a contributory in its winding up;

(b) in proceedings with respect to a voluntary arrangement proposed by a debtor under Part VIII of the Act, by the debtor;

(c) in bankruptcy proceedings, by–
  (i) the bankrupt,
  (ii) any person against whom, or by whom, a bankruptcy petition has been presented, and
  (iii) any person who has been served, in accordance with Chapter 1 of Part 6 of the Rules, with a statutory demand.

**7.31(3) [Authority to inspect]** The right of inspection conferred as above on any person may be exercised on his behalf by a person properly authorised by him.

**7.31(4) [Leave to inspect]** Any person may, by special leave of the court, inspect the file.

**7.31(5) [When right not exercisable etc.]** The right of inspection conferred by this Rule is not exercisable in the case of documents, or parts of documents, as to which the court directs (either generally or specially) that they are not to be made open to inspection without the court's leave.

An application for a direction of the court under this paragraph may be made by the official receiver, by the person who in relation to any proceedings is the responsible insolvency practitioner, or by any party appearing to the court to have an interest.

**7.31(6) [If Secretary of State etc. requires to inspect]** If, for the purpose of powers conferred by the Act or the Rules, the Secretary of State, the Department or the official receiver requires to inspect the file of any insolvency proceedings, and requests the transmission of the file, the court shall comply with the request (unless the file is for the time being in use for the court's own purposes).

**7.31(7) [Application of r. 7.28]** Paragraphs (2) and (3) of Rule 7.28 apply in respect of the court's file of any proceedings as they apply in respect of court records.

## 7.32 Filing of Gazette notices and advertisements

**7.32(1) [Filing by officer of the court]** In any court in which insolvency proceedings are pending, an officer of the court shall file a copy of every issue of the Gazette which contains an advertisement relating to those proceedings.

**7.32(2) [Filing by advertiser]** Where there appears in a newspaper an advertisement relating to insolvency proceedings pending in any court, the person inserting the advertisement shall file a copy of it in that court.

The copy of the advertisement shall be accompanied by, or have endorsed on it, such particulars as are necessary to identify the proceedings and the date of the advertisement's appearance.

**7.32(3) [Court officer's memorandum]** An officer of any court in which insolvency proceedings are pending shall from time to time file a memorandum giving the dates of, and other particulars relating to, any notice published in the Gazette, and any newspaper advertisements, which relate to proceedings so pending.

The officer's memorandum is prima facie evidence that any notice or advertisement mentioned in it was duly inserted in the issue of the newspaper or the Gazette which is specified in the memorandum.

# Chapter 6 – Costs and Detailed Assessment

## 7.33 Application of the CPR

**7.33** Subject to provision to inconsistent effect made as follows in this Chapter, CPR Part 43 (scope of costs rules and definitions), Part 44 (general rules about costs), Part 45 (fixed costs),

Part 47 (procedure for detailed assessment of costs and default provisions) and Part 48 (costs – special cases) shall apply to insolvency proceedings with any necessary modifications.

## 7.34 Requirement to assess costs by the detailed procedure

**7.34(1) [Costs, charges, expenses]** Subject as follows, where the costs, charges or expenses of any person are payable out of the insolvent estate, the amount of those costs, charges or expenses shall be decided by detailed assessment unless agreed between the responsible insolvency practitioner and the person entitled to payment, and in the absence of such agreement the responsible insolvency practitioner may serve notice in writing requiring that person to commence detailed assessment proceedings in accordance with CPR Part 47 (procedure for detailed assessment of costs and default provisions) in the court to which the insolvency proceedings are allocated or, where in relation to a company there is no such court, that in relation to any court having jurisdiction to wind up the company.

**7.34(2) [Assessment of costs, charges, expenses]** If a liquidation or creditors' committee established in insolvency proceedings (except administrative receivership) resolves that the amount of any such costs, charges or expenses should be decided by detailed assessment, the insolvency practitioner shall require detailed assessment in accordance with CPR Part 47.

**7.34(3) [Payments on account]** Where the amount of the costs, charges or expenses of any person employed by an insolvency practitioner in insolvency proceedings are required to be decided by detailed assessment or fixed by order of the court this does not preclude the insolvency practitioner from making payments on account to such person on the basis of an undertaking by that person to repay immediately any money which may, when detailed assessment is made, prove to have been overpaid, with interest at the rate specified in section 17 of the Judgments Act 1838 on the date payment was made and for the period from the date of payment to that of repayment.

**7.34(4) [Power of court re costs]** In any proceedings before the court, including proceedings on a petition, the court may order costs to be decided by detailed assessment.

**7.34(5) [Costs of trustee in bankruptcy, liquidator]** Unless otherwise directed or authorised, the costs of a trustee in bankruptcy or a liquidator are to be allowed on the standard basis for which provision is made in CPR rule 44.4 (basis of assessment) and rule 44.5 (factors to be taken into account in deciding the amount of costs).

**7.34(6) [Application of Rule]** This Rule applies additionally (with any necessary modifications) to winding-up and bankruptcy proceedings commenced before the coming into force of the Rules.

## 7.35 Procedure where detailed assessment required

**7.35(1) [Requirements of costs officer]** Before making a detailed assessment of the costs of any person employed in insolvency proceedings by a responsible insolvency practitioner, the costs officer shall require a certificate of employment, which shall be endorsed on the bill and signed by the insolvency practitioner.

**7.35(2) [Information on certificate]** The certificate shall include–

(a) the name and address of the person employed,

(b) details of the functions to be carried out under the employment, and

(c) a note of any special terms of remuneration which have been agreed.

**7.35(3) [Detailed assessment proceedings]** Every person whose costs in insolvency proceedings are required to be decided by detailed assessment shall, on being required in writing to do so by the insolvency practitioner, commence detailed assessment proceedings in accordance with CPR Part 47 (procedure for detailed assessment of costs and default provisions).

**7.35(4) [Commencement of detailed assessment proceedings within three months]** If that person does not commence detailed assessment proceedings within 3 months of the requirement under paragraph (3), or within such further time as the court, on application, may permit, the insolvency practitioner may deal with the insolvent estate without regard to any claim by that person, whose claim is forfeited by such failure to commence proceedings.

**7.35(5) [Failure to commence proceedings]** Where in any such case such a claim lies additionally against an insolvency practitioner in his personal capacity, that claim is also forfeited by such failure to commence proceedings.

**7.35(6) [Assessment of costs by High Court]** Where costs have been incurred in insolvency proceedings in the High Court and those proceedings are subsequently transferred to a county court, all costs of those proceedings directed by the court or otherwise required to be assessed may nevertheless, on the application of the person who incurred the costs, be ordered to be decided by detailed assessment in the High Court.

## 7.36 Costs of sheriff

**7.36(1) [Detailed assessment of sheriff's bill]** Where a sheriff–

(a) is required under section 184(2) or 346(2) to deliver up goods or money, or

(b) has under section 184(3) or 346(3) deducted costs from the proceeds of an execution or money paid to him,

the responsible insolvency practitioner may require in writing that the amount of the sheriff's bill of costs be decided by detailed assessment.

**7.36(2) [Application of r. 7.35(4)]** Where such a requirement is made, Rule 7.35(4) applies.

**7.36(3) [In case of r. 7.36(1)(b) deduction]** Where, in the case of a deduction under paragraph (1)(b), any amount deducted is disallowed at the conclusion of the detailed assessment proceedings, the sheriff shall forthwith pay a sum equal to that disallowed to the insolvency practitioner for the benefit of the insolvent estate.

## 7.37 Petitions presented by insolvents

**7.37(1) [Credit for security]** In any case where a petition is presented by a company or individual ("the insolvent") against himself, any solicitor acting for the insolvent shall in his bill of costs give credit for any sum or security received from the insolvent as a deposit on account of the costs and expenses to be incurred in respect of the filing and prosecution of the petition; and the deposit shall be noted by the costs officer on the final costs certificate.

**7.37(2) [Application of r. 7.37(3)]** Paragraph (3) applies where a petition is presented by a person other than the insolvent to whom the petition relates and before it is heard the insolvent presents a petition for the same order, and that order is made.

**7.37(3) [No costs allowed to insolvent, etc.]** Unless the court considers that the insolvent estate has benefited by the insolvent's conduct, or that there are otherwise special circumstances justifying the allowance of costs, no costs shall be allowed to the insolvent or his solicitor out of the insolvent estate.

## 7.38 Costs paid otherwise than out of the insolvent estate

**7.38** Where the amount of costs is decided by detailed assessment under an order of the court directing that those costs are to be paid otherwise than out of the insolvent estate, the costs officer shall note on the final costs certificate by whom, or the manner in which, the costs are to be paid.

## 7.39 Award of costs against official receiver or responsible insolvency practitioner

**7.39** Without prejudice to any provision of the Act or Rules by virtue of which the official receiver is not in any event to be liable for costs and expenses, where the official receiver or a responsible insolvency practitioner is made a party to any proceedings on the application of another party to the proceedings, he shall not be personally liable for costs unless the court otherwise directs.

## 7.40 Applications for costs

**7.40(1) [Application of Rule]** This Rule applies where a party to, or person affected by, any proceedings in an insolvency–

(a) applies to the court for an order allowing his costs, or part of them, incidental to the proceedings, and

(b) that application is not made at the time of the proceedings.

**7.40(2) [Copies of application]** The person concerned shall serve a sealed copy of his application on the responsible insolvency practitioner, and, in winding up by the court or bankruptcy, on the official receiver.

**7.40(3) [Appearances]** The insolvency practitioner and, where appropriate, the official receiver may appear on the application.

**7.40(4) [Costs]** No costs of or incidental to the application shall be allowed to the applicant unless the court is satisfied that the application could not have been made at the time of the proceedings.

## 7.41 Costs and expenses of witnesses

**7.41(1) [No allowance to bankrupt, etc.]** Except as directed by the court, no allowance as a witness in any examination or other proceedings before the court shall be made to the bankrupt or an officer of the insolvent company to which the proceedings relate.

**7.41(2) [Petitioner's expenses]** A person presenting any petition in insolvency proceedings shall not be regarded as a witness on the hearing of the petition, but the costs officer may allow his expenses of travelling and subsistence.

## 7.42 Final costs certificate

**7.42(1) [Certificate is final, etc.]** A final costs certificate of the costs officer is final and conclusive as to all matters which have not been objected to in the manner provided for under the rules of the court.

**7.42(2) [Duplicate certificate]** Where it is proved to the satisfaction of a costs officer that a final costs certificate has been lost or destroyed, he may issue a duplicate.

**History**

Chapter 6 substituted for the former Ch. 6 by the Insolvency (Amendment) (No.2) Rules 1999 (SI 1999/1022), r. 3, Sch., para. 3 as from 26 April 1999. The former Ch. 6 read as follows:

"Chapter 6 – Costs and Taxation

7.33 Application of Rules of Supreme Court and County Court Rules

Subject to provision to inconsistent effect made as follows in this Chapter–

(a) Order 62 of the Rules of the Supreme Court applies to insolvency proceedings in the High Court, and

(b) Order 38 of the County Court Rules applies to such proceedings in a county court,

in either case, with any necessary modifications.

7.34 Requirement to tax costs

7.34(1) Subject as follows, where the costs, charges or expenses of any person are payable out of the insolvent estate, those costs, charges or expenses shall be taxed unless agreed between the responsible insolvency practitioner and the person entitled to payment, and in the absence of such agreement the responsible insolvency practitioner may require taxation by notice in writing requiring that person to deliver his bill of costs to the appropriate taxing officer for taxation; the appropriate taxing officer is that in relation to the court to which the insolvency proceedings are allocated or, where in relation to a company there is no such court, that in relation to any court having jurisdiction to wind up the company.

7.34(2) If a liquidation or creditors' committee established in insolvency proceedings (except administrative receivership) resolves that any such costs, charges or expenses be taxed, the insolvency practitioner shall require taxation.

7.34(3) Where the costs, charges or expenses of any person employed by an insolvency practitioner in insolvency proceedings are required to be taxed or fixed by order of the court this does not preclude the insolvency practitioner from making payments on account to such person on the basis of an undertaking by that person to repay immediately any money which may, on taxation, prove to have been overpaid, with interest at the rate specified in section 17 of the Judgments Act 1838 on the date payment was made and for the period from the date of payment to that of repayment.

7.34(4) In any proceedings before the court, including proceedings on a petition, the court may order costs to be taxed.

7.34(5) Unless otherwise directed or authorised, the costs of a trustee in bankruptcy or a liquidator are to be allowed on the standard basis specified in Rule 12 of order 62 of the Rules of the Supreme Court.

7.34(6) This Rule applies additionally (with any necessary modifications) to winding-up and bankruptcy proceedings commenced before the coming into force of the Rules.

7.35 Procedure where taxation required

7.35(1) Before taxing the costs of any person employed in insolvency proceedings by a responsible insolvency practitioner, the taxing officer shall require a certificate of employment, which shall be endorsed on the bill and signed by the insolvency practitioner.

7.35(2) The certificate shall include–
(a) the name and address of the person employed,
(b) details of the functions to be carried out under the employment, and
(c) a note of any special terms of remuneration which have been agreed.
7.35(3) Every person whose costs are required to be taxed in insolvency proceedings shall, on being required in writing to do so by the insolvency practitioner, deliver his bill of costs to the taxing officer for taxation.
7.35(4) If that person does not so deliver his bill within 3 months of the requirement under paragraph (3), or within such further time as the court, on application, may grant, the insolvency practitioner may deal with the insolvent estate without regard to any claim by that person, whose claim is forfeited.
7.35(5) Where in any such case such a claim lies additionally against an insolvency practitioner in his personal capacity, that claim is also forfeited.
7.35(6) Where costs have been incurred in insolvency proceedings in the High Court and those proceedings are subsequently transferred to a county court, all costs of those proceedings directed by the court or otherwise required to be taxed may nevertheless, on the application of the person who incurred the costs, be ordered to be taxed in the High Court.
7.36 Costs of sheriff
7.36(1) Where a sheriff–
(a) is required under section 184(2) or 346(2) to deliver up goods or money, or
(b) has under section 184(3) or 346(3) deducted costs from the proceeds of an execution or money paid to him,
the responsible insolvency practitioner may require in writing that the sheriff's bill of costs be taxed.
7.36(2) Where such a requirement is made, Rule 7.35(4) applies.
7.36(3) Where, in the case of a deduction under paragraph (1)(b), any amount is disallowed on taxation, the sheriff shall forthwith pay a sum equal to that amount to the insolvency practitioner for the benefit of the insolvent estate.
7.37 Petitions presented by insolvents
7.37(1) In any case where a petition is presented by a company or individual ("the insolvent") against himself, any solicitor acting for the insolvent shall in his bill of costs give credit for any sum or security received from the insolvent as a deposit on account of the costs and expenses to be incurred in respect of the filing and prosecution of the petition; and the deposit shall be noted by the taxing officer on the taxing certificate.
7.37(2) Paragraph (3) applies where a petition is presented by a person other than the insolvent to whom the petition relates and before it is heard the insolvent presents a petition for the same order, and that order is made.
7.37(3) Unless the court considers that the insolvent estate has benefitted by the insolvent's conduct, or that there are otherwise special circumstances justifying the allowance of costs, no costs shall be allowed to the insolvent or his solicitor out of the insolvent estate.
7.38 Costs paid otherwise than out of the insolvent estate
Where a bill of costs is taxed under an order of the court directing that the costs are to be paid otherwise than out of the insolvent estate, the taxing officer shall note on the certificate of taxation by whom, or the manner in which, the costs are to be paid.
7.39 Award of costs against official receiver or responsible insolvency practitioner
Without prejudice to any provision of the Act or Rules by virtue of which the official receiver is not in any event to be liable for costs and expenses, where the official receiver or a responsible insolvency practitioner is made a party to any proceedings on the application of another party to the proceedings, he shall not be personally liable for costs unless the court otherwise directs.
7.40 Applications for costs
7.40(1) This Rule applies where a party to, or person affected by, any proceedings in an insolvency–
(a) applies to the court for an order allowing his costs, or part of them, incidental to the proceedings, and
(b) that application is not made at the time of the proceedings.
7.40(2) The person concerned shall serve a sealed copy of his application on the responsible insolvency practitioner, and, in winding up by the court or bankruptcy, on the official receiver.
7.40(3) The insolvency practitioner and, where appropriate, the official receiver may appear on the application.
7.40(4) No costs of or incidental to the application shall be allowed to the applicant unless the court is satisfied that the application could not have been made at the time of the proceedings.
7.41 Costs and expenses of witnesses
7.41(1) Except as directed by the court, no allowance as a witness in any examination or other proceedings before the court shall be made to the bankrupt or an officer of the insolvent company to which the proceedings relate.
7.41(2) A person presenting any petition in insolvency proceedings shall not be regarded as a witness on the hearing of the petition, but the taxing officer may allow his expenses of travelling and subsistence.
7.42 Certificate of taxation
7.42(1) A certificate of taxation of the taxing officer is final and conclusive as to all matters which have not been objected to in the manner provided for under the rules of the court.
7.42(2) Where it is proved to the satisfaction of a taxing officer that a certificate of taxation has been lost or destroyed, he may issue a duplicate.
7.42(3) **"Certificate of taxation"** includes, for the purposes of the Rules, an order of the registrar in a county court."

# Chapter 7 – Persons Incapable of Managing Their Affairs

## 7.43 Introductory

**7.43(1) [Application of Ch. 7 Rules]** The Rules in this Chapter apply where in insolvency proceedings it appears to the court that a person affected by the proceedings is one who is incapable of managing and administering his property and affairs either–

(a) by reason of mental disorder within the meaning of the Mental Health Act 1983, or

(b) due to physical affliction or disability.

**7.43(2) ["The incapacitated person"]** The person concerned is referred to as "the incapacitated person".

## 7.44 Appointment of another person to act

**7.44(1) [Power of court]** The court may appoint such person as it thinks fit to appear for, represent or act for the incapacitated person. [FORM 7.19]

**7.44(2) [General or particular appointment]** The appointment may be made either generally or for the purpose of any particular application or proceeding, or for the exercise of particular rights or powers which the incapacitated person might have exercised but for his incapacity.

**7.44(3) [Appointment by court or on application]** The court may make the appointment either of its own motion or on application by–

(a) a person who has been appointed by a court in the United Kingdom or elsewhere to manage the affairs of, or to represent, the incapacitated person, or

(b) any relative or friend of the incapacitated person who appears to the court to be a proper person to make the application, or

(c) the official receiver, or

(d) the person who, in relation to the proceedings, is the responsible insolvency practitioner.

**7.44(4) [Ex parte application, powers of court]** Application under paragraph (3) may be made *ex parte*; but the court may require such notice of the application as it thinks necessary to be given to the person alleged to be incapacitated, or any other person, and may adjourn the hearing of the application to enable the notice to be given.

## 7.45 Affidavit in support of application

**7.45(1) [Affidavit of registered medical practitioner]** Except where made by the official receiver, an application under Rule 7.44(3) shall be supported by an affidavit of a registered medical practitioner as to the mental or physical condition of the incapacitated person.

**7.45(2) [Official receiver's report]** In the excepted case, a report made by the official receiver is sufficient.

## 7.46 Service of notices following appointment

**7.46** Any notice served on, or sent to, a person appointed under Rule 7.44 has the same effect as if it had been served on, or given to, the incapacitated person.

# Chapter 8 – Appeals in Insolvency Proceedings

## 7.47 Appeals and reviews of court orders (winding up)

**7.47(1) [Powers of courts]** Every court having jurisdiction under the Act to wind up companies may review, rescind or vary any order made by it in the exercise of that jurisdiction.

**7.47(2) [Appeal to High Court etc.]** An appeal from a decision made in the exercise of that jurisdiction by a county court or by a registrar of the High Court lies to a single judge of the High Court; and an appeal from a decision of that judge on such an appeal lies, with the leave of that judge or the Court of Appeal, to the Court of Appeal.

**7.47(3) [County court not to be restrained etc.]** A county court is not, in the exercise of its jurisdiction to wind up companies, subject to be restrained by the order of any other court, and no appeal lies from its decision in the exercise of that jurisdiction except as provided by this Rule.

**7.47(4) [Application for rescission of winding-up order]** Any application for the rescission of a winding-up order shall be made within 7 days after the date on which the order was made.

## 7.48 Appeals in bankruptcy

**7.48(1) [Appeal at instance of Secretary of State]** In bankruptcy proceedings, an appeal lies at the instance of the Secretary of State from any order of the court made on an application for the rescission or annulment of a bankruptcy order, or for a bankrupt's discharge.

**7.48(2) [Appeal to High Court, etc.]** In the case of an order made by a county court or by a registrar of the High Court, the appeal lies to a single judge of the High Court; and an appeal from a decision of that judge on such an appeal lies, with the leave of that judge or the Court of Appeal, to the Court of Appeal.

## 7.49 Procedure on appeal

**7.49(1) [Application of Supreme Court procedure, etc.]** Subject as follows, the procedure and practice of the Supreme Court relating to appeals to the Court of Appeal apply to appeals in insolvency proceedings.

**7.49(2) [Re appeal to single judge]** In relation to any appeal to a single judge of the High Court under section 375(2) (individual insolvency) or Rule 7.47(2) above (company insolvency), any reference in the CPR to the Court of Appeal is replaced by a reference to that judge and any reference to the registrar of civil appeals is replaced by a reference to the registrar of the High Court who deals with insolvency proceedings of the kind involved.

**7.49(3) [Appeal by ordinary application]** In insolvency proceedings, the procedure under RSC Order 59 (appeals to the Court of Appeal) is by ordinary application and not by application notice.

**History**
Rule 7.49 substituted by the Insolvency (Amendment) (No.2) Rules 1999 (SI 1999/1022), r. 3, Sch., para. 4 as from 26 April 1999. Rule 7.49 formerly read as follows:

"7.49 Procedure on appeal
**7.49(1)** Subject as follows, the procedure and practice of the Supreme Court relating to appeals to the Court of Appeal apply to appeals in insolvency proceedings.
**7.49(2)** In relation to any appeal to a single judge of the High Court under section 375(2) (individual insolvency) or Rule 7.47(2) above (company insolvency), any reference in the Rules of the Supreme Court to the Court of Appeal is replaced by a reference to that judge and any reference to the registrar of civil appeals is replaced by a reference to the registrar of the High Court who deals with insolvency proceedings of the kind involved.
**7.49(3)** In insolvency proceedings, the procedure under Order 59 of the Rules of the Supreme Court (appeal to the Court of Appeal) is by application, and not by summons."

## 7.50 Appeal against decision of Secretary of State or official receiver

**7.50** An appeal under the Act or the Rules against a decision of the Secretary of State or the official receiver shall be brought within 28 days of the notification of the decision.

# Chapter 9 – General

## 7.51 Principal court rules and practice to apply

**7.51(1) [Application of CPR, etc.]** The CPR, the practice and procedure of the High Court and of the county court (including any practice direction) apply to insolvency proceedings in the High Court and county court as the case may be, in either case with any necessary modifications, except so far as inconsistent with the Rules.

**7.51(2) [Allocations to CPR multi-track, etc.]** All insolvency proceedings shall be allocated to the multi-track for which CPR Part 29 (the multi-track) makes provision, accordingly those provisions of the CPR which provide for allocation questionnaires and track allocation will not apply.

**History**
Rule 7.51 substituted by the Insolvency (Amendment) (No.2) Rules 1999 (SI 1999/1022), r. 3, Sch., para. 5 as from 26 April 1999. Rule 7.51 formerly read as follows:

"**7.51** Except so far as inconsistent with the Insolvency Rules, the Rules of the Supreme Court and the practice of the High Court apply to insolvency proceedings in the High Court, and the County Court Rules and the practice of the county court apply to insolvency proceedings in a county court, in either case with any necessary modifications."

## 7.52 Right of audience

**7.52(1) [Official receivers and their deputies]** Official receivers and deputy official receivers have right of audience in insolvency proceedings, whether in the High Court or a county court.

**7.52(2) [Rights as obtained before Rules]** Subject as above, rights of audience in insolvency proceedings are the same as obtained before the coming into force of the Rules.

## 7.53 Right of attendance (company insolvency)

**7.53(1) [Creditor or member or contributory]** Subject as follows, in company insolvency proceedings any person stating himself in writing, in records kept by the court for that purpose, to be a creditor or member of the company or, where the company is being wound up, a contributory, is entitled, at his own cost, to attend in court or in chambers at any stage of the proceedings.

**7.53(2) [Attendance in person etc.]** Attendance may be by the person himself, or his solicitor.

**7.53(3) [Notice of proceedings]** A person so entitled may request the court in writing to give him notice of any step in the proceedings; and, subject to his paying the costs involved and keeping the court informed as to his address, the court shall comply with the request.

**7.53(4) [Costs]** If the court is satisfied that the exercise by a person of his rights under this Rule has given rise to costs for the insolvent estate which would not otherwise have been incurred and ought not, in the circumstances, to fall on that estate, it may direct that the costs be paid by the person concerned, to an amount specified.

The person's rights under this Rule are in abeyance so long as those costs are not paid.

**7.53(5) [Power of court to appoint representatives etc.]** The court may appoint one or more persons to represent the creditors, the members or the contributories of an insolvent company, or any class of them, to have the rights conferred by this Rule, instead of the rights being exercisable by any or all of them individually.

If two or more persons are appointed under this paragraph to represent the same interest, they must (if at all) instruct the same solicitor.

## 7.54 Insolvency practitioner's solicitor

7.54 Where in any proceedings the attendance of the responsible insolvency practitioner's solicitor is required, whether in court or in chambers, the insolvency practitioner himself need not attend, unless directed by the court.

## 7.55 Formal defects

7.55 No insolvency proceedings shall be invalidated by any formal defect or by any irregularity, unless the court before which objection is made considers that substantial injustice has been caused by the defect or irregularity, and that the injustice cannot be remedied by any order of the court.

## 7.56 Restriction on concurrent proceedings and remedies

7.56 Where, in insolvency proceedings the court makes an order staying any action, execution or other legal process against the property of a company, or against the property or person of an individual debtor or bankrupt, service of the order may be effected by sending a sealed copy of the order to whatever is the address for service of the plaintiff or other party having the carriage of the proceedings to be stayed.

## 7.57 Affidavits

**7.57(1) [Application of High Court practice and procedure]** Subject to the following paragraphs of this Rule the practice and procedure of the High Court with regard to affidavits, their form and contents and the procedure governing their use are to apply to all insolvency proceedings.

**7.57(2) [Affidavit by official receiver or responsible insolvency practitioner]** Where, in insolvency proceedings, an affidavit is made by the official receiver or the responsible insolvency practitioner, the deponent shall state the capacity in which he makes it, the position which he holds, and the address at which he works.

**7.57(3) [Swearing creditor's affidavit of debt]** A creditor's affidavit of debt may be sworn before his own solicitor.

**7.57(4) [Power of official receiver, etc.]** The official receiver, any deputy official receiver, or any officer of the court duly authorised in that behalf, may take affidavits and declarations.

**7.57(5) [Witness statement, etc.]** Subject to paragraph (6), where the Rules provide for the use of an affidavit, a witness statement verified by a statement of truth may be used as an alternative.

**7.57(6) [Non application of r. 7.57(5)]** Paragraph (5) does not apply to Rules 2.12., 3.4., 4.33., 6.60. (statement of affairs), 4.42., 6.66., 6.72. (further disclosure), 4.39., 4.40., 6.65; 6.70. (accounts), 4.73., 4.77., 6.96; 6.99. (claims) and 9.3., 9.4. (examinations).

**7.57(7) [Application of r. 7.57(5)]** Where paragraph (5) applies any form prescribed by Rule 12.7 of these Rules shall be modified as necessary.

**History**
Rule 7.57 substituted by the Insolvency (Amendment) (No.2) Rules 1999 (SI 1999/1022), r. 3, Sch., para. 6 as from 26 April 1999. Rule 7.57 formerly read as follows:

"**7.57(1)** Subject as follows, the rules and practice obtaining in the High Court with regard to affidavits, their form and contents, and the procedure governing their use, are to be taken as applicable in all insolvency proceedings in any court.
**7.57(2)** In applying RSC Order 41 (which relates to affidavits generally), there are to be disregarded provisions which are inconsistent with, or necessarily excluded by, the following paragraphs of this Rule.
**7.57(3)** Where in insolvency proceedings an affidavit is made by the official receiver or the responsible insolvency practitioner, the deponent shall state the capacity in which he makes it, the position which he holds, and the address at which he works.
**7.57(4)** Notwithstanding RSC Order 41 Rule 8 (affidavit not to be sworn before party's own solicitor), a creditor's affidavit of debt may be sworn before his own solicitor.
**7.57(5)** The official receiver, any deputy official receiver, or any officer of the court duly authorised in that behalf, may take affidavits and declarations."

## 7.58 Security in court

**7.58(1) [Form of security]** Where security has to be given to the court (otherwise than in relation to costs), it may be given by guarantee, bond or the payment of money into court.

**7.58(2) [Notice re bond]** A person proposing to give a bond as security shall give notice to the party in whose favour the security is required, and to the court, naming those who are to be sureties to the bond.

**7.58(3) [Court to give notice]** The court shall forthwith give notice to both the parties concerned of a venue for the execution of the bond and the making of any objection to the sureties.

**7.58(4) [Sureties' affidavits etc.]** The sureties shall make an affidavit of their sufficiency (unless dispensed with by the party in whose favour the security is required) and shall, if required by the court, attend the court to be cross-examined.

## 7.59 Payment into court

**7.59** The CPR relating to payment into and out of court of money lodged in court as security for costs apply to money lodged in court under the Rules.

**History**
Rule 7.59 substituted by the Insolvency (Amendment) (No.2) Rules 1999 (SI 1999/1022), r. 3, Sch., para. 7 as from 26 April 1999. Rule 7.59 formerly read as follows:

"**7.59** The Rules of the Supreme Court and the County Court Rules relating to payment into and out of court of money lodged in court as security for costs apply, in the High Court and a county court respectively, to money lodged in court under the Rules."

## 7.60 Further information and disclosure

**7.60(1) [Clarification, additional information, etc.]** Any party to insolvency proceedings may apply to the court for an order–

(a) that any other party
  (i) clarify any matter which is in dispute in the proceedings, or
  (ii) give additional information in relation to any such matter;

  in accordance with CPR Part 18 (further information); or

(b) to obtain disclosure from any other party in accordance with CPR Part 31 (disclosure and inspection of documents).

**7.60(2) [Application under Rule]** An application under this Rule may be made without notice being served on any other party.

**History**
Rule 7.60 substituted by the Insolvency (Amendment) (No.2) Rules 1999 (SI 1999/1022), r. 3, Sch., para. 8 as from 26 April 1999. Rule 7.60 formerly read as follows:

**"7.60 Discovery**

**7.60(1)** Any party to insolvency proceedings may, with the leave of the court, administer interrogatories to, or obtain discovery from, any other party to those proceedings.

**7.60(2)** Application under this Rule may be made *ex parte*."

## 7.61 Office copies of documents

**7.61(1) [Right to require office copy]** Any person who has under the Rules the right to inspect the court file of insolvency proceedings may require the court to provide him with an office copy of any document from the file.

**7.61(2) [Exercise of right]** A person's rights under this Rule may be exercised on his behalf by his solicitor.

**7.61(3) [Form of copy]** An office copy provided by the court under this Rule shall be in such form as the registrar thinks appropriate, and shall bear the court's seal.

# PART 8 – PROXIES AND COMPANY REPRESENTATION

## 8.1 Definition of "proxy"

**8.1(1) [Definition]** For the purposes of the Rules, a proxy is an authority given by a person (**"the principal"**) to another person (**"the proxy-holder"**) to attend a meeting and speak and vote as his representative. [FORMS 8.1 to 8.5]

**8.1(2) [Use of proxies]** Proxies are for use at creditors', company or contributories' meetings summoned or called under the Act or the Rules.

**History**
In r. 8.1(2) the words "summoned or called" inserted by the Insolvency (Amendment) Rules 1987 (SI 1987/1919), r. 3(1), Sch., Pt. 1, para. 134(1) as from 11 January 1988.

**8.1(3) [Giving proxies]** Only one proxy may be given by a person for any one meeting at which he desires to be represented; and it may only be given to one person, being an individual aged 18 or over. But the principal may specify one or more other such individuals to be proxy-holder in the alternative, in the order in which they are named in the proxy.

**8.1(4) [Chairman etc. as proxy-holder]** Without prejudice to the generality of paragraph (3), a proxy for a particular meeting may be given to whoever is to be the chairman of the meeting; and for a meeting held as part of the proceedings in a winding up by the court, or in a bankruptcy, it may be given to the official receiver.

**8.1(5) [Chairman etc. cannot decline]** A person given a proxy under paragraph (4) cannot decline to be the proxy-holder in relation to that proxy.

**8.1(6) [Conduct of proxy-holder]** A proxy requires the holder to give the principal's vote on matters arising for determination at the meeting, or to abstain, or to propose, in the principal's name, a resolution to be voted on by the meeting, either as directed or in accordance with the holder's own discretion.

**History**
R. 8.1(5) and (6) substituted for the former r. 8.1(5) by the Insolvency (Amendment) Rules 1987 (SI 1987/1919), r. 3(1), Sch., Pt. 1, para. 134(2) as from 11 January 1988; the former r. 8.1(5) read as follows:

"A proxy requires the holder to give the principal's vote on matters arising for determination at the meeting, or to abstain, either as directed or in accordance with the holder's own discretion; and it may authorise or require the holder to propose, in the principal's name, a resolution to be voted on by the meeting."

## 8.2 Issue and use of forms

**8.2(1) [When forms are sent with notice]** When notice is given of a meeting to be held in insolvency proceedings, and forms of proxy are sent out with the notice, no form so sent out shall have inserted in it the name or description of any person.

**8.2(2) [Forms of proxy]** No form of proxy shall be used at any meeting except that which is sent out with the notice summoning the meeting, or a substantially similar form.

**8.2(3) [Proxy to be signed etc.]** A form of proxy shall be signed by the principal, or by some person authorised by him (either generally or with reference to a particular meeting). If the form is signed by a person other than the principal, the nature of the person's authority shall be stated.

## 8.3 Use of proxies at meetings

**8.3(1) [Use at adjournment]** A proxy given for a particular meeting may be used at any adjournment of that meeting.

**8.3(2) [Official receiver etc. as proxy-holder]** Where the official receiver holds proxies for use at any meeting, his deputy, or any other official receiver, may act as proxy-holder in his place.

Alternatively, the official receiver may in writing authorise another officer of the Department to act for him at the meeting and use the proxies as if that other officer were himself proxy-holder.

**8.3(3) [Chairman etc. as proxy-holder]** Where the responsible insolvency practitioner holds proxies to be used by him as chairman of a meeting, and some other person acts as chairman, the other person may use the insolvency practitioner's proxies as if he were himself proxy-holder.

**8.3(4) [Appointment of responsible insolvency practitioner]** Where a proxy directs a proxy-holder to vote for or against a resolution for the nomination or appointment of a person as the responsible insolvency practitioner, the proxy-holder may, unless the proxy states otherwise, vote for or against (as he thinks fit) any resolution for the nomination or appointment of that person jointly with another or others.

**8.3(5) [Proposal by proxy-holder]** A proxy-holder may propose any resolution which, if proposed by another, would be a resolution in favour of which by virtue of the proxy he would be entitled to vote.

**8.3(6) [Specific directions to proxy-holder]** Where a proxy gives specific directions as to voting, this does not, unless the proxy states otherwise, preclude the proxy-holder from voting at his discretion on resolutions put to the meeting which are not dealt with in the proxy.

**History**

R. 8.3(4), (5) and (6) added by the Insolvency (Amendment) Rules 1987 (SI 1987/1919), r. 3(1), Sch., Pt. 1, para. 135 as from 11 January 1988.

## 8.4 Retention of proxies

**8.4(1) [Chairman to retain proxies]** Subject as follows, proxies used for voting at any meeting shall be retained by the chairman of the meeting.

**8.4(2) [Delivery]** The chairman shall deliver the proxies, forthwith after the meeting, to the responsible insolvency practitioner (where that is someone other than himself).

## 8.5 Right of inspection

**8.5(1) [Who may inspect]** The responsible insolvency practitioner shall, so long as proxies lodged with him are in his hands, allow them to be inspected, at all reasonable times on any business day, by–

(a) the creditors, in the case of proxies used at a meeting of creditors, and

(b) a company's members or contributories, in the case of proxies used at a meeting of the company or of its contributories.

**8.5(2) [Who are r. 8.5(1) creditors]** The reference in paragraph (1) to creditors is–

(a) in the case of a company in liquidation or of an individual's bankruptcy, those creditors who have proved their debts, and

(b) in any other case, persons who have submitted in writing a claim to be creditors of the company or individual concerned;

but in neither case does it include a person whose proof or claim has been wholly rejected for purposes of voting, dividend or otherwise.

**8.5(3) [Who may also inspect]** The right of inspection given by this Rule is also exercisable–

(a) in the case of an insolvent company, by its directors, and

(b) in the case of an insolvent individual, by him.

**8.5(4) [Person attending meeting]** Any person attending a meeting in insolvency proceedings is entitled, immediately before or in the course of the meeting, to inspect proxies and associated documents (including proofs) sent or given, in accordance with directions contained in any notice convening the meeting, to the chairman of that meeting or to any other person by a creditor, member or contributory for the purpose of that meeting.

**History**

In r. 8.5(4) the words from "(including proofs)" to the end substituted for the former words "to be used in connection with that meeting" by the Insolvency (Amendment) Rules 1987 (SI 1987/1919), r. 3(1), Sch., Pt. 1, para. 136 as from 11 January 1988.

## 8.6 Proxy-holder with financial interest

**8.6(1) [Limitation on voting by proxy-holder]** A proxy-holder shall not vote in favour of any resolution which would directly or indirectly place him, or any associate of his, in a position to receive any remuneration out of the insolvent estate, unless the proxy specifically directs him to vote in that way.

**8.6(1A) [Written authorisation]** Where a proxy-holder has signed the proxy as being authorised to do so by his principal and the proxy specifically directs him to vote in the way mentioned in paragraph (1), he shall nevertheless not vote in that way unless he produces to the chairman of the meeting written authorisation from his principal sufficient to show that the proxy-holder was entitled so to sign the proxy.

**History**

R. 8.6(1A) inserted by the Insolvency (Amendment) Rules 1987 (SI 1987/1919), r. 3(1), Sch., Pt. 1, para. 137(1) as from 11 January 1988.

**8.6(2) [Application of Rule]** This Rule applies also to any person acting as chairman of a meeting and using proxies in that capacity under Rule 8.3; and in its application to him, the proxy-holder is deemed an associate of his.

**History**

In r. 8.6(2) the words "under Rule 8.3" inserted by the Insolvency (Amendment) Rules 1987 (SI 1987/1919), r. 3(1), Sch., Pt. 1, para. 137(2) as from 11 January 1988.

## 8.7 Company representation

**8.7(1) [Production of copy of resolution]** Where a person is authorised under section 375 of the Companies Act to represent a corporation at a meeting of creditors or of the company or its contributories, he shall produce to the chairman of the meeting a copy of the resolution from which he derives his authority.

**8.7(2) [Copy of resolution to be sealed or certified]** The copy resolution must be under the seal of the corporation, or certified by the secretary or a director of the corporation to be a true copy.

**8.7(3) [Authority to sign proxy]** Nothing in this Rule requires the authority of a person to sign a proxy on behalf of a principal which is a corporation to be in the form of a resolution of that corporation.

**History**

R. 8.7(3) added by the Insolvency (Amendment) Rules 1987 (SI 1987/1919), r. 3(1), Sch., Pt. 1, para. 138 as from 11 January 1988.

# PART 9 – EXAMINATION OF PERSONS CONCERNED IN COMPANY AND INDIVIDUAL INSOLVENCY

## 9.1 Preliminary

**9.1(1) [Application of Pt. 9 Rules]** The Rules in this Part relate to applications to the court for an order under–

(a) section 236 (inquiry into company's dealings when it is, or is alleged to be, insolvent), or [FORM 9.1]

(b) section 366 (inquiry in bankruptcy, with respect to the bankrupt's dealings). [FORM 9.1]

**9.1(2) [Definitions]** The following definitions apply–

(a) the person in respect of whom an order is applied for is "the respondent";

(b) "the applicable section" is section 236 or section 366, according to whether the affairs of a company or those of a bankrupt or (where the application under section 366 is made by virtue of section 368) a debtor are in question;

(c) the company or, as the case may be, the bankrupt or debtor concerned is "the insolvent".

## 9.2 Form and contents of application

**9.2(1) [In writing, statement of grounds]** The application shall be in writing, and be accompanied by a brief statement of the grounds on which it is made.

**9.2(2) [Respondent sufficiently identified]** The respondent must be sufficiently identified in the application.

**9.2(3) [Purpose to be stated]** It shall be stated whether the application is for the respondent–

(a) to be ordered to appear before the court, or

(b) to be ordered to clarify any matter which is in dispute in the proceedings or to give additional information in relation to any such matter and if so CPR Part 18 (further information) shall apply to any such order, or

(c) to submit affidavits (if so, particulars to be given of the matters to which he is required to swear), or

(d) to produce books, papers or other records (if so, the items in question to be specified),

or for any two or more of those purposes.

**History**

Rule 9.2(3)(b) substituted by the Insolvency (Amendment) (No.2) Rules 1999 (SI 1999/1022), r. 3, Sch., para. 9 as from 26 April 1999. Rule 9.2(3)(b) formerly read as follows:

"to answer interrogatories (if so, particulars to be given of the matters in respect of which answers are required), or".

**9.2(4) [Ex parte application]** The application may be made *ex parte*.

## 9.3 Order for examination, etc.

**9.3(1) [Powers of court]** The court may, whatever the purpose of the application, make any order which it has power to make under the applicable section.

**9.3(2) [Venue]** The court, if it orders the respondent to appear before it, shall specify a venue for his appearance, which shall be not less than 14 days from the date of the order.

**9.3(3) [Order to submit affidavits]** If he is ordered to submit affidavits, the order shall specify–

(a) the matters which are to be dealt with in his affidavits, and

(b) the time within which they are to be submitted to the court.

**9.3(4) [Order to produce books etc.]** If the order is to produce books, papers or other records, the time and manner of compliance shall be specified.

**9.3(5) [Service]** The order must be served forthwith on the respondent; and it must be served personally, unless the court otherwise orders.

## 9.4 Procedure for examination

**9.4(1) [Applicant may attend etc.]** At any examination of the respondent, the applicant may attend in person, or be represented by a solicitor with or without counsel, and may put such questions to the respondent as the court may allow.

**9.4(2) [Other attendances etc.]** Any other person who could have applied for an order under the applicable section in respect of the insolvent's affairs may, with the leave of the court and if the applicant does not object, attend the examination and put questions to the respondent (but only through the applicant).

**9.4(3) [Clarification, additional information]** If the respondent is ordered to clarify any matter or to give additional information, the court shall direct him as to the questions which he is required to answer, and as to whether his answers (if any) are to be made on affidavit.

**History**
Rule 9.4(3) substituted by the Insolvency (Amendment) (No.2) Rules 1999 (SI 1999/1022), r. 3, Sch., para. 10 as from 26 April 1999. Rule 9.4(3) formerly read as follows:

"**9.4(3)** If the respondent is ordered to answer interrogatories, the court shall direct him as to the questions which he is required to answer, and as to whether his answers (if any) are to be made on affidavit."

**9.4(4) [Attendance etc. of creditor]** Where application has been made under the applicable section on information provided by a creditor of the insolvent, that creditor may, with the leave of the court and if the applicant does not object, attend the examination and put questions to the respondent (but only through the applicant).

**9.4(5) [Representation of respondent]** The respondent may at his own expense employ a solicitor with or without counsel, who may put to him such questions as the court may allow for the purpose of enabling him to explain or qualify any answers given by him, and may make representations on his behalf.

**9.4(6) [Record of examination]** There shall be made in writing such record of the examination as the court thinks proper. The record shall be read over either to or by the respondent and signed by him at a venue fixed by the court.

**9.4(7) [Record as evidence]** The written record may, in any proceedings (whether under the Act or otherwise) be used as evidence against the respondent of any statement made by him in the course of his examination.

## 9.5 Record of examination

**9.5(1) [Record etc. not to be filed]** Unless the court otherwise directs, the written record of the respondent's examination, and any answer given by him to interrogatories, and any affidavits submitted by him in compliance with an order of the court under the applicable section, shall not be filed in court.

**9.5(2) [Inspection]** The written record, answers and affidavits shall not be open to inspection, without an order of the court, by any person other than–

(a) the applicant for an order under the applicable section, or

(b) any person who could have applied for such an order in respect of the affairs of the same insolvent.

**9.5(3) [Application of r. 9.5(2)]** Paragraph (2) applies also to so much of the court file as shows the grounds of the application for an order under the applicable section and to any copy of proposed interrogatories.

**9.5(4) [Powers of court]** The court may from time to time give directions as to the custody and inspection of any documents to which this Rule applies, and as to the furnishing of copies of, or extracts from, such documents.

## 9.6 Costs of proceedings under s. 236, 366

**9.6(1) [Power of court]** Where the court has ordered an examination of any person under the applicable section, and it appears to it that the examination was made necessary because information had been unjustifiably refused by the respondent, it may order that the costs of the examination be paid by him.

**9.6(2) [Further power]** Where the court makes an order against a person under–

(a) section 237(1) or 367(1) (to deliver up property in his possession which belongs to the insolvent), or

(b) section 237(2) or 367(2) (to pay any amount in discharge of a debt due to the insolvent),

the costs of the application for the order may be ordered by the court to be paid by the respondent.

**9.6(3) [Applicant's costs]** Subject to paragraphs (1) and (2) above, the applicant's costs shall, unless the court otherwise orders, be paid out of the insolvent estate.

**9.6(4) [Travelling expenses etc.]** A person summoned to attend for examination under this Chapter shall be tendered a reasonable sum in respect of travelling expenses incurred in connection with his attendance. Other costs falling on him are at the court's discretion.

**9.6(5) [No order against official receiver]** Where the examination is on the application of the official receiver otherwise than in the capacity of liquidator or trustee, no order shall be made for the payment of costs by him.

# PART 10 – OFFICIAL RECEIVERS

## 10.1 Appointment of official receivers

**10.1** Judicial notice shall be taken of the appointment under sections 399 to 401 of official receivers and deputy official receivers.

## 10.2 Persons entitled to act on official receiver's behalf

**10.2(1) [In absence of official receiver]** In the absence of the official receiver authorised to act in a particular case, an officer authorised in writing for the purpose by the Secretary of State, or by the official receiver himself, may, with the leave of the court, act on the official receiver's behalf and in his place–

(a) in any examination under section 133, 236, 290 or 366, and

(b) in respect of any application to the court.

**10.2(2) [In case of emergency]** In case of emergency, where there is no official receiver capable of acting, anything to be done by, to or before the official receiver may be done by, to or before the registrar of the court.

## 10.3 Application for directions

**10.3** The official receiver may apply to the court for directions in relation to any matter arising in insolvency proceedings.

## 10.4 Official receiver's expenses

**10.4(1) ["Expenses"]** Any expenses incurred by the official receiver (in whatever capacity he may be acting) in connection with proceedings taken against him in insolvency proceedings are to be treated as expenses of the insolvency proceedings.

"Expenses" includes damages.

**10.4(2) [Official receiver's charge]** In respect of any sums due to him under paragraph (1), the official receiver has a charge on the insolvent estate.

# PART 11 – DECLARATION AND PAYMENT OF DIVIDEND (WINDING UP AND BANKRUPTCY)

## 11.1 Preliminary

**11.1(1) [Application of Pt. 11 Rules]** The Rules in this Part relate to the declaration and payment of dividends in companies winding up and in bankruptcy.

**11.1(2) [Definitions]** The following definitions apply–

(a) **"the insolvent"** means the company in liquidation or, as the case may be, the bankrupt; and

(b) **"creditors"** means those creditors of the insolvent of whom the responsible practitioner is aware, or who are identified in the insolvent's statement of affairs.

## 11.2 Notice of intended dividend

**11.2(1) [Before declaring dividend]** Before declaring a dividend, the responsible insolvency practitioner shall give notice of his intention to do so to all creditors whose addresses are known to him and who have not proved their debts.

**History**
In r. 11.2(1) the words "whose addresses are known to him and" inserted by the Insolvency (Amendment) Rules 1987 (SI 1987/1919), r. 3(1), Sch., Pt. 1, para. 139(1) as from 11 January 1988.

**11.2(1A) [Public advertisement]** Before declaring a first dividend, the responsible insolvency practitioner shall, unless he has previously by public advertisement invited creditors to prove their debts, give notice of the intended dividend by public advertisement.

**History**
R. 11.2(1A) inserted by the Insolvency (Amendment) Rules 1987 (SI 1987/1919), r. 3(1), Sch., Pt. 1, para. 139(2) as from 11 January 1988.

**11.2(2) ["The last date for proving"]** Any notice under paragraph (1) and any notice of a first dividend under paragraph (1A) shall specify a date ("the last date for proving") up to which proofs may be lodged. The date shall be the same for all creditors, and not less than 21 days from that of the notice.

**History**
In r. 11.2(2) the words from "Any notice" to "paragraph (1A)" substituted for the former words "The notice" by the Insolvency (Amendment) Rules 1987 (SI 1987/ 1919), r. 3(1), Sch., Pt. 1, para. 139(3) as from 11 January 1988.

**11.2(3) [Contents of notice]** The insolvency practitioner shall in the notice state his intention to declare a dividend (specified as interim or final, as the case may be) within the period of 4 months from the last date for proving.

## 11.3 Final admission/rejection of proofs

**11.3(1) [Dealing with every proof]** The responsible insolvency practitioner shall, within 7 days from the last date for proving, deal with every creditor's proof (in so far as not already dealt with) by admitting or rejecting it in whole or in part, or by making such provision as he thinks fit in respect of it.

**11.3(2) [Proofs lodged out of time]** The insolvency practitioner is not obliged to deal with proofs lodged after the date for proving; but he may do so, if he thinks fit.

## 11.4 Postponement or cancellation of dividend

**11.4** If in the period of 4 months referred to in Rule 11.2(3)–

(a) the responsible insolvency practitioner has rejected a proof in whole or in part and application is made to the court for his decision to be reversed or varied, or

(b) application is made to the court for the insolvency practitioner's decision on a proof to be reversed or varied, or for a proof to be expunged, or for a reduction of the amount claimed,

the insolvency practitioner may postpone or cancel the dividend.

## 11.5 Decision to declare dividend

**11.5(1) [Proceeding to declare dividend]** If the responsible insolvency practitioner has not, in the 4-month period referred to in Rule 11.2(3), had cause to postpone or cancel the dividend, he shall within that period proceed to declare the dividend of which he gave notice under that Rule.

**11.5(2) [Pending application re proof etc.]** Except with the leave of the court, the insolvency practitioner shall not declare the dividend so long as there is pending any application to the court to reverse or vary a decision of his on a proof, or to expunge a proof or to reduce the amount claimed.

If the court gives leave under this paragraph, the insolvency practitioner shall make such provision in respect of the proof in question as the court directs.

## 11.6 Notice of declaration

**11.6(1) [Notice to all creditors who have proved]** The responsible insolvency practitioner shall give notice of the dividend to all creditors who have proved their debts.

**11.6(2) [Particulars in notice]** The notice shall include the following particulars relating to the insolvency and the administration of the insolvent estate–

(a) amounts realised from the sale of assets, indicating (so far as practicable) amounts raised by the sale of particular assets;

(b) payments made by the insolvency practitioner in the administration of the insolvent estate;

(c) provision (if any) made for unsettled claims, and funds (if any) retained for particular purposes;

(d) the total amount to be distributed, and the rate of dividend;

(e) whether, and if so when, any further dividend is expected to be declared.

**11.6(3) [Simultaneous distribution]** The dividend may be distributed simultaneously with the notice declaring it.

**11.6(4) [Method of payment]** Payment of dividend may be made by post, or arrangements may be made with any creditor for it to be paid to him in another way, or held for his collection.

**11.6(5) [Endorsement in negotiable instrument]** Where a dividend is paid on a bill of exchange or other negotiable instrument, the amount of the dividend shall be endorsed on the instrument, or on a certified copy of it, if required to be produced by the holder for that purpose.

## 11.7 Notice of no, or no further, dividend

**11.7** If the responsible insolvency practitioner gives notice to creditors that he is unable to declare any dividend or (as the case may be) any further dividend, the notice shall contain a statement to the effect either–

(a) that no funds have been realised, or

(b) that the funds realised have already been distributed or used or allocated for defraying the expenses of administration.

## 11.8 Proof altered after payment of dividend

**11.8(1) [If amount claimed in proof increased]** If after payment of dividend the amount claimed by a creditor in his proof is increased, the creditor is not entitled to disturb the distribution of the dividend; but he is entitled to be paid, out of any money for the time being available for the payment of any further dividend, any dividend or dividends which he has failed to receive.

**11.8(2) [Payments under r. 11.8(1)]** Any dividend or dividends payable under paragraph (1) shall be paid before the money there referred to is applied to the payment of any such further dividend.

**11.8(3) [Proof withdrawn etc.]** If, after a creditor's proof has been admitted, the proof is withdrawn or expunged, or the amount of it is reduced, the creditor is liable to repay to the responsible insolvency practitioner, for the credit of the insolvent estate, any amount overpaid by way of dividend.

## 11.9 Secured creditors

**11.9(1) [Application of Rule]** The following applies where a creditor re-values his security at a time when a dividend has been declared.

**11.9(2) [Reduction of unsecured claim]** If the revaluation results in a reduction of his unsecured claim ranking for dividend, the creditor shall forthwith repay to the responsible insolvency practitioner, for the credit of the insolvent estate, any amount received by him as dividend in excess of that to which he would be entitled having regard to the revaluation of the security.

**11.9(3) [Increase of unsecured claim]** If the revaluation results in an increase of his unsecured claim, the creditor is entitled to receive from the insolvency practitioner, out of any money for the time being available for the payment of a further dividend, before any such further dividend is paid, any dividend or dividends which he has failed to receive, having regard to the revaluation of the security.

However, the creditor is not entitled to disturb any dividend declared (whether or not distributed) before the date of the revaluation.

## 11.10 Disqualification from dividend

**11.10** If a creditor contravenes any provision of the Act or the Rules relating to the valuation of securities, the court may, on the application of the responsible insolvency practitioner, order that the creditor be wholly or partly disqualified from participation in any dividend.

## 11.11 Assignment of right to dividend

**11.11(1) [Notice of assignment etc.]** If a person entitled to a dividend gives notice to the responsible insolvency practitioner that he wishes the dividend to be paid to another person, or that he has assigned his entitlement to another person, the insolvency practitioner shall pay the dividend to that other accordingly.

**11.11(2) [Contents of notice]** A notice given under this Rule must specify the name and address of the person to whom payment is to be made.

## 11.12 Preferential creditors

**11.12(1) [Application of Pt. 11 Rules]** Subject as follows, the Rules in this Part apply with respect to any distribution made in the insolvency to preferential creditors, with such adaptions as are appropriate considering that such creditors are of a limited class.

**11.12(2) [Rule 11.2 notice]** The notice by the responsible insolvency practitioner under Rule 11.2, where a dividend is to be declared for preferential creditors, need only be given to those creditors in whose case he has reason to believe that their debts are preferential and public advertisement of the intended dividend need only be given if the insolvency practitioner thinks fit.

**History**

In r. 11.12(2) the words from "and public advertisement" to the end added by the Insolvency (Amendment) Rules 1987 (SI 1987/1919), r. 3(1), Sch., Pt. 1, para. 140 as from 11 January 1988.

## 11.13 Debt payable at future time

**11.13(1) [Entitlement to dividend]** Where a creditor has proved for a debt of which payment is not due at the date of the declaration of dividend, he is entitled to dividend equally with other creditors, but subject as follows.

**11.13(2) [Calculation of amount of reduction]** For the purpose of dividend (and for no other purpose), the amount of the creditor's admitted proof (or, if a distribution has previously been made to him, the amount remaining outstanding in respect of his admitted proof) shall be reduced by a percentage calculated as follows–

$$\frac{I \times M}{12}$$

where I is 5 per cent. and M is the number of months (expressed, if need be, as, or as including, fractions of months) between the declaration of dividend and the date when payment of the creditor's debt would otherwise be due.

**History**

In r. 11.13(2) the words "a percentage" substituted for the former words "an amount" by the Insolvency (Amendment) Rules 1987 (SI 1987/1919), r. 3(1), Sch., Pt. 1, para. 141 as from 11 January 1988.

**11.13(3) [Other creditors' entitlement to interest]** Other creditors are not entitled to interest out of surplus funds under section 189(2) or (as the case may be) 328(4) until any creditor to whom paragraphs (1) and (2) apply has been paid the full amount of his debt.

# PART 12 – MISCELLANEOUS AND GENERAL

## 12.1 Power of Secretary of State to regulate certain matters

**12.1(1) [Power to make regulations]** Pursuant to paragraph 27 of Schedule 8 to the Act, and paragraph 30 of Schedule 9 to the Act, the Secretary of State may, subject to the Act and the Rules, make regulations with respect to any matter provided for in the Rules as relates to the carrying out of the functions of a liquidator, provisional liquidator, administrator or administrative receiver of a company, an interim receiver appointed under section 286, of the official receiver while acting as receiver or manager under section 287 or of a trustee of a bankrupt's estate, including, without prejudice to the generality of the foregoing, provision with respect to the following matters arising in companies winding up and individual bankruptcy–

(a) the preparation and keeping by liquidators, trustees, provisional liquidators, interim receivers and the official receiver, of books, accounts and other records, and their production to such persons as may be authorised or required to inspect them.

(b) the auditing of liquidators' and trustees' accounts;

(c) the manner in which liquidators and trustees are to act in relation to the insolvent company's or bankrupt's books, papers and other records, and the manner of their disposal by the responsible insolvency practitioner or others;

(d) the supply–
  (i) in company insolvency, by the liquidator to creditors and members of the company, contributories in its winding up and the liquidation committee, and
  (ii) in individual insolvency, by the trustee to creditors and the creditors' committee,

  of copies of documents relating to the insolvency and the affairs of the insolvent company or individual (on payment, in such cases as may be specified by the regulations, of the specified fee);

(e) the manner in which insolvent estates are to be distributed by liquidators and trustees, including provision with respect to unclaimed funds and dividends;

(f) the manner in which moneys coming into the hands of a liquidator or trustee in the course of his administration are to be handled and, in the case of a liquidator, invested, and the payment of interest on sums which, in pursuance of regulations made by virtue of this sub-paragraph, have been paid into the Insolvency Services Account;

(g) the amount (or the manner of determining the amount) to be paid to the official receiver by way of remuneration when acting as provisional liquidator, liquidator, interim receiver or trustee.

**History**
In r. 12.1(1) the words from ", subject to the Act and the Rules" to "generality of the foregoing, provision" substituted for the former words "make regulations" by the Insolvency (Amendment) Rules 1987 (SI 1987/1919), r. 3(1), Sch., Pt. 1, para. 142(1) as from 11 January 1988.

**12.1(2) [Reference to trustee in r. 12.1(1)]** Any reference in paragraph (1) to a trustee includes a reference to the official receiver when acting as receiver and manager under section 287.

**12.1(3) [Contents of regulations]** Regulations made pursuant to paragraph (1) may–

(a) confer a discretion on the court;

(b) make non-compliance with any of the regulations a criminal offence;

(c) make different provision for different cases, including different provision for different areas; and

(d) contain such incidental, supplemental and transitional provisions as may appear to the Secretary of State necessary or expedient.

**History**
In r. 12.1(3) the word ", and" and para. (d) added by the Insolvency (Amendment) Rules 1987 (SI 1987/1919), r. 3(1), Sch., Pt. 1, para. 142(2) as from 11 January 1988.

**Note**
See the Insolvency Regulations 1994 (SI 1994/2507) as amended.

## 12.2 Costs, expenses, etc.

**12.2** All fees, costs, charges and other expenses incurred in the course of winding up or bankruptcy proceedings are to be regarded as expenses of the winding up or, as the case may be, of the bankruptcy.

## 12.3 Provable debts

**12.3(1) [What is provable]** Subject as follows, in both winding up and bankruptcy, all claims by creditors are provable as debts against the company or, as the case may be, the bankrupt, whether they are present or future, certain or contingent, ascertained or sounding only in damages.

**12.3(2) [What is not provable]** The following are not provable–

(a) in bankruptcy, any fine imposed for an offence, and any obligation arising under an order made in family proceedings or under a maintenance assessment made under the Child Support Act 1991;

(b) in winding up or bankruptcy, any obligation arising under a confiscation order made under section 1 of the Drug Trafficking Offences Act 1986 or section 1 of the Criminal Justice (Scotland) Act 1987 or section 71 of the Criminal Justice Act 1988.

**"Fine"** and **"family proceedings"** have the meanings given by section 281(8) of the Act (which applies the Magistrates' Courts Act 1980 and the Matrimonial and Family Proceedings Act 1984).

**History**

In r. 12.3(2)(a) the words "or domestic" formerly appearing before the word "proceedings" deleted and the words "or under a maintenance assessment made under the Child Support Act 1991" added by the Insolvency (Amendment) Rules 1993 (SI 1993/602), r. 3, Sch., para. 2 as from 5 April 1993.

In r. 12.3(2)(b) the words "or section 71 of the Criminal Justice Act 1988" added by the Insolvency (Amendment) Rules 1989 (SI 1989/397), r. 3(1), Sch. as from 3 April 1989.

Previously the words "or section 1 of the Criminal Justice (Scotland) Act 1987" added by the Insolvency (Amendment) Rules 1987 (SI 1987/1919), r. 3(1), Sch., Pt. 1, para. 143(1) as from 11 January 1988.

At the end of r. 12.3(2) the words **"domestic proceedings"** formerly appearing after the word **"fine"** deleted by the Insolvency (Amendment) Rules 1993 (SI 1993/602), r. 3, Sch., para. 3 as from 5 April 1993.

**12.3(2A) [Postponed debts]** The following are not provable except at a time when all other claims of creditors in the insolvency proceedings (other than any of a kind mentioned in this paragraph) have been paid in full with interest under section 189(2) or, as the case may be, section 328(4)–

(a) in a winding up or a bankruptcy, any claim arising by virtue of–

(i) section 6(3)(a) of the Financial Services Act 1986, not being a claim also arising by virtue of section 6(3)(b) of that Act, or

(ii) section 61(3)(a) of that Act, not being a claim also arising by virtue of section 61(3)(b) of that Act;

(b) in a winding up or a bankruptcy, any claim arising by virtue of section 49 of the Banking Act 1987;

(c) in a winding up, any claim which by virtue of the Act or any other enactment is a claim the payment of which in a bankruptcy or a winding up is to be postponed.

**History**

R. 12.3(2A) inserted by the Insolvency (Amendment) Rules 1987 (SI 1987/1919), r. 3(1), Sch., Pt. 1, para. 143(2) as from 11 January 1988.

**12.3(3) [Effect of Rule]** Nothing in this Rule prejudices any enactment or rule of law under which a particular kind of debt is not provable, whether on grounds of public policy or otherwise.

## 12.4 Notices

**12.4(1) [Notices in writing etc.]** All notices required or authorised by or under the Act or the Rules to be given must be in writing, unless it is otherwise provided, or the court allows the notice to be given in some other way.

**12.4(2) [Proof of posting]** Where in any proceedings a notice is required to be sent or given by the official receiver or by the responsible insolvency practitioner, the sending or giving of it may be proved by means of a certificate–

(a) in the case of the official receiver, by him or a member of his staff, and

(b) in the case of the insolvency practitioner, by him, or his solicitor, or a partner or an employee of either of them,

that the notice was duly posted.

**12.4(3) [Certificates of posting]** In the case of a notice to be sent or given by a person other than the official receiver or insolvency practitioner, the sending or giving of it may be proved by means of a certificate by that person that he posted the notice, or instructed another person (naming him) to do so.

**12.4(4) [Certificate endorsed on copy of notice]** A certificate under this Rule may be endorsed on a copy or specimen of the notice to which it relates.

## 12.4A Quorum at meeting of creditors or contributories

**12.4A(1) [Meeting competent]** Any meeting of creditors or contributories in insolvency proceedings is competent to act if a quorum is present.

**12.4A(2) [Quorum]** Subject to the next paragraph, a quorum is–

(a) in the case of a creditors' meeting, at least one creditor entitled to vote;

(b) in the case of a meeting of contributories, at least 2 contributories so entitled, or all the contributories, if their number does not exceed 2.

**12.4A(3) [Persons present or represented]** For the purposes of this Rule, the reference to the creditor or contributories necessary to constitute a quorum is to those persons present or represented by proxy by any person (including the chairman) and in the case of any proceedings under Parts I–VII of the Act includes persons duly represented under section 375 of the Companies Act.

**12.4A(4) [Meeting to be delayed]** Where at any meeting of creditors or contributories–

(a) the provisions of this Rule as to a quorum being present are satisfied by the attendance of–
   (i) the chairman alone, or
   (ii) one other person in addition to the chairman, and

(b) the chairman is aware, by virtue of proofs and proxies received or otherwise, that one or more additional persons would, if attending, be entitled to vote,

the meeting shall not commence until at least the expiry of 15 minutes after the time appointed for its commencement.

**History**
R. 12.4A inserted by the Insolvency (Amendment) Rules 1987 (SI 1987/1919), r. 3(1), Sch., Pt. 1, para. 144 as from 11 January 1988.

## 12.5 Evidence of proceedings at meetings

**12.5(1) [Minute of proceedings admissible]** A minute of proceedings at a meeting (held under the Act or the Rules) of a person's creditors, or of the members of a company, or of the contributories in a company's liquidation, signed by a person describing himself as, or appearing to be, the chairman of that meeting is admissible in insolvency proceedings without further proof.

**12.5(2) [Minute as prima facie evidence]** The minute is prima facie evidence that–

(a) the meeting was duly convened and held,

(b) all resolutions passed at the meeting were duly passed, and

(c) all proceedings at the meeting duly took place.

## 12.6 Documents issuing from Secretary of State

**12.6(1) [Presumption re documents]** Any document purporting to be, or to contain, any order, directions or certificate issued by the Secretary of State shall be received in evidence and deemed to be or (as the case may be) contain that order or certificate, or those directions, without further proof, unless the contrary is shown.

**12.6(2) [Application of r. 12.6(1)]** Paragraph (1) applies whether the document is signed by the Secretary of State himself or an officer on his behalf.

**12.6(3) [Certificate as conclusive evidence]** Without prejudice to the foregoing, a certificate signed by the Secretary of State or an officer on his behalf and confirming–

(a) the making of any order,

(b) the issuing of any document, or

(c) the exercise of any discretion, power or obligation arising or imposed under the Act or the Rules,

is conclusive evidence of the matters dealt with in the certificate.

## 12.7 Forms for use in insolvency proceedings

**12.7(1) [Sch. 4 forms]** The forms contained in Schedule 4 to the Rules shall be used in and in connection with, insolvency proceedings, whether in the High Court or a county court.

**12.7(2) [Variations]** The forms shall be used with such variations, if any, as the circumstances may require.

**12.7(3) [Use of old forms]** Where any form contained in Schedule 4 is substantially the same as one used for a corresponding purpose under either–

(a) the law and practice obtaining before the coming into force of the Rules; or

(b) if the form was first required to be used after the coming into force of the Rules, the law and practice obtaining before the making of the requirement,

whichever shall be appropriate in any case, the latter may continue to be used (with the necessary modifications) until 1 March 1988.

**History**

R. 12.7(3) substituted by the Insolvency (Amendment) Rules 1987 (SI 1987/1919), r. 3(1), Sch., Pt. 1, para. 145 as from 11 January 1988; r. 12.7(3) formerly read as follows:

"Where any form contained in Schedule 4 is substantially the same as one used for a corresponding purpose under the law and practice obtaining before the coming into force of the Rules, the latter may continue to be used (with the necessary modifications) until the Lord Chancellor otherwise directs."

## 12.8 Insolvency practitioner's security

**12.8(1) [Duty re appointee's security]** Wherever under the Rules any person has to appoint, or certify the appointment of, an insolvency practitioner to any office, he is under a duty to satisfy himself that the person appointed or to be appointed has security for the proper performance of his functions.

**12.8(2) [Duty to review adequacy of security]** It is the duty–

(a) of the creditors' committee in companies administration, administrative receivership and bankruptcy,

(b) of the liquidation committee in companies winding up, and

(c) of any committe of creditors established for the purposes of a voluntary arrangement under Part I or VIII of the Act,

to review from time to time the adequacy of the responsible insolvency practitioner's security.

**12.8(3) [Cost of security]** In any insolvency proceedings the cost of the responsible insolvency practitioner's security shall be defrayed as an expense of the proceedings.

## 12.9 Time-limits

**12.9(1) [Application of CPR r. 2.8]** The provisions of CPR rule 2.8 (time) apply, as regards computation of time, to anything required or authorised to be done by the Rules.

**12.9(2) [Application of CPR r. 3.1(2)(a)]** The provisions of CPR rule 3.1(2)(a) (the court's general powers of management) apply so as to enable the court to extend or shorten the time for compliance with anything required or authorised to be done by the Rules.

**History**

Rule 12.9 substituted by the Insolvency (Amendment) (No.2) Rules 1999 (SI 1999/1022), r. 3, Sch., para. 11 as from 26 April 1999. Rule 12.9 formerly read as follows:

"**12.9** The provisions of Order 3 of the Rules of the Supreme Court, except Rules 3 and 6, apply as regards computation of time in respect of anything required or authorised by the Rules to be done."

## 12.10 Service by post

**12.10(1) [Proper service by post]** For a document to be properly served by post, it must be contained in an envelope addressed to the person on whom service is to be effected, and pre-paid for either first or second class post.

**12.10(1A) [Where to be served]** A document to be served by post may be sent to the last known address of the person to be served.

**History**
R. 12.10(1A) inserted by the Insolvency (Amendment) Rules 1987 (SI 1987/1919) r. 3(1), Sch., Pt. 1, para. 146 as from 11 January 1988.

**12.10(2) [First class post]** Where first class post is used, the document is treated as served on the second business day after the date of posting, unless the contrary is shown.

**12.10(3) [Second class post]** Where second class post is used, the document is treated as served on the fourth business day after the date of posting, unless the contrary is shown.

**12.10(4) [Presumed date of posting]** The date of posting is presumed, unless the contrary is shown, to be the date shown in the post-mark on the envelope in which the document is contained.

## 12.11 General provisions as to service

**12.11** Subject to Rule 12.10, CPR Part 6 (service of documents) applies as regards any matter relating to the service of documents and the giving of notice in insolvency proceedings.

**History**
Rule 12.11 substituted by the Insolvency (Amendment) (No.2) Rules 1999 (SI 1999/1022), r. 3, Sch., para. 12 as from 26 April 1999. Rule 12.11 formerly read as follows:

"**12.11(1)** Subject to Rule 12.10 and as follows, Order 65 of the Rules of the Supreme Court applies as regards any matter relating to the service of documents and the giving of notice in insolvency proceedings.
**12.11(2)** In Order 65 Rule 7, the expression "other originating process" does not include any application in insolvency proceedings.
**12.11(3)** Order 65 Rule 9 does not apply.
**12.11(4)** In Order 65 Rule 10, the expression "process" includes any application in insolvency proceedings."

## 12.12 Service outside the jurisdiction

**12.12(1) [Non-application of RSC, O.11 etc.]** RSC Order 11 (service of process, etc., out of the jurisdiction) does not apply in insolvency proceedings.

**History**
Rule 12.12(1) substituted by the Insolvency (Amendment) (No.2) Rules 1999 (SI 1999/1022), r. 3, Sch., para. 13 as from 26 April 1999. Rule 12.12(1) formerly read as follows:

"**12.12(1)** Order 11 of the Rules of the Supreme Court, and the corresponding County Court Rules, do not apply in insolvency proceedings."

**12.12(2) [Service of bankruptcy petition outside England and Wales]** A bankruptcy petition may, with the leave of the court, be served outside England and Wales in such manner as the court may direct.

**12.12(3) [Service on a person not in England and Wales]** Where for the purposes of insolvency proceedings any process or order of the court, or other document, is required to be served on a person who is not in England and Wales, the court may order service to be effected within such time, on such person, at such place and in such manner as it thinks fit, and may also require such proof of service as it thinks fit.

**12.12(4) [Supporting affidavit]** An application under this Rule shall be supported by an affidavit stating–

(a) the grounds on which the application is made, and
(b) in what place or country the person to be served is, or probably may be found.

## 12.13 Confidentiality of documents

**12.13(1) [Power of responsible insolvency practitioner]** Where in insolvency proceedings the responsible insolvency practitioner considers, in the case of a document forming part of the records of the insolvency, that–

(a) it should be treated as confidential, or
(b) it is of such a nature that its disclosure would be calculated to be injurious to the interests of the insolvent's creditors or, in the case of a company's insolvency, its members or the contributories in its winding up,

he may decline to allow it to be inspected by a person who would otherwise be entitled to inspect it.

**12.13(2) [Who may be refused inspection]** The persons to whom the insolvency practitioner may under this Rule refuse inspection include the members of a liquidation committee or a creditors' committee.

**12.13(3) [Application to court etc.]** Where under this Rule the insolvency practitioner determines to refuse inspection of a document, the person wishing to inspect it may apply to the court for that determination to be overruled; and the court may either overrule it altogether, or sustain it subject to such conditions (if any) as it thinks fit to impose.

**12.13(4) [Inspection of proof or proxy]** Nothing in this Rule entitles the insolvency practitioner to decline to allow the inspection of any proof or proxy.

**History**
R. 12.13(4) added by the Insolvency (Amendment) Rules 1987 (SI 1987/1919), r. 3(1), Sch., Pt. 1, para. 148 as from 11 January 1988.

# 12.14 Notices sent simultaneously to the same person

**12.14** Where under the Act or the Rules a document of any description is to be sent to a person (whether or not as a member of a class of persons to whom that same document is to be sent), it may be sent as an accompaniment to any other document or information which the person is to receive, with or without modification or adaption of the form applicable to that document.

# 12.15 Right to copy documents

**12.15** Where the Act or the Rules confer a right for any person to inspect documents, the right includes that of taking copies of those documents, on payment–

(a) in the case of documents on the court's file of proceedings, of the fee chargeable under any order made under section 130 of the Supreme Court Act 1981 or under section 128 of the County Courts Act 1984, and

(b) otherwise, of the appropriate fee.

**History**
In r. 12.15 the words "Act or the" inserted by the Insolvency (Amendment) Rules 1987 (SI 1987/1919), r. 3(1), Sch., Pt. 1, para. 149 as from 11 January 1988.

# 12.15A Charge for copy documents

**12.15A** Where the responsible insolvency practitioner or the official receiver is requested by a creditor, member, contributory or member of a liquidation or creditors' committee to supply copies of any documents he is entitled to require the payment of the appropriate fee in respect of the supply of the documents.

**History**
R. 12.15A inserted by the Insolvency (Amendment) Rules 1987 (SI 1987/1919), r. 3(1), Sch., Pt. 1, para. 150 as from 11 January 1988.

# 12.16 Non-receipt of notice of meeting

**12.16** Where in accordance with the Act or the Rules a meeting of creditors or other persons is summoned by notice, the meeting is presumed to have been duly summoned and held, notwithstanding that not all those to whom the notice is to be given have received it.

# 12.17 Right to have list of creditors

**12.17(1) [Application of Rule]** This Rule applies in any of the following proceedings–

(a) proceedings under Part II of the Act (company administration),

(b) a creditors' voluntary winding up, or a winding up by the court, and

(c) proceedings in bankruptcy.

**12.17(2) [Creditor's right to list etc.]** In any such proceedings a creditor who under the Rules has the right to inspect documents on the court file also has the right to require the responsible insolvency practitioner to furnish him with a list of the insolvent's creditors and the amounts of their respective debts.

This does not apply if a statement of the insolvent's affairs has been filed in court or, in the case of a creditors' voluntary winding up, been delivered to the registrar of companies.

**12.17(3)** **[Fee for sending list]** The insolvency practitioner, on being required by any person to furnish the list, shall send it to him, but is entitled to charge the appropriate fee for doing so.

## 12.18 False claim of status as creditor, etc.

**12.18(1)** **[Offence]** Where the Rules provide for creditors, members of a company or contributories in a company's winding up a right to inspect any documents, whether on the court's file or in the hands of a responsible insolvency practitioner or other person, it is an offence for a person, with the intention of obtaining a sight of documents which he has not under the Rules any right to inspect, falsely to claim a status which would entitle him to inspect them.

**12.18(2)** **[Penalties]** A person guilty of an offence under this Rule is liable to imprisonment or a fine, or both.

## 12.19 Execution overtaken by judgment debtor's insolvency

**12.19(1)** **[Application of Rule]** This Rule applies where execution has been taken out against property of a judgment debtor, and notice is given to the sheriff or other officer charged with the execution–

(a) under section 184(1) (that a winding-up order has been made against the debtor, or that a provisional liquidator has been appointed, or that a resolution for voluntary winding up has been passed); or

(b) under section 184(4) (that a winding-up petition has been presented or a winding-up order made, or that a meeting has been called at which there is to be proposed a resolution for voluntary winding up, or that such a resolution has been passed); or

(c) under section 346(2) (that the judgment debtor has been adjudged bankrupt); or

(d) under section 346(3)(b) (that a bankruptcy petition has been presented in respect of him).

**12.19(2)** **[Notice]** Subject as follows, the notice shall be in writing and be delivered by hand at, or sent by recorded delivery to, the office of the under-sheriff or (as the case may be) of the officer charged with the execution.

**12.19(3)** **[Execution in county court etc.]** Where the execution is in a county court, and the officer in charge of it is the registrar of that court, then if–

(a) there is filed in that court in respect of the judgment debtor a winding-up or bankruptcy petition, or

(b) there is made by that court in respect of him a winding-up order or an order appointing a provisional liquidator, or a bankruptcy order or an order appointing an interim receiver,

section 184 or (as the case may be) 346 is deemed satisfied as regards the requirement of a notice to be served on, or given to, the officer in charge of the execution.

## 12.20 The Gazette

**12.20(1)** **[Gazetted notice as evidence]** A copy of the Gazette containing any notice required by the Act or the Rules to be gazetted is evidence of any facts stated in the notice.

**12.20(2)** **[Gazetted notice of court order as conclusive evidence]** In the case of an order of the court notice of which is required by the Act or the Rules to be gazetted, a copy of the Gazette containing the notice may in any proceedings be produced as conclusive evidence that the order was made on the date specified in the notice.

**12.20(3)** **[Where gazetted order varied etc.]** Where an order of the court which is gazetted has been varied, and where any matter has been erroneously or inaccurately gazetted, the person whose responsibility it was to procure the requisite entry in the Gazette shall forthwith cause the variation of the order to be gazetted or, as the case may be, a further entry to be made in the Gazette for the purpose of correcting the error or inaccuracy.

## 12.21 Punishment of offences

**12.21(1) [Effect of Sch. 5]** Schedule 5 to the Rules has effect with respect to the way in which contraventions of the Rules are punishable on conviction.

**12.21(2) [First, second and third columns of Schedule]** In relation to an offence under a provision of the Rules specified in the first column of the Schedule (the general nature of the offence being described in the second column), the third column shows whether the offence is punishable on conviction on indictment, or on summary conviction, or either in the one way or the other.

**12.21(3) [Fourth column]** The fourth column shows, in relation to an offence, the maximum punishment by way of fine or imprisonment which may be imposed on a person convicted of the offence in the way specified in relation to it in the third column (that is to say, on indictment or summarily), a reference to a period of years or months being to a term of imprisonment of that duration.

**12.21(4) [Fifth column]** The fifth column shows (in relation to an offence for which there is an entry in that column) that a person convicted of the offence after continued contravention is liable to a daily default fine; that is to say, he is liable on a second or subsequent conviction of the offence to the fine specified in that column for each day on which the contravention is continued (instead of the penalty specified for the offence in the fourth column of the Schedule).

**12.21(5) [Application of s. 431]** Section 431 (summary proceedings), as it applies to England and Wales, has effect in relation to offences under the Rules as to offences under the Act.

# PART 13 – INTERPRETATION AND APPLICATION

## 13.1 Introductory

**13.1** This Part of the Rules has effect for their interpretation and application; and any definition given in this Part applies except, and in so far as, the context otherwise requires.

## 13.2 "The court"; "the registrar"

**13.2(1) ["The court"]** Anything to be done under or by virtue of the Act or the Rules by, to or before the court may be done by, to or before a judge or the registrar.

**13.2(2) ["The registrar"]** The registrar may authorise any act of a formal or administrative character which is not by statute his responsibility to be carried out by the chief clerk or any other officer of the court acting on his behalf, in accordance with directions given by the Lord Chancellor.

**Note**

See practice direction [1987] 1 All ER 107.

**13.2(3) ["The registrar" in individual insolvency proceedings]** In individual insolvency proceedings, **"the registrar"** means a Registrar in Bankruptcy of the High Court, or the registrar or deputy registrar of a county court.

**13.2(4) [In company insolvency proceedings in High Court]** In company insolvency proceedings in the High Court, **"the registrar"** means–

(a) subject to the following paragraph, a Registrar in Bankruptcy of the High Court;

(b) where the proceedings are in the District Registry of Birmingham, Bristol, Cardiff, Leeds, Liverpool, Manchester, Newcastle-upon-Tyne or Preston, the District Registrar.

**13.2(5) [In a county court]** In company insolvency proceedings in a county court, **"the registrar"** means the officer of the court whose duty it is to exercise the functions which in the High Court are exercised by a registrar.

## 13.3 "Give notice", etc.

**13.3(1) [Sending by post]** A reference in the Rules to giving notice, or to delivering, sending or serving any document, means that the notice or document may be sent by post, unless under a particular Rule personal service is expressly required.

**13.3(2) [Form of post]** Any form of post may be used, unless under a particular Rule a specified form is expressly required.

**13.3(3) [Personal service]** Personal service of a document is permissible in all cases.

**13.3(4) [Notice of venue]** Notice of the venue fixed for an application may be given by service of the sealed copy of the application under Rule 7.4(3).

## 13.4 Notice, etc. to solicitors

**13.4** Where under the Act or the Rules a notice or other document is required or authorised to be given to a person, it may, if he has indicated that his solicitor is authorised to accept service on his behalf, be given instead to the solicitor.

## 13.5 Notice to joint liquidators, joint trustees, etc.

**13.5** Where two or more persons are acting jointly as the responsible insolvency practitioner in any proceedings, delivery of a document to one of them is to be treated as delivery to them all.

## 13.6 "Venue"

**13.6** References to the **"venue"** for any proceeding or attendance before the court, or for a meeting, are to the time, date and place for the proceeding, attendance or meeting.

## 13.7 "Insolvency proceedings"

**13.7** **"Insolvency proceedings"** means any proceedings under the Act or the Rules.

## 13.8 "Insolvent estate"

**13.8** References to **"the insolvent estate"** are–

(a) in relation to a company insolvency, the company's assets, and

(b) in relation to an individual insolvency, the bankrupt's estate or (as the case may be) the debtor's property.

## 13.9 "Responsible insolvency practitioner", etc.

**13.9(1) [Definition]** In relation to any insolvency proceedings, **"the responsible insolvency practitioner"** means–

(a) the person acting in a company insolvency, as supervisor of a voluntary arrangement under Part I of the Act, or as administrator, administrative receiver, liquidator or provisional liquidator;

(b) the person acting in an individual insolvency, as the supervisor of a voluntary arrangement under Part VIII of the Act, or as trustee or interim receiver;

(c) the official receiver acting as receiver and manager of a bankrupt's estate.

**13.9(2) [Official receiver acting in relevant capacity]** Any reference to the liquidator, provisional liquidator, trustee or interim receiver includes the official receiver when acting in the relevant capacity.

## 13.10 "Petitioner"

**13.10** In winding up and bankruptcy, references to **"the petitioner"** or **"the petitioning creditor"** include any person who has been substituted as such, or been given carriage of the petition.

## 13.11 "The appropriate fee"

**13.11** **"The appropriate fee"** means–

(a) in Rule 6.192(2) (payor under income payments order entitled to clerical etc. costs), 50 pence; and

(b) in other cases, 15 pence per A4 or A5 page, and 30 pence per A3 page.

## 13.12 "Debt", "liability" (winding up)

**13.12(1) [Definition] "Debt"**, in relation to the winding up of a company, means (subject to the next paragraph) any of the following–

(a) any debt or liability to which the company is subject at the date on which it goes into liquidation;

(b) any debt or liability to which the company may become subject after that date by reason of any obligation incurred before that date; and

(c) any interest provable as mentioned in Rule 4.93(1).

**13.12(2) [Liability in tort]** In determining for the purposes of any provision of the Act or the Rules about winding up, whether any liability in tort is a debt provable in the winding up, the company is deemed to become subject to that liability by reason of an obligation incurred at the time when the cause of action accrued.

**13.12(3) [Debt or liability]** For the purposes of references in any provision of the Act or the Rules about winding up to a debt or liability, it is immaterial whether the debt or liability is present or future, whether it is certain or contingent, or whether its amount is fixed or liquidated, or is capable of being ascertained by fixed rules or as a matter of opinion; and references in any such provision to owing a debt are to be read accordingly.

**13.12(4) ["Liability"]** In any provision of the Act or the Rules about winding up, except in so far as the context otherwise requires, **"liability"** means (subject to paragraph (3) above) a liability to pay money or money's worth, including any liability under an enactment, any liability for breach of trust, any liability in contract, tort or bailment, and any liability arising out of an obligation to make restitution.

## 13.13 Expressions used generally

**13.13(1) ["Business day"] "Business day"** means any day other than a Saturday, a Sunday, Christmas Day, Good Friday or a day which is a bank holiday in any part of Great Britain under or by virtue of the Banking and Financial Dealings Act 1971 except in Rules 1.7., 4.10., 4.11., 4.16., 4.20., 5.10. and 6.23. where **"business day"** shall include any day which is a bank holiday in Scotland but not in England and Wales.

**History**

Rule 13.13(1) substituted by the Insolvency (Amendment) (No. 2) Rules 1999 (SI 1999/1022), r. 3, Sch., para. 14(a) as from 26 April 1999. Rule 13.13(1) formerly read as follows:

"**13.13(1) "Business day"** has the same meaning as in section 251 of the Act except in Rules 1.7, 4.10, 4.11, 4.16, 4.20, 5.10 and 6.23, where, if the court is the High Court, it has the same meaning as is given in Order 65, Rule 5(4) of the Rules of the Supreme Court, and, in relation to a county court, it means any day on which the court office is open in accordance with Order 2, Rule 2 of the County Court Rules."

**13.13(2) ["The Department"] "The Department"** means the Department of Trade and Industry.

**13.13(3) ["File in court"] "File in court"** means deliver to the court for filing.

**13.13(4) ["The Gazette"] "The Gazette"** means the London Gazette.

**13.13(5) ["General regulations"] "General regulations"** means regulations made by the Secretary of State under Rule 12.1.

**13.13(6) ["Practice direction"] "Practice direction"** means a direction as to the practice and procedure of any court within the scope of the CPR.

**13.13(7) ["Prescribed order of priority"] "Prescribed order of priority"** means the order of priority of payments laid down by Chapter 20 of Part 4 of the Rules, or Chapter 23 of Part 6.

**History**

Rule 13.13(6), (7) substituted for the former r. 13.13(6) by the Insolvency (Amendment) (No. 2) Rules 1999 (SI 1999/1022), r. 3, Sch., para. 14(b) as from 26 April 1999. Rule 13.13(6) formerly read as follows:

"**13.13(6) "Prescribed order of priority"** means the order of priority of payments laid down by Chapter 20 of Part 4 of the Rules, or Chapter 23 of Part 6."

## 13.14 Application

**13.14(1) [Application of Rules]** Subject to paragraph (2) of this Rule, and save where otherwise expressly provided, the Rules apply–

(a) to receivers appointed on or after the day on which the Rules come into force,

(b) to bankruptcy proceedings where the bankruptcy petition is presented on or after the day on which the Rules come into force, and

(c) to all other insolvency proceedings commenced on or after that day.

**History**

In r. 13.14(1)(a) the word "administrative" formerly appearing before the word "receiver" omitted by the Insolvency (Amendment) Rules 1987 (SI 1987/1919), r. 3(1), Sch., Pt. 1, para. 152 as from 11 January 1988.

**13.14(2) [Further application]** The Rules also apply to winding-up and bankruptcy proceedings commenced before that day to which provisions of the Act are applied by Schedule 11 to the Act, to the extent necessary to give effect to those provisions.

# Schedule 1 – Deposit Protection Board's Voting Rights

Rule 4.72(7)

**1** This Schedule applies as does Rule 4.72.

**2** In relation to any meeting at which the Deposit Protection Board is under Rule 4.72 entitled to be represented, the Board may submit in the liquidation, instead of a proof, a written statement of voting rights ("the statement").

**3** The statement shall contain details of–

(a) the names of creditors of the company in respect of whom an obligation of the Board has arisen or may reasonably be expected to arise as a result of the liquidation or proposed liquidation;

(b) the amount of the obligation so arising; and

(c) the total amount of all such obligations specified in the statement.

**4** The Board's statement shall, for the purpose of voting at a meeting (but for no other purpose), be treated in all respects as if it were a proof.

**5** Any voting rights which a creditor might otherwise exercise at a meeting in respect of a claim against the company are reduced by a sum equal to the amount of that claim in relation to which the Board, by virtue of its having submitted a statement, is entitled to exercise voting rights at that meeting.

**6** The Board may from time to time submit a further statement, and, if it does so, that statement supersedes any statement previously submitted.

# Schedule 2 – Alternative Courts for Debtors' Petitions in Bankruptcy

Rule 6.40(3)

| *Debtor's own county court* | *Nearest full-time court* |
|---|---|
| ABERDARE | CARDIFF |
| ABERYSTWYTH | CARDIFF |
| AYLESBURY | LUTON |
| BANBURY | LUTON or GLOUCESTER or READING |
| BANGOR | BIRKENHEAD or CHESTER |
| BARNSLEY | SHEFFIELD |
| BARNSTAPLE | EXETER |
| BARROW IN FURNESS | BLACKPOOL or PRESTON |
| BATH | BRISTOL |

| *Debtor's own county court* | *Nearest full-time court* |
|---|---|
| BEDFORD | LUTON |
| BLACKBURN | PRESTON |
| BLACKWOOD | CARDIFF |
| BOSTON | NOTTINGHAM |
| BRIDGEND | CARDIFF |
| BRIDGWATER | BRISTOL |
| BURNLEY | BOLTON or PRESTON |
| BURTON ON TRENT | LEICESTER or DERBY or NOTTINGHAM |
| BURY ST. EDMUNDS | CAMBRIDGE |
| CANTERBURY | CROYDON or THE HIGH COURT (LONDON) |
| CARLISLE | PRESTON or BLACKPOOL |
| CARMARTHEN | CARDIFF |
| CHELMSFORD | SOUTHEND or THE HIGH COURT (LONDON) |
| CHELTENHAM | GLOUCESTER |
| CHESTERFIELD | SHEFFIELD |
| COLCHESTER | SOUTHEND or THE HIGH COURT (LONDON) |
| COVENTRY | BIRMINGHAM |
| CREWE | STOKE or CHESTER |
| DARLINGTON | MIDDLESBROUGH |
| DEWSBURY | LEEDS |
| DONCASTER | SHEFFIELD |
| DUDLEY | BIRMINGHAM |
| DURHAM | NEWCASTLE |
| EASTBOURNE | BRIGHTON |
| GREAT GRIMSBY | HULL |
| GREAT YARMOUTH | NORWICH |
| GUILDFORD | CROYDON |
| HALIFAX | LEEDS |
| HARROGATE | LEEDS |
| HASTINGS | BRIGHTON |
| HAVERFORDWEST | CARDIFF |
| HEREFORD | GLOUCESTER |
| HERTFORD | LUTON |
| HUDDERSFIELD | LEEDS |
| IPSWICH | NORWICH or SOUTHEND |
| KENDAL | BLACKPOOL or PRESTON |
| KIDDERMINSTER | BIRMINGHAM |
| KING'S LYNN | NORWICH or CAMBRIDGE |
| LANCASTER | BLACKPOOL or PRESTON |
| LINCOLN | NOTTINGHAM |
| MACCLESFIELD | STOKE or MANCHESTER |
| MAIDSTONE | CROYDON or THE HIGH COURT (LONDON) |
| MEDWAY | CROYDON or THE HIGH COURT (LONDON) |
| MERTHYR TYDFIL | CARDIFF |
| MILTON KEYNES | LUTON |
| NEATH | CARDIFF |
| NEWBURY | READING |
| NEWPORT (GWENT) | CARDIFF |

| *Debtor's own county court* | *Nearest full-time court* |
|---|---|
| NEWPORT (I.O.W.) | SOUTHAMPTON or PORTSMOUTH |
| NORTHAMPTON | LUTON |
| OXFORD | READING |
| PETERBOROUGH | CAMBRIDGE |
| PONTYPRIDD | CARDIFF |
| PORTMADOC | BIRKENHEAD or STOKE or CHESTER |
| RHYL | BIRKENHEAD or CHESTER |
| ROCHDALE | OLDHAM or MANCHESTER |
| SALISBURY | BOURNEMOUTH or SOUTHAMPTON |
| SCARBOROUGH | YORK or HULL or MIDDLESBROUGH |
| SCUNTHORPE | HULL or SHEFFIELD |
| SHREWSBURY | STOKE |
| ST. ALBANS | LUTON |
| STAFFORD | STOKE |
| STOCKTON ON TEES | MIDDLESBROUGH |
| STOCKPORT | MANCHESTER |
| STOURBRIDGE | BIRMINGHAM |
| SUNDERLAND | NEWCASTLE |
| SWANSEA | CARDIFF |
| SWINDON | GLOUCESTER or READING |
| TAMESIDE | MANCHESTER |
| TAUNTON | EXETER or BRISTOL |
| TORQUAY | EXETER |
| TRURO | PLYMOUTH |
| TUNBRIDGE WELLS | CROYDON |
| WAKEFIELD | LEEDS |
| WARRINGTON | CHESTER or LIVERPOOL or MANCHESTER |
| WARWICK | BIRMINGHAM |
| WELSHPOOL | STOKE or CHESTER |
| WEST BROMWICH | BIRMINGHAM |
| WEYMOUTH | BOURNEMOUTH |
| WIGAN | BOLTON or MANCHESTER or PRESTON |
| WINCHESTER | SOUTHAMPTON |
| WORCESTER | GLOUCESTER |
| WORKINGTON | PRESTON or BLACKPOOL |
| WREXHAM | BIRKENHEAD or STOKE or CHESTER |
| YEOVIL | EXETER or BRISTOL |

**History**
Sch. 2 replaced by the Insolvency (Amendment) Rules 1987 (SI 1987/1919), r. 3(1), Sch., Pt. 2, para. 153 and Pt. 3 as from 11 January 1988; Sch. 2 formerly read as follows:

**"Schedule 2 – Alternative Courts for Debtors' Petitions in Bankruptcy**

Rule 6.40(3)

| *Debtor's own county court* | *Nearest full-time court* | *Debtor's own county court* | *Nearest full-time court* |
|---|---|---|---|
| ABERDARE | CARDIFF | BEDFORD | LUTON |
| ABERYSTWYTH | CARDIFF | BLACKBURN | PRESTON |
| ASHTON UNDER LYNE & STALYBRIDGE | MANCHESTER | BLACKWOOD | CARDIFF |
| AYLESBURY | LUTON | BOSTON | NOTTINGHAM |
| BANBURY | LUTON or GLOUCESTER | BRIDGEND | CARDIFF |
| BANGOR | BIRKENHEAD | BRIDGWATER | BRISTOL |
| BARNSLEY | SHEFFIELD | BURNLEY | BOLTON or PRESTON |
| BARNSTAPLE | EXETER | BURTON ON TRENT | LEICESTER |
| BARROW IN FURNESS | BLACKPOOL | BURY ST. EDMUNDS | CAMBRIDGE |
| BATH | BRISTOL | CANTERBURY | CROYDON |
| | | CARLISLE | PRESTON or BLACKPOOL |
| | | CARMARTHEN | CARDIFF |

| *Debtor's own county court* | *Nearest full-time court* |
|---|---|
| CHELMSFORD | SOUTHEND |
| CHELTENHAM | GLOUCESTER |
| CHESTER | BIRKENHEAD |
| CHESTERFIELD | SHEFFIELD |
| COLCHESTER | SOUTHEND |
| COVENTRY | BIRMINGHAM |
| CREWE | STOKE |
| DARLINGTON | MIDDLESBROUGH |
| DERBY | NOTTINGHAM |
| DEWSBURY | LEEDS |
| DONCASTER | SHEFFIELD |
| DUDLEY | BIRMINGHAM |
| DURHAM | NEWCASTLE |
| EASTBOURNE | BRIGHTON |
| GREAT GRIMSBY | HULL |
| GREAT YARMOUTH | NORWICH |
| GUILDFORD | CROYDON |
| HALIFAX | LEEDS |
| HARROGATE | LEEDS |
| HASTINGS | BRIGHTON |
| HAVERFORDWEST | CARDIFF |
| HEREFORD | GLOUCESTER |
| HERTFORD | LUTON |
| HUDDERSFIELD | LEEDS |
| IPSWICH | NORWICH or SOUTHEND |
| KENDAL | BLACKPOOL |
| KIDDERMINSTER | BIRMINGHAM |
| KING'S LYNN | NORWICH |
| LANCASTER | BLACKPOOL |
| LEOMINSTER | GLOUCESTER |
| LINCOLN | NOTTINGHAM |
| MACCLESFIELD | STOKE |
| MAIDSTONE | CROYDON |
| MEDWAY | CROYDON |
| MERTHYR TYDFIL | CARDIFF |
| MILTON KEYNES | LUTON |
| NEATH | CARDIFF |
| NEWBURY | READING |
| NEWPORT (GWENT) | CARDIFF |
| NEWPORT (I.O.W.) | SOUTHAMPTON |
| NORTHAMPTON | LUTON |
| OXFORD | READING |
| PETERBOROUGH | CAMBRIDGE |
| PONTYPRIDD | CARDIFF |
| PORTMADOC | BIRKENHEAD or STOKE |
| ROCHDALE | BOLTON |
| RHYL | BIRMINGHAM |
| SALISBURY | BOURNEMOUTH or SOUTHAMPTON |
| SCARBOROUGH | YORK, HULL or MIDDLESBROUGH |
| SCUNTHORPE | HULL |
| SHREWSBURY | STOKE |
| ST. ALBANS | LUTON |
| STAFFORD | STOKE |
| STOCKTON ON TEES | MIDDLESBROUGH |
| STOCKPORT | MANCHESTER |
| STOURBRIDGE | BIRMINGHAM |
| SUNDERLAND | NEWCASTLE |
| SWANSEA | CARDIFF |
| SWINDON | GLOUCESTER |
| TAUNTON | EXETER |
| TORQUAY | EXETER |
| TRURO | PLYMOUTH |
| TUNBRIDGE WELLS | CROYDON |
| WAKEFIELD | LEEDS |
| WARRINGTON | SALFORD |
| WARWICK | BIRMINGHAM |
| WELSHPOOL | STOKE |
| WEST BROMWICH | BIRMINGHAM |
| WEYMOUTH | BOURNEMOUTH |
| WIGAN | BOLTON |
| WINCHESTER | SOUTHAMPTON |
| WORCESTER | GLOUCESTER |
| WORKINGTON | PRESTON |
| WREXHAM | BIRKENHEAD or STOKE |
| YEOVIL | EXETER or BRISTOL" |

# Schedule 3 – Shorthand Writers' Remuneration

Rule 7.17

(Deleted by the Insolvency (Amendment) Rules 1993 (SI 1993/602), r. 3, Sch., para. 4 as from 5 April 1993.)

**History**

Sch. 3 formerly read as follows:

| | | |
|---|---|---|
| "1 | For attendance | £66.20. |
| 2 | Per folio of written record | 92.4p plus 5p per folio for all copies. |
| 3 | Travelling time | £7.00 per hour after first hour of each journey. |

4 In addition to the items in paragraphs 1 to 3, the following London weighting allowances (see note below) are payable in relation to the location of the court or other place concerned—

| Inner | Intermediate | Outer |
|---|---|---|
| £8.74 per day | £5.00 per day | £3.63 per day. |

5 The amounts shown in paragraph 4 are subject to a maximum annual allowance of—

| Inner | Intermediate | Outer |
|---|---|---|
| £1,750 | £1,000 | £725 |

The rate at which London weighting allowances are payable is determined as follows:

*(a) Inner*

The area within a radius of 5 miles from Charing Cross (statue of King Charles I).

*(b) Intermediate*

The area outside that specified in paragraph (a) but within a radius of 10 miles from Charing Cross.

*(c) Outer*

(i) The area outside those specified in paragraphs (a) and (b) but within a radius of 18 miles from Charing Cross; or

(ii) the former Borough of St Albans, Herts; or

(iii) the former Urban District of Slough, Bucks; or

(iv) the following towns whose boundary is intersected by the 18 miles radius from Charing Cross:–

| | |
|---|---|
| Abbots Langley | Redhill |
| Chertsey | Rickmansworth |

Egham
Fetcham
Godstone
Hatfield
South Ockenden
Stone
Swanscombe
Weybridge"

Previously Sch. 3, para. 1–3 substituted by the Insolvency (Amendment) Rules 1991 (SI 1991/495), r. 3, Sch., para. 4 as from 2 April 1991; para. 1–3 formerly read as follows:

| | | |
|---|---|---|
| "1 | For attendance | £56.43 |
| 2 | Per folio of written record | 78.8p plus 4p per folio for all copies. |
| 3 | Travelling time | £5.93 per hour after first hour of each journey." |

Prior the that Sch. 3, para. 1–5 subsituted by the Insolvency (Amendment) Rules 1989 (SI 1989/397), r. 3(1), Sch. as from 3 April 1989; para 1–5 formerly read as follows:

| | | |
|---|---|---|
| "1 | For attendance | £54.00 |
| 2 | Per folio of written record | 75.4p plus 4p per folio for all copies. |
| 3 | Travelling time | £5.67 per hour after first hour of each journey. |

**4** In addition to the items in paragraphs 1 to 3, the following London weighting allowances (see note below) are payable in relation to the location of the court or other place concerned—

| Inner | Intermediate | Outer |
|---|---|---|
| £7.33 per day | £4.20 per day | £3.08 per day |

**5** The amounts shown in paragraph 4 are subject to a maximum annual allowance of—

| Inner | Intermediate | Outer |
|---|---|---|
| £1,465 | £840 | £615" |

Originally Sch. 3, para. 1–3 substituted by the Insolvency (Amendment) Rules 1987 (SI 1987/1919), r. 3(1), Sch., Pt. 2, para. 154 as from 11 January 1988: para. 1–3 originally read as follows:

| | | |
|---|---|---|
| "1 | For attendance | £51.80 |
| 2 | Per folio of written record | 72.3p plus 4p per folio for all copies. |
| 3 | Travelling time | £5.44 per hour after first hour of each journey." |

# Schedule 4 – Forms

Rule 12.7

## Index

### Part 1: Company Voluntary Arrangements



### Part 2: Administration Procedure

| FORM NO. | TITLE |
|---|---|
| 2.14 | Notice by administrator of a change in committee membership |
| 2.15 | Administrator's abstract of receipts and payments |
| 2.16 | Notice to court of resignation by administrator under Rule 2.53(1) of the Insolvency Rules 1986 |
| 2.17 | Notice to court of resignation by administrator under Rule 2.53(2) of the Insolvency Rules 1986 |
| 2.18 | Notice of order to deal with charged property |
| 2.19 | Notice of discharge of administration order |
| 2.20 | Notice of variation of administration order |
| 2.21 | Statement of administrator's proposals |
| 2.22 | Statement of revised proposals and notice of meeting to consider them |
| 2.23 | Notice of result of meeting of creditors |

## Part 3: Administrative Receivership

| | |
|---|---|
| 3.1 | Written acceptance of appointment by receiver |
| 3.1A | Notice of appointment of administrative receiver (for newspaper or London Gazette) |
| 3.1B | Notice requiring preparation and submission of administrative receivership statement of affairs |
| 3.2 | Statement of affairs |
| 3.3 | Statement of affairs in administrative receivership following report to creditors |
| 3.4 | Certificate of constitution [amended certificate] of creditors' committee |
| 3.5 | Administrative receiver's report as to change in membership of creditors' committee |
| 3.6 | Receiver or manager or administrative receiver's abstract of receipts and payments |
| 3.7 | Notice of administrative receiver's death |
| 3.8 | Notice of order to dispose of charged property |
| 3.9 | Notice of resignation of administrative receiver pursuant to section 45(1) of Insolvency Act 1986 |
| 3.10 | Administrative receiver's report |

## Part 4: Companies Winding Up

| | |
|---|---|
| 4.1 | Statutory demand under section 123(1)(a) or 222(1)(a) of the Insolvency Act 1986 |
| 4.2 | Winding-up petition |
| 4.3 | Affidavit verifying winding-up petition |
| 4.4 | Affidavit of service of winding-up petition at registered office |
| 4.5 | Affidavit of service of winding-up petition other than at registered office or on an oversea company |
| 4.6 | Advertisement of winding-up petition |
| 4.7 | Certificate that relevant provision of Rules have been complied with |
| 4.8 | Order for leave to withdraw winding-up petition |
| 4.9 | Notice of intention to appear on petition |
| 4.10 | List of persons intending to appear on the hearing of the petition |
| 4.11 | Order for winding up by the court |
| 4.12 | Order for winding up by the court following upon the discharge of an administration order |
| 4.13 | Notice to official receiver of winding-up order |
| 4.14 | Petition by contributory |
| 4.14A | Notice to official receiver of appointment of provisional liquidator |
| 4.15 | Order of appointment of provisional liquidator |
| 4.16 | Notice requiring preparation and submission of statement of company's affairs |
| 4.17 | Statement of affairs [s. 131 IA86–winding up by court] |
| 4.18 | Statement of affairs [s. 95 IA86–voluntary liquidator] |
| 4.19 | Statement of affairs [s. 99 IA86–creditors' voluntary winding up] |

| FORM NO. | TITLE |
|---|---|
| 4.20 | Statement of affairs under s. 95/s. 99 to registrar of companies |
| 4.21 | Request by creditors for a meeting of the company's creditors [and contributories] |
| 4.22 | Notice to creditors of meeting of creditors |
| 4.23 | Notice to contributories of meeting of contributories |
| 4.24 | Request by contributory/contributories for a meeting of the company's contributories |
| 4.25 | Proof of debt–general form |
| 4.26 | Affidavit of debt |
| 4.27 | Certificate of appointment of liquidator by meeting |
| 4.28 | Certificate of appointment of two or more liquidators by meeting |
| 4.29 | Order of court appointing liquidator |
| 4.30 | Order of court appointing two or more liquidators |
| 4.31 | Notice of appointment of liquidator in winding up by the court (for registrar of companies) |
| 4.32 | Notice to court of resignation of liquidator following meeting of creditors |
| 4.33 | Notice of resignation as voluntary liquidator under s. 171(5) of the Insolvency Act 1986 |
| 4.34 | Order of court giving liquidator leave to resign |
| 4.35 | Order of court granting voluntary liquidator leave to resign |
| 4.36 | Notice to court of resignation of liquidator following leave of the court |
| 4.37 | Certificate of removal of liquidator |
| 4.38 | Certificate of removal of voluntary liquidator |
| 4.39 | Order of court removing liquidator or directing liquidator to summon a meeting of creditors for purpose of his removal |
| 4.40 | Notice of ceasing to act as voluntary liquidator |
| 4.41 | Liquidator's application to the Secretary of State for his release |
| 4.42 | Notice to court of final meeting of creditors |
| 4.43 | Notice to registrar of companies of final meeting of creditors |
| 4.44 | Notice of death of liquidator |
| 4.45 | Notice to official receiver or Secretary of State by liquidator on loss of qualification as insolvency practitioner |
| 4.46 | Notice of vacation of office by voluntary liquidator |
| 4.47 | Certificate of constitution [amended certificate] of liquidation committee |
| 4.48 | Notice of constitution of liquidation committee |
| 4.49 | Report by liquidator of any change in membership of liquidation committee |
| 4.50 | Liquidator's certificate that creditors paid in full |
| 4.51 | Certificate that creditors have been paid in full |
| 4.52 | Liquidator's certificate of continuance of liquidation committee |
| 4.53 | Notice of disclaimer under section 178 of the Insolvency Act 1986 |
| 4.54 | Notice to elect |
| 4.55 | Notice of intended disclaimer to interested party |
| 4.56 | Affidavit of liquidator in support of application for call |
| 4.57 | Order giving leave to make a call |
| 4.58 | Notice of call sanctioned by the court or the liquidation committee to be sent to contributory |
| 4.59 | Order for payment of call due from contributory |
| 4.60 | Order of appointment of special manager |
| 4.61 | Order of public examination |
| 4.62 | Notice to official receiver by creditor requesting him to make application for the holding of a public examination |
| 4.63 | Notice to official receiver by contributory requesting him to make application for the holding of a public examination |
| 4.64 | Order as to examination of person who is suffering from mental disorder or physical affliction or disability |
| 4.65 | Affidavit of verification of record of the public examination |

FORM NO. TITLE

4.66 Order of adjournment of public examination
4.67 Order appointing time for proceeding with public examination adjourned generally
4.68 Liquidator's statement of receipts and payments
4.69 Order of court on appeal against Secretary of State's decision under section 203(4) or 205(4) of the Insolvency Act 1986
4.70 Members' voluntary winding up declaration of solvency embodying a statement of assets and liabilities
4.71 Return of final meeting in a members' voluntary winding up
4.72 Return of final meeting in a creditors' voluntary winding up

## Part 5: Individual Voluntary Arrangements

5.1 Order for stay pending hearing of application for interim order
5.2 Interim order of court under section 252 of the Insolvency Act 1986
5.3 Order extending effect of interim order
5.4 Alternative orders to be made at hearing to consider chairman's report

## Part 6: Bankruptcy

6.1 Statutory demand under section 268(1)(a) of the Insolvency Act 1986–debt for liquidated sum payable immediately
6.2 Statutory demand under section 268(1)(a) of the Insolvency Act 1986–debt for liquidated sum payable immediately following a judgment or order of the court
6.3 Statutory demand under section 268(2) of the Insolvency Act 1986–debt payable at future date
6.4 Application to set aside statutory demand
6.5 Affidavit in support of application to set aside statutory demand
6.6 Order setting aside statutory demand
6.7 Creditor's bankruptcy petition on failure to comply with a statutory demand for a liquidated sum payable immediately
6.8 Creditor's bankruptcy petition on failure to comply with a statutory demand for a liquidated sum payable at a future date.
6.9 Creditor's bankruptcy petition where execution or other process on a judgment has been returned unsatisfied in whole or part
6.10 Bankruptcy petition for default in connection with voluntary arrangement
6.11 Affidavit of personal service of statutory demand
6.12 Affidavit of substituted service of statutory demand
6.13 Affidavit of truth of statements in bankruptcy petition
6.14 Application for registration of a petition in bankruptcy against an individual under Land Charges Act 1972
6.15 Order for substituted service of a bankruptcy petition
6.16 Substituted service of bankruptcy petition–notice in Gazette
6.17 Affidavit of personal service of bankruptcy petition
6.18 Affidavit of substituted service of bankruptcy petition
6.19 Notice by debtor of intention to oppose bankruptcy petition
6.20 Notice of intention to appear on bankruptcy petition
6.21 List of creditors intending to appear on hearing of the bankruptcy petition
6.22 Dismissal or withdrawal of bankruptcy petition
6.23 Order of adjournment of bankruptcy petition
6.24 Notice to debtor and creditors of order of adjournment of bankruptcy petition
6.24A Order for substitution of petitioner on creditor's petition
6.24B Change of carriage order
6.25 Bankruptcy order on creditor's petition
6.26 Application for registration of a bankruptcy order against an individual under the Land Charges Act 1972

| FORM NO. | TITLE |
|---|---|
| 6.27 | Debtor's bankruptcy petition |
| 6.28 | Debtor's petition statement of affairs |
| 6.29 | Order of appointment of insolvency practitioner to prepare a report under section 274(1) of the Insolvency Act 1986 |
| 6.30 | Bankruptcy order on debtor's petition |
| 6.31 | Revocation of certificate of summary administration |
| 6.32 | Order of appointment of interim receiver |
| 6.33 | Bankrupt's statement of affairs |
| 6.34 | Request by creditor(s) for a meeting of the bankrupt's creditors |
| 6.35 | Notice to creditors of meeting of creditors |
| 6.36 | Notice to bankrupt of meeting of creditors |
| 6.37 | Proof of debt |
| 6.38 | Proof by an existing trustee as a claim in later bankruptcy |
| 6.39 | Affidavit of debt |
| 6.40 | Certificate of appointment of trustee by creditors' meeting |
| 6.41 | Certificate of appointment of two or more trustees by creditors' meeting |
| 6.42 | Order of court appointing trustee |
| 6.43 | Order of court appointing two or more trustees |
| 6.44 | Notice to court of resignation of trustee following meeting of creditors |
| 6.45 | Order of court giving trustee leave to resign |
| 6.46 | Notice to court of resignation of trustee following leave of the court |
| 6.47 | Certificate of removal of trustee |
| 6.48 | Order of court removing trustee or directing trustee to summon a meeting of creditors for the purpose of his removal |
| 6.49 | Trustee's application to the Secretary of State for his release |
| 6.50 | Notice to court of final meeting of creditors |
| 6.51 | Notice to official receiver by trustee on loss of qualification as insolvency practitioner |
| 6.52 | Certificate of constitution [amended certificate] of creditors' committee |
| 6.53 | Report by trustee of any change in membership of creditors' committee |
| 6.54 | Order of appointment of special manager |
| 6.55 | Order for public examination of bankrupt |
| 6.56 | Request by creditor(s) for the holding of a public examination of the bankrupt |
| 6.57 | Order as to examination of bankrupt who is suffering from mental disorder or physical affliction or disability |
| 6.58 | Affidavit of verification of record of the public examination of the bankrupt |
| 6.59 | Order of adjournment of public examination of bankrupt |
| 6.60 | Order appointing time for proceeding with public examination of bankrupt adjourned generally |
| 6.61 | Notice of disclaimer under section 315 of the Insolvency Act 1986 |
| 6.62 | Notice to elect |
| 6.63 | Notice of intended disclaimer to interested party |
| 6.64 | Notice to bankrupt of an application under section 310 of the Insolvency Act 1986 for an income payments order |
| 6.65 | Order for income claimed under section 310(3)(a) of the Insolvency Act 1986 |
| 6.66 | Order for income claimed under section 310(3)(b) of the Insolvency Act1986 |
| 6.67 | Order converting income payments order made under section 310(1)(a) to an order under section 310(3)(b) of the Insolvency Act 1986 |
| 6.68 | Discharge or variation of order for income claimed under section 310 of the Insolvency Act 1986. |
| 6.69 | Order under section 369(1) of the Insolvency Act 1986 |
| 6.70 | Order under section 369(2) of the Insolvency Act 1986 |
| 6.71 | Order of annulment under section 282 of the Insolvency Act 1986 |
| 6.72 | Order of suspension of discharge under section 279(3) of the Insolvency Act 1986 |

| FORM NO. | TITLE |
|---|---|
| 6.73 | Order of court lifting suspension of discharge |
| 6.74 | Certificate that order suspending discharge has been lifted |
| 6.75 | Notice to court by bankrupt that he intends to dispute statements made by official receiver in his report under section 289(2) of the Insolvency Act 1986 |
| 6.76 | Order granting absolute/suspended discharge under section 280(2)(b) or (c) of the Insolvency Act 1986 |
| 6.77 | Certificate of discharge |
| 6.78 | Notice to existing trustee of the presentation of a petition for a later bankruptcy |
| 6.79 | Criminal bankruptcy petition |
| 6.79A | Charging order under section 313 of the Insolvency Act 1986 |
| 6.80 | Order to Post Office under section 371 of the Insolvency Act 1986 |

## Part 7: Court Procedure and Practice

| | |
|---|---|
| 7.1 | Originating application |
| 7.2 | Ordinary application |
| 7.3 | Declaration by official shorthand writer |
| 7.4 | Appointment of shorthand writer to take examination under the Insolvency Act 1986 |
| 7.5 | Declaration by shorthand writer |
| 7.6 | Warrant for failure to attend examination under section 133 of the Insolvency Act 1986 |
| 7.7 | Warrant of arrest etc under section 364 of the Insolvency Act 1986 |
| 7.8 | Warrant of arrest etc under section 236 or 366 of the Insolvency Act 1986 |
| 7.9 | Order for production of person arrested under warrant issued under section 134, 236, 364 or 366 of the Insolvency Act 1986 |
| 7.10 | Warrant to registrar of court in whose district a person against whom a warrant of arrest has been issued is believed to be |
| 7.11 | Endorsement of warrant of arrest issued by a court to which the same has been sent for execution by the court which originally issued it |
| 7.12 | Warrant of seizure of property under section 365 of the Insolvency Act 1986 |
| 7.13 | Search warrant under section 365 of the Insolvency Act 1986 |
| 7.14 | Order of discharge from custody under the Insolvency Act 1986 [General] |
| 7.15 | Affidavit in support of application for committal for contempt of court |
| 7.17 | Warrant of committal for contempt |
| 7.18 | Order of discharge from custody on contempt |
| 7.19 | Order appointing person to act for incapacitated person |

## Part 8: Proxies and Company Representation

| | |
|---|---|
| 8.1 | Proxy–company or individual voluntary arrangements |
| 8.2 | Proxy–administration |
| 8.3 | Proxy–administrative receivership |
| 8.4 | Proxy–winding up by the court or bankruptcy |
| 8.5 | Proxy–members' or creditors' voluntary winding up |

## Part 9: Examination of Persons Concerned in Company and Individual Insolvency

| | |
|---|---|
| 9.1 | Order under section 236 or 366 of the Insolvency Act 1986 |

**History**

A number of changes to the forms were made by the Insolvency (Amendment) Rules 1987 (SI 1987/1919), r. 3(1), Sch., Pt. 2, para. 157–159 as from 11 January 1988:

- Forms 2.4A, 3.1, 3.1A, 4.14A, 5.1, 5.2, 5.3, 5.4, 6.24A, 6.24B and 6.79A added;
- Forms 1.1, 2.1, 2.5, 2.8, 2.11, 2.12, 2.16, 2.17, 4.1, 4.12, 4.13, 4.14, 4.16, 4.53, 4.61, 4.64, 4.66, 4.67, 4.68, 4.70, 6.1, 6.2, 6.3, 6.11, 6.14, 6.26, 6.30, 6.55, 6.57, 6.59, 6.60, 6.61, 6.78, 7.9, 7.15, substituted for the former forms with identical numbers;

- Form 3.1B substituted for the former Form 3.1;
- Form 7.16 omitted.

Further changes were made by the Insolvency (Amendment) Rules 1991 (SI 1991/495), r. 3, Sch., para. 5, 6: the forms affected are Forms 4.71, 4.72, 6.71, 6.76 and 6.77.

**Note**
Sch. 4 also sets out the prescribed forms referred to in the above list. The forms are not reproduced here.

# Schedule 5 – Punishment of Offences under the Rules

Rule 12.21

*Note:* In the fourth and fifth columns of this Schedule, **"the statutory maximum"** means the prescribed sum under section 32 of the Magistrates Courts Act 1980 (c.43).

| Rule creating offence | General nature of offence | Mode of prosecution | Punishment | Daily default fine (where applicable) |
|---|---|---|---|---|
| In Part 1, Rule 1.30. | False representation or fraud for purpose of obtaining members' or creditors' consent to proposal for voluntary arrangement. | 1. On indictment.<br>2. Summary. | 7 years or a fine, or both.<br>6 months or the statutory maximum, or both. | |
| In Part 2, Rule 2.52(4). | Administrator failing to send notification as to progress of administration. | Summary. | One-fifth of the statutory maximum. | One-fiftieth of the statutory maximum. |
| In Part 3, Rule 3.32(5). | Administrative receiver failing to send notification as to progress of receivership. | Summary. | One-fifth of the statutory maximum. | One fiftieth of the statutory maximum. |
| In Part 5, Rule 5.30. | False representation or fraud for purpose of obtaining creditors' consent to proposal for voluntary arrangement. | 1. On indictment.<br>2. Summary. | 7 years or a fine, or both.<br>6 months or the statutory maximum, or both. | |
| In Part 12, Rule 12.18. | False representation of status for purpose of inspecting documents. | 1. On indictment.<br>2. Summary. | 2 years or a fine, or both.<br>6 months or the statutory maximum, or both. | |

**Note**
For "the statutory maximum", see note to Insolvency Act 1986, Sch. 10.



CCH.New Law
bbcl inru 1986b Mp 3474—98bcl 175

## EXPLANATORY NOTE

*(This Note does not form part of the Rules)*

These Rules set out the detailed procedure for the conduct of all company and individual insolvency proceedings in England and Wales under the Insolvency Act 1986 and otherwise give effect to that Act. The insolvency proceedings concerned are–

company voluntary arrangements (Part 1 of the Rules),
administration (Part 2),
administrative receivership (Part 3),
companies winding up (Part 4),
individual voluntary arrangements (Part 5),and
bankruptcy (Part 6).

Parts 7 to 13 of the Rules apply to both company and individual insolvency proceedings and are concerned with the following matters–

court procedure and practice (Part 7),
proxies and company representation (Part 8),
examination of persons concerned in company and individual insolvency (Part 9),
official receivers (Part 10),
declaration and payment of dividend (winding up and bankruptcy) (Part 11),
miscellaneous and general (Part 12), and interpretation and application (Part 13).

The Arrangement of Rules at the beginning of the statutory instrument lists the number and contents of all the Rules and Schedules. The Rules come into force on 29 December 1986 and generally apply to all insolvency proceedings commenced on or after that date. The Rules also apply to such proceedings commenced before that date to which provisions of the Insolvency Act 1986 are applied by Schedule 11 of the Act to the extent necessary to give effect to those provisions. In addition, Rules 6.36, 7.11 and 7.34 expressly provide for their application to insolvency proceedings, whenever commenced.

# THE INSOLVENCY (AMENDMENT) RULES 1987

(SI 1987/1919)

*Made on 9 November 1987 by the Lord Chancellor under s. 411 and 412 of the Insolvency Act 1986. Operative from 11 January 1988.*

## CITATION AND COMMENCEMENT

**1** These Rules may be cited as the Insolvency (Amendment) Rules 1987 and shall come into force on 11th January 1988, and that day is referred to in these Rules as the "commencement date".

## INTERPRETATION

**2(1)** In these Rules references to **"the principal Rules"** are to the Insolvency Rules 1986 and a Rule or Schedule or Form referred to by number means the Rule or Schedule or Form so numbered in the principal Rules.

**2(2)** These Rules shall be read and construed as one with the principal Rules.

## APPLICATION

**3(1)** Subject to paragraph (2), the principal Rules have effect in relation to insolvency proceedings to which the principal Rules apply by virtue of Rule 13.14 with the amendments set out in the Schedule to these Rules.

**3(2)** The principal Rules as so amended apply to all such proceedings on and after the commencement date whenever those proceedings were commenced.

**3(3)** Rule 4.223-CVL as so amended also applies to any winding up as is mentioned in paragraph 4(1) of Schedule 11 to the Insolvency Act 1986 on and after the commencement date.

## Schedule

Rule 3(1)

**Note**
Amendments not reproduced here–see the principal Rules.

### EXPLANATORY NOTE

(*This Note is not part of the Rules*)

These Rules make detailed amendments to the Insolvency Rules 1986, which set out detailed procedures for the conduct of all company and individual insolvency proceedings in England and Wales under the Insolvency Act 1986. These Rules apply to all insolvency proceedings to which the Insolvency Rules 1986 apply on and after 11 January 1988, whether or not those proceedings were commenced before, on or after that date.

Rule 3(3) also applies Rule 4.223-CVL of the Insolvency Rules 1986 as amended to those insolvency proceedings specified in paragraph 4(1) of Schedule 11 to the Insolvency Act 1986.

# THE INSOLVENCY (AMENDMENT) RULES 1989

(SI 1989/397)

*Made on 8 March 1989 by the Lord Chancellor under s. 411 and 412 of the Insolvency Act 1986. Operative from 3 April 1989.*

### CITATION AND COMMENCEMENT

**1** These Rules may be cited as the Insolvency (Amendment) Rules 1989 and shall come into force on 3rd April 1989, and that day is referred to in these Rules as "the commencement date".

### INTERPRETATION

**2(1)** In these Rules references to **"the principal Rules"** are to the Insolvency Rules 1986 and a Rule or Schedule so numbered in the principal Rules.

**2(2)** These Rules shall be read and construed as one with the principal Rules.

### APPLICATION

**3(1)** Subject to paragraph (2), the principal Rules have effect in relation to insolvency proceedings to which the principal Rules apply by virtue of Rule 13.14 with the amendments set out in the Schedule to these Rules.

**3(2)** The principal Rules as so amended apply to all such proceedings on and after the commencement whenever those proceedings were commenced.

## Schedule

Rule 3(1)

**Note**
Amendments not reproduced here–se the principal Rules.

### EXPLANATORY NOTE

(*This Note is not part of the Rules*)

These Rules make detailed amendments to the Insolvency Rules 1986 (as amended by the Insolvency (Amendment) Rules 1987), which set out detailed procedures for the conduct of all company and individual insolvency proceedings in England and Wales under the Insolvency Act 1986. These Rules apply to all insolvency proceedings to which the Insolvency Rules 1986 apply on and after 3rd April 1989, whether or not those proceedings were commenced before, on or after that date.

The amendments–

(a) are consequential on the coming into force on 3rd April 1989 of section 71 of the Criminal Justice Act 1988 (c. 33); and

(b) provide for an increase in the remuneration payable to shorthand writers appointed in insolvency proceedings.

# THE INSOLVENCY (AMENDMENT) RULES 1991

(SI 1991/495)

*Made on 4 March 1991 by the Lord Chancellor under s. 411 and 412 of the Insolvency Act 1986. Operative from 2 April 1991.*

## CITATION AND COMMENCEMENT

**1** These Rules may be cited as the Insolvency (Amendment) Rules 1991 and shall come into force on 2nd April 1991.

## INTERPRETATION

**2** In these Rules references to **"the principal Rules"** are to the Insolvency Rules 1986 and a Rule or Schedule referred to by number means the Rule or Schedule so numbered in the principal Rules.

## APPLICATION

**3** The principal Rules shall effect subject to the amendments set out in the Schedule to these Rules.

# Schedule

**Note**
Amendments not reproduced here–see the principal Rules.

## EXPLANATORY NOTE

(*This Note is not part of the Rules*)

These Rules further amend the Insolvency Rules 1986, which set out detailed procedures for the conduct of all company and individual insolvency proceedings in England and Wales under the Insolvency Act 1986, with effect from 2nd April 1991. The amendments increase the rates of remuneration for shorthand writers in insolvency proceedings from £56.43 to £66.20 for attendance, from 78.8p per folio of written record plus 4p per folio for all copies to 92.4p and 5p respectively and from £5.93 per hour travelling time to £7.00. They also amend provisions requiring or referring to advertisement in newspapers so that such advertisement can be in any newspaper.

# THE INSOLVENCY (AMENDMENT) RULES 1993

(SI 1993/602)

*Made on 4 March 1991 by the Lord Chancellor under s. 411–413 of the Insolvency Act 1986. Operative from 5 April 1993.*

## CITATION AND COMMENCEMENT

**1** These Rules may be cited as the Insolvency (Amendment) Rules 1991 and shall come into force on 5th April 1991.

INTERPRETATION

**2** In these Rules references to **"the principal Rules"** are to the Insolvency Rules 1986 and a Rule or Schedule referred to by number means the Rule or Schedule so numbered in the principal Rules.

APPLICATION

**3** The principal Rules shall have effect subject to the amendments set out in the Schedule to these Rules.

**Note**
Amendments not reproduced here – see r. 7.17, 12.3 of and Sch. 3 to the principal Rules.

**EXPLANATORY NOTE**

(*This Note is not part of the Rules*)

These Rules further amend the Insolvency Rules 1986, which set out detailed procedures for the conduct of all company and individual insolvency proceedings in England and Wales under the Insolvency Act 1986, with effect from 5th April 1991. The amendments delete the provisions setting out the remuneration of shorthand writers appointed in insolvency proceedings but provide that any question arising as to the rates of remuneration payable under Insolvency Rule 7.17 shall be determined by the court in its discretion. The Rules also amend the definition of obligations arising which are not provable as debts in a bankruptcy, in the light of amendments made to section 281 of the Insolvency Act 1986 by the Children Act 1989 (c. 41), which redefines "family proceedings" and the Child Support Act 1991, which introduces maintenance assessments.

# THE INSOLVENCY (AMENDMENT) RULES 1995

(SI 1995/586)

*Made on 6 March 1995 by the Lord Chancellor under s. 411–413 of the Insolvency Act 1986. Operative from 1 April 1995.*

CITATION AND COMMENCEMENT

**1** These Rules may be cited as the Insolvency (Amendment) Rules 1991 and shall come into force on 1 April 1991.

INTERPRETATION

**2** In these Rules references to **"the principal Rules"** are to the Insolvency Rules 1986 and a Rule referred to by number means the Rule so numbered in the principal Rules.

APPLICATION

**3(1)** Subject to paragraph (2), the principal Rules shall have effect subject to the amendments set out in the Schedule to these Rules.

**3(2)** The amendments to the principal Rules set out in the Schedule to these Rules shall not apply in relation to–

(a) winding-up proceedings commenced before 1 April 1995, or

(b) bankruptcy proceedings where the bankruptcy petition was presented before that day.

## Schedule

**Note**
Amendments not reproduced here–see r. 4.218 and 6.224 of the principal Rules.

## EXPLANATORY NOTE

(*This Note is not part of the Rules*)

These Rules further amend the Insolvency Rules 1986, which set out detailed procedures for the conduct of all company and individual insolvency proceedings in England and Wales under the Insolvency Act 1986, with effect from 1 April 1995. The amendments alter the order of priority in which the expenses of a winding up by the court and a bankruptcy are payable. The fee payable (under any fees order made under sections 414 and 415 respectively of the Insolvency Act) for the performance by the official receiver of his general duties as official receiver, and the repayable deposit lodged as security for that fee, are moved in the order of priority of payment from immediately before to immediately after the payment of the other fees payable under any such fees order and the remuneration of the official receiver under general regulations.

# THE INSOLVENCY (AMENDMENT) RULES 1999

(SI 1999/359)

*Made on 16 February 1999 by the Lord Chancellor under s. 412 and 413 of the Insolvency Act 1986. Operative from 22 March 1999.*

## CITATION AND COMMENCEMENT

**1** These Rules may be cited as the Insolvency (Amendment) Rules 1999 and shall come into force on 22nd March 1999.

## INTERPRETATION

**2** In these Rules references to **"the principal Rules"** are to the Insolvency Rules 1986 and a Rule referred to by number means the Rule so numbered in the principal Rules.

## APPLICATION

**3** The principal Rules shall have effect subject to the amendments set out in the Schedule to these Rules.

# Schedule

Rule 3

**Note**
Amendments not reproduced here – see the principal rules.

## EXPLANATORY NOTE

(*This Note is not part of the Rules*)

These Rules further amend the Insolvency Rules 1986 (SI 1986/1925), which set out detailed procedures for the conduct of all company and individual insolvency proceedings in England and Wales under the Insolvency Act 1986 (c. 45) (**"the Act"**), with effect from 22nd March 1999.

These Rules provide for the maintenance by the Secretary of State of a register of bankruptcy orders which shall be open to public inspection.

These Rules require the official receiver to enter in the register the specified bankruptcy information (as defined in Rule 6.223(B)(5)) received by him relating to any bankruptcy order. Subject to the exceptions provided in Rule 6.223(A)(3)(a)–(c), the Secretary of State is also under an obligation to enter in the register such specified bankruptcy information relating to any bankruptcy order made in the period of five years prior to 22nd March 1999 as is in his possession on that date.



bbcl inru 1986b Mp 3479—98bcl 175

Provision is made for the deletion of information entered in the register in the following circumstances:

(a) upon receipt by the Secretary of State of notice of an annulment order under section 282(1)(a) of the Act or of a copy of an order rescinding a bankruptcy order under section 375 of the Act;

(b) upon the expiry of two years after the date on which a bankrupt is discharged or, where a certificate for the summary administration of the bankrupt's estate is issued under section 275(1) of the Act, upon the expiry of three years after the bankrupt is discharged; and

(c) upon the expiry of two years after the date of an annulment order under section 261(1)(a) or 282(1)(b) of the Act.

These Rules also amend Rule 5.23 to provide for the deletion from the register of individual voluntary arrangements of information entered in it relating to any individual voluntary arrangement in respect of which the Secretary of State has received notice of the making of a revocation order made prior to 22nd March 1999 or of the final completion or termination of an arrangement more than two years prior to 22nd March 1999. Provision is also made for the deletion of information entered in the register relating to any individual voluntary arrangement upon the expiry of two years following the final completion or termination of such arrangement and following receipt by the Secretary of State of notice of the making of a revocation order. Rule 5.29 is amended so as to apply in the event of the completion or termination of an arrangement.

A Regulatory Impact Assessment is available, copies of which have also been placed in the libraries of both Houses of Parliament. Copies are also available from the Insolvency Service of the Department of Trade and Industry, PO Box 203, Room 5.1, 21 Bloomsbury Street, London WC1B 3QW.

# THE INSOLVENCY (AMENDMENT) (No. 2) RULES 1999

(SI 1999/1022)

*Made on 29 March 1999 by the Lord Chancellor under s. 411–413 of the Insolvency Act 1986. Operative from 22 March 1999.*

## CITATION AND COMMENCEMENT

**1** These Rules may be cited as the Insolvency (Amendment) (No. 2) Rules 1999 and shall come into force on 26th April 1999.

## INTERPRETATION

**2** In these Rules references to **"the principal Rules"** are to the Insolvency Rules 1986 and a Rule referred to by number means the Rule so numbered in the principal Rules.

## APPLICATION

**3** The principal Rules shall have effect subject to the amendments set out in the Schedule to these Rules.

# Schedule

Rule 3

**Note**

Amendments not reproduced here – see the principal rules.

## EXPLANATORY NOTE

(*This Note is not part of the Rules*)

These Rules further amend the Insolvency Rules 1986 (**"the Rules"**) which provide detailed procedures for the conduct of all company and individual insolvency proceedings in England and Wales under the Insolvency Act 1986.

The amendments come into force on 26th April 1999 to coincide with the coming into force of the Civil Procedure Rules 1998 (**"the CPR"**) which provide a new code of civil procedure for the civil courts which replaces the Rules of the Supreme Court 1986 and the County Court Rules 1981.

Although, by rule 2.1 of the CPR, the new civil procedure does not apply to insolvency proceedings, the Rules themselves apply all those provisions of the CPR and such practice of the High Court and County Court as is not inconsistent with provisions made by the Rules to such proceedings.

In addition to the application of the CPR and court practice, detailed amendment is made of such of the Rules as use language in relation to insolvency proceedings no longer to be used in civil procedure. Reference to "*ex parte* hearings" and to the "taxation" of costs are, for example, to be read, respectively, respectively, as references to "hearings without notice being given to any other party" and to "detailed assessment".

Consistent with the CPR, the amendments also bring practice in insolvency proceedings into line with the new civil procedure by permitting, for example, the use of witness statements verified by statements of truth in a number of situations where affidavit evidence was, before amendment of the Rules, obligatory.

# RULES AND REGULATIONS

## Table of Contents

**Note:** Statutory instruments which do no more than amend other provisions or provide for the coming into force of other provisions are not reproduced in full text here.



**continued over**

continued over

STATUTORY INSTRUMENT Page



continued over

STATUTORY INSTRUMENT Page



continued over

STATUTORY INSTRUMENT Page



continued over

STATUTORY INSTRUMENT



continued over

STATUTORY INSTRUMENT Page



continued over

STATUTORY INSTRUMENT Page



continued over

# THE STOCK TRANSFER (ADDITION OF FORMS) ORDER 1979

(SI 1979/277)

*Made on 7 March 1979 by the Treasury under s. 3(2) of the Stock Transfer Act 1963.*

**1** This Order may be cited as the Stock Transfer (Addition of Forms) Order 1979 and shall come into operation on 4th April 1979.

**2** Schedule 1 to the Stock Transfer Act 1963 shall be amended by adding thereto:–

(a) the form set out in Schedule 1 to this Order (hereinafter referred to as a sold transfer form), for use where registered securities to which section 1 of that Act applies are transferred to a stock exchange nominee as an alternative to the stock transfer form set out in Schedule 1 to that Act;

(b) the form set out in Schedule 2 to this Order (hereinafter referred to as a bought transfer form), for use where such securities are transferred from a stock exchange nominee as an alternative to the stock transfer form set out in Schedule 1 to that Act.

**3(1)** Section 1 of the Stock Transfer Act 1963 shall have effect subject to the amendment that a sold transfer form, and a stock transfer form used to transfer securities to a stock exchange nominee, need not specify–

(a) particulars of the consideration;

(b) the address of the transferee.

**3(2)** Section 1 of that Act shall have effect subject to the further amendment that a bought transfer form, and a stock transfer form used to transfer securities from a stock exchange nominee, need not, in the case of a transferor which is a body corporate, be executed under hand but shall be sufficiently executed by or on behalf of such transferor if they bear a facsimile of the corporate seal of the transferor, authenticated by the signature (whether actual or facsimile) of a director or the secretary of the transferor.

**4** In this Order **"stock exchange nominee"** has the same meaning as that given to it by section 7(2) of the Stock Exchange (Completion of Bargains) Act 1976.

# Schedule 1

**TALISMAN SOLD TRANSFER**

This transfer is pursuant to a Stock Exchange transaction, and is exempt from Transfer Stamp Duty.

Above this line for Registrar's use only

Bargain Reference No:

Name of Undertaking

Certificate lodged with Registrar

Description of Security

(for completion by the Registrars/Stock Exchange)

Amount of Stock or number of Stock units or shares or other security in words

Figures

In the name(s) of

Account Designation (if any)

Name(s) of registered holder(s) should be given in full; the address should be given where there is only one holder

If the transfer is not made by the registered holder(s) insert also the name(s) and capacity (e.g., Executor(s)) of the person(s) making the transfer.

I/We hereby transfer the above security out of the name(s) aforesaid into the name of and request the necessary entries to be made in the register.

Balance Certificate Required for (amount or number in figures)

*Bodies corporate should affix their common seal and each signatory should state his/her representative capacity (e.g. "Company Secretary" "Director") against his/her signature*

Stamp and Firm Code of Selling Broker

PLEASE SIGN HERE

1 ______

2 ______

3 ______

4 ______

Date

is lodging this transfer at the direction and on behalf of the Member Firm whose stamp appears herein ("the Original Lodging Agent") and does not in any manner or to any extent warrant or represent the validity, genuineness or correctness of the transfer instructions contained herein or the genuineness of the signature(s) of the transferor(s). The Original Lodging Agent by delivering this transfer to authorises to lodge this transfer for registration and agrees to be deemed for all purposes to be the person(s) actually lodging this transfer for registration.

Stock Exchange Operating Account Number (if applicable)

**Note**

For new Talisman Sold Transfer see Stock Transfer Act 1963, Sch. 1 and Stock Transfer (Substitution of Forms) Order 1990 (SI 1990/18).

## Schedule 2

Transfer Number

**TALISMAN BOUGHT TRANSFER**

Above this line for Registrar's use only

Name of Undertaking

| Rate | Description of Security |
|---|---|
| | |

| Stamp Duty | Bargain Date | Settlement | Price | Transfer Consideration | Figures |
|---|---|---|---|---|---|
| | | | | | |

Amount of Stock or Number of Stock Units or Shares or Other Security in Words

| Hundred Millions | Ten Millions | Millions | Hundred Thousands | Ten Thousands | Thousands | Hundreds | Tens | Units |
|---|---|---|---|---|---|---|---|---|
| | | | | | | | | |

Transferee Details

Account Designation

Apportionment Date

| Registrar | Batch | Company | Security | Bargain Reference | Firm | Transfer Number | Quantity |
|---|---|---|---|---|---|---|---|
| | | | | | | | |

hereby transfers the above security to the person(s) named under "Transferee Details" and requests the necessary entries to be made in the register. It confirms that the price and transfer consideration have been derived from information supplied by Member Firms.

is lodging this transfer at the direction and on behalf of the Member Firm whose code number appears herein ('the Original Lodging Agent') and does not in any manner or to any extent warrant or represent the validity or correctness of the transfer instructions contained herein. The Original Lodging Agent by instructing to deliver this transfer for registration agrees to be deemed for all purposes to be the person(s) actually lodging this transfer for registration

It is hereby certified on behalf of The Stock Exchange that the Stamp Duty indicated hereon has been or will be accounted for to the Commissioners of Inland Revenue pursuant to an agreement under Section 33 of the Finance Act 1970 as amended.

Dated

## EXPLANATORY NOTE

*(This Note is not part of the Order)*

This Order amends Schedule 1 to the Stock Transfer Act 1963 by adding forms for use, as alternative to the stock transfer form prescribed therein, where securities are transferred to and from a nominee of The Stock Exchange. The Order also amends section 1 of that Act by providing that neither particulars of the consideration nor the address of the transferee need be inserted in a form used to transfer securities to a stock exchange nominee and by providing that a form used to transfer securities from a stock exchange nominee which is a body corporate need not be executed under hand but shall be sufficiently executed if it bears a facsimile of the corporate seal authenticated by the actual or facsimile signature of a director or the secretary of the transferor. These changes are required in order to facilitate the "Talisman" settlement system for transactions in securities on The Stock Exchange.

# THE COMPANY AND BUSINESS NAMES REGULATIONS 1981

(SI 1981/1685)

*Made on 24 November 1981 by the Secretary of State under s. 31 and 32 of the Companies Act 1981. Operative from 26 February 1982.*

[**Notes:** (1) The current relevant provisions are CA 1985, s. 26, 29 and BNA 1985, s. 2, 3, 6.

(2) Amendments made by the Company and Business Names (Amendment) Regulations 1982 (SI 1982/1653) (operative from 1 January 1983); the Company and Business Names (Amendment) Regulations 1992 (SI 1992/1196) (operative from 5 and 12 June 1992) and the Company and Business Names (Amendment) Regulations 1995 (SI 1995/3022) (operative from 1 January 1996) have been included.]

**1** These Regulations may be cited as the Company and Business Names Regulations 1981 and shall come into operation on 26th February 1982.

**2** In these Regulations, unless the context otherwise requires, **"the Act"** means the Companies Act 1981.

**3** The words and expressions stated in column (1) of the Schedule hereto (together with the plural and possessive forms of those words and expressions) are hereby specified as words and expressions for the registration of which as or as part of a company's corporate name the approval of the Secretary of State is required by section 22(2)(b) of the Act or for the use of which as or as part of a business name his approval is required by section 28(2)(b) of the Act.

**History**

In reg. 3 the words "(together with the plural and possessive forms of those words and expressions)" inserted by the Company and Business Names (Amendment) Regulations 1992 (SI 1992/1196), reg. 1, 2(1), (2) as from 12 June 1992.

**4** Subject to Regulation 5, each Government department or other body stated in column (2) of the Schedule hereto is hereby specified as the relevant body for the purposes of section 31(2) and (3) of the Act in relation to the word or expression (and the plural and possessive forms of that word or expression) opposite to it in column (1).

**History**

In reg. 4 the words "(and the plural and the possessive forms of that word or expression)" inserted by the Company and Business Names (Amendment) Regulations 1992 (SI 1992/1196), reg. 1, 2(1), (3) as from 12 June 1992.

**5** Where two Government departments or other bodies are specified in the alternative in Column (2) of the Schedule hereto the second alternative is to be treated as specified,

(a) in the case of the corporate name of a company,

(i) if the company has not yet been registered and its principal or only place of business in Great Britain is to be Scotland or, if it will have no place of business in Great Britain, its proposed registered office is in Scotland, and

(ii) if the company is already registered and its principal or only place of business in

Great Britain is in Scotland or, if it has no place of business in Great Britain, its registered office is in Scotland, and

(b) in the case of a business name, if the principal or only place of the business carried on or to be carried on in Great Britain is or is to be in Scotland,

and the first alternative is to be treated as specified in any other case.

# Schedule – Specification of Words, Expressions and Relevant Bodies

Regulations 3, 4, and 5

| Column (1) | Column (2) |
|---|---|
| Word or expression | Relevant body |
| Abortion | Department of Health and Social Security |
| Apothecary | Worshipful Society of Apothecaries of London or Pharmaceutical Society of Great Britain |
| Association | |
| Assurance | |
| Assurer | |
| Authority | |
| Benevolent | |
| Board | |
| British | |
| Chamber of Commerce | |
| Chamber of Commerce, Training and Enterprise | |
| Chamber of Industry | |
| Chamber of Trade | |
| Charitable | Charity Commission or the Scottish Ministers |
| Charity | |
| Charter | |
| Chartered | |
| Chemist | |
| Chemistry | |
| Contact Lens | General Optical Council |
| Co-operative | |
| Council | |
| Dental | General Dental Council |
| Dentistry | |
| District Nurse | Panel of Assessors in District Nurse Training |
| Duke | Home Office or the Scottish Ministers |
| England | |
| English | |
| European | |
| Federation | |
| Friendly Society | |
| Foundation | |
| Fund | |
| Giro | |
| Great Britain | |
| Group | |
| Health Centre | Department of Health and Social Security |
| Health Service | |
| Health Visitor | Council for the Education and Training of Health Visitors |

| Column (1) | Column (2) |
|---|---|
| Word or expression | Relevant body |
| Her Majesty | Home Office or the Scottish Ministers |
| His Majesty | |
| Holding | |
| Industrial and Provident Society | |
| Institute | |
| Institution | |
| Insurance | |
| Insurer | |
| International | |
| Ireland | |
| Irish | |
| King | Home Office or the Scottish Ministers |
| Midwife | Central Midwives Board or Central Midwives Board for Scotland |
| Midwifery | |
| National | |
| Nurse | General Nursing Council for England and Wales or General Nursing Council for Scotland |
| Nursing | |
| Patent | |
| Patentee | |
| Police | Home Office or the Scottish Ministers |
| Polytechnic | Department for Education and Employment |
| Post Office | |
| Pregnancy Termination | Department of Health and Social Security |
| Prince | |
| Princess | Home Office or the Scottish Ministers |
| Queen | |
| Reassurance | |
| Reassurer | |
| Register | |
| Registered | |
| Reinsurance | |
| Reinsurer | |
| Royal | |
| Royale | Home Office or the Scottish Ministers |
| Royalty | |
| Scotland | |
| Scottish | |
| Sheffield | |
| Society | |
| Special School | Department for Education and Employment |
| Stock Exchange | |
| Trade Union | |
| Trust | |
| United Kingdom | |
| University | The Privy Council |
| Wales | |
| Welsh | |
| Windsor | Home Office or the Scottish Ministers |

**History**

In Sch. note the following amendments:

- in col. 2, the words "the Scottish Ministers" where they occur replaced the former words "Scottish Home and Health Department" with effect from 1 July 1999 by virtue of the Scotland Act 1998 (Consequential Modifications) (No. 2) Order 1999 (SI 1999/1820), art. 1(2), 4 and Sch. 2, para. 139 and the Scotland Act 1998 (Commencement) Order 1998 (SI 1998/3178), art. 3;
- in col. (2) the words "Worshipful Society of Apothecaries of London" substituted for the former words

"Worshipful Company of Apothecaries" by the Company and Business Names (Amendment) Regulations 1982 (SI 1982/1653), reg. 1, 2(a) as from 1 January 1983;

- in col. (1) the words "Breed", "Breeder" and "Breeding" formerly appearing before the word "British" and the words "Ministry of Agriculture, Fisheries and Food" formerly appearing opposite them in col. (2) deleted by the Company and Business Names (Amendment) Regulations 1995 (SI 1995/3022), reg. 1, 3(b) as from 1 January 1996;
- in col. (1) the words "Building Society" formerly appearing after the word "British" omitted by the Company and Business Names (Amendment) Regulations 1992 (SI 1992/1196), reg. 1, 2(1), (4) as from 12 June 1992;
- in col. (1) the words "Chemist" and "Chemistry" inserted by the Company and Business Names (Amendment) Regulations 1982 (SI 1982/1653), reg. 1, 2(b) as from 1 January 1983;
- in col. (1) the words "Chamber of Commerce, Training and Enterprise" inserted by the Company and Business Names (Amendment) Regulations 1995 (SI 1995/3022), reg. 1, 3(a) as from 1 January 1996;
- in col. (2) the words "Department for Education and Employment" substituted for the former words "Department of Education and Science" by the Company and Business Names (Amendment) Regulations 1995 (SI 1995/3022), reg. 1, 3(c) as from 1 January 1996;
- in col. (1) the words "Nursing Home" formerly appearing before the word "Patent" and the words "Department of Health and Social Security" formerly appearing opposite them in col. (2) deleted by the Company and Business Names (Amendment) Regulations 1995 (SI 1995/3022), reg. 1, 3(b) as from 1 January 1996;
- in col. (1) the word "Polytechnic" and in col. (2) opposite the words "Department of Education and Science" inserted by the Company and Business Names (Amendment) Regulations 1982 (SI 1982/1653), reg. 1, 2(c) as from 1 January 1983;
- in col. (1) the word "University" inserted by the Company and Business Names (Amendment) Regulations 1982 (SI 1982/1653), reg. 1, 2(c) as from 1 January 1983;
- in col. (2) (opposite the word "University" in col. (1)) the words "The Privy Council" substituted for the former words "Department of Education and Science" by the Company and Business Names (Amendment) Regulations 1992 (SI 1992/1196), reg. 1, 2(1), (5) as from 5 June 1992; those later words were themselves previously inserted by the Company and Business Names (Amendment) Regulations 1982 (SI 1982/1653), reg. 1, 2(c) as from 1 January 1983.

## EXPLANATORY NOTE

(*This Note is not part of the Regulations*)

These Regulations specify those words and expressions for the use of which as or as part of a company or business name the approval of the Secretary of State is required pursuant to sections 22(2)(b) or 28(2)(b) of the Companies Act 1981. In the case of certain words or expressions, a Government department or other body is specified as the relevant body which must be requested in writing to indicate whether and if so why it has any objection to the use of a particular word or expression as or as part of a name pursuant to section 31(2) or (3) of the Act (a statement that such a request has been made and a copy of any response is required to be submitted to the Secretary of State by section 31(3) of the Act).

# THE COMPANIES (INSPECTORS' REPORTS) (FEES) REGULATIONS 1981

(SI 1981/1686)

*Made on 24 November 1981 by the Secretary of State under s. 168(2) and 455(1) of the Companies Act 1948. Operative from 22 December 1981.*

[**Note:** For current provisions, see CA 1985, s. 437, 443.]

**1** These Regulations may be cited as the Companies (Inspectors' Reports) (Fees) Regulations 1981 and shall come into operation on 22nd December 1981.

**2** The fee prescribed for the furnishing of a copy of a report under section 168(2) of the Companies Act 1948 or for furnishing a copy of a report or part of a report under that section as it applies for the purposes of section 172 of that Act shall be 10 pence for each page copied.

## EXPLANATORY NOTE

(*This Note is not part of the Regulations*)

The Companies (Inspectors' Reports) (Fees) Regulations 1981 provide that the fee charged by the Secretary of State for furnishing a copy of a report under section 168(2) of the Companies Act 1948 as amended by section 88 of the Companies Act 1981 or under that section as it applies for the purposes of section 172 of the Companies Act 1948 as amended by section 89 of the Companies Act 1981 is to be 10 pence for each page copied.

# THE COMPANIES ACTS (PRE-CONSOLIDATION AMENDMENTS) ORDER 1984

(SI 1984/134)

*Made on 8 February 1984. Operative in accordance with s. 116(2) of the Companies Act 1981.*

*A. Amendments of the Companies Act 1948*

**1** In section 2(4) of the Companies Act 1948, for paragraph (c) there shall be substituted the following paragraph–

"(c) there must be shown in the memorandum against the name of each subscriber the number of shares he takes.".

**2** In section 7 of the Companies Act 1948, for subsection (1) there shall be substituted–

"(1) In the case of an unlimited company having a share capital, the articles must state the amount of share capital with which the company proposes to be registered.";

and subsections (2) and (3) shall be omitted.

**3** In section 51 of the Companies Act 1948, in subsection (6), all the words following "in pursuance of the prospectus" in paragraph (a) shall be omitted; and after that subsection there shall be inserted–

"(7) Where a prospectus offers shares for sale–

(a) subsection (1) of this section applies as if the reference to allotment were a reference to sale;

(b) subsection (2) does not apply, but–

(i) if the permission referred to in subsection (1) has not been applied for as there mentioned, or has been refused as there mentioned, the offeror of the shares shall forthwith repay without interest all money received from applicants in pursuance of the prospectus, and

(ii) if any such money is not repaid within eight days after the offeror becomes liable to repay it, he shall become liable to pay interest on the money due at the rate of 5 per cent per annum from the end of the eighth day;

(c) subsections (3) to (6) apply, but in subsection (3) for the first reference to the company there shall be substituted a reference to the offeror, and for the reference to the company and every officer of the company who is in default there shall be substituted a reference to any person by or through whom the offer is made and who knowingly and wilfully authorises or permits the default.".

**4** In section 52 of the Companies Act 1948, in subsection (1)(a), for the words "names, addresses and descriptions" there shall be substituted the words "names and addresses".

**5** At the end of section 106 of the Companies Act 1948, there shall be added as a subsection (2)–

"(2) In relation to such a company sections 103 and 104 apply with the substitution, for the reference to the company's registered office, of a reference to its principal place of business in England and Wales.".

**6** At the end of section 106K of the Companies Act 1948, there shall be added as a subsection (2)–

"(2) In relation to such a company sections 106H and 106I apply with the substitution, for the reference to the company's registered office, of a reference to its principal place of business in Scotland.".

**7** In section 124(1) of the Companies Act 1948, for the words "the form set out in Part II of the Schedule or as near thereto as circumstances admit" there shall be substituted the words "the prescribed form".

**8** In section 125(2) of the Companies Act 1948, for the words "annexed to" there shall be substituted the words "included in".

**9** In section 125(2) of the Companies Act 1948, the words from "(or, in the case" to "would be required)" shall be omitted.

**10** In section 126(2) of the Companies Act 1948, for the words from the beginning to "default fine" there shall be substituted–

"If a company fails to comply with this section, the company and every officer of the company who is in default shall be liable on summary conviction to a fine not exceeding the statutory maximum or on conviction after continued contravention to a default fine (within the meaning of section 80(2) of the Companies Act 1980) not exceeding one-tenth of the statutory maximum.".

**11** In section 143 of the Companies Act 1948, in paragraph (c) of subsection (4), after the word "resolutions" (where it first appears) there shall be inserted the words "or agreements".

**12** In section 152 of the Companies Act 1948, in subsection (4), for the words from "the end of its financial year" to the end of the subsection there shall be substituted–

"the end of its relevant financial year, that is–

(a) if its financial year ends with that of the holding company, that financial year, and
(b) if not, the subsidiary's financial year ending last before the end of the financial year of the holding company dealt with in the group accounts,

and with the subsidiary's profit or loss for its relevant financial year.".

**13** In section 167(2) of the Companies Act 1948, for the word "business" there shall be substituted the word "affairs".

**14** In section 249 of the Companies Act 1948–

(a) in subsection (4), after the words "has been audited" there shall be inserted the words "(or, as the case may be, forthwith if the Secretary of State decides not to have an audit)", and
(b) in subsection (5), for the words "shall cause the account when audited or a summary thereof" there shall be substituted the words "shall, when the account has been audited (alternatively, when he has been notified of the Secretary of State's decision not to have an audit) cause the account or a summary of it".

**15** In section 320 of the Companies Act 1948, in subsection (3), the words from "the expression" to "notour bankruptcy" shall be omitted.

**16** In section 322 of the Companies Act 1948, in subsection (3), for the word "Act" there shall be substituted the word "section".

**17** In the Companies Act 1948, the following shall be substituted for section 348–

"*Commission for receiving evidence*

**348(1)** When a company is wound up in England and Wales or in Scotland, the court may refer the whole or any part of the examination of witnesses –

(a) to a specified county court in England and Wales, or
(b) to the sheriff principal for a specified sheriffdom in Scotland, or
(c) to the High Court in Northern Ireland or a specified Northern Ireland county court,

("specified" meaning specified in the order of the winding-up court).

**348(2)** Any person exercising jurisdiction as a judge of the court to which the reference is made (or, in Scotland, the sheriff principal to whom it is made) shall then, by virtue of this section, be a commissioner for the purpose of taking the evidence of those witnesses.

**348(3)** The judge or sheriff principal shall have in the matter referred the same power of summoning and examining witnesses, of requiring the production and delivery of documents, of punishing defaults by witnesses, and of allowing costs and expenses to witnesses, as the court which made the winding-up order.

These powers are in addition to any which the judge or sheriff principal might lawfully exercise apart from this section.

**348(4)** The examination so taken shall be returned or reported to the court which made the order in such manner as that court requests.

**348(5)** This section extends to Northern Ireland.".

**18** In section 372 of the Companies Act 1948, in subsection (2), after the words "the last preceding abstract related" there shall be inserted the words "(or, if no preceding abstract has been sent under this section, from the date of his appointment)".

**19** In section 374 of the Companies Act 1948, in subsection (1), after the words "the last preceding abstract related" there shall be inserted the words "(or, if no preceding abstract has been delivered under this section, from the date of his appointment)".

**20** In section 384 of the Companies Act 1948, before paragraph (a) there shall be inserted the following paragraph–

"(aa) a statement in the prescribed form specifying the name with which the company is proposed to be registered;".

**21** In section 384 of the Companies Act 1948, in paragraph (c), sub-paragraphs (iii), (iiia) and (iv) shall be omitted.

**22** In section 385 of the Companies Act 1948, before paragraph (a) there shall be inserted the following paragraph–

"(aa) a statement in the prescribed form specifying the name with which the company is proposed to be registered; and"

**23** In Part VIII of the Companies Act 1948, after section 387 the following section shall be inserted–

"*Requirements as to name of company registering*

**387A(1)** The following applies with respect to the name of a company registering under this Part (whether a joint stock company or not).

**387A(2)** If the company is to be registered as a public company, its name must end with the words "public limited company" or, if it is stated that the company's registered office is to be situated in Wales, with those words or their equivalent in Welsh ("cwmni cyfyngedig cyhoeddus"); and those words or that equivalent may not be preceded by the word "limited" or its equivalent in Welsh ("cyfyngedig").

**387A(3)** In the case of a company limited by shares or by guarantee (not being a public company), the name must have "limited" as its last word (or, if the company's registered office is to be situated in Wales, "cyfyngedig"); but this is subject to section 25 of the Companies Act 1981 (exempting, in certain circumstances, a company from the requirement to have "limited" as part of the name).".

**24** In section 384(a) of the Companies Act 1948, for the words "names, addresses and occupations" there shall be substituted the words "names and addresses".

**25** In section 407 of the Companies Act 1948, the following amendments shall be made–

(a) for subsection (1) there shall be substituted –

"(1) An oversea company which establishes a place of business in Great Britain shall, within one month of doing so, deliver to the registrar of companies for registration–

(a) a certified copy of the charter, statutes or memorandum and articles of the company, or other instrument constituting or defining the company's constitution and, if the instrument is not written in English, a certified translation of it; and

(b) a return in the prescribed form containing–

(i) a list of the directors and secretary of the company containing the particulars mentioned in subsection (2) below,

(ii) a list of the names and addresses of some one or more persons resident in Great Britain authorised to accept on behalf of the company service of process and any notices required to be served on the company,

(iii) a list of the documents delivered in compliance with paragraph (a) of this subsection, and

(iv) a statutory declaration (made by a director or secretary of the company or by any person whose name and address are given in the list required by sub-paragraph (ii)) stating the date on which the company's place of business in Great Britain was established.",

(b) in subsection (2), for the words "paragraph (b)" there shall be substituted the words "paragraph (b)(i)", and

(c) subsection (2A) shall cease to have effect.

**26** In section 409 of the Companies Act 1948, for the words "the prescribed time" (where they occur in each of subsections (1) and (2)) there shall be substituted the words "the time specified below"; and after subsection (2) there shall be inserted–

"(3) The time for delivery to the registrar of the return required by subsection (1) or (2) is –

(a) in the case of an alteration to which subsection (1)(c) applies, 21 days after the making of the alteration, and

(b) in any other case, 21 days after the date on which notice of the alteration or change in question could have been received in Great Britain in due course of post (if despatched with due diligence)."

**27** In section 455(1) of the Companies Act 1948, after the definition of "officer" there shall be inserted–

""place of business" includes a share transfer or share registration office",

and accordingly the definition of "place of business" shall be omitted from section 415 in part X of that Act.

**28** In Schedule 6 to the Companies Act 1948, in paragraph 4, the words from "(or, in the case" to "would be required)" shall be omitted.

**29** In Schedule 8 to the Companies Act 1948, in paragraph 38(2)(b), after the words "of the company" there shall be inserted the words "or of the shareholder".

**30** In Schedule 8A to the Companies Act 1948, in paragraph 2(a), after the words "at the option of the company" there shall be inserted the words "or of the shareholder".

*B. Amendments of the Companies Act 1967*

**31** In section 43 of the Companies Act 1967, the following shall be inserted after subsection (1)–

"(1A) A company cannot be re-registered under this section if it has previously been re-registered as unlimited.".

**32** In section 44 of the Companies Act 1967, the following shall be inserted after subsection (1)–

"(1A) A company cannot under this section be re-registered as a public company.".

**33** In section 46 of the Companies Act 1967, after subsection (3) there shall be inserted–

"(3A) Where a company changes its name under this section, the change has effect from the date on which the altered certificate of incorporation is issued by the registrar of companies.".

**34** In section 111(1) of the Companies Act 1967, in paragraph (d), for the reference to the Insurance Companies Act 1974 there shall be substituted a reference to the Insurance Companies Act 1982.

*C. Amendment of the Companies (Floating Charges and Receivers) (Scotland) Act 1972*

**35** In section 25 of the Companies (Floating Charges and Receivers) (Scotland) Act 1972, in subsection (2), after the words, "the last preceding abstract related" there shall be inserted the words "(or, if no preceding abstract has been sent under this section, from the date of his appointment)".

*D. Amendment of the European Communities Act 1972*

**36** In section 9(8) of the European Communities Act 1972, for the reference to section 107 of the Companies Act 1948 there shall be substituted a reference to section 23 of the Companies Act 1976.

*E. Amendments of the Companies Act 1976*

**37** In section 9 of the Companies Act 1976, the following shall be substituted for subsection (2)–

"(2) In respect of each accounting reference period of the company, an oversea company shall deliver to the registrar of companies copies of the accounts and other documents required by subsection (1); and, if any such account or document is in a language other than English, there shall be annexed to the copy so delivered a certified translation of it into English.";

and in subsection (3) for the words "any accounts" there shall be substituted the words "any accounts or other documents".

**38** In the Companies Act 1976, the following shall be substituted for section 29–

"*Register of disqualification orders*

**29(1)** The Secretary of State may make regulations requiring officers of courts to furnish him with such particulars as the regulations may specify of cases in which–

(a) a disqualification order is made under section 188 of the Act 1948 or section 9 of the Insolvency Act 1976, or

(b) any action is taken by a court in consequence of which such an order is varied or ceases to be in force, or

(c) leave is granted by a court for a person subject to such an order to do any thing which otherwise the order prohibits him from doing;

and the regulations may specify the time within which, and the form and manner in which, such particulars are to be furnished.

**29(2)** The Secretary of State shall, from the particulars so furnished, maintain a register of such orders and of cases in which leave has been granted as mentioned in subsection (1)(c).

**29(3)** When an order of which entry is made in the register ceases to be in force, the Secretary of State shall delete the entry from the register and all particulars relating to it which have been furnished to him under this section.

**29(4)** The register shall be open to inspection on payment of such fee as may be specified by the Secretary of State in regulations made by him.

**29(5)** Regulations under this section shall be made by statutory instrument subject to annulment in pursuance of a resolution of either House of Parliament.".

*F. Amendments of the Companies Act 1980*

**39** In section 5 of the Companies Act 1980, the following shall be inserted after subsection (1)–

"(1A) A company cannot be re-registered under this section if it has previously been re-registered as unlimited.".

**40** In section 5 of the Companies Act 1980, in subsection (5), for the words "subsections (2) to (7) and (11) and (12)" there shall be substituted the words "subsections (2) to (7), (11), (11A) and (12) (except paragraph (a))"; and at the end of the subsection there shall be added–

"In subsections (2) and (2A) of section 24, as applied by this subsection, "another company" includes any body corporate and any body to which letters patent have been issued under the Chartered Companies Act 1837.".

**41** In section 10 of the Companies Act 1980, after subsection (2) there shall be inserted–

"(2A) A company cannot under this section be re-registered otherwise than as a company limited by shares or by guarantee.".

**42** In section 14 of the Companies Act 1980, in subsection (10) after the words "such a right but" there shall be inserted the words "(subject to the following subsection)"; and after that subsection there shall be inserted–

"(11) In relation to authority under this section for the grant of such rights as are mentioned in subsection (10)(b), the reference in subsection (3) to the maximum amount of relevant securities that may be allotted under the authority (as also the corresponding reference in subsection (4)) is to the maximum amount of shares which may be allotted pursuant to the rights.".

**43** In section 17(13) of the Companies Act 1980, for the words from "as including" to the end of the subsection there shall be substituted–

"as references to whoever was at the close of business on a date, to be specified in the offer and to fall in the period of 28 days immediately before the date of the offer, the holder of shares of that description".

**44** In section 24(2A) of the Companies Act 1980, for the words "by a nominee" (where those words occur for the second time) there shall be substituted the words "by or by a nominee".

**45** In section 37 of the Companies Act 1980, in subsection (9), the words "are otherwise acquired by the company" shall be omitted from paragraph (a), and after that paragraph there shall be inserted–

"(aa) are acquired by the company (otherwise than by such surrender or forfeiture, and otherwise than by any of the methods mentioned in section 35(4) above), the company having a beneficial interest in the shares, or".

**46** In section 48(1) of the Companies Act 1980, in paragraph (a), after the words "with such a director" there shall be inserted the words "acquires or"; and in paragraph (b), after the words "the company acquires" there shall be inserted the words "or is to acquire".

**47** In section 48(3) of the Companies Act 1980, in paragraph (a), the words "or the person nominated by it" shall be omitted.

**48** In section 55 of the Companies Act 1980, in paragraph (f), for the words "any other transaction, arrangement or agreement" there shall be substituted the words "any transaction, arrangement or agreement other than those mentioned in paragraphs (d) and (e) above".

**49** In section 57 of the Companies Act 1980, in subsection (1), for the words "if such a transaction or arrangement" there shall be substituted the words "if such a transaction, arrangement or agreement".

**50** In section 63 of the Companies Act 1980, in subsection (3), for the words from "and section 145" to the end of the subsection there shall be substituted–

"and where a shadow director by means of such a notice declares an interest in a contract or proposed contract, section 145 of the 1948 Act shall apply, if it is a specific notice under paragraph (a) above, as if the declaration had been made at the meeting there referred to and otherwise as if it had been made at the meeting of the directors next following the giving of the notice, and the making of the declaration shall in either case be deemed to form part of the proceedings at the meeting.".

**51** In Schedule 2 to the Companies Act 1980, there shall be inserted after the references to the Companies Act 1967 the following:–

"COMPANIES (FLOATING CHARGES AND RECEIVERS) (SCOTLAND) ACT 1972 (c. 67)

| | | | |
|---|---|---|---|
| 11(4) | Body corporate or Scottish firm acting as receiver | On summary conviction a fine not exceeding level 3 on the standard scale as defined in section 289G of the Criminal Procedure (Scotland) Act 1975. | (a) On conviction on indictment a fine.<br>(b) On summary conviction a fine not exceeding the statutory maximum. |
| 13(2) | Failing to deliver to the registrar a copy instrument of appointment of a receiver. | On summary conviction a fine not exceeding £5 for every day during which the default continues. | On summary conviction a fine not exceeding one-fifth of the statutory maximum or, on conviction after continued contravention, a default fine not exceeding one-fiftieth of the statutory maximum. |
| 14(4) | Failing to deliver to the registrar the court's interlocutor making the appointment of a receiver. | On summary conviction a fine not exceeding £5 for every day during which the default continues. | On summary conviction a fine not exceeding one-fifth of the statutory maximum or, on conviction after continued contravention, a default fine not exceeding one-fiftieth of the statutory maximum. |
| 22(5) | Failing to give notice to the registrar of cessation or removal of receiver. | On summary conviction a fine not exceeding £5 for every day during which the default continues. | On summary conviction a fine not exceeding one-fifth of the statutory maximum or, on conviction after continued contravention, a default fine not exceeding one-fiftieth of the statutory maximum. |
| 24(2) | Not stating on company documents that a receiver has been appointed. | On summary conviction a fine not exceeding level 1 on the standard scale as defined in section 289G of the Criminal Procedure (Scotland) Act 1975. | On summary conviction a fine not exceeding one-fifth of the statutory maximum. |
| 25(7) | Receiver making default in complying with provisions as to information where receiver appointed. | On summary conviction a fine not exceeding £5 for every day during which the default continues. | On summary conviction a fine not exceeding one-fifth of the statutory maximum or, on conviction after continued contravention, a default fine not exceeding one-fiftieth of the statutory maximum. |
| 26(5) | Default in relation to provisions as to statement to be submitted to receiver. | On summary conviction a fine not exceeding £10 for every day during which the default continues. | On summary conviction a fine not exceeding one-fifth of the statutory maximum or, on conviction after continued contravention, a default fine not exceeding one-fiftieth of the statutory maximum." |



CCH.New Law
bbclrandr1 Mp 3724—bcl98 205a

*G. Amendments of the Companies Act 1981*

**52** In section 12 of the Companies Act 1981, the following shall be inserted at the end of subsection (5)–

"This subsection does not apply to a public company, or to a banking, insurance or shipping company (the definitions in paragraph 8 of Schedule 2 to this Act to apply).".

**53** In section 24 of the Companies Act 1981, for subsection (3) there shall be substituted–

"**(3)** If it appears to the Secretary of State that misleading information has been given for the purposes of a company's registration with a particular name, or that undertakings or assurances have been given for that purpose and have not been fulfilled, he may within 5 years of the date of its registration with that name in writing direct the company to change its name within such period as he may specify.".

**54** In section 26 of the Companies Act 1981, in subsection (3), for the words "section 384(c)" there shall be substituted the words "section 384(aa) or 385(aa)".

**55** In section 31(2) of the Companies Act 1981, after the words "any such word or expression" there shall be inserted the words "and a government department or other body is specified under subsection (1)(b) in relation to that word or expression".

**56** In section 31(3) of the Companies Act 1981, after the words "any such word or expression" there shall be inserted the words "and a Government department or other body is specified under subsection (1)(b) in relation to that word or expression".

**57** In section 43(6) of the Companies Act 1981, after the words "where the shares" there shall be inserted the words "acquired or".

**58** In section 77(7) of the Companies Act 1981, for the words "the shares held or to be held by him" there shall be substituted the words "any interest held or to be held by him in any shares".

*H. Amendment of the Companies (Beneficial Interests) Act 1983*

**59** In section 1 of the Companies (Beneficial Interests) Act 1983, after paragraph (d) there shall be inserted–

"and

(e) section 37(9)(aa) of that Act.".

*I. Citation and Commencement*

**60** This Order may be cited as the Companies Act, (Pre-Consolidation Amendments) Order 1984 and shall come into operation under and in accordance with section 116(2) of the Companies Act 1981.

## EXPLANATORY NOTE

(*This Note does not form part of the Order*)

This Order makes certain amendments of the Companies Acts 1948 to 1983, in connection with the consolidation of those Acts. The power to make these amendments derives from section 116 of the Companies Act 1981, and is exercisable on the basis of recommendations made by the Law Commission and the Scottish Law Commission acting jointly. The amendments will come into force simultaneously with the coming into force of the Consolidation Acts. Each of the amendments made by the Order is the subject of a recommendation by the two Commissions as published in their report (Cmnd 9114). For an explanation of any amendment reference may be had to the corresponding recommendation in that report.

# THE COMPANIES ACTS (PRE-CONSOLIDATION AMENDMENTS) (NO. 2) ORDER 1984

(SI 1984/1169)

*Made on 31 July 1984. Operative in accordance with s. 116(2) of the Companies Act 1981.*

*A. Amendments of the Companies Act 1948*

**1** In section 152A of the Companies Act 1948, in subsection (2), for the words from "the end of its financial year" to the end of the subsection there shall be substituted–

"the end of its relevant financial year, that is–

(a) if its financial year ends with that of the holding company, that financial year, and
(b) if not, the subsidiary's financial year ending last before the end of the financial year of the holding company dealt with in the group accounts,

and with the subsidiary's profit or loss for its relevant financial year."

2 At the end of section 187 of the Companies Act 1948, the following subsection shall be added–

"(5) The power under section 193(2) of the Criminal Procedure (Scotland) Act 1975 to substitute a fine for a period of imprisonment shall, in relation to a conviction on indictment under subsection (1) of this section, be construed as including a power to impose such fine in addition to that period of imprisonment.".

3 At the end of section 328 of the Companies Act 1948, the following subsection shall be added–

"(4) The power under section 193(2) of the Criminal Procedure (Scotland) Act 1975 to substitute a fine for a period of imprisonment shall, in relation to a conviction on indictment under subsection (2) of this section, be construed as including a power to impose such fine in addition to that period of imprisonment.".

*B. Amendments of the Companies (Floating Charges and Receivers) (Scotland) Act 1972*

4 At the end of section 11 of the Companies (Floating Charges and Receivers) (Scotland) Act 1972, the following subsection shall be added–

"(7) The power under section 193(2) of the Criminal Procedure (Scotland) Act 1975 to substitute a fine for a period of imprisonment shall, in relation to a conviction on indictment under subsection (4) of this section, be construed as including a power to impose such fine in addition to that period of imprisonment.".

5 In section 32 of the Companies (Floating Charges and Receivers) (Scotland) Act 1972, in subsection (2), after the word "Act" there shall be inserted the words "except section 6 and the Schedule".

*C. Amendments of the Companies Act 1980*

6 In section 53 of the Companies Act 1980, in subsection (4), after the word "transaction" there shall be inserted the words "or arrangement".

7 In section 64 of the Companies Act 1980, in subsection (1), at the end of paragraph (d) there shall be inserted–

"or

(e) a Scottish firm in which–
(i) that director is a partner,
(ii) a partner is a person who, by virtue of paragraph (a), (b) or (c) above, is connected with that director, or
(iii) a partner is a Scottish firm in which that director is a partner or in which there is a partner who, by virtue of paragraph (a), (b) or (c) above, is connected with that director,".

*D. Amendments of the Companies Act 1981*

8 In section 4 of the Companies Act 1981, in subsection (3), for the words from "(a) the aggregate amount" to the end of the subsection there shall be substituted–

"the aggregate amount of the capital and reserves of that body corporate as at the end of its relevant financial year, and its profit or loss for the financial year; and for this purpose the relevant financial year is–

(a) if the financial year of the body corporate ends with that of the company giving the information in a note to its accounts, that financial year, and
(b) if not, the body corporate's financial year ending last before the end of the financial year of the company giving that information.".

**9** In section 4 of the Companies Act 1981, in subsection (6)(a), for the words "the financial year mentioned in subsection (3)(a)" there shall be substituted the words "its relevant financial year mentioned in subsection (3)".

**10** In section 9 of the Companies Act 1981, in subsection (6), for the words "the financial year of the subsidiary ending with or last before that of the holding company to which the group accounts relate" there shall be substituted the words "its relevant financial year"; and after that subsection there shall be added–

"(7) For the purposes of subsection (6), the relevant financial year of the subsidiary is–

(a) if its financial year ends with that of the holding company to which the group accounts relate, that financial year, and

(b) if not, the subsidiary's financial year ending last before the end of the financial year of the holding company.".

*E. Citation and commencement*

**11** This Order may be cited as the Companies Acts (Pre-Consolidation Amendments) (No. 2) Order 1984 and shall come into operation under and in accordance with section 116(2) of the Companies Act 1981.

## EXPLANATORY NOTE

(*This Note does not form part of the Order*)

This Order makes certain further amendments of the Companies Acts 1948 to 1983, in connection with the consolidation of those Acts. The power to make such amendments (which has already been once exercised, in the Companies Acts (Pre-Consolidation Amendments) Order 1984 (S.I. 1984/ No. 134)) derives from section 116 of the Companies Act 1981, and is exercisable on the basis of recommendations made by the Law Commission and the Scottish Law Commission acting jointly. The amendments will come into force simultaneously with the coming into force of the Consolidation Acts. Each of the amendments made by the Order is the subject of a recommendation by the two Commissions as published in their report (Cmnd. 9272). For an explanation of any amendment reference may be had to the corresponding recommendation in that report.

# THE COMPANIES (UNREGISTERED COMPANIES) REGULATIONS 1985

(SI 1985/680)

*Made on 29 April 1985 by the Secretary of State for Trade and Industry under s. 718 of and Sch. 22 to the Companies Act 1985. Operative from 1 July 1985.*

[**Note:** Amendments by the Companies (Unregistered Companies) (Amendment) Regulations 1990 (SI 1990/438) (operative from 1 April 1990), the Companies (Unregistered Companies) (Amendment No. 2) Regulations 1990 (SI 1990/1394) (operative from 31 July 1990) and the Companies (Unregistered Companies) (Amendment No. 3) Regulations 1990 (SI 1990/2571) (operative from 4 February 1991) have been included.]

**1** These Regulations may be cited as the Companies (Unregistered Companies) Regulations 1985 and shall come into operation on 1st July 1985.

**2** In these Regulations–

**"the Act"** means the Companies Act 1985;

**"instrument constituting or regulating the company"** means any Act of Parliament, royal charter, letters patent, deed of settlement, contract of copartnery, or other instrument constituting or regulating the company; and

**"unregistered company"** means any body corporate, incorporated in and having a principle place of business in Great Britain, other than a body corporate mentioned in section 718(2) of the Act.

**3** The Companies (Unregistered Companies) (Completion of Stock Exchange Bargains) Regulations 1980 and the Companies (Unregistered Companies) Regulations 1984 are hereby revoked.

**4** Subject to Regulation 5 below, the provisions of the Act specified in the Schedule to these Regulations shall apply to any unregistered company.

**5** For the purposes of the application to any unregistered company of the provisions which apply to it by virtue of Regulation 4 above–

(a) that the company shall be deemed to be–

(i) a company registered in England and Wales if its principal office on 5th January 1976 or, in the case of a company incorporated after that date, immediately after its incorporation was situated in England or Wales; or

(ii) a company registered in Scotland if its principle office on 5th January 1976 or, in the case of a company incorporated after that date, immediately after its incorporation was situated in Scotland;

and **"registrar of companies"** shall be construed accordingly;

(b) references to the registered office of a company shall be construed as references to the principal office of the company in England, Wales or Scotland, as the case may be;

(c) references to a public company shall be construed as references to an unregistered company which has power under the instrument constituting or regulating it to offer its shares or debentures to the public, and references to a private company shall be construed as references to an unregistered company which does not have power so to offer its shares or debentures;

(d) in relation to expenses and commissions incurred before 1st January 1985, Schedule 4 to the Act shall have effect, for the purposes of accounts of the company for any financial year beginning before 1st January 1990, as though paragraphs 3(2)(a) and (b) were omitted; and

(e) the said provisions shall be subject to the modifications and extensions set out in Regulation 6 below.

**6** The modifications and extensions referred to in Regulation 5(e) above are the following–

(a) for references to the memorandum or articles of association of a company there shall be substituted references to any instrument constituting or regulating the company;

(b) section 18 of the Act shall have effect as if:

(i) for the words "by any statutory provision, whether contained in an Act of Parliament or in an instrument made under an Act, a printed copy of the Act or instrument" there were substituted the words "a printed copy of the instrument effecting the alteration" and for the words "that provision comes into force" there were substituted the words "that instrument comes into effect"; and

(ii) in the case of a company incorporated on or after 5th January 1976, it required a printed copy of any instrument constituting or regulating the company to be forwarded to the registrar of companies not later than fifteen days after the date of the incorporation of the company and recorded by him, notwithstanding that such instrument has not been the subject of any alteration;

(c) sections 35 and 35B of the Act shall have effect as though they were expressed to be without prejudice to any rule of law which gives to a person dealing with a company incorporated by letters patent or by royal charter any greater protection in relation to the capacity of such a company than that afforded by those sections;

(d) in sections 36 to 36B, 40 and 186, for the references to the common seal of the company there shall be substituted references to the common or other authorised seal of the company;

(e) section 185(4) shall have effect as if for the words "subsection (1)" there were substituted "any provision of any instrument constituting or regulating the company";

(f) in section 351(1) of the Act for paragraphs (a) to (d) there shall be substituted the following:–

"(a) whether the company has its municipal office in England, Wales or Scotland, as the case may be, and the number which has been allocated to the company by the registrar of companies;
(b) the address of its principal office; and
(c) the manner in which it was incorporated and, if it is a limited company, that fact";

(g) notice of the receipt by the registrar of companies of
(i) any instrument constituting or regulating the company; and
(ii) any notice of the situation of the company's principal office shall be included in the matters which the registrar is required to cause to be published in the Gazette by virtue of section 711 of the Act;

(h) Schedule 4 to the Act shall have effect as if:–
(i) item K, II in balance sheet format 1 and liability item A, II in balance sheet format 2;
(ii) paragraph 51(2);
(iii) Part V;
were omitted;

(hh) Schedule 5 to the Act shall have effect as if paragraphs 10 and 29 were omitted;

(i) Schedule 9 to the Act shall have effect as if paragraph 13(4) was omitted.

**History**
In reg. 6(c) the words "sections 35 and 35B", "they" and "those sections" substituted for the former words "section 35", "it" and "that section" respectively by the Companies (Unregistered Companies) (Amendment No. 3) Regulations 1990 (SI 1990/2571), reg. 2(a) as from 4 February 1991.
In reg. 6(d) the words "36 to 36B" inserted by the Companies (Unregistered Companies) (Amendment No. 2) Regulations 1990 (SI 1990/1394), reg. 2(a) as from 31 July 1990.
In reg. 6(h) the words "(iv) Part VI" omitted, reg. 6(hh) inserted and in para. 6(i) the words "paragraph 13(4) was" substituted for the former words "paragraph 13(3) and (4) and paragraph 31 were" by the Companies (Unregistered Companies) (Amendment) Regulations 1990 (SI 1990/438), reg. 2(a), (b) as from 1 April 1990.

# Schedule – Provisions of the Act applied to Unregistered Companies by Regulation 4

Regulation 4

| Provisions of the Act applied | Subject matter |
|---|---|
| In Part I— | |
| section 18 ........................................ | Statutory and other amendments of memorandum and articles to be registered. |
| section 35 to 35B ................................ | Company's capacity; power of directors to bind it. |
| sections 36 to 36C ............................. | Company contracts and execution of documents by companies. |
| section 40 ........................................ | Official seal for share certificates etc. |
| section 42 ........................................ | Events affecting a company's status to be officially notified. |
| In Part III, Chapter I (with Schedule 3) | Prospectus and requirements in connection with it. |
| In Part IV, sections 82, 86 and 87................. | Allotments |
| In Part V— | |

| Provisions of the Act applied | Subject matter |
|---|---|
| section 185(4) ........................................ | Exemption from duty to prepare certificates where shares etc., issued to stock exchange nominee. |
| section 186 ............................................ | Certificate as evidence of title. |
| Part VII (except sections 252 and 253), with—<br>Schedules 4 to 6 ...................................<br>Schedule 7 (except paragraphs 2 to 2B, 7 and 8) ......................................................<br>Schedule 8 ............................................<br>Schedule 9 (except sub-paragraphs (a) to (d) of paragraph 2, sub-paragraphs (c), (d) and (e) of paragraph 3 and sub-paragraph (1)(c) of paragraph 10), and<br>Schedules 10 and 10A ........................... | Accounts and Audit |
| In Part IX—<br>section 287 ........................................... | Registered office |
| In Part X—<br>section 322A ........................................ | Invalidity of certain transactions involving directors, etc. |
| sections 343 to 347 ................................ | Register to be kept of certain transactions not disclosed in accounts; other related matters. |
| In Part XI—<br>sections 35(1), (2) and (5)(a) .................... | Particulars of company to be given in correspondence. |
| sections 363 (with Schedule 15) to 365 | Annual return. |
| sections 384 to 394A (except sections 385A, 386 and 393) ........................................ | Appointment, etc., of auditors. |
| In Part XXIV—<br>section 711 ........................................... | Public notice by registrar of companies with respect to certain documents. |
| In Part XXV—<br>section 720 ........................................... | Companies to publish periodical statement. |

**History**
In Sch.:

- in the entries relating to Pt. I, the entry relating to s. 35 to 35B substituted for the former entry relating to s. 35 by the Companies (Unregistered Companies) (Amendment No. 3) Regulations 1990 (SI 1990/2571), reg. 2(b) as from 4 February 1991; the former entry read as follows:

| Provisions of the Act applied | Subject matter |
|---|---|
| "section 35 .............................................. | Company's capacity; power of directors to bind it." |

- the entry relating to s. 36–36C substituted by the Companies (Unregistered Companies) (Amendment No. 2) Regulations 1990 (SI 1990/1394), reg. 2(b) as from 31 July 1990; the former entry read as follows:

| Provisions of the Act applied | Subject matter |
|---|---|
| "section 36(4) .......................................... | Binding effect of contract made for company before its formation." |

- in the entry relating to Pt. VII the words "(except sections 252 and 253)," inserted and in column 1 the words "paragraphs 2 to 2B, 7 and 8" substituted for the former words "paragraphs 2, 7 and 8" and the words "Schedules 10 and 10A" substituted for the former words "Schedule 10" by the Companies (Unregistered Companies) (Amendment) Regulations 1990 (SI 1990/438), reg. 2(c) as from 1 April 1990.
- in the entries relating to Pt. X, the entry relating to s. 322A inserted by the Companies (Unregistered Companies) (Amendment No. 3) Regulations 1990 (SI 1990/2571), reg. 2(c) as from 4 February 1991.
- in the entry relating to Pt. XI in column 1 the words "sections 384 to 394A (except sections 385A, 386 and 393)" substituted for the former words "sections 384 to 393" and in column 2 the word "qualifications" formerly appearing after the word "Appointment," omitted by the Companies (Unregistered Companies) (Amendment) Regulations 1990 (SI 1990/438), reg. 2(d) as from 1 April 1990.

## EXPLANATORY NOTE

*(This Note is not part of the Regulations)*

These Regulations replace the Companies (Unregistered Companies) Regulations 1984. They provide, consequent upon consolidation of the Companies Acts 1948 to 1983, for the application to unregistered companies of certain provisions of the Companies Act 1985.

They also incorporate provisions formerly in the Companies (Unregistered Companies) (Completion of Stock Exchange Bargains) Regulations 1980, and adapt section 186 dealing with the use of company seals.

# THE COMPANIES (REGISTERS AND OTHER RECORDS) REGULATIONS 1985

(SI 1985/724)

*Made on 8 May 1985 by the Secretary of State for Trade and Industry under s. 723(4) of the Companies Act 1985. Operative from 1 July 1985.*

## CITATION, COMMENCEMENT, REVOCATION AND INTERPRETATION

**1(1)** These Regulations may be cited as the Companies (Registers and other Records) Regulations 1985 and shall come into operation on 1st July 1985.

**1(2)** In these Regulations, unless the context otherwise requires–

**"the Act"** means the Companies Act 1985;

**"the place for inspection"** means, in relation to a register, or a register of holders of debentures of a company, which is kept by recording the matters in question otherwise than in a legible form, the place where the duty to allow inspection of the register is for the time being performed in accordance with these Regulations;

**"register"** means a register or other record as is mentioned in section 722(1) of the Act;

**"the register of directors' interests"** means the register required to be kept under section 325(1) of the Act.

**1(3)** Any reference in these Regulations to the duty to allow inspection of a register, or of the register of holders of debentures, is a reference to the duty provided for in section 723(3) of the Act to allow inspection of, or to furnish, a reproduction of the recording of the register, or of the relevant part of the recording in a legible form.

**1(4)** Any reference in these Regulations to the register of interests in voting shares shall be construed as including a reference to the separate part of that register referred to in section 213(1) of the Act.

**1(5)** The Companies (Registers and other Records) Regulations 1979 are hereby revoked.

## REQUIREMENTS WITH RESPECT TO REGISTERS KEPT OTHERWISE THAN IN A LEGIBLE FORM

**2(1)** This Regulation applies with respect to any register specified in Schedule 1 to these Regulations which is kept by a company by recording the matters in question otherwise than in a legible form.

**2(2)** The company shall perform the duty to allow inspection of any register to which this Regulation applies at a place specified in the said Schedule 1 in relation to that register.

**2(3)** In the case of any register to which this Regulation applies, the company shall not be required–

(a) to keep the register in any place where it is required to be kept under the Act,

(b) to give any notice to the registrar of companies required to be given under the Act of the place where the register is kept, or of any change in that place, or

(c) to include in its annual return any statement required to be given under the Act of the address of the place where the register is kept.

**2(4)** Where provision is made in the Act with respect to default in complying with any requirement of that Act regarding the place where a register specified in Schedule 1 to these Regulations is to be kept, that provision shall have effect in relation to any such register to which this Regulation applies as if there were substituted for the reference therein to such default, a reference to default in complying with the requirements of paragraph (2) above.

## NOTIFICATION OF PLACE FOR INSPECTION OF REGISTERS

**3(1)** Subject to the provisions of paragraph (3) below, where a company keeps any register specified in paragraph (2) below by recording the matters in question otherwise than in a legible form, the company shall send to the registrar of companies notice, in the form indicated in Part I of Schedule 2 to these Regulations, of the place for inspection of that register and of any change in that place.

**3(2)** The registers referred to in paragraph (1) above are

(a) the register of members,

(b) an overseas branch register, and

(c) the register of directors' interests.

**3(3)** The company shall not be obliged to give notice under paragraph (1) above–

(a) where the company changes from keeping a register in a legible form to keeping it otherwise than in a legible form and the place for inspection of the register immediately following the change is the same as the place where the register was kept in a legible form immediately prior to the change, or

(b) in the case of a register specified in paragraph 2(a) or (c) above, where since the register first came into existence–

(i) it has been kept by recording the matters in question otherwise than in a legible form, and

(ii) the place for inspection has been the registered office of the company.

**3(4)** Where the register of members of a company is kept by recording the matters in question otherwise than in a legible form and the place for inspection of that register is elsewhere than at the registered office, the company shall include in its annual return a statement of the address of the place for inspection of that register.

**3(5)** Subsection (4) of section 353 of the Act shall apply with respect to any default in complying with paragraph (1) above as it applies in relation to a default in complying with subsection (2) of that section; and subsection (7) of section 363 of the Act shall apply with respect to any failure to comply with paragraph (4) above as it applies in relation to a failure to comply with that section.

## REQUIREMENTS WITH RESPECT TO A REGISTER OF DEBENTURE HOLDERS KEPT OTHERWISE THAN IN A LEGIBLE FORM

**4(1)** This Regulation applies to any register of holders of debentures of a company which is kept by a company by recording the matters in question otherwise than in a legible form.

**4(2)** A company registered in England and Wales shall not perform the duty to allow inspection of a register to which this Regulation applies in Scotland and a company registered in Scotland shall not perform such duty in England and Wales.

**4(3)** A company shall not perform the duty to allow inspection of a register to which this regulation applies in England and Wales, in the case of a company registered in England and Wales, or in Scotland, in the case of a company registered in Scotland, elsewhere than at–

(a) the registered office of the company,

(b) any other office of the company at which the work of ensuring that the register is duly made up is done, or

(c) if the company arranges with some other person for the carrying out of the work referred to in (b) above to be undertaken on behalf of the company by that other person, the office of that other person at which the work is done.

**4(4)** The requirements of section 190 of the Act (provisions as to registers of debenture holders) and sections 363 and 364 of and Schedule 15 to that Act (annual returns) shall not apply to a register to which this Regulation applies insofar as they relate to any of the following matters–

(a) the place where the register is permitted to be kept,

(b) the giving of notice to the registrar of companies of the place where the register is kept, or of any change in that place, and

(c) the inclusion in the annual return of a statement of the address of the place where the register is kept.

## NOTIFICATION OF THE PLACE FOR INSPECTION OF REGISTERS OF DEBENTURE HOLDERS

**5(1)** Subject to paragraph (2) below, where the place for inspection of a register to which Regulation 4 above applies is in England and Wales or Scotland, the company shall send to the registrar of companies, notice in the form indicated in Part II of Schedule 2 to these Regulations of the place for inspection of that register and of any change in that place.

**5(2)** The company shall not be obliged to give notice under paragraph (1) above–

(a) where a company changes from keeping the register in a legible form to keeping it otherwise than in a legible form and the place for inspection of the register immediately following the change is the same as the place where the register was kept in a legible form immediately prior to the change, or

(b) where since the register first came into existence–

(i) it has been kept by recording the matters in question otherwise than in a legible form, and

(ii) the place for inspection has been the registered office of the company.

**5(3)** Where the place for inspection of a register to which Regulation 4 above applies is situated in England and Wales, in the case of a company registered in England and Wales, or in Scotland, in the case of a company registered in Scotland, elsewhere than at the registered office of the company, the company shall include in its annual return a statement of the address of that place.

**5(4)** Subsection (7) of section 363 of the Act shall apply with respect to any failure to comply with paragraph (3) above as it applies in relation to a failure to comply with that section.

## OTHER PROVISIONS RELATING TO REGISTERS KEPT OTHERWISE THAN IN A LEGIBLE FORM

**6(1)** Where a register or a register of holders of debentures is kept by recording the matters in question otherwise than in a legible form, any reference to such register in any provision of the Act relating to the place where a duplicate of such register, another register or duplicate of another register is required to be kept, shall be construed as a reference to the place for inspection of the first mentioned register.

**6(2)** Where the place for inspection of the register of members is the office of some person other than the company and by reason of any default of that person the company fails to comply with–

(a) the provisions of Regulation 2 above relating to the duty to allow inspection of the index of the register of members, or

(b) the provisons of Regulation 3 above relating to the register of members, section 357 of the Act (consequences of failure to comply with requirements as to register owing to agent's default) shall apply with respect to such failure as it applies in relation to a failure to comply with the provisions specified in that section by reason of any default of the person other than the company, at whose office the register of members is kept.

**6(3)** Where an overseas branch register is kept by a company by recording the matters in question otherwise than in a legible form, paragraphs 2(2) and 3(1) of Schedule 14 to the Act shall have effect as if, for the references to the country or territory where that register is kept, there were substituted references to the country or territory where the place for inspection of the register is situated.

**6(4)** Where the register of directors' interests is kept by a company by recording the matters in question otherwise than in a legible form, paragraph 29 of Schedule 13 to the Act shall have effect as if, for the reference to that register, there were substituted a reference to a reproduction of the recording of that register in a legible form.

**6(5)** Where the accounting records of a company are kept otherwise than in a legible form and the place for inspection of such records is outside Great Britain, section 222(2) of the Act shall have effect as if, for the references to the accounting records being kept at a place outside Great Britain, there were substituted references to the place for inspection of such records being at a place outside Great Britain.

# Schedule 1 – Places For Performance of Duty to Allow Inspection of Registers Kept Otherwise than in a Legible Form

Regulation 2

| Statutory Provision | Register | Place |
|---|---|---|
| COMPANIES ACT 1985 | | |
| Section 211(8) | Register and any associated index of interests in voting shares | (a) Where the register of directors' interests is kept otherwise than in a legible form, the place for inspection of that register.<br>(b) Where the register of directors' interests is kept in a legible form, the place where it is so kept. |
| Section 222(1) | Accounting records | The registered office of the company or such other place as the directors of the company think fit. |
| Section 288(1) | Register of directors and secretaries | The registered office of the company. |
| Section 353(1) | Register of members | The registered office of the company provided that—<br>(a) if the work of ensuring that the requirements of the Act with regard to entries in the register are complied with is done at another office of the company, the place for inspection may be that other office and |

| Statutory Provision | Register | Place |
|---|---|---|
| | | (b) if the company arranges with some other person for the carrying out of the work referred to in (a) above to be undertaken on behalf of the company by that other person, the place for inspection may be the office of that other person at which the work is done;<br>so however that the place for inspection shall not, in the case of a company registered in England and Wales, be at a place outside England and Wales and, in the case of a company registered in Scotland, be at a place outside Scotland. |
| Section 354(3) | Index of the register of members | (a) Where the register of members is kept otherwise than in a legible form, the place for inspection of that register.<br>(b) Where the register of members is kept in a legible form, the place where it is so kept. |
| Section 362(1) | Overseas branch register | Any place where, but for these Regulations, the register would be permitted to be kept under section 362(1) of the Act. |
| Sections 407(1) and 422(1) | Register of charges | The registered office of the company. |
| Schedule 13, paragraph 25 | Register of directors' interests . | (a) Where the register of members is kept otherwise than in a legible form:<br>(i) if the place for inspection of that register is the registered office of the company, that office, and<br>(ii) if not, the place for inspection of that register or the registered office of the company.<br>(b) Where the register of members is kept in a legible form:<br>(i) if that register is kept at the registered office of the company, that office, and<br>(ii) if that register is not so kept, the place where that register is kept or the registered office of the company. |

| Statutory Provision | Register | Place |
|---|---|---|
| Schedule 13, paragraph 28 | Index of the register of directors' interests | (a) Where the register of directors' interests is kept otherwise than in a legible form, the place for inspection of that register.<br>(b) Where the register of directors' interests is kept in a legible form, the place where it is so kept. |
| Schedule 14, paragraph 4(1) | Duplicate of overseas branch register | (a) Where the register of members is kept otherwise than in a legible form, the place for inspection of that register.<br>(b) Where the register of members is kept in a legible form, the place where it is so kept. |

## Schedule 2

**Note**
This Schedule sets out the prescribed forms – No. 325a, 353a, 362a and 190a – referred to in reg. 3(1) and 5(1). The forms are not reproduced here.

### EXPLANATORY NOTE

(*This Note is not part of the Regulations*)

Following the consolidation of the Companies Acts 1948 to 1983, these Regulations replace the Companies (Registers and other Records) Regulations 1979. They make the same provisions with respect to registers and other records which are kept under the Companies Act 1985 by recording the matters in question otherwise than in a legible form. Schedule 2 contains new forms of notice to be given to the Registrar of Companies.

# THE COMPANIES (DISCLOSURE OF DIRECTORS' INTERESTS) (EXCEPTIONS) REGULATIONS 1985

(SI 1985/802)

*Made on 21 May 1985 by the Secretary of State for Trade and Industry under s. 324(3) of the Companies Act 1985. Operative from 1 July 1985.*

**1** These Regulations may be cited as the Companies (Disclosure of Directors' Interests) (Exceptions) Regulations 1985 and shall come into operation on 1st July 1985.

**2** Section 324(1) and (2) of the Companies Act 1985 shall not require notification of–

(a) interests in shares or debentures of any person in his capacity as trustee or personal representative of any trust or estate of which the Public Trustee is also a trustee (otherwise than as custodian trustee) or, as the case may be, a personal representative;

(b) interests in shares in, or debentures of, a society registered under the Industrial and Provident Societies Act 1965 or deemed to be so registered by virtue of section 4 of that Act;

(c) interests in shares or debentures of a person in his capacity as trustee of, or as beneficiary under, a trust relating exclusively to–

(i) any retirement benefits scheme which is an approved scheme or a statutory scheme as defined in section 26(1) of the Finance Act 1970, and any retirement benefit scheme which is treated as being two or more separate retirement benefit schemes under section 25(3) of that Act where any of those separate schemes is an approved scheme or a statutory scheme, or

(ii) a superannuation fund to which section 36 of the Finance Act 1980 applies;

(d) any event occurring in relation to any person in any such capacity as is mentioned in paragraph (a) or (c) of this Regulation or in relation to any such shares or debentures as are mentioned in paragraph (b);

(e) interests in shares or debentures which a person is taken to have under paragraph 4 of Part I of Schedule 13 to the Companies Act 1985 where the body corporate referred to in that paragraph is interested in those shares or debentures in its capacity as trustee of any such trust as is mentioned in paragraph (c) of this Regulation;

(f) any event occurring in relation to any person as a result of which he is taken to have any such interest as is mentioned in paragraph (e) of this Regulation;

(g) interests in shares in a body corporate which arise solely on account of any limitation imposed by the memorandum or articles of association of the body corporate on a person's right to dispose of a share.

**3(1)** The said section 324(1) and (2) shall not require notification–

(a) to a company which is the wholly owned subsidiary of a body corporate incorporated outside Great Britain of interests in shares in, or debentures of, that body corporate or any other body corporate so incorporated, or of any event occurring in relation to any such shares or debentures;

(b) to a company by a director of the company who is also the director of a body corporate of which the company is the wholly owned subsidiary and which is itself required to keep a register under section 325(1) of the Companies Act 1985, of interests in any shares or debentures or of any event occurring in relation to any shares or debentures.

**3(2)** For the purposes of paragraph (1) of this Regulation, a company shall be deemed to be the wholly owned subsidiary of another body corporate if it has no members but that other and that other's wholly owned subsidiaries and its or their nominees.

**4** The Companies (Disclosure of Directors' Interests) (Exceptions) No. 1 Regulations 1967, the Companies (Disclosure of Directors' Interests) (Exceptions) No. 2 Regulations 1968 and the Companies (Disclosure of Directors' Interests) (Exceptions) No. 3 Regulations 1968 are hereby revoked.

## EXPLANATORY NOTE

(*This Note is not part of the Regulations*)

Section 324 of the Companies Act 1985 imposes on a director of a company the obligation to disclose interests in, and matters connected with, shares and debentures of the company and certain associated companies. These Regulations supersede the three previous Companies (Disclosure of Directors' Interests) (Exceptions) Regulations (listed in Regulation 4) which are revoked.

The Regulations except from the requirement of disclosure under section 324 specified interests in shares or debentures of–

(a) trusts or estates of which the Public Trustee is joint trustee or personal representative;

(b) a society registered under the Industrial and Provident Societies Act 1965;

(c) trusts relating exclusively to approved or statutory schemes as defined in section 26(1) of the Finance Act 1970 and superannuation funds to which section 36 of the Finance Act 1980 applies.

The Regulations also except from the requirement of disclosure interests in shares or debentures which a person is taken to have in certain circumstances under paragraph 4 of Part I of Schedule 13 to the Companies Act 1985 and interests in shares in a body corporate which arise only on account of any limitation imposed by the memorandum or articles of association of the body corporate on a person's right to dispose of a share. In addition they dispense with notification of certain interests by directors of some wholly owned subsidiary companies and with notification of certain other matters relating to the specified interests and the persons holding them.

# THE COMPANIES (TABLES A TO F) REGULATIONS 1985

(SI 1985/805)

*Made by the Secretary of State for Trade and Industry under s. 454(2) of the Companies Act 1948 – s. 3 and 8 of the Companies Act 1985 – on 22 May 1985. Operative from 1 July 1985.*

[**Note:** Amendments by SI 1985/1052 (operative from 1 August 1985) have been included – also the former Table A (as amended), as contained in First Sch. to former Companies Act 1948, has been reproduced at the end of these Regulations as it continues to be relevant for a large number of companies incorporated before 1 July 1985.]

**1** These Regulations may be cited as the Companies (Tables A to F) Regulations 1985 and shall come into operation on 1st July 1985.

**2** The regulations in Table A and the forms in Tables B, C, D, E and F in the Schedule to these Regulations shall be the regulations and forms of memorandum and articles of association for the purposes of sections 3 and 8 of the Companies Act 1985.

**3** The Companies (Alteration of Table A etc) Regulations 1984 are hereby revoked.

## Schedule

## Table A – Regulations for Management of a Company Limited by Shares

### INTERPRETATION

**1** In these regulations–

**"the Act"** means the Companies Act 1985 including any statutory modification or re-enactment thereof for the time being in force.

**"the articles"** means the articles of the company.

**"clear days"** in relation to the period of a notice means that period excluding the day when the notice is given or deemed to be given and the day for which it is given or on which it is to take effect.

**"executed"** includes any mode of execution.

**"office"** means the registered office of the company.

**"the holder"** in relation to shares means the member whose name is entered in the register of members as the holder of the shares.

**"the seal"** means the common seal of the company.

**"secretary"** means the secretary of the company or any other person appointed to perform the duties of the secretary of the company, including a joint, assistant or deputy secretary.

**"the United Kingdom"** means Great Britain and Northern Ireland.

Unless the context otherwise requires, words or expressions contained in these regulations bear the same meaning as in the Act but excluding any statutory modification thereof not in force when these regulations become binding on the company.

### SHARE CAPITAL

**2** Subject to the provisions of the Act and without prejudice to any rights attached to any existing shares, any share may be issued with such rights or restrictions as the company may by ordinary resolution determine.

**3** Subject to the provisions of the Act, shares may be issued which are to be redeemed or are to be liable to be redeemed at the option of the company or the holder on such terms and in such manner as may be provided by the articles.

**4** The company may exercise the powers of paying commissions conferred by the Act. Subject to the provisions of the Act, any such commission may be satisfied by the payment of cash or by the allotment of fully or partly paid shares or partly in one way and partly in the other.

**History**
Reg. 4 amended by substituting the word "provisions" for the former word "provision" by SI 1985/1052 as from 1 August 1985.

**5** Except as required by law, no person shall be recognised by the company as holding any share upon any trust and (except as otherwise provided by the articles or by law) the company shall not be bound by or recognise any interest in any share except an absolute right to the entirety thereof in the holder.

## SHARE CERTIFICATES

**6** Every member, upon becoming the holder of any shares, shall be entitled without payment to one certificate for all the shares of each class held by him (and, upon transferring a part of his holding of shares of any class, to a certificate for the balance of such holding) or several certificates each for one or more of his shares upon payment for every certificate after the first of such reasonable sum as the directors may determine. Every certificate shall be sealed with the seal and shall specify the number, class and distinguishing numbers (if any) of the shares to which it relates and the amount or respective amounts paid up thereon. The company shall not be bound to issue more than one certificate for shares held jointly by several persons and delivery of a certificate to one joint holder shall be a sufficient delivery to all of them.

**7** If a share certificate is defaced, worn-out, lost or destroyed, it may be renewed on such terms (if any) as to evidence and indemnity and payment of the expenses reasonably incurred by the company in investigating evidence as the directors may determine but otherwise free of charge, and (in the case of defacement or wearing-out) on delivery up of the old certificate.

## LIEN

**8** The company shall have a first and paramount lien on every share (not being a fully paid share) for all moneys (whether presently payable or not) payable at a fixed time or called in respect of that share. The directors may at any time declare any share to be wholly or in part exempt from the provisions of this regulation. The company's lien on a share shall extend to any amount payable in respect of it.

**9** The company may sell in such manner as the directors determine any shares on which the company has a lien if a sum in respect of which the lien exists is presently payable and is not paid within fourteen clear days after notice has been given to the holder of the share or to the person entitled to it in consequence of the death or bankruptcy of the holder, demanding payment and stating that if the notice is not complied with the shares may be sold.

**10** To give effect to a sale the directors may authorise some person to execute an instrument of transfer of the shares sold to, or in accordance with the directions of, the purchaser. The title of the transferee to the shares shall not be affected by any irregularity in or invalidity of the proceedings in reference to the sale.

**11** The net proceeds of the sale, after payment of the costs, shall be applied in payment of so much of the sum for which the lien exists as is presently payable, and any residue shall (upon surrender to the company for cancellation of the certificate for the shares sold and subject to a like lien for any moneys not presently payable as existed upon the shares before the sale) be paid to the person entitled to the shares at the date of the sale.

## CALLS ON SHARES AND FORFEITURE

**12** Subject to the terms of allotment, the directors may make calls upon the members in respect of any moneys unpaid on their shares (whether in respect of nominal value or premium) and each member shall (subject to receiving at least fourteen clear days' notice specifying when and where payment is to be made) pay to the company as required by the notice the amount called on his shares. A call may be required to be paid by instalments. A call may, before receipt by the company of any sum due thereunder, be revoked in whole or part and payment of a call may be postponed in whole or part. A person upon whom a call is made shall remain liable for calls made upon him notwithstanding the subsequent transfer of the shares in respect whereof the call was made.

**13** A call shall be deemed to have been made at the time when the resolution of the directors authorising the call was passed.

**14** The joint holders of a share shall be jointly and severally liable to pay all calls in respect thereof.

**15** If a call remains unpaid after it has become due and payable the person from whom it is due and payable shall pay interest on the amount unpaid from the day it became due and payable until it is paid at the rate fixed by the terms of allotment of the share or in the notice of the call or, if no rate is fixed, at the appropriate rate (as defined by the Act) but the directors may waive payment of the interest wholly or in part.

**16** An amount payable in respect of a share on allotment or at any fixed date, whether in respect of nominal value or premium or as an instalment of a call, shall be deemed to be a call and if it is not paid the provisions of the articles shall apply as if that amount had become due and payable by virtue of a call.

**17** Subject to the terms of allotment, the directors may make arrangements on the issue of shares for a difference between the holders in the amounts and times of payment of calls on their shares.

**18** If a call remains unpaid after it has become due and payable the directors may give to the person from whom it is due not less than fourteen clear days' notice requiring payment of the amount unpaid together with any interest which may have accrued. The notice shall name the place where payment is to be made and shall state that if the notice is not complied with the shares in respect of which the call was made will be liable to be forfeited.

**19** If the notice is not complied with any share in respect of which it was given may, before the payment required by the notice has been made, be forfeited by a resolution of the directors and the forfeiture shall include all dividends or other moneys payable in respect of the forfeited shares and not paid before the forfeiture.

**20** Subject to the provisions of the Act, a forfeited share may be sold, re-allotted or otherwise disposed of on such terms and in such manner as the directors determine either to the person who was before the forfeiture the holder or to any other person and at any time before sale, re-allotment or other disposition, the forfeiture may be cancelled on such terms as the directors think fit. Where for the purposes of its disposal a forfeited share is to be transferred to any person the directors may authorise some person to execute an instrument of transfer of the share to that person.

**21** A person any of whose shares have been forfeited shall cease to be a member in respect of them and shall surrender to the company for cancellation the certificate for the shares forfeited but shall remain liable to the company for all moneys which at the date of forfeiture were presently payable by him to the company in respect of those shares with interest at the rate at which interest was payable on those moneys before the forfeiture or, if no interest was so payable, at the appropriate rate (as defined in the Act) from the date of forfeiture until payment but the directors may waive payment wholly or in part or enforce payment without any allowance for the value of the shares at the time of forfeiture or for any consideration received on their disposal.

**22** A statutory declaration by a director or the secretary that a share has been forfeited on a specified date shall be conclusive evidence of the facts stated in it as against all persons claiming to be entitled to the share and the declaration shall (subject to the execution of an instrument of transfer if necessary) constitute a good title to the share and the person to whom the share is disposed of shall not be bound to see to the application of the consideration, if any, nor shall his title to the share be affected by any irregularity in or invalidity of the proceedings in reference to the forfeiture or disposal of the share.



bbcl randr1 Mp 3740—bcl98 205a

## [illegible]ANSFER OF SHARES

**23** The instrument of tran[illegible]hare may be in any usual form or in any other form which the directors may approve a[illegible] be executed by or on behalf of the transferor and, unless the share is fully paid, by or [illegible] of the transferee.

**24** The directors may refuse[illegible]ter the transfer of a share which is not fully paid to a person of whom they do not appro[illegible]and they may refuse to register the transfer of a share on which the company has a lien. They may also refuse to register a transfer unless–

(a) it is lodged at the office or at such other place as the directors may appoint and is accompanied by the certificate for the shares to which it relates and such other evidence as the directors may reasonably require to show the right of the transferor to make the transfer;

(b) it is in respect of only one class of shares; and

(c) it is in favour of not more than four transferees.

**25** If the directors refuse to register a transfer of a share, they shall within two months after the date on which the transfer was lodged with the company send to the transferee notice of the refusal.

**26** The registration of transfers of shares or of transfers of any class of shares may be suspended at such times and for such periods (not exceeding thirty days in any year) as the directors may determine.

**27** No fee shall be charged for the registration of any instrument of transfer or other document relating to or affecting the title to any share.

**28** The company shall be entitled to retain any instrument of transfer which is registered, but any instrument of transfer which the directors refuse to register shall be returned to the person lodging it when notice of the refusal is given.

## TRANSMISSION OF SHARES

**29** If a member dies the survivor or survivors where he was a joint holder, and his personal representatives where he was a sole holder or the only survivor of joint holders, shall be the only persons recognised by the company as having any title to his interest; but nothing herein contained shall release the estate of a deceased member from any liability in respect of any share which had been jointly held by him.

**30** A person becoming entitled to a share in consequence of the death or bankruptcy of a member may, upon such evidence being produced as the directors may properly require, elect either to become the holder of the share or to have some person nominated by him registered as the transferee. If he elects to become the holder he shall give notice to the company to that effect. If he elects to have another person registered he shall execute an instrument of transfer of the share to that person. All the articles relating to the transfer of shares shall apply to the notice or instrument of transfer as if it were an instrument of transfer executed by the member and the death or bankruptcy of the member had not occurred.

**31** A person becoming entitled to a share in consequence of the death or bankruptcy of a member shall have the rights to which he would be entitled if he were the holder of the share, except that he shall not, before being registered as the holder of the share, be entitled in respect of it to attend or vote at any meeting of the company or at any separate meeting of the holders of any class of shares in the company.

## ALTERATION OF SHARE CAPITAL

**32** The company may by ordinary resolution–

(a) increase its share capital by new shares of such amount as the resolution prescribes;

(b) consolidate and divide all or any of its share capital into shares of larger amount than its existing shares;

(c) subject to the provisions of the Act, sub-divide its shares, or any of them, into shares of smaller amount and the resolution may determine that, as between the shares resulting from the sub-division, any of them may have any preference or advantage as compared with the others; and

(d) cancel shares which, at the date of the passing of the resolution, have not been taken or agreed to be taken by any person and diminish the amount of its share capital by the amount of the shares so cancelled.

**33** Whenever as a result of a consolidation of shares any members would become entitled to fractions of a share, the directors may, on behalf of those members, sell the shares representing the fractions for the best price reasonably obtainable to any person (including, subject to the provisions of the Act, the company) and distribute the net proceeds of sale in due proportion among those members, and the directors may authorise some person to execute an instrument of transfer of the shares to, or in accordance with the directions of, the purchaser. The transferee shall not be bound to see to the application of the purchase money nor shall his title to the shares be affected by any irregularity in or invalidity of the proceedings in reference to the sale.

**34** Subject to the provisions of the Act, the company may by special resolution reduce its share capital, any capital redemption reserve and any share premium account in any way.

## PURCHASE OF OWN SHARES

**35** Subject to the provisions of the Act, the company may purchase its own shares (including any redeemable shares) and, if it is a private company, make a payment in respect of the redemption or purchase of its own shares otherwise than out of distributable profits of the company or the proceeds of a fresh issue of shares.

## GENERAL MEETINGS

**36** All general meetings other than annual general meetings shall be called extraordinary general meetings.

**37** The directors may call general meetings and, on the requisition of members pursuant to the provisions of the Act, shall forthwith proceed to convene an extraordinary general meeting for a date not later than eight weeks after receipt of the requisition. If there are not within the United Kingdom sufficient directors to call a general meeting, any director or any member of the company may call a general meeting.

## NOTICE OF GENERAL MEETINGS

**38** An annual general meeting and an extraordinary general meeting called for the passing of a special resolution or a resolution appointing a person as a director shall be called by at least twenty-one clear days' notice. All other extraordinary general meetings shall be called by at least fourteen clear days' notice but a general meeting may be called by shorter notice if it is so agreed–

(a) in the case of an annual general meeting, by all the members entitled to attend and vote thereat; and

(b) in the case of any other meeting by a majority in number of the members having a right to attend and vote being a majority together holding not less than ninety-five per cent in nominal value of the shares giving that right.

The notice shall specify the time and place of the meeting and the general nature of the business to be transacted and, in the case of an annual general meeting, shall specify the meeting as such. Subject to the provisions of the articles and to any restrictions imposed on any shares, the notice shall be given to all the members, to all persons entitled to a share in consequence of the death or bankruptcy of a member and to the directors and auditors.

**39** The accidental omission to give notice of a meeting to, or the non-receipt of notice of a meeting by, any person entitled to receive notice shall not invalidate the proceedings at that meeting.

## PROCEEDINGS AT GENERAL MEETINGS

**40** No business shall be transacted at any meeting unless a quorum is present. Two persons entitled to vote upon the business to be transacted, each being a member or a proxy for a member or a duly authorised representative of a corporation, shall be a quorum.

**41** If such a quorum is not present within half an hour from the time appointed for the meeting, or if during a meeting such a quorum ceases to be present, the meeting shall stand adjourned to the same day in the next week at the same time and place or to such time and place as the directors may determine.

**History**
Reg. 41 amended by SI 1985/1052 as from 1 August 1985.

**42** The chairman, if any, of the board of directors or in his absence some other director nominated by the directors shall preside as chairman of the meeting, but if neither the chairman nor such other director (if any) be present within fifteen minutes after the time appointed for holding the meeting and willing to act, the directors present shall elect one of their number to be chairman and, if there is only one director present and willing to act, he shall be chairman.

**43** If no director is willing to act as chairman, or if no director is present within fifteen minutes after the time appointed for holding the meeting, the members present and entitled to vote shall choose one of their number to be chairman.

**44** A director shall, notwithstanding that he is not a member, be entitled to attend and speak at any general meeting and at any separate meeting of the holders of any class of shares in the company.

**45** The chairman may, with the consent of a meeting at which a quorum is present (and shall if so directed by the meeting), adjourn the meeting from time to time and from place to place, but no business shall be transacted at an adjourned meeting other than business which might properly have been transacted at the meeting had the adjournment not taken place. When a meeting is adjourned for fourteen days or more, at least seven clear days' notice shall be given specifying the time and place of the adjourned meeting and the general nature of the business to be transacted. Otherwise it shall not be necessary to give any such notice.

**46** A resolution put to the vote of a meeting shall be decided on a show of hands unless before, or on the declaration of the result of, the show of hands a poll is duly demanded. Subject to the provisions of the Act, a poll may be demanded–

(a) by the chairman; or

(b) by at least two members having the right to vote at the meeting; or

(c) by a member or members representing not less than one-tenth of the total voting rights of all the members having the right to vote at the meeting; or

(d) by a member or members holding shares conferring a right to vote at the meeting being shares on which an aggregate sum has been paid up equal to not less than one-tenth of the total sum paid up on all the shares conferring that right;

and a demand by a person as proxy for a member shall be the same as a demand by the member.

**47** Unless a poll is duly demanded a declaration by the chairman that a resolution has been carried or carried unanimously, or by a particular majority, or lost, or not carried by a particular majority and an entry to that effect in the minutes of the meeting shall be conclusive evidence of the fact without proof of the number or proportion of the votes recorded in favour of or against the resolution.

**48** The demand for a poll may, before the poll is taken, be withdrawn but only with the consent of the chairman and a demand so withdrawn shall not be taken to have invalidated the result of a show of hands declared before the demand was made.

**49** A poll shall be taken as the chairman directs and he may appoint scrutineers (who need not be members) and fix a time and place for declaring the result of the poll. The result of the poll shall be deemed to be the resolution of the meeting at which the poll was demanded.

**50** In the case of an equality of votes, whether on a show of hands or on a poll, the chairman shall be entitled to a casting vote in addition to any other vote he may have.

**51** A poll demanded on the election of a chairman or on a question of adjournment shall be taken forthwith. A poll demanded on any other question shall be taken either forthwith or at such time and place as the chairman directs not being more than thirty days after the poll is demanded. The demand for a poll shall not prevent the continuance of a meeting for the transaction of any business other than the question on which the poll was demanded. If a poll is demanded before the declaration of the result of a show of hands and the demand is duly withdrawn, the meeting shall continue as if the demand had not been made.

**52** No notice need be given of a poll not taken forthwith if the time and place at which it is to be taken are announced at the meeting at which it is demanded. In any other case at least seven clear days' notice shall be given specifying the time and place at which the poll is to be taken.

**53** A resolution in writing executed by or on behalf of each member who would have been entitled to vote upon it if it had been proposed at a general meeting at which he was present shall be as effectual as if it had been passed at a general meeting duly convened and held and may consist of several instruments in the like form each executed by or on behalf of one or more members.

## VOTES OF MEMBERS

**54** Subject to any rights or restrictions attached to any shares, on a show of hands every member who (being an individual) is present in person or (being a corporation) is present by a duly authorised representative, not being himself a member entitled to vote, shall have one vote and on a poll every member shall have one vote for every share of which he is the holder.

**55** In the case of joint holders the vote of the senior who tenders a vote, whether in person or by proxy, shall be accepted to the exclusion of the votes of the other joint holders; and seniority shall be determined by the order in which the names of the holders stand in the register of members.

**56** A member in respect of whom an order has been made by any court having jurisdiction (whether in the United Kingdom or elsewhere) in matters concerning mental disorder may vote, whether on a show of hands or on a poll, by his receiver, curator bonis or other person authorised in that behalf appointed by that court, and any such receiver, curator bonis or other person may, on a poll, vote by proxy. Evidence to the satisfaction of the directors of the authority of the person claiming to exercise the right to vote shall be deposited at the office, or at such other place as is specified in accordance with the articles for the deposit of instruments of proxy, not less than 48 hours before the time appointed for holding the meeting or adjourned meeting at which the right to vote is to be exercised and in default the right to vote shall not be exercisable.

**57** No member shall vote at any general meeting or at any separate meeting of the holders of any class of shares in the company, either in person or by proxy, in respect of any share held by him unless all moneys presently payable by him in respect of that share have been paid.

**58** No objection shall be raised to the qualification of any voter except at the meeting or adjourned meeting at which the vote objected to is tendered, and every vote not disallowed at the meeting shall be valid. Any objection made in due time shall be referred to the chairman whose decision shall be final and conclusive.

**59** On a poll votes may be given either personally or by proxy. A member may appoint more than one proxy to attend on the same occasion.

**60** An instrument appointing a proxy shall be in writing, executed by or on behalf of the appointor and shall be in the following form (or in a form as near thereto as circumstances allow or in any other form which is usual or which the directors may approve)–

> "                    PLC/Limited
>
> I/We,                    , of                    , being a member/members of the above-named company, hereby appoint                    of                    , or failing him, of                    , as my/our proxy to vote in my/our name[s] and on my/our behalf at the annual/extraordinary general meeting of the company to be held on                    19    , and at any adjournment thereof.
>
> Signed on                    19    ."

**61** Where it is desired to afford members an opportunity of instructing the proxy how he shall act the instrument appointing a proxy shall be in the following form (or in a form as near thereto as circumstances allow or in any other form which is usual or which the directors may approve)–

" PLC/Limited

I/We, , of being a member/members of the above-named company, hereby appoint of , or failing him, of , as my/our proxy to vote in my/our name[s] and on my/our behalf at the annual/extraordinary general meeting of the company to be held on 19 , and at any adjournment thereof.

This form is to be used in respect of the resolutions mentioned below as follows:

Resolution No. 1 *for *against

Resolution No. 2 *for *against.

*Strike out whichever is not desired.

Unless otherwise instructed, the proxy may vote as he thinks fit or abstain from voting.

Signed this day of 19 ."

**62** The instrument appointing a proxy and any authority under which it is executed or a copy of such authority certified notarially or in some other way approved by the directors may–

(a) be deposited at the office or at such other place within the United Kingdom as is specified in the notice convening the meeting or in any instrument of proxy sent out by the company in relation to the meeting not less than 48 hours before the time for holding the meeting or adjourned meeting at which the person named in the instrument proposes to vote; or

(b) in the case of a poll taken more than 48 hours after it is demanded, be deposited as aforesaid after the poll has been demanded and not less than 24 hours before the time appointed for the taking of the poll; or

(c) where the poll is not taken forthwith but is taken not more than 48 hours after it was demanded, be delivered at the meeting at which the poll was demanded to the chairman or to the secretary or to any director;

and an instrument of proxy which is not deposited or delivered in a manner so permitted shall be invalid.

**63** A vote given or poll demanded by proxy or by the duly authorised representative of a corporation shall be valid notwithstanding the previous determination of the authority of the person voting or demanding a poll unless notice of the determination was received by the company at the office or at such other place at which the instrument of proxy was duly deposited before the commencement of the meeting or adjourned meeting at which the vote is given or the poll demanded or (in the case of a poll taken otherwise than on the same day as the meeting or adjourned meeting) the time appointed for taking the poll.

## NUMBER OF DIRECTORS

**64** Unless otherwise determined by ordinary resolution, the number of directors (other than alternate directors) shall not be subject to any maximum but shall be not less than two.

## ALTERNATE DIRECTORS

**65** Any director (other than an alternate director) may appoint any other director, or any other person approved by resolution of the directors and willing to act, to be an alternate director and may remove from office an alternate director so appointed by him.

**66** An alternate director shall be entitled to receive notice of all meetings of directors and of all meetings of committees of directors of which his appointor is a member, to attend and vote at any such meeting at which the director appointing him is not personally present, and generally to perform all the functions of his appointor as a director in his absence but shall not be entitled to receive any remuneration from the company for his services as an alternate director. But it shall not be necessary to give notice of such a meeting to an alternate director who is absent from the United Kingdom.

**67** An alternate director shall cease to be an alternate director if his appointor ceases to be a director; but, if a director retires by rotation or otherwise but is reappointed or deemed to have been reappointed at the meeting at which he retires, any appointment of an alternate director made by him which was in force immediately prior to his retirement shall continue after his reappointment.

**68** Any appointment or removal of an alternate director shall be by notice to the company signed by the director making or revoking the appointment or in any other manner approved by the directors.

**69** Save as otherwise provided in the articles, an alternate director shall be deemed for all purposes to be a director and shall alone be responsible for his own acts and defaults and he shall not be deemed to be the agent of the director appointing him.

## POWERS OF DIRECTORS

**70** Subject to the provisions of the Act, the memorandum and the articles and to any directions given by special resolution, the business of the company shall be managed by the directors who may exercise all the powers of the company. No alteration of the memorandum or articles and no such direction shall invalidate any prior act of the directors which would have been valid if that alteration had not been made or that direction had not been given. The powers given by this regulation shall not be limited by any special power given to the directors by the articles and a meeting of directors at which a quorum is present may exercise all powers exercisable by the directors.

**71** The directors may, by power of attorney or otherwise, appoint any person to be the agent of the company for such purposes and on such conditions as they determine, including authority for the agent to delegate all or any of his powers.

## DELEGATION OF DIRECTORS' POWERS

**72** The directors may delegate any of their powers to any committee consisting of one or more directors. They may also delegate to any managing director or any director holding any other executive office such of their powers as they consider desirable to be exercised by him. Any such delegation may be made subject to any conditions the directors may impose, and either collaterally with or to the exclusion of their own powers and may be revoked or altered. Subject to any such conditions, the proceedings of a committee with two or more members shall be governed by the articles regulating the proceedings of directors so far as they are capable of applying.

## APPOINTMENT AND RETIREMENT OF DIRECTORS

**73** At the first annual general meeting all the directors shall retire from office, and at every subsequent annual general meeting one-third of the directors who are subject to retirement by rotation or, if their number is not three or a multiple of three, the number nearest to one-third shall retire from office; but, if there is only one director who is subject to retirement by rotation, he shall retire.

**74** Subject to the provisions of the Act, the directors to retire by rotation shall be those who have been longest in office since their last appointment or reappointment, but as between persons who became or were last reappointed directors on the same day those to retire shall (unless they otherwise agree among themselves) be determined by lot.

**75** If the company, at the meeting at which a director retires by rotation, does not fill the vacancy the retiring director shall, if willing to act, be deemed to have been reappointed unless at the meeting it is resolved not to fill the vacancy or unless a resolution for the reappointment of the director is put to the meeting and lost.

**76** No person other than a director retiring by rotation shall be appointed or reappointed a director at any general meeting unless–

(a) he is recommended by the directors; or

(b) not less than fourteen nor more than thirty-five clear days before the date appointed for the meeting, notice executed by a member qualified to vote at the meeting has been given to the company of the intention to propose that person for appointment or reappointment stating the particulars which would, if he were so appointed or reappointed, be required to be included in the company's register of directors together with notice executed by that person of his willingness to be appointed or reappointed.

**77** Not less than seven nor more than twenty-eight clear days before the date appointed for holding a general meeting notice shall be given to all who are entitled to receive notice of the meeting of any person (other than a director retiring by rotation at the meeting) who is recommended by the directors for appointment or reappointment as a director at the meeting or in respect of whom notice has been duly given to the company of the intention to propose him at the meeting for appointment or reappointment as a director. The notice shall give the particulars of that person which would, if he were so appointed or reappointed, be required to be included in the company's register of directors.

**78** Subject as aforesaid, the company may by ordinary resolution appoint a person who is willing to act to be a director either to fill a vacancy or as an additional director and may also determine the rotation in which any additional directors are to retire.

**79** The directors may appoint a person who is willing to act to be a director, either to fill a vacancy or as an additional director, provided that the appointment does not cause the number of directors to exceed any number fixed by or in accordance with the articles as the maximum number of directors. A director so appointed shall hold office only until the next following annual general meeting and shall not be taken into account in determining the directors who are to retire by rotation at the meeting. If not reappointed at such annual general meeting, he shall vacate office at the conclusion thereof.

**80** Subject as aforesaid, a director who retires at an annual general meeting may, if willing to act, be reappointed. If he is not reappointed, he shall retain office until the meeting appoints someone in his place, or if it does not do so, until the end of the meeting.

## DISQUALIFICATION AND REMOVAL OF DIRECTORS

**81** The office of a director shall be vacated if–

(a) he ceases to be a director by virtue of any provision of the Act or he becomes prohibited by law from being a director; or

(b) he becomes bankrupt or makes any arrangement or composition with his creditors generally; or

(c) he is, or may be, suffering from mental disorder and either–
  (i) he is admitted to hospital in pursuance of an application for admission for treatment under the Mental Health Act 1983 or, in Scotland, an application for admission under the Mental Health (Scotland) Act 1960, or
  (ii) an order is made by a court having jurisdiction (whether in the United Kingdom or elsewhere) in matters concerning mental disorder for his detention or for the appointment of a receiver, curator bonis or other person to exercise powers with respect to his property or affairs; or

(d) he resigns his office by notice to the company; or

(e) he shall for more than six consecutive months have been absent without permission of the directors from meetings of directors held during that period and the directors resolve that his office be vacated.

## REMUNERATION OF DIRECTORS

**82** The directors shall be entitled to such remuneration as the company may by ordinary resolution determine and, unless the resolution provides otherwise, the remuneration shall be deemed to accrue from day to day.

## DIRECTORS' EXPENSES

**83** The directors may be paid all travelling, hotel, and other expenses properly incurred by them in connection with their attendance at meetings of directors or committees of directors or general meetings or separate meetings of the holders of any class of shares or of debentures of the company or otherwise in connection with the discharge of their duties.

## DIRECTORS' APPOINTMENTS AND INTERESTS

**84** Subject to the provisions of the Act, the directors may appoint one or more of their number to the office of managing director or to any other executive office under the company and may enter into an agreement or arrangement with any director for his employment by the company or for the provision by him of any services outside the scope of the ordinary duties of a director. Any such appointment, agreement or arrangement may be made upon such terms as the directors determine and they may remunerate any such director for his services as they think fit. Any appointment of a director to an executive office shall terminate if he ceases to be a director but without prejudice to any claim to damages for breach of the contract of service between the director and the company. A managing director and a director holding any other executive office shall not be subject to retirement by rotation.

**85** Subject to the provisions of the Act, and provided that he has disclosed to the directors the nature and extent of any material interest of his, a director notwithstanding his office–

(a) may be a party to, or otherwise interested in, any transaction or arrangement with the company or in which the company is otherwise interested;

(b) may be a director or other officer of, or employed by, or a party to any transaction or arrangement with, or otherwise interested in, any body corporate promoted by the company or in which the company is otherwise interested; and

(c) shall not, by reason of his office, be accountable to the company for any benefit which he derives from any such office or employment or from any such transaction or arrangement or from any interest in any such body corporate and no such transaction or arrangement shall be liable to be avoided on the ground of any such interest or benefit.

**86** For the purposes of regulation 85–

(a) a general notice given to the directors that a director is to be regarded as having an interest of the nature and extent specified in the notice in any transaction or arrangement in which a specified person or class of persons is interested shall be deemed to be a disclosure that the director has an interest in any such transaction of the nature and extent so specified; and

(b) an interest of which a director has no knowledge and of which it is unreasonable to expect him to have knowledge shall not be treated as an interest of his.

## DIRECTORS' GRATUITIES AND PENSIONS

**87** The directors may provide benefits, whether by the payment of gratuities or pensions or by insurance or otherwise, for any director who has held but no longer holds any executive office or employment with the company or with any body corporate which is or has been a subsidiary of the company or a predecessor in business of the company or of any such subsidiary, and for any member of his family (including a spouse and a former spouse) or any person who is or was dependent on him, and may (as well before as after he ceases to hold such office or employment) contribute to any fund and pay premiums for the purchase or provision of any such benefit.

## PROCEEDINGS OF DIRECTORS

**88** Subject to the provisions of the articles, the directors may regulate their proceedings as they think fit. A director may, and the secretary at the request of a director shall, call a meeting of the directors. It shall not be necessary to give notice of a meeting to a director who is absent from the United Kingdom. Questions arising at a meeting shall be decided by a majority of votes. In the case of an equality of votes, the chairman shall have a second or casting vote. A director who is also an alternate director shall be entitled in the absence of his appointor to a separate vote on behalf of his appointor in addition to his own vote.

**89** The quorum for the transaction of the business of the directors may be fixed by the directors and unless so fixed at any other number shall be two. A person who holds office only as an alternate director shall, if his appointor is not present, be counted in the quorum.

**90** The continuing directors or a sole continuing director may act notwithstanding any vacancies in their number, but, if the number of directors is less than the number fixed as the quorum, the continuing directors or director may act only for the purpose of filling vacancies or of calling a general meeting.

**91** The directors may appoint one of their number to be the chairman of the board of directors and may at any time remove him from that office. Unless he is unwilling to do so, the director so appointed shall preside at every meeting of directors at which he is present. But if there is no director holding that office, or if the director holding it is unwilling to preside or is not present within five minutes after the time appointed for the meeting, the directors present may appoint one of their number to be chairman of the meeting.

**92** All acts done by a meeting of directors, or of a committee of directors, or by a person acting as a director shall, notwithstanding that it be afterwards discovered that there was a defect in the appointment of any director or that any of them were disqualified from holding office, or had vacated office, or were not entitled to vote, be as valid as if every such person had been duly appointed and was qualified and had continued to be a director and had been entitled to vote.

**93** A resolution in writing signed by all the directors entitled to receive notice of a meeting of directors or of a committee of directors shall be as valid and effectual as if it had been passed at a meeting of directors or (as the case may be) a committee of directors duly convened and held and may consist of several documents in the like form each signed by one or more directors; but a resolution signed by an alternate director need not also be signed by his appointor and, if it is signed by a director who has appointed an alternate director, it need not be signed by the alternate director in that capacity.

**94** Save as otherwise provided by the articles, a director shall not vote at a meeting of directors or of a committee of directors on any resolution concerning a matter in which he has, directly or indirectly, an interest or duty which is material and which conflicts or may conflict with the interests of the company unless his interest or duty arises only because the case falls within one or more of the following paragraphs–

(a) the resolution relates to the giving to him of a guarantee, security, or indemnity in respect of money lent to, or an obligation incurred by him for the benefit of, the company or any of its subsidiaries;

(b) the resolution relates to the giving to a third party of a guarantee, security, or indemnity in respect of an obligation of the company or any of its subsidiaries for which the director has assumed responsibility in whole or part and whether alone or jointly with others under a guarantee or indemnity or by the giving of security;

(c) his interest arises by virtue of his subscribing or agreeing to subscribe for any shares, debentures or other securities of the company or any of its subsidiaries, or by virtue of his being, or intending to become, a participant in the underwriting or sub-underwriting of an offer of any such shares, debentures, or other securities by the company or any of its subsidiaries for subscription, purchase or exchange;

(d) the resolution relates in any way to a retirement benefits scheme which has been approved, or is conditional upon approval, by the Board of Inland Revenue for taxation purposes.

For the purposes of this regulation, an interest of a person who is, for any purpose of the Act (excluding any statutory modification thereof not in force when this regulation becomes binding on the company), connected with a director shall be treated as an interest of the director and, in relation to an alternate director, an interest of his appointor shall be treated as an interest of the alternate director without prejudice to any interest which the alternate director has otherwise.

**95** A director shall not be counted in the quorum present at a meeting in relation to a resolution on which he is not entitled to vote.

**96** The company may by ordinary resolution suspend or relax to any extent, either generally or in respect of any particular matter, any provision of the articles prohibiting a director from voting at a meeting of directors or of a committee of directors.

**97** Where proposals are under consideration concerning the appointment of two or more directors to offices or employments with the company or any body corporate in which the company is interested the proposals may be divided and considered in relation to each director separately and (provided he is not for another reason precluded from voting) each of the directors concerned shall be entitled to vote and be counted in the quorum in respect of each resolution except that concerning his own appointment.

**98** If a question arises at a meeting of directors or of a committee of directors as to the right of a director to vote, the question may, before the conclusion of the meeting, be referred to the chairman of the meeting and his ruling in relation to any director other than himself shall be final and conclusive.

## SECRETARY

**99** Subject to the provisions of the Act, the secretary shall be appointed by the directors for such term, at such remuneration and upon such conditions as they may think fit; and any secretary so appointed may be removed by them.

## MINUTES

**100** The directors shall cause minutes to be made in books kept for the purpose–

(a) of all appointments of officers made by the directors; and

(b) of all proceedings at meetings of the company, of the holders of any class of shares in the company, and of the directors, and of committees of directors, including the names of the directors present at each such meeting.

## THE SEAL

**101** The seal shall only be used by the authority of the directors or of a committee of directors authorised by the directors. The directors may determine who shall sign any instrument to which the seal is affixed and unless otherwise so determined it shall be signed by a director and by the secretary or by a second director.

## DIVIDENDS

**102** Subject to the provisions of the Act, the company may by ordinary resolution declare dividends in accordance with the respective rights of the members, but no dividend shall exceed the amount recommended by the directors.

**103** Subject to the provisions of the Act, the directors may pay interim dividends if it appears to them that they are justified by the profits of the company available for distribution. If the share capital is divided into different classes, the directors may pay interim dividends on shares which confer deferred or non-preferred rights with regard to dividend as well as on shares which confer preferential rights with regard to dividend, but no interim dividend shall be paid on shares carrying deferred or non-preferred rights if, at the time of payment, any preferential dividend is in arrear. The directors may also pay at intervals settled by them any dividend payable at a fixed rate if it appears to them that the profits available for distribution justify the payment. Provided the directors act in good faith they shall not incur any liability to the holders of shares conferring preferred rights for any loss they may suffer by the lawful payment of an interim dividend on any shares having deferred or non-preferred rights.

**104** Except as otherwise provided by the rights attached to shares, all dividends shall be declared and paid according to the amounts paid up on the shares on which the dividend is paid. All dividends shall be apportioned and paid proportionately to the amounts paid up on the shares during any portion or portions of the period in respect of which the dividend is paid; but, if any share is issued on terms providing that it shall rank for dividend as from a particular date, that share shall rank for dividend accordingly.

**105** A general meeting declaring a dividend may, upon the recommendation of the directors, direct that it shall be satisfied wholly or partly by the distribution of assets and, where any difficulty arises in regard to the distribution, the directors may settle the same and in particular may issue fractional certificates and fix the value for distribution of any assets and may determine that cash shall be paid to any member upon the footing of the value so fixed in order to adjust the rights of members and may vest any assets in trustees.

**106** Any dividend or other moneys payable in respect of a share may be paid by cheque sent by post to the registered address of the person entitled or, if two or more persons are the holders of the share or are jointly entitled to it by reason of the death or bankruptcy of the holder, to the registered address of that one of those persons who is first named in the register of members or to such person and to such address as the person or persons entitled may in writing direct. Every cheque shall be made payable to the order of the person or persons entitled or to such other person as the person or persons entitled may in writing direct and payment of the cheque shall be a good discharge to the company. Any joint holder or other person jointly entitled to a share as aforesaid may give receipts for any dividend or other moneys payable in respect of the share.

**107** No dividend or other moneys payable in respect of a share shall bear interest against the company unless otherwise provided by the rights attached to the share.

**108** Any dividend which has remained unclaimed for twelve years from the date when it became due for payment shall, if the directors so resolve, be forfeited and cease to remain owing by the company.

## ACCOUNTS

**109** No member shall (as such) have any right of inspecting any accounting records or other book or document of the company except as conferred by statute or authorised by the directors or by ordinary resolution of the company.

## CAPITALISATION OF PROFITS

**110** The directors may with the authority of an ordinary resolution of the company–

(a) subject as hereinafter provided, resolve to capitalise any undivided profits of the company not required for paying any preferential dividend (whether or not they are available for distribution) or any sum standing to the credit of the company's share premium account or capital redemption reserve;

(b) appropriate the sum resolved to be capitalised to the members who would have been entitled to it if it were distributed by way of dividend and in the same proportions and apply such sum on their behalf either in or towards paying up the amounts, if any, for the time being unpaid on any shares held by them respectively, or in paying up in full unissued shares or debentures of the company of a nominal amount equal to that sum, and allot the shares or debentures credited as fully paid to those members, or as they may direct, in those proportions, or partly in one way and partly in the other: but the share premium account, the capital redemption reserve, and any profits which are not available for distribution may, for the purposes of this regulation, only be applied in paying up unissued shares to be allotted to members credited as fully paid;

(c) make such provision by the issue of fractional certificates or by payment in cash or otherwise as they determine in the case of shares or debentures becoming distributable under this regulation in fractions; and

(d) authorise any person to enter on behalf of all the members concerned into an agreement with the company providing for the allotment to them respectively, credited as fully paid, of any shares or debentures to which they are entitled upon such capitalisation, any agreement made under such authority being binding on all such members.

## NOTICES

**111** Any notice to be given to or by any person pursuant to the articles shall be in writing except that a notice calling a meeting of the directors need not be in writing.

**112** The company may give any notice to a member either personally or by sending it by post in a prepaid envelope addressed to the member at his registered address or by leaving it at that address. In the case of joint holders of a share, all notices shall be given to the joint holder whose name stands first in the register of members in respect of the joint holding and notice so given shall be sufficient notice to all the joint holders. A member whose registered address is not within the United Kingdom and who gives to the company an address within the United Kingdom at which notices may be given to him shall be entitled to have notices given to him at that address, but otherwise no such member shall be entitled to receive any notice from the company.

**113** A member present, either in person or by proxy, at any meeting of the company or of the holders of any class of shares in the company shall be deemed to have received notice of the meeting and, where requisite, of the purposes for which it was called.

**114** Every person who becomes entitled to a share shall be bound by any notice in respect of that share which, before his name is entered in the register of members, has been duly given to a person from whom he derives his title.

**115** Proof that an envelope containing a notice was properly addressed, prepaid and posted shall be conclusive evidence that the notice was given. A notice shall be deemed to be given at the expiration of 48 hours after the envelope containing it was posted.

**History**

In reg. 115 the words "unless the contrary is proved" formerly appearing after "A notice shall" deleted by SI 1985/1052 as from 1 August 1985.

**116** A notice may be given by the company to the persons entitled to a share in consequence of the death or bankruptcy of a member by sending or delivering it, in any manner authorised by the articles for the giving of notice to a member, addressed to them by name, or by the title of representatives of the deceased, or trustee of the bankrupt or by any like description at the address, if any, within the United Kingdom supplied for that purpose by the persons claiming to be so entitled. Until such an address has been supplied, a notice may be given in any manner in which it might have been given if the death or bankruptcy had not occurred.

## WINDING UP

**117** If the company is wound up, the liquidator may, with the sanction of an extraordinary resolution of the company and any other sanction required by the Act, divide among the members in specie the whole or any part of the assets of the company and may, for that purpose, value any assets and determine how the division shall be carried out as between the members or different classes of members. The liquidator may, with the like sanction, vest the whole or any part of the assets in trustees upon such trusts for the benefit of the members as he with the like sanction determines, but no member shall be compelled to accept any assets upon which there is a liability.

## INDEMNITY

**118** Subject to the provisions of the Act but without prejudice to any indemnity to which a director may otherwise be entitled, every director or other officer or auditor of the company shall be indemnified out of the assets of the company against any liability incurred by him in defending any proceedings, whether civil or criminal, in which judgment is given in his favour or in which he is acquitted or in connection with any application in which relief is granted to him by the court from liability for negligence, default, breach of duty or breach of trust in relation to the affairs of the company.

**Note**

For text of former Table A (contained in First Sch. to former Companies Act 1948) see note at end of the Regulations.

# Table B – A Private Company Limited by Shares

## MEMORANDUM OF ASSOCIATION

**1** The company's name is "The South Wales Motor Transport Company cyfyngedig".

**2** The company's registered office is to be situated in Wales.

**3** The company's objects are the carriage of passengers and goods in motor vehicles between such places as the company may from time to time determine and the doing of all such other things as are incidental or conducive to the attainment of that object.

4 The liability of the members is limited.

5 The company's share capital is £50,000 divided into 50,000 shares of £1 each.

We, the subscribers to this memorandum of association, wish to be formed into a company pursuant to this memorandum; and we agree to take the number of shares shown opposite our respective names.

| Names and Addresses of Subscribers | Number of shares taken by each Subscriber |
|---|---|
| 1 Thomas Jones, 138 Mountfield Street, Tredegar. | 1 |
| 2 Mary Evans, 19 Merthyr Road, Aberystwyth. | 1 |
| Total shares taken | 2 |

Dated 19 .

Witness to the above signatures,
Anne Brown, "Woodlands",
Fieldside Road, Bryn Mawr.

# Table C – A Company Limited by Guarantee and not having a Share Capital

## MEMORANDUM OF ASSOCIATION

1 The company's name is "The Dundee School Association Limited".

2 The company's registered office is to be situated in Scotland.

3 The company's objects are the carrying on of a school for boys and girls in Dundee and the doing of all such other things as are incidental or conducive to the attainment of that object.

4 The liability of the members is limited.

5 Every member of the company undertakes to contribute such amount as may be required (not exceeding £100) to the company's assets if it should be wound up while he is a member or within one year after he ceases to be a member, for payment of the company's debts and liabilities contracted before he ceases to be a member, and of the costs, charges and expenses of winding up, and for the adjustment of the rights of the contributories among themselves.

We, the subscribers to this memorandum of association, wish to be formed into a company pursuant to this memorandum.

Names and Addresses of Subscribers.

1 Kenneth Brodie, 14 Bute Street, Dundee.

2 Ian Davis, 2 Burns Avenue, Dundee.

Dated 19 .

Witness to the above signatures,

Anne Brown, 149 Princes Street, Edinburgh.

## ARTICLES OF ASSOCIATION

### PRELIMINARY

1 Regulations 2 to 35 inclusive, 54, 55, 57, 59, 102 to 108 inclusive, 110, 114, 116 and 117 of Table A, shall not apply to the company but the articles hereinafter contained and, subject to the modifications hereinafter expressed, the remaining regulations of Table A shall constitute the articles of association of the company.

### INTERPRETATION

2 In regulation 1 of Table A, the definition of "the holder" shall be omitted.

### MEMBERS

3 The subscribers to the memorandum of association of the company and such other persons as are admitted to membership in accordance with the articles shall be members of the company. No person shall be admitted a member of the company unless he is approved by the directors. Every person who wishes to become a member shall deliver to the company an application for membership in such form as the directors require executed by him.

4 A member may at any time withdraw from the company by giving at least seven clear days' notice to the company. Membership shall not be transferable and shall cease on death.

### NOTICE OF GENERAL MEETINGS

5 In regulation 38 of Table A –

(a) in paragraph (b) the words "of the total voting rights at the meeting of all the members" shall be substituted for "in nominal value of the shares giving that right" and

(b) the words "The notice shall be given to all the members and to the directors and auditors" shall be substituted for the last sentence.

### PROCEEDINGS AT GENERAL MEETINGS

6 The words "and at any separate meeting of the holders of any class of shares in the company" shall be omitted from regulation 44 of Table A.

7 Paragraph (d) of regulation 46 of Table A shall be omitted.

### VOTES OF MEMBERS

8 On a show of hands every member present in person shall have one vote. On a poll every member present in person or by proxy shall have one vote.

### DIRECTORS' EXPENSES

9 The words "of any class of shares or" shall be omitted from regulation 83 of Table A.

### PROCEEDINGS OF DIRECTORS

10 In paragraph (c) of regulation 94 of Table A the word "debentures" shall be substituted for the words "shares, debentures or other securities" in both places where they occur.

### MINUTES

11 The words "of the holders of any class of shares in the company" shall be omitted from regulation 100 of Table A.

### NOTICES

12 The second sentence of regulation 112 of Table A shall be omitted.

13 The words "or of the holders of any class of shares in the company" shall be omitted from regulation 113 of Table A.

# Table D

## Part I – A Public Company Limited by Guarantee and having a Share Capital

### MEMORANDUM OF ASSOCIATION

1 The company's name is "Gwestai Glyndwr, cwmni cyfyngedig cyhoeddus".

2 The company is to be a public company.

3 The company's registered office is to be situated in Wales.

4 The company's objects are facilitating travelling in Wales by providing hotels and conveyances by sea and by land for the accommodation of travellers and the doing of all such other things as are incidental or conducive to the attainment of those objects.

5 The liability of the members is limited.

6 Every member of the company undertakes to contribute such amount as may be required (not exceeding £100) to the company's assets if it should be wound up while he is a member or within one year after he ceases to be a member, for payment of the company's debts and liabilities contracted before he ceases to be a member, and of the costs, charges and expenses of winding up, and for the adjustment of the rights of the contributories among themselves.

7 The company's share capital is £50,000 divided into 50,000 shares of £1 each.

We, the subscribers to this memorandum of association, wish to be formed into a company pursuant to this memorandum; and we agree to take the number of shares shown opposite our respective names.

| Names and Addresses of Subscribers | Number of shares taken by each Subscriber |
|---|---|
| 1 Thomas Jones, 138 Mountfield Street, Tredegar. | 1 |
| 2 Mary Evans, 19 Merthyr Road, Aberystwyth. | 1 |
| Total shares taken | 2 |

Dated 19 .

Witness to the above signatures,
Anne Brown, "Woodlands",
Fieldside Road, Bryn Mawr.

# Part II – A Private Company Limited by Guarantee and having a Share Capital

## MEMORANDUM OF ASSOCIATION

1 The company's name is "The Highland Hotel Company Limited".

2 The company's registered office is to be situated in Scotland.

3 The company's objects are facilitating travelling in the Highlands of Scotland by providing hotels and conveyances by sea and by land for the accommodation of travellers and the doing of all such other things as are incidental or conducive to the attainment of those objects.

4 The liability of the members is limited.

5 Every member of the company undertakes to contribute such amount as may be required (not exceeding £100) to the company's assets if it should be wound up while he is a member or within one year after he ceases to be a member, for payment of the company's debts and liabilities contracted before he ceases to be a member, and of the costs, charges and expenses of winding up, and for the adjustment of the rights of the contributories among themselves.

6 The company's share capital is £50,000 divided into 50,000 shares of £1 each.

We, the subscribers to this memorandum of association, wish to be formed into a company pursuant to this memorandum; and we agree to take the number of shares shown opposite our respective names.

| Names and Addresses of Subscribers | Number of shares taken by each Subscriber |
|---|---|
| Kenneth Brodie, 14 Bute Street, Dundee. | 1 |
| Ian Davis, 2 Burns Avenue, Dundee. | 1 |
| Total shares taken | 2 |

Dated 19 .

Witness to the above signatures,
Anne Brown, 149 Princes Street, Edinburgh.

# Part III – A Company (Public or Private) Limited by Guarantee and having a Share Capital

## ARTICLES OF ASSOCIATION

The regulations of Table A shall constitute the articles of association of the company.

# Table E – An Unlimited Company having a Share Capital

## MEMORANDUM OF ASSOCIATION

**1** The company's name is "The Woodford Engineering Company".

**2** The company's registered office is to be situated in England and Wales.

**3** The company's objects are the working of certain patented inventions relating to the application of microchip technology to the improvement of food processing, and the doing of all such other things as are incidental or conducive to the attainment of that object.

We, the subscribers to this memorandum of association, wish to be formed into a company pursuant to this memorandum; and we agree to take the number of shares shown opposite our respective names.

| Names and Addresses of Subscribers | Number of shares taken by each Subscriber |
|---|---|
| 1 Brian Smith, 24 Nibley Road, Wotton-under-Edge, Gloucestershire. | 3 |
| 2 William Green, 278 High Street, Chipping Sodbury, Avon. | 5 |
| Total shares taken | 8 |

Dated 19 .

Witness to the above signatures,
Anne Brown, 108 Park Way, Bristol 8.

## ARTICLES OF ASSOCIATION

**1** Regulations 3, 32, 34 and 35 of Table A shall not apply to the company, but the articles hereinafter contained and, subject to the modification hereinafter expressed, the remaining regulations of Table A shall constitute the articles of association of the company.

**2** The words "at least seven clear days' notice" shall be substituted for the words "at least fourteen clear days" notice in regulation 38 of Table A.

**3** The share capital of the company is £20,000 divided into 20,000 shares of £1 each.

**4** The company may by special resolution –

(a) increase the share capital by such sum to be divided into shares of such amount as the resolution may prescribe;
(b) consolidate and divide all or any of its share capital into shares of a larger amount than its existing shares;
(c) subdivide its shares, or any of them, into shares of a smaller amount than its existing shares;
(d) cancel any shares which at the date of the passing of the resolution have not been taken or agreed to be taken by any person;
(e) reduce its share capital and any share premium account in any way.

# Table F – A Public Company Limited by Shares

## MEMORANDUM OF ASSOCIATION

**1** The company's name is "Western Electronics Public Limited Company".

**2** The company is to be a public company.

**3** The company's registered office is to be situated in England and Wales.

**4** The company's objects are the manufacture and development of such descriptions of electronic equipment, instruments and appliances as the company may from time to time determine, and the doing of all such other things as are incidental or conducive to the attainment of that object.

**5** The liability of the members is limited.

**6** The company's share capital is £5,000,000 divided into 5,000,000 shares of £1 each.

We, the subscribers to this memorandum of association, wish to be formed into a company pursuant to this memorandum; and we agree to take the number of shares shown opposite our respective names.

| Names and Addresses of Subscribers | Number of shares taken by each Subscriber |
|---|---|
| 1 James White, 12 Broadmead, Birmingham. | 1 |
| 2 Patrick Smith, 145A Huntley House, London Wall, London EC2. | 1 |
| Total shares taken | 2 |

Dated 19 .

Witness to the above signatures,
Anne Brown, 13 Hute Street, London WC2.

## EXPLANATORY NOTE

*(This Note is not part of the Regulations)*

These Regulations replace the Companies (Alteration of Table A etc.) Regulations 1984 which are revoked. They provide the regulations (Table A) and the forms of memorandum and articles of association (Tables B, C, D, E and F) for the purposes of sections 3 and 8 of the Companies Act 1985.

Certain amendments have been made to Tables A and C. Table A has been amended as follows. The reference to "the Companies Act 1948 to 1983" has been converted to "the Companies Act 1985" and the references to "the Acts" to "the Act". In regulation 33, the words "subject to the provisions of the Act" have been inserted after the word "including" in the words in parenthesis. In regulation 65, the words "resolution of" have been inserted after "approved by". In regulation 87, "directors" replaces "company" as the second word of this regulation. In regulation 90, the words "the continuing directors or director" are substituted for the word "they". In regulation 111, in the first sentence the words "to or by any person" have been inserted after "given" and the words "except that a notice calling a meeting of the directors need not be in writing" after the word "writing". The remainder of the first sentence (with the deletion of the words "and" and "such") and the second sentence of regulation 111 are removed and become the first and second sentence of regulation 112. In regulation 116, the words "by them" have been deleted.

The following amendments have been made to the Articles of Association in Table C. In regulation 1, the word "inclusive" has been deleted in the third place where it appeared. In regulation 10, the words "in both places where they occur" have been substituted for the words "where they twice occur". Regulation 12 has been amended to refer to regulation 112 of Table A.

The Regulations will come into operation simultaneously with the coming into force of the Companies Act 1985.

**Note**

Reproduced below is the text of the former Table A (as amended, and contained in First Sch. to former Companies Act 1948). This table is included as it continues to be relevant for a large number of companies incorporated before 1 July 1985. See also CA 1985, s. 8.

**"COMPANIES ACT 1948, FIRST SCHEDULE, TABLE A**

Part I – Regulations for Management of a Company limited by Shares, not being a Private Company

INTERPRETATION

**1** In these regulations:–

**"the Act"** means the Companies Act, 1948.

**"the seal"** means the common seal of the company.

**"secretary"** means any person appointed to perform the duties of the secretary of the company.

**"the United Kingdom"** means Great Britain and Northern Ireland.

Expressions referring to writing shall, unless the contrary intention appears, be construed as including references to printing, lithography, photography, and other modes of representing or reproducing words in a visible form.

Unless the context otherwise requires, words or expressions contained in these regulations shall bear the same meaning as in the Act or any statutory modification thereof in force at the date at which these regulations become binding on the company.

SHARE CAPITAL AND VARIATION OF RIGHTS

**2** Without prejudice to any special rights previously conferred on the holders of any existing shares or class of shares, any share in the company may be issued with such preferred, deferred or other special rights or such restrictions, whether in regard to dividend, voting, return of capital or otherwise as the company may from time to time by ordinary resolution determine.

**3** Subject to the provisions of Part III of the Companies Act 1981, any shares may, with the sanction of an ordinary resolution, be issued on the terms that they are, or at the option of the company are liable, to be redeemed on such terms and in such manner as the company before the issue of the shares may by special resolution determine.

**4** If at any time the share capital is divided into different classes of shares, the rights attached to any class may, whether or not the company is being wound up, be varied with the consent in writing of the holders of three-fourths of the issued shares of that class, or with the sanction of an extraordinary resolution passed at a separate general meeting of the holders of the shares of the class.

**5** The rights conferred upon the holders of the shares of any class issued with preferred or other rights shall not, unless otherwise expressly provided by the terms of issue of the shares of that class, be deemed to be varied by the creation or issue of further shares ranking pari passu therewith.

**6** The company may exercise the powers of paying commissions conferred by section 53 of the Act, provided that the rate per cent or the amount of the commission paid or agreed to be paid shall be disclosed in the manner required by the said section and the rate of the commission shall not exceed the rate of 10 per cent of the price at which the shares in respect whereof the same is paid are issued or an amount equal to 10 per cent of such price (as the case may be). Such commission may be satisfied by the payment of cash or the allotment of fully or partly paid shares or partly in one way and partly in the other. The company may also on any issue of shares pay such brokerage as may be lawful.

**7** Except as required by law, no person shall be recognised by the company as holding any share upon any trust, and the company shall not be bound by or be compelled in any way to recognise (even when having notice thereof) any equitable, contingent, future or partial interest in any share or any interest in any fractional part of a share or (except only as by these regulations or by law otherwise provided) any other rights in respect of any share except an absolute right to the entirety thereof in the registered holder.

**8** Every person whose name is entered as a member in the register of members shall be entitled without payment to receive within two months after allotment or lodgment of transfer (or within such other period as the conditions of issue shall provide) one certificate for all his shares or several certificates each for one or more of his shares upon payment of 2s. 6d. for every certificate after the first or such less sum as the directors shall from time to time determine. Every certificate shall be under the seal or under the official seal kept by the company by virtue of section 2 of the Stock Exchange (Completion of Bargains) Act 1976 and shall specify the shares to which it relates and the amount paid up thereon. Provided that in respect of a share or shares held jointly by several persons the company shall not be bound to issue more than one certificate, and delivery of a certificate for a share to one of several joint holders shall be sufficient delivery to all such holders.

**9** If a share certificate be defaced, lost or destroyed, it may be renewed on payment of a fee of 2s. 6d. or such less sum and on such terms (if any) as to evidence and indemnity and the payment of out-of-pocket expenses of the company of investigating evidence as the directors think fit.

**10** (Repealed by Companies Act 1981, Sch. 4.)

LIEN

**11** The company shall have a first and paramount lien on every share (not being a fully paid share) for all moneys (whether presently payable or not) called or payable at a fixed time in respect of that share; but the directors may at any time declare any share to be wholly or in part exempt from the provisions of this regulation. The company's lien, if any, on a share shall extend to all dividends payable thereon.

**12** The company may sell, in such manner as the directors think fit, any shares on which the company has a lien, but no sale shall be made unless a sum in respect of which the lien exists is presently payable, nor until the expiration of fourteen days after a notice in writing, stating and demanding payment of such part of the amount in respect of which the lien exists as is presently payable, has been given to the registered holder for the time being of the share, or the person entitled thereto by reason of his death or bankruptcy.

**13** To give effect to any such sale the directors may authorise some person to transfer the shares sold to the purchaser thereof. The purchaser shall be registered as the holder of the shares comprised in any such transfer, and he shall not be bound to see to the application of the purchase money, nor shall his title to the shares be affected by any irregularity or invalidity in the proceedings in reference to the sale.

**14** The proceeds of the sale shall be received by the company and applied in payment of such part of the amount in respect of which the lien exists as is presently payable, and the residue, if any, shall (subject to a like lien for sums not presently payable as existed upon the shares before the sale) be paid to the person entitled to the shares at the date of the sale.

## CALLS ON SHARES

**15** The directors may from time to time make calls upon the members in respect of any moneys unpaid on their shares (whether on account of the nominal value of the shares or by way or premium) and not by the conditions of allotment thereof made payable at fixed times, provided that no call shall exceed one-fourth of the nominal value of the share or be payable at less than one month from the date fixed for the payment of the last preceding call, and each member shall (subject to receiving at least fourteen days' notice specifying the time or times and place of payment) pay to the company at the time or times and place so specified the amount called on his shares. A call may be revoked or postponed as the directors may determine.

**16** A call shall be deemed to have been made at the time when the resolution of the directors authorising the call was passed and may be required to be paid by instalments.

**17** The joint holders of a share shall be jointly and severally liable to pay all calls in respect thereof.

**18** If a sum called in respect of a share is not paid before or on the day appointed for payment thereof, the person from whom the sum is due shall pay interest on the sum from the day appointed for payment thereof to the time of actual payment at such rate not exceeding 5 per cent per annum as the directors may determine, but the directors shall be at liberty to waive payment of such interest wholly or in part.

**19** Any sum which by the terms of issue of a share becomes payable on allotment or at any fixed date, whether on account of the nominal value of the share or by way of premium, shall for the purposes of these regulations be deemed to be a call duly made and payable on the date on which by the terms of issue the same becomes payable, and in case of non-payment all the relevant provisions of these regulations as to payment of interest and expenses, forfeiture or otherwise shall apply as if such sum had become payable by virtue of a call duly made and notified.

**20** The directors may, on the issue of shares, differentiate between the holders as to the amount of calls to be paid and the times of payment.

**21** The directors may, if they think fit, receive from any member willing to advance the same, all or any part of the moneys uncalled and unpaid upon any shares held by him, and upon all or any of the moneys so advanced may (until the same would, but for such advance, become payable) pay interest at such rate not exceeding (unless the company in general meeting shall otherwise direct) 5 per cent per annum, as may be agreed upon between the directors and the member paying such sum in advance.

## TRANSFER OF SHARES

**22** The instrument of transfer of any share shall be executed by or on behalf of the transferor and transferee, and the transferor shall be deemed to remain a holder of the share until the name of the transferee is entered in the register of members in respect thereof.

**23** Subject to such of the restrictions of these regulations as may be applicable, any member may transfer all or any of his shares by instrument in writing in any usual or common form or any other form which the directors may approve.

**24** The directors may decline to register the transfer of a share (not being a fully paid share) to a person of whom they shall not approve, and they may also decline to register the transfer of a share on which the company has a lien.

**25** The directors may also decline to recognise any instrument of transfer unless:–

(a) fee of 2s. 6d. or such lesser sum as the directors may from time to time require is paid to the company in respect thereof;

(b) the instrument of transfer is accompanied by the certificate of the shares to which it relates, and such other evidence as the directors may reasonably require to show the right of the transferor to make the transfer; and

(c) the instrument of transfer is in respect of only one class of share.

**26** If the directors refuse to register a transfer they shall within two months after the date on which the transfer was lodged with the company send to the transferee notice of the refusal.

**27** The registration of transfers may be suspended at such times and for such periods as the directors may from time to time determine, provided always that such registration shall not be suspended for more than thirty days in any year.

**28** The company shall be entitled to charge a fee not exceeding 2s. 6d. on the registration of every probate, letters of administration, certificate of death or marriage, power of attorney, notice in lieu of distringas, or other instrument.

## TRANSMISSION OF SHARES

**29** In case of the death of a member the survivor or survivors where the deceased was a joint holder, and the legal personal representatives of the deceased where he was a sole holder, shall be the only persons recognised by the company as having any title to his interest in the shares; but nothing herein contained shall release the estate of a deceased joint holder from any liability in respect of any share which had been jointly held by him with other persons.

**30** Any person becoming entitled to a share in consequence of the death or bankruptcy of a member may, upon such evidence being produced as may from time to time properly be required by the directors and subject as hereinafter provided, elect either to be registered himself as holder of the share or to have some person nominated by him registered as the transferee thereof, but the directors shall, in either case, have the same right to decline or suspend registration as they would have had in the case of a transfer of the share by that member before his death or bankruptcy, as the case may be.

**31** If the person so becoming entitled shall elect to be registered himself, he shall deliver or send to the company a notice in writing signed by him stating that he so elects. If he shall elect to have another person registered he shall testify his election by executing to that person a transfer of the share. All the limitations, restrictions and provisions of these regulations relating to the right to transfer and the registration of transfers of shares shall be applicable to any such notice or transfer as aforesaid as if the death or bankruptcy of the member had not occurred and the notice or transfer were a transfer signed by that member.

**32** A person becoming entitled to a share by reason of the death or bankruptcy of the holder shall be entitled to the same dividends and other advantages to which he would be entitled if he were the registered holder of the share, except that he shall not, before being registered as a member in respect of the share, be entitled in respect of it to exercise any right conferred by membership in relation to meetings of the company:

Provided always that the directors may at any time give notice requiring any such person to elect either to be registered himself or to transfer the share, and if the notice is not complied with within ninety days the directors may thereafter withhold payment of all dividends, bonuses or other moneys payable in respect of the share until the requirements of the notice have been complied with.

## FORFEITURE OF SHARES

**33** If a member fails to pay any call or instalment of a call on the day appointed for payment thereof, the directors may, at any time thereafter during such time as any part of the call or instalment remains unpaid, serve a notice on him requiring payment of so much of the call or instalment as is unpaid, together with any interest which may have accrued.

**34** The notice shall name a further day (not earlier than the expiration of fourteen days from the date of service of the notice) on or before which the payment required by the notice is to be made, and shall state that in the event of non-payment at or before the time appointed the shares in respect of which the call was made will be liable to be forfeited.

**35** If the requirements of any such notice as aforesaid are not complied with, any share in respect of which the notice has been given may at any time thereafter, before the payment required by the notice has been made, be forfeited by a resolution of the directors to that effect.

**36** A forfeited share may be sold or otherwise disposed of on such terms and in such manner as the directors think fit, and at any time before a sale or disposition the forfeiture may be cancelled on such terms as the directors think fit.

**37** A person whose shares have been forfeited shall cease to be a member in respect of the forfeited shares, but shall, notwithstanding, remain liable to pay to the company all moneys which, at the date of forfeiture, were payable by him to the company in respect of the shares, but his liability shall cease if and when the company shall have received payment in full of all such moneys in respect of the shares.

**38** A statutory declaration in writing that the declarant is a director or the secretary of the company, and that a share in the company has been duly forfeited on a date stated in the declaration, shall be conclusive evidence of the facts therein stated as against all persons claiming to be entitled to the share. The company may receive the consideration, if any, given for the share on any sale or disposition thereof and may execute a transfer of the share in favour of the person to whom the share is sold or disposed of and he shall thereupon be registered as the holder of the share, and shall not be bound to see to the application of the purchase money, if any, nor shall his title to the share be affected by any irregularity or invalidity in the proceedings in reference to the forfeiture, sale or disposal of the share.

**39** The provisions of these regulations as to forfeiture shall apply in the case of non-payment of any sum which, by the terms of issue of a share, becomes payable at a fixed time, whether on account of the nominal value of the share or by way of premium, as if the same had been payable by virtue of a call duly made and notified.

## CONVERSION OF SHARES INTO STOCK

**40** The company may by ordinary resolution convert any paid-up shares into stock, and reconvert any stock into paid-up shares of any denomination.

**41** The holders of stock may transfer the same, or any part thereof, in the same manner, and subject to the same regulations, as and subject to which the shares from which the stock arose might previously to conversion have been transferred, or as near thereto as circumstances admit; and the directors may from time to time fix the minimum amount of stock transferable but so that such minimum shall not exceed the nominal amount of the shares from which the stock arose.

**42** The holders of stock shall, according to the amount of stock held by them, have the same rights, privileges and advantages as regards dividends, voting at meetings of the company and other matters as if they held the shares from which the stock arose, but no such privilege or advantage (except participation in the dividends and profits of the company and in the assets on winding up) shall be conferred by an amount of stock which would not, if existing in shares, have conferred that privilege or advantage.

**43** Such of the regulations of the company as are applicable to paid-up shares shall apply to stock, and the words "share" and "shareholder" therein shall include "stock" and "stockholder".

## ALTERATION OF CAPITAL

**44** The company may from time to time by ordinary resolution increase the share capital by such sum, to be divided into shares of such amount, as the resolution shall prescribe.

**45** The company may by ordinary resolution–

(a) consolidate and divide all or any of its share capital into shares of larger amount than its existing shares;

(b) sub-divide its existing shares, or any of them, into shares of smaller amount than is fixed by the memorandum of association subject, nevertheless, to the provisions of section 61(1)(d) of the Act;

(c) cancel any shares which, at the date of the passing of the resolution, have not been taken or agreed to be taken by any person.

**46** The company may by special resolution reduce its share capital, any capital redemption reserve fund or any share premium account in any manner and with, and subject to, any incident authorised, and consent required, by law.

## GENERAL MEETINGS

**47** The company shall in each year hold a general meeting as its annual general meeting in addition to any other meetings in that year, and shall specify the meeting as such in the notices calling it; and not more than fifteen months shall elapse between the date of one annual general meeting of the company and that of the next. Provided that so long as the company holds its first annual general meeting within eighteen months of its incorporation, it need not hold it in the year of its incorporation, or in the following year. The annual general meeting shall be held at such time and place as the directors shall appoint.

**48** All general meetings other than annual general meetings shall be called extraordinary general meetings.

**49** The directors may, whenever they think fit, convene an extraordinary general meeting, and extraordinary general meetings shall also be convened on such requisition, or, in default, may be convened by such requisitionists, as provided by section 132 of the Act. If at any time there are not within the United Kingdom sufficient directors capable of acting to form a quorum, any director or any two members of the company may convene an extraordinary general meeting in the same manner as nearly as possible as that in which meetings may be convened by the directors.

## NOTICE OF GENERAL MEETINGS

**50** An annual general meeting and a meeting called for the passing of a special resolution shall be called by twenty-one days' notice in writing at the least, and a meeting of the company other than an annual general meeting or a meeting for the passing of a special resolution shall be called by fourteen days' notice in writing at the least. The notice shall be exclusive of the day on which it is served or deemed to be served and of the day for which it is given, and shall specify the place, the day and the hour of meeting and, in the case of special business, the general nature of that business, and shall be given, in manner hereinafter mentioned or in such other manner, if any, as may be prescribed by the company in general meeting, to such persons as are, under the regulations of the company, entitled to receive such notices from the company: Provided that a meeting of the company shall, notwithstanding that it is called by shorter notice than that specified in this regulation, be deemed to have been duly called if it is so agreed–

(a) in the case of a meeting called as the annual general meeting, by all the members entitled to attend and vote thereat; and

(b) in the case of any other meeting, by majority in number of the members having a right to attend and vote at the meeting, being a majority together holding not less than 95 per cent in nominal value of the shares giving that right.

**51** The accidental omission to give notice of a meeting to, or the non-receipt of notice of a meeting by, any person entitled to receive notice shall not invalidate the proceedings at that meeting.

## PROCEEDINGS AT GENERAL MEETINGS

**52** All business shall be deemed special that is transacted at an extraordinary general meeting, and also all that is transacted at an annual general meeting, with the exception of declaring a dividend, the consideration of the accounts, balance sheets, and the reports of the directors and auditors, the election of directors in the place of those retiring and the appointment of, and the fixing of the remuneration of, the auditors.

**53** No business shall be transacted at any general meeting unless a quorum of members is present at the time when the meeting proceeds to business; save as herein otherwise provided, two members present in person or by proxy shall be a quorum.

**54** If within half an hour from the time appointed for the meeting a quorum is not present, the meeting, if convened upon the requisition of members, shall be dissolved; in any other case it shall stand adjourned to the same day in the next week, at the same time and place or to such other day and at such other time and place as the directors may determine.

**55** The chairman, if any, of the board of directors shall preside as chairman at every general meeting of the company, or if there is no such chairman, or if he shall not be present within fifteen minutes after the time appointed for the holding of the meeting or is unwilling to act the directors present shall elect one of their number to be chairman of the meeting.

**56** If at any meeting no director is willing to act as chairman or if no director is present within fifteen minutes after the time appointed for holding the meeting, the members present shall choose one of their number to be chairman of the meeting.

**57** The chairman may, with the consent of any meeting at which a quorum is present (and shall if so directed by the meeting), adjourn the meeting from time to time and from place to place, but no business shall be transacted at any adjourned meeting other than the business left unfinished at the meeting from which the adjournment took place. When a meeting is adjourned for thirty days or more, notice of the adjourned meeting shall be given as in the case of an original meeting. Save as aforesaid it shall not be necessary to give any notice of an adjournment or of the business to be transacted at an adjourned meeting.

**58** At any general meeting a resolution put to the vote of the meeting shall be decided on a show of hands unless a poll is (before or on the declaration of the result of the show of hands) demanded–

(a) by the chairman; or

(b) by at least two members present in person or by proxy; or

(c) by any member or members present in person or by proxy and representing not less than one-tenth of the total voting rights of all the members having the right to vote at the meeting; or

(d) by a member or members holding shares in the company conferring a right to vote at the meeting being shares on which an aggregate sum has been paid up equal to not less than one-tenth of the total sum paid up on all the shares conferring that right.

Unless a poll be so demanded a declaration by the chairman that a resolution has on a show of hands been carried or carried unanimously, or by a particular majority, or lost and an entry to that effect in the book containing the minutes of the proceedings of the company shall be conclusive evidence of the fact without proof of the number or proportion of the votes recorded in favour of or against such resolution.

The demand for a poll may be withdrawn.

**59** Except as provided in regulation 61, if a poll is duly demanded it shall be taken in such manner as the chairman directs, and the result of the poll shall be deemed to be the resolution of the meeting at which the poll was demanded.

**60** In the case of an equality of votes, whether on a show of hands or on a poll, the chairman of the meeting at which the show of hands takes place or at which the poll is demanded, shall be entitled to a second or casting vote.

**61** A poll demanded on the election of a chairman or on a question of adjournment shall be taken forthwith. A poll demanded on any other question shall be taken at such time as the chairman of the meeting directs, and any business other than that upon which a poll has been demanded may be proceeded with pending the taking of the poll.

## VOTES OF MEMBERS

**62** Subject to any rights or restrictions for the time being attached to any class or classes of shares, on a show of hands every member present in person shall have one vote, and on a poll every member shall have one vote for each share of which he is the holder.

**63** In the case of joint holders the vote of the senior who tenders a vote, whether in person or by proxy, shall be accepted to the exclusion of the votes of the other joint holders; and for this purpose seniority shall be determined by the order in which the names stand in the register of members.

**64** A member of unsound mind, or in respect of whom an order has been made by any court having jurisdiction in lunacy, may vote, whether on a show of hands or on a poll, by his committee, receiver, curator bonis, or other person in the nature of a committee, receiver or curator bonis appointed by that court, and any such committee, receiver, curator bonis or other person may, on a poll, vote by proxy.

**65** No member shall be entitled to vote at any general meeting unless all calls or other sums presently payable by him in respect of shares in the company have been paid.

**66** No objection shall be raised to the qualification of any voter except at the meeting or adjourned meeting at which the vote objected to is given or tendered, and every vote not disallowed at such meeting shall be valid for all purposes. Any such objection made in due time shall be referred to the chairman of the meeting, whose decision shall be final and conclusive.

**67** On a poll votes may be given either personally or by proxy.

**68** The instrument appointing a proxy shall be in writing under the hand of the appointer or of his attorney duly authorised in writing, or, if the appointer is a corporation, either under seal, or under the hand of an officer or attorney duly authorised. A proxy need not be a member of the company.

**69** The instrument appointing a proxy and the power of attorney or other authority, if any, under which it is signed or a notarially certified copy of that power or authority shall be deposited at the registered office of the company or at such other place within the United Kingdom as is specified for that purpose in the notice convening the meeting, not less than 48 hours before the time for holding the meeting or adjourned meeting, at which the person named in the instrument proposes to vote, or, in the case of a poll, not less than 24 hours before the time appointed for the taking of the poll, and in default the instrument of proxy shall not be treated as valid.

**70** An instrument appointing a proxy shall be in the following form or a form as near thereto as circumstances admit–

" Limited

I/We , of , in the county of , being a member/members of the above-named company, hereby appoint of , or failing him, of , as my/our proxy to vote for me/us on my/our behalf at the [annual or extraordinary, as the case may be] general meeting of the company to be held on the day of 19 , and at any adjournment thereof.

Signed this day of 19 ."

**71** Where it is desired to afford members an opportunity of voting for or against a resolution the instrument appointing a proxy shall be in the following form or a form as near thereto as circumstances admit–

" Limited

I/We , of , in the county of , being a member/members of the above-named company, hereby appoint of , or failing him, of , as my/our proxy to vote for me/us on my/our behalf at the [annual or extraordinary, as the case may be] general meeting of the company to be held on the day of 19 , and at any adjournment thereof.

Signed this day of 19 .

This form is to be used *in favour of / against the resolution.

Unless otherwise instructed the proxy will vote as he thinks fit.

*Strike out whichever is not desired."

**72** The instrument appointing a proxy shall be deemed to confer authority to demand or join in demanding a poll.

**73** A vote given in accordance with the terms of an instrument of proxy shall be valid notwithstanding the previous death or insanity of the principal or revocation of the proxy or of the authority under which the proxy was executed, or the transfer of the share in respect of which the proxy is given, provided that no intimation in writing of such death, insanity, revocation or transfer as aforesaid shall have been received by the company at the office before the commencement of the meeting or adjourned meeting at which the proxy is used.

**73A** Subject to the provisions of the Companies Acts 1948 to 1981, a resolution in writing signed by all the members for the time being entitled to receive notice of and to attend and vote at general meetings (or being corporations by their duly authorised representatives) shall be as valid and effective as if the same had been passed at a general meeting of the company duly convened and held.

### CORPORATIONS ACTING BY REPRESENTATIVES AT MEETINGS

**74** Any corporation which is a member of the company may by resolution of its directors or other governing body authorise such person as it thinks fit to act as its representative at any meeting of the company or of any class of members of the company, and the person so authorised shall be entitled to exercise the same powers on behalf of the corporation which he represents as that corporation could exercise if it were an individual member of the company.

### DIRECTORS

**75** The number of the directors and the names of the first directors shall be determined in writing by the subscribers of the memorandum of association or a majority of them.

**76** The remuneration of the directors shall from time to time be determined by the company in general meeting. Such remuneration shall be deemed to accrue from day to day. The directors may also be paid all travelling, hotel and other expenses properly incurred by them in attending and returning from meetings of the directors or any committee of the directors or general meetings of the company or in connection with the business of the company.

**77** The shareholding qualification for directors may be fixed by the company in general meeting, and unless and until so fixed no qualification shall be required.

**78** A director of the company may be or become a director or other officer of, or otherwise interested in, any company promoted by the company or in which the company may be interested as shareholder or otherwise, and no such director shall be accountable to the company for any remuneration or other benefits received by him as a director or officer of, or from his interest in, such other company unless the company otherwise direct.

### BORROWING POWERS

**79** The directors may exercise all the powers of the company to borrow money, and to mortgage or charge its undertaking, property and uncalled capital, or any part thereof, and subject to section 14 of the Companies Act 1980 to issue debentures, debenture stock, and other securities whether outright or as security for any debt, liability or obligation of the company or of any third party:

Provided that the amount for the time being remaining undischarged of moneys borrowed or secured by the directors as aforesaid (apart from temporary loans obtained from the company's bankers in the ordinary course of business) shall not at any time, without the previous sanction of the company in general meeting, exceed the nominal amount of the share capital of the company for the time being issued, but nevertheless no lender or other person dealing with the company shall be concerned to see or inquire whether this limit is observed. No debt incurred or security given in excess of such limit shall be invalid or ineffectual except in the case of express notice to the lender or the recipient of the security at the time when the debt was incurred or security given that the limit hereby imposed had been or was thereby exceeded.

### POWERS AND DUTIES OF DIRECTORS

**80** The business of the company shall be managed by the directors, who may pay all expenses incurred in promoting and registering the company, and may exercise all such powers of the company as are not, by the Companies Acts 1948 to 1981 or by these regulations, required to be exercised by the company in general meeting, subject, nevertheless, to any of these regulations, to the provisions of the Companies Acts 1948 to 1981 and to such regulations, being not inconsistent with the aforesaid regulations or provisions, as may be prescribed by the company in general meeting; but no regulation made by the company in general meeting shall invalidate any prior act of the directors which would have been valid if that regulation had not been made.

**81** The directors may from time to time and at any time by power of attorney appoint any company, firm or person or body of persons, whether nominated directly or indirectly by the directors, to be the attorney or attorneys of the company for such purposes and with such powers, authorities and discretions (not exceeding those vested in or exercisable by the directors under these regulations) and for such period and subject to such conditions as they may think fit, and any such powers of attorney may contain such provisions for the protection and convenience of persons dealing with any such attorney as the directors may think fit and may also authorise any such attorney to delegate all or any of the powers, authorities and discretions vested in him.

**82** The company may exercise the powers conferred by section 35 of the Act with regard to having an official seal for use abroad, and such powers shall be vested in the directors.

**83** The company may exercise the powers conferred upon the company by sections 119 to 123 (both inclusive) of the Act with regard to the keeping of a dominion register, and the directors may (subject to the provisions of those sections) make and vary such regulations as they may think fit respecting the keeping of any such register.

**84(1)** A director who is in any way, whether directly or indirectly, interested in a contract or proposed contract with the company shall declare the nature of his interest at a meeting of the directors in accordance with section 199 of the Act.

**84(2)** A director shall not vote in respect of any contract or arrangement in which he is interested, and if he shall do so his vote shall not be counted, nor shall he be counted in the quorum present at the meeting, but neither of these prohibitions shall apply to–

(a) any arrangement for giving any director any security or indemnity in respect of money lent by him to or obligations undertaken by him for the benefit of the company; or

(b) to any arrangement for the giving by the company of any security to a third party in respect of a debt or obligation of the company for which the director himself has assumed responsibility in whole or in part under a guarantee or indemnity or by the deposit of a security; or

(c) any contract by a director to subscribe for or underwrite shares or debentures of the company; or

(d) any contract or arrangement with any other company in which he is interested only as an officer of the company or as holder of shares or other securities;

and these prohibitions may at any time be suspended or relaxed to any extent, and either generally or in respect of any particular contract, arrangement or transaction, by the company in general meeting.

**84(3)** A director may hold any other office or place of profit under the company (other than the office of auditor) in conjunction with his office of director for such period and on such terms (as to remuneration and otherwise) as the directors may determine and no director or intending director shall be disqualified by his office from contracting with the company either with regard to his tenure of any such other office or place of profit or as vendor, purchaser or otherwise, nor shall any such contract, or any contract or arrangement entered into by or on behalf of the company in which any director is in any way interested, be liable to be avoided, nor shall any director so contracting or being so interested be liable to account to the company for any profit realised by any such contract or arrangement by reason of such director holding that office or of the fiduciary relation thereby established.

**84(4)** A director, notwithstanding his interest, may be counted in the quorum present at any meeting whereat he or any other director is appointed to hold any such office or place of profit under the company or whereat the terms of any such appointment are arranged, and he may vote on any such appointment or arrangement other than his own appointment or the arrangement of the terms thereof.

**84(5)** Any director may act by himself or his firm in a professional capacity for the company, and he or his firm shall be entitled to remuneration for professional services as if he were not a director; provided that nothing herein contained shall authorise a director or his firm to act as auditor to the company.

**85** All cheques, promissory notes, drafts, bills of exchange and other negotiable instruments, and all receipts for moneys paid to the company, shall be signed, drawn, accepted, endorsed, or otherwise executed, as the case may be, in such manner as the directors shall from time to time by resolution determine.

**86** The directors shall cause minutes to be made in books provided for the purpose–

(a) of all appointments of officers made by the directors;

(b) of the names of the directors present at each meeting of the directors and of any committee of the directors;

(c) of all resolutions and proceedings at all meetings of the company, and of the directors, and of committees of directors;

and every director present at any meeting of directors or committee of directors shall sign his name in a book to be kept for that purpose.

**87** The directors on behalf of the company may pay a gratuity or pension or allowance on retirement to any director who has held any other salaried office or place of profit with the company or to his widow or dependants and may make contributions to any fund and pay premiums for the purchase or provision of any such gratuity, pension or allowance.

## DISQUALIFICATION OF DIRECTORS

**88** The office of director shall be vacated if the director–

(a) ceases to be a director by virtue of section 182 or 185 of the Act; or

(b) becomes bankrupt or makes any arrangement or composition with his creditors generally; or

(c) becomes prohibited from being a director by reason of any order made under section 188 of the Act; or

(d) becomes of unsound mind; or

(e) resigns his office by notice in writing to the company; or

(f) shall for more than six months have been absent without permission of the directors from meetings of the directors held during that period.

## ROTATION OF DIRECTORS

**89** At the first annual general meeting of the company all the directors shall retire from office, and at the annual general meeting in every subsequent year one-third of the directors for the time being, or, if their number is not three or a multiple of three, then the number nearest one-third, shall retire from office.

**90** The directors to retire in every year shall be those who have been longest in office since their last election, but as between persons who become directors on the same day those to retire shall (unless they otherwise agree among themselves) be determined by lot.

**91** A retiring director shall be eligible for re-election.

**92** The company at the meeting at which a director retires in manner aforesaid may fill the vacated office by electing a person thereto, and in default the retiring director shall if offering himself for re-election be deemed to have been re-elected, unless at such meeting it is expressly resolved not to fill such vacated office or unless a resolution for the re-election of such director shall have been put to the meeting and lost.

**93** No person other than a director retiring at the meeting shall unless recommended by the directors be eligible for election to the office of director at any general meeting unless not less than three nor more than twenty-one days before the date appointed for the meeting there shall have been left at the registered office of the company notice in writing, signed by a member duly qualified to attend and vote at the meeting for which such notice is given, of his intention to propose such person for election, and also notice in writing signed by that person of his willingness to be elected.

**94** The company may from time to time by ordinary resolution increase or reduce the number of directors, and may also determine in what rotation the increased or reduced number is to go out of office.

**95** The directors shall have power at any time, and from time to time, to appoint any person to be a director, either to fill a casual vacancy or as an addition to the existing directors, but so that the total number of directors shall not at any time exceed the number fixed in accordance with these regulations. Any director so appointed shall hold office only until the next following annual general meeting, and shall then be eligible for re-election but shall not be taken into account in determining the directors who are to retire by rotation at such meeting.

**96** The company may by ordinary resolution, of which special notice has been given in accordance with section 142 of the Act, remove any director before the expiration of his period of office notwithstanding anything in these regulations or in any agreement between the company and such director. Such removal shall be without prejudice to any claim such director may have for damages for breach of any contract of service between him and the company.

**97** The company may by ordinary resolution appoint another person in place of a director removed from office under the immediately preceding regulation, and without prejudice to the powers of the directors under regulation 95 the company in general meeting may appoint any person to be a director either to fill a casual vacancy or as an additional director. A person appointed in place of a director so removed or to fill such a vacancy shall be subject to retirement at the same time as if he had become a director on the day on which the director in whose place he is appointed was last elected a director.

## PROCEEDINGS OF DIRECTORS

**98** The directors may meet together for the despatch of business, adjourn, and otherwise regulate their meetings, as they think fit. Questions arising at any meeting shall be decided by a majority of votes. In case of an equality of votes, the chairman shall have a second or casting vote. A director may, and the secretary on the requisition of a director shall, at any time summon a meeting of the directors. It shall not be necessary to give notice of a meeting of directors to any director for the time being absent from the United Kingdom.

**99** The quorum necessary for the transaction of the business of the directors may be fixed by the directors, and unless so fixed shall be two.

**100** The continuing directors may act notwithstanding any vacancy in their body, but, if and so long as their number is reduced below the number fixed by or pursuant to the regulations of the company as the necessary quorum of directors, the continuing directors or director may act for the purpose of increasing the number of directors to that number, or of summoning a general meeting of the company, but for no other purpose.

**101** The directors may elect a chairman of their meetings and determine the period for which he is to hold office; but if no such chairman is elected, or if at any meeting the chairman is not present within five minutes after the time appointed for holding the same, the directors present may choose one of their number to be chairman of the meeting.

**102** The directors may delegate any of their powers to committees consisting of such member or members of their body as they think fit; any committee so formed shall in the exercise of the powers so delegated conform to any regulations that may be imposed on it by the directors.

**103** A committee may elect a chairman of its meetings; if no such chairman is elected, or if at any meeting the chairman is not present within five minutes after the time appointed for holding the same, the members present may choose one of their number to be chairman of the meeting.

**104** A committee may meet and adjourn as it thinks proper. Questions arising at any meeting shall be determined by a majority of votes of the members present, and in the case of an equality of votes the chairman shall have a second or casting vote.

**105** All acts done by any meeting of the directors or of a committee of directors or by any person acting as a director shall, notwithstanding that it be afterwards discovered that there was some defect in the appointment of any such director or person acting as aforesaid, or that they or any of them were disqualified, be as valid as if every such person had been duly appointed and was qualified to be a director.

**106** A resolution in writing, signed by all the directors for the time being entitled to receive notice of a meeting of the directors, shall be as valid and effectual as if it had been passed at a meeting of the directors duly convened and held.

## MANAGING DIRECTOR

**107** The directors may from time to time appoint one or more of their body to the office of managing director for such period and on such terms as they think fit, and, subject to the terms of any agreement entered into in any particular case, may revoke such appointment. A director so appointed shall not, whilst holding that office, be subject to retirement by rotation or be taken into account in determining the rotation of retirement of directors, but his appointment shall be automatically determined if he cease from any cause to be a director.

**108** A managing director shall receive such remuneration (whether by way of salary, commission or participation in profits, or partly in one way and partly in another) as the directors may determine.

**109** The directors may entrust to and confer upon a managing director any of the powers exercisable by them upon such terms and conditions and with such restrictions as they may think fit, and either collaterally with or to the exclusion of their own powers and may from time to time revoke, withdraw, alter or vary all or any of such powers.

## SECRETARY

**110** Subject to section 21(5) of the Companies Act 1976 the secretary shall be appointed by the directors for such term, at such remuneration and upon such conditions as they may think fit; and any secretary so appointed may be removed by them.

**111** No person shall be appointed or hold office as secretary who is–

(a) the sole director of the company; or
(b) a corporation the sole director of which is the sole director of the company; or
(c) the sole director of a corporation which is the sole director of the company.

**112** A provision of the Act or these regulations requiring or authorising a thing to be done by or to a director and the secretary shall not be satisfied by its being done by or to the same person acting both as director and as, or in place of, the secretary.

## THE SEAL

**113** The directors shall provide for the safe custody of the seal, which shall only be used by the authority of the directors or of a committee of the directors authorised by the directors in that behalf, and every instrument to which the seal shall be affixed shall be signed by a director and shall be countersigned by the secretary or by a second director or by some other person appointed by the directors for the purpose.

## DIVIDENDS AND RESERVE

**114** The company in general meeting may declare dividends, but no dividend shall exceed the amount recommended by the directors.

**115** The directors may from time to time pay to the members such interim dividends as appear to the directors to be justified by the profits of the company.
**116** No dividend or interim dividend shall be paid otherwise than in accordance with the provisions of Part III of the Companies Act 1980 which apply to the company.
**117** The directors may, before recommending any dividend, set aside out of the profits of the company such sums as they think proper as a reserve or reserves which shall, at the discretion of the directors, be applicable for any purpose to which the profits of the company may be properly applied, and pending such application may, at the like discretion, either be employed in the business of the company or be invested in such investments (other than shares of the company) as the directors may from time to time think fit. The directors may also without placing the same to reserve carry forward any profits which they may think prudent not to divide.
**118** Subject to the rights of persons, if any, entitled to shares with special rights as to dividend, all dividends shall be declared and paid according to the amounts paid or credited as paid on the shares in respect whereof the dividend is paid, but no amount paid or credited as paid on a share in advance of calls shall be treated for the purposes of this regulation as paid on the share. All dividends shall be apportioned and paid proportionately to the amounts paid or credited as paid on the shares during any portion or portions of the period in respect of which the dividend is paid; but if any share is issued on terms providing that it shall rank for dividend as from a particular date such share shall rank for dividend accordingly.
**119** The directors may deduct from any dividend payable to any member all sums of money (if any) presently payable by him to the company on account of calls or otherwise in relation to the shares of the company.
**120** Any general meeting declaring a dividend or bonus may direct payment of such dividend or bonus wholly or partly by the distribution of specific assets and in particular of paid up shares, debentures or debenture stock of any other company or in any one or more of such ways, and the directors shall give effect to such resolution, and where any difficulty arises in regard to such distribution, the directors may settle the same as they think expedient, and in particular may issue fractional certificates and fix the value for distribution of such specific assets or any part thereof and may determine that cash payments shall be made to any members upon the footing of the value so fixed in order to adjust the rights of all parties, and may vest any such specific assets in trustees as may seem expedient to the directors.
**121** Any dividend, interest or other moneys payable in cash in respect of shares may be paid by cheque or warrant sent through the post directed to the registered address of the holder or, in the case of joint holders, to the registered address of that one of the joint holders who is first named on the register of members or to such person and to such address as the holder or joint holders may in writing direct. Every such cheque or warrant shall be made payable to the order of the person to whom it is sent. Any one of two or more joint holders may give effectual receipts for any dividends, bonuses or other moneys payable in respect of the shares held by them as joint holders.
**122** No dividend shall bear interest against the company.

## ACCOUNTS

**123** The directors shall cause accounting records to be kept in accordance with section 12 of the Companies Act 1976.
**124** The accounting records shall be kept at the registered office of the company or, subject to section 12(6) and (7) of the Companies Act 1976, at such other place or places as the directors think fit, and shall always be open to the inspection of the officers of the company.
**125** The directors shall from time to time determine whether and to what extent and at what times and places and under what conditions or regulations the accounts and books of the company or any of them shall be open to the inspection of members not being directors, and no member (not being a director) shall have any right of inspecting any account or book or document of the company except as conferred by statute or authorised by the directors or by the company in general meeting.
**126** The directors shall from time to time, in accordance with sections 150 and 157 of the Act and sections 1, 6 and 7 of the Companies Act 1976, cause to be prepared and to be laid before the company in general meeting such profit and loss accounts, balance sheets, group accounts (if any) and reports as are referred to in those sections.
**127** A copy of every balance sheet (including every document required by law to be annexed thereto) which is to be laid before the company in general meeting, together with a copy of the auditors' report and directors' report, shall not less than twenty-one days before the date of the meeting be sent to every member of, and every holder of debentures of, the company and to every person registered under regulation 31. Provided that this regulation shall not require a copy of those documents to be sent to any person of whose address the company is not aware or to more than one of the joint holders of any shares or debentures.

## CAPITALISATION OF PROFITS

**128** The company in general meeting may upon the recommendation of the directors resolve that it is desirable to capitalise any part of the amount for the time being standing to the credit of any of the company's reserve accounts or to the credit of the profit and loss account or otherwise available for distribution, and accordingly that such sum be set free for distribution amongst the members who would have been entitled thereto if distributed by way of dividend and in the same proportions on condition that the same be not paid in cash but be applied either in or towards paying up any amounts for the time being unpaid on any shares held by such members respectively or paying up in full unissued shares or debentures of the company to be allotted and distributed credited as fully paid up to and amongst such members in the proportion aforesaid, or partly in the one way and partly in the other, and the directors shall give effect to such resolution:
Provided that a share premium account and a capital redemption reserve fund may, for the purposes of this regulation, only be applied in the paying up of unissued shares to be allotted to members of the company as fully paid bonus shares.
**128A** The company in general meeting may on the recommendation of the directors resolve that it is desirable to capitalise any part of the amount for the time being standing to the credit of any of the company's reserve accounts or to the credit of the profit and loss account which is not available for distribution by applying such sum in paying up in full unissued shares to be allotted as fully paid bonus shares to those members of the company who would have been entitled to that sum if it were distributed by way of dividend (and in the same proportions), and the directors shall give effect to such resolution.
**129** Whenever a resolution is passed in pursuance of regulation 128 or 128A above the directors shall make all appropriations and applications of the undivided profits resolved to be capitalised thereby, and all allotments and issues of fully-paid shares or debentures, if any, and generally shall do all acts and things required to give effect thereto, with full power to the directors to make such provision by the issue of fractional certificates or by payment in cash or otherwise as they think fit for the case of shares or debentures becoming distributable in fractions, and also to authorise any person to enter on behalf of all the members entitled thereto into an agreement with the company providing for the allotment to them respectively, credited as fully paid up, of any further shares or debentures to which they may be entitled upon such capitalisation, or (as the case may require) for the payment up by the company on their behalf, by the application thereto of their respective proportions of the profits resolved to be capitalised, of the amounts or any part of the amounts

remaining unpaid on their existing shares, and any agreement made under such authority shall be effective and binding on all such members.

AUDIT

**130** Auditors shall be appointed and their duties regulated in accordance with section 161 of the Act, sections 14 and 23A of the Companies Act 1967 and sections 13 to 18 of the Companies Act 1976 and sections 7 and 12 of the Companies Act 1981.

NOTICES

**131** A notice may be given by the company to any member either personally or by sending it by post to him or to his registered address, or (if he has no registered address within the United Kingdom) to the address, if any, within the United Kingdom supplied by him to the company for the giving of notice to him. Where a notice is sent by post, service of the notice shall be deemed to be effected by properly addressing, prepaying, and posting a letter containing the notice, and to have been effected in the case of a notice of a meeting at the expiration of 24 hours after the letter containing the same is posted, and in any other case at the time at which the letter would be delivered in the ordinary course of post.

**132** A notice may be given by the company to the joint holders of a share by giving the notice to the joint holder first named in the register of members in respect of the share.

**133** A notice may be given by the company to the persons entitled to a share in consequence of the death or bankruptcy of a member by sending it through the post in a prepaid letter addressed to them by name, or by the title of representatives of the deceased, or trustee of the bankrupt, or by any like description, at the address, if any, within the United Kingdom supplied for the purpose by the persons claiming to be so entitled, or (until such an address has been so supplied) by giving the notice in any manner in which the same might have been given if the death or bankruptcy had not occurred.

**134** Notice of every general meeting shall be given in any manner hereinbefore authorised to–

(a) every member except those members who (having no registered address within the United Kingdom) have not supplied to the company an address within the United Kingdom for the giving of notices to them;

(b) every person upon whom the ownership of a share devolves by reason of his being a legal personal representative or a trustee in bankruptcy of a member where the member but for his death or bankruptcy would be entitled to receive notice of the meeting; and

(c) the auditor for the time being of the company.

No other person shall be entitled to receive notices of general meetings.

WINDING UP

**135** If the company shall be wound up the liquidator may, with the sanction of an extraordinary resolution of the company and any other sanction required by the Act, divide amongst the members in specie or kind the whole or any part of the assets of the company (whether they shall consist of property of the same kind or not) and may, for such purpose set such value as he deems fair upon any property to be divided as aforesaid and may determine how such division shall be carried out as between the members or different classes of members. The liquidator may, with the like sanction, vest the whole or any part of such assets in trustees upon such trusts for the benefit of the contributories as the liquidator, with the like sanction, shall think fit, but so that no member shall be compelled to accept any shares or other securities whereon there is any liability.

INDEMNITY

**136** Every director, managing director, agent, auditor, secretary and other officer for the time being of the company shall be indemnified out of the assets of the company against any liability incurred by him in defending any proceedings, whether civil or criminal, in which judgment is given in his favour or in which he is acquitted or in connection with any application under section 448 of the Act in which relief is granted to him by the court."

Part II – Regulations for the Management of a Private Company limited by Shares

**1–6** (Repealed by Companies Act 1980, s. 88 and Sch. 4. Repeal not applicable to private companies registered before 22 December 1980.

Part II of Table A formerly reads as follows:

"**1** The regulations contained in Part I of Table A (with the exception of regulations 24 and 53) shall apply.

**2** The company is a private company and accordingly–

(a) the right to transfer shares is restricted in manner hereinafter prescribed;

(b) the number of members of the company (exclusive of persons who are in the employment of the company and of persons who having been formerly in the employment of the company were while in such employment and have continued after the determination of such employment to be members of the company) is limited to fifty. Provided that where two or more persons hold one or more shares in the company jointly they shall for the purpose of this regulation be treated as a single member;

(c) any invitation to the public to subscribe for any shares or debentures of the company is prohibited;

(d) the company shall not have power to issue share warrants to bearer.

**3** The directors may, in their absolute discretion and without assigning any reason therefor, decline to register any transfer of any share, whether or not it is a fully paid share.

**4** No business shall be transacted at any general meeting unless a quorum of members is present at the time when the meeting proceeds to business; save as herein otherwise provided two members present in person or by proxy shall be a quorum.

**5** Subject to the provisions of the Act, a resolution in writing signed by all the members for the time being entitled to receive notice of and to attend and vote at general meetings (or being corporations by their duly authorised representatives) shall be as valid and effective as if the same had been passed at a general meeting of the company duly convened and held.

**6** The directors may at any time require any person whose name is entered in the register of members of the company to furnish them with any information, supported (if the directors so require) by a statutory declaration, which they may consider necessary for the purpose of determining whether or not the company is an exempt private company within the meaning of subsection (4) of section 129 of the Act.

*Note*: Regulations 3 and 4 of this Part are alternative to regulations 24 and 53 respectively of Part I."

From the repeal of Pt. II of Table A, Pt. I of Table A, in accordance with CA 1980, Sch. 3, para. 36(1), is to apply in relation to private companies limited by shares as it applies in relation to public companies so limited. It should be noted however that variations to Pt. I of Table A will be desirable in the case of private companies, if only to place restrictions on the freedom to transfer shares. See in particular Table A, Pt. I, reg. 73A.)

# THE STOCK EXCHANGE (DESIGNATION OF NOMINEES) ORDER 1985

(SI 1985/806)

*Made on 22 May 1985 by the Secretary of State for Trade and Industry under s. 185(4) of the Companies Act 1985. Operative from 1 July 1985.*

**1** This Order may be cited as the Stock Exchange (Designation of Nominees) Order 1985 and shall come into operation on 1st July 1985.

**2** The Stock Exchange (Designation of Nominees) Order 1979 is hereby revoked.

**3** The Secretary of State hereby designates SEPON Limited as a nominee of The Stock Exchange for the purposes of section 185 of the Companies Act 1985.

## EXPLANATORY NOTE

(*This Note is not part of the Order*)

Following the consolidation of the Companies Acts 1948 to 1983, this Order replaces the Stock Exchange (Designation of Nominees) Order 1979; it effects no change in the law.

# THE COMPANIES (FORMS) REGULATIONS 1985

(SI 1985/854)

*Made on 4 June 1985 by the Secretary of State for Trade and Industry under the enactments specified in Sch. 1 to the Regulations. Operative from 1 July 1985.*

[**Note:** Note the amendments to these Regulations by the Companies (Forms) (Amendment) Regulations 1986 (SI 1986/2097) as from 29 December 1986 (in particular the saving in reg. 2(2) of the latter Regulations), by the Companies (Forms) (Amendment) Regulations 1987 (SI 1987/752) as from 30 April 1987, by the Companies (Forms) (Amendment) Regulations 1988 (SI 1988/1359) as from 1 August 1988, by the Companies (Forms) (Amendment) Regulations 1990 (SI 1990/572) as from 8 March 1990, by the Companies (Forms Amendment No. 2 and Company's Type and Principal Business Activities) Regulations 1990 (SI 1990/1766) as from 1 October 1990 and 1 January 1991 and by the Companies (Forms) (Amendment) Regulations 1992 (SI 1992/3006) as from 1 January 1993.]

**1** These Regulations may be cited as the Companies (Forms) Regulations 1985 and shall come into operation on 1st July 1985.

**2** In these Regulations –

> **"the new Acts"** mean the Companies Act 1985 and the Companies Consolidation (Consequential Provisions) Act 1985,
> **"the old Acts"** mean the Companies Act 1948, Parts I and III of the Companies Act 1967, the Companies (Floating Charges and Receivers) (Scotland) Act 1972, the Companies Act 1976, the Companies Act 1980 and the Companies Act 1981, and
> **"the Act"** means the Companies Act 1985.

**3** The instruments specified in Schedule 2 are revoked.

**4(1)** The forms set out in Schedule 3, other than those listed in Part I of Schedule 4, with such variations as circumstances require, are the forms prescribed for the purposes of the provisions of the new Acts which are referred to in those forms.

**4(2)** The particulars contained in the forms listed in Parts I and II of Schedule 4 are the particulars prescribed for the purposes of the provisions of the Act which are referred to in those forms.

**5** (Revoked by SI 1988/1359, reg. 2(3) as from 1 August 1988).

**History**
Reg. 5 formerly read as follows:
"**5** For the purposes of section 88(2) of the Act, such part of any form from time to time prescribed under section 47(1) of the Finance Act 1973 as relates to the matters required to be stated by section 88(2)(a) of the Act is a form prescribed for the purposes of that subsection, even though the form prescribed under section 47(1) of the Finance Act 1973 is not set out in Schedule 3."

**Note**
Revocation of reg. 5 is excepted to the extent that the forms prescribed therein–

- shall, in any case where the allotment of shares was made before 16 March 1988, be used for the purposes of Companies Act 1985, s. 88(2) instead of the form prescribed by SI 1988/1359; and
- may, in any other case, in relation to documents received by the registrar of companies before 1 August 1988, be used for those purposes instead of the form prescribed by SI 1988/1359.

(See SI 1988/1359, reg. 3.)

**6** For the purposes of sections 21, 65(3), 72(2)(c), 77(5)(a), 241(3)(b), 272(5), 273(7), 691(1)(a), 698 and 700(2) of the Act, a translation of a document into English shall be certified to be a correct translation:–

(a) if the translation was made in the United Kingdom, by
  (i) a notary public in any part of the United Kingdom;
  (ii) a solicitor (if the translation was made in Scotland), a solicitor of the Supreme Court of Judicature of England and Wales (if it was made in England or Wales), or a solicitor of the Supreme Court of Judicature of Northern Ireland (if it was made in Northern Ireland); or
  (iii) a person certified by a person mentioned above to be known to him to be competent to translate the document into English; or

(b) if the translation was made outside the United Kingdom, by
  (i) a notary public;
  (ii) a person authorised in the place where the translation was made to administer an oath;
  (iii) any of the British officials mentioned in section 6 of the Commissioners for Oaths Act 1889;
  (iv) a person certified by a person mentioned in subparagraph (i), (ii) or (iii) of this paragraph to be known to him to be competent to translate the document into English.

**Note**
Reg. 6 revoked as from 1 April 1990 so far as it refers to CA 1985, s. 241(3)(b), 700(2) but this revocation shall not apply in relation to the accounts of a company in respect of a financial year or accounting reference period of the company which began before 23 December 1989, as the case may be (see SI 1990/572, reg. 5(3)).

**7(1)** For the purposes of sections 398(1) and (4), 400(2), 410(2) and 416(1) of the Act, a certificate or verification (as the case may be) that a copy of an instrument by which a charge is created or evidenced is a correct copy shall be given by the company which has created the charge, or (where that person is different) by the person who has delivered or sent the copy to the registrar.

**7(2)** (Revoked by SI 1986/2097, reg. 2 as from 29 December 1986.)

**History**
Reg. 7(2) formerly read as follows:
"For the purposes of section 469(1) of the Act, a certificate that a copy of an instrument of appointment is a correct copy shall be given by the person who has made the appointment."

**7(3)** A certificate referred to in paragraph (1) shall be signed by or on behalf of the person giving it. Where that person is a body corporate the person signing the certificate on behalf of the body shall be an officer of it.

**History**
In reg. 7(3) the words "or (2)" formerly appearing after the words "paragraph (1)" revoked by SI 1986/2097, reg. 2 as from 29 December 1986.

**7(4)** For the purposes of section 691(1)(a) of the Act, a copy of an instrument constituting or defining a company's constitution shall be certified, in the place of incorporation of the company, to be a true copy:–

(a) by an official of the Government to whose custody the original is committed; or

(b) by a notary public; or

(c) by an officer of the company on oath taken before:

(i) a person having authority in that place to administer an oath; or

(ii) any of the British officials mentioned in section 6 of the Commissioners for Oaths Act 1889.

**8(1)** Notwithstanding the provisions of regulation 3, but subject to paragraphs (2) and (4), the forms, the particulars and the manners of certifying or verifying copies and translations which were prescribed for the purposes of the old Acts by the instruments revoked by that regulation may be used or given for the purposes of the corresponding provisions of the new Acts instead of the forms, particulars and manners prescribed for those purposes by these Regulations.

**8(2)** Paragraph (1) does not apply to:

(a) Form PUC 7 prescribed under section 52(1) of the Companies Act 1948;

(b) Forms 15, 16, 17, 18 and 19 prescribed under sections 382, 384 and 386 of that Act;

(c) Forms F1, F2, F3 and F14 prescribed under section 407 of that Act; or

(d) Form 17e prescribed under section 13(4) of the Companies Act 1980.

**8(3)** Notwithstanding the repeal of the Companies Act 1948, but subject to paragraph (4), the form set out in Part II of the Sixth Schedule to that Act may be used as the form of the annual return of a company having a share capital instead of the form prescribed by these Regulations.

**8(4)** Paragraphs (1) and (3) apply only in relation to documents received by the registrar of companies, or by other recipients, before 1st July 1986.

**9** (Revoked by SI 1987/752, reg. 3 as from 30 April 1987.)

**History**

Reg. 9 formerly read as follows:

"**9(1)** For the purposes of sections 428(2) and 429(2) of the Act, a notice to a shareholder in a transferor company shall be given to him, in the form prescribed by regulation 4(1), either personally or by sending it to him by post.

**(2)** Where such a notice cannot be given personally or by post because the shareholder is the holder of a share warrant to bearer, the notice shall be given:–

(a) in a case where the articles of association or the regulations of the transferor company provide that notice to such shareholders may be given by advertisement, by advertisement in the manner so provided, and

(b) in any other case, by an advertisement in the Gazette.

**(3)** Where in accordance with paragraph (1) a notice is sent to a shareholder by post it shall be sent to him:–

(a) at his address in the United Kingdom registered in the books of the transferor company;

(b) if no such address is registered, to the address (if any) in the United Kingdom given by him to the transferor company for the giving of notices to him; or

(c) if no address in the United Kingdom is registered or has been so notified, to his address outside the United Kingdom registered in the books of the transferor company.

**(4)** Where in accordance with paragraph (1) a notice is sent to a shareholder by post:–

(a) if it is sent to an address in the United Kingdom it shall be sent by recorded delivery; and

(b) if it is sent to an address outside the United Kingdom it shall be sent by airmail, if that form of post is available."

# Schedule 1

The Companies Act 1985:

sections 6(1)(b)(i), 10(2), 12(3), 21(5), 30(5), 43(3) and (3)(e), 49(4) and (8)(a), 51(4), 53(1)(b), 54(4), 65(3)(b), 72(2)(c), 77(5)(a), 88(2)(a) and (3), 97(3)(a), 117(2) and (3), 122(1), 123(2), 128(1), (3) and (4), 129(1), (2) and (3), 139(4), 147(3), 155(6), 156(1), 157(3), 169(1), 173(5), 176(3)(a), 190(5), 224(2), 225(1) and (2), 241(3)(b), 242(3), 266(1) and (3), 272(5), 273(7), 287(2), 288(2), 318(4), 325(5), 353(2), 362(3), 363(2), 364(1), 386(2), 395(1), 397(1), 398(1) and (4), 400(2), 401(1), 403(1), 405(3), 409(1), 410(2), 413(2), 416(1), 417(1), 419(1) and (5), 424(1), 428(2), 429(2) and (3), 466(4) and (5), [469(1), 470(3), 481(1)(b) and (2), 482(1), 485(1)] 486, [495(2)(a) and (b), 496(1)(e), 497(2), 498(3), 600(1)], 680(1), 681(6), 684(1)(a) and (b) and (2), 685(4) and (4)(e), 686(1)(a) and (2), 690(2), 691(1)(a) and (b), 692(1) and (2), 694(4)(a) and (b), 698, 700(2), 701(2) and (6), and 744.

Schedule 13, paragraph 27 and Schedule 14, paragraph 1(1).

The Companies Consolidation (Consequential Provisions) Act 1985:

sections 2(1)(b) and (4)(b) and 4(1) and (4).

**Note**
Nos. 469(1), 470(3), 481(1)(b), (2), 482(1), 485(1), 495(2)(a), (b), 496(1)(e), 497(2), 498(3), 600(1), repealed by virtue of Insolvency Act 1986, s. 438 and Sch. 12.

# Schedule 2

Regulation 3

| Regulations Revoked | References |
|---|---|
| The Companies (Forms) Regulations 1979 | SI 1979/1547 |
| The Companies (Forms) Regulations 1980 | SI 1980/1826 |
| The Companies (Forms) (Amendment) Regulations 1980 | SI 1980/2016 |
| The Companies (Forms) Regulations 1981 | SI 1981/1622 |
| The Companies (Forms) Regulations 1982 | SI 1982/104 |
| The Companies (Forms No. 2) Regulations 1982 | SI 1982/674 |
| The Companies (Forms) Regulations 1983 | SI 1983/1021 |

# Schedule 3

**Note**
This schedule sets out the following prescribed forms (referred to in reg. 4(1) above): Form no. 6, 10, 12, 30(5)(a), 30(5)(b), 30(5)(c), 43(3), 43(3)(e), 49(1), 49(8)(a), 51, 53, 54, 88(2), 88(3), 97, 117, 122, 123, 128(1), 128(3), 128(4), 129(1), 129(2), 129(3), 139, 147, 155(6)a, 155(6)b, 157, 169, 173, 176, 190, 224, 225(1), 225(2), 242, 166(1), 266(3), 287, 288, 318, 325, 353, 362, 363, 386, 395, 397, 397a, 398, 400, 401, 403a, 403b, 405(1), 405(2), 410 (Scot), 413 (Scot), 413a (Scot), 416 (Scot), 417 (Scot), 419a (Scot), 419b (Scot), 428, 429(2), 429(3), 466 (Scot), 469 (Scot), 470 (Scot), 478 (Scot), 481 (Scot), 482 (Scot), 495(2)(a), 495(3)a, 495(3)b, 497, 600, 600a, 680a, 680b, 684, 685, 686, 691, 692(1)(a), 692(1)(b), 692(1)(c), 692(2), 694(a), 694(b), 701(2), 701(6)a, 701(6)b, R7, R7a, R8 and R9.
Also note that:
(1) Some of the forms were revoked by SI 1986/2097, reg. 2 as from 29 December 1986. They are no. 469(Scot), 470(Scot), 478(Scot), 481(Scot), 482(Scot), 495(2)(a), 495(3)a, 495(3)b and 497.
(2) Form no. 169, 225(1), 225(2), 428, 429(2), 429(3), 600 and 600a revoked, new form no. 169, 225(1), 225(2), 429(4), 429 dec, 430A, 600 and 600a included and form no. 6, 54, 88(2), (3), 122, 123, 128(1), 128(3), 128(4), 129(1), 129(2), 129(3), 157, 176, 190, 224, 266(1), 266(3), 287, 288, 318, 325, 353, 362, 386, 403a, 403b, 416(Scot), 419a(Scot), 419b(Scot) and R7a amended by SI 1987/752, reg. 5, 6 as from 30 April 1987.
(3) Form no. 88(2) revoked by SI 1988/1359, reg. 2(2), except to the extent specified in SI 1988/1359, reg. 3, as from 1 August 1988. A new Form no. 88(2) prescribed by SI 1988/1359, reg. 2(1).
(4) Note the new forms as from 1 April 1990 – see SI 1990/572, reg. 3, Sch. 2. Some forms in Sch. 3 were also revoked by SI 1990/572, reg. 4: no. 242 and 287 as from 1 April 1990 and no. 224, 701(2), 701(6)a and 701(6)b as from 1 April 1991 – note the various transitional arrangements.
(5) Note new forms as from 1 October 1990 – see SI 1990/1766, reg. 3, 4, Sch. 2. Some forms in Sch. 3 were revoked by SI 1990/1766, reg. 3, 4: no. 10, 288, 363, 691, 692(1)(b).
(6) Forms 691, 694(a) and 694(b) revoked by SI 1992/3006, reg. 5(1) as from 1 January 1993 (subject to transitional provisions in reg. 5(2) and 5(3)).

# Schedule 4

Regulation 4(2)

## Part I – Prescribed Particulars

Forms 88, 123, 395, 400, 410, 416, 466, 692(1)(a), 692(1)(c) and 692(2).

## Part II – Prescribed Particulars in Prescribed Forms

Forms 155(6)a, 155(6)b, 173.

**History**
In Sch. 4, Pt. I "482" and in Pt. II "493(3)a and 495(3)b" revoked by SI 1986/2097, reg. 2 as from 29 December 1986 and in Pt. I "692(1)(b)" revoked by SI 1990/1766, reg. 3(2) as from 1 October 1990.

## EXPLANATORY NOTE

*(This Note is not part of the Regulations)*

These Regulations provide for the forms set out in Schedule 3 to the Regulations (other than those listed in Part I of Schedule 4) to be the forms prescribed for the purposes of the provisions of the Companies Act 1985 and the Companies Consolidation (Consequential Provisions) Act 1985 which are referred to in those forms. The forms have all been amended, and most of them have been re-numbered. The numbers of the forms prescribed under the Companies Act 1985 now relate to the relevant sections of that Act.

The Regulations provide that the particulars contained in the forms listed in Schedule 4 are the particulars prescribed for the purposes of the Companies Act 1985 referred to in those forms. They make special provision for the use of appropriate Inland Revenue forms in certain circumstances. They prescribe the ways in which translations and copies of documents required to be delivered to the registrar of companies are to be certified or verified, and they prescribe the manner of giving notice by a transferee company to dissenting shareholders.

The Regulations also revoke the Companies (Forms) Regulations 1979 and the various other instruments specified in Schedule 2. But the Regulations permit the continued use of most of the various forms and ways of certifying or verifying copies and translations prescribed by the Regulations which are revoked, and also the continued use of the annual return form set out in the Schedule to the Companies (Annual Return) Regulations 1983, provided that the documents are received before 1st July 1986.

# THE COMPANIES (DEPARTMENT OF TRADE AND INDUSTRY) FEES ORDER 1985

(SI 1985/1784)

*Made on 18 November 1985 by the Lord Chancellor and the Treasury under s. 663(4) of the Companies Act 1985 and s. 2 of the Public Offices Fees Act 1879. Operative from 1 December 1985.*

[**Note:** This Order to a great extent has been superseded by the Insolvency Fees Order 1986 (SI 1986/2030) as from 29 December 1986. However this Order is still relevant where the winding up commenced before that date and for such windings up amendments made by the Bankruptcy and Companies (Department of Trade and Industry) Fees (Amendment) Order 1990 (SI 1990/559 (L 8)) and the Bankruptcy and Companies (Department of Trade and Industry) Fees (Amendment) Order 1991 (SI 1991/494) have been included.]

**1(1)** This Order may be cited as the Companies (Department of Trade and Industry) Fees Order 1985 and shall come into operation on 1st December 1985.

**1(2)** Unless the context otherwise requires, a fee referred to by number in this Order means a fee so numbered in the Schedule to this Order.

**2** The fees and percentages to be charged for and in respect of proceedings in the winding-up of companies shall be those set out in the Schedule to this Order.

**3(1)** All fees shall be taken in cash.

**3(2)** When a fee is paid to an officer of a court the person paying the fee shall inform the officer that the fee relates to a proceeding for or in the winding-up of a company.

**4** Where Value Added Tax is chargeable in respect of the provision of any service for which a fee is prescribed in the Schedule, there shall be payable in addition to that fee the amount of the Value Added Tax.

**5** Where the head office of the company being wound up is situated out of England, and the liquidation takes place partly in England and partly elsewhere, or where the court has sanctioned a reconstruction of the company or a scheme of arrangement of its affairs, or where for any other reason the Secretary of State is satisfied that the fees would be excessive, such reduction may be made in the said fees as may, on the application of the Secretary of State, be sanctioned by the Treasury.

**6** The Companies (Department of Trade and Industry) Fees Order 1984, is hereby revoked save as to any fee or percentage due or payable before the commencement of this Order.

## Schedule

Rule 2

| *No. of Fee* | *Description of Proceeding* | *Amount* £ |
|---|---|---|
| 1 | On application to the Secretary of State under section 15 of the Companies (Winding-up) Act 1890, section 224 of the Companies (Consolidation) Act 1908, or section 642 of the Companies Act 1985 for the payment of money out of the Insolvency Services Account or for the reissue of a cheque, money order or payable order in respect of money standing to the credit of the Insolvency Services Account. | 4.00 |
| 2 | On payments out of money which was paid into the Insolvency Services Account before 1 December 1985 and on payments of money into the Insolvency Services Account on and after 1 December 1985 under section 15 of the Companies (Winding-up) Act 1890, section 224 of the Companies (Consolidation) Act 1908, or section 642 of the Companies Act 1985: | |
| | (1) Where the money consists of unclaimed dividends:— ........per cent | 1.25 |
| | (2) Where the money consists of undistributed funds or balances:— | |
| | (i) on the first £50,000 or fraction thereof ........per cent | 1.25 |
| | (ii) on all further amounts ........per cent | 0.75 |
| | but so that— (a) the total fee payable under this sub-paragraph shall not exceed £7,500, (b) this fee and Fee No. 5 shall be disregarded in calculating the fee payable under this sub-paragraph. | |
| 3 | On the amounts paid by liquidators (including the Official Receiver when he is liquidator) into the Insolvency Services Account under section 542 of the Companies Act 1985 (after deducting any sums paid to secured creditors, other than holders of floating charges, in respect of their securities and any sums spent out of money received in carrying on the business of the company) a fee in accordance with the following scale— | |
| | (a) on the first £50,000 or fraction thereof ........per cent | 10.00 |
| | (b) on the next £50,000 or fraction thereof ........per cent | 7.50 |
| | (c) on the next £400,000 or fraction thereof ........per cent | 6.50 |
| | (d) on the next £500,000 or fraction thereof ........per cent | 3.75 |
| | (e) on the next £4,000,000 or fraction thereof ........per cent | 2.00 |
| | (f) on all further amounts ........per cent | 1.00 |

| No. of Fee | Description of Proceeding | Amount £ |
|---|---|---|
| 4 | On an application by a liquidator to the Secretary of State or to an Official Receiver to exercise the powers of a Committee of Inspection under section 548 of the Companies Act 1985 and Rule 214 of the Companies (Winding-up) Rule 1949—<br>for each separate item therein ............................................................... | 21.00 |
| 5 | On the amount expended on any purchase of Government securities (including the renewal of Treasury Bills) pursuant to a request made under section 660(2) of the Companies Act 1985 ...............per cent | 0.375 |
| 6 | When the Official Receiver is provisional liquidator pursuant to section 532 of the Companies Act 1985, such amount as the Court, on the application of the Official Receiver, may consider it reasonable to direct the petitioner or the company to pay to him. | |
| 7 | For the performance by the Official Receiver of his general duties as Official Receiver and in addition to any other fee payable hereunder— | |
| | (1) Where the winding-up order was made on or after 13 July 1982 but before 1 December 1985 ........................... | 222.00 |
| | (2) Where the winding-up order was made on or after 1 December 1985 ................................................................... | 490.00 |
| 8 | Where a winding-up order is made: | |
| | (1) On the payments made by the Official Receiver into the Insolvency Services Account (after deducting any sums on which fees are payable under Fees No. 9 and 10 and any sums spent in carrying on the business of the company) a fee in accordance with the following scale: | |
| | (i) on the first £5,000 or fraction thereof ............per cent | 20.00 |
| | (ii) on the next £5,000 or fraction thereof ............per cent | 15.00 |
| | (iii) on the next £90,000 or fraction thereof ...........per cent | 10.00 |
| | (iv) on all further amounts ..............................per cent | 5.00 |
| | (2) On the amount distributed in dividends or paid to preferential creditors and contributories by the Official Receiver:<br>half of the percentage prescribed in paragraph (1) above, calculated on the amount so distributed. | |
| 9 | On the payments made by the Official Receiver into the Insolvency Services Account from the realisation of property for secured creditors (other than holders of floating charges)—<br>the scale fees calculated under Fee No. 8(1) on that amount. | |
| 10 | On the payments made by the Official Receiver into the Insolvency Services Account from the realisation of property for holders of floating charges—<br>the scale fees calculated under Fee No. 8(1) and (2) on that amount. | |

| No. of Fee | Description of Proceeding | Amount £ |
|---|---|---|
| 11 | For travelling, keeping possession, legal costs and other reasonable expenses of the Official Receiver—<br>the amount disbursed. | |
| 12 | Where the Official Receiver as liquidator on or after 1 December 1985 at the request of a secured creditor or a receiver appointed by him, transfers or conveys property subject to any charge created thereon by the company — on the sale price of the property .................per cent | 0.50<br>Minimum fee<br>110.00 |
| 13 | For all official stationery, printing, postage and telephones, including notices to creditors and contributories of meetings and sittings of the court and room hire: | |
| | (a) for a number of creditors and contributories not exceeding 25 ............................................ | 129.00 |
| | (b) for every additional 10 creditors and contributories or part thereof ............................................ | 37.00 |
| | *This fee does not include the charge made by the Official Receiver or liquidator calling a meeting of creditors or contributories, for which provision is made in Rule 132 of the Companies (Winding-up) Rules 1949.* | |
| 14 | On the insertion in the *London Gazette* of a notice relating to a company which is being wound up by the court ............................ | 19.55 |
| | Provided that:—<br>(i) Where the winding-up order was made before 1 January 1980 only one fee of £12 shall be charged in respect of all insertions in the *London Gazette* after that date; and<br>(ii) Where the winding-up order was made on or after 1 January 1980 and before 18 August 1980 no fee shall be charged in respect of any insertions in the *London Gazette* made on or after 1 January 1980. | |
| 15 | On each dividend payable order issued by the Department. | 0.30 |
| 16 | Where the Official Receiver performs any duty not provided for in this Schedule, such amount as the Court, on the application of the Official Receiver with the sanction of the Secretary of State, may consider reasonable. | |

**History**

In the Schedule the figure "19.55" shown in relation to fee no. 14 substituted for the former figure "17.83" by the Bankruptcy and Companies (Department of Trade and Industry) Fees (Amendment) Order 1991 (SI 1991/494), art. 3 as from 2 April 1991. Previously the figure "17.83" substituted for the original figure "16.25" by the Bankruptcy and Companies (Department of Trade and Industry) Fees (Amendment) Order 1990 (SI 1990/559 (L 8)), art. 3 as from 2 April 1990.

## EXPLANATORY NOTE

(*This Note is not part of the Order*)

This Order replaces the Companies (Department of Trade and Industry) Fees Order 1984. It increases with effect from 1 December 1985 Fees No. 1, 4, 12, 13 and 14 set out in the Schedule to the 1984 Order in respect of certain winding-up proceedings from which it is estimated that the total amount of fees collected per annum at the new levels will be 10 per cent greater than the amount collected per annum at the existing levels. Fee No. 7 (which is in respect of the Official Receiver's general duties in compulsory liquidations) is increased from £222 to £490 where the winding-up order is made after 1 December 1985. (Fee 13(1), (2) and (3) has been amended and renumbered as Fees 13 and 14(i) and (ii), and subsequent Fees have been renumbered accordingly.)

The Order also changes the time at which Fees No. 2 and 3 are charged to the time when payment is made into the Insolvency Services Account. At present Fee No. 2 is charged when money is paid out of the Account, and Fee No. 3 after the submission of the liquidator's six monthly accounts. The level of Fees No. 2 and 3 remains the same.

# THE INSOLVENCY ACT 1985 (COMMENCEMENT NO. 1) ORDER 1986

(SI 1986/6 (C 1))

*Made on 1 January 1986 by the Secretary of State for Trade and Industry under s. 236(2) of the Insolvency Act 1985.*

**1** This Order may be cited as the Insolvency Act 1985 (Commencement No. 1) Order 1986.

**2** The provisions of the Insolvency Act 1985 specified in Schedule 1 hereto shall come into operation on 1 February 1986.

**3** The provisions of the Insolvency Act 1985 specified in Schedule 2 hereto shall come into operation on 1 March 1986.

## Schedule 1 – Provisions Coming into Operation on 1st February 1986

Article 2

| Provisions of the Act | Subject matter of provisions |
|---|---|
| Section 10 | Regulations rules and orders |
| Section 11 | Interpretation of Part I |
| Section 106 in so far as it relates to the making of rules in relation to administrative receivers | Company insolvency rules |
| Section 108(1) and (3) in so far as they relate to the provisions of the Act herein specified | Construction of Part II |
| Section 213(2) (7) (8) and (9) | Co-operation between courts exercising jurisdiction in relation to insolvency law |
| Section 226 in so far as it relates to the making of the rules in relation to administrative receivers under section 106 | Insolvency Rules Committee |
| Section 232 | Interpretation |
| Section 236(1) (2) (3) and (4) | Short title commencement and extent |
| Schedule 5 in so far as it relates to the making of rules in relation to administrative receivers | Provisions capable of inclusion in company insolvency rules. |

## Schedule 2 – Provisions Coming into Operation on 1st March 1986

Article 3

| Provisions of the Act | Subject matter of provisions |
|---|---|
| Section 45 | Preliminary to Part II Chapter IV |
| Section 108(1) and (3) in so far as they relate to provisions of the Act herein specified | Construction of Part II |
| Section 109(3) | Minor and consequential amendments of 1985 Act |
| Section 235(2) | Transitional provisions and savings |
| Schedule 9 paragraphs 7 and 8 | Transitional provisions and savings. |

### EXPLANATORY NOTE

(*This Note is not part of the Order*)

This Order brings into force on 1st February 1986 those provisions of the Insolvency Act 1985 specified in Schedule 1 to the Order and on 1st March 1986 those further provisions of that Act specified in Schedule 2 to the Order.

The provisions brought into force on 1st February 1986 are:

the rule-making power contained in section 10 together with section 11 in so far as it makes provision for interpretation of that section;

the rule-making power contained in section 106 as far as it confers power to make rules in respect of administrative receivers together with such of the list of specific provisions that can be made under that power contained in Schedule 5 as relates thereto;

sections 108(1) and (3) and 232 providing for the construction and interpretation of the provisions brought into force;

the rule-making power and interpretation provision contained in section 213(2) (7) (8) and (9);

section 226 in so far as it relates to the enabling of the Insolvency Rules Committee to be consulted on rules made in respect of administrative receivers under section 106;

section 236(1) to (4) providing for the short title, commencement and territorial extent of the Act;

The provisions brought into force on 1st March 1986 are:

section 45 providing for the definition of "administrative receiver";

sections 108(1) and (3) and 109(3) in so far as they provide for the construction of section 45 and the term "administrative receiver";

section 235(2) and paragraphs 7 and 8 of Schedule 9 making transitional provision in respect of the commencement of section 45.

# THE INSOLVENCY ACT 1985 (COMMENCEMENT NO. 2) ORDER 1986

(SI 1986/185 (C 7))

*Made on 6 February 1986 by the Secretary of State for Trade and Industry, under s. 236(2) of the Insolvency Act 1985.*

**1** This Order may be cited as the Insolvency Act 1985 (Commencement No. 2) Order 1986.

**2** The provisions of the Insolvency Act specified in Schedule 1 hereto shall come into operation on 1st March 1986.

**3** The provisions of the Insolvency Act 1985 specified in Schedule 2 hereto shall come into operation on 1st April 1986.

# Schedule 1 – Provisions Coming into Operation on 1st March 1986

Article 2

| Provisions of the Act | Subject matter of Provision |
|---|---|
| Section 106 in so far as it relates to:— (a) the making of rules in relation to England and Wales: and (b) the making of rules in relation to Scotland in respect of the matters specified in paragraphs 26, 28, 29, 30 and 31 of Schedule 5 to the Act | Company insolvency rules |
| Section 108(1) and (3) in so far as they relate to the provisions of the Act herein specified | Construction of Part II |
| Section 109(1) | Minor and consequential amendments of the Companies Act 1985 |
| Section 109(2) in so far as it relates to general rules under section 663(1) of the Companies Act 1985. | |
| Section 226 in so far as it relates to the making of rules under section 106 | Insolvency Rules Committee |
| Section 235(1) and (3) | Consequential amendments transitional provisions savings and repeals |
| Schedule 5 in so far as it relates to:— (a) the making of rules in relation to England and Wales: and (b) the making of rules in relation to Scotland in respect of the matters specified in paragraphs 26, 28, 29, 30 and 31 of the Schedule | Provisions capable of inclusion in company insolvency rules |
| Schedule 6 paragraph 24 in so far as it relates to the making of rules under section 106 in relation to England and Wales | Amendment to section 461 of the Companies Act 1985 |
| Schedule 8 paragraphs 32(4)(a) and 37(4) in so far as they relate to the making of rules under section 106 in relation to England and Wales | Consequential amendments to section 31 of the Banking Act 1979 and to section 59 of the Insurance Companies Act 1982 |
| Schedule 10 in so far as it provides for the repeal of or words in the following enactments:— (a) Section 663 of the Companies Act 1985 in so far as it relates to the making of general rules in relation to England and Wales. | Repeals |

| Provisions of the Act | Subject matter of Provision |
|---|---|
| (b) Section 744 of the Companies Act 1985 in so far as the words repealed relate to the making of general rules in relation to England and Wales.<br>(c) Section 10 of the Insolvency Act 1976 in so far as it relates to the making of rules under section 663 of the Companies Act 1985.<br>(d) The entries in Schedule 2 to the Companies Consolidation (Consequential Provisions) Act 1985(b) relating to:—<br>(i) section 31 of the Banking Act 1979 in so far as the entry in respect thereof repeals the reference to section 663 of the Companies Act 1985 in section 31(7)(a) of the Banking Act 1979.<br>(ii) section 59 of the Insurance Companies Act 1982 in so far as the entries in respect thereof repeal the references therein to section 663 of the Companies Act 1985 as that section applies to the making of general rules in England and Wales.<br>(iii) section 10(1) of the Insolvency Act 1976 in so far as the entry in respect thereof repeals the reference to section 663 of the Companies Act 1985 in section 10(1)(b) of the Insolvency Act 1976. | |

# Schedule 2 – Provisions Coming into Operation on 1st April 1986

Article 3

| Provisions of the Act | Subject matter of Provision |
|---|---|
| Section 213(1) (3) (4) (5) and (6) save in so far as they relate to the assisting of the courts of any relevant country or territory | Co-operation between courts exercising jurisdiction in relation to insolvency law |
| Section 234 | Crown application |
| Schedule 8 paragraph 36 | Consequential amendments |
| Schedule 10 in so far as it provides for the repeal of or words in the following enactments:—<br>(a) The Irish Bankrupt and Insolvent Act 1857 | Repeals |

| Provisions of the Act | Subject matter of Provision |
|---|---|
| (b) sections 65 and 121(7) of the Bankruptcy (Ireland) Amendment Act 1872 | |
| (c) section 121 of the Bankruptcy Act 1914 | |
| (d) section 122 of the Bankruptcy Act 1914 except in so far as it relates to courts in the United Kingdom acting in aid of and being auxiliary to British courts elsewhere | |
| (e) section 123 of the Bankruptcy Act 1914 | |
| (f) section 38(5) of the Criminal Law Act 1977 | |
| (g) section 570 of the Companies Act 1985 | |
| (h) section 246 of the Companies Act (Northern Ireland) 1960 | |

## EXPLANATORY NOTE

*(This Note is not part of the Order)*

This Order brings into force on 1st March 1986 those provisions of the Insolvency Act 1985 specified in Schedule 1 to the Order and on 1st April 1986 those further provisions of that Act specified in Schedule 2 to this Order.

The provisions brought into force on 1st March 1986 are:

the rule-making power contained in section 106 as far as it confers power to make rules generally in relation to England and Wales together with Schedule 5 in respect thereof and in relation to Scotland in respect of the matters specified in paragraphs 26, 28, 29, 30 and 31 of Schedule 5.

section 108(1) and (3) providing for the construction and interpretation of the provisions brought into force.

section 109(1) and paragraph 24 of Schedule 6 making amendments to the Companies Act 1985 consequential upon the commencement of section 106 generally in respect of England and Wales.

section 109(2) to the extent that it provides for references in the Companies Act 1985 to general rules under section 663(1) to have effect as references to rules under section 106 of the Act.

section 226 in so far as it relates to the enabling of the Insolvency Rules Committee to be consulted on the making of rules under section 106.

section 235(1) and paragraphs 32(4)(a) and 34(4) of Schedule 8 making amendments consequential upon the commencement of section 106 in relation to England and Wales under this instrument.

section 235(3) and the provisions of Schedule 10 to the Act specified in Schedule 1 hereto making repeals consequential upon the commencement of section 106 in relation to England and Wales and of section 226 under this instrument.

The provisions brought into force on 1st April 1986 are:

section 213 to the extent that it provides for co-operation between the courts of the three insolvency jurisdictions within the United Kingdom, England and Wales, Scotland and Northern Ireland.

section 234 making provision in respect of the application of the Act to the Crown.

Schedule 8 paragraph 36 and the provisions of Schedule 10 to the Act specified in Schedule 2 hereto making amendments and repeals consequential upon the commencement of section 213 under this instrument.

## NOTE AS TO EARLIER COMMENCEMENT ORDERS

(*This Note is not part of the Order*)

The following provisions of the Act have been brought into force by commencement order made before the date of this Order.

| Provision | Date of Commencement | S.I. No. |
|---|---|---|
| s. 10 | 1.2.86 | 1986/6 |
| s. 11 | 1.2.86 | 1986/6 |
| s. 106 partially | 1.2.86 | 1986/6 |
| s. 108(1) and (3) partially | 1.2.86 | 1986/6 |
| s. 213(2) (7) (8) and (9) | 1.2.86 | 1986/6 |
| s. 226 partially | 1.2.86 | 1986/6 |
| s. 232 | 1.2.86 | 1986/6 |
| s. 236(1)–(4) | 1.2.86 | 1986/6 |
| Sched 5 partially | 1.2.86 | 1986/6 |

The following provisions of the Act will be brought into force after the making of this order by a commencement order made before the date of this order.

| Provision | Date of Commencement | S.I. No. |
|---|---|---|
| s. 45 | 1.3.86 | 1986/6 |
| s. 108(1) and (3) partially | 1.3.86 | 1986/6 |
| s. 109(3) | 1.3.86 | 1986/6 |
| s. 235(2) | 1.3.86 | 1986/6 |
| Sched 9 paragraphs 7 and 8 | 1.3.86 | 1986/6 |

# THE ADMINISTRATIVE RECEIVERS (VALUE ADDED TAX CERTIFICATES) RULES 1986

(SI 1986/385)

*Made on 27 February 1986 by the Lord Chancellor under s. 106 and 226 of the Insolvency Act 1985.*

## CITATION AND COMMENCEMENT

**1(1)** These Rules may be cited as the Administrative Receivers (Value Added Tax Certificates) Rules 1986 and shall come into force on 1st April 1986.

**1(2)** In these Rules references to "the 1983 Act" are to the Value Added Tax Act 1983.

## APPLICATION OF THESE RULES

**2** These Rules apply to a company for the purposes of section 22 of the 1983 Act where a person is appointed to act as its administrative receiver except where such a person is appointed under section 467 of the Companies Act 1985 (power to appoint receivers under the law of Scotland).

## ISSUE OF CERTIFICATE OF INSOLVENCY

**3** In accordance with this Rule, it is the duty of the administrative receiver to issue a certificate in the terms of paragraph (b) of section 22(3) of the 1983 Act (which specifies the circumstances in which a company is deemed insolvent for the purposes of the section) forthwith upon his forming the opinion described in that paragraph.

## FORM OF CERTIFICATE

**4(1)** There shall in the certificate be specified:–

(a) the name of the company and its registered number;

(b) the full name of the administrative receiver and the date of his appointment as such; and

(c) the date on which the certificate is issued.

**4(2)** The certificate shall be intituled "CERTIFICATE OF INSOLVENCY FOR THE PURPOSES OF SECTION 22(3)(b) OF THE VALUE ADDED TAX ACT 1983".

## NOTIFICATION TO CREDITORS

**5(1)** Notice of the issue of the certificate shall be given by the administrative receiver within 3 months of his appointment or within 2 months of issuing the certificate, whichever is the later, to all of the company's unsecured creditors of whose address he is then aware and who have, to his knowledge, made supplies to the company, with a charge to value added tax, at any time before his appointment.

**5(2)** Thereafter, he shall give the notice to any such creditor of whose address and supplies to the company he becomes aware.

**5(3)** He is not under obligation to provide any creditor with a copy of the certificate.

## PRESERVATION OF CERTIFICATE WITH COMPANY'S RECORDS

**6** The certificate shall be retained with the company's accounting records, and section 222 of the Companies Act 1985 (where and for how long records are to be kept) applies to the certificate as it applies to those records.

## EXPLANATORY NOTE

*(This Note does not form part of the Rules)*

These Rules make provision in relation to England and Wales for the administrative receiver of a company to issue certificates under section 22 of the Value Added Tax Act 1983. That section enables an unpaid creditor of a company who has accounted for value added tax charged on the debt claimed from the company to claim a refund of the tax paid following the issue of a certificate by the administrative receiver that the assets of the company, in his opinion, would be insufficient to cover the payment of any dividend in respect of debts which are neither secured nor preferential.

# THE INSOLVENCY ACT 1985 (COMMENCEMENT NO. 3) ORDER 1986

(SI 1986/463 (C 14))

*Made on 10 March 1986 by the Secretary of State for Trade and Industry under s. 236(2) of the Insolvency Act 1985.*

**1** This Order may be cited as the Insolvency Act 1985 (Commencement No. 3) Order 1986.

**2** The provisions of the Insolvency Act 1985 specified in Schedule 1 hereto shall come into operation on 1st April 1986.

**3** The provisions of the Insolvency Act 1985 specified in Schedule 2 hereto shall come into operation on 28th April 1986.

# Schedule 1 – Provisions Coming into Operation on 1st April 1986

Article 2

| Provisions of the Act | Subject matter of Provision |
|---|---|
| Section 214 in so far as it relates to the awarding by a court in Scotland of the sequestration of an individual's estate | Parliamentary disqualification etc. |
| Schedule 8 paragraph 27 in so far as it relates to the awarding by a court in Scotland of the sequestration of an individual's estate | Consequential amendments. |
| Schedule 10 in so far as it provides for the repeal of, or words in, the following enactments all in so far as they relate to the awarding by a court in Scotland of the sequestration of an individual's estate:— (a) the Bankruptcy Disqualification Act 1871, (b) sections 32, 33 and 34 of the Bankruptcy Act 1883, (c) section 9 of the Bankruptcy Act 1890, (d) Section 1(2) of the Recess Elections Act 1975 | Repeals. |
| Schedule 10 in so far as it provides for the repeal of sub-paragraphs (i) and (ii) of section 18(3)(c) of the Civil Jurisdiction and Judgments Act 1982 | |

# Schedule 2 – Provisions Coming into Operation on 28th April 1986

Article 3

| Provisions of the Act | Subject matter of Provision |
|---|---|
| Section 12 | Duty of court to disqualify unfit directors of insolvent companies. |
| Section 13 | Disqualification after investigation of company. |
| Section 14 | Matters for determining unfitness of directors. |
| Section 15 | Responsibility for company's wrongful trading. |
| Section 16 | Disqualification of persons held to be liable to contribute to company's assets. |
| Section 18 | Personal liability of persons acting while disqualified. |

| Provisions of the Act | Subject matter of Provision |
|---|---|
| Section 108 in so far as not already in operation | Construction of Part II. |
| Section 216 | Repeal of section 152(4) of the Social Security Act 1975. |
| Schedule 2 | Matters for determining unfitness of directors. |
| Schedule 6:—<br>(a) paragraphs 1 to 7,<br>(b) paragraph 15(1) and (2) | Consequential amendments to the Companies Act 1985. |
| Schedule 9 paragraphs 2 to 4 | Transitional Provisions and Savings. |
| Schedule 10 in so far as it provides for the repeal of, or words in, the following enactments:—<br>(a) section 300 of the Companies Act 1985, | Repeals. |
| (b) in Schedule 12 to the Companies Act 1985, Part II and paragraphs 15 and 16,<br>(c) section 152(4) of the Social Security Act 1975. | Repeals. |

## EXPLANATORY NOTE

(*This Note is not part of the Order*)

This Order brings into force on 1st April 1986 those provisions of the Insolvency Act 1985 specified in Schedule 1 to the Order and on 28th April 1986 those further provisions of that Act specified in Schedule 2 to this Order.

The provisions brought into force on 1st April 1986 are:

section 214 which provides for the effect of bankruptcy on an individual's right to sit in the House of Commons or the House of Lords in so far as it regulates the effect of sequestration proceedings in Scotland and provisions in Schedules 8 and 10 to the Act consequential upon the commencement of section 214 under this instrument.

the repeal of provisions in section 18 of the Civil Jurisdiction and Judgments Act 1982 consequent upon the commencement of section 213 under the Insolvency Act 1985 (Commencement No. 2) Order 1986.

The provisions brought into force on 28th April 1986 are:

section 12 which provides for the disqualification of directors of insolvent companies on the grounds of unfitness.

section 13 which provides for the disqualifications of directors on the grounds of unfitness after a report on or an investigation of their companies' affairs under the powers contained in sections 437, 447 or 448 of the Companies Act 1985.

section 14 and Schedule 2 which provide for matters for determining the unfitness of directors.

section 15 which provides for persons responsible for a company's wrongful trading to be liable to contribute to its assets on a winding up.

section 16 which enables a court to disqualify persons held liable to contribute to a company's assets on winding up.

section 18 which imposes personal liability for a company's debts on a person who participates in the management of a company while disqualified.
section 108 which provides for the construction and interpretation of the provisions of Part II of the Act.
section 216 which provides for the repeal of section 152(4) of the Social Security Act 1975.
paragraph 15(1) and (2) of Schedule 6 which amends section 196 of the Companies Act 1985.
Schedules 6, 9 and 10 to the Act to the extent that they make consequential and transitional provision in respect of the provisions commenced under this instrument.

## NOTE AS TO EARLIER COMMENCEMENT ORDERS

(*This Note is not part of the Order*)

The following provisions of the Act have been brought into force by commencement order made before the date of this Order.

| Provision | Date of Commencement | S.I. No. |
|---|---|---|
| s. 10 | 1.2.86 | 1986/6 |
| s. 11 | 1.2.86 | 1986/6 |
| s. 106 partially | 1.2.86 | 1986/6 |
| s. 108(1) and (3) partially | 1.2.86 | 1986/6 |
| s. 213(2), (7), (8) and (9) | 1.2.86 | 1986/6 |
| s. 226 partially | 1.2.86 | 1986/6 |
| s. 232 | 1.2.86 | 1986/6 |
| s. 236(1)–(4) | 1.2.86 | 1986/6 |
| Sched 5 partially | 1.2.86 | 1986/6 |
| s. 45 | 1.3.86 | 1986/6 |
| s. 108(1) and (3) partially | 1.3.86 | 1986/6 |
| s. 109(3) | 1.3.86 | 1986/6 |
| s. 235(2) | 1.3.86 | 1986/6 |
| Sched 9 partially | 1.3.86 | 1986/6 |
| s. 106 partially | 1.3.86 | 1986/185 |
| s. 108(1) and (3) partially | 1.3.86 | 1986/185 |
| s. 109(1) | 1.3.86 | 1986/185 |
| s. 109(2) partially | 1.3.86 | 1986/185 |
| s. 226 partially | 1.3.86 | 1986/185 |
| s. 235(1) and (3) | 1.3.86 | 1986/185 |
| Sched 5 partially | 1.3.86 | 1986/185 |
| Sched 6 partially | 1.3.86 | 1986/185 |
| Sched 8 partially | 1.3.86 | 1986/185 |
| Sched 10 partially | 1.3.86 | 1986/185 |

The following provisions of the Act will be brought into force after the making of this Order by a commencement order made before the date of this Order.

| Provision | Date of Commencement | S.I. No. |
|---|---|---|
| s. 213(1), (3), (4), (5) and (6) partially | 1.4.86 | 1986/185 |

| Provision | Date of Commencement | S.I. No. |
|---|---|---|
| s. 234 | 1.4.86 | 1986/185 |
| Sched 8 partially | 1.4.86 | 1986/185 |
| Sched 10 partially | 1.4.86 | 1986/185 |

# THE INSOLVENCY ACT 1985 (COMMENCEMENT NO. 4) ORDER 1986

(SI 1986/840 (C 22))

*Made on 7 May 1986 by the Secretary of State for Trade and Industry under s. 236(2) of the Insolvency Act 1985.*

**1** This Order may be cited as the Insolvency Act 1985 (Commencement No. 4) Order 1986.

**2** The provisions of the Insolvency Act 1985 specified in Schedule 1 hereto shall come into force on 1st June 1986.

**3** The provisions of the Insolvency Act 1985 specified in Schedule 2 hereto shall come in force on 1st July 1986.

## Schedule 1 – Provisions Coming Into Force on 1st June 1986

Article 2

| Provision of the Act | Subject matter of provision |
|---|---|
| Section 3(2) | Power of the Secretary of State to declare by order that a professional body be recognised for the purposes of the section. |
| Section 4(1)(c) | Power of the Secretary of State to prescribe a fee for applications under section 5. |
| Section 5(2)(b) | Power of the Secretary of State to prescribe education and practical training and experience requirements. |
| Section 5(3) | Power of the Secretary of State to prescribe the maximum period for authorisation. |
| Schedule 1 paragraph 4(4) | Power of the Secretary of State to make rules regulating the procedure on any investigation by the Tribunal. |

## Schedule 2 – Provisions Coming Into Force on 1st July 1986

Article 3

| Provision of the Act | Subject matter of provision |
|---|---|
| Section 3 in so far as not already in force | Authorisation of members of recognised professional bodies. |

| | |
|---|---|
| Section 4 in so far as not already in force | Application for authorisation by a relevant authority. |
| Section 5 in so far as not already in force | Grant, refusal and withdrawal of authorisation by a relevant authority. |
| Section 6 | Notices. |
| Section 7 | Right to make representations. |
| Section 8 | Reference to Tribunal. |
| Section 9 | Refusal or withdrawal of an authorisation without reference to Tribunal. |
| Schedule 1 in so far as not already in force | Insolvency Practitioners Tribunal. |

## EXPLANATORY NOTE

(*This Note is not part of the Order*)

This Order brings into force on 1st June 1986 those provisions of the Insolvency Act 1985 specified in Schedule 1 to the Order and on 1st July 1986 those further provisions of the Act specified in Schedule 2 to the Order.

The provisions brought into force on 1st June 1986 are the following rule-making powers:

section 3(2) which enables the Secretary of State to recognise professional bodies which meet the criteria set out in section 3(3) as being entitled to authorise their members to act as insolvency practitioners.

section 4(1)(c) which enables the Secretary of State to prescribe fees to be paid by applicants to him for authorisation to act as insolvency practitioners.

section 5(2)(b) which enables the Secretary of State to prescribe the standards of education and experience that must be achieved by applicants to him for authorisation.

section 5(3) which enables the Secretary of State to prescribe the maximum period of duration for authorisations granted by him.

Schedule 1 paragraph 4(4) which enables the Secretary of State to make procedural rules governing investigations by the Insolvency Practitioners Tribunal.

The provisions brought into force on 1st July 1986 are:

the remainder of section 3, 4 and 5, sections 6 to 9 and the remainder of Schedule 1 which together with the rule-making powers commenced on 1st June provide for:

the recognition of professional bodies entitled to authorise their members to act as insolvency practitioners;

the establishment of the procedure by which the Secretary of State as the relevant authority may grant, refuse or withdraw authorisation to act as an insolvency practitioner; and

the establishment of an investigatory tribunal, the Insolvency Practitioners Tribunal, to which cases may be referred in the circumstances set out in section 8 of the Act.

## NOTE AS TO EARLIER COMMENCEMENT ORDERS

(*This Note is not part of the Order*)

The following provisions of the Act have been brought into force by commencement orders made before the date of this Order.

| Provision | Date of Commencement | S.I. No. |
|---|---|---|
| s. 10 | 1.2.86 | 1986/6 |
| s. 11 | 1.2.86 | 1986/6 |
| s. 106 partially | 1.2.86 | 1986/6 |

| Provision | Date of Commencement | S.I. No. |
|---|---|---|
| s. 108(1) and (3) partially | 1.2.86 | 1986/6 |
| s. 213(2), (7), (8) and (9) | 1.2.86 | 1986/6 |
| s. 226 partially | 1.2.86 | 1986/6 |
| s. 232 | 1.2.86 | 1986/6 |
| s. 236(1)–(4) | 1.2.86 | 1986/6 |
| Sched. 5 partially | 1.2.86 | 1986/6 |
| s. 45 | 1.3.86 | 1986/6 |
| s. 108(1) and (3) partially | 1.3.86 | 1986/6 |
| s. 109(3) | 1.3.86 | 1986/6 |
| s. 235(2) | 1.3.86 | 1986/6 |
| Sched. 9 partially | 1.3.86 | 1986/6 |
| s. 106 partially | 1.3.86 | 1986/185 |
| s. 108(1) and (3) partially | 1.3.86 | 1986/185 |
| s. 109(1) | 1.3.86 | 1986/185 |
| s. 109(2) partially | 1.3.86 | 1986/185 |
| s. 226 partially | 1.3.86 | 1986/185 |
| s. 235(1) and (3) | 1.3.86 | 1986/185 |
| Sched. 5 partially | 1.3.86 | 1986/185 |
| Sched. 6 partially | 1.3.86 | 1986/185 |
| Sched. 8 partially | 1.3.86 | 1986/185 |
| Sched. 10 partially | 1.3.86 | 1986/185 |
| s. 213(1), (3), (4), (5) and (6) partially | 1.4.86 | 1986/185 |
| s. 234 | 1.4.86 | 1986/185 |
| Sched. 8 partially | 1.4.86 | 1986/185 |
| Sched. 10 partially | 1.4.86 | 1986/185 |
| s. 214 partially | 1.4.86 | 1986/463 |
| Sched. 8 partially | 1.4.86 | 1986/463 |
| Sched. 10 partially | 1.4.86 | 1986/463 |
| s. 12 | 28.4.86 | 1986/463 |
| s. 13 | 28.4.86 | 1986/463 |
| s. 14 | 28.4.86 | 1986/463 |
| s. 15 | 28.4.86 | 1986/463 |
| s. 16 | 28.4.86 | 1986/463 |
| s. 18 | 28.4.86 | 1986/463 |
| s. 108 partially | 28.4.86 | 1986/463 |
| s. 216 | 28.4.86 | 1986/463 |
| Sched. 2 | 28.4.86 | 1986/463 |
| Sched. 6 partially | 28.4.86 | 1986/463 |
| Sched. 9 partially | 28.4.86 | 1986/463 |
| Sched. 10 partially | 28.4.86 | 1986/463 |

# THE INSOLVENCY PRACTITIONERS TRIBUNAL (CONDUCT OF INVESTIGATIONS) RULES 1986

(SI 1986/952)

*Made on 5 June 1986 by the Secretary of State for Trade and Industry under para. 4(4) of Sch. 1 to the Insolvency Act 1985 after consulting the Council on Tribunals in accordance with s. 10 of the Tribunals and Inquiries Act 1971. Operative from 1 July 1986.*

[**Note:** Although these Rules were made under the former Insolvency Act 1985 they continue for the purposes of the consolidated legislation – see Sch. 7, para. 4(4) to the Insolvency Act 1986.]

## CITATION COMMENCEMENT AND INTERPRETATION

**1(1)** These Rules may be cited as the Insolvency Practitioners Tribunal (Conduct of Investigations) Rules 1986 and shall come into force on 1st July 1986.

**1(2)** In these Rules:

(a) references to **"the Act"** are references to the Insolvency Act 1985;

(b) **"the applicant"** means an applicant for authorisation under section 5 of the Act or, where it is proposed to withdraw an authorisation granted under that section, the holder of the authorisation;

(c) **"Treasury Solicitor"** means the Solicitor for the affairs of Her Majesty's Treasury as provided in the Treasury Solicitor Act 1876; and

(d) **"a Scottish case"** means any case where at the time of the reference of the case to the Tribunal the applicant is either habitually resident in or has his principal place of business in Scotland.

## REFERENCE TO THE TRIBUNAL

**2(1)** On referring a case to the tribunal under section 8(2) of the Act the relevant authority shall–

(a) send to the tribunal a copy of the written notice served by it on the applicant in pursuance of section 6(2) of the Act, together with a copy of the notification by the applicant that he wishes the case to be referred to the tribunal, and

(b) give notice to the applicant of the date on which the case has been referred by it to the tribunal and of the address to which any statement notice or other document required by these Rules to be given or sent to the tribunal is to be given or sent.

**2(2)** Within 21 days of referring the case to the tribunal the relevant authority shall send to the tribunal such further information and copies of such other documents and records as it considers would be of assistance to the tribunal and shall, at the same time, send to the applicant such further information and copies of such other documents and records; or, if there is no such information or copies, the relevant authority shall within the said period notify the tribunal and the applicant to that effect.

## STATEMENT OF THE APPLICANT

**3(1)** Within 21 days after the relevant authority has sent to the applicant the material mentioned in Rule 2(2) or, as the case may be, after it has sent to him the notification mentioned in that Rule, the applicant shall send to the tribunal a statement of his grounds for requiring the case to be investigated by the tribunal specifying–

(a) which matters of fact (if any) contained in the written notice served on him under section 6(2) of the Act he disputes,

(b) any other matters which he considers should be drawn to the attention of the tribunal, and

(c) the names and addresses of any witnesses whose evidence he wishes the tribunal to hear.

**3(2)** The applicant shall, on sending the statement referred to in paragraph (1) of this Rule to the tribunal, send a copy to to the relevant authority.

## APPOINTMENT OF SOLICITORS AND COUNSEL TO THE TRIBUNAL

**4** At any time after the case has been referred to it the tribunal may appoint the Treasury Solicitor and Counsel, or, in Scottish cases, may request the Treasury Solicitor to appoint a solicitor and may appoint Counsel, to exercise the functions of:

(a) assisting the tribunal in seeking and presenting evidence in accordance with the requirements of the tribunal; and

(b) representing the public interest in relation to the matters before the tribunal.

## INVESTIGATION BY THE TRIBUNAL

**5** After the receipt of the statement referred to in Rule 3 or, if no such statement is received, after the expiry of the period referred to in that Rule the tribunal shall investigate the case and make a report by carrying out such inquiries as it thinks appropriate for that purpose into and concerning the information, documents, records and matters placed before it under the provisions of Rules 2 and 3 above; and in carrying out such inquiries the requirements set out in the following Rules shall apply.

## METHODS OF INQUIRY BY THE TRIBUNAL

**6(1)** As soon as practicable after the tribunal has considered the subject matter of the investigation it shall notify the relevant authority and the applicant of the manner in which it proposes to conduct its inquiries and in particular whether oral evidence is to be taken.

**6(2)** The tribunal shall give the relevant authority and the applicant a reasonable opportunity of making representations on the manner in which it proposes to conduct its inquiries and such representations may be made orally or in writing at the option of the relevant authority or the applicant as the case may be.

**6(3)** After considering any representations that may be made under paragraph (2) above the tribunal shall notify the relevant authority and the applicant whether and, if so, in what respects, it has decided to alter the manner in which it proposes to carry out its inquiries.

**6(4)** If at any subsequent stage in the investigation the tribunal proposes to make any material change in the manner in which its inquiries are to be carried out it shall notify the relevant authority and the applicant and the provisions of paragraphs (2) and (3) above shall apply accordingly.

## TAKING OF EVIDENCE

**7** When in the carrying out of its inquiries the tribunal:

(a) wishes to examine a witness orally:

  (i) it shall give notice to the applicant and the relevant authority of the time and place at which the examination will be held, and

  (ii) the applicant and the relevant authority shall be entitled to be present at the examination by the tribunal of any witness and to put such additional questions to him as may appear to the tribunal to be relevant to the subject matter of the investigation; or

(b) takes into consideration documentary evidence or evidence in the form of computer or other non documentary records not placed before the tribunal under the provisions of Rules 2 and 3 above, the tribunal shall give the applicant and the relevant authority an opportunity of inspecting that evidence and taking copies or an appropriate record thereof.

## FINAL REPRESENTATIONS

**8** After the tribunal has completed the taking of such evidence as it considers necessary for the purpose of the investigation it shall give the applicant and the relevant authority a reasonable opportunity of making representations on the evidence and on the subject matter of the investigation generally. Such representations may be made orally or in writing at the option of the applicant or, as the case may be, of the relevant authority.

## REPRESENTATION AT A HEARING

**9** At the hearing of oral representations or the taking of oral evidence–

(a) the applicant may be represented by Counsel or solicitor, or by any other person allowed by the tribunal to appear on his behalf; and

(b) the relevant authority may be represented by Counsel or solicitor or by any officer of the relevant authority.

## SERVICE OF WRITTEN REPRESENTATIONS

**10** Where the relevant authority or the applicant makes any written representations to the tribunal in the course of its investigation the relevant authority or, as the case may be, the applicant shall send a copy of such representations to the other.

## HEARINGS IN PUBLIC OR IN PRIVATE

**11(1)** The tribunal shall conduct its investigation in private and, save to the extent that these Rules provide for the hearing of oral representations or for the taking of oral evidence and the applicant requests that any such hearing be in public, no person other than those specified in Rule 9 above or having the leave of the tribunal shall be entitled to be present at any such hearing.

**11(2)** Nothing in this Rule shall prevent a member of the Council on Tribunals or of its Scottish Committee from attending in his capacity as such a member any such hearing.

## NOTICES

**12** Any notice or other document required by these Rules to be given or sent may be given or sent by first class post.

## TIME LIMITS

**13** The tribunal may in any investigation permit the relevant authority or the applicant to send any document or perform any act after the time prescribed in the Rules for so sending or performing and such permission may be granted after any such time has expired.

## POWERS OF CHAIRMAN

**14** Anything required or authorised to be done by the tribunal in the course of an investigation may be done by the chairman except–

(a) the settling of the manner in which the tribunal is to conduct its investigation,

(b) the hearing or consideration of any representations made by the relevant authority or the applicant, and

(c) the taking of evidence, whether orally or in the form of documents or non-documentary records.

## PERIOD WITHIN WHICH REPORT IS TO BE MADE

**15(1)** The tribunal shall make its report on the case to the relevant authority no later than four months after the date on which the case is referred to it under section 8(2) of the Act unless the relevant authority, on the application of the tribunal, permits the report to be made within such further period as the relevant authority may notify in writing to the tribunal.

**15(2)** The relevant authority may only permit the report to be made with the further period referred to in paragraph (1) above where it appears to that authority that, through exceptional circumstances, the tribunal will be unable to make its report within the period of four months referred to in paragraph (1) above.

## SCOTTISH CASES

**16** Any hearing or oral representations under Rule 6(2) or 8 or any examination of a witness under Rule 7(a) in a Scottish case shall be made or held in Scotland unless the applicant consents to any such hearing or examination taking place elsewhere.

## EXPLANATORY NOTE

(*This Note does not form part of the Rules*)

These Rules set out the procedure under which the Insolvency Practitioners Tribunal established under section 8 of the Act is to conduct the investigation of a case referred to it under that section.

The Rules provide for:

(a) the manner in which information and documents are to be made available by the relevant authority and the applicant for the purposes of the investigation;
(b) the appointment of solicitors and counsel to the tribunal;
(c) the manner in which the tribunal is to take oral evidence and to hear oral representations;
(d) the powers of the chairman of the tribunal; and
(e) the period within which the tribunal must make its report.

# THE INSOLVENCY PRACTITIONERS (RECOGNISED PROFESSIONAL BODIES) ORDER 1986

(SI 1986/1764)

*Made on 10 October 1986 by the Secretary of State for Trade and Industry under s. 3(2) and 10 of the Insolvency Act 1985. Operative from 10 November 1986.*

[**Note:** Although this order was made under the former Insolvency Act 1985, it continues for the purpose of the Insolvency Act 1986 – see s. 391, 491 of that Act.]

**1** This Order may be cited as the Insolvency Practitioners (Recognised Professional Bodies) Order 1986 and shall come into force on 10th November 1986.

**2** The bodies specified in the Schedule to this Order are hereby declared to be recognised professional bodies for the purposes of section 3 of the Insolvency Act 1985.

## Schedule – Recognised Professional Bodies

Article 2

The Chartered Association of Certified Accountants
The Insolvency Practitioners Association
The Institute of Chartered Accountants in England and Wales
The Institute of Chartered Accountants in Ireland
The Institute of Chartered Accountants of Scotland
The Law Society
The Law Society of Scotland

## EXPLANATORY NOTE

(*This Note is not part of the Order*)

This Order declares the bodies specified in the Schedule to the Order to be recognised professional bodies under section 3 of the Insolvency Act 1985 membership of which will entitle an individual to act as an insolvency practitioner under the Act where he is permitted to do so by or under the rules of the body concerned.

# THE INSOLVENCY (SCOTLAND) RULES 1986

(SI 1986/1915 (S 139))

*Made on 10 November 1986 by the Secretary of State under s. 411 of the Insolvency Act 1986. Operative from 29 December 1986.*

[**Note:** Amendments by the Insolvency (Scotland) Amendment Rules 1987 (SI 1987/1921 (S 132)) (operative from 11 January 1988) have been included.]

# ARRANGEMENT OF RULES

## INTRODUCTORY PROVISIONS



## PART 1 – COMPANY VOLUNTARY ARRANGEMENTS

### CHAPTER 1 – PRELIMINARY



### CHAPTER 2 – PROPOSAL BY DIRECTORS



### CHAPTER 3 – PROPOSAL BY ADMINISTRATOR OR LIQUIDATOR WHERE HE IS THE NOMINEE



### CHAPTER 4 – PROPOSAL BY ADMINISTRATOR OR LIQUIDATOR WHERE ANOTHER INSOLVENCY PRACTITIONER IS THE NOMINEE



### CHAPTER 5 – MEETINGS



### CHAPTER 6 – IMPLEMENTATION OF THE VOLUNTARY ARRANGEMENT



## PART 2 – ADMINISTRATION PROCEDURE

### CHAPTER 1 – APPLICATION FOR, AND MAKING OF, THE ORDER

| | |
|---|---|
| Form 2.3 (Scot) | Notice of dismissal of petition for administration order. |
| Form 2.4 (Scot) | Notice of discharge of administration order. |
| Form 2.5 (Scot) | Notice requiring submission of administration statement of affairs. |
| Form 2.6 (Scot) | Statement of affairs. |
| Form 2.7 (Scot) | Notice of statement of administrator's proposals. |
| Form 2.8 (Scot) | Notice of result of meeting of creditors. |
| Form 2.9 (Scot) | Administrator's abstract of receipts and payments. |
| Form 2.10 (Scot) | Statement of administrator's proposed revisions and notice of meeting to consider them. |
| Form 2.11 (Scot) | Notice of order to deal with secured property. |
| Form 2.12 (Scot) | Notice of variation of administration order. |
| Form 2.13 (Scot) | Notice to court of resignation of administrator. |
| *Part 3:* | *Receivers* |
| Form 3.1 (Scot) | Notice requiring submission of receivership statement of affairs. |
| Form 3.2 (Scot) | Receiver's abstract of receipts and payments. |
| Form 3.3 (Scot) | Notice of receiver's death. |
| Form 3.4 (Scot) | Notice of authorisation to dispose of secured property. |
| Form 3.5 (Scot) | Notice of receiver's report. |
| *Part 4:* | *Winding up* |
| Form 4.1 (Scot) | Statutory demand. |
| Form 4.2 (Scot) | Notice of winding up order. |
| Form 4.3 (Scot) | Notice requiring submission of Statement of Affairs in a liquidation. |
| Form 4.4 (Scot) | Statement of Affairs. |
| Form 4.5 (Scot) | Liquidator's statement of receipts and payments. |
| Form 4.6 (Scot) | Notice of liquidator's statement of receipts and payments. |
| Form 4.7 (Scot) | Statement of claim by creditor. |
| Form 4.8 (Scot) | Certificate of appointment of liquidator. |
| Form 4.9 (Scot) | Notice of appointment of liquidator. |
| Form 4.10 (Scot) | Certificate of removal of liquidator. |
| Form 4.11 (Scot) | Notice of removal of liquidator. |
| Form 4.12 (Scot) | Application by liquidator to the Accountant of Court for his release. |
| Form 4.13 (Scot) | Certificate by the Accountant of Court of release of the liquidator. |
| Form 4.14 (Scot) | Notice of certificate of release of liquidator. |
| Form 4.15 (Scot) | Notice of court of resignation of liquidator. |
| Form 4.16 (Scot) | Notice of resignation of liquidator. |
| Form 4.17 (Scot) | Notice of final meeting of creditors. |
| Form 4.18 (Scot) | Notice of death of liquidator. |
| Form 4.19 (Scot) | Notice of vacation of office by liquidator. |
| Form 4.20 (Scot) | Certificate of constitution of creditors'/liquidation committee. |
| Form 4.21 (Scot) | Liquidator's certificate of continuance of liquidation committee. |
| Form 4.22 (Scot) | Notice of constitution/continuance of liquidation/creditors' committee. |
| Form 4.23 (Scot) | Liquidator's certificate that creditors paid in full. |
| Form 4.24 (Scot) | Notice of certificate that creditors have been paid in full. |
| Form 4.25 (Scot) | Declaration of solvency. |
| Form 4.26 (Scot) | Return of final meeting in a voluntary winding up. |
| Form 4.27 (Scot) | Notice of court's order sisting proceedings in winding up by the Court. |
| Form 4.28 (Scot) | Notice under section 204(6) or 205(6). |
| [Form 4.29 (Scot) | Proxy.] |

## INTRODUCTORY PROVISIONS

### CITATION AND COMMENCEMENT

**0.1** These Rules may be cited as the Insolvency (Scotland) Rules 1986 and shall come into operation on 29th December 1986.

### INTERPRETATION

**0.2(1)** In these Rules

**"the Act"** means the Insolvency Act 1986;
**"the Companies Act"** means the Companies Act 1985;
**"the Banking Act"** means the Banking Act 1987;
**"the Bankruptcy Act"** means the Bankruptcy (Scotland) Act 1985;
**"the Rules"** means the Insolvency (Scotland) Rules 1986;
**"accounting period"** in relation to the winding up of a company, shall be construed in accordance with section 52(1) and (6) of the Bankruptcy Act as applied by Rule 4.68;
**"business day"** means any day other than a Saturday, a Sunday, Christmas Day, Good Friday or a day which is a bank holiday in any part of Great Britain;
**"company"** means a company which the courts in Scotland have jurisdiction to wind up;
**"insolvency proceedings"** means any proceedings under the first group of Parts in the Act or under these Rules;
**"proxy-holder"** shall be construed in accordance with Rule 7.14;
**"receiver"** means a receiver appointed under section 51 (Receivers (Scotland)); and
**"responsible insolvency practitioner"** means, in relation to any insolvency proceedings, the person acting as supervisor of a voluntary arrangement under Part I of the Act, or as administrator, receiver, liquidator or provisional liquidator.

**History**
In r. 0.2(1) the definitions of "the Banking Act" and "proxy-holder" inserted by the Insolvency (Scotland) Amendment Rules 1987 (SI 1987/1921 (S 132)), r. 3, Sch., Pt. I, para. 1 as from 11 January 1988.

**0.2(2)** In these Rules, unless the context otherwise requires, any reference–

(a) to a section is a reference to a section of the Act;
(b) to a Rule is a reference to a Rule of the Rules;
(c) to a Part or a Schedule is a reference to a Part of, or Schedule to, the Rules;
(d) to a Chapter is a reference to a Chapter of the Part in which that reference is made.

### APPLICATION

**0.3** These Rules apply–

(a) to receivers appointed, and
(b) to all other insolvency proceedings which are commenced, on or after the date on which the Rules come into operation.

# PART 1 – COMPANY VOLUNTARY ARRANGEMENTS

## Chapter 1 – Preliminary

### SCOPE OF THIS PART; INTERPRETATION

**1.1(1)** The Rules in this Part apply where, pursuant to Part I of the Act, it is intended to make and there is made a proposal to a company and to its creditors for a voluntary arrangement, that is to say, a composition in satisfaction of its debts or a scheme of arrangement of its affairs.

**1.1(2)** In this Part–

(a) Chapter 2 applies where the proposal for a voluntary arrangement is made by the directors of the company, and neither is the company in liquidation nor is an administration order under Part II of the Act in force in relation to it;
(b) Chapter 3 applies where the company is in liquidation or an administration order is in

force and the proposal is made by the liquidator or (as the case may be) the administrator, he in either case being the nominee for the purposes of the proposal;

(c) Chapter 4 applies in the same case as Chapter 3, but where the nominee is an insolvency practitioner other than the liquidator or administrator; and

(d) Chapters 5 and 6 apply in all of the three cases mentioned in sub-paragraphs (a) to (c) above.

**1.1(3)** In Chapters 3, 4 and 5 the liquidator or the administrator is referred to as the "responsible insolvency practitioner".

## Chapter 2 – Proposal by Directors

### PREPARATION OF PROPOSAL

**1.2** The directors shall prepare for the intended nominee a proposal on which (with or without amendments to be made under Rule 1.3 below) to make his report to the court under section 2.

### CONTENTS OF PROPOSAL

**1.3(1)** The directors' proposal shall provide a short explanation why, in their opinion, a voluntary arrangement under Part I of the Act is desirable, and give reasons why the company's creditors may be expected to concur with such an arrangement.

**1.3(2)** The following matters shall be stated, or otherwise dealt with, in the directors' proposal–

(a) the following matters, so far as within the directors' immediate knowledge–
  (i) the company's assets, with an estimate of their respective values;
  (ii) the extent (if any) to which the assets are subject to any security in favour of any creditors;
  (iii) the extent (if any) to which particular assets of the company are to be excluded from the voluntary arrangement;

(b) particulars of any property other than assets of the company itself, which is proposed to be included in the arrangement, the source of such property and the terms on which it is to be made available for inclusion;

(c) the nature and amount of the company's liabilities (so far as within the directors' immediate knowledge), the manner in which they are proposed to be met, modified, postponed or otherwise dealt with by means of the arrangement, and (in particular)–
  (i) how it is proposed to deal with preferential creditors (defined in section 386) and creditors who are, or claim to be secured;
  (ii) how persons connected with the company (being creditors) are proposed to be treated under the arrangement; and
  (iii) whether there are, to the directors' knowledge, any circumstances giving rise to the possibility, in the event that the company should go into liquidation, of claims under–

    section 242 (gratuitous alienations),
    section 243 (unfair preferences),
    section 244 (extortionate credit transactions), or
    section 245 (floating charges invalid);

  and, where any such circumstances are present, whether, and if so how, it is proposed under the voluntary arrangement to make provision for wholly or partly indemnifying the company in respect of such claims;

(d) whether any, and if so what, cautionary obligations (including guarantees) have been given of the company's debts by other persons, specifying which (if any) of the cautioners are persons connected with the company;

(e) the proposed duration of the voluntary arrangement;

(f) the proposed dates of distributions to creditors, with estimates of their amounts;

(g) the amount proposed to be paid to the nominee (as such) by way of remuneration and expenses;

(h) the manner in which it is proposed that the supervisor of the arrangement should be remunerated and his expenses defrayed;

(i) whether, for the purposes of the arrangement, any cautionary obligations (including guarantees) are to be offered by directors, or other persons, and whether (if so) any security is to be given or sought;

(j) the manner in which funds held for the purposes of the arrangement are to be banked, invested or otherwise dealt with pending distribution to creditors;

(k) the manner in which funds held for the purpose of payment to creditors, and not so paid on the termination of the arrangement, are to be dealt with;

(l) the manner in which the business of the company is being and is proposed to be conducted during the course of the arrangement;

(m) details of any further credit facilities which it is intended to arrange for the company and how the debts so arising are to be paid;

(n) the functions which are to be undertaken by the supervisor of the arrangement;

(o) the name, address and qualification of the person proposed as supervisor of the voluntary arrangement, and confirmation that he is (so far as the directors are aware) qualified to act as an insolvency practitioner in relation to the company.

**1.3(3)** With the agreement in writing of the nominee, the directors' proposal may be amended at any time up to delivery of the former's report to the court under section 2(2).

## NOTICE TO INTENDED NOMINEE

**1.4(1)** The directors shall give to the intended nominee written notice of their proposal.

**1.4(2)** The notice accompanied by a copy of the proposal, shall be delivered either to the nominee himself, or to a person authorised to take delivery of documents on his behalf.

**1.4(3)** If the intended nominee agrees to act, he shall cause a copy of the notice to be endorsed to the effect that it has been received by him on a specified date; and the period of 28 days referred to in section 2(2) then runs from that date.

**1.4(4)** The copy of the notice so endorsed shall be returned by the nominee forthwith to the directors at an address specified by them in the notice for that purpose.

## STATEMENT OF AFFAIRS

**1.5(1)** The directors shall, within 7 days after their proposal is delivered to the nominee, or within such longer time as he may allow, deliver to him a statement of the company's affairs.

**1.5(2)** The statement shall comprise the following particulars (supplementing or amplifying, so far as is necessary for clarifying the state of the company's affairs, those already given in the directors' proposal)–

(a) a list of the company's assets, divided into such categories as are appropriate for easy identification, with estimated values assigned to each category;

(b) in the case of any property on which a claim against the company is wholly or partly secured, particulars of the claim and its amount and of how and when the security was created;

(c) the names and addresses of the company's preferential creditors (defined in section 386), with the amounts of their respective claims;

(d) the names and addresses of the company's unsecured creditors, with the amounts of their respective claims;

(e) particulars of any debts owed by or to the company to or by persons connected with it;

(f) the names and addresses of the company's members and details of their respective shareholdings; and

(g) such other particulars (if any) as the nominee may in writing require to be furnished for the purposes of making his report to the court on the directors' proposal.

**1.5(3)** The statement of affairs shall be made up to a date not earlier than 2 weeks before the date of the notice given by the directors to the nominee under Rule 1.4. However the nominee may allow an extension of that period to the nearest practicable date (not earlier than 2 months before the date of the notice under Rule 1.4); and if he does so, he shall give his reasons in his report to the court on the directors' proposal.

**1.5(4)** The statement shall be certified as correct, to the best of their knowledge and belief, by two or more directors of the company or by the company secretary and at least one director (other than the secretary himself).

## ADDITIONAL DISCLOSURE FOR ASSISTANCE OF NOMINEE

**1.6(1)** If it appears to the nominee that he cannot properly prepare his report on the basis of information in the directors' proposal and statement of affairs, he may call on the directors to provide him with–

(a) further and better particulars as to the circumstances in which, and the reasons why, the company is insolvent or (as the case may be) threatened with insolvency;

(b) particulars of any previous proposals which have been made in respect of the company under Part I of the Act;

(c) any further information with respect to the company's affairs which the nominee thinks necessary for the purposes of his report.

**1.6(2)** The nominee may call on the directors to inform him, with respect to any person who is, or at any time in the 2 years preceding the notice under Rule 1.4 has been, a director or officer of the company, whether and in what circumstances (in those 2 years or previously) that person–

(a) has been concerned in the affairs of any other company (whether or not incorporated in Scotland) which has become insolvent, or

(b) has had his estate sequestrated, granted a trust deed for his creditors, been adjudged bankrupt or compounded or entered into an arrangement with his creditors.

**1.6(3)** For the purpose of enabling the nominee to consider their proposal and prepare his report on it, the directors must give him access to the company's accounts and records.

## NOMINEE'S REPORT ON THE PROPOSAL

**1.7(1)** With his report to the court under section 2 the nominee shall lodge–

(a) a copy of the directors' proposal (with amendments, if any, authorised under Rule 1.3(3));

(b) a copy or summary of the company's statement of affairs.

**1.7(2)** If the nominee makes known his opinion that meetings of the company and its creditors should be summoned under section 3, his report shall have annexed to it his comments on the proposal. If his opinion is otherwise, he shall give his reasons for that opinion.

**1.7(3)** The nominee shall send a copy of his report and of his comments (if any) to the company. Any director, member or creditor of the company is entitled, at all reasonable times on any business day, to inspect the report and comments.

## REPLACEMENT OF NOMINEE

**1.8** Where any person intends to apply to the court under section 2(4) for the nominee to be replaced he shall give to the nominee at least 7 days' notice of his application.

## SUMMONING OF MEETINGS UNDER SECTION 3

**1.9(1)** If in his report the nominee states that in his opinion meetings of the company and its creditors should be summoned to consider the directors' proposal, the date on which the meetings are to be held shall be not less than 14, nor more than 28 days from the date on which he lodged his report in court under section 2.

**1.9(2)** The notice summoning the meeting shall specify the court in which the nominee's report under section 2 has been lodged and with each notice there shall be sent–

(a) a copy of the directors' proposal;

(b) a copy of the statement of affairs or, if the nominee thinks fit, a summary of it (the summary to include a list of creditors and the amount of their debts); and

(c) the nominee's comments on the proposal.

## Chapter 3 – Proposal by Administrator or Liquidator where he is the Nominee

### PREPARATION OF PROPOSAL

**1.10** The responsible insolvency practitioner's proposal shall specify–

(a) all such matters as under Rule 1.3 in Chapter 2 the directors of the company would be required to include in a proposal by them with, in addition, where the company is subject to an administration order, the names and addresses of the company's preferential creditors (defined in section 386), with the amounts of their respective claims, and

(b) such other matters (if any) as the insolvency practitioner considers appropriate for ensuring that members and creditors of the company are enabled to reach an informed decision on the proposal.

**History**

In r. 1.10(a) the words from "with, in addition, where the company is subject" to "the amounts of their respective claims", inserted by the Insolvency (Scotland) Amendment Rules 1987 (SI 1987/1921 (S 132)), r. 3, Sch., Pt. I, para. 2 as from 11 January 1988.

### SUMMONING OF MEETINGS UNDER SECTION 3

**1.11(1)** The responsible insolvency practitioner shall give at least 14 days' notice of the meetings of the company and of its creditors under section 3(2).

**1.11(2)** With each notice summoning the meeting, there shall be sent–

(a) a copy of the responsible insolvency practitioner's proposal; and

(b) a copy of the company's statement of affairs or, if he thinks fit, a summary of it (the summary to include a list of the creditors and the amount of their debts).

## Chapter 4 – Proposal by Administrator or Liquidator where Another Insolvency Practitioner is the Nominee

### PREPARATION OF PROPOSAL AND NOTICE TO NOMINEE

**1.12(1)** The responsible insolvency practitioner shall give notice to the intended nominee, and prepare his proposal for a voluntary arrangement, in the same manner as is required of the directors in the case of a proposal by them, under Chapter 2.

**1.12(2)** Rule 1.2 applies to the responsible insolvency practitioner as it applies to the directors; and Rule 1.4 applies as regards the action to be taken by the nominee.

**1.12(3)** The content of the proposal shall be as required by Rule 1.10, reading references to the directors as referring to the responsible insolvency practitioner.

**History**

In r. 1.12(3) the words "Rule 1.10" substituted for the former words "Rule 1.3" by the Insolvency (Scotland) Amendment Rules 1987 (SI 1987/1921 (S 132)), r. 3, Sch., Pt. I, para. 3 as from 11 January 1988.

**1.12(4)** Rule 1.6 applies, in respect of the information to be provided to the nominee, reading references to the directors as referring to the responsible insolvency practitoner.

**1.12(5)** With the proposal the responsible insolvency practitioner shall provide a copy of the company's statement of affairs.

**1.12(6)** Rules 1.7 to 1.9 apply as regards a proposal under this Chapter as they apply to a proposal under Chapter 2.

## Chapter 5 – Meetings

### GENERAL

**1.13** The provisions of Chapter 1 of Part 7 (Meetings) shall apply with regard to the meetings of the company and of the creditors which are summoned under section 3, subject to Rules 1.9, 1.11 and 1.12(6) and the provisions in this Chapter.

## SUMMONING OF MEETINGS

**1.14(1)** In fixing the date, time and place for the creditors' meeting and the company meeting, the person summoning the meetings ("the convenor") shall have regard primarily to the convenience of the creditors.

**1.14(2)** The meetings shall be held on the same day and in the same place, but the creditors' meetings shall be fixed for a time in advance of the company meeting.

## ATTENDANCE BY COMPANY OFFICERS

**1.15(1)** At least 14 days' notice to attend the meetings shall be given by the convenor to–

(a) all directors of the company, and

(b) any persons in whose case the convenor thinks that their presence is required as being officers of the company or as having been directors or officers of it at any time in the 2 years immediately preceding the date of the notice.

**1.15(2)** The chairman may, if he thinks fit, exclude any present or former director or officer from attendance at a meeting, either completely or for any part of it; and this applies whether or not a notice under this Rule has been sent to the person excluded.

## ADJOURNMENTS

**1.16(1)** On the day on which the meetings are held, they may from time to time be adjourned; and, if the chairman thinks fit for the purpose of obtaining the simultaneous agreement of the meetings to the proposal (with the same modifications, if any), the meetings may be held together.

**1.16(2)** If on that day the requisite majority for the approval of the voluntary arrangement (with the same modifications, if any) has not been obtained from both creditors and members of the company, the chairman may, and shall, if it is so resolved, adjourn the meetings for not more than 14 days.

**1.16(3)** If there are subsequently further adournments, the final adjournment shall not be to a day later than 14 days after the date on which the meetings were originally held.

**1.16(4)** There shall be no adjournment of either meeting unless the other is also adjourned to the same business day.

**1.16(5)** In the case of a proposal by the directors, if the meetings are adjourned under paragraph (2), notice of the fact shall be given by the nominee forthwith to the court.

**1.16(6)** If following any final adjournment of the meetings the proposal (with the same modifications, if any) is not agreed by both meetings, it is deemed rejected.

## REPORT OF MEETINGS

**1.17(1)** A report of the meetings shall be prepared by the person who was chairman of them.

**1.17(2)** The report shall–

(a) state whether the proposal for a voluntary arrangement was approved or rejected and, if approved, with what (if any) modifications;

(b) set out the resolutions which were taken at each meeting, and the decision on each one;

(c) list the creditors and members of the company (with their respective values) who were present or represented at the meeting, and how they voted on each resolution; and

(d) include such further information (if any) as the chairman thinks it appropriate to make known to the court.

**1.17(3)** A copy of the chairman's report shall, within 4 days of the meetings being held, be lodged in court.

**1.17(4)** In respect of each of the meetings the persons to whom notice of the result of the meetings is to be sent under section 4(6) are all those who were sent notice of the meeting. The notice shall be sent immediately after a copy of the chairman's report is lodged in court under paragraph (3).

**1.17(5)** If the voluntary arrangement has been approved by the meetings (whether or not in the form proposed) the chairman shall forthwith send a copy of the report to the registrar of companies.

## Chapter 6 – Implementation of the Voluntary Arrangement

### RESOLUTIONS TO FOLLOW APPROVAL

**1.18(1)** If the voluntary arrangement is approved (with or without modifications) by the two meetings, a resolution may be taken by the creditors, where two or more insolvency practitioners are appointed to act as supervisor, on the question whether acts to be done in connection with the arrangement may be done by one of them or are to be done by both or all.

**1.18(2)** A resolution under paragraph (1) may be passed in anticipation of the approval of the voluntary arrangement by the company meeting if such meeting has not at that time been concluded.

**1.18(3)** If at either meeting a resolution is moved for the appointment of some person other than the nominee to be supervisor of the arrangement, there must be produced to the chairman, at or before the meeting–

(a) that person's written consent to act (unless the person is present and then and there signifies his consent), and

(b) his written confirmation that he is qualified to act as an insolvency practitioner in relation to the company.

### HAND-OVER OF PROPERTY, ETC. TO SUPERVISOR

**1.19(1)** After the approval of the voluntary arrangement, the directors or, where–

(a) the company is in liquidation or is subject to an administration order, and

(b) a person other than the responsible insolvency practitioner is appointed as supervisor of the voluntary arangement,

the responsible insolvency practitioner, shall forthwith do all that is required for putting the supervisor into possession of the assets included in the arrangement.

**1.19(2)** Where paragraph 1(a) and (b) applies, the supervisor shall, on taking possession of the assets, discharge any balance due to the responsible insolvency practitioner by way of remuneration or on account of–

(a) fees, costs, charges and expenses properly incurred and payable under the Act or the Rules, and

(b) any advances made in respect of the company, together with interest on such advances at the official rate (within the meaning of Rule 4.66(2)(b)) ruling at the date on which the company went into liquidation or (as the case may be) became subject to the administration order.

**1.19(3)** Alternatively, the supervisor shall, before taking possession, give the responsible insolvency practitioner a written undertaking to discharge any such balance out of the first realisation of assets.

**1.19(4)** The sums due to the responsible insolvency practitioner as above shall be paid out of the assets included in the arrangement in priority to all other sums payable out of those assets, subject only to the deduction from realisations by the supervisor of the proper costs and expenses of such realisations.

**1.19(5)** The supervisor shall from time to time out of the realisation of assets discharge all cautionary obligations (including guarantees) properly given by the responsible insolvency practitioner for the benefit of the company and shall pay all the responsible insolvency practitioner's expenses.

### REVOCATION OR SUSPENSION OF THE ARRANGEMENT

**1.20(1)** This Rule applies where the court makes an order of revocation or suspension under section 6.

**1.20(2)** The person who applied for the order shall serve copies of it–

(a) on the supervisor of the voluntary arrangement, and

(b) on the directors of the company or the administrator or liquidator (according to who made the proposal for the arrangement).

Service on the directors may be effected by service of a single copy of the order on the company at its registered office.

**1.20(3)** If the order includes a direction given by the court, under section 6(4)(b), for any further meetings to be summoned, notice shall also be given by the person who applied for the order to whoever is, in accordance with the direction, required to summon the meetings.

**1.20(4)** The directors or (as the case may be) the administrator or liquidator shall–

(a) forthwith after receiving a copy of the court's order, give notice of it to all persons who were sent notice of the creditors' and the company meetings or who, not having been sent that notice, appear to be affected by the order; and

(b) within 7 days of their receiving a copy of the order (or within such longer period as the court may allow), give notice to the court whether it is intended to make a revised proposal to the company and its creditors, or to invite re-consideration of the original proposal.

**1.20(5)** The person on whose application the order of revocation or suspension was made shall, within 7 days after the making of the order, deliver a copy of the order to the registrar of companies.

## SUPERVISOR'S ACCOUNTS AND REPORTS

**1.21(1)** Where the voluntary arrangement authorises or requires the supervisor–

(a) to carry on the business of the company, or to trade on its behalf or in its name, or

(b) to realise assets of the company, or

(c) otherwise to administer or dispose of any of its funds,

he shall keep accounts and records of his acts and dealings in and in connection with the arrangement, including in particular records of all receipts and payments of money.

**1.21(2)** The supervisor shall, not less often than once in every 12 months beginning with the date of his appointment, prepare an abstract of such receipts and payments and send copies of it, accompanied by his comments on the progress and efficacy of the arrangement, to–

(a) the court,

(b) the registrar of companies,

(c) the company,

(d) all those of the company's creditors who are bound by the arrangement,

(e) subject to paragraph (5) below, the members of the company who are so bound, and

(f) where the company is not in liquidation, the company's auditors for the time being.

If in any period of 12 months he has made no payments and had no receipts, he shall at the end of that period send a statement to that effect to all those specified in sub-paragraphs (a) to (f) above.

**1.21(3)** An abstract provided under paragraph (2) shall relate to a period beginning with the date of the supervisor's appointment or (as the case may be) the day following the end of the last period for which an abstract was prepared under this Rule; and copies of the abstract shall be sent out, as required by paragraph (2), within the two months following the end of the period to which the abstract relates.

**1.21(4)** If the supervisor is not authorised as mentioned in paragraph (1), he shall, not less often than once in every 12 months beginning with the date of his appointment, send to all those specified in paragraphs 2(a) to (f) a report on the progress and efficacy of the voluntary arrangement.

**1.21(5)** The court may, on application by the supervisor,–

(a) dispense with the sending under this Rule of abstracts or reports to members of the company, either altogether or on the basis that the availability of the abstract or report to members on request is to be advertised by the supervisor in a specified manner;

(b) vary the dates on which the obligation to send abstracts or reports arises.

## FEES, COSTS, CHARGES AND EXPENSES

**1.22** The fees, costs, charges and expenses that may be incurred for any of the purposes of a voluntary arrangement are–

(a) any disbursements made by the nominee prior to the approval of the arrangement, and any remuneration for his services as is agreed between himself and the company (or, as the case may be, the administrator or liquidator);

(b) any fees, costs, charges or expenses which–

(i) are sanctioned by the terms of the arrangement, or

(ii) would be payable, or correspond to those which would be payable, in an administration or winding up.

## COMPLETION OF THE ARRANGEMENT

**1.23(1)** Not more than 28 days after the final completion of the voluntary arrangement, the supervisor shall send to all the creditors and members of the company who are bound by it a notice that the voluntary arrangement has been fully implemented.

**1.23(2)** With the notice there shall be sent to each creditor and member a copy of a report by the supervisor, summarising all receipts and payments made by him in pursuance of the arrangement, and explaining any difference in the actual implementation of it as compared with the proposal approved by the creditors' and company meetings.

**1.23(3)** The supervisor shall, within the 28 days mentioned above, send to the registrar of companies and to the court a copy of the notice to creditors and members under paragraph (1), together with a copy of the report under paragraph (2).

**1.23(4)** The court may, on application by the supervisor, extend the period of 28 days under paragraphs (1) or (3).

## FALSE REPRESENTATIONS, ETC.

**1.24(1)** A person being a past or present officer of a company commits an offence if he make any false representation or commits any other fraud for the purpose of obtaining the approval of the company's members or creditors to a proposal for a voluntary arrangement under Part I of the Act.

**1.24(2)** For this purpose **"officer"** includes a shadow director.

**1.24(3)** A person guilty of an offence under this Rule is liable to imprisonment or a fine, or both.

# PART 2 – ADMINISTRATION PROCEDURE

## Chapter 1 – Application for, and Making of, the Order

### INDEPENDENT REPORT ON COMPANY'S AFFAIRS

**2.1(1)** Where it is proposed to apply to the court by way of petition for an administration order to be made under section 8 in relation to a company, there may be prepared in support of the petition a report by an independent person to the effect that the appointment of an administrator for the company is expedient.

**2.1(2)** The report may be by the person proposed as administrator, or by any other person having adequate knowledge of the company's affairs, not being a director, secretary, manager, member or employee of the company.

**2.1(3)** The report shall specify which of the purposes specified in section 8(3) may, in the opinion of the person preparing it, be achieved for the company by the making of an administration order in relation to it.

## NOTICE OF PETITION

**2.2(1)** Under section 9(2)(a), notice of the petition shall forthwith be given by the petitioner to any person who has appointed, or is or may be entitled to appoint, an administrative receiver, and to the following persons–

(a) an administrative receiver, if appointed;

(b) if a petition for the winding up of the company has been presented but no order for winding up has yet been made, the petitioner under that petition;

(c) a provisional liquidator, if appointed;

(d) the person proposed in the petition to be the administrator;

(e) the registrar of companies;

(f) the Keeper of the Register of Inhibitions and Adjudications for recording in that register; and

(g) the company, if the petition for the making of an administration order is presented by the directors or by a creditor or creditors of the company.

**History**
In r. 2.2(1) the words "to any person" substituted for the former words "to the person" by the Insolvency (Scotland) Amendment Rules 1987 (SI 1987/1921 (S 132)), r. 3, Sch., Pt. I, para. 4 as from 11 January 1988.

**2.2(2)** Notice of the petition shall also be given to the persons upon whom the court orders that the petition be served.

## NOTICE AND ADVERTISEMENT OF ADMINISTRATION ORDER

**2.3(1)** If the court makes an administration order, it shall forthwith give notice of the order to the person appointed as administrator.

**2.3(2)** Under section 21(1)(a) the administrator shall forthwith after the order is made, advertise the making of the order once in the Edinburgh Gazette and once in a newspaper circulating in the area where the company has its principal place of business or in such newspapers as he thinks most appropriate for ensuring that the order comes to the notice of the company's creditors.

**2.3(3)** Under section 21(2), the administrator shall send a notice with a copy of the court's order certified by the clerk of court to the registrar of companies, and in addition shall send a copy of the order to the following persons–

(a) any person who has appointed, or is or may be entitled to appoint, an administrative receiver;

(b) an administrative receiver, if appointed;

(c) a petitioner in a petition for the winding up of the company; if that petition is pending;

(d) any provisional liquidator of the company, if appointed; and

(e) the Keeper of the Register of Inhibitions and Adjudications for recording in that register.

**History**
R. 2.3(3)(a) substituted by the Insolvency (Scotland) Amendment Rules 1987 (SI 1987/1921 (S 132)), r. 3, Sch., Pt. I, para. 5 as from 11 January 1988; r. 2.3(3)(a) formerly read as follows:

"(a) any person who has appointed an administrative receiver, or has power to do so;"

**2.3(4)** If the court dismisses the petition under section 9(4) or discharges the administration order under section 18(3) or 24(5), the petitioner or, as the case may be, the administrator shall–

(a) forthwith send a copy of the court's order dismissing the petition or effecting the discharge to the Keeper of the Register of Inhibitions and Adjudications for recording in that register; and

(b) within 14 days after the date of making of the order, send a notice with a copy, certified by the clerk of the court, of the court's order dismissing the petition or effecting the discharge to the registrar of companies.

**2.3(5)** Paragraph (4) is without prejudice to any order of the court as to the persons by and to whom, and how, notice of any order made by the court under section 9(4), 18 or 24 is to be given and to section 18(4) or 24(6) (notice by administrator of court's order discharging administration order).

## Chapter 2 – Statement of Affairs and Proposals to Creditors

### NOTICE REQUIRING STATEMENT OF AFFAIRS

**2.4(1)** This Rule and Rules 2.5 and 2.6 apply where the administrator decides to require a statement as to the affairs of the company to be made out and submitted to him in accordance with section 22.

**2.4(2)** The administrator shall send to each of the persons upon whom he decides to make such a requirement under section 22, a notice in the form required by Rule 7.30 and Schedule 5 requiring him to make out and submit a statement of affairs.

**2.4(3)** Any person to whom a notice is sent under this Rule is referred to in this Chapter as "a deponent".

### FORM OF THE STATEMENT OF AFFAIRS

**2.5(1)** The statement of affairs shall be in the form required by Rule 7.30 and Schedule 5.

**2.5(2)** The administrator shall insert any statement of affairs submitted to him in the sederunt book.

### EXPENSES OF STATEMENT OF AFFAIRS

**2.6(1)** A deponent who makes up and submits to the administrator a statement of affairs shall be allowed and be paid by the administrator out of his receipts, any expenses incurred by the deponent in so doing which the administrator considers to be reasonable.

**2.6(2)** Any decision by the administrator under this Rule is subject to appeal to the court.

**2.6(3)** Nothing in this Rule relieves a deponent from any obligation to make up and submit a statement of affairs, or to provide information to the administrator.

### STATEMENT TO BE ANNEXED TO PROPOSALS

**2.7(1)** There shall be annexed to the administrator's proposals, when sent to the registrar of companies under section 23 and laid before the creditors' meeting to be summoned under that section, a statement by him showing–

(a) details relating to his appointment as administrator, the purposes for which an administration order was applied for and made, and any subsequent variation of those purposes;

(b) the names of the directors and secretary of the company;

(c) an account of the circumstances giving rise to the application for an administration order;

(d) if a statement of affairs has been submitted, a copy or summary of it with the administrator's comments, if any;

(e) if no statement of affairs has been submitted, details of the financial position of the company at the latest practicable date (which must, unless the court otherwise orders, be a date not earlier than that of the administration order);

(f) the manner in which the affairs and business of the company–
  (i) have, since the date of the administrator's appointment, been managed and financed, and
  (ii) will, if the administrator's proposals are approved, continue to be managed and financed; and

(g) such other information (if any) as the adminstrator thinks necessary to enable creditors to decide whether or not to vote for the adoption of the proposals.

**History**

R. 2.7(1) renumbered as such and para. (f) substituted by the Insolvency (Scotland) Amendment Rules 1987 (SI 1987/1921 (S 132)), r. 3, Sch., Pt. I, para. 6(1), (2) as from 11 January 1988; para. (f) formerly read as follows:

"(f) the manner in which the affairs of the company will be managed and its business financed, if the administrator's proposals are approved; and"

**2.7(2)** Where the administrator intends to apply to the court under section 18 for the administration order to be discharged at a time before he has sent a statement of his proposals to creditors, in accordance with section 23(1), he shall, at least 10 days before he makes such an application, send to all creditors of the company of whom he is aware, a report containing the information required by paragraph (1)(a) to (f)(i) of this Rule.

**History**

R. 2.7(2) inserted by the Insolvency (Scotland) Amendment Rules 1987 (SI 1987/1921 (S 132)), r. 3, Sch., Pt. I, para. 6(3) as from 11 January 1988.

### NOTICE OF PROPOSALS TO MEMBERS

**2.8** Any notice required to be published by the administrator–

(a) under section 23(2)(b) (notice of address for members of the company to write for a copy of the administrator's statement of proposals), and

(b) under section 25(3)(b) (notice of address for members of the company to write for a copy of the administrator's statement of proposed revisions to the proposals),

shall be inserted once in the Edinburgh Gazette and once in the newspaper in which the administrator's appointment was advertised.

## Chapter 3 – Meetings and Notices

### GENERAL

**2.9** The provisions of Chapter 1 of Part 7 (Meetings) shall apply with regard to meetings of the company's creditors or members which are summoned by the administrator, subject to the provisions in this Chapter.

### MEETING TO CONSIDER ADMINISTRATOR'S PROPOSALS

**2.10(1)** The administrator shall give at least 14 days' notice to attend the meeting of the creditors under section 23(1) to any directors or officers of the company (including persons who have been directors or officers in the past) whose presence at the meeting is, in the administrator's opinion, required.

**2.10(2)** If at the meeting there is not the requisite majority for approval of the administrator's proposals (with modifications, if any), the chairman may, and shall if a resolution is passed to that effect, adjourn the meeting for not more than 14 days.

### RETENTION OF TITLE CREDITORS

**2.11** For the purpose of entitlement to vote at a creditors' meeting in administration proceedings, a seller of goods to the company under a retention of title agreement shall deduct from his claim the value, as estimated by him, of any rights arising under that agreement in respect of goods in the possession of the company.

### HIRE-PURCHASE, CONDITIONAL SALE AND HIRING AGREEMENTS

**2.12(1)** Subject as follows, an owner of goods under a hire-purchase agreement or under an agreement for the hire of goods for more than 3 months, or a seller of goods under a conditional sale agreement, is entitled to vote in respect of the amount of the debt due and payable to him by the company as at the date of the administration order.

**2.12(2)** In calculating the amount of any debt for this purpose, no account shall be taken of any amount attributable to the exercise of any right under the relevant agreement, so far as the right has become exercisable solely by virtue of the presentation of the petition for an administration order or any mater arising in consequence of that or of the making of the order.

### REPORT AND NOTICE OF MEETINGS

**2.13** Any report or notice by the administrator of the result of creditors' meetings held under section 23(1) or 25(2) shall have annexed to it details of the proposals which were considered by the meeting in question and of any revisions and modifications to the proposals which were also considered.

**History**

R. 2.13 substituted by the Insolvency (Scotland) Amendment Rules 1987 (SI 1987/1921 (S 132)), r. 3, Sch., Pt. I, para. 7 as from 11 January 1988; r. 2.13 formerly read as follows:

"REPORT OF MEETINGS
Any report by the administrator of the proceedings of creditors' meetings held under section 23(1) or 25(2) shall have annexed to it details of the proposals which were considered by the meeting in question and of any modifications which were also considered."

## NOTICES TO CREDITORS

**2.14(1)** Within 14 days after the conclusion of a meeting of creditors to consider the administrator's proposals or proposed revisions under section 23(1) or 25(2), the administrator shall send notice of the result of the meeting (including, where appropriate, details of the proposals as approved) to every creditor to whom notice of the meeting was sent and to any other creditor of whom the administrator has become aware since the notice was sent.

**2.14(2)** Within 14 days after the end of every period of 6 months beginning with the date of approval of the administrator's proposals or proposed revisions, the administrator shall send to all creditors of the company a report on the progress of the administration.

**2.14(3)** On vacating office, the administrator shall send to creditors a report on the administration up to that time. This does not apply where the administration is immediately followed by the company going into liquidation, nor where the administrator is removed from office by the court or ceases to be qualified to act as an insolvency practitioner.

# Chapter 4 – The Creditors' Committee

## APPLICATION OF PROVISIONS IN PART 3 (RECEIVERS)

**2.15(1)** Chapter 3 of Part 3 (The creditors'committee) shall apply with regard to the creditors' committee in the administration as it applies to the creditors' committee in receivership, subject to the modifications specified below and to any other necessary modifications.

**2.15(2)** For any reference in the said Chapter 3, or in any provision of Chapter 7 of Part 4 as applied by Rule 3.6, to the receiver, receivership or the creditors' committee in receivership, there shall be substituted a reference to the administrator, the administration and the creditors' committee in the administration.

**2.15(3)** In Rule 3.4(1) and 3.7(1), for the reference to section 68 or 68(2), there shall be substituted a reference to section 26 or 26(2).

**2.15(4)** For Rule 3.5 there shall be substituted the following Rule–

"*Functions of the committee*

**3.5** The creditors' committee shall assist the administrator in discharging his functions and shall act in relation to him in such manner as may be agreed from time to time.".

# Chapter 5 – The Administrator

## REMUNERATION

**2.16(1)** The administrator's remuneration shall be determined from time to time by the creditors' committee or, if there is no creditors' committee, by the court, and shall be paid out of the assets as an expense of the administration.

**2.16(2)** The basis for determining the amount of the remuneration payable to the administrator may be a commission calculated by reference to the value of the company's property with which he has to deal, but there shall in any event be taken into account–

(a) the work which, having regard to that value, was reasonably undertaken by him; and

(b) the extent of his responsibilities in administering the company's assets.

**2.16(3)** Rules 4.32 to 4.34 of Chapter 6 of Part 4 shall apply to an administration as they apply to a liquidation but as if for any reference to the liquidator or the liquidation committee there was substituted a reference to the administrator or the creditors committee.

## ABSTRACT OF RECEIPTS AND PAYMENTS

**2.17(1)** The administrator shall–

(a) within 2 months after the end of 6 months from the date of his appointment, and of every subsequent period of 6 months, and

(b) within 2 months after he ceases to act as administrator,

send to the court, and to the registrar of companies, and to each member of the creditors' committee, the requisite accounts of the receipts and payments of the company.

**2.17(2)** The court may, on the administrator's application, extend the period of 2 months mentioned in paragraph (1).

**2.17(3)** The accounts are to be in the form of an abstract showing–

(a) receipts and payments during the relevant period of 6 months, or

(b) where the administrator has ceased to act, receipts and payments during the period from the end of the last 6 month period to the time when he so ceased (alternatively, if there has been no previous abstract, receipts and payments in the period since his appointment as administrator).

**2.17(4)** If the administrator makes default in complying with this Rule, he is liable to a fine and, for continued contravention, to a daily default fine.

## RESIGNATION FROM OFFICE

**2.18(1)** The administrator may give notice of his resignation on grounds of ill health or because–

(a) he intends ceasing to be in practice as an insolvency practitioner, or

(b) there is some conflict of interest or change of personal circumstances, which precludes or makes impracticable the further discharge by him of the duties of administrator.

**2.18(2)** The administrator may, with the leave of the court, give notice of his resignation on grounds other than those specified in paragraph (1).

**2.18(3)** The administrator must give to the persons specified below at least 7 days' notice of his intention to resign, or to apply for the court's leave to do so–

(a) if there is a continuing administrator of the company, to him;

(b) if there is no such administrator, to the creditors' committee; and

(c) if there is no such administrator and no creditors' committee, to the company and its creditors.

## ADMINISTRATOR DECEASED

**2.19(1)** Subject to the following paragraph, where the administrator has died, it is the duty of his executors or, where the deceased administrator was a partner in a firm, of a partner of that firm to give notice of that fact to the court, specifying the date of the death. This does not apply if notice has been given under the following paragraph.

**2.19(2)** Notice of the death may also be given by any person producing to the court a copy of the death certificate.

## ORDER FILLING VACANCY

**2.20** Where the court makes an order filling a vacancy in the office of administrator, the same provisions apply in respect of giving notice of, and advertising, the appointment as in the case of the administration order.

**History**

In r. 2.20 the words "administration order" substituted for the former words "original appointment of an administrator" by the Insolvency (Scotland) Amendment Rules 1987 (SI 1987/1921 (S 132)), r. 3, Sch., Pt. I, para. 8 as from 11 January 1988.

# Chapter 6 – VAT Bad Debt Relief

## APPLICATION OF PROVISIONS IN PART 3 (RECEIVERS)

**2.21** Chapter 5 of Part 3 (VAT bad debt relief) shall apply to an administrator as it applies to an administrative receiver, subject to the modification that, for any reference to the administrative receiver, there shall be substituted a reference to the administrator.

# PART 3 – RECEIVERS

## Chapter 1 – Appointment

### ACCEPTANCE OF APPOINTMENT

**3.1(1)** Where a person has been appointed a receiver by the holder of a floating charge under section 53, his acceptance (which need not be in writing) of that appointment for the purposes of paragraph (a) of section 53(6) shall be intimated by him to the holder of the floating charge or his agent within the period specified in that paragraph and he shall, as soon as possible after his acceptance, endorse a written docquet to that effect on the instrument of appointment.

**3.1(2)** The written docquet evidencing receipt of the instrument of appointment, which is required by section 53(6)(b), shall also be endorsed on the instrument of appointment.

**3.1(3)** The receiver shall, as soon as possible after his acceptance of the appointment, deliver a copy of the endorsed instrument of appointment to the holder of the floating charge or his agent.

**3.1(4)** This Rule shall apply in the case of the appointment of joint receivers as it applies to the appointment of a receiver, except that, where the docquet of acceptance required by paragraph (1) is endorsed by each of the joint receivers, or two or more of them, on the same instrument of appointment, it is the joint receiver who last endorses his docquet of acceptance who is required to send a copy of the instrument of appointment to the holder of the floating charge or his agent under paragraph (3).

## Chapter 2 – Statement of Affairs

### NOTICE REQUIRING STATEMENT OF AFFAIRS

**3.2(1)** Where the receiver decides to require from any person or persons a statement as to the affairs of the company to be made out and submitted to him in accordance with section 66, he shall send to each of those persons a notice in the form required by Rule 7.30 and Schedule 5 requiring him to make out and submit a statement of affairs in the form prescribed by the Receivers (Scotland) Regulations 1986.

**3.2(2)** Any person to whom a notice is sent under this Rule is referred to in this Chapter as "a deponent".

**3.2(3)** The receiver shall insert any statement of affairs submitted to him in the sederunt book.

### EXPENSES OF STATEMENT OF AFFAIRS

**3.3(1)** A deponent who makes up and submits to the receiver a statement of affairs shall be allowed and be paid by the receiver, as an expense of the receivership, any expenses incurred by the deponent in so doing which the receiver considers to be reasonable.

**3.3(2)** Any decision by the receiver under this Rule is subject to appeal to the court.

**3.3(3)** Nothing in this Rule relieves a deponent from any obligation to make up and submit a statement of affairs, or to provide information to the receiver.

## Chapter 3 – The Creditors' Committee

### CONSTITUTION OF COMMITTEE

**3.4(1)** Where it is resolved by the creditors' meeting to establish a creditors' committee under section 68, the committee shall consist of at least 3 and not more than 5 creditors of the company elected at the meeting.

**3.4(2)** Any creditor of the company who has lodged a claim is eligible to be a member of the committee, so long as his claim has not been rejected for the purpose of his entitlement to vote.

**3.4(3)** A body corporate or a partnership may be a member of the committee, but it cannot act as such otherwise than by a representative appointed under Rule 7.20, as applied by Rule 3.6.

## FUNCTIONS OF THE COMMITTEE

**3.5** In addition to the functions conferred on it by the Act, the creditors' committee shall represent to the receiver the views of the unsecured creditors and shall act in relation to him in such manner as may be agreed from time to time.

## APPLICATION OF PROVISIONS RELATING TO LIQUIDATION COMMITTEE

**3.6(1)** Chapter 7 of Part 4 (The liquidation committee) shall apply with regard to the creditors' committee in the receivership and its members as it applies to the liquidation committee and the creditor members thereof, subject to the modifications specified below and to any other necessary modifications.

**3.6(2)** For any reference in the said Chapter 7 to–

(a) the liquidator or the liquidation committee, there shall be substituted a reference to the receiver or the creditors' committee;

(b) to the creditor member, there shall be substituted a reference to a creditor,

and any reference to a contributory member shall be disregarded.

**3.6(3)** In Rule 4.42(3) and 4.52(2), for the reference to Rule 4.41(1), there shall be substituted a reference to Rule 3.4(1).

**3.6(4)** In Rule 4.57,

(a) for the reference to an expense of the liquidation, there shall be substituted a reference to an expense of the receivership;

(b) at the end of that Rule there shall be inserted the following–

"This does not apply to any meeting of the committee held within 3 months of a previous meeting, unless the meeting in question is summoned at the instance of the receiver.".

**3.6(5)** The following Rules shall not apply, namely–

Rules 4.40, 4.41, 4.43 to 4.44, 4.53, 4.56, 4.58 and 4.59.

## INFORMATION FROM RECEIVER

**3.7(1)** Where the committee resolves to require the attendance of the receiver under section 68(2), the notice to him shall be in writing signed by the majority of the members of the committee for the time being or their representatives.

**3.7(2)** The meeting at which the receiver's attendance is required shall be fixed by the committee for a business day, and shall be held at such time and place as he determines.

**3.7(3)** Where the receiver so attends, the members of the committee may elect any one of their number to be chairman of the meeting, in place of the receiver or any nominee of his.

## MEMBERS' DEALINGS WITH THE COMPANY

**3.8(1)** Membership of the committee does not prevent a person from dealing with the company while the receiver is acting, provided that any transactions in the course of such dealings are entered into on normal commercial terms.

**3.8(2)** The court may, on the application of any person interested, set aside a transaction which appears to it to be contrary to the requirements of this Rule, and may give such consequential directions as it thinks fit for compensating the company for any loss which it may have incurred in consequence of the transaction.

# Chapter 4 – Miscellaneous

## ABSTRACT OF RECEIPTS AND PAYMENTS

**3.9(1)** The receiver shall–

(a) within 2 months after the end of 12 months from the date of his appointment, and of every subsequent period of 12 months, and

(b) within 2 months after he ceases to act as receiver,

send the requisite accounts of his receipts and payments as receiver to–

(i) the Accountant in Bankruptcy,

(ii) the holder of the floating charge by virtue of which he was appointed,

(iii) the members of the creditors' committee (if any),

(iv) the company or, if it is in liquidation, the liquidator.

**History**

In r. 3.9(1)(b), sub-para. (i) substituted with effect from 1 July 1999 by virtue of the Scotland Act 1998 (Consequential Modifications) (No. 2) Order 1999 (SI 1999/1820), art. 1(2), 4 and Sch. 2, para. 141(1), (2) and the Scotland Act 1998 (Commencement) Order 1998 (SI 1998/3178), art. 3. Sub-para. (i) formerly read "the registrar of companies".

**3.9(2)** The court may, on the receiver's application, extend the period of 2 months referred to in paragraph (1).

**3.9(3)** The accounts are to be in the form of an abstract showing–

(a) receipts and payments during the relevant period of 12 months, or

(b) where the receiver has ceased to act, receipts and payments during the period from the end of the last 12-month period to the time when he so ceased (alternatively, if there has been no previous abstract, receipts and payments in the period since his appointment as receiver).

**3.9(4)** This Rule is without prejudice to the receiver's duty to render proper accounts required otherwise than as above.

**3.9(5)** If the receiver makes default in complying with this Rule, he is liable to a fine and, for continued contravention, to a daily default fine.

## RECEIVER DECEASED

**3.10** If the receiver dies, the holder of the floating charge by virtue of which he was appointed shall, forthwith on his becoming aware of the death, give notice of it to–

(a) the registrar of companies,

(b) the members of the creditors' committee (if any),

(c) the company or, if it is in liquidation, the liquidator,

(d) the holder of any other floating charge and any receiver appointed by him,

(e) the Accountant in Bankruptcy.

**History**

R. 3.10(e) inserted with effect from 1 July 1999 by virtue of the Scotland Act 1998 (Consequential Modifications) (No. 2) Order 1999 (SI 1999/1820), art. 1(2), 4 and Sch. 2, para. 141(1), (3) and the Scotland Act 1998 (Commencement) Order 1998 (SI 1998/3178), art. 3.

## VACATION OF OFFICE

**3.11** The receiver, on vacating office on completion of the receivership or in consequence of his ceasing to be qualified as an insolvency practitioner, shall, in addition to giving notice to the registrar of companies and the Accountant in Bankruptcy under section 62(5), give notice of his vacating office, within 14 days thereof, to–

(a) the holder of the floating charge by virtue of which he was appointed,

(b) the members of the creditor's committee (if any),

(c) the company or, if it is in liquidation, the liquidator,

(d) the holder of any other floating charge and any receiver appointed by him.

**History**

In r. 3.11, the words "and the Accountant in Bankruptcy" inserted with effect from 1 July 1999 by virtue of the Scotland Act 1998 (Consequential Modifications) (No. 2) Order 1999 (SI 1999/1820), art. 1(2), 4 and Sch. 2, para. 141(1), (4) and the Scotland Act 1998 (Commencement) Order 1998 (SI 1998/3178), art. 3.

# Chapter 5 – VAT Bad Debt Relief

## ISSUE OF CERTIFICATE OF INSOLVENCY

**3.12(1)** In accordance with this Rule, it is the duty of the administrative receiver to issue a certificate in the terms of paragraph (b) of section 22(3) of the Value Added Tax Act 1983 (which specifies the circumstances in which a company is deemed insolvent for the purposes of that section) forthwith upon his forming the opinion described in that paragraph.

**3.12(2)** There shall in the certificate be specified–

(a) the name of the company and its registered number;

(b) the name of the administrative receiver and the date of this appointment; and

(c) the date on which the certificate is issued.

**3.12(3)** The certificate shall be entitled "CERTIFICATE OF INSOLVENCY FOR THE PURPOSES OF SECTION 22(3)(b) OF THE VALUE ADDED TAX ACT 1983".

### NOTICE TO CREDITORS

**3.13(1)** Notice of the issue of the certificate shall be given by the administrative receiver within 3 months of his appointment or within 2 months of issuing the certificate, whichever is the later, to all of the company's unsecured creditors of whose address he is then aware and who have, to his knowledge, made supplies to the company, with a charge to value added tax, at any time before his appointment.

**3.13(2)** Thereafter, he shall give the notice to any such creditor of whose address and supplies to the company he becomes aware.

**3.13(3)** He is not under obligation to provide any creditor with a copy of the certificate.

### PRESERVATION OF CERTIFICATE WITH COMPANY'S RECORDS

**3.14(1)** The certificate shall be retained with the company's accounting records, and section 222 of the Companies Act (where and for how long records are to be kept) shall apply to the certificate as it applies to those records.

**3.14(2)** It is the duty of the administrative receiver, on vacating office to bring this Rule to the attention of the directors or (as the case may be) any successor of his as receiver.

# PART 4 – WINDING UP BY THE COURT

## Chapter 1 – Provisional Liquidator

### APPOINTMENT OF PROVISIONAL LIQUIDATOR

**4.1(1)** An application to the court for the appointment of a provisional liquidator under section 135 may be made by the petitioner in the winding up, or by a creditor of the company, or by a contributory, or by the company itself, or by any person who under any enactment would be entitled to present a petition for the winding up of the company.

**History**

R. 4.1(1) renumbered as such by the Insolvency (Scotland) Amendment Rules 1987 (SI 1987/1921 (S 132)), r. 3, Sch., Pt. I, para. 9 as from 11 January 1988.

**4.1(2)** The court shall be satisfied that a person has caution for the proper performance of his functions as provisional liquidator if a statement is lodged in court or it is averred in the winding-up petition that the person to be appointed is an insolvency practitioner, duly qualified under the Act to act as liquidator, and that he consents so to act.

**History**

R. 4.1(2) inserted by the Insolvency (Scotland) Amendment Rules 1987 (SI 1987/1921 (S 132)), r. 3, Sch., Pt. I, para. 9 as from 11 January 1988.

### ORDER OF APPOINTMENT

**4.2(1)** The provisional liquidator shall forthwith after the order appointing him is made, give notice of his appointment to–

(a) the registrar of companies;

(aa) the Accountant in Bankruptcy;

(b) the company; and

(c) any receiver of the whole or any part of the property of the company.

**History**
R. 4.2(aa) inserted with effect from 1 July 1999 by virtue of the Scotland Act 1998 (Consequential Modifications) (No. 2) Order 1999 (SI 1999/1820), art. 1(2), 4 and Sch. 2, para. 141(1), (5) and the Scotland Act 1998 (Commencement) Order 1998 (SI 1998/3178), art. 3.

**4.2(2)** The provisional liquidator shall advertise his appointment in accordance with any directions of the court.

## CAUTION

**4.3** The cost of providing the caution required by the provisional liquidator under the Act shall unless the court otherwise directs be–

(a) if a winding up order is not made, reimbursed to him out of the property of the company, and the court may make an order against the company accordingly, and

(b) if a winding up order is made, reimbursed to him as an expense of the liquidation.

## FAILURE TO FIND OR TO MAINTAIN CAUTION

**4.4(1)** If the provisional liquidator fails to find or to maintain his caution, the court may remove him and make such order as it thinks fit as to expenses.

**4.4(2)** If an order is made under this Rule removing the provisional liquidator, or discharging the order appointing him, the court shall give directions as to whether any, and if so what, steps should be taken for the appointment of another person in his place.

## REMUNERATION

**4.5(1)** The remuneration of the provisional liquidator shall be fixed by the court from time to time.

**4.5(2)** Section 53(4) of the Bankruptcy Act shall apply to determine the basis for fixing the amount of the remuneration of the provisional liquidator, subject to the modifications specified in Rule 4.16(2) and to any other necessary modifications.

**4.5(3)** Without prejudice to any order of the court as to expenses, the provisional liquidator's remuneration shall be paid to him, and the amount of any expenses incurred by him (including the remuneration and expenses of any special manager appointed under section 177) reimbursed–

(a) if a winding up order is not made, out of the property of the company;

(b) if a winding up order is made, as an expense of the liquidation.

**History**
In r. 4.5(3) the words from the beginning to "out of the property of the company" substituted by the Insolvency (Scotland) Amendment Rules 1987 (SI 1987/1921 (S 132)), r. 3, Sch., Pt. I, para. 10(1) as from 11 January 1988; the former words read as follows:

"The provisional liquidator's remuneration shall, unless the court otherwise directs, be paid to him, and the amount of any expenses incurred by him reimbursed–

(a) if a winding up order is not made, out of the property of the company (and the court may make an order against the company accordingly), and"

**4.5(4)** Unless the court otherwise directs, in a case falling within paragraph (3)(a) above, the provisional liquidator may retain out of the company's property such sums or property as are or may be required for meeting his remuneration and expenses.

**History**
R. 4.5(4) inserted by the Insolvency (Scotland) Amendment Rules 1987 (SI 1987/1921 (S 132)), r. 3, Sch., Pt. I, para. 10(2) as from 11 January 1988.

## TERMINATION OF APPOINTMENT

**4.6(1)** The appointment of the provisional liquidator may be terminated by the court on his application, or on that of any of the persons entitled to make application for his appointment under Rule 4.1.

**4.6(2)** If the provisional liquidator's appointment terminates, in consequence of the dismissal of the winding up petition or otherwise, the court may give such directions as it thinks fit with respect to–

(a) the accounts of his administration;

(b) the expenses properly incurred by the provisional liquidator; or

(c) any other matters which it thinks appropriate.

**History**

In r. 4.6(2) words formerly appearing at the end deleted by the Insolvency (Scotland) Amendment Rules 1987 (SI 1987/1921 (S 132)), r. 3, Sch., Pt. I, para. 11 as from 11 January 1988; the former words read as follows:

"and, without prejudice to the power of the court to make an order against any other person, may direct that any expenses properly incurred by the provisional liquidator during the period of his appointment, including any remuneration to which he is entitled, be paid out of the property of the company, and authorise him to retain out of that property such sums as are required for meeting those expenses."

## Chapter 2 – Statement of Affairs

### NOTICE REQUIRING STATEMENT OF AFFAIRS

**4.7(1)** This Chapter applies where the liquidator or, in a case where a provisional liquidator is appointed, the provisional liquidator decides to require a statement as to the affairs of the company to be made out and submitted to him in accordance with section 131.

**4.7(2)** In this Chapter the expression "Liquidator" includes "provisional liquidator".

**4.7(3)** The liquidator shall send to each of the persons upon whom he decides to make such a requirement under section 131, a notice in the form required by Rule 7.30 and Schedule 5 requiring him to make out and submit a statement of affairs.

**4.7(4)** Any person to whom a notice is sent under this Rule is referred to in this Chapter as **"a deponent"**.

### FORM OF THE STATEMENT OF AFFAIRS

**4.8(1)** The statement of affair shall be in the form required by Rule 7.30 and Schedule 5.

**4.8(2)** The liquidator shall insert any statement of affairs submitted to him in the sederunt book.

### EXPENSES OF STATEMENT OF AFFAIRS

**4.9(1)** At the request of any deponent, made on the grounds that he cannot himself prepare a proper statement of affairs, the liquidator may authorise an allowance towards expenses to be incurred by the deponent in employing some person or persons to be approved by the liquidator to assist the deponent in preparing it.

**4.9(2)** Any such request by the deponent shall be accompanied by an estimate of the expenses involved.

**4.9(3)** An authorisation given by the liquidator under this Rule shall be subject to such conditions (if any) as he thinks fit to impose with respect to the manner in which any person may obtain access to relevant books and papers.

**4.9(4)** Nothing in this Rule relieves a deponent from any obligation to make up and submit a statement of affairs, or to provide information to the liquidator.

**4.9(5)** Any allowance by the liquidator under this Rule shall be an expense of the liquidation.

**4.9(6)** The liquidator shall intimate to the deponent whether he grants or refuses his request for an allowance under this Rule and where such request is refused the deponent affected by the refusal may appeal to the court not later than 14 days from the date intimation of such refusal is made to him.

## Chapter 3 – Information

### INFORMATION TO CREDITORS AND CONTRIBUTORIES

**4.10(1)** The liquidator shall report to the creditors and, except where he considers it would be inappropriate to do so, the contributories with respect to the proceedings in the winding up within six weeks after the end of each accounting period or he may submit such a report to a meeting of creditors or of contributories held within such period.

**4.10(2)** Any reference in this Rule to creditors is to persons known to the liquidator to be creditors of the company.

**4.19(3)** The appointment of the liquidator takes effect upon the passing of the resolution for his appointment and the date of his appointment shall be stated in the certificate.

**History**

In r. 4.19(3) the words "takes effect upon the passing of the resolution for his appointment" substituted for the former words "shall be effective as from the date when his appointment is certified under paragraph (2) by the chairman of the meeting of the creditors or, where no person has been nominated to be liquidator by that meeting, the chairman of the meeting of the contributories" and the words "the date of his appointment" substituted for the former words "this date" by the Insolvency (Scotland) Amendment Rules 1987 (SI 1987/1921 (S 132)), r. 3, Sch., Pt. I, para. 17(1) as from 11 January 1988.

**4.19(4)** The liquidator shall–

(a) within 7 days of his appointment, give notice of his appointment to the court and to the Accountant in Bankruptcy; and

(b) within 28 days of his appointment, give notice of it in a newspaper circulating in the area where the company has its principal place of business, or in such newspaper as he thinks most appropriate for ensuring that it comes to the notice of the company's creditors and contributories.

**History**

In r. 4.19(4)(a), the words "the Accountant in Bankruptcy" substituted for the former words " the registrar of companies" with effect from 1 July 1999 by virtue of the Scotland Act 1998 (Consequential Modifications) (No. 2) Order 1999 (SI 1999/1820), art. 1(2), 4 and Sch. 2, para. 141(1), (8) and the Scotland Act 1998 (Commencement) Order 1998 (SI 1998/3178), art. 3.

**4.19(5)** The provisions of Rule 4.18(5) shall apply to any notice given by the liquidator under this Rule.

**4.19(6)** Paragraphs (4) and (5) need not be complied with in the case of a liquidator appointed by a meeting of contributories and replaced by another liquidator appointed on the same day by a creditors' meeting.

**History**

In r. 4.19(6) the words "a meeting of contributories" substituted for the former words "a company meeting" by the Insolvency (Scotland) Amendment Rules 1987 (SI 1987/1921 (S 132)), r. 3, Sch., Pt. I, para. 17(2) as from 11 January 1988.

## AUTHENTICATION OF LIQUIDATOR'S APPOINTMENT

**4.20** A copy certified by the clerk of court of any order of court appointing the liquidator or, as the case may be, a copy, certified by the chairman of the meeting which appointed the liquidator, of the certificate of the liquidator's appointment under Rule 4.19(2), shall be sufficient evidence for all purposes and in any proceedings that he has been appointed to exercise the powers and perform the duties of liquidator in the winding up of the company.

## HAND-OVER OF ASSETS TO LIQUIDATOR

**4.21(1)** This Rule applies where a person appointed as liquidator ("the succeeding liquidator") succeeds a previous liquidator ("the former liquidator") as the liquidator.

**4.21(2)** When the succeeding liquidator's appointment takes effect, the former liquidator shall forthwith do all that is required for putting the succeeding liquidator into possession of the assets.

**4.21(3)** The former liquidator shall give to the succeeding liquidator all such information, relating to the affairs of the company and the course of the winding up, as the succeeding liquidator considers to be reasonably required for the effective discharge by him of his duties as such and shall hand over all books, accounts, statements of affairs, statements of claim and other records and documents in his possession relating to the affairs of the company and its winding up.

## TAKING POSSESSION AND REALISATION OF THE COMPANY'S ASSETS

**4.22(1)** The liquidator shall–

(a) as soon as may be after his appointment take possession of the whole assets of the company and any property, books, papers or records in the possession or control of the company or to which the company appears to be entitled; and

(b) make up and maintain an inventory and valuation of the assets which he shall retain in the sederunt book.

**4.22(2)** The liquidator shall be entitled to have access to all documents or records relating to the assets or the property or the business or financial affairs of the company sent by or on behalf of the company to a third party and in that third party's hands and to make copies of any such documents or records.

**4.22(3)** If any person obstructs a liquidator who is exercising, or attempting to exercise, a power conferred by sub-section (2) above, the court, on the application of the liquidator, may order that person to cease so to obstruct the liquidator.

**4.22(4)** The liquidator may require delivery to him of any title deed or other document or record of the company, notwithstanding that a right of lien is claimed over the title deed or document or record, but this paragraph is without prejudice to any preference of the holder of the lien.

**4.22(5)** Section 39(4) and (7) of the Bankruptcy Act shall apply in relation to a liquidation of a company as it applies in relation to a sequestration of a debtor's estate, subject to the modifications specified in Rule 4.16(2) and to any other necessary modifications.

**History**

R. 4.22 substituted by the Insolvency (Scotland) Amendment Rules 1987 (SI 1987/1921 (S 132)), r. 3, Sch., Pt. I, para. 18 as from 11 January 1988: r. 4.22 formerly read as follows:

"TAKING POSSESSION AND REALISATION OF THE COMPANY'S ASSETS

**4.22(1)** Sections 38 and 39(4) and (7) of the Bankruptcy Act shall apply in relation to a liquidation of a company as it applies in relation to a sequestration of a debtor's estate, subject to the modifications specified in paragraph (2) and Rule 4.16(2) and to any other necessary modifications.

**(2)** For subsection (1) of sections 38, there shall be substituted the following section–

"(1) The liquidator shall–

(a) as soon as may be after his appointment take possession of the whole assets of the company and any property, books, papers or records in the possession or control of the company or to which the company appears to be entitled; and

(b) make up and maintain an inventory and valuation of the asset which he shall retain in the sederunt book.""

## Section B: Removal and Resignation; Vacation of Office

### SUMMONING OF MEETING FOR REMOVAL OF LIQUIDATOR

**4.23(1)** Subject to section 172(3) and without prejudice to any other method of summoning the meeting, a meeting of creditors for the removal of the liquidator in accordance with section 172(2) shall be summoned by the liquidator if requested to do so by not less than one quarter in value of the creditors.

**4.23(2)** Where a meeting of creditors is summoned especially for the purpose of removing the liquidator in accordance with section 172(2), the notice summoning it shall draw attention to section 174(4)(a) or (b) with respect to the liquidator's release.

**4.23(3)** At the meeting, a person other than the liquidator or his nominee may be elected to act as chairman; but if the liquidator or his nominee is chairman and a resolution has been proposed for the liquidator's removal, the chairman shall not adjourn the meeting without the consent of at least one-half (in value) of the creditors present (in person or by proxy) and entitled to vote.

**4.23(4)** Where a meeting is to be held or is proposed to be summoned under this Rule, the court may, on the application of any creditor, give directions as to the mode of summoning it, the sending out and return of forms of proxy, the conduct of the meeting, and any other matter which appears to the court to require regulation or control under this Rule.

### PROCEDURE ON LIQUIDATOR'S REMOVAL

**4.24(1)** Where the creditors have resolved that the liquidator be removed, the chairman of the creditors' meeting shall forthwith–

(a) if, at the meeting, another liquidator was not appointed, send a certificate of the liquidator's removal to the court and a copy of the certificate to the Accountant in Bankruptcy, and

(b) otherwise, deliver the certificate to the new liquidator, who shall forthwith send a copy of the certificate to the court and to the Accountant in Bankruptcy.

**4.36(2)** Notice of the death may also be given by any person producing to the court and to the Accountant in Bankruptcy a copy of the death certificate.

**History**
In r. 4.36(2), the words "the Accountant in Bankruptcy" substituted for the former words " the registrar of companies" with effect from 1 July 1999 by virtue of the Scotland Act 1998 (Consequential Modifications) (No. 2) Order 1999 (SI 1999/1820), art. 1(2), 4 and Sch. 2, para. 141(1), (15) and the Scotland Act 1998 (Commencement) Order 1998 (SI 1998/3178), art. 3.

## LOSS OF QUALIFICATION AS INSOLVENCY PRACTITIONER

**4.37(1)** This Rules applies where the liquidator vacates office on ceasing to be qualified to act as an insolvency practitioner in relation to the company.

**4.37(2)** He shall forthwith give notice of his doing so to the court and to the Accountant in Bankruptcy.

**History**
In r. 4.37(2), the words "the Accountant in Bankruptcy" substituted for the former words " the registrar of companies" with effect from 1 July 1999 by virtue of the Scotland Act 1998 (Consequential Modifications) (No. 2) Order 1999 (SI 1999/1820), art. 1(2), 4 and Sch. 2, para. 141(1), (16) and the Scotland Act 1998 (Commencement) Order 1998 (SI 1998/3178), art. 3.

**4.37(3)** Rule 4.25(2) and (3) apply as regards the liquidator obtaining his release as if he had been removed by the court.

## POWER OF COURT TO SET ASIDE CERTAIN TRANSACTIONS

**4.38(1)** If in the course of the liquidation the liquidator enters into any transaction with a person who is an associate of his, the court may, on application of any person interested, set the transaction aside and order the liquidator to compensate the company for any loss suffered in consequence of it.

**4.38(2)** This does not apply if either–

(a) the transaction was entered into with the prior consent of the court, or

(b) it is shown to the court's satisfaction that the transaction was for value, and that it was entered into by the liquidator without knowing, or having any reason to suppose, that the person concerned was an associate.

**4.38(3)** Nothing in this Rule is to be taken as prejudicing the operation of any rule of law with respect to a trustee's dealings with trust property, or the fiduciary obligations of any person.

## RULE AGAINST SOLICITATION

**4.39(1)** Where the court is satisfied that any improper solicitation has been used by or on behalf of the liquidator in obtaining proxies or procuring his appointment, it may order that no remuneration be allowed as an expense of the liquidation to any person by whom, or on whose behalf, the solicitation was exercised.

**4.39(2)** An order of the court under this Rule overrides any resolution of the liquidation committee or the creditors, or any other provision of the Rules relating to the liquidator's remuneration.

# Chapter 7 – The Liquidation Committee

## PRELIMINARY

**4.40** For the purposes of this Chapter–

(a) an "insolvent winding up" takes place where a company is being wound up on grounds which include its inability to pay its debts, and

(b) a "solvent winding up" takes place where a company is being wound up on grounds which do not include that one.

## MEMBERSHIP OF COMMITTEE

**4.41(1)** Subject to Rule 4.34 below, the liquidation committee shall consist as follows:–

(a) in the case of any winding up, of at least 3 and not more than 5 creditors of the company, elected by the meeting of creditors held under section 138 or 142 of the Act, and also

(b) in the case of a solvent winding up where the contributories' meeting held under either of those sections so decides, of up to 3 contributories, elected by that meeting.

**History**

In r. 4.41(1)(b) the word "of" inserted after the word "decides," by the Insolvency (Scotland) Amendment Rules 1987 (SI 1987/1921 (S 132)), r. 3, Sch., Pt. I, para. 23(1) as from 11 January 1988.

**4.41(2)** Any creditor of the company (other than one whose debt is fully secured and who has not agreed to surrender his security to the liquidator) is eligible to be a member of the committee, so long as–

(a) he has lodged a claim of his debt in the liquidation, and

(b) his claim has neither been wholly rejected for voting purposes, nor wholly rejected for the purposes of his entitlement so far as funds are available to a dividend.

**4.41(3)** No person can be a member as both a creditor and a contributory.

**4.41(4)** A body corporate or a partnership may be a member of the committee, but it cannot act as such otherwise than by a member's representative appointed under Rule 4.48 below.

**4.41(5)** In this Chapter, members of the committee elected or appointed by a creditors' meeting are called "creditor members", and those elected or appointed by a contributories' meeting are called "contributory members".

**4.41(6)** Where the Deposit Protection Board exercises the right (under section 58 of the Banking Act to be a member of the committee, the Board is to be regarded as an additional creditor member.

**History**

In r. 4.41(6) the words "section 58 of the Banking Act" substituted for the former words "section 28 of the Banking Act 1979" by the Insolvency (Scotland) Amendment Rules 1987 (SI 1987/1921 (S 132)), r. 3, Sch., Pt. I, para. 23(2) as from 11 January 1988.

## FORMALITIES OF ESTABLISHMENT

**4.42(1)** The liquidation committee shall not come into being, and accordingly cannot act, until the liquidator has issued a certificate of its due constitution.

**4.42(2)** If the chairman of the meeting which resolves to establish the committee is not the liquidator, he shall forthwith give notice of the resolution to the liquidator (or, as the case may be, the person appointed as liquidator by the same meeting), and inform him of the names and addresses of the persons elected to be members of the committee.

**4.42(3)** No person may act as a member of the committee unless and until he has agreed to do so and, unless the relevant proxy or authorisation contains a statement to the contrary, such agreement may be given on behalf of the member by his proxy-holder or any representative under section 375 of the Companies Act who is present at the meeting at which the committee is established; and the liquidator's certificate of the committee's due constitution shall not be issued until at least the minimum number of persons in accordance with Rule 4.41 who are to be members of it have agreed to act, but shall be issued forthwith thereafter.

**History**

In r. 4.42(3) the words from "and, unless the relevant proxy or authorisation" to "at which the committee is established" inserted by the Insolvency (Scotland) Amendment Rules 1987 (SI 1987/1921 (S 132)), r. 3, Sch., Pt. I, para. 24 as from 11 January 1988.

**4.42(4)** As and when the others (if any) agree to act, the liquidator shall issue an amended certificate.

**4.42(5)** The certificate (and any amended certificate) shall be sent by the liquidator to the Accountant in Bankruptcy.

**History**

In r. 4.42(5), the words "the Accountant in Bankruptcy" substituted for the former words " the registrar of companies" with effect from 1 July 1999 by virtue of the Scotland Act 1998 (Consequential Modifications) (No. 2) Order 1999 (SI 1999/1820), art. 1(2), 4 and Sch. 2, para. 141(1), (17) and the Scotland Act 1998 (Commencement) Order 1998 (SI 1998/3178), art. 3.

**4.42(6)** If after the first establishment of the committee there is any change in its membership, the liquidator shall report the change to the Accountant in Bankruptcy.

**History**
In r. 4.42(6), the words "the Accountant in Bankruptcy" substituted for the former words " the registrar of companies" with effect from 1 July 1999 by virtue of the Scotland Act 1998 (Consequential Modifications) (No. 2) Order 1999 (SI 1999/1820), art. 1(2), 4 and Sch. 2, para. 141(1), (17) and the Scotland Act 1998 (Commencement) Order 1998 (SI 1998/3178), art. 3.

## COMMITTEE ESTABLISHED BY CONTRIBUTORIES

**4.43(1)** The following applies where the creditors' meeting under section 138 or 142 of the Act does not decide that a liquidation committee should be established or decides that a liquidation committee should not be established.

**4.43(2)** A meeting of contributories under section 138 or 142 may appoint one of their number to make application to the court for an order to the liquidator that a further creditors' meeting be summoned for the purpose of establishing a liquidation committee; and–

(a) the court may, if it thinks that there are special circumstances to justify it, make that order, and

(b) the creditors' meeting summoned by the liquidator in compliance with the order is deemed to have been summoned under section 142.

**4.43(3)** If the creditors' meeting so summoned does not establish a liquidation committee, a meeting of contributories may do so.

**4.43(4)** The committee shall then consist of at least 3, and not more than 5, contributories elected by that meeting; and Rule 4.42 shall apply to such a committee with the substitution of the reference to Rule 4.41 in paragraph (3) of that Rule by reference to this paragraph.

**History**
In r. 4.43(4) the words from "with the substitution" to the end substituted for the former words "with the substitution of references to contributories for references to creditors" by the Insolvency (Scotland) Amendment Rules 1987 (SI 1987/1921 (S 132)), r. 3, Sch., Pt. I, para. 25 as from 11 January 1988.

## OBLIGATIONS OF LIQUIDATOR TO COMMITTEE

**4.44(1)** Subject as follows, it is the duty of the liquidator to report to the members of the liquidation committee all such matters as appear to him to be, or as they have indicated to him as being, of concern to them with respect to the winding up.

**4.44(2)** In this case of matters so indicated to him by the committee, the liquidator need not comply with any request for information where it appears to him that–

(a) the request is frivolous or unreasonable, or

(b) the cost of complying would be excessive, having regard to the relative importance of the information, or

(c) there are not sufficient assets to enable him to comply.

**4.44(3)** Where the committee has come into being more than 28 days after the appointment of the liquidator, he shall report to them, in summary form, what actions he has taken since his appointment, and shall answer all such questions as they may put to him regarding his conduct of the winding up hitherto.

**4.44(4)** A person who becomes a member of the committee at any time after its first establishment is not entitled to require a report to him by the liquidator, otherwise than in summary form, of any matters previously arising.

**4.44(5)** Nothing in this Rule disentitles the committee, or any member of it, from having access to the liquidator's cash book and sederunt book, or from seeking an explanation of any matter within the committee's responsibility.

## MEETINGS OF THE COMMITTEE

**4.45(1)** Subject as follows, meetings of the liquidation committee shall be held when and where determined by the liquidator.

**4.45(2)** The liquidator shall call a first meeting of the committee to take place within 3 months of his appointment or of the committee's establishment (whichever is the later); and thereafter he shall call a meeting–

(a) if so requested by a creditor member of the committee or his representative (the meeting then to be held within 21 days of the request being received by the liquidator), and

(b) for a specified date, if the committee has previously resolved that a meeting be held on that date.

**4.45(3)** The liquidator shall give 7 days' written notice of the time and place of any meeting to every member of the committee (or his representative, if designated for that purpose), unless in any case the requirement of the notice has been waived by or on behalf of any member. Waiver may be signified either at or before the meeting.

## THE CHAIRMAN AT MEETINGS

**4.46(1)** The chairman at any meeting of the liquidation committee shall be the liquidator, or a person nominated by him to act.

**4.46(2)** A person so nominated must be either–

(a) a person who is qualified to act as an insolvency practitioner in relation to the company, or

(b) an employee of the liquidator or his firm who is experienced in insolvency matters.

## QUORUM

**4.47** A meeting of the committee is duly constituted if due notice of it has been given to all the members, and at least 2 creditor members or, in the case of a committee of contributories, 2 contributory members are present or represented.

## COMMITTEE MEMBERS' REPRESENTATIVES

**4.48(1)** A member of the liquidation committee may, in relation to the business of the committee, be represented by another person duly authorised by him for that purpose.

**4.48(2)** A person acting as a committee-member's representative must hold a mandate entitling him so to act (either generally or specially) and signed by or on behalf of the committee-member, and for this purpose any proxy or authorisation under section 375 of the Companies Act in relation to any meeting of creditors (or, as the case may be, members or contributories) of the company shall, unless it contains a statement to the contrary, be treated as such a mandate to act generally signed by or on behalf of the committee-member.

**History**

In r. 4.48(2) the words from ", and for this purpose any proxy or authorisation" to the end added by the Insolvency (Scotland) Amendment Rules 1987 (SI 1987/1921 (S 132)), r. 3, Sch., Pt. I, para. 26 as from 11 January 1988.

**4.48(3)** The chairman at any meeting of the committee may call on a person claiming to act as a committee-member's representative to produce his mandate and may exclude him if it appears that his mandate is deficient.

**4.48(4)** No member may be represented by a body corporate or by a partnership, or by an undischarged bankrupt.

**4.48(5)** No person shall–

(a) on the same committee, act at one and the same time as representative of more than one committee-member, or

(b) act both as a member of the committee and as representative of another member.

**4.48(6)** Where a member's representative signs any document on the member's behalf, the fact that he so signs must be stated below his signature.

## RESIGNATION

**4.49** A member of the liquidation committee may resign by notice in writing delivered to the liquidator.

## TERMINATION OF MEMBERSHIP

**4.50** Membership of the liquidation committee of any person is automatically terminated if–

(a) his estate is sequestrated or he becomes bankrupt or grants a trust deed for the benefit of or makes a composition with his creditors, or

(b) at 3 consecutive meetings of the committee he is neither present nor represented (unless at the third of those meetings it is resolved that this Rule is not to apply in his case), or

(c) that creditor being a creditor member, he ceases to be, or is found never to have been a creditor.

## REMOVAL

**4.51** A creditor member of the committee may be removed by resolution at a meeting of creditors; and a contributory member may be removed by a resolution of a meeting of contributories.

## VACANCY (CREDITOR MEMBERS)

**4.52(1)** The following applies if there is a vacancy among the creditor members of the committee.

**4.52(2)** The vacancy need not be filled if the liquidator and a majority of the remaining creditor members so agree, provided that the total number of members does not fall below the minimum required by Rule 4.41(1).

**4.52(3)** The liquidator may appoint any creditor, who is qualified under the Rules to be a member of the committee, to fill the vacancy, if a majority of the other creditor members agrees to the appointment, and the creditor concerned consents to act.

**4.52(4)** Alternatively, a meeting of creditors may resolve that a creditor be appointed (with his consent) to fill the vacancy. In this case, at least 14 days' notice must have been given of the resolution to make such an appointment (whether or not of a person named in the notice).

**4.52(5)** Where the vacancy is filled by an appointment made by a creditors' meeting at which the liquidator is not present, the chairman of the meeting shall report to the liquidator the appointment which has been made.

## VACANCY (CONTRIBUTORY MEMBERS)

**4.53(1)** The following applies if there is a vacancy among the contributory members of the committee.

**4.53(2)** The vacancy need not be filled if the liquidator and a majority of the remaining contributory members so agree, provided that, in the case of a committee of contributory members only, the total number of members does not fall below the minimum required by Rule 4.43(4) or, as the case may be, 4.59(4).

**History**
In r. 4.53(2) the reference to "Rule 4.43(4)" substituted for the former reference to "Rule 4.41(1)" by the Insolvency (Scotland) Amendment Rules 1987 (SI 1987/1921 (S 132)), r. 3, Sch., Pt. I, para. 27 as from 11 January 1988.

**4.53(3)** The liquidator may appoint any contributory member (being qualified under the Rules to be a member of the committee) to fill the vacancy, if a majority of the other contributory members agree to the appointment, and the contributory concerned consents to act.

**4.53(4)** Alternatively, a meeting of contributories may resolve that a contributory be appointed (with his consent) to fill the vacancy. In this case, at least 14 days' notice must have been given of the resolution to make such an appointment (whether or not of a person named in the notice).

**4.53(5)** Where the vacancy is filled by an appointment made by a contributories' meeting at which the liquidator is not present, the chairman of the meeting shall report to the liquidator the appointment which has been made.

## VOTING RIGHTS AND RESOLUTIONS

**4.54(1)** At any meeting of the committee, each member of it (whether present himself, or by his representative) has one vote; and a resolution is passed when a majority of the creditor members present or represented have voted in favour of it.

**4.54(2)** Subject to the next paragraph, the votes of contributory members do not count towards the number required for passing a resolution, but the way in which they vote on any resolution shall be recorded.

**4.54(3)** Paragraph (2) does not apply where, by virtue of Rule 4.43(4) or 4.59, the only members of the committee are contributories. In that case the committee is to be treated for voting purposes as if all its members were creditors.

**4.54(4)** Every resolution passed shall be recorded in writing, either separately or as part of the minutes of the meeting. The record shall be signed by the chairman and kept as part of the sederunt book.

## RESOLUTIONS BY POST

**4.55(1)** In accordance with this Rule, the liquidator may seek to obtain the agreement of members of the liquidation committee to a resolution by sending to every member (or his representative designated for the purpose) a copy of the proposed resolution.

**4.55(2)** Where the liquidator makes use of the procedure allowed by this Rule, he shall send out to members of the committee or their representatives (as the case may be) a copy of any proposed resolution on which a decision is sought, which shall be set out in such a way that agreement with or dissent from each separate resolution may be indicated by the recipient on the copy so sent.

**History**

In r. 4.55(2) the words from "a copy of any proposed resolution" to the end substituted by the Insolvency (Scotland) Amendment Rules 1987 (SI 1987/1921 (S 132)), r. 3, Sch., Pt. I, para. 28 as from 11 January 1988; the former words read as follows:

"a statement incorporating the resolution to which their agreement is sought, each resolution (if more than one) being set out in a separate document."

**4.55(3)** Any creditor member of the committee may, within 7 business days from the date of the liquidator sending out a resolution, require him to summon a meeting of the committee to consider the matters raised by the resolution.

**4.55(4)** In the absence of such a request, the resolution is deemed to have been passed by the committee if and when the liquidator is notified in writing by a majority of the creditor members that they concur with it.

**4.55(5)** A copy of every resolution passed under this Rule, and a note that the committee's concurrence was obtained, shall be kept in the sederunt book.

## LIQUIDATOR'S REPORTS

**4.56(1)** The liquidator shall, as and when directed by the liquidation committee (but not more often than once in any period of 2 months), send a written report to every member of the committee setting out the position generally as regards the progress of the winding up and matters arising in connection with it, to which the liquidator considers the committee's attention should be drawn.

**4.56(2)** In the absence of such directions by the committee, the liquidator shall send such a report not less often than once in every period of 6 months.

**4.56(3)** The obligations of the liquidator under this Rule are without prejudice to those imposed by Rule 4.44.

## EXPENSES OF MEMBERS, ETC.

**4.57(1)** The liquidator shall defray any reasonable travelling expenses directly incurred by members of the liquidation committee or their representatives in respect of their attendance at the committee's meetings, or otherwise on the committee's business, as an expense of the liquidation.

**4.57(2)** Paragraph (1) does not apply to any meeting of the committee held within 3 months of a previous meeting.

## DEALINGS BY COMMITTEE-MEMBERS AND OTHERS

**4.58(1)** This Rule applies to–

(a) any member of the liquidation committee:

(b) any committee-member's representative;

(c) any person who is an associate of a member of the committee or of a committee-member's representative; and

(d) any person who has been a member of the committee at any time in the last 12 months.

**4.58(2)** Subject as follows, a person to whom this Rule applies shall not enter into any transaction whereby he–

(a) receives out of the company's assets any payment for services given or goods supplied in connection with the liquidation, or
(b) obtains any profit from the liquidation, or
(c) acquires any part of the company's assets.

**4.58(3)** Such a transaction may be entered into by a person to whom this Rule applies–
(a) with the prior leave of the court, or
(b) if he does so as a matter of urgency, or by way of performance of a contract in force before the date on which the company went into liquidation, and obtains the court's leave for the transaction, having applied for it without undue delay, or
(c) with the prior sanction of the liquidation committee, where it is satisfied (after full disclosure of the circumstances) that the transaction will be on normal commercial terms.

**4.58(4)** Where in the committee a resolution is proposed that sanction be accorded for a transaction to be entered into which, without that sanction or the leave of the court, would be in contravention of this Rule, no member of the committee, and no representative of a member, shall vote if he is to participate directly or indirectly in the transaction.

**4.58(5)** The court may, on the application of any person interested–
(a) set aside a transaction on the ground that it has been entered into in contravention of this Rule, and
(b) make with respect to it such other order as it thinks fit, including (subject to the following paragraph) an order requiring a person to whom this Rule applies to account for any profit obtained from the transaction and compensate the company's assets for any resultant loss.

**4.58(6)** In the case of a person to whom this Rule applies as an associate of a member of the committee or of a committee-member's representative, the court shall not make any order under paragraph (5), if satisfied that he entered into the relevant transaction without having any reason to suppose that in doing so he would contravene this Rule.

**4.58(7)** The expenses of an application to the court for leave under this Rule are not payable as an expense of the liquidation, unless the court so orders.

## COMPOSITION OF COMMITTEE WHEN CREDITORS PAID IN FULL

**4.59(1)** This Rule applies if the liquidator issues a certificate that the creditors have been paid in full, with interest in accordance with section 189.

**4.59(2)** The liquidator shall forthwith send a copy of the certificate to the Accountant in Bankruptcy.

**History**
In r. 4.59(2), the words "the Accountant in Bankruptcy" substituted for the former words " the registrar of companies" with effect from 1 July 1999 by virtue of the Scotland Act 1998 (Consequential Modifications) (No. 2) Order 1999 (SI 1999/1820), art. 1(2), 4 and Sch. 2, para. 141(1), (18) and the Scotland Act 1998 (Commencement) Order 1998 (SI 1998/3178), art. 3.

**4.59(3)** The creditor members of the liquidation committee shall cease to be members of the committee.

**4.59(4)** The committee continues in being unless and until abolished by decision of a meeting of contributories, and (subject to the next paragraph) so long as it consists of at least 2 contributory members.

**4.59(5)** The committee does not cease to exist on account of the number of contributory members falling below 2, unless and until 28 days have elapsed since the issue of the liquidator's certificate under paragraph (1), but at any time when the committee consists of less than 2 contributory members, it is suspended and cannot act.

**4.59(6)** Contributories may be co-opted by the liquidator, or appointed by a contributories meeting, to be members of the committee; but the maximum number of members is 5.

**4.59(7)** The foregoing Rules in this Chapter continue to apply to the liquidation committee (with any necessary modifications) as if all the members of the committee were creditor members.

## FORMAL DEFECTS

**4.59A** The acts of the liquidation committee established for any winding up are valid notwithstanding any defect in the appointment, election or qualifications of any member of the committee or any committee-member's representative or in the formalities of its establishment.

**History**
R. 4.59A inserted by the Insolvency (Scotland) Amendment Rules 1987 (SI 1987/1921 (S 132)), r. 3, Sch., Pt. I, para. 29 as from 11 January 1988.

# Chapter 8 – The Liquidation Committee where Winding Up Follows Immediately on Administration

## PRELIMINARY

**4.60(1)** The Rules in this Chapter apply where–

(a) the winding up order has been made immediately upon the discharge of an administration order under Part II of the Act, and

(b) the court makes an order under section 140(1) appointing as liquidator the person who was previously the administrator.

**4.60(2)** In this Chapter the expressions **"insolvent winding up"**, **"solvent winding up"**, **"credit member"**, and **"contributory member"** each have the same meaning as in Chapter 7.

## CONTINUATION OF CREDITORS' COMMITTEE

**4.61(1)** If under section 26 a creditors' committee has been established for the purposes of the administration, then (subject as follows in this Chapter) that committee continues in being as the liquidation committee for the purposes of the winding up, and–

(a) it is deemed to be a committee established as such under section 142, and

(b) no action shall be taken under subsections (1) to (4) of that section to establish any other.

**4.61(2)** This Rule does not apply if, at the time when the court's order under section 140(1) is made, the committee under section 26 consists of less than 3 members; and a creditor who was, immediately before the date of that order, a member of such a committee ceases to be a member on the making of the order if his debt is fully secured (and he has not agreed to surrender his security to the liquidator).

## MEMBERSHIP OF COMMITTEE

**4.62(1)** Subject as follows, the liquidation committee shall consist of at least 3, and not more than 5, creditors of the company, elected by the creditors' meeting held under section 26 or (in order to make up numbers or fill vacancies) by a creditors' meeting summoned by the liquidator after the company goes into liquidation.

**4.62(2)** In the case of a solvent winding up, the liquidator shall, on not less than 21 days' notice, summon a meeting of contributories, in order to elect (if it so wishes) contributory members of the liquidation committee, up to 3 in number.

## LIQUIDATOR'S CERTIFICATE

**4.63(1)** The liquidator shall issue a certificate of the liquidation committee's continuance specifying the persons who are, or are to be, members of it.

**4.63(2)** It shall be stated in the certificate whether or not the liquidator has summoned a meeting of contributories under Rule 4.62(2), and whether (if so) the meeting has elected contributories to be members of the committee.

**4.63(3)** Pending the issue of the liquidator's certificate, the committee is suspended and cannot act.

**4.63(4)** No person may act, or continue to act, as a member of the committee unless and until he has agreed to do so; and the liquidator's certificate shall not be issued until at least the minimum number of persons required under Rule 4.62 to form a committee elected, whether under Rule 4.62 above or under section 26, have signified their agreement.

**4.63(5)** As and when the others signify their agreement, the liquidator shall issue an amended certificate.

**4.63(6)** The liquidator's certificate (or, as the case may be, the amended certificate) shall be sent by him to the Accountant in Bankruptcy.

**History**
In r. 4.63(6), the words "the Accountant in Bankruptcy" substituted for the former words " the registrar of companies" with effect from 1 July 1999 by virtue of the Scotland Act 1998 (Consequential Modifications) (No. 2) Order 1999 (SI 1999/1820), art. 1(2), 4 and Sch. 2, para. 141(1), (19) and the Scotland Act 1998 (Commencement) Order 1998 (SI 1998/3178), art. 3.

**4.63(7)** If subsequently there is any change in the committee's membership, the liquidator shall report the change to the Accountant in Bankruptcy.

**History**
In r. 4.63(7), the words "the Accountant in Bankruptcy" substituted for the former words " the registrar of companies" with effect from 1 July 1999 by virtue of the Scotland Act 1998 (Consequential Modifications) (No. 2) Order 1999 (SI 1999/1820), art. 1(2), 4 and Sch. 2, para. 141(1), (19) and the Scotland Act 1998 (Commencement) Order 1998 (SI 1998/3178), art. 3.

## OBLIGATIONS OF LIQUIDATOR TO COMMITTEE

**4.64(1)** As soon as may be after the issue of the liquidator's certificate under rule 4.63, the liquidator shall report to the liquidation committee what actions he has taken since the date on which the company went into liquidation.

**4.64(2)** A person who becomes a member of the committee after that date is not entitled to require a report to him by the liquidator, otherwise than in a summary form, of any matters previously arising.

**4.64(3)** Nothing in this Rule disentitles the committee, or any member of it, from having access to the sederunt book (whether relating to the period when he was administrator, or to any subsequent period), or from seeking an explanation of any matter within the committee's responsibility.

## APPLICATION OF CHAPTER 7

**4.65** Except as provided elsewhere in this Chapter, Rules 4.44 to 4.59A of Chapter 7 shall apply to a liquidation committee established under this Chapter from the date of issue of the certificate under Rule 4.63 as if it had been established under section 142.

**History**
In r. 4.65 the reference to "Rules 4.44 to 4.59A" substituted for the former reference to "Rules 4.44 to 4.59" by the Insolvency (Scotland) Amendment Rules 1987 (SI 1987/1921 (S 132)), r. 3, Sch., Pt. I, para. 30 as from 11 January 1988.

# Chapter 9 – Distribution of Company's Assets by Liquidator

## ORDER OF PRIORITY IN DISTRIBUTION

**4.66(1)** The funds of the company's assets shall be distributed by the liquidator to meet the following expenses and debts in the order in which they are mentioned–

(a) the expenses of the liquidation;

(aa) where the court makes a winding up order in relation to a company and, at the time when the petition for winding up was first presented to the court, there was in force in relation to the company a voluntary arrangement under Part 1 of the Act, any expenses properly incurred as expenses of the administration of that arrangement;

(b) any preferential debts within the meaning of section 386 (excluding any interest which has been accrued thereon to the date of commencement of the winding up within the meaning of section 129);

(c) ordinary debts, that is to say a debt which is neither a secured debt nor a debt mentioned in any other sub-paragraph of this paragraph;

(d) interest at the official rate on–
  (i) the preferential debts, and
  (ii) the ordinary debts,
between the said date of commencement of the winding up and the date of payment of the debt; and

(e) any postponed debt.

**History**
R. 4.66(1)(aa) inserted by the Insolvency (Scotland) Amendment Rules 1987 (SI 1987/1921 (S 132)), r. 3, Sch., Pt. I, para. 31(1) as from 11 January 1988.

**4.66(2)** In the above paragraph–

(a) **"postponed debt"** means a creditor's right to any alienation which has been reduced or restored to the company's assets under section 242 or to the proceeds of sale of such an alienation; and

(b) **"official rate"** shall be construed in accordance with subsection (4) of section 189 and, for the purposes of paragraph (a) of that subsection, as applied to Scotland by subsection (5), the rate specified in the Rules shall be 15 per centum per annum.

**4.66(3)** The expenses of the liquidation mentioned in sub-paragraph (a) of paragraph (1) are payable in the order of priority mentioned in Rule 4.67.

**4.66(4)** Subject to the provisions of section 175, any debt falling within any of sub-paragraphs (b) to (e) of paragraph (1) shall have the same priority as any other debt falling within the same sub-paragraph and, where the funds of the company's assets are inadequate to enable the debts mentioned in this sub-paragraph to be paid in full, they shall abate in equal proportions.

**4.66(5)** Any surplus remaining, after all expenses and debts mentioned in paragraph (1) have been paid in full, shall (unless the articles of the company otherwise provide) be distributed among the members according to their rights and interests in the company.

**4.66(6)** Nothing in this Rule shall affect–

(a) the right of a secured creditor which is preferable to the rights of the liquidator; or

(b) any preference of the holder of a lien over a title deed or other document which has been delivered to the liquidator in accordance with a requirement under Rule 4.22(4).

**History**
In r. 4.66(6)(b) the words "the liquidator" substituted for the former words "the permanent trustee" and the words "Rule 4.22(4)" substituted for the former words "section 38(4) of the Bankruptcy Act, as applied by Rule 4.22" by the Insolvency (Scotland) Amendment Rules 1987 (SI 1987/1921 (S 132)), r. 3, Sch., Pt. I, para. 31(1) as from 11 January 1988.

## ORDER OF PRIORITY OF EXPENSES OF LIQUIDATION

**4.67(1)** Subject to section 156 and paragraph (2), the expenses of the liquidation are payable out of the assets in the following order of priority–

(a) any outlays properly chargeable or incurred by the provisional liquidator or liquidator in carrying out his functions in the liquidation, except those outlays specifically mentioned in the following sub-paragraphs;

(b) the cost, or proportionate cost, of any caution provided by a provisional liquidator, liquidator or special manager in accordance with the Act or the Rules;

(c) the remuneration of the provisional liquidator (if any);

(d) the expenses of the petitioner in the liquidation, and of any person appearing in the petition whose expenses are allowed by the court;

(e) the remuneration of the special manager (if any);

(f) any allowance made by the liquidator under Rule 4.9(1) (expenses of statement of affairs);

(g) the remuneration or emoluments of any person who has been employed by the liquidator to perform any services for the company, as required or authorised by or under the Act or the Rules;

(h) the remuneration of the liquidator determined in accordance with Rule 4.32;

(i) the amount of any corporation tax on chargeable gains accruing on the realisation of any asset of the company (without regard to whether the realisation is effected by the liquidator, a secured creditor or otherwise).

**History**
In r. 4.67(1)(i) the word "corporation" substituted for the former words "capital gains" by the Insolvency (Scotland) Amendment Rules 1987 (SI 1987/1921 (S 132)), r. 3, Sch., Pt. I, para. 32 as from 11 January 1988.

**4.67(2)** In any winding up by the court which follows immediately on a voluntary winding up (whether members' voluntary or creditors' voluntary), such outlays and remuneration of the voluntary liquidator as the court may allow, shall have the same priority as the outlays mentioned in sub-paragraph (a) of paragraph (1).

**4.67(3)** Nothing in this Rule applies to or affects the power of any court, in proceedings by or against the company, to order expenses to be paid by the company, or the liquidator; nor does it affect the rights of any person to whom such expenses are ordered to be paid.

### APPLICATION OF THE BANKRUPTCY ACT

**4.68(1)** Sections 52, 53 and 58 of the Bankruptcy Act shall apply in relation to the liquidation of a company as they apply in relation to a sequestration of a debtor's estate, subject to the modifications specified in Rules 4.16(2) and 4.32(2) and (3) and the following paragraph and to any other necessary modifications.

**4.68(2)** In section 52, the following modifications shall be made–

(a) in subsection (4)(a) for the reference to "the debts mentioned in subsection (1)(a) to (d)", there shall be substituted a reference to the expenses of the winding up mentioned in Rule 4.67(1)(a);

(b) in subsection (5), the words "with the consent of the commissioners or if there are no commissioners of the Accountant in Bankruptcy" should be deleted; and

(c) in subsection (7) and (8) for the references to section 48(5) and 49(6)(b) there should be substituted a reference to those sections as applied by Rule 4.16(1).

## Chapter 10 – Special Manager

### APPOINTMENT AND REMUNERATION

**4.69(1)** This Chapter applies to an application under section 177 by the liquidator or, where one has been appointed, by the provisional liquidator for the appointment of a person to be special manager (references in this Chapter to the liquidator shall be read as including the provisional liquidator).

**4.69(2)** An application shall be supported by a report setting out the reasons for the appointment. The report shall include the applicant's estimate of the value of the assets in respect of which the special manager is to be appointed.

**4.69(3)** The order of the court appointing the special manager shall specify the duration of his appointment, which may be for a period of time or until the occurrence of a specified event. Alternatively the order may specify that the duration of the appointment is to be subject to a further order of the court.

**4.69(4)** The appointment of a special manager may be renewed by order of the court.

**4.69(5)** The special manager's remuneration shall be fixed from time to time by the court.

**4.69(6)** The acts of the special manager are valid notwithstanding any defect in his appointment or qualifications.

### CAUTION

**4.70(1)** The appointment of the special manager does not take effect until the person appointed has found (or, being allowed by the court to do so, has undertaken to find) caution to the person who applies for him to be appointed.

**4.70(2)** It is not necessary that caution be found for each separate company liquidation; but it may be found either specially for a particular liquidation, or generally for any liquidation in relation to which the special manager may be employed as such.

**4.70(3)** The amount of the caution shall be not less than the value of the assets in respect of which he is appointed, as estimated by the applicant in his report under Rule 4.69.

**4.70(4)** When the special manager has found caution to the person applying for his appointment, that person shall certify the adequacy of the security and notify the court accordingly.

**4.70(5)** The cost of finding caution shall be paid in the first instance by the special manager; but–

(a) where a winding up order is not made, he is entitled to be reimbursed out of the property of the company, and the court may make an order on the company accordingly, and
(b) where a winding up order has been or is subsequently made, he is entitled to be reimbursed as an expense of the liquidation.

### FAILURE TO FIND OR TO MAINTAIN CAUTION

**4.71(1)** If the special manager fails to find the required caution within the time stated for that purpose by the order appointing him, or any extension of that time that may be allowed, the liquidator shall report the failure to the court, which may thereupon discharge the order appointing the special manager.

**4.71(2)** If the special manager fails to maintain his caution the liquidator shall report his failure to the court, which may thereupon remove the special manager and make such order as it thinks fit as to expenses.

**4.71(3)** If an order is made under this Rule removing the special manager, or recalling the order appointing him, the court shall give directions as to whether any, and if so what, steps should be taken to appoint another special manager in his place.

### ACCOUNTING

**4.72(1)** The special manager shall produce accounts containing details of his receipts and payments for the approval of the liquidator.

**4.72(2)** The accounts shall be in respect of 3-month periods for the duration of the special manager's appointment (or for a lesser period if his appointment terminates less than 3 months from its date, or from the date to which the last accounts were made up).

**4.72(3)** When the accounts have been approved, the special manager's receipts and payments shall be added to those of the liquidator.

### TERMINATION OF APPOINTMENT

**4.73(1)** The special manager's appointment terminates if the winding up petition is dismissed or, if a provisional liquidator having been appointed, he is discharged without a winding up order having been made.

**4.73(2)** If the liquidator is of opinion that the employment of the special manager is no longer necessary or profitable for the company, he shall apply to the court for directions, and the court may order the special manager's appointment to be terminated.

**4.73(3)** The liquidator shall make the same application if a resolution of the creditors is passed, requesting that the appointment be terminated.

## Chapter 11 – Public Examination of Company Officers and Others

### NOTICE OF ORDER FOR PUBLIC EXAMINATION

**4.74** Where the court orders the public examination of any person under section 133(1), then, unless the court otherwise directs, the liquidator shall give at least 14 days' notice of the time and place of the examination to the persons specified in paragraphs (c) to (e) of section 133(4) and the liquidator may, if he thinks fit, cause notice of the order to be given, by public advertisement in one or more newspapers circulating in the area of the principal place of business of the company, at least 14 days before the date fixed for the examination but there shall be no such advertisement before at least 7 days have elapsed from the date when the person to be examined was served with the order.

### ORDER ON REQUEST BY CREDITORS OR CONTRIBUTORIES

**4.75(1)** A request to the liquidator by a creditor or creditors or contributory or contributories under section 133(2) shall be made in writing and be accompanied by–
(a) a list of the creditors (if any) concurring with the request and the amounts of their respective claims in the liquidation, or (as the case may be) of the contributories (if any) so concurring, with their respective values, and

(b) from each creditor or contributory concurring, written confirmation of his concurrence.

**4.75(2)** The request must specify the name of the proposed examinee, the relationship which he has, or has had, to the company and the reasons why his examination is requested.

**4.75(3)** Before an application to the court is made on the request, the requisitionists shall deposit with the liquidator such sum as the latter may determine to be appropriate by way of caution for the expenses of the hearing of a public examination, if ordered.

**4.75(4)** Subject as follows, the liquidator shall, within 28 days of receiving the request, make the application to the court required by section 133(2).

**4.75(5)** If the liquidator is of opinion that the request is an unreasonable one in the circumstances, he may apply to the court for an order relieving him from the obligation to make the application otherwise required by that subsection.

**4.75(6)** If the court so orders, and the application for the order was made *ex parte*, notice of the order shall be given forthwith by the liquidator to the requisitionists. If the application for an order is dismissed, the liquidator's application under section 133(2) shall be made forthwith on conclusion of the hearing of the application first mentioned.

**4.75(7)** Where a public examination of the examinee has been ordered by the court on a creditors' or contributories' requisiton under this Rule the court may order that the expenses of the examination are to be paid, as to a specified proportion, out of the caution under paragraph (3), instead of out of the assets.

## Chapter 12 – Miscellaneous

### LIMITATION

**4.76** The provisions of section 8(5) and 22(8), as read with section 73(5), of the Bankruptcy (Scotland) Act 1985 (presentation of petition or submission of claim to bar effect of limitation of actions) shall apply in relation to the liquidation as they apply in relation to a sequestration, subject to the modifications specified in Rule 4.16(2) and to any other necessary modifications.

### DISSOLUTION AFTER WINDING UP

**4.77** Where the court makes an order under section 204(5) or 205(5), the person on whose application the order was made shall deliver to the registrar of companies a copy of the order.

## Chapter 13 – Company with Prohibited Name

### PRELIMINARY

**4.78** The Rules in this Chapter–

(a) relate to the leave required under section 216 (restriction on re-use of name of company in insolvent liquidation) for a person to act as mentioned in section 216(3) in relation to a company with a prohibited name,

(b) prescribe the cases excepted from that provision, that is to say, those in which a person to whom the section applies may so act without that leave, and

(c) apply to all windings up to which section 216 applies, whether or not the winding up commenced before or after the coming into force of the Insolvency (Scotland) Amendment Rules 1987.

**History**

In r. 4.78 the former word "and" omitted at the end of para. (a) and the word ", and" and para. (c) inserted at the end of para. (b) by the Insolvency (Scotland) Amendment Rules 1987 (SI 1987/1921 (S 132)), r. 3, Sch., Pt. I, para. 33 as from 11 January 1988.

### APPLICATION FOR LEAVE UNDER SECTION 216(3)

**4.79** When considering an application for leave under section 216, the court may call on the liquidator, or any former liquidator, of the liquidating company for a report of the circumstances in which that company became insolvent, and the extent (if any) of the applicant's apparent responsibility for its doing so.

## FIRST EXCEPTED CASE

**4.80(1)** Where a company ("the successor company") acquires the whole, or substantially the whole, of the business of an insolvent company, under arrangements made by an insolvency practitioner acting as its liquidator, administrator or receiver, or as supervisor of a voluntary arrangement under Part I of the Act, the successor company may for the purposes of section 216 give notice under this Rule to the insolvent company's creditors.

**4.80(2)** To be effective, the notice must be given within 28 days from the completion of the arrangements to all creditors of the insolvent company of whose addresses the successor is aware in that period; and it must specify–

(a) the name and registered number of the insolvent company and the circumstances in which its business has been acquired by the successor company,

(b) the name which the successor company has assumed, or proposes to assume for the purpose of carrying on the business, if that name is or will be a prohibited name under section 216, and

(c) any change of name which it has made, or proposes to make, for that purpose under section 28 of the Companies Act.

**4.80(3)** The notice may name a person to whom section 216 may apply as having been a director or shadow director of the insolvent company, and give particulars as to the nature and duration of that directorship, with a view to his being a director of the successor company or being otherwise associated with its management.

**4.80(4)** If the successor company has effectively given notice under this Rule to the insolvent company's creditors, a person who is so named in the notice may act in relation to the successor company in any of the ways mentioned in section 216(3), notwithstanding that he has not the leave of the court under that section.

## SECOND EXCEPTED CASE

**4.81(1)** Where a person to whom section 216 applies as having been a director or shadow director of the liquidating company applies for leave of the court under that section not later than 7 days from the date on which the company went into liquidation, he may, during the period specified in paragraph (2) below, act in any of the ways mentioned in section 216(3), notwithstanding that he has not the leave of the court under that section.

**4.81(2)** The period referred to in paragraph (1) begins with the day in which the company goes into liquidation and ends either on the day falling 6 weeks after that date or on the day on which the court disposes of the application for leave under section 216, whichever of those days occurs first.

**History**

R. 4.81 substituted by the Insolvency (Scotland) Amendment Rules 1987 (SI 1987/1921 (S 132)), r. 3, Sch., Pt. I, para. 34 as from 11 January 1988; r. 4.81 formerly read as follows:

"SECOND EXCEPTED CASE

**4.81(1)** In the circumstances specified below, a person to whom section 216 applies as having been a director or shadow director of the liquidating company may act in any of the ways mentioned in section 216(3), notwithstanding that he has not the leave of the court under that section.

**4.81(2)** Those circumstances are that–

(a) he applies to the court for leave, not later than 7 days from the date on which the company went into liquidation, and

(b) leave is granted by the court not later than 6 weeks from that date."

## THIRD EXCEPTED CASE

**4.82** The court's leave under section 216(3) is not required where the company there referred to, though known by a prohibited name within the meaning of the section,–

(a) has been known by that name for the whole of the period of 12 months ending with the day before the liquidating company went into liquidation, and

(b) has not at any time in those 12 months been dormant within the meaning of section 252(5) of the Companies Act.

# PART 5 – CREDITORS' VOLUNTARY WINDING UP

## APPLICATION OF PART 4

**5** The provisions of Part 4 shall apply in a creditors' voluntary winding up of a company as they apply in a winding up by the court subject to the modifications specified in Schedule 1 and to any other necessary modifications.

# PART 6 – MEMBERS' VOLUNTARY WINDING UP

## APPLICATION OF PART 4

**6** The provisions of Part 4, which are specified in Schedule 2, shall apply in relation to a members' voluntary winding up of a company as they apply in a winding up by the court, subject to the modifications specified in Schedule 2 and to any other necessary modifications.

# PART 7 – PROVISIONS OF GENERAL APPLICATION

## Chapter 1 – Meetings

### SCOPE OF CHAPTER

**7.1(1)** This Chapter applies to any meetings held in insolvency proceedings other than meetings of a creditors' committee in administration or receivership, or of a liquidation committee.

**7.1(2)** The Rules in this Chapter shall apply to any such meeting subject to any contrary provision in the Act or in the Rules, or to any direction of the court.

### SUMMONING OF MEETINGS

**7.2(1)** In fixing the date, time and place for a meeting, the person summoning the meeting (**"the convenor"**) shall have regard to the convenience of the persons who are to attend.

**7.2(2)** Meetings shall in all cases be summoned for commencement between 10.00 and 16.00 hours on a business day, unless the court otherwise directs.

### NOTICE OF MEETING

**7.3(1)** The convenor shall give not less than 21 days' notice of the date, time and place of the meeting to every person known to him as being entitled to attend the meeting.

**7.3(2)** In paragraph (1), for the reference to 21 days, there shall be substituted a reference to 14 days in the following cases:–

(a) any meeting of the company or of its creditors summoned under section 3 (to consider directors' proposal for voluntary arrangement);

(b) a meeting of the creditors under section 23(1)(b) or 25(2)(b) (to consider administrator's proposals or proposed revisions);

(c) a meeting of creditors under section 67(2) (meeting of unsecured creditors in receivership); and

(d) a meeting of creditors or contributories under section 138(3) or (4).

**History**

In r. 7.3(2) the word "and" formerly appearing at the end of para. (b) omitted and the words "; and" and para. (d) inserted at the end of para. (c) by the Insolvency (Scotland) Amendment Rules 1987 (SI 1987/1921 (S 132)), r. 3, Sch., Pt. I, para. 35(1) as from 11 January 1988.

**7.3(3)** The convenor may also publish notice of the date, time and place of the meeting in a newspaper circulating in the area of the principal place of business of the company or in such other newspaper as he thinks most appropriate for ensuring that it comes to the notice of the persons who are entitled to attend the meeting. In the case of a creditors' meeting summoned by the administrator under section 23(1)(b), the administrator shall publish such a notice.

**7.3(3A)** Any notice under this paragraph shall be published not less than 21 days or, in cases to which paragraph (2) above applies, 14 days before the meeting.

**History**
R. 7.3(3A) inserted by the Insolvency (Scotland) Amendment Rules 1987 (SI 1987/1921 (S 132)), r. 3, Sch., Pt. I, para. 35(2) as from 11 January 1988.

**7.3(4)** Any notice under this Rule shall state–

(a) the purpose of the meeting;

(b) the persons who are entitled to attend and vote at the meeting;

(c) the effects of Rule 7.9 or, as the case may be, 7.10 (Entitlement to Vote) and of the relevant provisions of Rule 7.12 (Resolutions);

(d) in the case of a meeting of creditors or contributories, that proxies may be lodged at or before the meeting and the place where they may be lodged; and

(e) in the case of a meeting of creditors, that claims may be lodged by those who have not already done so at or before the meeting and the place where they may be lodged.

Where a meeting of creditors is summoned specially for the purpose of removing the liquidator in accordance with section 171(2) or 172(2), or of receiving his resignation under Rule 4.28, the notice summoning it shall also include the information required by Rule 4.23(2) or, as the case may be, 4.28(2).

**7.3(5)** With the notice given under paragraph (1), the convenor shall also send out a proxy form.

**7.3(6)** In the case of any meeting of creditors or contributories, the court may order that notice of the meeting be given by public advertisement in such form as may be specified in the order and not by individual notice to the persons concerned. In considering whether to make such an order, the court shall have regard to the cost of the public advertisement, to the amount of the assets available and to the extent of the interest of creditors or contributories or any particular class of either.

**7.3(7)** The provisions of this Rule shall not apply to a meeting of creditors summoned under section 95 or 98 but any notice advertised in accordance with section 95(2)(c) or 98(1)(c) shall give not less than 7 days' notice of the meeting.

**History**
R. 7.3(7) inserted by the Insolvency (Scotland) Amendment Rules 1987 (SI 1987/1921 (S 132)), r. 3, Sch., Pt. I, para. 35(3) as from 11 January 1988.

## ADDITIONAL NOTICES IN CERTAIN CASES

**7.4(1)** This Rule applies where a company goes, or proposes to go, into liquidation and it is an authorised institution or a former authorised institution within the meaning of the Banking Act.

**History**
R. 7.4(1) substituted by the Insolvency (Scotland) Amendment Rules 1987 (SI 1987/1921 (S 132)), r. 3, Sch., Pt. I, para. 36 as from 11 January 1988; r. 7.4(1) formerly read as follows:

"This Rule applies where a company goes, or proposes to go, into liquidation and it is–

(a) a recognised bank or licensed institution within the meaning of the Banking Act 1979, or

(b) an institution to which sections 16 and 18 of that Act apply as if it were a licensed institution."

**7.4(2)** Notice of any meeting of the company at which it is intended to propose a resolution for its voluntary winding up shall be given by the directors to the Bank of England ("the Bank") and to the Deposit Protection Board ("the Board") as such notice is given to members of the company.

**7.4(3)** Where a creditors' meeting is summoned by the liquidator under section 95 or 98, the same notice of meeting must be given to the Bank and Board as is given to the creditors under this Chapter.

**7.4(4)** Where the company is being wound up by the court, notice of the first meetings of creditors and contributories within the meaning of Rule 4.12 shall be given to the Bank and the Board by the liquidator.

**7.4(5)** Where in any winding up a meeting of creditors or contributories is summoned for the purpose of–

(a) receiving the liquidator's resignation, or

(b) removing the liquidator, or

(c) appointing a new liquidator,

the person summoning the meeting and giving notice of it shall also give notice to the Bank and the Board.

**7.4(6)** The Board is entitled to be represented at any meeting of which it is required by this Rule to be given notice; and Schedule 3 has effect with respect to the voting rights of the Board at such a meeting.

## CHAIRMAN OF MEETINGS

**7.5(1)** The chairman at any meeting of creditors in insolvency proceedings, other than at a meeting of creditors summoned under section 98, shall be the responsible insolvency practitioner, or except at a meeting of creditors under section 95 a person nominated by him in writing.

**History**

In r. 7.5(1) the words ", other than at a meeting of creditors summoned under section 98," and "except at a meeting of creditors under section 95" inserted by the Insolvency (Scotland) Amendment Rules 1987 (SI 1987/1921 (S 132)), r. 3, Sch., Pt. I, para. 37 as from 11 January 1988.

**7.5(2)** A person nominated under this Rule must be either–

(a) a person who is qualified to act as an insolvency practitioner in relation to the company, or

(b) an employee of the administrator, receiver or liquidator, as the case may be, or his firm who is experienced in insolvency matters.

**7.5(3)** This Rule also applies to meetings of contributories in a liquidation.

**7.5(4)** At the first meeting of creditors or contributories in a winding up by the court, the interim liquidator shall be the chairman except that, where a resolution is proposed to appoint the interim liquidator to be the liquidator, another person may be elected to act as chairman for the purpose of choosing the liquidator.

**7.5(5)** This Rule is subject to Rule 4.23(3) (meeting for removal of liquidator).

## MEETINGS REQUISITIONED

**7.6(1)** Subject to paragraph (8), this Rule applies to any request by a creditor or creditors–

(a) to–

(i) an administrator under section 17(3), or

(ii) a liquidator under section 171(3) or 172(3),

for a meeting of creditors; or

(b) to a liquidator under section 142(3) for separate meetings of creditors and contributories, or for any other meeting under any other provision of the Act or the Rules.

**History**

R. 7.6(1) substituted by the Insolvency (Scotland) Amendment Rules 1987 (SI 1987/1921 (S 132)), r. 3, Sch., Pt. I, para. 38(1) as from 11 January 1988; r. 7.6(1) formerly read as follows:

"Subject to paragraph (8), this Rule applies to any request by a creditor or creditors for a meeting of creditors–

(a) to an administrator under section 17(3), or

(b) to a liquidator under section 142(3), 171(3) or 172(3),

or under any other provision of the Act or the Rules."

**7.6(2)** Any such request shall be accompanied by–

(a) a list of any creditors concurring with the request, showing the amounts of the respective claims against the company of the creditor making the request and the concurring creditors;

(b) from each creditor concurring, written confirmation of his concurrence; and

(c) a statement of the purpose of the proposed meeting.

**7.6(3)** If the administrator or, as the case may be, the liquidator considers the request to be properly made in accordance with the Act or the Rules, he shall summon a meeting of the creditors to be held on a date not more than 35 days from the date of his receipt of the request.

**7.6(4)** Expenses of summoning and holding a meeting under this Rule shall be paid by the creditor or creditors making the request, who shall deposit with the administrator, or, as the case may be, the liquidator caution for their payment.

**History**
In r. 7.6(4) the words ", or, as the case may be, the liquidator" inserted by the Insolvency (Scotland) Amendment Rules 1987 (SI 1987/1921 (S 132)), r. 3, Sch., Pt. I, para. 38(2) as from 11 January 1988.

**7.6(5)** The sum to be deposited shall be such as the administrator or, as the case may be, the liquidator may determine and he shall not act without the deposit having been made.

**7.6(6)** The meeting may resolve that the expenses of summoning and holding it are to be payable out of the assets of the company as an expense of the administration or, as the case may be, the liquidation.

**7.6(7)** To the extent that any caution deposited under this Rule is not required for the payment of expenses of summoning and holding the meeting, it shall be repaid to the person or persons who made it.

**7.6(8)** This Rule applies to requests by a contributory or contributories for a meeting of contributories, with the modification that, for the reference in paragraph (2) to the creditors' respective claims, there shall be substituted a reference to the contributories' respective values (being the amounts for which they may vote at any meeting).

**7.6(9)** This Rule is without prejudice to the powers of the court under Rule 4.67(2) (voluntary winding up succeeded by winding up by the court).

## QUORUM

**7.7(1)** Subject to the next paragraph, a quorum is–

(a) in the case of a creditors' meeting, at least one creditor entitled to vote;

(b) in the case of a meeting of contributories, at least 2 contributories so entitled, or all the contributories, if their number does not exceed 2.

**7.7(2)** For the purposes of this Rule, the reference to the creditor or contributories necessary to constitute a quorum is not confined to those persons present or duly represented under section 375 of the Companies Act but includes those represented by proxy by any person (including the chairman).

**7.7(3)** Where at any meeting of creditors or contributories–

(a) the provisions of this Rule as to a quorum being present are satisfied by the attendance of–
  (i) the chairman alone, or
  (ii) one other person in addition to the chairman, and

(b) the chairman is aware, by virtue of claims and proxies received or otherwise, that one or more additional persons would, if attending, be entitled to vote,

the meeting shall not commence until at least the expiry of 15 minutes after the time appointed for its commencement.

**History**
R. 7.7(3) inserted by the Insolvency (Scotland) Amendment Rules 1987 (SI 1987/1921 (S 132)), r. 3, Sch., Pt. I, para. 39 as from 11 January 1988.

## ADJOURNMENT

**7.8(1)** This Rule applies to meetings of creditors and to meetings of contributories.

**7.8(2)** If, within a period of 30 minutes from the time appointed for the commencement of a meeting, a quorum is not present, then, unless the chairman otherwise decides, the meeting shall be adjourned to the same time and place in the following week or, if that is not a business day, to the business day immediately following.

**7.8(3)** In the course of any meeting, the chairman may, in his discretion, and shall, if the meeting so resolves, adjourn it to such date, time and place as seems to him to be appropriate in the circumstances.

**7.8(4)** Paragraph (3) is subject to Rule 4.23(3) where the liquidator or his nominee is chairman and a resolution has been proposed for the liquidator's removal.

**7.8(5)** An adjournment under paragraph (2) or (3) shall not be for a period of more than 21 days and notice of the adjourned meeting may be given by the chairman.

**History**
In r. 7.8(5) the words "(2) or (3)" substituted for the former words "(1) or (2)" and the words "and notice of the adjourned meeting may be given by the chairman" inserted at the end by the Insolvency (Scotland) Amendment Rules 1987 (SI 1987/1921 (S 132)), r. 3, Sch., Pt. I, para. 40(1) as from 11 January 1988.

**7.8(6)** Where a meeting is adjourned, any proxies given for the original meeting may be used at the adjourned meeting.

**7.8(7)** Where a company meeting at which a resolution for voluntary winding up is to be proposed is adjourned without that resolution having been passed, any resolution passed at a meeting under section 98 held before the holding of the adjourned company meeting only has effect on and from the passing by the company of a resolution for winding up.

**History**
R. 7.8(7) inserted by the Insolvency (Scotland) Amendment Rules 1987 (SI 1987/1921 (S 132)), r. 3, Sch., Pt. I, para. 40(2) as from 11 January 1988.

## ENTITLEMENT TO VOTE (CREDITORS)

**7.9(1)** This Rule applies to a creditors' meeting in any insolvency proceedings.

**7.9(2)** A creditor is entitled to vote at any meeting if he has submitted his claim to the responsible insolvency practitioner and his claim has been accepted in whole or in part.

**7.9(3)** Chapter 5 of Part 4 (claims in liquidation) shall apply for the purpose of determining a creditor's entitlement to vote at any creditors' meeting in any insolvency proceedings as it applies for the purpose of determining a creditor's entitlement to vote at a meeting of creditors in a liquidation, subject to the modifications specified in the following paragraphs and to any other necessary modification.

**7.9(4)** For any reference in the said Chapter 5, or in any provision of the Bankruptcy Act as applied by Rule 4.16(1), to–

(a) the liquidator, there shall be substituted a reference to the supervisor, administrator or receiver, as the case may be;

(b) the liquidation, there shall be substituted a reference to the voluntary arrangement, administration or receivership as the case may be;

(c) the date of commencement of winding up, there shall be substituted a reference–

 (i) in the case of a meeting in a voluntary arrangement, to the date of the meeting or, where the company is being wound up or is subject to an administration order, the date of its going into liquidation or, as the case may be, of the administration order; and

 (ii) in the case of a meeting in the administration or receivership, to the date of the administration order or, as the case may be, the date of appointment of the receiver.

**7.9(5)** In the application to meetings of creditors other than in liquidation proceedings of Schedule 1 to the Bankruptcy Act, paragraph 5(2) and (3) (secured creditors) shall not apply.

**7.9(6)** This Rule is subject to Rule 7.4(6) and Schedule 3.

## ENTITLEMENT TO VOTE (MEMBERS AND CONTRIBUTORIES)

**7.10(1)** Members of a company or contributories at their meetings shall vote according to their rights attaching to their shares respectively in accordance with the articles of association.

**7.10(2)** In the case of a meeting of members of the company in a voluntary arrangement, where no voting rights attach to a member's share, he is nevertheless entitled to vote either for or against the proposal or any modification of it.

**7.10(3)** Reference in this Rule to a person's share include any other interests which he may have as a member of the company.

## CHAIRMAN OF MEETING AS PROXY HOLDER

**7.11(1)** Where the chairman at a meeting of creditors or contributories holds a proxy which requires him to vote for a particular resolution and no other person proposes that resolution–

(a) he shall propose it himself, unless he considers that there is good reason for not doing so, and

(b) if he does not propose it, he shall forthwith after the meeting notify the person who granted him the proxy of the reason why he did not do so.

**7.11(2)** At any meeting in a voluntary arrangement, the chairman shall not, by virtue of any proxy held by him, vote to increase or reduce the amount of the remuneration or expenses of the nominee or the supervisor of the proposed arrangement, unless the proxy specifically directs him to vote in that way.

## RESOLUTIONS

**7.12(1)** Subject to any contrary provision in the Act or the Rules, at any meeting of creditors, contributories or members of a company, a resolution is passed when a majority in value of those voting, in person or by proxy, have voted in favour of it.

**7.12(2)** In a voluntary arrangement, at a creditors' meeting for any resolution to pass approving any proposal or modification, there must be at least three quarters in value of the creditors present or represented and voting, in person or by proxy, in favour of the resolution.

**7.12(3)** In a liquidation, in the case of a resolution for the appointment of a liquidator–

(a) if, on any vote, there are two nominees for appointment, the person for whom a majority in value has voted shall be appointed;

(b) if there are three or more nominees, and one of them has a clear majority over both or all the others together, that one is appointed; and

(c) in any other case, the chairman of the meeting shall continue to take votes (disregarding at each vote any nominee who has withdrawn and, if no nominee has withdrawn, the nominee who obtained the least support last time), until a clear majority is obtained for any one nominee.

The chairman may, at any time, put to the meeting a resolution for the joint appointment of any two or more nominees.

**7.12(4)** Where a resolution is proposed which affects a person in respect of his remuneration or conduct as a responsible insolvency practitioner, the vote of that person, or of his firm or of any partner or employee of his shall not be reckoned in the majority required for passing the resolution. This paragraph applies with respect to a vote given by a person (whether personally or on his behalf by a proxy-holder) either as creditor or contributory or member or as proxy-holder for a creditor, contributory, or member.

**History**

In r. 7.12(4) the words "(whether personally or on his behalf by a proxy-holder)" inserted and the word "proxy-holder" (before the words "for a creditor") substituted for the former word "proxy" by the Insolvency (Scotland) Amendment Rules 1987 (SI 1987/1921 (S 132)), r. 3, Sch., Pt. I, para. 41 as from 11 January 1988.

## REPORT OF MEETING

**7.13(1)** The chairman at any meeting shall cause a report to be made of the proceedings at the meeting which shall be signed by him.

**7.13(2)** The report of the meeting shall include–

(a) a list of all the creditors or, as the case may be, contributories who attended the meeting, either in person or by proxy;

(b) a copy of every resolution passed; and

(c) if the meeting established a creditors' committee or a liquidation committee, as the case may be, a list of the names and addresses of those elected to be members of the committee.

**7.13(3)** The chairman shall keep a copy of the report of the meeting as part of the sederunt book in the insolvency proceedings.

# Chapter 2 – Proxies and Company Representation

## DEFINITION OF "PROXY"

**7.14(1)** For the purposes of the Rules, a person "the principal" may authorise another person ("the proxy-holder") to attend, speak and vote as his representative at meetings of creditors or contributories or of the company in insolvency proceedings, and any such authority is referred to as a proxy.

**7.14(2)** A proxy may be given either generally for all meetings in insolvency proceedings or specifically for any meeting or class of meetings.

**7.14(3)** Only one proxy may be given by the principal for any one meeting; and it may only be given to one person, being an individual aged 18 or over. The principal may nevertheless nominate one or more other such persons to be proxy-holder in the alternative in the order in which they are named in the proxy.

**7.14(4)** Without prejudice to the generality of paragraph (3), a proxy for a particular meeting may be given to whoever is to be the chairman of the meeting and any person to whom such a proxy is given cannot decline to be the proxy-holder in relation to that proxy.

**History**
In r. 7.14(4) the words from "and any person to whom" to the end inserted by the Insolvency (Scotland) Amendment Rules 1987 (SI 1987/1921 (S 132)), r. 3, Sch., Pt. I, para. 42 as from 11 January 1988.

**7.14(5)** A proxy may require the holder to vote on behalf of the principal on matters arising for determination at any meeting, or to abstain, either as directed or in accordance with the holder's own discretion; and it may authorise or require the holder to propose, in the principal's name, a resolution to be voted on by the meeting.

## FORM OF PROXY

**7.15(1)** With every notice summoning a meeting of creditors or contributories or of the company in insolvency proceedings there shall be sent out forms of proxy.

**7.15(2)** A form of proxy shall not be sent out with the name or description of any person inserted in it.

**7.15(3)** A proxy shall be in the form sent out with the notice summoning the meeting or in a form substantially to the same effect.

**7.15(4)** A form of proxy shall be filled out and signed by the principal, or by some person acting under his authority and, where it is signed by someone other than the principal, the nature of his authority shall be stated on the form.

## USE OF PROXY AT MEETING

**7.16(1)** A proxy given for a particular meeting may be used at any adjournment of that meeting.

**7.16(2)** A proxy may be lodged at or before the meeting at which it is to be used.

**7.16(3)** Where the responsible insolvency practitioner holds proxies to be used by him as chairman of the meeting, and some other person acts as chairman, the other person may use the insolvency practitioner's proxies as if he were himself proxy-holder.

**7.16(4)** Where a proxy directs a proxy-holder to vote for or against a resolution for the nomination or appointment of a person to be the responsible insolvency practitioner, the proxy-holder may, unless the proxy states otherwise, vote for or against (as he thinks fit) any resolution for the nomination or appointment of that person jointly with another or others.

**7.16(5)** A proxy-holder may propose any resolution which, if proposed by another, would be a resolution in favour of which he would be entitled to vote by virtue of the proxy.

**7.16(6)** Where a proxy gives specific directions as to voting, this does not, unless the proxy states otherwise, preclude the proxy-holder from voting at his discretion on resolutions put to the meeting which are not dealt with in the proxy.

**History**
R. 7.16(4)–(6) added by the Insolvency (Scotland) Amendment Rules 1987 (SI 1987/1921 (S 132)), r. 3, Sch., Pt. I, para. 43 as from 11 January 1988.

## RETENTION OF PROXIES

**7.17(1)** Proxies used for voting at any meeting shall be retained by the chairman of the meeting.

**7.17(2)** The chairman shall deliver the proxies forthwith after the meeting to the responsible insolvency practitioner (where he was not the chairman).

**7.17(3)** The responsible insolvency practitioner shall retain all proxies in the sederunt book.

## RIGHT OF INSPECTION

**7.18(1)** The responsible insolvency practitioner shall, so long as proxies lodged with him are in his hands, allow them to be inspected at all reasonable times on any business day, by–

(a) the creditors, in the case of proxies used at a meeting of creditors,

(b) a company's members or contributories, in the case of proxies used at a meeting of the company or of its contributories.

**7.18(2)** The reference in paragraph (1) to creditors is–

(a) in the case of a company in liquidation, those creditors whose claims have been accepted in whole or in part, and

(b) in any other case, persons who have submitted in writing a claim to be creditors of the company concerned,

but in neither case does it include a person whose claim has been wholly rejected for purposes of voting, dividend or otherwise.

**7.18(3)** The right of inspection given by this Rule is also exercisable, in the case of an insolvent company, by its directors.

**7.18(4)** Any person attending a meeting in insolvency proceedings is entitled, immediately before or in the course of the meeting, to inspect proxies and associated documents (including claims)–

(a) to be used in connection with that meeting, or

(b) sent or given to the chairman of that meeting or to any other person by a creditor, member or contributory for the purpose of that meeting, whether or not they are to be used at it.

**History**

In r. 7.18(4) the words from "(including claims)" to the end substituted for the former words "to be used in connection with that meeting" by the Insolvency (Scotland) Amendment Rules 1987 (SI 1987/1921 (S 132)), r. 3, Sch., Pt. I, para. 44 as from 11 January 1988.

## PROXY-HOLDER WITH FINANCIAL INTEREST

**7.19(1)** A proxy-holder shall not vote in favour of any resolution which would directly or indirectly place him, or any associate of his, in a position to receive any remuneration out of the insolvent estate, unless the proxy specifically directs him to vote in that way.

**7.19(1A)** Where a proxy-holder has signed the proxy as being authorised to do so by his principal and the proxy specifically directs him to vote in the way mentioned in paragraph (1), he shall nevertheless not vote in that way unless he produces to the chairman of the meeting written authorisation from his principal sufficient to show that the proxy-holder was entitled so to sign the proxy.

**History**

R. 7.19(1A) inserted by the Insolvency (Scotland) Amendment Rules 1987 (SI 1987/1921 (S 132)), r. 3, Sch., Pt. I, para. 45(1) as from 11 January 1988.

**7.19(2)** This Rule applies also to any person acting as chairman of a meeting and using proxies in that capacity in accordance with Rule 7.16(3); and in the application of this Rule to any such person, the proxy-holder is deemed an associate of his.

**History**

In r. 7.19(2) the words "in accordance with Rule 7.16(3)" inserted and the words "in the application of this Rule to any such person" substituted for the former words "in its application to him" by the Insolvency (Scotland) Amendment Rules 1987 (SI 1987/1921 (S 132)), r. 3, Sch., Pt. I, para. 45(2) as from 11 January 1988.

## REPRESENTATION OF CORPORATIONS

**7.20(1)** Where a person is authorised under section 375 of the Companies Act to represent a corporation at a meeting of creditors or contributories, he shall produce to the chairman of the meeting a copy of the resolution from which he derives his authority.

**7.20(2)** The copy resolution must be executed in accordance with the provisions of section 36(3) of the Companies Act, or certified by the secretary or a director of the corporation to be a true copy.

**7.20(3)** Nothing in this Rule requires the authority of a person to sign a proxy on behalf of a principal which is a corporation to be in the form of a resolution of that corporation.

**History**
R. 7.20(3) added by the Insolvency (Scotland) Amendment Rules 1987 (SI 1987/1921 (S 132)), r. 3, Sch., Pt. I, para. 46 as from 11 January 1988.

## Chapter 3 – Miscellaneous

### GIVING OF NOTICES, ETC.

**7.21(1)** All notices required or authorised by or under the Act or the Rules to be given, sent or delivered must be in writing, unless it is otherwise provided, or the court allows the notice to be sent or given in some other way.

**7.21(2)** Any reference in the Act or the Rules to giving, sending or delivering a notice or any such document means, without prejudice to any other way and unless it is otherwise provided, that the notice or document may be sent by post, and that, subject to Rule 7.22, any form of post may be used. Personal service of the notice or document is permissible in all cases.

**History**
In r. 7.21(2) the words "Act or the" inserted by the Insolvency (Scotland) Amendment Rules 1987 (SI 1987/1921 (S 132)), r. 3, Sch., Pt. I, para. 47 as from 11 January 1988.

**7.21(3)** Where under the Act or the Rules a notice or other document is required or authorised to be given, sent or delivered by a person ("the sender") to another ("the recipient"), it may be given, sent or delivered by any person duly authorised by the sender to do so to any person duly authorised by the recipient to receive or accept it.

**7.21(4)** Where two or more persons are acting jointly as the responsible insolvency practitioner in any proceedings, the giving, sending or delivering of a notice or document to one of them is to be treated as the giving, sending or delivering of a notice or document to each or all.

### SENDING BY POST

**7.22(1)** For a document to be properly sent by post, it must be contained in an envelope addressed to the person to whom it is to be sent, and pre-paid for either first or second class post.

**7.22(1A)** Any document to be sent by post may be sent to the last known address of the person to whom the document is to be sent.

**History**
R. 7.22(1A) inserted by the Insolvency (Scotland) Amendment Rules 1987 (SI 1987/1921 (S 132)), r. 3, Sch., Pt. I, para. 48 as from 11 January 1988.

**7.22(2)** Where first class post is used, the document is to be deemed to be received on the second business day after the date of posting, unless the contrary is shown.

**7.22(3)** Where second class post is used, the document is to be deemed to be received on the fourth business day after the date of posting, unless the contrary is shown.

### CERTIFICATE OF GIVING NOTICE, ETC.

**7.23(1)** Where in any proceedings a notice or document is required to be given, sent or delivered by the responsible insolvency practitioner, the date of giving, sending or delivery of it may be proved by means of a certificate signed by him or on his behalf by his solicitor, or a partner or an employee of either of them, that the notice or document was duly given, posted or otherwise sent, or delivered on the date stated in the certificate.

**7.23(2)** In the case of a notice or document to be given, sent or delivered by a person other than the responsible insolvency practitioner, the date of giving, sending or delivery of it may be proved by means of a certificate by that person that he gave, posted or otherwise sent or delivered the notice or document on the date stated in the certificate, or that he instructed another person (naming him) to do so.

**7.23(3)** A certificate under this Rule may be endorsed on a copy of the notice to which it relates.

**7.23(4)** A certificate purporting to be signed by or on behalf of the responsible insolvency practitioner, or by the person mentioned in paragraph (2), shall be deemed, unless the contrary is shown, to be sufficient evidence of the matters stated therein.

## VALIDITY OF PROCEEDINGS

**7.24** Where in accordance with the Act or the Rules a meeting of creditors or other persons is summoned by notice, the meeting is presumed to have been duly summoned and held, notwithstanding that not all those to whom the notice is to be given have received it.

## EVIDENCE OF PROCEEDINGS AT MEETINGS

**7.25** A report of proceedings at a meeting of the company or of the company's creditors or contributories in any insolvency proceedings, which is signed by a person describing himself as the chairman of that meeting, shall be deemed, unless the contrary is shown, to be sufficient evidence of the matters contained in that report.

## RIGHT TO LIST OF CREDITORS AND COPY DOCUMENTS

**7.26(1)** Paragraph (2) applies to–

(a) proceedings under Part II of the Act (company administration), and

(b) proceedings in a creditors' voluntary winding up, or a winding up by the court.

**7.26(2)** Subject to Rule 7.27, in any such proceedings, a creditor who has the right to inspect documents also has the right to require the responsible insolvency practitioner to furnish him with a list of the company's creditors and the amounts of their respective debts.

**7.26(2A)** Where the responsible insolvency practitioner is requested by a creditor, member, contributory or by a member of a liquidation committee or of a creditors' committee to supply a copy of any document, he is entitled to require payment of the appropriate fee in respect of the supply of that copy.

**History**
R. 7.26(2A) inserted by the Insolvency (Scotland) Amendment Rules 1987 (SI 1987/1921 (S 132)), r. 3, Sch., Pt. I, para. 49 as from 11 January 1988.

**7.26(3)** Subject to Rule 7.27, where a person has the right to inspect documents, the right includes that of taking copies of those documents, on payment of the appropriate fee.

**7.26(4)** In this Rule, the appropriate fee means 15 pence per A4 or A5 page and 30 pence per A3 page.

## CONFIDENTIALITY OF DOCUMENTS

**7.27(1)** Where, in any insolvency proceedings, the responsible insolvency practitioner considers, in the case of a document forming part of the records of those proceedings,–

(a) that it should be treated as confidential, or

(b) that it is of such a nature that its disclosure would be calculated to be injurious to the interests of the company's creditors or, in the case of the winding up of a company, its members or the contributories in its winding up,

he may decline to allow it to be inspected by a person who would otherwise be entitled to inspect it.

**7.27(2)** The persons who may be refused the right to inspect documents under this Rule by the responsible insolvency practitioner include the members of a creditors' committee in administration or in receivership, or of a liquidation committee.

**7.27(3)** Where under this Rule the responsible insolvency practitioner refuses inspection of a document, the person who made that request may apply to the court for an order to overrule the refusal and the court may either overrule it altogether, or sustain it, either unconditionally or subject to such conditions, if any, as it thinks fit to impose.

**7.27(4)** Nothing in this Rule entitles the responsible insolvency practitioner to decline to allow inspection of any claim or proxy.

**History**
R. 7.27(4) inserted by the Insolvency (Scotland) Amendment Rules 1987 (SI 1987/1921 (S 132)), r. 3, Sch., Pt. I, para. 50 as from 11 January 1988.

## INSOLVENCY PRACTITIONER'S CAUTION

**7.28(1)** Wherever under the Rules any person has to appoint, or certify the appointment of, an insolvency practitioner to any office, he is under a duty to satisfy himself that the person appointed or to be appointed has caution for the proper performance of his functions.

**7.28(2)** It is the duty–

(a) of the creditors' committee in administration or in receivership,

(b) of the liquidation committee in companies winding up, and

(c) of any committee of creditors established for the purposes of a voluntary arrangement under Part I of the Act,

to review from time to time the adequacy of the responsible insolvency practitioner's caution.

**7.28(3)** In any insolvency proceedings the cost of the responsible insolvency practitioner's caution shall be paid as an expense of the proceedings.

## PUNISHMENT OF OFFENCES

**7.29(1)** Schedule 4 has effect with respect to the way in which contraventions of the Rules are punishable on conviction.

**7.29(2)** In that Schedule–

(a) the first column specifies the provision of the Rules which creates an offence;

(b) in relation to each such offence, the second column describes the general nature of the offence;

(c) the third column indicates its mode of trial, that is to say whether the offence is punishable on conviction on indictment, or on summary conviction, or either in the one way or the other;

(d) the fourth column shows the maximum punishment by way of fine or imprisonment which may be imposed on a person convicted of the offence in the mode of trial specified in relation to it in the third column (that is to say, on indictment or summarily), a reference to a period of years or months being to a maximum term of imprisonment of that duration; and

(e) the fifth column shows (in relation to an offence for which there is an entry in that column) that a person convicted of the offence after continued contravention is liable to a daily default fine; that is to say, he is liable on a second or subsequent conviction of the offence to the fine specified in that column for each day on which the contravention is continued (instead of the penalty specified for the offence in the fourth column of that Schedule).

**7.29(3)** Section 431 (summary proceedings), as it applies to Scotland, has effect in relation to offences under the Rules as to offences under the Act.

## FORMS FOR USE IN INSOLVENCY PROCEEDINGS

**7.30** The forms contained in Schedule 5, with such variations as circumstances require, are the forms to be used for the purposes of the provisions of the Act or the Rules which are referred to in those forms.

## FEES, EXPENSES, ETC.

**7.31** All fees, costs, charges and other expenses incurred in the course of insolvency proceedings are to be regarded as expenses of those proceedings.

## POWER OF COURT TO CURE DEFECTS IN PROCEDURE

**7.32(1)** Section 63 of the Bankruptcy Act (power of court to cure defects in procedure) shall apply in relation to any insolvency proceedings as it applies in relation to sequestration, subject to the modifications specified in paragraph (2) and to any other necessary modifications.

**7.32(2)** For any reference in the said section 63 to any expression in column 1 below, there shall be substituted a reference to the expression in column 2 opposite thereto–

| *Column 1* | *Column 2* |
|---|---|
| This Act or any regulations made under it | The Act or the Rules |
| Permanent trustee | Responsible insolvency practitioner |
| Sequestration process | Insolvency proceedings |

| | |
|---|---|
| Debtor | Company |
| Sheriff | The court |
| Person who would be eligible to be elected under section 24 of this Act | Person who would be eligible to act as a responsible insolvency practitioner |

## SEDERUNT BOOK

**7.33(1)** The responsible insolvency practitioner shall maintain a sederunt book during his term of office for the purpose of providing an accurate record of the administration of each insolvency proceedings.

**7.33(2)** Without prejudice to the generality of the above paragraph, there shall be inserted in the sederunt book a copy of anything required to be recorded in it by any provision of the Act or of the Rules.

**7.33(3)** The responsible insolvency practitioner shall make the sederunt book available for inspection at all reasonable hours by any interested person.

**7.33(4)** Any entry in the sederunt book shall be sufficient evidence of the facts stated therein, except where it is founded on by the responsible insolvency practitioner in his own interest.

**7.33(5)** Without prejudice to paragraph (3), the responsible insolvency practitioner shall retain, or shall make arrangements for retention of, the sederunt book for a period of ten years from the relevant date.

**7.33(6)** Where the sederunt book is maintained in non-documentary form it shall be capable of reproduction in legible form.

**7.33(7)** In this Rule **"the relevant date"** has the following meanings:–

(a) in the case of a company voluntary arrangement under Part I of the Act, the date of final completion of the voluntary arrangement;

(b) in the case of an administration order under Part II of the Act, the date on which the administration order is discharged;

(c) in the case of a receivership under Part III of the Act, the date on which the receiver resigns and the receivership terminates without a further receiver being appointed; and

(d) in the case of a winding-up, the date of dissolution of the company.

**History**

R. 7.33(5)–(7) inserted by the Insolvency (Scotland) Amendment Rules 1987 (SI 1987/1921 (S 132)), r. 3, Sch., Pt. I, para. 51 as from 11 January 1988.

## DISPOSAL OF COMPANY'S BOOKS, PAPERS AND OTHER RECORDS

**7.34(1)** Where a company has been the subject of insolvency proceedings ("the original proceedings") which have terminated and other insolvency proceedings ("the subsequent proceedings") have commenced in relation to that company, the responsible insolvency practitioner appointed in relation to the original proceedings, shall, before the expiry of the later of–

(a) the period of 30 days following a request to him to do so by the responsible insolvency practitioner appointed in relation to the subsequent proceedings, or

(b) the period of 6 months after the relevant date (within the meaning of Rule 7.33),

deliver to the responsible insolvency practitioner appointed in relation to the subsequent proceedings the books, papers and other records of the company.

**7.34(2)** In the case of insolvency proceedings, other than winding up, where–

(a) the original proceedings have terminated, and

(b) no subsequent proceedings have commenced within the period of 6 months after the relevant date in relation to the original proceedings,

the responsible insolvency practitioner appointed in relation to the original proceedings may dispose of the books, papers and records of the company after the expiry of the period of 6 months referred to in sub-paragraph (b), but only in accordance with directions given by–

(i) the creditors' committee (if any) appointed in the original proceedings,

(ii) the members of the company by extraordinary resolution, or

(iii) the court.

**7.34(3)** Where a company is being wound up the liquidator shall dispose of the books, papers and records of the company either in accordance with–

(a) in the case of a winding up by the court, directions of the liquidation committee, or, if there is no such committee, directions of the court;

(b) in the case of a members' voluntary winding up, directions of the members by extraordinary resolution; and

(c) in the case of a creditors' voluntary winding up, directions of the liquidation committee, or, if there is no such committee, of the creditors given at or before the final meeting under section 106,

or, if, by the date which is 12 months after the dissolution of the company, no such directions have been given, he may do so after that date in such a way as he deems appropriate.

**History**
R. 7.34 inserted by the Insolvency (Scotland) Amendment Rules 1987 (SI 1987/1921 (S 132)), r. 3, Sch., Pt. I, para. 52 as from 11 January 1988.

# Schedule 1 – Modifications of Part 4 in Relation to Creditors' Voluntary Winding up

Rule 5

**1** The following paragraphs describe the modifications to be made to the provisions of Part 4 in their application by Rule 5 to a creditors' voluntary winding up of a company.

## GENERAL

**2** Any reference, in any provision in Part 4, which is applied to a creditors' voluntary winding up, to any other Rule is a reference to that Rule as so applied.

## CHAPTER 1 (PROVISIONAL LIQUIDATOR)

**3** This Chapter shall not apply.

## CHAPTER 2 (STATEMENT OF AFFAIRS)

**Rules 4.7 and 4.8**

**4** For these Rules, there shall be substituted the following–

"**4.7(1)** This Rule applies with respect to the statement of affairs made out by the liquidator under section 95(3) (or as the case may be) by the directors under section 99(1).

**4.7(2)** The statement of affairs shall be in the form required by Rule 7.30 and Schedule 5.

**4.7(3)** Where the statement of affairs is made out by the directors under section 99(1), it shall be sent by them to the liquidator, when appointed.

**4.7(3A)** Where a liquidator is nominated by the company at a general meeting held on a day prior to that on which the creditors' meeting summoned under section 98 is held, the directors shall forthwith after his nomination or the making of the statement of affairs, whichever is the later, deliver to him a copy of the statement of affairs.

**4.7(4)** The liquidator shall insert a copy of the statement of affairs made out under this Rule in the sederunt book.

**4.7(5)** The statement of affairs under section 99(1) shall be made up to the nearest practicable date before the date of the meeting of creditors under section 98 or to a date not more than 14 days before that on which the resolution for voluntary winding up is passed by the company, whichever is the later.

**4.7(6)** At any meeting held under section 98 where the statement of affairs laid before the meeting does not state the company's affairs as at the date of the meeting, the directors of the company shall cause to be made to the meeting, either by the director presiding at the meeting or by another person with knowledge of the relevant matters, a report (written or oral) on any material transactions relating to the company occurring between the date of the making of the statement of affairs and that of the meeting and any such report shall be recorded in the report of the meeting kept under Rule 7.13."

**History**

In para. 4, r. 4.7(3A), (5) and (6) inserted by the Insolvency (Scotland) Amendment Rules 1987 (SI 1987/1921 (S 132)), r. 3, Sch., Pt. I, para. 53, as from 11 January 1988.

**Rule 4.9**

**5** For this Rule, there shall be substituted

"*Expenses of statement of affairs,*

**4.9(1)** Payment may be made as an expense of the liquidation, either before or after the commencement of the winding up, of any reasonable and necessary expenses of preparing the statement of affairs under section 99.

**4.9(2)** Where such a payment is made before the commencement of the winding up, the director presiding at the creditors' meeting held under section 98 shall inform the meeting of the amount of the payment and the identity of the person to whom it was made.

**4.9(3)** The liquidator appointed under section 100 may make such a payment (subject to the next paragraph); but if there is a liquidation committee, he must give the committee at least 7 days' notice of his intention to make it.

**4.9(4)** Such a payment shall not be made by the liquidator to himself, or to any associate of his, otherwise than with the approval of the liquidation committee, the creditors, or the court.

**4.9(5)** This Rule is without prejudice to the powers of the court under Rule 4.67(2) (voluntary winding up succeeded by winding up by the court).".

## CHAPTER 3 (INFORMATION)

**Rule 4.10**

**6** For this Rule, there shall be substituted the following:–

"*Information to creditors and contributories*

**4.10** The liquidator shall, within 28 days of a meeting held under section 95 or 98, send to creditors and contributories of the company–

(a) a copy or summary of the statement of affairs, and
(b) a report of the proceedings at the meeting.".

## CHAPTER 4 (MEETINGS OF CREDITORS AND CONTRIBUTORIES)

**Rule 4.12**

**7** This Rule shall not apply.

**Rule 4.14**

**8** After this Rule, there shall be inserted the following:–

"*Expenses of meeting under section 98*

**4.14A(1)** Payment may be made out of the company's assets as an expense of the liquidation, either before or after the commencement of the winding up, of any reasonable and necessary expenses incurred in connection with the summoning, advertisement and holding of a creditors' meeting under section 98.

**4.41A(2)** Where any such payments are made before the commencement of the winding up, the director presiding at the creditors' meeting shall inform the meeting of their amount and the identity of the persons to whom they were made.

**4.41A(3)** The liquidator appointed under section 100 may make such a payment (subject to the next paragraph); but if there is a liquidation committee, he must give the committee at least 7 days' notice of his intention to make the payment.

**4.41A(4)** Such a payment shall not be made by the liquidator to himself, or to any associate of his, otherwise than with the approval of the liquidation committee, the creditors, or the court.

**4.41A(5)** This Rule is without prejudice to the powers of the court under Rule 4.67(2) (voluntary winding up succeeded by winding up by the court).".

**Rule 4.15**

**9(1)** In paragraph (5), for the reference to section 129, there shall be substituted a reference to section 86.

**9(2)** In paragraph (6) there shall be inserted at the end the following:–

"and to the director who presides over any meeting of creditors as provided by section 99(1)."

**History**
Para. 9(1) renumbered as such and para. 9(2) inserted by the Insolvency (Scotland) Amendment Rules 1987 (SI 1987/1921 (S 132)), r. 3, Sch., Pt. I, para. 54 as from 11 January 1988.

**Rule 4.16**

**10** In paragraph (2), for the reference to section 129, there shall be substituted a reference to section 86.

## CHAPTER 6 (THE LIQUIDATOR)

**Rule 4.18**

**11(1)** For paragraph (1), there shall be substituted the following:–

"**4.18(1)** This Rule applies where the liquidator is appointed by the court under section 100(3) or 108.".

**11(2)** Paragraphs 4(a) and 5 shall be deleted.

**Rule 4.19**

**12(1)** For paragraphs (1) to (3) there shall be substituted the following:–

"**4.19(1)** This Rule applies where a person is nominated forv appointment as liquidator under section 100(1) either by a meeting of the creditors or by a meeting of the company.

**4.19(2)** Subject as follows, the chairman of the meeting shall certify the appointment, but not unless and until the person to be appointed has provided him with a written statement to the effect that he is an insolvency practitioner, duly qualified under the Act to be the liquidator and that he consents so to act. The liquidator's appointment takes effect on the passing of the resolution for his appointment.

**4.19(3)** The chairman shall forthwith send the certificate to the liquidator, who shall keep it in the sederunt book.".

**History**
In para. 12(1), in the substituted r. 4.19(2) the words "takes effect on the passing of the resolution for his appointment" substituted for the former words "is effective from the date of the certificate" by the Insolvency (Scotland) Amendment Rules 1987 (SI 1987/1921 (S 132)), r. 3, Sch., Pt. I, para. 55(a) as from 11 January 1988.

**12(2)** Paragraphs (4)(a) and (5) shall not apply.

**12(3)** In paragraph (6), for the reference to paragraphs (4) and (5), there shall be substituted a reference to paragraphs (3) and (4).

**12(4)** After paragraph 6 there shall be inserted the following sub-paragraph:–

"**4.19(7)** Where a vacancy in the office of liquidator occurs in the manner mentioned in section 104, a meeting of creditors to fill the vacancy may be convened by any creditor or, if there were more liquidators than one, by any continuing liquidator."

**History**
Para. 12(4) inserted by the Insolvency (Scotland) Amendment Rules 1987 (SI 1987/1921 (S 132)), r. 3, Sch., Pt. I, para. 55(b) as from 11 January 1988.

**Rule 4.23**

**13(1)** In paragraph (1), for the references to section 172(2) and (3), there shall be substituted a reference to section 171(2) and (3).

**13(2)** In paragraph (2), for the references to section 172(2) and 174(4)(a) or (b), there shall be substituted a reference to section 171(2) and 173(2)(a) or (b).

**Rule 4.24**

**14** In this Rule the references to the court shall be deleted.

**Rule 4.25**

**15** In paragraph (1), for the reference to section 174(4)(a), there shall be substituted a reference to section 173(2)(a), and the reference to the court shall be deleted.

**Rule 4.28**

**16(1)** In paragraph (1), for the reference to section 172(6), there shall be substituted a reference to section 171(5).

**16(2)** In paragraph (2), for the reference to section 174(4)(c), there shall be substituted a reference to section 173(2)(c).

**Rule 4.29**

**17(1)** In this Rule for paragraph (3) there shall be substituted the following:–

"**4.29(3)** The liquidator, whose resignation is accepted, shall forthwith after the meeting give notice of his resignation to the Accountant in Bankruptcy as required by section 171(5).".

**History**
In Sch. 1, para. 17, in the modification of r. 4.29(3), the words "the Accountant in Bankruptcy" substituted for the former words " the registrar of companies" with effect from 1 July 1999 by virtue of the Scotland Act 1998 (Consequential Modifications) (No. 2) Order 1999 (SI 1999/1820), art. 1(2), 4 and Sch. 2, para. 141(1), (20) and the Scotland Act 1998 (Commencement) Order 1998 (SI 1998/3178), art. 3.

**Rule 4.31**

**18(1)** For this Rule, substitute the following:–

"*Final Meeting*

**4.31(1)** The liquidator shall give at least 28 days' notice of the final meeting of creditors to be held under section 106. The notice shall be sent to all creditors whose claims in the liquidation have been accepted.

**4.31(2)** At the final meeting, the creditors may question the liquidator with respect to any matter contained in the account required under that section and may resolve against the liquidator having his release.

**4.31(3)** The liquidator shall, within 7 days of the meeting, give notice to the registrar of companies under section 171(6) that the final meeting has been held. The notice shall state whether or not he has been released.

**4.31(4)** If the creditors at the final meeting have not resolved against the liquidator having his release, he is released in terms of section 173(2)(e)(ii) when he vacates office under section 171(6). If they have so resolved, he must obtain his release from the Accountant of Court and Rule 4.25(2) and (3) shall apply accordingly subject to the modifications that in Rule 4.25(3) sub-paragraph (a) shall apply with the word "new" replaced by the word "former" and sub-paragraph (b) shall not apply."

**History**
In para. 18 in the substituted r. 4.31(4) the words "subject to the modifications" to the end inserted by the Insolvency (Scotland) Amendment Rules 1987 (SI 1987/1921 (S 132)), r. 3, Sch., Pt. I, para. 56 as from 11 January 1988.

**Rule 4.36**

**19** For the reference to the court there shall be substituted a reference to the liquidation committee (if any) or a member of that committee.

**Rule 4.37**

**20(1)** In paragraph (2), the reference to the court shall be omitted.

**20(2)** At the end of this Rule, there shall be inserted the following:–

"*Vacation of office on making of winding up order*

**4.37A** Where the liquidator vacates office in consequence of the court making a winding up order against the company, Rule 4.25(2) and (3) apply as regards the liquidator obtaining his release, as if he had been removed by the court.".

## CHAPTER 7 (THE LIQUIDATION COMMITTEE)

**Rule 4.40**

21 This Rule shall not apply.

**Rule 4.41**

22 For paragraph (1) there shall be substituted the following:–

"**4.41(1)** The committee must have at least 3 members before it can be established.".

**Rule 4.43**

23 This Rule shall not apply.

**Rule 4.47**

24 For this Rule, there shall be substituted the following:–

"*Quorum*

**4.47** A meeting of the committee is duly constituted if due notice of it has been given to all the members and at least 2 members are present or represented.".

**Rule 4.53**

25 After paragraph (4) there shall be inserted the following:–

"**4.53(4A)** Where the contributories make an appointment under paragraph (4), the creditor members of the committee may, if they think fit, resolve that the person appointed ought not to be a member of the committee; and–

(a) that person is not then, unless the court otherwise directs, qualified to act as a member of the committee, and

(b) on any application to the court for a direction under this paragraph the court may, if it thinks fit, appoint another person (being a contributory) to fill the vacancy on the committee.".

**Rule 4.54**

26 Paragraphs (2) and (3) shall not apply.

**Rule 4.55**

27 In paragraphs (3) and (4), the word **"creditor"** shall be omitted.

## CHAPTER 8 (THE LIQUIDATION COMMITTEE WHERE WINDING UP FOLLOWS IMMEDIATELY ON ADMINISTRATION)

28 This Chapter shall not apply.

## CHAPTER 9 (DISTRIBUTION OF COMPANY'S ASSETS BY LIQUIDATOR)

**Rule 4.66**

**29(1)** At the beginning of paragraph (1), insert the following:–

"Subject to the provision of section 107,".

**29(2)** In paragraph (1)(b), for the reference to section 129, there shall be substituted a reference to section 86.

## CHAPTER 10 (SPECIAL MANAGER)

**Rule 4.70**

30 For paragraph (5), there shall be substituted the following:–

"**4.70(5)** The cost of finding caution shall be paid in the first instance by the special manager; but he is entitled to be reimbursed out of the assets as an expense of the liquidation.".

**Rule 4.71**

31 Paragraph (1) shall not apply.

CHAPTER 11 (PUBLIC EXAMINATION OF COMPANY OFFICERS AND OTHERS)

32 This Chapter shall not apply.

CHAPTER 12 (MISCELLANEOUS)

**Rule 4.77**

33 This Rule shall not apply.

# Schedule 2 – Application of Part 4 in Relation to Members' Voluntary Winding Up

Rule 6

1 The following paragraphs describe the provisions of Part 4 which, subject to the modifications set out in those paragraphs and any other necessary modifications, apply to a members' voluntary winding up.

GENERAL

2 Any reference in any provision of Part 4, which is applied to a members' voluntary winding up, to any other Rule is a reference to that Rule as so applied.

CHAPTER 3 (INFORMATION)

**Rule 4.11**

3 This Rule shall apply subject to the modifications that for the words "accounting period" where they occur, there shall be substituted the words "period of twenty six weeks".

**History**

In para. 3 the words from "subject to" to the end inserted by the Insolvency (Scotland) Amendment Rules 1987 (SI 1987/1921 (S 132)), r. 3, Sch., Pt. I, para. 57 as from 11 January 1988.

CHAPTER 6 (THE LIQUIDATOR)

**Rule 4.18**

**4(1)** This Rule shall apply subject to the following modifications.

**4(2)** For paragraph (1), there shall be substituted the following:–

"**4.18(1)** This Rule applies where the liquidator is appointed by the court under section 108.".

**4(3)** Paragraphs 4 and 5 shall be deleted.

**Rule 4.19**

**5(1)** This Rule shall apply subject to the following modifications.

**5(2)** For paragraphs (1) to (3) there shall be substituted the following:–

"**4.19(1)** This Rule applies where the liquidator is appointed by a meeting of the company.

**4.19(2)** Subject as follows, the chairman of the meeting shall certify the appointment, but not unless and until the person to be appointed has provided him with a written statement to the effect that he is an insolvency practitioner, duly qualified under the Act to be the liquidator and that he consents so to act. The liquidator's appointment takes effect on the passing of the resolution for his appointment.

**4.19(3)** The chairman shall forthwith send the certificate to the liquidator, who shall keep it in the sederunt book.".

**History**

In para. 5(2) in the substituted Rule 4.19(2) the words "takes effect on the passing of the resolution for his appointment" substituted for the former words "is effective from the date of the certificate" by the Insolvency (Scotland) Amendment Rules 1987 (SI 1987/1921 (S 132)), r. 3, Sch., Pt. I, para. 58 as from 11 January 1988.

**5(3)** Paragraphs 4(a), (5) and (6) shall be deleted.

**Rule 4.20 to 4.22**

6 These Rules shall apply.

**Rule 4.26**

7 This Rule shall apply except that in paragraph (1) for the reference to "creditors" there shall be substituted the words "the company".

**Rule 4.27**

8 This Rule shall apply.

**Rule 4.28**

**9(1)** This Rule shall apply subject to the following modifications.

**9(2)** In paragraph (1)–

(a) for the reference to section 172(6), there shall be substituted a reference to section 171(5), and

(b) for the reference to a meeting of creditors, there shall be substituted a reference to a meeting of the company.

**9(3)** In paragraph (2)–

(a) for reference to section 174(4)(c) there shall be substituted a reference to section 173(2)(c), and

(b) for the reference to Rule 4.29(4), there shall be substituted a reference to Rule 4.28A.

**9(4)** After paragraph (4) there shall be inserted the following paragraphs:–

"**4.28(5)** The notice of the liquidator's resignation required by section 171(5) shall be given by him to the Accountant in Bankruptcy forthwith after the meeting.

**4.28(6)** Where a new liquidator is appointed in place of the one who has resigned, the former shall, in giving notice of his appointment, state that his predecessor has resigned and whether he has been released.

**4.28(7)** If there is no quorum present at the meeting summoned to receive the liquidator's resignation the meeting is deemed to have been held."

**History**

In para 9(4), in r. 4.28(5), the words "the Accountant in Bankruptcy" substituted for the former words " the registrar of companies" with effect from 1 July 1999 by virtue of the Scotland Act 1998 (Consequential Modifications) (No. 2) Order 1999 (SI 1999/1820), art. 1(2), 4 and Sch. 2, para. 141(1), (21) and the Scotland Act 1998 (Commencement) Order 1998 (SI 1998/3178), art. 3.

In para. 9(4), r. 4.28(7) inserted by the Insolvency (Scotland) Amendment Rules 1987 (SI 1987/1921 (S 132)), r. 3, Sch., Pt. I, para. 59 as from 11 January 1988.

**9(5)** After this Rule, there shall be inserted the following Rule:–

"*Release of resigning or removed liquidator*

**4.28A(1)** Where the liquidator resigns, he has his release from the date on which he gives notice of his resignation to the Accountant in Bankruptcy.

**4.28A(2)** Where the liquidator is removed by a meeting of the company, he shall forthwith give notice to the Accountant in Bankruptcy of his ceasing to act.

**4.28A(3)** Where the liquidator is removed by the court, he must apply to the Accountant of Court for his release.

**4.28A(4)** Where the Accountant of Court gives the release, he shall certify it accordingly, and send the certificate to the Accountant in Bankruptcy.

**4.28A(5)** A copy of the certificate shall be sent by the Accountant of Court to the former liquidator, whose release is effective from the date of the certificate.".

**History**

In inserted r. 4.28 the words "the Accountant in Bankruptcy" where they occur were substituted for the former words "the registrar of companies" with effect from 1 July 1999 by virtue of the Scotland Act 1998 (Consequential Modifications) (No. 2) Order 1999 (SI 1999/1820), art. 1(2), 4 and Sch. 2, para. 141(1), (22) and the Scotland Act 1998 (Commencement) Order 1998 (SI 1998/3178), art. 3.

**Rule 4.36**

10 This Rule shall apply, except that for any reference to the court, there shall be substituted a reference to the directors of the company or any one of them.

**Rule 4.37**

**11(1)** This Rule shall apply subject to the following modifications.

**11(2)** In paragraph (2), the reference to the court shall be omitted.

**11(3)** For paragraph (3), there shall be substituted the following:

"**(3)** Rule 4.28A applies as regards the liquidator obtaining his release, as if he had been removed by the court.".

**11(4)** At the end of this Rule, there shall be inserted the following:–

"*Vacation of office on making of winding up order*

**4.37A** Where the liquidator vacates office in consequence of the court making a winding up order against the company, Rule 4.28A applies as regards the liquidator obtaining his release, as if he had been removed by the court.".

**Rule 4.38**

**12** This Rule shall apply.

**Rule 4.39**

**13** This Rule shall apply.

### CHAPTER 10 (SPECIAL MANAGER)

**14(1)** This Chapter shall apply subject to the following modifications.

**14(2)** In Rule 4.70 for paragraph (5), there shall be substituted the following:–

"**(5)** The cost of finding caution shall be paid in the first instance by the special manager; but he is entitled to be reimbursed out of the assets as an expense of the liquidation.".

**14(3)** In Rule 4.71, paragraph (1) shall not apply.

## Schedule 3 – Deposit Protection Board's Voting Rights

Rule 7.4(6)

**1** This Schedule applies where Rule 7.4 does.

**2** In relation to any meeting at which the Deposit Protection Board is under Rule 7.4 entitled to be represented, the Board may submit in the liquidation, instead of a claim, a written statement of voting rights ("the statement").

**3** The statement shall contain details of:–

(a) the names of creditors of the company in respect of whom an obligation of the Board has arisen or may reasonably be expected to arise as a result of the liquidation or proposed liquidation;

(b) the amount of the obligation so arising; and

(c) the total amount of all such obligations specified in the statement.

**4** The Board's statement shall, for the purpose of voting at a meeting (but for no other purpose), be treated in all respects as if it were a claim.

**5** Any voting rights which a creditor might otherwise exercise at a meeting in respect of a claim against the company are reduced by a sum equal to the amount of that claim in relation to which the Board, by virtue of its having submitted a statement, is entitled to exercise voting rights at that meeting.

**6** The Board may from time to time submit a further statement, and, if it does so, that statement supersedes any statement previously submitted.

## Schedule 4 – Punishment of Offences Under the Rules

Rule 7.29

**Note:** In the fourth and fifth columns of this Schedule, **"the statutory maximum"** means the prescribed sum under section 289B(6) of the Criminal Procedure (Scotland) Act 1975 (c. 21).

| *Rule creating offence* | *General nature of offence* | *Mode of prosecution* | *Punishment* | *Daily default fine (where applicable)* |
|---|---|---|---|---|
| In Part 1, Rule 1.24 | False representation or fraud for purpose of obtaining members' or creditors' consent to proposal for voluntary arrangement | 1. On indictment | 7 years or a fine, or both | |
| | | 2. Summary | 6 months or the statutory maximum, or both | |
| In Part 2, Rule 2.17(4) | Administrator failing to send notification as to progress of administration | Summary | One-fifth of the statutory maximum | One-fiftieth of the statutory maximum |
| In Part 3, Rule 3.9(5) | Receiver failing to send notification as to progress of receivership | Summary | One-fifth of the statutory maximum | One-fiftieth of the statutory maximum |

# Schedule 5 – Forms

Rule 7.30

**Note**

The forms are not reproduced here but are as follows:

| *Form* | *Title* |
|---|---|
| 1.1 (Scot) | Notice of Report of a Meeting Approving Voluntary Arrangement<br>Pursuant to section 416 of the Insolvency Act 1986 and Rule 1.17(5) of the Insolvency (Scotland) Rules 1986. |
| 1.2 (Scot) | Notice of Order of Revocation or Suspension of Voluntary Arrangement<br>Pursuant to section 6 of the Insolvency Act 1986 and Rule 1.20(5) of the Insolvency (Scotland) Rules 1986. |
| 1.3 (Scot) | Notice of Voluntary Arrangement Supervisor's Abstract of Receipts and Payments<br>Pursuant to Rule 1.21(2)(b) of the Insolvency (Scotland) Rules 1986. |
| 1.4 (Scot) | Notice of Completion of Voluntary Arrangement<br>Pursuant to Rule 1.23(3) of the Insolvency (Scotland) Rules 1986. |
| 2.1 (Scot) | Notice of Petition for Administration Order<br>Pursuant to section 9(2)(a) of the Insolvency Act 1986 and Rule 2.2(1) of the Insolvency (Scotland) Rules 1986. |
| 2.2 (Scot) | Notice of Administration Order<br>Pursuant to section 21(2) of the Insolvency Act 1986 and Rule 2.3(3) of the Insolvency (Scotland) Rules 1986. |
| 2.3 (Scot) | Notice of Dismissal of Petition for Administration Order<br>Pursuant to Rule 2.3(4) of the Insolvency (Scotland) Rules 1986. |
| 2.4 (Scot) | Notice of Discharge of Administration Order<br>Pursuant to sections 18(4) and 24(5) of the Insolvency Act 1986 and Rule 2.3(4) of the Insolvency (Scotland) Rules 1986. |
| 2.5 (Scot) | Notice Requiring Submission of Administration Statement of Affairs<br>Pursuant to section 22(4) of the Insolvency Act 1986 and Rule 2.4(2) of the Insolvency (Scotland) Rules 1986. |
| 2.6 (Scot) | Statement of Affairs<br>Pursuant to section 22(1) of the Insolvency Act 1986 and Rule 25(1) of the Insolvency (Scotland) Rules 1986. |
| 2.7 (Scot) | Notice of Statement of Administrator's proposals<br>Pursuant to section 23(1)(a) of the Insolvency Act 1986 and Rule 2.7 of the Insolvency (Scotland) Rules 1986. |
| 2.8 (Scot) | Notice of Result of Meeting of Creditors<br>Pursuant to section 24(4)/25(6) of the Insolvency Act 1986. |

| *Form* | *Title* |
|---|---|
| 2.9 (Scot) | Administrator's Abstract of Receipts and Payments<br>Pursuant to Rule 2.17(1) of the Insolvency (Scotland) Rules 1986. |
| 2.10 (Scot) | Statement of Administrator's Proposed Revisions and Notice of Meeting to Consider Them<br>Pursuant to section 25(2)(a) of the Insolvency Act 1986. |
| 2.11 (Scot) | Notice of Order to Deal with Secured Property<br>Pursuant to sections 15(7) of the Insolvency Act 1986. |
| 2.12 (Scot) | Notice of Variation of Administration Order<br>Pursuant to section 18(4) of the Insolvency Act 1986. |
| 2.13 (Scot) | Notice to Court of Resignation of Administrator<br>Pursuant to section 19(1) of the Insolvency Act 1986 and Rule 2.18 of the Insolvency (Scotland) Rules 1986. |
| 3.1 (Scot) | Notice Requiring Submission of Receivership Statement of Affairs<br>Pursuant to section 66(1) and (4) of the Insolvency Act 1986 and Rule 3.2(1) of the Insolvency (Scotland) Rules 1986. |
| 3.2 (Scot) | Receiver's Abstract of Receipts and Payments<br>Pursuant to Rule 3.9(1) and (3) of the Insolvency (Scotland) Rules 1986. |
| 3.3 (Scot) | Notice of Receiver's Death<br>Pursuant to Rule 3.10 of the Insolvency (Scotland) Rules 1986. |
| 3.4 (Scot) | Notice of Authorisation to Dispose of Secured Property<br>Pursuant to section 61(6) of the Insolvency Act 1986. |
| 3.5 (Scot) | Notice of Receiver's Report.<br>Pursuant to section 67(1) of the Insolvency Act 1986. |
| 4.1 (Scot) | Statutory Demand for Payment of Debt<br>Pursuant to section 123(1)(a) or section 222(1)(a) of the Insolvency Act 1986. |
| 4.2 (Scot) | Notice of Winding up Order<br>Pursuant to section 130 of the Insolvency Act 1986. |
| 4.3 (Scot) | Notice Requiring Submission of Statement of Affairs<br>Pursuant to section 131(4) of the Insolvency Act 1986 and Rule 4.7(3) of the Insolvency (Scotland) Rules 1986. |
| 4.4 (Scot) | Statement of Affairs<br>Pursuant to sections 95, 99 and 131 of the Insolvency Act 1986 and Rules 4.7 and 4.8 of the Insolvency (Scotland) Rules 1986. |
| 4.5 (Scot) | Liquidator's Statement of Receipts and Payments<br>Pursuant to section 192 of the Insolvency Act 1986 and Rule 4.11 of the Insolvency (Scotland) Rules 1986. |
| 4.6 (Scot) | Notice of Liquidator's Statement of Receipts and Payments<br>Pursuant to section 192 of the Insolvency Act 1986 and Rule 4.11 of the Insolvency (Scotland) Rules 1986. |
| 4.7 (Scot) | Statement of Claim by Creditor<br>Pursuant to Rule 4.15(2)(a) of the Insolvency (Scotland) Rules 1986. |
| 4.8 (Scot) | Certificate of Appointment of Liquidator<br>Pursuant to Rule 4.19 of the Insolvency (Scotland) Rules 1986. |
| 4.9 (Scot) | Notice of Appointment of Liquidator<br>Pursuant to Rules 4.2, 4.18, 4.19 and 4.27 of the Insolvency (Scotland) Rules 1986. |
| 4.10 (Scot) | Certificate of Removal of Liquidator<br>Pursuant to sections 171(2) and 172(2) of the Insolvency Act 1986 and Rules 4.24(1) and 4.25(1) of the Insolvency (Scotland) Rules 1986. |
| 4.11 (Scot) | Notice of Removal of Liquidator<br>Pursuant to sections 171(2) and 172(2) of the Insolvency Act 1986 and Rules 4.24, 4.26 and 4.28A of the Insolvency (Scotland) Rules 1986. |
| 4.12 (Scot) | Application by Liquidator to the Accountant of Court for his Release<br>Pursuant to section 173(2)(b), (e)(i) and (3), and section 174(4)(b), (d)(i) and (7) of the Insolvency Act 1986 and Rules 4.25 and 4.28A of the Insolvency (Scotland) Rules 1986. |
| 4.13 (Scot) | Certificate by the Accountant of Court of Release of Liquidator<br>Pursuant to section 173(2)(b), (e)(i) and (3), and section 174(4)(b), (d)(i) and (7) of the Insolvency Act 1986 and Rules 4.25(3)(a) and 4.28A of the Insolvency (Scotland) Rules 1986. |
| 4.14 (Scot) | Certificate of Release of Liquidator<br>Pursuant to Rules 4.25 and 4.28A of the Insolvency (Scotland) Rules 1986. |
| 4.15 (Scot) | Notice to Court of Resignation of Liquidator<br>Pursuant to section 172(6) of the Insolvency Act 1986 and Rule 4.29 of the Insolvency (Scotland) Rules 1986. |
| 4.16 (Scot) | Notice of Resignation of Liquidator<br>Pursuant to sections 171(5) and 172(6) of the Insolvency Act 1986 and Rules 4.28A, 4.29 and 4.30 of the Insolvency (Scotland) Rules 1986. |
| 4.17 (Scot) | Notice of Final Meeting of Creditors<br>Pursuant to sections 171(6) and 172(8) of the Insolvency Act 1986 and Rule 4.31(4) of the Insolvency (Scotland) Rules 1986. |
| 4.18 (Scot) | Notice of Death of Liquidator<br>Pursuant to Rule 4.36 of the Insolvency (Scotland) Rules 1986. |
| 4.19 (Scot) | Notice of Vacation of Office by Liquidator<br>Pursuant to Rule 4.37(2) of the Insolvency (Scotland) Rules 1986. |
| 4.20 (Scot) | Certificate of Constitution of Creditors'/Liquidation Committee<br>Pursuant to Rule 4.42 and that Rule as applied by Rules 2.15 and 3.6, of the Insolvency (Scotland) Rules 1986. |
| 4.21 (Scot) | Liquidator's Certificate of Continuance of Liquidation Committee<br>Pursuant to Rule 4.63(1) of the Insolvency (Scotland) Rules 1986. |

| Form | Title |
|---|---|
| 4.22 (Scot) | Notice of Constitution/Continuance of Liquidation/Creditors' Committee Pursuant to Rules 2.15, 3.6, 4.42(5) and (6) and 4.63(6) and (7) of the Insolvency (Scotland) Rules 1986. |
| 4.23 (Scot) | Liquidator's Certificate that Creditors Paid in Full Pursuant to Rule 4.59(1) of the Insolvency (Scotland) Rules 1986. |
| 4.24 (Scot) | Notice of Certificate that Creditors Have Been Paid in Full Pursuant to Rule 4.59(2) of the Insolvency (Scotland) Rules 1986. |
| 4.25 (Scot) | Declaration of Solvency Pursuant to section 89(3) of the Insolvency Act 1986. |
| 4.26 (Scot) | Return of Final Meeting in a Voluntary Winding Up Pursuant to sections 94 and 106 of the Insolvency Act 1986. |
| 4.27 (Scot) | Notice of Court's Order Sisting Proceedings in Winding Up by the Court Pursuant to sections 112(3) and 147(3) of the Insolvency Act 1986. |
| 4.28 (Scot) | Notice under section 204(6) or 205(6) Pursuant to section 204(6) or 205(6) of the Insolvency Act 1986 and Rule 4.77 of the Insolvency (Scotland) Rules 1986. |
| 4.29 (Scot) | Proxy Pursuant to Rules 7.14 and 7.15 of the Insolvency (Scotland) Rules 1986. |

**History**
In Sch. 5, Forms 2.13 (Scot), 4.1 (Scot), 4.7 (Scot) substituted and Form 4.29 (Scot) added by the Insolvency (Scotland) Amendment Rules 1987 (SI 1987/1921 (s. 132)), Sch., Pt. III and II as from 11 January 1988.

## EXPLANATORY NOTE

(*This Note does not form part of the Rules*)

These Rules set out the detailed procedure for the conduct of insolvency proceedings under the Insolvency Act 1986 ("the Act") relating to companies registered in Scotland and other companies which the Scottish courts have jurisdiction to wind up and otherwise give effect to that Act in relation to Scotland.

Part 1 of the Rules sets out the procedure relating to company voluntary arrangements under Part I of the Act.

Part 2 of the Rules sets out the procedure relating to the administration procedure in Part II of the Act (Administration Orders).

Part 3 of the Rules sets out the procedure relating to receivers in Chapter II of part III of the Act (Receivers (Scotland)). In addition, the Receivers (Scotland) Regulations 1986 (S.I. 1986/1917) prescribe matters which expressly fall to be prescribed in terms of that Chapter.

Parts 4–6 of the Rules set out the procedure relating to winding up of companies in Part IV of the Act. Part 4 of the Rules deals with winding up by the court. Parts 5 and 6 of, and Schedules 1 and 2 to, the Rules apply the provisions of Part 4, with modifications, to creditors' voluntary winding up and members' voluntary winding up respectively.

Part 7 of the Rules contains provisions of general application to insolvency proceedings. They include provisions relating to meetings (Chapter 1), proxies and company representation (Chapter 2) and miscellaneous matters (Chapter 3). In particular, Schedule 5 contains the forms which are to be used for the purposes of the provisions of the Act or the Rules which are referred to in those forms.

The Rules come into force on 29th December 1986 when the Act comes into force and will apply to insolvency proceedings which are commenced on or after that day.

# THE RECEIVERS (SCOTLAND) REGULATIONS 1986

(SI 1986/1917 (S 141))

*Made on 10 November 1986 by the Secretary of State for Trade and Industry under s. 53(1), (6), 54(3), 62(1), (5), 65(1)(a), 66(1), 67(2), (6), 70(1) and 71 of the Insolvency Act 1986. Operative from 29 December 1986.*

## CITATION AND COMMENCEMENT

**1** These regulations may be cited as the Receivers (Scotland) Regulations 1986 and shall come into operation on 29th December 1986.

## INTERPRETATION

**2** In these regulations, **"the Act"** means the Insolvency Act 1986.

## FORMS

**3** The forms set out in the Schedule to these regulations, with such variations as circumstances require, are the forms prescribed for the purposes of the provisions of the Act which are referred to in those forms.

## INSTRUMENT OF APPOINTMENT

**4** The certified copy instrument of appointment of a receiver which is required to be submitted to the registrar of companies and the Accountant in Bankruptcy by or on behalf of the person making the appointment under section 53(1) of the Act shall be certified to be a correct copy by or on behalf of that person.

**History**

In r. 4, the words "and the Accountant in Bankruptcy" inserted with effect from 1 July 1999 by virtue of the Scotland Act 1998 (Consequential Modifications) (No. 2) Order 1999 (SI 1999/1820), art. 1(2), 4 and Sch. 2, para. 142(1), (2) and the Scotland Act 1998 (Commencement) Order 1998 (SI 1998/3178), art. 3.

## JOINT RECEIVERS

**5** Where two or more persons are appointed joint receivers by the holder of a floating charge under section 53 of the Act, subsection (6) of that section shall apply subject to the following modifications:–

(a) the appointment of any of the joint receivers shall be of no effect unless the appointment is accepted by all of them in accordance with paragraph (a) of that subsection and Rule 3.1 of the Insolvency (Scotland) Rules 1986; and

(b) their appointment as joint receivers shall be deemed to be made on the day on and at the time at which the instrument of appointment is received by the last of them, as evidenced by the written docquet required by paragraph (b) of that subsection.

## RESIGNATION

**6** For the purposes of section 62(1) of the Act, a receiver, who wishes to resign his office, shall give at least 7 days' notice of his resignation to–

(a) the holder of the floating charge by virtue of which he was appointed;

(b) the holder of any other floating charge and any receiver appointed by him;

(c) the members of any committee of creditors established under section 68 of the Act; and

(d) the company, or if it is then in liquidation, its liquidator,

and the notice shall specify the date on which the resignation takes effect.

## REPORT TO CREDITORS

**7** Where the receiver determines to publish a notice under paragraph (b) of section 67(2) of the Act, the notice shall be published in a newspaper circulating in the area where the company has its principal place of business or in such other newspaper as he thinks most appropriate for ensuring that it comes to the notice of the unsecured creditors of the company.

# Schedule – Forms

Regulation 3

**Note**

The forms are not reproduced here but are as follows:

| *Form* | *Title* |
|---|---|
| 1 (Scot) | Notice of appointment of a Receiver by the Holder of a Floating Charge: Pursuant to section 53(1) of the Insolvency Act 1986 and Regulation 3 of the Receivers (Scotland) Regulations 1986. |
| 2 (Scot) | Notice of appointment of a Receiver by the Court Pursuant to section 54(3) of the Insolvency Act 1986. |
| 3 (Scot) | Notice of the Receiver ceasing to act or of his removal Pursuant to section 62(5) of the Insolvency Act 1986. |

(c) paragraph 1(b) shall be omitted;

(d) in paragraph 1(c) after the words "Part VIII" there shall be added the words "in Form 2 set out in the said Schedule 3";

(e) at the end of paragraph 1(d) there shall be added the words "in Form 3 set out in the said Schedule 3 in any case where a creditor could present such a petition under paragraph (a) above"; and

(f) at the end of subsection (2) there shall be added the words "in Form 4 set out in the said Schedule 3".

**2** Section 266 with the following modifications:–

(a) for subsection (1) there shall be substituted the following:–

"(1) An insolvency administration petition shall, unless the court otherwise directs, be served on the personal representative and shall be served on such other persons as the court may direct."; and

(b) in subsection (3) for the words "bankruptcy petition" there shall be substituted the words "petition to the court for an insolvency administration order with or without costs".

**3** Section 267 with the following modifications to subsection (2):–

(a) before the words "at the time" there shall be inserted the words "had the debtor been alive"; and

(b) for paragraphs (a) to (d) there shall be substituted the following:–

"(a) the amount of the debt, or the aggregate amount of the debts, owed by the debtor would have been equal to or exceeded the bankruptcy level, or

(b) the debt, or each of the debts, owed by the debtor would have been for a liquidated sum payable to the petitioning creditor, or one or more of the petitioning creditors, either immediately or at some certain future time, and would have been unsecured.".

**4** Section 269 with the modification that in subsection (2) for the words "sections 267 to 270" there shall be substituted the words "section 267 and this section".

**5** Section 271 as if for that section there were substituted the following:–

"**271(1)** The court may make an insolvency administration order on a petition for such an order under section 264(1) if it is satisfied–

(a) that the debt, or one of the debts, in respect of which the petition was presented is a debt which,

(i) having been payable at the date of the petition or having since become payable, has neither been paid nor secured or compounded for; or

(ii) has no reasonable prospect of being able to be paid when it falls due; and

(b) that there is a reasonable probability that the estate will be insolvent.

**271(2)** A petition for an insolvency administration order shall not be presented to the court after proceedings have been commenced in any court of justice for the administration of the deceased debtor's estate.

**271(3)** Where proceedings have been commenced in any such court for the administration of the deceased debtor's estate, that court may, if satisfied that the estate is insolvent, transfer the proceedings to the court exercising jurisdiction for the purposes of the Parts in the second Group of Parts.

**271(4)** Where proceedings have been transferred to the court exercising jurisdiction for the purposes of the Parts in the second Group of Parts, that court may make an insolvency administration order in Form 5 set out in Schedule 3 to the Administration of Insolvent Estates of Deceased Persons Order 1986 as if a petition for such an order had been presented under section 264.

**271(5)** Nothing in sections 264, 266, 267, 269 or 271 to 273 shall invalidate any payment made or any act or thing done in good faith by the personal representative before the date of the insolvency administration order.".

**6** Section 272(1) with the following modifications:–

(a) after the word "petition" there shall be inserted the words "in Form 6 set out in Schedule 3 to the Administration of Insolvent Estates of Deceased Persons Order 1986"; and

(b) for the words "debtor is unable to pay his debts" there shall be substituted the words "estate of a deceased debtor is insolvent".

**7** Section 273 as if for that section there were substituted the following:–

"**273** The court shall make an insolvency administration order in Form 4 set out in Schedule 3 to the Administration of Insolvent Estates of Deceased Persons Order 1986 on the hearing of a petition presented under section 272 if it is satisfied that the deceased debtor's estate is insolvent.".

**8** Section 276(2).

**9** Section 277.

**10** Section 278 except paragraph (b) as if for paragraph (a) there were substituted the following:–

"(a) commences with the day on which the insolvency administration order is made;".

**11** Section 282(1) and (4).

**12** Sections 283 to 285 with the modification that they shall have effect as if the petition had been presented and the insolvency administration order had been made on the date of death of the deceased debtor, and with the following modifications to section 283:–

(a) in subsection (2)(b), for the words "bankrupt and his family" there shall be substituted the words "family of the deceased debtor"; and

(b) after subsection (4) there shall be added the following subsection:–

"**(4A)** References in any of this Group of Parts to property, in relation to a deceased debtor, include the capacity to exercise and take proceedings for exercising all such powers over or in respect of property as might have been exercised by his personal representative for the benefit of the estate on the date of the insolvency administration order and as are specified in subsection (4) above.".

**13** Section 286(1) and (3) to (8).

**14** Section 287.

**15** Section 288 with the modification that for subsections (1) and (2) there shall be substituted the following:–

"**(1)** Where an insolvency administration order has been made, the personal representative, or if there is no personal representative such person as the court may on the application of the official receiver direct, shall submit to the official receiver a statement of the deceased debtor's affairs containing particulars of the assets and liabilities of the estate as at the date of the insolvency administration order together with other particulars of the affairs of the deceased debtor in Form 7 set out in Schedule 3 to the Administration of Insolvent Estates of Deceased Persons Order 1986 or as the official receiver may require.

**(2)** The statement shall be submitted before the end of the period of fifty-six days beginning with the date of a request by the official receiver for the statement or such longer period as he or the court may allow.".

**16** Section 289 as if for that section there were substituted the following:–

"**289** The official receiver is not under any duty to investigate the conduct and affairs of the deceased debtor unless he thinks fit but may make such report (if any) to the court as he thinks fit.".

**17** Section 291.

**18** Sections 292 to 302, except section 297(4), with the modification that, where a meeting of creditors is summoned for the purposes of any provision in those sections, the rules regarding the trustee in bankruptcy and the creditors' committee shall apply accordingly.

(b) in the case of individual insolvency, extends to England and Wales only.

## INTERPRETATION

**2(1)** In this Order–

**"the Act"** means the Insolvency Act 1986;

**"corporate member"** means an insolvent member which is a company;

**"individual member"** means an insolvent member who is an individual;

**"insolvent member"** means a member of an insolvent partnership, against whom an insolvency petition is being or has been presented;

**"insolvency order"** means–

(a) in the case of an insolvent partnership or a corporate member, a winding-up order; and

(b) in the case of an individual member, a bankruptcy order;

**"insolvency petition"** means–

(a) in the case of a petition presented against a corporate member, a petition for its winding up by the court; and

(b) in the case of a petition presented against an individual member, a petiton to the court for a bankruptcy order to be made against the individual,

where the petition is presented in conjunction with a petition for the winding up of the partnership by the court as an unregistered company under the Act; and

**"responsible insolvency practitioner"** means–

(a) in winding up, the liquidator; and

(b) in bankruptcy, the trustee,

and in either case includes the official receiver when so acting.

**2(2)** The definitions in paragraph (1) above other than the first definition shall be added to those in section 436 of the Act.

**2(3)** A Form referred to in this Order by number means the Form so numbered in Schedule 3 to this Order.

## MEMBERS OR OTHER PERSONS HAVING CONTROL OR MANAGEMENT OF BUSINESS OF INSOLVENT PARTNERSHIP

**3** Where an insolvent partnership is being wound up under Part V of the Act as an unregistered company, any member or former member of the partnership or any other person who has or has had control or management of the partnership business–

(a) shall for the purposes of the provisions of the Act and the Company Directors Disqualification Act 1986 applied by this Order be deemed to be an officer and director of the company; and

(b) shall deliver up to the liquidator of the partnership for the purposes of the exercise of the liquidator's functions under the provisions referred to in paragraph (a) above possession of any partnership property within the meaning of the Partnership Act 1890 which he holds for the purposes of the partnership.

## VERIFICATION OF PETITION FOR WINDING UP INSOLVENT PARTNERSHIP

**4** Every affidavit verifying the petition for the winding up of an insolvent partnership under Part V of the Act shall include the names in full and addresses of all members of the partnership so far as known to the petitioner.

## APPLICATION OF INSOLVENCY RULES, INSOLVENCY REGULATIONS AND INSOLVENCY FEES ORDER TO PROVISIONS OF THE ACT APPLIED IN RELATION TO INSOLVENT PARTNERSHIPS

**5(1)** The Insolvency Rules 1986, the Insolvency Regulations 1986 and the Insolvency Fees Order 1986 apply with the necessary modifications for the purpose of giving effect to the provisions of Parts I and IV to XI of the Act which are applied in relation to insolvent partnerships with the modifications specified in this Order.

**5(2)** In the case of any conflict between any provision of the Insolvency Rules 1986 and any provision of this Order, the latter provision shall prevail.

**5(3)** Sections 414(4) and 415(3) of the Act shall apply with the following modifications:–

(a) where an order provides for any sum to be deposited on presentation of a winding-up or bankruptcy petition, that sum shall, in the case of an insolvent partnership, only be required to be deposited in respect of the petition for winding up the partnership; and

(b) production of any receipt for the sum deposited upon presentation of the petition for winding up the partnership shall suffice for the filing in court of an insolvency petition against an insolvent member.

### APPLICATION OF PROVISIONS OF THE COMPANY DIRECTORS DISQUALIFICATION ACT 1986 IN RELATION TO INSOLVENT PARTNERSHIPS

**6** Where an insolvent partnership is wound up as an unregistered company under Part V of the Act, the provisions of sections 6 to 10, 15, 19(c) and 20 of, and Schedule 1 to, the Company Directors Disqualification Act 1986 apply in relation to the partnership as if any member of the partnership were a director of a company, and the partnership were a company as defined by section 22(2)(b) of that Act.

## PART 2 – WINDING UP OF INSOLVENT PARTNERSHIP ONLY

**7** The provisions of Part V of the Act specified in Schedule 1 to this Order shall apply in relation to the winding up of insolvent partnerships as unregistered companies with the modifications specified in that Schedule where no insolvency petition is presented by the petitioner against an insolvent member.

## PART 3 – WINDING UP OF INSOLVENT PARTNERSHIP INVOLVING INSOLVENCY PETITIONS AGAINST TWO OR MORE INSOLVENT MEMBERS

### APPLICATION OF PROVISIONS OF THE ACT WITH MODIFICATIONS

**8(1)** Sections 220(1) and 221 of the Act shall apply in relation to the winding up of insolvent partnerships as unregistered companies where an insolvency petition is presented by the petitioner against two or more insolvent members, with the following modifications:–

(a) in section 220(1), before the words "any association" there shall be inserted the words "any insolvent partnership,";

(b) for section 221(1) there shall be substituted the following:–

"**(1)** Subject to the provisions of this Part, any insolvent partnership which has a principal place of business in England and Wales may be wound up as an unregistered company under this Act; and all the provisions of this Act and the Companies Act about winding up apply to the winding up of such a partnership as an unregistered company with the exceptions and additions mentioned in the following subsections and in Part I of Schedule 2 to the Insolvency Partnerships Order 1986."; and

(c) for section 221(5) there shall be substituted the following:–

"**(5)** The circumstances in which an insolvent partnership may be wound up are that the partnership is unable to pay its debts.".

**8(2)** All the provisions of the Act and the Companies Act about winding up of companies by the court shall apply in relation to the winding up of a corporate member where the insolvent partnership is wound up as an unregistered company under paragraph (1) above, with the

Member States' laws governing companies. Nor must a grouping be used for the transfer of any property between a company and a director, or any person connected with him, except to the extent allowed by the Member States' laws governing companies. For the purposes of this provision the making of a loan includes entering into any transaction or arrangement of similar effect, and property includes moveable and immoveable property;

(e) be a member of another European Economic Interest Grouping.

## ARTICLE 4

1 Only the following may be members of a grouping:

(a) companies or firms within the meaning of the second paragraph of Article 58 of the Treaty and other legal bodies governed by public or private law, which have been formed in accordance with the law of a Member State and which have their registered or statutory office and central administration in the Community; where, under the law of a Member State, a company, firm or other legal body is not obliged to have a registered or statutory office, it shall be sufficient for such a company, firm or other legal body to have its central administration in the Community;

(b) natural persons who carry on any industrial, commercial, craft or agricultural activity or who provide professional or other services in the Community.

2 A grouping must comprise at least:

(a) two companies, firms or other legal bodies, within the meaning of paragraph 1, which have their central administrations in different Member States, or

(b) two natural persons, within the meaning of paragraph 1, who carry on their principal activities in different Member States, or

(c) a company, firm or other legal body within the meaning of paragraph 1 and a natural person, of which the first has its central administration in one Member State and the second carries on his principal activity in another Member State.

3 A Member State may provide that groupings registered at its registries in accordance with Article 6 may have no more than 20 members. For this purpose, that Member State may provide that, in accordance with its laws, each member of a legal body formed under its laws, other than a registered company, shall be treated as a separate member of a grouping.

4 Any Member State may, on grounds of that State's public interest, prohibit or restrict participation in groupings by certain classes of natural persons, companies, firms, or other legal bodies.

## ARTICLE 5

A contract for the formation of a grouping shall include at least:

(a) the name of the grouping preceded or followed either by the words "European Economic Interest Grouping" or by the initials "EEIG", unless those words or initials already form part of the name;

(b) the official address of the grouping;

(c) the objects for which the grouping is formed;

(d) the name, business name, legal form, permanent address or registered office, and the number and place of registration, if any, of each member of the grouping;

(e) the duration of the grouping, except where this is indefinite.

## ARTICLE 6

A grouping shall be registered in the State in which it has its official address, at the registry designated pursuant to Article 39(1).

## ARTICLE 7

A contract for the formation of a grouping shall be filed at the registry referred to in Article 6.

The following documents and particulars must also be filed at that registry:

(a) any amendment to the contract for the formation of a grouping, including any change in the composition of a grouping;
(b) notice of the setting up or closure of any establishment of the grouping;
(c) any judicial decision establishing or declaring the nullity of a grouping, in accordance with Article 15;
(d) notice of the appointment of the manager or managers of a grouping, their names and any other identification particulars required by the law of the Member State in which the register is kept, notification that they may act alone or must act jointly, and the termination of any manager's appointment;
(e) notice of a member's assignment of his participation in a grouping or a proportion thereof, in accordance with Article 22(1);
(f) any decision by members ordering or establishing the winding up of a grouping, in accordance with Article 31, or any judicial decision ordering such winding up, in accordance with Articles 31 or 32;
(g) notice of the appointment of the liquidator or liquidators of a grouping, as referred to in Article 35, their names and any other identification particulars required by the law of the Member State in which the register is kept, and the termination of any liquidator's appointment;
(h) notice of the conclusion of a grouping's liquidation, as referred to in Article 35(2);
(i) any proposal to transfer the official address, as referred to in Article 14(1);
(j) any clause exempting a new member from the payment of debts and other liabilities which originated prior to his admission, in accordance with Article 26(2).

## ARTICLE 8

The following must be published, as laid down in Article 39, in the gazette referred to in paragraph 1 of that Article:
(a) the particulars which must be included in the contract for the formation of a grouping pursuant to Article 5, and any amendments thereto;
(b) the number, date and place of registration as well as notice of the termination of that registration;
(c) the documents and particulars referred to in Article 7(b) to (j).

The particulars referred to in (a) and (b) must be published in full. The documents and particulars referred to in (c) may be published either in full or in extract form or by means of a reference to their filing at the registry, in accordance with the national legislation applicable.

## ARTICLE 9

**1** The documents and particulars which must be published pursuant to this Regulation may be relied on by a grouping as against third parties under the conditions laid down by the national law applicable pursuant to Article 3(5) and (7) of Council Directive 68EEC of 9 March 1968 on co-ordination of safeguards which, for the protection of the interests of members and others, are required by Member States of companies within the meaning of the second paragraph of Article 58 of the Treaty, with a view to making such safeguards equivalent throughout the Community.

**2** If activities have been carried on on behalf of a grouping before its registration in accordance with Article 6 and if the grouping does not, after its registration, assume the obligations arising out of such activities, the natural persons, companies, firms or other legal bodies which carried on those activities shall bear unlimited joint and several liability for them.

## ARTICLE 10

Any grouping establishment situated in a Member State other than that in which the official address is situated shall be registered in that State. For the purpose of such registration, a grouping shall file, at the appropriate registry in that Member State, copies of the documents which must be filed at the registry of the Member State in which the official address is situated, together, if necessary, with a translation which conforms with the practice of the registry where the establishment is registered.

accordance with the conditions laid down in the contract for the formation of the grouping or determined by unanimous decision of the members in question.

## ARTICLE 31

**1** A grouping may be wound up by a decision of its members ordering its winding up. Such a decision shall be taken unanimously, unless otherwise laid down in the contract for the formation of the grouping.

**2** A grouping must be wound up by a decision of its members:

(a) noting the expiry of the period fixed in the contract for the formation of the grouping or the existence of any other cause for winding up provided for in the contract, or

(b) noting the accomplishment of the grouping's purpose or the impossibility of pursuing it further.

Where, three months after one of the situations referred to in the first subparagraph has occurred, a members' decision establishing the winding up of the grouping has not been taken, any member may petition the court to order winding up.

**3** A grouping must also be wound up by a decision of its members or of the remaining member when the conditions laid down in Article 4(2) are no longer fulfilled.

**4** After a grouping has been wound up by decision of its members, the manager or managers must take the steps required as listed in Articles 7 and 8. In addition, any person concerned may take those steps.

## ARTICLE 32

**1** On application by any person concerned or by a competent authority, in the event of the infringement of Articles 3, 12 or 31(3), the court must order a grouping to be wound up, unless its affairs can be and are put in order before the court has delivered a substantive ruling.

**2** On application by a member, the court may order a grouping to be wound up on just and proper grounds.

**3** A Member State may provide that the court may, on application by a competent authority, order the winding up of a grouping which has its official address in the State to which that authority belongs, wherever the grouping acts in contravention of that State's public interest, if the law of that State provides for such a possibility in respect of registered companies or other legal bodies subject to it.

## ARTICLE 33

When a member ceases to belong to a grouping for any reason other than the assignment of his rights in acordance with the conditions laid down in Article 22(1), the value of his rights and obligations shall be determined taking into account the assets and liabilities of the grouping as they stand when he ceases to belong to it.

The value of the rights and obligations of a departing member may not be fixed in advance.

## ARTICLE 34

Without prejudice to Article 37(1), any member who ceases to belong to a grouping shall remain answerable, in accordance with the conditions laid down in Article 24, for the debts and other liabilities arising out of the grouping's activities before he ceased to be a member.

## ARTICLE 35

**1** The winding up of a grouping shall entail its liquidation.

**2** The liquidation of a grouping and the conclusion of its liquidation shall be governed by national law.

**3** A grouping shall retain its capacity, within the meaning of Article 1(2), until its liquidation is concluded.

**4** The liquidator or liquidators shall take the steps required as listed in Articles 7 and 8.

## ARTICLE 36

Groupings shall be subject to national laws governing insolvency and cessation of payments. The commencement of proceedings against a grouping on grounds of its insolvency or cessation of payments shall not by itself cause the commencement of such proceedings against its members.

## ARTICLE 37

**1** A period of limitation of five years after the publication, pursuant to Article 8, of notice of a member's ceasing to belong to a grouping shall be substituted for any longer period which may be laid down by the relevant national law for actions against that member in connection with debts and other liabilities arising out of the grouping's activities before he ceased to be a member.

**2** A period of limitation of five years after the publication, pursuant to Article 8, of notice of the conclusion of the liquidation of a grouping shall be substituted for any longer period which may be laid down by the relevant national law for actions against a member of the grouping in connection with debts and other liabilities arising out of the grouping's activities.

## ARTICLE 38

Where a grouping carries on any activity in a Member State in contravention of that State's public interest, a competent authority of that State may prohibit that activity. Review of that competent authority's decision by a judicial authority shall be possible.

## ARTICLE 39

**1** The Member States shall designate the registry or registries responsible for effecting the registration referred to in Articles 6 and 10 and shall lay down the rules governing registration. They shall prescribe the conditions under which the documents referred to in Articles 7 and 10 shall be filed. They shall ensure that the documents and particulars referred to in Article 8 are published in the appropriate official gazette of the Member State in which the grouping has its official address, and may prescribe the manner of publication of the documents and particulars referred to in Article 8(c).

The Member States shall also ensure that anyone may, at the appropriate registry pursuant to Article 6 or, where appropriate, Article 10, inspect the documents referred to in Article 7 and obtain, even by post, full or partial copies thereof.

The Member States may provide for the payment of fees in connection with the operations referred to in the preceding subparagraphs; those fees may not, however, exceed the administrative cost thereof.

**2** The Member States shall ensure that the information to be published in the *Official Journal of the European Communities* pursuant to Article 11 is forwarded to the Office for Official Publications of the European Communities within one month of its publication in the official gazette referred to in paragraph 1.

**3** The Member States shall provide for appropriate penalties in the event of failure to comply with the provisions of Articles 7, 8 and 10 on disclosure and in the event of failure to comply with Article 25.

## ARTICLE 40

The profits or losses resulting from the activities of a grouping shall be taxable only in the hands of its members.

## ARTICLE 41

**1** The Member States shall take the measures required by virtue of Article 39 before 1 July 1989. They shall immediately communicate them to the Commission.

**2** For information purposes, the Member States shall inform the Commission of the classes of natural persons, companies, firms and other legal bodies which they prohibit from participating in groupings pursuant to Article 4(4). The Commission shall inform the other Member States.

ARTICLE 42

1 Upon the adoption of this Regulation, a Contact Committee shall be set up under the auspices of the Commission. Its function shall be:

(a) to facilitate, without prejudice to Articles 169 and 170 of the Treaty, application of this Regulation through regular consultation dealing in particular with practical problems arising in connection with its application;

(b) to advise the Commission, if necessary, on additions or amendments to this Regulation.

2 The Contact Committee shall be composed of representatives of the Member States and representatives of the Commission. The chairman shall be a representative of the Commission. The Commission shall provide the secretariat.

3 The Contact Committee shall be convened by its chairman either on his own initiative or at the request of one of its members.

ARTICLE 43

This Regulation shall enter into force on the third day following its publication in the *Official Journal of the European Communities*.

It shall apply from 1 July 1989, with the exception of Articles 39, 41 and 42 which shall apply as from the entry into force of the Regulation.

This Regulation shall be binding in its entirety and directly applicable in all Member States.

# Schedule 2 – Forms Relating to EEIGs

Regulations 2(2), 4(1), 5(1), 9(2), (3), (9) and (10), 12(2) and (4), 13(1) and 18, and Schedule 4, paragraph 14

**Note**

The following forms are set out in Sch. 2 but not reproduced here:

| | |
|---|---|
| EEIG 1 | Statement of name, official address, members, objects and duration for EEIG whose official address is in Great Britain |
| EEIG 2 | Statement of name, establishment address in Great Britain and members of an EEIG whose official address is outside the UK |
| EEIG 3 | Notice of manager's particulars, and of termination of appointment where the official address of the EEIG is in Great Britain |
| EEIG 4 | Notice of documents and particulars required to be filed |
| EEIG 5 | Notice of setting up or closure of an establishment of an EEIG |
| EEIG 6 | Statement of name, other than registered name, under which an EEIG whose official address is outside Great Britain proposes to carry on business in Great Britain |
| EEIG 7 | Statement of name, other than registered name, under which an EEIG whose official address is outside Great Britain proposes to carry on business in substitution for name previously approved |

# Schedule 3 – Authorised Equivalents in other Community Official Languages of "European Economic Interest Grouping" and "EEIG"

| | |
|---|---|
| DANISH: | Europæiske Økonomiske Firmagruppe (EØFG) |
| DUTCH: | Europese Economische Samenwerkingsverbanden (EESV) |
| FRENCH: | Groupement Européen d'intérêt économique (GEIE) |
| GERMAN: | Europäische Wirtschaftliche Interessenvereinigung (EWIV) |

| | |
|---|---|
| GREEK: | (written phonetically in letters of the Latin alphabet as "Evropaikos omilos economicou skopou (EOOS)") |
| IRISH: | Grupail Eorpach um Leas Eacnamaioch (GELE) |
| ITALIAN: | Gruppo Europeo di Interesse Economico (GEIE) |
| PORTUGUESE: | Agrupamento Europeu de Interesse Econômico (AEIE) |
| SPANISH: | Agrupación Europea de Interés Económico (AEIE) |

# Schedule 4 – Provisions of Companies Act 1985 applying to EEIGs and their establishments

Regulation 18

**1** section 26(1)(c) to (e), (2) and (3).

**2** section 28(2) to (5) and (7) so far as it relates to a direction given under subsection (2).

**3** section 29(1)(a).

**4** Part XII for the purpose of the creation and registration of charges to which it applies.

**5** section 432(1) and (2).

**6** section 434 so far as it refers to inspectors appointed under section 432 as applied by regulation 18 above and this Schedule.

**7** section 436 so far as it refers to inspectors appointed under section 432, and to section 434, as applied by regulation 18 above and this Schedule.

**8** sections 437 to 439.

**9** section 441 so far as it applies to inspectors appointed under section 432 as applied by regulation 18 above and this Schedule.

**10** section 447, as if paragraph (1)(d) referred to any EEIG which is carrying on business in Great Britain or has at any time carried on business there, whether or not any such EEIG is a body corporate.

**11** sections 448 to 452.

**12** section 458.

**13** Part XVIII relating to floating charges and receivers (Scotland).

**14** section 694 as if it referred to–

(a) the registered name of an EEIG whose establishment is registered or is in the process of being registered under regulation 12 above with the necessary modifications;

(b) regulation 10 above as applied by regulation 12(7) in addition to section 26;

(c) in subsection (4)(a), a statement in Form EEIG 6; and

(d) in subsection (4)(b), a statement in Form EEIG 7.

**15** section 697(2) as if it referred to an EEIG whose establishment is registered or is in the process of being registered under regulation 12 above.

**16** section 704(5), (7) and (8).

**17** section 705(2).

**18** sections 706, 707 and 710(1) to (3) and (5) as if they referred to documents and particulars delivered to or furnished by the registrar under these Regulations.

**19** section 714(1) as if it referred to EEIGs or their establishments registered under these Regulations or in Northern Ireland.

**20** section 718(2) as if it included a reference to an EEIG registered in Great Britain under these Regulations.

**21** section 725.

**22** section 730 and Schedule 24 so far as they refer to offences under sections applied by regulation 18 above and this Schedule.

**23** section 731.

**24** sections 732 and 733 so far as they refer to sections 447 to 451 as applied by regulation 18 above and this Schedule.

**History**

In Sch. 4, para. 16, the words "section 704(5), (7) and (8)" substituted for the former words "section 704(5)" by Deregulation and Contracting Out Act 1994, s. 76, 82(2)(f) and Sch. 16, para. 15 with effect from 3 January 1995.

## EXPLANATORY NOTE

(*This Note is not part of the Regulations*)

These Regulations make provisions in respect of European Economic Interest Groupings formed under article 1 of the Council Regulation (EEC) No. 2137/85, which provides a legal framework for groupings of natural persons, companies, firms and other legal entities to enable them to co-operate effectively when carrying on business activities across national frontiers within the European Community. Such groupings, which have their official address in Great Britain, when registered there under these Regulations are bodies corporate and their members have unlimited joint and several liability for the debts and liabilities of such groupings.

The EC Regulation is directly applicable in UK law but these Regulations are necessary for implementation in part of the Community obligations and for other purposes mentioned in section 2(2) of the European Communities Act 1972. In particular certain provisions are left for national law by the EC Regulation. Articles 35 and 36 provide that groupings shall be subject to national laws governing their winding up and the conclusion of their liquidation and insolvency and cessation of payments. Regulation 8 of these Regulations provides for modifications to Part V of the Insolvency Act 1986, where a grouping is wound up as an unregistered company under Part V. Accordingly the Court has power to wind up a grouping in the circumstances set out in articles 31 and 32 or the grouping may be wound up voluntarily in the circumstances set out in article 31; and a grouping is dissolved after 3 months of the receipt by the registrar of a notice of the conclusion of the liquidation, whether or not the grouping has been wound up by the Court.

# THE RESTRICTIVE TRADE PRACTICES (SALE AND PURCHASE AND SHARE SUBSCRIPTION AGREEMENTS) (GOODS) ORDER 1989

(SI 1989/1081)

*Made on 29 June 1989 by the Secretary of State for Trade and Industry under s. 2(3) and (5) of the Restrictive Trade Practices Act 1977. Operative from 30 June 1989.*

## CITATION AND COMMENCEMENT

**1** This Order may be cited as the Restrictive Trade Practices (Sale and Purchase and Share Subscription Agreements) (Goods) Order 1989 and shall come into force on the day after the day on which it is made.

## INTERPRETATION

**2** In this Order–

**"the Act of 1976"** means the Restrictive Trade Practices Act 1976;

**"acquired enterprise"** means a company in which shares are acquired or a business an interest in which is acquired;

**"business"** means any undertaking which is, or any part of an undertaking which part is–

(a) carried on as a going concern for gain or reward; or
(b) carried on as a going concern in the course of which goods or services are supplied otherwise than free of charge;

**"company"** means a company as defined in section 735 of the Companies Act 1985 and an oversea company as defined in section 744 of that Act;

**"contract of employment"** means a contract of service whether it is express or implied and (if it is express) whether it is oral or in writing;

**"goods"** has the same meaning as in section 43(1) of the Act of 1976;

**"group"** means a group of interconnected bodies corporate within the meaning of section 43(1) of the Act of 1976;

**"member of the issuing company"** is to be construed in accordance with section 22 of the Companies Act 1985;

**"purchaser"** means a person acquiring shares in a company, or acquiring an interest in a business, whether for cash or otherwise;

**"relevant restriction"** means a restriction described in section 6(1) of the Act of 1976;

**"services"** has the same meaning as in section 20 of the Act of 1976.

## SALE AND PURCHASE AGREEMENTS

**3(1)** This article applies to an agreement made on or after the date on which this Order comes into force–

(a) the parties to which include a person (the **"vendor"**) who agrees to transfer shares in a company or the whole of his interest in a business to a purchaser;

(b) under which, in the case of an agreement for the transfer of shares in a company, more than 50 per cent in nominal value of the issued share capital of that company is transferred or agreed to be transferred to one purchaser or to more than one purchaser each of which is a member of the same group;

(c) under which no relevant restriction in respect of any of the matters described in section 6(1)(a) or (b) of the Act of 1976 is accepted by a person; and

(d) under which no relevant restriction in respect of any of the matters described in section 6(1)(c) to (f) of that Act is accepted by a person other than such a person as is described in paragraph (2) below.

**3(2)** Persons by whom a relevant restriction may be accepted for the purpose of paragraph (1)(d) above are–

(a) any vendor;

(b) any member of the same group as any vendor; and

(c) any individual;

other than a body corporate or unincorporate which is also a purchaser under the agreement in question, or a member of the same group as such a body.

**4(1)** In determining whether an agreement to which article 3 applies is an agreement to which the Act of 1976 applies by virtue of section 6 of that Act, no account shall be taken of any relevant restriction–

(a) which is accepted for a period not exceeding that permitted under paragraph (2) below; and

(b) which limits the extent to which the person accepting the restriction may compete with the acquired enterprise, or may be engaged or interested in, disclose information to, or otherwise assist any business which so competes.

**4(2)** For the purpose of paragraph (1)(a) above, a permitted period is:–

(a) a period of 5 years beginning with the date of the agreement; or

(b) in the case of restrictions accepted by an individual who is to have a contract of employment with or a contract for the supply of services to the acquired enterprise, the purchaser, or a member of the same group as the purchaser, a period beginning with the date of the agreement and ending 2 years after the date of expiry or termination of the contract, whichever ends the later.

## SHARE SUBSCRIPTION AGREEMENTS

**5** This article applies to an agreement made on or after the date on which this Order comes into force–

(a) which provides for a person (the **"subscriber"**) to subscribe (whether or not in cash) for shares in a company (the **"issuing company"**);

(b) under which no relevant restriction in respect of any of the matters described in section 6(1)(a) or (b) of the Act of 1976 is accepted by a person; and

(c) under which no relevant restriction in respect of any of the matters described in section 6(1)(c) to (f) of that Act is accepted by a body corporate or unincorporate.

**6(1)** In determining whether an agreement to which article 5 applies is an agreement to which the Act of 1976 applies by virtue of section 6 of that Act, no account shall be taken of any relevant restriction–

(a) which is accepted for a period not exceeding that permitted under paragraph (2) below; and

(b) which limits the extent to which the person accepting the restriction may compete with the issuing company, or may be engaged or interested in, disclose information to, or otherwise assist any business which so competes.

**6(2)** For the purpose of paragraph (1)(a) above, a permitted period is:–

(a) a period of 5 years beginning with the date of the agreement; or

(b) in the case of restrictions accepted–

(i) by a member of the issuing company, a period beginning with the date of the agreement and ending 2 years after the date on which that person ceases to be a member; or

(ii) by an individual who is to have a contract of employment with or a contract for the supply of services to the issuing company, a period beginning with the date of the agreement and ending 2 years after the date of expiry or termination of the contract,

whichever ends the later.

## EXPLANATORY NOTE

(*This Note is not part of the Order*)

The Restrictive Trade Practices Act 1976 requires that restrictive agreements between two or more persons carrying on business in the United Kingdom in the supply of goods be furnished to the Director General of Fair Trading for registration.

This Order exempts from the registration requirements of the 1976 Act agreements for the sale and purchase of shares in a company or of a business ("sale and purchase agreements") and agreements for the subscription of shares in a company ("share subscription agreements") provided that the agreements satisfy certain conditions.

In the case of sale and purchase agreements the main conditions are (articles 3 and 4)–

(a) that more than 50 per cent in nominal value of the issued share capital of the company be transferred to one purchaser or to more than one where they are all members of the same group of companies, or (as the case may be) that the whole of the vendor's interest in a business be transferred to one or more purchasers;

(b) that the agreements only contain registrable restrictions of the type described in section 6(1)(c) to (f) of the 1976 Act;

(c) that such restrictions only be accepted by vendors, their associated companies or by individuals (save that bodies corporate or unincorporate cannot accept such restrictions where they are also purchasers under the agreement in question);

(d) that the restrictions to be disregarded only limit the extent to which the persons accepting them may compete with the company or business which is the subject of the sale, or be involved in or assist any business which so competes; and

(e) that the restrictions to be disregarded only be operative for a period not exceeding 5 years beginning with the date of the agreement or a period beginning with the date of the agreement and ending 2 years after the date of expiry or termination of the relevant employment or services contract, whichever is the later.

In the case of share subscription agreements the main conditions are (articles 5 and 6)–

(a) that the agreements only contain registrable restrictions of the type described in section 6(1)(c) to (f) of the 1976 Act;

(b) that such restrictions only be accepted by individuals;

(c) that the restrictions to be disregarded only limit the extent to which the persons accepting them may compete with the issuing company or be involved in or assist any business which so competes; and

(d) that the restrictions to be disregarded only be operative for a period exceeding 5 years beginning with the date of the agreement or a period beginning with the date of the agreement and ending 2 years after the relevant person ceases to be a member of the issuing company or after the date of expiry or termination of the relevant employment or services contract, whichever is the later.

# THE BANKS (ADMINISTRATION PROCEEDINGS) ORDER 1989

(SI 1989/1276)

*Made on 24 July 1989 by the Secretary of State for Trade and Industry under s. 422 of the Insolvency Act 1986. Operative from 23 August 1989.*

## CITATION AND COMMENCEMENT

**1** This Order may be cited as the Banks (Administration Proceedings) Order 1989 and shall come into force on 23rd August 1989.

## APPLICATION OF PROVISIONS IN THE INSOLVENCY ACT 1986 WITH MODIFICATIONS IN RELATION TO COMPANIES WHICH ARE AUTHORISED OR FORMER AUTHORISED INSTITUTIONS UNDER THE BANKING ACT 1987

**2** The provisions in Part II of the Insolvency Act 1986 shall apply in relation to those authorised institutions and former authorised institutions within the meaning of the Banking Act 1987 which are companies within the meaning of section 735 of the Companies Act 1985 with the modifications specified in the Schedule to this Order (any reference to a numbered section in the Schedule being, unless otherwise provided, to a section of the Insolvency Act 1986) and accordingly the provisions of the first Group of Parts of the Insolvency Act 1986 apply in relation to such institutions with such modifications.

## APPLICATION

**3** This Order shall not apply in relation to petitions for administration orders presented before it comes into force or in relation to administration orders made upon such petitions.

# Schedule – Modifications of Part II of the Insolvency Act 1986 in relation to companies which are authorised or former authorised institutions under the Banking Act 1987

Article 2

**1** In section 8, after subsection (1) there shall be inserted the following subsection:–

"**(1A)** For the purposes of a petition presented by the Bank of England alone or together with any other party an authorised institution or former authorised institution within the meaning of the Banking Act 1987 which defaults in an obligation to pay any sum due and payable in respect of a deposit within the meaning of section 92 of that Act shall be deemed to be unable to pay its debts as mentioned in subsection (1) above.".

2 In section 8(4) paragraph (b) shall be omitted.

3 In section 9(1), after the words "the directors," there shall be inserted the words "or by the Bank of England,".

4 In section 9(2)(a), after the word "company," there shall be inserted the words "to the Bank of England (unless it is a petitioner),".

5 At the end of section 13(3)(c) there shall be added the words "or (d) by the Bank of England.".

6 In section 23(1)(a), after the words "registrar of companies" there shall be inserted the words ", the Bank of England".

7 In section 25(2)(a), after the words "their addresses)" there shall be inserted the words "and the Bank of England".

8 In section 27(1), after the words "in force," there shall be inserted the words "the Bank of England, the Deposit Protection Board, or".

9 In section 27(1)(a), for the words "(including at least himself)" there shall be substituted the words "(including, where the applicant is a creditor or member, at least himself)".

## EXPLANATORY NOTE

(*This Note is not part of the Order*)

This Order applies provisions in Part II of the Insolvency Act 1986 with modifications to companies which are authorised institutions or former authorised institutions under the Banking Act 1987. The Order enables administration orders to be made in relation to such bodies, and makes special provision to permit the Bank of England to petition for such orders and for the involvement of the Bank of England and the Deposit Protection Board in the conduct of administration proceedings.

# THE COMPANIES ACT 1985 (MODIFICATIONS FOR STATUTORY WATER COMPANIES) REGULATIONS 1989

(SI 1989/1461)

*Made on 8 August 1989 by the Secretary of State for the Environment and the Secretary of State for Wales, under s. 185(2)(d) of, and para. 71(2) of Sch. 25 to, the Water Act 1989. Operative from 1 September 1989.*

## CITATION AND COMMENCEMENT

1 These Regulations may be cited as the Companies Act 1985 (Modifications for Statutory Water Companies) Regulations 1989 and shall come into force on 1st September 1989.

## MODIFICATIONS OF PART XIII OF THE COMPANIES ACT 1985

2 Where a statutory water company applies to the court under section 425(1) of the Companies Act 1985 ("the 1985 Act") with a view to securing an order of the court in respect of a compromise or arrangement in anticipation of provision contained in a memorandum and articles having effect as mentioned in section 101(2)(b) of the Water Act 1989, Part XIII of the 1985 Act shall apply–

(a) with the insertion after the words "no effect until" in section 425(3) of the words "the memorandum and articles come into force by virtue of an order made by the Secretary of State under section 101(2)(c) of the Water Act 1989 and"; and

(b) as if sections 427 to 430 were omitted.

## EXPLANATORY NOTE

(*This Note is not part of the Regulations*)

Paragraph 71(2) of Schedule 25 to the Water Act 1989 provides that Part XIII of the Companies Act 1985 (arrangements and reconstructions) shall have effect in relation to statutory water companies that are not limited companies with prescribed modifications. These Regulations specify the modifications which have the effect of applying only sections 425 and 426 of Part XIII.

The modifications apply where a statutory water company applies to the court under section 425 with a view to securing an order in respect of a compromise or arrangement with its creditors or members in anticipation of a change in the provisions for its constitution and regulation. The modification to section 425(3) has the effect of postponing the effect of the court's order under section 425(2) sanctioning the compromise or arrangement until the new memorandum and articles come into force by virtue of an order made by the Secretary of State under section 101(2)(c) of the Water Act 1989 and a copy of the court's order has been delivered to the registrar of companies.

# THE INSIDER DEALING (PUBLIC SERVANTS) ORDER 1989

(SI 1989/2164)

*Made on 19 November 1989 by the Secretary of State for Trade and Industry under s. 2(5) of the Company Securities (Insider Dealing) Act 1985. Operative from 1 January 1990.*

[**Note:** See note to SI 1989/2165 below.]

**1** This Order may be cited as the Insider Dealing (Public Servants) Order 1989 and shall come into force on 1 January 1990.

**2** It is hereby declared that the following persons are to be public servants for the purposes of section 2 of the Company Securities (Insider Dealing) Act 1985–

(a) the Governor, Deputy Governor, Directors, employees and individuals acting as employees of the Bank of England, and members of the Board of Banking Supervision;

(b) members of the Council, Committee, Appeal Tribunal or Disciplinary Committees or any Disciplinary Committee of Lloyd's, individuals by whom any such body acts, and officers and employees of Lloyd's;

(c) members of the Monopolies and Mergers Commission and individuals employed by, or engaged in work for or on behalf of, the Commission or employed by, or engaged in that work or on behalf of, persons so engaged.

## EXPLANATORY NOTE

(*This Note is not part of the Order*)

This Order extends the definition of public servant for the purposes of section 2 of the Companies Securities (Insider Dealing) Act 1985 ("the Act") to the following persons:

(a) the Governor, Deputy Governor, Directors, employees and individuals acting as employees of the Bank of England, and members of the Board of Banking Supervision;

(b) members of the Council, Committee, Appeal Tribunal or Disciplinary Committees or any Disciplinary Committee of Lloyd's, individuals by whom any such body acts, and officers and employees of Lloyd's;

(c) members of the Monopolies and Mergers Commission and individuals employed by, or engaged in work for or on behalf of, the Commission or employed by, or engaged in that work for or on behalf of, persons so engaged.

Section 2 of the Act provides among other matters that it shall be an offence for a public servant holding, in an official capacity, unpublished price sensitive information (as defined in section 10 of the Act) about securities of a particular company to deal in those securities, or to counsel or procure dealing in those securities by another.

# THE INSIDER DEALING (RECOGNISED STOCK EXCHANGE) ORDER 1989

(SI 1989/2165)

*Made on 19 November 1989 by the Secretary of State for Trade and Industry under s. 16(1) and (1A) of the Company Securities (Insider Dealing) Act 1985. Operative from 1 Janaury 1990.*

[**CCH Note:** The Company Securities (Insider Dealing) Act 1985 has been replaced by s. 79(14) and Sch. 6, Pt. I of the Criminal Justice Act 1993. See now the Insider Dealing (Securities and Regulated Markets) Order 1994 (SI 1994/187).]

**1** This Order may be cited as the Insider Dealing (Recognised Stock Exchange) Order 1989 and shall come into force on 1 January 1990.

**2** The Secretary of State hereby declares the investment exchange known as NASDAQ, which is an unincorporated association consisting of the National Association of Securities Dealers Inc., NASDAQ Inc., NASD Market Services Inc., and NASDAQ International Ltd., to be a recognised stock exchange for the purposes of the Company Securities (Insider Dealing) Act 1985.

## EXPLANATORY NOTE

(*This Note is not part of the Order*)

This Order declares the investment exchange known as NASDAQ to be a recognised stock exchange for the purposes of the Company Securities (Insider Dealing) Act 1985 ("the Act"). The Act provides, amongst other matters, that it shall be an offence to deal in securities on a recognised stock exchange whilst in possession of unpublished price sensitive information (as defined in section 10) in relation to those securities, or to counsel or procure such dealing.

# THE INSOLVENCY ACT 1986 (GUERNSEY) ORDER 1989

(SI 1989/2409)

*Made on 19 December 1989 under s. 442 of the Insolvency Act 1986. Operative from 1 February 1990.*

**1** This Order may be cited as the Insolvency Act 1986 (Guernsey) Order 1989 and shall come into force on 1st February 1990.

**2** Subsections (4), (5), (10) and (11) of section 426 of the Insolvency Act 1986 shall extend to the Bailiwick of Guernsey with the modifications specified in the Schedule to this Order.

## Schedule – Modifications in the Extension of Provisions of the Insolvency Act 1986 to the Bailiwick of Guernsey

Article 2

**1** Any reference to any provision of section 426 of the Insolvency Act 1986 shall be construed as a reference to that provision as it has effect in the Bailiwick of Guernsey.

**2** In subsections (4) and (5), for "United Kingdom" there shall be substituted "Bailiwick of Guernsey."

3 For paragraphs (a), (b) and (c) of subsection (10) there shall be substituted the following paragraphs:

"(a) in relation to Guernsey:

(i) Titres II to V of the Law entitled "Loi ayant rapport aux Débiteurs et à la Renonciation" of 1929;

(ii) the Ordinance entitled "Ordonnance relative à la Renonciation" of 1929;

(iii) articles LXXI to LXXXI of the Law entitled "Loi relative aux Sociétés Anonymes ou à Responsabilité Limitée" of 1908;

(iv) sections 1, 3(3) and 4(2) of the Law of Property (Miscellaneous Provisions) (Guersey) Law 1979;

(v) the Preferred Debts (Guernsey) Law 1983;

(vi) sections 12 and 32 to 39 of the Insurance Business (Guernsey) Law 1986;

(vii) the rules of the customary law of Guernsey concerning persons who are unable to pay their judgment debts;

(viii) any enactment for the time being in force in Guernsey which amends, modifies, supplements or replaces any of those rules or provisions;

(b) in relation to Alderney:

(i) Part I of the Companies (Amendment) (Alderney) Law 1962;

(ii) the Preferred Debts (Guernsey) Law 1983;

(iii) sections 12, 32 to 39, 68(2) and 68(5) of the Insurance Business (Guernsey) Law 1986;

(iv) the rules of the customary law of Alderney concerning persons who are unable to pay their judgment debts;

(v) any enactment for the time being in force in Alderney which amends, modifies, supplements or replaces any of those rules or provisions;

(c) in relation to Sark:

(i) the rules of the customary law of Sark concerning persons who are unable to pay their judgment debts;

(ii) any enactment for the time being in force in Sark which amends, modifies, supplements or replaces any of those rules;".

4 For paragraphs (a) and (b) of subsection (11) there shall be substituted "the United Kingdom, the Bailiwick of Jersey or the Isle of Man".

## EXPLANATORY NOTE

(*This Note is not part of the Order*)

This Order extends certain provisions of section 426 of the Insolvency Act 1986 (co-operation between courts) to the Bailiwick of Guernsey with the modifications specified in the Schedule to the Order.

# THE STOCK TRANSFER (SUBSTITUTION OF FORMS) ORDER 1990

(SI 1990/18)

*Made on 8 January 1990 by the Treasury under s. 3(2) of the Stock Transfer Act 1963. Operative from 31 January 1990.*

1 This Order may be cited as the Stock Transfer (Substitution of Forms) Order 1990 and shall come into force on 31st January 1990.

2 Schedule 1 to the Stock Transfer Act 1963 ("the Act") shall be amended by substituting for the form entitled "Talisman Sold Transfer" the form set out in the Schedule to this Order.

3 Section 1(3) of the Act shall apply in relation to the form for which the form set out in the Schedule to this Order is substituted as it applies to any form which was common or usual

# Schedule 1 – Provisions of Part I of the Companies Act 1989 to be brought into force by this Order

Article 3

| *Provision of Part I* | *Purposes for which to be in force* |
|---|---|
| Section 1 (Introduction). | For the purposes of any section or part thereof brought into force by this Order. |
| Section 2 (Accounting records). | For all purposes. |
| Section 3 (A company's financial year and accounting reference periods). | For all purposes. |
| Section 4 (Individual company accounts). | For all purposes. |
| Section 5 (Group accounts). | For all purposes. |
| Section 6 (Additional disclosure required in notes to accounts). | For all purposes. |
| Section 7 (Approval and signing of accounts). | For all purposes except the insertion of section 233(5) into Part VII of the 1985 Act. |
| Section 8 (Directors' report). | For all purposes. |
| Section 9 (Auditors' report). | For all purposes. |
| Section 10 (Publication of accounts and reports). | For all purposes. |
| Section 11 (Laying and delivery of accounts and reports). | For all purposes except the insertion of section 242A into the 1985 Act. |
| Section 13 (Small and medium-sized companies and groups). | For all purposes. |
| Section 14 (Dormant companies). | For all purposes. |
| Section 16 (Private companies: election to dispense with laying of accounts and reports before general meeting). | For all purposes. |
| Section 17 (Unlimited companies: exemption from requirement to deliver accounts and reports). | For all purposes. |
| Section 18 (Banking and insurance companies and groups: special provisions). | For all purposes. |
| Section 19 (Accounting standards). | For all purposes. |
| Section 20 (Power to alter accounting requirements). | For all purposes. |
| Section 21 (Parent and subsidiary undertakings). | For all purposes. |
| Section 22 (Other interpretation provisions). | For all purposes. |
| Section 23 and Schedule 10 (Consequential amendments). | For all purposes except in so far as paragraph 24(2) of Schedule 10 omits the entries relating to section 245(1) and (2), in so far as paragraph 24(3) inserts an entry for section 233(5) and in so far as paragraph 35(2)(b) amends section 3(3) of the Company Directors Disqualification Act 1986. |

# Schedule 2

Article 7

## Part I – General Transitional and Saving Provisions

### GENERAL RULES

**1(1)** The provisions of this paragraph have effect, in addition to the provisions of the Interpretation Act 1978, for securing the continuity of the law so far as Part I of the 1989 Act re-enacts (with or without modification) provisions of the old Part VII in the new Part VII.

**1(2)** References (express or implied) in a provision of the new Part VII or in any other enactment (including in any subordinate legislation within the meaning of section 21(1) of the Interpretation Act 1978) to any provision of the new Part VII shall, so far as the context permits, be construed as including, in connection with a relevant financial year of a company or otherwise in connection with events, circumstances or purposes occurring before the coming into force of the provisions of the 1989 Act, a reference to the corresponding provision of the old Part VII.

**1(3)** Where an offence has been committed for the continuance of which a penalty was provided for under any provision of the old Part VII, proceedings may be taken under the corresponding provision of the new Part VII in respect of the continuance of the offence on and after 1st April 1990 in the like manner as if the offence had been committed under the corresponding provision.

**1(4)** Where any period of time specified in any provision of the old Part VII is current immediately prior to 1st April 1990, and there is a corresponding provision of the new Part VII, the new Part VII shall have effect as if that corresponding provision had been in force when that period began to run.

**1(5)** The provisions of this paragraph have effect subject to any specific transitional or saving provisions made by this Order.

### APPLICATION OF SECTION 245 OF THE OLD PART VII

**2** (Revoked by SI 1990/2569 (C 68), art. 8 as from 7 January 1991.)

**History**

The revocation of para. 2 applies save to the extent that CA 1985, s. 245 as originally enacted is continued in force by SI 1990/2569 (C 68), art. 6; para. 2 formerly read as follows:

"Section 245 of the old Part VII shall have effect for any financial year of a company other than a relevant financial year as if the references in sub-section (2) thereof to sections 229(5) to (7) and section 230 were references to sections 227, 231 and 232 of the new Part VII and to paragraph 3 of this Schedule."

### INSURANCE GROUPS

**3(1)** Notwithstanding any provision of the new Part VII, the directors of the parent company of an insurance group (within the meaning of section 255A(4) thereof) which is required by section 227 thereof to prepare group accounts may prepare those accounts for any financial year commencing before 23rd December 1994 in other than consolidated form, if:

(a) an undertaking within the group is authorised to carry on both long term and general business (those expressions having the meaning ascribed to them by section 1 of the Insurance Companies Act 1982) or the group comprises one or more undertakings authorised to carry on long term business and one or more undertakings authorised to carry on general business; and

(b) that form would have been permitted by section 229(6) of the old Part VII.

**History**

In para. 3(1) the words "commencing before 23rd December 1994" substituted for the former words "ending prior to 1st January 1994" by the Companies Act 1985 (Insurance Companies Accounts) Regulations 1993 (SI 1993/3246), reg. 1, 5 as from 19 December 1993.

**3(2)** Where the parent company of an insurance group takes advantage of sub-paragraph (1), the provisions of the new Part VII shall apply with respect to such alternate-form group accounts (and in particular their content) with any necessary modifications as a consequence of their being other than in consolidated form.

| Provision | Date of Commencement | S.I. No. |
|---|---|---|
| S. 75(6) | 21.2.1990 | S.I. 1990/142 |
| S. 75(7) | 25.1.1990 | S.I. 1990/98 |
| Ss. 76 to 79 | 21.2.1990 | S.I. 1990/142 |
| S. 80 except to the extent that it refers to Part VII of the 1989 Act | 21.2.1990 | S.I. 1990/142 |
| S. 81(1) | 21.2.1990 | S.I. 1990/142 |
| S. 81(2) except to the extent that it refers to Part VII of the 1989 Act | 21.2.1990 | S.I. 1990/142 |
| S. 81(3) and (4) | 21.2.1990 | S.I. 1990/142 |
| S. 81(5) except to the extent that it refers to Part VII of the 1989 Act | 21.2.1990 | S.I. 1990/142 |
| Ss. 82 to 86 | 21.2.1990 | S.I. 1990/142 |
| S. 87(1) to (3) | 21.2.1990 | S.I. 1990/142 |
| S. 87(4) except to the extent that it refers to Part VII of the 1989 Act | 21.2.1990 | S.I. 1990/142 |
| S. 87(5) and (6) | 21.2.1990 | S.I. 1990/142 |
| Ss. 88 to 91 | 21.2.1990 | S.I. 1990/142 |
| S. 145 but only in so far as it relates to paragraphs 1, 8, 9, 12, 19 and 21 of Schedule 19 to the 1989 Act | 1.3.1990 | S.I. 1990/142 |
| S. 146 | 1.4.1990 | S.I. 1990/142 |
| S. 151 | 1.4.1990 | S.I. 1990/142 |
| S. 152 | 1.3.1990 | S.I. 1990/142 |
| S. 153 but only in so far as it relates to paragraphs 1, 13, 17, 21 and 26 of Schedule 20 to the 1989 Act | 1.4.1990 | S.I. 1990/142 |
| S. 192 in so far as it inserts section 47A into the Financial Services Act 1986 | 15.3.1990 | S.I. 1990/354 |
| S. 193 in so far as is necessary in order to enable regulations to be made under section 62A of, and paragraph 22A of Schedule 11 to, the Financial Services Act 1986 | 15.3.1990 | S.I.1990/354 |
| Sections 194 to 200 | 15.3.1990 | S.I. 1990/354 |
| Sections 203 to 205 | 15.3.1990 | S.I. 1990/354 |
| S. 206(1) except in so far as it relates to the insertion by paragraph 32 of Schedule 23 to the 1989 Act of paragraph 13B into Schedule 11 of the Financial Services Act 1986 | 15.3.1990 | S.I. 1990/354 |
| S. 206(2) to (4) | 15.3.1990 | S.I. 1990/354 |
| S. 208 | 1.3.1990 | S.I. 1990/142 |
| S. 209 | 21.2.1990 | S.I. 1990/142 |
| S. 210 | 1.4.1990 | S.I. 1990/142 |

| *Provision* | *Date of Commencement* | *S.I. No.* |
|---|---|---|
| S. 212 in so far as it relates to the repeals effected by Schedule 24 to the 1989 Act referred to below | On the dates referred to below in connection with Schedule 24 | In the S.I.s listed below in connection with Schedule 24 |
| Ss. 213 to 215 in so far as they were not already in force at the time of the making of S.I. 1990/142 | 2.2.1990 | S.I. 1990/142 |
| S. 216 | 25.1.1990 | S.I. 1990/98 |
| Schedules 11 and 12 | 1.3.1990 | S.I. 1990/142 |
| Schedule 14 | 1.3.1990 | S.I. 1990/142 |
| Schedule 19, paragraphs 1, 8, 9, 12, 19 and 21 | 1.3.1990 | S.I. 1990/142 |
| Schedule 20, paragraphs 1, 13, 17, 21 and 26 | 1.4.1990 | S.I. 1990/142 |
| Schedule 24 in so far as it relates to repeals in or of ss. 435, 440, 443, 446, 447, 449, 452 and 735A of the Companies Act 1985, ss.94, 105, 179, 180, 198(1) and 199(9) of the Financial Services Act 1986 and s.84(l) of the Banking Act 1987 | 21.2.1990 | S.I. 1990/142 |
| Schedule 24 in so far as it relates to the repeal in s. 21(2) of the Company Directors Disqualification Act 1986 | 1.3.1990 | S.I. 1990/142 |
| Schedule 24 in so far as it relates to the repeals in, or of, sections 48, 55, 119, 159 and 160 of, and paragraphs 4, 10 and 14 of Schedule 11 to the Financial Services Act 1986 | 15.3.1990 | S.I. 1990/354 |
| Schedule 24 in so far as it relates to repeals in or of ss. 46(3) and 85 of the Fair Trading Act 1973 | 1.4.1990 | S.I. 1990/142 |

# THE COMPANIES (UNREGISTERED COMPANIES) (AMENDMENT) REGULATIONS 1990

(SI 1990/438)

*Made on 5 March 1990 by the Secretary of State for Trade and Industry under s. 718 of and Sch. 22 to the Companies Act 1985. Operative from 1 April 1990.*

**1** These Regulations may be cited as the Companies (Unregistered Companies) (Amendment) Regulations 1990 and shall come into force on 1st April 1990.

**2** [Amendments to Companies (Unregistered Companies) Regulations 1985, reg. 6, Sch. not reproduced here.]

## EXPLANATORY NOTE

(*This Note is not part of the Regulations*)

The Companies (Unregistered Companies) (Amendment) Regulations 1985 applied certain provisions of the Companies Act 1985 to unregistered companies.

These Regulations amend the 1985 Regulations to reflect the amendments made by the Companies Act 1989 to those 1985 Act provisions which relate to the preparation of accounts

**8(5)** For the purposes of paragraph (1) above, the reference to an insolvency practitioner in the definition of office-holder in regulation 1(3) shall be construed in accordance with section 388 of the Act but without regard to subsection (5) of that section and references to an office-holder who has been appointed or to a person who has been appointed an office-holder shall include the official receiver in any case where the official receiver is or has been an office-holder whether by virtue of his office or otherwise.

**8(6)** For the purposes of paragraph (1) above a person carrying on insolvency practice includes a firm or partnership.

### FEES

**9** The fee to accompany an application to which the Regulations in this Part apply shall be:–

(a) in a case where, at the relevant time, the applicant is the holder of an authorisation, £100; and

(b) in any other case, £200.

### MAXIMUM PERIOD OF AUTHORISATION

**10** No authorisation granted pursuant to an application to which the Regulations in this Part apply shall continue in force for a period of more than 3 years from the date on which it is granted.

## PART III – THE REQUIREMENTS FOR SECURITY AND CAUTION FOR THE PROPER PERFORMANCE OF THE FUNCTIONS OF AN INSOLVENCY PRACTITIONER

### APPLICATION OF THIS PART

**11** Save as provided in regulation 2(3) above, the Regulations in this Part apply in relation to any person appointed on or after the commencement date to act as an insolvency practitioner in relation to any person.

### REQUIREMENTS FOR SECURITY OR CAUTION

**12(1)** For the purposes of section 390(3)(b) of the Act the requirements in respect of security or caution for the proper performance of the functions of an insolvency practitioner are that:–

(a) there is in force at the time when an insolvency practitioner is appointed to act in relation to any person a bond which complies with the requirements set out in Part I of Schedule 2 to these Regulations under which the surety or cautioner is liable in the general penalty sum of £250,000; and

(b) there is in force in relation to that bond with effect from the time when an insolvency practitioner is appointed to act in relation to any person a specific penalty in respect of the practitioner acting in relation to that person under which the specific penalty sum is not less than the value of that person's assets estimated in accordance with Part II of the said Schedule; and

(c) where, at any time before the practitioner obtains his release or discharge in respect of his acting in relation to that person, he forms the opinion that the value of the assets comprised in the estate of that person is higher than the penalty sum under the current specific penalty (being a penalty sum less than £5,000,000), there is obtained by the practitioner a further specific penalty in respect of his acting in relation to that person under which the penalty sum is at least equal to that higher value or £5,000,000 (whichever shall be the less).

**History**

In reg. 12(1)(b) the words from the beginning to "in relation to any person a" substituted for the former words "there is issued under that bond as soon as reasonably possible after the appointment of the practitioner a certificate of", and in reg. 12(1)(c) the words "certificate of" formerly appearing after the words "under the current" deleted and the words "obtained by the practitioner a further specific penalty in respect of his" substituted for the former words "issued forthwith a further certificate of specific penalty in respect of the practitioner" by the Insolvency Practitioners (Amendment) Regulations 1993 (SI 1993/221), reg. 1, 2, 5(a), (b) as from 1 April 1993.

**Note**

For transitional provision, see the Insolvency Practitioners (Amendment) Regulations 1993 (SI 1993/221), reg. 4(2).

**12(2)** In paragraph (1)(c), "**the current specific penalty**" means the specific penalty for the time being in force which has been obtained pursuant to paragraph (1)(b) or (c), as the case may be.

**History**

In reg. 12(2) the words "**certificate of**" formerly appearing after the words "**the current**" deleted, the words "the specific penalty" substituted for the former words "the certificate" and the word "obtained" substituted for the former word "issued" by the Insolvency Practitioners (Amendment) Regulations 1993 (SI 1993/221), reg. 1, 2, 5(c) as from 1 April 1993.

**Note**

For transitional provision, see the Insolvency Practitioners (Amendment) Regulations 1993 (SI 1993/221), reg. 4(2).

**12(3)** The bond referred to in paragraph (1) shall be retained by the recognised professional body or, as the case may be, the competent authority by which the practitioner has been authorised to act as an insolvency practitioner.

## EXCEPTIONS IN RELATION TO REQUIREMENTS FOR SECURITY OR CAUTION

**13** Where an insolvency practitioner who is appointed to be:–

(a) provisional liquidator in the winding up by the court of a company is subsequently appointed to be liquidator of that company; or

(b) liquidator in a voluntary winding up of a company is subsequently appointed to be liquidator in the winding up of that company by the court; or

(c) interim trustee in the sequestration of the estate of any person is subsequently appointed to be permanent trustee in the sequestration of the estate of that person; or

(d) an administrator of a company is subsequently appointed to be a liquidator of that company pursuant to section 140 of the Act;

and a specific penalty is obtained under regulation 12(1) in respect of the earlier or earliest such appointment, it shall not be necessary for such a specific penalty to be obtained in respect of the subsequent appointment of the practitioner in any of those circumstances.

**History**

In reg. 13 the words "specific penalty is obtained" substituted for the former words "certificate of specific penalty is issued" and the words "a specific penalty to be obtained" substituted for the former words "a certificate to be issued" by the Insolvency Practitioners (Amendment) Regulations 1993 (SI 1993/221), reg. 1, 2, 6 as from 1 April 1993.

**Note**

For transitional provision, see the Insolvency Practitioners (Amendment) Regulations 1993 (SI 1993/221), reg. 4(2).

## INSPECTION AND RETENTION REQUIREMENTS IN ENGLAND AND WALES

**14(1)** Where an insolvency practitioner is appointed to act in relation to any person, he shall retain a copy of the bordereau containing the entry evidencing the specific penalty obtained by him in respect of that appointment or any further specific penalty obtained by him in respect of so acting and shall produce it on demand for inspection to any person reasonably appearing to him to be a creditor or contributory of the person to whom he has been appointed, to the person (being an individual) to whom he has been appointed, to any partner in the partnership to which he has been appointed and, where the person to whom he has been appointed is a company, to any director or other officer of the company, and to the Secretary of State.

**14(2)** The insolvency practitioner shall retain the copy of the bordereau containing the entry required to be produced under paragraph (1) above for a period of two years from the date on which he is granted his release or discharge in respect of that appointment.

**Note**

Re reg. 14(1), (2) "bordereau" is defined under the Insolvency Practitioners (Amendment) Regulations 1993 (SI 1993/221), reg. 1(3) as follows:

"**"bordereau"** means a form upon which an insolvency practitioner enters certain details in relation to his appointment as insolvency practitioner in relation to a person, including the name of that person, the date of appointment, the value of the assets comprised in the estate of the person estimated in accordance with Part II of Schedule 2 to the 1990 Regulations, any increase in his estimation of the value of those assets and the date of his release or discharge fromthe appointment, for the purposes of evidencing those matters."

**14(3)** In this regulation "**company**" means a company which the courts in England and Wales have jurisdiction to wind up.

**3** General accounting.

**4** Cost and management accounting.

**5** Consolidated accounts.

**6** Internal control.

**7** Standards relating to the preparation of annual and consolidated accounts and to methods of valuing balance sheet items and of computing profits and losses.

**8** Legal and professional standards and professional guidance relating to the statutory auditing of accounting documents and to those carrying out such audits.

**9** Those aspects of the following which are relevant to auditing–

(a) company law;

(b) the law of insolvency and similar procedures;

(c) tax law;

(d) civil and commercial law;

(e) social security law and law of employment;

(f) information and computer systems;

(g) business, general and financial economics;

(h) mathematics and statistics; and

(i) basic principles of financial management of undertakings.

## EXPLANATORY NOTE

(*This Note is not part of the Regulations*)

These Regulations prescribe the subjects listed in the Schedule as the subjects which are relevant for the purposes of paragraph 7 of Schedule 12 to the Companies Act 1989. That paragraph provides that a qualification may not be recognised for the purposes of Part II of the Companies Act 1989 (Eligibility for Appointment as Company Auditor) unless it is restricted to persons who have passed an examination testing subjects prescribed for the purposes of the paragraph.

The regulations also complete the legislative implementation of the obligations imposed by Article 6 of the Directive 84/253/EEC (No. L126/20) on the approval of persons responsible for carrying out the statutory audits of accounting documents.

# THE COMPANY AUDITORS (RECOGNITION ORDERS) (APPLICATION FEES) REGULATIONS 1990

(SI 1990/1206)

*Made on 7 June 1990 by the Secretary of State for Trade and Industry under s. 45 of the Companies Act 1989. Operative from 2 July 1990.*

## CITATION AND COMMENCEMENT

**1** These Regulations may be cited as the Company Auditors (Recognition Orders) (Application Fees) Regulations 1990 and shall come into force on 2nd July 1990.

**2(1)** An applicant for a recognition order declaring the applicant to be a recognised supervisory body for the purposes of Part II of the Companies Act 1989 shall pay a fee of £6,500 in respect of its application.

**2(2)** An applicant for a recognition order declaring a qualification offered by it to be a recognised professional qualification for the purposes of Part II of the Companies Act 1989 shall pay a fee of £6,000 in respect of its applicant.

## EXPLANATORY NOTE

(*This Note is not part of the Regulations*)

These Regulations prescribe the fees payable by applicants for recognition orders under Part II of the Companies Act 1989.

# THE COMPANIES ACT 1989 (COMMENCEMENT NO. 6 AND TRANSITIONAL AND SAVING PROVISIONS) ORDER 1990

(SI 1990/1392 (C 41))

*Made on 9 July 1990 by the Secretary of State for Trade and Industry under s. 215(2), (3) and (4) of the Companies Act 1989.*

## CITATION

**1** This Order may be cited as the Companies Act 1989 (Commencement No. 6 and Transitional and Saving Provisions) Order 1990.

## PROVISIONS OF THE COMPANIES ACT 1989 COMMENCED BY THIS ORDER

**2** In Part V of the Companies Act 1989:–

(a) section 129 shall come into force on 1st November 1990;

(b) section 130 and Schedule 17 shall come into force on 31st July 1990;

(c) section 138 shall come into force on 31st July 1990 subject to the saving provision set out in article 5 below; and

(d) section 144 and Schedule 18 shall come into force on 1st November 1990, subject to the transitional provisions set out in article 6 below.

**3** Part IX of the Companies Act 1989 shall come into force on 1st November 1990.

**4** Part X of the Companies Act 1989:–

(a) section 211(2), subject to the saving provision set out in article 7 below, and section 211(3) shall come into force on 31st July 1990; and

(b) the repeals effected by Schedule 24 in or of:

(i) section 651(1) and Schedule 22 (in so far as Schedule 24 effects a repeal of the entry relating to section 36(4)) of the Companies Act 1985; and

(ii) Schedules 15 and 18 to the Building Societies Act 1986.

together with section 212 so far as relating to those repeals, shall come into force on 31st July 1990.

## SAVING PROVISION RELATING TO SECTION 138 OF THE COMPANIES ACT 1989

**5** For the avoidance of doubt, section 345(3) of the Companies Act 1985 shall apply to section 138 of the Companies Act 1989 as it applies to an order made under section 345 of the Companies Act 1985.

## TRANSITIONAL PROVISIONS RELATING TO SECTION 144 OF THE COMPANIES ACT 1989

**6(1)** The new section 736 of the Companies Act 1985, inserted by section 144(1) of the Companies Act 1989 shall not have effect for the purposes of the provisions of the unamended Companies Act 1985 continued in force by paragraph 13 of Part II of Schedule 2 and paragraph 3 of Schedule 3 to the Companies Act 1989 (Commencement No. 4 and Transitional and Saving

| Provision | Date of Commencement | S.I. No. |
|---|---|---|
| S. 206(2) to (4) (subject to transitional and saving provisions) | 15.3.1990 | S.I. 1990/354 |
| S. 208 | 1.3.1990 | S.I. 1990/142 |
| S. 209 | 21.2.1990 | S.I. 1990/142 |
| S. 210 | 1.4.1990 | S.I. 1990/142 |
| S. 212 insofar as it relates to the repeals effected by Schedule 24 to the 1989 Act referred to below | On the dates referred to below in connection with Schedule 24 | In the SIs listed below in connection with Schedule 24 |
| Schedule 24 insofar as it relates to repeals in or of ss. 435, 440, 443, 446, 447, 449, 452 and 735A of the Companies Act 1985, ss. 94, 105, 179, 180, 198(1) and 199(9) of the Financial Services Act 1986 and s. 84(1) of the Banking Act 1987 | 21.2.1990 | S.I. 1990/142 |
| Schedule 24 insofar as it relates to the repeal in s. 21(2) of the Company Directors Disqualification Act 1986 | 1.3.1990 | S.I. 1990/142 |
| Schedule 24 insofar as it relates to the repeals in, or of, sections 48, 55, 119, 159 and 160 of, and paragraphs 4, 10 and 14 of Schedule 11 to the Financial Services Act 1986 | 15.3.1990 | S.I. 1990/354 |
| Schedule 24 insofar as it relates to repeals in or of ss. 46(3) and 85 of the Fair Trading Act 1973 | 1.4.1990 | S.I. 1990/142 |
| Schedule 24 insofar as it relates to repeals in or of section 42(6) of the Harbours Act 1964; sections 716, 717, 744 (in part) and 746 of, and Schedules 2, 4, 9, 11, 22 (in part) and 24 (in part) to, the Companies Act 1985: paragraphs 23 and 45 of Schedule 6 to the Insolvency Act 1985: and the entries in Part 1 of Schedule 13 to the Insolvency Act 1986 relating to sections 222(4) and 225 | 1.4.1990 | S.I. 1990/355 |
| Schedule 24 insofar as it relates to repeals in or of section 199(9) of, and paragraph 22 of Schedule 16 to, the Financial Services Act 1986 | 1.4.1990 | S.I. 1990/355 |
| Schedule 24 insofar as it relates to repeals in or of sections 201, 202(1) and 209(1)(j) of the Companies Act 1985 | 31.5.1990 | S.I. 1990/713 |
| Ss. 213 to 215 insofar as they were not already in force at the time of the making of S.I. 1990/142 | 2.2.1990 | S.I. 1990/142 |
| S. 216 | 25.1.1990 | S.I. 1990/98 |

# THE COMPANIES (FAIR DEALING BY DIRECTORS) (INCREASE IN FINANCIAL LIMITS) ORDER 1990

(SI 1990/1393)

*Made on 9 July 1990 by the Secretary of State for Trade and Industry under s. 345(1) of the Companies Act 1985. Operative from 31 July 1990.*

## CITATION AND COMMENCEMENT

**1** This Order may be cited as the Companies (Fair Dealing by Directors) (Increase in Financial Limits) Order 1990 and shall come into force on 31st July 1990.

## INCREASE IN FINANCIAL LIMITS

**2** [Amendments to Part X of the Companies Act 1985 (enforcement of fair dealing by directors), s. 320(2), 335(1), 337(3), 340(7), 344(1).]

## EXPLANATORY NOTE

(*This Note is not part of the Order*)

This Order increases certain of the financial limits specified in Part X of the Companies Act 1985 (enforcement of fair dealing by directors). The limits in question are the sums specified in sections 320(2), 335(1), 337(3), 340(7), and 344(1). In each case, the sum specified is doubled. Section 138 of the Companies Act 1989 (c.40) provides for increases in the other financial limits (relating to loans etc. to directors) specified in Part X of the Companies Act 1985.

# THE COMPANIES (UNREGISTERED COMPANIES) (AMENDMENT NO. 2) REGULATIONS 1990

(SI 1990/1394)

*Made on 9 July 1990 by the Secretary of State for Trade and Industry under s. 718 of and Sch. 22 to the Companies Act 1985. Operative from 31 July 1990.*

**1** These Regulations may be cited as the Companies (Unregistered Companies) (Amendment No. 2) Regulations 1990 and shall come into force on 31st July 1990.

**2** [Amendment to the Companies (Unregistered Companies) Regulations 1985, reg. 6(d) and Sch.]

## EXPLANATORY NOTE

(*This Note is not part of the Regulations*)

These Regulations amend the Companies (Unregistered Companies) Regulations 1985, which apply certain provisions of the Companies Act 1985 to unregistered companies. The amendments have the effect of applying to such companies the new provisions relating to company contracts and execution of documents inserted into the Companies Act 1985 by the Companies Act 1989. These provisions include the abolition of the requirement to have a corporate seal.

# THE DEFINITION OF SUBSIDIARY (CONSEQUENTIAL AMENDMENTS) REGULATIONS 1990

(SI 1990/1395)

*Made on 9 July 1990 by the Secretary of State for Trade and Industry under s. 144(4) of the Companies Act 1989. Operative from 1 November 1990.*

**1** These Regulations may be cited as the Definition of Subsidiary (Consequential Amendments) Regulations 1990 and shall come into force on 1st November 1990.

**2** In section 77(3) of the Electricity Act 1989, in the definition of "subsidiary", for the words "has the same meaning as in" substitute "has the meaning given by section 736 of".

## EXPLANATORY NOTE

(*This Note is not part of the Regulations*)

These Regulations effect a minor amendment to the Electricity Act 1989, consequential on the new definition of "subsidiary" inserted by section 144 of the Companies Act 1989 into the Companies Act 1985 (c.6).

# THE EEC MERGER CONTROL (CONSEQUENTIAL PROVISIONS) REGULATIONS 1990

(SI 1990/1563)

*Made on 27 July 1990 by the Secretary of State for Trade and Industry under s. 2(2) of the European Communities Act 1972 and s. 75F(1), (2) of the Fair Trading Act 1973. Operative from 21 September 1990.*

**1(1)** These Regulations may be cited as the EEC Merger Control (Consequential Provisions) Regulations 1990 and shall come into force on 21st September 1990.

**1(2)** In these Regulations, **"the Merger Control Regulation"** means Council Regulation (EEC) No. 4064/89 on the control of concentrations between undertakings, and expressions used in that Regulation shall bear the same meaning in these Regulations.

**2** For the purpose of determining the effect of giving a merger notice and the steps which may be or are to be taken by any person in connection with such a notice in a case in which the arrangements in question are or would result in a concentration with a Community dimension, section 75B of the Fair Trading Act 1973 is amended by omitting the word "or" at the end of paragraph (b) of subsection (7) and adding the following at the end of that subsection:

"or,

(d) appears to him that the notified arrangements are, or if carried into effect would result in, a concentration with a Community dimension within the meaning of Council Regulation (EEC) No. 4064/89 of 21st December 1989 on the control of concentrations between undertakings."

**3** A merger reference may be made under section 64 of the Fair Trading Act 1973 in a case in which the relevant enterprises ceased to be distinct enterprises at a time and in circumstances not falling within subsection (4) of that section if by reason of the Merger Control Regulation or anything done under or in accordance with it the reference could not have been made earlier than six months before the date on which it is to be made.

## EXPLANATORY NOTE

(*This Note is not part of the Regulations*)

These Regulations make provision consequential upon Council Regulation (EEC) No. 4064/89 on the control of concentrations between undertakings ("the Merger Control Regulation").

Regulation 2 amends the provision of the Fair Trading Act 1973 about restriction on the power to make a merger reference where prior notice has been given (inserted by the Companies Act 1989) by providing that the Director General of Fair Trading may reject a merger notice where it appears to him that the merger is also a "concentration with a Community dimension" within the Merger Control Regulation.

Regulation 3 enables a merger reference to be made later than the time limit in section 64(4) of the Fair Trading Act 1973 if it is made within six months of the removal of any restriction on the making of the reference created by the Merger Control Regulation.

# THE LIMITED PARTNERSHIP (UNRESTRICTED SIZE) NO. 2 REGULATIONS 1990

(SI 1990/1580)

*Made on 30 July 1990 by the Secretary of State for Trade and Industry under s. 717(1)(d) and 744 of the Companies Act 1985. Operative from 21 August 1990.*

**1** These Regulations may be cited as the Limited Partnership (Unrestricted Size) No. 2 Regulations 1990, and shall come into force on 21st August 1990.

**2(1)** So much of the Limited Partnerships Act 1907 as provides that a limited partnership shall not consist of more than twenty persons shall not apply to a partnership carrying on business as insurance brokers and consisting of persons each of whom is a registered insurance broker or an enrolled body corporate.

**2(2)** In these Regulations, **"registered insurance broker"** and **"enrolled"** have the meanings given in section 29(1) of the Insurance Brokers (Registration) Act 1977.

## EXPLANATORY NOTE

(*This Note does not form part of the Regulations*)

The Limited Partnerships Act 1907 provides that a limited partnership shall not consist of more than twenty persons. These Regulations exempt from that prohibition partnerships formed for the purpose of carrying on business as insurance brokers where each partner is either a registered insurance broker or an enrolled body corporate within the meaning of the Insurance Brokers (Registration) Act 1977.

# THE PARTNERSHIPS (UNRESTRICTED SIZE) NO. 6 REGULATIONS 1990

(SI 1990/1581)

*Made on 30 July 1990 by the Secretary of State for Trade and Industry under s. 716(2)(d) and 744 of the Companies Act 1985. Operative from 21 August 1990.*

**1** These Regulations may be cited as the Partnerships (Unrestricted Size) No. 6 Regulations 1990, and shall come into force on 21st August 1990.

**2(1)** Section 716(1) of the Companies Act 1985 does not prohibit the formation for the purpose of carrying on business as insurance brokers of a partnership consisting of persons each of whom is a registered insurance broker or an enrolled body corporate.

**2(2)** In these Regulations, **"registered insurance broker"** and **"enrolled"** have the meanings given in section 29(1) of the Insurance Brokers (Registration) Act 1977.

## EXPLANATORY NOTE

(*This Note does not form part of the Regulations*)

Section 716(1) of the Companies Act 1985 prohibits the formation of partnerships consisting of more than twenty persons. These Regulations exempt from that prohibition partnerships formed for the purpose of carrying on business as insurance brokers where each partner is either a registered insurance broker or an enrolled body corporate within the meaning of the Insurance Brokers (Registration) Act 1977.

## NOTE AS TO EARLIER COMMENCEMENT ORDERS

(*This Note is not part of the Order*)

The following provisions of the Companies Act 1989 have been brought into force by commencement order made before the date of this Order:

| *Provision* | *Date of Commencement* | *S.I. No.* |
|---|---|---|
| Ss. 1 and 15 but only for the purpose of inserting a new section 251 into the Companies Act 1985 (subject to certain transitional and saving provisions) | 1.3.1990 | S.I. 1990/142 |
| The remaining provisions of Part I (subject to important transitional and saving provisions) other than section 7 (in so far as it inserts a new section 233(5) into the Companies Act 1985), 11 (in so far as it inserts a new section 242A into the Companies Act 1985), 12 and 23 (in part) | 1.4.1990 (save paragraph 19 of Schedule 10 which is commenced on 1.8.1990) | S.I. 1990/355 |
| The remaining provisions of Part I (subject to transitional and savings provisions) except sections 1 and 11 in so far as they insert a new section 242A into the Companies Act 1985 | 7.1.1991 | S.I. 1990/2569 |
| S. 24 but only for the purposes of any provision brought into force by Article 3 of S.I. 1990/142 | 1.3.1990 | S.I. 1990/142 |
| S. 30 | 1.3.1990 | S.I. 1990/142 |
| S. 31 but only for purposes relating to the recognition of supervisory bodies under Schedule 11 to the Companies Act 1989 ("the 1989 Act") and for the purpose of enabling the Secretary of State to approve a qualification under section 31(4) and (5) of the 1989 Act | 1.3.1990 | S.I. 1990/142 |
| Ss. 32 and 33 | 1.3.1990 | S.I. 1990/142 |
| Ss. 37 to 40 | 1.3.1990 | S.I. 1990/142 |
| S. 41(1) and (4) but only for the purposes of an application under any provision brought into force by article 3 of S.I. 1990/142 or of any requirement imposed under any such provision | 1.3.1990 | S.I. 1990/142 |
| S. 41(3) | 1.3.1990 | S.I. 1990/142 |
| S. 41(5) and (6) but only for the purposes of s. 41(3) of the 1989 Act | 1.3.1990 | S.I. 1990/142 |
| Ss. 42 to 44 but only for the purposes of any provisions brought into force by article 3 of S.I. 1990/142 | 1.3.1990 | S.I. 1990/142 |
| S. 45 | 1.3.1990 | S.I. 1990/142 |
| S.47(1) | 1.3.1990 | S.I. 1990/142 |
| S. 48(1) and (2) | 1.3.1990 | S.I. 1990/142 |
| S. 49 but only for the purposes of any provision brought into force by article 3 of S.I. 1990/142 | 1.3.1990 | S.I. 1990/142 |
| Ss. 50 and 51 | 1.3.1990 | S.I. 1990/142 |

| *Provision* | *Date of Commencement* | *S.I. No.* |
|---|---|---|
| Ss. 52 to 54 but only for the purposes of any provision brought into force by article 3 of S.I. 1990/142 | 1.3.1990 | S.I. 1990/142 |
| Ss. 55 to 64 | 21.2.1990 | S.I. 1990/142 |
| S. 65(1) | 21.2.1990 | S.I. 1990/142 |
| S. 65(2) except to the extent that it refers to Part VII of the 1989 Act and except, in the case of s. 65(2)(g), to the extent that the said paragraph refers to a body established under s. 46 of the 1989 Act | 21.2.1990 | S.I. 1990/142 |
| S. 65(2) in so far as not yet in force but only to the extent that it refers to Part VIII of the 1989 Act | 25.4.1991 | S.I. 1991/878 |
| S. 65(3) to (7) | 21.2.1990 | S.I. 1990/142 |
| S. 66 to 74 | 21.2.1990 | S.I. 1990/142 |
| S. 75(1) | 21.2.1990 | S.I. 1990/142 |
| S. 75(2) | 25.1.1990 | S.I. 1990/98 |
| S. 75(3), in so far as it provides for the insertion in s. 180(1) of the Financial Services Act 1986 of a new paragraph (oo) | 25.1.1990 | S.I. 1990/98 |
| S. 75(3) except in so far as brought into force as referred to above, except to the extent that it refers to Part VII of the 1989 Act and except, in the case of s. 75(3)(c), to the extent that it refers to a body established by order under s. 46 of the 1989 Act | 21.2.1990 | S.I. 1990/142 |
| S. 75(3) in so far as not yet in force but only to the extent that it refers to Part VII of the 1989 Act | 24.4.1991 | S.I. 1991/878 |
| S. 75(4) in so far as it provides a definition of "public servant" for the purposes of the new s. 180(1) (oo) of the Financial Services Act 1986 | 25.1.1990 | S.I. 1990/98 |
| S. 75(4) except in so far as brought into force as referred to above | 21.2.1990 | S.I. 1990/142 |
| S. 75(6) | 21.2.1990 | S.I. 1990/142 |
| S. 75(7) | 25.1.1990 | S.I. 1990/98 |
| Ss. 76 to 79 | 21.2.1990 | S.I. 1990/142 |
| S. 80 except to the extent that it refers to Part VII of the 1989 Act | 21.2.1990 | S.I. 1990/142 |
| S. 80 in so far as not in force | 25.4.1991 | S.I. 1991/878 |
| S. 81(1) | 21.2.1990 | S.I. 1990/142 |
| S. 81(2) except to the extent that it refers to Part VII of the 1989 Act | 21.2.1990 | S.I. 1990/142 |
| S. 81(2) in so far as not in force | 25.4.1991 | S.I. 1991/878 |
| S. 81(3) and (4) | 21.2.1990 | S.I. 1990/142 |
| S. 81(5) except to the extent that it refers to Part VII of the 1989 Act | 21.2.1990 | S.I. 1990/142 |

| Provision | Date of Commencement | S.I. No. |
|---|---|---|
| S. 81(5) in so far as not in force | 25.4.1991 | S.I. 1991/878 |
| Ss. 82 to 86 | 21.2.1990 | S.I. 1990/142 |
| S. 87(1) to (3) | 21.2.1990 | S.I. 1990/142 |
| S. 87(4) except to the extent that it refers to Part VII of the 1989 Act | 21.2.1990 | S.I. 1990/142 |
| S. 87(4) in so far as not in force | 25.4.1991 | S.I. 1991/878 |
| S. 87(5) and (6) | 21.2.1990 | S.I. 1990/142 |
| Ss. 88 to 91 | 21.2.1990 | S.I. 1990/142 |
| Sections 108 to 112 (subject to transitional and savings provisions) | 4.2.1991 | S.I. 1990/2569 |
| Sections 113 to 124 (subject to transitional and saving provisions) | 1.4.1990 | S.I. 1990/355 |
| Sections 125 and 127(1), (2) and (4), and section 127(7) to the extent necessary to insert into Schedule 22 of the Companies Act 1985 a reference to the new sections 706, 707 and 715A of that Act | 7.1.1991 | S.I. 1990/2569 |
| Section 126 and, in so far as not yet in force, section 127 (subject, in the case of the former, to a transitional provision) | 1.7.1991 | S.I. 1991/488 |
| S. 129 | 1.11.1990 | S.I. 1990/1392 |
| S. 130 (and Schedule 17) | 31.7.1990 | S.I. 1990/1392 |
| Sections 131 and 132 (subject, in the case of the former, to a saving provision) | 1.4.1990 | S.I. 1990/355 |
| Section 134(1) to (3), (5) and (6) (subject to certain provisions) | 31.5.1990 | S.I. 1990/713 |
| Section 135 | 7.1.1991 | S.I. 1990/2569 |
| Section 136 (subject to a transitional provision) | 1.4.1990 | S.I. 1990/355 |
| Section 137(1); section 137(2) in part (subject to a transitional provision) | 1.4.1990 | S.I. 1990/355 |
| S. 138 (subject to saving provision) | 31.7.1990 | S.I. 1990/1392 |
| S. 139 (subject to transitional and saving provisions) | 1.10.1990 | S.I. 1990/1707 |
| S. 144 (and Schedule 18) (subject to transitional provisions) | 1.11.1990 | S.I. 1990/1392 |
| S. 145 but only in so far as it relates to paragraphs 1, 8, 9, 12, 19 and 21 of Schedule 19 to the 1989 Act | 1.3.1990 | S.I. 1990/142 |
| Section 145 but only in so far as it extends to paragraph 10 of Schedule 19 to the 1989 Act | 7.1.1991 | S.I. 1990/2569 |
| Section 145 but only in so far as it extends to paragraph 11 of Schedule 19 to the 1989 Act | 4.2.1991 | S.I. 1990/2569 |
| S. 145 but only in so far as it relates to paragraphs 15 to 18 of Schedule 19 to the 1989 Act | 1.4.1990 | S.I. 1990/355 |

| *Provision* | *Date of Commencement* | *S.I. No.* |
|---|---|---|
| S. 145 but only in so far as it relates to paragraphs 2 to 7 and 14 of Schedule 19 to the 1989 Act (subject, in the case of paragraphs 2 and 6, to transitional and saving provisions) | 1.10.1990 | S.I. 1990/1707 |
| S. 146 | 1.4.1990 | S.I. 1990/142 |
| S. 151 | 1.4.1990 | S.I. 1990/142 |
| S. 152 | 1.3.1990 | S.I. 1990/142 |
| S. 153 but only in so far as it relates to paragraphs 1, 13, 17, 21 and 26 of Schedule 20 to the 1989 Act | 1.4.1990 | S.I. 1990/142 |
| Part VII in so far as necessary to enable regulations to be made under sections 155(4) and (5), 158(4) and (5), 160(5), 173(4) and (5), 174(2) to (4), 185, 186 and 187(3) and paragraph 2(3) of Schedule 21 | 25.4.1991 | S.I. 1991/488 |
| S. 154 | 25.4.1991 | S.I. 1991/878 |
| S. 155, 156 and Schedule 21 in so far as not in force | 25.4.1991 | S.I. 1991/878 |
| S. 157 subject to certain provisions | 25.4.1991 | S.I. 1991/878 |
| S. 158 in so far as not in force | 25.4.1991 | S.I. 1991/878 |
| S. 159 | 25.4.1991 | S.I. 1991/878 |
| S. 160 in so far as not yet in force but subject to certain provisions concerning insolvency proceedings begun before the coming into force of the section and to provisions concerning its application in Northern Ireland | 25.4.1991 | S.I. 1991/878 |
| S. 161 | 25.4.1991 | S.I. 1991/878 |
| S. 162 subject to certain provisions concerning its application in Northern Ireland | 25.4.1991 | S.I. 1991/878 |
| S. 163 to 165 | 25.4.1991 | S.I. 1991/878 |
| S. 166 subject to certain provisions concerning insolvency proceedings begun before the section comes into force and to provisions concerning its application in Northern Ireland | 25.4.1991 | S.I. 1991/878 |
| S. 167 subject to provisions concerning its application in Northern Ireland | 25.4.1991 | S.I. 1991/878 |
| S. 168 and 169 except section 169(4) | 25.4.1991 | S.I. 1991/878 |
| S. 173 in so far as not in force | 25.4.1991 | S.I. 1991/878 |
| S. 174 in so far as not in force but subject to certain provisions concerning insolvency proceedings begun before the section comes into force | 25.4.1991 | S.I. 1991/878 |
| S. 175 subject to certain provisions concerning insolvency proceedings begun before the section comes into force | 25.4.1991 | S.I. 1991/878 |
| S. 177 except in so far as it would have effect where the property is held as margin at the time the section comes into force | 25.4.1991 | S.I. 1991/878 |

| Provision | Date of Commencement | S.I. No. |
|---|---|---|
| S. 179 except in so far as it would have effect where the property is subject to the relevant market charge at the time the section comes into force | 25.4.1991 | S.I. 1991/878 |
| S. 180 except in so far as it would effect certain procedures commenced or begun before the section comes into force | 25.4.1991 | S.I. 1991/878 |
| S. 182 and Schedule 22 and s. 183 | 25.4.1991 | S.I. 1991/878 |
| S. 184 subject to provisions concerning its application in Northern Ireland | 25.4.1991 | S.I. 1991/878 |
| S. 187 in so far as not in force | 25.4.1991 | S.I. 1991/878 |
| Ss. 188 to 191 | 25.4.1991 | S.I. 1991/878 |
| S. 192 in so far as it inserts section 47A into the Financial Services Act 1986 (subject to transitional and saving provisions) | 15.3.1990 | S.I. 1990/354 |
| S. 193 in so far as is necessary in order to enable regulations to be made under section 62A of, and paragraph 22A of Schedule 11 to, the Financial Services Act 1986 (subject to transitional and saving provisions) | 15.3.1990 | S.I. 1990/354 |
| Section 193 in so far as not in force (subject to a saving provision) | 1.4.1991 | S.I. 1991/488 |
| Sections 194 to 200 (subject to transitional and saving provisions) | 15.3.1990 | S.I. 1990/354 |
| S. 201 | 25.4.1991 | S.I. 1991/878 |
| Sections 203 to 205 (subject to transitional and saving provisions) | 15.3.1990 | S.I. 1990/354 |
| S. 206(1) except in so far as it relates to the insertion by paragraph 32 of Schedule 23 to the 1989 Act of paragraph 13B into Schedule 11 of the Financial Services Act 1986 (subject to transitional and saving provisions) | 15.3.1990 | S.I. 1990/354 |
| S. 206(2) to (4) (subject to transitional and saving provisions) | 15.3.1990 | S.I. 1990/354 |
| S. 207 | 1.11.1990 | S.I. 1990/1392 |
| S. 208 | 1.3.1990 | S.I. 1990/142 |
| S. 209 | 21.2.1990 | S.I. 1990/142 |
| S. 210 | 1.4.1990 | S.I. 1990/142 |
| S. 211(2) (subject to a saving provision) and (3) | 31.7.1990 | S.I. 1990/1392 |
| S. 212 in so far as it relates to the repeals effected by Schedule 24 to the 1989 Act referred to below | On the dates referred to below in connection with Schedule 24 | In the SIs listed below in connection with Schedule 24 |

| Provision | Date of Commencement | S.I. No. |
|---|---|---|
| Schedule 24 in so far as it relates to repeals in or of ss. 435, 440, 443, 446, 447, 449, 452 and 735A of the Companies Act 1985, ss. 94, 105, 179, 180, 198(1) and 199(9) of the Financial Services Act 1986 and s. 84(1) of the Banking Act 1987 | 21.2.1990 | S.I. 1990/142 |
| Schedule 24 in so far as it relates to the repeal in s. 21(2) of the Company Directors Disqualification Act 1986 | 1.3.1990 | S.I. 1990/142 |
| Schedule 24 in so far as it relates to the repeals in, or of, sections 48, 55, 119, 159 and 160 of, and paragraphs 4, 10 and 14 of Schedule 11 to the Financial Services Act 1986 | 15.3.1990 | S.I. 1990/354 |
| Schedule 24 in so far as it relates to repeals in or of ss. 46(3) and 85 of the Fair Trading Act 1973 | 1.4.1990 | S.I. 1990/142 |
| Schedule 24 in so far as it relates to repeals in or of section 42(6) of the Harbours Act 1964; sections 716, 717, 744 (in part) and 746 of, and Schedules 2, 4, 9, 11, 22 (in part) and 24 (in part) to, the Companies Act 1985; paragraphs 23 and 45 of Schedule 6 to the Insolvency Act 1985; and the entries in Part I of Schedule 13 to the Insolvency Act 1986 relating to sections 222(4) and 225 | 15.3.1990 | S.I. 1990/354 |
| Schedule 24 in so far as it relates to repeals in or of section 119(9) of, and paragraph 22 of Schedule 16 to, the Financial Services Act 1986 | 1.4.1990 | S.I. 1990/355 |
| Schedule 24 in so far as it relates to repeals in or of sections 201, 202(1) and 209(1)(j) of the Companies Act 1985 | 31.5.1990 | S.I. 1990/713 |
| Schedule 24 in so far as it relates to repeals in or of section 651(1) and Schedule 22 (in part) of the Companies Act 1985 | 31.7.1990 | S.I. 1990/1392 |
| Schedule 24 in so far as it relates to repeals in or of Schedules 15 and 18 to the Building Societies Act 1986 | 31.7.1990 | S.I. 1990/1392 |
| Schedule 24 in so far as it relates to repeals in or of sections 466(2) and 733(3) of and Schedules 22 (in part) and 24 (in part) to the Companies Act 1985 (subject, in the case of Schedules 22 and 24, to transitional and saving provisions) | 1.10.1990 | S.I. 1990/1707 |
| Schedule 24 in so far as it relates to Part I of Schedule 13 to the Insolvency Act 1986 (in part) | 1.10.1990 | S.I. 1990/1707 |
| Schedule 24 in so far as it relates to section 708(1)(b) of the 1985 Act | 7.1.1991 | S.I. 1990/2569 |

| Provision | Date of Commencement | S.I. No. |
|---|---|---|
| Schedule 24 in so far as it repeals Schedule 15 to the 1985 Act (subject to the transitional and savings provisions made by articles 4 and 5 of the Companies Act 1989 (Commencement No. 7 and Transitional and Savings Provisions) Order 1990) | 7.1.1991 | S.I. 1990/2569 |
| Schedule 24 in so far as it repeals the entries relating to section 245(1) and (2) in Schedule 24 to the 1985 Act (subject to the transitional and savings provisions made by article 6 of the Companies Act 1989 (Commencement No. 8 and Transitional and Savings Provisions) Order 1990) | 7.1.1991 | S.I. 1990/2569 |
| Ss. 213 to 215 in so far as they were not already in force at the time of the making of S.I. 1990/142 | 2.2.1990 | S.I. 1990/142 |
| S. 216 | 25.1.1990 | S.I. 1990/98 |

# THE COMPANIES ACT 1989 (REGISTER OF AUDITORS AND INFORMATION ABOUT AUDIT FIRMS) REGULATIONS 1991

(SI 1991/1566)

*Made on 7 July 1991 by the Secretary of State for Trade and Industry under s. 35 and 36 of the Companies Act 1989. Operative from 1 October 1991.*

## CITATION, COMMENCEMENT AND INTERPRETATION

**1(1)** These Regulations may be cited as the Companies Act 1989 (Register of Auditors and Information about Audit Firms) Regulations 1991 and shall come into force on 1st October 1991.

**1(2)** In these Regulations, unless the context otherwise requires–

**"the Act"** means the Companies Act 1989;

**"business day"** means any day which is not Saturday, Sunday, Christmas Day, Good Friday or a bank holiday within the meaning of the Banking and Financial Dealings Act 1971; and

**"the register"** means the register to be kept by virtue of regulation 2 below.

## RECOGNISED SUPERVISORY BODIES TO KEEP REGISTER OF AUDITORS

**2(1)** The recognised supervisory bodies, or, if there is only one recognised supervisory body, that recognised supervisory body, shall keep a register of–

(a) the individuals and firms eligible for appointment as company auditor, and

(b) the individuals holding an appropriate qualification who are responsible for company audit work on behalf of such firms.

**2(2)** Each person's entry in the register shall give–

(a) his name and address; and

(b) in the case of a person eligible as mentioned in paragraph (1)(a) of this regulation, the name of the relevant supervisory body.

2(3) The responsibilities of each supervisory body, or, if there is only one supervisory body, of that supervisory body, in connection with the obligation imposed by paragraph (1) of this regulation shall be determined in accordance with regulation 3 of these Regulations.

## OBLIGATIONS OF RECOGNISED SUPERVISORY BODIES WITH RESPECT TO MAINTENANCE OF REGISTER

3(1) Where there is more than one recognised supervisory body, each recognised supervisory body shall co-operate with each other recognised supervisory body for the purpose of ensuring that each enter information on the register.

3(2) Each recognised supervisory body, or if there is only one recognised supervisory body, that supervisory body, shall take reasonable care to ensure that, at all times–

(a) the register accurately states the individuals and firms eligible for appointment as company auditor under its rules and the individuals holding an appropriate qualification who are responsible for company audit work on behalf of such firms;

(b) the names and addresses shown on the register relating to persons falling within (a) above are correct; and

(c) its name appears on the register by virtue of regulation 2(2)(b) above only if the person in question is eligible for appointment as company auditor under its rules.

3(3) To the extent that paragraph (2) of this regulation imposes a duty on a recognised supervisory body to take reasonable care to ensure that the register is amended to reflect changes in the information specified in that paragraph, the recognised supervisory body in question shall be regarded as having discharged that duty if it ensures that the register is appropriately amended within the period of 10 business days beginning with the day on which it becomes aware of the relevant change.

## INFORMATION ABOUT FIRMS TO BE AVAILABLE TO THE PUBLIC

4 A recognised supervisory body shall, in accordance with these Regulations, keep and make available to the public the following information in relation to each firm eligible under its rules for appointment as company auditor–

(a) where the firm is a body corporate, the name and address of each person who is a director of the body or holds any shares in it; and

(b) where the firm is a partnership, the name and address of each partner,

indicating which of the persons mentioned in sub-paragraphs (a) and (b) above is responsible for company audit work on behalf of the firm.

## PLACE OF KEEPING AND INSPECTION OF REGISTER

5(1) The register shall be kept at the principal office in the United Kingdom of one of the recognised supervisory bodies, or, if there is only one recognised supervisory body, at the principal office in the United Kingdom of that body.

5(2) The recognised supervisory body at whose principal office the register is kept shall ensure that it is open to inspection by any person during a period of at least two hours between the hours of 9am and 5pm in any business day.

5(3) The recognised supervisory bodies, or, if there is only one recognised supervisory body, that recognised supervisory body, shall ensure that the register may be inspected in each of the following ways–

(a) alphabetically; and

(b) by reference to recognised supervisory bodies.

5(4) The recognised supervisory bodies, or, if there is only one recognised supervisory body, that recognised supervisory body, may charge a fee for inspection of the register or any part of it not exceeding £2.50 for each hour, or part of an hour, that is spent in conducting an inspection.

## INSPECTION OF INFORMATION KEPT UNDER REGULATION 4

6(1) Subject to paragraph (3), a recognised supervisory body shall ensure that the information it is required to keep and make available to the public by virtue of regulation 4 of these regulations is open to inspection by any person during a period of at least two hours between the hours of 9am and 5pm in every business day at its principal office in the United Kingdom.

**6(2)** A recognised supervisory body shall ensure that the information may be inspected in each of the following ways–

(a) alphabetically; and

(b) by reference to firm.

**6(3)** A recognised supervisory body may charge a fee for inspection of the information or any part of it not exceeding £2.50 for each hour, or part of an hour, spent by a person in conducting an inspection.

## COPIES OF ENTRIES ON REGISTER

**7(1)** Subject to paragraph (2), the recognised supervisory bodies, or, if there is only one recognised supervisory body, that recognised supervisory body, shall ensure that any person may obtain a copy of any entry in the register, being a copy which is certified to be a true copy of the relevant entry by or on behalf of a recognised supervisory body.

**7(2)** The recognised supervisory bodies, or, if there is only one recognised supervisory body, that recognised supervisory body, may charge a person a fee not exceeding 5p for a copy of an entry in the register.

**7(3)** The recognised supervisory bodies, or, if there is only one recognised supervisory body, that recognised supervisory body, shall ensure that it is possible for a person to require copies of entries by each of the means mentioned in regulation 5(3) of these Regulations.

## COPIES OF INFORMATION KEPT UNDER REGULATION 4

**8(1)** Subject to paragraph (2), a recognised supervisory body shall ensure that any person may obtain a copy of the whole or any part of the information which it is required to keep by virtue of regulation 4 of these Regulations certified by the body to be a true copy of the relevant information.

**8(2)** A recognised supervisory body may charge a person a fee not exceeding 5p for a copy of the information it keeps relating to any director of or shareholder in a firm which is a body corporate or any partner in a firm which is a partnership.

**8(3)** A recognised supervisory body shall ensure that it is possible for a person to require copies of information by each of the means mentioned in regulation 6(2) of the Regulations.

## EXPLANATORY NOTE

(*This Note is not part of the Regulations*)

Regulation 2 of the regulations obliges supervisory bodies recognised under Part II of the Companies Act 1989 (eligibility for appointment as company auditor) to keep a register containing the information specified in the regulation. Regulation 3 of the regulations imposes certain obligations on recognised supervisory bodies in connection with the keeping of the register. Regulation 4 of the regulations obliges each recognised supervisory body to make the information specified in the regulation available to the public. Regulations 5 to 8 of the regulations make provision as to the keeping of the register; as to the inspection of it or of information kept by virtue of regulation 4 and as to the obtaining of copies of entries on the register or of information kept by virtue of regulation 4. Regulations 7 and 8 authorise the charging of fees for inspection and obtaining copies. The regulations implement article 28 of the Eighth Council Directive of 10 April 1984 on the approval of persons responsible for carrying out the statutory audits of accounting documents (84/253/EEC) (L. 126/20).

# THE COMPANIES (DISCLOSURE OF INTERESTS IN SHARES) (ORDERS IMPOSING RESTRICTIONS ON SHARES) REGULATIONS 1991

(SI 1991/1646)

*Made on 17 July 1991 by the Secretary of State for Trade and Industry under s. 135(4) of the Companies Act 1989. Operative from 18 July 1991.*

## CITATION AND COMMENCEMENT

**1** These Regulations may be cited as the Companies (Disclosure of Interests in Shares) (Orders imposing restrictions on shares) Regulations 1991 and shall come into force on the day after the day on which they are made.

## INTERPRETATION

**2** In these Regulations unless the context otherwise requires reference to a numbered section shall be construed as a reference to a numbered section of the Companies Act 1985.

## AMENDMENTS OF PART VI, COMPANIES ACT 1985

**3** [Insertion of s. 210(5A).]

**4** [Insertion of s. 216(1A), (1B); substitution in s. 216(2).]

## AMENDMENTS OF PART XIV, COMPANIES ACT 1985

**5** [Insertion of s. 445(1A); substitution in s. 445(2).]

## AMENDMENTS OF PART XV, COMPANIES ACT 1985

**6** [Insertions in s. 454.]

**7** [Insertions in s. 455(1), (2).]

**8** [Insertion of s. 456(1A); insertion in s. 456(4).]

## EXPLANATORY NOTE

(*This Note is not part of the Regulations*)

These Regulations amend sections 210, 216 and 445 and Part XV (orders imposing restrictions on shares) of the Companies Act 1985, so as to permit orders imposing restrictions on shares to be made in a form protecting the rights of third parties. The Regulations also amend Part VI with respect to the making of interim orders by a court and further amend Part XV with respect to the circumstances in which restrictions imposed upon shares may be relaxed or removed.

Transitional provision is made with respect to subsisting orders of the court or of the Secretary of State which impose restrictions on shares.

# THE COMPANIES HOUSE TRADING FUND ORDER 1991

(SI 1991/1795)

*Made on 31 July by the Secretary of State for Trade and Industry. Operative from 1 October 1991.*

Whereas:

(1) It appears to the Secretary of State for Trade and Industry ("the Secretary of State") that–

(a) those operations described in Schedule 1 to this Order (being operations of a Department of the Government for which the Secretary of State is responsible) are suitable to be financed by means of a fund established under the Government Trading Funds Act 1973 and, in particular, to be so managed that the revenue of such a fund would consist principally of receipts in respect of goods or services provided in the course of the operations in question; and

(b) the financing of the operations in question by means of such a fund would be in the interests of improved efficiency and effectiveness of the management of those operations;

(2) In accordance with sections 1(3) and 6(4) of the Act of 1973, the Secretary of State has taken such steps as appear to him to be appropriate to give an opportunity to such persons as appear to him appropriate to make representations to him and has laid before Parliament a report about the representations received and his conclusions;

(3) In accordance with section 2 of the Act of 1973, the Secretary of State has determined with the concurrence of the Treasury that the assets and liabilities set out in Schedule 2 to this Order are properly attributable to the operations for which a fund is to be established by this Order and are suitable to be appropriated to that fund;

(4) In accordance with section 6(2) of the Act of 1973, a draft of this Order has been laid before the House of Commons and has been approved by a resolution of that House.

Now, therefore, the Secretary of State in exercise of the powers conferred upon him by sections 1, 2 and 2B(6) of the Act of 1973, and all other powers enabling him in that behalf, with the concurrence of the Treasury hereby makes the following Order:

### CITATION AND COMMENCEMENT

**1** This Order may be cited as the Companies House Trading Fund Order 1991 and shall come into force on 1st October 1991.

### INTERPRETATION

**2** In this Order:–

**"the Act of 1973"** means the Government Trading Funds Act 1973 as amended by the Government Trading Act 1990 and the Finance Act 1991;

**"Companies House"** means that part of the Department of Trade and Industry known as the Companies House Executive Agency;

**"the fund"** means the fund established by article 3 of this Order;

**"the funded operations"** means the operations of Companies House as described in Schedule 1 to this Order; and

**"the registrar of companies"** has the same meaning as in the Companies Act 1985.

### ESTABLISHMENT OF THE FUND

**3** There shall be established as from 1st October 1991 a fund for the funded operations.

### SOURCE OF LOANS

**4** The Secretary of State is designated as the source of issues to the fund by way of loan.

### ASSETS, LIABILITIES AND PUBLIC DIVIDEND CAPITAL

**5(1)** The Crown assets and liabilities set out in Schedule 2 to this Order shall be appropriated as assets and liabilities of the fund.

**5(2)** The sum of £18,454,000 shall be treated as public dividend capital.

### LIMITATION OF INDEBTEDNESS

**6** The maximum amount that may be issued to the fund by way of loan under section 2B of the Act of 1973 shall be £40,000,000.

## Schedule 1 – The Funded Operations

Article 2

**1** The following operations with respect to companies and other forms of business organisation required by law to register, or register information, with the registrar of companies:

(a) the registration and striking off the register of such entities;

(b) the regulation of the registered names of such entities;

(c) the registration or recording of information required by law to be submitted to the registrar in respect of such entities;

(d) the maintenance of records required by law to be kept by the registrar concerning such entities;

(e) the making available for inspection of those records and the provision of copies of such records or of any information contained in or based upon those records;

(f) the administration and enforcement of laws relating to such entites, including the consideration and pursuit of complaints about the breach of such laws;

(g) the provision of guidance on matters relating to the law and practice governing such entities.

**2** The regulation of business names, including the administration and enforcement of laws governing the use of business names (including the consideration and pursuit of complaints about the breach of such laws) and the provision of guidance on matters relating to the law and practice governing the use of business names.

**3** Without prejudice to the foregoing, the performance by the registrar of companies of any function of his imposed on him by law as at 1st October1991 and the performance of any functions of the Secretary of State as are performed as at that date by any officer employed within Companies House.

**4** Operations incidental, conducive or otherwise ancillary to the foregoing.

# Schedule 2 – Assets and Liabilities

Article 5

## ASSETS

Freehold land and building at Crown Way, Cardiff.

Plant and computers as at 1st October 1991 used or allocated for use in the funded operations.

Intangible assets arising from the funded operations as carried on up to that date.

Current assets as at that date used or allocated for use in, or arising from, the funded operations.

## LIABILITIES

Creditors as at that date arising from the funded operations.

## EXPLANATORY NOTE

(*This Note is not part of the Order*)

This Order provides for the setting up as from 1st October 1991 of a fund with public money under the Government Trading Funds Act 1973 for the operations of Companies House as described in Schedule 1 to the Order. It designates the Secretary of State for Trade and Industry as the authorised lender to the fund and imposes a limit of £40,000,000 on the amount which may be lent to the fund. It provides for the assets and liabilities set out in Schedule 2 to the Order to be appropriated to the fund and for £18,454,000 to be treated as public dividend capital.

# THE COMPANIES ACT 1989 (COMMENCEMENT NO. 12 AND TRANSITIONAL PROVISION) ORDER 1991

(SI 1991/1996 (C 57))

*Made on 2 September 1991 by the Secretary of State for Trade and Industry under s. 215(2) and (3) of the Companies Act 1989.*

## CITATION AND INTERPRETATION

**1(1)** This Order may be cited as the Companies Act 1989 (Commencement No. 12 and Transitional Provision) Order 1991.

**1(2)** In this Order, **"the Act"** means the Companies Act 1989.

## PROVISIONS OF THE ACT BROUGHT INTO FORCE BY THE ORDER

**2(1)** Subject to the provisions of article 3 of this Order, the following provisions of the Act shall, insofar as they are not yet in force, come into force on 1st October 1991–

(a) Part II (eligibility for appointment as company auditor) except section 46 and Schedule 13 (delegation of functions of Secretary of State), section 47(2) to (6) (power for Secretary of State to make provisions as to discharge of certain functions under Schedule 14 (restrictive practices) when delegation order in force) and section 48(3) (exemption from liability for damages for body established by delegation order);

(b) section 211(1) (building societies: miscellaneous amendments); and

(c) section 212 and Schedule 24 insofar as is necessary to effect the repeal of, or of words in, the following provisions–

  (i) section 389 of the Companies Act 1985;

  (ii) section 460(1) of the Companies Act 1985;

  (iii) section 196(3) of the Financial Services Act 1986; and

  (iv) section 565(6)(b) of the Income and Corporation Taxes Act 1988.

**2(2)** The following provisions of the Act shall come into force on 1st November 1991–

(a) section 134(4) (disclosure of interests in shares – particulars to be contained in notification);

(b) section 143 (rights of inspection and related matters); and

(c) section 212 and Schedule 24 insofar as is necessary to effect the repeal of, or of words in, the following provisions, that is to say, sections 169(5), 175(6)(b), 191(1), (3)(a) and (3)(b), 219(1), 288(3), 318(7), 356(1), (2) and (4) and 383(1), (2) and (3) of the Companies Act 1985 and paragraph 25 of Schedule 13 to that Act.

## TRANSITIONAL PROVISION RELATING TO THE COMING INTO FORCE OF SECTION 28 OF THE ACT

**3(1)** A person who, on the date that section 28 of the Act comes into force, is ineligible for appointment as a company auditor by reason of not being a member of a recognised supervisory body but who then holds office as auditor of a company under an appointment for which he was not disqualified by virtue of section 389 of the Companies Act 1985 and for which he is not ineligible by virtue of section 27 of the Act may, notwithstanding the coming into force of section 28 of the Act, continue to act, and hold office, as auditor of the company until whichever of the following first occurs–

(a) the expiry of his term of office as determined in accordance with paragraph (2) of this article; or

(b) his becoming ineligible for appointment as auditor of the company by virtue of section 27 of the Act.

**3(2)** For the purposes of paragraph (1) of this article a person's term of office shall expire–

(a) in a case in which the appointment is as auditor of a company which has elected to dispense with the obligation to appoint auditors annually, at the time at which he would, in accordance with section 386 of the Companies Act 1985, cease to hold office if the election ceased to be in force on 1st October 1991; and

(b) in any other case, at the end of the time within which the company must, in accordance with whichever is applicable of section 385(2) or 385A(2) of the Companies Act 1985, next appoint auditors after 1st October 1991.

## EXPLANATORY NOTE

(*This Note is not part of the Order*)

Subject to the exceptions mentioned below, the Order brings into force on 1st October 1991 the remaining provisions of Part II of the Companies Act 1989 ("the Act") which is concerned with eligibility for appointment as company auditor. The provisions not brought into force are those conferring power on the Secretary of State to transfer functions of his under the Part to a body established by order under section 46 of the Act and certain related provisions.

The Order also brings into force on 1st October 1991 section 211(1) of the Companies Act 1989 which contains provisions making miscellaneous amendments concerning building societies.

The Order brings sections 134(4) and 143 of the Companies Act 1989 into force on 1st November 1991 together with certain related repeals. Section 134(4) concerns the particulars which must be contained in a notification disclosing an interest in shares. Section 143 concerns rights of inspection of company registers and related matters.

The Order repeals section 389 of the Companies Act 1985 concerning qualifications for appointment as auditor on 1st October 1991 and also repeals, on the same date, the provisions of, or of words in, section 460(1) of the Companies Act 1985, section 196(3) of the Financial Services Act 1986 and section 565(6)(b) of the Income and Corporation Taxes Act 1988.

Article 3 of the Order contains a transitional provision concerning the position of persons holding office as auditor of a company on 1st October 1991.

## NOTE AS TO EARLIER COMMENCEMENT ORDERS

(*This Note is not part of the Order*)

The provisions of the Companies Act 1989 brought into force by Orders made before the making of the Companies Act 1989 (Commencement No. 11) Order 1991 (SI 1991/1452) are listed in a note appended to that Order. That Order itself brought into force the provisions of sections 35 and 36 of the Companies Act 1989 which oblige the Secretary of State to make regulations requiring the keeping of a register of company auditors (section 35) and requiring recognised supervisory bodies under Part II of the Companies Act 1989 to make available to the public information about firms eligible under their rules for appointment as a company auditor (section 36).

# THE COMPANIES ACT 1989 (ELIGIBILITY FOR APPOINTMENT AS COMPANY AUDITOR) (CONSEQUENTIAL AMENDMENTS) REGULATIONS 1991

(SI 1991/1997)

*Made on 3 September 1991 by the Secretary of State for Trade and Industry under s. 50 of the Companies Act 1989. Operative from 1 October 1991.*

## CITATION AND INTERPRETATION

**1(1)** These Regulations may be cited as the Companies Act 1989 (Eligibility for Appointment as Company Auditor) (Consequential Amendments) Regulations 1991 and shall come into force on 1st October 1991.

**1(2)** In these Regulations, **"the Act"** means the Companies Act 1989.

## CONSEQUENTIAL AMENDMENTS

**2** The enactments mentioned in the Schedule to these Regulations shall have effect with the amendments specified therein.

**3** Where a partnership constituted under the law of England and Wales or under the law of any other country or territory in which a partnership is not a legal person is appointed under any enactment as amended by these Regulations, the provisions of section 26 of the Act apply to the appointment in the same way as they apply to the appointment as company auditor of such a partnership.

## TRANSITIONAL PROVISION

**4** None of the amendments specified in the Schedule to these Regulations shall have the effect that a person is required to resign from or otherwise surrender an appointment, or that the appointment of a person must be terminated, before the date on which the person's appointment would, apart from these Regulations, have expired.

# Schedule – Amendments to Enactments

Regulation 2

**Note**

Amendments not reproduced – relevant amendments have been incorporated elsewhere.

## EXPLANATORY NOTE

*(This Note is not part of the Regulations)*

Regulation 2 of the regulations and the Schedule to them make amendments to the enactments mentioned in the Schedule which are consequential upon the provisions of Part II of the Companies Act 1989 (eligibility for appointment as company auditor) having effect in place of section 389 of the Companies Act 1985 (qualification for appointment as auditor). Section 389 of the Companies Act 1985 is repealed on 1st October 1991.

Regulation 3 of the regulations makes provision as to what the effect is when a partnership which is not a legal person is appointed under an enactment amended by the regulations and regulation 4 of the regulations contains a transitional provision concerning the position of persons holding an appointment when the regulations come into force.

# THE COMPANIES (INSPECTION AND COPYING OF REGISTERS, INDICES AND DOCUMENTS) REGULATIONS 1991

(SI 1991/1998)

*Made on 2 September 1991 by the Secretary of State for Trade and Industry under s. 723A of the Companies Act 1985 and the provisions in Sch. 1 to these Regulations. Operative from 1 November 1991.*

## CITATION AND COMMENCEMENT

**1** These Regulations may be cited as the Companies (Inspection and Copying of Registers, Indices and Documents) Regulations 1991 and shall come into force on 1st November 1991.

## INTERPRETATION

**2** In these Regulations:

**"the Act"** means the Companies Act 1985;

**"business day"** means, in relation to a company subject to any provision of these Regulations, any day except a Saturday or Sunday, Christmas Day, Good Friday and any other day which is a bank holiday in the part of Great Britain where that company is registered (or in the case of a company that is a body corporate to which section 723A of the Act is applied by section 718 thereof, the part of Great Britain where its principal office was situated on 5th January 1976 or if it was incorporated after that date, the part of Great Britain where its principal office was situated immediately after incorporation); and

**"company"** includes a body corporate to which section 723A of the Act is applied by any enactment.

## INSPECTION

**3(1)** This Regulation applies to an obligation to make a register, index or document available for inspection imposed on a company by sections 169(5) (contract for purchase by company of its own shares), 175(6) (statutory declaration and auditors' report relating to payment out of capital), 191(1) (register of debenture holders), 219(1) (register of interests in shares &c), 288(3) (register of directors and secretaries), 318(7) (directors' service contracts), 356(1) (register and index of members) and 383(1) (minute books) of the Act, as well as to section 325 of, and paragraph 25 of Part IV of Schedule 13 to, the Act (register of directors' interests).

**3(2)** The company shall:

(a) make the register, index or document available for such inspection for not less than two hours during the period between 9 a.m. and 5 p.m. on each business day; and

(b) permit a person inspecting the register, index or document to copy any information made available for inspection by means of the taking of notes or the transcription of the information.

**3(3)** Paragraph (2)(b) shall not be construed as obliging a company to provide any facilities additional to those provided for the purposes of facilitating inspection.

## REGISTERS OF MEMBERS AND DEBENTURE HOLDERS: PRESENTATION AND EXTRACTION OF ENTRIES

**4(1)** This Regulation applies to a company's register of members maintained under section 352 of the Act, to an index of the names of the company's members maintained under section 354 thereof and to a register of debenture holders maintained under section 190 thereof.

**4(2)** A company is not obliged:

(a) by virtue of section 356(1) of the Act to present for inspection its register of members or an index of members' names; or

(b) by virtue of section 191(1) of the Act to present for inspection a register of debenture holders maintained by it,

in a manner which groups together entries by reference to whether a member or (as the case may be) a debenture holder has given an address in a particular geographical location, is of a particular nationality, has a holding of a certain size, is a natural person or not or is of a particular gender.

**4(3)** Nor is a company obliged:

(a) by virtue of section 356(3) of the Act, in providing a copy of a part of its register of members; or

(b) by virtue of section 191(2) of the Act, in providing a copy of a part of a register of debenture holders,

to extract entries from the register by reference to whether a member or (as the case may be) a debenture holder has given an address in a particular geographical location, is of a particular nationality, has a holding of a certain size, is a natural person or not or is of a particular gender.

## FEES

**5** Schedule 2 to these Regulations prescribes the fees payable for the purposes of the provisions of the Act listed therein.

# Schedule 1

Sections 191(1), 191(2), 191(3), 219(2), 288(3), 325(5) (together with paragraphs 25 and 26(1) of Part IV of Schedule 13), 356(1), 356(3) and 383(3).

# Schedule 2

Regulation 5

## FEES IN RESPECT OF INSPECTIONS OF REGISTERS BY NON-MEMBERS

**1** The fee prescribed for the purposes of the following provisions of the Act:

(a) section 191(1) (Fee for inspection of register of debenture holders);

(b) section 288(3) (Fee for inspection of register of directors and secretaries);

(c) section 325(5) and paragraph 25 of Part IV of Schedule 13 (Fee for inspection of register of directors' interests in shares or debentures); and

(d) section 356(1) (Fee for inspection of register of members and index);

is £2.50 for each hour or part thereof during which the right of inspection is exercised.

## FEES FOR PROVISION COPIES AND ENTRIES IN REGISTERS AND COPIES OF REPORTS

**2** The fee prescribed for the purposes of the following provisions of the Act:

(a) section 191(2) (Fee for copies of entries in the register of debentures);

(b) section 219(2) (Fees for copies of entries in the register of interests in shares or copies of reports or part of reports made pursuant to section 215(7));

(c) section 325(5) and paragraph 26(1) of Part IV of Schedule 13 (Fee for copies of entries in the register of directors' interests in shares or debentures); and

(d) section 356(3) (Fee for copies of entries in the register of members);

is:

(i) for the first 100 entries, or part thereof copied, .................................... £2.50;

(ii) for the next 1000 entries, or part thereof copied, ................................ £20.00; and

(iii) for every subsequent 1000 entries, or part thereof copied, ...................... £15.00.

## FEES FOR COPIES OF OTHER DOCUMENTS

**3** The fee prescribed for the purposes of the following provisions of the Act–

(a) section 191(3) (Fee for copies of trust deeds); and

(b) section 383(3) (Fee for copies of minutes)

is 10 pence per hundred words, or part thereof, copied.

## EXPLANATORY NOTE

(*This Note is not part of the Regulations*)

These Regulations set out certain obligations of companies in relation to the inspection and copying of their records by members and non-members. They set out the circumstances in which companies are not obliged to provide copies of entries on the various registers and prescribe the fees that they may charge for the provision of copies of entries on registers and for copies of other documents.

Section 723A(6) of the Companies Act 1985 (as inserted by section 143(1) of the Companies Act 1989) provides that companies can provide more extensive facilities than they are obliged to provide under these Regulations or charge fees that are less than those prescribed under these Regulations.

# THE COMPANIES ACT 1985 (DISCLOSURE OF REMUNERATION FOR NON-AUDIT WORK) REGULATIONS 1991

(SI 1991/2128)

*Made on 21 September 1991 by the Secretary of State for Trade and Industry under s. 390B of the Companies Act 1985. Operative from 14 October 1991.*

[**Note:** Amendments by the Companies Act (Disclosure of Remuneration for Non-Audit Work) (Amendment) Regulations 1995 (SI 1995/1520) (operative from 10 July 1995) have been included.]

## CITATION AND COMMENCEMENT

**1** These Regulations may be cited as the Companies Act 1985 (Disclosure of Remuneration for Non-Audit Work) Regulations 1991 and shall come into force on 14th October 1991.

## INTERPRETATION

**2** In these Regulations, unless the context otherwise requires–

**"the 1985 Act"** means the Companies Act 1985;

**"the 1989 Act"** means the Companies Act 1989;

**"annual accounts"** has the meaning given in section 262(1) of the 1985 Act;

**"associate"** in relation to a company's auditors, means a person who is to be regarded as an associate of those auditors by virtue of regulation 3 of these Regulations;

**"associated undertaking"** in relation to a company means any undertaking which, in accordance with section 258 of the 1985 Act, is a subsidiary undertaking of the company other than a subsidiary undertaking formed under the law of a country or territory outside the United Kingdom;

**"director"** and **"group"** have the respective meanings given in section 53(1) of the 1989 Act; and

**"remuneration"** includes sums paid in respect of expenses.

## PERSONS WHO ARE TO BE REGARDED AS ASSOCIATES OF A COMPANY'S AUDITORS

**3(1)** This regulation applies, subject to regulation 7 below, in order to determine whether a person is to be regarded as an associate of a company's auditors in any financial year of a company in relation to which disclosure must be made in the annual accounts of that company relating to that year by virtue of regulation 5 of these Regulations.

**History**

In reg. 3(1) the words ", subject to regulation 7 below," inserted by the Companies Act 1985 (Disclosure of Remuneration for Non-Audit Work) (Amendment) Regulations 1995 (SI 1995/1520), reg. 1, 3 as from 10 July 1995.

**3(2)** Where a company's auditors are a body corporate, each of the following shall be regarded as an associate of theirs in a relevant financial year–

(a) any partnership in which the auditors were, at any time in the financial year, a partner;

(b) any partnership in which a director of the auditors was, at any time in the financial year, a partner;

(c) any body corporate which was, at any time in the financial year, in the same group as the auditors;

(d) any body corporate which was an associated undertaking of the auditors or of a body corporate in the same group as the auditors at any time in the financial year;

(e) any body corporate in which any director of the auditors either alone or with any associate of the auditors was, at any time in the financial year, entitled to exercise, or control the exercise of, 20% or more of the voting rights at any general meeting and any body corporate which was, at any time in the financial year, in the same group as any such body corporate; and

(f) any director of the auditors.

**3(3)** Where a company's auditors are a partnership, each of the following shall be regarded as an associate of theirs in a relevant financial year–

(a) any other partnership which had, at any time in the financial year, a partner in common with the auditors;

(b) any body corporate which was, at any time in the financial year, a partner in the auditors;

(c) any body corporate in which, whether alone or with any associate of the auditors, the auditors or any partner in the auditors was, at any time in the financial year, entitled to exercise, or control the exercise of, 20% or more of the voting rights at any general meeting;

(d) any body corporate which was, at any time in the financial year, in the same group as any such body corporate as is mentioned in sub-paragraph (b) or (c) above; and

(e) any partner in the auditors.

**3(4)** Where a company's auditor is an individual, each of the following shall be regarded as an associate of his in a relevant financial year–

(a) any partnership in which the auditor was, at any time in the financial year, a partner; and

(b) any body corporate in which the auditor or any associate of his was, at any time in the financial year, entitled to exercise or control the exercise of 20% or more of the voting rights at any general meeting and any body corporate which was, at any time in that year, in the same group as any such body corporate.

**3(5)** Each of the following shall be regarded as an associate of a company's auditors in a relevant financial year whether the auditors are a body corporate, a partnership or an individual, that is to say, any person who was, at any time in that financial year, entitled to receive 20% or more of the auditors' profits and any person of whose profits the auditors were, in that financial year entitled to receive 20% or more.

## APPLICATION TO SMALL OR MEDIUM SIZED COMPANIES

**4** In relation to a company which qualifies as small or medium sized by virtue of section 247 of the 1985 Act, these regulations shall not require the information specified in regulation 5 below to be disclosed in notes to the annual accounts of the company relating to a financial year in respect of which the company is entitled to the exemptions mentioned in section 246 of the 1985 Act.

## DISCLOSURE OF REMUNERATION FOR NON-AUDIT WORK

**5(1)** Subject to paragraph (3) below, there shall be disclosed in notes to the annual accounts of a company relating to each financial year beginning on or after 1st October 1991–

(a) the aggregate of the remuneration, if any, in respect of work carried out in that year of the company's auditors during that year and of any person who is treated, by virtue of regulation 3, as having been an associate of the company's auditors in that year; and

(b) the aggregate of the remuneration, if any, in respect of work carried out during the previous financial year of the company's auditors and of any person who is treated, by virtue of regulation 3, as having been an associate of the company's auditors in that previous financial year

for services other than those of the auditors in their capacity as such supplied–

(i) to the company; and

(ii) to an associated undertaking of the company in any case in which the company's auditors or any associates of the company's auditors are auditors of the relevant associated undertaking.

**5(2)** This regulation applies to benefits in kind as to payments in cash, and, in relation to any such benefit, its nature and its estimated money value shall also be disclosed in the note.

**5(3)** Paragraph (1) above does not require disclosure of remuneration for a financial year beginning before 1st October 1991.

**5(4)** Where more than one person has been appointed as a company's auditor in a single financial year, paragraph (1) above has effect to require separate disclosure in respect of remuneration of each such person and their associates.

## DUTY OF AUDITORS TO SUPPLY INFORMATION

**6** The auditors of a company shall supply the directors of the company with such information as is necessary to enable relevant associates of the auditors to be identified for the purposes of regulation 5 of these Regulations.

## PERSONS WHO ARE NOT TO BE REGARDED AS ASSOCIATES OF A COMPANY'S AUDITORS

**7** For the purposes of these Regulations a body corporate shall not be regarded as an associate of a company's auditors in a relevant financial year–

(a) by virtue of regulation 3(2)(e) of these Regulations if the relevant director of the auditors was entitled to exercise, or control the exercise of, 20% or more of the voting rights at any general meeting of such body corporate solely by virtue of acting as an insolvency practitioner in relation to any person, or in his capacity as a receiver, or a receiver or manager, of the property of a company, or a judicial factor on the estate of any person;

(b) by virtue of regulation 3(3)(c) of these Regulations if the auditors or the relevant partner in the auditors were or was entitled to exercise, or control the exercise of, 20% or more of the voting rights at any general meeting of such body corporate solely by virtue of acting as an insolvency pratitioner in relation to any person, or in his capacity as an receiver, or a receiver or manager, of the property of a company, or a judicial factor on the estate of any person;

(c) by virtue of regulation 3(4)(b) of these Regulations if neither the auditor nor any associate of his was entitled to exercise, or control the exercise of, 20% or more of the voting rights at any general meeting of such body corporate otherwise than by virtue of acting as an insolvency practitioner in relation to any person, or in his capacity as a receiver, or a receiver or manager, of the property of a company, or a judicial factor on the estate of any person.

**History**
Reg. 7 inserted by the Companies Act 1985 (Disclosure of Remuneration for Non-Audit Work) (Amendment) Regulations 1995 (SI 1995/1520) reg. 1, 4 as from 10 July 1995.

## EXPLANATORY NOTE

(*This Note is not part of the Regulations*)

The Regulations require remuneration of a company's auditors and their associates for non-audit work done for a company and its associated undertakings to be disclosed in notes to the company's annual accounts prepared in respect of financial years beginning on or after 1st October 1991. The Regulations place the auditors of a company under a duty to provide the company's directors with the information necessary to enable the relevant associates to be identified. Article 4 of the Regulations contains a limited exemption for small and medium-sized companies.

# THE COMPANIES ACT 1989 (COMMENCEMENT NO. 13) ORDER 1991

(SI 1991/2173 (C 65))

*Made on 28 September 1991 by the Secretary of State for Trade and Industry under s. 215 of the Companies Act 1989.*

## CITATION

**1** This Order may be cited as the Companies Act 1989 (Commencement No. 13) Order 1991.

## PROVISIONS OF THE COMPANIES ACT 1989 BROUGHT INTO FORCE BY THE ORDER

**2** In so far as they are not yet in force, the provisions of sections 160, 162, 166, 167 and 184 of the Companies Act 1989 shall come into force on 1st October 1991.

## EXPLANATORY NOTE

*(This Note is not part of the Regulations)*

The Order brings the provisions of sections 160 (duty to give assistance for purposes of default proceedings), 162 (duty to report on completion of default proceedings), 166 (powers of Secretary of State to give directions), 167 (application to determine whether default proceedings to be taken) and 184 (indemnity for certain acts etc.) of the Companies Act 1989 into force on 1st October 1991 insofar as they are not already in force. The relevant provisions were brought into force on 25th April 1991 by the Companies Act 1989 (Commencement No. 10 and Saving Provisions) Order 1991 (SI 1991/878) except insofar as they had effect for certain purposes concerning office-holders appointed under Northern Ireland insolvency legislation and other matters which might affect the operation of Northern Ireland insolvency law.

The provisions brought into force by the Order are contained in Part VII of the Companies Act 1989 which is concerned principally with the effects of insolvency law on certain financial markets. Provisions of the Companies (No. 2) (Northern Ireland) Order 1990 (SI 1990/1504 (NI 10)) corresponding to those of Part VII of the Companies Act 1989 will come into force on the same date as the provisions brought into force by the Order.

## NOTE AS TO EARLIER COMMENCEMENT ORDERS

*(This Note is not part of the Order)*

The provisions of the Companies Act 1989 brought into force by Orders made before the making of the Companies Act 1989 (Commencement No. 11) Order 1991 (SI 1991/1452) are listed in a note appended to that Order. The following provisions of the Companies Act 1989 are brought into force by commencement order made before the date of the Order–

| *Provisions* | *Date of Commencement* | *S.I. No.* |
|---|---|---|
| Sections 35 and 36 | 26.6.1991 | S.I. 1991/1452 |
| Part II in so far as not yet in force, except sections 46, 47(2) to (6), 48(3) and Schedule 13, and subject to a saving provision concerning the coming into force of section 28 | 1.10.1991 | S.I. 1991/1996 |
| Section 134(4) | 1.11.1991 | S.I. 1991/1996 |
| Section 143 | 1.11.1991 | S.I. 1991/1996 |
| Section 212 and Schedule 24 in so far as is necessary to effect the repeal of, or of words in, sections 389 and 460(1) of the Companies Act 1985, section 196(3) of the Financial Services Act 1986 and section 565(6)(b) of the Income and Corporation Taxes Act 1988 | 1.10.1991 | S.I. 1991/1996 |
| Section 212 and Schedule 24 in so far as is necessary to effect the repeal of, or of words in, sections 169(5), 175(6)(b), 191(1), (3)(a) and (3)(b), 219(1), 288(3), 318(7), 356(1), (2) and (4) and 383(1), (2) and (3) of the Companies Act 1985 and paragraph 25 of Schedule 13 to that Act | 1.11.1991 | S.I. 1991/1996 |

# THE BANK ACCOUNTS DIRECTIVE (MISCELLANEOUS BANKS) REGULATIONS 1991

(SI 1991/2704)

*Made on 1 December 1991 by the Secretary of State for Trade and Industry under s. 2(2) of and Sch. 2, para. 2(2) to the European Communities Act 1972. Operative from 2 December 1991.*

## CITATION, COMMENCEMENT AND EXTENT

**1** These Regulations, which extend to Great Britain, may be cited as the Bank Accounts Directive (Miscellaneous Banks) Regulations 1991 and shall come into force on the day after the day on which they are made.

## INTERPRETATION

**2** In these Regulations–

**"the 1985 Act"** means the Companies Act 1985;

**"accounts"** means the annual accounts, the directors' report and the auditors' report required by Regulation 4(1);

**"director"** includes, in the case of a body which is not a company, any corresponding officer of that body;

**"enactment"** includes any subordinate legislation within the meaning of section 21(1) of the Interpretation Act 1978, other than these Regulations;

**"financial year"**, in relation to a body to which these Regulations apply, means any period in respect of which a profit and loss account of the undertaking is required to be made up by its constitution or by any enactment (whether that period is a year or not) or, failing any such requirement, a period of 12 months beginning on 1st April;

and other expressions shall have the meanings ascribed to them by the 1985 Act.

## SCOPE OF APPLICATION

**3** These Regulations apply to any body of persons, whether incorporated or unincorporated, which:–

(a) is incorporated or formed by or established under any public general Act of Parliament passed before the year 1837;

(b) has a principal place of business within Great Britain;

(c) is an authorised institution within the meaning of the Banking Act 1987; and

(d) is not required by any enactment to prepare accounts under Part VII of the 1985 Act.

## PREPARATION OF ACCOUNTS

**4(1)** The directors of a body of persons to which these Regulations apply shall in respect of each financial year of the body prepare such annual accounts and directors' report, and cause to be prepared such auditors' report, as would be required under Part VII of the 1985 Act if the body were a banking company formed and registered under that Act, subject to the provisions of the Schedule to these Regulations.

**4(2)** The accounts required by paragraph (1) shall be prepared within a period of 7 months beginning immediately after the end of the body's financial year.

## PUBLICATION OF ACCOUNTS

**5(1)** A body of persons to which these Regulations apply shall make available the latest accounts prepared under Regulation 4 for inspection by any person, without charge and during business hours, at the body's principal place of business within Great Britain.

**5(2)** The body shall supply to any person upon request a copy of those accounts (or such part of those accounts as may be requested) at a price not exceeding the administrative cost of making the copy.

**5(3)** Paragraph (2) applies whether the request for a copy is made orally during inspection under paragraph (1) above, by post or otherwise.

**5(4)** The annual accounts prepared under Regulation 4 shall be the body's accounts for the purposes of section 45 of the Banking Act 1987 (Audited accounts to be open to inspection) and the auditors' report prepared under that Regulation shall be the auditors' report on the accounts or report of the auditors for the purposes of that section.

### PENALTIES FOR NON-COMPLIANCE

**6(1)** If the directors of a body of persons to which these Regulations apply fail to prepare, or (in the case of the auditors' report) fail to cause to be prepared, the accounts required by Regulation 4(1) within the period referred to in Regulation 4(2), every person who, immediately before the end of the period referred to in Regulation 4(2), was a director of the body is guilty of an offence and liable on summary conviction to a fine not exceeding the statutory maximum.

**6(2)** If any annual accounts or a directors' report are made available for inspection under Regulation 5 which do not comply with the requirements of Regulation 4(1) as to the matters to be included therein, every person who, at the time the annual accounts or report were first made available for inspection, was a director of the body is guilty of an offence and liable on summary conviction to a fine not exceeding the statutory maximum.

**6(3)** In proceedings against a person for an offence under this Regulation, it is a defence for him to prove that he took all reasonable steps for securing compliance with the requirements in question.

**7(1)** If a body of persons to which these Regulations apply fails to comply with Regulation 5 it is guilty of an offence and liable on summary conviction to a fine not exceeding the statutory maximum.

**7(2)** Sections 733(2) and (3) and 734(1) to (4) and (6) of the 1985 Act shall apply to an offence under paragraph (1) as they do to an offence under section 394A(1) of that Act.

### TRANSITIONAL PROVISIONS

**8(1)** The directors of a body of persons to which these Regulations apply need not prepare accounts in accordance with Regulation 4 with respect to a financial year of the body commencing on a date prior to 23rd December 1992.

**8(2)** Where advantage is taken of paragraph (1), Regulation 5 shall not apply.

## Schedule – Modifications and Adaptations of Part VII of the 1985 Act

Regulation 4

**1** Where a body of persons subject to these Regulations is unincorporated, the accounts shall comply with the requirements of Part VII of the 1985 Act (Accounts and Audit) subject to any necessary modifications to take account of that fact; in particular the accounts shall comply with Part VII of the 1985 Act subject to the provisions of section 259(2) and (3) of that Act.

**2** Accounts prepared under these Regulations shall state they are so prepared.

**3** Accounts prepared under these Regulations shall comply with the provisions of Schedule 4A to the 1985 Act (as modified by Part II of Schedule 9 to that Act) as if paragraphs 13(3) to (5), 14 and 15 were omitted and paragraph 13(6) only required a statement of any adjustments to consolidated reserves.

**4** Accounts prepared under these Regulations shall comply with the provisions of Schedule 5 to the 1985 Act (as modified by Part III of Schedule 9 to that Act) as if paragraphs 4, 5, 10, 18, 19 and 29 were omitted.

**5** Accounts prepared under these Regulations shall comply with the provisions of Schedule 6 to the 1985 Act (as modified by Part IV of Schedule 9 to that Act) as if paragraphs 2 to 6, 8 and 9 were omitted.

**6(1)** Accounts prepared under these Regulations shall comply with paragraph 6 of Schedule 7 to the 1985 Act, but otherwise that Schedule shall not apply to such a body.

**6(2)** Where a body subject to these Regulations has a share capital and may lawfully acquire its own shares, the directors' report of that body shall, in addition to the matters referred to in sub-paragraph (1), state:

(a) the reasons for any acquisition of such shares during the financial year;

(b) the number and nominal value of any such shares acquired during the financial year and the number and nominal value of any such shares disposed of during the financial year, together, in each case, with the percentage of the total issued share capital of the body that they represent;

(c) the value and nature of any consideration given for the acquisition of such shares and the value and nature of any consideration received for the disposal of such shares during the financial year; and

(d) the number and nominal value of all such shares held by the body at the end of the financial year, together with the percentage they represent of the total issued share capital of the body.

**7** Accounts prepared under these Regulations shall comply with the provisions of Part I of Schedule 9 to the 1985 Act subject to the following modifications:

(a) in Section B of Chapter I of that Part, the profit and loss account formats there prescribed shall apply as if item 15 of format 1 and Charges item 9 and Income item 8 of format 2 were omitted; and

(b) in Chapter III of that Part, paragraphs 49, 54, 56, 57, 66(1)(b), 68(1)(b) and (2), 73(2), 74 and 75 shall not apply.

**8** For the purposes of the provisions of Part VII of the 1985 Act as applied by these Regulations, these Regulations shall be regarded as part of the requirements of that Act.

**9** Paragraphs 3 to 7 of this Schedule shall not be construed as affecting the requirement to give a true and fair view under sections 226 and 227 of the 1985 Act, as applied by these Regulations.

## EXPLANATORY NOTE

(*This Note is not part of the Regulations*)

1. These Regulations implement Council Directive 86/635/EEC Official Journal No L372 of 31.12.1986 pages 1–17 on the Annual Accounts and Consolidated Accounts of Banks and Other Financial Institutions, in so far as that Directive is applicable to bodies corporate or unincorporate other than (a) bodies corporate to which Part VII of the Companies Act 1985 ("the 1985 Act") applies and (b) building societies. (The Companies Act 1985 (Bank Accounts) Regulations 1991 (SI 1991/2705) implement Directive 86/635/EEC in respect of bodies corporate to which Part VII of the 1985 Act applies. Separate Regulations will deal with building societies.)

2. The scope of application of the Regulations is set out in Regulation 3. They apply, in effect, to certain institutions authorised under the Banking Act 1987 to carry on a deposit taking business which were incorporated or formed by or under Public General Acts which predate modern legislation governing the legal forms in which business may be carried on.

3. The directors of bodies of persons to which the Regulations apply are required by Regulation 4 to prepare accounts and a directors' report, and to obtain an auditors' report on such accounts, in accordance with the provisions of Part VII of the 1985 Act which are applicable to banking companies and groups, subject to certain modifications set out in the Schedule to the Regulations. The Schedule disapplies requirements of Part VII which do not derive from the European Community Directives on Accounts.

4. Regulation 5 requires the documents prepared under Regulation 4 to be made available for inspection without charge at the body's principal place of business within Great Britain; the documents are also to be those to which section 45 of the Banking Act 1987 applies. That section requires the accounts of an institution authorised under that Act to be open to inspection at any of its branches.

5. Regulations 6 and 7 impose criminal penalties for failure to comply with the Regulations.

6. Regulation 8 permits the directors of a body of persons to which the Regulations apply not to prepare accounts and a directors' report (and obtain an auditors' report on the accounts) under the Regulations for financial years commencing on a date prior to 23rd December 1992. This transitional provision mirrors the transitional provision contained in the Companies Act 1985 (Bank Accounts) Regulations 1991.

# THE COMPANIES ACT 1985 (BANK ACCOUNTS) REGULATIONS 1991

(SI 1991/2705)

*Made on 1 December 1991 by the Secretary of State for Trade and Industry under s. 257 of the Companies Act 1985. Operative from 2 December 1991.*

## CITATION AND INTERPRETATION

**1** These Regulations may be cited as the Companies Act 1985 (Bank Accounts) Regulations 1991 and shall come into force on the day after the day on which they are made.

**2** In these Regulations **"the 1985 Act"** means the Companies Act 1985 and **"the 1989 Act"** means the Companies Act 1989.

## AMENDMENTS OF SECTIONS

**3** [Insertion of new s. 255–255B into Pt. VII of the 1985 Act.]

**4** [Amendment of s. 255C of the 1985 Act.]

## INSERTION OF NEW SCHEDULE

**5(1)** Parts I and II of Schedule 9 to the 1985 Act shall form a new Schedule to that Act numbered "Schedule 9A" and entitled "Special Provisions For Insurance Companies And Groups", which shall be inserted after Schedule 9.

**5(2)** Part III of Schedule 9 to the 1985 Act is repealed.

**5(3)** The following is substituted for the heading of Schedule 9 to the 1985 Act: "Special Provisions For Banking Companies And Groups".

**5(4)** Parts I to III of Schedule 1 to these Regulations (Form and content of accounts of banking companies and groups) are inserted into the 1985 Act as Parts I to III of Schedule 9 to that Act.

## OTHER AMENDMENTS

**6** Part VII of the 1985 Act shall be further amended in accordance with the provisions of Schedule 2 to these Regulations.

**7** The 1985 Act shall be further amended in accordance with the provisions of Schedule 3 to these Regulations, which are consequential on the amendments made by the foregoing Regulations.

**8** In section 32 of the Housing Subsidies Act 1967 (Interpretation), in the definition of "insurance company", the words "Schedule 9A" shall be substituted for the words "Schedule 9".

## TRANSITIONAL PROVISIONS

**9(1)** A company (including any body corporate to which Part VII is applied by any enactment) may, with respect to a financial year of the company commencing on a date prior to 23rd December 1992, prepare such annual accounts as it would have been required to prepare had the modifications to the 1985 Act effected by these Regulations not been made.

**9(2)** The amendments effected by Regulations 3 to 8 above shall, where a company prepares accounts under paragraph (1) of this Regulation, be treated (as regards that company) as not having been made.

# Schedule 1 – Form and Content of Accounts of Banking Companies and Groups

Regulation 5

[**Note:** This schedule sets out the new Pt. I–III of Sch. 9 to the 1985 Act.]

# Schedule 2 – Further Amendments to Part VII of the 1985 Act

Regulation 6

[**Note:** Amendment re s. 254(3), 260(6), 262A of and new Pt. I and II of Sch. 9 and Sch. 10 to the 1985 Act.]

# Schedule 3 – Further (Consequential) Amendments of the Companies Act 1985

Regulation 7

[**Note:** Amendments re Sch. 11 and Sch. 22 to the 1985 Act.]

## EXPLANATORY NOTE

(*This Note is not part of the Regulations*)

1. These Regulations implement Council Directive 86/635/EEC Official Journal N.O. L372 of 31.12.1986, pages 1–17 on the Annual Accounts and Consolidated Accounts of Banks and Other Financial Institutions, in so far as that Directive is applicable to bodies corporate to which Part VII of the Companies Act 1985 ("the 1985 Act") applies.

2. The Regulations firstly amend Schedule 9 to the 1985 Act, which makes special provision for the accounts of banking and insurance companies and groups. The existing Parts I and II of that Schedule are formed by the Regulations into a new Schedule 9A (Regulation 5(1)) and confined in their operation to insurance companies and groups. The existing Part III of Schedule 9 is repealed (Regulation 5(2)). New Parts I to III are inserted into Schedule 9 by Regulation 5(4) and are set out in Parts I to III of Schedule 1 to the Regulations. The new Part I lays down rules governing the content of the individual accounts of banking companies, including prescribed formats to be followed, the valuation rules to be applied and the disclosures to be made in the notes to the accounts. The new Part II adapts the general rules of Part VII of the 1985 Act with respect to the consolidated accounts of a company to the special circumstances of banking groups. The new Part III makes special provision with respect to the disclosures required of banking companies and the parent companies of banking groups in respect of undertakings in which they, or members of their group of companies, have invested.

3. Regulation 3 substitutes new sections 255 to 255B for the existing sections of those numbers in Part VII of the 1985 Act. These sections introduce the new provisions of Schedule 9 and the new Schedule 9A. Inter alia, they define which companies are to prepare group accounts under the special provisions with respect to banking groups.

4. Regulation 4 also amends section 255C of the 1985 Act, which sets out special rules on the content of the directors' report and presently applies to banking and insurance companies and groups, so that for the future it will only apply to insurance companies and groups.

5. Regulations 6 to 8 make further and consequential amendments.

6. Regulation 9 sets out a transitional provision whereby a company may prepare accounts in accordance with the unamended Part VII, as that Part applies to banking companies and groups, rather than under the amended provisions for a financial year commencing prior to 23rd December 1992.

# THE PARTNERSHIPS (UNRESTRICTED SIZE) NO. 8 REGULATIONS 1991

(SI 1991/2729)

*Made on 2 December 1991 by the Secretary of State for Trade and Industry under s. 716(2)(d) and 744 of the Companies Act 1985. Operative from 1 January 1992.*

**1** These Regulations may be cited as the Partnerships (Unrestricted Size) No. 8 Regulations 1991 and shall come into force on 1st January 1992.

**2** Section 716(1) of the Companies Act 1985 does not prohibit the formation for the purpose of carrying on practice as lawyers of a partnership which is a multi-national partnership within the meaning of section 89(9) of the Courts and Legal Services Act 1990.

## EXPLANATORY NOTE

(*This Note is not part of the Regulations*)

Section 716 of the Companies Act 1985 prohibits the formation of partnerships of more than 20 persons. These regulations exempt from that prohibition partnerships formed for the purpose of carrying on practice as lawyers which are multi-national partnerships within the meaning of the Courts and Legal Services Act 1990.

# THE COMPANIES ACT 1989 (COMMENCEMENT NO. 14 AND TRANSITIONAL PROVISION) ORDER 1991

(SI 1991/2945 (C 92))

*Made on 20 December 1991 by the Secretary of State for Trade and Industry under s. 215(2), (3) of the Companies Act 1989.*

**1** This Order may be cited as the Companies Act 1989 (Commencement No. 14 and Transitional Provision) Order 1991.

**2** Sections 1 and 11 in Part I of the Companies Act 1989 shall come into force on 1st July 1992 for the purpose of inserting the new section 242A into Part VII of the Companies Act 1985, subject to the transitional provision set out in article 3 below.

**3(1)** This article applies where –

(a) the requirements of section 242 of the Companies Act 1985 as to the delivering of accounts and reports before the end of the period allowed for so doing have not been complied with before 1st July 1992, and

(b) those requirements have still not been complied with on that date.

**3(2)** In such a case, the period by reference to the length of which the amount of the penalty is determined under section 242A(2) of the Companies Act 1985 shall be deemed to commence on 1st July 1992.

## EXPLANATORY NOTE

(*This Note is not part of the Order*)

This Order brings into force on 1st July 1992 sections 1 and 11 in Part I of the Companies Act 1989 (Company Accounts) for the purpose of inserting a new section 242A (liability to civil penalty for failure to deliver accounts under section 242) into Part VII of the Companies Act 1985.

Article 3 makes transitional provision in cases where the requirements of section 242 of the Companies Act 1985 as to the delivering of accounts and reports have not been complied with before 1st July 1992, and have still not been complied with on that date. In such cases the period by reference to which the amount of the civil penalty is calculated under section 242A(2) is deemed to commence on 1st July 1992.

### NOTE AS TO EARLIER COMMENCEMENT ORDERS

*(This Note is not part of the Order)*

The provisions of the Companies Act 1989 brought into force by Orders made before the making of the Companies Act 1989 (Commencement No. 13) Order 1991 (SI 1991/2173) are set out in a note appended to that Order.

That Order itself brought into force on 1st October 1991 (in so far as they were not already in force) the provisions of sections 160 (duty to give assistance for purposes of default proceedings), 162 (duty to report on completion of default proceedings), 166 (powers of secretary of state to give directions), 167 (application to determine whether default proceedings to be taken) and 184 (indemnity for certain acts etc.) of the Companies Act 1989.

## THE INSIDER DEALING (RECOGNISED STOCK EXCHANGE) ORDER 1992

(SI 1992/451)

*Made on 1 March 1992 by the Secretary of State for Trade and Industry under s. 16(1) and (1A) of the Company Securities (Insider Dealing) Act 1985. Operative from 23 March 1992.*

**1** This Order may be cited as the Insider Dealing (Recognised Stock Exchange) Order 1992 and shall come into force on 23rd March 1992.

**2** The Secretary of State hereby declares the investment exchange known as The London International Financial Futures Exchange (Administration and Management), an unlimited company having a share capital, to be a recognised stock exchange for the purposes of the Company Securities (Insider Dealing) Act 1985.

### EXPLANATORY NOTE

*(This Note is not part of the Order)*

This Order declares the investment exchange known as The London International Financial Futures Exchange (Administration and Management) to be a recognised stock exchange for the purposes of the Company Securities (Insider Dealing) Act 1985 ("the Act"). The exchange administers a market called "The London International Financial Futures and Options Exchange" of "LIFFE". The Act provides, amongst other matters, that it shall be an offence to deal in securities on a recognised stock exchange whilst in possession of unpublished price sensitive information (as defined in section 10) in relation to those securities, or to counsel or procure such dealing.

## THE FINANCIAL MARKETS AND INSOLVENCY (AMENDMENT) REGULATIONS 1992

(SI 1992/716)

*Made on 11 March 1992 by the Secretary of State for Trade and Industry under s. 187(3) of the Companies Act 1989. Operative from 1 May 1992.*

**1** These Regulations may be cited as the Financial Markets and Insolvency (Amendment) Regulations 1992 and shall come into force on 1st May 1992.


bbcl randr3 Mp 4122—bcl98 215a

**2** In Regulation 16(1)(a)(ii) of the Financial Markets and Insolvency Regulations 1991, for the reference to the Financial Services (Clients' Money) Regulations 1987 there shall be substituted a reference to the Financial Services (Client Money) Regulations 1991.

### EXPLANATORY NOTE

(*This Note is not part of the Regulations*)

The Regulations amend the Financial Markets and Insolvency Regulations 1991 to bring up to date the reference to Clients' Money regulations. This does not result in any material change to the arrangements. Regulation 16 of the Financial Markets and Insolvency Regulations 1991 makes provision as to the circumstances in which certain contracts effected by a member or designated non-member of a recognised investment exchange or by a member of a recognised clearing house as principal are to be treated as having been effected in a different capacity from other contracts he has effected as principal.

# THE LIMITED PARTNERSHIPS (UNRESTRICTED SIZE) NO. 3 REGULATIONS 1992

(SI 1992/1027)

*Made on 24 April 1992 by the Secretary of State for Trade and Industry under s. 717(1)(d) and 744 of the Companies Act 1985. Operative from 30 April 1992.*

**1** These Regulations may be cited as the Limited Partnerships (Unrestricted Size) No. 3 Regulations 1992, and shall come into force on 30th April 1992.

**2** So much of the Limited Partnerships Act 1907 as provides that a limited partnership shall not consist of more than twenty persons does not apply to a partnership which is, and is carrying on business as, a member firm of The International Stock Exchange of the United Kingdom and the Republic of Ireland Limited.

### EXPLANATORY NOTE

(*This Note is not part of the Regulations*)

The Limited Partnerships Act 1907 provides that a limited partnership shall not consist of more than 20 persons. These Regulations exempt from that prohibition partnerships which are, and are carrying on business as, member firms of The International Stock Exchange of the United Kingdom and the Republic of Ireland Limited.

# THE PARTNERSHIPS (UNRESTRICTED SIZE) NO. 9 REGULATIONS 1992

(SI 1992/1028)

*Made on 24 April 1992 by the Secretary of State for Trade and Industry under s. 716(2)(d) and 744 of the Companies Act 1985. Operative from 30 April 1992.*

**1** These Regulations may be cited as the Partnerships (Unrestricted Size) No. 9 Regulations 1992, and shall come into force on 30th April 1992.

**2(1)** Section 716(1) of the Companies Act 1985 does not prohibit the formation for the purpose of carrying on business as a member firm of the London Stock Exchange of a partnership consisting of more than 20 persons which is upon formation a member firm of the London Stock Exchange by virtue of succeeding to the business of another partnership which was such a member firm.

**2(2)** In these Regulations, **"the London Stock Exchange"** means The International Stock Exchange of the United Kingdom and the Republic of Ireland Limited.

## EXPLANATORY NOTE

(*This Note is not part of the Regulations*)

Section 716 of the Companies Act 1985 prohibits the formation of partnerships consisting of more than 20 persons. These Regulations exempt from that prohibition any partnership formed for the purpose of carrying on business as a member firm of The International Stock Exchange of the United Kingdom and the Republic of Ireland Limited which is a member firm of that body by virtue of succeeding to the business of another partnership which was also a member firm.

# THE COMPANY AND BUSINESS NAMES (AMENDMENT) REGULATIONS 1992

(SI 1992/1196)

*Made on 19 May 1992 by the Secretary of State for Trade and Industry under s. 29 of the Companies Act 1985 and s. 3 and 6 of the Business Names Act 1985. Operative from 5 and 12 June 1992.*

**1** These Regulations may be cited as the Company and Business Names (Amendment) Regulations 1992 and shall come into force in the case of this regulation and regulation 2(5) on 5th June 1992 and in the case of the remainder of the Regulations on 12th June 1992.

**2** [Amendments to reg. 3 and 4 of and Sch. to the Company and Business Names Regulations 1981.]

**3(1)** Sections 2 and 3 of the Business Names Act 1985 shall not prohibit a person from carrying on any business under a name which includes any word or expression specified for the purposes of those sections by virtue of the amendments made by regulation 2(2) and (3) above to the Company and Business Names Regulations 1981, if–

(a) he carried on that business immediately before 12th June 1992, and

(b) he continues to carry it on under the name which immediately before that day was its lawful business name.

**3(2)** Nor shall sections 2 and 3 of the Business Names Act 1985 prohibit a person to whom a business has been transferred on or after 12th June 1992 from carrying on that business during the period of twelve months beginning with the date of transfer so long as he continues to carry it on under the name which was its lawful business name immediately before that date.

## EXPLANATORY NOTE

(*This Note is not part of the Regulations*)

These Regulations amend the Company and Business Names Regulations 1981 (as amended by the Company and Business Names (Amendment) Regulations 1982) (the "1981 Regulations"). The 1981 Regulations specify certain words and expressions for the purposes of section 26 of the Companies Act 1985 and section 2 of the Business Names Act 1985. Under those sections the Secretary of State's approval is required for the use of such words and expressions in (respectively) a company or a business name.

In relation to certain of the words or expressions so specified, a Government department or other body is specified to which a request has to be made to indicate whether it objects to the use of the word or expression.

These Regulations amend the 1981 Regulations by specifying (regulation 2(2) and (3)) the plural and possessive forms of the words or expressions specified in the Schedule to the 1981 Regulations and by substituting (regulation 2(5)) The Privy Council for the Department of Education and Science as the relevant body which must be requested to give an indication of any objection to the use of the word "University" as part of a company or business name.

These Regulations also amend the Schedule to the 1981 Regulations (regulation 2(4)) by omitting the words "Building Society" from column (1) as words that require the Secretary of State's approval for use as part of a company or business name. Use of such words as part of a company or business name is regulated by section 107 of the Building Societies Act 1986 (c. 53).

The amendments to the 1981 Regulations made by regulation 2(2) and (3) are subject to transitional provisions in regulation 3. These allow the continued use of a business name lawfully used prior to the coming into force of regulation 2(2) and (3) until 12 months after any sale of the business concerned.

# THE TRANSFER OF FUNCTIONS (FINANCIAL SERVICES) ORDER 1992

(SI 1992/1315)

*Made on 4 June 1992 by the Privy Council under s. 1 and 2 of the Ministers of the Crown Act 1975 and s. 2(2) of the European Communities Act 1972. Operative from 7 June 1992.*

## CITATION AND COMMENCEMENT

**1(1)** This Order may be cited as the Transfer of Functions (Financial Services) Order 1992.

**1(2)** This Order shall come into force on 7th June 1992.

## TRANSFER OF FUNCTIONS FROM THE SECRETARY OF STATE TO THE TREASURY

**2(1)** Subject to the following provisions of this Order, the functions of the Secretary of State under–

(a) the Company Securities (Insider Dealing) Act 1985,

(b) the Financial Services Act 1986,

(c) Parts VII (financial markets and insolvency) and IX (transfer of securities) of the Companies Act 1989, and

(d) the Uncertificated Securities Regulations 1992,

are hereby transferred to the Treasury.

**2(2)** The functions of the Secretary of State under the following provisions of the Companies Act 1989 are also hereby transferred to the Treasury–

(a) section 203(3), so far as it concerns the making of an order specifying when the transitional period referred to in that section is to end;

(b) section 206(2) (power to make a delegation order on bringing into force any provision of Part VIII of the Act which amends the Financial Services Act 1986); and

(c) section 215(2), (3) and (4) so far as it relates to the bringing into force of–

(i) any provision of Part VII; or

(ii) any provision of Part VIII of the Act which amends the Financial Services Act 1986.

**2(3)** Subject to the following provisions of this Order, in so far as the Secretary of State retains any functions under Part III of the Companies Act 1985 and the Prevention of Fraud (Investments) Act 1958 (which enactments have been repealed with savings) those functions are also hereby transferred to the Treasury.

**2(4)** In relation to the enactments referred to in paragraph (3) above, references in this Order to the Secretary of State or to the Secretary of State for Trade and Industry include references to the Board of Trade.

## FUNCTIONS RETAINED BY THE SECRETARY OF STATE

**3** The functions of the Secretary of State mentioned in Schedule 1 to this Order are not transferred to the Treasury.

## FUNCTIONS TO BE EXERCISABLE JOINTLY BY THE SECRETARY OF STATE AND THE TREASURY

**4** The functions of the Secretary of State mentioned in Schedule 2 to this Order shall be exercisable by the Secretary of State jointly with the Treasury.

## FUNCTIONS TO BE EXERCISABLE BY THE SECRETARY OF STATE AND THE TREASURY CONCURRENTLY

**5** The functions of the Secretary of State mentioned in Schedule 3 to this Order shall be exercisable by the Secretary of State and the Treasury concurrently.

## FUNCTIONS TRANSFERRED TO DESIGNATED AGENCY

**6(1)** Nothing in this Order affects the exercise (including any exercise concurrently with the Secretary of State) of any function which, before the coming into force of this Order, has been transferred from the Secretary of State to a designated agency by an order (in this Article referred to as a "delegation order") under section 114 of the Financial Services Act 1986 or section 168(2) or section 206(2) of the Companies Act 1989.

**6(2)** Where, before the coming into force of this Order, any function has been so transferred, the powers under section 115 of the Financial Services Act 1986 or section 168(3) of the Companies Act 1989 to make an order resuming that function shall be construed as powers of the Treasury to make an order assuming that function; and references in those sections to the resumption of functions shall be construed accordingly.

**6(3)** The transfer to the Treasury by virtue of this Order of the power to make a delegation order does not affect the operation of any enactment under which such an order may be subject to a reservation that the function which is transferred is to be exercisable concurrently by the Secretary of State.

## BARLOW CLOWES EX GRATIA PAYMENTS SCHEME

**7(1)** The functions of the Secretary of State for Trade and Industry with respect to the Barlow Clowes ex gratia payments scheme are hereby transferred to the Treasury.

**7(2)** In this Order **"the Barlow Clowes ex gratia payments scheme"** means the scheme announced in a statement made in the House of Commons on 19th December 1989 by the Secretary of State for Trade and Industry.

## TRANSFERS OF PROPERTY, RIGHTS AND LIABILITIES

**8** There are hereby transferred–

(a) to the Solicitor for the affairs of Her Majesty's Treasury any property, rights and liabilities to which, immediately before the coming into force of this Order, the Secretary of State for Trade and Industry is entitled or subject in connection with the Barlow Clowes ex gratia payments scheme; and

(b) to the Treasury all other property, rights and liabilities to which, immediately before the coming into force of this Order, the Secretary of State for Trade and Industry is entitled or subject in connection with any functions transferred by this Order.

## DESIGNATION FOR PURPOSES OF EUROPEAN COMMUNITIES ACT 1972

**9** For the purposes of section 2(2) of the European Communities Act 1972, the Treasury is hereby designated (in place of the Secretary of State) in relation to–

(a) matters relating to listing of securities on a stock exchange and information concerning listed securities,

(b) measures relating to open-ended collective investment schemes which have as their purpose investment in transferable securities, with the aim of spreading investment risk of funds raised from the public, and

(c) measures relating to prospectuses on offers of transferable securities to the public,

and in relation to anything supplemental or incidental to those matters or measures.

## SUPPLEMENTARY

**10(1)** The enactments mentioned in Schedule 4 to this Order shall be amended in accordance with that Schedule.

**10(2)** Subject to paragraph (1) above, in any enactment or instrument passed or made before the coming into force of this Order, any reference to the Secretary of State shall be construed, so far as necessary in consequence of any transfers effected by this Order as if it were a reference to the Treasury, to the Secretary of State and the Treasury acting jointly, to the Secretary of State or the Treasury or, as the case may be, to the Solicitor for the affairs of Her Majesty's Treasury.

**10(3)** In this Order **"instrument"** includes (without prejudice to the generality of that expression) regulations, rules, orders, contracts, memoranda and articles of association and other documents.

**10(4)** Any legal proceedings to which the Secretary of State for Trade and Industry or his Department is a party at the coming into force of this Order may–

(a) if they relate to any property, rights and liabilities transferred by Article 8(a) above, be continued by or against the Treasury and the Solicitor for the affairs of Her Majesty's Treasury;

(b) if they relate to any other transfer effected by this Order, be continued by or against the Treasury.

**10(5)** This Order shall not affect the validity of anything done (or having effect as if done) by or in relation to the Secretary of State for Trade and Industry before the coming into force of this Order, and (subject to paragraph (4) above) anything which at that date is in process of being done by or in relation to him may, if it relates to any function or any property, rights and liabilities transferred by this Order, be continued by or in relation to the Treasury.

**10(6)** Anything done (or having effect as if done) by the Secretary of State for Trade and Industry for the purpose of or in connection with anything transferred by this Order which immediately before the coming into force of this Order is in force shall have effect, so far as required for continuing its effect on and after that date, as if done by the Treasury.

# Schedule 1 – Functions Retained by the Secretary of State

Article 3

### THE PREVENTION OF FRAUD (INVESTMENTS) ACT 1958

**1** The function under section 14(8) (consent to prosecutions).

### THE COMPANIES ACT 1985

**2** The functions under sections 65(3)(b) and 77(5)(a) (prescribing manner in which translation to be certified as correct translation).

### THE COMPANY SECURITIES (INSIDER DEALING) ACT 1985

**3** The function under section 8 (punishment of contraventions).

### THE FINANCIAL SERVICES ACT 1986

**4** The functions under section 6 (injunctions and restitution orders).

**5** The function of taking disciplinary action under section 47A (in respect of failure to comply with statements of principle) in so far as the action consists of a function specified in this Schedule.

**6** The function of giving a direction under section 59 (employment of prohibited persons) and associated functions, where the direction would have the effect of prohibiting the employment of an individual in connection with investment business carried on in connection with or for the purpose of insurance business at Lloyd's, being employment by any person who is an exempted person as respects such business.

**Note**

See Note after Sch. 1, para. 26.

See the Contracting Out (Functions in Relation to Insurance) Order 1998 (SI 1998/2842), art. 1, 2, 3 and Sch.1, para. 64(a).

**7** The functions under section 60 (public statements as to person's misconduct) and 61(1) (injunctions) in any case in which those functions are exercisable by virtue of a contravention of a direction of the kind described in paragraph 6 above.

**Note**

See Note after Sch. 1, para. 26.

See the Contracting Out (Functions in Relation to Insurance) Order 1998 (SI 1998/2842), art. 1, 2, 3 and Sch.1, para. 64(a).

**8** The functions under section 61(1)–

(a) with respect to a person who is an exempted person by virtue of section 42 in any case in which the contravention or proposed contravention arises or is likely to arise in the course of investment business as respects which the person is exempt; or

(b) exercisable by virtue of section 61(1)(a)(ii) or (iii) (injunctions relating to contraventions of sections 47, 56, 57 or 59 or of requirements imposed under section 58(3)).

**Note**

See Note after Sch. 1, para. 26.

See the Contracting Out (Functions in Relation to Insurance) Order 1998 (SI 1998/2842), art. 1, 2, 3 and Sch.1, para. 64(a).

**9** The functions under section 61(3) in relation to a contravention of a provision referred to in section 61(1)(a)(ii) or (iii) by a person who neither is, nor has ever been, an authorised person or appointed representative.

**10** The functions under section 61 in relation to a contravention or proposed contravention of section 130.

**Note**

See Note after Sch. 1, para. 26.

See the Contracting Out (Functions in Relation to Insurance) Order 1998 (SI 1998/2842), art. 1, 2, 3 and Sch.1, para. 64(a).

**11** The functions under sections 72 and 73 (winding up orders).

**12** The functions under section 94 (investigations).

**13** The functions under sections 97 to 101 (references to Tribunal) in so far as they arise out of a notice or a copy of a notice which, by virtue of any other paragraph of this Schedule, falls, after the coming into force of this Order, to be served by the Secretary of State.

**14** The functions under section 105 (investigation powers).

**15** The functions under section 106 (exercise of investigative powers by officer etc.).

**16** The functions under section 128B (relevance of information given and action taken by other regulatory authorities) and subsections (1), (4) and (5) of section 128C (enforcement in support of overseas regulatory authority) in so far as they relate to any other function specified in this Schedule.

**17** The function under subsection (3)(c) of section 128C.

**18** The functions under subsections (3) and (4) of section 130 (restriction on promotion of contracts of insurance).

**Note**

See Note after Sch. 1, para. 26.

**19** The functions under section 138 (insurance brokers).

**Note**

See Note after Sch. 1, para. 26.

**20** The functions under subsection (3) of section 148 (exemptions from disclosure) but without prejudice to the existing concurrent power of the Treasury under that subsection.

**21** The functions under subsection (3) of section 165 (exemptions from disclosure) but without prejudice to the existing concurrent power of the Treasury under that subsection).

**22** The functions under sections 177 and 178 (investigations into insider dealing and penalties for failure to co-operate).

**23** In so far as they relate to insurance business which is not also investment business, the functions under–

(a) section 183 (reciprocal facilities for financial business),

(b) section 184 (investment and insurance business), or

(c) section 186 (variation and revocation of notices).

**Note**

See Note after Sch. 1, para. 26.

**24** The functions under section 199 (powers of entry).

**25** The functions under section 201 (prosecutions).

**26** The following functions under Schedule 10 (regulated insurance companies)–

(a) the function under sub-paragraph (2) of paragraph 3 (certification as to requirement in sub-paragraph (1));

(b) the function under paragraph 4(6) of determining (before a delegation order is made transferring functions of making rules and regulations in relation to a regulated insurance company) whether the rules and regulations will take proper account of Part II of the Insurance Companies Act 1982 or, as the case may be, of the provisions for corresponding purposes in the law of the member State in which the company is established;

(c) functions under paragraph 6 (procedure on exercise of powers of intervention);

(d) functions under paragraph 10 (consultation with designated agency).

**Note**

The functions of the Secretary of State mentioned in Sch. 1, para. 6, 7, 8(a), 10, 18, 19, 23 and 26 transferred to the Treasury by the Transfer of Functions (Insurance) Order 1997 (SI 1997/2781), art. 1, 2(2) as from 5 January 1998.

### THE UNCERTIFICATED SECURITIES REGULATIONS 1992

**27** The functions under regulations 26(2) (inspection of registers) and 110 (investigations).

# Schedule 2 – Functions Exercisable Jointly by the Secretary of State and the Treasury

Article 4

### THE FINANCIAL SERVICES ACT 1986

**1** The function of revoking a recognition order in respect of a recognised self-regulating organisation whose members include or may include regulated insurance companies on the ground that–

(a) the requirement specified in paragraph 3(1) of Schedule 10 is not satisfied; or

(b) the organisation has contravened sub-paragraph (3) or (4) of paragraph 6 of that Schedule as applied by sub-paragraph (5) of paragraph 6.

**Note**

See Note after Sch. 2, para. 6.

See the Contracting Out (Functions in Relation to Insurance) Order 1998 (SI 1998/2842), art. 1, 2, 3 and Sch. 1, para. 64(b).

**2** The function of giving a direction under subsection (1) of section 33, where the function–

(a) falls within paragraph (a) of that subsection, and

(b) is made in respect of a regulated insurance company.

**Note**

See Note after Sch. 2, para. 6.

See the Contracting Out (Functions in Relation to Insurance) Order 1998 (SI 1998/2842), art. 1, 2, 3 and Sch. 1, para. 64(b).

**3** The function of taking disciplinary action under section 47A (in respect of failure to comply with statements of principle) in so far as the action consists of a function specified in this Schedule.

**4** In so far as they relate to investment business which is also insurance business, the functions under–

(a) section 183 (reciprocal facilities for financial business),
(b) section 184 (investment and insurance business),
(c) sections 28, 29, 33, 34, 60, 61 and 97 to 101 in relation to a contravention of a partial restriction notice under section 184(4), or
(d) section 186 (variation and revocation of notices).

**Note**

See Note after Sch. 2, para. 6.

**5** The functions under section 128B (relevance of information given and action taken by other regulatory authorities) and subsections (1), (4) and (5) of section 128C (enforcement in support of overseas regulatory authority) in so far as they relate to any other function specified in this Schedule.

**6** In Schedule 10 (regulated insurance companies) the functions under paragraph 8(2) to (5) in so far as they relate to a direction of a description mentioned in paragraph 2 above.

**Note**

The functions mentioned in Sch. 2, para. 1, 2, 4 and 6 as exercisable by the Secretary of State jointly with the Treasury transferred to the Treasury by the Transfer of Functions (Insurance) Order 1997 (SI 1997/2781), art. 1, 2(3) from 5 January 1998.

See the Contracting Out (Functions in Relation to Insurance) Order 1998 (SI 1998/2842), art. 1, 2, 3 and Sch. 1, para. 64(b).

THE COMPANIES ACT 1989

**7(1)** Subject to sub-paragraphs (2) and (3) below, functions under the following provisions of Part VII, namely, sections 158(4) and (5), 160(5), 170 to 174, 176, 181, 185 and 186.

**7(2)** The reference in sub-paragraph (1) above to the functions under section 170 does not include a reference to the function under subsection (1) of that section of approving an overseas investment exchange.

**7(3)** The reference in sub-paragraph (1) above to functions under section 186 is a reference only to so much of the functions under that section as relates to any function under the other enactments specified in sub-paragraph (1) above.

# Schedule 3 – Functions Exercisable Concurrently by the Secretary of State and the Treasury

Article 5

**1** The functions under section 180 and 181 of the Financial Services Act 1986 (restrictions on disclosure).

**2** In Schedule 9 to that Act (designated agency status etc.), the function under paragraph 13 (communication of information).

**3** In section 82 of the Companies Act 1989 (request for assistance by overseas regulatory authority), the function under subsection (3) of being satisfied as to whether assistance requested by an overseas regulatory authority is for the purpose of its regulatory functions.

# Schedule 4 – Modifications of Enactments

Article 10(1)

THE COMPANIES ACT 1985

**1** In section 449(1)(d) of the Companies Act 1985 for the words "Secretary of State to exercise any of his functions" there shall be substituted "Secretary of State or the Treasury to exercise any of their functions".

**2** Section 744 of that Act shall have effect, in relation to any provision of that Act conferring a function transferred to the Treasury by this Order, as if "prescribed" meant prescribed by statutory instrument made by the Treasury.

## THE FINANCIAL SERVICES ACT 1986

**3** In sections 178(10), 199(7) and 201(4) of the Financial Services Act 1986 (which extend the functions to which a delegation order may apply) for the words "Secretary of State", in the last place where they occur in each of those provisions, there shall be substituted "Treasury".

**4** In section 179(3) of that Act, before paragraph (a) there shall be inserted the following paragraph–

"(aa) the Treasury."

**5** In section 180(1) of that Act, after paragraph (b) there shall be inserted the following paragraph–

"(bb) for the purpose of enabling or assisting the Treasury to exercise any of their powers under this Act or under Part III or VII of the Companies Act 1989."

**6** In section 186 of that Act at the end of subsection (7) there shall be inserted " which varies or revokes a notice relating to the carrying on of a deposit-taking business as mentioned in section 185 above".

**7** In section 205 of that Act, after the words "Secretary of State" there shall be inserted "or the Treasury".

**8** In section 205A(1) of that Act, after the words "Secretary of State" there shall be inserted "or the Treasury".

**9** In section 207(1) of that Act, at the end of the definition of "prescribed", there shall be inserted "or the Treasury".

**10** In Schedule 7 to that Act, in paragraph 1(2), for the words "Secretary of State" there shall be substituted "Treasury".

## THE BANKING ACT 1987

**11(1)** In section 84 of the Banking Act 1987, in subsection (1), in the Table, after the entry relating to the Secretary of State there shall be inserted–

"The Treasury Functions under the Financial Services Act 1986 or under Part III or VII of the Companies Act 1989."

**11(2)** In subsection (6)(a)(ii) of that section after the words "Secretary of State" there shall be inserted "or the Treasury".

## THE COMPANIES ACT 1989

**12** In section 87(4) of the Companies Act 1989, in the Table, after the entry relating to the Secretary of State there shall be inserted–

"The Treasury Functions under the Financial Services Act 1986 or under this Part or Part VII of this Act."

**13** In each of the following provisions of Part VII of that Act (which provide for the Secretary of State to consult the Treasury and the Bank of England)–

(a) section 171(6),
(b) section 172(3),
(c) section 173(6),
(d) section 174(5), and
(e) section 176(6),

for the words "shall consult the Treasury and" there shall be substituted "and the Treasury shall consult".

## THE FRIENDLY SOCIETIES ACT 1992

**14** In section 64 of the Friendly Societies Act 1992 after subsection (3) there shall be inserted the following subsection–

"(3A) Nothing in section 63 above prohibits the disclosure of information to the Treasury in circumstances where it is desirable or expedient that the information should be disclosed for the purpose of facilitating the discharge by the Treasury of any functions of theirs under the Financial Services Act 1986 or under Part III or Part VII of the Companies Act 1989 nor does that section prohibit further disclosure of the information by the Treasury with the consent of the Commission."

## EXPLANATORY NOTE

(*This Note is not part of the Order*)

This Order transfers a number of functions currently exercisable by the Secretary of State to the Treasury with effect from 7th June, so as to be exercisable by the Treasury alone, by the Secretary of State and the Treasury acting jointly or by the Secretary of State and the Treasury acting concurrently. It also makes a number of ancillary and supplementary provisions.

The main functions transferred are functions under the Company Securities (Insider Dealing) Act 1985, the Financial Services Act 1986, Parts VII (financial markets and insolvency) and IX (transfer of securities) of the Companies Act 1989, the Uncertificated Securities Regulations 1992 and the Barlow Clowes *ex gratia* payments scheme. The statutory powers are transferred by virtue of Article 2, which is subject to Articles 3 to 5. Article 3 excludes functions specified in Schedule 1 from the transfer so that they remain exercisable by the Secretary of State. The functions that thus remain with the Secretary of State are in the main functions connected with the prudential supervision of insurance undertakings and enforcement (including investigations and prosecutions). Article 4 provides that functions specified in Schedule 2 are to be exercisable by the Secretary of State and the Treasury acting jointly. These joint functions consist, essentially, of certain functions in connection with the prudential supervision of insurance companies and the imposition of restrictions on grounds of reciprocity where investment business which is also insurance business is carried on, together with functions of making secondary legislation under Part VII of the Companies Act 1989 which affects the operation of insolvency law. Article 5 provides that certain minor functions set out in Schedule 3 to the Order are to be exercisable concurrently. The functions under the Barlow Clowes *ex gratia* payments scheme are transferred by Article 7.

To a considerable extent the functions of the Secretary of State under the Financial Services Act 1986 and to a lesser degree under Part VII of the Companies Act 1989 have been transferred, under powers contained in those Acts, in whole or in part to a "designated agency" (at the date of this Order, The Securities and Investments Board) so as to be exercisable by that agency alone or concurrently with the Secretary of State. This Order operates on the functions of the Secretary of State so far as they remain vested in him following those transfers. Article 6 both preserves the effect of those transfers and ensures that the Treasury can assume the powers from the designated agency in circumstances where the Secretary of State would have been entitled to resume them.

Article 9 designates the Treasury as the appropriate authority to make Regulations implementing certain EC Directives in the area of financial services, in place of the Secretary of State.

Articles 8 and 10 (together with Schedule 4) make ancillary and supplemental provision, in particular provision in relation to property rights and liabilities held by the Secretary of State in connection with the functions transferred by the Order and provision enabling enactments and instruments to be interpreted correctly in consequence of the transfers effected by the Order.

# THE PARTNERSHIPS (UNRESTRICTED SIZE) NO. 10 REGULATIONS 1992

(SI 1992/1439)

*Made on 16 June 1992 by the Secretary of State for Trade and Industry under s. 716(2)(d) and 744 of the Companies Act 1985. Operative from 10 July 1992.*

**1** These Regulations may be cited as the Partnerships (Unrestricted Size) No. 10 Regulations 1992 and shall come into force on 10th July 1992.


bbcl randr3 Mp 4132—bcl98 215a

**2** Section 716(1) of the Companies Act 1985 does not prohibit the formation for the purpose of carrying on practice as consulting engineers of a partnership consisting of persons the majority of whom are recognised by The Engineering Council as chartered engineers.

**3** The Partnerships (Unrestricted Size) No. 3 Regulations 1970 are hereby revoked.

## EXPLANATORY NOTE

(*This Note is not part of the Regulations*)

Section 716 of the Companies Act 1985 prohibits the formation of partnerships consisting of more than 20 persons. These Regulations exempt from that prohibition any partnership formed for the purpose of carrying on practice as consulting engineers and consisting of persons the majority of whom are recognised by The Engineering Council as chartered engineers. They replace, and revoke, earlier Regulations (S.I. 1970/992) which provided for an exemption in relation to engineers recognised as chartered engineers by The Engineering Council's predecessor, the Council of Engineering Institutions.

# THE COMPANIES (SINGLE MEMBER PRIVATE LIMITED COMPANIES) REGULATIONS 1992

(SI 1992/1699)

*Made on 14 July 1992 by the Secretary of State for Trade and Industry under s. 2(2) of and para. 2(2) of Sch. 2 to the European Communities Act 1972. Operative from 15 July 1992.*

## CITATION AND COMMENCEMENT

**1** These Regulations may be cited as the Companies (Single Member Private Limited Companies) Regulations 1992 and shall come into force on the day after the day on which they were made.

## SINGLE MEMBER PRIVATE COMPANIES LIMITED BY SHARES OR BY GUARANTEE

**2(1)** Notwithstanding any enactment or rule of law to the contrary, a private company limited by shares or by guarantee within the meaning of section 1 of the Companies Act 1985 may be formed by one person (in so far as permitted by that section as amended by these Regulations) and may have one member; and accordingly–

(a) any enactment or rule of law which applies in relation to a private company limited by shares or by guarantee shall, in the absence of any express provision to the contrary, apply with such modification as may be necessary in relation to such a company which is formed by one person or which has only one person as a member as it does in relation to such a company which is formed by two or more persons or which has two or more persons as members; and

(b) without prejudice to the generality of the foregoing, the Companies Act 1985 and the Insolvency Act 1986 shall have effect with the amendments specified in the Schedule to these Regulations.

**2(2)** In this regulation **"enactment"** shall include an enactment comprised in subordinate legislation and **"subordinate legislation"** shall have the same meaning as in section 21(1) of the Interpretation Act 1978.

## TRANSITIONAL PROVISION

**3** A person who, before the coming into force of these Regulations, is liable by virtue of section 24 of the Companies Act 1985 for the payment of the debts of a private company limited by shares or by guarantee, shall not be so liable for the payment of the company's debts contracted on or after the day on which these Regulations come into force.

## Schedule – Amendments to the Companies Act 1985 and the Insolvency Act 1986

Regulation 2

[The amendments are not reproduced here but see CA 1985, s. 1(3A), 24, 322B, 352A, 370A, 382B, 680(1A), 741(3), Sch. 24 and IA 1986, s. 122(1)(e).]

### EXPLANATORY NOTE

(*This Note is not part of the Regulations*)

1. These Regulations implement Council Directive No. 89/667/EEC on single-member private limited-liability companies (OJ No. L395, 30.12.89, p. 40). The directive requires Member States to provide for the formation of a company having one member and to permit a company to be a single member company, subject to certain safeguards. In relation to the UK, it applies to private companies limited by shares or by guarantee.

2. Regulation 2(1) provides that a private company limited by shares or by guarantee may be formed by one person (in so far as permitted by section 1 of the Companies Act 1985 as amended by the Regulations) and may have one member. It also provides that any enactment or rule of law applying to a private company limited by shares or by guarantee shall, in the absence of any express provision to the contrary, apply with any necessary modification to such a company which has been formed by one person or which has only one member.

3. Without prejudice to the generality of Regulation 2(1), Regulation 2(2) also makes specific amendments to the Companies Act 1985 and the Insolvency Act 1986 as set out in the Schedule to the Regulations. The following sections of the Companies Act 1985 are amended: section 1 (mode of forming an incorporated company), section 24 (minimum membership for carrying on business) and section 680 (companies capable of being registered under Chapter II of Part XXII). The following new provisions are inserted into the Companies Act 1985: section 322B (contracts with sole members who are directors), section 352A (statement that company has only one member), section 370A (quorum at meetings of the sole member) and section 382B (recording of decisions by the sole member). Consequential amendments are made to section 741 of the Companies Act 1985 and to Schedule 24 to that Act. Section 122 of the Insolvency Act 1986 (circumstances in which company may be would up by the court) is also amended.

4. Regulation 3 contains a transitional provision.

# THE COMPANIES ACT 1985 (ACCOUNTS OF SMALL AND MEDIUM-SIZED ENTERPRISES AND PUBLICATION OF ACCOUNTS IN ECUs) REGULATIONS 1992

(SI 1992/2452)

*Made on 15 October 1992 by the Secretary of State for Trade and Industry under s. 257 of the Companies Act 1985. Operative from 16 November 1992.*

### CITATION AND INTERPRETATION

**1** These Regulations may be cited as the Companies Act 1985 (Accounts of Small and Medium-Sized Enterprises and Publication of Accounts in ECUs) Regulations 1992 and shall come into force on 16th November 1992.

**2** In these Regulations "**the 1985 Act**" means the Companies Act 1985.

### DELIVERY AND PUBLICATION OF ACCOUNTS IN ECUS

**3** [Insertion of s. 242B into 1985 Act.]

## MODIFICATIONS OF PART VII OF THE 1985 ACT WITH RESPECT TO SMALL AND MEDIUM-SIZED COMPANIES AND GROUPS

**4(1), (2)** [Modifications to s. 246 of 1985 Act.]

**4(3)** Schedule 8 to the 1985 Act is modified in accordance with the provisions of the Schedule to these Regulations.

**5** [Modifications to s. 247 of 1985 Act.]

**6** [Modifications to s. 249 of 1985 Act.]

## TRANSITIONAL PROVISIONS

**7(1)** These Regulations shall apply to annual accounts in respect of financial years ending on or after the date of coming into force of these Regulations, and to directors' and auditors' reports on those accounts.

**7(2)** In determining under section 247 or 249 of the 1985 Act whether a company or group qualifies as small or medium-sized in relation to financial years subsequent to its first financial year which end on or after the date of coming into force of these Regulations:

(a) the company or group shall be treated as having qualified as small or medium-sized (as the case may be) in each previous financial year ending on or after 9th November 1990 in which it would have so qualified under section 247(3) or 249(3) as amended by these Regulations; and

(b) the company or group shall be treated as having qualified as small or medium-sized in any such financial year if they would have been so entitled had the company or group had the qualification it is treated as having had under sub-paragraph (a) above.

# Schedule – Modifications of Schedule 8

Regulation 4(3)

## REORGANISATION OF THE SCHEDULE

**1(1)** Parts I, II and III of Schedule 8 shall become, respectively, Section A, Section B and Section C of Part III of Schedule 8.

**1(2)** Paragraphs 1 to 10 of Schedule 8, as modified by paragraph 4 below, shall be renumbered as paragraphs 17 to 26 of Schedule 8.

**1(3)** The provisions set out in paragraph 2 below shall be inserted in Schedule 8 as a new Part I.

**1(4)** The provisions set out in paragraph 3 below shall be inserted in Schedule 8 as a new Part II.

**1(5)** The following shall be inserted in Schedule 8, immediately after the new Part II–

[Pt. III not reproduced here.]

## THE NEW PART I

**2** The following shall be inserted in Schedule 8, immediately after the heading, as Part I of that Schedule–

[Pt. I not reproduced here.]

## THE NEW PART II

**3** The following shall be inserted in Schedule 8 as Part II immediately after the Part inserted by paragraph 2 above–

[Pt. II not reproduced here.]

## THE MODIFICATIONS REFERRED TO IN PARAGRAPH 1(2)

**4(1)** Paragraphs 1 to 10 of Schedule 8 shall be modified as follows.

**4(2)** In paragraph 3(1) for the words "paragraph 48(1) and (4)" there shall be substituted the words "paragraph 48(1) and (4)(a)".

**4(3)** After paragraph 3(3) there shall be inserted the following sub-paragraph–

"(4) The information required by section 390A(3) (amount of auditors' remuneration) need not be given.".

**4(4)** In paragraphs 7(1), 8(1) and 10(1), for the words "Part I or II" there shall be substituted in each case the words "Section A or Section B of this Part".

**4(5)** In paragraph 7(1)(a), for the words "Part I or, as the case may be, Part II" there shall be substituted the words "Section A or, as the case may be, Section B of this Part".

**4(6)** In paragraph 7(2), there shall be inserted at the end "or, where section 246(1A) applies, immediately above the statements required by that section".

**4(7)** In paragraph 9, for the words "Paragraphs 7 and 8" there shall be substituted the words "Paragraphs 23 and 24".

**4(8)** In paragraph 10(2) and (3), for the words "this Schedule", wherever they occur, there shall be substituted the words "this Part of this Schedule".

## EXPLANATORY NOTE

*(This Note is not part of the Regulations)*

1. These Regulations implement Council Directive 90/604/EEC (OJ No L317, 16.11.1990, pages 57 to 59) which amends Directive 78/660/EEC on annual accounts (OJ No. L222, 14.8.1978, pages 11 to 31) (the Fourth EC Company Law Directive) and Directive 83/349/EEC on consolidated accounts (OJ No. L193, 18.7.1983, pages 1 to 17) (the Seventh EC Company Law Directive) as concerns the exemptions for small and medium-sized companies and the publication of accounts in ECUs. It also takes advantage of some existing Member State options in Directive 78/660/EEC on annual accounts and makes some minor amendments to Part VII of the Companies Act 1985 (Accounts and Audit).

2. Regulation 3 permits delivery to the registrar of companies and publication of accounts translated into European Currency Units (ECUs).

3. Regulation 4 and the Schedule to the Regulations modify the requirements of Part VII of the Companies Act 1985 and Schedule 8 to that Act (Exemptions for small and medium-sized companies) in respect of the content of the annual accounts and directors' reports of small companies. These exemptions apply not only to the individual accounts of such companies but also to the group accounts where a small company prepares them. After the application of all the exemptions conferred by paragraph 3 of the Schedule, the individual balance sheet, of a small company which adopts format 1 would be as follows:

*Format 1*

A. Called up share capital not paid

B. Fixed assets

I Intangible assets

1. Goodwill
2. Other tangible assets

II Tangible assets

1. Land and buildings
2. Plant and machinery etc.

III Investments

1. Shares in group undertakings and participating interests
2. Loans to group undertakings in which the company has a participating interest
3. Other investments other than loans
4. Others

C. Current Assets

I Stocks

1. Stocks

2. Payments on account

II Debtors

1. Trade debtors
2. Amounts owed by group undertakings and undertakings in which the company has a participating interest
3. Others

III Investments

(1) Shares in group undertakings
2. Other investments

IV Cash at bank and in hand

D. Prepayments and accrued income

E. Creditors: amounts falling due within one year

1. Bank loans and overdrafts
2. Trade creditors
3. Amounts owed to group undertakings and undertakings in which the company has a participating interest
4. Other creditors

F. Net current assets (liabilities)

G. Total assets less current liabilities

H. Creditors: amounts falling due after more than one year

1. Bank loans and overdrafts
2. Trade creditors
3. Amounts owed to group undertakings and undertakings in which the company has a participating interest
4. Other creditors

I. Provisions for liabilities and charges

J. Accruals and deferred income

K. Capital and reserves

I Called up share capital

II Share premium account

III Revaluation reserve

IV Other reserves

V Profit and loss account

4. Regulations 5 and 6 raise the thresholds contained in sections 247 and 249 of the Companies Act 1985 for the exemptions applicable to small and medium-sized companies and groups.

5. Regulation 7 contains transitional provisions. Regulation 7(1) provides for the Regulations to apply to accounts for financial years ending on or after the date of coming into force of the Regulations. Regulation 7(2) makes transitional provision to enable companies to take early advantage of the new thresholds for small and medium-sized companies.

6. The Regulations also correct two minor defects in the Companies Act 1985. Regulations 5(2) and 6(2) correct the position whereby certain small and medium-sized companies were technically precluded from filing abbreviated accounts with the registrar of companies. Paragraph 4(3) of the Schedule to the Regulations restores the exemption for small companies from the requirement to disclose the auditors' remuneration in the abbreviated accounts they may deliver to the registrar of companies. This exemption was inadvertently removed by the Companies Act 1989.

# THE COMPANIES (FEES) (AMENDMENT) REGULATIONS 1992

(SI 1992/2876)

*Made on 17 November 1992 by the Secretary of State for Trade and Industry under s. 708 of the Companies Act 1985. Operative from 1 January 1993.*

**1** These Regulations may be cited as the Companies (Fees) (Regulations 1992, and shall come into force on the 1st January 1993.

**2** In these Regulations, "**the 1991 Regulations**" means the Companies (Fees) Regulations 1991.

**3** [Amendments to reg. 2 of 1991 Regulations.]

**4** [Amendments to Sch. of 1991 Regulations.]

**5(1)** The fee prescribed in entry 1A of the Schedule to the 1991 Regulations (as inserted by regulation 4(a) above) shall not be payable in respect of the registration of a branch of an oversea company under paragraph 1 of Schedule 21A to the Companies Act 1985 where:

(a) the particulars required by paragraph 1 have been delivered to the registrar prior to 1 July 1993; and

(b) that company was registered in the same part of Great Britain immediately prior to 1 January 1993.

**5(2)** For the purpose of paragraph (1)(b) above, an oversea company is a registered company if it has duly delivered documents under section 691 to the registrar for that part of Great Britain in which it has established its place of business, and has not given notice to him under section 696(4) that it has ceased to have an established place of business in that part of Great Britain.

## EXPLANATORY NOTE

(*This Note is not part of the Regulations*)

These Regulations amend the Companies (Fees) Regulations 1991, following amendments to the Companies Act 1985 to be introduced by the Oversea Companies and Credit and Financial Institutions (Branch Disclosure) Regulations 1992 (SI 1992/3179) , which create a new regime for the registration of branches of oversea companies. The amendments to these Regulations will take effect from 1st January 1993 which is at the same time as the amendments to the 1985 Act introduced by SI 1992/3179.

*Regulation 3* makes a number of amendments to the definitions in the 1991 Regulations. The purpose of the amendments is to take account of the fact that, as a result of the 1992 Regulations, the registrar of companies will be receiving and recording, under the Companies Acts, documents and particulars relating to particular branches of oversea companies and to entities which are undertakings but not necessarily companies (for example partnerships).

*Regulation 4* amends the Schedule to the 1991 Regulations by introducing certain new fees payable in respect of oversea companies and (by use of the new definitions introduced by regulation 2) extends existing fees so as to cover branches and undertakings.

A new fee of £50.00 in respect of registering a place of business or a branch of an oversea company is introduced. No fee shall be payable, however, in respect of the registration of a branch of an oversea company prior to 1st July 1993 where that company had a place of business registered in the same part of Great Britain immediately prior to 1st January 1993 (*Regulation 5*).

A new fee of £50.00 is also prescribed in respect of registration or re-registration of a name under which an oversea company proposes carrying on business in Great Britain.

Given the new register of branches of oversea companies will be kept in computerised form, for inspection of information on the register of a branch of an oversea company via the registrar's computer a new fee of £1.00 is payable. For obtaining paper copies of information obtained from such an inquiry, a further fee of 50p per screen of information is payable.

The existing Schedule of fees prescribed in respect of searching and obtaining information about a company is amended to include branches of an oversea company and undertakings in general. The fee for registration of the accounts of an oversea company is consequentially amended so as to extend to any accounts registered by a company or other undertaking under Part II of Chapter XXIII of the Companies Act 1985.

# THE COMPANIES ACT 1985 (AMENDMENT OF SECTIONS 250 AND 251) REGULATIONS 1992

(SI 1992/3003)

*Made on 2 December 1992 by the Secretary of State for Trade and Industry under s. 257 of the Companies Act 1985. Operative from 4 and 31 December 1992.*

## CITATION

**1** These Regulations may be cited as the Companies Act 1985 (Amendment of Sections 250 and 251) Regulations 1992 and shall come into force in the case of this regulation and regulation 3 on 4th December 1992 and in the case of regulation 2 on 31st December 1992.

## AMENDMENT OF SECTION 250

**2** [Omission and substitution in s. 250(1).]

## AMENDMENT OF SECTION 251

**3** [Insertions and substitutions in s. 251(1), (2), (7).]

## EXPLANATORY NOTE

(*This Note is not part of the Regulations*)

These Regulations amend sections 250 and 251 of the Companies Act 1985.

Section 250 enables a private company which is dormant, subject to certain conditions, to exempt itself by special resolution from the audit requirements of Part VII of the 1985 Act. Regulation 2 amends section 250(1) by removing the references in that subsection to general meetings of the company at which annual accounts are laid. Under section 250(1)(a) as amended the special resolution required by the section can be passed at any time, provided that the company has been dormant from the time of its formation. Under section 250(1)(b) as amended the special resolution must be passed after copies of the annual accounts and reports for the previous financial year have been sent out under section 238 of the 1985 Act.

Section 251 permits certain public companies to send out summary financial statements to members of the company instead of the full accounts and reports where the requirements of regulations made under the section are satisfied. Regulation 3 of these Regulations extends the scope of section 251 so that it applies not only to public companies whose shares, or any class of whose shares, are listed on the International Stock Exchange of the United Kingdom and the Republic of Ireland Limited, but also to public companies whose debentures, or any class of whose debentures, are so listed. The scope of section 251 is also extended so that that section and any regulations made under it apply not only to the members of a company but to any person entitled under section 238 to receive copies of a company's accounts and reports.

Finally, regulation 3(4)(b) amends section 251(2) to enable regulations to be made as to the ascertainment of the wishes of persons regarding the receipt of full accounts and reports before they become entitled persons (as defined).

# THE COMPANIES (FORMS) (AMENDMENT) REGULATIONS 1992

(SI 1992/3006)

*Made on 20 November 1992 by the Secretary of State for Trade and Industry under the enactments specified in Sch. 1 to the Regulations. Operative from 1 January 1993.*

**1** These Regulations may be cited as the Companies (Forms) (Amendment) Regulations 1992, and shall come into force on 1st January 1993.

**2** In these Regulations–

**"the Act"** means the Companies Act 1985;

**"the 1985 Regulations"** means the Companies (Forms) Regulations 1985.

**3** For the purpose of paragraphs 5(b), 6(1)(b) and 7(1) of Schedule 21A, paragraphs 2(b), 3(b) and 12(2) of Schedule 21C, and paragraphs 2(4) and 10(2) of Schedule 21D to the Act, a translation of a document into English shall be certified to be a correct translation–

(a) if the translation was made in the United Kingdom, by–

(i) a notary public in any part of the United Kingdom;

(ii) a solicitor (if the translation was made in Scotland), a solicitor of the Supreme Court of Judicature of England and Wales (if it was made in England or Wales), or a solicitor of the Supreme Court of Judicature of Northern Ireland (if it was made in Northern Ireland); or

(iii) a person certified by a person mentioned in sub-paragraphs (i) and (ii) above to be known to him to be competent to translate the document into English; or

(b) if the translation was made outside the United Kingdom, by–

(i) a notary public;

(ii) a person authorised in the place where the translation was made to administer an oath;

(iii) any of the British officials mentioned in section 6 of the Commissioner for Oaths Act 1889; or

(iv) a person certified by a person mentioned in sub-paragraphs (i) to (iii) above to be known to him to be competent to translate the document into English.

**4(1)** The forms set out in Schedule 2, with such variation as circumstances require, are the forms prescribed for the purpose of the provisions of the 1985 Act which are referred to in those forms.

**4(2)** The particulars contained in the forms listed in Schedule 3 are the particulars prescribed for the purpose of the provisions of the Act which are referred to in those forms.

**5(1)** Forms 691, 694(a) and 694(b) in Schedule 3 to the 1985 Regulations are revoked except to the extent specified in paragraph (2) below.

**5(2)** Notwithstanding paragraph (1) above or regulation 4(1), Forms 691 in Schedule 3 to the 1985 Regulations may continue to be used in relation to a return and declaration delivered for registration of a place of business of an oversea company made before 1st January 1994.

**5(3)** Notwithstanding paragraph (1) or regulation 4(1), Forms 694(a) and 694(b) in Schedule 3 to the 1985 Regulations may continue to be used in relation to a return of a statement of name under which an oversea company proposes to carry on business in Great Britain made before 1st January 1994.

# Schedule 1

The Companies Act 1985–

sections 691; 694(4)(a) and (b); 703P(1), (3) and (5); 703Q(1) and (2); and 744.
Schedule 21A, paragraphs 1(1), 7(1) and 8(2).

# Schedule 2 – Prescribed Forms

Regulation 4(1)

**Note**
This schedule sets out the following prescribed forms referred to in reg. 4(1) above – forms 691, 694(4)(a), 694(4)(b), 703P(1), 703P(3), 703P(5), 703Q(1), 703Q(2), BR1, BR2, BR3, BR4, BR5, BR6, BR7. They are not reproduced here.

# Schedule 3 – Prescribed Particulars in Prescribed Forms

Regulation 4(2)

Forms BR2; BR3; BR4; BR5; and BR6.

## EXPLANATORY NOTE

*(This Note is not part of the Regulations)*

These Regulations prescribe forms to be used in filing particulars with the registrar of companies in connection with the new regime for the registration of branches of oversea companies, introduced by the Oversea Companies and Credit and Financial Institutions (Branch Disclosure) Regulations 1992 (SI 1992/3179).

They also prescribe amended forms (Forms 691, 694(4)(a) and 694(4)(b)) in connection with the registration of a place of business of an oversea company pursuant to section 691, and the registration of names of oversea companies. There is, however, a transitional provision permitting the continued use of the existing forms for a period of 12 months following the commencement of these Regulations.

The Regulations also provide how certain translations of documents, required to be filed with the registrar of companies in respect of the branches of oversea companies, are to be certified.

# THE COMPANIES ACT 1985 (DISCLOSURE OF BRANCHES AND BANK ACCOUNTS) REGULATIONS 1992

(SI 1992/3178)

*Made on 13 December 1992 by the Secretary of State for Trade and Industry under s. 257 of the Companies Act 1985. Operative from 1 January 1993.*

## CITATION AND INTERPRETATION

**1** These Regulations may be cited as the Companies Act 1985 (Disclosure of Branches and Bank Accounts) Regulations 1992 and shall come into force on 1st January 1993.

**2** In these Regulations **"the 1985 Act"** means the Companies Act 1985.

## AMENDMENTS OF THE 1985 ACT

### DISCLOSURE OF BRANCHES

**3** [Omission in para. 6(b) and insertion of para. 6(d) in Sch. 7 to 1985 Act.]

### OTHER AMENDMENTS

**4–7** [Amendments to s. 228, 255A, 255B and 262 of 1985 Act.]

## TRANSITIONAL PROVISIONS

**8** The directors of a company (including a body corporate, or unincorporated body of persons, to which part VII of the 1985 Act is applied by virtue of any enactment, including any subordinate legislation within the meaning of section 21 of the Interpretation Act 1978:

(a) need not comply with paragraph 6(d) of Schedule 7 to the 1985 Act (as inserted by regulation 3) in preparing a directors' report under section 234 of that Act for a financial year of the company commencing on a date prior to 1st January 1993; and

(b) may prepare annual accounts under Part VII of the 1985 Act for a financial year of the company commencing on a date prior to 23rd December 1992 as if the amendments to sections 255A, 255B and 262 of the 1985 Act effected by regulations 5, 6 and 7 had not been made.

## EXPLANATORY NOTE

(*This Note is not part of the Regulations*)

1. The principal purpose of these Regulations is to implement Article 11 of the Eleventh Company Law Directive 89/666/EEC (OJ No. L395 30.12.89, pp. 36–39). In accordance with that provision, Regulation 3 amends Schedule 7 to the Companies Act 1985, which deal with the content of the directors' report which accompanies a company's annual accounts, by inserting into paragraph 6 an additional requirement, sub-paragraph (d), that the directors' report of a company (unless it is an unlimited company) contain an indication of the existence of any branches of the company outside the United Kingdom.

2. Regulation 4 makes a minor amendment to section 228 of the Companies Act 1985 so as to clarify that group accounts drawn up in accordance with the Seventh Directive as applied by the Bank Accounts Directive (86/635/EEC, OJ No. L372 31.12.1986 pp 1–17) are acceptable for the purposes of the exemption conferred (subject to conditions) by that section from the requirement to prepare group accounts if the company is consolidated in the group accounts of an EC company.

3. Regulations 5 and 6 make two minor amendments to the special provisions of Part VII of the Companies Act 1985 applicable to the accounts of banking companies and groups, to align more closely those provisions with the Bank Accounts Directive.

4. Regulation 7 substitutes a new definition of "credit institution" into section 262 of the Companies Act 1985, reflecting the new definition to be introduced into Part XXIII of that Act by the Oversea Companies and Credit and Financial Institutions (Branch Disclosure) Regulations 1992 (SI 1992/3179).

5. Regulation 8 sets out transitional arrangements.

# THE OVERSEA COMPANIES AND CREDIT AND FINANCIAL INSTITUTIONS (BRANCH DISCLOSURE) REGULATIONS 1992

(SI 1992/3179)

*Made on 13 December 1992 by the Secretary of State for Trade and Industry under s. 2(2) of and para. 2(2) of Sch. 2 to the European Communities Act 1972. Operative from 1 January 1993.*

## CITATION ETC.

**1(1)** These Regulations may be cited as the Oversea Companies and Credit and Financial Institutions (Branch Disclosure) Regulations 1992.

**1(2)** In these Regulations, **"the principal Act"** means the Companies Act 1985 and **"the 1989 Act"** means the Companies Act 1989.

**1(3)** These Regulations shall come into force on 1st January 1993.

**1(4)** These Regulations extend to England and Wales and Scotland.

## IMPLEMENTATION OF THE BANK BRANCHES DIRECTIVE

**2** [Insertion of new s. 699A, 699B and Sch. 21C in principal Act.]

## IMPLEMENTATION OF THE ELEVENTH COMPANY LAW DIRECTIVE

**3** [Amendments in Pt. XXIII of principal Act, insertion of new s. 705A in principal Act.]

## CONSEQUENTIAL AMENDMENTS

**4** Schedule 3 to these Regulations (consequential amendments) shall have effect.

TRANSITION

**5** Schedule 4 to these Regulations (transitional provisions) shall have effect.

# Schedule 1 – Delivery of Reports and Accounts: Credit and Financial Institutions to which the Bank Branches Directive (89/117/EEC) Applies

Regulation 2

**Note**

New Sch. 21C to principal Act not reproduced here.

# Schedule 2 – Amendments of Part XXIII of the Principal Act

Regulation 3

**Note**

These amendments are not reproduced here – see Pt. XXIII of principal Act including Sch. 21A, 21B and 21D.

# Schedule 3 – Consequential Amendments

Regulation 4

**Note**

Amendments not reproduced here – those relevant have been incorporated elsewhere.

# Schedule 4 – Transitional Provisions

Regulation 5

BRANCH REGISTRATION

**1(1)** This paragraph applies to any limited company incorporated outside the United Kingdom and Gibraltar which, immediately after 31st December 1992, has a branch in England and Wales which it had there immediately before 1st January 1993.

**1(2)** A company to which this paragraph applies shall be treated for the purposes of paragraph 1(1) of Schedule 21A to the principal Act as having opened on 1st January 1993 any branch which it has in England and Wales immediately after 31st December 1992 and had there immediately before 1st January 1993.

**1(3)** Where a company to which this paragraph applies was a registered oversea company in relation to England and Wales immediately before 1st January 1993, paragraph 1(1) of Schedule 21A to the principal Act shall have effect, in its application by virtue of sub-paragraph (2) above, with the substitution for "one month" of "six months".

**1(4)** For the purposes of sub-paragraph (3) above, a company is a registered oversea company in relation to England and Wales if it has duly delivered documents to the registrar for England and Wales under section 691 of the principal Act and has not subsequently given notice to him under section 696(4) of that Act that it has ceased to have an established place of business there.

**1(5)** Subject to sub-paragraph (6), sections 691 and 692 of the principal Act shall, in relation to England and Wales, continue to apply to a company to which this paragraph applies (notwithstanding section 690B of that Act) until such time as it has–

(a) complied with paragraph 1 of Schedule 21A to the principal Act in respect of a branch in England and Wales, or

(b) ceased to have a branch there.

**1(6)** Sections 691 and 692 of the principal Act shall not however apply to any company to which this paragraph applies, if the company had no place of business in England and Wales immediately prior to 1st December 1992.

**1(7)** This paragraph shall also apply with the substitution for references to England and Wales of references to Scotland.

**1(8)** For the purposes of this paragraph "branch" has the same meaning as in section 698(2) of the principal Act and whether a branch is in England and Wales or Scotland is to be determined in accordance with that section.

**2(1)** This paragraph applies to any limited company incorporated outside the United Kingdom and Gibraltar which–

(a) has an established place of business in England and Wales both immediately before 1st January 1993 and immediately after 31st December 1992, and

(b) does not have a branch there immediately after 31st December 1992.

**2(2)** Where, immediately after 31st December 1992, a company to which this paragraph applies has a branch elsewhere in the United Kingdom, sections 691 and 692 of the principal Act shall, in relation to England and Wales, continue to apply to the company (notwithstanding section 690B of that Act) until such time as it gives the registrar for England and Wales notice of the fact that it is a company to which section 690A applies.

**2(3)** In sub-paragraph (2) above, **"registrar"** has the same meaning as in the principal Act.

**2(4)** This paragraph shall also apply with the substitution for references to England and Wales of references to Scotland.

**2(5)** For the purposes of this paragraph **"branch"** has the same meaning as in section 698(2) of the principal Act and whether a branch is in England and Wales or Scotland or Northern Ireland is to be determined in accordance with that section.

**3(1)** Where–

(a) a company to which paragraph 1 above applies delivers a return under paragraph 1(1) of Schedule 21A to the principal Act in respect of a branch in England and Wales or Scotland,

(b) the return is the first which the company has delivered under that provision in respect of a branch in that part of Great Britain,

(c) immediately before delivering the return, the company was a registered oversea company in relation to that part of Great Britain, and

(d) the company states in the return that the particulars have previously been delivered in respect of a place of business of the company in that part, giving the company's registered number,

the documents previously registered under section 691(1)(a) of that Act shall be treated as registered under paragraph 1 of Schedule 21A to that Act in respect of the branch to which the return relates.

**3(2)** For the purposes of this paragraph, a company is a registered oversea company in relation to England and Wales or Scotland if–

(a) it has duly delivered documents to the registrar for that part of Great Britain under section 691 of the principal Act,

(b) it has duly complied with any obligation to make a return to that registrar under section 692(1)(a) of that Act, and

(c) it has not subsequently given notice to that registrar under section 696(4) of that Act that it has ceased to have an established place of business in that part.

**3(3)** For the purposes of this paragraph **"branch"** has the same meaning as in section 698(2) of the principal Act.

## DELIVERY OF ACCOUNTS AND REPORTS: INSTITUTIONS AND COMPANIES PREVIOUSLY SUBJECT TO SECTION 700

**4(1)** This paragraph applies to any company which–

(a) immediately after 31st December 1992, is an institution to which Part I of Schedule 21C to the principal Act applies, and

(b) immediately before 1st January 1993, was a company to which section 700 of that Act applies.

**4(2)** Notwithstanding section 699B of the principal Act, sections 700 to 703 of that Act shall continue to apply in relation to any financial year of a company to which this paragraph applies beginning before 1st January 1993.

**4(3)** Schedule 21C to the principal Act shall only have effect to require a company to which this paragraph applies to deliver accounting documents for registration if they have been prepared with reference to a period ending after the end of the last financial year of the company in relation to which sections 700 to 703 of that Act apply.

**4(4)** In this paragraph, **"financial year"** has the same meaning as in section 700 of the principal Act.

**5(1)** This paragraph applies to any company which–

(a) immediately after 31st December 1992, is an institution to which Part II of Schedule 21C to the principal Act applies, and

(b) immediately before 1st January 1993, was a company to which section 700 of that Act applies.

**5(2)** Paragraphs 10 and 12(1) of Schedule 21C to the principal Act shall have effect, in relation to any company to which this paragraph applies, with the insertion after "each financial year of the institution" of "ending after 31st December 1992".

**5(3)** Any date which, immediately before 1st January 1993, is established for the purposes of sections 224 and 225 of the principal Act, as applied by section 701 of that Act, as the accounting reference date of a company to which this paragraph applies shall, immediately after 31st December 1992, be treated as established as the accounting reference date of the company for the purposes of those sections, as applied by paragraph 11 of Schedule 21C to that Act.

**5(4)** In their application to a company to which this paragraph applies, paragraphs 11(a) and 13(2) of Schedule 21C to the principal Act shall have effect with the substitution for "becoming an institution to which this Part of this Schedule applies" of "establishing a place of business in Great Britain".

**6(1)** This paragraph applies to any company which–

(a) immediately after 31st December 1992, is a company to which Part I of Schedule 21D to the principal Act applies, and

(b) immediately before 1st January 1993, was a company to which Chapter II of Part XXIII of that Act applies.

**6(2)** Notwithstanding section 699B of the principal Act, sections 700 to 703 of that Act shall continue to apply in relation to any financial year of a company to which this paragraph applies beginning before 1st January 1993.

**6(3)** Schedule 21D to the principal Act shall only have effect to require a company to which this paragraph applies to deliver accounting documents for registration if they have been prepared with reference to a period ending after the end of the last financial year of the company in relation to which sections 700 to 703 of that Act apply.

**6(4)** In this paragraph, **"financial year"** has the same meaning as in section 700 of the principal Act.

**7(1)** This paragraph applies to any company which–

(a) immediately after 31st December 1992, is a company to which Part II of Schedule 21D to the principal Act applies, and

(b) immediately before 1st January 1993, was a company to which section 700 of that Act applies.

**7(2)** Paragraphs 8 and 10(1) of Schedule 21D to the principal Act shall have effect, in relation to a company to which this paragraph applies, with the insertion after "each financial year of the company" of "ending after 31st December 1992".

**7(3)** Any date which, immediately before 1st January 1993, is established for the purposes of sections 224 and 225 of the principal Act, as applied by section 701 of that Act, as the accounting reference date of a company to which this paragraph applies shall, immediately after 31st December 1992, be treated as established as the accounting reference date of the company for the purposes of those sections, as applied by paragraph 9 of Schedule 21D to that Act.

**7(4)** In its application to a company to which this paragraph applies, paragraphs 9(a) and 12(2) of Schedule 21D to the principal Act shall have effect with the substitution for "becoming a company to which this Part of this Schedule applies" of "establishing a place of business in Great Britain".

## DELIVERY OF ACCOUNTS AND REPORTS: OTHER INSTITUTIONS AND COMPANIES

**8(1)** This paragraph applies to an institution to which Part I of Schedule 21C applies and to a company to which Part I of Schedule 21D applies, other than a company to which paragraphs 4 to 7 apply.

**8(2)** Paragraph 1(2) of Schedule 21A and the provisions of Schedules 21C and 21D to the principal Act shall only have effect to require a company to which this paragraph applies to deliver accounting documents for registration if they have been prepared with reference to a period commencing on or after 1st January 1993.

## REFERENCES TO ENACTMENTS AND CONTINUANCE OF LAW

**9(1)** Any reference in any enactment (including any subordinate legislation within the meaning of section 21 of the Interpretation Act 1978) to any provision in Part XXIII of the principal Act as unamended by these Regulations shall be construed as including a reference to the corresponding provision inserted by these Regulations with respect to companies to which section 690A and 699A or (as the case may be) section 699AA of that Act applies, unless the context otherwise requires.

**9(2)** This provision made by this paragraph is without prejudice to the operation of the Interpretation Act 1978 or to any amendments effected by Schedule 3 to these Regulations.

## EXPLANATORY NOTE

(*This Note is not part of the Regulations*)

1. These Regulations implement, through a number of amendments to the Companies Act 1985 ("the Act"), Council Directive 89/666/89 (the "Eleventh Company Law Directive") on the disclosure requirements in respect of branches opened by certain companies in a Member State (OJ No. L395 30.12.89, pp. 36–39) and Council Directive 89/117/EEC (the "Bank Branches Directive") on publication of annual accounting documents by credit and financial institutions (OJ No. L44 16.2.89, pp.40–42).

2. The Eleventh Company Law Directive deals with disclosures (including disclosure of accounting documents) required to be made by branches established in a Member State of limited companies incorporated in another Member State or a non-EC country. The Bank Branches Directive complements this by establishing special rules on the disclosure of accounting documents of a branch of a credit or financial institution in a Member State which has its head office outside that state.

3. The branch registration regime created by these Regulations complements the existing place of business registration regime set out in Part XXIII of the Act. If a company within the scope of the Eleventh Directive establishes a place of business that is not a branch and has no

other branch in the United Kingdom, it will be subject to the place of business registration regime. That regime will also remain applicable to companies not within the scope of the Eleventh Directive.

4. *Regulation 2 and Schedule 1* implement the Bank Branches Directive by inserting new sections 699A and 699B, together with a new Schedule 21C, into the Act. Section 699A applies the new accounts disclosure requirements of Schedule 21C to a branch (as defined), established in Great Britain, of a credit or financial institution (as defined) which is incorporated outside the United Kingdom or Gibraltar and also has its head office outside these places. Section 699B disapplies the accounting disclosure requirements of sections 700 to 703, applicable to companies subject to the place of business registration regime, to any institution to which section 699A applies. Schedule 21C sets out the requirements for delivery of reports and accounts of credit and financial institutions to which the Bank Branches Directive applies. Part I of the Schedule applies to an institution which is required by its parent law to prepare and have audited accounts for its financial period, and whose principal or only branch within the United Kingdom is in Great Britain. Such institutions are required to deliver to the registrar of companies all the accounting documents (with certified translations, if necessary), which it prepares in accordance with its parent law (modified where permitted). Where the parent law does not require registration of these documents, the institution may instead make the documents available for inspection at each branch of the institution in Great Britain and make copies available on request. Part II of the Schedule applies to incorporated institutions which are not required by the law of the country in which the head office resides to prepare and have audited accounts. Such an institution is required to prepare accounts and a directors' report as if it were a company to which section 700 applies (which sets out the accounting regime for companies subject to place of business registration).

5. *Regulation 3 and Schedule 2* implement the Eleventh Company Law Directive. Regulation 3 inserts new section 705A into the Act, which requires the establishment and maintenance of a register of branches of oversea companies. Schedule 2 makes a number of amendments to Part XXIII of the Act, the most important of which are:

(a) *Paragraph 2 of Schedule 2* inserts new sections 690A and 690B into the Act. Section 690A imposes the branch registration requirements of the new Schedule 21A on any limited company which is incorporated outside the United Kingdom and Gibraltar and which has a branch in Great Britain. Section 690B provides that the requirements of section 691 (place of business registration regime) shall not apply to a limited company to which section 690A applies.

(b) *Paragraph 3 of Schedule 2* inserts Schedule 21A into the Act, which sets out the particulars which must be disclosed by a company registering a branch. A return must also be made in respect of any alteration to any particulars registered.

(c) *Paragraphs 4 and 5 of Schedule 2* insert section 692A and Schedule 21B into the Act which provide for certain transitional arrangements where a company moves from the place of business registration regime to the branch registration regime and *vice versa*.

(d) *Paragraph 6 of Schedule 2* amends section 693 of the Act by setting out certain particulars which must be disclosed about a branch and the company on the letterheads etc. used in the business of the branch. Additional particulars must be disclosed where the company is not one incorporated in an EC Member State.

(e) *Paragraph 8 of Schedule 2* inserts section 694A into the Act, which makes parallel provision for service of documents to that made by existing section 695 in respect of companies subject to the place of business registration regime.

(f) *Paragraph 10 of Schedule 2* inserts section 695A into the Act, which provides that an oversea company shall deliver documents under the branch registration regime to the registrar for that part of Great Britain where the branch is situated. If a branch is closed notice must be given of that fact to the relevant registrar.

(g) *Paragraph 13 of Schedule 2* amends Section 698 of the Act so as to provide for the interpretation of "branch" for the purposes of the branch registration regime and to provide a rule to determine in which part of the United Kingdom a branch is to be regarded as located where it comprises places of business in more than one such part.

(h) *Paragraph 18 of Schedule 2* inserts Schedule 21D into the Act. It sets out the reports and accounts which must be delivered by a company subject to branch registration in respect of a branch, other than a branch which is subject to Schedule 21C. Part I of the Schedule applies to companies which are required by their parent law to prepare, have audited and disclose accounts. Such companies must deliver to the registrar all accounting documents (modified where permitted), and certified translations where necessary, disclosed in accordance with the parent law. Delivery is not required in respect of a branch where those documents have been delivered by the company in respect of another branch in the United Kingdom and where this fact has been disclosed by the branch in its return under Schedule 21A. Part II applies to companies that do not have such requirements under their parent law. Such companies are required to prepare accounts, a directors' report and an auditors' report as if they were a company to which section 700 applies. As with Part I, provision is made for these documents to be returned by a company in respect of more than one branch.

(i) *Paragraph 19 of Schedule 2* inserts sections 703O to 703R into the Act. These sections require particulars to be delivered in respect of winding up or other insolvency proceedings against a company which is subject to the branch registration regime. Section 703P requires a return to be made where such a company is being wound up, where a liquidator is appointed, and upon the termination of the winding up. Returns are not required, however, where winding up proceedings under Part V of the Insolvency Act 1986 have been commenced (as that Act contains separate requirements to file returns with the registrar of companies). Section 703Q requires a return where insolvency proceedings, other than that for the winding up of the company, are commenced. If the company ceases to be subject to such proceedings a further return is required.

6. *Regulation 4 and Schedule 3* make a number of amendments consequential upon the implementation of the two Directives.

7. *Regulation 5 and Schedule 4* set out transitional arrangements.

# THE BANKING COORDINATION (SECOND COUNCIL DIRECTIVE) REGULATIONS 1992

(SI 1992/3218)

*Made on 16 December 1992 by the Treasury under s. 2(2) of the European Communities Act 1972. Operative from 1 January 1993.*

[**Note:** The functions of the Bank of England under these regulations transferred to the Financial Services Authority by the Bank of England Act 1998, s. 21(a)(ii), 45 as from 1 June 1998 (see SI 1998/1120 (C 25), art. 2). Relevant amendments by the Banking Coordination (Second Council Directive) (Amendment) Regulations 1993 (SI 1993/3225) (operative from 1 January 1994); the Banking Coordination (Second Council Directive) (Amendment) Regulations 1995 (SI 1995/1217) (operative from 1 June 1995) and the Banking (Gibraltar) Regulations 1999 (SI 1999/2094) (operative from 20 August 1999) have been included.]

## ARRANGEMENT OF REGULATIONS

### PART I – GENERAL

REGULATION

- The definition of "relevant EFTA State" inserted by the Banking Coordination (Second Council Directive) (Amendment) Regulations 1993 (SI 1993/3225), reg. 1, 2(a) as from 1 January 1994.
- In the definition of "home-regulated investment business" the words "(subject to regulation 2B(3) below)" inserted by the Banking (Gibraltar) Regulations 1999 (SI 1999/2094), reg. 1, 2(2)(c) as from 20 August 1999.
- In the definition of "home-regulated activity" the words "regulation 2B(3), 3(7) or" substituted for the former words "regulation 3(7) or" by the Banking (Gibraltar) Regulations 1999 (SI 1999/2094) reg. 1, 2(2)(b) as from 20 August 1999.
- The definitions of "member state" inserted by the Banking Coordination (Second Council Directive) (Amendment) Regulations 1993 (SI 1993/3225), reg. 1, 2(a) as from 1 January 1994.

**2(2B)** Any reference in these Regulations to the First Council Directive or the Second Council Directive is a reference to that Directive as amended by the Prudential Supervision Directive (within the meaning of the Financial Institutions (Prudential Supervision) Regulations 1996).

**History**

Reg. 2(2B) inserted by the Financial Institutions (Prudential Supervision) Regulations 1996 (SI 1996/1669), reg. 1, 23 and Sch. 5, para. 11 as from 18 July 1996.

**2(2)** In these Regulations **"parent undertaking"**, **"share"**, **"subsidiary undertaking"** and **"undertaking"** have the same meanings as in Part VII of the Companies Act 1985 or Part VIII the Companies (Northern Ireland) Order 1986 except that–

(a) **"subsidiary undertaking"** also includes, in relation to an institution incorporated in or formed under the law of another member State, any undertaking which is a subsidiary undertaking within the meaning of any rule of law in force in that State for purposes connected with the implementation of the Seventh Company Law Directive based on article 54(3)(g) of the Treaty on consolidated accounts (No. 83/349/EEC); and

(b) **"parent undertaking"** shall be construed accordingly.

**2(3)** For the purposes of these Regulations a subsidiary undertaking of an institution is a 90 per cent subsidiary undertaking of the institution if the institution holds 90 per cent or more of the voting rights in the subsidiary undertaking.

**2(4)** Any reference in these Regulations to the carrying on of home-regulated investment business in the United Kingdom–

(a) is a reference to the carrying on of such business in reliance on regulation 5(1)(b) below; and

(b) shall be construed in accordance with section 1(3) of the Financial Services Act.

## ICELAND

**2A(1)** For the period commencing with 1st January 1994 and ending on the implementation date and subject to paragraph (2) below, wherever the expressions **"another member State"**, **"member State"** and **"relevant EFTA State"** are used in these Regulations they have effect for the purposes of these Regulations as if they did not include a reference to Iceland.

**2A(2)** Paragraph (1) above does not apply to–

(a) the definition of **"the commencement date"** in regulation 2(1) above where it has effect in relation to the provisions described in sub-paragraph (e) below;

(b) regulation 22(1), (2) and (3) below;

(c) regulation 24(1) and (3) below;

(d) paragraphs 1 to 7 of Schedule 6 to these Regulations;

(e) paragraphs 2 and 3 of Schedule 11 to these Regulations;

(f) the definitions of **"another member State"**, **"relevant supervisory authority"** and **"supervisory authority"** in section 106 of the Banking Act as inserted by regulation 45 below in so far as those definitions are used in the following provisions of the Banking Act–

(i) section 9(7) as inserted by regulation 26 below;

(ii) section 11(1A)(f)as inserted by regulation 28(1) below;

(iii) section 12A(1) and (3)(b) as inserted by regulation 29 below;

(iv) section 13(3A) as inserted by regulation 30(1) below;

(v) section 15(4) as insertd by regulation 30(2) below;

(vi) section 22(1A) as inserted by regulation 31(2) below; and

(vii) section 86(1)(b), (3) and (4) as substituted by regulation 41 below;

(g) the definitions of **"another member State"**, **"relevant supervisory authority"** and **"supervisory authority"** in section 119(2A) of the Building Societies Act as inserted by regulation 81 below in so far as those definitions are used in the following provisions of the Building Societies Act–

(i) section 43(1A)(f) as inserted by regulation 71(1) below;

(ii) section 45A(1) and 3(b) as inserted by regulation 74 below;

(iii) section 54(3B) as inserted by regulation 77(1) below; and

(iv) section 54(6) as inserted by regulation 77(2) below.

**2A(3)** In relation to a credit institution incorporated in or formed under the law of Iceland, any reference to the commencement date in paragraphs 1, 6 and 7 of Schedule 11 to these Regulations is construed as a reference to the implementation date.

**2A(4)** In this regulation **"the implementation date"** means the date, to be notified in the London, Edinburgh and Belfast Gazettes, on which the EFTA Surveillance Authority to be established under Article 108 of the Agreement on the European Economic Area is notified by Iceland that it has implemented the Second Council Directive, or 1st January 1995, whichever is the sooner.

**History**

Reg. 2A added by the Banking Coordination (Second Council Directive) (Amendment) Regulations 1993 (SI 1993/3225), reg. 1, 2(d) as from 1 January 1994.

## GIBRALTAR

**2B(1)** Except as otherwise provided by regulation 2C below, these Regulations shall apply as if Gibraltar were another member State.

**2B(2)** In relation to–

(a) the carrying on by credit institutions and financial institutions incorporated in or formed under the law of Gibraltar (referred to in this regulation and regulation 2C below as "Gibraltar institutions") of listed activities in the United Kingdom; and

(b) the carrying on by credit institutions and financial institutions incorporated in or formed under the law of the United Kingdom of listed activities in Gibraltar,

any reference in these Regulations to "the commencement date" shall be taken to be a reference to 20th August 1999.

**2B(3)** In these Regulations–

(a) **"home-regulated activity"**, in relation to a Gibraltar institution, means any listed activity falling within items 1 to 6 in the Annex to the Second Council Directive which that institution is authorised by the relevant supervisory authority in Gibraltar to carry on in the United Kingdom;

(b) **"home-regulated investment business"**, in relation to such an institution, means investment business which consists in carrying on one or more listed activities falling within items 1 to 6 in the Annex to the Second Council Directive–

(i) in relation to which a supervisory authority in Gibraltar has regulatory functions; and

(ii) which, in the case of a Gibraltar institution which is a European subsidiary, it is carrying on in Gibraltar; and

(c) any reference to a listed activity which a European institution is authorised or permitted to carry on in its home state shall be treated, in relation to a Gibraltar institution, as a reference to any such listed activity as is mentioned in sub-paragraph (a) above.

**2B(4)** Regulations 11(5) and 17(5) shall each have effect, in relation to Gibraltar institutions, as if the words "and the European Commission" were omitted.

**History**

See history note after reg. 2C.

## REQUIREMENTS AS RESPECTS EUROPEAN INTSTITUTIONS

**2C(1)** Except in their application to a Gibraltar institution, Part II of, and Schedule 2 to, these Regulations shall apply as if Gibraltar were part of the United Kingdom.

**2C(2)** In the case of an institution other than a Gibraltar institution, the requirements of paragraph 1 or 4 of Schedule 2 to these Regulations shall be taken to have been complied with in respect of an activity or branch if corresponding requirements under the law of Gibraltar have been complied with in respect of that activity or branch.

**2C(3)** Where, in the case of an institution other than a Gibraltar institution, the Authority receives from the relevant supervisory authority in the institution's home State a notice given in accordance with paragraph 3 of Schedule 2 to these Regulations, if either–

(a) the notice states that the institution intends to establish a place of business in Gibraltar; or

(b) the notice states that the institution intends to carry on home-regulated activities by the provision of services in the United Kingdom or Gibraltar,

the Authority shall send a copy of the notice to the supervisory authority in Gibraltar.

**2C(4)** Where, in the case of an institution other than a Gibraltar institution, the Authority receives from the relevant supervisory authority in the institution's home State a notice given in accordance with paragraph 4 of Schedule 2 to these Regulations in respect of a place of business established in Gibraltar, the Authority shall send a copy of the notice to the supervisory authority in Gibraltar.

**History**
Reg. 2B and 2C inserted by the Banking (Gibraltar) Regulations 1999 (SI 1999/2094), reg. 1, 2(3) as from 20 August 1999.

## PART II – RECOGNITION OF EUROPEAN INSTITUTIONS

### PRELIMINARY

### EUROPEAN INSTITUTIONS

**3(1)** In these Regulations **"European institution"** means a European authorised institution or a European subsidiary.

**3(2)** A credit institution is a European authorised institution for the purposes of these Regulations if–

(a) it is incorporated in or formed under the law of another member State;

(b) its principal place of business is in that State;

(c) it is for the time being authorised to act as a credit institution by the relevant supervisory authority in that State; and

(d) the requirements of paragraph 1 of Schedule 2 to these Regulations have been complied with in relation to its carrying on of an activity or its establishment of a branch.

**3(3)** A financial institution is a European subsidiary for the purposes of these Regulations if–

(a) it is incorporated in or formed under the law of another member State;

(b) it is a 90 per cent. subsidiary undertaking of a credit institution which–
  (i) is incorporated in or formed under the law of that State; and
  (ii) is a European authorised institution or a quasi-European authorised institution;

(c) the conditions mentioned in paragraph (6) below are fulfilled in relation to it; and

(d) the requirements of paragraph 1 of Schedule 2 to these Regulations have been (and continue to be) complied with in relation to its carrying on of an activity or its establishment of a branch.

**3(4)** In these Regulations **"quasi-European institution"** means an institution–

(a) which is not a European institution; but

(b) which would be such an institution if the requirements of paragraph 1 of Schedule 2 to these Regulations had been (and continued to be) complied with in relation to its carrying on of an activity or its establishment of a branch;

and **"quasi-European authorised institution"** and **"quasi-European subsidiary"** shall be construed accordingly.

**3(5)** For the purposes of paragraph (3)(b) above, any two or more European authorised institutions or quasi-European authorised institutions which–

(a) are incorporated in or formed under the law of the same member State; and

(b) hold voting rights in the same undertaking,

shall be regarded as a single institution; and in these Regulations **"parent undertaking"**, in relation to an institution which is a European subsidiary or quasi-European subsidiary by virtue of this paragraph, shall be construed accordingly.

**3(6)** The conditions referred to in paragraph (3)(c) above are–

(a) that each home-regulated activity stated in the institution's recognition notice is carried on by it in its home State;

(b) that the constituent instrument of the institution permits it to carry on each such activity;

(c) that the consolidated supervision of the institution's parent undertaking or, if more than one, any of them effectively includes supervision of the institution; and

(d) that the institution's parent undertaking has guaranteed or, if more than one, they have jointly and severally guaranteed, with the consent of the relevant supervisory authority in its or their home State, the institution's obligations;

and in this paragraph **"recognition notice"**, in relation to an institution, means a notice given by it in accordance with paragraph 2 of Schedule 2 to these Regulations.

**3(7)** Subject to regulation 2B(3) above, in these Regulations **"home-regulated activity"**, in relation to a European institution or quasi-European authorised institution, means any listed activity–

(a) in relation to which a supervisory authority in its home State has regulatory functions; and

(b) which, in the case of a European subsidiary, it is carrying on its home State.

**History**

In reg. 3(7) the words "Subject to regulation 2B(3) above," inserted by the Banking (Gibraltar) Regulations 1999 (SI 1999/2094), reg. 2(1), (4) as from 20 August 1999.

**3(8)** Schedule 2 to these Regulations (which contains requirements to be complied with by or in relation to European institutions) shall have effect.

## AUTHORISED AND PERMITTED ACTIVITIES

**4(1)** For the purposes of these Regulations a European authorised institution (other than one incorporated in or formed under the law of Gibraltar) is authorised to carry on in its home State any listed activity which its authorisation as a credit institution authorises it to carry on.

**History**

In reg. 4(1) the words "(other than one incorporated in or formed under the law of Gibraltar)" inserted by the Banking (Gibraltar) Regulations 1999 (SI 1999/2094), reg. 2(1), (5) as from 20 August 1999.

**4(2)** For the purposes of these Regulations a European subsidiary (other than one incorporated in or formed under the law of Gibraltar)is permitted to carry on in its home State any listed activity which it is lawful for it to carry on, and it is carrying on, in that State.

**History**

In reg. 4(2) the words "(other than one incorporated in or formed under the law of Gibraltar)" inserted by the Banking (Gibraltar) Regulations 1999 (SI 1999/2094), reg. 2(1), (6) as from 20 August 1999.

## EFFECT OF RECOGNITION

### AUTHORISATIONS AND LICENCES NOT REQUIRED

**5(1)** Subject to paragraph (2) and (3) below, nothing in the following enactments, namely–

(a) section 3 of the Banking Act (restriction on acceptance of deposits);

(b) sections 3 and 4 of the Financial Services Act (restrictions on carrying on investment business);

(c) sections 21, 39(1) and 147(1) of the Consumer Credit Act (Consumer Credit Act businesses needing a licence); and

(d) section 2 of the Insurance Companies Act (restriction on carrying on insurance business), shall prevent a European institution from carrying on in the United Kingdom any listed activity which it is authorised or permitted to carry on in its home State.

**History**
See history note after reg. 5(3).

**5(2)** In relation to a European institution in respect of which a prohibition under these Regulations is in force–

(a) paragraph (1)(a) above shall not apply if the prohibition is under regulation 9 below;

(b) paragraph (1)(b) above shall not apply if the prohibition is under regulation 15 below; and

(c) paragraph (1)(c) above shall not apply if the prohibition is under regulation 18 below.

**5(3)** Paragraph (1)(a) above shall not apply in relation to a European institution in respect of which a determination under regulation 13A below is in force.

**History**
in reg. 5(1) the words "paragraphs (2) and (3)" substituted for the former words "paragraph (2)" and reg. 5(3) added by the Banking Coordination (Second Council Directive) (Amendment) Regulations 1993 (SI 1993/3225), reg. 1, 2(e), (f) as from 1 January 1994.

## PROCEDURAL REQUIREMENTS FOR CARRYING ON LISTED ACTIVITIES

**6(1)** A European institution shall not–

(a) carry on in the United Kingdom by the provision of services any home-regulated activity; or

(b) establish a branch in the United Kingdom for the purpose of carrying on such an activity,

unless the requirements of paragraph 1 of Schedule 2 to these Regulations have been (and, in the case of a European subsidiary, continue to be) complied with in relation to its carrying on of the activity or, as the case may be, its establishment of the branch.

**6(2)** A European institution shall not change the requisite details of a branch established by it in the United Kingdom unless the requirements of paragraph 4 of Schedule 2 to these Regulations have been complied with in relation to its making of the change.

**6(3)** An institution which contravenes paragraph (1) or (2) above shall be guilty of an offence and liable on summary conviction to a fine not exceeding level 5 on the standard scale; but such a contravention shall not invalidate any transaction.

**6(4)** In proceedings brought against an institution for an offence under paragraph (3) above it shall be a defence for the institution to show that it took all reasonable precautions and exercised all due diligence to avoid the commission of the offence.

## EFFECT OF NON-RECOGNITION

## PROHIBITION ON CARRYING ON CERTAIN LISTED ACTIVITIES

**7(1)** A quasi-European authorised institution shall not–

(a) carry on in the United Kingdom by the provision of services any home-regulated activity; or

(b) establish a branch in the United Kingdom for the purpose of carrying on such an activity.

**7(2)** An institution which contravenes paragraph (1) above shall be guilty of an offence and liable on summary conviction to a fine not exceeding level 5 on the standard scale; but such a contravention shall not invalidate any transaction.

**7(3)** In proceedings brought against an institution for an offence under paragraph (2) above it shall be a defence for the institution to show that it took all reasonable precautions and exercised all due diligence to avoid the commission of the offence.

## FUNCTIONS OF AUTHORITY

[**Note:** The heading to reg. 8 technically not amended by the Bank of England Act 1998, Sch. 5, para. 21, 23 as from 1 June 1998; amendment made by CCH.New Law; heading formerly read "FUNCTIONS OF BANK".]

## DUTY TO PREPARE FOR SUPERVISION

**8(1)** In any case where–

(a) the Authority receives from the relevant supervisory authority in an institution's home State a notice given in accordance with paragraph 3 of Schedule 2 to these Regulations; and

(b) the notice states that the institution intends to establish a branch in the United Kingdom,

the Authority shall, before the expiry of the period of two months beginning with the day on which it received the notice, draw to the attention of the institution such provisions of these Regulations, the relevant Acts or regulations or rules made under those Acts as, having regard to the activities mentioned in the notice, the Authority considers appropriate.

**8(2)** In any case where the Authority receives from the relevant supervisory authority in an institution's home State such a notice as is mentioned in paragraph (1) above–

(a) the Authority shall also, before the expiry of the said period of two months, consider whether the situation as respects the institution is such that the powers conferred by paragraph (2) of regulation 9 below are likely to become exercisable; and

(b) if it considers that the situation is such as is mentioned in sub-paragraph (a) above, the Authority may impose, as soon as the requirements of paragraph 1 of Schedule 2 to these Regulations have been complied with in relation to the institution, such restriction under regulation 10 below as appears to it desirable.

**8(3)** In any case where the Authority receives from an institution a notice given in accordance with paragraph 4 of Schedule 2 to these Regulations, the Authority shall, before the expiry of the period of one month beginning with the day on which it received the notice, draw to the attention of the institution such provisions of these Regulations, the relevant Acts or regulations or rules made under those Acts as, having regard to the proposed change mentioned in the notice, the Authority considers appropriate.

**8(4)** Nothing in this regulation shall require the Authority to draw to the attention of an institution any provision which, in connection with the same notice, has been or will be drawn to its attention under regulation 14 below.

**8(5)** In this regulation and regulation 9 below **"the relevant Acts"** means the Banking Act, the Financial Services Act, the Consumer Credit Act and the Insurance Companies Act.

**History**
See history note after reg. 10.

**Note**
The heading to reg. 8–13A not in fact amended by the Bank of England Act 1998, Sch. 5, para. 23. It is however submitted that the heading should have been so amended and thus CCH has made the relevant substitution for "Bank".

## POWER TO PROHIBIT THE ACCEPTANCE OF DEPOSITS

**9(1)** In this regulation **"prohibition"** means a prohibition on accepting deposits in the United Kingdom.

**9(2)** Subject to paragraph (3) and regulation 11 below, the Authority may impose a prohibition on a European institution if–

(a) the institution is a European authorised institution which has established a branch in the United Kingdom and it appears to the Authority that the branch is not or may not be maintaining or, as the case may be, will not or may not maintain adequate liquidity;

(b) the Authority is informed by the relevant supervisory authority in the institution's home State that it has failed to take any or sufficient steps to cover risks arising from its open positions on financial markets in the United Kingdom;

(c) it appears to the Authority that the institution has failed to comply with any obligation imposed on it by these Regulations or by or under any of the relevant Acts;

(d) the Authority is informed by a supervisory authority in the institution's home State that it has failed to comply with any obligation imposed on it by or under any rule of law in force in that State for purposes connected with the implementation of the Second Council Directive;

(e) it appears to the Authority that it has been provided with false, misleading or inaccurate information by or on behalf of the institution or by or on behalf of a person who is or is to be a director, controller or manager of the institution; or

(f) it appears to the Authority that the situation as respects the institution is such that, if it were authorised by the Authority under the Banking Act, the Authority could revoke the authorisation.

**9(3)** The Authority may not impose a prohibition on a European institution on the ground mentioned in paragraph (2)(f) above unless–

(a) the Authority has requested the relevant supervisory authority in the institution's home State to take all appropriate measures for the purpose of securing that the institution remedies the situation; and

(b) the Authority is satisfied either–

(i) that that authority has failed or refused to take measures for that purpose; or

(ii) that the measures taken by that authority have proved inadequate for that purpose.

**9(4)** Any prohibition imposed under this regulation may be withdrawn by written notice served by the Authority on the institution concerned; and any such notice shall take effect on such date as is specified in the notice.

**9(5)** In the case of a European institution which is a member of a self-regulating organisation, the reference in paragraph (2)(c) above to any obligation imposed by or under the relevant Acts shall be taken to include a reference to any obligation imposed by the rules of that organisation.

**9(6)** In this regulation **"controller"**, **"director"** and **"manager"** have the same meanings as in the Banking Act.

**9(7)** Schedule 3 to these Regulations (which makes supplemental provision with respect to prohibitions imposed under this regulation and restrictions imposed under regulation 10 below) shall have effect.

**History**

See history note after reg. 10.

## POWER TO RESTRICT LISTED ACTIVITIES

**10(1)** In this regulation **"restriction"** means a direction that a European institution or former European institution–

(a) may not carry on in the United Kingdom any home-regulated activity (other than the acceptance of deposits) which is specified in the direction; or

(b) may not carry on in the United Kingdom, otherwise than in accordance with such condition or conditions as may be specified in the direction, any home-regulated activity which is so specified.

**10(2)** Where it appears to the Authority that the situation as respects a European institution is such that the powers conferred by paragraph (2) of regulation 9 above are exercisable, the Authority may, instead of or as well as imposing a prohibition, impose such restriction as appears to it desirable.

**10(3)** Where it appears to the Authority that the situation as respects a former European authorised institution is such that the powers conferred by paragraph (2) of regulation 9 above would be exercisable if the institution were still a European authorised institution, the Authority may impose such restriction as appears to it desirable.

**10(4)** Subsection (4) of section 12 of the Banking Act (examples of conditions that may be imposed) applies for the purposes of this regulation as it applies for the purposes of that section.

**10(5)** Any restriction imposed under this regulation–

(a) may be withdrawn; or

(b) may be varied with the agreement of the institution concerned,

by written notice served by the Authority on the institution; and any such notice shall take effect on such date as is specified in the notice.

**10(6)** An institution which fails to comply with a restriction shall be guilty of an offence and liable–

(a) on conviction on indictment, to a fine;

(b) on summary conviction, to a fine not exceeding the statutory maximum.

**10(7)** The fact that a restriction has not been complied with (whether or not constituting an offence under paragraph (6) above) shall not invalidate any transaction but, in the case of a European institution, shall be a ground for the imposition of a prohibition under regulation 9 above.

**10(8)** In this regulation **"former European authorised institution"** means an institution which was formerly a European authorised institution and continues to have a liability in respect of any deposit for which it had a liability when it was a European authorised institution.

**History**

In reg. 8 to 10, the word "Authority" wherever occurring substituted for the former word "Bank" by the Bank of England Act 1998, s. 23(1), 45 and Sch. 5, para. 21, 23 as from 1 June 1998 (see SI 1998/1120 (C 25), art. 2).

## LIMITATIONS ON AUTHORITY'S POWERS

[**Note:** The heading to reg. 11 technically not amended by the Bank of England Act 1998, Sch. 5, para. 21, 24 as from 1 June 1998; amendment made by CCH.New Law; heading formerly read "LIMITATIONS ON BANK'S POWERS".]

**11(1)** This regulation applies where it appears to the Authority that the situation as respects a European institution is such that the Authority's power–

(a) to impose a prohibition or restriction on the institution; or

(b) to vary otherwise than with the agreement of the institution any restriction imposed on the institution,

is exercisable by virtue of regulation 9(2)(a) above, or by virtue of any failure to comply with a requirement imposed under section 39 of the Banking Act (information and production of documents) for statistical purposes.

**History**

In reg. 11(1), the word "Authority's" substituted for the former word "Bank's" by the Bank of England Act 1998, s. 23(1), 45 and Sch. 5, para. 21, 24(b) as from 1 June 1998 (see SI 1998/1120 (C 25), art. 2).

**11(2)** The Authority shall require the institution in writing to remedy the situation.

**11(3)** If the institution fails to comply with the requirement under paragraph (2) above within a reasonable time, the Authority shall give a notice to that effect to the relevant supervisory authority in the institution's home State requesting that authority–

(a) to take all appropriate measures for the purpose of ensuring that the institution remedies the situation; and

(b) to inform the Authority of the measures it proposes to take or has taken or the reasons for not taking any such measures.

**11(4)** Subject to paragraph (5) below, the Authority shall not take any steps to impose a prohibition or restriction on a European institution, or to vary otherwise than with the agreement of a European institution any restriction imposed on the institution, unless it is satisfied–

(a) that the relevant supervisory authority has failed or refused to take measures for the purpose mentioned in sub-paragraph (a) of paragraph (3) above; or

(b) that the measures taken by that authority have proved inadequate for that purpose.

**11(5)** Where the Authority considers that the prohibition, restriction or variation should be imposed as a matter of urgency, it may take steps to impose the prohibition, restriction or variation–

(a) before complying with paragraphs (2) and (3) above; or

(b) where it has complied with those paragraphs, without being satisfied as mentioned in paragraph (4) above;

but in such a case the Authority shall, at the earliest opportunity, inform the relevant supervisory authority in the institution's home State and the European Commission of the steps taken.

**11(6)** In any case where–

(a) by virtue of paragraph (5) above, the Authority has imposed a prohibition or restriction on a European institution, or varied a restriction imposed on such an institution, before complying with paragraphs (2) and (3) above or, as the case may be, before it is satisfied as mentioned in paragraph (4) above; and

(b) the European Commission decides under the Second Council Directive that the Authority must withdraw or vary the prohibition, restriction or variation,

the Authority shall in accordance with the decision withdraw or vary the prohibition, restriction or variation.

**11(7)** In any case where–

(a) the Authority has given notice to a European institution under paragraph 2 of Schedule 3 to these Regulations of a proposal to impose a prohibition or restriction or vary a restriction;

(b) the prohibition, restriction or variation has not taken effect; and

(c) the European Commission decides under the Second Council Directive that the Authority must withdraw or vary the notice,

the Authority shall in accordance with the decision withdraw or vary the notice.

**11(8)** This regulation shall not apply–

(a) as respects the imposition of a restriction in pursuance of regulation 8(2) above; or

(b) in any case where regulation 12 below applies.

**History**

In reg. 11, the word "Authority" wherever occurring substituted for the former word "Bank" by the Bank of England Act 1998, s. 23(1), 45 and Sch. 5, para. 21, 24(a) as from 1 June 1998 (see SI 1998/1120 (C 25), art. 2).

**Note**

The heading to reg. 11 not in fact amended by the Bank of England Act 1998, Sch. 5, para. 24. It is however submitted that the heading should have been so amended and thus CCH has made the relevant substitution for "Bank's".

## PROHIBITION OR RESTRICTION ON INFORMATION FROM SUPERVISORY AUTHORITY

**12(1)** This regulation applies where in the case of a European institution–

(a) the Authority is informed by the relevant supervisory authority in the institution's home State that it has failed to take any or sufficient steps to cover risks arising from its open positions on financial markets in the United Kingdom; or

(b) the Authority is informed by a supervisory authority in that State that the institution is failing to comply with an obligation imposed by or under any rule of law in force in that State for purposes connected with the implementation of the Second Council Directive.

**12(2)** The Authority shall as soon as practicable send a copy of the information received by it to every other authority which it knows is a connected UK authority.

**12(3)** The Authority shall also–

(a) consider whether to exercise its powers under regulation 9 or 10 above; and

(b) notify its decision, and any action which it has taken or intends to take, to the supervisory authority and to every other authority which it knows is a connected UK authority.

**History**

See history note after reg. 13A.

## OBLIGATION OF AUTHORITY WHERE INSTITUTION CEASES TO BE A EUROPEAN INSTITUTION ETC.

[**Note:** The heading to reg. 13 technically not amended by the Bank of England Act 1998, Sch. 5, para. 21, 25 as from 1 June 1998; amendment made by CCH.New Law; heading formerly read "OBLIGATION OF BANK WHERE INSTITUTION CEASES TO BE A EUROPEAN INSTITUTION ETC.".]

**13(1)** Where the Authority is informed that–

(a) an institution has ceased to be a European institution; or

(b) a European institution has ceased to carry on any particular home-regulated activity in the United Kingdom, the Authority shall inform every other authority which it knows is a connected UK authority of that fact.

**History**
See history note after reg. 13A.

**Note**
The heading to reg. 13 not in fact specifically amended by the Bank of England Act 1998, Sch. 5, para. 25. It is however submitted that the heading should have been so amended and thus CCH has made the relevant substitution for "Bank".

## TREASURY DETERMINATIONS FOR IMPLEMENTING DECISIONS

**13A(1)** For the purpose of implementing a relevant decision within the meaning of section 26A(1) of the Banking Act the Treasury may following consultation with the Authority make a determination in respect of a credit institution if–

(a) it is incorporated in or formed under the law of a relevant EFTA State;

(b) it is the subsidiary undertaking of a parent undertaking governed by the laws of a third country whose treatment of credit institutions from the European Economic Area of any part of it gave rise to the relevant decision; and

(c) it conforms to regulation 3(2)(b) and (c) above but not to regulation 3(2)(d).

**13A(2)** A determination made under paragraph (1) shall prohibit a credit institution in respect of which it is made from thereafter carrying on in the United Kingdom by the provision of services any home-regulated activity or establishing a branch in the United Kingdom for the purpose of carrying on such an activity notwithstanding that the requirements of paragraph 1 of Schedule 2 to these Regulations are at any time complied with in relation to its carrying on of the activity or, as the case may be, its establishment of the branch.

**13A(3)** A determination made under paragraph (1) above may relate to a particular institution or class of institution.

**13A(4)** A determination made under paragraph (1) above may be withdrawn at any time by the Treasury, but such withdrawal shall not affect anything done in accordance with the determination before it was withdrawn.

**13A(5)** Notice of a determination made under paragraph (1) above in respect of a particular institution or of the withdrawal of such a determination shall be given in writing by the Treasury to that institution and notice of any determination made under paragraph (1) or of the withdrawal of any determination shall be published in the London, Edinburgh and Belfast Gazettes on the date of the determination or, as the case may be, on the date of the withdrawal, or as soon as practicable thereafter.

**13A(6)** A credit institution which fails to comply with a determination made under paragraph (1) shall be guilty of an offence and liable on sumary conviction to a fine not exceeding level 5 on the standard scale; but such a contravention shall not invalidate any transaction.

**13A(7)** In proceedings brought against a credit institution for an offence under paragraph (6) above it shall be a defence for the institution to show that it took all reasonable precautions and exercised all due diligence to avoid the commission of the offence.

**History**
In reg. 12 to 13A the word "Authority" wherever occurring substituted for the former word "Bank" by the Bank of England Act 1998, s. 23(1), 45 and Sch. 5, para. 21, 25 as from 1 June 1998 (see SI 1998/1120 (C 25), art. 2).
Previously, reg. 13A added by the Banking Coordination (Second Council Directive) (Amendment) Regulations 1993 (SI 1993/3225), reg. 1, 2(g) as from 1 January 1994.

## FUNCTIONS OF BOARD

### DUTY TO PREPARE FOR SUPERVISION

**14(1)** In any case where–

(a) the Authority receives a notice under paragraph 3 of Schedule 2 to these Regulations; and

(b) the notice states that the institution concerned intends to establish a branch in the United Kingdom for the purpose of carrying on a home-regulated activity appearing to the Authority to constitute investment business,

the Authority shall, before the expiry of the period of two months beginning with the day on which it received the notice, draw to the attention of the institution such provisions of these

Regulations, the Financial Services Act or rules or regulations made under that Act as, having regard to the activities mentioned in the notice, it considers appropriate.

**14(2)** In any case where–

(a) the Authority receives a notice under paragraph 4 of Schedule 2 to these Regulations; and

(b) the institution concerned is, or as a result of the proposed change mentioned in the notice will be, carrying on in the United Kingdom a home-regulated activity appearing to the Authority to constitute investment business,

the Authority shall, before the expiry of the period of one month beginning with the day on which it received the notice, draw to the attention of the institution such provisions of these Regulations, the Financial Services Act or rules or regulations made under that Act as, having regard to the proposed change mentioned in the notice, it considers appropriate.

**History**

Reg. 14 substituted by the Bank of England Act 1998, s. 23(1), 45 and Sch. 5, para. 21, 26 as from 1 June 1998 (see SI 1998/1120 (C 25), art. 2). The former reg. 14 read as follows:

"**14(1)** In any case where–

(a) the Board receives from the Bank under paragraph 3 of Schedule 2 to these Regulations a copy of a notice given in accordance with that paragraph; and

(b) the notice states that the institution concerned intends to establish a branch in the United Kingdom for the purpose of carrying on a home-regulated activity appearing to the Board to constitute investment business,

the Board shall, before the expiry of the period of two months beginning with the day on which the Bank received the notice, draw to the attention of the institution such provisions of these Regulations, the Financial Services Act or rules or regulations made under that Act as, having regard to the activities mentioned in the notice, it considers appropriate.

**(2)** In any case where–

(a) the Board receives from the Bank under paragraph 4 of Schedule 2 to these Regulations a copy of a notice given in accordance with that paragraph; and

(b) the institution concerned is, or as a result of the proposed change mentioned in the notice will be, carrying on in the United Kingdom a home-regulated activity appearing to the Board to constitute investment business,

the Board shall, before the expiry of the period of one month beginning with the day on which the Bank received the notice, draw to the attention of the institution such provisions of these Regulations, the Financial Services Act or rules or regulations made under that Act as, having regard to the proposed change mentioned in the notice, it considers appropriate."

## POWER TO PROHIBIT THE CARRYING ON OF INVESTMENT BUSINESS

**15(1)** If it appears to the Board that a European institution–

(a) has contravened or is likely to contravene any provision of the Financial Services Act or any rules or regulations made under it;

(b) in purported compliance with any such provision, has furnished it with false, inaccurate or misleading information;

(c) has contravened or is likely to contravene any prohibition or requirement imposed under that Act; or

(d) has failed to comply with any statement of principle issued under that Act,

it may impose on the institution a prohibition under this regulation, that is to say, a prohibition on carrying on, or purporting to carry on, home-regulated investment business in the United Kingdom.

**15(2)** Where the institution is a member of a recognised self-regulating organisation–

(a) the reference in paragraph (1) above to rules made under the Financial Services Act shall be taken to include a reference to the rules of that organisation; and

(b) the reference in that paragraph to any prohibition or requirement imposed under that Act shall be taken to include a reference to any prohibition or requirement imposed by virtue of the rules of that organisation.

**15(3)** A prohibition under this regulation–

(a) may be absolute; or

(b) may be limited, that is to say, imposed for a specified period or until the occurrence of a specified event or until specified conditions are complied with;

and any period, event or conditions specified in the case of a limited prohibition may be varied by the Board on the application of the institution concerned.

**15(4)** Any prohibition imposed under this regulation may be withdrawn by written notice served by the Board on the institution concerned; and any such notice shall take effect on such date as is specified in the notice.

**15(5)** Schedule 4 to these Regulations (which makes supplemental provision with respect to prohibitions imposed under this regulation) shall have effect.

## POWER TO RESTRICT THE CARRYING ON OF INVESTMENT BUSINESS

**16(1)** Where it appears to the Board that the situation as respects a European institution carrying on home-regulated investment business in the United Kingdom is such that the power conferred by regulation 15(1) above is exercisable, the Board may, instead of or as well as imposing a prohibition, exercise–

(a) in relation to the institution; or

(b) except in the case of the power conferred by section 65 of that Act, in relation to any appointed representative of the institution,

the powers conferred on the Board by Chapter VI of Part I of the Financial Services Act.

**16(2)** Except where they are required to be exercised by virtue of section 128C of that Act (enforcement in support of overseas regulatory authority), the powers conferred by that Chapter shall not, subject to paragraph (3) below, be exercisable in relation to–

(a) a European institution carrying on home-regulated investment business in the United Kingdom which is a member of a recognised self-regulating organisation and is subject to the rules of such an organisation in carrying on all the home-regulated investment business carried on by it; or

(b) an appointed representative whose principal or, in the case of such a representative with more than one principal, each of whose principals is–
  (i) a member of a recognised self-regulating organisation; and
  (ii) subject to the rules of such an organisation in carrying on the home-regulated investment business in respect of which it has accepted responsibility for the appointed representative's activities.

**16(3)** The powers conferred by section 67(1)(b) of the Financial Services Act may on any of the grounds specified in regulation 15(1) above be exercised in relation to a person mentioned in paragraph (2) above at the request of any recognised self-regulating organisation of which he or, in the case of an appointed representative, any of his principals is a member.

## LIMITATIONS ON BOARD'S POWERS

**17(1)** This regulation applies where it appears to the Board that the situation is such that its power–

(a) to impose a prohibition under regulation 15 above;

(b) to publish a statement with respect to a European institution under section 60 of the Financial Services Act;

(c) to make an application with respect to such an institution under section 61(1) of that Act;

(d) to impose a prohibition or requirement on such an institution under Chapter VI of Part I of that Act;

(e) to vary a prohibition or requirement imposed on such an institution under that Chapter; or

(f) to refuse an application for the variation or rescission of such a prohibition or requirement,

is exercisable by virtue of any contravention of a requirement to furnish information for statistical purposes imposed under that Act.

**17(2)** The Board shall require the institution in writing to remedy the situation.

**17(3)** If the institution fails to comply with the requirement under paragraph (2) above within a reasonable time, the Board shall give a notice to that effect to the relevant supervisory authority in the institution's home State requesting that authority–

(a) to take all appropriate measures for the purpose of ensuring that the institution concerned remedies the situation which has given rise to the issue of the notice; and

(b) to inform the Board of the measures it proposes to take or has taken or the reasons for not taking such measures.

**17(4)** Subject to paragraph (5) below, the Board shall not take any such action as is mentioned in sub-paragraphs (a) to (f) of paragraph (1) above with respect to a European institution unless it is satisfied–

(a) that the relevant supervisory authority has failed or refused to take measures for the purpose mentioned in sub-paragraph (a) of paragraph (3) above; or

(b) that the measures taken by that authority have proved inadequate for that purpose.

**17(5)** Where the Board decides that it should take action as mentioned in any of sub-paragraphs (a) to (e) of paragraph (1) above with respect to a European institution as a matter of urgency in order to protect the interests of investors, it may take that action–

(a) before complying with paragraphs (2) and (3) above; or

(b) where it has complied with those requirements, before it is satisfied as mentioned in paragraph (4) above;

but in such a case it shall, at the earliest opportunity, inform the relevant supervisory authority in the institution's home State and the European Commission of the action taken.

**17(6)** In any case where–

(a) by virtue of paragraph (5) above, the Board has–

(i) imposed a prohibition under regulation 15 above;

(ii) published a statement with respect to a European institution under section 60 of the Financial Services Act;

(iii) made an application under section 61(1) of that Act with respect to such an institution;

(iv) imposed on such an institution a prohibition or requirement under Chapter VI of Part I of that Act; or

(v) varied a prohibition or requirement imposed on such an institution under that Chapter,

before complying with paragraphs (2) and (3) above or, as the case may be, before it is satisfied as mentioned in paragraph (4) above; and

(b) the European Commission decides under the Second Council Directive that the Board must withdraw or amend the statement, withdraw the application, or rescind or vary the prohibition or requirement,

the Board shall in accordance with the decision withdraw or amend the statement, withdraw the application, or rescind or vary the prohibition or requirement.

**17(7)** For the purposes of paragraph (6)(b) above the Board shall be taken to withdraw or amend a statement if it publishes a further statement retracting or, as the case may be, correcting it; and the Board shall after publication of the further statement send a copy of it to any person to whom a copy of the previous statement was sent under section 60(5) of the Financial Services Act.

**17(8)** In any case where–

(a) the Board has, by virtue of sub-paragraph (5) above, given notice to a European institution under subsection (2) of section 60 of the Financial Services Act before complying with paragraphs (2) and (3) above or, as the case may be, before it is satisfied as mentioned in paragraph (4) above;

(b) the statement to which the notice relates has not been published; and

(c) the European Commission decides under the Second Council Directive that the Board must not publish the statement, or must publish a different statement under that section,

the Board shall in accordance with the decision withdraw the notice or give a different notice in substitution.

## FUNCTIONS OF DIRECTOR

### POWER TO PROHIBIT THE CARRYING ON OF CONSUMER CREDIT ACT BUSINESS

**18(1)** If it appears to the Director that paragraph (2) below has been or is likely to be contravened as respects a European institution, he may impose on the institution a prohibition under this regulation, that is to say, a prohibition on carrying on, or purporting to carry on, in the United Kingdom any Consumer Credit Act business which consists of or includes carrying on one or more home-regulated activities.

**18(2)** This paragraph is contravened as respects a European institution if–

(a) the institution or any of the institution's employees, agents or associates (whether past or present); or

(b) where the institution is a body corporate, any controller of the institution or an associate of any such controller,

does any of the things specified in paragraphs (a) to (d) of section 25(2) of the Consumer Credit Act.

**18(3)** A prohibition under this regulation may be absolute or may be imposed for a specified period or until the occurrence of a specified event or until specified conditions are complied with; and any period, event or conditions specified in the case of a prohibition may be varied by the Director on the application of the institution concerned.

**18(4)** Any prohibition imposed under this regulation may be withdrawn by written notice served by the Director on the institution concerned; and any such notice shall take effect on such date as is specified in the notice.

**18(5)** In this regulation **"associate"** has the same meaning as in section 25(2) of the Consumer Credit Act and **"controller"** has the meaning given by section 189(1) of that Act.

**18(6)** Schedule 5 to these Regulations (which makes supplemental provision with respect to prohibitions imposed under this regulation and restrictions imposed under regulation 19 below) shall have effect.

### POWER TO RESTRICT THE CARRYING ON OF CONSUMER CREDIT ACT BUSINESS

**19(1)** In this regulation **"restriction"** means a direction that a European institution may not carry on in the United Kingdom, otherwise than in accordance with such condition or conditions as may be specified in the direction, any Consumer Credit Act business which–

(a) consists of or includes carrying on one or more home-regulated activities; and

(b) is specified in the direction.

**19(2)** Where it appears to the Director that the situation as respects a European institution is such that the powers conferred by paragraph (1) of regulation 18 above are exercisable, the Director may, instead of imposing a prohibition, impose such restriction as appears to him desirable.

**19(3)** Any restriction imposed under this regulation–

(a) may be withdrawn; or

(b) may be varied with the agreement of the institution concerned,

by written notice served by the Director on the institution; and any such notice shall take effect on such date as is specified in the notice.

**19(4)** An institution which contravenes or fails to comply with a restriction shall be guilty of an offence and liable–

(a) on conviction on indictment, to a fine;

(b) on summary conviction, to a fine not exceeding the statutory maximum.

**19(5)** The fact that a restriction has not been complied with (whether or not constituting an offence under paragraph (4) above) shall be a ground for the imposition of a prohibition under regulation 18 above.

# PART III – RECOGNITION IN OTHER MEMBER STATES OF UK INSTITUTIONS

## PRELIMINARY

### UK INSTITUTIONS ETC.

**20(1)** In these Regulations **"UK institution"** means a UK authorised institution or a UK subsidiary.

**20(2)** A credit institution is a UK authorised institution for the purposes of these Regulations if–

(a) it is incorporated in or formed under the law of any part of the United Kingdom;

(b) its principal place of business is in the United Kingdom; and

(c) it is for the time being authorised by the Authority under the Banking Act or by the Commission under the Building Societies Act.

**History**
See history note after reg. 20(9).

**20(3)** A financial institution is a UK subsidiary for the purposes of these Regulations if–

(a) it is incorporated in or formed under the law of any part of the United Kingdom;

(b) it is a 90 per cent. subsidiary undertaking of a UK authorised institution; and

(c) the conditions mentioned in paragraph (5) below are fulfilled in relation to it.

**20(4)** For the purposes of paragraph (3)(b) above, any two or more UK authorised institutions which hold voting rights in the same undertaking shall be regarded as a single institution; and in these Regulations **"parent undertaking"**, in relation to an institution which is a UK subsidiary by virtue of this paragraph, shall be construed accordingly.

**20(5)** The conditions referred to in paragraph (3)(c) above are–

(a) that each listed activity stated in the institution's recognition notice is carried on by it in the United Kingdom;

(b) that the constituent instrument of the institution permits it to carry on each such activity;

(c) that the consolidated supervision of the institution's parent undertaking or, if more than one, any of them effectively includes supervision of the institution; and

(d) that the institution's parent undertaking has guaranteed or, if more than one, they have each jointly and severally guaranteed, with the consent of the UK authority, the institution's obligations;

and in this paragraph and regulation 23(1) below **"recognition notice"**, in relation to an institution, means a notice given by it in accordance with paragraph 2 of Schedule 6 to these Regulations.

**20(6)** In these Regulations **"home-regulated activity"**–

(a) in relation to a UK authorised institution, means any listed activity;

(b) in relation to a UK subsidiary, means any listed activity which it is carrying on in the United Kingdom.

**20(7)** In these Regulations **"the UK authority"**–

(a) in relation to a UK authorised institution which is authorised by the Authority under the Banking Act or a UK subsidiary whose parent undertaking (or each of whose parent undertakings) is so authorised, means the Authority;

(b) in relation to a UK authorised institution which is authorised by the Commission under the Building Societies Act or a UK subsidiary whose parent undertaking (or each of whose parent undertakings) is so authorised, means the Commission;

(c) in relation to a UK subsidiary of whose parent undertakings one is authorised by the Authority under the Banking Act and another is authorised by the Commission under the Building Societies Act, means such one of the Authority and the Commission as may be agreed between them.

**History**
See history note after reg. 20(9).

**20(8)** An agreement made for the purposes of sub-paragraph (c) of paragraph (7) above–

(a) may relate to particular UK subsidiaries or to UK subsidiaries of particular descriptions; and

(b) shall provide that the UK authority in relation to any UK subsidiary falling within that sub-paragraph shall keep the other party informed of anything done by it in relation to that subsidiary.

**20(9)** In the case of a UK authorised institution which is authorised by the Commission under the Building Societies Act, the power conferred by section 18(1)(b) of that Act to guarantee the discharge of the liabilities of the bodies corporate there mentioned includes power, with the consent of the Commission, to guarantee their obligations for the purposes of this regulation.

**History**
In reg. 20, the word "Authority" wherever occurring substituted for the former word "Bank" by the Bank of England Act 1998, s. 23(1), 45 and Sch. 5, para. 21, 27 as from 1 June 1998 (see SI 1998/1120 (C 25), art. 2).

### AUTHORISED AND PERMITTED ACTIVITIES

**21(1)** For the purposes of these Regulations a UK authorised institution is authorised to carry on in the United Kingdom any listed activity which it is lawful for it to carry on in the United Kingdom.

**21(2)** For the purposes of these Regulations a UK subsidiary is permitted to carry on in the United Kingdom any listed activity which it is lawful for it to carry on, and it is carrying on, in the United Kingdom.

## PROCEDURAL REQUIREMENTS

### PROCEDURAL REQUIREMENTS FOR CARRYING ON CERTAIN LISTED ACTIVITIES

**22(1)** Subject to paragraph (2) below, a UK institution shall not–

(a) carry on in another member State by the provision of services any listed activity which it is authorised or permitted to carry on in the United Kingdom; or

(b) establish a branch in another member State for the purpose of carrying on such an activity,

unless the requirements of paragraph 1 of Schedule 6 to these Regulations have been (and, in the case of a UK subsidiary, continue to be) complied with in relation to its carrying on of the activity or, as the case may be, its establishment of the branch.

**22(2)** Paragraph (1) above shall not apply in relation to a UK subsidiary if–

(a) there has been no compliance with the requirements of paragraph 1 of Schedule 6 to these Regulations in relation to its carrying on of an activity or its establishment of a branch; or

(b) each such compliance has ceased to have effect.

**22(3)** A UK institution shall not change the requisite details of a branch established by it in another member State unless the requirements of paragraph 5 of Schedule 6 to these Regulations have been complied with in relation to its making of the change.

**22(4)** An institution which contravenes paragraph (1) or (3) above shall be guilty of an offence and liable on summary conviction to a fine not exceeding level 5 on the standard scale.

**22(5)** In proceedings brought against an institution for an offence under paragraph (4) above it shall be a defence for the institution to show that it took all reasonable precautions and exercised all due diligence to avoid the commission of the offence.

**22(6)** Schedule 6 to these Regulations (which contains requirements to be complied with by or in relation to UK institutions) shall have effect.

## REGULATION OF UK SUBSIDIARIES FOR RECOGNITION PURPOSES

### RESTRICTION ON ACTIVITIES OF UK SUBSIDIARIES

**23(1)** In this regulation **"restriction"** means a direction that a UK subsidiary to which section 22(l) above applies–

(a) may not carry on in the United Kingdom any listed activity stated in its recognition notice which is specified in the direction; or

(b) may not carry on in the United Kingdom, otherwise than in accordance with such condition or conditions as may be specified in the direction, any such activity which is so specified.

**23(2)** Where it appears to the UK authority that the situation as respects a UK subsidiary is such that, if it were authorised by the Authority under the Banking Act, the Authority could revoke its authorisation on the ground specified in section 11(1)(a) of that Act, the UK authority may impose on the institution such restriction as appears to it desirable.

**History**

See history note after reg. 23(7).

**23(3)** Subsection (4) of section 12 of the Banking Act (examples of conditions that may be imposed) applies for the purposes of this regulation as it applies for the purposes of that section; and Schedule 3 to that Act (minimum criteria for authorisation) as applied by this regulation shall have effect as if–

(a) paragraph 6 (minimum initial capital) were omitted; and

(b) where the Commission is the UK authority, the reference to that Act in paragraph 4(8) were a reference to the Building Societies Act.

**23(4)** Any restriction imposed under this regulation–

(a) may be withdrawn; or

(b) may be varied with the agreement of the institution concerned,

by written notice served by the UK authority on the institution; and any such notice shall take effect on such date as is specified in the notice.

**23(5)** An institution which contravenes or fails to comply with a restriction shall be guilty of an offence and liable–

(a) on conviction on indictment, to a fine;

(b) on summary conviction, to a fine not exceeding the statutory maximum.

**23(6)** The fact that a restriction has not been complied with (whether or not constituting an offence under paragraph (5) above) shall not invalidate any transaction.

**23(7)** Schedule 7 to these Regulations (which makes supplemental provision with respect to restrictions imposed under this regulation) shall have effect.

**History**

In reg. 23, the word "Authority" wherever occurring substituted for the former word "Bank" by the Bank of England Act 1998, s. 23(1), 45 and Sch. 5, para. 21, 27 as from 1 June 1998 (see SI 1998/1120 (C 25), art. 2).

### RESTRICTION ON INFORMATION FROM SUPERVISORY AUTHORITY

**24(1)** This regulation applies where in the case of a UK subsidiary the UK authority is informed by a supervisory authority in another member State that the institution is failing to comply with an obligation imposed by or under any rule of law in force in that State for purposes connected with the implementation of the Second Council Directive.

**24(2)** The UK authority shall as soon as practicable send a copy of the information received by it to every other authority which it knows is a connected UK authority.

**24(3)** The UK authority shall also–

(a) consider whether to exercise its powers under regulation 23 above; and

(b) notify its decision, and any action which it has taken or intends to take, to the supervisory authority and to every other authority which it knows is a connected UK authority.

## PART V – AMENDMENTS OF FINANCIAL SERVICES ACT

### AUTHORISATION BY MEMBERSHIP OF RECOGNISED SELF-REGULATING ORGANISATIONS

**48(1)** Section 7 of the Financial Services Act (authorisation by membership of recognised self-regulating organisation) shall have effect as if it included provision that an institution which–

(a) is a European institution or quasi-European authorised institution; and

(b) is a member of a recognised self-regulating organisation,

is not, by virtue of its membership of that organisation, an authorised person as respects any home-regulated investment business.

**48(2)** Paragraph 2 of Schedule 2 to that Act (requirements for recognition of self-regulating organisations) shall have effect as if it included provision that the rules and practices of the organisation must be such as to secure that where–

(a) a UK authorised institution applies for admission as a member of the organisation; and

(b) the institution states in its application that it proposes to carry on investment business which consists of or includes a listed activity,

the institution shall not be admitted as a member unless the UK authority has notified the organisation that, were the institution so admitted, the UK authority would not by reason of that proposal exercise any of its relevant powers.

**48(3)** In this regulation **"relevant powers"** means–

(a) in relation to the Authority, the powers conferred on it by section 11 or 12 of the Banking Act (power to revoke or restrict authorisations);

(b) in relation to the Commission, the powers conferred on it by section 42 or 43 of the Building Societies Act (power to impose conditions on or revoke authorisations).

**History**

In reg. 48, the word "Authority" wherever occurring substituted for the former word "Bank" by the Bank of England Act 1998, s. 23(1), 45 and Sch. 5, para. 21, 27 as from 1 June 1998 (see SI 1998/1120 (C 25), art. 2).

## APPLICATIONS FOR AUTHORISATION

**49** Section 26 of the Financial Services Act (applications for authorisation) shall have effect as if it included provision that an application for authorisation in respect of any home-regulated investment business may not be made by–

(a) a European authorised institution or quasi-European authorised institution; or

(b) a European subsidiary which has not applied for a direction under paragraph 5 of Schedule 2 to these Regulations.

## GRANT AND REFUSAL OF AUTHORISATION

**50(1)** Section 27 of the Financial Services Act (grant and refusal of authorisation) shall have effect as if it included provision that–

(a) where a European institution or quasi-European authorised institution holds an authorisation granted under that section, the institution is not by virtue of that authorisation an authorised person as respects any home-regulated investment business;

(b) where an application for authorisation in respect of any home-regulated investment business is made by a European subsidiary which has applied for a direction under paragraph 5 of Schedule 2 of these Regulations, the Secretary of State shall not grant the application unless he is satisfied that the institution will cease to be a European subsidiary on or before the date when the authorisation takes effect; and

(c) for the purposes of determining whether to grant or refuse an application in respect of any other investment business made by a European subsidiary, the fact that the subsidiary is subject to supervision pursuant to article 18(2) of the Second Council Directive shall be taken into account.

**50(2)** That section shall also have effect as if it included provision that where–

(a) a UK authorised institution applies for authorisation; and

(b) the institution states in its application that it proposes to carry on investment business which consists of or includes a listed activity,

the Board shall not grant the authorisation unless the UK authority has notified the Board that, were the authorisation granted, the UK authority would not by reason of that proposal exercise any of its relevant powers.

**50(3)** In this regulation **"relevant powers"** has the same meaning as in regulation 48 above.

## AUTHORISATION IN OTHER MEMBER STATE

**51** Section 31 of the Financial Services Act (authorisation in other member State) shall have effect as if it included provision that an institution to which that section applies and which is a European institution or quasi-European authorised institution is not, by virtue of that section, an authorised person as respects any home-regulated investment business.

## EXEMPTED PERSONS

**52(1)** Section 43 of the Financial Services Act (listed money market institutions) shall have effect as if it included provision that an institution which–

(a) is a European institution or quasi-European authorised institution; and

(b) is for the time being included in a list maintained for the purposes of that section,

is not, by virtue of its inclusion in that list, an exempted person as respects any home-regulated investment business.

**52(2)** That section shall also have effect as if it included provision that the conditions and arrangements referred to in subsection (2) must be such as to secure that no European institution, other than one on which an absolute prohibition has been imposed under regulation 15 of these Regulations, is refused admission to the list, or removed from it, for reasons relating to–

(a) the fitness of the institution to be included in the list;

(b) the financial standing of the institution; or

(c) any other matter for which, under the Second Council Directive, responsibility is reserved to a supervisory authority in the institution's home State.

## RECIPROCAL FACILITIES FOR BANKING BUSINESS

**53(1)** No notice shall be served under section 183 of the Financial Services Act (reciprocal facilities for financial business) on a credit institution incorporated in or formed under the law of any part of the United Kingdom which–

(a) appears to the Secretary of State or the Treasury to be a subsidiary undertaking of a person connected with a country outside the United Kingdom; and

(b) is carrying on, or appears to the Secretary of State or the Treasury to intend to carry on, any investment, insurance or banking business in, or in relation to, the United Kingdom,

if the sole ground for giving that notice is the ground specified in paragraph (2) below.

**53(2)** The ground referred to in paragraph (1) above is that it appears to the Secretary of State or the Treasury that by reason of–

(a) the law of the country concerned; or

(b) any action taken by, or the practices of, the government or any other authority or body in that country,

credit institutions connected with the United Kingdom are unable to carry on banking business in, or in relation to, that country on terms as favourable as those on which credit institutions connected with that country are able to carry on such business in, or in relation to, the United Kingdom.

## THE BOARD'S FUNCTIONS UNDER THE REGULATIONS

**54** The functions of the Board under these Regulations shall be treated for the purposes of the Financial Services Act and the Transfer of Functions (Financial Services) Order 1992 as if they were functions under Chapter VI of Part I of that Act which–

(a) had been functions of the Secretary of State; and

(b) had been transferred to the Board by the Financial Services Act 1986 (Delegation) Order 1987.

## OTHER AMENDMENTS OF FINANCIAL SERVICES ACT

**55** The provisions of the Financial Services Act which are mentioned in Schedule 9 to these Regulations shall have effect subject to the amendments there specified.

## CONSTRUCTION OF PART V

**56(1)** In this Part of these Regulations **"authorised person"** has the same meaning as in the Financial Services Act.

**56(2)** If and to the extent that a European institution is an authorised person, nothing in this Part of these Regulations, except regulations 48(1), 50(1) and 51 and paragraphs 5, 6, 11(2), 20 and 30 of Schedule 9, shall affect the operation of the Financial Services Act in relation to it.

# PART IX – SUPPLEMENTAL

## MINOR AND CONSEQUENTIAL AMENDMENTS

**82(1)** The provisions mentioned in Schedule 10 to these Regulations shall have effect subject to the amendments there specified, being minor amendments or amendments consequential on the provisions of these Regulations.

**82(2)** Any deed, contract or other instrument made before the commencement date shall have effect, unless the context otherwise requires, as if any reference to an institution authorised by the Bank under the Banking Act (however expressed) included a reference to a European deposit-taker.

**82(3)** In this regulation and Schedule 10 to these Regulations **"European deposit-taker"** means a European authorised institution which has lawfully established a branch in the United Kingdom for the purpose of accepting deposits.

## TRANSITIONAL PROVISIONS AND SAVINGS

**83** Schedule 11 to these Regulations shall have effect with respect to the transitional and other matters there mentioned.

# Schedule 1 – Annex to the Second Council Directive

Regulation 2(1)

"ANNEX – LIST OF ACTIVITIES SUBJECT TO MUTUAL RECOGNITION

1. Acceptance of deposits and other repayable funds from the public.
2. Lending (1).
3. Financial leasing.
4. Money transmission services.
5. Issuing and administering means of payment (e.g. credit cards, travellers' cheques and bankers' drafts).
6. Guarantees and commitments.
7. Trading for own account or for account of customers in:
   - (a) money market instruments (cheques, bills, CDs, etc.);
   - (b) foreign exchange;
   - (c) financial futures and options;
   - (d) exchange and interest rate instruments;
   - (e) transferable securities.
8. Participation in securities issues and the provision of services relating to such issues.
9. Advice to undertakings on capital structure, industrial strategy and related questions and advice and services relating to mergers and the purchase of undertakings.
10. Moneybroking.

11. Portfolio management and advice.
12. Safekeeping and administration of securities.
13. Credit reference services.
14. Safe custody services.

(1) Including inter alia:
- consumer credit,
- mortgage credit,
- factoring, with or without recourse,
- financing of commercial transactions (including forfaiting)."

# Schedule 2 – Requirements as Respects European Institutions

Regulation 3(8)

## REQUIREMENTS FOR CARRYING ON ACTIVITIES ETC.

**1(1)** In relation to the carrying on of a home-regulated activity by the provision of services, the requirements of this paragraph are that the institution has given to the relevant supervisory authority in its home State a notice in accordance with paragraph 2 below.

**1(2)** In relation to the establishment of a branch, the requirements of this paragraph are–

(a) that the institution has given to the relevant supervisory authority in its home State a notice in accordance with paragraph 2 below;

(b) that the Authority has received from that authority a notice in accordance with paragraph 3 below; and

(c) that either–
  (i) the Authority has informed the institution that it may establish the branch; or
  (ii) the period of two months beginning with the day on which the Authority received the notice mentioned in paragraph (b) above has elapsed.

**History**
See history note after para. 5(4).

**2** A notice given by an institution to the relevant supervisory authority in its home State is given in accordance with this paragraph if it states–

(a) the United Kingdom to be a member State in which the institution proposes to carry on home-regulated activities;

(b) whether the institution intends to establish a branch in the United Kingdom;

(c) if the notice states that the institution does not intend to establish such a branch, the home-regulated activities in relation to which the notice is given; and

(d) if the notice states that the institution intends to establish such a branch, the requisite details of the branch.

**3(1)** A notice given in respect of a European authorised institution or quasi-European authorised institution by the relevant supervisory authority in its home State is in accordance with this paragraph if it–

(a) certifies that the institution is a credit institution which is for the time being authorised to act as such an institution by the authority;

(b) contains the information stated in the institution's notice; and

(c) if the institution intends to establish a branch in the United Kingdom, contains–
  (i) a statement of the amount of the institution's own funds and the solvency ratio of the institution (calculated in accordance with the Solvency Ratio Directive); and
  (ii) details of any deposit guarantee scheme which is intended to secure the protection of depositors in the branch.

**3(2)** A notice given in respect of a European subsidiary or quasi-European subsidiary by the relevant supervisory authority in its home State is in accordance with this paragraph if it–

(a) certifies that the institution is a financial institution which is a 90 per cent subsidiary undertaking of a European institution incorporated in or formed under the law of that State;

(b) certifies that the conditions mentioned in regulation 3(6) of these Regulations are fulfilled in relation to the institution;

(c) certifies that the institution's business is being conducted in a prudent manner;

(d) contains the information stated in the institution's notice; and

(e) if the institution intends to establish a branch in the United Kingdom, contains a statement of the amount of the institution's own funds and the consolidated solvency ratio of the institution's parent undertaking (calculated in accordance with the Solvency Ratio Directive).

**3(3)** The Authority shall as soon as practicable send a copy of any notice received by it in accordance with this paragraph, and a note of the date of its receipt, to every other authority which it knows is a connected UK authority.

**History**
See history note after para. 5(4).

## REQUIREMENTS FOR CHANGING REQUISITE DETAILS OF BRANCH

**4(1)** Subject to sub-paragraph (2) below, the requirements of this paragraph are–

(a) that the institution has given a notice to the Authority, and to the relevant supervisory authority in its home State, stating the details of the proposed change;

(b) that the Authority has received from that authority a notice stating those details; and

(c) that either the Authority has informed the institution that it may make the change, or the period of one month beginning with the day on which it gave the Authority the notice mentioned in paragraph (a) above has elapsed.

**4(2)** In the case of a change occasioned by circumstances beyond the institution's control, the requirements of this paragraph are that the institution has, as soon as practicable (whether before or after the change), given a notice to the Authority, and to the relevant supervisory authority in its home State, stating the details of the change.

**4(3)** The Authority shall as soon as practicable send a copy of any notice received by it in accordance with this paragraph, and a note of the date of its receipt, to every other authority which it knows is a connected UK authority.

## CANCELLATION OF COMPLIANCE WITH CERTAIN REQUIREMENTS

**5(1)** The Authority may, on an application by a European subsidiary, direct that any compliance with the requirements of paragraph 1 above in relation to–

(a) its carrying on of any activity; or

(b) its establishment of a branch,

shall cease to have effect as from such date as may be specified in the direction.

**5(2)** The Authority shall not give a direction under this paragraph unless–

(a) the applicant has given notice of the application to the relevant supervisory authority in its home State; and

(b) the Authority has agreed with that authority that the direction should be given.

**5(3)** The date specified in a direction under this paragraph–

(a) shall not be earlier than the date requested in the application; but

(b) subject to that, shall be such date as may be agreed between the Authority and the relevant supervisory authority.

**5(4)** The Authority shall as soon as practicable send a copy of any direction given under this paragraph to the applicant, to the relevant supervisory authority and to every other authority which it knows is a connected UK authority.

**History**
In Sch. 2 the word "Authority" wherever occurring substituted for the former word "Bank" by the Bank of England Act 1998, s. 23(1), 45 and Sch. 5, para. 21, 29 as from 1 June 1998 (see SI 1998/1120 (C 25), art. 2).

# Schedule 3 – Prohibitions and Restrictions by the Authority

Regulation 9(7)

## PRELIMINARY

**1** In this Schedule–

**"prohibition"** means a prohibition under regulation 9 of these Regulations;

**"restriction"** means a restriction under regulation 10 of these Regulations.

## NOTICE OF PROHIBITION OR RESTRICTION IN NON-URGENT CASES

**2(1)** Subject to paragraph 3 below, where the Authority proposes, in relation to a European institution–

(a) to impose a prohibition;

(b) to impose a restriction; or

(c) to vary a restriction otherwise than with the agreement of the institution,

the Authority shall give notice of its proposal to the institution and to every other authority which it knows is a connected UK authority.

**History**
See history note after para. 5(2).

**2(2)** If the proposed action is within paragraph (b) or (c) of sub-paragraph (1) above, the notice under that sub-paragraph shall specify the proposed restriction or, as the case may be, the proposed variation.

**2(3)** A notice under sub-paragraph (1) above shall state the grounds on which the Authority proposes to act and give particulars of the institution's rights under sub-paragraph (5) below.

**History**
See history note after para. 5(2).

**2(4)** Where a proposed restriction consists of or includes a condition requiring the removal of any person as director, controller or manager, the Authority shall give that person a copy of the notice mentioned in sub-paragraph (1) above, together with a statement of his rights under sub-paragraph (5) below.

**History**
See history note after para. 5(2).

**2(5)** An institution which is given a notice under sub-paragraph (1) above and a person who is given a copy under sub-paragraph (4) above may, within the period of 14 days beginning with the day on which the notice was given, make representations to the Authority.

**History**
See history note after para. 5(2).

**2(6)** After giving a notice under sub-paragraph (1) above and taking into account any representations made under sub-paragraph (5) above, the Authority shall decide whether–

(a) to proceed with the action proposed in the notice;

(b) to take no further action;

(c) if the proposed action was the imposition of a prohibition, to impose a restriction instead of or in addition to the prohibition; or

(d) if the proposed action was the imposition or variation of a restriction, to impose a different restriction or make a different variation.

**History**
See history note after para. 5(2).

**2(7)** The Authority shall give–

(a) the institution;

(b) any such person as is mentioned in sub-paragraph (4) above; and

(c) the relevant supervisory authority in the institution's home State,

written notice of its decision and, except where the decision is to take no further action, the notice shall state the reasons for the decision and give particulars of the rights conferred by sub-paragraph (11) below and section 27 of the Banking Act.

**History**

See history note after para. 5(2).

**2(8)** A notice under sub-paragraph (7) above shall be given–

(a) within the period of 28 days beginning with the day on which the notice under sub-paragraph (1) above was given; or

(b) where a reply of the relevant supervisory authority to a notice under regulation 11(3) of these Regulations was received during the second half of that period, within the period of 14 days beginning with the day on which that reply was so received;

and where such a reply was so received, the Authority shall give notice of that fact to the institution and to any such person as is mentioned in sub-paragraph (4) above.

**History**

See history note after para. 5(2).

**2(9)** If no notice under sub-paragraph (7) above is given within the period mentioned in sub-paragraph (8) above, the Authority shall be treated as having at the end of that period given a notice under that sub-paragraph to the effect that no further action is to be taken.

**History**

See history note after para. 5(2).

**2(10)** A notice under sub-paragraph (7) above imposing a prohibition or a restriction on an institution or varying a restriction shall, subject to section 27(4) of the Banking Act, have the effect of prohibiting the institution from accepting deposits in the United Kingdom or restricting its activities or varying the restriction in the manner specified in the notice.

**2(11)** Where the decision notified under sub-paragraph (7) above is to impose or vary a restriction otherwise than as stated in the notice given under sub-paragraph (1) above–

(a) the institution concerned; and

(b) in the case of a European institution, the relevant supervisory authority,

may, within the period of seven days beginning with the day on which the notice was given under sub-paragraph (7) above, make written representations to the Authority with respect to the restriction or variation and the Authority may, after taking those representations into account, alter the restriction.

**History**

See history note after para. 5(2).

**2(12)** The Authority may omit from the copy given to a person under sub-paragraph (4) above and from a notice given to him under sub-paragraph (7) above any matter which does not relate to him.

**History**

See history note after para. 5(2).

## NOTICE OF PROHIBITION OR RESTRICTION IN URGENT CASES

**3(1)** No notice need be given in accordance with paragraph 2 above in respect of–

(a) the imposition of a prohibition;

(b) the imposition of a restriction; or

(c) the variation of a restriction otherwise than with the agreement of the institution concerned,

in any case in which the Authority considers that the prohibition or restriction should be imposed, or the variation should be made, as a matter of urgency.

**History**
See history note after para. 5(2).

**3(2)** In any such case the Authority may by written notice to the institution impose the prohibition or restriction or make the variation.

**History**
See history note after para. 5(2).

**3(3)** Any such notice shall state the reasons for which the Authority has acted and particulars of the rights conferred by sub-paragraph (5) below and by section 27 of the Banking Act.

**History**
See history note after para. 5(2).

**3(4)** Where a restriction consists of or includes a condition requiring the removal of any person as director, controller or manager, the Authority shall give that person a copy of the notice mentioned in sub-paragraph (2) above, together with a statement of his rights under sub-paragraph (5) below.

**History**
See history note after para. 5(2).

**3(5)** An institution to which a notice is given under this paragraph and a person who is given a copy of it by virtue of sub-paragraph (4) above may within the period of 14 days beginning with the day on which the notice was given make representations to the Authority.

**History**
See history note after para. 5(2).

**3(6)** After giving a notice under sub-paragraph (2) above and taking into account any representations made in accordance with sub-paragraph (5) above, the Authority shall decide whether–

(a) to confirm or rescind its original decision; or

(b) to impose a different restriction or to vary the restriction in a different manner.

**History**
See history note after para. 5(2).

**3(7)** The Authority shall, within the period of 28 days beginning with the day on which the notice was given under sub-paragraph (2) above, give–

(a) the institution; and

(b) the relevant supervisory authority in the institution's home State,

written notice of its decision under sub-paragraph (6) above and, except where the decision is to rescind the original decision, the notice shall state the reasons for the decision.

**History**
See history note after para. 5(2).

**3(8)** Where the notice under sub-paragraph (7) above is of a decision to take the action specified in sub-paragraph (6)(b) above, the notice under sub-paragraph (7) shall have the effect of imposing the prohibition or restriction, or making the variation specified in the notice, with effect from the date on which it is given.

## APPEALS

**4(1)** Section 27 of the Banking Act (rights of appeal) shall have effect as if–

(a) the decisions mentioned in subsection (1) included a decision of the Authority to impose a prohibition or impose or vary a restriction; and

(b) the reference in subsection (4) to the revocation of an institution's authorisation included a reference to the imposition of a prohibition on the institution.

**History**
See history note after para. 5(2).

**4(2)** Section 29 of that Act (determination of appeals) shall have effect as if in subsection (2)(a)–

(a) the reference to revoking an authorisation included a reference to imposing a prohibition; and

(b) the reference to restricting an authorisation instead included a reference to imposing instead a restriction.

**4(3)** That section shall also have effect as if it included provision that, in the case of any appeal by a European institution, notice of the tribunal's determination, together with a statement of its reasons, shall be given to the relevant supervisory authority in the institution's home State.

## STATEMENT OF PRINCIPLES

**5(1)** The Authority shall, as soon as practicable after the coming into force of these Regulations, publish in such manner as it thinks appropriate a statement of the principles in accordance with which it is acting or proposing to act in exercising its power to impose a prohibition on or to restrict the listed activities of a European institution.

**History**
See history note after para. 5(2).

**5(2)** Subsection (2) of section 16 of the Banking Act (statement of principles) shall apply for the purposes of sub-paragraph (1) above as it applies for the purpose of subsection (1) of that section.

**History**
In Sch. 3, the word "Authority" wherever occurring substituted for the former word "Bank" by the Bank of England Act 1998, s. 23(1), 45 and Sch. 5, para. 21, 29 as from 1 June 1998 (see SI 1998/1120 (C 25), art. 2).

**Note**
Note that the same substitution has been made in the heading to Sch. 3, although not technically required by above amendment.

# Schedule 4 – Prohibitions by the Board

Regulation 15(5)

## NOTICE OF PROHIBITION

**1(1)** Where the Board proposes–

(a) to impose a prohibition on a European institution under regulation 15 of these Regulations; or

(b) to refuse an application made by a European institution under paragraph (3) of that regulation,

it shall give the institution on which it proposes to impose the prohibition, or whose application it proposes to refuse, written notice of its intention to do so, stating the reasons for which it proposes to act.

**1(2)** In the case of a proposed prohibition the notice shall state the date on which it is proposed that the prohibition should take effect and, in the case of a limited prohibition, its proposed duration.

**1(3)** Where the reasons stated in a notice under sub-paragraph (1) above relate specifically to matters which–

(a) refer to a person identified in the notice other than the institution concerned; and

(b) are in the opinion of the Board prejudicial to that person in any office or employment,

the Board shall, unless it considers it impracticable to do so, serve a copy of the notice on that person.

**1(4)** A notice under sub-paragraph (1) above shall give particulars of the right to require the case to be referred to the Financial Services Tribunal under section 97 of the Financial Services Act.

**1(5)** Where a case is not required to be referred to that Tribunal by an institution on whom a notice is served under sub-paragraph (1) above, the Board shall, at the expiration of the period within which such a requirement can be made–

(a) give that institution written notice of the prohibition or refusal; or

(b) give that institution written notice that the prohibition is not to be imposed or, as the case may be, written notice of the grant of the application, and the Board may give public notice of any decision notified by it under paragraph (a) or (b) above and the reasons for the decision, except that it shall not do so in the case of a decision notified under paragraph (b) unless the institution concerned consents to its doing so.

**1(6)** Where the Board gives a notice under sub-paragraph (1) or (5)(a) or (b) above, it shall serve a copy of the notice–

(b) on the relevant supervisory authority in the institution's home State.

**History**

Para. 1(6)(a) omitted and revoked by the Bank of England Act 1998, s. 23(1), 43, 45 and Sch. 5, para. 21, 20 and Sch. 9, Pt. II as from 1 June 1998 (see SI 1998/1120 (C 25), art. 2). The former para. 1(6)(a) read as follows:

"(a) on the Bank; and"

## REFERENCES TO THE FINANCIAL SERVICES TRIBUNAL

**2** Section 97 of the Financial Services Act (references to the Tribunal) shall have effect as if–

(a) any reference to a notice served under section 29 of that Act included a reference to a notice served under paragraph 1 above;

(b) any reference to a copy of a notice served under the said section 29 included a reference to a copy of a notice served under sub-paragraph (3) of that paragraph;

(c) any reference to the withdrawal of an authorisation included a reference to the imposition of an absolute prohibition under regulation 15 of these Regulations; and

(d) any reference to the suspension of an authorisation included a reference to the imposition of a limited prohibition under regulation 15 of these Regulations,

and any reference in that section to a decision not to withdraw or suspend an authorisation shall be construed accordingly.

**3(1)** Section 98 of the Financial Services Act (decisions on references by applicant or authorised person etc.) shall have effect as if–

(a) the applications mentioned in paragraph (a) of subsection (2) included an application for the variation of a limited prohibition imposed under regulation 15 of these Regulations; but

(b) as if the applications mentioned in paragraph (b) of that subsection did not include an application for the rescission of any prohibition imposed under that regulation.

**3(2)** Subsection (3)(b) of that section shall have effect as if the provisions there referred to included regulation 15 of these Regulations.

**3(3)** That section shall have effect as if it included provision that paragraph 1 above shall not apply to any action taken by the Board in accordance with the Tribunal's report.

**4(1)** Subsection (2) of section 100 of the Financial Services Act (withdrawal of references) shall have effect as if the reference to the provisions mentioned in section 97(1)(a) of that Act included a reference to paragraph 1 above.

**4(2)** That section shall have effect as if it included provision that where a person on whom a notice was served under paragraph 1 above withdraws a case from the Tribunal, sub-paragraph (5) of that paragraph shall apply to him as if he had not required the case to be referred.

# Schedule 5 – Prohibitions and Restrictions by the Director

Regulation 18(6)

## PRELIMINARY

**1** In this Schedule–

**"appeal period"** has the same meaning as in the Consumer Credit Act;

**"prohibition"** means a prohibition under regulation 18 of these Regulations;

**"restriction"** means a restriction under regulation 19 of these Regulations.

## NOTICE OF PROHIBITION OR RESTRICTION

**2(1)** This paragraph applies where the Director proposes, in relation to a European institution–

(a) to impose a prohibition;

(b) to impose a restriction; or

(c) to vary a restriction otherwise than with the agreement of the institution.

**2(2)** The Director shall, by notice–

(a) inform the institution that, as the case may be, the Director proposes to impose the prohibition or restriction or vary the restriction, stating his reasons; and

(b) invite the institution to submit representations to the proposal in accordance with paragraph 4 below.

**2(3)** If he imposes the prohibition or restriction or varies the restriction, the Director may give directions authorising the institution to carry into effect agreements made before the coming into force of the prohibition, restriction or variation.

**2(4)** A prohibition, restriction or variation shall not come into force before the end of the appeal period.

**2(5)** Where the Director imposes a prohibition or restriction or varies a restriction, he shall serve a copy of the prohibition, restriction or variation–

(a) on the Authority; and

(b) on the relevant supervisory authority in the institution's home State.

**History**
See history note after para. 5.

## APPLICATION TO REVOKE PROHIBITION OR RESTRICTION

**3(1)** This paragraph applies where the Director proposes to refuse an application made by a European institution for the revocation of a prohibition or restriction.

**3(2)** The Director shall, by notice–

(a) inform the institution that the Director proposes to refuse the application, stating his reasons; and

(b) invite the institution to submit representations in support of the application in accordance with paragraph 4 below.

## REPRESENTATIONS TO DIRECTOR

**4(1)** Where this paragraph applies to an invitation by the Director to an institution to submit representations, the Director shall invite the institution, within 21 days after the notice containing the invitation is given to it, or such longer period as the Director may allow–

(a) to submit its representations in writing to the Director; and

(b) to give notice to the Director, if it thinks fit, that it wishes to make representations orally;

and where notice is given under paragraph (b) above the Director shall arrange for the oral representations to be heard.

**4(2)** In reaching his determination the Director shall take into account any representations submitted or made under this paragraph.

**4(3)** The Director shall give notice of his determination to the institution.

## APPEALS

**5** Section 41 of the Consumer Credit Act (appeals to the Secretary of State) shall have effect as if–

(a) the following determinations were mentioned in column 1 of the table set out at the end of that section, namely–

(i) imposition of a prohibition or restriction or the variation of a restriction; and

(ii) refusal of an application for the revocation of a prohibition or restriction; and

(b) the European institution concerned were mentioned in column 2 of that table in relation to those determinations.

**History**
In Sch. 5, the word "Authority" wherever occurring substituted for the former word "Bank" by the Bank of England Act 1998, s. 23(1), 45 and Sch. 5, para. 21, 31 as from 1 June 1998 (see SI 1998/1120 (C 25), art. 2).

# Schedule 6 – Requirements as Respects UK Institutions

Regulation 22(6)

## REQUIREMENTS FOR CARRYING ON ACTIVITIES ETC.

**1(1)** In relation to the carrying on of a home-regulated activity by the provision of services, the requirements of this paragraph are that the institution has given to the UK authority a notice in accordance with paragraph 2 below.

**1(2)** In relation to the establishment of a branch, the requirements of this paragraph are–

(a) that the institution has given to the UK authority a notice in accordance with paragraph 2 below;

(b) that the UK authority has given to the relevant supervisory authority in the member State concerned the notice which, subject to paragraph 4 below, it is required by paragraph 3(1) or (2) below to give; and

(c) that either–

(i) the relevant supervisory authority has informed the institution that it may establish the branch; or

(ii) the period of two months beginning with the day on which the UK authority gave the relevant supervisory authority the notice mentioned in paragraph (b) above has elapsed.

**2** A notice given by an institution to the UK authority is given in accordance with this paragraph if it states–

(a) the member State in which the institution proposes to carry on home-regulated activities;

(b) whether the institution intends to establish a branch in that member State;

(c) if the notice states that the institution does not intend to establish such a branch, the home-regulated activities in relation to which the notice is given; and

(d) if the notice states that the institution intends to establish such a branch, the requisite details of the branch.

**3(1)** The notice which, subject to paragraph 4 below, the UK authority is required to give in respect of a UK authorised institution is a notice which is addressed to the relevant supervisory authority in the member State identified in the institution's notice under paragraph 2 above and which–

(a) certifies that the institution is a credit institution which is for the time being authorised by the UK authority under the Banking Act or, as the case may be, the Building Societies Act;

(b) contains the information stated in the institution's notice; and

(c) if the institution intends to establish a branch in the member State, contains–

(i) a statement of the amount of the institution's own funds and the solvency ratio of the institution (calculated in accordance with the Solvency Ratio Directive); and

(ii) details of any deposit guarantee scheme which is intended to secure the protection of depositors in the branch.

**3(2)** The notice which, subject to paragraph 4 below, the UK authority is required to give in respect of a UK subsidiary is a notice which is addressed to the relevant supervisory authority in the member State identified in the institution's notice under paragraph 2 above and which–

(a) certifies that the institution is a financial institution which is a 90 per cent subsidiary undertaking of a UK authorised institution;

(b) certifies that the conditions mentioned in regulation 20(5) of these Regulations are fulfilled in relation to the institution;

(c) certifies that the institution's business is being conducted in a prudent manner;

(d) contains the information stated in the institution's notice; and

(e) if the institution intends to establish a branch in the member State, contains a statement of the amount of the institution's own funds and the consolidated solvency ratio of the institution's parent undertaking (calculated in accordance with the Solvency Ratio Directive).

**4(1)** Where the institution's notice under paragraph 2 above states that the institution does not intend to establish a branch in the member State, the notice referred to in paragraph 3(1) or (2) above shall be given within the period of one month beginning with the date on which the institution's notice was received by the UK authority.

**4(2)** Where the institution's notice under paragraph 2 above states that the institution intends to establish a branch in the member State, the UK authority shall, within the period of three months beginning with the date on which the institution's notice was received–

(a) give the notice referred to in paragraph 3(1) or (2) above; or

(b) refuse to give such a notice.

**4(3)** The UK authority may not refuse to give such a notice unless, having regard to the home-regulated activities proposed to be carried on, the UK authority doubts the adequacy of the administrative structure or the financial situation of the institution.

**4(4)** Before determining to give or to refuse to give such a notice, the UK authority–

(a) shall seek and take into account the views of every other authority which it knows is a connected UK authority in relation to any of the home-regulated activities proposed to be carried on; and

(b) may regard itself as satisfied in relation to any matter relating to those activities which is relevant to the decision if any such authority informs the UK authority that it is so satisfied.

**4(5)** In reaching a determination as to the adequacy of the administrative structure, the UK authority may have regard to the adequacy of management, systems and controls and the presence of relevant skills needed for the activities proposed to be carried on.

**4(6)** Where the institution's notice under paragraph 2 above states that the institution proposes to establish a branch, the UK authority shall, within the period of three months referred to in sub-paragraph (2) above, notify the institution–

(a) that it has given the notice referred to in paragraph 3(l) or (2) above, stating the date on which it did so; or

(b) that it has refused to give the notice, stating the reasons for the refusal and giving particulars of the rights conferred by section 27 of the Banking Act or, as the case may be, section 46 of the Building Societies Act.

## REQUIREMENTS FOR CHANGING REQUISITE DETAILS OF BRANCH

**5(1)** Subject to sub-paragraph (2) below, the requirements of this paragraph are–

(a) that the institution has given a notice to the UK authority, and to the relevant supervisory authority in the member State in which it has established the branch, stating the details of the proposed change;

(b) that that authority has received from the UK authority a notice under paragraph 6(1) below; and

(c) that either that authority has informed the institution that it may make the change, or the period of one month beginning with the day on which it gave that authority the notice mentioned in paragraph (a) above has elapsed.

**5(2)** In the case of a change occasioned by circumstances beyond the institution's control, the requirements of this paragraph are that the institution has, as soon as practicable (whether before or after the change), given a notice to the UK authority, and to the relevant supervisory authority in the member State in which it has established the branch, stating the details of the change.

**6(1)** The UK authority shall, within the period of one month beginning with the date on which the notice under paragraph 5(1) above was received–

(a) give a notice to the relevant supervisory authority informing it of the details of the proposed change; or

(b) refuse to give such a notice.

**6(2)** The UK authority may not refuse to give a notice under sub-paragraph (1) above unless, having regard to the changes and to the home-regulated activities proposed to be carried on, the UK authority doubts the adequacy of the administrative structure or the financial situation of the institution.

**6(3)** Before determining to give or to refuse to give such a notice, the UK authority–

(a) shall seek and take into account the views of any connected UK authority in relation to any changes to the home-regulated activities proposed to be carried on; and

(b) may regard itself as satisfied in relation to any matter relating to those activities which is relevant to the decision if any such authority informs the UK authority that it is so satisfied.

**6(4)** In reaching a determination as to the adequacy of the administrative structure, the UK authority may have regard to the adequacy of management, systems and controls and the presence of relevant skills needed for the activities proposed to be carried on.

**6(5)** The UK authority shall, within the period of one month referred to in sub-paragraph (1) above, notify the institution–

(a) that it has given the notice referred to in that sub-paragraph, stating the date on which it did so; or

(b) that it refused to give the notice, stating the reasons for the refusal and giving particulars of the rights conferred by section 27 of the Banking Act or, as the case may be, section 46 of the Building Societies Act.

## CANCELLATION OF COMPLIANCE WITH CERTAIN REQUIREMENTS

**7(1)** The UK authority may, on an application by a UK subsidiary, direct that any compliance with the requirements of paragraph 1 above in relation to–

(a) its carrying on of any activity in another member State; or

(b) its establishment of a branch in another member State,

shall cease to have effect as from such date as may be specified in the direction.

**7(2)** The UK authority shall not give a direction under this paragraph unless–

(a) the applicant has given notice of the application to the relevant supervisory authority in the member State concerned; and

(b) the UK authority has agreed with the relevant supervisory authority that the direction should be given.

**7(3)** The date specified in a direction under this paragraph–

(a) shall not be earlier than the date requested in the application; but

(b) subject to that, shall be such date as may be agreed between the UK authority and the relevant supervisory authority.

**7(4)** The UK authority shall as soon as practicable send a copy of any direction given under this paragraph to the applicant, to the relevant supervisory authority and to every other authority which it knows is a connected UK authority.

## APPEALS

**8(1)** Section 27 of the Banking Act (rights of appeal) shall have effect as if the decisions mentioned in subsection (1) included a decision of the Authority to refuse to give a notice under paragraph 3(1) or (2) or 6(1) above.

**History**
See history note after para. 9(2).

**8(2)** Section 29 of the Banking Act (determination of appeals) shall have effect as if it included provision that, where the tribunal reverses a decision of the Authority to refuse to give a notice under paragraph 3(1) or (2) or 6(1) above, the tribunal shall direct the Authority to give the notice.

**History**
See history note after para. 9(2).

**9(1)** Section 46 of the Building Societies Act (rights of appeal) shall have effect as if–

(a) the decisions mentioned in subsection (1) included a decision of the Commission to refuse to give a notice under paragraph 3(1) or (2) or 6(1) above; and

(b) in relation to such a decision, the reference in that subsection to a building society included a reference to a UK subsidiary.

**9(2)** Section 47 of the Building Societies Act (determination of appeals) shall have effect as if it included provision that, where the tribunal reverses a decision of the Commission to refuse to give a notice under paragraph 3(1) or (2) or 6(1) above, the tribunal shall direct the Commission to give the notice.

**History**

In Sch. 6, the word "Authority" wherever occurring substituted for the former word "Bank" by the Bank of England Act 1998, s. 23(1), 45 and Sch. 5, para. 21, 31 as from 1 June 1998 (see SI 1998/1120 (C 25), art. 2).

# Schedule 7 – Restrictions by the UK Authority

Regulation 23(7)

## PRELIMINARY

**1** In this Schedule **"restriction"** means a restriction under regulation 23 of these Regulations.

## NOTICE OF RESTRICTION IN NON-URGENT CASES

**2(1)** Subject to paragraph 3 below, where the UK authority proposes, in relation to a UK subsidiary–

(a) to impose a restriction; or

(b) to vary a restriction otherwise than with the agreement of the institution,

the UK authority shall give notice of its proposal to the institution and to every other authority which it knows is a connected UK authority.

**2(2)** A notice under sub-paragraph (1) above shall–

(a) specify the proposed restriction or, as the case may be, the proposed variation; and

(b) state the grounds on which the UK authority proposes to act and give particulars of the institution's rights under sub-paragraph (4) below.

**2(3)** Where–

(a) a proposed restriction consists of or includes a condition requiring the removal of any person as director, controller or manager; or

(b) the ground or a ground for a proposal to impose or vary a restriction is that it appears to the UK authority that the criterion in paragraph 1 of Schedule 3 to the Banking Act is not or has not been fulfilled, or may not or may not have been fulfilled, in the case of any person,

the UK authority shall give that person a copy of the notice mentioned in sub-paragraph (1) above, together with a statement of his rights under sub-paragraph (4) below.

**2(4)** An institution which is given a notice under sub-paragraph (1) above and a person who is given a copy under sub-paragraph (3) above may, within the period of 14 days beginning with the day on which the notice was given, make representations to the UK authority.

**2(5)** After giving a notice under sub-paragraph (1) above and taking into account any representations made under sub-paragraph (4) above, the UK authority shall decide whether–

(a) to proceed with the action proposed in the notice;

(b) to take no further action; or

(c) to impose a different restriction or, as the case may be, make a different variation.

**2(6)** The UK authority shall give–

(a) the institution; and

(b) any such person as is mentioned in sub-paragraph (4) above,

written notice of its decision and, except where the decision is to take no further action, the notice shall state the reasons for the decision and give particulars of the rights conferred by sub-paragraph (10) below and section 27 of the Banking Act or, as the case may be, section 46 of the Building Societies Act.

**2(7)** A notice under sub-paragraph (6) above shall be given within the period of 28 days beginning with the day on which the notice under sub-paragraph (1) above was given.

**2(8)** If no notice under sub-paragraph (6) above is given within the period mentioned in sub-paragraph (7) above, the UK authority shall be treated as having at the end of that period given a notice under that sub-paragraph to the effect that no further action is to be taken.

**2(9)** A notice under sub-paragraph (6) above imposing a restriction on an institution or varying a restriction shall have the effect of restricting the institution's activities or varying the restriction in the manner specified in the notice.

**2(10)** Where the decision notified under sub-paragraph (6) above is to impose or vary a restriction otherwise than as stated in the notice given under sub-paragraph (1) above–

(a) the institution concerned may, within the period of seven days beginning with the day on which the notice was given under sub-paragraph (6) above, make written representations to the UK authority with respect to the restriction or variation; and

(b) the UK authority may, after taking those representations into account, alter the restriction.

**2(11)** The UK authority may omit from the copy given to a person under sub-paragraph (4) above and from a notice given to him under sub-paragraph (6) above any matter which does not relate to him.

## NOTICE OF RESTRICTION IN URGENT CASES

**3(1)** No notice need be given in accordance with paragraph 2 above in respect of–

(a) the imposition of a restriction; or

(b) the variation of a restriction otherwise than with the agreement of the institution concerned,

in any case in which the UK authority considers that the restriction should be imposed, or the variation should be made, as a matter of urgency.

**3(2)** In any such case the UK authority may by written notice to the institution impose the restriction or make the variation.

**3(3)** Any such notice shall state the reasons for which the UK authority has acted and particulars of the rights conferred by sub-paragraph (5) below and by section 27 of the Banking Act or, as the case may be, section 46 of the Building Societies Act.

**3(4)** Where–

(a) a restriction consists of or includes a condition requiring the removal of any person as director, controller or manager; or

(b) the ground or a ground for a restriction or variation ofa restriction is that it appears to the UK authority that the criterion in paragraph 1 of Schedule 3 to the Banking Act is not or has not been fulfilled, or may not or may not have been fulfilled, in the case of any person,

the UK authority shall give that person a copy of the notice mentioned in sub-paragraph (2) above, together with a statement of his rights under sub-paragraph (5) below.

**3(5)** An institution to which a notice is given under this paragraph and a person who is given a copy of it by virtue of sub-paragraph (4) above may within the period of 14 days beginning with the day on which the notice was given make representations to the UK authority.

**3(6)** After giving a notice under sub-paragraph (2) above and taking into account any representations made in accordance with sub-paragraph (5) above, the UK authority shall decide whether–

(a) to confirm or rescind its original decision; or

(b) to impose a different restriction or to vary the restriction in a different manner.

**3(7)** The UK authority shall, within the period of 28 days beginning with the day on which the notice was given under sub-paragraph (2) above, give the institution written notice of its decision under sub-paragraph (6) above and, except where the decision is to rescind the original decision, the notice shall state the reasons for the decision.

**3(8)** Where the notice under sub-paragraph (7) above is of a decision to take the action specified in sub-paragraph (6)(b) above, the notice under sub-paragraph (7) shall have the effect of imposing the restriction, or making the variation specified in the notice, with effect from the date on which it is given.

### APPEALS

**4** Section 27 of the Banking Act (rights of appeal) shall have effect as if the decisions mentioned in subsection (1) included a decision of the Authority to impose or vary a restriction.

**5(1)** Section 46 of the Building Societies Act (rights of appeal) shall have effect as if–

(a) the decisions mentioned in subsection (1) included a decision of the Commission to impose or vary a restriction; and

(b) in relation to such a decision, the reference in that subsection to a building society included a reference to a UK subsidiary.

**5(2)** Section 47 of that Act (determination of appeals) shall have effect as if it included provision enabling the tribunal to vary any decision of the Commission to impose or vary a restriction by directing the Commission to impose a different restriction or make a different variation.

### STATEMENT OF PRINCIPLES

**6(1)** The Authority shall, as soon as practicable after the coming into force of these Regulations, publish in such manner as it thinks appropriate a statement of the principles in accordance with which it is acting or proposing to act in exercising its power to restrict the listed activities of a UK subsidiary.

**History**

In para. 6(1) the word "Authority" substituted for the former word "Bank" by the Bank of England Act 1998, s. 23(1), 45 and Sch. 5, para. 21, 31 as from 1 June 1998 (see SI 1998/1120 (C 25), art. 2).

**6(2)** Subsection (2) of section 16 of the Banking Act (statement of principles) shall apply for the purposes of sub-paragraph (1) above as it applies for the purpose of subsection (1) of that section.

## Schedule 9 – Amendments of Financial Services Act

Regulation 55

### PRELIMINARY

**1** In this Schedule–

**"the Act"** means the Financial Services Act;

**"investment agreement"** has the same meaning as in the Act.

### RESTRICTION ON CARRYING ON BUSINESS

**2** Section 5 of the Act (agreements made by or through unauthorised persons) shall have effect as if the persons mentioned in subsection (1)(b)(i) included a European institution acting in the course of home-regulated investment business carried on by it in the United Kingdom.

### AUTHORISED PERSONS

**3** Section 10 of the Act (grant and refusal of recognition of self-regulating organisations) shall have effect as if the excepted cases mentioned in subsection (3) included the case where the member is a European institution and the business is home-regulated investment business.

**4** Section 13 of the Act (alteration of rules of recognised self-regulating organisation for protection of investors) shall have effect as if the excepted cases mentioned in subsection (2) (both as amended and as originally enacted) included the case where the member is a European institution and the business is home-regulated investment business.

**5** Section 28 of the Act (withdrawal and suspension of authorisation) shall have effect in relation to an authorisation granted to a European institution as if the reference in subsection (1)(a) to the investment business which the holder of the authorisation is carrying on or proposing to carry on did not include a reference to any home-regulated investment business.

**6** Section 32 of the Act (notice of commencement of business) shall have effect in relation to a notice given under subsection (1) by a European institution or quasi-European authorised institution as if the reference in subsection (2)(a) to the investment business which is proposed to be carried on did not include a reference to any home-regulated investment business.

## EXEMPTED PERSONS

**7** Section 44 of the Act (appointed representatives) shall have effect as if any reference to an authorised person included a reference to a European institution carrying on home-regulated investment business in the United Kingdom.

**8** Section 45 of the Act (miscellaneous exemptions) shall have effect as if the reference in subsection (2) to a partnership which is an authorised person included a reference to a partnership which is or was a European institution carrying on home-regulated investment business in the United Kingdom.

## CONDUCT OF BUSINESS

**9(1)** Section 47A of the Act (statements of principle) shall have effect as if–

(a) the reference in subsection (1) to the conduct expected of persons authorised to carry on investment business included a reference to the conduct expected of European institutions carrying on home-regulated investment business in the United Kingdom; and

(b) the reference in subsection (4) to the withdrawal or suspension of authorisation under section 28 of the Act included a reference to the imposition of a prohibition under regulation 15 of these Regulations.

**9(2)** That section shall also have effect as if it included provision that a statement of principle issued under that section shall not include, as respects any European institution–

(a) provision as to the fitness of the institution to carry on any home-regulated investment business; or

(b) provision as to any other matter for which, under the Second Council Directive, responsibility is reserved to the relevant supervisory authority in the institution's home State.

**10(1)** Section 48 of the Act (conduct of business rules) shall have effect as if–

(a) the reference in subsection (1) to the conduct of investment business by authorised persons included a reference to the conduct of home-regulated investment business carried on in the United Kingdom by European institutions; and

(b) the reference in subsection (2) to an authorised person included a reference to a European institution carrying on home-regulated investment business in the United Kingdom.

**10(2)** That section shall have effect as if it included provision that rules under that section shall not include, as respects any European institution–

(a) provision prohibiting the institution from carrying on, or holding itself out as carrying on, any home-regulated investment business; or

(b) provision as to any matter for which, under the Second Council Directive, responsibility is reserved to the relevant supervisory authority in the institution's home State.

**11(1)** Section 49 of the Act (financial resources rules) shall have effect as if it included provision that rules under that section shall not include, as respects any European institution which is a member of a recognised self-regulating organisation, provision requiring the institution to have and maintain financial resources in respect of any home-regulated investment business carried on by it.

**11(2)** Subsection (2) of that section shall also have effect in relation to an authorised person who is a European institution as if the reference in paragraph (b) to any business (whether or not investment business) carried on by the person concerned did not include a reference to any home-regulated investment business.

**12(1)** Section 51 of the Act (cancellation rules) shall have effect as if the reference in subsection (1) to a person who has entered or offered to enter into an investment agreement with an authorised person included a reference to a person who has entered or offered to enter into an investment agreement to which sub-paragraph (2) below applies.

**12(2)** This sub-paragraph applies to an investment agreement which is made by a European institution in the course of the carrying on by it of home-regulated investment business in the United Kingdom.

**13(1)** Section 52 of the Act (notification regulations) shall have effect as if any reference to authorised persons, or an authorised person, included a reference to European institutions, or a European institution, carrying on home-regulated investment business in the United Kingdom.

**13(2)** That section shall also have effect as if it included provision that regulations under that section shall not require European institutions to furnish information which is not reasonably required for purposes connected with the exercise of functions under the Act or these Regulations.

**14** Section 53 of the Act (indemnity rules) shall have effect as if the reference in subsection (1) to civil liability incurred by an authorised person in connection with his investment business included a reference to civil liability incurred by a European institution in connection with home-regulated investment business carried on by it in the United Kingdom.

**15** Section 54 of the Act (compensation fund) shall have effect as if–

(a) it included provision that rules establishing a scheme under that section may include in the scheme provision for compensating investors in cases where persons who are or have been European institutions are unable, or likely to be unable, to satisfy claims in respect of any civil liability incurred by them in connection with home-regulated investment business carried on by them in the United Kingdom; and

(b) any reference in subsection (2) to authorised persons included a reference to European institutions carrying on home-regulated investment business in the United Kingdom.

**16** Section 55 of the Act (clients' money) shall have effect as if any reference to authorised persons, or an authorised person, included a reference to European institutions, or a European institution, carrying on home-regulated investment business in the United Kingdom.

**17** Section 57 of the Act (restrictions on advertising) shall have effect as if any reference to an authorised person included a reference to a European institution carrying on home-regulated investment business in the United Kingdom.

**18** Section 59 of the Act (employment of prohibited persons) shall have effect as if any reference to authorised persons, or an authorised person, included a reference to European institutions, or a European institution, carrying on home-regulated investment business in the United Kingdom.

**19** Section 60 of the Act (public statement as to person's misconduct) shall have effect as if–

(a) the reference in subsection (1) to a person who is or was an authorised person by virtue of section 25 of that Act included a reference to a person who is or was a European institution carrying on home-regulated investment business in the United Kingdom;

(b) the reference in subsection (3) to the authorised person included a reference to the European institution; and

(c) it included provision that where any notice under that section is given to a person who is or was a European institution, a copy of the notice shall be served on the Authority.

**History**
In para. 19(c), the word "Authority" substituted for the former word "Bank" by the Bank of England Act 1998, s. 23(1), 45 and Sch. 5, para. 21, 33 as from 1 June 1998 (see SI 1998/1120 (C 25), art. 2).

**20** Section 64 of the Act (scope of powers of intervention) shall have effect in relation to an authorised person who is a European institution as if the reference in subsection (1) to investment business of a particular kind did not include a reference to any home-regulated investment business which the authorised person is carrying on or proposing to carry on.

**21** Section 65 of the Act (restriction of business) shall have effect as if the reference in subsection (1) to an authorised person included a reference to a European institution carrying on home-regulated investment business in the United Kingdom.

**22** Section 66 of the Act (restriction on dealing with assets) shall have effect as if–

(a) the reference in subsection (1) to an authorised person included a reference to a European institution carrying on home-regulated investment business in the United Kingdom; and

(b) it included provision that a prohibition may not be imposed under that section in relation to a European institution unless the relevant supervisory authority in the institution's home State has requested that measures be taken for the purpose of ensuring that the institution has sufficient assets available to cover risks arising from open positions on financial markets in the United Kingdom.

**23** Section 67 of the Act (vesting of assets in trustee) shall have effect as if–

(a) any reference to an authorised person included a reference to a European institution carrying on home-regulated investment business in the United Kingdom; and

(b) it included provision that a requirement may not be imposed under that section in relation to a European institution unless the relevant supervisory authority in the institution's home State has requested that measures be taken for the purpose of ensuring that the institution has sufficient assets available to cover risks arising from open positions on financial markets in the United Kingdom.

## COLLECTIVE INVESTMENT SCHEMES

**24** Section 75 of the Act (collective investment schemes: interpretation) shall have effect as if the reference in subsection (6) to an authorised person included a reference to a European institution carrying on home-regulated investment business in the United Kingdom.

**25** Section 76 of the Act (restrictions on promotion) shall have effect as if any reference to an authorised person included a reference to a European institution carrying on home-regulated investment business in the United Kingdom.

**26** Section 93 of the Act (applications to the court) shall have effect as if the reference in subsection (1) to an authorised person included a reference to a European institution.

## INFORMATION

**27** Section 102 of the Act (register of authorised persons etc.) shall have effect as if it included provision that–

(a) the register kept under that section shall contain an entry in respect of each institution which appears to the Board to be a European institution carrying on home-regulated investment business in the United Kingdom;

(b) the entry in respect of each such institution shall consist of–

  (i) information as to the services which the institution holds itself out as able to provide; and

  (ii) such other information as the Board may determine;

(c) where it appears to the Board that any person in respect of whom there is an entry in the register by virtue of paragraph (a) above has ceased to be a European institution carrying on home-regulated investment business in the United Kingdom, the Board shall make a note to that effect in the entry together with the reason why the person in question is no longer such an institution; and

(d) an entry in respect of which a note is made by virtue of paragraph (c) above may be removed from the register at the end of such period as the Board thinks fit.

**28** Section 104 of the Act (power to call for information) shall have effect as if–

(a) the reference in subsection (1) to a person who is authorised to carry on investment business by virtue of any of the provisions there mentioned included a reference to a European institution carrying on home-regulated investment business in the United Kingdom; and

(b) references to functions under the Act included references to functions under these Regulations.

**29** Section 106 of the Act (exercise of investigation powers by officer etc.) shall have effect as if it included provision that–

(a) where the Secretary of State or the Board authorises a person other than one of his or its officers to exercise any powers under section 105 of the Act (investigation powers) in relation to any home-regulated investment business of a European institution, the Secretary of State or, as the case may be, the Board may determine that subsection (3) of section 106 shall not apply; and

(b) where such a determination is made, the person authorised to exercise the powers shall make a report to the relevant supervisory authority in the institution's home State, in such manner as that authority may require, on the exercise of those powers and the results of exercising them.

## AUDITORS

**30** Subsection (3) of section 107 of the Act (appointment of auditors) shall have effect in relation to an auditor appointed by an authorised person which is a European institution as if the reference to the accounts of the authorised person did not include a reference to any accounts relating to a home-regulated activity.

**31** Section 109 of the Act (communication by auditor with supervisory authorities) shall have effect as if in subsection (1)–

(a) the reference to an authorised person included a reference to a European institution; and

(b) the reference to functions under the Act included a reference to functions under these Regulations.

**32** Subsection (3) of section 110 of the Act (overseas business) shall have effect in relation to a European institution as if any reference to investment business did not include a reference to home-regulated investment business; and the reference in paragraph (b) of that subsection to the powers and duties of an auditor shall be construed accordingly.

## FEES

**33** Section 113 of the Act (periodical fees) shall have effect as if it included provision that a European institution carrying on home-regulated investment business in the United Kingdom shall pay such periodical fees to the Board as may be prescribed by regulations made under that section.

## PREVENTION OF RESTRICTIVE PRACTICES

**34** Section 119 of the Act (recognised self-regulating organisations, investment exchanges and clearing houses) shall have effect as if any reference in subsections (1) and (2) to the protection of investors included a reference to compliance with the Second Council Directive.

**35** Section 121 of the Act (designated agencies) shall have effect as if any reference in subsections (1) and (2) to the protection of investors included a reference to compliance with the Second Council Directive.

## RELATIONS WITH OTHER REGULATORY AUTHORITIES

**36(1)** Section 128C of the Act (enforcement in support of overseas regulatory authority) shall have effect as if it–

(a) required the powers mentioned in subsection (1) to be exercised at the request of the relevant supervisory authority in another member State if their exercise is necessary for the purposes of complying with the Second Council Directive; and

(b) included provision that, in relation to the exercise of those powers in such a case, subsections (4) and (5) shall not apply and the Board shall notify the action taken by it to that authority.

**36(2)** That section shall also have effect as if the reference in subsection (2) to the power to withdraw or suspend authorisation under section 28 of the Act included a reference to the power to impose a prohibition under regulation 15 of these Regulations.

## OFFICIAL LISTING OF SECURITIES

**37** Section 154 of the Act (advertisements etc. in connection with listing applications) shall have effect as if–

(a) it included provision that, where a European institution carrying on home-regulated investment business in the United Kingdom contravenes that section, it shall be treated as having contravened rules made under Chapter V of Part I of the Act, or in the case of an institution which is a member of a recognised self-regulating organisation, the rules of that organisation; and

(b) the reference in subsection (3) to a person other than an authorised person did not include a reference to such an institution.

## OFFERS OF UNLISTED SECURITIES

**38** Section 171 of the Act (contraventions in relation to offers of unlisted securities) shall have effect as if–

(a) it included provision that, where a European institution carrying on home-regulated investment business in the United Kingdom does any of the things specified in paragraphs (a) to (c) of subsection (1), it shall be treated as having contravened rules made under Chapter V of Part I of the Act, or in the case of an institution which is a member of a recognised self-regulating organisation, the rules of that organisation; and

(b) the reference in subsection (3) to a person other than an authorised person did not include a reference to such an institution.

## INSIDER DEALING

**39(1)** Section 178 of the Act (penalty for failure to co-operate with section 177 investigations) shall have effect as if–

(a) the reference in subsection (3) to an authorised person included a reference to a European institution; and

(b) the notices which may be served on a European institution under that subsection included a notice–

(i) directing that regulation 5(1)(b) of these Regulations shall not apply in relation to the institution after the expiry of a specified period after the service of the notice; or

(ii) directing that during a specified period that provision shall apply in relation to the institution only as respects the performance of contracts entered into before the notice comes into force;

(c) the reference in subsection (4) to the period mentioned in paragraphs (a) and (c) of subsection (3) included a reference to the period mentioned in paragraph (b)(i) and (ii) above;

(d) any reference in subsection (5) to an unauthorised person did not include a reference to a European institution carrying on home-regulated investment business in the United Kingdom; and

(e) the reference in that subsection to any authorised person included a reference to such a European institution.

**39(2)** That section shall also have effect as if it included provision that if, it appears to the Secretary of State–

(a) that a person on whom he serves a notice under subsection (3) is a European institution carrying on home-regulated investment business in the United Kingdom; or

(b) that a person on whom he serves a revocation notice under subsection (7) was such an institution at the time when the notice which is being revoked was served,

he shall serve a copy of the notice on the Board or, in the case of an institution which is a member of a recognised self-regulating organisation, that organisation.

## RESTRICTIONS ON DISCLOSURE OF INFORMATION

**40** Section 179 of the Act (restrictions on disclosure of information) shall have effect as if the reference in subsection (2) to functions under the Act included a reference to functions under these Regulations.

**41** Section 180 of the Act (exceptions from restriction on disclosure of information) shall have effect as if–

(a) the reference in paragraph (g) of subsection (1) to functions under the Banking Act included a reference to functions under these Regulations;

(b) the reference in that subsection to functions under the Building Societies Act included a reference to functions under these Regulations; and

(c) the reference in that subsection to an authorised person included a reference to a European institution carrying on home-regulated investment business in the United Kingdom.

## MISCELLANEOUS AND SUPPLEMENTARY

**42** Section 191 of the Act (occupational pension schemes) shall have effect as if any reference to an authorised person included a reference to a European institution carrying on home-regulated investment business in the United Kingdom.

**43** Section 206 of the Act shall have effect as if the reference in subsection (1) to authorised persons included a reference to European institutions.

## ACTIVITIES CONSTITUTING INVESTMENT BUSINESS

**44(1)** Paragraph 17 of Schedule 1 to the Act (investments and investment business) shall have effect as if any reference to authorised persons, or an authorised person, included a reference to European institutions, or a European institution, carrying on home-regulated investment business in the United Kingdom.

**44(2)** Paragraph 18 of that Schedule shall have effect as if the reference in sub-paragraph (2) to an authorised person included a reference to a European institution carrying on home-regulated investment business in the United Kingdom.

**44(3)** Paragraph 26 of that Schedule shall have effect as if any reference to an authorised person, or authorised persons, included a reference to a European institution, or European institutions, carrying on home-regulated investment business in the United Kingdom.

## REQUIREMENTS FOR RECOGNITION OF SELF-REGULATING ORGANISATION

**45(1)** Paragraph 2 of Schedule 2 to the Act (requirements for recognition of self-regulating organisation) shall have effect as if it included provision that the rules and practices of the organisation must be such as to secure that no European institution, other than one on which an absolute prohibition has been imposed under regulation 15 of these Regulations, is refused admission to the organisation, or expelled from it, for reasons relating to the institution's fitness to carry on any home-regulated investment business.

**45(2)** Paragraph 3 of that Schedule shall have effect as if it included provision that the rules of the organisation must not include, as respects any European institution–

(a) provision requiring the institution to have and maintain financial resources in respect of any home-regulated investment business carried on by it; or

(b) provision as to any other matter for which, under the Second Council Directive, responsibility is reserved to a supervisory authority in the institution's home State.

**45(3)** That paragraph shall also have effect as if–

(a) the reference in sub-paragraph (3) to Chapter VI of Part I of the Act included a reference to regulation 16 of these Regulations; and

(b) it included provision that the rules of the organisation must be such as to secure that, where a power falling within that sub-paragraph is exercisable by virtue of a European institution's contravention of a requirement to furnish information for statistical purposes, the exercise of the power shall be subject to such restrictions as are necessary for the purposes of complying with article 21 of the Second Council Directive.

**45(4)** Paragraph 7 of that Schedule shall have effect as if it included provision that, for the purposes of complying with the Second Council Directive, the organisation must be able and willing to co-operate, by the sharing of information and otherwise, with supervisory authorities in other member States.

### QUALIFICATIONS OF DESIGNATED AGENCY

**46(1)** Paragraph 4 of Schedule 7 to the Act (qualifications of designated agency) shall have effect as if any reference to authorised persons included a reference to European institutions carrying on home-regulated investment business in the United Kingdom.

**46(2)** Paragraph 5 of that Schedule shall have effect as if it included provision that, for the purposes of complying with the Second Council Directive, the agency must be able and willing to co-operate, by the sharing of information and otherwise, with supervisory authorities in other member States.

### PRINCIPLES APPLICABLE TO DESIGNATED AGENCY'S LEGISLATIVE PROVISIONS

**47** Schedule 8 to the Act (principles applicable to designated agency's legislative provisions) shall have effect as if any reference to an authorised person included a reference to a European institution carrying on home-regulated investment business in the United Kingdom.

# Schedule 10 – Minor and Consequential Amendments

Regulation 82(1)

## Part I – Primary Legislation

**1–15** [Not reproduced]

### COMPANIES ACT 1985 (c.6)

**16** Section 446 of the Companies Act 1985 (investigation of share dealings) shall have effect as if the references in subsection (4)(c) to (e) to an authorised person within the meaning of the Financial Services Act included a reference to a European institution carrying on home-regulated investment business in the United Kingdom.

### COMPANY SECURITIES (INSIDER DEALING) ACT 1985 (c.8)

**17** (Revoked by Criminal Justice Act 1993, s. 79(14) and Sch. 6, Pt. II as from 1 March 1994.)

**History**
In regard to the date of the above repeal see SI 1994/242 (C.7), art. 2 and Sch.; para. 17 formerly read as follows:

"Section 13 of the Company Securities (Insider Dealing) Act 1985 (definition of **"off-market dealer"** etc.) shall have effect as if the reference in subsection (3) to an authorised person within the meaning of the Financial Services Act included a reference to a European institution carrying on home-regulated investment business in the United Kingdom."

**18–22** [Not reproduced]

### FINANCIAL SERVICES ACT 1986 (c.60)

**23** In Part I of Schedule 5 to the Financial Services Act (listed money market institutions), paragraph 2(2) shall have effect as if the reference to an authorised institution within the meaning of the Banking Act included a reference to a European deposit-taker.

**24–28** [Not reproduced]

### COMPANIES ACT 1989 (c.40)

**29** Section 176 of the Companies Act 1989 (power to make provision about certain charges) shall have effect as if the reference in subsection (2) to an authorised person within the meaning of the Financial Services Act included a reference to a European institution carrying on home-regulated investment business in the United Kingdom.

**30–33** [Not reproduced]

## Part II – Subordinate Legislation

**34–36** [Not reproduced]

### INSOLVENCY REGULATIONS 1986 (SI 1986/1994)

**37** Regulation 2 of the Insolvency Regulations 1986 (interpretation) shall have effect as if, in the definition of **"bank"**, the reference to any authorised institution in England and Wales within the meaning of the Banking Act included a reference to a European deposit-taker in England and Wales.

**38–47** [Not reproduced]

### PUBLIC COMPANIES (DISCLOSURE OF INTERESTS IN SHARES) (INVESTMENT MANAGEMENT EXCLUSION) REGULATIONS 1988 (SI 1988/706)

**48** (Revoked by the Disclosure of Interests in Shares (Amendment) Regulations 1993 (SI 1993/1819), reg. 10(2) as from 18 September 1993.)

**History**
Para. 48 formerly read as follows:
"Regulation 3 of the Public Companies (Disclosure of Interests in Shares) (Investment Management Exclusion) Regulations 1988 shall have effect as if the reference in paragraph (b) to an authorised person under Chapter III of Part I of the Financial Services Act included a reference to a European institution carrying on home-regulated investment business in the United Kingdom."

**49–68** [Not reproduced]

# Schedule 11 – Transitional Provisions and Savings

Regulation 83

## Part I – Recognition of Institutions

### EUROPEAN AUTHORISED INSTITUTIONS

**1(1)** This paragraph applies to a credit institution incorporated in or formed under the law of another member State which immediately before the commencement date is authorised to act as a credit institution by the relevant supervisory authority in that State.

**1(2)** If an institution to which this paragraph applies–

(a) is immediately before the commencement date carrying on in the United Kingdom by the provision of services any home-regulated activity; or

(b) has established in the United Kingdom for the purpose of carrying on such an activity a branch which immediately before that date is in existence,

it shall be treated for all purposes of these Regulations as if the requirements of paragraph 1 of Schedule 2 to these Regulations had been complied with in relation to its carrying on of the activity or, as the case may be, its establishment of the branch.

### UK AUTHORISED INSTITUTIONS

**2(1)** This paragraph applies to a credit institution incorporated in or formed under the law of any part of the United Kingdom which immediately before the commencement date is authorised by the Bank under the Banking Act or by the Commission under the Building Societies Act.

**2(2)** If an institution to which this paragraph applies–

(a) is immediately before the commencement date carrying on in another member State by the provision of services any listed activity; or

(b) has established in another member State for the purpose of carrying on such an activity a branch which immediately before that date is in existence,

it shall be treated for all purposes of these Regulations as if the requirements of paragraph 1 of Schedule 6 to these Regulations had been complied with in relation to its carrying on of the activity or, as the case may be, its establishment of the branch.

**3(1)** An institution which by virtue of paragraph 2 above is treated as if the requirements of paragraph 1 of Schedule 6 to these Regulations had been complied with in relation to its carrying on of one or more listed activities shall, before the end of the period of three months beginning with the commencement date, give to the UK authority a notice stating the activity or activities in question.

**3(2)** An institution which by virtue of paragraph 2 above is treated as if the requirements of paragraph 1 of Schedule 6 to these Regulations had been complied with in relation to its establishment of a branch shall, before the end of the period of three months beginning with the commencement date, give to the UK authority a notice stating the requisite details of the branch.

**3(3)** (Revoked by the Banking Coordination (Second Council Directive) (Amendment) Regulations 1993 (SI 1993/3225), reg. 1, 2(h) as from 1 January 1994.)

**History**

Reg. 3(3) formerly read as follows:

"An institution which fails to comply with sub-paragraph (1) or (2) above shall be guilty of an offence and liable on summary conviction to a fine not exceeding level 5 on the standard scale."

# Part II – Amendments of Banking Act

**4–7** [Not reproduced]

# Part III – Amendments of Financial Services Act

## PRELIMINARY

**8(1)** Any reference in this Part of this Schedule to a statement of principle or to rules or regulations is a reference to a statement of principle issued, or to rules or regulations made, before the commencement date.

**8(2)** Expressions used in this Part of this Schedule which are also used in Schedule 9 to these Regulations have the same meanings as in that Schedule.

## STATEMENTS OF PRINCIPLE

**9(1)** A statement of principle issued under section 47A of the Financial Services Act shall, unless the contrary intention appears, apply to a European institution carrying on home-regulated investment business in the United Kingdom to the same extent as it would apply if the institution were an authorised person as respects that business.

**9(2)** If the Board is satisfied that it is necessary to do so for the purpose of implementing the Second Council Directive so far as relating to any particular European institution, the Board may, on the application or with the consent of the institution, by order direct that all or any of the provisions of such a statement–

(a) shall not apply to the institution; or

(b) shall apply to it with such modifications as may be specified in the order.

## CONDUCT OF BUSINESS RULES

**10(1)** Rules made under section 48 of the Financial Services Act (conduct of business rules) shall, unless the contrary intention appears, apply in relation to the conduct of home-regulated investment business carried on by a European institution in the United Kingdom to the same extent as they would apply if the institution were an authorised person as respects that business.

**10(2)** If the Board is satisfied that it is necessary to do so for the purpose of implementing the Second Council Directive so far as relating to any particular European institution, the Board may, on the application or with the consent of the institution, by order direct that all or any of the provisions of such rules–

(a) shall not apply in relation to the conduct of home-regulated investment business carried on by the institution; or

(b) shall apply in relation to the conduct of such business with such modifications as may be specified in the order.

**10(3)** A member of a recognised self-regulating organisation who contravenes a rule applying to him by virtue of this paragraph shall be treated as having contravened the rules of the organisation.

## FINANCIAL RESOURCES RULES

**11** If the Board is satisfied that it is necessary to do so for the purpose of implementing the Second Council Directive so far as relating to any particular institution which is a European institution and an authorised person, the Board may, on the application or with the consent of the institution, by order direct that all or any of the provisions of rules under section 49 of the Financial Services Act (financial resources rules)–

(a) shall not apply to the institution; or

(b) shall apply to it with such modifications as may be specified in the order.

## CANCELLATION RULES

**12(1)** Rules made under section 51 of the Financial Services Act (cancellation rules) shall, unless the contrary intention appears, apply in relation to a person who has entered or offered to enter into an investment agreement to which sub-paragraph (2) below applies as they apply in relation to a person mentioned in that section.

**12(2)** This sub-paragraph applies to an investment agreement which is made by a European institution in the course of the carrying on by it of home-regulated investment business in the United Kingdom.

## NOTIFICATION REGULATIONS

**13(1)** Regulations made under section 52 of the Financial Services Act (notification regulations) shall, unless the contrary intention appears, apply in relation to a European institution carrying on home-regulated investment business in the United Kingdom to the same extent as they would apply if the institution were an authorised person as respects that business.

**13(2)** If the Board is satisfied that it is necessary to do so for the purpose of implementing the Second Council Directive so far as relating to any particular European institution, the Board may, on the application or with the consent of the institution, by order direct that all or any of the provisions of such regulations–

(a) shall not apply to the institution; or

(b) shall apply to it with such modifications as may be specified in the order.

## COMPENSATION FUND

**14(1)** Rules under section 54 of the Financial Services Act (compensation fund) shall, unless the contrary intention appears, apply in cases where a person who is or has been a European institution is unable, or likely to be unable, to satisfy claims in respect of any description of civil liability incurred by it in connection with home-regulated investment business carried on by it in the United Kingdom to the same extent as they would apply if the institution were an authorised person as respects that business.

**14(2)** If the Board is satisfied that it is necessary to do so for the purpose of implementing the Second Council Directive so far as relating to any particular person who is or has been a European institution, the Board may, on the application or with the consent of that person, by order direct that all or any of the provisions of such rules–

(a) shall not apply in relation to cases where that person is unable, or likely to be unable, to satisfy claims in respect of any description of civil liability incurred by it in connection with home-regulated investment business carried on by it; or

(b) shall apply in relation to such cases with such modifications as may be specified in the order.

## CLIENTS' MONEY

**15(1)** Regulations under section 55 of the Financial Services Act (clients' money) shall, unless the contrary intention appears, apply in relation to money which a European institution holds in the course of home-regulated investment business carried on by it in the United Kingdom to the same extent as they would apply if the institution were an authorised person as respects that business.

**15(2)** If the Board is satisfied that it is necessary to do so for the purpose of implementing the Second Council Directive so far as relating to any particular European institution, the Board may, on the application or with the consent of the institution, by order direct that all or any of the provisions of such regulations–

(a) shall not apply in relation to money which the institution holds in the course of home-regulated investment business carried on by it; or

(b) shall apply in relation to such money with such modifications as may be specified in the order.

**15(3)** A member of a recognised self-regulating organisation who contravenes a regulation applying to him by virtue of this paragraph shall be treated as having contravened the rules of the organisation.

## UNSOLICITED CALLS

**16(1)** Regulations under section 56 of the Financial Services Act (unsolicited calls) shall, unless the contrary intention appears, apply in relation to a European institution carrying on home-regulated investment business in the United Kingdom to the same extent as they would apply if the institution were an authorised person.

**16(2)** A member of a recognised self-regulating organisation who contravenes a regulation applying to him by virtue of this paragraph shall be treated as having contravened the rules of the organisation.

## SUPPLEMENTAL

**17(1)** An order under this Part of this Schedule may be subject to conditions.

**17(2)** Such an order may be revoked at any time by the Board; and the Board may at any time vary any such order on the application or with the consent of the European institution to which it applies.

# Part IV – Amendments of Building Societies Act

**18–19** [Not reproduced]

## EXPLANATORY NOTE

(*This Note is not part of the Regulations*)

These Regulations give effect to the Second Council Directive 89/646/EEC on the coordination of laws, regulations and administrative provisions relating to the taking up and pursuit of the business of credit institutions (OJ No. L386, 30.12.89, p. 1), and to certain provisions of Council Directive 77/780/EEC (OJ No. L322, 17.12.77, p. 30), which is amended by the Second Council Directive. They also give effect to the Council Directive 92/30/EEC on the supervision of credit institutions on a consolidated basis (OJ No. L110, 28.4.92, p. 52). The Regulations come into force on 1st January 1993.

Part I of the Regulations defines various words and expressions for the purposes of the Regulations.

Part II of the Regulations makes provision for the recognition of certain credit institutions authorised in other member States, and of certain subsidiaries of such institutions, for the purposes of carrying on listed activities in the United Kingdom. "Listed activities" are the activities which are set out in Schedule 1. Subject to compliance with the notification requirements contained in Schedule 2, nothing in certain specified provisions of the Banking Act 1987 (c.22), the Financial Services Act 1986 (c.60), the Consumer Credit Act 1974 (c.39) and the Insurance Companies Act 1982 (c.50) is to prevent a "European institution" (regulation 3) from carrying on in the United Kingdom, whether by the provision of services or the establishment of a branch, any listed activity which it is authorised or permitted to carry on in its "home state" (regulation 5). Certain offences in connection with carrying on listed activities and the establishment of branches are created by regulations 5 and 6. There are requirements concerning changes to the "requisite details" of a branch of a European institution (regulation 6(2)). Prohibitions and restrictions on a European institution in relation to carrying on listed activities may be imposed by the Bank of England (regulations 8 to 12), the Securities and Investment Board (regulations 15 to 17) and the Director General of Fair Trading (regulations 18 and 19), in the circumstances and in accordance with the conditions set out in the Regulations. Schedules 3, 4 and 5 make supplemental provision in connection with such prohibitions and restrictions imposed by the Bank, the Board and the Director General respectively. The Bank (regulation 8) and the Board (regulation 14) also have certain duties to prepare for supervision when a European institution is establishing a branch in the United Kingdom pursuant to the Regulations.

Part III of the Regulations makes provision for the carrying on of listed activities in other member States by "UK Institutions", which means certain credit institutions ("UK authorised institutions") which are authorised under the Banking Act or Building Societies Act, and certain subsidiaries ("UK subsidiaries") of such institutions (regulation 20). For the purposes of the Regulations, a UK authorised institution is authorised to carry on in the UK any listed activity which it is lawful for it to carry on in the UK; a UK subsidiary is permitted to carry on in the UK any listed activity which it is lawful for it to carry on, and it is carrying on in the UK (regulation 21). Subject to certain qualifications relating to UK subsidiaries, a UK institution is not to carry on in another member State by the provision of services any listed activity which it is authorised or permitted to carry on in the UK, or establish a branch for the purpose of carrying on such an activity, unless the notification requirements of Schedule 6 have been complied with (regulation 22). There are also requirements concerning changes to the "requisite details" of a branch of a UK institution established in another member State. The "UK authority" (regulation 20(7)) – which will be the Bank of England or the Building Societies Commission – is given powers to impose a restriction on the carrying on in the UK of any listed activities by a UK subsidiary (regulations 23 and 24), and Schedule 7 makes supplemental provision in that regard.

Part IV of the Regulations amends the Banking Act 1987 in relation to credit institutions authorised by the Bank of England. The principal changes relate to applications for authorisation (regulation 25), "own funds" and initial capital requirements for authorisation (regulation 27), powers of revocation, including powers in relation to the carrying on of listed activities without having given the Bank prior notice (regulation 28), powers of revocation following information from a supervisory authority in another member State (regulation 29), implementation of certain EC decisions relating to third countries (regulation 32), holdings in credit institutions (regulations 31, and 33 to 35), information and investigations (regulations 36 and 37), and disclosure of information (regulations 38 to 42). Further amendments to the Banking Act 1987 are made by Schedule 8, in particular in relation to European institutions.

Part V of the Regulations amends the Financial Services Act 1986. The principal changes relate to membership of self-regulating organisations (regulation 48), applications for, and grant and refusal of, authorisation under that Act (regulations 49 and 50), and reciprocal facilities for banking business (regulation 53). Further amendments to the Financial Services Act 1986 are made by Schedule 9, in particular in relation to European institutions.

Part VI of the Regulations amends the Consumer Credit Act 1974. The principal changes relate to the effect of standard licences (regulation 57), the grant of standard licences (regulation 58), conduct of business (regulation 59), disclosure of information (regulation 62), and modification of subordinate legislation in relation to European institutions (regulation 63).

Part VII of the Regulations amends the Insurance Companies Act 1982, principally in relation to the withdrawal of authorisation under that Act of a European subsidiary (regulation 64), and the application of Part II of the Act to a European institution (regulation 65).

Part VIII of the Regulations amends the Building Societies Act 1986. The principal changes relate to the establishment of building societies (regulation 67), minimum capital requirements (regulation 68), powers in respect of "qualifying holdings" in building societies (regulations 68 to 70 and 72), revocation powers, including powers in relation to the carrying on of listed activities without having given the Building Societies Commission prior notice (regulation 71), powers of revocation following information from a supervisory authority in another member State (regulation 74), disclosure of information (regulations 76 and 77), and accounting records and systems of business control (regulation 78).

Schedule 2 sets out procedural requirements as respects European institutions relating to the carrying on in the UK of listed activities by the provision of services, the establishment of a branch, and changes to the requisite details of a branch. It also specifies the procedure whereby cancellation of compliance with notification requirements by a European subsidiary may be effected.

Schedule 6 sets out procedural requirements as respects UK institutions relating to the carrying on in another member State of listed activities by the provision of services, the establishment of a branch, and changes to the requisite details of a branch. It also specifies the procedure whereby cancellation of compliance with notification requirements by a UK subsidiary may be effected.

Schedule 10 contains minor and consequential amendments to primary and secondary legislation.

Schedule 11 contains transitional provisions and savings, making further amendments to the Banking Act 1987, the Financial Services Act 1986, and the Building Societies Act 1986.

# THE INSOLVENCY PRACTITIONERS (AMENDMENT) REGULATIONS 1993

(SI 1993/221)

*Made on 9 February 1993 by the Secretary of State for Trade and Industry under s. 390, 393 and 419 of the Insolvency Act 1986. Operative from 1 April 1993.*

## CITATION, COMMENCEMENT AND OPERATION

**1(1)** These Regulations may be cited as the Insolvency Practitioners (Amendment) Regulations 1993.

**1(2)** These Regulations shall come into force on 1st April 1993.

**1(3)** In these Regulations:–

**"bordereau"** means a form upon which an insolvency practitioner enters certain details in relation to his appointment as insolvency practitioner in relation to a person, including the name of that person, the date of appointment, the value of the assets comprised in the estate of the person estimated in accordance with Part II of Schedule 2 to the 1990 Regulations, any increase in his estimation of the value of those assets and the date of his release or discharge from the appointment, for the purposes of evidencing those matters;

**"the commencement date"** means the date on which these Regulations come into force;

**"the 1990 Regulations"** means the Insolvency Practitioners Regulations 1990 and any regulation or Schedule referred to by number means, unless the context otherwise requires, the regulation or Schedule so numbered in the 1990 Regulations.

## AMENDMENTS TO 1990 REGULATIONS

**2** The 1990 Regulations shall be amended as specified in regulations 3 to 11 below.

**3(1)** Paragraph (2) below shall apply to any application made to a competent authority on or after the commencement date.

**3(2)** [Addition to Sch. 1, Pt. I, para. 1.]

**4(1)** Regulations 5 to 11 of these Regulations have effect in relation to any person appointed on or after the commencement date to act as an insolvency practitioner in relation to any person.

**4(2)** Without prejudice to regulation 2(3) of the 1990 Regulations, the 1990 Regulations shall continue to apply and have effect without the amendments provided for in regulations 5 to 11 of these Regulations in relation to any person appointed to act as insolvency practitioner in relation to any person before the commencement date insofar as he continues so to act in relation to that person on or after the commencement date pursuant to that appointment or (notwithstanding paragraph (1) above) to a subsequent appointment to act as an insolvency practitioner within the scope of regulation 13 of the 1990 Regulations made on or after the commencement date.

**5** [Amendments to reg. 12.]

**6** [Substitutions in reg. 13.]

**7** [Substitutions in reg. 14.]

**8** [Amendments to reg. 15.]

**9** [Insertion of new reg. 15A.]

**10** [Amendments to Sch. 2, Pt. I.]

**11** [Amendments to Sch. 3, para. 7.]

## EXPLANATORY NOTE

*(This Note does not form part of the Regulations)*

These Regulations amend the Insolvency Practitioners Regulations 1990 with effect from 1st April 1993. They amend the prescribed requirements in respect of security or caution for the proper performance of the functions of an insolvency practitioner where he is appointed to act in relation to a person on or after that date, except for certain savings, and the records in respect of such security or caution to be kept for inspection or submitted to his authorising body by an insolvency practitioner in respect of the estate of each person in relation to whom the practitioner acts.

The Regulations also amend the prescribed educational requirements in relation to insolvency practitioners to include degrees conferred by certain institutions specified by Order of the Privy Council under section 76(1) of the Further and Higher Education Act 1992 or section 48(1) of the Further and Higher Education (Scotland) Act 1992.

# THE DISCLOSURE OF INTERESTS IN SHARES (AMENDMENT) REGULATIONS 1993

(SI 1993/1819)

*Made on 20 July 1993 by the Secretary of State for Trade and Industry under s. 210A of the Companies Act 1985. Operative from 18 September 1993.*

## CITATION AND COMMENCEMENT

**1** These Regulations may be cited as the Disclosure of Interests in Shares (Amendment) Regulations 1993 and shall come into force on the sixtieth day after the day on which they are made.

## AMENDMENTS OF PART VI OF THE COMPANIES ACT 1985

**2** Part VI of the Companies Act 1985 shall be amended in accordance with regulations 3 to 9 below.

**3** [Substitution in s. 198.]

**4** [Amendments to s. 199.]

**5** [Substitution for s. 200.]

**6** [Amendments to s. 202.]

**7** [Amendments to s. 206.]

**8** [Substitution for s. 209.]

**9** [Substitution for s. 220(1).]

## REVOCATIONS

**10(1)** The following Regulations are hereby revoked–

(a) the Public Companies (Disclosure of Interests in Shares) (Exclusions) Regulations 1982; and

(b) the Public Companies (Disclosure of Interests in Shares) (Investment Management Exclusion) Regulations 1988.

**10(2)** In the Banking Coordination (Second Council Directive) Regulations 1992, in Schedule 10, paragraph 48 is hereby revoked.

## TRANSITIONAL PROVISIONS

**11(1)** In this regulation **"commencement"** means the commencement of these Regulations.

**11(2)** Where a person–

(a) has a notifiable interest immediately after commencement, but did not have such an interest immediately before commencement, or

(b) had a notifiable interest immediately before commencement, but does not have such an interest immediately after commencement, or

(c) had a notifiable interest immediately before commencement and has such an interest immediately after commencement but the percentage levels of his interest immediately before and immediately after commencement are not the same,

then he comes under an obligation to notify the company with respect to the interest which he has or had in its shares; and the provisions of Part VI of the Companies Act 1985 shall apply as if that obligation arose under section 198 of that Act.

## EXPLANATORY NOTE

*(This Note is not part of the Regulations)*

These Regulations amend Part VI of the Companies Act 1985, which imposes an obligation to disclose certain interests in shares comprised in certain issued share capital of public companies. Exemptions from that obligation, contained in that Part and in the Public Company (Disclosure of Interests in Shares) (Exclusions) Regulations 1982 (SI 1982/677) and the Public Company (Disclosure of Interests in Shares) (Investment Management Exclusion) Regulations 1988 (SI 1988/706) and paragraph 48 of Schedule 10 to the Banking Coordination (Second Council Directive) Regulations 1992 (SI 1992/3218, which amended SI 1988/706) are amended or superseded. In some cases the changes made are because continuance of certain exemptions in their present form would be incompatible with Council Directive 88/627/EEC on the information to be published when a major holding in a listed company is acquired or disposed of. The Regulations come into force on the sixtieth day after the day on which they are made.

Regulation 4 amends section 199 of that Act to make special provision for certain interests in relation to the percentage level of interest constituting a notifiable interest within the meaning of that Part. Amendments to section 198 (regulation 3), section 202 (regulation 6) and section 206 (regulation 7) and the substitution of section 200 (regulation 5) are amendments consequential upon the amendment to section 199 of the Act.

Regulation 8 supersedes section 209 of the Act (interests in shares to be disregarded for the purposes of sections 198 to 202) and the above mentioned Regulations by substituting a new section 209. Exemptions provided under new subsections (1) and (8) are subject to certain conditions as to the control of voting rights attaching to the shares concerned (see subsections (5), (6) and (7)). The exemption provided under subsection (8) is subject to a condition as to intervention in the management of the company. Subsection (10) provides for additional classes of interest to be exempted where the company concerned is not a listed company. Subsection (12) continues the exemption for proxy holders formerly contained in subsection (2) of section 209.

Regulation 9 substitutes a new section for section 220 of the Act (definitions to be applied for Part VI).

Regulation 10 revokes the Public Company (Disclosure of Interests in Shares) (Exclusions) Regulations 1982 (SI 1982/677) and the Public Company (Disclosure of Interests in Shares) (Investment Management Exclusion) Regulations 1988 (SI 1988/706) and paragraph 48 of Schedule 10 to the Banking Coordination (Second Council Directive) Regulations 1992 (SI 1992/3218).

Regulation 11 makes transitional provisions to impose an obligation of disclosure in relation to interests which become notifiable as a result of the coming into force of these Regulations.

# THE PARTNERSHIPS AND UNLIMITED COMPANIES (ACCOUNTS) REGULATIONS 1993

(SI 1993/1820)

*Made on 20 July 1993 by the Secretary of State for Trade and Industry under s. 2(2) of and para. 2(2) of Sch. 2 to the European Communities Act 1972 and s. 257 of the Companies Act 1985. Operative from 21 July 1993.*

## CITATION, COMMENCEMENT AND EXTENT

**1(1)** These Regulations may be cited as the Partnerships and Unlimited Companies (Accounts) Regulations 1993.

**1(2)** These Regulations shall come into force on the day after the day on which they are made.

**1(3)** These Regulations do not extend to Northern Ireland.

## INTERPRETATION

**2(1)** In these Regulations, unless the context otherwise requires–

**"the 1985 Act"** means the Companies Act 1985;

**"the accounts"**, in relation to a qualifying partnership, means the annual accounts, the annual report and the auditors' report required by regulation 4 below;

**"dealt with on a consolidated basis"** means dealt with by the method of full consolidation, the method of proportional consolidation or the equity method of accounting;

**"financial year"**, in relation to a qualifying partnership, means any period of not more than 18 months in respect of which a profit and loss account of the partnership is required to be made up by or in accordance with its constitution or, failing any such requirement, each period of 12 months beginning with 1st April;

**"the Fourth Directive"** means the Fourth Council Directive (78/660/EEC) of 25th July 1978 on the annual accounts of certain types of companies, as amended;

**"general partner"** has the same meaning as in the Limited Partnerships Act 1907;

**"limited company"** means a company limited by shares or limited by guarantee;

**"limited partnership"** means a partnership formed in accordance with the Limited Partnerships Act 1907;

**"qualifying company"** has the meaning given by regulation 9 below;

**"qualifying partnership"** has the meaning given by regulation 3 below;

**"the Seventh Directive"** means the Seventh Council Directive (83/349/EEC) of 13th June 1983 on consolidated accounts, as amended;

and other expressions shall have the meanings ascribed to them by the 1985 Act.

**2(2)** Any reference in these Regulations to the members of a qualifying partnership shall be construed, in relation to a limited partnership, as a reference to its general partner or partners.

## QUALIFYING PARTNERSHIPS

**3(1)** A partnership which is governed by the laws of any part of Great Britain is a qualifying partnership for the purposes of these Regulations if each of its members is–

(a) a limited company, or

(b) an unlimited company, or a Scottish firm, each of whose members is a limited company.

**3(2)** Where the members of a qualifying partnership include–

(a) an unlimited company, or a Scottish firm, each of whose members is a limited company, or

(b) a member of another partnership each of whose members is–

(i) a limited company, or

(ii) an unlimited company, or a Scottish firm, each of whose members is a limited company,

any reference in regulations 4 to 8 below to the members of the qualifying partnership includes a reference to the members of that company, firm or other partnership.

**3(3)** The requirements of regulations 4 to 8 below shall apply without regard to any change in the members of a qualifying partnership which does not result in it ceasing to be such a partnership.

**3(4)** Any reference in paragraph (1) or (2) above to a limited company, an unlimited company, a Scottish firm or another partnership includes a reference to any comparable undertaking incorporated in or formed under the law of any country or territory outside Great Britain.

## PREPARATION OF ACCOUNTS OF QUALIFYING PARTNERSHIPS

**4(1)** Subject to regulation 7 below, the persons who are members of a qualifying partnership at the end of any financial year of the partnership shall, in respect of that year–

(a) prepare the like annual accounts and annual report, and

(b) cause to be prepared such an auditors' report,

as would be required under Part VII of the 1985 Act (accounts and audit) if the partnership were a company formed and registered under that Act.

**4(2)** The accounts required by this regulation–

(a) shall be prepared within a period of 10 months beginning immediately after the end of the financial year, and

(b) shall state that they are prepared under this regulation.

**4(3)** The Schedule to these Regulations (which makes certain modifications and adaptations for the purposes of this regulation) shall have effect.

## DELIVERY OF ACCOUNTS OF QUALIFYING PARTNERSHIPS TO REGISTRAR ETC.

**5(1)** Subject to regulation 7 below, each limited company which is a member of a qualifying partnership at the end of any financial year of the partnership shall append to the copy of its annual accounts which is next delivered to the registrar in accordance with section 242 of the 1985 Act a copy of the accounts of the partnership prepared for that year under regulation 4 above.

**5(2)** Subject to regulation 7 below, a limited company which is a member of a qualifying partnership shall supply to any person upon request–

(a) the name of each member which is to deliver, or has delivered, a copy of the latest accounts of the partnership to the registrar under paragraph (1) above, and

(b) the name of each member incorporated in a member State other than the United Kingdom which is to publish, or has published, the latest accounts of the partnership in accordance with the provisions of the Fourth or Seventh Directive.

## PUBLICATION OF ACCOUNTS OF QUALIFYING PARTNERSHIPS AT HEAD OFFICE

**6(1)** Subject to paragraph (2) and regulation 7 below, this regulation applies where a qualifying partnership's head office is in Great Britain and each of its members is–

(a) an undertaking comparable to a limited company which is incorporated in a country or territory outside the United Kingdom, or

(b) an undertaking comparable to an unlimited company or partnership–

(i) which is incorporated in or formed under the law of such a country or territory, and

(ii) each of whose members is such an undertaking as is mentioned in paragraph (a) above.

**6(2)** Paragraph (1) above does not apply where any member of a qualifying partnership is–

(a) an undertaking comparable to a limited company which is incorporated in a member State other than the United Kingdom, or

(b) an undertaking comparable to an unlimited company or partnership–

(i) which is incorporated in or formed under the law of such a State, and

(ii) each of whose members is such an undertaking as is mentioned in paragraph (a) above,

and (in either case) the latest accounts of the qualifying partnership have been or are to be appended to the accounts of any member of the partnership and published under the law of that State and in accordance with the provisions of the Fourth or Seventh Directive.

**6(3)** The members of the qualifying partnership–

(a) shall make the latest accounts of the partnership available for inspection by any person, without charge and during business hours, at the head office of the partnership, and

(b) if any document comprised in those accounts is in a language other than English, shall annex to that document a translation of it into English, certified in accordance with regulation 5 of the Companies (Forms) (Amendment) Regulations 1990 to be a correct translation.

**6(4)** A member of the qualifying partnership shall supply to any person upon request–

(a) a copy of the accounts required by paragraph (3)(a) above to be made available for inspection, and

(b) a copy of any translation required by paragraph (3)(b) above to be annexed to any document comprised in those accounts,

at a price not exceeding the administrative cost of making the copy.

## EXEMPTION FROM REGULATIONS 4 TO 6 WHERE ACCOUNTS CONSOLIDATED

**7(1)** The members of a qualifying partnership are exempt from the requirements of regulations 4 to 6 above if the partnership is dealt with on a consolidated basis in group accounts prepared by–

(a) a member of the partnership which is established under the law of a member State, or

(b) a parent undertaking of such a member which is so established,

and (in either case) the conditions mentioned in paragraph (2) below are complied with.

**7(2)** The conditions are–

(a) that the group accounts are prepared and audited under the law of the member State concerned in accordance with the provisions of the Seventh Directive, and

(b) the notes to those accounts disclose that advantage has been taken of the exemption conferred by this regulation.

**7(3)** Where advantage is taken of the exemption conferred by this regulation, any member of the qualifying partnership which is a limited company must disclose on request the name of at least one member or parent undertaking in whose group accounts the partnership has been or is to be dealt with on a consolidated basis.

## PENALTIES FOR NON-COMPLIANCE WITH REGULATIONS 4 TO 6

**8(1)** If, in respect of a financial year of a qualifying partnership, the requirements of paragraph (1) of regulation 4 above are not complied with within the period referred to in paragraph (2) of that regulation, every person who was a member of the partnership or a director of such a member at the end of that year is guilty of an offence and liable on summary conviction to a fine not exceeding level 5 on the standard scale.

**8(2)** If the accounts of a qualifying partnership–

(a) a copy of which is delivered to the registrar under regulation 5 above, or

(b) which are made available for inspection under regulation 6 above,

do not comply with the requirements of regulation 4(1) above, every person who, at the time when the copy was so delivered or (as the case may be) the accounts were first made available for inspection, was a member of the partnership or a director of such a member is guilty of an offence and liable on summary conviction to a fine not exceeding level 5 on the standard scale.

**8(3)** If a member of a qualifying partnership fails to comply with regulation 5, 6 or 7(3) above, that member and any director of that member is guilty of an offence and liable on summary conviction to a fine not exceeding level 5 on the standard scale.

**8(4)** It is a defence for a person charged with an offence under this regulation to show that he took all reasonable steps for securing that the requirements in question would be complied with.

**8(5)** The following provisions of the 1985 Act, namely–

(a) section 731 (summary proceedings),

(b) section 733 (offences by bodies corporate), and

(c) section 734 (criminal proceedings against unincorporated bodies),

shall apply to an offence under this regulation.

## QUALIFYING COMPANIES

**9(1)** An unlimited company incorporated in Great Britain is a qualifying company for the purposes of these Regulations if each of its members is–

(a) a limited company, or

(b) another unlimited company, or a Scottish firm, each of whose members is a limited company.

**9(2)** Any reference in paragraph (1) above to a limited company, another unlimited company or a Scottish firm includes a reference to any comparable undertaking incorporated in or formed under the law of any country or territory outside Great Britain.

## DELIVERY OF ACCOUNTS OF QUALIFYING COMPANIES TO REGISTRAR

**10** [Substitution in s. 254(3) of 1985 Act.]

## NOTES TO COMPANY ACCOUNTS OF MEMBERSHIP OF QUALIFYING PARTNERSHIPS OR COMPANIES

**11** [Substitution in s. 231(3) of 1985 Act; insertion of para. 9A and 28A in Sch. 5 to 1985 Act.]

## TRANSITIONAL PROVISIONS

**12(1)** The members of a qualifying partnership need not prepare accounts in accordance with regulation 4 above for a financial year commencing before 23rd December 1994.

**12(2)** Where advantage is taken of the exemption conferred by paragraph (1) above, regulations 5 and 6 above shall not apply, and the amendments to the 1985 Act effected by regulation 11 above shall be treated as not having been made.

# Schedule – Modifications and Adaptations for Purposes of Regulation 4

Regulation 4

**1(1)** Accounts prepared under regulation 4 of these Regulations shall comply with the requirements of Part VII of the 1985 Act as to the content of accounts subject to the following, namely–

(a) the provisions of section 259(2) and (3) of that Act (meaning of "undertaking" and related expressions),

(b) the omission of the provisions mentioned in paragraph 2(1) below, and

(c) any necessary modifications to take account of the fact that partnerships are unincorporated.

**1(2)** For the purposes of the provisions of Part VII of the 1985 Act as applied to accounts so prepared, these Regulations shall be regarded as part of the requirements of that Act.

**2(1)** The provisions referred to in paragraph 1(1)(b) above are–

(a) in Part I of Schedule 4 to the 1985 Act, paragraph 3(6) and, in paragraph 3(2), the words from "adopted" to the end;

(b) in Part II of that Schedule, paragraph 20;

(c) in Part III of that Schedule, paragraphs 36A, 41, 43, 44, 45, 50(3)(b), 51(2), 53 and 54;

(d) in Schedule 4A to that Act, paragraphs 13(3) to (5), 14 and 15;

(e) in Schedule 5 to that Act, paragraphs 4, 5, 10, 12, 18, 19 and 29;

(f) in Schedule 6 to that Act, paragraphs 2 to 6, 8 and 9; and

(g) Schedule 7 to that Act except paragraph 6.

**2(2)** Sub-paragraph (1) above shall not be construed as affecting the requirement to give a true and fair view under sections 226 and 227 of the 1985 Act.

**2(3)** Part II of the Companies Act 1989 (eligibility for appointment as auditors) shall apply to auditors appointed for the purposes of regulation 4 of these Regulations as if qualifying partnerships were companies formed and registered under the 1985 Act, subject to any necessary modifications to take account of the fact that partnerships are unincorporated.

## EXPLANATORY NOTE

*(This Note is not part of the Regulations)*

1. These Regulations implement Council Directive 90/605/EEC (Official Journal No. L317 of 16.11.1990, pages 60 to 62) which amends Directive 78/660/EEC on annual accounts (O.J. No. L222 of 14.8.1978, pages 11 to 31) (the Fourth EC Company Law Directive) and Directive 83/349/EEC on consolidated accounts (O.J. No. L193 of 18.7.1983, pages 1 to 17) (the Seventh EC Company Law Directive) as regards the scope of those Directives.

2. The scope of application of the Regulations is set out in regulations 3 (qualifying partnerships) and 9 (qualifying companies). They apply, in effect, to partnerships, limited partnerships and unlimited companies all of whose members having unlimited liability are limited companies.

3. Members of a qualifying partnership (general partners in the case of limited partnerships) are required by regulation 4 to prepare accounts and a directors' report, and to obtain an auditors' report on such accounts, in accordance with the provisions of Part VII of the Companies Act 1985 (the 1985 Act), subject to certain modifications set out in the Schedule to

the Regulations. The Schedule disapplies requirements of Part VII which do not derive from the European Community Directives on accounts.

4. Regulations 5 and 6 contain requirements about the publication of accounts prepared under the Regulations by members of qualifying partnerships.

5. Regulation 7 provides an exemption from the Regulations where the partnership has been dealt with in consolidated group accounts prepared by a member of the partnership established under the law of a member State of the EEC (or a parent of such a member), by the method of full or proportional consolidation or by the equity method of accounting.

6. Regulation 8 imposes criminal penalties for failure to comply with the Regulations.

7. Regulation 10 requires that unlimited companies which are qualifying companies deliver their accounts to the registrar of companies (they are already required to prepare accounts under Part VII of the 1985 Act).

8. Regulation 11 imposes additional disclosure requirements in the notes to the accounts of companies which are members of qualifying partnerships or qualifying companies.

9. Regulation 12 permits the members of a qualifying partnership not to prepare accounts and a directors' report (and obtain an auditors' report on the accounts) under the Regulations for financial years commencing on a date prior to 23rd December 1994.

# THE FINANCIAL SERVICES (DISCLOSURE OF INFORMATION) (DESIGNATED AUTHORITIES) (NO. 7) ORDER 1993

(SI 1993/1826)

*Made on 21 July 1993 by the Secretary of State for Trade and Industry under s. 180(3), (4) of the Financial Services Act 1986, s. 449(1B), (1C) of the Companies Act 1985 and s. 87(5) of the Companies Act 1989. Operative from 16 August 1993.*

## CITATION AND COMMENCEMENT

**1** This Order may be cited as the Financial Services (Disclosure of Information) (Designated Authorities) (No. 7) Order 1993 and shall come into force on 16th August 1993.

## DESIGNATION OF AUTHORITIES AND SPECIFICATION OF FUNCTIONS

**2** For the purposes of section 180(3) of the Financial Services Act 1986 and section 449(1B) of the Companies Act 1985, a person authorised by the Secretary of State under section 245C of the Companies Act 1985 is designated as an authority in relation to that person's functions relating to the securing of compliance by companies with the accounting requirements of the Companies Act 1985.

**3** [Insertion at end of table in s. 87(4) of Companies Act 1989.]

## EXPLANATORY NOTE

(*This Note is not part of the Order*)

This Order designates a person authorised by the Secretary of State under section 245C of the Companies Act 1985, as an authority (in relation to that person's functions in securing compliance by companies with the accounting requirements of that Act), for the purposes of section 180(3) of the Financial Services Act 1986, section 449(1B) of the Companies Act 1985 and section 87 of the Companies Act 1989. Under section 245B of the Companies Act 1985, the Secretary of State or a person authorised by him under section 245C of that Act may apply to the court for a declaration or declarator that the annual accounts of a company do not comply with the requirements of the Companies Act 1985 and an order requiring the directors of the company to prepare revised accounts. The Financial Reporting Review Panel Limited was so authorised with effect from 1st February 1991 (SI 1991/13). The effect of the designation is to permit the disclosure of information which would otherwise be restricted if disclosure is for the purposes of enabling or assisting the designated authority to discharge the specified functions. There have been seven previous orders designating public or other authorities for the purposes of either or both of section 180 of the Financial Services Act 1986 and section 449 of the Companies Act 1985 (SI 1986/2046, 1987/859, 1141, 1988/1058, 1334, 1989/940, 2009). No previous orders have been made under section 87 of the Companies Act 1989.

# THE COMPANIES ACT 1989 (RECOGNISED SUPERVISORY BODIES) (PERIODICAL FEES) REGULATIONS 1993

(SI 1993/1881)

*Made on 20 July 1993 by the Secretary of State for Trade and Industry under s. 45 of the Companies Act 1989. Operative from 16 August 1993.*

## CITATION AND COMMENCEMENT

**1** These Regulations may be cited as the Companies Act 1989 (Recognised Supervisory Bodies) (Periodical Fees) Regulations 1993 and shall come into force on 16th August 1993.

## PRESCRIPTION OF PERIODICAL FEES

**2(1)** On 1st October 1993 a recognised supervisory body shall pay to the Secretary of State a periodical fee of £440 in respect of the period from 16th August 1993 to 30th September 1993.

**2(2)** On 1st October 1993 and 1st October of each succeeding year a recognised supervisory body shall pay to the Secretary of State a periodical fee of £3,500.

## NEW RECOGNISED SUPERVISORY BODIES

**3(1)** The first periodical fee payable by a body which becomes a recognised supervisory body after the commencement of these Regulations shall be payable on the date on which it becomes a recognised supervisory body and each subsequent periodical fee shall be payable in accordance with regulation 2(2).

**3(2)** The amount of the first periodical fee payable in accordance with paragraph (1) shall be equal to

$$\frac{A \times £3,500}{365}$$

where A is the number of days from the date when the body becomes a recognised supervisory body to the following 30th September, inclusive of both dates.

**3(3)** Where the amount of the periodical fee calculated in accordance with paragraph (2) is not a multiple of £10 it shall be rounded down to the next multiple of £10.

## EXPLANATORY NOTE

(*This Note is not part of the Regulations*)

These Regulations are made under section 45 of the Companies Act 1989 and prescribe the fees payable by a recognised supervisory body. A fee of £440 is payable for the period from 16th August 1993 to 30th September 1993. Thereafter, a recognised supervisory body is to pay a periodical fee of £3,500 each year. For a body that becomes a recognised supervisory body after the commencement of these Regulations a pro rata fee is payable for the period from the date of its recognition to the following 30th September (inclusive).

A recognised supervisory body is a body recognised by the Secretary of State for the purposes of Part II of the Companies Act 1989 (eligibility for appointment as company auditor).



CCH.New Law

bbcl randr4 Mp 4208—bcl98 220a

# THE DISCLOSURE OF INTERESTS IN SHARES (AMENDMENT) (NO. 2) REGULATIONS 1993

(SI 1993/2689)

*Made on 28 October 1993 by the Secretary of State for Trade and Industry under s. 210A of the Companies Act 1985. Operative from 29 October 1993.*

## CITATION AND COMMENCEMENT

**1** These Regulations may be cited as the Disclosure of Interests in Shares (Amendment) (No. 2) Regulations 1993 and shall come into force on the day after the day on which they are made.

## AMENDMENTS OF PART VI OF THE COMPANIES ACT 1985

**2** Part VI of the Companies Act 1985 shall be amended in accordance with Regulation 3 below.

**3** [Amendments to s. 209(2)(a).]

## TRANSITIONAL PROVISIONS

**4(1)** In this Regulation **"commencement"** means the commencement of these Regulations.

**4(2)** Where a person–

(a) had a notifiable interest immediately before commencement, but does not have such an interest immediately after commencement, or

(b) had a notifiable interest immediately before commencement and has such an interest immediately after commencement but the percentage levels of his interest immediately before and immediately after commencement are not the same,

then he comes under an obligation to notify the company with respect to the interest which he has or had in its shares; and the provisions of Part VI of the Companies Act 1985 shall apply as if that obligation arose under section 198 of that Act.

## EXPLANATORY NOTE

(*This Note is not part of the Regulations*)

These Regulations amend section 209 of the Companies Act 1985. Subsection (2) of that section provides for certain interests held by way of security to be disregarded for the purposes of the obligation to disclose interests in shares comprised in certain issued share capital of public companies which is imposed by sections 198 to 202 of that Act. These Regulations amend that subsection to make similar provision for interests held by way of security by stock exchanges situated or operating in a member State and by persons who deal in securities or derivatives (as defined in section 220 of the Companies Act 1985) on an exchange situated or operating in a member State. Article 4 also makes transitional provisions in order to impose an obligation to notify upon persons who, as a result of the coming into force of the Regulations, no longer have a notifiable interest within the meaning of Part VI of the Companies Act 1985 or whose notifiable interest is reduced.

Part VI of the Companies Act 1985 was amended by the Disclosure of Interests in Shares (Amendment) Regulations 1993 (SI 1993/1819), which came into force on 18th September 1993.

# THE COMPANIES ACT 1985 (INSURANCE COMPANIES ACCOUNTS) REGULATIONS 1993

(SI 1993/3246)

*Made on 18 December 1993 by the Secretary of State for Trade and Industry under s. 257 of the Companies Act 1985. Operative from 19 December 1993.*

## ARRANGEMENT OF REGULATIONS

## SCHEDULES



## CITATION AND COMMMENCEMENT

**1(1)** These Regulations may be cited as the Companies Act 1985 (Insurance Companies Accounts) Regulations 1993 shall come into force on the day after the day on which they are made.

**1(2)** In these regulations**"the 1985 Act"** means the Companies Act 1985.

## INSURANCE COMPANIES

**2** [Amendment of s. 255 of the 1985 Act.]

## INSURANCE GROUPS

**3** [Amendment of s. 255A of the 1985 Act.]

## FORM AND CONTENT OF ACCOUNTS

**4** For Schedule 9A to the 1985 Act there shall be substituted Schedule 1 to these Regulations (form and content of accounts of insurance companies and groups).

## MINOR AND CONSEQUENTIAL AMENDMENTS

**5(1)** The 1985 Act shall have effect subject to the amendments specified in Schedule 2 to these Regulations (being minor amendments and amendments consequential on the provisions of these Regulations).

**5(2)** In paragraph 3(1) of Part I of Schedule 2 to the Companies Act 1989 (Commencement No. 4 and Transitional and Saving Provisions) Order 1990, for the words "ending prior to 1st January 1994" there shall be substituted the words "commencing before 23rd December 1994".

## EXEMPTED COMPANIES

**6(1)** A company to which paragraph (2) below applies may, with respect to any financial year, prepare such annual accounts as it would have been required to prepare had the modifications to the 1985 Act effected by these Regulations not been made.

**6(2)** This paragraph applies to–

(a) any company which is excluded from the scope of Council Directive 73/239/EEC by Article 3 of that Directive, and

(b) any company referred to in Article 2(2) or (3) or 3 of Council Directive 79/267/EEC.

**6(3)** The modifications effected by regulations 2 to 5 above shall, where a company prepares accounts under paragraph (1) of this Regulation, be treated (as regards that company) as not having been made.

## TRANSITIONAL PROVISIONS

**7(1)** A company (including any body corporate to which Part VII of the 1985 Act is applied by any enactment) may, with respect to a financial year of the company commencing before 23rd December 1994, prepare such annual accounts as it would have been required to prepare had the modifications to the 1985 Act effected by these Regulations not been made.

7(2) The modifications effected by regulations 2 to 5 above shall, where a company prepares accounts under paragraph (1) of this Regulation, be treated (as regards that company) as not having been made.

# Schedule 1 – Form and Content of Accounts of Insurance Companies and Groups

Regulation 4

**Note**

This Schedule sets out the new Sch. 9A to the 1985 Act.

# Schedule 2 – Minor and Consequential Amendments of 1985 Act

Regulation 5

**Note**

Amendment re s. 228(2)(b), 254(3), 255C, 260(6), 262A, 268(1) of and Sch. 10, 11, 22 to the 1985 Act.

## EXPLANATORY NOTE

(*This Note is not part of the Regulations*)

1. These Regulations implement Council Directive 91/674 EEC Official Journal No. L374 of 31.12.91, pages 7 to 31, on the annual accounts and consolidated accounts of insurance undertakings, in so far as that Directive is applicable to bodies corporate to which Part VII of the Companies Act 1985 ("the 1985 Act") applies.

2. Regulations 2 and 3 amend sections 255 and 255A of the 1985 Act which make special provisions for the accounts of banking and insurance companies and groups. They introduce a requirement for insurance companies to prepare accounts in accordance with the new Schedule 9A, and define which companies are to prepare group accounts under the special provisions with respect to insurance groups.

3. Regulation 4 substitutes as new Schedule 9A to the 1985 Act, Schedule 1 to the Regulations. The new Schedule 9A sets out the form and content of accounts of insurance companies and groups. Part I lays down rules governing the content of the individual accounts of insurance companies, including prescribed formats to be followed, the valuation rules to be applied, the rules for determining provisions and the disclosures to be made in the notes to the accounts. Part II of new Schedule 9A adapts the general rules of Part VII of the 1985 Act with respect to the consolidated accounts of a company to the special circumstances of insurance groups.

4. Regulation 5 of, and Schedule 2 to, the Regulations make minor and consequential amendments to the 1985 Act and to the Companies Act 1989 (Commencement No. 4 and Transitional and Saving Provisions) Order 1990 (SI 1990/355).

5. Regulation 6 specifies certain companies which, under the terms of the Directive, may continue to prepare accounts under Part VII of the 1985 Act, as it applies to insurance companies and groups, without the amendments effected by these Regulations.

6. Regulation 7 sets out a transitional provision whereby a company may prepare accounts in accordance with the unamended Part VII, as the Part applies to insurance companies and groups, rather than under the amended provisions for a financial year commencing before 23rd December 1994.

# THE COMPANIES (WELSH LANGUAGE FORMS AND DOCUMENTS) REGULATIONS 1994

(SI 1994/117)

*Made on 25 January 1994 by the Secretary of State for Trade and Industry under s. 287(3), 288(2), 363(2), 710B(3),(8) and 744 of the Companies Act 1985. Operative from 1 February 1994.*

[**Note:** Amendments by the Companies (Welsh Language Forms and Documents) (Amendment) Regulations 1994 (SI 1994/727) (operative from 1 April 1994) and the Companies (Welsh Language Forms and Documents) (Amendment) Regulations 1995 (SI 1995/734) (operative from 1 April 1995) have been included.]

**1** These Regulations may be cited as the Companies (Welsh Language Forms and Documents) Regulations 1994, and shall come into force on 1st February 1994.

**2** In these Regulations a reference to a numbered section, part or schedule is a reference to a section, part or schedule of the Companies Act 1985.

**3** Forms 287 CYM, 288 CYM and 363 CYM in the Schedule to these Regulations, with such variations as circumstances may require, are additional forms prescribed for the purposes of sections 287(3), 288(2) and 363(2) respectively.

**4(1)** The documents described in paragraph (2) are prescribed for the purpose of section 710B(3)(a) (documents which may be delivered to the registrar of companies in Welsh by a company, whose memorandum states that its registered office is to be situated in Wales, without an accompanying English translation).

**4(2)** The documents referred to in paragraph (1) are:

(a) a copy of the memorandum and articles of a relevant company as delivered, or as altered;

(b) a copy of the annual accounts of a relevant company;

(c) a copy of the annual report (within the meaning of Part VII) of the directors of a relevant company;

(d) a copy of the auditors' report (within the meaning of Part VII) on the accounts of a relevant company; and

(e) any document appended, by virtue of section 243(2) (accounts of subsidiary undertakings to be appended in certain cases) or paragraph 7(2) of Part II of Schedule 9 (banking groups: information as to undertaking in which shares held as a result of financial assistance operation), to the annual accounts of a relevant company.

**History**

In reg. 4(2) para. (a) inserted and former para. (a)–(d) renumbered para. (b)–(e) by the Companies (Welsh Language Forms and Documents) (Amendment) Regulations 1995 (SI 1995/734), reg. 6 as from 1 April 1995.

**4(3)** For the purpose of paragraph (2), a **"relevant company"** is such a company as is mentioned in section 710B(1)(b), other than a public company whose shares or debentures, or any class of whose shares or debentures, are listed within the meaning of section 251(1).

**History**

Reg. 4(3) substituted by the Companies (Welsh Language Forms and Documents) (Amendment) Regulations 1994 (SI 1994/727) as from 1 April 1994; reg. 4(3) formerly read as follows:

"For the purpose of paragraph (2), a **"relevant company"** is any company to which section 710B(1) applies, other than a listed company as defined in section 251(1)."

**5** For the purpose of section 710B(8), a translation of a document into English shall be certified to be a correct translation–

(a) if the translation was made in the United Kingdom, by–

 (i) a notary public in any part of the United Kingdom;

 (ii) a solicitor (if the translation was made in Scotland), a solicitor of the Supreme Court of Judicature of England and Wales (if it was made in England or Wales), or a solicitor of the Supreme Court of Judicature of Northern Ireland (if it was made in Northern Ireland);

 (iii) a person certified by a person mentioned in sub-paragraphs (i) and (ii) above to be known to him to be competent to translate the document into English; or

(iv) in the case of a translation obtained by the registrar of companies pursuant to section 710B(4), the person who has translated the document into English; or

(b) if the translation was made outside the United Kingdom, by–

(i) a notary public;

(ii) a person authorised in the place where the translation was made to administer an oath;

(iii) any of the British officials mentioned in section 6 of the Commissioners for Oaths Act 1889; or

(iv) a person certified by a person mentioned in sub-paragraphs (i) to (iii) above, to be known to him to be competent to translate the document into English.

# Schedule

Regulation 3

**Note**
This Schedule sets out forms 287 CYM, 288 CYM and 363 CYM. They are not reproduced here.

## EXPLANATORY NOTE

(*This Note is not part of the Regulations*)

These Regulations are made following the commencement of the Welsh Language Act 1993. That Act makes provision for the use of the Welsh language generally for official purposes, but contains specific provisions concerning documents to be delivered to the registrar of companies.

The Regulations prescribe additional forms which are in Welsh as well as in English, namely:

– an additional form for giving notice to the registrar of companies of a change in the situation of a company's registered office address, under section 287 of the Companies Act 1985 (**"the Act"**);

– an additional form for giving notice to the registrar of companies of particulars of appointment and resignation of directors and secretaries, and of any change in the particulars contained in the register, under section 288 of the Act; and

– an additional annual return form, for the purpose of section 363 of the Act (delivery of annual returns).

As a result of section 710B(3)(b) of the Act, inserted by the Welsh Language Act 1993, these forms may be filled out in Welsh without an accompanying certified English translation where a company's memorandum states that its registered office is to be situated in Wales. (The registrar himself is required to obtain a translation in such cases.)

The Regulations also prescribe, for the purpose of section 710B(3)(a) of the Act, certain accounting documents which may be delivered to the registrar of companies in Welsh without being accompanied by a certified English translation (the registrar again being required to obtain a translation). This provision preserves the effect of section 255E (Delivery of accounting documents in Welsh only) which is repealed by the Welsh Language Act 1993. It also extends the scope of this provision to public companies which are not listed companies.

The Regulations also prescribe the manner of certifying a correct translation of a document into English for the purpose of section 710B(8) of the Act – that is, for cases where a document may be delivered to the registrar in Welsh, but with an English translation. In the case of a translation obtained by the registrar pursuant to section 710B(4), the regulations prescribe that the translation may be certified by the person from whom the registrar has obtained the translation.

# THE INSIDER DEALING (SECURITIES AND REGULATED MARKETS) ORDER 1994

(SI 1994/187)

*Made on 1 February 1994 by the Treasury under s. 54(1), 60(1), 62(1) and 64(3) of the Criminal Justice Act 1993. Operative from 1 March 1994.*

## TITLE, COMMENCEMENT AND INTERPRETATION

**1** This Order may be cited as the Insider Dealing (Securities and Regulated Markets) Order 1994 and shall come into force on the twenty eighth day after the day on which it is made.

**2** In this Order a "State within the European Economic Area" means a State which is a member of the European Communities and the Republics of Austria, Finland and Iceland, the Kingdoms of Norway and Sweden and the Principality of Liechtenstein.

## SECURITIES

**3** Articles 4 to 8 set out conditions for the purposes of section 54(1) of the Criminal Justice Act 1993 (securities to which Part V of the Act of 1993 applies).

**4** The following condition applies in relation to any security which falls within any paragraph of Schedule 2 to the Act of 1993, that is, that it is officially listed in a State within the European Economic Area or that it is admitted to dealing on, or has its price quoted on or under the rules of, a regulated market.

**5** The following alternative condition applies in relation to a warrant, that is, that the right under it is a right to subscribe for any share or debt security of the same class as a share or debt security which satisfies the condition in article 4.

**6** The following alternative condition applies in relation to a depositary receipt, that is, that the rights under it are in respect of any share or debt security which satisfies the condition in article 4.

**7** The following alternative conditions apply in relation to an option or a future, that is, that the option or rights under the future are in respect of–

(a) any share or debt security which satisfies the condition in article 4, or

(b) any depositary receipt which satisfies the condition in article 4 or article 6.

**8** The following alternative condition applies in relation to a contract for differences, that is, that the purpose or pretended purpose of the contract is to secure a profit or avoid a loss by reference to fluctuations in–

(a) the price of any shares or debt securities which satisfy the condition in article 4, or

(b) an index of the price of such shares or debt securities.

## REGULATED MARKETS

**9** The following markets are regulated markets for the purposes of Part V of the Act of 1993–

(a) any market which is established under the rules of an investment exchange specified in the Schedule to this Order;

(b) the market known as OFEX, operated by J. P. Jenkins Limited.

**History**

In art. 9, "(a)" and para. (b) inserted by Insider Dealing (Securities and Regulated Markets) (Amendment) Order 2000 (SI 2000/1923), art. 1, 2(2), with effect from 20 July 2000.

## UNITED KINGDOM REGULATED MARKETS

**10** The regulated markets which are regulated in the United Kingdom for the purposes of Part V of the Act of 1993 are any market which is established under the rules of–

(a) the London Stock Exchange Limited;

(b) LIFFE Administration & Management;

(c) OMLX, the London Securities and Derivatives Exchange Limited;

(d) Tradepoint Financial Networks plc;

(e) COREDEAL Limited;

together with the market known as OFEX, operated by J. P. Jenkins limited.

**History**

In art. 10 para (c), the word "and" omitted and para. (e) and final paragraph inserted by Insider Dealing (Securities and Regulated Markets) (Amendment) Order 2000 (SI 2000/1923), art. 1, 2(3), with effect from 20 July 2000.

Previously, art. 10, para. (a) substituted; in para. (b) the word "and" omitted; after para. (c) the word "and" inserted; para. (d) inserted by the Insider Dealing (Securities and Regulated Markets) (Amendment) Order 1996 (SI 1996/1561), art. 1, 3 as from 1 July 1996. Art. 10, para. (a) formerly read as follows:

"the International Stock Exchange of the United Kingdom and the Republic of Ireland Limited, other than the market which operates in the Republic of Ireland known as the Irish Unit of the International Stock Exchange of the United Kingdom and the Republic of Ireland Limited."

# Schedule – Regulated Markets

Article 9

Any market which is established under the rules of one of the following investment exchanges:

Amsterdam Stock Exchange.
Antwerp Stock Exchange.
Athens Stock Exchange.
Barcelona Stock Exchange.
Bavarian Stock Exchange.
Berlin Stock Exchange.
Bilbao Stock Exchange.
Bologna Stock Exchange.
Bremen Stock Exchange.
Brussels Stock Exchange.
Copenhagen Stock Exchange.
COREDEAL Limited.
Dusseldorf Stock Exchange.
The exchange known as EASDAQ.
Florence Stock Exchange.
Frankfurt Stock Exchange.
Genoa Stock Exchange.
Hamburg Stock Exchange.
Hanover Stock Exchange.
Helsinki Stock Exchange.
Iceland Stock Exchange.
The Irish Stock Exchange Limited.
Lisbon Stock Exchange.
LIFFE Administration & Management.
The London Stock Exchange Limited.
Luxembourg Stock Exchange.
Lyon Stock Exchange.
Madrid Stock Exchange.
Milan Stock Exchange.
Naples Stock Exchange.
The exchange known as NASDAQ.
The exchange known as the Nouveau Marché.
OMLX, the London Securities and Derivatives Exchange Limited.
Oporto Stock Exchange.
Oslo Stock Exchange.
Palermo Stock Exchange.
Paris Stock Exchange.

Rome Stock Exchange.
Stockholm Stock Exchange.
Stuttgart Stock Exchange.
Tradepoint Financial Networks plc.
Trieste Stock Exchange.
Turin Stock Exchange.
Valencia Stock Exchange.
Venice Stock Exchange.
Vienna Stock Exchange.

**History**

In Sch. to 1994 Order, "COREDEAL Limited" and "the exchange known as EASDAQ" inserted and "Securitries Exchange of Iceland" omitted by Insider Dealing (Securities and Regulated Markets) (Amendment) Order 2000 (SI 2000/1923), art. 1, 2(4), with effect from 20 July 2000.

Previously,"Bordeaux Stock Exchange" and "Ghent Stock Exchange" omitted; "The International Stock Exchange of the United Kingdom and the Republic of Ireland Limited" substituted by "Iceland Stock Exchange" and "The Irish Stock Exchange"; "Liege Stock Exchange" and "Lille Stock Exchange" omitted; "The London Stock Exchange Limited" inserted; "Marseille Stock Exchange", "Nancy Stock Exchange" and "Nantes Stock Exchange" omitted; "The exchange known as the Nouveau Marché" and "Tradepoint Financial Networks plc." inserted by the Insider Dealing (Securities and Regulated Markets) (Amendment) Order 1996 (SI 1996/1561), art. 1, 4 as from 1 July 1996.

## EXPLANATORY NOTE

*(This Note is not part of the Order)*

Part V of the Criminal Justice Act 1993 (**"the Act"**) establishes the offence of insider dealing. It is an offence for an individual who has information as an insider to deal on a "regulated market" or through or as a professional intermediary in "securities" whose price would be significantly affected if the inside information were made public. It is also an offence to encourage insider dealing and to disclose inside information. No offence is committed unless there is some connection with the United Kingdom which includes dealing on a regulated market which has been identified as being "regulated in the United Kingdom".

This Order specifies the securities to which the insider dealing provisions apply and identifies what is a regulated market and a market regulated in the United Kingdom. The Act defines other terms used.

Section 54(1) of the Act provides that Part V applies to any security which falls within any paragraph of Schedule 2 to the Act which satisfies any condition applying to it under an order made by the Treasury for the purposes of section 54(1). Articles 4 to 8 of this Order set out those conditions.

The first condition applies to any security falling within Schedule 2: shares, debt securities, warrants, depositary receipts, options, futures and contracts for differences. Any security of those types which is officially listed in a State within the European Economic Area or which is admitted to dealing on, or has its price quoted on or under the rules of, a regulated market is a security for the purposes of insider dealing.

Alternative conditions apply to securities listed in Schedule 2 to the Act other than shares and debt securities. A depositary receipt is a security for the purposes of insider dealing if the rights under it are in respect of shares or debt securities which satisfy the first condition i.e. that the shares or debt securities are officially listed in a State within the European Economic Area or are admitted to dealing on or have their price quoted on or under the rules of a regulated market. A warrant is a security for the purposes of insider dealing if the right under it is a right to subscribe for any share or debt security of the same class as a share or debt security which satisfies the first condition.

An option or a future is a security for the purposes of insider dealing if the option or rights under the future are in respect of shares, debt securities or depositary receipts which satisfy the first condition or are in respect of a depositary receipt which satisfies the first condition or the rights under which are in respect of shares or debt securities which satisfy the first condition.

A contract for differences is a security for the purpose of insider dealing if the purpose or pretended purpose of the contract is to secure a profit or avoid a loss by reference to fluctuations in the price or an index of the price of shares or debt securities which meet the first condition.

Article 9 and the Schedule to the Order identify which markets are "regulated markets" for the purposes of insider dealing. They are the markets which are established under the rules of an investment exchange specified in that Schedule.

Article 10 identifies the regulated markets which are "regulated in the United Kingdom" for the purposes of the territorial scope of the offence of insider dealing. These are markets established under the rules of the International Stock Exchange of the United Kingdom and the Republic of Ireland Limited (other than the market operating in the Republic of Ireland known as the Irish Unit), of LIFFE and OMLX.

# THE TRADED SECURITIES (DISCLOSURE) REGULATIONS 1994

(SI 1994/188)

*Made on 1 February 1994 by the Treasury under s. 2(2) of the European Communities Act 1972. Operative from 1 March 1994.*

## CITATION AND COMMENCEMENT

**1(1)** These Regulations may be cited as the Traded Securities (Disclosure) Regulations 1994.

**1(2)** These Regulations shall come into force on 1st March 1994.

## INTERPRETATION

**2** In these Regulations:

**"the Official List"** has the meaning given by section 142(7) of the Financial Services Act 1986;

**"overseas investment exchange"** and **"recognised investment exchange"** have the meaning given by section 207(1) of the Financial Services Act 1986;

**"regulated market"** means any market in the United Kingdom on which securities are admitted to trading being a market which is regulated and supervised by a recognised investment exchange and which operates regularly and is accessible directly or indirectly to the public; and

**"security"** means any security which falls within any paragraph of the Schedule to these Regulations but does not include an investment which is admitted to the Official List in accordance with Part IV of the Financial Services Act 1986.

and the expressions **"admitting to trading"** and **"company"** and **"undertaking"** have the same meaning as in the Council Directive of 13th November 1989 co-ordinating regulations on insider dealing (89/592/EEC).

## OBLIGATION TO DISCLOSE INFORMATION

**3(1)** Subject to paragraph (2) below, a company or undertaking which is an issuer of a security admitted to trading on a regulated market (an "issuer") shall inform the public as soon as possible of any major new developments in the issuer's sphere of activity which are not public knowledge and which may, by virtue of their effect on the issuer's assets and liabilities or financial position or on the general course of its business, lead to substantial movements in the price of that security.

**3(2)** A recognised investment exchange which regulates and supervises a regulated market on which an issuer's securities are admitted to trading may exempt the issuer from the obligation imposed by paragraph (1) above if satisfied that the disclosure of the particular information would prejudice the legitimate interests of that issuer.

**3(3)** The rules of a recognised investment exchange must, at least, enable the exchange, in the event of a failure by an issuer whose securities are admitted to trading on a regulated market which the exchange regulates and supervises to comply with the obligation imposed by paragraph (1) above, to do any of the following, that is to say–

(a) discontinue the admission of the securities to trading;
(b) suspend trading in the securities;
(c) publish the fact that the issuer has failed to comply with the obligation; and
(d) itself make public any information which the issuer has failed to publish.

**4** The Financial Services Act 1986 shall have effect as if the requirement set out in paragraph (3) of regulation 3 above was–

(a) in the case of a recognised investment exchange which is not an overseas investment exchange, among those specified in Schedule 4 to that Act (requirements for recognition of UK investment exchange); and
(b) in the case of an overseas investment exchange, among those mentioned in section 37(7)(a) of that Act (revocation of recognition order) and specified in section 40(2) of that Act (requirements for recognition of overseas investment exchange etc.).

# Schedule

Regulation 2

**1** Shares and stock in the share capital of a company (**"shares"**).

**2** Any instrument creating or acknowledging indebtedness which is issued by a company or undertaking, including, in particular, debentures, debenture stock, loan stock, bonds and certificates of deposit (**"debt securities"**).

**3** Any right (whether conferred by warrant or otherwise) to subscribe for shares or debt securities (**"warrants"**).

**4(1)** The rights under any depositary receipt.

**4(2)** For the purposes of sub-paragraph (1) above a **"depositary receipt"** means a certificate or other record (whether or not in the form of a document)–

(a) which is issued by or on behalf of a person who holds any relevant securities of a particular issuer; and
(b) which acknowledges that another person is entitled to rights in relation to the relevant securities or relevant securities of the same kind.

**4(3)** In sub-paragraph (2) above **"relevant securities"** means shares, debt securities and warrants.

**5** Any option to acquire or dispose of any security falling within any other paragraph of this Schedule.

**6(1)** Rights under a contract for the acquisition or disposal of relevant securities under which delivery is to be made at a future date and at a price agreed when the contract is made.

**6(2)** In sub-paragraph (1) above–

(a) the references to a future date and to a price agreed when the contract is made include references to a date and a price determined in accordance with the terms of the contract; and
(b) **"relevant securities"** means any security falling within any other paragraph of this Schedule.

**7(1)** Rights under a contract which does not provide for the delivery of securities but whose purpose or pretended purpose is to secure a profit or avoid a loss by reference to fluctuations in–

(a) a share index or other similar factor connected with relevant securities; or
(b) the price of particular relevant securities.

**7(2)** In sub-paragraph (1) above **"relevant securities"** means any security falling within any other paragraph of this Schedule.

## EXPLANATORY NOTE

*(This Note is not part of the Regulations)*

The Regulations give effect to the provisions of article 7 of the Council Directive of 13th November 1989 co-ordinating regulations on insider dealing (89/592/EEC OJ No. L334/30). Article 7 requires that all companies and undertakings, the transferable securities of which are, whatever their nature, admitted to trading on a market which is regulated and supervised by bodies recognised by public bodies, operates regularly and is accessible directly or indirectly to the public, should be under an obligation to inform the public as soon as possible of any major new developments in the issuer's sphere of activity which are not public knowledge and which may, by virtue of their effect on the issuer's assets and liabilities or financial position or on the general course of its business, lead to substantial movements in the price of the securities admitted to trading. The authorities responsible for the market on which securities are admitted to trading may exempt a company or undertaking from compliance with the requirement if the disclosure of the information would prejudice the legitimate interests of that company or undertaking. In the United Kingdom, the obligation extends to companies and undertakings whose securities are admitted to trading on an investment exchange recognised under the Financial Services Act 1986.

Regulation 2 of, and the Schedule to, the Regulations contain definitions which are relevant for the purposes of the Regulations.

Regulation 3(1) imposes the obligation required by article 7 except where the securities in question are admitted to listing in accordance with Part IV of the Financial Services Act. Listing rules made under that Part impose the obligation in relation to such securities.

Regulation 3(2) enables an investment exchange recognised under the Financial Services Act to dispense an issuer from compliance with the obligation in the circumstances permitted by article 7 and regulation 3(3) requires that each recognised investment exchange must have rules which enable it, at least, to discontinue or suspend trading in the relevant securities where there has been a failure to comply with the obligation.

Regulation 4 makes the obligation imposed on recognised investment exchanges by regulation 3(3) one of the requirements which an exchange must meet if it is to continue to be recognised under the Financial Services Act.

# THE COMPANIES ACT 1985 (BANK ACCOUNTS) REGULATIONS 1994

(SI 1994/233)

*Made on 2 February 1994 by the Secretary of State for Trade and Industry under s. 257 of the Companies Act 1985. Operative from 11 and 28 February 1994.*

## CITATION, COMMENCEMENT AND INTERPRETATION

**1(1)** These Regulations may be cited as the Companies Act 1985 (Bank Accounts) Regulations 1994.

**1(2)** This regulation and regulations 2, 4 and 7 shall come into force on 11th February 1994, and the remainder of the regulations shall come into force on 28th February 1994.

**2** In these Regulations **"the 1985 Act"** means the Companies Act 1985.

## AMENDMENT OF SECTION 255B

**3** [Substitution in s. 255B(2) of the 1985 Act.]

## AMENDMENT OF SCHEDULE 9 ETC

**4** [Repeals in s. 262A of and Pt. I, para. 89 of Sch. 9 to the 1985 Act.]

**5** [Amendments of Pt. IV, para. 1, 2, 3(1), (4), (5) of Sch. 9 to the 1985 Act.]

## CONSEQUENTIAL AMENDMENT OF SECTION 343 ETC.

**6** [Amendments in s. 343(1)(a), (2), (4) of and in para. 10 and 11 of Sch. 10 to the Companies Act 1989.]

## TRANSITIONAL PROVISIONS

**7** The directors of a company (including a body corporate, or unincorporated body of persons, to which Part VII of the 1985 Act is applied by virtue of any enactment, including any subordinate legislation within the meaning of section 21 of the Interpretation Act 1978, may prepare annual accounts under Part VII of the 1985 Act for a financial year of the company commencing on a date prior to 23rd December 1992 as if the amendments effected by regulation 4 of these Regulations had not been made.

**8** A company to which section 343 of the 1985 Act applied before it was amended by these Regulations shall be regarded, for the purposes of subsection (2) of that section as amended by these Regulations, as having taken advantage of the provisions of paragraph 2 of Part IV of Schedule 9 to the 1985 Act in relation to any financial year for which accounts were prepared under Part VII of that Act prior to its amendment by these Regulations.

## EXPLANATORY NOTE

(*This Note is not part of the Regulations*)

1. These Regulations amend the special provisions in Part VII of the Companies Act 1985 ("the 1985 Act") applicable to the accounts of banking companies and groups.

2. Regulations 3 and 5 amend section 255B of, and Part IV of Schedule 9 to, the 1985 Act to extend the provisions relating to companies which are holding companies of banking companies, to companies which are holding companies of credit institutions (as defined in section 262 of the 1985 Act). Part IV is also amended so that companies to which it applies can if they so wish comply with Schedule 6 to the 1985 Act for the purposes of their accounts for a financial year, without the special adaptations made by Part IV of Schedule 9. Regulation 6 amends section 343 of the 1985 Act consequentially upon the amendments to Part IV and makes consequential repeals in Schedule 10 to the Companies Act 1989.

3. Regulation 4 repeals the definitions of "Banking activities" and "Banking transactions" in Part I of Schedule 9 to the 1985 Act, so as to align the provisions of that Part of the Schedule more closely with the provisions of the Bank Accounts Directive (86/635/EEC, O.J. No. L372 of 31.12.1986, pages 1–17).

4. Regulations 7 and 8 contain transitional provisions.

5. A Compliance Cost Assessment is available, copies of which have been placed in the libraries of both Houses of Parliament. Copies are also available from the Companies Division of the Department of Trade and Industry, Room 519 10–18 Victoria Street, London SW1H 0NN.

# THE PARTNERSHIPS (UNRESTRICTED SIZE) NO. 11 REGULATIONS 1994

(SI 1994/644)

*Made on 7 March 1994 by the Secretary of State for Trade and Industry under s. 716(2)(d) and 744 of the Companies Act 1985. Operative from 29 March 1994.*

**1** These Regulations may be cited as the Partnerships (Unrestricted Size) No. 11 Regulations 1994, and shall come into force on 29th March 1994.

**2(1)** Section 716(1) of the Companies Act 1985 does not prohibit the formation of partnerships consisting of more than 20 persons–

(a) for the purpose of carrying on business as patent agents, where each such person is a patent agent,

(b) for the purpose of carrying on business as registered trade mark agents, where each such person is a registered trade mark agent, or

(c) for the purpose of carrying on business as either patent agents or registered trade mark agents, or as both patent agents and registered trade mark agents, where the partnership concerned satisfies the conditions prescribed by paragraphs (a) and (b) of Rule 3 of the Patent Agents (Mixed Partnerships and Bodies Corporate) Rules 1994 or Rule 3 of the Registered Trade Mark Agents (Mixed Partnerships and Bodies Corporate) Rules 1994.

**2(2)** In these Regulations,

(a) **"patent agent"** means a person whose name is entered in the register kept pursuant to rules made under section 275 of the Copyright, Designs and Patents Act 1988, and

(b) **"registered trade mark agent"** means a person whose name is entered in the register kept pursuant to rules made under section 282 of that Act.

**3** In Regulation 1 of the Partnerships (Unrestricted Size) No. 1 Regulations 1968, paragraph (a) is revoked.

## EXPLANATORY NOTE

(*This Note is not part of the Regulations*)

Section 716 of the Companies Act 1985 prohibits the formation of partnerships consisting of more than 20 persons. The Regulations exempt from that prohibition any partnership formed for the purpose of carrying on business as patent or registered trade mark agents where each partner is entered on the register of patent agents or registered trade mark agents, kept pursuant to section 275 or 282 of the Copyright, Designs and Patents Act 1988 (see SI 1990/1457 and SI 1990/1458 for rules made under those sections). It also exempts mixed partnerships of patent agents and registered trade mark agents where the partnership concerned satisfies conditions prescribed pursuant to the Secretary of State's powers under that Act (SI 1994/362 and 1994/363).

The Regulations also revoke that part of SI 1968/1222 (the Partnerships (Unrestricted Size) No. 1 Regulations) which related to partnerships carrying on business as patent agents.

# THE FOREIGN COMPANIES (EXECUTION OF DOCUMENTS) REGULATIONS 1994

(SI 1994/950)

*Made on 24 March 1994 by the Secretary of State for Trade and Industry under s. 130(6) of the Companies Act 1989. Operative from 16 May 1994.*

[**Note:** Amendments by the Foreign Companies (Execution of Documents) (Amendment) Regulations 1995 (SI 1995/1729) (operative from 1 August 1995) have been included.]

## CITATION AND COMMENCEMENT

**1** These Regulations may be cited as the Foreign Companies (Execution of Documents) Regulations 1994 and shall come into force on 16th May 1994.

## APPLICATION OF SECTIONS 36 TO 36C COMPANIES ACT 1985

**2** Sections 36, 36A, 36B and 36C of the Companies Act 1985 shall apply to companies incorporated outside Great Britain with the adaptations and modifications set out in regulations 3 to 6 below.

**History**

In reg. 2 the words "Sections 36, 36A, 36B and 36C" substituted for the former words "Sections 36 to 36C" and the words "regulations 3 to 5 below" substituted for the former words "regulations 3 to 6 below" by the Foreign Companies (Execution of Documents) (Amendment) Regulations 1995 (SI 1995/1729), reg. 1, 3(a), (b) as from 1 August 1995.

**3** References in the said sections 36, 36A, 36B and 36C to a company shall be construed as references to a company incorporated outside Great Britain.

**History**
In reg. 3 the words "sections 36, 36A, 36B and 36C" substituted for the former words "sections 36 to 36C" by the Foreign Companies (Execution of Documents) (Amendment) Regulations 1995 (SI 1995/1729), reg. 1, 4 as from 1 August 1995.

## ADAPTATION OF SECTION 36

**4** Section 36 shall apply as if–

(a) after the words "common seal," in paragraph (a) there were inserted "or in any manner permitted by the laws of the territory in which the company is incorporated for the execution of documents by such a company,", and

(b) for paragraph (b) there were substituted–

"(b) on behalf of a company, by any person who, in accordance with the laws of the territory in which the company is incorporated, is acting under the authority (express or implied) of that company;".

## ADAPTATION OF SECTION 36A

**5** Section 36A shall apply as if–

(a) at the end of subsection (2) there were inserted–

", or if it is executed in any manner permitted by the laws of the territory in which the company is incorporated for the execution of documents by such a company.",

(b) for subsection (4) there were substituted–

"(4) A document which–

(a) is signed by a person or persons who, in accordance with the laws of the territory in which the company is incorporated, is or are acting under the authority (express or implied) of that company, and

(b) is expressed (in whatever form of words) to be executed by the company,

has the same effect in relation to that company as it would have in relation to a company incorporated in England and Wales if executed under the common seal of a company so incorporated.", and

(c) in subsection (6) for the words from a "director" to "directors of the company" there were substituted "a person or persons who, in accordance with the laws of the territory in which the company is incorporated, is or are acting under the authority (express or implied) of that company".

## ADAPTATION OF SECTION 36B

**6** (Revoked by the Foreign Companies (Execution of Documents) (Amendment) Regulations 1995 (SI 1995/1729), reg. 1, 5 as from 1 August 1995).

**History**
Reg. 6 formerly read as follows:

"Section 36B shall apply as if–

(a) in subsection (3)(c) for the reference to "two persons", there were substituted a reference to "a person",

(b) in subsection (6)(c), for the reference to "two persons", there were substituted a reference to "a person", and

(c) at the end of subsection (7) there were inserted–

"and any reference in this section to a person authorised to sign or to subscribe a document on behalf of a company is a reference to a person who, in accordance with the laws of the territory in which the company is incorporated, is acting under the authority (express or implied) of that company"."

## EXPLANATORY NOTE

(*This Note is not part of the Regulations*)

These Regulations, made under section 130(6) of the Companies Act 1989, apply the following provisions of the Companies Act 1985 to companies incorporated outside Great Britain, with the adaptations and modifications set out in regulations 3 to 6–

(a) section 36 (company contracts: England and Wales),

(b) section 36A (execution of documents: England and Wales),

(c) section 36B (execution of documents: Scotland), and

(d) section 36C (pre-incorporation contracts, deeds and obligations).

# THE COMPANIES ACT 1985 (AUDIT EXEMPTION) REGULATIONS 1994

(SI 1994/1935)

*Made on 19 July 1994 by the Secretary of State for Trade and Industry under s. 245(3)–(5) and 257 of the Companies Act 1985. Operative from 11 August 1994.*

[**Note**: Amendments by the Companies Act 1985 (Audit Exemption) (Amendment) Regulations 1994 (SI 1994/2879) (operative from 12 November 1994) have been included.]

## CITATION, COMMENCEMENT AND INTERPRETATION

**1(1)** These Regulations may be cited as the Companies Act 1985 (Audit Exemption) Regulations 1994 and shall come into force on 11th August 1994.

**1(2)** In these Regulations **"the 1985 Act"** means the Companies Act 1985.

## AUDIT EXEMPTION FOR CERTAIN CATEGORIES OF SMALL COMPANIES

**2** [Insertion of s. 249A–E of the 1985 Act.]

## EXEMPTION FROM REQUIREMENT TO APPOINT AUDITORS

**3** [Substitution of s. 388A of the 1985 Act.]

## CONSEQUENTIAL AMENDMENTS OF ENACTMENTS

**4** Schedule 1 to these Regulations (which makes consequential amendments of the 1985 Act and the Charities Act 1993) shall have effect.

## CONSEQUENTIAL AMENDMENTS OF COMPANIES (REVISION OF DEFECTIVE ACCOUNTS AND REPORT) REGULATIONS 1990

**5** The Companies (Revision of Defective Accounts and Report) Regulations 1990 shall be amended in accordance with Schedule 2 to these Regulations.

## APPLICATION AND TRANSITIONAL PROVISIONS

**6(1)** Subject to paragraph (2) below, the provisions of these Regulations shall apply to any annual accounts of a company which are approved by the board of directors on or after the day on which these Regulations come into force (**"the commencement date"**).

**History**
See history note after reg. 6(2).

**6(2)** The provisions of these Regulations do not apply to any annual accounts the period for laying and delivering of which expired before 11th August 1994.

**History**
In reg. 6(1) the words "Subject to paragraph (2) below" substituted for the former words "Subject to paragraphs (2) to (4) below" and reg. 6(2) substituted for former reg. 6(2)–(4) by the Companies Act 1985 (Audit Exemption) (Amendment) Regulations 1994 (SI 1994/2879), reg. 1, 2 as from 12 November 1994; reg. 6(2)–(4) formerly read as follows:

"**6(2)** Where–
(a) the accounts for a financial year which has ended have not been approved by the board of directors before the commencement date, or
(b) the financial year to which any accounts relate ends less than one month after the commencement date,
the provisions of these Regulations do not apply unless a copy of those accounts is delivered to the registrar before the end of the period allowed for laying and delivering them.

**(3)** In any case falling within paragraph (2) above, any member or members holding not less in the aggregate than 10 per cent in nominal value of the company's issued share capital or any class of it or, if the company does not have a share capital, not less than 10 per cent in number of the members of the company, may by notice in writing deposited at the registered office of the company before the end of the period of one month beginning with the commencement date require that the company obtains an audit of its accounts for the financial year in question.

**(4)** Where a notice is deposited under paragraph (3) above, the company shall not be exempt from the provisions of Part VII of the 1985 Act relating to the audit of accounts in respect of the financial year to which the notice relates."

## Schedule 1 – Consequential Amendments of Enactments

Regulation 4

### Part I – Amendments of Companies Act 1985

**1(1)** Section 240 of the 1985 Act (requirements in connection with publication of accounts) shall be amended as follows.

**1(2)** [Amendment to s. 240(1).]

**1(3)** [Amendments to s. 240(3).]

**2** [Amendment to s. 245(4)(b).]

**3** [Amendment to s. 262A.]

**4** [Amendment to s. 384(1).]

**5** [Insertion of Sch. 8, para. 25A.]

### Part II – Amendments of Charities Act 1993

**6** In section 45 of the Charities Act 1993 (annual reports), in subsection (5), for the words "the auditors' report" there shall be substituted the words "any auditors' report or report made for the purposes of section 249A(2) of that Act".

**7** In section 47 of that Act (public inspection of annual reports etc.), in subsection (3) for paragraph (c) there shall be substituted the following paragraph–

"(c) in the case of a charity which is a company, a reference to the most recent annual accounts of the company prepared under Part VII of the Companies Act 1985 in relation to which any of the following conditions is satisfied–

(i) they have been audited;

(ii) a report required for the purposes of section 249A(2) of that Act has been made in respect of them; or

(iii) they relate to a year in respect of which the company is exempt from audit by virtue of section 249A(1) of that Act; and".

## Schedule 2 – Consequential Amendments of the Companies (Revision of Defective Accounts and Report) Regulations 1990

Regulation 5

**1** The Companies (Revision of Defective Accounts and Report) Regulations 1990 shall be amended as follows.

**2** [Insertion of reg. 6A and 6B.]

**3** [Insertion of reg. 14A.]

### EXPLANATORY NOTE

*(This Note is not part of the Regulations)*

These Regulations amend the provisions of Part VII of the Companies Act 1985 (accounts and audit) by inserting new sections 249A to 249E into that Part (regulation 2).

The new provisions exempt small companies which satisfy specified conditions from the obligation to have their annual accounts audited (section 249A). Slightly different criteria apply to small companies which are charities (section 249A(5)). Section 249B sets out the cases where the exemptions are not available.

In certain circumstances the audit report is to be replaced by a report to be made by a suitably qualified person (defined as a "reporting accountant") (sections 249C and 249D).

Section 249E sets out the effect of the exemption from the audit requirement on other provisions of Part VII of the 1985 Act.

Regulation 3 substitutes a new section 388A which provides that a company exempt from the audit requirements is also exempt from the obligation to appoint auditors, and gives power to the directors to appoint auditors if that exemption ceases.

Regulation 4 and Schedule 1 make consequential amendments of the 1985 Act and the Charities Act 1993. Regulation 5 and Schedule 2 make consequential amendments of the Companies (Revision of Defective Accounts and Report) Regulations 1990.

Regulation 6 determines the application of the regulations and contains transitional provisions.

# THE COMPANIES (FEES) (AMENDMENT) REGULATIONS 1994

(SI 1994/2217)

*Made on 23 August 1994 by the Secretary of State for Trade and Industry under s. 708 of the Companies Act 1985. Operative from 20 September 1994.*

**1** These Regulations may be cited as the Companies (Fees) (Amendment) Regulations 1994 and shall come into force on 20th September 1994.

**2** In these Regulations, **"the 1991 Regulations"** means the Companies (Fees) Regulations 1991.

**3** [Amendments to Sch. to the 1991 Regulations]

**4(1)** The fees prescribed by regulation 3 above (other than the fee specified in paragraph (2) below) apply to any registration, re-registration or entering on the register in respect of which every document necessary for the registrar of companies to effect such an act is delivered to the registrar on or after 1st October 1994.

**4(2)** The fee prescribed in relation to entry 2 by regulation 3 above in respect of the registration of an annual return applies to any annual return which the company

(a) is required to deliver to the registrar made up to a date not later than a return date occurring on or after 1st October 1994; and

(b) which is delivered on or after 20th September 1994.

**4(3)** For the purposes of paragraph (2) above a "return date" in relation to any company is ascertained in accordance with section 363(1) of the Companies Act 1985.

## EXPLANATORY NOTE

(*This Note is not part of the Regulations*)

These Regulations amend the Companies (Fees) Regulations 1991, as amended by the Companies (Fees) (Amendment) Regulations 1992 which require the payment of fees in respect of functions performed by the registrar of companies under the Companies Act 1985.

*Regulation 3* amends those Regulations by:

(1) reducing the fees applicable in respect of:

- (i) the registration of a company, on its formation under the Companies Act 1985, or in pursuance of Chapter II of Part XXII of that Act, or for its re-registration under that Act;
- (ii) the registration of the particulars required by section 691 of or paragraph 1 of Schedule 21A to the Companies Act 1985 in respect of the establishment of a place of business or a branch of an oversea company; and
- (iii) the entering on the register of the name assumed by a company by virtue of a special resolution under section 28 of the Companies Act 1985;

from £50.00 to £20.00;

(2) reducing the fees applicable in respect of:

(i) the registration of an annual return; and

(ii) the registration of copy accounts of an oversea company, from £32.00 to £18.00;

(3) abolishing the fee applicable in respect of the registration or re-registration of a name under which an oversea company proposes to carry on business in Great Britain; and

(4) removing, in respect of the fee applicable to annual returns, an obsolete reference to "copy annual returns".

*Regulation 4* applies the new fees (with the exception of the fees for the delivery of an annaul return) to any registration, re-registration or entering on the register where all the relevant documents are delivered to the registrar on or after 1st October 1994. In relation to annual returns the new fee is applied to all annual returns which are made up to a date not later than a return date (ascertained for each company in accordance with section 363(1) of the Companies Act 1985) on or after 1st October 1994 and which are delivered on or after 20th September 1994.

# THE INSOLVENT PARTNERSHIPS ORDER 1994

(SI 1994/2421)

*Made on 13 September 1994 by the Secretary of State for Trade and Industry under s. 420(1), (2) of the Insolvency Act 1986 and s. 21(2) of the Company Directors Disqualification Act 1986. Operative from 1 December 1994.*

## ARRANGEMENT OF ARTICLES

### PART I – GENERAL



### PART II – VOLUNTARY ARRANGEMENTS



### PART III – ADMINISTRATION ORDERS



### PART IV – CREDITORS' ETC. WINDING-UP PETITIONS



### PART V – MEMBERS' PETITIONS

## PART VI – PROVISIONS APPLYING IN INSOLVENCY PROCEEDINGS IN RELATION TO INSOLVENT PARTNERSHIPS



## PART VII – DISQUALIFICATION



## PART VIII – MISCELLANEOUS



## SCHEDULES




bbcl randr4 Mp 4227—bcl98 220b

# PART I – GENERAL

## CITATION, COMMENCEMENT AND EXTENT

**1(1)** This Order may be cited as the Insolvent Partnerships Order 1994 and shall come into force on 1st December 1994.

**1(2)** This Order–

(a) in the case of insolvency proceedings in relation to companies and partnerships, relates to companies and partnerships which the courts in England and Wales have jurisdiction to wind up; and

(b) in the case of insolvency proceedings in relation to individuals, extends to England and Wales only.

**1(3)** In paragraph (2) the term **"insolvency proceedings"** has the meaning ascribed to it by article 2 below.

## INTERPRETATION: DEFINITIONS

**2(1)** In this Order, except in so far as the context otherwise requires–

**"the Act"** means the Insolvency Act 1986;

**"agricultural charge"** has the same meaning as in the Agricultural Credits Act 1928;

**"agricultural receiver"** means a receiver appointed under an agricultural charge;

**"corporate member"** means an insolvent member which is a company;

**"the court"**, in relation to an insolvent partnership, means the court which has jurisdiction to wind up the partnership;

**"individual member"** means an insolvent member who is an individual;

**"insolvency order"** means–

(a) in the case of an insolvent partnership or a corporate member, a winding-up order; and

(b) in the case of an individual member, a bankruptcy order;

**"insolvency petition"** means, in the case of a petition presented to the court–

(a) against a corporate member, a petition for its winding up by the court;

(b) against an individual member, a petition for a bankruptcy order to be made against that individual,

where the petition is presented in conjunction with a petition for the winding up of the partnership by the court as an unregistered company under the Act;

**"insolvency proceedings"** means any proceedings under the Act, this Order or the Insolvency Rules 1986;

**"insolvent member"** means a member of an insolvent partnership, against whom an insolvency petition is being or has been presented;

**"joint bankruptcy petition"** means a petition by virtue of article 11 of this Order;

**"joint debt"** means a debt of an insolvent partnership in respect of which an order is made by virtue of Part IV or V of this Order;

**"joint estate"** means the partnership property of an insolvent partnership in respect of which an order is made by virtue of Part IV or V of this Order;

**"joint expenses"** means expenses incurred in the winding up of an insolvent partnership or in the winding up of the business of an insolvent partnership and the administration of its property;

**"limited partner"** has the same meaning as in the Limited Partnerships Act 1907;

**"member"** means a member of a partnership and any person who is liable as a partner within the meaning of section 14 of the Partnership Act 1890;

**"officer"**, in relation to an insolvent partnership, means–

(a) a member; or

(b) a person who has management or control of the partnership business;

**"partnership property"** has the same meaning as in the Partnership Act 1890;

**"postponed debt"** means a debt the payment of which is postponed by or under any provision of the Act or of any other enactment;

**"responsible insolvency practitioner"** means–

(a) in winding up, the liquidator of an insolvent partnership or corporate member; and
(b) in bankruptcy, the trustee of the estate of an individual member,

and in either case includes the official receiver when so acting;

**"separate debt"** means a debt for which a member of a partnership is liable, other than a joint debt;

**"separate estate"** means the property of an insolvent member against whom an insolvency order has been made;

**"separate expenses"** means expenses incurred in the winding up of a corporate member, or in the bankruptcy of an individual member; and

**"trustee of the partnership"** means a person authorised by order made by virtue of article 11 of this Order to wind up the business of an insolvent partnership and to administer its property.

**2(2)** The definitions in paragraph (1), other than the first definition, shall be added to those in section 436 of the Act.

**2(3)** References in provisions of the Act applied by this Order to any provision of the Act so applied shall, unless the context otherwise requires, be construed as references to the provision as so applied.

**2(4)** Where, in any Schedule to this Order, all or any of the provisions of two or more sections of the Act are expressed to be modified by a single paragraph of the Schedule, the modification includes the combination of the provisions of those sections into the one or more sections set out in that paragraph.

### INTERPRETATION: EXPRESSIONS APPROPRIATE TO COMPANIES

**3(1)** This article applies for the interpretation in relation to insolvent partnerships of expressions appropriate to companies in provisions of the Act and of the Company Directors Disqualification Act 1986 applied by this Order, unless the contrary intention appears.

**3(2)** References to companies shall be construed as references to insolvent partnerships and all references to the registrar of companies shall be omitted.

**3(3)** References to shares of a company shall be construed–

(a) in relation to an insolvent partnership with capital, as references to rights to share in that capital; and

(b) in relation to an insolvent partnership without capital, as references to interests–
  (i) conferring any right to share in the profits or liability to contribute to the losses of the partnership, or
  (ii) giving rise to an obligation to contribute to the debts or expenses of the partnership in the event of a winding up.

**3(4)** Other expressions appropriate to companies shall be construed, in relation to an insolvent partnership, as references to the corresponding persons, officers, documents or organs (as the case may be) appropriate to a partnership.

## PART II – VOLUNTARY ARRANGEMENTS

### VOLUNTARY ARRANGEMENT OF INSOLVENT PARTNERSHIP

**4(1)** The provisions of Part I of the Act shall apply in relation to an insolvent partnership, those provisions being modified in such manner that, after modification, they are as set out in Schedule 1 to this Order.

**4(2)** For the purposes of the provisions of the Act applied by paragraph (1), the provisions of the Act specified in paragraph (3) below, insofar as they relate to company voluntary arrangements, shall also apply in relation to insolvent partnerships.

**4(3)** The provisions referred to in paragraph (2) are–

(a) section 233 in Part VI,

(b) Part VII, with the exception of section 250,

(c) Part XII,

(d) Part XIII,

(e) sections 411, 413, 414 and 419 in Part XV, and

(f) Parts XVI to XIX.

### VOLUNTARY ARRANGEMENTS OF MEMBERS OF INSOLVENT PARTNERSHIP

**5(1)** Where insolvency orders are made against an insolvent partnership and an insolvent member of that partnership in his capacity as such, Part I of the Act shall apply to corporate members and Part VIII to individual members of that partnership, with the modification that any reference to the creditors of the company or of the debtor, as the case may be, includes a reference to the creditors of the partnership.

**5(2)** Paragraph (1) is not to be construed as preventing the application of Part I or (as the case may be) Part VIII of the Act to any person who is a member of an insolvent partnership (whether or not a winding-up order has been made against that partnership) and against whom an insolvency order has not been made under this Order or under the Act.

## PART III – ADMINISTRATION ORDERS

### ADMINISTRATION ORDER IN RELATION TO INSOLVENT PARTNERSHIP

**6(1)** The provisions of Part II of the Act shall apply in relation to an insolvent partnership, certain of those provisions being modified in such manner that, after modification, they are as set out in Schedule 2 to this Order.

**6(2)** For the purposes of the provisions of the Act applied by paragraph (1), the provisions of the Act specified in paragraph (3) below, insofar as they relate to administration orders, shall also apply in relation to insolvent partnerships.

**6(3)** The provisions referred to in paragraph (2) are–

(a) section 212 in Part IV,

(b) Part VI,

(c) Part VII, with the exception of section 250,

(d) Part XIII,

(e) sections 411, 413, 414 and 419 in Part XV, and

(f) Parts XVI to XIX.

## PART IV – CREDITORS' ETC. WINDING-UP PETITIONS

### WINDING UP OF INSOLVENT PARTNERSHIP AS UNREGISTERED COMPANY ON PETITION OF CREDITOR ETC. WHERE NO CONCURRENT PETITION PRESENTED AGAINST MEMBER

**7(1)** Subject to paragraph (2) below, the provisions of Part V of the Act shall apply in relation to the winding up of an insolvent partnership as an unregistered company on the petition of a creditor, of a responsible insolvency practitioner, of the Secretary of State or of any other person other than a member, where no insolvency petition is presented by the petitioner against a member or former member of that partnership in his capacity as such.

**History**
In art. 7(1) the words ", of the Secretary of State or of any other person other than a member," substituted for the former words "or of the Secretary of State," by the Insolvent Partnerships (Amendment) Order 1996 (SI 1996/1308), art. 1, 2 as from 14 June 1996.

**7(2)** Certain of the provisions referred to in paragraph (1) are modified in their application in relation to insolvent partnerships which are being wound up by virtue of that paragraph in such manner that, after modification, they are as set out in Part I of Schedule 3 to this Order.

**7(3)** The provisions of the Act specified in Part II of Schedule 3 to this Order shall apply as set out in that Part for the purposes of section 221(5) of the Act, as modified by Part I of that Schedule.

## WINDING UP OF INSOLVENT PARTNERSHIP AS UNREGISTERED COMPANY ON CREDITOR'S PETITION WHERE CONCURRENT PETITIONS PRESENTED AGAINST ONE OR MORE MEMBERS

**8(1)** Subject to paragraph (2) below, the provisions of Part V of the Act (other than sections 223 and 224), shall apply in relation to the winding up of an insolvent partnership as an unregistered company on a creditor's petition where insolvency petitions are presented by the petitioner against the partnership and against one or more members or former members of the partnership in their capacity as such.

**8(2)** Certain of the provisions referred to in paragraph (1) are modified in their application in relation to insolvent partnerships which are being wound up by virtue of that paragraph in such manner that, after modification, they are as set out in Part I of Schedule 4 to this Order.

**8(3)** The provisions of the Act specified in Part II of Schedule 4 to this Order shall apply as set out in that Part for the purposes of section 221(5) of the Act, as modified by Part I of that Schedule.

**8(4)** The provisions of the Act specified in paragraph (5) below, insofar as they relate to winding up of companies by the court in England and Wales on a creditor's petition, shall apply in relation to the winding up of a corporate member or former corporate member (in its capacity as such) of an insolvent partnership which is being wound up by virtue of paragraph (1).

**8(5)** The provisions referred to in paragraph (4) are–

(a) Part IV,

(b) Part VI,

(c) Part VII, and

(d) Parts XII to XIX.

**8(6)** The provisions of the Act specified in paragraph (7) below, insofar as they relate to the bankruptcy of individuals in England and Wales on a petition presented by a creditor, shall apply in relation to the bankruptcy of an individual member or former individual member (in his capacity as such) of an insolvent partnership which is being wound up by virtue of paragraph (1).

**8(7)** The provisions referred to in paragraph (6) are–

(a) Part IX (other than sections 269, 270, 287 and 297), and

(b) Parts X to XIX.

**8(8)** Certain of the provisions referred to in paragraphs (4) and (6) are modified in their application in relation to the corporate or individual members or former corporate or individual members of insolvent partnerships in such manner that, after modification, they are as set out in Part II of Schedule 4 to this Order.

**8(9)** The provisions of the Act applied by this Article shall further be modified so that references to a corporate or individual member include any former such member against whom an insolvency petition is being or has been presented by virtue of this Article.

# PART V – MEMBERS' PETITIONS

## WINDING UP OF INSOLVENT PARTNERSHIP AS UNREGISTERED COMPANY ON MEMBER'S PETITION WHERE NO CONCURRENT PETITION PRESENTED AGAINST MEMBER

**9** The following provisions of the Act shall apply in relation to the winding up of an insolvent partnership as an unregistered company on the petition of a member where no insolvency petition is presented by the petitioner against a member of that partnership in his capacity as such–

(a) sections 117 and 221, modified in such manner that, after modification, they are as set out in Schedule 5 to this Order; and

(b) the other provisions of Part V of the Act, certain of those provisions being modified in such manner that, after modification, they are as set out in Part I of Schedule 3 to this Order.

## WINDING UP OF INSOLVENT PARTNERSHIP AS UNREGISTERED COMPANY ON MEMBER'S PETITION WHERE CONCURRENT PETITIONS PRESENTED AGAINST ALL MEMBERS

**10(1)** The following provisions of the Act shall apply in relation to the winding up of an insolvent partnership as an unregistered company on a member's petition where insolvency petitions are presented by the petitioner against the partnership and against all its members in their capacity as such–

(a) sections 117, 124, 125, 221, 264, 265, 271 and 272 of the Act, modified in such manner that, after modification, they are as set out in Schedule 6 to this Order; and

(b) sections 220, 225 and 227 to 229 in Part V of the Act, section 220 being modified in such manner that, after modification, it is as set out in Part I of Schedule 4 to this Order.

**10(2)** The provisions of the Act specified in paragraph (3) below, insofar as they relate to winding up of companies by the court in England and Wales on a member's petition, shall apply in relation to the winding up of a corporate member (in its capacity as such) of an insolvent partnership which is wound up by virtue of paragraph (1).

**10(3)** The provisions referred to in paragraph (2) are–

(a) Part IV,

(b) Part VI,

(c) Part VII, and

(d) Parts XII to XIX.

**10(4)** The provisions of the Act specified in paragraph (5) below, insofar as they relate to the bankruptcy of individuals in England and Wales where a bankruptcy petition is presented by a debtor, shall apply in relation to the bankruptcy of an individual member (in his capacity as such) of an insolvent partnership which is being wound up by virtue of paragraph (1).

**10(5)** The provisions referred to in paragraph (4) are–

(a) Part IX (other than sections 273, 274, 287 and 297), and

(b) Parts X to XIX.

**10(6)** Certain of the provisions referred to in paragraphs (2) and (4) are modified in their application in relation to the corporate or individual members of insolvent partnerships in such manner that, after modification, they are as set out in Part II of Schedule 4 to this Order, save that the provisions on summary administration of a debtor's estate shall apply in relation to the individual members of insolvent partnerships in such manner that, after modification, those provisions are as set out in Schedule 7 to this Order.

## INSOLVENCY PROCEEDINGS NOT INVOLVING WINDING UP OF INSOLVENT PARTNERSHIP AS UNREGISTERED COMPANY WHERE INDIVIDUAL MEMBERS PRESENT JOINT BANKRUPTCY PETITION

**11(1)** The provisions of the Act specified in paragraph (2) below shall apply in relation to the bankruptcy of the individual members of an insolvent partnership where those members jointly present a petition to the court for orders to be made for the bankruptcy of each of them in his capacity as a member of the partnership, and the winding up of the partnership business and administration of its property, without the partnership being wound up as an unregistered company under Part V of the Act.

**11(2)** The provisions referred to in paragraph (1) are–

(a) Part IX (other than sections 273, 274 and 287), and

(b) Parts X to XIX,

insofar as they relate to the insolvency of individuals in England and Wales where a bankruptcy petition is presented by a debtor.

**11(3)** Certain of the provisions referred to in paragraph (1) are modified in their application in relation to the individual members of insolvent partnerships in such manner that, after modification, they are as set out in Schedule 7 to this Order.

# PART VI – PROVISIONS APPLYING IN INSOLVENCY PROCEEDINGS IN RELATION TO INSOLVENT PARTNERSHIPS

## WINDING UP OF UNREGISTERED COMPANY WHICH IS A MEMBER OF INSOLVENT PARTNERSHIP BEING WOUND UP BY VIRTUE OF THIS ORDER

**12** Where an insolvent partnership or other body which may be wound up under Part V of the Act as an unregistered company is itself a member of an insolvent partnership being so wound up, articles 8 and 10 above shall apply in relation to the latter insolvent partnership as though the former body were a corporate member of that partnership.

## DEPOSIT ON PETITIONS

**13(1)** Where an order under section 414(4) or 415(3) of the Act (security for fees) provides for any sum to be deposited on presentation of a winding-up or bankruptcy petition, that sum shall, in the case of petitions presented by virtue of articles 8 and 10 above, only be required to be deposited in respect of the petition for winding up the partnership, but shall be treated as a deposit in respect of all those petitions.

**13(2)** Production of evidence as to the sum deposited on presentation of the petition for winding up the partnership shall suffice for the filing in court of an insolvency petition against an insolvent member.

## SUPPLEMENTAL POWERS OF COURT

**14(1)** At the end of section 168 of the Act there shall be inserted the following subsections:–

"**(5A)** Where at any time after a winding-up petition has been presented to the court against any person (including an insolvent partnership or other body which may be wound up under Part V of the Act as an unregistered company), whether by virtue of the provisions of the Insolvent Partnerships Order 1994 or not, the attention of the court is drawn to the fact that the person in question is a member of an insolvent partnership, the court may make an order as to the future conduct of the insolvency proceedings and any such order may apply any provisions of that Order with any necessary modifications.

**(5B)** Any order or directions under subsection (5A) may be made or given on the application of the official receiver, any responsible insolvency practitioner, the trustee of the partnership or any other interested person and may include provisions as to the administration of the joint estate of the partnership, and in particular how it and the separate estate of any member are to be administered.

**(5C)** Where the court makes an order under section 72(1)(a) of the Financial Services Act 1986 or section 92(1)(a) of the Banking Act 1987 for the winding up of an insolvent partnership, the court may make an order as to the future conduct of the winding-up proceedings, and any such order may apply any provisions of the Insolvent Partnerships Order 1994 with any necessary modifications.".

**14(2)** At the end of section 303 of the Act there shall be inserted the following subsections:–

"**(2A)** Where at any time after a bankruptcy petition has been presented to the court against any person, whether under the provisions of the Insolvent Partnerships Order 1994 or not, the attention of the court is drawn to the fact that the person in question is a member of an insolvent partnership, the court may make an order as to the future conduct of the insolvency proceedings and any such order may apply any provisions of that Order with any necessary modifications.

**(2B)** Where a bankruptcy petition has been presented against more than one individual in the circumstances mentioned in subsection (2A) above, the court may give such directions for consolidating the proceedings, or any of them, as it thinks just.

**(2C)** Any order or directions under subsection (2A) or (2B) may be made or given on the application of the official receiver, any responsible insolvency practitioner, the trustee of the partnership or any other interested person and may include provisions as to the administration of the joint estate of the partnership, and in particular how it and the separate estate of any member are to be administered.".

### MEANING OF "ACT AS INSOLVENCY PRACTITIONER"

**15(1)** After section 388(2) of the Act there shall be inserted the following–

"**(2A)** A person acts as an insolvency practitioner in relation to an insolvent partnership by acting–

(a) as its liquidator, provisional liquidator or administrator, or

(b) as trustee of the partnership under article 11 of the Insolvent Partnerships Order 1994, or

(c) as supervisor of a voluntary arrangement approved in relation to it under Part I of this Act.".

**15(2)** In section 388(3) the words "to a partnership and" shall be omitted.

## PART VII – DISQUALIFICATION

### APPLICATION OF COMPANY DIRECTORS DISQUALIFICATION ACT 1986

**16** Where an insolvent partnership is wound up as an unregistered company under Part V of the Act, the provisions of sections 6 to 10, 15, 19(c) and 20 of, and Schedule 1 to, the Company Directors Disqualification Act 1986 shall apply, certain of those provisions being modified in such manner that, after modification, they are as set out in Schedule 8 to this Order.

## PART VIII – MISCELLANEOUS

### FORMS

**17(1)** The forms contained in Schedule 9 to this Order shall be used in and in connection with proceedings by virtue of this Order, whether in the High Court or a county court.

**17(2)** The forms shall be used with such variations, if any, as the circumstances may require.

### APPLICATION OF SUBORDINATE LEGISLATION

**18(1)** The subordinate legislation specified in Schedule 10 to this Order shall apply as from time to time in force and with such modifications as the context requires for the purpose of giving effect to the provisions of the Act and of the Company Directors Disqualification Act 1986 which are applied by this Order.

**18(2)** In the case of any conflict between any provision of the subordinate legislation applied by paragraph (1) and any provision of this Order, the latter provision shall prevail.



CCH.New Law
bbcl randr4 Mp 4234—bcl98 220b

## SUPPLEMENTAL AND TRANSITIONAL PROVISIONS

**19(1)** This Order does not apply in relation to any case in which a winding-up or a bankruptcy order was made under the Insolvent Partnerships Order 1986 in relation to a partnership or an insolvent member of a partnership, and where this Order does not apply the law in force immediately before this Order came into force continues to have effect.

**19(2)** Where winding-up or bankruptcy proceedings commenced under the provisions of the Insolvent Partnerships Order 1986 were pending in relation to a partnership or an insolvent member of a partnership immediately before this Order came into force, either–

(a) those proceedings shall be continued, after the coming into force of this Order, in accordance with the provisions of this Order, or

(b) if the court so directs, they shall be continued under the provisions of the 1986 Order, in which case the law in force immediately before this Order came into force continues to have effect.

**19(3)** For the purpose of paragraph (2) above, winding-up or bankruptcy proceedings are pending if a statutory or written demand has been served or a winding-up or bankruptcy petition has been presented.

**19(4)** Nothing in this Order is to be taken as preventing a petition being presented against an insolvent partnership under–

(a) section 53 or 54 of the Insurance Companies Act 1982(a) (winding up: insurance companies),

(b) section 72(2)(d) of the Financial Services Act 1986 (winding up: investment business),

(c) section 92 of the Banking Act 1987 (winding up: authorised institutions), or

(d) any other enactment.

**19(5)** Nothing in this Order is to be taken as preventing any creditor or creditors owed one or more debts by an insolvent partnership from presenting a petition under the Act against one or more members of the partnership liable for that debt or those debts (as the case may be) without including the others and without presenting a petition for the winding up of the partnership as an unregistered company.

**19(6)** Bankruptcy proceedings may be consolidated by virtue of article 14(2) above irrespective of whether they were commenced under the Bankruptcy Act 1914 or the Insolvency Act 1986 or by virtue of the Insolvent Partnerships Order 1986 or this Order, and the court shall, in the case of proceedings commenced under or by virtue of different enactments, make provision for the manner in which the consolidated proceedings are to be conducted.

## REVOCATION

**20** The Insolvent Partnerships Order 1986 is hereby revoked.

# Schedule 1 – Modified Provisions of Part I of the Act (Company Voluntary Arrangements) as applied by Article 4

Article 4

For Part I of the Act there shall be substituted:–

## "PART I – PARTNERSHIP VOLUNTARY ARRANGEMENTS

## THE PROPOSAL

*Those who may propose an arrangement*

**1(1)** The members of an insolvent partnership (other than one for which an administration order is in force, or which is being wound up as an unregistered company, or in respect of which an order has been made by virtue of article 11 of the Insolvent

Partnerships Order 1994) may make a proposal under this Part to the partnership's creditors for a composition in satisfaction of the debts of the partnership or a scheme of arrangement of its affairs (from here on referred to, in either case, as a "voluntary arrangement").

**1(2)** A proposal under this Part is one which provides for some person ("the nominee") to act in relation to the voluntary arrangement either as trustee or otherwise for the purpose of supervising its implementation; and the nominee must be a person who is qualified to act as an insolvency practitioner in relation to the insolvent partnership.

**1(3)** Such a proposal may also be made–

(a) where an administration order is in force in relation to the partnership, by the administrator,

(b) where the partnership is being wound up as an unregistered company, by the liquidator, and

(c) where an order has been made by virtue of article 11 of the Insolvent Partnerships Order 1994, by the trustee of the partnership.

*Procedure where nominee is not the liquidator, administrator or trustee*

**2(1)** This section applies where the nominee under section 1 is not the liquidator, administrator or trustee of the insolvent partnership.

**2(2)** The nominee shall, within 28 days (or such longer period as the court may allow) after he is given notice of the proposal for a voluntary arrangement, submit a report to the court stating–

(a) whether, in his opinion, meetings of the members of the partnership and of the partnership's creditors should be summoned to consider the proposal, and

(b) if in his opinion such meetings should be summoned, the date on which, and time and place at which, he proposes the meetings should be held.

**2(3)** The nominee shall also state in his report whether there are in existence any insolvency proceedings in respect of the insolvent partnership or any of its members.

**2(4)** For the purposes of enabling the nominee to prepare his report, the person intending to make the proposal shall submit to the nominee–

(a) a document setting out the terms of the proposed voluntary arrangement, and

(b) a statement of the partnership's affairs containing–

(i) such particulars of the partnership's creditors and of the partnership's debts and other liabilities and of the partnership property as may be prescribed, and

(ii) such other information as may be prescribed.

**2(5)** The court may, on an application made by the person intending to make the proposal, in a case where the nominee has failed to submit the report required by this section, direct that the nominee be replaced as such by another person qualified to act as an insolvency practitioner in relation to the insolvent partnership.

*Summoning of meetings*

**3(1)** Where the nominee under section 1 is not the liquidator, administrator or trustee of the insolvent partnership, and it has been reported to the court that such meetings as are mentioned in section 2(2) should be summoned, the person making the report shall (unless the court otherwise directs) summon those meetings for the time, date and place proposed in the report.

**3(2)** Where the nominee is the liquidator, administrator or trustee of the insolvent partnership, he shall summon meetings of the members of the partnership and of the partnership's creditors to consider the proposal for such a time, date and place as he thinks fit.

**3(3)** The persons to be summoned to a creditors' meeting under this section are every creditor of the partnership of whose claim and address the person summoning the meeting is aware.

## CONSIDERATION AND IMPLEMENTATION OF PROPOSAL

*Decisions of meetings*

**4(1)** The meetings summoned under section 3 shall decide whether to approve the proposed voluntary arrangement (with or without modifications).

**4(2)** The modifications may include one conferring the functions proposed to be conferred on the nominee on another person qualified to act as an insolvency practitioner in relation to the insolvent partnership.

But they shall not include any modification by virtue of which the proposal ceases to be a proposal such as is mentioned in section 1.

**4(3)** A meeting so summoned shall not approve any proposal or modification which affects the right of a secured creditor of the partnership to enforce his security, except with the concurrence of the creditor concerned.

**4(4)** Subject as follows, a meeting so summoned shall not approve any proposal or modification under which–

(a) any preferential debt of the partnership is to be paid otherwise than in priority to such of its debts as are not preferential debts, or

(b) a preferential creditor of the partnership is to be paid an amount in respect of a preferential debt that bears to that debt a smaller proportion than is borne to another preferential debt by the amount that is to be paid in respect of that other debt.

However, the meeting may approve such a proposal or modification with the concurrence of the preferential creditor concerned.

**4(5)** Subject as above, each of the meetings shall be conducted in accordance with the rules.

**4(6)** After the conclusion of either meeting in accordance with the rules, the chairman of the meeting shall report the result of the meeting to the court, and, immediately after reporting to the court, shall give notice of the result of the meeting to all those who were sent notice of the meeting in accordance with the rules.

**4(7)** References in this section to preferential debts and preferential creditors are to be read in accordance with section 386 in Part XII of this Act.

*Effect of approval*

**5(1)** This section has effect where each of the meetings summoned under section 3 approves the proposed voluntary arrangement either with the same modifications or without modifications.

**5(2)** The approved voluntary arrangement–

(a) takes effect as if made by the members of the partnership at the creditors' meeting, and

(b) binds every person who in accordance with the rules had notice of, and was entitled to vote at, that meeting (whether or not he was present or represented at the meeting) as if he were a party to the voluntary arrangement.

**5(3)** Subject as follows, if the partnership is being wound up as an unregistered company, or an administration order or an order by virtue of article 11 of the Insolvent Partnerships Order 1994 is in force, the court may do one or both of the following, namely–

(a) by order–

   (i) stay all proceedings in the winding up or in the proceedings under the order made by virtue of the said article 11 (as the case may be), including any related insolvency proceedings of a member of the partnership in his capacity as such, or

   (ii) discharge the administration order;

(b) give such directions as it thinks appropriate for facilitating the implementation of the approved voluntary arrangement with respect to–

   (i) the conduct of the winding up, of the proceedings by virtue of the said article 11 or of the administration (as the case may be), and

(ii) the conduct of any related insolvency proceedings as referred to in paragraph (a)(i) above.

**5(4)** The court shall not make an order under subsection (3)(a)–

(a) at any time before the end of the period of 28 days beginning with the first day on which each of the reports required by section 4(6) has been made to the court, or

(b) at any time when an application under the next section or an appeal in respect of such an application is pending, or at any time in the period within which such an appeal may be brought.

*Challenge of decisions*

**6(1)** Subject to this section, an application to the court may be made, by any of the persons specified below, on one or both of the following grounds, namely–

(a) that a voluntary arrangement approved at the meetings summoned under section 3 unfairly prejudices the interests of a creditor, member or contributory of the partnership;

(b) that there has been some material irregularity at or in relation to either of the meetings.

**6(2)** The persons who may apply under this section are–

(a) a person entitled, in accordance with the rules, to vote at either of the meetings;

(b) the nominee or any person who has replaced him under section 2(5) or 4(2); and

(c) if the partnership is being wound up as an unregistered company or an administration order or order by virtue of article 11 of the Insolvent Partnerships Order 1994 is in force, the liquidator, administrator or trustee of the partnership.

**6(3)** An application under this section shall not be made after the end of the period of 28 days beginning with the first day on which each of the reports required by section 4(6) has been made to the court.

**6(4)** Where on such an application the court is satisfied as to either of the grounds mentioned in subsection (1), it may do one or both of the following, namely–

(a) revoke or suspend the approvals given by the meetings or, in a case falling within subsection (1)(b), any approval given by the meeting in question;

(b) give a direction to any person for the summoning of further meetings to consider any revised proposal the person who made the original proposal may make or, in a case falling within subsection (1)(b), a further meeting of the members of the partnership or (as the case may be) of the partnership's creditors to reconsider the original proposal.

**6(5)** Where at any time after giving a direction under subsection (4)(b) for the summoning of meetings to consider a revised proposal the court is satisfied that the person who made the original proposal does not intend to submit a revised proposal, the court shall revoke the direction and revoke or suspend any approval given at the previous meetings.

**6(6)** In a case where the court, on an application under this section with respect to any meeting–

(a) gives a direction under subsection (4)(b), or

(b) revokes or suspends an approval under subsection (4)(a) or (5),

the court may give such supplemental directions as it thinks fit, and, in particular, directions with respect to things done since the meeting under any voluntary arrangement approved by the meeting.

**6(7)** Except in pursuance of the preceding provisions of this section, an approval given at a meeting summoned under section 3 is not invalidated by any irregularity at or in relation to the meeting.

*Implementation of proposal*

**7(1)** This section applies where a voluntary arrangement approved by the meetings summoned under section 3 has taken effect.

**7(2)** The person who is for the time being carrying out in relation to the voluntary arrangement the functions conferred–

(a) by virtue of the approval on the nominee, or

(b) by virtue of section 2(5) or 4(2) on a person other than the nominee,

shall be known as the supervisor of the voluntary arrangement.

**7(3)** if any of the partnership's creditors or any other person is dissatisfied by any act, omission or decision of the supervisor, he may apply to the court; and on the application the court may–

(a) confirm, reverse or modify any act or decision of the supervisor,

(b) give him directions, or

(c) make such other order as it thinks fit.

**7(4)** The supervisor–

(a) may apply to the court for directions in relation to any particular matter arising under the voluntary arrangement, and

(b) is included among the persons who may apply to the court for the winding up of the partnership as an unregistered company or for an administration order to be made in relation to it.

**7(5)** The court may, whenever–

(a) it is expedient to appoint a person to carry out the functions of the supervisor, and

(b) it is inexpedient, difficult or impracticable for an appointment to be made without the assistance of the court,

make an order appointing a person who is qualified to act as an insolvency practitioner in relation to the partnership, either in substitution for the existing supervisor or to fill a vacancy.

**7(6)** The power conferred by subsection (5) is exercisable so as to increase the number of persons exercising the functions of supervisor or, where there is more than one person exercising those functions, so as to replace one or more of those persons."

# Schedule 2 – Modified Provisions of Part II of the Act (Administration Orders) as applied by Article 6

**1** Sections 8 to 15 of, and Schedule 1 to, the Act are set out as modified in this Schedule.

## SECTION 8: POWER OF COURT TO MAKE ORDER

**2** Section 8 is modified so as to read as follows:–

"**8(1)** Subject to this section, if the court–

(a) is satisfied that a partnership is unable to pay its debts (within the meaning given to that expression by section 222, 223 or 224 of this Act), and

(b) considers that the making of an order under this section would be likely to achieve one or more of the purposes mentioned below,

the court may make an administration order in relation to the partnership.

**8(2)** An administration order is an order directing that, during the period for which the order is in force, the affairs and business of the partnership and the partnership property shall be managed by a person ("the administrator") appointed for the purpose by the court.

**8(3)** The purposes for whose achievement an administration order may be made are–

(a) the survival of the whole or any part of the undertaking of the partnership as a going concern;

(b) the approval of a voluntary arrangement under Part I; and

(c) a more advantageous realisation of the partnership property than would be effected on a winding up;

and the order shall specify the purpose or purposes for which it is made.

**8(4)** An administration order shall not be made in relation to a partnership after an order has been made for it to be wound up by the court as an unregistered company, nor after an order has been made in relation to it by virtue of article 11 of the Insolvent Partnerships Order 1994, nor where it is–

(a) an insurance company within the meaning of the Insurance Companies Act 1982, or

(b) an authorised institution or former authorised institution within the meaning of the Banking Act 1987.".

## SECTION 9: APPLICATION FOR ORDER

3 Section 9 is modified so as to read as follows:–

"**9(1)** An application to the court for an administration order shall be by petition in Form 1 in Schedule 9 to the Insolvent Partnerships Order 1994 presented either by the members of the insolvent partnership in their capacity as such, or by a creditor or creditors (including any contingent or prospective creditor or creditors), or by all or any of those parties, together or separately.

**9(2)** Where a petition is presented to the court–

(a) notice of the petition shall be given forthwith to any person who has appointed, or is or may be entitled to appoint, an agricultural receiver of the partnership, and to such other persons as may be prescribed, and

(b) the petition shall not be withdrawn except with the leave of the court.

**9(3)** Where the court is satisfied that there is an agricultural receiver of the partnership, the court shall dismiss the petition unless it is also satisfied either–

(a) that the person by whom or on whose behalf the receiver was appointed has consented to the making of the order, or

(b) that, if an administration order were made, any security by virtue of which the receiver was appointed would–

(i) be liable to be released or discharged under sections 238 to 240 in Part VI (transactions at an undervalue and preferences),

(ii) be avoided under section 245 in that Part (avoidance of floating charges), or

(iii) be challengeable under section 242 (gratuitous alienations) or 243 (unfair preferences) in that Part, or under any rule of law in Scotland.

**9(4)** Subject to subsection (3), on hearing a petition the court may dismiss it, or adjourn the hearing conditionally or unconditionally, or make an interim order or any other order that it thinks fit.

**9(5)** Without prejudice to the generality of subsection (4), an interim order under that subsection may restrict the exercise of any powers of the officers of the partnership (whether by reference to the consent of the court or of a person qualified to act as an insolvency practitioner in relation to the partnership, or otherwise).".

## SECTION 10: EFFECT OF APPLICATION

4 Section 10 is modified so as to read as follows:–

"**10(1)** During the period beginning with the presentation of a petition for an administration order and ending with the making of such an order or the dismissal of the petition–

(a) no order may be made for the winding up of the insolvent partnership, nor may any order be made by virtue of article 11 of the Insolvent Partnerships Order 1994 or under section 35 of the Partnership Act 1890 in respect of the partnership;

(b) no steps may be taken to enforce any security over the partnership property, or to repossess goods in the possession, under any hire-purchase agreement, of one or more of the officers of the partnership in their capacity as such, except with the leave of the court and subject to such terms as the court may impose; and

(c) no other proceedings and no execution or other legal process may be commenced or continued, and no distress may be levied, against the partnership or the partnership property except with the leave of the court and subject to such terms as aforesaid.

**10(2)** Nothing in subsection (1) requires the leave of the court–

(a) for the presentation of a petition for the winding up of the partnership,

(b) for the presentation of a petition by virtue of article 11 of the Insolvent Partnerships Order 1994 in respect of the partnership,

(c) for the appointment of an agricultural receiver of the partnership, or

(d) for the carrying out by such a receiver (whenever appointed) of any of his functions.

**10(3)** Where–

(a) a petition for an administration order is presented at a time when there is an agricultural receiver of the partnership, and

(b) the person by or on whose behalf the receiver was appointed has not consented to the making of the order,

the period mentioned in subsection (1) is deemed not to begin unless and until that person so consents.

**10(4)** References in this section and the next to hire-purchase agreements include conditional sale agreements, chattel leasing agreements and retention of title agreements.

**10(5)** In the application of this section and the next to Scotland, references to execution being commenced or continued include references to diligence being carried out or continued, and references to distress being levied shall be omitted.".

## SECTION 11: EFFECT OF ORDER

5 Section 11 is modified so as to read as follows:–

"**11(1)** On the making of an administration order, any petition for the winding up of the insolvent partnership and any petition for an order to be made by virtue of article 11 of the Insolvent Partnerships Order 1994 shall be dismissed.

**11(2)** Where an administration order has been made, any agricultural receiver of the partnership and any receiver of the partnership property shall vacate office on being required to do so by the administrator.

**11(3)** During the period for which an administration order is in force–

(a) no order may be made for the winding up of the partnership;

(b) no order may be made by virtue of article 11 of the Insolvent Partnerships Order 1994 in respect of the partnership;

(c) no order may be made under section 35 of the Partnership Act 1890 in respect of the partnership;

(d) no agricultural receiver of the partnership may be appointed except with the consent of the administrator or the leave of the court and subject (where the court gives leave) to such terms as the court may impose;

(e) no other steps may be taken to enforce any security over the partnership property, or to repossess goods in the possession, under any hire-purchase agreement, of one or more of the officers of the partnership in their capacity as such, except with the consent of the administrator or the leave of the court and subject (where the court gives leave) to such terms as the court may impose; and

(f) no other proceedings and no execution or other legal process may be commenced or continued, and no distress may be levied, against the partnership or the partnership property except with the consent of the administrator or the leave of the court and subject (where the court gives leave) to such terms as aforesaid.

**11(4)** Where at any time an agricultural receiver or a receiver of part of the partnership property has vacated office under subsection (2)–

(a) his remuneration and any expenses properly incurred by him, and

(b) any indemnity to which he is entitled out of the partnership property,

shall be charged on and (subject to subsection (3) above) paid out of any partnership property which was in his custody or under his control at that time in priority to any security held by the person by or on whose behalf he was appointed.".

## SECTION 12: NOTIFICATION OF ORDER

6 Section 12 is modified so as to read as follows:–

"**12(1)** Every invoice, order for goods or business letter which, at a time when an administration order is in force in relation to an insolvent partnership, is issued by or on behalf of the partnership or the administrator, being a document on or in which the name under which the partnership carries on business appears, shall also contain the administrator's name and a statement that the affairs and business of the partnership and the partnership property are being managed by the administrator.

**12(2)** If default is made in complying with this section, any of the following persons who without reasonable excuse authorises or permits the default, namely, the administrator and any officer of the partnership, is liable to a fine.".

## SECTION 13: APPOINTMENT OF ADMINISTRATOR

7 Section 13 is modified so as to read as follows:–

"**13(1)** The administrator of a partnership shall be appointed either by the administration order or by an order under the next subsection.

**13(2)** If a vacancy occurs by death, resignation or otherwise in the office of the administrator, the court may by order fill the vacancy.

**13(3)** An application for an order under subsection (2) may be made–

(a) by any continuing administrator of the partnership; or

(b) where there is no such administrator, by a creditors' committee established under section 26 below; or

(c) where there is no such administrator and no such committee, by the members of the partnership or by any creditor or creditors of the partnership.".

## SECTION 14: GENERAL POWERS

8 Section 14 is modified so as to read as follows:–

"**14(1)** The administrator of an insolvent partnership–

(a) may do all such things as may be necessary for the management of the affairs and business of the partnership and of the partnership property, and

(b) without prejudice to the generality of paragraph (a), has the powers specified in Schedule 1 to this Act;

and in the application of that Schedule to the administrator of a partnership the words "he" and "him" refer to the administrator.

**14(2)** The administrator also has power–

(a) to prevent any person from taking part in the management of the partnership business and to appoint any person to be a manager of that business, and

(b) to call any meeting of the members or creditors of the partnership.

**14(3)** The administrator may apply to the court for directions in relation to any particular matter arising in connection with the carrying out of his functions.

**14(4)** Any power exercisable by the officers of the partnership, whether under the Partnership Act 1890, the partnership agreement or otherwise, which could be exercised in such a way as to interfere with the exercise by the administrator of his powers is not exercisable except with the consent of the administrator, which may be given either generally or in relation to particular cases.

**14(5)** Subject to subsection (6) below, in exercising his powers the administrator is deemed to act as the agent of the members of the partnership in their capacity as such.

**14(6)** An officer of the partnership shall not, unless he otherwise consents, be personally liable for the debts and obligations of the partnership incurred during the period when the administration order is in force.


bbcl randr4 Mp 4242—bcl98 220b

**14(7)** A person dealing with the administrator in good faith and for value is not concerned to inquire whether the administrator is acting within his powers.".

SECTION 15: POWER TO DEAL WITH CHARGED PROPERTY, ETC.

**9** Section 15 is modified so as to read as follows:–

"**15(1)** The administrator of a partnership may dispose of or otherwise exercise his powers in relation to any partnership property which is subject to a security to which this subsection applies as if the property were not subject to the security.

**15(2)** Where, on an application by the administrator, the court is satisfied that the disposal (with or without other assets) of–

(a) any partnership property subject to a security to which this subsection applies, or
(b) any goods in the possession of one or more officers of the partnership in their capacity as such under a hire-purchase agreement,

would be likely to promote the purpose or one or more of the purposes specified in the administration order, the court may by order authorise the administrator to dispose of the property as if it were not subject to the security or to dispose of the goods as if all rights of the owner under the hire-purchase agreement were vested in the members of the partnership.

**15(3)** Subsection (1) applies to any security which, as created, was a floating charge unless an agricultural receiver has been appointed under that security; and subsection (2) applies to any other security.

**15(4)** Where property is disposed of under subsection (1), the holder of the security has the same priority in respect of any partnership property directly or indirectly representing the property disposed of as he would have had in respect of the property subject to the security.

**15(5)** It shall be a condition of an order under subsection (2) that–

(a) the net proceeds of the disposal, and
(b) where those proceeds are less than such amount as may be determined by the court to be the net amount which would be realised on a sale of the property or goods in the open market by a willing vendor, such sums as may be required to make good the deficiency,

shall be applied towards discharging the sums secured by the security or payable under the hire-purchase agreement.

**15(6)** Where a condition imposed in pursuance of subsection (5) relates to two or more securities, that condition requires the net proceeds of the disposal and, where paragraph (b) of that subsection applies, the sums mentioned in that paragraph to be applied towards discharging the sums secured by those securities in the order of their priorities.

**15(7)** References in this section to hire-purchase agreements include conditional sale agreements, chattel leasing agreements and retention of title agreements.".

**10** Schedule 1 is modified so as to read as follows:–

## "Schedule 1 – Powers of Administrator

Section 14

**1** Power to take possession of, collect and get in the partnership property and, for that purpose, to take such proceedings as may seem to him expedient.

**2** Power to sell or otherwise dispose of the partnership property by public auction or private auction or private contract or, in Scotland, to sell, feu, hire out or otherwise dispose of the partnership property by public roup or private bargain.

**3** Power to raise or borrow money and grant security therefor over the partnership property.

**4** Power to appoint a solicitor or accountant or other professionally qualified person to assist him in the performance of his functions.

**5** Power to bring or defend any action or other legal proceedings in the name and on behalf of any member of the partnership in his capacity as such or of the partnership.

**6** Power to refer to arbitration any question affecting the partnership.

**7** Power to effect and maintain insurances in respect of the partnership business and property.

**8** Power to do all acts and execute, in the name and on behalf of the partnership or of any member of the partnership in his capacity as such, any deed, receipt or other document.

**9** Power to draw, accept, make and endorse any bill of exchange or promissory note in the name and on behalf of any member of the partnership in his capacity as such or of the partnership.

**10** Power to appoint any agent to do any business which he is unable to do himself or which can more conveniently be done by an agent and power to employ and dismiss employees.

**11** Power to do all such things (including the carrying out of works) as may be necessary for the realisation of the partnership property.

**12** Power to make any payment which is necessary or incidental to the performance of his functions.

**13** Power to carry on the business of the partnership.

**14** Power to establish subsidiary undertakings of the partnership.

**15** Power to transfer to subsidiary undertakings of the partnership the whole or any part of the business of the partnership or of the partnership property.

**16** Power to grant or accept a surrender of a lease or tenancy of any of the partnership property, and to take a lease or tenancy of any property required or convenient for the business of the partnership.

**17** Power to make any arrangement or compromise on behalf of the partnership or of its members in their capacity as such.

**18** Power to rank and claim in the bankruptcy, insolvency, sequestration or liquidation of any person indebted to the partnership and to receive dividends, and to accede to trust deeds for the creditors of any such person.

**19** Power to present or defend a petition for the winding up of the partnership under the Insolvent Partnerships Order 1994.

**20** Power to do all other things incidental to the exercise of the foregoing powers.".

# Schedule 3 – Provisions of the Act which apply with Modifications for the Purposes of Article 7 to Winding Up of Insolvent Partnership on Petition of Creditor etc. where no Concurrent Petition Presented against Member

Article 7

## PART I – MODIFIED PROVISIONS OF PART V OF THE ACT

**1** Sections 220 to 223 of the Act are set out as modified in Part I of this Schedule, and sections 117, 131, 133, 234 and Schedule 4 are set out as modified in Part II.

### SECTION 220: MEANING OF "UNREGISTERED COMPANY"

**2** Section 220 is modified so as to read as follows:–

"**220** For the purposes of this Part, the expression "unregistered company" includes any insolvent partnership.".

## SECTION 221: WINDING UP OF UNREGISTERED COMPANIES

3 Section 221 is modified so as to read as follows:–

"**221(1)** Subject to subsections (2) and (3) below and to the provisions of this Part, any insolvent partnership may be wound up under this Act if it has, or at any time had, in England and Wales either–

(a) a principal place of business, or
(b) a place of business at which business is or has been carried on in the course of which the debt (or part of the debt) arose which forms the basis of the petition for winding up the partnership.

**221(2)** Subject to subsection (3) below, an insolvent partnership shall not be wound up under this Act if the business of the partnership has not been carried on in England and Wales at any time in the period of 3 years ending with the day on which the winding-up petition is presented.

**221(3)** If an insolvent partnership has a principal place of business situated in Scotland or in Northern Ireland, the court shall not have jurisdiction to wind up the partnership unless it had a principal place of business in England and Wales–

(a) in the case of a partnership with a principal place of business in Scotland, at any time in the period of 1 year, or
(b) in the case of a partnership with a principal place of business in Northern Ireland, at any time in the period of 3 years, ending with the day on which the winding-up petition is presented.

**221(4)** No insolvent partnership shall be wound up under this Act voluntarily.

**221(5)** To the extent that they are applicable to the winding up of a company by the court in England and Wales on the petition of a creditor or of the Secretary of State, all the provisions of this Act and the Companies Act about winding up apply to the winding up of an insolvent partnership as an unregistered company–

(a) with the exceptions and additions mentioned in the following subsections of this section and in section 221A, and
(b) with the modifications specified in Part II of Schedule 3 to the Insolvent Partnerships Order 1994.

**221(6)** Sections 73(1), 74(2)(a) to (d) and (3), 75 to 78, 83, 122, 123, 202, 203, 205 and 250 shall not apply.

**221(7)** The circumstances in which an insolvent partnership may be wound up as an unregistered company are as follows–

(a) if the partnership is dissolved, or has ceased to carry on business, or is carrying on business only for the purpose of winding up its affairs;
(b) if the partnership is unable to pay its debts;
(c) if the court is of the opinion that it is just and equitable that the partnership should be wound up.

**221(8)** Every petition for the winding up of an insolvent partnership under Part V of this Act shall be verified by affidavit in Form 2 in Schedule 9 to the Insolvent Partnerships Order 1994.

*Petition by liquidator, administrator, trustee or supervisor to wind up insolvent partnership as unregistered company*

**221A(1)** A petition in Form 3 in Schedule 9 to the Insolvent Partnerships Order 1994 for winding up an insolvent partnership may be presented by–

(a) the liquidator or administrator of a corporate member or of a former corporate member, or
(b) the administrator of the partnership, or
(c) the trustee of an individual member's, or of a former individual member's, estate, or
(d) the supervisor of a voluntary arrangement approved under Part I of this Act in

relation to a corporate member or the partnership, or under Part VIII of this Act in relation to an individual member,

if the ground of the petition is one of the circumstances set out in section 221(7).

**221A(2)** In this section "petitioning insolvency practitioner" means a person who has presented a petition under subsection (1).

**221A(3)** If the ground of the petition presented under subsection (1) is that the partnership is unable to pay its debts and the petitioning insolvency practitioner is able to satisfy the court that an insolvency order has been made against the member whose liquidator or trustee he is because of that member's inability to pay a joint debt, that order shall, unless it is proved otherwise to the satisfaction of the court, be proof for the purposes of section 221(7) that the partnership is unable to pay its debts.

**221A(4)** Where a winding-up petition is presented under subsection (1), the court may appoint the petitioning insolvency practitioner as provisional liquidator of the partnership under section 135 (appointment and powers of provisional liquidator).

**221A(5)** Where a winding-up order is made against an insolvent partnership after the presentation of a petition under subsection (1), the court may appoint the petitioning insolvency practitioner as liquidator of the partnership; and where the court makes an appointment under this subsection, section 140(3) (official receiver not to become liquidator) applies as if an appointment had been made under that section.

**221A(6)** Where a winding-up petition is presented under subsection (1), in the event of the partnership property being insufficient to satisfy the costs of the petitioning insolvency practitioner the costs may be paid out of the assets of the corporate or individual member, as the case may be, as part of the expenses of the liquidation, administration, bankruptcy or voluntary arrangement of that member, in the same order of priority as expenses properly chargeable or incurred by the practitioner in getting in any of the assets of the member.".

## SECTION 222: INABILITY TO PAY DEBTS: UNPAID CREDITOR FOR £750 OR MORE

4 Section 222 is modified so as to read as follows:–

"**222(1)** An insolvent partnership is deemed (for the purposes of section 221) unable to pay its debts if there is a creditor, by assignment or otherwise, to whom the partnership is indebted in a sum exceeding £750 then due and–

(a) the creditor has served on the partnership, in the manner specified in subsection (2) below, a written demand in the prescribed form requiring the partnership to pay the sum so due, and

(b) the partnership has for 3 weeks after the service of the demand neglected to pay the sum or to secure or compound for it to the creditor's satisfaction.

**222(2)** Service of the demand referred to in subsection (1)(a) shall be effected–

(a) by leaving it at a principal place of business of the partnership in England and Wales, or

(b) by leaving it at a place of business of the partnership in England and Wales at which business is carried on in the course of which the debt (or part of the debt) referred to in subsection (1) arose, or

(c) by delivering it to an officer of the partnership, or

(d) by otherwise serving it in such manner as the court may approve or direct.

**222(3)** The money sum for the time being specified in subsection (1) is subject to increase or reduction by regulations under section 417 in Part XV; but no increase in the sum so specified affects any case in which the winding-up petition was presented before the coming into force of the increase.".

## SECTION 223: INABILITY TO PAY DEBTS: DEBT REMAINING UNSATISFIED AFTER ACTION BROUGHT

5 Section 223 is modified so as to read as follows:–

"**223(1)** An insolvent partnership is deemed (for the purposes of section 221) unable to pay its debts if an action or other proceeding has been instituted against any member for any debt or demand due, or claimed to be due, from the partnership, or from him in his character of member, and–

(a) notice in writing of the institution of the action or proceeding has been served on the partnership in the manner specified in subsection (2) below, and
(b) the partnership has not within 3 weeks after service of the notice paid, secured or compounded for the debt or demand, or procured the action or proceeding to be stayed or sisted, or indemnified the defendant or defender to his reasonable satisfaction against the action or proceeding, and against all costs, damages and expenses to be incurred by him because of it.

**223(2)** Service of the notice referred to in subsection (1)(a) shall be effected–

(a) by leaving it at a principal place of business of the partnership in England and Wales, or
(b) by leaving it at a place of business of the partnership in England and Wales at which business is carried on in the course of which the debt or demand (or part of the debt or demand) referred to in subsection (1) arose, or
(c) by delivering it to an officer of the partnership, or
(d) by otherwise serving it in such manner as the court may approve or direct.".

# PART II – OTHER MODIFIED PROVISIONS OF THE ACT ABOUT WINDING UP BY THE COURT

## SECTION 117: HIGH COURT AND COUNTY COURT JURISDICTION

**6** Section 117 is modified so as to read as follows:–

"**117(1)** Subject to subsections (3) and (4) below, the High Court has jurisdiction to wind up any insolvent partnership as an unregistered company by virtue of article 7 of the Insolvent Partnerships Order 1994 if the partnership has, or at any time had, in England and Wales either–

(a) a principal place of business, or
(b) a place of business at which business is or has been carried on in the course of which the debt (or part of the debt) arose which forms the basis of the petition for winding up the partnership.

**117(2)** Subject to subsections (3) and (4) below, a petition for the winding up of an insolvent partnership by virtue of the said article 7 may be presented to a county court in England and Wales if the partnership has, or at any time had, within the insolvency district of that court either–

(a) a principal place of business, or
(b) a place of business at which business is or has been carried on in the course of which the debt (or part of the debt) arose which forms the basis of the winding-up petition.

**117(3)** Subject to subsection (4) below, the court only has jurisdiction to wind up an insolvent partnership if the business of the partnership has been carried on in England and Wales at any time in the period of 3 years ending with the day on which the petition for winding it up is presented.

**117(4)** If an insolvent partnership has a principal place of business situated in Scotland or in Northern Ireland, the court shall not have jurisdiction to wind up the partnership unless it had a principal place of business in England and Wales–

(a) in the case of a partnership with a principal place of business in Scotland, at any time in the period of 1 year, or
(b) in the case of a partnership with a principal place of business in Northern Ireland, at any time in the period of 3 years,

ending with the day on which the petition for winding it up is presented.

**117(5)** The Lord Chancellor may by order in a statutory instrument exclude a county court from having winding-up jurisdiction, and for the purposes of that jurisdiction may attach its district, or any part thereof, to any other county court, and may by statutory instrument revoke or vary any such order.

In exercising the powers of this section, the Lord Chancellor shall provide that a county court is not to have winding-up jurisdiction unless it has for the time being jurisdiction for the purposes of Parts VIII to XI of this Act (individual insolvency).

**117(6)** Every court in England and Wales having winding-up jurisdiction has for the purposes of that jurisdiction all the powers of the High Court; and every prescribed officer of the court shall perform any duties which an officer of the High Court may discharge by order of a judge of that court or otherwise in relation to winding up.".

## SECTION 131: STATEMENT OF AFFAIRS OF INSOLVENT PARTNERSHIP

7 Section 131 is modified so as to read as follows:–

"**131(1)** Where the court has, by virtue of article 7 of the Insolvent Partnerships Order 1994, made a winding-up order or appointed a provisional liquidator in respect of an insolvent partnership, the official receiver may require some or all of the persons mentioned in subsection (3) below to make out and submit to him a statement in the prescribed form as to the affairs of the partnership.

**131(2)** The statement shall be verified by affidavit by the persons required to submit it and shall show–

(a) particulars of the debts and liabilities of the partnership and of the partnership property;
(b) the names and addresses of the partnership's creditors;
(c) the securities held by them respectively;
(d) the dates when the securities were respectively given; and
(e) such further or other information as may be prescribed or as the official receiver may require.

**131(3)** The persons referred to in subsection (1) are–

(a) those who are or have been officers of the partnership;
(b) those who have taken part in the formation of the partnership at any time within one year before the relevant date;
(c) those who are in the employment of the partnership, or have been in its employment within that year, and are in the official receiver's opinion capable of giving the information required;
(d) those who are or have been within that year officers of, or in the employment of, a company which is, or within that year was, an officer of the partnership.

**131(4)** Where any persons are required under this section to submit a statement of affairs to the official receiver, they shall do so (subject to the next subsection) before the end of the period of 21 days beginning with the day after that on which the prescribed notice of the requirement is given to them by the official receiver.

**131(5)** The official receiver, if he thinks fit, may–

(a) at any time release a person from an obligation imposed on him under subsection (1) or (2) above; or
(b) either when giving the notice mentioned in subsection (4) or subsequently, extend the period so mentioned;

and where the official receiver has refused to exercise a power conferred by this subsection, the court, if it thinks fit, may exercise it.

**131(6)** In this section–

**"employment"** includes employment under a contract for services; and

**"the relevant date"** means–

(a) in a case where a provisional liquidator is appointed, the date of his appointment; and

(b) in a case where no such appointment is made, the date of the winding-up order.

**131(7)** If a person without reasonable excuse fails to comply with any obligation imposed under this section, he is liable to a fine and, for continued contravention, to a daily default fine.".

## SECTION 133: PUBLIC EXAMINATION OF OFFICERS OF INSOLVENT PARTNERSHIPS

**8** Section 133 is modified so as to read as follows:–

"**133(1)** Where an insolvent partnership is being wound up by virtue of article 7 of the Insolvent Partnerships Order 1994, the official receiver may at any time before the winding up is complete apply to the court for the public examination of any person who–

(a) is or has been an officer of the partnership; or

(b) has acted as liquidator or administrator of the partnership or as receiver or manager or, in Scotland, receiver of its property; or

(c) not being a person falling within paragraph (a) or (b), is or has been concerned, or has taken part, in the formation of the partnership.

**133(2)** Unless the court otherwise orders, the official receiver shall make an application under subsection (1) if he is requested in accordance with the rules to do so by one-half, in value, of the creditors of the partnership.

**133(3)** On an application under subsection (1), the court shall direct that a public examination of the person to whom the application relates shall be held on a day appointed by the court; and that person shall attend on that day and be publicly examined as to the formation or management of the partnership or as to the conduct of its business and affairs, or his conduct or dealings in relation to the partnership.

**133(4)** The following may take part in the public examination of a person under this section and may question that person concerning the matters mentioned in subsection (3), namely–

(a) the official receiver;

(b) the liquidator of the partnership;

(c) any person who has been appointed as special manager of the partnership's property or business;

(d) any creditor of the partnership who has tendered a proof in the winding up.".

## SECTION 234: GETTING IN THE PARTNERSHIP PROPERTY

**9** Section 234 is modified so as to read as follows:–

"**234(1)** This section applies where, by virtue of article 7 of the Insolvent Partnerships Order 1994–

(a) an insolvent partnership is being wound up, or

(b) a provisional liquidator of an insolvent partnership is appointed;

and "the office-holder" means the liquidator or the provisional liquidator, as the case may be.

**234(2)** Any person who is or has been an officer of the partnership, or who is an executor or administrator of the estate of a deceased officer of the partnership, shall deliver up to the office-holder, for the purposes of the exercise of the office-holder's functions under this Act and (where applicable) the Company Directors Disqualification Act 1986, possession of any partnership property which he holds for the purposes of the partnership.

**234(3)** Where any person has in his possession or control any property, books, papers or records to which the partnership appears to be entitled, the court may require that person forthwith (or within such period as the court may direct) to pay, deliver, convey, surrender or transfer the property, books, papers or records to the office-holder or as the court may direct.

**234(4)** Where the office-holder–

(a) seizes or disposes of any property which is not partnership property, and

(b) at the time of seizure or disposal believes, and has reasonable grounds for believing, that he is entitled (whether in pursuance of an order of the court or otherwise) to seize or dispose of that property,

the next subsection has effect.

**234(5)** In that case the office-holder–

(a) is not liable to any person in respect of any loss or damage resulting from the seizure or disposal except in so far as that loss or damage is caused by the office-holder's own negligence, and

(b) has a lien on the property, or the proceeds of its sale, for such expenses as were incurred in connection with the seizure or disposal.".

**10** Schedule 4 is modified so as to read as follows:–

# "Schedule 4 – Powers of Liquidator in a Winding Up

Section 167

## PART I – POWERS EXERCISABLE WITH SANCTION

**1** Power to pay any class of creditors in full.

**2** Power to make any compromise or arrangement with creditors or persons claiming to be creditors, or having or alleging themselves to have any claim (present or future, certain or contingent, ascertained or sounding only in damages) against the partnership, or whereby the partnership may be rendered liable.

**3** Power to compromise, on such terms as may be agreed–

(a) all debts and liabilities capable of resulting in debts, and all claims (present or future, certain or contingent, ascertained or sounding only in damages) subsisting or supposed to subsist between the partnership and a contributory or alleged contributory or other debtor or person apprehending liability to the partnership, and

(b) all questions in any way relating to or affecting the partnership property or the winding up of the partnership,

and take any security for the discharge of any such debt, liability or claim and give a complete discharge in respect of it.

**4** Power to bring or defend any action or other legal proceeding in the name and on behalf of any member of the partnership in his capacity as such or of the partnership.

**5** Power to carry on the business of the partnership so far as may be necessary for its beneficial winding up.

## PART II – POWERS EXERCISABLE WITHOUT SANCTION

**6** Power to sell any of the partnership property by public auction or private contract, with power to transfer the whole of it to any person or to sell the same in parcels.

**7** Power to do all acts and execute, in the name and on behalf of the partnership or of any member of the partnership in his capacity as such, all deeds, receipts and other documents.

**8** Power to prove, rank and claim in the bankruptcy, insolvency or sequestration of any contributory for any balance against his estate, and to receive dividends in the bankruptcy, insolvency or sequestration in respect of that balance, as a separate debt due from the bankrupt or insolvent, and rateably with the other separate creditors.

**9** Power to draw, accept, make and endorse any bill of exchange or promissory note in the name and on behalf of any member of the partnership in his capacity as such or of the partnership, with the same effect with respect to the liability of the partnership or of any member of the partnership in his capacity as such as if the bill or note had been drawn, accepted, made or endorsed in the course of the partnership's business.

**10** Power to raise on the security of the partnership property any money requisite.

**11** Power to take out in his official name letters of administration to any deceased contributory, and to do in his official name any other act necessary for obtaining payment of any money due from a contributory or his estate which cannot conveniently be done in the name of the partnership.

In all such cases the money due is deemed, for the purpose of enabling the liquidator to take out the letters of administration or recover the money, to be due to the liquidator himself.

**12** Power to appoint an agent to do any business which the liquidator is unable to do himself.

**13** Power to do all such other things as may be necessary for winding up the partnership's affairs and distributing its property.".

# Schedule 4 – Provisions of the Act which apply with Modifications for the Purposes of Article 8 to Winding Up of Insolvent Partnership on Creditor's Petition where Concurrent Petitions are Presented against One or More Members

Article 8

## PART I – MODIFIED PROVISIONS OF PART V OF THE ACT

**1(1)** Sections 220 to 222 of the Act are set out as modified in Part I of this Schedule, and the provisions of the Act specified in sub-paragraph (2) below are set out as modified in Part II.

**1(2)** The provisions referred to in sub-paragraph (1) are sections 117, 122 to 125, 131, 133, 136, 137, 139 to 141, 143, 146, 147, 168, 172, 174, 175, 189, 211, 230, 231, 234, 264, 265, 267, 268, 271, 283, 284, 288, 292 to 296, 298 to 303, 305, 314, 328, 331 and 356, and Schedule 4.

### SECTION 220: MEANING OF "UNREGISTERED COMPANY"

**2** Section 220 is modified so as to read as follows:–

"**220** For the purposes of this Part, the expression **"unregistered company"** includes any insolvent partnership.".

### SECTION 221: WINDING UP OF UNREGISTERED COMPANIES

**3** Section 221 is modified so as to read as follows:–

"**221(1)** Subject to subsections (2) and (3) below and to the provisions of this Part, any insolvent partnership may be wound up under this Act if it has, or at any time had, in England and Wales either–

(a) a principal place of business, or

(b) a place of business at which business is or has been carried on in the course of which the debt (or part of the debt) arose which forms the basis of the petition for winding up the partnership.

**221(2)** Subject to subsection (3) below, an insolvent partnership shall not be wound up under this Act if the business of the partnership has not been carried on in England and Wales at any time in the period of 3 years ending with the day on which the winding-up petition is presented.

**221(3)** If an insolvent partnership has a principal place of business situated in Scotland or in Northern Ireland, the court shall not have jurisdiction to wind up the partnership unless it had a principal place of business in England and Wales–

(a) in the case of a partnership with a principal place of business in Scotland, at any time in the period of 1 year, or

(b) in the case of a partnership with a principal place of business in Northern Ireland, at any time in the period of 3 years,

ending with the day on which the winding-up petition is presented.

**221(4)** No insolvent partnership shall be wound up under this Act voluntarily.

**221(5)** To the extent that they are applicable to the winding up of a company by the court in England and Wales on a creditor's petition, all the provisions of this Act and the Companies Act about winding up apply to the winding up of an insolvent partnership as an unregistered company–

(a) with the exceptions and additions mentioned in the following subsections of this section, and

(b) with the modifications specified in Part II of Schedule 4 to the Insolvent Partnerships Order 1994.

**221(6)** Sections 73(1), 74(2)(a) to (d) and (3), 75 to 78, 83, 154, 202, 203, 205 and 250 shall not apply.

**221(7)** Unless the contrary intention appears, a member of a partnership against whom an insolvency order has been made by virtue of article 8 of the Insolvent Partnerships Order 1994 shall not be treated as a contributory for the purposes of this Act.

**221(8)** The circumstance in which an insolvent partnership may be wound up as an unregistered company is that the partnership is unable to pay its debts.

**221(9)** Every petition for the winding up of an insolvent partnership under Part V of this Act shall be verified by affidavit in Form 2 in Schedule 9 to the Insolvent Partnerships Order 1994.".

## SECTION 222: INABILITY TO PAY DEBTS: UNPAID CREDITOR FOR £750 OR MORE

**4** Section 222 is modified so as to read as follows:–

"**222(1)** An insolvent partnership is deemed (for the purposes of section 221) unable to pay its debts if there is a creditor, by assignment or otherwise, to whom the partnership is indebted in a sum exceeding £750 then due and–

(a) the creditor has served on the partnership, in the manner specified in subsection (2) below, a written demand in Form 4 in Schedule 9 to the Insolvent Partnerships Order 1994 requiring the partnership to pay the sum so due,

(b) the creditor has also served on any one or more members or former members of the partnership liable to pay the sum due (in the case of a corporate member by leaving it at its registered office and in the case of an individual member by serving it in accordance with the rules) a demand in Form 4 in Schedule 9 to that Order, requiring that member or those members to pay the sum so due, and

(c) the partnership and its members have for 3 weeks after the service of the demands, or the service of the last of them if served at different times, neglected to pay the sum or to secure or compound for it to the creditor's satisfaction.

**222(2)** Service of the demand referred to in subsection (1)(a) shall be effected–

(a) by leaving it at a principal place of business of the partnership in England and Wales, or

(b) by leaving it at a place of business of the partnership in England and Wales at which business is cariied on in the course of which the debt (or part of the debt) referred to in subsection (1) arose, or

(c) by delivering it to an officer of the partnership, or

(d) by otherwise serving it in such manner as the court may approve or direct.

**222(3)** The money sum for the time being specified in subsection (1) is subject to increase or reduction by regulations under section 417 in Part XV; but no increase in the sum so specified affects any case in which the winding-up petition was presented before the coming into force of the increase.".

# PART II – OTHER MODIFIED PROVISIONS OF THE ACT ABOUT WINDING UP BY THE COURT AND BANKRUPTCY OF INDIVIDUALS

## SECTIONS 117 AND 265: HIGH COURT AND COUNTY COURT JURISDICTION

**5** Sections 117 and 265 are modified so as to read as follows:–

"**117(1)** Subject to the provisions of this section, the High Court has jurisdiction to wind up any insolvent partnership as an unregistered company by virtue of article 8 of the Insolvent Partnerships Order 1994 if the partnership has, or at any time had, in England and Wales either–

(a) a principal place of business, or

(b) a place of business at which business is or has been carried on in the course of which the debt (or part of the debt) arose which forms the basis of the petition for winding up the partnership.

**117(2)** Subject to subsections (3) and (4) below, a petition for the winding up of an insolvent partnership by virtue of the said article 8 may be presented to a county court in England and Wales if the partnership has, or at any time had, within the insolvency district of that court either–

(a) a principal place of business, or

(b) a place of business at which business is or has been carried on in the course of which the debt (or part of the debt) arose which forms the basis of the winding-up petition.

**117(3)** Subject to subsection (4) below, the court only has jurisdiction to wind up an insolvent partnership if the business of the partnership has been carried on in England and Wales at any time in the period of 3 years ending with the day on which the petition for winding it up is presented.

**117(4)** If an insolvent partnership has a principal place of business situated in Scotland or in Northern Ireland, the court shall not have jurisdiction to wind up the partnership unless it had a principal place of business in England and Wales–

(a) in the case of a partnership with a principal place of business in Scotland, at any time in the period of 1 year, or

(b) in the case of a partnership with a principal place of business in Northern Ireland, at any time in the period of 3 years,

ending with the day on which the petition for winding it up is presented.

**117(5)** Subject to subsection (6) below, the court has jurisdiction to wind up a corporate member or former corporate member, or make a bankruptcy order against an individual member or former individual member, of a partnership against which a petition has been presented by virtue of article 8 of the Insolvent Partnerships Order 1994 if it has jurisdiction in respect of the partnership.

**117(6)** Petitions by virtue of the said article 8 for the winding up of an insolvent partnership and the bankruptcy of one or more members or former members of that partnership may not presented to a district registry of the High Court.

**117(7)** The Lord Chancellor may by order in a statutory instrument exclude a county court from having winding-up jurisdiction, and for the purposes of that jurisdiction may attach its district, or any part thereof, to any other county court, and may by statutory instrument revoke or vary any such order.



bbcl randr4 Mp 4253—bcl98 220b

In exercising the powers of this section, the Lord Chancellor shall provide that a county court is not to have winding-up jurisdiction unless it has for the time being jurisdiction for the purposes of Parts VIII to XI of this Act (individual insolvency).

**117(8)** Every court in England and Wales having winding-up jurisdiction has for the purposes of that jurisdiction all the powers of the High Court; and every prescribed officer of the court shall perform any duties which an officer of the High Court may discharge by order of a judge of that court or otherwise in relation to winding up.".

## CIRCUMSTANCES IN WHICH MEMBERS OF INSOLVENT PARTNERSHIPS MAY BE WOUND UP OR MADE BANKRUPT BY THE COURT:

## SECTION 122 – CORPORATE MEMBER SECTION 267 – INDIVIDUAL MEMBER

**6(a)** Section 122 is modified so as to read as follows:–

"**122** A corporate member or former corporate member may be wound up by the court if it is unable to pay its debts.".

**6(b)** Section 267 is modified so as to read as follows:–

"**267(1)** Where a petition for the winding up of an insolvent partnership has been presented to the court by virtue of article 8 of the Insolvent Partnerships Order 1994, a creditor's petition against any individual member or former individual member of that partnership by virtue of that article must be in respect of one or more joint debts owed by the insolvent partnership, and the petitioning creditor or each of the petitioning creditors must be a person to whom the debt or (as the case may be) at least one of the debts is owed.

**267(2)** Subject to section 268, a creditor's petition may be presented to the court in respect of a joint debt or debts only if, at the time the petition is presented–

(a) the amount of the debt, or the aggregate amount of the debts, is equal to or exceeds the bankruptcy level,

(b) the debt, or each of the debts, is for a liquidated sum payable to the petitioning creditor, or one or more of the petitioning creditors, immediately, and is unsecured,

(c) the debt, or each of the debts, is a debt for which the individual member or former member is liable and which he appears to be unable to pay, and

(d) there is no outstanding application to set aside a statutory demand served (under section 268 below) in respect of the debt or any of the debts.

**267(3)** "The bankruptcy level" is £750; but the Secretary of State may by order in a statutory instrument substitute any amount specified in the order for that amount or (as the case may be) for the amount which by virtue of such an order is for the time being the amount of the bankruptcy level.

**267(4)** An order shall not be made under subsection (3) unless a draft of it has been laid before, and approved by a resolution of, each House of Parliament.".

## DEFINITION OF INABILITY TO PAY DEBTS: SECTION 123 – CORPORATE MEMBER

## SECTION 268 – INDIVIDUAL MEMBER

**7(a)** Section 123 is modified so as to read as follows:–

"**123(1)** A corporate member or former member is deemed unable to pay its debts if there is a creditor, by assignment or otherwise, to whom the partnership is indebted in a sum exceeding £750 then due for which the member or former member is liable and–

(a) the creditor has served on that member or former member and the partnership, in the manner specified in subsection (2) below, a written demand in Form 4 in Schedule 9 to the Insolvent Partnerships Order 1994 requiring that member or former member and the partnership to pay the sum so due, and

(b) the corporate member or former member and the partnership have for 3 weeks after the service of the demands, or the service of the last of them if served at different times, neglected to pay the sum or to secure or compound for it to the creditor's satisfaction.

**123(2)** Service of the demand referred to in subsection (1)(a) shall be effected, in the case of the corporate member or former corporate member, by leaving it at its registered office, and, in the case of the partnership–

(a) by leaving it at a principal place of business of the partnership in England and Wales, or
(b) by leaving it at a place of business of the partnership in England and Wales at which business is carried on in the course of which the debt (or part of the debt) referred in subsection (1) arose, or
(c) by delivering it to an officer of the partnership, or
(d) by otherwise serving it in such manner as the court may approve or direct.

**123(3)** The money sum for the time being specified in subsection (1) is subject to increase or reduction by order under section 416 in Part XV.".

**7(b)** Section 268 is modified so as to read as follows:–

"**268(1)** For the purposes of section 267(2)(c), an individual member or former individual member appears to be unable to pay a joint debt for which he is liable if the debt is payable immediately and the petitioning creditor to whom the insolvent partnership owes the joint debt has served–

(a) on the individual member or former individual member in accordance with the rules a demand (known as "the statutory demand"), in Form 4 in Schedule 9 to the Insolvent Partnerships Order 1994, and
(b) on the partnership in the manner specified in subsection (2) below a demand (known as "the written demand") in the same form,

requiring the member or former member and the partnership to pay the debt or to secure or compound for it to the creditor's satisfaction, and at least 3 weeks have elapsed since the service of the demands, or the service of the last of them if served at different times, and neither demand has been complied with nor the demand against the member set aside in accordance with the rules.

**268(2)** Service of the demand referred to in subsection (1)(b) shall be effected–

(a) by leaving it at a principal place of business of the partnership in England and Wales, or
(b) by leaving it at a place of business of the partnership in England and Wales at which business is carried on in the course of which the debt (or part of the debt) referred to in subsection (1) arose, or
(c) by delivering it to an officer of the partnership, or
(d) by otherwise serving it in such manner as the court may approve or direct.".

## SECTIONS 124 AND 264: APPLICATIONS TO WIND UP INSOLVENT PARTNERSHIP AND TO WIND UP OR BANKRUPT INSOLVENT MEMBER

**8** Sections 124 and 264 are modified so as to read as follows:–

"**124(1)** An application to the court by virtue of article 8 of the Insolvent Partnerships Order 1994 for the winding up of an insolvent partnership as an unregistered company and the winding up or bankruptcy (as the case may be) of at least one of its members or former members shall–

(a) in the case of the partnership, be by petition in Form 5 in Schedule 9 to that Order,
(b) in the case of a corporate member or former corporate member, be by petition in Form 6 in that Schedule, and
(c) in the case of an individual member or former individual member, be by petition in Form 7 in that Schedule.

**124(2)** Each of the petitions mentioned in subsection (1) may be presented by any creditor or creditors to whom the partnership and the member or former member in question is indebted in respect of a liquidated sum payable immediately.

**124(3)** The petitions mentioned in subsection (1)–

(a) shall all be presented to the same court and, except as the court otherwise permits or directs, on the same day, and

(b) except in the case of the petition mentioned in subsection (1)

(c) shall be advertised in Form 8 in the said Schedule 9.

**124(4)** At any time after presentation of a petition under this section the petitioner may, with the leave of the court obtained on application and on such terms as it thinks just, add other members or former members of the partnership as parties to the proceedings in relation to the insolvent partnership.

**124(5)** Each petition presented under this section shall contain particulars of other petitions being presented in relation to the partnership, identifying the partnership and members concerned.

**124(6)** The hearing of the petition against the partnership fixed by the court shall be in advance of the hearing of any petition against an insolvent member.

**124(7)** On the day appointed for the hearing of the petition against the partnership, the petitioner shall, before the commencement of the hearing, hand to the court Form 9 in Schedule 9 to the Insolvent Partnerships Order 1994, duly completed.

**124(8)** Any member of the partnership or any person against whom a winding-up or bankruptcy petition has been presented in relation to the insolvent partnership is entitled to appear and to be heard on any petition for the winding up of the partnership.

**124(9)** A petitioner under this section may at the hearing withdraw a petition if–

(a) subject to subsection (10) below, he withdraws at the same time every other petition which he has presented under this section; and

(b) he gives notice to the court at least 3 days before the date appointed for the hearing of the relevant petition of his intention to withdraw the petition.

**124(10)** A petitioner need not comply with the provisions of subsection (9)(a) in the case of a petition against an insolvent member if the court is satisfied on application made to it by the petitioner that, because of difficulties in serving the petition or for any other reason, the continuance of that petition would be likely to prejudice or delay the proceedings on the petition which he has presented against the partnership or on any petition which he has presented against any other insolvent member.

**124(11)** Where notice is given under subsection (9)(b), the court may, on such terms as it thinks just, substitute as petitioner, both in respect of the partnership and in respect of each insolvent member against whom a petition has been presented, any creditor of the partnership who in its opinion would have a right to present the petitions, and if the court makes such a substitution the petitions in question will not be withdrawn.

**124(12)** Reference in subsection (11) to substitution of a petitioner includes reference to change of carriage of the petition in accordance with the rules.".

## SECTIONS 125 AND 271: POWERS OF COURT ON HEARING OF PETITIONS AGAINST INSOLVENT PARTNERSHIP AND MEMBERS

**9** Sections 125 and 271 are modified so as to read as follows:–

"**125(1)** Subject to the provisions of section 125A, on hearing a petition under section 124 against an insolvent partnership or any of its insolvent members, the court may dismiss it, or adjourn the hearing conditionally or unconditionally or make any other order that it thinks fit; but the court shall not refuse to make a winding-up order against the partnership or a corporate member on the ground only that the partnership property or (as the case may be) the member's assets have been mortgaged to an amount equal to or in excess of that property or those assets, or that the partnership has no property or the member no assets.

**125(2)** An order under subsection (1) in respect of an insolvent partnership may contain directions as to the future conduct of any insolvency proceedings in existence against any insolvent member in respect of whom an insolvency order has been made.

*Hearing of petitions against members*

**125A(1)** On the hearing of a petition against an insolvent member the petitioner shall draw the court's attention to the result of the hearing of the winding-up petition against the partnership and the following subsections of this section shall apply.

**125A(2)** If the court has neither made a winding-up order, nor dismissed the winding-up petition, against the partnership the court may adjourn the hearing of the petition against the member until either event has occurred.

**125A(3)** Subject to subsection (4) below, if a winding-up order has been made against the partnership, the court may make a winding-up order against the corporate member in respect of which, or (as the case may be) a bankruptcy order against the individual member in respect of whom, the insolvency petition was presented.

**125A(4)** If no insolvency order is made under subsection (3) against any member within 28 days of the making of the winding-up order against the partnership, the proceedings against the partnership shall be conducted as if the winding-up petition against the partnership had been presented by virtue of article 7 of the Insolvent Partnerships Order 1994 and the proceedings against any member shall be conducted under this Act without the modifications made by that Order (other than the modifications made to sections 168 and 303 by article 14).

**125A(5)** If the court has dismissed the winding-up petition against the partnership, the court may dismiss the winding-up petition against the corporate member or (as the case may be) the bankruptcy petition against the individual member. However, if an insolvency order is made against a member, the proceedings against that member shall be conducted under this Act without the modifications made by the Insolvent Partnerships Order 1994 (other than the modifications made to sections 168 and 303 of this Act by article 14 of that Order).

**125A(6)** The court may dismiss a petition against an insolvent member if it considers it just to do so because of a change in circumstances since the making of the winding-up order against the partnership.

**125A(7)** The court may dismiss a petition against an insolvent member who is a limited partner, if–

(a) the member lodges in court for the benefit of the creditors of the partnership sufficient money or security to the court's satisfaction to meet his liability for the debts and obligations of the partnership; or

(b) the member satisfies the court that he is no longer under any liability in respect of the debts and obligations of the partnership.

**125A(8)** Nothing in sections 125 and 125A or in sections 267 and 268 prejudices the power of the court, in accordance with the rules, to authorise a creditor's petition to be amended by the omission of any creditor or debt and to be proceeded with as if things done for the purposes of those sections had been done only by or in relation to the remaining creditors or debts.".

## SECTIONS 131 AND 288: STATEMENTS OF AFFAIRS – INSOLVENT PARTNERSHIPS; CORPORATE MEMBERS; INDIVIDUAL MEMBERS

**10** Sections 131 and 288 are modified so as to read as follows:–

"**131(1)** This section applies where the court has, by virtue of article 8 of the Insolvent Partnerships Order 1994–

(a) made a winding-up order or appointed a provisional liquidator in respect of an insolvent partnership, or

(b) made a winding-up order or appointed a provisional liquidator in respect of any corporate member of that partnership, or

(c) made a bankruptcy order in respect of any individual member of that partnership.

**131(2)** The official receiver may require some or all of the persons mentioned in subsection (4) below to make out and submit to him a statement as to the affairs of the partnership or member in the prescribed form.

**131(3)** The statement shall be verified by affidavit by the persons required to submit it and shall show–

(a) particulars of the debts and liabilities of the partnership or of the member (as the case may be), and of the partnership property and member's assets;
(b) the names and addresses of the creditors of the partnership or of the member (as the case may be);
(c) the securities held by them respectively;
(d) the dates when the securities were respectively given; and
(e) such further or other information as may be prescribed or as the official receiver may require.

**131(4)** The persons referred to in subsection (2) are–

(a) those who are or have been officers of the partnership;
(b) those who are or have been officers of the corporate member;
(c) those who have taken part in the formation of the partnership or of the corporate member at any time within one year before the relevant date;
(d) those who are in the employment of the partnership or of the corporate member, or have been in such employment within that year, and are in the official receiver's opinion capable of giving the information required;
(e) those who are or have been within that year officers of, or in the employment of, a company which is, or within that year was, an officer of the partnership or an officer of the corporate member.

**131(5)** Where any persons are required under this section to submit a statement of affairs to the official receiver, they shall do so (subject to the next subsection) before the end of the period of 21 days beginning with the day after that on which the prescribed notice of the requirement is given to them by the official receiver.

**131(6)** The official receiver, if he thinks fit, may–

(a) at any time release a person from an obligation imposed on him under subsection (2) or (3) above; or
(b) either when giving the notice mentioned in subsection (5) or subsequently, extend the period so mentioned;

and where the official receiver has refused to exercise a power conferred by this subsection, the court, if it thinks fit, may exercise it.

**131(7)** In this section–

**"employment"** includes employment under a contract for services; and

**"the relevant date"** means–

(a) in a case where a provisional liquidator is appointed, the date of his appointment; and
(b) in a case where no such appointment is made, the date of the winding-up order.

**131(8)** Any person who without reasonable excuse fails to comply with any obligation imposed under this section (other than, in the case of an individual member, an obligation in respect of his own statement of affairs), is liable to a fine and, for continued contravention, to a daily default fine.

**131(9)** An individual member who without reasonable excuse fails to comply with any obligation imposed under this section in respect of his own statement of affairs, is guilty of a contempt of court and liable to be punished accordingly (in addition to any other punishment to which he may be subject).".

## SECTION 133: PUBLIC EXAMINATION OF OFFICERS OF INSOLVENT PARTNERSHIPS

**11** Section 133 is modified so far as insolvent partnerships are concerned so as to read as follows:–

"**133(1)** Where an insolvent partnership is being wound up by virtue of article 8 of the Insolvent Partnerships Order 1994, the official receiver may at any time before the winding up is complete apply to the court for the public examination of any person who–

(a) is or has been an officer of the partnership; or

(b) has acted as liquidator or administrator of the partnership or as receiver or manager or, in Scotland, receiver of its property;

(c) not being a person falling within paragraph (a) or (b), is or has been concerned, or has taken part, in the formation of the partnership.

**133(2)** Unless the court otherwise orders, the official receiver shall make an application under subsection (1) if he is requested in accordance with the rules to do so by one-half, in value,of the creditors of the partnership.

**133(3)** On an application under subsection (1), the court shall direct that a public examination of the person to whom the application relates shall be held on a day appointed by the court; and that person shall attend on that day and be publicly examined as to the formation or management of the partnership or as to the conduct of its business and affairs, or his conduct or dealings in relation to the partnership.

**133(4)** The following may take part in the public examination of a person under this section and may question that person concerning the matters mentioned in subsection (3), namely–

(a) the official receiver;

(b) the liquidator of the partnership;

(c) any person who has been appointed as special manager of the partnership's property or business;

(d) any creditor of the partnership who has tendered a proof in the winding up.

**133(5)** On an application under subsection (1), the court may direct that the public examination of any person under this section in relation to the affairs of an insolvent partnership be combined with the public examination of any person under this Act in relation to the affairs of a corporate member of that partnership against which, or an individual member of the partnership against whom, an insolvency order has been made.".

## SECTIONS 136, 293 AND 294: FUNCTIONS OF OFFICIAL RECEIVER IN RELATION TO OFFICE OF RESPONSIBLE INSOLVENCY PRACTITIONER

**12** Sections 136, 293 and 294 are modified so as to read as follows:–

"**136(1)** The following provisions of this section and of section 136A have effect, subject to section 140 below, where insolvency orders are made in respect of an insolvent partnership and one or more of its insolvent members by virtue of article 8 of the Insolvent Partnerships Order 1994.

**136(2)** The official receiver, by virtue of his office, becomes the responsible insolvency practitioner of the partnership and of any insolvent member and continues in office until another person becomes responsible insolvency practitioner under the provisions of this Part.

**136(3)** The official receiver is, by virtue of his office, the responsible insolvency practitioner of the partnership and of any insolvent member during any vacancy.

**136(4)** At any time when he is the responsible insolvency practitioner of the insolvent partnership and of any insolvent member, the official receiver may summon a combined meeting of the creditors of the partnership and the creditors of such member, for the purpose of choosing a person to be responsible insolvency practitioner in place of the official receiver.

*Duty of official receiver to summon meetings*

**136A(1)** It is the duty of the official receiver–

(a) as soon as practicable in the period of 12 weeks beginning with the day on which the insolvency order was made against the partnership, to decide whether to exercise his power under section 136(4) to summon a meeting, and

(b) if in pursuance of paragraph (a) he decides not to exercise that power, to give notice of his decision, before the end of that period, to the court and to the creditors of the partnership and the creditors of any insolvent member against whom an insolvency order has been made, and

(c) (whether or not he has decided to exercise that power) to exercise his power to summon a meeting under section 136(4) if he is at any time requested to do so in accordance with the rules by one-quarter, in value, of either–

(i) the partnership's creditors, or

(ii) the creditors of any insolvent member against whom an insolvency order has been made,

and accordingly, where the duty imposed by paragraph (c) arises before the official receiver has performed a duty imposed by paragraph (a) or (b), he is not required to perform the latter duty.

**136A(2)** A notice given under subsection (1)(b) to the creditors shall contain an explanation of the creditors' power under subsection (1)(c) to require the official receiver to summon a combined meeting of the creditors of the partnership and of any insolvent member.

**136A(3)** If the official receiver, in pursuance of subsection (1)(a), has decided to exercise his power under section 136(4) to summon a meeting, he shall hold that meeting in the period of 4 months beginning with the day on which the insolvency order was made against the partnership.

**136A(4)** If (whether or not he has decided to exercise that power) the official receiver is requested, in accordance with the provisions of subsection (1)(c), to exercise his power under section 136(4) to summon a meeting, he shall hold that meeting in accordance with the rules.

**136A(5)** Where a meeting of creditors of the partnership and of any insolvent member has been held under section 136(4), and an insolvency order is subsequently made against a further insolvent member by virtue of article 8 of the Insolvent Partnerships Order 1994–

(a) any person chosen at that meeting to be responsible insolvency practitioner in place of the official receiver shall also be the responsible insolvency practitioner of the member against whom the subsequent order is made, and

(b) subsection (1) of this section shall not apply.".

## SECTIONS 137, 295, 296 AND 300: APPOINTMENT OF RESPONSIBLE INSOLVENCY PRACTITIONER BY SECRETARY OF STATE

**13** Sections 137, 295, 296 and 300 are modified so as to read as follows:–

"**137(1)** This section and the next apply where the court has made insolvency orders in respect of an insolvent partnership and one or more of its insolvent members by virtue of article 8 of the Insolvent Partnerships Order 1994.

**137(2)** The official receiver may, at any time when he is the responsible insolvency practitioner of the partnership and of any insolvent member, apply to the Secretary of State for the appointment of a person as responsible insolvency practitioner of both the partnership and of such member in his place.

**137(3)** If a meeting is held in pursuance of a decision under section 136A(1)(a), but no person is chosen to be responsible insolvency practitioner as a result of that meeting, it is the duty of the official receiver to decide whether to refer the need for an appointment to the Secretary of State.

*Consequences of section 137 application*

**137A(1)** On an application under section 137(2), or a reference made in pursuance of a decision under section 137(3), the Secretary of State shall either make an appointment or decline to make one.

**137A(2)** If on an application under section 137(2), or a reference made in pursuance of a decision under section 137(3), no appointment is made, the official receiver shall continue to be responsible insolvency practitioner of the partnership and its insolvent member or members,but without prejudice to his power to make a further application or reference.

**137A(3)** Where a responsible insolvency practitioner has been appointed by the Secretary of State under subsection (1) of this section, and an insolvency order is subsequently made against a further insolvent member by virtue of article 8 of the Insolvent Partnerships Order 1994, then the practitioner so appointed shall also be the responsible insolvency practitioner of the member against whom the subsequent order is made.

**137A(4)** Where a responsible insolvency practitioner has been appointed by the Secretary of State under subsection (1), or has become responsible insolvency practitioner of a further insolvent member under subsection (3), that practitioner shall give notice of his appointment or further appointment (as the case may be) to the creditors of the insolvent partnership and the creditors of the insolvent member or members against whom insolvency orders have been made or, if the court so allows, shall advertise his appointment in accordance with the directions of the court.

**137A(5)** Subject to subsection (6) below, in that notice or advertisement the responsible insolvency practitioner shall–

(a) state whether he proposes to summon, under section 141 below, a combined meeting of the creditors of the insolvent partnership and of the insolvent member or members against whom insolvency orders have been made, for the purpose of determining whether a creditors' committee should be established under that section, and

(b) if he does not propose to summon such a meeting, set out the power under that section of the creditors of the partnership and of the insolvent member or members to require him to summon one.

**137A(6)** Where in a case where subsection (3) applies a meeting has already been held under section 141 below, the responsible insolvency practitioner shall state in the notice or advertisement whether a creditors' committee was established at that meeting and–

(a) if such a committee was established, shall state whether he proposes to appoint additional members of the committee under section 141A(3), and

(b) if such a committee was not established, shall set out the power under section 141 of the creditors of the partnership and of the insolvent member or members to require him to summon a meeting for the purpose of determining whether a creditors' committee should be established under that section.".

## SECTION 139: RULES APPLICABLE TO MEETINGS OF CREDITORS

**14** Section 139 is modified so as to read as follows:–

"**139(1)** This section applies where the court has made insolvency orders against an insolvent partnership and one or more of its insolvent members by virtue of article 8 of the Insolvent Partnerships Order 1994.

**139(2)** Subject to subsection (4) below, the rules relating to the requisitioning, summoning, holding and conducting of meetings on the winding up of a company are to apply (with the necessary modifications) to the requisitioning, summoning, holding and conducting of–

(a) separate meetings of the creditors of the partnership or of any corporate member against which an insolvency order has been made, and

(b) combined meetings of the creditors of the partnership and the creditors of the insolvent member or members.

**139(3)** Subject to subsection (4) below, the rules relating to the requisitioning, summoning, holding and conducting of meetings on the bankruptcy of an individual are to apply (with the necessary modifications) to the requisitioning, summoning, holding and conducting of separate meetings of the creditors of any individual member against whom an insolvency order has been made.

**139(4)** Any combined meeting of creditors shall be conducted as if the creditors of the partnership and of the insolvent member or members were a single set of creditors.".

## SECTION 140: APPOINTMENT BY THE COURT FOLLOWING ADMINISTRATION OR VOLUNTARY ARRANGEMENT

**15** Section 140 is modified so as to read as follows:–

"**140(1)** This section applies where insolvency orders are made in respect of an insolvent partnership and one or more of its insolvent members by virtue of article 8 of the Insolvent Partnerships Order 1994.

**140(2)** Where the orders referred to in subsection (1) are made immediately upon the discharge of an administration order in respect of the partnership, the court may appoint as responsible insolvency practitioner the person who has ceased on the discharge of the administration order to be the administrator of the partnership.

**140(3)** Where the orders referred to in subsection (1) are made at a time when there is a supervisor of a voluntary arrangement approved in relation to the partnership under Part I, the court may appoint as responsible insolvency practitioner the person who is the supervisor at the time when the winding-up order against the partnership is made.

**140(4)** Where the court makes an appointment under this section, the official receiver does not become the responsible insolvency practitioner as otherwise provided by section 136(2), and he has no duty under section 136A(1)(a) or (b) in respect of the summoning of creditors' meetings.".

## SECTIONS 141, 301 AND 302: CREDITORS' COMMITTEE: INSOLVENT PARTNERSHIP AND MEMBERS

**16** Sections 141, 301 and 302 are modified so as to read as follows:–

"**141(1)** This section applies where–

(a) insolvency orders are made in respect of an insolvent partnership and one or more of its insolvent members by virtue of article 8 of the Insolvent Partnerships Order 1994, and

(b) a combined meeting of creditors has been summoned for the purpose of choosing a person to be responsible insolvency practitioner of the partnership and of any such insolvent member or members.

**141(2)** The meeting of creditors may establish a committee ("the creditors' committee") which shall consist of creditors of the partnership or creditors of any insolvent member against whom an insolvency order has been made, or both.

**141(3)** The responsible insolvency practitioner of the partnership and of its insolvent member or members (not being the official receiver) may at any time, if he thinks fit, summon a combined general meeting of the creditors of the partnership and of such member or members for the purpose of determining whether a creditors' committee should be established and, if it is so determined, of establishing it.

The responsible insolvency practitioner (not being the official receiver) shall summon such a meeting if he is requested, in accordance with the rules, to do so by one-tenth, in value, of either–

(a) the partnership's creditors, or

(b) the creditors of any insolvent member against whom an insolvency order has been made.

*Functions and membership of creditors' committee*

**141A(1)** The committee established under section 141 shall act as liquidation committee for the partnership and for any corporate member against which an insolvency order has been made, and as creditors' committee for any individual member against whom an insolvency order has been made, and shall as appropriate exercise the functions conferred on liquidation and creditors' committees in a winding up or bankruptcy by or under this Act.

**141A(2)** The rules relating to liquidation committees are to apply (with the necessary modifications and with the exclusion of all references to contributories) to a committee established under section 141.

**141A(3)** Where the appointment of the responsible insolvency practitioner also takes effect in relation to a further insolvent member under section 136A(5) or 137A(3), the practitioner may appoint any creditor of that member (being qualified under the rules to be a member of the committee) to be an additional member of any creditors' committee already established under section 141, provided that the creditor concerned consents to act.

**141A(4)** The court may at any time, on application by a creditor of the partnership or of any insolvent member against whom an insolvency order has been made, appoint additional members of the creditors' committee.

**141A(5)** If additional members of the creditors' committee are appointed under subsection (3) or (4), the limit on the maximum number of members of the committee specified in the rules shale increased by the number of additional members so appointed.

**141A(6)** The creditors' committee is not to be able or required to carry out its functions at any time when the official receiver is responsible insolvency practitioner of the partnership and of its insolvent member or members; but at any such time its functions are vested in the Secretary of State except to the extent that the rules otherwise provide.

**141A(7)** Where there is for the time being no creditors' committee, and the responsible insolvency practitioner is a person other than the official receiver, the functions of such a committee are vested in the Secretary of State except to the extent that the rules otherwise provide.".

## SECTIONS 143, 168(4) AND 305: GENERAL FUNCTIONS OF RESPONSIBLE INSOLVENCY PRACTITIONER

17 Sections 143, 168(4) and 305 are modified so as to read as follows:–

"**143(1)** The functions of the responsible insolvency practitioner of an insolvent partnership and of its insolvent member or members against whom insolvency orders have been made by virtue of article 8 of the Insolvent Partnerships Order 1994, are to secure that the partnership property and the assets of any such corporate member, and the estate of any such individual member, are got in, realised and distributed to their respective creditors and, if there is a surplus of such property or assets or in such estate, to the persons entitled to it.

**143(2)** In the carrying out of those functions, and in the management of the partnership property and of the assets of any corporate member and of the estate of any individual member, the responsible insolvency practitioner is entitled, subject to the provisions of this Act, to use his own discretion.

**143(3)** It is the duty of the responsible insolvency practitioner, if he is not the official receiver–

(a) to furnish the official receiver with such information,

(b) to produce to the official receiver, and permit inspection by the official receiver of, such books, papers and other records, and

(c) to give the official receiver such other assistance,

as the official receiver may reasonably require for the purposes of carrying out his functions in relation to the winding up of the partnership and any corporate member or the bankruptcy of any individual member.

**143(4)** The official name of the responsible insolvency practitioner in his capacity as trustee of an individual member shall be "the trustee of the estate of..........., a bankrupt" (inserting the name of the individual member); but he may be referred to as "the trustee in bankruptcy" of the particular member.".

## SECTIONS 146 AND 331: DUTY TO SUMMON FINAL MEETING OF CREDITORS

**18** Sections 146 and 331 are modified so as to read as follows:–

"**146(1)** This section applies, subject to subsection (3) of this section and section 332 below, if it appears to the responsible insolvency practitioner of an insolvent partnership which is being wound up by virtue of article 8 of the Insolvent Partnerships Order 1994 and of its insolvent member or members that the winding up of the partnership or of any corporate member, or the administration of any individual member's estate, is for practical purposes complete and the practitioner is not the official receiver.

**146(2)** The responsible insolvency practitioner shall summon a final general meeting of the creditors of the partnership or of the insolvent member or members (as the case may be) or a combined final general meeting of the creditors of the partnership and of the insolvent member or members which–

(a) shall as appropriate receive the practitioner's report of the winding up of the insolvent partnership or of any corporate member or of the administration of the estate of any individual member, and

(b) shall determine whether the practitioner should have his release under section 174 in Chapter VII of this Part in respect of the winding up of the partnership or of the corporate member, or the administration of the individual member's estate (as the case may be).

**146(3)** The responsible insolvency practitioner may, if he thinks fit, give the notice summoning the final general meeting at the same time as giving notice of any final distribution of the partnership property or the property of the insolvent member or members; but, if summoned for an earlier date, that meeting shall be adjourned (and, if necessary, further adjourned) until a date on which the practitioner is able to report to the meeting that the winding up of the partnership or of any corporate member, or the administration of any individual member's estate, is for practical purposes complete.

**146(4)** In the carrying out of his functions in the winding up of the partnership and of any corporate member and the administration of any individual member's estate, it is the duty of the responsible insolvency practitioner to retain sufficient sums from the partnership property and the property of any such insolvent member to cover the expenses of summoning and holding any meeting required by this section.".

## SECTION 147: POWER OF COURT TO STAY PROCEEDINGS

**19** Section 147 is modified, so far as insolvent partnerships are concerned, so as to read as follows:–

"**147(1)** The court may, at any time after an order has been made by virtue of article 8 of the Insolvent Partnerships Order 1994 for winding up an insolvent partnership, on the application either of the responsible insolvency practitioner or the official receiver or any creditor or contributory, and on proof to the satisfaction of the court that all proceedings in the winding up of the partnership ought to be stayed, make an order staying the proceedings, either altogether or for a limited time, on such terms and conditions as the court thinks fit.

**147(2)** If, in the course of hearing an insolvency petition presented against a member of an insolvent partnership, the court is satisfied that an application has been or will be made under subsection (1) in respect of a winding-up order made against the partnership, the court may adjourn the petition against the insolvent member, either conditionally or unconditionally.

**147(3)** Where the court makes an order under subsection (1) staying all proceedings on the order for winding up an insolvent partnership–

(a) the court may, on hearing any insolvency petition presented against an insolvent member of the partnership, dismiss that petition; and

(b) if any insolvency order has already been made by virtue of article 8 of the Insolvent Partnerships Order 1994 in relation to an insolvent member of the partnership, the court may make an order annulling or rescinding that insolvency order, or may make any other order that it thinks fit.

**147(4)** The court may, before making any order under this section, require the official receiver to furnish to it a report with respect to any facts or matters which are in his opinion relevant to the application.".

## SECTIONS 168, 303 AND 314(7): SUPPLEMENTARY POWERS OF RESPONSIBLE INSOLVENCY PRACTITIONER

**20** Sections 168(1) to (3) and (5), 303 and 314(7) are modified so as to read as follows:–

"**168(1)** This section applies where the court has made insolvency orders in respect of an insolvent partnership and one or more of its insolvent members by virtue of article 8 of the Insolvent Partnerships Order 1994.

**168(2)** The responsible insolvency practitioner of the partnership and of such member or members may at any time summon either separate or combined general meetings of–

(a) the creditors or contributories of the partnership, and

(b) the creditors or contributories of the member or members, for the purpose of ascertaining their wishes.

**168(3)** It is the duty of the responsible insolvency practitioner–

(a) to summon separate meetings at such times as the creditors of the partnership or of the member (as the case may be), or the contributories of any corporate member, by resolution (either at the meeting appointing the responsible insolvency practitioner or otherwise) may direct, or whenever requested in writing to do so by one-tenth in value of such creditors or contributories (as the case may be); and

(b) to summon combined meetings at such times as the creditors of the partnership and of the member or members by resolution (either at the meeting appointing the responsible insolvency practitioner or otherwise) may direct, or whenever requested in writing to do so by one-tenth in value of such creditors.

**168(4)** The responsible insolvency practitioner may apply to the court (in the prescribed manner) for directions in relation to any particular matter arising in the winding up of the insolvent partnership or in the winding up or bankruptcy of an insolvent member.

**168(5)** If any person is aggrieved by an act or decision of the responsible insolvency practitioner, that person may apply to the court; and the court may confirm, reverse or modify the act or decision complained of, and make such order in the case as it thinks just.".

## SECTIONS 172 AND 298: REMOVAL ETC. OF RESPONSIBLE INSOLVENCY PRACTITIONER OR OF PROVISIONAL LIQUIDATOR

**21** Sections 172 and 298 are modified so as to read as follows:–

"**172(1)** This section applies with respect to the removal from office and vacation of office of–

(a) the responsible insolvency practitioner of an insolvent partnership which is being wound up by virtue of article 8 of the Insolvent Partnerships Order 1994 and of its insolvent member or members against whom insolvency orders have been made, or

(b) a provisional liquidator of an insolvent partnership, and of any corporate member of that partnership, against which a winding-up petition is presented by virtue of that article,

and, subject to subsections (6) and (7) below, any removal from or vacation of office under this section relates to all offices held in the proceedings relating to the partnership.

**172(2)** Subject as follows, the responsible insolvency practitioner or provisional liquidator may be removed from office only by an order of the court.

**172(3)** If appointed by the Secretary of State, the responsible insolvency practitioner may be removed from office by a direction of the Secretary of State.

**172(4)** A responsible insolvency practitioner or provisional liquidator, not being the official receiver, shall vacate office if he ceases to be a person who is qualified to act as an insolvency practitioner in relation to the insolvent partnership or any insolvent member of it against whom an insolvency order has been made.

**172(5)** The responsible insolvency practitioner may, with the leave of the court (or, if appointed by the Secretary of State, with the leave of the court or the Secretary of State), resign his office by giving notice of his resignation to the court.

**172(6)** Where a final meeting has been held under section 146 (final meeting of creditors of insolvent partnership or of insolvent members), the responsible insolvency practitioner whose report was considered at the meeting shall vacate office as liquidator of the insolvent partnership or of any corporate member or as trustee of the estate of any individual member (as the case may be) as soon as he has given notice to the court (and, in the case of a corporate member, to the registrar of companies) that the meeting has been held and of the decisions (if any) of the meeting.

**172(7)** The responsible insolvency practitioner shall vacate office as trustee of the estate of an individual member if the insolvency order against that member is annulled.".

## SECTIONS 174 AND 299: RELEASE OF RESPONSIBLE INSOLVENCY PRACTITIONER OR OF PROVISIONAL LIQUIDATOR

**22** Sections 174 and 299 are modified so as to read as follows:–

"**174(1)** This section applies with respect to the release of–

(a) the responsible insolvency practitioner of an insolvent partnership which is being wound up by virtue of article 8 of the Insolvent Partnerships Order 1994 and of its insolvent member or members against whom insolvency orders have been made, or

(b) a provisional liquidator of an insolvent partnership, and of any corporate member of that partnership, against which a winding-up petition is presented by virtue of that article.

**174(2)** Where the official receiver has ceased to be the responsible insolvency practitioner and a person is appointed in his stead, the official receiver has his release with effect from the following time, that is to say–

(a) in a case where that person was nominated by a combined general meeting of creditors of the partnership and of any insolvent member or members, or was appointed by the Secretary of State, the time at which the official receiver gives notice to the court that he has been replaced;

(b) in a case where that person is appointed by the court, such time as the court may determine.

**174(3)** If the official receiver while he is a responsible insolvency practitioner gives notice to the Secretary of State that the winding up of the partnership or of any corporate member or the administration of the estate of any individual member is for practical purposes complete, he has his release as liquidator or trustee (as the case may be) with effect from such time as the Secretary of State may determine.

**174(4)** A person other than the official receiver who has ceased to be a responsible insolvency practitioner has his release with effect from the following time, that is to say–

(a) in the case of a person who has died, the time at which notice is given to the court in accordance with the rules that that person has ceased to hold office;

(b) in the case of a person who has been removed from office by the court or by the Secretary of State, or who has vacated office under section 172(4), such time as the Secretary of State may, on an application by that person, determine;

(c) in the case of a person who has resigned, such time as may be directed by the court (or, if he was appointed by the Secretary of State, such time as may be directed by the court or as the Secretary of State may, on an application by that person, determine);

(d) in the case of a person who has vacated office under section 172(6)–

(i) if the final meeting referred to in that subsection has resolved against that person's release, such time as the Secretary of State may, on an application by that person, determine, and

(ii) if that meeting has not so resolved, the time at which that person vacated office.

**174(5)** A person who has ceased to hold office as a provisional liquidator has his release with effect from such time as the court may, on an application by him, determine.

**174(6)** Where a bankruptcy order in respect of an individual member is annulled, the responsible insolvency practitioner at the time of the annulment has his release with effect from such time as the court may determine.

**174(7)** Where the responsible insolvency practitioner or provisional liquidator (including in both cases the official receiver when so acting) has his release under this section, he is, with effect from the time specified in the preceding provisions of this section, discharged from liability both in respect of acts or omissions of his in the winding up of the insolvent partnership or any corporate member or the administration of the estate of any individual member (as the case may be) and otherwise in relation to his conduct as responsible insolvency practitioner or provisional liquidator.

But nothing in this section prevents the exercise, in relation to a person who has had his release under this section, of the court's powers under section 212 (summary remedy against delinquent directors, liquidators, etc.) or section 304 (liability of trustee).".

## SECTIONS 175 AND 328: PRIORITY OF EXPENSES AND DEBTS

23 Sections 175 and 328(1) to (3) and (6) are modified so as to read as follows:–

"*Priority of expenses*

**175(1)** The provisions of this section shall apply in a case where article 8 of the Insolvent Partnerships Order 1994 applies, as regards priority of expenses incurred by a responsible insolvency practitioner of an insolvent partnership, and of any insolvent member of that partnership against whom an insolvency order has been made.

**175(2)** The joint estate of the partnership shall be applicable in the first instance in payment of the joint expenses and the separate estate of each insolvent member shall be applicable in the first instance in payment of the separate expenses relating to that member.

**175(3)** Where the joint estate is insufficient for the payment in full of the joint expenses, the unpaid balance shall be apportioned equally between the separate estates of the insolvent members against whom insolvency orders have been made and shall form of the expenses to be paid out of those estates.

**175(4)** Where any separate estate of an insolvent member is insufficient for the payment in full of the separate expenses to be paid out of that estate, the unpaid balance shall form part of the expenses to be paid out of the joint estate.

**175(5)** Where after the transfer of any unpaid balance in accordance with subsection (3) or (4)any estate is insufficient for the payment in full of the expenses to be paid out of that estate, the balance then remaining unpaid shall be apportioned equally between the other estates.

**175(6)** Where after an apportionment under subsection (5) one or more estates are insufficient for the payment in full of the expenses to be paid out of those estates, the total of the unpaid balances of the expenses to be paid out of those estates shall continue to be apportioned equally between the other estates until provision is made for the payment in full of the expenses or there is no estate available for the payment of the balance finally remaining unpaid, in which case it abates in equal proportions between all the estates.

**175(7)** Without prejudice to subsections (3) to (6) above, the responsible insolvency practitioner may, with the sanction of any creditors' committee established under section 141 or with the leave of the court obtained on application–

(a) pay out of the joint estate as part of the expenses to be paid out of that estate any expenses incurred for any separate estate of an insolvent member; or

(b) pay out of any separate estate of an insolvent member any part of the expenses incurred for the joint estate which affects that separate estate.

*Priority of debts in joint estate*

**175A(1)** The provisions of this section and the next (which are subject to the provisions section 9 of the Partnership Act 1890 as respects the liability of the estate of a deceased member) shall apply as regards priority of debts in a case where article 8 of the Insolvent Partnerships Order 1994 applies.

**175A(2)** After payment of expenses in accordance with section 175 and subject to section 175C(2), the joint debts of the partnership shall be paid out of its joint estate in the following order of priority–

(a) the preferential debts;

(b) the debts which are neither preferential debts nor postponed debts;

(c) interest under section 189 on the joint debts (other than postponed debts);

(d) the postponed debts;

(e) interest under section 189 on the postponed debts.

**175A(3)** The responsible insolvency practitioner shall adjust the rights among themselves of the members of the partnership as contributories and shall distribute any surplus to the members or, where applicable, to the separate estates of the members, according to their respective rights and interests in it.

**175A(4)** The debts referred to in each of paragraphs (a) and (b) of subsection (2) rank equally between themselves, and in each case if the joint estate is insufficient for meeting them, they abate in equal proportions between themselves.

**175A(5)** Where the joint estate is not sufficient for the payment of the joint debts in accordance with paragraphs (a) and (b) of subsection (2), the responsible insolvency practitioner shall aggregate the value of those debts to the extent that they have not been satisfied or are not capable of being satisfied, and that aggregate amount shall be a claim against the separate estate of each member of the partnership against whom an insolvency order has been made which–

(a) shall be a debt provable by the responsible insolvency practitioner in each such estate, and

(b) shall rank equally with the debts of the member referred to in section 175B(1)(b) below.

**175A(6)** Where the joint estate is sufficient for the payment of the joint debts in accordance with paragraphs (a) and (b) of subsection (2) but not for the payment of interest under paragraph (c) of that subsection, the responsible insolvency practitioner shall aggregate the value of that interest to the extent that it has not been satisfied or is not capable of being satisfied, and that aggregate amount shall be a claim against the separate estate of each member of the partnership against whom an insolvency order has been made which–

(a) shall be a debt provable by the responsible insolvency practitioner in each such estate, and

(b) shall rank equally with the interest on the separate debts referred to in section 175B(1)(c) below.

**175A(7)** Where the joint estate is not sufficient for the payment of the postponed joint debts in accordance with paragraph (d) of subsection (2), the responsible insolvency practitioner shall aggregate the value of those debts to the extent that they have not been satisfied or are not capable being satisfied, and that aggregate amount shall be a claim against the separate estate of each member of the partnership against whom an insolvency order has been made which–

(a) shall be a debt provable by the responsible insolvency practitioner in each such estate, and

(b) shall rank equally with the postponed debts of the member referred to in section 175B(1)(d) below.

**175A(8)** Where the joint estate is sufficient for the payment of the postponed joint debts in accordance with paragraph (d) of subsection (2) but not for the payment of interest under paragraph (e) of that subsection, the responsible insolvency practitioner shall aggregate the value of that interest to the extent that it has not been satisfied or is not capable of being satisfied, and that aggregate amount shall be a claim against the separate estate of each member of the partnership against whom an insolvency order has been made which–

(a) shall be a debt provable by the responsible insolvency practitioner in each such estate, and

(b) shall rank equally with the interest on the postponed debts referred to in section 175B(1)(e) below.

**175A(9)** Where the responsible insolvency practitioner receives any distribution from the separate estate of a member in respect of a debt referred to in paragraph (a) of subsection (5), (6), (7) or (8) above, that distribution shall become part of the joint estate and shall be distributed in accordance with the order of priority set out in subsection (2) above.

*Priority of debts in separate estate*

**175B(1)** The separate estate of each member of the partnership against whom an insolvency order has been made shall be applicable, after payment of expenses in accordance with section 175 and subject to section 175C(2) below, in payment of the separate debts of that member in the following order of priority–

(a) the preferential debts;

(b) the debts which are neither preferential debts nor postponed debts (including any debt referred to in section 175A(5)(a));

(c) interest under section 189 on the separate debts and under section 175A(6);

(d) the postponed debts of the member (including any debt referred to in section 175A(7)(a));

(e) interest under section 189 on the postponed debts of the member and under section 175A(8).

**175B(2)** The debts referred to in each of paragraphs (a) and (b) of subsection (1) rank equally between themselves, and in each case if the separate estate is insufficient for meeting them, they abate in equal proportions between themselves.

**175B(3)** Where the responsible insolvency practitioner receives any distribution from the joint estate or from the separate estate of another member of the partnership against whom an insolvency order has been made, that distribution shall become part of the separate estate and shall be distributed in accordance with the order of priority set out in subsection (1) of this section.

*Provisions generally applicable in distribution of joint and separate estates*

**175C(1)** Distinct accounts shall be kept of the joint estate of the partnership and of the separate estate of each member of that partnership against whom an insolvency order is made.

**175C(2)** No member of the partnership shall prove for a joint or separate debt in competition with the joint creditors, unless the debt has arisen–


bbcl randr4 Mp 4269—bcl98 220b

(a) as a result of fraud, or
(b) in the ordinary course of a business carried on separately from the partnership business.

**175C(3)** For the purpose of establishing the value of any debt referred to in section 175A(5)(a) or (7)(a), that value may be estimated by the responsible insolvency practitioner in accordance with section 322 or (as the case may be) in accordance with the rules.

**175C(4)** Interest under section 189 on preferential debts ranks equally with interest on debts which are neither preferential debts nor postponed debts.

**175C(5)** Sections 175A and 175B are without prejudice to any provision of this Act or of another enactment concerning the ranking between themselves of postponed debts and interest thereon, but in the absence of any such provision postponed debts and interest there on rank equally between themselves.

**175C(6)** If any two or more members of an insolvent partnership constitute a separate partnership, the creditors of such separate partnership shall be deemed to be a separate set of creditors and subject to the same statutory provisions as the separate creditors of any member of the insolvent partnership.

**175C(7)** Where any surplus remains after the administration of the estate of a separate partnership, the surplus shall be distributed to the members or, where applicable, to the separate estates of the members of that partnership according to their respective rights and interests in it.

**175C(8)** Neither the official receiver, the Secretary of State nor a responsible insolvency practitioner shall be entitled to remuneration or fees under the Insolvency Rules 1986, the Insolvency Regulations 1986 or the Insolvency Fees Order 1986 for his services in connection with–

(a) the transfer of a surplus from the joint estate to a separate estate under section 175A(3),
(b) a distribution from a separate estate to the joint estate in respect of a claim referred to in section 175A(5), (6), (7) or (8), or
(c) a distribution from the estate of a separate partnership to the separate estates of the members of that partnership under subsection (7) above.".

## SECTIONS 189 AND 328: INTEREST ON DEBTS

**24** Sections 189 and 328(4) and (5) are modified so as to read as follows:–

"**189(1)** In the winding up of an insolvent partnership or the winding up or bankruptcy (as the case may be) of any of its insolvent members interest is payable in accordance with this section, in the order of priority laid down by sections 175A and 175B, on any debt proved in the winding up or bankruptcy, including so much of any such debt as represents interest on the remainder.

**189(2)** Interest under this section is payable on the debts in question in respect of the periods during which they have been outstanding since the winding-up order was made against the partnership or any corporate member (as the case may be) or the bankruptcy order was made against any individual member.

**189(3)** The rate of interest payable under this section in respect of any debt ("the official rate" for the purposes of any provision of this Act in which that expression is used) is whichever the greater of–

(a) the rate specified in section 17 of the Judgments Act 1838 on the day on which the winding-up or bankruptcy order (as the case may be) was made, and
(b) the rate applicable to that debt apart from the winding up or bankruptcy.".

## SECTIONS 211 AND 356: FALSE REPRESENTATIONS TO CREDITORS

**25** Sections 211 and 356(2)(d) are modified so as to read as follows:–

"**211(1)** This section applies where insolvency orders are made against an insolvent partnership and any insolvent member or members of it by virtue of article 8 of the Insolvent Partnerships Order 1994.

**211(2)** Any person, being a past or present officer of the partnership or a past or present officer (which for these purposes includes a shadow director) of a corporate member against which an insolvency order has been made–

(a) commits an offence if he makes any false representation or commits any other fraud for the purpose of obtaining the consent of the creditors of the partnership (or any of them) or of the creditors of any of its members (or any of such creditors) to an agreement with reference to the affairs of the partnership or of any of its members or to the winding up of the partnership or of a corporate member, or the bankruptcy of an individual member, and

(b) is deemed to have committed that offence if, prior to the winding up or bankruptcy (as the case may be), he has made any false representation, or committed any other fraud, for that purpose.

**211(3)** A person guilty of an offence under this section is liable to imprisonment or a fine, or both.".

## SECTIONS 230, 231 AND 292: APPOINTMENT TO OFFICE OF RESPONSIBLE INSOLVENCY PRACTITIONER OR PROVISIONAL LIQUIDATOR

**26** Sections 230, 231 and 292 are modified so as to read as follows:–

"**230(1)** This section applies with respect to the appointment of–

(a) the responsible insolvency practitioner of an insolvent partnership which is being wound up by virtue of article 8 of the Insolvent Partnerships Order 1994 and of one or more of its insolvent members, or

(b) a provisional liquidator of an insolvent partnership, or of any of its corporate members, against which a winding-up petition is presented by virtue of that article,

but is without prejudice to any enactment under which the official receiver is to be, or maybe, responsible insolvency practitioner or provisional liquidator.

**230(2)** No person may be appointed as responsible insolvency practitioner unless he is, at the time of the appointment, qualified to act as an insolvency practitioner both in relation to the insolvent partnership and to the insolvent member or members.

**230(3)** No person may be appointed as provisional liquidator unless he is, at the time of the appointment, qualified to act as an insolvency practitioner both in relation to the insolvent partnership and to any corporate member in respect of which he is appointed.

**230(4)** If the appointment or nomination of any person to the office of responsible insolvency practitioner or provisional liquidator relates to more than one person, or has the effect that the office is to be held by more than one person, then subsection (5) below applies.

**230(5)** The appointment or nomination shall declare whether any act required or authorised under any enactment to be done by the responsible insolvency practitioner or by the provisional liquidator is to be done by all or any one or more of the persons for the time being holding the office in question.

**230(6)** The appointment of any person as responsible insolvency practitioner takes effect only if that person accepts the appointment in accordance with the rules. Subject to this, the appointment of any person as responsible insolvency practitioner takes effect at the time specified in his certificate of appointment.

*Conflicts of interest*

**230A(1)** If the responsible insolvency practitioner of an insolvent partnership being wound up by virtue of article 8 of the Insolvent Partnerships Order 1994 and of one or more of its insolvent members is of the opinion at any time that there is a conflict of interest between his functions as liquidator of the partnership and his functions as responsible insolvency practitioner of any insolvent member, or between his functions as responsible insolvency practitioner of two or more insolvent members, he may apply to the court for directions.

**230A(2)** On an application under subsection (1), the court may, without prejudice to the generality of its power to give directions, appoint one or more insolvency practitioners either in place of the applicant to act as responsible insolvency practitioner of both the partnership and its insolvent member or members or to act as joint responsible insolvency practitioner with the applicant.".

## SECTION 234: GETTING IN THE PARTNERSHIP PROPERTY

**27** Section 234 is modified, so far as insolvent partnerships are concerned, so as to read as follows:–

"**234(1)** This section applies where–

(a) insolvency orders are made by virtue of article 8 of the Insolvent Partnerships Order 1994 in respect of an insolvent partnership and its insolvent member or members, or

(b) a provisional liquidator of an insolvent partnership and any of its corporate members is appointed by virtue of that article;

and "the office-holder" means the liquidator or the provisional liquidator, as the case may be.

**234(2)** Any person who is or has been an officer of the partnership, or who is an executor or administrator of the estate of a deceased officer of the partnership, shall deliver up to the office-holder, for the purposes of the exercise of the office-holder's functions under this Act and (where applicable) the Company Directors Disqualification Act 1986, possession of any partnership property which he holds for the purposes of the partnership.

**234(3)** Where any person has in his possession or control any property, books, papers or records to which the partnership appears to be entitled, the court may require that person forthwith (or within such period as the court may direct) to pay, deliver, convey, surrender or transfer the property, books, papers or records to the office-holder or as the court may direct.

**234(4)** Where the office-holder–

(a) seizes or disposes of any property which is not partnership property, and

(b) at the time of seizure or disposal believes, and has reasonable grounds for believing,that he is entitled (whether in pursuance of an order of the court or otherwise) to seize or dispose of that property,

the next subsection has effect.

**234(5)** In that case the office-holder–

(a) is not liable to any person in respect of any loss or damage resulting from the seizure or disposal except in so far as that loss or damage is caused by the office-holder's own negligence, and

(b) has a lien on the property, or the proceeds of its sale, for such expenses as were incurred in connection with the seizure or disposal.".

## SECTION 283: DEFINITION OF INDIVIDUAL MEMBER'S ESTATE

**28** Section 283 is modified so as to read as follows:–

"**283(1)** Subject as follows, the estate of an individual member for the purposes of this Act comprises–

(a) all property belonging to or vested in the individual member at the commencement of the bankruptcy, and

(b) any property which by virtue of any of the provisions of this Act is comprised in that estate or is treated as falling within the preceding paragraph.

**283(2)** Subsection (1) does not apply to–

(a) such tools, books, vehicles and other items of equipment as are not partnership property and as are necessary to the individual member for use personally by him in his employment, business or vocation;

(b) such clothing, bedding, furniture, household equipment and provisions as are not partnership property and as are necessary for satisfying the basic domestic needs of the individual member and his family.

This subsection is subject to section 308 in Chapter IV (certain excluded property reclaimable by trustee).

**283(3)** Subsection (1) does not apply to–

(a) property held by the individual member on trust for any other person, or

(b) the right of nomination to a vacant ecclesiastical benefice.

**283(4)** References in any provision of this Act to property, in relation to an individual member, include references to any power exercisable by him over or in respect of property except in so far as the power is exercisable over or in respect of property not for the time being comprised in the estate of the individual member and–

(a) is so exercisable at a time after either the official receiver has had his release in respect of that estate under section 174(3) or a meeting summoned by the trustee of that estate under section 146 has been held, or

(b) cannot be so exercised for the benefit of the individual member;

and a power exercisable over or in respect of property is deemed for the purposes of any provision of this Act to vest in the person entitled to exercise it at the time of the transaction or event by virtue of which it is exercisable by that person (whether or not it becomes so exercisable at that time).

**283(5)** For the purposes of any such provision of this Act, property comprised in an individual member's estate is so comprised subject to the rights of any person other than the individual member (whether as a secured creditor of the individual member or otherwise) in relation thereto, but disregarding any rights which have been given up in accordance with the rules.

**283(6)** This section has effect subject to the provisions of any enactment not contained in this Act under which any property is to be excluded from a bankrupt's estate.".

## SECTION 284: INDIVIDUAL MEMBER: RESTRICTIONS ON DISPOSITIONS OF PROPERTY

**29** Section 284 is modified so as to read as follows:–

"**284(1)** Where an individual member is adjudged bankrupt by virtue of article 8 of the Insolvent Partnerships Order 1994, any disposition of property made by that member in the period to which this section applies is void except to the extent that it is or was made with the consent of the court, or is or was subsequently ratified by the court.

**284(2)** Subsection (1) applies to a payment (whether in cash or otherwise) as it applies to a disposition of property and, accordingly, where any payment is void by virtue of that subsection, the person paid shall hold the sum paid for the individual member as part of his estate.

**284(3)** This section applies to the period beginning with the day of the presentation of the petition for the bankruptcy order and ending with the vesting, under Chapter IV of this Part, of the individual member's estate in a trustee.

**284(4)** The preceding provisions of this section do not give a remedy against any person–

(a) in respect of any property or payment which he received before the commencement of the bankruptcy in good faith, for value and without notice that the petition had been presented, or

(b) in respect of any interest in property which derives from an interest in respect of which there is, by virtue of this subsection, no remedy.

**284(5)** Where after the commencement of his bankruptcy the individual member has incurred a debt to a banker or other person by reason of the making of a payment which is void under this section, that debt is deemed for the purposes of any provision of this Act to have been incurred before the commencement of the bankruptcy unless–

(a) that banker or person had notice of the bankruptcy before the debt was incurred, or

(b) it is not reasonably practicable for the amount of the payment to be recovered from the person to whom it was made.

**284(6)** A disposition of property is void under this section notwithstanding that the property is not or, as the case may be, would not be comprised in the individual member's estate; but nothing in this section affects any disposition made by a person of property held by him on trust for any other person other than a disposition made by an individual member of property held by him on trust for the partnership.".

**30** Schedule 4 is modified so as to read as follows:–

# "Schedule 4 – Powers of Liquidator in a Winding up

## PART I – POWERS EXERCISABLE WITH SANCTION

**1** Power to pay any class of creditors in full.

**2** Power to make any compromise or arrangement with creditors or persons claiming to be creditors, or having or alleging themselves to have any claim (present or future, certain or contingent, ascertained or sounding only in damages) against the partnership, or whereby the partnership may be rendered liable.

**3** Power to compromise, on such terms as may be agreed–

(a) all debts and liabilities capable of resulting in debts, and all claims (present or future, certain or contingent, ascertained or sounding only in damages) subsisting or supposed to subsist between the partnership and a contributory or alleged contributory or other debtor or person apprehending liability to the partnership, and

(b) all questions in any way relating to or affecting the partnership property or the winding up of the partnership,

and take any security for the discharge of any such debt, liability or claim and give a complete discharge in respect of it.

**4** Power to bring or defend any action or other legal proceeding in the name and on behalf of any member of the partnership in his capacity as such or of the partnership.

**5** Power to carry on the business of the partnership so far as may be necessary for its beneficial winding up.

## PART II – POWERS EXERCISABLE WITHOUT SANCTION

**6** Power to sell any of the partnership property by public auction or private contract, with power to transfer the whole of it to any person or to sell the same in parcels.

**7** Power to do all acts and execute, in the name and on behalf of the partnership or of any member of the partnership in his capacity as such, all deeds, receipts and other documents.

**8** Power to prove, rank and claim in the bankruptcy, insolvency or sequestration of any contributory for any balance against his estate, and to receive dividends in the bankruptcy, insolvency or sequestration in respect of that balance, as a separate debt due from the bankrupt or insolvent, and rateably with the other separate creditors.

**9** Power to draw, accept, make and endorse any bill of exchange or promissory note in the name and on behalf of any member of the partnership in his capacity as such or of the partnership, with the same effect with respect to the liability of the partnership or of any member of the partnership in his capacity as such as if the bill or note had been drawn, accepted, made or endorsed in the course of the partnership's business.

**10** Power to raise on the security of the partnership property any money requisite.

**11** Power to take out in his official name letters of administration to any deceased contributory, and to do in his official name any other act necessary for obtaining payment of any money due from a contributory or his estate which cannot conveniently be done in the name of the partnership.

In all such cases the money due is deemed, for the purpose of enabling the liquidator to take out the letters of administration or recover the money, to be due to the liquidator himself.

**12** Power to appoint an agent to do any business which the liquidator is unable to do himself.

**13** Power to do all such other things as may be necessary for winding up the partnership's affairs and distributing its property.".

# Schedule 5 – Provisions of the Act which apply with Modifications for the Purposes of Article 9 to Winding Up of Insolvent Partnership on Member's Petition where No Concurrent Petition Presented against Member

Article 9

## SECTION 117: HIGH COURT AND COUNTY COURT JURISDICTION

**1** Section 117 is modified so as to read as follows:–

"**117(1)** Subject to subsections (3) and (4) below, the High Court has jurisdiction to wind up any insolvent partnership as an unregistered company by virtue of article 9 of the Insolvent Partnerships Order 1994 if the partnership has, or at any time had, a principal place of business in England and Wales.

**117(2)** Subject to subsections (3) and (4) below, a petition for the winding up of an insolvent partnership by virtue of the said article 9 may be presented to a county court in England and Wales if the partnership has, or at any time had, a principal place of business within the insolvency district of that court.

**117(3)** Subject to subsection (4) below, the court only has jurisdiction to wind up an insolvent partnership if the business of the partnership has been carried on in England and Wales at any time in the period of 3 years ending with the day on which the petition for winding it up is presented.

**117(4)** If an insolvent partnership has a principal place of business situated in Scotland or in Northern Ireland, the court shall not have jurisdiction to wind up the partnership unless it had a principal place of business in England and Wales–

(a) in the case of a partnership with a principal place of business in Scotland, at any time in the period of 1 year, or

(b) in the case of a partnership with a principal place of business in Northern Ireland, at any time in the period of 3 years,

ending with the day on which the petition for winding it up is presented.

**117(5)** The Lord Chancellor may by order in a statutory instrument exclude a county court from having winding-up jurisdiction, and for the purposes of that jurisdiction may attach its district, or any part thereof, to any other county court, and may by statutory instrument revoke or vary any such order.

In exercising the powers of this section, the Lord Chancellor shall provide that a county court is not to have winding-up jurisdiction unless it has for the time being jurisdiction for the purposes of Parts VIII to XI of this Act (individual insolvency).

**117(6)** Every court in England and Wales having winding-up jurisdiction has for the purposes of that jurisdiction all the powers of the High Court; and every prescribed officer of the court shall perform any duties which an officer of the High Court may discharge by order of a judge of that court or otherwise in relation to winding up.".

## SECTION 221: WINDING UP OF UNREGISTERED COMPANIES

2 Section 221 is modified so as to read as follows:–

"**221(1)** Subject to subsections (2) and (3) below and to the provisions of this Part, any insolvent partnership which has, or at any time had, a principal place of business in England and Wales may be wound up under this Act.

**221(2)** Subject to subsection (3) below an insolvent partnership shall not be wound up under this Act if the business of the partnership has not been carried on in England and Wales at any time in the period of 3 years ending with the day on which the winding-up petition is presented.

**221(3)** If an insolvent partnership has a principal place of business situated in Scotland or in Northern Ireland, the court shall not have jurisdiction to wind up the partnership unless it had a principal place of business in England and Wales–

(a) in the case of a partnership with a principal place of business in Scotland, at any time in the period of 1 year, or

(b) in the case of a partnership with a principal place of business in Northern Ireland, at any time in the period of 3 years,

ending with the day on which the winding-up petition is presented.

**221(4)** No insolvent partnership shall be wound up under this Act voluntarily.

**221(5)** To the extent that they are applicable to the winding up of a company by the court in England and Wales on a member's petition or on a petition by the company, all the provisions of this Act and the Companies Act about winding up apply to the winding up of an insolvent partnership as an unregistered company–

(a) with the exceptions and additions mentioned in the following subsections of this section and in section 221A, and

(b) with the modifications specified in Part II of Schedule 3 to the Insolvent Partnerships Order 1994.

**221(6)** Sections 73(1), 74(2)(a) to (d) and (3), 75 to 78, 83, 122, 123, 124(2) and (3), 202, 203, 205 and 250 shall not apply.

**221(7)** The circumstances in which an insolvent partnership may be wound up as an unregistered company are as follows–

(a) if the partnership is dissolved, or has ceased to carry on business, or is carrying on business only for the purpose of winding up its affairs;

(b) if the partnership is unable to pay its debts;

(c) if the court is of the opinion that it is just and equitable that the partnership should be wound up.

**221(8)** Every petition for the winding up of an insolvent partnership under Part V of this Act shall be verified by affidavit in Form 2 in Schedule 9 to the Insolvent Partnerships Order 1994.

*Who may present petition*

**221A(1)** A petition for winding up an insolvent partnership may be presented by any member of the partnership if the partnership consists of not less than 8 members.

**221A(2)** A petition for winding up an insolvent partnership may also be presented by any member of it with the leave of the court (obtained on his application) if the court is satisfied that–

(a) the member has served on the partnership, by leaving at a principal place of business of the partnership in England and Wales, or by delivering to an officer of the partnership, or by otherwise serving in such manner as the court may approve or direct, a written demand in Form 10 in Schedule 9 to the Insolvent Partnerships Order 1994 in respect of a joint debt or debts exceeding £750 then due from the partnership but paid by the member, other than out of partnership property;

(b) the partnership has for 3 weeks after the service of the demand neglected to pay the sum or to secure or compound for it to the member's satisfaction; and

(c) the member has obtained a judgment, decree or order of any court against the partnership for reimbursement to him of the amount of the joint debt or debts so paid and all reasonable steps (other than insolvency proceedings) have been taken by the member to enforce that judgment, decree or order.

**221A(3)** Subsection (2)(a) above is deemed included in the list of provisions specified in subsection (1) of section 416 of this Act for the purposes of the Secretary of State's order-making power under that section.".

# Schedule 6 – Provisions of the Act which apply with Modifications for the Purposes of Article 10 to Winding up of Insolvent Partnership on Member's Petition Where Concurrent Petitions are Presented against all the Members

Article 10

## SECTIONS 117 AND 265: HIGH COURT AND COUNTY COURT JURISDICTION

**1** Sections 117 and 265 are modified so as to read as follows:–

"**117(1)** Subject to the provisions of this section, the High Court has jurisdiction to wind up any insolvent partnership as an unregistered company by virtue of article 10 of the Insolvent Partnerships Order 1994 if the partnership has, or at any time had, a principal place of business in England and Wales.

**117(2)** Subject to the provisions of this section, a petition for the winding up of an insolvent partnership by virtue of the said article 10 may be presented to a county court in England and Wales if the partnership has, or at any time had, a principal place of business within the insolvency district of that court.

**117(3)** Subject to subsection (4) below, the court only has jurisdiction to wind up an insolvent partnership if the business of the partnership has been carried on in England and Wales at any time in the period of 3 years ending with the day on which the petition for winding it up is presented.

**117(4)** If an insolvent partnership has a principal place of business situated in Scotland or in Northern Ireland, the court shall not have jurisdiction to wind up the partnership unless it had a principal place of business in England and Wales–

(a) in the case of a partnership with a principal place of business in Scotland, at any time in the period of 1 year, or

(b) in the case of a partnership with a principal place of business in Northern Ireland, at any time in the period of 3 years,

ending with the day on which the petition for winding it up is presented.

**117(5)** Subject to subsection (6) below, the court has jurisdiction to wind up a corporate member, or make a bankruptcy order against an individual member, of a partnership against which a petition has been presented by virtue of article 10 of the Insolvent Partnerships Order 1994 if it has jurisdiction in respect of the partnership.

**117(6)** Petitions by virtue of the said article 10 for the winding up of an insolvent partnership and the bankruptcy of one or more members of that partnership may not be presented to a district registry of the High Court.

**117(7)** The Lord Chancellor may by order in a statutory instrument exclude a county court from having winding-up jurisdiction, and for the purposes of that jurisdiction may attach its district, or any thereof, to any other county court, and may by statutory instrument revoke or vary any such order.

In exercising the powers of this section, the Lord Chancellor shall provide that a county court is not to have winding-up jurisdiction unless it has for the time being jurisdiction for the purposes of Parts VIII to XI of this Act (individual insolvency).

**117(8)** Every court in England and Wales having winding-up jurisdiction has for the purposes of that jurisdiction all the powers of the High Court; and every prescribed officer of the court shall perform any duties which an officer of the High Court may discharge by order of a judge of that court or otherwise in relation to winding up.".

## SECTIONS 124, 264 AND 272: APPLICATIONS TO WIND UP INSOLVENT PARTNERSHIP AND TO WIND UP OR BANKRUPT INSOLVENT MEMBERS

**2** Sections 124, 264 and 272 are modified so as to read as follows:–

"**124(1)** An application to the court by a member of an insolvent partnership by virtue of article 10 of the Insolvent Partnerships Order 1994 for the winding up of the partnership as an unregistered company and the winding up or bankruptcy (as the case may be) of all its members shall–

(a) in the case of the partnership, be by petition in Form 11 in Schedule 9 to that Order,
(b) in the case of a corporate member, be by petition in Form 12 in that Schedule, and
(c) in the case of an individual member, be by petition in Form 13 in that Schedule.

**124(2)** Subject to subsection (3) below, a petition under subsection (1)(a) may only be presented by a member of the partnership on the grounds that the partnership is unable to pay its debts and if–

(a) petitions are at the same time presented by that member for insolvency orders against every member of the partnership (including himself or itself); and
(b) each member is willing for an insolvency order to be made against him or it and the petition against him or it contains a statement to this effect.

**124(3)** If the court is satisfied, on application by any member of an insolvent partnership, that presentation of petitions under subsection (1) against the partnership and every member of it would be impracticable, the court may direct that petitions be presented against the partnership and such member or members of it as are specified by the court.

**124(4)** The petitions mentioned in subsection (1)–

(a) shall all be presented to the same court and, except as the court otherwise permits or directs, on the same day, and
(b) except in the case of the petition mentioned in subsection (1)(c) shall be advertised in Form 8 in the said Schedule 9.

**124(5)** Each petition presented under this section shall contain particulars of the other petitions being presented in relation to the partnership, identifying the partnership and members concerned.

**124(6)** The hearing of the petition against the partnership fixed by the court shall be in advance of the hearing of the petitions against the insolvent members.

**124(7)** On the day appointed for the hearing of the petition against the partnership, the petitioner shall, before the commencement of the hearing, hand to the court Form 9 in Schedule 9 to the Insolvent Partnerships Order 1994, duly completed.

**124(8)** Any person against whom a winding-up or bankruptcy petition has been presented in relation to the insolvent partnership is entitled to appear and to be heard on any petition for the winding up of the partnership.

**124(9)** A petitioner under this section may at the hearing withdraw the petition if–

(a) subject to subsection (10) below, he withdraws at the same time every other petition which he has presented under this section; and

(b) he gives notice to the court at least 3 days before the date appointed for the hearing of the relevant petition of his intention to withdraw the petition.

**124(10)** A petitioner need not comply with the provisions of subsection (9)(a) in the case of a petition against a member, if the court is satisfied on application made to it by the petitioner that, because of difficulties in serving the petition or for any other reason, the continuance of that petition would be likely to prejudice or delay the proceedings on the petition which he has presented against the partnership or on any petition which he has presented against another insolvent member.".

## SECTIONS 125 AND 271: POWERS OF COURT ON HEARING OF PETITIONS AGAINST INSOLVENT PARTNERSHIP AND MEMBERS

**3** Sections 125 and 271 are modified so as to read as follows:–

"**125(1)** Subject to the provisions of section 125A, on hearing a petition under section 124 against an insolvent partnership or any of its insolvent members, the court may dismiss it, or adjourn the hearing conditionally or unconditionally or make any other order that it thinks fit; but the court shall not refuse to make a winding-up order against the partnership or a corporate member on the ground only that the partnership property or (as the case may be) the member's assets have been mortgaged to an amount equal to or in excess of that property or those assets, or that the partnership has no property or the member no assets.

**125(2)** An order under subsection (1) in respect of an insolvent partnership may contain directions as to the future conduct of any insolvency proceedings in existence against any insolvent member in respect of whom an insolvency order has been made.

*Hearing of petitions against members*

**125A(1)** On the hearing of a petition against an insolvent member the petitioner shall draw the court's attention to the result of the hearing of the winding-up petition against the partnership and the following subsections of this section shall apply.

**125A(2)** If the court has neither made a winding-up order, nor dismissed the winding-up petition, against the partnership the court may adjourn the hearing of the petition against the member until either event has occurred.

**125A(3)** Subject to subsection (4) below, if a winding-up order has been made against the partnership, the court may make a winding-up order against the corporate member in respect of which, or (as the case may be) a bankruptcy order against the individual member in respect of whom, the insolvency petition was presented.

**125A(4)** If no insolvency order is made under subsection (3) against any member within 28 days of the making of the winding-up order against the partnership, the proceedings against the partnership shall be conducted as if the winding-up petition against the partnership had been presented by virtue of article 7 of the Insolvent Partnerships Order 1994, and the proceedings against any member shall be conducted under this Act without the modifications made by that Order (other than the modifications made to sections 168 and 303 by article 14).

**125A(5)** If the court has dismissed the winding-up petition against the partnership, the court may dismiss the winding-up petition against the corporate member or (as the case may be) the bankruptcy petition against the individual member. However, if an insolvency order is made against a member, the proceedings against that member shall be conducted under this Act without the modifications made by the Insolvent Partnerships Order 1994 (other than the modifications made to sections 168 and 303 of this Act by article 14 of that Order).

**125A(6)** The court may dismiss a petition against an insolvent member if it considers it just to do so because of a change in circumstances since the making of the winding-up order against the partnership.

**125A(7)** The court may dismiss a petition against an insolvent member who is a limited partner, if–

(a) the member lodges in court for the benefit of the creditors of the partnership sufficient money or security to the court's satisfaction to meet his liability for the debts and obligations of the partnership; or

(b) the member satisfies the court that he is no longer under any liability in respect of the debts and obligations of the partnership.."

## SECTION 221: WINDING UP OF UNREGISTERED COMPANIES

**4** Section 221 is modified so as to read as follows:–

"**221(1)** Subject to subsections (2) and (3) below and to the provisions of this Part, any insolvent partnership which has, or at any time had, a principal place of business in England and Wales may be wound up under this Act.

**221(2)** Subject to subsection (3) below, an insolvent partnership shall not be wound up under this Act if the business of the partnership has not been carried on in England and Wales at any time in the period of 3 years ending with the day on which the winding-up petition is presented.

**221(3)** If an insolvent partnership has a principal place of business situated in Scotland or in Northern Ireland, the court shall not have jurisdiction to wind up the partnership unless it had a principal place of business in England and Wales–

(a) in the case of a partnership with a principal place of business in Scotland, at any time in the period of 1 year, or

(b) in the case of a partnership with a principal place of business in Northern Ireland, at any time in the period of 3 years,

ending with the day on which the winding-up petition is presented.

**221(4)** No insolvent partnership shall be wound up under this Act voluntarily.

**221(5)** To the extent that they are applicable to the winding up of a company by the court in England and Wales on a member's petition, all the provisions of this Act and the Companies Act about winding up apply to the winding up of an insolvent partnership as an unregistered company–

(a) with the exceptions and additions mentioned in the following subsections of this section, and

(b) with the modifications specified in Part II of Schedule 4 to the Insolvent Partnerships Order 1994.

**221(6)** Sections 73(1), 74(2)(a) to (d) and (3), 75 to 78, 83, 124(2) and (3), 154, 202, 203, 205 and 250 shall not apply.

**221(7)** Unless the contrary intention appears, the members of the partnership against whom insolvency orders are made by virtue of article 10 of the Insolvent Partnerships Order 1994 shall not be treated as contributories for the purposes of this Act.

**221(8)** The circumstances in which an insolvent partnership may be wound up as an unregistered company are that the partnership is unable to pay its debts.

**221(9)** Every petition for the winding up of an insolvent partnership under Part V of this Act shall be verified by affidavit in Form 2 in Schedule 9 to the Insolvent Partnerships Order 1994.".

# Schedule 7 – Provisions of the Act which apply with Modifications for the Purposes of Article 11 where Joint Bankruptcy Petition Presented by Individual Members without Winding Up Partnership as Unregistered Company

Article 11

**1(1)** The provisions of the Act specified in sub-paragraph (2) below, are set out as modified in this Schedule.

**1(2)** The provisions referred to in sub-paragraph (1) above are sections 264 to 266, 272, 275, 283, 284, 290, 292 to 301, 305, 312, 328, 331 and 387.

## SECTION 264: PRESENTATION OF JOINT BANKRUPTCY PETITION

2 Section 264 is modified so as to read as follows:–

"**264(1)** Subject to section 266(1) below, a joint bankruptcy petition may be presented to the court by virtue of article 11 of the Insolvent Partnerships Order 1994 by all the members of an insolvent partnership in their capacity as such provided that all the members are individuals and none of them is a limited partner.

**264(2)** A petition may not be presented under paragraph (1) by the members of an insolvent partnership which is an authorised institution or former authorised institution within the meaning of the Banking Act 1987.

**264(3)** The petition–

(a) shall be in Form 14 in Schedule 9 to the Insolvent Partnerships Order 1994; and
(b) shall contain a request that the trustee shall wind up the partnership business and administer the partnership property without the partnership being wound up as an unregistered company under Part V of this Act.

**264(4)** The petition shall either–

(a) be accompanied by an affidavit in Form 15 in Schedule 9 to the Insolvent Partnerships Order 1994 made by the member who signs the petition, showing that all the members are individual members (and that none of them is a limited partner) and concur in the presentation of the petition, or
(b) contain a statement that all the members are individual members and be signed by all the members.

**264(5)** On presentation of a petition under this section, the court may make orders in Form 16 in Schedule 9 to the Insolvent Partnerships Order 1994 for the bankruptcy of the members and the winding up of the partnership business and administration of its property.".

## SECTION 265: CONDITIONS TO BE SATISFIED IN RESPECT OF MEMBERS

3 Section 265 is modified so as to read as follows:–

"**265(1)** Subject to the provisions of this section, a joint bankruptcy petition by virtue of article 11 of the Insolvent Partnerships Order 1994 may be presented–

(a) to the High Court (other than to a district registry of that Court) if the partnership has, or at any time had, a principal place of business in England and Wales, or
(b) to a county court in England and Wales if the partnership has, or at any time had, a principal place of business within the insolvency district of that court.

**265(2)** A joint bankruptcy petition shall not be presented to the court by virtue of article 11 unless the business of the partnership has been carried on in England and Wales at any time in the period of 3 years ending with the day on which the joint bankruptcy petition is presented.".

## SECTION 266: OTHER PRELIMINARY CONDITIONS

4 Section 266 is modified so as to read as follows:–

"**266(1)** If the court is satisfied, on application by any member of an insolvent partnership, that the presentation of the petition under section 264(1) by all the members of the partnership would be impracticable, the court may direct that the petition be presented by such member or members as are specified by the court.

**266(2)** A joint bankruptcy petition shall not be withdrawn without the leave of the court.

**266(3)** The court has a general power, if it appears to it appropriate to do so on the grounds that there has been a contravention of the rules or for any other reason, to dismiss a joint bankruptcy petition or to stay proceedings on such a petition; and, where it stays proceedings on a petition, it may do so on such terms and conditions as it thinks fit.".

## SECTION 272: GROUNDS OF JOINT BANKRUPTCY PETITION

5 Section 272 is modified so as to read as follows:–

"**272(1)** A joint bankruptcy petition may be presented to the court by the members of a partnership only on the grounds that the partnership is unable to pay its debts.

**272(2)** The petition shall be accompanied by–

(a) a statement of each member's affairs in Form 17 in Schedule 9 to the Insolvent Partnerships Order 1994, and

(b) a statement of the affairs of the partnership in Form 18 in that Schedule, sworn by one or more members of the partnership.

**272(3)** The statements of affairs required by subsection (2) shall contain–

(a) particulars of the member's or (as the case may be) partnership's creditors, debts and other liabilities and of their assets, and

(b) such other information as is required by the relevant form.."

## SECTION 275: SUMMARY ADMINISTRATION

6 Section 275 is modified so as to read as follows:–

"**275(1)** Where orders have been made against the members of an insolvent partnership by virtue of article 11 of the Insolvent Partnerships Order 1994, and the case is as specified in the next subsection, the court shall, if it appears to it appropriate to do so, issue a certificate for the summary administration of any member's estate.

**275(2)** That case is where it appears to the court–

(a) that the aggregate amount of the unsecured joint debts of the partnership and unsecured separate debts of the member concerned is less than the small bankruptcies level prescribed for the purposes of section 273 (as that section applies apart from the Insolvent Partnerships Order 1994), and

(b) that within the period of 5 years ending with the presentation of the joint bankruptcy petition the member concerned has neither been adjudged bankrupt nor made a composition with his creditors in satisfaction of his debts or a scheme of arrangement of his affairs.

**275(3)** The court may at any time revoke a certificate issued under this section if it appears to it that, on any grounds existing at the time the certificate was issued, the certificate ought not to have been issued.".

## SECTION 283: DEFINITION OF MEMBER'S ESTATE

7 Section 283 is modified so as to read as follows:–

"**283(1)** Subject as follows, a member's estate for the purposes of this Act comprises–

(a) all property belonging to or vested in the member at the commencement of the bankruptcy, and

(b) any property which by virtue of any of the provisions of this Act is comprised in that estate or is treated as falling within the preceding paragraph.

partnership takes effect only if that person accepts the appointment in accordance with the rules. Subject to this, the appointment of any person as trustee takes effect at the time specified in his certificate of appointment.

**292(5)** This section is without prejudice to the provisions of this Chapter under which the official receiver is, in certain circumstances, to be trustee of the members' estates and of the partnership.

*Conflicts of interest*

**292A(1)** If the trustee of the members' estates and of the partnership is of the opinion at any time that there is a conflict of interest between his functions as trustee of the members' estates and his functions as trustee of the partnership, or between his functions as trustee of the estates of two or more members, he may apply to the court for directions.

**292A(2)** On an application under subsection (1), the court may, without prejudice to the generality of its power to give directions, appoint one or more insolvency practitioners either in place of the applicant to act both as trustee of the members' estates and as trustee of the partnership,or to act as joint trustee with the applicant.".

## SECTIONS 293 AND 294: SUMMONING OF MEETING TO APPOINT TRUSTEE

**11** Sections 293 and 294 are modified so as to read as follows:–

"**293(1)** Where orders are made by virtue of article 11 of the Insolvent Partnerships Order 1994, the official receiver, by virtue of his office, becomes the trustee of the estates of the members and the trustee

of the partnership and continues in office until another person becomes trustee under the provisions of this Part.

**293(2)** The official receiver is, by virtue of his office, the trustee of the estates of the members and the trustee of the partnership during any vacancy.

**293(3)** At any time when he is trustee, the official receiver may summon a combined meeting of the creditors of the members and the creditors of the partnership, for the purpose of appointing a trustee in place of the official receiver.

**293(4)** It is the duty of the official receiver–

(a) as soon as practicable in the period of 12 weeks beginning with the day on which the first order was made by virtue of article 11 of the Insolvent Partnerships Order 1994, to decide whether to exercise his power under subsection (3) to summon a meeting, and

(b) if in pursuance of paragraph (a) he decides not to exercise that power, to give notice of his decision, before the end of that period, to the court and to those creditors of the members and those of the partnership who are known to the official receiver or identified in a statement of affairs submitted under section 272, and

(c) (whether or not he has decided to exercise that power) to exercise his power to summon a meeting under subsection (3) if he is at any time requested to do so by one-quarter, in value, of either–

(i) the creditors of any member against whom an insolvency order has been made, or

(ii) the partnership's creditors,

and accordingly, where the duty imposed by paragraph (c) arises before the official receiver has performed a duty imposed by paragraph (a) or (b), he is not required to perform the latter duty.

**293(5)** A notice given under subsection (4)(b) to the creditors shall contain an explanation of the creditors' power under subsection (4)(c) to require the official receiver to summon a combined meeting of the creditors of the partnership and of the members against whom insolvency orders have been made.

**293(6)** If the official receiver, in pursuance of subsection (4)(a), has decided to exercise his power under subsection (3) to summon a meeting, he shall hold that meeting in the period of 4 months beginning with the day on which the first order was made by virtue of article 11 of the Insolvent Partnerships Order 1994.

**293(7)** If (whether or not he has decided to exercise that power) the official receiver is requested, in accordance with the provisions of subsection (4)(c), to exercise his power under subsection (3) to summon a meeting, he shall hold that meeting in accordance with the rules.

**293(8)** Where a meeting of creditors of the partnership and of the members has been held, and an insolvency order is subsequently made against a further insolvent member by virtue of article 11 of the Insolvent Partnerships Order 1994–

(a) any person chosen at the meeting to be responsible insolvency practitioner in place of the official receiver shall also be the responsible insolvency practitioner of the member against whom the subsequent order is made, and

(b) subsection (4) of this section shall not apply..”

## SECTION 295: FAILURE OF MEETING TO APPOINT TRUSTEE

**12** Section 295 is modified so as to read as follows:–

“**295(1)** If a meeting of creditors summoned under section 293 is held but no appointment of a person as trustee is made, it is the duty of the official receiver to decide whether to refer the need for an appointment to the Secretary of State.

**295(2)** On a reference made in pursuance of that decision, the Secretary of State shall either make an appointment or decline to make one.

**295(3)** If–

(a) the official receiver decides not to refer the need for an appointment to the Secretary of State, or

(b) on such a reference the Secretary of State declines to make an appointment, the official receiver shall give notice of his decision or, as the case may be, of the Secretary of State’s decision to the court.”.

## SECTION 296: APPOINTMENT OF TRUSTEE BY SECRETARY OF STATE

**13** Section 296 is modified so as to read as follows:–

“**296(1)** At any time when the official receiver is the trustee of the members’ estates and of the partnership by virtue of any provision of this Chapter he may apply to the Secretary of State for the appointment of a person as trustee instead of the official receiver.

**296(2)** On an application under subsection (1) the Secretary of State shall either make an appointment or decline to make one.

**296(3)** Such an application may be made notwithstanding that the Secretary of State has declined to make an appointment either on a previous application under subsection (1) or on a reference under section 295 or under section 300(2) below.

**296(4)** Where a trustee has been appointed by the Secretary of State under subsection (2) of this section, and an insolvency order is subsequently made against a further insolvent member by virtue of article 11 of the Insolvent Partnerships Order 1994, then the trustee so appointed shall also be the trustee of the member against whom the subsequent order is made.

**296(5)** Where the trustee of the members’ estates and of the partnership has been appointed by the Secretary of State (whether under this section or otherwise) or has become trustee of a further insolvent member under subsection (4), the trustee shall give notice of his appointment or further appointment (as the case may be) to the creditors of the members and the creditors of the partnership or, if the court so allows, shall advertise his appointment in accordance with the court’s directions.

**296(6)** Subject to subsection (7) below, in that notice or advertisement the trustee shall–

(a) state whether he proposes to summon a combined general meeting of the creditors of the members and of the creditors of the partnership for the purpose of establishing a creditors' committee under section 301, and

(b) if he does not propose to summon such a meeting, set out the power of the creditors under this to require him to summon one.

**296(7)** Where in a case where subsection (4) applies a meeting referred to in subsection (6)(a) has already been held, the trustee shall state in the notice or advertisement whether a creditors' committee was established at that meeting and

(a) if such a committee was established, shall state whether he proposes to appoint additional members of the committee under section 301A(3), and

(b) if such a committee was not established, shall set out the power of the creditors to require him to summon a meeting for the purpose of determining whether a creditors' committee should be established.".

## SECTION 297: RULES APPLICABLE TO MEETINGS OF CREDITORS

**14** Section 297 is modified so as to read as follows:–

"**297(1)** This section applies where the court has made orders by virtue of article 11 of the Insolvent Partnerships Order 1994.

**297(2)** Subject to subsection (3) below, the rules relating to the requisitioning, summoning, holding and conducting of meetings on the bankruptcy of an individual are to apply (with the necessary modifications) to the requisitioning, summoning, holding and conducting of separate meetings of the creditors of each member and of combined meetings of the creditors of the partnership and the creditors of the members.

**297(3)** Any combined meeting of creditors shall be conducted as if the creditors of the members and of the partnership were a single set of creditors.".

## SECTION 298: REMOVAL OF TRUSTEE; VACATION OF OFFICE

**15** Section 298 is modified so as to read as follows:–

"**298(1)** Subject as follows, the trustee of the estates of the members and of the partnership may be removed from office only by an order of the court.

**298(2)** If the trustee was appointed by the Secretary of State, he may be removed by a direction of the Secretary of State.

**298(3)** The trustee (not being the official receiver) shall vacate office if he ceases to be a person who is for the time being qualified to act as an insolvency practitioner in relation to any member or to the partnership.

**298(4)** The trustee may, with the leave of the court (or, if appointed by the Secretary of State, with the leave of the court or the Secretary of State), resign his office by giving notice of his resignation to the court.

**298(5)** Subject to subsections (6) and (7) below, any removal from or vacation of office under this section relates to all offices held in the proceedings by virtue of article 11 of the Insolvent Partnerships Order 1994.

**298(6)** The trustee shall vacate office on giving notice to the court that a final meeting has been held under section 331 in Chapter IV (final meeting of creditors of insolvent partnership or of members) and of the decision (if any) of that meeting.

**298(7)** The trustee shall vacate office as trustee of a member if the order made by virtue of article 11 of the Insolvent Partnerships Order 1994 in relation to that member is annulled.".

## SECTION 299: RELEASE OF TRUSTEE

**16** Section 299 is modified so as to read as follows:–

"**299(1)** Where the official receiver has ceased to be the trustee of the members' estates and of the partnership and a person is appointed in his stead, the official receiver shall have his release with effect from the following time, that is to say–

(a) where that person is appointed by a combined general meeting of creditors of the members and of the partnership or by the Secretary of State, the time at which the official receiver gives notice to the court that he has been replaced, and

(b) where that person is appointed by the court, such time as the court may determine.

**299(2)** If the official receiver while he is the trustee gives notice to the Secretary of State that the administration of the estate of any member, or the winding up of the partnership business and administration of its affairs, is for practical purposes complete, he shall have his release as trustee of any member or as trustee of the partnership (as the case may be) with effect from such time as the Secretary of State may determine.

**299(3)** A person other than the official receiver who has ceased to be the trustee of the estate of any member or of the partnership shall have his release with effect from the following time, that is to say–

(a) in the case of a person who has died, the time at which notice is given to the court in accordance with the rules that that person has ceased to hold office;

(b) in the case of a person who has been removed from office by the court or by the Secretary of State, or who has vacated office under section 298(3), such time as the Secretary of State may, on an application by that person, determine;

(c) in the case of a person who has resigned, such time as may be directed by the court (or, if he was appointed by the Secretary of State, such time as may be directed by the court or as the Secretary of State may, on an application by that person, determine);

(d) in the case of a person who has vacated office under section 298(6)–

(i) if the final meeting referred to in that subsection has resolved against that person's release, such time as the Secretary of State may, on an application by that person, determine; and

(ii) if that meeting has not so resolved, the time at which the person vacated office.

**299(4)** Where an order by virtue of article 11 of the Insolvent Partnerships Order 1994 is annulled in so far as it relates to any member, the trustee at the time of the annulment has his release in respect of that member with effect from such time as the court may determine.

**299(5)** Where the trustee (including the official receiver when so acting) has his release under this section, he shall, with effect from the time specified in the preceding provisions of this section, be discharged from all liability both in respect of acts or omissions of his in the administration of the estates of the members and in the winding up of the partnership business and administration of its affairs and otherwise in relation to his conduct as trustee.

But nothing in this section prevents the exercise, in relation to a person who has had his release under this section, of the court's powers under section 304 (liability of trustee).".

## SECTION 300: VACANCY IN OFFICE OF TRUSTEE

17 Section 300 is modified so as to read as follows:–

"**300(1)** This section applies where the appointment of any person as trustee of the members' estates and of the partnership fails to take effect or, such an appointment having taken effect, there is otherwise a vacancy in the office of trustee.

**300(2)** The official receiver may refer the need for an appointment to the Secretary of State and shall be trustee until the vacancy is filled.

**300(3)** On a reference to the Secretary of State under subsection (2) the Secretary of State shall either make an appointment or decline to make one.

**300(4)** If on a reference under subsection (2) no appointment is made, the official receiver shall continue to be trustee, but without prejudice to his power to make a further reference.

**300(5)** References in this section to a vacancy include a case where it is necessary, in

(a) that he is or has been an officer of a partnership which has at any time become insolvent (whether while he was an officer or subsequently), and
(b) that his conduct as an officer of that partnership (either taken alone or taken together with his conduct as an officer of any other partnership or partnerships, or as a director of any company or companies) makes him unfit to be concerned in the management of a company.

**6(2)** For the purposes of this section and the next–
(a) a partnership becomes insolvent if–
 (i) the court makes an order for it to be wound up as an unregistered company at a time when its assets are insufficient for the payment of its debts and other liabilities and the expenses of the winding up; or
 (ii) an administration order is made in relation to the partnership; and
(b) a company becomes insolvent if–
 (i) the company goes into liquidation at a time when its assets are insufficient for the payment of its debts and other liabilities and the expenses of the winding up,
 (ii) an administration order is made in relation to the company, or
 (iii) an administrative receiver of the company is appointed.

**6(3)** For the purposes of this section and the next, references to a person's conduct as an officer of any partnership or partnerships, or as a director of any company or companies, include, where the partnership or company concerned or any of the partnerships or companies concerned has become insolvent, that person's conduct in relation to any matter connected with or arising out of the insolvency of that partnership or company.

**6(4)** In this section and the next "the court" means–
(a) in the case of a person who is or has been an officer of a partnership which is being wound up as an unregistered company by the court, the court by which the partnership is being wound up,
(b) in the case of a person who is or has been an officer of a partnership in relation to which an administration order is in force, the court by which that order was made, and
(c) in any other case, the High Court;
and in both sections "director" includes a shadow director.

**6(5)** Under this section the minimum period of disqualification is 2 years, and the maximum period is 15 years.

*Section 7: applications to court under s. 6; reporting provisions*

**7(1)** If it appears to the Secretary of State that it is expedient in the public interest that a disqualification order under section 6 should be made against any person, an application for the making of such an order against that person may be made–
(a) by the Secretary of State, or
(b) if the Secretary of State so directs in the case of a person who is or has been an officer of a partnership which is being wound up by the court as an unregistered company, by the official receiver.

**7(2)** Except with the leave of the court, an application for the making under that section of a disqualification order against any person shall not be made after the end of the period of 2 years beginning with the day on which the partnership of which that person is or has been an officer became insolvent.

**7(3)** If it appears to the office-holder responsible under this section, that is to say–
(a) in the case of a partnership which is being wound up by the court as an unregistered company, the official receiver, or
(b) in the case of a partnership in relation to which an administration order is in force, the administrator, that the conditions mentioned in section 6(1) are satisfied as respects a person who is or has been an officer of that partnership, the office-holder shall forthwith report the matter to the Secretary of State.

**7(4)** The Secretary of State or the official receiver may require any of the persons mentioned in subsection (5) below–

(a) to furnish him with such information with respect to any person's conduct as an officer of a partnership or as a director of a company, and

(b) to produce and permit inspection of such books, papers and other records relevant to that person's conduct as such an officer or director, as the Secretary of State or the official receiver may reasonably require for the purpose of determining whether to exercise, or of exercising, any function of his under this section.

**7(5)** The persons referred to in subsection (4) are–

(a) the liquidator or administrator, or former liquidator or administrator of the partnership,

(b) the liquidator, administrator or administrative receiver, or former liquidator, administrator or administrative receiver, of the company.

*Section 8: disqualification after investigation*

**8(1)** If it appears to the Secretary of State from a report made by inspectors under section 437 of the Companies Act or section 94 or 177 of the Financial Services Act 1986, or from information or documents obtained under–

(a) section 447 or 448 of the Companies Act,
(b) section 105 of the Financial Services Act 1986,
(c) section 2 of the Criminal Justice Act 1987,
(d) section 52 of the Criminal Justice (Scotland) Act 1987, or
(e) section 83 of the Companies Act 1989,

that it is expedient in the public interest that a disqualification order should be made against any person who is or has been an officer of any insolvent partnership, he may apply to the court for such an order to be made against that person.

**8(2)** The court may make a disqualification order against a person where, on an application under this section, it is satisfied that his conduct in relation to the partnership makes him unfit to be concerned in the management of a company.

**8(3)** In this section "the court" means the High Court.

**8(4)** The maximum period of disqualification under this section is 15 years.

*Section 9: matters for determining unfitness of officers of partnerships*

**9(1)** This section applies where it falls to a court to determine whether a person's conduct as an officer of a partnership (either taken alone or taken together with his conduct as an officer of any other partnership or partnerships or as a director or shadow director of any company or companies) makes him unfit to be concerned in the management of a company.

**9(2)** The court shall, as respects that person's conduct as an officer of that partnership or each of those partnerships or as a director of that company or each of those companies, have regard in particular–

(a) to the matters mentioned in Part I of Schedule 1 to this Act, and

(b) where the partnership or company (as the case may be) has become insolvent, to the matters mentioned in Part II of that Schedule;

and references in that Schedule to the officer and the partnership or, as the case may be, to the director and the company, are to be read accordingly.

**9(3)** Subsections (2) and (3) of section 6 apply for the purposes of this section and Schedule 1 as they apply for the purposes of sections 6 and 7.

**9(4)** Subject to the next subsection, any reference in Schedule 1 to an enactment contained in the Companies Act or the Insolvency Act includes, in relation to any time before the coming into force of that enactment, the corresponding enactment in force at that time.

**9(5)** The Secretary of State may by order modify any of the provisions of Schedule 1; and such an order may contain such transitional provisions as may appear to the Secretary of State necessary or expedient.

**9(6)** The power to make orders under this section is exercisable by statutory instrument subject to annulment in pursuance of a resolution of either House of Parliament.

# Schedule 1 – Matters for Determining Unfitness of Officers of Partnerships

Section 9

## PART I – MATTERS APPLICABLE IN ALL CASES

**1** Any misfeasance or breach of any fiduciary or other duty by the officer in relation to the partnership or, as the case may be, by the director in relation to the company.

**2** Any misapplication or retention by the officer or the director of, or any conduct by the officer or the director giving rise to an obligation to account for, any money or other property of the partnership or, as the case may be, of the company.

**3** The extent of the officer's or the director's responsibility for the partnership or, as the case may be, the company entering into any transaction liable to be set aside under Part XVI of the Insolvency Act (provisions against debt avoidance).

**4** The extent of the director's responsibility for any failure by the company to comply with any of the following provisions of the Companies Act, namely–

(a) section 221 (companies to keep accounting records);
(b) section 222 (where and for how long records to be kept);
(c) section 288 (register of directors and secretaries);
(d) section 352 (obligation to keep and enter up register of members);
(e) section 353 (location of register of members);
(f) section 363 (duty of company to make annual returns); and
(g) sections 399 and 415 (company's duty to register charges it creates).

**5** The extent of the director's responsibility for any failure by the directors of the company to comply with–

(a) section 226 or 227 of the Companies Act (duty to prepare annual accounts), or
(b) section 233 of that Act (approval and signature of accounts).

**6** Any failure by the officer to comply with any obligation imposed on him by or under any of the following provisions of the Limited Partnerships Act 1907–

(a) section 8 (registration of particulars of limited partnership);
(b) section 9 (registration of changes in particulars);
(c) section 10 (advertisement of general partner becoming limited partner and of assignment of share of limited partner).

## PART II – MATTERS APPLICABLE WHERE PARTNERSHIP OR COMPANY HAS BECOME INSOLVENT

**7** The extent of the officer's or the director's responsibility for the causes of the partnership or (as the case may be) the company becoming insolvent.

**8** The extent of the officer's or the director's responsibility for any failure by the partnership or (as the case may be) the company to supply any goods or services which have been paid for (in whole or in part).

**9** The extent of the officer's or the director's responsibility for the partnership or (as the case may be) the company entering into any transaction or giving any preference, being a transaction or preference–

(a) liable to be set aside under section 127 or sections 238 to 240 of the Insolvency Act, or
(b) challengeable under section 242 or 243 of that Act or under any rule of law in Scotland.

**10** The extent of the director's responsibility for any failure by the directors of the company to comply with section 98 of the Insolvency Act (duty to call creditors' meeting in creditors' voluntary winding up).

**11** Any failure by the director to comply with any obligation imposed on him by or under any of the following provisions of the Insolvency Act–

(a) section 47 (statement of affairs to administrative receiver);
(b) section 66 (statement of affairs in Scottish receivership);
(c) section 99 (directors' duty to attend meeting; statement of affairs in creditors' voluntary winding up).

**12** Any failure by the officer or the director to comply with any obligation imposed on him by or under any of the following provisions of the Insolvency Act (both as they apply in relation to companies and as they apply in relation to insolvent partnerships by virtue of the provisions of the Insolvent Partnerships Order 1994)–

(a) section 22 (statement of affairs in administration);
(b) section 131 (statement of affairs in winding up by the court);
(c) section 234 (duty of any one with property to deliver it up);
(d) section 235 (duty to co-operate with liquidator, etc.).""".

# Schedule 9 – Forms

Article 17

| Form No. | Description |
|---|---|
| 1 | Petition for administration order. |
| 2 | Affidavit verifying petition to wind up partnership. |
| 3 | Petition to wind up partnership by liquidator, administrator, trustee or supervisor. |
| 4 | Written/statutory demand by creditor. |
| 5 | Creditor's petition to wind up partnership (presented in conjunction with petitions against members). |
| 6 | Creditor's petition to wind up corporate member (presented in conjunction with petition against partnership). |
| 7 | Creditor's bankruptcy petition against individual member (presented in conjunction with petition against partnership). |
| 8 | Advertisement of winding-up petition (s) against partnership (and any corporate members). |
| 9 | Notice to court of progress on petitions presented. |
| 10 | Demand by member. |
| 11 | Members' petition to wind up partnership (presented in conjunction with petitions against members). |
| 12 | Members' petition to wind up corporate member (presented in conjunction with petition against partnership). |
| 13 | Member's bankruptcy petition against individual member (presented in conjunction with petition against partnership). |
| 14 | Joint bankruptcy petition against individual members. |
| 15 | Affidavit of individual member(s) as to concurrence of all members in presentation of joint bankruptcy petition against individual members. |
| 16 | Bankruptcy orders on joint bankruptcy petition presented by individual members. |
| 17 | Statement of affairs of member of partnership. |
| 18 | Statement of affairs of partnership. |

**Note**
The forms are not reproduced here.

# Schedule 10 – Subordinate Legislation Applied

Article 18

The Insolvency Practitioners Tribunal (Conduct of Investigations) Rules 1986
The Insolvency Practitioners (Recognised Professional Bodies) Order 1986

The Insolvency Rules 1986
The Insolvency Regulations 1986
The Insolvency Proceedings (Monetary Limits) Order 1986
The Administration of Insolvent Estates of Deceased Persons Order 1986
The Insolvency (Amendment of Subordinate Legislation) Order 1986
The Insolvency Fees Order 1986
The Companies (Disqualification Orders) Regulations 1986
The Co-operation of Insolvency Courts (Designation of Relevant Countries and Territories) Order 1986
The Insolvent Companies (Reports on Conduct of Directors) No. 2 Rules 1986
The Insolvent Companies (Disqualification of Unfit Directors) Proceedings Rules 1987
The Insolvency Practitioners Regulations 1990

## EXPLANATORY NOTE

*(This Note is not part of the Order)*

This Order revokes and replaces the Insolvent Partnerships Order 1986 (SI 1986/2142) ("the 1986 Order"). Like the 1986 Order it provides a code for the winding up of insolvent partnerships, but it also introduces two new procedures – voluntary arrangements and administrations – for insolvent partnerships.

The Order differs in form from the 1986 Order in that, rather than making textual amendments to the provisions of the Insolvency Act 1986 (c.45) ("the Act") applied by the Order with modifications, it sets the modified provisions out in full in the Schedules to the Order. In so doing, many of the provisions applying to partnerships, individual members and corporate members (as defined in article 2) have been amalgamated.

The following are the main provisions of the Order, and the main changes made to the 1986 Order:–

1 *Article 4 and Schedule 1* apply Part I of the Act (company voluntary arrangements) to insolvent partnerships for the first time, with appropriate modifications.

2 *Article 6 and Schedule 2* apply Part II of the Act (administration orders) to insolvent partnerships for the first time, with appropriate modifications.

3 Where an insolvent partnership is wound up under Part V of the Act as an unregistered company without involving the concurrent insolvency of any of its members, separate provision is now made depending on whether the winding up is on the petition of a creditor, a responsible insolvency practitioner or the Secretary of State (*article 7 and Schedule 3*) or a member's petition (*article 9 and Schedule 5*). A main change from the corresponding provisions in the 1986 Order is that the jurisdictional requirements of the 1986 Order have been modified so far as creditors' petitions are concerned. Under the 1986 Order the courts in England and Wales only had jurisdiction if the partnership had a *principal* place of business in England and Wales. Under the Order, whilst that remains the case on a member's petition, the court also has jurisdiction on a creditor's petition if the insolvent partnership has a place of business in England and Wales (which in the case of the county court must be in the relevant insolvency district) at which business is carried on in the course of which the petition debt arose (*Schedule 3 paragraphs 3 and 6; Schedule 5, paragraphs 1 and 2*). Special rules apply for partnerships which also have a principal place of business in Scotland or Northern Ireland.

4 Where the winding up of an insolvent partnership involves the concurrent insolvency of its members, separate provision is now made depending on whether the appropriate petitions are presented by a creditor (*article 8 and Schedule 4*) or a member (*article 10 and Schedules 4 and 6*). Other main changes from the 1986 Order are:–

(a) on a creditors' petition, a miminum of one member (rather than two as previously) needs to be made insolvent concurrently with the partnership (*article 8(1)*);

(b) the jurisdictional requirements are as set out in paragraph 3 of this Note (*Schedule 4, paragraphs 3 and 5; Schedule 6, paragraphs 1 and 4*);

(c) the Order makes further modifications to section 271 of the Act which was the subject of a decision of the Court of Appeal in *In Re Marr (A Bankrupt)* (1990 2 WLR 1264) (*Schedule 4 paragraph 9; Schedule 6, paragraph 3*);

(d) on the making of a bankruptcy order against an individual member the official receiver no longer becomes receiver and manager pending the appointment of a trustee, but becomes trustee unless and until another responsible insolvency practitioner (as defined in *article 2*) is appointed in his place (*Schedule 4, paragraph 12*);

(e) the Order removes the mandatory requirement under section 136 of the Act as modified by the 1986 Order for the official receiver to summon a meeting of creditors to choose a person to be responsible insolvency practitioner in his place and replaces it with a discretion to do so, as is the case in section 136 in unmodified form. The official receiver is however under duty to consider the exercise of that discretion under section 136A (*Schedule 4, paragraph 12*); and

(f) *Schedule 4, paragraphs 23 and 24* contain modified provisions on the order of priority of payment of expenses and debts out of the joint and separate estates. In particular, where the joint estate is not sufficient for the payment of the joint debts, it provides for the responsible insolvency practitioner to lodge a claim representing the aggregate value of the outstanding amount of those debts in the separate estate of each member against whom an insolvency order has been made.

**5** Provision for the individual members of an insolvent partnership to present petitions for their bankruptcy (provided there are no corporate or limited partners) is now made by *article II and Schedule 7.* Main changes from the 1986 Order are:–

(a) the court may issue a certificate of summary administration of the estate of any qualifying member (*Schedule 7, paragraph 6*); and

(b) *Schedule 7, paragraph 21* contains modified provisions on the order of priority of payment of expenses and debts out of the joint and separate estates. In particular it makes provisions similar to those referred to in paragraph 4(f) above.

**6** *Article 16 and Schedule 8* apply specified provisions of the Company Directors Disqualification Act 1986 (c.45) where an insolvent partnership is wound up as an unregistered company under Part V of the Act.

**7** The relevant forms for use in proceedings under the Order are contained in *Schedule 9 (article 17)*.

**8** *Article 18 and Schedule 10* specify the subordinate legislation which is to apply for the purposes of giving effect to the provisions of the Act and of the Company Directors Disqualification Act 1986 applied by the Order.

**9** *Article 19* of the Order contains supplemental and transitional provisions.

**10** A Compliance Cost Assessment is available, copies of which have been placed in the libraries of both Houses of Parliament. Copies are also available from The Insolvency Service of the Department of Trade and Industry, PO Box 203, Room 5.1, 21 Bloomsbury Street, London WC1B 3QW.

# THE INSOLVENCY REGULATIONS 1994

(SI 1994/2507)

*Made on 26 September 1994 by the Secretary of State for Trade and Industry under r. 12.1 of the Insolvency Rules 1986 and s. 411, 412 of and para. 27 of Sch. 8 and para. 30 of Sch. 9 to the Insolvency Act 1986. Operative from 24 October 1994.*

[**Note:** These Regulations are amended by the Insolvency (Amendment) Regulations 2000 (SI 2000/485) as from 31 March 2000.]

## PART 1 – GENERAL

### CITATION AND COMMENCEMENT

**1** These Regulations may he cited as the Insolvency Regulations 1994 and shall come into force on 24th October 1994.

## REVOCATIONS

**2** Subject to regulation 37 below, the Regulations listed in Schedule 1 to these Regulations are hereby revoked.

## INTERPRETATION AND APPLICATION

**3(1)** In these Regulations, except where the context otherwise requires–

**"bank"** means any authorised institution in England and Wales within the meaning of the Banking Act 1987 or a European deposit-taker as defined in regulation 82(3) of the Banking Coordination (Second Council Directive) Regulations 1992 that is to say a European authorised institution which has lawfully established a branch in the United Kingdom for the purpose of accepting deposits;

**"bankrupt"** means the bankrupt or his estate;

**"company"** means the company which is being wound up;

**"creditors' committee"** means any committee established under section 301;

**"electronic transfer"** means transmission by any electronic means;

**"liquidation committee"** means, in the case of a winding up by the court, any committee established under section 141 and, in the case of a creditors' voluntary winding up, any committee established under section 101;

**"liquidator"** includes, in the case of a company being wound up by the court, the official receiver when so acting;

**"local bank"** means any bank in, or in the neighbourhood of, the insolvency district, or the district in respect of which the court has winding-up jurisdiction, in which the proceedings are taken, or in the locality in which any business of the company or, as the case may be, the bankrupt is carried on;

**"local bank account"** means, in the case of a winding up by the court, a current account opened with a local bank under regulation 6(2) below and, in the case of a bankruptcy, a current account opened with a local bank under regulation 21(1) below;

**"payment instrument"** means a cheque or payable order;

**"the Rules"** means the Insolvency Rules 1986; and

**"trustee"**, subject to regulation 19(2) below, means trustee of a bankrupt's estate including the official receiver when so acting;

and other expressions used in these Regulations and defined by the Rules have the meanings which they bear in the Rules.

**History**

In reg. 3(1) the definition of "electronic transfer" inserted by the Insolvency (Amendment) Regulations 2000 (SI 2000/485), reg. 1, 3 and Sch., para. 1 as from 31 March 2000.

**3(2)** A Rule referred to in these Regulations by number means the Rule so numbered in the Rules.

**3(3)** Any application to be made to the Secretary of State or to the Department or anything required to be sent to the Secretary of State or to the Department under these Regulations shall be addressed to the Department of Trade and Industry, The Insolvency Service, PO Box 3690, Birmingham B2 4UY.

**3(4)** Where a regulation makes provision for the use of a form obtainable from the Department, the Department may provide different forms for different cases arising under that regulation.

**3(5)** Subject to regulation 37 below, these Regulations apply–

(a) to winding-up proceedings commenced on or after 29th December 1986; and

(b) to bankruptcy proceedings where the bankruptcy petition is or was presented on or after that day.

# PART 2 – WINDING UP

## INTRODUCTORY

**4** This Part of these Regulations relates to–

(a) voluntary winding up and

(b) winding up by the court

of companies which the courts in England and Wales have jurisdiction to wind up.

## Payments into and out of the Insolvency Services Account

### PAYMENTS INTO THE INSOLVENCY SERVICES ACCOUNT

**5(1)** In the case of a winding up by the court, subject to regulation 6 below, the liquidator shall pay all money received by him in the course of carrying out his functions as such without any deduction into the Insolvency Services Account kept by the Secretary of State with the Bank of England to the credit of the company once every 14 days or forthwith if £5,000 or more has been received.

**5(2)** In the case of a voluntary winding up, the liquidator shall, within 14 days of the expiration of the period of 6 months from the date of his appointment and of every period of six months thereafter until he vacates office, pay into the Insolvency Services Account to the credit of the company the balance of funds in his hands or under his control relating to the company, including any unclaimed or undistributed assets or dividends, but excluding such part (if any) as he considers necessary to retain for the immediate purposes of the winding up.

**5(3)** Every payment of money into the Insolvency Services Account under this regulation shall be–

(a) made through the Bank Giro system; or

(b) sent direct to the Bank of England, Threadneedle Street, London EC2R 8AH by cheque drawn in favour of the "Insolvency Services Account" and crossed "A/c payee only" "Bank of England"; or

(c) made by electronic transfer,

and the liquidator shall on request be given by the Department a receipt for the money so paid.

**History**

Reg. 5(3) substituted by the Insolvency (Amendment) Regulations 2000 (SI 2000/485), reg. 1, 3 and Sch., para. 2 as from 31 March 2000; the former reg. 5(3) read as follows:

"Every payment of money into the Insolvency Services Account under this regulation shall be–

(a) made through the Bank Giro system; or

(b) sent direct to the Bank of England, PO Box 3, Birmingham B2 5EY by cheque drawn in favour of the "Insolvency Services Account" and crossed "A/c payee only" "Bank of England",

and the liquidator shall on request be given by the Department a receipt for the money so paid."

**5(4)** Every payment of money made under sub-paragraph (a) or (b) of paragraph (3) above shall be accompanied by a form obtainable from the Department for that purpose or by a form that is substantially similar. Every payment of money made under sub-paragraph (c) of paragraph (3) above shall specify the name of the liquidator making the payment and the name of the company to whose credit such payment is made.

**History**

In reg. 5(4) the words "made under sub-paragraph (a) or (b) of paragraph (3) above" substituted for the former words "under paragraph (1) and (2) above" and the words "Every payment of money made under sub-paragraph (c)" to the end inserted by the Insolvency (Amendment) Regulations 2000 (SI 2000/485), reg. 1, 3 and Sch., para. 3 as from 31 March 2000.

**5(5)** Where in a voluntary winding up a liquidator pays any unclaimed dividend into the Insolvency Services Account, he shall at the same time give notice to the Secretary of State, on a form obtainable from the Department or on one that is substantially similar, of the name and address of the person to whom the dividend is payable and the amount of the dividend.

### LOCAL BANK ACCOUNT AND HANDLING OF FUNDS NOT BELONGING TO THE COMPANY

**6(1)** This regulation does not apply in the case of a voluntary winding up.

**6(2)** Where the liquidator intends to exercise his power to carry on the business of the company, he may apply to the Secretary of State for authorisation to open a local bank account, and the Secretary of State may authorise him to make his payments into and out of a specified bank, subject to a limit, instead of into and out of the Insolvency Services Account if satisfied that an administrative advantage will be derived from having such an account.

**6(3)** Money received by the liquidator relating to the purpose for which the account was opened may be paid into the local bank account to the credit of the company to which the account relates.

**6(4)** Where the liquidator opens a local bank account pursuant to an authorisation granted under paragraph (2) above, he shall open and maintain the account in the name of the company.

**6(5)** Where money which is not an asset of the company is provided to the liquidator for a specific purpose, it shall be clearly identifiable in a separate account.

**6(6)** The liquidator shall keep proper records, including documentary evidence of all money paid into and out of every local bank account opened and maintained under this regulation.

**6(7)** The liquidator shall pay without deduction any surplus over any limit imposed by an authorisation granted under paragraph (2) above into the Insolvency Services Account in accordance with regulation 5 above as that regulation applies in the case of a winding up by the court.

**6(8)** As soon as the liquidator ceases to carry on the business of the company or vacates office or an authorisation given in pursuance of an application under paragraph (2) above is withdrawn, he shall close the account and pay any balance into the Insolvency Services Account in accordance with regulation 5 above as that regulation applies in the case of a winding up by the court.

## PAYMENT OF DISBURSEMENTS ETC. OUT OF THE INSOLVENCY SERVICES ACCOUNT

**7(A1)** Paragraphs (1) to (3) of this regulation are subject to paragraph (3A).

**History**
Reg. 7(A1) inserted by the Insolvency (Amendment) Regulations 2000 (SI 2000/485), reg. 1, 3 and Sch., para. 4 as from 31 March 2000.

**7(1)** In the case of a winding up by the court, on application to the Department, the liquidator shall be repaid all necessary disbursements made by him, and expenses properly incurred by him, in the course of his administration to the date of his vacation of office out of any money standing to the credit of the company in the Insolvency Services Account.

**7(2)** In the case of a winding up by the court, the liquidator shall on application to the Department obtain payment instruments to the order of the payee for sums which become payable on account of the company for delivery by the liquidator to the persons to whom the payments are to be made.

**7(3A)** In respect of an application made by the liquidator under paragraphs (1) to (3) above, the Secretary of State, if requested to do so by the liquidator, may, at his discretion,

(a) make the payment which is the subject of the application to the liquidator by electronic transfer; or

(b) as an alternative to the issue of payment instruments, make payment by electronic transfer to the persons to whom the liquidator would otherwise deliver payment instruments.

**History**
Reg. 7(3A) inserted by the Insolvency (Amendment) Regulations 2000 (SI 2000/485), reg. 1, 3 and Sch., para. 5 as from 31 March 2000.

**7(4)** Any application under this regulation shall be made by the liquidator on a form obtainable from the Department for the purpose or on a form that is substantially similar.

**7(5)** In the case of a winding up by the court, on the liquidator vacating office, he shall be repaid by any succeeding liquidator out of any funds available for the purpose any necessary disbursements made by him and any expenses properly incurred by him but not repaid before he vacates office.

## Dividends to Creditors and returns of Capital to Contributories of a Company

### PAYMENT

**8(A1)** Paragraphs (1) to (3) of this regulation are subject to paragraph (3A).

**History**
Reg. 8(A1) inserted by the Insolvency (Amendment) Regulations 2000 (SI 2000/485), reg. 1, 3 and Sch., para. 6 as from 31 March 2000.

**8(1)** In the case of a winding up by the court, the liquidator shall pay every dividend by payment instruments which shall be prepared by the Department on the application of the liquidator and transmitted to him for distribution amongst the creditors.

**8(2)** In the case of a winding up by the court, the liquidator shall pay every return of capital to contributories by payment instruments which shall be prepared by the Department on application.

**8(3)** In the case of a voluntary winding up, where the liquidator requires to make payments out of any money standing to the credit of the company in the Insolvency Services Account by way of distribution, he shall apply in writing to the Secretary of State who may either authorise payment to the liquidator of the sum required by him, or may direct payment instruments to be issued to the liquidator for delivery by him to the persons to whom the payments are to be made.

**8(3A)** In respect of an application made by the liquidator under paragraphs (1) to (3) above, the Secretary of State, if requested to do so by the liquidator, may, at his discretion,

(a) as an alternative to the issue of payment instruments, make payment by electronic transfer to the persons to whom the liquidator would otherwise deliver payment instruments; or

(b) make the payment which is the subject of the application to the liquidator by electronic transfer.

**History**
Reg. 8(3A) inserted by the Insolvency (Amendment) Regulations 2000 (SI 2000/485), reg. 1, 3 and Sch., para. 7 as from 31 March 2000.

**8(4)** Any application under this regulation for a payment instrument or payment by electronic transfer shall be made by the liquidator on a form obtainable from the Department for the purpose or on a form which is substantially similar.

**History**
In reg. 8(4) the words "or payment by electronic transfer" appearing after the word "instrument" inserted by the Insolvency (Amendment) Regulations 2000 (SI 2000/485), reg. 1, 3 and Sch., para. 8 as from 31 March 2000.

**8(5)** In the case of a winding up by the court, the liquidator shall enter the total amount of every dividend and of every return to contributories that he desires to pay under this regulation in the records to be kept under regulation 10 below in one sum.

**8(6)** On the liquidator vacating office, he shall send to the Department any valid unclaimed or undelivered payment instruments for dividends or returns to contributories after endorsing them with the word "cancelled."

## Investment or Otherwise Handling of Funds in Winding Up of Companies and Payment of Interest

**9(1)** When the cash balance standing to the credit of the company in the account in respect of that company kept by the Secretary of State is in excess of the amount which, in the opinion of the liquidator, is required for the immediate purposes of the winding up and should be invested, he may request the Secretary of State to invest the amount not so required in Government securities, to be placed to the credit of that account for the company's benefit.

**9(2)** When any of the money so invested is, in the opinion of the liquidator, required for the immediate purposes of the winding up, he may request the Secretary of State to raise such sum as may be required by the sale of such of those securities as may be necessary.

**9(3)** In cases where investments have been made at the request of the liquidator in pursuance of paragraph (1) above and additional sums to the amounts so invested, including money received under paragraph (7) below, are paid into the Insolvency Services Account to the credit of the company, a request shall be made to the Secretary of State by the liquidator if it is desired that these additional sums should be invested.

**9(4)** Any request relating to the investment in, or sale of, as the case may be, Treasury Bills made under paragraphs (1), (2) or (3) above shall be made on a form obtainable from the

Department or on one that is substantially similar and any request relating to the purchase or sale, as the case may be, of any other type of Government security made under the provisions of those paragraphs shall be made in writing.

**9(5)** Any request made under paragraphs (1), (2) or (3) above shall be sufficient authority to the Secretary of State for the investment or sale as the case may be.

**9(6)** Whenever the amount standing to the credit of a company in the Insolvency Services Account on or after 24th October 1994 exceeds £2,000, the company shall be entitled to interest on the excess at the rate of $3^1/_2$ per cent per annum provided that:

(a) where, in the opinion of the liquidator, it is necessary or expedient in order to facilitate the conclusion of the winding up that interest should cease to accrue, he may give notice in writing to the Secretary of State to that effect and interest shall cease to accrue from the date of receipt of that notice by the Secretary of State; and

(b) at any time after receipt by the Secretary of State of a notice under sub-paragraph (a) above, provided that the balance standing to the credit of the company exceeds £2,000, the liquidator may give notice in writing to the Secretary of State requesting that interest should accrue on the excess and interest shall start to accrue on the excess at the rate of $3^1/_2$ per cent per annum from the date of receipt of the notice by the Secretary of State.

**9(7)** All money received in respect of investments and interest earned under this regulation shall be paid into the Insolvency Services Account to the credit of the company.

**9(8)** In addition to the application of paragraphs (1) to (7) above, in a voluntary winding up:

(a) any money invested or deposited at interest by the liquidator shall be deemed to be money under his control, and when such money forms part of the balance of funds in his hands or under his control relating to the company required to be paid into the Insolvency Services Account under regulation 5 above, the liquidator shall realise the investment or withdraw the deposit and shall pay the proceeds into that Account: Provided that where the money is invested in Government securities, such securities may, with the permission of the Secretary of State, be transferred to the control of the Secretary of State instead of being forthwith realised and the proceeds paid into the Insolvency Services Account; and

(b) where any of the money represented by securities transferred to the control of the Secretary of State pursuant to sub-paragraph (a) above is, in the opinion of the liquidator, required for the immediate purposes of the winding up he may request the Secretary of State to raise such sums as may be required by the sale of such of those securities as may be necessary and such request shall be sufficient authority to the Secretary of State for the sale and the Secretary of State shall pay the proceeds of the realisation into the Insolvency Services Account in accordance with paragraph (7) above and deal with them in the same way as other money paid into that Account may be dealt with.

## Records to be Maintained by Liquidators and the Provision of Information

### FINANCIAL RECORDS

**10(1)** This regulation does not apply in the case of a members' voluntary winding up.

**10(2)** The liquidator shall prepare and keep–

(a) separate financial records in respect of each company; and

(b) such other financial records as are required to explain the receipts and payments entered in the records described in sub-paragraph (a) above or regulation 12(2) below, including an explanation of the source of any receipts and the destination of any payments;

and shall, subject to regulation 12(2) below as to trading accounts, from day to day enter in those records all the receipts and payments (including, in the case of a voluntary winding up, those relating to the Insolvency Services Account) made by him.

**10(3)** In the case of a winding up by the court, the liquidator shall obtain and keep bank statements relating to any local bank account in the name of the company.

**10(4)** The liquidator shall submit financial records to the liquidation committee when required for inspection.

**10(5)** In the case of a winding up by the court, if the liquidation committee is not satisfied with the contents of the financial records submitted under paragraph (4) above it may so inform the Secretary of State, giving the reasons for its dissatisfaction, and the Secretary of State may take such action as he thinks fit.

## PROVISION OF INFORMATION BY LIQUIDATOR

**11(1)** In the case of a winding up by the court, the liquidator shall, within 14 days of the receipt of a request for a statement of his receipts and payments as liquidator from any creditor, contributory or director of the company, supply free of charge to the person making the request, a statement of his receipts and payments as liquidator during the period of one year ending on the most recent anniversary of his becoming liquidator which preceded the request.

**11(2)** In the case of a voluntary winding up, the liquidator shall, on request from any creditor, contributory or director of the company for a copy of a statement for any period, including future periods, sent to the registrar of companies under section 192, send such copy free of charge to the person making the request and the copy of the statement shall be sent within 14 days of the liquidator sending the statement to the registrar or the receipt of the request whichever is the later.

## LIQUIDATOR CARRYING ON BUSINESS

**12(1)** This regulation does not apply in the case of a members' voluntary winding up.

**12(2)** Where the liquidator carries on any business of the company, he shall–

(a) keep a separate and distinct account of the trading, including, where appropriate, in the case of a winding up by the court, particulars of all local bank account transactions; and

(b) incorporate in the financial records required to be kept under regulation 10 above the total weekly amounts of the receipts and payments made by him in relation to the account kept under sub-paragraph (a) above.

## RETENTION AND DELIVERY OF RECORDS

**13(1)** All records kept by the liquidator under regulations 10 and 12(2) and any such records received by him from a predecessor in that office shall be retained by him for a period of 6 years following–

(a) his vacation of office, or

(b) in the case of the official receiver, his release as liquidator under section 174,

unless he delivers them to another liquidator who succeeds him in office.

**13(2)** Where the liquidator is succeeded in office by another liquidator, the records referred to in paragraph (1) above shall be delivered to that successor forthwith, unless, in the case of a winding up by the court, the winding up is for practical purposes complete and the successor is the official receiver, in which case the records are only to be delivered to the official receiver if the latter so requests.

## PROVISION OF ACCOUNTS BY LIQUIDATOR AND AUDIT OF ACCOUNTS

**14(1)** The liquidator shall, if required by the Secretary of State at any time, send to the Secretary of State an account in relation to the company of the liquidator's receipts and payments covering such period as the Secretary of State may direct and such account shall, if so required by the Secretary of State, be certified by the liquidator.

**14(2)** Where the liquidator in a winding up by the court vacates office prior to the holding of the final general meeting of creditors under section 146, he shall within 14 days of vacating office send to the Secretary of State an account of his receipts and payments as liquidator for any period not covered by an account previously so sent by him or if no such account has been sent, an account of his receipts and payments in respect of the whole period of his office.

**14(3)** In the case of a winding up by the court, where:

(a) a final general meeting of creditors has been held pursuant to section 146, or

(b) a final general meeting is deemed to have been held by virtue of Rule 4.125(5),

the liquidator shall send to the Secretary of State, in case (a), within 14 days of the holding of the final general meeting of creditors and, in case (b), within 14 days of his report to the court pursuant to Rule 4.125(5), an account of his receipts and payments as liquidator which are not covered by any previous account so sent by him, or if no such account has been sent an account of his receipts and payments in respect of the whole period of his office.

**14(4)** In the case of a winding up by the court, where a statement of affairs has been submitted under the Act, any account sent under this regulation shall be accompanied by a summary of that statement of affairs and shall show the amount of any assets realised and explain the reasons for any non-realisation of any assets not realised.

**14(5)** In the case of a winding up by the court, where a statement of affairs has not been submitted under the Act, any account sent under this regulation shall be accompanied by a summary of all known assets and their estimated values and shall show the amounts actually realised and explain the reasons for any non-realisation of any assets not realised.

**14(6)** Any account sent to the Secretary of State shall, if he so requires, be audited, but whether or not the Secretary of State requires the account to be audited, the liquidator shall send to the Secretary of State on demand any documents (including vouchers and bank statements) and any information relating to the account.

## PRODUCTION AND INSPECTION OF RECORDS

**15(1)** The liquidator shall produce on demand to the Secretary of State, and allow him to inspect, any accounts, books and other records kept by him (including any passed to him by a predecessor in office), and this duty to produce and allow inspection shall extend–

(a) to producing and allowing inspection at the premises of the liquidator; and

(b) to producing and allowing inspection of any financial records of the kind described in regulation 10(2)(b) above prepared by the liquidator (or any predecessor in office of his) before 24th October 1994 and kept by the liquidator;

and any such demand may–

(i) require the liquidator to produce any such accounts, books or other records to the Secretary of State, and allow him to inspect them–

(A) at the same time as any account is sent to the Secretary of State under regulation 14 above; or

(B) at any time after such account is sent to the Secretary of State;

whether or not the Secretary of State requires the account to be audited; or

(ii) where it is made for the purpose of ascertaining whether the provisions of these Regulations relating to the handling of money received by the liquidator in the course of carrying out his functions have been or are likely to be complied with, be made at any time, whether or not an account has been sent or should have been sent to the Secretary of State under regulation 14 above and whether or not the Secretary of State has required any account to be audited.

**15(2)** The liquidator shall allow the Secretary of State on demand to remove and take copies of any accounts, books and other records kept by the liquidator (including any passed to him by a predecessor in office), whether or not they are kept at the premises of the liquidator.

## DISPOSAL OF COMPANY'S BOOKS, PAPERS AND OTHER RECORDS

**16(1)** The liquidator in a winding up by the court, on the authorisation of the official receiver, during his tenure of office or on vacating office, or the official receiver while acting as liquidator, may at any time sell, destroy or otherwise dispose of the books, papers and other records of the company.

**16(2)** In the case of a voluntary winding up, the person who was the last liquidator of a company which has been dissolved may, at any time after the expiration of a period of one year from the date of dissolution, destroy or otherwise dispose of the books, papers and other records of the company.

### VOLUNTARY LIQUIDATOR TO PROVIDE INFORMATION TO SECRETARY OF STATE

**17(1)** In the case of a voluntary winding up, a liquidator or former liquidator, whether the winding up has been concluded under Rule 4.223 or not, shall, within 14 days of a request by the Secretary of State, give the Secretary of State particulars of any money in his hands or under his control representing unclaimed or undistributed assets of the company or dividends or other sums due to any person as a member or former member of the company and such other particulars as the Secretary of State may require for the purpose of ascertaining or getting in any money payable into the Insolvency Services Account.

**17(2)** The particulars referred to in paragraph (1) above shall, if the Secretary of State so requires, be certified by the liquidator, or former liquidator, as the case may be.

### PAYMENT OF UNCLAIMED OR UNDISTRIBUTED ASSETS, DIVIDENDS OR OTHER MONEY ON DISSOLUTION OF COMPANY

**18** In the case of a company which has been dissolved, notwithstanding anything in these Regulations, any money in the hands of any or any former liquidator at the date of dissolution of the company or his earlier vacation of office, representing unclaimed or undistributed assets of the company or dividends or held by the company in trust in respect of dividends or other sums due to any person as a member or former member of the company, shall forthwith be paid by him into the Insolvency Services Account.

# PART 3 – BANKRUPTCY

### INTRODUCTORY

**19(1)** This Part of these Regulations relates to bankruptcy and extends to England and Wales only.

**19(2)** In addition to the application of the provisions of this Part to the official receiver when acting as trustee, the provisions of this Part (other than regulations 30 and 31) shall also apply to him when acting as receiver or manager under section 287 and the term **"trustee"** shall be construed accordingly.

## Payments Into and Out of the Insolvency Services Account

### PAYMENTS INTO THE INSOLVENCY SERVICES ACCOUNT

**20(1)** Subject to regulation 21 below, the trustee shall pay all money received by him in the course of carrying out his functions as such without any deduction into the Insolvency Services Account kept by the Secretary of State with the Bank of England to the credit of the bankrupt once every 14 days or forthwith if £5,000 or more has been received.

**20(2)** Every payment of money into the Insolvency Services Account under this regulation shall be–

(a) made through the Bank Giro system; or

(b) sent direct to the Bank of England, Threadneedle Street, London EC2R 8AH by cheque drawn in favour of the "Insolvency Services Account" and crossed "A/c payee only" "Bank of England"; or

(c) made by electronic transfer,

and the trustee shall on request be given by the Department a receipt for the money so paid.

**History**

Reg. 20(2) substituted by the Insolvency (Amendment) Regulations 2000 (SI 2000/485), reg. 1, 3 and Sch., para. 9 as from 31 March 2000; the former reg. 20(2) read as follows:

"Every payment of money into the Insolvency Services Account under this regulation shall be–

(a) made through the Bank Giro system; or
(b) sent direct to the Bank of England, PO Box 3, Birmingham B2 5EY by cheque drawn in favour of the "Insolvency Services Account" and crossed "A/c payee only" "Bank of England",

and the liquidator shall on request be given by the Department a receipt for the money so paid."

**20(3)** Every payment of money made under sub-paragraph (a) or (b) of paragraph (2) above shall be accompanied by a form obtainable from the Department for that purpose or by a form that is substantially similar. Every payment of money made under sub-paragraph (c) of paragraph (2) above shall specify the name of the trustee making the payment and the name of the bankrupt to whose credit such payment is made.

**History**
In reg. 20(3) the words "made under sub-paragraph (a) or (b) of paragraph (2) above" substituted for the former words "under paragraph (1) above" and the words "Every payment of money made under sub-paragraph (c)" to the end inserted by the Insolvency (Amendment) Regulations 2000 (SI 2000/485), reg. 1, 3 and Sch., para. 10 as from 31 March 2000.

## LOCAL BANK ACCOUNT AND HANDLING OF FUNDS NOT FORMING PART OF THE BANKRUPT'S ESTATE

**21(1)** Where the trustee intends to exercise his power to carry on the business of the bankrupt, he may apply to the Secretary of State for authorisation to open a local bank account, and the Secretary of State may authorise him to make his payments into and out of a specified bank, subject to a limit, instead of into and out of the Insolvency Services Account if satisfied that an administrative advantage will be derived from having such an account.

**21(2)** Money received by the trustee relating to the purpose for which the account was opened may be paid into the local bank account to the credit of the bankrupt to whom the account relates.

**21(3)** Where the trustee opens a local bank account pursuant to an authorisation granted under paragraph (1) above he shall open and maintain the account in the name of the bankrupt.

**21(4)** Where money which does not form part of the bankrupt's estate is provided to the trustee for a specific purpose it shall be clearly identifiable in a separate account.

**21(5)** The trustee shall keep proper records, including documentary evidence of all money paid into and out of every local bank account opened and maintained under this regulation.

**21(6)** The trustee shall pay without deduction any surplus over any limit imposed by an authorisation granted under paragraph (1) above into the Insolvency Services Account in accordance with regulation 20(1) above.

**21(7)** As soon as the trustee ceases to carry on the business of the bankrupt or vacates office or an authorisation given in pursuance of an application under paragraph (1) above is withdrawn, he shall close the account and pay any balance into the Insolvency Services Account in accordance with regulation 20(1) above.

## PAYMENT OF DISBURSEMENTS ETC. OUT OF THE INSOLVENCY SERVICES ACCOUNT

**22(A1)** Paragraphs (1) and (2) of this regulation are subject to paragraph (2A).

**History**
Reg. 22(A1) inserted by the Insolvency (Amendment)Regulations 2000 (SI 2000/485), reg. 1, 3 and Sch., para. 11 as from 31 March 2000.

**22(1)** On application to the Department, the trustee shall be repaid all necessary disbursements made by him, and expenses properly incurred by him, in the course of his administration to the date of his vacation of office out of any money standing to the credit of the bankrupt in the Insolvency Services Account.

**22(2)** The trustee shall on application to the Department obtain payment instruments to the order of the payee for sums which become payable on account of the bankrupt for delivery by the trustee to the persons to whom the payments are to be made.

**22(2A)** In respect of an application made by the trustee under paragraph (1) or (2) above, the Secretary of State, if requested to do so by the trustee, may, at his discretion,

(a) make the payment which is the subject of the application to the trustee by electronic transfer; or
(b) as an alternative to the issue of payment instruments, make payment by electronic transfer to the persons to whom the trustee would otherwise deliver payment instruments.

**History**
Reg. 22(2A) inserted by the Insolvency (Amendment) Regulations 2000 (SI 2000/485), reg. 1, 3 and Sch., para. 12 as from 31 March 2000.

**22(3)** Any application under this regulation shall be made on a form obtainable from the Department or on one that is substantially similar.

**22(4)** On the trustee vacating office, he shall be repaid by any succeeding trustee out of any funds available for the purpose any necessary disbursements made by him and any expenses properly incurred by him but not repaid before he vacates office.

## Dividends to Creditors

### PAYMENT

**23(1)** Subject to paragraph (1A), the trustee shall pay every dividend by payment instruments which shall be prepared by the Department on the application of the trustee and transmitted to him for distribution amongst the creditors.

**History**
In reg. 23(1) the words "Subject to paragraph (1A)," inserted by the Insolvency (Amendment) Regulations 2000 (SI 2000/485), reg. 1, 3 and Sch., para. 13 as from 31 March 2000.

**23(1A)** In respect of an application made by the trustee under paragraph (1) above, the Secretary of State, if requested to do so by the trustee, may, at his discretion, as an alternative to the issue of payment instruments, make payment by electronic transfer to the persons to whom the trustee would otherwise deliver payment instruments.

**History**
Reg. 23(1A) inserted by the Insolvency (Amendment) Regulations 2000 (SI 2000/485), reg. 1, 3 and Sch., para. 14 as from 31 March 2000.

**23(2)** Any application under this regulation for a payment instrument or payment by electronic transfer shall be made by the trustee on a form obtainable from the Department for the purpose or on a form which is substantially similar.

**History**
In reg. 23(2) the words "or payment by electronic transfer" appearing after the word "instrument" inserted by the Insolvency (Amendment) Regulations 2000 (SI 2000/485), reg. 1, 3 and Sch., para. 15 as from 31 March 2000.

**23(3)** The trustee shall enter the total amount of every dividend that he desires to pay under this regulation in the records to be kept under regulation 24 below in one sum.

**23(4)** On the trustee vacating office, he shall send to the Department any valid unclaimed or undelivered payment instruments for dividends after endorsing them with the word "cancelled."

## Records to be Maintained by Trustees and the Provision of Information

### FINANCIAL RECORDS

**24(1)** The trustee shall prepare and keep–

(a) separate financial records in respect of each bankrupt; and

(b) such other financial records as are required to explain the receipts and payments entered in the records described in sub-paragraph (a) above or regulation 26 below, including an explanation of the source of any receipts and the destination of any payments;

and shall, subject to regulation 26 below as to trading accounts, from day to day enter in those records all the receipts and payments made by him.

**24(2)** The trustee shall obtain and keep bank statements relating to any local bank account in the name of the bankrupt.

**24(3)** The trustee shall submit financial records to the creditors' committee when required for inspection.

**24(4)** If the creditors' committee is not satisfied with the contents of the financial records submitted under paragraph (3) above it may so inform the Secretary of State, giving the reasons for its dissatisfaction and the Secretary of State may take such action as he thinks fit.

### PROVISION OF INFORMATION BY TRUSTEE

**25** The trustee shall, within 14 days of the receipt of a request from any creditor or the bankrupt for a statement of his receipts and payments as trustee, supply free of charge to the person making the request, a statement of his receipts and payments as trustee during the period of one year ending on the most recent anniversary of his becoming trustee which preceded the request.

## TRUSTEE CARRYING ON BUSINESS

**26** Subject to paragraph (2) below, where the trustee carries on any business of the bankrupt, he shall–

(a) keep a separate and distinct account of the trading, including, where appropriate, particulars of all local bank account transactions; and

(b) incorporate in the financial records required to be kept under regulation 24 above the total weekly amounts of the receipts and payments made by him in relation to the account kept under paragraph (a) above.

## RETENTION AND DELIVERY OF RECORDS

**27(1)** All records kept by the trustee under regulations 24 and 26 and any such records received by him from a predecessor in that office shall be retained by him for a period of 6 years following–

(a) his vacation of office, or

(b) in the case of the official receiver, his release as trustee under section 299,

unless he delivers them to another trustee who succeeds him in office.

**27(2)** Where the trustee is succeeded in office by another trustee, the records referred to in paragraph (1) above shall be delivered to that successor forthwith, unless the bankruptcy is for practical purposes complete and the successor is the official receiver, in which case the records are only to be delivered to the official receiver if the latter so requests.

## PROVISION OF ACCOUNTS BY TRUSTEE AND AUDIT OF ACCOUNTS

**28(1)** The trustee shall, if required by the Secretary of State at any time, send to the Secretary of State an account of his receipts and payments as trustee of the bankrupt covering such period as the Secretary of State may direct and such account shall, if so required by the Secretary of State, be certified by the trustee.

**28(2)** Where the trustee vacates office prior to the holding of the final general meeting of creditors under section 331, he shall within 14 days of vacating office send to the Secretary of State an account of his receipts and payments as trustee for any period not covered by an account previously so sent by him, or if no such account has been sent, an account of his receipts and payments in respect of the whole period of his office.

**28(3)** Where:

(a) a final general meeting of creditors has been held pursuant to section 331, or

(b) a final general meeting is deemed to have been held by virtue of Rule 6.137(5),

the trustee shall send to the Secretary of State, in case (a), within 14 days of the holding of the final general meeting of creditors and, in case (b), within 14 days of his report to the court pursuant to Rule 6.137(5), an account of his receipts and payments as trustee which are not covered by any previous account so sent by him, or if no such account has been sent, an account of his receipts and payments in respect of the whole period of his office.

**28(4)** Where a statement of affairs has been submitted under the Act, any account sent under this regulation shall be accompanied by a summary of that statement of affairs and shall show the amount of any assets realised and explain the reasons for any non-realisation of any assets not realised.

**28(5)** Where a statement of affairs has not been submitted under the Act, any account sent under this regulation shall be accompanied by a summary of all known assets and their estimated values and shall show the amounts actually realised and explain the reasons for any non-realisation of any assets not realised.

**28(6)** Any account sent to the Secretary of State shall, if he so requires, be audited, but whether or not the Secretary of State requires the account to be audited, the trustee shall send to the Secretary of State on demand any documents (including vouchers and bank statements) and any information relating to the account.

### PRODUCTION AND INSPECTION OF RECORDS

**29(1)** The trustee shall produce on demand to the Secretary of State, and allow him to inspect, any accounts, books and other records kept by him (including any passed to him by a predecessor in office), and this duty to produce and allow inspection shall extend–

(a) to producing and allowing inspection at the premises of the trustee; and

(b) to producing and allowing inspection of any financial records of the kind described in regulation 24(1)(b) above prepared by the trustee before 24th October 1994 and kept by him;

and any such demand may–

(i) require the trustee to produce any such accounts, books or other records to the Secretary of State, and allow him to inspect them–

(A) at the same time as any account is sent to the Secretary of State under regulation 28 above; or

(B) at any time after such account is sent to the Secretary of State;

whether or not the Secretary of State requires the account to be audited; or

(ii) where it is made for the purpose of ascertaining whether the provisions of these Regulations relating to the handling of money received by the trustee in the course of carrying out his functions have been or are likely to be complied with, be made at any time, whether or not an account has been sent or should have been sent to the Secretary of State under regulation 28 above and whether or not the Secretary of State has required any account to be audited.

**29(2)** The trustee shall allow the Secretary of State on demand to remove and take copies of any accounts, books and other records kept by the trustee (including any passed to him by a predecessor in office), whether or not they are kept at the premises of the trustee.

### DISPOSAL OF BANKRUPT'S BOOKS, PAPERS AND OTHER RECORDS

**30** The trustee, on the authorisation of the official receiver, during his tenure of office or on vacating office, or the official receiver while acting as trustee, may at any time sell, destroy or otherwise dispose of the books, papers and other records of the bankrupt.

### PAYMENT OF UNCLAIMED OR UNDISTRIBUTED ASSETS, DIVIDENDS OR OTHER MONEY

**31** Notwithstanding anything in these Regulations, any money–

(a) in the hands of the trustee at the date of his vacation of office, or

(b) which comes into the hands of any former trustee at any time after his vacation of office,

representing, in either case, unclaimed or undistributed assets of the bankrupt or dividends, shall forthwith be paid by him into the Insolvency Services Account.

## PART 4 – CLAIMING MONEY PAID INTO THE INSOLVENCY SERVICES ACCOUNT

**32(1)** Any person claiming to be entitled to any money paid into the Insolvency Services Account may apply to the Secretary of State for payment and shall provide such evidence of his claim as the Secretary of State may require.

**32(2)** Any person dissatisfied with the decision of the Secretary of State in respect of his claim made under this regulation may appeal to the court.

| *Provision* | *Date of Commencement* | *SI No* |
|---|---|---|
| S. 47(1) | 1.3.1990 | SI 1990/142 |
| S. 48(1) and (2) | 1.3.1990 | SI 1990/142 |
| S. 49 but only for the purposes of any provisions brought into force by article 3 of SI 1990/142 | 1.3.1990 | SI 1990/142 |
| Ss. 50 and 51 | 1.3.1990 | SI 1990/142 |
| Ss. 52 to 54 but only for the purposes of any provisions brought into force by article 3 of SI 1990/142 | 1.3.1990 | SI 1990/142 |
| The remaining provisions of Part II (subject to transitional and saving provisions) with the exception of those conferring powers on the Secretary of State to transfer functions of his under this Part to a body corporate established under s. 46 of the Act | 1.10.1991 | SI 1991/1996 |
| Ss. 55 to 64 | 21.2.1990 | SI 1990/142 |
| S. 65(1) | 21.2.1990 | SI 1990/142 |
| S. 65(2) except to the extent that it refers to Part VII of the 1989 Act and except, in the case of s. 65(2)(g), to the extent that the said paragraph refers to a body established under s. 46 of the 1989 Act | 21.2.1990 | SI 1990/142 |
| S. 65(2) insofar as not yet in force but only to the extent that it refers to Part VIII of the 1989 Act | 25.4.1991 | SI 1991/878 |
| S. 65(3) to (7) | 21.2.1990 | SI 1990/142 |
| S. 66 to 74 | 21.2.1990 | SI 1990/142 |
| S. 75(1) | 21.2.1990 | SI 1990/142 |
| S. 75(2) | 25.1.1990 | SI 1990/98 |
| S. 75(3), insofar as it provides for the insertion in S. 180(1) of the Financial Services Act 1986 of a new paragraph (oo) | | |
| S. 75(3) except insofar as brought into force as referred to above, except to the extent that it refers to Part VII of the 1989 Act and except, in the case of s. 75(3)(c), to the extent that it refers to a body established by order under s. 46 of the 1989 Act | 21.2.1990 | SI 1990/142 |
| S. 75(3) insofar as not yet in force but only to the extent that it refers to Part VII of the 1989 Act | 24.4.1991 | SI 1991/878 |
| S. 75(4) insofar as it provides a definition of "public servant" for the purposes of the new s. 180(1) (oo) of the Financial Services Act 1986 | 25.1.1990 | SI 1990/98 |
| S. 75(4) except insofar as brought into force as referred to above | 21.2.1990 | SI 1990/142 |
| S. 75(5) | 21.2.1990 | SI 1990/142 |
| S. 75(6) | 21.2.1990 | SI 1990/142 |
| S. 75(7) | 25.1.1990 | SI 1990/98 |
| Ss. 76 to 79 | 21.2.1990 | SI 1990/142 |

| *Provision* | *Date of Commencement* | *SI No* |
|---|---|---|
| S. 80 except to the extent that it refers to Part VII of the 1989 Act | 21.2.1990 | SI 1990/142 |
| S. 80 insofar as not in force | 25.4.1991 | SI 1991/878 |
| S. 81(1) | 21.2.1990 | SI 1990/142 |
| S. 81(2) except to the extent that it refers to Part VII of the 1989 Act | 21.2.1990 | SI 1990/142 |
| S. 81(2) insofar as not in force | 25.4.1991 | SI 1991/878 |
| S. 81(3) and (4) | 21.2.1990 | SI 1990/142 |
| S. 81(5) except to the extent that it refers to Part VII of the 1989 Act | 21.2.1990 | SI 1990/142 |
| S. 81(5) insofar as not in force | 25.4.1991 | SI 1991/878 |
| Ss. 82 to 86 | 21.2.1990 | SI 1990/142 |
| S. 87(1) to (3) | 21.2.1990 | SI 1990/142 |
| S. 87(4) except to the extent that it refers to Part VII of the 1989 Act | 21.2.1990 | SI 1990/142 |
| S. 87(4) insofar as not in force | 25.4.1991 | SI 1991/878 |
| S. 87(5) and (6) | 21.2.1990 | SI 1990/142 |
| Ss. 88 to 91 | 21.2.1990 | SI 1990/142 |
| Ss. 108 to 112 (subject to transitional and savings provisions) | 4.2.1990 | SI 1990/2569 |
| Ss. 113 to 124 (subject to transitional and saving provisions) | 1.4.1990 | SI 1990/355 |
| Ss. 125 and 127(1), (2) and (4), and section 127(7) to the extent necessary to insert into Schedule 22 of the Companies Act 1985 a reference to the new sections 706, 707 and 715A of that Act | 7.1.1991 | SI 1990/2569 |
| S. 126 and, insofar as not yet in force, section 127 (subject, in the case of the former, to a transitional provision) | 1.7.1991 | SI 1991/488 |
| S. 129 | 1.11.1990 | SI 1990/1392 |
| S. 130 (and Schedule 17) | 31.7.1990 | SI 1990/1392 |
| Ss. 131 and 132 (subject, in the case of the former, to a saving provision) | 1.4.1990 | SI 1990/355 |
| S. 134(1) to (3), (5) and (6) (subject to transitional and saving provisions) | 31.5.1990 | SI 1990/713 |
| S. 134(4) | 1.11.1991 | SI 1991/1996 |
| S. 135 | 7.1.1991 | SI 1990/2569 |
| S. 136 (subject to a transitional provision) | 1.4.1990 | SI 1990/355 |
| S. 137(1); section 137(2) in part (subject to a transitional provision) | 1.4.1990 | SI 1990/355 |
| S. 138 (subject to saving provision) | 31.7.1990 | SI 1990/1392 |
| S. 139 (subject to transitional and saving provisions) | 1.10.1990 | SI 1990/1707 |
| S. 143 | 1.11.1991 | SI 1991/1996 |
| S. 144 (and Schedule 18) (subject to transitional provisions) | 1.11.1990 | SI 1990/1392 |

| *Provision* | *Date of Commencement* | *SI No* |
|---|---|---|
| S. 145 but only insofar as it relates to paragraphs 1, 8, 9, 12, 19, and 21 of Schedule 19 to the 1989 Act | 1.3.1990 | SI 1990/142 |
| S. 145 but only insofar as it extends to paragraph 10 of Schedule 19 to the 1989 Act | 7.1.1991 | SI 1990/2569 |
| S. 145 but only insofar as it extends to paragraph 11 of Schedule 19 to the 1989 Act | 4.2.1991 | SI 1990/2569 |
| S. 145 but only insofar as it relates to paragraphs 15 to 18 of Schedule 19 to the 1989 Act | 1.4.1990 | SI 1990/355 |
| S. 145 but only insofar as it relates to paragraphs 2 to 7 and 14 of Schedule 19 to the 1989 Act (subject, in the case of paragraphs 2 and 6, to transitional and saving provisions) | 1.10.1990 | SI 1990/1707 |
| S. 146 | 1.4.1990 | SI 1990/142 |
| S. 151 | 1.4.1990 | SI 1990/142 |
| S. 152 | 1.3.1990 | SI 1990/142 |
| S. 153 but only insofar as it relates to paragraphs 1, 13, 17, 21 and 26 of Schedule 20 to the 1989 Act | 1.4.1990 | SI 1990/142 |
| Part VII insofar as necessary to enable regulations to be made under sections 155(4) and (5), 158(4) and (5), 160(5), 173(4) and (5), 174(2) to (4), 185, 186 and 187(3) and paragraph 2(3) of Schedule 21 | 25.4.1991 | SI 1991/488 |
| S. 154 | 25.4.1991 | SI 1991/878 |
| S. 155, 156 and Schedule 21 insofar as not in force | 25.4.1991 | SI 1991/878 |
| S. 157 subject to certain provisions | 25.4.1991 | SI 1991 878 |
| S. 158 insofar as not in force | 25.4.1991 | SI 1991/878 |
| S. 159 | 25.4.1991 | SI 1991/878 |
| S. 160 insofar as not yet in force but subject to certain provisions concerning insolvency proceedings begun before the coming into force of the section and to provisions concerning its application in Northern Ireland | 25.4.1991 | SI 1991/878 |
| S. 160 insofar as not yet in force | 1.10.1991 | SI 1991/2173 |
| S. 161 | 25.4.1991 | SI 1991/878 |
| S. 162 subject to certain provisions concerning its application in Northern Ireland | 25.4.1991 | SI 1991/878 |
| S. 162 insofar as not yet in force | 1.10.1991 | SI 1991/2173 |
| S. 163 to 165 | 25.4.1991 | SI 1991/878 |
| S. 166 subject to certain provisions concerning insolvency proceedings begun before the section comes into force and to provisions concerning its application in Northern Ireland | 25.4.1991 | SI 1991/878 |
| S. 166 insofar as not yet in force | 1.10.1991 | SI 1991/2173 |
| S. 167 subject to provisions concerning its application in Northern Ireland | 25.4.1991 | SI 1991/878 |
| S. 167 insofar as not yet in force | 1.10.1991 | SI 1991/2173 |
| S. 168 and 169 except section 169(4) | 25.4.1991 | SI 1991/878 |

| *Provision* | *Date of Commencement* | *SI No* |
|---|---|---|
| S. 173 insofar as not in force | 25.4.1991 | SI 1991/878 |
| S. 174 insofar as not in force but subject to certain provisions concerning insolvency proceedings begun before the section comes into force | 25.4.1991 | SI 1991/878 |
| S. 175 subject to certain provisions concerning insolvency proceedings begun before the section comes into force | 25.4.1991 | SI 1991/878 |
| S. 177 except insofar as it would have effect where the property is held as margin at the time the section comes into force | 25.4.1991 | SI 1991/878 |
| S. 179 except insofar as it would have effect where the property is subject to the relevant market charge at the time the section comes into force | 25.4.1991 | SI 1991/878 |
| S. 180 except insofar as it would affect certain procedures commenced or begun before the section comes into force | 25.4.1991 | SI 1991/878 |
| S. 182 and Schedule 22 and s. 183 | 25.4.1991 | SI 1991/878 |
| S. 184 subject to provisions concerning its application in Northern Ireland | 25.4.1991 | SI 1991/878 |
| S. 184 insofar as not yet in force | 1.10.1991 | SI 1991/2173 |
| S. 187 insofar as not in force | 25.4.1991 | SI 1991/878 |
| Ss. 188 to 191 | 25.4.1991 | SI 1991/878 |
| S. 192 insofar as it inserts section 47A into the Financial Services Act 1986 (subject to transitional and saving provisions) | 15.3.1990 | SI 1990/354 |
| S. 193 insofar as is necessary in order to enable regulations to be made under section 62A of, and paragraph 22A of Schedule 11 to, the Financial Services Act 1986 (subject to transitional and saving provisions) | 15.3.1990 | SI 1990/354 |
| S. 193 insofar as not in force (subject to a saving provision) | 1.4.1991 | SI 1991/488 |
| Ss. 194 to 200 (subject to transitional and saving provisions) | 15.3.1990 | SI 1990/354 |
| S. 201 | 25.4.1991 | SI 1991/878 |
| Ss. 203 to 205 (subject to transitional and saving provisions) | 15.3.1990 | SI 1990/354 |
| S. 206(1) except insofar as it relates to the insertion by paragraph 32 of Schedule 23 to the 1989 Act of paragraph 1 3B into Schedule 11 of the Financial Services Act 1986 (subject to transitional and saving provisions) | 15.3.1990 | SI 1990/354 |
| S. 206(2) to (4) (subject to transitional and saving provisions) | 15.3.1990 | SI 1990/354 |
| S. 207 | 1.11.1990 | SI 1990/1392 |
| S. 208 | 1.3.1990 | SI 1990/142 |
| S. 209 | 21.2.1990 | SI 1990/142 |
| S. 210 | 1.4.1990 | SI 1990/142 |

| *Provision* | *Date of Commencement* | *SI No* |
|---|---|---|
| S. 211(1) | 1.10.1991 | SI 1991/1996 |
| S. 211(2) (subject to a saving provision) and (3) | 31.7.1990 | SI 1990/1392 |
| S. 212 insofar as it relates to the repeals effected by Schedule 24 to the 1989 Act referred to below | On the dates referred to below in connection with Schedule 24 | In the SIs listed below in connection with Schedule 24 |
| Schedule 24 insofar as it relates to repeals in, or of, ss. 435, 440, 443, 446, 447, 449, 452 and 735A of the Companies Act 1985, ss. 94, 105, 179, 180, 198(1) and 199(9) of the Financial Services Act 1986 and s. 84(1) of the Banking Act 1987 | 21.2.1990 | SI 1990/142 |
| Schedule 24 insofar as it relates to the repeal in s. 21(2) of the Company Directors Disqualification Act 1986 | 1.3.1990 | SI 1990/142 |
| Schedule 24 insofar as it relates to the repeals in, or of, sections 48, 55, 159 and 160 of, and paragraphs 4, 10 and 14 of Schedule 11, to the Financial Services Act 1986 | 15.3.1990 | SI 1990/354 |
| Schedule 24 insofar as it relates to repeals in, or of, ss. 46(3) and 85 of the Fair Trading Act 1973 | 1.4.1990 | SI 1990/142 |
| Schedule 24 insofar as it relates to repeals in, or of, section 42(6) of the Harbours Act 1964; sections 716, 717, 744 (in part) and 746 of, and Schedule 2, 4, 9, 11, 22 (in part) and 24 (in part) to, the Companies Act 1985; paragraphs 23 and 45 of Schedule 6 to the Insolvency Act 1985; and the entries in Part I of Schedule 13 to the Insolvency Act 1986 relating to sections 222 (4) and 225 | 15.3.1990 | SI 1990/354 |
| Schedule 24 insofar as it relates to repeals in, or of, section 119(9) of, and paragraph 22 of Schedule 16 to, the Financial Services Act 1986 | 1.4.1990 | SI 1990/355 |
| Schedule 24 insofar as it relates to repeals in, or of, sections 201, 202(1) and 209(1)(j) of the Companies Act 1985 | 31.5.1990 | SI 1990/713 |
| Schedule 24 insofar as it relates to repeals in, or of, section 651(l) and Schedule 22 (in part) of the Companies Act 1985 | 31.7.1990 | SI 1990/1392 |
| Schedule 24 insofar as it relates to repeals in, or of, Schedules 15 and 18 to the Building Societies Act 1986 | 31.7.1990 | SI 1990/1392 |
| Schedule 24 insofar as it relates to repeals in, or of, sections 466(2) and 733(3) of and Schedules 22 (in part) and 24 (in part) to the Companies Act 1985 (subject, in the case of Schedules 22 and 24, to transitional and saving provisions) | 1.10.1990 | SI 1990/1707 |
| Schedule 24 insofar as it relates to Part I of Schedule 13 to the Insolvency Act 1986 (in part) | 1.10.1990 | SI 1990/1707 |

| *Provision* | *Date of Commencement* | *SI No* |
|---|---|---|
| Schedule 24 insofar as it relates to section 708(1)(b) of the 1985 Act | 7.1.1991 | SI 1990/2569 |
| Schedule 24 insofar as it repeals Schedule 15 to the 1985 Act (subject to the transitional and savings provisions made by articles 4 and 5 of the Companies Act 1989 (Commencement No. 7 and Transitional and Savings Provisions) Order 1990) | 7.1.1991 | SI 1990/2569 |
| Schedule 24 insofar as it repeals the entries relating to section 245(1) and (2) in Schedule 24 to the 1985 Act (subject to the transitional and savings provisions made by article 6 of the Companies Act 1989 (Commencement No. 8 and Transitional and Savings Provisions) Order 1990) | 7.1.1991 | SI 1990/2569 |
| Schedule 24 insofar as is necessary to effect the repeal of, or words in, sections 389 and 460(1) of the Companies Act 1985, section 196(3) of the Financial Services Act 1986 and section 565(6)(b) of the Income and Corporation Taxes Act 1988 | 1.10.1991 | SI 1991/1996 |
| Schedule 24 insofar as it relates to the repeals in, or of, ss. 169(5), 175(6)(b), 191(1), (3)(a) and (3)(b), 219(1), 288(3), 318(7), 356(1), (2) and (4), 383(1), (2) and (3) of the Companies Act 1985 and paragraph 25 of Schedule 13 to that Act | 1.11.1991 | SI 1991/1996 |
| Ss. 213 to 215 insofar as they were not already in force at the time of the making of SI 1990/142 | 2.2.1990 | SI 1990/142 |
| S. 216 | 25.1.1990 | SI 1990/98 |

# THE COMPANIES (FEES) (AMENDMENT) REGULATIONS 1995

(SI 1995/1423)

*Made on 27 May 1995 by the Secretary of State for Trade and Industry under s. 708(1) and (2) of the Companies Act 1985. Operative from 1 July 1995.*

**1** These Regulations may be cited as the Companies (Fees) (Amendment) Regulations 1995 and shall come into force on 1st July 1995.

**2** [Insertion of entry 20A into Sch. to the 1991 Regulations.]

## EXPLANATORY NOTE

(*This Note is not part of the Regulations*)

These Regulations amend the Companies (Fees) Regulations 1991, following amendments to the Companies Act 1985 to be made by section 13(1) of, and Schedule 5 to, the Deregulation and Contracting Out Act 1994 (c. 40) which provide a new procedure for the directors of a non-trading private company to apply to the registrar of companies for the company's name to be struck off the register. A new fee of £10.00 is prescribed in respect of the making of such an application. These Regulations will come into force on 1st July 1995, the same date on which the relevant provisions of the Deregulation and Contracting Out Act 1994 will be brought into force.

# THE COMPANIES (FORMS) (NO. 2) REGULATIONS 1995

(SI 1995/1479)

*Made on 31 May 1995 by the Secretary of State for Trade and Industry under s. 652A(2), 652D(6) and 744 of the Companies Act 1985. Operative from 1 July 1995.*

**1** These Regulations may be cited as the Companies (Forms) (No. 2) Regulations 1995 and shall come into force on 1st July 1995.

**2** Forms 652a and 652c in the Schedule to these Regulations, with such variations as circumstances require, are forms prescribed for the purposes of sections 652A(2) and 652D(6) of the Companies Act 1985.

## Schedule

Regulation 2

**Note**
The forms are not reproduced here.

### EXPLANATORY NOTE

(*This Note is not part of the Regulations*)

These Regulations prescribe two forms to be used for the purposes of the new provisions for the directors of a non-trading private company to apply to the registrar of companies for the company's name to be struck off the register, which are to be inserted into the Companies Act 1985 by section 13(1) of, and Schedule 5 to, the Deregulation and Contracting Out Act 1994 (c. 40). The forms will take effect on 1st July 1995, the date on which the relevant provisions of the 1994 Act will be brought into force. The forms are form 652a (application for striking off) and 652c (withdrawal of application for striking off).

# THE COMPANIES (WELSH LANGUAGE FORMS AND DOCUMENTS) (NO. 2) REGULATIONS 1995

(SI 1995/1480)

*Made on 31 May 1995 by the Secretary of State for Trade and Industry under s. 652A(2), 652D(6) and 744 of the Companies Act 1985, as extended by s. 26(3) of the Welsh Language Act 1993. Operative from 1 July 1995.*

**1** The Regulations may be cited as the Companies (Welsh Language Forms and Documents) (No. 2) Regulations 1995 and shall come into force on 1st July 1995.

**2** Forms 652aCYM and 652cCYM in the Schedule to these Regulations, with such variations as circumstances require, are forms prescribed for the purposes of sections 652A(2) and 652D(6) of the Companies Act 1985.

## Schedule

Regulation 2

**Note**
This Schedule sets out forms 652aCYM and 652cCYM. They are not reproduced here.

### EXPLANATORY NOTE

(*This Note is not part of the Regulations*)

These Regulations prescribe two forms which are in Welsh as well as in English to be used for the purposes of the new provisions for the directors of a non-trading private company to apply to the registrar of companies for the company's name to be struck off the register. The new provisions are to be inserted into the Companies Act 1985 by section 13(1) of, and Schedule 5 to, the Deregulation and Contracting Out Act 1994 (c. 40). The forms will take effect on 1st July 1995, the date on which the relevant provisions of the 1994 Act will be brought into force. The forms are form 652aCYM (application for striking off) and 652cCYM (withdrawal of application for striking off).

# THE COMPANIES (WELSH LANGUAGE FORMS AND DOCUMENTS) (NO. 3) REGULATIONS 1995

(SI 1995/1508)

*Made on 8 June 1995 by the Secretary of State for Trade and Industry under s. 12, 30 and 744 of the Companies Act 1985, as extended by s. 26(3) of the Welsh Language Act 1993. Operative from 1 July 1995.*

**1** These Regulations may be cited as the Companies (Welsh Language Forms and Documents) (No. 3) Regulations 1995 and shall come into force on 1st July 1995.

**2** Forms 12CYM, 30(5)(a)CYM, 30(5)(b)CYM and 30(5)(c)CYM in the Schedule to these Regulations, with such variations as circumstances require, are forms prescribed in the purposes of sections 12 and 30(5)(a), 30(5)(b) and 30(5)(c) respectively of the Companies Act 1985.

**3** Form 12CYM in the Schedule to the Companies (Welsh Language Forms and Documents) (Amendment) Regulations 1995 shall be revoked with effect from 1st July 1995.

## Schedule

Regulation 2

**Note**

This Schedule sets out forms 12CYM, 30(5)(a)CYM, 30(5)(b)CYM and 30(5)(c)CYM. They are not reproduced here.

### EXPLANATORY NOTE

(*This Note is not part of the Regulations*)

These Regulations prescribe new forms which are in Welsh as well as in English. The forms prescribed for the purposes of section 30 of the Companies Act 1985 are prescribed for use when making statutory declarations under sub-section (5) of that section (exemption from requirement of "limited" as part of the name of a company). Equivalent English forms were prescribed by the Companies Form (Amendment) Regulations 1995 (SI 1995/736).

New form 12CYM replaces form 12CYM prescribed in the Companies (Welsh Language Forms and Documents) (Amendment) Regulations 1995 (SI 1995/734). The form 12CYM prescribed by SI 1995/734 contained a mistake in that it referred to "consent signature" instead of to "declarant's signature". Form 12CYM is a form for the statutory declaration of compliance with the requirements on application for registration of a company, under section 12 of the Companies Act 1995. The previously prescribed form 12CYM is revoked with effect from 1st July 1995.

# THE COMPANIES (DISQUALIFICATION ORDERS) (AMENDMENT) REGULATIONS 1995

(SI 1995/1509)

*Made on 8 June 1995 by the Secretary of State for Trade and Industry under s. 18 of the Company Directors Disqualification Act 1986. Operative from 1 July 1995.*

### CITATION AND COMMENCEMENT

**1** These Regulations may be cited as the Companies (Disqualification Orders) (Amendment) Regulations 1995 and shall come into force on 1st July 1995.

## APPLICATION

2 These Regulations amend the Companies (Disqualification Orders) Regulations 1986 and shall apply in relation to a disqualification order made after the coming into force of these Regulations and to a grant of leave, or any action taken by a court in consequence of which a disqualification order is varied or ceases to be in force, made or taken after that date, in relation to a disqualification order made before, on or after that date.

## AMENDMENT OF THE COMPANIES (DISQUALIFICATION ORDERS) REGULATIONS 1986

3 The Schedules numbered 1 to 4 set out in the Schedule to these Regulations shall be substituted for Schedules 1 to 4 respectively to the Companies (Disqualification Orders) Regulations 1986.

# Schedule

Regulation 3

**Note**

Sch. 1–4 set out the relevant forms. They are not reproduced here – see the 1986 regulations (SI 1986/2067).

## EXPLANATORY NOTE

*(This Note is not part of the Regulations)*

These Regulations amend the Companies (Disqualification Orders) Regulations 1986 (SI 1986/2067) (the "1986 Regulations").

The Company Directors Disqualification Act 1986 gives specified courts power to make a disqualification order against a person which provides that he shall not, without leave of the court, be a director, or liquidator or administrator of a company, or receiver or manager of a company's property, or be concerned or take part in the promotion, formation or management of a company, for a specified period.

The 1986 Regulations require certain court officers to provide the Secretary of State with particulars of disqualification orders and the granting of leave in relation to such orders, and of any action taken by a court in consequence of which such orders are varied or cease to be in force. They also specify the form and time in which they must be given.

These Regulations substitute new forms for those prescribed by the 1986 Regulations.

# THE COMPANIES ACT 1985 (DISCLOSURE OF REMUNERATION FOR NON-AUDIT WORK) (AMENDMENT) REGULATIONS 1995

(SI 1995/1520)

*Made on 8 June 1995 by the Secretary of State for Trade and Industry under s. 390B of the Companies Act 1985. Operative from 10 July 1995.*

## CITATION AND COMMENCEMENT

1 These Regulations may be cited as the Companies Act 1985 (Disclosure of Remuneration for Non-Audit Work) (Amendment) Regulations 1995 and shall come into force on 10th July 1995.

## INTERPRETATION

2 In these Regulations–

**"the 1991 Regulations"** means the Companies Act 1985 (Disclosure of Remuneration for Non-Audit Work) Regulations 1991;

**"acting as an insolvency practitioner"** shall be construed in accordance with section 388 of the Insolvency Act 1986;

any reference to **"a receiver, or a receiver or manager, of the property of a company"** includes a receiver, or (as the case may be) a receiver or manager, of part only of that property.

## AMENDMENT OF THE 1991 REGULATIONS

**3, 4** [Amendment of reg. 3 and insertion of new reg. 7 in 1991 Regulations (SI 1991/2128).]

## EXPLANATORY NOTE

(*This Note is not part of the Regulations*)

These Regulations amend the Companies Act 1985 (Disclosure of Remuneration for Non-Audit Work) Regulations 1991 (the "1991 Regulations") which require disclosure in notes to a company's annual accounts of remuneration of a company's auditors and their associates for non-audit work done for the company and its associated undertakings.

Regulation 4 amends the definition of "associate" of a company's auditors contained in the 1991 Regulations to exclude any body corporate in respect of which any partner in or director of the company's auditors, was at any time in the relevant financial year entitled to exercise, or control the exercise of, 20 per cent or more of the voting rights at any general meeting solely in his capacity as an insolvency practitioner, a receiver, a receiver or manager, or a judicial factor.

# THE FINANCIAL SERVICES ACT 1986 (INVESTMENT ADVERTISEMENTS) (EXEMPTIONS) (No. 2) ORDER 1995

(SI 1995/1536)

*Made on 14 June 1995 by the Treasury under s. 58(3)(d) and (4) and s. 205A of the Financial Services Act 1986. Operative from 19 June 1995.*

## CITATION AND COMMENCEMENT

**1** This Order may be cited as the Financial Services Act 1986 (Investment Advertisements) (Exemptions) (No. 2) Order 1995 and shall come into force on 19th June 1995.

## INTERPRETATION

**2** In this Order and in the Schedules hereto–

**"the Act"** means the Financial Services Act 1986;

**"the 1985 Act"** means the Companies Act 1985;

**"the 1986 Order"** means the Companies (Northern Ireland) Order 1986;

**"EEA State"** means a State which is a Contracting Party to the Agreement on the European Economic Area signed at Oporto on 2nd May 1992, as adjusted by the Protocol signed at Brussels on 17th March 1993, but until that Agreement comes into force in relation to Liechtenstein does not include the State of Liechtenstein;

**"private company"**, in relation to a body corporate which is a company within the meaning of the 1985 Act, means a private company within the meaning of section 1(3) of the 1985 Act and, in relation to a body corporate which is a company within the meaning of the 1986 Order, means a private company within the meaning of article 12(3) of the 1986 Order; and

**"relevant EEA market"** means a market in an EEA State which is established under the rules of an investment exchange specified in Part I of Schedule 1 to this Order or which meets the criteria specified in Part II of that Schedule.

## INVESTMENT ADVERTISEMENTS ISSUED FOR THE PURPOSE OF PROMOTING OR ENCOURAGING INDUSTRIAL OR COMMERCIAL ACTIVITY OR ENTERPRISE

**3(1)** Section 57 of the Act shall not apply to an investment advertisement issued or caused to be issued by a body corporate of the kind described in paragraph (2) below which–

(a) relates to shares in or debentures of a private company;

(b) contains no invitation or information which would make it an investment advertisement other than an invitation or information which it is reasonable to expect a person engaged in an activity of the kind described in that paragraph to give in the course of engaging in that activity; and

(c) complies with the requirements of paragraph (3) of this article.

**3(2)** A body corporate falls within this paragraph if–

(a) it is a body corporate which has as its principal object or one of its principal objects the promotion or encouragement of industrial or commercial activity or enterprise in the United Kingdom or in any particular area of it or the dissemination of information concerning persons engaged in such activity or enterprise or requiring capital in order to become so engaged; and

(b) it has no direct or indirect pecuniary interest in any matters which are the subject of any investment advertisement it issues which is exempt by virtue of this article or in any investment agreement which may be entered into following such an advertisement.

**3(3)** The requirements referred to in paragraph (1)(c) of this article are that the advertisement should contain the following statements presented in a manner which, depending upon the medium through which the advertisement is issued, are calculated to bring the contents of the statements prominently to the attention of recipients of the advertisement–

"Investment in new business carries high risks, as well as the possibility of high rewards. It is highly speculative and potential investors should be aware that no established market exists for the trading of shares in private companies. Before investing in a project about which information is given, potential investors are strongly advised to take advice from a person authorised under the Financial Services Act 1986 who specialises in advising on investments of this kind.

The persons to whose order this advertisement has been issued have taken reasonable steps to ensure that the information it contains is neither inaccurate nor misleading.".

## TAKE-OVERS OF PRIVATE COMPANIES

**4(1)** In this article and in Schedule 4 to this Order–

(a) the expressions **"debentures"** and **"shares"**, when used–

(i) in relation to a body corporate which is a company within the meaning of the 1985 Act have the same meaning as in that Act;

(ii) in relation to a body corporate which is a company within the meaning of the 1986 Order have the same meaning as in that Order; and

(iii) in relation to any other body corporate, mean investments falling within paragraph 1 or 2 of Schedule 1 to the Act issued by that body corporate; and

(b) **"relevant offer"** means an offer of the kind described in Part II of Schedule 4 to this Order for shares in or debentures of a body corporate of the kind described in Part III of that Schedule.

**4(2)** Section 57 of the Act shall not apply to an investment advertisement if it falls within paragraph (3), (4), or (5) below.

**4(3)** An investment advertisement falls within this paragraph if–

(a) it is issued in connection with a relevant offer;

(b) it fulfils the conditions specified in Part IV of Schedule 4 to this Order; and

(c) it contains no invitation or information which would make it an investment advertisement other than–

(i) an invitation or information relating to a relevant offer; or

(ii) an invitation or information relating to a relevant offer and an invitation or information relating to an offer for investments falling within paragraph 4 or 5 of Schedule 1 to the Act which confer an entitlement or rights with respect to shares or debentures which are the subject of that relevant offer.

**4(4)** An investment advertisement falls within this paragraph if–

(a) it either accompanies or is issued after the issue of an investment advertisement which contains a relevant offer and which falls within paragraph (3) above; and

(b) it contains no invitation or information which would make it an investment advertisement other than an invitation or information relating to investments falling within paragraph 4 or 5 of Schedule 1 to the Act which confer an entitlement or rights with respect to shares or debentures which are the subject of that relevant offer.

**4(5)** An investment advertisement falls within this paragraph if it is issued in connection with a relevant offer and is a form of application for shares or debentures or for investments falling within paragraph 4 or 5 of Schedule 1 to the Act.

## SALE OF BODY CORPORATE

**5(1)** In this article–

(a) **"a group of connected individuals"**, in relation to the party disposing of shares in a body corporate, means persons each of whom is, or is a close relative of, a director or manager of the body corporate and, in relation to the party acquiring the shares, means persons each of whom is, or is a close relative of, a person who is to be a director or manager of the body corporate;

(b) **"close relative"** means a person's spouse, his children (including, in Northern Ireland, his adopted children) and step-children, his parents and step-parents, his brothers and sisters, and his step-brothers and step-sisters and includes a person acting in the capacity of trustee or personal representative of any such relative; and

(c) **"single individual"** includes two or more persons acting in their capacity as the personal representatives of a single individual.

**5(2)** Section 57 of the Act shall not apply to an investment advertisement if the invitation is made or the information is given by or on behalf of a body corporate, a partnership, a single individual or a group of connected individuals for the purposes of or with a view to the acquisition or disposal of shares in a body corporate other than an open-ended investment company between parties each of whom is a body corporate, a partnership, a single individual or a group of connected individuals, being shares which–

(a) consist of or include shares carrying 75 per cent or more of the voting rights attributable to share capital which are exercisable in all circumstances at any general meeting of the body corporate; or

(b) would, together with any shares already held by the person or persons by or on whose behalf the advertisement is issued, carry not less than that percentage of those voting rights.

## DEALINGS IN COURSE OF NON-INVESTMENT BUSINESS

**6** Section 57 shall not apply to an investment advertisement issued or caused to be issued by a person who holds a permission granted under paragraph 23 of Schedule 1 to the Act if the only reason why the advertisement would be subject to the provisions of section 57 of the Act is because it contains an invitation or information given for the purposes of or in connection with anything done in accordance with the terms and conditions of the permission.

## ADVERTISEMENTS ISSUED TO PERSONS OF PARTICULAR KINDS

**7(1)** In this article **"relevant person"** means a person who is not an authorised person and who is not unlawfully carrying on investment business in the United Kingdom.

**Note**
Concerning European investment firms, see the Investment Services Regulations 1995 (SI 1995/3275), reg. 57 and Sch. 10, para. 21.

**7(2)** Section 57 of the Act shall not apply to an investment advertisement issued or caused to be issued by a relevant person in circumstances in which either–

(a) it is contained in a copy of a publication being a copy which is issued to a particular person by reason of his having placed an advertisement in that publication; or

(b) it is issued to a person whose business it is to place, or arrange for the placing of, advertising and who is sent the advertisement for the purposes of that business.

## ADVERTISEMENTS DIRECTED AT INFORMING OR INFLUENCING PERSONS OF A PARTICULAR KIND

**8(1)** Section 57 of the Act shall not apply to an investment advertisement to which it would, apart from this article or other applicable exemption, otherwise apply if the advertisement may reasonably be regarded as being directed at informing or influencing only persons who fall within any one or more of the following categories–

(a) a government, local authority or public authority, or the Scottish Administration or any part thereof;

(b) persons whose ordinary activities involve them, as principal or as agent, in acquiring, holding, managing or disposing of investments for the purposes of a business carried on by them or whom it is reasonable to expect will, as principal or agent, acquire, hold, manage or dispose of investments for the purposes of such a business;

(c) persons whose ordinary business involves the giving of advice which may lead to another person acquiring or disposing of an investment or refraining from so doing; and

(d) persons whose ordinary business involves making arrangements with a view to another person acquiring or disposing of investments.

**History**
In art. 8(1)(a) the words ", or the Scottish Administration or any part thereof" inserted by the Scotland Act 1998 (Consequential Modifications) (No. 2) Order 1999 (SI 1999/1820), art. 1(2), 4, Sch. 2, Pt. I, para. 79 as from 1 July 1999.

**8(2)** For the purposes of paragraph (1) of this article–

(a) the expression **"government, local authority or public authority"** has the meaning given in Note (1) to paragraph 3 of Schedule 1 to the Act; and

(b) an advertisement may be regarded as directed at informing or influencing a person of a kind specified in paragraph (1) if it is addressed to some other person in his capacity as an employee of that person, and, for these purposes, employment includes employment otherwise than under a contract of service.

**9(1)** For the purposes of article 8 of this Order, each of the following is an indication that an advertisement is directed at informing or influencing persons of a kind specified in paragraph (1) of that article–

(a) the advertisement expressly states that it is directed at persons of a kind specified in article 8(1) of this Order and that it would be imprudent for persons of any other kind to respond to it;

(b) the advertisement expressly states that any investment or service to which it relates is available only to persons having professional experience in matters relating to investment;

(c) the manner in which the advertisement is disseminated is such that it is unlikely to come to the attention of persons who are not professionally experienced in matters relating to investment; and

(d) any invitation or information contained in the advertisement is unlikely to appeal to persons who do not have professional experience in matters relating to investment.

**9(2)** None of the indications given in paragraph (1) above is to be taken as showing conclusively that an advertisement is directed as there mentioned and, equally, the fact that an advertisement contains none of those indications is not to be taken to indicate that it is not so directed.

**10(1)** For the purposes of article 8 of this Order, each of the following is an indication that an advertisement is directed at informing or influencing persons of a kind not specified in paragraph (1) of that article–

(a) the advertisement concerns an investment which is likely to be of interest mainly to persons acting in their personal capacity;

(b) the minimum amount which may be expended in order to enter into any transaction to which the advertisement relates is sufficiently small that it is unlikely to deter persons who do not have professional experience in matters relating to investment from responding to the advertisement; and

(c) the advertisement is a direct offer advertisement within the meaning given to that expression for the purposes of the core rules for the conduct of investment business.

**10(2)** None of the indications given in paragraph (1) above is to be taken as showing conclusively that an advertisement is directed as there mentioned and, equally, the fact that an advertisement contains none of those indications is not to be taken to indicate that it is not so directed.

## ADVERTISEMENTS REQUIRED OR PERMITTED TO BE PUBLISHED BY EXCHANGE OR MARKET RULES

**11** Section 57 of the Act shall not apply to any advertisement relating to any investment falling within any of paragraphs 1 to 5 of Schedule 1 to the Act which is permitted to be traded or dealt in on a relevant EEA market or a market established under the rules of an investment exchange specified in Schedule 2 to this Order, if the advertisement consists of or of any part of a document which is required or permitted to be published by the rules of the relevant market, or by a body which regulates such a market or which regulates offers or issues of investments to be traded on such a market.

## ADVERTISEMENTS BY CERTAIN MARKETS

**12** Section 57 of the Act shall not apply to an investment advertisement which is issued or caused to be issued by a market which is a relevant EEA market or is established under the rules of an investment exchange specified in Schedule 2 or 3 to this Order if the only reason why section 57 would otherwise apply to the advertisement is that it contains information which identifies a particular investment falling within paragraph 7, 8 or 9 of Schedule 1 to the Act as one which may be traded or dealt in on the market.

## INDUSTRIAL AND PROVIDENT SOCIETIES

**13** Section 57 of the Act shall not apply to an investment advertisement which is issued or caused to be issued by an industrial and provident society with respect to investments falling within paragraph 2 of Schedule 1 to the Act which it has issued or proposes to issue.

## PUBLIC OFFERS OF SECURITIES

**14** Section 57 of the Act shall not apply to an investment advertisement which–

(a) is a prospectus, or supplementary prospectus, issued in accordance with Part II of the Public Offers of Securities Regulations 1995;

(b) relates to a prospectus or supplementary prospectus published or to be published in accordance with Part II of the Public Offers of Securities Regulations 1995, and which contains no invitation or information which would make it an investment advertisement other than–

  (i) the name and address of the person by whom the investments to which the prospectus or supplementary prospectus relates are to be offered (within the meaning of the Public Offers of Securities Regulations 1995), or other particulars for communicating with him;

  (ii) the nature and the nominal value of the investments to which the prospectus or supplementary prospectus relates, the number offered and the price at which they are offered;

(iii) a statement that a prospectus or supplementary prospectus issued in accordance with Part II of the Public Offers of Securities Regulations 1995 is or will be available and, if it is not yet available, when it is expected to be; and

(iv) instructions for obtaining a copy of the prospectus or supplementary prospectus; or

(c) is required by a relevant EEA market for admission of an investment to trading on that market which–

(i) contains the information which would be required by Part II of the Public Offers of Securities Regulations 1995 if it were a prospectus; and

(ii) does not contain any information other than information required or permitted to be published by the rules of the relevant EEA market.

### ADVERTISEMENTS REQUIRED OR AUTHORISED UNDER ENACTMENTS

**15** Section 57 of the Act shall not apply to an investment advertisement if its issue is required or authorised by or under any enactment other than the Act.

### REVOCATIONS

**16** The Financial Services Act 1986 (Investment Advertisements) (Exemptions) (No. 2) Order 1988 and the Financial Services Act 1986 (Investment Advertisements) (Exemptions) (No. 2) Order 1992 are hereby revoked.

# Schedule 1 – Relevant EEA Markets

Article 2

## Part I – Exchanges Operating Relevant EEA Markets

Asociacion de Intermediarios de Activos Financieros.
Amsterdam Financial Futures Market.
Amsterdam Pork and Potato Terminal Market (NLKKAS-Amsterdam Clearing House).
Amsterdam Stock Exchange.
Antwerp Stock Exchange.
Athens Stock Exchange.
Barcelona Stock Exchange.
Berlin Stock Exchange.
Bilbao Stock Exchange.
Bologna Stock Exchange.
Bremen Stock Exchange.
Brussels Stock Exchange.
Copenhagen Stock Exchange (including FUTOP).
Deutsche Terminboerse.
Dusseldorf Stock Exchange.
European Options Exchange.
Finnish Options Market.
Florence Stock Exchange.
Frankfurt Stock Exchange.
Genoa Stock Exchange.
Hamburg Stock Exchange.
Hanover Stock Exchange.
Helsinki Stock Exchange.
The International Stock Exchange of the United Kingdom and the Republic of Ireland Limited.
Irish Futures and Options Exchange.
Lisbon Stock Exchange.

Luxembourg Stock Exchange.
Madrid Stock Exchange.
Marche a Terme International de France (MATIF).
MEFF Renta Fija.
MEFF Renta Variable.
Milan Stock Exchange.
Marche des Options Negociables de Paris (MONEP).
Munich Stock Exchange.
Naples Stock Exchange.
OM Stockholm AB.
Oporto Stock Exchange.
Oslo Stock Exchange.
Palermo Stock Exchange.
Paris Stock Exchange.
Rome Stock Exchange.
Stockholm Stock Exchange.
Stuttgart Stock Exchange.
Trieste Stock Exchange.
Turin Stock Exchange.
Valencia Stock Exchange.
Venice Stock Exchange.
Wiener Bourse.

## Part II – Criteria Relevant to Definition of "Relevant EEA Market"

The criteria relevant for the purposes of the definition of **"relevant EEA market"** in article 2 of this Order are the following–

(a) the head office of the market must be situated in an EEA State; and
(b) the market must he subject to requirements in the EEA State in which its head office is situated as to–
  (i) the manner in which it operates;
  (ii) the means by which access may be had to the facilities it provides;
  (iii) the conditions to be satisfied before an investment may be traded or dealt in by means of its facilities; and
  (iv) the reporting and publication of transactions effected by means of its facilities.

# Schedule 2 – Non-EEA Exchanges Relevant for the Purposes of Articles 11 and 12

Articles 11 and 12

Alberta Stock Exchange.
American Stock Exchange.
Australian Stock Exchange Limited.
Basler Effektenbourse.
Bolsa Mexicana de Valores.
Boston Stock Exchange.
Bourse de Geneve.
Chicago Board Options Exchange.

Cincinnati Stock Exchange.
Effektenborsenverein Zurich.
Fukuoka Stock Exchange.
Hiroshima Stock Exchange.
Johannesburg Stock Exchange.
Korea Stock Exchange.
Kuala Lumpur Stock Exchange.
Kyoto Securities Exchange.
Midwest Stock Exchange.
The Montreal Exchange.
Nagoya Stock Exchange.
NASDAQ.
New York Stock Exchange.
New Zealand Stock Exchange.
Niigata Stock Exchange.
Osaka Securities Exchange.
Pacific Stock Exchange.
Philadelphia Stock Exchange.
Sapporo Securities Exchange.
Securities Exchange of Thailand.
Singapore Stock Exchange.
Stock Exchange of Hong Kong Limited.
Tokyo Stock Exchange.
Toronto Stock Exchange.
Vancouver Stock Exchange.
Winnipeg Stock Exchange.

## Schedule 3 – Non-EEA Exchanges Relevant for the Purposes of Article 12

Article 12

Australian Financial Futures Market.
Chicago Board of Trade.
Chicago Mercantile Exchange.
Coffee, Sugar and Cocoa Exchange, Inc.
Commodity Exchange, Inc.
Hong Kong Futures Exchange.
International Securities Market Association.
Kansas City Board of Trade.
Mid-America Commodity Exchange.
Minneapolis Grain Exchange.
New York Cotton Exchange (including the Citrus Associates of the New York Cotton Exchange).
New York Futures Exchange.
New York Mercantile Exchange.
New Zealand Futures Exchange.

Philadelphia Board of Trade.
Singapore International Monetary Exchange.
South African Futures Exchange (SAFEX).
Swiss Options and Financial Futures Exchange (SOFFEX).
Sydney Futures Exchange.
Toronto Futures Exchange.

# Schedule 4

Article 4

## PART I

**1** In this Schedule–

**"date of the offer"** means the date specified in an investment advertisement to which article 4(3) of this Order applies as the date on which the advertisement was issued to recipients of the offer;

**"equity share capital"**, **"holding company"**, **"subsidiary"**, and **"wholly owned subsidiary"**have the same meanings as in the 1985 Act when used in relatIon to a body corporate which is a company within the meaning of that Act and have the same meanings as in the 1986 Order when used in relation to a body corporate which is a company within the meaning of that Order;

**"offer document"** means an investment advertisement to which article 4(3) of this Order applies;

**"offeree company"** means a body corporate of the kind specified in paragraph 3 of this Schedule shares in or debentures of which are the subject of an offer; and

**"offeror"** means a person by or on behalf of whom an offer is made;

and for the purposes of this Schedule shares or debentures are to be regarded as being held by or on behalf of an offeror if the person who holds them, or on whose behalf they are held, has agreed that an offer should not be made in respect of them.

## PART II

**2** An offer is an offer of the kind referred to in article 4(1)(b) of the Order if it is an offer for all the shares in, or all the shares comprised in the equity or non-equity share capital of, an offeree company or is an offer for all the debentures of an offeree company other than, in each case, shares or debentures held by or on behalf of the offeror, and–

(a) terms have been recommended by all the directors of the offeree company other than any director who is the offeror or a director of the offeror;

(b) in the case of an offer for debentures or for non-equity share capital where, at the date of the offer, shares carrying 50 per cent or less of the voting rights attributable to the equity share capital are held by or on behalf of the offeror, the offer includes or is accompanied by an offer made by the offeror for the rest of the shares comprised in the equity share capital;

(c) in the case of an offer for shares comprised in the equity share capital where, at the date of the offer–

(i) shares carrying 50 per cent or less of the voting rights then exercisable in general meetings of the offeree company; and

(ii) shares carrying 50 per cent or less of the voting rights attributable to the equity share capital;

are held by or on behalf of the offeror, it is a condition of the offer that sufficient shares be acquired or be agreed to be acquired by the offeror pursuant to or during the offer to result in shares carrying more than the said percentages of voting rights being held by him or on his behalf;

(d) except insofar as it may be totally withdrawn and all persons released from any obligation incurred under it, the offer is open for acceptance by every recipient for the period of at least 21 days beginning with the day after the day on which the document was issued to recipients of the offer;

(e) the acquisition of the shares or debentures to which the offer relates is not conditional upon the recipients approving, or consenting to, any payment or other benefit being made or given to any director or former director of the offeree company in connection with, or as compensation or consideration for, his ceasing to be a director or to hold any office held in conjunction with any directorship or, in the case of a former director, to hold any office which he held in conjunction with his former directorship and continued to hold after ceasing to be a director;

(f) the consideration for the shares or debentures is cash or, in the case of an offeror which is a body corporate other than an open-ended investment company, is either cash or shares in or debentures of the offeror or any combination of cash, such shares and such debentures; and

(g) copies of the following documents are available during normal office hours and free of charge at the place specified in the offer document by virtue of paragraph 10 of this Schedule–

  (i) the memorandum and articles of association of the offeree company and, if the offeror is a body corporate, the memorandum and articles of association of the offeror or, if it has no memorandum and articles of association, any instrument constituting or defining the constitution of the offeror, and, if such document is not written in English, a certified English translation of the instrument;

  (ii) in the case of an offeree company which does not fall within subparagraph (iv) below, the audited accounts of the offeree company in respect of the last two accounting reference periods for which the laying and delivering of accounts under the 1985 Act or the 1986 Order has passed and, if accounts have been delivered to the relevant registrar of companies in respect of a later accounting reference period, copies of those accounts;

  (iii) in the case of an offeror which is required to deliver accounts to the registrar of companies and which does not fall within subparagraph (iv) below, the audited accounts of the offeror in respect of the last two accounting reference periods for which the laying and delivering of accounts under the 1985 Act or the 1986 Order has passed and, if accounts have been delivered to the relevant registrar of companies in respect of a later accounting reference period, copies of those accounts;

  (iv) in the case of an offeree company or an offeror which was incorporated during the period of three years immediately preceding the date of the offer or which has, at any time during that period, passed a resolution in accordance with section 252 of the 1985 Act or Article 260 of the 1986 Order, the information described in whichever is relevant of sub-paragraph (ii) or (iii) with respect to that body corporate need be included only in relation to the period since its incorporation or since it last ceased to be exempt from the obligation to appoint auditors as the case may be;

  (v) all existing contracts of service entered into for a period of more than a year between the offeree company and any of its directors and, if the offeror is a body corporate. between the offeror and any of its directors;

  (vi) any report, letter, valuation or other document any part of which is exhibited or referred to in the offer document;

  (vii) if the offer document contains any statement purporting to have been made by an expert, that expert's written consent to the inclusion of that statement; and

  (viii) all material contracts (if any) of the offeree company and of the offeror (not, in either case, being contracts which were entered into in the ordinary course of business) entered into during the period of two years immediately preceding the date of the offer.

## PART III

**3** A body corporate is a body corporate of the kind referred to in article 4(1)(b) of this Order if–

(a) it is a private company; and

(b) no shares comprised in the equity share capital of the company are or have, at any time within the period of ten years immediately preceding the date of the offer, been–

(i) listed or quoted on an investment exchange whether in the United Kingdom or elsewhere; or

(ii) shares in respect of which information has, with the agreement or approval of any officer of the company, been published for the purpose of facilitating deals in them, indicating prices at which persons have dealt or were willing to deal in them other than persons who were, at the time the information was published, existing members of a relevant class; or

(iii) subject to a marketing arrangement which accorded to the company the facilities referred to in section 163(2)(b) of the 1985 Act or article 173(2)(b) of the 1986 Order; or

(iv) the subject of an offer (whether in the United Kingdom or elsewhere) in relation to which a copy of a prospectus was delivered to the relevant registrar of companies in accordance with section 41 of the Companies Act 1948, section 41 of the Companies Act (Northern Ireland) 1960, section 64 of the 1985 Act or article 74 of the 1986 Order or Part II of the Public Offers of Securities Regulations 1995.

**4** For the purposes of paragraph 3(b)(ii) of this Schedule a person shall be regarded as being a member of a relevant class if he was, at the relevant time, an existing member or debenture holder of the offeree company, or an existing employee of that company, or a member of the family of such a member or employee and for these purposes **"family"** in relation to a person means that person's husband or wife, widow or widower and children (including step-children and, in Northern Ireland, adopted children) and their descendants and any trustee (acting in his capacity as such) of a trust the principal beneficiary of which is that person or any of those relatives.

## PART IV

**5** An advertisement fulfils the conditions specified in article 4(3)(b) of this Order if it takes the form of a document which complies with the requirements of paragraphs 6 to 11 of this Schedule and is accompanied by the material specified in paragraph 12.

**6** The document must state on its face the identity of the offeror and, if the offer is being made on behalf of another person, the identity of that person.

**7** The document must state on its face the fact that the terms of the offer are recommended by all the directors of the offeree company other than (if that is the case) any director who is the offeror or a director of the offeror.

**8** The document must contain prominently the following words: "If you are in any doubt about this offer you should consult a person authorised under the Financial Services Act 1986 who specialises in advising on the sale of shares and debentures" or other words to like effect.

**9** The document must state clearly the matters referred to in paragraph 2(d) and (e) of this Schedule and the date on which it was issued to recipients of the offer.

**10** The document must name a place in the United Kingdom at which copies of the documents specified in paragraph 2(g) of this Schedule may be inspected and state that those documents may be inspected at that place free of charge.

**11** The document must contain the following information–

(a) particulars of all shares in or debentures of the offeree company and of all investments falling within paragraphs 4, 5 or 7 of Schedule 1 to the Act which relate to shares in or debentures of the offeree company held by or on behalf of the offeror or each offeror if there is more than one or, if none are so held, an appropriate negative statement;

(b) a statement as to whether or not the offer is conditional upon acceptances in respect of a minimum number of shares or debentures being received and, if the offer is so conditional, what the minimum number is;

(c) where the offer is conditional upon acceptances, the date which is the latest date on which it can become unconditional;

(d) if the offer is, or has become, unconditional the fact that it will remain open until further notice and that at least 14 days' notice will be given before it is closed;

(e) if applicable, a statement as to whether or not, if circumstances arise in which an offeror is able compulsorily to acquire shares of any dissenting minority under Part XIIIA of the 1985 Act or articles 421 to 423 of the 1986 Order, that offeror intends so to acquire those shares;

(f) if shares or debentures are to be acquired for cash, the period within which payment will be made and the method of payment;

(g) if the consideration or any part of the consideration for the shares or debentures to be acquired is shares in or debentures of an offeror–

(i) the nature and particulars of the offeror's business, its financial and trading prospects and its place of incorporation;

(ii) in respect of any offeror which is a body corporate, and in respect of the offeree company, its turnover, profit on ordinary activities before and after tax, extraordinary items, tax on extraordinary items and its profit and loss and the rate per cent of any dividends paid adjusted as appropriate to take account of relevant changes over the period and the total amount absorbed thereby for, in each case, the period of five years immediately preceding the date of the offer; provided that in the case of a body corporate which was incorporated during the period of five years immediately preceding the date of the offer or which has, at any time during that period, passed a resolution in accordance with section 252 of the 1985 Act or article 260 of the 1986 Order, the information described in this subparagraph with respect to that body corporate need be included only in relation to the period since its incorporation or since it last ceased to be exempt from the obligation to appoint auditors, as the case may be;

(iii) particulars of the first dividend in which any such shares or debentures will participate and of the rights attaching to them (including, in the case of debentures, rights as to interest) and of any restrictions of their transfer;

(iv) an indication of the effect of acceptance on the capital and income position of the holder of shares in or debentures of the offeree company; and

(v) particulars of all material contracts (not being contracts which were entered into in the normal course of business) which were entered into by each of the offeree company and the offeror during the period of two years immediately preceding the date of the offer;

(h) particulars of the terms on which shares in or debentures of the offeree company acquired in pursuance of the offer will be transferred and of any restrictions on their transfer;

(i) whether or not it is proposed, in connection with the offer, that any payment or other benefit be made or given to any director or former director of the offeree company in connection with or as compensation or consideration for his ceasing to be a director or to hold any office held in conjunction with a directorship or, in the case of a former director, to hold any office which he held in conjunction with his former directorship and which he continued to hold after ceasing to be a director and, if it is so proposed, details of each such payment or benefit;

(j) whether or not there exists any agreement or arrangement between the offeror or any person with whom the offeror has an agreement of the kind described in section 204 of the 1985 Act or article 212 of the 1986 Order and any director or shareholder of the offeree company or any person who has been such a director or shareholder at any time during the period of twelve months immediately preceding the date of the offer, being an agreement or arrangement which is connected with or dependent on the offer, and if there is any such agreement or arrangement particulars of it;

(k) whether or not the offeror has reason to believe that there has been any material change in the financial position or prospects of the offeree company since the end of the accounting reference period to which the accounts referred to in paragraph 12 of this Schedule relate, and if the offeror has reason to believe that there has been any such change particulars of it;

(l) whether or not there is any agreement or arrangement whereby any shares or debentures acquired by the offeror in pursuance of the offer will or may be transferred to any other person together with the names of the parties to any such agreement or arrangement and particulars of all shares and debentures in the offeree company held by such persons;

(m) particulars of any dealings in the shares in or debentures of the offeree company, and, if the offeror is a body corporate, the offeror during the period of twelve months immediately preceding the date of the offer by every person who was a director of either of them at any time during that period, or, if there have been no such dealings, an appropriate negative statement;

(n) in a case where the offeror is a body corporate which is required to deliver accounts under the 1985 Act or the 1986 Order, particulars of the assets and liabilities as shown in its audited accounts in respect of the latest accounting reference period for which the period for laying and delivering accounts under the relevant legislation has passed or, if accounts in respect of a later accounting reference period have been delivered under the relevant legislation, as shown in those accounts and not the earlier accounts;

(o) where valuations of assets are given in connection with the offer, the basis on which the valuation was made and the names and addresses of the persons who valued them and particulars of any relevant qualifications; and

(p) if any profit forecast is given in connection with the offer, a statement of the assumptions on which the forecast is based.

12 The document must be accompanied by the following–

(a) the audited accounts of the offeree company in respect of the latest accounting reference period for which the period for laying and delivering accounts under the 1985 Act or the 1986 Order has passed, or, if accounts in respect of a later accounting reference period have been delivered under the relevant legislation, those accounts and not the earlier ones;

(b) a letter advising the directors of the offeree company on the financial implications of the offer from a competent person who is independent of and has no substantial financial interest in the offeree company or the offeror, being a letter which sets out the advice that person has given in relation to the offer;

(c) a statement by the directors of the offeree company, acting as a board, stating–

(i) whether or not there has been any material change in the financial position or prospects of the offeree company since the end of the accounting reference period to which the accounts accompanying the offer document relate and, if there has been any such change, particulars of it;

(ii) any interests, in percentage terms, which any of the directors have in the shares in or debentures of the offeree company or any offeror which is a body corporate being interests which, in the case of the offeree company, are required to be entered in the register kept by the company under section 325 of the 1985 Act or article 333 of the 1986 Order or, in the case of an offeror, would be required to be so entered if the director were a director of the offeror and in the case of an offeror which is not a company within the meaning of the 1985 Act or the 1986 Order if the offeror were such a company;

(iii) any material interest which any director has in any contract entered into by the offeror and in any contract entered into by any member of any group of which the offeror is a member;

(d) a statement as to whether or not each director intends to accept the offer in respect of his own beneficial holdings in the offeree company;

(e) a statement by the directors of any offeror which is a body corporate shares in or debentures of which are the consideration or any part of the consideration for the offer that the information concerning the offeror and those shares or debentures contained in the document is correct;

(f) if the offeror is making the offer on behalf of another person, a statement by the offeror as to whether or not he has taken any steps to ascertain whether that person will be in a position to implement the offer and, if he has taken any such steps, what those steps are and his opinion as to whether that person will be in a position to implement the offer; and

(g) a statement that each of the directors of the offeree company, the offeror or, if the offeror is a body corporate, each of the directors of the offeror, are responsible for the information contained in the document insofar as it relates to themselves or their respective bodies corporate and that, to the best of their knowledge and belief (having taken all reasonable care to ensure that such is the case), the information is in accordance with the facts and that no material fact has been omitted.

## EXPLANATORY NOTE

(*This Note is not part of the Order*)

This Order consolidates, amends and adds to the various exemptions from the restrictions on advertising imposed by section 57 of the Financial Services Act 1986 provided by the Financial Services Act 1986 (Investment Advertisements) (Exemptions) (No. 2) Order 1988 and the Financial Services Act 1986 (Investment Advertisements) (Exemptions) (No. 2) Order 1992.

Article 3 of the Order concerns advertisements issued by certain bodies corporate in connection with the promotion or encouragement of industrial or commercial activity or enterprise in the United Kingdom. Article 4 concerns certain advertisements issued in connection with takeovers of private companies. Article 5 concerns advertisements which are issued in connection with certain sales of shares in a body corporate. Article 6 concerns advertisements issued by persons holding permissions granted under paragraph 23 of Schedule 1 to the Financial Services Act 1986. Article 7 concerns the position where a publication is sent to a person who has placed an advertisement in it and with advertisements issued to person involved in advertising. Article 8 concerns advertisements directed at informing or influencing persons of the kind described in the article. Articles 9 and 10 give certain indications as to whether an advertisement may be regarded as being directed at informing or influencing persons of the relevant kind. Article 11 concerns advertisements relating to an investment falling within any of the paragraphs 1 to 5 of Schedule 1 to the Financial Services Act 1986 which is traded or dealt in on a market of the kind referred to in the article, or which is permitted by a body which reglates such a market or the offer or issue of such investments on such a market. Article 12 concerns advertisements issued or caused to be issued by a market of the kind referred to in the article. Article 13 concerns the issue by industrial and provident societies of advertisements relating to their debentures. Article 14 concerns advertisements which are prospectuses issued in accordance with the Public Offers of Securities Regulations 1995, publications publicising such prospectuses, or documents required for admission to trading on a market of the kind referred to in the article. Article 15 concerns advertisements the issue of which is required or authorised under other legislation.

# THE PUBLIC OFFERS OF SECURITIES REGULATIONS 1995

(SI 1995/1537)

*Made on 14 June 1995 by the Treasury under s. 2(2) and Sch. 2 to the European Communities Act 1972. Operative from 19 June 1995.*

[**Note:** Amendments to these Regulations by the Public Offers of Securities (Amendment) Regulations 1999 (SI 1999/734) and the Public Offers of Securities (Amendment) (No. 2) Regulations 1999 (SI 1999/1146) (both operative from 10 May 1999) have been included.]

## PART I – GENERAL

### CITATION, COMMENCEMENT AND EXTENT

**1(1)** These Regulations may be cited as the Public Offers of Securities Regulations 1995 and shall come into force on 19th June 1995.

**1(2)** These Regulations extend to Northern Ireland.

### INTERPRETATION

**2(1)** In these Regulations, except where the context otherwise requires–

**"the Act"** means the Financial Services Act 1986;

**"approved exchange"** means, in relation to dealings in securities, a recognised investment exchange approved by the Treasury for the purposes of these Regulations either generally or in relation to such dealings, and the Treasury shall give notice in such manner as they think appropriate of the exchanges which are for the time being approved;

**"body corporate"** shall be construed in accordance with section 207(1) of the Act;

**"convertible securities"** means–

(i) securities falling within paragraph 2 of Schedule 1 to the Act which can be converted into or exchanged for, or which confer rights to acquire, securities; or

(ii) securities falling within paragraph 4 or 5 of that Schedule;

and **"conversion"** in relation to convertible securities means their conversion into or exchange for, or the exercise of rights conferred by them to acquire, other securities (**"underlying securities"**);

**"credit institution"** has the same meaning as it has for the purposes of paragraph 3 of Schedule 11A to the Act;

**"director"** shall be construed in accordance with section 207(1) of the Act;

**"ecu"** has the same meaning as it has for the purposes of paragraph 3 of Schedule 11A to the Act;

**"European institution"** has the same meaning as in the Banking Coordination (Second Council Directive) Regulations 1992;

**"Euro-securities"** means securities which–

(a) are to be underwritten (by whatever means, including acquisition or subscription, with a view to resale) and distributed by a syndicate at least two of the members of which have their registered offices in different countries or territories;

(b) are to be offered on a significant scale in one or more countries or territories other than the country or territory in which the issuer has its registered office; and

(c) may be acquired pursuant to the offer only through a credit institution or other financial institution;

**"financial institution"** has the same meaning as it has for the purposes of paragraph 3 of Schedule 11A to the Act;

**"group"** has the meaning given in section 207(1) of the Act;

**"home-regulated investment business"** has the same meaning as in the Banking Coordination (Second Council Directive) Regulations 1992;

**"issuer"**, in relation to any securities, means the person by whom they have been or are to be issued;

**"member State"** means a State which is a Contracting Party to the Agreement on the European Economic Area signed at Oporto on 2nd May 1992 as adjusted by the Protocol signed at Brussels on 17th March 1993;

**"private company"** has the meaning given in section 1(3) of the Companies Act 1985;

**"the registrar of companies"**, in relation to a prospectus relating to any securities, means–

(a) if the securities are or are to be issued by a company incorporated in Great Britain, the registrar of companies in England and Wales or the registrar of companies in Scotland according to whether the company's registered office is in England and Wales or in Scotland;

(b) if the securities are or are to be issued by a company incorporated in Northern Ireland, the registrar of companies for Northern Ireland;

(c) in any other case, any of those registrars;

**"recognised investment exchange"** has the meaning given in section 207(1) of the Act;

**"securities"** means investments to which Part II of these Regulations applies; and

**"sale"** includes any disposal for valuable consideration.

**History**

In reg. 2(1) the definition of **"Euro-securities"** substituted by the Public Offers of Securities (Amendment) Regulations 1999 (SI 1999/734), reg.1, 2(a) as from 10 May 1999. The former definition read as follows:

""**Euro-securities**" has the same meaning as it has for the purposes of paragraph 3 of Schedule 11A to the Act;".

**2(2)** In the application of these Regulations to Scotland, references to a matter being actionable at the suit of a person shall be construed as references to the matter being actionable at the instance of that person.

**2(3)** References to the Companies Act 1985 include references to the corresponding Northern Ireland provision.

## PART II – PUBLIC OFFERS OF UNLISTED SECURITIES

### INVESTMENTS TO WHICH THIS PART APPLIES

**3(1)** This Part of these Regulations applies to any investment which–

(a) is not admitted to official listing, nor the subject of an application for listing, in accordance with Part IV of the Act; and

(b) falls within paragraph 1, 2, 4 or 5 of Schedule 1 to the Act.

**3(2)** In the application of those paragraphs for the purposes of these Regulations–

(a) debentures having a maturity of less than one year from their date of issue shall be deemed to be excluded from paragraph 2;

(b) the note to paragraph 1 shall have effect with the omission of the words ", except in relation to any shares of a class defined as deferred shares for the purposes of section 119 of the Building Societies Act 1986,";

(c) paragraphs 4 and 5 shall have effect with the omission of references to investments falling within paragraph 3; and

(d) paragraph 4 shall have effect as though after the words "subscribe for" there were inserted "or acquire."

**Note**

Reg. 3 has effect from 19 June 1995 as if transferable shares in a body corporate incorporated under the law of, or any part of, the UK relating to industrial and provident societies, and bills of exchange accepted by a banker, were not investments to which Pt. II applies: see the Investment Services Regulations 1995 (SI 1995/3275), reg. 1(1), Sch. 10, para. 22.

### REGISTRATION AND PUBLICATION OF PROSPECTUS

**4(1)** When securities are offered to the public in the United Kingdom for the first time the offeror shall publish a prospectus by making it available to the public, free of charge, at an address in the United Kingdom, from the time he first offers the securities until the end of the period during which the offer remains open.

**4(2)** The offeror shall, before the time of publication of the prospectus, deliver a copy of it to the registrar of companies for registration.

**4(3)** Paragraph (2) and regulations 5, 6 and 8 to 15 shall not apply to a prospectus submitted for approval in accordance with listing rules made under section 156A of the Act.

## OFFERS OF SECURITIES

**5** A person is to be regarded as offering securities if, as principal–

(a) he makes an offer which, if accepted, would give rise to a contract for the issue or sale of the securities by him or by another person with whom he has made arrangements for the issue or sale of the securities; or

(b) he invites a person to make such an offer;

but not otherwise; and, except where the context otherwise requires, in this Part of these Regulations **"offer"** and **"offeror"** shall be construed accordingly.

## OFFERS TO THE PUBLIC IN THE UNITED KINGDOM

**6** A person offers securities to the public in the United Kingdom if, to the extent that the offer is made to persons in the United Kingdom, it is made to the public; and, for this purpose, an offer which is made to any section of the public, whether selected as members or debenture holders of a body corporate, or as clients of the person making the offer, or in any other manner, is to be regarded as made to the public.

## EXEMPTIONS

**7(1)** For the purposes of these Regulations, an offer of securities shall be deemed not to be an offer to the public in the United Kingdom if, to the extent that the offer is made to persons in the United Kingdom–

(a) the condition specified in any one of the sub-paragraphs of paragraph (2) is satisfied in relation to the offer; or

(b) paragraph (3) applies in relation to the offer.

**7(2)** The following are the conditions specified in this paragraph–

(a) the securities are offered to persons–

  (i) whose ordinary activities involve them in acquiring, holding, managing or disposing of investments (as principal or agent) for the purposes of their businesses; or

  (ii) who it is reasonable to expect will acquire, hold, manage or dispose of investments (as principal or agent) for the purposes of their businesses;

 or are otherwise offered to persons in the context of their trades, professions or occupations;

(b) the securities are offered to no more than fifty persons;

(c) the securities are offered to the members of a club or association (whether or not incorporated) and the members can reasonably be regarded as having a common interest with each other and with the club or association in the affairs of the club or association and in what is to be done with the proceeds of the offer;

(d) the securities are offered to a restricted circle of persons whom the offeror reasonably believes to be sufficiently knowledgeable to understand the risks involved in accepting the offer;

(e) the securities are offered in connection with a bona fide invitation to enter into an underwriting agreement with respect to them;

(f) the securities are the securities of a private company and are offered by that company to–

  (i) members or employees of the company;

  (ii) members of the families of any such members or employees; or

  (iii) holders of securities issued by the company which fall within paragraph 2 of Schedule 1 to the Act;

(ff) the securities are the securities of a private company and are offered to holders of other securities in that company (whether or not of the same class) in pursuance of a requirement imposed by a provision in its articles of association or in an agreement between all the holders of securities, or all the holders of one or more classes of security, of that company;

(g) the securities are offered to a government, local authority or public authority, as defined in paragraph 3 of Schedule 1 to the Act;

(h) the total consideration payable for the securities cannot exceed ecu 40,000 (or an equivalent amount);

(i) the minimum consideration which may be paid by any person for securities acquired by him pursuant to the offer is at least ecu 40,000 (or an equivalent amount);

(j) the securities are denominated in amounts of at least ecu 40,000 (or an equivalent amount);

(k) the securities are offered in connection with a takeover offer;

(l) the securities are offered in connection with a merger within the meaning of Council Directive No. 78/855/EEC;

(m) the securities are shares and are offered free of charge to any or all of the holders of shares in the issuer;

(n) the securities are shares, or investments falling within paragraph 4 or 5 of Schedule 1 to the Act relating to shares, in a body corporate and are offered in exchange for shares in the same body corporate, and the offer cannot result in any increase in the issued share capital of the body corporate;

(o) the securities are issued by a body corporate and offered–

(i) by the issuer, by a body corporate connected with the issuer or by a relevant trustee;

(ii) only to qualifying persons; and

(iii) on terms that a contract to acquire any such securities may be entered into only by the qualifying person to whom they were offered or, if the terms of the offer so permit, any qualifying person;

(p) the securities result from the conversion of convertible securities and listing particulars or a prospectus relating to the convertible securities were or was published in the United Kingdom under or by virtue of Part IV of the Act, Part III of the Companies Act 1985 or these Regulations;

(q) the securities are issued by–

(i) a charity within the meaning of section 96(1) of the Charities Act 1993;

(ii) a housing association within the meaning of section 5(1) of the Housing Act 1985;

(iii) an industrial or provident society registered in accordance with section 1(2)(b) of the Industrial and Provident Societies Act 1965; or

(iv) a non-profit making association or body, recognised by the country or territory in which it is established, with objectives similar to those of a body falling within any of paragraphs (i) to (iii);

and the proceeds of the offer will be used for the purposes of the issuer's objectives;

(r) the securities offered are shares and ownership of the securities entitles the holder–

(i) to obtain the benefit of services provided by a building society within the meaning of section 119(1) of the Building Societies Act, an industrial or provident society registered in accordance with section 1(2) of the Industrial and Provident Societies Act 1965 or a body of a like nature established in a Member State; or

(ii) to membership of such a body;

(s) the securities offered are Euro-securities, and no advertisement relating to the offer is issued in the United Kingdom (within the meaning of the Act), or is caused to be issued, by the issuer of the Euro-securities or by any credit institution or other financial institution through which the Euro-securities may be acquired pursuant to the offer, or by any body corporate which is a member of the same group as that issuer or any of those institutions, other than–

(i) an advertisement falling within article 8 of the Financial Services Act 1986 (Investments Advertisements) (Exemptions) (No. 2) Order 1995; or

(ii) an advertisement which would fall within article 11 of the Financial Services Act 1986 (Investment Advertisements) (Exemptions) Order 1996 if the person issuing the advertisement were a relevant person within the meaning of that article and there were added to the list of persons in paragraph (3) of that article a person with or for whom any credit institution or other financial institution through which the Euro-securities may be acquired pursuant to the offer has effected or arranged for the effecting of a transaction within the period of twelve months ending with the date on which the offer is first made;

(t) the securities are of the same class, and were issued at the same time, as securities in respect of which a prospectus has been published under or by virtue of Part IV of the Act, Part III of the Companies Act 1985 or these Regulations;

(u) the securities are not transferable.

**History**
In reg. 7(2):

- para. (ff) inserted by the Public Offers of Securities (Amendment) Regulations 1999 (SI 1999/734), reg. 1, 2(b), as from 10 May 1999.
- in para. (i) the words "paid by any person for securities acquired by him" appearing after the words "which may be" substituted for the former words "paid for securities acquired" by the Public Offers of Securities (Amendment) Regulations 1999 (SI 1999/734), reg. 1, 2(c), as from 10 May 1999.
- in para. (o)(i) the words from ", by a body" to the end inserted by the Public Offers of Securities (Amendment) Regulations 1999 (SI 1999/734), reg. 1, 2(d), as from 10 May 1999.
- para. (s) substituted by the Public Offers of Securities (Amendment) Regulations 1999 (SI 1999/734), reg. 1, 2(e), as from 10 May 1999. The former para. (s) read as follows:

"the securities offered are Euro-securities and are not the subject of advertising likely to come to the attention of persons who are not professionally experienced in matters relating to investment;"

**7(3)** This paragraph applies in relation to an offer where the condition specified in one relevant sub-paragraph is satisfied in relation to part, but not the whole, of the offer and, in relation to each other part of the offer, the condition specified in a different relevant sub-paragraph is satisfied.

**7(4)** For the purposes of paragraph (3), **"relevant sub-paragraph"** means any of sub-paragraphs (a) to (f), (g), (k) to (q) and (t) of paragraph (2).

**History**
In reg. 7(4) the words "sub-paragraphs (a) to (f), (g), (k) to (q) and (t)" substituted for the former words "sub-paragraphs (a) to (g), (k) to (n), (p), (q) and (t)" by the Public Offers of Securities (Amendment) Regulations 1999 (SI 1999/734), reg. 1, 2(f), as from 10 May 1999.

**7(5)** For the purposes of this regulation, **"shares"**, except in relation to a takeover offer, means investments falling within paragraph 1 of Schedule 1 to the Act.

**7(6)** For the purposes of determining whether the condition specified in sub-paragraph (b) or (h) of paragraph (2) is satisfied in relation to an offer, the offer shall be taken together with any other offer of securities of the same class which was–

(a) made by the same person;

(b) open at any time within the period of 12 months ending with the date on which the offer is first made; and

(c) deemed not to be an offer to the public in the United Kingdom by virtue of that condition being satisfied.

**7(6A)** For the purposes of paragraph (2)(b), the making of an offer of securities to trustees of a trust or members of a partnership in their capacity as such, or the making of such an offer to any other two or more persons jointly, shall be treated as the making of an offer to a single person.

**History**
Reg. (6A) inserted by the Public Offers of Securities (Amendment) Regulations 1999 (SI 1999/734), reg. 1, 2(g), as from 10 May 1999.

**7(7)** In determining for the purposes of paragraph (2)(d) whether a person is sufficiently knowledgeable to understand the risks involved in accepting an offer of securities, any information supplied by the offeror shall be disregarded, apart from information about–

(a) the issuer of the securities, or

(b) if the securities confer the right to acquire other securities, the issuer of those other securities.

**7(8)** For the purposes of paragraph (2)(f)–

(a) the members of a person's family are the person's husband or wife, widow or widower and children (including stepchildren) and their descendants, and any trustee (acting in his capacity as such) of a trust the principal beneficiary of which is the person himself or herself, or any of those relatives; and

(b) regulation 3(2)(a) shall not apply.

**7(9)** For the purposes of determining whether the condition mentioned in sub-paragraph (h), (i) or (j) of paragraph (2) is satisfied in relation to an offer, an amount, in relation to an amount denominated in ecu, is an **"equivalent amount"** if it is an amount of equal value, calculated at the latest practicable date before (but in any event not more than 3 days before) the date on which the offer is first made, denominated wholly or partly in another currency or unit of account.

**7(10)** For the purposes of paragraph (2)(k), **"takeover offer"** means–

(a) an offer to acquire shares in a body corporate incorporated in the United Kingdom which is a takeover offer within the meaning of Part XIIIA of the Companies Act 1985 (or would be such an offer if that Part of that Act applied in relation to any body corporate);

(b) an offer to acquire all or substantially all the shares, or the shares of a particular class, in a body corporate incorporated outside the United Kingdom; or

(c) an offer made to all the holders of shares, or of shares of a particular class, in a body corporate to acquire a specified proportion of those shares;

but in determining whether an offer falls within sub-paragraph (b) there shall be disregarded any shares which the offeror or any associate of his holds or has contracted to acquire; and in determining whether an offer falls within sub-paragraph (c) the offeror, any associate of his and any person whose shares the offeror or any such associate has contracted to acquire shall not be regarded as holders of the shares.

**History**
See history note after reg. 7(10A).

**7(10A)** In paragraph (10)–

**"associate"** has the same meaning as in section 430E of the Companies Act 1985; and

**"share"** has the same meaning as in section 428(1) of that Act.

**History**
Reg. 7(10), (10A) substituted for the former reg. 7(10) by the Public Offers of Securities (Amendment) Regulations 1999 (SI 1999/734), reg. 1, 2(h), as from 10 May 1999. The former reg. 7(10) read as follows:

"For the purposes of paragraph (2)(k), **"takeover offer"** means–

(a) an offer which is a takeover offer within the meaning of Part XIIIA of the Companies Act 1985 (or would be such an offer if that Part of that Act applied in relation to any body corporate); or

(b) an offer made to all the holders of shares, or of shares of a particular class, in a body corporate to acquire a specified proportion of those shares (**"holders"** and **"shares"** being construed in accordance with that Part);

but in determining for the purposes of sub-paragraph (b) whether an offer is made to all the holders of shares, or of shares of any class, the offeror, any associate of his (within the meaning of section 430E of that Act) and any person whose shares the offeror or any such associate has contracted to acquire shall not be regarded as holders of the shares."

**7(11)** For the purposes of paragraph (2)(m), **"holders of shares"** means the persons who, at the close of business on a date specified in the offer and falling within the period of 60 days ending with the date on which the offer is first made, were holders of such shares.

**History**
In reg. 7(11) the words "60 days" substituted for the former words "28 days" by the Public Offers of Securities (Amendment) Regulations 1999 (SI 1999/734), reg. 1, 2(i), as from 10 May 1999.

**7(12)** For the purposes of paragraph (2)(o), a person is a **"qualifying person"**, in relation to an issuer, if he is a bona fide employee or former employee of the issuer or of another body corporate in the same group (within the meaning of Schedule 1 to the Act) or the wife, husband, widow, widower or child or stepchild under the age of eighteen of such an employee or former employee.

**History**
In reg. 7(12) the words "(within the meaning of Schedule 1 to the Act)" appearing after the words "in the same group" inserted by the Public Offers of Securities (Amendment) Regulations 1999 (SI 1999/734), reg. 1, 2(j), as from 10 May 1999.

**7(13)** The references in paragraph (2)(o) to "a body corporate connected with the issuer" and to "a relevant trustee" shall be construed in accordance with paragraph 20 of Schedule 1 to the Act.

**History**
Reg. 7(13) inserted by the Public Offers of Securities (Amendment) Regulations 1999 (SI 1999/734), reg. 1, 2(k), as from 10 May 1999.

## FORM AND CONTENT OF PROSPECTUS

**8(1)** Subject to regulation 11 and to paragraphs (2), (4), (5) and (6), a prospectus shall contain the information specified in Parts II to X of Schedule 1 to these Regulations (which shall be construed in accordance with Part I of that Schedule).

**8(2)** Where the requirement to include in a prospectus any information (the **"required information"**) is inappropriate to the issuer's sphere of activity or to the legal form of the issuer or the offeror or to the securities to which the prospectus relates, the requirement–

(a) shall have effect as a requirement that the prospectus contain information equivalent to the required information; but

(b) if there is no such equivalent information, shall not apply.

**History**
In reg. 8(2) the words "the legal form of the issuer or the offeror" appearing after the words "sphere of activity or to" substituted for the former words "its legal form" by the Public Offers of Securities (Amendment) Regulations 1999 (SI 1999/734), reg. 1, 2(l), as from 10 May 1999.

**8(3)** The information in a prospectus shall be presented in as easily analysable and comprehensible a form as possible.

**8(4)** Where, on the occasion of their admission to dealings on an approved exchange, securities falling within paragraph 1 of Schedule 1 to the Act are offered on a pre-emptive basis to some or all of the existing holders of such securities, a body or person designated for the purposes of this paragraph by the Treasury shall have power to authorise the omission from a prospectus subject to this regulation of specified information provided that up-to-date information equivalent to that which would otherwise be required by this regulation is available as a result of the requirements of that approved exchange.

In this paragraph, **"specified information"** means information specified in paragraphs 41 to 47 of Schedule 1 to these Regulations.

**8(4A)** In determining for the purposes of paragraph (4) whether information is equivalent to that specified in paragraph 45 of Schedule 1, there shall be disregarded–

(a) the requirements of sub-paragraphs (1)(a)(i), (1)(a)(iv), (1)(b)(iii), (2)(a)(ii), (2)(a)(iv) and (8)(b) of that paragraph; and

(b) any requirement of sub-paragraph (10)(a), (10)(b) or (11)(c) to include a statement by the person responsible for the interim accounts or report.

**History**
Reg. 8(4A) inserted by the Public Offers of Securities (Amendment) Regulations 1999 (SI 1999/734), reg. 1, 2(m), as from 10 May 1999.

**8(5)** Where a class of securities falling within paragraph 1 of Schedule 1 to the Act has been admitted to dealings on an approved exchange, a body or person designated for the purposes of this paragraph by the Treasury shall have power to authorise the making of an offer without a prospectus, provided that–

(a) the number or estimated market value or the nominal value or, in the absence of a nominal value, the accounting par value of the securities offered amounts to less than ten per cent of the number or of the corresponding value of securities of the same class already admitted to dealings; and

(b) up-to-date information equivalent to that required by this regulation is available as a result of the requirements of that approved exchange.

**8(6)** Where a person–

(a) makes an offer to the public in the United Kingdom of securities which he proposes to issue; and

(b) has, within the 12 months preceding the date on which the offer is first made, published a full prospectus relating to a different class of securities which he has issued, or to an earlier issue of the same class of securities,

he may publish, instead of a full prospectus, a prospectus which contains only the differences which have arisen since the publication of the full prospectus mentioned in sub-paragraph (b) and any supplementary prospectus and which are likely to influence the value of the securities, provided that the prospectus is accompanied by that full prospectus and any supplementary prospectus or contains a reference to it or them; and, for this purpose, a full prospectus is one which contains the information specified in Parts II to X of Schedule 1 (other than any information whose omission is authorised by or under paragraph (2) or (4) or regulation 11).

## GENERAL DUTY OF DISCLOSURE IN PROSPECTUS

**9(1)** In addition to the information required to be included in a prospectus by virtue of regulation 8 a prospectus shall (subject to these Regulations) contain all such information as investors would reasonably require, and reasonably expect to find there, for the purpose of making an informed assessment of–

(a) the assets and liabilities, financial position, profits and losses, and prospects of the issuer of the securities; and

(b) the rights attaching to those securities.

**9(2)** The information to be included by virtue of this regulation shall be such information as is mentioned in paragraph (1) which is within the knowledge of any person responsible for the prospectus or which it would be reasonable for him to obtain by making enquiries.

**9(3)** In determining what information is required to be included in a prospectus by virtue of this regulation regard shall be had to the nature of the securities and of the issuer of the securities.

**9(4)** For the purposes of this regulation **"issuer"**, in relation to a certificate or other instrument falling within paragraph 5 of Schedule 1 to the Act, means the person who issued or is to issue the securities to which the certificate or instrument relates.

## SUPPLEMENTARY PROSPECTUS

**10(1)** Where a prospectus has been registered under this Part of these Regulations in respect of an offer of securities and at any time while an agreement in respect of those securities can be entered into in pursuance of that offer–

(a) there is a significant change affecting any matter contained in the prospectus whose inclusion was required by regulation 8 or 9; or

(b) a significant new matter arises the inclusion of information in respect of which would have been so required if it had arisen when the prospectus was prepared; or

(c) there is a significant inaccuracy in the prospectus,

the offeror shall deliver to the registrar of companies for registration, and publish in accordance with paragraph (3), a supplementary prospectus containing particulars of the change or new matter or, in the case of an inaccuracy, correcting it.

**10(2)** In paragraph (1) **"significant"** means significant for the purpose of making an informed assessment of the matters mentioned in regulation 9(1)(a) and (b).

**10(3)** Regulation 4(1) shall apply to a supplementary prospectus delivered for registration to the registrar of companies in the same way as it applies to a prospectus except that the obligation to publish the supplementary prospectus shall begin with the time it is delivered for registration to the registrar of companies.

**10(4)** Where the offeror is not aware of the change, new matter or inaccuracy in question he shall not be under any duty to comply with paragraphs (1) and (3) unless he is notified of it by a person responsible for the prospectus; but any person responsible for the prospectus who is aware of such a matter shall be under a duty to give him notice of it.

**10(5)** Where a supplementary prospectus has been registered under this regulation in respect of an offer, the preceding paragraphs of this regulation have effect as if any reference to a prospectus were a reference to the prospectus originally registered and that supplementary prospectus, taken together.

## EXCEPTIONS

**11(1)** The Treasury or the Secretary of State may authorise the omission from a prospectus or supplementary prospectus of information whose inclusion would otherwise be required by these Regulations if they or he consider that disclosure of that information would be contrary to the public interest.

**11(2)** An offeror may omit from a prospectus or supplementary prospectus information with respect to an issuer whose inclusion would otherwise be required by these Regulations if–

(a) he is not that issuer, nor acting in pursuance of an agreement with that issuer;

(b) the information is not available to him because he is not that issuer; and

(c) he has been unable, despite making such efforts (if any) as are reasonable, to obtain the information.

**11(3)** The competent authority for the purposes of Part IV of the Act ("the competent authority") may authorise the omission from a prospectus or supplementary prospectus of information whose inclusion would otherwise be required by these Regulations, if–

(a) the information is of minor importance only, and is not likely to influence assessment of the issuer's assets and liabilities, financial position, profits and losses and prospects; or

(b) disclosure of that information would be seriously detrimental to the issuer and its omission would not be likely to mislead investors with regard to facts and circumstances necessary for an informed assessment of the securities.

**11(4)** Paragraph (4) of regulation 9 applies for the purposes of paragraph (3) as it applies for the purposes of that regulation.

**11(5)** The competent authority may make rules providing for the payment of fees to it for the discharge of its functions under paragraph (3).

**11(6)** Section 156 of the Act shall apply to rules made under paragraph (5) as it applies to listing rules.

## ADVERTISEMENTS ETC. IN CONNECTION WITH OFFER OF SECURITIES

**12** An advertisement, notice, poster or document (other than a prospectus) announcing a public offer of securities for which a prospectus is or will be required under this Part of these Regulations shall not be issued to or caused to be issued to the public in the United Kingdom by the person proposing to make the offer unless it states that a prospectus is or will be published, as the case may be, and gives an address in the United Kingdom from which it can be obtained or will be obtainable.

## PERSONS RESPONSIBLE FOR PROSPECTUS

**13(1)** For the purpose of this Part of these Regulations the persons responsible for a prospectus or supplementary prospectus are–

(a) the issuer of the securities to which the prospectus or supplementary prospectus relates;

(b) where the issuer is a body corporate, each person who is a director of that body corporate at the time when the prospectus or supplementary prospectus is published;

(c) where the issuer is a body corporate, each person who has authorised himself to be named, and is named, in the prospectus or supplementary prospectus as a director or as having agreed to become a director of that body either immediately or at a future time;

(d) each person who accepts, and is stated in the prospectus or supplementary prospectus as accepting, responsibility for, or for any part of, the prospectus or supplementary prospectus;

(e) the offeror of the securities, where he is not the issuer;

(f) where the offeror is a body corporate, but is not the issuer and is not making the offer in association with the issuer, each person who is a director of that body corporate at the time when the prospectus or supplementary prospectus is published; and

(g) each person not falling within any of the foregoing paragraphs who has authorised the contents of, or of any part of, the prospectus or supplementary prospectus.

**13(2)** A person is not responsible under paragraph (1)(a), (b) or (c) unless the issuer has made or authorised the offer in relation to which the prospectus or supplementary prospectus was published; and a person is not responsible for a prospectus or supplementary prospectus by virtue of paragraph (1)(b) if it is published without his knowledge or consent and on becoming aware of its publication he forthwith gives reasonable public notice that it was published without his knowledge or consent.

**13(2A)** A person is not responsible under paragraph (1)(e) as the offeror of the securities if–

(a) the issuer is responsible for the prospectus or supplementary prospectus in accordance with this regulation;

(b) the prospectus or supplementary prospectus was drawn up primarily by the issuer, or by one or more persons acting on behalf of the issuer; and

(c) the offeror is making the offer in association with the issuer.

**History**
Reg. 13(2A) inserted by the Public Offers of Securities (Amendment) Regulations 1999 (SI 1999/734), reg. 1, 2(n), as from 10 May 1999.

**13(3)** Where a person has accepted responsibility for, or authorised, only part of the contents of any prospectus or supplementary prospectus, he is responsible under paragraph (1)(d) or (g) only for that part and only if it is included in (or substantially in) the form and context to which he has agreed.

**13(4)** Nothing in this regulation shall be construed as making a person responsible for any prospectus or supplementary prospectus by reason only of giving advice as to its contents in a professional capacity.

**13(5)** Where by virtue of this regulation the issuer of any shares pays or is liable to pay compensation under regulation 14 for loss suffered in respect of shares for which a person has subscribed no account shall be taken of that liability or payment in determining any question as to the amount paid on subscription for those shares or as to the amount paid up or deemed to be paid up on them.

## COMPENSATION FOR FALSE OR MISLEADING PROSPECTUS

**14(1)** Subject to regulation 15 the person or persons responsible for a prospectus or supplementary prospectus shall be liable to pay compensation to any person who has acquired the securities to which the prospectus relates and suffered loss in respect of them as a result of any untrue or misleading statement in the prospectus or supplementary prospectus or the omission from it of any matter required to be included by regulation 9 or 10.

**14(2)** Where regulation 8 requires a prospectus to include information as to any particular matter on the basis that the prospectus must include a statement either as to that matter or, if such is the case, that there is no such matter, the omission from the prospectus of the information shall be treated for the purposes of paragraph (1) as a statement that there is no such matter.

**14(3)** Subject to regulation 15, a person who fails to comply with regulation 10 shall be liable to pay compensation to any person who has acquired any of the securities in question and suffered loss in respect of them as a result of the failure.

**14(4)** This regulation does not affect any liability which any person may incur apart from this regulation.

**14(5)** References in this regulation to the acquisition by any person of securities include references to his contracting to acquire them or an interest in them.

## EXEMPTION FROM LIABILITY TO PAY COMPENSATION

**15(1)** A person shall not incur any liability under regulation 14(1) for any loss in respect of securities caused by any such statement or omission as is there mentioned if he satisfies the court that at the time when the prospectus or supplementary prospectus was delivered for registration he reasonably believed, having made such enquiries (if any) as were reasonable, that the statement was true and not misleading or that the matter whose omission caused the loss was properly omitted and–

(a) that he continued in that belief until the time when the securities were acquired; or

(b) that they were acquired before it was reasonably practicable to bring a correction to the attention of persons likely to acquire the securities in question; or

(c) that before the securities were acquired he had taken all such steps as it was reasonable for him to have taken to secure that a correction was forthwith brought to the attention of those persons; or

(d) that the securities were acquired after such a lapse of time that he ought in the circumstances to be reasonably excused, and, if the securities are dealt in on an approved exchange, that he continued in that belief until after the commencement of dealings in the securities on that exchange.

**15(2)** A person shall not incur any liability under regulation 14(1) for any loss in respect of securities caused by a statement purporting to be made by or on the authority of another person as an expert which is, and is stated to be, included in the prospectus or supplementary prospectus with that other person's consent if he satisfies the court that at the time when the prospectus or supplementary prospectus was delivered for registration he believed on reasonable grounds that the other person was competent to make or authorise the statement and had consented to its inclusion in the form and context in which it was included and–

(a) that he continued in that belief until the time when the securities were acquired; or

(b) that they were acquired before it was reasonably practicable to bring the fact that the expert was not competent or had not consented to the attention of persons likely to acquire the securities in question; or

(c) that before the securities were acquired he had taken all such steps as it was reasonable for him to have taken to secure that that fact was forthwith brought to the attention of those persons; or

(d) that the securities were acquired after such a lapse of time that he ought in the circumstances to be reasonably excused and, if the securities are dealt in on an approved exchange, that he continued in that belief until after the commencement of dealings in the securities on that exchange.

**15(3)** Without prejudice to paragraphs (1) and (2), a person shall not incur any liability under regulation 14(1) for any loss in respect of any securities caused by any such statement or omission as is there mentioned if he satisfies the court–

(a) that before the securities were acquired a correction or, where the statement was such as is mentioned in paragraph (2), the fact. that the expert was not competent or had not consented had been published in a manner calculated to bring it to the attention of persons likely to acquire the securities in question; or

(b) that he took all such steps as it was reasonable for him to take to secure such publication and reasonably believed that it had taken place before the securities were acquired.

**15(4)** A person shall not incur any liability under regulation 14(1) for any loss resulting from a statement made by an official person or contained in a public official document which is included in the prospectus or supplementary prospectus if he satisfies the court that the statement is accurately and fairly reproduced.

**15(5)** A person shall not incur any liability under regulation 14(1) or (3) if he satisfies the court that the person suffering the loss acquired the securities in question with knowledge that the statement was false or misleading, of the omitted matter or of the change, new matter or inaccuracy, as the case may be.

**15(6)** A person shall not incur any liability under regulation 14(3) if he satisfies the court that he reasonably believed that the change, new matter or inaccuracy in question was not such as to call for a supplementary prospectus.

**15(7)** In this regulation **"expert"** includes any engineer, valuer, accountant or other person whose profession, qualifications or experience give authority to a statement made by him; and references to the acquisition of securities include references to contracting to acquire them or an interest in them.

## CONTRAVENTIONS

**16(1)** An authorised person who contravenes regulation 4(1) or, where it applies, regulation 4(2), or who contravenes regulation 12, or who assists another person to contravene any of those provisions, shall be treated as having contravened rules made under Chapter V of Part I of the Act or, in the case of a person who is an authorised person by virtue of his membership of a recognised self-regulating organisation or certification by a recognised professional body, the rules of that organisation or body.

**16(2)** A person other than an authorised person who contravenes regulation 4(1) or, where it applies, regulation 4(2), or who contravenes regulation 12, or who assists another person to contravene any of those provisions, shall be guilty of an offence and liable–

(a) on conviction on indictment, to imprisonment for a term not exceeding two years or to a fine or to both;

(b) on summary conviction, to imprisonment for a term not exceeding three months or to a fine not exceeding level 5 on the standard scale.

**16(3)** Without prejudice to any liability under regulation 14, a person shall not be regarded as having contravened regulation 4 by reason only of a prospectus not having fully complied with the requirements of these Regulations as to its form or content.

**16(4)** Any contravention to which this regulation applies shall be actionable at the suit of a person who suffers loss as a result of the contravention subject to the defences and other incidents applying to actions for breach of statutory duty.

**16(5)** In this regulation **"authorised person"** means a person authorised under Chapter III of Part I of the Act and **"recognised professional body"** and **"recognised self-regulating organisation"** have the meanings given in section 207(1) of the Act.

**16(6)** A European institution carrying on home-regulated investment business in the United Kingdom which contravenes regulation 4(1) or, where it applies, 4(2) or which contravenes regulation 12, or which assists another person to contravene any of those provisions, shall be treated for all purposes–

(a) if it is not a member of a recognised self-regulating organisation, as having contravened rules made under Chapter V of Part I of the Act; or

(b) if it is a member of a recognised self-regulating organisation, as having contravened the rules of that organisation;

and the reference in paragraph (2) to a person other than an authorised person shall be treated as not including a reference to such an institution.

# PART III – AMENDMENTS TO PART IV OF THE ACT ETC.

## AMENDMENTS TO THE ACT AND OTHER MINOR AND CONSEQUENTIAL AMENDMENTS

**17** Schedule 2 to these Regulations shall have effect.

## PENALTIES

**18** Where these Regulations amend, extend the application of, or modify the effect of, a provision contained in Part IV of the Act and thereby create a new criminal offence which, but for this regulation, would be punishable to a greater extent than is permitted under paragraph (1)(d) of Schedule 2 to the European Communities Act 1972, the maximum punishment for the offence shall be the maximum permitted under that paragraph at the time the offence was committed, on conviction on indictment or on summary conviction, as the case may be.

## PART IV – MISCELLANEOUS

### DESIGNATIONS

**19** For the purposes of Articles 11, 12, 13, 14, 18, 19, 20, 21 and 22 of Council Directive No. 89/298/EEC the Treasury may designate such bodies as they think fit and they shall give notice in such manner as they think appropriate of the designations they have made.

### MUTUAL RECOGNITION

**20** Schedule 4 to these Regulations shall have effect to make provision for the recognition of prospectuses and listing particulars approved in other member States.

### REVOCATION

**21** The Companies Act 1985 (Mutual Recognition of Prospectuses) Regulations 1991 and the Companies (Northern Ireland) Order 1986 (Mutual Recognition of Prospectuses) Regulations (Northern Ireland) 1991 are hereby revoked.

### REGISTRATION OF DOCUMENTS BY THE REGISTRAR OF COMPANIES

**22** For the purposes of the provisions mentioned in section 735B of the Companies Act 1985, regulations 4(2) and 10(1) shall be regarded as provisions of the Companies Acts.

### APPLICATION OF PART X OF THE ACT

**23(1)** Section 187(4) of the Act shall apply to the competent authority in the discharge or purported discharge of its functions under these Regulations as it applies to it in the discharge or purported discharge of its functions under Part IV of the Act.

**23(2)** Section 188 of the Act shall apply to proceedings arising out of any act or omission (or proposed act-or omission) of the competent authority in the discharge or purported discharge of any function under regulation 11 as it applies to the proceedings mentioned in that section.

**23(3)** Section 192 of the Act shall apply to a person designated under regulation 19 in respect of any action which he proposes to take or has power to take by virtue of being so designated.

**23(4)** Section 199 of the Act shall apply in relation to an offence under these Regulations as it applies in relation to the offences mentioned in that section.

**23(5)** Subsections (1) and (5) of section 200 of the Act shall apply to applications under these Regulations as they apply to applications under the Act, and to requirements imposed on a person by or under these Regulations as they apply to requirements imposed on a person by or under the Act.

**23(6)** Sections 201(1), 202 and 203 of the Act shall apply to offences under these Regulations as they apply to offences under the Act.

### AMENDMENTS TO REGULATIONS MADE UNDER THE BANKING ACT 1987

**24** Schedule 5 to these Regulations shall have effect to amend regulations made under the Banking Act 1987.

# Schedule 1 – Form and Content of Prospectus

## Part I – Interpretation

**1** In this Schedule, except where the context otherwise requires–

**"annual accounts"** has the same meaning as in Part VII of the Companies Act 1985;

**"control"** means the ability, in practice, to determine the actions of the issuer; and **"joint control"** means control exercised by two or more persons who have an agreement or understanding (whether formal or informal) which may lead to their adopting a common policy in respect of the issuer;

**"debentures"** means securities falling within paragraph 2 of Schedule 1 to the Act;

**"financial year"** has the same meaning as in Part VII of the Companies Act 1985;

**"group accounts"** has the same meaning as in Part VII of the Companies Act 1985;

**"the last three years"**, in relation to an undertaking whose accounts are required to be dealt with in a prospectus, means three completed financial years which immediately precede the date on which the offer is first made and which cover a continuous period of at least 35 months, disregarding a financial year which ends less than three months before the date on which the offer is first made and for which accounts have not been prepared by that date;

**"parent undertaking"** and **"subsidiary undertaking"** have the same meaning as in Part VII of the Companies Act 1985;

**"state of affairs"** means the state of affairs of an undertaking, in relation to its balance sheet, at the end of a financial year;

**"subsidiary"** and **"holding company"** have the same meanings as in sections 736 and 736A of the Companies Act 1985; and

**"undertaking"** has the same meaning as in Part VII of the Companies Act 1985.

# Part II – General Requirements

**2** The name of the issuer and the address of its registered office.

**3** If different, the name and address of the person offering the securities.

**4** The names and functions of the directors of the issuer.

**5** The date of publication of the prospectus.

**6** A statement that a copy of the prospectus has been delivered for registration to the registrar of companies in accordance with regulation 4(2), indicating to which registrar of companies it has been delivered.

**7** A statement that the prospectus has been drawn up in accordance with these Regulations.

**8** The following words, "If you are in any doubt about the contents of this document you should consult a person authorised under the Financial Services Act 1986 who specialises in advising on the acquisition of shares and other securities", or words to the like effect.

# Part III – The Persons Responsible for the Prospectus and Advisers

**9** The names, addresses (home or business) and functions of those persons responsible (which in this Part of this Schedule has the same meaning as in regulation 13) for the prospectus or any part of the prospectus, specifying such part.

**10(1)** A declaration by the directors of the issuer (where it is responsible for the prospectus) or (in any other case) by the directors of the offeror, that to the best of their knowledge the information contained in the prospectus is in accordance with the facts and that the prospectus makes no omission likely to affect the import of such information.

**History**
Para. 10(1) substituted by the Public Offers of Securities (Amendment) Regulations 1999 (SI 1999/734), 1, 2(o), as from 10 May 1999. The former para. 10(1) read as follows:

"A declaration by the directors of the issuer (or, if the offeror is not the issuer, by the directors of the offeror) that to the best of their knowledge the information contained in the prospectus is in accordance with the facts and that the prospectus makes no omission likely to affect the import of such information."

**10(2)** Without prejudice to paragraph 45 of this Schedule, a statement by any person who accepts responsibility for the prospectus, or any part of it, that he does so.

## Part IV – The Securities to which the Prospectus Relates and the Offer

**11** A description of the securities being offered, including the class to which they belong and a description of the rights attaching to them including (where applicable)–

(a) if the securities are shares, rights as regards–
  (i) voting;
  (ii) dividends;
  (iii) return of capital on the winding up of the issuer;
  (iv) redemption;

  and a summary of the consents necessary for the variation of any of those rights;

(b) if the securities are debentures, rights as regards–
  (i) interest payable;
  (ii) repayment of principal;

(c) if the securities are convertible securities–
  (i) the terms and dates on which the holder of the convertible securities is entitled to acquire the related underlying securities;
  (ii) the procedures for exercising the entitlement to the underlying securities; and
  (iii) such information relating to the underlying securities as would have been required under paragraphs (a) or (b) if the securities being offered had been the underlying securities.

**12** The date(s) (if any) on which entitlement to dividends or interest arises.

**13** Particulars of tax on income from the securities withheld at source, including tax credits.

**14** The procedure for the exercise of any right of preemption attaching to the securities.

**15** Any restrictions on the free transferability of the securities being offered.

**16(1)** A statement as to whether–

(a) the securities being offered have been admitted to dealings on a recognised investment exchange; or

(b) an application for such admission has been made.

**16(2)** Where no such application for dealings has been made, or such an application has been made and refused, a statement as to whether or not there are, or are intended to be, any other arrangements for there to be dealings in the securities and, if there are, a brief description of such arrangements.

**17** The purpose for which the securities are being issued.

**18** The number of securities being issued.

**19** The number of securities being offered.

**20** The total proceeds which it is expected will be raised by the offer and the expected net proceeds, after deduction of the expenses, of the offer.

**21** Where the prospectus relates to shares which are offered for subscription, particulars as to–

(a) the minimum amount which, in the opinion of the directors of the issuer, must be raised by the issue of those shares in order to provide the sums (or, if any part of them is to be defrayed in any other manner, the balance of the sums) required to be provided in respect of each of the following–
  (i) the purchase price of any property purchased, or to be purchased, which is to be defrayed in whole or in part out of the proceeds of the issue;
  (ii) any preliminary expenses payable by the issuer and any commission so payable to any person in consideration of his agreeing to subscribe for, or of his procuring or agreeing to procure subscriptions for, any shares in the issuer;
  (iii) the repayment of any money borrowed by the issuer in respect of any of the foregoing matters;

(iv) working capital; and

(b) the amounts to be provided in respect of the matters mentioned otherwise than out of the proceeds of the issue and the sources out of which those amounts are to be provided.

**22** The names of any persons underwriting or guaranteeing the offer.

**23** The amount or the estimated amount of the expenses of the offer and by whom they are payable, including (except in so far as information is required to be included in the prospectus by section 97(3) of the Companies Act 1985) a statement as to any commission payable by the issuer to any person in consideration of his agreeing to subscribe for securities to which the prospectus relates or of his procuring or agreeing to procure subscriptions for such securities.

**24** The names and addresses of the paying agents (if any).

**25** The period during which the offer of the securities is open.

**26** The price at which the securities are offered or, if appropriate, the procedure, method and timetable for fixing the price.

**27** The arrangements for payment for the securities being offered and the arrangements and timetable for their delivery.

**28** The arrangements during the period prior to the delivery of the securities being offered relating to the moneys received from applicants including the arrangements for the return of moneys to applicants where their applications are not accepted in whole or in part and the timetable for the return of such moneys.

# Part V – General Information about the Issuer and the Capital

**29** The date and place of incorporation of the issuer. In the case of an issuer not incorporated in the United Kingdom, the address of its principal place of business in the United Kingdom (if any).

**30** The place of registration of the issuer and the number with which it is registered.

**31** The legal form of the issuer, the legislation under which it was formed and (if different) the legislation now applicable to it.

**32** A summary of the provisions in the issuer's memorandum of association determining its objects.

**33** If the liability of the members of the issuer is limited, a statement of that fact.

**34** The amount of the issuer's authorised share capital and any limit on the duration of the authorisation to issue such share capital.

**35** The amount of the issuer's issued share capital.

**36** The number and particulars of any listed and unlisted securities issued by the issuer not representing share capital.

**37** The number of shares of each class making up each of the authorised and issued share capital, the nominal value of such shares and, in the case of the issued share capital, the amount paid up on the shares.

**38** The amount of any outstanding listed and unlisted convertible securities issued by the issuer, the conditions and procedures for their conversion and the number of shares which would be issued as a result of their conversion.

**39** If the issuer is a member of a group, a brief description of the group and of the issuer's position in it, stating, where the issuer is a subsidiary, the name of its holding company.

**40** Insofar the offeror has the information, an indication of the persons, who, directly or indirectly, jointly or severally, exercise or could exercise control over the issuer and particulars of the proportion of the issuer's voting capital held by such persons.



bbcl randr5 Mp 4361—bcl98 225a

## Part VI – The Issuer's Principal Activities

**41** A description of the issuer's principal activities and of any exceptional factors which have influenced its activities.

**42** A statement of any dependence of the issuer on patents or other intellectual property rights, licences or particular contracts, where any of these are of fundamental importance to the issuer's business.

**43** Information regarding investments in progress where they are significant.

**44** Information on any legal or arbitration proceedings, active, pending or threatened against, or being brought by, the issuer or any member of its group which are having or may have a significant effect on the issuer's financial position.

## Part VII – The Issuer's Assets and Liabilities, Financial Position and Profits and Losses

**45(1)** If the issuer is a company to which Part VII of the Companies Act 1985 applies otherwise than by virtue of section 700 of that Act–

(a) the issuer's annual accounts for the last three years together with–

(i) a statement by the directors of the issuer that the accounts have been prepared in accordance with the law, and that they accept responsibility for them, or a statement why they are unable to make such a statement;

(ii) the names and addresses of the auditors of the accounts;

(iii) a copy of the auditors' reports on the accounts, within the meaning of section 235 of the Companies Act 1985; and

(iv) a statement by the auditors that they consent to the inclusion of their reports in the prospectus and accept responsibility for them, and have not become aware, since the date of any report, of any matter affecting the validity of that report at that date; or a statement why they are unable to make such a statement; or

(b) a report by a person qualified to act as an auditor with respect to the state of affairs and profit or loss shown by the issuer's annual accounts for the last three years together with–

(i) the name and address of the person responsible for the report;

(ii) if different, the name and address of the person who audited the accounts on which the report is based; and

(iii) a statement by the person responsible for the report that in his opinion the report gives a true and fair view of the state of affairs and profit or loss of the issuer and its subsidiary undertakings, and that he consents to the inclusion of his report in the prospectus and accepts responsibility for it; or a statement why he is unable to make such a statement.

**45(2)** If the issuer is not a company to which Part VII of the Companies Act 1985 applies (or is a company to which that Part of that Act applies by virtue of section 700 of that Act)–

(a) the issuer's accounts (and, if it is a parent undertaking, its subsidiary undertakings' accounts) for the last three years, prepared in accordance with the applicable law, together with–

(i) the name and address of the person responsible for the accounts;

(ii) a statement by the person responsible for the accounts that they have been properly prepared in accordance with the applicable law, and that he accepts responsibility for them, or statement why he is unable to make such a statement;

(iii) the names and addresses of the auditors of the accounts and their reports; and

(iv) a statement by the auditors that they consent to the inclusion of their reports in the prospectus and accept responsibility for them, and have not become aware, since the date of any report, of any matter affecting the validity of than report at that date; or a statement why they are unable to make such a statement; or

(b) a report by a person qualified to act as an auditor with respect to the state of affairs and profit or loss shown by the issuer's accounts (and, if the issuer is a parent undertaking, by its subsidiary undertakings' accounts) for the last three years, such report to be drawn up in accordance with the applicable law, or as if the provisions of the Companies Act 1985 relating to annual accounts applied to the issuer, together with–
  (i) the name and address of the person responsible for the report;
  (ii) if different, the name and address of the person who audited the accounts on which the report is based; and
  (iii) a statement by the person responsible for the report that in his opinion the report gives a true and fair view of the state of affairs and profit or loss of the issuer and its subsidiary undertakings and that he consents to the inclusion of his report in the prospectus and accepts responsibility for it; or a statement why he is unable to make such a statement.

**45(3)** If, in accordance with the law applicable to it, the accounts of an issuer failing within sub-paragraph (2) consist only of consolidated accounts with respect to itself and its subsidiary undertakings, the prospectus is not required by virtue of sub-paragraph (2) to include separate accounts for each undertaking, or to include a report which deals with the accounts of each undertaking separately.

**45(4)** If, in the case of an issuer falling within sub-paragraph (1) or (2), the prospectus would, but for this sub-paragraph, include both separate accounts for the issuer and its subsidiary undertakings and consolidated accounts, either the separate accounts or the consolidated accounts may be omitted from the prospectus if their inclusion would not provide any significant additional information.

**45(5)** If an issuer failing within sub-paragraph (2) is not required by the law applicable to it to have its accounts audited–

(a) if the accounts have not been audited–
  (i) the prospectus shall contain a statement to that effect; and
  (ii) paragraph (a)(iii) and (iv) or, as the case may be, paragraph (b)(ii) of sub-paragraph (2) shall not apply to the issuer; and

(b) if the accounts have nonetheless been audited, the prospectus shall contain a statement to that effect.

**45(6)** Sub-paragraphs (7) and (8) shall apply in so far as the issuer has not been in existence for the whole of the last three years.

**45(7)** Subject to sub-paragraph (8)–

(a) the requirement in sub-paragraphs (1)(a) and (2)(a) that the prospectus contain accounts for the last three years shall be construed as a requirement that the prospectus contain the accounts which the undertaking concerned was required (by its constitution or by the law under which it is established) to prepare for financial years during its existence, disregarding a financial year which ends less than three months before the date on which the offer is first made and for which accounts have not been prepared by that date; and

(b) the requirement in sub-paragraphs (1)(b) and (2)(b) that the prospectus contain a report with respect to the state of affairs and profit or loss for the last three years shall be construed as a requirement that the prospectus contain a report with respect to the accounts which the undertaking concerned was required (by its constitution or by the law under which it is established) to prepare for financial years during its existence, disregarding a financial year which ends less than three months before the date on which the offer is first made and for which accounts have not been prepared by that date.

**45(8)** If an undertaking has not been required (by its constitution or by the law under which it is established) to prepare any accounts for financial years, the requirement in sub-paragraphs (1) and (2) that the prospectus contain accounts for, or a report with respect to, the last three years shall be construed as a requirement that the prospectus contain a report by a person qualified to act as an auditor which includes–

(a) details of the profit or loss of the undertaking in respect of the period beginning with the date of its formation and ending on the latest practicable date before (but not in any event more than three months before) the date on which the offer is first made, and of its state of affairs at that latest practicable date; and

(b) a statement by the person responsible for the report that in his opinion it gives a true and fair view of the state of affairs and profit or loss of the undertaking and that he consents to the inclusion of his report in the prospectus and accepts responsibility for it; or a statement why he is unable to make such a statement.

**45(9)** If the issuer is a parent undertaking, the requirements of sub-paragraph (1) or, as the case may be, sub-paragraph (2), shall apply to each subsidiary undertaking in respect of any part of the last three years for which information is not otherwise required by those sub-paragraphs, and for this purpose any reference in sub-paragraphs (3) to (8) to the issuer shall have effect as a reference to the subsidiary undertaking.

**History**

In para. 45(9) the words from ", and for this purpose" to the end inserted by the Public Offers of Securities (Amendment) Regulations 1999 (SI 1999/734), reg. 1, 2(p)(i), as from 10 May 1999.

**45(9A)** Neither sub-paragraph (2) nor sub-paragraph (9) requires the inclusion in the prospectus of the accounts of a subsidiary undertaking, a report dealing with those accounts, or any other information relating to a subsidiary undertaking, if the accounts are not, or the report or the information is not, reasonably necessary for the purpose of making an informed assessment of the issuer's assets and liabilities, financial position, profits and losses and prospects, or of the securities being offered.

**History**

Para. 45(9A) inserted by the Public Offers of Securities (Amendment) Regulations 1999 (SI 1999/734), reg. 1, 2(p)(ii), as from 10 May 1999.

**45(10)** Where more than nine months have elapsed at the date on which the offer is first made since the end of the last financial year in respect of which accounts or a report are required to be included in the prospectus by this paragraph, there shall also be included in the prospectus—

(a) interim accounts of the undertaking concerned (which need not be audited but which must otherwise be prepared to the standard applicable to accounts required for each financial year) covering the period beginning at the end of the last financial year in respect of which accounts or a report are required to be included in the prospectus by this paragraph, and ending not less than six months after the end of that financial year, together with the name and address of the person responsible for the interim accounts and a statement by him that the interim accounts have been properly prepared in accordance with the law applicable to the undertaking, and that he consents to the inclusion of the accounts and statement in the prospectus and accepts responsibility for them; or a statement why he is unable to make such a statement; or

(b) a report by a person qualified to act as an auditor covering the same period with respect to the state of affairs and profit or loss of the undertaking concerned, prepared in accordance with the law applicable to the undertaking, together with the name and address of the person responsible for preparing the report, and a statement by him that he consents to the inclusion of the report in the prospectus and accepts responsibility for it; or a statement why he is unable to make such a statement.

**History**

In para. 45(10)(a) the words "and ending not less than six months after the end of that financial year" appearing after the words "by this paragraph," substituted for the former words "and ending on the latest practicable date before (but not in any event more than three months before) the date on which the offer is first made" by the Public Offers of Securities (Amendment) Regulations 1999 (SI 1999/734), reg. 1, 2(p)(iii), as from 10 May 1999.

**45(11)** If any interim accounts of the issuer have been published since the end of the last financial year of the issuer in respect of which accounts or a report are required to be included in the prospectus by this paragraph, other than interim accounts included in a prospectus in accordance with sub-paragraph (10), they shall be included in the prospectus, together with–

(a) an explanation of the purpose for which the accounts were prepared;

(b) a reference to the legislation in accordance with which they were prepared; and

(c) the name and address of the person responsible for them, and a statement from him that he consents to the inclusion of the accounts in the prospectus and accepts responsibility for them.

## Part VIII – The Issuer's Administration, Management and Supervision

**46** A concise description of the directors' existing or proposed service contracts with the issuer or any subsidiary of the issuer, excluding contracts expiring, or determinable by the employing company without payment of compensation within one year, or an appropriate negative statement.

**47(1)** The aggregate remuneration paid and benefits in kind granted to the directors of the issuer during the last completed financial year of the issuer, together with an estimate of the aggregate amount payable and benefits in kind to be granted to the directors, and proposed directors, for the current financial year under the arrangements in force at the date on which the offer is first made.

**47(2)** The interests of each director of the issuer in the share capital of the issuer, distinguishing between beneficial and non-beneficial interests, or an appropriate negative statement.

## Part IX – Recent Developments in the Issuer's Business and Prospects

**48** The significant recent trends concerning the development of the issuer's business since the end of the last completed financial year of the issuer.

**49** Information on the issuer's prospects for at least the current financial year of the issuer.

## Part X – Convertible Securities and Guaranteed Debentures

**50** Where the prospectus relates to convertible securities, and the issuer of the related underlying securities is not the same as the issuer of the convertible securities, the information specified in this Schedule must be given in respect of the issuer of the convertible securities, and the information specified in paragraph 2 and Parts V, VI, VII, VIII and IX of this Schedule must be given in respect of the issuer of the underlying securities.

**51** Where the prospectus relates to debentures which are guaranteed by one or more persons, the name and address and the information specified in Parts V, VI, VII, VIII and IX of this Schedule must also be given in respect of any guarantor who is not an individual.

# Schedule 2 – Amendments to the Financial Services Act 1986 and Minor and Consequential Amendments and Repeals

## Part I – Amendments to Part IV of the Financial Services Act 1986

Regulation 17

**1–2** [Amendment of s. 142 and 144; and insertion of s. 154A, 156A, 156B and Sch. 11A not reproduced here.]

**3** Subsection (3) of section 156B of the Act shall not apply to a European institution carrying on home-regulated investment business in the United Kingdom which contravenes subsection 3(1) of that section, but it shall be treated for all purposes–

(a) if it is not a member of a recognised self-regulating organisation, as having contravened rules made under Chapter V of Part I of the Act; or

(b) if it is a member of a recognised self-regulating organisation, as having contravened the rules of that organisation.

## Part II – Consequential Amendments and Repeals

**4–9** [Amendments and repeals affecting s. 48, 58, Pt. V, 192, 199, 207, Sch. 15 and Sch. 16 not reproduced here.]

**10** Sections 198 and 199 of the Companies Act 1989 are hereby repealed.

**11** In regulation 3 of the Control of Misleading Advertisements Regulations 1988–

(a) in paragraph (1)(b), the words from "except where" to the end of the paragraph; and

(b) in paragraph (2), the words ""approved exchange",";

shall be deleted.

**12** In Schedule 9 to the Banking Coordination (Second Council Directive) Regulations 1992), paragraph 38 is hereby revoked.

# Schedule 3 – Offers of Securities to the Public in the United Kingdom

Schedule 2, paragraph 3(2)

[Insertion of Sch. 11A not reproduced here.]

# Schedule 4 – Mutual Recognition of Prospectuses and Listing Particulars

Regulation 20

## Part I – Recognition for the Purposes of Part IV of the Financial Services Act 1986 of Prospectuses – and Listing Particulars Approved in Other Member States

**1** In this Part of this Schedule–

(a) the term **"competent authority"** includes a body designated by a member State pursuant to Article 12 of Council Directive No. 89/298/EEC;

(b) **"the UK authority"** means the competent authority for the purposes of Part IV of the Act.

(c) **"European document"** means–

(i) listing particulars which have been approved by the competent authority in another member State and which Article 24a of Council Directive No. 80/390/EEC requires or paragraph 5 of that article permits to be recognised as listing particulars;

(ii) a prospectus which has been approved by the competent authority in another member State and which Article 24b of Council Directive No. 80/390/EEC requires or which paragraph 2 of that article, in referring to paragraph 5 of article 24a of that Directive, permits to be recognised as listing particulars; or

(iii) a prospectus which has been approved by the competent authority in another member State, which Article 21 of Council Directive No. 89/298/EEC requiries or which paragraph 4 of that article permits to be recognised and which relates to securities which are the subject of an application for listing in the United Kingdom and which are to be offered in the United Kingdom prior to admission to listing in the United Kingdom by means of the prospectus;

including in each case any supplement to listing particulars or a prospectus which, before the completion of the preparation of the recognised document for submission to the UK authority pursuant to an application for listing, has been approved pursuant to Article 23 of Council Directive No. 80/390/EEC or Article 18 of Council Directive No. 89/298/EEC by the competent authorities which approved the listing particulars or prospectus.

Where the European document submitted to the UK authority is a translation into English of the document approved by the competent authorities in another member State then, unless the context otherwise requires, the document as translated shall be regarded as the European document rather than the document as approved.

**2** In this Part of this Schedule, **"recognised European document"** means a document consisting of a European document submitted to the UK authority pursuant to an application for listing under section 143 of the Act and, if information is required to be added to it in accordance with listing rules, including that information.

**3** Subject to paragraph 4, Part IV of the Act shall apply to a recognised European document as it applies–

(a) in relation to listing particulars, within the meaning of section 144(2) of the Act (in a case where the securities to which it relates will not be offered in the United Kingdom prior to admission to listing in the United Kingdom); or

(b) in relation to a prospectus to which section 144 of the Act applies (in a case where the recognised European document is a prospectus and the securities to which it relates are to be offered in the United Kingdom prior to admission to listing in the United Kingdom).

**4** Part IV of the Act shall apply to a recognised European document subject to the following modifications–

(a) nothing in Part IV shall require the approval by the UK authority of a recognised European document which has been approved as described in paragraph 1(c);

(b) in sections 146, 147(1)(a) and 150(2) of the Act, any reference to information specified or required by listing rules or required by the competent authority or to matter whose inclusion was required by listing rules or by the competent authority shall apply as if it were a reference to information required by or to matter whose inclusion was required by the legislation relating to the contents of prospectuses and listing particulars, or by the competent authorities, of the member State where the European document forming part of that recognised European document was approved;

(c) nothing in section 147 of the Act shall require the approval by the UK authority of supplementary listing particulars or a supplementary prospectus which is, or is a translation into English of, a supplement which has been approved pursuant to Article 23 of Council Directive No. 80/390/EEC or Article 18 of Council Directive No. 89/298/EEC by the competent authority which approved the listing particulars or prospectus to which the supplement relates.

**5** Subject to paragraphs 1 and 3, references in Part IV of the Act to supplementary listing particulars shall be taken to include references to supplementary prospectuses.

**6** This Part of this Schedule shall not apply to listing particulars or a prospectus approved in another member State prior to the coming into force of these Regulations.

## Part II – Recognition for the Purposes of Part II of these Regulations of Prospectuses Approved in Other Member States

**7** In this Part of this Schedule **"recognised prospectus"** means a prospectus which has been approved in accordance with Article 20 of Council Directive No. 89/298/EEC in another member State and satisfies the requirements of paragraphs (a) to (c) of paragraph 8(1); and where the prospectus has been translated into English, the English version shall be the recognised prospectus.

**8(1)** Where a prospectus has been approved in accordance with Article 20 of Council Directive No. 89/298/EEC in another member State it shall, subject to sub-paragraph (2), be deemed for the purposes of regulation 4(1) to comply with regulations 8 and 9 of these Regulations provided that–

(a) (revoked by the Public Offers of Securities (Amendment) Regulations 1999 (SI 1999/734), reg. 1, 2(q) as from 10 May 1999.)

(b) the offer of securities to which the prospectus relates is made in the United Kingdom simultaneously with the making of the offer in the member State where the prospectus was approved or within 3 months after the making of that offer;

(c) there is added to the information contained in the prospectus as approved in the other member State such of the following information as is not included in the prospectus as so approved–

(i) (revoked by the Public Offers of Securities (Amendment) Regulations 1999 (SI 1999/734), reg. 1, 2(q) as from 10 May 1999.)

(ii) the names and addresses of the paying agents for the securities in the United Kingdom (if any);

(iii) a statement of how notice of meetings and other notices from the issuer of the Securities will be given to United Kingdom resident holders of the securities; and

(d) where a partial exemption or partial derogation has been granted in the other member State pursuant to Council Directive No. 89/298/EEC–

(i) the partial exemption or partial derogation in question is of a type for which a corresponding partial exemption or partial derogation is made in these Regulations; and

(ii) the circumstances that justify the partial exemption or partial derogation also exist in the United Kingdom.

**History**
Para. 8(1)(a) formerly read as follows:
"where the prospectus as approved in the other member State was written in a language other than English, the prospectus has been translated into English and the translation has been certified to be a correct translation in the manner prescribed in regulation 6 of the Companies (Forms) Regulations 1985 or the corresponding Northern Ireland provision;"
Para. 8(1)(c)(i) formerly read as follows:
"a summary of the tax treatment relevant to United Kingdom resident holders of the securities;"

**8(2)** Where, prior to the delivery for registration to the registrar of companies of a prospectus which has been approved in another member State, a supplement to the prospectus has been approved pursuant to Article 23 of Council Directive No. 80/390/EEC or Article 18 of Council Directive No. 89/298/EEC in the member State where the prospectus was approved, the references in sub-paragraph (1) and in paragraph 7 to a prospectus shall be taken to be references to the prospectus taken together with the supplement.

**9** Subject to paragraph 8(2), Part II of these Regulations shall apply in relation to a recognised prospectus as it applies in relation to a prospectus to which the said Part II would apply apart from this paragraph except that in regulations 9(l), 10(l)(a) and 14(2) of these Regulations the references to information or any matter required to be included in a prospectus by these Regulations shall be taken to be references to information or any matter required to be included by virtue of the legislation relating to the contents of prospectuses of the member State where the recognised prospectus was approved and by virtue of paragraph 8(1)(c).

# Part III – Recognition for the Purposes of the Companies Act 1985 of Prospectuses Approved in Other Member States

**10** In this Part of this Schedule, **"recognised prospectus"** has the same meaning as in Part II of this Schedule.

**11** (Revoked by the Public Offers of Securities (Amendment) Regulations 1999 (SI 1999/734), reg. 1, 2(r), as from 10 May 1999.)

**History**
Para. 11 formerly read as follows:
"The provisions of the Companies Act 1985, other than–
(a) section 83; and
(b) in section 84, the words "This is without prejudice to section 83.",
shall apply to a recognised prospectus."

**12** A recognised prospectus shall be deemed to comply with sections 97(3) and 693(1)(a) and (d) of the Companies Act 1985.

# Schedule 5 – Amendments to Regulations made under the Banking Act 1987

Regulation 24

**1(1)** The Banking Act 1987 (Advertisements) Regulations 1988 shall be amended as follows.

**1(2)** In regulation 2(4)(a), for the words "to which section 56 of the Companies Act 1985 applies or would apply if not excluded by paragraph (a) or (b) of subsection (5) of that section" there shall be substituted–

"a prospectus to which regulation 8 of the Public Offers of Securities Regulations 1995 applies, or would apply but for regulation 7 of those regulations where–
(i) the prospectus is issued to existing members or debenture holders of a company; and
(ii) the prospectus relates to shares in or debentures of the company,
whether an applicant for shares or debentures will or will not have the right to renounce in favour of other persons."

**1(3)** (Revoked by the Public Offers of Securities (Amendment) Regulations 1999 (SI 1999/734), reg. 1, 2(s), as from 10 May 1999.)

**History**
Para. 1(3) formerly read as follows:
"In regulation 2(4)(b), for the words "a prospectus to which section 72 of that Act applies or would apply if not excluded by paragraph (a) or (b) of subsection (6) of that section" there shall be substituted–
"a prospectus to which regulation 8 of the Public Offers of Securities Regulations 1995 applies, or would apply but for regulation 7 of those regulations where–
(i) the prospectus is issued to existing members or debenture holders of a company; and
(ii) the prospectus relates to shares in or debentures of the company,
whether an applicant for shares or debentures will or will not have the right to renounce in favour of other persons.""

**1(4)** In regulation 2(4)(c), for the words from "together with" to the end there shall be substituted–

"together with a prospectus to which regulation 8 of the Public Offers of Securities Regulations 1995 applies, or would apply but for regulation 7 of those regulations where–
(i) the prospectus is issued to existing members or debenture holders of a company; and
(ii) the prospectus relates to shares in or debentures of the company,
whether an applicant for shares or debentures will or will not have the right to renounce in favour of other persons."

**2** In regulation 13(d)(iv) of the Banking Act 1987 (Exempt Transactions) Regulations 1988, for the words "section 56 or 72 of the Companies Act 1985 or the corresponding Northern Ireland legislation" there shall be substituted "regulation 8 of the Public Offers of Securities Regulations 1995".

## EXPLANATORY NOTE

*(This Note is not part of the Regulations)*

These Regulations (which will replace Part III of the Companies Act 1985 (c.6) (capital issues) for almost all purposes) provide for a person offering transferable securities to the public in certain circumstances to prepare and publish a prospectus according to requirements set out in the Regulations. The Regulations also amend Part IV of the Financial Services Act 1986 (c.60) so that a prospectus may, in certain circumstances, be prepared, scrutinised and approved, in accordance with listing rules. Part V of the Financial Services Act 1986 (offers of unlisted securities), which has not been brought into force, is repealed.

The Regulations, which come into force on 19th June 1995, give effect to Council Directive No. 89/298/EEC on the coordination of the requirements for the drawing-up, scrutiny and distribution of a prospectus when transferable securities are to be offered to the public (OJ No. L124, 5.5.89, p. 8). They also give effect, in relation to the mutual recognition of prospectuses and listing particulars, to certain provisions of Council Directive No. 80/390/EEC (OJ No. L100, 17.4.80, p. 1) which is amended by Council Directives 87/345/EEC (OJ No. L185, 4.7.87, p. 81), 90/211/EEC (OJ No. L112, 3.5.90, p. 24) and 94/18/EC (OJ No. L135, 31.5.94, p. 1).

Part I of the Regulations makes provision for the citation and commencement of the Regulations and contains interpretation provisions.

Part II of the Regulations makes provision for a prospectus to be prepared and published, without prior scrutiny and approval, where transferable securities which are not admitted to official listing, nor the subject of an application for official listing, are offered to the public for the first time. A prospectus must contain the information necessary for investors to make an informed assessment of the issuer's position and prospectus, and the rights attached to the securities, and must contain certain specified information (regulations 8 and 9; Schedule 1). A prospectus must be registered with the registrar of companies, and published, before an offer to the public is made. By regulation 7, certain sorts of offers of securities are deemed not to be offers to the public. Regulation 11 provides for information to be omitted from a prospectus in certain circumstances. Regulations 13 to 15 impose civil liability on persons responsible for a false or misleading prospectus. By regulation 16, contraventions of the requirement to publish a prospectus (and the requirement in regulation 12 to refer in advertisements to the availability of a prospectus) are subject to criminal or regulatory sanctions.

Part III of the Regulations gives effect to Schedule 2, which makes amendments to the Financial Services Act 1986 and other minor and consequential amendments. It also provides that where the Regulations create new criminal offences the maximum penalties shall not exceed those permitted under the European Communities Act 1972 (c.68).

Part IV of the Regulations gives effect to Schedule 4 (mutual recognition of prospectuses and listing particulars) and deals with other miscellaneous matters.

Schedule 1 to the Regulations specifies the information with a prospectus prepared under Part II must contain.

Schedule 2 to the Regulations makes amendments to Part IV of the Financial Services Act 1986. The amended provisions of the Act allow listing rules to be made so that a prospectus, rather than listing particulars, must be produced where an application for admission to the Official List has been made, and the securities in question are to be offered to the public before admission (section 144). They also allow listing rules to be made so that a prospectus may be produced where there is no application for listing (section 156A). Schedule 2 also gives effect to Schedule 3.

Schedule 3 to the Regulations inserts Schedule 11A into the Act. Schedule 11A defines what is an offer to the public for the purposes of the amended provisions in Part IV of the Act. Certain sorts of offers (with some differences, those listed in regulation 7) are not offers to the public.

Schedule 4 to the Regulations deals with the mutual recognition of prospectuses and listing particulars approved in other member States for the purposes of Part IV of the Financial Services Act 1986, the Regulations themselves, and the Companies Act 1985.

Schedule 5 to the Regulations deals with the amendment of regulations made under the Banking Act 1987.

# THE COMPANIES ACT 1989 (COMMENCEMENT NO. 16) ORDER 1995

(SI 1995/1591 (C 34))

*Made on 21 June 1995 by the Treasury under s. 215(2) of the Companies Act 1989.*

**1** This Order may be cited as the Companies Act 1989 (Commencement No. 16) Order 1995.

**2** Sections 171, 176 and 181 of the Companies Act 1989 shall come into force on 4th July 1995.

## EXPLANATORY NOTE

(*This Note is not part of the Order*)

The Order brings sections 171, 176 and 181 of the Companies Act 1989 (**"the 1989 Act"**) into force on 4th July 1995.

Section 171 enables the Treasury and the Secretary of State, acting jointly, to make regulations which provide that the provisions of Part VII of the 1989 Act applicable to contracts connected with a body that is a recognised investment exchange or a recognised clearing house under the Financial Services Act 1986 (c. 60) apply to contracts of any specified description in relation to which settlement arrangements are provided by a person for the time being included in a list maintained by the Bank of England for the purposes of section 171.

Section 176 enables the Treasury and the Secretary of State, acting jointly, to make regulations which provide that general law of insolvency has effect in relation to charges of any description specified in the regulations granted in favour of a person included in the list maintained by the Bank of England under section 171 of the 1989 Act, and in relation to any action taken in enforcing such charges, subject to such provisions as may be specified in the regulations.

Section 181 has the effect that the power to make regulations under sections 171 and 176 of the 1989 Act includes power to apply sections 177 to 179 of that Act (which concern the rights and remedies exercisable in relation to property provided as cover for margin or as security for a charge in connection with contracts connected with a recognised investment exchange or a recognised clearing house) to any contract in relation to which the power conferred by section 171 is exercised and to the property subject to any charge in relation to which the power conferred by section 176 is exercised.

## NOTE AS TO EARLIER COMMENCEMENT

(*This Note is not part of the Order*)

The provisions of the Companies Act 1989 ("the 1989 Act") brought into force by Orders made before the making of the Companies Act 1989 (Commencement No. 15 and Transitional and Savings Provisions) Order 1995 (SI 1995/1352) are set out in a note appended to that Order.

The Companies Act 1989 (Commencement No. 15 and Transitional and Savings Provisions) Order brings certain provisions of the 1989 Act into force on 3rd July 1995 subject to the transitional and savings provisions set out in the Order. The provisions in question are section 140(1) to (6) (which amends sections 463 and 464 of the Companies Act 1985 ("the 1985 Act") in relation to floating charges in Scotland), a consequential repeal made by Schedule 24 to the 1989 Act to section 464 of the 1985 Act, the repeal by Schedule 24 to the 1989 Act of the definition of "annual return" in section 744 of the 1985 Act, and paragraph 20 of Schedule 19 to the 1989 Act which inserts a new section 744A (index of defined expressions) into the 1985 Act.

# THE FOREIGN COMPANIES (EXECUTION OF DOCUMENTS) (AMENDMENT) REGULATIONS 1995

(SI 1995/1729)

*Made on 6 July 1995 by the Secretary of State for Trade and Industry under s. 130(6) of the Companies Act 1989. Operative from 1 August 1995.*

## CITATION AND COMMENCEMENT

**1** These Regulations may be cited as the Foreign Companies (Execution of Documents) (Amendment) Regulations 1995 and shall come into force on 1st August 1995.

INTERPRETATION

**2** In these Regulations **"the principal Regulations"** means the Foreign Companies (Execution of Documents) Regulations 1994.

**3–5** [Amendment of reg. 2, 3 of principal Regulations and revocation of reg. 6.]

## EXPLANATORY NOTE

*(This Note is not part of the Regulations)*

These Regulations amend the Foreign Companies (Execution of Documents) Regulations 1994 ("the 1994 Regulations").

The 1994 Regulations adapted section 36B (execution of a document by a company under the law of Scotland) of the Companies Act 1985 ("the 1985 Act") for the purpose of its application to a company incorporated outside Great Britain. With effect from 1st August 1995, however, paragraph 5 of Schedule 2 to the Requirements of Writing (Scotland) Act 1995 ("the 1995 Act") provides new rules for the signing of documents, in accordance with the law of Scotland, by all bodies corporate other than companies incorporated in Great Britain, or local authorities. From that date, therefore, those rules will apply to companies incorporated outside Great Britain. Moreover, paragraph 51 of Schedule 4 to the 1995 Act substitutes a new section 36B in the 1985 Act (providing that where an enactment requires a document to be executed by a company affixing its common seal, a document signed in accordance with the 1995 Act is to have effect as if so executed), for which the translations provided by regulation 6 of the 1994 Regulations are no longer relevant. In view of those changes, regulation 6 of the 1994 Regulations is revoked and a consequential amendment is made in regulation 2. It is also provided by virtue of amendments to regulations 2 and 3 of the 1994 Regulations that substituted section 36B of the 1985 Act shall apply to a company incorporated outside Great Britain, with the modification that references in that provision to a company shall be construed as references to a company incorporated outside Great Britain.

# THE FINANCIAL MARKETS AND INSOLVENCY (MONEY MARKET) REGULATIONS 1995

(SI 1995/2049)

*Made on 4 August 1995 by the Treasury and the Secretary of State for Trade and Industry under s. 171, 176, 181, 185 and 186 of the Companies Act 1989. Operative from 15 August 1995.*

## GENERAL

CITATION AND COMMENCEMENT

**1** These Regulations may be cited as the Financial Markets and Insolvency (Money Market) 1995 Regulations and shall come into force on 15th August 1995.

INTERPRETATION OF THE REGULATIONS

**2** In these Regulations–

**"the Act"** means the Companies Act 1989;

**"the 1986 Act"** means the Financial Services Act 1986;

**"business day"** has the same meaning as in section 167(3) of the Act;

**"defaulter"** means a person in respect of whom action has been taken by a listed person under his default rules, whether by declaring the person in respect of whom action has been taken to be a defaulter or otherwise;

**"default rules"** means the rules of a listed person which provide for the taking of action in the event of a person appearing to be unable, or likely to become unable, to meet his liabilities in respect of one or more money market contracts or related contracts;

**"ecu"**means the unit of account of that name defined in Council Regulation (EEC) No. 3320/94;

**"the list"** means the list maintained by the Financial Services Authority for the purposes of section 171 of the Act;

**"listed person"** means a person for the time being included in the list;

**"money market charge"** means a charge, whether fixed or floating, granted in favour of a listed person for the purpose of securing debts or liabilities arising in connection with the settlement of money market contracts or related contracts;

**"money market contract"** means a contract in relation to which a listed person provides settlement arrangements and which is a contract for the acquisition or disposal either of–

(a) currency of the United Kingdom or of any other country or territory; or

(b) rights under a contract the value of which is determined by reference to the value of the ecu;

**"Part VII"** means Part VII of the Act;

**"related contract"** means a contract other than a money market contract effected by a listed person under his default rules for the purpose of enabling the settlement of a money market contract or another related contract;

**"rules"** means the rules made or conditions imposed by a listed person with respect to the provision by that person of settlement arrangements.

**History**

In reg. 2 in the definition of **"the list"** the words "Financial Services Authority" substituted for the former words "Bank of England" by the Bank of England Act 1998 (Consequential Amendments of Subordinate Legislation) Order 1998 (SI 1998/1129), art. 1, 2 and Sch. 1, para. 20(1), (2).

Previously in reg. 2 the definition of **"ecu"** inserted and the definition of **"money market contract"** replaced by the Financial Markets and Insolvency (Ecu) Contracts Regulations 1998 (SI 1998/27), reg. 1, reg. 2(a) and (b) respectively as from 2 February 1998. The former definition of **"money market contract"** read as follows:

"**"money market contract"** means a contract for the acquisition or disposal of currency of the United Kingdom or of any other country or territory, being a contract in relation to which a listed person provides settlement arrangements;".

## INTERPRETATION OF PART VII AS APPLIED BY THE REGULATIONS

**3** References in the provisions of Part VII as they are applied by these Regulations–

(a) to a defaulter shall be taken to be to references to a defaulter within the meaning of these Regulations;

(b) to default proceedings shall be taken to be references to proceedings taken by a listed person under his default rules;

(c) to default rules shall be taken to be references to default rules within the meaning of these Regulations;

(d) to a market charge shall be taken to be references to a money market charge;

(e) to market contracts shall be taken to be references to money market contracts and related contracts;

(f) to a member of a recognised investment exchange or a recognised clearing house shall be taken to be references to a person using the settlement arrangements provided by a listed person;

(g) to a recognised investment exchange or a recognised clearing house shall be taken to be references to a listed person; and

(h) to rules shall be taken to be references to rules within the meaning of these Regulations.

## EXTENSION OF PART VII TO MONEY MARKET CONTRACTS AND RELATED CONTRACTS

EXTENSION OF PART VII TO MONEY MARKET CONTRACTS AND RELATED CONTRACTS

**4** Subject to the provisions of regulation 5 of these Regulations, Part VII shall apply to money market contracts and to related contracts as it applies to contracts connected with a recognised investment exchange or a recognised clearing house.

**5** In their application to money market contracts and related contracts, the provisions of Part VII shall apply as if references to designated non-members were omitted and as if references to property provided as margin or as cover for margin included references to any property provided to a listed person for the purposes of or in connection with the settlement of money market contracts or related contracts.

## APPLICATION OF CERTAIN PROVISIONS OF THE 1986 ACT IN RELATION TO A LISTED PERSON

APPLICATION OF CERTAIN PROVISIONS OF THE 1986 ACT IN RELATION TO A LISTED PERSON

**6** In relation to a listed person, the provisions of the 1986 Act mentioned in regulations 7 to 18 of these Regulations shall apply with the exceptions, additions and adaptations specified in relation to those provisions.

### COMPLIANCE ORDERS

**7** Section 12 of the 1986 Act (compliance orders) shall apply in relation to a listed person as if–

(a) the circumstances specified in subsection (1) of that section as those in which an application may be made to the court were the following, that is to say that it appears to the Financial Services Authority that the circumstances are such that it could take action to remove a person from the list in accordance with the arrangements made by it for that purpose;

(b) functions under the section were exercisable by the Financial Services Authority and not by any other person;

(c) the references to a recognised organisation were references to a listed person;

(d) the references to subsection (3) of section 10 of the 1986 Act (grant and refusal of recognition) to any requirement of Schedule 2 to that Act and to any obligation to which a recognised organisation is subject by virtue of that Act were references to the matters mentioned in sub-paragraph (a) of this paragraph;

(e) the reference in subsection (1) to the revocation of a recognition order under section 11 of the 1986 Act (revocation of recognition) were a reference to the removal of a person from the list; and

(f) the power conferred on the court by subsection (2) were a power to direct the listed person concerned to take such steps as the court may direct for securing that he ceases to be eligible for removal from the list.

**History**

In reg. 7(a), (b) the words "Financial Services Authority" substituted for the former words "Bank of England" by the Bank of England Act 1998 (Consequential Amendments of Subordinate Legislation) Order 1998 (SI 1998/1129), art. 1, 2 and Sch. 1, para. 20(1), (3)(a) as from 1 June 1998.

### POWERS OF INTERVENTION

**8** Section 64 of the 1986 Act (scope of powers of intervention) shall apply in relation to a listed person as if–

(a) subsections (2) to (4) were omitted;

(b) the exception in subsection (1) and the related reference in that subsection to an appointed representative were omitted;

(c) the reference in subsection (1) to the powers conferred by Chapter VI of Part I of the 1986 Act was a reference to the powers conferred on the Financial Services Authority by virtue of regulations 9 to 12 of these Regulations;

(d) the circumstances mentioned in subsection (1) as those in which the relevant powers are exercisable were the following, that is to say that it appears to the Financial Services Authority that the circumstances are such that it could take action to remove a person from the list in accordance with the arrangements made by it for that purpose; and

(e) the first reference in subsection (1) to any authorised person was a reference to any listed person.

**History**

In reg. 8(c), (d) the words "Financial Services Authority" substituted for the former words "Bank of England" by the Bank of England Act 1998 (Consequential Amendments of Subordinate Legislation) Order 1998 (SI 1998/1129), art. 1, 2 and Sch. 1, para. 20(1), (3)(b) as from 1 June 1998.

**9** Section 65 of the 1986 Act (restriction of business) shall apply in relation to a listed person as if–

(a) functions under that section were exercisable by the Financial Services Authority and not by any other person;

(b) the reference to an authorised person was a reference to a listed person;

(c) the references to investment business were references to the provision of settlement arrangements in relation to money market contracts; and

(d) the reference to the United Kingdom was a reference to Great Britain.

**History**

In reg. 9(a) the words "Financial Services Authority" substituted for the former words "Bank of England" by the Bank of England Act 1998 (Consequential Amendments of Subordinate Legislation) Order 1998 (SI 1998/1129), art. 1, 2 and Sch. 1, para. 20(1), (3)(c) as from 1 June 1998.

**10** Section 66 of the 1986 Act (restriction on dealing with assets) shall apply in relation to a listed person as if–

(a) functions under that section were exercisable by the Financial Services Authority and not by any other person;

(b) the references to an appointed representative were omitted;

(c) the references to an authorised person were references to a listed person; and

(d) the reference to the United Kingdom was a reference to Great Britain.

**History**

In reg. 10(a) the words "Financial Services Authority" substituted for the former words "Bank of England" by the Bank of England Act 1998 (Consequential Amendments of Subordinate Legislation) Order 1998 (SI 1998/1129), art. 1, 2 and Sch. 1, para. 20(1), (3)(d) as from 1 June 1998.

**11** Section 68 of the 1986 Act (maintenance of assets in United Kingdom) shall apply in relation to a listed person as if–

(a) functions under that section were exercisable by the Financial Services Authority and not by any other person;

(b) the reference to an appointed representative was omitted;

(c) the references to an authorised person were references to a listed person;

(d) the references to liabilities in respect of investment business were references to liabilities arising from the provision of settlement arrangements; and

(e) the references to the United Kingdom were references to Great Britain.

**History**

In reg. 11(a) the words "Financial Services Authority" substituted for the former words "Bank of England" by the Bank of England Act 1998 (Consequential Amendments of Subordinate Legislation) Order 1998 (SI 1998/1129), art. 1, 2 and Sch. 1, para. 20(1), (3)(e) as from 1 June 1998.

**12** Section 69 of the 1986 Act (rescission and variation) shall apply in relation to a listed person as if–

(a) functions under that section were exercisable by the Financial Services Authority and not by any other person; and

(b) the reference to a prohibition or requirement imposed under Chapter VI of Part I of the 1986 Act were a reference to a prohibition or requirement imposed under those provisions of that Chapter which apply in relation to a listed person by virtue of these Regulations.

**History**

In reg. 12(a) the words "Financial Services Authority" substituted for the former words "Bank of England" by the Bank of England Act 1998 (Consequential Amendments of Subordinate Legislation) Order 1998 (SI 1998/1129), art. 1, 2 and Sch. 1, para. 20(1), (3)(f) as from 1 June 1998.

**13** Section 70 of the 1986 Act (notices) shall apply in relation to a listed person as if–

(a) the reference to a prohibition or requirement imposed under Chapter VI of Part I of the

1986 Act were a reference to a prohibition or requirement imposed under those provisions of that Chapter which apply in relation to a listed person by virtue of these Regulations;

(b) functions under that section were exercisable by the Financial Services Authority and not by any other person; and

(c) subsection (5) was omitted.

**History**

In reg. 13(b) the words "Financial Services Authority" substituted for the former words "Bank of England" by the Bank of England Act 1998 (Consequential Amendments of Subordinate Legislation) Order 1998 (SI 1998/1129), art. 1, 2 and Sch. 1, para. 20(1), (3)(g) as from 1 June 1998.

**14** Section 72 of the 1986 Act (winding up orders) shall apply in relation to a listed person as if–

(a) the powers conferred on the court were exercisable only on the presentation of a petition by the Financial Services Authority;

(b) the references to an appointed representative were omitted;

(c) references to an authorised person, to any person whose authorisation is suspended under section 28 of the 1986 Act or who is the subject of a direction under section 33(1)(b) of that Act were references to a listed person; and

(d) the provisions of subsections (2)(d) and (3) to (5) were omitted.

**History**

In reg. 14(a) the words "Financial Services Authority" substituted for the former words "Bank of England" by the Bank of England Act 1998 (Consequential Amendments of Subordinate Legislation) Order 1998 (SI 1998/1129), art. 1, 2 and Sch. 1, para. 20(1), (3)(h) as fom 1 June 1998.

**15** Section 74 of the 1986 Act (administration orders) shall apply in relation to a listed person as if it enabled the Financial Services Authority to present a petition under section 9 of the Insolvency Act 1986 (applications for administration orders) in relation to a company to which section 8 of that Act applies which is a listed person.

**History**

In reg. 15 the words "Financial Services Authority" substituted for the former words "Bank of England" by the Bank of England Act 1998 (Consequential Amendments of Subordinate Legislation) Order 1998 (SI 1998/1129), art. 1, 2 and Sch. 1, para. 20(1), (3)(i) as from 1 June 1998.

**16** Section 105 of the 1986 Act (investigation powers) shall apply in relation to a listed person as if–

(a) functions under that section were exercisable by the Financial Services Authority and not by any other person;

(b) the circumstances mentioned in subsection (1) as those in which the powers under that section are exercisable were that it appeared to the Financial Services Authority that there is good reason to exercise those powers for the purpose of investigating the affairs, or any aspect of the affairs, of any listed person so far as relevant to settlement arrangements provided by that person in relation to money market contracts or related contracts; and

(c) subsections (2) and (9) were omitted.

**History**

In reg. 16(a), (b) the words "Financial Services Authority" substituted for the former words "Bank of England" by the Bank of England Act 1998 (Consequential Amendments of Subordinate Legislation) Order 1998 (SI 1998/1129), art. 1, 2 and Sch. 1, para. 20(1), (3)(j) as from 1 June 1998.

**17** Section 106 of the 1986 Act (exercise of investigation powers by officer etc.) shall apply in connection with the application, by regulation 16 of these Regulations, of section 105 of that Act in relation to a listed person as if–

(a) the references to the powers conferred by section 105 were references to the powers conferred by that section as it applies by virtue of these Regulations;

(b) functions under section 106 were functions of the Financial Services Authority and not of any other person;

(c) the references to any officer of a person exercising functions under the section were references to any officer of the Financial Services Authority; and

(d) the person to whom a report must be made by virtue of subsection (3) were the Financial Services Authority.

**History**
In reg. 17(b), (c), (d) the words "Financial Services Authority" substituted for the former words "Bank of England" by the Bank of England Act 1998 (Consequential Amendments of Subordinate Legislation) Order 1998 (SI 1998/1129), art. 1, 2 and Sch. 1, para. 20(1), (3)(k) as from 1 June 1998.

**18** Section 199 of the 1986 Act (powers of entry) shall apply in connection with the application, by regulation 16 of these Regulations, of section 105 of that Act in relation to a listed person as if–

(a) the circumstances mentioned in subsections (1) and (2) as those in which a justice of the peace may issue a warrant were that he is satisfied on information given on oath by or on behalf of the Financial Services Authority, or by a person authorised to exercise powers under section 105 of the 1986 Act as that section applies by virtue of these Regulations, that there are reasonable grounds for believing that there are on any premises documents whose production has been required under section 105 as it applies by virtue of these Regulations and which have not been produced in compliance with the requirement; and

(b) subsection (7) was omitted.

**History**
In reg. 18(a) the words "Financial Services Authority" substituted for the former words "Bank of England" by the Bank of England Act 1998 (Consequential Amendments of Subordinate Legislation) Order 1998 (SI 1998/1129), art. 1, 2 and Sch. 1, para. 20(1), (3)(l) as from 1 June 1998.

## APPLICATION OF PROVISIONS OF PART VII OF THE ACT IN RELATION TO A LISTED PERSON

## APPLICATION OF PROVISIONS OF PART VII OF THE ACT IN RELATION TO A LISTED PERSON

**19(1)** Subject to the following provisions of this Regulation, the provisions of Part VII shall apply in relation to a listed person.

**19(2)** In their application, by virtue of paragraph (1) of this Regulation, in relation to a listed person–

(a) sections 157 (change in default rules), 162 (duty to report on completion of default proceedings), 166 (powers to give directions) and 167 (application to determine whether default proceedings to be taken) of the Act shall apply as if functions under those sections were exercisable by the Financial Services Authority and not by any other person;

(b) sections 184(3) and (4) (indemnity for certain acts) shall apply as if the functions mentioned in section 184(3) were the functions of a listed person so far as relating to, or to matters arising out of–
  (i) his default rules; or
  (ii) any obligation to which he is subject by virtue of Part VII as it is applied by these Regulations; and

(c) section 184(5) shall apply as if the reference to paragraph 5 or 12 of Schedule 21 to the Act was a reference to paragraph 6 of the Schedule to these Regulations.

**History**
In reg. 19(2)(a) the words "Financial Services Authority" substituted for the former words "Bank of England" by the Bank of England Act 1998 (Consequential Amendments of Subordinate Legislation) Order 1998 (SI 1998/1129), art. 1, 2 and Sch. 1, para. 20(1), (3)(m) as from 1 June 1998.

## MONEY MARKET CHARGES

## MONEY MARKET CHARGES

**20** The general law of insolvency shall have effect in relation to a money market charge subject to the provisions of regulations 21 to 24 of these Regulations.

## ADMINISTRATION ORDERS, ETC.

**21(1)** The provisions of this regulation are subject to the provisions of regulations 22 to 24 below.

**21(2)** The following provisions of the Insolvency Act 1986 (which relate to administration orders and administrators) do not apply in relation to a money market charge–

(a) sections 10(1)(b) and 11(3)(c) (restriction on enforcement of security while petition for administration order pending or order in force); and

(b) section 15(1) and (2) (power of administrator to deal with charged property);

and section 11(2) of that Act (receiver to vacate office when so requested by administrator) does not apply to a receiver appointed under a money market charge.

**21(3)** However, where a money market charge falls to be enforced after an administration order has been made or a petition for an administration order has been presented, and there exists another charge over some or all of the same property ranking in priority to or *pari passu* with the market charge, the court may, on the application of any person interested, order that there shall be taken after enforcement of the money market charge such steps as the court may direct for the purpose of ensuring that the chargee under the other charge is not prejudiced by the enforcement of the money market charge.

**21(4)** The following provisions of the Insolvency Act 1986 (which relate to the powers of receivers) do not apply to a money market charge–

(a) section 43 (power of administrative receiver to dispose of charged property); and

(b) section 61 (power of receiver in Scotland to dispose of an interest in property).

**21(5)** Sections 127 and 284 of the Insolvency Act 1986 (avoidance of property dispositions effected after the commencement of winding up or presentation of a bankruptcy petition), and section 32(8) of the Bankruptcy (Scotland) Act 1985 (effect of dealing with debtor relating to estate vested in permanent trustee), do not apply to a disposition of property as a result of which the property becomes subject to a money market charge or any transaction pursuant to which that disposition is made.

**21(6)** However, if a person (other than the chargee under the money market charge) who is a party to a disposition mentioned in paragraph (5) above has notice at the time of the disposition that a petition has been presented for the winding up, bankruptcy or sequestration of the estate of the party making the disposition, the value of any profit to him arising from the disposition is recoverable by the relevant office-holder unless the court directs otherwise.

**21(7)** Any sum recoverable by virtue of paragraph (6) above ranks for priority, in the event of the insolvency of the person from whom it is due, immediately before preferential or, in Scotland, preferred debts.

**21(8)** In a case falling within paragraph (5) above (as a disposition of property as a result of which the property becomes subject to a money market charge) and section 164(3) of the Act as it has effect by virtue of these Regulations (as the provision of margin or other property in relation to money market contracts), section 164(4), as it has effect by virtue of these Regulations, applies with respect to the recovery of the amount or value of the margin or other property and paragraph (6) above does not apply.

## LIMITATIONS ON EXTENT TO WHICH CHARGE TO BE TREATED AS MONEY MARKET CHARGE

**22(1)** Where a money market charge is granted partly for purposes other than securing debts or liabilities arising in connection with the settlement of money market contracts or related contracts, the provisions of these Regulations apply in relation to it only in so far as it has effect for the purpose of securing such debts and liabilities.

**22(2)** The provisions of these Regulations shall not have effect in relation to any money market charge, whether fixed or floating, to the extent that it is a charge on land or any interest in land.

**22(3)** For the purposes of paragraph (2) above, a charge on a debenture forming part of a series shall not be treated as a charge on land or any interest in land by reason of the fact that the debenture is itself secured by a charge on land or any interest in land.

**22(4)** The provisions of these Regulations shall apply to a money market charge only to the extent that–

(a) it is a charge over property provided, whether as margin or otherwise, by a person to a

limited exemption from liability in damages on the Bank of England. Regulation 30 limits to Great Britain the territorial scope of the regulations and the provisions of Part VII of the 1989 Act applied by the regulations in modified form.

# THE COMPANIES (SUMMARY FINANCIAL STATEMENT) REGULATIONS 1995

(SI 1995/2092)

*Made on 4 August 1995 by the Secretary of State for Trade and Industry under s. 245(3) and (4) and s. 251(1), (2) and (3) of the Companies Act 1985. Operative from 1 September 1995.*

## ARRANGEMENT OF REGULATIONS

# PART I – GENERAL

## CITATION AND COMMENCEMENT

**1** These Regulations may be cited as the Companies (Summary Financial Statement) Regulations 1995 and shall come into force on 1st September 1995.

## INTERPRETATION

**2** In these Regulations, unless otherwise stated–

**"the 1985 Act"** means the Companies Act 1985;

**"banking company"** means a company the directors of which prepare accounts for a financial year in accordance with the special provisions of Part VII of the 1985 Act relating to banking companies;

**"EEA State"** means a State which is a Contracting Party to the Agreement on the European Economic Area signed at Oporto on 2nd May 1992, as adjusted by the Protocol signed at Brussels on 17th March 1993 and by EEA Council Decision Number 1/95 of 10th March 1995;

**"entitled persons"** means the same as in section 251 of the 1985 Act;

**"full accounts and reports"** means a company's annual accounts, the directors' report and the auditors' report on those accounts required to be sent to entitled persons under section 238(1) of the 1985 Act and **"full"** in relation to any balance sheet, profit and loss account, group accounts or directors' report means any such document comprised in the full accounts and reports;

**"insurance company"** means a company the directors of which prepare accounts for a financial year in accordance with the special provisions of Part VII of the 1985 Act relating to insurance companies;

**"listed public company"** means a public company whose shares or debentures, or any class of whose shares or debentures, are listed within the meaning of section 251(1) of the 1985 Act.

# PART II – CONDITIONS FOR SENDING OUT SUMMARY FINANCIAL STATEMENT

## CASES IN WHICH SENDING OF SUMMARY FINANCIAL STATEMENT PROHIBITED

**3(1)** A listed public company may not send a summary financial statement to an entitled person instead of copies of its full accounts and reports, in any case where it is prohibited from doing so by any relevant provision (within the meaning of paragraph (2) below)–

(a) in its memorandum or articles of association, or

(b) where the entitled person is a holder of the company's debentures, in any instrument constituting or otherwise governing any of the company's debentures of which that person is a holder.

**3(2)** For the purposes of paragraph (1) above, any provision (however expressed) which requires copies of the full accounts and reports to be sent to entitled persons, or which forbids the sending of summary financial statements under section 251 of the 1985 Act, is a relevant provision.

## ASCERTAINMENT OF ENTITLED PERSON'S WISHES

**4(1)** A listed public company may not send a summary financial statement to an entitled person in place of copies of its full accounts and reports, unless the company has ascertained that the entitled person does not wish to receive copies of those documents.

**4(2)** Whether or not an entitled person wishes to receive copies of the full accounts and reports for a financial year is to be ascertained–

(a) from any relevant notification in writing he has given to the company (either as an entitled person or as a person to whom paragraph (5) of this regulation applies) as to whether he wishes to receive copies of the full accounts and reports or as to whether he wishes, instead of copies of those documents, to receive summary financial statements; or

(b) failing any such express notification, from any failure to respond to an opportunity given to the entitled person (including for this purpose a person to whom paragraph (5) of this regulation applies) to elect to receive copies of the full accounts and reports either in response to a notice send by the company under regulation 5 below, or as part of a relevant consultation of his wishes by the company under regulation 6 below.

**4(3)** For the purposes of paragraph (2)(a) above, a notification is a relevant notification with respect to a financial year if it relates to that year (whether or not it has been given at the invitation of the company) and if it is received by the company not later than 28 days before the first date on which copies of the full accounts and reports are sent out to entitled persons in compliance with section 238(1) of the 1985 Act with respect to the financial year.

**4(4)** A company may not send a summary financial statement to an entitled person in relation to any financial year in place of copies of the full accounts and reports unless–

(a) the period allowed for laying and delivering full accounts and reports under section 244 of the 1985 Act for that year has not expired, and

(b) the summary financial statement has been approved by the board of directors and the original statement signed on behalf of the board by a director of the company.

**4(5)** This paragraph applies to a person who is entitled, whether conditionally or unconditionally, to become an entitled person in relation to the company, but who has not yet become such an entitled person.

## CONSULTATION BY NOTICE

**5(1)** A listed public company may give a notice to an entitled person (including for this purpose a person to whom regulation 4(5) above applies), by sending it by post or giving it in any other manner authorised by the company's articles, which shall–

(a) state that for the future, so long as he is an entitled person, he will be sent a summary financial statement for each financial year instead of a copy of the company's full accounts and reports, unless he notifies the company in writing that he wishes to receive full accounts and reports,

(b) state that the summary financial statement for a financial year will contain a summary of the company's or group's profit and loss account, balance sheet and directors' report for that year,

(c) state that the printed card or form accompanying the notice in accordance with paragraph (2) below must be returned by a date specified in the notice, being a date at least 21 days after service of the notice and not less than 28 days before the first date on which copies of the full accounts and reports for the next financial year for which the entitled person is entitled to receive them are sent out to entitled persons in compliance with section 238(1) of the 1985 Act,

(d) include a statement in a prominent position to the effect that a summary financial statement will not contain sufficient information to allow as full an understanding of the results and state of affairs of the company or group as would be provided by the full annual accounts and reports and that members and debenture holders requiring more detailed information have the right to obtain, free of charge, a copy of the company's last full accounts and reports, and

(e) state that the summary financial statement will contain a statement by the company's auditors as to whether the summary financial statement is consistent with the full accounts and reports for the year in question, whether it complies with the requirements of section 251 of the Act and of these Regulations and whether their report on the accounts was qualified.

**5(2)** Subject to paragraph (3) below, the notice shall be accompanied by a printed card or form, in respect of which any postage necessary for its return to the company has been, or will be, paid by the company, which is so worded as to enable an entitled person (including a person to whom regulation 4(5) above applies), by marking a box and returning the card or form, to notify the company that he wishes to receive full accounts and reports for the next financial year for which he is entitled to receive them as an entitled person and for all future financial years thereafter.

**5(3)** The company need not pay the postage in respect of the return of the printed card or form in the following circumstances–

(a) if the address of a member to which notices are sent in accordance with the company's articles is not within an EEA State,

(b) if the address of a debenture holder to which notices are sent in accordance with the terms of any instrument constituting or otherwise governing the debentures of which he is a holder is not within an EEA State, or

(c) if the address of a person to whom regulation 4(5) above applies to which notices are sent, in accordance with the contractual provisions whereunder he has a right (conditionally or unconditionally) to become an entitled person, is not within an EEA State.

### RELEVANT CONSULTATION

**6(1)** A listed public company may conduct a relevant consultation to ascertain the wishes of an entitled person.

**6(2)** For the purposes of this regulation, a relevant consultation of the wishes of an entitled person is a notice given to the entitled person (including for this purpose a person to whom regulation 4(5) above applies), by sending it by post or giving it in any other manner authorised by the company's articles, which–

(a) states that for the future, so long as he is an entitled person, he will be sent a summary financial statement instead of the full accounts and reports of the company, unless he notifies the company in writing that he wishes to continue to receive full accounts and reports;

(b) accompanies a copy of the full accounts and reports;

(c) accompanies a copy of a summary financial statement, prepared in accordance with section 251 of the 1985 Act and these Regulations, with respect to the financial year covered by those full accounts and reports and which is identified in the notice as an example of the document which the entitled person will receive for the future, so long as he is an entitled person, unless he notifies the company to the contrary; and

(d) subject to paragraph (3) below, is accompanied by a printed card or form, in respect of which any postage necessary for its return to the company has been, or will be, paid by the company, which is so worded as to enable an entitled person (including a person to whom regulation 4(5) above applies), by marking a box and returning the card or form, to notify the company that he wishes to receive full accounts and reports for the next financial year for which he is entitled to receive them as an entitled person and for all future financial years thereafter.

**6(3)** Regulation 5(3) above applies in respect of the payment of postage for the return of the printed card or form referred to in paragraph (2)(d) of this regulation.

## PART III – FORM AND CONTENT OF SUMMARY FINANCIAL STATEMENT

### PROVISIONS APPLYING TO ALL COMPANIES AND GROUPS

**7(1)** Every summary financial statement issued by a listed public company in place of the full accounts and reports must comply with this regulation.

**7(2)** The summary financial statement must state the name of the person who signed it on behalf of the board.

shown for the immediately preceding financial year; for this purpose "the corresponding amount" is the amount shown in the summary financial statement for that year or which would have been so shown had such a statement been prepared for that year, after any adjustments necessary to ensure that that amount is comparable with the item for the financial year in question.

# Schedule 2 – Form and Content of Summary Financial Statement of Banking Companies and Groups

Regulation 9

## FORM OF SUMMARY FINANCIAL STATEMENT

**1(1)** The summary financial statement shall contain the information prescribed by the following paragraphs of this Schedule, in such order and under such headings as the directors consider appropriate, together with any other information necessary to ensure that the summary financial statement is consistent with the full accounts and reports for the financial year in question.

**1(2)** Nothing in this Schedule shall be construed as prohibiting the inclusion in the summary financial statement of any additional information derived from the company's annual accounts and the directors' report.

## SUMMARY DIRECTORS' REPORT

**2(1)** The summary financial statement shall contain the whole of, or a summary of, that portion of the directors' report for the year in question which sets out the following matters–

(a) the matters required by section 234(1)(a) of the 1985 Act (business review);

(b) the amount recommended to be paid as dividend, if not disclosed in the summary profit and loss account;

(c) the matters required by paragraph 6(a) of Schedule 7 to the 1985 Act (important post-balance sheet events); and

(d) the matters required by paragraph 6(b) of that Schedule (likely future developments in the business).

**2(2)** The summary financial statement shall also contain the list of names of directors required by section 234(2) of the 1985 Act.

## SUMMARY PROFIT AND LOSS ACCOUNT: COMPANIES NOT REQUIRED TO PREPARE GROUP ACCOUNTS

**3(1)** The summary financial statement shall contain, in the case of a company the directors of which are not required to prepare group accounts for the financial year, a summary profit and loss account showing, in so far as they may be derived from the full profit and loss account, the items, or combinations of items, listed in sub-paragraph (3) below, in the order set out in that sub-paragraph.

**3(2)** The items or combinations of items listed in sub-paragraph (3) below may appear under such headings as the directors consider appropriate.

**3(3)** The items, or combinations of items, referred to in sub-paragraph (1) above are–

(a) interest receivable and payable:
the net figure resulting from the combination of the following two items–
– format 1, items 1 and 2
– format 2, items A1 and B1;

(b) dividend income, fees and commissions receivable and payable, dealing profits or losses and other operating income:
the net figure resulting from the combination of the following items–

– format 1, items 3, 4, 5, 6 and 7
– format 2, items A2, A3, B2, B3, B4 and B7;

(c) administrative expenses, depreciation and amortisation, other operating charges, amounts written off, and adjustments to amounts written off, fixed asset investments: the net figure resulting from the combination of the following items–
– format 1, items 8, 9, 10, 13 and 14
– format 2, items A4, A5, A6, A8 and B6;

(d) provisions and adjustments to provisions: the net figure resulting from the combination of the following two items–
– format 1, items 11 and 12
– format 2, items A7 and B5;

(e) profit or loss on ordinary activities before tax:
– format 1, item 15
– format 2, item A9 or B8;

(f) tax on profit or loss on ordinary activities:
– format 1, item 16
– format 2, item A10;

(g) profit or loss on ordinary activities after tax:
– format 1, item 17
– format 2, item A11 or B9;

(h) extraordinary profit or loss after tax:
– format 1, item 22
– the net figure resulting from the combination of format 2, items A14 and B11;

(i) other taxes not shown under the preceding items:
– format 1, item 23
– format 2, item A15;

(j) profit or loss for the financial year:
– format 1, item 24
– format 2, item A16 or B12; and

(k) the aggregate amount of dividends paid and, if not disclosed in the summary directors' report, proposed.

**3(4)** The summary profit and loss account shall also show, at the end thereof and under such heading as the directors consider appropriate, the figure required by paragraph 1(1) of Part I of Schedule 6 to the 1985 Act (directors' emoluments).

## SUMMARY PROFIT AND LOSS ACCOUNT: COMPANIES REQUIRED TO PREPARE GROUP ACCOUNTS

**4(1)** The summary financial statement shall contain, in the case of a company the directors of which are required to prepare group accounts for the financial year, a summary consolidated profit and loss account showing the items, or combinations of items, required by paragraph 3 above, in the order required by that paragraph and under such headings as the directors consider appropriate, but with the modifications specified in sub-paragraph (2) below.

**4(2)** The modifications referred to in sub-paragraph (1) above are as follows–

(a) between the information required by paragraph 3(3)(d) and that required by paragraph 3(3)(e) there shall in addition be shown, under such heading as the directors consider appropriate, the item "Income from associated undertakings" required to be shown in the Schedule 9 formats by paragraph 3(7)(ii) of Part II of Schedule 9 to the 1985 Act;

(b) between the information required by paragraph 3(3)(g) and that required by paragraph 3(3)(h) there shall in addition be shown, under such heading as the directors consider appropriate, the item "Minority interests" required to be shown in the Schedule 9 formats by paragraph 17(3) of Schedule 4A to the 1985 Act as adapted by paragraph 3(3) of Part II of Schedule 9 to that Act; and

(c) the figures required by paragraph 3(3)(h) and (i) shall each be shown after the deduction or the addition (as the case may be) of the item "Minority interests" required to be shown in the Schedule 9 formats by paragraph 17(4) of Schedule 4A to the 1985 Act as adapted by paragraph 3(4) of Part II of Schedule 9 to that Act.

## SUMMARY BALANCE SHEET: COMPANIES NOT REQUIRED TO PREPARE GROUP ACCOUNTS

**5(1)** The summary financial statement shall contain, in the case of a company the directors of which are not required to prepare group accounts for the financial year, a summary balance sheet which shall show, in so far as they may be derived from the full balance sheet, the items, or combinations of items, set out in sub-paragraph (2) below, in the order set out in that sub-paragraph and under such headings as the directors consider appropriate.

**5(2)** The items, or combinations of items, referred to in sub-paragraph (1) above are as follows:

(a) cash and balances at central [or post office] banks, treasury bills and other eligible bills:

– the aggregate of items 1 and 2 under the heading "ASSETS";

(b) loans and advances to banks:

– item 3 under the heading "ASSETS";

(c) loans and advances to customers:

– item 4 under the heading "ASSETS";

(d) debt securities [and other fixed income securities], equity shares [and other variable-yield securities], participating interests and shares in group undertakings:

– the aggregate of items 5, 6, 7 and 8 under the heading "ASSETS";

(e) intangible and tangible fixed assets:

– the aggregate of items 9 and 10 under the heading "ASSETS";

(f) called up capital not paid, own shares, other assets, prepayments and accrued income:

– the aggregate of items 11 (or 14), 12, 13 and 15 under the heading "ASSETS";

(g) total assets under the heading "ASSETS";

(h) deposits by banks:

– item 1 under the heading "LIABILITIES";

(i) customer accounts:

– item 2 under the heading "LIABILITIES";

(j) debt securities in issue:

– item 3 under the heading "LIABILITIES";

(k) other liabilities, accruals and deferred income and provisions for liabilities and charges:

– the aggregate of items 4, 5 and 6 under the heading "LIABILITIES";

(l) subordinated liabilities:

– item 7 under the heading "LIABILITIES";

(m) called up share capital, share premium account, reserves, revaluation reserve and profit and loss account:

– the aggregate of items 8, 9, 10, 11 and 12 under the heading "LIABILITIES";

(n) total liabilities under the heading "LIABILITIES";

(o) contingent liabilities:

– item 1 under the heading "MEMORANDUM ITEMS"; and

(p) commitments:

– item 2 under the heading "MEMORANDUM ITEMS".

### SUMMARY BALANCE SHEET: COMPANIES REQUIRED TO PREPARE GROUP ACCOUNTS

**6(1)** The summary financial statement shall contain, in the case of a company the directors of which are required to prepare group accounts for the financial year, a summary consolidated balance sheet showing the items required by paragraph 5 above, in the order required by that paragraph and under such headings as the directors consider appropriate, but with the addition specified in sub-paragraph (2) below.

**6(2)** Between the items required by paragraph 5(2)(l) and (m) or after the item required by paragraph 5(2)(m) (whichever is the position adopted for the full accounts), there shall in addition be shown under an appropriate heading the item "Minority interests" required to be shown in the Schedule 9 format by paragraph 17(2) of Schedule 4A to the 1985 Act, as adapted by paragraph 3(2) of Part II of Schedule 9 to the 1985 Act.

### CORRESPONDING AMOUNTS

**7** In respect of every item shown in the summary profit and loss account or summary consolidated profit and loss account (as the case may be), or in the summary balance sheet or summary consolidated balance sheet (as the case may be) the corresponding amount shall be shown for the immediately preceding financial year; for this purpose "the corresponding amount" is the amount shown in the summary financial statement for that year or which would have been so shown had such a statement been prepared for that year, after any adjustments necessary to ensure that that amount is comparable with the item for the financial year in question.

# Schedule 3 – Form and Content of Summary Financial Statement of Insurance Companies and Groups

Regulation 10

### APPLICATION OF SCHEDULE

**1(1)** Paragraphs 2 to 8 of this Schedule apply where the full annual accounts for the financial year have been prepared under Part VII of the 1985 Act as amended by the Companies Act 1985 (Insurance Companies Accounts) Regulations 1993.

**1(2)** Paragraphs 2 and 3 and 8 to 11 of this Schedule apply where the full annual accounts for the financial year have been prepared under the transitional arrangements (as defined in paragraph 9(1) of this Schedule).

**1(3)** Paragraph 12 applies where the directors of a parent company of an insurance group, being entitled to do so, prepare group accounts for the financial year in an alternative form as permitted by article 7 of, and paragraph 3 of Part I of Schedule 2 to, the Companies Act 1989 (Commencement No. 4 and Transitional and Saving Provisions) Order 1990.

### FORM OF SUMMARY FINANCIAL STATEMENT

**2(1)** The summary financial statement shall contain the information prescribed by the following paragraphs of this Schedule, in such order and under such headings as the directors consider appropriate, together with any other information necessary to ensure that the summary financial statement is consistent with the full accounts and reports for the financial year in question.

**2(2)** Nothing in this Schedule shall be construed as prohibiting the inclusion in the summary financial statement of any additional information derived from the company's annual accounts and the directors' report.

### SUMMARY DIRECTORS' REPORT

**3(1)** The summary financial statement shall contain the whole of, or a summary of, that portion of the directors' report for the year in question which sets out the following matters–

(a) regulation 4 sets out the manner in which a listed public company is to ascertain whether an entitled person (as defined in regulation 2) wishes to receive a summary financial statement ("SFS") in place of the full accounts and reports for the financial year. If such companies have not received an express written notification from the entitled person, they can conduct a relevant consultation under regulation 6 of these Regulations (a procedure similar to that previously set out in regulation 6(3) of the 1992 Regulations). Alternatively, regulation 5 introduces a new procedure of sending entitled persons an advance notice describing what an SFS will contain and enclosing a reply-paid card on which entitled persons can indicate whether they wish to receive full accounts and reports;

(b) regulation 6(2)(b) of the 1992 Regulations (under which a failure by an entitled person to respond to a relevant consultation under that regulation impliedly countermanded any previous notification of a wish to receive full accounts and reports) is not re-enacted in these Regulations;

(c) companies will only have to pay for the postage on cards sent to entitled persons under regulations 5(2) and 6(2)(d) of these Regulations if those persons have addresses in the European Economic Area (regulation 5(3) and 6(3));

(d) when an SFS is sent to an entitled person under the Regulations it will no longer be accompanied by a reply-paid card on which the entitled person can request the full accounts and reports. The SFS will, however, contain a clear statement of the right of entitled persons to obtain a free copy of a company's full accounts and reports and of how that copy can be obtained, and of how they may elect to receive such accounts and reports rather than SFSs for future years (regulation 7(4) and (5));

(e) the revisions to the law on the content of the full statutory accounts of insurance companies and groups contained in the Companies Act 1985 (Insurance Companies Accounts) Regulations 1993 (SI 1993/3246) (and the transitional arrangements contained in those Regulations) are reflected in regulation 10 of, and Schedule 3 to, these Regulations;

(f) listed public companies other than insurance companies may continue to comply with the 1992 Regulations with respect to financial years commencing prior to 23rd December 1994 (regulation 11(2)). Special transitional arrangements for insurance companies are contained in Schedule 3; and

(g) the transitional provisions contained in paragraphs 3 and 7 of Schedule 2 to the 1992 Regulations are not re-enacted as they are spent.

# THE COMPANIES ACT 1989 PART II (CONSEQUENTIAL AMENDMENT) (NO. 2) REGULATIONS 1995

(SI 1995/2723)

*Made on 17 October 1995 by the Secretary of State for Trade and Industry under s. 50 of the Companies Act 1989. Operative from 13 November 1995.*

## CITATION AND COMMENCEMENT

**1** These Regulations may be cited as the Companies Act 1989 Part II (Consequential Amendment) (No. 2) Regulations 1995 and shall come into force on 13th November 1995.

## CONSEQUENTIAL AMENDMENT

**2** In Schedule 11 to the Building Societies Act 1986, in paragraph 5(2), sub-paragraph (d) (body corporate not qualified for appointment as an auditor of a building society) is hereby repealed.

## EXPLANATORY NOTE

(*This Note is not part of the Regulations*)

Regulation 2 amends Schedule 11 to the Building Societies Act 1986, by repealing sub-paragraph 5(2)(d).

That provision excluded bodies corporate from appointment as an auditor of a building society.

By virtue of section 25 of the Companies Act 1989, a body corporate may be appointed as an auditor of a company under the Companies Act 1985, if that body corporate is otherwise eligible for appointment. The repeal of sub-paragraph 5(2)(d) of Schedule 11 to the Building Societies Act 1986 will mean that bodies corporate will be eligible for appointment as auditors of building societies to the same extent that they are so eligible in relation to companies.

# THE COMPANY AND BUSINESS NAMES (AMENDMENT) REGULATIONS 1995

(SI 1995/3022)

*Made on 23 November 1995 by the Secretary of State for Trade and Industry under s. 29 of the Companies Act 1985 and s. 3 and 6 of the Business Names Act 1985. Operative from 1 January 1996.*

**1** These Regulations may be cited as the Company and Business Names (Amendment) Regulations 1995 and shall come into force on 1st January 1996.

**2** In these Regulations:–

**"the 1981 Regulations"** means the Company and Business Names Regulations 1981;
**"the Act"** means the Business Names Act 1985.

**3** [Amendments to col. (1) and (2) of Sch. to the Company and Business Names (Amendment) Regulations 1981.]

**4(1)** Sections 2 and 3 of the Act shall not prohibit a person from carrying on any business under a name which includes any word or expression specified for the purposes of those sections by virtue of the amendment made by regulation 3(a) above to the 1981 Regulations, if–

(a) he carried on that business immediately before 1st January 1996; and

(b) he continues to carry it on under the name which immediately before that day was its lawful business name.

**4(2)** Nor shall sections 2 and 3 of the Act prohibit a person to whom a business has been transferred on or after 1st January 1996 from carrying on that business during the period of twelve months beginning with the date of transfer so long as he continues to carry it on under the name which was its lawful business name immediately before the date of transfer.

## EXPLANATORY NOTE

(*This Note is not part of the Regulations*)

These Regulations amend the Company and Business Names Regulations 1981, (SI 1981/1685, referred to here as the "1981 Regulations"), as amended by the Company and Business Names (Amendment) Regulations 1982 (SI 1982/1653) and the Company and Business Names (Amendment) Regulations 1992 (SI 1992/1196). The 1981 Regulations specify certain words and expressions for the purposes of section 26 of the Companies Act 1985 and section 2 of the Business Names Act 1985. Under those sections the Secretary of State's approval is required for the use of such words and expressions in (respectively) a company or business name.

These Regulations amend the 1981 Regulations by inserting (regulation 3(a)) the expression "Chamber of Commerce, Training and Enterprise" into the list of those expressions.

They also delete from that list the words "Breed", "Breeders" and "Breeding" and "Nursing Home" and the names of the relevant bodies which must be asked whether they have any objection to the use of those words.

The amendment to the 1981 Regulations made by regulation 3(a) is subject to transitional provisions in regulation 4. These allow the continued use of a business name lawfully used prior to the coming into force of regulation 3 until 12 months after any transfer of the business concerned.

# THE FINANCIAL SERVICES ACT 1986 (INVESTMENT SERVICES) (EXTENSION OF SCOPE OF ACT) ORDER 1995

(SI 1995/3271)

*Made on 18 December 1995 by the Treasury under s. 2 and 205A of the Financial Services Act 1986. Operative from 1 January 1996.*

## CITATION AND COMMENCEMENT

**1** This Order may be cited as the Financial Services Act 1986 (Investment Services) Extension of Scope of Act) Order 1995 and shall come into force on 1st January 1996.

## INTERPRETATION

**2(1)** In this Order–

**"the Act"** means the Financial Services Act 1986;

**"core investment service"** means a service listed in Section A of the Annex to the Investment Services Directive, the text of which is set out in Part I of Schedule 1 to this Order together with the text of Section B of that Annex which is relevant to the interpretation of Section A;

**"investment firm"** has the meaning given in paragraph (2) below;

**"the Investment Services Directive"** means the Council Directive on investment services in the securities field (No. 93/22/EEC); and

**"listed service"** means a service listed in Section A or C of the Annex to the Investment Services Directive.

**2(2)** In this Order references to an investment firm are references to any person, other than one within paragraph (3) below, whose regular occupation or business is the provision of any one or more core investment services to third parties on a professional basis.

**2(3)** The persons within this paragraph are persons to whom the Investment Services Directive does not apply by virtue of the provisions of Article 2(2) of that Directive, the text of which is set out in Schedule 2 to this Order.

## SHARES IN INDUSTRIAL AND PROVIDENT SOCIETIES

**3** Paragraph 1 of Schedule 1 to the Act shall have effect as if transferable shares in a body incorporated under the law of, or of any part of, the United Kingdom relating to industrial and provident societies fell within that paragraph.

## BILLS OF EXCHANGE

**4** Paragraph 2 of Schedule 1 to the Act shall have effect as if bills of exchange accepted by a banker fell within that paragraph.

## AMENDMENT OF PART II OF SCHEDULE 1 TO THE ACT FOR CERTAIN PURPOSES

**5** For the purposes of the provisions of sections 47A and 48 of the Act, Part II of Schedule 1 to the Act shall have effect as if amongst the activities falling within that Part of that Schedule were those listed services falling within Section C of the Annex to the Investment Services Directive; and for these purposes none of the exclusions in Part III of that Schedule shall have effect.

## AMENDMENT OF PART III OF SCHEDULE 1 TO THE ACT

**6(1)** (Revoked by the Financial Services Act 1986 (Restriction of Scope of Act and Meaning of Collective Investment Scheme) Order 1996 (SI 1996/2996), art. 1, 2(3) as from 1 January 1997.)

**History**

Para. 6(1) formerly read as follows:

"Nothing in paragraphs 17 to 19 and 21 of Schedule 1 to the Act shall have the effect that the provision of any core investment service to third parties on a professional basis is excluded from the activities which fall within the paragraphs in Part II of Schedule 1 to the Act."

**6(2)** Paragraph 23 of Schedule 1 to the Act shall have effect as if it precluded a permission being granted to any person who is an investment firm.

TRANSITIONAL PROVISIONS

7 The prohibitions in section 3 of the Act shall not, until 1st January 1997, extend to any person who is, by virtue only of any provision of this Order, carrying on, or purporting to carry on, investment business in the United Kingdom.

# Schedule 1 – Annex to the Investment Services Directive

Article 2(1)

**"ANNEX**

SECTION A – SERVICES

**1(a)** Reception and transmission, on behalf of investors, of orders in relation to one or more instruments listed in section B.
**1(b)** Execution of such orders other than for own account.
**2** Dealing in any of the instruments listed in Section B for own account.
**3** Managing portfolios of investments in accordance with mandates given by investors on a discretionary, client-by-client basis where such portfolios include one or more of the instruments listed in section B.
**4** Underwriting in respect of issues of any of the instruments listed in section B and/or the placing of such issues.

SECTION B – INSTRUMENTS

**1(a)** Transferable securities.
**1(b)** Units in collective investment undertakings.
**2** Money-market instruments.
**3** Financial-futures contracts, including equivalent cash-settled instruments.
**4** Forward interest-rate agreements (FRAs).
**5** Interest-rate, currency and equity swaps.
**6** Options to acquire or dispose of any instruments falling within this section of the Annex, including equivalent cash-settled instruments. This category includes in particular options on currency and on interest rates.

SECTION C – NON-CORE SERVICES

**1** Safekeeping and administration in relation to one or more of the instruments listed in Section B.
**2** Safe custody services.
**3** Granting credits or loans to an investor to allow him to carry out a transaction in one or more of the instruments listed in Section B, where the firm granting the credit or loan is involved in the transaction.
**4** Advice to undertakings on capital structure, industrial strategy and related matters and advice and service relating to mergers and the purchase of undertakings.
**5** Services related to underwriting.
**6** Investment advice concerning one or more of the instruments listed in Section B.
**7** Foreign-exchange service where these are connected with the provision of investment services."

# Schedule 2 – Article 2.2 of the Investment Services Directive

Article 2(3)

"This Directive shall not apply to:

(a) insurance undertakings as defined in article 1 of Directive 73/239/EEC or Article 1 or Directive 79/267/EEC or undertakings carrying on the reinsurance and retrocession activities referred to in Directive 64/225/EEC;

(b) firms which provide investment services exclusively for their parent undertakings, for their subsidiaries or for other subsidiaries of their parent undertakings;

(c) persons providing an investment service where that service is provided in an incidental manner in the course of a professional activity and that activity is regulated by legal or regulatory provisions or a code of ethics governing the profession which do not exclude the provision of that service;

(d) firms that provide investment services consisting exclusively in the administration of employee-participation schemes;

(e) firms that provide investment services that consist in providing both the services referred to in (b) and those referred to in (d);

(f) the central banks of Member States and other national bodies performing similar functions and other public bodies charged with or intervening in the management of the public debt;

(g) firms

– which may not hold clients' funds or securities and which for that reason may not at any time place themselves in debit with their clients, and

– which may not provide any investment service except the reception and transmission of orders in transferable securities and units in collective investment undertakings, and

– which in the course of providing that service may transmit orders only to

(i) investment firms authorized in accordance with this Directive;

(ii) credit institutions authorised in accordance with Directives 77/780/EEC and 89/646/EEC;

(iii) branches of investment firms or of credit institutions which are authorized in a third country and which are subject to and comply with prudential rules considered by the competent authorities as at least as stringent as those laid down in this Directive, in Directive 89/646/EEC or in Directive 93/6/EEC;

(iv) collective investment undertakings authorized under the law of a Member State to market units to the public and to the managers of such undertakings;

(v) investment companies with fixed capital, as defined in article 15(4) of Directive 79/91/EEC, the securities of which are listed or dealt in on a regulated market in a Member State;

– the activities of which are governed at national level by rules or by a code of ethics;

(h) collective investment undertakings whether coordinated at Community level or not and the depositaries and managers of such undertakings;

(i) persons whose main business is trading in commodities amongst themselves or with producers or professional users of such products and who provide investment services only for such producers and professional users to the extent necessary for their main business;

(j) firms that provide investment services consisting exclusively in dealing for their own account on financial-futures or options markets or which deal for the accounts of other members of those markets or make prices for them and which are guaranteed by clearing members of the same markets. Responsibility for ensuring the performance of contracts entered into by such firms must be assumed by clearing members of the same markets;

(k) associations set up by Danish pension funds with the sole aim of managing the assets of pension funds that are members of those associations;

(l) "agenti di cambio" whose activities and functions are governed by Italian Royal

Decree No 222 of 7 March 1925 and subsequent provisions amending it, and who are authorized to carry on their activities under Article 19 of Italian Law No. 1 of 2 January 1991."

## EXPLANATORY NOTE

(*This Note is not part of the Order*)

The Order makes amendments to the scope of the Financial Services Act 1986 ("the Act") required to give effect to Council Directive No. 93/22/EEC on investment services in the securities field (OJ No. L 141, 10.5.93, p. 27). In so far as other legislative provision is needed to implement the provisions of the directive, this is contained in the Act, in an Order to be made under section 46 of the Act and in Regulations to be made under section 2(2) of the European Communities Act 1972. The Order comes into force on 1 January 1996.

The scope of the Act is determined by section 1 of the Act. Section 2 confers power on the Treasury to make orders extending or restricting the scope of the Act for the purposes of all or any of its provisions. The exercise of this power is among the functions transferred to the Treasury by the Transfer of Functions (Financial Services) Order 1992 (SI 1992/1315).

Section 1 of the Act defines "investments" by reference to the instruments falling within Part I of Schedule 1. Articles 3 and 4 of the Order add certain instruments to the investments falling within Part I of that Schedule (certain shares in industrial and provident societies and certain bills of exchange).

Article 5 of the Order extends, for the purposes of sections 47A and 48 of the Act, the activities that are to constitute the carrying on of investment business. As required by article 11 of the directive, statements of principle and rules can now be made under those two sections in respect of all services covered by the directive.

Section 1 of the Act defines "investment business" by reference to activities which fall within Part II of Schedule 1 to the Act and which are not excluded by Part III of that Schedule. Article 6 of the Order amends the meaning of "investment business" to cover the provision of all investment services to which the directive applies.

# THE UNCERTIFICATED SECURITIES REGULATIONS 1995

(SI 1995/3272)

*Made on 18 December 1995 by the Treasury under the Transfer of Functions (Financial Services) Order 1992 and s. 207(9) of the Companies Act 1989. Operative from 19 December 1995.*

[**Note:** Amendments to these Regulations by the Open-Ended Investment Companies (Investment Companies with Variable Capital) Regulations 1996 (SI 1996/2827) (operative from 6 January 1997) and the Uncertificated Securities (Amendment) Regulations 2000 (SI 2000/1682) (operative from 1 July 2000) have been included.]

## ARRANGEMENT OF THE REGULATIONS

### PART I – CITATION, COMMENCEMENT AND INTERPRETATION



### PART II – THE OPERATOR

*Approval and compliance*

## THE SCHEDULES



# PART I – CITATION, COMMENCEMENT AND INTERPRETATION

## CITATION AND COMMENCEMENT

**1** These Regulations may be cited as the Uncertificated Securities Regulations 1995 and shall come into force the day after the day on which they are made.

## PURPOSES AND BASIC DEFINITIONS

**2(1)** These Regulations enable title to units of a security to be evidenced otherwise than by a certificate and transferred otherwise than by a written instrument, and make provision for certain supplementary and incidental matters; and in these Regulations **"relevant system"** means a computer-based system, and procedures, which enable title to units of a security to be evidenced and transferred without a written instrument, and which facilitate supplementary and incidental matters.

**2(2)** Where title to a unit of a security is evidenced otherwise than by a certificate by virtue of these Regulations, the transfer of title to such a unit of a security shall be subject to these Regulations.

**2(3)** Part II of these Regulations has effect for the purpose of securing–

(a) that the Operator of a relevant system is a person approved for the purpose by the Treasury; and

(b) that a person is only approved if it appears to the Treasury that certain requirements are satisfied with respect to that person, the relevant system and his rules and practices.

**2(4)** Part III of these Regulations has effect for the purpose–

(a) of enabling companies and other persons to become participating issuers in relation to a relevant system, that is to say, persons who permit–
   (i) the holding of units of securities issued by them in uncertificated form; and
   (ii) the transfer by means of the system of title to units of such of the securities issued by them as are held in that form; and

(b) of establishing the duties and obligations of participating issuers in relation to uncertificated units of a security with respect to the keeping of registers, the registration of transfers and other matters.

**2(5)** Part IV of these Regulations has effect for the purpose of securing–

(a) in certain circumstances–
   (i) that the persons expressed to have sent instructions by means of a relevant system which are properly authenticated, and the persons on whose behalf those instructions are expressed to have been sent, are prevented from denying to the persons to whom those instructions are addressed that certain information relating to them is correct; and
   (ii) that the persons to whom the instructions referred to in subparagraph (a)(i) are addressed may accept that certain information relating to them is correct; and

(b) in certain circumstances that persons suffering loss are compensated by the person approved under Part II of these Regulations.

## INTERPRETATION

**3(1)** In these Regulations–

**"the 1985 Act"** means the Companies Act 1985;

**"the 1986 Act"** means the Financial Services Act 1986;

**"certificate"** means any certificate, instrument or other document of, or evidencing, title to units of a security;

**"company"** means a company within the meaning of section 735(1) of the 1985 Act;

**"dematerialised instruction"** means an instruction sent or received by means of a relevant system;

**"designated agency"** has the meaning given by regulation 11(1);

**"enactment"** includes an enactment comprised in any subordinate legislation within the meaning of the Interpretation Act 1978;

**"generate"**, in relation to an Operator-instruction, means to initiate the procedures by which an Operator-instruction comes to be sent;

**"guidance"**, in relation to an Operator, means guidance issued by him which is intended to have continuing effect and is issued in writing or other legible form, which if it were a rule, would come within the definition of a rule;

**"instruction"** includes any instruction, election, acceptance or any other message of any kind;

**"interest in a security"** means any legal or equitable interest or right in relation to a security, including–

(a) an absolute or contingent right to acquire a security created, allotted or issued or to be created, allotted or issued; and

(b) the interests or rights of a person for whom a security is held by a custodian or depositary;

**"issue"**, in relation to a new unit of a security, means to confer title to a new unit on a person;

**"issuer-instruction"** means a properly authenticated dematerialised instruction attributable to a participating issuer;

**"officer"**, in relation to a participating issuer, includes–

(a) where the participating issuer is a company, such persons as are mentioned in section 744 of the 1985 Act;

(b) where the participating issuer is a partnership, a partner; or in the event that no partner is situated in the United Kingdom, a person in the United Kingdom who is acting on behalf of a partner; and

(c) where the participating issuer is neither a company nor a partnership, any member of its governing body; or in the event that no member of its governing body is situated in the United Kingdom, a person in the United Kingdom who is acting on behalf of any member of its governing body;

**"Operator"** means a person approved by the Treasury under these Regulations as Operator of a relevant system;

**"Operator-instruction"** means a properly authenticated dematerialised instruction attributable to an Operator;

**"Operator-system"** means those facilities and procedures which are part of the relevant system, which are maintained and operated by or for an Operator, by which he generates Operator-instructions and receives dematerialised instructions from system-participants and by which persons change the form in which units of a participating security are held;

**"the 1986 Order"** means the Companies (Northern Ireland) Order 1986;

**"participating issuer"** means a person who has issued a security which is a participating security;

**"participating security"** means a security title to units of which is permitted by an Operator to be transferred by means of a relevant system;

**"register of members"** means a register of members maintained by a company under section 352 of the 1985 Act;

**"register of securities"**–

(a) in relation to shares, means a register of members; and

(b) in relation to units of a security other than shares, means a register maintained by the issuer, whether by virtue of these Regulations or otherwise, of persons holding the units;

**"relevant system"** has the meaning given by regulation 2(1); and **"relevant system"** includes an Operator-system;

**"rules"**, in relation to an Operator, means rules made or conditions imposed by him with respect to the provision of the relevant system;

**"securities"** means shares, stock, debentures, debenture stock, loan stock, bonds, units of a collective investment scheme within the meaning of the 1986 Act, rights under a depositary receipt within the meaning of paragraph 4 of Schedule 2 to the Criminal Justice Act 1993, and other securities of any description, and interests in a security;

**"settlement bank"**, in relation to a relevant system, means a person who has contracted to make payments in connection with transfers of title to uncertificated units of a security by means of that system;

**"share"** means share (or stock) in the share capital of a company;

**"system-member"**, in relation to a relevant system, means a person who is permitted by an Operator to transfer by means of that system title to uncertificated units of a security held by him, and shall include, where relevant, two or more persons who are jointly so permitted;

**"system-member instruction"** means a properly authenticated dematerialised instruction attributable to a system-member;

**"system-participant"**, in relation to a relevant system, means a person who is permitted by an Operator to send and receive properly authenticated dematerialised instructions; and **"sponsoring system-participant"** means a system-participant who is permitted by an Operator to send properly authenticated dematerialised instructions attributable to another person and to receive properly authenticated dematerialised instructions on another person's behalf;

**"system-user"**, in relation to a relevant system, means a person who as regards that system is a participating issuer, system-member, system-participant or settlement bank;

**"uncertificated unit of a security"** means a unit of a security title to which is recorded on the relevant register of securities as being held in uncertificated form, and title to which, by virtue of these Regulations, may be transferred by means of a relevant system; and **"certificated unit of a security"** means a unit of a security which is not an uncertificated unit;

**"unit of a security"** means the smallest possible transferable unit of the security (for example a single share) and, in the case of any share–

(a) which is issued by an investment company with variable capital (within the meaning of the Open-Ended Investment Companies (Investment Companies with Variable Capital) Regulations 1996) which is a participating issuer; and

(b) to which are attached rights expressed in two denominations;

it includes any smaller denomination share and any larger denomination share (within the meaning, in the case of each such share, of the Open-Ended Investment Companies (Investment Companies with Variable Capital) Regulations 1996),

and other expressions have the meanings given to them by the 1985 Act.

**History**

In reg. 3(1) in the definition of "unit of security" the words beginning with "and, in the case of any share–" and ending with "Variable Capital) Regulations 1996)" inserted by the Open-Ended Investment Companies (Investment Companies with Variable Capital) Regulations 1996 (SI 1996/2827) reg.1, 75 and Sch. 8, para. 27 as from 6 January 1997.

**3(2)** For the purposes of these Regulations–

(a) a dematerialised instruction is properly authenticated if it complies with the specifications referred to in paragraph 5(b) of Schedule 1 to these Regulations; and

(b) a dematerialised instruction is attributable to a person if it is expressed to have been sent by that person, or if it is expressed to have been sent on behalf of that person, in accordance with the specifications of the Operator referred to in paragraph 5(c) of Schedule 1 to these Regulations; and a dematerialised instruction may be attributable to more than one person.

**3(3)** In these Regulations, except where otherwise indicated–

(a) a reference to a numbered regulation or Schedule is a reference to the regulation of or the Schedule to these Regulations so numbered;

(b) a reference in a regulation to a numbered paragraph is a reference to the paragraph of that regulation so numbered;

(c) a reference in a Schedule to a numbered paragraph is a reference to the paragraph of that Schedule so numbered; and

(d) a reference in a paragraph to a numbered subparagraph is a reference to the subparagraph of that paragraph so numbered.

# PART II – THE OPERATOR

## APPROVAL AND COMPLIANCE

### APPLICATIONS FOR APPROVAL

**4(1)** A person may apply to the Treasury for their approval of him as Operator of a relevant system.

**4(2)** Any such application–

(a) shall be made in such a manner as the Treasury may direct; and

(b) shall be accompanied by such information as the Treasury may reasonably require for the purpose of determining the application.

**4(3)** At any time after receiving an application and before determining it, the Treasury may require the applicant to furnish additional information.

**4(4)** The directions and requirements given or imposed under paragraphs (2) and (3) may differ as between different applications.

**4(5)** Any information to be furnished to the Treasury under this regulation shall, if they so require, be in such form or verified in such manner as they may specify.

**4(6)** Every application shall be accompanied by a copy of any rules and guidance to be issued by the applicant.

### GRANT AND REFUSAL OF APPROVAL

**5(1)** If, on an application made under regulation 4, it appears to the Treasury that the requirements of Schedule 1 are satisfied with respect to the application, they may–

(a) subject to the payment of any fee charged by virtue of regulation 6(1); and

(b) subject to the provisions of Schedule 2,

approve the applicant as Operator of a relevant system.

**5(2)** An approval under this regulation shall be by instrument in writing and shall state the date on which it takes effect.

**5(3)** Schedule 1 (which imposes requirements which must appear to the Treasury to be satisfied with respect to an Operator, the relevant system and his rules and practices) shall have effect.

**5(4)** Where the Treasury refuse an application for approval they shall give the applicant a written notice to that effect stating the reasons for the refusal.

### FEES

**6(1)** The Treasury may charge a fee to a person seeking approval as Operator of a relevant system.

**6(2)** The Treasury may charge an Operator a periodical fee.

**6(3)** Any fee chargeable by the Treasury under this regulation shall not exceed an amount which reasonably represents the amount of costs incurred–

(a) in the case of a fee charged to a person seeking approval, in determining whether approval ought to be granted; and

(b) in the case of a periodical fee, in satisfying themselves that the Operator and the relevant system in question continue to meet the requirements of Schedule 1 to these Regulations and that the Operator is complying with any obligations to which he is subject by virtue of them.

**6(4)** For the purposes of paragraph (3), the costs incurred by the Treasury shall be determined on the basis that they include such proportion of the following matters as are properly attributable to the performance of the relevant function–

(a) expenditure on staff, equipment, premises, facilities, research and development;

(b) the allocation, over a period of years, whether before or after the coming into force of these Regulations, of any initial expenditure incurred wholly and exclusively to perform the function or to prepare for its performance;

(c) any notional interest incurred on any capital expended on or in connection with the performance of the function or in preparing for its performance and, in a case in which any function is exercisable by a designated agency, any actual interest payable on any sums borrowed which have been so expended; and

(d) any other matter which, in accordance with generally accepted accounting principles, may properly be taken account of in ascertaining the costs properly attributable to the performance of the function.

**6(5)** For the purposes of paragraph (4)(c)–

(a) **"notional interest"** means any interest which that person might reasonably have been expected to have been liable to pay had the sums expended been borrowed at arm's length; and

(b) **"actual interest"** means the actual interest paid on sums borrowed in a transaction at arm's length and, where a sum has been borrowed otherwise than in such a transaction, means whichever is the lesser of the interest actually paid and the interest that might reasonably have been expected to be paid had the transaction been at arm's length.

**6(6)** Any fee received by the Treasury under this regulation shall be paid into the Consolidated Fund.

**6(7)** Any fee received by a designated agency under this regulation may be retained by it.

## SUPERVISION

### WITHDRAWAL OF APPROVAL

**7(1)** If at any time it appears to the Treasury that any requirement of Schedule 1 is not satisfied, or that an Operator has failed to comply with any obligation to which he is subject by virtue of these Regulations, they may, by written instrument, subject to paragraph (2), withdraw approval from that Operator.

**7(2)** Subsections (2) to (9) of section 11 of the 1986 Act shall apply in relation to the withdrawal of approval from an Operator under paragraph (1) as they apply in relation to the revocation of a recognition order under subsection (1) of that section; and in those subsections as they so apply–

(a) any reference to a recognised organisation shall be taken to be a reference to an Operator; and

(b) any reference to members of a recognised organisation shall be taken to be a reference to system-users.

### COMPLIANCE ORDERS AND DIRECTIONS

**8(1)** If at any time it appears to the Treasury that any requirement of Schedule 1 is not satisfied, or that an Operator has failed to comply with any obligation to which he is subject by virtue of these Regulations, they may–

(a) make an application to the court; or

(b) subject to paragraph (3), give to the Operator such directions as they think fit for securing that the relevant requirement is satisfied or obligation complied with.

**8(2)** If on any application by the Treasury under paragraph (1)(a) the court is satisfied that the requirement is not satisfied or, as the case may be, that the Operator has failed to comply with the obligation in question, it may order the Operator to take such steps as the court directs for securing that the requirement is satisfied or that the obligation is complied with.

**8(3)** Before giving a direction under paragraph (1)(b) the Treasury shall–

(a) if circumstances permit, consult the Operator and afford him an opportunity to make representations; and

(b) so far as it is practicable to estimate it, have regard to the cost to the Operator of complying with any term of any direction and to the costs to other persons resulting from the Operator's compliance.

**8(4)** The jurisdiction conferred by paragraph (2) shall be exercised by the High Court and the Court of Session.

INJUNCTIONS AND RESTITUTION ORDERS

**9(1)** If on the application of the Treasury the court is satisfied that–

(a) there is a reasonable likelihood that any person will contravene any provision of the rules of an Operator to which that person is subject and which regulate the carrying on by him of investment business within the meaning of the 1986 Act;

(b) any person has contravened any such rule, and that there is a reasonable likelihood that the contravention will continue or be repeated; or

(c) any person has contravened any such rule, and that there are steps that could be taken for remedying the contravention,

the court may grant an injunction restraining the contravention or, in Scotland, an interdict prohibiting the contravention or, as the case may be, make an order requiring that person and any other person who appears to the court to have been knowingly concerned in the contravention to take such steps as the court may direct to remedy it.

**9(2)** Subsections (2) to (9) of section 61 of the 1986 Act shall apply in relation to the application of the Treasury for an injunction or, in Scotland, an interdict under paragraph (1) as they have effect in relation to the application of the Secretary of State for an injunction or, in Scotland, an interdict under subsection (1) of that section; and in those subsections as they so apply–

(a) the reference to a recognised clearing house shall be taken to be a reference to an Operator;

(b) the reference in subsection (2) to such rules as are mentioned in subsection (1)(a)(iv) shall be taken to be a reference to the rules mentioned in paragraph (1)(a);

(c) the reference to such steps as are mentioned in subsection (1) shall be taken to be a reference to such steps as are mentioned in paragraph (1);

(d) the reference in subsection (3)(a) to profits having accrued to any person as a result of his contravention of any provision or condition mentioned in subsection (1)(a) shall be taken to be a reference to profits having accrued to any person as a result of his contravention of any rule mentioned in paragraph (1)(a);

(e) the references to subsection (3) shall be taken to be references to that subsection as it so applies.

PROVISION OF INFORMATION BY OPERATORS

**10(1)** The Treasury may, in writing, require an Operator to give them such information as they may specify.

**10(2)** The Treasury may, in writing, require an Operator to furnish them at such times or in respect of such periods as they may specify with such information relating to that Operator as is so specified.

**10(3)** Where an Operator amends, revokes or adds to his rules or guidance he shall within seven days give written notice to the Treasury of the amendment, revocation or addition.

**10(4)** The notices and information required to be given or furnished under the foregoing provisions of this regulation shall be such as the Treasury reasonably require for the exercise of their functions under these Regulations.

**10(5)** The Treasury may require information to be given by a specified time, in a specified form and to be verified in a specified manner.

## MISCELLANEOUS

### DELEGATION OF TREASURY FUNCTIONS

**11(1)** If it appears to the Treasury that there is a body corporate–

(a) to which functions have been transferred under section 114 of the 1986 Act; and

(b) which is able and willing to discharge all or any of the functions conferred by this Part of these Regulations,

they may, subject to paragraphs (2) and (3), by instrument in writing delegate all or any of those functions to that body; and a body to which functions are so delegated is referred to in these Regulations as a **"designated agency"**.

**11(2)** The functions conferred on the Treasury by regulation 12 may not be delegated.

**11(3)** A designated agency shall send to the Treasury a copy of any guidance issued by virtue of these Regulations and any requirements imposed by it on the Operator by virtue of regulation 10, and give them written notice of any amendment or revocation of or addition to any such guidance or requirements.

**11(4)** A designated agency shall–

(a) send to the Treasury a copy of any guidance issued by it which is intended to have continuing effect and is issued in writing or other legible form; and

(b) give them written notice of any amendment, revocation of or addition to guidance issued by it,

but notice need not be given of the revocation of guidance other than is mentioned in subparagraph (a) or of any amendment or addition which does not result in or consist of such guidance as is there mentioned.

**11(5)** The Treasury shall not delegate any function to a designated agency unless they are satisfied that–

(a) any guidance issued by it in the exercise of its functions under these Regulations;

(b) requirements imposed by it on the Operator by virtue of regulation 10;

(c) any guidance proposed to be issued by it in the exercise of its functions under these Regulations; or

(d) any requirements it proposes to impose on the Operator by virtue of regulation 10,

do not have, and are not intended or likely to have, to any significant extent the effect of restricting, distorting or preventing competition, or if they have or are intended or likely to have that effect to any significant extent, that the effect is not greater than is necessary for the protection of investors.

**11(6)** The powers conferred by paragraph (7) shall be exercisable by the Treasury if at any time it appears to them that–

(a) any guidance issued by the designated agency in the exercise of its functions under these Regulations;

(b) requirements imposed by the designated agency on the operator by virtue of regulation 10; or

(c) any practices of a designated agency followed in the exercise of its functions under these Regulations,

have, or are intended or are likely to have, to any significant extent the effect of restricting, distorting or preventing competition and that the effect is greater than is necessary for the protection of investors.

**11(7)** The powers exercisable under this paragraph are–

(a) to resume all or any of the functions delegated to the designated agency by the written instrument referred to in paragraph (1); or

(b) to direct the designated agency to take specified steps for the purpose of securing that the guidance, requirements or practices in question do not have the effect mentioned in paragraph (6).

**11(8)** The Treasury may by written instrument–

(a) at the request or with the consent of a designated agency; or

(b) if at any time it appears to them that a designated agency is unable or unwilling to discharge all or any of the functions delegated to it,

resume all or any of the functions delegated to the agency under paragraph (1).

**11(9)** Section 187(3) of the 1986 Act shall apply in relation to anything done or omitted in the discharge or purported discharge of functions delegated under paragraph (1) as it applies in relation to anything done or omitted to be done in the discharge or purported discharge of functions exercisable by virtue of a delegation order made by virtue of section 114 of the 1986 Act.

**11(10)** In this regulation–

(a) any reference to guidance issued to an Operator by a designated agency is a reference to any guidance issued or any recommendation made by the designated agency in writing, or other legible form, which is intended to have continuing effect, and is issued or made to an Operator; and

(b) references to the practices of the designated agency are references to the practices of the designated agency in its capacity as such.

## INTERNATIONAL OBLIGATIONS

**12(1)** If it appears to the Treasury–

(a) that any action proposed to be taken by an Operator or designated agency would be incompatible with Community obligations or any other international obligations of the United Kingdom; or

(b) that any action which an Operator or designated agency has power to take is required for the purpose of implementing any such obligation,

they may direct the Operator or designated agency not to take or, as the case may be, to take the action in question.

**12(2)** A direction under this regulation may include such supplementary or incidental requirements as the Treasury think necessary or expedient.

**12(3)** Where the function of granting under regulation 5, or withdrawing under regulation 7, an Operator's approval is exercisable by a designated agency, any direction under paragraph (1) in respect of that Operator shall be a direction requiring the agency to give the Operator such a direction as is specified in the direction by the Treasury.

**12(4)** Any direction under this regulation is enforceable on application of the person who gave it, by injunction or, in Scotland, by an order under section 45 of the Court of Session Act 1988.

## PREVENTION OF RESTRICTIVE PRACTICES

**13** Schedule 2 (which reproduces, with necessary modifications, the provisions of sections 119, 120 and 122 to 125 and 128 of the 1986 Act) shall have effect.

**History**

In reg. 13 the word "125" substituted for the former word "126" by Competition Act 1998 (Transitional, Consequential and Supplemental Provisions) 2000 (SI 2000/311), art. 1, 30(1), (2) as from 1 March 2000 subject to transitional provision in art. 4 of that order.

# PART III – PARTICIPATING ISSUERS

## PARTICIPATION BY ISSUERS

### PARTICIPATION IN RESPECT OF SHARES

**14(1)** Where an Operator permits a class of shares in relation to which regulation 15 applies, or in relation to which a directors' resolution passed in accordance with regulation 16 is effective, to be a participating security, title to shares of that class which are recorded on a register of members as being held in uncertificated form may be transferred by means of the relevant system to which the permission relates.

**14(2)** In paragraph (1) the reference to a register of members shall not include an overseas branch register.

**15(1)** This regulation applies to a class of shares if a company's articles of association in all respects are consistent with–

(a) the holding of shares in that class in uncertificated form;

(b) the transfer of title to shares in that class by means of a relevant system; and

(c) these Regulations.

**15(2)** A company may permit the holding of shares in a class to which this regulation applies in uncertificated form, and the transfer of title to any such shares by means of a relevant system.

**16(1)** This regulation applies to a class of shares if a company's articles of association in any respect are inconsistent with–

(a) the holding of shares in that class in uncertificated form;

(b) the transfer of title to shares in that class by means of a relevant system; or

(c) any provision of these Regulations.

**16(2)** A company may resolve, subject to paragraph (6)(a), by resolution of its directors (in this Part referred to as a **"directors' resolution"**) that title to shares of a class issued or to be issued by it may be transferred by means of a relevant system.

**16(3)** Upon a directors' resolution becoming effective in accordance with its terms, and for as long as it is in force, the articles of association in relation to the class of shares which were the subject of the directors' resolution shall not apply to any uncertificated shares of that class to the extent that they are inconsistent with–

(a) the holding of shares of that class in uncertificated form;

(b) the transfer of title to shares of that class by means of a relevant system; and

(c) any provision of these Regulations.

**16(4)** Unless a company has given notice to every member of the company in accordance with its articles of association of its intention to pass a directors' resolution before the passing of such a resolution, it shall give such notice within 60 days of the passing of the resolution.

**16(5)** Notice given by the company before the coming into force of these Regulations of its intention to pass a directors' resolution which, if it had been given after the coming into force of these Regulations would have satisfied the requirements of paragraph (4), shall be taken to satisfy the requirements of that paragraph.

**16(6)** In respect of a class of shares, the members of a company may by ordinary resolution–

(a) if a directors' resolution has not been passed, resolve that the directors of the company shall not pass a directors' resolution; or

(b) if a directors' resolution has been passed but not yet come into effect in accordance with its terms, resolve that it shall not come into effect; or

(c) if a directors' resolution has been passed and is effective in accordance with its terms but the class of shares has not yet been permitted by the Operator to be a participating security, resolve that the directors' resolution shall cease to have effect; or

(d) if a directors' resolution has been passed and is effective in accordance with its terms and the class of shares has been permitted by the Operator to be a participating security, resolve that the directors shall take the necessary steps to ensure that title to shares of the class that was the subject of the directors' resolution shall cease to be transferable by means of a relevant system and that the directors' resolution shall cease to have effect;

and the directors shall be bound by the terms of any such ordinary resolution.

**16(7)** Such sanctions as apply to a company and its officers in the event of a default in complying with section 376 of the 1985 Act shall apply to a participating issuer and his officers in the event of a default in complying with paragraph (4).

**16(8)** A company shall not permit the holding of shares in such a class as is referred to in paragraph (1) in uncertificated form, or the transfer of title to shares in such a class by means of a relevant system, unless in relation to that class of shares a directors' resolution is effective.

**16(9)** This regulation shall not be taken to exclude the right of the members of a company to amend the articles of association of the company, in accordance with the articles, to allow the holding of any class of its shares in uncertificated form and the transfer of title to shares in such a class by means of a relevant system.

INTERPRETATION OF REGULATIONS 15 AND 16

**17** For the purposes of regulations 15 and 16 any shares with respect to which share warrants to bearer are issued under section 188 of the 1985 Act shall be regarded as forming a separate class of shares.

PARTICIPATION IN RESPECT OF SECURITIES OTHER THAN SHARES

**18(1)** Subject to paragraph (2), where an Operator permits a security other than a share to be a participating security, title to units of that security which are recorded in a register of securities as being held in uncertificated form may be transferred by means of a relevant system.

**18(2)** In relation to any security (other than a share), if the law under which it is constituted is not a law of England and Wales, Northern Ireland or Scotland, or if a current term of its issue is in any respect inconsistent with–

(a) the holding of title to units of that security in uncertificated form;

(b) the transfer of title to units of that security by means of a relevant system; or

(c) these Regulations,

the issuer shall not permit the holding of units of that security in uncertificated form, or the transfer of title to units of that security by means of a relevant system.

**18(3)** In this regulation the terms of issue of a security shall be taken to include the terms prescribed by the issuer on which units of the security are held and title to them is transferred.

## KEEPING OF REGISTERS

### ENTRIES OF REGISTERS

**19(1)** A participating issuer which is a company shall enter on its register of members, in respect of any class of shares which is a participating security, how many shares each member holds in uncertificated form and certificated form respectively.

**19(2)** Without prejudice to sections 190 and 191 of the 1985 Act, a participating issuer who, apart from this regulation, is required by or under an enactment or instrument to maintain in the United Kingdom a register of persons holding securities (other than shares) issued by him, shall enter on that register in respect of any class of security which is a participating security–

(a) the names and addresses of the persons holding units of that security; and

(b) how many units of that security each person holds in uncertificated form and certificated form respectively.

**19(3)** A participating issuer who, apart from this regulation, is not required by or under an enactment or instrument to maintain in the United Kingdom in respect of a participating security issued by him a register of persons holding units of that participating security, shall maintain in the United Kingdom a register recording–

(a) the names and addresses of the persons holding units of that security in uncertificated form; and

(b) how many units of that security each person holds in that form.

**19(4)** Such sanctions as apply to a company and its officers in the event of a default in complying with section 352 of the 1985 Act shall apply to a participating issuer and his officers in the event of a default in complying with paragraph (1), (2) or (3).

**19(5)** Without prejudice to any lesser period of limitation and to any rule as to the prescription of rights, liability incurred by a participating issuer arising–

(a) from the making or deletion of an entry in a register of securities pursuant to paragraph (1), (2) or (3); or

(b) from a failure to make or delete any such entry,

shall not be enforceable more than 20 years after the date on which the entry was made or deleted or, in the case of a failure, the failure first occurred.

**19(6)** For the purposes of paragraph (1)–

(a) notwithstanding section 362 of, or paragraph 2(1) of Schedule 14 to, the 1985 Act, the reference to a company's register of members shall not be taken to include an overseas branch register;

(b) those members who hold shares in uncertificated form may not be entered as holders of those shares on an overseas branch register; and

(c) any shares with respect to which share warrants to bearer are issued under section 188 of the 1985 Act shall be regarded as forming a separate class of shares.

**19(7)** No notice of any trust, expressed, implied or constructive, shall be entered on a register of securities which is maintained by virtue of paragraph (3) in relation to uncertificated units of a security, or be receivable by the registrar of such a register.

**19(8)** Paragraph (7) shall not apply to a participating issuer constituted under the law of Scotland.

**19(9)** This regulation shall not apply to a participating issuer which is an investment company with variable capital (within the meaning of the Open-Ended Investment Companies (Investment Companies with Variable Capital) Regulations 1996).

**History**
Reg. 19(9) inserted by the Open-Ended Investment Companies (Investment Companies with Variable Capital) Regulations 1996 (SI 1996/2827) reg.1, 75 and Sch. 8, para. 28 as from 6 January 1997.

## EFFECT OF ENTRIES ON REGISTERS

**20(1)** Subject to regulation 23(7), an entry on such a register as is mentioned in regulation 19(1) or (2) which records a person as holding units of a security in uncertificated form shall be evidence of such title to the units as would be evidenced if the entry on the register related to units of that security held in certificated form.

**20(2)** Subject to regulation 23(7), an entry on a register maintained by virtue of regulation 19(3) shall be prima facie evidence, and in Scotland sufficient evidence unless the contrary is shown, that the person to whom the entry relates has such title to the units of the security which he is recorded as holding in uncertificated form as he would have if he held the units in certificated form.

## RECTIFICATION OF AND CHANGES TO REGISTERS OF SECURITIES

**21(1)** A participating issuer shall not rectify a register of securities in relation to uncertificated units of a security held by a system-member except–

(a) with the consent of the Operator; or

(b) by order of a court in the United Kingdom.

**21(2)** A participating issuer who rectifies or otherwise changes an entry on a register of securities in relation to uncertificated units of a security (except in response to an Operator-instruction) shall immediately–

(a) notify the Operator; and

had not given to the Operator or the sponsoring system-participant (as the case may be), identified in the properly authenticated dematerialised instruction as having sent it, his authority to send the properly authenticated dematerialised instruction on his behalf; or

(b) he was a participating issuer, or a sponsoring system-participant receiving properly authenticated dematerialised instructions on behalf of a participating issuer, and–

(i) he had actual notice from the Operator of any of the matters specified in subparagraph (a); or

(ii) the instruction was an Operator-instruction requiring the registration of title in the circumstances specified in regulation 23(1)(a), (b) or (c); or

(c) he was an Operator and the instruction related to a transfer of units of a security which was in excess of any limit imposed by virtue of paragraph 12 of Schedule 1.

**29(6)** Notwithstanding that an addressee has received in respect of a properly authenticated dematerialised instruction actual notice of the kind referred to in paragraph (5), the addressee may accept the matters specified in paragraph (4) if at the time that he received the actual notice it was not practicable for him to halt his processing of the instruction.

**29(7)** Subject to paragraph (8), a person who is permitted by this regulation to accept any matter shall not be liable in damages or otherwise to any person by reason of his having relied on the matter that he was permitted to accept.

**29(8)** The provisions of paragraph (7) do not affect–

(a) any liability of the Operator to pay compensation under regulation 30; or

(b) any liability of a participating issuer under regulation 37 arising by reason of a default in complying with, or contravention of, regulation 23(5).

**29(9)** Subject to paragraph (7), this regulation has effect without prejudice to the liability of any person for causing or permitting a dematerialised instruction–

(a) to be sent without authority; or

(b) to contain information which is incorrect; or

(c) to be expressed to have been sent by a person who did not send it.

**29(10)** For the purposes of this regulation–

(a) a properly authenticated dematerialised instruction is expressed to have been sent by a person or on behalf of a person if it is attributable to that person; and

(b) an addressee is the person to whom a properly authenticated dematerialised instruction indicates it is addressed in accordance with the specifications of the Operator drawn up in order to satisfy paragraph 5(d) of Schedule 1.

**29(11)** Nothing in this regulation shall be taken, in respect of any authority, to modify or derogate from the protections to a donee or third person given by or under any enactment or to prohibit a donee or third person so protected from accepting any of the matters specified in paragraph (4).

**History**

Reg. 29(11) inserted by the Uncertificated Securities (Amendment) Regulations 2000 (SI 2000/1682), reg. 1, 2(1), (3) as from 1 July 2000.

## LIABILITY FOR FORGED DEMATERIALISED INSTRUCTIONS AND INDUCED OPERATOR-INSTRUCTIONS

**30(1)** For the purpose of this regulation–

(a) a dematerialised instruction is a forged dematerialised instruction if–

(i) it was not sent from the computers of a system-participant or the computers comprising an Operator-system; or

(ii) it was not sent from the computers of the system-participant or the computers comprising an Operator-system (as the case may be) from which it is expressed to have been sent;

(b) an act is a causative act if, not being a dematerialised instruction and not being an act which causes a dematerialised instruction to be sent from the computer of a system-participant, it unlawfully causes the Operator to send an Operator-instruction to a participating issuer; and

(c) an Operator-instruction is an induced Operator-instruction if it is an Operator-instruction to a participating issuer which results from a causative act or a forged dematerialised instruction.

**30(2)** If, as a result of either a forged dematerialised instruction (not being one which results in an induced Operator-instruction) or an induced Operator-instruction any one of the following events occurs–

(a) the name of any person remains on, is entered on, or is removed or omitted from, a register of securities;

(b) the number of units of a security in relation to which the name of any person is entered on a register of securities is increased, reduced, or remains unaltered;

(c) the description of any units of a security in relation to which the name of any person is entered on a register of securities is changed or remains unaltered;

and that person suffers loss as a result, he may apply to the court for an order that the Operator compensate him for his loss.

**30(3)** It is immaterial for the purposes of paragraph (2)(a) to (c) whether the event is permanent or temporary.

**30(4)** The court shall not make an order under paragraph (2)–

(a) if the Operator identifies a person as being responsible (whether alone or with others) for the forged dematerialised instruction (not being one which results in an induced Operator-instruction) or the causative act or forged dematerialised instruction resulting in the induced Operator-instruction (as the case may be) notwithstanding that it is impossible (for whatever reason) for the applicant to obtain satisfactory compensation from that person; or

(b) if the Operator shows that a participating issuer would be liable under regulation 37 to compensate the applicant for the loss in respect of which the application is made, by reason of the participating issuer's default in complying with, or contravention of, regulation 23(5).

**30(5)** Subject to paragraph (6), the court may award to an applicant compensation for–

(a) each forged dematerialised instruction (not being one which results in an induced Operator-instruction); and

(b) each induced Operator-instruction,

resulting in an event mentioned in paragraph (2)(a) to (c); provided that the court shall not award to an applicant more than £50000 for each such forged dematerialised instruction or induced Operator-instruction.

**30(6)** In respect of liability arising under this regulation the court shall–

(a) in awarding compensation only order the Operator to pay such amount of compensation as it appears to it to be just and equitable in all the circumstances having regard to the loss sustained by the applicant as a result of the forged dematerialised instruction or induced Operator-instruction;

(b) in ascertaining the loss, apply the same rules concerning the duty of a person to mitigate his loss as apply to damages recoverable under the common law of England and Wales, Northern Ireland, or Scotland, (as the case may be); and

(c) where it finds that the loss was to any extent caused or contributed to by any act or omission of the applicant, reduce the amount of the award by such proportion as it thinks just and equitable having regard to that finding.

**30(7)** An application to a court for an order under paragraph (2) shall not prejudice any right of the Operator to recover from a third party any sum that he may be ordered to pay.

**30(8)** This regulation does not affect any liability or right which any person may incur or have apart from this regulation.

**30(9)** Where an application is made under paragraph (2), and the Operator receives from the applicant a request for information or documents relating to–

(a) a forged dematerialised instruction; or

(b) an induced Operator-instruction,

in respect of which the application is made, the Operator shall, in so far as he is able, and in so far as the request is reasonable, within one month furnish the applicant with the information and documents.

**30(10)** The applicant shall, in so far as he is able, within one month furnish the Operator with such information or documents as the Operator reasonably requests in connection with an application under paragraph (2) with respect to–

(a) steps taken by the applicant to prevent the giving of any forged dematerialised instruction (whether of the kind referred to in paragraph (2) or any other kind); and

(b) steps taken by the applicant to mitigate loss suffered by him;

provided that the applicant need not furnish information or documents pursuant to this paragraph until the Operator has complied with any request made by virtue of paragraph (9).

**30(11)** Neither the Operator nor the applicant shall be required to disclose any information by virtue of, respectively, paragraph (9) or (10) which would be privileged in the course of civil proceedings; and which in Scotland they would be entitled to refuse to disclose on grounds of confidentiality as between client and professional legal adviser in proceedings in the Court of Session.

**30(12)** The jurisdiction conferred by this regulation shall be exercisable, in the case of a participating security constituted under the law of England and Wales, or Northern Ireland, by the High Court; and in the case of a participating security constituted under the law of Scotland by the Court of Session.

# PART V – MISCELLANEOUS AND SUPPLEMENTAL

## MISCELLANEOUS

### CONSTRUCTION OF REFERENCES TO TRANSFERS ETC.

**31** References in any enactment or rule of law to a proper instrument of transfer or to a transfer with respect to securities, or any expression having like meaning, shall be taken to include a reference to an Operator-instruction to a participating issuer to register a transfer of title on the relevant register of securities in accordance with the Operator-instruction.

### CERTAIN FORMALITIES AND REQUIREMENTS NOT TO APPLY

**32(1)** Any requirements in an enactment or rule of law which apply in respect of the transfer of securities otherwise than by means of a relevant system shall not prevent an Operator-instruction from requiring a participating issuer to register a transfer of title to uncertificated units of a security.

**32(2)** Subject to regulation 26(2), notwithstanding any enactment, instrument or rule of law, a participating issuer shall not issue a certificate in relation to any uncertificated units of a participating security.

**32(3)** A document issued by or on behalf of a participating issuer purportedly evidencing title to an uncertificated unit of a participating security shall not be evidence of title to the unit of the security; and in particular section 186 of the 1985 Act shall not apply to any document issued with respect to uncertificated shares.

**32(4)** Any requirement in or under any enactment to endorse any statement or information on a certificate evidencing title to a unit of a security–

(a) shall not prohibit the conversion into, or issue of, units of the security in uncertificated form; and

(b) in relation to uncertificated units of the security, shall be taken to be a requirement to provide the holder of the units with the statement or information on request by him.

**32(5)** Sections 53(1)(c) and 136 of the Law of Property Act 1925 (which impose requirements for certain dispositions and assignments to be in writing) shall not apply (if they would otherwise do so) to–

(a) any transfer of title to uncertificated units of a security by means of a relevant system; and

(b) any disposition or assignment of an interest in uncertificated units of a security title to which is held by a relevant nominee, or in which the relevant nominee has an interest by virtue of regulation 25(1) or (2).

**32(6)** In paragraph (5) **"relevant nominee"** means a subsidiary undertaking of an Operator designated by him as a relevant nominee in accordance with such rules and practices as are mentioned in paragraph 19(d) of Schedule 1 to these Regulations.

TRUSTS, TRUSTEES AND PERSONAL REPRESENTATIVES ETC.

**33(1)** Unless expressly prohibited from transferring units of a security by means of any computer-based system, a trustee or personal representative shall not be chargeable with a breach of trust or, as the case may be, with default in administering the estate by reason only of the fact that–

(a) for the purpose of acquiring units of a security which he has the power to acquire in connection with the trust or estate, he has paid for the units under arrangements which provide for them to be transferred to him from a system-member but not to be so transferred until after the payment of the price;

(b) for the purpose of disposing of units of a security which he has power to dispose of in connection with the trust or estate, he has transferred the units to a system-member under arrangements which provide that the price is not to be paid to him until after the transfer is made; or

(c) for the purpose of holding units of a security belonging to the trust or estate in uncertificated form and for transferring title to them by means of a relevant system, he has become a system-member.

**33(2)** Notwithstanding section 192 of the 1985 Act, a trustee of a trust deed for securing an issue of debentures shall not be chargeable with a breach of trust by reason only of the fact that he has assented to an amendment of the trust deed only for the purposes of–

(a) allowing the holding of the debentures in uncertificated form;

(b) allowing the exercise of rights attaching to the debentures by means of a relevant system; or

(c) allowing the transfer of title to the debentures by means of a relevant system;

provided that he has given or caused to be given notice of the amendment in accordance with the trust deed not less than 30 days prior to its becoming effective to all persons registered as holding the debentures on a date not more than 21 days before the dispatch of the notice.

**33(3)** The Operator shall not be bound by or compelled to recognise any express, implied or constructive trust or other interest in respect of uncertificated units of a security, even if he has actual or constructive notice of the said trust or interest.

**33(4)** Paragraph (3) shall not prevent, in the case of a participating issuer constituted under the law of Scotland, the Operator giving notice of a trust to the participating issuer on behalf of the system-member.

NOTICES OF MEETINGS

**34(1)** For the purposes of determining which persons are entitled to attend or vote at a meeting, and how many votes such persons may cast, the participating issuer may specify in the notice of the meeting a time, not more than 48 hours before the time fixed for the meeting, by which a person must be entered on the relevant register of securities in order to have the right to attend or vote at the meeting.

**34(2)** Changes to entries on the relevant register of securities after the time specified by virtue of paragraph (1) shall be disregarded in determining the rights of any person to attend or vote at the meeting, notwithstanding any provisions in any enactment, articles of association or other instrument to the contrary.

**34(3)** For the purposes of serving notices of meetings, whether under section 370(2) of the 1985 Act, any other enactment, a provision in the articles of association or any other instrument, a participating issuer may determine that persons entitled to receive such notices are those persons entered on the relevant register of securities at the close of business on a day determined by him.

**34(4)** The day determined by a participating issuer under paragraph (3) may not be more than 21 days before the day that the notices of the meeting are sent.

## NOTICES TO MINORITY SHAREHOLDERS

**35(1)** This regulation shall apply in relation to any uncertificated units of a security to which a notice given pursuant to section 429 of the 1985 Act relates, in place of the provisions of section 430(6) of that Act.

**35(2)** On receipt of a notice sent pursuant to section 430(5)(a) of the 1985 Act, a company which is a participating issuer shall be under the same obligation to enter the offeror on its register of securities as the holder of the uncertificated units of the security to which the notice relates, in place of the system-member who was immediately prior to such entry registered as the holder of such units, as it would be if it had received an Operator-instruction requiring it to amend its register of securities in such manner; and regulation 23(9) shall have effect accordingly.

**35(3)** A company which amends its register of securities in accordance with paragraph (2) shall forthwith notify the Operator by issuer-instruction of the amendment.

**35(4)** The reference in section 430D(5) of the 1985 Act to section 430(6) shall be taken to include a reference to the provisions of paragraph (2).

**35(5)** In this regulation, **"offeror"** has the meaning given by section 428(8) of the 1985 Act as construed in accordance with section 430D(5) of that Act.

## IRREVOCABLE POWERS OF ATTORNEY

**36(1)** This regulation applies where the terms of an offer for all or any uncertificated units of a participating security provide that a person accepting the offer creates an irrevocable power of attorney in favour of the offeror, or a person nominated by the offeror, in the terms set out in the offer.

**36(2)** An acceptance communicated by properly authenticated dematerialised instruction in respect of uncertificated units of a security shall constitute a grant of an irrevocable power of attorney by the system-member accepting the offer in favour of the offeror, or person nominated by the offeror, in the terms set out in the offer.

**36(3)** Where the contract constituted by such offer and acceptance referred to in paragraphs (1) and (2) respectively is governed by the law of England and Wales, section 4 of the Powers of Attorney Act 1971 shall apply to a power of attorney constituted in accordance with this regulation.

**36(4)** A declaration in writing by the offeror stating the terms of a power of attorney and that it has been granted by virtue of this regulation and stating the name and address of the grantor shall be prima facie evidence, and in Scotland sufficient evidence unless the contrary is shown, of the grant; and any requirement in any enactment, rule of law, or instrument to produce a copy of the power of attorney, or such a copy certified in a particular manner, shall be satisfied by the production of the declaration or a copy of the declaration certified in that manner.

**36(5)** In the application of this regulation to an offer, acceptance or contract governed by the law of Scotland, any reference to an irrevocable power of attorney shall mean and include reference to an irrevocable mandate, however expressed.

## ACTUAL NOTICE

**36A** For the purpose of determining under these Regulations whether a person has actual notice of a fact, matter or thing that person shall not under any circumstances be taken to be concerned to establish whether or not it exists or has occurred.

**History**
Reg. 36A inserted by the Uncertificated Securities (Amendment) Regulations 2000 (SI 2000/1682), reg. 1, 2(1), (4) as from 1 July 2000.

## PARTICIPATING SECURITIES IN UNCERTIFICATED FORM

**36B** In respect of a participating security which is specified in Schedule 4 or whose terms of issue provide that its units may only be held in uncertificated form and title to them may only be transferred by means of a relevant system, nothing in these Regulations shall require a participating issuer or its officers to maintain a register which records how many units of the participating security are held in certificated form or to change a unit of such a participating security from uncertificated form to certificated form or vice versa.

**History**
Reg. 36B inserted by the Uncertificated Securities (Amendment) Regulations 2000 (SI 2000/1682), reg. 1, 2(1), (4) as from 1 July 2000.

## CGO SERVICE

**36C** No transfer of a participating security may be effected through the medium of the CGO Service, and in this regulation CGO Service means the computer-based system established under the Stock Transfer Act 1982.

**History**
Reg. 36C inserted by the Uncertificated Securities (Amendment) Regulations 2000 (SI 2000/1682), reg. 1, 2(1), (4) as from 1 July 2000.

## DEFAULTS AND CONTRAVENTIONS

### BREACHES OF STATUTORY DUTY

**37(1)** A default in complying with, or a contravention of, regulation 16(8), 18(2), 21(1) or (2), 22, 23(4) or (5), 26(1), 26(2)(a) or (c), 27(1), 28(3) or 35(3) shall be actionable at the suit of a person who suffers loss as a result of the default or contravention, or who is otherwise adversely affected by it, subject to the defences and other incidents applying to actions for breach of statutory duty.

**37(2)** Paragraph (1) shall not affect the liability which any person may incur, nor affect any right which any person may have, apart from paragraph (1).

**37(3)** Any action for default in compliance with or contravention of any regulation referred to in paragraph (1) in respect of a security for which the Bank of England by or under any enactment is registrar shall be brought against the Bank of England.

**History**
Reg. 37(3) inserted by the Uncertificated Securities (Amendment) Regulations 2000 (SI 2000/1682), reg. 1, 2(1), (5) as from 1 July 2000.

### LIABILITY OF OFFICERS FOR CONTRAVENTIONS

**38** In regulation 16(7), 19(4), 23(9), 26(4) or 27(8) an officer of a participating issuer shall be in default in complying with, or in contravention of, the provision mentioned in that regulation if, and only if, he knowingly and wilfully authorised or permitted the default or contravention.

### EXEMPTION FROM LIABILITY

**38A** Regulations 19(4) , 23(9), 26(4) and 27(8) shall not apply to any of the following or its officers–

(a) the Crown;

(b) any person acting on behalf of the Crown;

(c) the Bank of England; or

(d) in respect of a security which immediately before it became a participating security was transferable by exempt transfer within the meaning of the Stock Transfer Act 1982, a participating issuer.

**History**
Reg. 38A inserted by the Uncertificated Securities (Amendment) Regulations 2000 (SI 2000/1682), reg. 1, 2(1), (6) as from 1 July 2000.

## NORTHERN IRELAND

### APPLICATION TO NORTHERN IRELAND

**39(1)** In their application to Northern Ireland, these Regulations shall have effect with the following modifications.

**39(2)** In regulation 32(5)–

(a) for the reference to section 53(1)(c) of the Law of Property Act 1925 there shall be substituted a reference to section 6 of the Statute of Frauds (Ireland) 1695; and

(b) for the reference to section 136 of the Law of Property Act 1925 there shall be substituted a reference to section 87 of the Judicature (Northern Ireland) Act 1978.

**39(3)** In regulation 36(3) for the reference to section 4 of the Powers of Attorney Act 1971 there shall be substituted a reference to section 3 of the Powers of Attorney Act (Northern Ireland) 1971.

**39(4)** For references to provisions of the 1985 Act there shall be substituted references to the equivalent provisions of the 1986 Order and, in particular, for the references to the 1985 Act listed in column 1 of Schedule 3 in the provisions of these Regulations listed in column 2 of that Schedule, there shall be substituted the references to the 1986 Order listed in column 3 of that Schedule.

## AMENDMENTS AND REVOCATIONS

### MINOR AND CONSEQUENTIAL AMENDMENTS

**40(1)** [Amendment to s. 182(1)(b) of the Companies Act 1985.]

**40(2)** [Amendment to s. 183(1) of the Companies Act 1985.]

**40(3)** [Insertion of para. (l), (m) in s. 380(4) of the Companies Act 1985.]

**40(4)** [Insertion of para. (m) in s. 180(1) of the Financial Services Act 1986.]

### REVOCATIONS

**41** The Uncertificated Securities Regulations 1992 are hereby revoked.

# Schedule 1 – Requirements for Approval of a Person as Operator

Regulation 5(3)

### ARRANGEMENTS AND RESOURCES

**1** An Operator must have adequate arrangements and resources for the effective monitoring and enforcement of compliance with his rules or, as respects monitoring, arrangements providing for that function to be performed on his behalf (and without affecting his responsibility) by another body or person who is able and willing to perform it.

### FINANCIAL RESOURCES

**2** An Operator must have financial resources sufficient for the proper performance of his functions as an Operator.

### PROMOTION AND MAINTENANCE OF STANDARDS

**3** An Operator must be able and willing to promote and maintain high standards of integrity and fair dealing in the operation of the relevant system and to cooperate, by the sharing of information or otherwise, with the Treasury and any other authority, body or person having responsibility for the supervision or regulation of investment business or other financial services.

### OPERATION OF THE RELEVANT SYSTEM

**4** Where an Operator causes or permits a part of the relevant system which is not the Operator-system to be operated by another person (other than as his agent) the Operator–

(a) shall monitor compliance by the person and that part with the requirements of this Schedule; and

(b) shall have arrangements to ensure that the person provides him with such information and such assistance as he may require in order to meet his obligations under these Regulations.

## SYSTEM SECURITY

**5** A relevant system must be constructed and operate in such a way–

(a) so as to minimise the possibility of unauthorised access to, or modification of, any program or data held in any computer forming part of the Operator-system;

(b) that each dematerialised instruction is properly authenticated in accordance with the specifications of the Operator, which shall provide that each dematerialised instruction–
  (i) is identifiable as being from the computers of a particular system-participant; and
  (ii) is designed to minimise fraud and forgery;

(c) that each dematerialised instruction, in accordance with the specifications of the Operator, expresses by whom it has been sent and, where relevant, on whose behalf it has been sent;

(d) that each dematerialised instruction, in accordance with the specifications of the Operator, indicates–
  (i) where it is sent to a system-participant or the Operator, that it is addressed to that system-participant or the Operator; and
  (ii) where it is sent to a person who is using the facilities of a sponsoring system-participant to receive dematerialised instructions, that it is addressed to that person and the sponsoring system-participant; and
  (iii) where it is sent to the Operator in order for him to send an Operator-instruction to a system-participant, that it is addressed to the Operator, to the system-participant and, if the system-participant is acting as a sponsoring system-participant, to the relevant person on whose behalf the sponsoring system-participant receives dematerialised instructions; and

(e) that the possibility for a system-participant to send a dematerialised instruction on behalf of a person from whom he has no authority is minimised.

## SYSTEM CAPABILITIES

**6** A relevant system must ensure that the Operator-system can send and respond to properly authenticated dematerialised instructions in sufficient volume and speed.

**7** Before an Operator-instruction to a participating issuer to register a transfer of uncertificated units of a security is generated, a relevant system must–

(a) be able to establish that the transferor is likely to have title to or, by virtue of regulation 25(1) or (2), an interest in, such number of units of the security as is in aggregate at least equal to the number to be transferred; or

(b) be able to notify the participating issuer in accordance with regulation 24(1) that the transfer is one of two or more transfers which may be registered in accordance with regulation 24(2).

**8** A relevant system must maintain adequate records of all dematerialised instructions.

**9** A relevant system must be able–

(a) to permit each system-member to obtain a copy of any records relating to him as are maintained by the relevant system in order to comply with paragraph 7(a) or 8; and

(b) to make correcting entries in such records as are maintained in order to comply with paragraph 7(a) which are inaccurate.

**10** A relevant system must be able to establish, where there is a transfer of uncertificated units of a security to a system-member for value, that a settlement bank has agreed to make payment in respect of the transfer, whether alone or taken together with another transfer for value.

**11** A relevant system must ensure that the Operator-system is able to generate Operator-instructions–

(a) requiring participating issuers to amend the appropriate registers of securities kept by them; and

(b) informing settlement banks of their payment obligations.

**12** A relevant system must–

(a) enable a system-member–

(i) to grant authority to a sponsoring system-participant to send properly authenticated dematerialised instructions on his behalf; and

(ii) to limit such authority by reference to the net value of the units of securities to be transferred in any one day; and

(b) prevent the transfer of units in excess of that limit.

**12A** For the purposes of paragraph 12(a)(ii), once authority is granted pursuant to a system charge (within the meaning of regulation 3 of the Financial Markets and Insolvency Regulations 1996) a limit of such authority shall not be imposed or changed without the consent of the donee of that authority.

**History**

Sch. 1, para. 12A inserted by the Uncertificated Securities (Amendment) Regulations 2000 (SI 2000/1682), reg. 1, 2(1), (7)(a) as from 1 July 2000.

**12B** Nothing in paragraph 12 or 12A shall be taken, in respect of an authority, to modify or derogate from the protections given by or under any enactment to a donee of the authority or a third person.

**History**

Sch. 1, para. 12B inserted by the Uncertificated Securities (Amendment) Regulations 2000 (SI 2000/1682), reg. 1, 2(1), (7)(a) as from 1 July 2000.

**13** A relevant system must enable system-members–

(a) to change the form in which they hold or are to hold units of a participating security; and

(b) where appropriate, to require participating issuers to issue certificates relating to units of a participating security held or to be held by them.

**13A** Paragraph 13 shall not apply to any participating security specified in Schedule 4 or whose terms of issue provide that its units may only be held in uncertificated form and title to them may only be transferred by means of a relevant system.

**History**

Sch. 1, para. 13A inserted by the Uncertificated Securities (Amendment) Regulations 2000 (SI 2000/1682), reg. 1, 2(1), (7)(b) as from 1 July 2000.

## OPERATING PROCEDURES

**14** A relevant system must comprise procedures which provide that it responds only to properly authenticated dematerialised instructions which are attributable to a system-user or an Operator.

**15(1)** Subject to subparagraph (2), a relevant system must comprise procedures which provide that an Operator-instruction requiring a participating issuer to register a transfer of uncertificated units of a security, or informing a settlement bank of its payment obligations in respect of such a transfer, is generated only if–

(a) it has–

(i) received a system-member instruction from the transferor; or

(ii) been required to do so by a court in the United Kingdom or by or under an enactment;

(b) it has–

(i) established that the transferor is likely to have title to, or is likely to have by virtue of regulation 25(1) or (2) an interest in, such number of units as is in aggregate at least equal to the number to be transferred; or

(ii) established that the transfer is one of two or more transfers which may be notified to the participating issuer in accordance with regulation 24(1);

(c) in the case of a transfer to a system-member for value, it has established that a settlement bank has agreed to make payment in respect of the transfer, whether alone or taken together with another transfer for value; and

(d) the transfer is not in excess of any limit which by virtue of paragraph 12(a)(ii) the transferor has set on an authority given by him to a sponsoring system-participant.

**15(1A)** Nothing in paragraph 15(1) shall prevent the generation of an Operator-instruction in accordance with procedures agreed between the Operator and the transferor to enable the transfer by means of a relevant system of uncertificated units of a security which immediately before their conversion into uncertificated form were transferable by exempt transfer within the meaning of the Stock Transfer Act 1982.

**History**

Sch. 1, para. 15(1A) inserted by the Uncertificated Securities (Amendment) Regulations 2000 (SI 2000/1682), reg. 1, 2(1), (7)(c) as from 1 July 2000.

**15(2)** A relevant system must comprise procedures which provide that an Operator-instruction requiring a participating issuer to register a transfer of uncertificated units of a security, or informing a settlement bank of its payment obligations in respect of such a transfer, may be generated if necessary to correct an error and if in accordance with the rules and practices of an Operator instituted in order to comply with this Schedule.

**16(1)** Subject to subparagraph (2), a relevant system must comprise procedures which provide that an Operator-instruction to a participating issuer relating to a right, privilege or benefit attaching to or arising from an uncertificated unit of a security, is generated only if it has–

(a) received a properly authenticated dematerialised instruction attributable to the system-member having the right, privilege or benefit requiring the Operator to generate an Operator-instruction to the participating issuer; or

(b) been required to do so by a court in the United Kingdom or by or under an enactment.

**16(2)** A relevant system must comprise procedures which provide that an Operator-instruction to a participating issuer relating to a right, privilege or benefit attaching to or arising from an uncertificated unit of a security, may be generated if necessary to correct an error and if in accordance with the rules and practices of an Operator instituted in order to comply with this Schedule.

**17** A relevant system must comprise procedures which ensure that, where the relevant system maintains records in order to comply with paragraph 15(1)(b)(i), the records are regularly reconciled with the registers of securities maintained by participating issuers.

**18** A relevant system must comprise procedures which–

(a) enable system-users to notify the Operator of an error in or relating to a dematerialised instruction; and

(b) ensure that, where the Operator becomes aware of an error in or relating to a dematerialised instruction, he takes appropriate corrective action.

## RULES AND PRACTICES

**19** An Operator's rules and practices–

(a) must bind system-members and participating issuers–

  (i) so as to ensure the efficient processing of transfers of title to uncertificated units of a security in response to Operator-instructions; and

  (ii) as to the action to be taken where transfer of title in response to an Operator-instruction cannot be effected;

(b) must make provision for a participating issuer to cease to participate in respect of a participating security so as–

  (i) to minimise so far as practicable any disruption to system-members in respect of their ability to transfer the relevant security; and

  (ii) to provide the participating issuer with any relevant information held by the Operator relating to uncertificated units of the relevant security held by system-members;

(c) must make provision for the orderly termination of participation by system-members and system-participants whose participation is disruptive to other system-members or system-participants or to participating issuers; and

(d) if they make provision for the designation of a subsidiary undertaking as a relevant nominee, must require that the relevant nominee maintain adequate records of–

(i) the names of the persons who have an interest in the securities it holds; and

(ii) the nature and extent of their interests.

**20** An Operator's rules and practices must require–

(a) that each system-participant is able to send and receive properly authenticated dematerialised instructions;

(b) that each system-member has arrangements–

(i) for properly authenticated dematerialised instructions attributable to him to be sent;

(ii) for properly authenticated dematerialised instructions to be received by or for him; and

(iii) with a settlement bank for payments to be made, where appropriate, for units of a security transferred by means of the relevant system; and

(c) that each participating issuer is able to respond with sufficient speed to Operator-instructions.

**21** An Operator must have rules which require system-users and former system-users to provide him with such information in their possession as he may require in order to meet his obligations under these Regulations.

# Schedule 2 – Prevention of Restrictive Practices

Regulation 13

## EXAMINATION OF RULES AND PRACTICES

**1(1)** The Treasury shall not approve a person as Operator of a relevant system unless they are satisfied that the rules and any guidance of which copies are furnished with the application for approval–

(a) do not have, and are not intended or likely to have, to any significant extent the effect of restricting, distorting or preventing competition; or

(b) if they have or are intended to have that effect to any significant extent, that the effect is not greater than is necessary for the protection of investors, or for compliance with Council Directive 89/646/EEC.

**1(2)** The powers conferred by subparagraph (3) shall be exercisable by the Treasury if at any time it appears to them that–

(a) any rules made or guidance issued by an Operator;

(b) any practices of an Operator; or

(c) any practices of a system-user,

have, or are intended or likely to have, to a significant extent the effect of restricting, distorting or preventing competition and that the effect is greater than is necessary for the protection of investors or for compliance with Council Directive 89/646/EEC.

**1(3)** The powers exercisable under this paragraph are–

(a) to withdraw approval from the Operator;

(b) to direct the Operator to take specified steps for the purpose of securing that the rules, guidance or practices in question do not have the effect mentioned in subparagraph (2); or

(c) to make alterations in the rules of the Operator for that purpose.

**1(4)** Subsections (2) to (5), (7) and (9) of section 11 of the 1986 Act shall apply in relation to the withdrawal of approval under subparagraph (3) as they apply in relation to the revocation of an order under subsection (1) of that section; and in those subsections as they so apply–

(a) any reference to a recognised organisation shall be taken to be a reference to the Operator; and

(b) any reference to members of a recognised organisation shall be taken to be a reference to system-users.

**1(5)** The practices referred to in subparagraph (2)(b) are practices of the Operator in his capacity as such.

**1(6)** The practices referred to in subparagraph 2(c) are practices in relation to business in respect of which system-users are subject to the rules of the Operator and which are required or contemplated by his rules or guidance or otherwise attributable to his conduct in his capacity as Operator.

## MODIFICATION OF PARAGRAPH 1 WHERE DELEGATION ORDER IS MADE

**2(1)** This paragraph applies instead of paragraph 1 where the function of approving a person as Operator has been delegated to a designated agency by virtue of regulation 11.

**2(2)** The designated agency–

(a) shall send to the Treasury a copy of the rules and any guidance copies of which are furnished with the application for approval together with any other information supplied with or in connection with the application; and

(b) shall not grant the approval without the leave of the Treasury,

and the Treasury shall not give leave in any case in which they would (apart from the delegation of functions to a designated agency) have been precluded by paragraph 1(1) from granting approval.

**2(3)** A designated agency shall send to the Treasury a copy of any notice received by it from an Operator under regulation 10(3).

**2(4)** If at any time it appears to the Treasury that there are circumstances such that (apart from a delegation order) they would have been able to exercise any of the powers conferred by paragraph 1(3) they may, notwithstanding the delegation order–

(a) themselves exercise the power conferred by paragraph 1(3)(a); or

(b) direct the designated agency to exercise the power conferred by paragraph 1(3)(b) or (c) in such manner as they may specify.

**2(5)** In this paragraph **"delegation order"** means an instrument in writing under regulation 11.

## REPORTS BY THE DIRECTOR GENERAL OF FAIR TRADING

**3(1)** The Treasury shall before deciding–

(a) whether to refuse to grant an approval in pursuance of paragraph 1(1); or

(b) whether to refuse leave for the granting of an approval in pursuance of paragraph 2(2),

send to the Director General of Fair Trading (in this Schedule referred to as "the Director") a copy of the rules and of any guidance which the Treasury are required to consider in making that decision together with such other infornnation as the Treasury consider will assist in discharging his functions under subparagraph (2).

**3(2)** The Director shall report to the Treasury whether, in his opinion, the rules and guidance copies of which are sent to him under subparagraph (1) have, or are intended or likely to have, to any significant extent the effect of restricting, distorting or preventing competition and, if so, what that effect is likely to be; and in making any decision as is mentioned in subparagraph (1) the Treasury shall have regard to the Director's report.

**3(3)** The Treasury shall send to the Director copies of any notice received by them under regulation 10(3) or paragraph 2(3) together with such other information as the Treasury consider will assist the Director in discharging his functions under subparagraphs (4) and (5).

**3(4)** The Director shall keep under review–

(a) the rules, guidance and practices mentioned in paragraph 1(2); and

(b) the matters specified in the notices of which copies are sent to him under subparagraph (3),

and if at any time he is of the opinion that any such rules or guidance taken together with any such matters, have, or are intended or likely to have, to any significant extent the effect mentioned in subparagraph (2), he shall report his opinion to the Treasury stating what in his opinion that effect is or is likely to be.

**3(5)** The Director may report to the Treasury his opinion that any such matter as is mentioned in subparagraph (4)(b) does not in his opinion have, and is not intended or likely to have, to any significant extent the effect mentioned in subparagraph (2).

**3(6)** The Director may from time to time consider whether any such practices as are mentioned in paragraph 1(2) have, or are intended or likely to have, to any significant extent the effect mentioned in subparagraph (2) and, if so, what that effect is or is likely to be; and if he is of that opinion he shall make a report to the Treasury stating his opinion and what the effect is or is likely to be.

**3(7)** The Treasury shall not exercise their powers under paragraph 1(3) or 2(4) except after receiving a report from the Director under subparagraph (4) or (6).

**3(8)** The Director may, if he thinks fit, publish any report made by him under this paragraph but shall exclude from a published report, so far as practicable, any matter which relates to the affairs of a particular person (other than the person seeking approval as an Operator) the publication of which would or might in his opinion seriously and prejudiciaily affect the interests of that person.

## INVESTIGATIONS BY THE DIRECTOR GENERAL OF FAIR TRADING

**4(1)** For the purpose of investigating any matter with a view to his consideration under paragraph 3 the Director may by a notice in writing–

(a) require any person to produce, at any time and place specified in the notice, to the Director or to any person appointed by him for the purpose, any documents which are specified or described in the notice and which are documents in his custody or under his control and relating to any matter relevant to the investigation; or

(b) require any person carrying on business to furnish to the Director such information as may be specified or described in the notice, and specify the time within which, and the manner and form in which, any such information is to be furnished.

**4(2)** A person shall not under this paragraph be required to produce any document or disclose any information which he would be entitled to refuse to produce or disclose on grounds of legal professional privilege in proceedings in the High Court or on grounds of confidentiality as between client and professional legal adviser in proceedings in the Court of Session.

**4(3)** Subsections (6) to (8) of section 85 of the Fair Trading Act 1973 (enforcement provisions) shall apply in relation to a notice under this paragraph as they apply in relation to a notice under subsection (1) of that section but as if in subsection (7) of that section, for the words from "any one" to "the Commission" there were substituted "the Director."

## EXEMPTIONS FROM THE FAIR TRADING ACT 1973

**5(1)** For the purpose of determining whether a monopoly situation within the meaning of the Fair Trading Act 1973 exists by reason of the circumstances mentioned in section 7(1)(c) of that Act, no account shall be taken of–

(a) the rules or guidance issued by an Operator or any conduct constituting such a practice as is mentioned in paragraph 1(2); or

(b) any guidance issued by a designated agency in the exercise of its functions under these Regulations or any practices of a designated agency in the exercise of its functions under these Regulations.

**5(2)** Where approval is withdrawn there shall be disregarded for the purpose mentioned in subparagraph (1) any such conduct as is mentioned in that subparagraph which occurred while the approval was in force.

**5(3)** Where on a monopoly reference under section 50 or 51 of said Act of 1973 falling within section 49 of that Act the Competition Commission find that a monopoly situation within the meaning of that Act exists and–

(a) that the person (or, if more than one, any of the persons) in whose favour it exists is subject to the rules of an Operator or to the requirements imposed and guidance issued by a designated agency in the exercise of functions delegated to it under regulation 11(1); or

(b) that any such person's conduct in carrying on any business to which those rules relate is the subject of guidance issued by an Operator or designated agency; or

(c) that the person (or, if more than one, any of the persons) in whose favour the monopoly situation exists is an Operator or designated agency,

the Commission, in making their report on that reference, shall exclude from their consideration the question whether the rules, guidance or any acts or omissions of such an Operator or agency as is mentioned in subparagraph (c) in his or its capacity as such operate, or may be expected to operate, against the public interest; and section 54(3) of that Act shall apply subject to the provisions of this paragraph.

**History**
In para. 5(3) the words "Competition Commission" substituted for the former words "Monopolies and Mergers Commission" by the Competition Act 1998 (Competition Commission) Transitional, Consequential and Supplemental Provisions Order 1999 (SI 1999/506), art. 1, 36 as from 1 April 1999.

## EXEMPTIONS FROM RESTRICTIVE TRADE PRACTICES ACT 1976

**6** (Revoked by Competition Act 1998 (Transitional, Consequential and Supplemental Provisions) 2000 (SI 2000/311), art. 1, 30(1), (3) as from 1 March 2000 subject to transitional provision in art. 4 of that order.)

**History**
Para. 6 formerly read as follows:

"**(1)** The Restrictive Trade Practices Act 1976 shall not apply to any agreement for the constitution of an Operator, including any term deemed to be contained in it by virtue of section 8(2) or 16(3) of that Act.

**(2)** The said Act of 1976 shall not apply to any agreement the parties to which consist of or include–

(a) an Operator; or

(b) a person who is subject to the rules of an Operator,

by reason of any term the inclusion of which in the agreement is required or contemplated by the rules or guidance of the Operator.

**(3)** Where approval is withdrawn from an Operator the foregoing provisions shall have effect as if the Operator had continued to have approval until the end of the period of six months beginning with the day on which the withdrawal takes effect.

**(4)** Where an agreement ceases by virtue of this paragraph to be subject to registration–

(a) the Director shall remove from the register maintained by him under the said Act of 1976 any particulars which are entered or filed in that register in respect of the agreement; and

(b) any proceedings in respect of the agreement which are pending before the Restrictive Practices Court shall be discontinued.

**(5)** Where an agreement which has been exempt from registration by virtue of this paragraph ceases to be exempt in consequence of a withdrawal of approval from an Operator, the time within which particulars of the agreement are to be furnished in accordance with section 24 of, and Schedule 2 to, the said Act of 1976 shall be the period of one month beginning with the day on which the agreement ceased to be exempt from registration.

**(6)** Where in the case of an agreement registered under the said Act of 1976 a term ceases to fall within subparagraph (2) in consequence of the withdrawal of approval from an Operator and particulars of that term have not previously been furnished to the Director under section 24 of that Act, those particulars shall be furnished to him within the period of one month beginning with the day on which the term ceased to fall within that subparagraph."

## EXEMPTIONS FROM COMPETITION ACT 1980

**7** (Revoked by Competition Act 1998 (Transitional, Consequential and Supplemental Provisions) 2000 (SI 2000/311), art. 1, 30(1), (3) as from 1 March 2000 subject to transitional provision in art. 4 of that order.)

**History**
Reg. 7 formerly read as follows:

"**(1)** No course of conduct constituting any such practice as is mentioned in paragraph 1(2) shall constitute an anti-competitive practice for the purpose of the Competition Act 1980.

**(2)** Where approval is withdrawn from an Operator, there shall not be treated as an anti-competitive practice for the purposes of that Act any such course of conduct as is mentioned in subparagraph (1) which occurred while the approval was effective."

## SUPPLEMENTARY PROVISIONS

**8(1)** Before the Treasury exercise a power under paragraph 1(3)(b) or (c), or their power to refuse leave under paragraph 2(2), or their power to give a direction under paragraph 2(4), in respect of an Operator, they shall–

(a) give written notice of their intention to do so to the Operator and take such steps (whether by publication or otherwise) as they think appropriate for bringing the notice to the attention of any other person who in their opinion is likely to be affected by the exercise of the power; and

(b) have regard to any representation made within such time as they consider reasonable by the Operator or by any such other person.

**8(2)** A notice under subparagraph (1) shall give particulars of the manner in which the Treasury propose to exercise the power in question and state the reasons for which they propose to act; and the statement of reasons may include matters contained in any report received by them under paragraph 3.

**8(3)** Any direction given under this Schedule shall, on the application of the person by whom it was given, be enforceable by injunction or, in Scotland, by an order for specific performance under section 45 of the Court of Session Act 1988.

**8(4)** The fact that any rules made by an Operator have been altered by or pursuant to a direction given by the Treasury under this Schedule shall not preclude their subsequent alteration or revocation by the Operator.

**8(5)** In determining under this Schedule whether any guidance has, or is likely to have, any particular effect the Treasury and the Director may assume that the persons to whom it is addressed will act in conformity with it.

# Schedule 3 – Adaptations in Respect of Northern Ireland

Regulation 39(4)

| Column 1<br>Reference to the 1985 Act | Column 2<br>Provisions of these Regulations | Column 3<br>Reference to the 1986 Order |
|---|---|---|
| Section 182 | Regulation 40(1) | Article 192 |
| Section 183 | Regulation 23(8)<br>Regulation 27(8)<br>Regulation 40(2) | Article 193 |
| Section 185 | Regulation 26(3) | Article 195 |
| Section 186 | Regulation 32(3) | Article 196 |
| Section 188 | Regulation 17<br>Regulation 19(6) | Article 198 |
| Section 190 | Regulation 19(2) | Article 199 |
| Section 191 | Regulation 19(2) | Article 200 |
| Section 192 | Regulation 33(2) | Article 201 |
| Section 352 | Regulation 3(1)<br>Regulation 19(4) | Article 360 |
| Section 358 | Regulation 22 | Article 366 |
| Section 362 | Regulation 19(6) | Article 370 |
| Section 370 | Regulation 34(3) | Article 378 |
| Section 376 | Regulation 16(7) | Article 384 |
| Section 380 | Regulation 40(3) | Article 388 |

| Column 1 Reference to the 1985 Act | Column 2 Provisions of these Regulations | Column 3 Reference to the 1986 Order |
|---|---|---|
| Section 428 | Regulation 35(5) | Article 421 |
| Section 429 | Regulation 35(1) | Article 422 |
| Section 430 | Regulation 35(1)<br>Regulation 35(2)<br>Regulation 35(4) | Article 423 |
| Section 430D | Regulation 35(4)<br>Regulation 35(5) | Article 423D |
| Section 735 | Regulation 3(1) | Article 3 |
| Section 744 | Regulation 3(1) | Article 2 |
| Paragraph (2) of Schedule 14 | Regulation 19(6) | Paragraph (2) of Schedule 14 |

# Schedule 4 – The participating securities specified in regulation 36B and Schedule 1 paragraph 13A

FLOATING RATE TREASURY STOCK 2001

A strip in relation to any stock or bond within the meaning of section 47(1B) of the Finance Act 1942.

**History**
Sch. 4 inserted by the Uncertificated Securities (Amendment) Regulations 2000 (SI 2000/1682), reg. 1, 2(1), (8) as from 1 July 2000.

## EXPLANATORY NOTE

(*This Note is not part of the Regulations*)

1. These Regulations make provision for the transfer without a written instrument, and the evidencing otherwise than by a certificate, of title to a unit of a security, in accordance with a computer-based system and procedures known as the "relevant system". The relevant system centres on a person known as the "Operator". The legal framework underlying the operation of the relevant system, together with the criteria which the Operator and the relevant system must meet, are enshrined in these Regulations.

2. Regulations 2 and 3 set out the purposes and definitions of the Regulations. A unit of a security which may be transferred by means of the relevant system is referred to as an "uncertificated unit". A security, the units of which may become uncertificated, is referred to as a "participating security". An issuer who issues a participating security is, in relation to that security, referred to as a "participating issuer". Instructions sent by means of the relevant system are referred to as "dematerialised instructions".

3. Regulations 4 to 13 make provision for the approval of the Operator by the Treasury if it appears to them that he and any relevant system meet certain criteria specified in Schedule 1. The Regulations give the Treasury certain powers in relation to the Operator if he, or the relevant system, fails to meet the criteria, or if necessary for the performance of their functions under the Regulations. Provision is also made for the delegation by the Treasury of their functions under the Regulations to a designated agency. Schedule 2 provides for oversight by the Director General of Fair Trading of the rules and guidance of the Operator to ensure that they do not distort competition.

4. Regulations 14 to 17 set out the conditions on which issuers may allow securities issued by them to become participating securities and hence to be held in uncertificated form and transferred by means of the relevant system. Provision is made for a class of shares governed by articles of association which are in all respects consistent with the Regulations to become a

participating security. Provision is also made for the directors of a company to pass a "directors' resolution" so that other classes of shares can become participating securities notwithstanding any contrary provisions in the articles of association, and for the members of the company to prevent or reverse a directors' resolution. Conditions are specified for securities other than shares to become participating securities.

5. Regulations 18 to 22 make provision for the keeping by participating issuers of "registers of securities" recording persons holding in uncertificated form units of a security issued by them, and for the title that such entries confer. Provision is also made for the notification to the Operator of changes to entries on registers of securities and also for the Operator to give his consent to the rectification or closing of such registers.

6. Regulations 23 and 24 make provision for a participating issuer, subject to a number of exceptions, to register the transfer of title to an uncertificated unit of a security following an Operator-instruction to do so. Provision is also made to allow participating issuers to register two or more transfers on a net basis, or simultaneously, in certain circumstances.

7. Regulation 25 makes provision for a transferee to acquire a property right in uncertificated units transferred by means of the relevant system before his name appears on the register of securities. Other than in the case of Scottish securities, the transferee acquires an equitable interest in a number of units calculated in accordance with the regulation. In relation to Scottish securities, the transferor is deemed to hold on trust for the transferee a number of units which is calculated in the same way.

8. Regulations 26 to 28 make provision for the conversion of units of a participating security between certificated and uncertificated form, and for the issue of new units of a participating security in uncertificated form.

9. Regulation 29 makes provision to prevent persons sending certain dematerialised instructions, and to prevent persons on whose behalf they are sent, from denying particular matters relating to the instructions. It also makes provision for persons receiving such instructions to accept, with certain exceptions, that the information contained in them and matters relating to them are correct.

10. Regulation 30 provides that the Operator is liable, in certain circumstances, if as a result of the sending of certain dematerialised instructions a person suffers loss.

11. Regulations 31 and 32 amend certain references in enactments and rules of law, and disapply certain formalities and requirements.

12. Regulation 33 makes provision for trustees to use the relevant system and for debentures to be held in uncertificated form and transferred by means of the relevant system.

13. Regulation 34 makes provision for giving notices of meetings.

14. Regulations 35 and 36 make provisions relating to take-overs of companies with shares held in uncertificated form.

15. Regulations 37 and 38 provide for the liability of participating issuers and their officers for contravening certain regulations.

16. Regulation 39 and Schedule 3 adapt the Regulations as they apply to Northern Ireland.

17. Regulation 40 makes certain minor and consequential amendments to the Companies Act 1985 and the Financial Services Act 1986.

18. Regulation 41 revokes the Uncertificated Securities Regulations 1992.

# THE FINANCIAL SERVICES ACT 1986 (EEA REGULATED MARKETS) (EXEMPTION) ORDER 1995

(SI 1995/3273)

*Made on 18 December 1995 by the Treasury under s. 46 of the Financial Services Act 1986. Operative from 1 January 1996.*

## CITATION, COMMENCEMENT AND INTERPRETATION

**1(1)** This Order may be cited as the Financial Services Act 1986 (EEA Regulated Markets) (Exemption) order 1995 and shall come into force on 1st January 1996.

**1(2)** In this Order–

**"EEA State"** means a State which is a contracting party to the agreement on the European Economic Area signed at Oporto on the 2nd May 1992 as adjusted by the Protocol signed at Brussels on 17th March 1993;

**"the Investment Services Directive"** means the Council Directive on investment services in the securities field (No. 93/22/EEC).

## EXEMPTION OF CERTAIN EUROPEAN MARKETS

**2** A person who provides the trading facilities constituting a market which–

(a) appears on the list drawn up by an EEA State other than the United Kingdom pursuant to article 16 of the Investment Services Directive; and

(b) operates without any requirement that a person dealing on the market should have a physical presence in the EEA State from which the trading facilities are provided or on any trading floor that the market may have,

is an exempted person as respects anything done in connection with or for the purposes of the provision of those trading facilities.

## EXPLANATORY NOTE

(*This Note is not part of the Order*)

The Order makes provision for an exemption from the scope of the authorisation requirement imposed by Part I of the Financial Services Act 1986. The exemption is needed because Article 15.4 of Council Directive No. 93/22/EEC on investment services in the securities field (OJ No. L 141, 10.5.93, p. 27) ("the Investment Services Directive") has the effect that an EEA State must allow a market of the kind described in the Order to place within the territory of the State the facilities necessary to enable investment firms from that State to become members of the market or to have access to it.

The exemption has the effect that a person may, without having to obtain authorisation under the Financial Services Act, provide within the United Kingdom trading facilities constituting a market which operates without any requirement for a person dealing on the market to have a physical presence either in the EEA State from which the trading facilities are provided or on any physical floor that the market may have provided that the market appears on a list drawn up by another EEA State pursuant to the provisions of Article 16 of the Investment Services Directive. An EEA State may enter a market on the list only if the market concerned is a regulated market within the meaning of Article 1.13 of the Investment Services Directive and only if the EEA State is the home member State of the market within the meaning of article 1.6(c) of that Directive.

# THE INVESTMENT SERVICES REGULATIONS 1995

(SI 1995/3275)

*Made on 18 December 1995 by the Treasury under s. 2(2) of the European Communities Act 1972. Operative from 1 January 1996 (except reg. 27 and 31 which become operative from 1 January 1997).*

[**Note:** The functions of the Bank of England under these regulations transferred to the Financial Services Authority by s. 21(b)(ii), 45 of the Bank of England Act 1998 as from 1 June 1998 (see SI 1998/1120 (C 25), art. 2). Amendments to the regulations by the Bank of England Act 1998 operative from that date have been included.]

## ARRANGEMENT OF REGULATIONS

### PART I – GENERAL

## PART I – GENERAL

### CITATION AND COMMENCEMENT

**1(1)** These Regulations may be cited as the Investment Services Regulations 1995.

**1(2)** These Regulations, except regulations 27 and 31, shall come into force on 1st January 1996, and those regulations shall come into force on 1st January 1997.

### INTERPRETATION: GENERAL

**2(1)** In these Regulations–

**"the Consumer Credit Act"** means the Consumer Credit Act 1974;

**"the Financial Services Act"** means the Financial Services Act 1986;

**"another EEA State"** means an EEA State other than the United Kingdom;

**"appointed representative"** has the same meaning as in the Financial Services Act;

**"authorised"**, in relation to the provision of a listed activity, shall be construed in accordance with regulation 4 or, as the case may be, regulation 19 below;

**"authorised person"** has the same meaning as in the Financial Services Act;

**"the Authority"** means the Financial Services Authority (formerly known as the Securities and Investments Board);

**"the Bank"** means the Bank of England;

**"the Board"** means The Securities and Investments Board (now known as the Financial Services Authority);

**"branch"** means one or more places of business established or proposed to be established in the same EEA State for the purpose of providing listed services;

**"the Capital Adequacy Directive"** means the Council Directive on the capital adequacy of investment firms and credit institutions (No. 93/6/EEC);

**"the commencement date"** means 1st January 1996;

**"connected UK authority"**, in relation to an investment firm providing or proposing to provide any listed service in the United Kingdom, means an authority in the United Kingdom which has regulatory functions in relation to that service;

**"Consumer Credit Act business"** means consumer credit business, consumer hire business or ancillary credit business;

**"consumer credit business"**, **"consumer hire business"** and **"ancillary credit business"** have the same meanings as in the Consumer Credit Act;

**"core investment service"** means a service listed in Section A of the Annex to the Investment Services Directive, the text of which is set out in Schedule 1 to these Regulations together with the text of Section B of that Annex which is relevant to the interpretation of Section A;

**"credit institution"** means a credit institution as defined in article 1 of the First Council Directive, that is to say, an undertaking whose business is to receive deposits or other repayable funds from the public and to grant credits for its own account;

**"designated agency"** has the same meaning as in the Financial Services Act;

**"the Director"** means the Director General of Fair Trading;
**"EEA State"** means a State which is a contracting party to the agreement on the European Economic Area signed at Oporto on the 2nd May 1992 as adjusted by the Protocol signed at Brussels on 17th March 1993;
**"establish"**, in relation to a branch, means establish the place of business or, as the case may be, the first place of business which constitutes the branch;
**"European authorised institution"** means a credit institution whose authorisation under the First Council Directive and the Second Council Directive covers one or more core investment services;
**"the European Commission"** means the Commission of the Communities;
**"European investment firm"** has the meaning given by regulation 3 below;
**"European subsidiary"** has the same meaning as in the Banking Coordination (Second Council Directive) Regulations 1992, as those regulations have effect immediately before the commencement date;
**"exempted person"** has the same meaning as in the Financial Services Act;
**"50 per cent controller"** has the same meaning as in regulation 46;
**"firm"** includes an individual and a body corporate;
**"the First Council Directive"** means the First Council Directive on the coordination of laws, regulations and administrative provisions relating to the taking up and pursuit of the business of credit institutions (No. 77/780/EEC);
**"home-regulated investment business"**, in relation to a European investment firm, means investment business which consists in the provision of one or more listed services which its authorisation as an investment firm authorises it to provide;
**"home State"**, in relation to–

(a) an investment firm which has no registered office, means the EEA State in which the firm's head office is situated; and
(b) an investment firm which has a registered office, means the EEA state in which that office is situated;

**"investment business"** has the same meaning as in the Financial Services Act;
**"investment firm"** has the meaning given in paragraph (2) below;
**"the Investment Services Directive"** means the Council Directive on investment services in the securities field (No. 93/22/EEC);
**"listed service"** means a service listed in Section A or C of the Annex to the Investment Services Directive;
**"member"** and **"rules"**, in relation to a recognised self-regulating organisation, have the same meanings as in the Financial Services Act;
**"quasi-European investment firm"** has the meaning given by regulation 3(2) below;
**"recognised self-regulating organisation"** has the same meaning as in the Financial Services Act;
**"relevant supervisory authority"**, in relation to another EEA State, means the authority in that State which has regulatory functions in relation to any core investment service, whether or not it also has such functions in relation to any non-core investment service;
**"requisite details"**, in relation to an investment firm means–

(a) particulars of the programme of operations of the business to be carried on by the firm, including a description of the particular core investment services and non-core investment services to be provided; and
(b) where a branch is established or proposed to be established–
(i) particulars of the structural organisation of the branch;
(ii) the address in the EEA State in which the branch is or is to be established from which information about the business may be obtained; and
(iii) the names of the managers of the business;

**"the Second Council Directive"** means the Second Council Directive on the coordination of laws, regulations and administrative provisions relating to the taking up and pursuit of the business of credit institutions and amending the First Council Directive (No. 89/646/EEC);

**"supervisory authority"**, in relation to another EEA State, means an authority in that State which has regulatory functions in relation to one or more listed services;

**"UK authorised institution"** and **"UK subsidiary"** have the same meanings as in the Banking Coordination (Second Council Directive) Regulations 1992;

**"UK investment firm"** and **"UK authorised investment firm"** have the meaning given by regulation 18 below; and

**"UK regulatory authority"**, in relation to an investment firm providing or proposing to provide a core or non-core investment service in the United Kingdom, means an authority in the United Kingdom which has regulatory functions in relation to that service.

**History**

In reg. 2(1), the entry relating to the Authority inserted by the Bank of England Act 1998, s. 23(1), 45 and Sch. 5, para. 45(1), (2)(a) as from 1 June 1998 (see SI 1998/1120 (C 25), art. 2). In the entry relating to the Board, the words "(now known as the Financial Services Authority)" inserted by the Bank of England Act 1998, s. 23(1), 45 and Sch. 5, para. 45(1), (2)(b) as from 1 June 1998 (see SI 1998/1120 (C 25), art. 2).

**2(2B)** Any reference in these Regulations to the First Council Directive or the Second Council Directive is a reference to that Directive as amended by the Prudential Supervision Directive (within the meaning of the Financial Institutions (Prudential Supervision) Regulations 1996).

**History**

Reg. 2(2B) inserted by the Financial Institutions (Prudential Supervision) Regulations 1996 (SI 1996/1669), reg. 1, 23 and Sch. 5, para. 12 as from 18 July 1996.

**2(2)** In these Regulations, **"investment firm"** means any person, other than one within paragraph (3) below, whose regular occupation or business is the provision of any one or more core investment services to third parties on a professional basis.

**2(3)** The persons within this paragraph are persons to whom the Investment Services Directive does not apply by virtue of the provisions of paragraph 2 of article 2 of that directive, the text of which is set out in Schedule 2 to these Regulations.

**2(4)** For the purposes of paragraph (2) above, where a person (the first person) provides one of the services referred to in paragraph 1(a) of Section A of the Annex to the Investment Services Directive (reception and transmission of orders) solely for the account of and under the full and unconditional responsibility of another person (the second person), that service shall be regarded as a service provided not by the first person but by the second person.

**2(5)** In these Regulations **"parent undertaking"**, **"share"**, **"subsidiary undertaking"** and **"undertaking"** have the same meanings as in Part VII of the Companies Act 1985 or Part VIII the Companies (Northern Ireland) Order 1986 except that–

(a) **"subsidiary undertaking"** also includes, in relation to an investment firm incorporated in or formed under the law of another EEA State, any undertaking which is a subsidiary undertaking within the meaning of any rule of law in force in that State for purposes connected with the implementation of the Seventh Company Law Directive based on article 54(3)(g) of the Treaty on consolidated accounts (No. 83/349/EEC); and

(b) **"parent undertaking"** shall be construed accordingly.

**2(6)** Any reference in these Regulations to the carrying on of home-regulated investment business in the United Kingdom–

(a) is a reference to the carrying on of such business in reliance on regulation 5(1)(a) below; and

(b) shall be construed in accordance with section 1(3) of the Financial Services Act.

## PART II – RECOGNITION IN UK OF EUROPEAN INVESTMENT FIRMS

### PRELIMINARY

### EUROPEAN INVESTMENT FIRMS

**3(1)** An investment firm is a European investment firm for the purposes of these regulations if–

(a) it is incorporated in or formed under the law of another EEA State;

(b) its head office is in that State;

(c) it is for the time being, either a European authorised institution or authorised to act as an investment firm by a relevant supervisory authority in that State; and

(d) in the case of an investment firm which is not a European authorised institution and was not on the commencement date a European subsidiary, the requirements of paragraph 1 of Schedule 3 to these Regulations have been complied with in relation to its provision of a service or its establishment of a branch.

**3(2)** In these Regulations **"quasi-European investment firm"** means an investment firm other than a European authorised institution–

(a) which is not a European investment firm; but

(b) which would be such an investment firm if the requirements of paragraph 1 of Schedule 3 to these Regulations had been complied with in relation to its provision of a service or its establishment of a branch.

**3(3)** Schedule 3 to these Regulations (which contains requirements to be complied with by or in relation to European investment firms) shall have effect.

### AUTHORISED SERVICES

**4** For the purposes of these Regulations a European investment firm is authorised to provide in its home State any listed service which its authorisation as an investment firm or as a credit institution authorises it to provide.

## EFFECT OF RECOGNITION

### AUTHORISATIONS AND LICENCES NOT REQUIRED

**5(1)** Subject to paragraph (2) below, nothing in the following enactments, namely–

(a) sections 3 and 4 of the Financial Services Act (restrictions on carrying on investment business); and

(b) sections 21, 39(1) and 147(1) of the Consumer Credit Act (Consumer Credit Act businesses needing a licence),

shall prevent a European investment firm from providing in the United Kingdom any listed service which it is authorised to provide in its home State.

**5(2)** In relation to a European investment firm in respect of which a prohibition under these Regulations is in force–

(a) paragraph (1)(a) above shall not apply if the prohibition is under regulation 9 below; and

(b) paragraph (1)(b) above shall not apply if the prohibition is under regulation 15 below.

### PROCEDURAL REQUIREMENTS FOR CARRYING ON LISTED SERVICES

**6(1)** A European investment firm (other than a credit institution authorised in its home State to provide one or more core investment services) shall not–

(a) provide in the United Kingdom by the provision of services any listed service; or

(b) establish a branch in the United Kingdom for the purpose of providing such a service,

unless the requirements of paragraph 1 of Schedule 3 to these Regulations have been complied with in relation to its provision of the service or, as the case may be, its establishment of the branch.

**6(2)** A European investment firm (other than a credit institution authorised in its home State to provide one or more core investment services) which does not have a branch in the United Kingdom shall not change the requisite details of its activities in the United Kingdom unless the requirements of paragraph 4 of Schedule 3 to these regulations have been complied with in relation to its making of the change.

**6(3)** A European investment firm (other than a credit institution authorised in its home member state to provide one or more core investment services) shall not change the requisite details of a branch established by it in the United Kingdom unless the requirements of paragraph 5 of Schedule 3 to these Regulations have been complied with in relation to its making of the change.

**6(4)** An investment firm which contravenes paragraph (1), (2) or (3) above shall be guilty of an offence and liable on summary conviction to a fine not exceeding level 5 on the standard scale; but such a contravention shall not invalidate any transaction.

**6(5)** In proceedings brought against an investment firm for an offence under paragraph (4) above it shall be a defence for the investment firm to show that it took all reasonable precautions and exercised all due diligence to avoid the commission of the offence.

**6(6)** Proceedings in respect of an offence under any provision of this regulation shall not be instituted–

(a) in England and Wales, except by the Board or by or with the consent of the Secretary of State or the Director of Public Prosecutions; or

(b) in Northern Ireland, except by the Board or by or with the consent of the Secretary of State or the Director of Public Prosecutions for Northern Ireland.

## EFFECT OF NON-RECOGNITION

### PROHIBITION ON CARRYING ON CERTAIN LISTED SERVICES

**7(1)** A quasi-European investment firm shall not–

(a) provide in the United Kingdom by the provision of services any listed service; or

(b) establish a branch in the United Kingdom for the purpose of providing such a service.

**7(2)** An investment firm which contravenes paragraph (1) above shall be guilty of an offence and liable on summary conviction to a fine not exceeding level 5 on the standard scale; but such a contravention shall not invalidate any transaction.

**7(3)** In proceedings brought against an investment firm for an offence under paragraph (2) above it shall be a defence for the investment firm to show that it took all reasonable precautions and exercised all due diligence to avoid the commission of the offence.

**7(4)** Proceedings in respect of an offence under this regulation shall not be instituted–

(a) in England and Wales, except by the Board or by or with the consent of the Secretary of State or the Director of Public Prosecutions; or

(b) in Northern Ireland, except by the Board or by or with the consent of the Secretary of State or the Director of Public Prosecutions for Northern Ireland.

## FUNCTIONS OF BOARD

### DUTY TO PREPARE FOR SUPERVISION

**8(1)** In any case where the Board receives from a relevant supervisory authority in an investment firm's home State a notice given in accordance with paragraph 3 of Schedule 3 to these Regulations, the Board shall, before the expiry of the relevant period draw to the attention of the firm such provisions of these Regulations, the relevant Acts or regulations or rules made under those Acts as, having regard to the services mentioned in the notice, the Board considers appropriate.

**8(2)** In any case where the Board receives from the relevant supervisory authority in an investment firm's home State such a notice as is mentioned in paragraph (1) above stating that the firm intends to establish a branch in the United Kingdom–

(a) the Board shall also, before the expiry of the relevant period, consider whether the situation as respects the investment firm is such that the powers conferred by regulation 9(1) below are likely to become exercisable; and

(b) if so, the Board may impose, as soon as the requirements of paragraph 1 of Schedule 3 to these Regulations have been complied with in relation to the firm, such restriction under regulation 10 below as appears to it desirable.

**8(3)** (Revoked by the Bank of England Act 1998, s. 43, 45 and Sch. 9, Pt. II as from 1 June 1998).

**History**
In regard to the date of the above revocation, see SI 1998/1120 (C 25), art. 2. The former para. 8(3) read as follows:
"**8(3)** In any case where the Bank receives from the relevant supervisory authority in an investment firm's home State such a notice as is mentioned in regulation 13(1) below stating that the firm intends to establish a branch in the United Kingdom, the Bank may request the Board to exercise the powers conferred on it by regulation 10 below in relation to the firm and, if the Board is satisfied that the situation with respect to the firm is such that the powers conferred by regulation 9(1) below are likely to become exercisable, the Board may impose, as soon as the requirements of paragraph 1 of Schedule 3 to these Regulations have been complied with in relation to the firm, such restriction under regulation 10 as appears to it, after consulting the Bank, to be desirable."

**8(4)** In any case where the Board receives from an investment firm a notice given in accordance with paragraph 4 or 5 of Schedule 3 to these Regulations, the Board shall draw to the attention of the firm such provisions of these Regulations, the relevant Acts or regulations or rules made under those Acts as, having regard to the proposed change mentioned in the notice, the Board considers appropriate.

**8(5)** In this regulation–

(a) **"the relevant Acts"** means the Financial Services Act and the Consumer Credit Act; and

(b) **"the relevant period"** means–

(i) in relation to a notice given in accordance with paragraph 3 of Schedule 3 to these Regulations which states that the investment firm intends to establish a branch in the United Kingdom, the period of two months beginning with the day on which the Board received the notice;

(ii) in any other case, the period of one month beginning with the day on which the Board received the notice.

## POWER TO PROHIBIT THE PROVISION OF LISTED SERVICES

**9(1)** If it appears to the Board that a European investment firm–

(a) has contravened or is likely to contravene any provision of the Financial Services Act or any rules or regulations made under it;

(b) in purported compliance with any such provision, has furnished it with false, inaccurate or misleading information;

(c) has contravened or is likely to contravene any prohibition or requirement imposed under that Act; or

(d) has failed to comply with any statement of principle issued under that Act,

it may impose on the investment firm a prohibition under this regulation, that is to say, a prohibition on providing or purporting to provide in the United Kingdom any listed services.

**9(2)** Where the investment firm is a member of a recognised self-regulating organisation–

(a) the reference in paragraph (1) above to rules made under the Financial Services Act shall be taken to include a reference to the rules of that organisation; and

(b) the reference in that paragraph to any prohibition or requirement imposed under that Act shall be taken to include a reference to any prohibition or requirement imposed by virtue of the rules of that organisation.

**9(3)** A prohibition under this regulation–

(a) may be absolute; or

(b) may be limited, that is to say, imposed for a specified period or until the occurrence of a specified event or until specified conditions are complied with;

and any period, event or conditions specified in the case of a limited prohibition may be varied by the Board on the application of the investment firm concerned.

**9(4)** Any prohibition imposed under this regulation may be withdrawn by written notice served by the Board on the investment firm concerned; and any such notice shall take effect on such date as is specified in the notice.

**9(5)** Schedule 4 to these Regulations (which makes supplemental provision with respect to prohibitions imposed under this regulation and restrictions imposed under regulation 10 below) shall have effect.

POWER TO RESTRICT PROVISION OF LISTED SERVICES

**10(1)** Where it appears to the Board that the situation as respects a European investment firm providing any listed service in the United Kingdom is such that the powers conferred by regulation 9(1) above are exercisable, the Board may, instead of or as well as imposing a prohibition, exercise–

(a) in relation to the investment firm; or

(b) except in the case of the power conferred by section 65 of the Financial Services Act, in relation to any appointed representative of the investment firm,

the powers conferred on the Board by Chapter VI of Part I of that Act (powers of intervention).

**10(2)** Except where they are required to be exercised by virtue of section 128C of that Act (enforcement in support of overseas regulatory authority), the powers conferred by that Chapter shall not, subject to paragraph (3) below, be exercisable in relation to–

(a) a European investment firm providing any listed service in the United Kingdom which is a member of a recognised self-regulating organisation and is subject to the rules of such an organisation in the provision of listed services provided by it in the United Kingdom; or

(b) an appointed representative whose principal or, in the case of such a representative with more than one principal, each of whose principals is–

(i) a member of a recognised self-regulating organisation; and

(ii) subject to the rules of such an organisation in providing the listed service in respect of which it has accepted responsibility for the appointed representative's activities.

**10(3)** The powers conferred by section 67(1)(b) of the Financial Services Act may on any of the grounds specified in regulation 9(1) above be exercised in relation to a person mentioned in paragraph (2) above at the request of any recognised self-regulating organisation of which he or, in the case of an appointed representative, any of his principals is a member.

**10(4)** In this regulation, **"principal"** has the same meaning as in the Financial Services Act.

LIMITATIONS ON BOARD'S POWERS

**11(1)** This regulation applies where it appears to the Board that the situation is such that its power–

(a) to impose a prohibition on a European investment firm under regulation 9 above;

(b) to publish a statement with respect to such a firm under section 60 (public statement as to person's misconduct) of the Financial Services Act;

(c) to make an application with respect to such a firm under section 61(1) (injunctions) of that Act;

(d) to impose a prohibition or requirement on such an investment firm under Chapter VI of Part I of that Act (powers of intervention);

(e) to vary a prohibition or requirement imposed on such an investment firm under that Chapter; or

(f) to refuse an application for the variation or rescission of a prohibition or requirement so imposed,

is exercisable by virtue of any contravention of any provision which is made pursuant to a provision of the Investment Services Directive that confers power on the host States and which is conferred under that Act.

**11(2)** The Board shall require the investment firm in writing to remedy the situation.

**11(3)** If the investment firm fails to comply with the requirement under paragraph (2) above within a reasonable time, the Board shall give a notice to that effect to the relevant supervisory authority in the investment firm's home State requesting that authority–

(a) to take all appropriate measures for the purpose of ensuring that the investment firm concerned remedies the situation which has given rise to the issue of the notice; and

(b) to inform the Board of the measures it proposes to take or has taken or the reasons for not taking such measures.

**11(4)** Subject to paragraph (5) below, the Board shall not take any such action as is mentioned in sub-paragraph (a) to (f) of paragraph (1) above with respect to a European investment firm unless it is satisfied–

(a) that the relevant supervisory authority has failed or refused to take measures for the purpose mentioned in paragraph (3)(a) above; or

(b) that the measures taken by that authority have proved inadequate for that purpose.

**11(5)** Where the Board decides that it should take action as mentioned in any of sub-paragraphs (a) to (e) of paragraph (1) above with respect to a European investment firm as a matter of urgency in order to protect the interests of investors, it may take that action–

(a) before complying with paragraphs (2) and (3) above; or

(b) where it has complied with those requirements, before it is satisfied as mentioned in paragraph (4) above;

but in such a case it shall, at the earliest opportunity, inform the relevant supervisory authority in the investment firm's home State and the European Commission of the action taken.

**11(6)** In any case where–

(a) by virtue of paragraph (5) above, the Board has taken action as mentioned in any of sub-paragraphs (a) to (e) of paragraph (1) above before complying with paragraphs (2) and (3) above or, as the case may be, before it is satisfied as mentioned in paragraph (4) above; and

(b) the European Commission decides under the Investment Services Directive that the Board must withdraw or amend the statement, withdraw the application, or rescind or vary the prohibition or requirement,

the Board shall in accordance with the decision withdraw or amend the statement, withdraw the application, or rescind or vary the prohibition or requirement.

**11(7)** For the purposes of paragraph (6)(b) above the Board shall be taken to withdraw or amend a statement if it publishes a further statement retracting or, as the case may be, correcting it; and the Board shall after publication of the further statement send a copy of it to any person to whom a copy of the previous statement was sent under section 60(5) of the Financial Services Act.

**11(8)** In any case where–

(a) the Board has, by virtue of sub-paragraph (5) above, given notice to a European investment firm under section 60(2) of the Financial Services Act before complying with paragraphs (2) and (3) above or, as the case may be, before it is satisfied as mentioned in paragraph (4) above;

(b) the statement to which the notice relates has not been published; and

(c) the European Commission decides under the Investment Services Directive that the Board must not publish the statement, or must publish a different statement under that section, the Board shall in accordance with the decision withdraw the notice or give a different notice in substitution.

### OBLIGATION OF BOARD WHERE INVESTMENT FIRM CEASES TO BE A EUROPEAN INVESTMENT FIRM ETC.

**12** Where the Board is informed that–

(a) a person has ceased to be a European investment firm; or–

(b) a European investment firm has ceased to provide any particular listed service in the United Kingdom,

the Board shall inform every other authority which it knows is a connected UK authority of that fact.

## FUNCTIONS OF THE BANK

### DUTY TO PREPARE FOR SUPERVISION

**13** (Revoked by the Bank of England Act 1998, s. 43, 45 and Sch. 9, Pt. II as from 1 June 1998).

## PART V – AMENDMENTS OF FINANCIAL SERVICES ACT

### AUTHORISATION BY MEMBERSHIP OF RECOGNISED SELF-REGULATING ORGANISATIONS

**21(1)** Section 7 of the Financial Services Act (authorisation by membership of recognised self-regulating organisation) shall have effect as if it included provision that a person who–

(a) is a European investment firm or quasi-European investment firm; and

(b) is a member of a recognised self-regulating organisation,

is not, by virtue of its membership of that organisation, an authorised person as respects any home-regulated investment business.

**21(2)** Paragraph 1 of Schedule 2 to that Act (requiremnts for recognition of self-regulating organisations) shall have effect as if it included provision that the rules and practices of the organisation must be such as to secure–

(a) that the requirements of paragraph (3) below are met with respect to each member which is a UK investment firm and is not a UK authorised institution; and

(b) that a UK investment firm (other than a UK authorised institution) is admitted to membership only if the requirements of paragraph (4) below are met with respect to the firm.

**21(3)** The requirements of this paragraph are that–

(a) the head office of the firm, and, if the firm has a registered office, its registered office, must be situated in the United Kingdom;

(b) in the case of a firm which is neither a body corporate nor a partnership constituted under the law of Scotland, the firm must carry on business in the United Kingdom;

(c) the firm must have adequate capital to meet the requirements of any rules applicable to it requiring the maintenance of financial resources; and

(d) except in the case of a firm which is subject to rules of the organisation making provision with respect to the matters dealt with in section 48(2)(1) of the Financial Services Act (protection of investors on death etc. of natural person), its business is effectively directed by two or more persons.

**21(4)** The requirements of this paragraph are that–

(a) the firm has submitted to the organisation concerned a programme of operations containing at least the following information–
 (i) a description of the listed services that the firm proposes to provide; and
 (ii) a description of the firm's structure; and

(b) in a case in which the firm is–
 (i) a subsidiary undertaking;
 (ii) a subsidiary undertaking of the parent undertaking; or
 (iii) controlled by the 50 per cent controller,

of an investment firm or credit institution which is for the time being authorised to act as such a firm or institution by the relevant supervisory authority in another EEA State, the organisation concerned has consulted that authority.

**21(5)** Paragraph 2 of Schedule 2 to the Financial Services Act shall have effect as if it included provision that the rules and practices of the organisation relating to the admission of members must be such as to secure that each applicant for membership that is a UK investment firm is informed of the organisation's decision on the application not later than six months after the date on which the application was received.

### APPLICATIONS FOR AUTHORISATION

**22** Section 26 of the Financial Services Act (applications for authorisation) shall have effect as if it included provision that an application for authorisation in respect of any home-regulated investment business may not be made by a European investment firm or quasi-European investment firm.

## GRANT AND REFUSAL OF AUTHORISATION

**23(1)** Section 27 of the Financial Services Act (grant and refusal of authorisation) shall have effect as if it included provision that where a European investment firm or a quasi-European investment firm holds an authorisation granted under that section, the firm is not by virtue of that authorisation an authorised person as respects any home-regulated investment business.

**23(2)** That section shall also have effect in relation to a relevant firm, that is to say, a UK investment firm which is not a UK authorised institution, as if it included provision–

(a) that the Board may not grant authorisation to a relevant firm unless the Board is satisfied that the requirements of paragraph (3) below are met;

(b) that the Board may not grant authorisation to a relevant firm where it is–
  (i) a subsidiary undertaking;
  (ii) a subsidiary undertaking of the parent undertaking; or
  (iii) controlled by the 50 per cent controller,

of an investment firm or credit institution which is for the time being authorised to act as such a firm or institution by the relevant supervisory authority in another EEA State, unless the Board has consulted that authority;

(c) that the Board is required to specify, in a notice given under section 27(8) of the Financial Services Act to a relevant firm, that the date on which authorisation takes effect is the date upon which the notice is given; and

(d) that the Board is under an obligation to notify each applicant who is a relevant firm of the Board's decision on the application not later than six months after the date on which the application was received.

**23(3)** The requirements of this paragraph are that–

(a) the head office of the firm, and, if the firm has a registered office, its registered office, must be situated in the United Kingdom;

(b) in the case of a firm which is neither a body corporate nor a partnership constituted under the law of Scotland, the firm must carry on business in the United Kingdom;

(c) the firm must have adequate capital to meet the requirements of any rules applicable to it requiring the maintenance of financial resources; and

(d) except in the case of a firm which is subject to rules of the organisation making provision with respect to the matters dealt with in section 48(2)(1) of the Financial Services Act (protection of investors on death etc. of natural person), its business is effectively directed by two or more persons.

## AUTHORISATION IN OTHER EEA STATE

**24** Section 31 of the Financial Services Act (authorisation in other EEA State) shall have effect as if it included provision that an investment firm to which that section applies and which is a European investment firm or a quasi-European investment firm is not, by virtue of that section, an authorised person as respects any home-regulated investment business.

## CERTAIN EEA REGULATED MARKETS

**25** A person who provides the trading facilities constituting a market which–

(a) appears on the list drawn up by another EEA State pursuant to Article 16 of the Investment Services Directive; and

(b) operates without any requirement that a person dealing on the market should have a physical presence in the EEA State from which the trading facilities are provided or on any trading floor that the market may have,

shall not be an exempted person by virtue of section 36 of the Financial Services Act as respects anything done in connection with or for the purposes of the provision of those trading facilities which constitutes investment business.

## EXEMPTED PERSONS

**26(1)** Section 43 of the Financial Services Act (listed money market institutions) shall have effect as if it included provision that an investment firm which–

(a) is a European investment firm or quasi-European investment firm; and
(b) is for the time being included in a list maintained for the purposes of that section,

is not, by virtue of its inclusion in that list, an exempted person as respects any home-regulated investment business.

**26(2)** That section shall also have effect as if it included provision that the conditions and arrangements referred to in subsection (2) must be such as to secure that–

(a) no European investment firm, other than one on which an absolute prohibition has been imposed under regulation 9 of these Regulations or under regulation 15 of the Banking Coordination (Second Council Directive) Regulations, is refused admission to the list, or removed from it, for reasons relating to–
  (i) the fitness of the firm to provide listed services;
  (ii) the financial standing of the firm; or
  (iii) any other matter for which, under the Investment Services Directive, responsibility is reserved to a supervisory authority in the firm's home State;
(b) where any power that the Authority has by virtue of those conditions and arrangements is exercisable by virtue of a European investment firm's contravention of any provision made pursuant to any provision of the Investment Services Directive that confers power on host States, the exercise of the power is subject to such restrictions as are necessary for the purposes of complying with article 19 of the Investment Services Directive;
(c) the Authority is under an obligation–
  (i) upon admitting a UK investment firm which is neither an authorised person nor a UK authorised institution to the list, to issue the firm with a written statement specifying the core investment services which that firm is permitted to provide by virtue of its inclusion in the list;
  (ii) upon becoming aware of the occurrence of any change in the range of core investment services which such a firm is permitted to provide by virtue of its inclusion in the list, to withdraw the previous statement and to issue the firm in question with a further written statement reflecting the change;
  (iii) upon becoming aware that such a firm has become an authorised person or a UK authorised institution, to withdraw from the firm the written statement specifying the core investment services which the firm is permitted to provide by virtue of its inclusion in the list; and
  (iv) to inform each applicant for admission to the list who is a UK investment firm but who is neither an authorised person nor a UK authorised institution of the Authority's decision on the application not later than six months after the date on which the application was received; and
(d) no UK investment firm which is neither an authorised person nor a UK authorised institution is admitted to the list unless the requirements of paragraph (3) below are met.

**History**
In reg. 26(2)(b) the word "Authority" substituted for the former word "Bank" in the first place where it occurred and the words "by the Bank" omitted and revoked by the Bank of England Act 1998, s. 23(1), 43, 45 and Sch. 5, para. 43, 45(1), (4)(a)(i) and Sch. 9, Pt. II as from 1 June 1998 (see SI 1998/1120 (C 25), art. 2).
In reg. 26(2)(c) the word "Authority" substituted for the former word "Bank" and the word "Authority's" substituted for the former word "Bank's" by the Bank of England Act 1998, s. 23(1), 45 and Sch. 5, para. 45(1), (4)(a)(ii) as from 1 June 1998 (see SI 1998/1120 (C 25), art. 2).

**26(3)** The requirements of this paragraph are that–

(a) the head office of the firm, and if the firm has a registered office, its registered office, must be situated in the United Kingdom;
(b) the firm must be a fit and proper person to carry on listed services;
(c) in the case of a firm which is neither a body corporate nor a partnership constituted under the law of Scotland, the firm must carry on business in the United Kingdom;
(d) the firm must have adequate capital to meet the requirements of any rules applicable to it requiring the maintenance of financial resources;
(e) either the firm will, if admitted to the list, be subject to conditions making provision with

respect to the matters mentioned in section 48(2)(1) of the Financial Services Act (protection of investor on death etc. of natural person) or its business will be effectively directed by two or more persons of sufficiently good repute and experience to provide listed services;

(f) the firm must have submitted to the Authority a programme of operations of the business to be carried on by the firm containing at least the following information–
  (i) a description of the particular listed services that the firm proposes to provide; and
  (ii) particulars of the firm's structure; and

(g) in the case of a firm which is not and is not seeking to become, an authorised person but which is–
  (i) a subsidiary undertaking;
  (ii) a subsidiary undertaking of the parent undertaking; or
  (iii) controlled by the 50 per cent controller,

of an investment firm or credit institution which is for the time being authorised to act as such a firm or institution by a relevant supervisory authority in another EEA State, the Authority has consulted that authority.

**History**
See history note after reg. 26(4).

**26(4)** That section shall also have effect as if it enabled the Authority to regard itself as satisfied with respect to any matter relevant for the purposes of its supervision of a person admitted to the list maintained for the purposes of section 43 of that Act who is a UK investment firm or a European authorised investment firm if–

(a) any relevant regulatory authority informs the Authority that it is satisfied with respect to the matter; and

(b) the Authority is satisfied as to the nature and scope of the supervision exercised by that regulatory authority.

**History**
In reg. 26(3) and (4) the word "Authority" wherever occurring substituted for the former word "Bank" by the Bank of England Act 1998, s. 23(1), 45 and Sch. 5, para. 45(1), (4)(b) as from 1 June 1998 (see SI 1998/1120 (C 25), art. 2).

**26(5)** In paragraph (4) above, **"relevant regulatory authority"**–

(a) in relation to a UK investment firm means any UK regulatory authority; and

(b) in relation to a European investment firm means a supervisory authority in the firm's home State.

## APPOINTED REPRESENTATIVES

**27** Section 44 of the Financial Services Act (appointed representatives) shall have effect as if it included provision that a UK investment firm is not, by virtue of that section, an exempted person as respects a service specified in paragraph 1(a) of Section A of the Annex to the Investment Services Directive (reception and transmission of orders) unless that activity is carried out solely for the account of an investment firm.

## STATEMENT OF SERVICES COVERED BY AUTHORISATION

**28(1)** Section 102 of the Financial Services Act (register of authorised persons and recognised organisations etc.) shall have effect as if it required the Board–

(a) upon it first appearing to it that a UK investment firm is a UK authorised investment firm to which this regulation applies, to issue the firm with a written statement specifying the core investment services which that firm is permitted to provide;

(b) upon becoming aware of the occurrence of any change in the range of core investment services which such a UK authorised investment firm is permitted to provide, to withdraw the previous statement and issue the firm in question with a further written statement reflecting the change; and

(c) upon a UK authorised investment firm ceasing to be a UK authorised investment firm to which this regulation applies, to withdraw from the firm the statement specifying the core investment services it was permitted to provide.

**28(2)** This regulation applies to a UK authorised investment firm which is an authorised person.

## RECIPROCAL FACILITIES FOR INVESTMENT BUSINESS

**29(1)** No notice shall be served under section 183 of the Financial Services Act (reciprocal facilities for financial business) on a UK investment firm which–

(a) appears to the Secretary of State or the Treasury to be a subsidiary undertaking of a person connected with a country outside the United Kingdom; and

(b) is carrying on, or appears to the Secretary of State or the Treasury to intend to carry on, any investment, insurance or banking business in, or in relation to, the United Kingdom,

if the sole ground for giving that notice is the ground specified in paragraph (2) below.

**29(2)** The ground referred to in paragraph (1) above is that it appears to the Secretary of State or the Treasury that by reason of–

(a) the law of the country concerned; or

(b) any action taken by, or the practices of, the government or any other authority or body in that country,

investment firms connected with the United Kingdom are unable to provide core investment services in, or in relation to, that country on terms as favourable as those on which investment firms connected with that country are able to provide such services in, or in relation to, the United Kingdom.

## EXEMPTION FROM LIABILITY FOR DAMAGES

**30** No recognised self-regulating organisation which is a competent authority designated by the United Kingdom for the purposes of Article 22 of the Investment Services Directive or for the purposes of Article 9 of the Capital Adequacy Directive and none of the officers, servants or members of the governing body of such an organisation shall be liable in damages for anything done or omitted in the discharge or purported discharge of its functions as such an authority unless the act or omission is shown to have been in bad faith.

## RECOGNISED PROFESSIONAL BODIES

**31** Paragraph 2 of Schedule 3 to the Financial Services Act (requirements for recognition of recognised professional bodies) shall have effect as if it included provision that the rules, practices and arrangements of a recognised professional body must be such as to secure that no UK investment firm can be certified by the body for the purposes of Part I of the Financial Services Act if it appears to the body that any core investment services provided by the firm are provided by it otherwise than in an incidental manner in the course of a professional activity.

## OTHER AMENDMENTS OF FINANCIAL SERVICES ACT

**32** The provisions of the Financial Services Act which are mentioned in Schedule 7 to these Regulations shall have effect subject to the amendments there specified.

## CONSTRUCTION OF PART V

**33** If and to the extent that a European investment firm is an authorised person, nothing in this Part of these Regulations, except regulations 21(1), 23(1) and 24 and paragraphs 5, 6, 11(2), 20 and 28 of Schedule 7, shall affect the operation of the Financial Services Act in relation to it.

# PART VI – AMENDMENTS OF CONSUMER CREDIT ACT

## EFFECT OF STANDARD LICENCE

**34(1)** Section 22 of the Consumer Credit Act (standard and group licences) shall have effect as if it included provision that a standard licence held by a European investment firm or quasi-European investment firm does not cover the provision by that firm of any listed services.

**34(2)** In this regulation and regulation 35 below **"standard licence"** has the meaning given by section 22(1)(a) of the Consumer Credit Act.

## GRANT OF STANDARD LICENCE

**35** Section 25 of the Consumer Credit Act (licensee to be a fit person) shall have effect as if–

(a) it included provision that a standard licence shall not be issued to a European investment firm or quasi-European investment firm in respect of any listed services; and

(b) the reference in subsection (2)(b) to any provision made by or under that Act, or by or under any enactment regulating the provision of credit to individuals or other transactions with individuals, included a reference to any corresponding provision in force in another EEA State.

## CONDUCT OF BUSINESS

**36(1)** Section 26 of the Consumer Credit Act (conduct of business), and any existing regulations made otherwise than by virtue of section 54 of that Act, shall have effect as if any reference to a licensee included a reference to a European investment firm carrying on any Consumer Credit Act business where that business consists of the provision of a listed service.

**36(2)** Section 54 of that Act (conduct of business regulations), and any existing regulations made by virtue of that section, shall have effect as if any reference to a licensee who carries on a consumer credit business included a reference to a European investment firm which carries on such a business.

**36(3)** In this regulation **"existing regulations"** means regulations made under section 26 of that Act before the commencement date.

## THE REGISTER

**37** Section 35 of the Consumer Credit Act (the register) shall have effect as if the particulars to be included in the register included–

(a) particulars of information received by the Director under regulation 12 or 14 above;

(b) particulars of prohibitions and restrictions imposed by him under regulation 15 or 16 above;

(c) such particulars of documents received by him under paragraph 3(2), 4(3) or 5(3) of Schedule 3 to these Regulations as he thinks fit; and

(d) particulars of such other matters (if any) arising under these Regulations as he thinks fit.

## ENFORCEMENT OF AGREEMENTS

**38(1)** Section 40 of the Consumer Credit Act (enforcement of agreements by unlicensed trader) shall have effect as if the reference in subsection (1) to a regulated agreement, other than a non-commercial agreement, made when the creditor or owner was unlicensed did not include a reference to such an agreement made when the creditor or owner was a relevant firm.

**38(2)** Section 148 of that Act (enforcement of agreement for services of unlicensed trader) shall have effect as if the reference in subsection (1) to an agreement for the services of a person carrying on an ancillary credit business made when that person was unlicensed did not include a reference to such an agreement made when that person was a relevant firm.

**38(3)** Section 149 of that Act (enforcement of regulated agreements made on the introduction of an unlicensed credit-broker) shall have effect as if references in subsections (1) and (2) to introductions by an unlicensed credit-broker did not include references to introductions by a credit-broker who was a relevant firm.

**38(4)** In this regulation **"relevant firm"** means a European investment firm–

(a) to which paragraph (1) of regulation 5 above applies by virtue of sub-paragraph (b) of that paragraph; and

(b) which is not precluded from making the agreement or introductions in question by a restriction imposed under regulation 16 above.

## RESTRICTIONS ON DISCLOSURE OF INFORMATION

**39** Section 174 of the Consumer Credit Act (restrictions on disclosure of information) shall have effect as if in subsection (3A) the reference to the Director's functions under the Consumer Credit Act included a reference to his functions under these Regulations.

## POWER TO MODIFY SUBORDINATE LEGISLATION IN RELATION TO EUROPEAN INVESTMENT FIRMS

**40(1)** If the Secretary of State is satisfied that it is necessary to do so for the purpose of implementing the Investment Services Directive so far as relating to any particular European investment firm, he may, on the application or with the consent of the firm, by order direct that all or any of the provisions of–

(a) any regulations made under section 26 of the Consumer Credit Act; or

(b) any regulations or orders made under Parts IV to VIII of that Act,

shall not apply to the firm or shall apply to it with such modifications as may be specified in the order.

**40(2)** An order under this regulation may be subject to conditions.

**40(3)** An order under this regulation may be revoked at any time by the Secretary of State; and the Secretary of State may at any time vary any such order on the application or with the consent of the European investment firm to which it applies.

## PART VII – NOTIFICATION OF CONTROLLERS

## NOTIFICATION OF NEW OR INCREASED CONTROL

**41(1)** No person shall become a minority, 10 per cent, 20 per cent, 33 per cent or 50 per cent controller of a UK authorised investment firm which is not a UK authorised institution unless–

(a) he has served on each relevant regulator written notice that he intends to become such a controller of the firm; and

(b) each relevant regulator has done one of the following, that is to say–

(i) has notified him in writing before the end of the period of three months beginning with the date of service of that notice on the regulator that there is no objection to his becoming such a controller of the firm; or

(ii) has allowed that period to elapse without serving on him under regulation 42 below a written notice of objection to his becoming such a controller.

**41(2)** Paragraph (1) above applies also in relation to a person becoming a partner in a UK authorised investment firm which is not a UK authorised institution but is a partnership formed under the law of any part of the United Kingdom.

**41(3)** A relevant regulator may, after receiving a notice under paragraph (1)(a) above from any person, by notice in writing require him to provide such additional information or documents as the regulator concerned may reasonably require for deciding whether to serve a notice of objection.

**41(4)** Where additional information or documents are required from any person by a notice under paragraph (3) above the time between the giving of the notice and the receipt of the information or documents shall be added to the period mentioned in paragraph (1)(b) above.

**41(5)** A notice given by a person under paragraph (1)(a) above shall not be regarded as compliance with that paragraph except as respects his becoming a controller of the firm in question within the period of one year beginning–

(a) in a case where a person has become a controller without his having been served with a notice of objection, with the date on which he became such a controller; and

(b) in a case in which he has been served with one or more notices of objection and the notice or, as the case may be, each of them, has been quashed, with the date upon which the notice is quashed or, if more than one notice was served, with the date of the quashing of the last such notice to be quashed.

## OBJECTION TO NEW OR INCREASED CONTROL

**42(1)** A relevant regulator may serve a notice of objection on a person who has given a notice under regulation 41 above unless the regulator concerned is satisfied, having regard to the need to ensure the sound and prudent management of the firm, that the person in question is a fit and proper person to become a controller of the description in question.

**42(2)** Before deciding whether to serve a notice of objection under this regulation in any case where–

(a) the person concerned is, or is a 50 per cent controller of, an investment firm which is for the time being authorised to act as such by the relevant supervisory authority in another EEA State; and

(b) the notice under regulation 41 above stated the intention to become a 50 per cent controller,

each relevant regulator shall consult the relevant supervisory authority in the investment firm's home State.

**42(3)** Before serving a notice of objection under this regulation, a relevant regulator shall serve the person concerned with a preliminary written notice stating that the regulator is considering the service on that person of a notice of objection; and that preliminary notice–

(a) shall specify the reasons why the regulator is not satisfied as mentioned in paragraph (1) above; and

(b) shall give particulars of the rights conferred by paragraph (4) below.

**42(4)** A person served with a notice under paragraph (3) above may, within the period of one month beginning with the day on which the notice is served, make written representations to the regulator who served the notice; and where such representations are made, that regulator shall take them into account in deciding whether to serve a notice of objection.

**42(5)** Where a person required to give notice under regulation 41 above in relation to his becoming a controller of any description becomes a controller of that description without having given notice as required by that regulation, any regulator to whom the person concerned failed to give notice may serve him with a notice of objection under this regulation at any time within three months after becoming aware of his having done so and may, for the purpose of deciding whether to serve him with such notice, require him by notice in writing to provide such information or documents as the regulator concerned may reasonably require.

**42(6)** The period mentioned in regulation 41(1)(b) above (with any extension under paragraph (4) of that regulation) and the period mentioned in paragraph (5) above shall not expire, if it would otherwise do so, until fourteen days after the end of the period within which representations can be made under paragraph (4) above.

**42(7)** Where the reasons stated in a notice of objection under this regulation relate specifically to matters which–

(a) refer to a person identified in the notice other than the person seeking to become a controller of the relevant description; and

(b) are in the opinion of the regulator serving the notice prejudicial to that person in relation to any office or employment,

the regulator concerned shall, unless it considers it impracticable to do so, serve a copy of the notice on that person.

**42(8)** A notice of objection under this regulation shall–

(a) specify the reasons why the regulator concerned is not satisfied as mentioned in paragraph (1) above; and

(b) given particulars of the right to require the matter to be referred to the Financial Services Tribunal under the provisions of section 97 of the Financial Services Act or, as the case may be, of any right that the person concerned may have to appeal against the notice under any rules or arrangements made by the regulator concerned.

**42(9)** Where a case is not required by the person on whom a notice of objection has been served to be referred to the Financial Services Tribunal or, as the case may be, an appeal is not made by him against the notice, the regulator concerned may give public notice that he has objected to that person becoming a controller of the relevant description and the reasons for the objection.

**42(10)** Section 97 of the Financial Services Act (references to the Tribunal) shall have effect as if any reference to a notice served under section 59(4) of that Act included a reference to a notice of objection served by the Board under this regulation in a case in which it is the relevant regulator by virtue of regulation 46(5)(b)(i) below.

**History**

In reg. 42(10) the words "in a case" to the end inserted by the Bank of England Act 1998, s. 23(1), 45 and Sch. 5, para. 45(1), (5) as from 1 June 1998 (see SI 1998/1120 (C 25), art. 2).

## CONTRAVENTIONS OF REGULATION 41

**43(1)** Subject to paragraph (2) below, any person who contravenes regulation 41 above by

(a) failing to give the notice required by sub-paragraph (a) of paragraph (1) of that regulation; or

(b) becoming a controller of any description to which that regulation applies before the end of the period mentioned in sub-paragraph (b) of that paragraph in a case in which no relevant regulator has served him with the preliminary notice under regulation 42(3) above,

shall be guilty of an offence.

**43(2)** A person shall not be guilty of an offence under paragraph (1) above if he shows that he did not know the acts or circumstances by virtue of which he became a controller of the relevant description; but where a person becomes a controller of any such description without such knowledge and subsequently becomes aware of the fact that he has become such a controller he shall be guilty of an offence unless he gives each relevant regulator written notice of the fact that he has become such a controller within fourteen days of becoming aware of that fact.

**43(3)** Any person who–

(a) before the end of the period mentioned in paragraph (1)(b) of regulation 41 above becomes a controller of any description to which that paragraph applies after being served with a preliminary notice under regulation 42(3) above;

(b) contravenes regulation 41 above by becoming a controller of any description after having been served with a notice of objection to his becoming a controller of that description; or

(c) having become a controller of any description in contravention of that regulation (whether before or after being served with such a notice of objection) continues to be such a controller after such a notice has been served on him,

shall be guilty of an offence.

**43(4)** A person guilty of an offence under paragraph (1) or (2) above shall be liable on summary conviction to a fine not exceeding level 5 on the standard scale.

**43(5)** A person guilty of an offence under paragraph (3) above shall be liable–

(a) on conviction on indictment, to imprisonment for a term not exceeding two years or to a fine or to both;

(b) on summary conviction, to a fine not exceeding level 5 on the standard scale and, in respect of an offence under sub-paragraph (c) of that paragraph, to a fine not exceeding £100 for each day on which the offence has continued.

## RESTRICTIONS ON VOTING RIGHTS

**44(1)** The powers conferred by this regulation shall be exercisable where a person–

(a) has contravened regulation 41 above by becoming a controller of any description after being served with a notice of objection to his becoming a controller of that description; or

(b) having become a controller of any description in contravention of that regulation continues to be one after such a notice has been served on him.

**44(2)** The Authority may, by notice in writing served on the person concerned direct that any specified shares to which this regulation applies shall, until further notice, be subject to the restriction that no voting rights shall be exercisable in respect of the shares.

**History**

In reg. 44(2) the words "The Authority" substituted for the former words " The Board or, in a case in which the person concerned is a controller of a UK authorised investment firm which is an exempted person by virtue of being admitted to the list maintained by the Bank for the purposes of section 43 of the Financial Services Act and is not an authorised person, the Bank," by the Bank of England Act 1998, s. 23(1), 45 and Sch. 5, para. 45(1), (6) as from 1 June 1998 (see SI 1998/1120 (C 25), art. 2).

**44(3)** This regulation applies–

(a) to all the shares in the firm of which the person in question is a controller of the relevant description which are held by him or any associate of his and which were not so held immediately before he became such a controller of the firm; and

(b) where the person in question became a controller of the relevant description of a firm as a result of the acquisition by him or any associate of his of shares in another company, to all the shares in that company which are held by him or any associate of his and which were not so held before he became such a controller of that firm.

**44(4)** A copy of any notice served on the person concerned under paragraph (2) above shall be served on the firm or company to whose shares it relates and, if it relates to shares held by an associate of that person, on that associate.

## PRIOR NOTIFICATION OF CEASING TO BE A RELEVANT CONTROLLER

**45(1)** A person shall not cease to be a minority, 10 per cent, 20 per cent, 33 per cent or 50 per cent controller of a UK authorised investment firm which is not a UK authorised institution unless he has first given to each relevant regulator written notice of his intention to cease to be such a controller of the firm.

**45(2)** If, after ceasing to be such a controller of such a firm, a person will, either alone or with any associate or associates–

(a) still hold 10 per cent or more of the shares in the firm or another person of whom it is a subsidiary undertaking;

(b) still be entitled to exercise or control the exercise of 10 per cent or more of the voting power at any general meeting of the firm or of another person of whom it is such an undertaking; or

(c) still be able to exercise a significant influence over the management of the firm or another person of whom it is such an undertaking by virtue of–

(i) a holding of shares in; or

(ii) an entitlement to exercise, or control the exercise of, the voting power at any general meeting of,

the firm or, as the case may be, the other person concerned,

his notice under paragraph (1) above shall state the percentage of the shares or voting power which he will (alone or with any associate or associates) hold or be entitled to exercise or control.

**45(3)** Subject to paragraph (4) below, any person who contravenes paragraph (1) or (2) above shall be guilty of an offence.

**45(4)** Subject to paragraph (5) below, a person shall not be guilty of an offence under paragraph (3) above if he shows that he did not know of the acts or circumstances by virtue of which he ceased to be a controller of the relevant description in sufficient time to enable him to comply with paragraph (1) above.

**45(5)** Notwithstanding anything in paragraph (4) above, a person who ceases to be a controller of a relevant description without having complied with paragraph (1) above shall be guilty of an offence if, within fourteen days of becoming aware of the fact that he has ceased to be such a controller–

(a) he fails to give each relevant regulator written notice of that fact; or

(b) he gives each relevant regulator such a notice but any such notice fails to comply with paragraph (2) above.

**45(6)** A person guilty of an offence under this regulation shall be liable on summary conviction to a fine not exceeding level 5 on the standard scale.

## CONSTRUCTION OF PART VII

**46(1)** In this Part of these Regulations–

(a) a **"minority controller"** means a controller not falling within sub-paragraph (a) or (b) of paragraph (2) below;

(b) a **"10 per cent controller"** means a controller in whose case the percentage referred to in the relevant paragraph is 10 or more but less than 20;

(c) a **"20 per cent controller"** means a controller in whose case the percentage referred to in the relevant paragraph is 20 or more but less than 33;

(d) a **"33 per cent controller"** means a controller in whose case the percentage referred to in the relevant paragraph is 33 or more but less than 50; and

(e) a **"50 per cent controller"** means a controller in whose case the percentage referred to in the relevant paragraph is 50 or more,

and for these purposes **"controller"** has the meaning given in paragraph (2) below and **"the relevant paragraph"**, in relation to a controller, means whichever one of sub-paragraph (a) or (b) of paragraph (2) below gives the greater percentage of his case.

**46(2)** A **"controller"**, in relation to an investment firm, means a person who, either alone or with any associate or associates–

(a) holds 10 per cent or more of the shares in the firm or another person of whom the firm is a subsidiary undertaking;

(b) is entitled to exercise, or control the exercise of, 10 per cent or more of the voting power at any general meeting of the firm or another person of whom the firm is such an undertaking; or

(c) is able to exercise a significant influence over the management of the firm or another person of whom the firm is such an undertaking by virtue of–

  (i) a holding of shares in; or

  (ii) an entitlement to exercise, or control the exercise of, the voting power at any general meeting of,

the firm or, as the case may be, the other person concerned.

**46(3)** In this Part of these Regulations **"associate"**, in relation to a person entitled to exercise or control the exercise of voting power in relation to, or holding shares in, an undertaking, means–

(a) the wife or husband or son or daughter of that person;

(b) the trustees of any settlement under which that person has a life interest in possession or, in Scotland, a life interest;

(c) any company of which that person is a director;

(d) any person who is an employee or partner of that person;

(e) if that person is a company–

  (i) any director of that company;

  (ii) any subsidiary undertaking of that company;

  (iii) any director or employee of any such subsidiary undertaking; and

(f) if that person has with any other person an agreement or arrangement with respect to the acquisition, holding or disposal of shares or other interests in that undertaking or body corporate or under which they undertake to act together in exercising their voting power in relation to it, that other person.

**46(4)** For the purposes of paragraph (3) above–

**"son"** includes stepson and **"daughter"** includes stepdaughter; and

**"settlement"** includes any disposition or arrangement under which property is held on trust.

**46(5)** References in this Part of these Regulations to a **"relevant regulator"**, in relation to an investment firm, are references to–

(a) any recognised self-regulating organisation to whose rules the firm is subject in providing core investment services;

(b) the Authority, in a case in which the firm in question–
  (i) is subject, in providing core services, to rules made by the Authority, or
  (ii) is not an authorised person and is an exempted person by virtue of being admitted to the list maintained for the purposes of section 43 of the Financial Services Act.

**History**

Reg. 46(5)(b) substituted for the former reg. 46(5)(b), (c) by the Bank of England Act 1998, s. 23(1), 45 and Sch. 5, para. 45(1), (7) as from 1 June 1998 (see SI 1998/1120 (C 25), art. 2). The former reg. 46(5)(b), (c) read as follows:

"(b) the Board, in a case in which the firm in question is subject, in providing core services, to rules made by the Board; and

(c) the Bank, in a case in which the firm in question is not an authorised person and is an exempted person by virtue of being admitted to the list maintained for the purposes of section 43 of the Financial Services Act."

**46(6)** References in this Part of these Regulations to **"voting rights"**, in relation to an undertaking, shall be construed in accordance with paragraph 2 of Schedule 10A to the Companies Act 1985 or paragraph 2 of Schedule 10A to the Companies (Northern Ireland) Order 1986.

**46(7)** Nothing in this Part of these Regulations shall require a person to give notice of his intention to become or to cease to be a controller of any description pursuant to an agreement entered into before the commencement date to acquire or dispose of a holding of shares or an entitlement to exercise or control the exercise of voting power.

### PROSECUTION OF OFFENCES UNDER PART VII

**47** Proceedings in respect of an offence under any provision of this Part of these Regulations shall not be instituted–

(a) in England and Wales, except by the Board or by or with the consent of the Secretary of State or the Director of Public Prosecutions; or

(b) in Northern Ireland, except by the Board or by or with the consent of the Secretary of State or the Director of Public Prosecutions for Northern Ireland.

## PART VIII – MISCELLANEOUS

### RESTRICTIONS ON DISCLOSURE OF INFORMATION

**48(1)** This paragraph applies to any confidential information which–

(a) any person who works or has worked for any person designated by the United Kingdom as a competent authority for the purposes of Article 22 of the Investment Services Directive or Article 9 of the Capital Adequacy Directive; or

(b) any auditor or expert instructed by such an authority,

has received in the course of discharging his duties as such a person, auditor or expert in relation to an investment firm having its head or registered office in an EEA State.

**48(2)** Section 179 of the Financial Services Act shall not apply to information to which paragraph (1) above applies.

**48(3)** Information to which paragraph (1) above applies shall not be disclosed by any person referred to in sub-paragraph (a) or (b) of that paragraph, or by any person receiving it directly or indirectly from such a person, except in any of the circumstances specified in Article 25 of the Investment Services Directive (as amended by the Prudential Supervision Directive), the text of which (as so amended) is set out in Schedule 8 to these Regulations; and for these purposes such information–

(a) may, subject to the provisions of paragraph (5) below, be disclosed in the circumstances described in Article 25.8 of the Investment Services Directive; and

(b) may, until 2nd July 1996, be disclosed in the circumstances described in Article 25.9 of that Directive.

**History**

In reg. 48(3) the words from "the Investment Services Directive" to "(as so amended)" substituted for the former words "the Investment Services Directive, the text of which" by the Financial Institutions (Prudential Supervision) Regulations 1996 (SI 1996/1669), reg. 1, 11(1) as from 18 July 1996.



bbcl randr5 Mp 4466—bcl98 225b

**48(4)** Information received under Article 25.2 of the Investment Services Directive may not be communicated in the circumstances referred to in Article 25.7 of that Directive without the express consent of the supervisory authority from whom it was obtained.

**48(5)** Information of the kind described in the third paragraph of Article 25.8 of the Investment Services Directive may not be disclosed in the cases referred to in Article 25.8 except with the express consent of whichever is relevant of the authorities mentioned in the third paragraph of Article 25.8.

**48(6)** Information which is obtained from the supervisory authorities of another EEA State may not be disclosed for any of the purposes mentioned in the first paragraph of Article 25.9 of the Investment Services Directive without the express consent of the authorities that disclosed the information; and such information may be used only for the purposes that caused those authorities to agree to disclose it.

**48(7)** Any person who contravenes any provision of this regulation shall be guilty of an offence and liable–

(a) on conviction on indictment, to imprisonment for a term not exceeding two years or to a fine or to both;

(b) on summary conviction, to imprisonment for a term not exceeding three months or to a fine not exceeding level 5 on the standard scale or to both.

**48(8)** Proceedings in respect of an offence under this Regulation shall not be instituted–

(a) in England and Wales, except by or with the consent of the Secretary of State or the Director of Public Prosecutions; or

(b) in Northern Ireland, except by or with the consent of the Secretary of State or the Director of Public Prosecutions for Northern Ireland.

**48(9)** In proceedings brought against any person for an offence under this regulation, it shall be a defence for him to prove that he took all reasonable precautions and exercised all due diligence to avoid the commission of the offence.

**48(10)** In this regulation **"the Prudential Supervision Directive"** has the same meaning as in the Financial Institutions (Prudential Supervision) Regulations 1996.

**History**

Reg. 48(10) inserted by the Financial Institutions (Prudential Supervision) Regulations 1996 (SI 1996/1669), reg. 1, 11(2) as from 18 July 1996.

## REGULATED MARKETS

**49(1)** The Board shall keep a list upon which it shall enter the name of each market of which the United Kingdom is the home State and which appears to the Board to satisfy the conditions set out in paragraph (2) below,

**49(2)** The conditions referred to in paragraph (1) above are that the market in question–

(a) is a market for instruments of a kind listed in section B of the Annex to the Investment Services Directive (the text of which is set out in Schedule 1 to these Regulations);

(b) functions regularly;

(c) is subject to rules made or approved by a UK regulatory authority that define–

  (i) the conditions for the operation of the market;

  (ii) the conditions for access to the market;

  (iii) where the Council Directive coordinating the conditions for the admission of securities to official stock exchange listing (No. 79/279/EEC) is applicable, the conditions governing admission to listing imposed in that directive; and

  (iv) where that directive is not applicable, the conditions that must be satisfied by an instrument before it can effectively be dealt in on the market; and

(d) has rules that give effect to the provisions of articles 20 and 21 of the Investment Services Directive.

**49(3)** If it appears to the Board that a market the name of which the Board has entered on the list kept by it by virtue of this regulation has ceased to comply with any of the conditions set out in paragraph (2) above, the Board shall forthwith remove the name of the market in question from the list.

**49(4)** In this Regulation–

(a) **"home State"**, in relation to a market, means the EEA State in which the registered office of the person providing trading facilities is situated or, if that person has no registered office, the EEA State in which his head office is situated; and

(b) **"UK regulatory authority"**, in relation to a regulated market, means an authority in the United Kingdom which has regulatory functions in relation to that market.

## POWER OF BOARD TO GIVE DIRECTIONS

**50(1)** If, on the application of a UK authorised investment firm other than a UK authorised institution, it appears to the Board that–

(a) compliance by that firm with any provision of any rules made by the Board under section 49 of the Financial Services Act (financial resources rules) is, on any particular occasion, not required by any provisions of the Capital Adequacy Directive; and

(b) the Board may, consistently with the provisions of that Directive, exempt the firm from complying with the relevant provision,

it may direct that the firm need not, on the occasion in question, comply with such requirements as it may specify in writing.

**50(2)** The power conferred by paragraph (1) above may be exercised unconditionally or subject to conditions.

**50(3)** If it appears to the Board that, having regard to any change in the circumstances of a UK authorised investment firm other than a UK authorised institution since the end of the period for which the firm last prepared annual accounts, the firm requires financial resources additional to those which it is required to maintain by virtue of rules made under section 49 of the Financial Services Act that give effect to the provisions of Annex IV to the Capital Adequacy Directive, it may direct the firm to increase the amount of its financial resources so that they are equivalent to such proportion of its fixed overheads for the twelve months preceding the date of the direction as the Board considers appropriate.

**50(4)** Any failure by a firm to comply with any condition imposed under paragraph (2) above or with any direction given under paragraph (3) above shall be treated as a failure by the firm to comply with an obligation imposed on it under the Financial Services Act or, in the case of a firm which is a member of a recognised self-regulating organisation, with the rules of that organisation.

## BOARD'S POWER TO OBTAIN INFORMATION FROM GROUP MEMBERS

**51(1)** Subject to paragraph (2) below, the Board may require a UK authorised investment firm (other than a UK authorised institution) which is a member of a group to supply it, or, in a case in which the requirement is imposed at the request of a recognised self-regulating organisation, the organisation concerned, with such information as the Board may reasonably require in order to assess, or enable the assessment of, the adequacy of the financial resources available to a group of which the firm concerned is a member.

**51(2)** The powers conferred by this regulation shall not be exercisable in relation to an investment firm which is a member of a recognised self-regulating organisation and is subject to the rules of such an organisation in carrying on all the investment business carried on by it unless such an organisation has requested the exercise of the powers.

**51(3)** If it appears to the Board to be necessary to do so for the purpose of assessing, or enabling the assessment of, the adequacy of the financial resources available to a group which includes amongst its members a UK authorised investment firm which is not a UK authorised institution, it may also exercise the powers conferred by paragraph (1) above in relation to any of the persons mentioned in paragraph (4) below.

**51(4)** The persons referred to in paragraph (3) above are any person who is or has at any relevant time been–

(a) a partnership of which the investment firm in question is or was a member;

(b) a parent undertaking, subsidiary undertaking or related company of that firm;

(c) a subsidiary undertaking of a parent undertaking of that firm;

(d) a parent undertaking of a subsidiary undertaking of that firm; or

(e) any undertaking which is a 50 per cent controller of that firm.

**51(5)** The Board may exercise the powers conferred by this regulation at the request of the relevant supervisory authority in the home State of a European investment firm for the purpose of assisting that authority to assess the adequacy of the financial resources available to a group of which the firm is a member or to enable such an assessment to be made.

**51(6)** In this Regulation, **"related company"** means any body corporate in which a member of a group of which an investment firm is a member has a qualifying interest; and for these purposes what constitutes a qualifying interest shall be determined in accordance with sub-paragraphs (2) to (4) of paragraph 30 of Schedule 1 to the Financial Services Act.

## POWERS OF ENTRY

**52** Any officer, servant or agent of the Board may, on producing (if required to do so) evidence of his authority, enter upon any premises occupied by a person on whom a requirement has been imposed under regulation 51 above for any of the following purposes–

(a) obtaining any information that the person has been required to give under that regulation;

(b) verifying the accuracy of any information that the person has given in pursuance of such a requirement;

(c) verifying that the person is able to give any information that he may reasonably be required to give under that regulation.

## CONTRAVENTION OF REGULATION 51 OR 52

**53(1)** Any authorised person who fails to comply with a requirement imposed on it under regulation 51 above or who intentionally obstructs a person exercising rights conferred by regulation 52 above shall be treated as having failed to comply with a requirement imposed on it under the Financial Services Act, or, in the case of a person who is a member of a recognised self-regulating organisation, the rules of that organisation.

**53(2)** Any person, other than an authorised person, who, without reasonable excuse, fails to comply with a requirement imposed on him under regulation 51 above or intentionally obstructs a person exercising rights under regulation 52 above shall be guilty of an offence and liable on summary conviction to imprisonment for a term not exceeding three months or to a fine not exceeding level 5 on the standard scale or to both.

**53(3)** Proceedings in respect of an offence under this regulation shall not be instituted–

(a) in England and Wales, except by the Board or by or with the consent of the Secretary of State or the Director of Public Prosecutions; or

(b) in Northern Ireland, except by the Board or by or with the consent of the Secretary of State or the Director of Public Prosecutions for Northern Ireland.

## DIRECTIONS TO THE BANK

**54(1)** If it appears to the Treasury–

(a) that any action proposed to be taken by the Authority would be incompatible with the provisions of the Investment Services Directive or the Capital Adequacy Directive; or

(b) that any action which the Authority has power to take is required for the purpose of implementing any provision of those Directives, they may direct the Authority not to take or, as the case may be, to take the action in question.

**History**

In reg. 54(1) the word "Authority" wherever occurring substituted for the former word "Bank" by the Bank of England Act 1998, s. 23(1), 45 and Sch. 5, para. 45(1), (8) as from 1 June 1998 (see SI 1998/1120 (C 25), art. 2).

[**Note:** The heading to reg. 54 not amended by the Bank of England Act 1998, Sch. 5, para. 45(8). It is submitted that the heading should read "DIRECTIONS TO THE AUTHORITY".]

**54(2)** A direction under this regulation may contain such supplementary or incidental requirements as the Treasury think necessary or expedient.

**54(3)** A direction under this regulation is enforceable by injunction or, in Scotland, by an order under section 45 of the Courts of Session Act 1988.

### POSITION OF EUROPEAN SUBSIDIARIES

**55** The provisions of Schedule 9 to these Regulations (which makes provision with respect to certain European subsidiaries) shall have effect.

## PART IX – SUPPLEMENTAL

### THE BOARD'S FUNCTIONS UNDER THE REGULATIONS

**56(1)** The functions of the Board under these Regulations, except its function of instituting proceedings, shall be treated for the purposes of the Financial Services Act and the Transfer of Functions (Financial Services) Order 1992 as if they were functions under Chapter VI of Part I of that Act which–

(a) had been functions of the Secretary of State; and

(b) had been transferred to the Board by the Financial Services Act 1986 (Delegation) Order 1987.

**56(2)** The function of the Board of instituting proceedings under these Regulations shall be treated for the purposes of the Financial Services Act and the Transfer of Functions (Financial Services) Order 1992 as if it were a function to which section 114 of the Financial Services Act applies by virtue of the provisions of section 201(4) of that Act which had been transferred to the Board by the Financial Services Act 1986 (Delegation) Order 1987 so as to be exercisable concurrently with the Secretary of State.

**56(3)** Paragraph (1) above does not have effect in relation to –

(a) any function acquired by virtue of the Bank of England Act 1998, or

(b) so much of any function as is exercisable by virtue of that Act.

**History**

Reg. 56(3) inserted by the Bank of England Act 1998, s. 23(1), 45 and Sch. 5, para. 45(1), (9) as from 1 June 1998 (see SI 1998/1120 (C 25), art. 2).

### MINOR AND CONSEQUENTIAL AMENDMENTS

**57(1)** The provisions mentioned in Schedule 10 to these Regulations shall have effect subject to the amendments there specified, being minor amendments or amendments consequential on the provisions of these Regulations.

**57(2)** Any deed, contract or other instrument made before the commencement date shall have effect, unless the context otherwise requires, as if any reference to a person authorised under the Financial Services Act (however expressed) included a reference to a European investment firm.

### TRANSITIONAL PROVISIONS AND SAVINGS

**58** Schedule 11 to these Regulations shall have effect with respect to the transitional and other matters there mentioned.

# Schedule 1 – Annex to the Investment Services Directive

Regulation 2(1)

"ANNEX – SECTION A

*Services*

**1(a)** Reception and transmission, on behalf of investors, of orders in relation to oneor more of the instruments listed in section B.

**1(b)** Execution of such orders other than for own account.

**2** Dealing in any of the instruments listed in Section B for own account.

**3** Managing portfolios of investments in accordance with mandates given by investors on a discretionary, client-by-client basis where such portfolios include oneor more of the instruments listed in section B.

**4** Underwriting in respect of issues of any of the instruments listed in section B and/or the placing of such issues.

SECTION B

*Instruments*

**1(a)** Transferable securities.

**1(b)** Units in collective investment undertakings.

**2** Money market instruments.

**3** Financial-futures contracts, including equivalent cash-settled instruments.

**4** Forward interest-rate agreements (FRAs).

**5** Interest-rate, currency and equity swaps.

**6** Options to acquire or dispose of any instruments falling within this section of the Annex, including equivalent cash-settled instruments. This category includes in particular options on currency and on interest rates.

SECTION C

*Non-core services*

**1** Safekeeping and administration in relation to one or more of the instruments listed in Section B.

**2** Safe custody services.

**3** Granting credits or loans to an investor to allow him to carry out a transaction in one or more of the instruments listed in Section B, where the firm granting the credit or loan is involved in the transaction.

**4** Advice to undertakings on capital structure, industrial strategy and related matters and advice and service relating to mergers and the purchase of undertakings.

**5** Services related to underwriting.

**6** Investment advice concerning one or more of the instruments listed in Section B.

**7** Foreign-exchange service where these are connected with the provision of investment services."

# Schedule 2 – Article 2.2 of the Investment Services Directive

Regulation 2(3)

"This Directive shall not apply to:

(a) insurance undertakings as defined in article 1 of Directive 73/239/EEC or article 1 of Directive 79/267/EEC or undertakings carrying on the reinsurance and retrocession activities referred to in Directive 64EEC;

(b) firms which provide investment services exclusively for their parent undertakings, for their subsidiaries or for other subsidiaries of their parent undertakings;

(c) persons providing an investment service where that service is provided in an incidental manner in the course of a professional activity and that activity is regulated by legal or regulatory provisions or a code of ethics governing the profession which do not exclude the provision of that service;

(d) firms that provide investment services consisting exclusively in the administration of employee-participation schemes;

(e) firms that provide investment services that consist in providing both the services referred to in (b) and those referred to in (d);

(f) the central banks of Member States and other national bodies performing similar functions and other public bodies charged with or intervening in the management of the public debt;

(g) firms

– which may not hold clients' funds or securities and which for that reason may not at any time place themselves in debit with their clients, and

– which may not provide any investment service except the reception and transmission of orders in transferable securities and units in collective investment undertakings, and

– which in the course of providing that service may transmit orders only to

(i) investment firms authorised in accordance with this Directive;

(ii) credit institutions authorised in accordance with Directives 77/780/EEC and 89/646/EEC;

(iii) branches of investment firms or of credit institutions which are authorized in a third country and which are subject to and comply with prudential rules considered by the competent authorities as at least as stringent as those laid down in this Directive, in Directive 89/646/EEC or in Directive 93/6/EEC;

(iv) collective investment undertakings authorized under the law of a Member State to market units to the public and to the managers of such undertakings;

(v) investment companies with fixed capital, as defined in article 15(4) of Directive 79/91/EEC, the securities of which are listed or dealt in on a regulated market in a Member State;

– the activities of which are governed at national level by rules or by a code of ethics;

(h) collective investment undertakings whether coordinated at Community level or not and the depositaries and managers of such undertakings;

(i) persons whose main business is trading in commodities amongst themselves or with producers or professional users of such products and who provide investment services only for such producers and professional users to the extent necessary for their main business;

(j) firms that provide investment services consisting exclusively in dealing for their own account on financial-futures or options markets or which deal for the accounts of other members of those markets or make prices for them and which are guaranteed by clearing members of the same markets. Responsibility for ensuring the performance of contracts entered into by such firms must be assumed by clearing members of the same markets;

(k) associations set up by Danish funds with the sole aim of managing the assets of pension funds that are members of those associations;

(l) "agenti di cambio" whose activities and functions are governed by Italian Royal Decree No. 222 of 7 March 1925 and subsequent provisions amending it, and who are authorized to carry on their activities under article 19 of Italian Law No. 1 of 2 January 1991."

# Schedule 3 – Requirements as Respects European Investment Firms

Regulation 3(3)

## REQUIREMENTS FOR PROVIDING SERVICES ETC.

**1(1)** In relation to the provision by the provision of services of any listed service, the requirements of this paragraph are–

(a) that the firm has given to the relevant supervisory authority in its home State a notice in accordance with paragraph 2 below; and

(b) that the Board has received from that authority a notice in accordance with paragraph 3 below.

**History**

In para. 1(1)(b) the former words ", or, in the case of a listed firm, the Bank,", appearing after the words "that the Board" revoked by the Bank of England Act 1998, s. 43, 45 and Sch. 9, Pt. II as from 1 June 1998 (see SI 1998/1120 (C 25), art. 2).

**1(2)** In relation to the establishment of a branch, the requirements of this paragraph are–

(a) that the firm has given to the relevant supervisory authority in its home State a notice in accordance with paragraph 2 below;

(b) that the Board has received from that authority a notice in accordance with paragraph 3 below; and

(c) that either–

(i) the Board has informed the firm that it may establish the branch; or

(ii) the period of two months beginning with the day on which the Board received the notice mentioned in paragraph (b) above has elapsed.

**History**

In para. 1(2)(b) the former words ", or, in the case of a listed firm, the Bank,", appearing after the words "that the Board" revoked by the Bank of England Act 1998, s. 43, 45 and Sch. 9, Pt. II as from 1 June 1998 (see SI 1998/1120 (C 25), art. 2).
In para. 1(2)(c) the former words "or, as the case may be, the Bank", appearing after the words "the Board" in both places revoked by the Bank of England Act 1998, s. 43, 45 and Sch. 9, Pt. II as from 1 June 1998 (see SI 1998/1120 (C 25), art. 2).

**2** A notice given by a firm to the relevant supervisory authority in its home State is given in accordance with this paragraph if it states–

(a) the United Kingdom to be an EEA State in which the firm proposes to provide listed services;

(b) whether the firm intends to establish a branch in the United Kingdom; and

(c) the requisite details.

**3(1)** A notice given in respect of a European investment firm or quasi-European investment firm by the relevant supervisory authority in its home State is in accordance with this paragraph if it–

(a) certifies that the firm is an investment firm which is for the time being authorised to act as such a firm by the authority;

(b) contains the information stated in the firm's notice; and

(c) if the firm intends to establish a branch in the United Kingdom, contains details of any compensation scheme which is intended to protect the branch's investors.

**3(2)** The Board shall as soon as practicable send a copy of any notice received by it in accordance with this paragraph, and a note of the date of its receipt, to every other authority which it knows is a connected UK authority.

**History**

In para. 3(2) the former words "or, as the case may be, the Bank", appearing after the words "The Board" revoked by the Bank of England Act 1998, s. 43, 45 and Sch. 9, Pt. II as from 1 June 1998 (see SI 1998/1120 (C 25), art. 2).

## REQUIREMENTS FOR CHANGING REQUISITE DETAILS WHERE SERVICES ARE PROVIDED

**4(1)** Subject to sub-paragraph (2) below, the requirements of this paragraph are that the firm has given a notice to the Board and to the relevant supervisory authority in its home State, stating the details of the proposed change.

**History**

In para. 4(1) the former words ", or, in the case of a listed firm, to the Bank,", appearing after the words "the Board" revoked by the Bank of England Act 1998, s. 43, 45 and Sch. 9, Pt. II as from 1 June 1998 (see SI 1998/1120 (C 25), art. 2).

**4(2)** In the case of a change occasioned by circumstances beyond the firm's control, the requirements of this paragraph are that the firm has, as soon as practicable (whether before or after the change), given a notice to the Board, and to the relevant supervisory authority in its home State, stating the details of the change.

**History**

In para. 4(2) the former words "or, as the case may be to the Bank,", appearing after the words "the Board" revoked by the Bank of England Act 1998, s. 43, 45 and Sch. 9, Pt. II as from 1 June 1998 (see SI 1998/1120 (C 25), art. 2).

**4(3)** The Board shall as soon as practicable send a copy of any notice received by it in accordance with this paragraph, and a note of the date of its receipt, to every other authority which it knows is a connected UK authority.

**History**
In para. 4(3) the former words "or, as the case may be, the Bank", appearing after the words "The Board" revoked by the Bank of England Act 1998, s. 43, 45 and Sch. 9, Pt. II as from 1 June 1998 (see SI 1998/1120 (C 25), art. 2).

## REQUIREMENTS FOR CHANGING REQUISITE DETAILS OF BRANCH

**5(1)** Subject to sub-paragraph (2) below, the requirements of this paragraph are–

(a) that the firm has given a notice to the Board and to the relevant supervisory authority in its home State, stating the details of the proposed change;

(b) that the Board has received from that authority a notice stating those details; and

(c) that either the Board has informed the firm that it may make the change, or the period of one month beginning with the day on which it gave the Board the notice mentioned in paragraph (a) above has elapsed.

**History**
In para. 5(1)(a) the former words "or, in the case of a listed firm, to the Bank,", appearing after the words "the Board" revoked by the Bank of England Act 1998, s. 43, 45 and Sch. 9, Pt. II as from 1 June 1998 (see SI 1998/1120 (C 25), art. 2).
In para. 5(1)(b) and (c) the former words "or, as the case may be, the Bank", wherever appearing after the words "the Board" revoked by the Bank of England Act 1998, s. 43, 45 and Sch. 9, Pt. II as from 1 June 1998 (see SI 1998/1120 (C 25), art. 2).

**5(2)** In the case of a change occasioned by circumstances beyond the firm's control, the requirements of this paragraph are that the firm has, as soon as practicable (whether before or after the change), given a notice to the Board, and to the relevant supervisory authority in its home State, stating the details of the change.

**History**
In para. 5(2) the former words "or, as the case may be, to the Bank", appearing after the words "the Board" revoked by the Bank of England Act 1998, s. 43, 45 and Sch. 9, Pt. II as from 1 June 1998 (see SI 1998/1120 (C 25), art. 2).

**5(3)** The Board shall as soon as practicable send a copy of any notice received by it in accordance with this paragraph, and a note of the date of its receipt, to every other authority which it knows is a connected UK authority.

**History**
In para. 5(3) the former words "or, as the case may be, the Bank", appearing after the words "The Board" revoked by the Bank of England Act 1998, s. 43, 45 and Sch. 9, Pt. II as from 1 June 1998 (see SI 1998/1120 (C 25), art. 2).

## MEANING OF "LISTED FIRM"

**6** (Revoked by the Bank of England Act 1998, s. 43, 45 and Sch. 9, Pt. II as from 1 June 1998).

**History**
In regard to the date of the above revocation, see SI 1998/1120 (C 25), art. 2. Para. 6 formerly read as follows:
"**(6)** In this Schedule, references to a **"listed firm"** are references to a European investment firm which is admitted, or is seeking admission, to the list maintained by the Bank for the purposes of section 43 of the Financial Services Act and is not carrying on, or proposing to carry on home-regulated investment business in the United Kingdom otherwise than by means of transactions or arrangements to which Schedule 5 to that Act applies."

# Schedule 4 – Prohibitions by the Board

Regulation 9(5)

## NOTICE OF PROHIBITION

**1(1)** Where the Board proposes–

(a) to impose a prohibition on a European investment firm under regulation 9 of these Regulations; or

(b) to refuse an application made by a European investment firm under paragraph (3) of that regulation,

it shall give the firm on which it proposes to impose the prohibition, or whose application it proposes to refuse, written notice of its intention to do so, stating the reasons for which it proposes to act.

**1(2)** In the case of a proposed prohibition the notice shall state the date on which it is proposed that the prohibition should take effect and, in the case of a limited prohibition, its proposed duration.

**1(3)** Where the reasons stated in a notice under this paragraph relate specifically to matters which–

(a) refer to a person identified in the notice other than the firm concerned; and

(b) are in the opinion of the Board prejudicial to that person in relation to any office or employment,

the Board shall, unless it considers it impracticable to do so, serve a copy of the notice on that person.

**1(4)** A notice under this paragraph shall give particulars of the right to require the case to be referred to the Financial Services Tribunal under section 97 of the Financial Services Act.

**1(5)** Where a case is not required to be referred to that Tribunal by a person on whom a notice is served under this paragraph, the Board shall, at the expiration of the period within which such a requirement can be made–

(a) give that person written notice of the prohibition or refusal; or

(b) give that person written notice that the prohibition is not to be imposed or, as the case may be, written notice of the grant of the application;

and the Board may give public notice of any decision notified by it under paragraph (a) or (b) above and the reasons for the decision, except that it shall not do so in the case of a decision notified under paragraph (b) unless the person concerned consents to its doing so.

**1(6)** Where the Board gives a notice under sub-paragraph (1) or (5)(a) or (b) above, it shall serve a copy of the notice on the relevant supervisory authority in the firm's home State.

## REFERENCES TO THE FINANCIAL SERVICES TRIBUNAL

**2** Section 97 of the Financial Services Act (references to the Tribunal) shall have effect as if–

(a) any reference to a notice served under section 29 of that Act included a reference to a notice served under paragraph 1 above;

(b) any reference to a copy of a notice served under that section included a reference to a copy of a notice served under sub-paragraph (3) of that paragraph;

(c) any reference to the withdrawal of an authorisation included a reference to the imposition of an absolute prohibition under regulation 9 of these Regulations; and

(d) any reference to the suspension of an authorisation included a reference to the imposition of a limited prohibition under regulation 9 of these Regulations;

and any reference in that section to a decision not to withdraw or suspend an authorisation shall be construed accordingly.

**3(1)** Section 98 of the Financial Services Act (decisions on references by applicant or authorised person etc.) shall have effect as if–

(a) the applications mentioned in paragraph (a) of subsection (2) included an application for the variation of a limited prohibition imposed under regulation 9 of these Regulations; but

(b) the applications mentioned in paragraph (b) of that subsection did not include an application for the rescission of any prohibition imposed under that regulation.

**3(2)** Subsection (3)(b) of that section shall have effect as if the provisions there referred to included regulation 9 of these Regulations.

**3(3)** That section shall have effect as if it included provision that paragraph 1 above shall not apply to any action taken by the Board in accordance with the Tribunal's report.

**4(1)** Section 100(2) of the Financial Services Act (withdrawal of references) shall have effect as if the reference to the provisions mentioned in section 97(1)(a) of that Act included a reference to paragraph 1 above.

**4(2)** Section 100 of the Financial Services Act shall also have effect as if it included provision that where a person on whom a notice was served under paragraph 1 above withdraws a case from the Tribunal, sub-paragraph (5) of that paragraph shall apply to him as if he had not required the case to be referred.

# Schedule 5 – Prohibitions and Restrictions by the Director

Regulation 15(6)

## PRELIMINARY

**1** In this Schedule–

**"appeal period"** has the same meaning as in the Consumer Credit Act;
**"prohibition"** means a prohibition under regulation 15 of these Regulations;
**"restriction"** means a restriction under regulation 16 of these Regulations.

## NOTICE OF PROHIBITION OR RESTRICTION

**2(1)** This paragraph applies where the Director proposes, in relation to a European investment firm–

(a) to impose a prohibition;

(b) to impose a restriction; or

(c) to vary a restriction otherwise than with the agreement of the firm.

**2(2)** The Director shall, by notice–

(a) inform the firm that, as the case may be, the Director proposes to impose the prohibition or restriction or vary the restriction, stating his reasons; and

(b) invite the firm to submit representation as to the proposal in accordance with paragraph 4 below.

**2(3)** If he imposes the prohibition or restriction or varies the restriction, the Director may give directions authorising the firm to carry into effect agreements made before the coming into force of the prohibition, restriction or variation.

**2(4)** A prohibition, restriction or variation shall not come into force before the end of the appeal period.

**2(5)** Where the Director imposes a prohibition or restriction or varies a restriction, he shall serve a copy of the prohibition, restriction or variation–

(a) on the Board; and

(b) on the relevant supervisory authority in the firm's home State.

## APPLICATION TO REVOKE PROHIBITION OR RESTRICTION

**3(1)** This paragraph applies where the Director proposes to refuse an application made by a European investment firm for the revocation of a prohibition or restriction.

**3(2)** The Director shall, by notice–

(a) inform the firm that the Director proposes to refuse the application, stating his reasons; and

(b) invite the firm to submit representations in support of the application in accordance with paragraph 4 below.

## REPRESENTATIONS TO DIRECTOR

**4(1)** Where this paragraph applies to an invitation by the Director to a firm to submit representations, the Director shall invite the firm, within 21 days after the notice containing the invitation is given to it, or such longer period as the Director may allow–

(a) to submit its representations in writing to the Director; and

(b) to give notice to the Director, if it thinks fit, that it wishes to make representations orally;

and where notice is given under paragraph (b) above the Director shall arrange for the oral representations to be heard.

4(2) In reaching his determination the Director shall take into account any representations submitted or made under this paragraph.

4(3) The Director shall give notice of his determination to the firm.

APPEALS

5 Section 41 of the Consumer Credit Act (appeals to the Secretary of State) shall have effect as if–

(a) the following determinations were mentioned in column 1 of the table set out at the end of that section, namely–
   (i) imposition of a prohibition or restriction or the variation of a restriction; and
   (ii) refusal of an application for the revocation of a prohibition or restriction; and

(b) the European investment firm concerned were mentioned in column 2 of that table in relation to those determinations.

# Schedule 6 – Requirements as Respects UK Authorised Investment Firms

Regulation 20

REQUIREMENTS FOR PROVIDING LISTED SERVICES ETC.

1(1) In relation to the provision by the provision of services of any listed service, the requirements of this paragraph are that the firm has given to the Board a notice in accordance with paragraph 2 below.

**History**

In para. 6(1) the former words ", or, in the case of a listed person, to the Bank,", appearing after the words "the Board" revoked by the Bank of England Act 1998, s. 43, 45 and Sch. 9, Pt. II as from 1 June 1998 (see SI 1998/1120 (C 25), art. 2).

1(2) In relation to the establishment of a branch, the requirements of this paragraph are–

(a) that the firm has given to the Board a notice in accordance with paragraph 2 below;

(b) that the Board has given to the relevant supervisory authority in the EEA State concerned the notice which, subject to paragraph 4(2) below, it is required by paragraph 3 below to give; and

(c) that either–
   (i) the relevant supervisory authority has informed the firm that it may establish the branch; or
   (ii) the period of two months beginning with the day on which the Board gave the relevant supervisory authority the notice mentioned in paragraph (b) above has elapsed.

**History**

In para. 1(2)(a) the former words ", or, in the case of a listed firm, to the Bank,", appearing after the words "the Board" revoked by the Bank of England Act 1998, s. 43, 45 and Sch. 9, Pt. II as from 1 June 1998 (see SI 1998/1120 (C 25), art. 2).
In para. 1(2)(b) and (c)(ii) the former words "or, as the case may be, the Bank", appearing after the words "the Board" revoked by the Bank of England Act 1998, s. 43, 45 and Sch. 9, Pt. II as from 1 June 1998 (see SI 1998/1120 (C 25), art. 2).

2 A notice given by a firm to the Board is given in accordance with this paragraph if it states–

(a) the EEA State in which the firm proposes to carry on listed services;

(b) whether the firm intends to establish a branch in that EEA State; and

(c) in either case, the requisite details.

**History**

In para. 2 the former words "or, as the case may be, to the Bank,", appearing after the words "the Board" revoked by the Bank of England Act 1998, s. 43, 45 and Sch. 9, Pt. II as from 1 June 1998 (see SI 1998/1120 (C 25), art. 2).

3 The notice which, subject to paragraph 4(2) below, the Board is required to give in respect of a UK authorised investment firm is a notice which is addressed to the relevant supervisory authority in the EEA State identified in the firm's notice under paragraph 2 above and which–

(a) certifies that the firm is an authorised person, or, as the case may be, an exempted person, under the Financial Services Act;

(b) contains the information stated in the firm's notice; and

(c) if the firm intends to establish a branch in the EEA State, contains details of any compensation scheme which is intended to protect the branch's investors.

**History**
In para. 3 the former words "or, as the case may be, the Bank,", appearing after the words "the Board" revoked by the Bank of England Act 1998, s. 43, 45 and Sch. 9, Pt. II as from 1 June 1998 (see SI 1998/1120 (C 25), art. 2).

**4(1)** Where the firm's notice under paragraph 2 above states that the firm does not intend to establish a branch in the EEA State, the notice referred to in paragraph 3 above shall be given within the period of one month beginning with the date on which the firm's notice was received by the Board.

**History**
In para. 4(1) the former words "or, as the case may be, the Bank", appearing after the words "the Board" revoked by the Bank of England Act 1998, s. 43, 45 and Sch. 9, Pt. II as from 1 June 1998 (see SI 1998/1120 (C 25), art. 2).

**4(2)** Where the firm's notice under paragraph 2 above states that the firm intends to establish a branch in the EEA State, the Board shall, within the period of three months beginning with the date on which the firm's notice was received–

(a) give the notice referred to in paragraph 3 above; or

(b) refuse to give such a notice.

**History**
In para. 4(2) the former words "or, as the case may be, the Bank", appearing after the words "the Board" revoked by the Bank of England Act 1998, s. 43, 45 and Sch. 9, Pt. II as from 1 June 1998 (see SI 1998/1120 (C 25), art. 2).

**4(3)** The Board or, as the case may be, the Bank may not refuse to give such a notice unless, having regard to the listed services proposed to be provided, the Board doubts the adequacy of the administrative structure or the financial situation of the firm.

**History**
In para. 4(3) the former words "or, as the case may be, the Bank", appearing after the words "the Board" revoked by the Bank of England Act 1998, s. 43, 45 and Sch. 9, Pt. II as from 1 June 1998 (see SI 1998/1120 (C 25), art. 2).

**4(4)** Before determining to give or to refuse to give such a notice, the Board –

(a) shall seek and take into account the views of every other authority which it knows is a connected UK authority in relation to any of the listed services proposed to be provided; and

(b) may regard itself as satisfied in relation to any matter relating to those services which is relevant to the decision if any such authority informs the Board that it is so satisfied.

**History**
In para. 4(4) and 4(4)(b) the former words "or, as the case may be, the Bank", appearing after the words "the Board" revoked by the Bank of England Act 1998, s. 43, 45 and Sch. 9, Pt. II as from 1 June 1998 (see SI 1998/1120 (C 25), art. 2).

**4(5)** In reaching a determination as to the adequacy of the administrative structure, the Board may have regard to the adequacy of management, systems and controls and the presence of relevant skills needed for the services proposed to be provided.

**History**
In para. 4(5) the former words "or, as the case may be, the Bank", appearing after the words "the Board" revoked by the Bank of England Act 1998, s. 43, 45 and Sch. 9, Pt. II as from 1 June 1998 (see SI 1998/1120 (C 25), art. 2).

**4(6)** Where the firm's notice under paragraph 2 above states that the firm proposes to establish a branch, the Board , shall, within the period of three months referred to in sub-paragraph (2) above, notify the firm–

(a) that it has given the notice referred to in paragraph 3 above, stating the date on which it did so; or

(b) that it has refused to give the notice, stating the reasons for the refusal and giving particulars of the right to refer the case to the Financial Services Tribunal under section 97 of the Financial Services Act or, as the case may be, of any relevant arrangements made by it for a review of its decision.

**History**
In para. 4(6) the former words "or, as the case may be, the Bank", appearing after the words "the Board" revoked by the Bank of England Act 1998, s. 43, 45 and Sch. 9, Pt. II as from 1 June 1998 (see SI 1998/1120 (C 25), art. 2).

In para. 4(6)(b) the word "it" substituted for the former words "the Bank" by the Bank of England Act 1998, s. 23(1), 45 and Sch. 5, para. 45(1), (10) as from 1 June 1998 (see SI 1998/1120 (C 25), art. 2).

## RESTRICTION ON CARRYING ON BUSINESS

**2** Section 5 of the Act (agreements made by or through unauthorised persons) shall have effect as if the persons mentioned in subsection (1)(b)(i) included a European investment firm acting in the course of home-regulated investment business carried on by it in the United Kingdom.

## AUTHORISED PERSONS

**3** Section 10 of the Act (grant and refusal of recognition of self-regulating organisations) shall have effect as if the excepted cases mentioned in subsection (3) included the case where the member is a European investment firm and the business is home-regulated investment business.

**4** Section 13 of the Act (alteration of rules of recognised self-regulating organisation for protection of investors) shall have effect as if the excepted cases mentioned in subsection (2) (both as amended and as originally enacted) included the case where the member is a European investment firm and the business is home-regulated investment business.

**5** Section 28 of the Act (withdrawal and suspension of authorisation) shall have effect in relation to an authorisation granted to a European investment firm as if the reference in subsection (1)(a) to the investment business which the holder of the authorisation is carrying on or proposing to carry on did not include a reference to any home-regulated investment business.

**6** Section 32 of the Act (notice of commencement of business) shall have effect in relation to a notice given under subsection (1) by a European investment firm or quasi-European investment firm as if the reference in subsection (2)(a) to the investment business which is proposed to be carried on did not include a reference to any home-regulated investment business.

## EXEMPTED PERSONS

**7** Section 44 of the Act (appointed representatives) shall have effect as if any reference to an authorised person included a reference to a European investment firm carrying on home-regulated investment business in the United Kingdom.

**8** Section 45 of the Act (miscellaneous exemptions) shall have effect as if the reference in subsection (2) to a partnership which is an authorised person included a reference to a partnership which is or was a European investment firm carrying on home-regulated investment business in the United Kingdom.

## CONDUCT OF BUSINESS

**9(1)** Section 47A of the Act (statements of principle) shall have effect as if–

(a) the reference in subsection (1) to the conduct expected of persons authorised to carry on investment business included a reference to the conduct expected of European investment firms carrying on home-regulated investment business in the United Kingdom; and

(b) the reference in subsection (4) to the withdrawal or suspension of authorisation under section 28 of the Act included a reference to the imposition of a prohibition under regulation 9 of these Regulations.

**9(2)** That section shall also have effect as if it included provision that a statement of principle issued under that section shall not include, as respects any European investment firm–

(a) provision as to the fitness of the firm to carry on any home-regulated investment business; or

(b) provision as to any other matter for which, under the Investment Services Directive, responsibility is reserved to the relevant supervisory authority in the firm's home State.

**10(1)** Section 48 of the Act (conduct of business rules) shall have effect as if–

(a) the reference in subsection (1) to the conduct of investment business by authorised persons included a reference to the conduct of home-regulated investment business carried on in the United Kingdom by European investment firms; and

(b) the reference in subsection (2) to an authorised person included a reference to a European investment firm carrying on home-regulated investment business in the United Kingdom.

**10(2)** That section shall have effect as if it included provision that rules under that section shall not include, as respects any European investment firm–

(a) provision prohibiting the firm from carrying on, or holding itself out as carrying on, any home-regulated investment business; or

(b) provision as to any matter for which, under the Investment Services Directive, responsibility is reserved to the relevant supervisory authority in the firm's home State.

**11(1)** Section 49 of the Act (financial resources rules) shall have effect as if it included provision that rules under that section shall not include, as respects any European investment firm which is a member of a recognised self-regulating organisation, provision requiring the firm to have and maintain financial resources in respect of any home-regulated investment business carried on by it.

**11(2)** Subsection (2) of that section shall also have effect in relation to an authorised person who is a European investment firm as if the reference in paragraph (b) to any business (whether or not investment business) carried on by the person concerned did not include a reference to any home-regulated investment business.

**12(1)** Section 51 of the Act (cancellation rules) shall have effect as if the reference in subsection (1) to a person who has entered or offered to enter into an investment agreement with an authorised person included a reference to a person who has entered or offered to enter into an investment agreement to which sub-paragraph (2) below applies.

**12(2)** This sub-paragraph applies to an investment agreement which is made by a European investment firm in the course of the carrying on by it of home-regulated investment business in the United Kingdom.

**13(1)** Section 52 of the Act (notification regulations) shall have effect as if any reference to authorised persons, or an authorised person, included a reference to European investment firms, or a European investment firm, carrying on home-regulated investment business in the United Kingdom.

**13(2)** That section shall also have effect as if it included provision that regulations under that section shall not require European investment firms to furnish information which is not reasonably required for purposes connected with the exercise of functions under the Act or these Regulations.

**14** Section 53 of the Act (indemnity rules) shall have effect as if the reference in subsection (1) to civil liability incurred by an authorised person in connection with his investment business included a reference to civil liability incurred by a European investment firm in connection with home-regulated investment business carried on by it in the United Kingdom.

**15** Section 54 of the Act (compensation fund) shall have effect as if–

(a) it included provision that rules establishing a scheme under that section may include in the scheme provision for compensating investors in cases where persons who are or have been European investment firms are unable, or likely to be unable, to satisfy claims in respect of any civil liability incurred by them in connection with home-regulated investment business carried on by them in the United Kingdom; and

(b) any reference in subsection (2) to authorised persons included a reference to European investment firms carrying on home-regulated investment business in the United Kingdom.

**16** Section 55 of the Act (clients' money) shall have effect as if any reference to authorised persons, or an authorised person, included a reference to European investment firms, or a European investment firm, carrying on home-regulated investment business in the United Kingdom.

**17** Section 57 of the Act (restrictions on advertising) shall have effect as if any reference to an authorised person included a reference to a European investment firm carrying on home-regulated investment business in the United Kingdom.

**18** Section 59 of the Act (employment of prohibited persons) shall have effect as if any reference to authorised persons, or an authorised person, included a reference to European investment firms, or a European investment firm, carrying on home-regulated investment business in the United Kingdom.

19 Section 60 of the Act (public statement as to a person's misconduct) shall have effect as if–

(a) the reference in subsection (1) to a person who is or was an authorised person by virtue of section 25 of that Act included a reference to a person who is or was a European investment firm carrying on home-regulated investment business in the United Kingdom; and

(b) the reference in subsection (3) to the authorised person included a reference to the European investment firm.

20 Section 64 of the Act (scope of powers of intervention) shall have effect in relation to an authorised person who is a European investment firm as if the reference in subsection (1) to investment business of a particular kind did not include a reference to any home-regulated investment business which the authorised person is carrying on or proposing to carry on.

21 Section 65 of the Act (restriction of business) shall have effect as if the reference in subsection (1) to an authorised person included a reference to a European investment firm carrying on home-regulated investment business in the United Kingdom.

## COLLECTIVE INVESTMENT SCHEMES

22 Section 75 of the Act (collective investment schemes: interpretation) shall have effect as if the reference in subsection (6) to an authorised person included a reference to a European investment firm carrying on home-regulated investment business in the United Kingdom.

23 Section 76 of the Act (restrictions on promotion) shall have effect as if any reference to an authorised person included a reference to a European investment firm carrying on home-regulated investment business in the United Kingdom.

24 Section 93 of the Act (applications to the court) shall have effect as if the reference in subsection (1) to an authorised person included a reference to a European investment firm.

## INFORMATION

25 Section 102 of the Act (register of authorised persons etc.) shall have effect as if it included provision that–

(a) the register kept under that section shall contain an entry in respect of each firm which appears to the Board to be a European investment firm carrying on home-regulated investment business in the United Kingdom;

(b) the entry in respect of each such firm shall consist of–

(i) information as to the services which the firm holds itself out as able to provide; and

(ii) such other information as the Board may determine;

(c) where it appears to the Board that any person in respect of whom there is an entry in the register by virtue of paragraph (a) above has ceased to be a European investment firm carrying on home-regulated investment business in the United Kingdom, the Board shall make a note to that effect in the entry together with the reason why the person in question is no longer such a firm; and

(d) an entry in respect of which a note is made by virtue of paragraph (c) above may be removed from the register at the end of such period as the Board thinks fit.

26 Section 104 of the Act (power to call for information) shall have effect as if–

(a) the reference in subsection (1) to a person who is authorised to carry on investment business by virtue of any of the provisions there mentioned included a reference to a European investment firm carrying on home-related investment business in the United Kingdom; and

(b) references to functions under the Act included references to functions under these Regulations.

27 Section 106 of the Act (exercise of investigation powers by officer etc.) shall have effect as if it included provision that–

(a) where the Secretary of State or the Board authorises a person other than one of his or its officers to exercise any powers under section 105 of the Act (investigation powers) in relation to any home-regulated investment business of a European investment firm, the Secretary of State or, as the case may be, the Board may determine that subsection (3) of section 106 shall not apply; and

(b) where such a determination is made, the person authorised to exercise the powers shall make a report to the relevant supervisory authority in the firm's home State, in such manner as that authority may require, on the exercise of those powers and the results of exercising them.

## AUDITORS

**28** Subsection (3) of section 107 of the Act (appointment of auditors) shall have effect in relation to an auditor appointed by an authorised person which is a European investment firm as if the reference to the accounts of the authorised person did not include a reference to any accounts relating to home-regulated investment business.

**29** Section 109 of the Act (communication by auditor with supervisory authorities) shall have effect as if in subsection (1)–

(a) the reference to an authorised person included a reference to a European investment firm; and

(b) the reference to functions under the Act included a reference to functions under these Regulations.

**30** Subsection (3) of section 110 of the Act (overseas business) shall have effect in relation to a European investment firm as if any reference to investment business did not include a reference to home-regulated investment business; and the reference in paragraph (b) of that subsection to the powers and duties of an auditor shall be construed accordingly.

## FEES

**31** Section 113 of the Act (periodical fees) shall have effect as if it included provision that a European investment firm carrying on home-regulated investment business in the United Kingdom shall pay such periodical fees to the Board as may be prescribed by regulations made under that section.

## PREVENTION OF RESTRICTIVE PRACTICES

**32** Section 119 of the Act (recognised self-regulating organisations, investment exchanges and clearing houses) shall have effect as if any reference in subsections (1) and (2) to the protection of investors included a reference to compliance with the Investment Services Directive.

**33** Section 121 of the Act (designated agencies) shall have effect as if any reference in subsections (1) and (2) to the protection of investors included a reference to compliance with the Investment Services Directive.

## RELATIONS WITH OTHER REGULATORY AUTHORITIES

**34(1)** Section 128C of the Act (enforcement in support of overseas regulatory authority) shall have effect as if it–

(a) required the powers mentioned in subsection (1) to be exercised at the request of the relevant supervisory authority in another EEA State if their exercise is necessary for the purposes of complying with the Investment Services Directive; and

(b) included provision that, in relation to the exercise of those powers in such a case, subsections (4) and (5) shall not apply and the Board shall notify the action taken by it to that authority.

**34(2)** That section shall also have effect as if the reference in subsection (2) to the power to withdraw or suspend authorisation under section 28 of the Act included a reference to the power to impose a prohibition under regulation 9 of these Regulations.

## OFFICIAL LISTING OF SECURITIES

**35** Section 142 of the Act (official listing) shall have effect as if–

(a) transferable shares in a body incorporated under the law of, or of any part of, the United Kingdom relating to industrial and provident societies; and

(b) bills of exchange accepted by a banker,

were not investments to which that section applies.

**36** Section 154 of the Act (advertisements etc. in connection with listing applications) shall have effect as if–

(a) it included provision that, where a European investment firm carrying on home-regulated investment business in the United Kingdom contravenes that section, it shall be treated as having contravened rules made under Chapter V of Part I of the Act, or in the case of a firm which is a member of a recognised self-regulating organisation, the rules of that organisation; and

(b) the reference in subsection (3) to a person other than an authorised person did not include a reference to such a firm.

## INSIDER DEALING

**37(1)** Section 178 of the Act (penalty for failure to co-operate with section 177 investigations) shall have effect as if–

(a) the reference in subsection (3) to an authorised person included a reference to a European investment firm; and

(b) the notices which may be served on a European investment firm under that subsection included a notice–

(i) directing that regulation 5(1)(a) of these Regulations shall not apply in relation to the firm after the expiry of a specified period after the service of the notice; or

(ii) directing that during a specified period that provision shall apply in relation to the firm only as respects the performance of contracts entered into before the notice comes into force;

(c) the reference in subsection (4) to the period mentioned in paragraphs (a) and (c) of subsection (3) included a reference to the period mentioned in paragraph (b)(i) and (ii) above;

(d) any reference in subsection (5) to an unauthorised person did not include a reference to a European investment firm carrying on home-regulated investment business in the United Kingdom; and

(e) the reference in that subsection to any authorised person included a reference to such a European investment firm.

**37(2)** That section shall also have effect as if it included provision that, if it appears to the Secretary of State–

(a) that a person on whom he serves a notice under subsection (3) is a European investment firm carrying on home-regulated investment business in the United Kingdom; or

(b) that a person on whom he serves a revocation notice under subsection (7) was such a firm at the time when the notice which is being revoked was served,

he shall serve a copy of the notice on the Board or, in the case of a firm which is a member of a recognised self-regulating organisation, that organisation.

**38** Section 180 of the Act (exceptions from restriction on disclosure of information) shall have effect as if–

(a) the reference in section 180(1)(e) to functions under the Act included functions under these Regulations; and

(b) the reference in section 180(1) to an authorised person included a reference to a European investment firm carrying on home-regulated investment business in the United Kingdom.

## MISCELLANEOUS AND SUPPLEMENTARY

**39** Section 191 of the Act (occupational pension schemes) shall have effect as if any reference to an authorised person included a reference to a European investment firm carrying on home-regulated investment business in the United Kingdom.

**40** Section 206 of the Act (publication of information and advice) shall have effect as if the reference in subsection (1) to authorised persons included a reference to European investment firms.

**41** Section 207(5) of the Act (interpretation: definition of controller) as it has effect in relation to a UK investment firm shall have effect as if the reference in section 207(5)(a) to 15 per cent were a reference to 10 per cent.

## ACTIVITIES CONSTITUTING INVESTMENT BUSINESS

**42(1)** Paragraph 17 of Schedule 1 to the Act (investments and investment business) shall have effect as if any reference to authorised persons, or an authorised person, included a reference to European investment firms, or a European investment firm, carrying on home-regulated investment business in the United Kingdom.

**42(2)** Paragraph 18 of that Schedule shall have effect as if the reference in sub-paragraph (2) to an authorised person included a reference to a European investment firm carrying on home-regulated investment business in the United Kingdom.

**42(3)** Paragraph 26 of that Schedule shall have effect as if any reference to an authorised person, or authorised persons, included a reference to a European investment firm, or European investment firms, carrying on home-regulated investment business in the United Kingdom.

## REQUIREMENTS FOR RECOGNITION OF SELF-REGULATING ORGANISATION

**43(1)** Paragraph 2 of Schedule 2 to the Act (requirements for recognition of self-regulating organisation) shall have effect as if it included provision that the rules and practices of the organisation must be such as to secure that no European investment firm, other than one on which an absolute prohibition has been imposed under regulation 9 of these Regulations, is refused admission to the organisation, or expelled from it, for reasons relating to the firm's fitness to carry on any home-regulated investment business.

**43(2)** Paragraph 3 of that Schedule shall have effect as if it included provision that the rules of the organisation must not include, as respects any European investment firm–

(a) provision requiring the firm to have and maintain financial resources in respect of any home-regulated investment business carried on by it; or

(b) provision as to any other matter for which, under the Investment Services Directive, responsibility is reserved to a supervisory authority in the firm's home State.

**43(3)** That paragraph shall also have effect as if–

(a) the reference in sub-paragraph (3) to Chapter VI of Part I of the Act included a reference to regulation 10 of these Regulations; and

(b) it included provision that the rules of the organisation must be such as to secure that, where a power falling within that sub-paragraph is exercisable by virtue of a European investment firm's contravention of a requirement of any provision made pursuant to any provision of the Investment Services Directive that confers power on host States, the exercise of the power shall be subject to such restrictions as are necessary for the purposes of complying with article 19 of the Investment Services Directive.

**43(4)** Paragraph 7 of that Schedule shall have effect as if it included provision that, for the purposes of complying with the Investment Services Directive, the organisation must be able and willing to co-operate, by the sharing of information and otherwise, with supervisory authorities in other EEA States.

## QUALIFICATIONS OF DESIGNATED AGENCY

**44(1)** Paragraph 4 of Schedule 7 to the Act (qualifications of designated agency) shall have effect as if any reference to authorised persons included a reference to European investment firms carrying on home-regulated investment business in the United Kingdom.

**44(2)** Paragraph 5 of that Schedule shall have effect as if it included provision that, for the purposes of complying with the Investment Services Directive, the agency must be able and willing to co-operate, by the sharing of information and otherwise, with supervisory authorities in other EEA States.

PRINCIPLES APPLICABLE TO DESIGNATED AGENCY'S LEGISLATIVE PROVISIONS

**45** Schedule 8 to the Act (principles applicable to designated agency's legislative provisions) shall have effect as if any reference to an authorised person included a reference to a European investment firm carrying on home-regulated investment business in the United Kingdom.

# Schedule 8 – Article 25 of the Investment Services Directive

Regulation 48(3)

"*Article 25*

**1** Member States shall provide that all persons who work or who have worked for the competent authorities, as well as auditors and experts instructed by the competent authorities, shall be bound by the obligation of professional secrecy. Accordingly, no confidential information which they may receive in the course of their duties may be divulged to any person or authority whatsoever, save in summary or aggregate form such that individual investment firms cannot be identified, without prejudice to cases covered by criminal law.

Nevertheless, where an investment firm has been declared bankrupt or is being compulsorily wound up, confidential information which does not concern third parties involved in attempts to rescue that investment firm may be divulged in civil or commercial proceedings.

**2** Paragraph 1 shall not prevent the competent authorities of different Member States from exchanging information in accordance with this Directive or other Directives applicable to investment firms. That information shall be subject to the conditions of professional secrecy imposed in paragraph 1.

**3** Member States may conclude cooperation agreements providing for exchanges of information with the competent authorities of third countries only if the information disclosed is covered by guarantees of professional secrecy at least equivalent to those provided for in this Article.

**4** Competent authorities receiving confidential information under paragraph 1 or 2 may use it only in the course of their duties:

- to check that the conditions governing the taking up of the business of investment firms are met and to facilitate the monitoring, on a non-consolidated or consolidated basis, of the conduct of that business, especially with regard to the capital adequacy requirements imposed in Directive 93/6/EEC, administrative and accounting procedures and internal control mechanisms,
- to impose sanctions,
- in administrative appeals against decisions by the competent authorities, or
- in court proceedings initiated under article 26.

**5** Paragraphs 1 and 4 shall not preclude the exchange of information:

(a) within a Member State, where there are two or more competent authorities, or

(b) within a Member State or between Member States, between competent authorities and

- authorities responsible for the supervision of credit institutions, other financial organizations and insurance undertakings and the authorities responsible for the supervision of financial markets,
- bodies responsible for the liquidation and bankruptcy of investment firms and other similar procedures; and
- persons responsible for carrying out statutory audits of the accounts of investment firms and other financial institutions,

in the performance of their supervisory functions, or the disclosure to bodies which administer compensation schemes of information necessary for the performance of their functions. Such information shall be subject to the conditions of professional secrecy imposed in paragraph 1.

**5a** Notwithstanding paragraphs 1 to 4, Member States may authorize exchanges of information between the competent authorities and:

- the authorities responsible for overseeing the bodies involved in the liquidation and bankruptcy of financial undertakings and other similar procedures, or
- the authorities responsible for overseeing persons charged with carrying out statutory audits of the accounts of insurance undertakings, credit institutions, investment firms and other financial institutions.

Member States which have recourse to the option provided for in the first subparagraph shall require at least that the following conditions are met:

- the information shall be for the purpose of performing the task of overseeing referred to in the first subparagraph,
- information received in this context shall be subject to the conditions of professional secrecy imposed in paragraph 1,
- where the information originates in another Member State, it may not be disclosed without the express agreement of the competent authorities which have disclosed it and, where appropriate, solely for the purposes for which those authorities gave their agreement.

Member States shall communicate to the Commission and to the other Member States the names of the authorities which may receive information pursuant to this paragraph.

**History**

See history note after para. 6.

**5b** Notwithstanding paragraphs 1 to 4, Member States may, with the aim of strengthening the stability, including integrity, of the financial system, authorize the exchange of information between the competent authorities and the authorities or bodies responsible under the law for the detection and investigation of breaches of company law.

Member States which have recourse to the option provided for in the first subparagraph shall require at least that the following conditions are met:

- the information shall be for the purpose of performing the task referred to in the first subparagraph,
- information received in this context shall be subject to the conditions of professional secrecy imposed in paragraph 1,
- where the information originates in another Member State, it may not be disclosed without the express agreement of the competent authorities which have disclosed it and, where appropriate, solely for the purposes for which those authorities gave their agreement.

Where, in a Member State, the authorities or bodies referred to in the first subparagraph perform their task of detection or investigation with the aid, in view of their specific competence, of persons appointed for that purpose and not employed in the public sector, the possibility of exchanging information provided for in the first subparagraph may be extended to such persons under the conditions stipulated in the second subparagraph.

In order to implement the final indent of the second subparagraph, the authorities or bodies referred to in the first subparagraph shall communicate to the competent authorities which have disclosed the information, the names and precise responsibilities of the persons to whom it is to be sent.

Member States shall communicate to the Commission and to the other Member States the names of the authorities or bodies which may receive information pursuant to this paragraph.

Before 31 December 2000, the Commission shall draw up a report on the application of the provisions of this paragraph.

**History**

See history note after para. 6.

6 This Article shall not prevent a competent authority from transmitting:

- to central banks and other bodies with a similar function in their capacity as monetary authorities,
- where appropriate, to other public authorities responsible for overseeing payment systems,

information intended for the performance of their task, nor shall it prevent such authorities or bodies from communicating to the competent authorities such information as they may need for the purposes of paragraph 4. Information received in this context shall be subject to the conditions of professional secrecy imposed in this Article.

**History**

Para. 5a, 5b and 6 substituted for the former para. 6 by the Financial Institutions (Prudential Supervision) Regulations 1996 (SI 1996/1669), reg. 1, 11(3), Sch. 2 as from 18 July 1996; the former para. 6 read as follows:

"This Article shall not prevent a competent authority from disclosing to those central banks which do not supervise credit institutions or investment firms individually such information as they may need to act as monetary authorities. Information received in this context shall be subject to the conditions of professional secrecy imposed in paragraph 1."

7 This Article shall not prevent the competent authorities from communicating the information referred to in paragraphs 1 to 4 to a clearing house or other similar body recognised under national law for the provision of clearing or settlement services for one of their Member State's markets if they consider that it is necessary to communicate the information in other to ensure the proper functioning of those bodies in relation to defaults or potential defaults by market participants. The information received shall be subject to the conditions of professional secrecy imposed in paragraph 1. The Member States shall, however, ensure that information received under paragraph 2 may not be disclosed in the circumstances referred to in this paragraph without the express consent of the competent authorities which disclosed it.

8 In addition, notwithstanding the provisions referred to in paragraphs 1 and 4, Member States may, by virtue of provisions laid down by law, authorize the disclosure of certain information to other departments of their central government administrations responsible for legislation on the supervision of credit institutions, financial institutions, investment firms and insurance undertakings and to inspectors instructed by those departments.

Such disclosures may, however, be made only where necessary for reasons of prudential control.

Member States shall, however, provide that information received under paragraphs 2 and 5 and that obtained by means of the on-the-spot verifications referred to in Article 24 may never be disclosed in the cases referred to in this paragraph except with the express consent of the competent authorities which disclosed the information or of the competent authorities of the Member State in which the on-the-spot verification was carried out.

9 If, at the time of adoption of this Directive, a Member State provides for the exchange of information between authorities in order to check compliance with the laws on prudential supervision, on the organization, operation and conduct of commercial companies and on the regulation of financial markets, that Member State may continue to authorize the forwarding of such information pending coordination of all the provisions governing the exchange of information between authorities for the entire financial sector but not in any case after 11 July 1996.

Member States shall, however, ensure that, where information comes from another Member State, it may not be disclosed in the circumstances referred to in the first sub-paragraph without the express consent of the competent authorities which disclosed it and it may be used only for the purpose for which those authorities gave their agreement.

The Council shall effect the coordination referred to in the first sub-paragraph on the basis of a Commission proposal. The Council notes the Commission's statement to the effect that it will submit proposals by 31 July 1993 at the latest. The Council will act on those proposals within the shortest possible time with the intention of bringing the rules proposed into effect on the same date as this Directive."

# Schedule 9 – Position of European Subsidiaries

Regulation 55

**1** In this Schedule–

**"the Banking Regulations"** means the Banking Coordination (Second Council Directive) Regulations 1992;
**"financial institution"** has the same meaning as in the Banking Regulations;
**"listed activity"** has the same meaning as in the Banking Regulations;
**"non-ISD activity"** means any listed activity other than a listed service.

## MODIFICATIONS OF THE BANKING REGULATIONS

**2** Regulation 3(3) of the Banking Regulations (requirements for being European subsidiary) shall cease to have effect except in so far as it relates to any financial institution–

(a) which immediately before the commencement date, is a European subsidiary and which, after that date, carries on in the United Kingdom (by whatever means and whether or not in conjunction with the provision by it of any listed service) any non-ISD activity in relation to which the requirements of paragraph 1 of Schedule 2 to those Regulations continue to be complied with; or

(b) which after the commencement date satisfies (and continues to satisfy) the requirements of regulation 3(3) in relation to the carrying on by it (by whatever means and whether or not in conjunction with the provision by it of any listed service) of any non-ISD activity;

and the meaning of **"European institution"** given by regulation 3(1) of those Regulations shall be modified accordingly.

**3** The following provisions of the Banking Regulations, that is to say–

(a) definitions of **"authorised or permitted"**, **"connected UK authority"** and **"home-regulated investment business"** in regulation 2(1) (interpretation: general);

(b) regulation 3(7) (meaning of home-regulated activity);

(c) regulation 4(2) (permitted activities);

(d) regulation 5(1) (authorisations and licences not required);

(e) regulation 65 (application of Part II of the Insurance Companies Act 1982);

(f) regulation 66 (meaning of insurance business),

shall have effect, in relation to any financial institution falling within paragraph (a) or (b) of paragraph 2 above, as if any reference to a listed activity were a reference to any non-ISD activity.

## PROCEDURAL REQUIREMENTS FOR EXISTING EUROPEAN SUBSIDIARIES CARRYING ON LISTED SERVICES

**4** Nothing in regulation 6(1) of these Regulations shall require a European investment firm which, immediately before the commencement date, is a European subsidiary to give further notice of any matter of which it has already given notice under paragraph 1 of Schedule 2 to the Banking Regulations.

**5** In respect of any listed service (whether or not provided in conjunction with the carrying on of any listed activity), regulation 6(3) of these Regulations (and not regulation 6(2) of the Banking Regulations) applies in respect of changes to the requisite details of any branch established in the United Kingdom by a European investment firm which, immediately before the commencement date, is a European subsidiary.

# Part II – Amendments of Financial Services Act

## PRELIMINARY

**3(1)** Any reference in this Part of this Schedule to a statement of principle or to rules or regulations is a reference to a statement of principle issued, or to rules or regulations made, before the commencement date.

**3(2)** Expressions used in this Part of this Schedule which are also used in Schedule 7 to these Regulations have the same meanings as in that Schedule.

## STATEMENTS OF PRINCIPLE

**4(1)** A statement of principle issued under section 47A of the Financial Services Act (statements of principle with respect to conduct and financial standing) shall, unless the contrary intention appears, apply to a European investment firm carrying on home-regulated investment business in the United Kingdom to the same extent as it would apply if the investment firm were an authorised person as respects that business.

**4(2)** If the Board is satisfied that it is necessary to do so for the purpose of implementing the Investment Services Directive or the Capital Adequacy Directive so far as relating to any particular European investment firm, the Board may, on the application or with the consent of the firm, by order direct that all or any of the provisions of such a statement–

(a) shall not apply to the firm; or

(b) shall apply to it with such modifications as may be specified in the order.

## CONDUCT OF BUSINESS RULES

**5(1)** Rules made under section 48 of the Financial Services Act (conduct of business rules) shall, unless the contrary intention appears, apply in relation to the conduct of home-regulated investment business carried on by a European investment firm in the United Kingdom to the same extent as they would apply if the investment firm were an authorised person as respects that business.

**5(2)** If the Board is satisfied that it is necessary to do so for the purpose of implementing the Investment Services Directive so far as relating to any particular European investment firm, the Board may, on the application or with the consent of the firm, by order direct that all or any of the provisions of such rules–

(a) shall not apply in relation to the conduct of home-regulated investment business carried on by the firm; or

(b) shall apply in relation to the conduct of such business with such modifications as may be specified in the order.

**5(3)** A member of a recognised self-regulating organisation who contravenes a rule applying to him by virtue of this paragraph shall be treated as having contravened the rules of the organisation.

## FINANCIAL RESOURCES RULES

**6** If the Board is satisfied that it is necessary to do so for the purpose of implementing the Capital Adequacy Directive so far as relating to any particular firm which is a European investment firm and an authorised person, the Board may, on the application or with the consent of the firm, by order direct that all or any of the provisions of rules under section 49 of the Financial Services Act (financial resources rules)–

(a) shall not apply to the firm; or

(b) shall apply to it with such modifications as may be specified in the order.

## CANCELLATION RULES

**7(1)** Rules made under section 51 of the Financial Services Act (cancellation rules) shall, unless the contrary intention appears, apply in relation to a person who has entered or offered to enter into an investment agreement to which sub-paragraph (2) below applies as they apply in relation to a person mentioned in that section.

**7(2)** This sub-paragraph applies to an investment agreement which is made by a European investment firm in the course of the carrying on by it of home-regulated investment business in the United Kingdom.

## NOTIFICATION REGULATIONS

**8(1)** Regulations made under section 52 of the Financial Services Act (notification regulations) shall, unless the contrary intention appears, apply in relation to a European investment firm carrying on home-regulated investment business in the United Kingdom to the same extent as they would apply if the investment firm were an authorised person as respects that business.

**8(2)** If the Board is satisfied that it is necessary to do so for the purpose of implementing the Investment Services Directive or the Capital Adequacy Directive so far as relating to any particular European investment firm, the Board may, on the application or with the consent of the firm, by order direct that all or any of the provisions of such regulations–

(a) shall not apply to the firm; or

(b) shall apply to it with such modifications as may be specified in the order.

## COMPENSATION FUND

**9(1)** Rules under section 54 of the Financial Services Act (compensation fund) shall, unless the contrary intention appears, apply in cases where a person who is or has been a European investment firm is unable, or likely to be unable, to satisfy claims in respect of any description of civil liability incurred by it in connection with home-regulated investment business carried on by it in the United Kingdom to the same extent as they would apply if the investment firm were an authorised person as respects that business.

**9(2)** If the Board is satisfied that it is necessary to do so for the purpose of implementing the Investment Services Directive so far as relating to any particular person who is or has been a European investment firm, the Board may, on the application or with the consent of that person, by order direct that all or any of the provisions of such rules–

(a) shall not apply in relation to cases where that person is unable, or likely to be unable, to satisfy claims in respect of any description of civil liability incurred by it in connection with home-regulated investment business carried on by it; or

(b) shall apply in relation to such cases with such modifications as may be specified in the order.

## UNSOLICITED CALLS

**10(1)** Regulations under section 56 of the Financial Services Act (unsolicited calls) shall, unless the contrary intention appears, apply in relation to European investment firm carrying on home-regulated investment business in the United Kingdom to the same extent as they would apply if the investment firm were an authorised person.

**10(2)** A member of a recognised self-regulating organisation who contravenes a regulation applying to him by virtue of this paragraph shall be treated as having contravened the rules of the organisation.

## SUPPLEMENTAL

**11(1)** An order under this Part of this Schedule may be subject to conditions.

**11(2)** Such an order may be revoked at any time by the Board; and the Board may at any time vary any such order on the application or with the consent of the European investment firm to which it applies.

## EXPLANATORY NOTE

*(This Note is not part of the Regulations)*

The Regulations give effect to provisions of Council Directive 93/22/EEC on investment services in the securities field (OJ No. L141, 10.5.93, p. 27) ("the Investment Services Directive"). They also give effect to provisions of Council Directive 93/6/EEC on the capital adequacy of investment firms and credit institutions (OJ No. L141, 15.3.93, p. 1). Most of the Regulations come into force on 1st January 1996. Two of them (one relating to the position of appointed representatives under the Financial Services Act 1986 and the other relating to the position of recognised professional bodies under that Act) come into force of 1st January 1997.

Part I of the Regulations defines various words and expressions for the purposes of the Regulations. Schedules 1 and 2 to the Regulations are relevant to the construction of Part I.

Part II of the Regulations makes provision for the recognition of certain investment firms authorised in other EEA States for the purposes of providing listed services in the United Kingdom. "Listed services" are the services which are set out in Schedule 1. Subject to compliance with the notification requirements contained in Schedule 3, nothing in certain specified provisions of the Financial Services Act 1986 (c.60) and the Consumer Credit Act 1974 (c.39) is to prevent a "European investment firm" (regulation 3) from providing in the United Kingdom, whether by the provision of services or the establishment of a branch, any listed service which its authorisation as an investment firm in its "home state" authorises it to provide (regulation 5). Certain offences in connection with provision of listed services and the establishment of branches are created by regulations 6 and 7. There are requirements concerning changes to the "requisite details" of a European investment firm (regulation 6(2) and (3)). Prohibitions and restrictions on a European investment firm in relation to the provision of listed services may be imposed by the Securities and Investments Board (regulations 9 to 11) and the Director General of Fair Trading (regulations 15 and 16), in the circumstances and in accordance with the conditions set out in the Regulations. Schedules 4 and 5 make supplemental provision in connection with such prohibitions and restrictions imposed by the Board and the Director General respectively. The Board (regulation 8) and the Bank (regulation 13) also have certain duties to prepare for supervision when a European investment firm is proposing to commence activities in the United Kingdom pursuant to the Regulations.

Part III of the Regulations makes provision for the implementation of certain decisions by the Council or the Commission.

Part IV of the Regulations makes provision for the carrying on of listed activities in other member States by "UK authorised investment firms", which means certain persons who are authorised under the Financial Services Act 1986 or exempted under that Act by virtue of being admitted to the list maintained by the Bank of England for the purposes of section 43 (regulation 18). A UK authorised investment firm is not to provide any listed service by the provision of services nor establish a branch in another EEA State in order to provide such a service unless the notification requirements of Schedule 6 have been complied with (regulation 20). There are also requirements concerning changes to the "requisite details" of a UK authorised investment firm.

Part V of the Regulations amends the Financial Services Act 1986. The principal changes relate to membership of self-regulating organisations (regulation 21), applications for, and grant and refusal of, authorisation by' the Securities and Investments Board under that Act (regulations 22 and 23), the granting of exemption to certain EEA markets (regulation 25), the conditions for admission to and removal from the list maintained by the Bank of England for the purposes of section 43 of that Act (regulation 26), appointed representatives (regulation 27), reciprocal facilities for investment business (regulation 29) and certification by recognised professional bodies (regulation 31). Other amendments to the Financial Services Act 1986 are made by Schedule 7, in particular in relation to European investment firms.

Part VI of the Regulations amends the Consumer Credit Act 1974. The principal changes relate to the effect of standard licences (regulation 34), the grant of standard licences (regulation 35), conduct of business (regulation 36), disclosure of information (regulation 39), and modification of subordinate legislation in relation to European investment firms (regulation 40).

Part VII of the Regulations introduces new requirements obliging persons who wish to acquire or increase holdings in UK authorised investment firms in excess of certain specified sizes to notify the relevant regulators before doing so. The regulators concerned are given power to object to the proposed acquisition. Certain offences in connection with notification are created by regulation 43. The Part contains transitional provisions relating to agreements entered into before the date on which the requirements of the Part come into force.

Part VIII of the Regulations makes provision as to certain miscellaneous matters. It contains provisions restricting the disclosure of confidential information relating to investment firms (regulation 48 and Schedule 8). It also contains provisions requiring the Securities and Investments Board to maintain a list of UK markets which meet certain requirements (regulation 49). It confers powers on the Board relating to the maintenance of financial resources by investment firms (regulation 50) and for the purpose of facilitating the assessment of the financial resources available to a group the members of which include an investment firm (regulations 51 to 53). The Part also confers powers on the Treasury to give directions to the Bank of England if such directions are necessary to ensure compliance with Investment Services Directive or the Capital Adequacy Directive (regulation 54). Finally, Part VIII (regulation 55 and Schedule 9) contains provisions relating to the position of certain EEA subsidiaries of EEA credit institutions. Prior to the coming into force of the Regulations, the ability of those subsidiaries to provide listed services in the United Kingdom was dealt with by the provisions of the Banking Coordination (Second Council Directive) Regulations 1992 (SI 1992/3218). From 1st January 1996, the ability of such subsidiaries to provide such services will be dealt with under the Regulations.

Part IX (including Schedules 10 and 11) makes provision in relation to the functions conferred on the Securities and Investments Board by the Regulations and contains minor and consequential amendments to primary and secondary legislation as well as transitional provisions and savings.

# THE COMPANIES ACT 1985 (MISCELLANEOUS ACCOUNTING AMENDMENTS) REGULATIONS 1996

(SI 1996/189)

*Made on 1 February 1996 by the Secretary of State for Trade and Industry under s. 257 of the Companies Act 1985. Operative from 2 February 1996 (except reg. 2 and 3 which are operative from 1 April 1996).*

## CITATION, INTERPRETATION AND COMMENCEMENT

**1(1)** These Regulations may be cited as the Companies Act 1985 (Miscellaneous Accounting Amendments) Regulations 1996 and, subject to paragraph (2) below, shall come into force on the day after the day on which they are made.

**1(2)** Regulations 2 and 3 shall come into force on 1st April 1996.

**1(3)** In these Regulations, **"the 1985 Act"** means the Companies Act 1985.

**2–13** [Amendments of s. 224, 225, 228, 234, 237, 246–248, 249B, 250, 262, 262A, 268.]

## AMENDENT OF SCHEDULES

**14** [Amendments of Sch. 4, 4A, 5, 7, 9, 9A, 11.]

## MINOR AND CONSEQUENTIAL AMENDENTS

**15** [Amendments of s. 231(3), (5), 255A(6)(b), Sch. 7, para. 1(2), Sch. 8, para. 15, 23(2), 26(3).]

## APPLICATION AND TRANSITIONAL PROVISIONS

**16(1)** Subject to the following provisions of this regulation, these Regulations apply to the annual accounts and annual report of any company (including any body corporate to which Part VII of the 1985 Act is applied by any enactment) for any financial year ending on or after the date of coming into force of the Regulations in accordance with regulation 1(1).

**16(2)** Subject to paragraphs (3) to (6) below, a company may, with respect to a financial year of the company ending on or before 24th March 1996, prepare and deliver to the registrar of companies such annual accounts and annual report as it would have been required to prepare and deliver had the amendments to the 1985 Act effected by these Regulations not been made.

**16(3)** The amendments effected by regulations 2 and 3 come into force in accordance with regulation 1(2).

**16(4)** A public company may pass a special resolution in accordance with section 250 of the 1985 Act as amended by regulation 11(2) at any time after the coming into force of these Regulations.

**16(5)** The amendments to the 1985 Act effected by regulations 6, 8 and 10(1) to (3), and by paragraphs 3, 4, 6, 10 and 18 of Schedule 5 to these Regulations apply to any annual accounts of a company which are approved by the board of directors on or after the day on which these Regulations come into force.

**16(6)** The amendments to the 1985 Act effected by regulations 13 and 14(8) apply in respect of any distribution made on or after the day on which these Regulations come into force.

# Schedule 1 – Form and Content of Company Accounts

Regulation 14(1)

**1-16** [Amendments of Sch. 4, para. 3(7), note (13) on the balance sheet formats in Pt. 1, section B, para. 34(3), (3A), 39, 41(1)(a), (2), 45(1), 48(1), 50(3)(b), 51(3), 53(2)(a), (3)–(6), 54(1), 55(1), (3), 56(2), (3), 59, 94(2), (3)].

# Schedule 2 – Form and Content of Group Accounts

Regulation 14(2)

**1-5** [Amendments of Sch. 4A, para. 1(1), 2(2), 13(4), (7), 14(1).]

# Schedule 3 – Disclosure of Information: Related Undertakings

Regulation 14(3)

**1-25** [Amendments of Sch. 5, para. 1(3)(b), 3–5, 6(1)–(3), 7(2), 8(2)(b), 9(1), 10, 11(3)(b), 12(3)(b), 13(2), 15(3)(b), 18, 19, 20(1)–(3), 22(3)(b), 23(2), 24(2)(b), 25(1), 26(2), 27(2)(b), 28(1), 29, 30(3)(b), 31(3)(b).]

# Schedule 4 – Form and Content of Accounts of Banking Companies and Groups

Regulation 14(6)

**1-13** [Amendments of Sch. 9, Pt. I, para. 8, 44(3), (4), 47(1), 52(a), 54(1)(a), (2), 66(1)(b), 68(1)(b), 73(3), 74, 75(1), 77(2), (3), 87(b), (c).]

# Schedule 5 – Form and Content of Accounts of Insurance Companies and Groups

Regulation 14(7)

**1-19** [Amendments of Sch. 9A, Pt. I, para. 5, profit and loss account format in Ch. I, section B, para. 21, 29(3), (4), 54, 59(a), 61(1)(a), (2), 65(b), 66(1), 68(1), 70(3), 71, 72(3), 73(2)(a), (3)–(5), 74(1), 79(2), (3), 84(c), 86(b), (c).]

# Schedule 6 – Modifications of Part VIII of the 1985 Act where Company's Accounts Prepared in Accordance with Special Provisions for Insurance Companies

Regulation 14(8)

**1-3** [Amendments of Sch. 11, para. 7, 9.]

## EXPLANATORY NOTE

(*This Note does not form part of the Regulations*)

These Regulations make a number of miscellaneous amendments to the provisions of the Companies Act 1985 (c. 6) (**"the 1985 Act"**) concerning accounts and audit. The principal changes are as follows:

(a) Regulation 2 amends section 224 of the 1985 Act (accounting reference periods and accounting reference date) to alter the method by which the accounting reference date of companies incorporated on or after 1st April 1996 is calculated.

(b) Regulation 3 amends section 225 of the 1985 Act (alteration of accounting reference date) to widen the circumstaces in which the accounting reference date of a company may be changed.

(c) Regulation 5(3) amends section 234 of the 1985 Act (duty to prepare directors' report) by inserting in subsection (4) a reference to new Part VI of Schedule 7 to the 1985 Act. Regulation 14(5) amends Schedule 7 to the 1985 Act by the insertion of a new Part VI. Part VI provides that the directors' report of public companies and large private companies which are subsidiaries of a public company must contain a statement of the company's policy on payment of its suppliers. Companies which follow any code or standard on payment practice must state what code or standard is followed and where information about it can be found; companies which do not follow such codes or standards must give a fuller statement on their payment practices.

(d) Regulation 10 amends section 249B of the 1985 Act (cases where exemption from audit not available). The amendment enables a company which would otherwise be disqualified from claiming exemption from audit under section 249A of the 1985 Act for a financial year because it was a subsidiary undertaking for any period in that year, to claim that exemption provided it was dormant throughout that period.

(e) Regulation 13 and paragraphs 3, 4, 6, 10 and 18 of Schedule 5 to the Regulations make certain amendments to the provisions of the 1985 Act concerning the accounts of insurance companies and groups so as to align those provisions more closely with the provisions of the Insurance Accounts Directive (Council Directive 91/674/EEC Official Journal No. L374 of 31.12.91, pages 7 to 31). Regulation 14(8) and Schedule 6 to the Regulations contain amendments to Schedule 11 to the 1985 Act (modifications of Part VIII where company's accounts prepared in accordance with special provisions for banking or insurance companies) consequential on those amendments.

(f) Regulation 14(1) and Schedule 1 to the Regulations contain amendments to Schedule 4 to the 1985 Act (form and content of company accounts).

(g) Regulation 14(2) and Schedule 2 to the Regulations contain amendments to Schedule 4A to the 1985 Act (form and content of group accounts).

(h) Regulation 14(3) and Schedule 3 to the Regulations contain amendments to Schedule 5 to the 1985 Act (disclosure of information: related undertakings).

(i) Regulation 14(4) repeals certain provisions in Schedule 7 to the 1985 Act concerning the matters to be dealt with in the directors' report.

(j) Regulation 14(6) and Schedule 4 to the Regulations contain amendments to Schedule 9 to the 1985 Act (form and content of accounts of banking companies and groups).

(k) Regulation 14(7) and Schedule 5 to the Regulations contain amendments to Schedule 9A to the 1985 Act (form and content of accounts of insurance companies and groups) in addition to those mentioned in paragraph (e) above.

(l) Regulation 15 makes certain minor and consequential amendments to sections 231 and 255A of, and Schedules 7 and 8 to, the 1985 Act, and regulation 16 makes provision concerning the application of the Regulations and contains transitional provisions.

# THE CO-OPERATION OF INSOLVENCY COURTS (DESIGNATION OF RELEVANT COUNTRIES) ORDER 1996

(SI 1996/253)

*Made on 8 February 1996 by the Secretary of State for Trade and Industry under s. 426(11) of the Insolvency Act 1986. Operative from 1 March 1996.*

**1** This Order may be cited as the Co-operation of Insolvency Courts (Designation of Relevant Countries) Order 1996 and shall come into force on 1st March 1996.

**2** The countries specified in the Schedule to this Order are hereby designated relevant countries for the purposes of section 426 of the Insolvency Act 1986.

## Schedule – Relevant Countries

Article 2

Malaysia
Republic of South Africa

### EXPLANATORY NOTE

(*This Note is not part of the Order*)

This Order designates as relevant countries for the purposes of section 426 of the Insolvency Act 1986 the countries specified in the Schedule to the Order. The courts of the countries so designated will have the right under section 426 to request assistance in matters of insolvency law from courts having jurisdiction in relation to insolvency law in any part of the United Kingdom. The Order comes into force on 1st March 1996. One other Order has been made under section 426(11) (the Co-operation of Insolvency Courts (Designation of Relevant Countries and Territories) Order 1986, SI 1986/2123).

A Compliance Cost Assessment is available, copies of which have been placed in the Libraries of both Houses of Parliament. Copies are also available from the Insolvency Service of the Department of Trade and Industry, PO Box 203, Room 5.1, 21 Bloomsbury Street, London WC1B 3QW.

# THE PARTNERSHIPS (UNRESTRICTED SIZE) NO. 11 REGULATIONS 1996

(SI 1996/262)

*Made on 8 February 1996 by the Secretary of State for Trade and Industry under s. 716(2)(d) and 744 of the Companies Act 1985. Operative from 15 March 1996.*

**1** These Regulations may be cited as the Partnerships (Unrestricted Size) No. 11 Regulations 1996 and shall come into force on 15th March 1996.

**2** Section 716(1) of the Companies Act 1985 does not prohibit the formation for the purpose of carrying on practice as actuaries of a partnership consisting of persons not less than three-quarters of the total number of whom are either Fellows of the Institute of Actuaries or Fellows of the Faculty of Actuaries.

**3** The Partnerships (Unrestricted Size) No. 2 Regulations 1970 are hereby revoked.

## EXPLANATORY NOTE

(*This Note is not part of the Regulations*)

Section 716 of the Companies Act 1985 prohibits the formation of partnerships of more than 20 persons. These Regulations exempt from that prohibition partnerships formed for the purpose of carrying on practice as actuaries and consisting of persons at least three-quarters of whom are Fellows of the Institute of Actuaries or Fellows of the Faculty of Actuaries. They replace, and revoke, earlier Regulations (SI 1970/835) which provided for an exemption in relation to partnerships consisting of persons all of whom were Fellows of either the Institute of Actuaries or Faculty of Actuaries.

# THE COMPANIES (REVISION OF DEFECTIVE ACCOUNTS AND REPORT) (AMENDMENT) REGULATIONS 1996

(SI 1996/315)

*Made on 13 February 1996 by the Secretary of State for Trade and Industry under s. 245 of the Companies Act 1985. Operative from 1 April 1996.*

**1** These Regulations may be cited as the Companies (Revision of Defective Accounts and Report) (Amendment) Regulations 1996 and shall come into force on 1st April 1996.

**2** The Companies (Revision of Defective Accounts and Report) Regulations 1990 (**"the 1990 Regulations"**) are amended in accordance with regulations 3 to 7 below.

**3** [Amendment of reg. 6(1), 7(1).]

**4** [Amendment of reg. 9(1).]

**5** [Amendment of reg. 10(3).]

**6** [Insertion of reg. 13A.]

**7** [Amendment of reg. 16(2).]

## EXPLANATORY NOTE

(*This Note is not part of the Regulations*)

These Regulations, which are made under section 245 of the Companies Act 1985 (c. 6), make certain amendments to the Companies (Revision of Defective Accounts and Report) Regulations 1990 (SI 1990/2570). In particular–

(a) regulation 3 amends regulations 6(1) and 7(1) of the 1990 Regulations to make it clear that a company's current auditors are required to report on any revised accounts (or revised directors' report) prepared under section 245 unless the directors engage the former auditors under regulation 6(2) or 7(2);

(b) regulation 5 amends regulation 10(3) of the 1990 Regulations to make it clear that the obligation under that provision must be complied with not more than 28 days after the date of revsion of the accounts (or directors' report) under section 245; and

(c) regulation 6 inserts a new regulation 13A into the 1990 Regulations which provides for the preparation and delivery to the registrar of companies of revised abbreviated accounts (as defined in regulation 13(1) of the 1990 Regulations) in addition to the provision already made by regulation 13.

# THE COMPANIES (FORMS) (AMENDMENT) REGULATIONS 1996

(SI 1996/594)

*Made on 5 March 1996 by the Secretary of State for Trade and Industry under s. 224(2), 225(1), (2), 701 and 704 of the Companies Act 1985. Operative from 1 April 1996.*

**1(1)** These Regulations may be cited as the Companies (Forms) (Amendment) Regulations 1996 and shall come into force on 1st April 1996.

**1(2)** In these Regulations–

**"the 1985 Act"** means the Companies Act 1985; and

**"the 1990 Regulations"** means the Companies (Forms) (Amendment) Regulations 1990.

**2** With effect from 1st April 1996, form 225 in the Schedule to these Regulations, with such variations as circumstances require, is the form prescribed for the purposes of section 225 of the 1985 Act, including that section as applied by section 701 of the 1985 Act.

**3(1)** With effect from 1st April 1996, forms 225(1), 225(2), 701b and 701c in Schedule 2 to the 1990 Regulations are revoked, save that those forms may be used until 1st April 1997 for those purposes of section 225 of the 1985 Act (including that section as applied by section 701) which correspond to the purposes for which the forms were originally prescribed.

## Schedule

Regulation 2

**Note**
This Schedule sets out the prescribed form (Form 255) referred to in reg. 2. Form 225 is not reproduced here.

### EXPLANATORY NOTE

(*This Note is not part of the Regulations*)

These Regulations prescribe a new form 225 to be used by companies (including certain oversea companies) in order to change their accounting reference date under section 225 of the Companies Act 1985. The new form reflects amendments to section 225 to be made by regulation 3 of the Companies Act 1985 (Miscellaneous Accounting Amendments) Regulations 1996, and will take effect on 1st April 1996, the date on which those amendments come into force.

The Regulations revoke existing forms 225(1), 225(2), 701b and 701c with effect from 1st April 1996. Those forms will be replaced by new form 225. There is, however, transitional provision permitting the existing form to be used until 1st April 1997 in certain circumstances.

The Regulations revoke existing forms 224 and 701a with effect from 1st January 1997, after which they become obsolete due to amendments to section 224 of the Companies Act 1985 to be made by regulation 2 of the Companies Act 1985 (Miscellaneous Accounting Amendments) Regulations 1996.

# THE COMPANIES (PRINCIPAL BUSINESS ACTIVITIES) (AMENDMENT) REGULATIONS 1996

(SI 1996/1105)

*Made on 9 April 1996 by the Secretary of State for Trade and Industry under s. 364(3) and 744 of the Companies Act 1985. Operative from 6 May 1996.*

**1** These Regulations may be cited as the Companies (Principal Business Activities) (Amendment) Regulations 1996 and shall come into force on 6th May 1996.

**2(1)** The Companies (Forms Amendment No. 2 and Company's Type and Principal Business Activities) Regulations 1990) ("**the 1990 Regulations**") are amended as follows.

**2(2)–(4)** [Amendments of reg. 2, 5(2) and Sch. 3, Pt. II of the 1990 Regulations not reproduced here.]

**3** Notwithstanding the provisions of regulation 2 above, the system of classifying business activities which was prescribed for the purpose of section 364(3) of the Companies Act 1985 by regulation 5(2) of the 1990 Regulations may continue to be used in relation to an annual return delivered to the registrar on or before 5th May 1997 instead of the system prescribed for that purpose by these Regulations.

### EXPLANATORY NOTE

(*This Note is not part of the Regulations*)

These Regulations amend the Companies (Forms Amendment No. 2 and Company's Type and Principal Business Activities) Regulations 1990 ("the 1990 Regulations"). The 1990 Regulations prescribe the system of classifying business activities for the purposes of section 364(1)(b) of the Companies Act 1985 (as substituted by the Companies Act 1989) which requires a company to give its principal business activities in its annual return. These Regulations amend the 1990 Regulations by prescribing (regulation 2) for this purpose the Standard Industrial Classification of Economic Activities 1992. Copies of the Standard Industrial Classification of Economic Activities 1992 are available from Her Majesty's Stationery Office. The amendment made by regulation 2 is subject to a transitional provision in regulation 3. This allows the continued use of the VAT Trade Classification system in an annual return delivered to the Registrar of Companies on or before 5th May 1997.

# THE INSOLVENT PARTNERSHIPS (AMENDMENT) ORDER 1996

(SI 1996/1308)

*Made on 14 May 1996 by the Lord Chancellor, with the concurrence of the Secretary of State for Trade and Industry, under s. 420(1) and (2) of the Insolvency Act 1986 and s. 21(2) of the Company Directors Disqualification Act 1986. Operative from 14 June 1996.*

## CITATION AND COMMENCEMENT

**1** This Order may be cited as the Insolvent Partnerships (Amendment) Order 1996 and shall come into force on 14th June 1996.

## AMENDMENT OF ARTICLE 7

**2** [Amendment to art. 7 of the Insolvent Partnerships Order 1994 (SI 1994/2421).]

### EXPLANATORY NOTE

(*This Note is not part of the Order*)

This Order amends article 7 of the Insolvent Partnerships Order 1994 (S.I. 1994/2421) ("the Order") with effect from 14th June 1996. The Order provides a code for the winding up of insolvent partnerships.

The amendment to article 7 of the Order (which provides for the winding up of an insolvent partnership as an unregistered company on the petition of a creditor, of a responsible insolvency practitioner or of the Secretary of State where no concurrent petition is presented against a member) extends the list of petitioners to include any other person other than a member. This will include the Bank of England and the Securities and Investments Board who are entitled under the Banking Act 1987 (c. 22) and the Financial Services Act 1986 (c. 60) respectively to present a petition for the winding up of an insolvent partnership.

# THE FINANCIAL SERVICES ACT 1986 (UNCERTIFICATED SECURITIES) (EXTENSION OF SCOPE OF ACT) ORDER 1996

(SI 1996/1322)

*Made on 16 May 1996 by the Treasury under s. 2 and 205A of the Financial Services Act 1986. Operative from 15 July 1996.*

## CITATION, COMMENCEMENT AND INTERPRETATION

**1(1)** This Order may be cited as the Financial Services Act 1986 (Uncertificated Securities) (Extension of Scope of Act) Order 1996 and shall come into force on 15th July 1996.

**1(2)** In this Order **"the Act"** means the Financial Services Act 1986.

## AMENDMENTS TO THE ACT

**2(1)** [Addition of para. 16A of Sch. 1 to the Act.]

**2(2)** [Addition of para. 18(5A), 18(5B) of Sch. 1 to the Act.]

**2(3)** [Addition of para. 22(4A) of Sch. 1 to the Act.]

**2(4)** [Addition of para. 27(3) of Sch. 1 to the Act.]

## EXPLANATORY NOTE

(*This Note is not part of the Regulations*)

The Order amends the scope of the Financial Services Act 1986 ("the Act") by extending the activities which constitute the carrying on of investment business.

Article 1 of the Order adds a new paragraph (paragraph 16A) to Part II of Schedule 1 to the Act. (Part II of Schedule 1 sets out the activities which constitute investment business.) The new paragraph is concerned with the sending on behalf of another person dematerialised instructions relating to an investment by means of a relevant system (within the meaning of the Uncertificated Securities Regulations 1995 – SI 1995/3272). The paragraph also concerns offers or agreements to send such instructions. The activities of certain persons are expressly excluded from the new paragraph.

Article 2 adds a sub-paragraph to paragraph 18 of Schedule 1 to the Act. It provides an exclusion in respect of activities falling within the new paragraph 16A in which one body corporate in a group engages on behalf of another body corporate in the same group.

Article 3 adds a sub-paragraph to paragraph 22 of Schedule 1 to the Act. It provides an exclusion in respect of activities falling within the new paragraph 16A engaged in by a trustee or personal representative.

Article 4 adds a sub-paragraph to paragraph 27 of Schedule 1 to the Act. It provides an exclusion in respect of offers or agreements by overseas persons to engage in activities falling within the new paragraph 16A where the offer or agreement is the result of an unsolicited approach made to the overseas person or is the result of an approach or solicitation by the overseas person which did not contravene the provisions of the Act relating to unsolicited calls and advertising.

# THE COMPANIES (FEES) (AMENDMENT) REGULATIONS 1996

(SI 1996/1444)

*Made on 5 June 1996 by the Secretary of State for Trade and Industry under s. 708(1) and (2) of the Companies Act 1985. Operative from 20 September 1996.*

**1** These Regulations may be cited as the Companies (Fees) (Amendment) Regulations 1996 and shall come into force on 20th September 1996.

**2** In these Regulations, **"the 1991 Regulations"** means the Companies (Fees) Regulations 1991.

**3** [Amendments to Sch. to the 1991 Regulations.]

**4(1)** Subject to paragraph (2) below, the fees prescribed by regulation 3 come into effect on 1st October 1996.

**4(2)** The fee prescribed in relation to entry 2 by regulation 3(a) above in respect of the registration of an annual return applies to any annual return which the company–

(a) is required to deliver to the registrar made up to a date not later than a return date occurring on or after 1st October 1996; and

(b) which is delivered on or after 20th September 1996.

**4(3)** For the purposes of paragraph (2) above, a **"return date"** in relation to any company is ascertained in accordance with section 363(1) of the Companies Act 1985.

## EXPLANATORY NOTE

(*This Note is not part of the Regulations*)

These Regulations amend the Companies (Fees) Regulations 1991, as amended by the Companies (Fees) (Amendment) Regulations 1992, the Companies (Fees) (Amendment) Regulations 1994 and the Companies (Fees) (Amendment) Regulations 1995, which require the payment of fees in respect of functions performed by the registrar of companies under the Companies Act 1985.

Regulation 3 amends these Regulations by:

(1) reducing the fees applicable in respect of:

(a) the registration of an annual return, and the registration of copy accounts delivered by an oversea company otherwise than at the time of a branch registration,

(b) the registration of a change of name by a company,

(c) the delivery by post pursuant to any form of request other than one on-line, of a basic set of microfiche copies,

(d) the delivery by post pursuant to any form of request other than one on-line, of the excluded documents of a branch or undertaking recorded and kept by the registrar in the form of a microfiche copy (regulation 3(a));

(2) increasing the fees applicable in respect of the following matters from £3.00 to £3.50:

(a) the inspection of a basic set of microfiche copies,

(b) the inspection of the excluded documents of a branch or undertaking recorded and kept by the registrar of companies in the form of a microfiche copy,

(c) the inspection of a list of members of a company consisting of more than 10 pages, other than an inspection requested on the same occasion as a request to inspect the basic set of microfiche copies relating to that company,

(d) the delivery, at an office of the registrar, of a basic set of microfiche copies,

(e) the delivery, at an office of the registrar, of microfiche copies of the excluded documents of a branch or undertaking recorded and kept by the registrar in the form of a microfiche copy (regulation 3(a));

(3) increasing the fees applicable in respect of certified copies of, or extracts from, any record and, when the record is a list of members consisting of more than 10 pages, in respect of the first ten pages, from £12.00 to £15.00 (regulation 3(a));

(4) increasing the fees applicable in respect of the supply of a first certificate of incorporation on any occasion from £12.00 to £15.00 and for each additional certificate supplied on the same occasion from £9.50 to £10.00 (regulation 3(a));

(5) abolishing the fee applicable in respect of the inspection of entries in the register relating to one company (regulation 3(b));

(6) prescribing a new fee of £10.00 in relation to the registration of a change of the corporate name of an oversea company (regulation 3(c));

(7) replacing entry 11 with a new provision requiring the payment of fees by reference only to whether the relevant copies (lists of members consisting of more than 10 pages) were delivered by post or at an office of the registrar. In the first case a fee of £5.00 is charged, in the latter a fixed fee of £3.50 is payable in place of a fee of £3.00 for the first five sheets of microfiche and 10p for each subsequent sheet (regulation 3(d));

(8) replacing entry 12 with a new entry under which a new fee is charged in relation to the delivery of paper copies of records, other than a list of members, relating to a company at an office of the registrar where those records are requested otherwise than on the occasion of the inspection of the records of that company or of a request for a basic set of microfiche copies relating to that company. The new fee is £3.50 plus £1 for each document of these records supplied. The fee for copies requested on the specified occasions remains the same (regulation 3(e));

(9) replacing entry 13 with a new entry under which new fees are charged, in respect of paper copies of a company's records, kept by the registrar in the form of a microfiche copy, other than a list of members, by reference to the number of documents requested rather than the mode of request. The fee is £6.00 in respect of one document and £2.50 in respect of each further document requested on the same occasion (regulation 3(f));

(10) replacing entries 16, 16A and 16B by a new entry 16 under which new fees are charged in respect of paper copies of particulars registered in respect of a branch or undertaking by reference to the means of delivery. The new fee is 10p per screen of information on a computer terminal where the copies are delivered at an office of the registrar or £1 per screen where delivered by post (regulation 3(g)).

Regulation 4 provides for the new fees (with the exception of the fees for the registration of an annual return) to come into effect on 1st October 1996. In relation to annual returns the new fee is applied to all annual returns which are made up to a date not later than a return date (ascertained for each company in accordance with section 363(1) of the Companies Act 1985) on or after 1st October 1996 and which are delivered on or after 20th September 1996.

# THE FINANCIAL MARKETS AND INSOLVENCY REGULATIONS 1996

(SI 1996/1469)

*Made on 5 June 1996 by the Treasury and the Secretary of State for Trade and Industry under s. 185 and 186 of the Companies Act 1989. Operative from 15 July 1996.*

## PART I – GENERAL

### CITATION AND COMMENCEMENT

**1** These Regulations may be cited as the Financial Markets and Insolvency Regulations 1996 and shall come into force on 15th July 1996.

### INTERPRETATION

**2(1)** In these Regulations–

**"the Act"** means the Companies Act 1989;

**"business day"** means any day which is not a Saturday or Sunday, Christmas Day, Good Friday or a bank holiday in any part of the United Kingdom under the Banking and Financial Dealings Act 1971;

**"issue"**, in relation to an uncertificated unit of a security, means to confer on a person title to a new unit;

**"register of securities"**–

(a) in relation to shares, means a register of members; and
(b) in relation to units of a security other than shares, means a register maintained by the issuer, whether by virtue of the 1995 Regulations or otherwise, of persons holding the units;

**"the 1995 Regulations"** means the Uncertificated Securities Regulations 1995;

**"relevant nominee"** means a system-member who is a subsidiary undertaking of the Operator designated by him as such in accordance with such rules and practices as are mentioned in paragraph 19(d) of Schedule 1 to the 1995 Regulations;

**"settlement bank"** means a person who has contracted with an Operator to make payments in connection with transfers, by means of a relevant system, of title to uncertificated units of a security and of interests of system-beneficiaries in relation to such units;

**"system-beneficiary"** means a person on whose behalf a system-member or former system-member holds or held uncertificated units of a security;

**"system-charge"** means a charge of a kind to which regulation 3(2) applies;

**"system-member"** means a person who is permitted by an Operator to transfer by means of a relevant system title to uncertificated units of a security held by him; and **"former system-member"** means a person whose participation in the relevant system is terminated or suspended;

**"transfer"**, in relation to title to uncertificated units of a security, means the generation of an Operator-instruction requiring a participating issuer to register a system-member on the relevant register of securities as the holder of those units; and in relation to an interest of a system-beneficiary in relation to uncertificated units of a security, means the transfer of the interest to another system-beneficiary by means of a relevant system; and

other expressions used in these Regulations which are also used in the 1995 Regulations have the same meanings as in those Regulations.

**2(2)** For the purposes of these Regulations, a person holds a unit of a security if–

(a) in the case of an uncertificated unit, he is entered on a register of securities in relation to the unit in accordance with regulation 19 of the 1995 Regulations; and

(b) in the case of a certificated unit, he has title to the unit.

**2(3)** A reference in any of these Regulations to a numbered regulation shall be construed as a reference to the regulation bearing that number in these Regulations.

**2(4)** A reference in any of these Regulations to a numbered paragraph shall, unless the reference is to a paragraph of a specified regulation, be construed as a reference to the paragraph bearing that number in the regulation in which the reference is made.

## PART II – SYSTEM-CHARGES

### APPLICATION OF PART VII OF THE ACT IN RELATION TO SYSTEM-CHARGES

**3(1)** Subject to the provisions of these Regulations, Part VII of the Act shall apply in relation to–

(a) a charge to which paragraph (2) applies (**"a system-charge"**) and any action taken to enforce such a charge; and

(b) any property subject to a system-charge,

in the same way as it applies in relation to a market charge, any action taken to enforce a market charge and any property subject to a market charge.

**3(2)** This paragraph applies in relation to a charge granted in favour of a settlement bank for the purpose of securing debts or liabilities arising in connection with any of the following–

(a) a transfer of uncertificated units of a security to a system-member by means of a relevant system whether the system-member is acting for himself or on behalf of a system-beneficiary;

(b) a transfer, by one system-beneficiary to another and by means of a relevant system, of his interests in relation to uncertificated units of a security held by a relevant nominee where the relevant nominee will continue to hold the units;

(c) an agreement to make a transfer of the kind specified in paragraph (a);

(d) an agreement to make a transfer of the kind specified in paragraph (b): and

(e) an issue of uncertificated units of a security to a system-member by means of a relevant system whether the system-member is acting for himself or on behalf of a system-beneficiary.

**3(3)** In its application, by virtue of these Regulations, in relation to a system-charge, section 173(2) of the Act shall have effect as if the references to "purposes specified" and "specified purposes" were references to any one or more of the purposes specified in paragraph (2).

## CIRCUMSTANCES IN WHICH PART VII APPLIES IN RELATION TO SYSTEM-CHARGE

**4(1)** Part VII of the Act shall apply in relation to a system-charge granted by a system-member and in relation to property subject to such a charge only if–

(a) it is granted to a settlement bank by a system-member for the purpose of securing debts or liabilities arising in connection with any of the transactions specified in regulation 3(2), being debts or liabilities incurred by that system-member or by a system-beneficiary on whose behalf he holds uncertificated units of a security; and

(b) it contains provisions which refer expressly to the relevant system in relation to which the grantor is a system-member.

**4(2)** Part VII of the Act shall apply in relation to a system-charge granted by a system-beneficiary and in relation to property subject to such a charge only if–

(a) it is granted to a settlement bank by a system-beneficiary for the purpose of securing debts or liabilities arising in connection with any of the transactions specified in regulation 3(2), incurred by that system-beneficiary or by a system-member who holds uncertificated units of a security on his behalf; and

(b) it contains provisions which refer expressly to the relevant system in relation to which the system-member who holds the uncertificated units of a security in relation to which the system-beneficiary has the interest is a system-member.

## EXTENT TO WHICH PART VII APPLIES TO A SYSTEM-CHARGE

**5** Part VII of the Act shall apply in relation to a system-charge only to the extent that–

(a) it is a charge over any one or more of the following–

(i) uncertificated units of a security held by a system-member or a former system-member;

(ii) interests of a kind specified in regulation 25(1)(a) or 25(2)(a) of the 1995 Regulations in uncertificated units of a security in favour of a system-member or a former system-member;

(iii) interests of a system-beneficiary in relation to uncertificated units of a security;

(iv) units of a security which are no longer in uncertificated form because the person holding the units has become a former system-member;

(v) sums or other benefits receivable by a system-member or former system-member by reason of his holding uncertificated units of a security, or units which are no longer in uncertificated form because the person holding the units has become a former system-member;

(vi) sums or other benefits receivable by a system-beneficiary by reason of his having an interest in relation to uncertificated units of a security or in relation to units which are no longer in uncertificated form because the person holding the units has become a former system-member;

(vii) sums or other benefits receivable by a system-member or former system-member by way of repayment, bonus, preference, redemption, conversion or accruing or offered in respect of uncertificated units of a security, or units which are no longer in uncertificated form because the person holding the units has become a former system-member;

(viii) sums or other benefits receivable by a system-beneficiary by way of repayment, bonus, preference, redemption, conversion or accruing or offered in respect of uncertificated units of a security in relation to which he has an interest or in respect of units in relation to which the system-beneficiary has an interest and which are no longer in uncertificated form because the person holding the units has become a former system-member;

(ix) sums or other benefits receivable by a system-member or former system-member in respect of the transfer of uncertificated units of a security by or to him by means of a relevant system;

(x) sums or other benefits receivable by a system-member or former system-member in respect of an agreement to transfer uncertificated units of a security by or to him by means of a relevant system;

(xi) sums or other benefits receivable by a system-beneficiary in respect of the transfer of the interest of a system-beneficiary in relation to uncertificated units of a security by or to him by means of a relevant system or in respect of the transfer of uncertificated units of a security by or to a system-member acting on his behalf by means of a relevant system;

(xii) sums or other benefits receivable by a system-beneficiary in respect of an agreement to transfer the interest of a system-beneficiary in relation to uncertificated units of a security by or to him by means of a relevant system, or in respect of an agreement to transfer uncertificated units of a security by or to a system-member acting on his behalf by means of a relevant system; and

(b) it secures–

(i) the obligation of a system-member or former system-member to reimburse a settlement bank, being an obligation which arises in connection with any of the transactions specified in regulation 3(2) and whether the obligation was incurred by the system-member when acting for himself or when acting on behalf of a system-beneficiary; or

(ii) the obligation of a system-beneficiary to reimburse a settlement bank, being an obligation which arises in connection with any of the transactions specified in regulation 3(2) and whether the obligation was incurred by the system-beneficiary when acting for himself or by reason of a system-member acting on his behalf.

## LIMITATION ON DISAPPLICATION OF SECTIONS 10(1)(B) AND 11(3)(C) OF INSOLVENCY ACT 1986 IN RELATION TO SYSTEM-CHARGES

**6(1)** This regulation applies where an administration order is made in relation to a system-member or former system-member.

**6(2)** The disapplication of sections 10(1)(b) and 11(3)(c) of the Insolvency Act 1986 by section 175(1)(a) of the Act shall have effect, in relation to a system-charge granted by a system-member or former system-member, only to the extent necessary to enable there to be realised, whether through the sale of uncertificated units of a security or otherwise, the lesser of the two sums specified in paragraphs (3) and (4).

**6(3)** The first sum of the two sums referred to in paragraph (2) is the net sum of–

(a) all payment obligations discharged by the settlement bank in connection with–

(i) transfers of uncertificated units of a security by means of a relevant system made during the qualifying period to or by the relevant system-member or former system-member, whether acting for himself or on behalf of a system-beneficiary;

(ii) agreements made during the qualifying period to transfer uncertificated units of a security by means of a relevant system to or from the relevant system-member or former system-member, whether acting for himself or on behalf of a system-beneficiary; and

(iii) issues of uncertificated units of a security by means of a relevant system made during the qualifying period to the relevant system-member or former system-member, whether acting for himself or on behalf of a system-beneficiary; less

(b) all payment obligations discharged to the settlement bank in connection with transactions of any kind described in paragraph (3)(a)(i) and (ii).

**6(4)** The second of the two sums referred to in paragraph (2) is the sum (if any) due to the settlement bank from the relevant system-member or former system-member by reason of an obligation of the kind described in regulation 5(b)(i).

**6(5)** In this regulation and regulation 7, **"qualifying period"** means the period–

(a) beginning with the fifth business day before the day on which the petition for the making of the administration order was presented; and

(b) ending with the second business day after the day on which the administration order is made.

## LIMITATION ON DISAPPLICATION OF SECTIONS 10(1)(B) AND 11(3)(C) OF INSOLVENCY ACT 1986 IN RELATION TO SYSTEM-CHARGES GRANTED BY A SYSTEM-BENEFICIARY

**7(1)** This regulation applies where an administration order is made in relation to a system-beneficiary.

**7(2)** The disapplication of sections 10(1)(b) and 11(3)(c) of the Insolvency Act 1986 by section 175(1)(a) of the Act shall have effect, in relation to a system-charge granted by a system-beneficiary, only to the extent necessary to enable there to be realised, whether through the sale of interests of a system-beneficiary in relation to uncertificated units of a security or otherwise, the lesser of the two sums specified in paragraphs (3) and (4).

**7(3)** The first of the two sums referred to in paragraph (2) is the net sum of–

(a) all payment obligations discharged by the settlement bank in connection with–

(i) transfers, to or by the relevant system-beneficiary by means of a relevant system made during the qualifying period, of interests of the system- beneficiary in relation to uncertificated units of a security held by a relevant nominee, where the relevant nominee has continued to hold the units;

(ii) agreements made during the qualifying period to transfer, to or from the relevant system-beneficiary by means of a relevant system, interests of the system-beneficiary in relation to uncertificated units of a security held by a relevant nominee, where the relevant nominee will continue to hold the units;

(iii) transfers, during the qualifying period and by means of a relevant system, of uncertificated units of a security, being transfers made to or by a system-member acting on behalf of the relevant system-beneficiary;

(iv) agreements made during the qualifying period to transfer uncertificated units of a security by means of a relevant system to or from a system-member acting on behalf of the relevant system-beneficiary; and

(v) issues of uncertificated units of a security made during the qualifying period and by means of a relevant system, being issues to a system-member acting on behalf of the relevant system-beneficiary; less

(b) all payment obligations discharged to the settlement bank in connection with transactions of any kind described in paragraph (3)(a)(i) to (iv).

**7(4)** The second of the two sums referred to in paragraph (2) is the sum (if any) due to the settlement bank from the relevant system-beneficiary by reason of an obligation of the kind described in regulation 5(b)(ii).

## ABILITY OF ADMINISTRATOR OR RECEIVER TO RECOVER ASSETS IN CASE OF PROPERTY SUBJECT TO SYSTEM-CHARGE

**8(1)** This regulation applies where an administration order is made or an administrator or an administrative receiver or a receiver is appointed, in relation to a system-member, former system-member or system-beneficiary.

**8(2)** The disapplication, by section 175(1)(b) and (3) of the Act, of sections 15(1) and (2), 43 and 61 of the Insolvency Act 1986 shall cease to have effect after the end of the relevant day in respect of any property which is subject to a system-charge granted by the system-member, former system-member or system-beneficiary if on the basis of a valuation in accordance with paragraph (3), the charge is not required for the realisation of the sum specified in paragraph (4) or (5).

**8(3)** For the purposes of paragraph (2), the value of property shall, except in a case falling within paragraph (6), be such as may be agreed between the administrator, administrative receiver or receiver on the one hand and the settlement bank on the other.

**8(4)** Where the system-charge has been granted by a system-member or former system-member, the sum referred to in paragraph (2) is whichever is the lesser of–

(a) the sum referred to in regulation 6(3);

(b) the sum referred to in regulation 6(4) due to the settlement bank at the close of business on the relevant day.

**8(5)** Where the system-charge has been granted by a system-beneficiary, the sum referred to in paragraph (2) is whichever is the lesser of–

(a) the sum referred to in regulation 7(3);

(b) the sum referred to in regulation 7(4) due to the settlement bank at the close of business on the relevant day.

**8(6)** For the purposes of paragraph (2), the value of any property for which a price for the relevant day is quoted in the Daily Official List of The London Stock Exchange Limited shall–

(a) in a case in which two prices are so quoted, be an amount equal to the average of those two prices, adjusted where appropriate to take account of any accrued dividend or interest; and

(b) in a case in which one price is so quoted, be an amount equal to that price, adjusted where appropriate to take account of any accrued dividend or interest.

**8(7)** In this regulation **"the relevant day"** means the second business day after the day on which the administration order is made, or the administrative receiver or receiver is appointed.

# PART III – MARKET CONTRACTS

## AMENDMENTS TO SECTION 156 OF THE ACT

**9** [Insertion of s. 156(3A) into the Act.]

## EXPLANATORY NOTE

*(This Note is not part of the Regulations)*

The Regulations apply with modifications certain provisions of Part VII of the Companies Act 1989 (c. 40) ("Part VII") to certain charges (and to property subject to those charges) granted in favour of those who undertake assured payment obligations in connection with the settlement of transactions through a relevant system in respect of which an Operator has been approved under the Uncertificated Securities Regulations 1995 (SI 1995/3272). The provisions applied are ones which modify the way in which the charges in question are treated in the event of an administration or certain kinds of receivership under the Insolvency Act 1986 (c. 45) and ones which modify the way in which rights of persons other than the chargee may be exercised in relation to property subject to those charges.

Regulation 2 defines certain expressions used elsewhere in the regulations. It provides that a charge to which the relevant provisions of Part VII are extended is referred to in the regulations as a "system-charge". Regulation 2 also provides that certain of the expressions used in the regulations have the same meaning as in the Uncertificated Securities Regulations 1995.

Regulations 3 and 4 apply the relevant provisions of Part VII (as modified by the regulations) in relation to system-charges and to property subject to such charges if the conditions mentioned in regulation 4 are met.

Regulation 5 provides that Part VII applies in relation to a system-charge only to the extent that it is a charge over property of particular kinds and is granted to secure obligations of particular kinds.

Regulations 6 and 7 limit the disapplication of certain provisions of the Insolvency Act 1986 in relation to system-charges. The provisions in question are ones which restrict the ability of persons to take steps to enforce any security they have over the property of a company during the course of administration proceedings under the Insolvency Act.

Regulation 8 makes provision as to the ability of an administrator and certain kinds of receiver to recover property subject to a system-charge after a particular period if the property is not required for one of the purposes specified in the regulation.

The Regulations (regulation 9) also make provision clarifying the effect of those provisions of Part VII which require investment exchanges and clearing houses recognised under the Financial Services Act 1986 to have default rules enabling them to deal with certain contracts into which they enter on recognised investment exchanges and recognised clearing houses which do not enter into contracts of the relevant kind.

# THE DEREGULATION (RESOLUTIONS OF PRIVATE COMPANIES) ORDER 1996

(SI 1996/1471)

*Made on 5 June 1996 by the Secretary of State for Trade and Industry under s. 1 of the Deregulation and Contracting Out Act 1994. Operative from 19 June 1996.*

## CITATION, COMMENCEMENT AND INTERPRETATION

**1(1)** This Order may be cited as the Deregulation (Resolutions of Private Companies) Order 1996 and shall come into force 14 days after the day on which it is made.

**1(2)** In this Order **"the 1985 Act"** means the Companies Act 1985.

## ELECTIVE RESOLUTIONS: EFFECT WHEN PASSED AT MEETINGS CONVENED AT SHORT NOTICE

**2** [Insertion of s. 379A(2A).]

## WRITTEN RESOLUTIONS: AUDITORS

**3(1)** [Substitution of s. 381B.]

**3(2)** [Amendments of s. 381A(5); s. 390(2); and Sch. 24.]

**3(3)** This article has effect in relation to written resolutions first proposed on or after the day on which this Order comes into force.

## WRITTEN RESOLUTIONS: RELATIONSHIP OF STATUTORY PROCEDURE AND COMPANY'S CONSTITUTION

**4** [Insertion of words at the end of s. 381C(1).]

## EXPLANATORY NOTE

*(This Note is not part of the Order)*

This Order, which is made under section 1 of the Deregulation and Contracting Out Act 1994 (c. 40), amends certain provisions of the Companies Act 1985 (c. 6) concerning the resolutions of private companies.

Article 2 amends section 379A (elective resolution of private company) by enabling less than 21 days' notice to be given of a meeting at which an elective resolution is to be proposed, provided that all members entitled to attend and vote at that meeting agree to the short notice.

Article 3(1) substitutes a new section 381B (duty to notify auditors of proposed written resolution). The new section imposes a duty on the directors and secretary of a company to send the company's auditors a copy, or otherwise inform them of the contents, of any written resolution proposed under section 381A (written resolutions of private companies) at or before the time that resolution is supplied to a member for signature. Breach of the duty will result in the commission of a criminal offence (for which the new section provides certain defences), but will not affect the validity of any resolution passed under section 381A. Article 3(2) makes amendments consequential on the substitution of the new section. Article 3(3) provides for the new section to apply to written resolutions first proposed on or after the day on which this Order comes into force.

Article 4 amends section 381C(1) (written resolutions: supplementary provisions) to make clear that the statutory written resolution procedure under sections 381A and 381B may be used notwithstanding any provision in a private company's memorandum or articles, but does not prejudice any power conferred by any such provision.

# THE DISCLOSURE OF INTERESTS IN SHARES (AMENDMENT) REGULATIONS 1996

(SI 1996/1560)

*Made on 14 June 1996 by the Secretary of State for Trade and Industry under s. 210A of the Companies Act 1985. Operative from 15 July 1996.*

## CITATION AND COMMENCEMENT

1 These Regulations may be cited as the Disclosure of Interests in Shares (Amendment) Regulations 1996 and shall come into force on 15th July 1996.

## INTERESTS TO BE DISREGARDED FOR DISCLOSURE PURPOSES

2 [Insertion of s. 209(9A), (9B) into the Companies Act 1985.]

## EXPLANATORY NOTE

(*This Note is not part of the Regulations*)

These Regulations make provision for disregarding, for the purposes of the disclosure of interests in shares pursuant to sections 198 to 202 of the Companies Act 1985, certain interests in shares arising from arrangements effected under a computer-based system for the transfer of title to securities otherwise than by a written instrument where the operator of the system is approved by the Treasury under the Uncertificated Securities Regulations 1995 ("the system").

Where:

(a) securities of a particular aggregate value are transferred by one person ("the transferor") to another person ("the transferee") under the system;

(b) those securities are of kinds and amounts determined by the facilities and procedures maintained and operated by the operator of the system; and

(c) those securities, or securities of the same kinds and amounts are returned to the transferor on the next day on which the system is in operation,

any interest of the transferee in those securities is disregarded for the purposes of sections 198 to 202 of the Companies Act 1985.

or potential participator in the same joint enterprise if the only reason why the advertisement would be subject to the provisions of section 57 of the Act is because it contains an invitation or information of the kind described in section 57(2) of the Act which is made or given in connection with, or for the purposes of, the joint enterprise.

## SALE OF GOODS AND SUPPLY OF SERVICES

**9(1)** For the purposes of this article–

(a) the expressions **"supplier"** and **"related sale or supply"** shall be construed in accordance with paragraph 19 of Schedule 1 to the Act and the expression **"customer"** shall also be construed in accordance with that paragraph except that it shall be construed as excluding references to an individual; and

(b) a group shall be treated as including any body corporate in which a member of the group holds a qualifying capital interest within the meaning of paragraph 30 of Schedule 1 to the Act.

**9(2)** Subject to paragraph (3) below, section 57 of the Act shall not apply to an investment advertisement issued or caused to be issued by a supplier or a body corporate in the same group as a supplier to a customer or a body corporate in the same group as a customer if the only reason why the advertisement would be subject to the provisions of section 57 of the Act is because it contains an invitation or information of the kind described in section 57(2) of the Act which is made or given for the purposes of or in connection with the supplier selling or offering or agreeing to sell goods to the customer or supplying or offering or agreeing to supply him with services or is given for the purposes of or in connection with a related sale or supply provided that the supplier's main business is to supply goods or services and not to engage in activities falling within Part II of Schedule 1 to the Act.

**9(3)** This article shall not apply to an advertisement which contains an invitation or information with respect to an investment falling within paragraph 6 or 10 of Schedule 1 to the Act or, so far as relevant to either of those paragraphs, paragraph 11 of that Schedule.

## OVERSEAS PERSONS

**10(1)** In this article **"overseas person"** means a person who does not fall within section 1(3)(a) of the Act.

**10(2)** Subject to the provisions of paragraph (3) below, section 57 of the Act shall not apply to an investment advertisement which an overseas person issues or causes to be issued to another person if that other person is either–

(a) a person with or for whom the overseas person has, in the course of carrying on investment business, effected or arranged for the effecting of a transaction within the period of twelve months ending with the date on which the investment advertisement was issued; or

(b) a person to whom the overseas person has, in the course of carrying on such business, provided custody services falling within paragraph 13A of Schedule 1 to the Act within that period; or

(c) a person to whom the overseas person has, in the course of carrying on such a business, given advice falling within paragraph 15 of Schedule 1 to the Act within that period; or

(d) a person on whose behalf the overseas person has, in the course of carrying on such business, sent or caused to be sent dematerialised instructions falling within paragraph 16A of Schedule 1 to the Act within that period.

**10(3)** The provisions of paragraph (2) shall not apply unless –

(a) in a case within paragraph (2)(a) above, the transaction was effected or arranged at a time when the other person was neither resident nor had a place of business in the United Kingdom; or

(b) in a case within paragraph (2)(b) above, the custody services were provided outside the United Kingdom at a time when the other person was neither resident nor had a place of business in the United Kingdom; or

(c) in a case within paragraph (2)(c) above, the advice was given outside the United Kingdom at a time when the other person was neither resident nor had a place of business in the United Kingdom; or

(d) in a case within paragraph (2)(d) above, the dematerialised instruction was sent, or caused to be sent when the other person was neither resident nor had a place of business in the United Kingdom; or

(e) in a case within paragraph (2)(a), (b), (c) or (d), if the transaction was effected or arranged, or the custody services were provided, or the advice was given or the dematerialised instruction was sent or caused to be sent otherwise than in the circumstances described in whichever is relevant of sub-paragraph (a), (b), (c) or (d) of this paragraph, the overseas person had, on a previous occasion and in the course of carrying on investment business –
   (i) effected or arranged for the effecting of a transaction with or for the other person in the circumstances described in sub-paragraph (a) of this paragraph; or
   (ii) provided to the other person custody services falling within paragraph 13A of Schedule 1 to the Act in the circumstances described in sub-paragraph (b) of this paragraph; or
   (iii) given the other person advice falling within paragraph 15 of Schedule 1 to the Act in the circumstances described in sub-paragraph (c) of this paragraph; or
   (iv) sent or caused to be sent, on behalf of the other person a dematerialised instruction falling within paragraph 16A of Schedule 1 to the Act in the circumstances described in sub-paragraph (d) of this paragraph.

**History**

Art. 10 substituted by the Financial Services Act 1986 (Investment Advertisements) (Exemptions) Order 1997 (SI 1997/963), art. 1, 2 and 3 as from 1 June 1997. Former art. 10 read as follows:

"(1) In this article **"overseas person"** means a person who does not fall within section 1(3)(a) of the Act.

(2) Subject to the provisions of paragraph (3) below, section 57 of the Act shall not apply to an investment advertisement which an overseas person issues or causes to be issued to another person if that other person is either–

(a) a person with or for whom the overseas person has, in the course of carrying on investment business, effected or arranged for the effecting of a transaction within the period of twelve months ending with the date on which the investment advertisement was issued; or

(b) a person to whom the overseas person has, in the course of carrying on such business, given advice falling within paragraph 15 of Schedule 1 to the Act within that period; or

(c) a person on whose behalf the overseas person has, in the course of carrying on such business, sent, or caused to be sent, dematerialised instructions falling within paragraph 16A of Schedule 1 to the Act within that period.

(3) The provisions of paragraph (2) above shall not apply unless–

(a) in a case within paragraph (2)(a) above, the transaction was effected or arranged at a time when the other person was neither resident nor had a place of business in the United Kingdom; or

(b) in a case within paragraph (2)(b) above, the advice was given outside the United Kingdom at a time when the other person was neither resident nor had a place of business in the United Kingdom; or

(c) in a case within paragraph (2)(c) above, the dematerialised instruction was sent, or caused to be sent, when the other person was neither resident nor had a place of business in the United Kingdom; or

(d) in a case within paragraph (2)(a), (b) or (c), if the transaction was effected or arranged or the advice was given or the dematerialised instruction was sent or caused to be sent otherwise than in the circumstances described in whichever is relevant of sub-paragraph (a), (b) or (c) of this paragraph, the overseas person had, on a previous occasion and in the course of carrying on investment business–

(i) effected or arranged for the effecting of a transaction with or for the other person in the circumstances described in sub-paragraph (a) of this paragraph; or

(ii) given the other person advice falling within paragraph 15 of Schedule 1 to the Act in the circumstances described in sub-paragraph (b) of this paragraph; or

(iii) sent or caused to be sent, on behalf of the other person a dematerialised instruction falling within paragraph 16A of Schedule 1 to the Act in the circumstances described in sub-paragraph (c) of this paragraph."

## ADVERTISEMENTS ISSUED TO PERSONS SUFFICIENTLY EXPERT TO UNDERSTAND THE RISKS INVOLVED

**11(1)** In this article **"relevant person"** means a person who is not an authorised person nor a European investment firm carrying on home-regulated investment business in the United Kingdom and who is not unlawfully carrying on investment business in the United Kingdom.

**History**

In art. 11(1) the words " nor a European investment firm carrying on home-regulated investment business in the United Kingdom" inserted by the Financial Services Act 1986 (Investment Advertisements) (Exemptions) Order 1997 (SI 1997/963), art. 1, 2 and 4(a) as from 1 June 1997.

**11(2)** Section 57 of the Act shall not apply to an investment advertisement issued or caused to be issued by a relevant person if either–

Australian Stock Exchange Limited.
Basler Effektenbourse.
Bolsa Mexicana de Valores.
Boston Stock Exchange.
Bourse de Geneve.
Chicago Board Options Exchange.
Cincinnati Stock Exchange.
Effektenborsenverein Zurich.
Fukuoka Stock Exchange.
Hiroshima Stock Exchange.
Johannesburg Stock Exchange.
Korea Stock Exchange.
Kuala Lumpur Stock Exchange.
Kyoto Securities Exchange.
Midwest Stock Exchange.
The Montreal Exchange.
Nagoya Stock Exchange.
NASDAQ.
New York Stock Exchange.
New Zealand Stock Exchange.
Niigata Stock Exchange.
Osaka Securities Exchange.
Pacific Stock Exchange.
Philadelphia Stock Exchange.
Sapporo Securities Exchange.
Securities Exchange of Thailand.
Singapore Stock Exchange.
Stock Exchange of Hong Kong Limited.
Tokyo Stock Exchange.
Toronto Stock Exchange.
Vancouver Stock Exchange.
Winnipeg Stock Exchange.

# Schedule 3 – Other Markets Relevant for the Purposes of Article 16

Article 16

Australian Financial Futures Market.
Chicago Board of Trade.
Chicago Mercantile Exchange.
Coffee, Sugar and Cocoa Exchange, Inc.
Commodity Exchange, Inc.
Hong Kong Futures Exchange.
International Securities Market Association.
Kansas City Board of Trade.

Mid-America Commodity Exchange.

Minneapolis Grain Exchange.

New York Cotton Exchange (including the Citrus Associates of the New York Cotton Exchange).

New York Futures Exchange.

New York Mercantile Exchange.

New Zealand Futures Exchange.

Philadelphia Board of Trade.

Singapore International Monetary Exchange.

South African Futures Exchange (SAFEX).

Swiss Options and Financial Futures Exchange (SOFFEX).

Sydney Futures Exchange.

Toronto Futures Exchange.

# Schedule 4 – Advertisements Relating to Matters of Common Interest

Article 12

**1** An advertisement complies with the requirements of this Schedule if it complies with the requirements of paragraphs 2, 3 and 4 below.

**2** An advertisement complies with the requirements of this paragraph if it contains a statement made by the directors or the persons named therein as promoters of the company accepting responsibility therefor without any limitation of liability on the basis that they have taken all reasonable care to ensure that every statement whether of fact or opinion which it contains is true and not misleading in the form and context in which it is included.

**3** An advertisement complies with the requirements of this paragraph if it contains either–

(a) a statement by the directors or the persons named therein as promoters of the company also accepting responsibility therefor without any limitation of liability that they have taken all reasonable care to ensure that the document contains all such information as a person such as the person or persons to whom the advertisement is addressed and their professional advisers would reasonably require and reasonably expect to find there for the purpose of making an informed assessment of the assets and liabilities, financial position, profits and losses, and prospects of the company and the rights attaching to the shares or debentures to which the document relates; or

(b) the words "you should regard any subscription for shares in or debentures of this company as made primarily to assist the furtherance of its objectives (other than any purely financial objectives) and only secondarily, if at all, as an investment".

**4** An advertisement complies with the requirements of this paragraph if it contains prominently the words "If you are in any doubt about this offer you should consult a person authorised under the Financial Services Act 1986 who specialises in advising on investments of the kind being offered" or other words to a like effect.

## EXPLANATORY NOTE

(*This Note is not part of the Order*)

This Order provides for certain exemptions from the restrictions on advertising imposed by section 57 of the Financial Services Act 1986. It revokes the Financial Services Act 1986 (Investment Advertisements) (Exemptions) Order 1995 and reproduces its provisions with amendments to articles 4 and 10 relating to the sending of dematerialised instructions and certain other minor amendments.

Article 3 of the Order concerns advertisements issued by bodies corporate to members and creditors. Article 4 concerns advertisements which are issued or caused to be issued by a body

(a) the reference in subsection (1) to an auditor of an authorised person included–
(i) a reference to an auditor of a body with which a qualifying person is closely linked by control who is also an auditor of that person; and
(ii) a reference to an auditor of a qualifying undertaking;

(b) the second reference in that subsection to the authorised person, and the reference in subsection (3) to that person, included a reference to such a body or undertaking.

**10(2)** In this regulation–

**"qualifying person"** means a UK investment firm, or a trustee or manager of a qualifying undertaking;

**"qualifying undertaking"** means an undertaking to which the UCITS Directive applies and which is, within the meaning of that Directive, situated in the United Kingdom;

**"trustee"**–
(a) in relation to a qualifying undertaking which is a unit trust scheme, means the person holding the property in question on trust for the participants;
(b) in relation to any other qualifying undertaking, means any person who (whether or not under a trust) is entrusted with the custody of the property in question;

**"the UCITS Directive"** means the Council Directive of 20th December 1985 on the coordination of laws, regulations and administrative provisions relating to undertakings for collective investment in transferable securities (No. 85/611/EEC);

**"UK investment firm"** has the same meaning as in the Investment Services Regulations 1995;

and other expressions which are also used in the Financial Services Act have the same meanings as in that Act.

## DISCLOSURE OF INFORMATION: INVESTMENT SERVICES

**11(1)** [Amendment of reg. 48(3) of the Investment Services Regulations 1995.]

**11(2)** [Insertion of reg. 48(10) into the 1995 Regulations.]

**11(3)** [Substitution of para. 6 of Sch. 8 to the 1995 Regulations by paras. set out in Sch. 2.]

## DISCLOSURE OF INFORMATION: UCITS

**12(1)** This paragraph applies to any confidential information which–

(a) any person who works or has worked for any person designated by the United Kingdom as a competent authority for the purposes of Article 49 of the UCITS Directive; or

(b) any auditor or expert instructed by such an authority,

has received in the course of discharging his duties as such a person, auditor or expert in relation to an undertaking to which the UCITS Directive applies and which is, within the meaning of that Directive, situated in an EEA State.

**12(2)** Section 179 of the Financial Services Act shall not apply to information to which paragraph (1) above applies.

**12(3)** Information to which paragraph (1) above applies shall not be disclosed by any person referred to in sub-paragraph (a) or (b) of that paragraph, or by any person receiving it directly or indirectly from such a person, except in any of the circumstances specified in paragraphs 2 to 11 of Article 50 of the UCITS Directive (as inserted by the Prudential Supervision Directive), the text of which (as so inserted) is set out in Schedule 3 to these Regulations.

**12(4)** For the purposes of paragraph (3) above information to which paragraph (1) above applies may, subject to the provisions of paragraph (6) below, be disclosed in the circumstances described in Article 50.11 of the UCITS Directive.

**12(5)** Information received under Article 50.3 of the UCITS Directive may not be communicated in the circumstances referred to in Article 50.10 of that Directive without the express consent of the supervisory authority from whom it was obtained.

**12(6)** Information of the kind described in the third paragraph of Article 50.11 of the UCITS Directive may not be disclosed in the cases referred to in Article 50.11 except with the express consent of whichever is relevant of the authorities mentioned in the third paragraph of Article 50.11.

**12(7)** Any person who contravenes any provision of this regulation shall be guilty of an offence and liable–

(a) on conviction on indictment, to imprisonment for a term not exceeding two years or to a fine or to both;

(b) on summary conviction, to imprisonment for a term not exceeding three months or to a fine not exceeding the statutory maximum or to both.

**12(8)** Proceedings in respect of an offence under this Regulation shall not be instituted–

(a) in England and Wales, except by or with the consent of the Secretary of State or the Director of Public Prosecutions; or

(b) in Northern Ireland, except by or with the consent of the Secretary of State or the Director of Public Prosecutions for Northern Ireland.

**12(9)** In proceedings brought against any person for an offence under this regulation, it shall be a defence for him to prove that he took all reasonable precautions and exercised all due diligence to avoid the commission of the offence.

**12(10)** In this regulation–

**"EEA State"** means a State which is a contracting party to the agreement on the European Economic Area signed at Oporto on 2nd May 1992 as adjusted by the Protocol signed at Brussels on 17th March 1993;

**"the UCITS Directive"** has the same meaning as in regulation 10 above.

### THE BOARD'S FUNCTIONS UNDER THE REGULATIONS

**13** The functions of the Board under these Regulations shall be treated for the purposes of the Financial Services Act and the Transfer of Functions (Financial Services) Order 1992 as if they were functions under Chapter VI of Part I of that Act which–

(a) had been functions of the Secretary of State; and

(b) had been transferred to the Board by the Financial Services Act 1986 (Delegation) Order 1987.

# Schedule 1 – Meaning of "Closely Linked": Modifications of Companies Act Provisions

Regulation 2(3)

### PRELIMINARY

**1** The modifications of sections 258 to 260 of and Schedule 10A to the Companies Act 1985 which are referred to in regulation 2(3) above are as follows.

### ABILITY TO APPOINT MAJORITY OF DIRECTORS

**2(1)** After subsection (2) of section 258 the insertion of the following subsection–

"(2A) An undertaking is also a parent undertaking in relation to another undertaking, a subsidiary undertaking, if–

(a) it is a member of the undertaking and, at all times since the beginning of the undertaking's immediately preceding financial year, a majority of the undertaking's board of directors have been directors who were appointed solely as a result of the exercise of its voting rights, and

(b) no other person is the undertaking's parent undertaking by virtue of paragraph (a), (b) or (c) of subsection (2)."

**2(2)** In subsection (3) of that section, after the words "subsection (2)" the insertion of the words "or 2A".

## PARTICIPATION WITHOUT CONTROL

**3(1)** After subsection (3) of section 258 the insertion of the following subsections–

"(3A) Subject to subsection (3B) below, an undertaking is also a parent undertaking in relation to another undertaking, a subsidiary undertaking, if it has a participating interest in the undertaking which–

(a) entitles it to 20 per cent or more of the voting rights in the undertaking, or

(b) comprises 20 per cent or more of the shares of the undertaking.

(3B) For the purpose of determining whether a person has a participating interest in an undertaking which is a building society (within the meaning of the Building Societies Act 1986), subsection (3A) above shall have effect as if the reference in paragraph (b) to shares were a reference to deferred shares (within the meaning of that Act)."

**3(2)** After subsection (5) of that section the insertion of the following subsection–

"(5A) An undertaking ("A") shall not be treated as a parent undertaking of an undertaking ("B") by reason only that another undertaking which is A's subsidiary undertaking by virtue of subsection (3A) is a parent undertaking of B."

**3(3)** After subsection (4) of section 259 the insertion of the following subsection–

"(4A) Two subsidiary undertakings of the same parent undertaking shall not be fellow subsidiary undertakings if either of them is a subsidiary undertaking by virtue of section 258(3A)."

**3(4)** In subsection (5) of section 260, for the words "section 258(4)" the substitution of the words "section 258(3A) or (4)".

**3(5)** In paragraph 2(1) of Schedule 10A, after the words "section 258(2)(a) and (d)" the insertion of the words "and (3A)(a)".

## EXPLANATORY NOTE

(*This Note is not part of the Regulations*)

These Regulations give effect to European Parliament and Council Directive 95/26/EC (OJ No. L168, 18.7.95, p.7) amending Directives 77/780/EEC and 89/646/EEC in the field of credit institutions, Directives 73/239/EEC and 92/49/EEC in the field of non-life insurance, Directives 79/267/EEC and 92/96/EEC in the field of life assurance, Directive 93/22/EEC in the field of investment firms and Directive 85/611/EEC in the field of undertakings for collective investment in transferable securities (UCITS) with a view to reinforcing prudential supervision.

Part I of the Regulations, together with Schedule 1, defines various words and phrases, including "closely linked", for the purposes of the Regulations.

Part II of the Regulations makes provision for banking institutions. It amends sections 9 and 11 of the Banking Act 1987 (c.22) so that the Bank of England must refuse an application for authorisation (and may revoke authorisation) where a credit institution is closely linked to another person and where those close links would prevent the effective exercise of the Bank's supervisory functions in relation to the institution. The protection given by section 47 of the Banking Act to certain auditors is extended. Part V of the Banking Act is amended so as to permit the disclosure of information in certain circumstances.

Part III of the Regulations makes provision for building societies. Amendments are made to the Building Societies Act 1986 (c. 53) which broadly correspond to those made to the Banking Act.

Part IV of and Schedules 2 and 3 to the Regulations make provision in relation to financial services. Sections 27, 28 and 43 of, and paragraph 2 of Schedule 2 to the Financial Services Act 1986 (c.60) are to have effect in such a way as to reflect the requirements of the Directive in relation to the grant and revocation of authorisation of investment firms and other authorised institutions, and the recognition of self-regulating organisations. The protection given by section 109 of the Act to certain auditors is extended. Provision is made for the disclosure of information in relation to investment firms and UCITS.

Part V of the Regulations makes provision for friendly societies to which section 37(2) or (3) of the Friendly Societies Act 1992 (c.40) applies ("Directive societies"). Amendments are made to the Friendly Societies Act 1992 which broadly correspond to those made to the Banking Act. Directive societies are required to have their principal place of business situated in the United Kingdom or, in the case of those Directive societies registered under the Friendly Societies Act 1974 (c.46), in the British Islands.

Part VI of the Regulations makes provision for insurance companies. Amendments are made to the Insurance Companies Act 1982 (c.50) which broadly correspond to those made to the Banking Act. In addition, Part VI imposes a duty on certain insurance companies to notify the Secretary of State if they become closely linked to another person.

Part VII of the Regulations deals with miscellaneous and supplemental matters, including transitory provisions for States which are parties to the European Economic Area Agreement but which may not have implemented the Directive fully before the coming into force of the Regulations.

Schedule 4 to the Regulations amends statutory instruments made in 1994 dealing with the duties of auditors of banks and other institutions to which the Directive applies.

Schedule 5 to the Regulations makes minor and consequential amendments to the Banking Act 1987, the Building Societies Act 1986, the Friendly Societies Act 1992 and the Insurance Companies Act 1982, the Banking Coordination (Second Council Directive) Regulations 1992 (SI 1992/3218) and the Investment Services Regulations 1995 (SI 1995/3275).

# THE INSOLVENT COMPANIES (REPORTS ON CONDUCT OF DIRECTORS) RULES 1996

(SI 1996/1909)

*Made on 22 July 1996 by the Lord Chancellor and the Secretary of State for Trade and Industry, under s. 411 and 413 of the Insolvency Act 1986 and s. 21(2) of the Company Directors Disqualification Act 1986. Operative from 30 September 1996.*

## CITATION, COMMENCEMENT AND INTERPRETATION

**1(1)** These Rules may be cited as the Insolvent Companies (Reports on Conduct of Directors) Rules 1996.

**1(2)** These Rules shall come into force on 30th September 1996.

**1(3)** In these Rules–

**"the Act"** means the Company Directors Disqualification Act 1986;

**"the former Rules"** means the Insolvent Companies (Reports on Conduct of Directors) No. 2 Rules 1986; and

**"the commencement date"** means 30th September 1996.

## REVOCATION

**2** Subject to rule 7 below the former Rules are hereby revoked.

## REPORTS REQUIRED UNDER SECTION 7(3) OF THE ACT

**3(1)** This rule applies to any report made to the Secretary of State under section 7(3) of the Act by:–

(a) the liquidator of a company which the courts in England and Wales have jurisdiction to wind up which passes a resolution for voluntary winding up on or after the commencement date;

(b) an administrative receiver of a company appointed otherwise than under section 51 of the Insolvency Act 1986 (power to appoint receiver under the law of Scotland) on or after the commencement date; or

(c) the administrator of a company which the courts in England and Wales have jurisdiction



CCH.New Law
bbcl randr5 Mp 4536—bcl98 225b

to wind up in relation to which the court makes an administration order on or after the commencement date.

**3(2)** Such a report shall be made in the Form D1 set out in the Schedule hereto, or in a form which is substantially similar, and in the manner and to the extent required by the Form D1.

## RETURN BY OFFICE-HOLDER

**4(1)** This rule applies where it appears to a liquidator of a company as mentioned in rule 3(1)(a), to an administrative receiver as mentioned in rule 3(l)(b), or to an administrator as mentioned in rule 3(1)(c) (each of whom is referred to hereinafter as **"an office-holder"**) that the company has at any time become insolvent within the meaning of section 6(2) of the Act.

**4(2)** Subject as follows there may be furnished to the Secretary of State by an office-holder at any time during the period of 6 months from the relevant date (defined in paragraph (4) below) a return with respect to every person who:–

(a) was, on the relevant date, a director or shadow director of the company, or

(b) had been a director or shadow director of the company at any time in the 3 years immediately preceding that date.

**4(3)** The return shall be made in the Form D2 set out in the Schedule hereto, or in a form which is substantially similar, and in the manner and to the extent required by the Form D2.

**4(4)** For the purposes of this rule, **"the relevant date"** means:–

(a) in the case of a company in creditors' voluntary winding up (there having been no declaration of solvency by the directors under section 89 of the Insolvency Act 1986), the date of the passing of the resolution for voluntary winding up,

(b) in the case of a company in members' voluntary winding up, the date on which the liquidator forms the opinion that, at the time when the company went into liquidation, its assets were insufficient for the payment of its debts and other liabilities and the expenses of winding up,

(c) in the case of the administrative receiver, the date of his appointment,

(d) in the case of the administrator, the date of the administration order made in relation to the company,

and for the purposes of sub-paragraph (c) above the only appointment of an administrative receiver to be taken into account in determining the relevant date shall be that appointment which is not that of a successor in office to an administrative receiver who has vacated office either by death or pursuant to section 45 of the Insolvency Act 1986.

**4(5)** Subject to paragraph (6) below, it shall be the duty of an office-holder to furnish a return complying with the provisions of paragraphs (3) and (4) of this rule to the Secretary of State:–

(a) where he is in office in relation to the company on the day one week before the expiry of the period of 6 months from the relevant date, not later than the expiry of such period;

(b) where he vacates office (otherwise than by death) before the day one week before the expiry of the period of 6 months from the relevant date, within 14 days after his vacation of office except where he has furnished such a return on or prior to the day one week before the expiry of such period.

**4(6)** A return need not be provided under this rule by an office-holder if he has, whilst holding that office in relation to the company, since the relevant date, made a report under rule 3 with respect to all persons falling within paragraph (2) of this rule and (apart from this paragraph) required to be the subject of a return.

**4(7)** If an office-holder without reasonable excuse fails to comply with the duty imposed by paragraph (5) of this rule, he is guilty of an offence and–

(a) on summary conviction ofthe offence, is liable to a fine not exceeding level 3 on the standard scale, and

(b) after continued contravention, is liable to a daily default fine; that is to say, he is liable on a second or subsequent summary conviction of the offence to a fine of one-tenth of level 3 on the standard scale for each day on which the contravention is continued (instead of the penalty specified in sub-paragraph (a)).

**4(8)** Section 431 of the Insolvency Act 1986 (summary proceedings), as it applies to England and Wales, has effect in relation to an offence under this rule as to offences under Parts I to VII of that Act.

## FORMS

**5** The forms referred to in rule 3(2) and rule 4(3) shall be used with such variations, if any, as the circumstances may require.

## ENFORCEMENT OF SECTION 7(4)

**6(1)** This rule applies where under section 7(4) of the Act (power to call on liquidators, former liquidators and others to provide information) the Secretary of State or the official receiver requires or has required a person:–

(a) to furnish him with information with respect to a person's conduct as director or shadow director of a company, and

(b) to produce and permit inspection of relevant books, papers and other records.

**6(2)** On the application of the Secretary of State or (as the case may be) the official receiver, the court may make an order directing compliance within such period as may be specified.

**6(3)** The court's order may provide that all costs of and incidental to the application shall be borne by the person to whom the order is directed.

## TRANSITIONAL AND SAVING PROVISIONS

**7(1)** Subject to paragraph (2) below, rules 3 and 4 of the former Rules shall continue to apply as if the former Rules had not been revoked when any of the events mentioned in sub-paragraphs (a), (b) or (c) of rule 3(1) of the former Rules (passing of resolution for voluntary winding up, appointment of administrative receiver, making of administration order) occurred on or after 29th December 1986 but before the commencement date.

**7(2)** Until 31st December 1996–

(a) the forms contained in the Schedule to the former Rules which were required to be used for the purpose of complying with those Rules, or

(b) the Form Dl or D2 as set out in the Schedule to these Rules, as appropriate, or a form which is substantially similar thereto, with such variations, if any, as the circumstances may require,

may be used for the purpose of complying with rules 3 and 4 of the former Rules as applied by paragraph (1) above; but after that date the forms mentioned in sub-paragraph (b) of this paragraph shall be used for that purpose.

**7(3)** When a period referred to in rule 5(2) of the former Rules is current immediately before the commencement date, these Rules have effect as if rule 6(2) of these Rules had been in force when the period began and the period is deemed to expire whenever it would have expired if these Rules had not been made and any right, obligation or power dependent on the beginning, duration or end of such period shall be under rule 6(2) of these Rules as it was or would have been under the said rule 5(2).

**7(4)** The provisions of this rule are to be without prejudice to the operation of section 16 of the Interpretation Act 1978 (saving from repeals) as it is applied by section 23 of that Act.

## Schedule

Rules 3(2), 4(3) and 7(2)

**Note**
The Forms are not reproduced here but are as follows:

| *Form* | *Title* |
|---|---|
| D1 | Report under section 7(3) of the Company Directors Disqualification Act 1986. |
| D2 | Return of office-holder under rule 4 of the Insolvent Companies (Reports on Conduct of Directors) Rules 1996. |

## EXPLANATORY NOTE

(*This Note is not part of the Rules*)

These Rules revoke and replace the Insolvent Companies (Reports on Conduct of Directors) No. 2 Rules 1986 (S.I. 1986/2134) (**"the 1986 Rules"**) subject to transitional and saving provisions.

The Rules make provision in relation to England and Wales for the manner in which a voluntary liquidator, administrative receiver or administrator of a company, (**"the office-holder"**), is to make a report to the Secretary of State, under section 7(3) of the Company Directors Disqualification Act 1986 (**"the Act"**) in relation to any person who has been a director or shadow director of an insolvent company and whose conduct appears to the office-holder to be such that he is unfit to be concerned in the management of a company. The Rules also provide for returns to be made to the Secretary of State by office-holders, in respect of directors or shadow directors of an insolvent company, where a report has not already been made in respect of such persons under section 7(3) of the Act.

Rules 3 and 4 apply in respect of reports and returns to be made where the relevant insolvency proceedings have commenced (that is, when one of the following events has occurred: the company has passed a resolution for it to be voluntarily wound up; an administrative receiver has been appointed; or an administration order has been made) on or after 30th September 1996.

Rule 3, taken with rule 5, provides that reports under section 7(3) of the Act should be made in Form Dl set out in the Schedule or in a substantially similar form, with any necessary variations.

Rule 4, taken with rule 5, provides for a return to be made in Form D2 set out in the Schedule or in a substantially similar form, with any necessary variations, in relation to every person who has been a director or shadow director of an insolvent company on, or within the three years prior to, the commencement of the relevant insolvency proceedings. The return is required to be made by the office-holder in office one week before the end of six months after the commencement of those insolvency proceedings, and by any office-holder who vacates office during that period, except where he has made a report under rule 3 covering every such person.

Rule 6 enables the Secretary of State or the official receiver to apply to the court to enforce compliance by the office-holder with a requirement under section 7(4) of the Act to furnish information and books, papers and other records relevant to the conduct of a person as a director.

Rule 7 contains transitional and saving provisions under which rules 3 and 4 of the 1986 Rules (which made provision for purposes similar to those for which rules 3 and 4 of these Rules provide) remain in force, with modifications relating to the forms to be used, for cases where the relevant insolvency proceedings commenced on or after 29th December 1986 and before 30th September 1996.

By virtue of the operation of sections 22A and 22B respectively of the Act, the Act applies to building societies within the meaning of the Building Societies Act 1986 (c. 53) and to incorporated friendly societies within the meaning of the Friendly Societies Act 1992 (c. 40) as it applies to companies and these Rules apply similarly.

Important changes made by these Rules are that:–

(a) only one form is now prescribed for a section 7(3) report and one for a return to be made under the Rules;

(b) every office-holder is now required by rule 4(5) to make a return to the Secretary of State in accordance with rule 4 (except where he has made a report as described under rule 4(6)).

A Compliance Cost Assessment is available copies of which have been placed in the libraries of both Houses of Parliament. Copies are also available from The Insolvency Service of the Department of Trade and Industry, P.O. Box 203, Room 5.1, 21 Bloomsbury Street, London WC1B 3QW.

# THE INSOLVENT COMPANIES (REPORTS ON CONDUCT OF DIRECTORS) (SCOTLAND) RULES 1996

(SI 1996/1910 (S 154))

*Made on 22 July 1996 by the Secretary of State for Trade and Industry under s. 411 of the Insolvency Act 1986 and s. 21(2) of the Company Directors Disqualification Act 1986. Operative from 30 September 1996.*

## CITATION, COMMENCEMENT AND INTERPRETATION

**1(1)** These Rules may be cited as the Insolvent Companies (Reports on Conduct of Directors) (Scotland) Rules 1996.

**1(2)** These Rules shall come into force on 30th September 1996.

**1(3)** In these Rules–

**"the Act"** means the Company Directors Disqualification Act 1986;

**"the former Rules"** means the Insolvent Companies (Reports on Conduct of Directors) (No. 2) (Scotland) Rules 1986;

**"the commencement date"** means 30th September 1996; and

**"a company"** means a company which the courts in Scotland have jurisdiction to wind up.

## REVOCATION

**2** Subject to rule 7 below the former Rules are hereby revoked.

## REPORTS REQUIRED UNDER SECTION 7(3) OF THE ACT

**3(1)** This rule applies to any report made to the Secretary of State under section 7(3) of the Act by:–

(a) the liquidator of a company which is being wound up by an order of the court made on or after the commencement date;

(b) the liquidator of a company which passes a resolution for voluntary winding up on or after that date;

(c) a receiver of a company appointed under section 51 of the Insolvency Act 1986 (power to appoint receiver under the law of Scotland) on or after that date, who is an administrative receiver; or

(d) the administrator of a company in relation to which the court makes an administration order on or after that date.

**3(2)** Such a report shall be made in the Form D1 (Scot) set out in the Schedule hereto, or in a form which is substantially similar, and in the manner and to the extent required by the Form D1 (Scot).

## RETURN BY OFFICE-HOLDER

**4(1)** This rule applies where it appears to a liquidator of a company as mentioned in rule 3(1)(a) or (b), to an administrative receiver as mentioned in rule 3(1)(c), or to an administrator as mentioned in rule 3(1)(d) (each of whom is referred to hereinafter as **"an office-holder"**) that the company has at any time become insolvent within the meaning of section 6(2) of the Act.

**4(2)** Subject as follows there may be furnished to the Secretary of State by an office-holder at any time during the period of 6 months from the relevant date (defined in paragraph (4) below) a return with respect to every person who:–

(a) was, on the relevant date, a director or shadow director of the company, or

(b) had been a director or shadow director of the company at any time in the 3 years immediately preceding that date.

**4(3)** The return shall be made in the Form D2 (Scot) set out in the Schedule hereto, or in a form which is substantially similar, and in the manner and to the extent required by the Form D2 (Scot).

**4(4)** For the purposes of this rule, **"the relevant date"** means:–

(a) in the case of a company in liquidation (except in the case mentioned in paragraph (4)(b) below), the date on which the company goes into liquidation within the meaning of section 247(2) of the Insolvency Act 1986,

(b) in the case of a company in members' voluntary winding up, the date on which the liquidator forms the opinion that, at the time when the company went into liquidation, its assets were insufficient for the payment of its debts and other liabilities and the expenses of winding up,

(c) in the case of the administrative receiver, the date of his appointment,

(d) in the case of the administrator, the date of the administration order made in relation to the company,

and for the purposes of sub-paragraph (c) above the only appointment of an administrative receiver to be taken into account in determining the relevant date shall be that appointment which is not that of a successor in office to an administrative receiver who has vacated office either by death or pursuant to section 62 of the Insolvency Act 1986.

**4(5)** Subject to paragraph (6) below, it shall be the duty of an office-holder to furnish a return complying with the provisions of paragraphs (3) and (4) of this rule to the Secretary of State:–

(a) where he is in office in relation to the company on the day one week before the expiry of the period of 6 months from the relevant date, not later than the expiry of such period;

(b) where he vacates office (otherwise than by death) before the day one week before the expiry of the period of 6 months from the relevant date, within 14 days after his vacation of office except where he has furnished such a return on or prior to the day one week before the expiry of such period.

**4(6)** A return need not be provided under this rule by an office-holder if he has, whilst holding that office in relation to the company, since the relevant date, made a report under rule 3 with respect to all persons falling within paragraph (2) of this rule and (apart from this paragraph) required to be the subject of a return.

**4(7)** If an office-holder without reasonable excuse fails to comply with the duty imposed by paragraph (5) of this rule, he is guilty of an offence and–

(a) on summary conviction of the offence, is liable to a fine not exceeding level 3 on the standard scale, and

(b) after continued contravention, is liable to a daily default fine; that is to say, he is liable on a second or subsequent summary conviction of the offence to a fine of one-tenth of level 3 on the standard scale for each day on which the contravention is continued (instead of the penalty specified in sub-paragraph (a)).

**4(8)** Section 431 of the Insolvency Act 1986 (summary proceedings), as it applies to Scotland, has effect in relation to an offence under this rule as to offences under Parts I to VII of that Act.

## FORMS

**5** The forms referred to in rule 3(2) and rule 4(3) shall be used with such variations, if any as the circumstances may require.

## ENFORCEMENT OF SECTION 7(4)

**6(1)** This rule applies where under section 7(4) of the Act (power to call on liquidators, former liquidators and others to provide information) the Secretary of State requires or has required a person:–

(a) to furnish him with information with respect to a person's conduct as director or shadow director of a company, and

(b) to produce and permit inspection of relevant books, papers and other records.

**6(2)** On the application of the Secretary of State, the court may make an order directing compliance within such period as may be specified.

**6(3)** The court's order may provide that all expenses of and incidental to the application shall be borne by the person to whom the order is directed.

## TRANSITIONAL AND SAVING PROVISIONS

**7(1)** Subject to paragraph (2) below, rules 3 and 4 of the former Rules shall continue to apply as if the former Rules had not been revoked when any of the events mentioned in sub-paragraphs (a), (b), (c) or (d) of rule 2(1) of the former Rules (order of the court for winding up, passing of resolution for voluntary winding up, appointment of administrative receiver, making of administration order) occurred on or after 29th December 1986 but before the commencement date.

**7(2)** Until 31st December 1996–

(a) the forms contained in the Schedule to the former Rules which were required to be used for the purpose of complying with those rules, or

(b) the Form Dl (Scot) or D2 (Scot) as set out in the Schedule to these rules, as appropriate, or a form which is substantially similar thereto, with such variations, if any, as the circumstances may require,

may be used for the purpose of complying with rules 3 and 4 of the former Rules as applied by paragraph (1) above; but after that date the forms mentioned in sub-paragraph (b) of this paragraph shall be used for that purpose.

**7(3)** When a period referred to in rule 5(2) of the former Rules is current immediately before the commencement date, these Rules have effect as if rule 6(2) of these Rules had been in force when the period began and the period is deemed to expire whenever it would have expired if these Rules had not been made and any right, obligation or power dependent on the beginning, duration or end of such period shall be under rule 6(2) of these Rules as it was or would have been under the said rule 5(2).

**7(4)** The provisions of this rule are to be without prejudice to the operation of section 16 of the Interpretation Act 1978 (saving from repeals) as it is applied by section 23 of that Act.

# Schedule

Rules 3(2) and 4(3) and 7(2)

**Note**
The Forms are not reproduced here but are as follows:

| *Form* | *Title* |
|---|---|
| D1 (Scot) | Report under section 7(3) of the Company Directors Disqualification Act 1986. |
| D2 (Scot) | Return by office-holder under rule 4 of the Insolvent Companies (Reports on Conduct of Directors) (Scotland) Rules 1996. |

## EXPLANATORY NOTE

(*This Note is not part of the Rules*)

These Rules revoke and replace the Insolvent Companies (Reports on Conduct of Directors) (No. 2) (Scotland) Rules 1986 (S.I. 1986/1916) (**"the 1986 Rules"**) subject to transitional and saving provisions.

The Rules make provision in relation to Scotland for the manner in which a liquidator, administrative receiver or administrator of a company (**"the office-holder"**), is to make a report to the Secretary of State, under section 7(3) of the Company Directors Disqualification Act 1986 (**"the Act"**) in relation to any person who has been a director or shadow director of an insolvent company and whose conduct appears to the office-holder to be such that he is unfit to be concerned in the management of a company.

The Rules also provide for returns to be made to the Secretary of State by office-holders, in respect of directors or shadow directors of an insolvent company, where a report has not already been made in respect of such persons under section 7(3) of the Act.

Rules 3 and 4 apply in respect of reports and returns to be made where the relevant insolvency proceedings have commenced (that is, when one of the following events has occurred: the court has ordered the company to be wound up; the company has passed a resolution for it to be voluntarily wound up; an administrative receiver has been appointed; or, an administration order has been made) on or after 30th September 1996.

Rule 3, taken with rule 5, provides that reports under section 7(3) of the Act should be made in Form D1 (Scot) set out in the Schedule or in a substantially similar form, with any necessary variations.

Rule 4, taken with rule 5, provides for a return to be made in Form D2 (Scot) set out in the Schedule or in a substantially similar form, with any necessary variations, in relation to every person who has been a director or shadow director of an insolvent company on, or within the three years prior to, the commencement of the relevant insolvency proceedings. The return is required to be made by the office-holder in office one week before the end of six months after the commencement of those insolvency proceedings, and by any office-holder who vacates office during that period, except where he has made a report under rule 3 covering every such person.

Rule 6 enables the Secretary of State to apply to the court to enforce compliance by the office-holder with a requirement under section 7(4) of the Act to furnish information and books, papers and other records relevant to the conduct of a person as a director.

Rule 7 contains transitional and saving provisions under which rule 3 and 4 of the 1986 Rules (which made provision for purposes similar to those for which rule 3 and 4 of these Rules provide) remain in force, with modifications relating to the forms to be used, for cases where the relevant insolvency proceedings commenced on or after 29th December 1986 and before 30th September 1996.

By virtue of the operation of section 22A and 22B respectively of the Act, the Act applies to building societies within the meaning of the Building Societies Act 1986 (c. 53) and to incorporated friendly societies within the meaning of the Friendly Societies Act 1992 (c. 40) as it applies to companies and these Rules apply similarly.

Important changes made by these Rules are that:–

(a) only one form is now prescribed for a section 7(3) report and one for a return to be made under the Rules;

(b) every office-holder is now required by rule 4(5) to make a return to the Secretary of State in accordance with rule 4 (except where he has made a report as described under rule 4(6)).

A Compliance Cost Assessment is available copies of which have been placed in the libraries of both Houses of Parliament. Copies are also available from The Insolvency Service of the Department of Trade and Industry, P.O. Box 203, Room 5.1, 21 Bloomsbury Street, London WC1B 3QW.

# THE OPEN-ENDED INVESTMENT COMPANIES (INVESTMENT COMPANIES WITH VARIABLE CAPITAL) REGULATIONS 1996

(SI 1996/2827)

*Made on 11 November 1996 by the Treasury under s. 2(2) of the European Communities Act 1972. Operative from 6 January 1997.*

## ARRANGEMENT OF REGULATIONS

### PART I – GENERAL



### PART II – FORMATION, SUPERVISION AND CONTROL

*General*

## PART III – CORPORATE CODE

*Organs*



*Shares*



*Operation*



*Reports*



*Mergers and divisions*

# PART I – GENERAL

## CITATION, COMMENCEMENT AND EXTENT

**1(1)** These Regulations may be cited as the Open-Ended Investment Companies (Investment Companies with Variable Capital) Regulations 1996.

**1(2)** These Regulations shall come into force on 6th January 1997.

**1(3)** Except for paragraph 7(b) of Schedule 1 to these Regulations which has effect in relation to certain collective investment schemes which have head offices in Northern Ireland, these Regulations shall have effect in relation to any investment company with variable capital which has its head office situated in Great Britain.

## INTERPRETATION

**2(1)** In these Regulations, except where the context otherwise requires–

**"the 1985 Act"** means the Companies Act 1985;

**"the 1986 Act"** means the Financial Services Act 1986;

**"annual general meeting"** has the meaning given in regulation 31(1) below;

**"annual report"** has the meaning given in regulation 60(1)(a) below;

**"authorisation order"** means an order made by SIB under regulation 9 below;

**"bearer shares"** has the meaning given in regulation 42 below;

**"court"**, in relation to any proceedings under these Regulations involving an investment company with variable capital the head office of which is situated in England and Wales, means the High Court and in relation to such a company the head office of which is situated in Scotland, means the Court of Session;

**"depositary"**, in relation to an investment company with variable capital, has the meaning given in regulation 5(1) below;

**"director"**, in relation to an investment company with variable capital, includes a person occupying in relation to it the position of director (by whatever name called);

**"investment company with variable capital"** has the meaning given in regulation 3(2) below;

**"larger denomination share"** has the meaning given in regulation 39(5) below;

**"officer"**, in relation to an investment company with variable capital, includes a director or any secretary or manager;

**"participating issuer"** and **"participating security"** have the same meaning as in the Uncertificated Securities Regulations 1995;

**"prospectus"** has the meaning given in regulation 6(2) below;

**"register of shareholders"** means the register kept under paragraph 1(1) of Schedule 4 to these Regulations;

**"scheme property"**, in relation to an investment company with variable capital, means the property subject to the collective investment scheme constituted by the company;

**"shadow director"**, in relation to an investment company with variable capital, means a person in accordance with whose directions or instructions (not being advice given in a professional capacity) the directors of that company are accustomed to act;

**"share certificate"** has the meaning given in regulation 40(1) below;

**"SIB"** means the body known as the Securities and Investments Board;

**"SIB regulations"** means any regulations made by SIB under regulation 6(1) below;

**"smaller denomination share"** has the meaning given in regulation 39(5) below;

**"transfer documents"** has the meaning given in paragraph 5(3) of Schedule 5 to these Regulations;

**"transferable securities"** has the same meaning as in the UCITS Directive;

**"UCITS Directive"** means the Council Directive co-ordinating the laws, regulations and administrative provisions relating to undertakings for collective investment in transferable securities (No. 85/611 EEC);

**"umbrella company"** means an investment company with variable capital whose instrument of incorporation provides for such pooling as is mentioned in subsection (3)(a) of section 75 of the 1986 Act (collective investment schemes: interpretation) in relation to separate parts of the scheme property and whose shareholders are entitled to exchange rights in one part for rights in another; and

**"uncertificated unit of a security"** has the same meaning as in the Uncertificated Securities Regulations 1995.

**2(2)** In these Regulations any reference to a shareholder of an investment company with variable capital is a reference to–

(a) the person who holds the share certificate, or other documentary evidence of title, mentioned in regulation 42 below; and

(b) the person whose name is entered on the company's register of shareholders in relation to any share or shares other than a bearer share.

**2(3)** In these Regulations, any reference to a controller shall be construed in accordance with subsection (5) of section 207 of the 1986 Act (interpretation); and any reference to a manager shall be construed in accordance with subsection (6) of that section.

**2(4)** In these Regulations, unless the contrary intention appears, expressions which are also used in the 1985 Act or the 1986 Act have the same meanings as in that Act.

## PART II – FORMATION, SUPERVISION AND CONTROL

### GENERAL

#### INVESTMENT COMPANY WITH VARIABLE CAPITAL

**3(1)** If SIB makes an authorisation order then, immediately upon the coming into effect of the order, a body shall be incorporated (notwithstanding that, at the point of its incorporation by virtue of this paragraph, the body will not have any shareholders or property).

**3(2)** Any body incorporated by virtue of paragraph (1) above shall be known as an investment company with variable capital.

**3(3)** The name of an investment company with variable capital shall be the name mentioned in the authorisation order made in respect of the company or, if it changes its name in accordance with these Regulations and SIB regulations, by its new name.

## REGISTRATION BY REGISTRAR OF COMPANIES

**4(1)** As soon as is reasonably practicable after the coming into effect of an authorisation order in respect of an investment company with variable capital, SIB shall send a copy of the order to–

(a) the registrar of companies for England and Wales, if the instrument of incorporation of the company states that the company's head office is to be situated in England and Wales, or that it is to be situated in Wales; or

(b) the registrar of companies for Scotland, if the instrument of incorporation of the company states that the head office of the company is to be situated in Scotland.

**4(2)** The registrar shall, upon receipt of the copy of the authorisation order, forthwith register–

(a) the instrument of incorporation of the company; and

(b) the details in relation to the company, its directors and its depositary which are contained in the other papers retained by him under regulation 13(3) below.

**4(3)** A company shall not carry on any business unless its instrument of incorporation has been registered under paragraph (2) above.

**4(4)** Schedule 1 to these Regulations (which makes provision with respect to the registration of, and the functions of the registrar of companies in relation to, investment companies with variable capital) shall have effect.

**4(5)** In this regulation any reference to the instrument of incorporation of a company is a reference to the instrument of incorporation which was supplied for the purposes of regulation 9(1)(a) below.

## SAFEKEEPING OF SCHEME PROPERTY BY DEPOSITARY

**5(1)** Subject to paragraph (2) below, all the scheme property of an investment company with variable capital shall be entrusted for safekeeping to a person appointed for the purpose ("a depositary").

**5(2)** Nothing in paragraph (1) above–

(a) shall apply to any scheme property designated for the purposes of this regulation by SIB regulations;

(b) shall prevent a depositary from–

(i) entrusting to a third party all or some of the assets in its safekeeping; or

(ii) in a case falling within paragraph (i) above, authorising the third party to entrust all or some of those assets to other specified persons.

**5(3)** Schedule 2 to these Regulations (which makes provision with respect to depositaries of investment companies with variable capital) shall have effect.

## SIB REGULATIONS

**6(1)** SIB's powers to make regulations under section 81 (constitution and management) and section 85 (publication of scheme particulars) of the 1986 Act in relation to authorised unit trust schemes shall be exercisable in relation to investment companies with variable capital–

(a) for like purposes; and

(b) subject to the same conditions.

**6(2)** In these Regulations any document complying with regulations made by SIB under paragraph (1) above for purposes of the like nature as the purposes for which power is conferred by section 85 of the 1986 Act shall be known as a prospectus.

"company" or its Welsh equivalent ("cwmni");
"and company" or its Welsh equivalent ("a'r cwmni");
"company limited" or its Welsh equivalent ("cwmni cyfyngedig");
"limited" or its Welsh equivalent ("cyfyngedig");
"unlimited" or its Welsh equivalent ("anghyfyngedig");
"public limited company" or its Welsh equivalent "cwmni cyfyngedig cyhoeddus");
"European Economic Interest Grouping" or any equivalent set out in Schedule 3 to the European Economic Interest Grouping Regulations 1989;
"investment company with variable capital" or its Welsh equivalent ("cwmni buddsoddi â chyfalaf newidiol");

(c) abbreviations of any of those words or expressions where they appear at the end of the name; and

(d) type and case of letters, accents, spaces between letters and punctuation marks;

and "and" and "&" are to be taken as the same.

## ALTERATIONS

### SIB APPROVAL FOR CERTAIN CHANGES IN RESPECT OF COMPANY

**15(1)** An investment company with variable capital shall give written notice to SIB of–

(a) any proposed alteration to the company's instrument of incorporation;

(b) any proposed alteration to the company's prospectus which, if made, would be significant;

(c) any proposed reconstruction or amalgamation involving the company;

(d) any proposal to wind up the affairs of the company otherwise than by the court;

(e) any proposal to replace a director of the company, to appoint any additional director or to decrease the number of directors in post; and

(f) any proposal to replace the depositary of the company.

**15(2)** Any notice given under paragraph (1)(a) above shall be accompanied by a certificate signed by a solicitor to the effect that the change in question will not affect the compliance of the instrument of incorporation with Schedule 3 to these Regulations and with such of the requirements of SIB regulations as relate to the contents of that instrument.

**15(3)** Effect shall not be given to any proposal falling within paragraph (1) above unless–

(a) SIB has given its approval to the proposal; or

(b) three months have elapsed since the date on which the notice was given under paragraph (1) above without SIB having notified the company that the proposal is not approved.

**15(4)** No change falling within paragraph (1)(e) above shall be made if any of the criteria set out in regulation 10(4) to (7) and (8)(f) would not be satisfied if the change were made and no change falling within paragraph (1)(f) above shall be made if any of the criteria set out in regulation 10(8) above would not be satisfied if the change were made.

## INTERVENTION

### REVOCATION OF AUTHORISATION

**16(1)** SIB may revoke an authorisation order if it appears to it–

(a) that any of the requirements for the making of the order are no longer satisfied;

(b) that it is undesirable in the interests of shareholders, or potential shareholders, of the investment company with variable capital concerned that it should continue to be authorised; or

(c) without prejudice to sub-paragraph (b) above, that the company, any of its directors or its depositary–

(i) has contravened any relevant provision;

(ii) in purported compliance with any such provision, has furnished SIB with false, inaccurate or misleading information; or

(iii) has contravened any prohibition or requirement imposed under a provision falling within paragraph (5)(a), (c) or (e) below.

**16(2)** For the purposes of paragraph (1)(b) above, SIB may take into account–

(a) any matter relating to the company or its depositary;

(b) any matter relating to any director or controller of the depositary of the company;

(c) any matter relating to any person employed by or associated, for the purposes of the business of the company, with the company or its depositary; or

(d) any matter relating to–

(i) any director of the company; or

(ii) any person who would be such a person as is mentioned in any of sub-paragraph (a) to (d) of paragraph (2) of regulation 9 above if that paragraph applied in respect of a director of the company as it applies in respect of a proposed director.

**16(3)** Before revoking any authorisation order that has come into effect, SIB shall ensure that such steps as are necessary and appropriate to secure the winding up of the company (whether by the court or otherwise) have been taken.

**16(4)** This regulation confers the same powers in relation to a shadow director of an investment company with variable capital as it confers in relation to a director of such a company.

**16(5)** In paragraph (1)(c) above, **"relevant provision"** means any provision of–

(a) the 1986 Act;

(b) any rules or regulations made under than Act;

(c) these Regulations;

(d) SIB regulations; and

(e) any rules of a recognised self-regulating organisation of which an investment company with variable capital, or any director or depositary of such a company, is a member.

## REPRESENTATIONS AGAINST REVOCATION

**17(1)** Where, in respect of an investment company with variable capital, SIB proposes to revoke an authorisation order on any of the grounds set out in regulation 16(1) above, SIB shall give the company, its depositary and any other person who appears to SIB to be interested written notice of its intention to do so.

**17(2)** A notice under paragraph (1) above shall state the reasons for which SIB proposes to revoke the order and give particulars of the rights conferred by paragraph (3) below.

**17(3)** A person on whom notice is served under paragraph (1) above may, within 21 days of the date of service, make written representations to SIB and, if desired, oral representations to a person appointed for that purpose by SIB.

**17(4)** SIB shall have regard to any representations made in accordance with paragraph (3) above in determining whether to revoke the authorisation order.

## DIRECTIONS

**18(1)** SIB may give a direction under this regulation in relation to an investment company with variable capital if it appears to it–

(a) that any of the requirements for the making of an authorisation order in respect of the company are no longer satisfied;

(b) that the exercise of the power conferred by this paragraph is desirable in the interests of shareholders, or potential shareholders, of the company; or

(c) without prejudice to sub-paragraph (b) above, that the company, any of its directors or its depositary–

(i) has contravened any relevant provision;

(ii) in purported compliance with any such provision, has furnished SIB with false, inaccurate or misleading information; or

## WINDING UP

### WINDING UP BY THE COURT

**25(1)** Where an investment company with variable capital is wound up as an unregistered company under Part V of the Insolvency Act 1986, the provisions of that Act shall apply for the purposes of the winding up with the following modifications.

**25(2)** A petition for the winding up of an investment company with variable capital may be presented by the depositary of the company as well as by any person authorised under section 124 or 124A of the Insolvency Act 1986 (as those sections apply by virtue of Part V of that Act) to present a petition for the winding up of the company.

**25(3)** Where a petition for the winding up of an investment company with variable capital is presented by a person other than SIB–

(a) that person shall serve a copy of the petition on SIB; and

(b) SIB shall be entitled to be heard on the petition.

**25(4)** If, before the presentation of a petition for the winding up by the court of an investment company with variable capital as an unregistered company under Part V of the Insolvency Act 1986, the affairs of the company are being wound up otherwise than by the court–

(a) section 129(2) of the Insolvency Act 1986 (commencement of winding up by the court) shall not apply; and

(b) any winding up of the company by the court shall be deemed to have commenced–

(i) at the time at which SIB gave its approval to a proposal mentioned in paragraph (1)(d) of regulation 15 above; or

(ii) in a case falling within paragraph (3)(b) of that regulation, on the day next following the end of the three month period mentioned in that paragraph.

### DISSOLUTION ON WINDING UP BY THE COURT

**26(1)** This regulation applies where, in respect of an investment company with variable capital, the registrar of companies receives–

(a) a notice served for the purposes of section 172(8) of the Insolvency Act 1986 (final meeting of creditors and vacation of office by liquidator), as that section applies by virtue of Part V of that Act; or

(b) a notice from the official receiver that the winding up by the court of the company is complete.

**26(2)** The registrar shall, on receipt of the notice, forthwith register it; and, subject as follows, at the end of the period of three months beginning with the day of the registration of the notice, the company shall be dissolved.

**26(3)** The Secretary of State may, on the application of the official receiver or any other person who appears to the Secretary of State to be interested, give a direction deferring the date at which the dissolution of the company is to take effect for such period as the Secretary of State thinks fit.

**26(4)** An appeal to the court lies from any decision of the Secretary of State on an application for a direction under paragraph (3) above.

**26(5)** Paragraph (3) above does not apply to a case where the winding up order was made by the court in Scotland, but in such a case the court may, on an application by any person appearing to the court to have an interest, order that the date at which the dissolution of the company is to take effect shall be deferred for such period as the court thinks fit.

**26(6)** It is the duty of the person–

(a) on whose application a direction is given under paragraph (3) above;

(b) in whose favour an appeal with respect to an application for such a direction is determined; or

(c) on whose application an order is made under paragraph (5) above;

not later than seven days after the giving of the direction, the determination of the appeal or the making of the order, to deliver to the registrar of companies for registration a copy of the direction or determination or, in respect of an order, a certified copy of the interlocutor.

**26(7)** If a person without reasonable excuse fails to deliver a copy as required by paragraph (6) above, he is guilty of an offence.

**26(8)** A person guilty of an offence under paragraph (7) above is liable, on summary conviction–

(a) to a fine not exceeding level 1 on the standard scale; and

(b) on a second or subsequent conviction, instead of the penalty set out in sub-paragraph (a) above, to a fine of £100 for each day on which the contravention is continued.

DISSOLUTION IN OTHER CIRCUMSTANCES

**27(1)** Where the affairs of an investment company with variable capital have been wound up otherwise than by the court, SIB shall ensure that, as soon as is reasonably practicable after the winding up is complete, the registrar of companies is sent notice of that fact.

**27(2)** The registrar shall, upon receipt of the notice, forthwith register it; and, subject as follows, at the end of the period of three months beginning with the day of the registration of the notice, the company shall be dissolved.

**27(3)** The court may on the application of SIB or the company make an order deferring the date at which the dissolution of the company is to take effect for such period as the court thinks fit.

**27(4)** It is the duty of the person on whose application an order of the court under paragraph (3) above is made to deliver, not later than seven days after the making of the order, to the registrar of companies a copy of the order for registration.

**27(5)** Where any company, the head office of which is situated in England and Wales, or Wales, is dissolved by virtue of paragraph (2) above, any sum of money (including unclaimed distributions) standing to the account of the company at the date of the dissolution shall, on such date as is determined in relation to the dissolution of that company in accordance with SIB regulations, be paid into court.

**27(6)** Where any company, the head office of which is situated in Scotland, is dissolved by virtue of paragraph (2) above, any sum of money (including unclaimed dividends and unapplied or undistributable balances) standing to the account of the company at the date of the dissolution shall–

(a) on such date as is determined in relation to the dissolution of that company in accordance with SIB regulations, be lodged in an appropriate bank or institution as defined in section 73(1) of the Bankruptcy (Scotland) Act 1985 (interpretation) in the name of the Accountant of the Court; and

(b) thereafter be treated as if it were a sum of money lodged in such an account by virtue of section 193 of the Insolvency Act 1986 (unclaimed distributions), as that section applies by virtue of Part V of that Act.

## PART III – CORPORATE CODE

### ORGANS

DIRECTORS

**28(1)** On the coming into effect of an authorisation order in respect of an investment company with variable capital, the persons named in the application under regulation 7 above as directors of the company shall be deemed to be appointed as its first directors.

**28(2)** Subject to regulations 15 and 20 above, any subsequent appointment as a director of a company shall be made by the company in general meeting; except that the directors of the company may appoint a person to act as director to fill any vacancy until such time as the next following annual general meeting of the company takes place.

**28(3)** Any act of a director is valid notwithstanding–

(a) any defect that may thereafter be discovered in his appointment or qualifications; or

(b) that it is afterwards discovered that his appointment had terminated by virtue of any provision contained in SIB regulations which requires a director to retire upon attaining a specified age.

**28(4)** The business of a company shall be managed–

(a) where a company has only one director, by that director; or

(b) where a company has more than one director, by the directors but subject to any provision contained in SIB regulations as to the allocation between the directors of responsibilities for the management of the company (including any provision there may be as to the allocation of such responsibility to one or more directors to the exclusion of others).

**28(5)** Subject to the provisions of these Regulations, SIB regulations and the company's instrument of incorporation, the directors of a company may exercise all the powers of the company.

## DIRECTORS TO HAVE REGARD TO INTERESTS OF EMPLOYEES

**29(1)** Without prejudice to the generality of the powers and duties that any director of an investment company with variable capital has apart from this regulation, the matters to which such a director is to have regard in the performance of his functions include the interests of the company's employees in general, as well as its shareholders.

**29(2)** Accordingly, the duty imposed by this regulation on any director of a company is owed by him to the company (and the company alone) and is enforceable in the same way as any other fiduciary duty owed to an investment company with variable capital by its directors.

**29(3)** This regulation applies to a shadow director of an investment company with variable capital as it applies to a director of such a company.

## INSPECTION OF DIRECTORS' SERVICE CONTRACTS

**30(1)** Every investment company with variable capital shall keep at an appropriate place–

(a) in the case of each director whose contract of service with the company is in writing, a copy of that contract; and

(b) in the case of each director whose contract of service with the company is not in writing, a written memorandum setting out its terms.

**30(2)** All copies and memoranda kept by a company in accordance with paragraph (1) above shall be kept in the same place.

**30(3)** The following are appropriate places for the purposes of paragraph (1) above–

(a) the company's head office;

(b) the place where the company's register of shareholders is kept; and

(c) where any person designated in the company's instrument of incorporation for the purposes of paragraph 4 of Schedule 5 to these Regulations is a director of the company and is a body corporate, the registered or principal office of that person.

**30(4)** Every copy and memorandum required by paragraph (1) above to be kept shall be open to the inspection of any shareholder of the company.

**30(5)** If such an inspection is refused, the court may by order compel an immediate inspection of the copy or memorandum concerned.

**30(6)** Every copy and memorandum required by paragraph (1) above to be kept shall be made available by the company for inspection by any shareholder at the company's annual general meeting.

**30(7)** Paragraph (1) above applies to a variation of a director's contract of service as it applies to the contract.

## GENERAL MEETINGS

**31(1)** Subject to paragraph (2) below, every investment company with variable capital shall in each year hold a general meeting ("annual general meeting") in addition to any other meetings, whether general or otherwise, it may hold in that year.

**31(2)** If a company holds its first annual general meeting within 18 months of the date on which the authorisation order made by SIB in respect of the company comes into effect, paragraph (1) above shall not require the company to hold any other meeting as its annual general meeting in the year of its incorporation or in the following year.

**31(3)** Subject to paragraph (2) above, not more than 15 months shall elapse between the date of one annual general meeting of a company and the date of the next.

## CAPACITY OF COMPANY

**32(1)** The validity of an act done by an investment company with variable capital shall not be called into question on the ground of lack of capacity by reason of anything in these Regulations, SIB regulations or the company's instrument of incorporation.

**32(2)** Nothing in paragraph (1) above shall affect the duty of the directors to observe any limitations on their powers.

## POWER OF DIRECTORS AND GENERAL MEETING TO BIND THE COMPANY

**33(1)** In favour of a person dealing in good faith, the following powers, that is to say–

(a) the power of the directors of an investment company with variable capital (whether or not acting as a board) to bind the company, or authorise others to do so; and

(b) the power of such a company in general meeting to bind the company, or authorise others to do so;

shall be deemed to be free of any limitation under the company's constitution.

**33(2)** For the purposes of this regulation–

(a) a person "deals with" a company if he is party to any transaction or other act to which the company is a party;

(b) subject to paragraph (4) below, a person shall not be regarded as acting in bad faith by reason only of his knowing that, under the company's constitution, an act is beyond any of the powers referred to in sub-paragraph (a) or (b) of paragraph (1) above; and

(c) subject to paragraph (4) below, a person shall be presumed to have acted in good faith unless the contrary is proved.

**33(3)** The reference in paragraph (1) above to any limitation under the company's constitution on the powers set out in sub-paragraph (a) or (b) of that paragraph shall include any limitation deriving from these Regulations, from SIB regulations or from a resolution of the company in general meeting or of a meeting of any class of shareholders.

**33(4)** Paragraph (2)(b) and (c) above do not apply where–

(a) by virtue of a limitation deriving from these Regulations or from SIB regulations, an act is beyond any of the powers referred to in paragraph (1)(a) or (b) above; and

(b) the person in question–

(i) has actual knowledge of that fact; or

(ii) has deliberately failed to make enquiries in circumstances in which a reasonable and honest person would have done so.

**33(5)** Paragraph (1) above does not affect any liability incurred by the directors or any other person by reason of the directors exceeding their powers.

## NO DUTY TO ENQUIRE AS TO CAPACITY ETC

**34** Subject to regulation 33(4)(b)(ii) above, a party to a transaction with an investment company with variable capital is not bound to enquire–

(a) as to whether the transaction is permitted by these Regulations, SIB regulations or the company's instrument of incorporation; or

**41(6)** Case 4 is any case where shares are issued or transferred to a nominee of a recognised investment exchange who is designated for the purposes of this paragraph in the rules of the investment exchange in question.

## BEARER SHARES

**42** An investment company with variable capital may, if its instrument of incorporation so provides, issue shares ("bearer shares") evidenced by a share certificate, or by any other documentary evidence of title for which provision is made in the instrument of incorporation, which indicates–

(a) that the holder of the document is entitled to the shares specified in it; and

(b) that no entry will be made on the register of shareholders identifying the holder of those shares.

## REGISTER OF SHAREHOLDERS

**43** Schedule 4 to these Regulations (which makes provision with respect to the register of shareholders of an investment company with variable capital) shall have effect.

## POWER TO CLOSE REGISTER

**44(1)** Subject as mentioned in paragraph (2) below, an investment company with variable capital may, on giving notice by advertisement in a national newspaper circulating in all the countries in which shares in the company are sold, close the register of shareholders for any time or times not exceeding in the whole 30 days in each year.

**44(2)** Sub-paragraph (1) above has effect–

(a) in the case of a company which is a participating issuer, subject to regulation 22 of the Uncertificated Securities Regulations 1995 (consent of Operator of system required to close register) and to any requirements contained in SIB regulations, in so far as such requirements are not inconsistent with that regulation; and

(b) in the case of any other company, subject to any requirements contained in SIB regulations.

## POWER OF COURT TO RECTIFY REGISTER

**45(1)** An application to the court may be made under this regulation if–

(a) the name of any person is, without sufficient cause, entered in or omitted from the register of shareholders of an investment company with variable capital;

(b) default is made as to the details contained in any entry on the register in respect of a person's holding of shares in the company; or

(c) default is made or unnecessary delay takes place in amending the register so as to reflect the fact of any person having ceased to be a shareholder.

**45(2)** An application under this regulation may be made by the person aggrieved, by any shareholder of the company or by the company itself.

**45(3)** The court may either refuse the application or may order rectification of the register of shareholders and payment by the company of any damages sustained by any party aggrieved.

**45(4)** On such an application the court may decide any question necessary or expedient to be decided for rectification of the register of shareholders including, in particular, any question relating to the right of a person who is a party to the application to have his name entered in or omitted from the register (whether the question arises as between shareholders and alleged shareholders or as between shareholders or alleged shareholders on the one hand and the company on the other hand).

## SHARE TRANSFERS

**46** Schedule 5 to these Regulations (which makes provision for the transfer of registered and bearer shares in an investment company with variable capital) shall have effect.

## OPERATION

### POWER INCIDENTAL TO CARRYING ON BUSINESS

**47** An investment company with variable capital shall have power to do all such things as are incidental or conducive to the carrying on of its business.

### NAME TO APPEAR IN CORRESPONDENCE ETC

**48(1)** Every investment company with variable capital shall have its name mentioned in legible characters in all letters of the company and in all other documents issued by the company in the course of business.

**48(2)** If an officer of a company or a person on the company's behalf signs or authorises to be signed on behalf of the company any cheque or order for money or goods in which the company's name is not mentioned as required by paragraph (1) above he is personally liable to the holder of the cheque or order for money or goods for the amount of it (unless it is duly paid by the company).

### PARTICULARS TO APPEAR IN CORRESPONDENCE ETC

**49(1)** Every investment company with variable capital shall have the following particulars mentioned in legible characters in all letters of the company and in all other documents issued by the company in the course of business, that is to say–

(a) the company's place of registration;
(b) the number with which it is registered;
(c) the address of its head office; and
(d) the fact that it is an investment company with variable capital.

**49(2)** Where, in accordance with section 705 of the 1985 Act (companies' registered numbers) (as that section has effect by virtue of Schedule 1 to these Regulations), the registrar of companies makes any change of existing registered numbers in respect of any investment company with variable capital then, for a period of three years beginning with the date on which the notification of the change is sent to the company by the registrar, the requirement of paragraph (1)(b) above is satisfied by the use of either the old number or the new.

### CONTRACTS: ENGLAND AND WALES

**50** Under the law of England and Wales a contract may be made–

(a) by an investment company with variable capital by writing under its common seal; or
(b) on behalf of such a company, by any person acting under its authority (whether express or implied);

and any formalities required by law in the case of a contract made by an individual also apply, unless a contrary intention appears, to a contract made by or on behalf of an investment company with variable capital.

### EXECUTION OF DOCUMENTS: ENGLAND AND WALES

**51(1)** Under the law of England and Wales the following provisions have effect with respect to the execution of documents by an investment company with variable capital.

**51(2)** A document is executed by a company by the affixing of its common seal.

**51(3)** A company need not have a common seal, however, and the following provisions of this regulation apply whether it does or not.

**51(4)** A document that is signed by at least one director and expressed (in whatever form of words) to be executed by the company has the same effect as if executed under the common seal of the company.

**51(5)** A document executed by a company which makes it clear on its face that it is intended by the person or persons making it to be a deed has effect, upon delivery, as a deed; and it shall be presumed, unless a contrary intention is proved, to be delivered upon its being executed.

**51(6)** In favour of a purchaser a document shall be deemed to have been duly executed by a company if it purports to be signed by at least one director or, in the case of a director which is

(a) a copy of that report; and

(b) a copy of the most recent revision of the company's prospectus.

**65(6)** A company shall not later than 14 days after the completion of a revised annual report under regulation 62 above send to the registrar of companies a copy of that revised report.

**65(7)** Where a resolution removing an auditor is passed at a general meeting of a company under paragraph 12 of Schedule 6 to these Regulations, a company shall not later than 14 days after the holding of the meeting notify the registrar of companies of the passing of the resolution.

**65(8)** Where an auditor of a company deposits a notice of his resignation from office under paragraph 15 of Schedule 6 to these Regulations, a company shall not later than 14 days after the deposit of the notice send a copy of the notice to the registrar of companies.

**65(9)** Where the affairs of a company are to be wound up otherwise than by the court, the company shall as soon as reasonably practicable after the commencement of the winding up notify the registrar of companies of that fact.

## CONTRAVENTIONS

**66** Any of the following persons, that is to say–

(a) a person who contravenes any provision of these Regulations; and

(b) an investment company with variable capital, or any director or depositary of such a company, which contravenes any provision of SIB regulations;

shall be treated as having contravened rules made under Chapter V of Part I of the 1986 Act or, in the case of a person who is an authorised person by virtue of his membership of a recognised self-regulating organisation or certification by a recognised professional body, the rules of that organisation or body.

## PROSECUTIONS

**67(1)** Proceedings in respect of an offence under regulation 26 above or paragraph 3(3) or 19(1) of Schedule 6 to these Regulations shall not be instituted, in England and Wales, except by or with the consent of the Secretary of State or the Director of Public Prosecutions.

**67(2)** Proceedings in respect of an offence under any other provision of these Regulations shall not be instituted, in England and Wales, except by SIB or by or with the consent of the Secretary of State or the Director of Public Prosecutions.

**67(3)** SIB shall exercise the function conferred by this regulation of instituting proceedings subject to such conditions or restrictions as the Treasury may from time to time impose.

## OFFENCES: BODIES CORPORATE, PARTNERSHIPS AND UNINCORPORATED ASSOCIATIONS

**68(1)** Where an offence under these Regulations committed by an investment company with variable capital is proved to have been committed with the consent or connivance of, or to be attributable to any neglect on the part of, a director of the company, or a person purporting to act in any such capacity, he, as well as the company, is guilty of the offence and liable to be proceeded against and punished accordingly.

This paragraph applies to a shadow director of an investment company with variable capital as it applies to a director of such a company.

**68(2)** Where an offence under these Regulations committed by any body corporate other than an investment company with variable capital is proved to have been committed with the consent or connivance of, or to be attributable to any neglect on the part of, a director, manager, secretary or other similar officer of the body, or a person purporting to act in any such capacity, he, as well as the body corporate, is guilty of the offence and liable to be proceeded against and punished accordingly.

**68(3)** Where the affairs of any body corporate other than an investment company with variable capital are managed by its members, paragraph (2) above applies in relation to the acts and defaults of a member in connection with his functions of management as it applies in relation to the acts and defaults of a director of a body corporate.

**68(4)** Where an offence under these Regulations committed by a partnership is proved to have been committed with the consent or connivance of, or to be attributable to any neglect on the part of, a partner, he, as well as the partnership is guilty of the offence and liable to be proceeded against and punished accordingly.

**68(5)** Where an offence under these Regulations committed by an unincorporated association (other than a partnership) is proved to have been committed with the consent or connivance of, or to be attributable to any neglect on the part of, any officer of the association or any member of its governing body, he, as well as the association is guilty of the offence and liable to be proceeded against and punished accordingly.

## TIME LIMITS FOR PROSECUTION OF OFFENCES

**69(1)** Any information relating to an offence under these Regulations which is triable by a magistrates' court in England and Wales may be so tried on an information laid at any time within 12 months after the date on which evidence sufficient in the opinion of the relevant authority to justify the proceedings comes to its knowledge.

**69(2)** Proceedings in Scotland for an offence triable only summarily which is alleged to have been committed under these Regulations may be commenced at any time within 12 months after the date on which evidence sufficient in the Lord Advocate's opinion to justify the proceedings came to his knowledge or, where such evidence was reported to him by the Secretary of State or SIB, within 12 months after the date on which it came to the knowledge of the Secretary of State or SIB (as the case may be).

For the purposes of this paragraph proceedings shall be deemed to be commenced on the date on which a warrant to apprehend or to cite the accused is granted, if the warrant is executed without undue delay.

**69(3)** Paragraph (1) above does not authorise the trial of an information laid, and paragraph (2) does not authorise the commencement of proceedings, more than three years after the commission of the offence.

**69(4)** For the purposes of these Regulations a certificate by the relevant authority or the Lord Advocate as to the date on which such evidence as is referred to above came to its or his knowledge is conclusive evidence of that fact.

**69(5)** Nothing in this regulation affects proceedings within the time limits prescribed by section 127(1) of the Magistrates' Courts Act 1980 or section 136 of the Criminal Procedure (Scotland) Act 1995 (the usual time limits for criminal proceedings).

**69(6)** In this regulation **"relevant authority"**, in relation to an offence means–

(a) in a case where the person instituting proceedings in respect of the offence is a person who, by virtue of regulation 67(1) or (2) above, may not do so without the consent of the Secretary of State or the Director of Public Prosecutions, the Secretary of State or the Director of Public Prosecutions; and

(b) in any other case where proceedings are instituted in England and Wales, the person instituting the proceedings.

## JURISDICTION AND PROCEDURE IN RESPECT OF OFFENCES

**70(1)** Summary proceedings for an offence under these Regulations may, without prejudice to any jurisdiction exercisable apart from this regulation, be taken against an investment company with variable capital or other body corporate, or an unincorporated association, at any place at which it has a place of business and against an individual at any place where he is for the time being.

**70(2)** Proceedings for an offence alleged to have been committed under these Regulations by an unincorporated association shall be brought in the name of the association (and not in that of any of its members), and for the purposes of any such proceedings any rules of court relating to the service of documents apply as in relation to a body corporate.

**70(3)** Section 33 of the Criminal Justice Act 1925 and Schedule 3 to the Magistrates' Courts Act 1980 (procedure on charge of offence against a corporation) apply in a case in which an unincorporated association is charged in England and Wales with an offence under these Regulations as they apply in the case of a corporation.

**70(4)** In relation to proceedings on indictment in Scotland for an offence alleged to have been committed under these Regulations by an unincorporated association, section 70 of the Criminal Procedure (Scotland) Act 1995 (proceedings on indictment against bodies corporate) applies as if the association were a body corporate.

**70(5)** A fine imposed on an unincorporated association on its conviction of such an offence shall be paid out of the funds of the association.

## SERVICE OF DOCUMENTS

**71(1)** This regulation has effect in relation to any notice, direction or other document required or authorised by these Regulations or SIB regulations to be given or served on any person other than the registrar of companies.

**71(2)** Any such document may be given to or served on the person in question–

(a) by delivering it to him;

(b) by leaving it at his proper address; or

(c) by sending it by post to him at that address.

**71(3)** Any such document may–

(a) in the case of an investment company with variable capital, be given to or served on any director of the company;

(b) in the case of any other body corporate (including any director referred to in sub-paragraph (a) above which is a body corporate) be given to or served on the secretary or clerk of that body;

(c) in the case of a partnership, be given to or served on any partner; and

(d) in the case of an unincorporated association other than a partnership, be given to or served on any member of the governing body of that association.

**71(4)** For the purposes of this regulation and section 7 of the Interpretation Act 1978 (service of documents by post) in its application to this regulation, the proper address of any person is his last known address (whether of his residence or of a place where he carries on business or is employed) and also–

(a) in the case of an investment company with variable capital or any of its directors, the company's head office;

(b) in the case of any other body corporate (including any director referred to in paragraph (3)(a) above which is a body corporate) or its secretary or clerk, the address of its registered or principal office in the United Kingdom;

(c) in the case of an unincorporated association (other than a partnership) or a member of its governing body, its principal office in the United Kingdom.

## EVIDENCE OF GRANT OF PROBATE ETC

**72** The production to a company of any document which is by law sufficient evidence of probate of the will, or letters of administration of the estate, or confirmation as executor, of a deceased person having been granted to some person shall be accepted by the company as sufficient evidence of the grant.

## SIB'S FUNCTIONS UNDER THE REGULATIONS

**73(1)** The functions of SIB under these Regulations, except its function of instituting proceedings, shall be treated for the purposes of the 1986 Act and the Transfer of Functions (Financial Services) Order 1992 as if they were functions to which section 114 of that Act applies which–

(a) had been functions of the Secretary of State; and

(b) had been transferred to SIB by the Financial Services Act 1986 (Delegation) Order 1987.

**73(2)** The function of SIB of instituting proceedings under these Regulations shall be treated for the purposes of the 1986 Act and the Transfer of Functions (Financial Services) Order 1992 as if it were a function to which section 114 of the 1986 Act applies by virtue of the provisions of section 201(4) of that Act which had been transferred to SIB by the Financial Services Act 1986 (Delegation) Order 1987 so as to be exercisable concurrently with the Secretary of State.

FEES

**74(1)** Every application under regulation 7 above shall be accompanied by such fee as may be prescribed by SIB by virtue of paragraph (3)(a) below; and no such application shall be regarded as duly made unless this paragraph is complied with.

**74(2)** Each investment company with variable capital shall pay such periodical fees to SIB as may be prescribed by SIB by virtue of paragraph (3)(b) below.

**74(3)** SIB may, with respect to investment companies with variable capital, make regulations prescribing fees for purposes of the like nature as the purposes for which power is conferred by–

(a) section 112(5) of the 1986 Act (application fees) in respect of applications under section 77 of that Act (applications for authorisation of unit trust scheme);

(b) section 113(8) of that Act (periodical fees) in respect of managers of authorised unit trust schemes and operators of recognised schemes.

MINOR AND CONSEQUENTIAL AMENDMENTS

**75** The enactments mentioned in Schedule 8 to these Regulations (being minor amendments and amendments consequential on the provisions of these Regulations) shall have effect subject to the amendments specified in that Schedule.

# Schedule 1 – Application of Part XXIV of 1985 Act

Regulation 4

**1** Part XXIV of the 1985 Act (the registrar of companies, his functions and offices) shall, subject to the modifications set out in paragraphs 2 to 8 below, apply for the purposes of the registration of, and the functions of the registrar of companies in relation to, investment companies with variable capital under these Regulations as it applies to the registration of, and the functions of the registrar in relation to, companies within the meaning given by section 735(1) of that Act.

**2** Except in the expressions "the registrar of companies" and "the Companies Acts", any reference to companies (including any such reference in section 711 of the 1985 Act as it applies with the modifications set out in paragraph 6 below) shall be taken to be a reference to investment companies with variable capital.

**3** Any reference to the Companies Acts (including any reference to the 1985 Act, however expressed) shall be taken to be a reference to these Regulations and SIB regulations.

**4** Any reference to the memorandum of a company shall be taken to be a reference to the instrument of incorporation of an investment company with variable capital; and any reference to the registered office of a company shall be taken to be a reference to the head office of an investment company with variable capital.

**5** Any power to make regulations under Part XXIV of the 1985 Act in relation to companies shall be exercisable in relation to investment companies with variable capital–

(a) for like purposes; and

(b) subject to the same conditions.

**6** Section 711 of the 1985 Act (public notice by registrar of receipt and issue of certain documents) shall apply as if for paragraphs (a) to (z) of subsection (1) there were substituted the following paragraphs–

(a) any document making or evidencing an alteration in a company's instrument of incorporation;

(b) any notice of a change in the address of a company's head office;

(c) any notice of a change in the directors of a company;
(d) any notice of a change in the depositary of a company;
(e) any annual report of a company delivered under regulation 65(5) or (6) above;
(f) any copy of an order in respect of a company made by virtue of regulation 64 above;
(g) any copy of a winding up order in respect of a company; and
(h) any copy of any instrument providing for the dissolution of a company on a winding up.

7 Section 714 (registrar's index of company and corporate names) shall have effect as if the bodies listed in subsection (1) of that section included–
(a) investment companies with variable capital in respect of which an authorisation order has come into effect; and
(b) collective investment schemes which are open-ended investment companies and which have head offices situated in Northern Ireland and which comply with the conditions necessary for them to enjoy the rights conferred by the UCITS Directive.

8 The following provisions of Part XXIV of the 1985 Act shall not apply, that is to say–
(a) in section 705. the words in subsection (4) from "but for a period" to the end and subsection (5);
(b) section 705A;
(c) section 707A(4);
(d) section 710;
(e) section 710B(6) and (7);
(f) section 711(2);
(g) in section 711A, in subsection (1) the words "or made available by the company for inspection" and subsection (4); and
(h) section 714(2).

# Schedule 2 – Depositaries

Regulation 5

## APPOINTMENT

1 On the coming into effect of an authorisation order in respect of an investment company with variable capital, the person named in the application under regulation 7 above as depositary of the company shall be deemed to be appointed as its first depositary.

2 Subject to regulations 15 and 20 above, any subsequent appointment of the depositary of a company shall be made by the directors of the company.

## RETIREMENT

3 The depositary of a company may not retire voluntarily except upon the appointment of a new depositary.

## RIGHTS

4(1) The depositary of a company is entitled–
(a) to receive all such notices of, and other communications relating to, any general meeting of the company as a shareholder of the company is entitled to receive;
(b) to attend any general meeting of the company;
(c) to be heard at any general meeting which it attends on any part of the business of the meeting which concerns it as depositary;
(d) to convene a general meeting of the company when it sees fit;
(e) to require from the company's officers such information and explanations as it thinks necessary for the performance of its functions as depositary; and

(f) to have access, except in so far as they concern its appointment or removal, to any reports, statements or other papers which are to be considered at any meeting held by the directors of the company (when acting in their capacity as such), at any general meeting of the company or at any meeting of holders of shares of any particular class.

**4(2)** Sub-paragraph (1)(e) above applies to a shadow director of an investment company with variable capital as it applies to an officer of such a company.

## STATEMENT BY DEPOSITARY CEASING TO HOLD OFFICE

**5(1)** Where the depositary of a company ceases, for any reason other than by virtue of a court order made under regulation 20 above, to hold office, it may deposit at the head office of the company a statement of any circumstances connected with its ceasing to hold office which it considers should be brought to the attention of the shareholders or creditors of the company or, if it considers that there are no such circumstances, a statement that there are none.

**5(2)** If the statement is of circumstances which the depositary considers should be brought to the attention of the shareholders or creditors of the company, the company shall not later than 14 days after the deposit of the statement either–

(a) send a copy of the statement to each of the shareholders whose name appears on the register of shareholders (other than the person who is designated in the company's instrument of incorporation for the purposes of paragraph 4 of Schedule 5 to these Regulations) and take such steps as SIB regulations may require for the purpose of bringing the fact that the statement has been made to the attention of the holders of any bearer shares; or

(b) apply to the court;

and, where an application is made under paragraph (b) above, the company shall notify the depositary.

**5(3)** Unless the depositary receives notice of an application to the court before the end of the period of 21 days beginning with the day on which it deposited the statement, it shall not later than seven days after the end of that period send a copy of the statement to each of the registrar of companies and SIB.

**5(4)** If the court is satisfied that the depositary is using the statement to secure needless publicity for defamatory matter–

(a) it shall direct that copies of the statement need not be sent out and that the steps required by SIB regulations need not be taken; and

(b) it may further order the company's costs on the application to be paid in whole or in part by the depositary notwithstanding that the depositary is not a party to the application;

and the company shall not later than 14 days after the court's decision take such steps in relation to a statement setting out the effect of the order as are required by sub-paragraph (2)(a) above in relation to the statement deposited under sub-paragraph (1) above.

**5(5)** If the court is not so satisfied, the company shall not later than 14 days after the court's decision take the steps required by sub-paragraph (2)(a) above and notify the depositary of the court's decision.

**5(6)** The depositary shall not later than seven days after receiving such a notice send a copy of the statement to each of the registrar of companies and SIB.

**5(7)** Where a notice of appeal is filed not later than 14 days after the court's decision, any reference to that decision in sub-paragraphs (4) and (5) above shall be construed as a reference to the final determination or withdrawal of that appeal, as the case may be.

**6(1)** This paragraph applies where copies of a statement have been sent to shareholders under paragraph 5 above.

**6(2)** The depositary who made the statement has, notwithstanding that it has ceased to hold office, the rights conferred by paragraph 4(1)(a) to (c) above in relation to the general meeting of the company next following the date on which the copies were sent out.

**6(3)** The reference in paragraph 4(1)(c) above to business concerning the depositary as depositary shall be construed in relation to a depositary who has ceased to hold office as a reference to business concerning it as former depositary.

# Schedule 3 – Instrument of Incorporation

Regulation 9

**1** The instrument of incorporation of an investment company with variable capital shall–

(a) contain the statements set out in paragraph 2 below; and

(b) contain provision made in accordance with paragraph 3 and 4 below.

**2** The statements referred to in paragraph 1(a) above are–

(a) the head office of the company is situated in England and Wales, Wales or Scotland (as the case may be);

(b) the company is an open-ended investment company with variable share capital;

(c) the shareholders are not liable for the debts of the company;

(d) the scheme property is entrusted to a depositary for safekeeping (subject to any exceptions permitted by SIB regulations); and

(e) charges or expenses of the company may be taken out of the scheme property.

**3(1)** The instrument of incorporation shall contain provision as to the following matters–

(a) the object of the company;

(b) any matter relating to the procedure for the appointment, retirement and removal of any director of the company for which provision is not made in these or SIB regulations; and

(c) the currency in which the accounts of the company are to be prepared.

**3(2)** Subject to sub-paragraph (3) below, the provision referred to in sub-paragraph (1)(a) above as to the object of an investment company with variable capital shall be a statement that the object of the company is to invest the scheme property in transferable securities with the aim of spreading investment risk and giving its shareholders the benefit of the results of the management of that property.

**3(3)** The object of the company may differ from that set out in sub-paragraph (2) above only to the extent that it provides for restriction of the range of transferable securities in which investment may be made.

**4(1)** The instrument of incorporation shall also contain provision as to the following matters–

(a) the name of the company;

(b) the category, as specified in SIB regulations, to which the company belongs;

(c) the maximum and minimum sizes of the company's capital;

(d) in the case of an umbrella company, the investment objectives applicable to each part of the scheme property that is pooled separately;

(e) the classes of shares that the company may issue indicating, in the case of an umbrella company, which class or classes of shares may be issued in respect of each part of the scheme property that is pooled separately;

(f) the rights attaching to shares of each class (including any provision for the expression in two denominations of such rights);

(g) if the company is to be able to issue bearer shares, a statement to that effect together with details of any limitations on the classes of the company's shares which are to include bearer shares;

(h) in the case of a company which is a participating issuer, a statement to that effect together with an indication of any class of shares in the company which is a class of participating securities;

(i) if the company is to dispense with the requirements of regulation 40 above, the details of any substituted procedures for evidencing title to the company's shares; and

(j) the form, custody and use of the company's common seal (if any).

**4(2)** For the purposes of sub-paragraph (1)(c) above, the size at any time of a company's capital shall be taken to be the value at that time, as determined in accordance with SIB regulations, of the scheme property of the company less the liabilities of the company.

**5(1)** Once an authorisation order has been made in respect of a company, no amendment may be made to the statements contained in the company's instrument of incorporation which are required by paragraph 2 above.

**5(2)** Subject to paragraph 3(3) above and to any restriction imposed by SIB regulations, a company may amend any other provision which is contained in its instrument of incorporation.

**5(3)** No amendment to a provision which is contained in a company's instrument of incorporation by virtue of paragraph 3 above may be made unless it has been approved by the shareholders of the company in general meeting.

**6(1)** The provisions of a company's instrument of incorporation shall be binding on the officers and depositary of the company and on each of its shareholders; and all such persons (but no others) shall be taken to have notice of the provisions of the instrument.

**6(2)** A person is not debarred from obtaining damages or other compensation from a company by reason only of his holding or having held shares in the company.

# Schedule 4 – Register of Shareholders

Regulation 43

## GENERAL

**1(1)** Subject to sub-paragraph (2) below, every investment company with variable capital shall keep a register of persons who hold shares in the company.

**1(2)** Except to the extent that the aggregate numbers of shares mentioned in paragraphs 5(1)(b) and 7 below include bearer shares, nothing in this Schedule requires any entry to be made in the register in respect of bearer shares.

**2(1)** Subject as mentioned in sub-paragraph (2) below, the register of shareholders shall be prima facie evidence of any matters which are by these Regulations directed or authorised to be contained in it.

**2(2)** In the case of a register kept by a company which is a participating issuer, sub-paragraph (1) above has effect subject to regulation 23(7) of the Uncertificated Securities Regulations 1995 (purported registration of transfer of title to uncertificated unit other than in accordance with that regulation to be of no effect).

**3** In the case of companies registered in England and Wales, no notice of any trust, express, implied or constructive, shall be entered on the company's register or be receivable by the company.

**4** A company shall exercise all due diligence and take all reasonable steps to ensure that the information contained in the register is at all times complete and up to date.

## CONTENTS

**5(1)** The register of shareholders shall contain an entry consisting of–

(a) the name of the person who is designated in the company's instrument of incorporation for the purposes of paragraph 4 of Schedule 5 to these Regulations (in this Schedule referred to as the designated person);

(b) a statement of the aggregate number of all shares in the company held by that person; and

(c) in the case of a company which is a participating issuer, a statement in respect of shares of any class that is a class of participating securities of how many shares of that class are held by that person in uncertificated form and certificated form respectively.

appointment of company auditors shall be exercisable in relation to the appointment of auditors of investment companies with variable capital–

(a) for like purposes; and

(b) subject to the same conditions.

**2(4)** Any reference in this paragraph to an officer of an investment company with variable capital shall include a reference to a shadow director of such a company.

**3(1)** No person shall act as auditor of a company if he is ineligible for appointment to the office.

**3(2)** If during his term of office an auditor of a company becomes ineligible for appointment to the office, he shall thereupon vacate office and shall forthwith give notice in writing to the company concerned that he has vacated it by reason of ineligibility.

**3(3)** A person who acts as auditor of a company in contravention of sub-paragraph (1) above or fails to give notice of vacating his office as required by sub-paragraph (2) above is guilty of an offence and liable–

(a) on conviction on indictment, to a fine;

(b) on summary conviction, to a fine not exceeding the statutory maximum.

**3(4)** In the case of continued contravention he is liable on a second or subsequent summary conviction (instead of the fine mentioned in sub-paragraph (3)(b) above) to a fine not exceeding £100 in respect of each day on which the contravention is continued.

**3(5)** In proceedings against a person for an offence under this paragraph it is a defence for him to show that he did not know and had no reason to believe that he was, or had become, ineligible for appointment.

## APPOINTMENT

**4(1)** Every company shall appoint an auditor or auditors in accordance with this paragraph.

**4(2)** A company shall, at each general meeting at which the company's annual report is laid, appoint an auditor or auditors to hold office from the conclusion of that meeting until the conclusion of the next general meeting at which an annual report is laid.

**4(3)** The first auditors of a company may be appointed by the directors of the company at any time before the first general meeting of the company at which an annual report is laid; and auditors so appointed shall hold office until the conclusion of that meeting.

**4(4)** Where no appointment is made under sub-paragraph (3) above, the first auditors of any company may be appointed by the company in general meeting.

**4(5)** No rules made under section 107 of the 1986 Act (appointment etc of auditors) shall apply in relation to investment companies with variable capital.

**5** If, in any case, no auditors are appointed as required in paragraph 4 above, SIB may appoint a person to fill the vacancy.

**6(1)** The directors of a company, or the company in general meeting, may fill a casual vacancy in the office of auditor.

**6(2)** While such a vacancy continues, any surviving or continuing auditor or auditors may continue to act.

**7(1)** Sub-paragraphs (2) to (5) below apply to the appointment as auditor of a company of a partnership constituted under the law of England and Wales or Northern Ireland, or under the law of any other country or territory in which a partnership is not a legal person; and sub-paragraphs (3) to (5) below apply to the appointment as such an auditor of a partnership constituted under the law of Scotland, or under the law of any other country or territory in which a partnership is a legal person.

**7(2)** The appointment is, unless the contrary intention appears, an appointment of the partnership as such and not of the partners.

**7(3)** Where the partnership ceases, the appointment shall be treated as extending to–

(a) any partnership which succeeds to the practice of that partnership and is eligible for the appointment; and

(b) any person who succeeds to that practice having previously carried it on in partnership and is eligible for the appointment.

**7(4)** For this purpose a partnership shall be regarded as succeeding to the practice of another partnership only if the members of the successor partnership are substantially the same as those of the former partnership; and a partnership or other person shall be regarded as succeeding to the practice of a partnership only if it or he succeeds to the whole or substantially the whole of the business of the former partnership.

**7(5)** Where the partnership ceases and no person succeeds to the appointment under sub-paragraph (3) above, the appointment may with the consent of the company be treated as extending to a partnership or other person eligible for the appointment who succeeds to the business of the former partnership or to such part of it as is agreed by the company shall be treated as comprising the appointment.

## RIGHTS

**8(1)** The auditors of a company shall have a right of access at all times to the company's books, accounts and vouchers and are entitled to require from the company's officers such information and explanations as they think necessary for the performance of their duties as auditors.

**8(2)** An officer of a company commits an offence if he knowingly or recklessly makes to the company's auditors a statement (whether written or oral) which–

(a) conveys or purports to convey any information or explanations which the auditors require, or are entitled to require, as auditors of the company; and

(b) is misleading, false or deceptive in a material particular.

**8(3)** A person guilty of an offence under sub-paragraph (2) above is liable–

(a) on conviction on indictment, to imprisonment not exceeding a term of two years or to a fine or to both;

(b) on summary conviction, to imprisonment not exceeding a term of three months or to a fine not exceeding the statutory maximum or to both.

**8(4)** This paragraph applies to a shadow director of an investment company with variable capital as it applies to an officer of such a company.

**9(1)** The auditors of a company are entitled–

(a) to receive all such notices of, and other communications relating to, any general meeting of the company as a shareholder of the company is entitled to receive;

(b) to attend any general meeting of the company; and

(c) to be heard at any general meeting which they attend on any part of the business of the meeting which concerns them as auditors.

**9(2)** The right to attend and be heard at a meeting is exercisable in the case of a body corporate or partnership by an individual authorised by it in writing to act as its representative at the meeting.

## REMUNERATION

**10(1)** The remuneration of auditors of a company who are appointed by the company in general meeting shall be fixed by the company in general meeting or in such manner as the company in general meeting may determine.

**10(2)** The remuneration of auditors who are appointed by the directors or SIB shall, as the case may be, be fixed by the directors or SIB (and shall be payable by the company even where it is fixed by SIB).

**11(1)** Subject to sub-paragraph (2) below, the power of the Secretary of State to make regulations under section 390B of the 1985 Act (remuneration of auditors and their associates for non-audit work) in relation to company auditors shall be exercisable in relation to auditors of investment companies with variable capital–

(a) for like purposes; and

(b) subject to the same conditions.

**11(2)** For the purposes of the exercise of the power to make regulations under section 390B of the 1985 Act, as extended by sub-paragraph (1) above, the reference in section 390B(3) to a note to a company's accounts shall be taken to be a reference to the annual report of an investment company with variable capital.

## REMOVAL

**12(1)** A company may by resolution remove an auditor from office notwithstanding anything in any agreement between it and him.

**12(2)** Where a resolution removing an auditor is passed at a general meeting of a company, the company shall not later than 14 days after the holding of the meeting notify SIB of the passing of the resolution.

**12(3)** Nothing in this paragraph shall be taken as depriving a person removed under it of compensation or damages payable to him in respect of the termination of his appointment as auditor or of any appointment terminating with that as auditor.

## RIGHTS ON REMOVAL OR NON-REAPPOINTMENT

**13(1)** A resolution at a general meeting of a company–

(a) removing an auditor before the expiration of his period of office; or

(b) appointing as auditor a person other than the retiring auditor;

is not effective unless notice of the intention to move it has been given to the investment company with variable capital at least 28 days before the meeting at which it is moved.

**13(2)** On receipt of notice of such an intended resolution, the company shall forthwith send a copy to the person proposed to be removed or, as the case may be, to the person proposed to be appointed and to the retiring auditor.

**13(3)** The auditor proposed to be removed or, as the case may be, the retiring auditor may make with respect to the intended resolution representations in writing to the company (not exceeding a reasonable length) and request their notification to the shareholders of the company.

**13(4)** The company shall (unless the representations are received by the company too late for it to do so)–

(a) in any notice of the resolution given to the shareholders of the company, state the fact of the representations having been made;

(b) send a copy of the representations to each of the shareholders whose name appears on the register of shareholders (other than the person who is designated in the company's instrument of incorporation for the purposes of paragraph 4 of Schedule 5 to these Regulations) and to whom notice of the meeting is or has been sent;

(c) take such steps as SIB regulations may require for the purpose of bringing the fact that the representations have been made to the attention of the holders of any bearer shares; and

(d) at the request of any holder of bearer shares, provide a copy of the representations.

**13(5)** If a copy of any such representations is not sent out as required because they were received too late or because of the company's default or if, for either of those reasons, any steps required by sub-paragraph (4)(c) or (d) above are not taken, the auditor may (without prejudice to his right to be heard orally) require that the representations be read out at the meeting.

**13(6)** Copies of the representations need not be sent out, the steps required by sub-paragraph (4)(c) or (d) above need not be taken and the representations need not be read out at the meeting if, on the application of the company or any other person claiming to be aggrieved, the court is satisfied that the rights conferred by this paragraph are being abused to secure needless publicity for defamatory matter; and the court may order the costs of the company on such an application to be paid in whole or in part by the auditor, notwithstanding that he is not a party to the application.

**14(1)** An auditor who has been removed from office has, notwithstanding his removal, the rights conferred by paragraph 9 above in relation to any general meeting of the company at which his term of office would otherwise have expired or at which it is proposed to fill the vacancy caused by his removal.

**14(2)** Any reference in paragraph 9 above to business concerning the auditors as auditors shall be construed in relation to an auditor who has been removed from office as a reference to business concerning him as former auditor.

## RESIGNATION

**15(1)** An auditor of a company may resign his office by depositing a notice in writing to that effect at the company's head office.

**15(2)** Such a notice is not effective unless it is accompanied by the statement required by paragraph 18 below.

**15(3)** An effective notice of resignation operates to bring the auditor's term of office to an end as of the date on which the notice is deposited or on such later date as may be specified in it.

**15(4)** The company shall not later than 14 days after the deposit of a notice of resignation send a copy of the notice to SIB.

**16(1)** This paragraph applies where a notice of resignation of an auditor is accompanied by a statement of circumstances which he considers ought to be brought to the attention of the shareholders or creditors of the company.

**16(2)** An auditor may deposit with the notice a signed requisition that a general meeting of the company be convened forthwith for the purpose of receiving and considering such explanation of the circumstances connected with his resignation as he may wish to place before the meeting.

**16(3)** The company shall, not later than 21 days after the date of the deposit of a requisition under this paragraph, proceed to convene a meeting for a day not more than 28 days after the date on which the notice convening the meeting is given.

**16(4)** The auditor may request the company to circulate to the shareholders of the company whose name appears on the register of shareholders (other than the person who is designated in the company's instrument of incorporation for the purposes of paragraph 4 of Schedule 5 to these Regulations)–

(a) before the meeting convened on his requisition; or

(b) before any general meeting at which his term of office would otherwise have expired or at which it is proposed to fill the vacancy caused by his resignation;

a statement in writing (not exceeding a reasonable length) of the circumstances connected with his resignation.

**16(5)** The company shall (unless the statement is received by it too late for it to do so)–

(a) in any notice or advertisement of the meeting given or made to shareholders of the company, state the fact of the statement having been made;

(b) send a copy of the statement to every shareholder of the company to whom notice of the meeting is or has been sent; and

(c) at the request of any holder of bearer shares, provide a copy of the statement.

**16(6)** If a copy of the statement is not sent out or provided as required because it was received too late or because of the company's default the auditor may (without prejudice to his right to be heard orally) require that the statement be read out at the meeting.

**16(7)** Copies of a statement need not be sent out or provided and the statement need not be read out at the meeting if, on the application of the company or any other person claiming to be aggrieved, the court is satisfied that the rights conferred by this paragraph are being abused to secure needless publicity for defamatory matter; and the court may order the costs of the company on such an application to be paid in whole or in part by the auditor, notwithstanding that he is not a party to the application.

**17(1)** An auditor who has resigned has, notwithstanding his removal, the rights conferred by paragraph 9 above in relation to any such general meeting of the company as is mentioned in paragraph 16(4)(a) or (b) above.

**17(2)** The reference in paragraph 9 above to business concerning the auditors as auditors shall be construed in relation to an auditor who has resigned as a reference to business concerning him as former auditor.

## STATEMENT BY AUDITOR CEASING TO HOLD OFFICE

**18(1)** Where an auditor ceases for any reason to hold office, he shall deposit at the head office of the company a statement of any circumstances connected with his ceasing to hold office which he considers should be brought to the attention of the shareholders or creditors of the company or, if he considers that there are no such circumstances, a statement that there are none.

**18(2)** The statement shall be deposited–

(a) in the case of resignation, along with the notice of resignation;

(b) in the case of failure to seek re-appointment, not less than 14 days before the end of the time allowed for next appointing auditors; and

(c) in any other case, not later than the end of the period of 14 days beginning with the date on which he ceases to hold office.

**18(3)** If the statement is of circumstances which the auditor considers should be brought to the attention of the shareholders or creditors of the company, the company shall not later than 14 days after the deposit of the statement either–

(a) send a copy of the statement to each of the shareholders whose name appears on the register of shareholders (other than the person who is designated in the company's instrument of incorporation for the purposes of paragraph 4 of Schedule 5 to these Regulations) and take such steps as SIB regulations may require for the purpose of bringing the fact that the statement has been made to the attention of the holders of any bearer shares; or

(b) apply to the court;

and, where an application is made under paragraph (b) above, the company shall notify the auditor.

**18(4)** Unless the auditor receives notice of an application to the court before the end of the period of 21 days beginning with the day on which he deposited the statement, he shall not later than seven days after the end of that period send a copy of the statement to each of the registrar of companies and SIB.

**18(5)** If the court is satisfied that the auditor is using the statement to secure needless publicity for defamatory matter–

(a) it shall direct that copies of the statement need not be sent out and that the steps required by SIB regulations need not be taken; and

(b) it may further order the company's costs on the application to be paid in whole or in part by the auditor notwithstanding that he is not a party to the application;

and the company shall not later than 14 days after the court's decision take such steps in relation to a statement setting out the effect of the order as are required by sub-paragraph (3)(a) above in relation to the statement deposited under sub-paragraph (1) above.

**18(6)** If the court is not so satisfied, the company shall not later than 14 days after the court's decision send to each of the shareholders a copy of the auditor's statement and notify the auditor of the court's decision.

**18(7)** The auditor shall not later than seven days after receiving such a notice send a copy of the statement to each of the registrar of companies and SIB.

**18(8)** Where a notice of appeal is filed not later than 14 days after the court's decision, any reference to that decision in sub-paragraphs (5) and (6) above shall be construed as a reference to the final determination or withdrawal of that appeal, as the case may be.

**19(1)** If a person ceasing to hold office as auditor fails to comply with paragraph 18 above, he is guilty of an offence and liable–

(a) on conviction on indictment, to a fine;

(b) on summary conviction, to a fine not exceeding the statutory maximum.

**19(2)** In proceedings for an offence under sub-paragraph (1) above, it is a defence for the person charged to show that he took all reasonable steps and exercised all due diligence to avoid the commission of the offence.

# Schedule 7 – Mergers and Divisions

Regulation 64

**1** This Schedule applies to any reconstruction or amalgamation involving an investment company with variable capital which takes the form of a scheme described in paragraph 4 below.

**2** An investment company with variable capital may apply to the court under section 425 of the 1985 Act (power of company to compromise with creditors or members) for an order sanctioning a scheme falling within any of paragraphs (a) to (c) of paragraph 4(1) below where–

(a) the scheme in question involves a compromise or arrangement with its shareholders or creditors or any class of its shareholders or creditors; and

(b) the consideration for the transfer or each of the transfers envisaged by the scheme is to be–

(i) shares in the transferee company receivable by shareholders of the transferor company; or

(ii) where there is more than one transferor company and any one or more of them is a public company, shares in the transferee company receivable by shareholders or members of the transferor companies (as the case may be);

in each case with or without any cash payment to shareholders.

**3** A public company may apply to the court under section 425 of the 1985 Act for an order sanctioning a scheme falling within any of paragraph (b) or (c) of paragraph 4(1) below where–

(a) the scheme in question involves a compromise or arrangement with its members or creditors or any class of its members or creditors; and

(b) the consideration for the transfer or each of the transfers envisaged by the scheme is to be–

(i) shares in the transferee company receivable by members of the transferor company; or

(ii) where there is more than one transferor company and any one or more of them is an investment company with variable capital, shares in the transferee company receivable by members or shareholders of the transferor companies (as the case may be);

in each case with or without any cash payment to shareholders.

**4(1)** The schemes falling within this paragraph are–

(a) any scheme under which the undertaking, property and liabilities of an investment company with variable capital are to be transferred to another such company, other than one formed for the purpose of, or in connection with, the scheme;

(b) any scheme under which the undertaking, property and liabilities of two or more bodies corporate, each of which is either–

(i) an investment company with variable capital; or

(ii) a public company;

are to be transferred to an investment company with variable capital formed for the purpose of, or in connection with, the scheme;

(c) any scheme under which the undertaking, property and liabilities of an investment company with variable capital or a public company are to be divided among and transferred to two or more investment companies with variable capital whether or not formed for the purpose of, or in connection with, the scheme.

**4(2)** Nothing in this Schedule shall be taken as enabling the court to sanction a scheme under which the whole or any part of the undertaking, property or liabilities of an investment company with variable capital may be transferred to any person other than an investment company with variable capital.

**5** For the purposes of this Schedule, sections 425 to 427 of the 1985 Act shall, subject to paragraph 6 below, have effect in respect of any application made by virtue of paragraph 2 or 3 above as they have effect in respect of applications falling within section 427A(1) of that Act (that is to say, subject to the provisions of section 427A of, and Schedule 15B to, that Act (mergers and divisions of public companies)).

**6(1)** All the provisions of the 1985 Act referred to in paragraph 5 above shall have effect with such modifications as are necessary or appropriate for the purposes of this Schedule.

**6(2)** In particular, any reference in those provisions to a Case 1 Scheme, a Case 2 Scheme or a Case 3 Scheme shall be taken to be a reference to a scheme falling within paragraphs (a), (b) or (c) of paragraph 4(1) above.

**6(3)** Without prejudice to the generality of sub-paragraph (1) above, the following references in those provisions shall, unless the context otherwise requires, have effect as indicated below, that is to say–

(a) any reference to a scheme shall be taken to be a reference to a scheme falling within any of paragraphs (a) to (c) of paragraph 4(1) above;

(b) any reference to a company shall be taken to be a reference to an investment company with variable capital;

(c) any reference to members shall be taken to be a reference to shareholders of an investment company with variable capital;

(d) any reference to the registered office of a company shall be taken to be a reference to the head office of an investment company with variable capital;

(e) any reference to the memorandum and Articles of a company shall be taken to be a reference to the instrument of incorporation of an investment company with variable capital;

(f) any reference to a report under section 103 of the 1985 Act shall be taken to be a reference to any report with respect to the valuation of any non-cash consideration given for shares in an investment company with variable capital which may be required by SIB regulations;

(g) any reference to annual accounts shall be taken to be a reference to the accounts contained in the annual report of an investment company with variable capital;

(h) any reference to a directors' report in relation to a company's annual accounts, shall be taken to be a reference to any report of the directors of an investment company with variable capital that is contained in the company's annual report;

(i) any reference to the requirements of the 1985 Act as to balance sheets forming part of a company's annual accounts shall be taken to be a reference to any requirements arising by virtue of SIB regulations as to balance sheets drawn up for the purposes of the accounts contained in the annual report of an investment company with variable capital;

(j) any reference to paid up capital shall be taken to be a reference to the share capital of an investment company with variable capital.

# Schedule 8 – Minor and Consequential Amendments

Regulation 75

## Part I – Primary Legislation

### TRUSTEE INVESTMENTS ACT 1961 (C. 62)

**1** [Insertion of paragraph 2A into Pt. III of Schedule 1 to the Trustee Investments Act 1961.]

### STOCK TRANSFER ACT 1963 (C. 18)

**2** [Insertion of s. 1(4)(f) into the Stock Transfer Act 1963.]

### DATA PROTECTION ACT 1984 (C. 35)

**3** Section 30 of the Data Protection Act 1984 (exemption for regulation of financial services etc) shall have effect as if the reference in subsection (2) to any enactment included these Regulations.

### COMPANIES ACT 1985 (C. 6)

**4** [Insertion of s. 26(1)(bb), amendment of s. 26(3)(b) of the 1985 Act.]

**5** [Insertion of s. 199(2A)(bb) into the 1985 Act.]

**6** [Insertion of s. 209(1)(h)(iii) into the 1985 Act.]

**7** [Amendment to s. 220(1) of the 1985 Act.]

**8** [Insertion of s. 716(2)(e) into the 1985 Act.]

**9** [Insertion of s. 718(2)(d) into the 1985 Act.]

### COMPANY DIRECTORS DISQUALIFICATION ACT 1986 (C. 46)

**10** [Insertion of paragraph 5A into Schedule 1 to the Company Directors Disqualification Act 1986.]

### FINANCIAL SERVICES ACT 1986 (C. 60)

**11** [Insertion of s. 24A into the 1986 Act.]

**12** [Insertion of s. 47A(4)(e) into the 1986 Act.]

**13** [Insertion of s. 72(6) into the 1986 Act.]

**14** [Amendment to s. 76(1) of the 1986 Act.]

**15** [Insertion of s. 83(2)(aa), amendment to s. 83(2) of the 1986 Act.]

**16** [Insertion of s. 87(2A), amendment to s. 87(2A), amendment to s. 87(2) of the 1986 Act.]

**17** [Insertion of s. 102(2)(bb), amendment to s. 102(6) of the 1986 Act.]

**18** [Amendment to s. 104(1) of the 1986 Act.]

**19** [Amendment to s. 108(1) of the 1986 Act.]

**20** [Amendment to s. 205A(1), insertion of s. 205A(1A) into the 1986 Act.]

**21** [Insertion of s. 206(1)(bb), (bc) into the 1986 Act.]

**22** [Amendment to s. 207(1) of the 1986 Act.]

**23** [Amendment to paragraph 1(1) of Schedule 8 to the 1986 Act.]

**24** [Amendment to paragraph 7 of Schedule 9 to the 1986 Act.]

### PENSION SCHEMES ACT 1993 (C. 48)

**25** [Insertion of s. 38(6)(d) into the Pension Schemes Act 1993.]

## Part II – Subordinate Legislation

### THE DATA PROTECTION (REGULATION OF FINANCIAL SERVICES ETC) (SUBJECT ACCESS EXEMPTION) ORDER 1987 (S.I. 1987/1905)

**26** [Amendment to Schedule 1 to the Data Protection (Regulation of Financial Services etc.) (Subject Access Exemption) Order 1987.]

## EXCESS RETIREMENT BENEFITS OF DIRECTORS AND PAST DIRECTORS

**4** [Substitution of paragraph 7 of Schedule 6 to the Act.]

## COMPENSATION TO DIRECTORS FOR LOSS OF OFFICE

**5(1)** [Amendment to sub-paragraph (2)(b) of paragraph 8 of Schedule 6 to the Act.]

**5(2)** [Substitution of sub-paragraph (4) of paragraph 8 of Schedule 6 to the Act.]

## MINOR AND CONSEQUENTIAL AMENDMENTS

**6(1)** [Substitution of s. 246(3) of the Act.]

**6(2)** [Amendment to paragraph 10 of Schedule 6 to the Act.]

**6(3)** [Amendment to paragraph 11(1) of Schedule 6 to the Act.]

**6(4)** [Amendment to sub-paragraph (2) of paragraph 13 of Schedule 6 to the Act.]

**6(5)** [Substitution of sub-paragraph (3) of paragraph 13 of Schedule 6 to the Act.]

## EXPLANATORY NOTE

*(This Note is not part of the Regulations)*

These Regulations amend provisions in Part I of Schedule 6 to the Companies Act 1985 (c. 6) (**"the 1985 Act"**) relating to the disclosure of directors' emoluments or other benefits in the notes to a company's annual accounts in respect of any financial year. They also make amendments to section 246 of the 1985 Act, as amended by the Companies Act 1985 (Accounts of Small and Medium-sized Companies and Minor Accounting Amendments) Regulations 1997 (SI 1997/220).

Regulation 1 provides for the citation, commencement and interpretation of the Regulations.

Regulation 2 substitutes a new paragraph 1 of Schedule 6 (aggregate amount of directors' emoluments etc.) which makes the following provision:–

(a) Companies are required to show, separately, the aggregate amount of directors' emoluments, the aggregate amount of gains made by directors from share options, the aggregate amount of money or other assets (other than share options) paid to or received by directors under long term incentive schemes and the aggregate value of company contributions in respect of directors to pension schemes where those contributions are in respect of money purchase benefits;

(b) Companies are also required to state the number of directors who are accruing benefits under, respectively, money purchase pension schemes and defined benefit pension schemes;

(c) An unlisted company is exempted from the requirement to show share option gains by its directors and the value of any shares receivable by them under long term incentive schemes, but must show the number of directors who exercised share options and who received or became entitled to shares under long term incentive schemes;

(d) Under paragraph 1(6)(a) a company need not show any information, other than that relating to share option gains, if it is readily ascertainable from other information which is shown.

Regulation 3 substitutes a new paragraph 2 (details of highest-paid director's emoluments etc.) for paragraphs 2 to 6 of Schedule 6. Firstly, the paragraph fixes the aggregate emoluments threshold above which disclosure in respect of the highest paid director is required at £200,000. Where those aggregates exceed £200,000 there shall be disclosed the proportion attributable to the highest paid director. Secondly, there is a requirement to disclose the amount of the highest paid director's accrued retirement benefits, if he is a member of a defined benefit scheme, other than money-purchase benefits or those benefits arising from voluntary contributions made by that director. Where the company is unlisted, whether the highest paid director exercised share options or received, or became entitled to shares, under long term incentive schemes, is also to be shown. The requirements previously imposed under paragraphs 2 to 6 of Schedule 6 are repealed.

Regulation 4 substitutes a new paragraph 7 of Schedule 6 (excess retirement benefits of directors and past directors). The effect of the paragraph is to require companies to disclose increases in the amount of retirement benefits paid to directors or past directors in excess of the amounts to which they were entitled when the benefits became payable unless those excess benefits were paid to all members of the relevant scheme on the same basis and were paid without recourse to additional contributions.

Regulation 5 makes amendments to paragraph 8 of Schedule 6 (compensation to directors for loss of office). The effect of the amendments is to include payments in respect of breach of contract within the scope of the meaning of the term **"compensation for loss of office"**.

Regulation 6 contains amendments to section 246 of the 1985 Act (special provisions for small companies) applying Schedule 6 as amended by these Regulations to small companies. It also makes other minor and consequential amendments to paragraphs 10, 11 and 13 of Schedule 6.

An assessment of compliance costs for companies is to be placed in the libraries of both Houses of Parliament. Copies can be obtained by post from the Company Law Directorate, Department of Trade and Industry, 5.M. 15, 1 Victoria Street, London SW1H 0ET.

# THE COMPANIES ACT 1985 (DIRECTORS' REPORT) (STATEMENT OF PAYMENT PRACTICE) REGULATIONS 1997

(SI 1997/571)

*Made on 3 March 1997 by the Secretary of State for Trade and Industry under s. 257 of the Companies Act 1985. Operative from 4 March 1997.*

## CITATION, COMMENCEMENT AND INTERPRETATION

**1(1)** These Regulations may be cited as the Companies Act 1985 (Directors' Report) (Statement of Payment Practice) Regulations 1997.

**1(2)** These Regulations shall come into force on the day after the day on which they are made.

**1(3)** In these Regulations **"the 1985 Act"** means the Companies Act 1985.

## INCLUSION OF PAYMENT PRACTICE IN REPORT

**2(1)** [Amendment to s. 234(4) of the 1985 Act.]

**2(2)** [Substitution of Part VI of Schedule 7 to the 1985 Act.]

## TRANSITIONAL PROVISION

**3** A company may, with respect to a financial year ending on or before 24th March 1997, prepare and deliver to the registrar of companies such annual accounts and annual report as it would have been required to prepare and deliver had these Regulations not been made.

## EXPLANATORY NOTE

(*This Note does not form part of the Regulations*)

These Regulations amend section 234 of the Companies Act 1985 (c. 6) (**"the 1985 Act"**) and Part VI of Schedule 7 to the 1985 Act.

The Regulations substitute for Part VI of Schedule 7 to the 1985 Act, with consequential amendments to section 234, a new Part set out in regulation 2(2). The new Part VI provides that the directors' report of public companies and large private companies which are subsidiaries of a public company must contain a statement of the company's policy and practice on payment of its suppliers.

The new Part VI restates the existing provisions of Part VI (statement of the company's policy on payment of its suppliers) and adds a new requirement to state the company's practice on payment of its suppliers. The directors' report must state the figure, expressed in days, which bears the same proportion to the number of days in the year as the amount owed to trade creditors at the year end bears to the amounts invoiced by suppliers during the year.

The Regulations will not apply to annual accounts and annual reports prepared and delivered to the registrar of companies in respect of financial years ending on or before 24th March 1997.

# THE FINANCIAL SERVICES ACT 1986 (CORPORATE DEBT EXEMPTION) ORDER 1997

(SI 1997/816)

*Made on 13 March 1997 by the Treasury under s. 46 of the Financial Services Act 1986. Operative from 3 April 1997.*

## CITATION, COMMENCEMENT AND INTERPRETATION

**1(1)** This Order may be cited as the Financial Services Act 1986 (Corporate Debt Exemption) Order 1997 and shall come into force on 3rd April 1997.

**1(2)** In this Order **"the Act"** means the Financial Services Act 1986.

## CORPORATE DEBT EXEMPTION

**2** [Amendments to Pt. I of Sch. 5 to the Act.]

**3** [Amendment of Sch. 5, Pt. II, para. 5(2) of the Act.]

## REVOCATION

**4** Articles 1(2) and 2 of the Financial Services Act 1986 (Listed Money Market Institutions and Miscellaneous Exemptions) Order 1990 are hereby revoked.

**5** Paragraph 23 of Schedule 10 to the Banking Coordination (Second Council Directive) Regulations 1992 is hereby revoked.

## EXPLANATORY NOTE

(*This Note is not part of the Order*)

This Order extends the range of corporate debt instruments which can be the subject of transactions which fall within Schedule 5 of the Financial Services Act 1986 (c.60) (**"FSA"**) and therefore benefit from the exemption granted in section 43 of the FSA. The order replaces the separate categories of investment currently set out in paragraphs 2(2)(a) and (b) of Schedule 5 of the FSA and in Article 2 of the Financial Services Act 1986 (Listed Money Market Institutions and Miscellaneous Exemptions) Order 1990 (S.I. 1990/696) with a single category of corporate debt instruments having a maturity date of not more than five years from the date of issue.

# THE COMPANIES ACT 1985 (AUDIT EXEMPTION) (AMENDMENT) REGULATIONS 1997

(SI 1997/936)

*Made on 18 March 1997 by the Secretary of State for Trade and Industry under s. 257 of the Companies Act 1985. Operative from 15 April 1997.*

## CITATION, APPLICATION AND INTERPRETATION

**1(1)** These Regulations may be cited as the Companies Act 1985 (Audit Exemption) (Amendment) Regulations 1997 and shall come into force on 15th April 1997.

**1(2)** These Regulations apply to the annual accounts of any company for any financial year ending two months or more after the coming into force of the Regulations.

**1(3)** In these Regulations, **"the 1985 Act"** means the Companies Act 1985.

## AMENDMENT OF SECTION 249A

**2(1)** Section 249A of the 1985 Act (exemptions from audit for certain categories of small company) is amended as follows.

**2(2)** [Amendment of s. 249A(2) of the 1985 Act.]

**2(3)** [Amendment of s. 249A(3)(b) of the 1985 Act.]

**2(4)** [Insertion of s. 249A(3A) into the 1985 Act.]

**2(5)** [Amendment of s. 249A(4) of the 1985 Act.]

**2(6)** [Repeal of s. 249A(5) of the 1985 Act.[

**2(7)** [Insertion of s. 249A(6A) into the 1985 Act.]

**2(8)** Section 249A shall be deemed, since the commencement of that section, to have had effect as amended by paragraph (7).

## AMENDMENT OF SECTION 249B

**3(1)** Section 249B of the 1985 Act (cases where exemption from audit not available) is amended as follows.

**3(2)** [Amendment of s. 249B(1) of the 1985 Act.]

**3(3)** [Insertions of s. 249B(1B) and (1C) into the 1985 Act.]

## AMENDMENT OF SECTION 249D

**4(1)** Section 249D of the 1985 Act (definition of reporting accountant) is amended as follows.

**4(2)** [Amendment of s. 249D(3)(d) of the 1985 Act.]

## EXPLANATORY NOTE

(*This Note does not form part of the Regulations*)

1. These Regulations amend provisions in Part VII of the Companies Act 1985 (c.6) (**"the 1985 Act"**) concerning the exemption of certain small companies from the requirement to have their annual accounts audited. The amendments are to apply to annual accounts for financial years ending two months or more after the coming into force of the Regulations (regulation 1(2)).

2. Regulation 2(3) increases the turnover limit in section 249A(3)(b) of the 1985 Act which a small company other than a small charitable company must not exceed in respect of a financial year if it is to be exempt from audit from £90,000 to £350,000 (for small charitable companies the gross income limit will remain at £90,000 – see regulation 2(4)). As a consequence of this increase, the requirement that small companies falling within section 249A(2) obtain a report from a reporting accountant is repealed except in the case of small charitable companies.

3. Regulation 2(7) inserts a new subsection (6A) into section 249A of the 1985 Act to make clear that companies which are dormant and which fall within paragraph (a) or (b) of section 250(1) of the 1985 Act may claim exemption from audit under either section 249A or section 250. Regulation 2(8) provides that that amendment shall be deemed to have had effect since the commencement of section 249A (on 11th August 1994).

4. Regulation 3(2) and (3) amends section 249B of the 1985 Act. The amendments enable a company which would otherwise be disqualified from claiming exemption from audit under section 249A for a financial year because it was a parent company or subsidiary undertaking for any period in that year, to claim the exemption, provided that the group of which it was a member was a small group satisfying the conditions specified in new section 249B(1C).

5. Regulation 4 amends section 249D(3)(d) of the 1985 Act as a consequence of the Chartered Association of Certified Accountants having changed its name to the Association of Chartered Certified Accountants.

# THE FINANCIAL SERVICES ACT 1986 (INVESTMENT ADVERTISEMENTS) (EXEMPTIONS) ORDER 1997

(SI 1997/963)

*Made on 19 March 1997 by the Treasury under s. 58(3)(a) to (c) and (4) and s. 205A of the Financial Services Act 1986. Operative from 1 June 1997.*

## CITATION AND COMMENCEMENT

**1** This Order may be cited as the Financial Services Act 1986 (Investment Advertisements) (Exemptions) Order 1997 and shall come into force on 1st June 1997.

## INTERPRETATION

**2** In this Order–

**"the Act"** means the Financial Services Act 1986;

**"the 1996 Order"** means the Financial Services Act 1986 (Investment Advertisements) (Exemptions) Order 1996.

## OVERSEAS PERSONS

**3** [Deletion and substitution of art. 10 of the 1996 Order.]

## ADVERTISEMENTS ISSUED TO PERSONS SUFFICIENTLY EXPERT TO UNDERSTAND THE RISKS INVOLVED

**4** [Amendments of art. 11 of the 1996 Order.]

## EXCHANGES OPERATING RELEVANT EEA MARKETS

**5** [Amendment of Pt. I of Schedule 1 to the 1996 Order.]

## EXPLANATORY NOTE

(*This Note is not part of the Order*)

This Order amends certain provisions of the Financial Services (Investment Advertisements) (Exemptions) Order 1996 (S.I. 1996/1586) (**"the 1996 Order"**) which sets out various exemptions from the restrictions on advertising imposed by section 57 of the Financial Services Act 1986 (**"the FSA"**).

Article 3 of this Order revokes article 10 of the 1996 Order and reproduces its provisions with amendments relating to the provision of custody services. According to article 10 of the 1996 Order, an overseas person who provides specified investment services to another person who is not resident and has no place of business in the United Kingdom may issue an investment advertisement to that other person if that other person subsequently resides in or establishes a place of business in the United Kingdom. The new article 10 substituted by this Order provides that custody services falling within paragraph 13A of Schedule 1 to the FSA are among the specified investment services for this purpose. Paragraph 13A was inserted in Schedule 1 by The Financial Services Act 1986 (Extension of Scope of Act) Order 1996 (S.I. 1996/2958).

Article 4 of this Order amends article 11 of the 1996 Order exempting investment advertisements issued to persons sufficiently expert to understand the risks involved. Article 4 provides that European investment firms carrying on home-regulated investment business in the United Kingdom are not relevant persons for the purpose of article 11 and that they fall within the category of persons who are sufficiently expert to understand the risks involved.

Article 5 amends the list of exchanges operating relevant EEA markets in Part I of Schedule 1 to the 1996 Order to take account of the merger of the Amsterdam Stock Exchange and European Options Exchange into the Amsterdam Exchanges AEX.

# THE COMPANIES OVERSEAS BRANCH REGISTERS (HONG KONG) ORDER 1997

(SI 1997/1313)

*Made on 20 May 1997 by Her Majesty the Queen with the advice of the Privy Council under para 3(2) of the Schedule to the Hong Kong Act 1985. Operative from 1 July 1997.*

**1** This Order may be cited as the Companies Overseas Branch Registers (Hong Kong) Order 1997 and shall come into force on 1st July 1997.

**2** [Amendment of Pt. I of Sch. 14 to the Companies Act 1985 and Pt. I of Sch. 14 to the Companies (Northern Ireland) Order 1986.]

**3** This Order extends to Northern Ireland.

## EXPLANATORY NOTE

(*This Note is not part of the Order*)

This Order, which comes into force on 1st July 1997, amends Part I of Schedule 14 to the Companies Act 1985, which specifies the countries and territories in which by virtue of section 362 of that Act a company may cause to be kept in such country or territory a branch register of members there resident, by inserting a reference to the Hong Kong Special Administrative Region of the People's Republic of China.

Part I of Schedule 14 will thereby continue to apply to Hong Kong after 30 June 1997 notwithstanding that the Region will not be a part of Her Majesty's dominions.

The Order makes a corresponding amendment to Part I of Schedule 14 to the Companies (Northern Ireland) Order 1986.

# THE PARTNERSHIPS (UNRESTRICTED SIZE) NO. 12 REGULATIONS 1997

(SI 1997/1937)

*Made on 31 July 1997 by the Secretary of State for Trade and Industry under s. 716(2)(d) and 744 of the Companies Act 1985. Operative from 1 September 1997.*

**1** These Regulations may be cited as the Partnerships (Unrestricted Size) No. 12 Regulations 1997 and shall come into force on 1st September 1997.

**2** Section 716(1) of the Companies Act 1985 does not prohibit the formation, for the purpose of carrying on practice in relation to matters connected with the European Patent Convention, of a partnership consisting of persons the majority of whom are members of the Institute of Professional Representatives before the European Patent Office.

**3** For the purposes of these Regulations the European Patent Convention is the Convention on the Grant of European Patents signed in Munich on 5th October 1973 as from time to time amended.

## EXPLANATORY NOTE

(*This Note is not part of the Regulations*)

Section 716 of the Companies Act 1985 prohibits the formation of partnerships consisting of more than 20 persons. These Regulations exempt from that prohibition any partnership formed for the purpose of carrying on practice in relation to matters connected with the European Patent Convention 1973 (Cmnd. 8510) where the majority of the partners are members of the Institute of Professional Representatives before the European Patent Office.

# THE COMPANIES (MEMBERSHIP OF HOLDING COMPANY) (DEALERS IN SECURITIES) REGULATIONS 1997

(SI 1997/2306)

*Made on 23 September 1997 by the Secretary of State for Trade and Industry under s. 2(2) of the European Communities Act 1972. Operative from 20 October 1997.*

## CITATION AND COMMENCEMENT

**1** These Regulations may be cited as the Companies (Membership of Holding Company) (Dealers in Securities) Regulations 1997 and shall come into force on 20th October 1997.

## AMENDMENT OF SECTION 23 OF THE COMPANIES ACT 1985

**2** [Substitution of s. 23(3) of the Companies Act 1985.]

**3** [Amendment of s. 23(4),(5) of the Companies Act 1985.]

**4(1)** [Insertion of definition of "EEA State" into s. 744 of the Companies Act 1985.]

**4(2)** [Omission of the definition of "EEA State" from s. 262(1) of the Companies Act 1985.]

**4(3)** [Insertion of definition of "EEA State" into s. 744 of the Companies Act 1985.]

**4(4)** [Omission of the definition of "EEA State" from s. 262A of the Companies Act 1985.]

## EXPLANATORY NOTE

(*This Note is not part of the Regulations*)

These Regulations further implement the provisions of Article 24a of Second Council Directive 77/91/EEC (OJ No. L26, 31.1.77, p. 1), on the co-ordination of safeguards in respect of the formation of public limited liability companies and the maintenance and alteration of their capital. Article 24a was inserted by Council Directive 92/101/EEC (OJ No. L347, 28.11.92, p. 64). Those Community provisions extend to the EEA by virtue of Annex XXII to the EEA Agreement and Decision No. 7/94 of the EEA Joint Committee.

The Regulations alter the scope of the exemption contained in section 23(3) of the Companies Act 1985, which excludes certain kinds of dealings in securities from the prohibition (laid down by section 23(1) of the Act) on the ownership by a body corporate of shares in its holding company The exemption for the benefit of **"market makers"** is replaced by an exemption for the benefit of **"intermediaries"**, defined as a certain class of dealers in securities. Excluded from that definition are persons who carry on various categories of **"excluded business"**, which correspond to those contained in section 80A(5) and section 88A(5) of the Finance Act 1986. Provision is also made for the consequences of a breach of the prohibition where the shares are subsequently acquired by a purchaser without notice of the breach. The amendments provided for by these Regulations are made following changes in the system of trading on certain regulated securities markets.

# THE FINANCIAL SERVICES ACT 1986 (EXTENSION OF SCOPE OF ACT) ORDER 1997

(SI 1997/2543)

*Made on 27 October 1997 by the Treasury under s. 2 and 205A of the Financial Services Act 1986. Operative from 10 November 1997.*

## CITATION AND COMMENCEMENT

**1(1)** This Order may be cited as the Financial Act 1986 (Extension of Scope of Act) Order 1997.

**1(2)** This Order shall come into force on 10th November 1997.

## DEMATERIALISED INSTRUCTIONS SENT ETC. THROUGH CGO SERVICE

**2(1)** Paragraph 16A of Schedule 1 to the Financial Services Act 1986 (sending dematerialised instructions etc. as activity constituting investment business) shall be amended as follows.

**2(2)** [Substitution of Sch. 1, para. 16A.]

**2(3)** [Amendment of Note (1) to Sch. 1. para. 16A.]

**2(4)** [Insertion on Note (1A) to Sch. 1, para. 16A.]

**2(5)** [Substitution of Notes (2) and (3) to Sch. 1, para. 16A.]

## CONSEQUENTIAL AMENDMENT

**3** [Substitution of Sch. 1, para. 18(5B).]

## EXPLANATORY NOTE

(*This Note is not part of the Order*)

The Order extends the activities that constitute the carrying on of investment business for the purposes of the Financial Services Act 1986 ("FSA") so as to include certain activities carried on in order to communicate through the computer-based system established under the Stock Transfer Act 1982. That system was established for the purposes of transferring or allotting certain Government and other securities without the need for a written instrument. The system and its associated procedures are sometimes referred to as the CGO (Central Gifts Office) Service.

Article 2 amends paragraph 16A of Schedule 1 to the FSA, and the Notes to that paragraph, to extend the activities listed in that paragraph so as to cover instructions sent by means of the system and to provide for certain exemptions. Paragraph 18 of Schedule 1 to the FSA is consequentially amended by Article 3.

# THE COMPANIES ACT 1985 (INSURANCE COMPANIES ACCOUNTS) (MINOR AMENDMENTS) REGULATIONS 1997

(SI 1997/2704)

*Made on 12 November 1997 by the Secretary of State for Trade and Industry under s. 257 of the Companies Act 1985. Operative from 31 December 1997.*

**1** These Regulations may be cited as the Companies Act 1985 (Insurance Companies Accounts) (Minor Amendments) Regulations 1997 and shall come into force on 31st December 1997.

**2(1)** Schedule 9A to the Companies Act 1985 is amended as follows.

**2(2)** [Amendment to heading to note 10 on the profit and loss account format set out in Section B of Ch. I of Pt. I.]

## EXPLANATORY NOTE

(*This Note does not form part of the Regulations*)

These Regulations make minor amendments to the heading to note (10) on the profit and loss account format for insurance companies set out in Schedule 9A to the Companies Act 1985. Regulation 2(2) corrects two incorrect references in the heading to note (10) which implements article 43 of the Council Directive 91/674/EEC (Official Journal No. L374 of 31.12.91, pages 7 to 31) on the annual and consolidated accounts of insurance undertakings. Article 43 itself contains an incorrect reference in its heading to item II.2.

(i) an advertisement falling within article 8 of the Financial Services Act 1986 (Investment Advertisements) (Exemptions) (No. 2) Order 1995; or

(ii) an advertisement which falls within article 11 of the Financial Services Act 1986 (Investment Advertisements) (Exemptions) Order 1996, or would do so if there were added to the list of persons in paragraph (3) of that article a person with or for whom any credit institution or other financial institution through which the Euro-securities may be acquired pursuant to the offer has effected or arranged for the effecting of a transaction within the period of twelve months ending with the date on which the offer is first made;"".

## AMENDMENT OF THE BANKING ACT 1987 (ADVERTISEMENTS) REGULATIONS 1988

**5** Regulation 2(4)(b) of the Banking Act 1987 (Advertisements) Regulations 1988 is revoked.

## EXPLANATORY NOTE

(*This Note is not part of the Regulations*)

These Regulations amend the Public Offers of Securities Regulations 1995 (**"the 1995 Regulations"**), which implement Council Directive 89/298/EEC, coordinating the requirements for the drawing-up, scrutiny and distribution of the prospectus to be published when transferable securities are offered to the public (OJ L124, 5.5.89, p8).

In relation to offers of unlisted securities, regulation 2(a) to (k) make changes to regulation 7 of the 1995 Regulations, which provides for exemptions from the requirement to publish a prospectus by deeming certain sorts of offers not to be offers to the public.

Regulation 4 makes equivalent changes (so far as relevant) to the exemptions contained in Schedule 11A to the Financial Services Act 1986, relating to offers where an application for admission to the Official List has been made, and the securities in question are to be offered to the public before admission.

Regulation 2(l), (m), (o) and (p) amend regulation 8 of, and Schedule 1 to, the 1995 Regulations, which prescribe the information which is to contained in a prospectus.

Regulations 2(n) and 3 provide that the offeror of securities is not to be treated as responsible for a prospectus in certain circumstances where he is making the offer in association with the issuer.

Regulation 2(q) removes the requirements for a prospectus approved in another Member State to be translated into English, and to contain a summary of the relevant tax treatment. Regulation 2(r) revokes paragraph 11 of Schedule 4 to the 1995 Regulations, which applied certain provisions of the Companies Act 1985 to prospectuses approved in other Member States.

Regulations 2(s) and 5 revoke a redundant provision in the Banking Act 1987 (Advertisements) Regulations 1988, and make a consequential revocation in the 1995 Regulations.

A regulatory impact assessment covering these Regulations is available from the Public Enquiry Unit, Room 89/2, HM Treasury, Parliament Street, London SW1P 3AG.

# THE INSOLVENT COMPANIES (DISQUALIFICATION OF UNFIT DIRECTORS) PROCEEDINGS (AMENDMENT) RULES 1999

(SI 1999/1023)

*Made on 29 March 1999 by the Lord Chancellor under s. 411 and 413 of the Insolvency Act 1986 and s. 21(2) of the Company Directors Disqualification Act 1986. Operative from 26 April 1999.*

## CITATION AND COMMENCEMENT

**1** These Rules may be cited as the Insolvent Companies (Disqualification of Unfit Directors) Proceedings (Amendment) Rules 1999 and shall come into force on 26th April 1999.

## INTERPRETATION

**2** In these Rules, references to **"the principal Rules"** are to the Insolvent Companies (Disqualification of Unfit Directors) Proceedings Rules 1987 and unless the context otherwise requires a rule (referred to by number) means the rule so numbered in the principal Rules.

**3** The principal Rules are amended as set out in the Schedule to these Rules.

# Schedule

Rule 3

**Note**

Amendments not reproduced here – see the principal rules.

## EXPLANATORY NOTE

(*This Note is not part of the Regulations*)

These Rules amend the Insolvent Companies (Disqualification of Unfit Directors) Proceedings Rules 1987 (**"the principal Rules"**) which provide procedures for applications by the Secretary of State or the official receiver for the disqualification of directors by courts in England and Wales under sections 7 and 8 of the Company Directors Disqualification Act 1986.

The amendments come into force on 26th April 1999 to coincide with the coming into force of the Civil Procedure Rules 1998 (**"the CPR"**) which provide a new code of civil procedure for the civil courts which replaces the Rules of the Supreme Court 1965 and the County Court Rules 1981.

Although, by rule 2.1 of the CPR the new civil procedure does not apply to proceedings for which rules may be made under section 411 of the Insolvency Act 1986, the principal Rules themselves (as amended by these Rules), apply all the provisions of the CPR and any relevant practice direction, except where the principal Rules make provision to inconsistent effect. Provision is made for the application or disapplication of certain rules of the CPR and for the application of certain of the Insolvency Rules 1986.

Adaptations are also made to take account of changes embodied in the CPR in the expressions used in relation to civil procedure.

# THE PUBLIC OFFERS OF SECURITIES (AMENDMENT) (NO. 2) REGULATIONS 1999

(SI 1999/1146)

*Made on 13 April 1999 by the Treasury under s. 2(2) of the European Communities Act 1972. Operative from 10 May 1999.*

## CITATION AND COMMENCEMENT

**1** These Regulations may be cited as the Public Offers of Securities (Amendment) (No. 2) Regulations 1999 and shall come into force on 10th May 1999.

## AMENDMENT OF THE 1995 REGULATIONS

**2** [Substitution of reg. 7(2)(s) of the Public Offers of Securities Regulations 1995 (SI 1995/1537).]

## AMENDMENT OF THE FINANCIAL SERVICES ACT 1986

**3** [Substitution of para. 3(1)(r) of Sch. 11A to the Financial Services Act 1986.]

## REVOCATIONS

**4** Regulations 2(e) and 4(c) of the Public Offers of Securities (Amendment) Regulations 1999 are revoked.

(b) an investment firm as defined in point 2 of Article 1 of Council Directive 93/22/EEC excluding the bodies set out in the list in Article 2(2)(a) to (k);
(c) a public authority or publicly guaranteed undertaking;
(d) any undertaking whose head office is outside the European Community and whose functions correspond to those of a credit institution or investment firm as defined in (a) and (b) above; or
(e) any undertaking which is treated by the designating authority as an institution in accordance with regulation 8(1),

which participates in a designated system and which is responsible for discharging the financial obligations arising from transfer orders which are effected through the system;

**"netting"** means the conversion into one net claim or obligation of different claims or obligations between participants resulting from the issue and receipt of transfer orders between them, whether on a bilateral or multilateral basis and whether through the interposition of a clearing house, central counterparty or settlement agent or otherwise;

**"Part VII"** means Part VII of the Companies Act 1989;

**"participant"** means–
(a) an institution,
(b) a body corporate or unincorporated association which carries out any combination of the functions of a central counterparty, a settlement agent or a clearing house, with respect to a system, or
(c) an indirect participant which is treated as a participant, or is a member of a class of indirect participants which are treated as participants, in accordance with regulation 9 9;

**"protected trust deed"** and **"trust deed"** shall be construed in accordance with section 73(1) of the Bankruptcy (Scotland) Act 1985 (interpretation);

**"relevant office-holder"** means–
(a) the official receiver;
(b) any person acting in relation to a company as its liquidator, provisional liquidator, or administrator;
(c) any person acting in relation to an individual (or, in Scotland, any debtor within the meaning of the Bankruptcy (Scotland) Act 1985) as his trustee in bankruptcy or interim receiver of his property or as permanent or interim trustee in the sequestration of his estate or as his trustee under a protected trust deed; or
(d) any person acting as administrator of an insolvent estate of a deceased person;

and in sub-paragraph (b),

**"company"** means any company, society, association, partnership or other body which may be wound up under the Insolvency Act 1986;

**"rules"**, in relation to a designated system, means rules or conditions governing the system with respect to the matters dealt with in these Regulations;

**"securities"** means (except for the purposes of the definition of "charge") any instruments referred to in section B of the Annex to Council Directive 93/22/EEC;

**"settlement account"** means an account at a central bank, a settlement agent or a central counterparty used to hold funds or securities (or both) and to settle transactions between participants in a designated system;

**"settlement agent"** means a body corporate or unincorporated association providing settlement accounts to the institutions and any central counterparty in a designated system for the settlement of transfer orders within the system and, as the case may be, for extending credit to such institutions and any such central counterparty for settlement purposes;

**"the Settlement Finality Directive"** means Directive 98/26/EC of the European Parliament and of the Council of 19th May 1998 on settlement finality in payment and securities settlement systems;

**"transfer order"** means–
(a) an instruction by a participant to place at the disposal of a recipient an amount of

money by means of a book entry on the accounts of a credit institution, a central bank or a settlement agent, or an instruction which results in the assumption or discharge of a payment obligation as defined by the rules of a designated system ("a payment transfer order"); or

(b) an instruction by a participant to transfer the title to, or interest in, securities by means of a book entry on a register, or otherwise ("a securities transfer order");

**"winding up"** means–

(a) winding up by the court, or

(b) creditors' voluntary winding up,

within the meaning of the Insolvency Act 1986 (but does not include members' voluntary winding up within the meaning of that Act).

**2(2)** In these Regulations–

(a) references to the law of insolvency include references to every provision made by or under the Insolvency Act 1986 or the Bankruptcy (Scotland) Act 1985; and in relation to a building society references to insolvency law or to any provision of the Insolvency Act 1986 are to that law or provision as modified by the Building Societies Act 1986;

(b) in relation to Scotland, references to–

(i) sequestration include references to the administration by a judicial factor of the insolvent estate of a deceased person,

(ii) an interim or permanent trustee include references to a judicial factor on the insolvent estate of a deceased person, and

(iii) "set off" include compensation.

**2(3)** Subject to paragraph (1), expressions used in these Regulations which are also used in the Settlement Finality Directive have the same meaning in these Regulations as they have in the Settlement Finality Directive.

**2(4)** References in these Regulations to things done, or required to be done, by or in relation to a designated system shall, in the case of a designated system which is neither a body corporate nor an unincorporated association, be treated as references to things done, or required to be done, by or in relation to the operator of that system.

## PART II – DESIGNATED SYSTEMS

### APPLICATION FOR DESIGNATION

**3(1)** Any body corporate or unincorporated association may apply to the designating authority for an order declaring it, or any system of which it is the operator, to be a designated system for the purposes of these Regulations.

**3(2)** Any such application–

(a) shall be made in such manner as the designating authority may direct; and

(b) shall be accompanied by such information as the designating authority may reasonably require for the purpose of determining the application.

**3(3)** At any time after receiving an application and before determining it, the designating authority may require the applicant to furnish additional information.

**3(4)** The directions and requirements given or imposed under paragraphs (2) and (3) may differ as between different applications.

**3(5)** Any information to be furnished to the designating authority under this regulation shall be in such form or verified in such manner as it may specify.

**3(6)** Every application shall be accompanied by copies of the rules of the system to which the application relates and any guidance relating to that system.

### GRANT AND REFUSAL OF DESIGNATION

**4(1)** Where–

(a) an application has been duly made under regulation 3;

**15(3)** If, in Scotland, an award of sequestration or a winding-up order has been made, or a creditors' voluntary winding-up resolution has been passed, or a trust deed has been granted and it has become a protected trust deed, the debt–

(a) may be claimed in the sequestration or winding up or under the protected trust deed or, as the case may be, is payable to the relevant office-holder; and

(b) shall be taken into account for the purposes of any rule of law relating to set-off applicable in sequestration, winding up or in respect of a protected trust deed;

in the same way as a debt due before the date of sequestration (within the meaning of section 73(1) of the Bankruptcy (Scotland) Act 1985) or the commencement of the winding up (within the meaning of section 129 of the Insolvency Act 1986) or the grant of the trust deed.

## DISCLAIMER OF PROPERTY, RESCISSION OF CONTRACTS, &C

**16(1)** Sections 178, 186, 315 and 345 of the Insolvency Act 1986 (power to disclaim onerous property and court's power to order rescission of contracts, &c) do not apply in relation to–

(a) a transfer order; or

(b) a contract for the purpose of realising collateral security.

In the application of this paragraph in Scotland, the reference to sections 178, 315 and 345 shall be construed as a reference to any rule of law having the like effect as those sections.

**16(2)** In Scotland, a permanent trustee on the sequestrated estate of a defaulter or a liquidator or a trustee under a protected trust deed granted by a defaulter is bound by any transfer order given by that defaulter and by any such contract as is mentioned in paragraph (1)(b) notwithstanding section 42 of the Bankruptcy (Scotland) Act 1985 or any rule of law having the like effect applying in liquidations or any like provision or rule of law affecting the protected trust deed.

**16(3)** Sections 127 and 284 of the Insolvency Act 1986 (avoidance of property dispositions effected after commencement of winding up or presentation of bankruptcy petition), section 32(8) of the Bankruptcy (Scotland) Act 1985 (effect of dealing with debtor relating to estate vested in permanent trustee) and any like provision or rule of law affecting a protected trust deed, do not apply to–

(a) a transfer order, or any disposition of property in pursuance of such an order;

(b) the provision of collateral security;

(c) a contract for the purpose of realising collateral security or any disposition of property in pursuance of such a contract; or

(d) any disposition of property in accordance with the rules of a designated system as to the application of collateral security.

## ADJUSTMENT OF PRIOR TRANSACTIONS

**17(1)** No order shall be made in relation to a transaction to which this regulation applies under–

(a) section 238 or 339 of the Insolvency Act 1986 (transactions at an undervalue);

(b) section 239 or 340 of that Act (preferences); or

(c) section 423 of that Act (transactions defrauding creditors).

**17(2)** As respects Scotland, no decree shall be granted in relation to any such transaction–

(a) under section 34 or 36 of the Bankruptcy (Scotland) Act 1985 or section 242 or 243 of the Insolvency Act 1986 (gratuitous alienations and unfair preferences); or

(b) at common law on grounds of gratuitous alienations or fraudulent preferences.

**17(3)** This regulation applies to–

(a) a transfer order, or any disposition of property in pursuance of such an order;

(b) the provision of collateral security;

(c) a contract for the purpose of realising collateral security or any disposition of property in pursuance of such a contract; or

(d) any disposition of property in accordance with the rules of a designated system as to the application of collateral security.

## COLLATERAL SECURITY CHARGES

### MODIFICATIONS OF THE LAW OF INSOLVENCY

**18** The general law of insolvency has effect in relation to a collateral security charge and the action taken to enforce such a charge, subject to the provisions of regulation 19.

### ADMINISTRATION ORDERS, &C

**19(1)** The following provisions of the Insolvency Act 1986 (which relate to administration orders and administrators) do not apply in relation to a collateral security charge–

(a) sections 10(1)(b) and 11(3)(c) (restriction on enforcement of security while petition for administration order pending or order in force); and

(b) section 15(1) and (2) (power of administrator to deal with charged property);

and section 11(2) of that Act (receiver to vacate office when so required by administrator) does not apply to a receiver appointed under such a charge.

**19(2)** However, where a collateral security charge falls to be enforced after an administration order has been made or a petition for an administration order has been presented, and there exists another charge over some or all of the same property ranking in priority to or *pari passu* with the collateral security charge, on the application of any person interested, the court may order that there shall be taken after enforcement of the collateral security charge such steps as the court may direct for the purpose of ensuring that the chargee under the other charge is not prejudiced by the enforcement of the collateral security charge.

**19(3)** Sections 127 and 284 of the Insolvency Act 1986 (avoidance of property dispositions effected after commencement of winding up or presentation of bankruptcy petition), section 32(8) of the Bankruptcy (Scotland) Act 1985 (effect of dealing with debtor relating to estate vested in permanent trustee) and any like provision or rule of law affecting a protected trust deed, do not apply to a disposition of property as a result of which the property becomes subject to a collateral security charge or any transactions pursuant to which that disposition is made.

## GENERAL

### TRANSFER ORDER ENTERED INTO DESIGNATED SYSTEM FOLLOWING INSOLVENCY

**20(1)** This Part does not apply in relation to any transfer order given by a participant which is entered into a designated system after–

(a) a court has made an order of a type referred to in regulation 22 in respect of that participant, or

(b) that participant has passed a creditors' voluntary winding-up resolution, or

(c) a trust deed granted by that participant has become a protected trust deed,

unless the conditions mentioned in paragraph (2) are satisfied.

**20(2)** The conditions referred to in paragraph (1) are that–

(a) the transfer order is carried out on the same day that the event specified in paragraph (1)(a), (b) or (c) occurs, and

(b) the settlement agent, the central counterparty or the clearing house can show that it did not have notice of that event at the time of settlement of the transfer order.

**20(3)** For the purposes of paragraph (2)(b), the relevant settlement agent, central counterparty or clearing house shall be taken to have notice of an event specified in paragraph (1)(a), (b) or (c) if it deliberately failed to make enquiries as to that matter in circumstances in which a reasonable and honest person would have done so.

## DISAPPLICATION OF CERTAIN PROVISIONS OF PART VII

**21(1)** The provisions of the Companies Act 1989 mentioned in paragraph (2) do not apply in relation to–

(a) a market contract which is also a transfer order effected through a designated system; or

(b) a market charge which is also a collateral security charge.

**21(2)** The provisions referred to in paragraph (1) are as follows–

(a) section 163(4) to (6) (net sum payable on completion of default proceedings);

(b) section 164(4) to (6) (disclaimer of property, rescission of contracts, &c); and

(c) section 175(5) and (6) (administration orders, &c).

## NOTIFICATION OF INSOLVENCY ORDER OR PASSING OF RESOLUTION FOR CREDITORS' VOLUNTARY WINDING UP

**22(1)** Upon the making of an order for bankruptcy, sequestration, administration or winding up in respect of a participant in a designated system, the court shall forthwith notify both the system and the designating authority that such an order has been made.

**22(2)** Following receipt of–

(a) such notification from the court, or

(b) notification from a participant of the passing of a creditors' voluntary winding-up resolution or of a trust deed becoming a protected trust deed, pursuant to paragraph 5(4) of the Schedule,

the designating authority shall forthwith inform the Treasury of the notification.

## APPLICABLE LAW RELATING TO SECURITIES HELD AS COLLATERAL SECURITY

**23** Where–

(a) securities (including rights in securities) are provided as collateral security to a participant or a central bank (including any nominee, agent or third party acting on behalf of the participant or the central bank), and

(b) a register, account or centralised deposit system located in an EEA State legally records the entitlement of that person to the collateral security,

the rights of that person as a holder of collateral security in relation to those securities shall be governed by the law of the EEA State or, where appropriate, the law of the part of the EEA State, where the register, account, or centralised deposit system is located.

## APPLICABLE LAW WHERE INSOLVENCY PROCEEDINGS ARE BROUGHT

**24** Where insolvency proceedings are brought in any jurisdiction against a person who participates, or has participated, in a system designated for the purposes of the Settlement Finality Directive, any question relating to the rights and obligations arising from, or in connection with, that participation and falling to be determined by a court in England and Wales or in Scotland shall (subject to regulation 23) be determined in accordance with the law governing that system.

## INSOLVENCY PROCEEDINGS IN OTHER JURISDICTIONS

**25(1)** The references to insolvency law in section 426 of the Insolvency Act 1986 (co-operation between courts exercising jurisdiction in relation to insolvency) include, in relation to a part of the United Kingdom, this Part and, in relation to a relevant country or territory within the meaning of that section, so much of the law of that country or territory as corresponds to this Part.

**25(2)** A court shall not, in pursuance of that section or any other enactment or rule of law, recognise or give effect to–

(a) any order of a court exercising jurisdiction in relation to insolvency law in a country or territory outside the United Kingdom, or

(b) any act of a person appointed in such a country or territory to discharge any functions under insolvency law,

in so far as the making of the order or the doing of the act would be prohibited in the case of a court in England and Wales or Scotland or a relevant office-holder by this Part.

**25(3)** Paragraph (2) does not affect the recognition or enforcement of a judgment required to be recognised or enforced under or by virtue of the Civil Jurisdiction and Judgments Act 1982.

### SYSTEMS DESIGNATED IN OTHER EEA STATES, NORTHERN IRELAND AND GIBRALTAR

**26(1)** Where an equivalent overseas order or equivalent overseas security is subject to the insolvency law of England and Wales or Scotland, this Part shall apply–

(a) in relation to the equivalent overseas order as it applies in relation to a transfer order; and

(b) in relation to the equivalent overseas security as it applies in relation to collateral security in connection with a designated system.

**26(2)** In paragraph (1)–

(a) **"equivalent overseas order"** means an order having the like effect as a transfer order which is effected through a system designated for the purposes of the Settlement Finality Directive in another EEA State, Northern Ireland or Gibraltar; and

(b) **"equivalent overseas security"** means any realisable assets provided under a charge or a repurchase or similar agreement, or otherwise (including money provided under a charge) for the purpose of securing rights and obligations potentially arising in connection with such a system.

## Schedule – Requirements for designation of system

Regulation 4(1)

### ESTABLISHMENT, PARTICIPATION AND GOVERNING LAW

**1(1)** The head office of at least one of the participants in the system must be in Great Britain and the law of England and Wales or Scotland must be the governing law of the system.

**1(2)** There must be not less than three institutions participating in the system, unless otherwise determined by the designating authority in any case where–

(a) there are two institutions participating in a system; and

(b) the designating authority considers that designation is required on the grounds of systemic risk.

**1(3)** The system must be a system through which transfer orders are effected.

**1(4)** Where orders relating to financial instruments other than securities are effected through the system–

(a) the system must primarily be a system through which securities transfer orders are effected; and

(b) the designating authority must consider that designation is required on grounds of systemic risk.

### ARRANGEMENTS AND RESOURCES

**2** The system must have adequate arrangements and resources for the effective monitoring and enforcement of compliance with its rules or, as respects monitoring, arrangements providing for that function to be performed on its behalf (and without affecting its responsibility) by another body or person who is able and willing to perform it.

and references to the exercise of the transferred functions include references to the exercise and enforcement of such rights and the discharge of such obligations.

**2(4)** No reference in these Regulations to the Official List maintained for the purposes of Part IV by the old competent authority shall be construed as extending to the Daily Official List published by The London Stock Exchange Limited.

## CHANGE OF COMPETENT AUTHORITY FOR THE PURPOSES OF PART IV OF THE ACT

**3** In section 142(6) of the Act, for the words "The International Stock Exchange of the United Kingdom and the Republic of Ireland Limited", there shall be substituted the words "The Financial Services Authority".

## REFERENCES TO THE OLD COMPETENT AUTHORITY

**4(1)** Any reference in an enactment to the old competent authority shall have effect as a reference to the new competent authority.

**4(2)** Any reference in an enactment to the Official List maintained for the purposes of Part IV by the old competent authority shall have effect as a reference to the Official List maintained for those purposes by the new competent authority.

**4(3)** Paragraphs (1) and (2) apply however the reference is expressed.

**4(4)** If a reference in a relevant provision is predicated on the continuing exercise by the old competent authority of any of the transferred functions, paragraphs (1) to (3) shall, in relation to any time after the transfer date, apply to the reference in the same way as they apply to a reference in an enactment.

**4(5)** In paragraph (4), "relevant provision" means a provision which–

(a) has effect before, as well as after, the transfer date, and

(b) is contained in a document other than an enactment.

## TRANSFER OF RIGHTS AND OBLIGATIONS IN RELATION TO NON-PART IV INVESTMENTS

**5** All rights and obligations of the old competent authority arising out of the admission by it of investments to the Official List otherwise than in accordance with Part IV are transferred to the new competent authority.

## TRANSITIONAL PROVISIONS

**6(1)** These Regulations shall not affect the validity of anything done before the transfer date–

(a) by the old competent authority in the exercise of the transferred functions, or

(b) by another person in relation to the exercise of the transferred functions by the old competent authority,

but subject to paragraph (2) any such thing shall have effect for all purposes as if done by the new competent authority in the exercise of those functions or (as the case may be) as if done in relation to the exercise by the new competent authority of those functions.

**6(2)** Paragraph (1) shall not affect any liability in damages of the old competent authority for anything done or omitted in the discharge or purported discharge of the transferred functions where such act or omission is shown to have been in bad faith.

**6(3)** Where any issue as to such liability arises in legal proceedings against the old competent authority, the new competent authority shall provide the old competent authority with such assistance, including access to staff and records, as is reasonably necessary in order to enable the old competent authority to deal with the proceedings.

**6(4)** The new competent authority shall be substituted for the old competent authority in all legal proceedings to which the old competent authority is, at the transfer date, a party in relation to its exercise of the transferred functions, other than proceedings in relation to any liability of the kind mentioned in paragraph (2).

**6(5)** Anything which, immediately before the transfer date, is in the process of being done–

(a) by the old competent authority in the exercise of the transferred functions, or

(b) by another person in relation to the exercise of the transferred functions by the old competent authority,

may be carried on and completed by the new competent authority in the exercise of those functions or (as the case may be) carried on and completed in relation to the exercise by the new competent authority of those functions.

**6(6)** Without prejudice to paragraph (1), listing rules made by the old competent authority or by any committee or sub-committee of the old competent authority in the exercise of the transferred functions shall be treated and have effect for all purposes as if made in the exercise of the transferred functions by the governing body of the new competent authority or, as the case may be, by a committee or sub-committee of that governing body.

**6(7)** Without prejudice to paragraph (1), investments which at the transfer date are listed on the Official List maintained for the purposes of Part IV by the old competent authority shall be treated for all purposes as if they were listed on the Official List maintained for those purposes by the new competent authority.

**6(8)** Securities the listing of which is suspended under section 145(2) of the Act, or in pursuance of rights of the old competent authority in relation to investments admitted to the Official List otherwise than in accordance with Part IV, shall nevertheless be regarded as listed for the purposes of paragraph (7).

## TRANSFER OF STAFF

**7** The transfer of functions effected by these Regulations shall be regarded for the purposes of the Transfer of Undertakings (Protection of Employment) Regulations 1981 as the transfer of part of an undertaking, whether or not it would be so regarded apart from this regulation.

## ANTICIPATORY EXERCISE OF POWER TO MAKE LISTING RULES

**8** For the purpose of bringing listing rules under section 142(6) of the Act into effect on the transfer date, the new competent authority may, prior to that date, exercise the power to make such rules as if these Regulations were fully in force, and may do anything which is necessary or expedient to enable it to exercise that power.

## REPEALS

**9** Paragraph 2(3) of Schedule 4 to the Act is repealed.

## EXPLANATORY NOTE

(*This Note is not part of the Regulations*)

These Regulations amend the Financial Services Act 1986 (c.60) ("the Act") so as to change the competent authority for the purposes of Part IV of the Act (official listing of securities). The competent authority for the purposes of Part IV was originally the Council of The Stock Exchange, but was changed by the Official Listing of Securities (Change of Competent Authority) Regulations 1991 (S.I. 1991/2000) to The International Stock Exchange of the United Kingdom and the Republic of Ireland Limited (since 9 December 1995 known simply as The London Stock Exchange Limited).

Regulation 3 of these Regulations substitutes the Financial Services Authority as the new competent authority, with effect from the transfer date of 1st May 2000 when these Regulations (apart from regulation 8) come into force.

Regulation 4 updates references to the competent authority or to the Official List maintained for the purposes of Part IV by the competent authority, whether those references appear in primary and secondary legislation or other documents. This applies however the references are expressed but has no effect on references to the Daily Official List published by The London Stock Exchange Limited (see regulation 2(4)).

Regulation 5 transfers to the new competent authority all rights and obligations of the old competent authority in relation to investments admitted to the Official List otherwise than in accordance with Part IV (the power to admit certain investments to the Official List otherwise than under Part IVis preserved by section 142(9)) of the Act).

Regulation 6 makes a number of transitional provisions. These carry forward existing listings and listing rules, and anything done or in the process of being done at the time of the transfer. They also substitute the new competent authority in legal proceedings (except in relation to liabilities for things done or omitted in bad faith). Regulation 7 has the effect of tranferring staff to the new competent authority. Regulation 8 (which comes into force on the day after the Regulations are made) allows the new competent authority to make listing rules in advance of the transfer date, to come into force on that date.

Consequential upon the transfer, regulation 9 repeals one provision in the Act concerning the conditions for recognition of an investment exchange.

# THE COMPANIES ACT 1985 (AUDIT EXEMPTION) (AMENDMENT) REGULATIONS 2000

(SI 2000/1430)

*Made on 25 May 2000 by the Secretary of State for Trade and Industry under s. 257 of the Companies Act 1985. Operative from 26 May 2000 and applying to annual accounts and reports in respect of financial years ending on or after 26 July 2000.*

## INTRODUCTION

### CITATION, APPLICATION AND INTERPRETATION

**1(1)** These Regulations may be cited as the Companies Act 1985 (Audit Exemption) (Amendment) Regulations 2000 and come into force on the day after the day on which they are made.

**1(2)** These Regulations apply to annual accounts and reports in respect of financial years ending two months or more after the date of coming into force of these Regulations.

**1(3)** In these Regulations, references to sections (or Schedules) are to sections of (or Schedules to) the Companies Act 1985.

## AUDIT EXEMPTION

### MODIFICATION OF SECTION 249A

**2** [Amendment of s. 249A.]

### INSERTION OF NEW SECTION 249AA

**3** [Insertion of s. 249AA.]

### MODIFICATION OF SECTION 249B

**4** [Amendment of s. 249B.]

## DISCLOSURE WHERE DORMANT COMPANY ACTING AS AGENT

### ADDITIONAL DISCLOSURES IN NOTES TO ACCOUNTS

**5** [Insertion of Sch. 4, para. 58A.]

**6** [Insertion of Sch. 8, para. 51A.]

**7** [Insertion of Sch. 8A, para. 9A.]

## MINOR AND CONSEQUENTIAL AMENDMENTS

### MINOR AND CONSEQUENTIAL AMENDMENTS

**8(1)** [Amendment of s. 246(9).]

**8(2)** [Amendment of s. 247B(1).]

**8(3)** [Amendment of s. 249C(3).]

**8(4)** [Amendment of s. 249E(1).]

**8(5)** [Insertion of s. 249E(1A).]

**8(6)** Section 250 (resolution not to appoint auditors) is hereby repealed.

**8(7)** [Amendment of s. 289(4)(a).]

**8(8)** [Substitution of s. 386(2)(a).]

**8(9)** [Amendment of s. 388A(1).]

**8(10)** [Amendment of Sch. 1, para. 2(2)(a).]

## EXPLANATORY NOTE

*(This Note is not part of the Regulations)*

1. These Regulations amend provisions in Part VII of the Companies Act 1985 (c. 6) ("the 1985 Act") concerning–

- the exemption of certain small companies from the requirement to have their annual accounts audited, and
- the conditions a company must satisfy in order to qualify as dormant.

The amendments effected by the Regulations will apply to annual accounts and reports in respect of financial years ending two months or more after the date of coming into force of the Regulations (regulation 1(2)).

2. Regulation 2 increases the turnover limit in section 249A(3)(b) of the 1985 Act which a small company other than a small charitable company must not exceed in respect of a financial year if it is to be exempt from audit. The turnover limit is increased from £350,000 to £1 million (for small charitable companies the gross income limit remains at £90,000).

3. Regulation 4(3)(b) increases the turnover limit for a group to qualify as a small group for the purposes of section 249B(1C) from £350,000 net (£420,000 gross) to £1 million net (£1.2 million gross) (the limit as it applies in relation to small charitable companies remains unchanged). A company which would otherwise be disqualified from claiming exemption from audit under section 249A for a financial year because it was a parent company or subsidiary undertaking for any period in that year, may nevertheless claim the exemption if it is a member of a small group which satisfies the conditions specified in section 249B(1C). Regulation 4(3)(a) amends section 249B(1C)(a) to provide for the exemption from audit for small groups to apply to groups where not all the bodies in the group are companies within the meaning of section 735 of the 1985 Act.

4. Regulation 3 inserts a new section 249AA making provision for dormant companies to replace that in section 250 (which is repealed by regulation 8(6)). Dormant companies as defined will no longer need to pass a special resolution in order to qualify for exemption from audit, but instead will so qualify automatically provided 10% of members do not request an audit. The definition of dormancy has also been amended (see new section 249AA(4) to (7) ).

5. Regulations 5 to 7 impose new requirements for companies which are claiming dormancy status under section 249AA for a financial year and which have during that year acted as agent for any person to disclose that fact in the notes to their accounts (the amendments are to Schedules 4, 8 and 8A).

6. Regulations 2(3), 4(2), (4) and (5) and 8 make minor and consequential amendments.

7. A Regulatory Impact Assessment of these Regulations is available from the Department of Trade and Industry, Company Law and Investigations Directorate, Room 4102, 1 Victoria Street, London SW1H 0ET. A copy has also been placed in the libraries of both Houses of Parliament.

# Alphabetical List of Statutory Instruments

All statutory instruments listed below are reproduced in this volume unless indicated otherwise. Where a statutory instrument is referred to, the relevant statutory provisions where the reference may be found are set out. References are to the Companies Act 1985 unless otherwise stated. Abbreviations used are the same as those in the index; see the list of abbreviations at p. 5,003.

Access to Justice Act 1999 (Commencement No. 4 and Transitional Provisions) Order 2000, SI 2000/1920 (C. 4) (not reproduced) .......... CJA87 s. 1(9)–(11)
Accounting Standards (Prescribed Body) Regulations 1990, SI 1990/1667 .......... 256(1)
Act of Sederunt (Applications under Part VII of the Companies Act 1989) 1991, SI 1991/145 (S. 10) .......... CA89 s. 161(3), 163(4), 164(4), 175(5), 182(4)
Act of Sederunt (Company Directors Disqualification) 1986, SI 1986/2296 (S. 168)
Act of Sederunt (Rules of Court Amendment No. 11) (Companies) 1986, SI 1986/2298 (S. 170)
Act of Sederunt (Sheriff Court Company Insolvency Rules) 1986, SI 1986/2297 (S. 169)
Administration of Insolvent Estates of Deceased Persons Order 1986, SI 1986/1999 .......... IA86 s. 421; SI 1986/1925 r. 0.1
Administrative Receivers (Value Added Tax Certificates) Rules 1986, SI 1986/385
Bank Accounts Directive (Miscellaneous Banks) Regulations 1991, SI 1991/2704 .......... 257
Banking Coordination (Second Council Directive) (Amendment) Regulations 1993, SI 1993/3225 (not reproduced) .......... SI 1992/3218 reg. 2(1), 2A, 5
Banking Coordination (Second Council Directive) Regulations 1992, SI 1992/3218 .......... 446(4); FSA86 s. 5(1), 7(2), 10, 13(2), 26(5), 27(8), 28(1), 32(1), 43, 44, 45(2), 47A, 48–57, 59, 60, 67, 75(6), 76(7), 93(1), 102, 104, 106, 107(3), 109(1), 110, 113, 119(2), 121(2), 128C(5), 154, 171, 178, 179(2), 180(1), 183, 191, 206(1), Sch. 1 para. 17, 18(2), 26, Sch. 2 para. 2, 3, 7, Sch. 5 para. 2, Sch. 7 para. 5, Sch. 8 para. 12; CA89 s. 176(2); CJA93 Sch. 6 Pt. II; BEA Sch. 9 Pt. II
Banking (Gibraltar) Regulations 1999, SI 1999/2094 (not reproduced) ... SI 1992/3218 reg. 2(1), 3(7), 4
Bank of England Act 1998 (Commencement) Order 1998, SI 1998/1120 (C. 25) (not reproduced) .......... 449(1), (3); IA86 s. 422(1); FSA86 s. 43(4), 128C(3), 179(3), 180(1), 185(4), Sch. 5 para. 1, 4(1), 9, Sch. 7 para. 1(2); CA89 s. 82(2), (5), 87(4), 171, 176, 207(10); BEA; SI 1992/3218 reg. 2(1), 11(1); SI 1995/3275 reg. 2(1), 13, 14, 17(4), 18(2), 26, 42(10), 44(2), 46(5), 54(1), 56(3), Sch. 3, Sch. 6
Bank of England Act 1998 (Consequential Amendments of Subordinate Legislation) Order 1998, SI 1998/1129 (not reproduced) .......... SI 1986/1925 r. 4.1(1), 4.7(4), 4.10(4), 4.72(2), (6); SI 1995/2049; SI 1996/1669 reg. 1(3), 9(3)
Bankruptcy and Companies (DTI) Fees (Amendment) Order 1991, SI 1991/494 (not reproduced) .......... SI 1985/1784
Banks (Administration Proceedings) Order 1989, SI 1989/1276 .......... IA86 s. 8(4), 422(3)
British Technology Group Act 1991 (Appointed Day) Order 1991, SI 1991/2721 (C. 83) (not reproduced) .......... CC(CP)A Sch. 2; FSA86 Sch. 16 para. 10; IndA 13(2), 14(1), (4), 16(1), (4), 19(3), 20(3), 37(1), (2), (4)

Companies (Revision of Defective Accounts and Report) (Amendment) Regulations 1996, SI 1996/315 .................................................. SI 1990/2570 reg. 6(1), 7(1), 9(1), 10(3), 13A, 16(2)

Companies (Revision of Defective Accounts and Report) Regulations 1990, SI 1990/2570 .................................................. 245(3)–(5); SI 1995/2092 reg. 12

Companies (Single Member Private Limited Companies) Regulations 1992, SI 1992/1699 .................................................. 1(3A), 24, 322B, 352A, 370A, 382B, 680(1A), 741(3), Sch. 24; IA86 s. 122(1)

Companies (Summary Financial Statement) Regulations 1992, SI 1992/3075 (not reproduced) .................................................. SI 1990/2570 reg. 10(3), 14(1), (2), (4), 16(3)

Companies (Summary Financial Statement) Regulations 1995, SI 1995/2092 .................................................. 245(3)–(5), 251(1)–(3); SI 1990/2570 reg. 14(2), (4), 16(3)

Companies (Tables A to F) Regulations 1985 (including Table A of First Sch. to former Companies Act 1948), SI 1985/805 8; CC(CP)A 27

Companies (Unfair Prejudice Applications) Proceedings Rules 1986, SI 1986/2000 .................................................. IA86 s. 411(2); SI 1986/1925 r. 0.1

Companies (Unregistered Companies) (Amendment) Regulations 1990, SI 1990/438 .................................................. SI 1985/680 reg. 6, Sch.

Companies (Unregistered Companies) (Amendment No. 2) Regulations 1990, SI 1990/1394 .................................................. SI 1985/680 reg. 6, Sch.

Companies (Unregistered Companies) (Amendment No. 3) Regulations 1990, SI 1990/2571 .................................................. SI 1985/680 reg. 6, Sch.

Companies (Unregistered Companies) Regulations 1985, SI 1985/680 ... 718

Companies (Welsh Language Forms)(Amendment) (No. 2) Regulations 1999, SI 1999/2679

Companies (Welsh Language Forms)(Amendment) Regulations 1999, SI 1999/2357 .................................................. 88(2), 363(2)

Companies (Welsh Language Forms and Documents) (Amendment) Regulations 1994, SI 1994/727 (not reproduced) .................................................. SI 1994/117 reg. 4(2), (3)

Companies (Welsh Language Forms and Documents) (Amendment) Regulations 1995, SI 1995/734 .................................................. 10(2), 12(3), 287(3), 288(2), 363(2), 710B; SI 1994/117 reg. 4(2)

Companies (Welsh Language Forms and Documents) (No. 2) Regulations 1995, SI 1995/1480 .................................................. 12(3), 30(7), 652A(2), 652D(6)

Companies (Welsh Language Forms and Documents) (No. 3) Regulations 1995, SI 1995/1508

Companies (Welsh Language Forms and Documents) Regulations 1994, SI 1994/117 .................................................. 287(3), 288(2), 363(2), 710B(3), 744

Company Accounts (Disclosure of Directors' Emoluments) Regulations 1997, SI 1997/570 .................................................. 246(3), 257(5), Sch. 6 Pt. I

Company and Business Names (Amendment) Regulations 1982, SI 1982/1653 (not reproduced) .................................................. SI 1981/1685 Sch.

Company and Business Names (Amendment) Regulations 1992, SI 1992/1196 .................................................. BNA 2(4), 3(2); SI 1981/1685 Sch.

Company and Business Names (Amendment) Regulations 1995, SI 1995/3022 ........ SI 1981/1685 Sch. 29(6); BNA 2(1), 3(1), 6(3)
Company and Business Names Regulations 1981, SI 1981/1685 ..........
Company Auditors (Examinations) Regulations 1990, SI 1990/1146 ..... CA89 Sch. 12 para. 7
Company Auditors (Recognition Orders) (Application Fees) Regulations 1990, SI 1990/1206 ........ CA89 s. 45(4)
Competition Act 1998 (Commencement No. 4) Order 1999, SI 1999/2859 (C. 74) (not reproduced) ........ FTA73 Sch. 8 para. 3(1), (2)
Competition Act 1998 (Commencement No. 5) Order 2000, SI 2000/344 (C. 9) (not reproduced)........ FSA86 s. 125–127, Sch. 11 para. 12(1), (2); CA89 Sch. 14 para. 9, Sch. 20 para. 21–24
Competition Act 1998 (Competition Commission) Transitional, Consequential and Supplemental Provisions Order 1999, SI 1999/506 (not reproduced) ........ SI 1995/3272 Sch. 2 para. 5(3)
Competition Act 1998 (Transitional, Consequential and Supplemental Provisions) Order 2000, SI 2000/311) (not reproduced) ........ IA86 s. 428; FSA86 s. 126, 180(7); CA89 Sch. 18 para. 14; FTA73 s. 93A(1); SI 1995/3272 reg. 13, Sch. 2 para. 6, 7
Co-operation of Insolvency Courts (Designation of Relevant Countries) Order 1996, SI 1996/253 ........ IA86 s. 426(11)
Co-operation of Insolvency Courts (Designation of Relevant Countries and Territories) Order 1986, SI 1986/2123 ........ IA86 s. 426(11); SI 1986/1925 r. 0.1
Co-operation of Insolvency Courts (Designation of Relevant Country) Order 1998, SI 1998/2766
County Court Fees Order 1999, SI 1999/689 ........ IA86 s. 414(1)
Criminal Justice Act 1993 (Commencement No. 5) Order 1994, SI 1994/242 (C. 7) (not reproduced) ........ CJA87 s. 3(6)
Definition of Subsidiary (Consequential Amendments) Regulations 1990, SI 1990/1395 ........ CA89 s. 144(4)
Department of Trade and Industry (Fees) Order 1988, SI 1988/93
Deregulation and Contracting Out Act 1994 (Commencement No. 2) Order 1994, SI 1994/3188 (C. 76) (not reproduced) ........ FTA73 s. 77(1), (5)
Deregulation (Resolutions of Private Companies) Order 1996, SI 1996/1471 ........ 379A(2A), 381A(5), 381B, 381C(1), 390(2), Sch. 24
Disclosure of Interests in Shares (Amendment) (No. 2) Regulations 1993, SI 1993/2689 ........ 209(2)
Disclosure of Interests in Shares (Amendment) Regulations 1993, SI 1993/1819 ........ 198(1), 199(2A), (5)–(8), 200, 202(2)–(2B), 206(3)–(3B), 209, 210A(1), 220(1)
Disclosure of Interests in Shares (Amendment) Regulations 1996, SI 1996/1560 ........ 209(9A), (9B), 210A(1), (4)
EEC Merger Control (Consequential Provisions) Regulations 1990, SI 1990/1563 ........ FTA73 s. 64(1), 75B(7), 75F(1), (2)
EEC Merger Control (Distinct Market Investigations) Regulations 1990, SI 1990/1715 ........ FTA73 s. 85(6)–(8), 93B(3)

Financial Services Act 1986 (Commencement) (No. 14) Order 1999, SI 1999/727 (not reproduced) ........ 82, 83, 86, 87
Financial Services Act 1986 (Corporate Debt Exemption) Order 1997, SI 1997/816 ........ FSA86 s. 46(2), Sch. 5 para. 2(2), 5(2)
Financial Services Act 1986 (EEA Regulated Markets) (Exemption) Order 1995, SI 1995/3273 ........ FSA86 s. 46(2)
Financial Services Act 1986 (Exemption) Order 1996, SI 1996/1587 ........ FSA86 s. 46(2), 205, 205A, Sch. 1 para. 16A
Financial Services Act 1986 (Extension of Scope of Act) Order 1996, SI 1996/2958 ........ FSA86 s. 2(6), 205, 205A, Sch. 1 para. 13A, 16, 18(3A), 19(4A), 20(1), 22(2A), 24(2A), (3), 24A, 27(1)
Financial Services Act 1986 (Extension of Scope of Act) Order 1997, SI 1997/2543 ........ FSA86 Sch. 1 para. 16A, 18(5B)
Financial Services Act 1986 (Investment Advertisements) (Exemptions) (No. 2) Order 1995, SI 1995/1536 ........ FSA86 s. 57(10), 205, 205A
Financial Services Act 1986 (Investment Advertisements) (Exemptions) Order 1996, SI 1996/1586 ........ FSA86 s. 57(10), 58(4), 87(6), 88(10), 205, 205A
Financial Services Act 1986 (Investment Advertisements) (Exemptions) Order 1997, SI 1997/963 ........ FSA86 s. 58(4), 205, 205A; SI 1996/1586 art. 10, Sch. 1 Pt. I
Financial Services Act 1986 (Investment Services) (Extension of Scope of Act) Order 1995, SI 1995/3271 ........ FSA86 s. 2(6), 205, 205A
Financial Services Act 1986 (Miscellaneous Exemptions) Order 1997, SI 1997/3024 ........ FSA86 s. 46(2)
Financial Services Act 1986 (Restriction of Scope of Act and Meaning of Collective Investment Scheme) Order 1990, SI 1990/349 (not reproduced) ........ FSA86 s. 75(5A), (5B), (6)
Financial Services Act 1986 (Restriction of Scope of Act and Meaning of Collective Investment Scheme) Order 1996, SI 1996/2996 ........ FSA86 s. 2(6), 75(6), (9), Sch. 1 para. 17–19, 21, 36; SI 1995/3271 art. 6(1)
Financial Services Act 1986 (Restriction of Scope of Act and Meaning of Collective Investment Scheme) Order 1997, SI 1997/32 ........ FSA86 s. 75(6), Sch. 1 para. 37
Financial Services Act 1986 (Uncertificated Securities) (Extension of Scope of Act) Order 1996, SI 1996/1322 ........ FSA86 s. 2(6), 205, 205A, Sch. 1 para. 16A, 18(5A), (5B), 22(4A), 27(3)
Financial Services and Markets (Transitional Provisions) (Designated Date for Certain Self-Regulating Organisations) Order 2000, SI 2000/1734 (not reproduced) ........ FSMA Sch. 21 para. 1(3), (5), 2(3), (4)
Financial Services (Disclosure of Information) (Designated Authorities) (No. 7) Order 1993, SI 1993/1826 ........ 449(1B), (1C); CA89 s. 87(4)
Foreign Companies (Execution of Documents) (Amendment) Regulations 1995, SI 1995/1729 ........ SI 1994/950 reg. 2, 3, 6
Foreign Companies (Execution of Documents) Regulations 1994, SI 1994/950 ........ 36–36C; CA89 s. 130(6)

Industry Act 1975 (Prohibition and Vesting Order) Regulations 1998, SI 1998/3035 (not reproduced) .......... IndA 13(7), (8)

Insider Dealing (Public Servants) Order 1989, SI 1989/2164

Insider Dealing (Recognised Stock Exchange) (No. 2) Order 1990, SI 1990/47 .......... CS(ID)A 16(2)

Insider Dealing (Recognised Stock Exchange) Order 1989, SI 1989/47

Insider Dealing (Recognised Stock Exchange) Order 1992, SI 1992/451 .. CS(ID)A 16(2)

Insider Dealing (Securities and Regulated Markets) (Amendment) Order 1996, SI 1996/1561 .......... SI 1994/187 art. 10, Sch.

Insider Dealing (Securities and Regulated Markets) (Amendment) Order 2000, SI 2000/1923 .......... SI 1994/187 art. 9, 10, Sch.

Insider Dealing (Securities and Regulated Markets) Order 1994, SI 1994/187 .......... CJA93 s. 54(1), 60(1), 62(1), 64(1), (3); SI 1989/2165

Insolvency Act 1985 (Commencement No. 1) Order 1986, SI 1986/6 (C. 1)

Insolvency Act 1985 (Commencement No. 2) Order 1986, SI 1986/185 (C. 7) .......... 461(6), 501–650, 744; CC(CP)A Sch. 2

Insolvency Act 1985 (Commencement No. 3) Order 1986), SI 1986/463 (C. 14) .......... 196, 300, 301, 449(1), 501–650

Insolvency Act 1985 (Commencement No. 4) Order 1986, SI 1986/840 (C. 22)

Insolvency Act 1985 (Commencement No. 5) Order 1986, SI 1986/1924 (C. 71) .......... 13(4), 44(7), 103(7), 131(7), 140(2), 153(3), 156(3), 173(4), 178(7), 196, former 222(4), former 225(8), 295–299, 301, 302, 380(4), 395(1), 410(2), 425(1), 426(6), 441(1), 449(1), 461(6), 462(5), 463(2)–(4), 464(6), 467–485, 486(1), Pt. XIX, 501–650, 651(1), 658(1), 659–664, Pt. XXI, former 709(4), former 710(4), 724, 733(1), (3), 744, Sch. 12, Sch. 16, Sch. 17, Sch. 18, Sch. 19, Sch. 20 Pt. I, Sch. 24; CC(CP)A Sch. 2; IA86 s. 443; CDDA 25

Insolvency Act 1986 (Guernsey) Order 1989, SI 1989/2409 .......... IA86 s. 462(4), (5), (10), (11), 442

Insolvency (Amendment) (No. 2) Rules 1999, SI 1999/1022 (not reproduced) .......... SI 1986/1925 r. 0.2, 6.197, 7.33–7.42, 7.49, 7.51, 7.51, 7.57, 7.59, 7.60, 9.2(3), 9.4(3), 12.9, 12.11, 12.12(1), 13.13(1), (6), (7)

Insolvency (Amendment of Subordinate Legislation) Order 1986, SI 1986/2001 .......... IA86 s. 439(4); SI 1986/1925 r. 0.1

Insolvency (Amendment of Subordinate Legislation) Order 1987, SI 1987/1398 .......... SI 1986/2001 art. 3 196, 300, 301, 449(1), 501–650

Insolvency (Amendment) Regulations 2000, SI 2000/485 .......... SI 1994/2507 reg. 3(1), 5(3), (4), 7(A1), (3A), 8(3A), (4), 20(2), (3), 22(A1), (2A), 23(1), (1A), (2)

Insolvency (Amendment) Rules 1987, SI 1987/1919 (not reproduced) .... SI 1986/1925 passim

Insolvency (Amendment) Rules 1989, SI 1989/397 (not reproduced) ..... SI 1986/1925 r. 6.223, 12.3(2), Sch. 3

Insolvency (Amendment) Rules 1991, SI 1991/495 (not reproduced) ..... SI 1986/1925 r. 4.11(3), 4.21(4), 6.34(2), 6.35(2), 6.46(2), 6.47(2), Sch. 3, Sch. 4

Insolvency (Amendment) Rules 1993, SI 1993/602 (not reproduced) ..... SI 1986/1925 r. 7.17(2), 12.3(2), Sch. 3

Insolvency (Amendment) Rules 1995, SI 1995/586 (not reproduced) ..... SI 1986/1925 r. 4.218(1), 6.224(1)
Insolvency (Amendment) Rules 1999, SI 1999/359 (not reproduced) ..... SI 1986/1925 r. 5.23(1), (1A)–(1C), 5.25(5), 5.29(1), (3), 6.34(3), 6.46(3), 6.216(7), 6.223(A)–(C)
Insolvency (ECSC Levy Debts) Regulations 1987, SI 1987/2093 ......... IA86 s. 386(1), Sch. 6 para. 15A
Insolvency Fees (Amendment) Order 1994, SI 1994/2541 (not reproduced) ......... SI 1986/2030 art. 2, 4, 4A, 9, 12, Sch.
Insolvency Fees Order 1986, SI 1986/2030 ......... IA86 s. 414(1); SI 1986/1925 r. 0.1; SI 1985/1784
Insolvency Practitioners (Amendment) Regulations 1993, SI 1993/221 ... SI 1990/439 reg. 12–15A
Insolvency Practitioners (Recognised Professional Bodies) Order 1986, SI 1986/1764 ......... IA86 s. 391(5)
Insolvency Practitioners Regulations 1990, SI 1990/439 ......... IA86 s. 390(4), 392(1), 419(4); SI 1986/1925 r. 0.1
Insolvency Practitioners Tribunal (Conduct of Investigations) Rules 1986, SI 1986/952 ......... IA86 s. 396(1)
Insolvency Regulations 1986, SI 1986/1994 ......... SI 1986/1925 r. 0.1
Insolvency Regulations 1994, SI 1994/2507 ......... IA86 s. 403(3), 411(5), 412(4), Sch. 8 para. 27, Sch. 9 para. 30; SI 1986/1925 r. 12.1(3)
Insolvency Rules 1986, SI 1986/1925 ......... IA86 s. 2, 4(5), (6), 6, 9(2), 17(3), 19(1), 20(1), 21(2), 22(1), 23(2), 24(3), (4), 33(2), 95(3), 99(3), 124(5), 133(4), 141(5), 160(2), 172(8), 174(4), 288(2), 289(2), 411(2); SI 1987/1919; SI 1989/397; SI 1991/495; SI 1993/602; SI 1995/586; SI 1999/359; SI 1999/1022
Insolvency (Scotland) Amendment Rules 1987, SI 1987/1921 (S. 132) .... SI 1986/1915 passim
Insolvency (Scotland) Rules 1986, SI 1986/1915 (S. 139) ......... IA86 s. 169(2), 189(5), 411(2); SI 1986/1925 r. 0.1; SI 1987/1921 Sch.
Insolvent Companies (Disqualification of Unfit Directors) Proceedings (Amendment) Rules 1999, SI 1999/1023 ......... SI 1987/2023 r. 1–8
Insolvent Companies (Disqualification of Unfit Directors) Proceedings Rules 1987, SI 1987/2023 ......... IA86 s. 411(2); CDDA 7(1), 21(2)
Insolvent Companies (Reports on Conduct of Directors) No. 2 Rules 1986, SI 1986/2134 (not reproduced) ......... CDDA 21(2); SI 1986/1925 r. 0.1
Insolvent Companies (Reports on Conduct of Directors) (No. 2) (Scotland) Rules 1986, SI 1986/1916 (S. 140) (not reproduced) ......... CDDA 21(2); SI 1986/1925 r. 0.1
Insolvent Companies (Reports on Conduct of Directors) Rules 1996, SI 1996/1909 ......... IA86 s. 411(2); CDDA 21(2); SI 1986/1925 r. 0.1
Insolvent Companies (Reports on Conduct of Directors) (Scotland) Rules 1996, SI 1996/1910 (S. 154) ......... IA86 s. 411(2); CDDA 21(2)
Insolvent Partnerships (Amendment) Order 1996, SI 1996/1308 ......... IA86 s. 420(2); CDDA 21(2); SI 1994/2421 art. 7(1)
Insolvent Partnerships Order 1986, SI 1986/2142 ......... SI 1986/1925 r. 0.1
Insolvent Partnerships Order 1994, SI 1994/2421 ......... IA86 Pt. I, II, IV, 168(5A)–(5C), Pt. V–VII, Pt. IX–XIII, 388(2A), (3), Pt. XIV, Pt. XV, 420(3), Pt. XVI–XIX; CDDA 21(2), Sch. 1; SI 1986/1925 r. 0.1; SI 1986/2142

Trade Marks Act 1994 (Commencement) Order 1994, SI 1994/2550 (not reproduced) .................... 396(3A), 410(4)
Transfer of Functions (Economic Statistics) Order 1989, SI 1989/992 (not reproduced) .................... IndA 37(1)
Transfer of Functions (Financial Services) Order 1992, SI 1992/1315 .... 449(1), 744; FSA86 s. 178(10), 179(3), 180(1), 186(7), 199(7), 201(4), 205, 207(1); CA89 s. 87(4), 171(6), 172(3), 173(6), 174(5)
Transfer of Functions (Insurance) Order 1997, SI 1997/2781 (not reproduced) .................... 438(1); FSA86 s. 180(1); CA89 s. 87(4); SI 1992/1315 Sch. 1 para. 6–8, 10, 18, 19, 23, 26, Sch. 2 para. 1, 2, 4, 6
Trusts of Land and Appointment of Trustees Act 1996 (Commencement) Order 1996, SI 1996/2974 (C. 91) (not reproduced) .................... IA86 s. 336(3), (4)
Uncertificated Securities (Amendment) Regulations 2000, SI 2000/1682 .................... SI 1995/3272 reg. 27(2), 29(11), 36A–37, 38A, Sch. 1 para. 12A, 12B, 13A, 15(1A), Sch. 4
Uncertificated Securities Regulations 1995, SI 1995/3272 .................. 182(1), 183(1), (4), 352(5), 380(4); FSA86 s. 119, 120, 122–126, 128, 180(1); CA89 s. 207
Welfare Reform and Pensions Act 1999 (Commencement No. 4) Order 2000, SI 2000/1047 (C. 29) (not reproduced) .................... PSA93 Sch. 4 para. 2
Welfare Reform and Pensions Act 1999 (Commencement No. 7) Order 2000, SI 2000/1382 (C. 41) (not reproduced) .................... IA86 s. 310(7)
Welsh Language Act 1993 (Commencement) Order 1994, SI 1994/115 (not reproduced) .................... 21, 228(2), 242(1), 243(4), 255E, 351(3)–(5), 710B, Sch. 9 Pt. II para. 7(3)
Youth Justice and Criminal Evidence Act 1999 (Commencement No. 2) Order 2000, SI 2000/1034 (C. 27) (not reproduced) .................... 434(5A), (5B), 447(8A), (8B), 709(3); CDDA 20; CA89 s. 83(6A), (6B); FSA86 s. 105(5A), (5B), 177(6A), (6B); CJA87 s. 2(8AA); IA86 s. 433

# List of Forms Statutory Instruments

The list below, prepared by CCH.New Law editorial staff, lists Companies Act forms, company voluntary arrangement forms, administration order forms, receivership forms, winding up forms, insolvency application forms, proxy forms, order for private examination, etc., report on conduct of directors forms, disqualification order forms, and European Economic Interest Grouping (EEIG) forms. For each form the number, title and relevant statutory instrument are indicated. The forms themselves are not reproduced in this publication.

| **Companies Act Forms** | | *SI No.* |
|---|---|---|
| 6 | Cancellation of alteration to the objects of a company | SI 1995/736 |
| 10 | First directors and secretary and intended situation of registered office (Welsh form available: 10 CYM) | SI 1995/736 |
| 12 | Declaration on application for registration (Welsh form available:12 CYM) | SI 1995/736 |
| 30(5)(a) | Declaration on application for registration of a company exempt from the requirement to use the word 'limited' or 'cyfyngedig' (Welsh form available: 30(5)(a) CYM) | SI 1995/736 |
| 30(5)(b) | Declaration on application for registration under s. 680 of the Companies Act 1985 of a company exempt from the requirement to use the word 'limited' or 'cyfyngedig' (Welsh form available: 30(5)(b) CYM) | SI 1995/736 |
| 30(5)(c) | Change of name omitting 'limited' or 'cyfyngedig' (Welsh form available: 30(5)(c) CYM) | SI 1995/736 |
| 43(3) | Application by a private company for re-registration as a public company | SI 1995/736 |
| 43(3)(e) | Declaration on application by a private company on application for re-registration as a public company | SI 1995/736 |
| 49(1) | Application by a limited company to be re-registered as unlimited | SI 1995/736 |
| 49(8)(a) | Members' assent to company being re-registered as unlimited | SI 1995/736 |
| 51 | Application by an unlimited company to be re-registered as limited | SI 1995/736 |
| 53 | Application by a public company for re-registration as a private company | SI 1995/736 |
| 54 | Application to the Court for cancellation of resolution for re-registration | SI 1995/736 |
| 88(2) | Return of allotments of shares (Welsh form availiable: 88(2) CYM) | SI 1999/2356; Welsh form: SI 1999/2679 |
| 88(3) | Particulars of a contract relating to shares allotted as fully or partly paid up otherwise than in cash | SI 1987/752 |
| 97 | Statement of the amount or rate per cent of any commission payable in connection with the subscription of shares | SI 1985/854 |
| 117 | Application by a public company for certificate to commence business | SI 1995/736 |
| 122 | Notice of consolidation, division, sub-division, redemption or cancellation of shares, or conversion, re-conversion of stock into shares | SI 1987/752 |
| 123 | Notice of increase in nominal capital | SI 1987/752 |
| 128(1) | Statement of rights attached to allotted shares | SI 1987/752 |
| 128(3) | Statement of particulars of variation of rights attached to shares | SI 1987/752 |
| 128(4) | Notice of assignment of name or new name to any class of shares | SI 1987/752 |

| Form | | SI No. |
|---|---|---|
| 129(1) | Statement by a company without share capital of rights attached to newly created class of members | SI 1987/752 |
| 129(2) | Statement by a company without share capital of particulars of a variation of members' class rights | SI 1987/752 |
| 129(3) | Notice by a company without share capital of assignment of a name or other designation to a class of members | SI 1987/752 |
| 139 | Application by a public company for re-registration as a private company following a court order reducing capital | SI 1985/854 |
| 147 | Application by a public company for re-registration as a private company following cancellation of shares and reduction of nominal value of issued capital | SI 1985/854 |
| 155(6)a | Declaration in relation to assistance for the acquisition of shares | SI 1985/854 |
| 155(6)b | Declaration by the directors of a holding company in relation to assistance for the acquisition of shares | SI 1985/854 |
| 157 | Notice of application made to the court for the cancellation of a special resolution regarding financial assistance for the acquisition of shares | SI 1987/752 |
| 169 | Return by a company purchasing its own shares | SI 1987/752 |
| 173 | Declaration in relation to the redemption or purchase of shares out of capital | SI 1985/854 |
| 176 | Notice of application to the court for the cancellation of a resolution for the redemption or purchase of shares out of capital | SI 1987/752 |
| 190 | Location of register of debenture holders | SI 1995/736 |
| 190a | Notice of a place for inspection of a register of holders of debentures which is kept in a non-legible form, or of any change in that place | SI 1985/724 |
| 224 | Notice of accounting reference date (to be delivered within 9 months of incorporation) | SI 1990/572 |
| 225 | Change of accounting reference date | SI 1996/594 |
| 244 | Notice of claim to extension of period allowed for laying and delivering accounts – oversea business or interests | SI 1990/572 |
| 266(1) | Notice of intention to carry on business as an investment company | SI 1995/736 |
| 266(3) | Notice that a company no longer wishes to be an investmentcompany | SI 1995/736 |
| 287 | Change in situation or address of registered office (Welsh form available: 287 CYM) | SI 1995/736 |
| 288a | Appointment of director or secretary (Welsh form available: 288a CYM) | SI 1995/736 |
| 288b | Resignation of director or secretary (Welsh form available: 288b CYM) | SI 1999/2356 |
| 288c | Change of particulars for director or secretary (Welsh form available: 288c CYM) | SI 1995/736 |
| 318 | Location of directors' service contracts | SI 1995/736 |
| 325 | Location of register of directors' interests in shares etc. | SI 1995/736 |
| 325a | Notice of place for inspection of a register of directors' interests in shares etc. which is kept in a non-legible form, or of any change in that place | SI 1985/724 |
| 353 | Register of members | SI 1995/736 |
| 353a | Notice of place for inspection of a register of members which is kept in a non-legible form, or of any change in that place | SI 1985/724 |